CALDENE
www.caldene.co.uk
the passion of equestrianism
e understands your love of riding like Caldene, which is why you'll love our exciting new ranges of equestrian clothing. Come along and see them
And remind yourself why you feel so passionate about life on horseback. For your nearest Caldene stockist, please call us on 01422 883393

CARR & DAY & MARTIN
For all your horse and leather care needs
200 YEARS OF EXCELLENCE
REPEL
BELVOIR
GALLOP PLUS
NEW
HOOF OIL
For further details and a brochure contact Quay Equestrian Ltd
Website: www.quayequestrian.com Free Advice Line: 0800 413136

EQUEST
moxidectin ORAL GEL

YOUR HORSE

Contents

Your Horse Directory

The Ultimate Equestrian Services Guide
for the UK and Ireland

Containing over 16,000 Equestrian Businesses and Service Providers.

Also available on CD-ROM
Updated daily on www.hccyourhorse.com

HCC Publishing
The next generation directories

Your Horse Directory

Publishing Director: Howard Cox

Sales Manager: Neil Stokes

Project Manager: Julian Grattidge

Design & Production Manager: Lucy Hibbert
Design & Production Assistant: Paul Harrison
Design & Production Assistant: Mathew Jennings

Data Research Manager: Claire Thorpe
Researchers: Michelle Malbon, Angela Evans, Lise Taylor, Sarah Martin, Sarah Lockett, Faye Jackson, James Lloyd, Marie Devaney, Sally Webster, Sarah Murray

Editorial Programmer: Matthew Corne
CD programming: Paul Crossley
Website design and programming: Martin Robinson

Publisher: HCC Publishing Ltd

ISBN: 1-903897-07-6

Whilst every effort has been made to ensure the contents of this publication are accurate at the time of publishing, HCC Publishing and those involved in producing the content cannot be held responsible for any errors, omissions or changes in the details of this guide or for the consequences of any reliance on the information provided in the same. We have tried to ensure accuracy in this directory but things do change and we would be grateful if readers would advise us of any inaccuracies they might encounter.

Cover Photographs:
Main Picture: Holme Park Stud, © Mrs Susan Atten
Top Left : Little Meadow Stud, © Mrs Tamsin Evans

Further Information:

Emails: yourhorse@hccpublishing.co.uk
contactus@hccpublishing.co.uk

Website: www.hccyourhorse.com

Address: Meaford Power Station, Meaford, Stone, Staffordshire, ST15 0UU.

Tel: 0870 7541666 (From outside the UK +441782 371184)
Fax: 0870 7541667 (From outside the UK +441782 371167)

Foreword

Having been an equestrian enthusiast for many years, like countless others, I have found it difficult to locate suitable equestrian services that meet my specific needs. There is so much confusing information that has been published in recent years.

My mother has kept and bred Arabian horses for as long as I can remember, and through the years we have participated in many types of horse related disciplines; dressage, jumping, racing, western riding, and even endurance, to name but a few. During this time we have called on the services of countless business and service providers with mixed results.

The problems start when you try to locate a business or service that suits your exact requirements. It seems we all have to rely so much on hearsay, the equestrian press, poorly updated directories, and the odd snippet of information on TV....

...... but now at last there is the Your Horse Directory

The prestigious magazine Your Horse has teamed up with HCC Publishing to bring you the ultimate equestrian guide. A clear, concise, and informative next generation directory with 'searchable' details for over 16,000 equestrian businesses and service providers throughout the UK & Ireland.

No matter what kind of product or service you are looking for, the Your Horse Directory has all the answers. For the first time, using this unique directory, you will be able to search for products and services in the way that you want to. The searchable sections in the directory will allow you to...

- Search for riding schools in Bedfordshire that can teach children under 10, senior citizens, and the disabled.
- Search for cross country course designers and builders in Northumberland.
- Search for animal behaviourists in Cambridgeshire.
- Search for stable builders in Cheshire who also offer a design service.
- Search for farrier services in Bedfordshire, or indoor schooling in Cornwall
- Search for 30 minute lessons in Pembrokeshire for under £10.00

The searchable aspects are endless. The directory lists useable information on business name, business profile, address, contacts with website and e-mail details, opening hours, services offered, brands supplied, and even prices for lessons or livery.

All the information you could possibly want in order to locate your preferred equestrian service....

In addition to this hard copy format, the Your Horse Directory is also available as a powerful interactive CD-ROM, containing additional business information, photographs, maps and a whole host of interactive features including an extensive horse breeds database, products database, and an interactive diary. By accessing the CD-ROM, you will discover even more ways to locate the business that meets your requirements.

Purchasing the Your Horse Directory in either form also allows membership to the searchable www.hccyourhorse.com website, giving access to a whole host of 'equestrian' information which is updated on a daily basis.

The CD and website give you a million extra ways to locate the equestrian service of your choice.

Michelle Malbon
Your Horse Directory

Background

A brief walk around any equestrian event is enough to tell you that we all want something different from equestrian businesses or service providers. From ridden or in-hand classes to jumping or point-to-point, each discipline has different resource requirements. With these and many other diverse sectors still emerging within our sport, it's no wonder that tracking down suitable products or service providers has become increasingly difficult.

How do you find stables with suitable livery, be it part, full or DIY? Where do you take your horsebox for effective repairs? How do you locate suitable farrier or veterinary services? Where can you find advice on bloodstock, breeding or herbal remedies?

This has been the age-old problem with the majority of conventional equestrian directories. They do not provide the enquirer with the information they want, in the way that they want it. Most directories set out with good intentions, however, as the modern equestrian becomes more discerning, sophisticated, and even demanding, these 'one-dimensional' directories tend to leave the enquirer 'short-changed' and invariably frustrated.

With years of expertise in market research, database management, and publishing, the team at HCC knew what was needed. A truly 'searchable' directory, structured in such a way that any equestrian, no matter what their requirements, would be able to pick up the directory and find 'useable' information, presented in a structured manner that was easy on the eye.

Welcome to the Your Horse Directory, one of the Next Generation Directories from HCC Publishing.

Searching Made Simple .....

Your Involvement

We welcome your input; in fact we positively encourage your comments about any inaccuracies that may be apparent. We also welcome your recommendations about equestrian businesses not currently covered in this directory. So let's hear your constructive criticism. It is our aim to continue to improve the most comprehensive source of information about UK & Irish equestrian businesses and service providers currently available to you. So please contact us about businesses included or not included in the Your Horse Directory.

Data issue points to be aware of whilst using the Your Horse Directory.

1. Information given by businesses is usually obtained using sophisticated "data collection" questionnaires. If you would like to receive one, please contact us by telephone on 0870 754 1666 or you can also email us at: yourhorse@hccpublishing.co.uk

2. London (Greater) is listed as a county (we know it is not). Sub-areas of London have been recognised as a locality and are entered when they are known (e.g. Camden, Waterloo etc).

3. The Channel Islands are listed under England.

4. Some areas of information are incomplete due to lack of any co-operation by a business representative. That person, for unclear reasoning, prefers that you do not know more than they want to divulge.

5. In certain sections some names have been shortened to enable a uniform layout, but remain recognisable.

6. All telephone numbers have been corrected to the British Telecom recommended layout, including international numbers (any changes to numbers after publication is in the hands of BT). Don't forget that the international code for the UK is +44 and Ireland is +353

7. All prices listed are in UK pounds. Irish Punts and Euros have been converted to UK pounds at the time of publishing.

Standard Abbreviations

Admin - Administration
Agrcltrl - Agricultural
Ass - Association
Ast - Associates
Ave - Avenue
BA - British Association
Cl - Close
Clge - College
Clnc - Clinic
Co - Company
Confed - Confederation
Coun - Council
Cres - Crescent
Ctre - Centre
Ctry - Country
Dept - Department
Dvlp - Development
Ed - Education
Equip - Equipment
Est - Establishment
Est - Estate
Expo - Exposition
Fed - Federation
GB - Great Britain
Gen - General
Gr - Grove
Grp - Group
Gt - Great
Hol - Holiday
Hols - Holidays
Hosp - Hospital
Hse - House
Ind - Industrial
Ins - Institute
Int - International
Manu - Manufacturing
Mngmt - Management
Nat - National
Nr - Near
Org - Organisation
Pk - Park
Pl - Place
Prac - Practice
Prde - Parade
Pro - Professional
Rd - Road
Reg - Register
S.P.V.Synd - Sarcoids Post Viral Syndrome
Sq - Square
St - Street
Sup - Supplies
Sv - Service
Svs - Services
Trad - Traditional
Trce - Terrace
UK - United Kingdom
Uni - University
Vetnry - Veterinary

YOUR HORSE

In Partnership with

HCC Publishing

Searching Made Simple

SECTION 1

A-Z of Equestrian Businesses

This is the main section of the directory. It can be used to locate Equestrian Services and Supplies you already know the name of. Alternatively, it can be used for finding out more information on a service you have located after accessing the other searchable sections of the book.

What information can I find?

An alphabetical listing of services, detailing name, address, useful contact details, business profile and opening times.

1ST CHOICE PET SUPPLIES

1st Choice Pet Supplies, Unit 2 Cavour St, Burnley, **Lancashire**, BB12 0BQ, **ENGLAND**.
(T) 01282 830382.
Contact/s
Owner: Mrs S Heap
Profile Saddlery Retailer. Ref: YH00001

2 XCEL

2 Xcel, Unit 3, Kilda Pl, North Muirton Ind Est, Arran Road, Perth, **Perth and Kinross**, PH1 3RL, **SCOTLAND**.
(T) 01738 444445 (F) 01783 444419
(W) www.2xcel.co.uk.
Contact/s
Owner: Miss N Cooper
Profile Supplies. Ref: YH00002

4 SEASONS MARQUEE & FURNITURE

4 Seasons Marquee & Furniture Hire, Moorside Farm, Tushingham, Whitchurch, **Shropshire**, SY13 4QN, **ENGLAND**.
(T) 01948 665142 (F) 01948 666708
(M) 07860 258044.
Contact/s
Owner: Mr S Kay
Profile Supplies. Marquee hire.
Marquee hire for equestrian events. Ref: YH00003

608 VETNRY GRP

608 Veterinary Group, 608 Warwick Rd, Solihull, **Midlands (West)**, B91 1AA, **ENGLAND**.
(T) 0121 7053044 (F) 0121 7112585.
Contact/s
Practice Manager: Mr V Hayward
Profile Medical Support. Ref: YH00004

A & A PEATE

A & A Peate Ltd, Maesbury Hall Mills, Oswestry, **Shropshire**, SY10 8BB, **ENGLAND**.
(T) 01691 653201.
Profile Supplies. Ref: YH00005

A & E WOODWARD

A & E Woodward Ltd, Northbridge Engineering Works, Lime St, Hull, **Yorkshire (East)**, HU8 7AB, **ENGLAND**.
(T) 01482 329185 (F) 01482 216619.
Profile Supplies.
Clipper Service & Repair, regrinding of old clipper blades
Opening Times
Sp: Open Mon - Fri 08:00. Closed Mon - Fri 16:30.
Su: Open Mon - Fri 08:00. Closed Mon - Fri 16:30.
Au: Open Mon - Fri 08:00. Closed Mon - Fri 16:30.
Wn: Open Mon - Fri 08:00. Closed Mon - Fri 16:30.
Ref: YH00006

A & F WILLIAMSON & SONS

A & F Williamson & Sons Ltd, Corn Mills, Endon, Stoke-on-Trent, **Staffordshire**, ST9 9AB, **ENGLAND**.
(T) 01782 503121.
Profile Supplies. Ref: YH00007

A & H FEEDS

A & H Feeds Ltd (Ashtead), 29 The Street, Ashtead, **Surrey**, KT21 1AA, **ENGLAND**.
(T) 01372 274154.
Profile Supplies. Ref: YH00008

A & H FEEDS

A & H Feeds Ltd (Leatherhead), 3 Highlands Rd, Leatherhead, **Surrey**, KT22 8NB, **ENGLAND**.
(T) 01372 378989.
Profile Supplies. Ref: YH00009

A & H GREEN HARNESSMAKERS

A & H Green Harnessmakers, 237 Forest Rd, Old Woodhouse, Loughborough, **Leicestershire**, LE12 8TZ, **ENGLAND**.
(T) 01509 890102.
Contact/s
Owner: Mr T Green
Profile Saddlery Retailer. Ref: YH00010

A & I SUPPLIES

A & I Supplies, Edger Rd, Elgin, **Moray**, IV30 6YQ, **SCOTLAND**.
(T) 01343 544293.
Profile Supplies. Ref: YH00011

A & J SADDLERY

A & J Saddlery & Country Clothing, Brewster's Corner, Pendicke St, Southam, **Warwickshire**, CV47 1PN, **ENGLAND**.
(T) 01926 812238 (F) 01926 810415
(W) www.ajsaddlery.com.
Profile Feed Merchant, Riding Wear Retailer, Saddlery Retailer.
Mobile Saddlery and Country Clothing Stand (attends events around the country). Also supply Equine and Pet Feed. No.Staff: 4 Yr. Est: 1983
Opening Times
Sp: Open Mon - Sun 09:00. Closed Mon, Wed - Sun 17:30, Tues 19:00.
Su: Open Mon - Sun 09:00. Closed Mon, Wed - Sun 17:30, Tues 19:00.
Au: Open Mon - Sun 09:00. Closed Mon, Wed - Sun 17:30, Tues 19:00.
Wn: Open Mon - Sun 09:00. Closed Mon, Wed - Sun 17:30, Tues 19:00. Ref: YH00012

A & J TRAILER MADE

A & J Trailer Made, Number 3 Arch Stepney Bank, Newcastle-upon-Tyne, **Tyne and Wear**, NE1 2PW, **ENGLAND**.
(T) 0191 2211711 (F) 0191 2211711.
Contact/s
Owner: Mr A Hitchins
Profile Transport/Horse Boxes. Ref: YH00013

A & M MARKETING

A & M Marketing, 34 Port St, Evesham, **Worcestershire**, WR11 6AW, **ENGLAND**.
(T) 01386 48974 (F) 01386 443245.
Profile Supplies. Ref: YH00014

A & M SADDLERY

A & M Saddlery, 2a Wharf Rd, Ellesmere, **Shropshire**, SY12 0EL, **ENGLAND**.
(T) 01691 622264 (F) 01691 622264.
Contact/s
Owner: Mrs N Clay Ref: YH00015

A & M TURNPIKE FORGE

A & M Turnpike Forge, Clifton Hampden, Abingdon, **Oxfordshire**, OX14 3DE, **ENGLAND**.
(T) 01865 407755 (F) 01865 407557.
Contact/s
Owner: Mr R Hanson
Profile Blacksmith. Ref: YH00016

A A SHERWOOD

A A Sherwood (Feeds), 23 The Maples, Cirencester, **Gloucestershire**, GL7 1TQ, **ENGLAND**.
(T) 01285 651943.
Profile Supplies. Ref: YH00017

A B B A S STUD

A B B A S Stud, Gosford Farm, Ottery St Mary, **Devon**, EX11 1LX, **ENGLAND**.
(T) 01404 814998.
Profile Breeder. Ref: YH00018

A B R FOODS

A B R Foods Ltd, Swallow Rd, Weldon Ind Est, Corby, **Northamptonshire**, NN17 5JX, **ENGLAND**.
(T) 01536 265291 (F) 01536 263873.
Contact/s
National Account Manager: Rod Debenham
Profile Medical Support. Ref: YH00019

A C BRIDDLECOMBE & SONS

A C Briddlecombe & Sons, Lower Hse Farm, Upleadon, Newent, **Gloucestershire**, GL18 1HL, **ENGLAND**.
(T) 01452 790365.
Contact/s
Owner: Mr A Biddlecombe
Profile Breeder. Ref: YH00020

A C BURN

A C Burn Ltd, High Gate Works, Tweed Mouth, Berwick-upon-Tweed, **Northumberland**, TD15 2AP, **ENGLAND**.
(T) 01289 307245 (F) 01289 305727
(E) acburn@btclick.com.
Contact/s
General Manager: Mr D Lauder
Profile Riding Wear Retailer, Supplies.
No.Staff: 15 Yr. Est: 1907
Opening Times
Sp: Open Mon - Sat 08:30. Closed Mon - Fri 17:00, Sat 12:00.
Su: Open Mon - Sat 08:30. Closed Mon - Fri 17:00, Sat 12:00.
Au: Open Mon - Sat 08:30. Closed Mon - Fri 17:00, Sat 12:00.
Wn: Open Mon - Sat 08:30. Closed Mon - Fri 17:00, Sat 12:00.
Closed Sundays Ref: YH00021

A C BURN

A C Burn Ltd, Mountahooly, Jedburgh, **Scottish Borders**, TD8 6TJ, **SCOTLAND**.
(T) 01835 850250 (F) 01835 850250.
Contact/s
General Manager: Mr D Lauder
Profile Riding Wear Retailer, Supplies.
No.Staff: 15 Yr. Est: 1907
Opening Times
Sp: Open Mon - Sat 08:30. Closed Mon - Fri 17:30, Sat 12:00.
Su: Open Mon - Sat 08:30. Closed Mon - Fri 17:30, Sat 12:00.
Au: Open Mon - Sat 08:30. Closed Mon - Fri 17:30, Sat 12:00.
Wn: Open Mon - Sat 08:30. Closed Mon - Fri 17:30, Sat 12:00.
Closed Sundays Ref: YH00022

A C DAWSON & SONS

A C Dawson & Sons, Little Orchard, Leechpond Hill, Lower Beeding, Horsham, **Sussex (West)**, RH13 6NR, **ENGLAND**.
(T) 01403 891314.
Contact/s
Owner: Mr A Dawson
Profile Transport/Horse Boxes. Ref: YH00023

A C F ANIMAL BEDDING

A C F Animal Bedding, Westcroft Farm, Vann Rd, Fernhurst, Haslemere, **Surrey**, GU27 3NJ, **ENGLAND**.
(T) 01428 652863.
Contact/s
Partner: Mr A Lawes
Profile Supplies. Yr. Est: 1999 C.Size: 1997 Acres
Opening Times
Sp: Open 08:00. Closed 18:00.
Su: Open 08:00. Closed 18:00.
Au: Open 08:00. Closed 18:00.
Wn: Open 08:00. Closed 18:00. Ref: YH00024

A C G S EQUESTRIAN

A C G S Equestrian, Prys-lor-Werth Ganol, Llangristiolus, Bodorgan, **Isle of Anglesey**, LL62 5EG, **WALES**.
(T) 01407 840722.
Contact/s
Owner: Mr H Leonard
Profile Saddlery Retailer. Ref: YH00025

A C TRAILERS

A C Trailers, Smithy Cottage, Newcastle Rd, Hough, Crewe, **Cheshire**, CW2 5JS, **ENGLAND**.
(T) 01270 842471.
Contact/s
Manager: Mr A Weaver
Profile Transport/Horse Boxes. Ref: YH00026

A D L TACK & SADDLERY

A D L Tack Repairs, 164 Forest Rd, London, **London (Greater)**, E11 1LF, **ENGLAND**.
(T) 020 85398100 (F) 020 85398100
(E) adltack@ukgateway.net
Affiliated Bodies BETA.
Contact/s
Partner: Ms D Liddle
Profile Saddlery Retailer.
Workshop is based on site. Ref: YH00027

A D MARKETING CONSULTANTS

A D Marketing Consultants, Barlochan Hse, Twynholm, Kirkcudbright, **Dumfries and Galloway**, DG6 4NP, **SCOTLAND**.
(T) 01557 860259. Ref: YH00028

A E C ENGINEERING

A E C Engineering, Parcel Trce, Derby, **Derbyshire**, DE1 1LY, **ENGLAND**.
(T) 01332 346646 (F) 01332 346646.
Contact/s
Owner: Mr D Holmes
Profile Blacksmith. Ref: YH00029

A E LOCKWOOD & SON

A E Lockwood & Son, Forge Cottage, Church Hill, Midhurst, **Sussex (West)**, GU29 9NX, **ENGLAND**.
(T) 01730 813208.
Contact/s
Owner: Mr A Lockwood
Profile Farrier. Ref: YH00030

A E S CONSULTANTS

A E S Consultants, Mews 4 Earlsleigh, Groby Rd, Altrincham, **Cheshire**, WA1 4BQ, **ENGLAND**.
(T) 0161 9283718 (F) 0161 9295565. Ref: YH00031

A FRENCH & SONS

A French & Sons (Mills), Gusto Mills, Huntingdon Rd, Cambridge, **Cambridgeshire**, CB3 0DL, **ENGLAND**.
(T) 01223 276638.
Contact/s
Manager: Mr C Barker

Profile Saddlery Retailer. **Ref: YH00032**

A GRIFFITHS & SON

A Griffiths & Son, Efail Shingrig, Trelewis, Treharris, **Glamorgan (Vale of)**, CF46 6DP, **WALES**.
(T) 01443 411080.
Contact/s
Owner: Mr A Griffiths
Profile Farrier. **Ref: YH00033**

A H B INSURANCE

Anglo Hibernian Bloodstock Insurance, Richmond Hse, 127 High St, Newmarket, **Suffolk**, CB8 9AE, **ENGLAND**.
(T) 01638 669930 **(F)** 01638 669940
(E) anglo.hibernian@dial.pipex.com.
Contact/s
Admin: Miss C Froggert
Profile Bloodstock Insurance Agents. **Ref: YH00034**

A H P TRAILERS

A H P Trailers Ltd, Heath Mill Rd, Wombourne, Wolverhampton, **Midlands (West)**, WV5 8AP, **ENGLAND**.
(T) 01902 895281 **(F)** 01902 894577.
Profile Transport/Horse Boxes. **Ref: YH00035**

A HILLSDON & SON

A Hillsdon & Son, The Forge, Wethered Rd, Marlow, **Buckinghamshire**, SL7 3AH, **ENGLAND**.
(T) 01628 483076.
Contact/s
Owner: Mr A Hillson
Profile Blacksmith. **Ref: YH00036**

A J B SPENCE & SON

A J B Spence & Son, Main St, Reston, Eyemouth, **Scottish Borders**, TD14 5JU, **SCOTLAND**.
(T) 01890 761212.
Contact/s
Owner: Mr G Spencer
Profile Supplies. **Ref: YH00037**

A J C LAMONT

A J C Lamont (Trailers) Ltd, 15 Quilly Rd, Coleraine, **County Londonderry**, BT51 3PE, **NORTHERN IRELAND**.
(T) 028 70343563 **(F)** 028 70320576.
Contact/s
Owner: Mr A Lamont
Profile Transport/Horse Boxes. **Ref: YH00038**

A J GRANT & SONS

A J Grant & Sons, 40A Seafield Rd, Inverness, **Highlands**, IV1 1SG, **SCOTLAND**.
(T) 01463 233751 **(F)** 01463 711212.
Contact/s
Owner: Mr I Grant
Profile Transport/Horse Boxes. **Ref: YH00039**

A J PLEDGER

A J Pledger & Co Ltd, West St, Stamford, **Lincolnshire**, PE9 2PN, **ENGLAND**.
(T) 01780 762245 **(F)** 01780 754531
(E) sales@pledger.co.uk.
Contact/s
Owner: Mr S Dale
Profile Farrier. **Yr. Est:** 2000
Opening Times
Sp: Open Mon - Fri 08:00. Closed Mon - Fri 17:00.
Su: Open Mon - Fri 08:00. Closed Mon - Fri 17:00.
Au: Open Mon - Fri 08:00. Closed Mon - Fri 17:00.
Wn: Open Mon - Fri 08:00. Closed Mon - Fri 17:00.
Ref: YH00040

A J S FARRIERY

A J S Farriery, 131 Brighton Rd, Redhill, **Surrey**, RH1 6PS, **ENGLAND**.
(T) 01737 760630.
Contact/s
Owner: Mr A Starling
Profile Farrier. **Ref: YH00041**

A J STABLES

A J Stables, Adstone, Towcester, **Northamptonshire**, NN12 8DS, **ENGLAND**.
(T) 01327 860893.
Contact/s
Owner: Mr C Marriott
Profile Riding School, Stable/Livery. **Ref: YH00042**

A J STOKES & SONS

A J Stokes & Sons, Green Rd, Codford, Warminster, **Wiltshire**, BA12 0NW, **ENGLAND**.
(T) 01985 850248.
Contact/s
Owner: Mr A Stokes
Profile Transport/Horse Boxes. **Ref: YH00043**

A K FEEDS

A K Feeds, 24 Birchbrook Ind Pk, Lynn Lane, Shenstone, **Staffordshire**, WS14 0DJ, **ENGLAND**.
(T) 01543 481521.
Contact/s
Manager: Mr S Levoi
Profile Supplies. **Ref: YH00044**

A KERR HAULAGE

A Kerr Haulage, Fagra Farm, Dundrennan, Kirkcudbright, **Dumfries and Galloway**, DG6 4QT, **SCOTLAND**.
(T) 01557 500232.
Profile Transport/Horse Boxes. **Ref: YH00045**

A L FRY & SON

A L Fry & Son, The Forge, High St, East Meon, Petersfield, **Hampshire**, GU32 1QD, **ENGLAND**.
(T) 01730 823527.
Contact/s
Partner: Mr D Mastchin
Profile Blacksmith. **Ref: YH00046**

A L G TRAILER HIRE

A L G Trailer Hire, Wincham Lane, Wincham, Northwich, **Cheshire**, CW9 6DE, **ENGLAND**.
(T) 01606 44200 **(F)** 01606 330642.
Contact/s
Partner: Mr A Hatton
Profile Transport/Horse Boxes. **Ref: YH00047**

A M C S

A M C S (UK) Ltd, 15 Brooksdale Cl, Kettering, **Northamptonshire**, NN16 9BJ, **ENGLAND**.
(T) 01536 512117 **(F)** 01536 512117.
Contact/s
Owner: Mr A Walker
Profile Blacksmith. **Ref: YH00048**

A M CARR & SONS

A M Carr & Sons, Main St, Longford, **County Longford**, **IRELAND**.
(T) 043 47930.
Profile Supplies. **Ref: YH00049**

A M FABRICATIONS

A M Fabrications, Sherwood Ind Est, Bonnyrigg, **Lothian (Mid)**, EH19 3LW, **SCOTLAND**.
(T) 0131 6634609 **(F)** 0131 6636121.
Contact/s
Owner: Mr A McLaughlin
Profile Blacksmith. **Ref: YH00050**

A M S

A M S Ltd, 29 Main St, Barton In The Beans, Nuneaton, **Warwickshire**, CV13 0DJ, **ENGLAND**.
(T) 01455 291226.
Profile Transport/Horse Boxes. **Ref: YH00051**

A MEALOR & SONS

A Mealor & Sons, Wash Hall Farm, Hermitage Rd, Saughall, Chester, **Cheshire**, CH1 6AE, **ENGLAND**.
(T) 01244 880229.
Contact/s
Owner: Mr A Mealor
Profile Breeder. **Ref: YH00052**

A N A AST

A N A Associates- Events Consultants, Gautby Hse, Girton, Newark, **Nottinghamshire**, NG23 7JA, **ENGLAND**.
(T) 01522 778251 **(F)** 01522 778251.
Contact/s
Partner: Mr N Armitage
Profile Club/Association. **Ref: YH00053**

A NICHOLS

A Nichols (Cow Mills) Ltd, Cow Mills, Chipping Sodbury, **Gloucestershire (South)**, BS37 4AD, **ENGLAND**.
(T) 01454 313788.
Profile Supplies. **Ref: YH00054**

A P E S ROCKING HORSES

A P E S Rocking Horses, Ty Gwyn, Llannefydd, Denbigh, **Denbighshire**, LL16 5HB, **WALES**.
(T) 01745 540365 **(F)** 01765 540365
(E) macphersons@apesrockinghorses.co.uk
Affiliated Bodies BTG.
Contact/s
Partner: Mr S Macpherson **(Q)** Dip AD(Painting), Dip AD(Sculpture)
Profile Rocking Horses.
Rocking Horse restoration available. **No.Staff:** 2
Yr. Est: 1978 **C.Size:** 1 Acres **Ref: YH00055**

A P M COMMERCIALS

A P M Commercials Ltd, A P M Hse, Manby Rd, Immingham, **Lincolnshire (North East)**, DN40 2LL, **ENGLAND**.
(T) 01469 574862 **(F)** 01469 574864.
Contact/s
General Manager: Mr S Gilboy
Profile Transport/Horse Boxes. **Ref: YH00056**

A RUDD & SON

A Rudd & Son, 97 Leadwell Lane, Rothwell, Leeds, **Yorkshire (West)**, LS26 0SR, **ENGLAND**.
(T) 0113 2824061.
Contact/s
Owner: Mr A Rudd
Profile Transport/Horse Boxes. **Ref: YH00057**

A S JOHNSON & SON

A S Johnson & Son Ltd, London Lode Farm, Lode Hall, Three Holes, Wisbech, **Cambridgeshire**, PE14 9JW, **ENGLAND**.
(T) 01354 638476.
Profile Breeder. **Ref: YH00058**

A T E GROUP

A T E Group Ltd, Stafford Rd, Wolverhampton, **Midlands (West)**, WV10 7ER, **ENGLAND**.
(T) 01902 784040.
Profile Transport/Horse Boxes. **Ref: YH00059**

A T F

A T F Ltd, Mossley Farm, Height Lane, Chipping, Preston, **Lancashire**, PR3 2NU, **ENGLAND**.
(T) 01995 61292 **(F)** 01995 61292
(E) atfltd@aol.com. **Ref: YH00060**

A T HOGG

A T Hogg (Fife) Ltd, Station Rd, Cupar, **Fife**, KY15 5HX, **SCOTLAND**.
(T) 01337 860202 **(F)** 01337 860547.
Profile Supplies. **Ref: YH00061**

A T VEATER & SONS

A T Veater & Sons, Saddlery & Sports Specialists, Station Rd, Clifton, Bristol, **Bristol**, BS39 5RD, **ENGLAND**.
(T) 01761 452460.
Profile Saddlery Retailer. **Ref: YH00062**

A TO B

A To B, Grantley, School Rd, Barkham, Wokingham, **Berkshire**, RG41 4TR, **ENGLAND**.
(T) 0118 9760466.
Contact/s
Partner: Mr M Fry
Profile Transport/Horse Boxes. **Ref: YH00063**

A V BAKER & SONS

A V Baker & Sons, Church Farm, Old Park Lane, Bosham, Chichester, **Sussex (West)**, PO18 8EX, **ENGLAND**.
(T) 01243 572521 **(F)** 01243 572605.
Contact/s
Owner: Mr A Baker **Ref: YH00064**

A V S

A V S, Farmcote, Nettlesworth Lane Rd, Old Heathfield, **Sussex (East)**, TN21 9AP, **ENGLAND**.
(T) 01435 863683 **(F)** 01435 863683.
Contact/s
Owner: Mr T Morris
Profile Club/Association. **Ref: YH00065**

A W HELME & PARTNER

A W Helme & Partner, 13-17 Freckleton St, Kirkham, Preston, **Lancashire**, PR4 2SP, **ENGLAND**.
(T) 01772 682677 **(F)** 01772 683972.
Profile Medical Support. **Ref: YH00066**

A W MIDGLEY & SON

A W Midgley & Son Ltd, 13 Cheddar Business Pk, Wedmore, Cheddar, **Somerset**, BS27 3EB, **ENGLAND**.
(T) 01934 741741 **(F)** 01934 741555
(E) awmidgley@aol.com
(W) www.leather-skins-saddlery.co.uk.
Profile Saddlery Retailer. **Ref: YH00067**

A W RHOADES SADDLERY

A W Rhoades Saddlery and Animal Feeds, Waterloo St, Market Rasen, **Lincolnshire**, LN8 3EP, **ENGLAND**.
(T) 01673 842219 **(F)** 01673 842219
(W) www.fonaby.com.
Contact/s
General Manager: Ms C Taylor
Profile Riding Wear Retailer, Saddlery Retailer, Supplies. **No.Staff:** 5 **Yr. Est:** 2001
Opening Times
Sp: Open 09:00. Closed 16:30.
Su: Open 09:00. Closed 16:30.

Au: Open 09:00. Closed 16:30.
Wn: Open 09:00. Closed 16:30. **Ref: YH00068**

AAGUS, D

Mr D Aagus, 338 Larkshall Rd,, Chingford, **London (Greater)**, E4 9JB, **ENGLAND**.
(T) 020 85275286.
Profile Breeder. **Ref: YH00069**

AAPS

AAPS Ltd, Earls Barton Rd, Great Doddington, Wellingborough, **Northamptonshire**, NN29 7TA, **ENGLAND**.
(T) 01933 223262 **(F)** 01933 227490.
Profile Transport/Horse Boxes. **Ref: YH00070**

AASEN, MORTEN

Morten Aasen, Brookhurst Farm Hse, Guildford Rd, Broadbridge Heath, Horsham, **Sussex (West)**, RH12 3PN, **ENGLAND**.
(T) 01403 270137 **(F)** 01403 218240.
Contact/s
Owner: Mr M Aasen
Profile Breeder. **Ref: YH00071**

AB KETTLEBY STUD

Ab Kettleby Stud, The Manor Hse, Ab Kettleby, Melton Mowbray, **Leicestershire**, LE16 5AQ, **ENGLAND**.
(T) 01664 822258 **(F)** 01664 823148.
Contact/s
Owner: Mr J Burridge
Profile Breeder. **Ref: YH00072**

ABBAS MARQUEE HIRE

Abbas Marquee Hire, Common Farmhouse, Charlton Musgrove, Wincanton, **Somerset**, BA9 8HN, **ENGLAND**.
(T) 01963 33300 **(F)** 01963 31914
(E) abbasmarq@aol.com.
Contact/s
Owner: Mr R Hayward
Profile Supplies. **Ref: YH00073**

ABBERVILLE & MEADOW CT STUD

Abberville & Meadow Court Stud, Maddenstown, The Curragh, **County Kildare**, **IRELAND**.
(T) 045 521366 **(F)** 045 521351
(E) meadow@iol.ie.
Contact/s
Key Contact: Ms E Mulhern
Profile Breeder. Yr. Est: 1976 **Ref: YH00074**

ABBEY ACRE

Abbey Acre Riding Centre, Abbey Cottage, Kilkenny, West Glasson, Westmeath, **County Westmeath**, **IRELAND**.
(T) 09 0285289.
Contact/s
Owner: Mary Malvers
Profile Riding School. **Ref: YH00075**

ABBEY EQUINE CTRE

Abbey Equine Centre (Crickhowell), Brecon Hse, Elvicta Business Pk, Crickhowell, **Powys**, NP8 1DN, **WALES**.
(T) 01873 810425.
Contact/s
Vet: Mr R Fisher
Profile Medical Support. **Ref: YH00076**

ABBEY GREEN VETNRY GRP

Abbey Green Veterinary Group (Winchcombe), Abbey Cottage, Abbey Trce, Winchcombe, Cheltenham, **Gloucestershire**, GL54 5LW, **ENGLAND**.
(T) 01242 602235 **(F)** 01242 604094.
Contact/s
Partner: Mr I Maisey
Profile Medical Support. **Ref: YH00077**

ABBEY GREEN VETNRY GRP

Abbey Green Veterinary Group (Broadway), Church Cl, Broadway, **Worcestershire**, WR12 7AH, **ENGLAND**.
(T) 01386 852421.
Contact/s
Admin: Ms L Bearcroft
Profile Medical Support. **Ref: YH00078**

ABBEY HAY & STRAW

Abbey Hay & Straw, Pick Hill, Waltham Abbey, **Essex**, EN9 3LE, **ENGLAND**.
(T) 01992 701031.
Contact/s
Partner: Mr K Bince **Ref: YH00079**

ABBEY HSE VETNRY CLINIC

Abbey House Veterinary Clinic, Unit 7 Commercial St, Morley, Leeds, **Yorkshire (West)**, LS27 8AG, **ENGLAND**.
(T) 0113 2525818.
Contact/s
Practice Manager: Mr P Speck
Profile Medical Support. **Ref: YH00080**

ABBEY HSE VETNRY CLINIC

Abbey House Veterinary Clinic (Cleckheaton), 1 Cross Church St, Cleckheaton, **Yorkshire (West)**, BD19 3RP, **ENGLAND**.
(T) 01274 876686.
Contact/s
Practice Manager: Mr P Speck
Profile Medical Support. **Ref: YH00081**

ABBEY HSE VETNRY CLINIC

Abbey House Veterinary Clinic (Rothwell), 1 Oulton Lane, Rothwell, Leeds, **Yorkshire (West)**, LS26 0EA, **ENGLAND**.
(T) 0113 2827117.
Contact/s
Practice Manager: Mr P Speck
Profile Medical Support. **Ref: YH00082**

ABBEY PHOTO

Abbey Photo, Pop Hall Farm, Bay Horse Lane, Catforth, Preston, **Lancashire**, PR4 0HN, **ENGLAND**.
(T) 01772 690447 **(F)** 01772 690447. **Ref: YH00083**

ABBEY RACING

Abbey Racing, 21 Blackmill St, Kilkenny, **County Kilkenny**, **IRELAND**.
(T) 056 64444.
Profile Supplies. **Ref: YH00084**

ABBEY SADDLERY & CRAFTS

Abbey Saddlery & Crafts, Haig Rd, Parkgate Ind Est, Knutsford, **Cheshire**, WA16 8DX, **ENGLAND**.
(T) 01565 650343
(E) sales@abbeysaddlery.co.uk.
Contact/s
Partner: Mr R Brown
Profile Supplies. Saddlery Material Wholesalers.
Ref: YH00085

ABBEY TRAILERS

Abbey Trailers Ltd, 199 Abbey St, Derby, **Derbyshire**, DE22 3ST, **ENGLAND**.
(T) 01332 348630 **(F)** 01332 348630.
Contact/s
Owner: Mrs J Wilson
Profile Transport/Horse Boxes. **Ref: YH00086**

ABBEY VET GRP

Abbey Vet Group (Greenoch), Greenock Surgery, 19A Union St, Greenock, **Inverclyde**, PA16 8DD, **SCOTLAND**.
(T) 01475 721155 **(F)** 01475 787511.
Contact/s
Partner: Mr N McIntosh
Profile Medical Support. **Ref: YH00087**

ABBEY VET GRP

Abbey Vet Group (Paisley), 71 Canal St, Paisley, **Renfrewshire**, PA1 2NP, **SCOTLAND**.
(T) 0141 8874111 **(F)** 0141 8870813.
Contact/s
Partner: Mr N McIntosh **(Q)** MRCVS
Profile Medical Support. **Ref: YH00088**

ABBEY VETNRY CTRE

Abbey Veterinary Centre (A'genny), The Surgery, St Arvans Chambers, Hereford Rd, Abergavenny, **Monmouthshire**, NP7 5RP, **WALES**.
(T) 01873 854308.
Contact/s
Partner: Mr R Fisher
Profile Medical Support. **Ref: YH00089**

ABBEY VETNRY CTRE

Abbey Veterinary Centre, 16 Holywell St, Abbey Foregate, Shrewsbury, **Shropshire**, SY2 5DB, **ENGLAND**.
(T) 01743 232713 **(F)** 01743 243240.
Contact/s
Owner: Mr W Adams
Profile Medical Support. **Ref: YH00090**

ABBEY VETNRY GRP

Abbey Veterinary Group, 161 Chaddesden Lane, Chaddesden, Derby, **Derbyshire**, DE21 6LJ, **ENGLAND**.
(T) 01332 661554.
Profile Medical Support. **Ref: YH00091**

ABBEYCROFT VETNRY CTRE

Abbeycroft Veterinary Centre, 38 Station Rd, Northwich, **Cheshire**, CW9 5RA, **ENGLAND**.
(T) 01606 40332 **(F)** 01606 40523.
Profile Medical Support. **Ref: YH00092**

ABBEYFIELD EQUESTRIAN FARM

Abbeyfield Equestrian Farm Centre, Abbeyfield Equestrian Farm Ctre, Clane, **County Kildare**, **IRELAND**.
(T) 045 868188 **(F)** 045 868188
(E) abbeyfield@kildarehorse.ie.
Contact/s
Key Contact: Mr C O'Neill
Profile Equestrian Centre.
The centre has a range of facilities, including clay pigeon shooting and archery. C.Size: 200 Acres
Ref: YH00093

ABBEYFIELD SHETLAND STUD

Abbeyfield Shetland Stud, Oak Tree Cottage, Main Rd, Milford, **Staffordshire**, ST17 0UL, **ENGLAND**.
(T) 01785 661903
Affiliated Bodies SPSBS.
Contact/s
Owner: Mrs D Tindale
Profile Breeder. No.Staff: 2 Yr. Est: 1978
C.Size: 50 Acres
Opening Times
Telephone for an appointment **Ref: YH00094**

ABBEYFIELDS

Abbeyfields, 139 Charville Lane, Hayes, **London (Greater)**, UB4 8PB, **ENGLAND**.
(T) 020 88413362 **(F)** 020 88413362.
Contact/s
Owner: Mrs S Abbott
Profile Riding School.
Opening Times
Sp: Open Mon - Thurs, Sat, Sun 10:00. Closed Mon - Thurs 20:00, Sat, Sun 16:00.
Su: Open Mon - Thurs, Sat, Sun 10:00. Closed Mon - Thurs 20:00, Sat, Sun 16:00.
Au: Open Mon - Thurs, Sat, Sun 10:00. Closed Mon - Thurs 20:00, Sat, Sun 16:00.
Wn: Open Mon - Thurs, Sat, Sun 10:00. Closed Mon - Thurs 20:00, Sat, Sun 16:00. **Ref: YH00095**

ABBEYFIELDS VETNRY CTRE

Abbeyfields Veterinary Centre, 17 High St, Tadcaster, **Yorkshire (North)**, LS24 9AP, **ENGLAND**.
(T) 01937 832815.
Profile Medical Support. **Ref: YH00096**

ABBEYGLEN

Abbeyglen Riding Stables, Lyre Rd, Milltown, **County Kerry**, **IRELAND**.
(T) 066 9767714
Affiliated Bodies ABRS.
Contact/s
Partner: Anna Griffen
Profile Riding School, Stable/Livery.
Telephone for details on livery services.
Opening Times
Sp: Open Mon - Sun 09:30. Closed Mon - Sun 22:00.
Su: Open Mon - Sun 09:30. Closed Mon - Sun 22:00.
Au: Open Tues - Sun 15:00. Closed Tues - Sun 22:00.
Wn: Open Tues - Sun 15:00. Closed Tues - Sun 22:00.
Closed Mondays in Autumn & Winter. Daytime lessons in Autumn & Winter can be arranged.
Ref: YH00097

ABBISS, R I

R I Abbiss, 21 Blundies Lane, Enville, Stourbridge, **Midlands (West)**, DY7 5HU, **ENGLAND**.
(T) 01384 873725.
Contact/s
Owner: Mr R Abbiss
Profile Farrier. **Ref: YH00098**

ABBISS, RICHARD P

Richard P Abbiss DWCF, 33 Foster St, Kinver, **Staffordshire**, DY7 6EB, **ENGLAND**.
(T) 01971 277380.
Profile Farrier. **Ref: YH00099**

ABBOTSWOOD SHOW JUMPS

Abbotswood Show Jumps, High Ash Farm, Abbots Bromley, Rugeley, **Staffordshire**, WS15 3DF, **ENGLAND**.
(T) 01283 840267 **(F)** 01283 840740
(M) 07860 252473.
Profile Supplies. **Ref: YH00100**

ABBOTSWOOD VETNRY CTRE

Abbotswood Veterinary Centre, 18 Abbotswood, Yate, **Gloucestershire**, BS37 4NG, **ENGLAND**.
(T) 01454 322449.

Contact/s
Vet: Mr P Murphy
Profile Medical Support. Ref: YH00101

ABBOTT

Abbott & Co (Wessex) Ltd, Abberley Hse(Head Office), Park St, Cirencester, **Gloucestershire**, GL7 2BX, **ENGLAND**.
(T) 01285 653738 (F) 01285 885134
(W) www.abbottwessex.co.uk.
Contact/s
Agent: Mr A Speight (T) 01472 841000
Profile Supplies. Hay and Straw Merchants. Agents are available to cover the whole country.
No.Staff: 3 Yr. Est: 1939 Ref: YH00102

ABBOTT

Abbott & Co (Wessex) Ltd (Hants), The Old Station, Farringdon, Alton, **Hampshire**, GU34 3DP, **ENGLAND**.
(T) 01420 588535.
Contact/s
Owner: Mr D Crockford
Profile Supplies. Ref: YH00103

ABBOTT

Abbott & Co (Wessex) Ltd, Caplor Farm, Fownhope, Hereford, **Herefordshire**, HR1 4PT, **ENGLAND**.
(T) 01432 860990 (F) 01432 860991.
Contact/s
Owner: Mr G Williams
Profile Supplies. Ref: YH00104

ABBOTT

Abbott & Co (Wessex) Ltd, Pontfaen, Newchurch, Kington, **Herefordshire**, HR5 3QG, **ENGLAND**.
(T) 01544 370350.
Contact/s
Manager: Mr M Thomas
Profile Supplies. Ref: YH00105

ABBOTT

Abbott & Co (Wessex) Ltd, Tumplands, Dingestow, Monmouth, **Monmouthshire**, NP25 4DX, **WALES**.
(T) 01600 740350.
Profile Supplies. Ref: YH00106

ABBOTT

Abbott & Co (Wessex) Ltd, Brick Kiln Farm, Kerdiston, Norwich, **Norfolk**, NR10 4RR, **ENGLAND**.
(T) 01603 870903. Ref: YH00107

ABBOTT

Abbott & Co (Wessex) Ltd (Oxon), Firs Farm, Over Norton, Chipping Norton, **Oxfordshire**, OX7 5PT, **ENGLAND**.
(T) 01608 643675 (F) 01608 643912
(M) 07860 273624.
Profile Supplies. Ref: YH00108

ABBOTT

Abbott & Co (Wessex) Ltd, Marland, Winthill, Banwell, **Somerset (North)**, BS29 6NG, **ENGLAND**.
(T) 01934 822177.
Profile Supplies. Ref: YH00109

ABBOTT

Abbott & Co (Wessex) Ltd, Fen Pl Farm, East St, Turners Hill, Crawley, **Sussex (West)**, RH10 4QA, **ENGLAND**.
(T) 01342 717238 (F) 01342 717455.
Contact/s
Owner: Mr J Givons
Profile Supplies. Ref: YH00110

ABBOTT

Abbott & Co (Wessex) Ltd, Bucklands Farm, Brantridge Lane, Balcombe, Haywards Heath, **Sussex (West)**, RH17 6JP, **ENGLAND**.
(T) 01444 400822 (F) 01444 400922.
Profile Supplies. Ref: YH00111

ABBOTT DRAPER & FRASER

Abbott Draper & Fraser, The Veterinary Surgery, Harleigh Rd, Bodmin, **Cornwall**, PL31 1AQ, **ENGLAND**.
(T) 01208 72323 (F) 01208 78735.
Profile Medical Support. Ref: YH00112

ABBOTT DRAPER & FRASER

Abbott Draper & Fraser, 4 Park Rd, Wadebridge, **Cornwall**, PL27 7EA, **ENGLAND**.
(T) 01208 812530.
Profile Medical Support. Ref: YH00113

ABBOTT STREET FORGE

Abbott Street Forge, The Old Forge, Abbott St, Pamphill, Wimborne, **Dorset**, BH21 4EF, **ENGLAND**.
(T) 01202 888573.
Contact/s
Owner: Mr G Stuart
Profile Blacksmith. Ref: YH00114

ABBOTTS MORTON LIVERY YARD

Abbotts Morton Livery Yard, Morton Wood Lane, Abbots Morton, Worcester, **Worcestershire**, WR7 4LU, **ENGLAND**.
(T) 01386 793183.
Contact/s
Owner: Ms R Harris
Profile Stable/Livery. Ref: YH00115

ABCIS

American Bashkir Curly International Society, Shenval, Glenlivet, Ballindalloch, **Moray**, AB37 9DP, **SCOTLAND**.
(T) 01807 590212 (F) 01807 590212
Affiliated Bodies ABCR.
Contact/s
General Manager: Ms L Dingwall
(E) shenval@glenlivet1.freeserve.co.uk
Profile Club/Association. Breed Register.
No.Staff: 3 Yr. Est: 2001 Ref: YH00116

ABEL ENGINEERING

Abel Engineering, 6 Grundieswell Rd, Edinburgh, **Edinburgh (City of)**, EH17 8UB, **SCOTLAND**.
(T) 0131 6581336 (F) 0131 6542468.
Profile Blacksmith. Ref: YH00117

ABEL ENGINEERING

Abel Engineering, Maulsford Ave, Danderhall, Dalkeith, **Lothian (Mid)**, EH22 1PJ, **SCOTLAND**.
(T) 0131 6541336 (F) 0131 6542468.
Contact/s
Owner: Mr D Glasgow
Profile Blacksmith. Ref: YH00118

ABERCONWY EQUESTRIAN CTRE

Aberconwy Equestrian Centre, Wern Bach Farm, Llangwstenin, Llandudno Junction, **Conwy**, LL31 9JF, **WALES**.
(T) 01492 544362.
Profile Riding School, Stable/Livery. Ref: YH00119

ABERCONWY STUD

Aberconwy Stud, Tyn-Y-Coed Farm, Glan-Conwy, Colwyn Bay, **Conwy**, LL28 5TN, **WALES**.
(T) 01492 580689.
Profile Breeder. Ref: YH00120

ABERDEEN & NORTHERN MARTS

Aberdeen & Northern Marts, Thainstone Agricultural Ctre, Inverurie, **Aberdeenshire**, AB51 9XZ, **SCOTLAND**.
(T) 01467 623700.
Contact/s
Office Manager: Mr I Finley
Profile Horse Sales Agency. Auctioneers. Ref: YH00121

ABERDEEN CLGE

Aberdeen College, Clinterty Ctre, Kinellar, Aberdeen, **Aberdeen (City of)**, AB21 0TN, **SCOTLAND**.
(T) 01224 612000 (F) 01224 612750.
Profile Equestrian Centre. Ref: YH00122

ABERDEEN DISTRICT COUNCIL

Aberdeen District Council, Arts & Recreation Division, St Nicholas Hse, Broad St, Aberdeen, **Aberdeen (City of)**, AB10 1XJ, **SCOTLAND**.
(T) 01224 875879
(W) www.aberdeenshire.gov.uk.
Contact/s
Manager: Mr G Lennox
Profile Club/Association. Ref: YH00123

ABERDEEN RARE BREEDS PK

Aberdeen Rare Breeds Park, St Nicholas Hse, Aberdeen, **Aberdeen (City of)**, **SCOTLAND**.
(T) 01224 276276.
Profile Breeder. Ref: YH00124

ABERDEEN TRAILERS

Aberdeen Trailers, Crichney Lade Croft, Fyvie, Turriff, **Aberdeenshire**, AB53 8QY, **SCOTLAND**.
(T) 01651 891002 (F) 01651 891538.
Contact/s
Owner: Mr B Miazek
Profile Transport/Horse Boxes. Ref: YH00125

ABERGWYNANT FARM

Abergwynant Farm & Trekking Centre, Penmaenpool, Dolgellau, **Gwynedd**, LL40 1YF, **WALES**.
(T) 01341 422377.
Profile Riding School. Ref: YH00126

ABERLOUR RIDING/TREKKING CTRE

Aberlour Riding & Trekking Centre, Aberlour Hse, Aberlour, **Moray**, AB38 9LJ, **SCOTLAND**.
(T) 01340 871467.
Profile Riding School. Ref: YH00127

ABERQUEST

Aberquest, South Oldmoss Croft, Fyvie, Turriff, **Aberdeenshire**, AB53 8NA, **SCOTLAND**.
(T) 01651 806615.
Contact/s
Partner: Mr D Lavery
Profile Horse/Rider Accom. Ref: YH00128

ABERSOCH MARCHROS STUD

Abersoch Marchros Stud, Tyddyn Talgoch Uchaf, Bwlchtocyn, Abersoch, **Gwynedd**, LL53 7BT, **WALES**.
(T) 01758 712285 (F) 01758 712285
(E) helen.abersoch@virgin.net
(W) www.abersochholidays.co.uk/equestrian.html.
Contact/s
Owner: Miss H Mills
Profile Breeder, Horse/Rider Accom, Stable/Livery. Full and DIY livery available. Grazing - temporary or long term No.Staff: 3 Yr. Est: 1983
C.Size: 30 Acres
Opening Times
Sp: Open Mon - Sun 06:00. Closed Mon - Sun 21:00.
Su: Open Mon - Sun 06:00. Closed Mon - Sun 21:00.
Au: Open Mon - Sun 06:00. Closed Mon - Sun 21:00.
Wn: Open Mon - Sun 06:00. Closed Mon - Sun 21:00. Ref: YH00129

ABERSOCH RIDING/TREKKING CTRE

Abersoch Riding & Trekking Centre, Golf Rd, Maes Gwydryn, Abersoch, Pwllheli, **Gwynedd**, LL53 7ED, **WALES**.
(T) 01758 712767.
Contact/s
Owner: Mrs C Evans
Profile Equestrian Centre. Ref: YH00130

ABEX HORSE & RIDER

Abex Horse & Rider, Cold Harbour Works, Cryers Hill, High Wycombe, **Buckinghamshire**, HP15 6LU, **ENGLAND**.
(T) 01494 715670 (F) 01494 715670.
Profile Saddlery Retailer. Ref: YH00131

ABINGER FOREST RIDING CLUB

Abinger Forest Riding Club, Danesmead, Forest Green, Dorking, **Surrey**, RH5 5SG, **ENGLAND**.
(T) 01306 70316.
Contact/s
Chairman: Mrs A Metson
Profile Club/Association, Riding Club. Ref: YH00132

ABNALLS FARM

Abnalls Farm, Cross In Hand Lane, Lichfield, **Staffordshire**, WS13 8DZ, **ENGLAND**.
(T) 01543 417075 (F) 01543 417226.
Contact/s
Owner: Mrs M Jones
Profile Saddlery Retailer, Stable/Livery.
Ref: YH00133

ABRAM HALL RIDING CTRE

Abram Hall Riding Centre, Abram Hall, Warrington Rd, Abram, Wigan, **Lancashire**, WN2 5XA, **ENGLAND**.
(T) 01942 707021
Affiliated Bodies Ponies Ass UK.
Contact/s
General Manager: Ms H Crawford
Profile Arena, Breeder, Riding Club, Stable/Livery, Trainer. No.Staff: 2 Yr. Est: 1987
C.Size: 21 Acres
Opening Times
Sp: Open 06:00. Closed 21:00.
Su: Open 06:00. Closed 21:00.
Au: Open 06:00. Closed 21:00.
Wn: Open 06:00. Closed 21:00. Ref: YH00134

ABRAM, DAVID

David Abram, Toughnane, Bohola, **County Mayo**, **IRELAND**.
(T) 087 2374616.
Profile Saddlery Retailer.
Wholesalers of Trotting harnesses and bridlewear. Also available is a mobile unit and warehouse.
Opening Times
Telephone for further information. Ref: YH00135

ABRAM, T M

T M Abram, Buskhill Farm & Stud, Westow, York, **Yorkshire (North)**, YO60 7LS, **ENGLAND**.
(T) 01653 658288 **(F)** 01653 658288.
Contact/s
Partner: Mrs J Abram
Profile Breeder. **Ref: YH00136**

ABRS

Association of British Riding Schools, Queen's Chambers, 38-40 Queens St, Penzance, **Cornwall**, TR18 4BH, **ENGLAND**.
(T) 01736 369440 **(F)** 01736 351390
(E) office@abrs.org
(W) www.abrs.org.
Contact/s
Chairman: Mrs P Harris
Profile Club/Association.
Advice on where to ride **Ref: YH00137**

ABSOLAM EVANS & SON

Absolam Evans & Son, Bryn Y Groes, Llwynmawr, Llangollen, **Denbighshire**, LL20 7BB, **WALES**.
(T) 01691 718363.
Contact/s
Owner: Mr T Evans
Profile Blacksmith. **Ref: YH00138**

ACCESS TRAVEL

Access Travel Co Ltd, Transferry Hse, Arterial Rd, Hornchurch, **Essex**, RM11 3UT, **ENGLAND**.
(T) 01708 471313 **(F)** 01708 477546
(E) accesstrv@aol.com.
Profile Breeder. **Ref: YH00139**

ACCIMASSU

Accimassu, 23 Johns Rd, Studley, **Warwickshire**, B80 7EQ, **ENGLAND**.
(M) 07976 367006
Affiliated Bodies IASMT.
Profile Breeder, Medical Support, Stable/Livery, Track/Course, Trainer. **No.Staff:** 3 **Yr. Est:** 1985
C.Size: 20 Acres
Opening Times
Sp: Open Mon - Sun 08:00. Closed Mon - Sun 19:00.
Su: Open Mon - Sun 08:00. Closed Mon - Sun 19:00.
Au: Open Mon - Sun 08:00. Closed Mon - Sun 19:00.
Wn: Open Mon - Sun 08:00. Closed Mon - Sun 19:00. **Ref: YH00140**

ACHALONE ACTIVITIES

Achalone Activities, North Achalone, Halkirk, **Highlands**, KW12 6XA, **SCOTLAND**.
(T) 01847 831326.
Contact/s
Owner: Mrs M Bain
Profile Riding School, Stable/Livery. **Ref: YH00141**

ACKERMANN & JOHNSON

Ackermann & Johnson Ltd, 27 Lowndes St, London, **London (Greater)**, SW1X 9HY, **ENGLAND**.
(T) 020 72356464 **(F)** 020 78231057
(E) ackermann.johnson@btinternet.com
(W) www.artnet.com.
Contact/s
Owner: Mr P Johnson
Profile Art Dealer.
Art dealer specialising in equine sporting pictures
Yr. Est: 1962
Opening Times
Sp: Open Mon - Fri 09:00. Closed Mon - Fri 17:00.
Su: Open Mon - Fri 09:00. Closed Mon - Fri 17:00.
Au: Open Mon - Fri 09:00. Closed Mon - Fri 17:00.
Wn: Open Mon - Fri 09:00. Closed Mon - Fri 17:00.
Saturday by appointment **Ref: YH00142**

ACKERMANN, D H W

D H W Ackermann, Spring Farm, Cold Overton Rd, Oakham, **Leicestershire**, LE15 8DA, **ENGLAND**.
(T) 01572 755919 **(F)** 01572 771150.
Contact/s
Owner: Mr D Ackermann
Profile Trainer. **Ref: YH00143**

ACKLAND, RICHARD J

Richard J Ackland DWCF, 152 Campden Cres, Dagenham, **Essex**, RM8 2SJ, **ENGLAND**.
(T) 020 85970106.
Profile Farrier. **Ref: YH00144**

ACONLEY, P & V

P & V Aconley, Stud Farm Low Rd, Westow, York, **Yorkshire (North)**, YO60 7LX, **ENGLAND**.
(T) 01653 618594.
Profile Breeder. **Ref: YH00145**

ACORN ACTIVITIES

Acorn Activities, P O Box 120, Hereford, **Herefordshire**, HR4 8YB, **ENGLAND**.
(T) 01432 830083 **(F)** 01423 830110
(E) info@acornactivities.co.uk.
Profile Holidays.
Offer pony trekking weekends. **Ref: YH00146**

ACORN EQUESTRIAN CTRE

Acorn Equestrian Centre Ltd, Barrockstown, Maynooth, **County Kildare**, **IRELAND**.
(T) 01 6289116
(E) acornequestrian@kildarehorse.ie.
Contact/s
Key Contact: Mr R Kinsella
Profile Equestrian Centre. **C.Size:** 100 Acres
Ref: YH00147

ACORN FEEDS

Acorn Feeds, 1 Rochdale Rd, Golcar, Huddersfield, **Yorkshire (West)**, HD7 4NN, **ENGLAND**.
(T) 01484 654209 **(F)** 01484 654209
(M) 07989 477919
(E) acornj@genie.co.uk.
Contact/s
Owner: Mrs J Pashley
Profile Feed Merchant, Supplies.
Shampoos, oils and accessories for tack and cleaning are kept in stock. Saddles can be ordered.
Yr. Est: 1995
Opening Times
Sp: Open Mon - Sun 11:00. Closed Mon - Sun 22:00.
Su: Open Mon - Sun 11:00. Closed Mon - Sun 22:00.
Au: Open Mon - Sun 11:00. Closed Mon - Sun 22:00.
Wn: Open Mon - Sun 11:00. Closed Mon - Sun 22:00. **Ref: YH00148**

ACORN PALOMINO SHETLAND

Acorn Palomino Shetland Pony Stud, Brockhills Farm, Sway Rd, Tiptoe, Lymington, **Hampshire**, SO41 6FQ, **ENGLAND**.
(T) 01425 611280 **(F)** 01425 611280.
Contact/s
Owner: Mrs J Oakhill
Profile Breeder. **Ref: YH00149**

ACORN RUGS

Acorn Rugs, Barff Vale Farm, North Kelsey, Market Rasen, **Lincolnshire**, LN7 6LG, **ENGLAND**.
(T) 07971 003523.
Profile Supplies. **Ref: YH00150**

ACORN SADDLERY

Acorn Saddlery, 76B South St, South Molton, **Devon**, EX36 4AG, **ENGLAND**.
(T) 01769 573847 **(F)** 01769 573847.
Contact/s
Owner: Mr A Edwards
Profile Saddlery Retailer. **Ref: YH00151**

ACORN TRAILER HIRE

Acorn Trailer Hire, Shalford Farm, Brimpton, Reading, **Berkshire**, RG7 4RD, **ENGLAND**.
(T) 0118 9712918 **(F)** 0118 9714918.
Contact/s
Owner: Mr M Harcourt
Profile Transport/Horse Boxes. **Ref: YH00152**

ACORN VETNRY CTRE

Acorn Veterinary Centre (South Lanarkshire), Oak Villa, Woodstock Rd, Lanark, **Lanarkshire (South)**, ML11 7DH, **SCOTLAND**.
(T) 01555 663127 **(F)** 01555 663975.
Profile Medical Support. **Ref: YH00153**

ACORN VETNRY CTRE

Acorn Veterinary Centre (Warwickshire), 21 Station Rd, Studley, **Warwickshire**, B80 7HR, **ENGLAND**.
(T) 01527 853304.
Contact/s
Vet: Mr P Haseler
Profile Medical Support. **Ref: YH00154**

ACP

Association of Chartered Physiotherapists in Animal Therapy, Morland Hse, Salters Lane, Winchester, **Hampshire**, SO22 5JP, **ENGLAND**.
(T) 01962 863801 **(F)** 01962 863801.
Profile Club/Association. **Ref: YH00155**

ACRE & ASHDOWN FEEDS

Acre & Ashdown Feeds Ltd (Crowborough), Unit 8 Beacon Business Pk, Wealden Ind Est, Farningham Rd, Jarvis Brook, Crowborough, **Sussex (East)**, TN6 2JR, **ENGLAND**.
(T) 01892 669660 **(F)** 01892 669660.
Profile Saddlery Retailer. **Ref: YH00156**

ACRE HSE EQUESTRIAN

Acre House Equestrian, Acre Hse, Bowers Rd, Acrefair, **Denbighshire**, LL14 3TG, **WALES**.
(T) 01978 820435.
Profile Supplies. **Ref: YH00157**

ACRE HSE EQUESTRIAN

Acre House Equestrian, The Plassey, Eyton, Wrexham, **Wrexham**, LL13 0SP, **WALES**.
(T) 01978 781242 **(F)** 01978 781242.
Contact/s
Owner: Ms L Box
Profile Riding Wear Retailer, Saddlery Retailer, Supplies. **No.Staff:** 2 **Yr. Est:** 1997
Opening Times
Sp: Open 10:00. Closed 17:00.
Su: Open 10:00. Closed 17:00.
Au: Open 10:00. Closed 17:00.
Wn: Open 10:00. Closed 17:00. **Ref: YH00158**

ACRELIFFE

Acrecliffe Equestrian Centre, Bradford Rd, Otley, **Yorkshire (West)**, LS21 3DN, **ENGLAND**.
(T) 01943 873912
Affiliated Bodies RDA.
Contact/s
Owner: Mrs A Everall
Profile Riding School. BHS Exam Centre.
Lesson prices vary depending on the instructor
Yr. Est: 1963 **C.Size:** 22 Acres
Opening Times
Telephone for further information. **Ref: YH00159**

ACRUM LODGE STUD

L Chamberlain (Acrum) Limited, Acrum Lodge, West Auckland, Bishop Auckland, **County Durham**, DL14 9PB, **ENGLAND**.
(T) 01388 834636 **(F)** 01388 834636
(E) stallions@acrumlodgestud.com
(W) www.acrumlodgestud.com.
Contact/s
Owner: Mr N Chamberlain
Profile Breeder, Transport/Horse Boxes.
No.Staff: 3 **Yr. Est:** 1961 **C.Size:** 100 Acres
Ref: YH00160

ACTON HILL RIDING SCHOOL

Acton Hill Riding School, Acton Hill Farm, Stafford, **Staffordshire**, ST17 0RZ, **ENGLAND**.
(T) 01785 661383.
Profile Riding School. **Ref: YH00161**

ACTON, J M

J M Acton, Horse Shoe Farm, Creake Rd, Fakenham, **Norfolk**, NR21 9HT, **ENGLAND**.
(T) 01328 823561 **(F)** 01328 823561.
Contact/s
Owner: Mr J Acton
Profile Farrier. **Ref: YH00162**

ADA COLE RESCUE STABLES

Ada Cole Rescue Stables, Broadlands, Broadley Common, Nr Nazeing, Waltham Abbey, **Essex**, EN9 2DH, **ENGLAND**.
(T) 01992 892133 **(F)** 01992 893841.
Contact/s
Animal Welfare Officer: Pauline Craven
Profile Medical Support.
Rescue, rehabilitate and re-home horses.
Ref: YH00163

ADAM, N

Neil Adam, Collins Stud Hse, 22 Ley Rd, Stetchworth, Newmarket, **Suffolk**, CB8 9TS, **ENGLAND**.
(T) 01638 507400.
Profile Breeder. **Ref: YH00164**

ADAMS, D C T

D C T Adams, Kinknall Hall Farm, Hob Hey Lane, Culcheth, Warrington, **Cheshire**, WA3 4NQ, **ENGLAND**.
(T) 01925 762500.
Profile Farrier. **Ref: YH00165**

ADAMS, GAVIN

Gavin Adams DWCF, The Forge, Hall Farm, Hall Lane, Ridgewell, **Essex**, CO9 4SE, **ENGLAND**.
(T) 07860 665587.
Profile Farrier. **Ref: YH00166**

ADAMS, J

J Adams, Forest Farm, Crow Hill, Crow, Ringwood, **Hampshire**, BH24 3DE, **ENGLAND**.
(T) 01425 476020.

Profile Farrier. Ref:YH00167

ADAMS, JAMES

James Adams, Arch 7 67 St Marks Rd, London, **London (Greater)**, W11 1RE, **ENGLAND**.
(T) 020 77276466.
Contact/s
Owner: Mr J Adams
Profile Blacksmith. Ref:YH00168

ADAMS, K

K Adams, 229 Rosalind St, Ashington, **Northumberland**, NE63 9BB, **ENGLAND**.
(T) 01670 811675.
Profile Farrier. Ref:YH00169

ADAMS, M

M Adams, Newlands Manor Farm Cottage, Everton, Lymington, **Hampshire**, SO41 0JH, **ENGLAND**.
(T) 01590 645780.
Profile Farrier. Ref:YH00170

ADAMS, MERVYN

Mervyn Adams, Farm Cottage, Newlands Manor Farm, Everton, Lymington, **Hampshire**, SO41 1JH, **ENGLAND**.
(T) 01590 645780.
Profile Farrier. Ref:YH00171

ADAMS, RICHARD A

Richard A Adams DWCF, Kinknall Hall, Hob-Hey Lane, Culcheth, Warrington, **Cheshire**, WA3 4NP, **ENGLAND**.
(T) 01925 762500.
Profile Farrier. Ref:YH00172

ADAMS, VAL

Mrs Val Adams, Church Farm, Laxton, Corby, **Northamptonshire**, NN17 3AX, **ENGLAND**.
(T) 01780 450254
(M) 07850 510761
(E) laxton.paint.horses@farmline.com.
Profile Breeder. Ref:YH00173

ADAMSON, J

J Adamson, West Plean Cottage, Plean, Stirling, **Stirling**, FK7 8AS, **SCOTLAND**.
(T) 01786 814729.
Contact/s
Owner: Mr J Adamson
Profile Farrier. Ref:YH00174

ADARE EQUESTRIAN CTRE

Adare Equestrian Centre, Kildimo Rd, Adare, **County Limerick**, **IRELAND**.
(T) 061 396373.
Contact/s
Owner: Sarah Geoghegan (Q) BHSII
Profile Equestrian Centre.
Ardare Equestrian Centre runs training courses to become a BHSAI. These courses are 12 weeks long, three days a week. Yr. Est: 1989
Opening Times
Sp: Open Mon - Sat 09:00. Closed Mon - Sat 20:00.
Su: Open Mon - Sat 09:00. Closed Mon - Sat 20:00.
Au: Open Mon - Sat 09:00. Closed Mon - Sat 18:00.
Wn: Open Mon - Sat 09:00. Closed Mon - Sat 18:00.
Closed Sundays Ref:YH00175

ADAS

ADAS, Oxford Spires Business Pk, Kidlington, **Oxfordshire**, OX5 1NZ, **ENGLAND**.
(T) 01522 521289 (F) 01522 589445
(E) equine@adas.co.uk
(W) www.adas.co.uk.
Contact/s
Key Contact: Geoff Fairfoull
Profile Supplies. Equine Advice.
An advisery service offering information to a broad range of the equine industry and answering queries from racehorse trainers to stud managers, to private horse owners and many more. Ref:YH00176

ADAS WESTERN

ADAS Western, Woodthorne, Wergs, Wolverhampton, **Midlands (West)**, WV6 8TQ, **ENGLAND**.
(T) 01902 693188 (F) 01902 693375.
Profile Medical Support. Ref:YH00177

ADCOCK, DOMINIC R

Dominic R Adcock DWCF BII, 1 Nobbscrook Cottage, Drift Rd, Winkfield, Windsor, **Berkshire**, SL4 4RS, **ENGLAND**.
(T) 01344 893763.
Profile Farrier. Ref:YH00178

ADDINGTON MANOR

Addington Manor Equestrian Centre, Addington, Buckingham, **Buckinghamshire**, MK18 2JR, **ENGLAND**.
(T) 01296 712402 (F) 01296 711721
(E) web_enquiries@addingtonuk.co.uk
(W) www.addingtonuk.co.uk.
Contact/s
For Bookings: Mr A Hill
(E) ad@addingtonuk.co.uk
Profile Arena, Equestrian Centre, Horse/Rider Accom.
Dressage, show jumping & eventing competitions are held. Accomodation for riders can be arranged.
No.Staff: 5 Yr. Est: 2001 C.Size: 100 Acres
Opening Times
Sp: Open Mon - Sun 09:30. Closed Mon - Sun 17:00.
Su: Open Mon - Sun 09:30. Closed Mon - Sun 17:00.
Au: Open Mon - Sun 09:30. Closed Mon - Sun 17:00.
Wn: Open Mon - Sun 09:30. Closed Mon - Sun 17:00. Ref:YH00179

ADDLESTONE HARDWARE

Addlestone Hardware, 116 Station Rd, Addlestone, **Surrey**, KT15 2BQ, **ENGLAND**.
(T) 01932 856855.
Profile Supplies. Ref:YH00180

ADDY, D L

D L Addy, 183 Rooley Moor Rd, Rochdale, **Lancashire**, OL12 7DQ, **ENGLAND**.
(T) 01706 647969.
Contact/s
Owner: Mr D Addy
Profile Farrier. Ref:YH00181

ADEL WOOD

Adel Wood, 34 Parkside Rd, Leeds, **Yorkshire (West)**, LS6 4NB, **ENGLAND**.
(T) 0113 2300469.
Contact/s
Manager: Kim Petty
Profile Riding School.
Opening Times
Sp: Open Tues - Sun 10:00. Closed Tues - Sun 16:00.
Su: Open Tues - Sun 10:00. Closed Tues - Sun 16:00.
Au: Open Tues - Sun 10:00. Closed Tues - Sun 16:00.
Wn: Open Tues - Sun 10:00. Closed Tues - Sun 16:00. Ref:YH00182

ADELAIDE VETNRY CTRE

Adelaide Cottage Veterinary Centre, 49 Mill St, Gamlingay, Sandy, **Bedfordshire**, SG19 3JW, **ENGLAND**.
(T) 01767 651569 (F) 01767 651534.
Profile Medical Support. Ref:YH00183

ADFAB FABRICATIONS

Adfab Fabrications, 1 Anderson St, Port Glasgow, **Renfrewshire**, PA14 5EP, **SCOTLAND**.
(T) 01475 744733.
Profile Blacksmith. Ref:YH00184

ADLINGTON EQUESTRIAN CTRE

Adlington Equestrian Centre, Street Lane, Adlington, Macclesfield, **Cheshire**, SK10 4NT, **ENGLAND**.
(T) 01625 874073.
Contact/s
Owner: Ms J Shaw
Profile Equestrian Centre. Ref:YH00185

ADLINGTON, D

D Adlington, Cartledge Hall Farm, 80 Cartledge Lane, Holmesfield, Dronfield, **Derbyshire**, S18 7SB, **ENGLAND**.
(T) 0114 2890760
(M) 0796 7914670.
Contact/s
Owner: Mr D Adlington
Profile Stable/Livery. Ref:YH00186

ADMIRAL TRAILERS

Admiral Trailers Ltd, Blundells Rd, Tiverton, **Devon**, EX16 4DA, **ENGLAND**.
(T) 01884 251577 (F) 01884 251578.
Profile Transport/Horse Boxes. Ref:YH00187

ADRENALINE SPORTS

Adrenaline Sports Ltd, 21 Scotlands Cl, Haslemere, **Surrey**, GU27 3AE, **ENGLAND**.
(T) 03068 85511 (F) 01306 882211
(E) sales@adrenaline-sports.com
(W) www.medi-wrap.com.
Profile Medical Support.
Injury Therapy Specialists. Manufacturers of magnetic and gel therapy products for horse, dog, cat and human use. Freephone 0800 698 3740.
Yr. Est: 1989 Ref:YH00188

ADSBOROUGH HSE STABLES

Adsborough House Stables, Adsborough Hse, Thurloxton, Taunton, **Somerset**, TA2 8RF, **ENGLAND**.
(T) 01823 412204.
Contact/s
Owner: Mrs T Franklin
Profile Riding School, Stable/Livery.
Specialise in training nervous and novice riders.
No.Staff: 3 Yr. Est: 1979 C.Size: 10 Acres
Ref:YH00189

ADSTONE LODGE STUD

Adstone Lodge Stud, Adstone, Towcester, **Northamptonshire**, NN12 8DS, **ENGLAND**.
(T) 01327 860301.
Profile Breeder. Ref:YH00190

ADUR VALLEY RIDING CLUB

Adur Valley Riding Club, 27 Busticle Lane, Sompting, Lancing, **Sussex (West)**, BN15 0DJ, **ENGLAND**.
(T) 01903 751475.
Contact/s
Chairman: Mr C White
Profile Club/Association, Riding Club. Ref:YH00191

ADVANCED EQUINE DENTISTRY

Advanced Equine Dentistry, Deildref, Llangurig, Llanidloes, **Powys**, SY18 6SL, **WALES**.
(T) 01686 440663
(E) equine-dentistry.co.uk@equestria.net.co.uk
(W) www.equine-dentistry.co.uk.
Profile Medical Support. Ref:YH00192

ADVANTA

Advanta Seeds UK, Sleaford, **Lincolnshire**, NG34 7HA, **ENGLAND**.
(T) 01529 304511 (F) 01529 303908
(E) monarch@advantaseeds.co.uk.
Contact/s
Marketing Services: Paul Lees
Profile Supplies. Grass Seed Producers.
Ref:YH00193

ADVERTISING ANSWERS

Advertising Answers, Savilles Cottage, Hatfield Pk Farm, Bush End, Takeley, Bishop's Stortford, **Hertfordshire**, CM22 6NE, **ENGLAND**.
(T) 01279 870043 (F) 01279 870043
(E) jane.watkins@breathemail.net
(W) www.advertising-answers.co.uk.
Contact/s
Owner: Miss J Watkins
Profile Advertising Agency. Ref:YH00194

AERBORN EQUESTRIAN

Aerborn Equestrian Ltd, Pegasus Hse, 198 Sneinton Dale, Nottingham, **Nottinghamshire**, NG2 4HJ, **ENGLAND**.
(T) 0115 9505631 (F) 0115 9483273
(W) www.aerborn.co.uk.
Contact/s
Owner: Mr J McGowan
Profile Supplies. Manufacturer of horse clothing.
Ref:YH00195

AESCWOOD

Aescwood, Rawlings Lane, Seer Green, Beaconsfield, **Buckinghamshire**, HP9 2RQ, **ENGLAND**.
(T) 01494 875048.
Profile Riding School, Saddlery Retailer.
Ref:YH00196

AESTHETE

Aesthete ARAB & Miniature Horses, Ramor Hse, North St, Doncaster, **Yorkshire (South)**, DN9 1AE, **ENGLAND**.
(T) 01427 728266 (F) 01427 728266
(E) jane@aesthete.freeserve.co.uk.
Profile Breeder. Ref:YH00197

AFON RIDING CLUB

Afon Riding Club, 19 Mansel St, Neath Port Talbot, **Neath Port Talbot**, SA13 1BL, **WALES**.
(T) 01639 886794.
Contact/s
Chairman: Mr S Roberts
Profile Club/Association. Ref:YH00198

AGNEW, R & A

R & A Agnew, West Dhuloch, Ervie, Stranraer, **Dumfries and Galloway**, **SCOTLAND**..
Profile Breeder. Ref:YH00199

AGRCLTRL SHOW EXHIBITORS AST
Agricultural Show Exhibitors Association, 7 Nursery Cl, Chadwell Heath, Romford, **Bedfordshire**, RM6 4LB, **ENGLAND**.
(T) 020 82200552.
Profile Club/Association. **Ref: YH00200**

AGRI SERVICES
Agri Services Ltd, Closutton, Bagenalstown, **County Carlow**, **IRELAND**.
(T) 087 2860662 **(F)** 050 322222
(E) kirsteenreid@unison.ie
(W) www.georgemullins.com.
Profile Transport/Horse Boxes. **Ref: YH00201**

AGRIQUESTRIAN CONSULTANTS
Agriquestrian Consultants, 129 Reigate Rd, Ewell, Epsom, **Surrey**, KT17 3DE, **ENGLAND**.
(T) 020 83930516 **(F)** 020 83930516.
Profile Architectural and planning. **Ref: YH00202**

AGRITRADERS
Agritraders Ltd, 16 Exeter Livestock Ctre, Matford Park Rd, Matford, Exeter, **Devon**, EX2 8FD, **ENGLAND**.
(T) 01392 467286.
Contact/s
Assistant: Mrs K Williams
Profile Supplies. **Ref: YH00203**

AGRIVET - KWG
Agrivet - KWG, Dorset Hse, Handcross, Haywards Heath, **Sussex (West)**, RH17 6BJ, **ENGLAND**.
(T) 01444 400104 **(F)** 01444 401007.
Profile Saddlery Retailer. **Ref: YH00204**

AHMET, M
Mr M Ahmet, Lambourne Pk Farm, Hoe Lane, Lambourne Pk, Romford, **Essex**, RM4 1NP, **ENGLAND**.
(T) 020 85006476.
Profile Breeder. **Ref: YH00205**

AIGLE INTERNATIONAL
Aigle International The Stirrup Trading Ltd, Ballymoney Pk, Kilbride, Wicklow, **County Wicklow**, **IRELAND**.
(T) 04 0448433.
Profile Supplies.
Agents for Aigle International. **Ref: YH00206**

AIKE GRANGE STUD
Aike Grange Stud Ltd, Aike, Driffield, **Yorkshire (East)**, YO25 9BG, **ENGLAND**.
(T) 01377 271271 **(F)** 01377 271384
(W) www.dressage-uk.co.uk.
Contact/s
Owner: Ms L Fry
Profile Stable/Livery.
Hold dressage competitions. £40.00 for a 45 minute one-to-one riding lesson. The cost of Livery varies from £70.00 - £140.00 Yr. Est: 1996
Opening Times
Sp: Open Mon - Sun 08:00. Closed Mon - Sun 21:00.
Su: Open Mon - Sun 08:00. Closed Mon - Sun 21:00.
Au: Open Mon - Sun 08:00. Closed Mon - Sun 21:00.
Wn: Open Mon - Sun 08:00. Closed Mon - Sun 21:00. **Ref: YH00207**

AIKEN, RONALD G
Ronald G Aiken DWCF, Cowsrieve Cottage, Blackhills, Peterhead, **Aberdeenshire**, AB42 3JS, **SCOTLAND**.
(T) 01779 472789.
Profile Farrier. **Ref: YH00208**

AIKENFIELD
Aikenfield, Aike, Driffield, **Yorkshire (East)**, YO25 9BG, **ENGLAND**.
(T) 01377 270326.
Profile Breeder. **Ref: YH00209**

AIKENS, MARK L
Mark L Aikens DWCF, Aotearoa Forge, Stocks Hill, Bawburgh, Norwich, **Norfolk**, NR9 3LJ, **ENGLAND**.
(T) 01603 813377
(M) 07850 709695.
Profile Farrier. **Ref: YH00210**

AILLECROSS EQUESTRIAN CTRE
Aillecross Equestrian Centre, Loughrea, **County Galway**, **IRELAND**.
(T) 091 841216.
Contact/s
Owner: Willie Leahy
Profile Riding School, Stable/Livery. **Ref: YH00211**

AILSA RIDING CLUB
Ailsa Riding Club, 12 Golf Course Rd, Girvan, **Ayrshire (South)**, KA26 9HW, **SCOTLAND**.
(T) 01465 3966.
Contact/s
Chairman: Ms M Logan
Profile Club/Association, Riding Club. **Ref: YH00212**

AINLEY, PETER D
Peter D Ainley DWCF, No 3 The Row, Stanton St Bernard, Marlborough, **Wiltshire**, SN8 4LR, **ENGLAND**.
(T) 01672 851156.
Profile Farrier. **Ref: YH00213**

AINSCOUGH F & J
Ainscough F & J & Co, Dam Lane, Rixton, Warrington, **Cheshire**, WA3 6LB, **ENGLAND**.
(T) 0161 7753453.
Contact/s
Owner: Mr D Conroy
Profile Blacksmith. **Ref: YH00214**

AINSWORTH, DARREN R
Darren R Ainsworth DWCF, 30 Alsop Way, Buxton, **Derbyshire**, SK17 7RJ, **ENGLAND**.
(T) 01298 27910.
Profile Farrier. **Ref: YH00215**

AINSWORTHS
Ainsworths, 38 New Cavendish St, London, **London (Greater)**, W1M 7LH, **ENGLAND**.
(T) 020 79355330 **(F)** 020 74864813.
Profile Medical Support. **Ref: YH00216**

AINTREE RACECOURSE
Aintree Racecourse Co Ltd, Aintree Racecourse, Aintree, **Merseyside**, L9 5AS, **ENGLAND**.
(T) 0151 5232600 **(F)** 0151 5222920.
Profile Track/Course. **Ref: YH00217**

AIR PURIFICATION SYSTEMS
Air Purification Systems, Ibs Hse, Dublin Rd, Portlaoise, **County Laois**, **IRELAND**.
(T) 050 260591
(E) airps@indigo.ie
(W) www.airpurification.ie.
Profile Supplies. **Ref: YH00218**

AIRBORNE SPORTS
Airborne Sports Horse & Rider Association, Lakeside Cottages, Shuttleworth College, Old Warden, Biggleswade, **Bedfordshire**, SG18 9DU, **ENGLAND**.
(T) 01767 627726.
Profile Club/Association. **Ref: YH00219**

AIRD, JOHN W
John W Aird, Whitesidehill Farm, Waterside, Lesmahagow, **Lanarkshire (South)**, ML11 0HL, **SCOTLAND**.
(T) 01555 894395.
Profile Farrier. **Ref: YH00220**

AIRE VALLEY RIDING CLUB
Aire Valley Riding Club, 100 Highgate, Heaton, Bradford, **Yorkshire (West)**, BD9 5PJ, **ENGLAND**.
(T) 01274 542729.
Contact/s
Secretary: Mrs J Pitts
Profile Club/Association, Riding Club. **Ref: YH00221**

AIRE VETNRY CTRE
Aire Veterinary Centre (Leeds), 177 Kirkstall Lane, Leeds, **Yorkshire (West)**, LS6 3EJ, **ENGLAND**.
(T) 0113 2786072.
Profile Medical Support. **Ref: YH00222**

AIRE VETNRY CTRE
Aire Veterinary Centre (W Yorkshire), 437A Harrogate Rd, Leeds, **Yorkshire (West)**, LS17 7AB, **ENGLAND**.
(T) 0113 2684304.
Profile Medical Support. **Ref: YH00223**

AIRLIE STUD
Airlie Stud, Grangewilliam, Maynooth, **County Kildare**, **IRELAND**.
(T) 01 6286336 **(F)** 01 6286674
(E) mail@airlie-stus.com
(W) www.airlie-stud.com.
Contact/s
Key Contact: Mr A Rogers
Profile Breeder.
Airlie Stud board mares for clients and also produce yearlings, for sales. **Ref: YH00224**

AIR-O-WEAR
Air-O-Wear Ltd, Aydon South Farm, Corbridge, **Northumberland**, NE45 5PL, **ENGLAND**.
(T) 01434 632816 **(F)** 01434 632849
(E) enquiries@airowear.co.uk
(W) www.airowear.co.uk.
Profile Riding Wear Retailer. **Ref: YH00225**

AISBY HSE RACING STABLES
Aisby House Racing Stables, Aisby Hse, Aisby, Grantham, **Lincolnshire**, NG32 3NF, **ENGLAND**.
(T) 01529 455260 **(F)** 01529 455260.
Contact/s
Owner: Mrs V Ward
Profile Stable/Livery.
Trains and breeds racehorses Yr. Est: 1990
Opening Times
Sp: Open Mon - Sun 18:00. Closed Mon - Sun 21:00.
Su: Open Mon - Sun 18:00. Closed Mon - Sun 21:00.
Au: Open Mon - Sun 18:00. Closed Mon - Sun 21:00.
Wn: Open Mon - Sun 18:00. Closed Mon - Sun 21:00.
Open during the day for owners, telephone during evening to make appointment **Ref: YH00226**

AISLABY GRANGE
Aislaby Grange, Aislaby Grange Farm, Eaglescliffe, Stockton-on-Tees, **Cleveland**, TS16 0QH, **ENGLAND**.
(T) 01642 788600 **(F)** 01642 788821.
Contact/s
Owner: Mrs P Macatier
Profile Breeder. **Ref: YH00227**

AITCHISON, G W
G W Aitchison, Castlemilk Smithy, Lockerbie, **Dumfries and Galloway**, DG11 1AB, **SCOTLAND**.
(T) 01576 510285.
Profile Farrier. **Ref: YH00228**

AKAL-TEKE SOCIETY
Akal-Teke Society of GB, Bodare Cottge, Daymer Lane, Trebetherick, Wadebridge, **Cornwall**, PL27 6SA, **ENGLAND**.
(T) 01208 862964.
Contact/s
Key Contact: Mrs S Waldock
Profile Club/Association. **Ref: YH00229**

AKBARY, H
H Akbary, Egerton Stud, Cambridge Rd, Newmarket, **Suffolk**, CB8 0TJ, **ENGLAND**.
(T) 01638 661118 **(F)** 01638 667154
(W) www.newmarketracehorsetrainers.co.uk
Affiliated Bodies Newmarket Trainers Fed.
Contact/s
Trainer: Mr H Akbary
Profile Trainer. **Ref: YH00230**

AKEHURST STUD
Akehurst Stud, Actons Farm, Buckholt Lane, Sidley, Bexhill-on-Sea, **Sussex (East)**, TN39 5AX, **ENGLAND**.
(T) 01424 830343.
Profile Breeder. **Ref: YH00231**

AKEHURST, JOHN
John Akehurst, South Hatch Stables, Burgh Heath Rd, Epsom, **Surrey**, KT17 4LX, **ENGLAND**.
(T) 01372 745880 **(F)** 01372 744231.
Contact/s
Owner: Mr J Akehurst
Profile Trainer. **Ref: YH00232**

AL MANZA STUD
Al Manza Stud, Whitehorse Cottage, East Rudham, King's Lynn, **Norfolk**, PE31 8RB, **ENGLAND**.
(T) 01485 528394 **(F)** 01485 528394.
Profile Breeder. **Ref: YH00233**

AL WAHA ARABIAN STUD
Al Waha Arabian Stud, Blackdown, Haslemere, **Surrey**, GU27 3BS, **ENGLAND**.
(T) 01428 644404.
Profile Breeder. **Ref: YH00234**

AL WAHA ARABIAN STUD
Al Waha Arabian Stud, Castle Copse, Fernden Lane, Haslemere, **Surrey**, GU27 3LA, **ENGLAND**.
(T) 01428 658242 **(F)** 01428 658871.
Contact/s
Manager: Mrs V Booth
Profile Breeder. **Ref: YH00235**

ALADDIN CAVE
Aladdin Cave, (equineeds) Park Nook, Lambley Rd, Lowdham, **Nottinghamshire**, NG14 7DF, **ENGLAND**.
(T) 0115 9313055.
Profile Saddlery Retailer. **Ref: YH00236**

ALAN BROWN/COUNTRY SPORTS

Alan Brown/Country Sports, 118 Nightingale Rd, Hitchin, **Hertfordshire**, SG5 1RG, **ENGLAND**.
(T) 01462 459918 **(F)** 01462 459918
(M) 07850 958114.
Profile Saddlery Retailer. **Ref: YH00237**

ALAN ELLISON

Alan Ellison Sporting Artist, Llwynpiod Farm, Trap, Llandeilo, **Carmarthenshire**, SA19 6RD, **WALES**.
(T) 01558 823280.
Profile Artist. **Ref: YH00238**

ALAN HADLEY

Alan Hadley Limited, Fenton Hse, 102 Grazeley Rd, Three Mile Cross, Reading, **Berkshire**, RG7 1BJ, **ENGLAND**.
(T) 0118 9883266 **(F)** 0118 9884538
(E) waste@hadleys.co.uk.
Profile Track/Course. **Ref: YH00239**

ALAN KING RACING

Alan King Racing Ltd, Barbary Castle Farm, Wroughton, Swindon, **Wiltshire**, SN4 0QZ, **ENGLAND**.
(T) 01793 815009 **(F)** 01793 845080.
Contact/s
Owner: Mr A King
Profile Trainer. **Ref: YH00240**

ALAN PRICE

Alan Price Saddler, 17 Twyn Pandy, Llangynidr, Crickhowell, **Powys**, NP8 1NF, **WALES**.
(T) 01874 730195.
Profile Saddlery Retailer. **Ref: YH00241**

ALASTAIR CRAIG NURSE

Alastair Craig Nurse, 1 Eastcliffe, Whitley Bay, **Tyne and Wear**, NE26 2BQ, **ENGLAND**.
(T) 0191 2514107.
Profile Farrier. **Ref: YH00242**

ALBANY FARM LIVERY STABLES

Albany Farm Livery Stables, Redfields Lane, Church Crookham, Fleet, **Hampshire**, GU13 0RB, **ENGLAND**.
(T) 01252 851682.
Contact/s
Owner: Ms B Pearce
Profile Stable/Livery. **Ref: YH00243**

ALBERT COTTAGE

Albert Cottage Veterinary Clinic, 66 Liskeard Rd, Saltash, **Cornwall**, PL12 4HG, **ENGLAND**.
(T) 01752 843397.
Profile Medical Support. **Ref: YH00244**

ALBERT E JAMES & SON

Albert E James & Son Ltd, Barrow Mill, Barrow Gurney, **Somerset (North)**, BS48 3RU, **ENGLAND**.
(T) 01275 463496 **(F)** 01275 463791.
Profile Supplies. **Ref: YH00245**

ALBINS, D J

Mrs D J Albins, Goldsmith's Cottage, Orwell Pk, Nacton, Ipswich, **Suffolk**, IP10 0JH, **ENGLAND**.
(T) 01473 659203.
Profile Breeder. **Ref: YH00246**

ALBION SADDLEMAKERS

Albion Saddlemakers, Albion Hse, Bridgeman St, Walsall, **Midlands (West)**, WS2 9PG, **ENGLAND**.
(T) 01922 646210 **(F)** 01922 643777
(E) sales@albion-saddlemakers.co.uk
(W) www.albionsaddlemakers.com.
Contact/s
Chairperson: Mr G Belton
Profile Saddle Manufacturer.
Sells to retailers only **Yr. Est:** 1983
Opening Times
Sp: Open Mon - Fri 09:00. Closed Mon - Fri 17:00.
Su: Open Mon - Fri 09:00. Closed Mon - Fri 17:00.
Au: Open Mon - Fri 09:00. Closed Mon - Fri 17:00.
Wn: Open Mon - Fri 09:00. Closed Mon - Fri 17:00.
Ref: YH00247

ALBOURNE EQUESTRIAN CTRE

Albourne Equestrian Centre, Henfield Rd, Albourne, Hassocks, **Sussex (West)**, BN6 9DE, **ENGLAND**.
(T) 01273 832989 **(F)** 01273 833392
Affiliated Bodies ABRS, BHS, RDA.
Contact/s
General Manager: Ms M Hughes
Profile Riding School, Stable/Livery.
Teaches Alexander Technique. **Yr. Est:** 1993
C.Size: 32 Acres
Opening Times
Sp: Open 09:00. Closed 18:00.
Su: Open 09:00. Closed 18:00.
Au: Open 09:00. Closed 18:00.
Wn: Open 09:00. Closed 18:00.
Closed Mondays **Ref: YH00248**

ALBRIGHTON FEEDS

Albrighton Feeds, Whiston Cross, Holyhead Rd, Albrighton, Wolverhampton, **Midlands (West)**, WV7 3BX, **ENGLAND**.
(T) 01902 372266 **(F)** 01902 372266.
Profile Saddlery Retailer. **Ref: YH00249**

ALBURY ANIMAL FEEDS

Albury Animal Feeds, Water Lane Farm, Water Lane, Albury, Guildford, **Surrey**, GU5 9BD, **ENGLAND**.
(T) 01483 203914 **(F)** 01483 203735.
Profile Supplies. **Ref: YH00250**

ALCESTER RIDING SUPPLIES

Alcester Riding Supplies, Grafton Hse, Bulls Head Yard, Alcester, **Warwickshire**, B49 5BX, **ENGLAND**.
(T) 01789 766155.
Contact/s
Owner: Mrs P Clarke
Profile Saddlery Retailer. **Ref: YH00251**

ALDBOROUGH HALL

Aldborough Hall Equestrian Centre Ltd, Aldborough Hatch, Aldborough Rd North, Ilford, **London (Greater)**, IG2 7TE, **ENGLAND**.
(T) 020 85901433 **(F)** 020 85901433
Affiliated Bodies BHS.
Contact/s
General Manager: Mr A Garrett
Profile Riding School.
One-to-one coaching for 40 minutes costs between £25.00 - £35.00 **No.Staff:** 12 **Yr. Est:** 1956
C.Size: 50 Acres
Opening Times
Tues - Sun by appointment **Ref: YH00252**

ALDEN EQUIFEEDS

Alden Equifeeds, Alden Farm, Upton, Didcot, **Oxfordshire**, OX11 9HS, **ENGLAND**.
(T) 01235 850188 **(F)** 01235 851225
(E) bucknell@aldenfarm.u-net.com.
Profile Supplies. **Ref: YH00253**

ALDER ROOT RIDING CTRE

Alder Root Riding Centre, Alder Root Farm, Alder Root Lane, Winwick, Warrington, **Cheshire**, WA2 8RZ, **ENGLAND**.
(T) 01925 226116 **(F)** 01925 226116
Affiliated Bodies BHS.
Contact/s
Owner: Mr E Lander
Profile Horse/Rider Accom, Riding School.
No.Staff: 2 **Yr. Est:** 1996 **C.Size:** 3 Acres
Opening Times
Sp: Open Mon - Sun 09:00. Closed Mon - Sun 20:00.
Su: Open Mon - Sun 09:00. Closed Mon - Sun 20:00.
Au: Open Mon - Sun 09:00. Closed Mon - Sun 20:00.
Wn: Open Mon - Sun 09:00. Closed Mon - Sun 20:00. **Ref: YH00254**

ALDER, D S

Mr D S Alder, Lucker Mill, Lucker, Belford, **Northumberland**, NE70 7JH, **ENGLAND**.
(T) 01668 213883.
Profile Supplies. **Ref: YH00255**

ALDER, R

R Alder, Manor Farm, Uxbridge, **London (Greater)**, UB8 3SD, **ENGLAND**.
(T) 01895 442737.
Contact/s
Owner: Mrs R Alder
Profile Stable/Livery. **Ref: YH00256**

ALDERSBROOK RIDING SCHOOL

Aldersbrook Riding School, Empress Ave, Manor Pk, London, **London (Greater)**, E12 5HW, **ENGLAND**.
(T) 020 85304648
Affiliated Bodies BHS.
Contact/s
Instructor: Mr M Doddimore
Profile Riding School, Stable/Livery. **Yr. Est:** 1972
Opening Times
Sp: Open 09:00. Closed 18:00.
Su: Open 09:00. Closed 18:00.
Au: Open 09:00. Closed 18:00.
Wn: Open 09:00. Closed 18:00.
Closed for lunch 13:00 - 14:00 **Ref: YH00257**

ALDERSHAWE LIVERY YARD

Aldershawe Livery Yard, Claypit Lane, Lichfield, **Staffordshire**, WS14 0AQ, **ENGLAND**.
(T) 01543 258645.
Contact/s
Owner: Miss S Busby
Profile Stable/Livery. **Ref: YH00258**

ALDERTON, BARRY D

Barry D Alderton DWCF, Brindledown, Edwards Hill, Lambourn, **Berkshire**, RG18 7NW, **ENGLAND**.
(T) 07831 594442.
Profile Farrier. **Ref: YH00259**

ALDERTON, JAMES

James Alderton DWCF, 1 Honeyhill Cottages, Little Saxham, Bury St Edmunds, **Suffolk**, IP29 5LA, **ENGLAND**.
(T) 01284 811024.
Profile Farrier. **Ref: YH00260**

ALDRED, J D

J D Aldred, Lynwood, Pine Ave, Little Hoole, Preston, **Lancashire**, PR4 5LB, **ENGLAND**.
(T) 01772 612333.
Contact/s
Owner: Mr D Aldred
Profile Trainer.
Buy and train horses on request - telephone for further information. **No.Staff:** 2 **Yr. Est:** 1971
C.Size: 25 Acres
Opening Times
By appointment only **Ref: YH00261**

ALDRETH VETNRY CTRE

Aldreth Veterinary Centre, 51 High St, Aldreth, Ely, **Cambridgeshire**, CB6 3PQ, **ENGLAND**.
(T) 01353 741485 **(F)** 01353 741318.
Profile Medical Support. **Ref: YH00262**

ALEX MCDERMID & SON

Alex McDermid & Son, 102 Duke St, Glasgow, **Glasgow (City of)**, G4 0UW, **SCOTLAND**.
(T) 0141 5520406 **(F)** 0141 5522503.
Contact/s
Owner: Mr I McDermid
Profile Blacksmith. **Ref: YH00263**

ALEXANDER

Alexander, 21A West Pilton Pl, Edinburgh, **Edinburgh (City of)**, EH4 4DG, **SCOTLAND**.
(T) 0131 3322001 **(F)** 0131 3321005.
Contact/s
Owner: Mr R Hogg
Profile Blacksmith. **Ref: YH00264**

ALEXANDER JAMES OF PENDLEBURY

Alexander James of Pendlebury, 6 Mossfield Rd, Swinton, Manchester, **Manchester (Greater)**, M27 6EN, **ENGLAND**.
(T) 0161 7936340 **(F)** 0161 7284661
(W) www.english-country-clothing.com
Affiliated Bodies BASC.
Contact/s
Owner: Mr A Little
Profile Riding Wear Retailer.
Clothes for country sports, (hunting, shooting, riding), all made to measure. **Yr. Est:** 1976
Opening Times
Sp: Open Mon - Sat 08:30. Closed Mon - Thurs 17:30, Fri 16:00, Sat 13:00.
Su: Open Mon - Sat 08:30. Closed Mon - Thurs 17:30, Fri 16:00, Sat 13:00.
Au: Open Mon - Sat 08:30. Closed Mon - Thurs 17:30, Fri 16:00, Sat 13:00.
Wn: Open Mon - Sat 08:30. Closed Mon - Thurs 17:30, Fri 16:00, Sat 13:00. **Ref: YH00265**

ALEXANDER TECHNIQUE

Society of Teachers of the Alexander Technique, 129 Camden Mews, London, **London (Greater)**, NW1 9AH, **ENGLAND**.
(T) 020 72843338 **(F)** 020 74825435
(E) info@stat.org.uk
(W) www.stat.org.uk.
Contact/s
Chairman: Mr J McDowell
Profile Club/Association.
It is the largest regulatory body for the Alexander Technique. **Yr. Est:** 1958
Opening Times
Sp: Open Mon - Fri 09:30. Closed Mon - Fri 15:30.
Su: Open Mon - Fri 09:30. Closed Mon - Fri 15:30.
Au: Open Mon - Fri 09:30. Closed Mon - Fri 15:30.
Wn: Open Mon - Fri 09:30. Closed Mon - Fri 15:30.
Ref: YH00266

ALEXANDER TECHNIQUE TEACHER

Alexander Technique Teacher, 2 Trumpeters

Court, West St, Wimborne, **Dorset**, BH21 1JS, **ENGLAND**.
(T) 01202 841789 (F) 01202 888581
Affiliated Bodies STAT.
Contact/s
Owner: Ruth Miller (Q) MSTAT (T) 01202 841789
Profile Medical Support, Medical Support. Alexander Technique teacher focusing on riders.
Ref: YH00267

ALEXANDER, D C S

D C S Alexander, 7 High St, Mauchline, **Ayrshire (South)**, KA5 6AJ, **SCOTLAND**.
(T) 01290 550200.
Profile Medical Support. Ref: YH00268

ALEXANDER, G & B

G & B Alexander, 9 Birch Cres, Blairgowrie, **Perth and Kinross**, **SCOTLAND**..
Profile Breeder. Ref: YH00269

ALEXANDER, HAMISH

Mr Hamish Alexander, Low Hse, Hanging Grimston, Kirby Underdale, York, **Yorkshire (North)**, YO41 1QZ, **ENGLAND**.
(T) 01759 368484
(M) 07774 214072.
Profile Trainer. Ref: YH00270

ALEXANDER, J E

J E Alexander, Howe Lane, Great Sampford, Saffron Walden, **Essex**, CB10 2NY, **ENGLAND**.
(T) 01799 586264 (F) 01799 586264.
Contact/s
Owner: Mr J Alexander
Profile Equestrian Centre, Riding School, Stable/Livery. Ref: YH00271

ALEXANDER, N W

Mr N W Alexander, Kinneston, Leslie, Glenrothes, **Fife**, KY6 3JJ, **SCOTLAND**.
(T) 01592 840223/840774 (F) 01592 84866.
Profile Breeder. Ref: YH00272

ALFORD, H J

H J Alford, Straight-Ash, Culmstock, Cullompton, **Devon**, EX15 3JX, **ENGLAND**.
(T) 01823 680283.
Profile Farrier. Ref: YH00273

ALFORD, STEVE

Steve Alford, Park Lodge, Brampton Bryan, Bucknell, **Shropshire**, SY7 0DH, **ENGLAND**.
(T) 01547 530664.
Profile Farrier. Ref: YH00274

ALFRED BULLER BLOODSTOCK

Alfred Buller Bloodstock Ltd, Scarvagh Hse, 32 Old Mill Rd, Scarvagh, Craigavon, **County Armagh**, BT63 6NL, **NORTHERN IRELAND**.
(T) 028 38832162 (F) 028 38832195
(W) www.scarvagh.com.
Contact/s
Owner: Mr A Buller
Profile Breeder, Stud Farm.
Opening Times
Sp: Open Mon - Sun 08:00. Closed Mon - Sun 17:00.
Su: Open Mon - Sun 08:00. Closed Mon - Sun 17:00.
Au: Open Mon - Sun 08:00. Closed Mon - Sun 17:00.
Wn: Open Mon - Sun 08:00. Closed Mon - Sun 17:00. Ref: YH00275

ALFRED HALES CARRIAGE LAMPS

Alfred Hales Carriage Lamps, Farley Cottage, Sibthorpe, Newark, **Nottinghamshire**, NG23 5PN, **ENGLAND**.
(T) 01636 525508. Ref: YH00276

ALGATE FABRACATES

Algate Fabracates, Mains Of Letham, St. Vigeans, Arbroath, **Angus**, DD11 4RF, **SCOTLAND**.
(T) 01241 431520 (F) 01241 431520.
Contact/s
Owner: Mr A Swankie
Profile Blacksmith. Ref: YH00277

ALGER, A

Mr A Alger, 16 Craddock St, Riverside, Cardiff, **Glamorgan (Vale of)**, CF11 8EU, **WALES**.
(T) 029 20388045.
Profile Breeder. Ref: YH00278

ALICE NUTTGENS SADDLERS

Alice Nuttgens Saddlers, Idlecombe Farm, Turville, Henley-on-Thames, **Oxfordshire**, RG9 6QU, **ENGLAND**.
(T) 01491 638700 (F) 01491 638700.
Contact/s
Owner: Mrs A Nuttgens
Profile Saddlery Retailer. Ref: YH00279

ALICHMORE RIDING/LIVERY CTRE

Alichmore Riding & Livery Centre, Strowan Rd, Crieff, **Perth and Kinross**, PH7 4HP, **SCOTLAND**.
(T) 01764 655567 (F) 01764 650113.
Contact/s
Owner: Mrs B Ramsey
Profile Riding School, Stable/Livery. Ref: YH00280

ALISTAIRE CLARKE TRANSPORT

Alistaire Clarke Transport, 19 Hall Rd, Scraptoft, **Leicestershire**, LE7 9SY, **ENGLAND**.
(T) 0116 2433709 (F) 0116 2419991
(M) 07831 454631.
Profile Transport/Horse Boxes. Ref: YH00281

ALKBOROUGH STABLES

Alkborough Stables, Front St, Alkborough, Scunthorpe, **Lincolnshire (North)**, DN15 9JP, **ENGLAND**.
(T) 01724 721387.
Profile Medical Support. Ref: YH00282

ALL 4 PETS

All 4 Pets Ltd, Beck Hse Farm Shop, Beck Hse, Scagglethorpe, Malton, **Yorkshire (North)**, YO17 8ED, **ENGLAND**.
(T) 01944 758717 (F) 01944 758137.
Profile Supplies. Ref: YH00283

ALL ENGLAND JUMPING COURSE

All England Jumping Course, London Rd, Hickstead, Haywards Heath, **Sussex (West)**, RH17 5NU, **ENGLAND**.
(T) 01273 834315 (F) 01273 834452.
Profile Arena. Ref: YH00284

ALL MANOR PK EQUESTRIAN CTRE

All Manor Park Equestrian Centre, Markedge Lane, Coulsdon, **Surrey**, CR5 3SL, **ENGLAND**.
(T) 01737 557014.
Profile Riding School, Stable/Livery. Ref: YH00285

ALL TIME EQUESTRIAN

All Time Equestrian Horse Rider Supplies, Unit F, Cophall Farm Business Pk, Effingham Rd, Copthorne, Crawley, **Sussex (West)**, RH10 3HZ, **ENGLAND**.
(T) 01342 718951 (F) 01342 717163.
Contact/s
General Manager: Ms S Compton
Profile Supplies.
Opening Times
Sp: Open 09:00. Closed 17:00.
Su: Open 09:00. Closed 17:00.
Au: Open 09:00. Closed 17:00.
Wn: Open 09:00. Closed 17:00.
Saturday 09:00 - 15:00 Ref: YH00286

ALLAN BLOODLINES

Allan Bloodlines, Blackthorn Hse, Pyrford Rd, West Byfleet, **Surrey**, KT14 6QY, **ENGLAND**.
(T) 01932 350660 (F) 01932 352906.
Profile Blood Stock Agency. Ref: YH00287

ALLAN, JAMES W

James W Allan DWCF, 23 Kingsway, Kirkconnel, **Dumfries and Galloway**, DG4 6PN, **SCOTLAND**.
(T) 01659 66154.
Profile Farrier. Ref: YH00288

ALLAN, W K A

W K A Allan, Culzean, High St, Freuchie, **Fife**, KY15 7EY, **SCOTLAND**.
(T) 01337 57531.
Profile Breeder. Ref: YH00289

ALLEN & PAGE

Allen & Page Ltd, Norfolk Mill, Shipdham, Thetford, **Norfolk**, IP25 7SD, **ENGLAND**.
(T) 01362 822900 (F) 01362 822910
(E) sales@allenandpage.com
(W) www.allenandpage.com.
Profile Feed Merchant, Medical Support.
Ref: YH00290

ALLEN & PARTNERS

Allen & Partners, The Veterinary Surgery, Millfield, Whitland, **Carmarthenshire**, SA34 0QN, **WALES**.
(T) 01994 240318 (F) 01994 241060.
Profile Medical Support. Ref: YH00291

ALLEN HOLLINGWORTH & SON

Allen Hollingworth & Son, Reins, Honley, Huddersfield, **Yorkshire (West)**, HD7 2LW, **ENGLAND**.
(T) 01484 661761.
Profile Blacksmith. Ref: YH00292

ALLEN, C N

C N Allen, Shadowfax Stables, Hamilton Rd, Newmarket, **Suffolk**, CB8 7JQ, **ENGLAND**.
(T) 01638 667870
(W) www.newmarketracehorsetrainers.co.uk
Affiliated Bodies Newmarket Trainers Fed.
Contact/s
Trainer: C N Allen
Profile Trainer. Ref: YH00293

ALLEN, D G

D G Allen, Barden Farm, Main Rd, Smalley, **Derbyshire**, DE7 6EE, **ENGLAND**.
(T) 01332 882066.
Profile Breeder. Ref: YH00294

ALLEN, DONNA

Donna Allen, Green Belt Bungalow, Nutts Lane, Leicester, **Leicestershire**, LE10 3EG, **ENGLAND**.
(T) 01455 634476.
Profile Trainer. Ref: YH00295

ALLEN, G

G Allen, 6 Willow Cottages, Lodge Rd, Bicknacre, Chelmsford, **Essex**, CM3 4HJ, **ENGLAND**.
(T) 01245 321219.
Contact/s
Owner: Mr G Allen
Profile Farrier. Ref: YH00296

ALLEN, J S

Mr J S Allen, Alne Pk, Park Lane, Great Alne, Alcester, **Warwickshire**, B49 6HU, **ENGLAND**.
(T) 01789 488469 (F) 01789 415330.
Profile Trainer. Ref: YH00297

ALLEN, LEE J

Lee J Allen DWCF, Oaklands, Lenton Rd, Ingoldsby, Grantham, **Lincolnshire**, NG33 4HA, **ENGLAND**.
(T) 01476 585732.
Profile Farrier. Ref: YH00298

ALLEN, MELVIN

Melvin Allen, 39 Duke Of York St, Wrenthorpe, Wakefield, **Yorkshire (West)**, WF2 0HX, **ENGLAND**.
(T) 01924 217453.
Profile Farrier. Ref: YH00299

ALLEN, P A

P A Allen, Allendale, Bury Green, Little Hadham, Ware, **Hertfordshire**, SG11 2HE, **ENGLAND**.
(T) 01279 655620.
Profile Breeder. Ref: YH00300

ALLEN, ROBERT T

Robert T Allen DWCF, Thatchers Rest, Rampisham, Dorchester, **Dorset**, DT2 0PR, **ENGLAND**.
(T) 01935 83456.
Profile Farrier. Ref: YH00301

ALLEN, SANDY

Sandy Allen, 5 Small Holding, Thornton Rd, Kirkcaldy, **Fife**, KY1 3NN, **SCOTLAND**.
(T) 01592 655444 (F) 01592 655656.
Contact/s
Owner: Mr S Allen
Profile Blacksmith. Ref: YH00302

ALLEN, SUZANNE

Mrs Suzanne Allen, Acrewood Lodge, The Glen, 46 Lenaderg Rd, Bainbridge, **County Down**, BT32 4PT, **NORTHERN IRELAND**.
(T) 028 40662425.
Profile Breeder. Ref: YH00303

ALLEN, T E

Mr T E Allen, Brynhywel, Efailwen, Clynderwen, **Pembrokeshire**, SA66 7JP, **WALES**.
(T) 01994 419483.
Profile Breeder. Ref: YH00304

ALLEN, T W

T W Allen, Bird Cage Cottage, Main St, Fleckney, Leicester, **Leicestershire**, LE8 8AQ, **ENGLAND**.
(T) 0116 2403213.
Contact/s
Partner: Mr T Allen
Profile Farrier. Ref: YH00305

ALLEN, W S

W S Allen, 30 Holtspur Way, Beaconsfield, **Buckinghamshire**, HP9 1DX, **ENGLAND**.
(T) 01494 673959.
Contact/s

Owner: Mr W Allen
Profile Breeder. Ref: YH00306

ALLENDALE, S

S Allendale, Newport Rd, Godshill, Ventnor, **Isle of Wight**, PO38 3LY, **ENGLAND**.
(T) 01983 840258.
Contact/s
Owner: Mr L Mills
Profile Riding School. Ref: YH00307

ALLENS SPORTINGMAN'S BOOKSHOP

Allens Sportingman's Bookshop, 119 Victor Rd, Solihull, **Midlands (West)**, B92 9DS, **ENGLAND**.
(T) 0121 7432285.
Profile Supplies. Ref: YH00308

ALLERFELDT, K M

K M Allerfeldt, Chapple Farm, Chapple Rd, Bovey Tracey, Newton Abbot, **Devon**, TQ13 9JX, **ENGLAND**.
(T) 01626 832284 **(F)** 01626 836818.
Contact/s
Owner: Mr K Allerfeldt Ref: YH00309

ALLERTON, S I

S I Allerton, Old Octon Farm Cottage, Octon, Thwing, Driffield, **Yorkshire (East)**, YO25 3EB, **ENGLAND**.
(T) 01262 470597.
Profile Farrier. Ref: YH00310

ALLEXTON EQUESTRIAN

Allexton Equestrian, The Old Coach Hse, Allexton Hall, Allexton, Oakham, **Rutland**, LE15 9AA, **ENGLAND**.
(T) 01572 717474.
Profile Breeder. Ref: YH00311

ALLIED TRAILER RENTAL

Allied Trailer Rental, Avenue Rd, Lasham, Alton, **Hampshire**, GU34 5SU, **ENGLAND**.
(T) 01256 381344 **(F)** 01256 381446.
Profile Transport/Horse Boxes. Ref: YH00312

ALLIGATOR SADDLERY

Alligator Saddlery, 1 South Lodge, East Tytherley Rd, Lockerley, Romsey, **Hampshire**, SO51 0LW, **ENGLAND**.
(T) 01794 341822. Ref: YH00313

ALLINGTON, JOHN W

John W Allington RSS, 22 Norfolk Drive, Melton Mowbray, **Leicestershire**, LE13 0AZ, **ENGLAND**.
(T) 01664 67053.
Profile Farrier. Ref: YH00314

ALLINGTON, JONATHAN D

Jonathan D Allington DWCF, 95 Burton Rd, Melton Mowbray, **Leicestershire**, LE13 1DN, **ENGLAND**.
(T) 07970 417037.
Profile Farrier. Ref: YH00315

ALLINSON, JONATHAN

Jonathan Allinson, Little Paddock Livery Yard, Frating Rd, Great Bromley, Colchester, **Essex**, CO7 7JL, **ENGLAND**.
(T) 01206 250921.
Contact/s
Trainer: Mr J Allinson **(Q)** AI
Profile Trainer.
Mobile trainer **Yr. Est:** 1991
Opening Times
Sp: Open Mon - Sun 08:00. Closed Mon - Sun 20:00.
Su: Open Mon - Sun 08:00. Closed Mon - Sun 20:00.
Au: Open Mon - Sun 08:00. Closed Mon - Sun 20:00.
Wn: Open Mon - Sun 08:00. Closed Mon - Sun 20:00.
Mobile Ref: YH00316

ALLISON & PARTNERS

Allison & Partners, The Old School Hse, 124 Newland St, Witham, **Essex**, CM8 1BA, **ENGLAND**.
(T) 01376 513638 **(F)** 01376 510509. Ref: YH00317

ALLISON, IAN TREVOR

Ian Trevor Allison DWCF, Calkin Cottage, Birmingham Rd, Stoneleigh, Coventry, **Warwickshire**, CV8 3DD, **ENGLAND**.
(T) 024 76419509.
Profile Farrier. Ref: YH00318

ALLISON, J

J Allison, Woodhead Farm, Uddingston, Glasgow, **Glasgow (City of)**, G71 5PJ, **SCOTLAND**.
(T) 01698 813362.
Contact/s
Owner: Mrs J Allison Ref: YH00319

ALLISON, W P

W P Allison, East Lodge, Cavers, Hawick, **Scottish Borders**, TD9 8LJ, **SCOTLAND**.
(T) 01450 373044.
Profile Farrier. Ref: YH00320

ALLMAN, R P & G E J

R P & G E J Allman, Far Poden, Honeybourne, Evesham, **Worcestershire**, WR11 5PS, **ENGLAND**.
(T) 01386 438281.
Profile Stable/Livery. Ref: YH00321

ALLMAN, RAY & MARK

Ray & Mark Allman, Madeley Heath Farm, Watering Trough Bank, Madeley Heath, Crewe, **Cheshire**, CW3 9LT, **ENGLAND**.
(T) 01782 750292.
Profile Breeder. Horse Dealers. Ref: YH00322

ALLONBY RIDING SCHOOL

Allonby Riding School, Rydal Mount Stables, Gilcrux, Wigton, **Cumbria**, CA7 2QD, **ENGLAND**.
(T) 01697 322889
(W) www.allonbyridingschool.fsnet.co.uk.
Contact/s
Owner: Mr P Carter
(E) peter@allonbyridingschool.fsnet.co.uk
Profile Arena, Riding School, Stable/Livery.
No.Staff: 2 **Yr. Est:** 1932 **C.Size:** 4 Acres
Opening Times
Open all year Ref: YH00323

ALLONBY, D

Mr D Allonby, The Court, Stanford-on-Soar, Loughborough, **Leicestershire**, LE12 5PY, **ENGLAND**.
(T) 01509 263782.
Profile Breeder. Ref: YH00324

ALLPRESS, BELGRAVE & PARTNERS

Allpress, Belgrave & Partners, The Equine Veterinary Hospital, Tortington, Arundel, **Sussex (West)**, BN18 0BG, **ENGLAND**.
(T) 01903 883050 **(F)** 01903 884590.
Profile Medical Support. Ref: YH00325

ALLTACK & ALLFEED

Alltack & Allfeed, New Shardelowes Farm, Balsham Rd, Fulbourn, Cambridge, **Cambridgeshire**, CB1 5DA, **ENGLAND**.
(T) 01223 882161 **(F)** 01223 882160.
Contact/s
Partner: Mrs J Allen
Profile Saddlery Retailer. Ref: YH00326

ALLTRUCK TRAILER RENTAL

Alltruck Trailer Rental PLC, Colthrop Lane, Thatcham, **Berkshire**, RG19 4NT, **ENGLAND**.
(T) 0870 5168781.
Profile Transport/Horse Boxes. Ref: YH00327

ALLWORK, S

S Allwork, Home Farm, Delapre Pk, Northampton, **Northamptonshire**, NN4 7BS, **ENGLAND**.
(T) 01604 764429.
Contact/s
Owner: Mr S Allwork
Profile Riding Club, Stable/Livery. Ref: YH00328

ALMOND RIDING CLUB

Almond Riding Club, The Mill, Hermand Est, West Calder, **Lothian (West)**, EH55 8QZ, **SCOTLAND**.
(T) 01506 872669.
Contact/s
Secretary: Mrs M Miller
Profile Club/Association, Riding Club. Ref: YH00329

ALMOND, M

Mr M Almond, 42 Wood Lane, Heskin, Chorley, **Lancashire**, PR7 5NU, **ENGLAND**.
(T) 01257 450012. Ref: YH00330

ALN VETNRY GRP

Aln Veterinary Group, Wagonway Rd, Alnwick, **Northumberland**, NE66 1QQ, **ENGLAND**.
(T) 01665 510999.
Profile Medical Support. Ref: YH00331

ALNER, R H

Mr R H Alner, Locketts Farm, Droop, Blandford, **Dorset**, DT11 0EZ, **ENGLAND**.
(T) 01258 817271 **(F)** 01258 817271
(M) 07767 436375.
Profile Trainer. Ref: YH00332

ALOE VERA EQUICARE

Aloe Vera Equicare, 15 Alders Rd, Edgware, **London (Greater)**, HA8 9QG, **ENGLAND**.
(T) 020 89592452.
Profile Medical Support. Ref: YH00333

ALSAGER & SANDBACH SADDLERY

Alsager & Sandbach Saddlery, Day Green Farm, Day Green, Hassall, Sandbach, **Cheshire**, CW11 4XU, **ENGLAND**.
(T) 01270 872095 **(F)** 01270 872095.
Contact/s
Owner: Mr A Whithy
Profile Saddlery Retailer. Ref: YH00334

ALSAGER EQUESTRIAN CTRE

Alsager Equestrian Centre, Lawton Heath End, Church Lawton, Stoke-on-Trent, **Staffordshire**, ST7 3RQ, **ENGLAND**.
(T) 01270 872994 **(F)** 01270 872994.
Contact/s
Owner: Mrs G Harrison
Profile Riding School, Stable/Livery, Track/Course.
Ref: YH00335

ALSCOT PARK STABLES

Alscot Park Stables, Alscot Pk, Atherstone On Stour, Stratford-upon-Avon, **Warwickshire**, CV37 8BL, **ENGLAND**.
(T) 01789 450052 **(F)** 01789 450053
(M) 07836 203079.
Profile Trainer. Ref: YH00336

ALSION THOM TRANSPORT

Alsion Thom Transport, Exeter Stables, Church St, Exning, Newmarket, **Suffolk**, CB8 7EH, **ENGLAND**.
(T) 01638 577675 **(F)** 01638 577675.
Contact/s
Owner: Mrs A Thom
Profile Transport/Horse Boxes. Ref: YH00337

ALSOP, D N

Mr D N Alsop, Hill Cottage, Wychnor, Burton-on-Trent, **Staffordshire**, DE13 8BY, **ENGLAND**.
(T) 01283 790803.
Profile Breeder. Ref: YH00338

ALSTON & KILLHOPE

Alston & Killhope Riding Centre, Low Cornriggs Farm, Cowshill, Bishop Auckland, **County Durham**, DL13 1AQ, **ENGLAND**.
(T) 01388 537600 **(F)** 01388 537777
(E) enquiries@lowcornriggsfarm.fsnet.co.uk
(W) www.britnett.com/lowcornriggsfarm
Affiliated Bodies ABRS, RDA.
Contact/s
Instructor: Mr A Senior **(Q)** BHS 2, BHSII, NCHM
(T) 01388 537089
Profile Holidays, Horse/Rider Accom, Riding Club, Riding School, Stable/Livery.
Childrens fun days, holidays for horses and day rides available. **No.Staff:** 5 **Yr. Est:** 1971
C.Size: 50 Acres
Opening Times
Sp: Open Mon - Sun 09:30. Closed Mon - Sun 21:30.
Su: Open Mon - Sun 09:30. Closed Mon - Sun 21:30.
Au: Open Mon - Sun 09:30. Closed Mon - Sun 21:30.
Wn: Open Mon - Sun 09:30. Closed Mon - Sun 21:30. Ref: YH00339

ALSTON, ERIC

Eric Alston, Edges Farm Racing Stables, Chapel Lane, Longton, Preston, **Lancashire**, PR4 5NA, **ENGLAND**.
(T) 01772 612120 **(F)** 01772 612120.
Contact/s
Partner: Mr E Alston
Profile Trainer. Ref: YH00340

ALSTON, HENRY CHARLES

Henry Charles Alston, 1 Greenfields, Sutton, Pulborough, **Sussex (West)**, RH20 1PP, **ENGLAND**.
(T) 01798 7302.
Profile Farrier. Ref: YH00341

ALSTONE COURT RIDING ESTB

Alstone Court Riding Establishment, Alstone Lane, Highbridge, **Somerset**, TA9 3DS, **ENGLAND**.
(T) 01278 789417.
Contact/s
Owner: Mrs S March
Profile Stable/Livery, Supplies.
Opening Times
Sp: Open Tues - Sun 09:00. Closed Tues - Sun 18:00.
Su: Open Tues - Sun 09:00. Closed Tues - Sun 18:00.
Au: Open Tues - Sun 09:00. Closed Tues - Sun

18:00.
Wn: Open Tues - Sun 09:00. Closed Tues - Sun 18:00. **Ref: YH00342**

ALTERNATIVE RIDING SCHOOL

Alternative Riding School (The), Doone Brae Farm, Windmill Rd, Pepperstock, Luton, **Bedfordshire**, LU1 4LQ, **ENGLAND**.
(T) 01582 841829.
Contact/s
General Manager: Ms T Lloyd
Profile Horse Rescue Centre. **C.Size:** 20 Acres
Ref: YH00343

ALTON RIDING SCHOOL

Alton Riding School, Alton, Chesterfield, **Derbyshire**, S42 6AW, **ENGLAND**.
(T) 01246 590267.
Contact/s
For Bookings: Mrs J Butler
Profile Breeder, Equestrian Centre, Riding School, Stable/Livery, Supplies. **No.Staff:** 6
Yr. Est: 1967 **C.Size:** 40 Acres
Opening Times
Sp: Open 09:00. Closed 21:00.
Su: Open 09:00. Closed 22:00.
Au: Open 09:00. Closed 21:00.
Wn: Open 09:00. Closed 21:00. **Ref: YH00344**

ALTON, JAMES

James Alton DWCF, 6 Orchard Ave, North Anston, Sheffield, **Yorkshire (South)**, S25 4BW, **ENGLAND**.
(T) 01909 563919.
Profile Farrier. **Ref: YH00345**

ALTRIES STABLES

Altries Stables, Back Mains Of Altries, Maryculter, Aberdeen, **Aberdeen (City of)**, AB12 0GJ, **SCOTLAND**.
(T) 01224 732005.
Profile Stable/Livery. **Ref: YH00346**

ALVANLEY HALL FARM

Alvanley Hall Farm, Manley Rd, Alvanley, Frodsham, **Cheshire**, WA6 9DN, **ENGLAND**.
(T) 01928 740753.
Contact/s
Owner: Mr S Pickering **Ref: YH00347**

ALVECHURCH RIDING CLUB

Alvechurch Riding Club, 27 Blythesway, Alvechurch, Birmingham, **Midlands (West)**, B48 7NB, **ENGLAND**.
(T) 0121 4455423.
Profile Riding Club. **Ref: YH00348**

ALVESCOT STUD

S J & A Hobbs, Alvescot Stud, Alvescot Field Farm, Carterton, **Oxfordshire**, OX18 1PD, **ENGLAND**.
(T) 01993 840044 **(F)** 01993 841344
(W) www.alvescotstud.co.uk.
Contact/s
Owner: Mr S Hobbs
Profile Breeder, Medical Support. **No.Staff:** 5
Yr. Est: 1981 **C.Size:** 360 Acres
Opening Times
Sp: Open Dawn. Closed Dusk.
Su: Open Dawn. Closed Dusk.
Au: Open Dawn. Closed Dusk.
Wn: Open Dawn. Closed Dusk. **Ref: YH00349**

ALVIE STABLES

Alvie Stables, Alvie Est, Kincraig, Kingussie, **Highlands**, PH21 1ND, **SCOTLAND**.
(T) 01540 651255.
Profile Riding School. **Ref: YH00350**

ALVINGHAM FORGE

Alvingham Forge, Yarburgh Rd, Alvingham, Louth, **Lincolnshire**, LN11 0QG, **ENGLAND**.
(T) 01507 327017.
Profile Blacksmith. **Ref: YH00351**

ALWYN HOLDEN

Alwyn Holder (Plant Hire) Ltd, Mallards Farm, Partridge Lane, Newdigate, **Surrey**, RH5 5BW, **ENGLAND**.
(T) 01293 862519.
Profile Track/Course. **Ref: YH00352**

ALYN BANK

Alyn Bank Riding School, Wrexham Rd, Pontblyddyn, Mold, **Flintshire**, CH7 4HG, **WALES**.
(T) 01352 770621.
Contact/s
Owner: Mrs E Chilton
Profile Riding School.
Teaches basic riding skills and has access to hacking country. **Yr. Est:** 1971 **C.Size:** 50 Acres

Opening Times
Sp: Open Tues - Sun 10:00. Closed Tues - Sun 18:00.
Su: Open Tues - Sun 10:00. Closed Tues - Sun 18:00.
Au: Open Tues - Sun 10:00. Closed Tues - Sun 18:00.
Wn: Open Tues - Sun 10:00. Closed Tues - Sun 18:00. **Ref: YH00353**

AMATEUR JOCKEYS AST OF GB

Amateur Jockeys Association of GB, Croft Cottage, 29 Manor Rd, Farnley Tyas, Huddersfield, **Yorkshire (West)**, HD4 6UL, **ENGLAND**.
(T) 01484 666507 **(F)** 01484 666507.
Profile Club/Association. **Ref: YH00354**

AMATEUR RIDERS ASS OF GB

Amateur Riders Association of GB, 40 Queen St, London, **London (Greater)**, EC4R 1DD, **ENGLAND**.
(T) 020 73322680.
Profile Club/Association. **Ref: YH00355**

AMBER HILLS EQUESTRIAN

Amber Hills Equestrian, Whitehouse Farm, 153 Belper Lane, Belper, **Derbyshire**, DE56 2UJ, **ENGLAND**.
(T) 01773 824080.
Contact/s
Owner: Mrs V Cooke
Profile Stable/Livery. **Ref: YH00356**

AMBERVALE

Ambervale Farm, North Common Lane, Sway, Lymington, **Hampshire**, SO41 8LL, **ENGLAND**.
(T) 01425 271313 **(F)** 01590 679782
(M) 07929 057537.
Contact/s
Owner: Mrs C Nicholson-Pike
Profile Stable/Livery, Trainer.
Give training to children between the ages of ten and twelve. Also train animals for films and advertising.
Opening Times
Telephone for an appointment. **Ref: YH00357**

AMBIVET VETNRY GRP

Ambivet Veterinary Group (Derbyshire), Ambivet Veterinary Clinic, Heage Rd, Ripley, **Derbyshire**, DE5 3GE, **ENGLAND**.
(T) 01773 747801.
Profile Medical Support. **Ref: YH00358**

AMBIVET VETNRY GRP

Ambivet Veterinary Group (Heanor), The Veterinary Clinic, 24 Mundy St, Heanor, **Derbyshire**, DE75 7EB, **ENGLAND**.
(T) 01773 717780 **(F)** 01773 712448.
Profile Medical Support. **Ref: YH00359**

AMBLECOTE TACK EXCHANGE

Amblecote Tack Exchange, 2 Dennis St, Amblecote, Stourbridge, **Midlands (West)**, DY8 4ED, **ENGLAND**.
(T) 01384 392681
(E) kjdl28312@blueyonder.co.uk.
Profile Saddlery Retailer. **Ref: YH00360**

AMBRIDGE SADDLERY

Ambridge Saddlery, 50 Marymead Drive, Stevenage, **Hertfordshire**, SG2 8AD, **ENGLAND**.
(T) 01438 315223.
Contact/s
Owner: Mr P Hendry
Profile Saddlery Retailer. **Ref: YH00361**

AMBRIDGE SADDLERY

Ambridge Saddlery, 23 Ash Cl, Watlington, **Oxfordshire**, OX9 5LW, **ENGLAND**.
(T) 01491 613622.
Profile Saddlery Retailer. **Ref: YH00362**

AMEGA SCIENCES

Amega Sciences, Royal Oak Ind Est, Lanchester Way, Daventry, **Northamptonshire**, NN11 5PH, **ENGLAND**.
(T) 01327 704444 **(F)** 01327 871154
(E) lis-middup@amega-sciences.com.
Profile Track/Course. **Ref: YH00363**

AMERICAN NAT SHOW

American National Show Horse Association, Birchwood Forge, Storridge, Malvern, **Worcestershire**, WR13 5RZ, **ENGLAND**.
(T) 01886 884285 **(F)** 01886 884285.
Profile Club/Association. **Ref: YH00364**

AMERICAN THOROUGHBRED

American Thoroughbred Products Ltd, Bay Tree Cottage, The Street, Kilmington, **Wiltshire**, BA12 6RG, **ENGLAND**.
(T) 01985 844613.
Profile Feed Merchant. **Ref: YH00365**

AMESBURY TRAILER HIRE

Amesbury Trailer Hire, Stockport Rd, Amesbury, Salisbury, **Wiltshire**, SP4 7LN, **ENGLAND**.
(T) 01980 624446.
Profile Transport/Horse Boxes. **Ref: YH00366**

AMHB

Association of Masters of Harriers & Beagles, P O Box 5682, Newbury, **Berkshire**, RG14 7JB, **ENGLAND**.
(T) 01635 41320 **(F)** 01635 582936
(E) amhb@newburynet.co.
Profile Club/Association. **Ref: YH00367**

AMMAN VALLEY PONY CLUB

Amman Valley Pony Club, Hillside, 81 Heol Y Mynydd, Garnswllt, Ammanford, **Carmarthenshire**, SA18 2SE, **WALES**.
(T) 01269 593252.
Profile Club/Association. **Ref: YH00368**

AMMAN VALLEY RACEWAY

Amman Valley Raceway, 16 Oakfield Rd, Garnant, Ammanford, **Carmarthenshire**, SA18 1JH, **WALES**.
(T) 01269 823734.
Profile Track/Course. **Ref: YH00369**

AMOS & PENNY

Amos & Penny, 1 Marine Cres, Falmouth, **Cornwall**, TR11 4BS, **ENGLAND**.
(T) 01326 313740.
Profile Medical Support. **Ref: YH00370**

AMOS, W

Mr W Amos, Broadhaugh Farm, Newmill, Hawick, **Scottish Borders**, TD9 0JX, **SCOTLAND**.
(T) 01450 850323.
Profile Supplies. **Ref: YH00371**

AMPORT RIDING SCHOOL

Amport Riding School, Furzedown Lane, Amport, Andover, **Hampshire**, SP11 8BE, **ENGLAND**.
(T) 01264 772972.
Contact/s
Owner: Mr R Hale
Profile Riding School, Stable/Livery. **Ref: YH00372**

AMRAK ENGINEERING

Amrak Engineering, Unit 14 Boden Streeet Ind Est, Glasgow, **Glasgow (City of)**, G40 3QF, **SCOTLAND**.
(T) 0141 5564754.
Profile Blacksmith. **Ref: YH00373**

AMTEX

Amtex Ltd, Pinsley Farm, Kingsland, Leominster, **Herefordshire**, HR6 9QT, **ENGLAND**.
(T) 01568 708926 **(F)** 01568 708121.
Profile Supplies. **Ref: YH00374**

AMY OXENBOULD

Amy Oxenbould (Sculpture), 10 Sandlea Pk, West Kirby, Wirral, **Merseyside**, CH48 0QF, **ENGLAND**.
(T) 0151 6256465. **Ref: YH00375**

ANCHOR TO NEEDLE FABRICATIONS

Anchor to Needle Fabrications Ltd, 1103 Argyle St, Glasgow, **Glasgow (City of)**, G3 8ND, **SCOTLAND**.
(T) 0141 2481616 **(F)** 0141 2481616.
Contact/s
Owner: Mr G Flemming
Profile Blacksmith. **Ref: YH00376**

ANCHOR TRAILERS

Anchor Trailers, 24 Lansdown Green, Kidderminster, **Worcestershire**, DY11 6PY, **ENGLAND**.
(T) 01562 755122.
Contact/s
Owner: Mr R Hodgkins
Profile Transport/Horse Boxes. **Ref: YH00377**

ANDALUSIANS

Maryss Andalusians, Church Farm, Church St, Semington, Trowbridge, **Wiltshire**, BA14 6JS, **ENGLAND**.
(T) 01380 870139 **(F)** 01380 870139.
Profile Breeder. **Ref: YH00378**

ANDERSON, D S

Mr & Mrs D S Anderson, Bents Farm, Summerbridge, Harrogate, **Yorkshire (North)**, HG3 4AN, **ENGLAND**.
(T) 01423 780975.
Profile Breeder. **Ref: YH00379**

ANDERSON, ALEC A
Alec A Anderson, Merrylaws, East Linton, **Lothian (East)**, EH40 3DX, **SCOTLAND**.
(T) 01620 870216.
Contact/s
Owner: Mr A Anderson
Profile Blacksmith. **Ref: YH00380**

ANDERSON, D
D Anderson, Park Smithy, Drumoak, Banchory, **Aberdeenshire**, AB31 5HB, **SCOTLAND**.
(T) 01330 811755 (F) 01330 811755.
Contact/s
Owner: Mr D Anderson
Profile Blacksmith. **Ref: YH00381**

ANDERSON, I F F
Mr I F F Anderson, Ty Canol, Guilsfield, Welshpool, **Powys**, SY21 9PS, **WALES**.
(T) 01938 590509
(M) 07889 896832.
Profile Supplies. **Ref: YH00382**

ANDERSON, IAN
Ian Anderson, 4 Shieldhill Gardens, Aberdeen, **Aberdeen (City of)**, AB12 3JY, **SCOTLAND**.
(T) 01224 248477.
Profile Blacksmith. **Ref: YH00383**

ANDERSON, JOHN C
John C Anderson, 89 Shenstone Rd, Sheffield, **Yorkshire (South)**, S6 1SP, **ENGLAND**.
(T) 0114 2333009.
Profile Farrier. **Ref: YH00384**

ANDERSON, JOHN F
John F Anderson RSS, 29 Highfield Ave, Mynydd Isa, Mold, **Flintshire**, CH7 6XY, **WALES**.
(T) 01244 545222.
Profile Farrier. **Ref: YH00385**

ANDERSON, P A
P A Anderson, Broomhill Farm, Fortrose, **Highlands**, IV10 8SH, **SCOTLAND**.
(T) 01381 620214.
Contact/s
Owner: Mrs C Anderson
Profile Riding School. **Ref: YH00386**

ANDERSON, SIMON H
Simon H Anderson DWCF, Holly Cottage, Wilstead Rd, Elstow, **Bedfordshire**, MK42 9YD, **ENGLAND**.
(T) 07778 616235.
Profile Farrier. **Ref: YH00387**

ANDMAR TRAILER CTRE
Andmar Trailer Centre, 24 Beechwood Pk, Strathfoyle, Londonderry, **County Londonderry**, BT47 6XD, **NORTHERN IRELAND**.
(T) 028 71860211 (F) 028 71860211.
Contact/s
Owner: Mr A Coyle
Profile Transport/Horse Boxes. **Ref: YH00388**

ANDREW BOTTERILL SADDLER
Andrew Botterill Saddler, Underwoods Yard, 57 High St, Wollaston, Wellingborough, **Northamptonshire**, NN29 7QF, **ENGLAND**.
(T) 01933 663514.
Profile Saddlery Retailer. **Ref: YH00389**

ANDREW GOOD VIDEO PRODUCERS
Andrew Good Video Producers, 63 Heathfield Rd, Sholing, **Hampshire**, SO2 8DL, **ENGLAND**.
(T) 023 80732705.
Profile Supplies. **Ref: YH00390**

ANDREW GRAY
Andrew Gray Trailers, Craighead Farm, Torrance, Glasgow, **Glasgow (City of)**, G64 4DR, **SCOTLAND**.
(T) 01360 620625.
Profile Transport/Horse Boxes. **Ref: YH00391**

ANDREW REILLY
Andrew Reilly Saddlers, Ashdown Works, Hartfield Rd, Forest Row, **Sussex (East)**, RH18 5LY, **ENGLAND**.
(T) 01342 825515 (F) 01342 825515.
Contact/s
Owner: Mr A Reilly (Q) Master Saddler, Saddle Fitter
Profile Saddlery Retailer.
Offers a mobile service to clients covering Sussex, Surrey, London and Kent. They carry a range of English made saddles: Ideal, Albion, and many more.
No.Staff: 2 Yr. Est: 1993 **Ref: YH00392**

ANDREW SIME
Andrew Sime & Co Ltd, 9 Woodditton Rd, Newmarket, **Suffolk**, CB8 9BQ, **ENGLAND**.
(T) 01638 663514 (F) 01638 663483.
Contact/s
Owner: Mr A Sime
Profile Blood Stock Agency. **Ref: YH00393**

ANDREW, M
Mrs M Andrew, 8 Northumberland Ave, Costhorpe, Worksop, **Nottinghamshire**, S81 9JP, **ENGLAND**.
(T) 01909 731292. **Ref: YH00394**

ANDREW, R M
Mrs R M Andrew, Bronheulog, Manafon, Welshpool, **Powys**, SY21 8BW, **WALES**.
(T) 01686 650285.
Profile Breeder. **Ref: YH00395**

ANDREWS MILLING
Andrews Milling Ltd, Percy St, Belfast, **County Antrim**, BT13 2HW, **NORTHERN IRELAND**.
(T) 028 90322451 (F) 028 90322451.
Profile Supplies. **Ref: YH00396**

ANDREWS, DAVID M
David M Andrews DWCF, Meetings Farm, Little Tew, Enstone, **Oxfordshire**, OX7 4JN, **ENGLAND**.
(T) 01608 683280.
Profile Farrier. **Ref: YH00397**

ANDREWS, DAVID V
David V Andrews DWCF, 17 Eastwood Cottages, Conyer, Teynham, Sittingbourne, **Kent**, ME9 9HD, **ENGLAND**.
(T) 01795 521321.
Profile Farrier. **Ref: YH00398**

ANDREWS, J
Mr J Andrews, Stratheden Hse, Ladybank, Cupar, **Fife**, KY7 7JS, **SCOTLAND**.
(T) 01337 830335.
Profile Supplies. **Ref: YH00399**

ANDREWS, JOHN
John Andrews, 51 Gloverstown Rd, Toomebridge, **County Antrim**, **NORTHERN IRELAND**.
Profile Breeder. **Ref: YH00400**

ANDREWS, JULIE
Julie Andrews, 12 Trelinnoe Cl, South Petherwin, Launceston, **Cornwall**, PL15 7JX, **ENGLAND**.
(T) 01566 774161 (F) 01566 774161
(M) 07721 903022
(E) julie@horseinsuranceservices.co.uk.
Profile Insurance Agents. **Ref: YH00401**

ANDREWS, R T
R T Andrews, Woolcotts Farm, Brompton Regis, Dulverton, **Somerset**, TA22 9NX, **ENGLAND**.
(T) 01398 371206.
Profile Breeder. **Ref: YH00402**

ANDREWS, SUE
Sue Andrews, Lypiatt Farm, Miserden, Stroud, **Gloucestershire**, GL6 7JA, **ENGLAND**.
(T) 01285 821576.
Profile Supplies. **Ref: YH00403**

ANDREWS, T
T Andrews, 1 Marsham Way, Halling, Rochester, **Kent**, ME2 1LY, **ENGLAND**.
(T) 01634 245535.
Contact/s
Owner: Mr T Andrews
Profile Farrier. **Ref: YH00404**

ANDY COOK RACING
Andy Cook Racing, Oakwood Stables, East Witton Rd, Middleham, Leyburn, **Yorkshire (North)**, DL8 4PT, **ENGLAND**.
(T) 01969 625223 (F) 01969 625224.
Contact/s
Owner: Mr A Cook
Profile Trainer.
45 box yard with treadmill, sand pen and gallops.
Yr. Est: 2001 C.Size: 1 Acres
Opening Times
Telephone for an appointment **Ref: YH00405**

ANFIELD HSE RACING STABLES
Anfield House Racing Stables, New Rd, Uttoxeter, **Staffordshire**, ST14 5DT, **ENGLAND**.
(T) 01889 568919.
Contact/s
Manager: Mr A Streeter
Profile Trainer. **Ref: YH00406**

ANGELA BROMWICH
Angela Bromwich Saddler, Westholme, Westfield Lane, Draycott, Cheddar, **Somerset**, BS27 3TP, **ENGLAND**.
(T) 01934 743141.
Contact/s
Owner: Ms A Bromwich
Profile Supplies. Saddlery.
Mrs Bromwich produces made-to-measure saddles.
Yr. Est: 1987
Opening Times
Telephone for an appointment **Ref: YH00407**

ANGELA MASKELL
Angela Maskell Bespoke Saddles, Meadow Edge, Silver St, Hordle, Lymington, **Hampshire**, SO41 0FN, **ENGLAND**.
(T) 01425 610785.
Profile Supplies. **Ref: YH00408**

ANGLE PARK
Angle Park Riding School and Livery Yard, Ladybank, Cupar, **Fife**, KY15 7UL, **SCOTLAND**.
(T) 01337 830641.
Contact/s
Owner: Ms J Wheatley (Q) BHSAI
Profile Riding School, Stable/Livery. No.Staff: 1
Yr. Est: 1990 C.Size: 12 Acres **Ref: YH00409**

ANGLESEY EQUESTRIAN CTRE
Anglesey Equestrian Centre, Tanrallt Newydd, Bodedern, Holyhead, **Isle of Anglesey**, LL65 3UE, **WALES**.
(T) 01407 741378 (F) 01407 741378
Affiliated Bodies BHS.
Contact/s
General Manager: Mr R Roberts
Profile Equestrian Centre, Riding School, Stable/Livery. No.Staff: 3 Yr. Est: 1999
C.Size: 12 Acres
Opening Times
Sp: Open 10:00. Closed 20:00.
Su: Open 10:00. Closed 20:00.
Au: Open 10:00. Closed 20:00.
Wn: Open 10:00. Closed 20:00. **Ref: YH00410**

ANGLEY STUD
Angley Stud, Angley Rd, Cranbrook, **Kent**, TN17 2PN, **ENGLAND**.
(T) 01580 715814 (F) 01580 714276.
Contact/s
Owner: Mr I Emes
Profile Breeder. **Ref: YH00411**

ANGLIA BLOODSTOCK
Anglia Bloodstock, Lark Hall Rd, Fordham, Ely, **Cambridgeshire**, CB7 5LS, **ENGLAND**.
(T) 01638 720590 (F) 01638 721206.
Contact/s
Owner: Mrs A Brudenell
Profile Blood Stock Agency. **Ref: YH00412**

ANGLIA HORSE TRANSPORT
Anglia Horse Transport, Dovesdale, Lower Rd, Westerfield, Ipswich, **Suffolk**, IP6 9AR, **ENGLAND**.
(T) 01473 255629
(M) 07850 253657.
Profile Transport/Horse Boxes. **Ref: YH00413**

ANGLIA TOWING EQUIPMENT
Anglia Towing Equipment, Unit 17 Grange Way Business Pk, Grange Way, Colchester, **Essex**, CO2 8HF, **ENGLAND**.
(T) 01206 795949.
Contact/s
General Manager: Mr S Bradshaw
Profile Transport/Horse Boxes. No.Staff: 7
Yr. Est: 1995
Opening Times
Sp: Open 08:00. Closed 17:30.
Su: Open 08:00. Closed 17:30.
Au: Open 08:00. Closed 17:30.
Wn: Open 08:00. Closed 17:30. **Ref: YH00414**

ANGLIA TRAILER MAILER
Anglia Trailer Mailer, 54 Damgate Lane, Martham, Great Yarmouth, **Norfolk**, NR29 4PZ, **ENGLAND**.
(T) 01493 748354.
Contact/s
Owner: Mr L Fearn
Profile Transport/Horse Boxes. **Ref: YH00415**

ANGLIA WOODCHIP
Anglia Woodchip Co Ltd, 3 Wingfield Court, Norwich Rd, Mulbarton, Norwich, **Norfolk**, NR14 8JP, **ENGLAND**.
(T) 01508 571452 (F) 01508 571453.
Contact/s

Assistant: Miss S Standley
Profile Track/Course. Ref: YH00416

ANGLIAN TRAILER CTRE

Anglian Trailer Centre Ltd, Oak Farm, Cockfield, Bury St Edmunds, **Suffolk**, IP30 0JH, **ENGLAND**.
(T) 01284 828415.
Profile Transport/Horse Boxes. Ref: YH00417

ANGLO & PART-BRED ARAB ASS

Anglo & Part-Bred Arab Owners Association, Gosford Farm, Ottery St Mary, **Devon**, EX11 1LX, **ENGLAND**.
(T) 01404 814998.
Profile Club/Association. Ref: YH00418

ANGLO EUROPEAN STUDBOOK

Anglo European Studbook Ltd, Flat 2 High Sussex, Beacon Rd, Crowborough, **Sussex (East)**, TN6 1AY, **ENGLAND**.
(T) 01892 610155 **(F)** 01892 610156.
Profile Supplies. Ref: YH00419

ANGMERING FORGE

Angmering Forge, Arundel Rd, Worthing, **Sussex (West)**, BN13 3EH, **ENGLAND**.
(T) 01903 776327.
Contact/s
Owner: Mr I Takasi
Profile Blacksmith. Ref: YH00420

ANGUS EQUESTRIAN

Angus Equestrian, Upper Balmachie Farm, Carnoustie, **Angus**, DD7 6LB, **SCOTLAND**.
(F) 01241 852953
(M) 07831 239396.
Contact/s
Owner: Mr J Lascelles Ref: YH00421

ANGUS MCMURTRIE

Angus McMurtrie Ltd, 1 Kellas Rd, Broughty Ferry, Dundee, **Angus**, DD5 3PE, **SCOTLAND**.
(T) 01382 350301 **(F)** 01382 350573.
Contact/s
Owner: Mr A McMurtrie
Profile Blacksmith. Ref: YH00422

ANGUS, S

S Angus, The Surgery, Tower Rd, Ramsey, **Isle of Man**, IM8 2EA, **ENGLAND**.
(T) 01624 812208.
Profile Medical Support. Ref: YH00423

ANIMAL AIRLINES

Animal Airlines, 35 Beatrice Ave, Manchester, **Manchester (Greater)**, M18 7JU, **ENGLAND**.
(T) 0161 2234035.
Profile Transport/Horse Boxes. Ref: YH00424

ANIMAL ALTERNATIVES

Animal ALTERNATIVES Ltd, P O Box 289, Richmond, **Surrey**, TW10 7XH, **ENGLAND**.
(T) 07002 264625 **(F)** 020 83322054
(E) info@animal-alternatives.co.uk
(W) www.horsefeeds.co.uk/animalalternatives.htm.
Contact/s
Key Contact: Miss C Liggett
Profile Medical Support.
Animal ALTERNATIVES produce products to aid animals natural body balances, from digestive stabilisers to immune support. Ref: YH00425

ANIMAL ARTISTRY

Animal Artistry, Stone Hse Farm, Thornbury, Bromyard, **Herefordshire**, HR7 4N7, **ENGLAND**.
(T) 01885 482484 **(F)** 01885 482484.
Profile Artist.
Animal artist. Ref: YH00426

ANIMAL BEDDING

Animal Bedding Co Ltd, Lavenham Farm, Nibley Lane, Iron Acton, Bristol, **Bristol**, BS37 9UR, **ENGLAND**.
(T) 01454 228171 **(F)** 01454 228171.
Contact/s
Administration: Ms C Horrill
Profile Medical Support, Supplies.
The shredded paper bedding supplied is dust and staple free. No.Staff: 5 Yr. Est: 1998
Opening Times
Sp: Open 08:30. Closed 17:00.
Su: Open 08:30. Closed 17:00.
Au: Open 08:30. Closed 17:00.
Wn: Open 08:30. Closed 17:00. Ref: YH00427

ANIMAL BEHAVIOUR CONSULTANTS

Animal Behaviour Consultants, Little Ash Eco-Farm, Throwleigh, Okehampton, **Devon**, EX20 2QG, **ENGLAND**.
(T) 01647 231394.
Contact/s
Owner: Dr M Kiley-Worthington
Profile Breeder, Medical Support. Animal Behaviourists. Ref: YH00428

ANIMAL CARE/EQUINE TRAIN ORG

Animal Care & Equine Training Organisation Ltd, Suite No 3, St Mary's Mews, St Mary's Pl, Stafford, **Staffordshire**, ST16 2AP, **ENGLAND**.
(T) 01785 608080 **(F)** 01785 608070.
Profile Equestrian Centre. Ref: YH00429

ANIMAL CRACKERS

Animal Crackers, Norwich Rd, Swardeston, Norwich, **Norfolk**, NR14 8DW, **ENGLAND**.
(T) 01508 570104.
Contact/s
Owner: Mr C Thompson
Profile Supplies. Ref: YH00430

ANIMAL EDIBLES

Animal Edibles, Hazeldene, Longdown, Exeter, **Devon**, EX6 7SR, **ENGLAND**.
(T) 01392 811264.
Profile Supplies. Ref: YH00431

ANIMAL FAYRE

Animal Fayre, The Coach Hse, Rags Lane, Cheshunt, **Hertfordshire**, EN7 6TE, **ENGLAND**.
(T) 01992 643025.
Profile Supplies. Ref: YH00432

ANIMAL FEED SHOP

Animal Feed Shop Ltd (The), Unit 8 Barhams Cl, Wylds Rd, Bridgwater, **Somerset**, TA6 4DS, **ENGLAND**.
(T) 01278 426386 **(F)** 01278 788142.
Profile Supplies. Ref: YH00433

ANIMAL HEALTH

Animal Health Distributord Association (UK), Gable Court, 8 Parsons Hill, Woodbridge, **Suffolk**, IP12 3RB, **ENGLAND**.
(T) 01394 410444 **(F)** 01394 410455.
Profile Club/Association. Ref: YH00434

ANIMAL HEALTH CTRE

Animal Health Centre, 2 Redcar Rd, Guisborough, **Cleveland**, TS14 6DB, **ENGLAND**.
(T) 01287 633255.
Profile Medical Support. Ref: YH00435

ANIMAL HEALTH CTRE

Animal Health Centre, 26 Station Rd, Filton, **Gloucestershire (South)**, BS12 7JQ, **ENGLAND**.
(T) 01179 693621.
Profile Medical Support. Ref: YH00436

ANIMAL HEALTH SUPPLIES

Animal Health Supplies, 1 Ivydene Trce, Boughton, **Northamptonshire**, NN14 1NJ, **ENGLAND**.
(T) 01536 790035 **(F)** 01536 790035.
Contact/s
Owner: Mr B Long
Profile Medical Support.
Rents, leases or sells endurance equipment, lasers, electrovets and ultrasounds. Can also provide most equipment for diagnostic, therapeutic or preventative purposes. Yr. Est: 1983
Opening Times
Sp: Open Mon - Sun 05:00. Closed Mon - Sun 22:00.
Su: Open Mon - Sun 05:00. Closed Mon - Sun 22:00.
Au: Open Mon - Sun 05:00. Closed Mon - Sun 22:00.
Wn: Open Mon - Sun 05:00. Closed Mon - Sun 22:00. Ref: YH00437

ANIMAL HEALTH TRUST

Animal Health Trust, P O Box 5, Newmarket, **Suffolk**, CB8 8JH, **ENGLAND**.
(T) 01638 751000 **(F)** 01638 751909.
Profile Medical Support. Ref: YH00438

ANIMAL HEALTH TRUST

Animal Health Trust, Lanwades Pk, Kentford, Newmarket, **Suffolk**, CB8 7UU, **ENGLAND**.
(T) 01638 751000 **(F)** 01638 750410.
Profile Club/Association. Ref: YH00439

ANIMAL INSURANCE

Animal Insurance Management Services Ltd, Aims Hse, Royal Oak Courtyard, Market Pl, Thirsk, **Yorkshire (North)**, YO7 1HQ, **ENGLAND**.
(T) 01845 526000 **(F)** 01845 525149.
Profile Club/Association. Ref: YH00440

ANIMAL MEDICINES

Animal Medicines Training Regulatory Authority, 8 Parsons Hill, Woodbridge, **Suffolk**, IP12 3RB, **ENGLAND**.
(T) 01394 411010 **(F)** 01394 411030.
Profile Club/Association. Ref: YH00441

ANIMAL PORTRAITURE

Animal Portraiture, 16 Strathdon Pk, Glenrothes, **Fife**, KY6 3NS, **SCOTLAND**.
(T) 01592 741314. Ref: YH00442

ANIMAL SCHOOL OF FARRIERY

Animal School of Farriery (The), The Animal Defence Ctre, Welby Lane, Melton Mowbray, **Leicestershire**, LE13 0SL, **ENGLAND**.
(T) 01664 411771.
Profile Farrier. Ref: YH00443

ANIMAL THERAPY

Animal Therapy Ltd, National Ass of Animal Therapists, Tyringham Hall, Cuddington, Aylesbury, **Buckinghamshire**, HP18 0AP, **ENGLAND**.
(T) 01844 291526 **(F)** 01844 290474
(M) 07831 353549
Affiliated Bodies NAAT.
Contact/s
Physiotherapist: Fred Lawrence
Profile Medical Support. Ref: YH00444

ANIMAL TRANSPORTATION

Animal Transportation, 70 Church Lane, London, **London (Greater)**, SW19 3PB, **ENGLAND**.
(T) 020 85426775.
Contact/s
Owner: Mr D Oldershaw
Profile Transport/Horse Boxes. Ref: YH00445

ANIMAL VETNRY SVS

Animal Veterinary Services, 18 Fore St, Copperhouse, Hayle, **Cornwall**, TR27 4DY, **ENGLAND**.
(T) 01736 755555.
Profile Medical Support. Ref: YH00446

ANIMAL WELFARE

Animal Welfare Company, Brookside, Corfe, Taunton, **Somerset**, TA3 7BU, **ENGLAND**.
(T) 01823 421267 **(F)** 01823 421898. Ref: YH00447

ANIMAL WORLD

Animal World, 16/18 Three Tuns Lane, Formby, Southport, **Merseyside**, L37 4AJ, **ENGLAND**.
(T) 01704 879008.
Profile Supplies. Ref: YH00448

ANIMALS IN DISTRESS

Animals in Distress, Field Of Dreams, Leach Farm, Swaindrod Lane, Blackstone Edge, Littleborough, **Lancashire**, OL15 0LE, **ENGLAND**.
(T) 01706 371731. Ref: YH00449

ANNAGHARVEY FARM

Annagharvey Farm, Annagharvey, Tullamore, **County Offaly**, **IRELAND**.
(T) 0506 43544 **(F)** 0506 43766
(M) 086 2512870
(E) annafarm@iol.ie
(W) www.annaharveyfarm.ie.
Contact/s
Equestrian Manager: Rachael Deverell
Profile Arena, Holidays.
Bi-annually hold Hunter Trials. Have a cross country centre. C.Size: 380 Acres Ref: YH00450

ANNAGHMORE SADDLERY

Annaghmore Saddlery and Countrywear, 35A Moss Rd, Portadown, Craigavon, **County Armagh**, BT62 1NB, **NORTHERN IRELAND**.
(T) 028 38851128 **(F)** 028 38852129.
Contact/s
Owner: Mr T McClealland **(Q)** Master Saddler
Profile Riding Wear Retailer, Saddlery Retailer.
Yr. Est: 1980
Opening Times
Sp: Open Mon - Sat 09:00. Closed Mon - Fri 20:00, Sat 18:00.
Su: Open Mon - Sat 09:00. Closed Mon - Fri 20:00, Sat 18:00.
Au: Open Mon - Sat 09:00. Closed Mon - Fri 20:00, Sat 18:00.
Wn: Open Mon - Sat 09:00. Closed Mon - Fri 20:00, Sat 18:00. Ref: YH00451

ANNAHILT SADDLERY

Annahilt Saddlery, 19 Ballykeel Rd, Hillsborough, **County Down**, BT26 6NW, **NORTHERN IRELAND**.
(T) 028 92638999.

Contact/s
Owner: Mr S Hunter
Profile Saddlery Retailer. **Ref: YH00452**

ANNANDALE EQUESTRIAN CTRE

Annandale Equestrian Centre, East Leys, Kininmonth, Peterhead, **Aberdeenshire**, AB42 4HT, **SCOTLAND**.
(T) 01771 622598.
Profile Riding School, Saddlery Retailer, Stable/Livery. **Ref: YH00453**

ANNANDALE SHETLAND PONY STUD

Annandale Shetland Pony Stud, Cottertown, Kilry, Alyth, **Perth and Kinross**, PH11 8JA, **SCOTLAND**..
Profile Breeder. **Ref: YH00454**

ANNA'S CTRY STORE

Anna's Country Store, Rushton Cottage, Tilford Rd, Rushmoor, Farnham, **Surrey**, GU10 2EP, **ENGLAND**.
(T) 01252 792044 **(F)** 01252 794512.
Profile Saddlery Retailer. **Ref: YH00455**

ANNE WAINWRIGHT SADDLERY

Anne Wainwright Saddlery & Feeds, The Croft, 41 Gringley Rd, Misterton, Doncaster, **Yorkshire (South)**, DN10 4AP, **ENGLAND**.
(T) 01427 890741.
Profile Saddlery Retailer. **Ref: YH00456**

ANNETTE YARROW

Annette Yarrow (Sculptor), North St Farm, Breamore, Fordingbridge, **Hampshire**, SP6 2DG, **ENGLAND**.
(T) 01725 512250 **(F)** 01725 512250.
Contact/s
Artist: Annette Yarrow **Ref: YH00457**

ANNINGSLEY PARK POLO

Anningsley Park Polo, Ash Farm, Bousley Rise, Ottershaw, **Surrey**, KT16 0LB, **ENGLAND**.
(T) 01932 872521 **(F)** 01932 872006.
Contact/s
Trainer: Paul Sweeney
Profile
Specialise in private tution of Polo lessons.
Ref: YH00458

ANSLOW, JENNIFER R

Mrs Jennifer R Anslow, The Poplars, Strawmoor Lane, Oaken, Wolverhampton, **Staffordshire**, WV8 2HY, **ENGLAND**.
(T) 01902 843951. **Ref: YH00459**

ANSTY POLO CLUB

Ansty Polo Club, New Barn Farm, Ansty, Salisbury, **Wiltshire**, SP3 5PX, **ENGLAND**.
(T) 01747 870245 **(F)** 01747 870488.
Profile Club/Association. Polo Club. **Ref: YH00460**

ANTHEL EQUINE SUPPLIES

Anthel Equine Supplies, Wimbourne Equestrian Ctre, Bambers Lane, Blackpool, **Lancashire**, FY4 5LH, **ENGLAND**.
(T) 01253 699090.
Contact/s
Owner: Mrs A Gisbourne
Profile Supplies. **Ref: YH00461**

ANTHONY D EVANS

Anthony D Evans & Co, 75 Moseley Ave, Coundon, Coventry, **Midlands (West)**, CV6 1HR, **ENGLAND**.
(T) 024 76595812 **(F)** 024 76601456. **Ref: YH00462**

ANTHONY WAKEHAM CONSULTING

Pulserate Partnership, Wothersome Grange, Bramham, Wetherby, **Yorkshire (West)**, LS23 6LY, **ENGLAND**.
(T) 0113 2893657 **(F)** 0113 2893842
Affiliated Bodies BETA.
Contact/s
Owner: Mr A Wakeham
(E) wakeham@emc.u-net.com
Profile Breeder. Equestrian Business Consultant.
No.Staff: 1 Yr. Est: 2001 C.Size: 55 Acres
Opening Times
Sp: Open 09:00. Closed 17:30.
Su: Open 09:00. Closed 17:30.
Au: Open 09:00. Closed 17:30.
Wn: Open 09:00. Closed 17:30. **Ref: YH00463**

ANTHONY WALLIS FARM/EQUINE

Anthony Wallis Farm / Equine Services, Brook Farm, Langridgeford, Umberleigh, **Devon**, EX37 9HR, **ENGLAND**.
(T) 01769 560740.
Profile Supplies. **Ref: YH00464**

ANTHONY, F J

F J Anthony BVMS, Fresh Acre Veterinary Surgery, Flaggeners Green, Bromyard, **Herefordshire**, HR7 4QR, **ENGLAND**.
(T) 01885 483427 **(F)** 01885 482169
(E) francis.anthony@virgin.net.
Contact/s
Principle of Practice: Mr F Anthony
Profile Medical Support. **Ref: YH00465**

ANTWICK STUD

Antwick Stud, Letcombe Regis, Wantage, **Oxfordshire**, OX12 9LH, **ENGLAND**.
(T) 01235 764456 **(F)** 01235 764456
(M) 07771 707474.
Profile Trainer. **Ref: YH00466**

ANVIL ENGINEERING

Anvil Engineering, Wardhead Pk, Kilmaurs Rd, Stewarton, Kilmarnock, **Ayrshire (East)**, KA3 5LH, **SCOTLAND**.
(T) 01563 525180.
Profile Blacksmith. **Ref: YH00467**

ANVIL FORGE

Anvil Forge, New Forge, Endon, Stoke-on-Trent, **Staffordshire**, ST9 9EX, **ENGLAND**.
(T) 01782 502358.
Profile Blacksmith. **Ref: YH00468**

ANVIL PRODUCTS

Anvil Products, Battleaxe Works, Heathery Rd, Wishaw, **Lanarkshire (North)**, ML2 7PT, **SCOTLAND**.
(T) 01698 351863 **(F)** 01698 372173.
Contact/s
Owner: Mr R McDonald
Profile Blacksmith. **Ref: YH00469**

ANVILCRAFT

Anvilcraft, Unit 5 Maws Craft Ctre, Ferry Rd, Jackfield, Telford, **Shropshire**, TF8 7LS, **ENGLAND**.
(T) 01952 882580.
Profile Blacksmith. **Ref: YH00470**

ANVILS BLACKSMITH

Anvils Blacksmith, Tyes Cross Farm, Grinstead Lane, East Grinstead, **Sussex (West)**, RH19 4HP, **ENGLAND**.
(T) 01342 811227 **(F)** 01342 811227.
Contact/s
Manager: Mr J Willie
Profile Blacksmith. **Ref: YH00471**

AON MCMILLEN

Aon McMillen Ltd, 31 Bedford St, Belfast, **County Antrim**, BT2 7FP, **NORTHERN IRELAND**.
(T) 028 90242771 **(F)** 028 90313644. **Ref: YH00472**

APACHE

Assoc for Promotion of Animal Complementary Health (The), Archers Wood Farm, Coppingford, Huntingdon, **Cambridgeshire**, PE28 5XY, **ENGLAND**.
(T) 07050 244196.
Contact/s
Owner: Miss K Zablotzky
Profile Medical Support. **Ref: YH00473**

APOLLO SADDLERY

Apollo Saddlery, Paulls Farm, Leire Lane, Ashby Parva, Lutterworth, **Leicestershire**, LE17 5HR, **ENGLAND**.
(T) 01455 202223 **(F)** 01455 202223.
Contact/s
Partner: Mr C Roberts
Profile Saddlery Retailer. **Ref: YH00474**

APPALOOSA HOLIDAYS

Ardfern Riding Centre, Craobh Haven, Lochgilphead, **Argyll and Bute**, PA31 8QR, **SCOTLAND**.
(T) 01852 500632 **(F)** 01852 500270
(E) appaloosaholidays@talk21.com
(W) www.aboutscotland.com/argyll/appaloosa.html.
Contact/s
Owner: Mr N Boase
Profile Breeder, Riding School, Trainer.
Training in Western and British riding available and also in Natural Horsemanship. Near by accommodation can be arranged. No.Staff: 3 Yr. Est: 1972
C.Size: 3000 Acres
Opening Times
Open all year, telephone or email to book
Ref: YH00475

APPALOOSAS, NOCONA

Nocona Appaloosas, Nantypwthly, Beguildy, Knighton, **Powys**, LD7 1YY, **WALES**.
(T) 01547 510275.
Profile Breeder. **Ref: YH00476**

APPALOOSAS, RODEGA

Rodega Appaloosas, Beck Farm, Cottenham Rd, Histon, **Cambridgeshire**, CB4 9ET, **ENGLAND**.
(T) 01223 237023.
Contact/s
Partner: Mr R Gale
(E) bob.gale@talk21.com
Profile Breeder.
Opening Times
Telephone for an appointment **Ref: YH00477**

APPIN EQUESTRIAN CTRE

Appin Equestrian Centre, 98 Abbots View, Haddington, **Lothian (East)**, EH39 5BL, **SCOTLAND**.
(T) 01620 880366 **(F)** 01620 880377
(E) appin@pcuk.org
Affiliated Bodies BHS.
Contact/s
Head Girl: Ms S Bowden **(Q)** BHS IT
Profile Riding School.
Specialists in dressage training. No.Staff: 4
Yr. Est: 1980
Opening Times
Sp: Open 08:30. Closed 20:30.
Su: Open 08:30. Closed 20:30.
Au: Open 08:30. Closed 20:30.
Wn: Open 08:30. Closed 20:30. **Ref: YH00478**

APPLEACRE DARTMOORS

Appleacre Dartmoors, Appleacre, The Hale, Wendover, **Buckinghamshire**, HP22 6NQ, **ENGLAND**.
(T) 01296 622062.
Profile Breeder. **Ref: YH00479**

APPLEMORE EQUITATION

Applemore Equitation, The Old Barn Dale Farm, Manor Rd, Dibden, Southampton, **Hampshire**, SO45 5TJ, **ENGLAND**.
(T) 023 80843180.
Profile Riding School. **Ref: YH00480**

APPLETREE STABLES/RIDING

Appletree Stables & Riding School, Starvenden Lane, Sissinghurst, Cranbrook, **Kent**, TN17 2AN, **ENGLAND**.
(T) 01580 713833.
Profile Riding School. **Ref: YH00481**

APPLEWELL INSURANCE BROKERS

Applewell Insurance Brokers, 3 Market Pl, Braintree, **Essex**, CM7 3HJ, **ENGLAND**.
(T) 01376 330624 **(F)** 01376 330004
(E) mail@event-assured.com.
Profile Club/Association. **Ref: YH00482**

APPLEWOOD & PERRY

Applewood & Perry, Honey Brook Forge, Cranborne Rd, Furzehill, Wimborne, **Dorset**, BH21 4HW, **ENGLAND**.
(T) 01202 848676.
Profile Blacksmith. **Ref: YH00483**

APPLEYARD TRAILERS

Appleyard Trailers, The Kennels, Main St, Strelley, Nottingham, **Nottinghamshire**, NG8 6PD, **ENGLAND**.
(T) 0115 9293901 **(F)** 0115 9293901.
Contact/s
Owner: Mr P Appleyard
Profile Transport/Horse Boxes. **Ref: YH00484**

APPS, S H

S H Apps, 8 Lady Garn Rd, West Hougham, Dover, **Kent**, CT15 7BA, **ENGLAND**.
(T) 01304 203480.
Profile Farrier. **Ref: YH00485**

APRIL COTTAGE STABLES

April Cottage Stables, April Cottage, Sturts Lane, Tadworth, **Surrey**, KT20 7RQ, **ENGLAND**.
(T) 01737 814301.
Contact/s
Owner: Mr T Staplehurst **Ref: YH00486**

AQHA

America Quarter Horse Association UK Ltd, 7 Whitehall Way, Sellindge, Ashford, **Kent**, TN25 6ET, **ENGLAND**.
(T) 01858 465892
(E) aqhauk@aol.com
(W) www.tslnet/aqhauk.
Contact/s
Key Contact: Miss J Muir
Profile Club/Association. **Ref: YH00487**

A-Z of COMPANIES

AQUAPLAST
Aquaplast, Penketh Pl, West Pimbo, Skelmersdale, **Lancashire**, WN8 9QX, **ENGLAND**.
(T) 01695 555523 **(F)** 01695 555513.
Profile Supplies. Ref: **YH00488**

AQUARIUS VETNRY CTRE
Aquarius Veterinary Centre, 30 George St, Brandon, **Suffolk**, IP27 0BX, **ENGLAND**.
(T) 01842 810480.
Profile Medical Support. Ref: **YH00489**

ARAB HORSE SOC
Arab Horse Society (The), Windsor Hse, The Square, Ramsbury, Marlborough, **Wiltshire**, SN8 2PE, **ENGLAND**.
(T) 01672 520782 **(F)** 01672 520880.
Contact/s
Chief Executive: Mr C Pickthall
Profile Club/Association. Ref: **YH00490**

ARABIAN BLOODSTOCK AGENCY
Arabian Bloodstock Agency, Water Farm, Raydon, **Suffolk**, IP7 5LW, **ENGLAND**.
(T) 01473 310407 **(F)** 01473 311206
(M) 07850 983916
(E) marybancroft@waterfarmarabians.freeserve.co.uk.
Contact/s
Assistant: Mr H Bancroft
Profile Blood Stock Agency. Ref: **YH00491**

ARABIAN SADDLE
Arabian Saddle Co (The), 10-14 Butts Rd, Walsall, **Midlands (West)**, WS4 2AR, **ENGLAND**.
(T) 01922 646677 **(F)** 01922 721149.
Profile Riding Wear Retailer, Saddlery Retailer, Supplies. Ref: **YH00492**

ARABLE FARM SUPPLIES
Arable Farm Supplies, South Rd Ind Est, Alnwick, **Northumberland**, NE66 2NN, **ENGLAND**.
(T) 01665 603345.
Profile Supplies. Ref: **YH00493**

ARAMSTONE STABLES
Aramstone Stables, Kings Caple, Hereford, **Herefordshire**, HR1 4TU, **ENGLAND**.
(T) 01432 840646 **(F)** 01432 840830
(M) 07770 627108.
Profile Trainer. Ref: **YH00494**

ARBON, D W
D W Arbon, Holmleigh, Pettistree, Woodbridge, **Suffolk**, IP13 0HU, **ENGLAND**.
(T) 01728 746133.
Profile Breeder. Ref: **YH00495**

ARBUTHNOT, D W P
D W P Arbuthnot, Saxon Gate Stables, Upper Lambourn, Hungerford, **Berkshire**, RG17 8QH, **ENGLAND**.
(T) 01488 72383 **(F)** 01488 72383.
Contact/s
Owner: Mr D Arbuthnot
Profile Trainer. Ref: **YH00496**

ARBUTHNOT, TIMOTHY R
Timothy R Arbuthnot RSS, Red Barn Farm, Deopham, Wymondham, **Norfolk**, NR18 9TW, **ENGLAND**.
(T) 01953 606369.
Profile Farrier. Ref: **YH00497**

ARCADE SADDLERY BEDFORD
Arcade Saddlery Bedford Ltd, 35 - 37 Roff Ave, Bedford, **Bedfordshire**, MK41 7TH, **ENGLAND**.
(T) 01234 212567.
Contact/s
Owner: Ms M Barker
Profile Riding Wear Retailer, Saddlery Retailer, Supplies. No.Staff: 2 Yr. Est: 1970
Ref: **YH00498**

ARCHIBALD
Archibald, 45 Sconce Rd, Articlave, Coleraine, **County Londonderry**, BT51 4JT, **NORTHERN IRELAND**.
(T) 028 70848247.
Profile Supplies. Ref: **YH00499**

ARCHWAY VETNRY PRACTICE
Archway Veterinary Practice, Station Sq, Grange-Over-Sands, **Cumbria**, LA11 6EH, **ENGLAND**.
(T) 01539 532669 **(F)** 07070 756606.
Contact/s
Vet: Mr T Boardman
Profile Medical Support. Ref: **YH00500**

ARCHWAY VETNRY SURGERY
Archway Veterinary Surgery, 21 High St, Highworth, **Wiltshire**, SN6 7AG, **ENGLAND**.
(T) 01793 765335 **(F)** 01793 861994.
Contact/s
Vet: Mr S Wolfensohn
Profile Medical Support. Ref: **YH00501**

ARDEN WOOD SHAVINGS
Arden Wood Shavings Limited, Kenilworth Rd, Hampton In Arden, Solihull, **Midlands (West)**, B92 0LP, **ENGLAND**.
(T) 01675 443888 **(F)** 01675 443873
(E) arden@dial.pipex.com.
Profile Supplies. Ref: **YH00502**

ARDENLEA ENTERPRISES
Ardenlea Enterprises Ltd, Aylesbury Rd, Princes Risborough, **Buckinghamshire**, HP27 0JP, **ENGLAND**.
(T) 01844 345572 **(F)** 01844 347080
(M) 07831 402121.
Profile Track/Course. Ref: **YH00503**

ARDENLEA ENTERPRISES
Ardenlea Enterprises Ltd (Epsom), 129 Reigate Rd, Ewell, Epsom, **Surrey**, KT17 3DE, **ENGLAND**.
(T) 020 83930516 **(F)** 020 83930516.
Profile Track/Course. Ref: **YH00504**

ARDENNES HORSE SOCIETY OF GB
Ardennes Horse Society of GB, White Ash Farm, Starvenden Lane, Sissinghurst, **Kent**, TN17 2AN, **ENGLAND**.
(T) 01580 715001 **(F)** 01580 715001.
Profile Breeder, Club/Association. Ref: **YH00505**

ARDERN HORSEBOXES
Ardern Horseboxes, Unit 12/Springbank Ind Est, Liverpool Rd, Platt Bridge, Wigan, **Lancashire**, WN2 3TY, **ENGLAND**.
(T) 01942 866659.
Contact/s
Owner: Mr D Godfell
Profile Transport/Horse Boxes. Ref: **YH00506**

ARDGOWAN
Ardgowan Riding Centre, Bankfoot, Inverkip, Greenock, **Inverclyde**, PA16 0DT, **SCOTLAND**.
(T) 01475 529288 **(F)** 01475 529288
(E) riding@ardgowan.co.uk
Affiliated Bodies ABRS, BHS.
Contact/s
General Manager: Miss E Wilson
Profile Riding School.
The centre has 3 flood lit outdoor schools and a show jumping course to BSJA standard. The riding centre is on a private estate so hacking is available on private land. No.Staff: 4 Yr. Est: 1989
Opening Times
Sp: Open Mon - Sun 10:00. Closed Mon - Sun 17:00.
Su: Open Mon - Sun 10:00. Closed Mon - Sun 17:00.
Au: Open Mon - Sun 10:00. Closed Mon - Sun 17:00.
Wn: Open Mon - Sun 10:00. Closed Mon - Sun 17:00.
Later times available due to flood lit areas.
Ref: **YH00507**

ARDMAIR STUD SHETLAND PONIES
Ardmair Stud of Shetland Ponies, Snipe Moss, Wyck Rd, Cheltenham, **Gloucestershire**, GL54 2EX, **ENGLAND**.
(T) 01451 820350.
Profile Breeder. Ref: **YH00508**

ARDMIDDLE LIVERY STABLES
Ardmiddle Livery Stables, Ardmiddle, Turriff, **Aberdeenshire**, AB53 4HJ, **SCOTLAND**.
(T) 01888 68098.
Profile Stable/Livery. Ref: **YH00509**

ARDMINNAN EQUESTRIAN CTRE
Ardminnan Equestrian Centre, 15 Ardminnan Rd, Portaferry, Newtownards, **County Down**, BT22 1QJ, **NORTHERN IRELAND**.
(T) 028 42771321 **(F)** 028 42771321.
Contact/s
Owner: Mrs I Gowan
Profile Equestrian Centre. Ref: **YH00510**

ARDMORE STABLES
Ardmore Stables, 8 Rushall Rd, Ardmore, Londonderry, **County Londonderry**, BT47 3UG, **NORTHERN IRELAND**.
(T) 028 71345187.
Contact/s
Owner: Mrs P McFall
Profile Arena, Riding School, Stable/Livery.
No.Staff: 3 Yr. Est: 1995
Opening Times
Sp: Open Mon - Fri 10:00. Closed Mon - Fri 17:00.
Su: Open Mon - Fri 10:00. Closed Mon - Fri 17:00.
Au: Open Mon - Fri 10:00. Closed Mon - Fri 17:00.
Wn: Open Mon - Fri 10:00. Closed Mon -Fri 17:00.
Ref: **YH00511**

ARDS RIDING CLUB
Ards Riding Club, 6 Primacy Drive, Bangor, **County Down**, BT19 7JB, **NORTHERN IRELAND**.
(T) 028 91451881.
Contact/s
Chairman: Miss F Warden
Profile Club/Association, Riding Club. Ref: **YH00512**

ARENA FARM & PET SUPPLIES
Arena Farm & Pet Supplies, Unit D, Palmers Brook Farm, Wootton, **Isle of Wight**, PO33 4NS, **ENGLAND**.
(T) 01983 884737 **(F)** 01983 884737.
Profile Supplies. Ref: **YH00513**

ARENA SADDLERY
Arena Saddlery, Bessels Way, Blewbury, Didcot, **Oxfordshire**, OX11 9NH, **ENGLAND**.
(T) 01235 850725 **(F)** 01235 850465.
Contact/s
Owner: Mrs A Deverteuil Ref: **YH00514**

ARENA SHOW JUMPS
Arena Show Jumps, 2 Mickley Lodge, Burley Rd, Langham, Oakham, **Leicestershire**, LE15 7JB, **ENGLAND**.
(T) 01572 771048.
Contact/s
Owner: Mrs P Barnet
Profile Supplies. Ref: **YH00515**

ARENA STRUCTURES
Arena Structures Ltd, Needingworth Rd, St Ives, **Cambridgeshire**, PE27 3ND, **ENGLAND**.
(T) 01480 468888 **(F)** 01480 462888. Ref: **YH00516**

ARENA UK
Arena UK, Willowtops, Allington, Grantham, **Lincolnshire**, NG32 2EF, **ENGLAND**.
(T) 01476 591569 **(F)** 01476 565442.
Profile Track/Course. Ref: **YH00517**

ARENASPRAY
Arenaspray, Rose Cottage, Thurgarton Lane, Hoveringham, **Nottinghamshire**, NG14 7JS, **ENGLAND**.
(T) 0115 9664644 **(F)** 0115 9664644
(E) phil@arenaspray.com.
Profile Supplies. Mobile Irrigation Unit.
Mobile sprinkler system for all types of arena.
Ref: **YH00518**

ARGAE HSE STABLES
Argae House Stables, St. Andrews Major, Dinas Powys, **Glamorgan (Vale of)**, CF64 4HD, **WALES**.
(T) 029 20515546.
Contact/s
Owner: Miss A Roberts
Profile Breeder, Stable/Livery, Track/Course.
Ref: **YH00519**

ARGO FEEDS
Argo Feeds Ltd (Ashton-under-Lyne), Unit 3, Woodend Mill No 2, Manchester Rd, Mossley, Ashton-under-Lyne, **Lancashire**, OL5 9BQ, **ENGLAND**.
(T) 01457 837749 **(F)** 01226 766707.
Profile Medical Support. Ref: **YH00520**

ARGO FEEDS
Argo Feeds Ltd, Kirkwood Mill, Sheffield Rd,, Penistone, Sheffield, **Yorkshire (South)**, S36 6HQ, **ENGLAND**.
(T) 01226 762341 **(F)** 01226 766707.
Profile Medical Support. Ref: **YH00521**

ARGYLL RIDING CLUB
Argyll Riding Club, Barnacriche Tarbert, Argyll, **Argyll and Bute**, PA29 6YA, **SCOTLAND**.
(T) 01880 820833.
Contact/s
Secretary: Mrs A Minshall
Profile Club/Association, Riding Club. Ref: **YH00522**

ARGYLL TRAIL RIDING
Argyll Trail Riding, Brenfield Farm, Ardrishaig, Lochgilphead, **Argyll and Bute**, PA30 8ER, **SCOTLAND**.
(T) 01546 603274 **(F)** 01546 603225.

Contact/s
Owner: Mrs T Grey-Stephens
Profile Riding School, Stable/Livery, Track/Course, Trainer. Ref: YH00523

ARGYLL WEATHERWISE

Argyll Weatherwise, Lagganmore, Kilinver, Oban, **Argyll and Bute**, PA34 4UU, **SCOTLAND**.
(T) 01852 316200
(E) asweatherwise@aol.com.
Profile Supplies. Agricultural Supplies.
Ref: YH00524

ARIAN TRAILERS

Arian Trailers, 15 Lockside Navigation Rd, Chelmsford, **Essex**, CM2 6HE, **ENGLAND**.
(T) 01245 491144.
Profile Transport/Horse Boxes. Ref: YH00525

ARIAT

Ariat, Faringdon, **Oxfordshire**, SN7 8LA, **ENGLAND**.
(T) 01367 244619 (F) 01367 242819. Ref: YH00526

ARIZONAS

GLN Retail Ltd T/A Arizonas, 55 Mount Pleasant Rd, Tunbridge Wells, **Kent**, TN1 1PT, **ENGLAND**.
(T) 01892 536666 (F) 01892 523237
(W) www.arizonas.co.uk.
Contact/s
General Manager: Ms K Exall
Profile Riding Wear Retailer, Saddlery Retailer, Supplies.
Suppliers of western saddlery and tack as well as associated goods i.e show apparel, boots, hats, shirts and gifts. No.Staff: 3 Yr. Est: 1997
Opening Times
Sp: Open Mon - Fri 10:00, Sat 09:30. Closed Mon - Fri 17:30, Sat 16:30.
Su: Open Mon - Fri 10:00, Sat 09:30. Closed Mon - Fri 17:30, Sat 16:30.
Au: Open Mon - Fri 10:00, Sat 09:30. Closed Mon - Fri 17:30, Sat 16:30.
Wn: Open Mon - Fri 10:00, Sat 09:30. Closed Mon - Fri 17:30, Sat 16:30. Ref: YH00527

ARK HSE VETNRY SURGERY

Ark House Veterinary Surgery, Ark Hse, 22 Hockliffe St, Leighton Buzzard, **Bedfordshire**, LU7 8HF, **ENGLAND**.
(T) 01525 373329 (F) 01525 852354.
Profile Medical Support. Ref: YH00528

ARK WROUGHT IRON WORK

Ark Wrought Iron Work, 34 Wild Green North, Slough, **Berkshire**, SL3 8NU, **ENGLAND**.
(T) 01753 717861 (F) 01753 670965.
Contact/s
Owner: Mrs Y Keates
Profile Blacksmith. Ref: YH00529

ARKENFIELD EQUESTRIAN CTRE

Arkenfield Equestrian Centre, Windmill Lane, Brindle, Chorley, **Lancashire**, PR6 8PG, **ENGLAND**.
(T) 01254 853002.
Contact/s
Owner: Mr W Burrow (T) 07944 888576
Profile Arena, Equestrian Centre, Riding School, Stable/Livery, Supplies, Trainer. No.Staff: 4
Yr. Est: 2001 C.Size: 15 Acres
Ref: YH00530

ARKENFIELD STABLES

Arkenfield Stables, Lowdham Rd, Gunthorpe, Nottingham, **Nottinghamshire**, NG14 7ES, **ENGLAND**.
(T) 0115 9664574 (F) 0115 9664574.
Contact/s
Owner: Mr D Pettifor
Profile Stable/Livery, Trainer. Ref: YH00531

ARKLEY LIVERY STABLES

Arkley Livery Stables, Barnet Rd, Barnet, **Hertfordshire**, EN5 3JT, **ENGLAND**.
(T) 020 84411299.
Contact/s
Partner: Mrs L Frame
Profile Stable/Livery. Ref: YH00532

ARLINGTON POLO

Arlington Polo, Heathfield, Bletchingdon, Kidlington, **Oxfordshire**, OX5 3DX, **ENGLAND**.
(T) 01869 351663.
Contact/s
Owner: Mrs P Dee
Profile Stable/Livery, Trainer. Ref: YH00533

ARMAC VETNRY GRP

Armac Veterinary Group, 4 Station Rd, Biggar, **Lanarkshire (South)**, ML12 6BW, **SCOTLAND**.
(T) 01899 220046.
Profile Medical Support. Ref: YH00534

ARMADILLO PRODUCTS

Armadillo Products Ltd, 18 Newton Tony, Salisbury, **Wiltshire**, SP4 0HA, **ENGLAND**.
(T) 01980 629796 (F) 01980 629250
(E) armadillo@horsetrading.co.uk
(W) www.armadilloproducts.co.uk.
Profile Medical Support.
Magnotherapy enhances the body's own ability to improve circulation. Ref: YH00535

ARMATHWAITE HALL

Armathwaite Hall Equestrian Centre, Coalbeck Farm, Bassenthwaite, Keswick, **Cumbria**, CA12 4RD, **ENGLAND**.
(T) 01768 776949 (F) 01768 776776
(E) armathwaite@equiworld.com.
Contact/s
Manager: Mr F Hewett-Smith
Profile Horse/Rider Accom. Ref: YH00536

ARMES, P J

P J Armes, The Firs, 27 Prince Of Wales Rd, Upton, Norwich, **Norfolk**, NR13 6BW, **ENGLAND**.
(T) 01493 751429.
Profile Farrier. Ref: YH00537

ARMITAGES TRAILERS

Armitages Trailers, 3-5 Kershaw Lane, Knottingley, **Yorkshire (West)**, WF11 0PG, **ENGLAND**.
(T) 01977 607155.
Profile Transport/Horse Boxes. Ref: YH00538

ARMOURY FARM LIVERY STABLES

Armoury Farm Livery Stables, Armoury Rd, West Bergholt, Colchester, **Essex**, CO6 3JP, **ENGLAND**.
(T) 01206 241939.
Contact/s
Owner: Mrs P West
Profile Stable/Livery. Ref: YH00539

ARMOURY STABLES

Armoury Stables, Armoury Rd, Pitlochry, **Perth and Kinross**, PH16 5AP, **SCOTLAND**.
(T) 01796 472102.
Profile Breeder. Ref: YH00540

ARMSON, RICHARD

Mr Richard Armson, Scotlands Farm, Burney Lane, Staunton-Harold, Melbourne, **Derbyshire**, DE73 1BH, **ENGLAND**.
(T) 01332 865293
(M) 07970 920149.
Profile Supplies. Ref: YH00541

ARMSTRONG BLACKSMITHS

Armstrong Blacksmiths, Lichfield Rd Ind Est, Tamworth, **Staffordshire**, B79 7TA, **ENGLAND**.
(T) 01827 316663.
Contact/s
Owner: Mr L Armstrong
Profile Blacksmith. Ref: YH00542

ARMSTRONG MOWERS

Armstrong Mowers, Ramswood, Crundale, Haverfordwest, **Pembrokeshire**, SA62 4EB, **WALES**.
(T) 01437 731362.
Profile Supplies. Ref: YH00543

ARMSTRONG RICHARDSON

Armstrong Richardson & Co Ltd, 47 Levenside, Stokesley, Middlesbrough, **Cleveland**, TS9 5BH, **ENGLAND**.
(T) 01642 710277 (F) 01642 710993
(E) enquiries@armstrongrichardson.co.uk
(W) www.armstrongrichardson.co.uk.
Profile Saddlery Retailer, Supplies.
Pet food and agricultural supplies. Yr. Est: 1925
Ref: YH00544

ARMSTRONG, BENJAMIN J

Benjamin J Armstrong DWCF, Top Coxmoor Farm, Kirkby In Ashfield, **Nottinghamshire**, NG17 7PR, **ENGLAND**.
(T) 01623 757316.
Profile Farrier. Ref: YH00545

ARMSTRONG, BRIAN

Brian Armstrong, Pantiles, Penselwood, Wincanton, **Somerset**, BA9 8NF, **ENGLAND**.
(T) 01747 841059 (F) 01747 841059. Ref: YH00546

ARMSTRONG, I & E

I & E Armstrong, Fiddlehall Farm, Fiddlehall, Falkland, **Fife**, KY15 7DD, **SCOTLAND**.
(T) 01337 857376 (F) 01337 857807.
Profile Supplies. Ref: YH00547

ARMSTRONG, J A

J A Armstrong, 12 Pitfour, Glencarse, **Perth and Kinross**, PH2 7NG, **SCOTLAND**.
(T) 01738 860298.
Profile Farrier. Ref: YH00548

ARMSTRONG, JOHN W

John W Armstrong DWCF, Salter Carr Farm, Sadbenge, Durham, **County Durham**, DL2 1SU, **ENGLAND**.
(T) 01325 332616.
Profile Farrier. Ref: YH00549

ARMSTRONG, LESLIE

Leslie Armstrong AWCF, Unit 29 Armstrong Rd, Lichfield Rd Ind Est, Tamworth, **Staffordshire**, B78 7NL, **ENGLAND**.
(T) 01827 316663.
Profile Farrier. Ref: YH00550

ARMSTRONG, PAUL J

Paul J Armstrong DWCF, 88 Austrey Rd, Warton, Tamworth, **Staffordshire**, B79 0HQ, **ENGLAND**.
(T) 07973 191879.
Profile Farrier. Ref: YH00551

ARMSTRONG, R

R Armstrong, East Rowden Farm, Sampford Courtenay, Okehampton, **Devon**, EX20 2SE, **ENGLAND**.
(T) 01837 82326. Ref: YH00552

ARMSTRONG, STEWART A

Stewart A Armstrong DWCF, 9 Dillarburn Rd, Lesmahagow, Lanark, **Lanarkshire (South)**, ML11 9PQ, **SCOTLAND**.
(T) 01555 892702.
Profile Farrier. Ref: YH00553

ARMY & NAVY STORES

Army & Navy Stores, 196 Stratford Rd, Shirley, Solihull, **Midlands (West)**, B90 3AG, **ENGLAND**.
(T) 0121 7445135.
Profile Saddlery Retailer. Ref: YH00554

ARNISS

Arniss Riding & Livery Stables, Godshill, Fordingbridge, **Hampshire**, SP6 2JX, **ENGLAND**.
(T) 01425 654114.
Contact/s
Manager: Mr I Pollack
Profile Riding School, Stable/Livery.
Opening Times
Closed Tuesdays Ref: YH00555

ARNISS RIDING STABLES

Arniss Riding Stables, Arniss Farm, Godshill, Fordingbridge, **Hampshire**, SP6 2JX, **ENGLAND**.
(T) 01425 654114.
Contact/s
Manageress: Miss A Finn Ref: YH00556

ARNOLD HITCHCOCK

Arnold Hitchcock & Co, Stocking Pelham Hall, Buntingford, **Hertfordshire**, SG9 0UT, **ENGLAND**.
(T) 01279 777445 (F) 01279 777445.
Profile Supplies. Ref: YH00557

ARNOLD, MATTHEW

Matthew Arnold, 1 Church View, Turkey Island, Shedfield, Southampton, **Hampshire**, SO3 2JE, **ENGLAND**.
(T) 01329 833344.
Profile Breeder. Ref: YH00558

ARNOLD, STEVEN

Steven Arnold DWCF, 78 Staney Cres, Uttoxeter, **Staffordshire**, ST14 7BD, **ENGLAND**.
(T) 01889 567868.
Profile Farrier. Ref: YH00559

ARNOLD, T J

Mr T J Arnold, Melodie Cottage, High Bar Lane, Thakeham, Pulborough, **Sussex (West)**, RH20 3EH, **ENGLAND**.
(T) 01403 741123.
Profile Trainer. Ref: YH00560

ARROW TRAILERS

Arrow Trailers, 1 Dixons Hill Cl, North Mymms, Hatfield, **Hertfordshire**, AL9 7EF, **ENGLAND**.
(T) 01707 262454 (F) 01707 261007.
Profile Transport/Horse Boxes. Ref: YH00561

ARROW TRAINING

Arrow Training, Weston Hse, Weston, Pembridge, Leominster, **Herefordshire**, HR6 9JE, **ENGLAND**.
(T) 01544 388321 (F) 01544 388111.

Profile Trainer. **Ref: YH00562**

ARROW VAULTING GRP

Arrow Vaulting Group, Curlew Cottage, Weston, Pembridge, Leominster, **Herefordshire**, HR6 9JE, **ENGLAND**.
(T) 01544 377321 **(F)** 01544 388111.
Profile Trainer. **Ref: YH00563**

ARTHERS, RICHARD A

Richard A Arthers DWCF, Brickmakers Cottage, 17 Main St, Newton Solney, Burton-on-Trent, **Staffordshire**, DE15 0SJ, **ENGLAND**.
(T) 01283 703451.
Profile Farrier. **Ref: YH00564**

ARTHUR COTTAM

Arthur Cottam & Co, The Double Grip Works/Carrwood Rd, Chesterfield Trading Est, Chesterfield, **Derbyshire**, S41 9QB, **ENGLAND**.
(T) 01246 453672 **(F)** 01246 260274.
Contact/s
Chairman: Mr A Cottam
Profile Blacksmith. **Ref: YH00565**

ARTHUR LODGE VETNRY HOSP

Arthur Lodge Veterinary Hospital, 17 Brighton Rd, Horsham, **Sussex (West)**, RH13 5BD, **ENGLAND**.
(T) 01403 252964 **(F)** 01403 732799.
Contact/s
Vet: Mr J Peters
Profile Medical Support. **Ref: YH00566**

ARTHUR, G H (PROF)

Prof G H Arthur, Fallowdene, Stone Allerton, Axbridge, **Somerset**, BS26 2NH, **ENGLAND**.
(T) 01934 712077.
Profile Medical Support. **Ref: YH00567**

ARTHUR, JOHN C

John C Arthur DWCF, 69 Ardrossan Gardens, Worcester Park, **Surrey**, KT4 7AX, **ENGLAND**.
(T) 020 83353101.
Profile Farrier. **Ref: YH00568**

ARTHUR, M R (HON)

Hon M R Arthur (The), Bingfield East Quarter, Hallington, Newcastle-upon-Tyne, **Tyne and Wear**, NE19 2LH, **ENGLAND**.
(T) 01434 672219 **(F)** 01434 672219.
Contact/s
Owner: Honourable M Arthur **(Q)** AMC, DC, MMCA
Profile Medical Support. **Ref: YH00569**

ARTHUR, STEPHEN

Mr Stephen Arthur, Hatherleigh, St Mary, **Jersey**, JE3 3AQ, **ENGLAND**.
(T) 01534 481385 **(F)** 01534 481455.
Profile Trainer. **Ref: YH00570**

ARTHUR, V R

Mrs V R Arthur, Bingfield East Quarter, Hallington, Newcastle-upon-Tyne, **Tyne and Wear**, NE19 2LH, **ENGLAND**.
(T) 01434 672219 **(F)** 01434 672219.
Profile Supplies. **Ref: YH00571**

ARTIC TRAILER SERVICES

Artic Trailer Services (Falkirk) Ltd, 49 Russel St, Falkirk, **Falkirk**, FK2 7HP, **SCOTLAND**.
(T) 01324 613533 **(F)** 01324 610660.
Contact/s
Manager: Mr W Scott
Profile Transport/Horse Boxes. **Ref: YH00572**

ARTIC TRAILER SERVICES

Artic Trailer Services Ltd, Unit 2B Bandeath Ind Est, Throsk, Stirling, **Stirling**, FK7 7NP, **SCOTLAND**.
(T) 01786 816005.
Profile Transport/Horse Boxes. **Ref: YH00573**

ARTIC TRAILERS

Artic Trailers, Holton Rd, Nettleton, Market Rasen, **Lincolnshire**, LN7 6AW, **ENGLAND**.
(T) 01472 851314.
Contact/s
Partner: Mr R Gissing
Profile Transport/Horse Boxes. **Ref: YH00574**

ARTIFICIAL INSEMINATION CTRE

Artificial Insemination Centre (The), Po Box 2, Kingswood, **Gloucestershire (South)**, BS15 9JN, **ENGLAND**.
(T) 01179 498118
(E) mike@aicentre.co.uk.
Profile Breeder, Medical Support. **Ref: YH00575**

ARTISTIC METAL DESIGN

Artistic Metal Design Ltd, Unit 1/7 Knutsford Way, Sealand Ind Est, Chester, **Cheshire**, CH1 4NS, **ENGLAND**.
(T) 01244 383938 **(F)** 01244 383938.
Profile Blacksmith. **Ref: YH00576**

ARUNDEL FARM

Arundel Farm Riding & Driving Centre, Park Pl, Arundel, **Sussex (West)**, BN18 9BE, **ENGLAND**.
(T) 01903 882668.
Contact/s
General Manager: Ms A Leggett **(Q)** BHSAI
Profile Riding School. No.Staff: 4
Yr. Est: 1960 **Ref: YH00577**

ARUNDEL RACING FARRIERS

Arundel Racing Farriers, The Forge, Castle Stables, Arundel, **Sussex (West)**, BN18 9AB, **ENGLAND**.
(T) 01903 882634.
Profile Blacksmith. **Ref: YH00578**

ARUNDELL ARMS

Arundell Arms (The), Lifton, **Devon**, PL16 0AA, **ENGLAND**.
(T) 01566 784666 **(F)** 01566 784494.
Profile Equestrian Centre. **Ref: YH00579**

ASA OF GB

American Saddlebred Association of GB, Uplands, Alfriston, **Sussex (East)**, BN26 5XE, **ENGLAND**.
(T) 01323 870977 **(F)** 01323 871375
(E) americansaddlebredsuk@compuserve.com
(W) www.americansaddlebreds.co.uk.
Profile Breeder, Club/Association.
Five-gaited display team - unique to Europe
Yr. Est: 1985 **Ref: YH00580**

ASCIACION DE CRIADORES

Asciacion de Criadores de Caballos Falabella, 1 Hambrook Hill Farm, Hambrook Hill, Hambrook, **Sussex (West)**, PO18 8UJ, **ENGLAND**.
(T) 01243 573469 **(F)** 01243 574416.
Contact/s
Key Contact: Mr A Shepherd **Ref: YH00581**

ASCOT HORSE BOXES INT

Ascot Horse Boxes International Ltd, The Ind Est, 26 Bonehurst Rd, Salfords, Redhill, **Surrey**, RH1 5ES, **ENGLAND**.
(T) 01293 773196 **(F)** 01293 773196.
Contact/s
Secretary: Mrs S Purnell
Profile Transport/Horse Boxes. **Ref: YH00582**

ASCOT PARK

Ascot Park Polo Club, Westcroft Pk Farm, Windlesham Rd, Chobham, Woking, **Surrey**, GU24 8SN, **ENGLAND**.
(T) 01276 858545 **(F)** 01276 858546
(E) info@polo.co.uk
(W) www.polo.co.uk.
Contact/s
Corporate Hospitality: Ms S Edwards
Profile Arena, Riding Club, Riding School, Riding Wear Retailer, Stable/Livery, Supplies, Trainer, Transport/Horse Boxes. Polo Club.
Corporate entertainment - 'Learn-to-Play' polo events
No.Staff: 25 Yr. Est: 1989 C.Size: 140 Acres

Opening Times
Sp: Open Tues - Sun 08:00. Closed Tues - Sun 18:00.
Su: Open Tues - Sun 08:00. Closed Tues - Sun 18:00.
Au: Open Tues - Sun 08:00. Closed Tues - Sun 18:00.
Wn: Open Tues - Sun 08:00. Closed Tues - Sun 18:00.
Closed Mondays **Ref: YH00583**

ASCOT RACECOURSE

Ascot Racecourse, High St, Ascot, **Berkshire**, SL5 5JN, **ENGLAND**.
(T) 01344 622211 **(F)** 01344 628299
(E) ascotraces@aol.com.
Contact/s
Clerk of Course: Nick Cheyne
Profile Track/Course. **Ref: YH00584**

ASCOT TIMBER BUILDINGS

Ascot Timber Buildings Ltd, T/A Ascot Stables & Windsor Stables, Fernhurst Saw Mill, Fernhurst, Haslemere, **Surrey**, GU27 3HB, **ENGLAND**.
(T) 01428 653107 **(F)** 01428 652362
(W) www.ascot-timber.co.uk.
Profile Transport/Horse Boxes. **Ref: YH00585**

ASGARD STUD

Asgard Stud, South Denhill, St Katherines, Inverurie, Inverurie, **Aberdeenshire**, AB51 8SU, **SCOTLAND**.
(T) 01651 891712 **(F)** 01651 891712
(E) david@asgardstud.com.
Profile Breeder. **Ref: YH00586**

ASH ROSETTES

Ash Rosettes, Broady Pk, Middle Filham, Ivybridge, **Devon**, PL21 0LR, **ENGLAND**.
(T) 01752 897059 **(F)** 01752 897059.
Profile Supplies. **Ref: YH00587**

ASH ROYD LIVERY STABLES

Ash Royd Livery Stables, Ash Royd Farm, Meltham, Huddersfield, **Yorkshire (West)**, HD7 3BG, **ENGLAND**.
(T) 01484 851747.
Contact/s
Owner: Mrs S Johnston
Profile Stable/Livery. **Ref: YH00588**

ASH, RICHARD W J

Richard W J Ash, Witherleigh Farm, Mill Rd, Barton St David, Somerton, **Somerset**, TA11 6DF, **ENGLAND**.
(T) 01458 850653.
Profile Blacksmith. **Ref: YH00589**

ASHBOURNE STABLES

Ashbourne Stables, Mortimers Lane, Upham, Southampton, **Hampshire**, SO32 1HF, **ENGLAND**.
(T) 01489 860502 **(F)** 01489 860502.
Contact/s
Owner: Mrs F Dunning
Profile Stable/Livery. **Ref: YH00590**

ASHBROOK EQUINE HOSP

Ashbrook Equine Hospital, Willows Veterinary Grp, Middlewich Rd, Allostock, Knutsford, **Cheshire**, WA16 9JQ, **ENGLAND**.
(T) 01565 723030 **(F)** 01606 783496.
Profile Medical Support. **Ref: YH00591**

ASHCRAFT EQUESTRIAN

Ashcraft Equestrian, Silver End Rd, Haynes, **Bedfordshire**, MK45 3TU, **ENGLAND**.
(T) 01234 381666 **(F)** 01234 381888
(M) 07850 062081.
Profile Transport/Horse Boxes. **Ref: YH00592**

ASHCROFT TRAILER HIRE

Ashcroft Trailer Hire Ltd, 11 Ormonde Ave, Newtownabbey, **County Antrim**, BT36 5AT, **NORTHERN IRELAND**.
(T) 028 90832641 **(F)** 028 90840291.
Contact/s
Manager: Mr E Anderson
Profile Transport/Horse Boxes. **Ref: YH00593**

ASHCROFT VETNRY SURGERY

Ashcroft Veterinary Surgery, 169 St Neots Rd, Hardwick, **Cambridgeshire**, CB3 7QJ, **ENGLAND**.
(T) 01954 210250.
Profile Medical Support. **Ref: YH00594**

ASHDOWN FOREST RIDING CTRE

Ashdown Forest Riding Centre, Whitehouse Farm, Duddleswell, Uckfield, **Sussex (East)**, TN22 3JA, **ENGLAND**.
(T) 01825 712108.
Contact/s
Owner: Mr S Petracopoulos
Profile Riding School, Stable/Livery. **Ref: YH00595**

ASHES EQUESTRIAN CTRE

Ashes Equestrian Centre, Ashe Rd, Mullingar, **County Westmeath**, **IRELAND**.
(T) 044 49533.
Profile Supplies. **Ref: YH00596**

ASHFIELD EQUESTRIAN

Ashfield Equestrian Centre, 9 Middle Rd, Islandmagee, Larne, **County Antrim**, BT40 3SL, **NORTHERN IRELAND**.
(T) 028 93373413.
Profile Stable/Livery. **Ref: YH00597**

ASHFIELD SUBS MANAGEMENT

Ashfield Subs Management Ltd, Bowden Hse, 36 Northampton Rd, Market Harborough, **Leicestershire**, LE16 9HE, **ENGLAND**.
(T) 01858 433432 **(F)** 01858 433715.
Profile Supplies. **Ref: YH00598**

ASHFIELDS EQUESTRIAN CTRE

Ashfields Equestrian Centre, Great Canfield,

Dunmow, **Essex**, CM6 1LD, **ENGLAND**.
(T) 01371 876060 **(F)** 01371 876386.
Profile Riding School, Stable/Livery. **Ref:YH00599**

ASHFORD EQUESTRIAN CTRE
Ashford Equestrian Centre, Cong, Mayo, **County Mayo**, **IRELAND**.
(T) 092 46507 **(F)** 092 46543
(W) www.rideatashford.com.
Contact/s
Owner: Brigid Clesham
Profile Breeder, Equestrian Centre, Trainer.
Within riding distance of the Connemara Mountains. The Equestrian Centre is only two minutes from the former ancestral home of the Guiness family where accommodation is now available. **Ref:YH00600**

ASHFORD FARM SUPPLIES
Ashford Farm Supplies & Saddlery, Mettams Yard, Milford, Bakewell, **Derbyshire**, DE45 1DX, **ENGLAND**.
(T) 01629 812072 **(F)** 01629 814540.
Profile Saddlery Retailer. **Ref:YH00601**

ASHFORD HILL RIDING SCHOOL
Ashford Hill Riding School, Goose Hill, Headley, Thatcham, **Berkshire**, RG19 8AS, **ENGLAND**.
(T) 01635 268587.
Contact/s
Partner: Mrs T Egan
Profile Riding School. **Ref:YH00602**

ASHFORD, A & W K
A & W K Ashford, 88 Ogley Rd, Brownhills, Walsall, **Midlands (West)**, WS8 6BB, **ENGLAND**.
(T) 01543 372693.
Contact/s
Farrier: Mr A Ashford
Profile Farrier. **Ref:YH00603**

ASHGILL STABLES
Ashgill Stables, Coverham, Leyburn, **Yorkshire (North)**, DL8 4TJ, **ENGLAND**.
(T) 01969 640420 **(F)** 01969 640505
(M) 07788 807569
(E) kirsty@johnwreymesracing.freeserve.co.uk.
Profile Trainer. **Ref:YH00604**

ASHINGDON RIDING CTRE
Ashingdon Riding Centre, Canewdon Rd, Rochford, **Essex**, SS4 3JL, **ENGLAND**.
(T) 01702 206531
Affiliated Bodies LGA.
Contact/s
Owner: Mrs S Alexandra
Profile Riding School. **No.Staff:** 6
Yr. Est: 1976
Opening Times
Sp: Open Sat, Sun 09:00. Closed Sat, Sun 16:00.
Su: Open Sat, Sun 09:00. Closed Sat, Sun 16:00.
Au: Open Sat, Sun 09:00. Closed Sat, Sun 16:00.
Wn: Open Sat, Sun 09:00. Closed Sat, Sun 16:00.
Open weekends only **Ref:YH00605**

ASHLANDS FARM
Ashlands Farm, Grenofen, Tavistock, **Devon**, PL19 9EW, **ENGLAND**.
(T) 01822 616881.
Contact/s
Owner: Ms J Spencer
Profile Horse/Rider Accom. **Ref:YH00606**

ASHLEY, J
Mrs J Ashley, Stanley Hse Farm, Teversal, **Nottinghamshire**, NG17 3JH, **ENGLAND**.
(T) 01773 872381.
Profile Breeder. **Ref:YH00607**

ASHMORE BLACKSMITHS
Ashmore Blacksmiths, Bretby Business Pk, Ashby Rd, Bretby, Burton-on-Trent, **Staffordshire**, DE15 0YZ, **ENGLAND**.
(T) 01283 553050.
Profile Blacksmith. **Ref:YH00608**

ASHMORE BROOK DAIRY FARM
Ashmore Brook Dairy Farm, Cross Hand Lane, Lichfield, **Staffordshire**, WS13 8DY, **ENGLAND**.
(T) 01543 254479.
Profile Stable/Livery. **Ref:YH00609**

ASHTON AGRICULTURE
Ashton Agriculture, Auction Mart, Lincoln Way, Clitheroe, **Lancashire**, BB7 1QD, **ENGLAND**.
(T) 01200 442500.
Profile Supplies. **Ref:YH00610**

ASHTON EQUESTRIAN CTRE
Ashton Equestrian Centre, Ashtown Castleknock, Dublin, **County Dublin**, **IRELAND**.
(T) 01 8387611.
Profile Stable/Livery.
Livery avaliable, prices on request. **Ref:YH00611**

ASHTON HALL EQUESTRIAN CTRE
Ashton Hall Equestrian Centre, Church Lane, Sale, **Cheshire**, M33 5QG, **ENGLAND**.
(T) 0161 9053160 **(F)** 0161 9051313.
Profile Supplies. **Ref:YH00612**

ASHTON SADDLERY
Ashton Saddlery, Lakeham Farm, Higher Ashton, Exeter, **Devon**, EX6 7RB, **ENGLAND**.
(T) 01647 252164.
Contact/s
Owner: Mrs P Turner
Profile Riding Wear Retailer, Saddlery Retailer, Supplies. **Ref:YH00613**

ASHTON STABLES
Ashton Stables, Stoke Rd, Ashton, Northampton, **Northamptonshire**, NN7 2JN, **ENGLAND**.
(T) 01604 864551 **(F)** 01604 858015.
Contact/s
General Manager: Mr M Townsend **(Q)** BHSI
Profile Stable/Livery, Trainer.
Ashton is a competition yard specialising in dressage. Training can be provided for people with their own horses. **Yr. Est:** 1997
Opening Times
Sp: Open Mon - Sun 07:30. Closed Mon - Sun 21:00.
Su: Open Mon - Sun 07:30. Closed Mon - Sun 21:00.
Au: Open Mon - Sun 07:30. Closed Mon - Sun 21:00.
Wn: Open Mon - Sun 07:30. Closed Mon - Sun 21:00. **Ref:YH00614**

ASHTON, STUART J
Stuart J Ashton DWCF, 9 Clarence Rd, Capel-Le-Ferne, Folkestone, **Kent**, CT18 7LW, **ENGLAND**.
(T) 01303 850056.
Profile Farrier. **Ref:YH00615**

ASHTREE EQUESTRIAN CTRE
Ashtree Equestrian Centre, Little Waltham, Little Waltham, Chelmsford, **Essex**, CM3 3PA, **ENGLAND**.
(T) 01245 362424.
Contact/s
Manager: Miss J Weal
Profile Riding School. **Ref:YH00616**

ASHWATER LIVERIES
Ashwater Liveries, Two Mile Ash, Horsham, **Sussex (West)**, RH13 7PG, **ENGLAND**.
(T) 01403 730250.
Contact/s
Partner: Mrs J Richmond
Profile Stable/Livery. **Ref:YH00617**

ASHWORTH VETNRY GRP
Ashworth Veterinary Group, Veterinary Ctre, Union Trce, Crieff, **Perth and Kinross**, PH7 4DE, **SCOTLAND**.
(T) 01764 652086 **(F)** 01764 655399.
Profile Medical Support. **Ref:YH00618**

ASKELL, VICTOR W J
Victor W J Askell RSS, Jubilee Farm, Dawlish, **Devon**, EX7 0PZ, **ENGLAND**.
(T) 01626 862482.
Profile Farrier. **Ref:YH00619**

ASKER HORSESPORTS
Asker Horsesports, 28 St Andrews Rd, Henley-on-Thames, **Oxfordshire**, RG9 1JB, **ENGLAND**.
(T) 01491 571400 **(F)** 01491 572566
(M) 07785 330705
(E) asker@compuserve.com.
Profile Trainer. **Ref:YH00620**

ASKEW, STEVEN
Steven Askew DWCF, 10 Fordside Ave, Clayton-Le-Moors, Accrington, **Lancashire**, BB5 5TH, **ENGLAND**.
(T) 01254 392347.
Profile Farrier. **Ref:YH00621**

ASKHAM BRYAN COLLEGE
Askham Bryan College, Askham Bryan, York, **Yorkshire (North)**, YO23 3PR, **ENGLAND**.
(T) 01904 772277 **(F)** 01904 772288.
Profile Equestrian Centre. **Ref:YH00622**

ASLETT, G
G Aslett, 2 Studley Farm Cottage, Studley Green, High Wycombe, **Buckinghamshire**, HP14 3XB, **ENGLAND**.
(T) 01494 485958.
Profile Farrier. **Ref:YH00623**

ASMALL HSE LIVERY STABLES
Asmall House Livery Stables, Asmall Lane, Scarisbrick, Ormskirk, **Lancashire**, L40 8JL, **ENGLAND**.
(T) 01695 570025.
Contact/s
Owner: Mrs S Dunn **Ref:YH00624**

ASOKA
Asoka Classical Stud, Barbrook Farm, Rock Bank, 278 Leigh Rd, Worsley, **Lancashire**, M28 1LH, **ENGLAND**.
(T) 0161 7904186
(W) www.asokaclassicalstud.co.uk.
Contact/s
Owner: Mrs P Litton
(E) peggy@asokaclassicalstud.co.uk
Profile Arena, Breeder, Equestrian Centre, Trainer.
Run classical & circus high schools, also classical equitation. Specialise in liberty & display work, including Becky's 'clicker' training. **No.Staff:** 3
Yr. Est: 1972 **C.Size:** 6 Acres
Opening Times
Open all year, telephone for an appointment
Ref:YH00625

ASPINALL AULD & CLARKSON
Aspinall Auld & Clarkson, 20 Glevum Way, Abbeydale, **Gloucestershire**, GL4 9BL, **ENGLAND**.
(T) 01452 300596.
Profile Medical Support. **Ref:YH00626**

ASPINWALL, LAWRENCE R
Lawrence R Aspinwall, Forest View, Llysty, Acton, Bishops Castle, **Shropshire**, SY9 5LA, **ENGLAND**.
(T) 01588 638830.
Profile Farrier. **Ref:YH00627**

ASPREY POLO
Asprey Polo Ltd, R C B P C, North St, Winkfield, Windsor, **Berkshire**, SL4 4TH, **ENGLAND**.
(T) 01344 890960 **(F)** 01344 890593.
Contact/s
Owner: Mr A Murray
(E) andrewmurray@showroom@aspreypolo.
Profile Riding Wear Retailer, Saddlery Retailer.
Sell polo equipment, including mallets.
Yr. Est: 1998
Opening Times
Sp: Open Mon - Sun 09:00. Closed Mon - Sun 17:30.
Su: Open Mon - Sun 09:00. Closed Mon - Sun 17:30.
Au: Open Mon - Sun 09:00. Closed Mon - Sun 17:30.
Wn: Open Mon - Sun 09:00. Closed Mon - Sun 17:30. **Ref:YH00628**

ASS BLOOD STOCK CONS
Associated Blood Stock Consultants Ltd, 3 Lily Lane, Flamborough, Bridlington, **Yorkshire (East)**, YO15 1PF, **ENGLAND**.
(T) 01262 851286.
Contact/s
Owner: Mr J Wilikinson
Profile Blood Stock Agency, Supplies. **Ref:YH00629**

ASS OF IRISH RACECOURSES
Association of Irish Racecourses, 12 Herbert St, Dublin, **County Dublin**, **IRELAND**.
(T) 01 6760911.
Profile Supplies. **Ref:YH00630**

ASS OF SHOW & AGRICULTURAL
Association of Show & Agricultural Organisations, The Showground, Shepton Mallet, **Somerset**, BA4 6QN, **ENGLAND**.
(T) 07711 205833 **(F)** 01749 823169.
Contact/s
Key Contact: Paul Hooper
Profile Club/Association. **Ref:YH00631**

ASSELBY GRANGE LIVERY YARD
Asselby Grange Livery Yard, Asselby Grange, Carr Lane, Eastrington, Goole, **Yorkshire (East)**, DN14 7QN, **ENGLAND**.
(T) 01430 410661.
Contact/s
Owner: Mrs J Atkinson **Ref:YH00632**

ASTI STUD & SADDLERY
Asti Stud & Saddlery (The), Millaway Farm, Goosey, Faringdon, **Oxfordshire**, SN7 8PA, **ENGLAND**.
(T) 01367 710288 **(F)** 01367 710218

(E) info@asti-stud.co.uk
(W) www.asti-stud.co.uk
Affiliated Bodies ABRS, BETA, BHS.
Contact/s
Owner: Mrs R Rowland
Profile Arena, Equestrian Centre, Riding School, Riding Wear Retailer, Saddlery Retailer, Stable/Livery, Supplies.
Opening Times
Sp: Open 08:00. Closed 18:00.
Su: Open 08:00. Closed 18:00.
Au: Open 08:00. Closed 18:00.
Wn: Open 08:00. Closed 18:00. Ref: YH00633

ASTILL, R E & D R

R E & D R Astill, 23 Flag Lane, Penwortham, Preston, **Lancashire**, PR1 9TQ, **ENGLAND**.
(T) 01772 336358.
Contact/s
Partner: Mr R Astill Ref: YH00634

ASTLEY RIDING CTRE

Astley Riding Centre, Astley Lane, Swillington, Leeds, **Yorkshire (West)**, LS26 8UD, **ENGLAND**.
(T) 0113 2873078 (F) 0113 2873078
Affiliated Bodies BHS.
Contact/s
Owner: Miss L Rafferty (Q) AI
Profile Breeder, Riding School, Saddlery Retailer, Stable/Livery. No.Staff: 4 Yr. Est: 1990
C.Size: 30 Acres
Opening Times
Sp: Open 10:00. Closed 20:00.
Su: Open 10:00. Closed 20:00.
Au: Open 10:00. Closed 19:00.
Wn: Open 10:00. Closed 19:00. Ref: YH00635

ASTLEY, D

Miss D Astley BHSII, Sea Dell, Gilly Lane, White Cross, Penzance, **Cornwall**, TR20 8BZ, **ENGLAND**.
(T) 01736 740813.
Profile Trainer. Ref: YH00636

ASTON HILL EQUESTRIAN

Aston Hill Equestrian, Aston Hill Farm, Aston By Doxey, Stafford, **Staffordshire**, ST16 1UF, **ENGLAND**.
(T) 01785 282274.
Contact/s
Owner: Mr E Foster
Profile Equestrian Centre. Ref: YH00637

ASTON HSE STUD

Aston House Stud Co, Aston Hse Stud, The Green, Aston Rowant, Watlington, **Oxfordshire**, OX9 5ST, **ENGLAND**.
(T) 01844 354140.
Profile Breeder. Ref: YH00638

ASTON, R K

R K Aston, Goldford Farm, Goldford Lane, Edge, Malpas, **Cheshire**, SY14 8LA, **ENGLAND**.
(T) 01829 782410.
Profile Breeder. Ref: YH00639

ASTOR HOUSE AST

Astor House Associates, White Pl Farm, Sutton Rd, Cookham, Maidenhead, **Berkshire**, SL6 9RA, **ENGLAND**.
(T) 01628 526332.
Contact/s
Owner: Mrs J Edwards
Profile Stable/Livery. Ref: YH00640

ATACK, MICHAEL J

Michael J Atack DWCF, 11 Cleveland Gr, Lupset Pk, Wakefield, **Yorkshire (West)**, WF2 8LB, **ENGLAND**.
(T) 01924 239195.
Profile Farrier. Ref: YH00641

ATHAG LTD

Athag Ltd UK, Carlyon Rd Ind Est, Atherstone, **Warwickshire**, CV9 1LQ, **ENGLAND**.
(T) 01827 713040 (F) 01827 717307.
Profile Supplies. Ref: YH00642

ATHERSTONE & DISTRICT

Atherstone & District Riding Club, Hillside Cottage, Clifton Rd, Netherseal, Swadlincote, **Derbyshire**, DE12 8BP, **ENGLAND**.
(T) 01827 373334.
Contact/s
Treasurer: Mr D Briggs
Profile Club/Association, Riding Club. Ref: YH00643

ATHERTON, JENNY

Jenny Atherton BHSI, Bullens Farm, Hurt's Lane, Bickerstaffe, **Lancashire**, L39 0EW, **ENGLAND**.
(T) 01695 422164
(M) 07831 800408.
Profile Trainer. Ref: YH00644

ATHERTON, P V J

P V J Atherton, Willow Farm, Twyford Lane, Bold, Widnes, **Cheshire**, WA8 3UT, **ENGLAND**.
(T) 0151 4242880.
Profile Farrier. Ref: YH00645

ATKIN, BARRY

Barry Atkin, Weathercock Farm, Chevington, **Suffolk**, IP29 5RG, **ENGLAND**.
(T) 01284 850511 (F) 01284 850911.
Profile Breeder. Ref: YH00646

ATKIN, M

Mrs M Atkin, Cattleholm Cottage, Cattleholmes, Wansford, Driffield, **Yorkshire (East)**, YO25 8NW, **ENGLAND**.
(T) 01377 241628.
Profile Breeder. Ref: YH00647

ATKIN, PETER ROBERT

Peter Robert Atkin, Roulee Farm, Snake Rd, Bamford, Sheffield, **Yorkshire (South)**, S30 2BJ, **ENGLAND**..
Profile Farrier. Ref: YH00648

ATKINS, PAUL

Paul Atkins, The Nest, Hamilton Rd, Little Canfield, Dunmow, **Essex**, CM6 1SY, **ENGLAND**.
(T) 01279 870805.
Profile Farrier. Ref: YH00649

ATKINSON & BURGESS

Atkinson & Burgess, Witten Lodge, Heywood Rd, Northam, Bideford, **Devon**, EX39 3QB, **ENGLAND**.
(T) 01237 473278.
Profile Medical Support. Ref: YH00650

ATKINSON LIVERIES/ARENA HIRE

Atkinson Liveries & Arena Hire, Mansion Hse Farm, Lightwood Lane, Sheffield, **Yorkshire (South)**, S8 8BG, **ENGLAND**.
(T) 0114 2391621. Ref: YH00651

ATKINSON, ROBERT W

Robert W Atkinson DWCF, Northbank Hse, Road Head, Carlisle, **Cumbria**, CA6 6NA, **ENGLAND**.
(T) 01697 7480780
(M) 07785 528711.
Profile Farrier. Ref: YH00652

ATLANTIC EQUINE

Atlantic Equine Ltd, Calcutt Hse, Flecknoe, Rugby, **Warwickshire**, CV23 8AU, **ENGLAND**.
(T) 01788 891406 (F) 01788 890793.
Contact/s
Owner: Mr T Lindsell
Profile Farrier. Ref: YH00653

ATLAS SHOWJUMPS

Atlas Showjumps, Foliejon, Goring Rd, Woodcote, Reading, **Berkshire**, RG8 0QD, **ENGLAND**.
(T) 01491 682104.
Contact/s
Owner: Mrs N Staniford
Profile Supplies. Ref: YH00654

ATREE, A L

Mrs A L Atree, Hernaford Farm, Harbertonford, Totnes, **Devon**, TQ9 7HY, **ENGLAND**.
(T) 01803 732687.
Profile Breeder. Ref: YH00655

ATTEW, P R & S B

Messrs P R & S B Attew, Holme Pk Stud, Ashwell, Baldock, **Hertfordshire**, SG7 5HY, **ENGLAND**.
(T) 01462 743206 (F) 01767 317945
(M) 07803 271110
(W) www.holmetrakehners.com.
Profile Breeder. Ref: YH00656

ATTINGTON STUD

Attington Stud, Tetsworth, Thame, **Oxfordshire**, OX9 7BY, **ENGLAND**.
(T) 01844 281206 (F) 01844 281365.
Contact/s
Partner: Mrs C Trotter
Profile Breeder. Ref: YH00657

AUBOISE

Aubiose (UK) Ltd, Grain Hse Farm, Chaceley, **Gloucestershire**, GL19 4EH, **ENGLAND**.
(T) 01452 780499 (F) 01452 780161
(M) 07774 140432
(E) info@aubiose.co.uk
(W) www.aubiose.co.uk.
Profile Medical Support. Ref: YH00658

AUBURN

Auburn Riding School, Auburn Moate Rd, Athlone, **County Westmeath**, **IRELAND**.
(T) 0902 74460.
Profile Riding School. Ref: YH00659

AUCHENHAMPER SUFFOLK

Auchenhamper Suffolk Tack Shop, South Cross Slacks, Gamrie, Banff, **Aberdeenshire**, AB45 3HB, **SCOTLAND**.
(T) 01261 851783.
Profile Saddlery Retailer. Ref: YH00660

AUDIBURN RIDING STABLES

Audiburn Riding Stables, Audiburn Farm, Ashcombe Lane, Kingston, Lewes, **Sussex (East)**, BN7 3JZ, **ENGLAND**.
(T) 01273 474398.
Profile Riding School. Ref: YH00661

AUGHEREA HOUSE

Augherea House Equestrian Centre, Augherea, **County Longford**, **IRELAND**.
(T) 043 41004. Ref: YH00662

AUGUST APPALOOSAS

August Appaloosas, Penucheldref, Llanddeusant, Holyhead, **Isle of Anglesey**, LL65 4BB, **WALES**.
(T) 01407 730849.
Contact/s
Owner: Mrs A McEachern
Profile Breeder.
Home of " August Harrier " 15.1hh, near Leopard Champion Appaloosa Stallion. Also registered and blood typed, with the BAPS and the APHC (USA).
No.Staff: 1 C.Size: 40 Acres Ref: YH00663

AULTON & BUTLER

Aulton & Butler Ltd, Ashtree Works/Bentley Lane Ind Pk, Bentley Lane, Walsall, **Midlands (West)**, WS2 8TL, **ENGLAND**.
(T) 01922 623297 (F) 01922 613586.
Contact/s
Owner: Mr K Aulton
Profile Supplies. Saddle Tree Manufacturer.
Sell to manufacturers only. Yr. Est: 1955
Opening Times
Sp: Open Mon - Fri 08:00. Closed Mon - Fri 17:00.
Su: Open Mon - Fri 08:00. Closed Mon - Fri 17:00.
Au: Open Mon - Fri 08:00. Closed Mon - Fri 17:00.
Wn: Open Mon - Fri 08:00. Closed Mon - Fri 17:00.
Ref: YH00664

AUSDAN STUD

Ausdan Stud, Cilyblaidd Manor, The Cilyblaidd Est, Pencarreg, Lampeter, **Carmarthenshire**, SA40 9QL, **WALES**.
(T) 01570 480090 (F) 01570 480012
(M) 07702 090906
(E) john.lyn@which.net.
Profile Breeder. Ref: YH00665

AUSTER LODGE LIVERY YARD

Auster Lodge Livery Yard, Auster Lodge, Dollan Lane, Edenham, Bourne, **Lincolnshire**, PE10 0LH, **ENGLAND**.
(T) 01778 591287.
Contact/s
General Manager: Mr R Haddow
Profile Stable/Livery. No.Staff: 2
Yr. Est: 1998
Opening Times
Sp: Open Mon - Sun 08:00. Closed Mon - Sun 20:00.
Su: Open Mon - Sun 08:00. Closed Mon - Sun 20:00.
Au: Open Mon - Sun 08:00. Closed Mon - Sun 20:00.
Wn: Open Mon - Sun 08:00. Closed Mon - Sun 20:00. Ref: YH00666

AUSTIN, GEORGE

George Austin, Kerswill Hse, Cornwood, Ivybridge, **Devon**, PL21 9HT, **ENGLAND**.
(T) 01752 892390 (F) 01752 894864.
Profile Medical Support. Ref: YH00667

AUSTIN, KATE

Kate Austin, Haslemere Hse, Lower St, Haslemere, **Surrey**, GU27 2PE, **ENGLAND**.
(T) 01428 651551 (F) 01428 653888
(E) djm@djmurphy.co.uk.
Profile Supplies. Ref: YH00668

AUTAUX-SEYMOUR

Autaux-Seymour, 1 Martindale Walk, Carcroft, Doncaster, **Yorkshire (South)**, DN6 8BX, **ENGLAND**.

(T) 01302 330749.
Contact/s
Owner: Mrs T Beedom
Profile Transport/Horse Boxes. Ref: YH00669

AUTO REPAIRS MECHANICAL
Auto Repairs Mechanical, Oxford Mews, Bexley, **Kent**, DA5 1BT, **ENGLAND**.
(T) 01322 554721.
Profile Transport/Horse Boxes. Ref: YH00670

AUTO TRAILER SERVICES
Auto Trailer Services, Old School Hse, Lower Seagry, Chippenham, **Wiltshire**, SN15 5EP, **ENGLAND**.
(T) 01249 721319.
Contact/s
Owner: Mr M Hicks
Profile Transport/Horse Boxes. Ref: YH00671

AUTODENTIFIED
Autodentified, Cedar Hse, Challock, Ashford, **Kent**, TN25 4DL, **ENGLAND**.
(T) 01233 740288.
Profile Security.
Autodentified produce security marks horse boxes and other equestrian hardware Ref: YH00672

AUTOTOW
Autotow, The Hamlet, Church Rd, Bradley Green, Redditch, **Worcestershire**, B96 6RN, **ENGLAND**.
(T) 01527 821675 (F) 01527 821675.
Contact/s
Owner: Mr N Keats
Profile Transport/Horse Boxes. Ref: YH00673

AUTOTRAK PORTABLE ROADWAYS
Autotrak Portable Roadways Limited, 48 Orchard Way, Bicester, **Oxfordshire**, OX6 8EJ, **ENGLAND**.
(T) 01869 248952 (F) 01869 248952
(M) 07885 281123.
Profile Track/Course. Ref: YH00674

AUTOW CTRE
Autow Centre Ltd, Arran Hse, Arran Rd, Perth, **Perth and Kinross**, PH1 3DZ, **SCOTLAND**.
(T) 01738 627272 (F) 01738 627273
(W) www.autow.co.uk
Affiliated Bodies NTTA.
Contact/s
Owner: Mr J Robertson
(E) jrr@autow.co.uk
Profile Transport/Horse Boxes. Ref: YH00675

AUTY, I
Mrs I Auty F B H S, 41 Oakleigh Ave, Hallow, **Worcestershire**, WR2 6NG, **ENGLAND**.
(T) 01905 640023
(M) 07850 972615.
Profile Trainer. Ref: YH00676

AVENUE EQUESTRIAN CTRE/STUD
Avenue Equestrian Centre & Stud, Hanley Rd, Malvern, **Worcestershire**, WR14 4PH, **ENGLAND**.
(T) 01684 310731.
Contact/s
Owner: Mrs S Wheelan Ref: YH00677

AVENUE RIDING CTRE
Avenue Riding Centre, Hanley Rd, Malvern, **Worcestershire**, WR14 1PH, **ENGLAND**.
(T) 01684 310731.
Contact/s
General Manager: Miss T Lloyd
Profile Horse/Rider Accom. Ref: YH00678

AVENUE VETNRY CTRE
Avenue Veterinary Centre, Pendennis Ave, Staple Hill, **Surrey**, BS16 5DW, **ENGLAND**.
(T) 01179 569038.
Profile Medical Support. Ref: YH00679

AVENUE VETNRY HOSP
Avenue Veterinary Hospital (The), 33 St Peters Ave, Kettering, **Northamptonshire**, NN16 0HB, **ENGLAND**.
(T) 01536 512200 (F) 01536 517408.
Profile Medical Support. Ref: YH00680

AVERHAM PK
Averham Park, Averham Pk Farm, Averham, Newark, **Nottinghamshire**, NG23 5RU, **ENGLAND**.
(T) 01636 611293.
Profile Trainer. Ref: YH00681

AVERY, J
J Avery, Felton Farm Hse, West Felton, Oswestry, **Shropshire**, SY11 4LE, **ENGLAND**.
(T) 01691 610264.
Contact/s
Owner: Mr J Avery
Profile Farrier. Ref: YH00682

AVERY, S B
Mr S B Avery, 2 West Marsh Cottage, West Marsh Lane, Barrow Haven, **Lincolnshire (North)**, DN19 7HA, **ENGLAND**.
(T) 01469 30998.
Profile Supplies. Ref: YH00683

AVERY, S R
S R Avery, Drumacre Hall Stud, Drumacre Lane West, Longton, Preston, **Lancashire**, PR4 4SB, **ENGLAND**.
(T) 01772 614572 (F) 01772 614572.
Contact/s
Owner: Mr S Avery
Profile Breeder. Ref: YH00684

AVIFORM
Aviform Ltd, P O Box 26, Forncett-St-Peter, Norwich, **Norfolk**, NR16 1LA, **ENGLAND**.
(T) 01508 530813 (F) 01508 530873
(E) robin@aviform.co.uk.
Profile Medical Support. Ref: YH00685

AVISON, PENNY
Mrs Penny Avison, Little Manor Farm, High Lane, Nawton, York, **Yorkshire (North)**, YO62 7TU, **ENGLAND**.
(T) 01439 771672
(M) 07989 133569.
Profile Stable/Livery. Ref: YH00686

AVON & WEST RACING CLUB
Avon & West Racing Club, Kendleshire Farm, Winterbourne, **Gloucestershire (South)**, BS36 1AU, **ENGLAND**.
(T) 01454 773274. Ref: YH00687

AVON FARMERS
Avon Farmers Ltd (Avon Centre), Wallingford Rd, Kingsbridge, **Devon**, TQ7 1ND, **ENGLAND**.
(T) 01548 857321 (F) 01548 852593.
Profile Saddlery Retailer. Ref: YH00688

AVON GALLERY
Avon Gallery, High St, Moreton In Marsh, **Gloucestershire**, GL54 2AA, **ENGLAND**.
(T) 01451 20443. Ref: YH00689

AVON RIDING CTRE
Avon Riding Centre, Kings Weston Rd, Henbury, Bristol, **Bristol**, BS10 7QT, **ENGLAND**.
(T) 01179 590266.
Contact/s
Manager: Mr N Woodfield
Profile Riding School. Ref: YH00690

AVON TRAILER TOWBAR CTRE
Avon Trailer Towbar Centre, Unit 1A First Ave, Westfield Ind Est, Midsomer Norton, Bath, **Bath & Somerset (North East)**, BA3 4BN, **ENGLAND**.
(T) 01761 411171.
Profile Transport/Horse Boxes. Ref: YH00691

AVONRIDE
Avonride Ltd, Spelter Site, Caerau, Maesteg, **Bridgend**, CF34 0AQ, **WALES**.
(T) 01656 739111 (F) 01656 737677
(W) www.avonride.com.
Profile Transport/Horse Boxes.
Avonride are manufacturers of horsebox and trailers axles. There are sixty Avonride agents throughout England. Yr. Est: 1961
Opening Times
Sp: Open Mon - Fri 08:30. Closed Mon - Fri 17:30.
Su: Open Mon - Fri 08:30. Closed Mon - Fri 17:30.
Au: Open Mon - Fri 08:30. Closed Mon - Fri 17:30.
Wn: Open Mon - Fri 08:30. Closed Mon - Fri 17:30.
Closed at weekends Ref: YH00692

AVONVALE VETNRY GRP
Avonvale Veterinary Group, Ratley Lodge, Ratley, Banbury, **Oxfordshire**, OX15 6DT, **ENGLAND**.
(T) 01295 670501 (F) 01295 670778.
Profile Medical Support. Ref: YH00693

AXECROFT
Axecroft Limited, Risehow Ind Est, Flimby, Maryport, **Cumbria**, CA15 8PD, **ENGLAND**.
(T) 01900 818010 (F) 01900 818225.
Profile Supplies. Ref: YH00694

AXIENT
Axient, Unit 20 Goldthorpe Ind Est, Commercial Rd, Goldthorpe, Rotherham, **Yorkshire (South)**, S63 9BL, **ENGLAND**.
(T) 01709 890222 (F) 01709 890444.
Profile Supplies. Ref: YH00695

AYLESBURY VALE RIDING CLUB
Aylesbury Vale Riding Club, Lamont, Dinton Rd, Upton, Aylesbury, **Buckinghamshire**, HP17 8UA, **ENGLAND**.
(T) 01525 379274.
Contact/s
Chairman: Ms D Summers
Profile Club/Association, Riding Club. Ref: YH00696

AYNSLEY, J W F
Mr J W F Aynsley, Ryehill, Thropton, Nr. Rothbury, Morpeth, **Northumberland**, NE65 7NG, **ENGLAND**.
(T) 01669 620271.
Profile Supplies. Ref: YH00697

AYR RACECOURSE
Ayr Racecourse, The Western Meeting Club, Ayr Racecourse Office, 2 Whitletts Rd, Ayr, **Ayrshire (South)**, KA8 0JE, **SCOTLAND**.
(T) 01292 264179 (F) 01292 610140.
Contact/s
General Manager/Clerk of Course: Richard Pridham
Profile Track/Course. Ref: YH00698

AYR RIDING CLUB
Ayr Riding Club, Reservoir Cottage, Ladykirk, Monkton, **Ayrshire (South)**, KA9 2SE, **SCOTLAND**.
(T) 01292 470033 (F) 01292 470033.
Contact/s
Chairman: Mrs J Belding
Profile Club/Association, Riding Club. Ref: YH00699

AYR RIDING CLUB DRESSAGE
Ayr Riding Club Dressage, Kilkerran, Maybole, **Ayrshire (South)**, KA19 7SJ, **SCOTLAND**.
(T) 01655 4207.
Profile Club/Association. Ref: YH00700

AYR TRAILER CTRE
Ayr Trailer Centre, 54 Crown St, Ayr, **Ayrshire (South)**, KA8 8AG, **SCOTLAND**.
(T) 01292 268401 (F) 01292 268401
Affiliated Bodies NTTA.
Contact/s
Owner: Mr F Beaton
Profile Transport/Horse Boxes.
Opening Times
Sp: Open 08:30. Closed 17:00.
Su: Open 08:30. Closed 17:00.
Au: Open 08:30. Closed 17:00.
Wn: Open 08:30. Closed 17:00. Ref: YH00701

AYRES, JOHN
John Ayres, 190 New Rd, Rumney, Cardiff, **Glamorgan (Vale of)**, CF3 3BN, **WALES**.
(T) 029 20793941 (F) 029 20793941.
Contact/s
Owner: Mr J Ayres
Profile Riding Wear Retailer, Saddlery Retailer, Supplies. Ref: YH00702

AYRES, OLIVIA
Mrs Olivia Ayres, 144 Bishop Rise, Hatfield, **Hertfordshire**, AL10 9QB, **ENGLAND**.
(T) 01707 260670.
Profile Breeder. Ref: YH00703

AYRSHIRE EQUITATION CTRE
Ayrshire Equitation Centre, South Mains, Corton Rd, Ayr, **Ayrshire (South)**, KA6 6BY, **SCOTLAND**.
(T) 01292 266267 (F) 01292 610323
(W) www.ayrequitation.co.uk
Affiliated Bodies ABRS, BHS, TRSS.
Contact/s
Owner: Mr K Galbraith
(E) kevin@ayrequitation.co.uk
Profile Equestrian Centre, Horse/Rider Accom, Riding School, Transport/Horse Boxes.
Full size all weather flood lit menage. Residential accomodation, can bring your own horse. The centre also hosts events, shows and competitions.
Yr. Est: 1996 C.Size: 75 Acres Ref: YH00704

AYTON CASTLE
Ayton Castle, Eyemouth, **Scottish Borders**, TD14 5RD, **SCOTLAND**.
(T) 01890 781212 (F) 01890 781550.
Profile Trainer. Ref: YH00705

A-ZEP TRANSPORT
A-Zep Transport, Little Chesters, Sandpit Lane, Dunsden, Reading, **Berkshire**, RG4 9PQ, **ENGLAND**.
(T) 0118 9731103.
Contact/s
Owner: Mrs M Vanreyk
Profile Transport/Horse Boxes. Ref: YH00706

AZTEC FENCING

Aztec Fencing, 70 Park Rd, Spalding, **Lincolnshire**, PE11 1NH, **ENGLAND**.
(T) 01775 724567. **Ref: YH00707**

AZTEC TRAILER

Aztec Trailer Manufacturers & Supplies, Unit 8 Sovereign Ctre, Lichfield Rd Neander, Tamworth, **Staffordshire**, B79 7XA, **ENGLAND**.
(T) 01827 310976.
Contact/s
Owner: Mr N Markidis
Profile Transport/Horse Boxes. **Ref: YH00708**

B & B LIVERY

B & B Livery, Fagdale Hall Farm, Potto, Northallerton, **Yorkshire (North)**, DL6 3EU, **ENGLAND**.
(T) 01642 700877 **(F)** 01642 701844.
Contact/s
Owner: Mr T Bainbridge
Profile Stable/Livery. **Ref: YH00709**

B & B TRAILERS

B & B Trailers, Splaynes Green, Uckfield, **Sussex (East)**, TN22 3TN, **ENGLAND**.
(T) 01825 713422.
Profile Transport/Horse Boxes. **Ref: YH00710**

B & D HORSE DRAWN

B & D Horse Drawn Corporate Carriages, Newbold, Black Firs Lane, Birmingham, **Midlands (West)**, B37 7JE, **ENGLAND**.
(T) 0121 7823493 **(F)** 0121 7823493.
Contact/s
Owner: Mrs D Skett
Profile Horse Drawn Carriages For Hire.
Harness repairs also carried out. Carriage hire for special occassions, ie. weddings etc. Yr. Est: 1973
Opening Times
Sp: Open 09:00. Closed 21:00.
Su: Open 09:00. Closed 21:00.
Au: Open 09:00. Closed 21:00.
Wn: Open 09:00. Closed 21:00.
Evenings are the best time to call **Ref: YH00711**

B & G SERVICES

B & G Services, 1 Orchard Pl, Mappleborough Green, Studley, **Warwickshire**, B80 7BP, **ENGLAND**.
(T) 01527 852672 **(F)** 01527 857305.
Profile Supplies. **Ref: YH00712**

B & M FENCING

B & M Fencing Ltd, Reading Rd, Hook, **Hampshire**, RG27 9DB, **ENGLAND**.
(T) 01256 762739 **(F)** 01256 766891. **Ref: YH00713**

B & R INT HORSE TRANSPORT

B & R International Horse Transport, Furze Hill Farm, Star Hill, Churt, Farnham, **Surrey**, GU10 2HS, **ENGLAND**.
(T) 01428 714313.
Contact/s
Partner: Mr B Ringrose
Profile Transport/Horse Boxes. **Ref: YH00714**

B 1ST RIDING SCHOOL

B 1st Riding School Ltd, 1 Higherfold Farm, Windlehurst Rd, High Lane, Stockport, **Cheshire**, SK6 8AQ, **ENGLAND**.
(T) 0161 4273737 **(F)** 0161 4273737.
Profile Riding School, Stable/Livery. **Ref: YH00715**

B B C RIDING CLUB

B B C Riding Club, 22 Dresden Rd, London, **London (Greater)**, N19 3BD, **ENGLAND**.
(T) 020 72720138.
Contact/s
Chairman: Mr J Salter
Profile Club/Association, Riding Club. **Ref: YH00716**

B B EQUESTRIAN

B B Equestrian, 16 Albrighton Cres, Lostock Hall, Preston, **Lancashire**, PR5 5LH, **ENGLAND**.
(T) 01772 467698
(M) 07930 224701.
Profile Supplies. **Ref: YH00717**

B B PRICE

B B Price Ltd, Newtown St, Cradley Heath, **Midlands (West)**, B64 5LD, **ENGLAND**.
(T) 01384 413341 **(F)** 01384 413311.
Profile Blacksmith. **Ref: YH00718**

B C M TRAILER HIRE

B C M Trailer Hire, Cowbeech Hill/Carters Corner, Cowbeech, Hailsham, **Sussex (East)**, BN27 4JA, **ENGLAND**.
(T) 01323 833821.
Profile Transport/Horse Boxes. **Ref: YH00719**

B F I WASTE SYSTEMS

B F I Waste Systems, 130 Millbank St, Northam, Southampton, **Hampshire**, SO14 5BB, **ENGLAND**.
(T) 023 80333553 **(F)** 023 80333819. **Ref: YH00720**

B G I BLOODSTOCK/INSURANCE

B G I Bloodstock & General Insurance Services Ltd, 162 High St, Newmarket, **Suffolk**, CB8 9AQ, **ENGLAND**.
(T) 01638 661411 **(F)** 01638 665013.
Profile Club/Association. **Ref: YH00721**

B G W SPECTRAFLECT

B G W Spectraflect Ltd, Unit 6 Churchill Ind Est, Churchill Rd, Cheltenham, **Gloucestershire**, GL53 7EG, **ENGLAND**.
(T) 01242 578748 **(F)** 01242 228969.
Profile Supplies. **Ref: YH00722**

B GREGSON & SON

B Gregson & Son, Manor Farm, South Stainley, Harrogate, **Yorkshire (North)**, HG3 3NE, **ENGLAND**.
(T) 01423 770171.
Profile Transport/Horse Boxes. **Ref: YH00723**

B H C COACH BUILDERS

B H C Coach Builders, The Stables, Stanwell New Rd, Staines, **Surrey**, TW18 4HZ, **ENGLAND**.
(T) 01784 453148.
Profile Transport/Horse Boxes. **Ref: YH00724**

B H S COUNTY BRIDLEWAYS

British Horse Society County Bridleways, Preston Farm, Drewsteignton, Exeter, **Devon**, EX6 6PR, **ENGLAND**.
(T) 01647 281231.
Profile Club/Association. **Ref: YH00725**

B H S SCOTLAND-HIGHLAND

British Horse Society Scotland Highland Region (North), Morven View, Spittal, **Highlands**, KW1 5XR, **SCOTLAND**.
(T) 01847 841255.
Profile Club/Association. **Ref: YH00726**

B H S WALES DEVELOP OFFICER

British Horse Society Development Officer (Wales), Clwydwaundwr, Sennybridge, **Powys**, LD3 8SP, **WALES**.
(T) 01874 836700.
Profile Club/Association. **Ref: YH00727**

B H S-N I CHAIRMAN

British Horse Society Chairman (Northern Ireland), The Drumlin, 49 Ballyworfy Rd, Hillsborough, **County Down**, BT26 6LR, **NORTHERN IRELAND**.
(T) 028 92682539.
Profile Club/Association. **Ref: YH00728**

B H S-SCOTLAND-HIGHLAND

British Horse Society Scotland (Highland Region), Achmonie Farm, Drumnadrochit, **Highlands**, IV63 6UX, **SCOTLAND**.
(T) 01456 450224 **(F)** 01456 450827.
Profile Club/Association. **Ref: YH00729**

B H S-WALES-POWYS REGION

British Horse Society Wales (Powys Region), Brithdin Farm, Llangurig, **Powys**, SY18 6SA, **WALES**.
(T) 01686 440675.
Profile Club/Association. **Ref: YH00730**

B I S

B I S (Trent), Units 7, Railway Enterprise Ctre, Shelton New Rd, Stoke-on-Trent, **Staffordshire**, ST4 7SH, **ENGLAND**.
(T) 01782 279797 **(F)** 01782 279797.
Profile Club/Association. **Ref: YH00731**

B J COMPONENTS

B J Components, 14 Floodgate St, Birmingham, **Midlands (West)**, B5 5ST, **ENGLAND**.
(T) 0121 6433295.
Contact/s
Owner: Mr B Cutts
Profile Transport/Horse Boxes. **Ref: YH00732**

B J LLEWELLYN

B J Llewellyn Racehorse Stables, Ffynonau-Duon Farm, Pentwyn, Fochriw, Bargoed, **Caerphilly**, CF81 9NR, **WALES**.
(T) 01685 841259 **(F)** 01685 843838.
Contact/s
Owner: Mr B Llewellyn
Profile Trainer. No.Staff: 5 Yr. Est: 1992
C.Size: 140 Acres
Opening Times
Sp: Open Mon - Fri 09:00. Closed Mon - Fri 17:00.
Su: Open Mon - Fri 09:00. Closed Mon - Fri 17:00.
Au: Open Mon - Fri 09:00. Closed Mon - Fri 17:00.
Wn: Open Mon - Fri 09:00. Closed Mon - Fri 17:00.
Outside these hours telephone for an appointment
Ref: YH00733

B J W EQUINE SVS

B J W Equine Services, Hill Farm Hse, Priory Rd, Thurgarton, **Nottinghamshire**, NG14 7GT, **ENGLAND**.
(T) 01636 830411.
Profile Supplies. **Ref: YH00734**

B K HILL TRAILERS

B K Hill Trailers Ltd, 47 Lea Rd, Stockport, **Manchester (Greater)**, SK4 4JT, **ENGLAND**.
(T) 0161 4324408.
Profile Transport/Horse Boxes. **Ref: YH00735**

B L R S

B L R S Ltd T/A Assured Engineering (1972), Stuart Hse, 97 Station Rd, Erdington, Birmingham, **Midlands (West)**, B23 6UG, **ENGLAND**.
(T) 0121 3737425 **(F)** 0121 3847412.
Profile Transport/Horse Boxes. **Ref: YH00736**

B M C PUBLIC RELATIONS

B M C Public Relations, 1 Market Cl, Poole, **Dorset**, BH15 1NQ, **ENGLAND**.
(T) 01202 669244 **(F)** 01202 672221.
Profile Club/Association. **Ref: YH00737**

B M ENGLISH & SON

B M English & Son, East Croft, East Rainton, Houghton Le Spring, **Tyne and Wear**, DH5 9QR, **ENGLAND**.
(T) 0191 5842153.
Profile Supplies. **Ref: YH00738**

B M F

B M F, Burton Park Rd, Petworth, **Sussex (West)**, GU28 0JR, **ENGLAND**.
(T) 01798 869496 **(F)** 01798 869497.
Profile Trainer. **Ref: YH00739**

B M H S

British Miniature Horse Society, Howick Farm, The Haven, Billingshurst, **Sussex (West)**, RH14 9BQ, **ENGLAND**.
(T) 01403 822639/823274 **(F)** 01403 822014
(W) www.toyhorse.co.uk.
Contact/s
Key Contact: Mrs T Adorian
Profile Club/Association.
The BHMS are official registers of all equines 34" and under. They are affiliated to the British Central Prefix Register and are also members of the BHS's Horse & Pony Breeds Committee. **Ref: YH00740**

B M H S

British Miniature Horse Society, Zeals Hse, Lower Zeal, Warminster, **Wiltshire**, BA12 6LG, **ENGLAND**.
(T) 01747 861786 **(F)** 01747 861786.
Contact/s
Registrar: Wendy Edgar
Profile Club/Association.
Opening Times
Telephone for further information **Ref: YH00741**

B M K FABRICATION

B M K Fabrication, 8 Cable Rd, Glenrothes, **Fife**, KY6 2SY, **SCOTLAND**.
(T) 01592 774052.
Contact/s
Owner: Mr B Kelly
Profile Blacksmith. **Ref: YH00742**

B M M LEATHERS

B M M Leathers, Oldhams Barn, Blackhouse Lane, Fox Hill, Petworth, **Sussex (West)**, GU28 9NU, **ENGLAND**.
(T) 01798 343364 **(F)** 01798 343364.
Profile Trainer. **Ref: YH00743**

B M VEALE & SON

B M Veale & Son, Forge Yard, Checkendon, Reading, **Berkshire**, RG8 0SP, **ENGLAND**.
(T) 01491 680151.
Profile Transport/Horse Boxes. **Ref: YH00744**

B P SVS

B P Services, Hale Manor Farm, Hale Common, Newport, **Isle of Wight**, PO30 3AR, **ENGLAND**.
(T) 01983 868158.
Profile Blacksmith. **Ref: YH00745**

B R I INT

B R I International LTd, (incorporating Border Rose Horse Transport), Swordwellrig, Annan, **Dumfries and Galloway**, DG12 6RA, **SCOTLAND**.
(T) 01461 40019.
Profile Transport/Horse Boxes. **Ref: YH00746**

B R ROUND

B R Round (Insurance Broker) B.I.I.B.A., 38 Moorend Rd, Mellor, Stockport, **Manchester (Greater)**, SK6 5PS, **ENGLAND**.
(T) 0161 4272808 **(F)** 0161 4497668.
Profile Club/Association. **Ref: YH00747**

B S I

B S I, Mr L Holyoak, Maylands Ave, Hemel Hempstead, **Hertfordshire**, HP2 4SQ, **ENGLAND**.
(T) 01442 230442 **(F)** 01442 231442.
Profile Club/Association. **Ref: YH00748**

B T H HIRE & SALES

B T H Hire & Sales, 251 Whitehall Rd, Leeds, **Yorkshire (West)**, LS12 6ER, **ENGLAND**.
(T) 08005 420794 **(F)** 0113 2794933.
Profile Transport/Horse Boxes. Trailer & Towing Equipment Specialists.
Supply accessories, including wheels, tyres, couplings, axles, lights, wheel clamps and other security products. **Ref: YH00749**

B W HILLS SOUTHBANK

B W Hills Southbank (Ltd), Southbank, Newbury Rd, Lambourn, Hungerford, **Berkshire**, RG17 7LL, **ENGLAND**.
(T) 01488 71548 **(F)** 01488 72823.
Profile Trainer.
Race horse trainer No.Staff: 1 Yr. Est: 1969
Opening Times
By appointment only **Ref: YH00750**

B WHEELWRIGHT & SON

B Wheelwright & Son, 143 Hollywood Lane, Hollywood, Birmingham, **Midlands (West)**, B47 5QJ, **ENGLAND**.
(T) 0121 4307102.
Profile Supplies. **Ref: YH00751**

B WORTLEY & SON

B Wortley & Son, Alder St, Off Bradford Rd, Huddersfield, **Yorkshire (West)**, HD1 6HZ, **ENGLAND**.
(T) 01484 422512.
Profile Supplies. **Ref: YH00752**

B, MCPHEE

McPhee B, Shotts Cottage, Kerse Rd, Fallin, Stirling, **Stirling**, FK7 7LU, **SCOTLAND**.
(T) 01786 461358.
Profile Blacksmith. **Ref: YH00753**

B.E.M.

B.E.M., Old Saw Mill, Station Rd, Newcastle Emlyn, **Carmarthenshire**, SA38 9BX, **WALES**.
(T) 01239 711337.
Profile Blacksmith. **Ref: YH00754**

B.E.V. A

British Equine Veterinary Association, 5 Finley St, London, **London (Greater)**, SW6 6HE, **ENGLAND**.
(T) 020 76106080 **(F)** 020 76106823
(E) info@beva.org.uk
(W) www.beva.org.uk.
Contact/s
Administration: Miss S Majendie
Profile Club/Association.
Opening Times
Sp: Open 09:00. Closed 17:00.
Su: Open 09:00. Closed 17:00.
Au: Open 09:00. Closed 17:00.
Wn: Open 09:00. Closed 17:00. **Ref: YH00755**

B.R.A.T.S. RIDING CLUB

B.R.A.T.S. (Cheshire) Riding Club, Radbroke Hall, Knutsford, **Cheshire**, WA16 9EU, **ENGLAND**.
(T) 01565 3888.
Contact/s
Secretary: Mrs P Trunkfield
Profile Club/Association, Riding Club. **Ref: YH00756**

B1' BRIDGE STUD

B1' Bridge Stud, 49 Studfold, Astley Village, Chorley, **Lancashire**, PR7 1UA, **ENGLAND**.
(T) 01257 415713.
Profile Breeder. **Ref: YH00757**

BA GREEN CROP DRIERS

British Association Green Crop Driers, Sliverwood, Stone St, Westenhanger, Hythe, **Kent**, CT21 4HT, **ENGLAND**.
(T) 01303 267317 **(F)** 01303 267317
(E) bagcd@compuserve.com.
Profile Club/Association. **Ref: YH00758**

BA GREEN CROP DRIERS

British Association of Green Crop Driers (The), 25 Frant Rd, Tunbridge Wells, **Kent**, TN2 5JT, **ENGLAND**.
(T) 01892 537777 **(F)** 01892 524593.
Profile Club/Association. **Ref: YH00759**

BA OF EQUINE SOC

British Association of Equine Societies, Home Farm, Priory Lane, Markfield, **Leicestershire**, LE67 9PH, **ENGLAND**.
(T) 01530 249371 **(F)** 01530 249371.
Profile Club/Association. **Ref: YH00760**

BABBAGE, N M

Mr N M Babbage, The Deer Pk, Brockhampton, Andoversford, Cheltenham, **Gloucestershire**, GL54 5SP, **ENGLAND**.
(T) 01242 821117 **(F)** 01242 821147
(M) 07976 262547.
Profile Trainer. **Ref: YH00761**

BABELL CROSS CTRY

Babell Cross Country, Babell, Holywell, **Flintshire**, CH8 8TZ, **WALES**.
(T) 01352 720442.
Profile Track/Course. **Ref: YH00762**

BABES, G

G Babes, Harelaw Farm, East Kilbride, Glasgow, **Lanarkshire (South)**, G75 9DR, **SCOTLAND**.
(T) 01355 238263.
Profile Breeder. **Ref: YH00763**

BABLEIGH RIDING SCHOOL

Bableigh Riding School, Bableigh Hse, Landkey, Barnstaple, **Devon**, EX32 0NT, **ENGLAND**.
(T) 01271 830242.
Profile Riding School. **Ref: YH00764**

BACHE, R E

R E Bache, Lyndon, Alveley, Bridgnorth, **Shropshire**, WV15 6LN, **ENGLAND**.
(T) 01746 780283 **(F)** 01746 780296.
Contact/s
Owner: Mr R Bache
Profile Transport/Horse Boxes. **Ref: YH00765**

BACHELORS LODGE

Bachelors Lodge Equestrian Centre, Bachelors Lodge, Kells Rd, Navan, **County Meath**, **IRELAND**.
(T) 046 21736 **(F)** 046 78299
(E) lowryfam@eircom.net.
Contact/s
Owner: Anthony Lowry
Profile Equestrian Centre, Riding School, Stable/Livery.
Full livery available, details on request. Has childrens riding holidays, residential courses and pony camps.
Opening Times
Sp: Open Tues - Sun 09:00. Closed Tues - Sat 18:00, Sun 13:00.
Su: Open Tues - Sun 09:00. Closed Tues - Sat 18:00, Sun 13:00.
Au: Open Tues - Sun 09:00. Closed Tues - Sat 18:00, Sun 13:00.
Wn: Open Tues - Sun 09:00. Closed Tues - Sat 18:00, Sun 13:00.
Closed Mondays & Sunday afternoons. Evening lessons by arrangement. **Ref: YH00766**

BACHMAN, T E

Mrs T E Bachman, Northbrook, Farnham, **Surrey**, GU10 5EU, **ENGLAND**.
(T) 01420 22188.
Profile Breeder. **Ref: YH00767**

BACKANDSIDES RIDING CTRE

Backandsides Riding Centre, Backandsides Farm, West Auckland, Bishop Auckland, **County Durham**, DL14 9PJ, **ENGLAND**.
(T) 01388 832202 **(F)** 01388 832202.
Contact/s
Partner: Mrs J Moffett **Ref: YH00768**

BACKHOUSE, J L & M C

J L & M C Backhouse, 1 Horsey Island, Kirby-Le-Soken, Frinton-on-Sea, **Essex**, CO13 0EZ, **ENGLAND**.
(T) 01255 672442.
Contact/s
Owner: Mr J Backhouse
Profile Breeder. **Ref: YH00769**

BACKHURST OF NORMANDY

Backhurst of Normandy, Strawberry Farm, Glaziers Lane, Normandy, Guildford, **Surrey**, GU3 2DF, **ENGLAND**.
(T) 01483 811360 **(F)** 01483 810888.
Profile Supplies. **Ref: YH00770**

BACKNOE END EQUESTRIAN CTRE

Backnoe End Equestrian Centre, Keysoe Rd, Thurleigh, Bedford, **Bedfordshire**, MK44 2EA, **ENGLAND**.
(T) 01234 772263.
Contact/s
Owner: Mrs S Jackson
Profile Riding School, Stable/Livery. **Ref: YH00771**

BACKWOOD LIVERY SERVICES

Backwood Livery Services, Backwood Hall Farm, Boathouse Lane, Parkgate, Neston, **Merseyside**, CH64 3SZ, **ENGLAND**.
(T) 0151 3364169.
Profile Stable/Livery. **Ref: YH00772**

BACUP & DISTRICT RIDING CLUB

Bacup & District Riding Club, 31 Ribble St, Bacup, **Lancashire**, OL13 9RH, **ENGLAND**.
(T) 01706 877564 **(F)** 01706 877564.
Contact/s
Secretary: Mrs S Smith
Profile Club/Association, Riding Club. **Ref: YH00773**

BADCOCK & EVERED

Badcock & Evered Ltd, Washford Mills, Washford, Watchet, **Somerset**, TA23 0JY, **ENGLAND**.
(T) 01984 640412.
Contact/s
Branch Manager: Mr I Robinson
Profile Saddlery Retailer. **Ref: YH00774**

BADEN POWELL STUD

Baden Powell Stud, Weston Farmhouse, The Street, Allury, Guildford, **Surrey**, GU5 9AY, **ENGLAND**.
(T) 01483 205087.
Profile Breeder. **Ref: YH00775**

BADENOCH RIDING CLUB

Badenoch Riding Club, Klondyke Cottage, Tullock, Nethybridge, **Highlands**, PH25 3EF, **SCOTLAND**.
(T) 01479 831615 **(F)** 01479 831587.
Contact/s
Treasurer: Mrs E Troup
Profile Club/Association, Riding Club. **Ref: YH00776**

BADGER WOOD FARM STABLES

Badger Wood Farm Stables, Clapers Lane, Fulking, **Sussex (West)**, BN5 9NJ, **ENGLAND**.
(T) 01273 857369.
Profile Stable/Livery. **Ref: YH00777**

BADGER WOOD TRAINING/LIVERY

Badger Wood Training & Livery Centre, Clappers Lane, Fulking, Henfield, **Sussex (West)**, BN5 9NJ, **ENGLAND**.
(T) 01273 857369.
Contact/s
Owner: Miss T Talbot
Profile Stable/Livery, Trainer. **Ref: YH00778**

BADGERS COURT LIVERY

Badgers Court Livery, Cackets Lane, Cudham, Sevenoaks, **Kent**, TN14 7QG, **ENGLAND**.
(T) 01959 533951.
Profile Stable/Livery. **Ref: YH00779**

BADGEWORTH LIVERY YARD

Badgeworth Livery Yard, Cold Pool Lane, Badgeworth, Cheltenham, **Gloucestershire**, GL51 5UP, **ENGLAND**.
(T) 01452 713818.
Contact/s
Owner: Mr G Pink
Profile Stable/Livery. **Ref: YH00780**

BADGWORTH ARENA

Badgworth Arena, Beech Tree Farm, Badgworth Lane, Axbridge, **Somerset**, BS26 2QU, **ENGLAND**.
(T) 01934 733514 **(F)** 01934 733514.
Contact/s
Owner: Mr C Andrews
Profile Equestrian Centre, Stable/Livery.
Livery available for horses in training only.
Yr. Est: 1996
Opening Times
Sp: Open Mon - Sun 09:00. Closed Mon - Sun 17:00.
Su: Open Mon - Sun 09:00. Closed Mon - Sun 17:00.
Au: Open Mon - Sun 09:00. Closed Mon - Sun

17:00.
Wn: Open Mon - Sun 09:00. Closed Mon - Sun 17:00. Ref: YH00781

BADMINTON HORSE FEEDS

Badminton Horse Feeds (N Ireland), 160 Moira Rd, Lisburn, **County Antrim**, BT28 1JB, **NORTHERN IRELAND**.
(T) 028 92662611 (F) 028 92677202.
Profile Supplies. Ref: YH00782

BADMINTON HORSE FEEDS

Badminton Horse Feeds (Lancashire), Whitebirk Ind Est, Blackburn, **Lancashire**, BB1 5GL, **ENGLAND**.
(T) 01254 59506.
Profile Supplies. Ref: YH00783

BADMINTON HORSE FEEDS

Badminton Horse Feeds, South St, Oakham, **Rutland**, LE15 6EA, **ENGLAND**.
(T) 01572 756091 (F) 01572 756021
(E) bsfeeds@compuserve.com
(W) www.badmintonfeeds.co.uk.
Profile Feed Merchant. Ref: YH00784

BADMINTON HORSE FEEDS

Badminton Horse Feeds (Somerset), Dunball Mill, Bristol Rd, Bridgwater, **Somerset**, TA6 4TB, **ENGLAND**.
(T) 01278 683551.
Profile Supplies. Ref: YH00785

BADMINTON HORSE FEEDS

Badminton Horse Feeds (North Yorkshire), Bishopsdyke Rd, Sherburn In Elmet, **Yorkshire (West)**, LS25 6JZ, **ENGLAND**.
(T) 01977 684784.
Profile Supplies. Ref: YH00786

BADMINTON HORSE TRIALS

Badminton Horse Trials (Mitsubishi Motors) (The), Badminton Horse Trials Office, Badminton, **Gloucestershire**, GL9 1DF, **ENGLAND**.
(T) 01454 218272 (F) 01454 218596
(E) info@badminton-horse.co.uk.
Contact/s
Secretary: Mrs J Tuckwell Ref: YH00787

BADMINTON SPORTING DIARY

Badminton Sporting Diary, Smythson Of Bond St, 40 New Bond St, London, **London (Greater)**, W1Y 0DE, **ENGLAND**.
(T) 09902 11311 (F) 01713 181500.
Profile Supplies. Ref: YH00788

BAGNALL, ANDREW J

Andrew J Bagnall DWCF, 3 Balmoral Rd, Erdington, Birmingham, **Midlands (West)**, B23 6NY, **ENGLAND**.
(T) 0121 3827915.
Profile Farrier. Ref: YH00789

BAGNUM LIVERY STABLES

Bagnum Livery Stables, Little Bagnum Farm, Bagnum, Ringwood, **Hampshire**, BH24 3BZ, **ENGLAND**.
(T) 01425 476263.
Contact/s
Owner: Mrs A Shelton Ref: YH00790

BAGSHAWS AGRICULTURAL

Bagshaws Agricultural, Vine Hse, Church St, Ashbourne, **Derbyshire**, DE6 1AE, **ENGLAND**.
(T) 01335 342201 (F) 01335 300542.
Contact/s
Consultant: Mr P Binder Ref: YH00791

BAHVS

British Association of Homeopathic Veterinary Surg (The), Chinham Hse, Standon-In-The-Vale, Faringdon, **Oxfordshire**, SN7 8NQ, **ENGLAND**.
(T) 01367 710324.
Contact/s
Key Contact: C Day
Profile Club/Association. Ref: YH00792

BAILEY ERNIE

Bailey Ernie, Arnestown, New Ross, **County Wexford**, **IRELAND**.
(T) 051 421870.
Profile Supplies. Ref: YH00793

BAILEY MILL

Bailey Mill Trekking Centre, Bailey, Newcastleton, **Scottish Borders**, TD9 0TR, **SCOTLAND**.
(T) 01697 748617
(W) www.holidaycottagescumbria.co.uk
Affiliated Bodies TRSS.
Contact/s
General Manager: Mr I Copeland (Q) TRSS
Profile Horse/Rider Accom, Riding School, Stable/Livery, Trekking, Leisure Centre.
On site jacuzzi, sauna, bar, meals and mountain bike hire. Ref: YH00794

BAILEY MOBILE

Bailey Mobile Shoeing & General Smith, 4 Manor Rd, Stourpaine, Blandford Forum, **Dorset**, DT11 8TQ, **ENGLAND**.
(T) 01258 452649.
Contact/s
Owner: Mr A Bailey
Profile Farrier. Ref: YH00795

BAILEY TRAILERS

Bailey Trailers Ltd, Aunsby, Sleaford, **Lincolnshire**, NG34 8TA, **ENGLAND**.
(T) 01529 455232 (F) 01529 455248.
Contact/s
Owner: Mr T Bailey
Profile Transport/Horse Boxes. Ref: YH00796

BAILEY, ALAN W

Alan W Bailey AFCL, The Oast Hse, Pomona Farm Barns, Bartestree, **Herefordshire**, HR1 4BQ, **ENGLAND**.
(T) 01432 851393.
Profile Farrier. Ref: YH00797

BAILEY, ANTHONY G

Anthony G Bailey AFCL, Smithy Hse, 29 Radmoor, Peplow, Hodnet, Market Drayton, **Shropshire**, **ENGLAND**.
(T) 01630 685585.
Profile Farrier. Ref: YH00798

BAILEY, DESMOND EARL

Desmond Earl Bailey RSS, Pantglas, Llanybydder, **Carmarthenshire**, SA40 9QZ, **WALES**.
(T) 01570 480860.
Profile Farrier. Ref: YH00799

BAILEY, ERNEST L

Ernest L Bailey RSS, 129 Pipering Lane, Bentley, Doncaster, **Yorkshire (South)**, DN5 9NB, **ENGLAND**.
(T) 01302 874340.
Profile Farrier. Ref: YH00800

BAILEY, JOHN ANDREW

John Andrew Bailey DWCF, 3 Tegsnose Mount, Langley, Macclesfield, **Cheshire**, SK11 0BX, **ENGLAND**.
(T) 01260 52873.
Profile Farrier. Ref: YH00801

BAILEY, K C

K C Bailey, Grange Farm, Preston Capes, Daventry, **Northamptonshire**, NN11 3TQ, **ENGLAND**.
(T) 01327 361733 (F) 01327 361703
(W) www.kcbaileyracing.com
Affiliated Bodies NTF.
Contact/s
Owner: Mr K Bailey
(E) kim@kcbaileyracing.com
Profile Trainer. No.Staff: 8 Yr. Est: 1978
Opening Times
Sp: Open Mon - Sat 08:00. Closed Mon - Fri 17:00, Sat 12:30.
Su: Open Mon - Sat 08:00. Closed Mon - Fri 17:00, Sat 12:30.
Au: Open Mon - Sat 08:00. Closed Mon - Fri 17:00, Sat 12:30.
Wn: Open Mon - Sat 08:00. Closed Mon - Fri 17:00, Sat 12:30.
Yard is closed on Sundays. Ref: YH00802

BAILEY, M F

M F Bailey, Hartwell Stud Farm, Hartwell Lane, Stone, **Staffordshire**, ST15 8TL, **ENGLAND**.
(T) 01782 372523.
Contact/s
Owner: Mr M Bailey
Profile Transport/Horse Boxes. Ref: YH00803

BAILEY, N E

N E Bailey, Black Greyhound Smithy, Macclesfield Rd, Over Alderley, Macclesfield, **Cheshire**, SK10 4SN, **ENGLAND**.
(T) 01625 827725.
Contact/s
Owner: Mr N Bailey
Profile Blacksmith. Ref: YH00804

BAILEY, RALPH

Ralph Bailey, Pear Tree Farm, 35 The Causeway, Woolavington, Bridgwater, **Somerset**, TA7 8DN, **ENGLAND**.
(T) 01278 683913 (F) 01278 683913.
Contact/s
Owner: Mr R Bailey
Profile Transport/Horse Boxes. Ref: YH00805

BAILEYS HORSE FEEDS

Baileys Horse Feeds, Four Elms Mills, Bardfield Saling, Braintree, **Essex**, CM7 5EJ, **ENGLAND**.
(T) 01371 850247 (F) 01371 851269
(E) info@baileyshorsefeeds.co.uk
(W) www.baileyshorsefeeds.co.uk.
Contact/s
Nuritionist: Miss K Lugsden
Profile Feed Merchant, Supplies.
Distributors of Buckeye nutritional feeds. Offer advice on feeding, equine nutrition and horsefeeds for your horse or pony.
Opening Times
Sp: Open Mon - Fri 09:00. Closed Mon - Fri 17:00.
Su: Open Mon - Fri 09:00. Closed Mon - Fri 17:00.
Au: Open Mon - Fri 09:00. Closed Mon - Fri 17:00.
Wn: Open Mon - Fri 09:00. Closed Mon - Fri 17:00. Ref: YH00806

BAILEYS HORSE FEEDS

Baileys Horse Feeds, Monkton Ind Est, Denby Dale Rd, Wakefield, **Yorkshire (West)**, WF2 7BP, **ENGLAND**.
(T) 01924 382820.
Profile Feed Merchant. Ref: YH00807

BAILEYS HORSE FEEDS

Baileys Horse Feeds, Unit 5, Headways Business Ctre, Denby Dale Rd, Wakefield, **Yorkshire (West)**, WF2 7AZ, **ENGLAND**.
(T) 01924 880600.
Profile Feed Merchant. Ref: YH00808

BAILY'S HUNTING DIRECTORY

Baily's Hunting Directory, Baily's, Chesterton Mill, French's Rd, Cambridge, **Cambridgeshire**, CB4 3NP, **ENGLAND**.
(T) 01223 350555 (F) 01223 356484
(E) karen@pearson.co.uk.
Profile Supplies. Ref: YH00809

BAIN, FIONA M

Fiona M Bain, 52 Briarwood Ave, Garden Village, Gosforth, **Tyne and Wear**, NE3 5DB, **ENGLAND**.
(T) 0191 2846685 (F) 0191 2846685. Ref: YH00810

BAINBRIDGE, BUTT & DALY

Bainbridge, Butt & Daly, Swanspool Veterinary Clinic, 1 London Rd, Wellingborough, **Northamptonshire**, NN8 2BT, **ENGLAND**.
(T) 01933 222145 (F) 01933 224163.
Profile Medical Support. Ref: YH00811

BAINBRIDGE, J S

Mr J S Bainbridge, Ploughlands, Littlemusgrave, Kirkby Stephen, **Cumbria**, CA17 4PQ, **ENGLAND**.
(T) 01768 341256.
Profile Trainer. Ref: YH00812

BAINBRIDGE, JULIAN

Julian Bainbridge BII Hons, Chapel Hse, Main St, York, **Yorkshire (North)**, YO1 4RR, **ENGLAND**.
(T) 07970 847488.
Profile Farrier. Ref: YH00813

BAINES, P

P Baines, 85 Eastgate, Louth, **Lincolnshire**, LN11 9TG, **ENGLAND**.
(T) 01507 602552.
Profile Supplies. Ref: YH00814

BAIRD, GEORGE M

George M Baird, West Whitefield, Burrelton, Blairgowrie, **Perth and Kinross**, PH13 9PT, **SCOTLAND**.
(T) 01821 650217.
Profile Breeder. Ref: YH00815

BAKER, COLETTE

Colette Baker, Sedgemead, 16 Braithewaite Pl, Burnham-on-Sea, **Somerset**, TA8 2PJ, **ENGLAND**.
(T) 01278 789954
Affiliated Bodies NAAT.
Contact/s
Physiotherapist: Colette Baker
Profile Medical Support. Ref: YH00816

BAKER, D J
Miss D J Baker, Walnut Farm, Hellidon Rd, Priors Marston, Rugby, **Warwickshire**, CV23 8RN, **ENGLAND**.
(T) 01327 260417.
Profile Supplies. **Ref: YH00817**

BAKER, GRAHAM J
Graham J Baker RSS, 7 Elm Cl, Shortgate Lane, Laughton, Lewes, **Sussex (East)**, BN8 6BW, **ENGLAND**.
(T) 01323 811615.
Profile Farrier. **Ref: YH00818**

BAKER, J
J Baker, Clare, Coldharbour Lane, Marlborough, **Wiltshire**, SN8 1BJ, **ENGLAND**.
(T) 01672 514013.
Contact/s
Owner: Mr J Baker
Profile Farrier. **Ref: YH00819**

BAKER, JENNY
Jenny Baker, Park Farm Lodge, Dedham, Colchester, **Essex**, CO7 6AX, **ENGLAND**.
(T) 01206 322553.
Profile Supplies. **Ref: YH00820**

BAKER, K D
K D Baker, 1 Big Allington, Broad St, Hollingbourne, Maidstone, **Kent**, ME17 1RD, **ENGLAND**.
(T) 01622 880655.
Profile Farrier. **Ref: YH00821**

BAKER, K M
K M Baker, Salix Hse, Hamerton Rd, Alconbury Weston, Huntingdon, **Cambridgeshire**, PE28 4JD, **ENGLAND**.
(T) 01480 890782.
Contact/s
Partner: Mr K Baker
Profile Stable/Livery. **Ref: YH00822**

BAKER, KEITH D
Keith D Baker RSS, 1 Big Allington Cottages, Broad St, Hollingbourne, Maidstone, **Kent**, ME17 1RD, **ENGLAND**.
(T) 01622 880098.
Profile Farrier. **Ref: YH00823**

BAKER, MARTYN D
Martyn D Baker DWCF, The Croft, Brookhill Rd, Coppathorne, **Cornwall**, RH10 3PR, **ENGLAND**.
(T) 01342 716324.
Profile Farrier. **Ref: YH00824**

BAKER, PETER N
Peter N Baker AWCF, 69 Whitley Rd, Aldbourne, Marlborough, **Wiltshire**, SN8 2BU, **ENGLAND**.
(T) 01672 540812
(M) 07836 501999.
Profile Farrier. **Ref: YH00825**

BAKER, RICHARD
Richard Baker, Catfoot Lane, Lambley, Nottingham, **Nottinghamshire**, NG4 4QH, **ENGLAND**.
(T) 0115 9267486.
Profile Stable/Livery. **Ref: YH00826**

BAKEWELL TRAILERS
Bakewell Trailers, Flint Hse, Calver, Hope Valley, **Derbyshire**, S32 3XH, **ENGLAND**.
(T) 01433 631333 **(F)** 01433 631333.
Profile Transport/Horse Boxes. **Ref: YH00827**

BAKEWELL TRAILERS
Bakewell Trailers Ltd, Flint Hse, Calver, Sheffield, **Yorkshire (South)**, S30 1XH, **ENGLAND**.
(T) 01433 631994 **(F)** 01433 631994.
Profile Transport/Horse Boxes. **Ref: YH00828**

BALANCE
Balance International, Westcott Venture Pk, Westcott, Aylesbury, **Buckinghamshire**, HP18 0XB, **ENGLAND**.
(T) 01296 658333 **(F)** 01296 658334
(E) contact@balanceinternational.com
(W) www.balanceinternational.com.
Contact/s
Partner: Carol Brett
Profile Saddle Consultants. Yr. Est: 1993
Ref: YH00829

BALANCED FEEDS
Balanced Horse Feeds, Byhurst Farm, Leatherhead Rd, Malden Rushett, **Surrey**, KT9 2NL, **ENGLAND**.
(T) 01372 721700 **(F)** 01372 745623
(E) neddy@neddynosh.co.uk
(W) www.balancedhorsefeeds.co.uk.
Contact/s
Assistant: Mr D Park
(E) doug@balancehorsefeeds.co.uk
Profile Feed Merchant. Feed Manufacturers.
Use a mixture of traditional & modern technology to produce feeds to maximise performance while providing the nutrition horses need. Yr. Est: 1985
Opening Times
Sp: Open Mon - Sat 08:00. Closed Mon - Sat 17:30.
Su: Open Mon - Sat 08:00. Closed Mon - Sat 17:30.
Au: Open Mon - Sat 08:00. Closed Mon - Sat 17:30.
Wn: Open Mon - Sat 08:00. Closed Mon - Sat 17:30.
Closed Sundays **Ref: YH00830**

BALCHIN, PETER W
Peter W Balchin DWCF, 1 Bickerstaff Cottage, Idlicote, Shipston-on-Stour, **Warwickshire**, CV36 5DX, **ENGLAND**.
(T) 01608 662077.
Profile Farrier. **Ref: YH00831**

BALCOMBE, JOHN A
John A Balcombe RSS, The Dolls Hse, Upper Pinewood Rd, Ash, Aldershot, **Hampshire**, GU12 6DL, **ENGLAND**..
Profile Farrier. **Ref: YH00832**

BALCOMBE, KEVIN P
Kevin P Balcombe DWCF, High Beeches, The Drive, Copthorne, **Cornwall**, RH10 3JZ, **ENGLAND**.
(T) 01342 712492.
Profile Farrier. **Ref: YH00833**

BALCUNNIN EQUESTRIAN CTRE
Balcunnin Equestrian Centre, Balcunnin, Skerries, **County Dublin**, **IRELAND**.
(T) 01 8490964. **Ref: YH00834**

BALDASERA, P
P Baldasera, Unit 4E Whitehouse Ctre, Stannington, Morpeth, **Northumberland**, NE61 6AW, **ENGLAND**.
(T) 01670 789563.
Contact/s
Owner: Mr P Baldesare
Profile Blacksmith. **Ref: YH00835**

BALDING, IAN
Ian Balding, Office, Pk Hse, Kingsclere, Newbury, **Berkshire**, RG20 5PY, **ENGLAND**.
(T) 01635 298210 **(F)** 01635 298305.
Contact/s
Owner: Mr I Balding
Profile Trainer. **Ref: YH00836**

BALDING, JOHN
John Balding, Mayflower Stables, Saracen Lane, Scrooby, Doncaster, **Yorkshire (South)**, DN10 6AS, **ENGLAND**.
(T) 01302 710096 **(F)** 01302 710096.
Contact/s
Owner: Mr J Balding
Profile Trainer. **Ref: YH00837**

BALDINGS
Baldings (Training) Ltd, Fyfield Stable, Fyfield, Andover, **Hampshire**, SP11 8EW, **ENGLAND**.
(T) 01264 772278 **(F)** 01264 771221.
Contact/s
Partner: Mrs S Geake
Profile Trainer. **Ref: YH00838**

BALDRAND VETNRY PRACTICE
Baldrand Veterinary Practice, Bowerham Rd, Lancaster, **Lancashire**, **ENGLAND**.
(T) 01524 60006.
Profile Medical Support. **Ref: YH00839**

BALDWIN, DAVID C
David C Baldwin, 20 King George Ave, Horsforth, Leeds, **Yorkshire (West)**, LS18 5NB, **ENGLAND**.
(T) 0113 2591301.
Profile Farrier. **Ref: YH00840**

BALDWYN, CHARLOTTE
Miss Charlotte Baldwyn MCSP.SRP Grad. Dip.Phys, Cannon Lodge, Ferry Rd, Bray, **Berkshire**, SL6 2AT, **ENGLAND**.
(T) 01628 627646 **(F)** 0118 9776655
(M) 07771 737009
(E) physio@gbdesigns.co.uk.
Profile Medical Support. **Ref: YH00841**

BALE-WILLIAMS, A M
Miss A M Bale-Williams, Lodge Farm Cottage, Halton, Chirk, **Denbighshire**, LL14 5AU, **WALES**.
(T) 01691 773396.
Profile Breeder. **Ref: YH00842**

BALFOUR, JAMES S
James S Balfour AWCF, 67 Woodend Drive, Northmuir, Kirriemuir, **Angus**, DD8 4TG, **SCOTLAND**.
(T) 01575 573980.
Profile Farrier. **Ref: YH00843**

BALFOUR, K P & P F
Kevin P Balfour DWCF & Peter F Balfour AFCL, 1 Woodside Cottages, Westmarch, Tealing, Dundee, **Angus**, DD4 0PW, **SCOTLAND**.
(T) 01382 380308.
Profile Farrier. **Ref: YH00844**

BALHALL RIDING STABLES
Balhall Riding Stables, Menmuir, Brechin, **Angus**, DD9 7RW, **SCOTLAND**.
(T) 01356 660284 **(F)** 01356 660284.
Profile Breeder, Riding School. **Ref: YH00845**

BALI HAI FARM
Bali Hai Farm, Cotman's Ash Lane, Kemsing, **Kent**, TN15 6RD, **ENGLAND**.
(T) 01959 524278.
Profile Stable/Livery, Track/Course. **Ref: YH00846**

BALL BROTHERS
Ball Brothers, 42 Church Rd, Aughnaskeagh, Dromara, **County Down**, BT25 2NS, **NORTHERN IRELAND**.
(T) 028 97532379.
Profile Supplies. **Ref: YH00847**

BALL OF MADLEY
Ball of Madley Ltd, Crossways, Clehonger, Hereford, **Herefordshire**, HR2 9QR, **ENGLAND**.
(T) 01981 250301.
Profile Feed Merchant. **Ref: YH00848**

BALL, A S
A S Ball DWCF, Pennti Lowarn, Mount, Bodmin, **Cornwall**, PL30 4ET, **ENGLAND**.
(T) 01208 821381.
Contact/s
Owner: Mr A Ball
Profile Farrier. **Ref: YH00849**

BALL, CHRISTINE
Christine Ball BHSAI (Reg), 15 Wimborne Ave, Orpington, **Kent**, BR5 2NS, **ENGLAND**.
(T) 01689 897746 **(F)** 01689 897746
(M) 07836 591250.
Profile Trainer. **Ref: YH00850**

BALL, H M & A H
H M & A H Ball, The Forge, High St, Winford, Bristol, **Bristol**, BS40 8EH, **ENGLAND**.
(T) 01275 472356.
Contact/s
Owner: Mr A Ball
Profile Farrier. **Ref: YH00851**

BALL, VIVIENNE
Vivienne Ball MCSP, SRP, Glen Hse, Harewood Rd, East Keswick, **Yorkshire (West)**, LS17 9HG, **ENGLAND**.
(T) 01937 572003.
Profile Medical Support. **Ref: YH00852**

BALLANTYNE, CLAIRE
Claire Ballantyne BHSI, 9 Beaconside Cl, Stafford, **Staffordshire**, ST16 3QS, **ENGLAND**.
(T) 01785 246047.
Profile Trainer. **Ref: YH00853**

BALLANTYNE, TONI
Toni Ballantyne, 3 Redhills, Eccleshall, **Staffordshire**, ST21 6JW, **ENGLAND**.
(T) 01785 850052 **(F)** 01782 859199
(M) 07774 697604
(E) toni@ballantyne.co.uk.
Profile Club/Association. **Ref: YH00854**

BALLINA EQUESTRIAN CTRE
Ballina Equestrian Centre, Corballa, Ballina, **County Sligo**, **IRELAND**.
(T) 096 45084 **(F)** 096 45084.
Contact/s
Owner: Mary Reape
Profile Equestrian Centre, Riding School, Stable/Livery. Horse dealers.
Full, part & DIY livery available, details on request. Horses and ponies are also for sale.
Opening Times
Sp: Open Mon - Sat 09:00. Closed Mon - Sat 18:00.
Su: Open Mon - Sat 09:00. Closed Mon - Sat 18:00.
Au: Open Mon - Sat 09:00. Closed Mon - Sat 18:00.
Wn: Open Mon - Sat 09:00. Closed Mon - Sat 18:00.
Closed Sundays, except between October - April when

showjumping is held. Ref: YH00855

BALLINADEE STABLES

Ballinadee Stables, Ballinadee, Bandon, **County Cork**, **IRELAND**.
(T) 021 4778152. Ref: YH00856

BALLINGDON SADDLERY

Ballingdon Saddlery, 82-83 Ballingdon St, Sudbury, **Suffolk**, CO10 2DA, **ENGLAND**.
(T) 01787 371325 (F) 01787 371325.
Contact/s
Owner: Mr J Wallace
Profile Saddlery Retailer. Yr. Est: 1976
Opening Times
Sp: Open Mon - Sat 09:00. Closed Mon - Sat 17:00.
Su: Open Mon - Sat 09:00. Closed Mon - Sat 17:00.
Au: Open Mon - Sat 09:00. Closed Mon - Sat 17:00.
Wn: Open Mon - Sat 09:00. Closed Mon - Sat 17:00.
Ref: YH00857

BALLINROBE RACECOURSE

Ballinrobe Racecourse, Ballinrobe, **County Mayo**, **IRELAND**.
(T) 092 41052 (F) 092 41406.
Profile Supplies. Ref: YH00858

BALLINROBE TRANSPORT

Ballinrobe Transport Ltd, Castleiney, Templemore, **County Tipperary**, **IRELAND**.
(T) 050 432280.
Profile Supplies. Ref: YH00859

BALLINTEGGART STUD

Ballinteggart Stud, Drumnasoo Rd, Portadown, **County Armagh**, BT62 4EX, **NORTHERN IRELAND**.
(T) 028 38358971 (F) 028 38330681.
Contact/s
Owner: Mrs H Troughton
Profile Breeder, Stable/Livery, Stud Farm.
E.U. approved semen collection centre.
Yr. Est: 1985
Opening Times
Sp: Open Mon - Sun 09:00. Closed Mon - Sun 18:00.
Su: Open Mon - Sun 09:00. Closed Mon - Sun 18:00.
Au: Open Mon - Sun 09:00. Closed Mon - Sun 18:00.
Wn: Open Mon - Sun 09:00. Closed Mon - Sun 18:00. Ref: YH00860

BALLINTESKIN TACK

Ballinteskin Tack Shop, Ballinteskin Farm, Wicklow, **County Wicklow**, **IRELAND**.
(T) 0404 69441.
Contact/s
Owner: Daniella O'Toole (T) 087 2503174
Profile Saddlery Retailer.
Stockist of french style Devoucoux tack. Ref: YH00861

BALLINTOHER EQUESTRIAN CTRE

Ballintoher Equestrian Centre, Nenagh, **County Tipperary**, **IRELAND**.
(T) 067 31400.
Contact/s
Owner: Mr R McDonnell
Profile Equestrian Centre, Riding School.
Opening Times
Telephone for further information Ref: YH00862

BALLIVICAR FARM

Ballivicar Farm, Port Ellen, Isle Of Islay, **Argyll and Bute**, PA42 7AW, **SCOTLAND**.
(T) 01496 302251 (F) 01496 302251.
Profile Equestrian Centre. Ref: YH00863

BALLOCHBROE LIVERY STABLES

Ballochbroe Livery Stables, Ballochbroe, Maybole, **Ayrshire (South)**, KA19 7PE, **SCOTLAND**.
(T) 01655 740400.
Contact/s
Owner: Ms C Geddes Ref: YH00864

BALLYBURDEN RIDING

Ballyburden Riding School, Ballyburden, Ballincollig, **County Cork**, **IRELAND**.
(T) 021 4871263.
Profile Riding School. Ref: YH00865

BALLYCLARE EQUESTRIAN CTRE

Ballyclare Equestrian Centre, 80 Collin Rd, Moorfields, Ballymena, **County Antrim**, BT42 3BY, **NORTHERN IRELAND**.
(T) 028 25831429. Ref: YH00866

BALLYCORR RIDING CLUB

Ballycorr Riding Club, 46 Lye Hill Rd, Templepatrick, Ballyclare, **County Antrim**, BT39 0ES, **NORTHERN IRELAND**.
(T) 028 93433692.
Contact/s
Chairman: Miss J McSeveny
Profile Club/Association, Riding Club. Ref: YH00867

BALLYKENLEY RIDING SCHOOL

Ballykenley Riding School, Ballykenley Glanworth, Cork, **County Cork**, **IRELAND**.
(T) 025 38417.
Profile Supplies. Ref: YH00868

BALLYKNOCK RIDING CLUB

Ballyknock Riding Club, Brook Cottage, 23 Bowens Manor, Lurgan, **County Armagh**, BT66 7RT, **NORTHERN IRELAND**.
(T) 028 28328378.
Contact/s
Chairman: Mr A Dewhurst
Profile Club/Association, Riding Club. Ref: YH00869

BALLYKNOCK RIDING SCHOOL

Ballyknock Riding School, 38 Ballyknock Rd, Hillsborough, **County Down**, BT26 6EF, **NORTHERN IRELAND**.
(T) 028 92692144.
Contact/s
Owner: Mrs J House
Profile Riding School, Stable/Livery. Ref: YH00870

BALLYMORE CONNEMARA STUD

Ballymore Connemara Stud, 14 Ditton Green, Woodditton, New Market, **Suffolk**, CB8 9SQ, **ENGLAND**.
(T) 01638 730248 (F) 01638 730248
(M) 07771 623775.
Profile Breeder. Ref: YH00871

BALLYNAHINCH & DISTRICT

Ballynahinch & District Riding Club, 9 The Pines, Culcavy Rd, Hillsborough, **County Down**, BT24 8LU, **NORTHERN IRELAND**.
(T) 028 92689397.
Contact/s
Chairman: Mr D Martin
Profile Club/Association, Riding Club. Ref: YH00872

BALLYNAHINCH RIDING CTRE

Ballynahinch Riding Centre, 13 Ballycreen Rd, Ballynahinch, **County Down**, BT24 8TZ, **NORTHERN IRELAND**.
(T) 028 97562883.
Profile Riding School, Stable/Livery. Ref: YH00873

BALNAKILLY RIDING CTRE

Balnakilly Riding Centre, Balnakilly Est, Kirkmichael, **Perth and Kinross**, PH10 7NB, **SCOTLAND**.
(T) 01250 81305 (F) 01250 81305.
Profile Riding School. Ref: YH00874

BALRUDDERY STABLES

Balruddery Stables, Balruddery Meadows, Invergowrie, Dundee, **Angus**, DD2 5LJ, **SCOTLAND**.
(T) 01382 360594.
Contact/s
Owner: Miss C McGreogor
Profile Stable/Livery. Ref: YH00875

BAMBERS GREEN RIDING CTRE

Bambers Green Riding Centre, Frogs Hall Farm, Bambers Green, Takeley, Bishop's Stortford, **Essex**, CM22 6PE, **ENGLAND**.
(T) 01279 870320.
Profile Riding School. Ref: YH00876

BAMFORTH, D

Miss D Bamforth, Thornleigh, 807 Manchester Rd, Linthwaite, Huddersfield, **Yorkshire (West)**, HD7 5NF, **ENGLAND**.
(T) 01484 843423.
Profile Breeder. Ref: YH00877

BAMPTON CATTLE TRANSPORT

Bampton Cattle Transport, Middle Rill Farm, Shillingford, Tiverton, **Devon**, EX16 9BD, **ENGLAND**.
(T) 01398 361295.
Profile Transport/Horse Boxes. Ref: YH00878

BANAGHER EQUESTRIAN CTRE

Banagher Equestrian Centre, Meenwaun, Banagher, **County Offaly**, **IRELAND**.
(T) 0509 51988. Ref: YH00879

BANBURY TRAILERS

Banbury Trailer & Towing Centre, Thorpe Way Ind Est, Banbury, **Oxfordshire**, OX16 4SP, **ENGLAND**.
(T) 01295 251526 (F) 01295 269163
(W) www.banburytrailers.co.uk.
Contact/s
Owner: Mr D Lunn
(E) sales@banburytrailers.co.uk
Profile Transport/Horse Boxes.
Horsebox servicing and sales No.Staff: 8
Yr. Est: 1981 C.Size: 0.5 Acres
Opening Times
Sp: Open 08:30. Closed 17:30.
Su: Open 08:30. Closed 17:30.
Au: Open 08:30. Closed 17:30.
Wn: Open 08:30. Closed 17:30. Ref: YH00880

BANCROFT GRACEY

Bancroft Gracey, 124 Appin Rd, Birkenhead, **Merseyside**, CH41 9HJ, **ENGLAND**.
(T) 0151 6781277.
Contact/s
Owner: Mr R Alexander
Profile Transport/Horse Boxes. Ref: YH00881

BANGOR-ON-DEE RACES

Bangor-on-Dee Races, The Racecourse, Bangor-on-Dee, **Wrexham**, LL13 0DA, **WALES**.
(T) 01978 780323 (F) 01978 780985
(E) racing@bangordee.sagehost.co.uk
(W) www.bangordee.co.uk.
Profile Track/Course.
Opening Times
Children under 16 get in free. There is free parking and a free bus service on the site Ref: YH00882

BANGORS PARK FARM

Bangors Park Farm, Bangors Rd South, Iver, **Buckinghamshire**, SL0 0AZ, **ENGLAND**.
(T) 01753 630264.
Profile Equestrian Centre, Riding School, Stable/Livery. Ref: YH00883

BANHAM, B D

Mr B D Banham, Broad Farm, Boat Dyke Lane, Acle, Norwich, **Norfolk**, NR13 3AZ, **ENGLAND**.
(T) 01493 751510.
Profile Breeder. Ref: YH00884

BANK FARM

Bank Farm, Middlewood Rd, Poynton, Stockport, **Manchester (Greater)**, SK12 1TU, **ENGLAND**.
(T) 01625 872656.
Contact/s
Owner: Mrs L Mitchell
Profile Riding School. Ref: YH00885

BANK FARM

Bank Farm, Raby, Mere Rd, Wirral, **Merseyside**, CH63 0LX, **ENGLAND**.
(T) 0151 3430067
(E) info@bankfarm-equestrian.co.uk
(W) www.bankfarm-equestrian.co.uk.
Profile Stable/Livery. Ref: YH00886

BANK FARM TRAILERS

Bank Farm Trailers, The Garage, Rear Of Green Cottage, Carmarthen, **Carmarthenshire**, SA31 2PD, **WALES**.
(T) 01267 231565 (F) 01267 222154.
Contact/s
Manager: Mr B Lacey
Profile Transport/Horse Boxes. Ref: YH00887

BANK FARM TRAILERS

Bank Farm Trailers, Bank Farm, Spytty Rd, Newport, **Newport**, NP19 4QW, **WALES**.
(T) 01633 279679 (F) 01633 270400.
Contact/s
Branch Manager: Mr G Turner
Profile Transport/Horse Boxes. Ref: YH00888

BANK FARM TRAILERS

Bank Farm Trailers, Robeston Wathen, Narberth, **Pembrokeshire**, SA67 8EN, **WALES**.
(T) 01834 860062 (F) 01834 861498.
Profile Transport/Horse Boxes. Ref: YH00889

BANK FARM TRAILERS

Bank Farm Trailers, Unit 1 Millbrook Yard, Landore, Swansea, **Swansea**, SA1 2JG, **WALES**.
(T) 01792 795834 (F) 01792 799251.
Profile Transport/Horse Boxes. Ref: YH00890

BANK HSE FARM

Bank House Farm, Wood Lane, Middlestown, Wakefield, **Yorkshire (West)**, WF4 4XD, **ENGLAND**.
(T) 01924 840614
Affiliated Bodies BHS.
Contact/s
General Manager: Mrs L Casey (Q) BHSII
Profile Riding School, Stable/Livery.
Opening Times
Sp: Open Tues - Thurs, Sat, Sun 08:30. Closed Tues -

Thurs 21:15, Sat 17:30, Sun 14:30.
Su: Open Tues - Thurs, Sat, Sun 08:30. Closed Tues - Thurs 21:15, Sat 17:30, Sun 14:30.
Au: Open Tues - Thurs, Sat, Sun 08:30. Closed Tues - Thurs 21:15, Sat 17:30, Sun 14:30.
Wn: Open Tues - Thurs, Sat, Sun 08:30. Closed Tues - Thurs 21:15, Sat 17:30, Sun 14:30.
No lessons on Friday Ref: YH00891

BANK TOP

Bank Top, Sowerby-under-Cotcliffe, Northallerton, **Yorkshire (North)**, DL6 3RE, **ENGLAND**.
(T) 01609 776127.
Contact/s
Owner: Mrs A Hart Ref: YH00892

BANKERS EQUINE DIRECT

Bankers Equine Direct, St Johns Pl, Easton St, High Wycombe, **Buckinghamshire**, HP11 1NL, **ENGLAND**.
(T) 01494 603603.
Profile Club/Association. Insurance Company.
Ref: YH00893

BANKFIELD RACING STABLES

Bankfield Racing Stables, Billesley Rd, Wilmcote, Stratford-upon-Avon, **Warwickshire**, CV37 9XG, **ENGLAND**.
(T) 01789 415607.
Profile Trainer. Ref: YH00894

BANKS BLACKSMITHS

Banks Blacksmiths, Duff St Lane, Edinburgh, **Edinburgh (City of)**, EH11 2HS, **SCOTLAND**.
(T) 0131 3372293 (F) 0131 3467993.
Profile Blacksmith. Ref: YH00895

BANKS CARGILL AGRICULTURE

Banks Cargill Agriculture, Eastern Mills, Bury Rd, Ramsey, Huntingdon, **Cambridgeshire**, PE26 1NF, **ENGLAND**.
(T) 01487 813361 (F) 01487 814600
(W) www.bankscargill.co.uk.
Contact/s
General Manager: Mr A Johston
Profile Supplies. No.Staff: 5
Opening Times
Sp: Open Mon - Fri 07:30. Closed Mon - Fri 17:00.
Su: Open Mon - Fri 07:30. Closed Mon - Fri 17:00.
Au: Open Mon - Fri 07:30. Closed Mon - Fri 17:00.
Wn: Open Mon - Fri 07:30. Closed Mon - Fri 17:00.
Ref: YH00896

BANKS OF SANDY

Banks of Sandy Ltd, 29 St Neots Rd, Sandy, **Bedfordshire**, SG19 1LD, **ENGLAND**.
(T) 01767 680351 (F) 01767 692412.
Profile Supplies. Ref: YH00897

BANKS SOUTHERN

Banks Southern, Red Shute Mill, Hermitage, Thatcham, **Berkshire**, RG18 9QU, **ENGLAND**.
(T) 01635 204100 (F) 01635 201417.
Profile Feed Merchant, Supplies. Ref: YH00898

BANKS, J

Mrs J Banks, Aikenfield, Aike, Driffield, **Yorkshire (East)**, YO25 9BG, **ENGLAND**.
(T) 01377 270326.
Contact/s
Owner: Mrs J Banks
Profile
Recuperates racing horses. Ref: YH00899

BANKS, J E

J E Banks, Jamesfield, Hamilton Rd, Newmarket, **Suffolk**, CB8 7JQ, **ENGLAND**.
(T) 01638 667997.
Profile Trainer. Ref: YH00900

BANKS, M C

Mr M C Banks, Manor Farm, Manor Farm Rd, Waresley, Sandy, **Bedfordshire**, SG19 3BX, **ENGLAND**.
(T) 01767 650563
(M) 07860 627370.
Profile Supplies. Ref: YH00901

BANKS, P A & C R

Messrs P A & C R Banks, Jermys, Duck St, Lt Easton, Great Dunmow, **Essex**, CM6 2JE, **ENGLAND**.
(T) 01371 870306.
Profile Breeder. Ref: YH00902

BANKS, R T

R T Banks, Dalegate Hse, Puddingate, Bishop Burton, Beverley, **Yorkshire (East)**, HU17 8QH, **ENGLAND**.
(T) 01964 550275 (F) 01964 551336.
Contact/s
Owner: Mr R Banks
Profile Breeder. Ref: YH00903

BANKSIDE SHIRE STUD

Bankside Shire Stud, The Old Brickworks, Top Of The Bank, Thurstonland, Huddersfield, **Yorkshire (West)**, HD4 6XZ, **ENGLAND**.
(T) 01484 661332.
Contact/s
Partner: Mrs C Parker
Profile Breeder. Ref: YH00904

BANN VALLEY RIDING CLUB

Bann Valley Riding Club, Ballintemple, 40 Churchtown Rd, Garvagh, Coleraine, **County Londonderry**, BT51 5BE, **NORTHERN IRELAND**.
(T) 028 70558209.
Contact/s
Chairman: Mrs W Moffett
Profile Club/Association, Riding Club. Ref: YH00905

BANNER EQUESTRIAN

Banner Equestrian, Toonagh, Fountain, Ennis, **County Clare**, **IRELAND**.
(T) 065 6823487
(M) 086 2772616.
Contact/s
Owner: Noel Barry
Profile Equestrian Centre, Riding School, Stable/Livery.
Trekking and jumping lessons available, as well as private lessons and livery
Opening Times
Closed Mondays, lesson times vary. Telephone for further information. Ref: YH00906

BANOGUE STUD

Banogue Stud, Callan, **County Kilkenny**, **IRELAND**.
(T) 056 25785.
Contact/s
Owner: Mary Carter
(E) marycarter@eircom.net
Profile Breeder.
Banogue Stud has a stallion standing
Opening Times
Telephone for further information Ref: YH00907

BANSOME WOOD STABLES

Bansome Wood Stables, Hawkwood Lane, Chislehurst, **Kent**, BR7 5PW, **ENGLAND**.
(T) 020 84673140.
Contact/s
Owner: Mrs P Bisley Ref: YH00908

BANSTEAD MANOR STUD

Banstead Manor Stud, Cheveley, Newmarket, **Suffolk**, CB8 9RD, **ENGLAND**.
(T) 01638 731115 (F) 01638 731117.
Contact/s
Stud Manager: Mr S Mockridge
Profile Breeder. Ref: YH00909

BANSTOCK HSE STABLES

Banstock House Stables, Cherry Garden Lane, Maidenhead, **Berkshire**, SL6 3QD, **ENGLAND**.
(T) 01628 822821 (F) 01628 823952.
Contact/s
Owner: Mrs S Meakin
Profile Riding School, Stable/Livery. Ref: YH00910

BANTRY BRIDLE

Bantry Bridle Ltd, Enterprise Cntr, Bantry, **County Cork**, **IRELAND**.
(T) 027 51144.
Profile Supplies. Ref: YH00911

BANTRY HORSE RIDING

Bantry Horse Riding Equestrian Centre, Coomanore South, Bantry, **County Cork**, **IRELAND**.
(T) 027 51412
(W) www.eventingireland.com/wehrli.htm.
Contact/s
Owner: Charlotte Wehrli
Profile Equestrian Centre, Riding School.
Self catering accommodation is available on site.
Opening Times
Sp: Open Mon - Sun 10:00. Closed Mon - Sun 20:00.
Su: Open Mon - Sun 10:00. Closed Mon - Sun 20:00.
Au: Open Mon - Sun 11:00. Closed Mon - Sun 18:00.
Wn: Open Mon - Sun 11:00. Closed Mon - Sun 18:00.
Times may vary depending on demand Ref: YH00912

BANWELL EQUESTRIAN CTRE

J Vosper, Downend Farm, Moor Rd, Banwell, Weston-Super-Mare, **Somerset (North)**, BS29 6ET, **ENGLAND**.
(T) 01934 822731.
Contact/s
Owner: Miss J Vosper
Profile Horse/Rider Accom.
Accommodation is self-catering. Yr. Est: 1984
Opening Times
Sp: Open 08:00. Closed 20:00.
Su: Open 08:00. Closed 20:00.
Au: Open 08:00. Closed 20:00.
Wn: Open 08:00. Closed 20:00. Ref: YH00913

BANWELL, D

D Banwell, Baytree Farm, Watchfield, Highbridge, **Somerset**, TA9 4RB, **ENGLAND**.
(T) 01278 783422.
Contact/s
Owner: Mr D Banwell
Profile Breeder. Horse Dealer. Ref: YH00914

BANWEN MINERS

Banwen Miners, 76 Clydach Rd, Craig Cefn Pk, Clydach, Swansea, **Swansea**, SA6 5TA, **WALES**.
(T) 01792 846329. Ref: YH00915

BAPBSH

British Association for the Pure Bred Spanish Horse, Church Farm, Church St, Semington, Trowbridge, **Wiltshire**, BA14 6JS, **ENGLAND**.
(T) 01380 870139.
Contact/s
Key Contact: Miss M McBryde
Profile Club/Association. Ref: YH00916

BAPSH

British Association for the Purebred Spanish Horse (The), 44 Fawcett Rd, New Milton, **Hampshire**, BH25 6SU, **ENGLAND**.
(T) 01425 638628 (F) 01425 638628.
Contact/s
Secretary: Maria Ward-Jones
Profile Breeder, Club/Association. Ref: YH00917

BAR - TEC

Bar - Tec, Bar-Tec Hse, Farnham Rd, Liss, **Hampshire**, GU33 6JU, **ENGLAND**.
(T) 01730 895598 (F) 01730 892088. Ref: YH00918

BARBARAFIELD RIDING SCHOOL

Barbarafield Riding School, Barbarafield Farm, Cupar, **Fife**, KY15 5PU, **SCOTLAND**.
(T) 01334 828223.
Contact/s
Owner: Mr G Berwick
Profile Riding School. Ref: YH00919

BARBER, A

A Barber, Farnova, Shorts Lane, Sheffield, **Yorkshire (South)**, S17 3AH, **ENGLAND**.
(T) 0114 2362899.
Profile Stable/Livery. Ref: YH00920

BARBER, F

F Barber, Woodcock Farm, Loughborough Rd, Rothley, **Leicestershire**, LE7 7NH, **ENGLAND**.
(T) 0116 2302215.
Profile Supplies. Ref: YH00921

BARBER, R

R Barber, Seaborough Manor, Beaminster, **Dorset**, DT8 3QY, **ENGLAND**.
(T) 01308 68272.
Profile Breeder. Ref: YH00922

BARCELONA FORGE

Barcelona Forge, Barcelona Forge, Barcelona, Looe, **Cornwall**, PL13 2JU, **ENGLAND**.
(T) 01503 272886.
Contact/s
Owner: Mr R Dodd
Profile Blacksmith. Ref: YH00923

BARCLAY, A

Mrs A Barclay, Fotherop, Oddington, Moreton In Marsh, **Gloucestershire**, GL56 0XF, **ENGLAND**.
(T) 01451 830680 (F) 01451 870572.
Profile Supplies. Ref: YH00924

BARCLAY, J

Mr J Barclay, Kinneston, Leslie, **Fife**, KY6 3JJ, **SCOTLAND**.
(T) 01592 840331 (F) 01592 840866.
Profile Trainer. Ref: YH00925

BARD VETNRY GRP

Bard Veterinary Group (The), Renwick Bank, 15 Catherine St, Dumfries, **Dumfries and Galloway**, DG1 1JF, **SCOTLAND**.

(T) 01387 255295 (F) 01387 266251.
Contact/s
Vet: Mr J Dickson (Q) MRCVS, MVB
Profile Medical Support. Ref: YH00926

BARDSEY MILLS

Bardsey Mills Ltd, Pool Mills Ind Est, Pool In Wharfedale, Otley, **Yorkshire (West)**, LS21 1EG, **ENGLAND**.
(T) 0113 2842057 (F) 0113 2842155
(E) sales@bardseymills.co.uk
(W) www.bardseymills.co.uk
Affiliated Bodies BETA.
Contact/s
Owner: Mr S Wetherald (Q) AMTRA
Profile Supplies. No.Staff: 4 Yr. Est: 1976
C.Size: 0.5 Acres
Opening Times
Sp: Open Mon - Sat 08:00. Closed Mon - Fri 17:00, Sat 12:00.
Su: Open Mon - Sat 08:00. Closed Mon - Fri 17:00, Sat 12:00.
Au: Open Mon - Sat 08:00. Closed Mon - Fri 17:00, Sat 12:00.
Wn: Open Mon - Sat 08:00. Closed Mon - Fri 17:00, Sat 12:00.
Closed Sundays Ref: YH00927

BARDWELL MANOR

Bardwell Manor Equestrian Centre, Ixworth Rd, Bardwell, Bury St Edmunds, **Suffolk**, IP31 1AU, **ENGLAND**.
(T) 01359 233010
(E) info@bardwell-equestrian.co.uk
(W) www.bardwell-equestrian.co.uk
Affiliated Bodies ABRS.
Contact/s
Owner: Ms S MacKinder (Q) ANCEBM, BHSAI
(E) shazmac@ic24.net
Profile Equestrian Centre, Riding Club, Riding School, Stable/Livery. No.Staff: 10
Yr. Est: 1996 C.Size: 150 Acres Ref: YH00928

BAREND RIDING CTRE

Barend Riding Centre, Barend, Sandyhills, Dalbeattie, **Dumfries and Galloway**, DG5 4NU, **SCOTLAND**.
(T) 01387 780648.
Profile Riding School, Stable/Livery. Ref: YH00929

BARETTE & GRUCHY

Barette & Gruchy Ltd, La Route Du Mont Mado, St John, **Jersey**, JE3 4DN, **ENGLAND**.
(T) 01534 864481 (F) 01534 864485.
Profile Saddlery Retailer. Ref: YH00930

BARFOOT, ROBERT L

Robert L Barfoot, 39 Longfield Rd, Desertmartin, Londonderry, **Yorkshire (North)**, **ENGLAND**..
Profile Breeder. Ref: YH00931

BARFORD PK RACING STABLES

Barford Park Racing Stables, Spaxton, Bridgwater, **Somerset**, TA5 1AF, **ENGLAND**.
(T) 01278 671437 (F) 01278 671437.
Profile Breeder, Trainer. Ref: YH00932

BARGOWER RIDING SCHOOL

Bargower Riding School, Fiveways, Hurlford, Kilmarnock, **Ayrshire (East)**, KA1 5JX, **SCOTLAND**.
(T) 01563 884223
Affiliated Bodies BHS, RDA.
Contact/s
Owner: Ms C Cano
Profile Riding School, Stable/Livery.
Childrens camps during the holidays. Teach children aged five years and upwards. Lessons are priced per hour. Yr. Est: 1987
Opening Times
Sp: Open 09:00. Closed 21:00.
Su: Open 09:00. Closed 21:00.
Au: Open 09:00. Closed 21:00.
Wn: Open 09:00. Closed 21:00. Ref: YH00933

BARHAM, KEVIN N A

Kevin N A Barham DWCF, 1 Claugbane Drive, Ramsey, **Isle of Man**, IM8 2AZ, **ENGLAND**.
(T) 01624 813014.
Profile Farrier. Ref: YH00934

BARK PRODUCTS

Bark Products, Divn Of William Sinclair Horticulture Ltd, Firth Rd, Lincoln, **Lincolnshire**, LN6 7AH, **ENGLAND**.
(T) 01522 537561 (F) 01522 513609.
Profile Supplies. Ref: YH00935

BARKER HICKMAN

Barker Hickman Ltd, Upton Mill, Shifnal, **Shropshire**, TF11 8NZ, **ENGLAND**.
(T) 01952 461111.
Profile Supplies. Ref: YH00936

BARKER SADDLERY OF WALSALL

Barker Saddlery of Walsall, Warstone Rd, Essington, Wolverhampton, **Midlands (West)**, WV11 2AR, **ENGLAND**.
(T) 01922 414144 (F) 01922 412400.
Contact/s
Owner: Mr B Barker
Profile Saddlery Retailer. Ref: YH00937

BARKER TRAINING

Barker Training, Greenbury Grange, Scorton, Richmond, **Yorkshire (North)**, DL10 6EP, **ENGLAND**.
(T) 01325 378266.
Contact/s
Owner: Mr D Barker
Profile Trainer. Ref: YH00938

BARKER, A C

A C Barker, The Helmsley Riding School, Helmsley, York, **Yorkshire (North)**, YO62 5AB, **ENGLAND**.
(T) 01439 770355.
Profile Riding School, Stable/Livery. Ref: YH00939

BARKER, C

Mrs C Barker, 32 Oaks Rd, Soothill, Batley, **Yorkshire (West)**, WF17 6NS, **ENGLAND**.
(T) 01924 359551.
Profile Breeder. Ref: YH00940

BARKER, DAVID

Mr David Barker, Tancred Grange, Scorton, Richmond, **Yorkshire (North)**, DL10 6AB, **ENGLAND**.
(T) 01325 378266 (F) 01748 818910.
Profile Trainer. Ref: YH00941

BARKER, E

Mrs E Barker, Manor Farm, Harrold, **Bedfordshire**, MK43 7EP, **ENGLAND**.
(T) 01234 720268.
Profile Breeder. Ref: YH00942

BARKER, J

J Barker, Barwell Ct Stables/Barwell Ct Farm, Leatherhead Rd, Chessington, **Surrey**, KT9 2LZ, **ENGLAND**.
(T) 01372 466528 (F) 01372 466528.
Contact/s
Owner: Mrs J Barker
Profile Stable/Livery. Ref: YH00943

BARKER, K J

Mr K J Barker, 118 Lent Green Lane, Burnham, **Buckinghamshire**, SL1 7AW, **ENGLAND**.
(T) 01628 660740.
Profile Breeder, Trainer. Ref: YH00944

BARKFOLD MANOR STUD

Barkfold Manor Stud, Kirdford, **Sussex (West)**, RH14 0JH, **ENGLAND**.
(T) 01403 820227 (F) 01403 820296.
Profile Breeder. Ref: YH00945

BARKING STUD

Barking Stud, Barkway, Royston, **Hertfordshire**, SG8 8EE, **ENGLAND**.
(T) 01763 848529 (F) 01763 849529.
Profile Breeder. Ref: YH00946

BARKSTON EQUESTRIAN CTRE

Barkston Equestrian Centre, 85 Cloghanramer Rd, Newry, **County Down**, BT34 1QG, **NORTHERN IRELAND**.
(T) 028 30252656. Ref: YH00947

BARKWAY EQUESTRIAN CTRE

Barkway Equestrian Centre, London Rd, Barkway, Royston, **Hertfordshire**, SG8 8EZ, **ENGLAND**.
(T) 01763 848880 (F) 01763 848027.
Contact/s
Owner: Mrs R Phillimore
Profile Breeder, Riding School, Stable/Livery.
Ref: YH00948

BARLASTON RIDING CTRE

Barlaston Riding Centre, Barlaston Old Rd, Barlaston, Stoke-on-Trent, **Staffordshire**, ST12 9ET, **ENGLAND**.
(T) 01782 373638 (F) 01782 657350
Affiliated Bodies BHS.
Contact/s
Owner: Mr J Hirrell
Profile Riding School, Stable/Livery.
Full, part, working and DIY livery available. There is a lecture room and secure tack room on site and hacking is also available. Cheques are not accepted.
Opening Times
Sp: Open 09:00. Closed 20:00.
Su: Open 09:00. Closed 20:00.
Au: Open 09:00. Closed 20:00.
Wn: Open 09:00. Closed 20:00. Ref: YH00949

BARLEY HALL STABLES

Barley Hall Stables, Barley Hall Stables/Barley Hall, Barnsley Rd, Thorpe Hesley, Rotherham, **Yorkshire (South)**, S61 2RX, **ENGLAND**.
(T) 0114 2455833.
Contact/s
Owner: Ms J Gibbs-Thompson Ref: YH00950

BARLEYFIELD SADDLERY

Barleyfield Saddlery, Ash Lane, Etwall, **Derbyshire**, DE65 6HT, **ENGLAND**.
(T) 01283 730166.
Contact/s
Owner: Mr R Holton
Profile Riding Wear Retailer, Saddlery Retailer, Supplies. No.Staff: 2 Yr. Est: 1997
Opening Times
Sp: Open Tues - Sun 09:00. Closed Tues - Sun 17:30.
Su: Open Tues - Sun 09:00. Closed Tues - Sun 17:30.
Au: Open Tues - Sun 09:00. Closed Tues - Sun 17:30.
Wn: Open Tues - Sun 09:00. Closed Tues - Sun 17:30.
Closed Mondays Ref: YH00951

BARLEYFIELDS

Barleyfields Equestrian Centre, Ash Lane, Etwall, Derby, **Derbyshire**, DE65 6HT, **ENGLAND**.
(T) 01283 734798
(W) www.barleyfields.com
Affiliated Bodies BHS.
Contact/s
Head Girl: Miss D Bates (Q) BHS SM, BHSII
Profile Arena, Equestrian Centre, Riding Club, Riding School, Riding Wear Retailer, Saddlery Retailer, Stable/Livery, Supplies, Track/Course, Trainer, Transport/Horse Boxes. No.Staff: 14
Yr. Est: 1994 C.Size: 35 Acres Ref: YH00952

BARLEYHILL PONY TREKKING

Barley Hill Pony Trekking Centre, Barleyhill, Bohola, **County Mayo**, **IRELAND**.
(T) 094 84128.
Contact/s
Owner: Olive Conlon
Profile Trekking Centre. Ref: YH00953

BARLEYTHORPE

Barleythorpe Stud & Highfield Stud Ltd, Main Rd, Barleythorpe, Oakham, **Leicestershire**, LE15 7EE, **ENGLAND**.
(T) 01572 722283.
Profile Breeder. Ref: YH00954

BARLING TACK SHOP

Barling Tack Shop, Shopland Hall Equesterian Ctre, Shopland Rd, Rochford, **Essex**, SS4 1LT, **ENGLAND**.
(T) 01702 530600 (F) 01702 530600.
Contact/s
Owner: Mrs A Murrell
Profile Supplies. Yr. Est: 1994
Opening Times
Sp: Open Tues - Sun 09:00. Closed Tues - Thurs 20:00, Fri, Sat, Sun 17:00.
Su: Open Tues - Sun 09:00. Closed Tues - Thurs 20:00, Fri, Sat, Sun 17:00.
Au: Open Tues - Sun 09:00. Closed Tues - Thurs 20:00, Fri, Sat, Sun 17:00.
Wn: Open Tues - Sun 09:00. Closed Tues - Thurs 20:00, Fri, Sat, Sun 17:00. Ref: YH00955

BARLOW, B S

Mr B S Barlow, 262 Oldham Rd, Rishworth, Ripponden, Halifax, **Yorkshire (West)**, HX6 4QB, **ENGLAND**.
(T) 01422 824238.
Profile Breeder. Ref: YH00956

BARLOW, E

Mrs E Barlow, Greenghyll Lodge, Demesne Lane, Camerton, Workington, **Cumbria**, CA14 1NF, **ENGLAND**.
(T) 07702 898275.
Profile Breeder. Ref: YH00957

BARLOW, JOHN (SIR)

Sir John Barlow, Ash Hse, Brindley, Nantwich, **Cheshire**, CW5 8HX, **ENGLAND**.
(T) 01270 524339 (F) 01270 524047.
Profile Supplies. Ref: YH00958

BARLOW, R

Mr R Barlow, Primrose Stud Farm, Denby Village, **Derbyshire**, DE5 8DT, **ENGLAND**.
(T) 01773 742249.
Profile Supplies. Ref: YH00959

BARMINSTER TRADING

Barminster Trading, The Old Livery Stable, The Street, Bethersden, Ashford, **Kent**, TN26 3AG, **ENGLAND**.
(T) 01233 820020 (F) 01233 820020.
Contact/s
Owner: Mrs K Humphries
Profile Riding Wear Retailer.
Sells second hand sadddles. No.Staff: 2
Yr. Est: 1993
Opening Times
Sp: Open Mon - Sun 09:00. Closed Mon - Sat 17:30, Sun 16:30.
Su: Open Mon - Sun 09:00. Closed Mon - Sat 17:30, Sun 16:30.
Au: Open Mon - Sun 09:00. Closed Mon - Sat 17:30, Sun 16:30.
Wn: Open Mon - Sun 09:00. Closed Mon - Sat 17:30, Sun 16:30. Ref: YH00960

BARN COTTAGE LIVERY STABLES

Barn Cottage Livery Stables, Haslucks Green Rd, Shirley, Solihull, **Midlands (West)**, B90 1EA, **ENGLAND**.
(T) 0121 4303060.
Profile Stable/Livery. Ref: YH00961

BARN TACK & TACKLE SHOP

Barn Tack & Tackle Shop (The), 83 High St, Edenbridge, **Kent**, TN8 5AU, **ENGLAND**.
(T) 01732 862260 (F) 01732 862260.
Contact/s
Partner: Mr J Proud
Profile Supplies. Ref: YH00962

BARN VETNRY PRACTICE

Barn Veterinary Practice (The), 2a Ashcroft Rd, Ipswich, **Suffolk**, IP1 6AA, **ENGLAND**.
(T) 01473 743460.
Profile Medical Support. Ref: YH00963

BARNACK CTRY STORE

Barnack Country Store, Manor Farm, Barnack, Stamford, **Lincolnshire**, PE9 3DY, **ENGLAND**.
(T) 01780 740115 (F) 01780 740115
(E) bcs@manorfarm.co.uk.
Contact/s
Owner: Mr H Brassey
Profile Saddlery Retailer. Ref: YH00964

BARNARD BROTHERS

Barnard Brothers (Ipswich) Ltd, 556 Woodbridge Rd, Ipswich, **Suffolk**, IP4 4PH, **ENGLAND**.
(T) 01473 727444 (F) 01473 727444.
Profile Supplies. Ref: YH00965

BARNBROOK, N

N Barnbrook RSS, 22 Hyperion Rd, Stourton, Stourbridge, **Staffordshire**, DY7 6SB, **ENGLAND**.
(T) 01384 374315.
Profile Farrier. Ref: YH00966

BARNBY MOOR STABLES

Barnby Moor Stables, Kennel Drive, Barnby Moor, Retford, **Nottinghamshire**, DN22 8QX, **ENGLAND**.
(T) 01777 711191.
Profile Farrier. Ref: YH00967

BARNCRAFT

Barncraft, Colboys, Hare Lane, Blindley Heath, Lingfield, **Surrey**, RH7 6JB, **ENGLAND**.
(T) 01342 834834 (F) 01342 835683.
Profile Transport/Horse Boxes. Ref: YH00968

BARNES & WINDER

Barnes & Winder Ltd, Victoria Works, White Cross, Guiseley, Leeds, **Yorkshire (West)**, LS20 8NJ, **ENGLAND**.
(T) 01943 872186.
Profile Transport/Horse Boxes. Ref: YH00969

BARNES FARM RETIREMENT

Barnes Farm Retirement & Rest Home, Barnes Farm, Poppinghole Lane, Robertsbridge, **Sussex (East)**, TN32 5BN, **ENGLAND**.
(T) 01580 830307 (F) 01580 830307.
Profile Stable/Livery. Ref: YH00970

BARNES GREEN

Barnes Green Riding School, Pennistone Rd, Grenoside, Sheffield, **Yorkshire (South)**, S35 8NA, **ENGLAND**.
(T) 0114 2402548
Affiliated Bodies ABRS, BHS.
Contact/s
Manager: Miss L Burgin (Q) BHSAI
Profile Riding School.
Full set of BSJ jumps. No.Staff: 7 Yr. Est: 1976
C.Size: 15 Acres
Opening Times
Sp: Open Mon - Sun 09:30. Closed Mon - Fri 20:00, Sat, Sun 16:30.
Su: Open Mon - Sun 09:30. Closed Mon - Fri 20:00, Sat, Sun 16:30.
Au: Open Mon - Sun 09:30. Closed Mon - Fri 20:00, Sat, Sun 16:30.
Wn: Open Mon - Sun 09:30. Closed Mon - Fri 20:00, Sat, Sun 16:30. Ref: YH00971

BARNES, A J

A J Barnes, Green Acres, High St, West Lydford, Somerton, **Somerset**, TA11 7BZ, **ENGLAND**.
(T) 01963 240373.
Profile Farrier. Ref: YH00972

BARNES, CLIFFORD

Clifford Barnes DWCF, 16 Bulbery, Abbotts Ann, Andover, **Hampshire**, SP11 7BN, **ENGLAND**.
(T) 01264 710059.
Profile Farrier. Ref: YH00973

BARNES, GEORGE EDWARD

George Edward Barnes, 3 Grange Farm Pk, Whitehall Rd, Colchester, **Essex**, CO2 8AL, **ENGLAND**.
(T) 01206 795950.
Profile Farrier. Ref: YH00974

BARNES, JONATHAN R H

Jonathan R H Barnes DWCF, Ashcoombe Farm, Steanbow, West Pennard, Glastonbury, **Somerset**, BA6 8ND, **ENGLAND**.
(T) 01749 890383.
Profile Farrier. Ref: YH00975

BARNES, LEE G

Lee G Barnes DWCF, Chellowdene, Horebeech Lane, Horam, **Sussex (East)**, TN21 0HR, **ENGLAND**.
(T) 01435 813721.
Profile Farrier. Ref: YH00976

BARNES, M A

M A Barnes, Bank Hse Farm, Little Salkeld, Penrith, **Cumbria**, CA10 1NN, **ENGLAND**.
(T) 01768 881257.
Contact/s
Owner: Mrs M Barnes
Profile Trainer. Ref: YH00977

BARNES, M A

Mr M A Barnes, Tarnside, Favlam, Brampton, Carlisle, **Cumbria**, CA8 1LA, **ENGLAND**.
(T) 01697 746675 (F) 01697 746675.
Profile Trainer. Ref: YH00978

BARNES, PAT

Pat Barnes, Shey Copse, Old Woking Rd, Woking, **Surrey**, GU22 8UA, **ENGLAND**.
(T) 01483 721708.
Contact/s
Owner: Mrs P Barnes
Profile Riding School, Stable/Livery, Track/Course.
Ref: YH00979

BARNES, RAYMOND

Raymond Barnes (Bloodstock) Ltd, Calendar Cottage, Cropley Gr, Ousden, Newmarket, **Suffolk**, CB8 8TL, **ENGLAND**.
(T) 01638 500405 (F) 01638 500586.
Profile Blood Stock Agency. Ref: YH00980

BARNET RIDING CTRE

Barnet Riding Centre, 106 Galley Lane, Homestead Farm, Barnet, **Hertfordshire**, EN5 4RA, **ENGLAND**.
(T) 020 84493531.
Contact/s
Manageress: Mrs J Johnson Ref: YH00981

BARNET, R

Mr R Barnet, Old Songhurst Farm, Loxwood, Billingshurst, **Sussex (West)**, RH14 0RA, **ENGLAND**.
(T) 01403 752792.
Profile Breeder. Ref: YH00982

BARNETT, G W

Mr G W Barnett, Blythe Hse Farm, Leek Rd, Weston Coyney, Stoke-on-Trent, **Staffordshire**, ST3 5BD, **ENGLAND**.
(T) 01782 316777.
Profile Trainer. Ref: YH00983

BARNFIELD EQUESTRIAN CTRE

Barnfield Equestrian Centre, Knockmore, Ballina, **County Mayo**, **IRELAND**.
(T) 094 58175. Ref: YH00984

BARNFIELD RIDING SCHOOL

Barnfield Riding School, Parkfields Rd, Kingston Upon Thames, **London (Greater)**, KT2 5LL, **ENGLAND**.
(T) 020 85463616.
Profile Riding School. Ref: YH00985

BARNFIELDS

Barnfields Stables, Sewardstone Rd, Chingford, London, **London (Greater)**, E4 7RH, **ENGLAND**.
(T) 020 85295200.
Contact/s
Owner: Miss L Wolsey (Q) BHSII
Profile Riding School, Stable/Livery. No.Staff: 4
Yr. Est: 1992 C.Size: 10 Acres
Opening Times
Sp: Open 09:30. Closed 18:00.
Su: Open 09:30. Closed 18:00.
Au: Open 09:30. Closed 18:00.
Wn: Open 09:30. Closed 18:00. Ref: YH00986

BARNFIELDS

Barnfields Farm Livery Stables, Nicker Hill, Keyworth, **Nottinghamshire**, NG12 5EB, **ENGLAND**.
(T) 0115 9374430 (F) 0115 9843169.
Profile Stable/Livery. Ref: YH00987

BARNHOUSE RACING STABLES

Barnhouse Racing Stables, Langdale, Melsonby, Richmond, **Yorkshire (North)**, DL10 5PW, **ENGLAND**.
(T) 01325 718046.
Profile Trainer. Ref: YH00988

BARNHOUSE VETNRY SURGERY

Barnhouse Veterinary Surgery, 1 Tarvin Rd, Littleton, Chester, **Cheshire**, CH3 7DD, **ENGLAND**.
(T) 01244 335550.
Profile Medical Support. Ref: YH00989

BARNSTAPLE HORSE/PET SUPP

Barnstaple Horse & Pet Supplies, Unit 1 The Square, Barnstaple, **Devon**, EX32 8LS, **ENGLAND**.
(T) 01271 344858.
Profile Saddlery Retailer. Ref: YH00990

BARNSTON RIDING CTRE

Barnston Riding Centre, Gills Lane, Wirral, **Merseyside**, CH61 1AH, **ENGLAND**.
(T) 0151 6482911 (F) 0151 6480375
Affiliated Bodies BHS.
Contact/s
Owner: Mr A Wlodarski
Profile Riding School.
Sells second hand saddles. Hacking and trekking can also be organised. Yr. Est: 1970
Opening Times
Sp: Open Tues - Sun 09:00. Closed Tues - Fri 20:00, Sat, Sun 18:00.
Su: Open Tues - Sun 09:00. Closed Tues - Fri 20:00, Sat, Sun 18:00.
Au: Open Tues - Sun 09:00. Closed Tues - Fri 20:00, Sat, Sun 18:00.
Wn: Open Tues - Sun 09:00. Closed Tues - Fri 20:00, Sat, Sun 18:00.
Closed Mondays Ref: YH00991

BARNWELL TRAILERS

Barnwell Trailers, Castle Farm, Barnwell, Peterborough, **Cambridgeshire**, PE8 5QD, **ENGLAND**.
(T) 01832 272218 (F) 01832 273290.
Contact/s
Owner: Mr S Berridge
Profile Transport/Horse Boxes. Ref: YH00992

BARODA STUD

Baroda Stud, Newbridge, **County Kildare**, **IRELAND**.
(T) 045 438888 (F) 045 438777
(E) baroda@eircom.net.
Contact/s
Key Contact: Mr P Myscercough
Profile Breeder. Ref: YH00993

BARON SADDLERY

Baron Saddlery, 28 Woodcote Way, Caversham, Reading, **Berkshire**, RG4 7HJ, **ENGLAND**.
(T) 0118 9464786.
Contact/s
Owner: Mrs M Snow Ref: YH00994

BARONS, D H

D H Barons, Hendham, Woodleigh, Kingsbridge, **Devon**, TQ7 4DP, **ENGLAND**.
(T) 01548 550326.
Profile Blood Stock Agency. **Ref: YH00995**

BAROSSA EQUESTRIAN

Barossa Equestrian, Devils Highway, Riseley, Reading, **Berkshire**, RG7 1XR, **ENGLAND**.
(T) 0118 9888180.
Contact/s
Manageress: Mrs H Fox **Ref: YH00996**

BAROSSA FARM RIDING STABLES

Barossa Farm Riding Stables, Devils Highway, Riseley, Reading, **Berkshire**, RG7 1XR, **ENGLAND**.
(T) 0118 9883776.
Contact/s
Owner: Mr P Cox
Profile Riding School, Stable/Livery. **Ref: YH00997**

BARR & LOCKHART

Barr & Lockhart, 93-95 High St, Kirkby Stephen, **Cumbria**, CA17 4SH, **ENGLAND**.
(T) 01768 371359.
Profile Medical Support. **Ref: YH00998**

BARR & MACMILLAN

Barr & MacMillan, 16 Kilmarnock Rd, Mauchline, **Ayrshire (South)**, KA5 5DE, **SCOTLAND**.
(T) 01290 50452.
Profile Medical Support. **Ref: YH00999**

BARR, ANGELINE

Mrs Angeline Barr, Bonnyton Moor, Eaglesham, Glasgow, **Glasgow (City of)**, G76 0PZ, **SCOTLAND**.
(T) 01355 303711.
Profile Breeder. **Ref: YH01000**

BARR, R E

Mr R E Barr, Carr Hse Farm, Seamer, Stokesley, **Cleveland**, TS9 5LL, **ENGLAND**.
(T) 01642 710687.
Profile Trainer. **Ref: YH01001**

BARRACA BLOODSTOCK

Barraca Bloodstock, Ripon Rd, Dishforth, Thirsk, **Yorkshire (North)**, YO7 3DB, **ENGLAND**.
(T) 01765 604073 **(F)** 01765 601601.
Contact/s
Owner: Mrs M Bean
Profile Blood Stock Agency. **Ref: YH01002**

BARRACLOUGH, A & S

Mr A & Mrs S Barraclough, Sentinels, St Stephens Hill, Launceston, **Cornwall**, PL15 8HR, **ENGLAND**.
(T) 01566 772043.
Profile Breeder. **Ref: YH01003**

BARRACLOUGH, M F

M F Barraclough, Arden Pk Stables, Manor Lane, Claverdon, Warwick, **Warwickshire**, CV35 8NH, **ENGLAND**.
(T) 01926 843332.
Profile Trainer. **Ref: YH01004**

BARRADALE FARM

Barradale Farm, Main Rd, Headcorn, **Kent**, TN27 9PJ, **ENGLAND**.
(T) 01622 890955 **(F)** 01622 890318.
Profile Supplies. **Ref: YH01005**

BARRADINE, ANN

Ann Barradine, 4 Pinbrook Ind Est, Chancel Lane, Pinhoe, Exeter, **Devon**, EX4 8JU, **ENGLAND**.
(T) 01392 469444 **(F)** 01392 467300.
Profile Advertising Agency. **Ref: YH01006**

BARRASS, J

J Barrass, Hayne Farm, Rawridge, Honiton, **Devon**, EX14 9QP, **ENGLAND**.
(T) 01404 861653.
Profile Farrier. **Ref: YH01007**

BARRATT, DAVID J

David J Barratt DWCF, 26 Church St, Haslingfield, **Cambridgeshire**, CB3 7JE, **ENGLAND**.
(T) 01223 872948.
Profile Farrier. **Ref: YH01008**

BARRATT, L J

Mr L J Barratt, Bromwich Pk, Maesbury, Oswestry, **Shropshire**, SY11 4JQ, **ENGLAND**.
(T) 01691 610209
(M) 07801 662383.
Profile Breeder, Trainer. **Ref: YH01009**

BARRATT, T

T Barratt, New Inn Hse, Glenferness, Nairn, **Highlands**, IV12 5UP, **SCOTLAND**.
(T) 01309 671305.
Contact/s
Owner: Mr T Barratt
Profile Farrier. **Ref: YH01010**

BARRETT, JEREMY J

Jeremy J Barrett BSc (Hons) DWCF, 4 Bridle Cl, Brafield On The Green, **Northamptonshire**, NN7 1AS, **ENGLAND**.
(T) 01604 696550.
Profile Farrier. **Ref: YH01011**

BARRETT, MARGARET

Margaret Barrett - Artist, Springfield, 4 Priory Rd, Market Bosworth, **Leicestershire**, CV13 0PB, **ENGLAND**.
(T) 01455 290112.
Contact/s
Owner: Mrs M Barrett
(E) margaret@spring-field.co.uk
Profile Artist.
Can paint horses at rest or in action. Also dogs, people and horse racing in oils or pastels. Designs for greetings cards and picture plates and calender sets of equestrian interest.
Opening Times
Telephone for an appointment. **Ref: YH01012**

BARRETT, R

R Barrett, Meadowside, 15B High St, Chatteris, **Cambridgeshire**, PE16 6BE, **ENGLAND**.
(T) 01354 692165.
Profile Breeder. **Ref: YH01013**

BARRETT, R J

R J Barrett, Radwell Farm, Mill Lane, Woburn Sands, Milton Keynes, **Buckinghamshire**, MK17 8SP, **ENGLAND**.
(T) 01908 584741.
Profile Breeder. **Ref: YH01014**

BARRETTS OF FECKENHAM

Barretts of Feckenham (Wolverhampton), 58-60 Victoria St, Wolverhampton, **Midlands (West)**, WV1 3NX, **ENGLAND**.
(T) 01902 421240.
Contact/s
Manager: Mr A Mansel
Profile Saddlery Retailer. **Ref: YH01015**

BARRETTS OF FECKENHAM

Barretts of Feckenham (Leeds), Selby Rd, Garforth, Leeds, **Yorkshire (West)**, LS25 2AQ, **ENGLAND**.
(T) 0113 2867976.
Profile Saddlery Retailer. **Ref: YH01016**

BARRETTSTOWN EST STUD FARM

Barrettstown Estate Stud Farm, Oving Rd, Whitchurch, Aylesbury, **Buckinghamshire**, HP22 4ES, **ENGLAND**.
(T) 01296 641313.
Contact/s
Manager: Mr J Eddery
Profile Breeder. **Ref: YH01017**

BARRETTSTOWN FARM

Barrettstown Farm House, Newbridge, **County Kildare**, **IRELAND**.
(T) 045 432023 **(F)** 045 432037.
Contact/s
Key Contact: Mr J Doyle
Profile Breeder.
Barrettstown has 15 boxes, a horse walker, all weather paddocks and a lunging ring. Yr. Est: 1983
C.Size: 105 Acres **Ref: YH01018**

BARRHEAD RIDING CLUB

Barrhead Riding Club, 15 Coylton Rd, Newlands, Glasgow, Glasgow, **Glasgow (City of)**, G43 2TA, **SCOTLAND**.
(T) 0141 6378788.
Contact/s
Secretary: Miss V Sneddon
Profile Club/Association, Riding Club. **Ref: YH01019**

BARRIBAL

Mr & Mrs Barribal, Morlyn Welsh Cobs, Incott Farm, Sampford Courtenay, Okehampton, **Devon**, EX20 2SR, **ENGLAND**.
(T) 01837 54696 **(F)** 01837 54696.
Contact/s
Owner: Mr W Barribal
Profile Breeder, Stable/Livery, Trainer. **Ref: YH01020**

BARRIER ANIMAL HEALTHCARE

Barrier Animal Healthcare, 36-37 Haverscroft Ind Est, New Rd, Attleborough, **Norfolk**, NR17 1YE, **ENGLAND**.
(T) 01953 456363 **(F)** 01953 455594
(E) sales@barrier-biotech.com
(W) www.barrier-biotech.com.
Contact/s
Marketing Manager: Mrs M Sargeant
Profile Medical Support, Supplies.
Other products available are herbicide, weed control and various non-toxic animal health care products.
No.Staff: 9 Yr. Est: 1989
Opening Times
Sp: Open 08:30. Closed 16:30.
Su: Open 08:30. Closed 16:30.
Au: Open 08:30. Closed 16:30.
Wn: Open 08:30. Closed 16:30. **Ref: YH01021**

BARRIERS INT

Barriers International Ltd, P O Box 999, Malmesbury, **Wiltshire**, SN16 0RX, **ENGLAND**.
(T) 01666 840819 **(F)** 01666 840988
(E) sales@barriersint.com. **Ref: YH01022**

BARRINGTON, J M

J M Barrington, The Old Rectory, Warmwell, **Dorset**, DT2 8HQ, **ENGLAND**.
(T) 01305 852104.
Profile Farrier. **Ref: YH01023**

BARROD HORSE BOXES

Barrod Horse Boxes Ltd, Unit 24 Wilden Ind Est, Stourport-on-Severn, **Worcestershire**, DY13 9JY, **ENGLAND**.
(T) 01299 822777.
Profile Transport/Horse Boxes. **Ref: YH01024**

BARRON, T D

Mr T D Barron, Maunby Hse, Maunby, Thirsk, **Yorkshire (North)**, YO7 4HD, **ENGLAND**.
(T) 01845 587435.
Profile Trainer. **Ref: YH01025**

BARRONS, HENRY A

Henry A Barrons RSS, 1 Cottage Farm, Mears Ashby Rd, Sywell, Northampton, **Northamptonshire**, NN6 0BJ, **ENGLAND**.
(T) 01604 646701.
Profile Farrier. **Ref: YH01026**

BARROW EQUESTRIAN CTRE

Barrow Equestrian Centre, Barrow Lane Farm, Great Barrow, Nr Tarvin, Chester, **Cheshire**, CH3 7LJ, **ENGLAND**.
(T) 01829 740325.
Contact/s
Owner: Mr E Coulter
Profile Arena, Equestrian Centre, Riding School, Stable/Livery. No.Staff: 2 Yr. Est: 1990
C.Size: 60 Acres **Ref: YH01027**

BARROW FARM

Barrow Farm Group Riding & RDA, Barrow Farm, Highwood, Chelmsford, **Essex**, CM1 3QR, **ENGLAND**.
(T) 01277 821538.
Profile Riding School. **Ref: YH01028**

BARROW SADDLERY & SUPPLIES

Barrow Saddlery & Supplies, 57 Friars Lane, Barrow-In-Furness, **Cumbria**, LA13 9NS, **ENGLAND**.
(T) 01229 835525 **(F)** 01229 835525.
Profile Saddlery Retailer. **Ref: YH01029**

BARROW STABLES

Barrow Stables, Barrow, Nr Cottesmore, Oakham, **Rutland**, LE15 7PE, **ENGLAND**.
(T) 01572 813331 **(F)** 01572 813306
(M) 07050 163688.
Contact/s
Owner: Miss R Matthews **(Q)** AI
Profile Arena, Breeder, Stable/Livery, Trainer. Schooling. No.Staff: 3 Yr. Est: 1983
C.Size: 40 Acres
Opening Times
Telephone for an appointment **Ref: YH01030**

BARROWBY FEEDS

Barrowby Feeds, The Bungalow, Recotry Lane, Barrowby, **Lincolnshire**, NG32 1BT, **ENGLAND**.
(T) 01476 564406.
Profile Supplies. **Ref: YH01031**

BARROWBY RIDING CTRE

Barrowby Riding Centre, Kirkby Overblow, Harrogate, **Yorkshire (North)**, HG3 1HU, **ENGLAND**.
(T) 0113 2886201 **(F)** 0113 2886152
(E) jencaley@gofree.co.uk.

Key: **(T)** telephone **(F)** fax **(M)** mobile **(E)** E-Mail Address **(W)** Website Address **(Q)** Qualifications
Yr. Est: Year Established C.Size: Complex Size Sp: Spring Su: Summer Au: Autumn Wn: Winter

Profile Trainer. Ref: YH01032

BARRY, DERMOT A

Dermot A Barry DWCF, 28 Warren Rd, Red Lodge, Bury St Edmunds, **Suffolk**, IP28 8JP, **ENGLAND**.
(T) 01638 552451
(M) 07778 168774.
Profile Farrier. Ref: YH01033

BARRY, JOHN F J

John F J Barry, Sharjah, 9 Paynesdown Rd, Thatcham, Newbury, **Berkshire**, RG13 4RT, **ENGLAND**.
(T) 01635 868196 **(F)** 01635 278758
(M) 07831 459371.
Profile Transport/Horse Boxes. Ref: YH01034

BARS R US

Bars R Us, Castleford Car Ctre, Barnsdale Rd, Allerton Bywater, Castleford, **Yorkshire (West)**, WF10 2AE, **ENGLAND**.
(T) 01977 604012.
Contact/s
Owner: Mr M Dennis
Profile Transport/Horse Boxes. Ref: YH01035

BARTHOLOMEWS

Bartholomews, Bognor Rd, Portfield, Chichester, **Sussex (West)**, PO19 2NT, **ENGLAND**.
(T) 01243 784171.
Profile Supplies. Ref: YH01036

BARTHORPE, JANE

Jane Barthorpe BHSAI, Jasmine Cottage, Mill Lane, Caunton, Newark, **Nottinghamshire**, NG23 6AJ, **ENGLAND**.
(T) 01636 86314.
Profile Medical Support. Ref: YH01037

BARTLE, G M

Mrs G M Bartle BHSI, Grimston Grange, Tadcaster, **Yorkshire (North)**, LS24 9BX, **ENGLAND**.
(T) 01937 834342.
Profile Trainer. Ref: YH01038

BARTLETT

Bartlett (Dorset) Ltd, 3-5 St Andrews Trading Est, St Andrews Rd, Bridport, **Dorset**, DT6 3EX, **ENGLAND**.
(T) 01308 422205 **(F)** 01308 422206.
Profile Supplies. Ref: YH01039

BARTLETT, R A

Mr R A Bartlett, Meikle Ben, Yetts Hole Rd, Glenmavis, Airdrie, **Lanarkshire (North)**, ML6 0PS, **SCOTLAND**.
(T) 01236 875278 **(F)** 01236 751791.
Profile Supplies. Ref: YH01040

BARTLETT, ROBERT S

Robert S Bartlett BII, 15 Nene Cl, Wansford, Peterborough, **Cambridgeshire**, PE8 6JJ, **ENGLAND**.
(T) 01780 782099.
Profile Farrier. Ref: YH01041

BARTLETT, W

Miss W Bartlett, Broadgate, 4 Hiatt Rd, Minchinhampton, Stroud, **Gloucestershire**, GL6 9DB, **ENGLAND**.
(T) 01453 883008.
Profile Breeder. Ref: YH01042

BARTLETT, WILLIAM G

William G Bartlett DWCF, 56 South St, South Normanton, **Derbyshire**, DE55 2DA, **ENGLAND**.
(T) 01773 581682.
Profile Farrier. Ref: YH01043

BARTON EQUESTRIAN CTRE

Barton Equestrian Centre, Green Lane Farm, Green Lane, Bilsborrow, Preston, **Lancashire**, PR3 0RR, **ENGLAND**.
(T) 01995 640033 **(F)** 01995 640033
Affiliated Bodies BSJA, BSPS.
Contact/s
Owner: Mrs J Martin **(Q)** BHS 1
Profile Breeder, Equestrian Centre.
Tuition available on own horses and ponies. BSJ and pony shows. Yr. Est: 1971
Opening Times
Lessons by appointment: Open all year for shows
Ref: YH01044

BARTON RIDING SCHOOL

Barton Riding School, Holy Cottage, Barton Stud, Newcastle-upon-Tyne, **Tyne and Wear**, NE3 5NA, **ENGLAND**.
(T) 0191 2362088.
Profile Riding School, Trainer. Ref: YH01045

BARTON STUD

Barton Stud, Great Barton, Bury St Edmunds, **Suffolk**, IP31 2SH, **ENGLAND**.
(T) 01284 787226 **(F)** 01284 787231.
Contact/s
Owner: Maj J Broughton
Profile Breeder. Ref: YH01046

BARTON, J M

J M Barton, 71 Worlaby Rd, Grimsby, **Lincolnshire (North East)**, DN33 3JR, **ENGLAND**.
(T) 01472 871091.
Profile Farrier. Ref: YH01047

BARTON, JOHN

John Barton, Rectory Farm, Little Chishill, Royston, **Hertfordshire**, SG8 8PB, **ENGLAND**.
(T) 01763 838205.
Profile Trainer. Ref: YH01048

BARTON, M A

M A Barton, 178 Warsash Rd, Warsash, Southampton, **Hampshire**, SO31 9JD, **ENGLAND**.
(T) 01489 577459.
Contact/s
Owner: Mr M Barton
Profile Farrier. Ref: YH01049

BARTON, R & J

R & J Barton, The Cottage, Moorside Farm, Wilsden, **Yorkshire (West)**, BD15 0LZ, **ENGLAND**.
(T) 01535 275452.
Profile Stable/Livery. Ref: YH01050

BARTONS CLOSE STABLES

Bartons Close Stables, Colway Cross Rd, Bishopsteignton, Teignmouth, **Devon**, TQ14 9TJ, **ENGLAND**.
(T) 01626 777988.
Profile Stable/Livery. Ref: YH01051

BARWELL, C R

C R Barwell, Ashfield, Stoodleigh, Tiverton, **Devon**, EX16 9QF, **ENGLAND**.
(T) 01398 351333.
Profile Blood Stock Agency, Trainer. Ref: YH01052

BASILDON EQUESTRIAN CLUB

Basildon Equestrian Club, 6 Kevin Cl, Billericay, **Essex**, CM11 2QW, **ENGLAND**.
(T) 01277 651920.
Profile Club/Association. Ref: YH01053

BASKERVILLE, R E

R E Baskerville, East Lodge, Aston Rowant, Watlington, **Oxfordshire**, OX9 5SN, **ENGLAND**.
(T) 01844 352090.
Profile Medical Support. Ref: YH01054

BASKEYFIELD, K & A

K & A Baskeyfield, The Fields Farm, Park Lane, Audley, Stoke-on-Trent, **Staffordshire**, **ENGLAND**.
(T) 01782 721949.
Profile Breeder. Ref: YH01055

BASSETT, A

Mrs A Bassett, Rhiwbina Farm, Rhiwbina Hill, Cardiff, **Powys**, CF14 6UP, **WALES**.
(T) 029 20692313.
Profile Breeder. Ref: YH01056

BASSINGFIELD RIDING SCHOOL

Bassingfield Riding School, Bassingfield, Radcliffe-on-Trent, Nottingham, **Nottinghamshire**, NG12 2LG, **ENGLAND**.
(T) 0115 9816806.
Contact/s
Owner: Mrs F Thomas
Profile Riding School. Ref: YH01057

BASTABLE M M

Bastable M M, Ringwood Rd, Fordingbridge, **Hampshire**, SP6 2ET, **ENGLAND**.
(T) 01425 653208.
Contact/s
Owner: Mrs M Bastables
Profile Stable/Livery. Ref: YH01058

BASTON & DISTRICT

Baston & District Horse & Pony Society, Spring View, 90 Northorpe, Bourne, **Lincolnshire**, PE10 0HZ, **ENGLAND**.
(T) 01778 425522.
Contact/s
Secretary: Mr J Pulford
Profile Club/Association. Ref: YH01059

BASTON & DISTRICT RIDING CLUB

Baston & District Riding Club, Burnside Hse, Witham On The Hill, Bourne, **Lincolnshire**, PE10 0JH, **ENGLAND**.
(T) 01775 820387.
Contact/s
Chairman: Mr F Knipe
Profile Club/Association. Ref: YH01060

BASTOW, ARTHUR R

Arthur R Bastow RSS, 12 Warwick Rd, Glascote, Tamworth, **Staffordshire**, B77 3EU, **ENGLAND**.
(T) 01827 66250.
Profile Farrier. Ref: YH01061

BATA

BATA (Lloyds of Beverley) Ltd, 7 Norwood, Beverley, **Yorkshire (East)**, HU17 9ET, **ENGLAND**.
(T) 01482 868135 **(F)** 01482 861173.
Contact/s
Manager: Ms S Grant
Profile Saddlery Retailer. Ref: YH01062

BATCHELOR, B

B Batchelor, The Forge, Stather Rd, Flixborough, Scunthorpe, **Lincolnshire (North)**, DN15 8RR, **ENGLAND**.
(T) 01724 859980 **(F)** 01724 859980.
Contact/s
Owner: Mr B Batchelor
Profile Blacksmith. Ref: YH01063

BATCHWORTH HEATH

Batchworth Heath Farm & Livery, Batchworth Heath, London Rd, Rickmansworth, **Hertfordshire**, WD3 1QB, **ENGLAND**.
(T) 01923 835457. Ref: YH01064

BATEMAN, BRETT

Brett Bateman, Glebe Farm, Tetford Rd, Greetham, Horncastle, **Lincolnshire**, LN9 6PT, **ENGLAND**.
(T) 01507 588229.
Profile Farrier. Ref: YH01065

BATES, AL

Al Bates, Lesbra Hse, Main St, Grendon Underwood, Aylesbury, **Buckinghamshire**, HP18 0SW, **ENGLAND**.
(T) 01296 770215.
Contact/s
Owner: Mr A Bates
Profile Transport/Horse Boxes.
Local and national transportation undertaken. Also transports sheep, pigs and cows.
Opening Times
By appointment only Ref: YH01066

BATES, D A

D A Bates, 10 Rookery Rd, Clenchwarton, King's Lynn, **Norfolk**, PE34 4EG, **ENGLAND**.
(T) 01553 773050.
Profile Breeder. Ref: YH01067

BATES, STEPHEN P

Stephen P Bates DWCF, Oyster Hill Forge, Clay Hill Lane, Headley, **Surrey**, KT18 6JX, **ENGLAND**.
(T) 01372 378543.
Profile Farrier. Ref: YH01068

BATESON TRAILERS

Bateson Trailers Ltd, Doodfield Works, Windlehurst Rd, Marple, Stockport, **Manchester (Greater)**, SK6 7EN, **ENGLAND**.
(T) 0161 4260500 **(F)** 0161 4260245
(W) www.bateson-trailers.co.uk.
Contact/s
General Manager: Mr J Smith
Profile Transport/Horse Boxes. Trailer Manufacturers.
Yr. Est: 1934
Opening Times
Sp: Open Mon - Sat 08:00. Closed Mon - Thurs 18:00, Fri 17:00, Sat 12:00.
Su: Open Mon - Sat 08:00. Closed Mon - Thurs 18:00, Fri 17:00, Sat 12:00.
Au: Open Mon - Sat 08:00. Closed Mon - Thurs 18:00, Fri 17:00, Sat 12:00.
Wn: Open Mon - Sat 08:00. Closed Mon - Thurs 18:00, Fri 17:00, Sat 12:00. Ref: YH01069

BATH EQUESTRIAN CTRE

Bath Equestrian Centre, Middle Hill, Weston, Bath, **Bath & Somerset (North East)**, BA1 4HL, **ENGLAND**.
(T) 01225 483483 **(F)** 01225 483483.
Contact/s
Owner: Mrs S Palmer
Profile Farrier. Ref: YH01070

BATH RACECOURSE

Bath Racecourse Co Ltd, Tylers Farm, Gravel Hill Rd, Yate, **Gloucestershire (South)**, BS37 7BN, **ENGLAND**.
(T) 01454 313186 (F) 01295 688030.
Contact/s
Clerk of Course: Mr R Farrant
Profile Track/Course. Ref: YH01071

BATH RACECOURSE STABLES

Bath Racecourse Stables, Chapel Farm, Lansdown, Bath, **Bath & Somerset (North East)**, BA1 9BS, **ENGLAND**.
(T) 01225 444274. Ref: YH01072

BATH RIDING CLUB

Bath Riding Club, 81 Audley Park Rd, Bath, **Bath & Somerset (North East)**, BA1 2XN, **ENGLAND**.
(T) 01225 426000.
Contact/s
Chairman: Mrs A Appleby
Profile Club/Association, Riding Club. Ref: YH01073

BATHER, D L

D L Bather, Barn Farm, Puddington Lane, Burton, Neston, **Merseyside**, CH64 5SF, **ENGLAND**.
(T) 0151 3367359.
Profile Transport/Horse Boxes. Ref: YH01074

BATT, F J

F J Batt, Porthllongdy Farm, Red Wharf Bay, Pentraeth, **Isle of Anglesey**, LL75 8RJ, **WALES**.
(T) 01248 852337.
Profile Riding Wear Retailer, Saddlery Retailer, Supplies. Ref: YH01075

BATT, J A

J A Batt, Garth Farm, Abergavenny, **Monmouthshire**, NP7 9SL, **WALES**.
(T) 01873 853420.
Contact/s
Partner: Mr J Batt
Profile Breeder. Ref: YH01076

BATTEN, HORACE

Horace Batten, The Cottage, 2 Coton Rd, Ravensthorpe, Northampton, **Northamptonshire**, NN6 8EG, **ENGLAND**.
(T) 01604 770287.
Contact/s
Owner: Mr H Batten
Profile Riding Wear Retailer, Supplies. Manufacturer of Riding Boots.
Makes made to measure boots and boot trees. You can visit him, he will come to you or you can use the mail order facility available. Yr. Est: 1830
Opening Times
Sp: Open Mon - Fri 09:00. Closed Mon - Fri 17:30.
Su: Open Mon - Fri 09:00. Closed Mon - Fri 17:30.
Au: Open Mon - Fri 09:00. Closed Mon - Fri 17:30.
Wn: Open Mon - Fri 09:00. Closed Mon - Fri 17:30.
Closed weekends. Hours may be reduced due to Foot and Mouth Ref: YH01077

BATTLE & DISTRICT RIDING CLUB

Battle & District Riding Club, 34 Frenches Farm Drive, Heathfield, **Sussex (East)**, TN21 8BW, **ENGLAND**.
(T) 01435 867423 (F) 01323 38060.
Contact/s
Chairman: Miss C Green
Profile Club/Association, Riding Club. Ref: YH01078

BATTLE EQUINE HEALTH

Battle Equine Health, Reeves Cottage, Kane Hythe Rd, Battle, **Sussex (East)**, TN33 9QU, **ENGLAND**.
(T) 01424 775051
(M) 07976 382469.
Profile Supplies. Ref: YH01079

BATTLE TRAILERS

Battle Trailers, Trailer Hse, Station Rd, Battle, **Sussex (East)**, TN33 0DE, **ENGLAND**.
(T) 01424 774439.
Contact/s
Owner: Mr P Doodes
Profile Transport/Horse Boxes. Ref: YH01080

BATTLE, HAYWARD & BOWER

Battle, Hayward & Bower Ltd, Victoria Chemical Works, Crofton Drive, Allenby Rd Ind Est, Lincoln, **Lincolnshire**, LN3 4NP, **ENGLAND**.
(T) 01522 529206 (F) 01522 538960
(E) bhb@battles.co.uk
(W) www.battles.co.uk.
Profile Riding Wear Retailer, Supplies.
Tack accessories and care products are also available.
Ref: YH01081

BATTLESBRIDGE HORSE & CTRY

Battlesbridge Mills Horse & Country Shop, The Mills, Wickford, **Essex**, SS11 8DP, **ENGLAND**.
(T) 01268 560008 (F) 01268 560008.
Contact/s
Manageress: Miss W Despy
Profile Riding Wear Retailer, Saddlery Retailer.
No.Staff: 5 Yr. Est: 1989
Opening Times
Sp: Open Mon - Fri 09:30, Sat 09:00, Sun 10:00. Closed Mon - Fri 17:30, Sat 17:00, Sun 16:00.
Su: Open Mon - Fri 09:30, Sat 09:00, Sun 10:00. Closed Mon - Fri 17:30, Sat 17:00, Sun 16:00.
Au: Open Mon - Fri 09:30, Sat 09:00, Sun 10:00. Closed Mon - Fri 17:30, Sat 17:00, Sun 16:00.
Wn: Open Mon - Fri 09:30, Sat 09:00, Sun 10:00. Closed Mon - Fri 17:30, Sat 17:00, Sun 16:00.
Ref: YH01082

BATY, FRANCIS JOSEPH

Francis Joseph Baty AFCL, Tyne Mills, Hexham, **Northumberland**, NE46 1XP, **ENGLAND**.
(T) 01434 603078.
Profile Farrier. Ref: YH01083

BAVERSTOCK CTRY SALES

Baverstock Country Sales, Baverstock Farm, Main Rd, Westerham Hill, **Kent**, TN16 2HL, **ENGLAND**.
(T) 01959 572604.
Profile Supplies. Ref: YH01084

BAXTER, ANN

Ms Ann Baxter, Ivy Farm, Roecliffe, Boroughbridge, **Yorkshire (North)**, YO51 9OY, **ENGLAND**.
(T) 01423 322986.
Profile Breeder. Ref: YH01085

BAXTER, DEREK MICHAEL

Derek Michael Baxter, Wood Farm, Whittington, Cheltenham, **Gloucestershire**, GL54 4EY, **ENGLAND**.
(T) 01242 820354.
Profile Farrier. Ref: YH01086

BAXTER, J S

J S Baxter BVMS, MRCVS, 2 Rose Ave, Horsforth, Leeds, **Yorkshire (West)**, LS18 4QE, **ENGLAND**.
(T) 0113 2583215.
Profile Medical Support. Ref: YH01087

BAXTER, S E

Miss S E Baxter, Church Farm, Whittington, Lichfield, **Staffordshire**, WS14 9JX, **ENGLAND**.
(T) 01543 432223 (F) 01543 432223
(M) 07977 0469576.
Profile Trainer. Ref: YH01088

BAXTERLEE

Baxterlee Equestrian & Training Centre, Main Rd, Atherstone, **Warwickshire**, CV9 1QT, **ENGLAND**.
(T) 01827 872222.
Contact/s
Owner: Miss D Smallman Ref: YH01089

BAXTERLEY

Baxterley Equestrian & Training Centre, 7 Repington Ave, Atherstone, **Warwickshire**, CV9 3AW, **ENGLAND**.
(T) 01827 872222 (F) 01827 711687.
Profile Equestrian Centre. Ref: YH01090

BAXTERS OF YARM

Baxters Of Yarm, 3 Fairfax Court, Yarm, **Cleveland**, TS15 9QZ, **ENGLAND**.
(T) 01642 888405 (F) 01642 888400.
Contact/s
Owner: Mrs P Baxter
Profile Supplies. Ref: YH01091

BAY HORSE SCHOOL EQUITATION

Bay Horse School Of Equitation, Cross Hill Farm, Wallace Lane, Forton, Preston, **Lancashire**, PR3 0BB, **ENGLAND**.
(T) 01524 791154. Ref: YH01092

BAY RIDING CLUB

Bay Riding Club, 124 Abbots Way, Preston Farm, North Shields, **Tyne and Wear**, NE29 8LY, **ENGLAND**.
(T) 0191 2595367.
Contact/s
Chairman: Mrs J Talligan
Profile Club/Association, Riding Club. Ref: YH01093

BAY VETNRY GRP

Bay Veterinary Group, 12 The Square, Milnthorpe, **Cumbria**, LA7 7QJ, **ENGLAND**.
(T) 01539 562770.
Profile Medical Support. Ref: YH01094

BAYER

Bayer plc, Veterinary Business Group, Eastern Way, Bury St Edmunds, **Suffolk**, IP32 7AH, **ENGLAND**.
(T) 01284 763200 (F) 01284 702810.
Profile Medical Support. Ref: YH01095

BAYLISS, M G

M G Bayliss, Kiln Bank, Evesham Rd, Stow On The Wold, Cheltenham, **Gloucestershire**, GL54 1EJ, **ENGLAND**.
(T) 01451 830714.
Profile Transport/Horse Boxes. Ref: YH01096

BAYLISS, RACHEL

Rachel Bayliss, Somerford Park Farm, Somerford, Congleton, **Cheshire**, CW12 4SW, **ENGLAND**.
(T) 01260 273288.
Contact/s
Owner: Miss R Bayliss
Profile Trainer. Ref: YH01097

BAYRAM, E

E Bayram, Inman Farm, King St, Sancton, York, **Yorkshire (North)**, YO43 4QR, **ENGLAND**.
(T) 01430 827495.
Contact/s
Owner: Mr E Bayram Ref: YH01098

BAYWOOD EQUESTRIAN

Baywood Equestrian, 12 Nightingales Corner, Cokes Lane, Amersham, **Buckinghamshire**, HP7 9PZ, **ENGLAND**.
(T) 01494 764325. Ref: YH01099

BAZIN, DARREN J

Darren J Bazin AWCF, Willowbrook Stud Farm, Rushton Rd, Kettering, **Northamptonshire**, NN14 2QN, **ENGLAND**.
(T) 01536 761310.
Profile Farrier. Ref: YH01100

BDS

British Driving Society, 27 Dugard Pl, Barford, Warwick, **Warwickshire**, CV35 8DX, **ENGLAND**.
(T) 01926 624420 (F) 01926 624633
(E) email@britishdrivingsociety.co.uk
(W) www.britishdrivingsociety.co.uk.
Contact/s
Secretary: Mrs J Dillon
Profile Club/Association, Supplies.
A national society for those who drive equines in harnesses. To encourage and assist those interested in driving horses/ponies/donkeys/mules Yr. Est: 1957
Ref: YH01101

BDS

BDS, Greenland Rd, Sheffield, **Yorkshire (South)**, S9 5FD, **ENGLAND**.
(T) 0114 2449736.
Profile Transport/Horse Boxes. Ref: YH01102

BEACH, L S

L S Beach B Vet Med FRCVS, 7 Park Rd, Fordingbridge, **Hampshire**, SP6 1EQ, **ENGLAND**.
(T) 01425 52221.
Profile Medical Support. Ref: YH01103

BEACH, WILLIAM C

William C Beach DWCF, Hurst Lodge, Hurst Lane, Egham, **Surrey**, TW20 8QJ, **ENGLAND**.
(T) 01344 841006.
Profile Farrier. Ref: YH01104

BEACHLEY STABLES

Beachley Stables, Special Needs Riding School, Harthill Rd, Liverpool, **Merseyside**, L18 3HU, **ENGLAND**.
(T) 0151 7244490.
Profile Stable/Livery. Ref: YH01105

BEACON COURT

Beacon Court, Bittaford, Ivybridge, **Devon**, PL21 0DS, **ENGLAND**.
(T) 01752 892260.
Contact/s
Owner: Ms C Booker
Profile Stable/Livery.
Opening Times
Telephone for an appointment and further information
Ref: YH01106

BEACON HILL SURGERY

Beacon Hill Surgery, Beacon Hill, Hindhead, **Surrey**, GU26 6NU, **ENGLAND**.
(T) 01428 606396 (F) 01428 608630.
Contact/s
Vet: Mr S Rodgers

Profile Medical Support. Ref:YH01107

BEACON VETNRY CTRE

Beacon Veterinary Centre, Station Rd, Aspatria, Wigton, **Cumbria**, CA7 2AL, **ENGLAND**.
(T) 01697 320242.
Profile Medical Support. Ref:YH01108

BEACONSFIELD EQUINE CTRE

Beaconfsield Equine Centre, London Rd, Godmanchester, Huntingdon, **Cambridgeshire**, PE18 8LH, **ENGLAND**.
(T) 01480 830688.
Contact/s
Owner: Mr T Wilson
Profile Equestrian Centre. Ref:YH01109

BEACONSFIELD PRODUCTS

Beaconsfield Products (Halesowen) Ltd, Foxoak St, Cradley Heath, **Midlands (West)**, B64 5DE, **ENGLAND**.
(T) 01384 569571 (F) 01384 566328.
Profile Blacksmith. Ref:YH01110

BEADLE, MARTIN

Martin Beadle DWCF BII, 6 Fastnet Cl, Haverhill, **Suffolk**, CB9 0LL, **ENGLAND**.
(T) 01440 707885.
Profile Farrier. Ref:YH01111

BEALBY, S M V

Mrs S M V Bealby, North Lodge, Barrowby, Grantham, **Lincolnshire**, NG32 1DH, **ENGLAND**.
(T) 01476 64568.
Profile Supplies. Ref:YH01112

BEALE FEEDS

Beale Feeds, Keys Farm, Lower Bentley, Bromsgrove, **Worcestershire**, B60 4JA, **ENGLAND**.
(T) 01527 821279.
Profile Supplies. Ref:YH01113

BEALE, C R

C R Beale, Hackney Pk, Mount Pleasant, Sway, Lymington, **Hampshire**, SO41 8LS, **ENGLAND**.
(T) 01590 682049.
Profile Farrier. Ref:YH01114

BEALES, K G

Mr K G Beales, Woodview Cottage, Claypitts Lane, Dibden, **Hampshire**, SO45 5TN, **ENGLAND**.
(T) 023 80840425.
Profile Breeder. Ref:YH01115

BEAMAN, J

J Beaman, Hurst Lea, Pedmore Rd, Brierley Hill, **Midlands (West)**, DY5 1TP, **ENGLAND**.
Profile Breeder. Ref:YH01116

BEAMISH RIDING CTRE

Beamish Riding Centre, Coppy Farm, Beamish, Stanley, **County Durham**, DH9 0RQ, **ENGLAND**.
(T) 01207 232993 (F) 01207 232993.
Contact/s
Owner: Mrs V Swinburn
Profile Riding School, Stable/Livery, Track/Course.
Ref:YH01117

BEAN, PHILLIPPA J

Phillippa J Bean DWCF, Les Mousettes, Rue De La Corderie, Vale, **Guernsey**, GY3 5BR, **ENGLAND**.
(T) 01481 44742.
Profile Farrier. Ref:YH01118

BEARDMORE FARRIER SV

David J Beardmore DWCF, 9 Cranshaw Drive, Pleckgate, Blackburn, **Lancashire**, BB1 8RE, **ENGLAND**.
(T) 01254 59904
Affiliated Bodies WCF.
Contact/s
Farrier: Mr D Beardmore (Q) DWCF
Profile Farrier. Ref:YH01119

BEARDSMORE, STEVEN M

Steven M Beardsmore DWCF, 5 South St, Ryde, **Isle of Wight**, PO33 2SD, **ENGLAND**.
(T) 01983 612082.
Profile Farrier. Ref:YH01120

BEARLEY CROSS STABLES

Bearley Cross Stables, Salters Lane, Wootton Wawen, Solihull, **Midlands (West)**, B95 6DN, **ENGLAND**.
(T) 01789 731432.
Contact/s
General Manager: Ms A King
Profile Arena, Equestrian Centre, Farrier, Saddlery Retailer, Stable/Livery, Trainer.
Clipping mane and tail pulling service and other various facilities available to hire. No.Staff: 3
Yr. Est: 1996 C.Size: 18.5 Acres
Opening Times
Sp: Open 07:00. Closed 20:00.
Su: Open 07:00. Closed 20:00.
Au: Open 07:00. Closed 20:00.
Wn: Open 07:00. Closed 20:00. Ref:YH01121

BEARSTONE STUD

Bearstone Stud, Bearstone Mill, Bearstone, Market Drayton, **Shropshire**, TF9 4HF, **ENGLAND**.
(T) 01630 647197 (F) 01630 647110.
Contact/s
Partner: Mr T Holcroft
Profile Breeder. Ref:YH01122

BEARWOOD RIDING CTRE

Bearwood Riding Centre, Bearwood Riding Ctre, Mole Rd, Sindlesham, Wokingham, **Berkshire**, RG41 5DB, **ENGLAND**.
(T) 0118 9760010.
Profile Riding School, Stable/Livery. Ref:YH01123

BEATTIE, T P

T P Beattie, Ratlingate Farm, Kirkandrews-on-Eden, Carlisle, **Cumbria**, **ENGLAND**..
Profile Breeder. Ref:YH01124

BEATY, R N

Mr R N Beaty, Stennerskeugh, Fell End, Ravenstonedale, Kirkby Stephen, **Cumbria**, CA17 4LL, **ENGLAND**.
(T) 01587 3682.
Profile Breeder. Ref:YH01125

BEAU COURT

Beau Court Stud & Riding School, Cwrt-Y-Mwnws Farm, Allt-Yr-Yn, Newport, **Caerphilly**, NP20 5EL, **WALES**.
(T) 01633 252004.
Contact/s
Owner: Miss L Morgan (Q) BHSAI
Profile Riding School, Stable/Livery. No.Staff: 2
Yr. Est: 1998
Opening Times
Sp: Open Mon - Sun 09:00. Closed Mon - Sun 18:00.
Su: Open Mon - Sun 09:00. Closed Mon - Sun 18:00.
Au: Open Mon - Sun 09:00. Closed Mon - Sun 18:00.
Wn: Open Mon - Sun 09:00. Closed Mon - Sun 18:00. Ref:YH01126

BEAUFORT COTTAGE

Beaufort Cottage Equine Hospital & Diagnostic Centre, Cotton End Rd, Exning, Newmarket, **Suffolk**, CB8 7NN, **ENGLAND**.
(T) 01638 577754 (F) 01638 577989.
Contact/s
Partner: Mr A McGladdery
Profile Medical Support. Ref:YH01127

BEAUFORT POLO CLUB

Beaufort Polo Club, Westonbirt, Tetbury, **Gloucestershire**, GL8 8QW, **ENGLAND**.
(T) 01666 880510 (F) 01666 880266
Affiliated Bodies HPA.
Contact/s
Chairperson: Mr S Tomlinson
Profile Polo Club & Polo Coaching Centre.
Beaufort trains polo players of all ages.
Yr. Est: 1989 C.Size: 70 Acres
Opening Times
Open May - September, Tuesday - Sunday, hours vary
Ref:YH01128

BEAULIEU PARK STUD

Beaulieu Park Stud, Staunton, Coleford, **Gloucestershire**, GL16 8PB, **ENGLAND**.
(T) 01600 714994.
Profile Breeder. Ref:YH01129

BEAUMONT AGRCLTRL & STUD FARM

Beaumont Agricultural & Stud Farm, Beaumont Rd, Broxbourne, **Hertfordshire**, EN10 7QJ, **ENGLAND**.
(T) 01992 462260.
Profile Breeder. Ref:YH01130

BEAUMONT EVENTS

Beaumont Events Ltd, 9 Bellingham Trading Est, Franthorne Way, **London (Greater)**, SE6 3BX, **ENGLAND**.
(T) 020 86986564 (F) 020 86986027. Ref:YH01131

BEAUMONT STABLES

Beaumont Stables, Ascot Paddocks, Winkfield Rd, Ascot, **Berkshire**, SL5 7LP, **ENGLAND**.
(T) 01344 627373.
Contact/s
Manager: Miss R Russell
Profile Stable/Livery. Ref:YH01132

BEAUMONT STABLES

Beaumont Stables, Forest Green Rd, Holyport, Maidenhead, **Berkshire**, SL6 2NN, **ENGLAND**.
(T) 01628 626116.
Profile Stable/Livery, Trainer. Ref:YH01133

BEAUMONT STUD

Beaumont Stud, Beaumont Manor Farm, Beaumont Rd, Broxbourne, **Hertfordshire**, EN10 7QJ, **ENGLAND**.
(T) 01992 451776.
Profile Breeder. Ref:YH01134

BEAUMONT, G L

Mrs G L Beaumont, Little Langley, Bardney Rd, Wragby, Market Rasen, **Lincolnshire**, LN8 5JE, **ENGLAND**.
(T) 01673 854387.
Profile Medical Support. Ref:YH01135

BEAUMONT, J A

J A Beaumont, Sunnyside, St Johns Rd, Bashley, New Milton, **Hampshire**, BH25 5SA, **ENGLAND**.
(T) 01425 614693.
Profile Farrier. Ref:YH01136

BEAUMONT, P

P Beaumont, Foulrice Farm, Stearsby, York, **Yorkshire (North)**, YO61 4SB, **ENGLAND**.
(T) 01347 888208 (F) 01347 888208.
Contact/s
Owner: Mr P Beaumont
Profile Trainer. Ref:YH01137

BEAUMONT, REBECCA

Rebecca Beaumont, Red Hse Farm, Govilon, Abergavenny, **Monmouthshire**, NP7 9RT, **WALES**.
(T) 01873 830644.
Contact/s
Owner: Miss R Beaumont
Profile Stable/Livery, Trainer. Ref:YH01138

BEAUPORT PK HOTEL

Beauport Park Hotel, Battle Rd, Hastings, **Sussex (East)**, TN38 8EA, **ENGLAND**.
(T) 01424 851222.
Profile Equestrian Centre. Ref:YH01139

BEAUPORT PK RIDING SCHOOL

Beauport Park Riding School, Hastings Rd, St Leonards-on-Sea, **Sussex (East)**, TN38 8EA, **ENGLAND**.
(T) 01424 851424.
Contact/s
Manager: Miss L Simes
Profile Riding School. Ref:YH01140

BEAUPORT PK RIDING STABLES

Beauport Park Riding Stables (Battle), Battle, **Sussex (East)**, **ENGLAND**.
(T) 01424 851424.
Profile Riding School. Ref:YH01141

BEAVER 84

Beaver 84 Ltd, Crompton Cl, Basildon, **Essex**, SS14 3AY, **ENGLAND**.
(T) 01268 530888. Ref:YH01142

BEAVER HORSE SHOP

Beaver Horse Shop, Windmill Farm, Otley Rd, Beckwithshaw, Harrogate, **Yorkshire (North)**, HG3 1QL, **ENGLAND**.
(T) 01423 566774 (F) 01423 528311
(W) www.countrysupplies.com.
Contact/s
Owner: Mrs J Fraser
Profile Riding Wear Retailer, Saddlery Retailer.
Yr. Est: 1988
Opening Times
Sp: Open Mon - Sun 09:00. Closed Mon - Sun 18:00.
Su: Open Mon - Sun 09:00. Closed Mon - Sun 18:00.
Au: Open Mon - Sun 09:00. Closed Mon - Sun 18:00.
Wn: Open Mon - Sun 09:00. Closed Mon - Sun 18:00. Ref:YH01143

BECCONSALL

Becconsall Farm Stables, Moss Hey Lane, Mere Brow, Preston, **Lancashire**, PR4 6LB, **ENGLAND**.
(T) 01772 813774
(W) www.newrider.com

Affiliated Bodies ABRS.
Contact/s
Owner: Miss G Walsh
Profile Equestrian Centre, Riding School, Stable/Livery.
Full, part and DIY livery available. **No.Staff:** 3
Yr. Est: 1975 **C.Size:** 42 Acres
Opening Times
Sp: Open Mon - Sun 09:30. Closed Mon - Sun 16:30.
Su: Open Mon - Sun 09:30. Closed Mon - Sun 16:30.
Au: Open Mon - Sun 09:30. Closed Mon - Sun 16:30.
Wn: Open Mon - Sun 09:30. Closed Mon - Sun 16:30.
Open all day everyday for livery **Ref:YH01144**

BECK VETNRY PRACTICE

Beck Veterinary Practice, 1 Liverton Rd, Loftus, **Cleveland**, TS13 4PY, **ENGLAND**.
(T) 01287 640269.
Profile Medical Support. **Ref:YH01145**

BECK, M

M Beck, Lakeside Paddocks, Lincombe, Lee, Ilfracombe, **Devon**, EX34 8LL, **ENGLAND**.
(T) 01271 862791.
Contact/s
Owner: Mr M Beck
Profile Breeder. **Ref:YH01146**

BECKERS EQUINE SVS

Beckers Equine Services, 3 Giles Travers Cl, Egham, **Surrey**, TW20 8UQ, **ENGLAND**.
(T) 01932 565204
Affiliated Bodies FRC.
Contact/s
Owner: Mr J Becker
Profile Farrier. **No.Staff:** 1 **Yr. Est:** 1982
Opening Times
Sp: Open 09:00. Closed 17:00.
Su: Open 09:00. Closed 17:00.
Au: Open 09:00. Closed 17:00.
Wn: Open 09:00. Closed 17:00. **Ref:YH01147**

BECKETT, R

Mr R Beckett, Windsor Hse, Lambourn, Hungerford, **Berkshire**, RG17 8NR, **ENGLAND**.
(T) 01488 71347 **(F)** 01488 72664.
Profile Trainer. **Ref:YH01148**

BECKHOUSE CARRIAGES

Beckhouse Carriages, Beckhouse Farm, Cropton, Pickering, **Yorkshire (North)**, YO18 8ER, **ENGLAND**.
(T) 01751 417235.
Profile Transport/Horse Boxes. **Ref:YH01149**

BEDALE & WEST OF YORE

Bedale & West of Yore, Manor Farm, Kirby Knowle, Thirsk, **Yorkshire (North)**, YO7 2JQ, **ENGLAND**.
(T) 01845 537321. **Ref:YH01150**

BEDALE COMBINED TRAINING GRP

Bedale Combined Training Group, Skerningham Farm, Harrogate Hill, Durham, **County Durham**, DL1 3JA, **ENGLAND**.
(T) 01325 730212.
Contact/s
Chairman: Mrs J Dent
Profile Club/Association. **Ref:YH01151**

BEDFORD RIDING BREECHES

Bedford Riding Breeches, 19 New Quebec St, London, **London (Greater)**, W1H 7DG, **ENGLAND**.
(T) 020 77239032.
Contact/s
Owner: Mr V MacInnes
Profile Riding Wear Retailer. **Ref:YH01152**

BEDFORD, LINDSEY

Miss Lindsey Bedford, 72 Victoria Rd, Roche, St Austell, **Cornwall**, PL26 8JG, **ENGLAND**.
(T) 01726 890295.
Profile Breeder. **Ref:YH01153**

BEDFORD, P & W

Messrs P & W Bedford, Sheepwalk Farm, New Rd, Escrick, York, **Yorkshire (North)**, YO19 6EZ, **ENGLAND**.
(T) 01904 728609 **(F)** 01904 728609.
Profile Breeder. **Ref:YH01154**

BEDGEBURY RIDING CTRE

Bedgebury Riding Centre, Bedgebury Pk, Goudhurst, **Kent**, TN17 2SH, **ENGLAND**.
(T) 01580 211602 **(F)** 01580 212296
(E) office@bedgeburyriding.ndo.co.uk
(W) www.bedgeburyridingcentre.co.uk
Affiliated Bodies BHS.
Contact/s
For Bookings: Mr S Gregory
(E) office@bedgeburyridingcentre.co.uk
Profile Equestrian Centre, Riding School, Stable/Livery.
Stabling available for up to 60 horses. There are two indoor and outdoor schools with access for hacking to 250 acres of parkland. **No.Staff:** 22
Yr. Est: 1974 **C.Size:** 200 Acres
Opening Times
Sp: Open 09:00. Closed 17:00.
Su: Open 09:00. Closed 17:00.
Au: Open 09:00. Closed 17:00.
Wn: Open 09:00. Closed 17:00. **Ref:YH01155**

BEDLINGTON BLYTH & DISTRICT

Bedlington Blyth & District Riding Club, 9 River View, Bedlington, **Northumberland**, NE22 5LR, **ENGLAND**.
(T) 01670 531884.
Contact/s
Chairman: Mrs J McClement
Profile Club/Association, Riding Club. **Ref:YH01156**

BEDMAX

Bedmax Ltd, Detchant, Belford, **Northumberland**, NE70 7PF, **ENGLAND**.
(T) 01668 213467 **(F)** 01668 213467
(W) www.bedmax.co.uk/ www.haymax.co.uk.
Contact/s
For Bookings: Mr P Forster
(E) peterforster@coastley.fsnet.co.uk
Profile Feed Merchant, Supplies. Bedding Manufacturers.
Producer Bedmax and Haymax. **No.Staff:** 11
Opening Times
See website or telephone for nearest stockists
Ref:YH01157

BEDWELLTY

Bedwellty Agricultural Society Ltd, Pantygwreiddyn Farm, Holly Bush, Blackwood, **Caerphilly**, NP12 0SD, **WALES**.
(T) 01495 224838 **(F)** 01495 224838.
Profile Club/Association. **Ref:YH01158**

BEE LINE TOWBAR/TRAILER CTRE

Bee Line Towbar & Trailer Centre, Unit 37 Honeyborough Ind Est, Neyland, Milford Haven, **Pembrokeshire**, SA73 1SE, **WALES**.
(T) 01646 601999.
Profile Transport/Horse Boxes. **Ref:YH01159**

BEE WOODCRAFT

Bee Woodcraft, 25 Farngarrett, Ardmore, **County Cork**, **IRELAND**.
(T) 024 94492 **(F)** 087-6881581
(E) bwoodcraft@esatclear.ie
(W) www.beewoodcraft.com.
Contact/s
Owner: Bryan Egan
Profile Supplies. Manufacture and supply stables and fencing.
Has a range of complimentary equestrian products, including mobile and static wooden shelters, hay barns, half doors, gates and fencing. **Yr. Est:** 1999
Ref:YH01160

BEE, M

Miss M Bee, Burnside of Meadaple, Rothienorman, Inverurie, **Aberdeenshire**, AB51 8UH, **SCOTLAND**.
(T) 01651 821398.
Profile Breeder. **Ref:YH01161**

BEEBEE & BEEBEE

Beebee & Beebee, 48 Lower Forster St, Walsall, **Midlands (West)**, WS1 1XB, **ENGLAND**.
(T) 01922 623407 **(F)** 01922 722575.
Contact/s
Chairman: Mrs J Hickton
Profile Riding Wear Retailer. **Ref:YH01162**

BEECH COTTAGE STUD

Beech Cottage Stud, Beech Cottage, Dromahair, **County Leitrim**, **IRELAND**.
(T) 071 64110. **Ref:YH01163**

BEECH HOUSE STUD

Beech House Stud, Newmarket Rd, Cheveley, Newmarket, **Suffolk**, CB8 9EH, **ENGLAND**.
(T) 01638 730335 **(F)** 01638 730457.
Contact/s
Manager: Mr E McFarling
Profile Breeder. **Ref:YH01164**

BEECH PARK RIDING CTRE

Beech Park Riding Centre, Rathcormac, **County Cork**, **IRELAND**.
(T) 025 36277. **Ref:YH01165**

BEECH TREE STUD & FARM

Beech Tree Stud & Farm, Upton Noble, Shepton Mallet, **Somerset**, BA4 6AX, **ENGLAND**.
(T) 01749 850245 **(F)** 01749 850932.
Contact/s
Owner: Mr G Griggs
Profile Breeder. **Ref:YH01166**

BEECHCROFT ANIMAL FEEDS

Beechcroft Animal Feeds, Flitwick Rd, Steppingley, **Bedfordshire**, MK45 5BA, **ENGLAND**.
(T) 01525 712685
(M) 07976 781553
(E) rmpreece@talk21.com
(W) www.beechcroftfeeds.co.uk.
Profile Supplies. **Ref:YH01167**

BEECHENER VETNRY SUPPLIES

Robin Beechener Veterinary Supplies, The Laurels, 80 Brize Norton Rd, Minster Lovell, **Oxfordshire**, OX8 5SG, **ENGLAND**.
(T) 01993 775215
(M) 07721 620442.
Profile Medical Support. **Ref:YH01168**

BEECHES EQUESTRIAN CTRE

Beeches Equestrian Centre (The), 171 Ballycore Rd, Ballyclare, **County Antrim**, BT39 9DF, **NORTHERN IRELAND**.
(T) 028 93352441.
Profile Riding School, Stable/Livery. **Ref:YH01169**

BEECHES RIDING CLUB

Beeches Riding Club (The), 37 Armoy Gardens, Rathcoole, Newtownabbey, **County Antrim**, BT36 8TH, **NORTHERN IRELAND**.
(T) 028 90853484.
Contact/s
Chairman: Mr T Boomer
Profile Club/Association. **Ref:YH01170**

BEECHEY, R F

R F Beechey RSS, Mansgate Cottage, Mansgate Hill, Nettleton, Lincoln, **Lincolnshire**, **ENGLAND**.
(T) 01472 852361.
Profile Farrier. **Ref:YH01171**

BEECHFIELD SADDLERY

Beechfield Saddlery, Beechfield, Shipton Lee, Grendon Underwood, **Buckinghamshire**, HP18 0QW, **ENGLAND**.
(T) 01296 770530.
Profile Saddlery Retailer. **Ref:YH01172**

BEECHGROVE STUD

Beechgrove Stud, The Grove, Scamblesby, Louth, **Lincolnshire**, LN11 9XT, **ENGLAND**.
(T) 01507 533223.
Profile Breeder. **Ref:YH01173**

BEECHMOUNT EQUITATION CTRE

Beechmount Equitation Centre, 67 Fleetwood Rd, Thornton-Cleveleys, **Lancashire**, FY5 1SB, **ENGLAND**.
(T) 01253 868310.
Profile Riding School, Stable/Livery. **Ref:YH01174**

BEECHVALE FARRIER SUPPLIES

Beechvale Farrier Supplies, 11 Quarterlands Rd, Lisburn, **County Antrim**, BT27 5TN, **NORTHERN IRELAND**.
(T) 028 90826423.
Contact/s
Company Secretary: Miss S Turner
Profile Farrier. **Ref:YH01175**

BEECHWOOD

Beechwood Riding School, Hillboxes Farm, Marden Pk, Woldingham, Caterham, **Surrey**, CR3 7JD, **ENGLAND**.
(T) 01883 342266
(W) www.beechwoodridingschool.co.uk
Affiliated Bodies ABRS, BHS.
Contact/s
Partner: Mr C Trace
Profile Riding School, Stable/Livery.
Pony club and pub rides available. Loan a pony and riding courses also available for adults and children.
Yr. Est: 1977 **C.Size:** 25 Acres
Opening Times
Sp: Open 09:00. Closed 16:00.
Su: Open 09:00. Closed 16:00.
Au: Open 09:00. Closed 16:00.
Wn: Open 09:00. Closed 16:00. **Ref:YH01176**

BEECHWOOD BLOODSTOCK

Beechwood Bloodstock, Beechwood Cottage,

Beechwood Ave, Weybridge, **Surrey**, KT13 9TE, **ENGLAND**.
(T) 01932 858034 **(F)** 01932 858034.
Profile Blood Stock Agency. **Ref: YH01177**

BEECHWOOD LIVERY/TRAINING

Beechwood Livery & Training Centre, Hodgetts Lane, Berkswell, **Warwickshire**, CV7 7DG, **ENGLAND**.
(T) 01676 534869 **(F)** 01676 534572.
Profile Stable/Livery. **Ref: YH01178**

BEECHWOOD VETNRY CTRE

Beechwood Veterinary Centre, 35 Beechwood Ave, Woodley, Reading, **Berkshire**, RG5 3DE, **ENGLAND**.
(T) 0118 9272999 **(F)** 0118 9272208.
Profile Medical Support. **Ref: YH01179**

BEECHWOOD VETNRY GRP

Beechwood Veterinary Group, 132 Austhorpe Rd, Leeds, **Yorkshire (West)**, LS15 8EJ, **ENGLAND**.
(T) 0113 2645422.
Profile Medical Support. **Ref: YH01180**

BEECHWOOD VETNRY GRP

Beechwood Veterinary Group, 335 Chapeltown Rd, Leeds, **Yorkshire (West)**, LS7 3LL, **ENGLAND**.
(T) 0113 2621189.
Profile Medical Support. **Ref: YH01181**

BEECHWOOD VETNRY GRP

Beechwood Veterinary Group, 430 Dewsbury Rd, Leeds, **Yorkshire (West)**, LS11 7LJ, **ENGLAND**.
(T) 0113 2700325.
Profile Medical Support. **Ref: YH01182**

BEECHWOOD VETNRY GRP

Beechwood Veterinary Group, 28 Springmead Drive, Garforth, Leeds, **Yorkshire (West)**, LS25 1JW, **ENGLAND**.
(T) 0113 2320030.
Profile Medical Support. **Ref: YH01183**

BEECROFT, PATRICK J

Patrick J Beecroft DWCF, 4 Nares Rd, Witton, Blackburn, **Lancashire**, BB2 2FH, **ENGLAND**.
(T) 01254 677571.
Profile Farrier. **Ref: YH01184**

BEEDIE BROS

Beedie Bros Ltd, Barnyards, Rosehearty, Fraserburgh, **Aberdeenshire**, AB43 7NU, **SCOTLAND**.
(T) 01346 571117 **(F)** 01346 571007.
Contact/s
Partner: Mr J Beedie
Profile Transport/Horse Boxes. **Ref: YH01185**

BEENBANE RIDING STABLES

Beenbane Riding Stables, Beenbane, Waterville, **County Kerry**, **IRELAND**.
(T) 066 9474391. **Ref: YH01186**

BEESLEY LIVESTOCK HAULAGE

B R & T Beesley Livestock Haulage, Howlands, Golford, Cranbrook, **Kent**, TN17 3PB, **ENGLAND**.
(T) 01580 715415.
Profile Transport/Horse Boxes. **Ref: YH01187**

BEESLEY, J A

J A Beesley, Monument Bungalow, Bucks Hill, Nuneaton, **Warwickshire**, CV10 9LS, **ENGLAND**.
(T) 07714 085242.
Contact/s
Owner: Mr J Beesley
Profile Farrier. **Ref: YH01188**

BEESLEY, JOSEPH A

Joseph A Beesley, Blacksmith Cottage, 22 Bauldington Rd, Shilton, Coventry, **Warwickshire**, CV7 9JT, **ENGLAND**.
(T) 07714 085242.
Profile Farrier. **Ref: YH01189**

BEESLEYS OF BALLAM

Beesleys of Ballam, The Stable Yard, West Moss Farm, West Moss Lane, Ballam, Lytham, **Lancashire**, FY8 4NH, **ENGLAND**.
(T) 07970 475177 **(F)** 01253 735465.
Contact/s
Owner: Mrs S Beesley
Profile Saddlery Retailer. **Ref: YH01190**

BEESONS

Beesons, 72 Railway St, Hertford, **Hertfordshire**, SG14 1BJ, **ENGLAND**.
(T) 01992 504020 **(F)** 01992 503838
(W) www.beesons.uk.com.
Contact/s
Partner: Mr G Beeson
(E) graham@beesons.fsbusiness.co.uk
Profile Chartered Surveyors.
Chartered surveyors, auctioneers and estate agents who are specialists in rural, agricultural sales and valuations. Yr. Est: 1992
Opening Times
Sp: Open Mon - Fri 09:00. Closed Mon - Fri 17:30.
Su: Open Mon - Fri 09:00. Closed Mon - Fri 17:30.
Au: Open Mon - Fri 09:00. Closed Mon - Fri 17:30.
Wn: Open Mon - Fri 09:00. Closed Mon - Fri 17:30.
Closed at weekends **Ref: YH01191**

BEESTON, MICHAEL GUY

Michael Guy Beeston DWCF, 1 Botts Way, Coalville, **Leicestershire**, LE67 4BT, **ENGLAND**.
(T) 01530 813718.
Profile Farrier. **Ref: YH01192**

BEEVER, C R

C R Beever, Kirby Hse, Woolsthorpe, Grantham, **Lincolnshire**, NG32 1NT, **ENGLAND**.
(T) 01476 870177 **(F)** 01476 870177.
Contact/s
Owner: Mr C Beever
Profile Transport/Horse Boxes. Yr. Est: 1997
Opening Times
Open by appointment only **Ref: YH01193**

BEGG & PARTNERS

Begg & Partners, 40 Stonehouse Rd, Strathaven, **Lanarkshire (South)**, ML10 6LF, **SCOTLAND**.
(T) 01357 520251.
Profile Medical Support. **Ref: YH01194**

BEGGARS ROOST SADDLERY

Beggars Roost Saddlery & Country Stores, Botley Rd, Fair Oak, Eastleigh, **Hampshire**, SO50 7AN, **ENGLAND**.
(T) 023 80692239 **(F)** 023 80893133.
Contact/s
Owner: Mrs J Jones
Profile Saddlery Retailer. **Ref: YH01195**

BEHAN D & E

Behan D & E Ltd, Moher, Pollerton Little, Carlow, **County Carlow**, **IRELAND**.
(M) 087 2578569.
Contact/s
Partner: David Behan
Profile All Weather Surface suppliers.
All weather surfaces for gallops and arenas. Non-slip granulated paving and white PVC running rails.
Opening Times
Telephone for further information **Ref: YH01196**

BEHAN, J J

J J Behan, 18 The Guillods Cottages, Graffham, Petworth, **Sussex (West)**, GU28 0NR, **ENGLAND**.
(T) 01798 867265.
Profile Farrier. **Ref: YH01197**

BEHAVIOUR & WELFARE

Behaviour & Welfare Consultancy Services, University Of Edinburgh, R(D)Svs Dept Vet Clinical Studies, Easter Bush Veterinary Centre, Roslin, **Lothian (Mid)**, EH25 9RG, **SCOTLAND**.
(T) 0131 6506281 **(F)** 0131 6506588.
Profile Club/Association. **Ref: YH01198**

BEIGHTON, G

G Beighton, Brookhouse Farm, Newbeggin-In-Bishopdale, Leyburn, **Yorkshire (North)**, DL8 3TD, **ENGLAND**.
(T) 01969 663483.
Profile Farrier. **Ref: YH01199**

BEKESBOURNE STABLES

Bekesbourne Stables, West Bungalow, Aerodrome Rd, Bekesbourne, Canterbury, **Kent**, CT4 5EX, **ENGLAND**.
(T) 01227 830910.
Contact/s
Owner: Mrs H Parren
Profile Stable/Livery. **Ref: YH01200**

BEKON HAFLINGER STUD

Bekon Haflinger Stud, Broomhill Farm, Cairnorrie, Methlick, **Aberdeenshire**, AB41 7BY, **SCOTLAND**.
(T) 01651 806265.
Profile Breeder. **Ref: YH01201**

BEL-AIR HOTEL & EQUESTRIAN

Bel-Air Hotel & Equestrian Club, Ashford, **County Wicklow**, **IRELAND**.
(T) 0404 40109 **(F)** 0404 40188
(E) bel-airhotel@eircom.net
(W) www.nci.ie/belair
Affiliated Bodies AIRE.
Contact/s
Assistant Manager: William Freeman Jnr
Profile Equestrian Centre, Horse/Rider Accom, Riding Club.
The hotel has been run by the Murphy Freeman family since 1937. The hotel offers bar and restaurant facilities with B&B rates from £35.00 per night.
C.Size: 200 Acres **Ref: YH01202**

BELASCO, STEPHEN R

Stephen R Belasco RSS Hons, Ashen Farm Hse, Southampton Rd, Dibden, **Hampshire**, SO4 5TA, **ENGLAND**.
(T) 023 80849648.
Profile Farrier. **Ref: YH01203**

BELCHER, A D

A D Belcher, Cummins Farm, New Rd, Aldham, Colchester, **Essex**, CO6 3PN, **ENGLAND**.
(T) 01206 240664 **(F)** 01206 577789.
Contact/s
Owner: Mr A Belcher
Profile Blacksmith. **Ref: YH01204**

BELCHER, IAN

Ian Belcher DWCF, Orchard Dene Cottage, South St, Blewbury, Didcot, **Oxfordshire**, OX11 9PR, **ENGLAND**.
(T) 01235 850029.
Profile Farrier. **Ref: YH01205**

BELCHER, MICHAEL E

Michael E Belcher BII, 34 Eastfields, Blewbury, Didcot, **Oxfordshire**, OX11 9NS, **ENGLAND**.
(T) 01235 850571.
Profile Farrier. **Ref: YH01206**

BELCHER, RACHAEL

Mrs Rachael Belcher, Batwell Farm, Shirenewton, Chepstow, **Monmouthshire**, NP16 6RX, **WALES**.
(T) 01291 641837.
Profile Breeder. **Ref: YH01207**

BELCHFORD STUD

Belchford Stud, Hemingby Rd, Belchford, Horncastle, **Lincolnshire**, LN9 5QN, **ENGLAND**.
(T) 01507 533331
(W) www.belchfordstud.com.
Contact/s
General Manager: Mrs J Stamp
(E) jennystamp@aol.com
Profile Breeder, Medical Support, Stable/Livery.
Equine Dentist. No.Staff: 2 Yr. Est: 1979
C.Size: 20 Acres
Opening Times
Telephone for an appointment **Ref: YH01208**

BELFAIRS RIDING SCHOOL

Belfairs Riding School Ltd, The Cottage, Eastwood Rd North, Leigh-on-Sea, **Essex**, SS9 4LR, **ENGLAND**.
(T) 01702 525571.
Contact/s
Manageress: Miss F Baker **Ref: YH01209**

BELGRAVE COACH BUILDERS

Belgrave Coach Builders Ltd, Unit 5 Davy Way, Llay Ind Est, Llay, Wrexham, **Wrexham**, LL12 0PG, **WALES**.
(T) 01978 855449 **(F)** 01978 855787.
Profile Transport/Horse Boxes. **Ref: YH01210**

BELGRAVE HSE VETNRY SURGERY

Belgrave House Veterinary Surgery, 139 High St, Linton, **Cambridgeshire**, CB1 6JT, **ENGLAND**.
(T) 01223 893720.
Profile Medical Support. **Ref: YH01211**

BELHAVEN ENGINEERING

Belhaven Engineering, 4 Campsie Rd, Wishaw, **Lanarkshire (North)**, ML2 7QG, **SCOTLAND**.
(T) 01698 372014 **(F)** 01698 372014.
Contact/s
Owner: Mr J Wilson
Profile Blacksmith. **Ref: YH01212**

BELL & PARTNERS

Bell & Partners, Grove Rise, Weston-under-Wetherley, Leamington Spa, **Warwickshire**, CV33 9BZ, **ENGLAND**.
(T) 01926 339090 **(F)** 01926 334352.
Profile Medical Support. **Ref: YH01213**

BELL EQUINE VETNRY CLINIC

Bell Equine Veterinary Clinic, Mereworth, Maidstone, **Kent**, ME18 5GS, **ENGLAND**.
(T) 01622 813700 **(F)** 01622 812233
(E) bevc@btinternet.com.
Profile Medical Support. **Ref: YH01214**

BELL FARM LIVERY STABLES
Bell Farm Livery Stables, Bell Lane, Eton Wick, Windsor, **Berkshire**, SL4 6LH, **ENGLAND**.
(T) 01753 830717. Ref: YH01215

BELL TRAILERS
Bell Trailers, Unit 16 Kirby Rd, Lomeshaye Ind Est, Nelson, **Lancashire**, BB9 6RS, **ENGLAND**.
(T) 01282 696343 (F) 01282 699260.
Profile Transport/Horse Boxes. Ref: YH01216

BELL, BROWN & BENTLEY
Bell, Brown & Bentley, 192 London Rd, Leicester, **Leicestershire**, LE2 1ND, **ENGLAND**.
(T) 0116 2661338.
Profile Medical Support. Ref: YH01217

BELL, D
Mr & Mrs D Bell, 80 Braepark Rd, Ballyclare, **County Antrim**, BT39 9SR, **NORTHERN IRELAND**.
(T) 028 93342363.
Profile Breeder. Ref: YH01218

BELL, HELEN
Helen Bell, Manor Farm, Newsham, Thirsk, **Yorkshire (North)**, YO7 4DJ, **ENGLAND**.
(T) 01845 587207. Ref: YH01219

BELL, IVON T
Ivon T Bell FWCF Hons, 19 Grantham Rd, Ropsley, Grantham, **Lincolnshire**, NG33 4BX, **ENGLAND**.
(T) 01476 585136.
Profile Farrier. Ref: YH01220

BELL, J
Mr J Bell, Waver Head, Brocklebank, Wigton, **Cumbria**, CA7 8DJ, **ENGLAND**.
(T) 01697 478644.
Profile Breeder. Ref: YH01221

BELL, J F & C R (ESQ)
J F & C R Bell Esq, Parks Farm Stud, Newsholme, Howden, **Yorkshire (East)**, DN14 7JR, **ENGLAND**.
(T) 01757 638281.
Profile Breeder. Ref: YH01222

BELL, JAKI
Ms Jaki Bell, Room 2303, Kings Reach Tower, Stamford St, London, **London (Greater)**, SE1 9LS, **ENGLAND**.
(T) 020 72617969
(E) jaki_bell@ipc.co.uk.
Profile Supplies. Ref: YH01223

BELL, JEFFREY
Jeffrey Bell, Greens Farm, Smithy Lane, Winmarleigh, Preston, **Lancashire**, PR3 0JU, **ENGLAND**.
(T) 01524 791491.
Profile Farrier. Ref: YH01224

BELL, JOHN
John Bell DWCF, 32 South St, Sunnybrow, Crook, **County Durham**, DL15 0NH, **ENGLAND**.
(T) 01388 747848.
Profile Farrier. Ref: YH01225

BELL, K J
K J Bell, Blooms Farm Cottages, Delvin End, Sible Hedingham, Halstead, **Essex**, CO9 3LN, **ENGLAND**.
(T) 01787 462473.
Profile Farrier. Ref: YH01226

BELL, M L
M L Bell, Fitzroy Hse, Black Bear Lane, Newmarket, **Suffolk**, CB8 0JT, **ENGLAND**.
(T) 01638 666567
(W) www.newmarketracehorsetrainers.co.uk
Affiliated Bodies Newmarket Trainers Fed.
Contact/s
Trainer: M L Bell
Profile Trainer. Ref: YH01227

BELL, MICHAEL D
Michael D Bell DWCF, The Flat, Badminton Farm, Badminton Farm, **Gloucestershire**, GL9 1ES, **ENGLAND**.
(T) 01454 218850.
Profile Farrier. Ref: YH01228

BELL, STEVEN A
Steven A Bell, Garybank Workshop, Bankfoot, Perth, **Perth and Kinross**, PH1 4DX, **SCOTLAND**.
(T) 01738 787354.
Profile Blacksmith. Ref: YH01229

BELL, T
Mr & Mrs T Bell, Beltoy, Glenoe, Larne, **County Antrim**, BT40 3LQ, **NORTHERN IRELAND**.
(T) 028 28378850.
Profile Breeder. Ref: YH01230

BELLCROWN
Bellcrown Ltd, Hampton Heath Ind Est, Hampton Heath, Malpas, **Cheshire**, SY14 8BZ, **ENGLAND**.
(T) 01948 820408 (F) 01948 820508
(E) info@bellcrown.com
(W) www.bellcrown.com.
Contact/s
Administration: Mrs N Huxley
Profile Carriage Manufacturers.
Handmade carriages built to personal specifications for any type of horses, from miniatures to 17 hands.
Opening Times
Sp: Open Mon - Fri 10:00. Closed Mon - Thurs 16:00, Fri 13:00.
Su: Open Mon - Fri 10:00. Closed Mon - Thurs 16:00, Fri 13:00.
Au: Open Mon - Fri 10:00. Closed Mon - Thurs 16:00, Fri 13:00.
Wn: Open Mon - Fri 10:00. Closed Mon - Thurs 16:00, Fri 13:00.
Weekends open by appointment. Ref: YH01231

BELLE LEATHER
Belle Leather, 3 Lumburn Cottages, Lumburn, Tavistock, **Devon**, PL19 8HT, **ENGLAND**.
(T) 01822 613711. Ref: YH01232

BELLE VUE STABLES
Belle Vue Stables, Carr Hse Rd, Doncaster, **Yorkshire (South)**, DN1 2BY, **ENGLAND**.
(T) 01302 349337.
Profile Stable/Livery. Ref: YH01233

BELLE VUE VALLEY
Belle Vue Valley, Argyll Rd, Exeter, **Devon**, EX4 4RY, **ENGLAND**.
(T) 01392 216928.
Contact/s
Owner: Mrs L Smedley
Profile Riding School. Ref: YH01234

BELLE VUE VETNRY PRACTICE
Belle Vue Veterinary Practice, Southend, Wigton, **Cumbria**, CA7 9QE, **ENGLAND**.
(T) 01697 342174.
Profile Medical Support. Ref: YH01235

BELLENIE, NICKI
Ms Nicki Bellenie, 74 Castle Rd, Wootton, Woodstock, **Oxfordshire**, OX20 1EG, **ENGLAND**.
(T) 01993 813362 (F) 01993 813362.
Profile Breeder. Ref: YH01236

BELLEVUE VETNRY GRP
Bellevue Veterinary Group, 43 Castle St, Banff, **Aberdeenshire**, AB4 1BJ, **SCOTLAND**.
(T) 01261 22168.
Profile Medical Support. Ref: YH01237

BELLINGDON END
Bellingdon End Farm Supplies, Bellingdon, Chesham, **Buckinghamshire**, HP5 2UR, **ENGLAND**.
(T) 01494 758239.
Contact/s
General Manager: Ms J Clark
Profile Riding Wear Retailer, Saddlery Retailer, Supplies. No.Staff: 6 Yr. Est: 1959
Opening Times
Sp: Open 09:00. Closed 17:00.
Su: Open 09:00. Closed 17:00.
Au: Open 09:00. Closed 17:00.
Wn: Open 09:00. Closed 17:00. Ref: YH01238

BELLINGHAM STABLES
Bellingham Stables, Farmyard Demesne, Castlebellingham, **County Louth**, **IRELAND**.
(T) 042 9372044. Ref: YH01239

BELLVIEW STABLES
Bellview Stables, 6 The Green, Snailwell, Newmarket, **Suffolk**, CB8 7LT, **ENGLAND**.
(T) 01638 577032 (F) 01638 578585.
Contact/s
Owner: Mr E Marshall Ref: YH01240

BELLWOOD
Bellwood Riding Stables & Liveries, Bellwood, Wellow Top Rd, Ningwood, Yarmouth, **Isle of Wight**, PO41 0TL, **ENGLAND**.
(T) 01983 531261.
Contact/s
Partner: Mr P Reynolds Ref: YH01241

BELLWOOD COTTAGE STABLES
Bellwood Cottage Stables, Settrington, Malton, **Yorkshire (North)**, YO17 8NP, **ENGLAND**.
(T) 01944 768370 (F) 01944 768370
(M) 07770 500028.
Profile Trainer. Ref: YH01242

BELLWOOD SADDLERY
Bellwood Saddlery, 8 Birmingham Rd, Cowes, **Isle of Wight**, PO31 7BH, **ENGLAND**.
(T) 01983 296644 (F) 01983 296655.
Contact/s
Owner: Mrs J Stafford
Profile Saddlery Retailer. Ref: YH01243

BELMONT BLACKSMITH
Belmont Blacksmith, Wellwood Cottage, Torphins, Banchory, **Aberdeenshire**, AB31 4JX, **SCOTLAND**.
(T) 01339 882099.
Contact/s
Owner: Mr I Cormack
Profile Blacksmith. Ref: YH01244

BELMONT COMMUNICATIONS
Belmont Communications Ltd, Unit 5 The Acorn Ctre, Roebuck Rd, Hainault, Ilford, **Essex**, IG6 3TU, **ENGLAND**.
(T) 01206 322349 (F) 020 85008124.
Profile Club/Association. Ref: YH01245

BELMONT HSE VETNRY SURGERY
Belmont House Veterinary Surgery, Salisbury Rd Business Pk, Salisbury Rd, Pewsey, **Wiltshire**, SN9 5PZ, **ENGLAND**.
(T) 01672 563413 (F) 01672 564671.
Contact/s
Vet: Miss E Thomas
Profile Medical Support. Ref: YH01246

BELMONT LIVERY STABLE
Belmont Livery Stable, 193 Forest Lane, Harrogate, **Yorkshire (North)**, HG2 7EF, **ENGLAND**.
(T) 01423 886997.
Contact/s
Owner: Mrs D Atkinson
Profile Breeder, Riding School, Stable/Livery.
Ref: YH01247

BELMONT RACING STABLES
Belmont Racing Stables, The Ridgeway, Mill Hill, **London (Greater)**, NW7 4BH, **ENGLAND**.
(T) 020 89063375
(M) 07836 214617.
Profile Trainer. Ref: YH01248

BELMONT RIDING CTRE
Belmont Riding Centre Ltd, Belmont Farm, The Ridgeway, London, **London (Greater)**, NW7 1QT, **ENGLAND**.
(T) 020 89061255 (F) 020 89061588.
Profile Riding School, Saddlery Retailer, Stable/Livery, Track/Course, Trainer. Ref: YH01249

BELMONT STABLING
Belmont Stabling, Pipers Farm, Lippitts Hill, Loughton, **Essex**, IG10 4AL, **ENGLAND**.
(T) 020 85020052 (F) 020 85023560.
Contact/s
Partner: Mrs F Bovis
Profile Supplies. Ref: YH01250

BELMOREDEAN
Belmoredean Stud & Livery Stables, Little Champions Farm, Maplehurst Rd, West Grinstead, **Sussex (West)**, RH13 6RN, **ENGLAND**.
(T) 01403 864635.
Profile Stable/Livery. Ref: YH01251

BELPER SADDLERY
Belper Saddlery, 21 Strutt St, Belper, **Derbyshire**, DE56 1UN, **ENGLAND**.
(T) 01773 823904.
Profile Saddlery Retailer. Ref: YH01252

BELSTANE RACING
Belstane Racing Stables, Belstane, Carluke, **Lanarkshire (South)**, ML8 5HN, **SCOTLAND**.
(T) 01555 773335 (F) 01555 772243.
Contact/s
Trainer: Mr I Simple
Profile Trainer. No.Staff: 7 Yr. Est: 1997
Opening Times
Telephone for an appointment Ref: YH01253

BELTON PK HORSE TRIALS
Belton Park Horse Trials (Pedigree Chum), Horse Trials Office, Beach Bank Farm, Surfleet, Spalding, **Lincolnshire**, PE11 4AX, **ENGLAND**.
(T) 01775 680613 (F) 01775 680613. Ref: YH01254

BELTON, C

Mrs C Belton, West View, Yarburgh, Louth, **Lincolnshire**, LN11 0TL, **ENGLAND**.
(T) 01507 363261.
Profile Trainer.
Mrs Belton is also a Dressage Judge **Ref: YH01255**

BELTONS COUNTRY SHOP

Beltons Country Shop, The Barn, Haycock Hotel, Peterborough, **Cambridgeshire**, PE8 6JA, **ENGLAND**.
(T) 01780 782530.
Contact/s
Owner: Mr D Belton
Profile Saddlery Retailer. **Ref: YH01256**

BELVEDERE EQUESTRIAN CTRE

Belvedere Equestrian Centre, 47A High Bangor Rd, Donaghadee, **County Down**, BT21 0PB, **NORTHERN IRELAND**.
(T) 028 91888249. **Ref: YH01257**

BELVOIR HORSE FEEDS

Belvoir Horse Feeds, Coleby Airfield, Boothby Graffoe Heath, **Lincolnshire**, LN5 0LR, **ENGLAND**.
(T) 01522 810741 **(F)** 01522 811201. **Ref: YH01258**

BELVOIR HORSE PRODUCTS

Belvoir Horse Products Ltd, South Lodge, Ropsley, Grantham, **Lincolnshire**, NG33 4AS, **ENGLAND**.
(T) 01476 585888 **(F)** 01476 585111
(E) belvoirbedding@btconnect.com.
Contact/s
For Bookings: Ms J Wiggins
Profile Supplies.
Producers of Belvoir Bedding, Flax-a-bed and Equi-lin.
Opening Times
Sp: Open Mon - Fri 09:00. Closed Mon - Fri 17:00.
Su: Open Mon - Fri 09:00. Closed Mon - Fri 17:00.
Au: Open Mon - Fri 09:00. Closed Mon - Fri 17:00.
Wn: Open Mon - Fri 09:00. Closed Mon - Fri 17:00.
Closed weekends **Ref: YH01259**

BELVOIR VALE HORSEBALL CLUB

Belvoir Vale Horseball Club, C/O 10 St Marys Cres, Ruddington, **Nottinghamshire**, NG11 6FQ, **ENGLAND**.
(T) 0115 9844522.
Profile Club/Association. **Ref: YH01260**

BEN BATES HYDRO BATH

Ben Bates Hydro Bath, 5 Krooner Rd, Camberley, **Surrey**, GU15 2QP, **ENGLAND**.
(T) 01276 670142 **(F)** 01276 670142.
Profile Medical Support. **Ref: YH01261**

BEN MAYES

Ben Mayes Equine Veterinary Practice, Durfold Cottage, Durfold Hill, Dorking Rd, Warnham, Horsham, **Sussex (West)**, RH12 3RY, **ENGLAND**.
(T) 01403 264831 **(F)** 01403 274207.
Profile Medical Support. **Ref: YH01262**

BENACRE THANET WAY

Benacre Thanet Way Riding Stables, Thanet Way, Whitstable, **Kent**, CT5 3DA, **ENGLAND**.
(T) 01227 770931.
Contact/s
Owner: Mrs A Oliver
Profile Riding School. **Ref: YH01263**

BENENSON, LESLIE

Leslie Benenson, Roseland, 138 Barnhorn Rd, Little Common, Bexhill-on-Sea, **Sussex (East)**, TN39 4QG, **ENGLAND**.
(T) 01424 33404. **Ref: YH01264**

BENFIELD, M

Mrs M Benfield, Teyrdan Hall Farm, Llanelian, Colwyn Bay, **Conwy**, LL29 8YU, **WALES**.
(T) 01492 518713 **(F)** 01492 518713.
Profile Breeder. **Ref: YH01265**

BENGOUGH, PIERS (LT COL SIR)

Lt Col Sir Piers Bengough, Arrow Farm & Stud, Canon Pyon, **Herefordshire**, HR4 8PD, **ENGLAND**.
(T) 01432 830220 **(F)** 01432 830516.
Profile Breeder. **Ref: YH01266**

BENHAM STUD

Benham Stud, Benham Stud Office, Finches Farm, Baydon, Marlborough, **Wiltshire**, SN8 2JN, **ENGLAND**.
(T) 01672 540680 **(F)** 01672 541088
(E) info@benhamstud.com.
Profile Breeder. **Ref: YH01267**

BENJAMIN BAKER

Benjamin Baker (Lye) Ltd, Baker Hse, The Hayes, Stourbridge, **Midlands (West)**, DY9 8RS, **ENGLAND**.
(T) 01384 422291 **(F)** 01384 893171.
Contact/s
Chairman: Mr R Byrne
Profile Blacksmith. **Ref: YH01268**

BENNETT, C J

Mr C J Bennett, Blacklands Farm, Normansland, Dymock, **Gloucestershire**, GL18 2BE, **ENGLAND**.
(T) 01531 890206.
Profile Supplies. **Ref: YH01269**

BENNETT, DANIEL J

Daniel J Bennett BII, Dac, Welby Lane, Melton Mowbray, **Leicestershire**, LE13 0SL, **ENGLAND**.
(T) 01664 411811.
Profile Farrier. **Ref: YH01270**

BENNETT, JAMES G

James G Bennett, 22 Hendry Trce, Buckie, **Moray**, AB56 1NS, **SCOTLAND**..
Profile Breeder. **Ref: YH01271**

BENNETT, R

Miss R Bennett, Flat 2 Oak Villa Farm, Stage Lane, Heatley, **Cheshire**, WA13 9JP, **ENGLAND**.
(T) 01925 754565.
Profile Breeder. **Ref: YH01272**

BENNETT, ROD

Mr Rod Bennett, Blue Bell Farm, Penton Grafton, Andover, **Hampshire**, SP11 0RR, **ENGLAND**.
(T) 01264 772341. **Ref: YH01273**

BENNEY TRAILERS

Benney Trailers, Unit 3 Bittaford Garage, Bittaford, Ivybridge, **Devon**, PL21 0ES, **ENGLAND**.
(T) 01752 691455.
Profile Transport/Horse Boxes. **Ref: YH01274**

BENNINGTON CARRIAGES

Bennington Carriages, Sparrow Lane, Long Bennington, Newark, **Nottinghamshire**, NG23 5DL, **ENGLAND**.
(T) 01400 281280 **(F)** 01400 282243
(E) bennington@proweb.co.uk.
Profile Transport/Horse Boxes. **Ref: YH01275**

BENNITT, CAROL

Carol Bennitt BHSI, Beacon Farm Hse, Ivinghoe Aston, Leighton Buzzard, **Bedfordshire**, LU7 9DP, **ENGLAND**.
(T) 01525 222293.
Profile Stable/Livery. **Ref: YH01276**

BENRIDGE RIDING CTRE

Benridge Riding Centre, Benridge Hagg, Morpeth, **Northumberland**, NE61 3SB, **ENGLAND**.
(T) 01670 518507.
Contact/s
Owner: Miss J Mancey
Profile Riding School, Stable/Livery. **Ref: YH01277**

BENSON STUD

Benson Stud, Harts Lane, Ardleigh, Colchester, **Essex**, CO7 7QE, **ENGLAND**.
(T) 01206 230779.
Profile Breeder. **Ref: YH01278**

BENSON, LAUREL

Laurel Benson, 91 School Drive, Flimby, Maryport, **Cumbria**, CA15 8PL, **ENGLAND**.
(T) 01900 813239 **(F)** 01768 899919
(E) laurelbenson@equestrianet.co.uk
(W) www.laurelbenson.co.uk.
Profile Supplies. **Ref: YH01279**

BENSON, SUE

Sue Benson, Ducks Farm, Eastcott, Devizes, **Wiltshire**, SN10 4PJ, **ENGLAND**.
(T) 01380 813448 **(F)** 01380 813448
(E) 101552.503@compuserve.com.
Profile Trainer. **Ref: YH01280**

BENSON, T F J

T F J Benson RSS, Fynnon-Newydd, Cross Inn, Llanon, **Ceredigion**, SY23 5NA, **WALES**.
(T) 01974 272309.
Profile Farrier. **Ref: YH01281**

BENT, BM & SA

BM & SA Bent, Bowers Hill, Badsey, Evesham, **Worcestershire**, WR11 5HG, **ENGLAND**.
(T) 01386 830234 **(F)** 01386 830234.
Contact/s
Owner: Miss S Bent
Profile Horse/Rider Accom, Stable/Livery.
B & B accomodation for horse and rider. Livery for ponies & horses is available and grazing is between £14.00 - £21.00 per week. **Yr. Est:** 1986
C.Size: 80 Acres
Opening Times
Open 7 days a week for livery, phone between 12:00 - 14:00 or in the evenings **Ref: YH01282**

BENT, R

R Bent, Hawkes Farm, Dores Lane, Braishfield, Romsey, **Hampshire**, S051 0QJ, **ENGLAND**.
(T) 01794 368971.
Contact/s
Owner: Mr R Bent
Profile Blacksmith. **Ref: YH01283**

BENTGATE EQUESTRIAN CTRE

Bentgate Equestrian Centre, Clod Lane, Haslingden, Rossendale, **Lancashire**, BB4 6LR, **ENGLAND**.
(T) 01706 224160.
Contact/s
Owner: Mrs C Cain
Profile Riding School. **Ref: YH01284**

BENTLEY HSE

Bentley House Stables, Newtown, Biddulph Park, **Staffordshire**, ST8 7SW, **ENGLAND**.
(T) 01782 517921
(E) noelle@bentleyhouse.co.uk.
Profile Riding School, Stable/Livery. **Ref: YH01285**

BENTLEY RIDING CTRE

Bentley Riding Centre, Bergholt Rd, Bentley, Ipswich, **Suffolk**, IP9 2DQ, **ENGLAND**.
(T) 01473 311715
(E) bently.ridingschool@btinternet.co.uk
(W) www.bentley.ridingschool.btinternet.co.uk
Affiliated Bodies BHS, BSJA.
Contact/s
Manager: Mr J Sutton
Profile Equestrian Centre, Riding School.
Pony days organised. **Yr. Est:** 1987
Opening Times
Sp: Open Tues - Sun 09:00. Closed Tues - Sun 21:00.
Su: Open Tues - Sun 09:00. Closed Tues - Sun 21:00.
Au: Open Tues - Sun 09:00. Closed Tues - Sun 21:00.
Wn: Open Tues - Sun 09:00. Closed Tues - Sun 21:00.
Closed Mondays **Ref: YH01286**

BENTLEY STABLES

Bentley Stables, Frog St, Kelvedon Hatch, Brentwood, **Essex**, CM15 0JH, **ENGLAND**.
(T) 01277 374664. **Ref: YH01287**

BENTONS

Bentons, 47 Nottingham St, Melton Mowbray, **Leicestershire**, LE13 1NN, **ENGLAND**.
(T) 01664 482525 **(F)** 01664 482526. **Ref: YH01288**

BENWELL, LIZ

Liz Benwell, Peartree Farm, Padgetts Rd, Wisbech, **Cambridgeshire**, PE14 9PL, **ENGLAND**.
(T) 01354 638291 **(F)** 01354 638542
(E) peartree@easynet.co.uk.
Profile Supplies. **Ref: YH01289**

BEOLEY EQUESTRIAN CTRE

Beoley Equestrian Centre, Icknield St, Beoley, Redditch, **Worcestershire**, B98 9AL, **ENGLAND**.
(T) 01527 65494 **(F)** 01527 597727.
Contact/s
Owner: Mr N Edmonds
Profile Riding School. **Ref: YH01290**

BERA

British Endurance Riding Association, National Agricultural Ctre, Stoneleigh Pk, Kenilworth, **Warwickshire**, CV8 2RP, **ENGLAND**.
(T) 024 76698863 **(F)** 024 76418429.
Profile Club/Association, Trainer. **Ref: YH01291**

BERA

British Endurance Riding Association, "olympus" 13, Brockhurst Rd, Monks Kirby, Rugby, **Warwickshire**, CV23 0RA, **ENGLAND**.
(T) 01788 832581.
Profile Club/Association. **Ref: YH01292**

BERESFORD BLOODSTOCK SERVICES

Beresford Bloodstock Services, Fairview Cottage, Wicks Green, Binfield, **Berkshire**, RG42 5PF, **ENGLAND**.

(T) 01344 860976 (F) 01344 455413.
Profile Blood Stock Agency. Ref: YH01293

BERESFORD, H B

H B Beresford, Chestnut Hse, School Lane, Brackenfield, **Derbyshire**, DE55 6DF, **ENGLAND**.
(T) 01773 832941.
Profile Breeder. Ref: YH01294

BERGENDORFF, FREDERICK

Frederick Bergendorff (SWE), Farnborough Hse, Strangers Hill, Banbury, **Oxfordshire**, OX17 1EQ, **ENGLAND**.
(T) 01295 690504. Ref: YH01295

BERGER, HANS

Hans Berger, Aysgarth, Limbersey Lane, Haynes, **Bedfordshire**, MK45 3QU, **ENGLAND**.
(T) 01234 740209.
Profile Farrier. Ref: YH01296

BERGH APTON STUD

Bergh Apton Stud, Bergh Apton, Norwich, **Norfolk**, NR15 1BN, **ENGLAND**.
(T) 01508 550480 (F) 01508 550747
(M) 07889 243236.
Profile Blood Stock Agency, Breeder. Ref: YH01297

BERGIN, TOM

Tom Bergin, Donoughmore, Johnstown, **County Kilkenny**, **IRELAND**.
(T) 056 31284.
Profile Supplies. Ref: YH01298

BERKELEY

Berkeley & Co Ltd, Stafford Park 18, Telford, **Shropshire**, TF3 3AW, **ENGLAND**.
(T) 01952 290446 (F) 01952 290094
(E) adrian@berkeley.ltd.uk
(W) www.berkeley.ltd.uk.
Contact/s
Marketing Manager: David Higgs
Profile Supplies. Metal Forming Manufacturer.
Berkeley produce buckles for riding equipment, such as head collars and girths. Ref: YH01299

BERKELEY & DISTRICT

Berkeley & District Riding Club, Old Manor Hse, West Littleton, Chippenham, **Wiltshire**, SN14 8JE, **ENGLAND**.
(T) 01225 891683.
Contact/s
Chairman: Mrs A Brown
Profile Club/Association, Riding Club. Ref: YH01300

BERKELEY EQUESTRIAN SVS

Berkeley Equestrian Services, Clock Tower Stables, Brighton Rd, Kingswood, **Surrey**, KT20 6SY, **ENGLAND**.
(T) 01737 832874.
Profile Stable/Livery. Ref: YH01301

BERKELEY STUDIOS

Berkeley Studios Ltd, Yew Tree Cottage, Burrington, Ludlow, **Shropshire**, SY8 2HT, **ENGLAND**.
(T) 01568 770117 (F) 01568 770199. Ref: YH01302

BERKS & BUCKS

Berks & Bucks Drag, Sapphire Cottage, Box Tree Lane, Postcombe, **Oxfordshire**, OX7 7DT, **ENGLAND**.
(T) 01844 281021. Ref: YH01303

BERKSHIRE CLGE OF AGRCLTRL

Berkshire College of Agriculture, Hall Pl, Burchetts Green, Maidenhead, **Berkshire**, SL6 6QR, **ENGLAND**.
(T) 01628 824444 (F) 01628 824695
(E) enquiries@bca.ac.uk
(W) www.berks-coll-ag.ac.uk.
Contact/s
Programme Area Manager: Mrs P Williams
Profile Stable/Livery. College. Ref: YH01304

BERKSHIRE DOWNS RIDING CLUB

Berkshire Downs Riding Club, Laburnum Cottage, South St, Letcombe Regis, **Oxfordshire**, OX12 9JY, **ENGLAND**.
(T) 01235 770560.
Contact/s
Chairman: Miss C Wensley
Profile Club/Association, Riding Club. Ref: YH01305

BERKSHIRE RIDING CTRE

Berkshire Riding Centre, Crouch Lane, Winkfield, Windsor, **Berkshire**, SL4 4TN, **ENGLAND**.
(T) 01344 884992.
Profile Stable/Livery. Ref: YH01306

BERKSHIRE ROSETTES

Berkshire Rosettes, 46 Redlands Rd, Reading, **Berkshire**, RG1 5HE, **ENGLAND**.
(T) 0118 9314446 (F) 0118 9863792.
Profile Supplies. Ref: YH01307

BERKSWELL FORGE WORKS

Berkswell Forge Works, Hornbrook Farm, Cornets End Lane, Meriden, Coventry, **Midlands (West)**, CV7 7LH, **ENGLAND**.
(T) 01675 443352.
Profile Blacksmith. Ref: YH01308

BERNARD CORBETT

Bernard Corbett & Co, Marston, Chester Rd, Malpas, **Cheshire**, SY14 8HT, **ENGLAND**.
(T) 01948 860272.
Profile Supplies. Ref: YH01309

BERNARD WEATHERILL

Bernard Weatherill Ltd, 8 Saville Row, London, **London (Greater)**, W1X 1AF, **ENGLAND**.
(T) 020 77346905 (F) 020 77346110.
Profile Saddlery Retailer. Ref: YH01310

BERNARD, JENNIFER

Mrs Jennifer Bernard, High Oaks, The Cwm, Forden, Montgomery, **Powys**, SY15 8NB, **WALES**.
(T) 01938 580563 (F) 01938 580563.
Profile Breeder. Ref: YH01311

BERNEY BROS

Berney Bros, Kilcullen, **County Kildare**, **IRELAND**.
(T) 045 481228 (F) 045 481094.
Profile Supplies. Ref: YH01312

BERRIEWOOD FARM

Berriewood Farm, Dorrington, Shrewsbury, **Shropshire**, SY5 7NN, **ENGLAND**.
(T) 01743 718252 (F) 01743 718163.
Contact/s
Secretary: Mrs P Cowdy
Profile Riding School, Stable/Livery. Ref: YH01313

BERRY ANIMAL FEEDS

Berry Animal Feeds, Morfa Bach Farm, Kidwelly, **Carmarthenshire**, SA17 4RN, **WALES**.
(T) 01554 890291 (F) 01554 890291.
Profile Feed Merchant. Ref: YH01314

BERRY, ANDREW I

Andrew I Berry DWCF, Bush Hse, Bury Rd, Hargrave, Bury St Edmunds, **Suffolk**, IP29 5HP, **ENGLAND**.
(T) 01284 850397
(M) 07774 601473.
Profile Farrier. Ref: YH01315

BERRY, FRANK

Frank Berry, Naas, Kilcullen, **County Kildare**, **IRELAND**.
(T) 045 481258 (F) 045 441557
(E) frankberrry@kildarehorse.ie
(W) www.kildarehorse.ie.
Contact/s
Trainer: Mr F Berry
Profile Trainer. Ref: YH01316

BERRY, N

Miss N Berry, Great Water Farm, Homestall Rd, Ashurst Wood, East Grinstead, **Sussex (West)**, RH19 3PQ, **ENGLAND**.
(T) 01342 824263.
Profile Supplies. Ref: YH01317

BERRYLANDS STABLES

Berrylands Stables, Berrylands Farm, Stanford Common, Pirbright, Woking, **Surrey**, GU24 0DG, **ENGLAND**.
(T) 01483 237642.
Contact/s
Owner: Mrs Y Gales Ref: YH01318

BERRYMAN-HORNE, A

Mrs A Berryman-Horne, Southlea Farm, Datchett, Slough, **Berkshire**, SL3 9BZ, **ENGLAND**.
(T) 01753 548541.
Profile Breeder. Ref: YH01319

BERRY'S HORSEFEEDS

Berry's Horsefeeds, Cattle Market Yard, Sumner St, Blackburn, **Lancashire**, BB2 2LD, **ENGLAND**.
(T) 01772 683276.
Profile Supplies. Ref: YH01320

BERTRAM, IAN

Ian Bertram, 7 Houston Mains, Uphall, Broxburn, **Lothian (West)**, EH52 6JU, **SCOTLAND**.
(T) 01506 811626.
Profile Supplies. Ref: YH01321

BERWICK, JOHN H

John H Berwick DWCF, Cullensmoor, North Bovey, Newton Abbot, **Devon**, TQ13 8RB, **ENGLAND**.
(T) 01647 440192.
Profile Farrier. Ref: YH01322

BEST & BEST

Best & Best, The Veterinary Surgery, 32 West Hill, Portishead, **Somerset (North)**, BS20 9LN, **ENGLAND**.
(T) 01275 847400.
Profile Medical Support. Ref: YH01323

BEST BOOTS

Best Boots Limited, Nettleton, Chippenham, **Wiltshire**, SN14 7NS, **ENGLAND**.
(T) 01249 783530 (F) 01249 782058
(E) info@bestboots.co.uk
(W) www.bestboots.co.uk.
Contact/s
Owner: Mr D Connors
(E) derry@bestboots.co.uk
Profile Riding Wear Retailer, Supplies. No.Staff: 2
Yr. Est: 1995
Opening Times
Sp: Open Appointment Only.
Su: Open Appointment Only.
Au: Open Appointment only.
Wn: Open Appointment only. Ref: YH01324

BEST CLEANING SV

Best Cleaning Service, Unit 2 Willow Farm, Finningham Rd, Rickinghall, Diss, **Norfolk**, IP22 1LQ, **ENGLAND**.
(T) 01379 890144.
Contact/s
Partner: Mr K Hare Ref: YH01325

BEST, J R

Mr J R Best, Scragged Oak Farm, Scragged Oak Rd, Hucking, Maidstone, **Kent**, ME17 1QU, **ENGLAND**.
(T) 01622 880276 (F) 01622 880904
(M) 07889 362154.
Profile Trainer. Ref: YH01326

BEST/THOROUGHBRED RACING GB

Bank End Stud Thoroughbreds, Bank End Stud, North Somercotes, Louth, **Lincolnshire**, LN11 7LN, **ENGLAND**.
(T) 01507 358146 (F) 01507 358824
(E) info@thoroughbredracinggb.co.uk
(W) www.thoroughbredracinggb.co.uk
Affiliated Bodies TBA.
Contact/s
General Manager: Ms J Powell
(E) powell447@btinternet.co.uk
Profile Blood Stock Agency, Breeder, Stable/Livery.
Racehorse Resting and Horse Rehabilitation
No.Staff: 7 Yr. Est: 1988 C.Size: 50 Acres
Ref: YH01327

BEST-TURNER, W DE

Mr W De Best-Turner, West Overton, Marlborough, **Wiltshire**, SN8 1QE, **ENGLAND**.
(T) 07977 910779 (F) 01249 813850
(E) northfarmracing@aol.com.
Profile Trainer. Ref: YH01328

BESWICK, H F

H F Beswick, Horton Head Farm, Horton, Leek, **Staffordshire**, ST13 8PQ, **ENGLAND**.
(T) 01538 306212.
Contact/s
Owner: Mr H Beswick
Profile Transport/Horse Boxes. Ref: YH01329

BETA

British Equestrian Trade Association Limited, East Wing, Stockeld Pk, Wetherby, **Yorkshire (West)**, LS22 4AW, **ENGLAND**.
(T) 01937 587062 (F) 01937 582728
(W) www.beta-uk.org.
Contact/s
Chief Executive: Ms C Williams
(E) claire@beta-uk.org
Profile Club/Association.
Safety Standards Agency. No.Staff: 3
Yr. Est: 1978 Ref: YH01330

BETCHWORTH FORGE

Betchworth Forge, The Street, Betchworth, **Surrey**, RH3 7DW, **ENGLAND**.
(T) 01737 844846 (F) 01737 844213.
Contact/s
Manager: Mr A Hazeltine
Profile Blacksmith. Ref: YH01331

BETHEL, J D W

J D W Bethel, Clarendon Hse, Market Pl, Middleham, Leyburn, **Yorkshire (North)**, DL8 4NP, **ENGLAND**.
(T) 01969 622962 (F) 01969 622157.
Contact/s
Owner: Mr J Bethel
Profile Trainer. **Ref: YH01332**

BETHELL, W A

Mr W A Bethell, Arnold Manor, Arnold, **Nottinghamshire**, HU11 5HP, **ENGLAND**.
(T) 01964 562996.
Profile Supplies. **Ref: YH01333**

BETTER-TACK

Better-Tack, Middledene, Surfleet Rd, Surfleet, Spalding, **Lincolnshire**, PE11 4AG, **ENGLAND**.
(T) 01775 680368.
Contact/s
Owner: Mrs M Bettinson
Profile Saddlery Retailer. **Ref: YH01334**

BETTING OFFICE LICENSEES

Betting Office Licensees Association, 3 A Lower James St, London, **London (Greater)**, WIF 9EH, **ENGLAND**.
(T) 020 74342111 (F) 020 74340444.
Contact/s
Chairman: Mr C Bell
Profile Club/Association. Yr. Est: 1975
Opening Times
Sp: Open Mon - Fri 09:00. Closed Mon - Fri 17:00.
Su: Open Mon - Fri 09:00. Closed Mon - Fri 17:00.
Au: Open Mon - Fri 09:00. Closed Mon - Fri 17:00.
Wn: Open Mon - Fri 09:00. Closed Mon - Fri 17:00.
Ref: YH01335

BETTISON, CARL

Carl Bettison AWCF Hons, 16 Ayleswater, Watermead, Aylesbury, **Buckinghamshire**, HP19 3FB, **ENGLAND**.
(T) 01296 395320.
Profile Farrier. **Ref: YH01336**

BEVAN, E G

Mr E G Bevan, Pullen Farm, Ullingswick, **Herefordshire**, HR1 3JQ, **ENGLAND**.
(T) 01432 820370.
Profile Supplies. **Ref: YH01337**

BEVAN, G W

G W Bevan, 38 St Neots Rd, Eltisley/St Neots, Huntingdon, **Cambridgeshire**, PE19 4TE, **ENGLAND**.
(T) 01480 880303.
Contact/s
Owner: Mr G Bevan
Profile Blacksmith. **Ref: YH01338**

BEVAN, LYNNE

Lynne Bevan, Cwmyoy Farm, Cwmyoy, Abergavenny, **Monmouthshire**, NP7 7NT, **WALES**.
(T) 01873 890288
(M) 07831 414667. **Ref: YH01339**

BEVAN, R E M

R E M Bevan, Little Langley, Bardney Rd, Wragby, Market Rasen, **Lincolnshire**, LN3 5JE, **ENGLAND**.
(T) 01673 858387.
Profile Farrier. **Ref: YH01340**

BEVERLEY HSE STABLES

Beverley House Stables, Exeter Rd, Newmarket, **Suffolk**, CB8 8LR, **ENGLAND**.
(T) 01638 601797 (F) 01638 663512
(M) 07802 663256
(W) www.newmarketracehorsetrainers.co.uk
Affiliated Bodies Newmarket Trainers Fed.
Profile Trainer. **Ref: YH01341**

BEVERLEY HYMERS SADDLERY

Beverley Hymers Saddlery Workshop, Achavrole, Halkirk, **Highlands**, KW12 6XQ, **SCOTLAND**.
(T) 01847 831750 (F) 01847 831750
Affiliated Bodies BETA, BHS.
Contact/s
Owner: Mrs B Hymers (Q) Saddle Fitter
(T) 01437 781238
Profile Equestrian Centre, Riding Wear Retailer, Saddlery Retailer. College.
North Highland College. Shetland and Highland Pony Show Headcollars (made to measure) No.Staff: 1
Yr. Est: 1994 C.Size: 300 Acres
Opening Times
Sp: Open 11:00. Closed 18:00.
Su: Open 11:00. Closed 18:00.
Au: Open 11:00. Closed 20:00.
Wn: Open 11:00. Closed 20:00. **Ref: YH01342**

BEVERLEY RACE

Beverley Race Co Ltd, The Racecourse, York Rd, Beverley, **Yorkshire (East)**, HU17 8QZ, **ENGLAND**.
(T) 01482 867488 (F) 01482 863892.
Profile Track/Course. **Ref: YH01343**

BEVIN BUTLER & DRUMMOND

Bevin Butler & Drummond, 124 Northampton Rd, Market Harborough, **Leicestershire**, LE16 9HF, **ENGLAND**.
(T) 01858 462839 (F) 01858 469127.
Profile Medical Support. **Ref: YH01344**

BEVIS, RICHARD

Mr Richard Bevis, Welsh View, Back Lane, Threapwood, Malpas, **Cheshire**, SY14 7AT, **ENGLAND**.
(T) 01948 770427
(M) 07802 446045.
Profile Trainer. **Ref: YH01345**

BEVRIDGE

Bevridge Farrier & Light Fabrication, Midtown Farm, Craigenhill Rd, Kilncadzow, Carluke, **Lanarkshire (South)**, ML8 4QS, **SCOTLAND**.
(T) 01555 771531.
Profile Farrier. **Ref: YH01346**

BEWERLEY

Bewerley School Of Horsemanship, Bewerley Old Hall, Bewerley, Harrogate, **Yorkshire (North)**, HG3 5JA, **ENGLAND**.
(T) 01423 712249 (F) 01423 712578.
Contact/s
Instructor: Ms R Dunn (Q) NVQ 2
Profile Riding School, Stable/Livery.
Full livery, hacking and trekking available.
No.Staff: 5 Yr. Est: 1964 C.Size: 35 Acres
Opening Times
Sp: Open Tues - Sun 08:00. Closed Tues - Sun 20:00.
Su: Open Tues - Sun 08:00. Closed Tues - Sun 20:00.
Au: Open Tues - Sun 08:00. Closed Tues - Sun 20:00.
Wn: Open Tues - Sun 08:00. Closed Tues - Sun 20:00. **Ref: YH01347**

BEWLEY, J R

Mr J R Bewley, Overton Bush, Camptown, Jedburgh, **Scottish Borders**, TD8 6RW, **SCOTLAND**.
(T) 01835 840273.
Profile Supplies. **Ref: YH01348**

BEXMINSTER

Bexminster Ltd, 21 Grove Rd, Emmer Green, Reading, **Berkshire**, RG4 8LJ, **ENGLAND**.
(T) 0118 9470654.
Profile Supplies.
Hay suppled has been analysed specifically for race horses. No.Staff: 2 Yr. Est: 1978
Opening Times
Sp: Open Mon - Sun 08:00. Closed Mon - Sun 20:00.
Su: Open Mon - Sun 08:00. Closed Mon - Sun 20:00.
Au: Open Mon - Sun 08:00. Closed Mon - Sun 20:00.
Wn: Open Mon - Sun 08:00. Closed Mon - Sun 20:00. **Ref: YH01349**

BEXWELL TRACTORS

Bexwell Tractors limited, Bexwell, Downham Market, **Norfolk**, PE38 9LU, **ENGLAND**.
(T) 01366 383301 (F) 01366 384930.
Profile Supplies. **Ref: YH01350**

BHDTA

British Horse Driving Trials Association (The), Dykeland Farm, Brandsby, York, **Yorkshire (North)**, YO61 4SF, **ENGLAND**.
(T) 01347 878789 (F) 01347 878776
(W) www.horsedrivingtrials.co.uk
Affiliated Bodies BEF.
Contact/s
Executive Officer: Mrs J Holah
(E) bhdta@dial.pipex.com
Profile Club/Association. **Ref: YH01351**

BHS

British Horse Society Scotland (Grampian Region), Newton Mhor, Methlick, Ellon, **Aberdeenshire**, AB42 8JN, **SCOTLAND**.
(T) 01358 761416
(W) www.bhsscotland.org.uk
Profile Club/Association. **Ref: YH01352**

BHS

British Horse Society (North East), Brynglas, Betws-Un-Rhos, Abergele, **Conwy**, LL22 9PY, **WALES**.
(T) 01745 720243
(W) www.bhs.org.uk.
Profile Club/Association. **Ref: YH01353**

BHS

British Horse Society (Dumfries & Galloway Region), Duncraig, Auchencaien, Castle Douglas, **Dumfries and Galloway**, DG7 1QV, **SCOTLAND**.
(T) 01556 640213
(E) dumfriesgalloway@bhsscotland.org.uk
(W) www.bhsscotland.org.uk.
Contact/s
Chairperson: Mrs P Culham
Profile Club/Association. **Ref: YH01354**

BHS

British Horse Society (Fife Region), Ingleside Hse, Leslie, **Fife**, KY6 3JA, **SCOTLAND**.
(T) 01592 741774
(W) www.bhsscotland.org.uk.
Profile Club/Association. **Ref: YH01355**

BHS

British Horse Society (North West), Bryn Llyn, Bodedern, **Gwynedd**, LL55 4TS, **WALES**.
(T) 01407 741106
(W) www.bhs.org.uk.
Profile Club/Association. **Ref: YH01356**

BHS

British Horse Society (Greater London Region), 92 Birkbeck Rd, Sidcup, **Kent**, DA14 4DW, **ENGLAND**.
(T) 020 83005656
(W) www.bhs.org.uk.
Profile Club/Association. **Ref: YH01357**

BHS

British Horse Society (Strathclyde Region), Muirsland, Lemahagowh, **Lanarkshire (South)**, ML11 OHY, **SCOTLAND**.
(T) 01555 893388
(W) www.bhs.org.uk.
Profile Club/Association. **Ref: YH01358**

BHS

British Horse Society (North West Region), New Croft, Whittingham Lane, Goosnargh, Preston, **Lancashire**, PR3 2JJ, **ENGLAND**.
(T) 01772 865680 (F) 01772 865680
(W) www.bhs.org.uk.
Contact/s
Chairperson: Mr M Sullivan
Profile Club/Association. **Ref: YH01359**

BHS

British Horse Society (East Midlands Region), Temple Grange, Navenby, **Lincolnshire**, LN5 OAU, **ENGLAND**.
(T) 01522 810203
(W) www.bhs.org.uk.
Contact/s
Chairperson: Mrs E Harding
Profile Club/Association. **Ref: YH01360**

BHS

British Horse Society (Lothian Region), Croft Dyke, Roslin Glen, Roslin, **Lothian (Mid)**, EH25 9PX, **SCOTLAND**.
(T) 0131 4402247 (F) 0131 4402247
(E) pipeat@aol.com
(W) www.bhs.org.uk.
Contact/s
Chairman: Mrs P Peat
Profile Club/Association. Yr. Est: 1947
Ref: YH01361

BHS

British Horse Society (Chairman), Wester Gormyre, Torpichen, Bathgate, **Lothian (West)**, EH48 4NA, **SCOTLAND**.
(T) 01506 652598 (F) 01506 652598
(W) www.bhsscotland.org.uk.
Profile Club/Association. **Ref: YH01362**

BHS

British Horse Society (Eastern Region), Rose Acre Riding Stables, Back Mundesley Rd, Gislingham, Norwich, **Norfolk**, NR11 8HN, **ENGLAND**.
(T) 01263 720671
(W) www.bhs.org.uk.
Contact/s
Chairperson: Mrs J Self
Profile Club/Association. **Ref: YH01363**

BHS

British Horse Society (North Region), High Leam, West Woodburn, Hexham, **Northumberland**, NE48 2SZ, **ENGLAND**.
(T) 01434 270236
(W) www.bhs.org.uk.
Contact/s
Chairperson: Lt Col R Cross OBE
Profile Club/Association. Ref: YH01364

BHS

British Horse Society (South Region), Downs Hollow, Burford Rd, Chipping Norton, **Oxfordshire**, OX7 5XB, **ENGLAND**.
(T) 01608 642643 **(F)** 01608 642648
(E) bhssouth@aol.com
(W) www.members.aol.com/bhssouth.
Contact/s
Development Officer: Mr L Denham
(T) 01285 810726
(E) lendenham@aol.com
Profile Club/Association. Ref: YH01365

BHS

British Horse Society (Development Officer), Woodburn Farm, Crieff, **Perth and Kinross**, PH7 3RG, **SCOTLAND**.
(T) 01764 654364 **(F)** 01764 654364
(W) www.bhsscotland.org.uk.
Profile Club/Association. Ref: YH01366

BHS

British Horse Society (Border Region), Easter Softlaw, Kelso, **Scottish Borders**, TD5 8BJ, **SCOTLAND**.
(T) 01573 224641
(W) www.bhs.org.uk.
Contact/s
Chairperson: Mrs V Scott-Watson
Profile Club/Association. Ref: YH01367

BHS

British Horse Society (Central Region), Meikle Canglour Farm, Strirling, **Stirling**, FK7 9QP, **SCOTLAND**.
(T) 01324 822696
(W) www.bhsscotland.org.uk.
Contact/s
Chairperson: Mrs P Whittaker
Profile Club/Association. Ref: YH01368

BHS

British Horse Society (South East Region), 23 Barn Cl, Albourne, Nr Hurstpierpoint, Hassocks, **Sussex (West)**, BN6 9DG, **ENGLAND**.
(T) 01273 834978 **(F)** 01273 834978
(W) www.bhs.org.uk.
Profile Club/Association. Ref: YH01369

BHS

British Horse Society (West Midlands Region), The Old Central Stores, Ulenhall, Solihull, **Warwickshire**, B95 5PB, **ENGLAND**.
(T) 01564 792655 **(F)** 01564 794980
(W) www.bhs.org.uk.
Profile Club/Association. Ref: YH01370

BHS

British Horse Society (The), Stoneleigh Deer Pk, Kenilworth, **Warwickshire**, CV8 2XZ, **ENGLAND**.
(T) 01926 707700 **(F)** 01926 707800
(W) www.bhs.org.uk.
Contact/s
Chief Executive: Ms K Driver **(T)** 0870 1202244
Profile Club/Association. Ref: YH01371

BHS

British Horse Society (South West Region), The Curates Egg, Dymocks Lane, Sutton Veny, Warminster, **Wiltshire**, BA12 7AX, **ENGLAND**.
(T) 01985 840515/213925 **(F)** 01985 840515
(W) www.bhs.org.uk.
Contact/s
Chairperson: Mr R Sullivan-Tailyour
Profile Club/Association. Ref: YH01372

BHS

British Horse Society (Yorkshire Region), Wassock Hse Farm, Langthorne, Badale, **Yorkshire (North)**, DL8 1PL, **ENGLAND**.
(T) 01677 422276 **(F)** 01677 427747
(W) www.bhs.org.uk.
Profile Club/Association. Ref: YH01373

BHS

British Horse Society Yorkshire Region, Long Lane Cl, Ackworth, Pontefract, **Yorkshire (West)**, WF7 7EY, **ENGLAND**.
(T) 01977 795450 **(F)** 01977 795470
(W) www.bhs.org.uk.
Contact/s
Administration: Mrs A Harris
Profile Club/Association. Ref: YH01374

BHS (SCOTLAND)

British Horse Society (Scotland), Woodburn, Crieff, **Perth and Kinross**, PH7 3RG, **SCOTLAND**.
(T) 01764 656334 **(F)** 01764 656334
(E) bhsscot@aol.com
(W) www.bhsscotland.org.uk.
Contact/s
Development Officer: Mrs H Mauchlen
Profile Club/Association. Charity. Ref: YH01375

BHS CHAIRMAN

British Horse Society Chairman (Wales), Fayre Oaks, Cefnllys Lane, Llandrindod Wells, **Powys**, LD1 5LE, **WALES**.
(T) 01597 822518.
Profile Club/Association. Ref: YH01376

BHS DEVELOPMENT (N IRE)

British Horse Society Development Officer (Northern Ireland), Hse Of Sport, Upper Malone Rd, Belfast, **County Antrim**, BT9 5LA, **NORTHERN IRELAND**.
(T) 028 90383816 **(F)** 028 90682757
(E) bhsireland@aol.com.
Profile Club/Association. Ref: YH01377

BHS INSURANCE HUNTER TRIALS

British Horse Society Insurance Hunter Trials (Compton), New Farm, Compton, Newbury, **Berkshire**, RG20 6NT, **ENGLAND**.
(T) 01844 281178 **(F)** 01844 281178.
Profile Club/Association. Ref: YH01378

BHS INSURANCE HUNTER TRIALS

British Horse Society Insurance Hunter Trials (Newbury), Kingsclere, Newbury, **Berkshire**, RG20 5PY, **ENGLAND**.
(T) 01844 281178 **(F)** 01844 281178.
Profile Club/Association. Ref: YH01379

BHS INSURANCE HUNTER TRIALS

British Horse Society Insurance Hunter Trials (Burnham), Snowball Farm, Dorney Wood Rd, Burnham, **Buckinghamshire**, SL1 8EH, **ENGLAND**.
(T) 01844 281178 **(F)** 01844 281178.
Profile Club/Association. Ref: YH01380

BHS INSURANCE HUNTER TRIALS

British Horse Society Insurance Hunter Trials (Great Missenden), Deep Mill Farm, London Rd, Little Kingshill, Great Missenden, **Buckinghamshire**, HP16 0DH, **ENGLAND**.
(T) 01844 281178 **(F)** 01844 281178.
Profile Club/Association. Ref: YH01381

BHS INSURANCE HUNTER TRIALS

British Horse Society Insurance Hunter Trials (East Meon), Bereleigh Est, East Meon, Petersfield, **Hampshire**, GU32 1PH, **ENGLAND**.
(T) 01844 281178 **(F)** 01844 281178.
Profile Club/Association. Ref: YH01382

BHS INSURANCE HUNTER TRIALS

British Horse Society Insurance Hunter Trials (Ascott under Wychwood), Crown Farm, Ascott Under Wychwood, **Oxfordshire**, **ENGLAND**.
(T) 01844 281178 **(F)** 01844 281178.
Profile Club/Association. Ref: YH01383

BHS INSURANCE HUNTER TRIALS

British Horse Society Insurance Hunter Trials (Henley on Thames), Rosehill, The Coach Hse, Henley-on-Thames, **Oxfordshire**, **ENGLAND**.
(T) 01844 281178 **(F)** 01844 281178.
Profile Club/Association. Ref: YH01384

BHS INSURANCE HUNTER TRIALS

British Horse Society Insurance Hunter Trials (Camberley), Sandhurst, R.M.A., Camberley, **Surrey**, GU15 4PQ, **ENGLAND**.
(T) 01844 281178 **(F)** 01844 281178.
Profile Club/Association. Ref: YH01385

BHS RIDING CLUBS

British Horse Society Riding Clubs, Monte Bre, Upper Malone Rd, Belfast, **County Antrim**, BT9 5PE, **NORTHERN IRELAND**.
(T) 028 90611567.
Contact/s
Chairman: Mrs S Laird
Profile Club/Association. Ref: YH01386

BHS WALES

British Horse Society (South East), Woodlands Farm, Caerphilly Mountain, Caerphilly, **Caerphilly**, CF83 1NF, **WALES**.
(T) 029 20885697 **(F)** 029 20888639
(W) www.bhs.org.uk.
Contact/s
Chairman: Mrs J Hyett
Profile Club/Association. Ref: YH01387

BHS WALES

British Horse Society (Wales), Rhydyfirian Cottage, Nanteos Lane, Aberystwyth, **Ceredigion**, SY23 4LU, **WALES**.
(T) 01970 617730 **(F)** 01970 617730
(E) bhswales@aol.com.
Contact/s
Development Officer: Mrs W Davies
Profile Club/Association, Trainer.
Ref: YH01388

BIAC

British Institute of Agricultural Consultants, The Estate Office, Torry Hill, Milstead, Sittingbourne, **Kent**, ME9 0SP, **ENGLAND**.
(T) 01795 830100 **(F)** 01795 830243.
Contact/s
Chief Executive: Mr C Hyde
Profile Medical Support. Ref: YH01389

BIBBY'S

Bibby's, 12 King St, Blackpool, **Lancashire**, FY1 3EJ, **ENGLAND**.
(T) 01253 20977. Ref: YH01390

BICESTER TRAILERS

Bicester Trailers, Troy, Somerton, Bicester, **Oxfordshire**, OX6 4NG, **ENGLAND**.
(T) 01869 345576.
Profile Transport/Horse Boxes. Ref: YH01391

BICKERSTAFFE HALL STABLE YARD

Bickerstaffe Hall Stable Yard, Hall Lane, Bickerstaffe, Ormskirk, **Lancashire**, L39 0EH, **ENGLAND**.
(T) 01695 722023.
Profile Stable/Livery. Ref: YH01392

BICKERTON, P E

Mrs P E Bickerton, 3 Pixley Cottages, Hinstock, Market Drayton, **Shropshire**, TF9 2TN, **ENGLAND**.
(T) 01952 550384
(M) 07966 441001.
Profile Supplies. Ref: YH01393

BICTON CLGE OF AGRICULTURE

Bicton College of Agriculture, East Budleigh, Budleigh Salterton, **Devon**, EX9 7BY, **ENGLAND**.
(T) 01395 562373 **(F)** 01395 567502
(W) www.bicton.ac.uk.
Profile Equestrian Centre. College.
College offering equine studies. Ref: YH01394

BICTON HORSE TRIALS

Bicton Horse Trials (Horse & Hound), St Giles Cottage, Northleigh, Colyton, **Devon**, EX24 6BL, **ENGLAND**.
(T) 01404 871296 **(F)** 01404 813276. Ref: YH01395

BIDDESDEN STUD

Biddesden Stud, Biddesden Hse, Andover, **Hampshire**, SP11 9DN, **ENGLAND**.
(T) 01264 790646 **(F)** 01264 791232.
Profile Breeder. Ref: YH01396

BIDDESTONE STUD

Biddestone Stud, Grooms Cottage, The Green, Biddestone, Chippenham, **Wiltshire**, SN14 7DG, **ENGLAND**.
(T) 01249 713349.
Contact/s
Manager: Mr I Bradbury
Profile Breeder. Ref: YH01397

BIDDY PALMER DESIGNS

Biddy Palmer Designs, 236 Courthouse Rd, Maidenhead, **Berkshire**, SL6 6HE, **ENGLAND**.
(T) 01628 781902. Ref: YH01398

BIDWELLS

Bidwells (Cambs), Trumpington Rd, Cambridge, **Cambridgeshire**, CB2 2LD, **ENGLAND**.
(T) 01223 841841 **(F)** 01223 845150. Ref: YH01399

BIDWELLS OF COGMILLS

Bidwells of Cogmills, Bristol Rd, Frampton Cotterell, **Gloucestershire (South)**, BS36 2AP, **ENGLAND**.

(T) 01454 772228.
Contact/s
Owner: Mr M Bidwell
Profile Saddlery Retailer. Ref: YH01400

BIELBYS OF SCARBOROUGH

Bielbys of Scarborough, 51 - 53 Victoria Rd, Scarborough, **Yorkshire (North)**, YO11 1SH, **ENGLAND**.
(T) 01723 361648 (F) 01723 361648. Ref: YH01401

BIG ARCH STABLES

Big Arch Stables, Castle Cottage, Castlewood, Talywain, Pontypool, **Monmouthshire**, NP4 7UF, **WALES**.
(T) 01495 774723. Ref: YH01402

BIGG, STEVEN N

Steven N Bigg DWCF, 68 Long Copse, Holbury, Southampton, **Hampshire**, SO45 2LA, **ENGLAND**.
(T) 023 80893255.
Profile Farrier. Ref: YH01403

BIGGLESWADE SADDLERY

Biggleswade Saddlery, South View, (off Hitchin St), Biggleswade, **Bedfordshire**, SG18 8BZ, **ENGLAND**.
(T) 01767 316089 (F) 01767 316089
(E) sales@biggleswadesaddlery.co.uk
(W) www.biggleswadesaddlery.co.uk.
Contact/s
Assistant Manager: Ms L Clifton
Profile Riding Wear Retailer, Saddlery Retailer, Supplies.
All ages and abilities are catered for. Clippers also available for hire. No.Staff: 3 Yr. Est: 1979
Opening Times
Sp: Open Mon - Sat 09:00, Sun 12:00. Closed Mon - Sat 18:00, Sun 16:00.
Su: Open Mon - Sat 09:00, Sun 12:00. Closed Mon - Sat 18:00, Sun 16:00.
Au: Open Mon - Sat 09:00, Sun 12:00. Closed Mon - Sat 18:00, Sun 16:00.
Wn: Open Mon - Sat 09:00, Sun 12:00. Closed Mon - Sat 18:00, Sun 16:00. Ref: YH01404

BIGLEY, L

Mr & Mrs L Bigley, The Quakers Farm, Michaelchurch, Eascley, **Hertfordshire**, HR2 0PT, **ENGLAND**.
(T) 01981 510667.
Profile Breeder. Ref: YH01405

BIGWOOD, FIONA

Fiona Bigwood, Charts Edge, Hosey Hill, Westerham, **Kent**, TN16 1PL, **ENGLAND**.
(T) 01959 561205 (F) 01959 565641. Ref: YH01406

BILL BIRD BOOTS & SHOES

Bill Bird Boots & Shoes, 49 Northwick Business Ctre, Blockley, Moreton In Marsh, **Gloucestershire**, GL56 9RF, **ENGLAND**.
(T) 01386 700855.
Profile Riding Wear Retailer. Ref: YH01407

BILL FELLOWES TRAILERS

Bill Fellowes Trailers, The Elms, Kennett, Newmarket, **Suffolk**, CB8 7QL, **ENGLAND**.
(T) 01440 820113.
Profile Transport/Horse Boxes. Ref: YH01408

BILLERICAY & DISTRICT

Billericay & District Riding Club, Red Roofs, Homestead Rd, Ramsden Bellhouse, Billericay, **Essex**, CM11 1RD, **ENGLAND**.
(T) 01268 710559.
Contact/s
Chairman: Mrs J Kemsley
Profile Club/Association, Riding Club. Ref: YH01409

BILLERICAY & DISTRICT

Billericay & District Riding Club Affiliated Dressage, Elm Tree Cottage, Oak Rd, Crays Hill, Billericay, **Essex**, CM11 2YL, **ENGLAND**.
(T) 01268 521040.
Profile Club/Association. Ref: YH01410

BILLERICAY FARM SVS

Billericay Farm Services Ltd, 12-14 School Rd, Downham, Billericay, **Essex**, CM11 1QU, **ENGLAND**.
(T) 01268 710237 (F) 01268 711040
(E) billericay@compuserve.com.
Profile Supplies. Ref: YH01411

BILLINGE, J N R

Mr J N R Billinge, Hilton Farm, Cupar, **Fife**, KY15 4QD, **SCOTLAND**.
(T) 01334 655180.
Profile Supplies. Ref: YH01412

BILLINGTON, G

G Billington, Tatham Farm Stables, Tatham Rd, Ruabon, Wrexham, **Wrexham**, LL14 6RF, **WALES**.
(T) 01978 821310.
Profile Stable/Livery. Ref: YH01413

BILLINGTON, GEOFF

Geoff Billington, Halle-Coole Stud, Heatley Lane, Newhall, Nantwich, **Cheshire**, CW5 8AZ, **ENGLAND**.
(T) 01270 780665 (F) 01270 780885
(M) 07785 301919.
Profile Trainer. Ref: YH01414

BILSDALE

Bilsdale, Hesketh Grange, Boltby, Thirsk, **Yorkshire (North)**, YO7 2HU, **ENGLAND**.
(T) 01845 537375. Ref: YH01415

BILSDALE RIDING CTRE

Bilsdale Riding Centre, Shaken Bridge Farm, Hawnby, York, **Yorkshire (North)**, YO62 5LT, **ENGLAND**.
(T) 01439 798252.
Contact/s
Owner: Mr A Cain
Profile Equestrian Centre, Riding School, Stable/Livery. Ref: YH01416

BILTON VETNRY CTRE

Bilton Veterinary Centre, 259 Bilton Rd, Rugby, **Warwickshire**, CV22 7EQ, **ENGLAND**.
(T) 01788 812650 (F) 01788 522439.
Contact/s
Manager: Mrs L Reece
Profile Medical Support. Ref: YH01417

BIMEDA

Bimeda, Bryn Cefni Ind Pk, Llangefni, **Isle of Anglesey**, LL77 7XA, **WALES**.
(T) 01248 725400 (F) 01248 725416.
Profile Medical Support. Ref: YH01418

BINCOMBE STUD

Bincombe Stud, Bincombe, Over Stowey, Bridgwater, **Somerset**, TA5 1EZ, **ENGLAND**.
(T) 01278 732273.
Profile Breeder. Ref: YH01419

BINFIELD HEATH POLO CLUB

Binfield Heath Polo Club, Mulberries, Dove Lane, Peppard Common, Henley-on-Thames, **Oxfordshire**, RG9 5RQ, **ENGLAND**.
(T) 01491 628727 (F) 01491 628727.
Profile Club/Association. Polo Club. Ref: YH01420

BINGHAM TRAILERS

Bingham Trailers, 107 Nottingham Rd, Cropwell Bishop, Nottingham, **Nottinghamshire**, NG12 3BA, **ENGLAND**.
(T) 0115 9894555 (F) 0115 9899033.
Profile Transport/Horse Boxes. Ref: YH01421

BINGHAM, R J

R J Bingham, Outovercott, Lynton, **Devon**, EX35 6JR, **ENGLAND**.
(T) 01598 753341.
Contact/s
Owner: Mrs S Bingham
Profile Riding School. Ref: YH01422

BINNS BOOKS

Binns Books, The Granary, Village Farm, Byram Cum Sutton, Knottingley, **Yorkshire (West)**, WF11 9NB, **ENGLAND**.
(T) 01977 607068.
Profile Supplies. Ref: YH01423

BINNS, A E G

A E G Binns, 62 The Garth, Cottingham, **Yorkshire (East)**, HU16 5BG, **ENGLAND**.
(T) 01482 843667.
Profile Farrier. Ref: YH01424

BINNS, ROSS BARRY

Ross Barry Binns, 18 West End Rd, Cottingham, **Yorkshire (East)**, HU16 5PN, **ENGLAND**.
(T) 01482 843662.
Profile Farrier. Ref: YH01425

BINNS, T J

T J Binns, Carr Hse Farm, Carr Lane, Weel, Beverley, **Yorkshire (East)**, HU17 0SH, **ENGLAND**.
(T) 01482 871792.
Profile Farrier. Ref: YH01426

BINTREE MANOR LIVERIES

Bintree Manor Liveries, Manor Hse, Bintree, Dereham, **Norfolk**, NR20 5NE, **ENGLAND**.
(T) 01362 684338.
Profile Stable/Livery. Ref: YH01427

BIRCH FARM

Birch Farm Livery & Equestrian School, White Stubbs Lane, Broxbourne, **Hertfordshire**, EN10 7QA, **ENGLAND**.
(T) 01992 467738.
Profile Riding School, Stable/Livery. Ref: YH01428

BIRCH, BRIAN

Brian Birch, Barn Cottage, Temple Guiting, Cheltenham, **Gloucestershire**, GL54 5XX, **ENGLAND**.
(T) 01386 852220.
Profile Farrier. Ref: YH01429

BIRCH, MICHAEL E

Michael E Birch, The Forge/Palmers Cross Farm, Codsall Rd, Wolverhampton, **Midlands (West)**, WV6 9QG, **ENGLAND**.
(T) 01902 751049.
Contact/s
Owner: Mrs C Birch
Profile Stable/Livery. Ref: YH01430

BIRCHALLS THE RIDING SHOP

Birchalls The Riding Shop, Pleasant View Garden Ctre, Plough Wents Rd, Chart Sutton, Maidstone, **Kent**, ME17 3SA, **ENGLAND**.
(T) 01622 844104 (F) 01622 844204.
Contact/s
Owner: Mr T Featherstone (Q) Saddle Fitter, SMS
Profile Riding Wear Retailer, Saddlery Retailer.
No.Staff: 5 Yr. Est: 1897
Opening Times
Sp: Open Mon - Sat 09:00, Sun 10:00. Closed Mon - Sat 17:30, Sun 16:00.
Su: Open Mon - Sat 09:00, Sun 10:00. Closed Mon - Sat 17:30, Sun 16:00.
Au: Open Mon - Sat 09:00, Sun 10:00. Closed Mon - Sat 17:30, Sun 16:00.
Wn: Open Mon - Sat 09:00, Sun 10:00. Closed Mon - Sat 17:30, Sun 16:00. Ref: YH01431

BIRCHER, ANDREW K

Andrew K Bircher, 32 Goat Lodge Rd, Great Totham, Maldon, **Essex**, CH9 8BT, **ENGLAND**.
(T) 01621 892712.
Profile Farrier. Ref: YH01432

BIRCHES LIVERY STABLES

Birches Livery Stables, The Birches, Radfall Rd, Whitstable, **Kent**, CT5 3ER, **ENGLAND**.
(T) 01227 792256.
Contact/s
Owner: Mr L Manz
Profile Stable/Livery. Ref: YH01433

BIRCHINLEY MANOR

Birchinley Manor Equestrian Centre Ltd, Wildhouse Lane, Milnrow, Rochdale, **Lancashire**, OL16 3TW, **ENGLAND**.
(T) 01706 644484.
Profile Equestrian Centre. Ref: YH01434

BIRCHWOOD

Birchwood Riding Centre & Saddlery, 140 Birchwood Lane, Somercotes, Alfreton, **Derbyshire**, DE55 4NE, **ENGLAND**.
(T) 01773 604305.
Contact/s
Owner: Mrs L Coyle
Profile Riding School, Stable/Livery. Ref: YH01435

BIRCHWOOD

Birchwood Equestrian Services, Bridgenorth Rd, Shatterford, Bewdley, **Worcestershire**, DY12 1TP, **ENGLAND**.
(T) 01299 861529 (F) 01299 861058
(E) birchcol@aol.com
(W) www.welcome.to/birchwood.
Contact/s
Partner: Mr J Colley
Profile Equestrian Centre.
Qualified and experienced care for the convalescent horse. Also able to accomodate mares and foals at foot, in spacious foaling boxes. Full livery with 24 hour supervision available, prices on request. Access to hacking country. Yr. Est: 1994 C.Size: 30 Acres
Opening Times
Telephone for further information between 17:00 - 22:00 Ref: YH01436

BIRD, CHARLES R S

Charles R S Bird DWCF, Cherry Tree Cottage, Brome Rd, Thrandeston, Eye, **Suffolk**, **ENGLAND**.
(T) 01379 783512.

Profile Farrier. Ref: YH01437

BIRDBROOK ROSETTES

Birdbrook Rosettes, P O Box 20, Saxilby, **Lincolnshire**, LN1 2QU, **ENGLAND**.
(T) 01522 702911 **(F)** 01522 703841
(E) rosettes@birdbrook.telme.com.
Profile Supplies. Ref: YH01438

BIRKBECK, H W

Mr H W Birkbeck, Castle Hill Farm, Soulby, Kirkby Stephen, **Cumbria**, CA17 4PL, **ENGLAND**.
(T) 01768 371554.
Profile Trainer. Ref: YH01439

BIRKBY HALL

Birkby Hall Riding School & Stables, Cartmel, Grange Over Sands, **Cumbria**, LA11 7NP, **ENGLAND**.
(T) 01539 536319.
Profile Riding School, Stable/Livery, Trainer.
Ref: YH01440

BIRKETT HALL LIVERY STABLE

Birkett Hall Livery Stable, Birkett Hall, Main Rd, Woodham Ferrers, Chelmsford, **Essex**, CM3 8RJ, **ENGLAND**.
(T) 01245 320205.
Contact/s
Owner: Mr P Richardson
Profile Stable/Livery. Ref: YH01441

BIRKLAND STUD

Birkland Stud, Broomfield Farm, Drumoak, Banchory, **Aberdeenshire**, AB31 5EP, **SCOTLAND**.
(T) 01330 811316.
Contact/s
Partner: Mrs A Ross
Profile Breeder. Ref: YH01442

BIRR EQUESTRIAN CTRE

Birr Equestrian Centre Ltd, Kingsborough Hse, Birr, **County Offaly**, **IRELAND**.
(T) 0509 21961
Affiliated Bodies AIRE.
Contact/s
Owner: Noel Cosgrave
Profile Equestrian Centre, Riding School.
Have week long summer camps for children in July and August. Hacking and trekking through the Slievebloom Mountains. Hunting is avaliable by arrangement. Yr. Est: 1978 C.Size: 160 Acres
Opening Times
Sp: Open Mon - Sun 09:00. Closed Mon - Sun 21:00.
Su: Open Mon - Sun 09:00. Closed Mon - Sun 21:00.
Au: Open Mon - Sun 09:00. Closed Mon - Sun 21:00.
Wn: Open Mon - Sun 09:00. Closed Mon - Sun 21:00. Ref: YH01443

BIRR HSE RIDING CTRE

Birr House Riding Centre, 81 Whinney Hill, Dundonald, Belfast, **County Antrim**, BT16 1UA, **NORTHERN IRELAND**.
(T) 028 90425858.
Contact/s
Owner: Mrs C McVaigh
Profile Riding School, Stable/Livery. Ref: YH01444

BIRT, JENNI

Jenni Birt, Paddock Farm, Red Ball, Wellington, **Somerset**, TA21 9RA, **ENGLAND**.
(T) 01823 673144
Affiliated Bodies NAAT.
Contact/s
Physiotherapist: Jenni Birt
Profile Medical Support. Ref: YH01445

BIRTILL ENGINEERING

Birtill Engineering, Little Bytham, Grantham, **Lincolnshire**, NG33 4QY, **ENGLAND**.
(T) 01780 410330 **(F)** 01780 410078.
Profile Transport/Horse Boxes. Ref: YH01446

BIRTLE RIDING CTRE

Birtle Riding Centre, Higher Elbut Farm, Elbut Lane, Birtle, Bury, **Lancashire**, BL9 7TU, **ENGLAND**.
(T) 0161 7646573.
Profile Riding School. Ref: YH01447

BISHOP BURTON COLLEGE

Bishop Burton College, Bishop Burton, Beverley, **Yorkshire (East)**, HU17 8QG, **ENGLAND**.
(T) 01964 553000 **(F)** 01964 553101
(W) www.bishopburton.ac.uk
Affiliated Bodies BD, BE, BHS, BSJA.
Contact/s
General Manager: Miss A Paling
Profile Equestrian Centre. College.
Horse trials and show jumping competitions are also offered
Opening Times
Sp: Open Mon - Fri 09:00. Closed Mon - Fri 16:00.
Su: Open Mon - Fri 09:00. Closed Mon - Fri 16:00.
Au: Open Mon - Fri 09:00. Closed Mon - Fri 16:00.
Wn: Open Mon - Fri 09:00. Closed Mon - Fri 16:00.
Ref: YH01448

BISHOP, PETER J

Peter J Bishop DWCF, 8 Woodcombe Cottages, Woodcombe, Minehead, **Somerset**, TA24 8SE, **ENGLAND**.
(T) 01643 704768.
Profile Farrier. Ref: YH01449

BISHOP'S DOWN FARM

Bishop's Down Farm, Dundridge Lane, Bishops's Waltham, Southampton, **Hampshire**, SO3 1GD, **ENGLAND**.
(T) 01489 893535.
Profile Breeder. Ref: YH01450

BISHOPS RIDING CLUB

Bishops Riding Club, 264 Finchale Rd, Newton Hall, Durham, **County Durham**, DH1 5PR, **ENGLAND**.
(T) 0191 3860456.
Contact/s
Chairman: Miss M Hedley
Profile Club/Association, Riding Club. Ref: YH01451

BISHOPTON VETNRY GRP

Bishopton Veterinary Group, Mill Farm, Studley Rd, Ripon, **Yorkshire (North)**, HG4 2QR, **ENGLAND**.
(T) 01765 602396 **(F)** 01765 690505
(E) sheenagh@bishoptonvets.demon.co.uk.
Profile Medical Support. Ref: YH01452

BISLEY TRANSPORT SVS

Bisley Transport Services, Dovedale, Stancombe, Stroud, **Gloucestershire**, GL6 7NF, **ENGLAND**.
(T) 01452 770732 **(F)** 01452 770732.
Contact/s
Owner: Mr A Jones
Profile Transport/Horse Boxes. Ref: YH01453

BIT BANK

Bit Bank, Carlton Bank Stud, Carlton-In-Cleveland, Stokesley, **Yorkshire (North)**, TS9 7DB, **ENGLAND**.
(T) 01642 710627
(E) info@magnolife.com
(W) www.bitbank.co.uk.
Contact/s
Owner: Ms H Hyde
(E) h.hyde@bitbank.co.uk
Profile Saddlery Retailer, Supplies.
Spurs, nosebands, SWC, kangaroo and sprenger bits available. Mail order catalogues and buy online. There is no hire charge involved and unsatisfied, any money, except postage, will be refunded. No.Staff: 3
Yr. Est: 1991
Opening Times
Sp: Open Mon - Fri 09:00. Closed Mon - Fri 17:30.
Su: Open Mon - Fri 09:00. Closed Mon - Fri 17:30.
Au: Open Mon - Fri 09:00. Closed Mon - Fri 17:30.
Wn: Open Mon - Fri 09:00. Closed Mon - Fri 17:30.
Open on Saturdays unless competing. Closed Sundays. Ref: YH01454

BITCHET FARM RIDING SCHOOL

Bitchet Farm Riding School, Bitchet Green, Seal, Sevenoaks, **Kent**, TN15 0NA, **ENGLAND**.
(T) 01732 762196.
Contact/s
Owner: Mrs J Thomson
Profile Riding School. Ref: YH01455

BITS & BOOTS

Bits & Boots, 21 Scrooby Rd, Bircotes, Doncaster, **Yorkshire (South)**, DN11 8JW, **ENGLAND**.
(T) 01302 751488.
Contact/s
Partner: Mrs C Sutcliffe
Profile Riding Wear Retailer, Saddlery Retailer.
Ref: YH01456

BITS & PIECES

Bits & Pieces (Sunbury on Thames), Vicarage Farm, Halliford Rd, Sunbury-on-Thames, **Surrey**, TW16 6DW, **ENGLAND**.
(T) 01932 765145 **(F)** 01932 765145
(M) 07711 214216.
Profile Saddlery Retailer. Ref: YH01457

BITS 'N' BOBS

Bits 'N' Bobs, Sibster Mains, Wick, Caithness, **Highlands**, KW1 4TB, **SCOTLAND**.
(T) 01955 603270.
Profile Saddlery Retailer. Ref: YH01458

BLABY MILL STABLES

Blaby Mill Stables, Blaby Mill, Mill Lane, Blaby, Leicester, **Leicestershire**, LE8 4FG, **ENGLAND**.
(T) 0116 2775576.
Contact/s
Owner: Mr K Hudson
Profile Stable/Livery.
DIY livery available, prices on request. Ref: YH01459

BLACK

Mr Black, Radio Hse, Pilley St, Pilley, Lymington, **Hampshire**, SO41 8QP, **ENGLAND**.
(T) 01590 672860.
Profile Breeder. Ref: YH01460

BLACK COUNTRY SADDLERY

Black Country Saddlery, 59-61 Wednesbury Rd, Walsall, **Midlands (West)**, WS1 4JL, **ENGLAND**.
(T) 01922 626936.
Contact/s
Partner: John Hartley
Profile Saddlery Retailer. Saddler.
Saddle fitters are available at weekends but the factory is closed. Sell to wholesalers and public.
No.Staff: 7 Yr. Est: 1993
Opening Times
Sp: Open Mon - Fri 08:30. Closed Mon - Fri 17:30.
Su: Open Mon - Fri 08:30. Closed Mon - Fri 17:30.
Au: Open Mon - Fri 08:30. Closed Mon - Fri 17:30.
Wn: Open Mon - Fri 08:30. Closed Mon - Fri 17:30.
Factory closed at weekends Ref: YH01461

BLACK FORGE ART

Black Forge Art, Weather Vanes & Hse Signs, Owley Farm, Wittersham, Tenterden, **Kent**, TN30 7HJ, **ENGLAND**.
(T) 01797 270073 **(F)** 01797 270073.
Contact/s
Owner: Mr R Fender
Profile Blacksmith.
Horse key signs, weather vanes and house signs are also available. Offer a one-off commission service.
Yr. Est: 1991
Opening Times
By appointment only Ref: YH01462

BLACK HORSE

Black Horse Saddlery & Pet Supplies, 153 Chorley Rd, Standish, Wigan, **Lancashire**, WN1 2TE, **ENGLAND**.
(T) 01257 423327.
Profile Saddlery Retailer. Ref: YH01463

BLACK HORSE ACCESSORIES

Black Horse Accessories, Black Horse Farm, Aberford, Leeds, **Yorkshire (West)**, LS25 3AU, **ENGLAND**.
(T) 0113 2813498 **(F)** 0113 2811036.
Profile Supplies. Ref: YH01464

BLACK HORSE STABLES

Black Horse Stables, Ballymaleel, Letterkenny, **County Donegal**, **IRELAND**.
(T) 074 51327. Ref: YH01465

BLACK ISLE RIDING CTRE

Black Isle Riding Centre, Eich-Lann, Drumsmittal, Inverness, **Highlands**, IV1 1AX, **SCOTLAND**.
(T) 01463 731707
Affiliated Bodies ABRS.
Profile Riding School. Trekking Centre.
Off road trekking through surrounding woodland available. Ref: YH01466

BLACK KNOLL HORSE SPORTS CTRE

Black Knoll Horse Sports Centre, Rhinefield Rd, Brockenhurst, **Hampshire**, SO42 7QE, **ENGLAND**.
(T) 01590 24400 **(F)** 01590 24433.
Profile Stable/Livery. Ref: YH01467

BLACK MOUNTAIN HOLIDAYS

Black Mountain Holidays, Castle Farm, Capel-Y-Ffin, Abergavenny, **Monmouthshire**, NP7 7NP, **WALES**.
(T) 01873 890961 **(F)** 01497 821058
(E) bmholidays@btopenworld.com
(W) www.hay-on-wye.co.uk/bmholidays/.
Profile Holidays. Ref: YH01468

BLACK, ARTHUR

Arthur Black (General Smiths) Ltd, Clay Lane, Oldbury, **Midlands (West)**, B69 4TH, **ENGLAND**.
(T) 0121 5524212.
Profile Blacksmith. Ref: YH01469

BLACK, AUDREY
Audrey Black, Simms Farm, Simms Lane, Mortimer Common, Reading, **Berkshire**, RG7 2JP, **ENGLAND**.
(T) 0118 9332384.
Contact/s
Owner: Mrs A Black
Profile Stable/Livery.
DIY livery yard, details on request. **Ref: YH01470**

BLACK, C J
Mrs C J Black, Tedsmore Hall, West Felton, Oswestry, **Shropshire**, SY11 4HD, **ENGLAND**.
(T) 01691 610208.
Profile Supplies. **Ref: YH01471**

BLACK, STUART B
Stuart B Black DWCF, 95 Cornwallis Rd, Bilton, Rugby, **Warwickshire**, CV22 7HL, **ENGLAND**.
(T) 01788 522117.
Profile Farrier. **Ref: YH01472**

BLACK, WENDY
Miss Wendy Black, High Fold, Troutbeck, Windermere, **Cumbria**, LA23 1PG, **ENGLAND**.
(T) 01539 433721.
Contact/s
Owner: Miss W Black
(E) wenandden@farming.co.uk
Profile Breeder.
All the ponies are kept in their natural habitat on the fell, except foals who are kept in for their first winter. Ponies are usually for sale as foals, although some older ones are available. No.Staff: 1
Yr. Est: 1961
Opening Times
Viewing by appointment, please telephone for further details **Ref: YH01473**

BLACKACRE RIDING STABLES
Blackacre Riding Stables, Blackacre, Castle-an-dinas Road, St Columb, **Cornwall**, TR9 6JA, **ENGLAND**.
(T) 01637 880628 **(F)** 01637 880628.
Contact/s
Partner: Mrs M Pearce
Profile Riding School, Stable/Livery. **Ref: YH01474**

BLACKBARN STABLES
Blackbarn Stables, Mentmore Rd, Leighton Buzzard, **Bedfordshire**, LU7 7NY, **ENGLAND**.
(T) 01525 852176. **Ref: YH01475**

BLACKBOAR FORGE
Blackboar Forge, Pendle Trading Est, Clitheroe Rd, Chatburn, Clitheroe, **Lancashire**, BB7 4JY, **ENGLAND**.
(T) 01200 440747 **(F)** 01200 440747.
Contact/s
Owner: Mr I Hogg
Profile Blacksmith. **Ref: YH01476**

BLACKBOROUGH END
Blackborough End Equestrian Centre, The Stables, East Winch Rd, Blackborough End, King's Lynn, **Norfolk**, PE32 1SF, **ENGLAND**.
(T) 01553 841212
Affiliated Bodies BHS.
Contact/s
Partner: Mrs E Nash
Profile Horse/Rider Accom, Riding School, Stable/Livery.
The centre offers something for riders of all abilities.
Ref: YH01477

BLACKDALE FARM LIVERIES
Blackdale Farm Liveries, 1 Blackdale Farm Cottages, Green St, Dartford, **Kent**, DA2 8DX, **ENGLAND**.
(T) 01322 228188.
Contact/s
Owner: Mr T Raven
Profile Stable/Livery. **Ref: YH01478**

BLACKDOWN LIVERY YARD
Blackdown Livery Yard, Blackdown Cross, Crediton, **Devon**, EX17 3QQ, **ENGLAND**.
(T) 01647 24096.
Contact/s
Owner: Miss E Harris
Profile Stable/Livery. **Ref: YH01479**

BLACKDOWN RIDING CLUB
Blackdown Riding Club, 25 Orchard Cl, Wrington, **Somerset (North)**, BS40 5ND, **ENGLAND**.
(T) 01934 862646.
Profile Club/Association, Riding Club. **Ref: YH01480**

BLACKDYKE FARM RIDING CTRE
Blackdyke Farm Riding Centre, Blackford, Carlisle, **Cumbria**, CA6 4EY, **ENGLAND**.
(T) 01228 674633.
Contact/s
Owner: Mrs J Collier
Profile Riding School. **Ref: YH01481**

BLACKER, P & S
P & S Blacker, Yeatmans Farm, Grafton, Bampton, **Oxfordshire**, OX18 2RY, **ENGLAND**..
Profile Breeder. **Ref: YH01482**

BLACKHALL EQUESTRIAN CTRE
Blackhall Equestrian Centre, Blackhall, Little Kilcloone, **County Meath**, **IRELAND**.
(T) 01 6290691.
Contact/s
Manager: Tom Walsh
Profile Riding School, Stable/Livery. Horse dealers. Livery is available, details on request. The school is 60m x 30m and has all weather gallops. C.Size: 25 Acres
Opening Times
Sp: Open Tues - Sun 09:00. Closed Tues, Fri 19:00, Wed, Thur 21:00, Sat, Sun 20:00.
Su: Open Tues - Sun 09:00. Closed Tues, Fri 19:00, Wed, Thur 21:00, Sat, Sun 20:00.
Au: Open Tues - Sun 09:00. Closed Tues, Fri 19:00, Wed, Thur 21:00, Sat, Sun 20:00.
Wn: Open Tues - Sun 09:00. Closed Tues, Fri 19:00, Wed, Thur 21:00, Sat, Sun 20:00.
Closed Mondays **Ref: YH01483**

BLACKHEATH LIVERY STABLES
Blackheath Livery Stables, Blackheath Farm, Milton-under-Wychwood, Burford, **Oxfordshire**, OX7 6HX, **ENGLAND**.
(T) 01993 823365.
Contact/s
Owner: Sarah Hazel
Profile Stable/Livery. **Ref: YH01484**

BLACKIE, G
Mr G Blackie, 84 Lanark Rd, Braidwood, Carluke, **Lanarkshire (South)**, ML8 5PG, **SCOTLAND**.
(T) 07831 657540 **(F)** 01555 72579. **Ref: YH01485**

BLACKLITE
R A Black Welding Engineers, Newlandhead, Tealing, Dundee, **Angus**, DD3 0QZ, **SCOTLAND**.
(T) 01382 380354 **(F)** 01382 380503.
Contact/s
Owner: Mr R Black
Profile Blacksmith, Supplies. Showjump Manufacturers.
Blacklite produce safety equipment.
Opening Times
Sp: Open Mon - Sat 08:00. Closed Mon - Sat 20:00.
Su: Open Mon - Sat 08:00. Closed Mon - Sat 20:00.
Au: Open Mon - Sat 08:00. Closed Mon - Sat 20:00.
Wn: Open Mon - Sat 08:00. Closed Mon - Sat 20:00.
Closed Sundays **Ref: YH01486**

BLACKMORE VALE STUD
Blackmore Vale Stud, Sandley Cottage, Sandley, Gillingham, **Dorset**, SP8 5DU, **ENGLAND**.
(T) 01747 823396.
Profile Breeder, Saddlery Retailer. **Ref: YH01487**

BLACKMORE VALEFORGE
Blackmore Valeforge, Blackmore Forge, Ring St, Stalbridge, Sturminster Newton, **Dorset**, DT10 2LL, **ENGLAND**.
(T) 01963 364116 **(F)** 01963 364116.
Contact/s
Owner: Mr R Dare
Profile Blacksmith. **Ref: YH01488**

BLACKMORE, A G
Mr A G Blackmore, Chasers, Stockings Lane, Little Berkhamsted, **Hertfordshire**, SG13 8LW, **ENGLAND**.
(T) 01707 875060.
Profile Supplies. **Ref: YH01489**

BLACKMORE, PAUL F
Paul F Blackmore DWCF, Westcot, Knowsley Lane, Prescot, **Merseyside**, L34 7HF, **ENGLAND**.
(T) 0151 4284000.
Profile Farrier. **Ref: YH01490**

BLACKNEST GATE RIDING CTRE
Blacknest Gate Riding Centre, Mill Lane, Sunninghill, Ascot, **Berkshire**, SL5 0PS, **ENGLAND**.
(T) 01344 876871. **Ref: YH01491**

BLACKPOOL EQUESTRIAN CTRE
Blackpool Equestrian Centre Ltd, 287 Midgeland Rd, Blackpool, **Lancashire**, FY4 5JA, **ENGLAND**.
(T) 01253 760641 **(F)** 01253 294002.
Contact/s
Owner: M. A Newman **(Q)** BHS 1
(E) avnewman@talk21.com
Profile Riding Club, Riding School, Stable/Livery.
Ref: YH01492

BLACKPOOL WORKSPACE
Blackpool Workspace, Unit 11, Fox's Ind Est, Holyoake Ave, Blackpool, **Lancashire**, FY2 0QX, **ENGLAND**.
(T) 01253 353301.
Contact/s
Machinist Trainer: Ms L Jolly
Profile Supplies.
Manufacturer of saddle cloths (not saddles or leather goods). No.Staff: 4 Yr. Est: 1999
Opening Times
Sp: Open Mon - Fri 09:00. Closed Mon - Fri 17:00.
Su: Open Mon - Fri 09:00. Closed Mon - Fri 17:00.
Au: Open Mon - Fri 09:00. Closed Mon - Fri 17:00.
Wn: Open Mon - Fri 09:00. Closed Mon - Fri 17:00.
Ref: YH01493

BLACKS LIVERY STABLES
Blacks Livery Stables, Stuckenduff Farm, Shandon, Helensburgh, **Argyll and Bute**, G84 8NW, **SCOTLAND**.
(T) 01436 820838.
Profile Stable/Livery. **Ref: YH01494**

BLACKSMITH
Blacksmith, Caudwells Mill, Bakewell Rd, Rowsley, Matlock, **Derbyshire**, DE4 2EB, **ENGLAND**.
(T) 01629 732220.
Contact/s
Manager: Mr B Brown
Profile Blacksmith. **Ref: YH01495**

BLACKSMITHS SHOP
Blacksmiths Shop (The), Easton Farm Pk, Easton, Woodbridge, **Suffolk**, IP13 0EQ, **ENGLAND**.
(T) 01728 747880.
Profile Breeder. **Ref: YH01496**

BLACKSMITHS SHOP
Blacksmiths Shop (The), Ifield Wood, Ifield, Crawley, **Sussex (West)**, RH11 0LE, **ENGLAND**.
(T) 01293 562029.
Profile Farrier. **Ref: YH01497**

BLACKSTOCK, L
L Blackstock, Threeply Farm, Torr Rd, Bridge Of Weir, **Renfrewshire**, PA11 3RT, **SCOTLAND**.
(T) 01505 612375.
Profile Blacksmith. **Ref: YH01498**

BLACKTHORN SHAVINGS
Blackthorn Shavings, Minstrals Farm, Withy Rd, East Huntspill, Highbridge, **Somerset**, TA9 3NW, **ENGLAND**.
(T) 01278 782349.
Contact/s
Owner: Mr D Webb
Profile Supplies. **Ref: YH01499**

BLACKVALLEY EQUESTRIAN
Blackvalley Equestrian, Beaufort, Derrycarna, **County Kerry**, **IRELAND**.
(T) 064 37133.
Contact/s
Partner: Mr F Tangney
Profile Equestrian Centre.
Rides are offered through the Black Valley, varying in time from a few hours to seven days. Accommodation is arranged on route.
Opening Times
Telephone for further information, prior booking is recommended. **Ref: YH01500**

BLACKWATER FARM
Blackwater Farm Cross Country Schooling, Sparham, Norwich, **Norfolk**, NR9 5PR, **ENGLAND**.
(T) 01362 688227.
Contact/s
Owner: Mr D Sayer
Profile Equestrian Centre. **Ref: YH01501**

BLACKWATER SADDLERY
Blackwater Saddlery, Glencairn, Tallow, **County Waterford**, **IRELAND**.
(T) 058 56075 **(F)** 058 56830.
Contact/s
Owner: Ms S Dahill **(Q)** QS
Profile Saddlery Retailer. No.Staff: 1
Yr. Est: 1999 C.Size: 0.25 Acres
Opening Times
Open all year **Ref: YH01502**

BLACKWOOD, LADY PERDITA
Lady Perdita Blackwood, Cavallo Farm Crawfordsburn Rd, Newtownards, **County Down**, BT23 4UJ, **NORTHERN IRELAND**.
(T) 028 91812603 **(F)** 028 91812603.
Contact/s
Owner: Mrs L Blackwood
Profile Trainer. **Ref: YH01503**

BLACUP TRAINING GRP
Blacup Training Group (The), Church View, Coley Rd, Northowram, Halifax, **Yorkshire (West)**, HX3 7SA, **ENGLAND**.
(T) 01422 203615 **(F)** 01422 200799.
Contact/s
Owner: Mr S Place
(E) steveplace@talk21.com
Profile Arena, Stable/Livery, Trainer. No.Staff: 10
Yr. Est: 1990 C.Size: 15 Acres **Ref: YH01504**

BLADES LIVESTOCK TRANSPORT
Blades Livestock Transport, 12 High St, Walcott, Lincoln, **Lincolnshire**, LN4 3SN, **ENGLAND**.
(T) 01526 860520 **(F)** 01526 860520.
Contact/s
Owner: Mr J White
Profile Transport/Horse Boxes. **Ref: YH01505**

BLAENAVON STIRRUP CLUB
Blaenavon Stirrup Club, 5 Railway Trce, Blaenavon, **Torfaen**, NP4 9BY, **WALES**.
(T) 01495 790718.
Profile Club/Association. **Ref: YH01506**

BLAENWAUN STUD
Blaenwaun Stud, Bwich-Tre-Banau, Porthyrhyd, Llanwrda, **Carmarthenshire**, SA19 8DN, **WALES**.
(T) 01558 650703.
Profile Breeder. **Ref: YH01507**

BLAIN'S TRAILERS & TYRES
Blain's Trailers & Tyres Ltd, St Margarets Farm, St Margarets, Great Gaddesden, Hemel Hempstead, **Hertfordshire**, HP1 3BZ, **ENGLAND**.
(T) 01442 842419 **(F)** 01442 843789.
Contact/s
Partner: Mr L Blain
Profile Transport/Horse Boxes. **Ref: YH01508**

BLAIR CASTLE TREKKING CTRE
Blair Castle Trekking Centre, Blair Castle Caravan Pk, Blair Atholl, Pitlochry, **Perth and Kinross**, PH18 5SR, **SCOTLAND**.
(T) 01796 481263.
Profile Breeder. **Ref: YH01509**

BLAIR, J K
J K Blair, 15 Wester Rd, Glasgow, **Glasgow (City of)**, G32 9JH, **SCOTLAND**.
(T) 0141 5565616 **(F)** 0141 7781065.
Contact/s
Owner: Mr J Blair
Profile Blacksmith. **Ref: YH01510**

BLAIR, J K
J K Blair, 424 Swanston St, Glasgow, **Glasgow (City of)**, G40 4HW, **SCOTLAND**.
(T) 0141 5565616.
Profile Blacksmith. **Ref: YH01511**

BLAIR, KENNETH O
Kenneth O Blair RSS, 8 Clare Pl, Crockfords Pk, Newmarket, **Suffolk**, CB8 8BH, **ENGLAND**.
(T) 01638 602564.
Profile Farrier. **Ref: YH01512**

BLAIR, R & K
R & K Blair, Main St, Straid, Ballyclare, **County Antrim**, BT39 9NE, **NORTHERN IRELAND**.
(T) 028 93352292.
Profile Supplies. **Ref: YH01513**

BLAIRFIELD FARM STUD
Blairfield Farm Stud, Blairfield Farm, Fenwick, Kilmarnock, **Ayrshire (East)**, KA3 6AR, **SCOTLAND**.
(T) 01560 482635.
Contact/s
Owner: Mr R Potie
Profile Stable/Livery, Stud Farm. Yr. Est: 1999
Opening Times
Sp: Open Mon - Sun 09:00. Closed Mon - Sun 20:00.
Su: Open Mon - Sun 09:00. Closed Mon - Sun 20:00.
Au: Open Mon - Sun 09:00. Closed Mon - Sun 20:00.
Wn: Open Mon - Sun 09:00. Closed Mon - Sun 20:00. **Ref: YH01514**

BLAIRHILL STUD
Blairhill Stud, Blairhill, Rumbling Bridge, Kinross, **Perth and Kinross**, **SCOTLAND**..
Profile Breeder. **Ref: YH01515**

BLAKE, JILL
Jill Blake Equine Shiatsu Practitioner, Newbrook Farm, Pound Lane, Upper Beeding, Steyning, **Sussex (West)**, BN44 3JD, **ENGLAND**.
(T) 01903 815924.
Contact/s
Owner: Mrs J Blake **(Q)** BHSAI
Profile Medical Support.
Shiatsu services also available. C.Size: 15 Acres
Opening Times
Sp: Open Mon - Sun 08:30. Closed Mon - Sun 18:00.
Su: Open Mon - Sun 08:30. Closed Mon - Sun 18:00.
Au: Open Mon - Sun 08:30. Closed Mon - Sun 18:00.
Wn: Open Mon - Sun 08:30. Closed Mon - Sun 18:00. **Ref: YH01516**

BLAKE, JOHN T
John T Blake DWCF, Rose Cottage, Lower Stow Bedon, Attleborough, **Norfolk**, NR17 1BZ, **ENGLAND**.
(T) 01953 498431.
Profile Farrier. **Ref: YH01517**

BLAKE, M
Mrs M Blake, Lippen Wood Farm, West Meon, Petersfield, **Hampshire**, GU32 1JW, **ENGLAND**.
(T) 01730 829251.
Profile Breeder. **Ref: YH01518**

BLAKELEY STUD FARM
Blakeley Stud Farm, Blakeley, Stanton Upon Hine Heath, Shrewsbury, **Shropshire**, SY4 4ND, **ENGLAND**.
(T) 01630 685374 **(F)** 01630 685374.
Contact/s
Partner: Mr R Edwards
Profile Breeder. **Ref: YH01519**

BLAKEMORE VALE SADDLERY
Blakemore Vale Saddlery, Four Winds, West Bourton, Gillingham, **Dorset**, SP8 5PE, **ENGLAND**.
(T) 01747 840741
(W) www.craft-fair.co.uk/BLACKMOREVALE.HTM.
Contact/s
Owner: Sue Harvey
Profile Supplies. Manufacture Bridles.
All bridles are hand made **Ref: YH01520**

BLAKES EQUESTRIAN
Blakes Equestrian, 64 Blakes Rd, Castlerock, Coleraine, **County Londonderry**, BT51 4UE, **NORTHERN IRELAND**.
(T) 028 70848972 **(F)** 028 70848972.
Contact/s
Owner: Mr I McKinney
Profile Riding Wear Retailer, Saddlery Retailer, Supplies. No.Staff: 3 Yr. Est: 1996
Opening Times
Sp: Open Mon - Sat 09:30. Closed Mon - Wed, Fri , Sat 17:30, Thurs 21:00.
Su: Open Mon - Sat 09:30. Closed Mon - Wed, Fri , Sat 17:30, Thurs 21:00.
Au: Open Mon - Sat 09:30. Closed Mon - Wed, Fri , Sat 17:30, Thurs 21:00.
Wn: Open Mon - Sat 09:30. Closed Mon - Wed, Fri , Sat 17:30, Thurs 21:00. **Ref: YH01521**

BLAKES OF FRILFORD
Blakes of Frilford, Grange Buildings, Kingston Rd, Frilford, Abingdon, **Oxfordshire**, OX13 5NX, **ENGLAND**.
(T) 01865 391254 **(F)** 01865 391022.
Profile Saddlery Retailer. **Ref: YH01522**

BLAND BLACKSMITH
Bland Blacksmith, Chestnut Rd, Windermere, **Cumbria**, LA23 2AL, **ENGLAND**.
(T) 01539 443987.
Profile Blacksmith. **Ref: YH01523**

BLANDFORD SADDLERY
Blandford Saddlery, Blandford Hse, 47 East St, Blandford Forum, **Dorset**, DT11 7DX, **ENGLAND**.
(T) 01258 455377 **(F)** 01258 455377.
Contact/s
Owner: Mrs A Willoughby
Profile Saddlery Retailer. **Ref: YH01524**

BLANKNEY
Blankney, Manor Farm, Darlton, Newark, **Nottinghamshire**, NG22 0TH, **ENGLAND**.
(T) 01777 228724. **Ref: YH01525**

BLANSHARD, M T W
M T W Blanshard, Lethornes Stables, Upper Lambourn, Hungerford, **Berkshire**, RG17 8QT, **ENGLAND**.
(T) 01488 71091.
Profile Trainer. **Ref: YH01526**

BLANT, M R
M R Blant, Swingate Farm, Swingate, Babbington, Nottingham, **Nottinghamshire**, NG16 2SU, **ENGLAND**.
(T) 0115 9382212 **(F)** 0115 9382212.
Contact/s
Owner: Mrs K Blant **Ref: YH01527**

BLARNEY RIDING CTRE
Blarney Riding Centre, The Paddock Killowen, Blarney, **County Cork**, **IRELAND**.
(T) 021 4385854.
Contact/s
Partner: Mrs A Lines
Profile Riding School.
The outdoor school is floodlit for evening lessons.
Yr. Est: 1986
Opening Times
Shows on Sundays. First lessons begin at 09:30. For closing times, telephone for further information.
Ref: YH01528

BLAYLOCK, J A
Mr J A Blaylock, Denton Hall, Low Row, Brampton, **Cumbria**, CA8 2JA, **ENGLAND**.
(T) 01697 746331.
Profile Breeder. **Ref: YH01529**

BLEACH FARM
Bleach Farm Stables, Bleach Farm Stables, Bridlington Rd, Stamford Bridge, York, **Yorkshire (North)**, YO41 1HA, **ENGLAND**.
(T) 01759 371846.
Contact/s
Owner: Mr J Hutchinson
Profile Riding School. No.Staff: 3
Yr. Est: 1990 C.Size: 40 Acres
Opening Times
Sp: Open Mon - Sun 08:00. Closed Mon - Sun 21:00.
Su: Open Mon - Sun 08:00. Closed Mon - Sun 21:00.
Au: Open Mon - Sun 08:00. Closed Mon - Sun 21:00.
Wn: Open Mon - Sun 08:00. Closed Mon - Sun 21:00. **Ref: YH01530**

BLEACH YARD STABLES
Bleach Yard Stables, Bleach Yard, The Paddock, Beverley, **Yorkshire (East)**, HU17 7HG, **ENGLAND**.
(T) 01482 882557.
Profile Riding School, Stable/Livery, Trainer.
Ref: YH01531

BLEAKHOLT ANIMAL SANCTUARY
Bleakholt Animal Sanctuary, Rochdale Rd, Edenfield, Ramsbottom, **Lancashire**, BL0 0RX, **ENGLAND**.
(T) 01706 822577.
Contact/s
Manager: Mr N Martin **Ref: YH01532**

BLEEKMAN, E & C
E & C Bleekman, Whorridge Farm Stud, Cullompton, **Devon**, EX15 1RX, **ENGLAND**.
(T) 01884 32274 **(F)** 01884 38006.
Contact/s
Partner: Mr E Bleekman
Profile Breeder, Trainer. **Ref: YH01533**

BLENDWORTH TRAILER CTRE
Blendworth Trailer Centre, Whichers Gate Garage, Whichers Gate Rd, Rowland's Castle, **Hampshire**, PO9 6BB, **ENGLAND**.
(T) 023 92413406.
Profile Transport/Horse Boxes. **Ref: YH01534**

BLENHEIM MARKETING
Blenheim Marketing, Church Farm, Coates, Cirencester, **Gloucestershire**, GL7 6NS, **ENGLAND**.
(T) 01285 770442 **(F)** 01285 770178.
Contact/s
Owner: Mr M Moseling **Ref: YH01535**

BLENHEIM RIDING CLUB
Blenheim Riding Club, 29 Chipstead St, London, **London (Greater)**, SW6 3SR, **ENGLAND**.
(T) 020 87362815.
Contact/s
Chairman: Mr M Sippitt

A-Z of COMPANIES

Profile Club/Association, Riding Club. Ref: YH01536

BLENHEIM STUD

Blenheim Stud, Blenheim Farm, Postcombe, **Oxfordshire**, OX9 7DX, **ENGLAND**.
(T) 01844 281248.
Profile Breeder. Ref: YH01537

BLETSOE BROWN

Bletsoe Brown Ltd, Sywell Hse, Sywell, Northampton, **Northamptonshire**, NN6 0BQ, **ENGLAND**.
(T) 01604 492956.
Profile Stable/Livery. Ref: YH01538

BLEWBURY RIDING/TRAINING CTRE

Blewbury Riding & Training Centre, Bessels Way, Blewbury, Didcot, **Oxfordshire**, OX11 9NH, **ENGLAND**.
(T) 01235 851016 (F) 01235 851016.
Contact/s
Owner: Miss J Dexter
(E) adev@kcc.co.uk
Profile Horse/Rider Accom, Riding School.
Camping facilities No.Staff: 8
Opening Times
Sp: Open Mon - Sun 09:30. Closed Mon - Sun 17:00.
Su: Open Mon - Sun 09:30. Closed Mon - Sun 17:00.
Au: Open Mon - Sun 09:30. Closed Mon - Sun 17:00.
Wn: Open Mon - Sun 09:30. Closed Mon - Sun 17:00. Ref: YH01539

BLINKERS EQUESTRIAN

Blinkers Equestrian Limited, Allied Hse, Bryn Lane, Wrexham Ind Est, Wrexham, **Wrexham**, LL13 9UT, **WALES**.
(T) 01978 661919
(E) sales@blinkersequine.com
(W) www.blinkersequine.com.
Profile Riding Wear Retailer, Saddlery Retailer, Supplies, Trainer.
Free mail order CD No.Staff: 3 Yr. Est: 1997
Opening Times
Sp: Open Tues - Fri 13:00, Sat 11:00. Closed Tues - Sat 17:00.
Su: Open Tues - Fri 13:00, Sat 11:00. Closed Tues - Sat 17:00.
Au: Open Tues - Fri 13:00, Sat 11:00. Closed Tues - Sat 17:00.
Wn: Open Tues - Fri 13:00, Sat 11:00. Closed Tues - Sat 17:00. Ref: YH01540

BLISLAND HARNESS MAKERS

Blisland Harness Makers, Higher Harrowbridge, Bolventur, Liskeard, **Cornwall**, PL14 6SD, **ENGLAND**.
(T) 01579 320593 (F) 01579 320593.
Contact/s
Saddler: Ms J Talbot-Smith (Q) Master Saddler
Profile Saddlery Retailer.
Other leather work, such mobile phone holders for the front of saddles, is also available. Yr. Est: 1980
C.Size: 1 Acres
Opening Times
Sp: Open 08:30. Closed 17:00.
Su: Open 08:30. Closed 17:00.
Au: Open 08:30. Closed 17:00.
Wn: Open 08:30. Closed 17:00. Ref: YH01541

BLIXEN-FINECKE, H (BARON)

Baron H Blixen-Finecke, Shenston Hse, Orchard Walk, Winscombe, **Somerset (North)**, BS25 5NF, **ENGLAND**.
(T) 01934 852521 (F) 01934 853198.
Profile Trainer. Ref: YH01542

BLOCK, P A

Mrs P A Block, Bentwitchen Hse, North Molton, **Devon**, EX36 3HA, **ENGLAND**.
(T) 01598 740258.
Profile Breeder. Ref: YH01543

BLOCKLEY, E

E Blockley, Hodgson Lane Farm, Whitehall Rd, Drighlington, Bradford, **Yorkshire (West)**, BD11 1BD, **ENGLAND**.
(T) 01274 852311.
Profile Breeder. Ref: YH01544

BLOFLOW MAGNOTHERAPY

Bloflow Magnotherapy, P O Box 523, Stoke-on-Trent, **Staffordshire**, ST10 2QL, **ENGLAND**.
(T) 01538 266113 (F) 01538 266113
(M) 07971 383431
(E) janeh@staffs77.freeserve.co.uk.
Profile Medical Support. Ref: YH01545

BLOND, A J LE

Mr A J Le Blond, South Lodge Farm, North Rd, Hetton-Le-Hole, Houghton Le Spring, **Tyne and Wear**, DH5 9JY, **ENGLAND**.
(T) 0191 5263442.
Profile Supplies. Ref: YH01546

BLOODHORSE INT

Bloodhorse International Ltd, 2 Church Cl, Upper Lambourn, Hungerford, **Berkshire**, RG17 8PU, **ENGLAND**.
(T) 01488 73595
Affiliated Bodies FBA.
Profile Blood Stock Agency. Yr. Est: 1993
Opening Times
Telephone for an appointment Ref: YH01547

BLOODLINES

Bloodlines Ltd, 17 Radley Mews, London, **London (Greater)**, W8 6JP, **ENGLAND**.
(T) 020 79383033 (F) 020 79383055.
Profile Club/Association. Ref: YH01548

BLOODSTOCK & STUD INVESTMENT

Bloodstock & Stud Investment Co Ltd, 1 The Green, Marlborough, **Wiltshire**, SN8 1AL, **ENGLAND**.
(T) 01672 512512 (F) 01672 516660.
Profile Club/Association. Ref: YH01549

BLOODSTOCK PUBLICATIONS

Bloodstock Publications, Kelston Hse, Little Bedwyn, Marlborough, **Wiltshire**, SN8 3JL, **ENGLAND**.
(T) 01672 870204 (F) 01672 870902.
Profile Supplies. Ref: YH01550

BLOOM, KATRYNA

Mrs Katryna Bloom MCSP, SRP, 108 Main St, Wressle, Selby, **Yorkshire (North)**, YO8 6ET, **ENGLAND**.
(T) 01757 638800 (F) 01757 630395.
Profile Medical Support. Ref: YH01551

BLOOM, M J

M J Bloom, Kimberley Home Farm, Wymondham, **Norfolk**, NR18 0RW, **ENGLAND**.
(T) 01953 603137.
Profile Breeder, Stable/Livery. Ref: YH01552

BLOOMFIELD, D E F

Mr D E F Bloomfield, Bowhayland, North Hill, Launceston, **Cornwall**, PL15 7PE, **ENGLAND**.
(T) 01566 782232.
Profile Supplies. Ref: YH01553

BLOOMFIELD, WARWICK J

Warwick J Bloomfield DWCF, 31 Chavey Down Rd, Winkfield Row, Bracknell, **Berkshire**, RG42 7PN, **ENGLAND**.
(T) 01344 890260.
Profile Farrier. Ref: YH01554

BLOOMSBURY STUD

Bloomsbury Stud, Woburn Abbey, Woburn, **Bedfordshire**, MK43 0TP, **ENGLAND**.
(T) 01525 290666 (F) 01525 290271.
Profile Breeder. Ref: YH01555

BLOOMSGORSE TREKKING CTRE

Bloomsgorse Trekking Centre, Bloomsgorse Farm, Bilsthorpe, Newark, **Nottinghamshire**, NG22 8TA, **ENGLAND**.
(T) 01623 870276.
Contact/s
Owner: Mrs Z Grant
Profile Riding School. Ref: YH01556

BLOOR, ANNE

Anne Bloor Saddler, Canalside Workshop, Williamscott Lane, Cropredy, Banbury, **Oxfordshire**, OX17 1PQ, **ENGLAND**.
(T) 01295 758297
Affiliated Bodies SMS.
Contact/s
Saddler: Ms A Bloor (Q) QS, SMS
(E) anne.blooreequestrianet.co.uk
Profile Saddlery Retailer. Yr. Est: 1981
Opening Times
Sp: Open 09:30. Closed 17:00.
Su: Open 09:30. Closed 17:00.
Au: Open 09:30. Closed 17:00.
Wn: Open 09:30. Closed 17:00. Ref: YH01557

BLOOR, J O

J O Bloor, Old Chapel Hse, High St, Glentham, Market Rasen, **Lincolnshire**, LN8 2EQ, **ENGLAND**.
(T) 01673 878452.
Contact/s
Owner: Mr J Bloor
Profile Farrier. Ref: YH01558

BLOOR, RAY

Ray Bloor, Cae Glas, Church Stoke, Montgomery, **Powys**, SY15 6TG, **WALES**.
(T) 01588 620021 (F) 01588 620021.
Contact/s
Owner: Mr R Bloor
Profile Supplies. Ref: YH01559

BLOSS, B

B Bloss, 51 Kirby Rise, Barham, Ipswich, **Suffolk**, IP6 0AX, **ENGLAND**.
(T) 01473 831833.
Contact/s
Owner: Mr B Bloss
Profile Transport/Horse Boxes. Ref: YH01560

BLT TRAILERS

BLT Trailers, Station Rd, Claverdon, Warwick, **Warwickshire**, CV35 8PE, **ENGLAND**.
(T) 01926 842445.
Profile Transport/Horse Boxes. Ref: YH01561

BLUE ASSOCIATES

Blue Associates, Juniper Cottage, Buckland Village, Aylesbury, **Buckinghamshire**, HP22 5HY, **ENGLAND**.
(T) 01296 630593 (F) 01296 631385
(E) blueassociates@compuserve.com.
Profile Club/Association. Ref: YH01562

BLUE BARN

Blue Barn (The), Otley Rd, Pool In Wharfedale, Otley, **Yorkshire (West)**, LS21 1EG, **ENGLAND**.
(T) 0113 2843121 (F) 0113 2843127.
Profile Supplies. Ref: YH01563

BLUE BARN EQUESTRIAN CTRE

Blue Barn Equestrian Centre, Blue Barn Farm, Great Chart, Ashford, **Kent**, TN23 3DH, **ENGLAND**.
(T) 01233 621183.
Contact/s
Partner: Mr A Draper
Profile Riding School, Stable/Livery. Ref: YH01564

BLUE CHIP

Blue Chip Feed Balancer, 504 Ecclesall Rd, Sheffield, **Yorkshire (South)**, S11 8PY, **ENGLAND**.
(T) 0114 2666200 (F) 0114 2685010
(E) sara@bluechipfeed.com
(W) www.bluechipfeed.com.
Contact/s
Administration: Ms S Fletcher
(E) sara@blue-chip-feed-balancer.co.uk
Profile Feed Merchant, Medical Support.
Feed Manufacturers & Distributors. Supply and distribute through Spillers. No limit to quantity you order via Mail Order. Blue Chip offer an advice line on 0114 2631200. Yr. Est: 1997
Opening Times
Sp: Open Mon - Fri 09:30. Closed Mon - Fri 17:00.
Su: Open Mon - Fri 09:30. Closed Mon - Fri 17:00.
Au: Open Mon - Fri 09:30. Closed Mon - Fri 17:00.
Wn: Open Mon - Fri 09:30. Closed Mon - Fri 17:00.
Closed at weekends but there is an answer phone. Ref: YH01565

BLUE CROSS ANIMAL

Blue Cross Animal Welfare Society, Equine Welfare Dept, Shilton Rd, Burford, **Oxfordshire**, OX18 4PF, **ENGLAND**.
(T) 01993 822651 (F) 01993 823083.
Contact/s
Key Contact: Major N Davenport
Profile Club/Association. Ref: YH01566

BLUE MOUNTAIN FARM

Blue Mountain Farm, Wells Hill Bottom, Haydon, Wells, **Somerset**, BA5 3EZ, **ENGLAND**.
(T) 01749 841011 (F) 01749 841011.
Contact/s
Owner: Mr M Saunders
Profile Trainer. Ref: YH01567

BLUE RIDGE WESTERN SADDLERY

Blue Ridge Western Saddlery, Honeycrocks Cottage, Honeycrocks Lane, Hailsham, **Sussex**

(East), BN27 2RN, **ENGLAND**.
(T) 01323 843905 **(F)** 01323 842728.
Profile Saddlery Retailer. Ref: YH01568

BLUE ROSE

Blue Rose, 105 Croston Rd, Garstang, Preston, **Lancashire**, PR3 1HQ, **ENGLAND**.
(T) 01995 601819 **(F)** 01995 601820.
Contact/s
Partner: Mrs E Iddon
Profile Transport/Horse Boxes. Ref: YH01569

BLUE SABRE RIDING SCHOOL

Blue Sabre Riding School, Bull Lane, Tiptree, Colchester, **Essex**, CO5 0BE, **ENGLAND**.
(T) 01621 816012
Affiliated Bodies ABRS.
Contact/s
Partner: Mrs J Elingford **(Q)** BHS 2
Profile Riding School, Stable/Livery. No.Staff: 1
Yr. Est: 1982 C.Size: 6 Acres Ref: YH01570

BLUE WELL RIDING CTRE

Blue Well Riding Centre, Ffynnonlas, Llanllwni, Pencader, **Carmarthenshire**, SA39 9AY, **WALES**.
(T) 01267 202274.
Profile Riding School. Ref: YH01571

BLUE ZEBRA PR

Blue Zebra Public Relations, The Power Hse, High St, Ardington, **Oxfordshire**, OX12 8PS, **ENGLAND**.
(T) 01235 833005 **(F)** 01235 833006
(E) blue.zebra@virgin.net.
Profile Club/Association. PR Agency. Ref: YH01572

BLUEGRASS HORSE FEEDS

Bluegrass Horse Feeds, Stilloga Mills, Eglish, Dungannon, **County Tyrone**, BT70 1LF, **NORTHERN IRELAND**.
(T) 028 87548276 **(F)** 028 87548308.
Profile Supplies. Ref: YH01573

BLUNDELL, REX G

Rex G Blundell, 34 Florence Rd, Woolston, Southampton, **Hampshire**, SO19 9BS, **ENGLAND**.
(T) 023 80448379. Ref: YH01574

BLUNT, ADRIEN

Adrien Blunt, 36 Rose Lane, Crewkerne, **Somerset**, TA18 7ER, **ENGLAND**.
(T) 01460 75974. Ref: YH01575

BLURTON, JAMES P

James P Blurton AWCF, Rose Hill, Kingswood Lane, Forden, Welshpool, **Powys**, SY21 8TR, **WALES**.
(T) 01938 580222.
Profile Farrier. Ref: YH01576

BLYTH MILL

Blyth Mill (Coleshill) Ltd, Blythe Rd, Coleshill, Birmingham, **Warwickshire**, B46 2AE, **ENGLAND**.
(T) 01675 462200.
Profile Supplies. Ref: YH01577

BLYTH, J

Mr J Blyth, Bogleys Farm, Kirkcaldy, **Fife**, KY1 3NY, **SCOTLAND**.
(T) 01592 651160.
Profile Trainer. Ref: YH01578

BLYTHE HAULAGE

Blythe Haulage, 2 Maplesden Cottages, Churchsettle Lane, Wadhurst, **Sussex (East)**, TN5 6NQ, **ENGLAND**.
(T) 01892 782471 **(F)** 01892 782471.
Contact/s
Owner: Mr P Jenner
Profile Transport/Horse Boxes. Ref: YH01579

BLYTHEMAN & PARTNERS

Blytheman & Partners, 202 Durham Rd, Gateshead, **Tyne and Wear**, NE8 4JR, **ENGLAND**.
(T) 0191 4784042.
Profile Medical Support. Ref: YH01580

BLYTHMAN & PARTNERS

Blythman & Partners, 16 Elsdon Rd, Gosforth, **Tyne and Wear**, NE3 1JD, **ENGLAND**.
(T) 0191 2841711 **(F)** 0191 2841081.
Profile Medical Support. Ref: YH01581

BOAG DESIGN BLACKSMITHS

Boag Design Blacksmiths, Bankfoot Cottages, Bankfoot Farm, Inverkip, Greenock, **Inverclyde**, PA16 0DT, **SCOTLAND**.
(T) 01475 521491.
Contact/s
Owner: Mr J Boag
Profile Blacksmith. Ref: YH01582

BOAK, D & J

D & J Boak, East Wold Farm, Langton, Malton, **Yorkshire (North)**, YO17 9QQ, **ENGLAND**.
(T) 01944 768221.
Profile Breeder. Ref: YH01583

BOARD-JONES, S

Mr & Mrs S Board-Jones, Willow Farm, Oakley Green Rd, Oakley Green, Windsor, **Berkshire**, SL4 4PZ, **ENGLAND**.
(T) 01753 842056.
Profile Breeder. Ref: YH01584

BOASE, N & L

Mr N & Mrs L Boase, Ardfern, Lochgilphead, **Argyll and Bute**, PA31 8QR, **SCOTLAND**.
(T) 01852 500270 **(F)** 01852 500270.
Profile Breeder. Ref: YH01585

BOB ELLIS EQUESTRIAN SVS

Bob Ellis Equestrian Services, 32 Whiteoaks Drive, Bishops Wood, Brewood, **Staffordshire**, ST19 9AH, **ENGLAND**.
(T) 01785 840430 **(F)** 01785 840430
(M) 07768 974688. Ref: YH01586

BOB JONES

Bob Jones Ltd, Boyden End Hse, Wickhambrook, Newmarket, **Suffolk**, CB8 8XX, **ENGLAND**.
(T) 01440 820664
(W) www.newmarketracehorsetrainers.co.uk
Affiliated Bodies Newmarket Trainers Fed.
Profile Trainer.
Quarantine Horses. Yr. Est: 1969 C.Size: 8 Acres Ref: YH01587

BOB PARRY

Bob Parry & Co Ltd, 22/23 Castle St, Caernarfon, **Gwynedd**, LL55 2NA, **WALES**.
(T) 01286 673286 **(F)** 01286 76322.
Contact/s
Chairperson: Mr R Pritchard-Jones Ref: YH01588

BOB PAULEY PA HIRE

Bob Pauley P A Hire, Lamplight, Casterton Lane, Tinwell, Stamford, **Lincolnshire**, PE9 3UQ, **ENGLAND**.
(T) 01780 766666 **(F)** 01780 766666
(M) 07889 601898. Ref: YH01589

BOCKMER LIVERY STABLES

Bockmer Livery Stables, 2 Bockmer End Cottage, Bockmer, Marlow, **Buckinghamshire**, SL7 2HL, **ENGLAND**.
(T) 01491 571284.
Profile Stable/Livery. Ref: YH01590

BOCKMER LIVERY STABLES

Bockmer Livery Stables, Bulbeck Lodge/2 Bockmer End Cottage, Bockmer, Marlow, **Buckinghamshire**, SL7 2HL, **ENGLAND**.
(T) 01491 571673.
Contact/s
Owner: Mr D Clarke
Profile Stable/Livery. Ref: YH01591

BOCM PAULS

BOCM Pauls Ltd (Exeter), Kestrel Way, Sowton Ind Est, Exeter, **Devon**, EX2 7LN, **ENGLAND**.
(T) 01392 50251 **(F)** 01392 50756.
Profile Supplies. Ref: YH01592

BOCM PAULS

BOCM Pauls Ltd (Newcastle-under-Lyme), Speedwell Rd, Parkhouse Ind Est, Chesterton, Newcastle-under-Lyme, **Staffordshire**, ST5 7RF, **ENGLAND**.
(T) 01782 565565 **(F)** 01782 564609.
Profile Supplies. Ref: YH01593

BODDY, STEPHEN M

Stephen M Boddy DWCF, 2 Downshire Cl, Great Shefford, Hungerford, **Berkshire**, RG17 7BS, **ENGLAND**.
(T) 01488 648624.
Profile Farrier. Ref: YH01594

BODEN & DAVIES

Boden & Davies, Mellor Hall Farm, Mellor, Stockport, **Cheshire**, SK6 5LU, **ENGLAND**.
(T) 0161 4271819 **(F)** 0161 4271012.
Profile Supplies. Ref: YH01595

BODICOTE FLYOVER FARM SHOP

Bodicote Flyover Farm Shop, Bodicote, Banbury, **Oxfordshire**, OX15 4BN, **ENGLAND**.
(T) 01295 270789 **(F)** 01295 264766.
Profile Supplies. Ref: YH01596

BODMIN TRAILER CTRE

Bodmin Trailer Centre, Treningle Hill, Bodmin, **Cornwall**, PL30 5JX, **ENGLAND**.
(T) 01208 831656.
Profile Transport/Horse Boxes. Ref: YH01597

BOGS HALL

Bogs Hall Stables, Bogs Hall Farm, Kirkby Malzeard, Ripon, **Yorkshire (North)**, HG4 3QL, **ENGLAND**.
(T) 01765 658184.
Contact/s
Owner: Mr R Botham
Profile Riding School, Stable/Livery.
Full livery available. Insured for children over four years of age. Yr. Est: 1994 C.Size: 15 Acres
Opening Times
Sp: Open Tues - Sun 08:00, Mon 12:00. Closed Mon - Sun 18:00.
Su: Open Tues - Sun 08:00, Mon 12:00. Closed Mon - Sun 18:00.
Au: Open Tues - Sun 08:00, Mon 12:00. Closed Mon - Sun 18:00.
Wn: Open Tues - Sun 08:00, Mon 12:00. Closed Mon - Sun 18:00.
Closed on Monday mornings Ref: YH01598

BOHEMIAN ARABIAN STUD

Bohemian Arabian Stud, The Bents, Field Lane, Leigh, Stoke-on-Trent, **Staffordshire**, ST10 4QD, **ENGLAND**.
(T) 01889 502247.
Contact/s
Owner: Mrs S Plant
Profile Breeder. Ref: YH01599

BOISSEAU, R

Mrs R Boisseau, Higher Hawksland Farm, Animal Therapy Ctre, St Issey, Wadebridge, **Cornwall**, PL27 7RG, **ENGLAND**.
(T) 01208 813199
(M) 07721 671633.
Profile Medical Support. Ref: YH01600

BOJAN AT WARREN KENNELS

Bojan at Warren Kennels, Britons Lane, Sheringham, **Norfolk**, NR26 8TP, **ENGLAND**.
(T) 01263 822640.
Profile Saddlery Retailer. Ref: YH01601

BOLD HEATH EQUESTRIAN

Bold Heath Equestrian Centre, Heath Hse Farm, Bold Heath, Widnes, **Cheshire**, WA8 3XT, **ENGLAND**.
(T) 0151 4245151 **(F)** 0151 4245583
Affiliated Bodies BHS.
Contact/s
Owner: Ms J Baker **(Q)** BHSII
Profile Arena, Equestrian Centre, Riding Club, Riding School, Riding Wear Retailer, Trainer. No.Staff: 5
Yr. Est: 1971 C.Size: 60 Acres
Opening Times
Sp: Open 09:00. Closed 19:30.
Su: Open 09:00. Closed 19:30.
Au: Open 09:00. Closed 19:30.
Wn: Open 09:00. Closed 19:30. Ref: YH01602

BOLD HEATH EQUESTRIAN CTRE

Bold Heath Equestrian Centre Dressage, 104 Clock Face Rd, Clock Face, St Helens, **Merseyside**, WA9 4LU, **ENGLAND**.
(T) 0151 4245151.
Contact/s
Secretary: Mrs S Lamb Ref: YH01603

BOLD RIDING CLUB

Bold Riding Club, Heath Hse Farm, Warrington Rd, Bold Heath, Widnes, **Cheshire**, WA8 3XT, **ENGLAND**.
(T) 0151 4236437.
Contact/s
Owner: Mr P Higham
Profile Riding Club. Ref: YH01604

BOLD VENTURE STUD

Bold Venture Stud, Stanbrook Farm, Staunton, **Gloucestershire**, GL19 3QR, **ENGLAND**.
(T) 01452 84264.
Profile Breeder. Ref: YH01605

BOLDTRY RIDING STABLES

Boldtry Riding Stables, Leigh Rd, Chulmleigh, **Devon**, EX18 7JW, **ENGLAND**.
(T) 01769 580366.
Contact/s
Owner: Mr N Brown
Profile Riding School. Ref: YH01606

BOLENOWE LIVERY STABLES

Bolenowe Livery Stables, Troon, Camborne,

Cornwall, TR14 9JA, **ENGLAND**.
(T) 01209 713690.
Profile Stable/Livery. **Ref: YH01607**

BOLGER, J S

Bolger J S, Glebe Hse, Coolcullen, **County Carlow**, **IRELAND**.
(T) 056 43150 **(F)** 056 43256
(E) jsb@iol.ie.
Profile Supplies. **Ref: YH01608**

BOLTON GATE SADDLERY

Bolton Gate Saddlery, Bolton Gate Farm, Leek Rd, Weston Coyney, Stoke-on-Trent, **Staffordshire**, ST3 5BD, **ENGLAND**.
(T) 01782 312824.
Contact/s
Owner: Mrs D Brandon
Profile Saddlery Retailer. **Ref: YH01609**

BOLTON RIDING CLUB

Bolton Riding Club, 18 Yates St, Tonge Moor, Bolton, **Manchester (Greater)**, BL2 2DX, **ENGLAND**.
(T) 01204 362584.
Profile Club/Association, Riding Club. **Ref: YH01610**

BOLTON, A

A Bolton, Stanworth Poultry Farm, Bolton Rd, Withnell, Chorley, **Lancashire**, PR6 8BP, **ENGLAND**.
(T) 01254 200684.
Contact/s
Owner: Miss A Bolton
Profile Breeder. **Ref: YH01611**

BOLTON, J

J Bolton, 5 Gainsborough Cres, Hillmorton, Rugby, **Warwickshire**, CV21 4DQ, **ENGLAND**.
(T) 01788 574667.
Profile Farrier. **Ref: YH01612**

BOLTON, M J

Mr M J Bolton, 41 Hurst Green Rd, Oxted, **Surrey**, RH8 9BS, **ENGLAND**.
(T) 01883 716492 **(F)** 01883 716193.
Profile Trainer. **Ref: YH01613**

BOLTWOOD STUD

Boltwood Stud, Boltwood Hse, Chiddingly, Lewes, **Sussex (East)**, BN8 6HH, **ENGLAND**.
(T) 01825 872412.
Contact/s
Owner: Mr A Giles
Profile Breeder. **Ref: YH01614**

BOND, CHRISTOPHER J

Christopher J Bond RSS, 58 Haughton Croft, Muckley Cross, Morville, Bridgnorth, **Shropshire**, WV16 4RP, **ENGLAND**.
(T) 01746 714010.
Profile Farrier. **Ref: YH01615**

BOND, CLIVE R

Clive R Bond, 7 Feast Cl, Fordham, Ely, **Cambridgeshire**, CB7 5PH, **ENGLAND**.
(T) 01638 721288.
Profile Farrier. **Ref: YH01616**

BOND, DAVID

David Bond DWCF, Old Chapel Forge, Upper Lambourn, Hungerford, **Berkshire**, RG17 8QP, **ENGLAND**.
(T) 01488 72613.
Profile Farrier. **Ref: YH01617**

BOND, J N

J N Bond, 2 Nash Elm Cottages, Duttons Lane, Arley, Bewdley, **Worcestershire**, DY12 1SS, **ENGLAND**.
(T) 01299 861316.
Profile Farrier. **Ref: YH01618**

BONE, HOUSTON

Houston Bone DWCF BII, 20 Linnet Drive, Barton Seagrave, Kettering, **Northamptonshire**, NN15 6SA, **ENGLAND**.
(T) 01536 420087.
Profile Farrier. **Ref: YH01619**

BONE, JOSEPH

Joseph Bone RSS, 59A Ceder Cres, Willington, Crook, Durham, **County Durham**, DL15 0DA, **ENGLAND**.
(T) 01388 745144.
Profile Farrier. **Ref: YH01620**

BONES

Bones, The Ind Est, Hatherleigh, Okehampton, **Devon**, EX20 3LP, **ENGLAND**.
(T) 01837 810888.
Profile Medical Support. **Ref: YH01621**

BONHAMS AUCTIONEERS

Bonhams Auctioneers, Montpelier Galleries, Montpelier St, London, **London (Greater)**, SW7 1HH, **ENGLAND**.
(T) 020 73933900 **(F)** 020 73933905
(E) bonhams@cityscape.co.uk. **Ref: YH01622**

BONIFACE, IAN

Ian Boniface DWCF, 1 Broad Croft, Chew Magna, **Bath & Somerset (North East)**, BS40 8QF, **ENGLAND**.
(T) 01275 333527.
Profile Farrier. **Ref: YH01623**

BONITA RACING STABLES

Bonita Racing Stables, Ogbourne Maisley, Marlborough, **Wiltshire**, SN8 1RY, **ENGLAND**.
(T) 01672 512973 **(F)** 01672 514166
(M) 07836 217825.
Profile Trainer. **Ref: YH01624**

BOOCOCK, MARC A

Marc A Boocock, 57 Westroyd Rd, Windhill, Shipley, **Yorkshire (West)**, BD18 2PG, **ENGLAND**.
(T) 01274 591180.
Profile Farrier. **Ref: YH01625**

BOOK STORE

Book Store (The), Southern Aviaries, Tinkers Lane, Hadlow Down, Ukfield, **Sussex (East)**, TN22 4EU, **ENGLAND**.
(T) 01825 85283 **(F)** 01825 85241.
Profile Supplies. **Ref: YH01626**

BOOKHAM LODGE STUD

Bookham Lodge Stud, Cobham Rd, Stoke D'abernon, Cobham, **Surrey**, KT11 3QJ, **ENGLAND**.
(T) 01932 867797.
Profile Farrier. **Ref: YH01627**

BOOKHAM RIDING CLUB

Bookham Riding Club, 4 Manor Court, Ave Elmers, Surbiton, **Surrey**, KT6 4SH, **ENGLAND**.
(T) 020 83900099.
Contact/s
Chairman: Ms J Millson
Profile Club/Association, Riding Club. **Ref: YH01628**

BOOKHAM RIDING CLUB

Bookham Riding Club, 12 Riverside Ave, East Molesey, **Surrey**, KT8 0AE, **ENGLAND**.
(T) 020 83987135.
Profile Club/Association, Riding Club. **Ref: YH01629**

BOOKLINE

Bookline, 35 Farranfad Rd, Downpatrick, **County Down**, BT30 8NH, **NORTHERN IRELAND**.
(T) 028 44811712.
Profile Supplies. **Ref: YH01630**

BOOL BY DESIGN

Bool By Design, Fishers Green Farm, Fishers Green, Utkinton, Tarporley, **Cheshire**, CW6 0JG, **ENGLAND**.
(T) 01829 732187 **(F)** 07092 201528
(W) www.boolbydesign.co.uk.
Contact/s
Partner: Mr R Bool
(E) ray@boolbydesign.co.uk
Profile Feed Merchant, Riding Wear Retailer, Saddlery Retailer, Supplies.
Orders can be placed either by telephone or on-line. Leather repairs are available, but must be brought to the shop. A laundry service is also offered.
No.Staff: 4 Yr. Est: 1997
Opening Times
Sp: Open Mon - Sat 09:00. Closed Mon - Sat 17:30.
Su: Open Mon - Sat 09:00. Closed Mon - Sat 17:30.
Au: Open Mon - Sat 09:00. Closed Mon - Sat 17:30.
Wn: Open Mon - Sat 09:00. Closed Mon - Sat 17:30.
Ref: YH01631

BOON, TERRY

Terry Boon, The Stables, The Moathouse, Rectory Lane, Hethel, Norwich, **Norfolk**, **ENGLAND**.
(T) 01508 578536. **Ref: YH01632**

BOOTH, A

Mr & Mrs A Booth, Long Acre Farm, Whitchurch, Reading, **Berkshire**, RG8 7QX, **ENGLAND**.
(T) 0118 9844587 **(F)** 0118 9841762.
Profile Breeder. **Ref: YH01633**

BOOTH, C B B

C B B Booth, Gravel Pit Farm, Foston, York, **Yorkshire (North)**, YO60 7QD, **ENGLAND**.
(T) 01653 618586.
Contact/s
Owner: Mr C Booth
Profile Trainer. **Ref: YH01634**

BOOTH, D C

Mrs D C Booth, Voakes Cottage, West Chiltington, Pulborough, **Sussex (West)**, RH20 2LU, **ENGLAND**.
(T) 01798 815765
(M) 07702 969919.
Profile Breeder. **Ref: YH01635**

BOOTH, NICHOLAS H

Nicholas H Booth DWCF, 184 Highfield Rd, Idle, Bradford, **Yorkshire (West)**, BD10 8QN, **ENGLAND**.
(T) 01274 612287.
Profile Farrier. **Ref: YH01636**

BOOTH, THOMAS M

Thomas M Booth DWCF, Ty-Lan, Nebo, Llanon, **Ceredigion**, SY23 5LE, **WALES**.
(T) 0113 272185.
Profile Farrier. **Ref: YH01637**

BOOTHROYD, A

A Boothroyd B Vet Med MRCVS, The Veterinary Ctre, 1 Station Ave, Filey, **Yorkshire (North)**, YO14 9AH, **ENGLAND**.
(T) 01723 513119.
Contact/s
Owner: Mrs J Hairsine **(Q)** MRCVS
Profile Medical Support. **Ref: YH01638**

BOOTS & SADDLES

Boots & Saddles, Langton Farm, Stewarton Rd, Newton Mearns, Glasgow, **Glasgow (City of)**, G77 6PU, **SCOTLAND**.
(T) 0141 6162082.
Contact/s
Owner: Mrs M Ferguson **Ref: YH01639**

BOOTS & SADDLES

Boots & Saddles, 277 Brithweunydd Rd, Tonypandy, **Rhondda Cynon Taff**, CF40 2NZ, **WALES**.
(T) 01443 432036 **(F)** 01443 432036.
Contact/s
Owner: Mr R Howells
Profile Riding Wear Retailer, Saddlery Retailer.
Yr. Est: 1975
Opening Times
Sp: Open Mon - Sat 09:00. Closed Mon - Sat 18:00.
Su: Open Mon - Sat 09:00. Closed Mon - Sat 18:00.
Au: Open Mon - Sat 09:00. Closed Mon - Sat 18:00.
Wn: Open Mon - Sat 09:00. Closed Mon - Sat 18:00.
Ref: YH01640

BOOTS 'N' SADDLES

Boots 'n' Saddles, 351 High St, Kirkcaldy, **Fife**, KY1 1JN, **SCOTLAND**.
(T) 01592 269782.
Contact/s
Owner: Mr J Thom **Ref: YH01641**

BORDER BRIDLEWAYS ASSOCIATION

Border Bridleways Association, Crossfields, Crossfields Lane, Mossley, Congleton, **Cheshire**, CW12 3BL, **ENGLAND**.
(T) 01260 273865.
Profile Club/Association. **Ref: YH01642**

BORDER ESTATES

Border Estates, Tudor Cottage, Hatfield, Leominster, **Herefordshire**, HR6 0SF, **ENGLAND**.
(T) 01568 760111 **(F)** 01568 760141
(E) property@bordersestates.co.uk
(W) www.bordersestates.co.uk.
Contact/s
Estate Agent: Mr R Lupton
(E) bordest@freenetname.co.uk
Profile Estate Agents.
The Midlands only specialist equestrian estate agents covering Gloucestershire, Herefordshire, Lincolnshire, Northamptonshire, Shropshire, Staffordshire, Warwickshire, Worcestershire and the Welsh Borders.
Ref: YH01643

BORDER SADDLERY

Border Saddlery, Ayton Mains, Eyemouth, **Scottish Borders**, TD14 5RE, **SCOTLAND**.
(T) 01890 781480 **(F)** 01890 781480.
Contact/s
Owner: Mr T Struthers **Ref: YH01644**

BORDER SHOWJUMPING EQUIPMENT

Border Showjumping Equipment, Fellcleugh, Cranshaws, Duns, **Scottish Borders**, TD11 3SH, **SCOTLAND**.
(T) 01361 890320
(M) 07831 162289.
Profile Supplies. **Ref: YH01645**

BORDER TRAILER WORKS
Border Trailer Works, The Old School, Welsh Frankton, Whittington, Oswestry, **Shropshire**, SY11 4NX, **ENGLAND**.
(T) 01691 622157.
Contact/s
Owner: Mr R Jones
Profile Transport/Horse Boxes. **Ref: YH01646**

BOREHAM SADDLERY
Boreham Saddlery, The Old Stove Shop, Main Rd, Boreham, Chelmsford, **Essex**, CM3 3HE, **ENGLAND**.
(T) 01245 450606.
Contact/s
Owner: Ms J Wisdom **Ref: YH01647**

BOREHARD LIVERY YARD
Borehard Livery Yard, Ardoon Stud, Newbridge, **County Kildare**, **IRELAND**.
(M) 087 2538944. **Ref: YH01648**

BORLAND, DAVID J
David J Borland DWCF, 17 Falkland Pk, Westmains, East Kilbride, **Lanarkshire (South)**, G74 1JD, **SCOTLAND**.
(T) 01355 276526.
Profile Farrier. **Ref: YH01649**

BORLAND, J S
Mr J S Borland, Elmhurst, Lichfield, **Staffordshire**, WS13 8HD, **ENGLAND**.
(T) 01543 251932.
Profile Breeder. **Ref: YH01650**

BORLEIGH MANOR STUD
Borleigh Manor Stud, Inch, Gorey, **County Wexford**, **IRELAND**.
(T) 040 237811.
Profile Supplies. **Ref: YH01651**

BOROHARD EQUESTRIAN CTRE
Borohard Equestrian Centre, Baysland, Naas, **County Kildare**, **IRELAND**.
(T) 045 895712
(E) borohardequestrian@kildarehorse.ie.
Contact/s
Key Contact: Ms J Soley
Profile Equestrian Centre, Stable/Livery.
Borohard is also a competition yard. **Ref: YH01652**

BORTHWICK, A J
A J Borthwick Vet & Agricultural Chemist, The Old Pump Hse, Ettrick Mill, Dunsdale Rd, Selkirk, **Scottish Borders**, TD7 5EB, **SCOTLAND**.
(T) 01750 20734 **(F)** 01750 22725.
Profile Medical Support.
Agricultural chemist. **Ref: YH01653**

BOSKELL RIDING CTRE
Boskell Riding Centre, Boskell Farm, Trenance Downs, St Austell, **Cornwall**, PL25 5RG, **ENGLAND**.
(T) 01726 73049.
Profile Riding School, Stable/Livery. **Ref: YH01654**

BOSLEY, M R
M R Bosley, Kingston Lisle Farm Racing Stables, Kingston Lisle, Wantage, **Oxfordshire**, OX12 9QL, **ENGLAND**.
(T) 01367 820115 **(F)** 01367 820115.
Contact/s
Manager: Mr M Bosley
Profile Trainer. **Ref: YH01655**

BOSSINGTON DRESSAGE STABLES
Bossington Dressage Stables, Porlock, Minehead, **Somerset**, TA24 8HB, **ENGLAND**.
(T) 01643 862020.
Profile Trainer. **Ref: YH01656**

BOSSY'S BIBS
Bossy's Bibs, 6 Beech Walk, Tring, **Hertfordshire**, HP23 5JQ, **ENGLAND**.
(T) 01442 824033
(E) bossy@bossysbibs.com
(W) www.bossysbibs.com.
Contact/s
Owner: Patsy Newton
Profile Supplies.
Bossy's produce bibs to help prevent rugs rubbing the shoulder area. **Ref: YH01657**

BOSTOCK, D R
D R Bostock DWCF, 3 Claughbane Ave, Ramsey, **Isle of Man**, IM8 2BE, **ENGLAND**.
(T) 01624 813996.
Profile Farrier. **Ref: YH01658**

BOSTON HORSE SUPPLIES
Boston Horse Supplies, 15 Emery Lane, Boston, **Lincolnshire**, PE21 8QA, **ENGLAND**.
(T) 01205 353829.
Contact/s
Owner: Mrs S Curtis
Profile Saddlery Retailer. **Ref: YH01659**

BOSTON MANOR RIDING CLUB
Boston Manor Riding Club, 51 Milton Rd, Hanwell, **London (Greater)**, W7 1LQ, **ENGLAND**.
(T) 020 88402489.
Profile Club/Association, Riding Club. **Ref: YH01660**

BOSVATHICK FARM
Bosvathick Farm Riding Stables, Bosvathick Farm, Constantine, Falmouth, **Cornwall**, TR11 5RD, **ENGLAND**.
(T) 01326 340367.
Contact/s
Owner: Ms A Badcock **Ref: YH01661**

BOSWELL STABLES
Boswell Stables, Ponsbourne Pk, Newgate St, Hertford, **Hertfordshire**, SG13 8QT, **ENGLAND**.
(T) 01707 875411.
Contact/s
Owner: Mr M Boswell
Profile Stable/Livery.
Full and part livery available, details on request.
Ref: YH01662

BOSWELL, J
J Boswell, Great Grounds Farm, Radway, **Warwickshire**, CV35 0UQ, **ENGLAND**.
(T) 01295 87265.
Profile Farrier. **Ref: YH01663**

BOSWORTH, CLIVE E
Clive E Bosworth RSS, Birds Holt Cottage, Waterloo Lane, Skellingthorpe, **Lincolnshire**, LN6 5SW, **ENGLAND**.
(T) 01522 685156.
Profile Farrier. **Ref: YH01664**

BOTTAMLEY, F D
F D Bottamley, East Butterwick, Scunthorpe, **Lincolnshire (North)**, DN17 3AG, **ENGLAND**.
(T) 01724 783001.
Profile Farrier. **Ref: YH01665**

BOTTING, ROBERT W
Robert W Botting AFCL, 2 Britten Cl, Horsham, **Sussex (West)**, RH13 6RL, **ENGLAND**.
(T) 01403 273400.
Profile Farrier. **Ref: YH01666**

BOTTISHAM HEATH STUD
Bottisham Heath Stud, Six Mile Bottom, Newmarket, **Suffolk**, CB8 0TT, **ENGLAND**.
(T) 01638 570272 **(F)** 01638 570246.
Contact/s
Owner: Mr R Cowell
Profile Breeder. **Ref: YH01667**

BOTTOMLEY, E
Mr & Mrs E Bottomley, 2 Lythwood Hall, Lythwood, Bayston Hill, Shrewsbury, **Shropshire**, SY3 0AD, **ENGLAND**.
(T) 01743 874747.
Profile Breeder. **Ref: YH01668**

BOUGHTON MILL RIDING SCHOOL
Boughton Mill Riding School, Boughton Mill, Welford Rd, Chapel Brampton, Northampton, **Northamptonshire**, NN6 8AB, **ENGLAND**.
(T) 01604 843319.
Contact/s
Owner: Mr C Robinson
Profile Riding School.
Opening Times
Sp: Open Mon - Sun 09:00. Closed Mon - Sun 20:00.
Su: Open Mon - Sun 09:00. Closed Mon - Sun 20:00.
Au: Open Mon - Sun 09:00. Closed Mon - Sun 20:00.
Wn: Open Mon - Sun 09:00. Closed Mon - Sun 20:00.
Answer phone service available. **Ref: YH01669**

BOUGOURD, W R
W R Bougourd, Broadmead Cottage, West End, Nailsea, Bristol, **Bristol**, BS48 2DD, **ENGLAND**.
(T) 01275 856456.
Profile Blacksmith. **Ref: YH01670**

BOUGOURD, WILLIAM R
William R Bougourd AWCF, Broadmead Cottage, West End, Nailsea, **Somerset (North)**, BS48 2BZ, **ENGLAND**.
(T) 01275 856456.
Profile Farrier. **Ref: YH01671**

BOULSTON
Boulston Equestrian Supplies, Unit 9, Withybush Trading Est, Haverfordwest, **Pembrokeshire**, SA62 4BS, **WALES**.
(T) 01437 769338 **(F)** 01437 779397
(E) beverly@boulston.freeserve.co.uk.
Profile Riding Wear Retailer, Saddlery Retailer, Supplies. **Ref: YH01672**

BOULTERS OF BANWELL
Boulters Of Banwell Ltd, Knightcott, Banwell, **Somerset (North)**, BS29 6HT, **ENGLAND**.
(T) 01934 822137 **(F)** 01934 823301.
Contact/s
General Manager: Mr P Boyes-Corkis
Profile Transport/Horse Boxes. **Ref: YH01673**

BOULTON & COOPER
Boulton & Cooper Ltd, St Michaels Hse, Malton, **Yorkshire (North)**, YO17 7LR, **ENGLAND**.
(T) 01653 692151 **(F)** 01653 600311.
Profile Property Agents. **Ref: YH01674**

BOULTON, ANDREA
Mrs Andrea Boulton, Joysons Hill Stables, Church Rd, Whyteleafe, **Surrey**, **ENGLAND**..
Profile Trainer. **Ref: YH01675**

BOUND, KEITH
Keith Bound, Cae Waen, Llangurig, Llanidloes, **Powys**, SY18 6SL, **WALES**.
(T) 01686 440606. **Ref: YH01676**

BOUNDARY FARM CARRIAGES
Boundary Farm Carriages, Boundary Farm Cottage, Boundary Lane, Wrightington, Wigan, **Lancashire**, WN6 0YX, **ENGLAND**.
(T) 01257 426145 **(F)** 01257 472222.
Profile Breeder, Stable/Livery, Trainer. **Ref: YH01677**

BOUNDARY GATE SADDLERY
Boundary Gate Saddlery, Hillside, Boundary Gate, Ditton Proprs, Bridgnorth, **Shropshire**, WV16 6TP, **ENGLAND**.
(T) 01746 712251
(M) 07702 326194.
Profile Supplies. **Ref: YH01678**

BOUNDARY ROAD STABLES
Boundary Road Stables, Boundary Rd, Taplow, Maidenhead, **Berkshire**, SL6 0EZ, **ENGLAND**.
(T) 01628 602869.
Contact/s
Manager: Miss A Manning
Profile Riding School. **Ref: YH01679**

BOUNDY, C J
C J Boundy RSS, Kilaganoon, Kerry Rd, Montgomery, **Powys**, SY15 6HW, **WALES**.
(T) 01686 668277.
Profile Farrier. **Ref: YH01680**

BOUNDY, TERRY
Terry Boundy, Tegfan, Montgomery, **Powys**, SY15 6HW, **WALES**.
(T) 01686 668505.
Profile Medical Support. **Ref: YH01681**

BOURNE PARK EQUESTRIAN CTRE
Bourne Park Equestrian Centre, Bourne Pk, Bridge, Canterbury, **Kent**, CT4 5BJ, **ENGLAND**.
(T) 01227 831927.
Contact/s
Owner: Miss K Hort **Ref: YH01682**

BOURNE VALE STABLES
Bourne Vale Stables, Little Hardwick Rd, Walsall, **Midlands (West)**, WS9 0SQ, **ENGLAND**.
(T) 0121 3537174.
Profile Riding School, Stable/Livery. **Ref: YH01683**

BOURNE, DAVID K
David K Bourne DWCF, 102 John St, Biddulph, Stoke-on-Trent, **Staffordshire**, ST8 6HW, **ENGLAND**.
(T) 01782 522627.
Profile Farrier. **Ref: YH01684**

BOURNE, SIMON S
Simon S Bourne, Day Green Farm, Day Green, Hassall Rd, Sandbach, **Cheshire**, CW11 4XU, **ENGLAND**.

(T) 01270 872095.
Contact/s
Farrier: Simon S Bourne **(Q)** DWCF
Profile Farrier. **Ref: YH01685**

BOURNEMOUTH BRONCOS

Bournemouth Broncos Horseball Club, C/O 15 Irving Rd, Southbourne, **Dorset**, BH6 5BG, **ENGLAND**.
(T) 01202 433135.
Profile Club/Association. **Ref: YH01686**

BOURNEMOUTH HORSE TRANSPORT

Bournemouth Horse Transport, 52 Wayside Rd, St. Leonards, Ringwood, **Hampshire**, BH24 2SJ, **ENGLAND**.
(T) 01202 891062.
Profile Transport/Horse Boxes. **Ref: YH01687**

BOURNEMOUTH TRAILER CTRE

Bournemouth Trailer Centre Ltd, 4 Old Forge Rd, Wimborne, **Dorset**, BH21 7RR, **ENGLAND**.
(T) 01202 893010 **(F)** 01202 897219.
Profile Transport/Horse Boxes. **Ref: YH01688**

BOURTON VALE EQUESTRIAN CTRE

Bourton Vale Equestrian Centre, Fosseway, Bourton-on-the-Water, Cheltenham, **Gloucestershire**, GL54 2HL, **ENGLAND**.
(T) 01451 820358.
Contact/s
Owner: Mr J Launchberry **Ref: YH01689**

BOURTON VALE EQUINE CLINIC

Bourton Vale Equine Clinic, The Veterinary Surgery, Wyck Rd, Lower Slaughter, Cheltenham, **Gloucestershire**, GL54 2EX, **ENGLAND**.
(T) 01451 820137 **(F)** 01451 822294.
Profile Medical Support. **Ref: YH01690**

BOUSFIELD, BRYAN

Mr Bryan Bousfield, Glaslyn Hse, Brough, Kirkby Stephen, **Cumbria**, CA17 4BT, **ENGLAND**.
(T) 01768 341391.
Profile Breeder. **Ref: YH01691**

BOUSFIELD, C J & J

C J & J Bousfield, Langrigg, Warcop, Appleby-In-Westmorland, **Cumbria**, CA16 6PT, **ENGLAND**.
(T) 01768 341395.
Contact/s
Owner: Mr C Bousfield
Profile Breeder. **Ref: YH01692**

BOUSFIELD, D

Mr D Bousfield, Trainlands, Maulds Meaburn, Penrith, **Cumbria**, CA10 3HX, **ENGLAND**.
(T) 01768 351249.
Profile Trainer. **Ref: YH01693**

BOW BRICKHILL TREKKING CTRE

Bow Brickhill Trekking Centre, Woburn Sands Rd, Bow Brickhill, Milton Keynes, **Buckinghamshire**, MK17 9JY, **ENGLAND**.
(T) 01908 373046.
Contact/s
Owner: Mrs L Skelton
Profile Equestrian Centre. Trekking Centre.
Ref: YH01694

BOW HOUSE FARM RIDING SCHOOL

Bow House Farm Riding School, Bow Hse, Bishops Castle, **Shropshire**, SY9 5HY, **ENGLAND**.
(T) 01588 638427.
Profile Riding School, Stable/Livery. **Ref: YH01695**

BOWDEN, JONATHAN D

Jonathan D Bowden DWCF, 3 Belle Vue Villas, Burton Row, Brent Knoll, Highbridge, **Somerset**, TA9 4BW, **ENGLAND**.
(T) 01278 760861.
Profile Farrier. **Ref: YH01696**

BOWDLER, T

T Bowdler, Cob Cottage, Lower Oulton, Norbury, Stafford, **Staffordshire**, ST20 0PG, **ENGLAND**.
(T) 01785 284363.
Profile Breeder. **Ref: YH01697**

BOWEN, ADRIAN R G

Adrian R G Bowen BII, Frondeg, 32 Brithwen Rd, Waunarlwydd, Swansea, **Swansea**, SA5 4QS, **WALES**.
(T) 01792 872868
(M) 07831 529089.
Profile Farrier. **Ref: YH01698**

BOWEN, DAVID & S D

David & S D Bowen, Moorham Hill Farm, Chapel Lane, Rawcliffe, Preston, **Lancashire**, PR3 6TB, **ENGLAND**.
(T) 01253 700376. **Ref: YH01699**

BOWEN, E & M

E & M Bowen, Eastwood, Derwydd Rd, Ammanford, **Carmarthenshire**, SA18 2TT, **WALES**.
(T) 01269 850495.
Profile Breeder. **Ref: YH01700**

BOWEN, JOHN

John Bowen, Old Farm Cottage, Hoggars Rd, Mendlesham, **Suffolk**, IP14 5SU, **ENGLAND**.
(T) 01449 766233
(E) johnsbowen@hotmail.com.
Profile Trainer.
British Eventing Coach. **Ref: YH01701**

BOWEN, PETER

Mr Peter Bowen, Yet-Y-Rhug, Letterston, Haverfordwest, **Pembrokeshire**, SA62 5TD, **WALES**.
(T) 01348 840118 **(F)** 01348 881373
(M) 07966 391196.
Profile Trainer. **Ref: YH01702**

BOWEN, S A

Mr S A Bowen, Plum Tree Cottage, 112 The Street, Adisham, Canterbury, **Kent**, CT3 3JR, **ENGLAND**.
(T) 01304 841876.
Profile Supplies. **Ref: YH01703**

BOWENS VICTOR

Bowens Victor, Grangecon, Colbinstown, **County Wicklow**, **IRELAND**.
(T) 045 403100.
Profile Supplies. **Ref: YH01704**

BOWENS, BARNABY

Barnaby Bowens DWCF, Smiths End Cottage, 72 Nunnery St, Castle Hedingham, **Essex**, CO9 3DP, **ENGLAND**.
(T) 01787 460508.
Profile Farrier. **Ref: YH01705**

BOWER, L J

Miss L J Bower, Greendowns, Preshaw Rd, Beauworth, Alresford, **Hampshire**, SO24 0PB, **ENGLAND**.
(T) 01962 771552.
Profile Trainer. **Ref: YH01706**

BOWERS, HENRY

Henry Bowers, Furnham Rd, Chard, **Somerset**, TA20 1AX, **ENGLAND**.
(T) 01460 62295.
Contact/s
Owner: Mr S Tolley
Profile Riding Club, Riding Wear Retailer, Saddlery Retailer.
Opening Times
Sp: Open Mon - Sat 09:00. Closed Mon - Sat 19:00.
Su: Open Mon - Sat 09:00. Closed Mon - Sat 19:00.
Au: Open Mon - Sat 09:00. Closed Mon - Sat 19:00.
Wn: Open Mon - Sat 09:00. Closed Mon - Sat 19:00.
Ref: YH01707

BOWERS, RICHARD

Richard Bowers, 15 Chequers Lane, Grendon, Northampton, **Northamptonshire**, NN7 1JP, **ENGLAND**.
(T) 01933 665900 **(F)** 01933 665901.
Contact/s
Partner: Mrs M Bowers
Profile Breeder. **Ref: YH01708**

BOWES MANOR EQUESTRIAN CTRE

Bowes Manor Equestrian Centre, Northside, Birtley, Chester Le Street, **County Durham**, DH3 1RF, **ENGLAND**.
(T) 0191 4109703 **(F)** 0191 4109703.
Contact/s
Owner: Mr S Gair
Profile Arena, Riding School, Stable/Livery, Transport/Horse Boxes. Horse Dealers.
Full and DIY livery available.
Opening Times
Sp: Open Mon - Sun 10:00. Closed Mon - Fri 18:00, Sat, Sun 19:00.
Su: Open Mon - Sun 10:00. Closed Mon - Fri 18:00, Sat, Sun 19:00.
Au: Open Mon - Sun 10:00. Closed Mon - Fri 16:00, Sat, Sun 17:00.
Wn: Open Mon - Sun 10:00. Closed Mon - Fri 16:00, Sat, Sun 17:00. **Ref: YH01709**

BOWHILL STABLES

Bowhill Stables, Bowhill Gardeners Cottage, Selkirk, **Scottish Borders**, TD7 5ET, **SCOTLAND**.
(T) 01750 20076 **(F)** 01750 20076
Affiliated Bodies BHS.
Contact/s
Owner: Mr A Black
(E) ali@bowhillstables.fsnet.co.uk
Profile Riding School, Stable/Livery, Track/Course.
Mr Black designed the Cross Country Event training course, alongside is a Le Trec course. Full livery, tuition and unlimited hacking through the surrounding estate available No.Staff: 2 **Ref: YH01710**

BOWLBY EQUINE

Bowlby Equine, Gurnsmead Farm, Kingston Lisle, Wantage, **Oxfordshire**, OX12 9QT, **ENGLAND**.
(T) 01367 820888 **(F)** 01367 820880.
Contact/s
Owner: Mr M Bowlby
Profile Trainer. **Ref: YH01711**

BOWLBY, P T S

Mr P T S Bowlby, Aisby Manor, Grantham, **Lincolnshire**, **ENGLAND**..
Profile Supplies. **Ref: YH01712**

BOWLEA TRAILERS

Bowlea Trailers, Bowlea Smithy, Howgate, Penicuik, **Lothian (Mid)**, EH26 8PX, **SCOTLAND**.
(T) 01968 673571 **(F)** 01968 673571.
Contact/s
Owner: Mr H McDonald - Smith
Profile Transport/Horse Boxes. No.Staff: 2
Yr. Est: 1991 C.Size: 7.5 Acres **Ref: YH01713**

BOWLER, A

A Bowler, Over Lane Farm, Over Lane, Hazelwood, Belper, **Derbyshire**, DE56 4AG, **ENGLAND**.
(T) 01773 550324 **(F)** 01773 550821.
Contact/s
Owner: Mr A Bowler
Profile Blacksmith. **Ref: YH01714**

BOWLERS

T W Bowler Ltd, Shady Oak Farm, Marple Rd, Offerton, Stockport, **Cheshire**, SK2 5HE, **ENGLAND**.
(T) 0161 4833375 **(F)** 0161 4873527.
Profile Riding Wear Retailer, Saddlery Retailer, Supplies. **Ref: YH01715**

BOWLERS RIDING SCHOOL

Bowlers Riding School, 35 Brewery Lane, Formby, Liverpool, **Merseyside**, L37 7DY, **ENGLAND**.
(T) 01704 872915
Affiliated Bodies BHS, RDA.
Contact/s
Owner: Miss M Bowler
Profile Riding School, Stable/Livery.
Driving and riding available for the disabled. Lessons are given for children from the age of three and a half years and upwards. Yr. Est: 1941
Opening Times
Sp: Open 09:00. Closed 22:00.
Su: Open 09:00. Closed 22:00.
Au: Open 09:00. Closed 22:00.
Wn: Open 09:00. Closed 22:00. **Ref: YH01716**

BOWLEY & COLEMAN TRUCKS

Bowley & Coleman Trucks Ltd, P O Box 25, Unit 73 Murdock Rd, Manton Lane Ind Est, Bedford, **Bedfordshire**, MK41 7PL, **ENGLAND**.
(T) 01234 349591 **(F)** 01234 356182.
Profile Supplies. **Ref: YH01717**

BOWLEY, HAZEL

Miss Hazel Bowley, 3 Corsehill View, Parkhill, Dyce, Aberdeen, **Aberdeen (City of)**, **SCOTLAND**..
Profile Breeder. **Ref: YH01718**

BOWLINGS RIDING SCHOOL

Bowlings Riding School, Meadow Farm, Rudbaxton, Haverfordwest, **Pembrokeshire**, SA62 4DB, **WALES**.
(T) 01437 741599.
Contact/s
Owner: Mrs J Gibson
Profile Riding School. **Ref: YH01719**

BOWMAN, CAROL

Mrs Carol Bowman, Stubbs Hall Farm, Wakefield Rd, Hampole, Doncaster, **Yorkshire (South)**, DN6 7EZ, **ENGLAND**.
(T) 01302 724659.
Profile Supplies. **Ref: YH01720**

BOWMAN, GEORGE

Mr George Bowman, Nine Chimneys, Red Hills, Penrith, **Cumbria**, CA11 0DR, **ENGLAND**.
(T) 01768 862676. **Ref: YH01721**

BOWNHILL EQUESTRIAN CTRE

Bownhill Equestrian Centre, Bownhill,

Woodchester, Stroud, **Gloucestershire**, GL5 5PW, **ENGLAND**.
(T) 01453 872144.
Contact/s
Owner: Mrs D Coles **Ref: YH01722**

BOWNHILL RIDING STABLES

Bownhill Riding Stables, Bownhill Lane, Lelley, Hull, **Yorkshire (East)**, HU12 8SS, **ENGLAND**.
(T) 01964 671913 **(F)** 01964 670641.
Contact/s
Owner: Mrs T Macintosh **Ref: YH01723**

BOWRING, S R

Mr S R Bowring, Fir Tree Farm, Edwinstowe, Mansfield, **Nottinghamshire**, NG21 9JG, **ENGLAND**.
(T) 01623 822451.
Profile Trainer. **Ref: YH01724**

BOWYER, D C

D C Bowyer, Hazeland Wood, Ratford, Calne, **Wiltshire**, SN11 9JX, **ENGLAND**.
(T) 01249 821839.
Profile Breeder. **Ref: YH01725**

BOXGROVE COMPETITION STABLES

Boxgrove Competition Stables, The Street, Boxgrove, Chichester, **Sussex (West)**, PO18 0DX, **ENGLAND**.
(T) 01243 775051.
Contact/s
Owner: Mr N Brookes
Profile Stable/Livery. **Ref: YH01726**

BOXMOOR SHOWJUMPS

Boxmoor Showjumps, Leighton Buzzard Rd, Piccotts End, Hemel Hempstead, **Hertfordshire**, HP1 3EJ, **ENGLAND**.
(T) 01442 267885
(M) 07836 291678.
Profile Supplies. **Ref: YH01727**

BOXTED HALL STUD

Boxted Hall Stud, Boxted Hall, Bury St Edmunds, **Suffolk**, IP29 4JT, **ENGLAND**.
(T) 01787 280226 **(F)** 01787 281663.
Profile Breeder. **Ref: YH01728**

BOYCE, DAVID J

David J Boyce RSS, Conamore, Old Post Office Rd, Chevington, Bury St Edmunds, **Suffolk**, IP29 5RD, **ENGLAND**.
(T) 01284 851059.
Profile Farrier. **Ref: YH01729**

BOYCE, P S

P S Boyce RSS, Lake View Cottage, Higher Priestacott, Belston, Okehampton, **Devon**, EX20 1QX, **ENGLAND**.
(T) 01837 840623.
Profile Farrier. **Ref: YH01730**

BOYD & PARTNERS

Boyd & Partners, 138 Kingston Rd, Staines, **Surrey**, TW18 1BL, **ENGLAND**.
(T) 01784 452048 **(F)** 01784 457232.
Profile Breeder. **Ref: YH01731**

BOYLE, M S

Mr M S Boyle, 143 Huntingdon Rd, Cambridge, **Cambridgeshire**, CB3 0DH, **ENGLAND**.
(T) 01223 368701.
Profile Medical Support. **Ref: YH01732**

BOYLES COURT

Boyles Court Farm, Dark Lane, Great Warley, Brentwood, **Essex**, CM14 5LL, **ENGLAND**.
(T) 01277 200989 **(F)** 01277 200989.
Contact/s
Owner: Mr R Waddington
Profile Stable/Livery. Yr. Est: 1991
C.Size: 109 Acres
Opening Times
Sp: Open 09:00. Closed 18:00.
Su: Open 09:00. Closed 18:00.
Au: Open 09:00. Closed 18:00.
Wn: Open 09:00. Closed 18:00. **Ref: YH01733**

BOYS, KEVIN

Kevin Boys, Surrey Docks Farm/South Wharf, Rotherhithe St, London, **London (Greater)**, SE16 5EY, **ENGLAND**.
(T) 020 72371408.
Profile Blacksmith. **Ref: YH01734**

BOYSON, R T

R T Boyson, Oakhanger Farm, Bordon, **Hampshire**, GU35 9JA, **ENGLAND**.
(T) 01420 474399.
Contact/s
Owner: Mr R Boyson **Ref: YH01735**

BRACKEN EQUESTRIAN

Bracken Equestrian, 87 Ballycoan Rd, Belfast, **County Antrim**, BT8 8LP, **NORTHERN IRELAND**.
(T) 028 90812485 **(F)** 028 90817413
Affiliated Bodies BETA, GMC, MSA.
Contact/s
Owner: Mr C Jackson
Profile Riding Wear Retailer, Saddlery Retailer.
Yr. Est: 1980
Opening Times
Sp: Open Mon - Sat 09:00. Closed Mon, Wed, Fri, 21:00, Tues, Thurs, Sat, 18:00.
Su: Open Mon - Sat 09:00. Closed Mon, Wed, Fri, 21:00, Tues: Thurs, Sat, 18:00.
Au: Open Mon - Sat 09:00. Closed Mon, Wed, Fri, 21:00, Tues: Thurs, Sat, 18:00.
Wn: Open Mon - Sat 09:00. Closed Mon, Wed, Fri, 21:00, Tues: Thurs, Sat, 18:00. **Ref: YH01736**

BRACKENBURY, R

Mrs R Brackenbury, The New Inn, Moreleigh, Totnes, **Devon**, TQ9 7JH, **ENGLAND**.
(T) 01548 821326.
Profile Supplies. **Ref: YH01737**

BRACKENDENE STUD

Brackendene Stud, Llanfair-Yn-Neubwll, Valley, Holyhead, Anglesey, **Isle of Anglesey**, LL65 3HF, **WALES**.
(T) 01407 740900.
Contact/s
Owner: Miss C Plews
Profile Breeder, Stable/Livery, Track/Course.
Ref: YH01738

BRACKENHILL STUD

Brackenhill Stud, Fawley, Henley-on-Thames, **Oxfordshire**, RG9 6JA, **ENGLAND**.
(T) 01491 575347 **(F)** 01491 579674.
Profile Breeder. **Ref: YH01739**

BRACKENHURST CLGE

Brackenhurst College Riding Club, Holly Farmhouse, Low St, Collingham, Newark, **Nottinghamshire**, NG23 7NL, **ENGLAND**.
(T) 01636 892957.
Contact/s
Chairman: Mr K Rodgerson
Profile Club/Association, Riding Club. **Ref: YH01740**

BRACKENHURST COLLEGE

Brackenhurst College, Student Administration, Department of Land-Based Studies, The Nottingham Trent University, Brackenhurst, Southwell, **Nottinghamshire**, NG25 0QF, **ENGLAND**.
(T) 01636 817000
(E) enquiries.lbs@ntu.ac.uk
(W) www.science.ntu.ac.uk/lbs.
Contact/s
Key Contact: David Butcher
Profile Equestrian Centre, College.
College offering equine studies. **Ref: YH01741**

BRACKNELL HORSE TRANSPORT

Bracknell Horse Transport, Rose Cottage Stables, Binfield Rd, Wokingham, **Berkshire**, RG40 5PP, **ENGLAND**.
(T) 01344 860566 **(F)** 01344 860566.
Contact/s
Owner: Ms S Scott
Profile Transport/Horse Boxes. **Ref: YH01742**

BRADBOURNE

Bradbourne Riding & Training Centre, Bradbourne Vale Rd, Sevenoaks, **Kent**, TN13 3DH, **ENGLAND**.
(T) 01732 453592.
Contact/s
Owner: Mr P Felgate
Profile Riding School, Trainer. **Ref: YH01743**

BRADBOURNE RIDING CLUB

Bradbourne Riding Club, Burrs Hill Barn, Burrs Hill, Brenchley, **Kent**, TN12 7AT, **ENGLAND**.
(T) 01892 723860.
Contact/s
Chairman: Mrs E Rushton
Profile Club/Association, Riding Club. **Ref: YH01744**

BRADBURNE, S

Mrs S Bradburne, Cunnoquhie Cottage, Ladybank, Cupar, **Fife**, KY15 7RU, **SCOTLAND**.
(T) 01337 810325 **(F)** 01337 810486
(M) 07768 705722.
Profile Trainer. **Ref: YH01745**

BRADBURY, DOUGLAS

Douglas Bradbury FWCF, 40 Thanet St, Clay Cross, Chesterfield, **Derbyshire**, S45 9JR, **ENGLAND**.
(T) 01246 863557.
Profile Farrier. **Ref: YH01746**

BRADBURY, NEAL

Neal Bradbury AWCF, 12 Linden Court, Clay Cross, Chesterfield, **Derbyshire**, S45 9HU, **ENGLAND**.
(T) 01246 861208.
Profile Farrier. **Ref: YH01747**

BRADFIELD RIDING CTRE

Bradfield Riding Centre, The Maltings, Bradfield, Reading, **Berkshire**, RG7 6AJ, **ENGLAND**.
(T) 0118 9744048.
Contact/s
Manager: Mrs J Edwards
Profile Riding School. **Ref: YH01748**

BRADLEY DOUBLELOCK

Bradley Doublelock Ltd, Victoria Works, Victoria St, Bingley, **Yorkshire (West)**, BD16 2NH, **ENGLAND**.
(T) 01274 560414 **(F)** 01274 551114.
Profile Transport/Horse Boxes. **Ref: YH01749**

BRADLEY DOUBLELOCK LTD

Bradley Doublelock Ltd, Unit 6, Monksland Trading Ctre, Galway Rd, Athlone, **County Roscommon**, **IRELAND**.
(T) 090 294628.
Contact/s
Branch Manager: Mr L Philips
Profile Transport/Horse Boxes. **Ref: YH01750**

BRADLEY MILL RIDING CTRE

Bradley Mill Riding Centre, Bradley Mill Farm, Wylam, **Northumberland**, NE41 8JD, **ENGLAND**.
(T) 01661 852707.
Contact/s
Owner: Mrs M Vallally **Ref: YH01751**

BRADLEY, A S

Miss A S Bradley, The Cottage, Tanners Lane, Berkswell, Coventry, **Warwickshire**, CV7 7DD, **ENGLAND**.
(T) 024 76470017.
Profile Trainer. **Ref: YH01752**

BRADLEY, D

D Bradley, Low Cockhow, Kinniside, Cleator, **Cumbria**, CA23 3AQ, **ENGLAND**.
(T) 01946 861354.
Profile Riding School. **Ref: YH01753**

BRADLEY, J M

Mr J M Bradley, Meads Farm, Sedbury Pk, Chepstow, **Monmouthshire**, NP16 7HN, **WALES**.
(T) 01291 622486 **(F)** 01291 626939.
Profile Trainer. **Ref: YH01754**

BRADLEY, JOHN

John Bradley, 5 Mereside, Soham, Ely, **Cambridgeshire**, CB7 5EE, **ENGLAND**.
(T) 01353 721367.
Profile Breeder. **Ref: YH01755**

BRADLEY, KEVIN

Kevin Bradley DWCF, 6 Ash Drive, Brackley, **Northamptonshire**, NN13 6EU, **ENGLAND**.
(T) 07976 711701.
Profile Farrier. **Ref: YH01756**

BRADLEY, M

Ms M Bradley, Waithe Close Farm, Thick Hollins Rd, Meltham, Huddersfield, **Yorkshire (West)**, HD7 1BN, **ENGLAND**.
(T) 01484 854138.
Profile Breeder. **Ref: YH01757**

BRADLEY, N

Mrs N Bradley, Mill Drove Farm, Mill Drove, Soham, **Cambridgeshire**, CB7 5HX, **ENGLAND**.
(T) 01353 720379.
Profile Breeder. **Ref: YH01758**

BRADLEY, PAUL

Mr Paul Bradley, New Pk, 117 Draycott Old Rd, Forsbrook, Stoke-on-Trent, **Staffordshire**, ST11 9AL, **ENGLAND**.
(T) 01782 392191 **(F)** 01782 598427
(M) 07711 965030.
Profile Supplies. **Ref: YH01759**

BRADLEY, S & J

Bradley S & J, Thorncliffe Stables, Thorncliffe Hall Farm, Hollingworth, Hyde, **Cheshire**, SK14 8JJ,

ENGLAND.
(T) 01457 762177.
Contact/s
Owner: Mrs S Bradley **Ref: YH01760**

BRADMAN, N

Mr N Bradman, Frandor, Waggon Lane, Upton, Pontefract, **Yorkshire (West)**, WF9 1JT, **ENGLAND**.
(T) 01977 642204.
Profile Breeder. **Ref: YH01761**

BRADSHAW, R J W

R J W Bradshaw, Hill Hse Farm, Ardingly Rd, Lindfield, Haywards Heath, **Sussex (West)**, RH16 2QY, **ENGLAND**.
(T) 01444 484057.
Profile Blacksmith. **Ref: YH01762**

BRADSTOCK HAMILTON & PARTNERS

Bradstock Hamilton & Partners Ltd, First Floor, 168 High St, Newmarket, **Suffolk**, CB8 9AJ, **ENGLAND**.
(T) 01638 676700 (F) 01638 664700.
Profile Club/Association. **Ref: YH01763**

BRADSTOCK, MARK

Mark Bradstock, Old Manor Hse, Letcombe Bassett, Wantage, **Oxfordshire**, OX12 9LP, **ENGLAND**.
(T) 01235 760780 (F) 01235 760754.
Profile Trainer. **Ref: YH01764**

BRADWELL, J

J Bradwell, Hall Cottage, High St, Holme, Newark, **Nottinghamshire**, NG23 7RZ, **ENGLAND**.
(T) 01636 703655 (F) 01636 703655.
Contact/s
Owner: Miss J Bradwell **Ref: YH01765**

BRADWELL, JANE

Jane Bradwell, Wolds Farm, Fosse Way, Cotgrave, **Nottinghamshire**, NG12 3HG, **ENGLAND**.
(T) 0115 9899717 (F) 0115 9899898.
Profile Trainer. **Ref: YH01766**

BRADY, R M S

Mr R M S Brady, West Langfaulds Farm, Saline, Dunfermline, **Fife**, KY12, **SCOTLAND**.. **Ref: YH01767**

BRADY, RON

Mr Ron Brady, West Langfaulds, Saline, **Fife**, KY12 9HR, **SCOTLAND**.
(T) 01383 851765.
Profile Breeder. **Ref: YH01768**

BRAEKMAN, HELENE

Helene Braekman, Green Pl, Ugley Green, Bishop's Stortford, **Essex**, CM22 6HL, **ENGLAND**.
(T) 01279 813286.
Profile Stable/Livery. **Ref: YH01769**

BRAEMAR

Braemar Equestrian, Fieldend Lane, Elstronwick, Hull, **Yorkshire (East)**, HU12 9BX, **ENGLAND**.
(T) 01964 670121
(E) info@braemarequestrian.com
(W) www.braemarequestrian.com.
Contact/s
Instructor: Mrs S Billany (Q) BHSAI
Profile Equestrian Centre, Horse/Rider Accom, Stable/Livery.
Regular shows and discipline clinics held. Private tuition is available with your own horse. No.Staff: 3 Yr. Est: 1999 C.Size: 15 Acres
Opening Times
Sp: Open Mon - Sun 09:00. Closed Mon - Sun 17:30.
Su: Open Mon - Sun 09:00. Closed Mon - Sun 17:30.
Au: Open Mon - Sun 09:00. Closed Mon - Sun 17:30.
Wn: Open Mon - Sun 09:00. Closed Mon - Sun 17:30.
Accommodation available May - September or by appointment **Ref: YH01770**

BRAES OF DERWENT

Braes Of Derwent, Beda Lodge, Hookergate, High Spen, Rowlands Gill, **Tyne and Wear**, NE39 2AF, **ENGLAND**.
(T) 01207 544476
(E) smithdj5@netscapeonline.co.uk
(W) www.braes-of-derwent.com. **Ref: YH01771**

BRAESIDE

Braeside Cross Country, Braeside Of Lindores, Newburgh, Cupar, **Fife**, KY14 6HU, **SCOTLAND**.
(T) 01337 840351
Affiliated Bodies BHS.
Contact/s
Owner: Mrs F Black
Profile Track/Course.
Course available for hire, £10.00 per horse per hour. Tuition with your own horse is also available.
No.Staff: 2 Yr. Est: 1987 C.Size: 70 Acres
Opening Times
Sp: Open Mon - Sun 09:00. Closed Mon - Sun 19:00.
Su: Open Mon - Sun 09:00. Closed Mon - Sun 19:00.
Au: Open Mon - Sun 09:00. Closed Mon - Sun 19:00.
Open March - October, closed through the winter
Ref: YH01772

BRAESIDE E.C

Braeside Equestrian Centre, Nelson Pk Rd, St. Margarets-At-Cliffe, Dover, **Kent**, CT15 6HH, **ENGLAND**.
(T) 01304 852959
Affiliated Bodies ABRS.
Contact/s
Owner: Miss J Driver (Q) BHSII
Profile Equestrian Centre, Riding School, Stable/Livery, Trainer. No.Staff: 6 Yr. Est: 1971 C.Size: 30 Acres **Ref: YH01773**

BRAESIDE EQUESTRIAN CTRE

Braeside Equestrian Centre, Durno, Pitcaphe, Inverurie, **Aberdeenshire**, AB51 5EN, **SCOTLAND**.
(T) 01467 681620.
Profile Stable/Livery. **Ref: YH01774**

BRAGG, MIRANDA

Miss Miranda Bragg, Rock Pk, Wotton Cross, Buckfastleigh, **Devon**, TQ11 0HB, **ENGLAND**.
(T) 01364 642137.
Profile Trainer. **Ref: YH01775**

BRAIDWOOD HSE EQUESTRIAN CTRE

Braidwood House Equestrian Centre, Braidwood Hse, Silverburn, **Lothian (Mid)**, EH26 9LP, **SCOTLAND**.
(T) 01968 676425 (F) 01968 676425.
Profile Equestrian Centre. **Ref: YH01776**

BRAILSFORD STABLES

Brailsford Stables Horsedrawn Carriages, The Cottage, Slack Lane, Brailsford, Ashbourne, **Derbyshire**, DE6 3BB, **ENGLAND**.
(T) 01335 360537
(E) brailsfordstables@yahoo.com
(W) www.brailsfordstables.co.uk.
Contact/s
Owner: Mr D Molloy
Profile Horse Drawn Carriages. Yr. Est: 1979
Ref: YH01777

BRAIN INTERNATIONAL

Brain International Ltd, P O Box 16, Woodstock, **Oxfordshire**, OX20 1NS, **ENGLAND**.
(T) 01993 812186 (F) 01993 813660.
Profile Blood Stock Agency. **Ref: YH01778**

BRAITHWAITE, C G

Mrs C G Braithwaite, Lochmalony, Cupar, **Fife**, KY15 4QF, **SCOTLAND**.
(T) 01337 870238.
Profile Breeder. **Ref: YH01779**

BRAKE, C J

C J Brake, Heazle Farm, Clayhidon, Cullompton, **Devon**, EX15 3TH, **ENGLAND**.
(T) 01823 680280.
Contact/s
Owner: Mr C Brake
Profile Riding School, Trainer. **Ref: YH01780**

BRAKE, DAVID & JANET

David & Janet Brake, 39 Eastville Rd, Tyllwyn, Ebbw Vale, **Blaenau Gwent**, NP23 6AH, **WALES**.
(T) 01495 305198.
Profile Breeder. **Ref: YH01781**

BRAKE, J R

J R Brake, Dingford Green, Buckland St. Mary, Chard, **Somerset**, TA20 3JW, **ENGLAND**.
(T) 01460 234295.
Profile Breeder. **Ref: YH01782**

BRAKE, R M

R M Brake, Fairlawn Farm, 20 Fairlawn Rd, Carshalton, **Surrey**, SM5 4HT, **ENGLAND**.
(T) 020 86420844. **Ref: YH01783**

BRAKE, V

Mr V Brake, Rapps Farm Cottage, Rapps, Ashill, Ilminster, **Somerset**, TA19 9LQ, **ENGLAND**.
(T) 01460 57128.
Profile Breeder. **Ref: YH01784**

BRAKEWELL, JEANETTE

Jeanette Brakewell, Oram Hse Farm, Oram Rd, Brindle, Chorley, **Lancashire**, PR6 8NT, **ENGLAND**.
(T) 01254 854238. **Ref: YH01785**

BRAMBER TRAILERS

Bramber Trailers, South View Rd, Willand, Cullompton, **Devon**, EX15 2RU, **ENGLAND**.
(T) 01884 820105 (F) 01884 821115.
Contact/s
Manager: Mr T Williams
Profile Transport/Horse Boxes. **Ref: YH01786**

BRAMBLES FARM ARABIANS

Brambles Farm Arabians, Brambles Farm, Gotham, Edmondsham, Wimborne, **Dorset**, BH21 5RJ, **ENGLAND**.
(T) 01202 822837.
Contact/s
Secretary: Miss S Coombs
Profile Saddlery Retailer.
Opening Times
Sp: Open Mon - Sun 24 Hours. Closed Mon - Sun 24 Hours.
Su: Open Mon - Sun 24 Hours. Closed Mon - Sun 24 Hours.
Au: Open Mon - Sun 24 Hours. Closed Mon - Sun 24 Hours.
Wn: Open Mon - Sun 24 Hours. Closed Mon - Sun 24 Hours. **Ref: YH01787**

BRAMBLES VETNRY SURGERY

Brambles Veterinary Surgery (The), 37 Albemarle Rd, Churchdown, **Gloucestershire**, GL3 2HE, **ENGLAND**.
(T) 01452 712194.
Contact/s
Owner: Mr N Savill (Q) BVSc, MRCVS
Profile Medical Support. **Ref: YH01788**

BRAMDON TREKKING CTRE

Bramdon Trekking Centre, Bramdon Lane, Portesham, Weymouth, **Dorset**, DT3 4HG, **ENGLAND**.
(T) 01305 871011.
Contact/s
Manager: Mr S George
Profile Equestrian Centre. Trekking Centre.
Ref: YH01789

BRAMLEY & WELLESLEY

Bramley & Wellesley Ltd, Unit C Chancel Close Trading Est, Eastern Ave, Gloucester, **Gloucestershire**, GL4 7SN, **ENGLAND**.
(T) 01452 300450 (F) 01452 308776
(E) bramley@wildnet.co.uk. **Ref: YH01790**

BRAMLEY, FRANCIS N

Francis N Bramley DWCF BII, C/O 123 High St, Barton Upon Humber, **Lincolnshire (North)**, DN18 5PU, **ENGLAND**..
Profile Farrier. **Ref: YH01791**

BRAMLEY, H

Mrs H Bramley, Station Farm, Bolton Percy, York, **Yorkshire (North)**, YO23 7AR, **ENGLAND**.
(T) 01904 744295.
Profile Breeder. **Ref: YH01792**

BRAMMALL, C A

C A Brammall, Bark Barn Forge, Graythwaite, Ulverston, **Cumbria**, LA12 8BB, **ENGLAND**.
(T) 01539 531833.
Profile Blacksmith. **Ref: YH01793**

BRAMPTON STABLES

Brampton Stables, Stable Lane, Church Brampton, Northampton, **Northamptonshire**, NN6 8BH, **ENGLAND**.
(T) 01604 842051 (F) 01604 842051.
Contact/s
Owner: Mr D Ward
Profile Riding School, Stable/Livery, Trainer.
Ref: YH01794

BRAND, J

Mr J Brand, Hereward Hse, Ely Rd, Witchford, **Cambridgeshire**, CB6 2HL, **ENGLAND**.
(T) 01353 663756.
Profile Breeder. **Ref: YH01795**

BRANDON FORGE SADDLERY

Brandon Forge Saddlery, Brandon Cres, Shadwell, Leeds, **Yorkshire (West)**, LS17 9JH, **ENGLAND**.
(T) 0113 2893374 (F) 0113 2893374
(W) www.brandonforgesaddlery.co.uk
Affiliated Bodies BETA.
Contact/s

General Manager: Ms R Mackie
Profile Saddlery Retailer. No.Staff: 2
Yr. Est: 1998 C.Size: 0.75 Acres
Opening Times
Sp: Open 09:30. Closed 17:30.
Su: Open 09:30. Closed 17:30.
Au: Open 09:30. Closed 17:30.
Wn: Open 09:30. Closed 17:30. Ref: YH01796

BRANDON RIDING ACADEMY

Brandon Riding Academy, Church Farm, Church Rd, Brandon, **Suffolk**, IP27 0JB, **ENGLAND**.
(T) 01842 810089.
Profile Stable/Livery. Ref: YH01797

BRANDON, E E (MRS)

Mrs E E Brandon, Shaw's Fold Farm, Boulton Rd, Aspull, Wigan, **Lancashire**, WN2 1PR, **ENGLAND**.
(T) 01942 831155.
Profile Breeder. Ref: YH01798

BRANDON-LODGE, C

Mrs C Brandon-Lodge, North Hill Farm, Cardington, Church Stretton, **Shropshire**, SY6 7LL, **ENGLAND**.
(T) 01694 771532.
Contact/s
Owner: George Brandon
Profile Horse/Rider Accom. Bed and Breakfast for Horses. Ref: YH01799

BRANDSBY AGRIC TRADING ASS

Brandsby Agric Trading Assoc Ltd (Driffield), Westgates, Nefferton, Driffield, **Yorkshire (East)**, YO25 4LJ, **ENGLAND**.
(T) 01377 254325.
Profile Supplies. Ref: YH01800

BRANDSBY AGRIC TRADING ASS

Brandsby Agric Trading Assoc Ltd (Kirkbymoorside), New Rd, Kirkbymoorside, **Yorkshire (North)**, YO62 6DT, **ENGLAND**.
(T) 01751 431302.
Profile Supplies. Ref: YH01801

BRANDSBY AGRIC TRADING ASS

Brandsby Agric Trading Assoc Ltd (Malton), Norton Rd, Malton, **Yorkshire (North)**, YO17 0NU, **ENGLAND**.
(T) 01653 693234 **(F)** 01653 696252. Ref: YH01802

BRANDSBY AGRIC TRADING ASSOC

Brandsby Agric Trading Assoc Ltd (Easingwold), Shire Bridge Mill, York Rd, Easingwold, **Yorkshire (North)**, YO61 3EQ, **ENGLAND**.
(T) 01347 21303.
Profile Supplies. Ref: YH01803

BRANDSBY AGRIC TRADING ASSOC

Brandsby Agric Trading Assoc Ltd (Egton), Kirkdale, Egton, Whitby, **Yorkshire (North)**, YO21 1UT, **ENGLAND**.
(T) 01947 85381.
Profile Supplies. Ref: YH01804

BRANDSBY AGRIC TRADING ASSOC

Brandsby Agric Trading Assoc Ltd (Helmsley), Station Rd, Helmsley, **Yorkshire (North)**, YO62 5DQ, **ENGLAND**.
(T) 01439 70372.
Profile Supplies. Ref: YH01805

BRANDSBY AGRIC TRADING ASSOC

Brandsby Agric Trading Assoc Ltd (Ruswarp), Station Yard, Ruswarp, Whitby, **Yorkshire (North)**, YO23 1NJ, **ENGLAND**.
(T) 01947 602522.
Profile Supplies. Ref: YH01806

BRANDSBY AGRIC TRADING ASSOC

Brandsby Agric Trading Assoc Ltd (Scarborough), Seamer, Scarborough, **Yorkshire (North)**, YO11 3PS, **ENGLAND**.
(T) 01723 584455.
Profile Supplies. Ref: YH01807

BRANDSBY AGRIC TRADING ASSOC

Brandsby Agric Trading Assoc Ltd (York), Gate Helmsley, York, **Yorkshire (North)**, YO41 1JS, **ENGLAND**.
(T) 01759 371291.
Profile Supplies. Ref: YH01808

BRANDSBY DARTMOORS

Brandsby Dartmoors, Lane Farm, Guilsfield, Welshpool, **Powys**, SY21 9DH, **WALES**.
(T) 01938 556315.
Profile Breeder. Ref: YH01809

BRANDSTONE FARM LIVERIES

Brandstone Farm Liveries, Brandstone Farm, Melton Brand, Doncaster, **Yorkshire (South)**, DN5 7EB, **ENGLAND**.
(T) 01302 789139 **(F)** 01302 783231.
Contact/s
Owner: Mrs S Middleton
Profile Stable/Livery.
DIY livery available for six horses only. Yr. Est: 1989
C.Size: 5 Acres
Opening Times
By appointment only Ref: YH01810

BRANSBY HOME

Bransby Home of Rest for Horses, Bransby, Saxilby, **Lincolnshire**, LN1 2PH, **ENGLAND**.
(T) 01427 788464 **(F)** 01427 787657.
Contact/s
Hon Secretary: Mr P Hunt
Profile Medical Support. Ref: YH01811

BRASH, DEAN

Dean Brash, Lea Lane, Great Braxted, Witham, **Essex**, CM8 3EP, **ENGLAND**.
(T) 01621 891376.
Profile Farrier. Ref: YH01812

BRASHILL, M

M Brashill, 42 Bannister St, Withernsea, **Yorkshire (East)**, HU19 2DT, **ENGLAND**.
(T) 01964 613928.
Profile Farrier. Ref: YH01813

BRASS TACKS

Brass Tacks, Garden Cottage, Little Somerford, Chippenham, **Wiltshire**, SN15 5BH, **ENGLAND**.
(T) 01666 826536
(M) 07775 943396. Ref: YH01814

BRASSIL, MARTIN

Martin Brassil, Beech Pk, Dunmurry, Kildare, **County Kildare**, **IRELAND**.
(T) 045 521042 **(F)** 045 521042
(W) www.kildarehorses.ie.
Contact/s
Trainer: Mr M Brassil
(E) martinbrassil@kildarehorse.ie
Profile Trainer. Ref: YH01815

BRASTOCK, R W

R W Brastock, Withymoor Cottage, Sodbury Rd, Badminton, **Gloucestershire**, GL9 1EV, **ENGLAND**.
(T) 01454 21465.
Profile Transport/Horse Boxes. Ref: YH01816

BRATTON STUD

Bratton Stud, Wooperton, Alnwick, **Northumberland**, NE66 4XJ, **ENGLAND**.
(T) 01665 578471.
Profile Breeder. Ref: YH01817

BRAVERY, G C

G C Bravery, Hamilton Rd, Newmarket, **Suffolk**, CB8 7JQ, **ENGLAND**.
(T) 01638 668985 **(F)** 01638 668985
(M) 07711 112345
(W) www.newmarketracehorsetrainers.co.uk
Affiliated Bodies Newmarket Trainers Fed.
Contact/s
Trainer: Mr G Bravery
Profile Trainer. Ref: YH01818

BRAWLINGS FARM RIDING CTRE

Brawlings Farm Riding Centre, Brawlings Lane, Chalfont St. Peter, Gerrards Cross, **Buckinghamshire**, SL9 0RE, **ENGLAND**.
(T) 01494 872132 **(F)** 01494 872611
Affiliated Bodies BHS, Pony Club UK.
Contact/s
Owner: Ms J Edwards **(Q)** BHSII **(T)** 01494 872377
(E) brawlingsfarm@aol.com
Profile Equestrian Centre, Riding Club, Riding School, Stable/Livery. No.Staff: 4 Yr. Est: 1990
C.Size: 15 Acres Ref: YH01819

BRAY, GEOFFREY A

Geoffrey A Bray DWCF, Woodstock, New Hse Lane, Pluckley, Ashford, **Kent**, TN27 0RX, **ENGLAND**..
Profile Farrier. Ref: YH01820

BRAYBAY COUNTRY KNITWEAR

Braybay Country Knitwear, Place Farm, Bardwell, Bury St Edmunds, **Suffolk**, IP31 1AQ, **ENGLAND**.
(T) 01359 251044.
Profile Supplies. Ref: YH01821

BRAYSIDE FARM DIY LIVERY

Brayside Farm DIY Livery, Clay Hill, Enfield, **London (Greater)**, EN2 9JL, **ENGLAND**.
(T) 020 83637064.
Contact/s
Owner: Mrs S Stevens
Profile Stable/Livery. Ref: YH01822

BRAZIER, JOHN F H

John F H Brazier MRCVS, Campbells Farm, Weston-under-Wetherley, Leamington Spa, **Warwickshire**, CV33 9BS, **ENGLAND**.
(T) 01926 632122 **(F)** 01926 632122.
Profile Medical Support. Ref: YH01823

BRAZINGTON, R G

Mr R G Brazington, Chapel Farm, Redmarley, **Gloucestershire**, GL19 3JF, **ENGLAND**.
(T) 01452 840384.
Profile Trainer. Ref: YH01824

BREAKSPEAR RIDING CLUB

Breakspear Riding Club, 31 Grayshott Laurels, Lindford, Bordon, **Hampshire**, GU35 0QB, **ENGLAND**.
(T) 01420 478247 **(F)** 01420 478247.
Contact/s
Chairman: Miss C Jensen
Profile Club/Association, Riding Club. Ref: YH01825

BREAKWELL, COLIN E

Colin E Breakwell RSS, 140 The Meadows, Green Lane, Leominster, **Herefordshire**, HR6 8RE, **ENGLAND**.
(T) 01568 612236.
Profile Farrier. Ref: YH01826

BREAKWELL, RON

Ron Breakwell, Blue Hse Farm, Aldridge Rd, Streetly, Sutton Coldfield, **Midlands (West)**, B74 2DX, **ENGLAND**.
(T) 0121 3534167 **(F)** 0121 3534167.
Contact/s
Partner: Mrs P Breakwell
Profile Blacksmith. Ref: YH01827

BREASTON EQUESTRIAN CTRE

Breaston Equestrian Centre, Sawley Rd, Breaston, Derby, **Derbyshire**, DE72 3EF, **ENGLAND**.
(T) 01332 872934.
Profile Riding School. Ref: YH01828

BRECON & TALYBONT

Brecon & Talybont, Glanafon, Fennifach, Brecon, **Powys**, LD3 9PH, **WALES**.
(T) 01874 623531. Ref: YH01829

BRECONGILL STABLES

Brecongill Stables, Brecongill, Middleham, Leyburn, **Yorkshire (North)**, DL8 4TJ, **ENGLAND**.
(T) 01969 640223 **(F)** 01969 640223.
Contact/s
Owner: Miss S Hall
Profile Trainer. Ref: YH01830

BREDY VETNRY CTRE

Bredy Veterinary Centre, Sea Rd North, Bridport, **Dorset**, DT6 4RR, **ENGLAND**.
(T) 01308 456771.
Profile Medical Support. Ref: YH01831

BREED EX EQUINE STUD

Breed EX Equine Stud (The), High Brow, Tirril, Penrith, **Cumbria**, CA10 2LS, **ENGLAND**.
(T) 01768 486986 **(F)** 01768 486986.
Profile Breeder, Stable/Livery, Supplies, Track/Course, Trainer. Ref: YH01832

BREESE, J C

Mrs J C Breese, Baddymarsh Farm, Lower Eggleton, Ledbury, **Herefordshire**, HR8 2UH, **ENGLAND**.
(T) 01531 670642 **(F)** 01531 670794.
Profile Supplies. Ref: YH01833

BREMNER, BLACK

Bremner, Black & Co, 21 Dunkeld St, Aberfeldy, **Perth and Kinross**, PH15 2AA, **SCOTLAND**.
(T) 01887 820616 **(F)** 01887 820616.
Profile Supplies. Ref: YH01834

BRENDON

Brendon Stud, London Rd, Pyecombe, Brighton, **Sussex (West)**, BN45 7ED, **ENGLAND**.
(T) 01273 844508/844697 **(F)** 01273 844322
(E) info@brendonstud.co.uk
(W) www.brendonstud.co.uk
Affiliated Bodies BD, BE, BEF, BERA, BETA, BHS, BSJA, Pony Club UK, RDA.

Contact/s
Assistant Manager: Ms E White
Profile Breeder, Equestrian Centre, Stud Farm, Trainer. No.Staff: 4 Yr. Est: 1982
C.Size: 90 Acres
Opening Times
Telephone for an appointment. During the evening please use the following number 01273 844697
Ref: YH01835

BRENDON HILL

Brendon Hill Farm, Brendon Hill, Watchet, **Somerset**, TA23 0LJ, **ENGLAND**.
(T) 01398 371222 (F) 01398 371481
(E) brendonhill@enterprise.net
(W) www.brendon-hill-event-horses.co.uk.
Profile Breeder. Ref: YH01836

BRENDON HORSE & RIDER

Brendon Horse & Rider Centre, London Rd, Pyecombe, Brighton, **Sussex (West)**, BN45 7ED, **ENGLAND**.
(T) 01273 845545 (F) 01273 844322
(W) www.brendon-pyecombe.co.uk
Affiliated Bodies BD, BE, BEF, BERA, BETA, BHS, BSJA, Pony Club UK, RDA.
Contact/s
Owner: Mr C Light
Profile Breeder, Equestrian Centre, Medical Support, Riding Wear Retailer, Saddlery Retailer, Stud Farm, Supplies, Trainer.
Veterinary products. No.Staff: 2 Yr. Est: 1980
Opening Times
Sp: Open Mon - Sat 09:00. Closed Mon - Sat 17:30.
Su: Open Mon - Sat 09:00. Closed Mon - Sat 17:30.
Au: Open Mon - Sat 09:00. Closed Mon - Sat 17:30.
Wn: Open Mon - Sat 09:00, Sun 10:00. Closed Mon - Sat 17:30, Sun 16:00.
Open on Show Sundays through the Winter.
Ref: YH01837

BRENDON MANOR FARM

Brendon Manor Farm & Riding Stables, Lynton, **Devon**, EX35 6LQ, **ENGLAND**.
(T) 01598 741246.
Profile Riding School, Stable/Livery. Ref: YH01838

BRENDON MANOR RIDING STABLES

Brendon Manor Riding Stables, Brendon, Lynton, **Devon**, EX35 6NX, **ENGLAND**.
(T) 01598 741246.
Profile Equestrian Centre. Ref: YH01839

BRENKLEY STABLES

Brenkley Stables, East Brenkley, Seaton Burn, Newcastle-upon-Tyne, **Tyne and Wear**, NE13 6BT, **ENGLAND**.
(T) 0191 2362145.
Contact/s
Owner: Mrs E Moscrop
Profile Breeder. Ref: YH01840

BRENLEY FARM LIVERY

Brenley Farm Livery, Brenley Farm Hse, Brenley Lane, Boughton-under-Blean, Faversham, **Kent**, ME13 9LY, **ENGLAND**.
(T) 01227 750552.
Contact/s
Owner: Miss K Vernon
Profile Stable/Livery. Ref: YH01841

BRENNAN RICHARD FENCING SV

Brennan Richard Fencing Service, Galbertstown Lr Holycross, Thurles, **County Tipperary**, **IRELAND**.
(T) 050 443236.
Profile Supplies. Ref: YH01842

BRENNAN, MICHAEL B

Michael B Brennan RSS, Ridgeland, Hallgate, Gedney, Spalding, **Lincolnshire**, PE12 0DA, **ENGLAND**.
(T) 01406 363484.
Profile Farrier. Ref: YH01843

BRENNAN, OWEN

Mr Owen Brennan, Sloswicks Farm, Broad Lane, Worksop, **Nottinghamshire**, S80 3NJ, **ENGLAND**.
(T) 01909 473950
(M) 07713 100041.
Profile Trainer. Ref: YH01844

BRENNAN, SHANE P

Shane P Brennan DWCF, Ridgeland, Hallgate, Gedney, Spalding, **Lincolnshire**, PE12 0DA, **ENGLAND**.
(T) 01406 363484.
Profile Farrier. Ref: YH01845

BRENNANSTOWN RIDING SCHOOL

Brennanstown Riding School Ltd, Hollybrook, Kilmacanogue, Bray, **County Wicklow**, **IRELAND**.
(T) 01 2863778 (F) 01 2829590.
Profile Riding School, Stable/Livery.
Offers ten week riding courses, both evening and day-time and gives training to BHS standard. Ref: YH01846

BRENT & BERROW RIDING CLUB

Brent & Berrow Riding Club, The Lodge, Shrub Farm, Burton Row, Brent Knoll, **Somerset**, TA9 4BX, **ENGLAND**.
(T) 01278 760787 (F) 01278 760787.
Profile Club/Association, Riding Club. Ref: YH01847

BRENT KNOLL RIDING CLUB

Brent Knoll Riding Club, Mendip View, Sparrow Hill Way, Upper Weare, Axbridge, **Somerset**, BS26 2LA, **ENGLAND**.
(T) 01934 732912.
Contact/s
Chairman: Mr E Scarlett
Profile Club/Association, Riding Club. Ref: YH01848

BRENTFORD RIDING SCHOOL

Brentford Riding School, Brentford, Ballydrain, Comber, **County Down**, **NORTHERN IRELAND**.
(T) 028 97 541259.
Profile Riding School. Ref: YH01849

BRENTON

Brenton, Penygarreg, Gwernogle, Carmarthen, **Carmarthenshire**, SA32 7SD, **WALES**.
(T) 01267 223248.
Contact/s
Owner: Mr P Brenton
Profile Breeder. Ref: YH01850

BRENTWOOD COMMUNICATIONS

Brentwood Communications Ltd, 180 Warley Hill, Brentwood, **Essex**, CM14 5HF, **ENGLAND**.
(T) 01277 225254 (F) 01277 223089. Ref: YH01851

BRETONS EQUESTRIAN CTRE

Bretons Equestrian Centre, Rainham Rd, Rainham, **Essex**, RM13 7LL, **ENGLAND**.
(T) 01708 524616.
Profile Equestrian Centre, Riding School.
Ref: YH01852

BRETT, CHRISTOPHER P J

Christopher P J Brett DWCF, 19 Keyford, Frome, **Somerset**, BA11 1JW, **ENGLAND**.
(T) 07973 360137.
Profile Farrier. Ref: YH01853

BREWIS, RHONA

Miss Rhona Brewis, Chester Hill, Belford, **Northumberland**, NE70 7EF, **ENGLAND**.
(T) 01668 213239
(M) 07718 390835.
Profile Breeder. Ref: YH01854

BREWSTER, J S

Mr J S Brewster, Garth Cottage Farm, Leeming Bar, Northallerton, **Yorkshire (North)**, DL7 9RS, **ENGLAND**.
(T) 01677 422893.
Profile Breeder. Ref: YH01855

BREWSTER, T & C

T & C Brewster, Bandirran Clydesdales, The Little Hse, Rait, Perth, **Perth and Kinross**, PH2 7RY, **SCOTLAND**.
(T) 01821 670798 (F) 01821 670798
(M) 07889 060495.
Profile Breeder. Ref: YH01856

BREYER MODEL HORSES

Breyer Model Horses, Utterly Horses, Bigods Hall, Bigods Lane, Great Dunmow, **Essex**, CM6 3BE, **ENGLAND**.
(T) 01371 875855 (F) 01371 872729
(E) enquiries@utterlyhorses.co.uk
(W) www.utterlyhorses.co.uk.
Contact/s
General Manager: Ms S Benfield
(E) sharon@utterlyhorses.co.uk
Profile Supplies.
Breyer produce model horses and giftware.
No.Staff: 2 Yr. Est: 2001
Opening Times
Telephone for further information Ref: YH01857

BRI - TAC

Bri - Tac (Synthetic Bridle Ware), Hill Farm, Lower Wood, Church Stretton, **Shropshire**, SY6 6LF, **ENGLAND**.
(T) 01694 751356.
Profile Supplies. Ref: YH01858

BRIAN CHAPMAN SPORTING ARTIST

Brian Chapman Sporting Artist, Skendleby Hall, Skendleby, Spilsby, **Lincolnshire**, PE23 4QA, **ENGLAND**.
(T) 01754 890490 (F) 01754 890490.
Contact/s
Owner: Mr B Chapman
Profile Artist. No.Staff: 1
Opening Times
By appointment only Ref: YH01859

BRIAN DAVIES MOTORS

Brian Davies Motors, Rear Of 18 Pontygwindy Rd, Caerphilly, **Caerphilly**, CF83 3AA, **WALES**.
(T) 029 20888684.
Profile Transport/Horse Boxes. Ref: YH01860

BRIAN JAMES TRAILERS

Brian James Trailers, Great Central Way Ind Est, Great Central Way, Woodford Halse, Daventry, **Northamptonshire**, NN11 3PZ, **ENGLAND**.
(T) 01327 260733.
Profile Transport/Horse Boxes. Ref: YH01861

BRIANA ELECTRONICS

Briana Electronics, Grey Mullets, Seaview Promenade, St Lawrence, Southminster, **Essex**, CM0 7NE, **ENGLAND**.
(T) 01621 779480 (F) 01621 778542. Ref: YH01862

BRIARS STUD

Briars Stud, 29 Shackleton Spring, Stevenage, **Hertfordshire**, **ENGLAND**..
Profile Breeder. Ref: YH01863

BRICK KILN STUD

Brick Kiln Stud, Fosse Way, Ettington, Stratford-upon-Avon, **Warwickshire**, CV37 7PA, **ENGLAND**.
(T) 01789 740233 (F) 01789 740871.
Contact/s
Owner: Mr M Anderson
Profile Breeder. Ref: YH01864

BRICKELL FARMS

Brickell Farms Ltd, Willow Farm, Crawley Rd, Witney, **Oxfordshire**, OX8 5TE, **ENGLAND**.
(T) 01993 772101.
Profile Breeder. Ref: YH01865

BRICKFIELDS

Brickfields Horse Country, Newnham Rd, Ryde, **Isle of Wight**, PO33 3TH, **ENGLAND**.
(T) 01983 566801 (F) 01983 562649
(W) www.brickfields.net
Affiliated Bodies BHS.
Contact/s
Owner: Mr P Legge
Profile Equestrian Centre, Riding School. Tourist Centre, Carriage Collection, B&B.
Wagon rides and pony rides for children available and hacking costs £15.00 per hour. Yr. Est: 1983
C.Size: 80 Acres
Opening Times
Sp: Open Mon - Sun 10:00. Closed Mon - Sun 17:00.
Su: Open Mon - Sun 10:00. Closed Mon - Sun 17:00.
Au: Open Mon - Sun 10:00. Closed Mon - Sun 17:00.
Wn: Open Mon - Sun 10:00. Closed Mon - Sun 17:00. Ref: YH01866

BRIDALWOOD

Bridalwood, Station Rd, Talacre, Holywell, **Flintshire**, CH8 9RD, **WALES**.
(T) 01745 888922.
Contact/s
Owner: Mrs C Jones Ref: YH01867

BRIDE, D

D Bride, 34 Foxholes Rd, Southbourne, Bournemouth, **Dorset**, BH6 3AT, **ENGLAND**.
(T) 01202 429341.
Profile Farrier. Ref: YH01868

BRIDESTOWE & DISTRICT

Bridestowe & District Riding Club, 25 Broad Park Rd, Bere Alston, Yelverton, **Devon**, PL20 7AH, **ENGLAND**.
(T) 01822 840573.
Contact/s
Chairman: Mrs M Wakeham
Profile Club/Association, Riding Club. Ref: YH01869

BRIDESWELL RIDING CTRE

Brideswell Riding Centre, Cushnie, Alford,

Aberdeenshire, AB33 8LD, SCOTLAND.
(T) 01975 581266.
Profile Riding School. Ref: YH01870

BRIDGE BARN RIDING CLUB

Bridge Barn Riding Club, 16 Barley Mow Cl, Knaphill, Woking, **Surrey**, GU21 2JA, **ENGLAND**.
(T) 01483 475200.
Contact/s
Chairman: Miss A Seyfang
Profile Club/Association, Riding Club. Ref: YH01871

BRIDGE FARM STABLES

Bridge Farm Stables, Windmill Rd, Gimingham, Mundesley, **Norfolk**, NR11 8HL, **ENGLAND**.
(T) 01263 720028.
Profile Riding School, Stable/Livery. Ref: YH01872

BRIDGE HOUSE VETNRY

Bridge House Veterinary Hospital, Pilton Bridge, Pilton, Barnstaple, **Devon**, EX31 1PG, **ENGLAND**.
(T) 01271 42119.
Profile Medical Support. Ref: YH01873

BRIDGE HSE EQUESTRIAN CTRE

Bridge House Equestrian Centre, Bridge Hse, Five Oaks Rd, Slinfold, Horsham, **Sussex (West)**, RH13 7QW, **ENGLAND**.
(T) 01403 790163 (F) 01403 791006.
Contact/s
Manager: Mrs E Maclleeraith
Profile Riding School, Stable/Livery. Ref: YH01874

BRIDGE OF DON EQUESTRIAN CTRE

Bridge Of Don Equestrian Centre & Ryovan Arabian Stud, Heath Farm/Whitestripes Rd, Park Hill, Dyce, Aberdeen, **Aberdeen (City of)**, AB21 7AP, **SCOTLAND**.
(T) 01224 724012. Ref: YH01875

BRIDGE OF DON EQUESTRIAN CTRE

Bridge of Don Equestrian Centre, Heath Farm, Whitestripes Rd, Parkhill, Dyce, **Aberdeen (City of)**, AB22 8AS, **SCOTLAND**.
(T) 01224 724012.
Profile Stable/Livery. Ref: YH01876

BRIDGE SADDLERY & COUNTRYWEAR

Bridge Saddlery & Countrywear, 30A Dale St, Milnrow, Rochdale, **Lancashire**, OL16 4HS, **ENGLAND**.
(T) 01706 645146. Ref: YH01877

BRIDGE WEAR TOWN & COUNTRY

Bridge Wear Town & Country, 1 Gryffe Pl, Main St, Bridge Of Weir, **Renfrewshire**, PA11 3PD, **SCOTLAND**.
(T) 01505 614000 (F) 01505 614000.
Contact/s
Owner: Mr K Bruce Ref: YH01878

BRIDGE, MARTIN S

Martin S Bridge RSS, 72 Haddon St, Tibshelf, **Derbyshire**, DE5 5QB, **ENGLAND**.
(T) 01773 874042.
Profile Farrier. Ref: YH01879

BRIDGEFOOT FARM

Bridgefoot Farm Riding Stables, Bridgefoot Farm, Ramsey, Harwich, **Essex**, **ENGLAND**..
Profile Riding School. Ref: YH01880

BRIDGEHILL PONY STUD

Bridgehill Pony Stud, Bridgehill Rd, Newborough, Peterborough, **Cambridgeshire**, PE6 7SA, **ENGLAND**.
(T) 01733 810316.
Profile Breeder. Ref: YH01881

BRIDGER, J J

J J Bridger, Upper Hatch Farm, Liphook, **Hampshire**, GU30 7EL, **ENGLAND**.
(T) 01428 722528.
Profile Trainer. No.Staff: 4 Yr. Est: 1970
C.Size: 160 Acres Ref: YH01882

BRIDGES, C & M

C & M Bridges, Queens Head Hse, Beech Hill Rd, Beech Hill, Reading, **Berkshire**, RG7 2AU, **ENGLAND**.
(T) 0118 9882162 (F) 0118 9882162. Ref: YH01883

BRIDGEWATER SHIPPING

Bridgewater Shipping, Bridgefoot Farm, Ramsey, Harwich, **Essex**, CO12 5HB, **ENGLAND**.
(T) 01255 880088 (F) 01255 880599
(M) 07860 581727.
Profile Transport/Horse Boxes. Ref: YH01884

BRIDGEWATER, CRAIG

Craig Bridgewater DWCF, 99 Toronto Rd, North End, Portsmouth, **Hampshire**, PO2 7QD, **ENGLAND**.
(T) 023 92358257.
Profile Farrier. Ref: YH01885

BRIDGIT DUERDEN & ASSOCIATES

Bridgit Duerden & Associates, 51 Main St, Whittington, Lichfield, **Staffordshire**, WS14 9JR, **ENGLAND**.
(T) 01543 432096 (F) 07070 602450
(M) 07971 362919. Ref: YH01886

BRIDGWATER TRAILER CTRE

Bridgwater Trailer Centre, Unit 7 Wireworks Est, Bristol Rd, Bridgwater, **Somerset**, TA6 4AP, **ENGLAND**.
(T) 01278 445000 (F) 01278 446641.
Contact/s
Owner: Mr J Manders
Profile Transport/Horse Boxes. Ref: YH01887

BRIDGWATER, MARY

Mrs Mary Bridgwater, Bear Hse Farm, Old Warwick Rd, Lapworth, **Warwickshire**, B94 6AZ, **ENGLAND**.
(T) 01564 782895 (F) 01564 782895.
Profile Trainer. Ref: YH01888

BRIDLE GROVE RIDING CTRE

Bridle Grove Riding Centre, Braggons Farm, Boxted, Bury St Edmunds, **Suffolk**, IP29 4LL, **ENGLAND**.
(T) 01787 280266.
Contact/s
Owner: Mrs D Laflin
Profile Hacking. Yr. Est: 1978 C.Size: 200 Acres
Opening Times
By appointment only Ref: YH01889

BRIDLE MOUNT STABLES

Bridle Mount Stables, Haws Lane, Haverigg, Millom, **Cumbria**, LA18 4LU, **ENGLAND**.
(T) 01229 770304. Ref: YH01890

BRIDLE PATH

Bridle Path, 31-32 St Johns St, Bury St Edmunds, **Suffolk**, IP33 1SN, **ENGLAND**.
(T) 01284 754124.
Contact/s
Owner: Mr P Hay
Profile Saddlery Retailer. Ref: YH01891

BRIDLE WAY & GAUNTLEYS

Bridle Way & Gauntleys (The), Mill Hse, Laneham Rd, Dunham-on-Trent, Newark, **Nottinghamshire**, NG22 0UW, **ENGLAND**.
(T) 01777 228040 (F) 01777 228977
Affiliated Bodies BETA.
Contact/s
General Manager: Ms S Collins
Profile Medical Support, Riding Wear Retailer, Saddlery Retailer, Supplies. No.Staff: 9
Yr. Est: 1990 C.Size: 3 Acres
Opening Times
Sp: Open Mon - Fri 08:30, Sat 09:00, Sun 10:00. Closed Mon - Fri 18:00, Sat 17:30, Sun 15:00.
Su: Open Mon - Fri 08:30, Sat 09:00, Sun 10:00. Closed Mon - Fri 18:00, Sat 17:30, Sun 15:00.
Au: Open Mon - Fri 08:30, Sat 09:00, Sun 10:00. Closed Mon - Fri 18:00, Sat 17:30, Sun 15:00.
Wn: Open Mon - Fri 08:30, Sat 09:00, Sun 10:00. Closed Mon - Fri 18:00, Sat 17:30, Sun 15:00.
Ref: YH01892

BRIDLES & BITS

Bridles & Bits, 15 Pembroke St, Tralee, **County Kerry**, **IRELAND**.
(T) 066 7129988 (F) 066 7129988
(E) bridlesandbits@eircom.net
(W) www.bridlesbits.com.
Contact/s
Owner: Ms S Forder
Profile Riding Wear Retailer, Saddlery Retailer, Supplies. No.Staff: 2 Yr. Est: 1995
Opening Times
Sp: Open Mon, Tues, Thurs - Sat 10:30, Wed 13:00. Closed Mon - Sat 18:00.
Su: Open Mon, Tues, Thurs - Sat 10:30, Wed 13:00. Closed Mon - Sat 18:00.
Au: Open Mon, Tues, Thurs - Sat 10:30, Wed 13:00. Closed Mon - Sat 18:00.
Wn: Open Mon, Tues, Thurs - Sat 10:30, Wed 13:00. Closed Mon - Sat 18:00.
Closed Sundays and Wednesday mornings
Ref: YH01893

BRIDLES TO BREECHES

Bridles To Breeches, 4 Castle Walk, Lower St, Stansted, **Essex**, CM24 8LY, **ENGLAND**.
(T) 01279 816097. Ref: YH01894

BRIDLEWAY

Bridleway, 25 Mardol, Shrewsbury, **Shropshire**, SY1 1PU, **ENGLAND**.
(T) 01743 354887 (F) 01743 354887. Ref: YH01895

BRIDLEWAYS

Bridleways, 12 Anslow Pl, Burnham, **Buckinghamshire**, SL1 6EA, **ENGLAND**.
(T) 01628 605218 (F) 01628 605218.
Profile Saddlery Retailer. Ref: YH01896

BRIDLEWAYS

Bridleways, Oborne Rd, Sherborne, **Dorset**, DT9 3RX, **ENGLAND**.
(T) 01935 814716 (F) 01935 814716.
Contact/s
Owner: Mrs R Diamonds
Profile Riding School. Ref: YH01897

BRIDLEWAYS EQUESTRIAN CTRE

Bridleways Equestrian Centre, Chapel Lane, Great Bookham, **Surrey**, KT23 4QG, **ENGLAND**.
(T) 01372 456385
Affiliated Bodies BHS.
Contact/s
Partner: Ms A Oppenheim
Profile Equestrian Centre, Riding School, Stable/Livery.
BHS approved livery yard and riding school.
No.Staff: 5 Yr. Est: 2001 C.Size: 12 Acres
Opening Times
Sp: Open 07:30. Closed 18:00.
Su: Open 07:30. Closed 18:00.
Au: Open 07:30. Closed 18:00.
Wn: Open 07:30. Closed 18:00. Ref: YH01898

BRIDLEWOOD EQUESTRIAN CTRE

Bridlewood Equestrian Centre, Tyn-Y-Morfa, Gwespyr, Holywell, **Flintshire**, CH8 9JW, **WALES**.
(T) 01745 888922.
Profile Riding School, Saddlery Retailer.
Ref: YH01899

BRIDLINGTON & DISTRICT

Bridlington & District Riding Club, 189 Sewerby Rd, Bridlington, **Yorkshire (East)**, YO16 7DD, **ENGLAND**.
(T) 01262 671131.
Contact/s
Chairman: Mrs D Smith
Profile Club/Association, Riding Club. Ref: YH01900

BRIDLINGTON HORSE PAGEANT

Bridlington Horse Pageant, The Parsonage, Bempton, Bridlington, **Yorkshire (East)**, YO15 1HL, **ENGLAND**.
(T) 01262 851052.
Contact/s
Secretary: G K Neely Ref: YH01901

BRIDPORT TRAILERS

Bridport Trailers, Unit 6, Magdalen Lane, Bridport, **Dorset**, DT6 5AA, **ENGLAND**.
(T) 01308 456070 (F) 01308 456070.
Contact/s
Owner: Mr A Horniblow
Profile Transport/Horse Boxes. Ref: YH01902

BRIERLEY BUSINESS SERVICES

Brierley Business Services, Dairy Hse, Clay Lane, Puncknowle, Dorchester, **Dorset**, DT2 9BG, **ENGLAND**.
(T) 01308 898283.
Profile Club/Association. Ref: YH01903

BRIERY CLOSE ARABIAN

Briery Close Arabian Stud Farm, Calgarth Hall, Troutbeck Bridge, Windermere, **Cumbria**, LA23 1HZ, **ENGLAND**.
(T) 01539 445489.
Contact/s
Manager: Mrs A Hill
Profile Breeder. Ref: YH01904

BRIERY CLOSE ARABIAN STUD

Briery Close Arabian Stud, Windermere, **Cumbria**, LA23 1LG, **ENGLAND**.
(T) 01539 445626 (F) 01539 488641.
Profile Breeder. Ref: YH01905

BRIGG VIEW

Brigg View Farm Stables, Sands Rd, Hunmanby Gap, Filey, **Yorkshire (North)**, YO14 9QW, **ENGLAND**.
(T) 01723 890205.
Contact/s

Owner: Mrs J Clemmit **(Q)** AI, BHS 1
Profile Riding School, Stable/Livery, Trainer. Competition Stable.
Brigg View Bishops John won a silver medal in the European 3 day event of Summer 2001. No.Staff: 4
Yr. Est: 1968 C.Size: 8 Acres
Opening Times
Sp: Open Mon - Sun 08:00. Closed Mon - Sun 19:00.
Su: Open Mon - Sun 08:00. Closed Mon - Sun 19:00.
Au: Open Mon - Sun 08:00. Closed Mon - Sun 19:00.
Wn: Open Mon - Sun 08:00. Closed Mon - Sun 19:00. **Ref: YH01906**

BRIGG, W NORRIS

W Norris Brigg, 14 Albert St, Wilsden, Bradford, **Yorkshire (West)**, BD15 0JJ, **ENGLAND**.
(T) 01535 272140.
Profile Transport/Horse Boxes. **Ref: YH01907**

BRIGGS-PRICE, ROYSTON M

Royston M Briggs-Price, 71 Millgate, Newark, **Nottinghamshire**, NG24 4TU, **ENGLAND**.
(T) 01636 705069.
Profile Farrier. **Ref: YH01908**

BRIGHTON RACECOURSE

Brighton Racecourse, Northern Racing, The Racecourse, Brighton, **Sussex (East)**, BN2 2XZ, **ENGLAND**.
(T) 01273 603580 **(F)** 01273 673267
(E) info@brighton-racecourse.co.uk.
Contact/s
Clerk of Course: Mr J Martin
Profile Track/Course. **Ref: YH01909**

BRIGHTWELLS BLOODSTOCK

Brightwells Bloodstock, The Mews, King St, Hereford, **Herefordshire**, HR4 9DB, **ENGLAND**.
(T) 01432 355300 **(F)** 01432 351028.
Contact/s
Manager: Mr A Elliott
Profile Blood Stock Agency. **Ref: YH01910**

BRILLS FARM

Brills Farm, Grants Lane, Oxted, **Surrey**, RH8 0RH, **ENGLAND**.
(T) 01883 722220.
Profile Stable/Livery. **Ref: YH01911**

BRIMINGTON EQUESTRIAN CTRE

Brimington Equestrian Centre, 130 Manor Rd, Brimington, Chesterfield, **Derbyshire**, S43 1NN, **ENGLAND**.
(T) 01246 235465.
Contact/s
Owner: Miss T Priest
Profile Riding School, Stable/Livery. **Ref: YH01912**

BRIMSMORE EQUESTRIAN CTRE

Brimsmore Equestrian Centre, Coppitts Hill Farm, Vagg Hill, Yeovil, **Somerset**, BA21 3PR, **ENGLAND**.
(T) 01935 410854 **(F)** 01935 410854.
Contact/s
General Manager: Ms H Barton Smith
(Q) BHS Int SM
Profile Equestrian Centre, Riding School, Stable/Livery.
Competitions, 3 hour hacks, pub rides, country park rides and childrens holiday weeks. Also hold lectures and demonstrations. Full, part and DIY Livery available. Yr. Est: 2000
Opening Times
Sp: Open Tues - Sun 07:30. Closed Tues - Sun 17:30.
Su: Open Tues - Sun 07:30. Closed Tues - Sun 17:30.
Au: Open Tues - Sun 07:30. Closed Tues - Sun 17:30.
Wn: Open Tues - Sun 07:30. Closed Tues - Sun 17:30.
Closed Monday **Ref: YH01913**

BRINDLE AND WHITE

Brindle and White (Rug-Tidy), Broad Carr, Strines, New Mills, **Derbyshire**, SK22 3BA, **ENGLAND**.
(T) 0161 4270404 **(F)** 0161 4270404
(E) info@rug-tidy.co.uk
(W) www.rug-tidy.co.uk.
Profile Supplies.
Brindle and White produce rug tidies for storing rugs.
Ref: YH01914

BRING YOUR HORSE ON HOLIDAY

Bring Your Horse On Holiday, Home Farm, Hallington, Louth, **Lincolnshire**, LN11 9QX, **ENGLAND**.
(T) 01507 605864 **(F)** 01472 250365
(E) canter.hallington@virginnet.co.uk.
Profile Stable/Livery. **Ref: YH01915**

BRINKLEY STUD

Brinkley Stud SRL Ltd, Burrough Green, Newmarket, **Suffolk**, CB8 9NE, **ENGLAND**.
(T) 01638 507066.
Contact/s
Manager: Mr L Kavanagh
Profile Breeder. **Ref: YH01916**

BRINSBURY COLLEGE

Brinsbury College, West Sussex College Of Agriculture & Horticulture, Brinsbury, North Heath, Pulborough, **Sussex (West)**, RH20 1DL, **ENGLAND**.
(T) 01798 877400 **(F)** 01798 875222.
Profile Equestrian Centre. **Ref: YH01917**

BRISBOURNE, MARK

Mark Brisbourne, Ness Strange Stables, Great Ness, Shrewsbury, **Shropshire**, SY4 2LE, **ENGLAND**.
(T) 01743 741536.
Contact/s
Owner: Mr M Brisbourne
Profile Trainer. **Ref: YH01918**

BRISLEY BOXES

Brisley Boxes, Bridge Cottage, Brisley Lane, Ruckinge, Ashford, **Kent**, TN26 2PN, **ENGLAND**.
(T) 01233 733881.
Contact/s
Owner: Mr R Tapp
Profile Transport/Horse Boxes. **Ref: YH01919**

BRISTOL FINE ART

Bristol Fine Art, 72/74 Park Row, Bristol, **Bristol**, BS1 5LE, **ENGLAND**.
(T) 01179 260344. **Ref: YH01920**

BRISTOL UNIVERSITY

Bristol University, Dept Of Animal Husbandry, Langford Hse, Langford, **Somerset**, BS40 5ER, **ENGLAND**.
(T) 01934 852581.
Profile Medical Support. **Ref: YH01921**

BRITANNIA TOWING CTRE

Britannia Towing Centre, Unit 2 Kensington Rd, Vauxhall Ind Est, Canterbury, **Kent**, CT1 1QZ, **ENGLAND**.
(T) 01277 457010.
Contact/s
Owner: Mr N Hutchins
Profile Transport/Horse Boxes. **Ref: YH01922**

BRITISH ANDALUSIAN SOCIETY

British Andalusian Society, High Oaks, The Cwm, Forden, Montgomery, **Powys**, SY1 8NB, **WALES**.
(T) 01938 580192.
Contact/s
Key Contact: Mrs J Bernard
Profile Club/Association. **Ref: YH01923**

BRITISH APPALOOSA SOCIETY

British Appaloosa Society, C/O 36 Clusterbolts, Stapleford, Hertford, **Hertfordshire**, SG14 3ND, **ENGLAND**.
(T) 01992 558657.
Contact/s
Key Contact: Mrs B George
Profile Club/Association. **Ref: YH01924**

BRITISH APPAREL & TEXTILE

British Apparel & Textile Confederation, 5 Portland Pl, London, **London (Greater)**, W1N 3AA, **ENGLAND**.
(T) 020 76367788 **(F)** 020 76367515.
Profile Club/Association. **Ref: YH01925**

BRITISH ARABIAN BLOODSTOCK

British Arabian Bloodstock Agency, 5 Bernard Pl, Birmingham, **Midlands (West)**, B18 7JQ, **ENGLAND**.
(T) 0121 5548803.
Profile Blood Stock Agency. **Ref: YH01926**

BRITISH BAVARIAN WARMBLOOD

British Bavarian Warmblood Association, Sittyton, Straloch, Newmachar, Aberdeen, **Aberdeen (City of)**, AB21 0RP, **SCOTLAND**.
(T) 01651 882226 **(F)** 01651 882313
(W) www.bbwa.co.uk.
Profile Breeder, Club/Association. **Ref: YH01927**

BRITISH BLOODSTOCK AGENCY

British Bloodstock Agency (UK) Ltd (The), 1 Chapel View, High St, Lambourn, Hungerford, **Berkshire**, RG17 8XL, **ENGLAND**.
(T) 01488 73111.
Contact/s
Accountant: Mr J Beazley
Profile Blood Stock Agency. **Ref: YH01928**

BRITISH BLOODSTOCK AGENCY

British Bloodstock Agency (UK) Ltd (The), Queensberry Hse, 129 High St, Newmarket, **Suffolk**, CB8 9BD, **ENGLAND**.
(T) 01638 665021 **(F)** 01638 660283
(E) bloodstock@bba.co.uk
(W) www.bba.co.uk.
Contact/s
Administration: Ms H Wargen
Profile Blood Stock Agency, Club/Association.
Yr. Est: 1911
Opening Times
Sp: Open 08:30. Closed 17:30.
Su: Open 08:30. Closed 17:30.
Au: Open 08:30. Closed 17:30.
Wn: Open 08:30. Closed 17:30. **Ref: YH01929**

BRITISH BLOODSTOCK AGENCY

British Bloodstock Agency (UK) Ltd (The), Doncaster Bloodstock Sales Ltd/Sales Paddock, Carr Hse Rd, Doncaster, **Yorkshire (South)**, DN4 5HP, **ENGLAND**.
(T) 01302 368144.
Profile Blood Stock Agency. **Ref: YH01930**

BRITISH BREEDER

British Breeder (The), 85 Fishers Field, Buckingham, **Buckinghamshire**, MK18 1SF, **ENGLAND**.
(T) 01280 824451 **(F)** 01280 824451
(E) celia@cwath.demon.co.uk.
Contact/s
Editorial: Celia Clarke
Profile Supplies. **Ref: YH01931**

BRITISH CAMARGUE HORSE SOC

British Camargue Horse Society, Valley Farm Riding & Driving Ctre, Valley Farm, Wickham Market, Woodbridge, **Suffolk**, IP13 0ND, **ENGLAND**.
(T) 01728 746916.
Contact/s
Owner: Sarah Ling
(E) sarah@valleyfarm.demon.co.uk
Profile Club/Association. **Ref: YH01932**

BRITISH CENTRAL PREFIX

British Central Prefix Registry, Home Farm, Priory Lane, Markfield, **Leicestershire**, LE67 9PH, **ENGLAND**.
(T) 01530 249371 **(F)** 01530 249371.
Contact/s
Secretary: Miss H Thomson
Profile Club/Association.
Opening Times
Contact between 12:00 - 15:00 **Ref: YH01933**

BRITISH DRESSAGE

British Dressage, Savilles Cottage, Hatfield Park Farm, Bush End, Takeley, Bishop's Stortford, **Essex**, CM22 6NE, **ENGLAND**.
(T) 01279 870043 **(F)** 01279 870043.
Contact/s
Advertising: Jane Watkins
Profile Supplies. **Ref: YH01934**

BRITISH DRESSAGE

British Dressage Ltd, National Agricultural Ctre, Stoneleigh Pk, Kenilworth, **Warwickshire**, CV8 2RJ, **ENGLAND**.
(T) 024 76698830 **(F)** 024 76690390
(W) www.britishdressage.co.uk.
Contact/s
Chief Executive: Mr D Holmes
(E) davidholmes@britishdressage.co.uk
Profile Club/Association. No.Staff: 16
Opening Times
Sp: Open 09:00. Closed 17:00.
Su: Open 09:00. Closed 17:00.
Au: Open 09:00. Closed 17:00.
Wn: Open 09:00. Closed 17:00. **Ref: YH01935**

BRITISH DRESSAGE SUPPORTERS

British Dressage Supporters Club, Savilles Cottage, Hatfield Park Farm, Bush End, Takeley, Bishop's Stortford, **Essex**, CM22 6NE, **ENGLAND**.
(T) 01279 870043 **(F)** 01279 870043.
Contact/s
Secretary: Mrs J Watkins
Profile Club/Association. **Ref: YH01936**

BRITISH EQUESTRIAN BROKERS

British Equestrian Insurance Brokers Ltd, Commercial & Equestrian Insurance, Hildenbrook Hse, The Slade, Tonbridge, **Kent**, TN9 1HR, **ENGLAND**.

(T) 01732 771719 (F) 01732 359982
(E) beib@globalnet.co.uk.
Contact/s
General Manager: Mr D Hall
Profile Club/Association. Insurance Company.
Ref: YH01937

BRITISH EQUESTRIAN FEDERATION

British Equestrian Federation, National Agricultural Ctre, Stoneleigh Pk, Kenilworth, **Warwickshire**, CV8 2RH, **ENGLAND**.
(T) 024 76698871 (F) 024 76696484.
Profile Club/Association. Ref: YH01938

BRITISH EQUESTRIAN TRADE

British Equestrian Trade Overseas, Twemlows Hall, Whitchurch, **Shropshire**, SY13 2EZ, **ENGLAND**.
(T) 01948 663239 (F) 01948 663836
(M) 07801 674242
(E) r.matson@virgin.net.
Profile Club/Association. Ref: YH01939

BRITISH EQUESTRIAN TRADE ASS

British Equestrian Trade Association, Stockeld Pk, Wetherby, **Yorkshire (West)**, LS22 4AW, **ENGLAND**.
(T) 01937 587062 (F) 01937 582728
(E) membership@emc.u-net.com
(W) www.beta-uk.org.
Contact/s
Chief Executive: Miss C Williams
Profile Club/Association. Ref: YH01940

BRITISH EQUESTRIAN WRITERS

British Equestrian Writers Association, Priory Hse, Station Rd, Swavesey, **Cambridgeshire**, CB4 5QJ, **ENGLAND**.
(T) 01954 232084 (F) 01954 231362.
Profile Club/Association. Ref: YH01941

BRITISH EQUINE COLLECTORS

British Equine Collectors Forum, 334 Browns Lane, Allesley, Coventry, **Midlands (West)**, CV5 9EE, **ENGLAND**.
(T) 024 76404425
(E) 101657.1155@compuserve.com.
Profile Supplies. Ref: YH01942

BRITISH GATES & TIMBER

British Gates & Timber Ltd, Biddenden, Ashford, **Kent**, TN27 8DD, **ENGLAND**.
(T) 01580 291555 (F) 01580 292011. Ref: YH01943

BRITISH HANOVERIAN HORSE SOC

British Hanoverian Horse Society (The), Ecton Field Plantation, Ecton Lane, Sywell, **Northamptonshire**, NN6 0BP, **ENGLAND**.
(T) 01604 492750
(W) www.hanoverian-gb.org.uk.
Contact/s
Hon Secretary: Mr J Shenfield
Profile Breeder, Club/Association. Ref: YH01944

BRITISH HARNESS RACING CLUB

British Harness Racing Club of GB, Burlington Cres, Goole, **Yorkshire (East)**, DN14 5EG, **ENGLAND**.
(T) 01405 766877 (F) 01405 766878
(E) harnessgb@aol.com.
Contact/s
Key Contact: Miss G Berry
Profile Club/Association. Ref: YH01945

BRITISH HAY & STRAW MERCHANTS

British Hay & Straw Merchants Association, 52 Park Meadow, Old Hatfield, **Hertfordshire**, AL9 5HB, **ENGLAND**.
(T) 01707 268807 (F) 01707 268807.
Contact/s
Key Contact: Miss A Dick
Profile Club/Association. Ref: YH01946

BRITISH HONOVERIAN HORSE REG

British Honoverian Horse Register (The), 1 Hare Pk, Alington Hill, Newmarket, **Suffolk**, CB8 0UW, **ENGLAND**.
(T) 01638 570288.
Profile Club/Association. Ref: YH01947

BRITISH HORSE

British Horse, P O Box 585, Leicester, **Leicestershire**, LE7 7XZ, **ENGLAND**.
(T) 07000 362636
(E) britishhorse@hotmail.com
(W) www.britishhorse.co.uk.
Contact/s
General Manager: Miss A Pateman
Profile Transport/Horse Boxes.
Transport - quote, source and arrange. Staffing agency.
No.Staff: 5 Yr. Est: 1992
Opening Times
All day everyday Ref: YH01948

BRITISH HORSE FEEDS

British Horse Feeds Ltd, Standon Mill, Standon, Stafford, **Staffordshire**, ST21 6RP, **ENGLAND**.
(T) 01782 791792 (F) 01782 791628. Ref: YH01949

BRITISH HORSE FOUNDATION

British Horse Foundation (The), East Of England Showground, Peterborough, **Cambridgeshire**, PE2 6XE, **ENGLAND**.
(T) 01733 234451 (F) 01733 370038.
Contact/s
Chief Executive: Mr A Mercer
Profile Club/Association. Ref: YH01950

BRITISH HORSE IND CONFED

British Horse Industry Confederation (The), National Agricultural Ctre, Kenilworth, **Warwickshire**, CV8 2RH, **ENGLAND**.
(T) 02476 696969.
Profile Club/Association. Ref: YH01951

BRITISH HORSE LOGGERS

British Horse Loggers/Forestry Contracting Association, Dalfling, Blairdaff, Inverurie, **Aberdeenshire**, AB51 5LA, **SCOTLAND**.
(T) 01467 651368 (F) 01467 651595
(E) members@fca.uk.
Profile Club/Association. Ref: YH01952

BRITISH HORSE TRIALS ASS

British Horse Trials Association, National Agruiculture Ctre, Stoneleigh Pk, Kenilworth, **Warwickshire**, CV8 2LR, **ENGLAND**.
(T) 024 76698856 (F) 024 76697235
(E) eventing@bhta.co.uk.
Contact/s
Key Contact: Miss J Brindley
Profile Club/Association. Ref: YH01953

BRITISH HORSEBALL ASSOCIATION

British Horseball Association, 67 Clifford Rd, New Barnet, **Hertfordshire**, EN5 5NZ, **ENGLAND**.
(T) 020 84411799 (F) 020 84411060
(E) horseball@showmobiles.demon.co.uk.
Profile Club/Association. Ref: YH01954

BRITISH HORSEBALL ASSOCIATION

British Horseball Association, 67 Clifford Rd, New Barnet, **Hertfordshire**, **ENGLAND**..
Contact/s
Key Contact: Mr J Copeland
Profile Club/Association. Ref: YH01955

BRITISH HORSERACING BOARD

British Horseracing Board (The), 42 Portman Sq, London, **London (Greater)**, W1H 6EN, **ENGLAND**.
(T) 020 73960011 (F) 020 79350131
(E) info@bhb.co.uk
(W) www.bhb.co.uk.
Profile Club/Association.
Governing authority for horseracing in Great Britain.
Yr. Est: 1993
Opening Times
Sp: Open Mon - Fri 09:00. Closed Mon - Fri 17:00.
Su: Open Mon - Fri 09:00. Closed Mon - Fri 17:00.
Au: Open Mon - Fri 09:00. Closed Mon - Fri 17:00.
Wn: Open Mon - Fri 09:00. Closed Mon - Fri 17:00.
Closed Saturdays and Sundays. Ref: YH01956

BRITISH HORSERACING BOARD

British Horseracing Board (The), 42 Portman Sq, London, **London (Greater)**, W1H 0EN, **ENGLAND**.
(T) 020 73960011 (F) 020 79353626.
Profile Club/Association. Ref: YH01957

BRITISH HORSERACING TRAINING

British Horseracing Training Board, Suite 16, Unit 8, King's Court, Newmarket, **Suffolk**, CB8 7SG, **ENGLAND**.
(T) 01638 560743 (F) 01638 660932
(E) info@rtbtb.keme.co.uk.
Profile Club/Association. Ref: YH01958

BRITISH LIVESTOCK

British Livestock Co (Wyddial) Ltd, Wyddial Bury, Wyddial, Buntingford, **Hertfordshire**, SG9 0EJ, **ENGLAND**.
(T) 01763 71770 (F) 01763 73276.
Profile Blood Stock Agency. Ref: YH01959

BRITISH LUGGAGE/LEATHERGOODS

British Luggage & Leathergoods Association, 10 Vyse St, Birmingham, **Midlands (West)**, B18 6LT, **ENGLAND**.
(T) 0121 2371107 (F) 0121 2363921
(E) enquiries@blla.org.uk.
Profile Club/Association. Ref: YH01960

BRITISH MORGAN HORSE SOCIETY

British Morgan Horse Society, P O Box 155, Godalming, **Surrey**, GU8 5YE, **ENGLAND**.
(T) 01483 861283 (F) 01483 861283
(E) bmhs@lineone.net.
Contact/s
Key Contact: Miss Q King
Profile Club/Association. Ref: YH01961

BRITISH MULE SOCIETY

British Mule Society, Hope Mount Farm, Top Of Hope, Alstonfield, Ashbourne, **Derbyshire**, DE6 2FR, **ENGLAND**.
(T) 01335 310353.
Contact/s
Key Contact: Mrs L Travis
(E) lorraine@ltravis.freeserve.co.uk
Profile Club/Association. Ref: YH01962

BRITISH OAT & BARLEY ASS

British Oat & Barley Association, 6 Catherine St, London, **London (Greater)**, WC2B 5JJ, **ENGLAND**.
(T) 020 78362460.
Profile Club/Association. Ref: YH01963

BRITISH PALOMINO SOCIETY

British Palomino Society (The), Penrhiwllan, Llandysul, **Carmarthenshire**, SA44 5NZ, **WALES**.
(T) 01239 851387 (F) 01289 851040.
Profile Club/Association. Ref: YH01964

BRITISH PERCHERON HORSE

British Percheron Horse Society, Lower Hse Barns, Bepton, Midhurst, **Sussex (West)**, GU29 0JB, **ENGLAND**.
(T) 01730 814185 (F) 01730 825061.
Profile Club/Association. Ref: YH01965

BRITISH RACING HERITAGE

British Racing Heritage, The Paddock, 58 Bury Rd, Newmarket, **Suffolk**, CB8 7BT, **ENGLAND**.
(T) 01638 666033.
Profile Supplies. Ref: YH01966

BRITISH RACING SCHOOL

British Racing School, Snailwell Rd, Newmarket, **Suffolk**, CB8 7NU, **ENGLAND**.
(T) 01638 665103 (F) 01638 560929
(E) britracesch@compuserve.com.
Profile Equestrian Centre. Ref: YH01967

BRITISH RACING SERVICES

British Racing Services, Beechwood Hse, Charlton, Malmesbury, **Wiltshire**, SN16 9RN, **ENGLAND**.
(T) 01666 860325 (F) 01666 860877.
Contact/s
Owner: Mr J Stevens
Profile Blood Stock Agency. Ref: YH01968

BRITISH RED CROSS

British Red Cross, 9 Grovesnor Cres, London, **London (Greater)**, SW1X 7EJ, **ENGLAND**.
(T) 020 72355454 (F) 020 72456315
(E) information@redcross.org.uk.
Profile Medical Support. Ref: YH01969

BRITISH RIDING CLUBS

British Riding Clubs, Stoneleigh Deer Pk, Kenilworth, **Warwickshire**, CV8 2XZ, **ENGLAND**.
(T) 01926 707700 (F) 01926 707800
(E) s.long@bhs.org.uk.
Profile Club/Association. Ref: YH01970

BRITISH SHOW HACK,

British Show Hack, Cob & Riding Horse Association (The), Chamberlain Walk, 88 High St, Coleshill, **Warwickshire**, B46 3BZ, **ENGLAND**.
(T) 01675 466211 (F) 01675 466242.
Profile Club/Association. Ref: YH01971

BRITISH SHOW JUMP STORES

British Show Jump Stores, British Show Jumping Assoc, Show Lane, Aldershot, **Hampshire**, GU11 2HE, **ENGLAND**.
(T) 01252 323164 (F) 01252 342528.
Profile Supplies. Ref: YH01972

BRITISH SHOW JUMPING ASS

British Show Jumping Association (Scotish Branch), Glenauld, Hamilton Rd, Strathaven, **Lanarkshire (South)**, ML10 6SX, **SCOTLAND**.
(T) 01357 522853 (F) 01357 520022
(E) bsjascot@aol.com
(W) www.bsja.co.uk/scottish.html.
Contact/s
Administration: Mrs J Mair

Profile Club/Association.
A governing body of show jumping in Great Britain. The purpose is to improve and maintain standards of show jumping while encouraging members of all standards and levels to enjoy fair competition over safe and attractive courses.
Opening Times
Sp: Open Mon - Fri 09:00. Closed Mon - Fri 17:00.
Su: Open Mon - Fri 09:00. Closed Mon - Fri 17:00.
Au: Open Mon - Fri 09:00. Closed Mon - Fri 17:00.
Wn: Open Mon - Fri 09:00. Closed Mon - Fri 17:00.
Ref: YH01973

BRITISH SHOW PONY SOCIETY

British Show Pony Society (Scottish Branch), Woodbank Farm, Armadale, Bathgate, **Lothian (West)**, EH48 3BE, **SCOTLAND**.
(T) 01501 733217 (F) 01501 733020
(E) info@britishshowponysociety.co.uk
(W) www.britishshowponysociety.co.uk.
Contact/s
Secretary: Mrs S Nixon
Profile Club/Association.
The main aim of the Society is to protect and improve the showing of childrens riding ponies.
Yr. Est: 1949
Opening Times
Sp: Open Mon - Fri 09:00. Closed Mon - Fri 17:00.
Su: Open Mon - Fri 09:00. Closed Mon - Fri 17:00.
Au: Open Mon - Fri 09:00. Closed Mon - Fri 17:00.
Wn: Open Mon - Fri 09:00. Closed Mon - Fri 17:00.
Ref: YH01974

BRITISH SKEWBALD/PIEBALD ASS

British Skewbald & Piebald Association, P O Box 67, Ely, **Cambridgeshire**, CB7 4FY, **ENGLAND**.
(T) 01353 860401
(W) www.ifield-park.co.uk/bspa.
Profile Breeder, Club/Association. Ref: YH01975

BRITISH SPORTING ART TRUST

British Sporting Art Trust, Picketts Cottage, Medmenham, Marlow, **Buckinghamshire**, SL7 2EZ, **ENGLAND**.
(T) 01491 571294. Ref: YH01976

BRITISH SPORTS HORSE REGISTER

British Sports Horse Register, Xis, 77 Throne Cres, Rowley Regis, Warley Town, **Midlands (West)**, B65 9JE, **ENGLAND**.
(T) 0121 5593975 (F) 0121 5590292.
Profile Club/Association. Ref: YH01977

BRITISH SPOTTED PONY SOCIETY

British Spotted Pony Society, Ramor Hse, North St, Owston Ferry, Doncaster, **Yorkshire (South)**, DN9 1AE, **ENGLAND**.
(T) 01427 728266 (F) 01427 728266
(E) bspps@spotted-pony.com.
Profile Club/Association. Ref: YH01978

BRITISH VETNRY ASS

British Veterinary Association, 7 Mansfield St, London, **London (Greater)**, W1G 9NQ, **ENGLAND**.
(T) 020 76366541 (F) 020 74362970
(E) bvahq@bva.co.uk
(W) www.bva.co.uk.
Profile Club/Association.
Provides advice and information for all members.
Yr. Est: 1883
Opening Times
Sp: Open 09:00. Closed 17:00.
Su: Open 09:00. Closed 17:00.
Au: Open 09:00. Closed 17:00.
Wn: Open 09:00. Closed 17:00. Ref: YH01979

BRITISH WARMBLOOD SOCIETY

British Warmblood Society, 77 Throne Cres, Rowley Regis, Warley, **Midlands (West)**, B65 9JE, **ENGLAND**.
(T) 0121 5595493.
Profile Club/Association. Ref: YH01980

BRITTAIN, C E

C E Brittain, Carlburg Stables, 49 Bury Rd, Newmarket, **Suffolk**, CB8 7BY, **ENGLAND**.
(T) 01638 664347 (F) 01638 661744
(W) www.newmarketracehorsetrainers.co.uk
Affiliated Bodies Newmarket Trainers Fed.
Contact/s
Owner: Mr C Brittain
Profile Trainer. Ref: YH01981

BRITTAIN, M

M Brittain, Northgate Lodge, Northgate Lane, Warthill, York, **Yorkshire (North)**, YO19 5XR, **ENGLAND**.
(T) 01759 371472.
Contact/s
Manager: Mr M Britton
Profile Breeder, Trainer. Ref: YH01982

BRITTON HOUSE STUD

Britton House Stud Ltd, Hewingbere, North Perrott, Crewkerne, **Somerset**, TA18 7TG, **ENGLAND**.
(T) 01935 891779 (F) 01935 891756.
Profile Breeder. Ref: YH01983

BRITTON, CHARLES

Charles Britton, Brookfield Hall, Longhill, Buxton, **Derbyshire**, SK17 6SU, **ENGLAND**.
(T) 01298 74388 (F) 01298 74388.
Profile Track/Course. Ref: YH01984

BRITTON, JOHN R

John R Britton DWCF, 2 Eastlaw, Ebchester, Consett, Durham, **County Durham**, DH8 0QH, **ENGLAND**.
(T) 01207 560669.
Profile Farrier. Ref: YH01985

BRITTON, VANESSA

Vanessa Britton, Lands End, Butters Hall Lane, Thompson, Thetford, **Norfolk**, IP24 1QQ, **ENGLAND**.
(T) 01953 483814 (F) 01953 483814. Ref: YH01986

BROAD ACRE

Broad Acre Stables & Saddlery, Broad Lanes, Six Ashes, Bridgnorth, **Shropshire**, WV15 6EG, **ENGLAND**.
(T) 01746 781019.
Contact/s
Owner: Mr M Wellings
Profile Trainer. Ref: YH01987

BROAD ACRES STABLES

Broad Acres Stables, Broadacres, Charlton Adam, Somerton, **Somerset**, TA11 7BA, **ENGLAND**.
(T) 01458 223161 (F) 01458 224099.
Contact/s
Owner: Mrs M Evans
Profile Stable/Livery. Ref: YH01988

BROAD REED MORGANS

Broad Reed Morgans, Broad Reed Farm, Five Ashes, Mayfield, **Sussex (East)**, TN20 6LG, **ENGLAND**.
(T) 01825 830403.
Profile Breeder. Ref: YH01989

BROAD, E P

E P Broad, Emral Hall, Wallington Lane, Bangor Isycoed, Wrexham, **Wrexham**, LL13 0BG, **WALES**.
(T) 01948 770576.
Contact/s
Owner: Mrs G Broad
Profile Breeder. Ref: YH01990

BROADACRES NURSERIES

Karina Hawkridge (Independent Ecoflow Distributor), Broadacres Stables, Old Coach Rd, Tadcaster, **Yorkshire (North)**, LS24 8HA, **ENGLAND**.
(T) 01937 833333
(E) support@choosehealthandhappiness.com
(W) www.choosehealthandhappiness.com.
Contact/s
Owner: Mrs K Hawkridge
(E) karinastevie@aol.com
Profile Medical Support. Magnetic Therapy.
Bioflow Magnetic Therapy products available for animals and people. No.Staff: 2 Yr. Est: 2001
Opening Times
Sp: Open 08:00. Closed 21:00.
Su: Open 08:00. Closed 21:00.
Au: Open 08:00. Closed 21:00.
Wn: Open 08:00. Closed 21:00. Ref: YH01991

BROADBRIDGE, P J

P J Broadbridge, Norwood Equestrian Ctre, Norwood Lane, Graffham, Petworth, **Sussex (West)**, GU28 0QG, **ENGLAND**.
(T) 01798 867338. Ref: YH01992

BROADCLOSE LIVERY

Broadclose Livery, Broadclose Farm, Broadclose Lane, Inkberrow, Worcester, **Worcestershire**, WR7 4JW, **ENGLAND**.
(T) 01386 792266.
Contact/s
Manager: Mr A Steele
Profile Riding School, Saddlery Retailer.
Ref: YH01993

BROADFEED

Broadfeed Limited, Unit 6 Spa Ind Pk, Longfield Rd, North Farm Ind Est, Tunbridge Wells, **Kent**, TN2 3EN, **ENGLAND**.
(T) 01892 532619 (F) 01892 517594.
Profile Supplies. Ref: YH01994

BROADFIELD STABLES

Broadfield Stables, Kings Barn Lane, Steyning, **Sussex (West)**, BN44 3YG, **ENGLAND**.
(T) 01903 816404 (F) 01903 814384.
Profile Stable/Livery. Ref: YH01995

BROADFIELD STUD

Broadfield Stud, Broadfield Stud, Naas, **County Kildare**, **IRELAND**.
(T) 045 897288.
Contact/s
Key Contact: Mrs A Whitehead
Profile Breeder. Yr. Est: 1959 C.Size: 150 Acres Ref: YH01996

BROADHEAD, G & J

G & J Broadhead, The Smithey, Huddersfield Rd, Elland, **Yorkshire (West)**, HX5 0EE, **ENGLAND**.
(T) 01422 372078.
Profile Farrier. Ref: YH01997

BROADHEATH SADDLERY

Broadheath Saddlery, 12 Woodcote Rd, Warwick, **Warwickshire**, CV34 5BZ, **ENGLAND**.
(T) 01926 495023.
Profile Saddlery Retailer. Ref: YH01998

BROADLANDS RIDING CTRE

Broadlands Riding Centre, Medstead, Alton, **Hampshire**, GU34 5PX, **ENGLAND**.
(T) 01420 563382.
Profile Riding School. Ref: YH01999

BROADLEYS VETNRY HOSPITAL

Broadleys Veterinary Hospital, Craig Leith Rd, Stirling, **Stirling**, FK7 7LE, **SCOTLAND**.
(T) 01786 445665 (F) 01786 445122.
Contact/s
Partner: Mr R Anderson
Profile Medical Support. Ref: YH02000

BROADMEADOW

Broadmeadow Country House & Equestrian Centre, Broadmeadow Country Hse, Bullstown, Ashbourne, **County Meath**, **IRELAND**.
(T) 01 8352823 (F) 01 8352819
(E) info@irelandequestrian.com
(W) www.irelandequestrian.com.
Contact/s
Instructor: Hazel O'Flynn
Profile Equestrian Centre, Horse/Rider Accom.
Livery is available, details on request. There are two outdoor schools and one indoor school with viewing areas and a coffee shop for spectators. Shows are held weekly. Yr. Est: 1996 CREDIT
Opening Times
Telephone for reservations Ref: YH02001

BROADSTONE STUD

Broadstone Stud, South Newington, Banbury, **Oxfordshire**, OX15 4JS, **ENGLAND**.
(T) 01608 737602 (F) 01608 730320.
Contact/s
Manager: Mrs J Bates
Profile Breeder. Ref: YH02002

BROADWAY FARM STABLES

Broadway Farm Stables, High St, Lolworth, Cambridge, **Cambridgeshire**, CB3 8HG, **ENGLAND**.
(T) 01954 780159.
Contact/s
Manager: Mrs J Rhodes Ref: YH02003

BROADWELL CROSS COUNTRY

L V Denham T/A Broadwell Cross Country Course, Broadwell Hse Farm, Broadwell, Rugby, **Warwickshire**, CV23 8HF, **ENGLAND**.
(T) 01926 812347 (F) 01926 812347
(E) broadwellhouse@ntlworld.com.
Contact/s
Owner: Mr A Denham
Profile Yr. Est: 1991 C.Size: 320 Acres
Ref: YH02004

BROBERG, J O

J O Broberg, The Croft, Weston, Stafford, **Staffordshire**, ST18 0HR, **ENGLAND**.
(T) 01889 270234 (F) 01889 271305.
Profile Medical Support. Ref: YH02005

BROCKADALE ARABIANS

Brockadale Arabians Est 1969, Jacksons Lane, Wentbridge, Pontefract, **Yorkshire (West)**, WF8 3HZ, **ENGLAND**.
(T) 01977 620505 (F) 01977 620505.
Contact/s
Owner: Mr T Fretwell

Profile Breeder, Stable/Livery. No.Staff: 2
Yr. Est: 1969 C.Size: 25 Acres
Opening Times
Sp: Open 08:00. Closed 19:00.
Su: Open 08:00. Closed 19:00.
Au: Open 08:00. Closed 16:00.
Wn: Open 08:00. Closed 16:00. **Ref: YH02006**

BROCKBANK, J E

Mr J E Brockbank, Westward Pk, Wigton, **Cumbria**, CA7 8AP, **ENGLAND**.
(T) 01697 342391.
Profile Supplies. **Ref: YH02007**

BROCKENCOTE SHETLAND

Brockencote Shetland Pony Stud, Bow Hills, Great Witley, **Worcestershire**, WR6 6HX, **ENGLAND**.
(T) 01299 896490 **(F)** 01299 896449.
Profile Breeder. **Ref: YH02008**

BROCKHAM & DISTRICT

Brockham & District Riding Club, Golden Lodge, Boxhill Rd, Tadworth, **Surrey**, KT20 7JS, **ENGLAND**.
(T) 01372 450301.
Contact/s
Chairman: Miss H Dart
Profile Club/Association, Riding Club. **Ref: YH02009**

BROCKHOLES FARM

Brockholes Farm Riding Centre, Brockholes Lane, Branton, Doncaster, **Yorkshire (South)**, DN3 3NH, **ENGLAND**.
(T) 01302 535057 **(F)** 01302 533187
(W) www.brockholesfarm.co.uk
Affiliated Bodies ABRS, Pony Club UK.
Contact/s
Owner: Mrs J Humphries
Profile Riding School.
Offers hacking and examination facilities as well as being a 'riding for the disabled' centre. Lesson prices vary according to time and ability. No.Staff: 25
Yr. Est: 1981 C.Size: 300 Acres
Opening Times
Sp: Open Mon 13:00, Tues, Wed 08:00, Thurs, Sat, Sun 09:00. Closed Mon, Wed, Thurs 20:00, Tues, Sat, Sun 17:00.
Su: Open Mon 13:00, Tues, Wed 08:00, Thurs, Sat, Sun 09:00. Closed Mon, Wed, Thurs 20:00, Tues, Sat, Sun 17:00.
Au: Open Mon 13:00, Tues, Wed 08:00, Thurs, Sat, Sun 09:00. Closed Mon, Wed, Thurs 20:00, Tues, Sat, Sun 17:00.
Wn: Open Mon 13:00, Tues, Wed 08:00, Thurs, Sat, Sun 09:00. Closed Mon, Wed, Thurs 20:00, Tues, Sat, Sun 17:00. **Ref: YH02010**

BROCKHURST STABLES

Brockhurst Stables, Brockhurst Pk Farm, 99 Brockhurst Lane, Canwell, Sutton Coldfield, **Midlands (West)**, B75 5SR, **ENGLAND**.
(T) 0121 3080788.
Contact/s
Owner: Mr D Prestridge **Ref: YH02011**

BROCKLEHURSTS OF BAKEWELL

Brocklehursts of Bakewell, Bridge St, Bakewell, **Derbyshire**, DE45 1DS, **ENGLAND**.
(T) 01629 812089 **(F)** 01629 814777
(E) sales@brocklehursts.com.
Contact/s
Owner: Mr J Brocklehurst **Ref: YH02012**

BROCKS FARM

Brocks Farm Livery & Training Centre, Brocks Farm, Longstock, Stockbridge, **Hampshire**, SO20 6DP, **ENGLAND**.
(T) 01264 810090 **(F)** 01264 810090.
Contact/s
Owner: Mrs J Burtenshaw
Profile Riding School, Stable/Livery.
Full and part livery available, prices on request.
Yr. Est: 1983
Opening Times
Sp: Open Tues - Sun 09:00. Closed Tues - Sun 17:00.
Su: Open Tues - Sun 09:00. Closed Tues - Sun 17:00.
Au: Open Tues - Sun 09:00. Closed Tues - Sun 17:00.
Wn: Open Tues - Sun 09:00. Closed Tues - Sun 17:00. **Ref: YH02013**

BROCKS, MICHAEL S

Michael S Brocks RSS, Oatmeal Cragg, 46 Greenfields Ave, Alton, **Hampshire**, GU34 2EE, **ENGLAND**.
(T) 01420 544129.
Profile Farrier. **Ref: YH02014**

BROCKWELL, P

P Brockwell, Unit R Block 2 Pocklington Ind Est, Pocklington, York, **Yorkshire (North)**, YO42 1NR, **ENGLAND**.
(T) 01759 304742.
Profile Blacksmith. **Ref: YH02015**

BROCKWOOD PARK HORSE TRIALS

Brockwood Park Horse Trials (Petersfield Saddlery), Noodcote Manor, Bramdean, Alresford, **Hampshire**, SO24 0LL, **ENGLAND**.
(T) 01962 771793.
Profile Track/Course. **Ref: YH02016**

BROCQ, JOAN LE

Mrs Joan Le Brocq, St Etienne, Rue D'lysee, St Peter, **Jersey**, JE3 7DT, **ENGLAND**.
(T) 01534 481461 **(F)** 01534 481461.
Profile Trainer. **Ref: YH02017**

BRODNAX, FRED

Fred Brodnax, 9 Sommerville Rd, Bristol, **Bristol**, BS7 9AD, **ENGLAND**.
(T) 01179 149460.
Contact/s
Owner: Mr F Brodnax
Profile Blacksmith. **Ref: YH02018**

BROGAR PONY STUD

Brogar Pony Stud, Emerald Bank, Burngrains, Methlick, **Aberdeenshire**, AB41 7EA, **SCOTLAND**.
(T) 01651 806275.
Profile Breeder. **Ref: YH02019**

BROGUESTOWN STUD

Broguestown Stud, Kill, **County Kildare**, **IRELAND**.
(T) 045 862176
(E) broguestownstud@kildarehorse.ie.
Contact/s
Key Contact: Mr M Doulton
Profile Breeder. **Ref: YH02020**

BROKEN SPOKE

Broken Spoke (The), Ruddenleys, Lamancha, West Linton, **Scottish Borders**, EH46 7BQ, **SCOTLAND**.
(T) 01968 661266 **(F)** 01968 661066
(M) 07768 515760.
Profile Breeder, Trainer. **Ref: YH02021**

BROKENSHIRE, ADRIAN KEITH

Adrian Keith Brokenshire, Shireokes Barn, Scarletts Well Rd, Bodmin, **Cornwall**, PL31 2PL, **ENGLAND**.
(T) 01208 74269.
Profile Farrier. **Ref: YH02022**

BROMLEY COMMON LIVERIES

Bromley Common Liveries, Bromley Common, Bromley, **Kent**, BR2 8HA, **ENGLAND**.
(T) 020 84620340.
Contact/s
Accountant: Mr C Atkin
Profile Stable/Livery. **Ref: YH02023**

BROMLEY TOWBARS & TRAILERS

Bromley Towbars & Trailers, 53-54 Palace Rd, Bromley, **Kent**, BR1 3JU, **ENGLAND**.
(T) 020 83131128.
Profile Transport/Horse Boxes. **Ref: YH02024**

BROMPTON HALL

Brompton Hall Equestrian Ltd, Brompton Hall, Churchstoke, Montgomery, **Powys**, SY15 6SP, **WALES**.
(T) 01588 620750 **(F)** 01588 620751
(M) 07979 795499
(E) bromptonequine@talk21.com.
Contact/s
General Manager: Mr T Ward
Profile Arena, Equestrian Centre, Riding School, Riding Wear Retailer, Saddlery Retailer, Stable/Livery, Supplies, Trainer, Transport/Horse Boxes.
No.Staff: 4 Yr. Est: 2000 C.Size: 8 Acres
Opening Times
Sp: Open Mon - Sun 08:00. Closed Mon - Sun 18:00.
Su: Open Mon - Sun 08:00. Closed Mon - Sun 18:00.
Au: Open Mon - Sun 08:00. Closed Mon - Sun 18:00.
Wn: Open Mon - Sun 08:00. Closed Mon - Sun 18:00. **Ref: YH02025**

BROMSGROVE SADDLERY

Bromsgrove Saddlery Limited, 148A New Rd, Aston Fields, Bromsgrove, **Worcestershire**, B60 2LE, **ENGLAND**.
(T) 01527 872704 **(F)** 01527 872704.
Contact/s
Owner: Mr M Pearson
Profile Riding Wear Retailer, Saddlery Retailer, Supplies.
Opening Times
Sp: Open Mon - Sat 09:00. Closed Mon - Sat 17:00.
Su: Open Mon - Sat 09:00. Closed Mon - Sat 17:00.
Au: Open Mon - Sat 09:00. Closed Mon - Sat 17:00.
Wn: Open Mon - Sat 09:00. Closed Mon - Sat 17:00.
Ref: YH02026

BROMYARD

Bromyard Equestrian Supplies & Tack, Linton Trading Est, Bromyard, **Herefordshire**, HR7 4QT, **ENGLAND**.
(T) 01885 488466 **(F)** 01885 483897.
Profile Saddlery Retailer. **Ref: YH02027**

BROMYARD & DISTRICT

Bromyard & District Riding Club, Stone Hse Farm, Thornbury, Bromyard, **Herefordshire**, HR6 9PH, **ENGLAND**.
(T) 01885 482484.
Contact/s
Chairman: Mr A Garrett
Profile Club/Association, Riding Club. **Ref: YH02028**

BRONALLT

Bronallt Equestrian Supplies, Chatham Works, Llandwrog, Caernarfon, **Gwynedd**, LL54 5TG, **WALES**.
(T) 01286 830031 **(F)** 01286 830031.
Contact/s
Owner: Mr M Coulson
Profile Riding Wear Retailer, Saddlery Retailer, Supplies. No.Staff: 4 Yr. Est: 1995
C.Size: 4 Acres
Opening Times
Sp: Open 09:00. Closed 17:00.
Su: Open 09:00. Closed 17:00.
Au: Open 09:00. Closed 17:00.
Wn: Open 09:00. Closed 17:00. **Ref: YH02029**

BRONANT LIVERY CTRE

Bronant Livery Centre, Ffordd Llanfynydd, Treuddyn, Mold, **Flintshire**, CH7 4LQ, **WALES**.
(T) 01352 770781.
Contact/s
Partner: Mr C Northall **Ref: YH02030**

BROOK BARN QUARTER HORSES

Brook Barn Quarter Horses, Redmires Rd, Sheffield, **Yorkshire (South)**, S10 4LJ, **ENGLAND**.
(T) 0114 2306032.
Profile Breeder. **Ref: YH02031**

BROOK END

Brook End Livery & Training Centre, North Brook End Farm, Steeple Morden, Royston, **Hertfordshire**, SG8 0PH, **ENGLAND**.
(T) 01763 853784.
Contact/s
Owner: Mrs D Crosby-Clark
Profile Stable/Livery. **Ref: YH02032**

BROOK FARM

Brook Farm Livery Yard, Brooks Rd, Raunds, Wellingborough, **Northamptonshire**, NN9 6NS, **ENGLAND**.
(T) 01933 624031.
Contact/s
Owner: Mr G Webster
Profile Stable/Livery.
DIY and part livery available. There is also off road riding on private tracks. Telephone for further information
No.Staff: 1 Yr. Est: 1985 C.Size: 30 Acres
Opening Times
Yard open to owners 7 days a week from 06:30 - 21:00. Floodlit arena for hire all year. **Ref: YH02033**

BROOK FARM EQUESTRIAN CTRE

Brook Farm Equestrian Centre, Brook Farm, Hempstead Rd, Radwinter, Saffron Walden, **Essex**, CB10 2TH, **ENGLAND**.
(T) 01799 599262.
Profile Riding School, Saddlery Retailer.
Ref: YH02034

BROOK FARM RIDING SCHOOL

Brook Farm Riding School, Stock Rd, Stock, Ingatestone, **Essex**, CM4 9PH, **ENGLAND**.
(T) 01277 840425.
Contact/s
Owner: Mrs P Stanbacka
Profile Riding School. **Ref: YH02035**

BROOK FARM STABLES

Brook Farm Livery/Riding Centre, Brook Farm Stables, Colchester Main Rd, Alresford, Colchester, **Essex**, CO7 8AP, **ENGLAND**.
(T) 01206 822502.
Contact/s
Owner: Mr B Christmas
Profile Riding School, Stable/Livery.
Full and DIY livery available. Also 'Loan a pony' and holiday rides. **Yr. Est:** 1984
Opening Times
Sp: Open Mon - Sun 07:30. Closed Mon - Sun 21:00.
Su: Open Mon - Sun 07:30. Closed Mon - Sun 21:00.
Au: Open Mon - Sun 07:30. Closed Mon - Sun 21:00.
Wn: Open Mon - Sun 07:30. Closed Mon - Sun 21:00. **Ref: YH02036**

BROOK HSE FARM

Brook House Farm Riding School, Watery Lane, Louth, **Lincolnshire**, LN11 9XL, **ENGLAND**.
(T) 01507 343266 **(F)** 01507 343266
(E) enquiry@brookhousefarm.com
(W) www.brookhousefarm.com.
Contact/s
Owner: Mr R Strawson
Profile Riding School, Stable/Livery.
Specialise in hacks through the countryside.
Yr. Est: 1996
Opening Times
Sp: Open Mon - Sun 09:00. Closed Mon - Sun 20:00.
Su: Open Mon - Sun 09:00. Closed Mon - Sun 20:00.
Au: Open Mon - Sun 09:00. Closed Mon - Sun 20:00.
Wn: Open Mon - Sun 09:00. Closed Mon - Sun 20:00. **Ref: YH02037**

BROOK STABLES

Brook Stables, Warren Farm, Cobblers Lane, Steppingley, Bedford, **Bedfordshire**, MK45 5AR, **ENGLAND**.
(T) 01525 712306.
Contact/s
Owner: Mrs J Halls
Profile Riding School, Stable/Livery.
Hacking and jumping facilities available.
Opening Times
Sp: Open Tue - Sun 09:00. Closed Tue - Fri 20:00, Sat, Sun 17:00.
Su: Open Tue - Sun 09:00. Closed Tue - Fri 20:00, Sat, Sun 17:00.
Au: Open Tue - Sun 09:00. Closed Tue - Fri 20:00, Sat, Sun 17:00.
Wn: Open Tue - Sun 09:00. Closed Tue - Fri 20:00, Sat, Sun 17:00.
Closed Mondays **Ref: YH02038**

BROOK STUD

Brook Stud Ltd, High St, Cheveley, Newmarket, **Suffolk**, CB8 9DG, **ENGLAND**.
(T) 01638 730212 **(F)** 01638 730819.
Contact/s
Accountant: M. W Higson
Profile Breeder. **Ref: YH02039**

BROOK, PHILIP J

Philip J Brook DWCF, Shrublands, 36 East Rd, Isleham, Ely, **Cambridgeshire**, CB7 5SN, **ENGLAND**.
(T) 01638 780496.
Profile Farrier. **Ref: YH02040**

BROOKE HOSPITAL FOR ANIMALS

Brooke Hospital for Animals, Broadmead Hse, Dept B E D, 21 Panton St, London, **London (Greater)**, SW1Y 4DR, **ENGLAND**.
(T) 020 79300210 **(F)** 020 79302386.
Profile Medical Support. **Ref: YH02041**

BROOKE LODGE

Brooke Lodge Riding Centre, Stepaside Stables, Stepaside, Sandyford, **County Dublin**, **IRELAND**.
(T) 01 2952153.
Profile Riding School.
Offer pony camps for children and weekly showjumping competitions, as well as trekking on Three Rock mountain.
Opening Times
Sp: Open Tues - Sun 09:00. Closed Tues - Sun 21:00.
Su: Open Tues - Sun 09:00. Closed Tues - Sun 21:00.
Au: Open Tues - Sun 09:00. Closed Tues - Sun 21:00.
Wn: Open Tues - Sun 09:00. Closed Tues - Sun 21:00.
Closed Mondays **Ref: YH02042**

BROOKE, G M

G M Brooke, York Rd Farm, Healaugh, Tadcaster, **Yorkshire (North)**, LS24 8DD, **ENGLAND**.
(T) 01937 834245.
Profile Farrier. **Ref: YH02043**

BROOKE, WILLIAM N

William N Brooke, 3 Breck Cottages, Wash, Chapel-En-Le-Frith, High Peak, **Cheshire**, SK22 4QN, **ENGLAND**.
(T) 01663 750432.
Profile Farrier. **Ref: YH02044**

BROOKES, JOSEPHINE

Mrs Josephine Brookes, Oldfords Farm, Seighford, Stafford, **Staffordshire**, ST18 9PE, **ENGLAND**.
(T) 01785 282257.
Profile Breeder. **Ref: YH02045**

BROOKES, REGINALD

Mr Reginald Brookes, Pipe Hall Farm, Abnalls Lane, Lichfield, **Staffordshire**, WS13 8BW, **ENGLAND**.
(T) 01543 223368.
Profile Supplies. **Ref: YH02046**

BROOKFIELD GREEN FARM

Brookfield Green Farm, 144 Brookfield Lane, Aughton, Ormskirk, **Lancashire**, L39 6SP, **ENGLAND**.
(T) 01695 423529.
Contact/s
Owner: Mrs M Johnson
Profile Stable/Livery.
Ample grazing and riding fields and DIY livery available. **No.Staff:** 1 **Yr. Est:** 1984 **C.Size:** 10 Acres **Ref: YH02047**

BROOKFIELD LIVERY

Brookfield Livery, Rampton Rd, Longstanton, Cambridge, **Cambridgeshire**, CB4 5EN, **ENGLAND**.
(T) 01954 780084.
Profile Stable/Livery. **Ref: YH02048**

BROOKFIELD SHIRES

Brookfield Shires Plc, New Farm, Buckworth Rd, Alconbury Weston, Huntingdon, **Cambridgeshire**, PE28 4JX, **ENGLAND**.
(T) 01480 891642 **(F)** 01480 890488.
Profile Breeder. **Ref: YH02049**

BROOKFIELD STABLES

Brookfield Stables, Northill Rd, Ickwell, Biggleswade, **Bedfordshire**, SG18 9ED, **ENGLAND**.
(T) 01767 627278.
Contact/s
Owner: Ms S Brinkley
Profile Stable/Livery. **Ref: YH02050**

BROOKFIELDS

M R J Blood Stock, Brookfields, Charity Lane, Westhead, Ormskirk, **Lancashire**, L40 6LG, **ENGLAND**.
(T) 01695 579334 **(F)** 01695 580473.
Contact/s
Manager: Mr R Wylie
Profile Blood Stock Agency, Breeder. **No.Staff:** 2 **Yr. Est:** 1992 **C.Size:** 20 Acres
Opening Times
By appointment only **Ref: YH02051**

BROOKFIELDS

Brookfields Riding & Livery Centre, Cannock Rd, Shareshill, Wolverhampton, **Midlands (West)**, WV10 7LZ, **ENGLAND**.
(T) 01922 414090 **(F)** 01922 414090.
Contact/s
Owner: Mrs M Blick
Profile Riding School, Stable/Livery. **Ref: YH02052**

BROOKFIELDS LIVERY STABLES

Brookfields Livery Stables, Brookfields Rd, Wyke, Bradford, **Yorkshire (West)**, BD12 9LU, **ENGLAND**.
(T) 01274 693494.
Profile Stable/Livery. **Ref: YH02053**

BROOKFIELDS STABLES

Brookfields Stables, Charity Lane, Westhead, **Lancashire**, L40 6LG, **ENGLAND**.
(T) 01695 579334.
Profile Trainer. **Ref: YH02054**

BROOKHOUSE FARM BUILDINGS

Brookhouse Farm Buildings, Brook Hse Farm, Brookhouse Lane, Congleton, **Cheshire**, CW12 3QP, **ENGLAND**.
(T) 01260 272556.
Contact/s
Owner: Mr D Wardle
Profile Breeder. **Ref: YH02055**

BROOKHOUSE FARM RIDING SCHOOL

Brookhouse Farm Riding School, Truemans Heath Lane, Shirley, Solihull, **Midlands (West)**, B90 1PG, **ENGLAND**.
(T) 0121 4742078 **(F)** 0121 4742078.
Contact/s
Manager: Mrs J Maynard
Profile Riding School. **Ref: YH02056**

BROOKLANDS EQUITARE

Brooklands Equitare, 11 Mullaghcarton Rd, Lisburn, **County Antrim**, BT28 2TE, **NORTHERN IRELAND**.
(T) 028 92622076.
Contact/s
Owner: Mrs S Scott
Profile Riding School. **Ref: YH02057**

BROOKLANDS FARM

Brooklands Farm, Wootton Lane, Balsall Common, Coventry, **Midlands (West)**, CU7 7BS, **ENGLAND**.
(T) 01676 532257.
Contact/s
General Manager: Miss L Newey
Profile Horse/Rider Accom. **Ref: YH02058**

BROOKLEIGH RIDING CTRE

Brookleigh Riding Centre, Sandwath Farm, Forcett, Richmond, **Yorkshire (North)**, DL11 7SE, **ENGLAND**.
(T) 01325 718286.
Contact/s
Owner: Mrs C Thompson **Ref: YH02059**

BROOKLYN FARM STABLES

Brooklyn Farm Stables, Cow Lane, Edlesborough, Dunstable, **Bedfordshire**, LU6 2HT, **ENGLAND**.
(T) 01525 220572 **(F)** 01525 220287.
Contact/s
Owner: Mrs S Yates
Profile Riding School, Stable/Livery. **Ref: YH02060**

BROOKS LANE SMITHY

Brooks Lane Smithy, Units 1 & 2 The Old Saltworks, Brooks Lane, Middlewich, **Cheshire**, CW10 0JH, **ENGLAND**.
(T) 01606 737155.
Profile Farrier. **Ref: YH02061**

BROOKS STABLES

Brooks Stables, Hilltop Ave, Benfleet, **Essex**, SS7 1PH, **ENGLAND**.
(T) 01268 753851.
Profile Saddlery Retailer, Stable/Livery.
Ref: YH02062

BROOKS, B R

Mr & Mrs B R Brooks, Great Hollanden Farm, Underriver, Sevenoaks, **Kent**, TN15 0SG, **ENGLAND**.
(T) 01732 832276.
Profile Breeder. **Ref: YH02063**

BROOKS, E M

Mrs E M Brooks, The Barton, Monkleigh, Bideford, **Devon**, EX39 5JX, **ENGLAND**.
(T) 01805 623156.
Profile Breeder. **Ref: YH02064**

BROOKS, J V

J V Brooks, Bank Farm/Melton Rd, Stanton-on-the-Wolds, Keyworth, Nottingham, **Nottinghamshire**, NG12 5PJ, **ENGLAND**.
(T) 0115 9375922.
Contact/s
Owner: Mr J Brooks
Profile Transport/Horse Boxes. **Ref: YH02065**

BROOKS, JONATHAN

Jonathan Brooks, Sinderland Lane, Dunham Massey, Altrincham, **Cheshire**, WA14 5SU, **ENGLAND**.
(T) 0161 9290509.
Contact/s
Owner: Mr J Brooks
Profile Farrier. **Ref: YH02066**

BROOKSBY EQUESTRIAN CTRE

Brooksby Equestrian Centre, Brooksby, Melton Mowbray, **Leicestershire**, LE14 2LJ, **ENGLAND**.
(T) 01664 424280 **(F)** 01664 424280.
Profile Breeder, Riding School, Stable/Livery, Track/Course. **Ref: YH02067**

BROOKSHAW, S A

S A Brookshaw, Preston Farm, Preston-on-Severn,

Uffington, Shrewsbury, **Shropshire**, SY4 4TB, **ENGLAND**.
(T) 01743 709227.
Contact/s
Owner: Mr S Brookshaw
Profile Trainer. **Ref: YH02068**

BROOKSIDE FORGE

Brookside Forge, Brookside, Gayton, Stafford, **Staffordshire**, ST18 0HJ, **ENGLAND**.
(T) 01889 271478.
Contact/s
Owner: Mr N Leech
Profile Blacksmith. **Ref: YH02069**

BROOKWICK WARD

Brookwick Ward & Co Ltd, 88 Westlaw Pl, Whitehill Ind Est, Glenrothes, **Fife**, KY6 2RZ, **SCOTLAND**.
(T) 01592 630052 **(F)** 01592 630109.
Profile Medical Support. **Ref: YH02070**

BROOM FARM RIDING SCHOOL

Broom Farm Riding School, Broom Farm, Stevenston, **Ayrshire (North)**, KA20 3DD, **SCOTLAND**.
(T) 01294 465437
Affiliated Bodies BHS.
Contact/s
Owner: Miss A Donaldson
Profile Riding School, Stable/Livery. Wedding carriages. **No.Staff:** 5 **Yr. Est:** 1974
Opening Times
Sp: Open 09:00. Closed 21:00.
Su: Open 09:00. Closed 21:00.
Au: Open 09:00. Closed 21:00.
Wn: Open 09:00. Closed 21:00. **Ref: YH02071**

BROOM HALL LIVERY YARD

Broom Hall Livery Yard and Stud, Broomhall Farm, Ushaw Moor, Durham, **County Durham**, DH7 7NB, **ENGLAND**.
(T) 0191 3736785.
Contact/s
For Bookings: Mr C Moore
Profile Breeder, Stable/Livery, Transport/Horse Boxes. **No.Staff:** 3 **Yr. Est:** 1995 **C.Size:** 44 Acres
Opening Times
Sp: Open 07:00. Closed 21:00.
Su: Open 07:00. Closed 21:00.
Au: Open 07:00. Closed 20:00.
Wn: Open 07:00. Closed 20:00. **Ref: YH02072**

BROOM LODGE

Broom Lodge Stables, Ashford, **County Wicklow**, **IRELAND**.
(T) 0404 40404. **Ref: YH02073**

BROOMBANK EQUESTRIAN

Broombank Equestrian, Broomhill Farm, Broomhill Rd, Old Whittington Rd, Chesterfield, **Derbyshire**, S41 9DA, **ENGLAND**.
(T) 01246 456488
(M) 07831 183567.
Profile Saddlery Retailer. **Ref: YH02074**

BROOME, DAVID

David Broome OBE, Mount Ballan Manor, Portskewett, Newport, **Monmouthshire**, NP16 6XP, **WALES**.
(T) 01291 420778 **(F)** 01291 422352. **Ref: YH02075**

BROOME, G W

G W Broome RSS, Yew Tree Cottage, Upton Magna, Shrewsbury, **Shropshire**, SY4 4TZ, **ENGLAND**.
(T) 01743 709296.
Profile Farrier. **Ref: YH02076**

BROOMELLS WORKSHOP

Broomells Workshop, Misbrook Yard, Misbrooks Green Rd, Capel, Dorking, **Surrey**, RH5 5HL, **ENGLAND**.
(T) 01306 711514 **(F)** 01306 711514
Affiliated Bodies MSA.
Contact/s
Owner: Ms P Thomas **(Q)** Master Saddler
Profile Saddlery Retailer. **No.Staff:** 2
Yr. Est: 1983
Opening Times
Sp: Open 09:00. Closed 17:00.
Su: Open 09:00. Closed 17:00.
Au: Open 09:00. Closed 17:00.
Wn: Open 09:00. Closed 17:00.
Saturday 09:00 - 13:00 **Ref: YH02077**

BROOMFIELD RIDING CTRE

Broomfield Riding Centre, Tinahely, **County Wicklow**, **IRELAND**.
(T) 0402 38117.
Contact/s
Owner: Pam Horn
Profile Riding School.
Hacks through beautiful scenic countryside and forestry. Tuition avaliable in riding and show jumping for all levels. **Ref: YH02078**

BROOMHALL RIDING SCHOOL

Broomhall Riding School, Harlequin Cottage, Heatley Lane, Broomhall, Nantwich, **Cheshire**, CW5 8BA, **ENGLAND**.
(T) 01270 780392.
Contact/s
Owner: Mr C Garside
Profile Riding School. **Ref: YH02079**

BROOMHILL

Broomhill Farm Equestrian Centre, Broomhill Farm, Smalden Lane, Grindleton, Clitheroe, **Lancashire**, BB7 4RX, **ENGLAND**.
(T) 01200 440462 **(F)** 01200 440900.
Contact/s
Instructor: Ms L Bridge
Profile Equestrian Centre, Riding School, Stable/Livery.
Full, part and DIY livery available. Escorted hacks and tuition on your own, or the schools horses. A 45 minute lessons cost £18.00 for children and £25.00 for adults. **No.Staff:** 7 **Yr. Est:** 1996
C.Size: 57 Acres
Opening Times
Sp: Open Mon - Sun 07:30. Closed Mon - Sun 20:30.
Su: Open Mon - Sun 07:30. Closed Mon - Sun 20:30.
Au: Open Mon - Sun 07:30. Closed Mon - Sun 20:30.
Wn: Open Mon - Sun 07:30. Closed Mon - Sun 20:30. **Ref: YH02080**

BROOMHILL STUD

Broomhill Stud, Swinford Mill Lane, Barrow, Chester, **Cheshire**, CH3 7LA, **ENGLAND**.
(T) 01829 741441 **(F)** 01829 741991.
Profile Breeder. **Ref: YH02081**

BROOMSIDE STUD

Broomside Stud, Shire Farm, Mansfield Lane, Calverton, **Nottinghamshire**, NG14 6HL, **ENGLAND**.
(T) 0115 9652590.
Profile Breeder, Saddlery Retailer, Stable/Livery, Supplies. **Ref: YH02082**

BROOTHOM PONIES

Broothom Ponies, Skelberry, Dunrossness, Shetland, **Shetland Islands**, ZE2 9JH, **SCOTLAND**.
(T) 01950 460464.
Contact/s
Owner: Mrs H Thompson
Profile Breeder, Riding School. **Ref: YH02083**

BROSHUIS TRAILERS

Broshuis Trailers Ltd, Wellington Hse, Lower Icknield Way, Longwick, Princes Risborough, **Buckinghamshire**, HP27 9RZ, **ENGLAND**.
(T) 01844 343582 **(F)** 01844 274071.
Contact/s
Manager: Mr R Vannaplldawn
Profile Transport/Horse Boxes. **Ref: YH02084**

BROSTER, R J

R J Broster, 21 Alamieu Gardens, Dartford, **Kent**, **ENGLAND**..
Profile Breeder. **Ref: YH02085**

BROUDEIN STUD FARM

Broudein Stud Farm (The), Burton Rd, Rosliston, Swadlincote, **Derbyshire**, DE12 8JX, **ENGLAND**.
(T) 01283 761107.
Contact/s
Partner: Mrs P Bartrem
Profile Breeder. **Ref: YH02086**

BROUGH, L E

Mrs L E Brough, Gables Lane, Middleton-In-Teesdale, Barnard Castle, Durham, **County Durham**, **ENGLAND**..
Profile Trainer. **Ref: YH02087**

BROUGHTON HALL

Broughton Hall Livery & Training Centre, Broughton Hall Farm, Broughton Rd, Lodge, Wrexham, **Wrexham**, LL11 5NF, **WALES**.
(T) 01978 757917.
Profile Equestrian Centre. **Ref: YH02088**

BROWING, MARY

Miss Mary Browing, Parish Hse, Greatworth, Bambury, **Oxfordshire**, OX17 2DX, **ENGLAND**.
(T) 01295 711532. **Ref: YH02089**

BROWN & PADDON

Brown & Paddon, 214 Elm Low Rd, Wisbech, **Cambridgeshire**, PE14 0DF, **ENGLAND**.
(T) 01945 583204.
Profile Medical Support. **Ref: YH02090**

BROWN ARABIANS

Brown Arabians, The Granary, Manor Farm, Aslacton, Norwich, **Norfolk**, NR15 2JS, **ENGLAND**.
(T) 01379 677550.
Contact/s
Owner: Mr D Brown
Profile Breeder. **Ref: YH02091**

BROWN BREAD HORSE RESCUE CTRE

Brown Bread Horse Rescue Centre, Ashburnham, Battle, **Sussex (East)**, TN33 9NX, **ENGLAND**.
(T) 01424 892381.
Contact/s
Admin: Mr D Steains
Profile Trainer. Welfare Centre.
Free advice line for any horse problems. Fund-raisers and helpers always welcome. The centre fights cruelty against horses hands-on, and is currently running the 'Free the Prisoners of Gender' campaign to help stallions and colts. They take in horses from all over the UK and lend them to private homes.
Opening Times
On call 24 hours a day. **Ref: YH02092**

BROWN RIGG RIDING SCHOOL

Brown Rigg Riding School, Bellingham, Hexham, **Northumberland**, NE48 2HR, **ENGLAND**.
(T) 01434 220272.
Contact/s
Key Contact: R B McLeod
Profile Holidays, Riding School.
Residential riding establishment (Riding holiday courses for children aged 9-16yrs) **Ref: YH02093**

BROWN TRAILERS

Brown Trailers, Weetslade Business Pk, Dudley, Cramlington, **Northumberland**, NE23 7PS, **ENGLAND**.
(T) 0191 2500187 **(F)** 0191 2502865.
Profile Transport/Horse Boxes. **Ref: YH02094**

BROWN, A

A Brown, Grey Goose Cottage, Little Compton, Moreton In Marsh, **Gloucestershire**, GL56 0SP, **ENGLAND**.
(T) 01608 674652.
Profile Farrier. **Ref: YH02095**

BROWN, A D

A D Brown, Little Barugh, Malton, **Yorkshire (North)**, YO17 6UY, **ENGLAND**.
(T) 01653 668626 **(F)** 01653 668626.
Contact/s
Partner: Mr A Brown
Profile Transport/Horse Boxes. **Ref: YH02096**

BROWN, A T

A T Brown, Unit 2 Camps Ind Est, Kirknewton, **Lothian (West)**, EH27 8DF, **SCOTLAND**.
(T) 01506 884517 **(F)** 01506 884517.
Contact/s
Partner: Mr T Brown
Profile Blacksmith. **Ref: YH02097**

BROWN, ALISTAIR

Mr Alistair Brown, Little Mondays, Upper Coberley, Cheltenham, **Gloucestershire**, GL53 9RD, **ENGLAND**.
(T) 01241 870238
(M) 07802 734319.
Profile Trainer. **Ref: YH02098**

BROWN, ANDREW N

Andrew N Brown AWCF, The Barn, Seagrave Grange, Seagrave, Sileby, **Leicestershire**, LE12 8HN, **ENGLAND**.
(T) 07836 570804.
Profile Farrier. **Ref: YH02099**

BROWN, ANDREW P

Andrew P Brown AFCL, 14 Birchwood Rd, Upton, Poole, **Dorset**, BH16 5LE, **ENGLAND**.
(T) 07710 821749.
Profile Farrier. **Ref: YH02100**

BROWN, ARTHUR H

Arthur H Brown RSS BII, 26 Winterway, Blockley, **Gloucestershire**, GL56 9EF, **ENGLAND**.
(T) 01386 700632.
Profile Farrier. **Ref: YH02101**

BROWN, C
C Brown, Pontgam Stud, Penheolddu, Wyllie Lane, Blackwood, **Caerphilly**, NP12 2NG, **WALES**.
(T) 01495 221474.
Profile Breeder. **Ref: YH02102**

BROWN, C N
C N Brown, Cherryvale, 92 Lough Rd, Boardmills, Lisburn, **County Antrim**, BT27 6TT, **NORTHERN IRELAND**.
(T) 028 92639300.
Profile Transport/Horse Boxes. **Ref: YH02103**

BROWN, CAROLINE
Miss Caroline Brown BHSII (Regd), Hanbury Pk, Needwood, Burton-on-Trent, **Staffordshire**, DE13 9PG, **ENGLAND**.
(T) 01283 75391.
Profile Trainer. **Ref: YH02104**

BROWN, D H
Mr D H Brown, The Grove, Blyth Rd, Roche Abbey, Maltby, **Yorkshire (South)**, S66 8NW, **ENGLAND**.
(T) 01709 812854.
Profile Supplies. **Ref: YH02105**

BROWN, DAVID R
David R Brown DWCF, Lochspout Cottage, Knapp Rd, Inchture, **Perth and Kinross**, PH14 9SN, **SCOTLAND**.
(T) 01828 686054.
Profile Farrier. **Ref: YH02106**

BROWN, DAVID V
David V Brown RSS BII, Badmondisfield End, Back St, Ousden, Newmarket, **Suffolk**, CB8 8TT, **ENGLAND**.
(T) 01638 500408.
Profile Farrier. **Ref: YH02107**

BROWN, GEOFF
Mr Geoff Brown, The Smallholding, Heugh, Stamfordham, **Northumberland**, NE18 0NH, **ENGLAND**.
(T) 01661 886819. **Ref: YH02108**

BROWN, I H
Mr I H Brown, Oakhouse, Ravenstonedale, Kirkby Stephen, **Cumbria**, CA17 4NQ, **ENGLAND**.
(T) 01539 623233.
Profile Trainer. **Ref: YH02109**

BROWN, I R
Mr I R Brown, Highview Farm, Upper Lye, Aymestrey, Leominster, **Herefordshire**, HR6 9SZ, **ENGLAND**.
(T) 01568 770231.
Profile Supplies. **Ref: YH02110**

BROWN, J
J Brown, Benbole Farm, St. Kew Highway, Bodmin, **Cornwall**, PL30 3EF, **ENGLAND**.
(T) 01208 841281.
Contact/s
Owner: Mr J Brown
Opening Times
Only open in the summer **Ref: YH02111**

BROWN, J
J Brown, Wilton, Egremont, **Cumbria**, CA22 2PJ, **ENGLAND**.
(T) 01946 820358.
Contact/s
Manager: Mr K Carr
Profile Breeder. **Ref: YH02112**

BROWN, J
Brown J., Block 3 Unit 2 Kirkintilloch Ind Est, Milton Rd, Kirkintilloch, Glasgow, **Glasgow (City of)**, G66 1SY, **SCOTLAND**.
(T) 0141 7760971.
Profile Blacksmith. **Ref: YH02113**

BROWN, J H W
J H W Brown, Church Farm, Pett Rd, Pett, Hastings, **Sussex (East)**, TN35 4HE, **ENGLAND**.
(T) 01424 813488 **(F)** 01424 813488.
Contact/s
Owner: Mr J Brown
Profile Farrier. **Ref: YH02114**

BROWN, J W
J W Brown, The Fosse Way, Upper Broughton, Melton Mowbray, **Leicestershire**, LE14 3QD, **ENGLAND**.
(T) 01664 823485.
Contact/s
Owner: Mr J Brown
Profile Saddlery Retailer. **Ref: YH02115**

BROWN, JAMES C
James C Brown, Forge Hse, 2 Newton Of Barr, Lochwinnoch, **Renfrewshire**, PA12 4AR, **SCOTLAND**.
(T) 01505 3365.
Profile Farrier. **Ref: YH02116**

BROWN, JOHN
Mr John Brown, Yn Yr Haul, Llansadwrn, Llanwrda, **Carmarthenshire**, SA19 8LH, **WALES**.
(T) 01550 777050
(M) 07967 230136
(E) annjon@tinyonline.co.uk. **Ref: YH02117**

BROWN, KARL J
Karl J Brown DWCF, 8 Mansfield Rd, Eston, Middlesbrough, **Cleveland**, TS6 9HG, **ENGLAND**.
(T) 01642 454685.
Profile Farrier. **Ref: YH02118**

BROWN, KELLY
Mrs Kelly Brown, Willowtree Cottage, Mountnessing Lane, Doddinghurst, Brentwood, **Essex**, CM15 0SP, **ENGLAND**.
(T) 01277 822951 **(F)** 01277 824227. **Ref: YH02119**

BROWN, LESLIE
Leslie Brown, Parkview, Carlton, Leyburn, **Yorkshire (North)**, DL8 4BD, **ENGLAND**.
(T) 01969 640274. **Ref: YH02120**

BROWN, LUKE R
Luke R Brown DWCF, 29 Windsor Cl, Mountsorrel, Loughborough, **Leicestershire**, LE12 7SS, **ENGLAND**.
(T) 07802 468316.
Profile Farrier. **Ref: YH02121**

BROWN, M A
M A Brown BHSI (Regd), 9 Barry Lynham Drive, Newmarket, **Suffolk**, CB8 8YU, **ENGLAND**.
(T) 01638 669729.
Profile Trainer. **Ref: YH02122**

BROWN, M IAN
M Ian Brown BHSII, The Stables, Manor Pk Farm, Hudswell, Richmond, **Yorkshire (North)**, DL11 6BL, **ENGLAND**.
(T) 07720 597614.
Profile Trainer. **Ref: YH02123**

BROWN, N & H
N & H Brown, 14 Chelmer Rd, Witham, **Essex**, CM8 2EU, **ENGLAND**.
(T) 01376 518663.
Profile Saddlery Retailer. **Ref: YH02124**

BROWN, NIGEL R
Nigel R Brown DWCF, Bleanllymon, Cross Ash, Abergavenny, **Monmouthshire**, NP7 8UA, **WALES**.
(T) 01873 821343.
Profile Farrier. **Ref: YH02125**

BROWN, OLIVER
Oliver Brown, 75 Lower Sloane St, London, **London (Greater)**, SW1W 8DA, **ENGLAND**.
(T) 020 72599494 **(F)** 020 72599444
(W) www.oliverbrown.org.uk.
Contact/s
Owner: Mr C Robson
Profile Riding Wear Retailer.
Sells clothing for hunting, shooting and riding.
Yr. Est: 1994
Opening Times
Sp: Open Mon - Sat 10:00. Closed Mon - Sat 18:30.
Su: Open Mon - Sat 10:00. Closed Mon - Sat 18:30.
Au: Open Mon - Sat 10:00. Closed Mon - Sat 18:30.
Wn: Open Mon - Sat 10:00. Closed Mon - Sat 18:30.
Ref: YH02126

BROWN, PIERCE R
Pierce R Brown DWCF, The Forge, Turgis Green, Hook, **Hampshire**, RG27 0AH, **ENGLAND**.
(T) 01256 883655.
Profile Farrier. **Ref: YH02127**

BROWN, R
R Brown, Blacksmiths Shop, Ash Magna, Whitchurch, **Shropshire**, SY13 4DR, **ENGLAND**.
(T) 01948 663188.
Profile Farrier. **Ref: YH02128**

BROWN, R & F
R & F Brown, Rose Cottage, Radernie, Cupar, **Fife**, KY15 7RZ, **SCOTLAND**.
(T) 01334 840525.
Profile Breeder. **Ref: YH02129**

BROWN, R L
Mr R L Brown, The Firs, Grosmont, Abergavenny, **Monmouthshire**, NP7 8LY, **WALES**.
(T) 01873 821278.
Profile Supplies. **Ref: YH02130**

BROWN, RAYMOND
Raymond Brown, 14 Esk Court, Forfar, **Angus**, **SCOTLAND**..
Profile Breeder. **Ref: YH02131**

BROWN, T
Mrs T Brown, Connemara Main St, East Ardsley, Wakefield, **Yorkshire (West)**, WF3 2AP, **ENGLAND**.
(T) 01924 828234.
Profile Supplies. **Ref: YH02132**

BROWN, YVETTE DU-LANEY
Mrs Yvette Du-Laney Brown, East Barton Farm, West Anstey, South Molton, **Devon**, EX36 3PN, **ENGLAND**.
(T) 01398 341380.
Profile Breeder. **Ref: YH02133**

BROWNBREAD
Brownbread Horse & Pony Rescue (The), Ashburnham, Battle, **Sussex (East)**, TN33 9NX, **ENGLAND**.
(T) 01424 892381
(W) www.brownbread.freeyellow.com/home.html.
Contact/s
Chairperson: Mr T Smith
Profile Club/Association. Registered charity.
Ref: YH02134

BROWNBREAD STUD
Brownbread Stud (The), Ashburnham, Battle, **Sussex (East)**, TN33 9NX, **ENGLAND**.
(T) 01424 892381.
Profile Breeder. **Ref: YH02135**

BROWNBRIDGE, JOSEPH
Joseph Brownbridge, Wheeland Villa, 36 Knottingley Rd, Pontefract, **Yorkshire (West)**, WF8 2LD, **ENGLAND**.
(T) 01977 703784.
Profile Transport/Horse Boxes. **Ref: YH02136**

BROWNE WILLES WHITE & GLIDDON
Browne Willes White & Gliddon, White Lodge Veterinary Clinic, Stephenson Rd, Minehead, **Somerset**, TA24 5EB, **ENGLAND**.
(T) 01643 703649 **(F)** 01643 704750
(E) whitlodvet@btinternet.com.
Profile Medical Support. **Ref: YH02137**

BROWNE, LIAM
Liam Browne, Pollardstown Stables The, Curragh, **County Kildare**, **IRELAND**.
(T) 045 486756.
Profile Supplies. **Ref: YH02138**

BROWNING, JARVIS
Jarvis Browning, Station Hse, Station Rd, Nawton, York, **Yorkshire (North)**, YO62 7RG, **ENGLAND**.
(T) 01439 771031.
Profile Farrier. **Ref: YH02139**

BROWNING, R P
Mr R P Browning, Woodhouse Farm Gravels, Minsterley, **Shropshire**, SY5 0JD, **ENGLAND**.
(T) 01743 791339.
Profile Breeder. **Ref: YH02140**

BROWNRIGG, RUSSELL P
Russell P Brownrigg DWCF, 37 Oakliegh Rd, Worthing, **Sussex (West)**, BN11 2QG, **ENGLAND**.
(T) 01903 200254.
Profile Farrier. **Ref: YH02141**

BROWNS
M E Brown Saddle & Harness Maker, 493 Chester Rd, Aldridge, Walsall, **Midlands (West)**, WS9 0PY, **ENGLAND**.
(T) 0121 3538040 **(F)** 0121 3538040.
Contact/s
Owner: Miss M Brown
Profile Saddlery Retailer.
Custom made saddles, bridles and harnesses.
Ref: YH02142

BROWNS COACHWORKS
Browns Coachworks Ltd, 282 Moira Rd, Maze, Lisburn, **County Antrim**, BT28 2TU, **NORTHERN IRELAND**.
(T) 028 92621711 **(F)** 028 92621962.
Profile Transport/Horse Boxes. **Ref: YH02143**

BROWNS FENCING

Browns Fencing, 381 Norristhorpe Lane, Liversedge, **Yorkshire (West)**, WF15 7BL, **ENGLAND**.
(T) 07768 762201. **Ref: YH02144**

BROWNS OF WEM

Browns of Wem Ltd, Four Lane Ends, Wem, Shrewsbury, **Shropshire**, SY4 5UQ, **ENGLAND**.
(T) 01939 232382 **(F)** 01939 234032
(E) info@brownsofwem.freeserve.co.uk. **Ref: YH02145**

BROWNS PET SHOP

Browns Pet Shop, Prebendal Farm, Grove Rd, Slipend, Luton, **Bedfordshire**, LU1 4DF, **ENGLAND**.
(T) 01582 725381.
Profile Supplies. **Ref: YH02146**

BROWNSTOWN STUD

Brownstown Stud, The Curragh, **County Kildare**, **IRELAND**.
(T) 045 441303 **(F)** 045 441215.
Contact/s
Key Contact: Mr N McGrath
(E) neilmcg@tinet.ie
Profile Breeder. **Ref: YH02147**

BROWSIDE PONY TREKKING CTRE

Browside Pony Trekking Centre, Ladysmith Farm, Browside, Ravenscar, Scarborough, **Yorkshire (North)**, YO13 0NH, **ENGLAND**.
(T) 01947 880295.
Profile Equestrian Centre. **Ref: YH02148**

BROWZERS

Browzers, 2 Buckingham Rd, Prestwich, Manchester, **Manchester (Greater)**, M25 9NE, **ENGLAND**.
(T) 0161 7732327 **(F)** 0161 7732327
(E) sales@browzersbooks.co.uk
(W) www.browzersbooks.co.uk.
Profile Supplies. Horse Racing Books & Memorabilia. Yr. Est: 1981
Opening Times
Telephone to confirm book details, can ring up to 19:00 **Ref: YH02149**

BROXBOURNEBURY RIDING SCHOOL

Broxbournebury Riding School, Allard Way, Broxbourne, **Hertfordshire**, EN10 7ER, **ENGLAND**.
(T) 01992 463301.
Contact/s
Partner: Mrs B Pallett
Profile Riding School. **Ref: YH02150**

BROXDOWN STUD

Broxdown Stud, 1 Furzedale, Bix Lane, Pinkneys Green, Maidenhead, **Berkshire**, SL6 6NY, **ENGLAND**.
(T) 01628 777384.
Profile Breeder. **Ref: YH02151**

BROYD, A E

Miss A E Broyd, Penrhiw Farm, Llangenny, Crickhowell, **Powys**, NP8 1HD, **WALES**.
(T) 01873 812292
(M) 07885 475492.
Profile Supplies. **Ref: YH02152**

BRSC

Balanced Registered Saddle Consultant, Dorville Hse, 98 High St, Riseley, Bedford, **Bedfordshire**, MK44 1DD, **ENGLAND**.
(T) 01234 709220
(W) www.ridersatplay.co.uk.
Contact/s
Consultant: Ms S Harris
(E) sarah@harri01.globalnet.co.uk
Profile Saddle Consultant.
The BRSC offer riding lessons and clinics, along with a saddle MOT service No.Staff: 1 Yr. Est: 1997
Opening Times
Telephone for an appointment **Ref: YH02153**

BRUCE WILCOCK

Bruce Wilcock Forgings, The Smithy, Hillswick, Shetland, **Shetland Islands**, ZE2 9RW, **SCOTLAND**.
(T) 01806 503300 **(F)** 01806 503300
(W) www.brucewilcockforgings.com
Affiliated Bodies FRC.
Profile Blacksmith, Farrier. Toolsmith.
Has both a mobile unit and facilities on-site for shoeing horses. A specialised forged toolsmith, blacksmith and farrier. No.Staff: 2 Yr. Est: 1968
Opening Times
Sp: Open Mon - Sat 09:00. Closed Mon - Fri 18:00, Sat 12:00.
Su: Open Mon - Sat 09:00. Closed Mon - Fri 18:00, Sat 12:00.
Au: Open Mon - Sat 09:00. Closed Mon - Fri 18:00, Sat 12:00.
Wn: Open Mon - Sat 09:00. Closed Mon - Fri 18:00, Sat 12:00.
Closed Sundays **Ref: YH02154**

BRUDENELL, MARC

Marc Brudenell DWCF, 1 Lime Trce, Irthlingborough, Wellingborough, **Northamptonshire**, NN9 5SJ, **ENGLAND**.
(T) 01933 651303.
Profile Farrier. **Ref: YH02155**

BRUNDALL SADDLERY

Brundall Saddlery, 2A Cucumber Lane, Brundall, Norwich, **Norfolk**, NR13 5QY, **ENGLAND**.
(T) 01603 717438.
Contact/s
Owner: Mr D Crickmore
Profile Riding Wear Retailer, Saddlery Retailer.
Ref: YH02156

BRUNDELL, M

Mrs M Brundell, 45 Parker Way, Halstead, **Essex**, CO9 1NT, **ENGLAND**.
(T) 01787 472728.
Profile Breeder. **Ref: YH02157**

BRUNEL UNIVERSITY RIDING CLUB

Brunel University Riding Club, Brunel University, Uxbridge, **London (Greater)**, UB8 3PH, **ENGLAND**.
(T) 01895 239125 **(F)** 01895 810477
(E) riding-club@brunel.ac.uk.
Profile Club/Association, Riding Club. **Ref: YH02158**

BRUNGER, ANTHONY R

Anthony R Brunger BI, 1 Trothy Way, Llantillio Crossenny, Abergavenny, **Monmouthshire**, NP7 8SY, **WALES**.
(T) 01600 780382.
Profile Farrier. **Ref: YH02159**

BRUNT, B

Mrs B Brunt, The Paddock, Bogg Lane, Walesby, Newark, **Nottinghamshire**, NG22 9NT, **ENGLAND**.
(T) 01623 860109.
Profile Breeder. **Ref: YH02160**

BRUNYEE, NIGEL

Nigel Brunyee, 171 Windsor Rd, Carlton-In-Lindrick, Worksop, **Nottinghamshire**, S81 9DH, **ENGLAND**.
(T) 01909 731692. **Ref: YH02161**

BRUTON KNOWLES

Bruton Knowles, Cattle Market, St Oswalds Rd, Gloucester, **Gloucestershire**, GL1 2SR, **ENGLAND**.
(T) 01452 303441 **(F)** 01452 307162.
Profile Art Dealers.
Art dealers specialising in equestrian events.
Ref: YH02162

BRYAN, B D

B D Bryan, West End, Llawhaden, Narberth, **Pembrokeshire**, SA67 8EA, **WALES**.
(T) 01437 541301.
Contact/s
Owner: Mr B Bryan
Profile Transport/Horse Boxes. **Ref: YH02163**

BRYAN, FRANCIS HAROLD

Francis Harold Bryan RSS, Allt View, Talyllyn, Brecon, **Powys**, LD3 7TD, **WALES**.
(T) 01874 658539.
Profile Farrier. **Ref: YH02164**

BRYAN, JOSEPH L

Joseph L Bryan DWCF, No 3 Carters Leaze, Great Wolford, Shipston-on-Stour, **Warwickshire**, CV36 5NS, **ENGLAND**.
(T) 01608 674069
(M) 07850 764259.
Profile Farrier. **Ref: YH02165**

BRYAN, R

Mr R Bryan, Birchwood Tree Farm, Appleton, Warrington, **Cheshire**, WA4 5AB, **ENGLAND**.
(T) 01925 263491.
Profile Breeder. **Ref: YH02166**

BRYAN, W & K

W & K Bryan, Stanley Villa, Kinnersley, Hereford, **Herefordshire**, HR3 6NY, **ENGLAND**.
(T) 01544 327323.
Contact/s
Owner: Mr W Bryan
Profile Trainer. **Ref: YH02167**

BRYANSTON RIDING CTRE

Bryanston Riding Centre, Bryanston School, Blandford Forum, **Dorset**, DT11 0PX, **ENGLAND**.
(T) 01258 452411.
Profile Riding School. **Ref: YH02168**

BRYANTS TRANSPORT

Bryants Transport, Mile Elm Farm, Mile Elm, Calne, **Wiltshire**, SN11 0NE, **ENGLAND**.
(T) 01249 813398.
Profile Transport/Horse Boxes. **Ref: YH02169**

BRYER, J

J Bryer, Princes Pl, Closworth, Yeovil, **Somerset**, BA22 9RH, **ENGLAND**.
(T) 01935 872268 **(F)** 01935 872268.
Contact/s
Partner: Mr R Bryer
Profile Breeder. **Ref: YH02170**

BRYERLEY SPRINGS FARM

Bryerley Springs Farm, Galley Lane, Great Brickhill, Milton Keynes, **Buckinghamshire**, MK17 9AA, **ENGLAND**.
(T) 01525 261823.
Contact/s
Owner: Mrs B Rumbold **(Q)** BHSAI
Profile Riding School, Stable/Livery. No.Staff: 2
Yr. Est: 1999 C.Size: 150 Acres **Ref: YH02171**

BRYLINE RIDING SURFACES

Bryline Riding Surfaces, Cottage Farm Buildings, Hartwell Rd, Roade, **Northamptonshire**, NN7 2NU, **ENGLAND**.
(T) 01604 864227.
Profile Track/Course. **Ref: YH02172**

BRYMPTON RIDING SCHOOL

Brympton Riding School, Common Rd, Whiteparish, Salisbury, **Wiltshire**, SP5 2RD, **ENGLAND**.
(T) 01794 884386.
Contact/s
Owner: Mrs S Near
Profile Riding School. **Ref: YH02173**

BRYN SION LIVERIES

Bryn Sion Liveries, Bryn Sion, Bryn Sion Hill, Afonwen, Mold, **Flintshire**, CH7 5UL, **WALES**.
(T) 01352 720705. **Ref: YH02174**

BRYNAVON AGENCIES

Brynavon Agencies, 7 Mayfield Ave, Laleston, **Bridgend**, CF32 0HL, **WALES**.
(T) 01656 645102. **Ref: YH02175**

BRYNGWYN RIDING CTRE

Bryngwyn Riding Centre, Old Rectory, Bryngwyn, Kington, **Herefordshire**, HR5 3QN, **ENGLAND**.
(T) 01497 851661.
Contact/s
Senior Partner: Miss R Miles
Profile Riding School. **Ref: YH02176**

BRYNORE STUD & LIVERY STABLES

Brynore Stud & Livery Stables, Criftins, Ellesmere, **Shropshire**, SY12 9HD, **ENGLAND**.
(T) 01691 690273.
Contact/s
Owner: Mrs N Wilson **Ref: YH02177**

BRYNORE STUD & LIVERY STABLES

Brynore Stud & Livery Stables, Dudleston Heath, Criftins, Ellesmere, **Shropshire**, SY12 9HD, **ENGLAND**.
(T) 01691 690273.
Contact/s
Owner: Ms M Gardner
(E) marion.gardner@btinternet.com
Profile Medical Support, Stable/Livery, Supplies. Horse Behaviourist.
Magnotherapy. Ms Marion Gardner trained with Kelly Marks and Monty Roberts in Intelligent Horsemanship
No.Staff: 2 Yr. Est: 1996 C.Size: 12 Acres
Opening Times
24 hours **Ref: YH02178**

BSPS

British Show Pony Society, 124 Green End Rd, Sawtry, Huntingdon, **Cambridgeshire**, PE28 5XS, **ENGLAND**.
(T) 01487 831376
(E) info@britishshowponysociety.co.uk
(W) www.britishshowponysociety.co.uk.
Contact/s
Chairperson: Mr J McTiffin
Profile Club/Association.
The main aim of the Society is to protect and improve the showing of childrens riding ponies.
Yr. Est: 1949
Opening Times
Sp: Open Mon - Fri 09:00. Closed Mon - Fri 17:00.
Su: Open Mon - Fri 09:00. Closed Mon - Fri 17:00.

Au: Open Mon - Fri 09:00. Closed Mon - Fri 17:00.
Wn: Open Mon - Fri 09:00. Closed Mon - Fri 17:00.
Ref: **YH02179**

BSPS AREA SCOTTISH BRANCH

BSPS Area Scottish Branch, Kirk Fauld, Kirkton Rd, Kilmaurs, **Ayrshire (East)**, KA3 2NW, **SCOTLAND**.
(T) 01563 38350.
Profile Club/Association. Ref: **YH02180**

BTC

B T C Ltd, Unit 8, Palmerston Rd, Aberdeen, **Aberdeen (City of)**, AB11 5RE, **SCOTLAND**.
(T) 01224 574737.
Contact/s
Owner: Mr C Donahue
Profile Blacksmith. Ref: **YH02181**

BUBBENHALL BRIDGE

Bubbenhall Bridge Equestrian Centre, Bubbenhall Rd, Baginton, Coventry, **Midlands (West)**, CV8 3BB, **ENGLAND**.
(T) 024 76301055
(W) www.newrider.com/riding-schools
Affiliated Bodies ABRS, BHS.
Contact/s
Partner: Miss M Mann **(Q)** ISM
Profile Riding School, Stable/Livery.
The centre has a secure tack room and lecture room. Clipping services are also available and a livery yard which offers both part & working livery.The working livery costs £42.50 for a horse and £32.50 for a pony. Part livery for a pony is £47.50. Yr. Est: 1991
Opening Times
Sp: Open Mon - Sun 08:00. Closed Mon - Sun 18:00.
Su: Open Mon - Sun 08:00. Closed Mon - Sun 18:00.
Au: Open Mon - Sun 08:00. Closed Mon - Sun 18:00.
Wn: Open Mon - Sun 08:00. Closed Mon - Sun 18:00. Ref: **YH02182**

BUBEAR & JONES

Bubear & Jones, Oyster Hill Forge, Clay Lane, Headley, Epsom, **Surrey**, KT18 6JX, **ENGLAND**.
(T) 01372 386417 **(F)** 01372 376615.
Contact/s
Owner: Mr S Scobell
Profile Blacksmith. Ref: **YH02183**

BUCAS

Bucas Ltd, Cork, **County Cork**, **IRELAND**.
(T) 021 4312200 **(F)** 021 4312941
(E) admin@bucas.com
(W) www.bucas.com.
Profile Riding Wear Retailer, Supplies. Ref: **YH02184**

BUCHAN RIDING CLUB

Buchan Riding Club, Mains Of Forest, Memsie, Fraserburgh, **Aberdeenshire**, AB43 7AT, **SCOTLAND**.
(T) 01346 541207.
Profile Club/Association, Riding Club. Ref: **YH02185**

BUCK, IAN

Ian Buck, Carters Cottage, Newbury St, Lambourn, Hungerford, **Berkshire**, RG17 8PB, **ENGLAND**.
(T) 01488 71811.
Profile Farrier. Ref: **YH02186**

BUCK, RICHARD

Richard Buck, Fairfield, The Mile, Pocklington, York, **Yorkshire (North)**, YO42 1TW, **ENGLAND**.
(T) 01759 303121.
Contact/s
Owner: Mr R Buck
Profile Farrier. Ref: **YH02187**

BUCKENHAM HORSE GROUP RDA

Buckenham Horse Group RDA, Blue Cedar, White Heath Rd, Thurton, **Norfolk**, NR14 6AF, **ENGLAND**.
(T) 01508 480386.
Profile Club/Association. Ref: **YH02188**

BUCKHATCH EQUESTRIAN CTRE

Buckhatch Equestrian Centre, Buckhatch Lane, Rettendon Common, Chelmsford, **Essex**, CM3 8ES, **ENGLAND**.
(T) 01245 400199.
Contact/s
Owner: Mrs P Gussin
Profile Equestrian Centre. Ref: **YH02189**

BUCKINGHAM HARNESS

Buckingham Harness, Goosey Wick Farm, Charney Bassett, Wantage, **Oxfordshire**, OX12 0EY, **ENGLAND**.
(T) 01367 710715 **(F)** 01367 718778. Ref: **YH02190**

BUCKINGHAM HSE

Buckingham House Just Equestrian Ltd, 29 Meeching Rise, Newhaven, **Sussex (East)**, BN9 9LB, **ENGLAND**.
(T) 01273 611555 **(F)** 01273 611666.
Profile Club/Association. Ref: **YH02191**

BUCKINGHAM RIDING CLUB

Buckingham Riding Club, Haven Cottage, Lower Boddington, Daventry, **Northamptonshire**, NN11 6XZ, **ENGLAND**.
(T) 01327 260621.
Contact/s
Chairman: Miss J Whitaker
Profile Club/Association, Riding Club. Ref: **YH02192**

BUCKINGHAM RIDING CLUB

Buckingham Riding Club CT & ODE, 3 The Row, Station Rd, Cropredy, Banbury, **Oxfordshire**, OX17 1PS, **ENGLAND**..
Contact/s
Secretary: Jackie Whitaker
Profile Club/Association. Ref: **YH02193**

BUCKLAND PR

Buckland PR and Design, Russet Farm, Robertsbridge, **Sussex (East)**, TN32 5NG, **ENGLAND**.
(T) 01580 881291 **(F)** 01580 881311
(E) tamara.strapp@farmline.com.
Profile Club/Association. Marketing Consultancy. Specialist in improving sales and permformance within the equine and agricultural industries. Ref: **YH02194**

BUCKLAND, LEE P

Lee P Buckland DWCF, 17 Rowhurst Ave, Addlestone, **Surrey**, KT15 1NF, **ENGLAND**.
(T) 01932 703245.
Profile Farrier. Ref: **YH02195**

BUCKLER, R H

R H Buckler, Melplash Court Farm, Melplash, Bridport, **Dorset**, DT6 3UH, **ENGLAND**.
(T) 01308 488318.
Profile Trainer. Ref: **YH02196**

BUCKLEY BITS

Buckley Bits, Unit 26 J B J Business Pk, Northampton Rd, Blisworth, Northampton, **Northamptonshire**, NN7 3DW, **ENGLAND**.
(T) 01604 858818 **(F)** 01604 858511
Affiliated Bodies BHTA.
Contact/s
General Manager: Ms R Field **(Q)** BSc(Hons)
Profile Supplies.
Wholesale. Yr. Est: 1996
Opening Times
Sp: Open Mon - Fri 09:00. Closed Mon - Fri 17:00.
Su: Open Mon - Fri 09:00. Closed Mon - Fri 17:00.
Au: Open Mon - Fri 09:00. Closed Mon - Fri 17:00.
Wn: Open Mon - Fri 09:00. Closed Mon - Fri 17:00.
Ref: **YH02197**

BUCKLEY, E H & J M

E H & J M Buckley, Hill Farm, Ings, Kendal, **Cumbria**, LA8 9QQ, **ENGLAND**.
(T) 01539 821746.
Profile Stable/Livery, Trainer. Ref: **YH02198**

BUCKLEY, J R

Mrs J R Buckley, Cabourne Hse, Cabourne, Caister, Lincoln, **Lincolnshire**, LN7 6HU, **ENGLAND**.
(T) 01472 852575 **(F)** 01472 852853
(M) 07974 175294.
Profile Supplies. Ref: **YH02199**

BUCKLEY'S IRONWORKS

Buckley's Ironworks, The Buildings, Stubhampton Farm, Tarrant Gunville, Blandford Forum, **Dorset**, DT11 8JS, **ENGLAND**.
(T) 01258 830359 **(F)** 01258 830359.
Contact/s
Partner: Miss S Carr
Profile Blacksmith. Ref: **YH02200**

BUCKMAN, VINCENT J

Vincent J Buckman DWCF, The Cottage, Ufford Rd, Bredfield, Woodbridge, **Suffolk**, IP13 6AR, **ENGLAND**.
(T) 01394 386858.
Profile Farrier. Ref: **YH02201**

BUCKMINSTER & DISTRICT

Buckminster & District Riding Club, 53 Redland Rd, Oakham, Rutland, **Rutland**, LE15 6PH, **ENGLAND**.
(T) 01572 722574.
Contact/s
Chairman: Mr G Thompson
Profile Club/Association, Riding Club. Ref: **YH02202**

BUCKMINSTER LODGE

Buckminster Lodge Equestrian Centre, Sewstern, Grantham, **Lincolnshire**, NG33 5RW, **ENGLAND**.
(T) 01572 787544 **(F)** 01572 787336.
Contact/s
General Manager: Miss A Gillingham
Profile Horse/Rider Accom. Yr. Est: 1985
Opening Times
Sp: Open Tues - Sun 08:00. Closed Tues - Sun 20:00.
Su: Open Tues - Sun 08:00. Closed Tues - Sun 20:00.
Au: Open Tues - Sun 08:00. Closed Tues - Sun 20:00.
Wn: Open Tues - Sun 08:00. Closed Tues - Sun 20:00.
Closed Monday. Answer phone service available.
Ref: **YH02203**

BUCKS FARM STUD

Bucks Farm Stud, Bucks Farm, Shorewell, Newport, **Isle of Wight**, PO30 3LP, **ENGLAND**.
(T) 01983 551206 **(F)** 01983 551206.
Contact/s
Owner: Mrs C Jones
Profile Horse/Rider Accom. Ref: **YH02204**

BUCKSTONES LIVERY YARD

Buckstones Livery Yard & Equestrian Centre, Lower Buckstone Farm, Sutton In Craven, **Yorkshire (West)**, BD20 7BD, **ENGLAND**.
(T) 01535 630593.
Profile Stable/Livery. Ref: **YH02205**

BUDD, EDWARDS & GLAS

Budd, Edwards & Glas, Regency Hse, Bow St, Langport, **Bath & Somerset (North East)**, TA10 9PS, **ENGLAND**.
(T) 01458 250459.
Profile Medical Support. Ref: **YH02206**

BUDD, M R

M R Budd, Oaken Lawn Riding School, Kingswood, Albrighton, Wolverhampton, **Midlands (West)**, WV7 3AL, **ENGLAND**.
(T) 01902 842551. Ref: **YH02207**

BUDLEIGH SALTERTON

Budleigh Salterton Riding School, Dalditch Lane, Budleigh Salterton, **Devon**, EX9 7AS, **ENGLAND**.
(T) 01395 442035 **(F)** 01395 443922.
Contact/s
Manager: Ms C Hallock
Profile Breeder, Riding School, Stable/Livery.
Ref: **YH02208**

BUDWORTH, G L

G L Budworth, The Smith/The Ferrers Ctre, Melbourne Rd, Staunton Harold, Ashby-De-La-Zouch, **Leicestershire**, LE65 1RU, **ENGLAND**.
(T) 07968 485201.
Contact/s
Owner: Mr G Budworth
Profile Blacksmith. Ref: **YH02209**

BUFFALO TRAILER SYSTEMS

Buffalo Trailer Systems Ltd, 22 Buckland Rd, Pen Mill Trading Est, Yeovil, **Somerset**, BA21 5HA, **ENGLAND**.
(T) 01935 411294 **(F)** 01935 411294.
Contact/s
Owner: Mrs E Foy
Profile Transport/Horse Boxes. Ref: **YH02210**

BULCOTE RIDING STABLES

Bulcote Riding Stables, Southwell Rd, Lowdham, Nottingham, **Nottinghamshire**, NG14 7DQ, **ENGLAND**.
(T) 0115 9312946 **(F)** 0115 9314353.
Contact/s
Owner: Mr K Ashworth
Profile Riding School. Ref: **YH02211**

BULKRITE TRUCK BODIES

Bulkrite Truck Bodies, Thorne Works, Dorrington, Shrewsbury, **Shropshire**, SY5 7EB, **ENGLAND**.
(T) 01743 718232 **(F)** 01743 718293.
Profile Transport/Horse Boxes. Ref: **YH02212**

BULL, A

Mr A Bull, Arclid Cottage Farm, Sandbach, **Cheshire**, CW11 0SU, **ENGLAND**.
(T) 01270 762129.
Profile Breeder. Ref: **YH02213**

BULLDOG SECURITY
Bulldog Security Products Limited, Units 2, 3, 4, Stretton Rd, Much Wenlock, **Shropshire**, TF13 6DH, **ENGLAND**.
(T) 01952 728171 **(F)** 01952 728117
(E) sales@bulldog-security-products.co.uk
(W) www.bulldog-security-products.co.uk.
Profile Manufacturers of Security Products.
Ref: YH02214

BULLEN, SARAH
Sarah Bullen, Avington Pk, Winchester, **Hampshire**, SO21 1DD, **ENGLAND**.
(T) 01962 779260 **(F)** 01962 779864. **Ref: YH02215**

BULLEN, SIMON
Simon Bullen DWCF, Meadowcroft Barn, Bury Rd, Edgworth, Bolton, **Manchester (Greater)**, BL7 0BS, **ENGLAND**.
(T) 01204 853270.
Profile Farrier. **Ref: YH02216**

BULLENS FARM EQUESTRIAN CTRE
Bullens Farm Equestrian Centre, North Perimeter Rd, Liverpool, **Merseyside**, L33 3AP, **ENGLAND**.
(T) 0151 5464800.
Contact/s
Owner: Mr B Stephens **Ref: YH02217**

BULLER, A W
A W Buller, 15 Fir Tree Lane, Scarva, Craigavon, **County Armagh**, BT63 6NY, **NORTHERN IRELAND**.
(T) 028 38831268.
Contact/s
Owner: Mr A Buller
Profile Breeder. **Ref: YH02218**

BULLOCK, J A & F
J A & F Bullock, Low Moor Acres, North Moor, Easingwold, York, **Yorkshire (North)**, YO61 3NB, **ENGLAND**.
(T) 01347 823430.
Contact/s
Owner: Mrs F Bullock
Profile Riding Wear Retailer, Saddlery Retailer, Supplies. **Ref: YH02219**

BULWER-LONG, T
T Bulwer-Long, 19 High St, Newmarket, **Suffolk**, CB8 8LX, **ENGLAND**.
(T) 01638 666168 **(F)** 01638 666273.
Contact/s
Owner: Mr T Bulwer-Long
Profile Blood Stock Agency. **Ref: YH02220**

BUNCE, ARTHUR LESLIE
Arthur Leslie Bunce, Trelanvean Farm Hse, St Keverne, Helston, **Cornwall**, TR12 6RN, **ENGLAND**.
(T) 01326 280265.
Profile Farrier. **Ref: YH02221**

BUNDOCK, PETER M
Peter M Bundock DWCF, 7 Second Ave, West Thurrock, **Essex**, RM20 3JB, **ENGLAND**.
(T) 01708 864753.
Profile Farrier. **Ref: YH02222**

BUNDY, JONATHAN P
Jonathan P Bundy BII, 34 Sambourne Rd, Warminster, **Wiltshire**, BA12 8LH, **ENGLAND**.
(T) 01985 847997.
Profile Farrier. **Ref: YH02223**

BUNGAY, PETER L
Peter L Bungay DWCF, Vernel Lewarne, Bathpool, Launceston, **Cornwall**, PL15 7NW, **ENGLAND**.
(T) 01579 363531.
Profile Farrier. **Ref: YH02224**

BUNN, CLAUDIA
Ms Claudia Bunn, Underwood Farm, Bishampton, Pershore, **London (Greater)**, W10, **ENGLAND**.
(T) 01386 860626.
Profile Trainer. **Ref: YH02225**

BUNTING, CHRISTOPHER JOHN
Christopher John Bunting DWCF, 31 High St, Spilsby, **Lincolnshire**, PE23 5JH, **ENGLAND**.
(T) 01790 752962.
Profile Farrier. **Ref: YH02226**

BUNTING, F
F Bunting, The Smithy, Alderwasley, Derby, **Derbyshire**, DE4 4GD, **ENGLAND**.
(T) 01629 822233.
Profile Farrier. **Ref: YH02227**

BUNTING, STANLEY G
Stanley G Bunting RSS, Old Lodge Farm, Moons Lane, Dormansland, Lingfield, **Surrey**, RH7 6PD, **ENGLAND**.
(T) 01342 870583.
Profile Breeder, Farrier. **Ref: YH02228**

BURCH, THOMAS A
Thomas A Burch RSS, Ranworth, The Hill, Charing, Ashford, **Kent**, TN27 0LU, **ENGLAND**.
(T) 01233 713654.
Profile Farrier. **Ref: YH02229**

BURCHELL, DAVID
David Burchell, Drysiog Farm, Briery Hill, Ebbw Vale, **Blaenau Gwent**, NP23 6BU, **WALES**.
(T) 01495 302551 **(F)** 01495 352464
Affiliated Bodies FRC.
Contact/s
Owner: Mr D Burchell **(Q)** Reg Farrier
Profile Trainer. Yr. Est: 1983
Opening Times
Sp: Open Mon - Sun 08:00. Closed Mon - Sun 22:00.
Su: Open Mon - Sun 08:00. Closed Mon - Sun 22:00.
Au: Open Mon - Sun 08:00. Closed Mon - Sun 22:00.
Wn: Open Mon - Sun 08:00. Closed Mon - Sun 22:00. **Ref: YH02230**

BURCHELL-SMALL & SHEMILT
Mrs A Burchell-Small & Mrs J Shemilt, White Rose Farm, Shovelstrode, East Grinstead, **Sussex (West)**, RH19 3PG, **ENGLAND**.
(T) 01342 302030.
Profile Breeder. **Ref: YH02231**

BURCHES RIDING SCHOOL
Burches Riding School, Great Burches Rd, Benfleet, **Essex**, SS7 3NF, **ENGLAND**.
(T) 01268 776654.
Contact/s
Owner: Mrs L Bush
Profile Riding School, Saddlery Retailer.
Ref: YH02232

BURCHWOOD STABLES
Burchwood Stables, Round St, Sole St, Cobham, **Kent**, DA13 9AY, **ENGLAND**.
(T) 01474 815156.
Profile Stable/Livery. **Ref: YH02233**

BURCOTT LIVERY
Burcott Livery, Bulls Lane, Wishaw, Sutton Coldfield, **Midlands (West)**, B76 9QW, **ENGLAND**.
(T) 0121 3132282. **Ref: YH02234**

BURCOTT RIDING CTRE
Burcott Riding Centre, Burcott, Wells, **Somerset**, BA5 1NQ, **ENGLAND**.
(T) 01749 673145.
Contact/s
Owner: Miss N Stephens
Profile Riding School, Stable/Livery. **Ref: YH02235**

BURCOTT RIDING CTRE
Burcott Riding Centre, Burcott Lane, Wells, **Somerset**, BAS 1NQ, **ENGLAND**.
(T) 01749 673145.
Contact/s
Instructor: Ms J Francis
Profile Riding School, Stable/Livery.
Floodlit outdoor school with lessons for children of 6 years of age and upwards. Working Livery also available. Yr. Est: 1966
Opening Times
Sp: Open Mon - Sun 08:00. Closed Mon - Sun 20:00.
Su: Open Mon - Sun 08:00. Closed Mon - Sun 20:00.
Au: Open Mon - Sun 08:00. Closed Mon - Sun 20:00.
Wn: Open Mon - Sun 08:00. Closed Mon - Sun 20:00. **Ref: YH02236**

BURE VALLEY STABLES
Bure Valley Stables, Birds Pl, Vicarage Lane, Buxton, Norwich, **Norfolk**, NR10 5HD, **ENGLAND**.
(T) 01603 279585. **Ref: YH02237**

BUREVALLEY FORGE
Burevalley Forge, Manor Farm, Heydon Rd, Aylsham, Norwich, **Norfolk**, NR11 6QT, **ENGLAND**.
(T) 01603 279773.
Contact/s
Owner: Mr C Howard
Profile Blacksmith. **Ref: YH02238**

BURFORD SCHOOL FARM
Burford School Farm Training Centre, Cheltenham Rd, Burford, **Oxfordshire**, OX18 4PL, **ENGLAND**.
(T) 01993 824172.
Profile Equestrian Centre. **Ref: YH02239**

BURGE, MARK
Mark Burge, 10 Blackhorse Mews, Borough Green, Sevenoaks, **Kent**, TN15 8SP, **ENGLAND**.
(T) 01732 780731 **(F)** 01732 884990
(M) 07901 852634. **Ref: YH02240**

BURGESS & GRAHAM
Burgess & Graham, Rose Cottage Farm, Weaverham Rd, Gorstage, Northwich, **Cheshire**, CW8 2SG, **ENGLAND**.
(T) 01606 883138.
Profile Medical Support. **Ref: YH02241**

BURGESS & RANDALL
Burgess & Randall, 1 Station Rd, Pulborough, **Sussex (West)**, RH20 1AH, **ENGLAND**.
(T) 01798 872506.
Profile Saddlery Retailer. **Ref: YH02242**

BURGESS ENDEAVOUR
Burgess Endeavour plc (Supafeeds Division), Woodlands, Priestmans Lane, Thornton-Le-Dale, Pickering, **Yorkshire (North)**, YO18 7RT, **ENGLAND**.
(T) 01751 474123 **(F)** 01751 477633.
Contact/s
Marketing Manager: Mrs S Riddolls
Ref: YH02243

BURGESS, GRAHAM G
Graham G Burgess DWCF, 16 Church Hall Rd, Rushden, **Northamptonshire**, NN10 9PA, **ENGLAND**.
(T) 01933 359719.
Profile Farrier. **Ref: YH02244**

BURGESS, JOHN
Mr John Burgess, Mill Lawn Farm, Golberdon, Callington, **Cornwall**, PL17 7NG, **ENGLAND**.
(T) 01579 62159.
Profile Breeder. **Ref: YH02245**

BURGESS, PAT
Mrs Pat Burgess, Coralie Cottage, Great Durnford, Salisbury, **Wiltshire**, SP4 6AZ, **ENGLAND**.
(T) 01722 782359.
Profile Trainer. **Ref: YH02246**

BURGH HILL FARM
Burgh Hill Farm, Burgh Hill, Bramshott, Liphook, **Hampshire**, GU30 7RQ, **ENGLAND**.
(T) 01428 751535.
Contact/s
Owner: Mr R Slingo **Ref: YH02247**

BURGHFIELD VETNRY SURGERY
Burghfield Veterinary Surgery, 1 Tarragon Way, Burghfield Common, Reading, **Berkshire**, RG7 3YU, **ENGLAND**.
(T) 0118 9832465 **(F)** 0118 9831767.
Profile Medical Support. **Ref: YH02248**

BURGHLEY VETNRY CTRE
Burghley Veterinary Centre, 3 Marville Court, Crowson Way, Deeping St James, Peterborough, **Cambridgeshire**, PE6 8EY, **ENGLAND**.
(T) 01778 344592.
Profile Medical Support. **Ref: YH02249**

BURGIN, KRISTOPHER
Kristopher Burgin DWCF, 3 Halfway Hse, Burnley Lane, Weir, Bacup, **Lancashire**, OL13 8QP, **ENGLAND**.
(T) 01706 874820.
Profile Farrier. **Ref: YH02250**

BURGOYNE, PAUL
Mr Paul Burgoyne, Frenchmans Lodge, Upper Lambourn, Hungerford, **Berkshire**, RG17 8QT, **ENGLAND**.
(T) 01488 71980.
Profile Trainer. **Ref: YH02251**

BURGOYNE, ROBERT
Robert Burgoyne DWCF, 28 Wood End Rd, Kempston, **Bedfordshire**, MK43 9BB, **ENGLAND**.
(T) 01234 855342.
Profile Farrier. **Ref: YH02252**

BURITON HORSE SVS
Buriton Horse Services, Homestead Farm, North Houghton, Stockbridge, **Hampshire**, SO20 6LG,

ENGLAND.
(T) 01264 810593.
Contact/s
Owner: Mr C Mulder
Profile Riding School. Western Riding Specialist.
No.Staff: 2 Yr. Est: 1970
Opening Times
Open all year. Ref: YH02253

BURKE BLOODSTOCK TRANSPORT

Burke Bloodstock Transport, 36 Owenmore Dr, Limerick, **County Limerick**, **IRELAND**.
(T) 061 228073.
Profile Supplies. Ref: YH02254

BURKE PATRICK

Burke Patrick, 2956 Maryville Gro, Kildare, **County Kildare**, **IRELAND**.
(T) 045 522078.
Profile Supplies. Ref: YH02255

BURKE'S HORSE TREKKING CTRE

Burke's Horse Trekking Centre, Rossnabeach Faha, Glenbeigh, **County Kerry**, **IRELAND**.
(T) 066 9768386
(M) 087 2379100
Affiliated Bodies AIRE.
Contact/s
Owner: Gerard Burke
Profile Trekking Centre.
Offer treks for all ages, children can trek around the farm attended by guides at all times. For adults and older children, there are treks along Rossbeigh Beach and through the Highlands of Kerry. Yr. Est: 2000
Opening Times
Open seven days a week through Spring & Summer and for bookings between November & February.
Ref: YH02256

BURLEY HILL STUD

Burley Hill Stud, Burley Hill, Allestree, **Derbyshire**, DE3 2ET, **ENGLAND**.
(T) 01332 840441 (F) 01332 840441.
Profile Breeder. Ref: YH02257

BURLEY LODGE STUD

Burley Lodge Stud, Hyde End Rd, Shinfield, Reading, **Berkshire**, RG2 9EP, **ENGLAND**.
(T) 0118 9885327 (F) 0118 9885327.
Profile Breeder. Ref: YH02258

BURLEY MANOR RIDING STABLES

Burley Manor Riding Stables, Burley Manor Hotel, Ringwood Rd, Burley, Ringwood, **Hampshire**, BH24 4BS, **ENGLAND**.
(T) 01425 403489.
Profile Riding School. Ref: YH02259

BURLEY VILLA EQUESTRIAN CTRE

Burley Villa Equestrian Centre, Bashley Common Rd, New Milton, **Hampshire**, BH25 5SQ, **ENGLAND**.
(T) 01425 610278 (F) 01425 614922
(E) burley@globalnet.co.uk
(W) www.users.globalnet.co.uk/~burleyv
Affiliated Bodies BHS.
Contact/s
General Manager: Mr P Cremer
Profile Riding Club, Riding School.
Local accommodation available. Western riding is a big part of life at Burley and there are four registered first aiders on site. Yr. Est: 1966
Opening Times
Sp: Open Tues - Thurs, Friday 12:00, Sat, Sun 08:00. Closed Tues - Sun 20:00.
Su: Open Tues - Thurs, Friday 12:00, Sat, Sun 08:00. Closed Tues - Sun 20:00.
Au: Open Tues - Thurs, Friday 12:00, Sat, Sun 08:00. Closed Tues - Sun 20:00.
Wn: Open Tues - Thurs, Friday 12:00, Sat, Sun 08:00. Closed Tues - Sun 20:00.
Closed on Mondays and Friday mornings. In high season the centre is open all day Fridays and Bank Holidays. It is closed Christmas Day and New Years Day. Ref: YH02260

BURLINGTON GALLERY

Burlington Gallery Ltd, 10 Burlington Gardens, London, **London (Greater)**, WIX 1LG, **ENGLAND**.
(T) 020 77349228 (F) 020 74943770. Ref: YH02261

BURMAN

Mr Burman, Home Farm, Ickwell, Biggleswade, **Bedfordshire**, SG18 9SS, **ENGLAND**.
(T) 01767 627409.
Profile Stable/Livery. Ref: YH02262

BURN EQUESTRIAN CLUB

Burn Equestrian Club, Knockbracken Healthcare Pk, Saintfield Rd, Belfast, **County Antrim**, BT8 8BH, **NORTHERN IRELAND**.
(T) 028 90402384 (F) 028 90402384
Affiliated Bodies BHS.
Contact/s
Manager: Mrs J Harper
Profile Equestrian Centre, Riding Club, Riding School, Stable/Livery.
Livery, full - £225 per month, DIY - £100 per month, grass - £60 per month, working (5 hours a day) - £165 per month
Opening Times
Sp: Open Mon - Sun 09:00. Closed Mon 17:00, Tues - Fri 21:00, Sat, Sun 18:00.
Su: Open Mon - Sun 09:00. Closed Mon 17:00, Tues - Fri 21:00, Sat, Sun 18:00.
Au: Open Mon - Sun 09:00. Closed Mon 17:00, Tues - Fri 21:00, Sat, Sun 18:00.
Wn: Open Mon - Sun 09:00. Closed Mon 17:00, Tues - Fri 21:00, Sat, Sun 18:00. Ref: YH02263

BURNETT, LEE

Lee Burnett DWCF, 29 Cwmgarw Rd, Brynamman, Ammanford, **Carmarthenshire**, SA18 1BY, **WALES**.
(T) 01269 823130.
Profile Farrier. Ref: YH02264

BURNETT, P A

P A Burnett, Roundhay Grange, Wetherby Rd, Leeds, **Yorkshire (West)**, LS8 2LW, **ENGLAND**.
(T) 0113 2653155.
Profile Stable/Livery. Ref: YH02265

BURNINGFOLD MANOR STUD FARM

Burningfold Manor Stud Farm Ltd, Plaistow Rd, Dunsfold, Godalming, **Surrey**, GU8 4PF, **ENGLAND**.
(T) 01483 200329 (F) 01483 200442.
Profile Breeder. Ref: YH02266

BURNS & WAKELY

Burns & Wakely, 60 St Johns St, Bedford, **Bedfordshire**, MK42 8ES, **ENGLAND**.
(T) 01234 853387.
Profile Medical Support. Ref: YH02267

BURNS & WAKELY

Burns & Wakely, Ridgway Veterinary Ctre, 47 The Ridgway, Flitwick, **Bedfordshire**, MK45 1DJ, **ENGLAND**.
(T) 01525 714892 (F) 01525 717024.
Profile Medical Support. Ref: YH02268

BURNS PET FOODS

Burns Pet Foods, Central Sq, 8 Irvine St, Workington, **Cumbria**, CA1 3BT, **ENGLAND**.
(T) 01900 604139.
Profile Supplies. Ref: YH02269

BURNS, DAVID H

David H Burns DWCF, Acre Cottage, Broughton, Biggar, **Lanarkshire (South)**, ML12 6QH, **SCOTLAND**.
(T) 01899 830417.
Profile Farrier. Ref: YH02270

BURNS, DAVID J MAHER

David J Maher Burns RSS, 42 Moor Lane, Woodford, **Cheshire**, SK7 1PP, **ENGLAND**.
(T) 0161 4398311.
Profile Farrier. Ref: YH02271

BURNS, G E

G E Burns, Tims Boatyard, Timsway, Staines, **Surrey**, TW18 3JY, **ENGLAND**.
(T) 01784 491424 (F) 01784 491424.
Contact/s
Owner: Mr G Burns
Profile Blacksmith. Ref: YH02272

BURNS, JAMES G

James G Burns, Landfall Paddocks, The Curragh, **County Kildare**, **IRELAND**.
(T) 045 441349 (F) 045 441213.
Contact/s
Trainer: Mr J Burns
(E) jamesgburns@kildarehorse.ie
Profile Trainer. Ref: YH02273

BURNSIDE STABLES

Burnside Stables, Kinellar, Aberdeen, **Aberdeen (City of)**, AB21 0TT, **SCOTLAND**.
(T) 01224 790284.
Profile Riding School, Stable/Livery. Ref: YH02274

BURNT HSE

Burnt House Arabian Stud, Greenacres, Burned Hse Lane, Preesall, Poulton-Le-Fylde, **Lancashire**, FY6 0PQ, **ENGLAND**.
(T) 01253 812690
(E) burnthouse@arabian.fsword.co.uk
Contact/s
General Manager: Miss S Helliwell
Profile Breeder. Yr. Est: 1989
Opening Times
By appointment only Ref: YH02275

BURR, C A

Mrs C A Burr, Holly Hill Farm, The Ridgeway, Enfield, **London (Greater)**, EN2 8AN, **ENGLAND**.
(T) 020 83633806.
Profile Breeder. Ref: YH02276

BURRELL, RAYMOND

Raymond Burrell, Penywern, New Cross, Aberystwyth, **Ceredigion**, SY23 4JT, **WALES**.
(T) 01974 261512 (F) 01974 261512.
Contact/s
Owner: Mr R Burrell
Profile Blacksmith. Ref: YH02277

BURREN RIDING CTRE

Burren Riding Centre Ltd, Fanore, Ballyvaughan, **County Clare**, **IRELAND**.
(T) 065 7076140 (F) 065 7076233
(E) burrenriding.ennis@eircom.net
Affiliated Bodies AIRE.
Contact/s
Manager: John Queally
(E) jjq@eircom.net
Profile Trail Riding Centre.
The riding centre overlooks Galway Bay. Treks can be arranged along Fanore Beach and through the sand dunes as well as through the 'Burren'. Daily, three day or weekly trail rides are on offer, with post to post trail rides as well. Ref: YH02278

BURRILL, RICHARD

Richard Burrill RSS, Clevland, Stane St, Ockley, **Surrey**, RH5 5TD, **ENGLAND**.
(T) 01306 711133.
Profile Farrier. Ref: YH02279

BURRINGTON, A W

Mrs A W Burrington, Blagdon Hse, Wheddon Cross, Minehead, **Somerset**, TA24 7EF, **ENGLAND**.
(T) 01643 841366.
Profile Breeder. Ref: YH02280

BURROUGH BLOODSTOCK

Burrough Bloodstock, 1 Henhaw Farm, Coopers Hill Rd, South Nutfield, Redhill, **Surrey**, RH1 5PD, **ENGLAND**.
(T) 01737 823160 (F) 01737 823161.
Contact/s
Partner: Mr C Martin
Profile Blood Stock Agency. Ref: YH02281

BURROWHAYES FARM

Burrowhayes Farm, West Luccombe, Porlock, **Somerset**, TA24 8HT, **ENGLAND**.
(T) 01643 862463.
Profile Equestrian Centre. Ref: YH02282

BURROWINE STABLES

Burrowine Stables, Burrowine Farm, Bogside, Alloa, **Clackmannanshire**, FK10 3QD, **SCOTLAND**.
(T) 01259 730316.
Contact/s
Partner: Mr J Farmer Ref: YH02283

BURROWS LEA FORGE

Burrows Lea Forge, Burrows Lea Farm, Hook Lane, Shere, Guildford, **Surrey**, GU5 9QQ, **ENGLAND**.
(T) 01483 203036.
Profile Blacksmith. Ref: YH02284

BURSTED MANOR RIDING CTRE

Bursted Manor Riding Centre, Pett Bottom, Canterbury, **Kent**, CT4 6EH, **ENGLAND**.
(T) 01227 830568.
Contact/s
Owner: Mrs P Toombs
Profile Riding School. Ref: YH02285

BURSTOW PK

Burstow Park Riding School, Antlands Lane, Horley, **Surrey**, RH6 9TF, **ENGLAND**.
(T) 01293 820766
Affiliated Bodies ABRS, BHS.
Contact/s
Head Girl: Ms J Smith (Q) AI
Profile Riding School. Yr. Est: 1987
C.Size: 25 Acres
Opening Times
Sp: Open 08:00. Closed 20:00.
Su: Open 08:00. Closed 20:00.
Au: Open 08:00. Closed 20:00.
Wn: Open 08:00. Closed 20:00. Ref: YH02286

BURT, GRAEME J

Graeme J Burt DWCF, 34 Chipstead Pk, Chipstead, Sevenoaks, **Kent**, TN13 2SN, **ENGLAND**.
(T) 01732 458108
(M) 07802 476700.
Profile Farrier. **Ref: YH02287**

BURT, S

Mrs S Burt, Tophill Farm, Withyham, Hartfield, **Sussex (East)**, TN7 4DB, **ENGLAND**.
(T) 01892 770019.
Profile Breeder. **Ref: YH02288**

BURT, THOMAS D

Thomas D Burt DWCF, 3 Oakbrook Drive, The Reddings, Cheltenham, **Gloucestershire**, GL51 6SB, **ENGLAND**.
(T) 01452 859511.
Profile Farrier. **Ref: YH02289**

BURTON AGNES STUD FARM

Burton Agnes Stud Farm, Burton Agnes Stud, Harpham, Driffield, **Yorkshire (East)**, YO25 8JB, **ENGLAND**.
(T) 01262 490441 **(F)** 01262 490333.
Contact/s
Manager: Mrs C Lister
Profile Breeder. **Ref: YH02290**

BURTON CONSTABLE RIDING CTRE

Burton Constable Riding Centre, Burton Constable, Hull, **Yorkshire (East)**, HU11 4LN, **ENGLAND**.
(T) 01964 562019 **(F)** 01964 562019.
Contact/s
Owner: Mr T Thompson
Profile Breeder, Riding School. Yr. Est: 1994
Opening Times
Sp: Open Tues - Sun 09:00. Closed Tues - Sun 17:00.
Su: Open Tues - Sun 09:00. Closed Tues - Sun 17:00.
Au: Open Tues - Sun 09:00. Closed Tues - Sun 17:00.
Wn: Open Tues - Sun 09:00. Closed Tues - Sun 17:00.
Closed Mondays **Ref: YH02291**

BURTON, GARY S

Gary S Burton DWCF, Folly Hatch, North Folly Rd, East Farleigh, **Kent**, ME15 0LT, **ENGLAND**.
(T) 01622 745071
(M) 07860 362208.
Profile Farrier. **Ref: YH02292**

BURTON, NICK

Nick Burton, Toad Hall, Hartpury, **Gloucestershire**, GL19 3BT, **ENGLAND**.
(T) 01452 700520 **(F)** 01452 700034. **Ref: YH02293**

BURTON, V & S

V & S Burton, Spinney Farm, Park Hill, Oulton, Lowestoft, **Suffolk**, NR32 5DQ, **ENGLAND**.
(T) 01502 564399.
Profile Supplies. **Ref: YH02294**

BURTON, W L

W L Burton, 15 Park Ave, Coundon Gate, Bishop Auckland, Durham, **County Durham**, DL14 8QH, **ENGLAND**.
(T) 01388 608400.
Profile Farrier. **Ref: YH02295**

BURTONWOOD RIDING SCHOOL

Burtonwood Riding School, Lumber Lane, Burtonwood, Warrington, **Cheshire**, WA5 4AS, **ENGLAND**.
(T) 01925 291899.
Profile Riding School. **Ref: YH02296**

BURWARTON EST TIMBER

Burwarton Estate Timber Co, Timber Yard, Ditton Priors, Bridgnorth, **Shropshire**, WV16 6TE, **ENGLAND**.
(T) 01746 712637 **(F)** 01746 787422. **Ref: YH02297**

BURWELL HILL GARAGES

Burwell Hill Garages Ltd, Burwell Hill, Brackley, **Northamptonshire**, NN13 7AY, **ENGLAND**.
(T) 01280 702268 **(F)** 01280 702478.
Profile Transport/Horse Boxes. **Ref: YH02298**

BURY FARM FODDER STORE

Bury Farm Fodder Store, Bury Farm, Edgwarebury Lane, Edgware, **London (Greater)**, HA8 8QS, **ENGLAND**.
(T) 020 8958 2932.
Contact/s
Owner: Mr C Baldwin
Profile Feed Merchant.
Opening Times
Sp: Open Tue - Sat 09:00, Sun 09:30. Closed Tue - Fri 18:00, Sat 17:00, Sun 16:00.
Su: Open Tue - Sat 09:00, Sun 09:30. Closed Tue - Fri 18:00, Sat 17:00, Sun 16:00.
Au: Open Tue - Sat 09:00, Sun 09:30. Closed Tue - Fri 18:00, Sat 17:00, Sun 16:00.
Wn: Open Tue - Sat 09:00, Sun 09:30. Closed Tue - Fri 18:00, Sat 17:00, Sun 16:00. **Ref: YH02299**

BURYFEEDS

Buryfeeds, 4 Osier Rd, Bury St Edmunds, **Suffolk**, IP33 1TA, **ENGLAND**.
(T) 01284 765683 **(F)** 01284 765683. **Ref: YH02300**

BURYWOOD LIVERY YARD

Burywood Livery Yard, Bury Farm, Bury Rd, London, **London (Greater)**, E4 7QL, **ENGLAND**.
(T) 020 85241949.
Contact/s
Owner: Mrs M Luesley **Ref: YH02301**

BUSBY EQUITATION CTRE

Busby Equitation Centre Ltd, Westerton Ave, Busby, **Glasgow (City of)**, G76 8JU, **SCOTLAND**.
(T) 0141 6441347 **(F)** 0141 6445193
Affiliated Bodies ABRS, BHS.
Contact/s
General Manager: Mr R Leitch **(Q)** BHSAI
Profile Arena, Breeder, Equestrian Centre, Riding School, Riding Wear Retailer, Saddlery Retailer, Stable/Livery, Supplies.
An embroidery service to personalise saddle pads, jackets, rugs and clothing is offered. No.Staff: 10
Yr. Est: 1968 C.Size: 48 Acres
Opening Times
Sp: Open Mon - Sun 08:00. Closed Mon - Sun 20:00.
Su: Open Mon - Sun 08:00. Closed Mon - Sun 20:00.
Au: Open Mon - Sun 08:00. Closed Mon - Sun 20:00.
Wn: Open Mon - Sun 08:00. Closed Mon - Sun 20:00. **Ref: YH02302**

BUSBY HALL TREKKING CTRE

Busby Hall Trekking Centre, Bagdale Farm, Carlton-In-Cleveland, Middlesbrough, **Cleveland**, TS9 7DH, **ENGLAND**.
(T) 01642 712403 **(F)** 01642 712403.
Contact/s
Owner: Mrs M Garbutt
Profile Equestrian Centre. **Ref: YH02303**

BUSBY SADDLERS

Busby Saddlers, Westerton Ave, Busby, **Glasgow (City of)**, G76 8JU, **SCOTLAND**.
(T) 0141 6445453. **Ref: YH02304**

BUSER, M

M Buser, 44 Braniel Rd, Lisburn, **County Antrim**, BT27 5JJ, **NORTHERN IRELAND**.
(T) 028 90826810 **(F)** 028 90826810.
Contact/s
Owner: Mr M Buser
Profile Blood Stock Agency. **Ref: YH02305**

BUSH LIVERY STABLES

Bush Livery Stables, Bush Farm, Saltash, **Cornwall**, PL12 6QY, **ENGLAND**.
(T) 01752 842148.
Profile Stable/Livery. **Ref: YH02306**

BUSH, KAREN

Karen Bush BHS.Int.T(Regd), 27 Hildreth Rd, Prestwood, Great Missenden, **Buckinghamshire**, HP16 0LZ, **ENGLAND**.
(T) 01494 890424.
Profile Trainer. **Ref: YH02307**

BUSH, N

Mr N Bush, Ebbdown Farm, North Wraxall, Chippenham, **Wiltshire**, SN14 7AT, **ENGLAND**.
(T) 01225 891293.
Profile Breeder, Track/Course. **Ref: YH02308**

BUSHELL, ANN

Ann Bushell, 6 Marske Hall, Marske In Swaldedale, Richmond, **Yorkshire (North)**, DL11 7NB, **ENGLAND**.
(T) 01748 850994 **(F)** 01748 850994
(E) abg@abgbushell.demon.co.uk. **Ref: YH02309**

BUSHELL, MARK

Mark Bushell, Manor Stables, Craft Workshop, Fulbeck, Grantham, **Lincolnshire**, NG32 3JN, **ENGLAND**.
(T) 01400 273711.
Contact/s
Owner: Mr M Bushell **Ref: YH02310**

BUSHY FARM EQUINE CLINIC

Bushy Farm Equine Clinic, Breadstone, Berkeley, **Gloucestershire**, GL13 9HG, **ENGLAND**.
(T) 01453 811867.
Profile Medical Support. **Ref: YH02311**

BUSHY PLAT LIVERY STABLES

Bushy Plat Livery Stables, Hole Hill, Westcott, Dorking, **Surrey**, RH4 3LU, **ENGLAND**.
(T) 01306 885301 **(F)** 01306 740833.
Contact/s
Owner: Mr J Brinsdon **Ref: YH02312**

BUSHY PLAT LIVERY STABLES

Bushy Plat Livery Stables, Hole Hill, Westcott, Dorking, **Surrey**, RH4 3LU, **ENGLAND**.
(T) 01306 740998 **(F)** 01306 740833.
Contact/s
Owner: Mr J Brinsdon
Profile Stable/Livery. **Ref: YH02313**

BUSINESS ADMIN SVS

Business Administration Services, The Stables, Yeld Rd, Bakewell, **Derbyshire**, DE45 1FJ, **ENGLAND**.
(T) 01629 812126.
Profile Club/Association. **Ref: YH02314**

BUSSELL, N E R

N E R Bussell, Carlin, Venn Rd, Barnstaple, **Devon**, EX32 0HT, **ENGLAND**.
(T) 01271 325050.
Profile Medical Support. **Ref: YH02315**

BUTCHER, K J

K J Butcher, 2 Home Farm Cottages, Betteshanger, Deal, **Kent**, CT14 0NT, **ENGLAND**.
(T) 01304 611349.
Profile Farrier. **Ref: YH02316**

BUTCHER, ROGER

Roger Butcher, 1 Broad Lane, Yate, Bristol, **Bristol**, BS37 7LD, **ENGLAND**.
(T) 01454 322645.
Contact/s
Owner: Mr R Butcher
Profile Blacksmith. **Ref: YH02317**

BUTE BLACKSMITHS

Bute Blacksmiths, 11 Castle St, Rothesay, **Argyll and Bute**, PA20 9HA, **SCOTLAND**.
(T) 01700 504235.
Profile Blacksmith. **Ref: YH02318**

BUTE PONY & RIDING CLUB

Bute Pony & Riding Club, Cranslagvourity Farm, Ettrick Bay, **Argyll and Bute**, PA20, **SCOTLAND**.
(T) 01700 502473.
Profile Club/Association, Riding Club. **Ref: YH02319**

BUTLER & ANTILL

Butler & Antill, Unit 4 Fieldgate Works, New St, Walsall, **Midlands (West)**, WS1 3DJ, **ENGLAND**.
(T) 01922 627192 **(F)** 01922 627192. **Ref: YH02320**

BUTLER TRAILERS

Butler Trailers, Stanier Rd, Calne, **Wiltshire**, SN11 9PX, **ENGLAND**.
(T) 01249 818886 **(F)** 01249 821639.
Profile Transport/Horse Boxes. **Ref: YH02321**

BUTLER, CARL S

Carl S Butler DWCF, 26 Marlborough Rd, Chelmsford, **Essex**, CM2 0JR, **ENGLAND**.
(T) 01245 266725.
Profile Farrier. **Ref: YH02322**

BUTLER, D A

Mrs D A Butler, Springholm, Napton Rd, Stockton, Rugby, **Warwickshire**, CV23 8HT, **ENGLAND**.
(T) 01926 815366.
Profile Supplies. **Ref: YH02323**

BUTLER, D J

D J Butler, Darrow Wood Farm, Shelfanger Rd, Diss, **Norfolk**, IP22 4XY, **ENGLAND**.
(T) 01379 640182 **(F)** 01379 640182.
Contact/s
Owner: Mr D Butler
Profile Blacksmith. **Ref: YH02324**

BUTLER, F L

F L Butler, Whitehouse Farm, Stryt Isa, Pen-Y-Ffordd, **Cheshire**, CH4 0JY, **ENGLAND**.
(T) 01978 760623.

Profile Supplies. Ref: YH02325

BUTLER, P

Mr P Butler, Homewoodgate Farm, Norrington Lane, East Chiltington, Lewes, **Sussex (East)**, BN7 3AU, **ENGLAND**.
(T) 01273 890124 (F) 01273 890124
(M) 07973 873846.
Profile Trainer. Ref: YH02326

BUTLER, SAMUEL

Samuel Butler, 5 Harewood Court, 299 Harrogate Rd, Leeds, **Yorkshire (West)**, LS17 6PA, **ENGLAND**.
(T) 0113 2663064. Ref: YH02327

BUTLER, W R

W R Butler, 4 Moores Cl, Debenham, Stowmarket, **Suffolk**, IP14 6RU, **ENGLAND**.
(T) 01728 861209 (F) 01728 861209.
Contact/s
Owner: Mr W Butler Ref: YH02328

BUTTERCUP FEEDS

Buttercup Feeds, Charlotte St, Melton Mowbray, **Leicestershire**, LE13 1NA, **ENGLAND**.
(T) 01664 410358 (F) 01664 481206.
Profile Supplies. Ref: YH02329

BUTTERFIELD, A

Mr A Butterfield, Hermit Hse Farm, Hermits Lane, Gawber, Barnsley, **Yorkshire (South)**, S75 2RW, **ENGLAND**.
(T) 01226 382001 (F) 01226 382001.
Profile Breeder. Ref: YH02330

BUTTERLAND

Butterland, Top Rd, Biddulph Moor, Stoke-on-Trent, **Staffordshire**, ST8 7LF, **ENGLAND**.
(T) 01782 522281.
Contact/s
Owner: Mrs R Attenborough
Profile Riding School. Ref: YH02331

BUTTERSTOCKS FARM

Butterstocks Farm, Butterstocks, Smithers Hill, Shipley, Horsham, **Sussex (West)**, RH13 8PE, **ENGLAND**.
(T) 01403 741606.
Contact/s
Manager: Mr K Richardson Ref: YH02332

BUTTERWORTH

Mr & Mrs Butterworth, Paddock Farm, Old Town, Hebden Bridge, **Yorkshire (West)**, HX7 8SW, **ENGLAND**.
(T) 01422 842441.
Profile Breeder. Ref: YH02333

BUTTERWORTH, B

Mrs B Butterworth, Bolton Mill, Bolton, Appleby-In-Westmorland, **Cumbria**, CA16 6AL, **ENGLAND**.
(T) 01768 361363 (F) 01768 361363.
Profile Supplies. Ref: YH02334

BUTTERWORTH, NINETTA

Ninetta Butterworth, Flat 5, 50 Sloane St, London, **London (Greater)**, SW1X 9SN, **ENGLAND**.
(T) 020 72354646.
Contact/s
Owner: Mrs N Butterworth
Profile Artist. No.Staff: 1 Yr. Est: 1950
Opening Times
By appointment only Ref: YH02335

BUTTON, PETER JOHN

Peter John Button, Selden Blacks, France Lane, Patching, **Sussex (West)**, BN13 3UP, **ENGLAND**.
(T) 01903 882634.
Profile Farrier. Ref: YH02336

BUTTONS SADDLERY

Buttons Saddlery, 44 Guildford Rd, West End, Woking, **Surrey**, GU24 9PW, **ENGLAND**.
(T) 01276 857771 (F) 01276 857771
(E) sales@buttonssaddlery.com
(W) www.buttonssaddlery.com
Affiliated Bodies SMS.
Contact/s
Partner: Mr A Benge (Q) Master Saddler
Profile Saddlery Retailer, Supplies.
Have made safety harnesses for the films Superman 2, 3 & 4. Yr. Est: 1973
Opening Times
Sp: Open 09:00. Closed 17:30.
Su: Open 09:00. Closed 17:30.
Au: Open 09:00. Closed 17:30.
Wn: Open 09:00. Closed 17:30. Ref: YH02337

BUTTS GREEN LIVERY

Butts Green Livery, Butts Green Rd, Sandon, Chelmsford, **Essex**, CM2 7RN, **ENGLAND**.
(T) 01245 222092.
Contact/s
Owner: Mr S Hall
Profile Stable/Livery. Ref: YH02338

BUXTON RIDING SCHOOL

Buxton Riding School, Fern Farm/Fern Rd, London Rd, Buxton, **Derbyshire**, SK17 9NP, **ENGLAND**.
(T) 01298 72319.
Contact/s
Owner: Mrs L Andrews
Profile Riding School, Stable/Livery. Ref: YH02339

BUZZARD, I A

I A Buzzard, Uplands Farm, Little Bourton, Banbury, **Oxfordshire**, OX17 1RF, **ENGLAND**.
(T) 01295 750240.
Contact/s
Owner: Mr I Buzzard Ref: YH02340

BWLCHGWYN FARM

Bwlchgwyn Farm Caravan Park & Pony Trekking Centre, Bwlchgwyn Farm, Arthog, **Gwynedd**, LL39 1BX, **WALES**.
(T) 01341 250107.
Contact/s
Owner: Mr J Evans
Profile Equestrian Centre. Trekking Centre. Caravan park. Yr. Est: 1976
Opening Times
Sp: Open Mon - Sun 09:00. Closed Mon - Sun 18:00.
Su: Open Mon - Sun 09:00. Closed Mon - Sun 18:00.
Au: Open Mon - Sun 09:00. Closed Mon - Sun 18:00.
Open Easter - October, closed through the Winter.
Ref: YH02341

BY HAMMER & HAND

By Hammer & Hand, Unit 5 J B J Business Pk, Northampton Rd, Blisworth, Northampton, **Northamptonshire**, NN7 3DW, **ENGLAND**.
(T) 01604 859252.
Profile Blacksmith. Ref: YH02342

BYAS MOSLEY

Byas Mosley & Co Ltd, 14-18 St Clair St, London, **London (Greater)**, EC3N 1JX, **ENGLAND**.
(T) 020 74810101 (F) 020 76233486. Ref: YH02343

BYCHAN STUD

Bychan Stud, Llwynbedw, Ffairfach, Llandeilo, **Carmarthenshire**, SA19 6TF, **WALES**.
(T) 01558 823405.
Profile Breeder. Ref: YH02344

BYCROFT, N

N Bycroft, Cotman Rise, Brandsby, York, **Yorkshire (North)**, YO61 4RN, **ENGLAND**.
(T) 01347 888641 (F) 01347 888641.
Contact/s
Owner: Mr N Bycroft
Profile Trainer. Ref: YH02345

BYERLEY STUD

Byerley Stud (The), Ingoe, Newcastle-upon-Tyne, **Tyne and Wear**, NE20 2SZ, **ENGLAND**.
(T) 01661 886356 (F) 01661 886484.
Profile Trainer. Ref: YH02346

BYRNE, J T

Mr J T Byrne DWCF, Moory Pk, Jeffreston, Kilgetty, **Pembrokeshire**, SA68 0RT, **WALES**.
(T) 01646 651708.
Profile Farrier. Ref: YH02347

BYRNE, MICHAEL J

Byrne Michael J, Knockgraffan, Cahir, **County Tipperary**, **IRELAND**.
(T) 052 62555.
Profile Supplies. Ref: YH02348

BYRNE, ROBERT

Robert Byrne DWCF BII, 29 Westland Court, West Rd, Bransgore, **Dorset**, BH23 8BY, **ENGLAND**.
(T) 01425 674327
(M) 07711 618691.
Profile Farrier. Ref: YH02349

BYRON VETNRY CLINIC

Byron Veterinary Clinic, 193 Derby Rd, Long Eaton, **Derbyshire**, NG10 4LQ, **ENGLAND**.
(T) 0115 9734659.
Profile Medical Support. Ref: YH02350

BYSTOCK PAPER BEDDING

Bystock Paper Bedding, Devon Sheltered Homes Trust, Bystock Court, Exmouth, **Devon**, EX8 5EQ, **ENGLAND**.
(T) 01395 266605.
Profile Supplies. Ref: YH02351

BYTHAN CASPIAN STUD

Bythan Caspian Stud (The), Potters Hill, Morkery Lane, Castle Bytham, Grantham, **Lincolnshire**, NG33 4SP, **ENGLAND**.
(T) 01780 410908 (F) 01780 410908
Affiliated Bodies CHS.
Contact/s
Owner: Mrs P Bowles
(E) patbowles@webleicester.co.uk
Profile Breeder.
Opening Times
Telephone for an appointment Ref: YH02352

C & C EQUINE SVS

C & C Equine Services Ltd, Old Helyers Farm, Kirdford Rd, Wisborough Green, Billingshurst, **Sussex (West)**, RH14 0DD, **ENGLAND**.
(T) 01403 700097.
Contact/s
Owner: Jane Cannon
Profile Stable/Livery. Freelance Instructors.
Opening Times
Telephone for an appointment Ref: YH02353

C & C HORSE TRANSPORT

C & C Horse Transport, Hesketh Grange, Boltby, Thirsk, **Yorkshire (North)**, YO7 2HU, **ENGLAND**.
(T) 01302 344342.
Profile Transport/Horse Boxes. Ref: YH02354

C & K EQUINE SVS

C & K Equine Services, Green Lane, Althorne, Chelmsford, **Essex**, CM3 6BJ, **ENGLAND**.
(T) 01621 740958 (F) 01621 741355.
Contact/s
Owner: Mrs C Nathan
Profile Transport/Horse Boxes. Ref: YH02355

C & L EQUESTRIAN

C & L Equestrian, Manor Farm, Beachampton, Milton Keynes, **Buckinghamshire**, MK19 6DT, **ENGLAND**.
(T) 01908 267154.
Contact/s
Owner: Mr C Strange
Profile Saddlery Retailer. Ref: YH02356

C & M TRAILERS

C & M Trailers Ltd, Wrangaton Motors, Wrangaton, South Brent, **Devon**, TQ10 9HD, **ENGLAND**.
(T) 01364 72204 (F) 01364 72205.
Profile Transport/Horse Boxes. Ref: YH02357

C & N ENGINEERING

C & N Engineering, Downhead Forge, St. Anns Chapel, Gunnislake, **Cornwall**, PL18 9HA, **ENGLAND**.
(T) 01822 832586.
Contact/s
Owner: Mr M Bickford
Profile Blacksmith. Ref: YH02358

C & S SWALWELL

C & S Swalwell, Foulsyke Farm, Loftus, Saltburn-by-the-Sea, **Cleveland**, TS13 4NB, **ENGLAND**.
(T) 01287 641732.
Profile Breeder. Ref: YH02359

C A BOWERS & SONS

C A Bowers & Sons Ltd, North St, Turners Hill, Crawley, **Sussex (West)**, RH10 4NP, **ENGLAND**.
(T) 01342 715225 (F) 01342 715501.
Profile Transport/Horse Boxes. Ref: YH02360

C A DAVIES & SONS

C A Davies & Sons Ltd, Dovefields Ind Est, Uttoxeter, **Staffordshire**, ST14 8AE, **ENGLAND**.
(T) 01889 564844 (F) 01889 568578.
Profile Saddlery Retailer. Ref: YH02361

C A J NICHOLAS

C A J Nicholas, Oakdale Vetnry Surgery, 8 Central Sq, Stanground, Peterborough, **Cambridgeshire**, PE2 8RH, **ENGLAND**.
(T) 01733 340021.
Profile Medical Support. Ref: YH02362

C A MARKETING

C A Marketing, Millfield, Alderford St, Sible Hedingham, **Essex**, CO9 3HX, **ENGLAND**.
(T) 01787 462524 (F) 01787 462524

(M) 07803 135275.
Profile Club/Association. Ref: YH02363

C B R

C B R, 2 Longlands Ave, Newtownabbey, **County Antrim**, BT36 7NE, **NORTHERN IRELAND**.
(T) 028 90865700.
Profile Transport/Horse Boxes. Ref: YH02364

C CARTER & SON

C Carter & Son, Glenside South, West Pinchbeck, Spalding, **Lincolnshire**, PE11 3NH, **ENGLAND**.
(T) 01775 640326.
Profile Blacksmith. Ref: YH02365

C DEAN & SON

C Dean & Son, The Forge, Mill Lane, Rodmell, Lewes, **Sussex (East)**, BN7 3HS, **ENGLAND**.
(T) 01273 474740 (F) 01273 474740.
Contact/s
Partner: Mr F Dean
Profile Blacksmith, Farrier. No.Staff: 4
Yr. Est: 1910 Ref: YH02366

C E ALDRIDGE

C E Aldridge & Co, Barningham Mill, Barningham, Bury St Edmunds, **Suffolk**, IP31 1BU, **ENGLAND**.
(T) 01359 221264.
Profile Supplies. Ref: YH02367

C E COBB & SONS

C E Cobb & Sons Ltd, Barrow Hse Farm, Woodcotes Lane, Darlton, Newark, **Nottinghamshire**, NG22 0TH, **ENGLAND**.
(T) 01777 228260 (F) 01777 228160.
Profile Supplies. Ref: YH02368

C E COOK & SONS

C E Cook & Sons, Lane End Farm, Markfield Lane, Newtown Linford, Leicester, **Leicestershire**, LE6 0AB, **ENGLAND**.
(T) 01530 242214 (F) 01530 245960.
Profile Saddlery Retailer. Ref: YH02369

C E S

Complete Equestrian Services (Derby), Grangefields Farm, Long Lane, Dalbury Lees, Ashbourne, **Derbyshire**, DE6 5BH, **ENGLAND**.
(T) 01332 824977 (F) 01332 824977
(M) 07971 177447
Affiliated Bodies BDS, BETA, BHS, BSJA.
Contact/s
For Bookings: Ms J Jones
Profile Blood Stock Agency, Breeder, Equestrian Centre, Riding School, Stable/Livery, Transport/Horse Boxes. Full Equestrian Agent.
Full Equestrian Agent. No.Staff: 4 Yr. Est: 1986
C.Size: 150 Acres
Opening Times
Sp: Open Mon - Sun 09:00. Closed Mon - Sun 21:00.
Su: Open Mon - Sun 09:00. Closed Mon - Sun 23:00.
Au: Open Mon - Sun 09:00. Closed Mon - Sun 22:00.
Wn: Open Mon - Sun 09:00. Closed Mon - Sun 20:00. Ref: YH02370

C FRANKS & SONS

C Franks & Sons, Firdale Farm, 197 Mildenhall Rd, Fordham, Ely, **Cambridgeshire**, CB7 5NT, **ENGLAND**.
(T) 01638 720822.
Contact/s
Partner: Mr C Franks
Profile Hay & Straw Merchants. Ref: YH02371

C H A O S

C H A O S, 204 Prestbury Rd, Cheltenham, **Gloucestershire**, GL52 3ER, **ENGLAND**.
(T) 01242 244677
(M) 07778 451630.
Profile Club/Association. Ref: YH02372

C H CURBISHLEY FARMS

C H Curbishley Farms Ltd, Brook Farm, Kermincham, Congleton, **Cheshire**, CW12 1LJ, **ENGLAND**.
(T) 01477 71328.
Profile Breeder. Ref: YH02373

C HANSON & SON

C Hanson & Son, Aynhams Hill Farm, Bracewell, Skipton, **Yorkshire (North)**, BD23 3JS, **ENGLAND**.
(T) 01200 445905. Ref: YH02374

C J BLACKSMITHS

C J Blacksmiths, The Smithy, Preston Brockhurst, Shrewsbury, **Shropshire**, SY4 5QA, **ENGLAND**.
(T) 01939 220357
(W) www.cjblacksmiths.co.uk.
Contact/s
General Manager: Mrs E Vago (Q) C&G 1(Forestry), C&G 2(Forestry), U.C
Profile Blacksmith.
Restoration of carriages and equipment, welding repairs and commissions. No.Staff: 3
Yr. Est: 1997
Opening Times
Sp: Open 08:30. Closed 17:30.
Su: Open 08:30. Closed 17:30.
Au: Open 08:30. Closed 17:30.
Wn: Open 08:30. Closed 17:30. Ref: YH02375

C J HAWKINS & SON

C J Hawkins & Son, School Rd, Kingswood, Bristol, **Bristol**, BS15 8BJ, **ENGLAND**.
(T) 01179 672477.
Contact/s
Owner: Mr C Hawkins
Profile Farrier. Ref: YH02376

C J HORSE TRANSPORT

C J Horse Transport, Lower Hill Farm, Lamerton, Tavistock, **Devon**, PL19 8RR, **ENGLAND**.
(T) 01822 612475 (F) 01822 612475.
Contact/s
Owner: Mr C Jenkins
Profile Breeder. Ref: YH02377

C J PUDDY SADDLERY

C J Puddy Saddlery, 474 Bath Rd, Saltford, Bristol, **Bristol**, BS31 3BA, **ENGLAND**.
(T) 01225 874760.
Contact/s
Owner: Mr C Puddy (Q) Saddle Fitter, SMS
Profile Saddlery Retailer.
Opening Times
Sp: Open 09:00. Closed 17:00.
Su: Open 09:00. Closed 17:00.
Au: Open 09:00. Closed 17:00.
Wn: Open 09:00. Closed 17:00. Ref: YH02378

C K TRAILERS

C K Trailers, Westwood, Organford Rd, Holton Heath, Poole, **Dorset**, BH16 6LA, **ENGLAND**.
(T) 01202 623384 (F) 01202 623384.
Contact/s
Owner: Mr C Corbin
Profile Transport/Horse Boxes. Ref: YH02379

C L H TRAILERS

C L H Trailers, Blegwyd, St. Clears, Carmarthen, **Carmarthenshire**, SA33 4LX, **WALES**.
(T) 01994 230055 (F) 01994 230052.
Contact/s
Owner: Mr C Hussell
Profile Transport/Horse Boxes. Ref: YH02380

C M TRAILERS

C M Trailers, Rear Of Hattons Hse, Flaunden Lane, Flaunden, Bovingdon, **Hertfordshire**, HP3 0PQ, **ENGLAND**.
(T) 01442 834343 (F) 01442 834343
(W) www.cmtrailers.co.uk.
Contact/s
Owner: Mr C Mash
(E) cmtrailers@lineone.net
Profile Transport/Horse Boxes.
Service trailers and provide parts. No.Staff: 1
Yr. Est: 1991 Ref: YH02381

C N HORSE BOX INT

C N Horse Box Int, 5 Green Acre Mount, Tilehurst, Reading, **Berkshire**, RG30 4UD, **ENGLAND**.
(T) 0118 9410077.
Profile Transport/Horse Boxes. Ref: YH02382

C P HUNT

C P Hunt, Malthouse Farm, Old Norwich Rd, Scottow, Norwich, **Norfolk**, NR10 5DB, **ENGLAND**.
(T) 01692 538687.
Contact/s
Owner: Mr C Hunt Ref: YH02383

C P S STAGING

C P S Staging, Station Yard, Station Rd, Bawtry, Doncaster, **Yorkshire (South)**, DN10 6QD, **ENGLAND**.
(T) 01302 711183. Ref: YH02384

C PILLOW & SON

C Pillow & Son Ltd, Boscombe Forge, Church Rd, Bookham, Leatherhead, **Surrey**, KT23 3JG, **ENGLAND**.
(T) 01372 457041.
Profile Blacksmith. Ref: YH02385

C R BLACK & SONS

C R Black & Sons Ltd, Padworth Saw Mills, Padworth, Reading, **Berkshire**, RG7 4NU, **ENGLAND**.
(T) 0118 9712175 (F) 0118 9713908.
Profile Transport/Horse Boxes. Ref: YH02386

C R DAY'S MOTORS

C R Day's Motors, Boastings Farm, Long Lane, Toddington, Dunstable, **Bedfordshire**, LU5 6HN, **ENGLAND**.
(T) 01525 875184 (F) 01525 874995.
Contact/s
Owner: Mr C Day
Profile Transport/Horse Boxes. Ref: YH02387

C R M

C R M Ltd, Unit G, White Herons Farm, Forest Rd, Colgate, Horsham, **Sussex (West)**, RH12 4TB, **ENGLAND**.
(T) 01293 851025 (F) 01293 851033.
Profile Club/Association. Ref: YH02388

C R SADDLERY

C R Saddlery Exercise Carts, 36 Close Hse, Bishop Auckland, **County Durham**, DL14 8RW, **ENGLAND**.
(T) 01388 450401 (F) 01388 450401
(E) info@equestria.net
(W) www.exercise-carts.co.uk.
Contact/s
Owner: Ms C Ramshaw
Profile Cart Manufacturers.
Tack security grading irons available. Ref: YH02389

C S HORSEBOXES

C S Horseboxes, Hay Barn, Cookshall Lane, High Wycombe, **Buckinghamshire**, HP12 4AP, **ENGLAND**.
(T) 01494 565618.
Contact/s
Owner: Mr K Rowe
Profile Transport/Horse Boxes. Ref: YH02390

C T C

C T C, Junction St, Carlisle, **Cumbria**, CA2 5XH, **ENGLAND**.
(T) 01228 549911 (F) 01228 549911.
Contact/s
Owner: Mr J Hall
Profile Transport/Horse Boxes. Ref: YH02391

C T C MARINE & LEISURE GROUP

C T C Marine & Leisure Group, Saltwater Hse, 16 Longlands Rd, Middlesbrough, **Cleveland**, TS4 2JR, **ENGLAND**.
(T) 01642 230123 (F) 01642 232007.
Profile Transport/Horse Boxes. Ref: YH02392

C T R

C T R, Waverley St, Central Orbital Trading Pk, Hull, **Yorkshire (East)**, HU1 2SH, **ENGLAND**.
(T) 01482 225591.
Contact/s
Manager: Mr C Gawthorpe
Profile Transport/Horse Boxes. Ref: YH02393

C U & PHOSCO

C U & Phosco Limited, Great Amwell, Ware, **Hertfordshire**, SG12 9TA, **ENGLAND**.
(T) 01920 860600 (F) 01920 485915.
Profile Supplies. Ref: YH02394

C V F

C V F, Coombe View Farm, Ansty Lane, Walsgrave On Sowe, Coventry, **Midlands (West)**, CV2 2DT, **ENGLAND**.
(T) 024 76610157.
Profile Saddlery Retailer. Ref: YH02395

C W G

C W G Ltd (Chelmorton), Unit A Brierlow Bar, Ashbourne Rd, Buxton, **Derbyshire**, SK17 9PY, **ENGLAND**.
(T) 01298 78228 (F) 01298 77313
(W) www.cwg.co.uk.
Profile Supplies. Ref: YH02396

C W G

C W G Ltd (Ongar), Stewarts Farm, Stanford Rivers, Ongar, **Essex**, CM5 9PT, **ENGLAND**.
(T) 01277 362434 (F) 01277 362332
(W) www.cwg.co.uk.
Contact/s
Manager: Mr S Cawley
Profile Supplies. Ref: YH02397

C W G

C W G Ltd (Melton Mowbray), Thorpe End, Melton

Mowbray, **Leicestershire**, LE13 1RB, **ENGLAND**.
(T) 01664 560217 **(F)** 01664 480165
(W) www.cwg.co.uk.
Profile Supplies.
A knowledgeable equestrian assistant. **Ref: YH02398**

C W G

C W G Ltd, Priory Dept, Uffington Rd, Stamford, **Lincolnshire**, PE9 2HD, **ENGLAND**.
(T) 01780 762543 **(F)** 01780 755152.
Profile Supplies. **Ref: YH02399**

C W G

C W G Ltd (Market Rasen), Gallamore Lane Ind Est, Market Rasen, **Lincolnshire**, LN8 3HZ, **ENGLAND**.
(T) 01673 843567 **(F)** 01673 844730
(W) www.cwg.co.uk.
Profile Supplies. **Ref: YH02400**

C W G

C W G Ltd (East Dereham), Hall Lane, Greens Rd Ind Est, East Dereham, **Norfolk**, NR20 3TQ, **ENGLAND**.
(T) 01362 692905 **(F)** 01362 698013
(W) www.cwg.co.uk.
Profile Supplies. **Ref: YH02401**

C W G

C W G Ltd (Towcester), Old Greens Norton Rd, Towcester, **Northamptonshire**, NN12 8AW, **ENGLAND**.
(T) 01327 350896 **(F)** 01327 359972
(W) www.cwg.co.uk.
Profile Supplies. **Ref: YH02402**

C W G

C W G Ltd (Newark), Unit 6 Worktown, Northern Rd, Newark, **Nottinghamshire**, NG24 2EU, **ENGLAND**.
(T) 01636 605560 **(F)** 01636 613281
(W) www.cwg.co.uk.
Profile Supplies. **Ref: YH02403**

C W G

C W G Ltd (Worksop), Claylands Ave, Dukeries Ind Est, Worksop, **Nottinghamshire**, S81 7DJ, **ENGLAND**.
(T) 01909 483753 **(F)** 01909 479279
(W) www.cwg.co.uk.
Profile Supplies. **Ref: YH02404**

C W G

C W G Ltd (Fauld), Fauld, Tutbury, Burton-on-Trent, **Staffordshire**, DE13 9HR, **ENGLAND**.
(T) 01283 813939 **(F)** 01283 520984
(W) www.cwg.co.uk.
Profile Supplies. **Ref: YH02405**

C W G

C W G Ltd (Bury), Chapel Pond Hill, Compiegne Way, Bury St Edmunds, **Suffolk**, IP32 7HT, **ENGLAND**.
(T) 01284 718100 **(F)** 01284 723444
(W) www.cwg.co.uk.
Profile Supplies. **Ref: YH02406**

C W LEE & SON

C W Lee & Son, Westonbirt Forge, Westonbirt, Tetbury, **Gloucestershire**, GL8 8QH, **ENGLAND**.
(T) 01666 880304 **(F)** 01666 880304.
Contact/s
Owner: Mr M Lee
Profile Blacksmith. **Ref: YH02407**

C W S HORSEBOX WINDOWS

C W S Horsebox Windows, 8 Kenneth St, Leeds, **Yorkshire (West)**, LS11 9RF, **ENGLAND**.
(T) 0113 2441288 **(F)** 0113 2441288.
Profile Transport/Horse Boxes. **Ref: YH02408**

CADARN TRAIL RIDING FARM

Cadarn Trail Riding Farm, Velindre, Brecon, **Powys**, LD3 0TB, **WALES**.
(T) 01497 847680 **(F)** 01497 847680.
Contact/s
Owner: Mr E Jones
Profile Equestrian Centre. Trekking Centre.
Ref: YH02409

CADDY TRAILORS

Caddy Trailors Ltd, 151-183 Holme Lane, Sheffield, **Yorkshire (South)**, S6 4JR, **ENGLAND**.
(T) 0114 2322000 **(F)** 0114 2326000.
Profile Transport/Horse Boxes. **Ref: YH02410**

CADMAN, S T

Mr S T Cadman, 13 Highcroft, Middlestone Moor, Spennymoor, Durham, **County Durham**, DL16 7AL, **ENGLAND**.
(T) 01388 813852.
Profile Breeder. **Ref: YH02411**

CADWALLENDER FORGE

Cadwallender Forge, Shucknall Court, Weston Beggard, Hereford, **Herefordshire**, HR1 4BH, **ENGLAND**.
(T) 01432 850515.
Contact/s
Owner: Mr P Cadwallender
Profile Blacksmith. **Ref: YH02412**

CAE IAGO RIDING CTRE

Cae Iago Riding Centre, Ffarmers, Llanwrda, **Carmarthenshire**, SA19 8LZ, **WALES**.
(T) 01558 650303.
Contact/s
Owner: Mr S Jones
Profile Riding School. **Ref: YH02413**

CAERDACH

Caerdach, Gartness Rd, Drymen, **Stirling**, G63 0BH, **SCOTLAND**.
(T) 01360 660596 **(F)** 01360 660596.
Profile Saddlery Retailer. **Ref: YH02414**

CAERNARFONSHIRE RIDING CLUB

Caernarfonshire Riding Club, Hafod-Y-Coed, Ceunant, Llandrug, Caernarfon, **Gwynedd**, LL55 4RY, **WALES**.
(T) 01286 650611.
Contact/s
Chairman: Lyn Hamer
Profile Club/Association, Riding Club. **Ref: YH02415**

CAHIR EQUESTRIAN CTRE

Cahir Equestrian Centre and Farmhouse, Grangemore, Ardfinnan Rd, Cahir, **County Tipperary**, **IRELAND**.
(T) 052 41426 **(F)** 052 41428
(M) 087 6762466
(E) cahirequestriancentre@eircom.net
Affiliated Bodies AIRE.
Contact/s
Owner: Fiona Hyland Ryan
Profile Equestrian Centre, Horse/Rider Accom, Stable/Livery.
Trekking and hacking in the surrounding countryside. Buy's and sell's horses. Livery is also available, details on request.
Opening Times
Sp: Open Tues - Sun 10:00. Closed Tues - Sun 18:00.
Su: Open Tues - Sun 10:00. Closed Tues - Sun 18:00.
Au: Open Tues - Sun 10:00. Closed Tues - Sun 16:30.
Wn: Open Tues - Sun 10:00. Closed Tues - Sun 16:30.
Closed Mondays **Ref: YH02416**

CAINE, E M

Mr E M Caine, High Crossett Farm, Fangdale Beck, Chop Gate, **Cleveland**, TS9 7LH, **ENGLAND**.
(T) 01439 798227.
Profile Supplies. **Ref: YH02417**

CAINES, GEOFFREY WILLIAM

Geoffrey William Caines, The Lee's, 21 Pound Bank Rd, Malvern, **Worcestershire**, WR14 2DW, **ENGLAND**.
(T) 01684 564226.
Profile Farrier. **Ref: YH02418**

CAIRNHOUSE RIDING CTRE

Cairnhouse Riding Centre, The Stables, Blackwaterfoot, Isle Of Arran, **Ayrshire (North)**, KA27 8EU, **SCOTLAND**.
(T) 01770 860466 **(F)** 01770 860466
(E) cairnhouse@stables70.freeserve.co.uk.
Contact/s
Owner: Ms D Murchie **(Q)** BHSAI, TRSS
Profile Arena, Equestrian Centre, Riding School, Stable/Livery. No.Staff: 5 Yr. Est: 1959
Opening Times
Sp: Open 08:00. Closed 18:00.
Su: Open 08:00. Closed 18:00.
Au: Open 08:00. Closed 18:00.
Wn: Open 08:00. Closed 18:00. **Ref: YH02419**

CAIRNS, PETER A

Peter A Cairns DWCF, 16 Rendcomb, Cirencester, **Gloucestershire**, GL7 7HB, **ENGLAND**.
(M) 07774 268577.
Profile Farrier. **Ref: YH02420**

CAISTER RIDING STABLES

Caister Riding Stables, Beech Hse Farm, Yarmouth Rd, Caister-on-Sea, Great Yarmouth, **Norfolk**, NR30 5TD, **ENGLAND**.
(T) 01493 720444.
Contact/s
Owner: Ms P Woolsley **Ref: YH02421**

CAISTER SADDLERY

Caister Saddlery, The Workshop, 97 Beach Rd, Caister On Sea, **Norfolk**, NR30 5HD, **ENGLAND**.
(T) 01493 721927.
Profile Saddlery Retailer. **Ref: YH02422**

CAITHNESS RIDING CLUB

Caithness Riding Club, Moss Of Halkirk, Halkirk, **Highlands**, KW12 6UJ, **SCOTLAND**.
(T) 01847 831355.
Contact/s
Secretary: Mrs D Binnie
Profile Club/Association, Riding Club. **Ref: YH02423**

CAKEHAM EQUESTRIAN CLUB

Cakeham Equestrian Club, Cakeham Stables, Cakeham Rd, West Wittering, Chichester, **Sussex (West)**, PO20 8LG, **ENGLAND**.
(T) 01243 672194. **Ref: YH02424**

CALCUTT & SONS

Calcutt & Sons Ltd, Bullington Lane, Sutton Scotney, Winchester, **Hampshire**, SO21 3RA, **ENGLAND**.
(T) 01962 760210 **(F)** 01962 760702
(E) calutts@msn.com
(W) www.calcuttandsons.co.uk.
Contact/s
Company Secretary: Mrs D Sherwood
Profile Riding Wear Retailer, Saddlery Retailer, Supplies. No.Staff: 10 Yr. Est: 1956
Opening Times
Sp: Open Mon - Sat 09:00. Closed Mon - Fri 18:00, Sat 17:00.
Su: Open Mon - Sat 09:00. Closed Mon - Fri 18:00, Sat 17:00.
Au: Open Mon - Sat 09:00. Closed Mon - Fri 18:00, Sat 17:00.
Wn: Open Mon - Sat 09:00. Closed Mon - Fri 18:00, Sat 17:00. **Ref: YH02425**

CALCUTT, A

A Calcutt, Exhall Hse Cottage, Blackberry Lane, Ash Green, Coventry, **Midlands (West)**, CV7 9AL, **ENGLAND**.
(T) 024 76360679. **Ref: YH02426**

CALDECOTE FARM LIVERY

Caldecote Farm Livery (Elstree) Ltd, Caldecote Lane, Bushey, Watford, **Hertfordshire**, WD2 3RL, **ENGLAND**.
(T) 020 89502314.
Contact/s
Manager: Mr E Brookes
Profile Stable/Livery. **Ref: YH02427**

CALDECOTE RIDING SCHOOL

Caldecote Riding School, Anker Cottage Farm, Caldecote Lane, Caldecote, Nuneaton, **Warwickshire**, CV10 0TN, **ENGLAND**.
(T) 024 76383103
Affiliated Bodies ABRS, BHS.
Contact/s
Owner: Mrs S Sandon
Profile Riding School, Stable/Livery, Supplies.
Rallies held for the Coventry District Branch of the Pony Club. No.Staff: 1 Yr. Est: 1988
C.Size: 12 Acres
Opening Times
Sp: Open Mon - Fri 09:00, Sat, Sun 08:30. Closed Mon - Sun 17:00.
Su: Open Mon - Fri 09:00, Sat, Sun 08:30. Closed Mon - Sun 17:00.
Au: Open Mon - Fri 09:00, Sat, Sun 08:30. Closed Mon - Sun 17:00.
Wn: Open Mon - Fri 09:00, Sat, Sun 08:30. Closed Mon - Sun 17:00. **Ref: YH02428**

CALDECOTT HALL

Caldecott Hall Equestrian Centre, Caldecott Hall, Fritton, Great Yarmouth, **Norfolk**, NR31 9EY, **ENGLAND**.
(T) 01493 488488 **(F)** 01493 488561.
Profile Riding School, Stable/Livery. **Ref: YH02429**

CALDENE CLOTHING

Caldene Clothing Co Ltd, Mytholmroyd, Hebden Bridge, Hebden Bridge, **Yorkshire (West)**, HX7 5QJ, **ENGLAND**.
(T) 01422 883393
(W) www.caldene.co.uk.
Contact/s
Owner: Mr C Uttley
Profile Riding Wear Retailer, Supplies.

No.Staff: 44 Yr. Est: 1922 **Ref: YH02430**

CALDER PARK STABLES

Calder Park Stables, Hamilton Rd, Newmarket, **Suffolk**, CB8 0HY, **ENGLAND**.
(M) 07885 674474
(W) www.newmarketracehorsetrainers.co.uk
Affiliated Bodies Newmarket Trainers Fed.
Contact/s
Trainer: Mr T Clement
Profile Trainer. **Ref: YH02431**

CALDER VETNRY GRP

Calder Veterinary Group, Bottoms Hse Vetnry Surgery, Savile Rd, Dewsbury, **Yorkshire (West)**, WF12 9LN, **ENGLAND**.
(T) 01924 465592 **(F)** 01924 450898.
Profile Medical Support. **Ref: YH02432**

CALDER VETNRY GRP

Calder Veterinary Group, 13 Doctor Lane, Mirfield, **Yorkshire (West)**, WF14 8DN, **ENGLAND**.
(T) 01924 492155.
Profile Medical Support. **Ref: YH02433**

CALDER VETNRY GRP

Calder Veterinary Group, 50 High St, Horbury, **Yorkshire (West)**, WF4 5LE, **ENGLAND**.
(T) 01924 281401.
Profile Medical Support. **Ref: YH02434**

CALDERDALE SADDLE CLUB

Calderdale Saddle Club, Clough Farm, Boulderclough, Sowerby Bridge, Halifax, **Yorkshire (West)**, HX6 1NJ, **ENGLAND**.
(T) 01422 883596.
Contact/s
Chairman: Mr G Cigan
Profile Club/Association. **Ref: YH02435**

CALDERS & GRANDIDGE

Calders & Grandidge, 194 London Rd, Boston, **Lincolnshire**, PE21 7HJ, **ENGLAND**.
(T) 01205 358866 **(F)** 01205 312400. **Ref: YH02436**

CALDEW VETNRY GRP

Caldew Veterinary Group, Carlisle Hse, Townhead Rd, Dalston, Carlisle, **Cumbria**, CA5 7JF, **ENGLAND**.
(T) 01228 710208 **(F)** 01228 711960
(E) caldewvet@bizonline.co.uk.
Profile Medical Support. **Ref: YH02437**

CALDICOT SADDLERY

Caldicot Saddlery, Little Oaks Stables, 43 Leechpool Holdings, Portskewett, **Newport**, NP26 5UB, **WALES**.
(T) 01291 422249 **(F)** 01291 422249.
Profile Saddlery Retailer. **Ref: YH02438**

CALDWELL, T H

Mr T H Caldwell, Burley Heyes Cottage, Arley Rd, Appleton, Warrington, **Cheshire**, WA4 4RR, **ENGLAND**.
(T) 01565 777275 **(F)** 01565 777275.
Profile Trainer. **Ref: YH02439**

CALEDONIAN EQUESTRIAN CTRE

Caledonian Equestrian Centre, Pitskelly Farm, Balbeggie, Perth, **Perth and Kinross**, PH2 6AR, **SCOTLAND**.
(T) 01821 640426.
Contact/s
Owner: Mrs S Bruce
Profile Riding School, Stable/Livery. **Ref: YH02440**

CALEDONIAN FENCING

Caledonian Fencing Ltd, Phoenix Works, North St, Lewes, **Sussex (East)**, BN7 2QJ, **ENGLAND**.
(T) 01273 477118 **(F)** 01273 473682. **Ref: YH02441**

CALEDONIAN RIDING CLUB

Caledonian Riding Club, Eight Acres, Culbokie, **Highlands**, IV7 8JH, **SCOTLAND**.
(T) 01349 877400.
Contact/s
Chairman: Mr I MacLeod
Profile Club/Association, Riding Club. **Ref: YH02442**

CALEY, MARK A

Mark A Caley DWCF, The Potting Shed, Edgemoor, Bishops Lane, Buxton, **Derbyshire**, SK17 6UP, **ENGLAND**.
(T) 01298 27470.
Profile Farrier. **Ref: YH02443**

CALICO LIVERY STABLES

Calico Livery Stables, 1A Miles Lane, Shevington, Wigan, **Lancashire**, WN6 8EB, **ENGLAND**.
(T) 01257 252156.
Profile Stable/Livery. **Ref: YH02444**

CALIFORNIA FARM RIDING SCHOOL

California Farm Riding School, Capel Lane, Charlton Kings, Cheltenham, **Gloucestershire**, GL54 4HQ, **ENGLAND**.
(T) 01242 244746.
Profile Riding School. **Ref: YH02445**

CALKE ABBEY RACING STABLES

Calke Abbey Racing Stables, Heath Lane, Boundary, Swadlincote, **Derbyshire**, DE11 7AY, **ENGLAND**.
(T) 01283 226046.
Contact/s
Owner: Mr T Donnilin
Profile Trainer. **Ref: YH02446**

CALLAGHAN, N A

N A Callaghan, 22 Hamilton Rd, Newmarket, **Suffolk**, CB8 0NY, **ENGLAND**.
(T) 01638 664040 **(F)** 01638 668446
(E) nacallaghan@aol.com
(W) www.newmarketracehorsetrainers.co.uk
Affiliated Bodies Newmarket Trainers Fed.
Contact/s
Trainer: Mr N Callaghan
Profile Trainer. **Ref: YH02447**

CALLAWAY, ELIZABETH

Elizabeth Callaway, 171 Bisops Rise, Hatfield, **Hertfordshire**, AL10 9EP, **ENGLAND**.
(T) 01707 264434
(E) e.callaway@deltaweb.demon.co.uk.
Profile Medical Support. **Ref: YH02448**

CALLIAGHSTOWN EQUESTRIAN

Calliaghstown Equestrian, Calliaghstown, Rathcoole, **County Dublin**, **IRELAND**.
(T) 01 4589236 **(F)** 014588171
(E) calliaghstownequestrian@kildarehorse.ie.
Contact/s
Key Contact: Gráinne Sugars
Profile Equestrian Centre, Riding School.
Calliaghstown Riding Centre is the beginning of the Wicklow Trail Ride, through the mountains and glens of the 'Garden of Ireland', finishing in the Monastic 7th Century village of Glendalough. Tuition holidays are available for adults and unaccompanied children with special instruction in cross country & show jumping. Irish hunters are bred at the centre.
Opening Times
Sp: Open Mon - Sun 09:00. Closed Mon - Thur 21:00, Fri - Sun 18:00.
Su: Open Mon - Sun 09:00. Closed Mon - Thur 21:00, Fri - Sun 18:00.
Au: Open Mon - Sun 09:00. Closed Mon - Thur 21:00, Fri - Sun 18:00.
Wn: Open Mon - Sun 09:00. Closed Mon - Thur 21:00, Fri - Sun 18:00. **Ref: YH02449**

CALLIAGHSTOWN RIDING CTRE

Calliaghstown Riding Centre, Rathcoole, **County Dublin**, **IRELAND**.
(T) 01 4589236 **(F)** 01 4588171. **Ref: YH02450**

CALLOW, W J

W J Callow, Netherclay Farm, Thurlbear, Taunton, **Somerset**, TA3 5AX, **ENGLAND**.
(T) 01823 276313.
Contact/s
Owner: Mr W Callow
Profile Stable/Livery. **Ref: YH02451**

CALLUM PARK RIDING CTRE

Callum Park Riding Centre, Lower Halstow, Sittingbourne, **Kent**, ME9 7ED, **ENGLAND**.
(T) 01795 844978.
Profile Riding School. **Ref: YH02452**

CALLWOOD, H S & A

Messrs H S & A Callwood, Manor Farm, Ollerton, Knutsford, **Cheshire**, WA16 8RC, **ENGLAND**.
(T) 01565 755893.
Profile Breeder. **Ref: YH02453**

CALTECH BIOTECHNOLOGY

Caltech Biotechnology, Solway Mills, Silloth, Carlisle, **Cumbria**, CA5 4AJ, **ENGLAND**.
(T) 01697 332592 **(F)** 01697 332339
(E) hilary@cmiplc.co.uk.
Profile Medical Support. **Ref: YH02454**

CALVERT TRUST ADVENTURE CTRE

Calvert Trust Adventure Centre, Riding Stables, Old Windebrowe, Keswick, **Cumbria**, CA12 4NT, **ENGLAND**.
(T) 01768 774395.
Contact/s
Stable Manager: Jane Whitehouse
Profile Riding School. **Ref: YH02455**

CALVERT TRUST KIELDER

Calvert Trust Kielder, Kielder Water, Hexham, **Northumberland**, NE48 1BS, **ENGLAND**.
(T) 01434 250232 **(F)** 01434 250015.
Profile Riding School. **Ref: YH02456**

CALVERT TRUST RIDING CTRE

Calvert Trust Riding Centre, Old Windebrow, Keswick, **Cumbria**, CA12 4QD, **ENGLAND**.
(T) 01768 774395.
Profile Riding School. **Ref: YH02457**

CALVERTON HORSE & PONY CLUB

Calverton Horse & Pony Club, Broomside Stud, Shire Farm, Mansfield Lane, Calverton, Nottingham, **Nottinghamshire**, NG14 6HL, **ENGLAND**.
(T) 0115 9652590.
Profile Club/Association.
Show Dates for 2002 are; April 21st, May 6th, May 27th, June 9th, July 7th, July 28th. **Ref: YH02458**

CALVIN

Calvin, 12 Stroma Court, Dreghorn, Irvine, **Ayrshire (North)**, KA11 4JF, **SCOTLAND**.
(T) 01294 214252.
Contact/s
Owner: Mr A Walker
Profile Blacksmith. **Ref: YH02459**

CALWETON VETNRY CTRE

Calweton Veterinary Centre, 79 Tavistock Rd, Callington, **Cornwall**, PL17 7RL, **ENGLAND**.
(T) 01579 383231 **(F)** 01579 383224.
Contact/s
Vet: Chris Luckhurst **(Q)** MRCVS
Profile Medical Support. **Ref: YH02460**

CALWETON VETNRY CTRE

Calweton Veterinary Centre, The Veterinary Surgery, The Millpool, Looe, **Cornwall**, PL13 2AF, **ENGLAND**.
(T) 01503 263773.
Profile Medical Support. **Ref: YH02461**

CALWETON VETNRY CTRE

Calweton Veterinary Centre, Unit 5 Gwel-Avon Ind Est, Saltash, **Cornwall**, PL12 6TW, **ENGLAND**.
(T) 01752 846805.
Profile Medical Support. **Ref: YH02462**

CAM EQUESTRIAN JOINERY/EQUIP

Cam Equestrian Joinery & Equipment Ltd, Cam Stables, Eardisley, Hereford, **Herefordshire**, HR3 6NS, **ENGLAND**.
(T) 01544 322000 **(F)** 01544 327210.
Contact/s
Marketing Manager: Paula Burrows
Profile Supplies. **Ref: YH02463**

CAMACHO RACING

Camacho Racing Ltd, Star Cottage, Welham Rd, Norton, Malton, **Yorkshire (North)**, YO17 9DU, **ENGLAND**.
(T) 01653 694901 **(F)** 01653 694901.
Contact/s
Administration: Ms S Camacho
Profile Trainer. **Ref: YH02464**

CAMBER, N B

N B Camber, Agricultural Merchant, Harley, Shrewsbury, **Shropshire**, SY5 6LN, **ENGLAND**.
(T) 01952 510481 **(F)** 01952 510222.
Contact/s
Owner: Mr N Camber
Profile Supplies. **Ref: YH02465**

CAMBIDGE, B R

Mr B R Cambidge, Park Oak Farm, Tong Rd, Bishopswood, Brewood, **Staffordshire**, ST19 9AP, **ENGLAND**.
(T) 01952 850249.
Profile Supplies. **Ref: YH02466**

CAMBRIAN HORSE TRAIL NETWORK

Cambrian Horse Trail Network, Coach Hse, Clyro, Hereford, **Herefordshire**, HR3 5LE, **ENGLAND**.
(T) 01497 821356
(E) will@free-rein.co.uk
(W) www.free-rein.co.uk.
Contact/s
Owner: Mr G Williams
(E) will@free-rein.co.uk
Profile Holidays, Horse/Rider Accom.
Cambrian Horse provides all that riders need on the Radnor Hills, including horses and ponies, maps and route descriptions, accommodation, baggage transfer,

Key: **(T)** telephone **(F)** fax **(M)** mobile **(E)** E-Mail Address **(W)** Website Address **(Q)** Qualifications
Yr. Est: Year Established C.Size: Complex Size Sp: Spring Su: Summer Au: Autumn Wn: Winter

helpline and full back-up. **Ref: YH02467**

CAMBRIDGE & DISTRICT
Cambridge & District Riding Club, Mowbray, Cottenham Rd, Histon, **Cambridgeshire**, CB4 9ET, **ENGLAND**.
(T) 01223 233398.
Contact/s
Chairman: Mrs J MacNab
Profile Club/Association, Riding Club. **Ref: YH02468**

CAMBRIDGE & NEWMARKET POLO
Cambridge & Newmarket Polo Club, 210 Victoria Rd, Cambridge, **Cambridgeshire**, CB4 3LG, **ENGLAND**.
(T) 01223 337659 **(F)** 01223 337610.
Contact/s
Polo Manager: Jeremy Allen
Profile Club/Association. Polo club. **Ref: YH02469**

CAMBRIDGE PET CREMATORIUM
Cambridge Pet Crematorium, A505 Main Rd, Thriplow Heath, Royston, **Hertfordshire**, SG8 7RR, **ENGLAND**.
(T) 01763 208295 **(F)** 01763 208885.
Profile Medical Support. **Ref: YH02470**

CAMBRIDGE TRAILERS
Cambridge Trailers Limited, Over Rd Corner, Longstanton, Cambridge, **Cambridgeshire**, CB4 5DW, **ENGLAND**.
(T) 01954 781905 **(F)** 01954 781905
(W) www.cambridgetrailers.co.uk.
Contact/s
Owner: Mr G Waters
(E) graham@cambridgetrailers.co.uk
Profile Transport/Horse Boxes. Trailer Manufacturer.
Repair and service trailers. **Ref: YH02471**

CAMBRIDGE UNIVERSITY
Cambridge University Riding Club, C/O Newnham College, Cambridge, **Cambridgeshire**, CB3 9DF, **ENGLAND**.
(T) 01223 335700.
Profile Club/Association, Riding Club. **Ref: YH02472**

CAMBRIDGE UNIVERSITY
Cambridge University Polo Club, St Edmunds College, Cambridge Or Brunswick, Woodditton Rd, Newmarket, **Suffolk**, CB8 9BQ, **ENGLAND**.
(T) 01638 662507.
Profile Club/Association. Polo Club. **Ref: YH02473**

CAMBRIDGE UNIVERSITY DRAG
Cambridge University Drag, The Green, Wardy Hill, Ely, **Cambridgeshire**, CB6 2DE, **ENGLAND**.
(T) 01353 777876. **Ref: YH02474**

CAMEL VALLEY RIDING CLUB
Camel Valley Riding Club, Cross Pk, Cardinham, **Cornwall**, PL30 4DJ, **ENGLAND**.
(T) 01566 86125 **(F)** 01566 86125
(E) bmeeson@compuserve.com.
Contact/s
Chairman: Liz Freeman
Profile Club/Association, Riding Club. **Ref: YH02475**

CAMERON & GREIG
Cameron & Greig, Ardmohr, Stirling Rd, Milnathort, **Perth and Kinross**, KY13 9XG, **SCOTLAND**.
(T) 01577 863494 **(F)** 01577 863494.
Profile Medical Support. **Ref: YH02476**

CAMERON HORSE TRANSPORT
Cameron Horse Transport, 62 Freame Cl, Chalford, Stroud, **Gloucestershire**, GL6 8HG, **ENGLAND**.
(T) 01453 885959.
Contact/s
Owner: Mr G Nelmes-Crocker
Profile Transport/Horse Boxes. **Ref: YH02477**

CAMERON, D N & R
Cameron D N & R, 11D Station Rd, Inverkeilor, Arbroath, **Angus**, DD11 5RT, **SCOTLAND**.
(T) 01241 830473.
Contact/s
Partner: Mrs N Cameron
Profile Blacksmith. **Ref: YH02478**

CAMERON, D N & R
D N & R Cameron, Chapelton Smiddy, Chapelton, Arbroath, **Angus**, DD11 4RT, **SCOTLAND**.
(T) 01241 828604 **(F)** 01241 828604.
Contact/s
Partner: Mr D Cameron
Profile Blacksmith. **Ref: YH02479**

CAMERON, DAVID
David Cameron, Tarras, Gartness Rd, Drymen, Glasgow, **Stirling**, G63 0BH, **SCOTLAND**.
(T) 01360 660323 **(F)** 01360 660000.
Contact/s
Owner: Mr D Cameron **Ref: YH02480**

CAMERON, JOHN
John Cameron, 41 Blackford Glen Rd, Edinburgh, **Edinburgh (City of)**, EH16 6TP, **SCOTLAND**.
(T) 0131 6649101 **(F)** 0131 6649101.
Contact/s
Owner: Mr J Cameron
Profile Blacksmith. **Ref: YH02481**

CAMM, J A
Mrs J A Camm, Brockhurst Farm, Oaks Lane, Brockhurst, Chesterfield, **Derbyshire**, S45 0HR, **ENGLAND**.
(T) 01246 590064.
Profile Breeder. **Ref: YH02482**

CAMPBELL, CARNET
Mrs Carnet Campbell, West Arnloss, Slamannan, **Falkirk**, FK1 3DH, **SCOTLAND**.
(T) 01324 851238.
Profile Riding School, Stable/Livery. **Ref: YH02483**

CAMPBELL, FINDLAY
Findlay Campbell, 15-19 Haddow St, Hamilton, **Lanarkshire (South)**, ML3 7HX, **SCOTLAND**.
(T) 01698 283491 **(F)** 01698 891955.
Contact/s
Owner: Mr F Campbell
Profile Blacksmith. **Ref: YH02484**

CAMPBELL, M
Miss M Campbell, Andbell Hse, Chuck Hatch, Hartfield, **Sussex (East)**, TN7 4EX, **ENGLAND**.
(T) 01342 823034. **Ref: YH02485**

CAMPBELL, NICHOLAS
Nicholas Campbell, Vale Hse, Burley St, Ringwood, **Hampshire**, BH24 4HQ, **ENGLAND**.
(T) 01425 403384 **(F)** 01425 480560. **Ref: YH02486**

CAMPBELL, SCOTT J
Scott J Campbell DWCF, 9 Victoria St, Forfar, **Angus**, DD8 3HU, **SCOTLAND**.
(T) 01307 463619.
Profile Farrier. **Ref: YH02487**

CAMPBELL, W M
Mrs W M Campbell, Honeysuckle Cottage, Penny Bridge, Pembroke, **Pembrokeshire**, SA72 4SP, **WALES**.
(T) 01646 687111.
Profile Breeder. **Ref: YH02488**

CAMPBELL-DIXON, D F A
D F A Campbell-Dixon, Church Moor Hall, Church Moor, Church Stretton, **Shropshire**, SY6 6PU, **ENGLAND**.
(T) 01694 781249.
Contact/s
Owner: Mrs D Campbell-Dixon
Profile Breeder. **Ref: YH02489**

CAMPERDOWN STABLES
Camperdown Stables, Camperdown Pk, Dundee, **Angus**, DD2 4TF, **SCOTLAND**.
(T) 01382 623879. **Ref: YH02490**

CAMPMUIR QUARTER HORSES
Campmuir Quarter Horses, Elmwood Hse, Campmuir, Coupar Angus, **Perth and Kinross**, PH13 9LN, **SCOTLAND**.
(T) 01828 670624 **(F)** 01828 670624
(M) 07774 480271.
Profile Breeder. **Ref: YH02491**

CAMROSA EQUESTRIAN
Camrosa Equestrian Ltd, Ladymeads Farm, Lower Cousley Wood, Wadhurst, **Sussex (East)**, TN5 6HH, **ENGLAND**.
(T) 01892 783240 **(F)** 01892 783240.
Profile Medical Support. **Ref: YH02492**

CANAAN FARM
Canaan Farm, Loughborough Rd, Costock, Loughborough, **Leicestershire**, LE12 6XB, **ENGLAND**.
(T) 01509 854264.
Contact/s
Owner: Mrs J Chiasserini **(T)** 01509 853351
Profile Stable/Livery. C.Size: 21 Acres
Opening Times
Sp: Open 07:00. Closed 22:00.
Su: Open 07:00. Closed 22:00.
Au: Open 07:00. Closed 22:00.
Wn: Open 07:00. Closed 22:00. **Ref: YH02493**

CANADA HAY
Canada Hay Co, Stonecross, North Stoke, Bath, **Bath & Somerset (North East)**, BA1 9AS, **ENGLAND**.
(T) 01179 322210.
Contact/s
Owner: Mr K Hill
Profile Hay Merchants.
Import Canadian and American hay. **Ref: YH02494**

CANDLER, B
Mr B Candler, 43 Bassleton Lane, Bassleton Court, Thornaby, **Cleveland**, TS17 0LB, **ENGLAND**.
(T) 01642 761722.
Profile Trainer. **Ref: YH02495**

CANDLERS
Candlers, 14 The Green, Writtle, Chelmsford, **Essex**, CM1 3DU, **ENGLAND**.
(T) 01245 421334.
Contact/s
Owner: Mr T Candler
Profile Riding Wear Retailer, Saddlery Retailer.
Have experts on-site in dressage and showing.
No.Staff: 2 Yr. Est: 1981
Opening Times
Sp: Open Mon - Sat 09:30. Closed Mon - Fri 17:30, Sat 17:00.
Su: Open Mon - Sat 09:30. Closed Mon - Fri 17:30, Sat 17:00.
Au: Open Mon - Sat 09:30. Closed Mon - Fri 17:30, Sat 17:00.
Wn: Open Mon - Sat 09:30. Closed Mon - Fri 17:30, Sat 17:00.
Closed on Wednesdays **Ref: YH02496**

CANDY, H
H Candy, Kingston Warren Farm, Kingston Warren, Wantage, **Oxfordshire**, OX12 9QF, **ENGLAND**.
(T) 01367 820276 **(F)** 01367 820500.
Contact/s
Owner: Mr H Candy
Profile Trainer. **Ref: YH02497**

CANE END STABLES
Cane End Stables, Cane End, Reading, **Berkshire**, RG4 9HH, **ENGLAND**.
(T) 07958 917061.
Profile Riding School, Stable/Livery. **Ref: YH02498**

CANN, ELIZABETH
Mrs Elizabeth Cann, Woodlands Farm, Morwenstow, Bude, **Cornwall**, EX23 9HU, **ENGLAND**.
(T) 01288 483387.
Profile Breeder. **Ref: YH02499**

CANN, STEPHEN J
Stephen J Cann DWCF, 3 Hayes Cl, Otterton, **Devon**, EX9 7JN, **ENGLAND**.
(T) 01395 568796.
Profile Farrier. **Ref: YH02500**

CANNEY, R
Mr R Canney, 3 Mill St, Greenock, **Renfrewshire**, PA15 4HG, **SCOTLAND**.
(T) 01475 783129. **Ref: YH02501**

CANNING, SUSAN
Susan Canning, 4 Stanlope Ave, Horsforth, Leeds, **Yorkshire (West)**, LS18 5AR, **ENGLAND**.
(T) 0113 2587391 **(F)** 0113 2587391.
Contact/s
Owner: Mrs S Canning
Profile Artist.
Commissions for horse and riders No.Staff: 1
Yr. Est: 1971
Opening Times
Sp: Open Mon - Sun 09:00. Closed Mon - Sun 18:00.
Su: Open Mon - Sun 09:00. Closed Mon - Sun 18:00.
Au: Open Mon - Sun 09:00. Closed Mon - Sun 18:00.
Wn: Open Mon - Sun 09:00. Closed Mon - Sun 18:00. **Ref: YH02502**

CANNINGTON COLLEGE
Cannington College Equestrian Centre, Rodway Hill, Cannington, Bridgwater, **Somerset**, TA5 2LS, **ENGLAND**.
(T) 01278 655000. **Ref: YH02503**

CANNOCK CHASE TREKKING CTRE
Cannock Chase Trekking Centre, Teddesley

Coppice, Penkridge, Stafford, **Staffordshire**, ST19 5RP, **ENGLAND**.
(T) 01785 711177.
Profile Equestrian Centre. **Ref: YH02504**

CANNON, DEVINA

Devina Cannon, The Limes, Little Everdon, Daventry, **Northamptonshire**, NN11 3BG, **ENGLAND**.
(T) 01327 361388 **(F)** 01327 361514
(M) 07836 246393. **Ref: YH02505**

CANNON, LINDA

Linda Cannon, White Lane Farm, White Lane, Albury, Guildford, **Surrey**, GU5 9BQ, **ENGLAND**.
(T) 01483 572502.
Contact/s
Owner: Mrs L Cannon
Profile Riding School. **Ref: YH02506**

CANTERBURY CARRIAGES

Canterbury Carriages, Highfield Stables, Stoneheap Rd, East Studdal, Dover, **Kent**, CT15 5BU, **ENGLAND**.
(T) 01304 364027 **(F)** 01304 375233
(M) 07976 440975.
Contact/s
Partner: Mr T Ledwith
Profile Trainer. **Ref: YH02507**

CANTERBURY CLGE

Canterbury College, New Dover Rd, Canterbury, **Kent**, CT1 3AJ, **ENGLAND**.
(T) 01227 811111 **(F)** 01227 811101
(E) admissions@cant-col.ac.uk.
Profile Equestrian Centre. **Ref: YH02508**

CANTERBURY RIDING CLUB

Canterbury Riding Club, The Hawthorns, St Andrews Gardens, Sheperdswell, Dover, **Kent**, CT15 7LT, **ENGLAND**.
(T) 01304 831510 **(F)** 01227 730026.
Contact/s
Chairman: Miss S Cox
Profile Club/Association, Riding Club. **Ref: YH02509**

CANTERBURY SADDLE CTRE

Canterbury Saddle Centre, 72 Wincheap, Canterbury, **Kent**, CT1 3RS, **ENGLAND**.
(T) 01227 767590 **(F)** 01227 767590.
Contact/s
Partner: Mr C Lloyd **Ref: YH02510**

CANTER-ON TACK SHOP

Canter-On Tack Shop, Unit 20 Albert Mill, Albert Pl, Lower Darwen, Darwen, **Lancashire**, BB3 0QE, **ENGLAND**.
(T) 01254 698980.
Profile Saddlery Retailer. **Ref: YH02511**

CANTERS END RIDING SCHOOL

Canters End Riding School, Wheelers Lane, Hadlow Down, Uckfield, **Sussex (East)**, TN22 4HR, **ENGLAND**.
(T) 01825 830213.
Contact/s
Owner: Ms V Grove
Profile Riding School, Stable/Livery. **Ref: YH02512**

CANTI, J

J Canti, Smiths Farm, Fivehead, Taunton, **Somerset**, TA3 6QX, **ENGLAND**.
(T) 01460 281793.
Contact/s
Owner: Jodi Canti
Profile Medical Support. **Ref: YH02513**

CANTILLON, DON

Mr Don Cantillon, Seymour Hse, 10 Rous Rd, Newmarket, **Suffolk**, CB8 8DL, **ENGLAND**.
(T) 01638 668507
(M) 07989 088524
(W) www.newmarketracehorsetrainers.co.uk
Affiliated Bodies Newmarket Trainers Fed.
Contact/s
Trainer: Mr D Cantillon
Profile Supplies, Trainer. **Ref: YH02514**

CANTLE, JOHN

John Cantle RSS, 81 Cherrydown Ave, Chingford, **London (Greater)**, E4 8DT, **ENGLAND**.
(T) 020 85247633.
Profile Farrier. **Ref: YH02515**

CANTREF

Cantref Trekking And Riding Centre, Cantref, Brecon, **Powys**, LD3 8LR, **WALES**.
(T) 01874 665223 **(F)** 01874 665223
(E) info@cantref.com
(W) www.cantref.com
Affiliated Bodies WTRA.
Contact/s
Owner: Mrs M Evans
Profile Arena, Blacksmith, Equestrian Centre, Holidays, Riding Club, Riding School, Track/Course.
No.Staff: 5 Yr. Est: 1961 C.Size: 200 Acres
Ref: YH02516

CANTY, JOSEPH M

Canty Joseph M, Collaghknock Glebe, Kildare, **County Kildare**, **IRELAND**.
(T) 045 521215.
Profile Supplies. **Ref: YH02517**

CANTY, PHILIP

Canty Philip, St Judes Frenchfurze Rd, Kildare, **County Kildare**, **IRELAND**.
(T) 045 521590.
Profile Supplies. **Ref: YH02518**

CAPALL RIDING CLUB

Capall Riding Club, Hillfarm, 31 Ballymaleddy Rd, Comber, **County Down**, BT23 5RD, **NORTHERN IRELAND**.
(T) 028 90791252.
Contact/s
Chairman: Mr R Bambridge
Profile Club/Association, Riding Club. **Ref: YH02519**

CAPES & SON

Capes & Son, 11 Old Boston Rd, Coningsby, Lincoln, **Lincolnshire**, LN4 4SZ, **ENGLAND**.
(T) 01526 342526.
Contact/s
Owner: Mr P Capes
Profile Blacksmith. **Ref: YH02520**

CAPITALL STUD

Capitall Stud, Donnett Farm, Whittington, Oswestry, **Shropshire**, SY11 4DB, **ENGLAND**.
(T) 01691 658645.
Profile Breeder. **Ref: YH02521**

CAPLE CRAFT

Caple Craft, Falcon Brook, How Caple, Hereford, **Herefordshire**, HR1 4TF, **ENGLAND**.
(T) 01989 740650 **(F)** 01989 740282.
Profile Blacksmith. **Ref: YH02522**

CAPRICORN FULTON HARRIS

Capricorn Fulton Harris, Capricorn Hse, Black Burn Rd, Rising Bridge, **Lancashire**, BB5 2AA, **ENGLAND**.
(T) 01706 211411 **(F)** 01706 215400
(E) cfh@cyberpublishing.co.uk. **Ref: YH02523**

CAPTAIN RUGWASH

Captain Rugwash, Penwern Fach, Ponthirwaun, Cardigan, **Ceredigion**, SA43 2RL, **WALES**.
(T) 01239 710694 **(F)** 01239 710694.
Profile Supplies. **Ref: YH02524**

CARADOC CLOTHING

Caradoc Clothing, Mor Brook Barn, Morville, Bridgnorth, **Shropshire**, WV16 5NR, **ENGLAND**.
(T) 01746 714275 **(F)** 01746 714275.
Profile Supplies. **Ref: YH02525**

CARAVAN CORNER

Caravan Corner, Hoo Hill Ind Est, Blackpool, **Lancashire**, FY3 7HJ, **ENGLAND**.
(T) 01253 394315.
Profile Transport/Horse Boxes.
Trailer repair. **Ref: YH02526**

CARD, REX T

Rex T Card, Homely, The Street, Northcove, Beccles, **Suffolk**, NR34 7PN, **ENGLAND**.
(T) 01502 476763.
Profile Farrier. **Ref: YH02527**

CARDEN, J

Mr J Carden, Woodside Farm, Smithy Lane, Mottram St. Andrew, Macclesfield, **Cheshire**, SK10 4QJ, **ENGLAND**.
(T) 01625 829748.
Profile Supplies. **Ref: YH02528**

CARDEN, SUSAN M M

Susan M M Carden, Keeper's Cottage, West Kington, Chippenham, **Wiltshire**, SN14 7JE, **ENGLAND**.
(T) 01249 783064 **(F)** 01249 783064
(M) 07970 413382. **Ref: YH02529**

CARDIFF CITY RIDING SCHOOL

Cardiff City Riding School, Pontcanna Fields, Fields Park Rd, Cardiff, **Glamorgan (Vale of)**, CF11 9JP, **WALES**.
(T) 029 20383908.
Profile Riding School. **Ref: YH02530**

CARDIFF RIDING SCHOOL

Cardiff Riding School, Pontcanna Fields, Cardiff, Cardiff, **Glamorgan (Vale of)**, CF1 9LB, **WALES**.
(T) 029 20383908.
Profile Riding School, Stable/Livery. **Ref: YH02531**

CARDIFF SPORTSGEAR

Cardiff Sportsgear Martial Arts Equipment, 192-194 Whitchurch Rd, Cardiff, **Glamorgan (Vale of)**, CF14 3JP, **WALES**.
(T) 029 20621207 **(F)** 029 20619343
(W) www.cardiffsportsgear.co.uk.
Contact/s
Manager: Mr B Barrett
Profile Riding Wear Retailer, Saddlery Retailer.
No.Staff: 2 Yr. Est: 1966
Opening Times
Sp: Open Mon - Sat 09:00. Closed Mon - Sat 18:00.
Su: Open Mon - Sat 09:00. Closed Mon - Sat 18:00.
Au: Open Mon - Sat 09:00. Closed Mon - Sat 18:00.
Wn: Open Mon - Sat 09:00. Closed Mon - Sat 18:00.
Ref: YH02532

CARDIFF TRAILER CTRE

Cardiff Trailer Centre, 641 Cowbridge Rd East, Cardiff, **Glamorgan (Vale of)**, CF5 1BH, **WALES**.
(T) 029 20565599 **(F)** 029 20575520.
Contact/s
Partner: Mr A Davies
Profile Transport/Horse Boxes. **Ref: YH02533**

CARENZA, JILL

Jill Carenza Riding & B & B, The Vine, Stanton, Broadway, **Worcestershire**, WR12 7NE, **ENGLAND**.
(T) 01386 584250 **(F)** 01386 584385
(E) info@cotswoldsriding.co.uk
(W) www.cotswoldsriding.co.uk.
Contact/s
Owner: Mrs J Gabb
Profile Horse/Rider Accom, Riding School. B & B. Offers hacking from £17.00 and a livery service, telephone for further information. Yr. Est: 1978
Opening Times
Sp: Open Mon - Sun 08:00. Closed Mon - Sun 18:00.
Su: Open Mon - Sun 08:00. Closed Mon - Sun 20:00.
Au: Open Mon - Sun 08:00. Closed Mon - Sun 18:00.
Wn: Open Mon - Sun 08:00. Closed Mon - Sun 17:00. **Ref: YH02534**

CAREY, D N

Mr D N Carey, Berllanhelyg Cottage, Tregare, Raglan, **Monmouthshire**, NP15 2BZ, **WALES**.
(T) 01495 310794
(M) 07889 248578.
Profile Supplies. **Ref: YH02535**

CAREY, R G

R G Carey, 2 Sawpits, Hooe, Battle, **Sussex (East)**, TN33 9HR, **ENGLAND**.
(T) 01424 892051.
Contact/s
Owner: Mr R Carey
Profile Wheelwright, Joiner, Indoor Driving Centre.
Ref: YH02536

CAREYS

Careys, Commercial Hse, King St, Southwell, **Nottinghamshire**, NG25 0EH, **ENGLAND**.
(T) 01636 813064 **(F)** 01636 813064.
Profile Supplies. **Ref: YH02537**

CARGO RIDING CTRE

Cargo Riding Centre, Cargo, Carlisle, **Cumbria**, CA6 4AW, **ENGLAND**.
(T) 01228 674300 **(F)** 01228 6743000
Affiliated Bodies BHS, Pony Club UK.
Contact/s
Owner: Miss J Weedall **(Q)** BHSAI
Profile Riding School, Stable/Livery.
Full livery available, prices on request. No.Staff: 5
Yr. Est: 1973 C.Size: 25 Acres
Opening Times
Sp: Open Mon - Sun 09:00. Closed Mon - Sun 17:00.
Su: Open Mon - Sun 09:00. Closed Mon - Sun 17:00.
Au: Open Mon - Sun 09:00. Closed Mon - Sun 17:00.
Wn: Open Mon - Sun 09:00. Closed Mon - Sun 17:00. **Ref: YH02538**

CARL BROWN HORSE TRANSPORT

Carl Brown Horse Transport, Cherry Tree Cottage,

Bilbrough, York, **Yorkshire (North)**, YO23 3PH, **ENGLAND**.
(T) 01937 530100 **(F)** 01937 530100
(M) 07860 307329.
Profile Transport/Horse Boxes. **Ref: YH02539**

CARLISLE RACECOURSE

Carlisle Racecourse Co Ltd, Durdar Rd, Carlisle, **Cumbria**, CA2 4TS, **ENGLAND**.
(T) 01228 522973 **(F)** 01228 591827.
Profile Track/Course. **Ref: YH02540**

CARLTON BANK STUD

Carlton Bank Stud, Carlton-In-Cleveland, Stokesley, **Yorkshire (North)**, TS9 7DB, **ENGLAND**.
(T) 01642 710627.
Profile Breeder. **Ref: YH02541**

CARLTON FOREST

Carlton Forest Equestrian Centre, Blyth Rd, Carlton Forest, Worksop, **Nottinghamshire**, S81 0TP, **ENGLAND**.
(T) 01909 731221.
Contact/s
Partner: Miss S Jowett
Profile Riding School, Saddlery Retailer, Stable/Livery. **Ref: YH02542**

CARLTON FORGE

Carlton Forge, 24 Hornsea Rd, Aldbrough, Hull, **Yorkshire (East)**, HU11 4QW, **ENGLAND**.
(T) 01964 527003 **(F)** 01964 527003.
Contact/s
Owner: Mr M Pugh-Roberts
Profile Blacksmith. **Ref: YH02543**

CARLTON STUD

Carlton Stud, Fields Farm, Egerton, Malpas, **Cheshire**, SY14 8AN, **ENGLAND**.
(T) 01829 720356.
Profile Breeder. **Ref: YH02544**

CARLTONS THE FEED MERCHANTS

Carltons The Feed Merchants, 1-3 Co-Operative Buildings, Seaton Delaval, Whitley Bay, **Tyne and Wear**, NE25 0AS, **ENGLAND**.
(T) 0191 2370615 **(F)** 0191 2374210.
Profile Feed Merchant. **Ref: YH02545**

CARMAN EQUESTRIAN SUPPLIES

Carman Equestrian Supplies, 593 Thornton Rd, Thornton, Bradford, **Yorkshire (West)**, BD13 3NW, **ENGLAND**.
(T) 01274 835333 **(F)** 01274 835222.
Contact/s
Owner: Mrs A Howell
Profile Supplies. **Ref: YH02546**

CARMARTHEN & PUMSAINT FARMERS

Carmarthen & Pumsaint Farmers Ltd (Llandeilo), The Stores, Ffairfach, Llandeilo, **Carmarthenshire**, SA19 6ST, **WALES**.
(T) 01558 822207.
Contact/s
Manager: Mr C Phillips
Profile Supplies. **Ref: YH02547**

CARMARTHEN & PUMSAINT FARMERS

Carmarthen & Pumsaint Farmers Ltd, Cawdor Stores, Car Pk, Kings Rd, Llandovery, **Carmarthenshire**, SA20 0AW, **WALES**.
(T) 01550 720347.
Contact/s
Manager: Mr E Phillips
Profile Supplies. **Ref: YH02548**

CARMARTHEN & PUMSAINT FARMERS

Carmarthen & Pumsaint Farmers Ltd, Cillefwr Ind Est, Johnstown, Carmarthen, **Carmarthenshire**, SA31 3RA, **WALES**.
(T) 01267 236794 **(F)** 01267 230721.
Contact/s
Manager: Mr H Morris
Profile Supplies. **Ref: YH02549**

CARMARTHEN & PUMSAINT FARMERS

Carmarthen & Pumsaint Farmers Ltd (Carmarthen), Town & Country Stores, Fair Lane, Carmarthen, **Carmarthenshire**, SA31 1RX, **WALES**.
(T) 01267 236185.
Profile Supplies. **Ref: YH02550**

CARMARTHEN & PUMSAINT FARMERS

Carmarthen & Pumsaint Farmers Ltd (Kidwelly), Pembrey Rd, Kidwelly, **Carmarthenshire**, SA17 4TF, **WALES**.
(T) 01554 890220.
Profile Supplies. **Ref: YH02551**

CARMARTHEN & PUMSAINT FARMERS

Carmarthen & Pumsaint Farmers Ltd (Llanbydder), Sheffield Stores, Llanybydder, **Carmarthenshire**, SA40 9XS, **WALES**.
(T) 01570 480207.
Profile Supplies. **Ref: YH02552**

CARMARTHEN & PUMSAINT FARMERS

Carmarthen & Pumsaint Farmers Ltd (Llangadog), Station Rd, Llangadog, **Carmarthenshire**, SA19 9LS, **WALES**.
(T) 01550 777281.
Contact/s
Manager: Mr L Morgan
Profile Supplies. **Ref: YH02553**

CARMARTHEN & PUMSAINT FARMERS

Carmarthen & Pumsaint Farmers Ltd (Nantgaredig), The Stores, Station Rd, Nantgaredig, Carmarthen, **Carmarthenshire**, SA32 7LQ, **WALES**.
(T) 01267 290202.
Profile Supplies. **Ref: YH02554**

CARMARTHEN & PUMSAINT FARMERS

Carmarthen & Pumsaint Farmers Ltd (Nr Talley), The Stores, Llansawel, Nr Talley, Llandeilo, **Carmarthenshire**, SA19 7JF, **WALES**.
(T) 01558 685203.
Profile Supplies. **Ref: YH02555**

CARMARTHEN & PUMSAINT FARMERS

Carmarthen & Pumsaint Farmers Ltd (St Clears), Market Stores, St Clears, **Carmarthenshire**, SA33 4AA, **WALES**.
(T) 01994 230208.
Contact/s
Manager: Mr M Jones
Profile Supplies. **Ref: YH02556**

CARMARTHEN & PUMSAINT FARMERS

Carmarthen & Pumsaint Farmers Ltd (Whitland), The Stores, Station Yard, Whitland, **Carmarthenshire**, SA34 0AP, **WALES**.
(T) 01994 240321.
Contact/s
Manager: Mr E Williams
Profile Supplies. **Ref: YH02557**

CARMARTHEN & PUMSAINT FARMERS

Carmarthen & Pumsaint Farmers Ltd (Pontardulais), Unit 1 Tyn Y Waun Trading Est, Hendy, Pontardulais, **Ceredigion**, SA4 1YL, **WALES**.
(T) 01792 884355.
Profile Supplies. **Ref: YH02558**

CARMARTHENSHIRE

Carmarthenshire Welsh Pony and Cob Association, Ffos-y-Bontbren, Penybryn, Cardigan, **Carmarthenshire**, SA43 3NN, **WALES**.
(T) 01239 615168
(W) www.welshponyandcob.com/~cwpca/indexm.htm.
Contact/s
Chairperson: Mr R Miller
(E) richard@heniarth.com
Profile Breeder, Club/Association. **Ref: YH02559**

CARMARTHENSHIRE CLGE

Carmarthenshire College, Sandy Rd, Pwll, Llanelli, **Carmarthenshire**, SA15 4DN, **WALES**.
(T) 01554 748000 **(F)** 01554 756088
(W) www.ccta.ac.uk.
Profile Equestrian Centre. College.
College offering equestrian related courses.
Ref: YH02560

CARMARTHENSHIRE CLGE

Carmarthenshire College of Technology & Art, Pibwrlwyd Campus, Carmarthen, **Carmarthenshire**, SA31 2NH, **WALES**.
(T) 01554 759165
(W) www.ccta.ac.uk.
Profile Equestrian Centre. College.
College offering equestrian related courses.
Ref: YH02561

CARNABY, IAN

Ian Carnaby, Abbotsbury Hse, 23 Station Rd, Nailsea, **Somerset (North)**, BS48 2PD, **ENGLAND**.
(T) 01275 855895 **(F)** 01275 855895. **Ref: YH02562**

CARNE RIDING STABLES

Carne Riding Stables, Ballask Carne, Kilrane, Wexford, **County Wexford**, **IRELAND**.
(T) 053 31185.
Contact/s
Owner: Desmond Ellard
Profile Equestrian Centre. Trekking Centre.
Offer half hour, hour and two hour treks along Carne Beach and through the surrounding countryside.
Opening Times
Open seven days a week between May - September.
Ref: YH02563

CARNEGIE & LINDSAY

Carnegie & Lindsay, Capontree Veterinary Ctre, Greenhill, Brampton, **Cumbria**, CA8 1SU, **ENGLAND**.
(T) 01697 72318 **(F)** 01697 741088.
Profile Medical Support. **Ref: YH02564**

CARNELL, R F

R F Carnell, Fairview, Park Hill, Ipplepen, Newton Abbot, **Devon**, TQ12 5TU, **ENGLAND**.
(T) 01803 812404 **(F)** 01803 812404.
Contact/s
Owner: Mr R Carnell
Profile Farrier. **Ref: YH02565**

CARO, D J

Mr D J Caro, Lilly Hill Farm, Little Marcle, Ledbury, **Herefordshire**, HR8 2LD, **ENGLAND**.
(T) 01531 631559 **(F)** 01531 634049.
Contact/s
Owner: Denis J Caro
Profile Trainer. **Ref: YH02566**

CAROE, C J E

Miss C J E Caroe, Park End Farm, Robins Folly, Thurleigh, **Bedfordshire**, MK44 2EQ, **ENGLAND**.
(T) 01234 771113
(M) 07974 483469.
Profile Trainer. **Ref: YH02567**

CARPENTER, E J

E J Carpenter, The Meads, Barnham Lane, Walberton, Arundel, **Sussex (West)**, BN18 0AX, **ENGLAND**.
(T) 01243 542016.
Contact/s
Owner: Mr E Carpenter
Profile Stable/Livery. **Ref: YH02568**

CARR & DAY & MARTIN

Carr & Day & Martin Ltd, Lloyds Hse, Alderley Rd, Wilmslow, **Cheshire**, SK9 1QT, **ENGLAND**.
(T) 01625 545200 **(F)** 01625 548488.
Contact/s
Manager: Mr R Donallon
Profile Riding Wear Retailer, Saddlery Retailer.
Ref: YH02569

CARR, J M

J M Carr, 18 Whitewall, Norton, Malton, **Yorkshire (North)**, YO17 9EH, **ENGLAND**.
(T) 01653 694671.
Contact/s
Owner: Mr J Carr
Profile Trainer. **Ref: YH02570**

CARR, PHILIP JOHN

Philip John Carr RSS, Greenhills, West Anstey, South Molton, **Devon**, EX36 3NU, **ENGLAND**.
(T) 01398 341300.
Profile Farrier. **Ref: YH02571**

CARR, R R

R R Carr, Northlands Farm, Northlands, Bodiam, Robertsbridge, **Sussex (East)**, TN32 5UX, **ENGLAND**.
(T) 01580 830789 **(F)** 01580 830789.
Contact/s
Owner: Mr R Carr
Profile Trainer. **Ref: YH02572**

CARR, RENEE

Mrs Renee Carr, Newstead Farm, Black Bank, Messingham Common, Susworth, Scunthorpe, **Lincolnshire**, DN17 3AX, **ENGLAND**.
(T) 01724 763233.
Profile Breeder. **Ref: YH02573**

CARR, S J

S J Carr, Brookside Farm, Sheffield Rd, Creswell, Worksop, **Nottinghamshire**, S80 4HN, **ENGLAND**.
(T) 01909 721279 **(F)** 01909 721279.
Contact/s
Owner: Mr S Carr
Profile Stable/Livery. **Ref: YH02574**

CARR, W

Mr W Carr, Greenhead Farm, Corporal Lane, Northowram, Halifax, **Yorkshire (West)**, HX3 7TE, **ENGLAND**.
(T) 01274 815263.
Profile Breeder. **Ref: YH02575**

CARRALEIGH DARTMOORS

Carraleigh Dartmoors, Churnmilk Farmhouse,

Brettenham Rd, Buxhall, Stowmarket, **Suffolk**, IP14 3DZ, **ENGLAND**.
(T) 01449 737668.
Profile Breeder. **Ref: YH02576**

CARRBRIDGE PONY TREKKING CTRE

Carrbridge Pony Trekking Centre, Ellan Hse, Carrbridge, **Highlands**, PH23 3AN, **SCOTLAND**.
(T) 01479 841602.
Profile Riding School. **Ref: YH02577**

CARREG DRESSAGE

Carreg Dressage, Penegoes, Machynlleth, **Powys**, SY20 8NW, **WALES**.
(T) 01650 511222 **(F)** 01650 511800.
Contact/s
Partner: Ms J Lloyd-Francis
Profile Trainer.
Dressage yard **Ref: YH02578**

CARR-EVANS, JEANETTE

Mrs Jeanette Carr-Evans, 8 Southbrook Cottages, Bayford, Wincanton, **Somerset**, BA9 9NL, **ENGLAND**.
(T) 01963 34860.
Profile Breeder. **Ref: YH02579**

CARRIAGE CONNECTIONS

Carriage Connections, Burrs Hill Farm, Hastings Rd, Marden, **Kent**, TN12 9BS, **ENGLAND**.
(T) 01622 831800 **(F)** 01622 831800.
Profile Horse Drawn Vehicles. **Ref: YH02580**

CARRIAGE OCCASIONS

Carriage Occasions, Conifers, Green Lane, Red Lodge, **Suffolk**, IP28 8LD, **ENGLAND**.
(T) 01638 751740 **(F)** 01638 751740
(E) button@freenet.co.uk
(W) www.carriage-occasions.co.uk.
Profile Horse Drawn Vehicles.
Carriage hire for Weddings and Special Occasions.
Yr. Est: 1991
Opening Times
Telephone for further information **Ref: YH02581**

CARRIAGEHOUSE INSURANCE

Carriagehouse Insurance Services, Spring Farm, Stratford St Mary, Colchester, **Essex**, CO7 6NB, **ENGLAND**.
(T) 01206 337388 **(F)** 01206 337422
(E) horseinsurance@carriagehouse.sagehost.co.uk.
Profile Supplies. Insurance service. **Ref: YH02582**

CARRIAGES

Carriages, Plumbersknowe Cottage, Innerleithen, **Scottish Borders**, EH44 6PS, **SCOTLAND**.
(T) 01721 722807.
Contact/s
Owner: Ms J Baine
Profile Transport/Horse Boxes. Horse drawn vehicles.
Ref: YH02583

CARRIAGEWAY STABLES

Carriageway Stables, Hamilton Rd, Newmarket, **Suffolk**, CB8 7JQ, **ENGLAND**.
(T) 01638 664292 **(F)** 01638 561186
(E) sarah.kelleway@virgin.net.
Contact/s
Trainer: Miss S Kelleway
Profile Breeder, Trainer. **Ref: YH02584**

CARRICK, CHARLES W

Mr Charles W Carrick, Easter Littleward, Kippen, **Stirling**, FK8 3QT, **SCOTLAND**.
(T) 01786 870308.
Profile Breeder. **Ref: YH02585**

CARRICKMACROSS SCHOOL

Carrickmacross School of Equitation, Drumconrath Rd, Carrickmacross, **County Monaghan**, **IRELAND**.
(T) 042 9661017. **Ref: YH02586**

CARRICKMINES EQUESTRIAN CTRE

Carrickmines Equestrian Centre, Glenamuck Rd, Foxrock, Dublin, **County Dublin**, **IRELAND**.
(T) 01 2955990
(E) info@carrickminesequestrian.ie
(W) www.carrickminesequestrian.ie.
Contact/s
Instructor: Bernadette Kennedy **(Q)** BHSAI
Profile Riding School, Stable/Livery.
The centre's outdoor ménage, at 100m by 50m, is one of the largest all weather equestrian arenas in Ireland.
C.Size: 80 Acres
Opening Times
Sp: Open Tues - Fri 15:30, Sat, Sun 10:00. Closed Tues, Thur 20:45, Wed 21:00, Fri 16:30, Sat 17:00, Sun 15:00.
Su: Open Tues - Fri 15:30, Sat, Sun 10:00. Closed Tues, Thur 20:45, Wed 21:00, Fri 16:30, Sat 17:00, Sun 15:00.
Au: Open Tues - Fri 15:30, Sat, Sun 10:00. Closed Tues, Thur 20:45, Wed 21:00, Fri 16:30, Sat 17:00, Sun 15:00.
Wn: Open Tues - Fri 15:30, Sat, Sun 10:00. Closed Tues, Thur 20:45, Wed 21:00, Fri 16:30, Sat 17:00, Sun 15:00.
Closed Mondays. Private tuition can be arranged on weekdays. **Ref: YH02587**

CARRIGBEG RIDING SCHOOL

Carrigbeg Riding School, Carrigbeg, Bagenalstown, **County Carlow**, **IRELAND**.
(T) 0503 21962.
Contact/s
Owner: Mrs S Patterson
Profile Riding School.
Telephone for further information and to book lesson times.
Opening Times
Closed Sundays **Ref: YH02588**

CARRINGTON RIDING

Carrington Riding Centre Ltd, Nursery Farm, Isherwood Rd, Carrington, Manchester, **Manchester (Greater)**, M31 4BH, **ENGLAND**.
(T) 0161 9695853 **(F)** 0161 9051416
(E) horseriding@supanet.com
Affiliated Bodies ABRS, BHS.
Contact/s
General Manager: Ms J Harrison
(Q) BA(Hons), BHSAI **(T)** 0161 9053006
(E) julia-h@supanet.com
Profile Arena, Equestrian Centre, Riding School, Stable/Livery.
Livery available, details on request. No.Staff: 8
Yr. Est: 1975 C.Size: 40 Acres
Opening Times
Sp: Open Mon - Sun 09:00. Closed Tues - Thurs 22:00, Fri 20:00, Sat, Sun 19:00.
Su: Open Mon - Sun 09:00. Closed Tues - Thurs 22:00, Fri 20:00, Sat, Sun 19:00.
Au: Open Mon - Sun 09:00. Closed Tues - Thurs 22:00, Fri 20:00, Sat, Sun 19:00.
Wn: Open Mon - Sun 09:00. Closed Tues - Thurs 22:00, Fri 20:00, Sat, Sun 19:00. **Ref: YH02589**

CARRINGTON, WALTER

Mr Walter Carrington MSTAT, 18 Lansdowne Rd, London, **London (Greater)**, W11 3LL, **ENGLAND**.
(T) 020 77277222.
Profile Trainer. **Ref: YH02590**

CARRINGTON-SYKES

Carrington-Sykes, Pentre Bach, Llandynog, Denbigh, **Denbighshire**, LL16 4LA, **WALES**.
(T) 01824 790725.
Profile Stable/Livery. **Ref: YH02591**

CARROLL, A W

Mr A W Carroll, Mill Hse, Kington, Ely Ford, Flavell, **Worcestershire**, WR7 4DG, **ENGLAND**.
(T) 01386 793459 **(F)** 01386 793459.
Profile Trainer. **Ref: YH02592**

CARROLL, MICHAEL J

Carroll Michael J, Sopwell, Cloughjordan, **County Tipperary**, **IRELAND**.
(T) 050 542109.
Profile Supplies. **Ref: YH02593**

CARRON ROW STABLES

Carron Row Stables, Carron Row Farm, 15 Segensworth Rd, Fareham, **Hampshire**, PO15 5DZ, **ENGLAND**.
(T) 01329 843452.
Contact/s
Manager: Miss K Bean
Profile Stable/Livery. Riding stables. **Ref: YH02594**

CARROWDORE SADDLERY

Carrowdore Saddlery, 24 Manse Rd, Carrowdore, Newtownards, **County Down**, BT22 2EZ, **NORTHERN IRELAND**.
(T) 028 91861578 **(F)** 028 91862311.
Contact/s
Owner: Mrs B Mekee
Profile Saddlery Retailer. **Ref: YH02595**

CARRS AGRICULTURE

Carrs Agriculture Ltd, Montgomery Way, Rosehill Est, Carlisle, **Cumbria**, CA1 2UY, **ENGLAND**.
(T) 01228 520212 **(F)** 01228 512572.
Profile Supplies. **Ref: YH02596**

CARRS AGRICULTURE

Carrs Agriculture Ltd (Penrith), Haweswater Rd, Penrith, **Cumbria**, CA11 9EH, **ENGLAND**.
(T) 01768 866354 **(F)** 01768 899345.
Profile Supplies. **Ref: YH02597**

CARRS BILLINGTON

Carrs Billington, Pendle Mill, Mill Lane, Gisburn, Clitheroe, **Lancashire**, BB7 4ES, **ENGLAND**.
(T) 01200 445491.
Contact/s
Store Supervisor: Mrs A Pye
Profile Supplies. **Ref: YH02598**

CARRS BILLINGTON

Carrs Billington, Unit 1 Brock Hols Way, Claughton-on-Brock, Preston, **Lancashire**, PR3 0PZ, **ENGLAND**.
(T) 01995 643200.
Contact/s
Store Supervisor: Miss H Rothwell
Profile Supplies. **Ref: YH02599**

CARRUTHERS ROSETTE

Carruthers Rosette Co, Garchell Farm, Balfron Station, **Stirling**, G63 0QY, **SCOTLAND**.
(T) 01360 850289.
Profile Supplies. **Ref: YH02600**

CARRUTHERS, RICHARD

Richard Carruthers BHSI, Forest Gate Farm, Delamare Rd, Norley, Frodsham, **Cheshire**, WA6 6NF, **ENGLAND**.
(T) 01928 787610.
Contact/s
Owner: Mr R Carruthers **(Q)** BHSI
Profile Trainer. C.Size: 30 Acres
Opening Times
Telephone for an appointment **Ref: YH02601**

CARRY ON RIDING STABLES

Carry on Riding Stables, 407 Birmingham Rd, Hertford Hill, Warwick, **Warwickshire**, CV35 7DZ, **ENGLAND**.
(T) 01926 492477.
Profile Stable/Livery. **Ref: YH02602**

CARRYON QUARTER HORSES

Carryon Quarter Horses, 7 Whitehall Way, Sellindge, Ashford, **Kent**, TN25 6ET, **ENGLAND**.
(T) 01303 814879 **(F)** 01303 814879
(E) jane@carryonqh.co.uk.
Profile Breeder. **Ref: YH02603**

CARSON, ROBERT

Mr Robert Carson, 58 Child St, Lambourn, Hungerford, **Berkshire**, RG17 8NZ, **ENGLAND**.
(T) 01488 72080.
Profile Supplies. **Ref: YH02604**

CARSTAIRS, H

Miss H Carstairs, Bargate Cottage, Gleneagles, Auchterarder, **Perth and Kinross**, PH3 1PJ, **SCOTLAND**.
(T) 01764 682207.
Profile Trainer. **Ref: YH02605**

CARTER, EDWARD

Edward Carter, Busherstown, **County Carlow**, **IRELAND**.
(T) 050 343538.
Contact/s
Owner: Edward Carter
Profile Breeder, Stable/Livery. **Ref: YH02606**

CARTER, J

Mr & Mrs J Carter, Millcroft Farm, Dawlish, **Devon**, EX7 0QU, **ENGLAND**.
(T) 01626 863154.
Profile Breeder, Supplies. **Ref: YH02607**

CARTER, S M

Mrs S M Carter, Billhay Farm, Semley, Shaftesbury, **Dorset**, SP7 9BP, **ENGLAND**.
(T) 01747 830540.
Profile Supplies. **Ref: YH02608**

CARTHORPE PONY TREKKING

Carthorpe Pony Trekking, Hall Garth Farm, Carthorpe, Bedale, **Yorkshire (North)**, DL8 2LD, **ENGLAND**.
(T) 01845 567204.
Contact/s
Owner: Mr M Trewhitt
Profile Equestrian Centre. Trekking centre.
Ref: YH02609

CARTMEL RACECOURSE

Cartmel Racecourse, Cartmel, Grange-Over-Sands, **Cumbria**, LA11 6QF, **ENGLAND**.
(T) 01539 536340 **(F)** 01539 536004.
Contact/s
General Manager: Mr C Barnett

Profile Track/Course. Ref:YH02610

CARTMELL, L A

L A Cartmell, 20 Newbury St, Lambourn, **Berkshire**, RG17 8PF, **ENGLAND**.
(T) 01488 71985.
Profile Farrier. Ref:YH02611

CARTWHEEL TRAILERS

Cartwheel Trailers, Lovel Rd, Chalfont St. Peter, Gerrards Cross, **Buckinghamshire**, SL9 9NW, **ENGLAND**.
(T) 01494 871262.
Contact/s
Owner: Mr L Savill
Profile Transport/Horse Boxes. Ref:YH02612

CASE, BENJAMIN

Mr Benjamin Case, Edgcote Hse, Edgcote, Banbury, **Oxfordshire**, OX17 1AG, **ENGLAND**.
(T) 01295 660909 (F) 01295 660908.
Contact/s
Owner: Mr B Case
Profile Trainer. Ref:YH02613

CASEY, DAVID L

David L Casey DWCF, Woodlands, Howfield Lane, Chartham Hatch, Canterbury, **Kent**, CT4 7LZ, **ENGLAND**.
(T) 01227 731046.
Profile Farrier. Ref:YH02614

CASEY, M L

M L Casey, Bigberry Farm, Bigberry Rd, Chartham Hatch, Canterbury, **Kent**, CT4 7NE, **ENGLAND**.
(T) 01227 738524.
Profile Equestrian Centre. Cross Country/Trekking Centre. Ref:YH02615

CASEY, W T

Mr W T Casey, Henfold Hse Cottage, Henfold Lane, Beare Green, Dorking, **Surrey**, RH5 4RW, **ENGLAND**.
(T) 01306 631529 (F) 01306 631529.
Profile Trainer. Ref:YH02616

CASON, P

P Cason, 18 Bertha St, Ferryhill, Durham, **County Durham**, DL17 8AZ, **ENGLAND**.
(T) 01740 652163.
Profile Farrier. Ref:YH02617

CASPIAN HORSE

Caspian Horse Society (The), 6 Nuns Walk, Virginia Water, **Surrey**, GU25 4RT, **ENGLAND**.
(T) 01344 843325.
Profile Breeder, Club/Association. Ref:YH02618

CASPIAN PONY SOC

Caspian Pony Society, Sparrow Farm, Lanhill, Chippenham, **Wiltshire**, SN14 6LX, **ENGLAND**.
(T) 01249 782246 (F) 01249 782256.
Contact/s
Key Contact: Mrs J Scott
Profile Club/Association. Ref:YH02619

CASSERLY, ANDREW

Andrew Casserly, Gunbanks Farm, Pounsley, Blackboys, Uckfield, **Sussex (East)**, TN22 5HS, **ENGLAND**.
(T) 01825 830627.
Profile Farrier. Ref:YH02620

CASSIDY EQUESTRIAN

Cassidy Equestrian, Warrington Rd, Comberbach, Northwich, **Cheshire**, CW9 6AY, **ENGLAND**.
(T) 01606 892700 (F) 01606 892700.
Contact/s
Partner: Mrs S Cassidy
Profile Saddlery Retailer. Ref:YH02621

CASSIE'S STORES

Cassie's Stores, Rolle Quay, Barnstaple, **Devon**, EX31 1JD, **ENGLAND**.
(T) 01271 346198.
Contact/s
Owner: Mr P Cassinelli Ref:YH02622

CASTELLAN RIDING ACADEMY

Castellan Riding Academy, Blaenffos, Boncath, **Pembrokeshire**, SA37 0HZ, **WALES**.
(T) 01239 841644.
Profile Equestrian Centre. Ref:YH02623

CASTLE FORGE

Castle Forge, New Rd, Sherborne, **Dorset**, DT9 5NR, **ENGLAND**.
(T) 01935 815357 (F) 01935 815357.
Contact/s
Owner: Mr N Willdig
Profile Blacksmith. Ref:YH02624

CASTLE FORGE

Castle Forge, Castle Farm, Wadhurst, **Sussex (East)**, TN5 6DA, **ENGLAND**.
(T) 01892 784482.
Contact/s
Owner: Mr A Powell
Profile Blacksmith. Ref:YH02625

CASTLE HILL EQUESTRIAN CTRE

Castle Hill Equestrian Centre Ltd, Briarlieas, Julianstown, **County Meath**, **IRELAND**.
(T) 041 9829430. Ref:YH02626

CASTLE HILL RIDING SCHOOL

Castle Hill Riding School, Main St, Brandon, Coventry, **Midlands (West)**, CV8 3HQ, **ENGLAND**.
(T) 024 76542762
Affiliated Bodies BHS.
Contact/s
Owner: Mrs P Potter
Profile Riding School, Stable/Livery.
Castle Hill has a range of facilities from changing rooms to lecture rooms. The school offers full/part livery and it has an all weather gallop. Training for exams to BHS level.
Opening Times
Sp: Open 09:00. Closed 17:00.
Su: Open 09:00. Closed 17:00.
Au: Open 09:00. Closed 17:00.
Wn: Open 09:00. Closed 17:00. Ref:YH02627

CASTLE HILL TRAILERS

Castle Hill Trailers, Homestead Farm, Palmers Green Lane, Brenchley, Tonbridge, **Kent**, TN12 7BH, **ENGLAND**.
(T) 01892 722186.
Contact/s
Partner: Mrs M McNulty
Profile Transport/Horse Boxes. Ref:YH02628

CASTLE HORSEBOXES

Castle Horseboxes Ltd, Whitehouse Farm, Beech Tree Lane, Ismere, Kidderminster, **Worcestershire**, DY10 3NT, **ENGLAND**.
(T) 01562 700003
(W) www.castlehorseboxes.co.uk.
Contact/s
Owner: Mr G Knight
Profile Transport/Horse Boxes. Ref:YH02629

CASTLE PIECE RACING STABLES

Castle Piece Racing Stables, Eastbury, Lambourn, Hungerford, **Berkshire**, RG17 7JR, **ENGLAND**.
(T) 01488 726637.
Profile Trainer. Ref:YH02630

CASTLE RIDING CTRE

Castle Riding Centre & Argyll Trail Riding, Brenfield, Ardrishaig, Lochgilphead, **Argyll and Bute**, PA30 8ER, **SCOTLAND**.
(T) 01546 603274 (F) 01546 603225
(E) info@brenfield.demon.co.uk
(W) www.brenfield.co.uk.
Contact/s
Instructor: Ms L McDonald
Profile Horse/Rider Accom, Riding School.
Opening Times
By appointment only Ref:YH02631

CASTLE ROSETTES

Castle Rosettes, 32 Atwell Cl, Wallingford, **Oxfordshire**, OX10 1LJ, **ENGLAND**.
(T) 01491 836192 (F) 01491 836192.
Profile Suppliers of Rosettes. Ref:YH02632

CASTLE SADDLERY

Castle Saddlery Ltd, Hendra Farm, Liskeard, **Cornwall**, PL14 3LJ, **ENGLAND**.
(T) 01579 344998.
Contact/s
Owner: Mr R Heaton
Profile Saddlery Retailer. Ref:YH02633

CASTLE SMITHY

Castle Smithy, Castle Chain Hse, Castle Chain, Pontefract, **Yorkshire (West)**, WF8 1QH, **ENGLAND**.
(T) 01977 602881.
Contact/s
Partner: Mr K Holden
Profile Blacksmith. Ref:YH02634

CASTLE STABLES

Castle Stables, Cholmondeley, Malpas, **Cheshire**, SY14 8AL, **ENGLAND**.
(T) 01829 720320 (F) 01829 720505.
Contact/s
Owner: Mrs J Hall
Profile Riding School, Stable/Livery. Ref:YH02635

CASTLE STABLES

Castle Stables, London Rd, Arundel, **Sussex (West)**, BN18 9LL, **ENGLAND**.
(T) 01903 882194.
Profile Breeder, Trainer. Ref:YH02636

CASTLE STABLES

Castle Stables, Gatherley Rd, Brompton On Swale, Richmond, **Yorkshire (North)**, DL10 7JN, **ENGLAND**.
(T) 01748 811570
(M) 07768 436678.
Profile Trainer. Ref:YH02637

CASTLE VETNRY GRP

Castle Veterinary Group, The Surgery, Pennygillam Way, Launceston, **Cornwall**, PL15 7ED, **ENGLAND**.
(T) 01566 772371 (F) 01566 777465.
Profile Medical Support. Ref:YH02638

CASTLE VETNRY SURGEONS

Castle Veterinary Surgeons, Montalbo Rd, Barnard Castle, Durham, **County Durham**, DL12 8ED, **ENGLAND**.
(T) 01833 695695 (F) 01833 690085.
Profile Medical Support. Ref:YH02639

CASTLEBROOK STABLES

Castlebrook Stables, Castle Rd, Bury, **Lancashire**, BL9 8QR, **ENGLAND**.
(T) 0161 7961066.
Contact/s
Owner: Mr A Dampier Ref:YH02640

CASTLECOOTE STORES

Castlecoote Stores, Castlecoote, Roscommon, **County Roscommon**, **IRELAND**.
(T) 090 363394.
Profile Supplies. Ref:YH02641

CASTLEFERGUS RIDING STABLES

Castlefergus Riding Stables, Quin, **County Clare**, **IRELAND**.
(T) 065 6825914.
Profile Supplies. Ref:YH02642

CASTLEHILL EQUESTRIAN CTRE

Castlehill Equestrian Centre, 86A Fenaghy Rd, Cullybackey, Ballymena, **County Antrim**, BT42 1EA, **NORTHERN IRELAND**.
(T) 028 25881222.
Contact/s
General Manager: Beverley Miller
Profile Riding School, Stable/Livery. Ref:YH02643

CASTLEMARTIN STUD

Castlemartin Stud, Kildare, **County Kildare**, **IRELAND**.
(T) 045 481335 (F) 045 481739
(E) cmstud@iol.ie
(W) www.castlemartinstud.com.
Contact/s
Key Contact: Mr J Kelly
Profile Breeder. Ref:YH02644

CASTLEMORRIS FEEDS

Castlemorris Feeds, Pencnwc Farm, Castlemorris, Haverfordwest, **Pembrokeshire**, SA62 5ER, **WALES**.
(T) 01348 840210 (F) 01248 840911.
Profile Feed Merchant, Saddlery Retailer.
Ref:YH02645

CASTLEWHITE

Castlewhite Riding Centre, The Viaduct, Waterfall, Cork, **County Cork**, **IRELAND**.
(T) 021 4870684
(M) 078 2747053
Affiliated Bodies AIRE.
Contact/s
Owner: Ms K Fitton
Profile Arena, Blacksmith, Breeder, Equestrian Centre, Farrier, Riding Club, Riding School, Stable/Livery, Trainer.
Have a battery operated wheelchair hoist for the RDAI
No.Staff: 3 Yr. Est: 1985 C.Size: 10 Acres
Opening Times
Open all year Ref:YH02646

CASTLEWOOD LIVERY

Castlewood Livery, Castlewood, Barrow Green, Teynham, Sittingbourne, **Kent**, ME9 9EA, **ENGLAND**.
(T) 01795 521959.
Contact/s
Owner: Ms I French
Profile Stable/Livery. Ref:YH02647

CASWELL, LESLEY
Ms Lesley Caswell, Henton Arabians, Henton, Chinnor, **Oxfordshire**, OX9 4AE, **ENGLAND**.
(T) 01844 353396
(M) 07831 877358.
Profile Supplies. **Ref: YH02648**

CATHERINE WRIGHT
Catherine Wright Limited, 2 Marsh Rd, Shabbington, Aylesbury, **Buckinghamshire**, HP18 9HF, **ENGLAND**.
(T) 01844 208041
(W) www.westerninstructor.co.uk.
Contact/s
Owner: Ms C Wright
(E) catherinelwright@netscapeonline.co.uk
Profile Trainer. Western Riding Instructor (Freelance). Show horses at Western competitions. **Ref: YH02649**

CATHERSTON
Catherston Stud, Croft Farm, Over Wallop, Stockbridge, **Hampshire**, SO20 8HX, **ENGLAND**.
(T) 01264 782716 **(F)** 01264 782717
(E) info@catherstonstud.com
(W) www.stallionsdirect.com/studs/catherston.
Contact/s
Owner: Mr A Loriston-Clarke **(Q)** BHS Int SM
Profile Trainer.
Offers training to Grand Prix level and above.Tuition and schooling (not breaking) on own horse.
Ref: YH02650

CATHIRON FARM LIVERY STABLES
Cathiron Farm Livery Stables, Cathiron Farm, Cathiron, Rugby, **Warwickshire**, CV23 0JH, **ENGLAND**.
(T) 01788 833039. **Ref: YH02651**

CATLEY'S FARM SUPPLIES
Catley's Farm Supplies, The Green, Devizes, **Wiltshire**, SN10 1LY, **ENGLAND**.
(T) 01380 723351.
Contact/s
Owner: G Day
Profile Feed Merchant. **Ref: YH02652**

CATLIPS FARM LIVERY STABLES
Catlips Farm Livery Stables, Catlips Farm, Berry Lane, Chorleywood, Rickmansworth, **Hertfordshire**, WD3 5EU, **ENGLAND**.
(T) 01923 282213.
Contact/s
Owner: Mrs S Betle
Profile Stable/Livery. **Ref: YH02653**

CATRIDGE FARM STUD
Catridge Farm Stud Ltd, Catridge Farm, Wick Lane, Lacock, Chippenham, **Wiltshire**, SN15 2LU, **ENGLAND**.
(T) 01249 730355 **(F)** 01249 730355.
Contact/s
Manager: Mr D Powell
Profile Breeder. **Ref: YH02654**

CATTERICK RACECOURSE
Catterick Racecourse Co Ltd, The Racecourse, Catterick Village, Richmond, **Yorkshire (North)**, DL10 7PE, **ENGLAND**.
(T) 01748 811478 **(F)** 01748 811082.
Profile Track/Course. **Ref: YH02655**

CATTON HALL COMBINED TRAINING
Catton Hall Combined Training, The Old Hse, Deans Lade Farm, Lichfield, **Staffordshire**, WS14 0AG, **ENGLAND**.
(T) 01543 256030. **Ref: YH02656**

CAUGHLEY PORCELAIN
Caughley Porcelain, Roden Hse, Shawbury, Shewsbury, **Shropshire**, SY4 4HP, **ENGLAND**.
(T) 01939 250337 **(F)** 01939 251019.
Profile Artist and sculptor. **Ref: YH02657**

CAULDWELL LIVERY STABLES
Cauldwell Livery Stables, Cauldwell Rd, Sutton-In-Ashfield, **Nottinghamshire**, NG17 5LB, **ENGLAND**.
(T) 01623 511547 **(F)** 01623 511547.
Contact/s
Owner: Mrs J Daddswell
Profile Stable/Livery. **Ref: YH02658**

CAULFIELD, ANDREW M
Andrew M Caulfield, 23 Thistledown Drv, Ixworth, Bury St Edmunds, **Suffolk**, IP31 2NH, **ENGLAND**.
(T) 01359 232629.
Profile Supplies. **Ref: YH02659**

CAUNTON GRASS DRIERS
Caunton Grass Driers Ltd, Hockerton Rd, Caunton, Newark, **Nottinghamshire**, NG23 6BA, **ENGLAND**.
(T) 01636 636889 **(F)** 01636 636698
(E) info@sherwoodestates.co.uk.
Profile Supplies. Bedding manufacturers.
Ref: YH02660

CAUSER, W H
W H Causer, Unit 12 Century Pk, Garrison Lane, Birmingham, **Midlands (West)**, B9 4NZ, **ENGLAND**.
(T) 0121 7721853.
Contact/s
Owner: Mr W Causer
Profile Blacksmith. **Ref: YH02661**

CAUSEWAY EQUESTRIAN
Causeway Equestrian, 95 Causeway Lane, Rufford, Ormskirk, **Lancashire**, L40 1SL, **ENGLAND**.
(T) 01704 821151 **(F)** 01704 821151.
Contact/s
Owner: Mr D Pettit
Profile Riding Wear Retailer, Saddlery Retailer.
Ref: YH02662

CAVALRY BARN
Cavalry Barn, Highlands, Mill Lane, Aldington, Ashford, **Kent**, TN25 7AJ, **ENGLAND**.
(T) 01233 720719.
Profile Equestrian Centre. **Ref: YH02663**

CAVAN EQUESTRIAN CTRE
Cavan Equestrian Centre Ltd, Shalom Stables, Latt, Cavan, **County Cavan**, **IRELAND**.
(T) 049 4332017/ 4362798 **(F)** 049 4331400
(M) 088 573118.
Profile
Cavan Equestrian Centre stage major international showjumping events throughout the year. Hold six International Performance Sales throughout the year. Can also arrange treks throught the Killykeen Forest Park. **Ref: YH02664**

CAVELLO PK FARM
Cavello Park Farm, Newtown, Linford, **Leicestershire**, LE6 0HB, **ENGLAND**.
(T) 01530 242993.
Profile Breeder. **Ref: YH02665**

CAVEWOOD GRANGE ARABIANS
Cavewood Grange Arabians, Cavewood Grange, North Cave, Brough, **Yorkshire (East)**, HU15 2PE, **ENGLAND**.
(T) 01430 421127.
Profile Breeder. **Ref: YH02666**

CAWLEY PARTNERS
Cawley Partners, New Fosse Farm, Stone, East Pennard, Shepton Mallet, **Somerset**, BA4 6RY, **ENGLAND**.
(T) 01749 860005 **(F)** 01749 860004.
Contact/s
Partner: Mr F Cawley
Profile Hay and straw merchants. **Ref: YH02667**

CAWOOD, WILLIAM
William Cawood, Old Tillage Farm, Kirby Grindalythe, Malton, **Yorkshire (North)**, YO17 8DF, **ENGLAND**.
(T) 01944 738228.
Contact/s
Owner: Mr W Cawood
Profile Transport/Horse Boxes. **Ref: YH02668**

CAXTON NAME PLATE MFG
Caxton Name Plate Mfg Co Ltd, Kew Green, Richmond, **Surrey**, TW9 3AR, **ENGLAND**.
(T) 020 89400041 **(F)** 020 89400642. **Ref: YH02669**

CAYBERRY STUD
Cayberry Stud, Fox Covert, Thornton Steward, Ripon, **Yorkshire (North)**, HG4 4BQ, **ENGLAND**.
(T) 01677 450493.
Profile Breeder. **Ref: YH02670**

CECIL, H R A
H R A Cecil, Warren Pl, Moulton Rd, Newmarket, **Suffolk**, CB8 8QQ, **ENGLAND**.
(T) 01638 662192 **(F)** 01638 669005
(E) henry.cecil@dial.pipex.com
(W) www.newmarketracehorsetrainers.co.uk
Affiliated Bodies Newmarket Trainers Fed.
Contact/s
Owner: Mr H Cecil
Profile Trainer. **Ref: YH02671**

CECIL, JULIE
Julie Cecil, Southgate, Hamilton Rd, Newmarket, **Suffolk**, CB8 0NQ, **ENGLAND**.
(T) 01638 560634.
Profile Trainer. **Ref: YH02672**

CEDAR HEALTH
Cedar Health Ltd, Pepper Rd, Hazel Grove, **Cheshire**, SK7 5BW, **ENGLAND**.
(T) 0161 4831235 **(F)** 0161 4564321.
Profile Medical Support. **Ref: YH02673**

CEDAR POINT STABLES
Cedar Point Stables, Headley, Epsom, **Surrey**, KT18 6BH, **ENGLAND**.
(T) 01372 270225 **(F)** 01372 270225.
Profile Trainer. **Ref: YH02674**

CEDAR TREE STUD
Cedar Tree Stud, Wilbraham Rd, Six Mile Bottom, Newmarket, **Suffolk**, CB8 0UW, **ENGLAND**.
(T) 01638 70211.
Profile Breeder. **Ref: YH02675**

CEDAR VETNRY GRP
Cedar Veterinary Group (Alton), Clifton Veterinary Surgery, Anstey Lane, Alton, **Hampshire**, GU34 2RH, **ENGLAND**.
(T) 01420 82163 **(F)** 01420 544373.
Profile Medical Support. **Ref: YH02676**

CEFN GLAN STUD
Cefn Glan Stud, Rock Hill, Llanarthney, Carmarthen, **Carmarthenshire**, SA32 8LJ, **WALES**.
(T) 01267 290376 **(F)** 01267 290823.
Contact/s
Owner: Miss H Underwood
Profile Breeder. **Ref: YH02677**

CEFN LLOGELL RACING STABLES
Cefn Llogell Racing Stables, Coed Kernew, **Newport**, NP1 9UD, **WALES**.
(T) 01633 680978 **(F)** 01633 680850.
Profile Trainer. **Ref: YH02678**

CELT 'N' GAEL CTRE
Celt 'n' Gael Centre, Celt N Gael Ctre, Gwalchmai, Holyhead, **Isle of Anglesey**, LL65 4RW, **WALES**.
(T) 01407 720072 **(F)** 01407 720880.
Profile Equestrian Centre. **Ref: YH02679**

CELTIC TRAILERS
Celtic Trailers Ltd, 25 New Rd, Skewen, Neath, **Glamorgan (Vale of)**, SA10 6UT, **WALES**.
(T) 01792 817777 **(F)** 01792 818333.
Profile Transport/Horse Boxes. **Ref: YH02680**

CENTAUR APPALOOSA STUD
Centaur Appaloosa Stud, Cold Newton Rd, Cold Newton, Leicester, **Leicestershire**, LE7 9DA, **ENGLAND**.
(T) 0116 2596443.
Contact/s
Owner: Mr J Dobson
Profile Breeder. **Ref: YH02681**

CENTAUR BLOODSTOCK
Centaur Bloodstock, 8 Warbank Lane, Kingston Upon Thames, **London (Greater)**, KT2 7ES, **ENGLAND**.
(T) 020 89498283 **(F)** 020 89498284
(M) 07785 733217.
Profile Blood Stock Agency, Breeder. **Ref: YH02682**

CENTAUR POLOCROSSE CLUB
Centaur Polocrosse Club, Ladyfields, Bayton, Kidderminster, **Worcestershire**, DY14 9HT, **ENGLAND**.
(T) 01299 832806.
Profile Club/Association. Polocrosse Club.
Ref: YH02683

CENTAUR TRANSPORT
Centaur Transport, Dairy Ground, Daisy Hill Farm, Duns Tew, Bicester, **Oxfordshire**, OX6 4JS, **ENGLAND**.
(T) 01869 349000 **(F)** 01869 349001.
Contact/s
Owner: Mr A Spatcher
Profile Transport/Horse Boxes. Horse drawn vehicles.
Ref: YH02684

CENTELL
Centell Saddlery, Little Heath Rd, Tilehurst, Reading, **Berkshire**, RG31 5TX, **ENGLAND**.
(T) 0118 9425168 **(F)** 0118 9425718.
Contact/s
Owner: Mrs J Vincent
Profile Riding Wear Retailer, Saddlery Retailer.
Sell horse wear. **Ref: YH02685**

CENTENNIAL ASIL ARABIAN STUD
Centennial Asil Arabian Stud Ltd, Pitchford Hall, Pitchford, Condover, Shrewsbury, **Shropshire**, SY5 7DN, **ENGLAND**.
(T) 01694 731315.
Profile Breeder. **Ref: YH02686**

CENTRAL COMMITTE FELL PACKS
Central Committee of Fell Packs, Sword Hse, Eskdale, Holmrook, **Cumbria**, CA19 1TT, **ENGLAND**.
(T) 01946 723295.
Profile Club/Association. **Ref: YH02687**

CENTRAL EQUESTRIAN WHOLESALE
Central Equestrian Wholesale, 19-21 Sandwell St, Walsall, **Midlands (West)**, WS1 3DR, **ENGLAND**.
(T) 01922 611553.
Profile Supplies. **Ref: YH02688**

CENTRAL PREFIX REGISTER
Central Prefix Register Ltd, Upper Marshes, Semley, Shaftesbury, **Dorset**, SP7 9AE, **ENGLAND**.
(T) 01747 850235 **(F)** 01747 850235
(E) centralprefixreg@aol.com
(W) www.centralprefixregister.com.
Contact/s
Secretary: Mrs G Dent
Profile Club/Association.
Registration of Breeders' prefixes and suffixes as a protection from duplication. Forty five breed societies are affiliated to the CPR. No.Staff: 1 Yr. Est: 1978
Opening Times
No visitors, please telephone, fax, e-mail or write.
Ref: YH02689

CENTRAL SADDLERY
Central Saddlery, Drumbroider Farm, Avonbridge, Falkirk, **Falkirk**, FK1 2HN, **SCOTLAND**.
(T) 01324 861229 **(F)** 01324 861462.
Contact/s
Owner: Mrs J Baird
Profile Saddlery Retailer. **Ref: YH02690**

CENTRAL TRAILER RENTCO
Central Trailer Rentco Ltd, Unit 3 Vale Ind Ctre, Southern Rd, Aylesbury, **Buckinghamshire**, HP19 9EW, **ENGLAND**.
(T) 01296 423885.
Profile Transport/Horse Boxes. **Ref: YH02691**

CENTRAL TRAILER RENTCO
Central Trailer Rentco Ltd, Yarm Rd, Middleton St. George, Darlington, **County Durham**, DL2 1HR, **ENGLAND**.
(T) 01325 333040 **(F)** 01325 333529.
Profile Transport/Horse Boxes. **Ref: YH02692**

CENTRAL TRAILER RENTCO
Central Trailer Rentco Ltd, Andes Rd, Nursling, Southampton, **Hampshire**, SO16 0YZ, **ENGLAND**.
(T) 023 80740666.
Profile Transport/Horse Boxes. **Ref: YH02693**

CENTRAL TRAILER RENTCO
Central Trailer Rentco Ltd, Whitehill Ind Est, 37 Inchmuir Rd, Whitehill Ind Est, Bathgate, **Lothian (West)**, EH48 2EP, **SCOTLAND**.
(T) 01506 632058.
Profile Transport/Horse Boxes. **Ref: YH02694**

CENTRAL TRAILER RENTCO
Central Trailer Rentco Ltd, Eleventh Ave, Team Valley Trading Est, Gateshead, **Tyne and Wear**, NE11 0JY, **ENGLAND**.
(T) 0191 4874117.
Profile Transport/Horse Boxes. **Ref: YH02695**

CENTRAL TRAILER RENTCO
Central Trailer Rentco Ltd, Ashfield Way/Whitehall Ind Est, Whitehall Rd, Leeds, **Yorkshire (West)**, LS12 5JB, **ENGLAND**.
(T) 0113 2797977 **(F)** 0113 2795703.
Contact/s
Manager: Mr P Lee
Profile Transport/Horse Boxes. **Ref: YH02696**

CENTRIFORCE
Centriforce, 8B Blackpole Trading Est, Worcester, **Worcestershire**, WR3 8SQ, **ENGLAND**.
(T) 01905 455410 **(F)** 01905 754708.
Profile Transport/Horse Boxes. **Ref: YH02697**

CENTURION EQUESTRIAN CTRE
Centurion Equestrian Centre, Birtley Lane, Hunwick, Bishop Auckland, Durham, **County Durham**, DL15 0SG, **ENGLAND**.
(T) 01388 606347.
Contact/s
Owner: Mr D Emmison
Profile Equestrian Centre, Riding School, Stable/Livery. **Ref: YH02698**

CENTURION INT HORSE TRANSPORT
Centurion International Horse Transport, Centurion Stables, 16 Swaffham Rd, Reach, **Cambridgeshire**, CB5 0HZ, **ENGLAND**.
(T) 01638 743440.
Profile Transport/Horse Boxes. **Ref: YH02699**

CERULLO, M
M Cerullo, The Old Granary Forge, Clarks Lane, Tatsfield, Westerham, **Kent**, TN16 2JU, **ENGLAND**.
(T) 01959 577501 **(F)** 01959 577501.
Contact/s
Owner: Mr M Cerullo
Profile Farrier. **Ref: YH02700**

CHADBOURNE, C
C Chadbourne, Gorsemoor Lodge, Clifton Rd, Netherseal, Swadlincote, **Derbyshire**, DE12 8BP, **ENGLAND**.
(T) 01283 760893.
Profile Farrier. **Ref: YH02701**

CHADWELL FARM
Chadwell Farm Stud, Chadwell Farm, Birdbrook, Halstead, **Essex**, CO9 4BE, **ENGLAND**.
(T) 01440 788123 **(F)** 01440 785331.
Contact/s
Owner: Mrs V Mustoe
Profile Breeder. Sell horses at auctions.
No.Staff: 4 Yr. Est: 1986
Opening Times
By appointment only **Ref: YH02702**

CHADWICK, R
Mrs R Chadwick, Chace Ct, Penstraze, Chacewater, Truro, **Cornwall**, TR4 8JY, **ENGLAND**.
(T) 01872 560904.
Profile Breeder. **Ref: YH02703**

CHADWICK, RUSSELL J
Russell J Chadwick DWCF, Hawthorne Farm, Bottomhouse, Leek, **Staffordshire**, ST13 7PB, **ENGLAND**.
(T) 01538 304376.
Profile Farrier. **Ref: YH02704**

CHADWICK, S G
Mr S G Chadwick, Eskrigg, Hayton, Aspatria, **Cumbria**, CA5 2PD, **ENGLAND**.
(T) 01697 321226.
Profile Supplies. **Ref: YH02705**

CHADWICK, SUE
Sue Chadwick, The Airfield, Crosland Moor, Huddersfield, **Yorkshire (West)**, HD4 7AG, **ENGLAND**.
(T) 01484 645784.
Profile Trainer. **Ref: YH02706**

CHAFF-CUTTERS ANIMAL SUPPLIES
Chaff-Cutters Animal Supplies, Little Paddocks, Bevan Cl, Carleton Rode, Norwich, **Norfolk**, NR16 1RE, **ENGLAND**.
(T) 01953 789792.
Profile Supplies. **Ref: YH02707**

CHAFFORD FARM
Chafford Farm Livery & Training Centre, Chafford Farm, Chafford Lane, Fordcombe, Tunbridge Wells, **Kent**, TN3 0SH, **ENGLAND**.
(T) 01892 740744 **(F)** 01892 740216.
Contact/s
Owner: Mr A Thompson
Profile Stable/Livery, Trainer. **Ref: YH02708**

CHALFONT HEIGHTS RIDING CLUB
Chalfont Heights Riding Club, The Old Vicarage, Old Long Gr, Seer Green, **Buckinghamshire**, HP9 2QH, **ENGLAND**.
(T) 01494 676548 **(F)** 01494 670968.
Contact/s
Chairman: Ms S Hogan
Profile Club/Association, Riding Club. **Ref: YH02709**

CHALGRAVE MANOR
Chalgrave Manor Livery Stables, Chalgrave Manor, Toddington, Dunstable, **Bedfordshire**, LU5 6HT, **ENGLAND**.
(T) 01525 872004.
Contact/s
Partner: Miss L Upchurch
Profile Stable/Livery. **Ref: YH02710**

CHALK PIT FARM STABLES
Chalk Pit Farm Stables, Challacot, Guildford Rd, Bookham, Leatherhead, **Surrey**, KT23 4HB, **ENGLAND**.
(T) 01372 456644.
Contact/s
Manager: Mrs S Core
Profile Stable/Livery. **Ref: YH02711**

CHALLENGER DISTRIBUTION
Challenger Distribution Ltd, Unit 1A Grange Farm, Newmarket Rd, Heydon, Royston, **Hertfordshire**, SG8 7PR, **ENGLAND**.
(T) 01763 208790.
Profile Supplies. **Ref: YH02712**

CHALLONER, JOHN
John Challoner, Bucknell, **Shropshire**, SY7 0AA, **ENGLAND**.
(T) 01547 530309 **(F)** 01547 530309.
Contact/s
Owner: Mr J Challoner
Profile Transport/Horse Boxes. **Ref: YH02713**

CHALLONER, TIMOTHY V
Timothy V Challoner AFCL, The Cotch, Corse Lawn, Gloucester, **Gloucestershire**, GL19 4ND, **ENGLAND**.
(T) 01452 780553.
Profile Farrier. **Ref: YH02714**

CHALMERS, ALEXANDER W
Alexander W Chalmers AFCL BI, 46 Lower Ashley Rd, Ashley, New Milton, **Hampshire**, BH25 5AD, **ENGLAND**.
(T) 01425 614531.
Profile Farrier. **Ref: YH02715**

CHALMERS, ALISTAIR N
Alistair N Chalmers DWCF, Raemoir, Kirkmichael, Blairgowrie, **Perth and Kinross**, PH10 7NX, **SCOTLAND**.
(T) 01250 881309.
Profile Farrier. **Ref: YH02716**

CHAMBERLAIN, A J
Mr A J Chamberlain, North End Farm, Ashton Keynes, Swindon, **Wiltshire**, SN6 6QR, **ENGLAND**.
(T) 01285 861347
(M) 07768 471719.
Profile Trainer. **Ref: YH02717**

CHAMBERS, G W
G W Chambers, Hurst Farm, Clay Lane, Jacobs Well, Guildford, **Surrey**, GU4 7PF, **ENGLAND**.
(T) 01483 576433 **(F)** 01483 454007.
Profile Abbatoirs. **Ref: YH02718**

CHAMBERS, IAN M
Ian M Chambers DWCF, 21 The Glebe, Hawley, Camberley, **Surrey**, GU17 9BB, **ENGLAND**.
(T) 01276 33040.
Profile Farrier. **Ref: YH02719**

CHAMBERS, J W
J W Chambers, Trowell Lane, Sutton Bonington, Loughborough, **Leicestershire**, LE12 5RW, **ENGLAND**.
(T) 01509 853199.
Profile Transport/Horse Boxes. **Ref: YH02720**

CHAMBERS, KEITH R
Keith R Chambers DWCF, 1 Trawden Way, Litherland, Liverpool, **Merseyside**, L21 0HX, **ENGLAND**.
(T) 0151 4761044.
Profile Farrier. **Ref: YH02721**

CHAMBERS, S C
S C Chambers, Higher Chilley Farm, East Allington, Totnes, **Devon**, TQ9 7QN, **ENGLAND**.
(T) 01548 521400.
Contact/s
Owner: Mrs S Chambers
Profile Transport/Horse Boxes. **Ref: YH02722**

CHAMBERS, W H
W H Chambers, Trinity Hse Farm, Swanland Dale, North Ferriby, **Yorkshire (East)**, HU14 3RA, **ENGLAND**.
(T) 01482 657089.
Profile Breeder. **Ref: YH02723**

CHAMELEON PHOTOGRAPHY
Chameleon Photography, 91 Forest Rd, Huddersfield, **Yorkshire (West)**, HD5 8ET, **ENGLAND**.
(T) 01484 539337.

Profile Photographer. Ref: YH02724

CHAMPFLEURIE STABLES

Champfleurie Stables, Brunton, Bathgate, **Lothian (West)**, EH48 4NE, **SCOTLAND**.
(T) 01506 655248.
Contact/s
Owner: Mrs L Ogilvy
Profile Riding School, Stable/Livery. Ref: YH02725

CHAMPION FEEDS EQUESTRIAN

Champion Feeds Equestrian, Pk Farm, Stoke Albany, Market Harborough, **Leicestershire**, LE16 8PT, **ENGLAND**.
(T) 0800 3288486.
Profile Feed Merchant, Supplies.
Offers a wide range of horse feeds, equipment and a delivery service
Opening Times
Opens Mon - Fri 08:30, Sat, Sun 09:00. Closes Mon - Fri 17:30, Sat, Sun 12:00 Ref: YH02726

CHAMPION SADDLERY

Champion Saddlery, Unit 3 Singers Yard, Torquay Rd, Paignton, **Devon**, TQ3 2AH, **ENGLAND**.
(T) 01803 521704.
Contact/s
Owner: Mr M Kowalski
Profile Saddlery Retailer. Ref: YH02727

CHAMPIONSHIP FOODS

Championship Foods Ltd, 50 Fishers Lane, Orwell, Royston, **Hertfordshire**, SG8 5QX, **ENGLAND**.
(T) 01223 208081 (F) 01223 207629.
Profile Feed Merchant. Ref: YH02728

CHANCE & HUNT NUTRITION

Chance & Hunt Nutrition, Alexander Hse, Crown Gate, Runcorn, **Cheshire**, WA7 2UP, **ENGLAND**.
(T) 01928 793088 (F) 01928 716997.
Profile Medical Support. Ref: YH02729

CHANCE, NOEL

Noel Chance, Top Yard, Saxon Hse Stables, Upper Lambourn, Hungerford, **Berkshire**, RG17 8QH, **ENGLAND**.
(T) 01488 73436 (F) 01488 72296.
Contact/s
Owner: Mr N Chance
Profile Trainer.
Trained 'Mr Mulligan' and 'Looks Like Trouble' both winners of the Tote Cheltenham Gold Cup.
Ref: YH02730

CHANDLERS CROSS RIDING CLUB

Chandlers Cross Riding Club, Anderley, Dunny Lane, Chipperfield, Kings Langley, **Hertfordshire**, WD4 9DQ, **ENGLAND**.
(T) 01923 267306.
Contact/s
Chairman: Mrs L Mitchell
Profile Club/Association, Riding Club. Ref: YH02731

CHANGING TACK

Changing Tack, Church Rd, Maidens Green, Winkfield, Windsor, **Berkshire**, SL4 4SJ, **ENGLAND**.
(T) 01344 883387.
Contact/s
Owner: Ms A Lyniskey
Profile Riding Wear Retailer, Saddlery Retailer.
Specialise in quality second hand equestrian equipment but also have a wide selection of new products. A cleaning service is also available.
Ref: YH02732

CHANIN, D

D Chanin, Lee Cross Farm, Thorverton, Exeter, **Devon**, EX5 5LN, **ENGLAND**.
(T) 01884 855494.
Contact/s
Owner: Mr N Chanin
Profile Breeder. Ref: YH02733

CHANNON, M

M Channon, West Ilsley Stables, West Ilsley, Newbury, **Berkshire**, RG20 7AE, **ENGLAND**.
(T) 01635 281166 (F) 01635 281177.
Contact/s
Owner: Mr M Channon
Profile Trainer. Ref: YH02734

CHANTRY VETNRY GRP

Chantry Veterinary Group, 13 Station Rd, Royston, Barnsley, **Yorkshire (South)**, S71 4EW, **ENGLAND**.
(T) 01226 722773.
Profile Medical Support. Ref: YH02735

CHANTRY VETNRY GRP

Chantry Veterinary Group, Gills Yard, Northgate, Wakefield, **Yorkshire (West)**, WF1 3BZ, **ENGLAND**.
(T) 01924 376858.
Profile Medical Support. Ref: YH02736

CHANTRY VETNRY GRP

Chantry Veterinary Group, 27 Lower Oxford St, Castleford, **Yorkshire (West)**, WF10 4AE, **ENGLAND**.
(T) 01977 554095.
Profile Medical Support. Ref: YH02737

CHAPEL FARM

Chapel Farm Equestrian Centre, Newbridge Rd, Newbridge, Wrexham, **Wrexham**, LL14 3AJ, **WALES**.
(T) 01978 823470.
Contact/s
General Manager: Miss L Teece
Profile Riding School, Stable/Livery.
Full and part livery available. Chapel Farm is also a pony club centre. No.Staff: 5 Yr. Est: 1986
C.Size: 25 Acres
Opening Times
Answer phone - messages answered within 24 hours
Ref: YH02738

CHAPEL FEEDS

Chapel Feeds, Old Silsoe Rd, Clophill, **Bedfordshire**, MK45 4AR, **ENGLAND**.
(T) 01525 860150.
Profile Feed Merchant. Ref: YH02739

CHAPEL FORGE

Chapel Forge Farriers, Old Chapel Forge, Upper Lambourn, Hungerford, **Berkshire**, RG17 8QP, **ENGLAND**.
(T) 01488 72613 (F) 01488 73835
Affiliated Bodies WCF.
Contact/s
Owner: Mr G Pickford (Q) FWCF
Profile Farrier.
Makes therapeutic and standard shoes. Has a workshop or can visit clients at home. No.Staff: 13
Yr. Est: 1981
Opening Times
Telephone for an appointment Ref: YH02740

CHAPELFIELD VETNRY

Chapelfield Veterinary Partnership, Mclintock Hse, 21 Chapel Field Rd, Norwich, **Norfolk**, NR2 1RR, **ENGLAND**.
(T) 01603 629046 (F) 01603 625060.
Contact/s
Practice Manager: Mrs E Sorrell
Profile Medical Support. Ref: YH02741

CHAPLIN, J

Miss J Chaplin, Blisbury Farm, Berkeley, **Gloucestershire**, GL13 9RB, **ENGLAND**.
(T) 01453 810335.
Profile Breeder. Ref: YH02742

CHAPMAN, COLIN

Chapman Colin, The Homestead, Fen Lane, East Keal, Spilsby, **Lincolnshire**, PE23 4AY, **ENGLAND**.
(T) 01790 753225.
Profile Transport/Horse Boxes. Ref: YH02743

CHAPMAN, D W

Mr D W Chapman, Mowbray Hse Farm, Stillington, York, **Yorkshire (North)**, YO61 1LT, **ENGLAND**.
(T) 01347 821683 (F) 01347 821683
(M) 07966 513866.
Profile Trainer. Ref: YH02744

CHAPMAN, DUNCAN

Duncan Chapman, Hardgate Smithy, Tarland, Aboyne, **Aberdeenshire**, AB3 4XQ, **SCOTLAND**.
(T) 01339 881356.
Profile Farrier. Ref: YH02745

CHAPMAN, K

Miss K Chapman, Wells Tye Farm, Barnston, Dunmow, **Essex**, CM6 1ND, **ENGLAND**.
(T) 01371 872875.
Profile Breeder. Ref: YH02746

CHAPMAN, WILLIAM

William Chapman, Sherwood, 41 Melgum Rd, Tarland, **Aberdeenshire**, AB34 4ZL, **SCOTLAND**.
(T) 01339 881480.
Profile Farrier. Ref: YH02747

CHAPPELOW, A

A Chappelow, Calder Court, Calder Farm, Sands Lane, Mirfield, **Yorkshire (West)**, WF14 8HJ, **ENGLAND**.
(T) 01924 493359.
Contact/s
Owner: Mr A Chappelow
Profile Stable/Livery.
Full and DIY livery available, prices on request.
Yr. Est: 1989 C.Size: 60 Acres
Opening Times
Sp: Open Mon - Sun 08:00. Closed Mon - Sun 20:00.
Su: Open Mon - Sun 08:00. Closed Mon - Sun 20:00.
Au: Open Mon - Sun 08:00. Closed Mon - Sun 20:00.
Wn: Open Mon - Sun 08:00. Closed Mon - Sun 20:00.
Telephone between these hours Ref: YH02748

CHARD, R J

R J Chard, 1 Hayleigh Farm Cottages, Streat Lane, Streat, Hassocks, **Sussex (West)**, BN6 8RU, **ENGLAND**.
(T) 01273 891033.
Contact/s
Owner: Mr R Chard
Profile Farrier. Ref: YH02749

CHARIOTS OF FIRE DRIVING CTRE

Chariots Of Fire Driving Centre, Nether Boreland, Boreland, Lockerbie, **Dumfries and Galloway**, DG11 2LL, **SCOTLAND**.
(T) 01576 610248 (F) 01576 610248
(E) amanda@chariots.org.uk
(W) www.chariots.org.uk.
Contact/s
Owner: Miss A Saville
Profile Equestrian Centre, Holidays, Horse/Rider Accom, Riding School, Stable/Livery, Trainer.
Prices range from £10.00 for one-one lessons to £320.00 for a week's B&B, livery and training. Also available is a display team and a driving centre with scenic carriage drives. Yr. Est: 1998 Ref: YH02750

CHARITY FARM LIVERY STABLES

Charity Farm Livery Stables, Charity Farm, Wrighington, Wigan, **Lancashire**, WN6 9PP, **ENGLAND**.
(T) 01257 451326.
Profile Stable/Livery. Ref: YH02751

CHARLBURY FARM

Charlbury Farm, Little Hinton Farm, Hinton, Hinton Parva, Swindon, **Wiltshire**, SN4 0DN, **ENGLAND**.
(T) 01793 790065.
Profile Stable/Livery. Ref: YH02752

CHARLBURY SADDLERY

Charlbury Saddlery, 26 Sturt Cl, Charlbury, Chipping Norton, **Oxfordshire**, OX7 3SS, **ENGLAND**.
(T) 01608 811254 (F) 01608 810511.
Contact/s
Owner: Mr C Clothier
Profile Saddlery Retailer. Ref: YH02753

CHARLES BRITTON CONSTRUCTION

Charles Britton Equestrian Construction Ltd, Gadlas Farm, Eastwick Lane, Dudleston Heath, Ellesmere, **Shropshire**, SY12 9DY, **ENGLAND**.
(T) 0870 0722321 (F) 0870 0722321.
Contact/s
Administration: Mr H Thomas
Profile Arena.
A complete turn-key design and build service of all equestrian facilities. No.Staff: 20 Yr. Est: 1979
Opening Times
Sp: Open Mon - Fri 09:00. Closed Mon - Fri 17:30.
Su: Open Mon - Fri 09:00. Closed Mon - Fri 17:30.
Au: Open Mon - Fri 09:00. Closed Mon - Fri 17:30.
Wn: Open Mon - Fri 09:00. Closed Mon - Fri 17:30.
Closed weekends Ref: YH02754

CHARLES EGERTON BLOODSTOCK

Charles Egerton Bloodstock, Heads Farm Stables, Chaddleworth, Newbury, **Berkshire**, RG16 0EE, **ENGLAND**.
(T) 01488 638771 (F) 01488 638832.
Profile Blood Stock Agency. Ref: YH02755

CHARLES HUNT & PARTNERS

Charles Hunt & Partners, Unit 1 Rockfort Ind Est, Hithercroft Rd, Wallingford, **Oxfordshire**, OX10 9DB, **ENGLAND**.
(T) 01491 837207 (F) 01491 837207.
Profile Saddlery Retailer. Ref: YH02756

CHARLES OWEN

Charles Owen & Co (Bow) Ltd, Royal Works, Croesfoel Ind Pk, Wrexham, **Wrexham**, LL14 4BJ, **WALES**.
(T) 01978 317777 (F) 01978 317778.
Contact/s
Owner: Mr R Burek
Profile Supplies.

Key: (T) telephone (F) fax (M) mobile (E) E-Mail Address (W) Website Address (Q) Qualifications
Yr. Est: Year Established C.Size: Complex Size Sp: Spring Su: Summer Au: Autumn Wn: Winter

Opening Times
Sp: Open Mon - Fri 08:00. Closed Mon - Fri 17:00.
Su: Open Mon - Fri 08:00. Closed Mon - Fri 17:00.
Au: Open Mon - Fri 08:00. Closed Mon - Fri 17:00.
Wn: Open Mon - Fri 08:00. Closed Mon - Fri 17:00.
Ref: YH02757

CHARLES, ANDREW JEREMY

Andrew Jeremy Charles DWCF, 1 Mill Field, Mill Lane, Lambourn, **Berkshire**, RG17 8YQ, **ENGLAND**.
(T) 01488 71310.
Profile Farrier. **Ref: YH02758**

CHARLES, D C

Mrs D C Charles, South Side Farm, High Mickley, Stocksfield, **Northumberland**, NE43 7LU, **ENGLAND**.
(T) 01661 843346.
Profile Breeder. **Ref: YH02759**

CHARLES, P

Mr P Charles, Heathcroft Farm, Bentworth, Alton, **Hampshire**, GU34 5JP, **ENGLAND**.
(T) 01420 561213 **(F)** 01420 561348.
Profile Breeder. **Ref: YH02760**

CHARLES-JONES, ALEXANDER

Alexander Charles- Jones, Pen Cottage, Fulbrook, Burford, **Oxfordshire**, OX18 4BU, **ENGLAND**.
(T) 01993 823265 **(F)** 01993 823265.
Profile Art Galleries and Auctions. **Ref: YH02761**

CHARLESLAND STUD

Charlesland Stud, Highfield Farm, London Rd, Figsbury, Salisbury, **Wiltshire**, FP4 6DT, **ENGLAND**.
(T) 01980 610963 **(F)** 01980 611104.
Profile Breeder. **Ref: YH02762**

CHARLEY, B

B Charley, Beanit Livery Farm, Hob Lane, Balsall Common, Coventry, **Midlands (West)**, CV7 7GX, **ENGLAND**.
(T) 01676 535115.
Profile Stable/Livery. **Ref: YH02763**

CHARLIE MANN RACING

Charlie Mann Racing Ltd, Whitcombe Hse, Upper Lambourn, Hungerford, **Berkshire**, RG17 8RA, **ENGLAND**.
(T) 01488 71717 **(F)** 01488 73223.
Contact/s
Owner: Mr C Mann
Profile Trainer. **Ref: YH02764**

CHARLTON DOWN STUD

Charlton Down Stud Ltd, Tetbury, **Gloucestershire**, GL8 8TZ, **ENGLAND**.
(T) 01666 880448.
Contact/s
Manager: F A Thomas
Profile Breeder. **Ref: YH02765**

CHARLTON, R B

Mr & Mrs R B Charlton, Linnel Wood, Hexham, **Northumberland**, NE46 1UB, **ENGLAND**.
(T) 01434 673262.
Profile Breeder, Stable/Livery, Track/Course.
Ref: YH02766

CHARLTON, J I A

Mr J I A Charlton, Mickley Grange Farm, Stocksfield, **Northumberland**, NE43 7TB, **ENGLAND**.
(T) 01661 843247
(M) 07850 007415.
Profile Trainer. **Ref: YH02767**

CHARLTON, ROGER J

Mr Roger J Charlton, Beckhampton Hse, Marlborough, **Wiltshire**, SN8 1QR, **ENGLAND**.
(T) 01672 539533 **(F)** 01672 539456
(M) 07710 784511.
Profile Trainer. **Ref: YH02768**

CHARLTON, S

S Charlton, Woodlands, Newcastle Emlyn, **Carmarthenshire**, SA38 9RA, **WALES**.
(T) 01239 710293.
Profile Breeder. **Ref: YH02769**

CHARLY'S YARD SMITHY

Charly's Yard Smithy, High Hesket, Carlisle, **Cumbria**, CA4 0JE, **ENGLAND**.
(T) 01697 473830
(M) 07860 507035.
Profile Farrier. **Ref: YH02770**

CHARMWOOD ARABIANS

Charmwood Arabians, 7 Gladsrone St, Anstey, Leicester, **Leicestershire**, LE7 7BT, **ENGLAND**.
(T) 0116 2356044.
Profile Breeder. **Ref: YH02771**

CHARNICAL RIDING CTRE

Charnical Riding Centre, Kirton Rd, Scotter, Gainsborough, **Lincolnshire**, DN21 3JA, **ENGLAND**.
(T) 01724 761760.
Contact/s
Owner: Mrs C Allan
Profile Riding School, Stable/Livery. Yr. Est: 1998
Ref: YH02772

CHARNWOOD MILLING

Charnwood Milling Co Ltd, Framlingham, Woodbridge, **Suffolk**, IP13 9PT, **ENGLAND**.
(T) 01728 723435 **(F)** 01728 724359
(E) feeds@charnwood-milling.co.uk
(W) www.charnwood-milling.co.uk.
Profile Feed Merchant.
Charnwood's horse feeds offer a choice of nearly twenty different diets including both pelleted and coarse mix rations. Those not sold as complete feeds, are designed to provide a total feed when hay is added. Yr. Est: 1960 **Ref: YH02773**

CHARNWOOD PET SUPPLIES

Charnwood Pet Supplies, 75 Town Green St, Rothley, **Leicestershire**, LE7 7AD, **ENGLAND**.
(T) 0116 2301955
(M) 07836 349456.
Profile Supplies. **Ref: YH02774**

CHART STABLES

Chart Stables Ltd, Bridgend Farmhouse, Hurstford Lane, Charing, Ashford, **Kent**, TN27 0ER, **ENGLAND**.
(T) 01233 713611/713778 **(F)** 01233 713598
(E) enquiries@chartstables.co.uk
(W) www.chartstables.co.uk.
Contact/s
Sales Manager: Mr A Norris
Profile Stabling (design and build).
A complete range of equestrian buildings, garages and workshops at very competitive prices available. The buildings can be delivered and erected throughout the UK and Europe. Yr. Est: 1994
Opening Times
Sp: Open Mon - Sat 08:00. Closed Mon - Fri 17:00, Sat 12:00.
Su: Open Mon - Sat 08:00. Closed Mon - Fri 17:00, Sat 12:00.
Au: Open Mon - Sat 08:00. Closed Mon - Fri 17:00, Sat 12:00.
Wn: Open Mon - Sat 08:00. Closed Mon - Fri 17:00, Sat 12:00.
Closed Sundays **Ref: YH02775**

CHARTERS, SUE

Sue Charters, Firs Farm, Knowbury, Ludlow, **Shropshire**, SY8 3JT, **ENGLAND**.
(T) 01584 891158 **(F)** 01584 891606
(E) firsfarm@netname.co.uk
Affiliated Bodies BD, BE, BHS.
Contact/s
Owner: Ms S Charters **(Q)** BHSI, NPS Dip
Profile Stable/Livery, Trainer.
Horse Schooling
Opening Times
Telephone for an appointment, there is an answer-phone **Ref: YH02776**

CHARTWELL STABLES

Chartwell Stables, Motts Hill Lane, Tadworth, Epsom, **Surrey**, KT20 6BA, **ENGLAND**.
(T) 01737 814847 **(F)** 01737 814847.
Profile Trainer. **Ref: YH02777**

CHAS MEDFORTH

Chas Medforth & Co, The Est Office, 38/40 Bridge St, Caernarfon, **Gwynedd**, LL55 1AF, **WALES**.
(T) 01286 672989 **(F)** 01286 672565.
Contact/s
Estate Agent: Mr C Medforth
Profile Estate agents.
Professional service offered covering sales, survey & valuation, auction and financial services.
Yr. Est: 1968 **Ref: YH02778**

CHASE FARM

Chase Farm, Llanmaes, Llantwit Major, **Glamorgan (Vale of)**, CF61 2XR, **WALES**.
(T) 01446 792725.
Profile Trainer. **Ref: YH02779**

CHASE FARM

Chase Farm Cross Country Schooling Course, Bramshott Chase, Hindhead, **Surrey**, GU26 6DG, **ENGLAND**.
(T) 01428 605322
(E) ashton@chase-farm.co.uk
(W) www.chase-farm.co.uk.
Contact/s
Owner: Mrs V Ashton
Profile Arena, Track/Course. Cross country and show jumping courses.
There is ample parking with good access for trailers and boxes. For Clubs and groups there is a large greenhouse which can be used for sheltering from the weather, with an electric point for boiling kettles.
C.Size: 20 Acres
Opening Times
The Course is on free draining sand which means we are able to stay open for most of the year.
Ref: YH02780

CHASE FARM STUD

Chase Farm Stud, The Warren, Ashtead, **Surrey**, KT21 2SH, **ENGLAND**.
(T) 01372 277639.
Contact/s
Owner: Mr J Shelton
Profile Stud Farm. **Ref: YH02781**

CHASE FENCING SUPPLIES

Chase Fencing Supplies (Kent), Penshurst Station Approach, Chiddingstone Causeway, Tonbridge, **Kent**, TN11 8JD, **ENGLAND**.
(T) 01892 870882 **(F)** 01892 870746.
Profile Supply and construct fencing. **Ref: YH02782**

CHASE FENCING SUPPLIES

Chase Fencing Supplies, Twickenham Ave, London Rd, Brandon, **Suffolk**, IP27 0PD, **ENGLAND**.
(T) 01842 810507 **(F)** 01842 812987.
Profile Supply and construct fencing. **Ref: YH02783**

CHASE RIDING SCHOOL

Chase Riding School, 352 Nuneaton Rd, Bulkington, Bedworth, **Warwickshire**, CV12 9RR, **ENGLAND**.
(T) 024 76312170.
Profile Riding School. **Ref: YH02784**

CHASE SADDLERY

Chase Saddlery, 76 Chase Side, Enfield, **London (Greater)**, EN2 6NX, **ENGLAND**.
(T) 020 83637238 **(F)** 020 83678190
(E) info@chasesaddlery.com
(W) www.chasesaddlery.com
Affiliated Bodies BETA, SMS.
Contact/s
Owner: Mrs V Georgiou
Profile Medical Support, Riding Wear Retailer, Saddlery Retailer, Supplies. Yr. Est: 1980
Opening Times
Sp: Open Mon - Sat 09:15. Closed Mon - Sat 17:15.
Su: Open Mon - Sat 09:15. Closed Mon - Sat 17:15.
Au: Open Mon - Sat 09:15. Closed Mon - Sat 17:15.
Wn: Open Mon - Sat 09:15. Closed Mon - Sat 17:15.
Closed Sundays **Ref: YH02785**

CHASE SIDE

Chase Side Stables & Riding School, Coppice Farm, Teddesley Coppice, Penkridge, Stafford, **Staffordshire**, ST19 5RP, **ENGLAND**.
(T) 01785 711177.
Contact/s
Owner: Mrs S Billingham
Profile Riding School. **Ref: YH02786**

CHASKIT HSE

Chaskit House Country Clothing and Saddlery, Chaskit Hse, Langton Rd, Langton Green, Tunbridge Wells, **Kent**, TN3 0EG, **ENGLAND**.
(T) 01892 863113 **(F)** 01892 863113.
Contact/s
Owner: Miss K Jones
Profile Riding Wear Retailer, Saddlery Retailer.
Ref: YH02787

CHATSWORTH SADDLERY

Chatsworth Saddlery, 424 Chatsworth Rd, Chesterfield, **Derbyshire**, S40 3BD, **ENGLAND**.
(T) 01246 237115.
Contact/s
Owner: Miss R Turner
Profile Saddlery Retailer. **Ref: YH02788**

CHATTERTON, M C

M C Chatterton, The Forge, Church St, Scawby, Brigg, **Lincolnshire (North)**, DN20 9AE, **ENGLAND**.
(T) 01652 654313.
Contact/s
Owner: Mr M Chatterton
Profile Farrier. **Ref: YH02789**

CHATTERTON, SHAUN MICHAEL

Shaun Michael Chatterton DWCF, Lowlands

Farm, Saxby, Market Rasen, **Lincolnshire**, LN8 2DP, **ENGLAND**.
(T) 01673 878375.
Profile Farrier. **Ref: YH02790**

CHAUCER RIDING/LIVERY STABLES

Chaucer Riding & Livery Stables, Kate St, Waltham, Canterbury, **Kent**, CT4 5SB, **ENGLAND**.
(T) 01227 700396.
Profile Riding School, Stable/Livery. **Ref: YH02791**

CHAVES HORSE TRANSPORT

Chaves Horse Transport, 36 Bath Rd, Corston, Bath, **Bath & Somerset (North East)**, BA2 9AA, **ENGLAND**.
(T) 01225 872675 **(F)** 01225 872675
(M) 07850 130205.
Profile Transport/Horse Boxes. **Ref: YH02792**

CHAVIC PK STABLES

Chavic Park Stables, Chavic Pk Farm, Jail Lane, Biggin Hill, Westerham, **Kent**, TN16 3AU, **ENGLAND**.
(T) 01959 572090 **(F)** 01959 572090.
Contact/s
Owner: Mrs G Palmer
Profile Riding School, Stable/Livery, Trainer.
Ref: YH02793

CHAWNER, P D

P D Chawner RSS, 66 Rough Rd, Kingstanding, Birmingham, **Midlands (West)**, B44 0UY, **ENGLAND**.
(T) 0121 3541416.
Profile Farrier. **Ref: YH02794**

CHEADLE EQUESTRIAN CTRE

Cheadle Equestrian Centre, Eaves Lane, Cheadle, Stoke-on-Trent, **Staffordshire**, ST10 1RB, **ENGLAND**.
(T) 01538 756400.
Contact/s
Partner: Mr P Cooke
Profile Stable/Livery. **Ref: YH02795**

CHECKENDON

Checkendon Equestrian Centre, Lovegroves Lane, Checkendon, Reading, **Berkshire**, RG8 0NE, **ENGLAND**.
(T) 01491 680225
(W) www.checkendon.f9.co.uk.
Contact/s
Owner: Miss L Tarrant
(E) linda@checkendon.f9.co.uk
Profile Horse/Rider Accom, Riding School, Stable/Livery.
Full, part and schooling Livery available, prices on request. Training for NVQ examinations.
No.Staff: 10 Yr. Est: 1994 C.Size: 40 Acres
Opening Times
Sp: Open Mon - Sun 09:00. Closed Mon - Sun 21:00.
Su: Open Mon - Sun 09:00. Closed Mon - Sun 21:00.
Au: Open Mon - Sun 09:00. Closed Mon - Sun 21:00.
Wn: Open Mon - Sun 09:00. Closed Mon - Sun 21:00. **Ref: YH02796**

CHECKLEY, PAUL N

Paul N Checkley DWCF, 499 Fox Hollies Rd, Hall Green, Birmingham, **Midlands (West)**, B28 6RJ, **ENGLAND**.
(T) 0121 2435896.
Profile Farrier. **Ref: YH02797**

CHEDDON FITZPAINE FORGE

Cheddon Fitzpaine Forge, Cheddon Fitzpaine, Taunton, **Somerset**, TA2 8JU, **ENGLAND**.
(T) 01823 413708 **(F)** 01823 413708.
Contact/s
Owner: Mr M Conlon
Profile Blacksmith. **Ref: YH02798**

CHELFORD FARM SUPPLIES

Chelford Farm Supplies Ltd, Knutsford Rd, Chelford, Macclesfield, **Cheshire**, SK11 9AS, **ENGLAND**.
(T) 01625 861588 **(F)** 01625 861235
(W) www.chelfordfarmsupplies.co.uk.
Contact/s
Manager: Ms H Beeson
Profile Feed Merchant, Riding Wear Retailer, Saddlery Retailer. **Ref: YH02799**

CHELMER TRAILERS

Chelmer Trailers, 3-4 Eckersley Rd Ind Est, Chelmsford, **Essex**, CM1 1SL, **ENGLAND**.
(T) 01245 259600 **(F)** 01245 263976.
Profile Transport/Horse Boxes. **Ref: YH02800**

CHELMSFORD EQUESTRIAN CTRE

Chelmsford Equestrian Centre, Carlton Farm, Beehive Lane, Chelmsford, **Essex**, CM2 8RJ, **ENGLAND**.
(T) 01245 358116 **(F)** 01245 358116.
Profile Riding School, Stable/Livery. **Ref: YH02801**

CHELSFIELD RIDING SCHOOL

Chelsfield Riding School, Church Rd, Chelsfield, Orpington, **Kent**, BR6 7SN, **ENGLAND**.
(T) 01689 855603.
Contact/s
Owner: Mr M Hamilton
Profile Riding School, Stable/Livery. **Ref: YH02802**

CHELTENHAM & DISTRICT

Cheltenham & District Riding Club, 28 Treelands Drv, Leckhampton, Cheltenham, **Gloucestershire**, GL53 0DE, **ENGLAND**.
(T) 01242 583673.
Contact/s
Chairman: Mrs J Potter
Profile Club/Association, Riding Club. **Ref: YH02803**

CHELTENHAM RACECOURSE

Cheltenham Racecourse, Prestbury Pk, Cheltenham, **Gloucestershire**, GL50 4SH, **ENGLAND**.
(T) 01242 513014 **(F)** 01242 224227.
Contact/s
Clerk of Course: Simon Claisse
Profile Track/Course. **Ref: YH02804**

CHELTENHAM SADDLERY

Cheltenham Saddlery, 262 London Rd, Charlton Kings, Cheltenham, **Gloucestershire**, GL52 6HS, **ENGLAND**.
(T) 01242 260157 **(F)** 01242 260157.
Profile Saddlery Retailer. **Ref: YH02805**

CHENIES STABLES

Chenies Stables, Lodge Farm, Lodge Lane, Chalfont St Giles, **Buckinghamshire**, HP8 4AH, **ENGLAND**.
(T) 01494 763197.
Contact/s
Owner: Ms J Madge
Profile Riding School. **Ref: YH02806**

CHEPHURST FARM LIVERIES

Chephurst Farm Liveries, Chedhurst Farm, Haven Rd, Rudgwick, Horsham, **Sussex (West)**, RH12 3JH, **ENGLAND**.
(T) 01403 822686.
Contact/s
Owner: Mr B Prime
Profile Stable/Livery. **Ref: YH02807**

CHEPSTOW RACECOURSE

Chepstow Racecourse PLC, 17 Welsh St, Chepstow, **Monmouthshire**, NP6 5YH, **WALES**.
(T) 01291 622260 **(F)** 01291 625550.
Contact/s
Clerk of Course: Mr J Martin
Profile Track/Course. **Ref: YH02808**

CHEPSTOW SADDLERY

Chepstow Saddlery Ltd, St. Arvans, Chepstow, **Monmouthshire**, NP16 6EJ, **WALES**.
(T) 01291 627072 **(F)** 01291 627993
(W) www.chepstowsaddlery.co.uk
Affiliated Bodies BETA.
Contact/s
General Manager: Mr I McNeil
Profile Riding Wear Retailer, Saddlery Retailer, Supplies. No.Staff: 4 Yr. Est: 1988
Opening Times
Sp: Open 09:30. Closed 18:00.
Su: Open 09:30. Closed 18:00.
Au: Open 09:30. Closed 18:00.
Wn: Open 09:30. Closed 18:00. **Ref: YH02809**

CHEQUER FARM STABLES

Chequer Farm Stables, Main St, Elvington, York, **Yorkshire (North)**, YO4 5AG, **ENGLAND**.
(T) 01904 608618.
Contact/s
Owner: Mr J Nicholson
Profile Riding School, Stable/Livery. Hacking. Instruction in Riding & Jumping. **Ref: YH02810**

CHEQUER HALL FARM

Chequer Hall Farm, Wheldrake Lane, Escrick, York, **Yorkshire (North)**, YO19 6EL, **ENGLAND**.
(T) 01904 728430.
Contact/s
Owner: Mr W Bedford
Profile Breeder. **Ref: YH02811**

CHEQUERS END EQUESTRIAN CTRE

Chequers End Equestrian Centre, Chequers Lane, Cadmore End, High Wycombe, **Buckinghamshire**, HP14 3PQ, **ENGLAND**.
(T) 01494 882161.
Contact/s
Owner: Mrs P Freeman
Profile Equestrian Centre, Riding School, Stable/Livery, Trainer.
Full, part and DIY livery, hacking, schooling, preparation for shows/competitions and fitness programmes available. Showjumps available for hire. **Ref: YH02812**

CHERRETT, TOM B

Tom B Cherrett, 18 Lydbrook Cl, Sittingbourne, **Kent**, ME10 1NW, **ENGLAND**.
(T) 01795 479883.
Profile Trainer. **Ref: YH02813**

CHERRY ANN WILE PHOTOGRAPHY

Cherry Ann Wile Photography, 47 Papplewick Lane, Hucknall, **Nottinghamshire**, NG15 7TN, **ENGLAND**.
(T) 0115 9527027.
Profile Photographer. **Ref: YH02814**

CHERRY TREE FARM

Cherry Tree Farm, New Rd, Coleshill, Amersham, **Buckinghamshire**, HP7 0LE, **ENGLAND**.
(T) 01494 722239 **(F)** 01494 432992.
Contact/s
Chairman: Mr J Joseph
Profile Blood Stock Agency. **Ref: YH02815**

CHERRY TREE LIVERY STABLES

Cherry Tree Livery Stables, Gill Lane, Kearby, Wetherby, **Yorkshire (West)**, LS22 4BS, **ENGLAND**.
(T) 0113 2886460.
Profile Stable/Livery. **Ref: YH02816**

CHERRY TREE RIDING CTRE

Cherry Tree Riding Centre, 28 Plainspot Rd, New Brinsley, **Nottinghamshire**, NG16 5BS, **ENGLAND**.
(T) 01773 712438.
Profile Stable/Livery. **Ref: YH02817**

CHERRY TREE STABLES

Cherry Tree Stables, Tower Rd, Coleshill, Amersham, **Buckinghamshire**, HP7 0LB, **ENGLAND**.
(T) 01494 724138.
Profile Breeder. **Ref: YH02818**

CHERRY, R J

R J Cherry RSS, Forge Side, Hastings Hill, Churchill, **Oxfordshire**, OX7 6NA, **ENGLAND**.
(T) 01608 658552.
Profile Farrier. **Ref: YH02819**

CHERRY-DOWNS BLOODSTOCK

Cherry-Downs Bloodstock, Murray Lodge Cottage, Queensberry Rd, Newmarket, **Suffolk**, CB8 9AU, **ENGLAND**.
(T) 01638 665756 **(F)** 01638 667621.
Contact/s
Owner: Mr A Cherry-Downs
Profile Blood Stock Agency, Breeder. **Ref: YH02820**

CHERRYWOOD LODGE

Cherrywood Lodge Riding Stables, Webbs Green, Soberton, Southampton, **Hampshire**, SO32 3PY, **ENGLAND**.
(T) 01489 877596.
Contact/s
Partner: Mr P Walker **Ref: YH02821**

CHERWELL VALLEY RIDING CLUB

Cherwell Valley Riding Club, 10 The Greenaway, Daventry, **Northamptonshire**, NN11 4EE, **ENGLAND**.
(T) 01327 878545
(E) buffalo@themutual.net.
Contact/s
Chairman: Mrs P Dowler
Profile Club/Association, Riding Club. **Ref: YH02822**

CHESFIELD EQUESTRIAN CTRE

Chesfield Equestrian Centre, Manor Farm, Chesfield, Graveley, Hitchin, **Hertfordshire**, SG4 7BN, **ENGLAND**.
(T) 01438 352654.
Profile Stable/Livery. **Ref: YH02823**

CHESHIRE

Cheshire, Whitegates, Main Rd, Worleston, Nantwich, **Cheshire**, CW5 6AN, **ENGLAND**.
(T) 01270 623311. **Ref: YH02824**

CHESHIRE EQUINE SVS

Cheshire Equine Services Ltd, Red Lion Abattoir, Sound Common, Nantwich, **Cheshire**, BN45 1NR, **ENGLAND**.
(T) 01629 640305 **(F)** 01629 640684.
Profile Abbatoir. **Ref: YH02825**

CHESHIRE MOBILE

Cheshire Mobile, Smoke Hall Lane, Winsford, **Cheshire**, CW7 3SB, **ENGLAND**.
(T) 01606 557591 **(F)** 01606 861387. **Ref: YH02826**

CHESHIRE POLO CLUB

Cheshire Polo Club (The), White Hall, Little Budworth, Tarporley, **Cheshire**, CW6 9EL, **ENGLAND**.
(T) 01829 760500.
Contact/s
Secretary: Ms L Taylor
Profile Club/Association. **Ref: YH02827**

CHESHIRE, RONALD

Ronald Cheshire RSS, 265 Cluny Pl, Glenrothes, **Fife**, KY7 4QU, **SCOTLAND**.
(T) 01592 771859.
Profile Farrier. **Ref: YH02828**

CHESNEY, DAVID (DR)

Dr David Chesney, Cowden, Charminster, Dorchester, **Dorset**, DT2 9RN, **ENGLAND**.
(T) 01305 265450 **(F)** 01305 250684.
Profile Breeder. **Ref: YH02829**

CHESSINGTON

Chessington Equestrian Centre, Off Clayton Rd, Chessington, **Surrey**, KT9 1NN, **ENGLAND**.
(T) 020 83987668.
Contact/s
General Manager: Mr S Banting **(Q)** BHSII
Profile Equestrian Centre, Riding School.
Hacking, day rides and 3 day trail rides. No.Staff: 4
Yr. Est: 1988 C.Size: 40 Acres
Opening Times
Sp: Open 08:00. Closed 20:30.
Su: Open 08:00. Closed 20:30.
Au: Open 08:00. Closed 20:30.
Wn: Open 08:00. Closed 20:30. **Ref: YH02830**

CHESTER RACE

Chester Race Co Ltd, The Racecourse, Chester, **Cheshire**, CH1 2LY, **ENGLAND**.
(T) 01244 323170 **(F)** 01244 344971.
Contact/s
Chief Executive: Richard Thomas
Profile Track/Course. **Ref: YH02831**

CHESTER SADDLERY

Chester Saddlery, 142A Christleton Rd, Chester, **Cheshire**, CH3 5TD, **ENGLAND**.
(T) 01244 318992.
Profile Saddlery Retailer. **Ref: YH02832**

CHESTERFIELD

Chesterfield Equestrian Centre, Crow Lane, Tapton, Chesterfield, **Derbyshire**, S41 0EQ, **ENGLAND**.
(T) 01246 206991
Affiliated Bodies BD.
Contact/s
Owner: Mrs D Thomas
Profile Arena, Equestrian Centre, Stable/Livery, Trainer, Transport/Horse Boxes. No.Staff: 3
C.Size: 12 Acres
Opening Times
Sp: Open Mon - Sun 07:00. Closed Mon - Sun 21:00.
Su: Open Mon - Sun 07:00. Closed Mon - Sun 21:00.
Au: Open Mon - Sun 07:00. Closed Mon - Sun 21:00.
Wn: Open Mon - Sun 07:00. Closed Mon - Sun 21:00.
Telephone for further details regarding horsebox & arena hire. **Ref: YH02833**

CHESTERMAN, DANIEL J

Daniel J Chesterman DWCF, 38 Mount Rd, Lanesfield, Wolverhampton, **Midlands (West)**, WV4 6NE, **ENGLAND**.
(T) 01902 885945.
Profile Farrier. **Ref: YH02834**

CHESTERS STUD

Chesters Stud, Humshaugh, Hexham, **Northumberland**, NE46 4EU, **ENGLAND**.
(T) 01434 681203 **(F)** 01434 681533.
Profile Stud Farm. **Ref: YH02835**

CHESTFIELD MORGANS STABLES

Chestfield Morgans Stables, 11 Beechcroft, Chestfield, Whitstable, **Kent**, CT5 3QF, **ENGLAND**.
(T) 01227 794250 **(F)** 01227 794205.
Contact/s
Owner: Mrs S Pamphilon
Profile Breeder. **Ref: YH02836**

CHESTNUT VETNRY GRP

Chestnut Veterinary Group (The), 1 Hoe Lane, Ware, **Hertfordshire**, SG12 9LS, **ENGLAND**.
(T) 01920 468874 **(F)** 01920 463115.
Contact/s
Partner: Mr A Buckling **(Q)** MRCVS
Profile Medical Support. **Ref: YH02837**

CHESTNUTS RIDING SCHOOL

Chestnuts Riding School, The Chestnuts, London Rd, Pyecombe, Brighton, **Sussex (West)**, BN45 7FJ, **ENGLAND**.
(T) 01273 503842.
Profile Riding School. **Ref: YH02838**

CHESTON EQUESTRIAN CTRE

Cheston Equestrian Centre, Cheston Farm, Wrangaton, South Brent, **Devon**, TQ10 9HL, **ENGLAND**.
(T) 01364 73266.
Contact/s
Partner: Mr D Christie
Profile Riding School. **Ref: YH02839**

CHEVAL ARMOIRE

Cheval Armoire, Shute Lane, Wrangaton, South Brent, **Devon**, TQ10 9HE, **ENGLAND**.
(T) 01364 73157 **(F)** 01364 73157.
Contact/s
Partner: Mrs C Wonnacott
Profile Riding Wear Retailer, Saddlery Retailer.
Ref: YH02840

CHEVAL D'OR

Cheval D'Or, Holly Hill Barn, Camps Heath, Oulton, Lowestoft, **Suffolk**, NR32 5DW, **ENGLAND**.
(T) 01502 500431.
Profile Supplies. **Ref: YH02841**

CHEVELEY PK

Cheveley Park Stud Ltd, Cheveley Pk, Cheveley, Newmarket, **Suffolk**, CB8 9DD, **ENGLAND**.
(T) 01638 730316 **(F)** 01638 730868.
Contact/s
Assistant Manager: Mr J Marsh
Profile Breeder, Stud Farm. **Ref: YH02842**

CHEVELEY PK STUD

Cheveley Park Stud Ltd, Sandwich Stud, Moulton Rd, Cheveley, Newmarket, **Suffolk**, CB8 9DN, **ENGLAND**.
(T) 01638 730245.
Profile Breeder. **Ref: YH02843**

CHEVINGTON STUD

Chevington Stud, Dependy Lane, Chevington, Bury St Edmunds, **Suffolk**, IP29 5RA, **ENGLAND**.
(T) 01284 850457 **(F)** 01284 850457.
Contact/s
Manager: Mr J Navrro
Profile Breeder. **Ref: YH02844**

CHEVRON EQUINE UK

Chevron Equine UK, 81 Cannock St, Leicester, **Leicestershire**, LE4 9HR, **ENGLAND**.
(T) 0116 2741134 **(F)** 0116 2764342.
Contact/s
Manager: Mr S Carter
Profile Supplies. **Ref: YH02845**

CHEZ NOUS

Chez Nous Riding School, Arva Rd, Drumlish, **County Longford**, **IRELAND**.
(T) 043 24368. **Ref: YH02846**

CHIBLEY FARM STUD

Chibley Farm Stud & Equestrian Centre, Stondon Rd, Shillington, Hitchin, **Hertfordshire**, SG5 3HG, **ENGLAND**.
(T) 01462 711583.
Contact/s
Owner: Mrs T Lewis
Profile Equestrian Centre, Stud Farm. **Ref: YH02847**

CHICHESTER, T A S

Mr T A S Chichester, Wiscombe Pk, Southleigh, Colyton, **Devon**, EX24 6JE, **ENGLAND**.
(T) 01404 871415.
Profile Breeder. **Ref: YH02848**

CHIDDOCK PONY STUD

Chiddock Pony Stud, The Barn, Salisbury, **Wiltshire**, SP5 2SG, **ENGLAND**.
(T) 01794 884470 **(F)** 01722 438666.
Profile Breeder. **Ref: YH02849**

CHIEVELEY MANOR STUD

Chieveley Manor Stud, Chieveley, Newbury, **Berkshire**, RG16 8UT, **ENGLAND**.
(T) 01635 248208 **(F)** 01635 248070.
Profile Breeder. **Ref: YH02850**

CHILD, RICHARD J

Richard J Child DWCF, Woodville, Beech Lane, Normandy, Guildford, **Surrey**, GU3 2JH, **ENGLAND**.
(T) 01483 811682.
Profile Farrier. **Ref: YH02851**

CHILDS, ADAM

Adam Childs DWCF, Tregonia, Green Lane, Tipton St John, Sidmouth, **Devon**, EX10 0AH, **ENGLAND**.
(T) 01404 812452.
Profile Farrier. **Ref: YH02852**

CHILDWICK BURY STUD

Childwick Bury Stud, The Office, Stud Lane, Childwick Bury, St Albans, **Hertfordshire**, AL3 6JW, **ENGLAND**.
(T) 01582 762752 **(F)** 01582 715356.
Profile Breeder. **Ref: YH02853**

CHILHAM FEEDS

Chilham Feeds, East Stour Farm, Godmersham, Canterbury, **Kent**, CT4 7DH, **ENGLAND**.
(T) 01227 731159.
Profile Feed Merchant, Supplies. **Ref: YH02854**

CHILLESFORD STABLES

Chillesford Stables, Church Farm, Woodbridge, **Suffolk**, IP12 3PS, **ENGLAND**.
(T) 01394 450087.
Contact/s
Owner: Mrs E Iliff
Profile Stable/Livery. **Ref: YH02855**

CHILLING BARN RIDING CTRE

Chilling Barn Riding Centre, Chilling Barn, Chilling Lane, Warsash, Southampton, **Hampshire**, SO31 9HF, **ENGLAND**.
(T) 01489 572232.
Contact/s
Owner: Mrs W Hewlett
Profile Equestrian Centre. **Ref: YH02856**

CHILMAN, J F

J F Chilman, Caldwell Mill, Mill Lane, Drakes Broughton, Pershore, **Worcestershire**, WR10 2AF, **ENGLAND**.
(T) 01905 840118.
Profile Farrier. **Ref: YH02857**

CHILTERN CONNEMARA

Chiltern Connemara Stud & Coombe Books, Combe Cottage, Presteigne, **Powys**, LD8 2LH, **WALES**.
(T) 01544 267026
(W) www.connemara-pony.net/.
Contact/s
Owner: Miss P Lyne
Profile Breeder. Author & Curator.
Supply books, video, posters and postcards via mail order Yr. Est: 1965
Opening Times
Books can be ordered by telephone, post or email, or from the Station House Museum **Ref: YH02858**

CHILTERN POLO CTRE

Chiltern Polo Centre, Lower Bassibones Farm, Lee Common, Great Missenden, **Buckinghamshire**, HP16 9LA, **ENGLAND**.
(T) 01494 837778 **(F)** 01494 791268.
Profile Polo Centre. **Ref: YH02859**

CHILTERN RIDING CLUB

Chiltern Riding Club, Furrows, Rosebery Rd, Tokers Green, Reading, **Berkshire**, RG4 9EL, **ENGLAND**.
(T) 0118 9478823.
Profile Club/Association, Riding Club. **Ref: YH02860**

CHILTON, S L

S L Chilton, 3 Holland Trce, Wrexham Rd, Pontblyddyn, Mold, **Flintshire**, CH7 4HJ, **WALES**.
(T) 01352 771592.
Contact/s
Owner: Mr S Chilton
Profile Farrier. **Ref: YH02861**

CHIMNEY MILL GALLERIES

Chimney Mill Galleries, Chimney Mill, West Stow, Bury St Edmunds, **Suffolk**, IP28 6ER, **ENGLAND**.
(T) 01284 728234.
Profile Stable/Livery. **Ref: YH02862**

CHING SADDLERS

Ching Saddlers, Golden Lion Hse, Crockernwell, Exeter, **Devon**, EX6 6NE, **ENGLAND**.
(T) 01647 24200.
Contact/s
Owner: Mr P Ching
Profile Saddlery Retailer. **Ref: YH02863**

CHIPPENHAM TRAILER HIRE

Chippenham Trailer Hire, 22 Erleigh Drive, Rowden Hill, Chippenham, **Wiltshire**, SN15 2NQ, **ENGLAND**.
(T) 01249 448988.
Profile Transport/Horse Boxes. **Ref: YH02864**

CHIPPINGS FARM

Chippings Farm Riding School & Livery Yard, West Lodge, Elvedon Rd, Cobham, **Surrey**, KT11 1BP, **ENGLAND**.
(T) 01932 860667.
Profile Riding School, Stable/Livery. **Ref: YH02865**

CHIPPINGS FARM STABLES

Chippings Farm Stables, Elvedon Rd, Norwood Farm Est, Cobham, **Surrey**, KT11 2BP, **ENGLAND**.
(T) 01932 860667.
Profile Riding School, Stable/Livery. **Ref: YH02866**

CHIPTRICK RIDING SCHOOL

Chiptrick Riding School, New Rd, Melksham, **Wiltshire**, SN12 7QY, **ENGLAND**.
(T) 01225 790047.
Profile Riding School. **Ref: YH02867**

CHIRON EQUESTRIAN BOOKS

Chiron Equestrian Books, 2 Andrews Way, Raunds, Wellingborough, **Northamptonshire**, NN9 6RD, **ENGLAND**.
(T) 01933 460715.
Profile Supplies. **Ref: YH02868**

CHISLEHURST & DISTRICT

Chislehurst & District Riding Club, 18 Padua Rd, Penge, **London (Greater)**, SE20 8HF, **ENGLAND**.
(T) 020 86590723.
Contact/s
Chairman: Miss J Morris
Profile Club/Association, Riding Club. **Ref: YH02869**

CHITCOMBE FARM SHOP

Chitcombe Farm Shop, Chitcombe Rd, Broad Oak, Rye, **Sussex (East)**, TN31 6EX, **ENGLAND**.
(T) 01424 883030 **(F)** 01424 883030.
Contact/s
Owner: Mr W Slinn **Ref: YH02870**

CHIVERTON RIDING CTRE

Chiverton Riding Centre, Blackwater, Truro, **Cornwall**, TR4 8HS, **ENGLAND**.
(T) 01872 560471.
Profile Riding School, Stable/Livery. **Ref: YH02871**

CHOBHAM & DISTRICT

Chobham & District Riding Club, 7 Wey Manor Flats, Byfleet Rd, New Haw, Weybridge, **Surrey**, KT15 3JR, **ENGLAND**.
(T) 01932 851126.
Contact/s
Chairman: Mr J Foss
Profile Club/Association, Riding Club. **Ref: YH02872**

CHOBHAM CHASERS CROSS COUNTRY

Chobham Chasers Cross Country Course, Berwin Pk, Chobham, Woking, **Surrey**, GU24 8JJ, **ENGLAND**.
(T) 01276 858479.
Profile Track/Course. **Ref: YH02873**

CHOBHAM RIDER

Chobham Rider (The), 98-100 High St, Chobham, Woking, **Surrey**, GU24 8LZ, **ENGLAND**.
(T) 01276 856738 **(F)** 01276 856738.
Contact/s
Owner: Mrs S Tomkins **Ref: YH02874**

CHODASIEWICZ, S

Mr S Chodasiewicz, Crabru, Backmuir Of Liff, Muirhead, Dundee, **Angus**, DD2 5QT, **SCOTLAND**.
(T) 01382 581498.
Profile Saddlery Retailer. **Ref: YH02875**

CHOICE SADDLERY

Choice Saddlery, 1 Broad St, Knighton, **Powys**, LD7 1AF, **WALES**.
(T) 01547 528385 **(F)** 01547 528385.
Contact/s
Owner: Ms L Higgins
Profile Riding Wear Retailer, Saddlery Retailer. Tack repairs. Made to measure bridles.
Opening Times
Sp: Open 09:30. Closed 16:00.
Su: Open 09:30. Closed 16:00.
Au: Open 09:30. Closed 16:00.
Wn: Open 09:30. Closed 16:00. **Ref: YH02876**

CHOLESBURY

Cholesbury Hay & Straw Supplies, Redwing Farm, Cholesbury Rd, Wigginton, Tring, **Hertfordshire**, HP23 6JH, **ENGLAND**.
(T) 01494 758288.
Profile Hay and Straw Merchants. **Ref: YH02877**

CHOLWELL EQUESTRIAN CTRE

Cholwell Equestrian Centre, Lewdown, Okehampton, **Devon**, EX20 4PT, **ENGLAND**.
(T) 01566 783215 **(F)** 01566 783215
(M) 07740 177120
(W) www.websouthwest.co.uk/allsorts/cholwell/.
Contact/s
Partner: Mrs J Clack
Profile Equestrian Centre, Stable/Livery. Dealers. Buy and sell horses and have a seven day money back warranty. Also liveries from £20 a week. All facilities are available for hire. **Ref: YH02878**

CHOLWELL FARM

Cholwell Farm & Riding Stables, Cholwell Farm, Mary Tavy, Tavistock, **Devon**, PL19 9QG, **ENGLAND**.
(T) 01822 810526.
Contact/s
Owner: Mrs D Penwill
Profile Riding School. **Ref: YH02879**

CHORLEY EQUESTRIAN CTRE

Chorley Equestrian Centre, Higher Garstang Farm, Chapel Lane, Heapey, Chorley, **Lancashire**, PR6 8TB, **ENGLAND**.
(T) 01257 268801
(E) chorleyec@freeuk.com
(W) www.chorleyec.freeuk.com
Affiliated Bodies BHS, Pony Club UK.
Contact/s
For Bookings: Miss A Berry **(Q)** BHSAI
Profile Arena, Club/Association, Equestrian Centre, Riding School, Stable/Livery. Pony Club.
'Own a pony' days are available in the holidays for children aged 8 and over. A two hour course is held for children under 8 years old, with one hour of riding and one hour pony care. The centre is 'pony club' registered and so this allows children who do not have their own pony to join and take part in the activities.
No.Staff: 6 Yr. Est: 1985 C.Size: 42 Acres
Ref: YH02880

CHRIS HAY

Chris Hall (Hay & Straw) Ltd, Green Lane Farm, Burnt Oak Lane, Newdigate, Dorking, **Surrey**, RH5 5BH, **ENGLAND**.
(T) 01306 631091 **(F)** 01306 631878.
Contact/s
Owner: Mr C Hall
Profile Hay and Straw Merchants. **Ref: YH02881**

CHRIS HAY

Chris Hall (Hay & Straw) Ltd, Parkgate Rd, Newdigate, Dorking, **Surrey**, RH5 5DZ, **ENGLAND**.
(T) 01306 631878.
Profile Hay and Straw Merchants. **Ref: YH02882**

CHRIS LEA

Chris Lea Insurance Services, 4 East Woodyards, Salisbury, **Wiltshire**, SP5 5QZ, **ENGLAND**.
(T) 01725 552821 **(F)** 01725 552045
(E) 105042.544@compuserve.com.
Profile Club/Association. Insurance Company.
Ref: YH02883

CHRISTIAN, M K

M K Christian, The Firs, Frodsham St, Kelsall, **Cheshire**, CW6 0RP, **ENGLAND**.
(T) 01829 751500.
Profile Medical Support. **Ref: YH02884**

CHRISTIAN, STEPHEN

Stephen Christian DWCF, Little Southernden, Southernden Lane, Headcorn, **Kent**, TN27 9LL, **ENGLAND**.
(T) 01622 891928.
Profile Farrier. **Ref: YH02885**

CHRISTIE

Messrs Christie, Dalfoil, Balfron, Glasgow, **Glasgow (City of)**, G63 0QD, **SCOTLAND**.
(T) 01360 440786.
Profile Breeder. **Ref: YH02886**

CHRISTIE & JEFFERS

Christie & Jeffers, 33 Market St, Ballymoney, **County Antrim**, BT53 6EA, **NORTHERN IRELAND**.
(T) 028 27663381 **(F)** 028 27663381.
Profile Supplies. **Ref: YH02887**

CHRISTIE, NORMAN

Norman Christie, Woodside Croft, Kinellar, Aberdeen, **Aberdeen (City of)**, AB21 0SE, **SCOTLAND**..
Profile Breeder. **Ref: YH02888**

CHRISTIE, RUPERT W W

Rupert W W Christie DWCF, 84 Frieth Rd, Marlow, **Buckinghamshire**, SL7 2QU, **ENGLAND**.
(T) 01628 482672.
Profile Farrier. **Ref: YH02889**

CHRISTIES

Christies, 8 King St, St James, London, **London (Greater)**, SW1 6QT, **ENGLAND**.
(T) 020 78399060 **(F)** 020 78391611
(W) www.christies.com.
Contact/s
Enquiries: Ms L Mitchell
Profile Art Dealers. Yr. Est: 1766
Opening Times
Sp: Open Mon - Fri 09:00. Closed Mon - Fri 18:00.
Su: Open Mon - Fri 09:00. Closed Mon - Fri 18:00.
Au: Open Mon - Fri 09:00. Closed Mon - Fri 18:00.
Wn: Open Mon - Fri 09:00. Closed Mon - Fri 18:00.
Ref: YH02890

CHRISTIES ANIMAL GROOMING

Christies Animal Grooming, 18 Greenhill Rd, Ballymoney, **County Antrim**, BT53 6LZ, **NORTHERN IRELAND**..
Profile Supplies. **Ref: YH02891**

CHRISTY'S EQUESTRIAN BUREAU

Christy's Equestrian Bureau, Rectory Farm, Foxcote, Radstock, Bath, **Bath & Somerset (North East)**, BA3 5YE, **ENGLAND**.
(T) 01373 834533.
Contact/s
Owner: Mrs C Yorke
Profile Equestrian Centre. **Ref: YH02892**

CHUKKA COVE

Chukka Cove Equestrian Supplies & Saddlery, Hardy's Farm Shop, Corner Farm, Farndon, Newark, **Nottinghamshire**, NG24 3SP, **ENGLAND**.
(T) 01636 705912 **(F)** 01636 705912.
Profile Saddlery Retailer, Supplies. **Ref: YH02893**

CHUKKA COVE SADDLERY

Chukka Cove Saddlery, Corner Hse Farm, Hawton Lane, Farndon, Newark, **Nottinghamshire**, NG24 3SD, **ENGLAND**.
(T) 01636 705912 **(F)** 01636 705912.
Contact/s
Owner: Mr J Digby **Ref: YH02894**

CHURCH FARM

Church Farm Holidays, Church Lane, Abenhall, Mitcheldean, **Gloucestershire**, GL17 0DX, **ENGLAND**.
(T) 01594 541211 **(F)** 01594 541212
(E) info@churchfarm.uk.net
(W) www.churchfarm.uk.net.
Contact/s
Partner: Mr J Verity
Profile Holidays, Horse/Rider Accom, Stable/Livery. Pets are welcome by prior appointment. Unrestricted hacking through the Forest of Dean. Holidays run from Saturday to Saturday, rooms must be vacated by 10:00 and you may not book in before 15:00. C.Size: 50 Acres
Opening Times
Open all year **Ref: YH02895**

CHURCH FARM & STUD

Church Farm & Stud, Church Farm, Church Lane, Ripe, Lewes, **Sussex (East)**, BN8 6AU, **ENGLAND**.
(T) 01323 811292.
Contact/s
Owner: Mrs L Phillips
Profile Breeder, Stable/Livery. **Ref: YH02896**

CHURCH FARM LIVERY STABLES

Church Farm Livery Stables, High St, Mawdesley, Ormskirk, **Lancashire**, L40 3TD, **ENGLAND**.

Key: **(T)** telephone **(F)** fax **(M)** mobile **(E)** E-Mail Address **(W)** Website Address **(Q)** Qualifications
Yr. Est: Year Established C.Size: Complex Size Sp: Spring Su: Summer Au: Autumn Wn: Winter

(T) 01704 821806 (F) 01704 821806.
Contact/s
Owner: Mrs H Millin
Profile Stable/Livery. Ref:YH02897

CHURCH FARM LIVERY STABLES

Church Farm Livery Stables, Church Walk, Bradwell, Great Yarmouth, **Norfolk**, NR31 9DX, **ENGLAND**.
(T) 01493 655074.
Profile Stable/Livery. Ref:YH02898

CHURCH FARM RIDING SCHOOL

Church Farm Riding School, Hilston, Hull, **Yorkshire (East)**, HU11 4QG, **ENGLAND**.
(T) 01964 670999.
Contact/s
Key Contact: Julie Nelson
Profile Riding School. Ref:YH02899

CHURCH FARM SMITHY

Church Farm Smithy, Church Farm, Marton, Macclesfield, **Cheshire**, SK11 9HF, **ENGLAND**.
(T) 01260 224727.
Profile Blacksmith. Ref:YH02900

CHURCH FARM STUD

Church Farm Stud, Guyler's Hse, Wattlefield, Wymondham, **Norfolk**, NR18 9JX, **ENGLAND**.
(T) 01953 789640 (F) 01953 789447.
Profile Breeder. Ref:YH02901

CHURCH FARM STUD

Church Farm Stud, Tytherington, Warminster, **Wiltshire**, BA12 7AE, **ENGLAND**.
(T) 01985 840229 (F) 01985 840568.
Profile Breeder. Ref:YH02902

CHURCH FARM TACK SHOP & FEEDS

Church Farm Tack Shop & Feeds, Hoxne Rd, Eye, **Suffolk**, IP23 7NJ, **ENGLAND**.
(T) 01379 871521.
Contact/s
Owner: Mrs J Thomson
Profile Equestrian Centre, Feed Merchant, Supplies.
Free local delivery Yr. Est: 2000
Opening Times
Sp: Open Mon - Sat 09:30. Closed Mon - Fri 17:00, Sat 16:30.
Su: Open Mon - Sat 09:30. Closed Mon - Fri 17:00, Sat 16:30.
Au: Open Mon - Sat 09:30. Closed Mon - Fri 17:00, Sat 16:30.
Wn: Open Mon - Sat 09:30. Closed Mon - Fri 17:00, Sat 16:30. Ref:YH02903

CHURCH FARMS

Church Farms, Church Farm, Main St, Etton, Beverley, **Yorkshire (East)**, HU17 7PQ, **ENGLAND**.
(T) 01430 810295.
Contact/s
Owner: Mr T Walker
Profile Stable/Livery, Trainer. Yr. Est: 1971
C.Size: 25 Acres
Opening Times
Sp: Open Mon - Sun 06:00. Closed Mon - Sun 20:00.
Su: Open Mon - Sun 06:00. Closed Mon - Sun 20:00.
Au: Open Mon - Sun 06:00. Closed Mon - Sun 20:00.
Wn: Open Mon - Sun 06:00. Closed Mon - Sun 20:00. Ref:YH02904

CHURCH ROAD RIDING SCHOOL

Church Road Riding School, 63 Springfield Rd, Weymouth, **Dorset**, DT3 5RN, **ENGLAND**.
(T) 01305 833272.
Profile Riding School. Ref:YH02905

CHURCH WALK VETNRY CTRE

Church Walk Veterinary Centre, 32 Crellin St, Barrow-In-Furness, **Cumbria**, LA14 1DU, **ENGLAND**.
(T) 01229 829863.
Profile Medical Support. Ref:YH02906

CHURCH WALK VETNRY CTRE

Church Walk Veterinary Centre, St Marys Pl, Church Walk, Ulverston, **Cumbria**, LA12 7EN, **ENGLAND**.
(T) 01229 583675.
Profile Medical Support. Ref:YH02907

CHURCH, D E

D E Church, 90 Abbots Rd, Hanham, **Gloucestershire (South)**, BS15 3NR, **ENGLAND**.
(T) 01179 679568.
Profile Farrier. Ref:YH02908

CHURCHES, M R

Mr M R Churches, The Oaks, Sticklynch, West Pennard, Glastonbury, **Somerset**, BA6 8NA, **ENGLAND**.
(T) 01749 890604.
Profile Supplies. Ref:YH02909

CHURCHFIELD FARM TACK SHOP

Churchfield Farm Tack Shop, Kings Dyke, Whittlesey, Peterborough, **Cambridgeshire**, PE7 2PA, **ENGLAND**.
(T) 01733 202257.
Profile Saddlery Retailer. Ref:YH02910

CHURCHFIELD VETNRY CTRE

Churchfield Veterinary Centre, 29 Sackville St, Barnsley, **Yorkshire (South)**, S70 2DB, **ENGLAND**.
(T) 01226 733333 (F) 01226 295660.
Contact/s
Vet: Mr P Dixon (Q) BVSc, MRCVS
Profile Medical Support. Ref:YH02911

CHURCHILL

Churchill Country & Equestrian Estate Agents, Event Hse, Wisborough Green, **Sussex (West)**, RH14 0DY, **ENGLAND**.
(T) 01403 700222 (F) 01403 700255
(E) churchillcountry@talk21.com
(W) www.churchillcountry.com.
Profile Estate Agents. Ref:YH02912

CHURCHILL SMITHY

Churchill Smithy Blacksmith & Engineers, Unit 17 Churchill Rd, Doncaster, **Yorkshire (South)**, DN1 2TF, **ENGLAND**.
(T) 01302 739839 (F) 01302 739839.
Contact/s
Manager: Mr A Durling
Profile Blacksmith. Ref:YH02913

CHURCHILL, J

J Churchill, Capton Mill, Capton, Dartmouth, **Devon**, TQ6 0JE, **ENGLAND**.
(T) 01803 712535 (F) 01803 712470.
Contact/s
Owner: Mr J Churchill
Profile Blacksmith. Ref:YH02914

CHURCHTOWN RIDING SCHOOL

Churchtown Riding School, Carrigeen, Churchtown, Mallow, **County Cork**, **IRELAND**.
(T) 022 48417
Affiliated Bodies AIRE.
Contact/s
Instructor: Norma Burke (Q) BHSII
Profile
Tuition is available for all abilities, both adults and children. Pony camps are available throughout the summer. Ref:YH02915

CHURN STABLES

Churn Stables, Blewbury, Didcot, **Oxfordshire**, OX11 9HF, **ENGLAND**.
(T) 01235 851997 (F) 01235 851998
(M) 07973 715122.
Profile Trainer. Ref:YH02916

CILWYCH FARM

Cilwych Farm, Bwlch, **Powys**, LD3 7JJ, **WALES**.
(T) 01597 83278.
Profile Stable/Livery. Ref:YH02917

CIMLA TREKKING

Cimla Trekking & Equestrian Holiday Centre, Hawdref Ganol Farm, Cimla, Neath, **Glamorgan (Vale of)**, SA12 9SL, **WALES**.
(T) 01639 644944 (F) 01639 899550
(W) www.ridingholidayswales.co.uk
Affiliated Bodies BHS, WTRA.
Contact/s
General Manager: Ms C Jones (Q) BHSAI
(E) caren@cimla.fsbusiness.co.uk
Profile Arena, Equestrian Centre, Riding School, Stable/Livery, Track/Course, Trainer. No.Staff: 8
Yr. Est: 1993 C.Size: 60 Acres Ref:YH02918

CINDER HILL VETNRY CLINIC

Cinder Hill Veterinary Clinic, Cinder Hill Lane, Horsted Keynes, Haywards Heath, **Sussex (West)**, RH17 7BA, **ENGLAND**.
(T) 01342 811335 (F) 01342 811404
(E) cginnett@cinderhillvet.com.
Profile Medical Support. Ref:YH02919

CINDERELLA CARRIAGES

Cinderella Carriages, Dummers Farm, Dunbridge Lane, Awbridge, Romsey, **Hampshire**, SO51 0GQ, **ENGLAND**.
(T) 01794 341047.
Contact/s
Owner: Mr G Fowle
Profile Transport/Horse Boxes. Horse drawn vehicles.
Ref:YH02920

CINQUE PORTS VETNRY ASS

Cinque Ports Veterinary Associates, Highlands Surgery, Ashford Rd, Tenterden, **Kent**, TN30 6LX, **ENGLAND**.
(T) 01580 763309.
Profile Medical Support. Ref:YH02921

CINQUE PORTS VETNRY ASS

Cinque Ports Veterinary Associates, Springfield Surgery, Cranbrook Rd, Hawkhurst, **Kent**, TN18 5EE, **ENGLAND**.
(T) 01580 752187 (F) 01580 753704.
Profile Medical Support. Ref:YH02922

CINQUE PORTS VETNRY ASS

Cinque Ports Veterinary Associates, Cinque Ports Sq, Rye, **Sussex (East)**, TN31 7AN, **ENGLAND**.
(T) 01797 222265.
Profile Medical Support. Ref:YH02923

CIRCLE D RIDING CTRE

Circle D Riding Centre (The), Cross, Axbridge, **Somerset**, BS26 2ED, **ENGLAND**.
(T) 01934 732577.
Profile Equestrian Centre. Ref:YH02924

CIRCUS HARLEQUIN

Circus Harlequin, Wasanga Manor, Hagneby Lane, Keal Cotes, Spilsby, **Lincolnshire**, PE23 4AW, **ENGLAND**.
(M) 07836 691110.
Profile Breeder. Ref:YH02925

CIRENCESTER GARAGE

Cirencester Garage Ltd, Love Lane Trading Est, Love Lane, Cirencester, **Gloucestershire**, GL7 1YG, **ENGLAND**.
(T) 01285 650909.
Profile Transport/Horse Boxes. Ref:YH02926

CIRENCESTER PK POLO CLUB

Cirencester Park Polo Club (The), Polo Office, The Old Kennels, Cirencester Park, **Gloucestershire**, GL7 1UR, **ENGLAND**.
(T) 01285 653225 (F) 01285 655003
(E) info@cirencesterpolo.co.uk.
Contact/s
Manager: Major N Musgrave
Profile Club/Association. Ref:YH02927

CITADEL TRAILERS

Citadel Trailers, 30 Holman Rd, Liskeard, **Cornwall**, PL14 3BE, **ENGLAND**.
(T) 01579 344877 (F) 01579 344844.
Contact/s
Owner: Mr A Stevenson
Profile Transport/Horse Boxes. Ref:YH02928

CITIGATE DEWE ROGERSON

Citigate Dewe Rogerson, 4th Floor, Yorkshire Hse, East Prde, Leeds, **Yorkshire (West)**, LS1 5SH, **ENGLAND**.
(T) 0113 2979899 (F) 0113 2442487. Ref:YH02929

CITY & GUILDS

City & Guilds, 1 Giltspur St, London, **London (Greater)**, EC1A 9DD, **ENGLAND**.
(T) 020 72942468 (F) 020 72942400
(W) www.city-and-guilds.co.uk.
Contact/s
Enquiries: Mr M Ormiston (T) 020 72942800
Profile Club/Association.
Examination/awarding body of NVQ's and City & Guilds vocational qualifications Ref:YH02930

CITY FORGE

City Forge, Fleet Way, Cardiff, **Glamorgan (Vale of)**, CF11 8TY, **WALES**.
(T) 029 20387906.
Contact/s
Owner: Mr A Murphy
Profile Blacksmith. Ref:YH02931

CITY TRUCK RENTALS

City Truck Rentals Ltd, 10 Northfield Drv, Woolstone, Milton Keynes, **Buckinghamshire**, MK15 0AA, **ENGLAND**.
(T) 01908 604024 (F) 01908 669378.
Contact/s
Area Manager: Mr S Bandy
Profile Transport/Horse Boxes. Ref:YH02932

CIVIL SV

Civil Service Riding Club, Royal Mews, London, **London (Greater)**, SW1W 0QH, **ENGLAND**.
(T) 020 79307232 **(F)** 020 79307233
(W) www.csrc.org.uk.
Contact/s
Chairperson: Mrs P Cooper
Profile Riding Club.
Civil Servants only. Lessons, hacks, competitions, courses, and examinations, available for members only
No.Staff: 4 Yr. Est: 1900
Opening Times
Sp: Open Mon - Sun 07:00. Closed Mon - Sun 21:00.
Su: Open Mon - Sun 07:00. Closed Mon - Sun 21:00.
Au: Open Mon - Sun 07:00. Closed Mon - Sun 21:00.
Wn: Open Mon - Sun 07:00. Closed Mon - Sun 21:00.
Lessons are on Mon, Tues, Weds, Fri, Sat, Sun and they begin at 17:30 **Ref: YH02933**

CIVIL SV (NORTHERN IRELAND)

Civil Service Riding Club (N Ireland), 15 Keel Pk, Moneyrea, **County Down**, BT23 6DE, **NORTHERN IRELAND**.
(T) 028 90449157.
Contact/s
Chairman: Mr T Watters
Profile Club/Association, Riding Club. **Ref: YH02934**

CLACK MILL RIDING STABLES

Clack Mill Riding Stables, Clack Mill, Keynsham Rd, Willsbridge, Bristol, **Bristol**, BS30 6EH, **ENGLAND**.
(T) 01179 328388.
Contact/s
Owner: Mrs M Gay
Profile Riding School. **Ref: YH02935**

CLAIFE/GRIZEDALE RIDING CTRE

Claife & Grizedale Riding Centre (The), Sawrey Knotts Est, Far Sawrey, Ambleside, **Cumbria**, LA22 0LG, **ENGLAND**.
(T) 01539 442105.
Profile Riding School. **Ref: YH02936**

CLAIRE HOWARTH

Claire Howarth Horse Transport, 2 Higher Marsh Row, Exminster, Exeter, **Devon**, EX6 8EB, **ENGLAND**.
(T) 01392 833380.
Profile Transport/Horse Boxes. **Ref: YH02937**

CLAIRE'S RIDING SCHOOL

Claire's Riding School, Moorfields, Furselands Rd, Three Legged Cross, Wimborne, **Dorset**, BH21 6RZ, **ENGLAND**.
(T) 01202 822975.
Profile Riding School. **Ref: YH02938**

CLAISH FARM PONY TREKKING

Claish Farm Pony Trekking, Claish Farm, Callander, **Perth and Kinross**, FK17 8JJ, **SCOTLAND**.
(T) 01877 330647.
Contact/s
Owner: Mrs V Gray
Profile Equestrian Centre. Trekking.
Offer treks through farmland with views of Ben Ledi and the River Teith. Horses and ponies available to suit everyone including complete beginners and children. Also there is a horse drawn cart and play area. Telephone for further price information
Opening Times
Sp: Open 09:00. Closed 18:00.
Su: Open 09:00. Closed 18:00.
Au: Open 09:00. Closed 18:00.
Wn: Open 09:00. Closed 18:00.
Apr - end Oct: Mon - Sat. Nov - Mar: weekends only.
Ref: YH02939

CLANCY DECLAN SADDLERY

Clancy Declan Saddlery Ltd, 11 Mount Carmel, Newbridge, **County Kildare**, **IRELAND**.
(T) 045 432606.
Profile Saddlery Retailer. **Ref: YH02940**

CLANDON FARM LIVERY STABLES

Clandon Farm Livery Stables, Clandon Farm, Martinstown, Dorchester, **Dorset**, DT2 9JF, **ENGLAND**.
(T) 01305 889363.
Profile Stable/Livery. **Ref: YH02941**

CLANDON MANOR SUPPLIES

Clandon Manor Supplies, Back Lane, East Clandon, Guildford, **Surrey**, GU4 7SA, **ENGLAND**.
(T) 01483 222765 **(F)** 01483 211411.
Profile Saddlery Retailer, Stable/Livery.
Ref: YH02942

CLANDON PK

Clandon Park Livery & Riding School, Temple Court, Clandon Pk, West Clandon, Guildford, **Surrey**, GU4 7RQ, **ENGLAND**.
(T) 01483 211400.
Profile Riding School, Stable/Livery. **Ref: YH02943**

CLANVILLE STUD

Clanville Stud, Clanville Lodge, Clanville, Andover, **Hampshire**, SP11 9HL, **ENGLAND**.
(T) 01264 772609 **(F)** 01264 771350.
Contact/s
Manager: Mr D Gravestock
Profile Breeder. **Ref: YH02944**

CLAPHAM, DIANA

Diana (Tiny) Clapham, South Lodge, Ropsley, Grantham, **Lincolnshire**, NG33 4AS, **ENGLAND**.
(T) 01476 585277 **(F)** 01476 585742
(M) 07836 672109.
Profile Trainer. **Ref: YH02945**

CLAPHAM, JENNIFER

Mrs Jennifer Clapham, Blue Hse Farm, Mattingley, Hook, **Hampshire**, RG27 8LJ, **ENGLAND**.
(T) 01256 882270.
Profile Breeder, Stable/Livery. **Ref: YH02946**

CLAPPER HSE RIDING CTRE

Clapper House Riding Centre, Maypark Hse, Clapper Farm, Wadebridge, **Cornwall**, PL27 6HZ, **ENGLAND**.
(T) 01208 812204.
Profile Equestrian Centre. **Ref: YH02947**

CLARA GUESTHOUSE

Clara Guesthouse & Trekking Centre, Knockrath Little, Clara Vale, Rathdrum, **County Wicklow**, **IRELAND**.
(T) 404 46318
(E) us@claratrekking.com
(W) www.claratrekking.com.
Contact/s
Owner: Miss M Phipps
Profile Horse/Rider Accom. Trekking Centre.
Experience off road riding at its best with panoramic views of the stunning Wicklow mountains, rivers and valleys. B & B accommodation with evening meal on request. All rooms are en-suite with prices from £25.00.
Opening Times
Open all year round, special offers at Christmas
Ref: YH02948

CLARE EQUESTRIAN CTRE

Clare Equestrian Centre, Deerpark, Doora, Ennis, **County Clare**, **IRELAND**.
(T) 065 6840136 **(F)** 065 6843607
(E) clareequestrian@esatclear.ie
(W) www.clareequestrian.com.
Contact/s
Owner: John Burke
Profile Horse/Rider Accom, Riding School, Stable/Livery.
Arrange treks to areas of local interest and also on the 'Burren'. Children are supervised at all times, childrens pony treks take place around the farm. Pony camps are available with emphasis on the holiday periods. Accommodation can be arranged nearby.
C.Size: 70 Acres **Ref: YH02949**

CLAREHAVEN STABLES

Clarehaven Stables Ltd, Bury Rd, Newmarket, **Suffolk**, CB8 7BY, **ENGLAND**.
(T) 01638 667323 **(F)** 01638 666389
(W) www.frontrunnerhorses.co.uk
Affiliated Bodies Newmarket Trainers Fed.
Contact/s
Trainer: Mr A Stewart
Profile Trainer. **Ref: YH02950**

CLAREMONT EQUESTRIAN CTRE

Claremont Equestrian Centre, Llanychan, Ruthin, **Denbighshire**, LL15 1UD, **WALES**.
(T) 01824 703324
Affiliated Bodies BHS.
Contact/s
Owner: Miss K Carman
Profile Stable/Livery.
Full, part and DIY livery available. Prices start at £33 plus feed per week No.Staff: 1 Yr. Est: 1976
Opening Times
Sp: Open Mon - Sun 09:00. Closed Mon - Sun 20:00.
Su: Open Mon - Sun 09:00. Closed Mon - Sun 20:00.
Au: Open Mon - Sun 09:00. Closed Mon - Sun 20:00.
Wn: Open Mon - Sun 09:00. Closed Mon - Sun 20:00. **Ref: YH02951**

CLAREMORRIS

Claremorris Saddlers & Equitation Centre, Galway Rd, Claremorris, **County Mayo**, **IRELAND**.
(T) 094 62292 **(F)** 094 62292
(M) 087 2533993
(E) hanleyhorses@esatclear.ie
(W) www.esatclear.ie/~hanley.
Contact/s
Owner: Charles Hanley **(Q)** BHSII
Profile Equestrian Centre, Stable/Livery.
Hunting & hacking is available through forests and farmland. Sole distributors of Equivalet in Ireland. Livery is avaliable, details on request.
Opening Times
Open seven days a week, telephone for further information **Ref: YH02952**

CLARENDON PK STUD

Clarendon Park Stud, Hindon Rd, Teffont, Salisbury, **Wiltshire**, SP3 5QU, **ENGLAND**.
(T) 01722 716436.
Profile Breeder. **Ref: YH02953**

CLARENDON VETNRY CTRE

Clarendon Veterinary Centre, 2 Clarendon Rd, Weston-Super-Mare, **Somerset (North)**, BS23 3EF, **ENGLAND**.
(T) 01934 629744.
Profile Medical Support. **Ref: YH02954**

CLARENDON VETNRY GRP

Clarendon Veterinary Group, The Veterinary Surgery, Clarendon Ave, Altrincham, **Cheshire**, WA15 8HD, **ENGLAND**.
(T) 0161 9280106 **(F)** 0161 9282059.
Profile Medical Support. **Ref: YH02955**

CLARENDON VETNRY GRP

Clarendon Veterinary Group, 237 Northenden Rd, Sale Moor, Sale, **Cheshire**, M33 2JD, **ENGLAND**.
(T) 0161 9052863.
Profile Medical Support. **Ref: YH02956**

CLARETON STUD

Clareton Stud, Throstle Nest Farm, Thornton-Le-Moor, Northallerton, **Yorkshire (North)**, DL6 3SD, **ENGLAND**.
(T) 01609 770300.
Profile Breeder. **Ref: YH02957**

CLARINA RIDING SCHOOL

Clarina Riding School, Clarina, **County Limerick**, **IRELAND**.
(T) 061 353087. **Ref: YH02958**

CLARION EVENTS

Clarion Events Ltd, Earls Court Exhibition Ctre, Warwick Rd, London, **London (Greater)**, SW5 9TA, **ENGLAND**.
(T) 020 73708206 **(F)** 020 73708347
(E) laura.heard@eco.co.uk.
Profile Club/Association. **Ref: YH02959**

CLARK & BUTCHER

Clark & Butcher Ltd, Lion Mills, Soham, Ely, **Cambridgeshire**, CB7 5HY, **ENGLAND**.
(T) 01353 720237 **(F)** 01353 723470
(E) etaylor@clarkandbutcher.co.uk.
Profile Supplies. Horse Feed Manufacturer.
Ref: YH02960

CLARK OF DOWLAIS

Clark of Dowlais, Pant Ind Est, Dowlais, Merthyr Tydfil, Merthyr, **Glamorgan (Vale of)**, CF48 3RN, **WALES**.
(T) 01873 854518.
Profile Supplies. **Ref: YH02961**

CLARK, CHRISTOPHER D

Christopher D Clark DWCF, 2 Chequers Cottages, Goudhurst, **Kent**, TN17 1DJ, **ENGLAND**.
(T) 01580 211591.
Profile Farrier. **Ref: YH02962**

CLARK, G

G Clark, Rushton Rd, Desborough, Kettering, **Northamptonshire**, NN14 2QN, **ENGLAND**.
(T) 01536 761310.
Profile Breeder. **Ref: YH02963**

CLARK, L M & GILMORE, TONY

Mrs L M Clark & Mr T Gilmore, Claywell Farm, Rempstone, Corfe Castle, Wareham, **Dorset**, BH20

5JJ, **ENGLAND**..
Contact/s
Partner: Mr T Gilmore (Q) AMC, DC, MMCA
(T) 01929 480332
Profile Medical Support. Ref: YH02964

CLARK, ROBERT
Robert Clark, Rymans Forge, Dell Quay Rd, Appledram, Chichester, **Sussex (West)**, PO20 7EE, **ENGLAND**.
(T) 01243 782692.
Profile Farrier. Ref: YH02965

CLARK, ROGER J
Roger J Clark FWCF Hons, The Garden Cottage, The Old Rectory, Barking, Ipswich, **Suffolk**, IP6 8HH, **ENGLAND**.
(T) 01449 720295.
Profile Breeder, Farrier. Ref: YH02966

CLARK, RON & JULIE
Ron & Julie Clark, 2 Honnington Cottages, Vauxhall Lane, Southborough, Tunbridge Wells, **Kent**, TN4 0XD, **ENGLAND**.
(T) 01892 29576.
Profile Trainer. Ref: YH02967

CLARK, SHEILA
W J Clark & Son, Fieldfare, Upper Bolton, Haddington, **Lothian (East)**, EH41 4HW, **SCOTLAND**.
(T) 01620 810346.
Contact/s
Owner: Mrs S Clark
Profile Horse/Rider Accom.
£18 per person per night, extra for horses
Yr. Est: 1986
Opening Times
Sp: Open Mon - Sun 08:00. Closed Mon - Sun 20:00.
Su: Open Mon - Sun 08:00. Closed Mon - Sun 20:00.
Au: Open Mon - Sun 08:00. Closed Mon - Sun 20:00.
Wn: Open Mon - Sun 08:00. Closed Mon - Sun 20:00. Ref: YH02968

CLARK, W L R & M E
W L R & M E Clark, Shortridge Hill Farm, Seven Crosses, Tiverton, **Devon**, EX16 8HH, **ENGLAND**.
(T) 01884 252632 (F) 01884 243233.
Contact/s
Partner: Mr W Clark
Profile Farrier. Ref: YH02969

CLARKE IRON
Clarke Iron, Arch 34 Popes Gr, Twickenham, **London (Greater)**, TW2 5TA, **ENGLAND**.
(T) 020 88942212.
Profile Blacksmith. Ref: YH02970

CLARKE, ALAN G
Alan G Clarke DWCF, 51 Downlands Ave, Broadwater, Worthing, **Sussex (West)**, BN14 9HG, **ENGLAND**.
(T) 01903 208638.
Profile Farrier. Ref: YH02971

CLARKE, CELIA
Celia Clarke, 85 Fishers Field, Buckingham, **Buckinghamshire**, MK18 1SF, **ENGLAND**.
(T) 01280 812281 (F) 01280 824451
(E) celia@cwath.demon.co.uk.
Profile Breeder. Ref: YH02972

CLARKE, CROCKETT & JAMISON
Clarke, Crockett & Jamison, 8 Glenmaquill Rd, Drumrainey, Magherafelt, **County Londonderry**, BT45 5EW, **NORTHERN IRELAND**.
(T) 028 79632841.
Profile Medical Support. Ref: YH02973

CLARKE, D
Mrs & Mrs D Clarke, 2 Bockmer End Cottages, Bockmer, Marlow, **Buckinghamshire**, SL7 2HL, **ENGLAND**.
(T) 01491 571673.
Profile Breeder. Ref: YH02974

CLARKE, P
P Clarke, B A T S Stud, Llansadwrn, **Carmarthenshire**, SA19 8BD, **WALES**.
(T) 01558 685573.
Profile Breeder. Ref: YH02975

CLARKE, W H
Mr W H Clarke, Broad Lee, Pickhill, Thirsk, **Yorkshire (North)**, YO7 4JU, **ENGLAND**.
(T) 01845 567234.
Profile Supplies. Ref: YH02976

CLARKE'S EQUINE COACHWORKS
Clarke's Equine Coachworks, Unit 416, Ash Rd North, Wrexham Ind Est, Wrexham, **Wrexham**, LL13 9UF, **WALES**.
(T) 01978 661939 (F) 01978 661939.
Contact/s
Owner: Mr A Clarke
Profile Transport/Horse Boxes. Ref: YH02977

CLARKE'S SPORTSDEN
Clarke's Sportsden, Trimgate St, Navan, **County Meath**, **IRELAND**.
(T) 046 21130.
Contact/s
Owner: Leslie Clarke
Profile Riding Wear Retailer, Saddlery Retailer, Supplies.
Opening Times
Sp: Open Mon - Sat 09:30. Closed Mon - Sat 18:00.
Su: Open Mon - Sat 09:30. Closed Mon - Sat 18:00.
Au: Open Mon - Sat 09:30. Closed Mon - Sat 18:00.
Wn: Open Mon - Sat 09:30. Closed Mon - Sat 18:00.
Closed Sundays Ref: YH02978

CLARK'S EQUESTRIAN
Clark's Equestrian, Poplar Farm, Long Lane, Aston End, Stevenage, **Hertfordshire**, SG2 7HF, **ENGLAND**.
(T) 01438 880226.
Contact/s
Owner: Mr M Clark
Profile Saddlery Retailer. Ref: YH02979

CLARKS HILL
Clarks Hill, School Rd, Evesham, **Worcestershire**, WR11 6PR, **ENGLAND**.
(T) 01386 443385 (F) 01386 443385.
Contact/s
Partner: Mrs M Cudd
Profile Riding School, Stable/Livery.
Offers part livery, and a riding school for children.
No.Staff: 2 Yr. Est: 1961 C.Size: 15 Acres
Opening Times
Sp: Open Sat, Sun 09:30. Closed Sat 14:30, Sun 12:00.
Su: Open Sat, Sun 09:30. Closed Sat 14:30, Sun 12:00.
Au: Open Sat, Sun 09:30. Closed Sat 14:30, Sun 12:00.
Wn: Open Sat, Sun 09:30. Closed Sat 14:30, Sun 12:00. Ref: YH02980

CLASSIC CARRIAGE
Classic Carriage Co, Flanders Farm, Silver St, Sway, Lymington, **Hampshire**, SO41 6DF, **ENGLAND**.
(T) 01590 682207.
Profile Horse drawn vehicles. Ref: YH02981

CLASSIC CARRIAGES
Classic Carriages, Flodden Edge Farm, Mindrum, **Northumberland**, TD12 4QG, **ENGLAND**.
(T) 01668 216287 (F) 01668 216287.
Contact/s
Partner: Mr T Fletcher
Profile Transport/Horse Boxes. Ref: YH02982

CLASSIC COLLECTION
Classic Collection Ltd, 4 Russet Cl, Alresford, **Hampshire**, SO24 9PS, **ENGLAND**.
(T) 01962 733533 (F) 01962 736103.
Contact/s
Owner: Miss C Smeeth
Profile Riding Wear Retailer, Saddlery Retailer.
Ref: YH02983

CLASSIC DRESSAGE COLLECTION
Classic Dressage Collection, Chilterns, Whelpley Hill, Chesham, **Buckinghamshire**, HP5 3RL, **ENGLAND**.
(T) 01442 834536 (F) 01442 833081.
Contact/s
Manageress: Mrs I Hudson
Profile Supplies. Ref: YH02984

CLASSIC EQUESTRIAN
Classic Equestrian, Narcot Lane, Chalfont St. Peter, Gerrards Cross, **Buckinghamshire**, SL9 8TR, **ENGLAND**.
(T) 01494 871298.
Contact/s
Manager: Mrs S Edwards
Profile Equestrian Centre. Ref: YH02985

CLASSIC EQUESTRIAN
Classic Equestrian, 98B Newbottle St, Houghton Le Spring, **Tyne and Wear**, DH4 4AJ, **ENGLAND**.
(T) 0191 5845195.
Contact/s
Owner: Miss L Key
Profile Riding Wear Retailer, Saddlery Retailer.
Ref: YH02986

CLASSIC EQUINE PRODUCTS
Classic Equine Products, PO Box 58, Beckenham, **Kent**, BR3 1WE, **ENGLAND**.
(T) 020 87781055 (F) 020 86594823.
Profile Riding Wear Retailer, Saddlery Retailer.
Ref: YH02987

CLASSIC RACING BOOKS
Classic Racing Books, 64 Stephen Way, Bignall End, Stoke-on-Trent, **Staffordshire**, ST7 8NL, **ENGLAND**.
(T) 01782 722394.
Profile Supplies. Ref: YH02988

CLASSICAL DRESSAGE
Classical Dressage, Bury Farm, St Marys Lane, Upminster, **Essex**, RM14 3PH, **ENGLAND**.
(T) 01708 640449.
Profile Trainer. Ref: YH02989

CLASSICAL RIDING SCHOOL
Classical Riding School & Display Team, Turville Valley Stud, Turville, Henley-on-Thames, **Oxfordshire**, RG9 6QU, **ENGLAND**.
(T) 01491 638338 (F) 01491 614896.
Profile Riding School. Display team. Ref: YH02990

CLASSY PONIES
Classy Ponies, 56 Cliffe St, Dewsbury, **Yorkshire (West)**, WF13 1RD, **ENGLAND**.
(T) 01924 466763
(E) andrew@abarrick.freeserve.co.uk.
Profile Supplies. Ref: YH02991

CLAVERDON
Claverdon Arabian Stud, Pinley Abbey, Claverdon, Warwick, **Warwickshire**, CV35 8ND, **ENGLAND**.
(T) 01926 842280 (F) 01926 842546.
Contact/s
Owner: Mrs J Lowe
Profile Breeder, Stud Farm.
Breed Performance Racehorses. Yr. Est: 1953
Opening Times
By appointment only. Answerphone service 09:00 - 21:00 Ref: YH02992

CLAVERING SADDLERY & LEATHER
Clavering Saddlery & Leather Workers, Leatside, Middle St, Clavering, Saffron Walden, **Essex**, CB11 4QL, **ENGLAND**.
(T) 01799 550297.
Contact/s
Owner: Mrs L Rhodes
Profile Saddlery Retailer. Ref: YH02993

CLAY HALL
Clay Hall Riding & Driving School, Days Lane, Pilgrims Hatch, Brentwood, **Essex**, CM15 9SJ, **ENGLAND**.
(T) 01277 374649 (F) 01277 372050
Affiliated Bodies ABRS.
Contact/s
Owner: Ms J Stewart (Q) BDS 2, BHS 4, BHSII
Profile Equestrian Centre, Riding School, Track/Course, Trainer. Horse & Carriage Hire.
Horse & Carriage Hire for Weddings. No.Staff: 4
Yr. Est: 1989 C.Size: 2 Acres
Opening Times
Sp: Open Mon - Sun 09:00. Closed Mon - Sun 19:00.
Su: Open Mon - Sun 09:00. Closed Mon - Sun 21:00.
Au: Open Mon - Sun 09:00. Closed Mon - Sun 19:00.
Wn: Open Mon - Sun 09:00. Closed Mon - Sun 19:00. Ref: YH02994

CLAY, W
Mr W Clay, Saverley Hse Farm, Saverley Green, Cresswell, Stoke-on-Trent, **Staffordshire**, ST11 9QX, **ENGLAND**.
(T) 01782 392131.
Profile Trainer. Ref: YH02995

CLAYBROOKE
Claybrooke Animal Feeds, Grange Farm, Frolesworth Lane, Claybrooke Magna, Lutterworth, **Leicestershire**, LE17 5DA, **ENGLAND**.
(T) 01455 202757 (F) 01455 202961
(E) claybrookeanimalfeeds@equestrianet.co.uk
(W) www.claybrookeanimalfeeds.co.uk.
Profile Feed Merchant. Ref: YH02996

CLAYBROOKE STABLES

Claybrooke Stables, Main Rd, Claybrooke Parva, Lutterworth, **Leicestershire**, LE17 5AE, **ENGLAND**.
(T) 01455 202511
(E) claybrooke@jbd.net
(W) www.claybrooke-stables.com.
Contact/s
Owner: Mrs D Clayton
Profile Riding School, Stable/Livery.
Claybrooke can arrange day courses for groups to spend a few hours learning the basics of looking after a horse, have a lesson, and then a hack. Claybrooke also have horses for sale. **Ref: YH02997**

CLAYDEN ENGINEERING

Clayden Engineering Ltd, Scandinavian Way, Stallingborough, Grimsby, **Lincolnshire (North East)**, DN41 8DU, **ENGLAND**.
(T) 01469 571203 **(F)** 01469 571574.
Profile Transport/Horse Boxes. **Ref: YH02998**

CLAYDON HORSE EXERCISERS

Claydon Horse Exercisers, Green Acres, Coventry Rd, Southam, **Warwickshire**, CV47 1BG, **ENGLAND**.
(T) 01926 811526 **(F)** 01926 811522.
Contact/s
Partner: Mrs B Funnell
Profile Trainer. **Ref: YH02999**

CLAYGATE SPORTS HORSES

Claygate Sports Horses, 103A Hare Lane, Claygate, Esher, **Surrey**, KT10 0QX, **ENGLAND**.
(T) 01372 466701
(W) www.claygatesportshorses.com.
Contact/s
Public Affairs and International officer: Aurélie Almedia
(E) aurelie@claygatesportshorses.com
Profile Blood Stock Agency.
Claygate Sports Horses sell the Selle Francais and Sport Horse breeds in the UK. The horses offered for sale are chosen for their superior athletic abilities and extremely kind and trainable temperament. This is also a free directory for the French and UK breeders of French competition horses. Therefore the breeders of these horses are able to register with them and receive a dedicated space on the Claygate website due to be launched January 2002.
Opening Times
Please telephone in the evening **Ref: YH03000**

CLAYSON-HASELWOOD

Clayson-Haselwood, 50 South Bar, Banbury, **Oxfordshire**, OX16 9AB, **ENGLAND**.
(T) 01295 271555 **(F)** 01295 258630
(E) property@claysonhaselwood.co.uk
(W) www.claysonhaselwood.co.uk.
Profile Estate Agents.
Auctioneers, planning & building advisors, covering North Oxfordshire, South Northamptonshire, North Buckinghamshire & South Warwickshire. **Ref: YH03001**

CLAYTON & COX

Clayton & Cox, Millpark Veterinary Ctre, Newent, **Gloucestershire**, GL18 1AZ, **ENGLAND**.
(T) 01531 820258 **(F)** 01531 822351.
Contact/s
Assistant: Miss K Gerhard
Profile Medical Support. **Ref: YH03002**

CLAYTON HILL STABLES

Clayton Hill Stables, Southdown Lodge, Clayton Hill, Clayton, Hassocks, **Sussex (West)**, BN6 9PQ, **ENGLAND**.
(T) 01273 844120.
Contact/s
Owner: Mrs P Gasson
Profile Riding School, Stable/Livery. **Ref: YH03003**

CLAYTON, J

J Clayton, Highfield Livery & Training Yard, Northop Hall, Sychdyn, Mold, **Flintshire**, CH7 6EG, **WALES**.
(T) 01352 840603.
Profile Stable/Livery. Training Yard. **Ref: YH03004**

CLAYTON, MICHAEL

Michael Clayton, Sunnyside Cottage, Braunston-In-Rutland, Oakham, **Rutland**, LE15 8QW, **ENGLAND**.
(T) 01572 724424 **(F)** 01572 770439.
Profile Supplies. **Ref: YH03005**

CLAYTON, PENNIE

Pennie Clayton, 48 Main Rd, Sutton At Hone, Dartford, **Kent**, DA4 9EU, **ENGLAND**.
(T) 01322 860337.
Contact/s
Owner: Ms P Clayton **(Q)** BHS IT
Profile Trainer.
Freelance dressage trainer
Opening Times
Telephone for further information **Ref: YH03006**

CLB

C L B Ltd, 42 Bartholomew St, Newbury, **Berkshire**, RG14 5QA, **ENGLAND**.
(T) 01635 569151 **(F)** 01635 253303.
Contact/s
Owner: Mr C Leafe
Profile Blood Stock Agency. **Ref: YH03007**

CLEAN, B

B Clean, 9-13 Hawkins Rd, Earlsdon, Coventry, **Midlands (West)**, CV5 6HZ, **ENGLAND**.
(T) 024 76714968 **(F)** 024 76772995.
Profile Supplies. **Ref: YH03008**

CLEAR HEIGHT STABLES

Clear Height Stables, Derby Stables Rd, Epsom, **Surrey**, KT18 5LB, **ENGLAND**.
(T) 01372 721490 **(F)** 01372 748099
(M) 07860 800109.
Profile Trainer. **Ref: YH03009**

CLEAR ROUND ORIGINALS

Clear Round Originals, 27 Hillhouse Ave, Bathgate, **Lothian (West)**, EH48 4BQ, **SCOTLAND**.
(T) 01506 632373.
Profile Supplies. **Ref: YH03010**

CLEARBROOK

Clearbrook Riding Stables, Riverslea, Clearbrook, Yelverton, **Devon**, PL20 6JB, **ENGLAND**.
(T) 01822 854208.
Contact/s
Owner: Mr B Searle **Ref: YH03011**

CLEATON, BRIAN E

Brian E Cleaton AFCL, Lion St, Hay-on-Wye, Hereford, **Herefordshire**, HR3 5AD, **ENGLAND**.
(T) 01497 820840.
Contact/s
Owner: Mr B Cleaton
Profile Farrier. **Ref: YH03012**

CLEE SADDLERY & LEATHERWORKS

Clee Saddlery & Leatherworks, 53 Cambridge St, Cleethorpes, **Lincolnshire (North East)**, DN35 8HD, **ENGLAND**.
(T) 01472 603918.
Contact/s
Owner: Mr K Tucker
Profile Saddlery Retailer. **Ref: YH03013**

CLEERE, NICHOLAS S P

Nicholas S P Cleere DWCF, 14 Goose Cottages, Chelmsford Rd, Battlesbridge, Wickford, **Essex**, SS11 8TB, **ENGLAND**.
(T) 01268 763795.
Profile Farrier. **Ref: YH03014**

CLEGGAN TREKKING CTRE

Cleggan Trekking Centre, Cleegan, Connemara, **County Galway**, **IRELAND**.
(T) 095 44746
Affiliated Bodies AIRE.
Contact/s
Owner: Judy Cazabon
Profile Equestrian Centre. Trekking Centre.
Organise treks to Omey Island, Cleggan and Sallema beaches. Riding holidays can also be arranged.
Ref: YH03015

CLEMENTS, D

D Clements, 30-40 Main St, Augher, **County Tyrone**, BT77 0BG, **NORTHERN IRELAND**.
(T) 028 82548248.
Profile Supplies. **Ref: YH03016**

CLEMENTS, D & R

D & R Clements, The Smithy, Castlebergh Lane, Settle, **Yorkshire (North)**, BD24 9ET, **ENGLAND**.
(T) 01729 825513.
Profile Blacksmith. **Ref: YH03017**

CLEMENTS, IAN A

Ian A Clements DWCF, The Lantern, North End Rd, Gestingthorpe, Halstead, **Essex**, CO9 3BW, **ENGLAND**.
(T) 01787 238488.
Profile Farrier. **Ref: YH03018**

CLEVEDALE VETNRY PRACTICE

Clevedale Veterinary Practice, The Old Sawmill, Home Farm, Upleatham, Redcar, **Cleveland**, TS11 8AG, **ENGLAND**.
(T) 01287 623802.
Profile Medical Support. **Ref: YH03019**

CLEVEDON RIDING

Clevedon Riding Centre, Clevedon Lane, Clevedon, **Somerset (North)**, BS21 7AG, **ENGLAND**.
(T) 01275 858699
(W) www.clevedonridingcentre.co.uk
Affiliated Bodies BHS.
Contact/s
Owner: Mrs J Sims
(E) judith@clevedonridingcentre.co.uk
Profile Riding School, Stable/Livery. **Yr. Est:** 1970
Opening Times
Sp: Open Mon - Sun 09:00. Closed Mon - Sun 21:00.
Su: Open Mon - Sun 09:00. Closed Mon - Sun 21:00.
Au: Open Mon - Sun 09:00. Closed Mon - Sun 21:00.
Wn: Open Mon - Sun 09:00. Closed Mon - Sun 21:00. **Ref: YH03020**

CLEVELAND BAY HORSE SOC

Cleveland Bay Horse Society, York Livestock Ctre, Murton, York, **Yorkshire (North)**, YO19 5UF, **ENGLAND**.
(T) 01904 489731 **(F)** 01904 489782.
Contact/s
Key Contact: Mr J Stephenson
Profile Club/Association. **Ref: YH03021**

CLEVELAND TRAILER CTRE

Cleveland Trailer Centre, Saltwater Hse, Longlands Rd, Middlesbrough, **Cleveland**, TS4 2JR, **ENGLAND**.
(T) 01642 230123.
Profile Transport/Horse Boxes. **Ref: YH03022**

CLEVELANDS STUD

Clevelands Stud, Oakley Green Rd, Oakley Green, Windsor, **Berkshire**, SL4 4QF, **ENGLAND**.
(T) 01628 25979.
Profile Breeder. **Ref: YH03023**

CLEVERLY, TANYA

Tanya Cleverly, Velmead Farm, Church Crookham, **Hampshire**, GU13 0RN, **ENGLAND**.
(T) 01252 850224
(M) 07860 391998.
Profile Trainer. **Ref: YH03024**

CLGE EQUESTRIAN CTRE

College Equestrian Centre (The), Clge Farm, Church Rd, Keysoe, Bedford, **Bedfordshire**, MK44 2JP, **ENGLAND**.
(T) 01234 708400 **(F)** 01234 708400
(E) info@thecollegeec.com
(W) www.thecollegeec.com.
Contact/s
Owner: Mr S Bates
(E) simon@thecollegeec.com
Profile Arena, Equestrian Centre, Riding Club, Stable/Livery, Track/Course. **No.Staff:** 10
Yr. Est: 1996 **C.Size:** 150 Acres
Opening Times
Sp: Open 09:00. Closed 17:00.
Su: Open 09:00. Closed 17:00.
Au: Open 09:00. Closed 17:00.
Wn: Open 09:00. Closed 17:00. **Ref: YH03025**

CLGE FARM

College Farm Equestrian Centre, West Markham, Tuxford, Newark, **Nottinghamshire**, NG22 0PN, **ENGLAND**.
(T) 01777 870886 **(F)** 01777 870880
(E) tuition@collegefarm.co.uk
(W) www.collegefarm.com
Affiliated Bodies BHS.
Contact/s
Owner: Ms V Hayton **(Q)** BHSII
(E) hayton@collegefarm.com
Profile Arena, Equestrian Centre, Horse/Rider Accom, Riding Club, Riding School, Stable/Livery, Track/Course, Trainer.
Full, semi-DIY, DIY and grass livery available, details on request. **No.Staff:** 10 **Yr. Est:** 1986
Opening Times
Sp: Open 08:00. Closed 19:00.
Su: Open 08:00. Closed 19:00.
Au: Open 08:00. Closed 17:00.
Wn: Open 08:00. Closed 17:00. **Ref: YH03026**

CLGE FARM SADDLERY & FEEDS

College Farm Saddlery & Feeds, 45 Fitzalan Rd, Finchley, **London (Greater)**, N3 3PG, **ENGLAND**.
(T) 020 83490690 **(F)** 020 83469988.
Profile Feed Merchant, Saddlery Retailer.
Ref: YH03027

CLGE HILL VETNRY GRP

College Hill Veterinary Group (Shawbury), High Ridge, Wem Rd, Shawbury, **Shropshire**, SY4 4NW,

A-Z of COMPANIES

ENGLAND.
(T) 01939 250655.
Profile Medical Support. Ref: YH03028

CLGE PRACT PHYTOTHERAPY

College of Practitioners of Phytotherapy, Bucksteep Manor, Bodle St Green, Hailsham, **Sussex (East)**, BN27 4RJ, **ENGLAND**.
(T) 01323 833869.
Profile Medical Support. Ref: YH03029

CLGE VALLEY

College Valley & North Northumberland, Sunilaws, Cornhill-on-Tweed, **Northumberland**, TD12 4RO, **ENGLAND**.
(T) 01890 882475. Ref: YH03030

CLIDDESDEN RIDING SCHOOL

Cliddesden Riding School, Station Rd, Cliddesden, Basingstoke, **Hampshire**, RG25 2JH, **ENGLAND**.
(T) 01256 330700.
Contact/s
Owner: Miss C Gibson
Profile Riding School. Ref: YH03031

CLIFF HATCH STABLES

Cliff Hatch Stables, Saunders Lane, Woking, **Surrey**, GU22 0NU, **ENGLAND**.
(T) 01483 747028.
Contact/s
Owner: Mrs D Passant
Profile Equestrian Centre. Ref: YH03032

CLIFF STUD

Cliff Stud, Helmsley, York, **Yorkshire (North)**, YO62 5HE, **ENGLAND**.
(T) 01439 770294 (F) 01439 770309.
Profile Breeder. Ref: YH03033

CLIFFE VETNRY GRP

Cliffe Veterinary Group, Radstock Hse, 21 Cliffe High St, Lewes, **Sussex (East)**, BN7 2AH, **ENGLAND**.
(T) 01273 473232 (F) 01273 472216.
Profile Medical Support. Ref: YH03034

CLIFFORD MOOR FARM

Clifford Moor Farm Riding School And Livery Stables, Clifford Moor Farm, Rhodes Lane, Clifford, Wetherby, **Yorkshire (West)**, LS23 6LQ, **ENGLAND**.
(T) 01937 844165 (F) 01937 844165
Affiliated Bodies ABRS.
Contact/s
Owner: Mrs P Gula-Walker
Profile Riding School, Stable/Livery. No.Staff: 3
Yr. Est: 1987 C.Size: 26 Acres
Opening Times
Sp: Open 08:00. Closed 21:00.
Su: Open 08:00. Closed 21:00.
Au: Open 08:00. Closed 21:00.
Wn: Open 08:00. Closed 21:00. Ref: YH03035

CLIFTON CARRIAGES

Clifton Carriages, 7 Rudthorpe Rd, Bristol, **Bristol**, BS7 9QG, **ENGLAND**.
(T) 01179 087458.
Contact/s
Owner: Ms I Rivas-Pile
Profile
Clifton Carriages provide a Victorian carriage with a driver and groom for safetyat public events such as weddings and funerals Yr. Est: 2000 Ref: YH03036

CLIFTON LODGE VETNRY GRP

Clifton Lodge Veterinary Group, 44 Station Rd, Billingham, Stockton-on-Tees, **Cleveland**, TS23 1AB, **ENGLAND**.
(T) 01642 555975.
Profile Medical Support. Ref: YH03037

CLIFTON LODGE VETNRY GRP

Clifton Lodge Veterinary Group, 24 Stockton Rd, Durham, **County Durham**, TS25 1RL, **ENGLAND**.
(T) 01429 272435.
Profile Medical Support. Ref: YH03038

CLIFTON LODGE VETRNRY GRP

Clifton Lodge Veterinary Group, 7 East End, Sedgefield, Durham, **County Durham**, TS21 3AU, **ENGLAND**.
(T) 01740 22126.
Profile Medical Support. Ref: YH03039

CLIFTON ON TEME

Clifton on Teme, The Saplings, Apple Cross, Stoke Bliss, Tenbury Wells, **Worcestershire**, WR15 8RZ, **ENGLAND**.
(T) 01885 410368. Ref: YH03040

CLIFTON VILLA

Clifton Villa Veterinary Surgery, 10 Cross St, Camborne, **Cornwall**, TR14 8EU, **ENGLAND**.
(T) 01209 711933 (F) 01872 247950.
Profile Medical Support. Ref: YH03041

CLIFTON VILLA

Clifton Villa Veterinary Surgery, Coronation Trce, Richmond Hill, Truro, **Cornwall**, TR1 3HJ, **ENGLAND**.
(T) 01872 273694 (F) 01872 274950.
Profile Medical Support. Ref: YH03042

CLINTON, P L

Mr P L Clinton, Lordlea Farm, Marston Lane, Doveridge, Ashbourne, **Derbyshire**, DE6 5JS, **ENGLAND**.
(T) 01889 566356.
Profile Trainer. Ref: YH03043

CLIP CLOP SHOP

Clip Clop Shop (The), The Shop/Cliffe Woods Garage, Town Rd, Cliffe Woods, Rochester, **Kent**, ME3 8JJ, **ENGLAND**.
(T) 01634 221023.
Profile Riding Wear Retailer, Saddlery Retailer.
Ref: YH03044

CLIP CLOPS SADDLERY

Clip Clops Saddlery, Beslyns Rd, Great Bardfield, Braintree, **Essex**, CM7 4TG, **ENGLAND**.
(T) 01371 810060 (F) 01371 810714.
Profile Saddlery Retailer. Ref: YH03045

CLIPPER SHARP

Clipper Sharp, Southwoods Farm, Culmstock, Cullompton, **Devon**, EX15 3JX, **ENGLAND**.
(T) 01823 681076 (F) 01823 681076
(E) richard@clippersharpservices.com
(W) www.clippersharpservices.com.
Profile Supplies.
New and serviced machines are sent 24 hour CITY LINK
Yr. Est: 1994 Ref: YH03046

CLIPPERS

Clippers (HG) Ltd, The Firs, Devauden, Chepstow, **Monmouthshire**, NP16 6PL, **WALES**.
(T) 01291 650543 (F) 01179 316151
(E) sales@clipperservices.co.uk
(W) www.clipperservices.co.uk.
Profile Supplies. Ref: YH03047

CLIPPETY CLOP

Clippety Clop, Tannoch Farm, Palacerigg, Cumbernauld, **Lanarkshire (North)**, G67 3HU, **SCOTLAND**.
(T) 01236 733424.
Profile Supplies. Ref: YH03048

CLITHEROE AUCTION MART

Clitheroe Auction Mart Co Ltd, The Ribblesdale Ctre, Clitheroe, **Lancashire**, BB7 1QD, **ENGLAND**.
(T) 01200 423325.
Profile Auctioneers. Ref: YH03049

CLIVE VALLEY VETNRY PRACTICE

Clive Valley Veterinary Practice, Whitelees Rd, Lanark, **Lanarkshire (South)**, ML11 7RX, **SCOTLAND**.
(T) 01555 663073.
Profile Medical Support. Ref: YH03050

CLIVEDEN STUD

Cliveden Stud, Cliveden Rd, Taplow, Maidenhead, **Berkshire**, SL6 0HU, **ENGLAND**.
(T) 01628 604145 (F) 01628 663635.
Contact/s
Manager: Mr P Friedman
Profile Breeder. Ref: YH03051

CLOCK TOWER RIDING CTRE

Clock Tower Riding Centre, Brighton Rd, Tadworth, **Surrey**, KT20 6QZ, **ENGLAND**.
(T) 01737 832874.
Profile Riding School, Stable/Livery. Ref: YH03052

CLONAKILTY EQUESTRIAN CTRE

Clonakilty Equestrian Centre, The Retreat, Clonakilty, **County Cork**, **IRELAND**.
(T) 023 33533 (F) 023 35012
(W) www.clonequestrian.com
Affiliated Bodies SJAI.
Contact/s
Owner: David O' Regan
(E) david@clonequestrian.com
Profile
Treks along the scenic Inchydoney Beach are available.
Ref: YH03053

CLONAKILTY SADDLERY

Clonakilty Saddlery, 4 Ashe St, Clonakilty, **County Cork**, **IRELAND**.
(T) 023 34425.
Profile Saddlery Retailer, Supplies. Ref: YH03054

CLONBOO RIDING SCHOOL

Clonboo Riding School, Clonboo Cross, Corrundulla, Galway, **County Galway**, **IRELAND**.
(T) 091 791362. Ref: YH03055

CLONLARA EQUESTRIAN CTRE

Clonlara Equestrian Centre, Oakfield, Main Killaloe Rd, Clonlara, **County Clare**, **IRELAND**.
(T) 061 354172
Affiliated Bodies AIRE.
Contact/s
Manager: Davnet Kiernan O'Brien
Profile Riding School.
Hacking, trekking and mini cross country course available. Ref: YH03056

CLONMEL EQUESTRIAN CTRE

Clonmel Equestrian Centre, Moangarriff, Clonmel, **County Tipperary**, **IRELAND**.
(T) 052 26580
(M) 087 2446302.
Contact/s
Owner: Mr T English
Profile Equestrian Centre, Riding School, Stable/Livery.
Livery available, details on request.
Opening Times
Sp: Open Mon - Fri 15:30, Sat 10:00. Closed Mon - Fri 20:00, Sat 18:00.
Su: Open Mon - Fri 15:30, Sat 10:00. Closed Mon - Fri 20:00, Sat 18:00.
Au: Open Mon - Fri 15:30, Sat 10:00. Closed Mon - Fri 20:00, Sat 18:00.
Wn: Open Mon - Fri 15:30, Sat 10:00. Closed Mon - Fri 20:00, Sat 18:00.
Treks take place on Sundays Ref: YH03057

CLONMORE RIDING CTRE

Clonmore Riding Centre, Clonmore, Rhode, **County Offaly**, **IRELAND**.
(T) 0405 39103. Ref: YH03058

CLONSHIRE EQUESTRIAN CTRE

Clonshire Equestrian Centre, Clonshire, Adare, **County Limerick**, **IRELAND**.
(T) 061 396770. Ref: YH03059

CLOSE, J

Mr J Close, Low Middlefield Cottage, Blakestone Lane, Norton, Stockton-on-Tees, **Cleveland**, TS21 3LE, **ENGLAND**.
(T) 01642 615235.
Profile Trainer. Ref: YH03060

CLOSE, M J

M J Close, Lowfield Farm, Bowes, Barnard Castle, **County Durham**, DL12 9JR, **ENGLAND**.
(T) 01833 628333 (F) 01833 628333.
Contact/s
Owner: Mr M Close
Profile Hay and Straw Merchant. Ref: YH03061

CLOTHES HORSE

Clothes Horse (The), Syston Grange Farm, Barkby Rd, Syston, Leicester, **Leicestershire**, LE7 2AJ, **ENGLAND**.
(T) 0116 2609801 (F) 0116 2609801
(W) www.the-clothes-horse.co.uk
Affiliated Bodies BETA.
Contact/s
General Manager: Miss C Andrews
(Q) AMTRA
Profile Riding Wear Retailer, Saddlery Retailer, Supplies. No.Staff: 6 Yr. Est: 1988
C.Size: 1 Acres
Opening Times
Sp: Open Mon - Sat 09:00. Closed Mon - Fri 17:30, Sat 17:00.
Su: Open Mon -Sat 09:00. Closed Mon - Fri 17:30, Sat 17:00.
Au: Open Mon - Sat 09:00. Closed Mon - Fri 17:30, Sat 17:00.
Wn: Open Mon - Sat 09:00. Closed Mon - Fri 17:30, Sat 17:00.
Closed Sundays Ref: YH03062

CLOTHES HORSE

Clothes Horse (2nd Hand Clothing) (The), The Old Laundry, Clifford Moor Rd, Boston Spa, **Yorkshire (West)**, LS23 6NZ, **ENGLAND**.
(T) 01937 832124 (F) 01937 832124.
Profile Riding Wear Retailer. Ref: YH03063

CLOTHES HORSE COMPANY
Clothes Horse Company (The), Bucks Farm Hoe Lane, Nazeing, **Essex**, EN9 2RW, **ENGLAND**.
(T) 01992 892142 **(F)** 01279 626893.
Profile Riding Wear Retailer, Supplies. **Ref: YH03064**

CLOTHIE SHETLAND PONY STUD
Clothie Shetland Pony Stud, Heugh Head, Cothal, Dyce, **Aberdeen (City of)**, AB21 0HT, **SCOTLAND**.
(T) 01224 722240.
Profile Breeder. **Ref: YH03065**

CLOUD STABLES
Cloud Stables, Church Lane, Arborfield, Reading, **Berkshire**, RG2 9JA, **ENGLAND**.
(T) 0118 9761522.
Contact/s
Manageress: Mrs S Pacey
Profile Riding School, Stable/Livery. **Ref: YH03066**

CLOUDBANK STABLES
Cloudbank Stables, 64 Downs Rd, South Wonston, Winchester, **Hampshire**, SO21 3EW, **ENGLAND**.
(T) 01962 881292.
Contact/s
Owner: Mr F Ward
Profile Riding School. **Ref: YH03067**

CLOUGH FIELDS STABLES
Clough Fields Stables, Clough Fields, Sheffield, **Yorkshire (South)**, S10 5PY, **ENGLAND**.
(T) 0114 2665162.
Contact/s
Owner: Mrs J Swift
Profile Stable/Livery. **Ref: YH03068**

CLOVER HILL SADDLERY
Clover Hill Saddlery, 1st Floor, 257 King Cross Rd, Halifax, **Yorkshire (West)**, HX1 3JL, **ENGLAND**.
(T) 01422 365890
(E) avdev58@yahoo.com.
Profile Saddlery Retailer. **Ref: YH03069**

CLOVERFIELD EQUESTRIAN CTRE
Cloverfield Equestrian Centre, Fairy Lane, Sale, **Cheshire**, M33 2JT, **ENGLAND**.
(T) 0161 9690701.
Contact/s
Owner: Mrs P Long
Profile Equestrian Centre, Riding School.
Ref: YH03070

CLOW, R A
R A Clow RSS, Caversham Farm, Burches Rd, Thundersley, Benfleet, **Essex**, SS7 3NE, **ENGLAND**.
(T) 01268 774144.
Profile Farrier. **Ref: YH03071**

CLOWES NASH & THURGAR
Clowes Nash & Thurgar, Norwich Livestock & Commercial Ctre, Hall Rd, Norwich, **Norfolk**, NR4 6EQ, **ENGLAND**.
(T) 01603 504488.
Profile Auctioneers of livestock and saddlery.
Ref: YH03072

CLOYBURN TREKKING CTRE
Cloyburn Trekking Centre, Glencloy, Brodick, **Ayrshire (North)**, KA27 8DA, **SCOTLAND**.
(T) 01770 302108.
Profile Equestrian Centre, Riding School. Trekking centre.
Treks cost £10 per hour. A children's programme is also offered.
Opening Times
Sp: Open 10:00. Closed 17:00.
Su: Open 10:00. Closed 17:00.
Au: Open 10:00. Closed 17:00.
Wn: Open 10:00. Closed 17:00.
Riding lessons are offered on Saturdays. **Ref: YH03073**

CLUB PRO-AM
Club Pro-Am (Polo Supplies) Ltd, Ham Polo Club, Petersham Rd, Richmond, **Surrey**, TW10 7AH, **ENGLAND**.
(T) 020 89483066 **(F)** 020 89483009.
Profile Polo supplies. **Ref: YH03074**

CLUB RACING
Club Racing Ltd, Ash Holm Lodge, Maunby, Thirsk, **Yorkshire (North)**, YO7 4HG, **ENGLAND**.
(T) 01845 587117 **(F)** 01845 587089.
Profile Club/Association. **Ref: YH03075**

CLUNY HACKNEY STUD
Cluny Hackney Stud, Millside Farm, Galston, **Ayrshire (East)**, K84 8NQ, **SCOTLAND**.
(T) 01563 820274.
Profile Breeder. **Ref: YH03076**

CLUTTON HILL AGRICULTURAL SVS
Clutton Hill Agricultural Services, Cash & Carry, Clutton Hill Farm, Clutton, **Bath & Somerset (North East)**, BS39 5QQ, **ENGLAND**.
(T) 01761 452458.
Profile Supplies. **Ref: YH03077**

CLWYD WELSH PONY & COB ASS
Clwyd Welsh Pony & Cob Association, Bryn Meibion, Clawddnewydd, Ruthin, **Denbighshire**, LL15 2NL, **WALES**.
(T) 01824 750256
Affiliated Bodies WPCS.
Contact/s
Secretary: Ms A Weaver
Profile Club/Association, Riding Club. **Ref: YH03078**

CLYDE VALLEY TREKKING CTRE
Clyde Valley Trekking Centre, Crossford, Carluke, **Lanarkshire (South)**, ML8 5NJ, **SCOTLAND**.
(T) 01555 860697.
Contact/s
Owner: Miss M McNair
Profile Equestrian Centre. Trekking centre.
Ref: YH03079

CLYDEBANK WELDING
Clydebank Welding & Fabrication Ltd, 102 Cable Depot Rd, Clydebank, **Argyll and Bute**, G81 1UF, **SCOTLAND**.
(T) 0141 9412552.
Profile Blacksmith. **Ref: YH03080**

CLYDESDALE HORSE SOC
Clydesdale Horse Society (The), 3 Grosvenor Gardens, Edinburgh, **Edinburgh (City of)**, EH12 5JU, **SCOTLAND**.
(T) 0131 3370923 **(F)** 0131 3377678
(E) secy@clydesdalehorse.co.uk
(W) www.clydesdalehorse.co.uk.
Contact/s
Key Contact: Mrs K Stephen
Profile Breeder, Club/Association. Yr. Est: 1877
Ref: YH03081

CLYDESDALE TIMBER PRODUCTS
Clydesdale Timber Products Ltd, Shedyard Farm, Laneside Rd, New Mills, High Peak, **Cheshire**, SK22 4QN, **ENGLAND**.
(T) 01663 746784 **(F)** 01663 747203
(W) www.clydesdale-timber.co.uk.
Profile Supplies. Stabling.
Clydesdale buildings are guaranteed for 7 years from the date of erection when installed by the Clydesdale team. There is a national delivery service and the stables are available in both standard and made to order sizes **Ref: YH03082**

CLYNDERWEN & CARDIGAN
Clynderwen & Cardiganshire Farmers, Llanglydwen Branch, Hebron, Whitland, **Carmarthenshire**, SA34 0XP, **WALES**.
(T) 01994 419238.
Profile Supplies. **Ref: YH03083**

CLYNDERWEN & CARDIGAN
Clynderwen & Cardiganshire Farmers, The Stores, Station Yard, Felinfach, Lampeter, **Ceredigion**, SA48 7HL, **WALES**.
(T) 01570 470327 **(F)** 01570 471412.
Profile Supplies. **Ref: YH03084**

CLYNDERWEN & CARDIGAN
Clynderwen & Cardiganshire Farmers, Talgarreg Yard, Llanbedr, **Gwynedd**, LL45 2NS, **WALES**.
(T) 01341 241204 **(F)** 01341 241204.
Profile Supplies. **Ref: YH03085**

CLYNDERWEN & CARDIGAN
Clynderwen & Cardiganshire Farmers, Station Rd, Johnston, **Pembrokeshire**, SA62 3PL, **WALES**.
(T) 01437 890473.
Profile Supplies. **Ref: YH03086**

CLYNDERWEN & CARDIGANSHIRE
Clynderwen & Cardiganshire Farmers, Bridge St, Newcastle Emlyn, **Carmarthenshire**, SA38 9DX, **WALES**.
(T) 01239 710443.
Profile Supplies. **Ref: YH03087**

CLYNDERWEN & CARDIGANSHIRE
Clynderwen & Cardiganshire Farmers, Parc-Y-Llyn, Llanbadarn, Aberystwyth, **Ceredigion**, SY23 3TL, **WALES**.
(T) 01970 612690.
Profile Supplies. **Ref: YH03088**

CLYNDERWEN & CARDIGANSHIRE
Clynderwen & Cardiganshire Farmers, Britannia Stores, Pwllhai, Cardigan, **Ceredigion**, SA43 1DB, **WALES**.
(T) 01239 612604.
Profile Supplies. **Ref: YH03089**

CLYNDERWEN & CARDIGANSHIRE
Clynderwen & Cardiganshire Farmers, The Stores, Station Yard, Tregaron, **Ceredigion**, SY25 6XX, **WALES**.
(T) 01974 298214.
Profile Supplies. **Ref: YH03090**

CLYNDERWEN & CARDIGANSHIRE
Clynderwen & Cardiganshire Farmers, Unit 10 Vale Business Pk, Lladon, **Glamorgan (Vale of)**, CF71 7PF, **WALES**.
(T) 01446 773203.
Profile Supplies. **Ref: YH03091**

CLYNDERWEN & CARDIGANSHIRE
Clynderwen & Cardiganshire Farmers, Bro Aran, Llanuwchllyn, Bala, **Gwynedd**, LL23 7UB, **WALES**.
(T) 01678 540224 **(F)** 01678 540250.
Profile Supplies. **Ref: YH03092**

CLYNDERWEN & CARDIGANSHIRE
Clynderwen & Cardiganshire Farmers, 76 High St, Bala, **Gwynedd**, LL23 7AD, **WALES**.
(T) 01678 520291.
Profile Supplies. **Ref: YH03093**

CLYNDERWEN & CARDIGANSHIRE
Clynderwen & Cardiganshire Farmers, Gaerwen Uchaf, Gaerwen, **Isle of Anglesey**, LL60 6DN, **WALES**.
(T) 01248 421154 **(F)** 01248 421035.
Profile Supplies. **Ref: YH03094**

CLYNDERWEN & CARDIGANSHIRE
Clynderwen & Cardiganshire Farmers, The Stores, Main St, Clynderwen, **Pembrokeshire**, SA66 7NW, **WALES**.
(T) 01437 563441 **(F)** 01437 563745.
Profile Supplies. **Ref: YH03095**

CLYNDERWEN & CARDIGANSHIRE
Clynderwen & Cardiganshire Farmers, Spring Gardens, Narberth, **Pembrokeshire**, SA67 7BT, **WALES**.
(T) 01834 860369.
Profile Supplies. **Ref: YH03096**

CLYNDERWEN & CARDIGANSHIRE
Clynderwen & Cardiganshire Farmers, Hermon Rd, Crymych, **Pembrokeshire**, SA41 3QE, **WALES**.
(T) 01239 831203.
Profile Supplies. **Ref: YH03097**

CLYNDERWEN & CARDIGANSHIRE
Clynderwen & Cardiganshire Farmers, Carew Branch, Milton, Tenby, **Pembrokeshire**, SA70 8SQ, **WALES**.
(T) 01646 651297.
Profile Supplies. **Ref: YH03098**

CLYNDERWEN & CARDIGANSHIRE
Clynderwen & Cardiganshire Farmers, The Stores, Maengwyn St, Machynlleth, **Powys**, SY20 8EA, **WALES**.
(T) 01654 702448.
Profile Supplies. **Ref: YH03099**

CLYN-DU RIDING CTRE
Clyn-Du Riding Centre, Clyndu, Graig, Burry Port, **Carmarthenshire**, SA16 0BZ, **WALES**.
(T) 01554 834084 **(F)** 01554 834235.
Contact/s
Owner: Mrs R Vaughan-Jones
Profile Riding School. **Ref: YH03100**

CLYNE ENGINEERING
Clyne Engineering, Milton Of Buntait, Glenurquhart, **Highlands**, IV63 6TW, **SCOTLAND**.
(T) 01456 476365 **(F)** 01456 476365.
Profile Supplies. Provide competition, marathon and exercise vehicles. **Ref: YH03101**

COACH HSE
Coach House Livery Stables, Little Gregories Lane, Theydon Bois, Epping, **Essex**, CM16 7JP, **ENGLAND**.
(T) 01992 813751.
Contact/s
Owner: Ms K Tullett
(E) karen@coachhousestables-freeserve.co.uk
Profile Arena, Equestrian Centre, Stable/Livery, Trainer, Transport/Horse Boxes.

There is miles of forest hacking within reach of the M25. Coach House offer an international dressage trainer and clinics held with a spanish riding school trainer. No.Staff: 6 Yr. Est: 1999 C.Size: 8 Acres
Opening Times
Sp: Open 07:30. Closed 21:30.
Su: Open 07:30. Closed 21:30.
Au: Open 07:30. Closed 21:30.
Wn: Open 07:30. Closed 21:30. Ref: YH03102

COACH HSE SADDLERY
Coach House Saddlery, Chestnuts Farm, Gilberts End, Hanley Castle, **Worcestershire**, WR8 0AS, **ENGLAND**.
(T) 01684 310980
(M) 07831 384332.
Profile Saddlery Retailer, Supplies. Ref: YH03103

COACH HSE STABLES
Coach House Stables (The), Old Coach Hse, High St, Chippenham, Ely, **Cambridgeshire**, CB7 5PP, **ENGLAND**.
(T) 01638 720415 (F) 01638 721970.
Contact/s
Owner: Mrs L Porter-Cohen
Profile Riding School. Ref: YH03104

COACH HSE STABLES
Coach House Stables (The), Letcombe Regis, Wantage, **Oxfordshire**, OX12 9LH, **ENGLAND**.
(T) 01235 767713
(M) 07836 275292.
Profile Trainer. Ref: YH03105

COACH HSE VETNRY CLINIC
Coach House Veterinary Clinic, Burlyns, East Woodhay, Newbury, **Berkshire**, RG20 0NU, **ENGLAND**.
(T) 01635 254143 (F) 01635 254272.
Profile Medical Support. Ref: YH03106

COACHLANE FEED STORES
Coachlane Feed Stores, Coachlane, Redruth, **Cornwall**, TR15 2TP, **ENGLAND**.
(T) 01209 219229 (F) 01209 315058.
Profile Feed Merchant. Ref: YH03107

COATES, MARGRIT
Margrit Coates, Red Gables, Whiteshoot, Redlynch, **Wiltshire**, SP5 2PR, **ENGLAND**.
(T) 01725 511904.
Contact/s
Author: Ms M Coates
Profile Medical Support. Ref: YH03108

COATS, A
A Coats, Dunrobin Stud, Dunes Rd, Greatstone, New Romney, **Kent**, TN28 8SP, **ENGLAND**.
(T) 01797 363335.
Contact/s
Owner: Mr A Coats
Profile Breeder. Ref: YH03109

COBB, I
Mr & Mrs I Cobb, Kilbrannan Farm, Gay St, Pulborough, **Sussex (West)**, RH20 2HJ, **ENGLAND**.
(T) 01798 812541.
Profile Breeder, Stable/Livery. Ref: YH03110

COBB, JASON R
Jason R Cobb DWCF, 39 Robert Dukeson Ave, Winthorpe Gardens, Newark, **Nottinghamshire**, NG24 2FF, **ENGLAND**.
(T) 01636 708633.
Profile Farrier. Ref: YH03111

COBBLETHORNS SADDLERY
Cobblethorns Saddlery, Cobblethorns, Glen Rd, Castle Bytham, Grantham, **Lincolnshire**, NG33 4RJ, **ENGLAND**.
(T) 01780 410489.
Profile Saddlery Retailer. Ref: YH03112

COBHAM MANOR
Cobham Manor Riding Centre, Water Lane, Thurnham, Maidstone, **Kent**, ME14 3LU, **ENGLAND**.
(T) 01622 738497/738871 (F) 01622 735600
(E) admin@cobham-manor.co.uk
(W) www.cobham-manor.co.uk
Affiliated Bodies BHS.
Contact/s
Owner: Mr J Brumer
Profile Equestrian Centre, Holidays, Riding School, Stable/Livery.
Facilities and services include regular clinics and demonstrations, discounted tuition when riding your own horse, coffee shop, club room, horseball games and affiliated/unaffiliated shows. Other facilities include clay shooting, archery and paintball. Corporate hospitality/team building events can be arranged. Children under 5 can have tuition on lead reins. Semi-private lessons (up to 3 people) also available for adults and children. (£16.50 for adults at weekends, for half an hour). Yr. Est: 1954 C.Size: 70 Acres
Opening Times
Sp: Open Tues - Sun 09:00. Closed Tues - Fri 21:00, Sat, Sun 17:00.
Su: Open Tues - Sun 09:00. Closed Tues - Fri 21:00, Sat, Sun 17:00.
Au: Open Tues - Sun 09:00. Closed Tues - Fri 21:00, Sat, Sun 17:00.
Wn: Open Tues - Sun 09:00. Closed Tues - Fri 21:00, Sat, Sun 17:00.
Closed Mondays Ref: YH03113

COBHAM MANOR
Cobham Manor Horseball Club, C/O 18 Lydbrook Cl, Sittingbourne, **Kent**, ME10 1NW, **ENGLAND**.
(T) 01795 479883.
Profile Club/Association. Ref: YH03114

COBHAMBURY FARM STUD
Cobhambury Farm Stud, Roman Rd, Marsh Green, Edenbridge, **Kent**, TN8 5PN, **ENGLAND**.
(T) 01732 863280 (F) 01732 867137.
Contact/s
Manager: Mr C Brockbank
Profile Breeder. Ref: YH03115

COBLEY, CHRIS & MARRIE
Chris & Marrie Cobley, 62 Commercial Rd, Talywain, Pontypool, **Torfaen**, NP4 7HT, **WALES**.
(T) 01495 772981.
Contact/s
Owner: Mr C Cobley
Profile Breeder.
Breeder of Welsh Section A ponies Ref: YH03116

COBRA SADDLEMAKERS
Cobra Saddlemakers Ltd, William Hse, Marsh Lane, Walsall, **Midlands (West)**, WS2 9AN, **ENGLAND**.
(T) 01922 630098.
Profile Saddlery Retailer. Ref: YH03117

COCHRANE, STUART M
Stuart M Cochrane, 3 Port St, Dalbeattie, **Dumfries and Galloway**, DG5 4BE, **SCOTLAND**.
(T) 01556 611854.
Profile Farrier. Ref: YH03118

COCKAIN, GODFREY J
Godfrey J Cockain DWCF, 16 Matlock Rd, The Triangle, Belper, **Derbyshire**, DE5 1BE, **ENGLAND**.
(T) 01773 820563.
Profile Farrier. Ref: YH03119

COCKBURN ENGINEERING
Cockburn Engineering, 17 West Harbour Rd, Edinburgh, **Edinburgh (City of)**, EH5 1PN, **SCOTLAND**.
(T) 0131 4677658 (F) 0131 4677022.
Profile Blacksmith. Ref: YH03120

COCKBURN, CHARLES KERR
Charles Kerr Cockburn, Crauchan, 15 High St, Earlston, **Scottish Borders**, TD4 6HQ, **SCOTLAND**.
(T) 01896 84778.
Profile Farrier. Ref: YH03121

COCKBURN, R G
Mr R G Cockburn, Stonecroft, High Ireby, Carlisle, **Cumbria**, CA5 1HF, **ENGLAND**.
(T) 01697 371751.
Profile Supplies. Ref: YH03122

COCKERTON SADDLERY
Cockerton Saddlery, 28A Cockerton Green, Darlington, **County Durham**, DL3 9EU, **ENGLAND**.
(T) 01325 240488
(E) tacksales@aol.com.
Profile Saddlery Retailer. Ref: YH03123

COCKING, R
R Cocking, Farm Lodge, Sezincote, Moreton In Marsh, **Gloucestershire**, GL56 9AB, **ENGLAND**.
(T) 01386 700662.
Profile Farrier. Ref: YH03124

COCKINGTON FORGE
Cockington Forge, Cockington Lane, Cockington Village, Torquay, **Devon**, TQ2 6XA, **ENGLAND**.
(T) 01803 605024.
Contact/s
Owner: Mr D Underhill
Profile Farrier. Ref: YH03125

COCKINGTON RIDING STABLES
Cockington Riding Stables, C/O Meadow Farm, Cockington Village, Torquay, **Devon**, TQ2 6XD, **ENGLAND**.
(T) 01803 606860.
Contact/s
Owner: Ms H Pitts
Profile Riding stables. Ref: YH03126

COCKRAM, R A
Mr R A Cockram, Deanhills Stud, The Grange Stables, Radway, **Warwickshire**, CV35 0UE, **ENGLAND**.
(T) 01295 670727 (F) 01295 670079.
Profile Breeder, Stable/Livery. Ref: YH03127

COCKS, L R
Mrs L R Cocks, 29 Pettits Rd, Dagenham, **Essex**, RM10 8NP, **ENGLAND**.
(T) 020 85956047.
Profile Transport/Horse Boxes. Horse drawn vehicles.
Ref: YH03128

COCKSCOMBE FARM LIVERY
Cockscombe Farm Livery, Cockscombe Farm, Twyford, Winchester, **Hampshire**, SO21 1QX, **ENGLAND**.
(T) 01962 712115.
Contact/s
Partner: Mrs G Davies
Profile Stable/Livery. Ref: YH03129

COCUM STUD
Cocum Stud, Upper Hse Farm, Hascombe, Godalming, **Surrey**, GU8 4JF, **ENGLAND**.
(T) 01483 208225 (F) 01483 208372.
Profile Breeder. Ref: YH03130

CODNER & CHALKLEY
Codner & Chalkley, Dragon Vetnry Ctre, 5 St Georges Trce, Cheltenham, **Gloucestershire**, GL50 3PT, **ENGLAND**.
(T) 01242 580324 (F) 01242 241908.
Profile Medical Support. Ref: YH03131

COE, ALAN R
Alan R Coe DWCF, 11 Birchwood Way, Tiptree, Colchester, **Essex**, CO5 0JR, **ENGLAND**.
(T) 01621 819875.
Profile Farrier. Ref: YH03132

COE, NICOLA
Nicola Coe (McIrvine), Ranmore Farm, Ranmore, Dorking, **Surrey**, RH5 6SY, **ENGLAND**.
(T) 01306 877823
(M) 07860 225443.
Profile Breeder. Ref: YH03133

COED Y WERN
Coed Y Wern Exmoor Ponies, Pwllgloyw, Brecon, **Powys**, LD3 9RA, **WALES**.
(T) 01874 690237.
Contact/s
Owner: Mr D Thomas
Profile Breeder. Ref: YH03134

COFFEY, D J
D J Coffey, 86 Hare Lane, Claygate, Esher, **Surrey**, KT10 0QU, **ENGLAND**.
(T) 01372 63148.
Profile Medical Support. Ref: YH03135

COGGINS MILL RIDING STABLES
Coggins Mill Riding Stables, Coggins Mill, Mayfield, **Sussex (East)**, TN20 6UR, **ENGLAND**.
(T) 01435 873289.
Contact/s
Owner: Mr C Perbrick
Profile Riding School. Ref: YH03136

COID, STEWART
Stewart Coid DWCF, Anvil Cottage, Daglingworth, Cirencester, **Gloucestershire**, GL7 7AE, **ENGLAND**.
(T) 01285 643915.
Profile Farrier. Ref: YH03137

COILESSAN
Coilessan Trekking & Riding Centre, Ardgartan Forest, Arrochar, **Argyll and Bute**, G83 7AR, **SCOTLAND**..
Profile Equestrian Centre. Trekking Centre.
Ref: YH03138

COILOG EVENTING
Coilog Eventing Ltd, Coilog Hse, Crosspatrick, Kilmeague, Naas, **County Kildare**, **IRELAND**.
(T) 045 860842 (F) 045 860843
(E) klsbyrne@tinet.ie

Affiliated Bodies AIRE.
Profile Equestrian Centre, Stable/Livery.
Ref: YH03139

COIS LINNE RIDING STABLE
Cois Linne Riding Stable, Deelis, Cahirciveen, **County Kerry**, **IRELAND**.
(T) 087 2364533. Ref: YH03140

COL, (LT) & STANFORD, E I
Lt Col & Mrs E I Stanford, Three Ashes, Stockland, Honiton, **Devon**, EX14 9EY, **ENGLAND**.
(T) 01404 881438.
Profile Breeder. Ref: YH03141

COLBERRY SADDLERY
Colberry Saddlery, Foxes Riding School, Badgers Rake Lane, Ledsham, Ellesmere Port, **Cheshire**, CH66 8PF, **ENGLAND**.
(T) 0151 3471853
Affiliated Bodies SMS.
Contact/s
Owner: Ms A Dodd (Q) QS, SMS
Profile Riding Wear Retailer, Saddlery Retailer, Supplies.
Own and experts in large/heavy-weight horses
No.Staff: 1 Yr. Est: 1990
Opening Times
Sp: Open Mon - Sat 10:00. Closed Mon - Sat 18:00.
Su: Open Mon - Sat 10:00. Closed Mon - Sat 18:00.
Au: Open Mon - Sat 10:00. Closed Mon - Sat 18:00.
Wn: Open Mon - Sat 10:00. Closed Mon - Sat 18:00.
Ref: YH03142

COLCHESTER EQUESTRIAN CTRE
Colchester Equestrian Centre, Pk Hse, Layer Rd, Kingsford, Colchester, **Essex**, CO2 0HT, **ENGLAND**.
(T) 01206 734516.
Contact/s
Owner: Mr D Merrett
Profile Equestrian Centre. Ref: YH03143

COLCHESTER GARRISON
Colchester Garrison Saddle Club, Butt Rd, Colchester, **Essex**, CO2 7TE, **ENGLAND**.
(T) 01206 782315.
Contact/s
Manageress: Mrs B Whittle
Profile Riding School.
Shows in dressage and show jumping. This is a military establishment. Yr. Est: 1951
Opening Times
Sp: Open 09:00. Closed 20:00.
Su: Open 09:00. Closed 20:00.
Au: Open 09:00. Closed 20:00.
Wn: Open 09:00. Closed 20:00. Ref: YH03144

COLDBECK, J D & N
J D & N Coldbeck, Dowson Garth, Egton Grange, Whitby, **Yorkshire (North)**, YO22 5AU, **ENGLAND**.
(T) 01947 895344.
Contact/s
Owner: Mr J Coldbeck
Profile Trainer. Ref: YH03145

COLDHARBOUR DRESSAGE
Coldharbour Dressage, Coldharbour Pk Farm, Rake, Liss, **Hampshire**, GU33 7JJ, **ENGLAND**.
(T) 01730 893100. Ref: YH03146

COLDICOTT, J H
J H Coldicott, 55 Barton St, Tewkesbury, **Gloucestershire**, GL20 5PX, **ENGLAND**.
(T) 01684 292177.
Profile Medical Support. Ref: YH03147

COLE AMBROSE
Cole Ambrose Limited, Stuntney Hall, Ely, **Cambridgeshire**, CB7 5TL, **ENGLAND**.
(T) 01353 662202.
Profile Breeder. Ref: YH03148

COLE, ANDREW CHARLES
Andrew Charles Cole AWCF, 963 Atherton Rd, Hindley Green, Wigan, **Lancashire**, WN2 4TA, **ENGLAND**.
(T) 07970 860946.
Profile Farrier. Ref: YH03149

COLE, ARTHUR
Arthur Cole, Unit D Ivy Rd Ind Est, Chippenham, **Wiltshire**, SN15 1SB, **ENGLAND**.
(T) 01249 659619 (F) 01249 659619.
Contact/s
Owner: Mr A Cole
Profile Blacksmith. Ref: YH03150

COLE, B
Miss B Cole, Market Rasen Stud Farm, Osgodby Lane, Middle Rasen, Market Rasen, **Lincolnshire**, LN8 3TX, **ENGLAND**.
(T) 01673 844812.
Profile Breeder. Ref: YH03151

COLE, DAVID B
David B Cole RSS, Oberry Flds, Bishops Hill, Lighthorne, **Warwickshire**, CV35 0BA, **ENGLAND**.
(T) 01926 651737.
Contact/s
Farrier: David B Cole (Q) RSS
Profile Farrier. Ref: YH03152

COLE, DEBORAH
Ms Deborah Cole, Westbridge Pk, Bishops Nympton, South Molton, **Devon**, EX36 3QT, **ENGLAND**.
(T) 01769 550842.
Profile Trainer. Ref: YH03153

COLE, DUNCAN L
Duncan L Cole DWCF Hons, Molecroft, Braughing Friars, Braughing, **Hertfordshire**, SG11 2NS, **ENGLAND**.
(T) 01279 771342
(M) 07973 625910.
Profile Farrier. Ref: YH03154

COLE, H T
Mr H T Cole, Frog St Farm, Beercrocombe, Taunton, **Somerset**, TA3 6AF, **ENGLAND**.
(T) 01823 480430.
Profile Supplies. Ref: YH03155

COLE, J A
J A Cole, Pound Green, Old School Lane, Lighthorne, **Warwickshire**, CV35 0AX, **ENGLAND**.
(T) 01926 651735.
Contact/s
Farrier: J A Cole
Profile Farrier. Ref: YH03156

COLE, J J
Mrs J J Cole, Saintjuliots Stud, Trevenn Farm, Marshgate, Camelford, **Cornwall**, PL32 9YN, **ENGLAND**.
(T) 01840 261247 (F) 01840 261247
(E) jcole27696@aol.com
(W) www.hometown.aol.com/jcole27696/index.html.
Profile Breeder, Stable/Livery. Ref: YH03157

COLE, JUSTIN
Justin Cole DWCF, 8 Hopkins St, Weston-Super-Mare, **Somerset (North)**, BS23 1RS, **ENGLAND**.
(T) 01934 635621.
Profile Farrier. Ref: YH03158

COLE, MELISSA
Melissa Cole, Couzens Farm, The Hill, Great Somerford, Chippenham, **Wiltshire**, SN15 5JB, **ENGLAND**.
(T) 01666 825794.
Profile Blacksmith. Ref: YH03159

COLE, S N
Mr S N Cole, West Batsworthy Farm, Rackenford, Tiverton, **Devon**, EX16 8EG, **ENGLAND**.
(T) 01884 881205 (F) 01884 881205
(M) 08350 38963.
Profile Trainer. Ref: YH03160

COLEBRIDGE STUD
Colebridge Stud (The), 5 Caesar Way, Coleshill, **Warwickshire**, B46 1UD, **ENGLAND**.
(T) 01675 462257.
Profile Breeder. Ref: YH03161

COLEG MEIRION-DWYFOR
Coleg Meirion-Dwyfor, Glynllifon Campus, Ffordd Clynnog, Caernarfon, **Gwynedd**, LL54 5DU, **WALES**.
(T) 01286 830261 (F) 01286 831597.
Profile Riding School. Ref: YH03162

COLEMAN CROFT
Coleman Croft Master Saddlers, Suttons Farm, Coopers Green, St Albans, **Hertfordshire**, AL4 9HJ, **ENGLAND**.
(T) 01707 274239 (F) 01707 271256
(W) www.colemancroft.com
Affiliated Bodies BETA.
Contact/s
Owner: Mrs P Gidden
Profile Riding Wear Retailer, Saddlery Retailer, Supplies. No.Staff: 10 Yr. Est: 1975
Opening Times
Sp: Open Mon - Sat 09:00. Closed Mon - Thurs, Sat 17:30, Fri 19:00.
Su: Open Mon - Sat 09:00. Closed Mon - Thurs, Sat 17:30, Fri 19:00.
Au: Open Mon - Sat 09:00. Closed Mon - Thurs, Sat 17:30, Fri 19:00.
Wn: Open Mon - Sat 09:00. Closed Mon - Thurs, Sat 17:30, Fri 19:00.
Closed on Sundays. Ref: YH03163

COLEMAN, ROBIN
Robin Coleman, Saddlers Cottage, 3 Chase Lane, Kenilworth, **Warwickshire**, CV8 1PR, **ENGLAND**.
(T) 01926 512368 (F) 01926 512368.
Contact/s
Owner: Mr R Coleman
Profile Saddlery Retailer. Ref: YH03164

COLEMANS FARM STABLES
Colemans Farm Stables, Colemans Farm, Theydon Mount, Epping, **Essex**, CM16 7PP, **ENGLAND**.
(T) 01708 688433.
Profile Breeder. Ref: YH03165

COLEMANS OF SANDYFORD
Colemans of Sandyford, Sandyford Village, Dublin, **County Dublin**, **IRELAND**.
(T) 01 2956047 (F) 01 2826311
(E) equestrian@latene.com
(W) www.latene.com/equestrian.
Profile Medical Support, Riding Wear Retailer, Supplies.
Veterinary chemists, although veterinary products are not available by mail order. Wide range of clothing and supplies for horse & rider available. Ref: YH03166

COLES KNAPP
Coles Knapp Halifax Agricultural, Ross-on-Wye, **Herefordshire**, HR9 7QF, **ENGLAND**.
(T) 01989 762225 (F) 01989 566082.
Profile Auctioneers. Ref: YH03167

COLESDALE FARM SVS
Colesdale Farm Services, Colesdale Farm, Northaw Rd West, Potters Bar, **Hertfordshire**, EN6 4QZ, **ENGLAND**.
(T) 01707 873353 (F) 01707 873353.
Profile Supplies. Ref: YH03168

COLGATE, T
T Colgate, Tilford Hse Farm, Tilford Rd, Tilford, Farnham, **Surrey**, GU10 2BX, **ENGLAND**.
(T) 01252 793335.
Contact/s
Owner: Mr T Colgate
Profile Hay and Straw Merchants. Ref: YH03169

COLGRAIN EQUESTRIAN CTRE
Colgrain Equestrian Centre, Cardross Rd, Cardross, Helensburgh, **Argyll and Bute**, G82 5HG, **SCOTLAND**.
(T) 01389 842022 (F) 01436 820035.
Contact/s
Partner: Mr W Hill
Profile Equestrian Centre, Riding School, Stable/Livery.
Fiona Spy has a wide range of competitive and teaching experience and is also a British Horse Society examiner. The centre offers tuition for all ages and abilities, as well as specialised competiton and career training. No.Staff: 5 Yr. Est: 1988
C.Size: 30 Acres
Opening Times
Sp: Open Mon - Sun 09:00. Closed Mon - Sun 21:00.
Su: Open Mon - Sun 09:00. Closed Mon - Sun 21:00.
Au: Open Mon - Sun 09:00. Closed Mon - Sun 21:00.
Wn: Open Mon - Sun 09:00. Closed Mon - Sun 21:00.
No lessons on a Monday Ref: YH03170

COLIN CLARK & AST
Colin Clark & Associates, 67 Meadrow, Farncombe, Godalming, **Surrey**, GU7 3HS, **ENGLAND**.
(T) 01483 421102.
Profile Medical Support. Ref: YH03171

COLLACOMBE FARM
Collacombe Farm Ltd, Collacombe Manor, Lamerton, Tavistock, **Devon**, PL19 8SB, **ENGLAND**.
(T) 01822 870231 (F) 01822 870530.
Profile Supplies. Ref: YH03172

COLLACOTT FARM
Collacott Farm, Kings Nympton, Umberleigh, **Devon**, EX37 9TP, **ENGLAND**.
(T) 01769 572491/572725
(W) www.collacott.co.uk
Affiliated Bodies BHS.
Profile Horse/Rider Accom, Riding School,

Track/Course.
2-3 day breaks including 4 hours riding - prices start at £55.00 per person. Riding prices start at £12.00 per hour. Yr. Est: 1983 C.Size: 20 Acres
Ref: YH03173

COLLAFORD FARM PARTNERSHIP

Collaford Farm Partnership, Collarford Farm, Plympton, Plymouth, **Devon**, PL7 5BD, **ENGLAND**.
(T) 01752 880339.
Contact/s
Owner: Mrs M Watts
Profile Stable/Livery. Ref: YH03174

COLLEASE TRAILER RENTALS

Collease Trailer Rentals Ltd, Collease Hse, Hauliers Rd, Felixstowe, **Suffolk**, IP11 3SF, **ENGLAND**.
(T) 01394 673289.
Contact/s
Manager: Mr A Bigmore
Profile Transport/Horse Boxes. Ref: YH03175

COLLETT, T W

T W Collett, 24 Queens Gr, Waterlooville, **Hampshire**, PO7 5HR, **ENGLAND**.
(T) 023 92261175.
Profile Blacksmith. Ref: YH03176

COLLEY, ANNE

Mrs Anne Colley, Birchwood Farm, Shatterford, Bewdley, **Worcestershire**, DY12 1TP, **ENGLAND**.
(T) 01299 861529.
Profile Stable/Livery, Trainer. Ref: YH03177

COLLEY, J M

J M Colley, Birchwood Farm, Bridgnorth Rd, Shatterford, Bewdley, **Worcestershire**, DY12 1TP, **ENGLAND**.
(T) 01299 861529.
Profile Farrier. Ref: YH03178

COLLIER, A M

Miss A M Collier, Stockwood Cottage, Forest Rd, Bream, Lydney, **Gloucestershire**, GL15 6LX, **ENGLAND**.
(T) 01594 562579.
Profile Breeder. Ref: YH03179

COLLIER, KATHY

Mrs Kathy Collier, 8 Bromsgrove Rd, Romsley, **Midlands (West)**, B62 0ET, **ENGLAND**.
(T) 01562 711196.
Profile Breeder. Ref: YH03180

COLLIER, W E

W E Collier, 12 Soham Rd, Fordham, Ely, **Cambridgeshire**, CB7 5LD, **ENGLAND**.
(T) 01638 720045.
Profile Transport/Horse Boxes. Ref: YH03181

COLLIER, W H

W H Collier, 1 Burloes Cottages, Newmarket Rd, Royston, **Hertfordshire**, SG8 7NJ, **ENGLAND**.
(T) 01763 244285.
Profile Farrier. Ref: YH03182

COLLINGHAM & DISTRICT SADDLE

Collingham & District Saddle Club, 3 Chainbridge Rd, Lound, Retford, **Nottinghamshire**, DN22 8RZ, **ENGLAND**.
(T) 01777 818453.
Contact/s
Chairman: Miss C Bingham
Profile Club/Association. Ref: YH03183

COLLINGRIDGE, H J

H J Collingridge, Harraton Court Stables, Chapel St, Exning, Newmarket, **Suffolk**, CB8 7HA, **ENGLAND**.
(T) 01638 577288
(W) www.newmarketracehorsetrainers.co.uk
Affiliated Bodies Newmarket Trainers Fed.
Contact/s
Owner: Mr H Collingridge
Profile Trainer. Ref: YH03184

COLLINGS, M A

M A Collings, Raven Crest, Impney, Droitwich, **Worcestershire**, WR9 0BL, **ENGLAND**.
(T) 01905 778085.
Contact/s
Owner: Mrs M Collings
Profile Breeder. Ref: YH03185

COLLINS PET FOODS

Collins Pet Foods, Blue Barns Farm, High St, Hardingstone, **Northamptonshire**, NN4 0DA, **ENGLAND**.
(T) 01604 762351 **(F)** 01604 702466.
Profile Feed Merchant. Ref: YH03186

COLLINS, E A

E A Collins, Station Hse, Castle Howard Station Rd, Welburn, York, **Yorkshire (North)**, YO60 7EW, **ENGLAND**.
(T) 01653 618303 **(F)** 01653 618159
(E) edmundcollins@stationhouse.demon.co.uk.
Profile Medical Support. Ref: YH03187

COLLINS, HANNAH

Mrs Hannah Collins, Barnards Farm Riding Ctre, Debden Green, Saffron Walden, **Essex**, CB11 3LU, **ENGLAND**.
(T) 01371 830043.
Profile Riding School, Saddlery Retailer.
Ref: YH03188

COLLINS, M J

Mr M J Collins, Meadow Cottage, Church Rd, Burstow, Horley, **Surrey**, RH6 9RG, **ENGLAND**.
(T) 01342 842507.
Profile Supplies. Ref: YH03189

COLLINS, STEPHEN A

Stephen A Collins DWCF, 38 Bryant Cl, Nettlestead, Maidstone, **Kent**, ME18 5EX, **ENGLAND**.
(T) 01622 813167.
Profile Farrier. Ref: YH03190

COLLIS, W K

W K Collis, 15 John French Way, Bulford Village, Salisbury, **Wiltshire**, SP4 9HP, **ENGLAND**.
(T) 01980 632234.
Profile Farrier. Ref: YH03191

COLLISTER, JOHN D

John D Collister RSS, The Forge, Burrow Hill, Chobham, Woking, **Surrey**, GU24 8QP, **ENGLAND**.
(T) 01276 856808.
Contact/s
Manager: Mr E Tedder
Profile Farrier. Ref: YH03192

COLMER STUD

Colmer Stud, Marshwood, Bridport, **Dorset**, DT6 5QA, **ENGLAND**.
(T) 01297 678652 **(F)** 01297 678791.
Contact/s
Owner: Mr S Bowditch
Profile Breeder, Stable/Livery.
Foaling facilities No.Staff: 2 Yr. Est: 1990
C.Size: 57 Acres Ref: YH03193

COLNE & DISTRICT RIDING CLUB

Colne & District Riding Club, 160 Birtwistle Ave, Colne, **Lancashire**, BB18 9RR, **ENGLAND**.
(T) 01282 862696.
Profile Club/Association, Riding Club. Ref: YH03194

COLNE CARGO TRANSPORT SVS

Colne Cargo Transport Services, Blackbatts Hse, Colne Engaine, Colchester, **Essex**, CO6 2HA, **ENGLAND**.
(T) 01206 795900 **(F)** 01206 795900
(M) 07970 852257
(E) le@colnecargo.demon.co.uk.
Profile Transport/Horse Boxes. Ref: YH03195

COLNE SADDLERY

Colne Saddlery, 1-3 Cattle Market, St Oswald Rd, Gloucester, **Gloucestershire**, GL1 2SG, **ENGLAND**.
(T) 01452 417184
Affiliated Bodies SMS.
Contact/s
Owner: Mr M Emtage
Profile Saddlery Retailer. Ref: YH03196

COLNE SADDLERY

Colne Saddlery, Greenbank Cottage, Kineton, Guiting Power, Cheltenham, **Gloucestershire**, GL54 5UG, **ENGLAND**.
(T) 01451 850570.
Profile Saddlery Retailer. Ref: YH03197

COLORLABS INT

Colorlabs International, The Maltings, Fordham Rd, Newmarket, **Suffolk**, CB8 7AG, **ENGLAND**.
(T) 01638 664444 **(F)** 01638 666360.
Profile Club/Association. Ref: YH03198

COLOURED HORSE & PONY SOC

Coloured Horse & Pony Society (UK), 1 Mclaren Cottages, Abertysswg, Rhymney, Tredegar, **Blaenau Gwent**, NP22 5BH, **WALES**.
(T) 01685 845045 **(F)** 01685 845045
(E) chapsuk@compuserve.com
(W) www.chapsuk.com
Affiliated Bodies BHS.
Contact/s
Secretary: Miss L Amor
Profile Club/Association.
CHAPS is a breed society which offer memberships, horse registrations, a stud book, stallion & mare gradings, showing, performance, issue journals and junior bursary. No.Staff: 1 Yr. Est: 1983
Opening Times
Sp: Open Mon - Fri 09:30. Closed Mon - Fri 12:30.
Su: Open Mon - Fri 09:30. Closed Mon - Fri 12:30.
Au: Open Mon - Fri 09:30. Closed Mon - Fri 12:30.
Wn: Open Mon - Fri 09:30. Closed Mon - Fri 12:30.
Office closed weekends. Telephone/fax enquires on 01685 845045 (18:00 - 20:00 Mon - Fri)
Ref: YH03199

COLQUHOUN, ELIZABETH

Miss Elizabeth Colquhoun, Little Tingewick Hse, Buckingham, **Buckinghamshire**, MK18 4AG, **ENGLAND**.
(T) 01280 4236.
Profile Breeder. Ref: YH03200

COLT SADDLERY

Colt Saddlery, 30 Navigation St, Walsall, **Midlands (West)**, WS2 9LT, **ENGLAND**.
(T) 01922 615015
(W) www.coltsaddlery.co.uk.
Contact/s
Owner: Mr S McCaige
Profile Saddlery Retailer. Saddle Manufacturer.
Supplies to traders. Yr. Est: 1987
Opening Times
Sp: Open Mon - Fri 08:00, Sat 09:00. Closed Mon - Fri 17:00, Sat 19:00.
Su: Open Mon - Fri 08:00, Sat 09:00. Closed Mon - Fri 17:00, Sat 19:00.
Au: Open Mon - Fri 08:00, Sat 09:00. Closed Mon - Fri 17:00, Sat 19:00.
Wn: Open Mon - Fri 08:00, Sat 09:00. Closed Mon - Fri 17:00, Sat 19:00. Ref: YH03201

COLTHERD, W S

Mr W S Coltherd, Clarilawmuir Farm, Selkirk, **Scottish Borders**, TD7 4QA, **SCOTLAND**.
(T) 01750 21251
(M) 07801 398199.
Profile Supplies. Ref: YH03202

COLTON, D W & J K

D W & J K Colton, Peek Hill Farm, Dousland, Yelverton, **Devon**, PL20 6PD, **ENGLAND**.
(T) 01822 852908.
Profile Breeder. Ref: YH03203

COLTSFOOT FARM LIVERY

Coltsfoot Farm Livery, Coltsfoot Farm, Coltsfoot Lane, Datchworth, Knebworth, **Hertfordshire**, SG3 6SB, **ENGLAND**.
(T) 01438 798001.
Profile Stable/Livery. Ref: YH03204

COLTSMOOR

Coltsmoor Equestrian Enterprises, Coltsmoor Farm, Coln St. Aldwyns, Cirencester, **Gloucestershire**, GL7 5AX, **ENGLAND**.
(T) 01285 750049.
Contact/s
Owner: Mr G Gee
Profile Riding School. Ref: YH03205

COLTSPRING SCHOOL OF RIDING

Coltspring School Of Riding, Sarratt Rd, Chandlers Cross, Rickmansworth, **Hertfordshire**, WD3 4LR, **ENGLAND**.
(T) 01923 774964.
Profile Riding School. Ref: YH03206

COLVIN, CLAIRE

Claire Colvin, 27 Park Rd, Hatherleigh, **Devon**, EX20 3JS, **ENGLAND**.
(T) 01837 811181 **(F)** 01837 811181. Ref: YH03207

COLWYN TACK CTRE

Colwyn Tack Centre, 50 Abergele Rd, Colwyn Bay, **Conwy**, LL29 7PA, **WALES**.
(T) 01492 533008.
Contact/s
Owner: Mr J Helme
Profile Saddlery Retailer. Ref: YH03208

COMBE STUD

Combe Stud, Gittisham, Honiton, **Devon**, EX14 0AD, **ENGLAND**.
(T) 01404 42334.
Profile Breeder. Ref: YH03209

COMBINED TRAINING DRESSAGE

East Cheshire Combined Training Group

Dressage, The White Cottage, Little Budworth, Tarporley, **Cheshire**, CW6 9EJ, **ENGLAND**.
(T) 01829 760277.
Profile Club/Association. **Ref: YH03210**

COMBINED TRAINING GRP

East Cheshire Combined Training Group, Ower Yam 222 Crewe Rd, Sandbach, **Cheshire**, CW11 0PY, **ENGLAND**.
(T) 01270 767260.
Profile Club/Association. **Ref: YH03211**

COMERFORD, MICHAEL J

Michael J Comerford DWCF, 6 Woodside, Fortis Green, Muswell Hill, **London (Greater)**, N10 3NY, **ENGLAND**.
(T) 07956 419180.
Profile Farrier. **Ref: YH03212**

COMFY PET & PEOPLE PRODUCTS

Comfy Pet & People Products, 2-4 Parsonage St, Bradninch, Exeter, **Devon**, EX5 4NW, **ENGLAND**.
(T) 01392 881285 **(F)** 01392 882188.
Profile Supplies. **Ref: YH03213**

COMHIRE

Comhire, 16-20 Boston Pl, Marylebone, **London (Greater)**, NW1 6HY, **ENGLAND**.
(T) 020 72627333 **(F)** 020 72621089. **Ref: YH03214**

COMMON FARM STABLES

Common Farm Stables, Upper Helmsley, York, **Yorkshire (North)**, YO4 1JX, **ENGLAND**.
(T) 01759 373508 **(F)** 01759 373509.
Profile Trainer. **Ref: YH03215**

COMPASS EQUESTRIAN PRODUCTS

Compass Equestrian Products, The Compass Stud, Porth-Y-Waen, Oswestry, **Shropshire**, SY10 8LY, **ENGLAND**.
(T) 01691 828576 **(F)** 01691 828576
(M) 07836 549488.
Profile Supplies. **Ref: YH03216**

COMPETITION HORSES

Competition Horses, Hibbits Lodge, Ridlington Rd, Braunston, Oakham, **Rutland**, LE15 8DB, **ENGLAND**.
(T) 01572 770606 **(F)** 01572 770606
(W) www.competition-horses.co.uk.
Contact/s
Owner: Mr M Williams
Profile Trainer.
Sells many young horses to compete in dressage and eventing.
Opening Times
By appointment only **Ref: YH03217**

COMPTON BEAUCHAMP ESTS

Compton Beauchamp Estates Ltd, Blewbury, Didcot, **Oxfordshire**, OX11 9HF, **ENGLAND**.
(T) 01235 851997 **(F)** 01235 851998.
Profile Trainer. **Ref: YH03218**

COMPTON, J C

Mrs J C Compton, Ward Of Turin, Forfar, **Angus**, DD8 2TE, **SCOTLAND**.
(T) 01307 830253 **(F)** 01307 830443.
Profile Breeder. **Ref: YH03219**

COMPTON, ROBIN D

Robin D Compton DWCF, Rosedene, Main St, Ulleskelf, Tadcaster, **Yorkshire (North)**, LS24 9DU, **ENGLAND**.
(T) 07836 219577.
Profile Farrier. **Ref: YH03220**

COMYN FARM RIDING STABLES

Comyn Farm Riding Stables, Comyn Farm, Ilfracombe, **Devon**, EX34 9RL, **ENGLAND**.
(T) 01271 865371.
Profile Riding stable. **Ref: YH03221**

CONANVET

Conanvet, Ardlair, Conon Bridge, Dingwall, **Highlands**, IV7 8AZ, **SCOTLAND**.
(T) 01349 861203 **(F)** 01349 865181.
Profile Medical Support. **Ref: YH03222**

CONCEPT SADDLERY

Concept Saddlery, Craftmasters Hall, Percival Hse, St Owen St, Hereford, **Herefordshire**, HR1 2JB, **ENGLAND**.
(T) 01432 274074.
Profile Saddlery Retailer. **Ref: YH03223**

CONCHIE, DAVID

David Conchie JNR (Saddlery), West Cotside, Barry, Carnoustie, **Angus**, DD7 7SA, **SCOTLAND**.
(T) 01382 532536 **(F)** 01382 532475
(W) www.conchie.com.
Contact/s
Owner: Mr D Conchie
(E) david@conchie.com
Profile Saddlery Retailer. **Ref: YH03224**

CONDRY, HUGH & SUE

Hugh & Sue Condry, Valley Cottage, Barford St Martin, Salisbury, **Wiltshire**, SP3 4BJ, **ENGLAND**.
(T) 01722 743427.
Contact/s
Owner: Hugh Condry
Profile Supplies. **Ref: YH03225**

CONDUIT FARM STUD

Conduit Farm Stud, Conduit Farm, Churchill, Chipping Norton, **Oxfordshire**, OX7 6NH, **ENGLAND**.
(T) 01608 658274 **(F)** 01608 659022.
Profile Breeder. **Ref: YH03226**

CONEY, T & K

T & K Coney, Lower End Town Farm, Lampeter Velfrey, Narberth, **Pembrokeshire**, SA67 8UJ, **WALES**.
(T) 01834 831236 **(F)** 01834 831236.
Contact/s
Partner: Mrs K Coney **Ref: YH03227**

CONGLETON TRAILER HIRE

Congleton Trailer Hire, King St, Buglawton, Congleton, **Cheshire**, CW12 2DS, **ENGLAND**.
(T) 01260 270380 **(F)** 01260 297380.
Profile Transport/Horse Boxes. **Ref: YH03228**

CONGLETON TRAILERS

Congleton Trailers Ltd, Havannah St, Congleton, **Cheshire**, CW12 2AH, **ENGLAND**.
(T) 01260 280588 **(F)** 01260 299408.
Profile Transport/Horse Boxes. **Ref: YH03229**

CONIBEAR, R H

R H Conibear, Ford Hill Forge, Hartland, Bideford, **Devon**, EX39 6EE, **ENGLAND**.
(T) 01237 441208.
Contact/s
Owner: Mr R Conibear
Profile Farrier. **Ref: YH03230**

CONISBROUGH PETS

Conisbrough Pets, 11B West St, Conisbrough, Doncaster, **Yorkshire (South)**, DN12 3JH, **ENGLAND**.
(T) 01709 867916 **(F)** 01709 867916.
Profile Supplies.
Opening Times
Mon, Tues 09:00 - 17:00, Weds 09:00 - 13:00, Thurs, 09:00 - 19:00, Fri, Sat 09:00 - 17:00 **Ref: YH03231**

CONKWELL GRANGE STUD

Conkwell Grange Stud Ltd, Conkwell, Limpley Stoke, Bath, **Bath & Somerset (North East)**, BA3 6HD, **ENGLAND**.
(T) 01225 722696 **(F)** 01225 722696.
Contact/s
Owner: Mrs E Harrington
Profile Breeder, Trainer. **Ref: YH03232**

CONNAUGHT HSE VETNRY HOSPITAL

Connaught House Veterinary Hospital, 61 Tettenhall Rd, Wolverhampton, **Midlands (West)**, WV3 9NB, **ENGLAND**.
(T) 01902 424725 **(F)** 01902 711330.
Contact/s
Vet: Ms S Taylor
Profile Medical Support. **Ref: YH03233**

CONNECTIONS PR

Connections PR, 29 Church St, Sawtry, **Cambridgeshire**, PE17 5SZ, **ENGLAND**.
(T) 01487 831031 **(F)** 01487 830792.
Profile Club/Association. **Ref: YH03234**

CONNEL HILL RIDING CTRE

Connel Hill Riding Centre, 48 Drumsough Rd, Randalstown, Antrim, **County Antrim**, BT41 2NW, **NORTHERN IRELAND**.
(T) 028 94472632.
Profile Equestrian Centre. **Ref: YH03235**

CONNELL, ANNE (LADY)

Lady Anne Connell, Steane Pk, Brackley, **Northamptonshire**, NN13 6DP, **ENGLAND**.
(T) 01280 705899.
Profile Supplies. **Ref: YH03236**

CONNEMARA PONY BREEDERS

Cumann Lucht Capaillini Chonamara, The Showgrounds, Clifden, **County Galway**, **IRELAND**.
(T) 095 21863 **(F)** 095 21005
(E) enquries@cpbs.ie
(W) www.cpbs.ie.
Contact/s
Secretary: Mr M Ward
Profile No.Staff: 2 Yr. Est: 1923
C.Size: 2 Acres
Opening Times
Sp: Open 09:30. Closed 17:00.
Su: Open 09:30. Closed 17:00.
Au: Open 09:30. Closed 17:00.
Wn: Open 09:30. Closed 17:00. **Ref: YH03237**

CONNEMARA PONY SOC

Connemara Pony Society, Woodlands St Mary Cottage, Woodlands St Mary, Lambourn, Hungerford, **Berkshire**, RG17 7SL, **ENGLAND**.
(T) 01488 73313 **(F)** 01488 73525.
Profile Club/Association. **Ref: YH03238**

CONNOLE, MARK J

Mark J Connole DWCF, 25 Barrel Nook, Old Great North Rd, Sutton-on-Trent, Newark, **Nottinghamshire**, NG23 6PW, **ENGLAND**.
(T) 01636 821569.
Profile Farrier. **Ref: YH03239**

CONNORS, MICK

Mick Connors, Pallas Stud, Woodstown, **County Waterford**, **IRELAND**.
(T) 051 382112.
Contact/s
Owner: Mick Connor
Profile Riding School.
Opening Times
Closed Mondays, telephone for further information
Ref: YH03240

CONOR FENELON

Conor Fenelon Equine Veterinary Clinic, Marks Farm, The Broadway, Great Dunmow, **Essex**, CM6 3BQ, **ENGLAND**.
(T) 01371 872102/878062 **(F)** 01371 874701.
Contact/s
Assistant: Ms L Hunt **(Q)** MRCVS
Profile Medical Support.
Consultations are by appointment and a 24 hour emergency service is also available. **Ref: YH03241**

CONQUEST

Conquest Livery & Riding Centre, Conquest Drove, Farcet Fen, **Cambridgeshire**, PE7 3DH, **ENGLAND**.
(T) 01733 240967.
Profile Riding School, Stable/Livery. **Ref: YH03242**

CONQUEST CTRE

Conquest Centre For Disabled Riders, Conquest Farm, Norton Fitzwarren, Taunton, **Somerset**, TA2 6PN, **ENGLAND**.
(T) 01823 433614.
Contact/s
Chairman: Mr M Babbage
Profile Equestrian Centre, Riding School.
Riding centre for the disabled only. A 45 minute lesson with one to one instruction costs £5.00.
Opening Times
Mon, Tues 10:30 - 15:00, Weds 10:00 - 18:30, Thurs 10:00 - 17:00, Fri 09:30 - 15:00, Sat 09:30 - 12:30
Ref: YH03243

CONSTANTINE, PAMELA

Pamela Constantine, Abingdon & Witney College, Witney Campus, Holloway Rd, Witney, **Oxfordshire**, OX28 6NE, **ENGLAND**.
(T) 01993 703464
Affiliated Bodies NAAT.
Contact/s
Physiotherapist: Pamela Constantine
Profile Medical Support.
Physiotherapist for horses & dogs. **Ref: YH03244**

CONSTERDINE, C J

C J Consterdine, Turnhurst Farm, Bosley, Macclesfield, **Cheshire**, SK11 0PX, **ENGLAND**.
(T) 01260 223306.
Profile Farrier. **Ref: YH03245**

CONTESSA

Contessa Riding Centre, Willow Tree Farm, Colliers End, Ware, **Hertfordshire**, SG11 1EN, **ENGLAND**.
(T) 01920 821496 **(F)** 01920 821496
(W) www.contessa-riding.co.uk
Affiliated Bodies ABRS, BHS.
Contact/s
General Manager: Miss T Layton **(Q)** BHSI
Profile Breeder, Horse/Rider Accom, Riding School.
Dressage and examination training specialist. One to one tuition is available. 30 minute sessions with a

BHS AI are £ 17.50, and £23.00 with a BHS I. Accommodation is also available either on site or nearby. **No.Staff:** 10 **Yr. Est:** 1977
C.Size: 35 Acres
Opening Times
Sp: Open Mon - Sun 09:00. Closed Mon - Sun 17:00.
Su: Open Mon - Sun 09:00. Closed Mon - Sun 17:00.
Au: Open Mon - Sun 09:00. Closed Mon - Sun 17:00.
Wn: Open Mon - Sun 09:00. Closed Mon - Sun 17:00.
Weekday evenings lessons are from 19:00 - 21:00. There is a childrens club on Friday evenings from 17:30 - 19:30. **Ref: YH03246**

CONTI, D & D
D & D Conti, 89 Ladysmith, East Gomeldon, Salisbury, **Wiltshire**, SP4 6LE, **ENGLAND**.
(T) 01980 610444 **(F)** 01980 610443.
Profile Breeder. **Ref: YH03247**

CONTINENTAL IND SUPPLIES
Continental Industrial Supplies Ltd, Princes Hse, 36/40 Jermyn St, London, **London (Greater)**, SW1Y 6DN, **ENGLAND**.
(T) 020 74375804.
Profile Supplies. **Ref: YH03248**

CONTROL TECHNIQUES
Control Techniques, Unit 79, Mochdre Ind Est, Newtown, **Powys**, SY16 4LE, **WALES**.
(T) 01686 612900.
Contact/s
Press Officer: Robyn Best
Profile Supplies.
Horse walkers made to order. **Ref: YH03249**

CONWAY PRODUCTS
Conway Products Ltd, Skull Hse Lane, Appley Bridge, Wigan, **Lancashire**, WN6 9DW, **ENGLAND**.
(T) 01257 254535.
Profile Transport/Horse Boxes. **Ref: YH03250**

CONWAY, PAUL A
Paul A Conway DWCF, Lyndale, Green Lane, Catforth, Preston, **Lancashire**, PR4 0HT, **ENGLAND**.
(T) 01772 690525.
Profile Farrier. **Ref: YH03251**

COOGAN, A B
Mr A B Coogan, 31 Hasse Rd, Soham, Ely, **Cambridgeshire**, CB7 5UW, **ENGLAND**.
(T) 01353 721673.
Profile Supplies. **Ref: YH03252**

COOGAN, JAMES
James Coogan, Stepping Stone Stables, Friarstown, Kildare, **County Kildare**, **IRELAND**.
(T) 045 521800.
Profile Supplies. **Ref: YH03253**

COOK & TIMSON
Cook & Timson, Veterinary Ctre, James St, Louth, **Lincolnshire**, LN11 0JW, **ENGLAND**.
(T) 01507 602828.
Profile Medical Support. **Ref: YH03254**

COOK, ANGELA
Angela Cook, Barton Cottage, Challick Lane, Wiveliscombe, **Somerset**, TA4 2SZ, **ENGLAND**.
(T) 01984 624453 **(F)** 01984 623934.
Profile Trainer. **Ref: YH03255**

COOK, COLIN
Colin Cook, 60 Swan St, Sileby, Loughborough, **Leicestershire**, LE12 7NW, **ENGLAND**.
(T) 01509 816969. **Ref: YH03256**

COOK, PHILIP MICHAEL
Philip Michael Cook AFCL, 12 Yew Tree Pk Homes, Ashford, Maidstone Rd, Charing, **Kent**, TN27 0DD, **ENGLAND**.
(T) 01233 712989.
Profile Farrier. **Ref: YH03257**

COOK, SAMUEL C
Samuel C Cook DWCF, 147 Bent Lane, Leyland, **Lancashire**, PR5 2HS, **ENGLAND**.
(T) 01772 499619.
Profile Farrier. **Ref: YH03258**

COOKE, DONALD
Donald Cooke (Corn Merchants), Bridge Mill, 3 Greasbrough Rd, Rotherham, **Yorkshire (South)**, S60 1RD, **ENGLAND**.
(T) 01709 365968 **(F)** 01709 377717.
Contact/s
Owner: Mr B Cooke
Profile Feed Merchant, Supplies. **Ref: YH03259**

COOKE, G A
Mrs G A Cooke, 28 Glyn Garth Ct, Menai Bridge, **Isle of Anglesey**, LL59 5PB, **WALES**.
(T) 01248 716734.
Profile Breeder. **Ref: YH03260**

COOKE, J & S
J & S Cooke, Heathfield Hse, North Cornelly, Bridgend, **Bridgend**, CF33 4HN, **WALES**.
(T) 01656 740844.
Profile Breeder. **Ref: YH03261**

COOKE, PAT
Pat Cooke, Bury Farm Hse, Dunstable Rd, Caddington, Luton, **Bedfordshire**, LU1 4AW, **ENGLAND**.
(T) 01582 732150.
Contact/s
Owner: Mrs P Cooke
Profile Horse Drawn Vehicles for hire for special occasions.
Carriages available for hire for any special occasion
Ref: YH03262

COOKE, PETER
Peter Cooke, The Poplars, Alsager Rd, Hassall, Sandbach, **Cheshire**, CW11 4SD, **ENGLAND**.
(T) 01270 760817.
Contact/s
Owner: Mr P Cooke
Profile Blacksmith. **Ref: YH03263**

COOKHAM EQUESTRIAN
Cookham Equestrian, The Thicket, Kiln Corner, Upper Basildon, **Berkshire**, RG8 8SU, **ENGLAND**.
(T) 01491 671150.
Profile Supplies. **Ref: YH03264**

COOK'S CASTLE FARM
Cook's Castle Farm, St Johns Rd, Wroxall, Ventnor, **Isle of Wight**, PO38 3AA, **ENGLAND**.
(T) 01983 852467.
Profile Stable/Livery. **Ref: YH03265**

COOKSLEY, BUZZ
Buzz Cooksley, The Forge, Allerford, Minehead, **Somerset**, TA24 8HN, **ENGLAND**.
(T) 01643 862446.
Contact/s
Owner: Mr B Cooksley
Profile Blacksmith. **Ref: YH03266**

COOKSON, LORRAINE
Lorraine Cookson, 30 Park Ave, Leeds, **Yorkshire (West)**, LS19 7EZ, **ENGLAND**.
(T) 0113 2509808 **(F)** 0113 2509508.
Profile Medical Support. **Ref: YH03267**

COOL RIDING STABLES
Cool Riding Stables, 68 Ballyhanedin Rd, Claudy, Londonderry, **County Londonderry**, BT47 4ER, **NORTHERN IRELAND**.
(T) 028 71338277.
Contact/s
Owner: Miss C Donaghy
Profile Equestrian Centre. **Ref: YH03268**

COOL SPORT
Cool Sport (UK) Ltd, PO Box 55, Brigg, **Lincolnshire**, DN38 6GE, **ENGLAND**.
(T) 01652 680920 **(F)** 01652 680930
(E) info@coolsport.com
(W) www.coolsport.com.
Profile Medical Support. **Ref: YH03269**

COOLADOYLE RIDING SCHOOL
Cooladoyle Riding School, Glen Hse, Cooladoyle, Newtownmountkennedy, **County Wicklow**, **IRELAND**.
(T) 01 2819906.
Contact/s
Instructor: Aideen Leveos
Profile Riding School.
During school holidays pony camps and treks are organised. The surrounding forest is ideal for hacking.
Opening Times
Sp: Open Tues - Sun 09:00. Closed Tues - Fri 18:00, Sat 15:00, Sun 13:00.
Su: Open Tues - Sun 09:00. Closed Tues - Fri 18:00, Sat 15:00, Sun 13:00.
Au: Open Tues - Sun 09:00. Closed Tues - Fri 17:00, Sat 15:00, Sun 13:00.
Wn: Open Tues - Sun 09:00. Closed Tues - Fri 16:00, Sat 15:00, Sun 13:00.
Closed Mondays **Ref: YH03270**

COOLMINE EQUESTRIAN CTRE
Coolmine Equestrian Centre, Saggart, **County Kildare**, **IRELAND**.
(T) 01 4588447. **Ref: YH03271**

COOMARA VETNRY PRACTICE
Coomara Veterinary Practice, Coomara, Carleton, Carlisle, **Cumbria**, CA4 0BU, **ENGLAND**.
(T) 01228 524740 **(F)** 01228 596986
(E) gbrooksvet@compuserve.com.
Profile Medical Support. **Ref: YH03272**

COOMBE PK EQUESTRIAN CTRE
Coombe Park Equestrian Centre, Littlehempston, Totnes, **Devon**, TQ9 6LW, **ENGLAND**.
(T) 01803 866615.
Profile Equestrian Centre. **Ref: YH03273**

COOMBE PK RACING STABLES
Coombe Park Racing Stables, Coombe Park Rd, Whitchurch On Thames, Reading, **Berkshire**, RG8 7QT, **ENGLAND**.
(T) 0118 9841317 **(F)** 0118 9841924
(M) 07976 748217.
Profile Trainer. **Ref: YH03274**

COOMBE STUDIO
Coombe Studio, Coombe Lane, Bovey Tracey, **Devon**, TQ13 9PH, **ENGLAND**.
(T) 01626 832914 **(F)** 01626 832914.
Contact/s
Owner: Mr K Ansell
Profile Animal Portrait Artist. **No.Staff:** 2
Yr. Est: 1981 **Ref: YH03275**

COOMBE WOOD STABLES
Coombe Wood Stables, Coombewood Lane, Hawkinge, Folkestone, **Kent**, CT18 7BZ, **ENGLAND**.
(T) 01303 893332 **(F)** 01303 893332.
Contact/s
Owner: Mrs G Fuller
Profile Riding School, Stable/Livery. **Ref: YH03276**

COOMBE, G A
G A Coombe, Sanham Farm, Great Dalby Rd, Kirby Bellars, Melton Mowbray, **Leicestershire**, LE14 2TN, **ENGLAND**.
(T) 01664 812289.
Contact/s
Owner: Mr G Coombe
Profile Breeder. **Ref: YH03277**

COOMBE, M J
Mr M J Coombe, Sea Barn Farm, Fleet, Weymouth, **Dorset**, DT3 4ED, **ENGLAND**.
(T) 01305 782218 **(F)** 01305 775396.
Profile Breeder. **Ref: YH03278**

COOMBEFIELD VETNRY HOSPITAL
Coombefield Veterinary Hospital, Coombe Lane, Axminster, **Devon**, EX13 5AX, **ENGLAND**.
(T) 01297 32156 **(F)** 01297 35793.
Profile Medical Support. **Ref: YH03279**

COOMBELANDS RACING STABLES
Coombelands Racing Stables, Coombelands Lane, Pulborough, **Sussex (West)**, RH20 1BP, **ENGLAND**.
(T) 01798 873011 **(F)** 01798 875163.
Contact/s
Owner: Mrs A Perrett
Profile Trainer. **Ref: YH03280**

COOMBES, P F
P F Coombes RSS, Red Roof, Shaftesbury Rd, Barford St Martin, Salisbury, **Wiltshire**, SP3 4BG, **ENGLAND**.
(T) 01722 742314.
Profile Farrier. **Ref: YH03281**

COOMBS, M
M Coombs, Bushes Farm, Bushes Rd, Stourpaine, Blandford Forum, **Dorset**, DT11 8SU, **ENGLAND**.
(T) 01258 455846.
Contact/s
Owner: Mrs M Coombs **Ref: YH03282**

COOPER & PARTNERS
Cooper & Partners, 95 High St, Repton, **Derbyshire**, DE6 6GF, **ENGLAND**.
(T) 01283 704067.
Profile Medical Support. **Ref: YH03283**

COOPER, CYRIL
Cyril Cooper AFCL, 86 Sandy Bank Ave, Rothwell, Leeds, **Yorkshire (West)**, LS26 0ER, **ENGLAND**.
(T) 0113 2822123.
Profile Farrier. **Ref: YH03284**

COOPER, D C

D C Cooper, Edgerley Farm, Clanfield, Bampton, **Oxfordshire**, OX18 2SB, **ENGLAND**.
(T) 01367 810317.
Profile Farrier. **Ref: YH03285**

COOPER, DAVID

David Cooper, Unit 7 Erith Small Business Ctre, Erith High St, Erith, **Kent**, DA8 1RT, **ENGLAND**.
(T) 01322 359393 **(F)** 01322 359393.
Contact/s
Owner: Mr D Cooper
Profile Transport/Horse Boxes. **Ref: YH03286**

COOPER, H J

H J Cooper, The Forge, Guildford Rd, Abinger Hammer, Dorking, **Surrey**, RH5 6SG, **ENGLAND**.
(T) 01306 730393.
Profile Farrier. **Ref: YH03287**

COOPER, JOHN

John Cooper, Rectory Rd, Meppershall, Shefford, **Bedfordshire**, SG17 5NB, **ENGLAND**.
(T) 01462 814282.
Profile Transport/Horse Boxes. **Ref: YH03288**

COOPER, PAUL H

Paul H Cooper DWCF, 5 Blacksmiths Lane, Wickham Bishops, Witham, **Essex**, CM8 3NR, **ENGLAND**.
(T) 01621 891191.
Profile Farrier. **Ref: YH03289**

COOPER, S & J M

S & J M Cooper, 24 Market Pl, Faringdon, **Oxfordshire**, SN7 7HU, **ENGLAND**.
(T) 01367 240517 **(F)** 01367 240517.
Contact/s
Owner: Mr S Cooper
Profile Saddlery Retailer. **Ref: YH03290**

COOPER, SIMON

Simon Cooper, 2 Tollbar Cottages, Styford, Stocksfield, **Northumberland**, NE43 7UA, **ENGLAND**.
(T) 01434 634193
(M) 07803 570079.
Profile Saddlery Retailer. **Ref: YH03291**

COPDOCK RIDING CTRE

Copdock Riding Centre, Mace Green Stud Farm, Wenham Rd, Copdock, Ipswich, **Suffolk**, IP8 3EY, **ENGLAND**.
(T) 01473 730678 **(F)** 01473 730678.
Contact/s
Owner: Mrs A Withy
Profile Equestrian Centre. **Ref: YH03292**

COPE, D M

D M Cope, Beckside Farm, Shawfield Head, Beckwithshaw, Harrogate, **Yorkshire (North)**, HG3 1QU, **ENGLAND**.
(T) 01423 560919.
Contact/s
Owner: Mrs D Cope
Profile Breeder. No.Staff: 2 Yr. Est: 1967
C.Size: 32 Acres
Opening Times
Telephone for an appointment **Ref: YH03293**

COPELAND, JIM

Jim Copeland, 67 Clifford Rd, New Barnet, **Hertfordshire**, EN5 5NZ, **ENGLAND**.
(T) 020 84401832.
Profile Trainer. **Ref: YH03294**

COPELAND, STUART

Stuart Copeland, 67 Clifford Rd, New Barnet, **Hertfordshire**, EN5 5NZ, **ENGLAND**.
(T) 020 84401832.
Profile Trainer. **Ref: YH03295**

COPGROVE HALL STUD

Copgrove Hall Stud, Occaney, Harrogate, **Yorkshire (North)**, HG3 3TH, **ENGLAND**.
(T) 01423 340596 **(F)** 01423 340696.
Contact/s
Owner: Mr G Reed
Profile Breeder. **Ref: YH03296**

COPLEY

Copley Stables, Copley, Bishopston, Swansea, **Swansea**, SA3 3JH, **WALES**.
(T) 01792 234428
Affiliated Bodies ABRS, BHS, WTRA.
Contact/s
Owner: Mrs W Hemns-Tucker **(Q)** BHSII
Profile Riding School, Stable/Livery.
Stable management courses available, 'Loan a Pony' weeks, breaking & schooling, show preparation and holiday courses. Telephone for further information.
No.Staff: 3 Yr. Est: 1975 C.Size: 10 Acres
Opening Times
Telephone for further information **Ref: YH03297**

COPLEY STABLES

Copley Stables, Copley, Swansea, **Swansea**, SA3 3JA, **WALES**.
(T) 01792 234428. **Ref: YH03298**

COPLEY, JOSEPHINE

Josephine Copley, 18 Forehill Ave, West Bessacar, Doncaster, **Yorkshire (South)**, DN4 7EX, **ENGLAND**.
(T) 01302 538425
(W) www.josephinecopley.co.uk.
Contact/s
Owner: Ms J Copley
Profile Artist.
Watercolour and pencil portraiture. Head studies and montages of horse and rider in various settings.
Yr. Est: 1986
Opening Times
Telephone for an appointment **Ref: YH03299**

COPPER HORSE STABLES

Copper Horse Stables, The Dell, Bishopsgate Rd, Englefield Green, Egham, **Surrey**, TW20 0AS, **ENGLAND**.
(T) 01784 434504 **(F)** 01784 434504.
Contact/s
Owner: Mr H Horst
Profile Stable/Livery. **Ref: YH03300**

COPPERALLEY EQUESTRIAN CTRE

Copperalley Equestrian Centre, Mayglare, Maynooth, **County Kildare**, **IRELAND**.
(T) 01 6286536
(E) copperalleyequestrian@kildarehorse.ie.
Contact/s
Key Contact: Mr J Connolly
Profile Equestrian Centre. **Ref: YH03301**

COPPERFIELD STABLES

Copperfield Stables, Haxton, Salisbury, **Wiltshire**, SP4 9PY, **ENGLAND**.
(T) 01980 670585.
Contact/s
Owner: Mr P Haynard
Profile Stable/Livery, Trainer, Transport/Horse Boxes.
No.Staff: 2 Yr. Est: 1978 C.Size: 10 Acres
Opening Times
Open all year **Ref: YH03302**

COPPICE EQUESTRIAN SADDLERY

Coppice Equestrian Saddlery, The Coppice, Farley Lane, Farley, **Staffordshire**, ST10 3BD, **ENGLAND**.
(T) 01538 703295
(M) 07768 442044.
Profile Saddlery Retailer, Stable/Livery.
Ref: YH03303

COPSEM STUD

Copsem Stud, Byhurst Farm, Malden Rushett, Chessington, **London (Greater)**, KT9 2NL, **ENGLAND**.
(T) 01372 721700 **(F)** 01372 745623
(W) www.balancedhorsefeeds.co.uk.
Contact/s
Owner: Mrs J Lane
(E) jane@balancedhorsefeeds.co.uk
Profile Breeder.
Standing Thoroughbred Stallion. Yr. Est: 1985
Opening Times
Telephone for an appointment **Ref: YH03304**

CORBETT OVINGTON STUD

Corbett Ovington Stud, Punsholt Farm, West Tisted, Alresford, **Hampshire**, SO24 0HN, **ENGLAND**.
(T) 01730 828281.
Contact/s
Owner: Mrs P Corbett
Profile Breeder. **Ref: YH03305**

CORBETT, MARK

Mark Corbett, Rawlins Farm, Charter Alley, Tadley, **Hampshire**, RG26 5PU, **ENGLAND**.
(T) 01256 851326 **(F)** 01256 850188
(M) 07860 347446.
Profile Breeder, Trainer. **Ref: YH03306**

CORBETT, R A C

Mr R A C Corbett, Holden Farm, Cheriton, **Hampshire**, SO24 0NX, **ENGLAND**.
(T) 01962 79267.
Profile Supplies. **Ref: YH03307**

CORBRIDGE & DISTRICT

Corbridge & District Riding Club, 2 Eastfield Cottages, Newcastle Rd, Corbridge, **Northumberland**, NE45 5LR, **ENGLAND**.
(T) 01434 633183 **(F)** 01434 633183.
Contact/s
Chairman: Miss R Fletcher
Profile Club/Association, Riding Club. **Ref: YH03308**

CORBRIDGE FABRICATIONS

Corbridge Fabrications, Unit 4, Bourne Works, East Grafton, Marlborough, **Wiltshire**, SN8 3DH, **ENGLAND**.
(T) 01264 850813.
Profile Transport/Horse Boxes. **Ref: YH03309**

CORDALL, I R

I R Cordall, 110 The Crossway, Fareham, **Hampshire**, PO16 8NH, **ENGLAND**.
(T) 023 92379282.
Profile Farrier. **Ref: YH03310**

CORDERY, PETER W

Peter W Cordery RSS, The Briars, Potmans Lane, Lunsford Cross, Bexhill-on-Sea, **Sussex (East)**, TN39 5JL, **ENGLAND**.
(T) 01424 892661.
Profile Farrier. **Ref: YH03311**

CORDINGLEY

Cordingley, Destrier Cottage, 24 High St, Steeton, Keighley, **Yorkshire (West)**, BD20 6NT, **ENGLAND**.
(T) 01535 654884 **(F)** 01254 301009. **Ref: YH03312**

CORDUFF STUD

Corduff Stud (The), Weston Pk, Kildare, **County Kildare**, **IRELAND**.
(T) 01 6280433
(E) corduffstud@kildarehorse.ie.
Contact/s
Key Contact: Mr J Egan
Profile Breeder. **Ref: YH03313**

CORDWAINERS CLGE

Cordwainers College, 182 Mare St, London, **London (Greater)**, E8 3RE, **ENGLAND**.
(T) 020 89850273 **(F)** 020 89859340
(E) info@cordwainers.ac.uk
(W) www.cordwainers.ac.uk.
Contact/s
Marketing Manager: Clare Groom
Profile Equestrian Centre. College.
Workshops for the leather based courses are equipped with a comprehensive range of machinery and equipment for making and testing footwear, fashion accessories, leather goods and saddlery. Yr. Est: 1887
Ref: YH03314

CORHAM STABLES

Corham Stables, Sandpit Lane, Bledlow, Princes Risborough, **Buckinghamshire**, HP27 9QQ, **ENGLAND**.
(T) 01844 342119.
Profile Riding School. **Ref: YH03315**

CORK RACECOURSE MALLOW

Cork Racecourse Mallow Ltd, Navigation Rd, Mallow, **County Cork**, **IRELAND**.
(T) 022 50207 **(F)** 022 50213.
Profile Supplies. **Ref: YH03316**

CORK SADDLERY

Cork Saddlery Ltd, 13 St Patricks Quay, Cork, **County Cork**, **IRELAND**.
(T) 021 4507542.
Profile Saddlery Retailer. **Ref: YH03317**

CORLEY, H V

Mr H V Corley BA (Oxon) DC (OSC) FBAAC, Pucketty Farm, Faringdon, **Oxfordshire**, SN7 8JP, **ENGLAND**.
(T) 01367 240181.
Profile Medical Support. **Ref: YH03318**

CORMAC MCCORMACK BLOODSTOCK

Cormac Mccormack Bloodstock Ltd, 47 The St, Kirtling, Newmarket, **Suffolk**, CB8 9PB, **ENGLAND**.
(T) 01638 731070.
Profile Blood Stock Agency. **Ref: YH03319**

CORMACK, ALEXANDER

Alexander Cormack, The Ha, Durran, Castletown, Caithness, **Hertfordshire**, **ENGLAND**..
Profile Breeder. **Ref: YH03320**

CORN STORES

Corn Stores (The), 360 Eversham Rd, Crabbs Cross, Redditch, **Worcestershire**, B97 5JB, **ENGLAND**.

A-Z of COMPANIES

(T) 01527 541982.
Profile Feed Merchant, Supplies. Ref: YH03321

CORNDALE ANIMAL FEEDS

Corndale Animal Feeds, Ivy Hse, 67 Seacoast Rd, Limavady, **County Londonderry**, BT49 9DW, **NORTHERN IRELAND**.
(T) 028 77722702 (F) 028 77722702.
Profile Feed Merchant. Ref: YH03322

CORNFIELD FARM

Cornfield Farm Equestrian Centre Ltd, Cornfield Gr, Burnley, **Lancashire**, BB12 8UB, **ENGLAND**.
(T) 01282 771328.
Contact/s
Owner: Mrs S Field
Profile Breeder, Equestrian Centre, Stable/Livery.
Ref: YH03323

CORNILO RIDING

Cornilo Riding, Sutton Ct Farm, Church Hill, Sutton, Dover, **Kent**, CT15 5DF, **ENGLAND**.
(T) 01304 380369 (F) 01304 364977.
Contact/s
Manageress: Mrs A Lemington
Profile Riding School. Ref: YH03324

CORNISH CALCIFIED SEAWEED

Cornish Calcified Seaweed, Newham, Truro, **Cornwall**, TR1 2ST, **ENGLAND**.
(T) 01872 78878.
Profile Supplies. Ref: YH03325

CORNISH EQUINE REGISTER

Cornish Equine Register (The), Bosahan Farm, Trewardreva, Falmouth, **Cornwall**, TR11 5QB, **ENGLAND**.
(T) 01326 340156.
Contact/s
Partner: Mrs B Olds
Profile Club/Association. Ref: YH03326

CORNISH RIDING HOLIDAYS

Cornish Riding Holidays, Buller Hill, Redruth, **Cornwall**, TR16 6ST, **ENGLAND**.
(T) 01209 211852 (F) 01209 211852
(E) bookings@cornish-riding-holidays.co.uk
(W) www.cornish-riding-holidays.co.uk
Affiliated Bodies ABRS, BHS.
Contact/s
General Manager: Ms K Dallimore
(E) mike@nofiveglobal.net
Profile Equestrian Centre, Holidays, Riding Club, Riding School, Stable/Livery.
The centre is set in the heart of the Cornish countryside. The family run centre has regular hacks out onto the beach, into the valleys or into the rugged moorlands. No.Staff: 10 Yr. Est: 1983
C.Size: 50 Acres
Opening Times
Sp: Open Mon - Sun 08:00. Closed Mon - Sun 20:00.
Su: Open Mon - Sun 08:00. Closed Mon - Sun 20:00.
Au: Open Mon - Sun 08:00. Closed Mon - Sun 20:00.
Wn: Open Mon - Sun 08:00. Closed Mon - Sun 20:00. Ref: YH03327

CORNISH SHIRE HORSE CTRE

Cornish Shire Horse Centre, Tredinnick, Wadebridge, **Cornwall**, PL27 7RA, **ENGLAND**.
(T) 01841 540276 (F) 01637 880936.
Profile Breeder. Tourist Attraction. Ref: YH03328

CORNWALL ANIMAL FEEDS

Cornwall Animal Feeds, 8 Central Sq, Newquay, **Cornwall**, TR7 1JH, **ENGLAND**.
(T) 01637 876652.
Profile Feed Merchant. Ref: YH03329

CORNWALL FARMERS

Cornwall Farmers Limited, Redmoor Rd, Kelly Bray, Callington, **Cornwall**, PL17 8EJ, **ENGLAND**.
(T) 01579 382292.
Profile Supplies. Ref: YH03330

CORNWALL FARMERS

Cornwall Farmers Limited, School Rd, Praze-An-Beeble, Camborne, **Cornwall**, TR14 0LB, **ENGLAND**.
(T) 01209 831431.
Profile Supplies. Ref: YH03331

CORNWALL FARMERS

Cornwall Farmers Limited, Otterham Station, Camelford, **Cornwall**, PL32 9SW, **ENGLAND**.
(T) 01840 261235.
Profile Supplies. Ref: YH03332

CORNWALL FARMERS

Cornwall Farmers Limited, Water-Ma-Trout Ind Est, Helston, **Cornwall**, TR13 0LW, **ENGLAND**.
(T) 01326 572345 (F) 01326 565505.
Profile Supplies. Ref: YH03333

CORNWALL FARMERS

Cornwall Farmers Limited, Station Yard, Liskeard, **Cornwall**, PL14 4DX, **ENGLAND**.
(T) 01579 343446.
Profile Supplies. Ref: YH03334

CORNWALL FARMERS

Cornwall Farmers Limited, Long Rock Ind Est, Poniou Rd, Penzance, **Cornwall**, TR20 8HX, **ENGLAND**.
(T) 01736 362839 (F) 01736 332519.
Profile Supplies. Ref: YH03335

CORNWALL FARMERS

Cornwall Farmers Limited, Victoria, Roche, St Austell, **Cornwall**, PL26 8LQ, **ENGLAND**.
(T) 01726 890666.
Profile Supplies. Ref: YH03336

CORNWALL FARMERS

Cornwall Farmers Limited, Threemilestone Ind Est, Threemilestone, Truro, **Cornwall**, TR4 9LD, **ENGLAND**.
(T) 01872 273044 (F) 01872 260484.
Profile Supplies. Ref: YH03337

CORNWALL FARMERS

Cornwall Farmers Limited, Trenant Trading Est, Wadebridge, **Cornwall**, PL27 6HB, **ENGLAND**.
(T) 01208 812444.
Profile Supplies. Ref: YH03338

CORNWALL FARMERS

Cornwall Farmers Limited, Market Pl, Hatherleigh, **Devon**, EX20 3JW, **ENGLAND**.
(T) 01837 810576.
Profile Supplies. Ref: YH03339

CORNWALL FARMERS

Cornwall Farmers Limited, Dobles Lane, Holsworthy, **Devon**, EX22 6HN, **ENGLAND**.
(T) 01409 253505 (F) 01409 253011.
Profile Supplies. Ref: YH03340

CORNWALL PAPER

Cornwall Paper Co Ltd, Wilson Way, Pool, Redruth, **Cornwall**, TR15 3RT, **ENGLAND**.
(T) 01209 212294 (F) 01209 313041.
Profile Supplies. Ref: YH03341

CORNWELL, RAYMOND T

Raymond T Cornwell AWCF, Cheesewring Farm, Minions, Liskeard, **Cornwall**, PL14 5LJ, **ENGLAND**.
(T) 01579 362200.
Profile Farrier. Ref: YH03342

CORROW TREKKING CTRE

Corrow Trekking Centre, Donich Pk, Lochgoilhead, Cairndow, **Argyll and Bute**, PA24 8AB, **SCOTLAND**.
(T) 01301 703247.
Profile Equestrian Centre. Trekking centre.
Beginners are welcome. Loch rides and forest treks are available need to be pre-booked. Riders of 10 years and over only.
Opening Times
Open mid-May to Oct, telephone for further details.
Ref: YH03343

CORRYLAIR FARM TREKKING CTRE

Corrylair Farm Trekking Centre, Corrylair, Gartly, Huntly, **Aberdeenshire**, AB54 4SB, **SCOTLAND**.
(T) 01466 720379.
Contact/s
Owner: Miss E Patterson
Profile Equestrian Centre. Trekking Centre.
Ref: YH03344

CORSCOMBE & HALSTOCK

Corscombe & Halstock Bridleway Group, Catsley Farmhouse, Corscombe, Dorchester, **Dorset**, DT2 0NR, **ENGLAND**.
(T) 01935 891220.
Profile Club/Association. Ref: YH03345

CORTEN, STEPHEN

Stephen Corten, 41 Whitedown Rd, Tadley, **Hampshire**, RG26 4BZ, **ENGLAND**.
(T) 0118 9820950.
Profile Farrier. Ref: YH03346

CORWEN & DISTRICT FARMERS

Corwen & District Farmers, Station Yard, Corwen, **Denbighshire**, LL21 0EG, **WALES**.
(T) 01490 412272.
Profile Supplies. Ref: YH03347

COSDON DARTMOORS

Cosdon Dartmoors, High View, South Zeal, Okehampton, **Devon**, EX20 2JL, **ENGLAND**.
(T) 01837 840508.
Profile Breeder. Ref: YH03348

COSFPS

Commons, Open Spaces and Footpaths Preservation Society, 25A Bell St, Henley-on-Thames, **Oxfordshire**, RG9 2BA, **ENGLAND**.
(T) 01491 573535.
Contact/s
Key Contact: Miss K Ashbrook
Profile Club/Association. Ref: YH03349

COSGROVE & SON

F Cosgrove & Son, North Walk Farm, Hainton, Market Rasen, **Lincolnshire**, LN8 6LD, **ENGLAND**.
(T) 01507 313727
Affiliated Bodies BHS, BSJA.
Contact/s
Owner: Mr D Cosgrove
Profile Breeder, Transport/Horse Boxes.
No.Staff: 3 Yr. Est: 1947 C.Size: 484 Acres
Opening Times
Telephone for an appointment Ref: YH03350

COSGROVE, D J S

D J S Cosgrove, Corner Hse Stables, Jamesfield Pl, Hamilton Rd, Newmarket, **Suffolk**, CB8 0TE, **ENGLAND**.
(T) 01638 661961 (F) 01638 661961
(W) www.newmarketracehorsetrainers.co.uk
Affiliated Bodies Newmarket Trainers Fed.
Contact/s
Owner: Mr D Cosgrove
Profile Trainer. Ref: YH03351

COSGROVE, SHONA

Shona Cosgrove, Skreen Rd, Dunshaughlin, **County Meath**, **IRELAND**.
(T) 01 8259842. Ref: YH03352

COSSENS, ANTHONY

Anthony Cossens, Will Farm, Peter Tavy, Tavistock, **Devon**, PL19 9NB, **ENGLAND**.
(T) 01822 810293.
Profile Farrier. Ref: YH03353

COSSINGTON

Cossington Stables, Syston Rd, Cossington, Leicester, **Leicestershire**, LE7 4UZ, **ENGLAND**.
(T) 0116 2608713.
Contact/s
Owner: Miss J Crawford
Profile Riding School, Stable/Livery. No.Staff: 3
Yr. Est: 1986
Opening Times
Sp: Open 08:00. Closed 18:30.
Su: Open 08:00. Closed 18:30.
Au: Open 08:00. Closed 18:30.
Wn: Open 08:00. Closed 18:30. Ref: YH03354

COSTELLO TOM

Costello Tom, Fenloe Hse, Newmarket-on-Fergus, **County Clare**, **IRELAND**.
(T) 061 368242.
Profile Supplies. Ref: YH03355

COSTER, NOEL

Noel Coster DWCF, 177 Southwood Rd, Rusthall, Tunbridge Wells, **Kent**, TN4 8UU, **ENGLAND**.
(T) 01892 540613.
Profile Farrier. Ref: YH03356

COTEBROOK STUD

Cotebrook Stud, Racecourse Lane, Cotebrook, Tarporley, **Cheshire**, CW6 9EF, **ENGLAND**.
(T) 01829 760221.
Contact/s
Owner: Mr T Stokes
Profile Riding School, Stud Farm. Ref: YH03357

COTON EQUITANA

Coton Equitana Ltd, Newton Lane, Newton, Rugby, **Warwickshire**, CV23 0TB, **ENGLAND**.
(T) 01788 860799.
Profile Trainer. Ref: YH03358

COTON, F

Mr F Coton, Chapel Farm, Epperstone, **Nottinghamshire**, NG14 6AE, **ENGLAND**.
(T) 0115 9663048.
Profile Supplies. Ref: YH03359

COTSWOLD EQUESTRIAN

Cotswold Equestrian Insurances, The Nags 7, Queens Mead, Worcester, **Worcestershire**, WR8 0ND, **ENGLAND**.
(T) 01684 594030.
Contact/s
Owner: Miss A Guy
Profile Insurance. **Ref: YH03360**

COTSWOLD EQUINE CTRE

Cotswold Equine Centre (The), Home Farm, Bradwell Gr, Burford, **Oxfordshire**, OX18 4JW, **ENGLAND**.
(T) 01993 823127 **(F)** 01993 823812.
Profile Medical Support. **Ref: YH03361**

COTSWOLD GRASS SEEDS

Cotswold Grass Seeds, Cotswold Business Village, London Rd, Moreton In Marsh, **Gloucestershire**, GL56 0JQ, **ENGLAND**.
(T) 08002 52211.
Profile Supplies. **Ref: YH03362**

COTSWOLD HORSE

Cotswold Horse, No 3 The Elliott Ctre, Elliott Rd, Cirencester, **Gloucestershire**, GL7 1YS, **ENGLAND**.
(T) 01285 655122 **(F)** 01285 655133
(E) nve@nve.co.uk.
Profile Medical Support. **Ref: YH03363**

COTSWOLD RIDING RAMBLES

Cotswold Riding Rambles, Upper Dale Cottage, Naunton, Cheltenham, **Gloucestershire**, GL54 3AJ, **ENGLAND**.
(T) 01451 850319.
Contact/s
Owner: Mrs C Adams
Profile Horse/Rider Accom.
Opening Times
Telephone for further information, there is an answer phone **Ref: YH03364**

COTSWOLD SADDLERY

Cotswold Saddlery, 46-48 Cricklade St, Cirencester, **Gloucestershire**, GL7 1JN, **ENGLAND**.
(T) 01285 651106.
Profile Saddlery Retailer. **Ref: YH03365**

COTSWOLD STUD

Cotswold Stud, Sezincote, Moreton In Marsh, **Gloucestershire**, GL56 9TB, **ENGLAND**.
(T) 01386 700700.
Profile Breeder. **Ref: YH03366**

COTSWOLD STUD

Cotswold Stud (Glocs), The Pk, Lower Slaughter, Cheltenham, **Gloucestershire**, GL54 2HY, **ENGLAND**.
(T) 01386 700700 **(F)** 01386 700701
(E) maryhambro@cotswoldstud.com.
Profile Breeder. **Ref: YH03367**

COTSWOLD TRAIL RIDING

Cotswold Trail Riding, Ongers Farm, Upton Lane, Brookthorpe, Gloucester, **Gloucestershire**, GL4 0UT, **ENGLAND**.
(T) 01452 813344.
Contact/s
Owner: Mr J Warner
Profile Riding School, Stable/Livery.
Hacking Yr. Est: 1990 C.Size: 360 Acres
Opening Times
Sp: Open 09:00. Closed 20:00.
Su: Open 09:00. Closed 20:00.
Au: Open 09:00. Closed 20:00.
Wn: Open 09:00. Closed 20:00. **Ref: YH03368**

COTSWOLD TRAILERS

Cotswold Trailers, Unit 1 Cambridge Mills, Cambridge, Gloucester, **Gloucestershire**, GL2 7AA, **ENGLAND**.
(T) 01453 890961 **(F)** 01453 890962.
Contact/s
Partner: Mr D Nelmes
Profile Transport/Horse Boxes. **Ref: YH03369**

COTSWOLD TRAILERS

Cotswold Trailers, Slaughter Pike Garage, Stow Rd, Bourton-on-the-Water, Cheltenham, **Gloucestershire**, GL54 2HW, **ENGLAND**.
(T) 01451 810200 **(F)** 01451 810400.
Contact/s
Owner: Mr D Nelmes
Profile Transport/Horse Boxes. **Ref: YH03370**

COTSWOLD VALE

Cotswold Vale Horseball Club, C/O Homestead Farm, Elmstone Hardwicke, Cheltenham, **Gloucestershire**, GL52 9TH, **ENGLAND**.
(T) 01242 680538.
Profile Club/Association. **Ref: YH03371**

COTTAGE ESTATES STABLES

Cottage Estates Stables, 'The Hollies', Loperwood, Whitemoor, Winsor, Southampton, **Hampshire**, S040 2HB, **ENGLAND**.
(T) 023 80812990 **(F)** 023 80813903
(E) alan@horsestabling.com
(W) www.horsestabling.com.
Contact/s
Key Contact: Mr A Brown
Profile Stable/Livery.
Manufacturer of Stabling, Loose Boxes, Tack Rooms, Hay Stores, Field Shelters, Mobile Field Shelters etc. Should their be a need to apply to local authorities for planning approval, we can supply the necessary elevated drawings. A small charge is made for these drawings, but this fee is deducted from the order total.
Yr. Est: 1980 **Ref: YH03372**

COTTAGE FARM

Cottage Farm, Cobbetts Lane, Blackwater, Camberley, **Hampshire**, GU17 9LW, **ENGLAND**.
(T) 01252 872224.
Profile Stable/Livery. **Ref: YH03373**

COTTAGE FARM RIDING STABLES

Cottage Farm Riding Stables, 100 Ilshaw Heath Rd, Warings Green, Hockley Heath, Solihull, **Warwickshire**, B94 6DL, **ENGLAND**.
(T) 01564 703314.
Profile Riding School. **Ref: YH03374**

COTTAGE FARM STABLES

Cottage Farm Stables, Bad Bargain Lane, Osbaldwick, York, **Yorkshire (North)**, YO31 0LA, **ENGLAND**.
(T) 01904 416245.
Profile Riding School, Stable/Livery.
Full livery service only, prices on request.
Opening Times
Open 24 hours **Ref: YH03375**

COTTAGE HOMES

Cottage Homes, Hammers Lane, London, **London (Greater)**, NW7 4EE, **ENGLAND**.
(T) 020 82010116. **Ref: YH03376**

COTTAGE INDUSTRIES

Cottage Industries (Equestrian) Ltd, Crown Lane, Wychbold, Droitwich, **Worcestershire**, WR9 0BX, **ENGLAND**.
(T) 01527 861753 **(F)** 01274 610181.
Profile Riding Wear Retailer, Saddlery Retailer.
Ref: YH03377

COTTAGE INDUSTRIES

Cottage Industries (Equestrian) Ltd, Hollybrook Mill, Harrogate Rd, Greengates, Bradford, **Yorkshire (West)**, BD10 0YY, **ENGLAND**.
(T) 01274 610000 **(F)** 01274 610181.
Profile Riding Wear Retailer, Saddlery Retailer.
Ref: YH03378

COTTAGE SADDLERY

Cottage Saddlery, Holly Farm, High Ferry Lane, Sibsey, Boston, **Lincolnshire**, PE22 0TA, **ENGLAND**.
(T) 01205 750257 **(F)** 01205 751160
Affiliated Bodies BETA.
Contact/s
Owner: Mrs D Briggs
Profile Riding Wear Retailer, Saddlery Retailer.
Yr. Est: 2000
Opening Times
Sp: Open Mon - Sat 10:00. Closed Mon - Sat 17:00.
Su: Open Mon - Sat 10:00. Closed Mon - Sat 17:00.
Au: Open Mon - Sat 10:00. Closed Mon - Sat 17:00.
Wn: Open Mon - Sat 10:00. Closed Mon - Sat 17:00.
Closed Sundays **Ref: YH03379**

COTTAGE STABLES

Cottage Stables, Little Hatherden, Andover, **Hampshire**, SP11 0HY, **ENGLAND**.
(T) 01264 735509 **(F)** 01264 735529
(M) 07774 993998.
Profile Trainer. **Ref: YH03380**

COTTAGE STUD

Cottage Stud (The), Hodgestown, Kilcock, **County Kildare**, **IRELAND**.
(T) 01 6287690
(E) cottagestud@kildarehorse.ie.
Contact/s
Key Contact: Mr P Monaghan
Profile Breeder. **Ref: YH03381**

COTTER, LLOYD J

Lloyd J Cotter DWCF, 9 Regency Gardens, Hornchurch, **Essex**, RM11 1PP, **ENGLAND**.
(T) 01708 474102.
Profile Farrier. **Ref: YH03382**

COTTERILL, B, C & A

B, C & A Cotterill, Hermitage Farm, Gr Lane, Wishaw, Sutton Coldfield, **Midlands (West)**, **ENGLAND**.
(T) 0121 3511318.
Profile Breeder. **Ref: YH03383**

COTTON EQUESTRIAN CTRE

Cotton Equestrian Centre, Holmes Chapel, Crewe, **Cheshire**, CW4 7ES, **ENGLAND**.
(T) 01477 537295.
Contact/s
Owner: Mr S Clarke
Profile Equestrian Centre, Trainer. **Ref: YH03384**

COTTON, SARAH

Sarah Cotton BHSI, The Flat, Skeggs Farm, Writtle, Chelmsford, **Essex**, CM1 3ET, **ENGLAND**.
(T) 01245 422860
(M) 07836 222104.
Profile Trainer. **Ref: YH03385**

COTTON, W J

Nuttys Livery Yard, Sainham Lane, Godshill, Ventnor, **Isle of Wight**, PO38 3JS, **ENGLAND**.
(T) 01983 840228.
Profile Stable/Livery. **Ref: YH03386**

COTTRELL, L G

Mr L G Cottrell, The Paddocks, Dulford, Cullompton, **Devon**, EX15 2DX, **ENGLAND**.
(T) 01884 266320.
Profile Trainer. **Ref: YH03387**

COTTRILL EQSTN VEHICLE SVS

H H Cottrill & Son (Cottrill Equestrian Vehicle Sales and Services), Little Parham Farm, Bredicot, Worcester, **Worcestershire**, WR7 4QB, **ENGLAND**.
(T) 01905 345377.
Contact/s
General Manager: Mr J Cottrill
Profile Transport/Horse Boxes.
Horsebox services **Ref: YH03388**

COULSDON CLGE

Coulsdon College, Placehouse Lane, Coulsdon, **Surrey**, CR5 1YA, **ENGLAND**.
(T) 01737 551176.
Profile Equestrian Centre. **Ref: YH03389**

COULSON, ROBERT G

Robert G Coulson DWCF, Flat 2, 43 Station Rd, New Barnet, **Hertfordshire**, EN5 1PR, **ENGLAND**.
(M) 07860 205834.
Profile Farrier. **Ref: YH03390**

COUNIHAN RACHEL

Counihan Rachel, Killeenlahan, Ballinagore, **County Westmeath**, **IRELAND**.
(T) 044 26383.
Profile Supplies. **Ref: YH03391**

COUNTASH TRAILERS

Countash Trailers, Rd 2 Hoobrook Ind Est, Worcester Rd, Kidderminster, **Worcestershire**, DY10 1HY, **ENGLAND**.
(T) 01562 824346 **(F)** 01562 824346.
Contact/s
Owner: Mr J Tew
Profile Transport/Horse Boxes. **Ref: YH03392**

COUNTESS OF ROTHES

Countess of Rothes, Tanglewood, West Tytherley, Salisbury, **Wiltshire**, SP5 1LX, **ENGLAND**.
(T) 01980 862314.
Profile Breeder. **Ref: YH03393**

COUNTESS OF SWINTON

Countess of Swinton (The), Dykes Hill Hse, Masham, Ripon, **Yorkshire (North)**, HG4 4NS, **ENGLAND**.
(T) 01765 689241 **(F)** 01765 689596.
Profile Breeder, Riding School. **Ref: YH03394**

COUNTIES EQUESTRIAN SVS

Counties Equestrian Services Ltd, PO Box 112, Knutsford, **Cheshire**, WA16 9BQ, **ENGLAND**.
(T) 07050 609110 **(F)** 07070 657517.
Contact/s
Manager: Mr S Garner
Profile Medical Support. **Ref: YH03395**

COUNTIES EQUESTRIAN SVS

Counties Equestrian Services Ltd, PO Box 2061, Wrexham, **Wrexham**, LL13 0ZL, **WALES**.
(T) 07050 609110 (F) 07070 657517
(E) sales@countiesequestrian.co.uk
(W) www.countiesequestrian.co.uk.
Profile Medical Support. Ref: YH03396

COUNTRY & DISTANCE RIDER

Country & Distance Rider, The Mill, Bearwalden Business Pk, Wendens Ambo, Saffron Walden, **Essex**, CB11 4JX, **ENGLAND**.
(T) 01799 544200.
Profile Supplies. Ref: YH03397

COUNTRY & EQUESTRIAN

Country & Equestrian Books & Gifts, 4A Clge Ct, Gloucester, **Gloucestershire**, GL1 2NJ, **ENGLAND**.
(T) 01452 502438 (F) 01452 332272
(E) sales@countryandequestrianbooks.co.uk
(W) www.countryandequestrianbooks.co.uk.
Profile Supplies. Ref: YH03398

COUNTRY CLASSICS

Country Classics, 68 Bow St, Lisburn, **County Antrim**, BT28 1AL, **NORTHERN IRELAND**.
(T) 028 92603383 (F) 028 92629079.
Contact/s
Owner: Mr R Saulters
Profile Riding Wear Retailer. Yr. Est: 1996
Opening Times
Sp: Open Mon - Sat 09:30. Closed Mon - Sat 17:00.
Su: Open Mon - Sat 09:30. Closed Mon - Sat 17:00.
Au: Open Mon - Sat 09:30. Closed Mon - Sat 17:00.
Wn: Open Mon - Sat 09:30. Closed Mon - Sat 17:00.
Ref: YH03399

COUNTRY CLASSICS

Country Classics, Green Acres, Trench Lane, Oddingly, Droitwich, **Worcestershire**, WR9 7ND, **ENGLAND**.
(T) 01905 795878 (F) 01905 795878.
Profile Saddlery Retailer. Ref: YH03400

COUNTRY COLLECTION

Country Collection Ltd, Crawhall, Brampton, **Cumbria**, CA8 1TN, **ENGLAND**.
(T) 01697 741735 (F) 01697 73838
(E) jane.tea@opermail.com.
Profile Supplies. Ref: YH03401

COUNTRY COVERS

Country Covers, 13 Arran Dri, Garforth, Leeds, **Yorkshire (West)**, LS25 2BU, **ENGLAND**.
(T) 0113 2862651.
Profile Supplies. Ref: YH03402

COUNTRY DRESSER

Country Dresser, Station Rd, Adare, **County Limerick**, **IRELAND**.
(T) 061 396915 (F) 061 395062
(E) countryd@iol.ie.
Contact/s
Owner: Mr R Carton
Profile Riding Wear Retailer, Saddlery Retailer, Supplies.
Country Dresser are clothing, rugs and fishing tackle, retailers No.Staff: 2 Yr. Est: 1995
Opening Times
Sp: Open Mon - Fri 09:00, Sat 09:30. Closed Mon - Fri 18:00, Sat 17:00.
Su: Open Mon - Fri 09:00, Sat 09:30. Closed Mon - Fri 18:00, Sat 17:00.
Au: Open Mon - Fri 09:00, Sat 09:30. Closed Mon - Fri 18:00, Sat 17:00.
Wn: Open Mon - Fri 09:00, Sat 09:30. Closed Mon - Fri 18:00, Sat 17:00.
Closed Sundays except in December, telephone for further details Ref: YH03403

COUNTRY EQUESTRIAN

Country Equestrian Ltd, Warren Farm, Warren Rd, Little Horwood, Milton Keynes, **Buckinghamshire**, MK17 0PT, **ENGLAND**.
(T) 01296 715700 (F) 01296 715900.
Profile Saddlery Retailer. Ref: YH03404

COUNTRY FARM LIVERY YARD

Country Farm Livery Yard, Yorley Farm, Upper Rd, Little Cornard, Sudbury, **Suffolk**, CO10 0NZ, **ENGLAND**.
(T) 01787 227353 (F) 01787 228395.
Contact/s
Owner: Mrs B Johnson
Profile Stable/Livery. Ref: YH03405

COUNTRY FEEDS

Country Feeds, Unit 12A Clyde View Shopping Ctre, Glasgow Rd, Blantyre, **Lanarkshire (South)**, G72 0QD, **SCOTLAND**.
(T) 01698 710215.
Profile Feed Merchant. Ref: YH03406

COUNTRY FEEDS

Country Feeds (Bradford), Wharf St, Shipley, Bradford, **Yorkshire (West)**, BD17 7DW, **ENGLAND**.
(T) 01274 593111.
Profile Feed Merchant. Ref: YH03407

COUNTRY FEEDS LARBERT

Country Feeds Larbert Ltd, Larbert Mill, Stirling Rd, Larbert, **Falkirk**, FK5 3NH, **SCOTLAND**.
(T) 01324 555535 (F) 01324 555535.
Profile Feed Merchant.
Wholesale enquiries welcome Ref: YH03408

COUNTRY GENTLEMEN'S ASS

Country Gentlemen's Association, Shuttleworth, Old Warden Pk, Biggleswade, **Bedfordshire**, SG18 9EA, **ENGLAND**.
(T) 01767 626242 (F) 01767 627158.
Contact/s
Key Contact: Mr C Page
Profile Club/Association. Ref: YH03409

COUNTRY ILLUSTRATED MAGAZINE

Country Illustrated Magazine, St Martins Magazines Plc, 3rd Floor Kent Hse, 14/17 Market Pl, London, **London (Greater)**, W1W 8AJ, **ENGLAND**.
(T) 020 72553331 (F) 020 72553332.
Profile Supplies. Ref: YH03410

COUNTRY JUMPKINS BAKER-MAC

Country Jumpkins Baker-Mac Ltd, Denmill, Tough, Alford, **Aberdeenshire**, AB33 8EP, **SCOTLAND**.
(T) 01975 562582 (F) 01975 562582
(E) bakermac@jumpkin.demon.co.uk.
Profile Supplies. Ref: YH03411

COUNTRY LANDOWNERS ASS

Country Landowners Association, 16 Belgrave Sq, London, **London (Greater)**, SW1X 8PQ, **ENGLAND**.
(T) 020 72350511 (F) 020 72354696
(W) www.clg.org.uk.
Contact/s
President: Mr A Bosanquet
Profile Club/Association.
Organisation that safeguards the interests of private landowners and rural business. Provides a free advisory service on rural issues. Provides publications on guidance for subjects such as tax, planning and economic issues. Organises CLA games fair and the premier festival of countryside sports. Yr. Est: 1907
Opening Times
Sp: Open Mon - Fri 09:30. Closed Mon - Fri 17:30.
Su: Open Mon - Fri 09:30. Closed Mon - Fri 17:30.
Au: Open Mon - Fri 09:30. Closed Mon - Fri 17:30.
Wn: Open Mon - Fri 09:30. Closed Mon - Fri 17:30.
Ref: YH03412

COUNTRY LAUNDRY SVS

Country Laundry Services, 48 The Old Mill, School Lane, Bamber Bridge, Preston, **Lancashire**, PR5 6PS, **ENGLAND**.
(T) 01772 330777.
Contact/s
Owner: Mr A Pollard
Profile Supplies. Laundry Service. Ref: YH03413

COUNTRY LEATHER SADDLERY

Country Leather Saddlery, Mount Pleasant Farm, 4 Wilson St, Stanley, Crook, **County Durham**, DL15 9RU, **ENGLAND**.
(T) 01388 768408.
Profile Saddlery Retailer. Ref: YH03414

COUNTRY LIFE

Country Life, 5 North St, Haverfordwest, **Pembrokeshire**, SA61 2JE, **WALES**.
(T) 01437 768415 (F) 01437 768415.
Contact/s
Owner: Mr T Curtis
Profile Riding Wear Retailer. Ref: YH03415

COUNTRY LIFE

Country Life, The Crossroads, Brompton, Northallerton, **Yorkshire (North)**, DL6 2RQ, **ENGLAND**.
(T) 01609 772124.
Contact/s
Owner: Mr M Pearson
Profile Riding Wear Retailer. Ref: YH03416

COUNTRY MATTERS

Country Matters, Whitworth Rd, Cirencester, **Gloucestershire**, GL7 1RT, **ENGLAND**.
(T) 01285 642425 (F) 01285 652151.
Profile Supplies. Ref: YH03417

COUNTRY METALCRAFT

Country Metalcraft, Bath Rd, Theale, Reading, **Berkshire**, RG7 5EE, **ENGLAND**.
(T) 0118 9302496.
Contact/s
Manager: Mr B Neal
Profile Blacksmith. Ref: YH03418

COUNTRY PADDOCKS

Country Paddocks, Germains Farm, Kelvedon Hall Lane, Kelvedon Hatch, Brentwood, **Essex**, CM14 5TL, **ENGLAND**.
(T) 01277 362056 (F) 01277 362460.
Profile Stable/Livery.
Full, part and DIY livery, prices on request.
Opening Times
Open 24 hours Ref: YH03419

COUNTRY PURSUIT

Country Pursuit, 1 Banbury St, Kineton, Warwick, **Warwickshire**, CV35 0JS, **ENGLAND**.
(T) 01926 641230.
Contact/s
Owner: Ms S Wixie
Profile Saddlery Retailer. Ref: YH03420

COUNTRY PURSUITS

Country Pursuits, Willow Grange, Ely Rd, Chittering, Cambridge, **Cambridgeshire**, CB5 9PL, **ENGLAND**.
(T) 01353 649573.
Contact/s
Owner: Ms F Dunne
(E) willowgrange@aol.com
Profile Equestrian Centre, Stable/Livery.
No.Staff: 4 Yr. Est: 1989 C.Size: 15 Acres
Ref: YH03421

COUNTRY PURSUITS

Country Pursuits, 36 High St, Cricklade, **Wiltshire**, SN6 6AY, **ENGLAND**.
(T) 01793 751946.
Profile Saddlery Retailer. Ref: YH03422

COUNTRY RIDER

Country Rider, The Old Mill, East Hill, Blackwater, Truro, **Cornwall**, TR4 8EG, **ENGLAND**.
(T) 01872 561172.
Profile Saddlery Retailer. Ref: YH03423

COUNTRY RIDING WEAR

Country Riding Wear, 4 Grand Prde, Station Rd, Hook, **Hampshire**, RG27 9HF, **ENGLAND**.
(T) 01256 762050 (F) 01256 762050
(E) sales@crwhook.fsnet.co.uk
(W) www.crwhook.fsnet.co.uk
Affiliated Bodies BETA, SMS.
Contact/s
Owner: Mr D Shorey
Profile Riding Wear Retailer.
Caters for most disciplines of riding including Dressage, Show Jumping, Eventing and Recreational. Numnahs, saddle cloths and travelling sets can be ordered in your own colours, with an embroidery service available for that special touch. Stock a wide range of clothing for riders of all ages and ability, from beginners to competitors at National level. Keep jodhpurs from sizes to fit children age 2 upwards to adult. Trained staff on hand to ensure the correct fit of your hat or body protector. Saddle fitting specialists who can fit any make or model. Stock a wide range of riding related gifts, books, videos and cards.
Ref: YH03424

COUNTRY SHOP

Country Shop (The), Rolls Mill, Sturminster Newton, **Dorset**, DT10 2HP, **ENGLAND**.
(T) 01258 473737 (F) 01258 471200.
Profile Riding Wear Retailer, Saddlery Retailer.
Ref: YH03425

COUNTRY SPORT

Country Sport, 31 Station Rd, Hadfield, Glossop, **Derbyshire**, SK13 1DB, **ENGLAND**.
(T) 01457 867643 (F) 01457 867643
(W) www.country-sport.co.uk.
Contact/s
Owner: Mr T Uttley
(E) country.sport@breathemail.net
Profile Riding Wear Retailer, Saddlery Retailer, Supplies.
Saddle checks can be carried out at own yard.
Yr. Est: 1982
Opening Times
Sp: Open Mon, Wed - Sat 09:00. Closed Mon, Wed - Fri 17:30, Sat 17:00.

Su: Open Mon, Wed - Sat 09:00. Closed Mon, Wed - Fri 17:30, Sat 17:00.
Au: Open Mon, Wed - Sat 09:00. Closed Mon, Wed - Fri 17:30, Sat 17:00.
Wn: Open Mon, Wed - Sat 09:00. Closed Mon, Wed - Fri 17:30, Sat 17:00.
Closed Tuesdays and Sundays **Ref: YH03426**

COUNTRY STABLING

Country Stabling, St. Erth Ind Est, Rose-An-Grouse, Canonstown, Hayle, **Cornwall**, TR27 6LP, **ENGLAND**.
(T) 01736 755540 **(F)** 01736 753190.
Contact/s
Owner: Mr M Bailey
Profile Supplies. **Ref: YH03427**

COUNTRY STILE CLOTHING

Country Stile Clothing, Dorset Hse Studfold, Horton-In-Ribblesdale, Settle, **Yorkshire (North)**, BD24 0ER, **ENGLAND**.
(T) 01729 860315.
Profile Riding Wear Retailer. **Ref: YH03428**

COUNTRY STYLE CLOTHING

Country Style Clothing, The Sidings Ind Est, Settle, **Yorkshire (North)**, BD24 9RP, **ENGLAND**.
(T) 01729 825446 **(F)** 01729 825664.
Profile Riding Wear Retailer. **Ref: YH03429**

COUNTRY STYLES

Country Styles, 169 Watling St, Towcester, **Northamptonshire**, NN12 6BX, **ENGLAND**.
(T) 01327 358200.
Contact/s
Owner: Mr M Fleming
Profile Riding Wear Retailer. Yr. Est: 1990
Opening Times
Sp: Open Mon - Sat 09:00. Closed Mon - Sat 18:00.
Su: Open Mon - Sat 09:00. Closed Mon - Sat 18:00.
Au: Open Mon - Sat 09:00. Closed Mon - Sat 18:00.
Wn: Open Mon - Sat 09:00. Closed Mon - Sat 18:00.
Ref: YH03430

COUNTRY SUPPLIES

Country Supplies, Jackson Hill Farm, Jackson Hill, Queensbury, Bradford, **Yorkshire (West)**, BD13 2LA, **ENGLAND**.
(T) 01274 884400 **(F)** 01274 884600.
Profile Saddlery Retailer. **Ref: YH03431**

COUNTRY TRADING

Country Trading, Tor View Garage, Edgarley, Glastonbury, **Somerset**, BA6 8LE, **ENGLAND**.
(T) 01458 833800 **(F)** 01458 833380.
Profile Saddlery Retailer. **Ref: YH03432**

COUNTRY TREKS

Country Treks, C/O The Vicarage Activity Ctre, The Bull Ring, Stottesdon, Kidderminster, **Worcestershire**, DY14 8UH, **ENGLAND**.
(T) 01746 718733.
Contact/s
Owner: Miss S Dobson
Profile Equestrian Centre. Trekking Centre.
Ref: YH03433

COUNTRY VEHICLES

Country Vehicles, Main St, Pymoor, Ely, **Cambridgeshire**, CB6 2DY, **ENGLAND**.
(T) 01353 698075.
Contact/s
Owner: Mr G Stapleton
Profile Transport/Horse Boxes. No.Staff: 3
Yr. Est: 1989 **Ref: YH03434**

COUNTRY VOGUE

Country Vogue, Garstang Rd, Claughton-on-Brock, Garstang, Preston, **Lancashire**, PR3 0PH, **ENGLAND**.
(T) 01995 640622 **(F)** 01995 640288.
Profile Supplies. **Ref: YH03435**

COUNTRY WAYS

Country Ways, 115 Holburn St, Aberdeen, **Aberdeen (City of)**, AB10 6BQ, **SCOTLAND**.
(T) 01224 585150.
Profile Riding Wear Retailer, Saddlery Retailer.
Ref: YH03436

COUNTRY YARNS & TACKROOM

Country Yarns & Tackroom, 3 The Sq, Bromyard, **Herefordshire**, HR7 4BP, **ENGLAND**.
(T) 01885 482035 **(F)** 01885 488115.
Contact/s
Owner: Mrs T Crae
Profile Riding Wear Retailer, Supplies. **Ref: YH03437**

COUNTRYMAN'S GALLERY

Countryman's Gallery (The), Kibworth Harcourt, Market Harborough, **Leicestershire**, LE8 0NE, **ENGLAND**.
(T) 0116 2793211 **(F)** 0116 2792437.
Profile Art Gallery.
Sporting Art Gallery. **Ref: YH03438**

COUNTRYSIDE

Countryside Showjumps, Bramford Rd, Bramford, Ipswich, **Suffolk**, IP8 4BA, **ENGLAND**.
(T) 01473 240340 **(F)** 01473 240350
(E) salses@countryside-sj.co.uk
(W) www.countryside-sj.co.uk.
Contact/s
Owner: Mr N MacDonald
Profile Supplies. Showjump Manufacturers.
Yr. Est: 1989
Opening Times
Sp: Open Mon - Fri 08:30. Closed Mon - Fri 16:30.
Su: Open Mon - Fri 08:30. Closed Mon - Fri 16:30.
Au: Open Mon - Fri 08:30. Closed Mon - Fri 16:30.
Wn: Open Mon - Fri 08:30. Closed Mon - Fri 16:30.
Outside of these opening hours the phone is redirected, calls are taken personally not by a machine
Ref: YH03439

COUNTRYSIDE ALLIANCE

Countryside Alliance, The Old Town Hall, 367 Kennington Rd, London, **London (Greater)**, SE11 4PT, **ENGLAND**.
(T) 020 78409200 **(F)** 020 77938484
(E) info@countryside-alliance.org
(W) www.countryside-alliance.org.
Contact/s
Chief Executive: Mr R Burge
Profile Club/Association.
Campaigns on rural issues that are important and relevant to people in the town and country.
Opening Times
Sp: Open 09:00. Closed 17:00.
Su: Open 09:00. Closed 17:00.
Au: Open 09:00. Closed 17:00.
Wn: Open 09:00. Closed 17:00. **Ref: YH03440**

COUNTRYSIDE COACHWORKS

Countryside Coachworks Ltd, Newmarket Rd, Heydon, Royston, **Hertfordshire**, SG8 7PR, **ENGLAND**.
(T) 01763 208908 **(F)** 01763 208430.
Contact/s
General Manager: Mr G Thopsom
Profile Transport/Horse Boxes. **Ref: YH03441**

COUNTRYWEAR

Countrywear, Trevadoc, Cusop, Hay On Wye, **Herefordshire**, HR3 5TP, **ENGLAND**.
(T) 01497 820896 **(F)** 01497 820896.
Profile Riding Wear Retailer. **Ref: YH03442**

COUNTRYWEAR BY LEWIS R LILLIE

Countrywear by Lewis R Lillie, Unit 1, Robinsons Way, Telford Way Ind Est, Kettering, **Northamptonshire**, NN16 8PT, **ENGLAND**.
(T) 01536 481558 **(F)** 01536 485218.
Profile Riding Wear Retailer. **Ref: YH03443**

COUNTRYWIDE

Countrywide, PO Box 1, Milland, Liphook, **Hampshire**, GU30 7NA, **ENGLAND**.
(T) 01428 741329.
Profile Supplies. **Ref: YH03444**

COUNTRYWIDE

Countrywide Stores (Hereford), Mortimer Rd, Hereford, **Herefordshire**, HR4 9SR, **ENGLAND**.
(T) 01432 352244 **(F)** 01432 352534
(W) www.countrywidefarmers.co.uk.
Contact/s
Head of Equine Department: Ms M Jones
Profile Medical Support, Riding Wear Retailer, Saddlery Retailer, Supplies.
Opening Times
Sp: Open Mon - Sat 08:30, Sun 10:00. Closed Mon - Sat 17:30, Sun 16:00.
Su: Open Mon - Sat 08:30, Sun 10:00. Closed Mon - Sat 17:30, Sun 16:00.
Au: Open Mon - Sat 08:30, Sun 10:00. Closed Mon - Sat 17:30, Sun 16:00.
Wn: Open Mon - Sat 08:30, Sun 10:00. Closed Mon - Sat 17:30, Sun 16:00. **Ref: YH03445**

COUNTRYWIDE

Countrywide Stores (Head Office), Countrywide Hse, The Butts, Worcester, **Worcestershire**, WR1 3NU, **ENGLAND**.
(T) 01905 25541 **(F)** 01905 723412
(E) enquiries@countrywidefarmers.co.uk
(W) www.countrywidefarmers.co.uk.
Profile Riding Wear Retailer, Saddlery Retailer, Supplies.
Also stock petfoods and garden sundries. Farmer and Equestrian evenings are run in the stores, see website or telephone for further information. **Ref: YH03446**

COUNTRYWIDE FEEDS

Countrywide Welland Valley Feeds, Leicester Rd, Market Harborough, **Leicestershire**, LE16 7AY, **ENGLAND**.
(T) 01858 461463 **(F)** 01858 461464.
Profile Feed Merchant. **Ref: YH03447**

COUNTRYWIDE STORES

Countrywide Stores (Twyford), London Rd, Twyford, Reading, **Berkshire**, RG10 9EQ, **ENGLAND**.
(T) 0118 9403770 **(F)** 0118 9403567.
Profile Supplies. **Ref: YH03448**

COUNTRYWIDE STORES

Countrywide Stores (Bridgend), South Rd, Bridgend Ind Est, Bridgend, **Bridgend**, CF31 3PT, **WALES**.
(T) 01656 652115 **(F)** 01656 647072.
Profile Supplies. **Ref: YH03449**

COUNTRYWIDE STORES

Countrywide Stores (Tingewick), Finmere Mill, Tingewick, **Buckinghamshire**, MK18 4BR, **ENGLAND**.
(T) 01280 848551 **(F)** 01280 847812.
Profile Supplies. **Ref: YH03450**

COUNTRYWIDE STORES

Countrywide Stores (Bourton), Station Rd, Bourton-on-The Water, **Gloucestershire**, GL54 2EP, **ENGLAND**.
(T) 01451 820551 **(F)** 01451 810183.
Profile Supplies. **Ref: YH03451**

COUNTRYWIDE STORES

Countrywide Stores (Cirencester), Stratton Mills, Cirencester, **Gloucestershire**, GL7 2HY, **ENGLAND**.
(T) 01285 653481.
Profile Supplies. **Ref: YH03452**

COUNTRYWIDE STORES

Countrywide Stores (Gloucester), Plot 4 The Cattle Market, St Oswolds Rd, Gloucester, **Gloucestershire**, GL1 2SR, **ENGLAND**.
(T) 01452 383083 **(F)** 01452 384296.
Profile Supplies. **Ref: YH03453**

COUNTRYWIDE STORES

Countrywide Stores (Gloucester), Animal Health Dept, 171 Westgate St, Gloucester, **Gloucestershire**, GL1 2RR, **ENGLAND**.
(T) 01452 526881 **(F)** 01452 529866.
Profile Supplies. **Ref: YH03454**

COUNTRYWIDE STORES

Countrywide Stores (Tewkesbury), Tredington, Tewkesbury, **Gloucestershire**, GL20 7BZ, **ENGLAND**.
(T) 01684 293368 **(F)** 01684 274377.
Profile Supplies. **Ref: YH03455**

COUNTRYWIDE STORES

Countrywide Stores (Thornbury), Eastwood, Old Gloucester Rd, The Knapp, Thornbury, **Gloucestershire (South)**, BS35 3UH, **ENGLAND**.
(T) 01454 260406 **(F)** 01454 260749.
Profile Supplies. **Ref: YH03456**

COUNTRYWIDE STORES

Countrywide Stores (Ledbury), Hazle Pk, Dymock Rd, Ledbury, **Herefordshire**, HR8 2JQ, **ENGLAND**.
(T) 01531 634601 **(F)** 01531 632552.
Profile Supplies. **Ref: YH03457**

COUNTRYWIDE STORES

Countrywide Stores (Bromyard), Tenbury Rd, Bromyard, **Herefordshire**, HR7 4LL, **ENGLAND**.
(T) 01885 483333 **(F)** 01885 483101.
Profile Supplies. **Ref: YH03458**

COUNTRYWIDE STORES

Countrywide Stores (Leominster), The Railway Ind Est (North), Worcester Rd, Leominster, **Herefordshire**, HR6 8AR, **ENGLAND**.
(T) 01568 612243 **(F)** 01568 610556.
Profile Supplies. **Ref: YH03459**

COUNTRYWIDE STORES

Countrywide Stores (Abergavenny), Lower Monk St, Abergavenny, **Monmouthshire**, NP7 5LU, **WALES**.
(T) 01873 855180 **(F)** 01873 856299.
Profile Supplies. **Ref: YH03460**

COUNTRYWIDE STORES

Countrywide Stores (Chepstow), The Backs,

Riverside Mill, Chepstow, **Monmouthshire**, NP16 5HS, **WALES**.
(T) 01291 622225 **(F)** 01291 627548.
Profile Supplies. **Ref: YH03461**

COUNTRYWIDE STORES

Countrywide Stores (Raglan), Grange Mill, Abergavenny Rd, Raglan, **Monmouthshire**, NP15 2AA, **WALES**.
(T) 01291 690056 **(F)** 01291 690378.
Profile Supplies. **Ref: YH03462**

COUNTRYWIDE STORES

Countrywide Stores (Chipping Norton), Banbury Rd, Chipping Norton, **Oxfordshire**, OX7 5TE, **ENGLAND**.
(T) 01608 642071 **(F)** 01608 645125.
Profile Supplies. **Ref: YH03463**

COUNTRYWIDE STORES

Countrywide Stores (Oxford), Stanton Harcourt Rd, Eynsham, Oxford, **Oxfordshire**, OX8 1HJ, **ENGLAND**.
(T) 01865 881556 **(F)** 01865 882880.
Profile Supplies. **Ref: YH03464**

COUNTRYWIDE STORES

Countrywide Stores (Llandrindod Wells), Tremont Rd, Llandrindod Wells, **Powys**, LD1 5BW, **WALES**.
(T) 01597 824851 **(F)** 01597 823914.
Profile Supplies. **Ref: YH03465**

COUNTRYWIDE STORES

Countrywide Stores (Presteigne), Presteigne Mill, Leominster Rd, Presteigne, **Powys**, LD8 2NH, **WALES**.
(T) 01544 267909 **(F)** 01544 260166.
Profile Supplies. **Ref: YH03466**

COUNTRYWIDE STORES

Countrywide Stores (Welshpool), Severn Rd, Welshpool, **Powys**, SY21 7AZ, **WALES**.
(T) 01938 554664 **(F)** 01938 554030.
Profile Supplies. **Ref: YH03467**

COUNTRYWIDE STORES

Countrywide Stores (Bishops Castle), Station St, Bishops Castle, **Shropshire**, SY9 5AQ, **ENGLAND**.
(T) 01588 638341 **(F)** 01588 630283.
Profile Supplies. **Ref: YH03468**

COUNTRYWIDE STORES

Countrywide Stores (Bridgnorth), Tasley Rd, Bridgnorth, **Shropshire**, WV16 4QB, **ENGLAND**.
(T) 01746 764411 **(F)** 01746 767864.
Profile Saddlery Retailer. **Ref: YH03469**

COUNTRYWIDE STORES

Countrywide Stores (Craven Arms), Farmore Mills, Shrewbury Rd, Craven Arms, **Shropshire**, SY7 9QG, **ENGLAND**.
(T) 01588 673013 **(F)** 01588 676806.
Profile Supplies. **Ref: YH03470**

COUNTRYWIDE STORES

Countrywide Stores (Marksbury), Westways Garage, Westway, Marksbury, **Somerset**, BA2 9HN, **ENGLAND**.
(T) 01761 470101 **(F)** 01761 472848.
Profile Supplies. **Ref: YH03471**

COUNTRYWIDE STORES

Countrywide Stores (Bridgwater), Huntsworth, Gate Mill, Marsh Lane, Bridgwater, **Somerset**, TA6 6LQ, **ENGLAND**.
(T) 01278 458481.
Profile Supplies. **Ref: YH03472**

COUNTRYWIDE STORES

Countrywide Stores (Redhill), Kingsmill Lane, South Nutfield, Redhill, **Surrey**, RH1 5NB, **ENGLAND**.
(T) 01737 823205 **(F)** 01737 822845.
Profile Supplies. **Ref: YH03473**

COUNTRYWIDE STORES

Countrywide Stores (Nuneaton), Redgate, Watling St, Nuneaton, **Warwickshire**, CV10 0RY, **ENGLAND**.
(T) 024 76384730 **(F)** 024 76375039.
Profile Supplies. **Ref: YH03474**

COUNTRYWIDE STORES

Countrywide Stores (Rugby), Station Mill, Stockton, Rugby, **Warwickshire**, CV23 8HA, **ENGLAND**.
(T) 01926 812513 **(F)** 01926 815105.
Profile Supplies. **Ref: YH03475**

COUNTRYWIDE STORES

Countrywide Stores (Stratford upon Avon), Bearley Mill, Bearley, Stratford-upon-Avon, **Warwickshire**, CV37 0SA, **ENGLAND**.
(T) 01789 731113 **(F)** 01789 731066.
Profile Supplies. **Ref: YH03476**

COUNTRYWIDE STORES

Countrywide Stores (Chippenham), Yatton Keynell, Castle Combe, Chippenham, **Wiltshire**, SN14 7BB, **ENGLAND**.
(T) 01249 782391 **(F)** 01249 782171.
Profile Supplies. **Ref: YH03477**

COUNTRYWIDE STORES

Countrywide Stores (Melksham), Bradford Rd, Melksham, **Wiltshire**, SN12 8LQ, **ENGLAND**.
(T) 01225 701470 **(F)** 01225 702318.
Profile Supplies. **Ref: YH03478**

COUNTRYWIDE STORES

Countrywide Stores (Swindon), Lady Lane, Blunsdon, Swindon, **Wiltshire**, SN2 4DN, **ENGLAND**.
(T) 01793 722888 **(F)** 01793 706011.
Profile Supplies. **Ref: YH03479**

COUNTRYWIDE STORES

Countrywide Stores (Kidderminster), Firs Ind Est, Stourport Rd, Kidderminster, **Worcestershire**, DY11 7QN, **ENGLAND**.
(T) 01562 820777 **(F)** 01562 829573.
Profile Supplies. **Ref: YH03480**

COUNTRYWIDE STORES

Countrywide Stores (Upton Upon Severn), Hanley Rd, Upton-upon-Severn, **Worcestershire**, WR8 0HU, **ENGLAND**.
(T) 01684 593131 **(F)** 01684 594873.
Profile Supplies. **Ref: YH03481**

COUNTRYWIDE STORES

Countrywide Stores (Bromsgrove), Brickhouse Lane, Stoke Prior, Bromsgrove, **Worcestershire**, B61 4LX, **ENGLAND**.
(T) 01527 831663 **(F)** 01527 570290.
Profile Supplies. **Ref: YH03482**

COUNTRYWIDE STORES

Countrywide Stores (Evesham), Worcester Rd, Evesham, **Worcestershire**, WR11 4QR, **ENGLAND**.
(T) 01386 442971 **(F)** 01386 765434.
Profile Saddlery Retailer. **Ref: YH03483**

COUNTRYWISE FEEDS & NEEDS

Countrywise Feeds & Needs, Shipman Joinery Yard, Station Rd, Rushton, Kettering, **Northamptonshire**, NN14 1RL, **ENGLAND**.
(T) 01536 713405 **(F)** 01536 713405.
Profile Feed Merchant, Supplies. **Ref: YH03484**

COUNTY COACHBUILDERS

County Coachbuilders, Yvans Hall, Hadleigh Heath, Hadleigh, **Suffolk**, IP7 5NX, **ENGLAND**.
(T) 01787 211555 **(F)** 01787 211200.
Profile Transport/Horse Boxes. **Ref: YH03485**

COUNTY COMPETITION STUD

County Competition Stud Livery & Training Yard, Home Farm, Munderfield Harold, Bromyard, **Herefordshire**, HR7 4SZ, **ENGLAND**.
(T) 01885 482062 **(F)** 01885 488464
(M) 07768 472882
Affiliated Bodies BHS.
Contact/s
Owner: Mrs Y Wall
Profile Arena, Breeder, Equestrian Centre, Stable/Livery, Trainer. No.Staff: 3 Yr. Est: 1977
C.Size: 30 Acres
Opening Times
Sp: Open Mon - Sun 08:00. Closed Mon - Sun 20:00.
Su: Open Mon - Sun 08:00. Closed Mon - Sun 20:00.
Au: Open Mon - Sun 08:00. Closed Mon - Sun 20:00.
Wn: Open Mon - Sun 08:00. Closed Mon - Sun 20:00.
Yard is open to livery owners seven days a week. Telephone for an appointment. **Ref: YH03486**

COUNTY FOOTWEAR

County Footwear Ltd - Allen & Caswell Ltd, Ll Regent Works, Cornwall Rd, Kettering, **Northamptonshire**, NN16 8PR, **ENGLAND**.
(T) 01536 512804 **(F)** 01536 519014
(E) sales@regentfootwear.co.uk.
Contact/s
Sales Manager: Michael S Cox
Profile Riding Wear Retailer. Footwear. **Ref: YH03487**

COUNTY GARAGE

County Garage, 42 York Rd, Strensall, York, **Yorkshire (North)**, YO3 5TG, **ENGLAND**.
(T) 01904 490162.
Profile Transport/Horse Boxes. **Ref: YH03488**

COUNTY LIVERY

County Livery, Long Meadow Stables, Ashendene Rd, Bayford, Hertford, **Hertfordshire**, SG13 8PX, **ENGLAND**.
(T) 01992 511423 **(F)** 01992 511423.
Contact/s
Owner: Mr K Patience
Profile Stable/Livery. **Ref: YH03489**

COUNTY ROSETTES

County Rosettes, The Double Hse, 22 Clge Lane, Hassocks, **Sussex (West)**, BN6 9AQ, **ENGLAND**.
(T) 01273 834079
(M) 07958 585840
(E) info@countyrosettes.co.uk
(W) www.countyrosettes.co.uk.
Profile Rosette Stockists.
County Rosettes offer a range of quality products in a variety of styles and colours, plus custom made rosettes and ribbons. Telephone for further information
Ref: YH03490

COUNTY SADDLERY

County Saddlery Ltd, New St, Walsall, **Midlands (West)**, WS1 3DF, **ENGLAND**.
(T) 01922 659080 **(F)** 01922 659089.
Contact/s
Company Secretary: Mrs M Holdcroft
Profile Saddlery Retailer.
There is an on-site Master Saddler. **Ref: YH03491**

COUNTY SLIGO RACES

County Sligo Races Ltd, Cleveragh Race Course, Sligo, **County Sligo**, **IRELAND**.
(T) 071 62484.
Profile Track/Course. **Ref: YH03492**

COUNTY TRAILERS

County Trailers, Hill Of Down, Enfield, **County Meath**, **IRELAND**.
(T) 040 541832.
Profile Transport/Horse Boxes. **Ref: YH03493**

COUNTY VETNRY GRP

County Veterinary Group, 12 Macclesfield Rd, Holmes Chapel, **Cheshire**, CW4 7NF, **ENGLAND**.
(T) 01477 535574.
Profile Medical Support. **Ref: YH03494**

COUNTY VETNRY GRP

County Veterinary Group, 30 Crewe Rd, Sandbach, **Cheshire**, CW11 0NE, **ENGLAND**.
(T) 01270 767455.
Profile Medical Support. **Ref: YH03495**

COUNTY VETNRY GRP

County Veterinary Group, 9 Lawton Rd, Alsager, Stoke-on-Trent, **Staffordshire**, ST7 2AA, **ENGLAND**.
(T) 01270 872670 **(F)** 01270 883122.
Profile Medical Support. **Ref: YH03496**

COUNTY WHIPS

County Whips Ltd, Hawkins Lane, Burton-on-Trent, **Staffordshire**, DE14 1PT, **ENGLAND**.
(T) 01283 565697.
Profile Whip Manufacturers. **Ref: YH03497**

COUPLAND, J

Mr J Coupland, Clge Farm, The Ave, East Ravendale, Grimsby, **Lincolnshire (North East)**, DN37 0RX, **ENGLAND**.
(T) 01472 827872 **(F)** 01472 827872
(M) 07831 555533.
Profile Supplies. **Ref: YH03498**

COURT FARM COUNTRY STORE

Court Farm Country Store, Ct Farm, Coleford Rd, Bream, Lydney, **Gloucestershire**, GL15 6ES, **ENGLAND**.
(T) 01594 564314.
Profile Saddlery Retailer. **Ref: YH03499**

COURT FARM LIVERY

Court Farm Livery, Pk Lane, Aveley, South Ockendon, **Essex**, RM15 4UD, **ENGLAND**.
(T) 01708 865659.
Contact/s
Owner: Mrs R Day
Profile Stable/Livery. **Ref: YH03500**

COURT FARM RIDING CTRE
Court Farm Riding Centre, Coventry Rd, Griff, Nuneaton, **Warwickshire**, CV10 7PJ, **ENGLAND**.
(T) 024 76313388 **(F)** 024 76313388.
Contact/s
Owner: Mr H Haddon
Profile Equestrian Centre. **Ref: YH03501**

COURT FARM STABLES
Court Farm Stables, Exford, **Somerset**, TA24 7LY, **ENGLAND**.
(T) 01643 831207.
Profile Stable/Livery. **Ref: YH03502**

COURTENAY, A L
A L Courtenay, Alma Farm, Leighton Rd, Toddington, **Bedfordshire**, LU5 6AP, **ENGLAND**.
(T) 01525 873592.
Profile Breeder, Farrier. **Ref: YH03503**

COURTHILL STABLES
Courthill Stables, Letcombe Regis, Wantage, **Oxfordshire**, OX12 9JL, **ENGLAND**.
(T) 01235 772481.
Profile Supplies. **Ref: YH03504**

COURTHOUSE STABLES
Courthouse Stables, The Courthouse, West Meon, Petersfield, **Hampshire**, GU32 1JG, **ENGLAND**.
(T) 01730 829572.
Profile Stable/Livery. **Ref: YH03505**

COURTLANDS
Courtlands Dressage, Fleet Lane, Finchampstead, Wokingham, **Berkshire**, RG40 4RN, **ENGLAND**.
(T) 0118 9731487 **(F)** 0118 9734347
Affiliated Bodies BHS.
Profile Arena, Stable/Livery, Trainer. Horse Dealers.
Yr. Est: 1986
Opening Times
Telephone for an appointment. Yard open to owners all day. **Ref: YH03506**

COURTLANDS
Courtlands Riding Academy, Todds Green, Stevenage, **Hertfordshire**, SG1 2JE, **ENGLAND**.
(T) 01438 726669.
Contact/s
Partner: Miss J Halling **(Q)** BHSAI
Profile Riding School.
Family run and family orientated stable. Train up to NVQ level 3. Yr. Est: 1979
Opening Times
Telephone for further information **Ref: YH03507**

COURTLANDS LIVERY STABLES
Courtlands Livery Stables, Chalmers Rd, Banstead, **Surrey**, SM7 3HF, **ENGLAND**.
(T) 01737 357259.
Contact/s
Manager: Mrs A Kestell
Profile Stable/Livery. **Ref: YH03508**

COURTLEA NUMNAHS
Courtlea Numnahs, PO Box 32, Ellesmere Port, **Cheshire**, CH66 7PF, **ENGLAND**.
(T) 0151 3393009 **(F)** 0151 3393009.
Contact/s
Owner: Mrs B Leather
Profile Supplies. **Ref: YH03509**

COURTNEY, S & WALLACE, D
S Courtney & D Wallace, Clements Cottage, Larch Ave, Holbury, **Hampshire**, SO45 2PB, **ENGLAND**.
(T) 023 80891882.
Profile Breeder. **Ref: YH03510**

COURTYARD FARM
Courtyard Farm, Ringstead, Hunstanton, **Norfolk**, PE36 5LQ, **ENGLAND**.
(T) 01485 525369.
Contact/s
Owner: Ms J Calvert
Profile Horse/Rider Accom. **Ref: YH03511**

COURTYARD SADDLERY
Courtyard Saddlery, Lilac Farm, Jewitt Lane, Collingham, **Yorkshire (West)**, LS22 5BA, **ENGLAND**.
(T) 01937 573162 **(F)** 01937 572084.
Profile Saddlery Retailer. **Ref: YH03512**

COUSINS, MAURICE C
Maurice C Cousins, Lower Farm, Church Lane, East Winch, King's Lynn, **Norfolk**, PE32 1NL, **ENGLAND**.
(T) 01553 840425
(M) 07836 287554.
Profile Breeder, Farrier. **Ref: YH03513**

COUSINS, S D J
S D J Cousins, Lower Farm Stud, Church Lane, East Winch, King's Lynn, **Norfolk**, PE32 1NL, **ENGLAND**.
(T) 01553 840425 **(F)** 01553 840425.
Profile Stable/Livery. **Ref: YH03514**

COUSLAND PK FARM
Cousland Park Farm, Equestrian Ctre, Cousland Pk Farm, Cousland, Dalkeith, **Lothian (Mid)**, EH22 2PD, **SCOTLAND**.
(T) 01875 616291 **(F)** 01875 616291
Affiliated Bodies BHS.
Contact/s
Groom: Ms A Stafford
Profile Horse/Rider Accom, Stable/Livery.
Yr. Est: 1997
Opening Times
Sp: Open 08:00. Closed 21:00.
Su: Open 08:00. Closed 21:00.
Au: Open 08:00. Closed 21:00.
Wn: Open 08:00. Closed 21:00. **Ref: YH03515**

COUTISSE
Coutisse, The Stables, 5 Duck St, Cerne Abbas, Dorchester, **Dorset**, DT2 7LA, **ENGLAND**.
(T) 01300 341718 **(F)** 01300 341718.
Profile Saddlery Retailer. **Ref: YH03516**

COUTTS, JANET
Janet Coutts, 40 King St, Beeston, Nottingham, **Nottinghamshire**, NG9 2DL, **ENGLAND**.
(T) 0115 9227917.
Profile Trainer. **Ref: YH03517**

COVENTRY SILVERCRAFT
Coventry Silvercraft Company Ltd (The), 6-8 Lamb St, Coventry, **Midlands (West)**, CV1 4AD, **ENGLAND**.
(T) 08700 106108 **(F)** 08700 106 104
(E) sales@coventry-silvercraft.co.uk
(W) www.coventry-silvercraft.com.
Profile Trophy Manufacturers.
The comprehensive Trophy Catalogue contains a wide choice of suitable awards & medals. All can be personalised and can include a figurine to depict your activity.
Yr. Est: 1945 **Ref: YH03518**

COVERT
Covert (The), East St, Petworth, **Sussex (West)**, GU28 0AB, **ENGLAND**.
(T) 01798 343118.
Profile Saddlery Retailer. **Ref: YH03519**

COWAN STABLES
Cowan Stables, Darnrigg Farm, Falkirk, **Falkirk**, FK1 3AS, **SCOTLAND**.
(T) 01324 851244 **(F)** 01324 851223.
Profile Breeder. **Ref: YH03520**

COWARD, J R
Mr J R Coward, Coed-Y-Paen, Pontypool, **Torfaen**, NP4 0TB, **WALES**.
(T) 01291 672733 **(F)** 01291 672733.
Profile Breeder. **Ref: YH03521**

COWDENKNOWES EQUI CTRE
Cowdenknowes Equi Centre, Cowdenknowes Stables, Earlston, **Scottish Borders**, TD4 6AA, **SCOTLAND**.
(T) 01896 848020.
Contact/s
Owner: Mrs F McQueen
Profile Equestrian Centre.
Trekking available. **Ref: YH03522**

COWDRAY PK POLO CLUB
Cowdray Park Polo Club, c/o Cowdray Est Office, Midhurst, **Sussex (West)**, GU29 0AQ, **ENGLAND**.
(T) 01730 813257
(E) enquiries@cowdraypolo.co.uk
(W) www.cowdraypolo.co.uk.
Contact/s
Coach: Mr C Atkinson **(T)** 01730 812941
(E) ckaa@talk21.com
Profile Club/Association. Polo Club.
Membership applications must be in writing and addressed to the Polo Manager. The annual subscription is currently £85 plus VAT(£99.88), plus joining fee of £25 plus VAT (£29.37) **Ref: YH03523**

COWELL, ROBERT
Robert Cowell, Cowell Farms, Six Mile Bottom, Newmarket, **Suffolk**, CB8 0TT, **ENGLAND**.
(T) 01638 570330 **(F)** 01638 570473
(W) www.newmarketracehorsetrainers.co.uk
Affiliated Bodies Newmarket Trainers Fed.
Contact/s
Owner: Mr R Cowell
Profile Breeder, Trainer. **Ref: YH03524**

COWIN EQUESTRIAN CTRE
Cowin Equestrian Centre, Pembrey Country Pk, Factory Rd, Burry Port, **Carmarthenshire**, SA16 0DZ, **WALES**.
(T) 01554 832160.
Contact/s
Owner: Mr D Fulcher
Profile Equestrian Centre, Riding School.
Ref: YH03525

COWLEY RIDING SCHOOL
Cowley Riding School, Four Acres, Cowley Lane, Holmesfield, Dronfield, **Derbyshire**, S18 7SD, **ENGLAND**.
(T) 0114 2890356.
Profile Riding School, Trainer. **Ref: YH03526**

COX & ROBINSON
Cox & Robinson (Agricultural) Ltd, The Creamery, Brackley Rd, Buckingham, **Buckinghamshire**, MK18 1JD, **ENGLAND**.
(T) 01280 816011 **(F)** 01280 822935.
Profile Saddlery Retailer. **Ref: YH03527**

COX, ADRIAN C S
Adrian C S Cox DWCF, 21 Springfield Cl, Lavant, Chichester, **Sussex (West)**, PO18 0AZ, **ENGLAND**.
(T) 01243 774345.
Profile Farrier. **Ref: YH03528**

COX, DAVE
Dave Cox, The Smithy, High St, Southwick, Fareham, **Hampshire**, PO17 6EB, **ENGLAND**.
(T) 023 92325744.
Profile Blacksmith. **Ref: YH03529**

COX, EDWARD J
Edward J Cox RSS BII, 186 Boswell Drv, Walsgrave on Sowe, Coventry, **Midlands (West)**, CV2 2GW, **ENGLAND**.
(T) 024 76621987.
Profile Farrier. **Ref: YH03530**

COX, J
Mrs J Cox, Meadow Hse, Coatham Mundeville, Darlington, **County Durham**, DL1 3LU, **ENGLAND**.
(T) 01325 314557 **(F)** 01325 301616.
Profile Stable/Livery. **Ref: YH03531**

COX, JAMES W
James W Cox DWCF, 157 Hinwick Rd, Wollaston, **Northamptonshire**, NN29 7QY, **ENGLAND**.
(T) 01933 663016.
Profile Farrier. **Ref: YH03532**

COX, JOHN H
John H Cox RSS, 79 Murcott Rd, Arncott, Bicester, **Oxfordshire**, OX6 0PL, **ENGLAND**.
(T) 01869 253624.
Profile Farrier. **Ref: YH03533**

COX, JOHN R
John R Cox, Lisnawilly, Dundalk, **County Louth**, **IRELAND**.
(T) 042 9334391.
Profile Supplies. **Ref: YH03534**

COX, P E
P E Cox, Thornsett Hey Farm, Birch Vale, High Peak, **Cheshire**, SK22 1AZ, **ENGLAND**.
(T) 01663 744226.
Profile Farrier. **Ref: YH03535**

COX, ROBERT
Robert Cox, 2 The Firs, Pinfold Lane, Stafford, **Staffordshire**, ST19 9PD, **ENGLAND**.
(T) 01785 840283.
Contact/s
Artist: Mr R Cox
Profile Artist. **Ref: YH03536**

COYLE, JAMES
Coyle James, Ferendale Stud Teltown Donaghpatrick, Navan, **County Meath**, **IRELAND**.
(T) 046 545193.
Profile Supplies. **Ref: YH03537**

CRACKENTHORPESTUD
Crackenthorpestud, Roger Head Farm, Appleby-In-Westmorland, **Cumbria**, CA16 6AD, **ENGLAND**.
(T) 01768 351845 **(F)** 01768 351845.
Contact/s
Owner: Mr A Chappelhow
Profile Breeder. **Ref: YH03538**

A-Z of COMPANIES

CRADDOCK, STEVE A

Steve A Craddock DWCF, Forge Cottage, Stowford, Lewdown, Okehampton, **Devon**, EX20 4BZ, **ENGLAND**.
(T) 01566 783112.
Profile Farrier. **Ref: YH03539**

CRADLEWELL FORGE

Cradlewell Forge (The), 123 Jesmond Rd, Newcastle-upon-Tyne, **Tyne and Wear**, NE2 1JY, **ENGLAND**.
(T) 0191 2817906.
Contact/s
Manager: Mr B Roberts
Profile Blacksmith. **Ref: YH03540**

CRADOC TACK

Cradoc Tack, The Old Smithy, Cradoc, Brecon, **Powys**, LD3 9PD, **WALES**.
(T) 01874 623466.
Contact/s
Manager: Mrs L Williams
Profile Saddlery Retailer. **Ref: YH03541**

CRAFTSMEN HORSE BOXES

Craftsmen Horse Boxes, 1A Kirkless Ind Est, Cale Lane, Aspull, Wigan, **Lancashire**, WN2 1HF, **ENGLAND**.
(T) 01942 492440.
Contact/s
Partner: Mr D Charlton
Profile Transport/Horse Boxes. **Ref: YH03542**

CRAGG, R

R Cragg, Silverwell Forge, Silverwell, Blackwater, Truro, **Cornwall**, TR4 8JG, **ENGLAND**.
(T) 01872 560658.
Contact/s
Owner: Mr C Cragg
Profile Farrier. **Ref: YH03543**

CRAGGS, R

Mr R Craggs, East Close Farm, Sedgefield, Durham, **County Durham**, TS21 3HW, **ENGLAND**.
(T) 01740 620239 **(F)** 01740 623476.
Profile Trainer. **Ref: YH03544**

CRAGINETHERTY

Craignetherty Highland Pony Stud, Craignethery Farm, Netherdale, Turriff, **Aberdeenshire**, AB53 4GT, **SCOTLAND**.
(T) 01466 780364
(E) craignetherty@hotmail.com
(W) www.craignetherty.batcave.net.
Contact/s
Owner: Mr H Duncan
Profile Blood Stock Agency, Breeder. No.Staff: 1
Yr. Est: 1960 C.Size: 180 Acres
Opening Times
Telephone for an appointment **Ref: YH03545**

CRAGO, KAREN

Mrs Karen Crago, Blandy's Farm, Blandy's Lane, Upper Basildon, Reading, **Berkshire**, RG8 8PH, **ENGLAND**.
(T) 01491 671214.
Profile Trainer. **Ref: YH03546**

CRAGO, PAUL

Mr Paul Crago, Blandy's Farm Cottage, Blandy's Lane, Upper Basildon, Reading, **Berkshire**, RG8 8PH, **ENGLAND**.
(T) 01491 671839.
Profile Stable/Livery. **Ref: YH03547**

CRAIB, MARGIE

Miss Margie Craib BHSI MC AMC MMCA BHSI, Ashridge Farm, Ringshall, Berkhamsted, **Hertfordshire**, HP4 1ND, **ENGLAND**.
(T) 01442 842729.
Profile Medical Support. **Ref: YH03548**

CRAIG & BUCHANAN

Craig & Buchanan, 23 Lochburn Rd, Glasgow, **Glasgow (City of)**, G20 9AE, **SCOTLAND**.
(T) 0141 9462007 **(F)** 0141 9452100.
Profile Blacksmith. **Ref: YH03549**

CRAIG BUILDERS ENGINEERS

Craig Builders Engineers Ltd, Craig Hse, 64 Darnley St, Glasgow, **Glasgow (City of)**, G41 2SE, **SCOTLAND**.
(T) 0141 4296355 **(F)** 0141 4292307.
Profile Blacksmith. **Ref: YH03550**

CRAIG ROBINSON & PARTNERS

Craig Robinson & Partners, 6 Wavell Drv, Rosehill, Carlisle, **Cumbria**, CA1 2ST, **ENGLAND**.
(T) 01228 521393.
Profile Medical Support. **Ref: YH03551**

CRAIGANTLET RIDING CLUB

Craigantlet Riding Club, 2 Laurelbank Ave, Newtownards, **County Down**, BT23 4AT, **NORTHERN IRELAND**.
(T) 028 91815028.
Contact/s
Chairman: Miss J Russell
Profile Riding Club. **Ref: YH03552**

CRAIGHEAD

Craighead Carriage & Driving Centre, Craighead Farm, Fauldhouse, **Lothian (West)**, EH47 9AB, **SCOTLAND**.
(T) 01501 771679 **(F)** 01501 771679.
Contact/s
Owner: Mrs E Cornish
Profile Horse/Rider Accom. Driving Centre.
Ref: YH03553

CRAIGIE BYRE RIDING SCHOOL

Craigie Byre Riding School, High Wardneuk, Monkton, Prestwick, **Ayrshire (South)**, KA9 2SL, **SCOTLAND**.
(T) 01563 830322.
Contact/s
Owner: Ms J Kemp
Profile Riding School. **Ref: YH03554**

CRAIGS STUD

Craigs Stud, Ballyclare, **County Antrim**, BT39 9DE, **NORTHERN IRELAND**.
(T) 028 93322327 **(F)** 028 25643459.
Profile Breeder. **Ref: YH03555**

CRAIGWEIL ARABIAN STUD

Craigweil Arabian Stud, East Balgray Hse, Balgray, Irvine, **Ayrshire (North)**, KA11 2AP, **SCOTLAND**.
(T) 01294 850273.
Profile Breeder. **Ref: YH03556**

CRAINE, A

A Craine, 53-55 Castle St, Bolton, **Manchester (Greater)**, BL2 1AD, **ENGLAND**.
(T) 01204 525830.
Profile Saddlery Retailer. **Ref: YH03557**

CRAMOND BRIG

Cramond Brig, Cramond Brig Farm, Edinburgh, **Edinburgh (City of)**, EH4 6DX, **SCOTLAND**.
(T) 0131 3395922.
Contact/s
Owner: Mr R Wishaw
Profile Blacksmith. **Ref: YH03558**

CRANE FORGE

Crane Forge, Bromely Green, Bamford, Hope Valley, **Derbyshire**, S33 0AA, **ENGLAND**.
(T) 0114 2848415.
Profile Blacksmith. **Ref: YH03559**

CRANE FRUEHAUF

Crane Fruehauf Ltd, Eastfield Rd, South Killingholme, Immingham, **Lincolnshire (North East)**, DN40 3EE, **ENGLAND**.
(T) 01469 572422 **(F)** 01469 571125.
Contact/s
Manager: Mr L Phipps
Profile Transport/Horse Boxes. **Ref: YH03560**

CRANE FRUEHAUF

Crane Fruehauf Ltd, Rashs Green, Dereham, **Norfolk**, NR19 1JF, **ENGLAND**.
(T) 01362 695353 **(F)** 01362 654312.
Profile Transport/Horse Boxes. **Ref: YH03561**

CRANE, LES

Les Crane, 9 Heskin Lane, Ormskirk, **Lancashire**, L39 1LR, **ENGLAND**.
(T) 01695 574132 **(F)** 01695 574132.
Contact/s
Owner: Mrs M Crane
Profile Transport/Horse Boxes. **Ref: YH03562**

CRANFORD HALL STUD

Cranford Hall Stud, Cranford, Kettering, **Northamptonshire**, NN14 4AD, **ENGLAND**.
(T) 01536 78692.
Profile Breeder. **Ref: YH03563**

CRANHAM, GERRY

Gerry Cranham, 80 Fairdene Rd, Coulsdon, **Surrey**, CR5 1RE, **ENGLAND**.
(T) 01737 553688 **(F)** 01737 553688
(E) cranhamphoto@btinternet.com.
Profile Photographer. **Ref: YH03564**

CRANLEIGH SCHOOL OF RIDING

Cranleigh School Of Riding (The), Horseshoe Lane, Cranleigh, **Surrey**, GU6 8QQ, **ENGLAND**.
(T) 01483 276426 **(F)** 01483 267398
Affiliated Bodies BHS, NAC, Pony Club UK.
Contact/s
General Manager: Ms E Lacey **(Q)** BHSII
Profile Equestrian Centre, Riding Club, Riding School, Stable/Livery, Trainer. No.Staff: 5
Yr. Est: 1979 C.Size: 60 Acres
Opening Times
Sp: Open 09:00. Closed 18:00.
Su: Open 09:00. Closed 18:00.
Au: Open 09:00. Closed 18:00.
Wn: Open 09:00. Closed 18:00. **Ref: YH03565**

CRANLEIGH STUD

Cranleigh Stud, Heiffers Farm, Rackenford, Tiverton, **Devon**, EX16 8EW, **ENGLAND**.
(T) 01884 881258 **(F)** 01884 881258
(E) marlyn@cranleighstud.freeserve.co.uk
(W) www.cranleighstud.cjb.net.
Profile Breeder. **Ref: YH03566**

CRANMORE VETNRY CTRE

Cranmore Veterinary Centre, 140 Chester Rd, Childer Thornton, **Cheshire**, CH66 1QN, **ENGLAND**.
(T) 0151 3399141.
Profile Medical Support. **Ref: YH03567**

CRANN, P F

Mrs P F Crann, Stone Haven, Halfway Hse Lane, Eardington, Bridgnorth, **Shropshire**, WV16 5JP, **ENGLAND**.
(T) 01746 768116 **(F)** 01746 768116
(M) 07836 533593.
Profile Breeder, Stable/Livery. **Ref: YH03568**

CRANNA, P

P Cranna, Knockandhu Riding School, Craigellachie, Aberlour, **Moray**, AB38 9RP, **SCOTLAND**.
(T) 01542 860302.
Contact/s
Owner: Mrs P Cranna
Profile Riding School, Stable/Livery. **Ref: YH03569**

CRANSWICK

Cranswick Warm Blood Stud, Shoby Priory, Main St, Shoby, Melton Mowbray, **Leicestershire**, LE14 3PJ, **ENGLAND**.
(T) 01664 813541 **(F)** 01664 813497
(E) info@cranswick-stud.com
(W) www.cranswick-stud.com.
Contact/s
Partner: Mr P Justason
Profile Blood Stock Agency, Breeder.
Frozen sperm importers. No.Staff: 1
Yr. Est: 1988 C.Size: 14 Acres
Opening Times
Visits by appointment only. **Ref: YH03570**

CRAVEN BRANCH

Craven Branch of the Pony Club, Lower Farm, Hayward Bottom, Hungerford, **Berkshire**, RG17 0PX, **ENGLAND**.
(T) 01488 682214.
Contact/s
Branch Secretary: Mrs M Chandler
Profile Club/Association. **Ref: YH03571**

CRAVEN CLGE

Craven College, High St, Skipton, **Yorkshire (North)**, BD23 1JY, **ENGLAND**.
(T) 01756 791411 **(F)** 01756 794872
(E) enquiries@craven-college.ac.uk
(W) www.craven-college.ac.uk.
Contact/s
Admin: Christine Bailey
Profile Equestrian Centre. College.
Craven College offers BHS Stages, First Aid at Work, Riding and Road Safety and Horse Owners Certificates. Courses have large emphasis on practical work
Ref: YH03572

CRAWFORD MESSENGER PUBLICITY

Crawford Messenger Publicity, Hop Garland Cottage, 3 Rock Farm Oast, Off Gibbs Hill, Nettlestead, **Kent**, ME18 5HT, **ENGLAND**.
(T) 01622 817319 **(F)** 01622 817319.
Profile Club/Association.
The Society of Master Saddlers have published a small booklet providing advice for horse owners considering purchasing a saddle. Copies of this booklet are available at £1. 50 each (inc. p and p) from Crawford Messenger Publicity. **Ref: YH03573**

CRAWFORD, DOUGLAS A

Douglas A Crawford DWCF, Heatherinch, Kettle

Rd, Ladybank, **Fife**, KY7 7PA, **SCOTLAND**.
(T) 01337 831042.
Profile Farrier. **Ref: YH03574**

CRAWFORD, MARTIN P

Martin P Crawford RSS, 2 Bailiffs Cottages, Sharsted Pk, Newnham, Sittingbourne, **Kent**, ME9 0JU, **ENGLAND**.
(T) 01795 890453.
Profile Farrier. **Ref: YH03575**

CRAWFORD, PAT

Pat Crawford, Hop Garland Cottage, 3 Rock Farm Oast, Off Gibbs Hill, Nettlestead, **Kent**, ME18 5HT, **ENGLAND**.
(T) 01622 817319 **(F)** 01622 817319.
Profile Supplies. **Ref: YH03576**

CRAWFORD-BROWN, FIONA

Fiona Crawford-Brown, Oak Lodge, Chilling Pl Farm, Ludgershall, **Buckinghamshire**, HP18 9UH, **ENGLAND**.
(T) 01844 238046
(M) 07711 640786
(E) crawfords.creations@virgin.net.
Profile Trainer. **Ref: YH03577**

CRAWLEY DOWN SADDLERY

Crawley Down Saddlery & Tack Exchange, The Corner Shop, 1 Bowers Pl, Crawley Down, Crawley, **Sussex (West)**, RH10 4HY, **ENGLAND**.
(T) 01342 716796.
Contact/s
Owner: Ms J Newton
Profile Supplies. No.Staff: 1
Opening Times
Sp: Open Tues - Sat 10:00. Closed Tues, Wed, Fri, Sat 17:30, Thurs 20:00.
Su: Open Tues - Sat 10:00. Closed Tues, Wed, Fri, Sat 17:30, Thurs 20:00.
Au: Open Tues - Sat 10:00. Closed Tues, Wed, Fri, Sat 17:30, Thurs 20:00.
Wn: Open Tues - Sat 10:00. Closed Tues, Wed, Fri, Sat 17:30, Thurs 20:00.
Closed Sunday, Monday and 11:45 - 12:15
Ref: YH03578

CRAWLEY, E & R

E & R Crawley, Holland Hse, The Rows, Newmarket, **Suffolk**, CB8 0NJ, **ENGLAND**.
(T) 01638 663332.
Contact/s
Partner: Mrs E Crawley
Profile Trainer. **Ref: YH03579**

CRAWSHAW, ALWYN

Alwyn Crawshaw, The Crawshaw Gallery, Priory Rd, Dawlish, **Devon**, EX7 9JF, **ENGLAND**.
(T) 01626 888027
Affiliated Bodies SEA.
Contact/s
Artist: Mr A Crawshaw
Profile Artist.
Alwyn works in watercolour, oils and acrylics. He has won the prize for the best watercolour at the society of Equestrian Artists Annual Exhibition on five occasions.
Ref: YH03580

CRAYSTON, R

Ms R Crayston, Weddingshaw Farm, Wilton, Egremont, **Cumbria**, CA22 2PJ, **ENGLAND**.
(T) 01946 823259.
Profile Breeder. **Ref: YH03581**

CRAZY HORSE SADDLERY

Crazy Horse Saddlery, 7 Lingen Rd, Ludlow Business Pk, Ludlow, **Shropshire**, SY8 1DX, **ENGLAND**.
(T) 01584 877366 **(F)** 01584 877366
(W) www.crazyhorsesaddlery.co.uk.
Profile Saddlery Retailer. **Ref: YH03582**

CREATON, N A

N A Creaton BHSI, 97 Ibstock Rd, Ellistown, Coalville, **Leicestershire**, LE67 1EE, **ENGLAND**.
(T) 01530 260272 **(F)** 01530 260272.
Profile Trainer. **Ref: YH03583**

CRECORA EQUESTRIAN CTRE

Crecora Equestrian Centre, Bettyville, Crecora, **County Limerick**, **IRELAND**.
(T) 061 355721. **Ref: YH03584**

CREDIT & FINANCIAL SVS

Credit & Financial Protection Services, 24/25 Bloomsbury Sq, London, **London (Greater)**, WC1A 2PL, **ENGLAND**.
(T) 020 76370661 **(F)** 020 74364663
(E) basma@basma.com.
Profile Club/Association. **Ref: YH03585**

CREDITON MILLING

Crediton Milling Co, Fordton Mills, Crediton, **Devon**, EX17 3DH, **ENGLAND**.
(T) 01363 772212.
Profile Supplies. **Ref: YH03586**

CREE LODGE

Cree Lodge, 47 Craigie Rd, Ayr, **Ayrshire (South)**, KA8 0HD, **SCOTLAND**.
(T) 01292 286958 **(F)** 01292 266232.
Contact/s
Owner: Mrs L Perritt
Profile Blood Stock Agency, Breeder, Trainer.
Ref: YH03587

CREE LODGE RACING STABLES

Nanostar Ltd, 47 Craigie Rd, Ayr, **Ayrshire (South)**, KA8 0HD, **SCOTLAND**.
(T) 01292 286958/266232 **(F)** 01292 286232
Affiliated Bodies NTF.
Contact/s
Owner: Miss L Perrat
Profile Trainer. Race Horse Trainer, Dealer.
Buys yearlings, trains and breaks them and then sells them on. Also able to train clients' horses, telephone for further information. Yr. Est: 1900
Opening Times
Sp: Open 09:00. Closed 19:00.
Su: Open 09:00. Closed 19:00.
Au: Open 09:00. Closed 19:00.
Wn: Open 09:00. Closed 19:00.
Office opening times **Ref: YH03588**

CREEDY, ROBERT RAYMOND

Robert Raymond Creedy DWCF, 15 Taunton Rd, Bishops Lydeard, Taunton, **Somerset**, TA4 3LW, **ENGLAND**.
(T) 01823 433972.
Profile Farrier. **Ref: YH03589**

CRENDON MANOR STABLES

Crendon Manor Stables, Long Crendon Manor, Frogmore Lane, Long Crendon, Aylesbury, **Buckinghamshire**, HP18 9DZ, **ENGLAND**.
(T) 01844 201526.
Contact/s
Owner: Mr D Myers **Ref: YH03590**

CRENDON SADDLERY

Crendon Saddlery, The Square, Long Crendon, Aylesbury, **Buckinghamshire**, HP18 9AA, **ENGLAND**.
(T) 01844 208572.
Contact/s
Saddler: Mr M Searle
Profile Saddlery Retailer. **Ref: YH03591**

CRESSWELL, J K S

Mr J K S Cresswell, Stoneydale Farm, Oakamoor, Stoke-on-Trent, **Staffordshire**, ST10 3AH, **ENGLAND**.
(T) 01538 702362 **(F)** 01782 324410.
Profile Supplies. **Ref: YH03592**

CREST-A-BED

Crest-A-Bed Ltd, Shemerra, Exchange St, Attleborough, **Norfolk**, NR17 2AB, **ENGLAND**.
(T) 01953 455339.
Contact/s
Owner: Mr J Crotty
Profile Supplies. **Ref: YH03593**

CREWE GARDENS

Crewe Gardens Animal Feeds, Crewe Gardens Farm, Crewe Lane, Kenilworth, **Warwickshire**, CV8 2LA, **ENGLAND**.
(T) 01926 852939.
Profile Feed Merchant.
Riding Clubs affiliated to the BHS receive a 5% discount at Crewe Gardens Animal Feeds. **Ref: YH03594**

CREWE SADDLERY

Crewe Saddlery Ltd, 97 Broughton Rd, Crewe, **Cheshire**, CW1 4NW, **ENGLAND**.
(T) 01270 584551 **(F)** 01270 256345
(E) sales@crewesaddlery.co.uk
(W) www.crewesaddlery.co.uk.
Contact/s
Owner: M. B Blakeman
Profile Riding Wear Retailer, Saddlery Retailer, Supplies. No.Staff: 12 Yr. Est: 1970
Opening Times
Sp: Open Mon - Sat 09:00. Closed Mon - Sat 19:00.
Su: Open Mon - Sat 09:00. Closed Mon - Sat 19:00.
Au: Open Mon - Sat 09:00. Closed Mon - Sat 19:00.
Wn: Open Mon - Sat 09:00. Closed Mon - Sat 19:00.
Closed Sundays & Bank Holidays **Ref: YH03595**

CRICKET HILL FEEDS

Cricket Hill Feeds, Cricket Hill Brow, Gildersome, Leeds, **Yorkshire (West)**, LS27 7LS, **ENGLAND**.
(T) 0113 2521552.
Profile Feed Merchant, Supplies. **Ref: YH03596**

CRIEFF HYDRO HOTEL STABLES

Crieff Hydro Hotel Stables, Stathearn Stables, Crieff Hydro Hotel, Crieff, **Perth and Kinross**, PH7 3LQ, **SCOTLAND**.
(T) 01764 651616.
Profile Riding School, Stable/Livery. **Ref: YH03597**

CRIGHTON, GJS & OLIVER, GA

George J S Crighton DWCF & Gary A Oliver DWCF, 12 Newtown Rd, Marlow, **Buckinghamshire**, SL7 1JU, **ENGLAND**.
(T) 01628 481255.
Contact/s
Partner: Gary A Oliver **(Q)** DWCF
Profile Farrier. **Ref: YH03598**

CRIMBOURNE STUD

Crimbourne Stud, Crimbourne Lane, Wisborough Green, Billingshurst, **Sussex (West)**, RH14 0HR, **ENGLAND**.
(T) 01403 700557 **(F)** 01403 700776.
Contact/s
Owner: Mr E Parker
Profile Breeder. **Ref: YH03599**

CRIMDON PARK EQUESTRIAN CTRE

Crimdon Park Equestrian Centre, Crimdon Pk, Blackhall Colliery, Hartlepool, **Cleveland**, TS27 4BQ, **ENGLAND**.
(T) 01429 267635.
Contact/s
Owner: Mrs C Ayre
Profile Equestrian Centre. **Ref: YH03600**

CRIMP, B A

B A Crimp, Alderford Farm, Halwill, Beaworthy, **Devon**, EX21 5TR, **ENGLAND**.
(T) 01409 221412.
Contact/s
Owner: Mr B Crimp
Profile Farrier. **Ref: YH03601**

CRIPPENDEN STUD

Crippenden Stud, 2 Crippenden Manor Cottages, Spode Lane, Cowden, Edenbridge, **Kent**, TN8 7HJ, **ENGLAND**.
(T) 01342 850638.
Profile Riding School. **Ref: YH03602**

CRIPPIN, I C

I C Crippin, Ashotts, Asheridge, Chesham, **Buckinghamshire**, HP5 2UU, **ENGLAND**.
(T) 01494 758609 **(F)** 01494 758609.
Contact/s
Partner: Mrs C Crippin
Profile Trainer. **Ref: YH03603**

CRISP, C (MISS)

Miss C Crisp, Oaklands Farm, Northwood Green, Westbury-on-Severn, **Gloucestershire**, GL14 1NA, **ENGLAND**.
(T) 01452 760963.
Contact/s
Partner: Mrs P Mason
Profile Equestrian Centre, Stable/Livery.
Full, part and DIY livery available, prices on request.
Ref: YH03604

CRIST, DAVID

David Crist DWCF, 11 The Glynde, Stevenage, **Hertfordshire**, SG2 8SY, **ENGLAND**.
(T) 01438 215219.
Profile Farrier. **Ref: YH03605**

CROCKET EQUESTRIAN

Crocket Equestrian & Outdoor, 3 Old Bridge Rd, Ayr, **Ayrshire (South)**, KA8 9SU, **SCOTLAND**.
(T) 01292 286377 **(F)** 01292 610444.
Contact/s
Owner: Mrs M Crocket
Profile Riding Wear Retailer, Saddlery Retailer.
Opening Times
Sp: Open Mon - Sat 09:00, Sun 11:00. Closed Mon - Sat 17:00, Sun 16:30.
Su: Open Mon - Sat 09:00, Sun 11:00. Closed Mon - Sat 17:00, Sun 16:30.
Au: Open Mon - Sat 09:00, Sun 11:00. Closed Mon - Sat 17:00, Sun 16:30.
Wn: Open Mon - Sat 09:00, Sun 11:00. Closed Mon - Sat 17:00, Sun 16:30. **Ref: YH03606**

A-Z of COMPANIES

A-Z of COMPANIES

CROCKFORDS STUD

Crockfords Stud, Crockfords Stud, Wooditton Rd, Newmarket, **Suffolk**, CB8 9BH, **ENGLAND**.
(T) 01638 561771 **(F)** 01638 666336
(E) crockfordstud@aol.com.
Contact/s
Owner: Mr J Crowhurst
Profile Stud Farm. Yr. Est: 1950 C.Size: 56 Acres
Opening Times
Sp: Open Mon - Fri 09:00. Closed Mon - Fri 17:00.
Su: Open Mon - Fri 09:00. Closed Mon - Fri 17:00.
Au: Open Mon - Fri 09:00. Closed Mon - Fri 17:00.
Wn: Open Mon - Fri 09:00. Closed Mon - Fri 17:00.
Ref: YH03607

CROCKSTEAD PK

Crockstead Park Equestrian Centre, Eastbourne Rd, Halland, Lewes, **Sussex (East)**, BN8 6PT, **ENGLAND**.
(T) 01825 840889 **(F)** 01227 830245
(E) crockstead@btconnect.com
(W) www.crocksteadpark.com
Affiliated Bodies BD, BSJA, BSPS, NPS, Ponies Ass UK.
Contact/s
Manager: Mr P Kemp
Profile Equestrian Centre.
Crockstead Park is a hotel, equestian & lesiure complex, with an on-site resturant. There is also an all weather surface track and two indoor schools. The centre sells European and Irish horses. No.Staff: 3 Yr. Est: 1998 C.Size: 300 Acres
Opening Times
Sp: Open 09:00. Closed 17:30.
Su: Open 09:00. Closed 17:30.
Au: Open 09:00. Closed 17:30.
Wn: Open 09:00. Closed 17:30.
Telephone for an appointment Ref: YH03608

CROFORD COACH BUILDERS

Croford Coach Builders Ltd, Dover Pl, Ashford, **Kent**, TN23 1HU, **ENGLAND**.
(T) 01233 623451.
Profile Horse Drawn Carriage Repair.
Repair horse drawn carriages and manufacturer of wooden carriage wheels. Ref: YH03609

CROFT & CO

Croft & Co (Brackley), High Point, Riding Rd, Buckingham Rd Ind Est, Brackley, **Northamptonshire**, NN13 7BH, **ENGLAND**.
(T) 01280 705457.
Profile Supplies. Ref: YH03610

CROFT & CO

Croft & Co (Banbury), Broad St, Banbury, **Oxfordshire**, OX16 8BT, **ENGLAND**.
(T) 01295 250131.
Profile Supplies. Ref: YH03611

CROFT BRIDLES

Croft Bridles, 12 Vicarage Pl, Walsall, **Midlands (West)**, WS1 3NA, **ENGLAND**.
(T) 01922 622549 **(F)** 01922 631603.
Contact/s
Owner: Mr R Beasley
Profile Supplies. Bridle Manufacturer.
Only sell to wholesalers. Yr. Est: 1979
Opening Times
Sp: Open 07:00. Closed 16:00.
Su: Open 07:00. Closed 16:00.
Au: Open 07:00. Closed 16:00.
Wn: Open 07:00. Closed 16:00. Ref: YH03612

CROFT END EQUESTRIAN CTRE

Croft End Equestrian Centre, Croft End Farm, Knott Lanes, Oldham, **Manchester (Greater)**, OL8 3JD, **ENGLAND**.
(T) 0161 6242849
Affiliated Bodies ABRS, BHS.
Contact/s
Key Contact: Mr S Kenworthy
Profile Equestrian Centre, Riding School, Stable/Livery.
More than 20 horses on-site. Full, part and DIY livery, prices on request. Specialities include: adult beginners, show-jumping, schooling, stable management, cross-country, hacking and dressage.
Opening Times
The horses have a day off on Mondays. Ref: YH03613

CROFT EQUESTRIAN CTRE

Croft Equestrian Centre, The Croft, Padworth Common, Reading, **Berkshire**, RG7 4QX, **ENGLAND**.
(T) 0118 9700261.
Profile Riding School, Saddlery Retailer, Stable/Livery. Ref: YH03614

CROFT FARM RIDING CTRE

Croft Farm Riding Centre, Croft Farm, Thrigby Rd, Filby, Great Yarmouth, **Norfolk**, NR29 3DP, **ENGLAND**.
(T) 01493 368275
Alt Contact Address
7 Pound Lane, Filby, Great Yarmouth, Norfolk, NR29 3HP, England. **(T)** 01493 369383
Contact/s
Owner: Ms H Cook **(Q)** BHSAI, NVQ 3, NVQ Ass
Profile Arena, Equestrian Centre, Riding Club, Riding School, Stable/Livery, Trainer. No.Staff: 6 Yr. Est: 1989 C.Size: 14 Acres Ref: YH03615

CROFT HSE VETNRY CLINIC

Croft House Veterinary Clinic, 378 Soothill Lane, Batley, **Yorkshire (West)**, WF17 6EU, **ENGLAND**.
(T) 01924 474300.
Profile Medical Support. Ref: YH03616

CROFT RIDING CTRE

Croft Riding Centre, Spring Lane, Croft, Warrington, **Cheshire**, WA3 7AS, **ENGLAND**.
(T) 01925 763715 **(F)** 01925 767847
(E) croftriding@go.to
Affiliated Bodies BHS.
Contact/s
Owner: Mrs J Daniels
Profile Equestrian Centre, Riding School, Stable/Livery.
Offers DIY livery only. Takes adult beginners (maximum weight 16 stone). Teaches children from 3 years of age and offers fun days and pony days. Exam training and centre. Stable management. No.Staff: 5
Ref: YH03617

CROFT STUD

Croft Stud (The), Severalls Lane, Colchester, **Essex**, CO4 5JB, **ENGLAND**.
(T) 01206 272736.
Profile Breeder. Ref: YH03618

CROFT VETNRY CTRE

Croft Veterinary Centre, 36 Market Pl, Bolsover, **Derbyshire**, S44 6PN, **ENGLAND**.
(T) 01246 823353 **(F)** 01246 241248.
Profile Medical Support. Ref: YH03619

CROFT VETNRY GRP

Croft Veterinary Group, West Croft, Brigham, Cockermouth, **Cumbria**, CA13 0TH, **ENGLAND**.
(T) 01900 825255.
Profile Medical Support. Ref: YH03620

CROFT VETNRY GRP

Croft Veterinary Group, 187 Harrington Rd, Workington, **Cumbria**, CA14 3XD, **ENGLAND**.
(T) 01900 602401.
Profile Medical Support. Ref: YH03621

CROFT WP & DESIGN

Croft WP & Design, The Paddocks, Croft Lane, Chipperfield, **Hertfordshire**, WD4 9DX, **ENGLAND**.
(T) 01923 266449.
Profile Club/Association. Ref: YH03622

CROFTON MANOR EQUESTRIAN CTRE

Crofton Manor Equestrian Centre, 213 Titchfield Rd, Stubbington, Fareham, **Hampshire**, PO14 3EW, **ENGLAND**.
(T) 01329 668855.
Profile Equestrian Centre, Trainer. Ref: YH03623

CROFTON RIDING STABLES

Crofton Riding & Livery Stables, 54 Pontefract Rd, Crofton, Wakefield, **Yorkshire (West)**, WF4 1LW, **ENGLAND**.
(T) 01924 863957.
Contact/s
Owner: Mrs J Dews
Profile Riding School, Stable/Livery.
Full livery available, prices on request No.Staff: 3 Yr. Est: 1976 C.Size: 5 Acres
Opening Times
Sp: Open Mon - Sat 09:30. Closed Mon - Sat 19:00.
Su: Open Mon - Sat 09:30. Closed Mon - Sat 19:00.
Au: Open Mon - Sat 09:30. Closed Mon - Sat 19:00.
Wn: Open Mon - Sat 09:30. Closed Mon - Sat 19:00.
Ref: YH03624

CROFTS, ANDY

Andy Crofts, Keepers Cottage, Winterfield Common, Albury, **Surrey**, GU5 9EN, **ENGLAND**.
(T) 01483 273656 **(F)** 01483 273656
(M) 07907 178998
(E) andycrofts@equestria.net
(W) www.andycrofts.co.uk.
Contact/s
Trainer: Mr A Crofts
Profile Trainer.
Offers introduction to riders & owners wishing to buy their own horses.
Opening Times
Telephone for further information Ref: YH03625

CROFTS, JOHN D

John D Crofts DWCF, 76 Washford Ave, Llanrumney, Cardiff, Cardiff, **Glamorgan (Vale of)**, CF3 5QB, **WALES**.
(T) 029 20799578.
Profile Farrier. Ref: YH03626

CROILA STABLES

Croila Stables, Golf Course Rd, Newtonmore, **Highlands**, PH20 1AT, **SCOTLAND**.
(T) 01540 673742.
Profile Breeder. Ref: YH03627

CROKE, MICHAEL

Croke Michael, Barrettsgrange, Fethard, **County Tipperary**, **IRELAND**.
(T) 052 31441.
Profile Supplies. Ref: YH03628

CROMER STUD

Cromer Stud, Cromer, Stevenage, **Hertfordshire**, SG2 7QA, **ENGLAND**.
(T) 01438 861276.
Profile Breeder. Ref: YH03629

CROMLECH MANOR FARM

Cromlech Manor Farm, Cromlech Manor, Tyn-Y-Gongl, **Isle of Anglesey**, LL74 8SB, **WALES**.
(T) 01248 853489.
Contact/s
Owner: Ms C Lomas
Profile Horse/Rider Accom. Ref: YH03630

CROMPTON, JOHN

John Crompton, Tile Farm, Asheridge, Chesham, **Buckinghamshire**, HP5 2XB, **ENGLAND**.
(T) 01494 758637.
Contact/s
Owner: Mr J Crompton **(Q)** DWCF
Profile Farrier. Ref: YH03631

CROMPTON, S W

S W Crompton, The Smithy, Neston Rd, Thornton Hough, Wirral, **Merseyside**, CH63 1JF, **ENGLAND**.
(T) 0151 3364833
Affiliated Bodies WCF.
Contact/s
Owner: Mr S Crompton **(Q)** DWCF
Profile Farrier. No.Staff: 2 Yr. Est: 1989
Ref: YH03632

CROMWELLS OF OLVESTON

Cromwells of Olveston, New Mills, Olveston, **Gloucestershire (South)**, BS35 4DT, **ENGLAND**.
(T) 01454 612540 **(F)** 01454 614308.
Profile Supplies. Ref: YH03633

CROOK BARN STABLES

Crook Barn Stables, Torver, Coniston, **Cumbria**, LA21 8BP, **ENGLAND**.
(T) 01539 441088
(E) carolebarr2@aol.com
Affiliated Bodies RDA.
Contact/s
Owner: Mrs C Barr
Profile Riding School. Trekking Centre.
All levels of riders welcome. Ref: YH03634

CROOK COTTAGE STABLES

Crook Cottage Stables, Bodens Lane, Walsall, **Midlands (West)**, WS9 0QZ, **ENGLAND**.
(T) 0121 3572349.
Contact/s
Partner: Mrs J Housley
Profile Stable/Livery. Ref: YH03635

CROOK, TRACY

Tracy Crook, 20 Clementi Ave, Holmer Green, High Wycombe, **Buckinghamshire**, HP15 6TN, **ENGLAND**.
(T) 01494 715114
(E) tccphysio@aol.com.
Profile Medical Support. Ref: YH03636

CROOKBANK STUD

Crookbank Stud, Lane Head, Tideswell, Buxton, **Derbyshire**, SK17 8RB, **ENGLAND**.
(T) 01298 872000.
Profile Breeder. Ref: YH03637

CROOKS TRAILERS

Crooks Trailers, 27 Hanover Sq, Coagh, Cookstown,

County Tyrone, BT80 0EF, **NORTHERN IRELAND**.
(T) 028 86737654.
Contact/s
Owner: Mr A Crooks
Profile Transport/Horse Boxes. **Ref: YH03638**

CROOKS TRAILERS

Crooks Trailers, Urbal Rd, Coagh, Cookstown, **County Tyrone**, BT80 0DP, **NORTHERN IRELAND**.
(T) 028 86737492.
Contact/s
Owner: Mr A Crooks
Profile Transport/Horse Boxes. **Ref: YH03639**

CROPTHORNE & EVESHAM VALE

Cropthorne & Evesham Vale Riding Club, Mill View Hse, Mill Lane, Drakes Broughton, Pershore, **Worcestershire**, WR10 2AF, **ENGLAND**.
(T) 01905 840286 **(F)** 01386 556652
(E) anne.martin@talk21.com.
Contact/s
Chairman: Mr P Worrall
Profile Riding Club. **Ref: YH03640**

CROSBY, HILARY & CAROLINE

Hilary & Caroline Crosby, Millbrook, Ballinasloe, **County Galway**, **IRELAND**.
(T) 0905 43683. **Ref: YH03641**

CROSBY, NICHOLAS

Nicholas Crosby DWCF, Eastfield Farm, Ulceby Rd, Wootton, **Lincolnshire (North)**, DN39 6SE, **ENGLAND**.
(T) 01469 588155.
Profile Farrier. **Ref: YH03642**

CROSS COUNTRY HORSE TRANSPORT

Cross Country Horse Transport, Brimlands Farm, Holcot Lane, Scaldwell, Northampton, **Northamptonshire**, NN6 9JR, **ENGLAND**.
(T) 01604 882883.
Contact/s
Owner: Antony Beck
Profile Trainer. **Ref: YH03643**

CROSS COUNTRY VEHICLES

Cross Country Vehicles Ltd, Hailey, Witney, **Oxfordshire**, OX8 5UF, **ENGLAND**.
(T) 01993 776622 **(F)** 01993 773218.
Profile Transport/Horse Boxes. **Ref: YH03644**

CROSS FOXES STUD

Cross Foxes Stud, Flutters Field Downside, Cobham, **Surrey**, KT11 3NY, **ENGLAND**.
(T) 01932 866840.
Profile Breeder. **Ref: YH03645**

CROSS GREEN VETNRY CTRE

Cross Green Veterinary Centre, 71 Cross Green, Otley, **Yorkshire (West)**, LS21 1HE, **ENGLAND**.
(T) 01943 462546.
Profile Medical Support. **Ref: YH03646**

CROSS HANDS TRAILER CTRE

Cross Hands Trailer Centre, 3 Llandeilo Rd, Cross Hands, Llanelli, **Carmarthenshire**, SA14 6NA, **WALES**.
(T) 01269 845165.
Contact/s
Owner: Mr T Vaughan
Profile Transport/Horse Boxes. **Ref: YH03647**

CROSS HSE STABLES

Cross House Stables, Cross Hse, Strathblane Rd, Campsie Glen, Glasgow, **Glasgow (City of)**, G66 7AR, **SCOTLAND**.
(T) 01360 311332. **Ref: YH03648**

CROSS KEYS FARM

Cross Keys Farm, Shire Lane, Chalfont St. Peter, Gerrards Cross, **Buckinghamshire**, SL9 0QY, **ENGLAND**.
(T) 01494 873218.
Contact/s
Owner: Mrs T Matthews
Profile Riding School, Stable/Livery. **Ref: YH03649**

CROSS LEYS FARM

Cross Leys Farm St John's Wood Livery Yard, Leicester Rd, Thornhaugh, Peterborough, **Cambridgeshire**, PE8 6NS, **ENGLAND**.
(T) 01780 782609.
Profile Riding School, Stable/Livery. **Ref: YH03650**

CROSS OAKS

Cross Oaks, Cross Oak Farmhouse Livery Stables, East Wellow, Romsey, **Hampshire**, SO51 6DR, **ENGLAND**.
(T) 01794 323499.
Profile Stable/Livery. **Ref: YH03651**

CROSS PK STUD

Cross Park Stud, Woodland, Newton Abbott, **Devon**, TQ13 7JU, **ENGLAND**.
(T) 01364 653453 **(F)** 01364 653593.
Profile Breeder. **Ref: YH03652**

CROSS STORES

Cross Stores, 1 Sterry Rd, Gowerton, Swansea, **Swansea**, SA4 3BS, **WALES**.
(T) 01792 874209.
Profile Saddlery Retailer. **Ref: YH03653**

CROSS, MICHAEL J

Michael J Cross DWCF, Primrose Cottage, 28 Main St, Lowick, Berwick-upon-Tweed, **Northumberland**, TD15 2UA, **ENGLAND**.
(T) 01289 388403.
Profile Farrier. **Ref: YH03654**

CROSSBANK RIDING SCHOOL

Crossbank Riding School, Cross Banks Cottage, Whorlton, Swainby, Northallerton, **Yorkshire (North)**, DL6 3HT, **ENGLAND**.
(T) 01642 701034.
Profile Riding School. **Ref: YH03655**

CROSSCOUNTRY EQUINE CLINIC

Crosscountry Equine Clinic, Devauden, Chepstow, **Monmouthshire**, NP16 5DB, **WALES**.
(T) 01291 625205 **(F)** 01291 626116
(E) johnmcewen1@compuserve.com.
Contact/s
Owner: David Thompson
Profile Medical Support. **Ref: YH03656**

CROSSCOUNTRY SCHOOLING GROUND

Crosscountry Schooling Ground, Danesbury Manor Farm, Flixton, Scarborough, **Yorkshire (North)**, YO11 3UL, **ENGLAND**.
(T) 01723 890242.
Contact/s
Owner: Mr R Mason
Profile Equestrian Centre. **Ref: YH03657**

CROSSLEY & GACHE

Crossley & Gache, 127A Marlpit Lane, Coulsdon, **Surrey**, CR5 2HH, **ENGLAND**.
(T) 01737 556446.
Profile Farrier. **Ref: YH03658**

CROSSLEY, IAN L

Ian L Crossley DWCF, 18 Woodfield Hill, Coulsdon, **Surrey**, CR5 3EN, **ENGLAND**.
(T) 01737 550228.
Profile Farrier. **Ref: YH03659**

CROSSLEY, NICHOLAS J

Nicholas J Crossley DWCF, Park Farm, High Rd, Chipstead, **Surrey**, CR3 3SH, **ENGLAND**.
(T) 01737 552933.
Profile Farrier. **Ref: YH03660**

CROSSLEY, RICHARD L

Richard L Crossley DWCF, Helena Church Rd, Ramsden Bellhouse, Billericay, **Essex**, CM11 1RR, **ENGLAND**.
(T) 01268 710304.
Profile Farrier. **Ref: YH03661**

CROSSOAKS FARM

Crossoaks Farm, Crossoaks Lane, Borehamwood, **Hertfordshire**, WD6 5PH, **ENGLAND**.
(T) 01707 651828.
Contact/s
Owner: Mrs W Aldred **Ref: YH03662**

CROSSRIGGS VETNRY CLINIC

Crossriggs Veterinary Clinic, 52 Townhead St, Cumnock, **Ayrshire (East)**, KA18 1LG, **SCOTLAND**.
(T) 01290 420255 **(F)** 01290 421086.
Profile Medical Support. **Ref: YH03663**

CROSSROADS RIDING CLUB

Crossroads Riding Club, 13 Crossway, Harpenden, **Hertfordshire**, AL5 4RA, **ENGLAND**.
(T) 01582 460654.
Contact/s
Chairman: Mrs A Piers
Profile Riding Club. **Ref: YH03664**

CROSSWAYS LIVERY YARD

Crossways Livery Yard, Axtown Lane, Yelverton, **Devon**, PL20 6BU, **ENGLAND**.
(T) 01822 853025.
Contact/s
Owner: Ms S Trafford
Profile Stable/Livery. **Ref: YH03665**

CROSSWAYS LIVERY YARD

Crossways Livery Yard, Lound Rd, Browston, Great Yarmouth, **Norfolk**, NR31 9DS, **ENGLAND**.
(T) 01493 781531.
Profile Stable/Livery. **Ref: YH03666**

CROSSWAYS SV CTRE

Crossways Service Centre, 99 Yarmouth Rd, Ellingham, Bungay, **Suffolk**, NR35 2PH, **ENGLAND**.
(T) 01508 518726 **(F)** 01508 518726.
Contact/s
Owner: Mr A Pickering
Profile Supplies. No.Staff: 2
Opening Times
Sp: Open Mon - Fri 08:30, Sat, Sun 09:00. Closed Mon - Fri 18:00, Sat 17:00, Sun 13:00.
Su: Open Mon - Fri 08:30, Sat, Sun 09:00. Closed Mon - Fri 18:00, Sat 17:00, Sun 13:00.
Au: Open Mon - Fri 08:30, Sat, Sun 09:00. Closed Mon - Fri 18:00, Sat 17:00, Sun 13:00.
Wn: Open Mon - Fri 08:30, Sat, Sun 09:00. Closed Mon - Fri 18:00, Sat 17:00, Sun 13:00. **Ref: YH03667**

CROSSWAYS TRANSPORT

Crossways Transport Ltd, 51 Wiltshire Ave, Crowthorne, **Berkshire**, RG45 6NH, **ENGLAND**.
(T) 01344 778714.
Profile Transport/Horse Boxes. **Ref: YH03668**

CROSSWELL

Crosswell Horse Agency, let Wen, Velindre, Crymych, **Pembrokeshire**, SA41 3XF, **WALES**.
(T) 01239 891262.
Contact/s
Owner: Miss C Morgan **(Q)** BHSAI
(E) crosswell.horse@amserve.net
Profile Riding School. Trekking Centre.
No.Staff: 2 Yr. Est: 1986 C.Size: 32 Acres
Opening Times
Open all year, please telephone for an appointment
Ref: YH03669

CROSSWINDS MORGANS

Crosswinds Morgans, Crosswinds Farm, Higher Bulstone, Branscombe, **Devon**, EX12 3BL, **ENGLAND**.
(T) 01297 680217.
Profile Breeder. **Ref: YH03670**

CROSTON CORN MILLS

Croston Corn Mills Ltd, Grape Lane, Croston, Preston, **Lancashire**, PR5 7HB, **ENGLAND**.
(T) 01772 600202 **(F)** 01772 601111.
Profile Supplies. **Ref: YH03671**

CROSTONS FARM RIDING & LIVERY

Crostons Farm Riding & Livery, Lucas Lane, Whittle-Le-Woods, Chorley, **Lancashire**, PR6 7DA, **ENGLAND**.
(T) 01257 274084.
Profile Riding School, Saddlery Retailer, Stable/Livery. **Ref: YH03672**

CROTHERS, BILLY

Billy Crothers, Woodlands, Crafton, Leighton Buzzard, **Bedfordshire**, LU7 0QJ, **ENGLAND**.
(T) 01296 662473 **(F)** 01296 660779.
Contact/s
Owner: Mr B Crowther
Profile Farrier. **Ref: YH03673**

CROUCHFIELD

Crouchfield Equestrian Club, Crouchfield Farm, Crouchfield, Chapmore End, Ware, **Hertfordshire**, SG12 0EX, **ENGLAND**.
(T) 01920 463057.
Contact/s
Owner: Mrs S Reeves-Smith
Profile Breeder, Riding School, Stable/Livery.
Full, part and DIY livery available, prices on request.
Also hold horse shows. Yr. Est: 1961 C.Size: 33 Acres
Opening Times
Sp: Open Mon - Sun 09:00. Closed Mon - Sun 18:00.
Su: Open Mon - Sun 09:00. Closed Mon - Sun 18:00.
Au: Open Mon - Sun 09:00. Closed Mon - Sun 18:00.
Wn: Open Mon - Sun 09:00. Closed Mon - Sun 18:00. **Ref: YH03674**

CROW, ANDREW M

Andrew M Crow AFCL, Monteviot Gardens, Ancrum, Jedburgh, **Scottish Borders**, TD8 6TU, **SCOTLAND**.
(T) 01835 830239.
Profile Farrier. **Ref: YH03675**

CROWDER, CHARLOTTE

Charlotte Crowder, Charbeck Hse, 34 Homefield Rd, Warlingham, **Surrey**, CR6 9HQ, **ENGLAND**.
(T) 01883 624103.
Profile Trainer. **Ref: YH03676**

CROWE, C D

C D Crowe, The Lodge, Garthmyl, Montgomery, **Powys**, SY15 6RS, **WALES**.
(T) 01686 640385 **(F)** 01686 640385.
Profile Supplies. **Ref: YH03677**

CROWFIELDS EQUESTRIAN SVS

Crowfields Equestrian Services, Fockbury Rd, Dodford, Bromsgrove, **Worcestershire**, B61 9AW, **ENGLAND**.
(T) 01527 833731.
Profile Stable/Livery. **Ref: YH03678**

CROWLEY, JOHN

John Crowley, Scariff Ballinacurra, Midleton, **County Cork**, **IRELAND**.
(T) 021 4631196.
Profile Supplies. **Ref: YH03679**

CROWN AXXESS

Crown Axxess Ltd, Horn Hatch Farm, Shalford, Guildford, **Surrey**, GU4 8HS, **ENGLAND**.
(T) 01483 450011 **(F)** 01483 569567
(E) sales@crownaxxess.co.uk
(W) www.crownaxxess.co.uk.
Contact/s
Manager: Miss S Roshanzamir
Profile Gate and Security Systems.
Design and manufacture automatic gate and barriers security systems. **Ref: YH03680**

CROWN HOTEL

Crown Hotel, Exmoor National Pk, Exford, Minehead, **Somerset**, TA24 7PP, **ENGLAND**.
(T) 01643 831554.
Contact/s
Owner: Michael Bradley
Profile Horse/Rider Accom, Riding School, Stable/Livery. **Ref: YH03681**

CROWN WELDING

Crown Welding & Fabrication, Blairtummock, Campsie Glen, Glasgow, **Glasgow (City of)**, G66 7AR, **SCOTLAND**.
(T) 0141 5501567.
Profile Blacksmith. **Ref: YH03682**

CROWSNEST RIDING CTRE

Crowsnest Riding Centre, Sticklepath, Okehampton, **Devon**, EX20 2PS, **ENGLAND**.
(T) 01837 840701.
Profile Riding School. **Ref: YH03683**

CROWSTONS

Crowstons Tack Shop, The Forge, Thealby, Scunthorpe, **Lincolnshire (North)**, DN15 9AE, **ENGLAND**.
(T) 01724 721808 **(F)** 01724 721808.
Contact/s
Owner: Ms L Crowston
Profile Riding Wear Retailer, Saddlery Retailer, Supplies. **No.Staff:** 2 **Yr. Est:** 1997
Opening Times
Sp: Open Mon, Tues, Thurs, Fri 09:00, Wed 09:30 Sat 10:00. Closed Mon - Fri 17:30, Sat 17:00.
Su: Open Mon, Tues, Thurs, Fri 09:00, Wed 09:30 Sat 10:00. Closed Mon - Fri 17:30, Sat 17:00.
Au: Open Mon, Tues, Thurs, Fri 09:00, Wed 09:30 Sat 10:00. Closed Mon - Fri 17:30, Sat 17:00.
Wn: Open Mon, Tues, Thurs, Fri 09:00, Wed 09:30 Sat 10:00. Closed Mon - Fri 17:30, Sat 17:00.
Closed Sundays **Ref: YH03684**

CROXTETH PK RIDING CTRE

Croxteth Park Riding Centre, Croxteth Hall Lane, West Derby, Liverpool, **Merseyside**, L12 0HA, **ENGLAND**.
(T) 0151 2209177
(E) croxteth@pcuk.org
Affiliated Bodies BHS, Pony Club UK.
Contact/s
Owner: Mrs V Stevens
Profile Riding School.
The centre has BHS qualified Instructors.
Opening Times
Sp: Open 09:00. Closed 17:30.
Su: Open 09:00. Closed 17:30.
Au: Open 09:00. Closed 17:30.
Wn: Open 09:00. Closed 17:30. **Ref: YH03685**

CROYDON HORSE & CATTLE

Croydon Horse & Cattle Transport, 249 Farleigh Rd, Warlingham, **Surrey**, CR6 9EL, **ENGLAND**.
(T) 01883 622584.
Contact/s
Owner: Mr E Yeoell
Profile Transport/Horse Boxes. **Ref: YH03686**

CRUACHAN STUD

Cruachan Stud, Watersmeet Farm, Five Oak Green, Tonbridge, **Kent**, TN12 6SE, **ENGLAND**.
(T) 01892 832654.
Profile Breeder. **Ref: YH03687**

CRUICKSHANK TRAILERS

Cruickshank Trailers, 52A Hermitage St, Crewkerne, **Somerset**, TA18 8ET, **ENGLAND**.
(T) 01460 73469 **(F)** 01460 74469.
Contact/s
Partner: Mrs M Cruickshank
Profile Transport/Horse Boxes. **Ref: YH03688**

CRUICKSHANKS, T & D

T & D Cruickshanks, Canal St, Kirkintilloch, Glasgow, **Glasgow (City of)**, G66 1QY, **SCOTLAND**.
(T) 0141 7762043.
Profile Blacksmith. **Ref: YH03689**

CRUMP, D G

D G Crump, Leaton Lodge, Crab Lane, Bobbington, Stourbridge, **Midlands (West)**, DY7 5DZ, **ENGLAND**.
(T) 01384 221212 **(F)** 01384 221212.
Contact/s
Owner: Mr D Crump
Profile Transport/Horse Boxes. **Ref: YH03690**

CRUMPLER, J G

Mr J G Crumpler, Clandon Farm, Beaminster, **Dorset**, DT8 3PT, **ENGLAND**.
(T) 01308 867578.
Contact/s
Owner: Mr J Crumpler
Profile Breeder. **Ref: YH03691**

CRUTCHER, STEPHEN J

Stephen J Crutcher DWCF, Bude Cottage, Bayford, Wincanton, **Somerset**, BA9 9NL, **ENGLAND**.
(T) 01963 34384.
Profile Farrier. **Ref: YH03692**

CRYER, ANDREW N

Andrew N Cryer DWCF, 47 Chapel St, Marlow, **Buckinghamshire**, SL7 3HN, **ENGLAND**.
(T) 01628 488927.
Profile Farrier. **Ref: YH03693**

CTRE - LINES

Centre - Lines, Potter Hill, Collingham, Newark, **Nottinghamshire**, NG23 7PZ, **ENGLAND**.
(T) 01636 892519
(E) admin@centrelines.co.uk
(W) www.centrelines.co.uk.
Contact/s
Horse Whisperer: Ms D Glennan **(Q)** MRPC
(E) debbie@centrelines.co.uk
Profile Riding School, Stable/Livery, Trainer.
No.Staff: 2 **Yr. Est:** 1986 **C.Size:** 6 Acres
Opening Times
Open all year round, telephone in the evening for appointments **Ref: YH03694**

CTRE RIDING SCHOOL

Centre Riding School (The), 143 Oldmixon Rd, Hutton, Weston-Super-Mare, **Somerset (North)**, BS24 9QA, **ENGLAND**.
(T) 01934 814666.
Profile Breeder, Riding School. **Ref: YH03695**

CTRE RIDING SCHOOL

Centre Riding School, Totterdown Farm, Oldmixon Rd, Hutton, Weston-Super-Mare, **Somerset (North)**, BS24 9QA, **ENGLAND**.
(T) 01934 814666.
Contact/s
Owner: Mrs M Williams **(Q)** BHSAI
Profile Breeder, Riding School. **Yr. Est:** 1967
Opening Times
Sp: Open Mon - Sun 08:00. Closed Mon - Sun 19:00.
Su: Open Mon - Sun 08:00. Closed Mon - Sun 19:00.
Au: Open Mon - Sun 08:00. Closed Mon - Sun 19:00.
Wn: Open Mon - Sun 08:00. Closed Mon - Sun 19:00. **Ref: YH03696**

CUCKMERE

Cuckmere Supplies Manufacturers, PO Box 1173, Station Rd, Polegate, **Sussex (East)**, BN26 6BW, **ENGLAND**.
(T) 01323 484575 **(F)** 01323 484575.
Contact/s
Partner: Ms J Streeter **Ref: YH03697**

CUCKOO HILL LIVERY CTRE

Cuckoo Hill Livery Centre, Melbury Rd, Yetminster, Sherborne, **Dorset**, DT9 6LX, **ENGLAND**.
(T) 01935 873399.
Contact/s
Owner: Miss V Chambers
Profile Stable/Livery. **Ref: YH03698**

CUCKSON CARRIAGE WHEELS

Cuckson Carriage Wheels, 6 Ormskirk Rd, Skelmersdale, **Lancashire**, WN8 8TP, **ENGLAND**.
(T) 01695 726275.
Profile Horse Drawn Vehicle Hire.
Horse drawn vehicle hire & services. **Ref: YH03699**

CUDDEFORD, DEREK (DR)

Dr Derek Cuddeford, Vetnry Field Station, Easter Bush, Roslin, **Lothian (Mid)**, EH25 9RG, **SCOTLAND**.
(T) 0131 6506221 **(F)** 0131 6506588.
Profile Medical Support. **Ref: YH03700**

CULFORD STABLES

Culford Riding & Livery Stable, Hengrave, Culford, Bury St Edmunds, **Suffolk**, IP28 6DX, **ENGLAND**.
(T) 01284 728119.
Contact/s
Owner: Mrs A French
Profile Riding School, Stable/Livery. **No.Staff:** 5
C.Size: 28 Acres **Ref: YH03701**

CULLEN

Cullen, Tuckingmill Farm, Brampton, **Devon**, EX16 9DX, **ENGLAND**.
(T) 01398 31750.
Profile Medical Support. **Ref: YH03702**

CULLEN, GLYN MITCHELL

Glyn Mitchell Cullen, Chase Farm, Little Burstead, Billericay, **Essex**, CM12 9SJ, **ENGLAND**.
(T) 01277 624979.
Profile Farrier. **Ref: YH03703**

CULLINAN, J

Mr J Cullinan, Ladymead Farm, Quainton, Aylesbury, **Buckinghamshire**, HP22 4AN, **ENGLAND**.
(T) 01296 655255 **(F)** 01296 655255
(M) 07768 661720.
Profile Trainer. **Ref: YH03704**

CULLINGHOOD FARM

Cullinghood Farm & Equestrian Centre, Herons Farm, Pangbourne, Reading, **Berkshire**, RG8 8QA, **ENGLAND**.
(T) 0118 9745228 **(F)** 0118 9745229
(E) enquiries@cullinghood.co.uk
(W) www.cullinghood.co.uk.
Contact/s
Owner: Miss M Culling
Profile Horse/Rider Accom, Riding School, Stable/Livery.
Breed own horses, there are between 40 - 50 horses and ponies. Livery is available, details on request. Lesson prices start from £10.00. Access to plenty of hacking with very little roadwork. Offer full, half board and B&B accommodation. **C.Size:** 400 Acres
Opening Times
Sp: Open Mon - Sun 09:00. Closed Mon - Fri 20:00, Sat, Sun 18:00.
Su: Open Mon - Sun 09:00. Closed Mon - Fri 20:00, Sat, Sun 18:00.
Au: Open Mon - Sun 09:00. Closed Mon - Fri 20:00, Sat, Sun 18:00.
Wn: Open Mon - Sun 09:00. Closed Mon - Fri 20:00, Sat, Sun 18:00. **Ref: YH03705**

CULLINGHURST ARABIAN STUD

Cullinghurst Arabian Stud, Heath Farm, Breckles Heath, Stow Bedon, Attleborough, **Norfolk**, NR17 1DR, **ENGLAND**.
(T) 01953 498790 **(F)** 01953 498790.
Contact/s
Owner: Mr H Price
Profile Breeder. **Ref: YH03706**

CULLYBURN EQUESTRIAN CTRE

Cullyburn Equestrian Centre, 18 Cullyburn Rd, Newtownabbey, **County Antrim**, BT36 5BN, **NORTHERN IRELAND**.
(T) 028 90842516.
Contact/s
Owner: Mr W Boyd
Profile Equestrian Centre. Trekking Centre.
Ref: YH03707

CULSHAW, D
Miss D Culshaw BHSI, Pound Farm, Edvin Ralph, Bromyard, **Herefordshire**, HR7 4LU, **ENGLAND**.
(T) 01885 483405.
Profile Trainer. **Ref: YH03708**

CULVERDEN VETNRY GRP
Culverden Veterinary Group, 11 Culverden Park Rd, Tunbridge Wells, **Kent**, TN4 9RD, **ENGLAND**.
(T) 01892 520296 **(F)** 01892 518290.
Contact/s
Owner: Mr J Sutton
Profile Medical Support. **Ref: YH03709**

CUMANI, L
L Cumani, Clare Hse, 3 Stetchworth Rd, Dullingham, Newmarket, **Suffolk**, CB8 9UJ, **ENGLAND**.
(T) 01638 508100.
Profile Trainer. **Ref: YH03710**

CUMANI, L M
L M Cumani, Bedford Hse Stables, 7 Bury Rd, Newmarket, **Suffolk**, CB8 7BX, **ENGLAND**.
(T) 01638 665432 **(F)** 01638 667160
(W) www.newarketracehorsetrainers.co.uk
Affiliated Bodies Newmarket Trainers Fed.
Contact/s
Owner: Mr L Cumani
Profile Trainer. **Ref: YH03711**

CUMBERLAND
Cumberland, Corbett Nook, Oulton, Wigton, **Cumbria**, CA7 0NR, **ENGLAND**.
(T) 01697 344415. **Ref: YH03712**

CUMBERLAND FARMERS
Cumberland Farmers, Round Hill, Welton, Carlisle, **Cumbria**, CA5 7HH, **ENGLAND**.
(T) 01697 476337.
Profile Club/Association. **Ref: YH03713**

CUMBOR, E S
E S Cumbor, School Garden Cottage, 21 Station Rd, Great Ayton, Middlesbrough, **Cleveland**, TS9 6HA, **ENGLAND**.
(T) 01642 722212.
Profile Breeder. **Ref: YH03714**

CUMBRIA SCHOOL OF SADDLERY
Cumbria School of Saddlery, Redhills Business Pk, Penrith, **Cumbria**, CA11 0DL, **ENGLAND**.
(T) 01768 899919 **(F)** 01768 899919
(W) www.saddlerycourses.com.
Contact/s
Owner: Mr D May **(Q)** Master Saddler
(E) davidmay@saddlerycourses.com
Profile Trainer. Education.
Saddlery Training. Five day courses - handstitching, intermediate and repairs. Tools and materials provided by the school. Courses cost £220 including a £50 deposit to be paid when booking. No.Staff: 1
Yr. Est: 1996
Opening Times
Sp: Open Mon - Fri 09:00. Closed Mon - Fri 17:00.
Su: Open Mon - Fri 09:00. Closed Mon - Fri 17:00.
Au: Open Mon - Fri 09:00. Closed Mon - Fri 17:00.
Wn: Open Mon - Fri 09:00. Closed Mon - Fri 17:00.
Ref: YH03715

CUMBRIA TOURIST BOARD
Cumbria Tourist Board, Ashleigh, Holly Rd, Windermere, **Cumbria**, LA23 2AQ, **ENGLAND**.
(T) 01539 444444 **(F)** 01539 444041.
Contact/s
Information Officer: Anita Peat
Profile Club/Association. **Ref: YH03716**

CUMBRIA WELDING & TRAILERS
Cumbria Welding & Trailers, Unit 7, Lake District Business Pk, Mint Bridge, Roa, Kendal, **Cumbria**, LA9 6NH, **ENGLAND**.
(T) 01539 732372 **(F)** 01539 732372.
Contact/s
Owner: Mr M Stonier
Profile Transport/Horse Boxes. **Ref: YH03717**

CUMINE, DENIS HAROLD
Denis Harold Cumine, Glandwr Bridge Cottage, Ambleston, Haverfordwest, **Pembrokeshire**, SA62 5DQ, **WALES**.
(T) 01437 741307.
Profile Farrier. **Ref: YH03718**

CUMMING, J W
J W Cumming, Keltneynurn Smithy, Keltneyburn, Aberfeldy, **Perth and Kinross**, PH15 2LF, **SCOTLAND**.
(T) 01887 830267.
Contact/s
Partner: Mr J Cumming
Profile Blacksmith. **Ref: YH03719**

CUMMINGS, G B & R
G B & R Cummings, Grove Fold Hse, Claughton-on-Brock, Preston, **Lancashire**, PR3 0PU, **ENGLAND**.
(T) 01995 640107.
Contact/s
Partner: Mr G Cummings
Profile Transport/Horse Boxes. **Ref: YH03720**

CUMMINGS, R C
R C Cummings, Southburn Grange, Chester Moor, Chester Le Street, **County Durham**, DH3 4QG, **ENGLAND**.
(T) 0191 3883329.
Contact/s
Owner: Mrs J Cummings
Profile Transport/Horse Boxes. **Ref: YH03721**

CUMMINS, M J
M J Cummins, The Forge, Ballinamullan Farms, Omagh, **County Tyrone**, BT79 0JP, **NORTHERN IRELAND**.
(T) 028 82249992.
Profile Farrier. **Ref: YH03722**

CUNNINGHAM & REED
Cunningham & Reed, 9 Melbourne Court, St Dials, Cwmbran, **Torfaen**, NP44 3AR, **WALES**.
(T) 01633 766796
(M) 07788 140153.
Profile Supplies. **Ref: YH03723**

CUNNINGHAM, M I
M I Cunningham, Gormanstown Stables Kildakey, Navan, **County Meath**, **IRELAND**.
(T) 046 31672.
Profile Supplies. **Ref: YH03724**

CUNNINGHAM, W S
Mr W S Cunningham, Embleton Farm, Garbutts Lane, Hutton Rudby, Yarm, **Tyne and Wear**, TS15 0DN, **ENGLAND**.
(T) 01642 701290
(M) 07885 158703.
Profile Trainer. **Ref: YH03725**

CUNNINGHAM-BROWN, K
Mr K Cunningham-Brown, Danebury Pl, Stockbridge, **Hampshire**, SO20 6JX, **ENGLAND**.
(T) 01264 781061 **(F)** 01264 781709.
Profile Trainer. **Ref: YH03726**

CURBAR RIDING STABLES
Curbar Riding Stables, Emberbrook/Bar Lane, Curbar, Calver, Hope Valley, **Derbyshire**, S32 3YA, **ENGLAND**.
(T) 01433 630584.
Contact/s
Owner: Mrs J Fox
Profile Riding School, Stable/Livery.
1-3 hour hacks across breathtaking moorland countryside. All ages/abilities are catered for. Each party is accompanied by 2 experienced trek leaders. For parties of 7+, hats are provided free of charge. DIY and full livery also offered. **Ref: YH03727**

CURLAND EQUESTRIAN CTRE
Curland Equestrian Centre, Crosses Farm, Curland, Taunton, **Somerset**, TA3 5SD, **ENGLAND**.
(T) 01460 234234.
Contact/s
Partner: Mrs K Gibson
Profile Equestrian Centre, Riding School.
Ref: YH03728

CURLEY, B J
B J Curley, Cleveland Hse Stables, Hamilton Rd, Newmarket, **Suffolk**, CB8 7JQ, **ENGLAND**.
(T) 01638 666546
(W) www.newmarketracehorsetrainers.co.uk
Affiliated Bodies Newmarket Trainers Fed.
Contact/s
Trainer: Mr B Curley
Profile Trainer. **Ref: YH03729**

CURLEY, B J
Mr B J Curley, 104A Ctre Drive, Newmarket, **Suffolk**, CB8 8AP, **ENGLAND**.
(T) 01638 668755.
Profile Trainer. **Ref: YH03730**

CURLEY, ERIC
Eric Curley, Convent View, Tallow, **County Waterford**, **IRELAND**.
(T) 058 56600.
Profile Supplies. **Ref: YH03731**

CURNOW, E M
E M Curnow, Five Acre Farm, West Rudham, King's Lynn, **Norfolk**, PE31 6TA, **ENGLAND**.
(T) 01485 528437.
Profile Medical Support. **Ref: YH03732**

CURRACLOE HOUSE
Curracloe House Equestrian Centre, Curracloe, Enniscorthy, **County Wexford**, **IRELAND**.
(T) 053 37582. **Ref: YH03733**

CURRAGH BLOODSTOCK AGENCY
Curragh Bloodstock Agency Ltd, Crossways, 23 The Avenue, Newmarket, **Suffolk**, CB8 9AA, **ENGLAND**.
(T) 01638 662620 **(F)** 01638 661658
(M) 07850 512035
(E) linda@curraghbloodstock.co.uk.
Profile Blood Stock Agency. **Ref: YH03734**

CURRAGH COTTAGE LEISURE
Curragh Cottage Leisure Riding & Pony Trekking Centre, The Spa, Tralee, **County Kerry**, **IRELAND**.
(T) 066 7136320
(M) 088 2120842
(E) curraghcottage@hotmail.com
Affiliated Bodies AIRE.
Contact/s
Owner: Fran McElligott
Profile Riding School. Trekking Centre.
Twice daily, hour and a half treks along the Kerry coast and over farmland. **Ref: YH03735**

CURRAGH EQUINE
Curragh Equine Ground Care, Ashcalushy Hse, Newtown, Suncroft, **County Kildare**, **IRELAND**.
(F) 045 441442
(M) 087 2041171.
Contact/s
Key Contact: Mr P Keatley
(E) peterkeatley@kildarehorse.ie
Profile Construction & Maintance.
Curragh Equine construct and maintain all weather gallops. **Ref: YH03736**

CURRAGH RACE COURSE OFFICE
Curragh Race Course Office, Curragh, **County Kildare**, **IRELAND**.
(T) 045 441205 **(F)** 045 441442
(E) info@curragh.ie
(W) www.curragh.ie.
Profile Track/Course. **Ref: YH03737**

CURRIDGE GREEN RIDING SCHOOL
Curridge Green Riding School, Curridge Green, Curridge, Thatcham, **Berkshire**, RG18 9EA, **ENGLAND**.
(T) 01635 200694.
Contact/s
Owner: Mr J Mills
Profile Riding School. **Ref: YH03738**

CURRIE, D P & J A
D P & J A Currie, Tilt Hammer Mill, Rathmell, Settle, **Yorkshire (North)**, BD24 0LA, **ENGLAND**.
(T) 01729 840506.
Contact/s
Owner: Mr S Currie
Profile Supplies. **Ref: YH03739**

CURRIE, G H
G H Currie, Vulcan Pl, Sandbank, Dunoon, **Argyll and Bute**, PA23 8PJ, **SCOTLAND**.
(T) 01369 706282.
Profile Blacksmith. **Ref: YH03740**

CURRIE, ROBERT J
Robert J Currie, Burnside Smithy, Beattock, Moffat, **Dumfries and Galloway**, DG10 9QU, **SCOTLAND**.
(T) 01683 300346 **(F)** 01683 300331.
Contact/s
Owner: Mr R Currie
Profile Blacksmith. **Ref: YH03741**

CURRY, COLIN J
Colin J Curry DWCF, 6 Pera Pl, Camden, Bath, **Bath & Somerset (North East)**, BA1 5NX, **ENGLAND**.
(T) 01225 311924.
Profile Farrier. **Ref: YH03742**

CURRY, JOAN
Joan Curry, Bedw Farm, Erwood, Builth Wells, **Powys**, LD2 3LQ, **WALES**.
(T) 01982 560416.
Profile Breeder. **Ref: YH03743**

CURTAINSIDER
Curtainsider, Congleton Rd, Sandbach, **Cheshire**, CW11 1HJ, **ENGLAND**.
(T) 01270 611259.
Profile Transport/Horse Boxes. **Ref: YH03744**

CURTIS, CARL
Mr Carl Curtis, The Paddocks, Snatchells Lane, Claybridge, Sykehouse, Goole, **Yorkshire (East)**, DN14 9AL, **ENGLAND**.
(T) 01405 785214.
Profile Trainer. **Ref: YH03745**

CURTIS, CHRISTOPHER
Christopher Curtis, Field Hse, Carthorpe, Bedale, **Yorkshire (North)**, DL8 2LF, **ENGLAND**.
(T) 01845 567381
(E) info@christophercurtis.co.uk
(W) www.christophercurtis.co.uk.
Profile Poet.
Humorous Country Sport Poet. The poems, accompanied by humorous illustrations, make ideal gifts, offered as tablemats, drink mats, or simply framed on their own. Yr. Est: 1974 **Ref: YH03746**

CURTIS, DERRICK
Derrick Curtis, Haygrove Farm Pk, 9 Mill Lane, Trull, Taunton, **Somerset**, TA3 7LD, **ENGLAND**.
(T) 01823 321971.
Profile Farrier. **Ref: YH03747**

CURTIS, J A
Mrs J A Curtis, Kingsmead Farm, Kingsmead, Wickham, **Hampshire**, PO17 5AU, **ENGLAND**.
(T) 01329 832312.
Profile Breeder. **Ref: YH03748**

CURTIS, J W P
Mr J W P Curtis, Manor Hse, Beeford, Driffield, **Yorkshire (East)**, YO25 8BD, **ENGLAND**.
(T) 01262 488225.
Profile Supplies. **Ref: YH03749**

CURTIS, MARK
Mark Curtis, 21 Lark Hill, Moulton, Newmarket, **Suffolk**, CB8 8RT, **ENGLAND**.
(T) 01638 751733.
Profile Farrier. **Ref: YH03750**

CURTIS, MAURICE JOHN
Maurice John Curtis RSS, Kinton Post Office Stores, 52 Falkenham Rd, Kinton, Ipswich, **Suffolk**, IP10 0NH, **ENGLAND**.
(T) 01394 448260.
Profile Farrier. **Ref: YH03751**

CURTIS, NICHOLAS
Nicholas Curtis DWCF, The Elms, 207 The St, Kirtling, Newmarket, **Suffolk**, CB8 9PD, **ENGLAND**.
(T) 01638 730041.
Profile Farrier. **Ref: YH03752**

CURTIS, P
P Curtis, 1 Brailes Ind Est, Winderton Rd, Lower Brailes, Banbury, **Oxfordshire**, OX15 5JW, **ENGLAND**.
(T) 01608 685631 **(F)** 01608 685631.
Contact/s
Owner: Mr P Curtis
Profile Blacksmith. **Ref: YH03753**

CURY RIDING STABLE
Cury Riding Stable, Churchtown, Cury Cross Lanes, Helston, **Cornwall**, TR12 7BW, **ENGLAND**.
(T) 01326 240591.
Contact/s
Partner: Mrs A Curnow
Profile Riding School. **Ref: YH03754**

CURZON, G E
Mr G E Curzon, Tythe Farm Hse, Wraysbury, Staines, **Surrey**, TW19 5QA, **ENGLAND**.
(T) 01784 483100.
Profile Supplies. **Ref: YH03755**

CUSACK, GERALD A
Gerald A Cusack, 4 Cill Corbain, Naas, **County Kildare**, **IRELAND**.
(T) 045 871713.
Contact/s
Trainer: Mr G Cusack
(E) gercusack@kildarehorse.ie
Profile Trainer. **Ref: YH03756**

CUSACK, OLIVER
Oliver Cusack, Ind Est, Rathangan, Bishopland, **County Kildare**, **IRELAND**.
(T) 045 521516.
Profile Supplies. **Ref: YH03757**

CUSTOM TRAILERS
Custom Trailers, Straight Furlong, Pymoor, Ely, **Cambridgeshire**, CB6 2EG, **ENGLAND**.
(T) 01353 699000 **(F)** 01353 699222.
Profile Transport/Horse Boxes. **Ref: YH03758**

CUT PRICE EQUESTRIAN
Cut Price Equestrian, Unit 20A Albert Pl, Lower Darwen, Darwen, **Lancashire**, BB3 0QE, **ENGLAND**.
(T) 01254 698980. **Ref: YH03759**

CUTHBERT, T A K
Mr T A K Cuthbert, 26 Eden Grange, Little Corby, Carlisle, **Cumbria**, CA4 8QW, **ENGLAND**.
(T) 01228 560822 **(F)** 01228 560822.
Profile Farrier, Trainer. **Ref: YH03760**

CUTTERIDGE, SARAH
Ms Sarah Cutteridge, Nunnerley Hse Farm, Leaveslake Drove, West Pinchbeck, Spalding, **Lincolnshire**, PE11 3QJ, **ENGLAND**.
(T) 01733 571271
(M) 07711 637041. **Ref: YH03761**

CUTTHORNE
Cutthorne, Luckell Bridge, Wheddon Cross, Minehead, **Somerset**, TA24 7EW, **ENGLAND**.
(T) 01643 83255.
Profile Stable/Livery. **Ref: YH03762**

CWM EQUESTRIAN CTRE
Cwm Equestrian Centre, Cwmnantffynnon, Rhydlewis, Handysur, Ceredigion, **Carmarthenshire**, SA44 5SH, **WALES**.
(T) 01239 851837.
Profile Equestrian Centre, Riding School.
Ref: YH03763

CWMTYDU RIDING STABLES
Cwmtydu Riding Stables, Pantrhyn Cymtydu, New Quay, **Carmarthenshire**, SA44 6LH, **WALES**.
(T) 01545 560494.
Profile Equestrian Centre.
Organise hacks.
Opening Times
Sp: Open Mon - Sun 11:00. Closed Mon - Sun 16:00.
Su: Open Mon - Sun 11:00. Closed Mon - Sun 11:00.
Au: Open Mon - Sun 11:00. Closed Mon - Sun 11:00.
Wn: Open Mon - Sun 11:00. Closed Mon - Sun 11:00. **Ref: YH03764**

CWRT ISAF FARM
Cwrt Isaf Farm, Llangattock, Brecon Becons National Pk, Crickhowell, **Powys**, NP8 1PH, **WALES**.
(T) 01873 812128/9.
Profile Stable/Livery. **Ref: YH03765**

CYZER, C
Mr C Cyzer, Elliotts, Maplehurst, Horsham, **Sussex (West)**, RH13 6QX, **ENGLAND**.
(T) 01403 730255 **(F)** 01403 730787.
Profile Trainer. **Ref: YH03766**

CZERPAK, J D
Mr J D Czerpak, Astley Grange Farm, Back Lane, East Langton, Market Harborough, **Leicestershire**, LE16 7TB, **ENGLAND**.
(T) 01858 545736.
Profile Trainer. **Ref: YH03767**

D & D EQUESTRIAN
D & D Equestrian, 6 Pound Farm Prde, Oulton Broad, Lowestoft, **Suffolk**, NR32 4SF, **ENGLAND**.
(T) 01502 568043 **(F)** 01502 517293
(E) email@company.com
(W) www.showclass.co.uk.
Profile Saddlery Retailer. **Ref: YH03768**

D & D JONES & SON
D & D Jones & Son, Ystrad Dewi Stud, Tregaron, **Ceredigion**, SY25 6UW, **WALES**.
(T) 01974 298286.
Profile Breeder. **Ref: YH03769**

D & F FEED SVS
D & F Feed Services, Lubbards Lodge Farm, Hullbridge Rd, Rayleigh, **Essex**, SS6 9QG, **ENGLAND**.
(T) 01268 642601
(E) dffeeds@copdockmill.co.uk
(W) www.copdockmill.co.uk.
Contact/s
Owner: Mr D Hopkins
Profile Feed Merchant, Riding Wear Retailer, Saddlery Retailer. No.Staff: 2 Yr. Est: 1983
Opening Times
Sp: Open Mon - Sat 09:00. Closed Mon - Sat 17:00.
Su: Open Mon - Sat 09:00. Closed Mon - Sat 17:00.
Au: Open Mon - Sat 09:00. Closed Mon - Sat 17:00.
Wn: Open Mon - Sat 09:00. Closed Mon - Sat 17:00.
Ref: YH03770

D & F HORSE SUPPLIES
D & F Horse Supplies, Bryncrin, Rhosgadfan, Caernarfon, **Gwynedd**, LL54 7HG, **WALES**.
(T) 01286 830166 **(F)** 01286 830166.
Profile Supplies. **Ref: YH03771**

D & G HORSE TRANSPORTATION
D & G Horse Transportation, Butterfly Flat, The Cliffs, Cheddar, **Somerset**, BS27 3QA, **ENGLAND**.
(T) 01934 744321.
Contact/s
Partner: Miss J Garratt
Profile Transport/Horse Boxes. **Ref: YH03772**

D & H ANIMAL HUSBANDRY
D & H Animal Husbandry, 30 Bower Hill, Epping, **Essex**, CM16 7AD, **ENGLAND**.
(T) 01992 572277.
Profile Supplies. **Ref: YH03773**

D A HARRISON & SONS
D A Harrison & Sons, Coppins Garage, Waverton, Carlisle, **Cumbria**, CA7 0AE, **ENGLAND**.
(T) 01697 344000.
Profile Supplies. **Ref: YH03774**

D A L E
D.A.L.E. Western Trading, 19 Mowbray Rd, Aylesbury, **Buckinghamshire**, HP20 2DQ, **ENGLAND**.
(T) 01296 421729
(E) sales@dalewestern.co.uk
(W) www.dalewestern.co.uk.
Contact/s
Partner: Mr D Evans
(E) dave@dalewestern.co.uk
Profile Saddlery Retailer. Western Riding Specialists.
Unusual 'western' style gifts for horse lovers.
Opening Times
E-mail or telephone orders. There is a 24 hour answer phone **Ref: YH03775**

D A W ENGINEERING
D A W Engineering, Fenton Barns, North Berwick, **Lothian (East)**, EH39 5BW, **SCOTLAND**.
(T) 01620 850420.
Profile Blacksmith. **Ref: YH03776**

D A WATTS
D A Watts Wheelwright, 10 Millers Cl, Finedon, Wellingborough, **Northamptonshire**, NN9 5DU, **ENGLAND**.
(T) 01933 680549.
Profile Supplies. **Ref: YH03777**

D B I INSURANCE
D B I Insurance Co Ltd, 9 St Stephens Ct, St Stephens Rd, Bournemouth, **Dorset**, BH2 6LG, **ENGLAND**.
(T) 08003 73218 **(F)** 01202 294522
(E) dbi@dbi-insurance.co.uk.
Profile Supplies. Insurance Company. **Ref: YH03778**

D B S FARM SUPPLIES
D B S Farm Supplies, 27 Dromore St, Dromara, **County Down**, BT25 2BJ, **NORTHERN IRELAND**.
(T) 028 97533232.
Profile Supplies. **Ref: YH03779**

D BLOWERS
D Blowers Ltd, 31 Bedingfield Cres, Halesworth, **Suffolk**, IP19 8EE, **ENGLAND**.
(T) 01986 872178.
Profile Transport/Horse Boxes. **Ref: YH03780**

D BLOWERS
D Blowers Ltd, High Croft, London Rd, Halesworth, **Suffolk**, IP19 8LR, **ENGLAND**.
(T) 01986 872861.
Profile Transport/Horse Boxes. **Ref: YH03781**

D BLOWERS
D Blowers Ltd, Willbank, Lodge Rd, Holton, Halesworth, **Suffolk**, IP19 8RZ, **ENGLAND**.
(T) 01986 872742.
Profile Transport/Horse Boxes. **Ref: YH03782**

D F ASSET SADDLERY
D F Asset Saddlery, Saddlers Farm, Beads Hall Lane, Pilgrims Hatch, Brentwood, **Essex**, CM15 9QP, **ENGLAND**.

(T) 01836 274411.
Profile Saddlery Retailer. Ref: YH03783

D H F ANIMAL FEEDS

D H F Animal Feeds, Dunmore Home Farm, Airth, **Falkirk**, FK2 8LX, **SCOTLAND**.
(T) 01324 831591 (F) 01324 831373.
Profile Feed Merchant. Ref: YH03784

D I Y LIVERY

D I Y Livery, Middle Grove Farm, Chesham Rd, Hyde End, Great Missenden, **Buckinghamshire**, HP16 0RD, **ENGLAND**.
(T) 01494 862985.
Profile Stable/Livery. Ref: YH03785

D I Y STABLING

D I Y Stabling, 7 Seething Old Hall Pk, Seething, Norwich, **Norfolk**, NR15 1DW, **ENGLAND**.
(T) 01508 528363 (F) 01508 528676.
Profile Stable/Livery. Ref: YH03786

D I Y TRAILERS

D I Y Trailers, Ffosyffin, Ffostrasol, Llandysul, **Carmarthenshire**, SA44 5JY, **WALES**.
(T) 01239 851675 (F) 01239 851675.
Contact/s
Owner: Mr C Richardson
Profile Transport/Horse Boxes. Ref: YH03787

D J SLATTER HORSE TRANSPORT

D J Slatter Horse Transport, 29 South St, Middle Barton, Chipping Norton, **Oxfordshire**, OX7 7BU, **ENGLAND**.
(T) 01869 340700
(M) 07885 6557409.
Profile Transport/Horse Boxes. Ref: YH03788

D L DAVIES & SON

D L Davies & Son, Blaengwenllan, Henllan, Llandysul, **Carmarthenshire**, SA44 5TY, **WALES**.
(T) 01239 851258.
Profile Breeder. Ref: YH03789

D L FABRICATIONS

D L Fabrications Ltd, Unit 30 Wallneuk Rd, Greenlaw Ind Est, Paisley, **Renfrewshire**, PA3 4BT, **SCOTLAND**.
(T) 0141 8401404.
Profile Blacksmith. Ref: YH03790

D L MORGAN & SON

D L Morgan & Son, Plasnewydd, Ffarmers, Llanwrda, **Carmarthenshire**, SA19 8JF, **WALES**.
(T) 01558 650771
Affiliated Bodies WCF.
Contact/s
Owner: Mr D Morgan
Profile Farrier.
Opening Times
By appointment only Ref: YH03791

D L P EQUINE CONSULTANTS

D L P Equine Consultants, Laneside Hse, Poles Lane, Otterbourne, **Hampshire**, SO21 2DS, **ENGLAND**.
(T) 01962 712708 (F) 01962 711997
(E) sarah.hamlyn@virgin.net.
Profile Medical Support. Ref: YH03792

D M E FABRICATIONS 1984

D M E Fabrications 1984, Unit 5 Clydebrae St, Glasgow, **Glasgow (City of)**, G51 2AJ, **SCOTLAND**.
(T) 0141 4400084.
Profile Blacksmith. Ref: YH03793

D M FARRIERY

D M Farriery, Lilac Cottage, Northorpe Rd, Halton Holegate, Spilsby, **Lincolnshire**, PE23 5NZ, **ENGLAND**.
(T) 01790 754060.
Contact/s
Owner: Mr D Brash
Profile Farrier. Ref: YH03794

D M P MACHINERY

D M P Machinery, Unit 24 Hardwick Ind Est, Bury St Edmunds, **Suffolk**, IP33 2QH, **ENGLAND**.
(T) 01284 755525 (F) 01284 755525.
Profile Supplies. Ref: YH03795

D MAY & SONS

D May & Sons, Barton Mill, Hewas Water, St Austell, **Cornwall**, PL26 7JE, **ENGLAND**.
(T) 01726 883838.
Profile Supplies. Ref: YH03796

D MCCULLOCH & SON

D McCulloch & Son, Redbrae, Maybole, **Ayrshire (South)**, KA19 7HJ, **SCOTLAND**.
(T) 01655 882290.
Contact/s
Partner: Mr G Armstrong
Profile Blacksmith. Ref: YH03797

D MORGAN & SON

D Morgan & Son Country Stores, Unit 24, Crofty Ind Est, Crofty, Swansea, **Swansea**, SA4 3RS, **WALES**.
(T) 01792 390011.
Contact/s
Owner: Mr J Gilchrist
Profile Supplies. Yr. Est: 1949
Opening Times
Sp: Open Mon - Fri 10:00, Sat 09:00, Sun 10:00.
Closed Mon - Fri 17:00, Sat 12:30, Sun 13:00.
Su: Open Mon - Fri 10:00, Sat 09:00, Sun 10:00.
Closed Mon - Fri 17:00, Sat 12:30, Sun 13:00.
Au: Open Mon - Fri 10:00, Sat 09:00, Sun 10:00.
Closed Mon - Fri 17:00, Sat 12:30, Sun 13:00.
Wn: Open Mon - Fri 10:00, Sat 09:00, Sun 10:00.
Closed Mon - Fri 17:00, Sat 12:30, Sun 13:00.
Ref: YH03798

D MORGAN & SONS

D Morgan & Sons (Farm Supplies) Ltd, Reynoldstown, Swansea, **Swansea**, SA3 1AQ, **WALES**.
(T) 01792 390011 (F) 01792 391015.
Profile Riding Wear Retailer, Supplies.
Country Store supplying riding wear and equestrian goods. Ref: YH03799

D M'S TACK SHACK

D M's Tack Shack, 7 Greendykes Rd, Broxburn, **Lothian (West)**, EH52 5AF, **SCOTLAND**.
(T) 01506 855440 (F) 01506 855440.
Contact/s
Owner: Mrs D Moir Ref: YH03800

D P CARRIAGES

D P Carriages, Church Farm, Fleggburgh Rd, Rollesby, Great Yarmouth, **Norfolk**, NR29 5HH, **ENGLAND**.
(T) 01493 748677.
Profile Horse Drawn Vehicles. Ref: YH03801

D P FENWICK

D P Fenwick Ltd, 2 Fairfield St, Dundee, **Angus**, DD3 8HY, **SCOTLAND**.
(T) 01382 825142.
Profile Blacksmith. Ref: YH03802

D P MULHOLLAND & SONS

D P Mulholland & Sons, Langarve Stores, 62 Glenavy Rd, Crumlin, **County Antrim**, BT29 4LA, **NORTHERN IRELAND**.
(T) 028 94452264.
Profile Supplies. Ref: YH03803

D R G TRAILERS

D R G Trailers, 11 Ivy Cl, Cannock, **Staffordshire**, WS11 1UZ, **ENGLAND**.
(T) 01543 504411.
Contact/s
Partner: Mr R Eaton
Profile Transport/Horse Boxes. Ref: YH03804

D R PATERSON GRP

D R Paterson Group Ltd (The), 79 Northinch St, Glasgow, **Glasgow (City of)**, G14 0RL, **SCOTLAND**.
(T) 0141 9591198 (F) 0141 9501458.
Profile Blacksmith. Ref: YH03805

D R W TRAILERS

D R W Trailers, The Woodlands, Gloucester Rd, Longhope, **Gloucestershire**, GL17 0RA, **ENGLAND**.
(T) 01452 830403 (F) 01452 831176.
Contact/s
Owner: Mr D Warwick
Profile Transport/Horse Boxes. Ref: YH03806

D S COOPER

D S Cooper Ltd, Shelley Bank Abattoir, Near Bank, Shelley, Huddersfield, **Yorkshire (West)**, HD8 8LT, **ENGLAND**.
(T) 01484 604599.
Profile Equine Crematorium. Ref: YH03807

D S PINCHES & SONS

D S Pinches & Sons, Meadowcroft, Habberley, Pontesbury, Shrewsbury, **Shropshire**, SY5 0TP, **ENGLAND**.
(T) 01743 792739.
Contact/s
Partner: Mr C Pinches
Profile Transport/Horse Boxes. Ref: YH03808

D THOMSON & SON

D Thomson & Son, 24 High St, Jedburgh, **Scottish Borders**, TD8 6AF, **SCOTLAND**.
(T) 01835 862448.
Profile Saddlery Retailer. Ref: YH03809

D TOBIAS

D Tobias (1995) Ltd, 50 Rogart St, Glasgow, **Glasgow (City of)**, G40 2AA, **SCOTLAND**.
(T) 0141 5542348 (F) 0141 5501090.
Profile Blacksmith. Ref: YH03810

D W AST

D W Associates, Sandpiper Hse, Frogmore, Kingsbridge, **Devon**, TQ7 2NR, **ENGLAND**.
(T) 01548 531770 (F) 01548 531110
(E) dwa@itnr.co.uk.
Profile Medical Support. Ref: YH03811

D WATSON & SONS

D Watson & Sons, The Smithy, Springfield Rd, Bigrigg, Egremont, **Cumbria**, CA22 2TG, **ENGLAND**.
(T) 01946 810598 (F) 01946 811258.
Contact/s
Owner: Mr D Watson
Profile Farrier. Ref: YH03812

DABBS

Dabbs Show & Active Centre, Arnot Hse, Giffordtown, Cupar, **Fife**, KY15 7UW, **SCOTLAND**.
(T) 01337 831244 (F) 01337 831880
(E) info@anique-sport-horses.co.uk
(W) www.anique-sport-horses.co.uk
Affiliated Bodies BHS, LGA, RDA.
Contact/s
Partner: Mr A Bonelli-Baird (T) 01337 831180
Profile Equestrian Centre, Riding School, Stable/Livery, Trainer, Transport/Horse Boxes.
Dog Shows and Vintage Rallys are sometimes held.
Yr. Est: 1995 C.Size: 20 Acres Ref: YH03813

DACE, L A

Mr L A Dace, Lee Place Racing Stables, Blackgate Lane, Pulborough, **Sussex (West)**, RH20 1DF, **ENGLAND**.
(T) 01403 701151 (F) 01403 701152
(M) 07802 368789.
Profile Trainer. Ref: YH03814

DADLYNGTON FIELD

Dadlyngton Field Equestrian Supplies, Broadlands Farm, Main St, Dadlington, Nuneaton, **Leicestershire**, CV13 6HX, **ENGLAND**.
(T) 01455 212586.
Contact/s
Owner: Mr L Mayne
Profile Saddlery Retailer. Ref: YH03815

DAISY LANE LIVERY YARD

Daisy Lane Livery Yard, Bagnalls Farm, Daisy Lane, Alrewas, Burton-on-Trent, **Staffordshire**, DE13 7DP, **ENGLAND**.
(T) 01543 419800.
Profile Stable/Livery. Ref: YH03816

DAISYCHAIN PHOTOGRAPHIC

Daisychain Photographic Products, 28 Feilden Court, Swan St, Kingsclere, Newbury, **Berkshire**, RG15 8AG, **ENGLAND**.
(T) 01635 298850 (F) 01635 298850
(E) daisychain@newbury.net.
Profile Photographer. Ref: YH03817

DALBLAIR VETNRY SURGERY

Dalblair Veterinary Surgery, 52/54 Dalblair Rd, Ayr, **Ayrshire (South)**, KA7 1UQ, **SCOTLAND**.
(T) 01292 63744.
Profile Medical Support. Ref: YH03818

DALBRACK HIGHLAND PONY STUD

Dalbrack Highland Pony Stud, Migvie, Glenesk, Brechin, **Angus**, DD9 7YY, **SCOTLAND**.
(T) 01356 670233.
Profile Breeder. Ref: YH03819

DALE COCHRANE

Dale Cochrane Equine Portraiture, 1 Silverdale Ave, Riddlesden, Keighley, **Yorkshire (West)**, BD20 5AR, **ENGLAND**.
(T) 01535 665988 (F) 01535 665988.
Contact/s
Owner: Mr D Cochrane
Profile Artist.
Opening Times
Telephone for an appointment Ref: YH03820

DALE FARM SADDLERY

Dale Farm Saddlery, Dale Farm Hse/Dale Farm,

Greensbridge Lane, Tarbock Green, Prescot, **Merseyside**, L35 1QB, **ENGLAND**.
(T) 0151 4870512.
Contact/s
Owner: Mr I Shacklady
Profile Saddlery Retailer. **Ref: YH03821**

DALE SCHOOL OF EQUITATION
Dale School Of Equitation, Whitehouse Farm, Bradley, Stafford, **Staffordshire**, ST18 9EA, **ENGLAND**.
(T) 01785 780279.
Profile Riding School. **Ref: YH03822**

DALE TRAILERS
Dale Trailers, South Middleton Hses, South Middleton, Alnwick, **Northumberland**, NE66 4YE, **ENGLAND**.
(T) 01668 217262.
Profile Transport/Horse Boxes. **Ref: YH03823**

DALE, MAURICE & RALPH M
Maurice & Ralph M Dale, The Forge, Gt Carlton, Louth, **Lincolnshire**, LN11 8JW, **ENGLAND**.
(T) 01507 450094.
Contact/s
Farrier: Maurice Dale **(Q)** RSS
Profile Farrier. **Ref: YH03824**

DALE, T
T Dale, Southern Cottage, Pursers Lane, Peaslake, Guildford, **Surrey**, GU5 9SJ, **ENGLAND**.
(T) 01306 730159.
Profile Farrier. **Ref: YH03825**

DALES FEED SUPPLIES
Dales Feed Supplies, Three Tuns Yard, Market Pl, Thirsk, **Yorkshire (North)**, YO7 3LH, **ENGLAND**.
(T) 01845 525947.
Profile Feed Merchant. **Ref: YH03826**

DALES HORSE BOXES
Dales Horse Boxes & Trailers Maintenance & Restoration, 48 Eshton Rd, Gargrave, Skipton, **Yorkshire (North)**, BD23 3PN, **ENGLAND**.
(T) 01756 749971.
Contact/s
Owner: Mr J De Berry
Profile Transport/Horse Boxes. Horse Box Construction/Conversion.
Repairs horse boxes and convert old wagons into horse boxes. Yr. Est: 1961
Opening Times
Telephone for further information **Ref: YH03827**

DALES PET FEED SUPPLIES
Dales Pet Feed Supplies, Water Skelgate, Ripon, **Yorkshire (North)**, HG4 1BQ, **ENGLAND**.
(T) 01765 608954.
Contact/s
Owner: Mr A Swales
Profile Feed Merchant, Supplies. **Ref: YH03828**

DALES PONY SOC
Dales Pony Society, Greystones, Glebe Ave, Great Longstone, Bakewell, **Devon**, DE45 1TY, **ENGLAND**.
(T) 01629 640439 **(F)** 01629 640439.
Contact/s
Key Contact: Mrs J Ashby
Profile Club/Association. **Ref: YH03829**

DALES VETNRY CTRE
Dales Veterinary Centre (The), 9 Courthouse St, Otley, **Yorkshire (West)**, LS21 3AN, **ENGLAND**.
(T) 01943 463447 **(F)** 01943 463105
(E) vets@vets4pets.co.uk.
Profile Medical Support. **Ref: YH03830**

DALES VIEW RIDING CTRE
Dales View Riding Centre, Higher Lane, Salterforth, Barnoldswick, **Lancashire**, BB18 5SH, **ENGLAND**.
(T) 01282 817300 **(F)** 01282 817300.
Contact/s
Owner: Mrs E Heath **(Q)** BHSII
Profile Riding School, Stable/Livery.
Offer tuition, breaking and schooling. No.Staff: 3
Yr. Est: 1991 C.Size: 8 Acres **Ref: YH03831**

DALESIDE EQUESTRIAN CTRE
Daleside Equestrian Centre, 4 The Cres, Eastriggs, Annan, **Dumfries and Galloway**, DG12 6NW, **SCOTLAND**.
(T) 01461 40409.
Profile Stable/Livery. **Ref: YH03832**

DALGETY AGRCLTRL
Dalgety Agriculture Ltd (Berks), Home Farm, Sulham Lane, Pangbourne, Reading, **Berkshire**, RG8 8DT, **ENGLAND**.
(T) 0118 9843360 **(F)** 0118 9842961.
Profile Supplies. **Ref: YH03833**

DALGETY AGRCLTRL
Dalgety Agriculture (Carmarthen), Llysonnen Mill, Travellers Rest, Carmarthen, **Carmarthenshire**, SA31 3RR, **WALES**.
(T) 01267 231341.
Profile Supplies. **Ref: YH03834**

DALGETY AGRCLTRL
Dalgety Agriculture, C/O V J Voyzey, 1 Woburn Rd, Launceston, **Cornwall**, PL15 7HL, **ENGLAND**.
(T) 01566 780231.
Profile Supplies. **Ref: YH03835**

DALGETY AGRCLTRL
Dalgety Agriculture (Knighton), Teme Mill, Station Rd, Knighton, **Powys**, LD7 1DT, **WALES**.
(T) 01547 528441.
Profile Supplies. **Ref: YH03836**

DALGETY AGRCLTRL
Dalgety Agriculture (Bury St Edmunds), 71/72 Eastern Way, Bury St Edmunds, **Suffolk**, IP32 7AB, **ENGLAND**.
(T) 01284 702633 **(F)** 01284 756104.
Profile Supplies. **Ref: YH03837**

DALGETY AGRCLTRL
Dalgety Agriculture Ltd (Newmarket), Cheveley Hse, Fordham Rd, Newmarket, **Suffolk**, CB8 7AH, **ENGLAND**.
(T) 01285 740777.
Profile Supplies. **Ref: YH03838**

DALGETY AGRCLTRL
Dalgety Agriculture Ltd (Fridaythorpe), Fridaythorpe, Driffield, **Yorkshire (East)**, YO25 9RT, **ENGLAND**.
(T) 01377 288441 **(F)** 01377 288441.
Profile Supplies. **Ref: YH03839**

DALGISH, S
Mrs S Dalgish, The Steading, Acomb, Hexham, **Northumberland**, N46 4RH, **ENGLAND**.
(T) 01434 602232.
Profile Stable/Livery. **Ref: YH03840**

DALLARS RIDING SCHOOL
Dallars Riding School, Dallars Hse, Hurlford, Kilmarnock, **Ayrshire (East)**, KA1 5JW, **SCOTLAND**.
(T) 01563 884231.
Contact/s
Owner: Mr A Richard
Profile Riding School. **Ref: YH03841**

DALLAS INDUSTRIES
Dallas Industries, 12 Park Rd, Market Lavington, **Wiltshire**, SN10 4ED, **ENGLAND**.
(T) 01380 818518.
Profile Saddlery Retailer. **Ref: YH03842**

DALLAS KEITH
Dallas Keith Ltd, Bromag Ind Est, Burford Rd, Witney, **Oxfordshire**, OX8 5SR, **ENGLAND**.
(T) 01993 773061.
Contact/s
Owner: Mr C Willett
Profile Medical Support. **Ref: YH03843**

DALMAKERRAN EQUESTRIAN CTRE
Dalmakerran Equestrian Centre, 2 Crossford Farm, By Moniaive, Thornhill, **Dumfries and Galloway**, DG3 4DZ, **SCOTLAND**.
(T) 01387 820435 **(F)** 01387 820435.
Contact/s
Owner: Ms D Wicks
Profile Equestrian Centre, Horse/Rider Accom.
Ref: YH03844

DALTON, B
Mrs B Dalton, Beechgrove, Spark Lane, Rufford, Ormskirk, **Lancashire**, L40 1SU, **ENGLAND**.
(T) 01704 821641 **(F)** 01704 821641
(E) daltonb@talk21.com.
Profile Breeder. **Ref: YH03845**

DALTON, HEATHER
Mrs Heather Dalton, Norton Hse, Norton, Shifnal, **Shropshire**, TF11 9ED, **ENGLAND**.
(T) 01952 730322 **(F)** 01952 730322.
Contact/s
Owner: Mrs H Dalton
Profile Trainer.
Mrs Dalton is a racehorse trainer.
Opening Times
Telephone for an appointment **Ref: YH03846**

DALTON, J N
Mr J N Dalton, Sutton Hse, Shifnal, **Shropshire**, TF11 9NF, **ENGLAND**.
(T) 01952 730656 **(F)** 01952 730261
(M) 07831 555351.
Profile Supplies. **Ref: YH03847**

DALTON, P T
Mr P T Dalton, Dovecote Cottage, Bretby Pk, Bretby, Burton-on-Trent, **Staffordshire**, DE15 0RB, **ENGLAND**.
(T) 01283 221922 **(F)** 01283 224679
(M) 07774 240753.
Profile Trainer. **Ref: YH03848**

DALTON, R
R Dalton, Union Farm, Litcham Rd, Gressenhall, Dereham, **Norfolk**, NR20 4AR, **ENGLAND**.
(T) 01362 860931.
Profile Breeder. **Ref: YH03849**

DALY, DAVID J
David J Daly RSS, 5 Denham Dri, Yateley, **Hampshire**, GU46 6LQ, **ENGLAND**.
(T) 01252 876070.
Profile Farrier. **Ref: YH03850**

DALY, G M
G M Daly, The Laurels, Ditton Green, Woodditton, Newmarket, **Suffolk**, CB8 9SQ, **ENGLAND**.
(T) 01638 730950.
Contact/s
Owner: Mr G Daly **Ref: YH03851**

DALY, PAT
Mr Pat Daly, Manor Farm, Hill, Berkley, **Gloucestershire**, GL13 9EE, **ENGLAND**.
(T) 01454 260341.
Profile Breeder. **Ref: YH03852**

DAM
Dam, 7-9 New Rd, Shoreham By Sea, **Sussex (West)**, BN43 6RA, **ENGLAND**.
(T) 01273 461469.
Contact/s
Owner: Mr N Whitley
Profile Supplies. **Ref: YH03853**

DAMART
Damart, Bowling Green Mills, Bingley, **Yorkshire (West)**, BD16 3ZD, **ENGLAND**.
(T) 01274 510000 **(F)** 01274 551130.
Profile Supplies. **Ref: YH03854**

DAMASTOWN STUD
Damastown Stud, Ballybrack, Kilcock, **County Kildare**, **IRELAND**.
(T) 01 6287423
(E) damastownstud@kildarehorse.ie.
Contact/s
Key Contact: Mr S Nolan
Profile Breeder. **Ref: YH03855**

DAMORY VETNRY CLINIC
Damory Veterinary Clinic, Edward St, Blandford, **Dorset**, DT11 7QT, **ENGLAND**.
(T) 01258 452626.
Profile Medical Support. **Ref: YH03856**

DAMPHAY PRODUCTS
Damphay Products (I W & L A Sant), Eastfields Farm, Slindon, Eccleshall, **Staffordshire**, ST21 6LX, **ENGLAND**.
(T) 01785 850678 **(F)** 01785 859500.
Profile Hay and Straw Merchants. **Ref: YH03857**

DAMPIER, J A
J A Dampier RSS, 41 Bury Old Rd, Ainsworth, Bolton, **Manchester (Greater)**, BL2 5PF, **ENGLAND**.
(T) 01204 361150.
Profile Farrier. **Ref: YH03858**

DAN Y LAN STUD
Dan Y Lan Stud, Howe Farm, Farley, Salisbury, **Wiltshire**, SP5 1AQ, **ENGLAND**.
(T) 01722 712246.
Profile Breeder. **Ref: YH03859**

DANBURY
Danbury Carriage Driving Centre (The), Chamberlains Farm, Sporehams Lane, Danbury, Chelmsford, **Essex**, CM3 4AJ, **ENGLAND**.
(T) 01245 226745 **(F)** 01245 226745
Affiliated Bodies BDS, BHS.
Contact/s
Owner: Mr T Selway
Profile Riding School, Trainer.

Breaks in horses for carriage driving and offers training in driving the carriages.
Opening Times
Sp: Open Mon - Sun 09:00. Closed Mon - Sun 18:00.
Su: Open Mon - Sun 09:00. Closed Mon - Sun 18:00.
Au: Open Mon - Sun 09:00. Closed Mon - Sun 18:00.
Wn: Open Mon - Sun 09:00. Closed Mon - Sun 18:00. **Ref: YH03860**

DANCESPORT & EQUESTRIAN

Dancesport & Equestrian, 56 Russell Way, The Metro Ctre, Gateshead, **Tyne and Wear**, NE11 9XX, **ENGLAND**.
(T) 0191 4601733.
Profile Saddlery Retailer. **Ref: YH03861**

DANCO INT

Danco International Plc, The Pavilion Ctre, Frog Lane, Coalpit Heath, **Gloucestershire (South)**, BS36 2NW, **ENGLAND**.
(T) 01454 250222 **(F)** 01454 250444.
Profile Club/Association. **Ref: YH03862**

DANDY BUSH SADDLERY

Dandy Brush Saddlery (The), School Farm, Hooe, Battle, **Sussex (East)**, TN33 9EY, **ENGLAND**.
(T) 01424 892962.
Contact/s
Owner: Ms M Cheese
Profile Riding Wear Retailer, Saddlery Retailer.
Yr. Est: 1979
Opening Times
Sp: Open 09:00. Closed 17:30.
Su: Open 09:00. Closed 17:30.
Au: Open 09:00. Closed 17:30.
Wn: Open 09:00. Closed 17:30. **Ref: YH03863**

DANE VALLEY

Dane Valley Baled Woodshavings, WTL Int Ltd, Bosley, Macclesfield, **Cheshire**, SK11 0PE, **ENGLAND**.
(T) 01260 223284 **(F)** 01260 223589.
Profile Supplies. **Ref: YH03864**

DANE VALLEY EQUESTRIAN CTRE

Dane Valley Equestrian Centre, Tanhouse Farm, Eaton, Congleton, **Cheshire**, CW12 2ND, **ENGLAND**.
(T) 01260 299454.
Profile Equestrian Centre. **Ref: YH03865**

DANECROFT RIDING

Danecroft Riding, Vera Lane, Welwyn, **Hertfordshire**, AL6 0EW, **ENGLAND**.
(T) 01438 717422
(M) 07979 347118.
Contact/s
Owner: Mrs Y Konig
Profile Riding School.
Courses in riding and stable management are run during half term and school holidays on weekdays from 9.00am-12noon (excluding Bank Holidays).
Ref: YH03866

DANES ANDALUSIAN STUD

Danes Andalusian Stud, Danes, Little Berkhamsted, Hertford, **Hertfordshire**, SG13 8LU, **ENGLAND**.
(T) 01707 875922.
Profile Breeder. **Ref: YH03867**

DANETHORPE LIVERY SVS

Danethorpe Livery Services, Danethorpe Hill Farm, Danethorpe Lane, Danethorpe, Newark, **Nottinghamshire**, NG24 2PB, **ENGLAND**.
(T) 01636 703980.
Contact/s
Owner: Mrs S Applewhite
Profile Stable/Livery. **Ref: YH03868**

DANGANELLY EQUESTRIAN CTRE

Danganelly Equestrian Centre, Danganelly Cooraclare, Kilrush, **County Clare**, **IRELAND**.
(T) 065 9059213. **Ref: YH03869**

DANIEL O'BRIEN RACING

Daniel O'Brien Racing Ltd, Knowles Bank, Half Moon Lane, Tudeley, Tonbridge, **Kent**, TN11 0PU, **ENGLAND**.
(T) 01892 824123 **(F)** 01892 823906.
Contact/s
Owner: Mr D O'Brien
Profile Trainer. **Ref: YH03870**

DANIEL THWAITES

Daniel Thwaites Plc, Star Brewery, Blackburn, **Lancashire**, BB1 5BU, **ENGLAND**.
(T) 01254 54431.
Contact/s
Owner: Mr P Baker
Profile Breeder. **Ref: YH03871**

DANIELS, ALISON

Alison Daniels, 89 Blackbrook Rd, Fareham, **Hampshire**, PO15 5DD, **ENGLAND**.
(T) 01329 847866.
Profile Breeder. **Ref: YH03872**

DANISH HORSES

Danish Horses, Hoad Farm, Acrise, Folkestone, **Kent**, CT18 8LP, **ENGLAND**.
(T) 01303 844377.
Profile Breeder. **Ref: YH03873**

DANL, KINANE

Kinane Danl, Kilvemnon Mullinahone, Thurles, **County Tipperary**, **IRELAND**.
(T) 052 53122.
Profile Supplies. **Ref: YH03874**

DAN-YR-OGOF

Dan-Yr-Ogof Riding Centre, Tygwidd, Brecon Rd, Penycae, Swansea, **Swansea**, SA9 1GJ, **WALES**.
(T) 01639 730049
(W) www.showcaves.co.uk.
Contact/s
Owner: Miss S Price
Profile Equestrian Centre. Trekking Centre.
Parking is available. Dan-yr-Ogof is part of the National Showcaves Centre. They offer two and a half hour and one hour treks on Welsh Cobs, in groups of five people. Basic tuition is given. Yr. Est: 1986
C.Size: 95 Acres
Opening Times
Open seven days a week from 1st April (or Easter if earlier) until October 31st. **Ref: YH03875**

DARBY ROSETTES

Darby Rosettes, 5 Goulburn Rd, Heartlease Est, Norwich, **Norfolk**, NR7 9UY, **ENGLAND**.
(T) 01603 440694 **(F)** 01603 440687. **Ref: YH03876**

DARBY, L W

L W Darby, 76 St Albans Rd, Hemel Hempstead, **Hertfordshire**, HP2 4BA, **ENGLAND**.
(T) 01442 256241.
Contact/s
Owner: Mr L Darby
Profile Farrier. **Ref: YH03877**

DARBY, MARTIN V

Martin V Darby RSS, Lower Poollands Farm, Titton, Stourport-on-Severn, **Worcestershire**, DY13 9QT, **ENGLAND**.
(T) 01299 822375.
Profile Farrier. **Ref: YH03878**

D'ARCY RIDING STABLES

D'Arcy Riding Stables, Chapel Rd, Tolleshunt D'arcy, Maldon, **Essex**, CM9 8TL, **ENGLAND**.
(T) 01621 860553 **(F)** 01621 869106
(E) info@ridingcentres.com
(W) www.ridingcentres.com.
Contact/s
Owner: Mrs V Hayes
Profile Riding School, Stable/Livery.
Livery, hacking and driving, prices available on request. No.Staff: 12 Yr. Est: 1973
Opening Times
Sp: Open Mon - Sun 09:00. Closed Mon - Sun 17:00.
Su: Open Mon - Sun 09:00. Closed Mon - Sun 17:00.
Au: Open Mon - Sun 09:00. Closed Mon - Sun 17:00.
Wn: Open Mon - Sun 09:00. Closed Mon - Sun 17:00. **Ref: YH03879**

D'ARCY SADDLERY

D'Arcy Saddlery Ltd, Chapel Rd, Tollshunt D'arcy, Maldon, **Essex**, CM9 8TL, **ENGLAND**.
(T) 01621 868858 **(F)** 01621 869106
(E) darcysaddlery@hotmail.com
(W) www.ridingcentres.com.
Contact/s
Owner: Mrs V Hayes
Profile Saddlery Retailer.
Make jodphurs, rugs and head collars to order.
No.Staff: 12 Yr. Est: 1973
Opening Times
Sp: Open Mon - Sun 09:00. Closed Mon - Sun 17:00.
Su: Open Mon - Sun 09:00. Closed Mon - Sun 17:00.
Au: Open Mon - Sun 09:00. Closed Mon - Sun 17:00.
Wn: Open Mon - Sun 09:00. Closed Mon - Sun 17:00. **Ref: YH03880**

D'ARCY STUD

D'Arcy Stud, Horseshoes, Kelvedon Rd, Tolleshunt D'arcy, Maldon, **Essex**, CM9 8EL, **ENGLAND**.
(T) 01621 816106.
Profile Breeder. **Ref: YH03881**

D'ARCY, DAVID C

David C D'Arcy DWCF, 42 Haslingden Old Rd, Knuzden, Blackburn, **Lancashire**, BB1 2DY, **ENGLAND**.
(T) 01254 264177.
Profile Farrier. **Ref: YH03882**

D'ARCY, PAUL

Paul D'Arcy, High Havens Stables, Hamilton Rd, Newmarket, **Suffolk**, CB8 0TE, **ENGLAND**.
(T) 01638 662000 **(F)** 01638 661100
(W) www.newmarketracehorsetrainers.co.uk
Affiliated Bodies Newmarket Trainers Fed.
Contact/s
Owner: Mr P D'Arcy
Profile Trainer. **Ref: YH03883**

DARENTH VALLEY FORGE

Darenth Valley Forge, Lower Austin Lodge Farm, Upper Austin Lodge Rd, Eynsford, Dartford, **Kent**, DA4 0HT, **ENGLAND**.
(T) 01322 866107.
Profile Blacksmith. **Ref: YH03884**

DARGUE, J S

Mr J S Dargue, Quarry Cottage, Dufton, Appleby-In-Westmorland, **Cumbria**, CA16 6DF, **ENGLAND**.
(T) 01768 351459.
Profile Breeder. **Ref: YH03885**

DARHO STUD & EQUESTRIAN SVS

Darho Stud & Equestrian Services, Millhill, Auchengray, **Lanarkshire (South)**, ML11 8LW, **SCOTLAND**.
(T) 01501 785392 **(F)** 01501 785392.
Profile Breeder. **Ref: YH03886**

DARK HORSE

Dark Horse, Close Hill, Bridestowe, Okehampton, **Devon**, EX20 4NT, **ENGLAND**.
(T) 01837 861675 **(F)** 01837 861675.
Contact/s
Partner: Mr R Reynolds
Profile Supplies. **Ref: YH03887**

DARKHORSE TINYTACK

Darkhorse Saddlery Caspian Stud, 26 Lee Lane, Royston, Barnsley, **Yorkshire (South)**, S71 4RT, **ENGLAND**.
(T) 01226 722449.
Contact/s
Owner: Ms D Thomson
Profile Breeder, Saddlery Retailer.
Manufacturer and retailer of everything for miniature horses, ponies & foals. No.Staff: 3
Yr. Est: 1981 C.Size: 50 Acres
Opening Times
Sp: Open 10:00. Closed 22:00.
Su: Open 10:00. Closed 22:00.
Au: Open 10:00. Closed 22:00.
Wn: Open 10:00. Closed 22:00. **Ref: YH03888**

DARLEY STUD MNGMT

Darley Stud Management Co Ltd, The Stud Hse, Hagbourne Rd, Aston Upthorpe, Didcot, **Oxfordshire**, OX11 9EE, **ENGLAND**.
(T) 01235 850300 **(F)** 01235 851137.
Contact/s
Manager: Mr D Marffy
Profile Breeder. **Ref: YH03889**

DARLEY STUD MNGMT

Darley Stud Management Co, Dalham Hall Stud, Duchess Dri, Newmarket, **Suffolk**, CB8 9HD, **ENGLAND**.
(T) 01638 730070 **(F)** 01638 730167.
Profile Breeder. **Ref: YH03890**

DARLINGTON & DISTRICT

Darlington & District Riding Club, Snotterton Hall, Staindrop, **County Durham**, DL2 3QZ, **ENGLAND**.
(T) 01833 660220.
Contact/s
Chairman: Mrs C I'Anson
Profile Club/Association, Riding Club. **Ref: YH03891**

DARLINGTON EQUESTRIAN CTRE

Darlington Equestrian Centre Ltd, Haughton Rd, Darlington, **County Durham**, DL1 2RJ, **ENGLAND**.
(T) 01325 468099 **(F)** 01325 468099.

A-Z of COMPANIES

Contact/s
Assistant: Mr G McWilliams
Profile Equestrian Centre, Riding School, Stable/Livery. No.Staff: 3 Yr. Est: 1999
C.Size: 8.5 Acres
Opening Times
Sp: Open 07:30. Closed 21:00.
Su: Open 07:30. Closed 21:00.
Au: Open 07:30. Closed 21:00.
Wn: Open 07:30. Closed 21:00. Ref: YH03892

DARLINGTON EQUESTRIAN CTRE
Darlington Equestrian Centre, Darlington Riding Ctre, Red Hall, Haughton, **County Durham**, DL1 2RJ, **ENGLAND**.
(T) 01325 468099.
Contact/s
Owner: Mr P McWilliams
Profile Equestrian Centre, Riding School, Stable/Livery. Ref: YH03893

DARLINGTON, JAMES
James Darlington DWCF, 32 Lower St, Merriot, Crewkerne, **Somerset**, TA16 5NN, **ENGLAND**.
(T) 01460 76037.
Profile Farrier. Ref: YH03894

DARLOW, G C
G C Darlow, Meadow Bank Farm, Holmes Chapel Rd, Over Peover, Knutsford, **Cheshire**, WA16 9JA, **ENGLAND**.
(T) 01565 722618.
Contact/s
Owner: Mr G Darlow
Profile Farrier. Ref: YH03895

DARLOWS
Darlow Rosettes, 8 Verney Cl, Butlers Marston, **Warwickshire**, CV35 0NP, **ENGLAND**.
(T) 01926 640050 (F) 01926 640050
(E) darlowro@supanet.com
(W) www.darlowrosettes.com.
Profile Supplies.
Rosette specialists Ref: YH03896

DARMADY, JOHN
Mr John Darmady, Camster Est, Lybster, **Highlands**, KW3 6BD, **SCOTLAND**.
(T) 01593 721251
(M) 07778 761323.
Profile Breeder. Ref: YH03897

DARNTON, A
Miss A Darnton, Rodlease Cottage, Boldre, Lymington, **Hampshire**, SO4 5QF, **ENGLAND**.
(T) 01590 672208.
Profile Breeder. Ref: YH03898

DARROW FARM SUPPLIES
Darrow Farm Supplies Ltd, Darrow Wood Farm, Shelfanger Rd, Diss, **Norfolk**, IP22 3XY, **ENGLAND**.
(T) 01379 640331 (F) 01379 641331.
Profile Feed Merchant, Supplies. Ref: YH03899

DARTMOOR CARRIAGES
Dartmoor Carriages Ltd, Lower Fenemere Court, Baschurch, Shrewsbury, **Shropshire**, SY4 2JF, **ENGLAND**.
(T) 01939 261011 (F) 01939 261011. Ref: YH03900

DARTMOOR DRIVING
Dartmoor Driving, Mitchelcombe, Holne, Newton Abbot, **Devon**, TQ13 7SP, **ENGLAND**.
(T) 01364 631438
(E) dartmoordriving@btinternet.com.
Profile Holidays, Horse/Rider Accom. Ref: YH03901

DARTMOOR HUNT SUPPORTERS
Dartmoor Hunt Supporters Club, Tetwell Farm, Ashford, Kingsbridge, **Devon**, TQ7 4NL, **ENGLAND**.
(T) 01548 550539.
Contact/s
Secretary: Mrs L Lucas
Profile Club/Association. Ref: YH03902

DARTMOOR LIVESTOCK PROTECTION
Dartmoor Livestock Protection Society, Hillbridge Farm, Peter Tavy, Tavistock, **Devon**, PL19 9NB, **ENGLAND**.
(T) 01822 810303.
Profile Club/Association. Ref: YH03903

DARTMOOR PONY SOC
Dartmoor Pony Society, 57 Pykes Down, Ivybridge, **Devon**, PL21 0BY, **ENGLAND**.
(T) 01752 897053 (F) 01752 897053.
Contact/s
Key Contact: Mrs L Setter
Profile Club/Association. Ref: YH03904

DARTMOOR ROSETTES
Dartmoor Rosettes, Freepost, Penton Chapel, Christow, Exeter, **Devon**, EX6 7YZ, **ENGLAND**.
(T) 01647 252411 (F) 01647 253109
(E) dartmoor@rosettes.u-net.com
(W) www.dartmoor-rosettes.com.
Profile Supplies.
Rosette manufacturers Ref: YH03905

DAUNT, A N
Mrs A N Daunt, Toad Hall, Wymondham, Melton Mowbray, **Leicestershire**, LE14 2BP, **ENGLAND**.
(T) 01572 767216.
Profile Breeder. Ref: YH03906

DAVDOR STUD
Davdor Stud, 95 Nether Currie Cres, Currie, **Edinburgh (City of)**, EH14 5JQ, **SCOTLAND**.
(T) 0131 4492507 (F) 0131 4492507.
Profile Breeder. Ref: YH03907

DAVE REGAN
Dave Regan Equine Dental Technician Services, 3 New Rd Cottages, Adlestrop, Moreton In Marsh, **Gloucestershire**, GL56 0YL, **ENGLAND**.
(T) 01608 659730 (F) 01608 684833
(E) davidregan@regannet.freeserve.co.uk
(W) www.equine-dental-tech.co.uk.
Profile Medical Support. Ref: YH03908

DAVENHILL, ADAM J
Adam J Davenhill DWCF, Crown Hill, Den Lane, Wrinehill, Crewe, **Cheshire**, CW3 9BT, **ENGLAND**.
(T) 01270 820472.
Profile Farrier. Ref: YH03909

DAVENPORT, P J
P J Davenport, 32 The Terrace, Cheadle, Stoke-on-Trent, **Staffordshire**, ST10 1PA, **ENGLAND**.
(T) 01538 754820.
Contact/s
Owner: Mr P Davenport
Profile Farrier. Ref: YH03910

DAVERN EQUESTRIAN CTRE
Davern Equestrian Centre, Tannersrath Lower, Clonmel, **County Tipperary**, **IRELAND**.
(T) 052 27327 (F) 052 29800
(M) 086 2520752.
Contact/s
Owner: Ann Marie Davern
Profile Holidays, Riding School.
Pony camp and residential riding holiday centre.
Ref: YH03911

DAVEY & DAVEY
Davey & Davey, The Vetnry Surgery, 39 Station Rd, Whittlesford, **Cambridgeshire**, CB2 4NL, **ENGLAND**.
(T) 01223 833651.
Profile Medical Support. Ref: YH03912

DAVEY, R
R Davey, Manor Farm, Moor Lane, Gotham, Nottingham, **Nottinghamshire**, NG11 0LH, **ENGLAND**.
(T) 0115 9830051.
Contact/s
Owner: Mr R Davey
Profile Stable/Livery.
Full, part and DIY livery available, prices on request.
Ref: YH03913

DAVEY'S LIVESTOCK TRANSPORT
Davey's Livestock Transport Ltd, Trecrogo, South Petherwin, Launceston, **Cornwall**, PL15 7LQ, **ENGLAND**.
(T) 01566 782233 (F) 01566 774251.
Profile Transport/Horse Boxes. Ref: YH03914

DAVID BAKER FARM SUPPLIES
David Baker Farm Supplies, Station Yard, Weston Rhyn, Oswestry, **Shropshire**, SY10 7TA, **ENGLAND**.
(T) 01691 773397.
Profile Supplies. Ref: YH03915

DAVID CATLIN
David Catlin - Saddler, Unit 2, Grange Farm Business Pk, Sandy Lane, Shedfield, Southampton, **Hampshire**, SO32 2HD, **ENGLAND**.
(T) 01329 835575 (F) 01329 835575.
Contact/s
General Manager: Ms P Andrews
Profile Saddlery Retailer. No.Staff: 2
Yr. Est: 1996
Opening Times
Sp: Open 09:00. Closed 17:00.
Su: Open 09:00. Closed 17:00.
Au: Open 09:00. Closed 17:00.
Wn: Open 09:00. Closed 17:00. Ref: YH03916

DAVID DUMOSCH
David Dumosch Ltd, Les Ruettes, St John, **Jersey**, JE3 4FN, **ENGLAND**.
(T) 01534 862333 (F) 01534 865152.
Profile Supplies. Ref: YH03917

DAVID ETON
David Eton, Clarke & Co, 103 High St, Eton, Windsor, **Berkshire**, SL4 6AF, **ENGLAND**.
(T) 01753 670170 (F) 01753 841773.
Profile Saddlery Retailer. Ref: YH03918

DAVID FARMER SADDLERY
David Farmer Saddlery, Lodge Farm, Brinkworth, Chippenham, **Wiltshire**, SN15 5DD, **ENGLAND**.
(T) 01666 830410
(M) 07831 830410.
Profile Riding Wear Retailer, Saddlery Retailer.
Specialises in riding chaps of all types. Ref: YH03919

DAVID FUNNELL CASUALTY SVS
David Funnell Casualty Services, Shipley Hatch, Mill Hill, Kingsnorth, Ashford, **Kent**, TN23 2EW, **ENGLAND**.
(T) 01233 625581.
Profile Abbatoir. Ref: YH03920

DAVID LEGGATE
David Leggate Specialist Surfaces Ltd, The Tythe Barn, Acton Turville, Badminton, **Gloucestershire**, GL9 1HW, **ENGLAND**.
(T) 01454 218060. Ref: YH03921

DAVID LEWIS INT
David Lewis International, Lyons Barn Farm, Barton Gate, Scotch Hill Lane, Barton Under Needwood, Burton-on-Trent, **Staffordshire**, DE13 8BP, **ENGLAND**.
(T) 01283 712939.
Profile Transport/Horse Boxes. Ref: YH03922

DAVID SMYLY
David Smyly (Bloodstock), The Bell Hse, Dorstone, **Herefordshire**, HR3 6AB, **ENGLAND**.
(T) 01981 550112 (F) 01981 550125.
Profile Blood Stock Agency. Ref: YH03923

DAVID THOMSON
David Thomson (Animal Feed Merchant), North Raw, East Calder, Livingston, **Lothian (West)**, EH53 0ET, **SCOTLAND**.
(T) 01506 881588 (F) 01506 884388.
Profile Supplies. Ref: YH03924

DAVID WILSON'S TRAILERS
David Wilson's Trailers Ltd, Hillsdown, Twyford Lane, Horsted Keynes, **Sussex (West)**, RH17 7DH, **ENGLAND**.
(T) 01825 740696 (F) 01825 740260
(E) info@dwt-exhibitions.co.uk.
Profile Transport/Horse Boxes. Ref: YH03925

DAVID, GLYN O
Glyn O David FWCF, 4 Greenfield Trce, Caerau, Maesteg, **Bridgend**, CF34 0RB, **WALES**.
(T) 01656 734387.
Profile Farrier. Ref: YH03926

DAVID, O J
O J David, 1 Evans Trce, Maesteg, **Bridgend**, CF34 0RH, **WALES**.
(T) 01656 735895.
Contact/s
Owner: Mr O David
Profile Farrier. Ref: YH03927

DAVIDSON, ALISTAIR
Alistair Davidson, 38 Duncan Rd, Tarland, Aboyne, **Aberdeenshire**, AB34 4YE, **SCOTLAND**.
(T) 01339 881405.
Profile Farrier. Ref: YH03928

DAVIDSON, C I
C I Davidson, Grey Cottage, Warwick-on-Eden, Carlisle, **Cumbria**, CA4 8PA, **ENGLAND**.
(T) 01228 561506 (F) 01228 561506.
Contact/s
Owner: Mr C Davidson
Profile Hay and Straw Merchants. Ref: YH03929

DAVIDSON, SCOTT G
Scott G Davidson DWCF, 52 Sharon St, Dalry, **Ayrshire (North)**, KA24 5DT, **SCOTLAND**.
(T) 01294 832418.
Profile Farrier. Ref: YH03930

DAVIDSONS VETNRY SUPPLIES
Davidsons Veterinary Supplies, Welton Rd, Blairgowrie, **Perth and Kinross**, PH10 6NB, **SCOTLAND**.
(T) 01350 725213 **(F)** 01350 725223
(E) info@wdavidson.sol.co.uk.
Contact/s
Equestrian Sales: Gillian Wilson
Profile Medical Support. **Ref: YH03931**

DAVIES & ANDERSON, J & C
J & C Davies & Anderson, 3 Caraway Cl, St Mellons, Cardiff, **Glamorgan (Vale of)**, CF3 0NF, **WALES**.
(T) 029 20259664 **(F)** 029 20259664
(E) tyntyla.stud@net.ntl.com.
Profile Breeder. **Ref: YH03932**

DAVIES & ROUTLEDGE
Davies & Routledge, Coed-Y-Brain, Newmarket Rd, Royston, **Hertfordshire**, SG8 7HD, **ENGLAND**.
(T) 01763 42221.
Profile Medical Support. **Ref: YH03933**

DAVIES BENAKI
Davies Benaki & Co Ltd, Abbot Davies Balancing Rein Stud, Hyde Rd, Roade, **Northamptonshire**, NN6 2LX, **ENGLAND**.
(T) 01604 863109.
Profile Supplies. **Ref: YH03934**

DAVIES RIDING BOOTS
Davies Riding Boots, Unit 6 Blaenant Ind Est, Blaenavon Rd, Brynmawr, Ebbw Vale, **Blaenau Gwent**, NP23 4BX, **WALES**.
(T) 01495 313045 **(F)** 01495 313045
(E) info@daviesridingboots.kickon.com
(W) www.daviesridingboots.co.uk.
Contact/s
Partner: Mr L Whitey
Profile Riding Wear Retailer.
Manufacturers of made to measure riding boots and trees. Appointments only. Self measuring forms can be sent out so you can measure your own feet.
Yr. Est: 1976
Opening Times
Sp: Open 09:00. Closed 15:00.
Su: Open 09:00. Closed 15:00.
Au: Open 09:00. Closed 15:00.
Wn: Open 09:00. Closed 15:00. **Ref: YH03935**

DAVIES, D
Mr D Davies, Blaenant Goch, Hermon, Cynwyl Elfed, Carmarthen, **Carmarthenshire**, **WALES**.
(T) 01267 233749.
Profile Breeder. **Ref: YH03936**

DAVIES, D A & H A
D A & H A Davies, Gadlys, Dinas, Caernarfon, **Gwynedd**, LL54 7YW, **WALES**.
(T) 01286 830586.
Contact/s
Partner: Mr D Davies
Profile Equestrian Centre. **Ref: YH03937**

DAVIES, D J
Mr D J Davies, Ynys Dwfnant Farm, Clyne, Resolven, **Glamorgan (Vale of)**, SA11 4BN, **WALES**.
(T) 01639 710774.
Profile Supplies. **Ref: YH03938**

DAVIES, E W (DR)
Dr E W Davies MBE, Ceulan, Miskin, Pontyclun, **Rhondda Cynon Taff**, CF72 8JU, **WALES**.
(T) 01443 224317 **(F)** 01443 223911
(E) ceulan@ukgateway.net.
Profile Breeder. **Ref: YH03939**

DAVIES, ERIC
Eric Davies, Maesmynach, Cribyn, Lampeter, **Ceredigion**, SA48 7LZ, **WALES**.
(T) 01570 470670 **(F)** 01570 470670.
Contact/s
Owner: Mr E Davies
Profile Breeder. **Ref: YH03940**

DAVIES, H L L
H L L Davies, Colsterworth, Grantham, **Lincolnshire**, NG33 5JJ, **ENGLAND**.
(T) 01476 861991 **(F)** 01476 861183.
Profile Transport/Horse Boxes. **Ref: YH03941**

DAVIES, J D J
Mr J D J Davies, Upperhouse Farm, Llanwenarth, Abergavenny, **Monmouthshire**, NP7 7LA, **WALES**.
(T) 01873 853458.
Profile Trainer. **Ref: YH03942**

DAVIES, JOHN W
John W Davies, The Curetage, Dunston, Stafford, **Staffordshire**, ST18 9AB, **ENGLAND**.
(T) 01785 712296.
Profile Farrier. **Ref: YH03943**

DAVIES, MARK
Mark Davies, Ysgubor Fach, Crwbin, Kidwelly, **Carmarthenshire**, SA17 5EB, **WALES**.
(T) 01269 870831.
Contact/s
Owner: Mr M Davies **(Q)** DWCF
Profile Farrier. **Ref: YH03944**

DAVIES, P S
Mr P S Davies, 19 Hatton Pk, Bromyard, **Herefordshire**, HR7 4EY, **ENGLAND**.
(T) 01885 482567.
Profile Supplies. **Ref: YH03945**

DAVIES, R
R Davies, Brick Yard Farm, Longwood, Eaton Constantine, Shrewsbury, **Shropshire**, SY5 6RF, **ENGLAND**.
(T) 01952 510582 **(F)** 01952 510682.
Contact/s
Owner: Mr R Davies
Profile Hay and Straw Merchants. **Ref: YH03946**

DAVIES, R & J
R & J Davies, Carreg Bica Farm, Hill Top, Ebbw Vale, **Blaenau Gwent**, NP3 6PJ, **WALES**.
(T) 01495 301569.
Profile Breeder. **Ref: YH03947**

DAVIES, TIGER
Tiger Davies, Coombe Farm, Puddington, Tiverton, **Devon**, EX16 8PF, **ENGLAND**.
(T) 01884 860503 **(F)** 01884 861029
(M) 07860 744734.
Profile Medical Support. **Ref: YH03948**

DAVIES, W B
W B Davies, Llwyn-Newydd Farm, Alltways Rd, Pontarsais, Carmarthen, **Carmarthenshire**, SA32 7DZ, **WALES**.
(T) 01267 253455.
Profile Breeder. **Ref: YH03949**

DAVIES, W D
W D Davies, Little Ease, Leddington, Dymock, **Gloucestershire**, GL18 2EG, **ENGLAND**.
(T) 01531 890631 **(F)** 01531 890631.
Contact/s
Owner: Mr W Williams
Profile Breeder. **Ref: YH03950**

DAVIES, ZOE
Zoe Davies BSc (Hons) MSc Eq.Sc., Parkside Farm, Broad Oak Lane, Mobberley, **Cheshire**, WA16 6JN, **ENGLAND**.
(T) 01565 873127.
Profile Medical Support. **Ref: YH03951**

DAVIS, J S & P A
J S & P A Davis, Lowland Farm Shop, West Mean, Petersfield, **Hampshire**, GU32 1JS, **ENGLAND**.
(T) 01730 829450.
Profile Supplies. **Ref: YH03952**

DAVIS, MEADE & PARTNERS
Davis, Meade & Partners, 8 Monmouth Pl, Bath, **Bath & Somerset (North East)**, BA1 2AU, **ENGLAND**.
(T) 01225 339700 **(F)** 01225 448761
(E) enquiries@davis-meade.co.uk
(W) www.davis-meade.co.uk.
Contact/s
Partner: Mr B Meade
Profile Estate Agents.
Estate Agents, Chartered Surveyors, Auctioneers and Valuers. **Ref: YH03953**

DAVIS, V C M
V C M Davis, The Forge, Aberystwyth, **Ceredigion**, SY23 4LL, **WALES**.
(T) 01974 261296
Affiliated Bodies WCF.
Contact/s
Owner: Mr V Davis
Profile Farrier. Yr. Est: 1971
Opening Times
Sp: Open Mon - Fri 08:30. Closed Mon - Fri 17:00.
Su: Open Mon - Fri 08:30. Closed Mon - Fri 17:00.
Au: Open Mon - Fri 08:30. Closed Mon - Fri 17:00.
Wn: Open Mon - Fri 08:30. Closed Mon - Fri 17:00.
Ref: YH03954

DAVISON VETNRY SURGEONS
Davison Veterinary Surgeons, 63-65 Ilkeston Rd, Nottingham, **Nottinghamshire**, NG7 3GR, **ENGLAND**.
(T) 0115 9786566 **(F)** 0115 9706886.
Profile Medical Support. **Ref: YH03955**

DAVISON, ANDREW PETER
Andrew Peter Davison DWCF, Garden Cottage, Wooley, Wantage, **Oxfordshire**, OX12 8NJ, **ENGLAND**.
Profile Farrier. **Ref: YH03956**

DAVISON, CATHERINE
Catherine Davison, 17 Gloucester Rd, Cirencester, **Gloucestershire**, GL7 2LB, **ENGLAND**.
(T) 01285 650275.
Profile Medical Support. **Ref: YH03957**

DAVISON, HOWARD
Howard Davison FWCF, Pandy Farm, Derwen Rd, Alltwen, Pontardawe, **Neath Port Talbot**, SA8 3AY, **WALES**.
(T) 01792 862515.
Profile Farrier. **Ref: YH03958**

DAVISON, RICHARD
Richard Davison FBHS, Combridge Farm, Combridge, Uttoxeter, **Staffordshire**, ST14 5BL, **ENGLAND**.
(T) 01889 507367.
Profile Stable/Livery, Trainer. **Ref: YH03959**

DAWE, N J
Mr N J Dawe, Chantry Cottage, Sea Lane, Kilve, Bridgwater, **Somerset**, TA5 1EG, **ENGLAND**.
(T) 01278 741457.
Profile Supplies. **Ref: YH03960**

DAWES, PHILIP A P
Philip A P Dawes RF, 12 Careswell Gardens, Idsall Green, Shifnal, **Shropshire**, TF11 8SQ, **ENGLAND**.
(T) 01952 462243.
Profile Farrier. **Ref: YH03961**

DAWSON, A
A Dawson, Moorside, 60 North End, Osmotherley, Northallerton, **Yorkshire (North)**, DL6 3BH, **ENGLAND**.
(T) 01609 883473.
Profile Farrier. **Ref: YH03962**

DAWSON, KARL
Karl Dawson DWCF, 17 Ashmore Cl, Middlewich, **Cheshire**, CW10 0QH, **ENGLAND**.
(T) 01606 836735.
Profile Farrier. **Ref: YH03963**

DAWSON, P G
Mr P G Dawson, 33 Valley Dri, Halton, **Yorkshire (West)**, LS15 7ES, **ENGLAND**.
(T) 0113 2602457.
Profile Trainer. **Ref: YH03964**

DAWSON, ROBERT
Robert Dawson, East View Cottage, Stakeford, Chappington, **Northumberland**, NE62 5UF, **ENGLAND**.
(T) 01670 852372.
Profile Farrier. **Ref: YH03965**

DAWSONSRENTALS
Dawsonsrentals Ltd, Pinfold Lane, Alltami, Mold, **Flintshire**, CH7 6NY, **WALES**.
(T) 01244 545000 **(F)** 01244 545444.
Contact/s
Branch Manager: Mr M Smith
Profile Transport/Horse Boxes. **Ref: YH03966**

DAY, H
Miss H Day, Pyleigh Court Farm, Lydeard St Lawrence, Taunton, **Somerset**, TA4 3QZ, **ENGLAND**.
(T) 01984 667229 **(F)** 01984 667428.
Profile Supplies. **Ref: YH03967**

DAY, NIGEL
Nigel Day, Manor Farm Buildings, Stoke Rd, Martock, **Somerset**, TA12 6AF, **ENGLAND**.
(T) 01935 824287.
Contact/s
Owner: Mr N Day **Ref: YH03968**

DAY, S
Mrs S Day, 4 Church Rd, Lyndon, Oakham, **Leicestershire**, LE15 8TU, **ENGLAND**.
(T) 01572 737403.
Profile Breeder. **Ref: YH03969**

DAYLESFORD STUD

Daylesford Stud, Moreton-in-Marsh, **Gloucestershire**, GL56 0YH, **ENGLAND**.
(T) 01608 658981.
Profile Breeder. **Ref: YH03970**

DAYS PET SHOP

Days Pet Shop & Saddlery Ltd, 250 Whitehall Rd, Drighlington, Bradford, **Yorkshire (West)**, BD11 1BB, **ENGLAND**.
(T) 0113 2852716 **(F)** 0113 2854744
(E) enquiries@dayspetshop.co.uk
(W) www.dayspetshop.co.uk.
Contact/s
Owner: Mr R Cook
Profile Riding Wear Retailer, Saddlery Retailer, Supplies. Yr. Est: 1978
Opening Times
Sp: Open Mon - Sat 09:00. Closed Mon - Fri 17:30, Sat 16:30.
Su: Open Mon - Sat 09:00. Closed Mon - Fri 17:30, Sat 16:30.
Au: Open Mon - Sat 09:00. Closed Mon - Fri 17:30, Sat 16:30.
Wn: Open Mon - Sat 09:00. Closed Mon - Fri 17:30, Sat 16:30.
Sun - by appointment **Ref: YH03971**

DAYTON, KYM

Kym Dayton, Wingland Farm, Walpole Marsh, Walpole St Andrew, Wisbech, **Cambridgeshire**, PE14 7JH, **ENGLAND**.
(T) 01945 780207.
Profile Breeder, Stable/Livery. **Ref: YH03972**

DE BEAUVOIR

De Beauvoir Farm Livery Yard, Church Rd, Ramsden Heath, Billericay, **Essex**, CM11 1PW, **ENGLAND**.
(T) 01268 711302.
Profile Stable/Livery. **Ref: YH03973**

DE BOIZ

De Boiz, Unit 2C Whitestone Business Pk, Saltwells Rd, Middlesbrough, **Cleveland**, TS4 2ED, **ENGLAND**.
(T) 01642 254034.
Contact/s
Owner: Mrs J Fowden
Profile Supplies. **Ref: YH03974**

DE BROMHEAD, HARRY

Harry De Bromhead, Knockeen, **County Waterford**, **IRELAND**.
(T) 051 375726.
Profile Supplies. **Ref: YH03975**

DE GILES, J A T

Mr J A T De Giles, South Farm, Stanton Fitzwarren, Swindon, **Wiltshire**, SN6 7RZ, **ENGLAND**.
(T) 01793 763094 **(F)** 01793 763094.
Profile Trainer. **Ref: YH03976**

DE GRAAFF TRAILERS

De Graaff Trailers, Langshot Stud Farm, Gracious Pond Rd, Chobham, Woking, **Surrey**, GU24 8HJ, **ENGLAND**.
(T) 01276 855566 **(F)** 01276 855577.
Contact/s
Owner: Mr A De Graaff
Profile Breeder. **Ref: YH03977**

DE HAAN, B

Mr B De Haan, Fairview, Longhedge, Lambourn, Hungerford, **Berkshire**, RG17 8NA, **ENGLAND**.
(T) 01488 72163
(M) 07831 104574.
Profile Trainer. **Ref: YH03978**

DE MONTFORT UNI

De Montfort University, School Of Agrcltrl, Caythorpe Court, Grantham, **Lincolnshire**, NG32 3EP, **ENGLAND**.
(T) 0845 9454647 **(F)** 0116 2577533
(E) enquiry@dmu.ac.uk
(W) www.dmu.ac.uk.
Profile Equestrian Centre. College.
The programme provides specialist skills in the production and training of sports horses leading to a BSc. Applicants must be able to ride to BHS/NVQ level two or above for the riding option and weigh no more than 13 stone. **Ref: YH03979**

DE SOUSA, NICOLA

Nicola de Sousa (BER), Tollgate, Shawford, Beckington, Bath, **Bath & Somerset (North East)**, BA3 6SQ, **ENGLAND**.
(T) 01373 830248. **Ref: YH03980**

DEACON, JOSEPH LYNDON

Joseph Lyndon Deacon RSS, The Rock Forge, Llanvaches, **Newport**, NP26 3AE, **WALES**.
(T) 01633 400747.
Profile Farrier. **Ref: YH03981**

DEACON, M J

M J Deacon, Hill Farm, Main St, Illston, Leicester, **Leicestershire**, LE7 9EG, **ENGLAND**.
(T) 0116 2596700 **(F)** 0116 2596700.
Contact/s
Partner: Mr M Deacon
Profile Farrier. **Ref: YH03982**

DEACON, NICHOLAS

Nicholas Deacon DWCF, 2 Velhurst Dri, Bussage, Stroud, **Gloucestershire**, GL6 8AF, **ENGLAND**.
(T) 01453 731761.
Profile Farrier. **Ref: YH03983**

DEACON, P J & K J

Mr P J & Mrs K J Deacon, 3 Middlebarn Cottages, Middlebarn Farm, Selhurst Pk, Chichester, **Sussex (West)**, PO18 0LY, **ENGLAND**.
(T) 01243 773551.
Profile Breeder. **Ref: YH03984**

DEAF HILL

Deaf Hill Riding Centre & Livery Yard, Thornley Rd, Trimdon Grange, Durham, **County Durham**, TS29 6DA, **ENGLAND**.
(T) 01429 882216.
Profile Riding School, Stable/Livery. **Ref: YH03985**

DEAKIN, SAMUEL E

Samuel E Deakin DWCF, 3 Chestnut Gr, Kirkby In Ashfield, Nottingham, **Nottinghamshire**, NG17 8BL, **ENGLAND**.
(T) 01623 722603.
Profile Farrier. **Ref: YH03986**

DEAKIN, STEWART E

Stewart E Deakin, 15 West Hill, Sutton-In-Ashfield, **Nottinghamshire**, NG17 3EP, **ENGLAND**.
(T) 01623 557987.
Contact/s
Owner: Mr S Deakin
Profile Transport/Horse Boxes. **Ref: YH03987**

DEAN CASTLE RIDING CTRE

Dean Castle Riding Centre Ltd, Assloss Rd, Dean Est, Kilmarnock, **Ayrshire (East)**, KA3 6BL, **SCOTLAND**.
(T) 01563 541123 **(F)** 01563 541123.
Contact/s
For Bookings: Miss D Jackson
Profile Arena, Riding School, Stable/Livery, Track/Course. No.Staff: 5 Yr. Est: 1983
C.Size: 50 Acres **Ref: YH03988**

DEAN RIDING STABLES

Dean Riding Stables, Lower Dean Farm, Trentishoe, Parracombe, Barnstaple, **Devon**, EX31 4PJ, **ENGLAND**.
(T) 01598 763565.
Profile Riding School, Stable/Livery. **Ref: YH03989**

DEAN, ANDREW M

Andrew M Dean DWCF, 17 Blackthorne Green, Colden Common, Winchester, **Hampshire**, SO21 1WL, **ENGLAND**.
(T) 01962 715034.
Profile Farrier. **Ref: YH03990**

DEAN, GEOFF

Geoff Dean, Kings Parade, 154 Findon Rd, Worthing, **Sussex (West)**, BN14 0EL, **ENGLAND**.
(T) 01903 264066
(E) geoff@geoff-dean.com
(W) www.geoff-dean.freeserve.co.uk.
Contact/s
Owner: Mr G Dean
Profile Saddler.
A Master member of the Society of Master Saddlers. His speciality is harness making. A catalogue is available on the website, and a 20% deposit is required with each order. Yr. Est: 1970 **Ref: YH03991**

DEAN, J G

Mr J G Dean, Cliff Ash Farm, Idridgehay, **Derbyshire**, DE4 4JE, **ENGLAND**.
(T) 01773 550300.
Profile Breeder. **Ref: YH03992**

DEAN, MARTYN

Martyn Dean, Jacks Bush, Lopcombe, Salisbury, **Wiltshire**, SP5 1BZ, **ENGLAND**.
(T) 01264 782200 **(F)** 01264 782200.
Contact/s
Owner: Mr M Dean
Profile Blacksmith. **Ref: YH03993**

DEAN, P

Mr & Mrs P Dean, Kirkhouse, Brampton, **Cumbria**, CA8 1JR, **ENGLAND**.
(T) 01697 746262 **(F)** 01697 746262.
Profile Breeder. **Ref: YH03994**

DEAN, RICHARD

Mr Richard Dean, Judge Hse Farm, Grafty Green, Maidstone, **Kent**, ME17 2AY, **ENGLAND**.
(T) 01622 850230.
Profile Supplies. **Ref: YH03995**

DEAN, ROGER S

Roger S Dean RSS, 49 Arundel Rd, Mount Pleasant, Newhaven, **Sussex (East)**, BN9 0NF, **ENGLAND**.
(T) 01273 517720.
Profile Farrier. **Ref: YH03996**

DEAN, T S

T S Dean, Heath Lodge Vetnry Hospital, St Bernards Rd, St Albans, **Hertfordshire**, AL3 5RA, **ENGLAND**.
(T) 01727 835294.
Profile Medical Support. **Ref: YH03997**

DEANDANE RIDING STABLES

Deandane Riding Stables, 397 Gathurst Rd, Shevington, Wigan, **Lancashire**, WN6 8JB, **ENGLAND**.
(T) 01257 253086 **(F)** 01257 253086
Affiliated Bodies ABRS, BHS.
Contact/s
Owner: Mr M Whalley
Profile Riding School.
Hacking is available. Lessons cost £13.00 for 45 minutes. No.Staff: 3 Yr. Est: 1966
Opening Times
Sp: Open Tues - Sun 10:00. Closed Tues - Fri 17:00, Sat, Sun 20:00.
Su: Open Tues - Sun 10:00. Closed Tues - Fri 17:00, Sat, Sun 20:00.
Au: Open Tues - Sun 10:00. Closed Tues - Fri 17:00, Sat, Sun 20:00.
Wn: Open Tues - Sun 10:00. Closed Tues - Fri 17:00, Sat, Sun 20:00.
Closed on Mondays **Ref: YH03998**

DEANE VETNRY CTRE

Deane Veterinary Centre, Wellington New Rd, Taunton, **Somerset**, TA1 5LU, **ENGLAND**.
(T) 01823 73722.
Profile Medical Support. **Ref: YH03999**

DEANE, A B

A B Deane, Bishops Down Stud Farm, Dundridge Lane, Bishops Waltham, Southampton, **Hampshire**, SO32 1GD, **ENGLAND**.
(T) 01489 893535.
Contact/s
Partner: Mrs M Deane
Profile Breeder. **Ref: YH04000**

DEARING, R

R Dearing, Manor Farm, Wilfholme, Driffield, **Yorkshire (East)**, YO25 9BQ, **ENGLAND**.
(T) 01377 270264.
Contact/s
Owner: Mr R Dearing
Profile Breeder.
Horse Supplier
Opening Times
By appointment **Ref: YH04001**

DEB GROVES ANIMAL FEEDS

Deb Groves Animal Feeds, Watching Well, Yarmouth Rd, Calbourne, **Isle of Wight**, PO30 4HZ, **ENGLAND**.
(T) 01983 531554.
Contact/s
Owner: Mrs D Groves
Profile Feed Merchant. **Ref: YH04002**

DEBDALE EQUINE CTRE

Debdale Equine Centre, Debdale Farm, Cookley, Kidderminster, **Worcestershire**, DY11 5YA, **ENGLAND**.
(T) 01562 850662.
Contact/s
Owner: Mr M Share
Profile Equestrian Centre. **Ref: YH04003**

DEBDALE HORSES

Debdale Horses, Chestnut Farm, Hallaton Rd, East Norton, Leicester, **Leicestershire**, LE7 9XF, **ENGLAND**.
(T) 01858 555795.

Contact/s
General Manager: Mrs M Cripps
Profile Equestrian Centre, Riding Club, Stable/Livery.
Yr. Est: 1987 C.Size: 20 Acres Ref: YH04004

DEBOIZ

Deboiz, Roman Castle Barn, Pickhill, Thirsk, **Yorkshire (North)**, YO7 4JR, **ENGLAND**.
(T) 01845 567840 (F) 01845 567840.
Contact/s
Partner: Mr S Fowden
Profile Supplies. Ref: YH04005

DEBROMHEAD, HARRY

Harry Debromhead, Knockeen, **County Waterford**, **IRELAND**.
(T) 051 375726.
Profile Trainer. Ref: YH04006

DECAL FORM

Decal Form Ltd, Unit G Boyn Valley Ind Est, Maidenhead, **Berkshire**, SL6 4EJ, **ENGLAND**.
(T) 01628 673833 (F) 01628 784002.
Profile Club/Association. Ref: YH04007

DECATHLON SPORTS & LEISURE

Decathlon UK Ltd, Georges Rd, Stockport, **Cheshire**, SK4 1DN, **ENGLAND**.
(T) 0161 4769600 (F) 0161 4769601
(W) www.decathlon.com.
Contact/s
Manager: Mr G Morgan
Profile Riding Wear Retailer, Saddlery Retailer.
Wide range of French and other international brands
Yr. Est: 1999
Opening Times
Sp: Open Mon - Fri 09:30, Sat 09:00, Sun 10:30. Closed Mon - Fri 20:00, Sat 19:00, Sun 16:30.
Su: Open Mon - Fri 09:30, Sat 09:00, Sun 10:30. Closed Mon - Fri 20:00, Sat 19:00, Sun 16:30.
Au: Open Mon - Fri 09:30, Sat 09:00, Sun 10:30. Closed Mon - Fri 20:00, Sat 19:00, Sun 16:30.
Wn: Open Mon - Fri 09:30, Sat 09:00, Sun 10:30. Closed Mon - Fri 20:00, Sat 19:00, Sun 16:30.
Ref: YH04008

DECATHLON SPORTS & LEISURE

Decathlon UK Ltd, Surrey Quays Rd, London, **London (Greater)**, SE16 2XU, **ENGLAND**.
(T) 020 23942000 (F) 020 73942010
(W) www.decathlon.com.
Contact/s
Manager: Mr E Poulet
Profile Riding Wear Retailer, Saddlery Retailer.
Wide range of French and other international brands
Yr. Est: 1999
Opening Times
Sp: Open Mon - Fri 10:00, Sat 09:00, Sun 11:00. Closed Mon - Thurs 19:30, Fri 20:00, Sat 19:00, Sun 17:00.
Su: Open Mon - Fri 10:00, Sat 09:00, Sun 11:00. Closed Mon - Thurs 19:30, Fri 20:00, Sat 19:00, Sun 17:00.
Au: Open Mon - Fri 10:00, Sat 09:00, Sun 11:00. Closed Mon - Thurs 19:30, Fri 20:00, Sat 19:00, Sun 17:00.
Wn: Open Mon - Fri 10:00, Sat 09:00, Sun 11:00. Closed Mon - Thurs 19:30, Fri 20:00, Sat 19:00, Sun 17:00.
Cafe opens at 08:45 on weekdays and is open on Saturday mornings Ref: YH04009

DECATHLON SPORTS & LEISURE

Decathlon UK Ltd, Ikea Retail Pk, Nottingham, **Nottinghamshire**, NG16 2RP, **ENGLAND**.
(T) 0115 9382020 (F) 0115 9387100
(W) www.decathlon.com.
Contact/s
Manager: Mr R Davies
Profile Riding Wear Retailer, Saddlery Retailer.
Wide range of French and other international brands
Yr. Est: 2000
Opening Times
Sp: Open Mon - Fri 10:00, Sat 09:00, Sun 11:00. Closed Mon - Fri 20:00, Sat 19:00, Sun 17:00.
Su: Open Mon - Fri 10:00, Sat 09:00, Sun 11:00. Closed Mon - Fri 20:00, Sat 19:00, Sun 17:00.
Au: Open Mon - Fri 10:00, Sat 09:00, Sun 11:00. Closed Mon - Fri 20:00, Sat 19:00, Sun 17:00.
Wn: Open Mon - Fri 10:00, Sat 09:00, Sun 11:00. Closed Mon - Fri 20:00, Sat 19:00, Sun 17:00.
Open Bank Holiday Mondays 10:00 - 18:00
Ref: YH04010

DECKER, P

P Decker, Stud Farm, Skirmett, Henley-on-Thames, **Oxfordshire**, RG9 6TD, **ENGLAND**.
(T) 01491 638460.
Contact/s
Owner: Miss P Decker
Profile Breeder. Ref: YH04011

DECOY POND FARM

Decoy Pond Farm, Beaulieu Rd, Beaulieu, Brockenhurst, **Hampshire**, SO42 7YQ, **ENGLAND**.
(T) 023 80292652.
Contact/s
Owner: Mr D Horton
Profile Stable/Livery, Track/Course. Ref: YH04012

DECOY POND SADDLERY

Decoy Pond Saddlery, Decoy Pond Farm, Beaulieu Rd, Beaulieu, **Hampshire**, SO42 7QL, **ENGLAND**.
(T) 023 80292652.
Profile Saddlery Retailer. Ref: YH04013

DEE FARM LIVERY STABLES

Dee Farm Livery Stables, Dee Farm, Laver, Heswell, Wirral, **Merseyside**, CH60 9JL, **ENGLAND**.
(T) 0151 3423905.
Contact/s
Owner: Mr E Waites
Profile Stable/Livery. Yr. Est: 1970
Opening Times
Sp: Open 09:00. Closed 18:00.
Su: Open 09:00. Closed 18:00.
Au: Open 09:00. Closed 18:00.
Wn: Open 09:00. Closed 18:00. Ref: YH04014

DEEBLE, BEN

Ben Deeble, 1 Challacombe Cottages, Postbridge, Yelverton, **Devon**, PL20 6TD, **ENGLAND**.
(T) 01822 880297.
Contact/s
Owner: Mr B Deeble
Profile Farrier. Ref: YH04015

DEEJAY ANIMAL FEED CTRE

Deejay Animal Feed Centre, Crown Farm Barn, Mill Rd, Burston, Diss, **Norfolk**, IP22 3TW, **ENGLAND**.
(T) 01379 741202.
Profile Feed Merchant, Supplies. Ref: YH04016

DEELEYS

Deeleys, Primary Works, Thorney Lanes, Hoar Cross, Burton-on-Trent, **Staffordshire**, DE13 8QT, **ENGLAND**.
(T) 01283 575268 (F) 01283 575369.
Contact/s
Owner: Ms L Deeley
Profile Transport/Horse Boxes. Ref: YH04017

DEEN CITY FARM

Deen City Farm, 39 Windsor Ave, Merton Abbey, London, **London (Greater)**, SW19 2RR, **ENGLAND**.
(T) 020 85435858.
Profile Riding School. Ref: YH04018

DEENY'S

Deeny's, 123 Learmount Rd, Ballyrory, Claudy, **County Londonderry**, BT47 4AL, **NORTHERN IRELAND**.
(T) 028 71338229 (F) 028 71338039.
Profile Saddlery Retailer. Ref: YH04019

DEEP WATER EQUITATION CTRE

Deep Water Equitation Centre, Deepwater, Dalskairth, Dumfries, **Dumfries and Galloway**, DG2 8ND, **SCOTLAND**.
(T) 01387 268311.
Contact/s
Owner: Mr J Slade
Profile Riding School, Saddlery Retailer.
Ref: YH04020

DEEPDENE STABLES

Deepdene Stables, Ashford Rd, Badlesmere Lees, Faversham, **Kent**, ME13 0NZ, **ENGLAND**.
(T) 01233 740228.
Contact/s
Owner: Mrs N Sunley
Profile Farrier, Riding School. Ref: YH04021

DEEPMILL STUD

Deepmill Stud, Deep Mill Farm, London Rd, Great Missenden, **Buckinghamshire**, HP16 0DH, **ENGLAND**.
(T) 01494 793800.
Profile Breeder. Ref: YH04022

DEER PARK RIDING STABLES

Deer Park Riding Stables, White Cliff Mill St, Blandford Forum, **Dorset**, DT11 7BN, **ENGLAND**.
(T) 01258 453283.
Contact/s
Assistant: Mrs D Kimber
Profile Riding School, Stable/Livery. Ref: YH04023

DEFENCE CLOTHING & TEXTILE

Defence Clothing & Textile Agency, Ministry Of Defence, Dct 7, Qpsd, Didcot, **Oxfordshire**, OX11 7HG, **ENGLAND**.
(T) 01235 513568 (F) 01235 815191.
Profile Saddlery Retailer. Ref: YH04024

DEFRA

Department for Environment, Food and Rural Affairs, Nobel Hse, 17 Smith Sq, London, **London (Greater)**, SW1P 3JR, **ENGLAND**.
(T) 020 72386000 (F) 020 72386591
(W) www.defra.gov.uk.
Profile Club/Association.
Taken over responsibility from M.A.F.F. Has responsibility for environmental issues, rural development, countryside, wildlife, animal welfare, hunting and many other issues.
Opening Times
Sp: Open Mon - Fri 09:00. Closed Mon - Fri 17:00.
Su: Open Mon - Fri 09:00. Closed Mon - Fri 17:00.
Au: Open Mon - Fri 09:00. Closed Mon - Fri 17:00.
Wn: Open Mon - Fri 09:00. Closed Mon - Fri 17:00.
Ref: YH04025

DEGE & SKINNER

Dege & Skinner, 10 Saville Row, London, **London (Greater)**, W1X 1AF, **ENGLAND**.
(T) 020 72872941 (F) 020 77348794
(E) info@dege-skinner.co.uk
(W) www.dege-skinner.co.uk.
Profile Riding Wear Retailer.
The company holds the Royal Warrant of Appointment to H.M. Queen Elizabeth II. Yr. Est: 1840
Opening Times
Mon - Fri 09:15 - 17:15, Sat 09:30 - 12:30, except for Public Holidays. Ref: YH04026

DELAHOOKE, JAMES STUART

James Stuart Delahooke, The Old Rectory, Barningham, Richmond, **Yorkshire (North)**, DL11 7DW, **ENGLAND**.
(T) 01833 621251 (F) 01833 621421.
Profile Blood Stock Agency. Ref: YH04027

DELAMERE COTTAGE STABLES

Delamere Cottage Stables, Folly Rd, Lambourn, Hungerford, **Berkshire**, RG17 8QE, **ENGLAND**.
(T) 01488 73999 (F) 01488 73888.
Contact/s
Owner: Mr K McAuliffe
Profile Trainer. Ref: YH04028

DELAWARE VETNRY GRP

Delaware Veterinary Group, Fulford Hse, Torbay Rd, Castle Cary, **Somerset**, BA7 7DT, **ENGLAND**.
(T) 01963 350307 (F) 01963 350396.
Profile Medical Support. Ref: YH04029

DELBRIDGE, G L

G L Delbridge, Comb & Cutter Resharpening Sv, Timberscombe, Minehead, **Somerset**, TA24 7TL, **ENGLAND**.
(T) 01643 841329.
Contact/s
Owner: Mrs D Delbridge
Profile Supplies. Ref: YH04030

DELL PK FARM

Dell Park Farm, Wick Lane, Englefield Green, Egham, **Surrey**, TW20 0XN, **ENGLAND**.
(T) 01784 436666.
Contact/s
Owner: Miss A Stone
Profile Stable/Livery. Ref: YH04031

DELL, STEPHEN

Stephen Dell DWCF, 20 The Green, Somerleyton, Lowestoft, **Suffolk**, NR32 5PY, **ENGLAND**.
(T) 01502 732036.
Profile Farrier. Ref: YH04032

DELOWEN LIVERY YARD

Delowen Livery Yard, 18 Queen St, Derby, **Derbyshire**, DE1 3DS, **ENGLAND**.
(T) 01332 842622.
Profile Stable/Livery. Ref: YH04033

DELROSA QUARTER HORSES

Delrosa Quarter Horses, Rose Cottage, Coombes Moor, Byton, Presteigne, **Powys**, LD8 2HY, **WALES**.
(T) 01544 267120.
Profile Breeder. Ref: YH04034

DELTA BLOOD STOCK MNGMT

Delta Blood Stock Management, 8 Belmont Ct, Newmarket, **Suffolk**, CB8 9BP, **ENGLAND**.
(T) 01638 668065.

A-Z of COMPANIES

Profile Blood Stock Agency, Breeder. Ref: YH04035

DELTA CONSTRUCTION
Delta Construction, Squires Farm, Easons Green, Uckfield, **Sussex (East)**, TN22 5RD, **ENGLAND**.
(T) 01825 840641 **(F)** 01825 840850.
Profile Stabling Construction. Ref: YH04036

DELTA ENGINEERING
Delta Engineering Co, Rear Of Fulwood Row, Ribbleton, Preston, **Lancashire**, PR2 6SL, **ENGLAND**.
(T) 01772 700713 **(F)** 01772 701138.
Profile Transport/Horse Boxes. Ref: YH04037

DELYSIA STUD STABLES
Delysia Stud Stables, Carpenters Rd, Brading, Sandown, **Isle of Wight**, PO36 0QA, **ENGLAND**.
(T) 01983 811404.
Contact/s
Owner: Mrs S Charlesworth
Profile Breeder. Ref: YH04038

DENBY RIDING STABLES
Denby Riding Stables, Denby Farm, Nanstallon, Bodmin, **Cornwall**, PL30 5LG, **ENGLAND**.
(T) 01208 72013 **(F)** 01208 72013.
Contact/s
Partner: Mrs D Moore
Profile Riding School, Stable/Livery. Ref: YH04039

DENCHWORTH
Denchworth Equestrian Supplies, Little Circourt, Denchworth, Wantage, **Oxfordshire**, OX12 0EB, **ENGLAND**.
(T) 01235 868175.
Profile Saddlery Retailer. Ref: YH04040

DENE COUNTRY STORES
Dene Country Stores, Iron Hill, Hollycombe, Liphook, **Hampshire**, GU30 7LP, **ENGLAND**.
(T) 01428 725137 **(F)** 01428 725091.
Profile Saddlery Retailer. Ref: YH04041

DENE HEAD LIVERY
Dene Head Livery, Dene Head Farm, Whiley Hill, Coatham Mundeville, Darlington, **County Durham**, DL3 0XN, **ENGLAND**.
(T) 01325 300448 **(F)** 01325 304374.
Contact/s
Owner: Mr S Middleton
Profile Arena, Blacksmith, Stable/Livery.
Yr. Est: 1999 C.Size: 30 Acres
Opening Times
Sp: Open 07:00. Closed 22:00.
Su: Open 07:00. Closed 22:00.
Au: Open 07:00. Closed 22:00.
Wn: Open 07:00. Closed 22:00. Ref: YH04042

DENE STUD
Dene Stud, Todridge, Great Whittington, **Tyne and Wear**, NE19 2HP, **ENGLAND**.
(T) 01434 672218.
Profile Breeder. Ref: YH04043

DENEWEAR
Denewear, Farm Farm, Higher Wraxall, Dorchester, **Dorset**, DT2 0HR, **ENGLAND**.
(T) 01935 83638 **(F)** 01935 83762
(E) mikedene@denewear.demon.co.uk.
Profile Supplies. Ref: YH04044

DENGIE
Dengie Crops Ltd, Heybridge Business Ctre, 110 The Causeway, Heybridge, Maldon, **Essex**, CM9 4ND, **ENGLAND**.
(T) 01621 841188 **(F)** 01621 842111
(E) feeds@dengie.com
(W) www.dengie.com.
Profile Feed Merchant. Ref: YH04045

DENHOLM, LESLIE
Leslie Denholm DWCF, 161 West Mainstreet, Whitburn, **Lothian (West)**, EH47 0QQ, **SCOTLAND**.
(T) 01501 745932.
Profile Farrier. Ref: YH04046

DENIS BRINICOMBE NUTRITION
Denis Brinicombe Nutrition, Fordton Ind Est, Crediton, **Devon**, EX17 3BZ, **ENGLAND**.
(T) 01363 775115 **(F)** 01363 772114.
Profile Medical Support. Ref: YH04047

DENMAR SUPPLIES
Denmar Supplies, Walford Lodge, Walford, Baschurch, Shrewsbury, **Shropshire**, SY4 2HL, **ENGLAND**.
(T) 01939 260471.
Profile Supplies. Ref: YH04048

DENMILL HIGHLAND PONY STUD
Denmill Highland Pony Stud, Tough, Alford, **Aberdeenshire**, AB33 8EP, **SCOTLAND**.
(T) 01975 562582 **(F)** 01975 562582
(E) denmill@highland-pony.demon.co.uk.
Profile Breeder. Ref: YH04049

DENMILL STABLES
Denmill Stables & Glenprosen Riding Centre, Denmill, Kirriemuir, **Angus**, DD8 5QQ, **SCOTLAND**.
(T) 01575 572757.
Profile Riding School. Ref: YH04050

DENNETT & PARKER
Dennett & Parker Ltd, Sydney Nursery, Dover Rd, Sandwich, **Kent**, CT13 0DA, **ENGLAND**.
(T) 01304 613240.
Contact/s
Partner: Mr D Parker
Profile Transport/Horse Boxes. Ref: YH04051

DENNIS, ANDREW F
Andrew F Dennis DWCF, Quantock Cottage, Hilltop Lane, Kilve, Bridgwater, **Somerset**, TA5 1SR, **ENGLAND**.
(T) 01278 741655
(M) 07768 210658.
Profile Farrier. Ref: YH04052

DENNIS, CHRISTOPHER J
Christopher J Dennis, Crosspass Hse, Lingerfield, Knaresborough, **Yorkshire (North)**, HG5 9JA, **ENGLAND**.
(T) 01423 864707 **(F)** 01423 864707
(E) c.j.dennis@btinternet.com. Ref: YH04053

DENNIS, EDWARD F
Edward F Dennis DWCF, 4 Bridgewater Pl, Leybourne, Maidstone, **Kent**, ME20 5QS, **ENGLAND**.
(T) 01732 822747.
Profile Farrier. Ref: YH04054

DENNIS, JUDY
Judy Dennis, Hamsterley Riding School & Livery Stables, Hamsterley, Bishop Auckland, **County Durham**, DL13 3NH, **ENGLAND**.
(T) 01388 488328
Affiliated Bodies ABRS.
Contact/s
Owner: Mrs J Dennis
Profile Riding School, Stable/Livery.
Teach children from the age of 3 upwards.
Opening Times
Telephone for an appointment Ref: YH04055

DENNIS, W W
Mr W W Dennis, Thorne Farm, Bude, **Cornwall**, EX23 0LU, **ENGLAND**.
(T) 01288 352849 **(F)** 01288 352849
(M) 07971 946011.
Profile Supplies. Ref: YH04056

DENNISON TRAILERS
Dennison Trailers Ltd, Caton Rd, Lancaster, **Lancashire**, LA1 3PE, **ENGLAND**.
(T) 01524 381808.
Profile Transport/Horse Boxes. Ref: YH04057

DENNISON, PAUL EDWARD
Paul Edward Dennison, 4 Greenside, Kirkby Lonsdale, Carnforth, **Lancashire**, LA6 2DQ, **ENGLAND**.
(T) 01524 272017.
Profile Farrier. Ref: YH04058

DENNIS'S SADDLERY/RIDING WEAR
Dennis's Saddlery & Riding Wear Ltd, Unit 21, Fleet Marston Farm, Fleet Marston, Aylesbury, **Buckinghamshire**, HP18 0PZ, **ENGLAND**.
(T) 01296 658660.
Contact/s
Manageress: Miss S Wallington
Profile Riding Wear Retailer, Saddlery Retailer.
Ref: YH04059

DENNIS'S SADDLERY/RIDING WEAR
Dennis's Saddlery & Riding Wear Ltd, 75 High St, Aylesbury, **Buckinghamshire**, HP20 1SA, **ENGLAND**.
(T) 01296 484752.
Profile Riding Wear Retailer, Saddlery Retailer.
Ref: YH04060

DENNY, D J B
D J B Denny B Vet Med MRCVS, 205 Henwick Rd, Worcester, **Worcestershire**, WR2 5PG, **ENGLAND**.
(T) 01905 424374.
Profile Medical Support. Ref: YH04061

DENNY, J E
J E Denny, 9 Market Cl, Brushford, Dulverton, **Somerset**, TA22 9AG, **ENGLAND**.
(T) 01398 323747.
Profile Farrier. Ref: YH04062

DENNY, L
Mrs L Denny, Foxcote Ct, Moreton-in-Marsh, **Gloucestershire**, GL56 0NJ, **ENGLAND**.
(T) 01608 650515.
Profile Breeder, Track/Course, Trainer. Ref: YH04063

DENSEM, R G
R G Densem, Old Hall Cottages, Birtles, Macclesfield, **Cheshire**, SK10 4RS, **ENGLAND**.
(T) 01625 861416.
Profile Breeder. Ref: YH04064

DENTEX (NORTH WEST)
Dentex (North West) Limited, 2-14 Mill St, Glossop, **Derbyshire**, SK13 8PT, **ENGLAND**.
(T) 01457 860456 **(F)** 01457 856963
(E) sales@new-dentex.co.uk
(W) www.new-dentex.co.uk.
Contact/s
Owner: Mr B Bramhall
Profile Supplies.
Drainage membranes and riding surfaces for arenas.
Ref: YH04065

DENTON RIDING CTRE
Denton Riding Centre, 93A Main St, Irton, Scarborough, **Yorkshire (North)**, YO12 4RJ, **ENGLAND**.
(T) 01723 863466.
Contact/s
Secretary: Mrs R Denton
Profile Farrier, Riding School. Ref: YH04066

DENTON VETNRY SURGERY
Denton Veterinary Surgery, 30 Denton Rd, Wokingham, **Berkshire**, RG11 2DX, **ENGLAND**.
(T) 0118 9781325.
Profile Medical Support. Ref: YH04067

DENTON, ROGER C
Roger C Denton, College Farmhouse, East Garston, Hungerford, **Berkshire**, RG17 7EX, **ENGLAND**.
(T) 01488 648904.
Profile Breeder. Ref: YH04068

DENYER, I D & C R M
I D & C R M Denyer, Haven Lodge, Cove, Tiverton, **Devon**, EX16 7RU, **ENGLAND**.
(T) 01398 331825.
Contact/s
Owner: Mr I Denyer
Profile Transport/Horse Boxes. Ref: YH04069

DEONE HART
Deone Hart Ltd, Worthy End Farm, Hornes End Rd, Flitwick, Bedford, **Bedfordshire**, MK45 1JL, **ENGLAND**.
(T) 01525 714469/712546.
Contact/s
Owner: Mrs B Smith
Profile Breeder. Horse Dealer.
Horses can be supplied to personal specifications.
Yr. Est: 1977
Opening Times
By appointment only Ref: YH04070

DERBY HSE SADDLERY
Derby House Saddlery Ltd, Newburgh, Parbold, Wigan, **Lancashire**, WN8 7NG, **ENGLAND**.
(T) 01257 462228 **(F)** 01257 464421
(W) www.equestrianmailorder.co.uk.
Contact/s
General Manager: Mr P Dickson
(E) sales@derbyhousesaddlery.co.uk
Profile Riding Wear Retailer, Saddlery Retailer, Supplies. No.Staff: 25 Yr. Est: 1968
Opening Times
Sp: Open 09:00. Closed 17:30.
Su: Open 09:00. Closed 17:30.
Au: Open 09:00. Closed 17:30.
Wn: Open 09:00. Closed 17:30. Ref: YH04071

DEREHAM CONVERSIONS
Dereham Conversions Ltd, Unit 3 52 London Rd, Dereham, **Norfolk**, NR19 1DF, **ENGLAND**.
(T) 01362 699977 **(F)** 01362 699977.
Profile Transport/Horse Boxes. Ref: YH04072

DEREHAM SADDLERY
Dereham Saddlery, The Chapel, Norwich Rd, Dereham, **Norfolk**, NR20 3AS, **ENGLAND**.
(T) 01362 692143.

Contact/s
Owner: Mr J Sayer
Profile Saddlery Retailer. Ref:YH04073

DEREK POINTON

Derek Pointon & Co, Harvest Hill Lane, Meriden, Coventry, **Midlands (West)**, CV7 7HW, **ENGLAND**.
(T) 01676 523456 (F) 01676 523455.
Profile Transport/Horse Boxes. Ref:YH04074

DERELOCHY SADDLER

Derelochy Saddler, Derelochy, Kingsteps, Lochloy Rd, Nairn, **Highlands**, IV12 5LF, **SCOTLAND**.
(T) 01667 452317 (F) 01667 452317.
Contact/s
Owner: Miss A Milne
Profile Saddlery Retailer. Ref:YH04075

DERMAX

Dermax, Unit G 7 Craigend Pl, Glasgow, **Glasgow (City of)**, G13 2UN, **SCOTLAND**.
(T) 0141 4005885 (F) 0141 4005886.
Contact/s
Owner: Mr G McAllister
Profile Blacksmith. Ref:YH04076

DERMAX IND SVS

Dermax Industrial Services, 31 Dalsholm Ave, Glasgow, **Glasgow (City of)**, G20 0TS, **SCOTLAND**.
(T) 0141 9466036 (F) 0141 9468111.
Contact/s
Owner: Mr G McAllister
Profile Blacksmith. Ref:YH04077

DERRINSTOWN STUD

Derrinstown Stud, Maynooth, **County Kildare**, **IRELAND**.
(T) 01 6286228 (F) 01 6286733
(E) info@derrinstown-stud.ie
(W) www.derrinstown-stud.com.
Contact/s
General Manager: Mr H De Burgh
Profile Breeder.
Derrinstown has its own resident vet. No.Staff: 83
Yr. Est: 1982 C.Size: 2000 Acres Ref:YH04078

DERRY & ANTRIM

Derry & Antrim Driving Club Ltd, 134 Portglenone Rd, Randalstown, Antrim, **County Antrim**, BT41 3EN, **NORTHERN IRELAND**.
(T) 028 94473706.
Contact/s
Chairman: Mr A McConnell
Profile Club/Association. Ref:YH04079

DERRYVARROGE STUD

Derryvarroge Stud, Donadea, Naas, **County Kildare**, **IRELAND**.
(T) 045 869005
(E) derryvarrogestud@kildarehorse.ie.
Contact/s
Key Contact: Mr J Jordan
Profile Breeder. Ref:YH04080

DERWENT OF LEEDS

Derwent of Leeds Ltd, Domestic Rd, Holbeck, **Yorkshire (West)**, LS12 6HS, **ENGLAND**.
(T) 0113 2443000 (F) 0113 2341033.
Contact/s
Manager: Mr J Welsh
Profile Saddlery Retailer. Ref:YH04081

DERWENTOAK RIDING CTRE

Derwentoak Riding Centre, Hagg Farm, Rowlands Gill, **Tyne and Wear**, NE39 1ND, **ENGLAND**.
(T) 01207 542140.
Profile Riding School. Ref:YH04082

DESIGN SVS

Design Services, Main St, Malham, Skipton, **Yorkshire (North)**, BD23 4DA, **ENGLAND**.
(T) 01729 830407 (F) 01729 830407.
Contact/s
Owner: Mr P Mason
Profile Blacksmith. Ref:YH04083

DESIGNER BROWBANDS

Designer Browbands, 186 Rayleigh Rd, Benfleet, **Essex**, SS7 3YP, **ENGLAND**.
(T) 01702 559876 (F) 01702 551765
(E) sales@designerbrowbands.co.uk
(W) www.designerbrowbands.co.uk.
Contact/s
Owner: Miss G Rassaelli
Profile Supplies. Ref:YH04084

DEVANEY, JOSEPH

Devaney Joseph, Frankford, Enniscrone, **County Mayo**, **IRELAND**.
(T) 096 36535.
Profile Supplies. Ref:YH04085

DEVANEYS

Devaneys, Eglinton St, Galway, **County Galway**, **IRELAND**.
(T) 091 539087.
Profile Supplies. Ref:YH04086

DEVENISH PITT

Devenish Pitt Riding School, Devenish Pitt, Honiton, **Devon**, EX24 6EG, **ENGLAND**.
(T) 01404 871355
(E) enqs@devenish-pittridingschool.co.uk
(W) www.devenish-pitt-ridingschool.co.uk
Affiliated Bodies BHS.
Contact/s
Owner: Mrs M Banks
Profile Horse/Rider Accom, Riding School.
Self catering cottages sleeping up to 6 people are available. Visitors have the use of a large garden to relax and enjoy the views. Devenish Pitt offers hacks and lessons from a friendly team of very experienced, qualified instructors. Regular riders can join the BHS Riding Proficiency Scheme, working towards different levels, receiving certificates and badges once these levels are achieved. The farm has many animals and pets, which willing volunteers can help to feed and look after. C.Size: 260 Acres
Opening Times
The riding school is normally closed on Mondays and Tuesdays, but will be open most Bank Holidays
Ref:YH04087

DEVEREUX, ADRIAN J

Adrian J Devereux DWCF, Heathfield, Thursley Rd, Elstead, **Surrey**, GU8 6EB, **ENGLAND**.
(T) 01252 703854.
Profile Farrier. Ref:YH04088

DEVICES WALKS & TALKS

Devices Walks & Talks, Canal Forge/Lower Wharf, Northgate St, Devizes, **Wiltshire**, SN10 1JN, **ENGLAND**.
(T) 01380 721759.
Contact/s
Owner: Mr J Girvan
Profile Blacksmith. Ref:YH04089

DEVILS HORSEMEN

Devils Horsemen (The), Wychwood Stud, Salden, Mursley, Milton Keynes, **Buckinghamshire**, MK17 0HX, **ENGLAND**.
(T) 01296 720854 (F) 01296 720855
(W) www.devilshorsemen.com.
Contact/s
For Bookings: Ms J Crow
(E) jo@thedevilshorsemen.com
Profile Breeder. Stunt Shows.
Gerard and Daniel Naprous have both worked with many famous people in film and television, including 'Last of the Summer Wine' and 'Jane Eyre', and many more. They have many horses to suit all needs, and have tack and carriages for period films and wild west shows. No.Staff: 3 Ref:YH04090

DEVIZES TRAILER CTRE

Devizes Trailer Centre, London Rd, Devizes, **Wiltshire**, SN10 2EP, **ENGLAND**.
(T) 01380 721758.
Contact/s
Owner: Mr A Card
Profile Transport/Horse Boxes. Ref:YH04091

DEVON & CORNWALL FARMS

West Devon & North Cornwall Farmers, West Devon Business Pk, Brook Rd, Tavistock, **Devon**, PL19 9DP, **ENGLAND**.
(T) 01822 614176 (F) 01822 614826.
Profile Supplies. Ref:YH04092

DEVON & SOMERSET STAGHOUNDS

Devon & Somerset Staghounds, Leigh, 42 Tower Hill, Williton, Taunton, **Somerset**, TA4 4NU, **ENGLAND**.
(T) 01984 632667.
Profile Club/Association. Ref:YH04093

DEVON EQUESTRIAN

Devon Equestrian Centre, Fishcross, Alloa, **Clackmannanshire**, FK10 3AN, **SCOTLAND**.
(T) 01259 769888 (F) 01259 769888
(W) www.clacksleisure.co.uk/facilities/dec.php
Affiliated Bodies BHS.
Profile Equestrian Centre.
Training and competition facilities and lessons given to people with own horses No.Staff: 11
C.Size: 100 Acres
Opening Times
Sp: Open Mon - Sun 09:00. Closed Mon - Sun 21:00.
Su: Open Mon - Sun 09:00. Closed Mon - Sun 21:00.
Au: Open Mon - Sun 09:00. Closed Mon - Sun 21:00.
Wn: Open Mon - Sun 09:00. Closed Mon - Sun 21:00. Ref:YH04094

DEVON HORSE & PONY SANCTUARY

Devon Horse & Pony Sanctuary, Hillside Cottage, Manaton, Newton Abbot, **Devon**, TQ13 9UY, **ENGLAND**.
(T) 01647 221209
(E) sanctuary@freeuk.com.
Contact/s
Key Contact: Mr T Phillips
Profile Welfare Centre.
Provide a home to retired, rescued and elderly horses, ponies and donkeys. Donations and legacies are always urgently needed to care for the residential animals. Yr. Est: 1976 Ref:YH04095

DEWDNEY, DEREK BARRIE

Derek Barrie Dewdney RSS, 107 Harpsden Rd, Henley-on-Thames, **Oxfordshire**, RG9 1ED, **ENGLAND**.
(T) 01491 572155.
Profile Farrier. Ref:YH04096

DEWHURST STABLING

Dewhurst Stabling, Dewhurst Farm, Wadhurst, **Sussex (East)**, TN5 6QE, **ENGLAND**.
(T) 01892 782494.
Profile Stabling. Ref:YH04097

DEWLAND SHETLAND PONY STUD

Dewland Shetland Pony Stud, Andross Manor, Ropley, **Hampshire**, SO24 0BZ, **ENGLAND**.
(T) 01962 773384 (F) 01962 773384.
Profile Breeder. Ref:YH04098

DEXTER, KIRK

Kirk Dexter DWCF, 44 Preston Rd, Oakdale, Poole, **Dorset**, BH15 3BL, **ENGLAND**.
(T) 01202 253398
(M) 07889 856462.
Profile Farrier. Ref:YH04099

DI CLARK FEEDS

Di Clark Feeds, Manor Farm, Whitfield, Brackley, **Northamptonshire**, NN13 5TQ, **ENGLAND**.
(T) 01280 850253.
Profile Feed Merchant. Ref:YH04100

DIAMOND CONSULTING SVS

Diamond Consulting Services Ltd, Chestnut Farm, Dinton, Aylesbury, **Buckinghamshire**, HP17 8UG, **ENGLAND**.
(T) 01296 747667 (F) 01296 747557
(E) frl@diamond.demon.co.uk.
Profile Supplies. Ref:YH04101

DIAMOND CTRE

Diamond Centre For Handicapped Riders (The), Woodmansterne Rd, Carshalton, **Surrey**, SM5 4DT, **ENGLAND**.
(T) 020 86437764 (F) 020 86438720.
Contact/s
Admin: Mrs C Frost
Profile Riding School. Ref:YH04102

DIAMOND FARM RIDING CTRE

Diamond Farm Riding Centre, Weston Rd, Brean, Burnham-on-Sea, **Somerset**, TA8 2RL, **ENGLAND**.
(T) 01278 751751.
Contact/s
Partner: Mrs J Spicer
Profile Equestrian Centre, Riding School.
Ref:YH04103

DIAMOND SADDLERY

Diamond Saddlery, Gunstone Hall, White Hse Lane, Gunstone, Codsall, Wolverhampton, **Midlands (West)**, WV8 1QQ, **ENGLAND**.
(T) 01902 842211.
Contact/s
Owner: Miss A Goodwin
Profile Saddlery Retailer, Supplies. Ref:YH04104

DIAMOND SADDLERY

Diamond Saddlery, The Barn, Malting Farm & Stud, Malting Lane, Hurstpierpoint, Hassocks, **Sussex (West)**, BN6 9JZ, **ENGLAND**.
(T) 01273 833114 (F) 01273 833114.
Contact/s
Owner: Mrs J Wheeler
Profile Saddlery Retailer. Ref:YH04105

DIAZ, FELIX

Felix Diaz DWCF, 142 Talbot Rd, South Shields, **Tyne and Wear**, NE34 0RG, **ENGLAND**.
(T) 0191 4218405.
Profile Farrier. **Ref: YH04106**

DIBDIN, D A

D A Dibdin, Ogdens Dairy Farm, Ogdens, Fordingbridge, **Hampshire**, SP6 2PZ, **ENGLAND**.
(T) 01425 653047.
Profile Transport/Horse Boxes. **Ref: YH04107**

DIBDIN, W O

W O Dibdin, Barn Cottage, Ogdens, Fordingbridge, **Hampshire**, SP6 2PZ, **ENGLAND**.
(T) 01425 655122.
Profile Breeder. **Ref: YH04108**

DICK, C

Mrs C Dick, Old Green End Farm, Common Rd, Kensworth, Dunstable, **Bedfordshire**, LU6 2PW, **ENGLAND**.
(T) 01582 872676.
Contact/s
Owner: Mr J Dick
Profile Horse Drawn Carriages.
Carriages are available for hire for weddings, funerals and other occasions. Mrs Dick is qualified to teach single and pair driving.
Ref: YH04109

DICKEN, ROBIN

Robin Dicken, Gardeners Cottage, Alscot Pk, Atherstone On Stour, Stratford-upon-Avon, **Warwickshire**, CV37 8BL, **ENGLAND**.
(T) 01789 450052 **(F)** 01789 450053.
Contact/s
Owner: Mr R Dicken
Profile Trainer. **Ref: YH04110**

DICKEY STEPS RIDING CTRE

Dickey Steps Riding Centre, Rakewood, Littleborough, **Lancashire**, OL15 0AT, **ENGLAND**.
(T) 01706 373919.
Contact/s
Partner: Mrs K Mills
Profile Riding School. **Ref: YH04111**

DICKIE'S FORGE

Dickie's Forge Ltd, 69 Hill Cot Rd, Bolton, **Manchester (Greater)**, BL1 8RL, **ENGLAND**.
(T) 01204 597990 **(F)** 01204 597990.
Contact/s
Sales Manager: Mr D Ryan
Profile Blacksmith. **Ref: YH04112**

DICKIE'S FORGE

Dickie's Forge Ltd, 25 Daniels Cross, Newport, **Shropshire**, TF10 7XJ, **ENGLAND**.
(T) 01952 820008 **(F)** 01952 850008.
Profile Blacksmith. **Ref: YH04113**

DICKINSON, T M

T M Dickinson, Whitridge Hse, Longwitton, Morpeth, **Northumberland**, NE61 4JS, **ENGLAND**.
(T) 01670 774293.
Contact/s
Owner: Mr T Dickinson
Profile Hay and Straw Merchants. **Ref: YH04114**

DICKSON & CHURCH

Dickson & Church Ltd, Elm Cottage, Lewes Rd, Forest Row, **Sussex (East)**, RH18 5AE, **ENGLAND**.
(T) 01342 822047 **(F)** 01342 824028.
Contact/s
Owner: Mr J Church
Profile Supplies. **Ref: YH04115**

DICKSON, F

Mrs F Dickson, 10 Birch Lane, Glenfarg, Perth, **Perth and Kinross**, PH2 9PG, **SCOTLAND**.
(T) 01577 830301.
Profile Breeder. **Ref: YH04116**

DICKSON, PENNY

Penny Dickson, 256A St Margarets Bank, High St, Rochester, **Kent**, ME1 1HY, **ENGLAND**.
(T) 01634 401983.
Contact/s
Saddler: Mrs P Dickson
Profile Saddlery Retailer.
Master Saddler **Ref: YH04117**

DICKSON, R

R Dickson, Newbridge Farm, Newbridge, Dumfries, **Dumfries and Galloway**, DG2 0QU, **SCOTLAND**.
(T) 01387 720360.
Contact/s
Owner: Mr R Dickson **Ref: YH04118**

DICKSONS

Dicksons (Hanley) Ltd, Myatt St, Far Green, Hanley, Stoke-on-Trent, **Staffordshire**, ST1 2LP, **ENGLAND**.
(T) 01782 212874 **(F)** 01782 214866.
Contact/s
Marketing Manager: Mr A Holding
Profile Feed Merchant. **Ref: YH04119**

DIJON STUD

Dijon Stud, Honeydon Rd, Colmworth, **Bedfordshire**, MK44 2ND, **ENGLAND**.
(T) 01234 376627.
Profile Breeder, Stable/Livery. **Ref: YH04120**

DILLON, JOHN E

John E Dillon DWCF, Threeways, 19 Townend, Somerby, **Leicestershire**, LE14 2QQ, **ENGLAND**.
(T) 01664 454194
(M) 07702 314085.
Profile Farrier. **Ref: YH04121**

DIMLANDS FARM RIDING SCHOOL

Dimlands Farm Riding School, Dimlands, Llantwit Major, **Glamorgan (Vale of)**, CF61 1YX, **WALES**.
(T) 01446 794943.
Profile Riding School. **Ref: YH04122**

DIMMOCK

Mr & Mrs Dimmock, Moor Cottage, Harwood Dale, Scarborough, **Yorkshire (North)**, YO13 0LA, **ENGLAND**.
(T) 01723 870263.
Profile Breeder. **Ref: YH04123**

DINESWR RIDING CTRE

Dineswr Riding Centre, Creigiau, Llandyfan, Ammanford, **Carmarthenshire**, SA18 2UD, **WALES**.
(T) 01269 850042 **(F)** 01269 850042.
Contact/s
Owner: Mr T Jenner
Profile Stable/Livery. **Ref: YH04124**

DINGLE BROOK FARM STABLES

Dingle Brook Farm Stables, Dingle Brook Farm, Dingle Lane, Rushton Spencer, Macclesfield, **Cheshire**, SK11 0RX, **ENGLAND**.
(T) 01260 226492.
Contact/s
Owner: Miss N Carman
(E) nicki@dinglebrook.fsnet.co.uk
Profile Horse/Rider Accom, Saddlery Retailer, Stable/Livery, Transport/Horse Boxes.
Full livery available, prices by arrangement
No.Staff: 2 Yr. Est: 1984 C.Size: 16 Acres
Opening Times
Sp: Open Mon - Sun 09:00. Closed Mon - Sun 21:00.
Su: Open Mon - Sun 09:00. Closed Mon - Sun 21:00.
Au: Open Mon - Sun 09:00. Closed Mon - Sun 21:00.
Wn: Open Mon - Sun 09:00. Closed Mon - Sun 21:00. **Ref: YH04125**

DIPTFORD STUD

Diptford Stud, Wonton Farm, Diptford, Totnes, **Devon**, TQ9 7LS, **ENGLAND**.
(T) 01364 72210.
Profile Breeder. **Ref: YH04126**

DIRECT FEEDS

Direct Feeds, The Old Cattle Market, Andover Rd, Winchester, **Hampshire**, SO23 7BT, **ENGLAND**.
(T) 01962 844181.
Contact/s
Owner: Mrs S Small
Profile Feed Merchant. **Ref: YH04127**

DIRTY DOBBINS

Dirty Dobbins, 6 Albert St, Mansfield Woodhouse, **Nottinghamshire**, NG19 8BH, **ENGLAND**.
(T) 01623 644626.
Profile Supplies. **Ref: YH04128**

DISCOUNT SADDLERY

Hey Farm Saddlery Ltd, Gawthorpe Lane, Huddersfield, **Yorkshire (West)**, HD5 0NZ, **ENGLAND**.
(T) 01484 428784 **(F)** 01484 532331
(E) sales@discountsaddlery.co.uk
(W) www.discountsaddlery.co.uk
Affiliated Bodies BETA.
Contact/s
Owner: Mr P Collins
Profile Riding Wear Retailer, Saddlery Retailer.
Also a retailer of bit accessories, dressage equipment, grooming equipment, polo items. Specialise in saddles, over 1000 in stock. No.Staff: 12
Yr. Est: 1981
Opening Times
Sp: Open Tues - Fri 09:00, Sat, Sun 10:00. Closed Tues - Fri 21:00, Sat, Sun 18:00.
Su: Open Tues - Fri 09:00, Sat, Sun 10:00. Closed Tues - Fri 21:00, Sat, Sun 18:00.
Au: Open Tues - Fri 09:00, Sat, Sun 10:00. Closed Tues - Fri 21:00, Sat, Sun 18:00.
Wn: Open Tues - Fri 09:00, Sat, Sun 10:00. Closed Tues - Fri 21:00, Sat, Sun 18:00. **Ref: YH04129**

DISCOUNT TOWBAR SUPPLIES

Discount Towbar Supplies, 327 Gallowgate, Glasgow, **Glasgow (City of)**, G40 2EF, **SCOTLAND**.
(T) 0141 5501750 **(F)** 0141 5502484.
Contact/s
Owner: Mr A McGough
Profile Transport/Horse Boxes. **Ref: YH04130**

DISNEY, SUE

Sue Disney, The Willows, Wolvershill, Banwell, **Somerset (North)**, BS29 6LE, **ENGLAND**.
(T) 01934 823934.
Profile Breeder. **Ref: YH04131**

DISS LIVERY CTRE

Diss Livery Centre, Westbrook Green Farm, Shelfanger Rd, Diss, **Norfolk**, IP22 4XX, **ENGLAND**.
(T) 01379 642464.
Contact/s
Owner: Mr G Debenham
Profile Stable/Livery. No.Staff: 2
Yr. Est: 1985 **Ref: YH04132**

DISTINCTIVE IRON WORK

Distinctive Iron Work, Forge Hse, Tewkesbury Rd, Uckington, Cheltenham, **Gloucestershire**, GL51 9SX, **ENGLAND**.
(T) 01242 680453 **(F)** 01242 680453.
Contact/s
Owner: Mr S Iddles
Profile Blacksmith. **Ref: YH04133**

DITCHAM, JANET

Janet Ditcham, Bluestone Morgans, Bluestone Farm, Cleeton St Mary, Kidderminster, **Worcestershire**, DY14 0QW, **ENGLAND**.
(T) 01584 891045.
Profile Breeder, Stable/Livery. **Ref: YH04134**

DITCHLING COMMON STUD

Ditchling Common Stud Riding School, Ditchling Common, Burgess Hill, **Sussex (West)**, RH15 0SE, **ENGLAND**.
(T) 01444 871900/236678.
Contact/s
Manager: Mr J Dudeney
Profile Riding School, Stable/Livery. **Ref: YH04135**

DITTISCOMBE EQUESTRIAN CTRE

Dittiscombe Equestrian Centre, Dittiscombe, Slapton, Kingsbridge, **Devon**, TQ7 2QF, **ENGLAND**.
(T) 01548 581049.
Contact/s
Owner: Mrs A Farley
Profile Riding School. **Ref: YH04136**

DIVOTS SADDLERY

Divots Saddlery (The), 34 Pardown, Oakley, Basingstoke, **Hampshire**, RG23 7DZ, **ENGLAND**.
(T) 01256 780265.
Profile Saddlery Retailer. **Ref: YH04137**

DIXON, F H

F H Dixon, The Forge, Staplefield, Haywards Heath, **Sussex (West)**, RH17 6ET, **ENGLAND**.
(T) 01444 400581.
Profile Supplies. **Ref: YH04138**

DIXON, GEOFFREY DAVID

Geoffrey David Dixon RSS, The Olde Bell Cottage, The Street, Freckenham, Bury St Edmunds, **Suffolk**, IP28 8HZ, **ENGLAND**.
(T) 01638 720635.
Profile Farrier. **Ref: YH04139**

DIXON, J B

Mrs J B Dixon, Grove Hse, Lyndhurst, **Hampshire**, SO43 7GG, **ENGLAND**.
(T) 023 80813211.
Profile Stable/Livery. **Ref: YH04140**

DIXON, JOHN

Mr John Dixon, Moorend, Thursby, Carlisle, **Cumbria**, CA5 6QP, **ENGLAND**.
(T) 01228 710318.
Profile Breeder. **Ref: YH04141**

DIXON, KAREN

Karen Dixon, Wycliffe Grange, Wycliffe, Barnard Castle, **County Durham**, DL12 9TS, **ENGLAND**.
(T) 01833 627526 **(F)** 01833 627526.
Profile Trainer. **Ref: YH04142**

DIXON, M L

M L Dixon, 32 Princes Rd, Kingston Upon Thames, **London (Greater)**, KT2 6AZ, **ENGLAND**.
(T) 020 85495399.
Profile Farrier. **Ref: YH04143**

DIXON-BATE

Dixon-Bate Ltd, Unit 45 First Ave, Deeside Ind Pk, Deeside, **Flintshire**, CH5 2LG, **WALES**.
(T) 01244 288925 **(F)** 01244 288462.
Profile Transport/Horse Boxes. **Ref: YH04144**

DIXONS DUSTLESS

Dixons Dustless, Porters Farm, Ricklinghall, Diss, **Norfolk**, IP22 1LY, **ENGLAND**.
(T) 01359 259341 **(F)** 01359 259185.
Profile Supplies. **Ref: YH04145**

DIXONS FORGE

Dixons Forge, Unit 47 Salthouse Mills Ind Est, Barrow-In-Furness, **Cumbria**, LA13 0DH, **ENGLAND**.
(T) 01229 431618.
Profile Blacksmith. **Ref: YH04146**

DOAGH FARM FEEDS

Doagh Farm Feeds, 10 Ballyclare Rd, Doagh, **County Antrim**, BT39 0PE, **NORTHERN IRELAND**.
(T) 028 93352282.
Profile Feed Merchant. **Ref: YH04147**

DOBBERSON, JAMES HENRY

James Henry Dobberson, 37 Shakespeare Ave, Tilbury, **Essex**, RM18 8AP, **ENGLAND**.
(T) 01375 406634.
Profile Farrier. **Ref: YH04148**

DOBBERSON, KEITH L

Keith L Dobberson, The Forge, 97 Pancroft, Bridge, **Essex**, RM4 1DA, **ENGLAND**.
(T) 01992 815543
(M) 07836 669842.
Profile Farrier. **Ref: YH04149**

DOBBINS CLOBBER

Dobbins Clobber, Penn Farm, Manor Rd, Towersey, Thame, **Oxfordshire**, OX9 3QX, **ENGLAND**.
(T) 01844 212324 **(F)** 01844 260767
(M) 07768 838386.
Profile Supplies. **Ref: YH04150**

DOBBINS DINER

Dobbins Diner incorporating Dobbins Direct, Station Rd Farm, Station Rd, Polesworth, Tamworth, **Staffordshire**, B79 0EH, **ENGLAND**.
(T) 01827 896019 **(F)** 01827 896019.
Contact/s
Owner: Mrs M Cook **(Q)** BHS 1
(E) mel@racingathome.fsnet.co.uk
Profile Breeder, Riding Wear Retailer, Supplies.
No.Staff: 5 Yr. Est: 1989 C.Size: 5 Acres
Opening Times
Sp: Open 10:00. Closed 16:00.
Su: Open 10:00. Closed 16:00.
Au: Open 10:00. Closed 16:00.
Wn: Open 10:00. Closed 16:00. **Ref: YH04151**

DOBBS, P J

P J Dobbs, Blaenau Farm, Llandeusant, Llangadog, **Carmarthenshire**, SA19 9UN, **WALES**.
(T) 01550 740277.
Profile Breeder. **Ref: YH04152**

DOBINSON, A W & A B

A W & A B Dobinson, Brierdene Farm, Whitley Bay, **Tyne and Wear**, NE26 4RP, **ENGLAND**.
(T) 0191 2524233.
Contact/s
Owner: Mr A Dobinson
Profile Breeder.
Breeder of Welsh Section A ponies **Ref: YH04153**

DOBSON, JOHN DAVID

John David Dobson DWCF, St Helens Farm, Common Rd, Thurnscoe, Rotherham, **Yorkshire (South)**, S63 0RJ, **ENGLAND**.
(T) 01709 892045.
Profile Farrier. **Ref: YH04154**

DOBSON, TERENCE FRANK

Terence Frank Dobson, 2 Furnace Pond Cottage, Dale Moor, Dale Abbey, Ilkeston, **Derbyshire**, DE7 4PF, **ENGLAND**.
(T) 0115 9309925.
Profile Farrier. **Ref: YH04155**

DOCKLANDS CARRIAGE DRIVING

Docklands Carriage Driving, 24 Langton Ave, East Ham, **London (Greater)**, E6 6AL, **ENGLAND**.
(T) 020 84715670.
Profile Trainer. **Ref: YH04156**

DOCKLANDS EQUESTRIAN CTRE

Docklands Equestrian Centre, 2 Claps Gate Lane, London, **London (Greater)**, E6 6JF, **ENGLAND**.
(T) 020 75113917.
Profile Equestrian Centre, Riding School, Stable/Livery.
Specialise in riding for disabled people. The centre offers class sessions, horse and pony riding in a covered arena, lunge lessons, Pony Club membership, private tuition and stable management instruction. The centre is fully accessible to disabled people.
Opening Times
Mon - Thurs 04:30 - 20:30, Sat, Sun 09:00 - 13:00
Ref: YH04157

DODD, C

Mr C Dodd, Sandy Lane Farm, Matlock Moor, Matlock, **Derbyshire**, DE4 5LD, **ENGLAND**.
(T) 01629 584586.
Profile Trainer. **Ref: YH04158**

DODDS, J P

Mr J P Dodds, South Hazelrigg, Chatton, Alnwick, **Northumberland**, NE66 5RZ, **ENGLAND**.
(T) 01668 215216
(M) 07710 346076.
Profile Trainer. **Ref: YH04159**

DODS, M

M Dods, Denton Hall Farm, Denton, Darlington, **County Durham**, DL2 3TY, **ENGLAND**.
(T) 01325 374270.
Profile Trainer. **Ref: YH04160**

DODSON & HORRELL

Dodson & Horrell Ltd, Lodge Farm, North Warnborough, Basingstoke, **Hampshire**, RG25 1HA, **ENGLAND**.
(T) 01832 737300 **(F)** 01832 737303
(E) enquiries@dodsonandhorrell.com
(W) www.dodsonandhorrellltd.com.
Contact/s
Area Manager: Mrs A Renouard
Profile Feed Merchant, Supplies. **Ref: YH04161**

DODSON & HORRELL

Dodson & Horrell Ltd, Spencer St, Ringstead, Kettering, **Northamptonshire**, NN14 4BX, **ENGLAND**.
(T) 01832 737300 **(F)** 01832 737303
(E) enquiries@dodsonandhorrell.com
(W) www.dodsonandhorrellltd.com.
Contact/s
Nutritionist: Teresa Hollands **(Q)** BSc, MSc
Profile Feed Merchant, Supplies. **Ref: YH04162**

DODSWORTH, KEITH D

Keith D Dodsworth DWCF, 43 Kents Hill Rd, South Benfleet, **Essex**, SS7 5PN, **ENGLAND**.
(T) 07710 435415.
Profile Farrier. **Ref: YH04163**

DOIDGE, T R

T R Doidge, Quarry Cres Pennygillam Ind Est, Pennygillam Ind Est, Launceston, **Cornwall**, PL15 7ED, **ENGLAND**.
(T) 01566 774431.
Contact/s
Owner: Mr T Doidge
Profile Hay and Straw Merchants. **Ref: YH04164**

DOIG, W G

W G Doig, 1 St Martin's Rd, Balbeggie, **Perth and Kinross**, PH2 6EX, **SCOTLAND**.
(T) 01821 640311.
Profile Farrier. **Ref: YH04165**

DOLBADARN TREKKING

Dolbadarn Trekking, Dolbadarn Hotel, Llanberis, **Gwynedd**, LL55 4SU, **WALES**.
(T) 01286 870277.
Profile Equestrian Centre. Trekking Centre.
Ref: YH04166

DOLFOR RIDING CLUB

Dolfor Riding Club, Lower Hill Farm, Marton, Welshpool, **Powys**, SY21 8JY, **WALES**.
(T) 01938 580277.
Contact/s
Chairman: Miss V Leeson
Profile Club/Association, Riding Club. **Ref: YH04167**

DOLGELLAU FARMERS

Dolgellau Farmers Ltd, Station Yard, Barmouth Rd, Dolgellau, **Gwynedd**, LL40 2YU, **WALES**.
(T) 01341 422253.
Profile Feed Merchant. **Ref: YH04168**

DOLGOED RIDING SCHOOL

Dolgoed Riding School, Dolgoed, Upper Denbigh Rd, St Asaph, **Denbighshire**, LL17 0LW, **WALES**.
(T) 01745 585330.
Contact/s
Owner: Mrs C Jelley
Profile Riding School. **Ref: YH04169**

DOLLIN & MORRIS

Dollin & Morris Limited, Standon Mill, Standon, Stafford, **Staffordshire**, ST21 6RP, **ENGLAND**.
(T) 01782 791209/791260 **(F)** 01782 791628
(E) info@dollinandmorris.co.uk
(W) www.dollinandmorris.co.uk.
Contact/s
Partner: Mr D Morris
Profile Feed Merchant. **Ref: YH04170**

DOLRHANOG RIDING CTRE

Dolrhanog Riding Centre, Dolrhanog Isaf, Cilgwyn, Trefdraeth, Sir Benfro, Newport, **Pembrokeshire**, SA42 0QH, **WALES**.
(T) 01239 820432.
Contact/s
Owner: Chia James
Profile Breeder, Equestrian Centre, Riding School.
A riding holiday centre for 8 - 80 year olds.
No.Staff: 5 Yr. Est: 1960 C.Size: 40 Acres
Opening Times
Sp: Open 10:00. Closed 16:00.
Su: Open 10:00. Closed 16:00.
Au: Open 10:00. Closed 16:00.
Wn: Open 10:00. Closed 16:00. **Ref: YH04171**

DOMINION RACING STABLES

Dominion Racing Stables, Hob Hill Farm, Seafield Lane, Alvechurch, **Midlands (West)**, B48 7HP, **ENGLAND**.
(T) 01564 822392 **(F)** 01564 822392
(M) 07971 594819.
Profile Trainer. **Ref: YH04172**

DON WEAR TEXTILES

Don Wear Textiles, Mayfield Hse, Bernard Lane, Green Hammerton, **Yorkshire (North)**, YO5 8BP, **ENGLAND**.
(T) 01423 330255 **(F)** 01423 330255
(E) nick@fullkit.com.
Profile Supplies. **Ref: YH04173**

DON, J S

J S Don, 1A Naughton Rd, Wormit, Newport-on-Tay, **Fife**, DD6 8NE, **SCOTLAND**.
(T) 01382 542379.
Profile Blacksmith. **Ref: YH04174**

DONALD, GEORGE

Mr George Donald, Corskie Cottage, Aberchirder, Huntly, **Aberdeenshire**, AB54 7TU, **SCOTLAND**.
(T) 01466 780401.
Profile Breeder. **Ref: YH04175**

DONALDSON, J & W

J & W Donaldson, Caledonian Pl, Moffat, **Dumfries and Galloway**, DG10 9EG, **SCOTLAND**.
(T) 01683 220321.
Profile Blacksmith. **Ref: YH04176**

DONALDSON, ROBERT

Robert Donaldson, 196 High St, Kinross, **Perth and Kinross**, KY13 8DE, **SCOTLAND**.
(T) 01577 863273.
Contact/s
Owner: Mr R Donaldson
Profile Blacksmith. **Ref: YH04177**

DONCASTER BLOODSTOCK SALES

Doncaster Bloodstock Sales Ltd, Auction Mart Offices, Hawick, **Scottish Borders**, TD9 9NN, **SCOTLAND**.
(T) 01450 372222 **(F)** 01450 378017.
Profile Blood Stock Agency. **Ref: YH04178**

DONCASTER RACECOURSE

Doncaster Racecourse, The Grandstand, Leger Way, Doncaster, **Yorkshire (South)**, DN2 6BB, **ENGLAND**.
(T) 01302 320066 **(F)** 01302 323271.
Profile Track/Course. **Ref: YH04179**

Key: **(T)** telephone **(F)** fax **(M)** mobile **(E)** E-Mail Address **(W)** Website Address **(Q)** Qualifications
Yr. Est: Year Established C.Size: Complex Size Sp: Spring Su: Summer Au: Autumn Wn: Winter

DONCASTER, R A

R A Doncaster, 49 Christchurch St, Ipswich, **Suffolk**, IP4 2DF, **ENGLAND**.
(T) 01473 255789.
Profile Medical Support. Ref: YH04180

DONEY, JON

Jon Doney, The Manor Hse, Bredon, Tewkesbury, **Gloucestershire**, GL20 7EQ, **ENGLAND**.
(T) 01684 773656 (F) 01684 773773
Affiliated Bodies BSJA.
Contact/s
Owner: Mr J Doney
Profile Show Jumps Supplier.
Awarded the BEF Medal of Honour for 1999. One of his most notable achievements was building the course for the European Show Jumping Championships at Hickstead. Any type of jump can be built to fit your requirements. Championship, Standard and Working Hunter sets are available for hire.
Ref: YH04181

DONISTHORPE & DISTRICT

Donisthorpe & District Riding Club, 4 Renshaw Drive, Newhall, Swadlincote, **Derbyshire**, DE11 0RY, **ENGLAND**.
(T) 01283 212575.
Contact/s
Chairman: Mrs C Charlton
Profile Riding Club. Ref: YH04182

DONKEY BREED SOC

Donkey Breed Society, The Hermitage, Pootings, Edenbridge, **Kent**, TN8 6SD, **ENGLAND**.
(T) 01732 864414 (F) 01732 864414.
Contact/s
Key Contact: Mrs C Morse
Profile Club/Association. Ref: YH04183

DONKEY SANCTUARY

Donkey Sanctuary (The), Slade Hse Farm, Salcombe Regis, Sidmouth, **Devon**, EX10 0NU, **ENGLAND**.
(T) 01395 578222 (F) 01395 579266
(E) thedonkeysanctuary@compuserve.com
(W) www.thedonkeysanctuary.org.uk.
Contact/s
Key Contact: Mr B Venn (T) 01395 578222
Profile Medical Support.
Ages range from one year to young adults, those over eight stones in weight are taught to drive a small cart. Offer riding therapy for the disabled. Yr. Est: 1975
Opening Times
During the summer months mobile units operate.
Ref: YH04184

DONNA LEIGH SADDLERY

Donna Leigh Saddlery, Unit 47 Meadowmill Ind Est, Dixon St, Kidderminster, **Worcestershire**, DY10 1HH, **ENGLAND**.
(T) 01562 746124 (F) 01562 752875.
Profile Saddlery Retailer. Ref: YH04185

DONNACHIE & TOWNLEY

Donnachie & Townley, The Vetnry Ctre, Market St, Rugeley, **Staffordshire**, WS15 2JH, **ENGLAND**.
(T) 01889 582023 (F) 01889 575533.
Profile Medical Support. Ref: YH04186

DONNELLY & SON

Donnelly & Son, 164 Ecclesville Rd, Fintona, **County Tyrone**, BT78 2EQ, **NORTHERN IRELAND**.
(T) 028 82841288 (F) 028 82840144.
Profile Supplies. Ref: YH04187

DONNINGTON SADDLE CLUB

Donnington Saddle Club, Donnington, Telford, **Shropshire**, TF2 8JX, **ENGLAND**.
(T) 01952 608423.
Profile Riding Club. Ref: YH04188

DONOGHUE, BARRY & KEVIN

Barry & Kevin Donoghue, Oldcastle, Meath, **County Meath**, **IRELAND**.
(T) 049 8541144. Ref: YH04189

DONVIEW VETNRY CTRE

Donview Veterinary Centre, 27 North St, Inverurie, **Aberdeenshire**, AB51 4RP, **SCOTLAND**.
(T) 01467 621429 (F) 01467 623012.
Profile Medical Support. Ref: YH04190

DOOK, C M A

Mrs C M A Dook, Woolthwaite Farm, Tickhill, Doncaster, **Yorkshire (South)**, DN11 9PJ, **ENGLAND**.
(T) 01302 742266.
Profile Supplies. Ref: YH04191

DOOLEY ANDREW FARRIER SV

Dooley Andrew Farrier Service, Halverstown, Kilcullen, **County Kildare**, **IRELAND**.
(T) 045 485477.
Profile Supplies. Ref: YH04192

DOOLEY, MICHAEL M

Mr Michael M Dooley, Four Winds, Broadmayne, **Dorset**, DT2 8LY, **ENGLAND**.
(T) 01305 854251 (F) 01305 854551
(M) 07831 344662
(E) michael.dooley4@virgin.net.
Profile Medical Support. Ref: YH04193

DOONE VALLEY RIDING STABLES

Doone Valley Riding Stables, Oare, Lynton, **Devon**, EX35 6NU, **ENGLAND**.
(T) 01598 741278 (F) 01598 741278.
Contact/s
Owner: Mr H Burge
Profile Holidays. Ref: YH04194

DORAN & GRADWELL

Doran & Gradwell, The Coppins, Kington Lane, Thornbury, **Gloucestershire (South)**, BS35 1NA, **ENGLAND**.
(T) 01454 413503 (F) 01454 419493.
Profile Medical Support. Ref: YH04195

DORAN, B N

Mr B N Doran, Stable Cottage, Peasebrook Farm, Cheltenham Rd, Broadway, **Worcestershire**, WR12 7LX, **ENGLAND**.
(T) 01386 858980.
Profile Trainer. Ref: YH04196

DORCHESTER RACING CLUB

Dorchester Racing Club, 39-41 North Rd, Islington, **London (Greater)**, N7 9DP, **ENGLAND**.
(T) 020 76079099.
Profile Club/Association. Ref: YH04197

DORCHESTER SADDLERY

Dorchester Saddlery, The Granary, Warmwell, Dorchester, **Dorset**, DT2 8HQ, **ENGLAND**.
(T) 01305 852270.
Contact/s
Owner: Mrs P Bush
Profile Saddlery Retailer. Ref: YH04198

DORE, S

Mrs S Dore, Old Rectory Cottage, Broughton Poggs, Lechlade, **Gloucestershire**, GL7 3JH, **ENGLAND**.
(T) 01367 860222.
Profile Breeder. Ref: YH04199

DORKING EQUESTRIAN CTRE

Dorking Equestrian Centre, Downs Meadow, Ranmore Rd, Dorking, **Surrey**, RH4 1HW, **ENGLAND**.
(T) 01306 881718
(E) dorkingec@hotmail.com
Affiliated Bodies BHS.
Profile Equestrian Centre, Riding School.
Pony days for children. Show jumping competitions.
Yr. Est: 1999
Opening Times
Sp: Open Tues - Sun 08:00. Closed Tues, Thurs 20:00, Wed, Fri - Sun 18:30.
Su: Open Tues - Sun 08:00. Closed Tues, Thurs 20:00, Wed, Fri - Sun 18:30.
Au: Open Tues - Sun 08:00. Closed Tues, Thurs 20:00, Wed, Fri - Sun 18:30.
Wn: Open Tues - Sun 08:00. Closed Tues, Thurs 20:00, Wed, Fri - Sun 18:30. Ref: YH04200

DORKING SADDLERY

Dorking Saddlery, 58 Dene St, Dorking, **Surrey**, RH4 2DP, **ENGLAND**.
(T) 01306 887665 (F) 01306 887665
Affiliated Bodies SMS.
Contact/s
Owner: Mrs J Forsyth
Profile Saddlery Retailer. Master Saddlers.
Ref: YH04201

DORMIT RIDING SURFACES

Dormit Riding Surfaces, Lakeside Sawmills, South Cerney, Cirencester, **Gloucestershire**, GL7 5UH, **ENGLAND**.
(T) 01285 860781 (F) 01285 861033.
Profile Track/Course. Ref: YH04202

DORNEY MEADOWS

Dorney Meadows, Old Marsh Lane, Taplow, Maidenhead, **Berkshire**, SL6 0DZ, **ENGLAND**.
(T) 01628 773843.
Contact/s
Owner: Mr B Cargin
Profile Stable/Livery. Ref: YH04203

DORSET BRIDLEWAYS

Dorset Bridleways, The Gardens, Woodlands, Wimborne, **Dorset**, BH21 6LT, **ENGLAND**.
(T) 01202 826867.
Profile Club/Association. Ref: YH04204

DORSET COUNTY SADDLERY

Dorset County Saddlery, Pamphill, Wimborne, **Dorset**, BH21 4ED, **ENGLAND**.
(T) 01202 888633 (F) 01202 888666
Affiliated Bodies SMS.
Contact/s
Owner: Mrs E Graeham
Profile Saddlery Retailer.
Approved Retailer of the SMS. Ref: YH04205

DORSET HEAVY HORSE CTRE

Dorset Heavy Horse Centre, Grains Hill, Edmondsham, Wimborne, **Dorset**, BH21 5RJ, **ENGLAND**.
(T) 01202 824040 (F) 01202 821407.
Profile Breeder, Riding School, Stable/Livery.
Ref: YH04206

DORSET RARE BREEDS CTRE

Dorset Rare Breeds Centre, Shaftesbury Rd, Gillingham, **Dorset**, SP8 5JG, **ENGLAND**.
(T) 01747 822169.
Profile Breeder. Ref: YH04207

DORTON GRANGE STABLES

Dorton Grange Stables, Brill, Aylesbury, **Buckinghamshire**, HP18 9UD, **ENGLAND**.
(T) 01844 238440
(M) 07801 752717.
Profile Trainer. Ref: YH04208

DOSTHILL SADDLERY

Dosthill Saddlery, 12 High St, Dosthill, Tamworth, **Staffordshire**, B77 1LF, **ENGLAND**.
(T) 01827 289251.
Profile Saddlery Retailer. Ref: YH04209

DOUCH, SELWYN

Mr Selwyn Douch, Glancellyn Farm, Nantgaredig, Carmarthen, **Carmarthenshire**, SA32 7NN, **WALES**.
(T) 01558 668497 (F) 01558 668497
(M) 07831 130456.
Profile Supplies. Ref: YH04210

DOUGLAS FARM RIDING SCHOOL

Douglas Farm Riding School, 21 Bradshaw Lane, Parbold, Wigan, **Lancashire**, WN8 7NQ, **ENGLAND**.
(T) 01257 462057
(W) www.horseweb-uk.com/stables/lanc.htm.
Contact/s
Owner: Mrs S Carr
Profile Riding School, Trainer. Ref: YH04211

DOUGLAS, EILEEN

Eileen Douglas, 295 Yorktown Rd, College Town, Sandhurst, **Berkshire**, GU47 0QA, **ENGLAND**.
(T) 01276 38196 (F) 01276 38196.
Contact/s
Owner: Mrs E Douglas
Profile Saddlery Retailer. Ref: YH04212

DOUGLAS, EILEEN

Eileen Douglas, Woods Farm, Easthampstead Rd, Wokingham, **Berkshire**, RG40 3AG, **ENGLAND**.
(T) 0118 9793593 (F) 0118 9796131.
Contact/s
Owner: Mrs E Douglas
Profile Saddlery Retailer. Ref: YH04213

DOUGLAS, JOHN L

John L Douglas, Balmesh Smithy, Glenluce, Newton Stewart, **Dumfries and Galloway**, DG8 0AG, **SCOTLAND**.
(T) 01581 300225 (F) 01581 300251.
Contact/s
Owner: Mr J Douglas
Profile Blacksmith.
Also have ATV motorbikes available. Ref: YH04214

DOUGLAS, W J

W J Douglas, Pleasants, Jedburgh, **Scottish Borders**, TD8 6QZ, **SCOTLAND**.
(T) 01835 863602.
Profile Breeder. Ref: YH04215

DOUTHWAITE, J D

Mr & Mrs J D Douthwaite, Parklands, Chapel Lane, Finghall, Leyburn, **Yorkshire (North)**, DL8 5LZ, **ENGLAND**.
(T) 01677 450741.
Profile Breeder. Ref: YH04216

DOVE STYLE

Dove Style, Dove Hse, Sumpter, Hoole Village, Chester, **Cheshire**, CH2 3JF, **ENGLAND**.
(T) 01244 313213 **(F)** 01244 343133.
Profile Breeder, Saddlery Retailer. Ref: **YH04217**

DOVECOTE FARM

Dovecote Farm Equestrian Centre, Dovecote Farm, Orston, **Nottinghamshire**, NG13 9NS, **ENGLAND**.
(T) 01949 851204.
Profile Riding School.
Dovecote Farm was recently featured on the Channel 4 show 'Faking It' in which they succeeded in training a dancer, who had never ridden before, to complete a show jumping course without error in only 28 days.
Ref: **YH04218**

DOVETAIL TRAILER

Dovetail Trailer Co Ltd, Donnington Pk, 85 Birdham Rd, Chichester, **Sussex (West)**, PO20 7DU, **ENGLAND**.
(T) 01243 533663 **(F)** 01243 783701.
Profile Transport/Horse Boxes. Ref: **YH04219**

DOW, S

S Dow, Clear Heights Stables, Derby Stables Rd, Epsom, **Surrey**, KT18 5LB, **ENGLAND**.
(T) 01372 721490 **(F)** 01372 748099.
Contact/s
Principal: Mr S Dow
Profile Trainer. Ref: **YH04220**

DOWDING, BRIAN H

Brian H Dowding, Markham, Blackwood, **Caerphilly**, NP12 0SA, **WALES**.
(T) 01495 224107.
Profile Breeder. Ref: **YH04221**

DOWN ROYAL CORPORATION

Down Royal Corporation of Horse Breeders, 71 Lismore Rd, Downpatrick, **County Down**, BT30 7EY, **NORTHERN IRELAND**.
(T) 028 44841125.
Profile Club/Association. Ref: **YH04222**

DOWN ROYAL RACECOURSE

Down Royal Racecourse, Maze, Lisburn, **County Antrim**, BT27 5BW, **NORTHERN IRELAND**.
(T) 028 92621256 **(F)** 028 92621433.
Contact/s
Admin Manager: Mrs M Murphy
Profile Track/Course. Ref: **YH04223**

DOWNE COURT RIDING CTRE

Downe Court Riding Centre, New Rd Hill, Orpington, **Kent**, BR6 7JA, **ENGLAND**.
(T) 01689 850283.
Profile Stable/Livery. Ref: **YH04224**

DOWNE FARM

Downe Farm, Downe Farm, Witheridge, Tiverton, **Devon**, EX16 8QF, **ENGLAND**.
(T) 01884 860465 **(F)** 01884 860465.
Contact/s
Owner: Miss V Cheffings
Profile Breeder, Stable/Livery. Ref: **YH04225**

DOWNE HALL STABLES

Downe Hall Stables, High Elms Rd, Downe, Orpington, **Kent**, BR6 7JL, **ENGLAND**.
(T) 01689 859127.
Contact/s
Owner: Mrs T Fisher
Profile Riding School. Ref: **YH04226**

DOWNEND TRAILOR SVS

Downend Trailor Services, 22 Graham Rd, Downend, Bristol, **Bristol**, BS16 6AN, **ENGLAND**.
(T) 01179 572060 **(F)** 01179 572060.
Contact/s
Owner: Mr A Summerill
Profile Transport/Horse Boxes. Ref: **YH04227**

DOWNES, T W

T W Downes, The Croft, 22 Fords Lane, Mow Cop, Stoke-on-Trent, **Staffordshire**, ST7 4NG, **ENGLAND**.
(T) 01782 516808.
Contact/s
Owner: Mrs C Downes
Profile Transport/Horse Boxes. Ref: **YH04228**

DOWNFIELD FARM SHOP

Downfield Farm Shop, Bridge Hse, Windy Bridge, Chilsworthy, Gunnislake, **Cornwall**, PL18 9AS, **ENGLAND**.
(T) 01822 833577.
Profile Supplies. Ref: **YH04229**

DOWNHAM, TREVOR I

Trevor I Downham DWCF, Mossbury, Pinchpools Rd, Manuden, Bishop's Stortford, **Hertfordshire**, CM23 1DX, **ENGLAND**.
(T) 01279 816843.
Profile Farrier. Ref: **YH04230**

DOWNIE, R

R Downie, Hebron, Morpeth, **Northumberland**, NE61 3LA, **ENGLAND**.
(T) 01670 512581.
Contact/s
Owner: Mr R Downie
Profile Blacksmith. Ref: **YH04231**

DOWNING, J

J Downing, 67 Wisbech Rd, Thorney, Peterborough, **Cambridgeshire**, PE6 0ST, **ENGLAND**.
(T) 01733 270469 **(F)** 01733 270469.
Contact/s
Owner: Mr J Downing
Profile Blacksmith. Ref: **YH04232**

DOWNLAND DONKEY STUD

Downland Donkey Stud, Hooley Farm, 15 Woodplace Lane, Coulsdon, **Surrey**, CR5 1NE, **ENGLAND**.
(T) 01737 553638. Ref: **YH04233**

DOWNLAND EQUESTRIAN

Downland Equestrian, Orpwood, Ardington, Wantage, **Oxfordshire**, OX12 8PN, **ENGLAND**.
(T) 01235 833300 **(F)** 01235 820950.
Contact/s
Owner: Mrs V Haigh
Profile Horse/Rider Accom. Ref: **YH04234**

DOWNLAND PONY STUD

Downland Pony Stud, Downland Pony Stud, Llangoedmor, **Ceredigion**, SA43 2LJ, **WALES**.
(T) 01239 613004.
Profile Breeder. Ref: **YH04235**

DOWNLAND VETNRY GRP

Downland Veterinary Group, Pk Vale Clinic, 71 Havant Rd, Emsworth, **Hampshire**, PO10 7NZ, **ENGLAND**.
(T) 01243 377141.
Contact/s
Partner: Mr R Grose
Profile Medical Support. Ref: **YH04236**

DOWNPATRICK RACECOURSE

Downpatrick Racecourse, 71 Lismore Rd, Downpatrick, **County Down**, BT30 7EY, **NORTHERN IRELAND**.
(T) 028 44841125 **(F)** 028 44842227.
Profile Track/Course. Ref: **YH04237**

DOWNS FENCING

Downs Fencing, Marlie Farm, The Broyle, Shortgate, Lewes, **Sussex (East)**, BN8 6PH, **ENGLAND**.
(T) 01825 840818.
Profile Fencing Specialists. Ref: **YH04238**

DOWNS HSE EQUINE

Downs House Equine, Combeleigh, Wheddon Cross, Minehead, **Somerset**, TA24 7AT, **ENGLAND**.
(T) 01643 841354 **(F)** 01643 841171.
Profile Medical Support. Ref: **YH04239**

DOWNS HSE REHABILITATION CTRE

Downs House Rehabilitation Centre, Baydon, Marlborough, **Wiltshire**, SN8 2JS, **ENGLAND**.
(T) 01672 540755 **(F)** 01672 541114.
Profile Medical Support. Ref: **YH04240**

DOWNS SIDE RIDING CTRE

Downs Side Riding Centre, Sully Rd, Penarth, **Glamorgan (Vale of)**, CF64 2TR, **WALES**.
(T) 029 20709719.
Profile Riding School. Ref: **YH04241**

DOWNTON HALL STABLES

Downton Hall Stables, Ludlow, **Shropshire**, SY8 3DX, **ENGLAND**.
(T) 01584 873688 **(F)** 01584 873525
(M) 07885 878056.
Profile Trainer. Ref: **YH04242**

DOWNTON, DANIEL A

Daniel A Downton DWCF, 81 Claverham Rd, Yatton, **Somerset (North)**, BS49 4LD, **ENGLAND**.
(T) 01934 838588.
Profile Farrier. Ref: **YH04243**

DOWSON, H B

Mrs H B Dowson, Lower Hill, Pershore, **Worcestershire**, WR10 3JR, **ENGLAND**.
(T) 01386 552029.
Profile Supplies. Ref: **YH04244**

DOYLE, DARREN L

Darren L Doyle DWCF, 3 Burnham Rd, Tadley, **Hampshire**, RG26 4QN, **ENGLAND**.
(T) 0118 9819085.
Profile Farrier. Ref: **YH04245**

DOYLE, JACK T

Doyle Jack T, Sales Paddock, Leger Way, Doncaster, **Yorkshire (South)**, DN2 6BB, **ENGLAND**.
(T) 01302 367473.
Profile Breeder. Ref: **YH04246**

DOYLE, JACQUELINE

Miss Jacqueline Doyle, Flemington, Upper Lambourn, Hungerford, **Berkshire**, RG17 8QH, **ENGLAND**.
(T) 01488 72223
(M) 07831 880678.
Contact/s
Owner: Miss J Doyle
Profile Trainer. Ref: **YH04247**

DOYLE, KEITH

Mr Keith Doyle, Brooklands, Marsh Lane, Eversley, **Hampshire**, RG27 0PD, **ENGLAND**.
(T) 01252 873368 **(F)** 01252 879853.
Profile Breeder. Ref: **YH04248**

DOYLE, MARK

Mark Doyle, C/O Little Acre, Newtown Lane, Leominster, **Herefordshire**, HR6 8QD, **ENGLAND**.
(T) 01568 614596
Alt Contact Address
317 Buckfield Rd, Leominster, Herefordshire, HR6 8SD, England. **(T)** 01568 612053
Contact/s
Owner: Mark Doyle **(T)** 01568 612053
Profile Stable/Livery, Trainer. Yr. Est: 1998
C.Size: 18 Acres Ref: **YH04249**

DOYLE, P.J.

Doyle P.J., Ramsgate, Gorey, **County Wexford**, **IRELAND**.
(T) 055 21357.
Profile Supplies. Ref: **YH04250**

DRAGON STUD

Dragon Stud, Bakers Farm, Bakers Lane, Shipley, Horsham, **Sussex (West)**, RH13 7JJ, **ENGLAND**.
(T) 01403 741764.
Contact/s
Senior Partner: Mrs M Burrell
Profile Breeder. Ref: **YH04251**

DRAGONFLY SADDLERY

Dragonfly Saddlery, Ditchling Crossroads, Ditchling, Hassocks, **Sussex (West)**, BN6 8UQ, **ENGLAND**.
(T) 01273 844606
(W) www.dragonflysaddlery.co.uk
Affiliated Bodies C & G, SMS.
Contact/s
Owner: Mr R Paine **(Q)** C&G
Profile Medical Support, Riding Wear Retailer, Saddlery Retailer, Supplies.
Saddle Fitting No.Staff: 2 Yr. Est: 1978
Opening Times
Sp: Open 09:15. Closed 17:15.
Su: Open 09:15. Closed 17:15.
Au: Open 09:15. Closed 17:15.
Wn: Open 09:15. Closed 17:15. Ref: **YH04252**

DRAGONHOLD STABLES

Dragonhold Stables, Ballyvolan Farm, Upper Newcastle, Newcastle, **County Wicklow**, **IRELAND**.
(T) 01 2819017.
Profile Supplies. Ref: **YH04253**

DRAKE HSE DIY STABLES

Drake House DIY Stables, Eaves Hall Lane, West Bradford, Clitheroe, **Lancashire**, BB7 3JG, **ENGLAND**.
(T) 01200 425494 **(F)** 01200 442013.
Contact/s
Owner: Mrs A Chippendale
Profile Stable/Livery. Ref: **YH04254**

DRAKE, PHILIP

Philip Drake DWCF, Bramble Hill Hotel, Bramshaw, Lyndhurst, **Hampshire**, SO43 7JG, **ENGLAND**.
(T) 023 80814461.
Profile Farrier. Ref: **YH04255**

DRAKES FARM

Drakes Farm Riding School & Livery Stables,

Drakes Farm, Ilton, Ilminster, **Somerset**, TA19 9EY, **ENGLAND**.
(T) 01460 53918 **(F)** 01460 53918
Affiliated Bodies ABRS.
Contact/s
Owner: Mrs P Matravers **(Q)** BHSAI
Profile Horse/Rider Accom, Riding School, Stable/Livery. C.Size: 70 Acres
Opening Times
Sp: Open Mon - Sun 09:00. Closed Mon - Sun 21:00.
Su: Open Mon - Sun 09:00. Closed Mon - Sun 21:00.
Au: Open Mon - Sun 09:00. Closed Mon - Sun 21:00.
Wn: Open Mon - Sun 09:00. Closed Mon - Sun 21:00. **Ref: YH04256**

DRAPER, GARY

Gary Draper, Claygate, The Lane, Chawston, **Bedfordshire**, MK44 3BH, **ENGLAND**.
(T) 01480 212383 **(F)** 01480 212383
(M) 07976 637815.
Profile Medical Support. **Ref: YH04257**

DRAPER, JUDITH

Judith Draper, West Barns, Low Cocklaw, Berwick-upon-Tweed, **Northumberland**, TD15 1UY, **ENGLAND**.
(T) 01289 386697 **(F)** 01289 386301.
Profile Supplies. **Ref: YH04258**

DRAPER, M

Miss M Draper, Kalamunda, Jordans Lane, Pilley, Lymington, **Hampshire**, SO41 5QW, **ENGLAND**.
(T) 01590 678217.
Profile Breeder. **Ref: YH04259**

DRAPER, MARTIN RAY

Martin Ray Draper DWCF, 16 Hopcott Cl, Minehead, **Somerset**, TA24 5HB, **ENGLAND**.
(T) 01643 706583.
Profile Farrier. **Ref: YH04260**

DRAUGHTON HEIGHT

Draughton Height Riding School, Height Lane, Draughton, Skipton, **Yorkshire (North)**, BD23 6DU, **ENGLAND**.
(T) 01756 710242.
Contact/s
Owner: Mrs N Halstead
Profile Riding School. **Ref: YH04261**

DRAYDON FARM

Draydon Farm, Dulverton, **Somerset**, TA22 9QE, **ENGLAND**.
(T) 01398 324345 **(F)** 01398 234338.
Profile Stable/Livery. **Ref: YH04262**

DREAPER JIM

Dreaper Jim, Greenogue Kilsallaghan, Dublin, **County Dublin**, **IRELAND**.
(T) 01 8350187 **(F)** 01 8353102.
Profile Supplies. **Ref: YH04263**

DREFACH EQUESTRIAN CTRE

Drefach Equestrian Centre, Cae Gwyn Rd, Drefach, Llanelli, **Carmarthenshire**, SA14 7BB, **WALES**.
(T) 01269 841224.
Profile Equestrian Centre. **Ref: YH04264**

DREGHORN, R

Mr R Dreghorn, 45 Church St, Lochwinnoch, **Renfrewshire**, PA12 4AE, **SCOTLAND**.
(T) 01505 842488. **Ref: YH04265**

DRESSAGE HORSE INT

Dressage Horse International Ltd, Moss Lea, Highfield Rd, Croston, Preston, **Lancashire**, PR5 7HH, **ENGLAND**.
(T) 01772 601753 **(F)** 01772 601331.
Profile Breeder. **Ref: YH04266**

DRESSAGE IRELAND

Dressage Ireland, 71 Killynure Rd West, Carryduff, **County Down**, BT8 8EA, **NORTHERN IRELAND**.
(T) 028 97563280.
Contact/s
Secretary: Mr R McCormick
Profile Club/Association. **Ref: YH04267**

DRESSAGE TRAINING CTRE

Dressage Training Centre, Watling St, Radlett, **Hertfordshire**, WD7 7AA, **ENGLAND**.
(T) 01923 440934.
Contact/s
Owner: Miss K McWhirter
Profile Trainer. **Ref: YH04268**

DREW, J R

J R Drew, Mildmay Vetnry Ctre, Eastgate St, Winchester, **Hampshire**, SO23 8DZ, **ENGLAND**.
(T) 01962 854088 **(F)** 01962 870844.
Profile Medical Support. **Ref: YH04269**

DREWE, C J

Mr C J Drewe, Lower Cross Farm, Blewbury Rd, East Hagbourne, Didcot, **Oxfordshire**, OX11 9ND, **ENGLAND**.
(T) 01235 813124
(M) 07979 903184.
Profile Trainer. **Ref: YH04270**

DREWITT

Drewitt Horse Drawn Vehicle Hire, 36 Hazon Way, Epsom, **Surrey**, KT19 8HN, **ENGLAND**.
(T) 01372 727153 **(F)** 01372 727153.
Contact/s
Owner: Mr A Drewitt
Profile Horse Drawn Vehicle Hire. **Ref: YH04271**

DRI-EX GALLOPS

Dri-Ex Gallops, Banks Plants Ltd, Frogham Hill, Fordingbridge, **Hampshire**, SP6 2HW, **ENGLAND**.
(T) 01425 654675 **(F)** 01425 655727.
Profile Track/Course. **Ref: YH04272**

DRIFFIELD DISCOUNT SADDLERY

Driffield Discount Saddlery, 91 Middle St South, Driffield, **Yorkshire (East)**, YO25 6QE, **ENGLAND**.
(T) 01377 240999.
Contact/s
Owner: Mr R Hoe
Profile Saddlery Retailer. **Ref: YH04273**

DRIFTEND STABLES

Driftend Stables, Driftwood Rd, Bourn, **Cambridgeshire**, CB3 7TP, **ENGLAND**.
(T) 01954 719565.
Profile Farrier. **Ref: YH04274**

DRINKWATER, J

Mrs J Drinkwater, 90 Farm Rd, Garden City, **Flintshire**, CH5 2HJ, **WALES**.
(T) 01244 811047.
Profile Breeder. **Ref: YH04275**

DRIVALL

Drivall Ltd, Narrow Lane, Hurst Green, Halesowen, **Midlands (West)**, B62 9PA, **ENGLAND**.
(T) 0121 4231122 **(F)** 0121 4232020.
Profile Fencing Supplier.
Supply electric fence systems for all types of livestock and pets, as well as a full range of fencing tools, fasteners and accessories. **Ref: YH04276**

DRIVER, J G & A S

J G & A S Driver, Meadow Farm, Cross Moor Lane, Haxby, **Yorkshire (North)**, YO32 2QR, **ENGLAND**.
(T) 01904 763400.
Contact/s
Owner: Mr J Driver
Profile Stable/Livery. **Ref: YH04277**

DRIVER, P R

P R Driver, 105A Harepath Rd, Seaton, **Devon**, EX12 2DX, **ENGLAND**.
(T) 01297 21109.
Profile Blacksmith. **Ref: YH04278**

DROVERS FORGE

Drovers Forge, Brooms Lane, Leadgate, Consett, **County Durham**, DH8 6RS, **ENGLAND**.
(T) 01207 506234 **(F)** 01207 506234.
Contact/s
Owner: Mr P Reid
Profile Blacksmith. **Ref: YH04279**

DRUM FEEDS

Drum Feeds, Todhills Farm, 684 Old Dalkeith Rd, Danderhall, Edinburgh, **Edinburgh (City of)**, EH22 1RR, **SCOTLAND**.
(T) 0131 6542185 **(F)** 0131 6634889.
Profile Saddlery Retailer. **Ref: YH04280**

DRUM MOORE FARM SHOP

Drum Moore Farm Shop, Todhills Farm, 684 Old Dalkeith Rd, Danderhall, Edinburgh, **Edinburgh (City of)**, EH22 1RR, **SCOTLAND**.
(T) 0131 6631504 **(F)** 0131 6634889.
Contact/s
General Manager: Mrs J Dipson
Profile Riding Wear Retailer, Saddlery Retailer.
Yr. Est: 1990
Opening Times
Sp: Open Mon - Sat 10:00. Closed Mon - Fri 17:00, Sat 16:00.
Su: Open Mon - Sat 10:00. Closed Mon - Fri 17:00, Sat 16:00.
Au: Open Mon - Sat 10:00. Closed Mon - Fri 17:00, Sat 16:00.
Wn: Open Mon - Sat 10:00. Closed Mon - Fri 17:00, Sat 16:00. **Ref: YH04281**

DRUM RIDING

Drum Riding For The Disabled Centre, Drum Est, Edinburgh, **Edinburgh (City of)**, EH17 8RX, **SCOTLAND**.
(T) 0131 6645803.
Profile Riding School. **Ref: YH04282**

DRUMAHEGLIS RIDING SCHOOL

Drumaheglis Riding School, 89 Glenstall Rd, Ballymoney, **County Antrim**, BT53 7NB, **NORTHERN IRELAND**.
(T) 028 27665500
Affiliated Bodies BHS.
Profile Riding School, Stable/Livery. **Ref: YH04283**

DRUM-A-HOY

Drum-a-Hoy Equestrian Feeds, 78A Carsonstown Rd, Saintfield, **County Down**, BT24 7AE, **NORTHERN IRELAND**.
(T) 028 97511394 **(F)** 028 97519229.
Profile Supplies. **Ref: YH04284**

DRUMAWHEY

Drumawhey Stud, 165 Whitehall Rd, Uxbridge, **London (Greater)**, UB8 2DS, **ENGLAND**.
(T) 01895 846606.
Contact/s
Owner: Mrs J Courtney-Phipps
Profile Breeder, Medical Support, Stable/Livery.
Yr. Est: 1960
Opening Times
Telephone for an appointment **Ref: YH04285**

DRUMBEG EQUINE CTRE

Drumbeg Equine Centre, Drumbeg, Drymen, Glasgow, **Lanarkshire (North)**, G63 0DW, **SCOTLAND**.
(T) 01360 660080 **(F)** 01360 660621.
Contact/s
Owner: Mrs S McKenzie
Profile Equestrian Centre, Stable/Livery.
Ref: YH04286

DRUMBRAE FARM AND RIDING CTRE

Drumbrae Farm and Riding Centre, Drumbrae Farm, Bridge Of Allan, Stirling, **Stirling**, FK9 4LT, **SCOTLAND**.
(T) 01786 832247.
Contact/s
Owner: Mr D McNicol
Profile Riding School. **Ref: YH04287**

DRUMCARROW

Drumcarrow Craig Livery Yard, Denhead, St Andrews, **Fife**, KY16 8PB, **SCOTLAND**.
(T) 01334 850115.
Contact/s
Owner: Mr H Lohoar
Profile Stable/Livery.
Full, part, DIY and grazing livery available, prices on request. Yr. Est: 1998 C.Size: 150 Acres
Opening Times
Sp: Open 07:00. Closed 21:00.
Su: Open 07:00. Closed 21:00.
Au: Open 07:00. Closed 21:00.
Wn: Open 07:00. Closed 21:00. **Ref: YH04288**

DRUMCOYLE LIVERY YARD

Drumcoyle Livery Yard, Drumcoyle Stables, Woodhead Rd, Coylton, Sundrum, Ayr, **Ayrshire (South)**, KA6 5JZ, **SCOTLAND**.
(T) 01292 570170.
Contact/s
Partner: Mr G Schuler
Profile Stable/Livery.
Livery - DIY costs £15.00 plus £10.00 for haylage. Full livery also available. Yr. Est: 1990
Opening Times
Sp: Open 08:00. Closed 20:00.
Su: Open 08:00. Closed 20:00.
Au: Open 08:00. Closed 20:00.
Wn: Open 08:00. Closed 20:00. **Ref: YH04289**

DRUMGOOLAND HOUSE

Drumgooland House & Equestrian Centre, 29 Dunnanew Rd, Seaforde, Downpatrick, **County Down**, BT30 8PJ, **NORTHERN IRELAND**.
(T) 028 44811956
(E) frank.mc_leigh@virgin.net.
Profile Riding School. **Ref: YH04290**

DRUMHONEY STABLES

Drumhoney Stables, Drumhoney, Irvinestown, Enniskillen, **County Fermanagh**, BT94 1NB, **NORTHERN IRELAND**.
(T) 028 68621892.
Profile Equestrian Centre. Trekking Centre.
The centre boasts one of the finest bridleways in the county, through Castle Archdale Country Park and the Mullies Forest, with 1000 acres of scenic riding. The stables caters for all, beginners, experienced and the disabled.
Opening Times
The stables are open all year round. **Ref: YH04291**

DRUMSAMNEY EQUESTRIAN CTRE

Drumsamney Equestrian Centre, 15 Drumsamney Rd, Desertmartin, Magherafelt, **County Londonderry**, BT45 5LA, **NORTHERN IRELAND**.
(T) 028 79642647 **(F)** 028 79642647.
Contact/s
Owner: Mrs V Johnson
Profile Equestrian Centre, Stable/Livery.
The cross country course is available for hire and there are also horse drawn carriages for hire for formal occasions. No.Staff: 2 Yr. Est: 1992
C.Size: 100 Acres
Opening Times
Sp: Open Mon - Sat 09:00. Closed Mon - Sat 21:00.
Su: Open Mon - Sat 09:00. Closed Mon - Sat 21:00.
Au: Open Mon - Sat 09:00. Closed Mon - Sat 21:00.
Wn: Open Mon - Sat 09:00. Closed Mon - Sat 21:00.
Ref: YH04292

DRURIDGE RIDING CLUB

Druridge Riding Club, 5 Marine St, Newbiggin, **Northumberland**, NE64 6BG, **ENGLAND**.
(T) 01670 852192.
Contact/s
Chairman: Mrs M Dodds
Profile Club/Association, Riding Club. **Ref: YH04293**

DRURY FARM SADDLERY

Drury Farm Saddlery, Drury Farm, 1 Hilltop Rd, Newmillerdam, Wakefield, **Yorkshire (West)**, WF2 6PY, **ENGLAND**.
(T) 01924 255015.
Profile Saddlery Retailer. **Ref: YH04294**

DRURY STUD FARM

Drury Stud Farm, Drury Lane, Bentworth, Alton, **Hampshire**, GU34 5RL, **ENGLAND**.
(T) 01420 562365.
Profile Breeder. **Ref: YH04295**

DRURY TRANSPORT

Drury Transport, Winksetter Farm, Harray, Orkney, **Orkney Isles**, KW17 2JR, **SCOTLAND**.
(T) 01856 771469.
Contact/s
Owner: Mr R Drury
Profile Transport/Horse Boxes. **Ref: YH04296**

DRYBRIDGE VETNRY CLINIC

Drybridge Veterinary Clinic, 2A Wonastow Rd, Monmouth, **Monmouthshire**, NP25 5AH, **WALES**.
(T) 01600 712206.
Profile Medical Support. **Ref: YH04297**

DRYDEN RIDING CTRE

Dryden Riding Centre, Dryden, Selkirk, **Scottish Borders**, TD7 4NT, **SCOTLAND**.
(T) 01750 32208
Affiliated Bodies BHS.
Profile Riding School.
Trekking and hacking available. **Ref: YH04298**

DRYDEN TRAILERS

Dryden Trailers, Orissa Hse, Dodford, Northampton, **Northamptonshire**, NN7 4SR, **ENGLAND**.
(T) 01327 341150 **(F)** 01327 341150.
Contact/s
Owner: Mrs E Fields
Profile Transport/Horse Boxes. **Ref: YH04299**

DRYSDALE, A

Mr A Drysdale, 1 New Row, Boreland, **Fife**, KY1 3YH, **SCOTLAND**.
(T) 01592 521666.
Profile Trainer. **Ref: YH04300**

DRYSDALE, G

Mr G Drysdale, Warroch Home Farm, Kinross, **Perth and Kinross**, KY13 0RG, **SCOTLAND**.
(T) 01577 62258.
Profile Trainer. **Ref: YH04301**

DRYSGOED FARM FEEDS

Drysgoed Farm Feeds, Drysgoed Farm, Efail Isaf, Pontypridd, **Rhondda Cynon Taff**, CF38 1SN, **WALES**.
(T) 01443 202089.
Profile Feed Merchant. **Ref: YH04302**

DTA

Desford Tack Agency, 88 Newbold Rd, Desford, Leicester, **Leicestershire**, LE9 9GS, **ENGLAND**.
(T) 01455 828660 **(F)** 01455 822522
(E) info@desfordtackagency.co.uk
(W) www.desfordtackagency.co.uk.
Contact/s
Owner: Mrs B Comer
Profile No.Staff: 1 Yr. Est: 2000
Opening Times
Sp: Open 09:00. Closed 17:00.
Su: Open 09:00. Closed 17:00.
Au: Open 09:00. Closed 17:00.
Wn: Open 09:00. Closed 17:00.
Closed Sunday and Monday **Ref: YH04303**

DU PLESSIS, J M

Miss J M Du Plessis, Higher Pill Farm, Saltash, **Cornwall**, PL12 6LS, **ENGLAND**.
(T) 01752 842362 **(F)** 01752 842362.
Profile Supplies. **Ref: YH04304**

DUBEY, STEPHEN M

Stephen M Dubey DWCF, Horseshoe Hse, Maynards Green, Heathfield, **Sussex (East)**, TN21 0DE, **ENGLAND**.
(T) 01435 812736.
Profile Farrier. **Ref: YH04305**

DUCKHAVEN STUD

Duckhaven Stud, Lornborough Rd, Westward Hse, Bideford, **Devon**, EX39 1AA, **ENGLAND**.
(T) 01237 478648 **(F)** 01237 476239.
Profile Breeder. **Ref: YH04306**

DUCKHURST FARM

Duckhurst Farm Equestrian Centre, Clapper Lane, Staplehurst, **Kent**, TN12 0JW, **ENGLAND**.
(T) 01580 891057.
Profile Stable/Livery. **Ref: YH04307**

DUDLEY DIE FORGINGS

Dudley Die Forgings Ltd, PO Box 18, Dudley, **Midlands (West)**, DY2 0SE, **ENGLAND**.
(T) 01384 342550 **(F)** 01384 481521.
Profile Blacksmith. **Ref: YH04308**

DUDLEY, G (ESQ)

G Dudley Esq, Woodside Farm, Southend Arterial Rd, West Horndon, Brentwood, **Essex**, CM13 3LN, **ENGLAND**.
(T) 01277 811044.
Profile Breeder. **Ref: YH04309**

DUDLEY, S & M C

Mr S & Miss M C Dudley, Sandhurst, 100 Main St, Sedgeberrow, Evesham, **Worcestershire**, WR11 6UF, **ENGLAND**.
(T) 01386 881978.
Profile Medical Support. **Ref: YH04310**

DUDMOOR FARM

Dudmoor Farm Riding School, Old Dudmoor Farm, Dudmoor Farm Rd, Fairmile, Christchurch, **Dorset**, BH23 6AQ, **ENGLAND**.
(T) 01202 473826 **(F)** 01202 480207.
Profile Riding School, Stable/Livery. **Ref: YH04311**

DUERDEN, BRIAN ROBERT

Brian Robert Duerden AFCL BI, 3 Michlow Cl, Bradwell, Hope Valley, **Derbyshire**, S33 9GF, **ENGLAND**.
(T) 01433 620972.
Profile Farrier. **Ref: YH04312**

DUFF, A

A Duff, The Smiddy, Pencaitland, Tranent, **Lothian (East)**, EH34 5EB, **SCOTLAND**.
(T) 01875 340411.
Profile Farrier. **Ref: YH04313**

DUFFIELD, ANN

Ann Duffield, Sun Hill Farm, Constable Burton, Leyburn, **Yorkshire (North)**, DL8 5RL, **ENGLAND**.
(T) 01677 450303 **(F)** 01677 450993.
Contact/s
Owner: Mrs A Duffield
Profile Trainer. **Ref: YH04314**

DUFFIELD, GILLIAN

Mrs Gillian Duffield, Cedar Cottage, Burrough Green, Newmarket, **Suffolk**, CB8 9NE, **ENGLAND**.
(T) 01638 507544 **(F)** 01638 507183.
Profile Trainer. **Ref: YH04315**

DUFFIN, CLIVE

Clive Duffin, 28 Cranford Ave, Church Crookham, Fleet, **Hampshire**, GU13 0QU, **ENGLAND**.
(T) 01252 625322.
Contact/s
Owner: Mr C Duffin
Profile Farrier. **Ref: YH04316**

DUFFIN, JULIA

Julia Duffin Saddler, 68 Windermere Rd, Ealing, **London (Greater)**, W5 4TD, **ENGLAND**.
(T) 0181 567 6596
(M) 07977 114896
Affiliated Bodies SMS.
Contact/s
Saddler: Ms J Duffin
Profile Saddle Fitter.
Approved by the Sidesaddle Association.
Yr. Est: 1988
Opening Times
Telephone for an appointment. Ms Duffin works as a mobile saddle fitter. **Ref: YH04317**

DUFFIN, W

W Duffin, 170 Largy Rd, Ahoghill, Ballymena, **County Antrim**, BT42 2RQ, **NORTHERN IRELAND**.
(T) 028 25871525.
Contact/s
Owner: Mr W Duffin
Profile Transport/Horse Boxes. **Ref: YH04318**

DUFFY, J A & P

J A & P Duffy, Perth-Y-Ber, Llanedwen, Llanfair, **Isle of Anglesey**, LL61 6PJ, **WALES**.
(T) 01248 430648 **(F)** 01248 430016.
Profile Supplies. **Ref: YH04319**

DUFFY, THOMAS

Thomas Duffy DWCF, Laggan Cottage, Carron, Arberlour, **Moray**, AB38 7QP, **SCOTLAND**.
(T) 01340 810684.
Profile Farrier. **Ref: YH04320**

DUFOSSE, TERESA

Teresa Dufosse, Nyland Farm, Kington, **Dorset**, SP8 5SG, **ENGLAND**.
(T) 01963 370422
Affiliated Bodies NAAT.
Contact/s
Physiotherapist: Teresa Dufosse
Profile Medical Support. **Ref: YH04321**

DUGGAN, RALPH B

Ralph B Duggan RSS, Hillcot, Brunton Bank, Wall, Hexham, **Northumberland**, NE46 4EQ, **ENGLAND**.
(T) 01434 681827.
Profile Farrier. **Ref: YH04322**

DUKES PLACE STABLES

Dukes Place Stables, Bishop Thornton, Harrogate, **Yorkshire (North)**, HG3 3JY, **ENGLAND**.
(T) 01765 620676.
Contact/s
Owner: Mr C Johnson
Profile Riding School. **Ref: YH04323**

DUKES STUD

Dukes Stud, 36 Newmarket Rd, Ashley, Newmarket, **Suffolk**, CB8 9DR, **ENGLAND**.
(T) 01638 730214 **(F)** 01638 730214.
Contact/s
Owner: Mr M Wyatt
Profile Breeder. **Ref: YH04324**

DULIEU, B R

Mr B R Dulieu, Bower Heath Farm, Bower Heath, Harpenden, **Hertfordshire**, AL5 5DZ, **ENGLAND**.
(T) 01582 767891.
Profile Breeder. **Ref: YH04325**

DULWICH RIDING SCHOOL

Dulwich Riding School, Dulwich Common, London, **London (Greater)**, SE21 7EX, **ENGLAND**.
(T) 020 86932944.
Contact/s
Manager: Mr J Bellman
Profile Riding School. **Ref: YH04326**

DUMBELL, LUCY

Lucy Dumbell, Knapp Farm, Aston Ingham, Ross On Wye, **Herefordshire**, HR9 7LS, **ENGLAND**.
(T) 01989 720429.
Profile Trainer. **Ref: YH04327**

DUMBRECK RIDING SCHOOL

Dumbreck Riding School, 82 Dumbreck Rd, Glasgow, **Glasgow (City of)**, G41 4SN, **SCOTLAND**.
(T) 0141 4270660.

Profile Riding School, Stable/Livery. Ref:YH04328

DUN HORSE & PONY SOC

Dun Horse & Pony Society (DHAPS), 7 Newton Cl, Deer Pk, Ledbury, **Herefordshire**, HR8 2XG, **ENGLAND**.
(T) 01531 632585.
Profile Club/Association. Ref:YH04329

DUN, J M

Mr J M Dun, Gilston, Heriot, **Scottish Borders**, EH38 5YS, **SCOTLAND**.
(T) 01875 835300
(M) 07889 022468.
Profile Breeder. Ref:YH04330

DUNBAR EQUINE

Dunbar Equine Osteopathic & Physical Therapy Practice, 2 High St, Dunbar, **Lothian (East)**, EH42 1EL, **SCOTLAND**.
(T) 01368 864989
(M) 07970 852349
(E) tom@equine-osteopathy.freeserve.co.uk.
Profile Medical Support. Ref:YH04331

DUNBAR, DEBBIE

Debbie Dunbar, The Studio, Pengwern Ganol, Cenarth, Newcastle Emlyn, **Carmarthenshire**, SA38 9RL, **WALES**.
(T) 01239 710020.
Profile Artist. Ref:YH04332

DUNCALF, ALAN W

Alan W Duncalf DWCF, Swan Cottage, Breech Moss, Norley, Warrington, **Cheshire**, WA6 8LR, **ENGLAND**.
(T) 01928 788151.
Profile Farrier. Ref:YH04333

DUNCAN ENGLAND ENTERPRISES

Duncan England Enterprises Ltd, Great Steeds Farm, Copsale Rd, Copsale, Horsham, **Sussex (West)**, RH13 6QX, **ENGLAND**.
(T) 01403 730244 **(F)** 01403 733893.
Contact/s
Owner: Mr D England
Profile Transport/Horse Boxes. Ref:YH04334

DUNCHURCH LODGE STUD

Dunchurch Lodge Stud, Duchess Drive, Newmarket, **Suffolk**, CB8 9HB, **ENGLAND**.
(T) 01638 662115.
Profile Breeder. Ref:YH04335

DUNCRAHILL STUD

Duncrahill Stud, Pencaitland, Tranent, **Lothian (East)**, EH34 5ER, **SCOTLAND**.
(T) 01875 340264 **(F)** 01875 340264
(E) duncrahill@email.msn.com
(W) www.duncrahillstud.co.uk.
Contact/s
Owner: Joan Cadzow
(E) jcadzow@duncrahillstud.co.uk
Profile Breeder. Ref:YH04336

DUNCRUE TRAILERS

Duncrue Trailers Ltd, 1 Hydepark Lane, Newtownabbey, **County Antrim**, BT36 4QD, **NORTHERN IRELAND**.
(T) 028 90838338 **(F)** 028 90838338.
Contact/s
Owner: Mr T Watson
Profile Transport/Horse Boxes. Ref:YH04337

DUNCRYNE

Duncryne Equitation & Trekking Centre, Gartocharn, Loch Lomond, Alexandria, **Dunbartonshire (West)**, G83 8NG, **SCOTLAND**.
(T) 01389 830425.
Profile Riding School. Trekking Centre. Ref:YH04338

DUNDALK RACE

Dundalk Race Co Ltd, Racecourse, Dundalk, **County Louth**, **IRELAND**.
(T) 042 9334419.
Profile Supplies. Ref:YH04339

DUNDEE & PERTH POLO CLUB

Dundee & Perth Polo Club, 3 Nelson Pl, Edinburgh, **Edinburgh (City of)**, EH3 6LH, **SCOTLAND**.
(T) 0131 5573313.
Profile Club/Association. Polo Club. Ref:YH04340

DUNEDIN TRAINING GRP

Dunedin Combined Training Group, 53 Meadowhouse Rd, Edinburgh, **Edinburgh (City of)**, EH12 7HW, **SCOTLAND**.
(T) 0131 3347111 **(F)** 0131 3345988.
Contact/s
Chairman: Ms J MacLean
Profile Club/Association. Ref:YH04341

DUNES RIDING

Dunes Riding Centre, Cott Lane, Martletwy, Narberth, **Pembrokeshire**, SA67 8AB, **WALES**.
(T) 01834 891398 **(F)** 01834 891473
(W) www.dunes-riding.co.uk
Affiliated Bodies ABRS, BHS, Pony Club UK.
Contact/s
General Manager: Ms S Weaver **(Q)** BHS 1
Profile Equestrian Centre, Riding Club, Riding School.
Pony Trekking available. No.Staff: 5
Yr. Est: 1989 C.Size: 20 Acres
Opening Times
Sp: Open Dawn. Closed Dusk.
Su: Open Dawn. Closed Dusk.
Au: Open Dawn. Closed Dusk.
Wn: Open Dawn. Closed Dusk. Ref:YH04342

DUNKERY

Dunkery Stud, Riverside Farm, Wooton Courtenay, Minehead, **Somerset**, TA24 8RE, **ENGLAND**.
(T) 01643 841215.
Contact/s
General Manager: Mrs J Webber **(T)** 01643 841596
Profile Breeder, Stable/Livery. No.Staff: 1
Yr. Est: 1935 C.Size: 50 Acres
Opening Times
Telephone for an appointment Ref:YH04343

DUNLOP, H F

H F Dunlop, 2 Craigs Rd, Cullybackey, Ballymena, **County Antrim**, BT42 1PF, **NORTHERN IRELAND**.
(T) 028 25880272.
Profile Breeder. Ref:YH04344

DUNLOPS

Dunlops, Ryedale Rd, Troqueer, **Dumfries and Galloway**, DG2 7EG, **SCOTLAND**.
(T) 01387 263733 **(F)** 01387 254326.
Profile Medical Support. Ref:YH04345

DUNMALL, PHILIP J

Philip J Dunmall FWCF, 17 Oast Ct, Yalding, Maidstone, **Kent**, ME18 6JY, **ENGLAND**.
(T) 01622 813210.
Profile Farrier. Ref:YH04346

DUNMANWAY RIDING SCHOOL

Dunmanway Riding School, Dunmanway Riding School, Dunmanway, **County Cork**, **IRELAND**.
(T) 023 45604.
Profile Riding School. Ref:YH04347

DUNMORE-FRANCIS, VALERIE

Mrs Valerie Dunmore-Francis, Bradmore Farm, Old Coulsdon, **Surrey**, CR5 2LQ, **ENGLAND**.
(T) 01737 557936 **(F)** 01737 557936.
Profile Trainer. Ref:YH04348

DUNN, ALLAN

Mr Allan Dunn, The Maltings, Lynch, Allerford, Minehead, **Somerset**, TA24 8HJ, **ENGLAND**.
(T) 01643 863124.
Profile Supplies. Ref:YH04349

DUNN, D

D Dunn, 19 Rock Village, Alnwick, **Northumberland**, NE66 3SD, **ENGLAND**.
(T) 01665 79237.
Profile Farrier. Ref:YH04350

DUNN, NIGEL

Nigel Dunn Animal Bedding Supplier, George's Farm, Cutsey, Trull, Taunton, **Somerset**, TA3 7NX, **ENGLAND**.
(T) 01823 421530 **(F)** 01823 421530.
Profile Supplies. Ref:YH04351

DUNN, P SCOTT

Mr P Scott Dunn, Straight Mile Farm, Billingbear, Wokingham, **Berkshire**, RG40 5RW, **ENGLAND**.
(T) 01344 426066 **(F)** 01344 861041.
Profile Medical Support. Ref:YH04352

DUNNETT, CATHERINE (DR)

Dr Catherine Dunnett BSC, PHD, Dengie-Main Ring, Heybridge Business Ctre, 110 The Causway, Maldon, **Essex**, CM9 4ND, **ENGLAND**.
(T) 01621 841188 **(F)** 01621 842111
(E) catherine.dunnett@dengie.com.
Profile Medical Support. Ref:YH04353

DUNNING, P L

P L Dunning RSS, Rozel Forge, Stapleford Lane, Durley, Southampton, **Hampshire**, SO32 2BU, **ENGLAND**.
(T) 023 80692519.
Profile Farrier. Ref:YH04354

DUNNING, T

T Dunning, Victoria Buildings, Victoria Rd, Bishops Waltham, Southampton, **Hampshire**, SO32 1BG, **ENGLAND**.
(T) 01489 894527.
Contact/s
Owner: Mr T Dunning
Profile Farrier. Ref:YH04355

DUNNS TRAILERS

Dunns Trailers, 36 Russell Drv, Nottingham, **Nottinghamshire**, NG8 2BH, **ENGLAND**.
(T) 0115 9281770 **(F)** 0115 9281770.
Contact/s
Owner: Mr J Dunn
Profile Transport/Horse Boxes. Ref:YH04356

DUNSFOLD RYSE STABLES

Dunsfold Ryse Stables, Dunsfold Ryse, Chiddingfold, **Surrey**, GU8 4YA, **ENGLAND**.
(T) 01483 200866 **(F)** 01483 200596.
Profile Stable/Livery, Track/Course. Ref:YH04357

DUNSMORE STABLES

Dunsmore Stables, Dunsmore Village, Wendover, **Buckinghamshire**, HP22 6QL, **ENGLAND**.
(T) 01296 622399.
Profile Horse/Rider Accom. Ref:YH04358

DUNSTON HEATH

Dunston Heath Racing Stables, Yewtree Cottage, Dunston Heath, Stafford, **Staffordshire**, ST18 9AQ, **ENGLAND**.
(T) 01785 714166.
Contact/s
Owner: Mr T Walker
Profile Trainer. Ref:YH04359

DUNSTON WEST FARM

Dunston West Farm Livery Stable, Whickham Highway, Whickham, Newcastle-upon-Tyne, **Tyne and Wear**, NE16 4EP, **ENGLAND**.
(T) 0191 4887170.
Profile Stable/Livery. Ref:YH04360

DUNTON STABLES

Dunton Stables, Kingsbury Rd, Curdworth, Sutton Coldfield, **Midlands (West)**, B76 0DF, **ENGLAND**.
(T) 01675 470330
(M) 07950 146740.
Contact/s
Owner: Mr J Richards Ref:YH04361

DUNVEGAN EQUESTRIAN CTRE

Dunvegan Equestrian Centre, Dunvegan, Cupar Rd, Newburgh, Cupar, **Fife**, KY14 6HA, **SCOTLAND**.
(T) 01337 841103.
Contact/s
Owner: Mrs C Calley
Profile Equestrian Centre. Ref:YH04362

DURAL FARM ENTERPRISES

Dural Farm Enterprises, Dural Farm, Bradworthy, Holsworthy, **Devon**, EX22 7RA, **ENGLAND**.
(T) 01409 241666.
Profile Breeder, Saddlery Retailer. Ref:YH04363

DURALOC

Duraloc Ltd, Unit 7 Carlton Miniott Business Pk, Carlton Rd, Carlton Miniott, Thirsk, **Yorkshire (North)**, YO7 4NF, **ENGLAND**.
(T) 01845 525250 **(F)** 01845 525200.
Contact/s
Owner: Mr K Reynard
Profile Transport/Horse Boxes. Ref:YH04364

DURALOCK

Duralock (UK) Ltd, 36 Springfield Rd, Elburton, Plymouth, **Devon**, PL9 8EN, **ENGLAND**.
(T) 01752 484085.
Profile Track/Course. Manufacture Surfaces.
Ref:YH04365

DURALOCK

Duralock (UK) Ltd, Barston Hse, Great Rollright, Chipping Norton, **Oxfordshire**, OX7 5RH, **ENGLAND**.
(T) 01608 730684 **(F)** 01608 737885
(M) 07860 668183
(E) jss@seel.demon.co.uk.
Contact/s
Sales Manager: Mr J Seel
Profile Track/Course. Manufacture Surfaces.
Ref:YH04366

DURBIN, J W
J W Durbin, Wayside, New Passage Rd, Pilning, Bristol, **Bristol**, BS35 4LZ, **ENGLAND**.
(T) 01454 632222 **(F)** 01454 632222.
Contact/s
Owner: Mrs H Durbin
Profile Farrier. Ref: **YH04367**

DURDANS STABLES
Durdans Stables (The), Chalk Lane, Epsom, **Surrey**, KT18 7AT, **ENGLAND**.
(T) 01372 745112 **(F)** 01372 741944.
Profile Trainer. Ref: **YH04368**

DURFEE WARM BLOOD STUD
Durfee Warm Blood Stud (The), Moorlands Farm, New Yatt, Witney, **Oxfordshire**, OX8 6TE, **ENGLAND**.
(T) 01993 868673.
Contact/s
Stud Manager: B A Wallin
Profile Breeder. Ref: **YH04369**

DURHAM LEYS FARM
Durham Leys Farm, Marsh Baldon, Oxford, **Oxfordshire**, OX44 9LP, **ENGLAND**.
(T) 01865 341311.
Contact/s
Owner: Mr R Wells Ref: **YH04370**

DURKIN, MICHAEL
Michael Durkin DWCF, Knowsley Farm, Bells Lane, Hoghton, Preston, **Lancashire**, PR5 0JJ, **ENGLAND**.
(T) 01254 853483.
Profile Farrier. Ref: **YH04371**

DURRANT, R C
R C Durrant, Bendyshehall, 84 High St, Bottisham, Cambridge, **Cambridgeshire**, CB5 9BA, **ENGLAND**.
(T) 01223 811455.
Contact/s
Owner: Mr R Durrant **(T)** 01223 812314
Profile Supplies. Ref: **YH04372**

DURRANT, R C & D A
R C & D A Durrant, Sunny Ridge Farm, Lode, Cambridge, **Cambridgeshire**, CB5 9EW, **ENGLAND**.
(T) 01223 811213.
Contact/s
Owner: Mr R Durrant
Profile Hay and Straw Merchants. Ref: **YH04373**

DURTNELL VETNRY CTRE
Durtnell Veterinary Centre, 255 Beeston Rd, Leeds, **Yorkshire (West)**, LS11 7LR, **ENGLAND**.
(T) 0113 2775350.
Profile Medical Support. Ref: **YH04374**

DURTNELL VETNRY CTRE
Durtnell Veterinary Centre, 260 Tong Rd, Leeds, **Yorkshire (West)**, LS12 3BG, **ENGLAND**.
(T) 0113 2791576.
Profile Medical Support. Ref: **YH04375**

DUTFIELD, P N
Mrs P N Dutfield, Crabhayne Farm, Axmouth, Seaton, **Devon**, EX12 4BW, **ENGLAND**.
(T) 01297 553560.
Profile Trainer. Ref: **YH04376**

DUTTON
Mr & Mrs Dutton, Barnshaw Hall Farm, Barnshaw, Holmes Chapel, **Cheshire**, CW4 8DE, **ENGLAND**.
(T) 01477 571301 **(F)** 01477 571301.
Profile Breeder. Ref: **YH04377**

DUTTON, G
G Dutton RSS, 9 Mornington Rd, Canvey Island, **Essex**, SS8 8DU, **ENGLAND**.
(T) 01268 27192.
Profile Farrier. Ref: **YH04378**

DUTTON, IAN J
Ian J Dutton DWCF, 2 Liskeard Way, Freshbrook, Swindon, **Wiltshire**, SN5 8NL, **ENGLAND**.
(T) 01793 618247.
Profile Farrier. Ref: **YH04379**

DUTTON, PHILLIP
Phillip Dutton (AUS), C/O Church Farm, Long Newnton, Tetbury, **Gloucestershire**, GL8 8RS, **ENGLAND**.
(T) 01666 502352 **(F)** 01666 504803. Ref: **YH04380**

DWYER, C A
Cedar Lodge Racing Stables, Hamilton Rd, Newmarket, **Suffolk**, CB8 0NQ, **ENGLAND**.
(T) 01638 667857 **(F)** 01638 667857
(M) 07831 579844
(W) www.newmarketracehorsetrainers.co.uk
Affiliated Bodies Newmarket Trainers Fed.
Contact/s
Trainer: Mr C Dwyer
Profile Trainer. Ref: **YH04381**

DWYFOR RIDING CTRE
Dwyfor Riding Centre, Llanystumdwy, Criccieth, **Gwynedd**, LL52 0LU, **WALES**.
(T) 01766 523349.
Profile Breeder, Riding School, Stable/Livery.
Ref: **YH04382**

DYAS-HARROLD, MARK
Mark Dyas-Harrold DWCF, 40 Oakwood Rd, Wollescote, Stourbridge, **Midlands (West)**, DY9 9DL, **ENGLAND**.
(T) 01384 897746.
Profile Farrier. Ref: **YH04383**

DYAS-HARROLD, P
P Dyas-Harrold, Lutley Forge, 59 Wychbury Rd, Pedmore, Stourbridge, **Midlands (West)**, DY9 9HP, **ENGLAND**.
(T) 01562 884524.
Profile Farrier. Ref: **YH04384**

DYER, H
H Dyer AWCF, The Forge, Londonderry, Northallerton, **Yorkshire (North)**, DL7 9NE, **ENGLAND**.
(T) 01677 422587.
Profile Farrier. Ref: **YH04385**

DYER, J
J Dyer, Walnut Tree Farm, Prickwillow Rd, Isleham, Ely, **Cambridgeshire**, CB7 5RG, **ENGLAND**.
(T) 01638 780680 **(F)** 01638 781500.
Contact/s
Owner: Mr J Dyer
Profile Transport/Horse Boxes. Ref: **YH04386**

DYER, NICHOLAS J
Nicholas J Dyer DWCF, 14 Lavers Oak, Martock, **Somerset**, TA12 6HG, **ENGLAND**.
(T) 01935 824852.
Profile Farrier. Ref: **YH04387**

DYFED RIDING CTRE
Dyfed Riding Centre, Maesyfelin, Bridell, Cardigan, **Ceredigion**, SA43 3DG, **WALES**.
(T) 01239 612594.
Contact/s
Owner: Mrs T Humfrey
Profile Riding School.
There is a paddock which is used for jumping and lessons throughout the summer and hacking is also available. The RDA meet at the stables on a regular basis.
Opening Times
Sp: Open Tues - Sat 10:00. Closed Tues - Sat 19:00.
Su: Open Tues - Sat 10:00. Closed Tues - Sat 19:00.
Au: Open Tues - Sat 10:00. Closed Tues - Sat 19:00.
Wn: Open Tues - Sat 10:00. Closed Tues - Sat 19:00.
Ref: **YH04388**

DYFFRYN CLETTWR RIDING CLUB
Dyffryn Clettwr Riding Club, Ty Lan Lawr, Ffos-Y-Ffin, Aberaeron, **Ceredigion**, SA46 0EL, **WALES**.
(T) 01545 570914.
Contact/s
Chairman: Mr P Day
Profile Club/Association, Riding Club. Ref: **YH04389**

DYFFRYN PAITH RIDING GRP
Dyffryn Paith Riding Group, Nevadd, Ciliau Aeron, Dyffryn Paith, Lampeter, **Ceredigion**, SA48 8DE, **WALES**.
(T) 01570 470100.
Contact/s
Chairman: Mrs A Blygh
Profile Club/Association. Ref: **YH04390**

DYKE, J D
Mr J D Dyke, Acresdyke, 63 Laughton Rd, Lubenham, Market Harborough, **Leicestershire**, LE16 9TE, **ENGLAND**.
(T) 01858 465892 **(F)** 01858 462772
(E) patandjohn@dyke.tslnet.co.uk. Ref: **YH04391**

DYKES, J H & D J
J H & D J Dykes, 55 Heol Onnen, North Cornelly, **Neath Port Talbot**, CF33 4DT, **WALES**.
(T) 01656 741484.
Contact/s
Owner: Mr D Dykes
Profile Breeder.
Breeder of Welsh Section A, D and C ponies
Ref: **YH04392**

E & L INSURANCE
E & L Insurance, PO Box 100, Ouseburn, **Yorkshire (North)**, YO26 9SZ, **ENGLAND**.
(T) 01423 330711 **(F)** 01423 331008.
Profile Insurance Company. Ref: **YH04393**

E & S FEEDS
E & S Feeds (Tillicoultry), 71 Ochil St, Tillicoultry, **Clackmannanshire**, FK13 6EJ, **SCOTLAND**.
(T) 01259 752002 **(F)** 01259 752002.
Profile Feed Merchant. Ref: **YH04394**

E A JAQUES
E A Jaques Willowcroft Livery, Willowcroft, Whitton Rd, Alkborough, Scunthorpe, **Lincolnshire (North)**, DN15 9JG, **ENGLAND**.
(T) 01724 721352.
Contact/s
Owner: Ms E Jaques
Profile Stable/Livery. Ref: **YH04395**

E ABINGTON & SONS
E Abington & Sons Ltd, 2 East St, Kimbolton, Huntingdon, **Cambridgeshire**, PE18 0HJ, **ENGLAND**.
(T) 01480 860224.
Profile Saddlery Retailer. Ref: **YH04396**

E ADAMS & SON
E Adams & Son, Smithy Cottage, Butterleigh, Cullompton, **Devon**, EX15 1PL, **ENGLAND**.
(T) 01884 855387 **(F)** 01884 855387.
Contact/s
Owner: Mr E Adams
Profile Blacksmith. Ref: **YH04397**

E B OWEN & SON
E B Owen & Son, Forge Mill, Templeton, Narberth, **Pembrokeshire**, SA67 8SG, **WALES**.
(T) 01834 860452 **(F)** 01834 860452.
Contact/s
Owner: Mr B Owen
Profile Blacksmith. Ref: **YH04398**

E C L MARKETING
E C L Marketing, 33 Mariner Gardens, Ham, Richmond, **Surrey**, TW10 7UU, **ENGLAND**.
(T) 020 89403725 **(F)** 020 83322054
(M) 07860 546687.
Profile Club/Association. Ref: **YH04399**

E D SIMPSON & SON
E D Simpson & Son Ltd, 7 Brook St, Shepshed, Leicester, **Leicestershire**, LE12 9RE, **ENGLAND**.
(T) 01509 503228.
Profile Medical Support. Ref: **YH04400**

E D T
Equine Dental Technician, 7 North View, Medomsley, Consett, **County Durham**, DH8 6PJ, **ENGLAND**.
(T) 01207 563169.
Contact/s
Owner: Mr N McCormack
Profile Medical Support, Trainer.
Mobile Equine Dental Technician.
Opening Times
Telephone for an appointment Ref: **YH04401**

E DODSWORTH & SON
E Dodsworth & Son, Overdale Hse, Main St, Harome, York, **Yorkshire (North)**, YO62 5JF, **ENGLAND**.
(T) 01439 770210.
Profile Transport/Horse Boxes. Ref: **YH04402**

E EDWARDS & SON
E Edwards & Son, Fron Bach, Lon Fron, Llangefni, **Isle of Anglesey**, LL77 7HB, **WALES**.
(T) 01248 750710.
Profile Breeder. Ref: **YH04403**

E F SVEIKUTIS BLACKSMITH
E F Sveikutis Traditional Blacksmith, Summit Locks, Stoke-on-Trent, **Staffordshire**, ST4 7AF, **ENGLAND**.
(T) 01782 204759.
Profile Blacksmith. Ref: **YH04404**

E G CAMPBELL
E G Campbell, 4 Ardlough Rd, Drumahoe, **County Londonderry**, BT47 5SW, **NORTHERN IRELAND**.
(T) 028 71311448.
Profile Medical Support. Ref: **YH04405**

E G WATSON & PARTNERS
E G Watson & Partners, West Farm, Front St, Earsdon, Whitley Bay, **Tyne and Wear**, NE25 9JU,

ENGLAND.
(T) 0191 2529386.
Contact/s
Partner: Mr E Watson
Profile Stable/Livery.
Full, part and DIY Livery available, prices on request.
Ref: YH04406

E H HUTTON

E H Hutton (Coachbuilders) Ltd, Coston, Melton Mowbray, **Leicestershire**, LE14 2RP, **ENGLAND**.
(T) 01476 860278 **(F)** 01476 861258.
Profile Transport/Horse Boxes. **Ref: YH04407**

E J A FROST

E J A Frost Ltd, The Forge, 22 Castle St, Eccleshall, Stafford, **Staffordshire**, ST21 6DF, **ENGLAND**.
(T) 01785 850312.
Contact/s
Owner: Mrs J Swinnerton
Profile Blacksmith. **Ref: YH04408**

E J SNELL & SONS

E J Snell & Sons, Paramount, Week, Harracott, Barnstaple, **Devon**, EX31 3JG, **ENGLAND**.
(T) 01271 858229 **(F)** 01271 858650.
Profile Supplies. **Ref: YH04409**

E JEFFRIES & SONS

E Jeffries & Sons, George St, Walsall, **Midlands (West)**, WS1 1SD, **ENGLAND**.
(T) 01922 642222 **(F)** 01922 615043
(E) sales@ejeffries.co.uk
Affiliated Bodies SMS.
Contact/s
Chief Executive: Mr D Kent
Profile Saddler. No.Staff: 100 **Ref: YH04410**

E K M EQUESTRIAN

E K M Equestrian, Willowbrook, Penybryn, Pyle, Bridgend, **Bridgend**, CF33 6RB, **WALES**.
(T) 01656 743950
Affiliated Bodies BHS.
Contact/s
Owner: Mrs K Milburn **(Q)** BHSI
(E) louis.kay@virgin.net
Profile Equestrian Centre, Riding School, Stable/Livery, Trainer. No.Staff: 5 Yr. Est: 1980
C.Size: 35 Acres **Ref: YH04411**

E K READMAN & SONS

E K Readman & Sons, High St, Cloughton, Scarborough, **Yorkshire (North)**, YO13 0AE, **ENGLAND**.
(T) 01723 870376 **(F)** 01723 870376.
Contact/s
Owner: Mr A Readman
Profile Saddlery Retailer. **Ref: YH04412**

E KENT & SON

E Kent & Son, The Forge, Exford, Minehead, **Somerset**, TA24 7PX, **ENGLAND**.
(T) 01643 831264.
Contact/s
Owner: Mr E Kent
Profile Farrier. **Ref: YH04413**

E L F FEEDS

E L F Feeds, East Luccombe Farm, Luccombe, Minehead, **Somerset**, TA24 8TE, **ENGLAND**.
(T) 01643 862493.
Profile Feed Merchant. **Ref: YH04414**

E M C

Equine Management Consultants, 17 Ormonde Way, Shoreham By Sea, **Sussex (West)**, BN43 5YB, **ENGLAND**.
(T) 01273 382354 **(F)** 01273 382354
(M) 07710 068876
(E) info@equineman.com
(W) www.equineman.com.
Contact/s
Owner: Mr S Biddlecombe
Profile Saddlery Retailer, Supplies.
Main distributor of 'Defy the Fly' products.
Ref: YH04415

E M JACOBS & SONS

E M Jacobs & Sons, The Forge, Bucklesham Rd, Kirton, Ipswich, **Suffolk**, IP10 0NU, **ENGLAND**.
(T) 01394 448253.
Profile Blacksmith. **Ref: YH04416**

E N ROBERTSON & SON

E N Robertson & Son, Queenswell Rd, Forfar, **Angus**, DD8 3JA, **SCOTLAND**.
(T) 01307 463331.
Contact/s
Owner: Mr B Robertson
Profile Blacksmith. **Ref: YH04417**

E P BARRUS

E P Barrus Ltd, Launton Rd, Bicester, **Oxfordshire**, OX6 0UR, **ENGLAND**.
(T) 01869 363636 **(F)** 01869 363600.
Profile Transport/Horse Boxes.
UK distributors of ATV's and light agricultural vehicles.
Ref: YH04418

E P C

E P C, Unit 1 Deverill Rd Trading Est, Deverill Rd, Sutton Veny, Warminster, **Wiltshire**, BA12 7BZ, **ENGLAND**.
(T) 01985 841144 **(F)** 01985 841188.
Contact/s
Owner: Mr C Reeves
Profile Supplies. **Ref: YH04419**

E P ISLES

E P Isles, Bensons Lane, Woodplumpton, Preston, **Lancashire**, PR4 0BL, **ENGLAND**.
(T) 01772 690245.
Contact/s
Owner: Mrs E Isles
Profile Breeder. **Ref: YH04420**

E P TOWING

E P Towing, 54 Darlington Cres, Saughall, Chester, **Cheshire**, CH1 6DB, **ENGLAND**.
(T) 01244 881609.
Profile Transport/Horse Boxes. **Ref: YH04421**

E Q

E Q, Church Farm, St Cross, Harleston, **Suffolk**, IP20 0NY, **ENGLAND**.
(T) 01986 782368 **(F)** 01986 782466
(E) fmw@eqmag.uk.co.
Contact/s
Equestrian Manager: F Wilmott
Profile Supplies. **Ref: YH04422**

E S EVERITT

E S Everitt Livestock Transport, Moat Farm, Stockwood, Redditch, **Worcestershire**, B96 6SX, **ENGLAND**.
(T) 01386 792267.
Profile Transport/Horse Boxes. **Ref: YH04423**

E S G SVS

E S G Services, Every St, Fernhill, Bury, **Lancashire**, BL9 5BE, **ENGLAND**.
(T) 0161 7642002 **(F)** 0161 7646552.
Profile Transport/Horse Boxes. **Ref: YH04424**

E STRACHAN

E Strachan, The Smiddy, Castlehill, Kintore, Inverurie, **Aberdeenshire**, AB51 0TZ, **SCOTLAND**.
(T) 01467 632374 **(F)** 01467 633013.
Contact/s
Owner: Mr E Strachan
Profile Blacksmith. **Ref: YH04425**

E SWINBURN & SON

E Swinburn & Son, Hedley West Farm, Marley Hill, Newcastle-upon-Tyne, **Tyne and Wear**, NE16 5EQ, **ENGLAND**.
(T) 01207 232893.
Profile Supplies. **Ref: YH04426**

E T A

East Thames Aggregates Ltd, Thameside Hse, Schoolfield Rd, West Thurrock, **Essex**, RM20 3HR, **ENGLAND**.
(T) 01708 869787 **(F)** 01708 861163.
Contact/s
General Manager: Mr B Tulip
Profile Arena, Supplies.
Silica sand and aggregate supplies for arena flooring and roofing. No.Staff: 7 Yr. Est: 1990
Ref: YH04427

E T C SAW MILLS

E T C Saw Mills Ltd, Ellesmere, **Shropshire**, SY12 9JW, **ENGLAND**.
(T) 01691 622441 **(F)** 01691 623468.
Contact/s
Sales Manager: Mr T Wakefield
Profile Transport/Horse Boxes. **Ref: YH04428**

E T M

E T M Ltd, White Farm, Wilton Lane, Culcheth, Warrington, **Cheshire**, WA3 4BA, **ENGLAND**.
(T) 01942 604979.
Contact/s
Owner: Mr M White
Profile Breeder. **Ref: YH04429**

E V J POSTAL BOOKSHOP

E V J Postal Bookshop, Graseby Hse, Exning Rd, Newmarket, **Suffolk**, CB8 0AU, **ENGLAND**.
(T) 01638 666160 **(F)** 01638 668665
(E) evj.subs@dial.pipex.com.
Profile Supplies. **Ref: YH04430**

E WARD & SON

E Ward & Son (Easingwold) Ltd, York Rd, Easingwold, York, **Yorkshire (North)**, YO61 3BB, **ENGLAND**.
(T) 01347 821359.
Profile Transport/Horse Boxes. **Ref: YH04431**

E WILLIAMS FARMERS

E Williams Farmers Ltd, Barn End Farm, Barn End Lane, Wilmington, Dartford, **Kent**, DA2 7QA, **ENGLAND**.
(T) 01322 223019.
Profile Supplies. **Ref: YH04432**

E, THOMAS & WILLIAMS, R

R Williams & E Thomas, Ty Wian, Llanfairynghornwy, Holyhead, **Isle of Anglesey**, LL65 4LL, **WALES**.
(T) 01407 710284.
Profile Breeder. **Ref: YH04433**

E.CO IRELAND

E.Co Ireland, 26 Whappstown Rd, Moorfields, Ballymena, **County Antrim**, BT42 3DA, **NORTHERN IRELAND**.
(T) 028 94432272 **(F)** 028 94433424.
Profile Supplies. **Ref: YH04434**

EACOCK, KAREN

Karen Eacock BHSI(SM), Fair Mile, Stoke Prior, Leominster, **Herefordshire**, HR6 0LR, **ENGLAND**.
(T) 01568 760310.
Profile Trainer. **Ref: YH04435**

EAGER, ROSS A

Ross A Eager DWCF, Manor Barn, Sands Farm, Dial Post, **Sussex (West)**, RH13 8NY, **ENGLAND**.
(T) 01403 711963.
Profile Farrier. **Ref: YH04436**

EAGLE HALL EST

Eagle Hall Estate Livery Yard Centre, Grange Farm, South Scarle Lane, North Scarle, Lincoln, **Lincolnshire**, LN6 9ER, **ENGLAND**.
(T) 01522 778204.
Contact/s
Owner: Mrs S Chennells **(Q)** BHS INT
Profile Stable/Livery.
Freelance instructor. Yr. Est: 1991
Opening Times
Sp: Open Mon - Sun 08:00. Closed Mon - Sun 20:00.
Su: Open Mon - Sun 08:00. Closed Mon - Sun 20:00.
Au: Open Mon - Sun 08:00. Closed Mon - Sun 20:00.
Wn: Open Mon - Sun 08:00. Closed Mon - Sun 20:00. **Ref: YH04437**

EAGLE LODGE EQUESTRIAN CTRE

Eagle Lodge Equestrian Centre, Gortalea, Tralee, **County Kerry**, **IRELAND**.
(T) 066 7137266.
Profile Equestrian Centre. **Ref: YH04438**

EAGLE TRAILERS

Eagle Trailers, 241A Blandford Rd, Poole, **Dorset**, BH15 4AZ, **ENGLAND**.
(T) 01202 671057.
Contact/s
Owner: Mr G Dilliway
Profile Transport/Horse Boxes. **Ref: YH04439**

EAGLE VETNRY GRP

Eagle Veterinary Group, The Vetnry Surgery, Norwich Rd, Halesworth, **Suffolk**, IP19 8HY, **ENGLAND**.
(T) 01986 873139 **(F)** 01986 874512.
Profile Medical Support. **Ref: YH04440**

EAGLESFIELD EQUESTRIAN CTRE

Eaglesfield Equestrian Centre Ltd, West Yoke, Ash, Sevenoaks, **Kent**, TN15 7HT, **ENGLAND**.
(T) 01474 872242 **(F)** 01474 873925.
Contact/s
Owner: Mrs J Clarke
Profile Equestrian Centre, Riding School, Stable/Livery. **Ref: YH04441**

EAKINS, S W

S W Eakins, Ravensbank Stables, 7 Icknield St,

Church Hill North, Redditch, **Worcestershire**, B98 9AD, **ENGLAND**.
(T) 01527 597354.
Contact/s
Partner: Mrs J Eakins
Profile Farrier. **Ref: YH04442**

EAKINS, SAMUEL W

Samuel W Eakins, Woodside Stud, Hilderstone Rd, Meir Heath, Stoke-on-Trent, **Staffordshire**, ST3 7NS, **ENGLAND**.
(T) 01782 394390.
Profile Farrier. **Ref: YH04443**

EALING RIDING SCHOOL

Ealing Riding School, 17-19 Gunnersbury Ave, London, **London (Greater)**, W5 3XD, **ENGLAND**.
(T) 020 89923808 **(F)** 020 88961716.
Contact/s
Owner: Miss I Lockyer
Profile Riding School. **Ref: YH04444**

EALSDON FARMS

Ealsdon Farms, Northmore Stud, Northend Rd, Exning, Newmarket, **Suffolk**, CB8 7JR, **ENGLAND**.
(T) 01638 577332.
Profile Breeder. **Ref: YH04445**

EAMES, J S

J S Eames, Tir Byw, Terfyn, Bodelwyddan, Rhyl, **Denbighshire**, LL18 5SW, **WALES**.
(T) 01745 833057.
Profile Farrier. **Ref: YH04446**

EAMONN RICE BLOOD STOCK

Eamonn Rice Blood Stock Agency, 14 Glenmont Pk, Dungannon, **County Tyrone**, BT71 7BB, **NORTHERN IRELAND**.
(T) 028 87723511 **(F)** 028 87722158
Affiliated Bodies SJAI.
Contact/s
Owner: Mr E Rice **(T)** 028 87723511
Profile Blood Stock Agency, Transport/Horse Boxes.
No.Staff: 5 Yr. Est: 1972 C.Size: 25 Acres
Opening Times
Sp: Open Mon - Sat 08:00. Closed Mon - Sat 17:00.
Su: Open Mon - Sat 08:00. Closed Mon - Sat 17:00.
Au: Open Mon - Sat 08:00. Closed Mon - Sat 17:00.
Wn: Open Mon - Sat 08:00. Closed Mon - Sat 17:00.
Ref: YH04447

EARDLEY, ANGELA

Angela Eardley, Holly Hedge Hse, Newcastle Rd, Hough, **Cheshire**, CW2 5JA, **ENGLAND**.
(T) 01270 842015.
Profile Breeder. **Ref: YH04448**

EARDLEY, LAWRENCE C

Lawrence C Eardley RSS, 56 Sheriffhales, Shifnal, **Shropshire**, TF11 8RD, **ENGLAND**.
(T) 01952 460495.
Profile Farrier. **Ref: YH04449**

EARL OF TYRONE

Cirencester Park Polo Club, C/O Cirencester Pk Polo Club, Polo Office, The Old Kennels, Cirencester Park, **Gloucestershire**, GL7 1UR, **ENGLAND**.
(T) 01285 653225
(W) www.cirencesterpolo.co.uk.
Profile Club/Association. Polo Club. **Ref: YH04450**

EARL, C L

C L Earl, Cropwell Lings Farm, Cropwell Butler, **Nottinghamshire**, NG12 2JS, **ENGLAND**.
(T) 01602 332796.
Profile Breeder. **Ref: YH04451**

EARLE, S A

Mr S A Earle, Fox Twitchen, East Kennett, Marlborough, **Wiltshire**, SN8 4EY, **ENGLAND**.
(T) 01672 861157 **(F)** 01672 861157
(M) 07850 350116.
Profile Trainer. **Ref: YH04452**

EARLSDON STUD

Earlsdon Stud, Brooklyn, 173 Duggins Lane, Tile Hill Village, Coventry, **Midlands (West)**, CV4 9GP, **ENGLAND**.
(T) 024 76462640.
Profile Breeder. **Ref: YH04453**

EARLSWAY FARM

Earlsway Farm, Bramfield, Halesworth, **Suffolk**, IP19 9AD, **ENGLAND**.
(T) 01986 784225 **(F)** 01986 784225.
Profile Stable/Livery. **Ref: YH04454**

EARLSWOOD RIDING CTRE

Earlswood Riding Centre, Upper Tump Farm, Earlswood, Chepstow, **Monmouthshire**, NP16 6AW, **WALES**.
(T) 01291 641381.
Profile Breeder, Riding School, Stable/Livery.
Ref: YH04455

EARLSWOOD STUD

Earlswood Stud, Earlswood, Chepstow, **Monmouthshire**, NP16 6AW, **WALES**.
(T) 01291 641381.
Profile Breeder. **Ref: YH04456**

EARLSWOOD SVS

Earlswood Services, 22 Nightingale Lane, Coventry, **Midlands (West)**, CV5 6AY, **ENGLAND**.
(T) 024 76670990.
Contact/s
Owner: Mr R Graham
Profile Supplies. **Ref: YH04457**

EARNSDALE FARM RIDING SCHOOL

Earnsdale Farm Riding School, Earnsdale Farm, Off Duddon Ave, Darwen, **Lancashire**, BB3 0LB, **ENGLAND**.
(T) 01254 702647.
Contact/s
Partner: Mrs M Comer
Profile Riding School, Saddlery Retailer, Stable/Livery. **Ref: YH04458**

EASAWAY

Easaway Ltd, Induna Stables, Fordham Rd, Newmarket, **Suffolk**, CB8 7AQ, **ENGLAND**.
(T) 01638 661999.
Profile Trainer. **Ref: YH04459**

EASI-LOADER

Easi-Loader, Fieldhouse, Main Rd, East Boldre, Brockenhurst, **Hampshire**, SO42 7WL, **ENGLAND**.
(T) 01425 652617.
Profile Supplies. **Ref: YH04460**

EASIRAMP SYSTEMS

Easiramp Systems, Dilltown Holdings Ltd, 3 The Martins Drv, Leighton Buzzard, **Bedfordshire**, LU7 7TQ, **ENGLAND**.
(T) 01525 373765 **(F)** 01525 373765
(E) nw50.hodges@tesco.net.
Profile Transport/Horse Boxes. **Ref: YH04461**

EAST ANGLIAN BLOODHOUNDS

East Anglian Bloodhounds, The Garden Cottage, The Old Rectory, Barking, Ipswich, **Suffolk**, IP6 8HH, **ENGLAND**.
(T) 01449 720295.
Profile Club/Association. **Ref: YH04462**

EAST ANGLIAN FARM RIDES

East Anglian Farm Rides, Highfield Farm, Kelvedon, **Essex**, CO5 9BJ, **ENGLAND**.
(T) 01206 251790 **(F)** 01206 251820.
Profile Stable/Livery. **Ref: YH04463**

EAST ANGLIAN RIDING CLUB

East Anglian Riding Club, Anchor Farm, Wood Lane, Little Ellingham, Attleborough, **Norfolk**, NR17 1JZ, **ENGLAND**.
(T) 01953 453057.
Contact/s
Secretary: Mr P Green
Profile Club/Association, Riding Club. **Ref: YH04464**

EAST ANGLIAN TRAILS

East Anglian Trails Ltd, Pip's Peace, Kenton, Stowmarket, **Suffolk**, IP14 6JS, **ENGLAND**.
(T) 01728 860429 **(F)** 01728 861712
(E) billbarrett@suffolkonline.net.
Contact/s
Partner: Mrs E Barrett
(E) eahorse@globalnet.co.uk
Profile Club/Association.
Also Bridleway Support Group - pleasure rides organised and equestrian routes researched. **Ref: YH04465**

EAST ANTRIM HOUNDS

East Antrim Hounds Branch of The Pony Club, 7 Lower Sizehill Rd, Ballyclare, **County Antrim**, BT39 9RP, **NORTHERN IRELAND**.
(T) 028 93352032.
Contact/s
Dist Comm: Mr J Andrews
Profile Club/Association. **Ref: YH04466**

EAST CHESHIRE TRAILERS

East Cheshire Trailers, Sandy Lane Garage, Sandy Lane, Macclesfield, **Cheshire**, SK10 4RJ, **ENGLAND**.
(T) 01625 611550.
Profile Transport/Horse Boxes. **Ref: YH04467**

EAST CLWYD RIDING CLUB

East Clwyd Riding Club, 15 Smelt Rd, Coedpoeth, **Wrexham**, LL11 3SH, **WALES**.
(T) 01978 757332.
Contact/s
Chairman: Mrs M Jones
Profile Club/Association, Riding Club. **Ref: YH04468**

EAST CORNWALL RIDING CLUB

East Cornwall Riding Club, Trebrownbridge, Horningtops, Liskeard, **Cornwall**, PL14 3PX, **ENGLAND**.
(T) 01503 240610.
Contact/s
Chairman: Mrs V Harding
Profile Club/Association, Riding Club. **Ref: YH04469**

EAST DEVON SADDLERY

East Devon Saddlery, Unit 3 Queen St, Honiton, **Devon**, EX14 1HB, **ENGLAND**.
(T) 01404 45599.
Contact/s
Owner: Mrs L Grant
Profile Saddlery Retailer. **Ref: YH04470**

EAST DOWN FOXHOUNDS

East Down Foxhounds Branch of The Pony Club, 77 Lisbane Rd, Saintfield, **County Down**, BT24 7BT, **NORTHERN IRELAND**.
(T) 028 97638731.
Contact/s
Dist Comm: Mrs M Newsam
Profile Club/Association. **Ref: YH04471**

EAST DURHAM

East Durham Equestrian Supplies, Snippersgate Farm, South Hetton, Durham, **County Durham**, DH6 2UQ, **ENGLAND**.
(T) 0191 5265888.
Profile Supplies. **Ref: YH04472**

EAST DURHAM & HOUGHALL

East Durham & Houghall Community College, Houghall Ctre, Houghall, **County Durham**, DH1 3SG, **ENGLAND**.
(T) 0191 3861351 **(F)** 0191 3860419.
Profile Equestrian Centre. College.
Training for Equine Business Management.
Ref: YH04473

EAST END FARM RIDING SCHOOL

East End Farm Riding School, 38 Wallingford Rd, Cholsey, Wallingford, **Oxfordshire**, OX10 9LB, **ENGLAND**.
(T) 01491 652515
Affiliated Bodies Pony Club UK
Alt Contact Address
20 Rothwell Cl, Chorley, Oxfordshire, OX10 9LF, England. **(T)** 01491 651831
Contact/s
Owner: Mrs C Carr **(Q)** BHS Int SM, BHSAI
Profile Riding School, Stable/Livery. No.Staff: 1
Opening Times
Sp: Open Mon - Sat 09:00. Closed Mon - Fri 19:00, Sat 16:00.
Su: Open Mon - Sat 09:00. Closed Mon - Fri 19:00, Sat 16:00.
Au: Open Mon - Sat 09:00. Closed Mon - Fri 19:00, Sat 16:00.
Wn: Open Mon - Sat 09:00. Closed Mon - Fri 19:00, Sat 16:00. **Ref: YH04474**

EAST ENGLAND AGRCLTRL SOC

East of England Agricultural Society, East Of England Showground, Peterborough, **Cambridgeshire**, PE2 6XE, **ENGLAND**.
(T) 01733 234451 **(F)** 01733 370038.
Contact/s
Chief Executive: Andrew Mercer
Profile Club/Association. **Ref: YH04475**

EAST KILBRIDE RIDING SCHOOL

East Kilbride Riding School, Newlandsmuir Farm, Jackton, East Kilbride, Glasgow, **Lanarkshire (South)**, G75 8RS, **SCOTLAND**.
(T) 01355 249955.
Profile Riding School. **Ref: YH04476**

EAST LAKE

East Lake, Eastlake, Belstone, Okehampton, **Devon**, EX20 1QT, **ENGLAND**.
(T) 01837 52513.
Contact/s
Owner: Mrs H Saunders
Profile Riding School, Stable/Livery. **Ref: YH04477**

EAST LODGE DONKEY STUD

East Lodge Donkey Stud, Hill View Farm,

Hambledon, Waterlooville, **Hampshire**, PO7 4RE, **ENGLAND**.
(T) 023 92632594.
Contact/s
Owner: Mrs S Horn
Profile Breeder. **Ref: YH04478**

EAST LODGE FARM RIDING EST

East Lodge Farm Riding Establishment, East Lodge, Washbrook Lane, Ecton, Northampton, **Northamptonshire**, NN6 0QU, **ENGLAND**.
(T) 01604 810244
Affiliated Bodies ABRS, BHS.
Contact/s
Owner: Mrs K White
Profile Riding School, Stable/Livery.
A coffee shop on site. There are regular organised hacks which take place. **Yr. Est:** 1989
Opening Times
Sp: Open Tues - Sun 08:00. Closed Tues - Sun 18:00.
Su: Open Tues - Sun 08:00. Closed Tues - Sun 18:00.
Au: Open Tues - Sun 08:00. Closed Tues - Sun 18:00.
Wn: Open Tues - Sun 08:00. Closed Tues - Sun 18:00.
Closed Mondays **Ref: YH04479**

EAST MANTON STABLES

East Manton Stables, Sparsholt, Wantage, **Oxfordshire**, OX12 9PJ, **ENGLAND**.
(T) 01235 751433 **(F)** 01235 751433
(M) 07973 260054.
Profile Trainer. **Ref: YH04480**

EAST MIDLANDS DRESSAGE GRP

East Midlands Dressage Group, The Old Cottage, Wilsic, Doncaster, **Yorkshire (South)**, DN11 9AG, **ENGLAND**.
(T) 01302 853482.
Contact/s
Chairman: Mrs J Youdon
Profile Club/Association. **Ref: YH04481**

EAST NOLTON RIDING STABLES

East Nolton Riding Stables, Nolton Haven, Haverfordwest, **Pembrokeshire**, SA62 3NW, **WALES**.
(T) 01437 710360 **(F)** 01437 710967.
Contact/s
Partner: Mr J Owen
Profile Breeder, Track/Course. **Ref: YH04482**

EAST RIDING

East Riding Equestrian Centre, Stony Carr Farm, Stony Lane, Newport, Brough, **Yorkshire (East)**, HU15 2RA, **ENGLAND**.
(T) 01430 440835.
Contact/s
Owner: Mrs J Elliot
Profile Equestrian Centre, Stable/Livery.
Yr. Est: 1983
Opening Times
Sp: Open Mon - Sun 09:00. Closed Mon - Sun 18:00.
Su: Open Mon - Sun 09:00. Closed Mon - Sun 18:00.
Au: Open Mon - Sun 09:00. Closed Mon - Sun 18:00.
Wn: Open Mon - Sun 09:00. Closed Mon - Sun 18:00.
Yard open to owners 24 hours a day. **Ref: YH04483**

EAST RIDING BRIDLEWAY ASS

East Riding Bridleway Association, Wisteria Cottage, 5 The Green, Cranswick, Driffield, **Yorkshire (East)**, YO25 9QU, **ENGLAND**.
(T) 01377 270057.
Profile Club/Association. **Ref: YH04484**

EAST SHROPSHIRE RIDING CLUB

East Shropshire Riding Club, 1 School Rd, Tettenhall Wood, **Midlands (West)**, WV6 8EJ, **ENGLAND**.
(T) 01902 565663.
Contact/s
Chairman: Mrs D Tandy
Profile Club/Association, Riding Club. **Ref: YH04485**

EAST SOLEY E C 2000

East Soley E C 2000, Stag Hill, Chilton Foliat, Hungerford, **Berkshire**, RG17 0TX, **ENGLAND**.
(T) 01488 686232 **(F)** 01488 686232
(W) www.eastsoleyec2000.co.uk.
Contact/s
Owner: Ms E Dove
(E) emma@eastsoleyec2000.co.uk
Profile Arena, Equestrian Centre, Stable/Livery, Trainer. Competition Centre, Show Centre.
No.Staff: 4 **Yr. Est:** 1999 **Ref: YH04486**

EAST STREET STABLES

East Street Stables, Pitmore Lane, Sway, Lymington, **Hampshire**, SO41 6BX, **ENGLAND**.
(T) 01590 683428.
Contact/s
Owner: Mrs J Chalk
Profile Track/Course.
Picnic areas and pub rides with forest access available.
Ref: YH04487

EAST VIEW FRUIT FARM

East View Fruit Farm & Riding Centre, Tanyard Lane, Danehill, Haywards Heath, **Sussex (West)**, RH17 7JL, **ENGLAND**.
(T) 01825 740240.
Contact/s
Partner: Mrs E Turner
Profile Equestrian Centre. Trekking Centre.
Private Farm and Country Lane Rides cost from £10.00. Ashdown Forest and Lakeland Treks from £16.00. 10 % discount for 6+ riders booked as a group. Please give prior notice if unable to make a booking or a charge may be incurred. **Ref: YH04488**

EASTBURY COTTAGE STABLES

Eastbury Cottage Stables, Lambourn, Hungerford, **Berkshire**, RG17 7JJ, **ENGLAND**.
(T) 01488 72258
(M) 07721 988439.
Profile Trainer. **Ref: YH04489**

EASTER BUSH VETNRY CTRE

Easter Bush Veterinary Centre, Easter Bush, Roslin, **Lothian (Mid)**, EH25 9RG, **SCOTLAND**.
(T) 0131 6506284
Affiliated Bodies BHS.
Contact/s
Instructor: Morag Neil **(Q)** BHSAI
Profile Medical Support, Riding School.
Riding lesson groups are comprised of no more than 5 people. The stables are part of a practising veterinary clinic. **No.Staff:** 4 **Yr. Est:** 1964
Opening Times
Sp: Open Tues - Sun 07:30. Closed Tues - Sun 17:00.
Su: Open Tues - Sun 07:30. Closed Tues - Sun 17:00.
Au: Open Tues - Sun 07:30. Closed Tues - Sun 17:00.
Wn: Open Tues - Sun 07:30. Closed Tues - Sun 17:00.
Closed Monday **Ref: YH04490**

EASTERBY TRAILERS

Easterby Trailers, Cottam Grange, Cottam, Driffield, **Yorkshire (East)**, YO25 3BY, **ENGLAND**.
(T) 01377 267415 **(F)** 01377 267416.
Profile Transport/Horse Boxes. **Ref: YH04491**

EASTERBY, M H

M H Easterby, The Cottage, Easthorpe Hall Stud, Easthorpe, Malton, **Yorkshire (North)**, YO17 6QX, **ENGLAND**.
(T) 01653 692593.
Profile Breeder. **Ref: YH04492**

EASTERBY, M H

M H Easterby, Habton Farm, Great Habton, Malton, **Yorkshire (North)**, YO17 6TY, **ENGLAND**.
(T) 01653 668566.
Profile Trainer. **Ref: YH04493**

EASTERBY, M W

M W Easterby, New Hse Farm, Stittenham, York, **Yorkshire (North)**, YO6 7TN, **ENGLAND**.
(T) 01347 878368 **(F)** 01347 878204.
Profile Trainer. **Ref: YH04494**

EASTERHILL

Easterhill Saddlery Centre, Easterhill Farm, Gartmore, **Stirling**, FK8 3SA, **SCOTLAND**.
(T) 01877 382875 **(F)** 01877 382875.
Contact/s
Owner: Mrs L Lovie
Profile Riding School, Saddlery Retailer, Stable/Livery. **Ref: YH04495**

EASTERN CASPIAN STUD

Eastern Caspian Stud, Eastern Hill, Astwood Bank, Redditch, **Worcestershire**, B96 6DZ, **ENGLAND**.
(T) 01527 892845.
Profile Breeder. **Ref: YH04496**

EASTERN CLGE EQUESTRIAN CTRE

Eastern College Equestrian Centre, Eastern Clge, New Costessey, Norwich, **Norfolk**, NR5 0TT, **ENGLAND**.
(T) 01603 741779.
Profile Equestrian Centre. **Ref: YH04497**

EASTERN WELSH PONY & COB ASS

Eastern Welsh Pony and Cob Association, Foxtons, 25 Barn Owl Cl, Langtoft, Peterborough, **Cambridgeshire**, PE6 9RG, **ENGLAND**.
(T) 01778 341130 **(F)** 01778 341130
(E) frances.sheffield@bun.com.
Profile Club/Association. **Ref: YH04498**

EASTERTON ARENAS

Easterton Arenas Ltd, Easterton Farm, Blackford, Auchterarder, **Perth and Kinross**, PH4 1RQ, **SCOTLAND**.
(T) 01764 682558 **(F)** 01764 682491.
Profile Arena, Breeder, Stable/Livery, Track/Course, Trainer. **Ref: YH04499**

EASTERTON FARM

Easterton Farm, Blackford, Auchterarder, **Perth and Kinross**, PH4 1RQ, **SCOTLAND**.
(T) 01764 682268 **(F)** 01764 682558.
Contact/s
General Manager: Mr G Hunt
Profile Horse/Rider Accom.
Opening Times
Sp: Open Mon - Sun 06:00. Closed Mon - Sun 21:00.
Su: Open Mon - Sun 06:00. Closed Mon - Sun 21:00.
Au: Open Mon - Sun 06:00. Closed Mon - Sun 21:00.
Wn: Open Mon - Sun 06:00. Closed Mon - Sun 21:00. **Ref: YH04500**

EASTERTON STABLES

Easterton Equitation Centre, Mugdock, Milngavie, Glasgow, **Glasgow (City of)**, G62 8LG, **SCOTLAND**.
(T) 0141 9561518
Affiliated Bodies ABRS, BHS.
Contact/s
Owner: Miss R Brown
Profile Riding School, Stable/Livery.
DIY and full livery available, prices on request.
No.Staff: 6 **Yr. Est:** 1991
Opening Times
Sp: Open Tues - Sun 10:00. Closed Tues - Sun 17:00.
Su: Open Tues - Sun 10:00. Closed Tues - Sun 17:00.
Au: Open Tues - Sun 10:00. Closed Tues - Sun 17:00.
Wn: Open Tues - Sun 10:00. Closed Tues - Sun 17:00.
Closed Mondays. Tuesday open late for lessons from 18:30 - 20:30, Thursday open late for lessons from 18:30 - 19:30. **Ref: YH04501**

EASTGATE VETNRY CTRE

Eastgate Veterinary Centre, 133 Eastgate, Pickering, **Yorkshire (North)**, YO18 7DW, **ENGLAND**.
(T) 01751 72204.
Profile Medical Support. **Ref: YH04502**

EASTGATE VETNRY PRACTICE

Eastgate Veterinary Practice, Millburn Rd, Inverness, **Highlands**, IV2 3PY, **SCOTLAND**.
(T) 01463 230893.
Profile Medical Support. **Ref: YH04503**

EASTHORPE HALL STUD

Easthorpe Hall Stud, Easthorpe, Malton, **Yorkshire (North)**, YO17 0QX, **ENGLAND**.
(T) 01653 668566 **(F)** 01653 668621.
Profile Breeder. **Ref: YH04504**

EASTLAKE & BEACHELL

Eastlake & Beachell Ltd, The Crescent, King St, Leicester, **Leicestershire**, LE1 6RX, **ENGLAND**.
(T) 0116 2544277 **(F)** 0116 2542512
(E) gb8bfp9j@ibmmail.com. **Ref: YH04505**

EASTLAKE INSURANCE

Eastlake Insurance, 36 Eastlake St, Plymouth, **Devon**, PL1 1BE, **ENGLAND**.
(T) 01752 222773.
Profile Insurance. **Ref: YH04506**

EASTLANDS

Eastlands Shetland & Connemara Pony Stud, Davington, Eskdalemuir, Langholm, **Dumfries and Galloway**, DG13 0QW, **SCOTLAND**.
(T) 01387 373246.
Profile Breeder. **Ref: YH04507**

EASTMAN, CHRISTOPHER M

Christopher M Eastman DWCF, 12 Hollinberry

Lane, Howbrook, High Green, Sheffield, **Yorkshire (South)**, S35 7EL, **ENGLAND**.
(T) 0114 2847159.
Profile Farrier. **Ref: YH04508**

EASTMERE STABLES

Eastmere Stables, Eastergate Lane, Eastergate, Chichester, **Sussex (West)**, PO20 6SJ, **ENGLAND**.
(T) 01243 543863 **(F)** 01243 543913.
Contact/s
For Bookings: Mr L Hedger
Profile Trainer. **Ref: YH04509**

EASTMINSTER SCHOOL OF RIDING

Eastminster School Of Riding, Hooks Hall Farm, The Chase, Rush Green, Romford, **Essex**, RM7 0SS, **ENGLAND**.
(T) 01708 447423.
Contact/s
Owner: Ms A Ackland
Profile Riding School, Stable/Livery. **Ref: YH04510**

EASTMOORS FARM

Eastmoors Farm, Eastmoor Farm, 236A Ringwood Rd, St. Leonards, Ringwood, **Hampshire**, BH24 2SB, **ENGLAND**.
(T) 01202 872302.
Contact/s
Owner: Mr N Hoare
Profile Stable/Livery. **Ref: YH04511**

EASTON & WANNOP

Easton & Wannop, Westgarth Vetnry Clinic, 62 Stonegate Rd, Leeds, **Yorkshire (West)**, LS6 4JG, **ENGLAND**.
(T) 0113 2756900.
Profile Medical Support. **Ref: YH04512**

EASTON CLGE

Easton College, Easton, Norwich, **Norfolk**, NR9 5BR, **ENGLAND**.
(T) 01603 731202 **(F)** 01603 741438
(W) www.easton-college.ac.uk.
Profile Equestrian Centre. College offering Equestrian Courses.
Facilities for equestrian students are regularly improved. There is an 18-horse stable block and both an outdoor and indoor riding school. **Ref: YH04513**

EASTON GREY SADDLERS

Easton Grey Saddlers, Pinkney Pk, Pinkney, Sherston, Malmesbury, **Wiltshire**, SN16 0NX, **ENGLAND**.
(T) 01666 840916 **(F)** 01666 311206
Affiliated Bodies SMS.
Contact/s
Owner: Mr C Whereatt **(Q)** Master Saddler
Profile Saddlery Retailer, Supplies. Driving Harness Specialists.
Bespoke Saddlery made to measure. **Ref: YH04514**

EASTON, N

Mr N Easton, 159 Newsham Rd, Blyth, **Northumberland**, NE24 5TL, **ENGLAND**.
(T) 01670 351791.
Profile Breeder. **Ref: YH04515**

EASTVIEW STABLES

Eastview Stables, Hillings Lane, Hawksworth, Guiseley, Leeds, **Yorkshire (West)**, LS20 8PB, **ENGLAND**.
(T) 01943 876619 **(F)** 01943 884886.
Contact/s
General Manager: Miss E Clark
Profile Stable/Livery.
Hunter and Competition livery available, prices and details on request. No.Staff: 1 Yr. Est: 1996
C.Size: 30 Acres **Ref: YH04516**

EASTWELL HALL STABLES

Eastwell Hall Stables, Eastwell, Melton Mowbray, **Leicestershire**, LE14 4EE, **ENGLAND**.
(T) 01949 860671 **(F)** 01949 860671
(M) 07860 277138.
Profile Trainer. **Ref: YH04517**

EASTWOOD STUD FARM

Eastwood Stud Farm, Graffham, Petworth, **Sussex (West)**, GU28 0QF, **ENGLAND**.
(T) 01798 867570
Affiliated Bodies BHS.
Contact/s
General Manager: Mrs S Walker
Profile Horse/Rider Accom. **Ref: YH04518**

EASTWOOD, D

Mrs D Eastwood, 4 Tun Lane, South Hiendley, Barnsley, **Yorkshire (South)**, S72 9BZ, **ENGLAND**.
(T) 01226 780459.
Profile Supplies. **Ref: YH04519**

EASTWOOD, M

Mr M Eastwood, Round Ings Hall, Round Ings Rd, Outlane, Huddersfield, **Yorkshire (West)**, HD3 3FQ, **ENGLAND**.
(T) 01422 379423.
Profile Breeder. **Ref: YH04520**

EASTWOOD, MATTHEW J

Matthew J Eastwood DWCF, 4 Tun Lane, South Hiendley, Barnsley, **Yorkshire (South)**, S72 9BZ, **ENGLAND**.
(T) 01226 780459.
Profile Farrier. **Ref: YH04521**

EASY FEEDS

Easy Feeds, Dyason, Main Rd, Broughton, Newark, **Nottinghamshire**, NG22 9JF, **ENGLAND**.
(T) 01623 860677 **(F)** 01623 860962.
Profile Feed Merchant. **Ref: YH04522**

EATON & HOLLIS

Eaton & Hollis, Cattle Market, Chequers Rd, Derby, **Derbyshire**, DE21 6EP, **ENGLAND**.
(T) 01332 349307 **(F)** 01332 385812.
Profile Chartered Surveyors, Auctioneers and Valuers.
Sales & Valuation of Agricultural Land, Farms, Implements & Stock. **Ref: YH04523**

EATON SMITHY

Eaton Smithy, Beech Lane, Eaton, Tarporley, **Cheshire**, CW6 9AH, **ENGLAND**.
(T) 01829 733902.
Profile Farrier. **Ref: YH04524**

EATON THORNE STABLES

Eaton Thorne Stables, Woodmancote, Henfield, **Sussex (West)**, BN5 9BH, **ENGLAND**.
(T) 01273 492591.
Contact/s
Owner: Mrs K Langhorne
Profile Riding School, Stable/Livery. **Ref: YH04525**

EATON, J M

Miss J M Eaton, Wenning Cottage, Wennington, **Lancashire**, LA2 8NN, **ENGLAND**.
(T) 01524 221374.
Profile Supplies. **Ref: YH04526**

EATON, STEPHEN G

Stephen G Eaton AWCF, The Smithy, Pontdolgoch, Caersws, **Powys**, SY17 5JE, **WALES**.
(T) 01686 688988.
Profile Farrier. **Ref: YH04527**

EBBISHAM FARM

Ebbisham Farm Livery Stables Ltd, Ebbisham Lane, Walton On The Hill, Tadworth, **Surrey**, KT20 7UP, **ENGLAND**.
(T) 01737 812568 **(F)** 01737 819513
Affiliated Bodies BHS.
Contact/s
General Manager: Robert Dibben
Profile Stable/Livery.
Full livery yard and training on own horses.
No.Staff: 10 Yr. Est: 1988 C.Size: 45 Acres
Opening Times
Sp: Open 07:30. Closed 21:00.
Su: Open 07:30. Closed 21:00.
Au: Open 07:30. Closed 21:00.
Wn: Open 07:30. Closed 21:00. **Ref: YH04528**

EBBORLANDS

Ebborlands Farm & Riding Centre, Wookey Hole, Wells, **Somerset**, BA5 1AY, **ENGLAND**.
(T) 01749 672550 **(F)** 01749 672550
Affiliated Bodies BHS.
Contact/s
Owner: Mrs E Gibbs
(E) eileengibbs@btinternet.co.uk
Profile Equestrian Centre, Riding School, Stable/Livery. No.Staff: 5 Yr. Est: 1974
C.Size: 150 Acres
Opening Times
Sp: Open 09:30. Closed 17:00.
Su: Open 09:30. Closed 17:00.
Au: Open 09:30. Closed 17:00.
Wn: Open 09:30. Closed 17:00. **Ref: YH04529**

EBEL, KARL WALTER GUSTAV

Karl Walter Gustav Ebel, The Hill, Glasgow Rd, Gretna, **Cumbria**, CA6 5HG, **ENGLAND**.
(T) 01461 337633.
Profile Farrier. **Ref: YH04530**

EBOR VALE RIDING CLUB

Ebor Vale Riding Club, Willow Tree Farm, Thornton, Melbourne, **Yorkshire (East)**, YO42 4RJ, **ENGLAND**.
(T) 01759 318355.
Contact/s
Chairman: Mrs G Greetham
Profile Club/Association, Riding Club. **Ref: YH04531**

ECCLESTON

Eccleston Equestrian Centre, Ulnes Walton Lane, Leyland, Preston, **Lancashire**, PR5 3LT, **ENGLAND**.
(T) 01772 600093
(E) sales@equestrian-northwest.co.uk
(W) www.equestrian-northwest.co.uk.
Contact/s
Owner: Ms K Green **(Q)** BHSII
Profile Equestrian Centre, Riding School.
Offers BHS education, training and lessons for children and adults. Full sized indoor and outdoor arenas.
Canteen facilities also available. **Ref: YH04532**

ECCLESVILLE CTRE

Fintona Regeneration Iniative Ltd., 11 Ecclesville Rd, Fintona, Omagh, **County Tyrone**, BT78 2BZ, **NORTHERN IRELAND**.
(T) 028 82840591
Affiliated Bodies BHS.
Contact/s
Administration: Mrs M King **(T)** 028 82840591
Profile Arena.
There is a health, fitness and leisure centre on site.
No.Staff: 7 Yr. Est: 1996
Opening Times
Sp: Open Mon - Fri 09:00. Closed Mon - Fri 17:00.
Su: Open Mon - Fri 09:00. Closed Mon - Fri 17:00.
Au: Open Mon - Fri 09:00. Closed Mon - Fri 17:00.
Wn: Open Mon - Fri 09:00. Closed Mon - Fri 17:00.
Ref: YH04533

ECKFORD, D A

D A Eckford, 12 Ayston Rd, Uppingham, Oakham, **Leicestershire**, LE19 9RL, **ENGLAND**.
(T) 01572 822399.
Contact/s
Owner: Mr P Houghton **(Q)** BVET, MRCVS
Profile Medical Support. **Ref: YH04534**

ECKLEY, B J

Mr B J Eckley, Closcedi Farm, Llanspyddid, Brecon, **Powys**, LD3 8NS, **WALES**.
(T) 01874 622422.
Profile Supplies. **Ref: YH04535**

ECKLEY, R J

R J Eckley, The Yeld, Lyonshall, Kington, **Herefordshire**, HR5 3LY, **ENGLAND**.
(T) 01544 340621 **(F)** 01544 340733.
Contact/s
Owner: Mr R Eckley
Profile Blood Stock Agency. **Ref: YH04536**

ECLIPSE

Eclipse, Long Rock, Penzance, **Cornwall**, TR20 8LD, **ENGLAND**.
(T) 01736 719170 **(F)** 01736 710872.
Contact/s
Partner: Mrs J Thomas
Profile Saddlery Retailer. **Ref: YH04537**

ECLIPSE MNGMT

Eclipse Management (Newmarket) Ltd, The Paddock, 58 Bury Rd, Newmarket, **Suffolk**, CB8 7LT, **ENGLAND**.
(T) 01638 668350 **(F)** 01638 668013.
Profile Blood Stock Agency. **Ref: YH04538**

ECTON CARRIAGES

Ecton Carriages, Park Hse, Reapsmoor, Longnor, Buxton, **Derbyshire**, SK17 0LG, **ENGLAND**.
(T) 01298 84423.
Profile Horse Drawn Vehicles. **Ref: YH04539**

EDDIE BRENNAN

Eddie Brennan Ltd, The Gate Lodge, Simmonscourt Rd, Dublin, **County Dublin**, **IRELAND**.
(T) 01 6609966 **(F)** 01 6609916.
Contact/s
Owner: Eddie Brennan
Profile Blood Stock Agency, Supplies, Transport/Horse Boxes. **Ref: YH04540**

EDDIE PALIN DISTRIBUTION

Eddie Palin Distribution Ltd, Unit 1A, Bert Smith Way, Market Drayton, **Shropshire**, TF9 3SN, **ENGLAND**.
(T) 01630 658488 **(F)** 01630 658280
(E) eddiepalin@west-midlands.com
(W) www.eddiepalin.com.
Profile Supplies. **Ref: YH04541**

EDDINS, J M & S M

J M & S M Eddins, Sluice Farm, Peterstone Wentlooge, Cardiff, **Glamorgan (Vale of)**, CF3 2TN, **WALES**.
(T) 029 20777079.
Contact/s
Partner: Mr S Eddins
Profile Breeder. **Ref: YH04542**

EDDLETHORPE EQUESTRIAN SVS

Eddlethorpe Equestrian Services (Malton) Ltd, Eddlethorpe Grange Farm, Malton, **Yorkshire (North)**, YO17 9QT, **ENGLAND**.
(T) 01653 658432 **(F)** 01653 658432.
Profile Riding School, Track/Course. **Ref: YH04543**

EDDY WILLIAMSON & PARTNERS

Eddy Williamson & Partners, North Rd Vetnry Ctre, 53 North Rd, Midsomer Norton, **Bath & Somerset (North East)**, BA3 2QE, **ENGLAND**.
(T) 01761 412132 **(F)** 01761 411660.
Profile Medical Support. **Ref: YH04544**

EDDY WILLIAMSON & PARTNERS

Eddy Williamson & Partners, The Vetnry Ctre, Allyn Saxon Drv, Shepton Mallet, **Somerset**, BA4 5QH, **ENGLAND**.
(T) 01749 342363.
Profile Medical Support. **Ref: YH04545**

EDEN EQUESTRIAN CTRE

Eden Equestrian Centre, Breedless Croft, Dunlugas, Turriff, **Aberdeenshire**, AB53 4NR, **SCOTLAND**.
(T) 01261 821214 **(F)** 01261 821214
Affiliated Bodies ABRS.
Contact/s
Owner: Ms J Whiteley **(Q)** BHSAI
(E) edenequestriancentre@btinternet.com
Profile Equestrian Centre, Riding School, Stable/Livery, Trainer, Transport/Horse Boxes.
No.Staff: 1 Yr. Est: 1994 C.Size: 13 Acres
Ref: YH04546

EDEN MEADOWS RIDING CTRE

Eden Meadows Riding Centre, Sandy Lane, Rocklands, Attleborough, **Norfolk**, NR17 1EN, **ENGLAND**.
(T) 01953 483545.
Contact/s
Owner: Mr J Dothie
Profile Riding School, Stable/Livery. **Ref: YH04547**

EDEN PRODUCE

Eden Produce, Eden Works, Colne Rd, Earby, Barnoldswick, **Lancashire**, BB18 6SY, **ENGLAND**.
(T) 01282 844213 **(F)** 01282 843336
(E) wolfendenconcrete@currantbun.com.
Profile Saddlery Retailer. **Ref: YH04548**

EDEN VALLEY TROTTING ASS

Eden Valley Trotting Association, 36 Castle View, Brough, Kirkby Stephen, **Cumbria**, CA17 4BA, **ENGLAND**.
(T) 01768 341586 **(F)** 01768 351975.
Profile Club/Association. **Ref: YH04549**

EDENGATE SADDLERY

Edengate Saddlery, 2A London Rd, Far Cotton, Northampton, **Northamptonshire**, NN4 8AH, **ENGLAND**.
(T) 01604 768675 **(F)** 01604 768675
Affiliated Bodies BETA.
Contact/s
Owner: Mrs A Halbert
(E) gary@home0197.freeserve.co.uk
Profile Riding Wear Retailer, Saddlery Retailer, Supplies. No.Staff: 2 Yr. Est: 1989
Opening Times
Sp: Open 09:30. Closed 17:30.
Su: Open 09:30. Closed 17:30.
Au: Open 09:30. Closed 17:30.
Wn: Open 09:30. Closed 17:30. **Ref: YH04550**

EDENSIDE

Edenside Stables, Edenside Stables, Edenside, St Andrews, **Fife**, KY16 9SQ, **SCOTLAND**.
(T) 01334 839592 **(F)** 01334 839592.
Contact/s
Owner: Mr R Gatherum
Profile Trainer. Train problem horses.
There are 7 acres of sand/woodchip indoor arenas.
No.Staff: 3 Yr. Est: 1981 C.Size: 32 Acres
Opening Times
Sp: Open 09:00. Closed 17:00.
Su: Open 09:00. Closed 17:00.
Au: Open 09:00. Closed 17:00.
Wn: Open 09:00. Closed 17:00.
Telephone for an appointment **Ref: YH04551**

EDENSOR LIVERY STABLES

Edensor Livery Stables, Chatsworth Pk, Bakewell, **Derbyshire**, DE4 1PP, **ENGLAND**.
(T) 01246 583463.
Profile Stable/Livery. **Ref: YH04552**

EDERGOLE RIDING CTRE

Edergole Riding Centre, 70 Moneymore Rd, Cookstown, **County Tyrone**, BT80 8PY, **NORTHERN IRELAND**.
(T) 028 86761133 **(F)** 028 86765572
Affiliated Bodies BHS.
Contact/s
Owner: Mr A Short **(Q)** BHSAI
Profile Equestrian Centre, Riding School.
No.Staff: 2 Yr. Est: 1981
Opening Times
Sp: Open Tues - Sat 09:00. Closed Tues - Sat 17:00.
Su: Open Tues - Sat 09:00. Closed Tues - Sat 17:00.
Au: Open Tues - Sat 09:00. Closed Tues - Sat 17:00.
Wn: Open Tues - Sat 09:00. Closed Tues - Sat 17:00.
Ref: YH04553

EDGCOTT HSE

Edgcott House, Exford, **Somerset**, TA24 7QG, **ENGLAND**.
(T) 01643 831495 **(F)** 01643 831495.
Profile Equestrian Centre. **Ref: YH04554**

EDGECOTE HSE STABLES

Edgecote House Stables, Edgecote, Chipping Warden, Banbury, **Oxfordshire**, OX17 1AG, **ENGLAND**.
(T) 01295 660909 **(F)** 01295 660908
(M) 07808 061223.
Profile Trainer. **Ref: YH04555**

EDGEWORTH POLO CLUB

Edgeworth Polo Club, Field Barn, Edgeworth, Stroud, **Gloucestershire**, GL6 7JF, **ENGLAND**.
(T) 01285 821550 **(F)** 01285 821756.
Profile Club/Association. Polo Club. **Ref: YH04556**

EDGINGTONS

Edgingtons, 6 Orion Prde, Hassocks, **Sussex (West)**, BN6 8QA, **ENGLAND**.
(T) 01273 844621 **(F)** 01273 843057.
Contact/s
Owner: Mrs N Edgington
Profile Saddlery Retailer. **Ref: YH04557**

EDINBURGH & DISTRICT

Edinburgh & District Riding Club, Nether Pentland, Loanhead, **Lothian (Mid)**, EH20 9QE, **SCOTLAND**.
(T) 0131 4401407.
Contact/s
Chairman: Mrs A MacLean
Profile Club/Association, Riding Club. **Ref: YH04558**

EDINBURGH & LASSWADE

Edinburgh & Lasswade Riding Centre, Kevock Rd, Lasswade, **Lothian (Mid)**, EH18 1HX, **SCOTLAND**.
(T) 0131 6637676.
Contact/s
Owner: Mrs M McNeughton
Profile Riding School, Stable/Livery.
Hacking available. No.Staff: 5 Yr. Est: 1980
Opening Times
Sp: Open 08:00. Closed 22:00.
Su: Open 08:00. Closed 22:00.
Au: Open 08:00. Closed 22:00.
Wn: Open 08:00. Closed 22:00. **Ref: YH04559**

EDINBURGH EQUESTRIAN CTRE

Edinburgh Equestrian Centre Ltd, Home Farm, Dalkeith, **Lothian (Mid)**, EH22 2NJ, **SCOTLAND**.
(T) 0131 6542563 **(F)** 0131 6542563.
Contact/s
Owner: Ms L Robertson
Profile Equestrian Centre, Riding Club, Stable/Livery.
Hacking available. No.Staff: 6 Yr. Est: 1994
Opening Times
Sp: Open 07:30. Closed 19:00.
Su: Open 07:30. Closed 19:00.
Au: Open 07:30. Closed 19:00.
Wn: Open 07:30. Closed 19:00. **Ref: YH04560**

EDINBURGH FABRICATION

Edinburgh Fabrication, 115D East Main St, Broxburn, **Lothian (West)**, EH52 5EJ, **SCOTLAND**.
(T) 01506 852247 **(F)** 01506 852247.
Contact/s
Owner: Mr D Fairgreaves
Profile Blacksmith. **Ref: YH04561**

EDINBURGH FABRICATIONS

Edinburgh Fabrications, 15 Gylemuir Rd, Edinburgh, **Edinburgh (City of)**, EH12 7UB, **SCOTLAND**.
(T) 0131 3344008.
Profile Blacksmith. **Ref: YH04562**

EDINBURGH POLO CLUB

Edinburgh Polo Club (The), Dalmohay Est Office, Kirknewton, **Lothian (West)**, EH27 8EB, **SCOTLAND**.
(T) 0131 3331331.
Profile Club/Association. **Ref: YH04563**

EDINBURGH SCHOOL

Edinburgh School Of Carriage Driving, Glenpark Stables, Balerno, **Edinburgh (City of)**, EH14 7BG, **SCOTLAND**.
(T) 0131 4495699 **(F)** 0131 4495699.
Contact/s
Owner: Mr J Cherry
Profile Carriage Driving School. **Ref: YH04564**

EDMUNDS, GARY

Gary Edmunds, Lillicot Farm, Icknield St, Alvechurch, **Midlands (West)**, B48 7EN, **ENGLAND**.
(T) 01564 826075.
Profile Farrier. **Ref: YH04565**

EDMUNDS, H

Mr H Edmunds, The Est Office, Cholderton, Salisbury, **Wiltshire**, SP4 0DR, **ENGLAND**.
(T) 01980 64203.
Profile Breeder. **Ref: YH04566**

EDMUNDSON, P W J

P W J Edmundson, 2 Apple Tree Cottages, Otley Rd, Grundisburgh, Woodbridge, **Suffolk**, IP13 6RY, **ENGLAND**.
(T) 01473 738868.
Profile Stable/Livery. **Ref: YH04567**

EDNIE, JAS P

Jas P Ednie, 36 Fairfield Rd, Colinsburgh, Leven, **Fife**, KY9 1LJ, **SCOTLAND**.
(T) 01333 340623 **(F)** 01333 340623.
Contact/s
Owner: Mr J Ednie
Profile Blacksmith. **Ref: YH04568**

EDWARD ROBERT SADDLERY

Edward Robert Saddlery Ltd, 4 Shelson Prde, Ashford Rd, Feltham, **London (Greater)**, TW13 4QZ, **ENGLAND**.
(T) 020 88909444 **(F)** 020 88442074.
Contact/s
Owner: Mrs K Brown
Profile Riding Wear Retailer, Saddlery Retailer.
Specialise in bespoke harnesses. Yr. Est: 1999
Opening Times
Sp: Open Mon - Fri 10:00, Sat 09:00. Closed Mon - Wed, Fri, Sat 18:00, Thurs 20:00.
Su: Open Mon - Fri 10:00, Sat 09:00. Closed Mon - Wed, Fri, Sat 18:00, Thurs 20:00.
Au: Open Mon - Fri 10:00, Sat 09:00. Closed Mon - Wed, Fri, Sat 18:00, Thurs 20:00.
Wn: Open Mon - Fri 10:00, Sat 09:00. Closed Mon - Wed, Fri, Sat 18:00, Thurs 20:00. **Ref: YH04569**

EDWARDS & TYLER

Edwards & Tyler, 2 Toatwood Bungalows, Blackgate Lane, Pulborough, **Sussex (West)**, RH20 1DD, **ENGLAND**.
(T) 01798 875790.
Profile Breeder. **Ref: YH04570**

EDWARDS BLACK SADDLERY

Edwards Black Saddlery, Blacks Filling Station, Foregates, Holmer, **Herefordshire**, HR4 9RJ, **ENGLAND**.
(T) 01432 264476 **(F)** 01432 352611.
Profile Saddlery Retailer. **Ref: YH04571**

EDWARDS MOBILE TOW BARS

Edwards Mobile Tow Bars, Vine Ind Est, Elland Rd, Brookfoot, Brighouse, **Yorkshire (West)**, HD6 2QS, **ENGLAND**.
(T) 01484 713335 **(F)** 01484 713335.
Contact/s
Owner: Mr S Dilley
Profile Transport/Horse Boxes. **Ref: YH04572**

EDWARDS SADDLERY

Edwards Saddlery, 51 Northwick Business Ctre, Northwick Pk, Blockley, Moreton In Marsh, **Gloucestershire**, GL56 9RF, **ENGLAND**.
(T) 01386 700606.

Profile Saddlery Retailer. **Ref: YH04573**

EDWARDS' SADDLERY

Edwards' Saddlery, Bidford Bridge Hse, High St, Bidford On Avon, **Warwickshire**, B50 4BG, **ENGLAND**.
(T) 01789 491222 **(F)** 01789 491222.
Contact/s
Owner: Mrs S Edwards
Profile Riding Wear Retailer, Saddlery Retailer, Supplies. Yr. Est: 1999
Opening Times
Sp: Open Mon - Sat 09:30. Closed Mon - Fri 17:00, Sat 16:00.
Su: Open Mon - Sat 09:30. Closed Mon - Fri 17:00, Sat 16:00.
Au: Open Mon - Sat 09:30. Closed Mon - Fri 17:00, Sat 16:00.
Wn: Open Mon - Sat 09:30. Closed Mon - Fri 17:00, Sat 16:00.
Closed on Sundays. **Ref: YH04574**

EDWARDS TRAILERS

Edwards Trailers, Hall Farm, Lackford, Bury St Edmunds, **Suffolk**, IP28 6HX, **ENGLAND**.
(T) 01284 728954 **(F)** 01284 728954.
Profile Transport/Horse Boxes. **Ref: YH04575**

EDWARDS, C C

Mr C C Edwards, Brynore Hall, Brynore, Criftins, Ellesmere, **Shropshire**, SY12 9LP, **ENGLAND**.
(T) 01691 690260. **Ref: YH04576**

EDWARDS, C J

C J Edwards, Mill Farm, Woodington Rd, East Wellow, Romsey, **Hampshire**, SO51 6DQ, **ENGLAND**.
(T) 01794 323226 **(F)** 01794 323226.
Contact/s
Owner: Mr C Edwards
Profile Transport/Horse Boxes. **Ref: YH04577**

EDWARDS, CHRISTOPHER R

Christopher R Edwards DWCF, 10 Kennett Cottages, Kennett, Newmarket, **Suffolk**, CB8 7QH, **ENGLAND**.
(T) 01638 750985.
Profile Farrier. **Ref: YH04578**

EDWARDS, ELWYN HARTLEY

Elwyn Hartley Edwards, Equestrian Trade News, Ty'n Rhos, Chwilog, Pwllheli, **Gwynedd**, LL53 6SG, **WALES**.
(T) 01766 810593 **(F)** 01766 810156
(E) elwyn@tynrhos23.freeserve.co.uk **Ref: YH04579**

EDWARDS, GORDON F

Gordon F Edwards RSS, Summering, Wheddon Cross, Minehead, **Somerset**, TA24 7AT, **ENGLAND**.
(T) 01643 831549
(M) 07970 059297.
Profile Farrier. **Ref: YH04580**

EDWARDS, J T

J T Edwards, Parc Le Breos Trekking Ctre, Parkmill, Swansea, **Swansea**, SA3 2HA, **WALES**.
(T) 01792 371636 **(F)** 01792 371287
(E) info@parc-le-breos.co.uk
(W) www.parc-le-breos.co.uk.
Contact/s
Owner: Mrs O Edwards
Profile Riding School. **Ref: YH04581**

EDWARDS, JOHN

John Edwards, 17 Bourneville Rd, Blaina, Abertillery, **Blaenau Gwent**, NP13 3EL, **WALES**.
(T) 01495 290722.
Profile Farrier. **Ref: YH04582**

EDWARDS, M C

M C Edwards, The Gables, Fiddling Lane, Stowting, Ashford, **Kent**, TN25 6AR, **ENGLAND**.
(T) 01303 813580.
Profile Farrier. **Ref: YH04583**

EDWARDS, MARCUS L

Marcus L Edwards BII, 168 St Leonard's Rd, Windsor, **Buckinghamshire**, SL2 5XD, **ENGLAND**.
(T) 01753 853837.
Profile Farrier. **Ref: YH04584**

EDWARDS, S

Miss S Edwards, Coldharbour Farm, Sutton, Pulborough, **Sussex (West)**, RH20 1PR, **ENGLAND**.
(T) 01798 869219
(M) 07778 023539.
Profile Trainer. **Ref: YH04585**

EDWIN TUCKER & SONS

Edwin Tucker & Sons Ltd, Brewery Meadow, Stonepark, Ashburton, Newton Abbott, **Devon**, TQ13 7DG, **ENGLAND**.
(T) 01364 652403 **(F)** 01364 654300.
Profile Saddlery Retailer. **Ref: YH04586**

EFFINGHAM R C

Effingham R C, 9 Budingham Dri, Fetcham, **Surrey**, KT22 9ES, **ENGLAND**.
(T) 01372 373840. **Ref: YH04587**

EFFORD DOWN RIDING STABLES

Efford Down Riding Stables, Vicarage Rd, Bude, **Cornwall**, EX23 8LT, **ENGLAND**.
(T) 01288 354244.
Profile Riding Stables. **Ref: YH04588**

EGAN, CHRISTINE

Egan Christine, Ballybad Lea Drangan, Ethard, **County Tipperary**, **IRELAND**.
(T) 052 52177.
Profile Supplies. **Ref: YH04589**

EGDON EQUINE

Egdon Equine, Egdon Hse, Nottington, Weymouth, **Dorset**, DT3 4BH, **ENGLAND**.
(T) 01305 813316 **(F)** 01305 816018.
Contact/s
Owner: Mrs G Smith **Ref: YH04590**

EGERDEN FARM STUD

Egerden Farm Stud, Egerton Farm, High Halden, Ashford, **Kent**, TN26 3JP, **ENGLAND**.
(T) 01233 850661.
Contact/s
Partner: Mrs J Dalton
Profile Breeder. **Ref: YH04591**

EGERTON STUD FARM

Egerton Stud Farm Ltd, Cambridge Rd, Newmarket, **Suffolk**, CB8 0NS, **ENGLAND**.
(T) 01638 661178 **(F)** 01638 667144.
Contact/s
Owner: Mr H Akbary
Profile Breeder. **Ref: YH04592**

EGGLESTON WOODCHIPS

Eggleston Woodchips, Malton Works, Lanchester, **County Durham**, DH7 0TP, **ENGLAND**.
(T) 01207 520869 **(F)** 01207 521941.
Profile Supplies. Woodchips. **Ref: YH04593**

EGHAM ANIMAL FOOD SUPPLIES

Egham Animal Food Supplies, 19/21 Station Rd, Egham, **Surrey**, TW20 0JG, **ENGLAND**.
(T) 01784 431616.
Contact/s
Owner: Mr C Tutin
Profile Feed Merchant. **Ref: YH04594**

EGLINTON EQUESTRIAN CLUB

Eglinton Equestrian Club, Lower Airfield Rd, Eglinton, **County Londonderry**, BT47 3PZ, **NORTHERN IRELAND**.
(T) 028 71810646
Alt Contact Address
5 Station Rd, Eglinton, County Londonderry, BT47 3PR, Northern Ireland.**(T)** 028 71810312
Profile Arena, Equestrian Centre, Riding Club.
Yr. Est: 1981 C.Size: 2 Acres **Ref: YH04595**

EIFIONYDD FARMERS

Eifionydd Farmers Ltd, New St, Pwllheli, **Gwynedd**, LL53 5HL, **WALES**.
(T) 01758 701111 **(F)** 01758 701012.
Contact/s
Sales Manager: Mr D Evans
Profile Saddlery Retailer. **Ref: YH04596**

EIGER SHETLANDS

Eiger Shetlands, Eiger Hse, Primrose Lane, Yeovil, **Somerset**, BA21 5SH, **ENGLAND**.
(T) 01935 412888.
Profile Breeder. **Ref: YH04597**

EILBERG, FERDI

Mr Ferdi Eilberg, Pink Green Farm, Beoley, Redditch, **Worcestershire**, B98 9AE, **ENGLAND**.
(T) 01564 742579.
Contact/s
Int Dressage Rider: Ferdi Eilberg
Profile Stable/Livery, Trainer. **Ref: YH04598**

EISENFARN STUD

Eisenfarn Stud, Pant Y Ddeuddwr, Pontardulais Rd, Cross Hands, Llanelli, **Carmarthenshire**, SA14 6NT, **WALES**.
(T) 01269 842346.
Contact/s
Owner: Mr M Watts
Profile Breeder. **Ref: YH04599**

EJECTORS UK

Ejectors UK Ltd, Unit 62 Anne Rd, Smethwick, **Midlands (West)**, B66 2NZ, **ENGLAND**.
(T) 0121 5558801.
Profile Transport/Horse Boxes. **Ref: YH04600**

ELDBERRY STUD

Eldberry Stud, 114 Winterhill Rd, Kimberworth, Rotherham, **Yorkshire (South)**, S61 2EW, **ENGLAND**.
(T) 01709 558955.
Profile Breeder. **Ref: YH04601**

ELECTRIC FENCING DIRECT

Electric Fencing Direct, Lodge Oast, Horns Lodge Lane, Tonbridge, **Kent**, TN11 9NJ, **ENGLAND**.
(T) 01732 833976 **(F)** 01732 838394.
Profile Fencing. **Ref: YH04602**

ELEDA STABLES

Eleda Stables (The), Somerley, Ringwood, **Hampshire**, BH24 3PL, **ENGLAND**.
(T) 01425 461744 **(F)** 01425 461810
(E) info@eleda.co.uk.
Profile Breeder, Stable/Livery, Trainer. **Ref: YH04603**

ELEY, JANET L

Janet L Eley, Hurstwood Cottage, Inwood, All Stretton, Church Stretton, **Shropshire**, SY6 6LA, **ENGLAND**.
(T) 01694 723203.
Profile Medical Support. **Ref: YH04604**

ELITE FORAGE

Elite Forage Co, 3 Cranford Cottages, Moulsford, Wallingford, **Oxfordshire**, OX10 9HR, **ENGLAND**.
(T) 01491 651055.
Contact/s
Partner: Mrs M Hill
Profile Hay and Straw Merchants. **Ref: YH04605**

ELITE RACING CLUB

Elite Racing Club, PO Box 100, Devizes, **Wiltshire**, SN10 4TE, **ENGLAND**.
(T) 01380 818181 **(F)** 01380 813446
(W) www.elite-racing-club.co.uk.
Profile Racing Club. **Ref: YH04606**

ELITE RIDING & EQUESTRIAN SVS

Elite Riding & Equestrian Services, West Cannock Farm, Cotswold Rd, Cannock, **Staffordshire**, WS12 5PZ, **ENGLAND**.
(T) 01543 422232.
Profile Riding School, Stable/Livery.
Offer lessons with own horse **Ref: YH04607**

ELIZABETH GREENWOOD

Elizabeth Greenwood (Equestrian Products) Ltd, Unit 1-3 Stoney Springs Ind Est, Brearley, Luddendenfoot, Halifax, **Yorkshire (West)**, HX2 6HP, **ENGLAND**.
(T) 01422 884866.
Profile Supplies. **Ref: YH04608**

ELKINGTON, ANDREW JAMES

Andrew James Elkington DWCF, 44 North St, Osbournby, Sleaford, **Lincolnshire**, NG34 0DR, **ENGLAND**.
(T) 01529 455730.
Profile Farrier. **Ref: YH04609**

ELLA, ANTHONY W

Anthony W Ella, Cleveland, Wyatts Green Lane, Doddinghurst, **Essex**, CM15 0PY, **ENGLAND**.
(T) 01277 823533.
Profile Farrier. **Ref: YH04610**

ELLBRIDGE EQUITATION CTRE

Ellbridge Equitation Centre, Lower South Wraxall, Bradford-on-Avon, **Wiltshire**, BA15 2RR, **ENGLAND**.
(T) 01225 864664 **(F)** 01225 864664.
Contact/s
Partner: Mr A Day **Ref: YH04611**

ELLE-DANI FARM

Elle-Dani Farm, Allum Lane, Elstree, Borehamwood, **Hertfordshire**, WD6 3NP, **ENGLAND**.
(T) 020 89532045 **(F)** 020 82070888.
Contact/s
Owner: Miss D Matock
Profile Riding School.
Pony & riding lessons **Ref: YH04612**

Key: **(T)** telephone **(F)** fax **(M)** mobile **(E)** E-Mail Address **(W)** Website Address **(Q)** Qualifications
Yr. Est: Year Established C.Size: Complex Size Sp: Spring Su: Summer Au: Autumn Wn: Winter

A-Z of COMPANIES

ELLERBY & WEBSTER

Ellerby & Webster, York Riding School, Wigginton Rd, Wigginton, York, **Yorkshire (North)**, YO32 2RJ, **ENGLAND**.
(T) 01904 750037.
Contact/s
Partner: Mr M Webster
Profile Riding School. **Ref: YH04613**

ELLESMERE

Ellesmere Riding & Trekking Centre, Ellesmere, Llangorse, Brecon, **Powys**, LD3 7UN, **WALES**.
(T) 01874 658252.
Profile Equestrian Centre. Trekking Centre.
Ref: YH04614

ELLIOT RIGHT WAY BOOKS

Elliot Right Way Books, Kingswood Buildings, Brighton Rd, Lower Kingswood, Tadworth, **Surrey**, KT20 6TD, **ENGLAND**.
(T) 01737 832202 **(F)** 01737 830311
(E) info@right-way.co.uk
(W) www.right-way.co.uk.
Profile Supplies. Publisher of Equestrian Books. Publish four equestrian books, 'In Harmony With Your Horse' and 'Riding and Schooling' both by Claire Albinson, 'The Right Way to Keep Ponies' by Hugh Venables and 'Solve Your Horse and Pony Problems' by Karen Bush and Sarah Viccars.
Opening Times
Sp: Open Mon - Sat 09:00. Closed Mon - Sat 17:00.
Su: Open Mon - Sat 09:00. Closed Mon - Sat 17:00.
Au: Open Mon - Sat 09:00. Closed Mon - Sat 17:00.
Wn: Open Mon - Sat 09:00. Closed Mon - Sat 17:00.
Ref: YH04615

ELLIOT, GINNY

Ginny Elliot MBE, Holliers Hse, Middle Barton, **Oxfordshire**, OX5 3DU, **ENGLAND**.
(T) 01869 340453. **Ref: YH04616**

ELLIOTT & FIELDHOUSE

Elliott & Fieldhouse, The Vetnry Ctre, Dulverton, **Somerset**, TA22 9NT, **ENGLAND**.
(T) 01398 323285.
Profile Medical Support. **Ref: YH04617**

ELLIOTT, BRIAN

Brian Elliott, 43 Spiller Rd, Chickerell, Weymouth, **Dorset**, DT3 4AX, **ENGLAND**.
(T) 01305 781361 **(F)** 01305 833900.
Profile Supplies. **Ref: YH04618**

ELLIOTT, D

Mrs D Elliott, Blaencathal, Pont-Sian, Llandysul, **Carmarthenshire**, SA44 4UE, **WALES**.
(T) 01545 590628.
Profile Trainer. **Ref: YH04619**

ELLIOTT, E A

Mr E A Elliott, Planting Hse, Windlestone Pk, Rushyford, **County Durham**, DL17 0LZ, **ENGLAND**.
(T) 01388 720383 **(F)** 01388 722355.
Profile Supplies. **Ref: YH04620**

ELLIS

Ellis & Co, 28 Normandy St, Alton, **Hampshire**, GU34 1BX, **ENGLAND**.
(T) 01420 84442 **(F)** 01420 541999
(W) www.home2view.co.uk/ellis.
Contact/s
Owner: Mr S Ellis
(E) simon@ellisco22.freeserve.co.uk
Profile Property Agents.
This company specialises in country, farm and equestrian property throughout Hampshire, Surrey and Sussex.
Opening Times
Sp: Open Mon - Sat 09:00. Closed Mon - Fri 17:30, Sat 12:30.
Su: Open Mon - Sat 09:00. Closed Mon - Fri 17:30, Sat 12:30.
Au: Open Mon - Sat 09:00. Closed Mon - Fri 17:30, Sat 12:30.
Wn: Open Mon - Sat 09:00. Closed Mon - Fri 17:30, Sat 12:30.
Closed Sundays **Ref: YH04621**

ELLIS ENGINEERING

Ellis Engineering, Rosedene, Coxes Farm Rd, Billericay, **Essex**, CM11 2UB, **ENGLAND**.
(T) 01277 631274 **(F)** 01277 631274.
Contact/s
Owner: Mr P Ellis
Profile Blacksmith. **Ref: YH04622**

ELLIS, ANDREW C

Andrew C Ellis RSS BII, Regalem, Saverley Green, Stoke-on-Trent, **Staffordshire**, ST11 9QX, **ENGLAND**.
(T) 01782 394980.
Profile Farrier. **Ref: YH04623**

ELLIS, D

D Ellis, Pensipple, Liskeard, **Cornwall**, PL14 4SP, **ENGLAND**.
(T) 01503 240245.
Profile Medical Support. **Ref: YH04624**

ELLIS, JANET B

Janet B Ellis Grad D.P., M.C.S.P., Burn Grange, Burn, Selby, **Yorkshire (North)**, YO8 8LA, **ENGLAND**.
(T) 01757 270475 **(F)** 01757 270605.
Profile Medical Support. **Ref: YH04625**

ELLIS, LEE R

Lee R Ellis DWCF, 30 Highfield Rd, Netherton, Wakefield, **Yorkshire (West)**, WF4 4NB, **ENGLAND**.
(T) 01924 266963.
Profile Farrier. **Ref: YH04626**

ELLIS, N

Miss N Ellis, Frankton Grange, Ellesmere, **Shropshire**, SY12 0JX, **ENGLAND**.
(T) 01939 270274.
Profile Breeder. **Ref: YH04627**

ELLISON COURT

Ellison Court Ltd, Sissinghurst Rd, Biddenden, Ashford, **Kent**, TN27 8EQ, **ENGLAND**.
(T) 01580 292290 **(F)** 01580 291687.
Contact/s
Owner: Mr C Burgess
Profile Trainer. **Ref: YH04628**

ELLISON RACEHORSE TRAINER

Ellison Racehorse Trainer, Low Meadows Farm, Lanchester, Durham, **County Durham**, DH7 0RE, **ENGLAND**.
(T) 01207 529991 **(F)** 01207 529991.
Contact/s
Owner: Mr B Ellison
Profile Trainer. **Ref: YH04629**

ELLMORE HORSE TRANSPORT

Ellmore Horse Transport, 5 Hill Hall Cottages, Old London Rd, Swinfen, Lichfield, **Staffordshire**, WS14 9QW, **ENGLAND**.
(T) 01543 481672
(M) 07768 056445.
Profile Transport/Horse Boxes. **Ref: YH04630**

ELM LEAZE STUD

Elm Leaze Stud & Equestrian Centre, The Street, Didmarton, Badminton, **Gloucestershire**, GL9 1DT, **ENGLAND**.
(T) 01454 238643.
Contact/s
Head Girl: Ms L Smith
Profile Equestrian Centre, Riding Club, Stable/Livery.
No.Staff: 4 Yr. Est: 1986 C.Size: 20 Acres
Ref: YH04631

ELM OF BURFORD

Elm of Burford, 48 High St, Burford, **Oxfordshire**, OX18 4QF, **ENGLAND**.
(T) 01993 841276 **(F)** 01993 841006.
Contact/s
Partner: Mr L Marshall
Profile Saddlery Retailer. **Ref: YH04632**

ELM PK EQUESTRIAN CTRE

Elm Park Equestrian Centre, Elm Pk, Boyton, Launceston, **Cornwall**, PL15 8NP, **ENGLAND**.
(T) 01566 785353.
Profile Equestrian Centre. **Ref: YH04633**

ELM TODD

Elm Todd Riding School, Little Clacton Rd, Great Holland, Frinton-on-Sea, **Essex**, CO13 0EX, **ENGLAND**.
(T) 01255 812194.
Contact/s
Owner: Mrs J McDougle
Profile Stable/Livery.
Full, part and DIY livery available, prices on request.
Yr. Est: 1976 C.Size: 26 Acres
Opening Times
Sp: Open Mon - Sun 09:00. Closed Mon - Sun 18:00.
Su: Open Mon - Sun 09:00. Closed Mon - Sun 18:00.
Au: Open Mon - Sun 09:00. Closed Mon - Sun 18:00.
Wn: Open Mon - Sun 09:00. Closed Mon - Sun 18:00. **Ref: YH04634**

ELM TREE TACK SHOP

Elm Tree Tack Shop, Halsham, **Yorkshire (East)**, HU12 0BS, **ENGLAND**.
(T) 01964 612391.
Profile Saddlery Retailer. Tack Shop. **Ref: YH04635**

ELMGROVE SADDLERY

Elmgrove Saddlery, Station Rd, Purton, Swindon, **Wiltshire**, SN5 4AH, **ENGLAND**.
(T) 01793 770613 **(F)** 01793 770613.
Contact/s
Owner: Mr C Croucher
Profile Riding Wear Retailer, Saddlery Retailer, Supplies. No.Staff: 3 Yr. Est: 1981
Opening Times
Sp: Open Mon - Fri 10:00, Sat 09:00, Sun 10:00. Closed Mon - Sat 17:00, Sun 13:00.
Su: Open Mon - Fri 10:00, Sat 09:00, Sun 10:00. Closed Mon - Sat 17:00, Sun 13:00.
Au: Open Mon - Fri 10:00, Sat 09:00, Sun 10:00. Closed Mon - Sat 17:00, Sun 13:00.
Wn: Open Mon - Fri 10:00, Sat 09:00, Sun 10:00. Closed Mon - Sat 17:00, Sun 13:00. **Ref: YH04636**

ELMHURST BLOODSTOCK

Elmhurst Bloodstock Ltd, Little Elmhurst, Church Cl, Brenchley, Tonbridge, **Kent**, TN12 7AA, **ENGLAND**.
(T) 01892 724741 **(F)** 01892 724742
(M) 07774 497279.
Profile Blood Stock Agency. **Ref: YH04637**

ELMS SADDLERY & LIVERIES

Elms Saddlery & Liveries (The), Elms Farm, Pett Lane, Icklesham, **Sussex (East)**, TN36 4AH, **ENGLAND**.
(T) 01797 225743.
Profile Saddlery Retailer, Stable/Livery.
Ref: YH04638

ELMS STUD

Elms Stud Co Ltd (The), The Elms, Horton Rd, Denton, Northampton, **Northamptonshire**, NN7 1DY, **ENGLAND**.
(T) 01604 696224 **(F)** 01604 696190.
Contact/s
Owner: Mr S Kenble
Profile Breeder.
Opening Times
Sp: Open Mon - Sun 09:00. Closed Mon - Sun 18:00.
Su: Open Mon - Sun 09:00. Closed Mon - Sun 18:00.
Au: Open Mon - Sun 09:00. Closed Mon - Sun 18:00.
Wn: Open Mon - Sun 09:00. Closed Mon - Sun 18:00. **Ref: YH04639**

ELMWOOD EQUESTRIAN CTRE

Elmwood Equestrian Centre, Maldon Rd, Burnham-on-Crouch, **Essex**, CM0 8NT, **ENGLAND**.
(T) 01621 783216 **(F)** 01621 784330.
Contact/s
Owner: Mrs A Hull
Profile Riding School, Stable/Livery.
Hacking available. Yr. Est: 1985 C.Size: 110 Acres
Opening Times
Sp: Open 08:00. Closed 17:00.
Su: Open 08:00. Closed 17:00.
Au: Open 08:00. Closed 17:00.
Wn: Open 08:00. Closed 17:00.
Closed Mondays **Ref: YH04640**

ELMWOOD FARM RIDING CTRE

Elmwood Farm Riding Centre, Elmwood Ave, Broadstairs, **Kent**, CT10 3PA, **ENGLAND**.
(T) 01843 602922.
Profile Riding School, Stable/Livery. **Ref: YH04641**

ELSENHAM STUD

Elsenham Stud, Fullers End, Elsenham, Bishop's Stortford, **Essex**, CM22 6EA, **ENGLAND**.
(T) 01279 816002.
Profile Breeder. **Ref: YH04642**

ELSON, H & M

H & M Elson, Top Farm, Ebrington, Chipping Campden, **Gloucestershire**, GL55 6NA, **ENGLAND**.
(T) 01386 593238.
Profile Breeder. **Ref: YH04643**

ELSWICK

Elswick Riding Centre Livery & Stablery, Bonds Lane, Elswick, Preston, **Lancashire**, PR4 3ZE, **ENGLAND**.
(T) 01995 670925.
Profile Riding School, Stable/Livery, Track/Course.
Ref: YH04644

ELVASTON CASTLE RIDING CTRE

Elvaston Castle Riding Centre, Elvaston Castle Country Pk, Elvaston, Thulston, Derby, **Derbyshire**, DE72 3EP, **ENGLAND**.
(T) 01332 751927.
Profile Riding School, Trainer. **Ref: YH04645**

ELVEDEN EQUESTRIAN CTRE

Elveden Equestrian Centre, Chalk Hall Farm, London Rd, Elveden, Thetford, **Norfolk**, IP24 3TZ, **ENGLAND**.
(T) 01842 890769 **(F)** 01842 890769.
Profile Equestrian Centre. **Ref: YH04646**

ELWELL, TERESA

Teresa Elwell, Lamberts Barn, Cropredy, Banbury, **Oxfordshire**, OX17 1QA, **ENGLAND**.
(T) 01295 750758 **(F)** 01295 750039
Affiliated Bodies MCA.
Contact/s
Owner: Teresa Elwell **(Q)** MC
(E) teresa_elwell@email.commom
Profile Medical Support.
Also offers EMRT (Equine Muscle Release Therapy).
Yr. Est: 1976
Opening Times
Telephone for an appointment. **Ref: YH04647**

ELWORTHY, S

S Elworthy, Buddles Hse, Dane Court Rd, Broadstairs, **Kent**, CT10 2QP, **ENGLAND**.
(T) 01843 865506.
Contact/s
Owner: Mrs S Elworthy
Profile Stable/Livery. **Ref: YH04648**

EMBLA STUD

Embla Stud, Swanpit Farm, Gnosall, **Staffordshire**, ST20 0EE, **ENGLAND**.
(T) 01785 822221.
Profile Breeder. **Ref: YH04649**

EMBLEN, JOHN G

John G Emblen DWCF, 159 Hermitage Woods Cres, St Johns, Woking, **Surrey**, GU21 1UJ, **ENGLAND**.
(T) 01276 855096.
Profile Farrier. **Ref: YH04650**

EMERGENCY RELIEF

Emergency Relief for Thoroughbreds, Fifth Floor, 60 St James's St, London, **London (Greater)**, SW1A 1LE, **ENGLAND**.
(T) 020 74080903.
Profile Club/Association. **Ref: YH04651**

EMERY

Emery, Brunswick St East, Maidstone, **Kent**, ME15 7UX, **ENGLAND**.
(T) 01622 751424.
Profile Blacksmith. **Ref: YH04652**

EMMA, CHARLOTTE

Charlotte Emma, Lark Hill Stud, Bell Hse Lane, Anslow, Burton-on-Trent, **Staffordshire**, DE13 9PA, **ENGLAND**.
(T) 01283 511766.
Contact/s
Owner: Mrs C Coxon **Ref: YH04653**

EMMERSON, S A

Mr & Mrs S A Emmerson, Gower Hall Farm, Foston, York, **Yorkshire (North)**, YO60 7QD, **ENGLAND**.
(T) 01653 618767.
Profile Breeder. **Ref: YH04654**

EMMERSONS

Emmersons, The Meadows, Kirkby, Stokesley, **Cleveland**, TS9 7AQ, **ENGLAND**.
(T) 01642 711640.
Profile Riding School. **Ref: YH04655**

EMMETT, ROBERT C

Robert C Emmett DWCF, 15 Withens Hill Croft, Illingworth, Halifax, **Yorkshire (West)**, HX2 9LJ, **ENGLAND**.
(T) 01422 248749.
Profile Farrier. **Ref: YH04656**

EMMOTT, G H

Mr G H Emmott, Currer Wood Farm, Steeton, Keighley, **Yorkshire (West)**, BD20 6PE, **ENGLAND**.
(T) 01535 653112.
Profile Breeder. **Ref: YH04657**

EMPIRE STABLES

Empire Stables, Ranby Hill, Ranby, Lincoln, **Lincolnshire**, LN8 5LN, **ENGLAND**.
(T) 01507 343365 **(F)** 01507 343365
(M) 07977 481650.
Profile Transport/Horse Boxes. **Ref: YH04658**

EMPORIUM

Emporium (The), 7 Wheeler St, Headcorn, Ashford, **Kent**, TN27 9SH, **ENGLAND**.
(T) 01622 890446
(E) info@theemporiumheadcorn.co.uk
(W) www.theemporiumheadcorn.co.uk.
Profile Saddlery Retailer. **Ref: YH04659**

EMRAL STUD

Emral Stud, Emral Hall Farm, Holly Bush, Bangor Isycoed, Worthenbury, **Wrexham**, LL13 0BG, **WALES**.
(T) 01948 81226.
Profile Breeder. **Ref: YH04660**

EMSLIE HORSE BOXES

Emslie Horse Boxes, The Conifers, Low Hill Rd, Roydon, Harlow, **Essex**, CM19 5JN, **ENGLAND**.
(T) 01279 792820 **(F)** 01279 792820.
Profile Transport/Horse Boxes. **Ref: YH04661**

EMSLIE, COLIN

Colin Emslie, 12 Meadows Vale, Oldmeldrum, Inverurie, **Aberdeenshire**, AB51 0GP, **SCOTLAND**.
(T) 01651 872333.
Profile Transport/Horse Boxes. **Ref: YH04662**

ENCOMPASS TRAINING SVS

Encompass Training Services, New Rd, Framlingham, **Suffolk**, IP13 9AT, **ENGLAND**.
(T) 01728 621037 **(F)** 01728 724306.
Profile Equestrian Centre. **Ref: YH04663**

END HSE

End House Stud, Gisburn, Clitheroe, **Lancashire**, BB7 4HW, **ENGLAND**.
(T) 01200 445426 **(F)** 01200 445426
(E) stallions@endhousestud.co.uk
(W) www.endhousestud.co.uk.
Contact/s
Owner: Ms T Goulding
Profile Blood Stock Agency, Breeder. No.Staff: 6
Yr. Est: 1998 C.Size: 60 Acres **Ref: YH04664**

ENDEAVOUR TOOLS

Endeavour Tools, Unit 7 First Stage Hse, Brimington Rd North, Chesterfield, **Derbyshire**, S41 9BE, **ENGLAND**.
(T) 01246 550193.
Contact/s
Manager: Mr A Purcell
Profile Blacksmith. **Ref: YH04665**

ENDELL VETNRY GRP

Endell Veterinary Group, 49 Endless St, Salisbury, **Wiltshire**, SP1 3UH, **ENGLAND**.
(T) 01722 710046 **(F)** 01722 711028.
Contact/s
Partner: Mr J Puzio
Profile Medical Support. **Ref: YH04666**

ENDON RIDING SCHOOL

Endon Riding School, Stanley Moss Lane, Stockton Brook, Stoke-on-Trent, **Staffordshire**, ST9 9LR, **ENGLAND**.
(T) 01782 502114.
Contact/s
Owner: Mrs D Machin
Profile Horse/Rider Accom, Riding School, Stable/Livery. **Ref: YH04667**

ENDURANCE HORSE AND PONY

Endurance Horse and Pony Society of GB, Tudor Nurseries, Chalk Pit Lane, Wool, Wareham, **Dorset**, BH20 6DW, **ENGLAND**.
(T) 01929 462316.
Contact/s
Key Contact: Mrs W Dunham
Profile Club/Association. **Ref: YH04668**

ENDURANCE RIDING SUPPORTERS

Endurance Riding Supporters Club, Graygill, Staunton, Coleford, **Gloucestershire**, GL16 8PD, **ENGLAND**.
(T) 01600 712536.
Contact/s
Key Contact: Mr D Bond
Profile Club/Association. **Ref: YH04669**

ENFIELD CHACE

Enfield Chace, Videne, Hawkshead Rd, Little Heath, Potters Bar, **Hertfordshire**, EN6 1LX, **ENGLAND**.
(T) 01707 654157. **Ref: YH04670**

ENGLAND, E M V

Miss E M V England, Grove Cottage, Priors Hardwick, Rugby, **Warwickshire**, CV23 8SN, **ENGLAND**.
(T) 01327 260437.
Profile Supplies. **Ref: YH04671**

ENGLISH BROTHERS

English Brothers Ltd, Salts Rd, Walton Highway, Wisbech, **Cambridgeshire**, PE14 7DU, **ENGLAND**.
(T) 01945 587500 **(F)** 01945 582576.
Profile Transport/Horse Boxes. **Ref: YH04672**

ENGLISH CHINA CLAYS

English China Clays Riding Club, 32 Trenarren View, Boscoppa, St Austell, **Cornwall**, PL25 3ER, **ENGLAND**.
(T) 01726 63753.
Contact/s
Chairman: Mr A Parker
Profile Club/Association, Riding Club. **Ref: YH04673**

ENGLISH CONNEMARA PONY SOC

English Connemara Pony Society (The), Glen Ferm, Waddicombe, Dulverton, **Somerset**, TA22 9RY, **ENGLAND**.
(T) 01398 341490 **(F)** 01398 341490
(E) connemaras@ecpsconnemaras.freeserve.co.uk
(W) www.ecpsconnemaras.freeserve.co.uk.
Profile Breeder, Club/Association. **Ref: YH04674**

ENGLISH INT HORSE TRANSPORT

English International Horse Transport, Horton View, Dartford Rd, South Darenth, Dartford, **Kent**, DA4 9HY, **ENGLAND**.
(T) 01322 862286.
Contact/s
Partner: Mrs A English
Profile Transport/Horse Boxes. **Ref: YH04675**

ENIGMA PHYSIOTHERAPY

Enigma Physiotherapy, The Old Chapel, Donnington, Moreton In Marsh, **Gloucestershire**, GL56 0XX, **ENGLAND**.
(T) 01451 831715.
Profile Medical Support. **Ref: YH04676**

ENNIS, FRANCIS

Francis Ennis, Emlagher Lodge, Ballyfair, The Curragh, **County Kildare**, **IRELAND**.
(T) 045 441462.
Contact/s
Trainer: Mr F Ennis
(E) francisennis@kildarehorse.ie
Profile Trainer. **Ref: YH04677**

ENNIS, FRANK

Frank Ennis, Elmagher Lodge, Ballyfair, Curragh Camp, Curragh, **County Kildare**, **IRELAND**.
(T) 045 441462.
Profile Trainer. **Ref: YH04678**

ENNISKILLEN CLGE

Enniskillen College of Agriculture, Levaghy, Enniskillen, **County Fermanagh**, BT74 4GF, **NORTHERN IRELAND**.
(T) 028 66344800 **(F)** 028 66344888
(W) www.enniskillencollege.ac.uk.
Profile Equestrian Centre. College offering Equestrian Courses. **Ref: YH04679**

ENRIGHT, G P

G P Enright, The Oaks Stables, The Old Racecourse, Lewes, **Sussex (East)**, BN7 1UR, **ENGLAND**.
(T) 01273 479183 **(F)** 01273 479183.
Contact/s
Owner: Mr G Enright
Profile Trainer. **Ref: YH04680**

EPPINGDENE EQUESTRIAN CTRE

Eppingdene Equestrian Centre, Ivy Chimneys Rd, Epping, **Essex**, CM16 4LE, **ENGLAND**.
(T) 01992 577757.
Contact/s
Owner: Miss L Jones
Profile Equestrian Centre. **Ref: YH04681**

EPSOM DOWNS RACECOURSE

Epsom Downs Racecourse, Epsom, **Surrey**, KT18 5LQ, **ENGLAND**.
(T) 01372 726311 **(F)** 01372 748253
(E) epsom@rht.net.
Contact/s
Director of Racing: Mr A Cooper
Profile Track/Course. **Ref: YH04682**

EPSOM POLO CLUB

Epsom Polo Club, Horton Country Pk, Horton Lane, Epsom, **Surrey**, KT19 8PL, **ENGLAND**.
(T) 01372 748200.
Profile Polo Club. **Ref: YH04683**

EPSOM VETNRY REMEDIES

Epsom Veterinary Remedies Ltd, Kingwood Stud, Lambourn Woodlands, Hungerford, **Berkshire**, RG17 7RS, **ENGLAND**.
(T) 01488 71657 **(F)** 01488 73434.
Profile Medical Support, Supplies. **Ref: YH04684**

EQUALLUS EQUESTRIAN

Equallus Equestrian Centre, Riverside Farm, Hares Lane, Hartley Wintney, Hook, **Hampshire**, RG27 8AD, **ENGLAND**.
(T) 01252 844554
(W) www.equallus.com.
Contact/s
Partner: Miss A Phillips **(Q)** AI
Profile Riding School, Stable/Livery.
The centre offers both part and full livery. Part livery includes everything except exercise. Lessons are available for riders with their own horses. Training for exams for BHS/ABRS and Pony Club are also available. No.Staff: 3 Yr. Est: 1998
Opening Times
Sp: Open Mon - Thurs 11:00, Sat - Sun 09:00. Closed Mon - Thurs 19:00, Sat - Sun 17:00.
Su: Open Mon - Thurs 11:00, Sat - Sun 09:00. Closed Mon - Thurs 19:00, Sat - Sun 17:00.
Au: Open Mon - Thurs 11:00, Sat - Sun 09:00. Closed Mon - Thurs 19:00, Sat - Sun 17:00.
Wn: Open Mon - Thurs 11:00, Sat - Sun 09:00. Closed Mon - Thurs 19:00, Sat - Sun 17:00.
Closed on Fridays **Ref: YH04685**

EQUARIUS

Equarius, 121 Chestnut Gr, New Malden, **Surrey**, KT3 3JT, **ENGLAND**.
(T) 020 89498740 **(F)** 020 89426497.
Profile Breeder. **Ref: YH04686**

EQUESPORT

Equesport, 10 London Rd, Calne, **Wiltshire**, SN11 0AB, **ENGLAND**.
(T) 01249 814443.
Contact/s
Owner: Mr W Griffiths
Profile Saddlery Retailer. **Ref: YH04687**

EQUEST

Equest, 3B The Old Creamery, Pipe Gate, Market Drayton, **Shropshire**, TF9 4HX, **ENGLAND**.
(T) 01630 647451 **(F)** 01630 647451.
Profile Breeder. **Ref: YH04688**

EQUESTRIA.NET

Equestria.net, Hawes Hill Court, Drift Rd, Windsor, **Berkshire**, SL4 4QQ, **ENGLAND**.
(T) 0870 7414590 **(F)** 0870 7414585
(E) info@equestria.net
(W) www.equestria.net.
Profile Supplies. **Ref: YH04689**

EQUESTRIAN

Equestrian (The), Stormer Hill Closes Farm, Cann St, Tottington, Bury, **Lancashire**, BL8 3PE, **ENGLAND**.
(T) 01204 882615
(M) 07976 265629.
Profile Supplies. **Ref: YH04690**

EQUESTRIAN & EXAM CTRE

Equestrian & Examination Centre, Christchurch Rd, West Parley, Ferndown, **Dorset**, BH22 8SQ, **ENGLAND**.
(T) 01202 570288 **(F)** 01202 570788.
Contact/s
Owner: Mr P Oliver
Profile Riding School, Stable/Livery, Track/Course, Trainer.
DIY livery available. Telephone for further price information. **Ref: YH04691**

EQUESTRIAN ASPECTS

Equestrian Aspects, 12 Carmelite Way, Hartley, **Kent**, DA3 8BP, **ENGLAND**.
(M) 07774 434912.
Profile Supplies. **Ref: YH04692**

EQUESTRIAN BRIDLE

Equestrian Bridle Co, 175 High St, Bloxwich, Walsall, **Midlands (West)**, WS3 3LH, **ENGLAND**.
(T) 01922 477823 **(F)** 01922 477823.
Contact/s
Owner: Mrs M Davies
Profile Supplies.
Sell mostly to retailers, but can sell to the public.
Yr. Est: 1970
Opening Times
Sp: Open Mon - Fri 09:00. Closed Mon - Thurs 16:00, Fri 14:00.
Su: Open Mon - Fri 09:00. Closed Mon - Thurs 16:00, Fri 14:00.
Au: Open Mon - Fri 09:00. Closed Mon - Thurs 16:00, Fri 14:00.
Wn: Open Mon - Fri 09:00. Closed Mon - Thurs 16:00, Fri 14:00.
Closed on weekends **Ref: YH04693**

EQUESTRIAN CLEARANCE CTRE

Equestrian Clearance Centre (The), Bull Green, Luddendenfoot, Halifax, **Yorkshire (West)**, HX2 6JJ, **ENGLAND**.
(T) 01422 882192 **(F)** 01422 881051
(E) equestrianclearance@excite.co.uk.
Contact/s
Owner: Ms L Meadowcroft
Profile Riding Wear Retailer, Saddlery Retailer.
Retailers of anything for horse and rider
Opening Times
Sp: Open Mon - Wed, Fri - Sun 10:00. Closed Mon - Wed, Fri 18:00, Sat, Sun 16:00.
Su: Open Mon - Wed, Fri - Sun 10:00. Closed Mon - Wed, Fri 18:00, Sat, Sun 16:00.
Au: Open Mon - Wed, Fri - Sun 10:00. Closed Mon - Wed, Fri 18:00, Sat, Sun 16:00.
Wn: Open Mon - Wed, Fri - Sun 10:00. Closed Mon - Wed, Fri 18:00, Sat, Sun 16:00.
Closed Thursdays **Ref: YH04694**

EQUESTRIAN COUNTRY LEISURE

Equestrian Country Leisure, 3 Collington Mansions, Collington Ave, Bexhill-on-Sea, **Sussex (East)**, TN39 3PU, **ENGLAND**.
(T) 01424 216657 **(F)** 01424 216657.
Contact/s
Owner: Miss K Pennall
Profile Riding Wear Retailer. **Ref: YH04695**

EQUESTRIAN CTRE

Equestrian Centre (The), Shardeloes Farm, Cherry Lane, Amersham, **Buckinghamshire**, HP7 0QF, **ENGLAND**.
(T) 01494 432577 **(F)** 01494 727004
(E) mail@shardeloesfarm.com
(W) www.shardeloesfarm.com.
Contact/s
For Bookings: Ms B Howard
(E) beckey@shardeloesfarm.com
Profile Arena, Equestrian Centre, Riding Club, Riding School, Stable/Livery, Track/Course.
Working livery available. Also offer a 'Horse Search' facility - can find you the perfect horse.
No.Staff: 10 Yr. Est: 1981 C.Size: 350 Acres
Ref: YH04696

EQUESTRIAN CTRE

Equestrian Centre (The), Gresford Rd, Hope, Wrexham, **Wrexham**, LL12 9SD, **WALES**.
(T) 01978 760356 **(F)** 01978 762388
(W) www.equestrian-centre.co.uk.
Contact/s
Owner: Mr M Tytherleigh
Profile Holidays, Horse/Rider Accom, Riding School.
No.Staff: 8 Yr. Est: 1988 C.Size: 70 Acres
Opening Times
Sp: Open Mon - Sun 08:30. Closed Mon - Wed 20:00, Thurs - Sun 18:00.
Su: Open Mon - Sun 08:30. Closed Mon - Wed 20:00, Thurs - Sun 18:00.
Au: Open Mon - Sun 08:30. Closed Mon - Wed 20:00, Thurs - Sun 18:00.
Wn: Open Mon - Sun 08:30. Closed Mon - Wed 20:00, Thurs - Sun 18:00. **Ref: YH04697**

EQUESTRIAN CTRE AT LOANHEAD

Equestrian Centre at Loanhead, Kingswells, Aberdeen, **Aberdeen (City of)**, AB15 8QD, **SCOTLAND**.
(T) 01224 742011.
Profile Equestrian Centre. **Ref: YH04698**

EQUESTRIAN DIRECT SALES

Equestrian Direct Sales, Beech Vista Garden Ctre, North Rd, Dublin, **County Dublin**, **IRELAND**.
(T) 01 8646707 **(F)** 01 8646707.
Contact/s
Owner: Christopher Grogan **(T)** 01 8259027
Profile Riding Wear Retailer, Saddlery Retailer, Supplies.
A mobile unit attends all the major shows, which also stocks horse clothing **Ref: YH04699**

EQUESTRIAN ENGINEERING

Equestrian Engineering, Pebble Orchard, 39 High St, Templecombe, **Somerset**, BA8 0JG, **ENGLAND**.
(T) 01963 33689.
Contact/s
Owner: Mr A Haskell
Profile Transport/Horse Boxes. **Ref: YH04700**

EQUESTRIAN EVENT INSURANCE

Equestrian Event Insurance Services, Event Hse, Deweys Lane, Ringwood, **Hampshire**, BH24 1AJ, **ENGLAND**.
(T) 01425 470360 **(F)** 01425 474905.
Profile Supplies. Insurance. **Ref: YH04701**

EQUESTRIAN FARM FEEDS

Equestrian Farm Feeds, 7 Flush Pk, Knockmore Rd, Lisburn, **County Antrim**, BT28 2DX, **NORTHERN IRELAND**.
(T) 028 92677640 **(F)** 028 92661803.
Profile Feed Merchant. **Ref: YH04702**

EQUESTRIAN FEDERATION

Equestrian Federation of Ireland, Ashton Hse, Castleknock, **County Dublin**, **IRELAND**.
(T) 01 868822 **(F)** 01 8683805
(E) efi@horsesport.ie
(W) www.horsesport.ie.
Contact/s
Administration: Ms A Chanarin
(E) annechanarin@horsesport.ie
Profile Club/Association. **Ref: YH04703**

EQUESTRIAN LEATHERS

Equestrian Leathers Ltd, Four Winds, Newcourt Ave, Bray, **County Wicklow**, **IRELAND**.
(T) 01 2867913.
Contact/s
Owner: Ms B Ryan
Profile Riding Wear Retailer, Saddlery Retailer.
Equestrian Leathers specialise in chaps and half chaps. Their products are made to measure, as well as imported.
Opening Times
Telephone for further information **Ref: YH04704**

EQUESTRIAN MANU & SUPPLY

Equestrian Manufacturing & Supply, 52 Mount St, Walsall, **Midlands (West)**, WS1 3PL, **ENGLAND**.
(T) 01922 613988. **Ref: YH04705**

EQUESTRIAN MATTING

Equestrian Matting, Pixton Green, Ashwicke, Chippenham, **Wiltshire**, SN14 8AL, **ENGLAND**.
(T) 01225 852552 **(F)** 01225 858986.
Profile Supplies. **Ref: YH04706**

EQUESTRIAN MNGMT CONSULTANTS

Equestrian Management Consultants Ltd, Wothersome Grange, Bramham, Wetherby, **Yorkshire (West)**, LS23 6LY, **ENGLAND**.
(T) 0113 2892267 **(F)** 0113 2893352
(E) wakeham@emc.u-net.com.
Profile Club/Association. **Ref: YH04707**

EQUESTRIAN RECORD BOOKS

Equestrian Record Books, The York Collection, 15 Elvaston Mews, London, **London (Greater)**, SW7 5HY, **ENGLAND**.
(T) 01953 851761
(M) 07956 487989
(E) p4york4@aol.com
(W) www.horse-web.com/sites/TheYorkCollection.
Profile Supplies.
The record books are specially designed for each discipline so that after each event you can simply enter results and comments, enabling a complete history of performance by horse & rider. **Ref: YH04708**

EQUESTRIAN REQUISITIES

Equestrian Requisities, 10-12 Queens Rd, Stonehouse, **Gloucestershire**, GL10 2QA, **ENGLAND**.
(T) 01453 791955 **(F)** 01453 821939.
Contact/s
Owner: Mrs S Birch
Profile Saddlery Retailer. **Ref: YH04709**

EQUESTRIAN SECURITY SVS

Equestrian Security Services (Freeze Marking), 17 St Johns Rd, Farnham, **Surrey**, GU9 8NU, **ENGLAND**.
(T) 01252 727053 **(F)** 01252 737738.
Contact/s
Manager: Mr C Larcombe
Profile Security.
Equestrian Security Services currently offer freeze branding **Ref: YH04710**

EQUESTRIAN SKILLS

Equestrian Skills, Madeley Heath Farm, Watering Trough Bank, Madeley Heath, Crewe, **Cheshire**, CW3 9LT, **ENGLAND**.
(T) 01782 750881 **(F)** 01782 750881.
Contact/s

Owner: Mrs J Allman
Profile Trainer. Ref: YH04711

EQUESTRIAN STOP

Equestrian Stop, Dolcoath Rd, Camborne, **Cornwall**, TR14 8RR, **ENGLAND**.
(T) 01209 716063 **(F)** 01209 716063
(M) 07967 653152
Alt Contact Address
Collingwood, South Tehidy, Camborne, Cornwall, TR14 0HU, England.**(T)** 01209 714696
Profile Saddlery Retailer, Supplies, Transport/Horse Boxes.
Free saddle fitting on new saddles. Second hand and made to measure saddles. Trailer hire. Bit library. Mobile shop.
Opening Times
Open 7 days a week. Ref: YH04712

EQUESTRIAN SURFACES

Equestrian Surfaces Ltd, St Tibbs Row, Cambridge, **Cambridgeshire**, CB2 3ET, **ENGLAND**.
(T) 01223 359940.
Profile Surfaces. Ref: YH04713

EQUESTRIAN SURFACES

Equestrian Surfaces Ltd, Station Rd, Padiham, Burnley, **Lancashire**, BB12 8EF, **ENGLAND**.
(T) 01282 680014 **(F)** 01282 618307
(E) equestriansurfaces@talk21.com
(W) www.pcbweb.co.uk/equestrian.
Contact/s
Owner: Mr P Harper
Profile Flooring specialists. Ref: YH04714

EQUESTRIAN SVS

Equestrian Services, Dauntsey, Chippenham, **Wiltshire**, SN15 4JH, **ENGLAND**.
(T) 01666 510217.
Profile Supplies. Ref: YH04715

EQUESTRIAN SVS FENCING

Equestrian Services Fencing, High Ridge Farm, Hospital Rd, Shirrell Heath, Southampton, **Hampshire**, SO32 2JR, **ENGLAND**.
(T) 01329 833870 **(F)** 01329 835157
(W) www.equestrianservicesfencing.co.uk.
Contact/s
Secretary: Miss V Dennis
(E) victoria-dennis@hotmail.com
Profile Supplies. Fencing. Ref: YH04716

EQUESTRIAN SVS THORNEY

Equestrian Services Thorney, Barroway Hse, English Drove, Thorney, Peterborough, **Cambridgeshire**, PE6 0PA, **ENGLAND**.
(T) 01733 270504 **(F)** 01733 270504.
Profile Club/Association. Ref: YH04717

EQUESTRIAN TRANSPORT SVS

Equestrian Transport Services Ltd, 66 Tollesbury Rd, Tolleshunt Darcy, Maldon, **Essex**, CM9 8UA, **ENGLAND**.
(T) 01621 869812 **(F)** 01621 860557.
Profile Transport/Horse Boxes. Ref: YH04718

EQUESTRIAN TRAVELLERS CLUB

Equestrian Travellers Club, 26A Collingham Pl, London, **London (Greater)**, SW5 0PZ, **ENGLAND**.
(T) 020 78351233 **(F)** 020 78351313
(E) lucy@etcfab.com.
Profile Club/Association. Ref: YH04719

EQUESTRIAN WORLD

Equestrian World, Doctors La, Maynooth, **County Kildare**, **IRELAND**.
(T) 01 6286853
(E) equestrianworld@eircom.net
(W) www.equine-net.com/.
Profile Supplies. Ref: YH04720

EQUESTRIAN WORLD

Equestrian World Ltd, 46 High St, Cowes, **Isle of Wight**, PO31 7RR, **ENGLAND**.
(T) 01983 291744 **(F)** 01983 297252.
Profile Saddlery Retailer. Ref: YH04721

EQUESTRIAN WORLD UK

Equestrian World UK Ltd, Twyford Farm Shop, London Rd, Ruscombe, Reading, **Berkshire**, RG10 9HW, **ENGLAND**.
(T) 0118 9403227 **(F)** 0118 9401176. Ref: YH04722

EQUESTRIAN WORLD UK

Equestrian World UK Ltd, Peppard Common, Henley-on-Thames, **Oxfordshire**, RG9 5LA, **ENGLAND**.
(T) 0118 9403227 **(F)** 0118 9401176. Ref: YH04723

EQUESTRIANA

Equestriana The Tack Shop At Osbaldene R.C, Osbaldeston Riding Ctre, Osbaldeston Lane, Osbaldeston, Blackburn, **Lancashire**, BB2 7LZ, **ENGLAND**.
(T) 01254 814000.
Contact/s
Owner: Mrs D McCullough
Profile Riding Wear Retailer, Saddlery Retailer, Supplies.
Embroidery service on rugs and saddle cloths.
No.Staff: 1 Yr. Est: 1998
Opening Times
Sp: Open Tues - Fri 15:30, Sat, Sun 10:00. Closed Tues - Fri 19:00, Sat, Sun 16:00.
Su: Open Tues - Fri 15:30, Sat, Sun 10:00. Closed Tues - Fri 19:00, Sat, Sun 16:00.
Au: Open Tues - Fri 15:30, Sat, Sun 10:00. Closed Tues - Fri 19:00, Sat, Sun 16:00.
Wn: Open Tues - Fri 15:30, Sat, Sun 10:00. Closed Tues - Fri 19:00, Sat, Sun 16:00. Ref: YH04724

EQUESTRUCT

Equestruct, Equestrian Property Repairs & Maintenance, 25 Lundwood Gr, Owthorpe, Sheffield, **Yorkshire (South)**, S20 6SR, **ENGLAND**.
(T) 0114 2471110.
Profile Property Repair and Maintenance.
Ref: YH04725

EQUETECH

Equetech, Unit 1, Aldenham Park Lodge, 126 Aldenham Rd, Bushey, **Hertfordshire**, WD2 2ET, **ENGLAND**.
(T) 01923 237524 **(F)** 01923 210592
(E) info@equetech.fsnet.co.uk.
Profile Supplies. Ref: YH04726

EQUI FILE

Equi File, 1 Warborne Lane, Pilley, Lymington, **Hampshire**, SO41 5QD, **ENGLAND**.
(T) 01590 678315 **(F)** 01590 670024.
Profile Supplies. Ref: YH04727

EQUI LIFE

Equi Life Ltd, Mead Hse Farm, Dauntsey, Chippenham, **Wiltshire**, SN15 4JA, **ENGLAND**.
(T) 0870 4440676 **(F)** 0870 4440677
(E) rae@equilife.co.uk
(W) www.equilife.co.uk.
Profile Supplies. Laminitis Helpline.
Farrier's Formula® Stockists Ref: YH04728

EQUI STUDY

Warwickshire College, Moreton Hall, Moreton Morrell, Warwick, **Warwickshire**, CV35 9BL, **ENGLAND**.
(T) 01926 318318 **(F)** 01926 318300
(E) enquires@warkscol.ac.uk
(W) www.warwickequine.ac.uk.
Contact/s
Equine Team Leader: Phillipa Francis
Profile Breeder, Stable/Livery.
Equine Studies features equine distance learning flexibility, ongoing research programmes, farriery training and the best equine studies library in the UK. Full-time, part-time and home study delivery is available.
Ref: YH14951

EQUI TEC

Equi Tec, 112 The Straits, Lower Gornal, Dudley, **Staffordshire**, DY3 3BD, **ENGLAND**.
(T) 01902 670878.
Profile Saddlery Retailer. Ref: YH04729

EQUI VENTURE

Equi Venture, Achinreir Farm, Barcaldine, **Argyll and Bute**, PA37 1SF, **SCOTLAND**.
(T) 01631 72320.
Profile Equestrian Centre. Ref: YH04730

EQUI VISION

Equi Vision, The Cottage, Glaston Rd, Bisbrooke, Oakham, **Rutland**, LE15 9EN, **ENGLAND**.
(T) 01572 821152. Ref: YH04731

EQUIBALE

Equibale, Sutton Lane, Langley Burrell, Chippenham, **Wiltshire**, SN15 4LW, **ENGLAND**.
(T) 01249 721500.
Contact/s
Owner: Mr P Miflin
Profile Supplies. Ref: YH04732

EQUIBOX

Equibox, Haddington, **Lothian (East)**, EH41 4PL, **SCOTLAND**.
(T) 01620 810850.
Contact/s
Owner: Mrs C Henderson
Profile Transport/Horse Boxes. Ref: YH04733

EQUIBRAND

Equibrand, Church St, Charwelton, **Northamptonshire**, NN11 3YT, **ENGLAND**.
(T) 01327 262444 **(F)** 01327 260771.
Profile Transport/Horse Boxes. Ref: YH04734

EQUIBRIEF

Equibrief Ltd, Green Lane Cottage, Green Lane, Finningham, Stowmarket, **Suffolk**, IP14 4TJ, **ENGLAND**.
(T) 01449 780153 **(F)** 01449 780153.
Profile Supplies. Ref: YH04735

EQUI-CARE

Equi-Care and Services, Pitskelly Farm, Balbeggie, Perth, **Perth and Kinross**, PH2 6AR, **SCOTLAND**.
(T) 01821 640726 **(F)** 01821 650469.
Contact/s
Retail Manager: Mrs A Bruce **(Q)** BHSII
Profile Riding Club, Riding School, Riding Wear Retailer, Saddlery Retailer, Stable/Livery, Supplies, Trainer. Rosette Manufacturer.
Lungeing and stable management sessions. Vaulting instructor available for lessons. No.Staff: 4
Ref: YH04736

EQUICENTRE

Equicentre, Blueys Farm, Twyford Rd, Waltham St Lawrence, **Berkshire**, RG10 0HE, **ENGLAND**.
(T) 0118 9341215.
Contact/s
Owner: Mr S Craig
Profile Breeder, Farrier, Saddlery Retailer, Trainer. Horse Shoe Suppliers.
Horse Recuperation for injured horses and grass livery also available. No.Staff: 4 Yr. Est: 1985
C.Size: 38 Acres
Opening Times
Sp: Open 07:00. Closed 20:00.
Su: Open 07:00. Closed 20:00.
Au: Open 07:00. Closed 20:00.
Wn: Open 07:00. Closed 20:00. Ref: YH04737

EQUICO

Equico, 36 Main St, Kilwinning, **Ayrshire (North)**, KA13 6AQ, **SCOTLAND**.
(T) 01294 559960.
Contact/s
Owner: Mrs E McManus
Profile Supplies. Ref: YH04738

EQUICRAFT SADDLERY

Equicraft Saddlery, 42 Rodney Rd, Backwell, Bristol, **Bristol**, BS48 3HW, **ENGLAND**.
(T) 01275 463933 **(F)** 01275 794414.
Contact/s
Owner: Mrs D Hillman
Profile Saddlery Retailer. Ref: YH04739

EQUICRUISER

Equicruiser UK Ltd, The Old Stables, Gosport Rd, Lower Farringdon, Alton, **Hampshire**, GU34 3DJ, **ENGLAND**.
(T) 01420 587074 **(F)** 01420 587090.
Profile Transport/Horse Boxes. Ref: YH04740

EQUICTRE

Equicentre, 84 Frieth Rd, Marlow, **Buckinghamshire**, SL7 2QU, **ENGLAND**.
(T) 01628 482672 **(F)** 01628 891184.
Contact/s
Owner: Mr C Craig
Profile Farrier. Ref: YH04741

EQUIDIRECT

Equidirect, PO Box 44, Alnwick, **Northumberland**, NE66 3YL, **ENGLAND**.
(T) 0870 7572263 **(F)** 0870 7572263
(E) sales@equidirect.co.uk
(W) www.equidirect.co.uk.
Contact/s
Owner: Ms K Morse
Profile Supplies. Equestrian Advertising.
An internet advertising service offering quality online advertising of everything equestrian. Photo gallery offers maximum sales opportunities for lead rein ponies to top class eventers, plus a services directory for trade advertisers. No.Staff: 3 Yr. Est: 1998
Opening Times

Sp: Open 10:00. Closed 17:00.
Su: Open 10:00. Closed 17:00.
Au: Open 10:00. Closed 17:00.
Wn: Open 10:00. Closed 17:00. Ref: YH04742

EQUI-DRENCH

Equi-Drench, Whalebones, Knossington, **Rutland**, LE15 8LU, **ENGLAND**.
(T) 01664 77875.
Profile Supplies. Ref: YH04743

EQUIFEEDS

Equifeeds, Holmecroft, Holme Lane, Rockley, Retford, **Nottinghamshire**, DN22 0QY, **ENGLAND**.
(T) 01777 838152 **(F)** 01909 484010.
Profile Feed Merchant. Ref: YH04744

EQUIFIELD SVS

Equifield Services, 2 Fairview, Marsh Lane, Leonard Stanley, Stonehouse, **Gloucestershire**, GL10 3NN, **ENGLAND**.
(T) 01453 825600 **(F)** 01453 825600.
Contact/s
Owner: Mrs D Breen
Profile Supplies. Ref: YH04745

EQUIFOR

Equifor, Totteridge Farm, Milton Lilbourne, Marlborough, **Wiltshire**, SN9 5LF, **ENGLAND**.
(T) 01672 563040 **(F)** 01672 562577
(E) info@equifor.com
(W) www.equifor.com
Affiliated Bodies BHDTA.
Contact/s
Owner: Mrs B Nadin
(E) barbara@equifor.com
Profile Riding Wear Retailer, Saddlery Retailer, Supplies. No.Staff: 2 Yr. Est: 1996
Opening Times
Sp: Open 10:00. Closed 18:00.
Su: Open 10:00. Closed 18:00.
Au: Open 10:00. Closed 18:00.
Wn: Open 10:00. Closed 18:00. Ref: YH04746

EQUIFORM NUTRITION

Equiform Nutrition Ltd, New Day Hse, First Ave, Weston Rd, Crewe, **Cheshire**, CW1 6BE, **ENGLAND**.
(T) 01270 252925 **(F)** 01270 251197.
Profile Medical Support. Ref: YH04747

EQUI-GRASS

Equi-Grass, Carnalea Kiltulla, Athenry, **County Galway**, **IRELAND**.
(T) 091 848330.
Profile Feed Merchant, Medical Support, Supplies.
Equi-Grass produce dust free horse forage, which is important because it has now been found that thoroughbred horses are becoming more and more sensitive to respiratory and allergy problems. Ref: YH04748

EQUI-GRASS

Equi-Grass, Winderton Farm, Brailes, Banbury, **Oxfordshire**, OX15 5JQ, **ENGLAND**.
(T) 01608 685241 **(F)** 01608 685241.
Profile Feed Merchant, Medical Support, Supplies.
Produce dust free horse forage, important because it has now been found that thoroughbred horses are becoming more and more sensitive to respiratory and allergy problems. Ref: YH04749

EQUIHERB

Equiherb, Herbal Dispensary For Horse & Rider, 103 High St, Syston, **Leicestershire**, LE7 1GQ, **ENGLAND**.
(T) 0116 2694590 **(F)** 0116 2602757.
Profile Medical Support. Ref: YH04750

EQUILINK

Equilink, Burnside Lodge, Embleton, Alnwick, **Northumberland**, NE66 3DW, **ENGLAND**.
(T) 0870 7572262 **(F)** 01665 576813
(E) sales@equilink.co.uk
(W) www.equilink.co.uk.
Contact/s
Owner: Mrs K Morse
Profile Breeder. Equestrian Database Bureau.
No.Staff: 4 Yr. Est: 1991
Opening Times
The database is accessible 24 hours a day, 7 days a week Ref: YH04751

EQUILUXE ENGINEERING

Equiluxe Engineering, Cherry Tree Farm, Barton Bendish, King's Lynn, **Norfolk**, PE33 9DJ, **ENGLAND**.
(T) 01366 347944 **(F)** 01366 347944.
Profile Transport/Horse Boxes. Ref: YH04752

EQUIMAC

Equimac Equestrian Laundry Services, Unit 4 Greenbank St, Preston, **Lancashire**, PR1 7PH, **ENGLAND**.
(T) 01772 884885 **(F)** 01772 884885.
Contact/s
Partner: Mrs W Cartwright
Profile Supplies. Ref: YH04753

EQUIMANIA RUSTICS

Equimania Rustics, 16 Lairgate, Beverley, **Yorkshire (East)**, HU17 8EE, **ENGLAND**.
(T) 01482 868869. Ref: YH04754

EQUIMAT

Equimat, Beatrice Rd, Kettering, **Northamptonshire**, NN16 9QS, **ENGLAND**.
(T) 01536 513456 **(F)** 01536 310080
(W) www.dinkie.com/equimat.
Profile Supplies.
Stable flooring and insulation specialists.
Ref: YH04755

EQUIMIX

Equimix Feeds Ltd, Sandy Lane Trading Est, Stourport-on-Severn, **Worcestershire**, DY13 9QA, **ENGLAND**.
(T) 01299 827744 **(F)** 01299 879470.
Contact/s
Owner: Mr J Doolittle
Profile Feed Merchant, Riding Wear Retailer, Saddlery Retailer, Supplies. No.Staff: 15
Yr. Est: 1975
Opening Times
Sp: Open Mon - Sat 08:30. Closed Mon - Sat 17:30.
Su: Open Mon - Sat 08:30. Closed Mon - Sat 17:30.
Au: Open Mon - Sat 08:30. Closed Mon - Sat 17:30.
Wn: Open Mon - Sat 08:30. Closed Mon - Sat 17:30.
Ref: YH04756

EQUINAME

Equiname Ltd, The Byerley Stud, Ingoe, Newcastle-upon-Tyne, **Tyne and Wear**, NE20 0SZ, **ENGLAND**.
(T) 01661 886356 **(F)** 01661 886484.
Contact/s
Trainer: Mr D Eddy
Profile Club/Association. Ref: YH04757

EQUINE & CANINE SUPPLIES

Equine & Canine Supplies, Knoll Farm, Ladywood Rd, Martin Hussingtree, Worcester, **Worcestershire**, WR3 7SX, **ENGLAND**.
(T) 01905 755773.
Profile Supplies. Ref: YH04758

EQUINE ADVISORY SV

Equine Advisory Service, Ronan Croft, Ogwell, Newton Abbot, **Devon**, TQ12 6BA, **ENGLAND**.
(T) 01626 360627.
Profile Supplies. Advice Service. Ref: YH04759

EQUINE AFFAIRS

Equine Affairs, Oakridge, 13 Orchard Cl, Gravenhurst, Bedford, **Bedfordshire**, MK45 4JF, **ENGLAND**.
(T) 01462 713848 **(F)** 01462 713848.
Contact/s
Owner: Miss V Lewis
Profile Supplies. Ref: YH04760

EQUINE AMERICA

Equine America, Unit 7 Lawson Hunt Business Pk, Guildford Rd, Broadbridge Heath, **Sussex (West)**, RH12 3JR, **ENGLAND**.
(T) 01403 255809 **(F)** 01403 241083
(E) equine.america@virgin.net
(W) www.equine-america.co.uk.
Profile Supplies. Ref: YH04761

EQUINE AMERICA

Equine America, High Close Cottage, Caldwell, Richmond, **Yorkshire (North)**, DL11 7UF, **ENGLAND**.
(T) 01325 730657.
Profile Supplies. Ref: YH04762

EQUINE AROMATHERAPY ASS

Equine Aromatherapy Association, PO Box 19, Hay On Wye, Hereford, **Herefordshire**, HR3 5AE, **ENGLAND**.
(T) 01455 619608.
Profile Club/Association. Ref: YH04763

EQUINE ART

Equine Art, 16 Reedfield, Clayton Brook, Bamber Bridge, Preston, **Lancashire**, PR5 8HT, **ENGLAND**.
(T) 01772 697902 **(F)** 01772 697902.
Contact/s
Owner: Mr D Bushnell
Profile Artist. Ref: YH04764

EQUINE BEHAVIOUR

Equine Behaviour Forum, Carmel Cottage, 50, Marsh Hse Lane, Darwen, **Lancashire**, BB3 3JB, **ENGLAND**.
(T) 01254 705487 **(F)** 01254 705487.
Profile Medical Support. Animal Behaviourists.
A voluntary organisation who produce a quarterly magazine 'Equine Behaviour' for their members..
Ref: YH04765

EQUINE BEHAVIOUR FORUM

Equine Behaviour Forum, The Moredun Foundation, Pentlands Science Pk, Bush Loan, Penicuik, **Lothian (Mid)**, EH26 0PZ, **SCOTLAND**.
(T) 0131 4456257 **(F)** 0131 4456235
(W) www.gla.ac.uk/external/EBF/.
Contact/s
Key Contact: Joyce McIntosh
Profile Club/Association. Animal Behaviourists.
Ref: YH04766

EQUINE BEHAVIOUR FORUM

Equine Behaviour Forum, Grove Cottages, Brinkley, Newmarket, **Suffolk**, CB8 0SF, **ENGLAND**.
(T) 01638 507502 **(F)** 01772 786037.
Contact/s
Key Contact: Mrs O Way
Profile Club/Association. Animal Behaviourists.
Ref: YH04767

EQUINE CHAUFFEUR SVS

Equine Chauffeur Services, 124 Kingfisher Drive, Woodley, Reading, **Berkshire**, RG5 3LQ, **ENGLAND**.
(T) 0118 9010138.
Profile Transport/Horse Boxes. Ref: YH04768

EQUINE CLEANING SVS

Equine Cleaning Services, Burton Cleaning Ctre, 97 Uxbridge St, Burton-on-Trent, **Staffordshire**, DE14 3JX, **ENGLAND**.
(T) 01283 511559.
Profile Supplies. Ref: YH04769

EQUINE CLOTHING

Equine Clothing Company, 14 Newbridge Rd, Upwell, Downham Market, **Norfolk**, PE14 9DT, **ENGLAND**.
(T) 01945 774312 **(F)** 01945 774312
(E) info@equineclothing.co.uk
(W) www.equineclothing.co.uk.
Contact/s
Owner: Ms C King
Profile Supplies. Horse Clothing Manufacturer.
Manufacturers of horse clothing. Provide an embroidery service for personalising clothing for you and your horse. No.Staff: 2 Yr. Est: 1992
Opening Times
Sp: Open Mon - Fri 08:00. Closed Mon - Fri 18:00.
Su: Open Mon - Fri 08:00. Closed Mon - Fri 18:00.
Au: Open Mon - Fri 08:00. Closed Mon - Fri 18:00.
Wn: Open Mon - Fri 08:00. Closed Mon - Fri 18:00.
Closed at weekends Ref: YH04770

EQUINE CONNECTIONS

Equine Connections Ltd, Unit 36 Landywood Enterprise Pk, Holly Lane, Great Wyrley, Walsall, **Midlands (West)**, WS6 6BD, **ENGLAND**.
(T) 01922 418780 **(F)** 01922 418782.
Contact/s
Owner: Mrs W Hunt Ref: YH04771

EQUINE DENTAL SVS

Equine Dental Services, Grapevine Farm, Puxton Rd, Rolestone, Hewish, Weston-Super-Mare, **Somerset (North)**, BS24 6UG, **ENGLAND**.
(T) 01934 820855
(M) 07768 323732.
Profile Medical Support. Ref: YH04772

EQUINE DENTAL TECHNICAL

Equine Dental Technical, 4 Regent Buildings, York Rd, York, **Yorkshire (North)**, YO26 4LT, **ENGLAND**.
(T) 01904 780511 **(F)** 01904 780511.
Contact/s
Owner: Mr R Ruddy
Profile Medical Support. Ref: YH04773

EQUINE DENTISTRY

Equine Dentistry Veterinary Surgeon Hanne Engstrom, 19 Gentian Court, Wakefield, **Yorkshire (West)**, WF2 0FE, **ENGLAND**.
(T) 07939 128374
(W) www.horsedentistry.info.hanne.com.
Contact/s
Owner: Ms H Engstrom
(E) hanne@hanne.com
Profile Medical Support.
Opening Times
Telephone for an appointment Ref: YH04774

EQUINE DESIGN INT

Equine Design International, 95 Ashford Rd, Iver, **Buckinghamshire**, SL0 0QF, **ENGLAND**.
(T) 01753 653832 **(F)** 01753 655159.
Contact/s
Partner: Mrs S Hill
Profile Saddlery Retailer. **Ref: YH04775**

EQUINE EASY CLEAR

Equine Easy Clear Ltd, Manor Hse, Briestfield Rd, Dewsbury, **Yorkshire (West)**, WF12 0PF, **ENGLAND**.
(T) 01924 488489.
Profile Supplies. **Ref: YH04776**

EQUINE ENTERPRISES

Equine Enterprises, Beckfield Farm, Gorse Lane, Newthorpe, South Milford, **Yorkshire (West)**, LS25 6JR, **ENGLAND**.
(M) 07957 545224.
Contact/s
Owner: Mrs L Thackray
Profile Stable/Livery.
Full and part livery available. Telephone for further price information No.Staff: 1 Yr. Est: 1991
C.Size: 14 Acres
Opening Times
Sp: Open Mon - Sun 08:00. Closed Mon - Sun 18:00.
Su: Open Mon - Sun 08:00. Closed Mon - Sun 18:00.
Au: Open Mon - Sun 08:00. Closed Mon - Sun 18:00.
Wn: Open Mon - Sun 08:00. Closed Mon - Sun 18:00.
Telephone between these hours **Ref: YH04777**

EQUINE EXTRAS

Equine Extras, Cleveland View, Blue Hse Farm, Claxton, Billingham, Stockton-on-Tees, **Cleveland**, TS22 5PW, **ENGLAND**.
(T) 01429 872050 **(F)** 01429 872050
(E) c.dryden@ukonline.co.uk.
Contact/s
Owner: Miss C Dryden
Profile Riding Wear Retailer, Supplies. **Ref: YH04778**

EQUINE HEALTH & HERBAL

S P Equine Health & Herbal, 32-40 Broton Est, Halstead, **Essex**, CO9 1HB, **ENGLAND**.
(T) 01787 476400 **(F)** 01787 475998
(E) vethealth@cwcom.net
(W) www.animal-health.co.uk.
Profile Medical Support, Supplies.
Orders can be e-mailed, faxed or telephoned
Ref: YH04779

EQUINE INDEX

Equine Index, 1 New Rd, Woolmer Green, Knebworth, **Hertfordshire**, SG3 6JX, **ENGLAND**.
(T) 01438 813690 **(F)** 01438 813014.
Profile Club/Association. **Ref: YH04780**

EQUINE INNOVATIONS

Equine Innovations, Alexandra St, Hyde, **Cheshire**, SK14 1DX, **ENGLAND**.
(T) 0161 3661001 **(F)** 0161 3661221
(E) sales@equineinnovations.com
(W) www.equineinnovations.com.
Contact/s
Owner: Miss J Hargreaves
Profile Supplies.
Developer of the 'Tri-Shield' rug system.
Yr. Est: 2000
Opening Times
Call the order line Mon - Fri 10:00 - 18:00 or leave a message on the 24 hour answering service.
Ref: YH04781

EQUINE INNOVATIONS

Equine Innovations, Knightsford Hse, Church Rd, Wombourne, Wolverhampton, **Midlands (West)**, WV5 9EX, **ENGLAND**.
(T) 01902 898031 **(F)** 01902 898031.
Contact/s
Owner: Mr A Thomas
Profile Supplies. **Ref: YH04782**

EQUINE LAUNDRY

Equine Laundry, 27 Freemantle Rd, Bristol, **Bristol**, BS5 6SY, **ENGLAND**.
(T) 01179 522775.
Profile Supplies. **Ref: YH04783**

EQUINE LAWYERS ASS

Equine Lawyers Association, P O Box 23, Brigg, **Lincolnshire (North)**, DN20 8TN, **ENGLAND**.
(T) 01652 688819.
Profile Club/Association. **Ref: YH04784**

EQUINE LIVERY SVS

Equine Livery Services, 22 Fairways, Weyhill, Andover, **Hampshire**, SP11 8DW, **ENGLAND**.
(T) 01264 773664.
Contact/s
Owner: Mr M Drinkwater
Profile Stable/Livery. **Ref: YH04785**

EQUINE MANIA

Equine Mania, Rear Of 30 Market St, Shaw, Oldham, **Lancashire**, OL2 8NH, **ENGLAND**.
(T) 01706 291414.
Contact/s
Partner: Mrs M Lockett **Ref: YH04786**

EQUINE MARKETING

Equine Marketing Ltd, The Hollies, Ledgemoor, Weobley, **Herefordshire**, HR4 8QH, **ENGLAND**.
(T) 01544 318196 **(F)** 01544 318770
(M) 07785 774739
(E) equinem1@wildnet.co.uk.
Profile Medical Support. **Ref: YH04787**

EQUINE MNGMT & TRAINING

Equine Management & Training Frederick A Cook Partnership, Marnham Hse, Pilsgate, Stamford, **Lincolnshire**, PE9 3HL, **ENGLAND**.
(T) 01780 740773 **(F)** 01780 740917
(E) enquiries@equine-training.co.uk
(W) www.equine-training.co.uk.
Profile Trainer.
Rehabilitation of racehorses and injured horses.
Ref: YH04788

EQUINE MNGMT SOLUTIONS

Equine Management Solutions Ltd, West Court Stables, West Court, Burbage, Marlborough, **Wiltshire**, SN8 3BN, **ENGLAND**.
(T) 01672 811423 **(F)** 01672 811416.
Profile Medical Support. **Ref: YH04789**

EQUINE NEWS

Equine News, The Moredun Foundation, Pentlands Science Pk, Bush Loan, Penicuik, **Lothian (Mid)**, EH26 0PZ, **SCOTLAND**.
(T) 0131 4456257 **(F)** 0131 4456235
(E) equine@mf.mri.sari.ac.uk.
Profile Supplies. **Ref: YH04790**

EQUINE NUTRITION

Equine Nutritional Consultancy Ltd, Jasmine Cottage, East Garston, Hungerford, **Berkshire**, RG17 7EX, **ENGLAND**.
(T) 01488 648683 **(F)** 01488 648047
(E) office@encltd.demon.co.uk.
Profile Medical Support. **Ref: YH04791**

EQUINE PICTURES

Equine Pictures, 11 Ferdi Lethert Hse, Ashford, **Kent**, TN24 9DF, **ENGLAND**.
(T) 01233 629349 **(F)** 01233 629349. **Ref: YH04792**

EQUINE PRODUCT MARKETING

Equine Product Marketing, Cranbrook Hse, 7 Flatts Rd, Barnard Castle, **County Durham**, DL12 8AB, **ENGLAND**.
(T) 01833 631153.
Profile Club/Association. **Ref: YH04793**

EQUINE PRODUCTS

Equine Products, The Pines, Baddington, Nantwich, **Cheshire**, CW5 8AD, **ENGLAND**.
(T) 01270 626257 **(F)** 01270 626257.
Profile Supplies. **Ref: YH04794**

EQUINE PRODUCTS

Equine Products UK Ltd, 22 Riversdale Ct, Newburn Haugh Ind Est, Newcastle-upon-Tyne, **Tyne and Wear**, NE15 8SG, **ENGLAND**.
(T) 0191 2645536 **(F)** 0191 2640487
(E) info@equine-camel.co.uk
(W) www.equine-camel.co.uk.
Profile Supplies. **Ref: YH04795**

EQUINE RESOURCES

Equine Resources, Sandlin Cottage, Sandlin, Leigh Sinton, Malvern, **Worcestershire**, WR13 5DN, **ENGLAND**.
(T) 01886 833893
(E) info@equineresources.co.uk.
Profile Breeder, Stable/Livery, Trainer. **Ref: YH04796**

EQUINE RESPONSE

Equine Response, Elm Leaze Stud, The Street, Didmarton, Badminton, **Gloucestershire**, GL9 1DT, **ENGLAND**.
(T) 01454 238849 **(F)** 01454 238395.
Profile Supplies. **Ref: YH04797**

EQUINE SEARCH

Equine Search, Bodyddon Fawr, Llanfyllin, **Powys**, SY22 5HJ, **WALES**.
(T) 01691 648916.
Contact/s
Owner: Miss J Downey
Profile Breeder. **Ref: YH04798**

EQUINE SHOP

Equine Shop (The), Cwrt Y Draenog, Llanddarog, Carmarthen, **Carmarthenshire**, SA32 8PG, **WALES**.
(T) 01267 275586 **(F)** 01267 275586.
Contact/s
Owner: Mrs M Challinor
Profile Supplies. **Ref: YH04799**

EQUINE SPORT THERAPY

Equine Sport Therapy, Syliards Farm, Five Fields Lane, Four Elms, Edenbridge, **Kent**, TN8 6NB, **ENGLAND**.
(T) 01732 700912 **(F)** 0870 0940134
(W) www.equine-sport-therapy.co.uk
Affiliated Bodies BE, NAAT.
Contact/s
Partner: Chris Caden-Parker
(E) chris@equine-sport-therapy.co.uk
Profile Breeder, Medical Support, Stable/Livery, Trainer. Rehabilitation Centre.
The treatments used for the drug free rehabilitation include ice, heat, exercise, massage, lasers, ultra-sound, electrical stimulation, and magnetic fields. A normal stay for a horse is a minimum of 10 - 14 days, at £30.00 per day, depending on treatment.
No.Staff: 4 Yr. Est: 1999 **Ref: YH04800**

EQUINE SPORTS MASSAGE ASS

Equine Sports Massage Association, 17 Gloucester Rd, Stratton, Cirencester, **Gloucestershire**, GL7 2LB, **ENGLAND**.
(T) 01285 650275.
Profile Club/Association, Medical Support.
Ref: YH04801

EQUINE SPORTS MASSAGE ASS

Equine Sports Massage Association Ltd, Haycroft Barn, Lower Wick, Dursley, **Gloucestershire**, GL11 6DD, **ENGLAND**.
(T) 01453 511814.
Contact/s
Chairman: Ms C Davison **(Q)** ITEC **(T)** 01285 831011
Profile Club/Association, Medical Support.
Ref: YH04802

EQUINE SVS

Equine Services, 30/32 Brook St, Raunds, Wellingborough, **Northamptonshire**, NN9 6LP, **ENGLAND**.
(T) 01933 623722 **(F)** 01933 460265.
Profile Blood Stock Agency. **Ref: YH04803**

EQUINE SVS INT

Equine Services International, 12 Kingston Ave, North Cheam, **Surrey**, SM3 9TZ, **ENGLAND**.
(T) 020 87153349 **(F)** 020 82869426.
Profile Club/Association. **Ref: YH04804**

EQUINE SWIMMING POOLS

Equine Swimming Pools Ltd, 3 The Riddings, Earlsdon, Coventry, **Midlands (West)**, CV5 6AT, **ENGLAND**.
(T) 024 76676467
(M) 07831 491339.
Profile Supplies. **Ref: YH04805**

EQUINE THERAPY

Equine Therapy, Northfield Farmhouse, Thornton Curtis, Ulceby, **Lincolnshire (North)**, DN39 6XW, **ENGLAND**.
(T) 01469 530131 **(F)** 01469 530131.
Contact/s
Owner: Mrs S Neville
Profile Medical Support.
Equipment for injured horses e.g lasers, aquatherapy, magnotherapy etc. **Ref: YH04806**

EQUINE VETNRY CLINIC

Equine Veterinary Clinic, Greyfriars Farm, Puttenham, Guildford, **Surrey**, GU3 1AQ, **ENGLAND**.
(T) 01483 811007 **(F)** 01483 811300.
Contact/s
Assistant: Mr E Garcia-Pego **(Q)** MRCVS
Profile Medical Support. **Ref: YH04807**

EQUINE VETNRY JOURNAL

Equine Veterinary Journal & Equine Veterinary Education, Graseby Hse, 351 Exning Rd, Newmarket, **Suffolk**, CB8 0AU, **ENGLAND**.

(T) 01638 666160 (F) 01638 668665
(E) evj.editorial@dial.pipex.com.
Contact/s
Professor: Dr P Rossdale (Q) FRCVS, MA, PhD
Profile Medical Support, Supplies. Ref: YH04808

EQUINES LIVERIES

Equines Equestrian Centre, Stanhope Farm, Scragged Oak Rd, Hucking, Maidstone, **Kent**, ME17 1QU, **ENGLAND**.
(T) 01622 880007.
Contact/s
Owner: Ms J Knight
Profile Breeder, Equestrian Centre, Stable/Livery, Trainer, Transport/Horse Boxes.
Coach transport to equine events. Yr. Est: 1998
C.Size: 53 Acres Ref: YH04809

EQUINIMITY

Equinimity, 102 Siddeley Ave, Coventry, **Midlands (West)**, CV3 1GD, **ENGLAND**.
(T) 024 76448076 (F) 024 76448076. Ref: YH04810

EQUINN

Equinn Ltd, Ringlands, Grays Rd, Westerham, **Kent**, TN16 2HX, **ENGLAND**.
(T) 01959 572293 (F) 01959 572509.
Contact/s
Partner: Mr W Van-Heyningen
Profile Supplies. Ref: YH04811

EQUINOMIC PRODUCTS

Equinomic Products Ltd, Willow Tree Barns, Passfield Hse Est, Headley Lane, Passfield, Liphook, **Hampshire**, GU30 7RN, **ENGLAND**.
(T) 01428 751110 (F) 01428 751140.
Contact/s
Manager: Mr J Sharp Ref: YH04812

EQUINOVA

EquiNova, Manor Farm, Norton Ferris, Warminster, **Wiltshire**, BA12 7HT, **ENGLAND**.
(T) 01985 844732 (F) 01985 844288.
Contact/s
Owner: Mrs A Penton
Profile Supplies. Ref: YH04813

EQUINOVA

EquiNova, The Old Dairy, Fonthill Bishop, Salisbury, **Wiltshire**, SP3 5SH, **ENGLAND**.
(T) 01747 820666 (F) 01747 820611.
Contact/s
Partner: Mr A Holford-Walker
Profile Riding Wear Retailer, Saddlery Retailer.
Ref: YH04814

EQUIPORT

Equiport, The Stables, Kennel Lane, Sandiway, Northwich, **Cheshire**, CW8 2EA, **ENGLAND**.
(T) 01606 889292 (F) 01606 888895.
Contact/s
Owner: Mr M Welsh
Profile Arena. Ref: YH04815

EQUISAVE HORSE AMBULANCES

Equisave Horse Ambulances Ltd, Bury Rd, Stradishall, Newmarket, **Suffolk**, CB8 8YN, **ENGLAND**.
(T) 01440 820113 (F) 01440 820113.
Contact/s
Owner: Mr B Fellowes
Profile Transport/Horse Boxes.
A horse ambulance service is provided for racing, point to points, polo and shows etc.
Opening Times
Sp: Open 09:00. Closed 17:30.
Su: Open 09:00. Closed 17:30.
Au: Open 09:00. Closed 17:30.
Wn: Open 09:00. Closed 17:30. Ref: YH04816

EQUISECRETS

Equisecrets, Hendrelas, Cumann, Lampeter, **Carmarthenshire**, SA48 8HA, **WALES**.
(T) 01570 421251 (F) 01570 421251
(W) www.equisecrets.co.uk.
Contact/s
Owner: Mr F Collins (Q) BHSI
Profile Trainer.
Train horses and riders of all levels as well as producing horses for film & TV. Also teach stunt performers, actors and actresses for equestrian roles.
Yr. Est: 2001
Opening Times
Best times to telephone are between 09:00 and 10:00. Otherwise there is an answer phone, please leave message and the call will be returned shortly.
Ref: YH04817

EQUISENSE

EquiSense Ltd, Brewham Lodge Farm, North Brewham, Bruton, **Somerset**, BA10 0JS, **ENGLAND**.
(T) 01749 850181 (F) 01749 850191.
Profile Trainer. Ref: YH04818

EQUISPORT

Equisport, 54 Walsall St, Willenhall, **Midlands (West)**, WV13 2DU, **ENGLAND**.
(T) 01902 630083 (F) 01902 609389. Ref: YH04819

EQUISSENTIAL

Equissential, Clge Equestrian Ctre, Church Rd, Keysoe, Bedford, **Bedfordshire**, MK44 2JP, **ENGLAND**.
(T) 01234 709399 (F) 01234 709399.
Contact/s
Partner: Mr P Williams
Profile Riding Wear Retailer. Yr. Est: 1999
Opening Times
Sp: Open Mon 14:00, Tues - Fri 10:00, Sat 09:00, Sun 10:00. Closed Mon - Fri 18:00, Sat 17:00, Sun 16:00.
Su: Open Mon 14:00, Tues - Fri 10:00, Sat 09:00, Sun 10:00. Closed Mon - Fri 18:00, Sat 17:00, Sun 16:00.
Au: Open Mon 14:00, Tues - Fri 10:00, Sat 09:00, Sun 10:00. Closed Mon - Fri 18:00, Sat 17:00, Sun 16:00.
Wn: Open Mon 14:00, Tues - Fri 10:00, Sat 09:00, Sun 10:00. Closed Mon - Fri 18:00, Sat 17:00, Sun 16:00. Ref: YH04820

EQUISTOCK

Equistock, The Square, Fethard, **County Tipperary**, **IRELAND**.
(T) 052 31020.
Profile Supplies. Ref: YH04821

EQUI-SURE

Equi-Sure Ltd, The Hayloft, Manor Farm, Wadswick, Corsham, **Wiltshire**, SN13 8JB, **ENGLAND**.
(T) 01225 810933/810938 (F) 01225 812563
(E) info@equisure.co.uk
(W) www.equisure.co.uk.
Profile Supplies.
Distributors of rubber matting. Specialises in finding new and innovative products for the outdoor person.
Ref: YH04822

EQUITACK

Equitack, 197 Lee Lane, Horwich, Bolton, **Manchester (Greater)**, BL6 7JD, **ENGLAND**.
(T) 01204 460730 (F) 01204 460730
Alt Contact Address
Wilderswood Barn, Wilderswood, Horwich, Bolton, Manchester (Greater), BL6 6SJ, England.
Contact/s
Owner: Miss S Gibson
Profile Breeder, Riding Wear Retailer, Saddlery Retailer, Supplies. No.Staff: 1 Yr. Est: 1999
Opening Times
Sp: Open 12:00. Closed 17:00.
Su: Open 12:00. Closed 17:00.
Au: Open 12:00. Closed 17:00.
Wn: Open 12:00. Closed 17:00. Ref: YH04823

EQUITACK

Equitack, 11 Springhill Gr, Crofton, Wakefield, **Yorkshire (West)**, WF4 1EY, **ENGLAND**.
(T) 01924 864942.
Profile Saddlery Retailer. Ref: YH04824

EQUITACK SADDLERY

Equitack Saddlery Ltd, Spring Green Nurseries, Pontefract Rd, Crofton, Wakefield, **Yorkshire (West)**, WF4 1LW, **ENGLAND**.
(T) 01924 864942 (F) 01924 864942.
Contact/s
Owner: Miss V Whittaker
Profile Riding Wear Retailer, Saddlery Retailer, Supplies. No.Staff: 4 Yr. Est: 1995
Opening Times
Sp: Open 10:00. Closed 18:00.
Su: Open 10:00. Closed 18:00.
Au: Open 10:00. Closed 18:00.
Wn: Open 10:00. Closed 17:30. Ref: YH04825

EQUITANA EQUESTIAN

Equitana Equestian, 3 Dodds Corners New Rd, Stokenchurch, High Wycombe, **Buckinghamshire**, HP14 3RZ, **ENGLAND**.
(T) 01494 484106.
Profile Saddlery Retailer. Ref: YH04826

EQUITANA HOLIDAYS

Equitana Holidays, Stocks Farm, Stocks Lane, Meonstoke, Southampton, **Hampshire**, SO32 3NQ, **ENGLAND**.
(T) 01489 877551.
Contact/s
Owner: Mr R Luxmore
Profile Holidays. Ref: YH04827

EQUITECHNICAL

Equitechnical Ltd, 4 Hammonds End Cottages, Redbourn Lane, Harpenden, **Hertfordshire**, AL5 2AY, **ENGLAND**.
(T) 01582 763994 (F) 01582 763551.
Profile Supplies. Ref: YH04828

EQUITOGS

Equitogs, Old Blacksmiths Yard, Water Lane, Angmering, Littlehampton, **Sussex (West)**, BN16 4EP, **ENGLAND**.
(T) 01903 770099 (F) 01903 770125
(E) angmering@equitogs.co.uk
(W) www.equitogs.co.uk.
Contact/s
Owner: Mr K Ewers
Profile Feed Merchant, Riding Wear Retailer, Saddlery Retailer, Supplies.
Delivery Service available No.Staff: 4
Yr. Est: 1986
Opening Times
Sp: Open Mon - Sat 09:00. Closed Mon - Sat 17:30.
Su: Open Mon - Sat 09:00. Closed Mon - Sat 17:30.
Au: Open Mon - Sat 09:00. Closed Mon - Sat 17:30.
Wn: Open Mon - Sat 09:00. Closed Mon - Sat 17:30.
Closed on Sundays Ref: YH04829

EQUITOGS

Equitogs, Wharf Farm, Wisborough Green, Newbridge, Billingshurst, **Sussex (West)**, RH14 0JG, **ENGLAND**.
(T) 01403 786021
(E) billingshurst@equitogs.co.uk
(W) www.equitogs.co.uk.
Contact/s
Owner: Mr K Ewers
Profile Riding Wear Retailer, Saddlery Retailer, Supplies.
Bedding and feed can be delivered. No.Staff: 4
Opening Times
Sp: Open Mon - Sat 09:00. Closed Mon - Sat 17:30.
Su: Open Mon - Sat 09:00. Closed Mon - Sat 17:30.
Au: Open Mon - Sat 09:00. Closed Mon - Sat 17:30.
Wn: Open Mon - Sat 09:00. Closed Mon - Sat 17:30.
Closed on Sundays Ref: YH04830

EQUITOPIA

Spirit of Exmoor, High Bullen Farm, Ilkerton, Barbrook, Lynton, **Devon**, EX35 6PH, **ENGLAND**.
(T) 01598 753318
(W) www.spiritofe.cjb.net.
Contact/s
Owner: Mr P Wood
(E) perry@highbullenfarm.fsnet.co.uk
Profile Breeder, Equestrian Centre, Holidays, Trainer.
Equitopia breed shire and lipizzaner cross horses.
No.Staff: 3 Yr. Est: 1987 C.Size: 13 Acres
Opening Times
To book your first visit, telephone to request a brochure
Ref: YH04831

EQUITOUR/PEREGRINE HOLIDAYS

Equitour/Peregrine Holidays, 41 South Prde, Summertown, **Oxfordshire**, OX2 7JP, **ENGLAND**.
(T) 01865 511642 (F) 01865 512583
(E) mail@equitour.co.uk
(W) www.peregrineholidays.co.uk.
Profile Holidays. Ref: YH04832

EQUITRED

Equitred Limited, Orchard Rise, White Hart Lane, Cadnam, Southampton, **Hampshire**, SO40 2NJ, **ENGLAND**.
(T) 023 80812327 (F) 023 80812327.
Profile Track/Course. Ref: YH04833

EQUI-VIDEO & EQUISETTE

Equi-Video & Equisette, Lynch Farm Equitation Ctre, Wistow Way, Orton Wistow, Peterborough, **Cambridgeshire**, PE2 6XA, **ENGLAND**.
(T) 01733 234445.
Profile Supplies. Ref: YH04834

EQUS HEALTH

EQUS Health, The Barn, Chequerswood Livery Stables, Wendover, Aylesbury, **Buckinghamshire**, HP22 6QL, **ENGLAND**.
(T) 01296 622399 (F) 01296 696687
Affiliated Bodies BHS, BSJA.
Contact/s
Owner: Ms S Franklin
Profile Arena, Medical Support, Stable/Livery,

Supplies. Equine Natural Remedies. Aromatherapy for horses available. **Ref: YH04835**

EQUUS

Equus - Equestrian Products and Country Clothing, John Browns Garden Ctre, Ringwood Rd, Three Legged Cross, Wimborne, **Dorset**, BH21 6RD, **ENGLAND**.
(T) 01202 828242 **(F)** 01202 828242.
Contact/s
Owner: M. N Pilley
Profile Riding Wear Retailer, Saddlery Retailer, Supplies. No.Staff: 2 Yr. Est: 1998
Opening Times
Sp: Open 09:30. Closed 17:00.
Su: Open 09:30. Closed 17:00.
Au: Open 09:30. Closed 17:00.
Wn: Open 09:30. Closed 17:00. **Ref: YH04836**

EQUUS

Equus Country & Equestrian, Equus Property, The Est Office, Barham Ct, Teston, Maidstone, **Kent**, ME18 5BZ, **ENGLAND**.
(T) 01622 618655
(W) www.equusproperty.co.uk.
Profile Property Services.
Country and equestrian property agents covering Kent, Sussex, Surrey and Hampshire. **Ref: YH04837**

EQUUS ELITE

Equus Elite, Blue Caps Stud Farm, Sleepers Stile Rd, Cousley Wood, Wadhurst, **Sussex (East)**, TN5 6QX, **ENGLAND**.
(T) 01892 785119
(M) 07711 663800.
Profile Breeder. **Ref: YH04838**

EQUUS EQUESTRIAN CTRES

Equus Equestrian Centres Ltd, Horton Lane, Epsom, **Surrey**, KT19 8PL, **ENGLAND**.
(T) 01372 749490/743084.
Profile Equestrian Centre, Riding School.
Ref: YH04839

EQUUS HEALTH

Equus Health, 2 Hawkmoor Farm Cottages, Newbridge, Gunnislake, **Cornwall**, PL18 9LH, **ENGLAND**.
(T) 01822 833356.
Profile Medical Support. **Ref: YH04840**

EQUUS HORSE & PONY

Equus Horse & Pony, The Old Cottage, Shortwood, Nailsworth, Stroud, **Gloucestershire**, GL6 0SJ, **ENGLAND**.
(T) 01453 833407 **(F)** 01453 833407.
Contact/s
Owner: Mrs C Beavan **Ref: YH04841**

EQUUS INSURANCE

Equus Insurance Services, PO Box 243, Orpington, **Kent**, BR6 8LL, **ENGLAND**.
(T) 01689 855522 **(F)** 01689 855544
(E) stephen@fryettinsurance.com
(W) www.equusinsurance.co.uk.
Profile Club/Association. Insurance Consultants.
Ref: YH04842

EQWEST VETNRY CTRE

Eqwest Veterinary Centre, Down Farm, Lamerton, Tavistock, **Devon**, PL19 8QA, **ENGLAND**.
(T) 01822 841370 **(F)** 01822 840067.
Profile Medical Support. **Ref: YH04843**

ERIC FIRKINS FARM SUPPLIES

Eric Firkins Farm Supplies, 16 Hanstone Rd, Stourport-on-Severn, **Worcestershire**, DY13 0HH, **ENGLAND**.
(T) 01299 823024 **(F)** 01299 877010.
Profile Supplies. **Ref: YH04844**

ERIC GILLIE

Eric Gillie Ltd (Horse Transport), Pottsclose Cottage, Kelso, **Scottish Borders**, TD5 8BN, **SCOTLAND**.
(T) 01573 430252 **(F)** 01573 430210.
Contact/s
Owner: Mr E Gillie
Profile Transport/Horse Boxes. No.Staff: 7 Yr. Est: 1974 **Ref: YH04845**

ERIC HIGNETT ENGINEERING

Eric Hignett Engineering, 49 Breezehill Rd, Neston, **Merseyside**, CH64 9PZ, **ENGLAND**.
(T) 0151 3361126.
Profile Transport/Horse Boxes. **Ref: YH04846**

ERIC WILLIAMS LEATHER-CRAFT

Eric Williams Leather-Craft, 1 Coed Bonwm, Corwen, **Denbighshire**, LL21 9EN, **WALES**.
(T) 01490 412489.
Profile Supplies. **Ref: YH04847**

ERIMUS STUD

Erimus Stud, The Moat Farm, Robertsbridge, **Sussex (East)**, TN32 5PR, **ENGLAND**.
(T) 01580 880459.
Profile Breeder. **Ref: YH04848**

ERISKAY PONY SOC

Eriskay Pony Society, Pokelly Hall, Fenwick, **Ayrshire (East)**, KA3 6BB, **SCOTLAND**.
(T) 01560 485970
(W) www.eriskaypony.com.
Contact/s
Chairperson: Mrs C Cochrane
(E) catrionam.cochrane@virgin.net
Profile Club/Association. **Ref: YH04849**

ERME VALLEY FARMERS

Erme Valley Farmers, Ermington, Ivybridge, **Devon**, PL21 9NT, **ENGLAND**.
(T) 01548 830410 **(F)** 01548 830980.
Contact/s
Owner: Mrs S West
Profile Medical Support, Riding Wear Retailer, Supplies. No.Staff: 2 Yr. Est: 1993
Opening Times
Sp: Open 09:00. Closed 17:30.
Su: Open 09:00. Closed 17:30.
Au: Open 09:00. Closed 17:30.
Wn: Open 09:00. Closed 17:30. **Ref: YH04850**

ERMIN ST STABLES

Ermin Street Stables, Ermin St, Lambourn Woodlands, Hungerford, **Berkshire**, RG17 7BL, **ENGLAND**.
(T) 01672 541189 **(F)** 01672 541108.
Profile Stable/Livery, Transport/Horse Boxes.
Ref: YH04851

ERNE LAKELAND RIDING CLUB

Erne Lakeland Riding Club, Derryscobe, Letterbreen, Enniskillen, **County Fermanagh**, BT74 9FD, **NORTHERN IRELAND**.
(T) 028 66341635.
Contact/s
Chairman: Mrs M Little
Profile Club/Association, Riding Club. **Ref: YH04852**

ERRAY

Golden Ducat Farming Co Ltd, Erray Farm, Tobermory, Isle Of Mull, **Argyll and Bute**, PA75 6PS, **SCOTLAND**.
(T) 01688 302331 **(F)** 01688 302331.
Contact/s
Owner: Mrs A Elwis
Profile Breeder.
Opening Times
Telephone for further information **Ref: YH04853**

ERROISTON EQUESTRIAN CTRE

Erroiston Equestrian Centre, Cruden Bay, Peterhead, **Aberdeenshire**, AB42 0PJ, **SCOTLAND**.
(T) 01779 812303.
Profile Riding School. **Ref: YH04854**

ERROL HUT SMITHY

Errol Hut Smithy & Woodwork, Cornhill-on-Tweed, **Northumberland**, TD12 4TP, **ENGLAND**.
(T) 01890 820317 **(F)** 01890 820317.
Contact/s
Owner: Mr N Smith
Profile Blacksmith. **Ref: YH04855**

ERROL RACEWAY

Errol Raceway, Flawcraig Farm, Rait, Perth, **Perth and Kinross**, PH2 7RY, **SCOTLAND**.
(T) 01821 670393.
Profile Track/Course. **Ref: YH04856**

ERSKINE, DOUGLAS J

Douglas J Erskine DWCF, Coldron Cottage, Gairney Bank, **Perth and Kinross**, KY13 9JZ, **SCOTLAND**.
(T) 01577 862601.
Profile Farrier. **Ref: YH04857**

ESCHEATLANDS STUD

Escheatlands Stud, Beckley, Rye, **Sussex (East)**, TN31 6SB, **ENGLAND**.
(T) 01424 882279.
Profile Breeder. **Ref: YH04858**

ESCRICK PK RIDEWAYS

Escrick Park Estate, The Estate Office, Escrick, York, **Yorkshire (North)**, YO19 6EA, **ENGLAND**.
(T) 01904 728252 **(F)** 01904 728831.
Contact/s
Administration: Mrs H Pentith
Profile Track/Course.
26 miles of hacking. 6 mile cross county course
No.Staff: 7 Yr. Est: 1991 C.Size: 100 Acres
Opening Times
Sp: Open Mon - Sun 09:00. Closed Mon - Sun 17:00.
Su: Open Mon - Sun 09:00. Closed Mon - Sun 17:00.
Au: Open Mon - Sun 09:00. Closed Mon - Sun 17:00.
Wn: Open Mon - Sun 09:00. Closed Mon - Sun 17:00.
Telephone during opening hours. **Ref: YH04859**

ESKDALE HARNESS

Eskdale Harness, Craigshaws, Eaglesfield, Lockerbie, **Dumfries and Galloway**, DG11 3AH, **SCOTLAND**.
(T) 01461 600224 **(F)** 01461 600224.
Contact/s
Owner: Mr D Britton
Profile Supplies. **Ref: YH04860**

ESKDALE SADDLERY

Eskdale Saddlery, 4 High St, Longtown, Carlisle, **Cumbria**, CA6 5UE, **ENGLAND**.
(T) 01228 792040.
Contact/s
Owner: Mr D Brittain
Profile Saddlery Retailer. **Ref: YH04861**

ESPRO EQUESTRIAN & SPORTSWEAR

Espro Equestrian & Sportswear Ltd, Units 1 Clayton St, Wigan, **Lancashire**, WN3 4DA, **ENGLAND**.
(T) 01942 321999 **(F)** 01942 231188.
Contact/s
Manager: Mr I Dulson
Profile Supplies. **Ref: YH04862**

ESS

Equestrian Support Services, PO Box 3376, Dorchester, **Dorset**, DT2 82A, **ENGLAND**.
(T) 01300 348997 **(F)** 01300 348736
(E) ess@hbgassist.com
(W) www.equestriansupport.co.uk.
Contact/s
Enquiries: Ms L McKenna
Profile Club/Association. Emergency Assistance System. No.Staff: 15
Opening Times
24 hour emergency support **Ref: YH04863**

ESSENDON & DISTRICT

Essendon & District Riding Club, Hunters Lodge, Brent Pelham, Buntingford, **Hertfordshire**, SG9 0AS, **ENGLAND**.
(T) 01920 821496.
Profile Club/Association, Riding Club. **Ref: YH04864**

ESSENTIALLY EQUINE

Essentially Equine, 25 School Ave, West Rainton, Houghton Le Spring, **Tyne and Wear**, DH4 6SA, **ENGLAND**.
(T) 0191 5121994.
Profile Supplies. **Ref: YH04865**

ESSEX ANIMAL FEEDS

Essex Animal Feeds Ltd, Noak Hill Rd, Noak Hill, Romford, **Essex**, RM3 7LS, **ENGLAND**.
(T) 01708 343363.
Profile Feed Merchant, Supplies. **Ref: YH04866**

ESSEX COUNTY SHOWGROUND

Essex County Showground Equestrian Club Ltd, Moulsham Hall Lane, Great Leighs, Chelmsford, **Essex**, CM3 1QP, **ENGLAND**.
(T) 01245 362412 **(F)** 01245 361850.
Contact/s
The Show Secretary: Sharon Soar
Profile Club/Association. **Ref: YH04867**

ESSEX FARMERS & UNION

Essex Farmers & Union (Easter), Park Gate Farm, Layer Marney, Colchester, **Essex**, CO5 9UH, **ENGLAND**.
(T) 01621 815470.
Profile Club/Association. **Ref: YH04868**

ESSEX FARMERS & UNION

Essex Farmers & Union (January), Langham Hall, Colchester, **Essex**, CO4 5PS, **ENGLAND**.
(T) 01206 322110.
Profile Club/Association. **Ref: YH04869**

ESSEX FENCING

Essex Fencing, The Old Bakery, Hawk Lane,

Battlesbridge, Wickford, **Essex**, SS11 7RL, **ENGLAND**.
(T) 01268 732184.
Profile Fencing. **Ref: YH04870**

ESSEX HAY & STRAW

Essex Hay & Straw Co Ltd, Cut Farm, Quay Lane, Beaumont, Clacton-on-Sea, **Essex**, CO16 0BB, **ENGLAND**.
(T) 01255 861996 **(F)** 01255 861996.
Profile Hay and Straw Merchants. **Ref: YH04871**

ESSEX RIDER

Essex Rider (The), 175 Waldegrave, Kingswood, Basildon, **Essex**, SS16 5EL, **ENGLAND**.
(T) 01268 288088.
Profile Supplies. **Ref: YH04872**

ESSEX TRAILER SALES

Essex Trailer Sales Ltd, Euro Base South, Hedley Ave, Grays, **Essex**, RM20 3JA, **ENGLAND**.
(T) 01375 385930 **(F)** 01375 391255.
Profile Transport/Horse Boxes. **Ref: YH04873**

ESSO RIDING CLUB

Esso (Fawley) Riding Club, Kennels Hse, 5 Long Lane, Fawley, **Hampshire**, SO45 2LF, **ENGLAND**.
(T) 023 80891275.
Contact/s
Secretary: Miss S Riley
Profile Club/Association, Riding Club. **Ref: YH04874**

ESTATE SUPPLIES & SVS

Estate Supplies & Services, Dairy Hse Farm, Ashley, Altrincham, **Cheshire**, WA15 0QG, **ENGLAND**.
(T) 0161 9283292 **(F)** 0161 9290287.
Profile Breeder, Supplies. **Ref: YH04875**

ESTON EQUESTRIAN CTRE

Eston Equestrian Centre, Jubilee Rd, Middlesbrough, **Cleveland**, TS6 9HA, **ENGLAND**.
(T) 01642 452260.
Profile Riding School. **Ref: YH04876**

ETAL MANOR

Etal Manor, Waltersteads, Ladykirk, Berwick-upon-Tweed, **Northumberland**, TD15 2PU, **ENGLAND**.
(T) 01890 820205. **Ref: YH04877**

ETCHES, C C

C C Etches, Brookwood Farm, Fenny Bentley, Ashbourne, **Derbyshire**, DE6 1LE, **ENGLAND**.
(T) 01335 350208.
Profile Breeder. **Ref: YH04878**

ETCHINGHAM STUD

Etchingham Stud, West Flatts, Slingsby, **Yorkshire (North)**, YO62 7AE, **ENGLAND**.
(T) 01653 628347 **(F)** 01653 628347.
Profile Breeder. **Ref: YH04879**

ETEK

Etek Equestrian Tec Riding School, Church Hse Farm Stables, Middleton St. George, Darlington, **County Durham**, DL2 1AY, **ENGLAND**.
(T) 01325 333332.
Profile Riding School. **Ref: YH04880**

ETHERIDGE, A G

A G Etheridge, Watermill Farm, The Moor, Middleton, Saxmundham, **Suffolk**, IP17 3LW, **ENGLAND**.
(T) 01728 648236.
Contact/s
Owner: Mr A Etheridge
Profile Breeder. **Ref: YH04881**

ETHERIDGE, DAVID H

David H Etheridge BII, 14 Ashton Cl, Bishops Waltham, **Hampshire**, SO3 1FP, **ENGLAND**.
(T) 01489 894258.
Profile Farrier. **Ref: YH04882**

ETHERINGTON, T J

Mr T J Etherington, Wold Hse, Norton, Malton, **Yorkshire (North)**, YO17 9QG, **ENGLAND**.
(T) 01653 692842.
Profile Trainer. **Ref: YH04883**

ETHERINGTON-SMITH, MICHAEL

Michael Etherington-Smith, The Dower Hse, Sibford Ferris, Banbury, **Oxfordshire**, OX15 5RA, **ENGLAND**.
(T) 01295 788492 **(F)** 01295 788659
(E) mikees@sibford.freeserve.co.uk. **Ref: YH04884**

ETS TRAILERS & TOWBARS

ETS Trailers & Towbars, 4 Chapel Rd, Rhiwceiliog Pencoed, Bridgend, **Bridgend**, CF35 6NN, **WALES**.
(T) 01656 864043 **(F)** 01656 864043.
Contact/s
Owner: Mr T Hill
Profile Transport/Horse Boxes. **Ref: YH04885**

ETTER SPORTS HORSES

Belmont House Stud, Belmont Hse, Bellmont, **County Offaly**, **IRELAND**.
(T) 090257353 **(F)** 090257353
(E) belmonthouse@esatclearie
(W) www.etterhorses.com.
Contact/s
General Manager: Ms A Etter
Profile Blood Stock Agency, Breeder. No.Staff: 6
Yr. Est: 1987 C.Size: 100 Acres **Ref: YH04886**

ETTINGTON PARK STABLES

Ettington Park Stables, Alderminster, Stratford-upon-Avon, **Warwickshire**, CV37 8BU, **ENGLAND**.
(T) 01789 450653.
Profile Riding School, Stable/Livery. **Ref: YH04887**

ETTINGTON PK RIDING CLUB

Ettington Park Riding Club, 11 Chapel Lane, Wellesbourne, **Warwickshire**, CV35 9QU, **ENGLAND**.
(T) 01789 840680.
Profile Club/Association, Riding Club. **Ref: YH04888**

ETTRICK FOREST RIDERS ASS

Ettrick Forest Riders Association, Timpendean Cottage, Jedburgh, **Scottish Borders**, TD8 6SS, **SCOTLAND**.
(T) 01835 830334.
Contact/s
Secretary: Mrs A Millar
Profile Club/Association. **Ref: YH04889**

ETTRICK STABLES

Ettrick Stables, Closeburn, Thornhill, **Dumfries and Galloway**, DG3 5HL, **SCOTLAND**.
(T) 01848 331346.
Profile Holidays, Riding School, Stable/Livery.
Ref: YH04890

EUBANK, A

Mr A Eubank, Barugh Farm, Waverton, Wigton, **Cumbria**, CA7 0AW, **ENGLAND**.
(T) 01697 342580.
Profile Breeder. **Ref: YH04891**

EURO MECH

Euro Mech, Bluebell Business Ctr, Old Naas Rd, Dublin, **County Dublin**, **IRELAND**.
(T) 01 4600655 **(F)** 01 4600659
(E) euromech@indigo.ie.
Profile Supplies. **Ref: YH04892**

EURO STYLE

Euro Style, Birchinley Manor, Wild Hse Lane, Milnrow, Rochdale, **Lancashire**, OL16 3TW, **ENGLAND**.
(T) 01706 633398 **(F)** 01706 632700.
Contact/s
Owner: Mr R Tsang
Profile Riding School. **Ref: YH04893**

EUROBALE

Eurobale Ltd, Hunters Lodge, Manor Farm Stud, Willoughby Lane, Keyworth, Nottingham, **Nottinghamshire**, NG12 5PU, **ENGLAND**.
(T) 0115 9372325 **(F)** 0115 9376020.
Profile Hay and Straw Merchants. **Ref: YH04894**

EUROCLIP 2000

Euroclip 2000 Ltd, 7 Riverside, Tramway Est, Banbury, **Oxfordshire**, OX16 8TU, **ENGLAND**.
(T) 01295 269056 **(F)** 01295 269036
(E) euroclip@weatherbeeta.com.
Profile Supplies. **Ref: YH04895**

EUROEJECTORS

Euroejectors Ltd, Unit D Atlas Trading Est, Cross St, Bilston, **Midlands (West)**, WV14 8TJ, **ENGLAND**.
(T) 01902 495195 **(F)** 01902 490012.
Profile Transport/Horse Boxes. **Ref: YH04896**

EUROENDURO

EuroEnduro, 20 Clover End, Witchford, Ely, **Cambridgeshire**, CB6 2XD, **ENGLAND**.
(T) 01353 663684 **(F)** 01353 663684
(E) euroenduro-owner@cee.hw.ac.uk. **Ref: YH04897**

EUROFARM

EuroFarm & Garden Supplies Ltd, Unit 3 Barrack St, Kilkenny, **County Kilkenny**, **IRELAND**.
(T) 056 23199.
Contact/s
Assistant Manager: Caroline Dargan
Profile Riding Wear Retailer, Saddlery Retailer, Supplies.
Some veterinary supplies are stocked as well as clothing and tack for horse and rider.
Opening Times
Sp: Open Mon - Sat 09:00. Closed Mon - Fri 18:00, Sat 16:00.
Su: Open Mon - Sat 09:00. Closed Mon - Fri 18:00, Sat 16:00.
Au: Open Mon - Sat 09:00. Closed Mon - Fri 18:00, Sat 16:00.
Wn: Open Mon - Sat 09:00. Closed Mon - Fri 18:00, Sat 16:00.
Closed Sundays **Ref: YH04898**

EUROFLEET RENTAL

Eurofleet Rental Ltd, Little Wigston, Appleby Magna, Swadlincote, **Derbyshire**, DE12 7BJ, **ENGLAND**.
(T) 01530 274700 **(F)** 01530 274600.
Profile Transport/Horse Boxes. **Ref: YH04899**

EUROFLEET RENTAL

Eurofleet Rental Ltd, Staniforth Rd, Sheffield, **Yorkshire (South)**, S9 4JE, **ENGLAND**.
(T) 0114 2430281.
Profile Transport/Horse Boxes. **Ref: YH04900**

EUROLEASE

Eurolease, PO Box 47, Thirsk, **Yorkshire (North)**, YO7 2YP, **ENGLAND**.
(T) 01845 597177 **(F)** 01845 597393.
Profile Transport/Horse Boxes. **Ref: YH04901**

EUROMEC

Euromec Ltd, A1 Valley Way, Market Harborough, **Leicestershire**, LE16 7PS, **ENGLAND**.
(T) 01858 434011 **(F)** 01858 464910.
Profile Supplies. **Ref: YH04902**

EURO-MECH

Euro-Mech Ltd, 164 Osbourne Rd, Brighton, **Sussex (East)**, BN1 6LS, **ENGLAND**.
(T) 01273 566294 **(F)** 01273 565732.
Profile Supplies. **Ref: YH04903**

EUROPA

Europa Saddlery, 1 New Farm Cottage, Cardenden, Lochgelly, **Fife**, KY5 9HP, **SCOTLAND**.
(T) 01592 784888.
Contact/s
Owner: Mrs P Cook
Profile Saddlery Retailer.
Small pony equipment and show equipment available by mail order. No.Staff: 2 Yr. Est: 1993
Opening Times
Telephone for further information **Ref: YH04904**

EUROPEAN & INT PEDIGREE

European & International Pedigree Research, Manor Farm, Higher Eype, Bridport, **Dorset**, DT6 6AT, **ENGLAND**.
(T) 01308 427080 **(F)** 01308 421145.
Profile Breeder, Club/Association. **Ref: YH04905**

EUROPEAN BREEDERS FUND

European Breeders Fund, Stanstead Hse, The Ave, Newmarket, **Suffolk**, CB8 9AA, **ENGLAND**.
(T) 01638 667960.
Contact/s
Chief Executive: Mr S Sheppard
Profile Blood Stock Agency. **Ref: YH04906**

EUROPEAN CONFERENCE

European Conference of Arabian Horse Organisations, Spring Hse, Marperton, Wincanton, **Somerset**, BA9 8EH, **ENGLAND**.
(T) 01963 32524 **(F)** 01963 32524.
Profile Club/Association. **Ref: YH04907**

EUROPEAN EQUESTRIAN

European Equestrian Co, Eardisley, Hereford, **Herefordshire**, HR3 6NS, **ENGLAND**.
(T) 01544 328484.
Profile Supplies. **Ref: YH04908**

EUROVET

Eurovet, 2 Ferriby High Rd, North Ferriby, **Yorkshire (East)**, HU14 3LE, **ENGLAND**.
(T) 01482 665783 **(F)** 01482 665782
(E) sales@osmonds.co.uk
(W) www.osmonds.co.uk.
Profile Medical Support. **Ref: YH04909**

EUR-O-WAY TRAILER HIRE

Eur-O-Way Specialist Trailer Hire, Moss Carr Farm, Moss Carr Rd, Keighley, **Yorkshire (West)**, BD21 4SD, **ENGLAND**.

(T) 01535 665912.
Contact/s
Owner: Mr S Ingham
Profile Transport/Horse Boxes. Ref: YH04910

EUSTACE, J M P

J M P Eustace, Pk Lodge Stables, Pk Lane, Newmarket, **Suffolk**, CB8 8AX, **ENGLAND**.
(T) 01638 664277 (F) 01638 664156
(W) www.newmarketracehorsetrainers.co.uk
Affiliated Bodies Newmarket Trainers Fed.
Contact/s
Trainer: Mr J Eustace
Profile Trainer. Ref: YH04911

EVANS & BROOKS

Evans & Brooks, Orleton Rd, Ludlow Business Pk, Ludlow, **Shropshire**, SY8 1XF, **ENGLAND**.
(T) 01584 875931.
Contact/s
Owner: Mr D Evans
Profile Transport/Horse Boxes. Ref: YH04912

EVANS BROS

Evans Bros (Dyfed), Mart Offices, Llanybyther, **Carmarthenshire**, SA40 9UE, **WALES**.
(T) 01570 480444 (F) 01570 480988.
Contact/s
Partner: Mr E Evans
Profile Auctioneers. Ref: YH04913

EVANS BROS

Evans Bros (Lampeter), 39 High St, Lampeter, **Ceredigion**, SA48 7BB, **WALES**.
(T) 01570 422395.
Contact/s
Partner: Mr D Evans
Profile Auctioneers. Ref: YH04914

EVANS, ALFRED D

Alfred D Evans, Kendelstown Stables, Delgany, **County Wicklow**, **IRELAND**.
(T) 01 2876792.
Profile Trainer. Ref: YH04915

EVANS, ANNE-MARIE & RICHARD

Anne-Marie & Richard Evans, The Stables, Borrego Stud, Sezincote, Moreton In Marsh, **Gloucestershire**, GL56 9TB, **ENGLAND**.
(T) 01386 701253.
Profile Trainer. Ref: YH04916

EVANS, DAVID T C

David T C Evans RSS, Cathedine Fawr, Bwlch, Brecon, **Powys**, LD3 7ZS, **WALES**.
(T) 01874 84454.
Profile Farrier. Ref: YH04917

EVANS, GARY B

Gary B Evans DWCF, 11 Jarvis Drv, Melton Mowbray, **Leicestershire**, LE13 0LF, **ENGLAND**.
(T) 01664 500398.
Profile Farrier. Ref: YH04918

EVANS, GORDON L

Gordon L Evans RSS, 6 Woodside, Fortis Green Rd, Muswell Hill, **London (Greater)**, **ENGLAND**.
(T) 020 88835976.
Profile Farrier. Ref: YH04919

EVANS, H J

Mr H J Evans, Nineveh Farm, Campden Rd, Mickleton, Chipping Campden, **Gloucestershire**, GL55 6PS, **ENGLAND**.
(T) 01386 438921.
Profile Supplies. Ref: YH04920

EVANS, IFOR WYN

Ifor Wyn Evans, Bryn Awelof, Ala Rd, Pwllheli, **Gwynedd**, LL53 5BN, **WALES**.
(T) 01758 612125.
Profile Farrier. Ref: YH04921

EVANS, J C

J C Evans, Holbrook Villa, Harmer Hill, Shrewsbury, **Shropshire**, SY4 3EW, **ENGLAND**.
(T) 01939 220605 (F) 01939 220534.
Contact/s
Owner: Miss J Evans
Profile Saddlery Retailer. Ref: YH04922

EVANS, J H

Mr J H Evans, Cwmiago, Cribyn, Lampeter, **Ceredigion**, SA4 87LY, **WALES**.
(T) 01570 434368.
Profile Breeder. Ref: YH04923

EVANS, J T

Mr J T Evans, Yew Tree Cottage, Red Hill Farm, Bredenbury, Bromyard, **Herefordshire**, HR7 4SY, **ENGLAND**.
(T) 01885 483535.
Profile Supplies. Ref: YH04924

EVANS, J T

J T Evans, Erddreiniog, Tregaian, Llangefni, **Isle of Anglesey**, LL77 7UH, **WALES**.
(T) 01248 722285.
Profile Breeder. Ref: YH04925

EVANS, M

Mrs M Evans, Hengoed, Clarbeston Rd, Pembroke, **Pembrokeshire**, SA63 4QL, **WALES**.
(T) 01437 731336.
Profile Supplies. Ref: YH04926

EVANS, M V

M V Evans, Huelva Lodge, Salem Rd, St Clears, Carmarthen, **Carmarthenshire**, SA33 4DH, **WALES**.
(T) 01994 230247.
Contact/s
Owner: Mr M Evans
Profile Supplies.
Opening Times
Sp: Open Mon - Sun 09:00. Closed Mon - Sun 18:00.
Su: Open Mon - Sun 09:00. Closed Mon - Sun 18:00.
Au: Open Mon - Sun 09:00. Closed Mon - Sun 18:00.
Wn: Open Mon - Sun 09:00. Closed Mon - Sun 18:00. Ref: YH04927

EVANS, MARTIN

Mr Martin Evans, The Hawthorns, Hurcott Lane, Kidderminster, **Worcestershire**, DY10 3PJ, **ENGLAND**.
(T) 01562 60970.
Profile Supplies. Ref: YH04928

EVANS, P D

Mr P D Evans, Long Mountain Farm, Leighton, Welshpool, **Powys**, SY21 8JB, **WALES**.
(T) 01938 570288
(M) 07860 668499.
Profile Trainer. Ref: YH04929

EVANS, R R

R R Evans, Oxstalls Farm, Warwick Rd, Stratford-upon-Avon, **Warwickshire**, CV37 0NS, **ENGLAND**.
(T) 01789 205277.
Profile Breeder. Ref: YH04930

EVANS, RHYS

Rhys Evans, 30 Brorhiwen, Rhiwlas, Bangor, **Gwynedd**, LL57 4EL, **WALES**.
(T) 01248 352835
(M) 07889 487810.
Profile Supplies. Ref: YH04931

EVANS, SALLYANN & LISA

Sallyann & Lisa Evans, Forest Farm, Forest Lane, Hanbury, Bromsgrove, **Worcestershire**, B60 4HP, **ENGLAND**.
(T) 01527 821526 (F) 01527 821084.
Profile Breeder, Trainer. Ref: YH04932

EVANS, T E

T E Evans, Gorwel, North Prde, Aberaeron, **Ceredigion**, SA46 0JP, **WALES**.
(T) 01545 570601.
Profile Breeder. Ref: YH04933

EVE LODGE STABLES

Eve Lodge Stables, Hamilton Rd, Newmarket, **Suffolk**, CB8 0NY, **ENGLAND**.
(T) 01638 669797.
Profile Trainer. Ref: YH04934

EVE TRAKWAY

Eve Trakway Ltd, Coxmoor Rd, Sutton-In-Ashfield, **Nottinghamshire**, NG17 5LA, **ENGLAND**.
(T) 01623 515333 (F) 01623 440154
(E) 106103.2724@compuserve.com.
Profile Club/Association. Ref: YH04935

EVENLODE RIDING CLUB

Evenlode Riding Club, 5 Eldersfield Cl, Gretton Rd, Winchcombe, **Gloucestershire**, GL54 5HW, **ENGLAND**.
(T) 01242 602263.
Profile Club/Association, Riding Club. Ref: YH04936

EVENT HORSE OWNERS ASS

Event Horse Owners Association, The White Hse, Crockerton, Warminster, **Wiltshire**, BA12 8AH, **ENGLAND**.
(T) 01985 212380 (F) 01985 212380.
Profile Club/Association. Ref: YH04937

EVENT SVS

Event Services Ltd, Unit 1 The Old Foundry, Brow Mills Ind Est, Brighouse Rd, Hipperholme, Halifax, **Yorkshire (West)**, HX3 8EF, **ENGLAND**.
(T) 01422 204114 (F) 01422 204431. Ref: YH04938

EVENTERS DIRECT

Eventers Direct, 20 Dobell Rd, Eltham, **London (Greater)**, SE9 1HE, **ENGLAND**.
(T) 020 88594414 (F) 020 88594414.
Profile Supplies. Ref: YH04939

EVENTERS INT

Eventers International, South Lodge, Ropsley, Grantham, **Lincolnshire**, NG33 4AS, **ENGLAND**.
(T) 01476 585277 (F) 01476 585742.
Profile Trainer. Ref: YH04940

EVENTING IRELAND

Eventing Ireland (Munster Region), 8 Amberly Gr, Grange, Douglas, **County Cork**, **IRELAND**.
(W) www.eventingireland.com.
Contact/s
Secretary: Ms M Connelly
Profile Club/Association. Ref: YH04941

EVENTING IRELAND

Eventing Ireland (Northern Region), Northern Region Mngmt Committee, 98 Shore St, Killyleagh, **County Down**, BT30 9QJ, **NORTHERN IRELAND**.
(T) 028 44828734 (F) 028 44821166
(E) eventingirelandnr@hotmail.com
(W) www.eventingireland.com.
Contact/s
Secretary: Miss M Spiers
Profile Club/Association.
Opening Times
Sp: Open Mon - Sat 09:00. Closed Mon - Sun 17:00.
Su: Open Mon - Sat 09:00. Closed Mon - Sun 17:00.
Au: Open Mon - Sat 09:00. Closed Mon - Sun 17:00.
Wn: Open Mon - Sat 09:00. Closed Mon - Sun 17:00.
24 hour answer phone and fax Ref: YH04942

EVENTING IRELAND

Eventing Ireland (Western Region), Tycooley, Caltra, Ballinasloe, **County Galway**, **IRELAND**.
(T) 090 578998
(W) www.eventingireland.com.
Contact/s
Secretary: Mr L Murphy
Profile Club/Association. Ref: YH04943

EVENTING IRELAND

Eventing Ireland, The Kildare Paddocks, Kill, **County Kildare**, **IRELAND**.
(T) 045 886674 (F) 045 886675
(W) www.eventingireland.com.
Contact/s
Secretary: Ms A Matheson
Profile Club/Association.
Opening Times
Sp: Open Mon - Fri 09:00. Closed Mon - Fri 17:00.
Su: Open Mon - Fri 09:00. Closed Mon - Fri 17:00.
Au: Open Mon - Fri 09:00. Closed Mon - Fri 17:00.
Wn: Open Mon - Fri 09:00. Closed Mon - Fri 17:00.
Ref: YH04944

EVENTING IRELAND

Eventing Ireland (North Leinster Region), C/O Dollandstown Stud, Kilcock, **County Kildare**, **IRELAND**.
(T) 01 6288329
(W) www.eventingireland.com.
Contact/s
Secretary: Mrs P Sharpe
Profile Club/Association. Ref: YH04945

EVENTING IRELAND

Eventing Ireland (South Leinster Region), C/O Carriagbeg Stud, Gorey, **County Wexford**, **IRELAND**.
(T) 087 2708577.
Contact/s
Secretary: Ms P Doyle
Profile Club/Association. Ref: YH04946

EVENTS MNGMT

Events Management, 6 Quarry Pk Cl, Moulton Park, **Northamptonshire**, NN3 6QB, **ENGLAND**.
(T) 01604 499662 (F) 01604 790445.
Profile Club/Association. Ref: YH04947

EVEQUE LEISURE EQUIPMENT

Eveque Leisure Equipment, Duttons Business Ctre, Dock Rd, Northwich, **Cheshire**, CW9 5HJ, **ENGLAND**.
(T) 01606 45611 (F) 01606 421257

(E) mail@eveque.co.uk
(W) www.eveque.co.uk.
Profile Supplies. Safety Equipment.
Safety mat manufacturers. **Yr. Est:** 1980
Ref: YH04948

EVERALL HORSE BOXES

Everall Horse Boxes, Acre Cliffe Stables, Bradford Rd, Otley, **Yorkshire (West)**, LS21 3DN, **ENGLAND**.
(T) 01943 870789.
Profile Transport/Horse Boxes. **Ref: YH04949**

EVERETT, ROGER H

Roger H Everett DWCF, The Beeches, Stone Cross, Exford, **Somerset**, TA24 7NX, **ENGLAND**.
(T) 01643 831248.
Profile Farrier. **Ref: YH04950**

EVERGREEN EQUESTIAN CTRE

Evergreen Equestian Centre, Evergreen, Old Lane, Tickenham, Clevedon, **Somerset (North)**, BS21 6RZ, **ENGLAND**.
(T) 01275 853400.
Contact/s
Owner: Mr P Stokes **Ref: YH04951**

EVERGREEN RIDING STABLES

Evergreen Riding Stables, 18 High St, Gayton, Northampton, **Northamptonshire**, NN7 3HD, **ENGLAND**.
(T) 01604 858247.
Contact/s
Owner: Mr M East
Profile Riding School. **Ref: YH04952**

EVERGREEN VETNRY SURGERY

Evergreen Veterinary Surgery, 63 London Rd South, Poynton, Stockport, **Cheshire**, SK12 1LA, **ENGLAND**.
(T) 01625 859019.
Profile Medical Support. **Ref: YH04953**

EVERITT, S & H

S & H Everitt, Brynglas, Llangadog, **Carmarthenshire**, SA19 9ES, **WALES**.
(T) 01550 740273.
Profile Breeder. **Ref: YH04954**

EVERKERRY

Everkerry, Redroofs, 106 Station Rd, Stanbridge, Leighton Buzzard, **Bedfordshire**, LU7 9JF, **ENGLAND**.
(T) 01525 210845.
Profile Breeder. **Ref: YH04955**

EVERY, LIZ

Liz Every, Bredon View, Manor Rd, Upper Bentley, Redditch, **Worcestershire**, B97 5TB, **ENGLAND**.
(T) 01527 542015
(M) 07759 212108. **Ref: YH04956**

EVERYTHING EQUESTRIAN

Busby Equitation Centre Ltd, Westerton Ave, Busby, **Glasgow (City of)**, G76 8JU, **SCOTLAND**.
(T) 0141 6442698 **(F)** 0141 4235733/6445193
(E) busby@pcuk.org
(W) www.scottishhorseshop.co.uk.
Contact/s
General Manager: Ms L Peat
Profile Riding Wear Retailer, Saddlery Retailer.
On-site embroidery service for saddle pads, rugs, jackets, clothing **No.Staff:** 4 **Yr. Est:** 1999
C.Size: 48 Acres
Opening Times
Sp: Open 08:00. Closed 20:00.
Su: Open 08:00. Closed 20:00.
Au: Open 08:00. Closed 20:00.
Wn: Open 08:00. Closed 20:00. **Ref: YH04957**

EVERYTHING EQUESTRIAN

Everything Equestrian, 3 Wingfield Ct, Norwich Rd, Mulbarton, Norwich, **Norfolk**, NR14 8JP, **ENGLAND**.
(T) 01508 571450 **(F)** 01508 571453.
Contact/s
Owner: Mr S Harris
Profile Saddlery Retailer. **Ref: YH04958**

EVILL, LIONEL ALAN

Lionel Alan Evill, 15 Manor Farm Cottage, Down Ampney, Cirencester, **Gloucestershire**, GL7 5QF, **ENGLAND**.
(T) 01793 750807.
Profile Farrier. **Ref: YH04959**

EWAR STUD FARM

Ewar Stud Farm, The Coach Hse, Bill Hill Pk, Wokingham, **Berkshire**, RG11 5QT, **ENGLAND**.
(T) 0118 9792076 **(F)** 0118 9785199.
Profile Breeder. **Ref: YH04960**

EWING & GIDLOW

Ewing & Gidlow MsRCVS, 29 Ryecroft Way, Wooler, **Northumberland**, NE71 6DY, **ENGLAND**.
(T) 01668 81323 **(F)** 01668 81226.
Profile Medical Support. **Ref: YH04961**

EWSHOT RIDING CLUB

Ewshot Riding Club, 2 Osier Bed Cottages, Old Pk Lane, Farnham, **Surrey**, GU9 0AJ, **ENGLAND**.
(T) 01252 726254.
Profile Club/Association, Riding Club. **Ref: YH04962**

EXBURY

Exbury Carriage & Wheel Builders, Exbury Est, Exbury, Southampton, **Hampshire**, SO45 1AZ, **ENGLAND**.
(T) 023 80897727.
Profile Carriage and Wheel Builders. **Ref: YH04963**

EXECUTIVE STUD

Executive Stud, Church Lane, Burrough Green, Newmarket, **Suffolk**, CB8 9LY, **ENGLAND**.
(T) 01638 507033 **(F)** 01638 507032.
Contact/s
Owner: Mrs C Sasse
Profile Breeder. **Ref: YH04964**

EXETER & DISTRICT

Exeter & District Riding Club, Hornets Castle, Sherril, Poundsgate, Newton Abbot, **Devon**, TQ13 7PS, **ENGLAND**.
(T) 01364 3352.
Profile Club/Association, Riding Club. **Ref: YH04965**

EXETER EQUESTRIAN CTRE

Exeter Equestrian Centre, Poltimore Barton, Moor Lane, Poltimore, Exeter, **Devon**, EX4 0AQ, **ENGLAND**.
(T) 01392 461067 **(F)** 01392 461067.
Contact/s
Partner: Mrs W Fuller
Profile Equestrian Centre. **Ref: YH04966**

EXETER STEEPLECHASE

Exeter Steeplechase Ltd, Haldon Racecourse, Kennford, Exeter, **Devon**, EX6 7XS, **ENGLAND**.
(T) 01392 832599 **(F)** 01392 833454.
Contact/s
Clerk of Course: Nick Ansell
Profile Track/Course. **Ref: YH04967**

EXMOOR NATIONAL PK AUTHORITY

Exmoor National Park Authority, Exmoor Hse, Dulverton, **Somerset**, TA22 9HL, **ENGLAND**.
(T) 01398 323665 **(F)** 01398 323150
(E) klwest@exmoor-nationalpark.gov.uk
(W) www.exmoor-nationalpark.gov.uk.
Profile Breeder, Club/Association. **Ref: YH04968**

EXMOOR PONY SOC

Exmoor Pony Society, Glenfern, Waddicombe, Dulverton, **Somerset**, TA22 9RY, **ENGLAND**.
(T) 01398 341490 **(F)** 01398 341490.
Profile Club/Association. **Ref: YH04969**

EXMOOR WHITE HORSE INN

Exmoor White Horse Inn, Exford, Exmoor, Minehead, **Somerset**, TA24 7PY, **ENGLAND**.
(T) 01643 831229.
Contact/s
Manager: Ms L Hendrie
Profile Holidays. **Ref: YH04970**

EXMOOR WHOLESALE

Exmoor Wholesale Supplies Ltd, Carnarvon Arms Garage, Brushford, Dulverton, **Somerset**, TA22 9AG, **ENGLAND**.
(T) 01398 323933 **(F)** 01398 323327
(E) gerald@exmoorsupplies.com.
Contact/s
Owner: Mr G Eva
Profile Supplies.
Agricultural Supplies **Yr. Est:** 1978
Opening Times
Sp: Open Mon - Fri 09:00. Closed Mon - Fri 17:00.
Su: Open Mon - Fri 09:00. Closed Mon - Fri 17:00.
Au: Open Mon - Fri 09:00. Closed Mon - Fri 17:00.
Wn: Open Mon - Fri 09:00. Closed Mon - Fri 17:00.
Closed weekends **Ref: YH04971**

EXPO LIFE

Expo Life, Beck Grange, Warwick Bridge, Carlisle, **Cumbria**, CA4 8RL, **ENGLAND**.
(T) 01228 561957 **(F)** 01228 561957
(E) expo.life@dial.pipex.com.
Profile Club/Association. **Ref: YH04972**

EXPRESS PET SUPPLIES

Express Pet Supplies, Gelligaer Ct, Hospital Rd, Hengoed, **Caerphilly**, CF82 8DG, **WALES**.
(T) 01443 838888 **(F)** 01443 839999.
Profile Supplies. **Ref: YH04973**

EXTON STUD

Exton Stud, Allens Farm, Exton, Southampton, **Hampshire**, SO32 3NW, **ENGLAND**.
(T) 01489 877432 **(F)** 01489 877187.
Contact/s
Owner: Miss A Ellington
Profile Breeder. **Ref: YH04974**

EYDON HALL FARM

Eydon Hall Farm, Eydon, Daventry, **Northamptonshire**, NN11 3QE, **ENGLAND**.
(T) 01327 261870 **(F)** 01327 260179.
Contact/s
Farm Manager: Mr T Campbell
Profile Breeder. **Ref: YH04975**

EYRE, J L

Mr J L Eyre, Hambleton Hse, Hambleton, Thirsk, **Yorkshire (North)**, YO7 2HA, **ENGLAND**.
(T) 01845 597481.
Profile Trainer. **Ref: YH04976**

EYRE, M G

Mrs M G Eyre, Cleeton Turn Cottage, Cleeton St Mary, Kidderminster, **Worcestershire**, DY14 0QT, **ENGLAND**.
(T) 01584 890797
(E) mgilleyre@compuserve.com.
Profile Breeder. **Ref: YH04977**

EYREFIELD LODGE STUD

Eyrefield Lodge Stud, The Curragh, **County Kildare**, **IRELAND**.
(T) 045 441211 **(F)** 045 441808
(E) eyrefield@tinet.ie.
Contact/s
Key Contact: Sir E Loder
Profile Breeder.
The stud sells foals and yearlings throughout England, Ireland and the USA. **Yr. Est:** 1901 **C.Size:** 160 Acres **Ref: YH04978**

F & A DUNBAR

F & A Dunbar Ltd, Two Bridges Rd, Milnrow, Rochdale, **Lancashire**, OL16 3SR, **ENGLAND**.
(T) 01706 847925 **(F)** 01706 845881.
Profile Blacksmith. **Ref: YH04979**

F & R CAWLEY

F & R Cawley (Toddington) Ltd, 59 Station Rd, Toddington, Dunstable, **Bedfordshire**, LU5 6BN, **ENGLAND**.
(T) 01525 55177.
Profile Transport/Horse Boxes. **Ref: YH04980**

F & STROKER & SONS

F Stroker & Sons, Rest Park Farm, Bishopdyke Rd, Sherburn In Elmet, Leeds, **Yorkshire (West)**, LS25 6HP, **ENGLAND**.
(T) 01977 683788
(E) vstoker@aol.com.
Contact/s
Owner: Mr M Stoker
Profile Supplies.
Haulage of hay and straw anywhere in the country
No.Staff: 5
Opening Times
Sp: Open Mon - Sun 07:30. Closed Mon - Sun 20:00.
Su: Open Mon - Sun 07:30. Closed Mon - Sun 20:00.
Au: Open Mon - Sun 07:30. Closed Mon - Sun 20:00.
Wn: Open Mon - Sun 07:30. Closed Mon - Sun 20:00. **Ref: YH04981**

F B FOREMAN & SONS

F B Foreman & Sons, Rotton Row, Theddlethorpe, St Helen, Mablethorpe, **Lincolnshire**, LN12 1NX, **ENGLAND**.
(T) 01507 473472 **(F)** 01507 473701.
Profile Supplies. **Ref: YH04982**

F B MARKETING

F B Marketing, 1 The Channel, Union St, Ashbourne, **Derbyshire**, DE6 1FB, **ENGLAND**.
(T) 01335 343729 **(F)** 01335 346009.
Profile Club/Association. **Ref: YH04983**

F BAYRAM & SONS

F Bayram & Sons, Townside Rd, North Newbald, York, **Yorkshire (North)**, YO43 4SL, **ENGLAND**.
(T) 01430 827291 **(F)** 01430 827292.
Contact/s
Owner: Mr P Bayram **Ref: YH04984**

F BLACKMORE & SON
F Blackmore & Son Ltd, 13A Quarry St, Liverpool, **Merseyside**, L25 6EY, **ENGLAND**.
(T) 0151 4281968 **(F)** 0151 4210084.
Profile Farrier. **Ref: YH04985**

F BRUNTON & SONS
F Brunton & Sons, Bruntons Forge, Newstead Farm, Guisborough, **Cleveland**, TS14 8DJ, **ENGLAND**.
(T) 01287 632558.
Profile Blacksmith. **Ref: YH04986**

F C HARRISS & SONS
F C Harriss & Sons, The Forge, Sturt Farm Ind Est, Burford, **Oxfordshire**, OX18 4ET, **ENGLAND**.
(T) 01993 822122 **(F)** 01993 822122.
Contact/s
Owner: Mr M Harriss
Profile Blacksmith. **Ref: YH04987**

F C ROBERTS & SON
F C Roberts & Son, Ashwood Fieldhouse Farm, Kingswinford, **Midlands (West)**, DY6 0AA, **ENGLAND**.
(T) 01384 273672.
Profile Supplies. **Ref: YH04988**

F CASWELL & SON
F Caswell & Son, 4 Chapel St, Badsey, Evesham, **Worcestershire**, WR11 5HA, **ENGLAND**.
(T) 01386 830646.
Contact/s
Owner: Mr R Caswell
Profile Farrier. **Ref: YH04989**

F DURRANT & SONS
F Durrant & Sons, 3 Mealcheapen St, Worcester, **Worcestershire**, WR1 2DH, **ENGLAND**.
(T) 01905 25247.
Contact/s
Owner: Mr T Smith
Profile Saddlery Retailer. **Ref: YH04990**

F E TOWE
F E Towe Ltd, 30 Navigation St, Walsall, **Midlands (West)**, WS2 9LT, **ENGLAND**.
(T) 01922 625907 **(F)** 01922 637178.
Contact/s
Chairman: Mr W Ward **Ref: YH04991**

F GREEN & SON
F Green & Son, Canal Warehouse, Eshton Rd, Gargrave, **Yorkshire (North)**, BD23 3DN, **ENGLAND**.
(T) 01756 749229.
Profile Supplies. **Ref: YH04992**

F H BURGESS
F H Burgess Ltd, St Peter's Way, Northampton, **Northamptonshire**, NN1 1QH, **ENGLAND**.
(T) 01604 32593 **(F)** 01604 36472.
Profile Transport/Horse Boxes. **Ref: YH04993**

F J LUCAS STABLES
F J Lucas Stables, West Dereham, King's Lynn, **Norfolk**, PE33 9RH, **ENGLAND**.
(T) 01366 500502 **(F)** 01366 501005.
Profile Stable/Livery. **Ref: YH04994**

F MARTIN & SON
F Martin & Son, Dorket Head Farm, St Georges Hill, Arnold, **Nottinghamshire**, NG5 8PU, **ENGLAND**.
(T) 0115 9268703 **(F)** 0115 9268703
(W) webstart.equestria.net/sites/martinsfarm.co.uk/.
Profile Feed Merchant, Supplies. No.Staff: 10
Yr. Est: 1911
Opening Times
Sp: Open Mon - Sat 08:00. Closed Mon - Fri 18:00, Sat 17:00.
Su: Open Mon - Sat 08:00. Closed Mon - Fri 18:00, Sat 17:00.
Au: Open Mon - Sat 08:00. Closed Mon - Fri 18:00, Sat 17:00.
Wn: Open Mon - Sat 08:00. Closed Mon - Fri 18:00, Sat 17:00.
Closed Sundays. **Ref: YH04995**

F N PILE & SON
F N Pile & Son, Fir Tree Farm, Warmington, Banbury, **Oxfordshire**, OX17 1BU, **ENGLAND**.
(T) 01295 690522 **(F)** 01295 690598.
Contact/s
Manager: Mr M Hughes
Profile Transport/Horse Boxes. **Ref: YH04996**

F NEWMAN & SONS
F Newman & Sons, The Limes, Station Approach, Medstead, Alton, **Hampshire**, GU34 5EN, **ENGLAND**.
(T) 01420 562163.
Contact/s
Owner: Mr F Newman
Profile Breeder, Farrier. **Ref: YH04997**

F P I
F P I (Sales), Wilds Lodge, Off Emphingham Rd, Stamford, **Lincolnshire**, PE9 4EB, **ENGLAND**.
(T) 01780 482200 **(F)** 01780 482112
(E) info@fpisales.com
(W) www.fpisales.com.
Profile Medical Support. **Ref: YH04998**

F S JUDGE & SONS
F S Judge & Sons, Wellington Farm, Kings Lane, Longcot, Faringdon, **Oxfordshire**, SN7 7SS, **ENGLAND**.
(T) 01793 782488 **(F)** 01793 784652.
Contact/s
Owner: Mrs B Judge
Profile Hay and Straw Merchants. **Ref: YH04999**

F S TRAILERS & TOWBARS CTRE
F S Trailers & Towbars Centre, 5D New Rd, St Ives, **Cambridgeshire**, PE27 5BG, **ENGLAND**.
(T) 01480 461303 **(F)** 01480 461304.
Contact/s
Partner: Mr F O'Carroll
Profile Transport/Horse Boxes. **Ref: YH05000**

F W HUME & SONS
F W Hume & Sons, Bridge Farm Hse, Ling Rd, Palgrave, Diss, **Norfolk**, IP22 1AA, **ENGLAND**.
(T) 01379 642620 **(F)** 01379 652738.
Contact/s
Owner: Mr R Hume
Profile Transport/Horse Boxes. **Ref: YH05001**

F W MASTERS & SON
F W Masters & Son, Panters Bridge, Mount, Bodmin, **Cornwall**, PL30 4DP, **ENGLAND**.
(T) 01208 821204.
Profile Supplies. **Ref: YH05002**

F W PERKINS
F W Perkins Ltd, Unit 17 Finnimore Trading Est, Ottery St Mary, **Devon**, EX11 1NR, **ENGLAND**.
(T) 01404 812605.
Profile Saddlery Retailer. **Ref: YH05003**

F W TINGLE & SONS
F W Tingle & Sons, 43 & 61 Warmfield Lane, Warmfield, Wakefield, **Yorkshire (West)**, WF1 5TL, **ENGLAND**.
(T) 01924 893234.
Profile Supplies. **Ref: YH05004**

F WILLIAMSON & SONS
F Williamson & Sons, Wood End Farm, Snelson, Chelford, Macclesfield, **Cheshire**, SK11 9BP, **ENGLAND**.
(T) 01625 861306.
Profile Breeder. **Ref: YH05005**

FACER, JAN
Jan Facer AFCL, Pothill Farm, The West Grinstead Pk Est, Honeybridge Lane, Ashurst, Partridge Green, **Sussex (West)**, RH13 8NX, **ENGLAND**.
(T) 01403 711949.
Profile Farrier. **Ref: YH05006**

FACTORY FARM
Factory Farm (Liveries), Factory Farm, Emley Moor, Huddersfield, **Yorkshire (West)**, HD8 9TE, **ENGLAND**.
(T) 01924 848219.
Contact/s
Secretary: Mrs J Hampshire
Profile Stable/Livery, Track/Course. **Ref: YH05007**

FAHEY, J
J Fahey, Blacksmiths Shop, High St, Brant Broughton, Lincoln, **Lincolnshire**, LN5 0SA, **ENGLAND**.
(T) 01400 272889.
Profile Farrier. **Ref: YH05008**

FAHEY, R
R Fahey, Manor Hse Farm, Butterwick, Brawby, Malton, **Yorkshire (North)**, YO17 6PS, **ENGLAND**.
(T) 01653 628001 **(F)** 01653 628001.
Contact/s
Owner: Mrs L Fahey
Profile Trainer. **Ref: YH05009**

FAIR CITY VETNRY GRP
Fair City Veterinary Group, 32 York Pl, Perth, **Perth and Kinross**, PH2 8EH, **SCOTLAND**.
(T) 01738 623210 **(F)** 01738 636692.
Profile Medical Support. **Ref: YH05010**

FAIR EARTH TRADING
Fair Earth Trading, 34 Oakridge, Little Oakley, **Essex**, CO12 5LL, **ENGLAND**.
(T) 01787 377725 **(F)** 01787 377725.
Profile Saddlery Retailer. **Ref: YH05011**

FAIR OAK BARN SADDLERY
Fair Oak Barn Saddlery, Country Gardens, Winchester Rd, Fair Oak, Eastleigh, **Hampshire**, SO50 7HD, **ENGLAND**.
(T) 023 80600450.
Profile Saddlery Retailer. **Ref: YH05012**

FAIR WINTER
Fair Winter Farm, Buckingham Rd, Singleborough, Milton Keynes, **Buckinghamshire**, MK17 0RB, **ENGLAND**.
(T) 01296 715664
Affiliated Bodies TBA.
Contact/s
General Manager: Mr W Edmeads
Profile Breeder.
Breed ten horses a year, and sell through auctions.
Yr. Est: 1995
Opening Times
By appointment only, written application.
Ref: YH05013

FAIRBOURNE CARRIAGES
Fairbourne Carriages, The Oast, Fairbourne Mill, Fairbourne Lane, Harrietsham, Maidstone, **Kent**, ME17 1LQ, **ENGLAND**.
(T) 01622 859502.
Contact/s
Owner: Mr N Wood
Profile Horse Drawn Vehicles. **Ref: YH05014**

FAIRBOURNE STABLES
Fairbourne Stables, Wyedale Lodge, Fairbourne Manor Farm, Harrietsham, Maidstone, **Kent**, ME17 1LH, **ENGLAND**.
(T) 01622 858554.
Profile Stable/Livery. **Ref: YH05015**

FAIRBURN, E J C
Miss E J C Fairburn, 28 Somersby Rd, Woodthorpe, **Nottinghamshire**, NG3 5QA, **ENGLAND**.
(T) 0115 9263126.
Profile Breeder.
Breeder of Welsh Section B ponies. **Ref: YH05016**

FAIRFIELD BLOODSTOCK
Fairfield Bloodstock, 21B Thoroughfare, Woodbridge, **Suffolk**, IP12 1AA, **ENGLAND**.
(T) 01394 380214 **(F)** 01394 380214.
Profile Blood Stock Agency, Breeder. **Ref: YH05017**

FAIRFIELD STABLES
Fairfield Stables, Newhouse Farm, Farm Rd, Chorleywood, Rickmansworth, **Hertfordshire**, WD3 5QB, **ENGLAND**.
(T) 01923 449971 **(F)** 01923 449971.
Contact/s
Owner: Miss A Pickess **Ref: YH05018**

FAIRFIELD STABLES
Fairfield Stables, Fairfield Hse Farm, Milwich, Stafford, **Staffordshire**, ST18 0EG, **ENGLAND**.
(T) 01889 505219. **Ref: YH05019**

FAIRFIELDS FARM
Fairfields Farm Livery Stables, Fairfields Farm, Stroud Wood Rd, Ryde, **Isle of Wight**, PO33 4BY, **ENGLAND**.
(T) 01983 616292.
Contact/s
Owner: Mr S Read
Profile Stable/Livery. **Ref: YH05020**

FAIRHAVEN FARM
Fairhaven Farm, Gooseford, Whiddon Down, Okehampton, **Devon**, EX20 2QH, **ENGLAND**.
(T) 01647 231261.
Profile Stable/Livery. **Ref: YH05021**

FAIRHOLME FARM
Fairholme Farm, 18 Bandon Rise, Wallington, **Surrey**, SM6 8PT, **ENGLAND**.
(T) 020 86694816.
Contact/s
Secretary: Mrs L Thompson **Ref: YH05022**

FAIRHOLME FARM LIVERY STABLE
Fairholme Farm Livery Stable, 14 Croydon Lane, Banstead, **Surrey**, SM7 3AN, **ENGLAND**.
(T) 01737 370377 **(F)** 01737 370377.
Contact/s

Owner: Mrs M McDonnell
Profile Stable/Livery. Ref: YH05023

FAIRHURST, C W

Mr C W Fairhurst, Glasgow Hse, Middleham, Leyburn, **Yorkshire (North)**, DL8 4QG, **ENGLAND**.
(T) 01969 622039 **(F)** 01969 622039
(M) 07889 410840.
Profile Trainer. Ref: YH05024

FAIRLEY STUD

Fairley Stud (The), Shute Hill, Chorley, Lichfield, **Staffordshire**, WS13 8BZ, **ENGLAND**.
(T) 01543 682707.
Profile Breeder. Ref: YH05025

FAIRMOOR VETNRY CTRE

Fairmoor Veterinary Centre, Fairmoor, Morpeth, **Northumberland**, NE65 3TN, **ENGLAND**.
(T) 01670 505321 **(F)** 01670 505330.
Profile Medical Support. Ref: YH05026

FAIRMOUNT STUDIOS

Fairmount Studios, Sunnydene, Wood Enderby, Boston, **Lincolnshire**, PE22 7PE, **ENGLAND**.
(T) 01507 568273.
Contact/s
Key Contact: Mrs G James
Profile Artist. Ref: YH05027

FAIRSPEAR EQUESTRIAN CTRE

Fairspear Equestrian Centre, Leafield, Witney, **Oxfordshire**, OX8 5NT, **ENGLAND**.
(T) 01993 878551 **(F)** 01993 844554
(M) 07971 205503.
Profile Equestrian Centre, Trainer. Ref: YH05028

FAIRTOWN RACING

Fairtown Racing, Fairtown Stud, Cotehill Rd, Cavan, **County Cavan**, **IRELAND**.
(T) 049 4338521.
Profile Supplies. Ref: YH05029

FAIRVIEW ARABIAN STUD

Fairview Arabian Stud, Stanneylands Rd, Styal, Wilmslow, **Cheshire**, SK9 4ER, **ENGLAND**.
(T) 01625 535976.
Profile Breeder. Ref: YH05030

FAIRVIEW FARM RIDING SCHOOL

Fairview Farm Riding School, Fairview Farm Stud, Main Rd, Ravenshead, Nottingham, **Nottinghamshire**, NG15 9GS, **ENGLAND**.
(T) 01623 793549.
Contact/s
Owner: Miss D Cox
Profile Riding School. Ref: YH05031

FAIRWAYS

Fairways, 20 Harriet Way, Bushey, Watford, **Hertfordshire**, WD2 3JH, **ENGLAND**.
(T) 020 89506922. Ref: YH05032

FAIRWAYS CLYDESDALE CTRE

Fairways Clydesdale Centre, Newton Farm, Glencarse, **Perth and Kinross**, PH2 7LX, **SCOTLAND**.
(T) 01738 632561.
Profile Breeder, Equestrian Centre. Ref: YH05033

FAIRYHOUSE RACE COURSE

Fairyhouse Race Course Ltd, Rathoath, Meath, **County Meath**, **IRELAND**.
(T) 01 8256167
(E) fairyhse@indigo.ie.
Profile Track/Course. Ref: YH05034

FAITHFULL, JEREMY B H

Jeremy B H Faithfull RSS, 2 Pembroke Trce, Dinton, Salisbury, **Wiltshire**, SP3 5EF, **ENGLAND**.
(T) 01722 716558.
Profile Farrier. Ref: YH05035

FAKENHAM RACECOURSE

Fakenham Racecourse Ltd, The Racecourse, Fakenham, **Norfolk**, NR21 7NY, **ENGLAND**.
(T) 01328 862388 **(F)** 01328 855908.
Contact/s
Clerk of Course: Mr D Hunter
Profile Track/Course. Ref: YH05036

FAKHOURI, ABDUL H O

Abdul H O Fakhouri DWCF, Wetwood Rough, High St Green, Chiddingfold, **Surrey**, GU8 4XY, **ENGLAND**.
(T) 01483 200339.
Profile Farrier. Ref: YH05037

FAL TEXTILE INDUSTRIES

Fal Textile Industries PLC, Unit 12, Ennerdale Rd, Rotary Parkway, Blyth, **Northumberland**, NE24 4RT, **ENGLAND**.
(T) 01670 357300 **(F)** 01670 357301
(E) sales@falpro.com
(W) www.falpro.com.
Profile Supplies.
Produces a range of rugs, including turnout, stable, target and active. Ref: YH05038

FALCON FORGE

Falcon Forge, The Chasewater Est, High St, Chasetown, Burntwood, **Staffordshire**, WS7 8XP, **ENGLAND**.
(T) 01543 677473.
Profile Blacksmith. Ref: YH05039

FALKLAND VETNRY CLINIC

Falkland Veterinary Clinic, 2 Essex St, Newbury, **Berkshire**, RG14 6QN, **ENGLAND**.
(T) 01635 46565.
Profile Medical Support. Ref: YH05040

FALLABELLA SOC

Fallabella Society, Marklye, Rushlake Green, Heathfield, **Sussex (East)**, TN21 9PN, **ENGLAND**.
(T) 01435 830270 **(F)** 01435 830767.
Profile Club/Association. Ref: YH05041

FAMILY AFFAIR

Family Affair, Pinkie Smithy, Crumstane, Duns, **Scottish Borders**, TD11 3LS, **SCOTLAND**.
(T) 01361 883113.
Contact/s
Owner: Mrs M Vernon Ref: YH05042

FANE VALLEY

Fane Valley, 1 Alexander Rd, Armagh, **County Armagh**, BT61 7JJ, **NORTHERN IRELAND**.
(T) 028 37522344.
Profile Supplies. Ref: YH05043

FANE VALLEY

Fane Valley Agricultural Store, 26 Rathfriland Rd, Banbridge, **County Down**, BT32 4LN, **NORTHERN IRELAND**.
(T) 028 40628778.
Profile Supplies. Ref: YH05044

FANSHAWE, J R

J R Fanshawe, The Office, Pegasus Stables, Snailwell Rd, Newmarket, **Suffolk**, CB8 7DJ, **ENGLAND**.
(T) 01638 664525 **(F)** 01638 664523
(W) www.newmarketracehorsetrainers.co.uk
Affiliated Bodies Newmarket Trainers Fed.
Contact/s
Owner: Mr J Fanshawe
Profile Trainer. Ref: YH05045

FANTASTIC FEATURES

Fantastic Features Ltd, 9 Nightingale Gardens, Sandhurst, **Berkshire**, GU47 9DQ, **ENGLAND**.
(T) 01252 872555 **(F)** 01252 890127
(M) 07774 730735
(E) info@fantasticfeatures.co.uk
(W) www.fantasticfeatures.co.uk/david.html.
Profile Equestrian/Sports Photographers.
PR Consultants who work both privately and commercially Ref: YH05046

FAR FOREST EQUESTRIAN CTRE

Far Forest Equestrian Centre, Far Forest Stables, Pound Bank, Far Forest, Kidderminster, **Worcestershire**, DY14 9DG, **ENGLAND**.
(T) 01299 266438.
Profile Equestrian Centre, Stable/Livery, Trainer.
Ref: YH05047

FAR FURLONG RIDING SCHOOL

Far Furlong Riding School, Far Furlong, Nether Westcote, Chipping Norton, **Oxfordshire**, OX7 6SD, **ENGLAND**.
(T) 01993 831193.
Profile Riding School. Ref: YH05048

FAR WESTFIELD STUD

Far Westfield Stud, Moreton Morrell, **Warwickshire**, CV35 9DB, **ENGLAND**.
(T) 01926 651296 **(F)** 01926 615186.
Profile Breeder. Ref: YH05049

FARAMUS, ANTOINETTE

Antoinette Faramus, 4 Croft Rd, Crowborough, **Sussex (East)**, TN6 3HD, **ENGLAND**.
(T) 01892 665664.
Profile Supplies. Ref: YH05050

FARES STABLES

Fares Stables Ltd, Newsells Pk, Barkway, Royston, **Hertfordshire**, SG8 8DA, **ENGLAND**.
(T) 01763 848396 **(F)** 01763 848986.
Contact/s
Manager: Mr C Oakshott
Profile Breeder. Ref: YH05051

FARFIELD LIVERY

Farfield Livery, Farfield Farm, Bolton Rd, Addingham, Ilkley, **Yorkshire (West)**, LS29 0RQ, **ENGLAND**.
(T) 01756 710267.
Profile Stable/Livery. Ref: YH05052

FARLAP EQUESTRIAN PHOTOGRAPHY

Farlap Equestrian Photography, Axworthy Cottage, Axworthy, Lewdown, **Devon**, EX20 4EB, **ENGLAND**.
(T) 01566 783233
(M) 07721 597926
(E) photos@farlap.co.uk.
Contact/s
Owner: Miss S Clark
Profile Photographer. Ref: YH05053

FARLEY HALL STUD

Farley Hall Stud, Farley Hall, Farley, Oakamoor, Stoke-on-Trent, **Staffordshire**, ST10 3BQ, **ENGLAND**.
(T) 01538 702637.
Profile Breeder. Ref: YH05054

FARM & COUNTRY

Farm & Country Ltd, 50 London Rd, Harleston, **Suffolk**, IP20 9BP, **ENGLAND**.
(T) 01379 853914.
Profile Supplies. Ref: YH05055

FARM EQUESTRIAN CTRE

Farm Equestrian Centre, Bride St, Loughrea, **County Galway**, **IRELAND**.
(T) 091 842712.
Profile Equestrian Centre. Ref: YH05056

FARMER, DAVID

David Farmer, Kingsdown Farm, Kingsdown Rd, Swindon, **Wiltshire**, SN2 6PB, **ENGLAND**.
(T) 01666 510080 **(F)** 01666 510080.
Contact/s
Owner: Mr D Farmer Ref: YH05057

FARMER, L J

L J Farmer, 54A Fore St, Kingsteignton, Newton Abbot, **Devon**, TQ12 3AU, **ENGLAND**.
(T) 01626 68153.
Profile Farrier. Ref: YH05058

FARMER, M J P

M J P Farmer, Brattle Farm, Five Oak Lane, Staplehurst, Tonbridge, **Kent**, TN12 0HE, **ENGLAND**.
(T) 01580 892560.
Contact/s
Saddler: Mr M Farmer **(Q)** Master Saddler
Profile Saddlery Retailer. Ref: YH05059

FARMERS DRAGHOUNDS

Farmers Draghounds, Garretts Barn, Tysoe Rd, Little Kineton, **Warwickshire**, CV35 0DZ, **ENGLAND**.
(M) 07831 603328. Ref: YH05060

FARMERS FRIEND

G Phillips & Sons (The Farmers Friend) Ltd, 17-18 Cowick St, Exeter, **Devon**, EX4 1AL, **ENGLAND**.
(T) 01392 277024 **(F)** 01392 277024.
Contact/s
General Manager: Mr A Marks
Profile Riding Wear Retailer, Saddlery Retailer.
Yr. Est: 1877
Opening Times
Sp: Open 09:00. Closed 17:00.
Su: Open 09:00. Closed 17:00.
Au: Open 09:00. Closed 17:00.
Wn: Open 09:00. Closed 17:00. Ref: YH05061

FARMERS HILL STUD

Farmers Hill Stud, Newmarket Rd, Cheveley, Newmarket, **Suffolk**, CB8 9EQ, **ENGLAND**.
(T) 01638 730368 **(F)** 01638 730368.
Profile Breeder. Ref: YH05062

FARMERS IMPLEMENT SUPPLY

Farmers Implement Supply Co, 10 Garden St, Off Ings Rd, Wakefield, **Yorkshire (West)**, WF1 1DX, **ENGLAND**.
(T) 01924 374908
(M) 07831 178828.
Profile Supplies. Ref: YH05063

FARMHOUSE STABLES

Farmhouse Stables, The Farmhouse, Kingsbury Rd,

Marston, Sutton Coldfield, **Midlands (West)**, B76 0DW, **ENGLAND**.
(T) 01675 475959.
Contact/s
Owner: Mr M Gee
Profile Riding School, Stable/Livery. Ref: YH05064

FARM-INSTALL
Farm-Install Ltd, 27 Levellers Lane, Eynesbury, St Neots, **Cambridgeshire**, PE19 2JL, **ENGLAND**.
(T) 01480 474736.
Profile Transport/Horse Boxes. Ref: YH05065

FARMIX
Farmix Ltd, Wadhurst Country Store, Washwell Lane, Wadhurst, **Sussex (East)**, TN5 6BN, **ENGLAND**.
(T) 01892 782026 (F) 01892 783422.
Profile Hay and Straw Merchants. Ref: YH05066

FARMKEY
Farmkey (Freeze Marking), England Hse, Beaumont Rd, Banbury, **Oxfordshire**, OX16 7RH, **ENGLAND**.
(T) 01295 252544 (F) 01295 251049.
Profile
Freeze marking security service. Ref: YH05067

FARMPET SUPPLIES
Farmpet Supplies, Old Blacksmith Shop, Cothelstone, Bishop Lydeard, Taunton, **Somerset**, TA4 3DS, **ENGLAND**.
(T) 01823 433316 (F) 01823 433316.
Profile Supplies. Ref: YH05068

FARMVIEW SYSTEMS
Farmview Systems, The Lindens Est Office, Friern Park, **London (Greater)**, N12 9DJ, **ENGLAND**.
(T) 020 84450452 (F) 020 84462761
(E) cctvcrew@btinternet.com.
Profile Supplies. Ref: YH05069

FARMWAY
Farmway Ltd (Stokesley), The Auction Mart, Station Rd, Stokesley, **Cleveland**, TS9 7AB, **ENGLAND**.
(T) 01642 710666 (F) 01642 710098.
Profile Supplies. Ref: YH05070

FARMWAY
Farmway Ltd, King St, Darlington, **County Durham**, DL3 6JL, **ENGLAND**.
(T) 01325 469131 (F) 01325 480456.
Profile Supplies. Ref: YH05071

FARMWAY
Farmway Ltd, Cock Lane, Piercebridge, Darlington, **County Durham**, DL2 3TJ, **ENGLAND**.
(T) 01325 374481 (F) 01325 374698
Affiliated Bodies BETA.
Contact/s
Equestrian Manager: Ms E Hopps
Profile Feed Merchant, Riding Wear Retailer, Saddlery Retailer, Supplies.
Opening Times
Sp: Open Mon - Sat 08:30. Closed Mon - Fri 17:00, Sat 12:00.
Su: Open Mon - Sat 08:30. Closed Mon - Fri 17:00, Sat 12:00.
Au: Open Mon - Sat 08:30. Closed Mon - Fri 17:00, Sat 12:00.
Wn: Open Mon - Sat 08:30. Closed Mon - Fri 17:00, Sat 12:00.
Closed Sundays Ref: YH05072

FARMWAY
Farmway Ltd, 5 South Rd, Wooler, **Northumberland**, NE71 6SN, **ENGLAND**.
(T) 01668 280000 (F) 01668 280009.
Profile Supplies. Ref: YH05073

FARMWAY
Farmway Ltd, Fairmoor, Morpeth, **Northumberland**, NE61 3JN, **ENGLAND**.
(T) 01670 500330 (F) 01670 500339
Affiliated Bodies BETA, MSA.
Contact/s
General Manager: Mr G Stephenson (Q) SMS
Profile Riding Wear Retailer, Saddlery Retailer, Supplies. No.Staff: 6 C.Size: 2 Acres
Opening Times
Sp: Open Mon - Sat 08:30. Closed Mon - Sat 17:00.
Su: Open Mon - Sat 08:30. Closed Mon - Sat 17:00.
Au: Open Mon - Sat 08:30. Closed Mon - Sat 17:00.
Wn: Open Mon - Sat 08:30. Closed Mon - Sat 17:00.
Closed Sundays Ref: YH05074

FARMWAY
Farmway Ltd (Hexham), Station Yard, Hexham, **Northumberland**, NE46 1EU, **ENGLAND**.
(T) 01434 602313 (F) 01434 601364.
Profile Supplies. Ref: YH05075

FARMWAY
Farmway Ltd (Driffield), Albion Mills, Driffield, **Yorkshire (East)**, YO25 6QA, **ENGLAND**.
(T) 01377 252531 (F) 01377 241159.
Profile Supplies. Ref: YH05076

FARMWAY
Farmway Ltd (Thirsk), Station Rd, Thirsk, **Yorkshire (North)**, YO7 1QH, **ENGLAND**.
(T) 01845 522338 (F) 01845 526326.
Profile Supplies. Ref: YH05077

FARMWAY
Farmway Ltd (Leyburn), Golden Lion Lane, Leyburn, **Yorkshire (North)**, DL8 5AS, **ENGLAND**.
(T) 01969 624454 (F) 01969 624554.
Profile Supplies. Ref: YH05078

FARMWELL
Farmwell Ltd (Hereford), Melrose Pl, White Cross Rd, Hereford, **Herefordshire**, HR4 0DN, **ENGLAND**.
(T) 01432 357357 (F) 01432 355554.
Profile Supplies. Ref: YH05079

FARNHAM CASTLE STABLES
Farnham Castle Stables Riding School, Old Pk Lane, Farnham, **Surrey**, GU9 0AL, **ENGLAND**.
(T) 01252 737747.
Profile Riding School. Ref: YH05080

FARNHAM RIDERS CLUB
Farnham Riders Club, 25 East Ring, Cardinals, Tongham, Farnham, **Surrey**, GU10 1EE, **ENGLAND**.
(T) 01428 723658.
Contact/s
Secretary: Ms J Strange (T) 01428 723658
Profile Club/Association, Riding Club. Ref: YH05081

FARNHAM SADDLERS
Farnham Saddlers, 7 West St, Farnham, **Surrey**, GU9 7DN, **ENGLAND**.
(T) 01252 713004 (F) 01252 737519.
Contact/s
Manageress: Mrs A Hemming
Profile Saddlery Retailer. Ref: YH05082

FARNINGHAM SADDLERY
Farningham Saddlery, Fernwood Hse, High St, Farningham, **Kent**, DA4 0DT, **ENGLAND**.
(T) 01322 864361 (F) 01322 861948
(M) 07968 940779.
Profile Saddlery Retailer, Transport/Horse Boxes.
Ref: YH05083

FARRALL, C A
Mrs C A Farrall, The Homestead, Dudleston, Ellesmere, **Shropshire**, SY12 9EH, **ENGLAND**.
(T) 01978 710324.
Profile Breeder. Ref: YH05084

FARRANT, TAMARA
Tamara Farrant, Russet Farm, Robertsbridge, **Sussex (East)**, TN32 5NG, **ENGLAND**.
(T) 01580 881291 (F) 01580 881311
(E) tamara.strapp@farmline.com. Ref: YH05085

FARRELL, P
P Farrell, Greenacre Stables, Blackwater, Buckland St. Mary, Chard, **Somerset**, TA20 3LE, **ENGLAND**.
(M) 07771 765210.
Profile Trainer. Ref: YH05086

FARRIER
Farrier, 14 Seagrim Rd, Wilton, Salisbury, **Wiltshire**, SP2 0JY, **ENGLAND**.
(T) 01722 742538.
Contact/s
Owner: Mr B Henry
Profile Farrier. Ref: YH05087

FARRIER SVS
Nigel R Stevens, Chy-Nessa, 29 Trewartha Est, Carbis Bay, St Ives, **Cornwall**, TR26 2TQ, **ENGLAND**.
(T) 01736 797642 (F) 01736 797642
Affiliated Bodies FRC.
Contact/s
Owner: Mr N Stevens (Q) DWCF
(E) n_stevens@hotmail.com
Profile Blacksmith, Farrier. No.Staff: 2
Yr. Est: 1986
Opening Times
Sp: Open 09:00. Closed 17:00.
Su: Open 09:00. Closed 17:00.
Au: Open 09:00. Closed 17:00.
Wn: Open 09:00. Closed 17:00. Ref: YH05088

FARRIER SVS
Pierce Brown, 74 Binfields Cl, Chineham, Basingstoke, **Hampshire**, RG24 8TP, **ENGLAND**.
(T) 01256 327108
Affiliated Bodies WCF.
Contact/s
Treasurer: Mr P Brown
Profile Farrier.
Comprehensive Equine Hoofcare. Ref: YH05089

FARRIERS EQUIPMENT
Farriers Equipment Ltd, Burrow Hill Green, Chobham, Woking, **Surrey**, GU24 8QP, **ENGLAND**.
(T) 01276 856808.
Profile Farrier. Ref: YH05090

FARRIERS REGISTRATION COUNCIL
Farriers Registration Council, Sefton Hse, Adam Court, Newick Rd, Peterborough, **Cambridgeshire**, PE1 5PP, **ENGLAND**.
(T) 01733 319911 (F) 01733 319910
(E) frc@farrier-reg.gov.uk
(W) www.farrier-reg.gov.uk.
Contact/s
Key Contact: Mr S Williamson-Noble
Profile Club/Association, Farrier.
Responsible for the regulation of farriers and management of farrier apprentices. No.Staff: 15
Yr. Est: 1975
Opening Times
Sp: Open 08:45. Closed 17:00.
Su: Open 08:45. Closed 17:00.
Au: Open 08:45. Closed 17:00.
Wn: Open 08:45. Closed 17:00. Ref: YH05091

FARRIERY CTRE
Haydn Price DWCF, The Forge, Little Pastures, Ty-Freeman Lane, Gwehelog, Usk, **Monmouthshire**, NP15 1RD, **WALES**.
(T) 01291 672826.
Profile Farrier. Ref: YH05092

FARRIERY PRACTICE
Farriery Practice (The), Unit One, Bramble Hill Farm, Toat Hill, Slinfold, Horsham, **Sussex (West)**, RH13 7RL, **ENGLAND**.
(T) 01403 791000.
Profile Farrier. Ref: YH05093

FARRINGDON FEEDS
Farringdon Feeds, The Old Station, Farringdon Ind Ctre, Lower Farringdon, Alton, **Hampshire**, GU34 3DP, **ENGLAND**.
(T) 01420 587202.
Contact/s
Partner: Mr B Larby
Profile Feed Merchant. Ref: YH05094

FARRINGTONS SADDLE
Farringtons Saddle Co, 72 Glebe St, Walsall, **Midlands (West)**, WS1 3NX, **ENGLAND**.
(T) 01922 634440 (F) 01922 634440.
Contact/s
Partner: Mr M Bailey
Profile Saddlery Retailer. Ref: YH05095

FARROW, C
C Farrow, Samways Stud, Alvediston, Salisbury, **Wiltshire**, SP5 5LQ, **ENGLAND**.
(T) 01722 780286.
Profile Stable/Livery. Ref: YH05096

FARROW, G M
G M Farrow, Waitwith Bank Farm, Hudswell, Richmond, **Surrey**, DL11 6DB, **ENGLAND**.
(T) 01748 823214.
Profile Breeder. Ref: YH05097

FARSYDE STUD & RIDING CTRE
Farsyde Stud & Riding Centre, Robin Hood Bay, Whitby, **Yorkshire (North)**, YO22 4UG, **ENGLAND**.
(T) 01947 880249 (F) 01947 880877
(E) farsydestud@talk21.com.
Contact/s
Owner: Miss H Green
Profile Horse/Rider Accom, Riding School.
No.Staff: 6 Yr. Est: 1971 C.Size: 70 Acres
Opening Times
Sp: Open Mon - Sun 09:00. Closed Mon - Sun 21:00.
Su: Open Mon - Sun 09:00. Closed Mon - Sun 21:00.
Au: Open Mon - Sun 09:00. Closed Mon - Sun 21:00.
Wn: Open Mon - Sun 09:00. Closed Mon - Sun 21:00. Ref: YH05098

A-Z of COMPANIES

FARTHING DOWNS STABLES

Farthing Downs Stables, Drive Rd, Coulsdon, **Surrey**, CR5 1BN, **ENGLAND**.
(T) 01737 551609.
Contact/s
Owner: Mrs J Kennedy
Profile Riding School, Stable/Livery. **Ref: YH05099**

FARTHING SADDLERY

Farthing Saddlery, Farthing Cottage, Back Lane, Cross In Hand, Heathfield, **Sussex (East)**, TN21 0QA, **ENGLAND**.
(T) 01435 867108 (F) 01435 867108.
Contact/s
Owner: Mr A Winchester
Profile Saddlery Retailer. **Ref: YH05100**

FARVIS & SONS

W J Farvis & Sons Ltd, Temple Works, Morley Rd, Southville, Bristol, **Bristol**, BS3 1DT, **ENGLAND**.
(T) 01179 666677 (F) 01179 669893
(E) sales@farvis.co.uk
(W) www.farvis.com.
Profile Medical Support. Boiler Manufacturers.
Manufacture electric linseed and barley boilers for feed. Yr. Est: 1840
Opening Times
Sp: Open Mon - Fri 08:00. Closed Mon - Fri 16:30.
Su: Open Mon - Fri 08:00. Closed Mon - Fri 16:30.
Au: Open Mon - Fri 08:00. Closed Mon - Fri 16:30.
Wn: Open Mon - Fri 08:00. Closed Mon - Fri 16:30.
Please telephone for further information. Office closed at weekends. **Ref: YH05101**

FAUGHANVALE STABLES

Faughanvale Stables, 9 Dunlade Rd, Greysteel, Londonderry, **County Londonderry**, BT47 3EF, **NORTHERN IRELAND**.
(T) 028 71811843 (F) 028 71811843
Affiliated Bodies BHS.
Contact/s
Owner: Mrs P Dalton
(E) daltonpatricia@hotmail.com
Profile Arena, Riding Club, Riding School, Stable/Livery, Trainer.
Train Racehorses on uphill gallop. No.Staff: 4
Yr. Est: 1995 C.Size: 70 Acres
Opening Times
Sp: Open Tues - Sun 10:00. Closed Wed, Fri, Sat, 18:00, Tues, Thurs 21:00, Sun 14:00.
Su: Open Tues - Sun 10:00. Closed Wed, Fri, Sat, 18:00, Tues, Thurs 21:00, Sun 14:00.
Au: Open Tues - Sun 10:00. Closed Wed, Fri, Sat, 18:00, Tues, Thurs 21:00, Sun 14:00.
Wn: Open Tues - Sun 10:00. Closed Wed, Fri, Sat, 18:00, Tues, Thurs 21:00, Sun 14:00. **Ref: YH05102**

FAULKNER, R M

R M Faulkner, Bryn Celyn, Pant, Llandegla, Wrexham, **Wrexham**, LL11 3AE, **WALES**.
(T) 01978 790421.
Profile Hay and Straw Merchants. **Ref: YH05103**

FAULKNERS FOOTWEAR

Faulkners Footwear, 5 Station Rd, Woodford Halse, Daventry, **Northamptonshire**, NN11 3RB, **ENGLAND**.
(T) 01327 260306.
Profile Riding Wear Retailer. **Ref: YH05104**

FAURIE, E

E Faurie, Heath Farm, Lyneham Rd, Milton-under-Wychwood, Chipping Norton, **Oxfordshire**, OX7 6LR, **ENGLAND**.
(T) 01993 830212.
Contact/s
Manager: Mr D Reynolds
Profile Trainer. **Ref: YH05105**

FAVERSHAM & DISTRICT

Faversham & District Riding Club, The Oast, Porters Lane, Sheldwich, Faversham, **Kent**, ME13 0DP, **ENGLAND**.
(T) 01795 536228.
Profile Club/Association, Riding Club. **Ref: YH05106**

FAVERSHAM RIDING CLUB

Faversham Riding Club, 18 Second Ave, Sheerness, **Kent**, ME12 1YG, **ENGLAND**.
(T) 01795 663660.
Contact/s
Chairman: Mr R Reid
Profile Club/Association, Riding Club. **Ref: YH05107**

FAWCETT, GEORGE

George Fawcett, 20 Craigy Rd, Saintfield, Ballynahinch, **County Down**, BT24 7BZ, **NORTHERN IRELAND**.
(T) 028 97511219 (F) 028 44511963.
Contact/s
Owner: Mr G Fawcett
Profile Transport/Horse Boxes. Horse Drawn Carriage Hire.
Horse and carriages supplied for weddings and funerals. **Ref: YH05108**

FAWCITT, ROBIN T

Robin T Fawcitt DWCF, Pk Farm, Red Hse Lane, Moor Monkton, **Yorkshire (North)**, YO26 8JQ, **ENGLAND**.
(T) 01904 738552.
Profile Farrier. **Ref: YH05109**

FAWLEY STUD

Fawley Stud, Fawley, Wantage, **Oxfordshire**, OX12 9NJ, **ENGLAND**.
(T) 01488 638243 (F) 01488 638865.
Profile Breeder. **Ref: YH05110**

FAYRELANDS

Fayrelands Palomino & Arabian Stud (The), Springhill Hse, Birmingham Rd, Kenilworth, **Warwickshire**, CV8 1PT, **ENGLAND**.
(T) 01676 34347.
Profile Breeder. **Ref: YH05111**

FAZ

FAZ, 11 Warwick Ave, Coventry, **Midlands (West)**, CV5 6DJ, **ENGLAND**.
(T) 024 76673944.
Profile Supplies. **Ref: YH05112**

FBA

Federation of Bloodstock Agents (GB) Ltd, Cuttings, 9 Paddocks Drive, Newmarket, **Suffolk**, CB8 9BE, **ENGLAND**.
(T) 01638 561116 (F) 01638 560332.
Contact/s
Key Contact: Mr A Mead
Profile Blood Stock Agency, Club/Association.
Ref: YH05113

FBHS HORSEWORLD

Friends of Bristol Horse Society Horseworld (Bristol), Staunton Manor Farm, Sleep Lane, Whitchurch, **Bath & Somerset (North East)**, BS14 0QJ, **ENGLAND**.
(T) 01275 540174 (F) 01275 540119.
Profile Club/Association. **Ref: YH05114**

FEARHEAD, DANIEL M

Daniel M Fearhead DWCF, Four Lane Ends Farm, Marthwaite, Sedbergh, **Cumbria**, LA10 5ES, **ENGLAND**.
(T) 01539 621184.
Profile Farrier. **Ref: YH05115**

FEARNALL

Fearnall Stud (The), Tilstone Fearnall, Tarporley, **Cheshire**, CW6 9HS, **ENGLAND**.
(T) 01829 733665
(E) sires@netlinkuk.net.
Contact/s
Owner: Mrs B Thomson
Profile Breeder.
The horses are sold through public auctions.
Opening Times
There is an answer phone, phone for details and directions **Ref: YH05116**

FEARNALL STUD

Fearnall Stud (The), Tilstone Fearnall, Tarporley, **Cheshire**, CW6 9HS, **ENGLAND**.
(T) 01829 733665
(M) 07860 634132.
Profile Farrier. **Ref: YH05117**

FEARNLEY, A

A Fearnley, Steadhall Farm, Woodhead, Burley In Wharfedale, Ilkley, **Yorkshire (West)**, LS29 7BH, **ENGLAND**.
(T) 01943 602086.
Profile Breeder. **Ref: YH05118**

FEDDERN, T A

T A Feddern, 31 Station Rd, Bow Brickhill, Milton Keynes, **Buckinghamshire**, MK17 9JU, **ENGLAND**.
(T) 01908 366400 (F) 01908 365125.
Profile Medical Support. **Ref: YH05119**

FEED BIN

Feed Bin (The), 5 Langford Dr, Luton, **Bedfordshire**, LU2 9AJ, **ENGLAND**.
(T) 01582 733339
(M) 07889 843890
(E) juliefisher@thefeedbin.freeserve.co.uk.
Contact/s
Owner: Miss J Fisher
Profile Feed Merchant, Supplies.
Mobile Feed Suppliers. **Ref: YH05120**

FEED-EM

Feed-Em, Unit 2 Morgan Drive, Guisborough, **Cleveland**, TS14 7DG, **ENGLAND**.
(T) 01287 636823.
Profile Supplies. **Ref: YH05121**

FEEDMARK

Feedmark, Church Farm, St Cross, Harleston, **Suffolk**, IP20 0NY, **ENGLAND**.
(T) 01986 782368 (F) 01986 782466
(E) ukoffice@feedmark.com
(W) www.feedmark.com
Affiliated Bodies BETA.
Contact/s
Customer Service Manager: Lucy Burman
Profile Feed Merchant.
UK deliveries do not include a delivery charge and are delivery on a 'next day' basis. Freephone 0800 585525. **Ref: YH05122**

FEEDMIX

Feedmix Ltd, Station Yard, Fyvie, Turriff, **Aberdeenshire**, AB53 8JQ, **SCOTLAND**.
(T) 01651 891227
(W) www.buchan.org.uk/business/bus_ffm.htm.
Profile Feed Merchant, Supplies. **Ref: YH05123**

FEEDMIX

Feedmix Limited, Mid Rd, Kirriemuir, **Angus**, DD8 4PJ, **SCOTLAND**.
(T) 01575 572252.
Profile Feed Merchant, Supplies. **Ref: YH05124**

FEEDSAFE

Feedsafe, Station Yard, Needham Market, Ipswich, **Suffolk**, IP6 8AT, **ENGLAND**.
(T) 01449 720821.
Profile Supplies. **Ref: YH05125**

FEEDWELL ANIMAL FOOD

Feedwell Animal Food Ltd, The Old Mill, Castlewellan, **County Down**, BT31 9NH, **NORTHERN IRELAND**.
(T) 028 44778765.
Profile Feed Merchant. **Ref: YH05126**

FEENEY'S EQUESTRIAN CTRE

Feeney's Equestrian Centre, Tonabruckey, Bushypark, Galway, **County Galway**, **IRELAND**.
(T) 091 527579 (F) 091 527579.
Contact/s
Owner: Gerard Feeney
Profile Horse/Rider Accom, Riding School.
Treks that vary in length from one to six hours can be arranged, taking in views of the Aran Isles, Galway Bay & the Burren. Holiday accommodation is on site as well as swimming, pitch & putt and overnight trips to the Aran Isles.
Opening Times
Sp: Open Mon - Sat 10:00. Closed Mon - Sat 18:00.
Su: Open Mon - Sat 10:00. Closed Mon - Sat 18:00.
Au: Open Mon - Sat 10:00. Closed Mon - Sat 18:00.
Wn: Open Mon - Sat 10:00. Closed Mon - Sat 18:00.
Closed Sundays **Ref: YH05127**

FELGATE, P S

P S Felgate, The Grimston Stud, Grimston, Melton Mowbray, **Leicestershire**, LE14 3BZ, **ENGLAND**.
(T) 01664 812019 (F) 01664 812019.
Contact/s
Owner: Mr P Felgate
Profile Trainer. **Ref: YH05128**

FELL PONY SOC

Fell Pony Society (The), Federation Hse, Gilwilly Ind Est, Penrith, **Cumbria**, CA11 9BL, **ENGLAND**.
(T) 01768 891001 (F) 01768 891001
(E) fpsoc@bhs-inter.net.
Profile Breeder, Club/Association. **Ref: YH05129**

FELL PONY SOC

Fell Pony Society, Brougham Hall, Penrith, **Cumbria**, CA10 2DE, **ENGLAND**.
(T) 01768 891001
(E) fpsoc@aol.com.
Contact/s
Key Contact: Mrs J Slattery
Profile Breeder, Club/Association. **Ref: YH05130**

FELL PONY SOC

Fell Pony Society (The), Keepers Cottage, Guyzance, Acklington, Morpeth, **Northumberland**, NE65 9AA, **ENGLAND**.
(T) 01670 761117 (F) 01670 761117.
Contact/s

Secretary: Ms S Wood
Profile Breeder, Club/Association. Ref: YH05131

FELL VIEW STABLES

Fell View Stables, Middleham, Leyburn, **Yorkshire (North)**, DL8 4SL, **ENGLAND**.
(T) 01969 623221 (F) 01969 624105
(M) 07715 29857.
Profile Trainer. Ref: YH05132

FELL, R S

Mrs R S Fell, Willake, Goodameavy, Roborough, Plymouth, **Devon**, PL6 7AP, **ENGLAND**.
(T) 01752 839322.
Profile Supplies. Ref: YH05133

FELLOWS & INSTRUCTORS

Fellows & Instructors of the BHS, Brampton Stables, Church Brampton, Northampton, **Northamptonshire**, NN6 8BH, **ENGLAND**.
(T) 01604 842051.
Contact/s
Key Contact: Mrs J Ward (Q) BHSI
Profile Club/Association. Ref: YH05134

FELLOWS & INSTRUCTORS

Fellows & Instructors of the BHS, C/O Mrs P Francis BHSI, Burton Dassett Vicarage, Northend, Leamington Spa, **Warwickshire**, CV33 0TH, **ENGLAND**.
(T) 01295 770400.
Profile Club/Association. Ref: YH05135

FELPHAM STABLES TACKROOM

Felpham Stables Tackroom, 37 Felpham Rd, Bognor Regis, **Sussex (West)**, PO22 7DA, **ENGLAND**.
(T) 01243 822223.
Contact/s
Owner: Mrs A Jones
Profile Riding Wear Retailer, Saddlery Retailer.
Riding equipment bought and sold. Part exchanges welcome. Ref: YH05136

FENBOURNE RIDING SCHOOL

Fenbourne Riding School, Grove Hse, Spalding Rd, Bourne, **Lincolnshire**, PE10 0AU, **ENGLAND**.
(T) 01778 425232.
Profile Breeder, Riding School. Ref: YH05137

FENCING CONTRACTOR

Fencing Contractor, Westwood Lodge, Glapthorn, Peterborough, **Cambridgeshire**, PE8 5BH, **ENGLAND**.
(T) 01832 205218 (F) 01832 205218.
Profile Fencing. Ref: YH05138

FENCING IN THE MIDLANDS

Fencing in the Midlands, Aston Magna, Moreton In Marsh, **Gloucestershire**, GL56 9QQ, **ENGLAND**.
(T) 01608 651096 (F) 01608 651879.
Profile Track/Course. Ref: YH05139

FENGATE DARTMOORS

Fengate Dartmoors, Forge Cottage, 65 High St, Warboys, **Cambridgeshire**, PE17 2TA, **ENGLAND**.
(T) 01487 822635.
Profile Breeder. Ref: YH05140

FENIX CARRIAGE DRIVING CTRE

Fenix Carriage Driving Centre, East Ruckham, Pennymoor, Tiverton, **Devon**, EX16 8LS, **ENGLAND**.
(T) 01363 866532.
Profile Carriage Driving Centre. Ref: YH05141

FENJAY STUD

Fenjay Stud, Fenhouses, Boston, **Lincolnshire**, PE20 3HN, **ENGLAND**.
(T) 01205 821259.
Profile Breeder. Ref: YH05142

FENLAND FEEDS

Fenland Feeds, 33 Spalding Rd, Bourne, **Lincolnshire**, PE10 0AT, **ENGLAND**.
(T) 01778 393409.
Profile Feed Merchant. Ref: YH05143

FENLAND TRAILER PARTS

Fenland Trailer Parts, Stirling Way, Market Deeping, Peterborough, **Cambridgeshire**, PE6 8AS, **ENGLAND**.
(T) 01778 346766 (F) 01778 346544.
Contact/s
Owner: Mr D Fox
Profile Transport/Horse Boxes. Ref: YH05144

FENLAND TRAILERS

Fenland Trailers, 31 Old Severalls Rd, Methwold Hythe, Thetford, **Norfolk**, IP26 4QR, **ENGLAND**.
(T) 01366 728426 (F) 01366 728243.
Contact/s
Owner: Mr C Workley
Profile Transport/Horse Boxes. Ref: YH05145

FENNELL, JOHN

John Fennell, Main St, Rathkeale, **County Limerick**, **IRELAND**.
(T) 069 64082.
Profile Supplies. Ref: YH05146

FENNELL, NIGEL D

Nigel D Fennell DWCF, Laurel Cottage, Whitehall, Odiham, **Hampshire**, RG29 1JP, **ENGLAND**.
(T) 01256 702908.
Profile Farrier. Ref: YH05147

FENNISCOURT STABLES

Fenniscourt Stables, Bagenalstown, **County Carlow**, **IRELAND**.
(T) 050 321250.
Contact/s
Trainer: Mr P Hughes
Profile Trainer. Ref: YH05148

FENNS FARM

Fenns Farm Riding & Livery Centre, Hunters Lodge, Fenns Farm, Fenns Lane, West End, Woking, **Surrey**, GU24 9QF, **ENGLAND**.
(T) 01483 797349.
Profile Riding School, Stable/Livery. Ref: YH05149

FENNSMITH, TONY

Tony Fennsmith, Market Fields, Kilkhampton, **Cornwall**, EX23 9QZ, **ENGLAND**.
(T) 01288 321777.
Profile Supplies. Ref: YH05150

FENTON

Messrs Fenton, Mains Of Duncrub, Dunning, **Perth and Kinross**, PH2 0QN, **SCOTLAND**.
(T) 01764 684700.
Profile Breeder. Ref: YH05151

FENTON FABRICATION

Fenton Fabrication, Lindifferon Farm, Ladybank, Cupar, **Fife**, KY15 7RX, **SCOTLAND**.
(T) 01337 810740.
Profile Blacksmith. Ref: YH05152

FENTON, PETER H

Peter H Fenton AFCL, Club Cottage, Top Rd, Arundel, **Sussex (West)**, BN18 0RP, **ENGLAND**.
(T) 01243 814492.
Profile Farrier. Ref: YH05153

FENWICK MOBILE EXHIBITIONS

Fenwick Mobile Exhibitions Ltd, Fenwick Bypass, Fenwick, Kilmarnock, **Ayrshire (East)**, KA3 6AW, **SCOTLAND**.
(T) 01560 600271 (F) 01560 600472.
Contact/s
Owner: Mr R MacGillivray
Profile Transport/Horse Boxes.
Hire, sell, service and repair horseboxes and trailers.
Opening Times
Sp: Open Mon - Fri 09:00. Closed Mon - Fri 17:00.
Su: Open Mon - Fri 09:00. Closed Mon - Fri 17:00.
Au: Open Mon - Fri 09:00. Closed Mon - Fri 17:00.
Wn: Open Mon - Fri 09:00. Closed Mon - Fri 17:00.
Ref: YH05154

FENWICK, S H

Mrs S H Fenwick, Lane End Hse, Eshton, Skipton, **Yorkshire (North)**, BD23 3QE, **ENGLAND**.
(T) 01756 749827.
Profile Breeder. Ref: YH05155

FENWICK, W J GODDARD

W J Goddard Fenwick, Cilyblaidd Manor, The Cilyblaidd Est, Pencarreg, Lampeter, **Carmarthenshire**, SA40 9QL, **WALES**.
(T) 01570 480090 (F) 01570 480012
(M) 07702 090906.
Contact/s
Owner: Mr W Goddard-Fenwick
Profile Club/Association. Ref: YH05156

FENWOLD VETNRY GRP

Fenwold Veterinary Group, Boston Rd, Spilsby, **Lincolnshire**, PE23 5HD, **ENGLAND**.
(T) 01790 752227.
Profile Medical Support. Ref: YH05157

FERENS, CUMMING & CORNISH

Ferens, Cumming & Cornish, Veterinary Surgery, Victoria Rd, Bicester, **Oxfordshire**, OX6 7PJ, **ENGLAND**.
(T) 01869 252077.
Profile Medical Support. Ref: YH05158

FERGUSHILL RIDING STABLES

Fergushill Riding Stables, Broomhill Farm, Fergushill, Kilwinning, **Ayrshire (North)**, KA13 7RF, **SCOTLAND**.
(T) 01294 552259
Affiliated Bodies RDA.
Contact/s
Owner: Mrs E Aitken
Profile Riding School.
Fergushill is a family run business. Limited one-to-one training is available. Children are taught from aged four and upwards. Games nights and competitions are also held. Yr. Est: 1964
Opening Times
Sp: Open Mon - Fri 18:00, Sat, Sun 09:00. Closed Mon - Fri 20:00, Sat, Sun 15:00.
Su: Open Mon - Fri 18:00, Sat, Sun 09:00. Closed Mon - Fri 20:00, Sat, Sun 15:00.
Au: Open Mon - Fri 18:00, Sat, Sun 09:00. Closed Mon - Fri 20:00, Sat, Sun 15:00.
Wn: Open Mon - Fri 18:00, Sat, Sun 09:00. Closed Mon - Fri 20:00, Sat, Sun 15:00. Ref: YH05159

FERMANAGH HARRIERS

Fermanagh Harriers Branch of the Pony Club, The Laurels, Moneykee, Irvinestown, Enniskillen, **County Fermanagh**, BT94 1FZ, **NORTHERN IRELAND**.
(T) 028 68621471.
Contact/s
Key Contact: Mrs I Thompson
Profile Club/Association. Ref: YH05160

FERN BANK RIDING SCHOOL

Fern Bank Riding School, Fern Bank, Carr Lane, Roughton, Norwich, **Norfolk**, NR11 8PG, **ENGLAND**.
(T) 01263 512796.
Contact/s
Partner: Mr J Fabb
Profile Riding School. Ref: YH05161

FERNDALE FARM SUPPLIES

Ferndale Farm Supplies, Stubbings Farm, The Ling, Garboldisham, Diss, **Norfolk**, IP22 2SW, **ENGLAND**.
(T) 01953 688200 (F) 01953 681577.
Profile Supplies. Ref: YH05162

FERNEYHOUGH, R J & OLIVER, A M

R J Ferneyhough & A M Oliver, Cross Farm, Colethrop, Stonehouse, **Gloucestershire**, GL10 3EW, **ENGLAND**.
(T) 01452 721405.
Profile Trainer. Ref: YH05163

FERNIE HUNT STABLES

Fernie Hunt Stables (The), Nether Green, Great Bowden, Market Harborough, **Leicestershire**, LE16 7HF, **ENGLAND**.
(T) 01858 462497. Ref: YH05164

FERNIE, A

A Fernie, 47 Norton Ave, Norton, **Cleveland**, TS20 2JR, **ENGLAND**.
(T) 01642 550669.
Profile Farrier. Ref: YH05165

FERNIEHAUGH LIVERY STABLES

Ferniehaugh Livery Stables, Ferniehaugh Est, Dolphinton, West Linton, Penicuik, **Lothian (West)**, EH46 7HJ, **SCOTLAND**.
(T) 01968 682332
(M) 07811 234168.
Profile Stable/Livery.
All weather floodlit school. 11 boxes and over 30 acres of all year turnout. Ref: YH05166

FERNIEHIRST MILL RIDING CTRE

Ferniehirst Mill Riding Centre, Ferniehirst Mill, Jedburgh, **Scottish Borders**, TD8 6PQ, **SCOTLAND**.
(T) 01835 863279 (F) 01835 863279
(E) ferniehirstmill@aol.com.
Contact/s
Owner: Mr A Swanson
Profile Horse/Rider Accom, Riding School.
No.Staff: 2 Yr. Est: 1971 C.Size: 25 Acres
Ref: YH05167

FERNLEA

Fernlea, Park Hill, Ipplepen, Newton Abbot, **Devon**, TQ12 5TU, **ENGLAND**.
(T) 01803 812328.
Profile Stable/Livery. Ref: YH05168

FERRIE, J & A

J & A Ferrie, The Smithy, High St, Newmilns,

Ayrshire (East), KA16 9EE, SCOTLAND.
(T) 01560 323002 (F) 01560 322382
(E) sales@j-aferrie.com
(W) www.j-aferrie.com
Affiliated Bodies WCF.
Contact/s
Partner: Mr A Ferrie (Q) FWCF, RSS
Profile Farrier. Farrier Retailers.
Shoeing of a variety of horses including games ponies, top eventers, show jumpers, hunters and dressage horses. Farrier supply business for any equipment, tools etc, these can be ordered online. There is also a tack shop for both the horse and rider, ranging from riding wear to rugs etc. No.Staff: 12
Opening Times
Sp: Open 08:00. Closed 17:30.
Su: Open 08:00. Closed 17:30.
Au: Open 08:00. Closed 17:30.
Wn: Open 08:00. Closed 17:30. Ref: YH05169

FERRIE, J C

J C Ferrie, 1 Norris St, Creetown, Newton Stewart, **Dumfries and Galloway**, DG8 7JL, **SCOTLAND**.
(T) 01671 820586.
Profile Farrier. Ref: YH05170

FERRING COUNTRY CTRE

Ferring Country Centre Riding Therapy Unit, Rife Way, Ferring, Worthing, **Sussex (West)**, BN12 5JZ, **ENGLAND**.
(T) 01903 245078.
Profile Equestrian Centre.
Farring Country offers riding instruction for the disabled, at minimum cost. This activity promotes improved balance, co-ordination and confidence.
Opening Times
Riding therapy is available seven days a week.
Ref: YH05171

FERRY FARM LIVERY YARD

Ferry Farm Livery Yard, Ferry Farm, Ferry Rd, Woodbastwick, Norwich, **Norfolk**, NR13 6HN, **ENGLAND**.
(T) 01603 721794.
Contact/s
Partner: Miss V Hill
Profile Stable/Livery. Ref: YH05172

FETHERSTON-GODLEY, M J

M J Fetherston-Godley, Kennet Hse, Broad St, East Ilsley, Newbury, **Berkshire**, RG20 7LW, **ENGLAND**.
(T) 01635 281250.
Profile Trainer. Ref: YH05173

FEU, DIANA DU

Mrs Diana Du Feu, Sedgecroft, Hawkchurch, Axminster, **Devon**, EX13 5XB, **ENGLAND**.
(T) 01297 678267.
Profile Breeder. Ref: YH05174

FFITCH-HEYES, J

J Ffitch-Heyes, County Stables, The Old Racecourse, Lewes, **Sussex (East)**, BN7 1UR, **ENGLAND**.
(T) 01273 480804.
Profile Trainer. Ref: YH05175

FFOOKS FLAGS

Ffooks Flags, 14 Little Dippers, Pulborough, **Sussex (West)**, RH20 2DB, **ENGLAND**.
(T) 01798 872888. Ref: YH05176

FFORDD GYRAITH LIVERY STABLES

Ffordd Gyraith Livery Stables, Ffordd Y Gyraith Farm, Cefn Cribwr, **Bridgend**, CF33 4PE, **WALES**.
(T) 01656 743983.
Profile Stable/Livery. Ref: YH05177

FFOREST UCHAF

Fforest Uchaf Horse & Pony Rehabilitation Centre, Maendy Rd, Penycoedcae, Pontypridd, **Rhondda Cynon Taff**, CF37 1PS, **WALES**.
(T) 01443 480327 (F) 01443 400110
(W) www.pitponies.co.uk.
Contact/s
Trustee: Roy Peckham
Profile Medical Support.
Provides a safe haven and tender loving care for horses and ponies who have suffered through neglect, ignorance or cruelty. A registered charity.
Ref: YH05178

FFOSLAS STUD

Ffoslas Stud, Bwlchllan, Lampeter, **Ceredigion**, SR48 8KH, **WALES**.
(T) 01974 821276.
Profile Breeder. Ref: YH05179

FFYNNOCYLL

Ffynnocyll, Hazelwell Farm, Cliffig, Whitland, **Carmarthenshire**, SA34 0LY, **WALES**.
(T) 01994 240879.
Profile Equestrian Centre. Ref: YH05180

FIELD

Field (The), King's Reach Tower, London, **London (Greater)**, SE1 9LS, **ENGLAND**.
(T) 020 72615198 (F) 020 72615358.
Profile Supplies. Ref: YH05181

FIELD & FARM SADDLERS

Field & Farm Saddlers, Newton Morrell Farm, Newton Morrell, Bicester, **Oxfordshire**, OX6 9AG, **ENGLAND**.
(T) 01280 848048.
Contact/s
Owner: Mr P Ray
Profile Saddlery Retailer. Ref: YH05182

FIELD BOTTOM RIDING STABLES

Field Bottom Riding Stables, Lower Shelf, Halifax, **Yorkshire (West)**, HX3 7SA, **ENGLAND**.
(T) 01422 201659.
Profile Riding School. Ref: YH05183

FIELD FARM

Field Farm Stables Riding Centre, The Field, Shipley, Heanor, **Derbyshire**, DE75 7JH, **ENGLAND**.
(T) 01773 713164.
Contact/s
Owner: Mrs G Barker
Profile Stable/Livery. Ref: YH05184

FIELD GALLERIES

Field Galleries Ltd, Low Hollins, Holm Cl, Woodham, Addlestone, **Surrey**, KT15 3QN, **ENGLAND**.
(T) 01932 342055 (F) 01932 342055
(E) info@field-galleries.co.uk.
Contact/s
Artist: Sue Wingate
Profile Art Gallery. Ref: YH05185

FIELD SPORTS

Field Sports, 99 Hartforde Rd, Borehamwood, **Hertfordshire**, WD6 5HY, **ENGLAND**.
(T) 020 82071300.
Contact/s
Owner: Mrs M Evans
Profile Riding Wear Retailer, Saddlery Retailer.
Ref: YH05186

FIELD, L E

Mrs L E Field, The Breach Farm, Teanford, Tean, **Staffordshire**, ST10 4EW, **ENGLAND**.
(T) 01538 722325.
Profile Breeder. Ref: YH05187

FIELD, LINDSEY

Lindsey Field, 64 New Lane, Croft, Warrington, **Cheshire**, WA3 7LW, **ENGLAND**.
(T) 01925 765851 (F) 01925 765851
(M) 07774 298452.
Profile Transport/Horse Boxes. Ref: YH05188

FIELD, MICHAEL P

Michael P Field, Littlebridge Hse, Barford St Michael, **Oxfordshire**, OX5 4RF, **ENGLAND**.
(T) 01869 338820.
Profile Medical Support. Ref: YH05189

FIELDER & JONES

Fielder & Jones, 10 Oxford St, Malmesbury, **Wiltshire**, SN16 9AZ, **ENGLAND**.
(T) 01666 822601 (F) 01666 822601.
Contact/s
Owner: Mr A Jones
Profile Art Gallery. Ref: YH05190

FIELDFARE

Fieldfare, 4 Jarvis Cleys, Cheshunt, Waltham Cross, **Hertfordshire**, EN7 6DN, **ENGLAND**.
(T) 01992 639933.
Contact/s
Partner: Mr R Hull
Profile Hay and Straw Merchants. Ref: YH05191

FIELDFARE TRAILERS

Fieldfare Trailers Ltd, Ford Farm, Old Malthouse Lane, Ford, Salisbury, **Wiltshire**, SP4 6DR, **ENGLAND**.
(T) 01980 611853.
Profile Transport/Horse Boxes. Ref: YH05192

FIELDGUARD

Fieldguard Ltd, Norley Farm, Horsham Rd, Cranleigh, **Surrey**, GU6 8EH, **ENGLAND**.
(T) 01483 275182/225224 (F) 01483 275341
(E) info@fieldguard.com
(W) www.fieldguard.com.
Profile Supplies.
Fieldguard supply barrows, shovels and plastics rivets which can be used with their products. Their mats are light and easy to handle, hard wearing, thermally efficient, cost effective and minimally absorbent. The mats can be used for bedding, under beddibedding and padding walls, rubber sheeting is available to cover floors and ramps. Yr. Est: 1984
Opening Times
Sp: Open Mon - Sat 08:30. Closed Mon - Fri 17:00, Sat 12:00.
Su: Open Mon - Sat 08:30. Closed Mon - Fri 17:00, Sat 12:00.
Au: Open Mon - Sat 08:30. Closed Mon - Fri 17:00, Sat 12:00.
Wn: Open Mon - Sat 08:30. Closed Mon - Fri 17:00, Sat 12:00.
Closed on Sundays. The company operate by mail order Ref: YH05193

FIELDHOUSE SADDLERY

Fieldhouse Saddlery Ltd, Unit 3/4, Green Lane, Birchills, Walsall, **Midlands (West)**, WS2 8LE, **ENGLAND**.
(T) 01922 638094 (F) 01922 622921.
Profile Saddlery Retailer. Ref: YH05194

FIELDING, M

M Fielding, 176/178 Chickerell Rd, Weymouth, **Dorset**, DT4 0QR, **ENGLAND**.
(T) 01305 784197.
Contact/s
Partner: Mr M Fielding
Profile Medical Support. Ref: YH05195

FIELDINGS EQUESTRIAN CTRE

Fieldings Equestrian Centre, Hens Nest Rd, East Whitburn, Bathgate, **Lothian (West)**, EH47 8EX, **SCOTLAND**.
(T) 01501 745986 (F) 01501 745683.
Contact/s
Owner: Mrs F Simpson
Profile Equestrian Centre. Ref: YH05196

FIELDWICK, T A

T A Fieldwick, Sackvile, Cowbeech, Hailsham, **Sussex (East)**, BN27 4JJ, **ENGLAND**.
(T) 01435 830540.
Contact/s
Owner: Mr T Fieldwick
Profile Breeder.
Breeder of Welsh Section C ponies Ref: YH05197

FIELDWICK, TIMOTHY

Timothy Fieldwick RSS, The Hollies, Three Leg Cross, Ticehurst, Wadhurst, **Sussex (East)**, TN5 7HL, **ENGLAND**.
(T) 01580 201167.
Profile Farrier. Ref: YH05198

FIESTA ROSETTES & TROPHIES

Fiesta Rosettes & Trophies, Unit 4, Vulcan Hse, Vulcan Rd, Norwich, **Norfolk**, NR6 6AQ, **ENGLAND**.
(T) 01603 426179 (F) 01603 410638.
Profile Supplies. Ref: YH05199

FIFE AGRICULTURAL ASS

Fife Agricultural Association, Chesterhill, Boarhills, St Andrews, **Fife**, KY16 8PP, **SCOTLAND**.
(T) 01334 880518.
Contact/s
Treasurer: Ms L Roger
Profile Club/Association.
Agricultural show with showing and show jumping classes. Ref: YH05200

FIFE FOXHOUNDS

Fife Foxhounds, Balcormo Mains, Leven, **Fife**, KY8 5QF, **SCOTLAND**.
(T) 01333 360229 (F) 01333 360540. Ref: YH05201

FIFE RIDING CLUB

Fife Riding Club, 16 Aboyne Gardens, Kirkcaldy, **Fife**, KY2 6EL, **SCOTLAND**.
(T) 01592 200430 (F) 01383 739714.
Profile Club/Association, Riding Club. Ref: YH05202

FILLINGHAM, T & P

T & P Fillingham, Stockham Pk, Chillybridge, Dulverton, **Somerset**, TA22 9JH, **ENGLAND**.
(T) 01398 323145.
Contact/s
Owner: Mr T Fillingham
Profile Breeder.
Breeder of Welsh Section B ponies Ref: YH05203

FILMSTONE FARM

Filmstone Farm, Narberth, **Pembrokeshire**, SA67 8AG, **WALES**.
(T) 01834 860518 (F) 01834 860518.
Contact/s
Owner: Mrs V Bradley (Q) BHSAI
(E) val.bradley@talk21.com
Profile Breeder, Stable/Livery, Trainer.
As well as breaking the following services are available: starting, rehabilitation, convalescence & retraining. No.Staff: 2 Yr. Est: 1976 C.Size: 21 Acres Ref: YH05204

FILTON CLGE

Filton College, Filton Ave, Bristol, **Bristol**, BS34 7AT, **ENGLAND**.
(T) 01179 312121 (F) 01179 312244
(W) www.filton-college.ac.uk.
Contact/s
Course Subject Manager: Mrs G Hannam
Profile Equestrian Centre. College.
BTEC National Certificate/ National Diploma/ First Diploma in Horse Management courses available.
Opening Times
Sp: Open Mon - Fri 08:00. Closed Mon - Thurs 21:00, Fri 16:45.
Su: Open Mon - Fri 08:00. Closed Mon - Thurs 21:00, Fri 16:45.
Au: Open Mon - Fri 08:00. Closed Mon - Thurs 21:00, Fri 16:45.
Wn: Open Mon - Fri 08:00. Closed Mon - Thurs 21:00, Fri 16:45. Ref: YH05205

FINANCIAL OMBUDSMAN SV

Financial Ombudsman Service (The), South Quay Plaza, 183 Marsh Wall, London, **London (Greater)**, E14 9SR, **ENGLAND**.
(T) 020 79641000/08450801800 (F) 020 79641001
(E) enquires@financial-ombudsman.org.uk
(W) www.financial-ombudsman.org.uk.
Profile Club/Association.
Provides customers with a free, independant service for resolving disputes about personnal finance matters, eg: insurance. Ref: YH05206

FINCH, A C & J J

A C & J J Finch, Cerrynt, Penmynydd Rd, Llangefni, **Isle of Anglesey**, LL77 7HR, **WALES**.
(T) 01248 750255 (F) 01248 722551.
Profile Medical Support. Ref: YH05207

FINCH, PAUL J

Paul J Finch DWCF, 4 Elm Pl, Worcester Rd, Harvington, Kidderminster, **Worcestershire**, DY10 4LU, **ENGLAND**.
(T) 07976 256775.
Profile Farrier. Ref: YH05208

FINDEISEN, M S

M S Findeisen, Whittington Mill, Great Whittington, Newcastle-upon-Tyne, **Tyne and Wear**, NE19 2HU, **ENGLAND**.
(T) 01434 672264.
Contact/s
Owner: Mr M Findeisen
Profile Riding School. Ref: YH05209

FINDON, EDWARD

Edward Findon DWCF, 72 St Phillips Rd, Newmarket, **Suffolk**, CB8 0EN, **ENGLAND**.
(T) 01638 560839.
Profile Farrier. Ref: YH05210

FINE ENGLISH BRIDLES

Fine English Bridles, Unit 2 Mayfield Workshops, 19 Wednesbury Rd, Walsall, **Midlands (West)**, WS1 3RU, **ENGLAND**.
(T) 01922 722033.
Profile Supplies. Bridle Workshop. Ref: YH05211

FININGS FARM LIVERY YARD

Finings Farm Livery Yard, Finings Lane, Lane End, High Wycombe, **Buckinghamshire**, HP14 3LP, **ENGLAND**.
(T) 01494 882156.
Contact/s
Owner: Mrs M Hebbourn
Profile Stable/Livery. Ref: YH05212

FINLAKE RIDING CTRE

Finlake Riding Centre, Chudleigh, Newton Abbot, **Devon**, TQ13 0EH, **ENGLAND**.
(T) 01626 852096.
Contact/s
Owner: Miss J Battams
Profile Equestrian Centre. Ref: YH05213

FINLOW HILL STABLES

Finlow Hill Stables, Finlow Hill Lane, Over Alderley, Macclesfield, **Cheshire**, SK10 4UG, **ENGLAND**.
(T) 01625 585470.
Profile Riding School, Stable/Livery. Ref: YH05214

FINN VALLEY RIDING CLUB

Finn Valley Riding Club, 8 The Queech, Capel St Mary, Ipswich, **Suffolk**, IP9 2UH, **ENGLAND**.
(T) 01394 270688.
Contact/s
Chairman: Mr A Smith
Profile Club/Association, Riding Club. Ref: YH05215

FINNEY, LIZ

Mrs Liz Finney, Manor Lodge, Ollerton, Knutsford, **Cheshire**, WA16 8RF, **ENGLAND**.
(T) 01565 633310 (F) 01565 632461. Ref: YH05216

FINNINGLEY LIVERY CTRE

Finningley Livery Centre, Old Bawtry Rd, Finningley, Doncaster, **Yorkshire (South)**, DN9 3BU, **ENGLAND**.
(T) 01302 771259 (F) 01302 773021.
Contact/s
Owner: Mrs J Cartwright
Profile Stable/Livery.
Full, part, DIY, stable and grass livery available. Telephone for further price information No.Staff: 2 Yr. Est: 1966 C.Size: 100 Acres
Opening Times
Sp: Open Mon - Sun 08:00. Closed Mon - Sun 19:00.
Su: Open Mon - Sun 08:00. Closed Mon - Sun 19:00.
Au: Open Mon - Sun 08:00. Closed Mon - Sun 19:00.
Wn: Open Mon - Sun 08:00. Closed Mon - Sun 19:00.
Answer phone service available Ref: YH05217

FINWOOD BARN

Finwood Barn, Finwood Rd, Rowington, Warwick, **Warwickshire**, CV35 7DL, **ENGLAND**.
(T) 01564 785104.
Contact/s
Owner: Mrs A Howkes
Profile Stable/Livery. Ref: YH05218

FIR TREE FARM

Fir Tree Farm, Fir Tree Farm, Ogdens, Fordingbridge, **Hampshire**, SP6 2PY, **ENGLAND**.
(T) 01425 654744.
Contact/s
Owner: Mrs J Simmons
Profile Riding School, Stable/Livery, Trainer.
Ref: YH05219

FIR TREE FARM EQUESTRIAN CTRE

Fir Tree Farm Equestrian Centre, Fir Tree Farm, Trumfleet Lane, Moss, Doncaster, **Yorkshire (South)**, DN6 0EB, **ENGLAND**.
(T) 01302 700574.
Profile Equestrian Centre. Ref: YH05220

FIR TREE RIDING CTRE

Fir Tree Riding Centre, Fir Tree Lane, Aughton, Ormskirk, **Lancashire**, L39 7HH, **ENGLAND**.
(T) 01695 423655.
Contact/s
Owner: Miss L Temme
Profile Equestrian Centre. Ref: YH05221

FIRBECK

Firbeck Equestrian Training Centre, Steetley, Worksop, **Nottinghamshire**, S80 3DZ, **ENGLAND**.
(T) 01909 720259 (F) 01909 720259
(M) 07775 912202
(E) annebondi@hotmail.com.
Profile Stable/Livery, Trainer. Ref: YH05222

FIRE ART

Fire Art, Powderham Pk, Powderham, Exeter, **Devon**, EX6 8JQ, **ENGLAND**.
(T) 01626 890997 (F) 01626 890997.
Contact/s
Owner: Mr P Gilbert
Profile Blacksmith. Ref: YH05223

FIRECRAFT

Firecraft, Catbrain Quarry, Painswick Beacon, Painswick, Stroud, **Gloucestershire**, GL6 6SU, **ENGLAND**.
(T) 01452 812589 (F) 01452 812589.
Contact/s
Owner: Mr R Overs
Profile Blacksmith. Ref: YH05224

FIRGO FARM CROSS CTRY COURSE

UK Chasers, Firgo Farm, Tufton, Whitchurch, **Hampshire**, RG28 7RE, **ENGLAND**.
(T) 01264 720863.
Profile Track/Course. Ref: YH05225

FIRS FARM EQUESTRIAN CTRE

Firs Farm Equestrian Centre, Woodside Lane, Hatfield, **Hertfordshire**, AL9 6DE, **ENGLAND**.
(T) 01707 662524.
Contact/s
Manager: Ms W Hayes
Profile Equestrian Centre. Ref: YH05226

FIRS VETNRY SURGERY

Firs Veterinary Surgery (The), 21 The Firs, Combe Down, Bath, **Bath & Somerset (North East)**, BA2 5ED, **ENGLAND**.
(T) 01225 832521 (F) 01225 835265.
Profile Medical Support. Ref: YH05227

FIRSEDGE

Firsedge Dartmoors, The Elms, Black Torrington, Beaworthy, **Devon**, EX21 5QD, **ENGLAND**.
(T) 01409 231285
(M) 07818 006081
(W) www.wendy.firsedge.btinternet.co.uk.
Contact/s
Key Contact: Jennifer Bridges
Profile Breeder.
Opening Times
Telephone for an appointment Ref: YH05228

FIRST ARTIST CORPORATION

First Artist Corporation, 87 Wembley Hill Rd, Wembley, **London (Greater)**, HA9 8BU, **ENGLAND**.
(T) 020 89001818 (F) 020 89032964.
Contact/s
Chairman: Jon Smith
Profile Club/Association. Ref: YH05229

FIRST EQUINE FINANCE

First Equine Finance, 179 Vauxhall Bridge Rd, London, **London (Greater)**, SW1V 1ER, **ENGLAND**.
(T) 020 78341111 (F) 020 78342244.
Profile Club/Association. Ref: YH05230

FIRTH RIXSON FORGINGS

Firth Rixson Forgings, Dale Rd North, Darley Dale, Matlock, **Derbyshire**, DE4 2JB, **ENGLAND**.
(T) 01629 733621.
Profile Blacksmith. Ref: YH05231

FIRTH VETNRY CTRE

Firth Veterinary Centre, 5 Ednam St, Annan, **Dumfries and Galloway**, DG12 6EF, **SCOTLAND**.
(T) 01461 202420 (F) 01461 201543.
Profile Medical Support. Ref: YH05232

FIRTH, ARTHUR

Arthur Firth, Wharf St, Dewsbury, **Yorkshire (West)**, WF12 9AT, **ENGLAND**.
(T) 01924 461722.
Profile Blacksmith. Ref: YH05233

FIRTH, IAN J

Ian J Firth DWCF, 32 Spa St, Ossett, **Yorkshire (West)**, WF5 0HJ, **ENGLAND**.
(T) 01924 270621.
Contact/s
Farrier: Ian J Firth (Q) DWCF
Profile Farrier. Ref: YH05234

FIRWOOD COURT STUD

Firwood Court Stud & Equestrian Centre, Bullockstone Rd, Herne Bay, **Kent**, CT6 7NN, **ENGLAND**.
(T) 01227 749404.
Contact/s
Manager: Mrs J Pritchard
Profile Breeder, Equestrian Centre, Stud Farm.
Ref: YH05235

FISHER FOUNDRIES

Fisher Foundries Ltd, Albion Rd, Greet, Birmingham, **Midlands (West)**, B11 2PB, **ENGLAND**.
(T) 0121 6240197 (F) 0121 6241242.
Contact/s
Owner: Mr H Groom
Profile Supplies. Ref: YH05236

FISHER, ANN

Ann Fisher, Lyndhurst, Four Winds, Bodmin, **Cornwall**, PL30 4HJ, **ENGLAND**.
(T) 01208 821294.
Contact/s
Owner: Mrs A Fisher

Profile Transport/Horse Boxes. **Ref: YH05237**

FISHER, ANNA

Anna Fisher, Owler Carr Farm, Eckington Rd, Coal Aston, Sheffield, **Yorkshire (South)**, S18 6BA, **ENGLAND**..
Profile Breeder. **Ref: YH05238**

FISHER, E P

Mrs E P Fisher, Sunnymeade, Houghton Lane, Sancton, **Yorkshire (East)**, YO43 4QX, **ENGLAND**.
(T) 01430 827236.
Profile Breeder. **Ref: YH05239**

FISHER, J T

Mr J T Fisher, Holme Pk Farm, Sonning, Reading, **Berkshire**, RG4 0SX, **ENGLAND**.
(T) 0118 9693485 **(F)** 0118 9693485
(M) 07785 296345.
Profile Breeder. **Ref: YH05240**

FISHER, R F

R F Fisher, Great Head Hse, Priory Rd, Ulverston, **Cumbria**, LA12 9RX, **ENGLAND**.
(T) 01229 585664.
Profile Trainer. **Ref: YH05241**

FISHER, STEPHEN R

Stephen R Fisher DWCF, Nutley Dell, High St, Nutley, **Sussex (East)**, TN22 3HE, **ENGLAND**.
(T) 01825 713387.
Profile Farrier. **Ref: YH05242**

FISHER, TONY P

Tony P Fisher DWCF, 7 Colin Cl, Shirley, Croydon, **Surrey**, CR0 8QD, **ENGLAND**.
(T) 020 87773126.
Profile Farrier. **Ref: YH05243**

FISHWICKS HORSEBOXES

Fishwicks Horseboxes, Longshaw Head Farm, Crowthorn Rd, Turton, Bolton, **Manchester (Greater)**, BL7 0JX, **ENGLAND**.
(T) 01204 852400.
Profile Transport/Horse Boxes. **Ref: YH05244**

FITT, MICHAEL

Michael Fitt, Fir Covert Rd, Felthorpe, Norwich, **Norfolk**, NR10 4DT, **ENGLAND**.
(T) 01603 868897 **(F)** 01603 868897.
Contact/s
Owner: Mr M Fitt
Profile Blacksmith. **Ref: YH05245**

FITTOCKS STUD

Fittocks Stud, High St, Cheveley, Newmarket, **Suffolk**, CB8 9DG, **ENGLAND**.
(T) 01638 730063.
Profile Breeder. **Ref: YH05246**

FITZGERALD, J G

J G Fitzgerald, Norton Grange, Pk Rd, Norton, Malton, **Yorkshire (North)**, YO17 9EA, **ENGLAND**.
(T) 01653 692718 **(F)** 01653 600214.
Contact/s
Owner: Mr J Fitzgerald
Profile Trainer. **Ref: YH05247**

FITZPATRICK, JAMES B

James B Fitzpatrick AFCL, Crosswinds, Llanddona, Beaumaris, **Isle of Anglesey**, LL58 8TW, **WALES**.
(T) 01248 811009.
Profile Farrier. **Ref: YH05248**

FITZROY TRAILERS

Fitzroy Trailers, Riverside Works, Bells Marsh Rd, Gorleston, Great Yarmouth, **Norfolk**, NR31 6QN, **ENGLAND**.
(T) 01493 655900.
Contact/s
Owner: Mr G Tovey
Profile Transport/Horse Boxes. **Ref: YH05249**

FITZSIMMONS, S & G

S & G Fitzsimmons, Crynmerlyn Ponies, Vendanwin, Low Rd, Wyberton, Boston, **Lincolnshire**, PE21 7AP, **ENGLAND**.
(T) 01205 361630.
Profile Breeder. **Ref: YH05250**

FITZWORTHY RIDING

Fitzworthy Riding, Fitzworthy, Cornwood, Ivybridge, **Devon**, PL21 9PH, **ENGLAND**.
(T) 01752 837836.
Contact/s
Owner: Mrs J Wilson
Profile Riding School. **Ref: YH05251**

FIVE HORSES

Five Horses Ltd, Stock, Gillingham, **Dorset**, SP8 5NR, **ENGLAND**.
(T) 01747 824566 **(F)** 01747 824566.
Contact/s
Manager: Mr I Fairbairn
Profile Breeder. **Ref: YH05252**

FIVE OAK GREEN STUD

Five Oak Green Stud, Whetsted Rd, Five Oak Green, Tonbridge, **Kent**, TN12 6RT, **ENGLAND**.
(T) 01892 836116.
Profile Breeder. **Ref: YH05253**

FIVE OAKS EQUESTRIAN CTRE

Five Oaks Equestrian Centre, Layhams Rd, Keston, **Kent**, BR2 6AR, **ENGLAND**.
(T) 01959 571856.
Contact/s
Owner: Mrs W Neil
Profile Equestrian Centre, Riding School, Stable/Livery. **Ref: YH05254**

FIVE SAINTS

Five Saints Riding & Trekking Centre, Gilfach Farm, Pumpsaint, Llanwrda, **Carmarthenshire**, SA19 8YN, **WALES**.
(T) 01558 650580.
Contact/s
Owner: Ms N Omar
Profile Equestrian Centre. Trekking Centre.
Ref: YH05255

FIVE SQUARE MOTORS

Five Square Motors Ltd, Salisbury Rd, Shaftesbury, **Dorset**, SP7 8BU, **ENGLAND**.
(T) 01747 852295.
Profile Transport/Horse Boxes. **Ref: YH05256**

FJORD HORSE REGISTRY

Fjord Horse Registry of Scotland (The), South Denhill, St Katherines, Inverurie, **Aberdeenshire**, AB51 8SU, **SCOTLAND**.
(T) 01651 891712
(E) fhrs@fdn.co.uk.
Contact/s
Key Contact: Mr D Stewart
Profile Club/Association. **Ref: YH05257**

FJORD HORSE SOC

Fjord Horse National Stud Book Association of GB, National Fjord Horse Ctre, Cilyblaidd Manor, Cilyblaidd Est, Pencarreg, Lampeter, **Carmarthenshire**, SA40 9QL, **WALES**.
(T) 01570 480090 **(F)** 01570 480012
(M) 07702 090906
(E) info@fjord-horse.co.uk
(W) www.fjord-horse.co.uk.
Contact/s
Key Contact: Miss L Moran
Profile Club/Association. **Ref: YH05258**

FLAGSTAFF STABLES

Flagstaff Stables, Sarum Rd, Winchester, **Hampshire**, SO22 5QT, **ENGLAND**.
(T) 01962 854051.
Contact/s
Owner: Mrs W Parkhurst
Profile Stable/Livery. **Ref: YH05259**

FLAMSTEAD HORSE LIVERY

Flamstead Horse Livery, Flamstead Farm, Chesham Rd, Ashley Green, Chesham, **Buckinghamshire**, HP5 3PH, **ENGLAND**.
(T) 01494 791362 **(F)** 01494 791946.
Contact/s
Owner: Mr T Robins-Brown
Profile Stable/Livery. **Ref: YH05260**

FLAT RACE JOCKEYS

Flat Race Jockeys' Valets Association of GB, West Hall, Kirby Hill, Richmond, **Yorkshire (North)**, DL11 7JH, **ENGLAND**.
(T) 01748 823939.
Contact/s
Secretary: Mr P Kingsley
Profile Club/Association. **Ref: YH05261**

FLATCHLEY FORGE

Flatchley Forge, The Forge, Flaxley, Newnham, **Gloucestershire**, GL14 1JR, **ENGLAND**.
(T) 01452 760245 **(F)** 01452 760245.
Contact/s
Owner: Mr J Watts
Profile Blacksmith. **Ref: YH05262**

FLATMOBILE

Flatmobile Ltd, Hogtrough Farm, Watchet Lane, Little Kingshill, Great Missenden, **Buckinghamshire**, HP16 0DR, **ENGLAND**.
(T) 01494 862581.
Profile Transport/Horse Boxes. **Ref: YH05263**

FLATTERS, B

B Flatters, 8 Church St, Baston, Peterborough, **Cambridgeshire**, PE6 9PE, **ENGLAND**.
(T) 01778 560316.
Contact/s
Owner: Mr B Flatters
Profile Farrier. **Ref: YH05264**

FLATTERS, MICHAEL J

Michael J Flatters DWCF, 56 St Leonards St, Stamford, **Lincolnshire**, PE9 2HN, **ENGLAND**.
(T) 01780 480087
(M) 07889 163331.
Profile Farrier. **Ref: YH05265**

FLAVIN & VERE

Flavin & Vere, Popes Lane Surgery, Lapford, Crediton, **Devon**, EX17 6PU, **ENGLAND**.
(T) 01363 83317 **(F)** 01363 83455.
Profile Medical Support. **Ref: YH05266**

FLEET, K L

Mrs K L Fleet, Meadowside, 430 Longford Rd, Thornford, Sherborne, **Dorset**, DT9 6QQ, **ENGLAND**.
(T) 01935 872815. **Ref: YH05267**

FLEETMEAD STUD

Fleetmead Stud, Blindley Heath, Lingfield, **Surrey**, RH7 6JX, **ENGLAND**.
(T) 01342 832796.
Profile Breeder. **Ref: YH05268**

FLEETWATER STUD

Fleetwater Stud, Minstead, Lyndhurst, **Hampshire**, SO43 7FY, **ENGLAND**.
(T) 023 80812534.
Profile Breeder, Stable/Livery, Supplies.
Ref: YH05269

FLEMING, BARBARA SLANE

Barbara Slane Fleming FBHS, Cockhall Cottages, Eglingham, Alnwick, **Northumberland**, NE66 2DN, **ENGLAND**.
(T) 01665 578471
(M) 07831 091218.
Profile Trainer. **Ref: YH05270**

FLEMING, J W

J W Fleming, Mill End Farm, Low Rd, Eyke, Woodbridge, **Suffolk**, IP12 2QF, **ENGLAND**.
(T) 01394 460510.
Profile Breeder. **Ref: YH05271**

FLETCHER TOOGOOD

Fletcher Toogood Ltd, St Margarets Farm, Great Brickhill, Milton Keynes, **Buckinghamshire**, MK17 9AY, **ENGLAND**.
(T) 01525 261224.
Profile Stable/Livery. **Ref: YH05272**

FLETCHER TRAILERS

Fletcher Trailers, Tank Bridge Workshop, Forcett, Richmond, **Yorkshire (North)**, DL11 7RZ, **ENGLAND**.
(T) 01325 718238.
Profile Transport/Horse Boxes. **Ref: YH05273**

FLETCHER, DAVID S

David S Fletcher DWCF, Abbeycroft, 77 Segensworth Rd, Titchfield, Fareham, **Hampshire**, PO15 5EA, **ENGLAND**.
(T) 01329 846316.
Profile Farrier. **Ref: YH05274**

FLETCHER, DESMOND EDWARD

Desmond Edward Fletcher RSS, Top Flat, Winson Mill Farm, Winson, Cirencester, **Gloucestershire**, GL7 5EP, **ENGLAND**.
(T) 01285 720380.
Profile Farrier. **Ref: YH05275**

FLETCHER, DOMINIC C

Dominic C Fletcher DWCF, Brynmor Byre, Tophill Farm, Groombridge Hill, **Kent**, TN3 9LY, **ENGLAND**.
(T) 01892 861773.
Profile Farrier. **Ref: YH05276**

FLETCHER, GRAHAM

Mr Graham Fletcher, Foxglade Farm, Woolstone, Farringdon, **Oxfordshire**, SN7 7QL, **ENGLAND**.
(T) 01367 820583.
Profile Trainer. **Ref: YH05277**

FLETCHER, H
Mrs H Fletcher, Ashlea, Prestwick Rd, Dinnington, Newcastle-upon-Tyne, **Tyne and Wear**, NE13 7AG, **ENGLAND**.
(T) 01661 22202.
Profile Breeder. **Ref: YH05278**

FLETCHER, JAN
Jan Fletcher, Livery Yard, Bournfield Farm Liveries, Union Rd, Bradfield, Reading, **Berkshire**, RG7 6AA, **ENGLAND**.
(T) 0118 9744780.
Profile Stable/Livery. **Ref: YH05279**

FLETCHER, KAREN
Karen Fletcher, Buttevant, Carlton Miniott, Thirsk, **Yorkshire (North)**, YO7 4NJ, **ENGLAND**.
(T) 01845 523482.
Profile Trainer. **Ref: YH05280**

FLETTNER VENTILATOR
Flettner Ventilator Limited, 2 Basing Hill, London, **London (Greater)**, NW11 8TH, **ENGLAND**.
(T) 020 84557711 **(F)** 020 84557710
(W) www.flettner.co.uk.
Contact/s
General Manager: Mr J Rouers
(E) sales@flettner.co.uk
Profile Transport/Horse Boxes. Horse Box Ventilation.
Ref: YH05281

FLEXTOL
Flextol Ltd, Cottage Lane Ind Est, Broughton, Astley, **Leicestershire**, LE9 6TU, **ENGLAND**.
(T) 01455 285333 **(F)** 01455 285238
(E) sales@flextol-ltd.demon.co.uk.
Profile Supplies. **Ref: YH05282**

FLIGHT VIEW
Flight View Riding Livery & Stud, Pilling Lane, Preesall, Poulton-Le-Fylde, **Lancashire**, FY6 0HH, **ENGLAND**.
(T) 01253 811777.
Profile Breeder, Stable/Livery, Stud Farm.
Ref: YH05283

FLIMWELL RIDING STABLES
Flimwell Riding Stables, Downash Farm, Rosemary Lane, Flimwell, Wadhurst, **Sussex (East)**, TN5 7PS, **ENGLAND**.
(T) 01580 879619.
Contact/s
Owner: Mr S Poland
Profile Riding School. **Ref: YH05284**

FLINT HALL FEEDS
Flint Hall Feeds, Flint Hall, Newbold Pacey, **Warwickshire**, CV35 9DY, **ENGLAND**.
(T) 01789 470470.
Contact/s
Manager: Mr P Tarver
Profile Feed Merchant. **Ref: YH05285**

FLINT, K M
Miss K M Flint, Thisker Cottage, Thimble Hill, Weston Underwood, **Derbyshire**, DE6 4PE, **ENGLAND**.
(T) 01335 60856.
Profile Breeder. **Ref: YH05286**

FLINTWYK ENGINEERING
Flintwyk Engineering Co, 15 Central Ave, Woodlands, Doncaster, **Yorkshire (South)**, DN6 7RU, **ENGLAND**.
(T) 01302 337947 **(F)** 01302 337947.
Profile Supplies. **Ref: YH05287**

FLOORS STUD
Floors Stud Co, Roxburgh Est, Floors Castle, Kelso, **Scottish Borders**, TD5 7RN, **SCOTLAND**.
(T) 01573 225302.
Profile Breeder. **Ref: YH05288**

FLOWER, M
Mr M Flower, Devonshire Hse, Willingdon Lane, Jevington, **Sussex (East)**, BN26 5QB, **ENGLAND**.
(T) 01323 488771 **(F)** 01323 488099.
Profile Trainer. **Ref: YH05289**

FLUOROCARBON BLOODSTOCK
Fluorocarbon Bloodstock Ltd, Chippenham Lodge, Chippenham, Ely, **Cambridgeshire**, CB7 5PX, **ENGLAND**.
(T) 01638 720705.
Profile Blood Stock Agency, Breeder. **Ref: YH05290**

FLY LAITHE STABLES
Fly Laithe Stables, Pepperhill, Shelf, Halifax, **Yorkshire (West)**, HX3 7TH, **ENGLAND**.
(T) 01274 672010.
Profile Riding School. **Ref: YH05291**

FLYAWAY
Flyaway, Lyne Hill Lane Equestian Ctre, Penkridge, Stafford, **Staffordshire**, ST19 5NT, **ENGLAND**.
(T) 01785 714009.
Profile Equestrian Centre, Supplies. **Ref: YH05292**

FLYING CHANGES
Flying Changes Saddlery & Clothing, Washbrook Farm, Aston Le Walls, Daventry, **Northamptonshire**, NN11 6RT, **ENGLAND**.
(T) 01327 264315 **(F)** 01327 264314.
Profile Riding Wear Retailer, Saddlery Retailer.
Ref: YH05293

FLYING M RANCH
Flying M Ranch, Henfwlch Rd, Carmarthen, **Carmarthenshire**, SA33 6AJ, **WALES**.
(T) 01267 238409.
Profile Horse/Rider Accom. **Ref: YH05294**

FLYING START RIDING CTRE
Flying Start Riding Centre, Parsonage Lane, Kingston St. Mary, Taunton, **Somerset**, TA2 8HL, **ENGLAND**.
(T) 01823 451506.
Contact/s
Partner: Mr S Jackman
Profile Equestrian Centre, Riding School.
Ref: YH05295

FOALE, D
Miss D Foale, Millfield, Street, **Somerset**, BA16 0YD, **ENGLAND**.
(T) 01458 442297 **(F)** 01458 447276.
Profile Trainer. **Ref: YH05296**

FOAMATION PRODUCTS
Foamation Products (Telford), 26 Heath Hill Ind Est, Dawley, Telford, **Shropshire**, TF4 2RH, **ENGLAND**.
(T) 01654 761269. **Ref: YH05297**

FOLKESTONE RACECOURSE
Folkestone Racecourse PLC, C/O Lingfield Park Racecourse, Lingfield, **Surrey**, RH7 6PQ, **ENGLAND**.
(T) 01342 834800 **(F)** 01342 832833.
Profile Track/Course. **Ref: YH05298**

FOLKINGTON MANOR STABLES
Folkington Manor Stables, Folkington, Polegate, **Sussex (East)**, BN26 5SD, **ENGLAND**.
(T) 01323 482437.
Contact/s
Manager: Mr A Saggers
Profile Riding School. **Ref: YH05299**

FOLLIFOOT PK
Follifoot Park Riding Centre, Pannal Rd, Follifoot, Harrogate, **Yorkshire (North)**, HG3 1DL, **ENGLAND**.
(T) 01423 870912 **(F)** 01423 870912
Affiliated Bodies ABRS, BHS.
Contact/s
Farrier: Mr C Pedley
Profile Arena, Equestrian Centre, Farrier, Riding School, Stable/Livery. No.Staff: 3 Yr. Est: 1985
C.Size: 50 Acres **Ref: YH05300**

FOLLY FARM STABLES
Folly Farm Stables, Forest Rd, Little Budworth, Tarporley, **Cheshire**, CW6 9ES, **ENGLAND**.
(T) 01829 760095 **(F)** 01829 760895
(M) 07976 522768.
Profile Trainer. **Ref: YH05301**

FOLLY FOOT FARM
Folly Foot Farm & Equestrian Centre, Lower Rd, Hockley, **Essex**, SS5 5NL, **ENGLAND**.
(T) 01702 232020.
Contact/s
Owner: Mr B Taylor
Profile Equestrian Centre. **Ref: YH05302**

FOLLY FOOT FARM
Folly Foot Farm, Los Pinares, Sandy Lane, Romsey, **Hampshire**, SO51 0PD, **ENGLAND**.
(T) 01794 367660.
Contact/s
Owner: Mrs C Bischof
Profile Riding School. **Ref: YH05303**

FOLLY, CHRISTOPHER C
Christopher C Folly DWCF, Quabbs Farm, Ryton, Dymock, **Gloucestershire**, GL18 2DW, **ENGLAND**.
(T) 01531 890330.
Profile Farrier. **Ref: YH05304**

FOLLYFOOT STABLES
Follyfoot Stables, Willow Pond Farm, Lower Rd, Hockley, **Essex**, SS5 5NL, **ENGLAND**.
(T) 01702 232456.
Contact/s
Manager: Ms L Gill **Ref: YH05305**

FONABY ANIMAL FEEDS
Fonaby Animal Feeds, 113 Brigg Rd, Caistor, **Lincolnshire**, LN7 6RX, **ENGLAND**.
(T) 01472 851115.
Profile Feed Merchant. **Ref: YH05306**

FONSECA, M & A
M & A Fonseca, Harbolets Gardens, Harbolets Rd, West Chiltington, Pulborough, **Sussex (West)**, RH20 2LG, **ENGLAND**.
(T) 01798 812375.
Profile Supplies. **Ref: YH05307**

FONTHILL STUD
Fonthill Stud, Fonthill Stables, Fonthill Gifford, Salisbury, **Wiltshire**, SP3 5RZ, **ENGLAND**.
(T) 01747 870507 **(F)** 01747 871763.
Contact/s
Groom: Mr M Stevenson
Profile Breeder. No.Staff: 5 Yr. Est: 1966
C.Size: 100 Acres
Opening Times
Telephone for an appointment **Ref: YH05308**

FONTWELL PK RACECOURSE
Fontwell Park Racecourse, Sussex Racecourses Mngmt, Fontwell Park Racecourse, Arundel, **Sussex (West)**, BN18 0SX, **ENGLAND**.
(T) 01243 543335 **(F)** 01243 543904
(E) enquiries@fontwellpark.co.uk.
Profile Track/Course. **Ref: YH05309**

FOOT FETISH
Foot Fetish, Jubilee Hse, John O'Gaunt, Melton Mowbray, **Leicestershire**, LE14 2RE, **ENGLAND**.
(T) 01664 454368.
Contact/s
Owner: Mr A Waldron
Profile Supplies. **Ref: YH05310**

FOOT, P B
P B Foot, Riverside, Rolls Mill, Sturminster Newton, **Dorset**, DT10 2HP, **ENGLAND**.
(T) 01258 472302.
Contact/s
Owner: Mr P Foot
Profile Transport/Horse Boxes. **Ref: YH05311**

FOOTE TRANSPORT
Foote Transport, 2 Elmhay Cottages, Middle St, Eastington, Stonehouse, **Gloucestershire**, GL10 3BD, **ENGLAND**.
(T) 01453 822041.
Contact/s
Owner: Mr R Foote
Profile Transport/Horse Boxes. **Ref: YH05312**

FOOTPRINT SADDLERY
Footprint Saddlery, Hobbans Farm, Moreton, Ongar, **Essex**, CM5 0LH, **ENGLAND**.
(T) 01277 890245 **(F)** 01277 890149.
Contact/s
Owner: Mr R Webster
Profile Saddlery Retailer. **Ref: YH05313**

FOR THE RECORD
For The Record Ltd, Puckshott Farm Stables, Weycombe Rd, Haslemere, **Surrey**, GU27 1AA, **ENGLAND**.
(T) 01428 654464 **(F)** 01428 643769.
Contact/s
Partner: Mr C Ashby **Ref: YH05314**

FORAGES, J T
J T Forages, Bull Farm, Glassenbury Rd, Hartley, Cranbrook, **Kent**, TN17 3QE, **ENGLAND**.
(T) 01580 715242 **(F)** 01580 715242.
Profile Hay and Straw Merchants. **Ref: YH05315**

FORBEK FARM
Forbek Farm, Godnow Rd, Crowle, Scunthorpe, **Lincolnshire (North)**, DN17 4EE, **ENGLAND**.
(T) 01724 712152.
Contact/s
Owner: Mrs J Chapman
Profile Training Centre.
BHS and NVQ Qualification Training **Ref: YH05316**

FORBES & SON
Forbes & Son, West Philpstoun Farm, Linlithgow, **Lothian (West)**, EH49 7RY, **SCOTLAND**.

(T) 01506 834209 **(F)** 01506 834209.
Contact/s
Owner: Mr G Forbes
Profile Stable/Livery. **Ref: YH05317**

FORBES COPPER

Forbes Copper, The Old Rectory, Farnham, Blandford, **Dorset**, DT11 8DE, **ENGLAND**.
(T) 01725 516474 **(F)** 01725 516484
(E) forbescopper@compuserve.com.
Profile Medical Support.
Manufacturers of copper chains and pastern straps for the relief of arthitic and injury pain. **Ref: YH05318**

FORBES, A L

Mr A L Forbes, Hill Hse Farm, Poppits Lane, Stramshall, Uttoxeter, **Staffordshire**, ST14 5EX, **ENGLAND**.
(T) 01889 568145 **(F)** 01782 599041.
Profile Trainer. **Ref: YH05319**

FORBES, JANE (LADY)

Lady Jane Forbes, Benevean, Kendoon, Castle Douglas, **Dumfries and Galloway**, DG7 3UB, **SCOTLAND**.
(T) 01644 460626. **Ref: YH05320**

FORBES, JOHN (SIR)

Sir John Forbes, Benevean, Kendoon, Dalry, Castle Douglas, **Dumfries and Galloway**, DG7 3UB, **SCOTLAND**.
(T) 01644 460626. **Ref: YH05321**

FORD CLOSE RIDING CTRE

Ford Close Riding Centre, Brass Castle Lane, Marton-In-Cleveland, Middlesbrough, **Cleveland**, TS8 9EE, **ENGLAND**.
(T) 01642 300257.
Contact/s
Owner: Miss S Ritchie
Profile Riding School. **Ref: YH05322**

FORD FARM STABLES

Ford Farm Stables, Hinton, Chippenham, **Wiltshire**, SN14 8HG, **ENGLAND**.
(T) 01179 372913.
Contact/s
Trainer: Miss A Wilson
Profile Stable/Livery, Trainer. **Ref: YH05323**

FORD, K

K Ford, New Barn Stables, Longfield Ave, Longfield, **Kent**, DA3 7LA, **ENGLAND**.
(T) 01474 706021.
Contact/s
Owner: Miss K Ford **Ref: YH05324**

FORD, NIGEL STEPHEN

Nigel Stephen Ford RSS, The Mount, Gurney Slade, Bath, **Bath & Somerset (North East)**, BA3 4UY, **ENGLAND**.
(T) 01749 840879.
Profile Farrier. **Ref: YH05325**

FORD, ROBIN

Robin Ford, Mainway, The Lizard, Helston, **Cornwall**, TR12 7NZ, **ENGLAND**.
(T) 01326 290755 **(F)** 01326 290755.
Contact/s
Owner: Mr R Ford
Profile Blacksmith. **Ref: YH05326**

FORD, RONALD SIMON

Ronald Simon Ford DWCF BII, Hillside Farm, Malmesbury Rd, Chippenham, **Wiltshire**, SN14 6BG, **ENGLAND**.
(T) 01249 750221.
Profile Farrier. **Ref: YH05327**

FORD, STEWART

Stewart Ford DWCF, 19 Lower Vellow, Williton, Taunton, **Somerset**, TA4 4LS, **ENGLAND**.
(T) 01984 656642.
Profile Farrier. **Ref: YH05328**

FORDBANK EQUE CTRE

Fordbank Eque Centre, Beith Rd, Milliken Pk, Johnstone, **Renfrewshire**, PA10 2NS, **SCOTLAND**.
(T) 01505 705829 **(F)** 01505 702818.
Contact/s
Owner: Mrs E Craig
Profile Riding School, Stable/Livery. **Ref: YH05329**

FOREMAN, DOUGLAS G

Douglas G Foreman AWCF, 1 Kennel Cottage, Hunt Kennels, Laughton Rd, Ringmer, Lewes, **Sussex (East)**, BN8 5NH, **ENGLAND**.
(T) 01273 812650.
Profile Farrier. **Ref: YH05330**

FORENAUGHTS STUD

Forenaughts Stud, Naas, **County Kildare**, **IRELAND**.
(T) 045 875330 **(F)** 045 866393.
Contact/s
Key Contact: Mr D Cantillon
(E) dermotcantillon@tinet.ie
Profile Breeder, Stud Farm. Yr. Est: 1986
Ref: YH05331

FOREST ARENA

Forest Arena, Forest Edge Stud, Drymere, Swaffham, **Norfolk**, PE37 8AS, **ENGLAND**.
(T) 01760 725448 **(F)** 01760 725884.
Profile Equestrian Centre. **Ref: YH05332**

FOREST COUNTRYWEAR

Forest Countrywear, 3 High St, Fordingbridge, **Hampshire**, SP6 1AS, **ENGLAND**.
(T) 01425 655393 **(F)** 01425 655393.
Contact/s
Owner: Mrs S Warden
Profile Saddlery Retailer. **Ref: YH05333**

FOREST EDGE RIDING STABLES

Forest Edge Riding Stables, Oakdene Holiday Pk, St. Leonards, Ringwood, **Hampshire**, BH24 2RZ, **ENGLAND**.
(T) 01202 865625. **Ref: YH05334**

FOREST FARM

Forest Farm Carriage Driving Centre, Barnes Lane, Milford On Sea, **Hampshire**, SO41 0RR, **ENGLAND**.
(T) 01590 644365 **(F)** 01590 644365
(E) driving@ffarm.fsnet.co.uk
(W) www.forestfarmdriving.com.
Contact/s
General Manager: Ms D Butler
Profile Arena, Horse/Rider Accom, Stable/Livery, Trainer.
Carriage driving tuition. No.Staff: 2
Yr. Est: 1992 C.Size: 30 Acres **Ref: YH05335**

FOREST FARM

Forest Farm Riding School & Livery Stables, Winterpit Lane, Mannings Heath, Horsham, **Sussex (West)**, RH13 6LZ, **ENGLAND**.
(T) 01403 251133.
Profile Riding School, Stable/Livery. **Ref: YH05336**

FOREST FEED

Forest Feed, Spa Ct, Spa Lane, Starbeck, Harrogate, **Yorkshire (North)**, HG2 7JF, **ENGLAND**.
(T) 01423 888188.
Profile Feed Merchant. **Ref: YH05337**

FOREST HARNESS

Forest Harness, Skeys Wood, Dowles Rd, Bewdley, **Worcestershire**, DY12 3AF, **ENGLAND**.
(T) 01299 403896.
Profile Supplies. **Ref: YH05338**

FOREST HOUSE VETNRY GRP

Forest House Veterinary Group, The Vetnry Hospital, 28 Clewer Hill Rd, Windsor, **Berkshire**, SL4 4BS, **ENGLAND**.
(T) 01753 858877 **(F)** 01753 853820.
Profile Medical Support. **Ref: YH05339**

FOREST HOUSE VETNRY SURGERY

Forest House Veterinary Surgery, 29 York Pl, Knaresborough, **Yorkshire (North)**, HG5 0AD, **ENGLAND**.
(T) 01423 862121 **(F)** 04123 869147.
Profile Medical Support. **Ref: YH05340**

FOREST INN

Forest Inn (The), Llanfihangel-Nant-Melan, New Radnor, **Powys**, LD8 2TN, **WALES**.
(T) 01544 350246 **(F)** 01544 350634
(E) fforestinn@aol.com.
Profile Stable/Livery. **Ref: YH05341**

FOREST LODGE

Forest Lodge, Motcombe, Shaftesbury, **Dorset**, SP7 9PL, **ENGLAND**.
(T) 01747 851685 **(F)** 01747 851685.
Contact/s
Manager: Mrs L Guy
Profile Riding School, Stable/Livery. **Ref: YH05342**

FOREST LODGE RIDING CTRE

Forest Lodge Riding Centre, Sandy Hill Lane, Weybourne, Holt, **Norfolk**, NR25 7HW, **ENGLAND**.
(T) 01263 588578.
Contact/s
Owner: Mrs L Davies
Profile Riding School, Stable/Livery. **Ref: YH05343**

FOREST LODGE RIDING SCHOOL

Forest Lodge Riding School, Forest Lodge, Epping New Rd, Epping, **Essex**, CM16 5HW, **ENGLAND**.
(T) 01992 812137.
Profile Riding School, Stable/Livery. **Ref: YH05344**

FOREST OF ARDEN RIDERS GRP

Forest of Arden Riders Group, Merryfields Farm, Wootton Wawen, **Warwickshire**, B95 6BS, **ENGLAND**.
(T) 01564 792720.
Profile Club/Association. **Ref: YH05345**

FOREST OF DEAN

Forest of Dean Equestrian Centre, Yorkley Wood Rd, Yorkley, Lydney, **Gloucestershire**, GL15 4TT, **ENGLAND**.
(T) 01594 562219.
Profile Riding School. **Ref: YH05346**

FOREST OF NEEDWOOD

Forest of Needwood Riding Club, Whitewood Hse, Sich Lane, Yoxall, Burton-on-Trent, **Staffordshire**, DE13 8NS, **ENGLAND**.
(T) 01543 472367.
Contact/s
Chairman: Miss C Jones
Profile Club/Association, Riding Club. **Ref: YH05347**

FOREST PARK

Forest Park Riding Stables, Rhinefield Rd, Brockenhurst, **Hampshire**, SO42 7ZG, **ENGLAND**.
(T) 01590 623429.
Contact/s
Owner: Mrs J Jackson
Profile Riding School. Hacking stables.
Yr. Est: 1986
Opening Times
Sp: Open Mon - Sun 08:00. Closed Mon - Sun 17:00.
Su: Open Mon - Sun 08:00. Closed Mon - Sun 17:00.
Au: Open Mon - Sun 08:00. Closed Mon - Sun 17:00.
Wn: Open Mon - Sun 08:00. Closed Mon - Sun 17:00. **Ref: YH05348**

FOREST PINES RIDING SCHOOL

Forest Pines Riding School, Wayside Rd, St. Leonards, Ringwood, **Hampshire**, BH24 2SJ, **ENGLAND**.
(T) 01202 871828.
Contact/s
Owner: Miss S Hayles
Profile Riding School. **Ref: YH05349**

FOREST PK

Forest Park Riding & Livery Centre, Lime Trees Ave, Santon Downham Rd, Santon Downham, Brandon, **Suffolk**, IP27 0TF, **ENGLAND**.
(T) 01842 815517. **Ref: YH05350**

FOREST RIDING CTRE

Forest Riding Centre, Yew Tree Farm, Llanvair Discoed, Chepstow, **Monmouthshire**, NP16 6LZ, **WALES**.
(T) 01633 400003.
Contact/s
Owner: Mrs J Platts **Ref: YH05351**

FOREST STABLES

Forest Stables, The Street, Great Hallingbury, Bishop's Stortford, **Essex**, CM22 7TR, **ENGLAND**.
(T) 01279 758051.
Contact/s
Owner: Mr L Glenn
Profile Riding School. **Ref: YH05352**

FOREST VIEW

Forest View Livery Stables, Parsonage Lane, Sidcup, **Kent**, DA14 5EZ, **ENGLAND**.
(T) 020 83008354.
Contact/s
Owner: Mrs S Burton
Profile Arena, Stable/Livery, Track/Course, Trainer, Transport/Horse Boxes.
Opening Times
Sp: Open 06:00. Closed 22:00.
Su: Open 06:00. Closed 22:00.
Au: Open 06:00. Closed 22:00.
Wn: Open 06:00. Closed 22:00. **Ref: YH05353**

FORESTER SADDLES

Forester Saddles, Sedgemore Farm, Furzley, Bramshaw, Lyndhurst, **Hampshire**, SO43 7JJ, **ENGLAND**.
(T) 01794 324013 **(F)** 01794 324013

(W) www.forester-saddles.co.uk
Affiliated Bodies BETA.
Contact/s
Owner: Ms G Huck
(E) gill@forestersaddles.ndo.co.uk
Profile Saddlery Retailer. No.Staff: 2
Yr. Est: 1981 Ref: YH05354

FORESTER SADDLES

Forester Saddles, Ermine Farm, Bridge St, Whaddon, Royston, **Hertfordshire**, SG8 5SN, **ENGLAND**.
(T) 01223 207358. Ref: YH05355

FORESTERS RIDING CLUB

Foresters Riding Club (The), Upshire Hall Lodge, Honey Lane, Waltham Abbey, **Essex**, EN9 3QT, **ENGLAND**.
(T) 01992 767152.
Profile Club/Association. Ref: YH05356

FORESTOKE HOLIDAYS

Forestoke Holidays, The Old Farmhouse, Forestoke, Holne, Newton Abbot, **Devon**, TQ13 7SS, **ENGLAND**.
(T) 01364 3361.
Profile Stable/Livery. Ref: YH05357

FOREVER LIVING PRODUCTS

Forever Living Products Ltd, Barrs Farm, High St, Soberton, **Hampshire**, SO32 3PN, **ENGLAND**.
(T) 01489 878548.
Profile Medical Support. Ref: YH05358

FORGE

Forge (The), 8 School Wynd, Largs, **Ayrshire (North)**, KA30 8NB, **SCOTLAND**.
(T) 01475 687362.
Profile Blacksmith. Ref: YH05359

FORGE

Forge (The), 1 St Margarets Steps, Bradford-on-Avon, **Wiltshire**, BA15 1DS, **ENGLAND**.
(T) 01225 862883.
Contact/s
Owner: Mr P Adams
Profile Blacksmith. Ref: YH05360

FORGE COTTAGE SADDLERY

Forge Cottage Saddlery, Horsedowns, Praze, Camborne, **Cornwall**, TR14 0NP, **ENGLAND**.
(T) 01209 831901.
Profile Supplies. Ref: YH05361

FORGE FEEDS

Forge Feeds (Ilston-on-the-Hill), The Forge, Ilston-on-the-Hill, **Leicestershire**, LE7 9EF, **ENGLAND**.
(T) 01537 55888.
Profile Feed Merchant. Ref: YH05362

FORGE SLINDON

Forge Slindon (The), Slindon Top Rd, Slindon, Arundel, **Sussex (West)**, BN18 0RP, **ENGLAND**.
(T) 01243 814276.
Profile Farrier. Ref: YH05363

FORGE STABLES

Forge Stables, Lowdham Laneoxton, Woodborough, **Nottinghamshire**, NG14 6DN, **ENGLAND**.
(T) 0115 9664374.
Profile Farrier. Ref: YH05364

FORGE TRADING

Forge Trading Co (The), Unit 5 Burcot Farm, East Stratton, Winchester, **Hampshire**, SO21 3DZ, **ENGLAND**.
(T) 01962 774111 (F) 01962 774110.
Profile Supplies. Ref: YH05365

FORGED AFFAIRS

Forged Affairs, Unit 3 Court Farm, Buckland Newton, Dorchester, **Dorset**, DT2 7BT, **ENGLAND**.
(T) 01300 345558 (F) 01300 345558.
Contact/s
Owner: Mr J Lacy
Profile Blacksmith. Ref: YH05366

FORGEHILL STUD

Forgehill Stud, South Godstone, **Surrey**, RH9 8LB, **ENGLAND**.
(T) 01342 893419.
Profile Trainer. Ref: YH05367

FORGEMILL

Forgemill Farm, Cilonen, Three Crosses, Gower, Swansea, **Swansea**, SA4 3UR, **WALES**.
(T) 01792 873760 (F) 01792 873760
(W) www.palominotrails.co.uk.
Contact/s
Owner: Ms E Morgan
(E) ellie_morgan@palominotrails.co.uk
Profile Riding School, Stable/Livery. No.Staff: 3
Yr. Est: 1971 C.Size: 80 Acres
Opening Times
Telephone for an appointment Ref: YH05368

FORGEWELD

Forgeweld, Forge Lane, Little Aston, Sutton Coldfield, **Midlands (West)**, B74 3BE, **ENGLAND**.
(T) 0121 3534988.
Profile Blacksmith. Ref: YH05369

FORGING AHEAD

Forging Ahead, Field Hse Farm, Dark Lane, Belbroughton, Stourbridge, **Midlands (West)**, DY9 9SS, **ENGLAND**.
(T) 01562 730003.
Contact/s
Owner: Mr P Margetts
Profile Blacksmith. Ref: YH05370

FORKE FARM & STUD

Forke Farm & Stud, Pennymoor, Tiverton, **Devon**, EX16 8LL, **ENGLAND**.
(T) 01363 866380 (F) 01363 866805.
Profile Breeder. Ref: YH05371

FORLAN STUD

Forlan Stud, Toplands, Slaughterford, Chippenham, **Wiltshire**, SN14 8RD, **ENGLAND**.
(T) 01249 782333 (F) 01249 782333
(W) www.forlanstud.co.uk.
Contact/s
Owner: Mrs E French
(E) betty@forlanstud.co.uk
Profile Breeder. Yr. Est: 1968 Ref: YH05372

FORMBY SADDLERY

Formby Saddlery, Warren Farm, Southport Old Rd, Formby, Liverpool, **Merseyside**, L37 0AN, **ENGLAND**.
(T) 01704 878140 (F) 01704 892280.
Contact/s
Owner: Mr J Goldbourne
Profile Riding Wear Retailer, Saddlery Retailer.
Yr. Est: 1994
Opening Times
Sp: Open Mon - Sun 10:00. Closed Mon, Wed, Fri 18:00, Thurs 19:00, Sat 17:00, Sun 16:00.
Su: Open Mon - Sun 10:00. Closed Mon, Wed, Fri 18:00, Thurs 19:00, Sat 17:00, Sun 16:00.
Au: Open Mon - Sun 10:00. Closed Mon, Wed, Fri 18:00, Thurs 19:00, Sat 17:00, Sun 16:00.
Wn: Open Mon - Sun 10:00. Closed Mon, Wed, Fri 18:00, Thurs 19:00, Sat 17:00, Sun 16:00.
Ref: YH05373

FORMBY TRAILERS

Formby Trailers, 6 Church Rd, Formby, Liverpool, **Merseyside**, L37 8BG, **ENGLAND**.
(T) 01704 871957.
Profile Transport/Horse Boxes. Ref: YH05374

FORMET

Formet Ltd, Wincomblee Rd, Walker, Newcastle-upon-Tyne, **Tyne and Wear**, NE6 3QQ, **ENGLAND**.
(T) 0191 2638686 (F) 0191 2626428.
Profile Blacksmith. Ref: YH05375

FORREST FEEDS

Forrest Feeds, The Mill, Edingley, Newark, **Nottinghamshire**, NG22 8BG, **ENGLAND**.
(T) 01623 882260
(E) forrest@feeds.fsnet.co.uk
(W) www.forrest-feeds.co.uk.
Contact/s
Partner: Mr J Forrest
Profile Feed Merchant. Ref: YH05376

FORREST HORSE TRANSPORT

Forrest Horse Transport, New Rd Farm, Tingrith, Milton Keynes, **Buckinghamshire**, MK17 9EN, **ENGLAND**.
(T) 01525 717546
(M) 07831 437147.
Profile Transport/Horse Boxes. Ref: YH05377

FORREST, W

Mr W Forrest, 1177 Tollcross Rd, Glasgow, **Glasgow (City of)**, G32 8HB, **SCOTLAND**.
(T) 0141 7781137.
Profile Trainer. Ref: YH05378

FORRYAN, NICHOLAS C W

Nicholas C W Forryan DWCF, 39 Main St, Whissending, **Rutland**, LE15 7ES, **ENGLAND**.
(T) 01664 474312.
Profile Farrier. Ref: YH05379

FORSTER, D M

Mr D M Forster, Todd Fall Farm, Heighington, **County Durham**, DL2 2XG, **ENGLAND**.
(T) 01388 772441.
Profile Supplies. Ref: YH05380

FORSYTH & MAZONAS

Forsyth & Mazonas, Holmefield Vetnry Ctre, Brayton Lane, Brayton, Selby, **Yorkshire (North)**, YO8 9DZ, **ENGLAND**.
(T) 01757 705562.
Profile Medical Support. Ref: YH05381

FORSYTH, GILLON S

Gillon S Forsyth DWCF, 56 Mill Hill, Newmarket, **Suffolk**, CB8 0JB, **ENGLAND**.
(T) 01638 602961.
Profile Farrier. Ref: YH05382

FORSYTH, MADELEINE

Madeleine Forsyth, The Bondgate Vetnry Surgery, 52 Bondgate, Helmsley, **Yorkshire (North)**, YO62 5EZ, **ENGLAND**.
(T) 01439 71019.
Profile Medical Support. Ref: YH05383

FORSYTH'S OF WOOLER

Forsyth's of Wooler Ltd, South Rd, Wooler, **Northumberland**, NE71 6QE, **ENGLAND**.
(T) 01668 281567 (F) 01668 281567.
Profile Saddlery Retailer. Ref: YH05384

FORT CTRE

Fort Centre Riding For Disabled, Craigmore Rd, Maghera, **County Londonderry**, BT46 5AN, **NORTHERN IRELAND**.
(T) 028 79644280
Affiliated Bodies NAC, RDA.
Contact/s
Manager: Mr J McCloskey (Q) RDAGI
Profile Equestrian Centre, Trainer.
Fort Centre is the largest purpose built equestrian centre in Ireland dealing solely with disabled children and adults. No.Staff: 7 Ref: YH05385

FORT DODGE ANIMAL HEALTH

Fort Dodge Animal Health, Flanders Rd, Hedge End, **Hampshire**, SO30 4QH, **ENGLAND**.
(T) 01489 781711 (F) 01489 788306.
Contact/s
Manager: Mr B Hardy
Profile Medical Support. Ref: YH05386

FORT WHEELBARROWS

Fort Wheelbarrows Ltd, P O Box 330, Woking, **Surrey**, GU22 9XS, **ENGLAND**.
(T) 01483 727898 (F) 01483 727808
(E) hub@fort-uk.com.
Profile Supplies. Ref: YH05387

FORT WIDLEY EQUESTRIAN CTRE

Fort Widley Equestrian Centre, Fort Widley, Portsdown Hill Rd, Cosham, **Hampshire**, PO6 3LS, **ENGLAND**.
(T) 023 92324553.
Profile Riding School, Stable/Livery. Ref: YH05388

FORT, J R

Mr J R Fort, 27 High Shaws, Brandon, **County Durham**, DH7 8QT, **ENGLAND**.
(T) 0191 3782319.
Profile Supplies. Ref: YH05389

FORTH VIEW RIDING CLUB

Forth View Riding Club, 42 Evershed Drive, Dunfermline, **Fife**, KY11 8RE, **SCOTLAND**.
(T) 01383 738993.
Profile Club/Association, Riding Club. Ref: YH05390

FORTHSIDE FABRICATION

Forthside Fabrication, Unit 2 Foundry Rd, Bonnybridge, **Falkirk**, FK4 2AP, **SCOTLAND**.
(T) 01324 814446 (F) 01324 814446.
Contact/s
Partner: Mr M Thomson
Profile Blacksmith. Ref: YH05391

FORTUNE CTRE

Fortune Centre of Riding Therapy (The), Avon Tyrrell, Bransgore, Christchurch, **Dorset**, BH23 8EE, **ENGLAND**.
(T) 01425 673297 (F) 01425 674320.
Profile Equestrian Centre. Ref: YH05392

FORWARD THINKING

Forward Thinking, Upper Dee Mill, Llangollen, **Denbighshire**, LL20 8SD, **WALES**.
(T) 01978 861105 (F) 01978 861173

(M) 07802 953401. Ref: YH05393

FOSKETT, RUSSELL WILLIAM

Russell William Foskett DWCF, Elm Cottage, Lycrome Rd, Chesham, **Buckinghamshire**, HP5 3LD, **ENGLAND**.
(T) 01494 785348.
Profile Farrier. Ref: YH05394

FOSS FEEDS

Foss Feeds, Foss Farm, Copmanthorpe Lane, Acaster Malbis, **Yorkshire (North)**, YO23 2UG, **ENGLAND**.
(T) 01904 706376.
Profile Supplies. Ref: YH05395

FOSSE DRYBED

Fosse Drybed, Whetstone Magna, Lutterworth Rd, Whetstone, **Leicestershire**, LE8 6NB, **ENGLAND**.
(T) 0116 2477907 (F) 0116 2477996
(E) milesh@fosse.co.uk.
Profile Supplies. Ref: YH05396

FOSTER & SEWARD

Foster & Seward, 90 Winchester Rd, Basingstoke, **Hampshire**, RG21 1UH, **ENGLAND**.
(T) 01256 473371.
Contact/s
Partner: Mr M Seward
Profile Medical Support. Ref: YH05397

FOSTER & SON

Foster & Son, 83 Jermyn St, St James's, London, **London (Greater)**, SW1Y 6JD, **ENGLAND**.
(T) 020 79305385. Ref: YH05398

FOSTER BLOODSTOCK

Foster Bloodstock, Mill Farm, Higham, Bury St Edmunds, **Suffolk**, IP28 6NZ, **ENGLAND**.
(T) 01284 811661 (F) 01284 811663.
Contact/s
Owner: Ms J Foster (Q) BSc(Hons)
Profile Blood Stock Agency.
Can offer valuation service of horses for insurance purposes. Ref: YH05399

FOSTER, A J

A J Foster, 22-23 Station St, Walsall, **Midlands (West)**, WS2 9JZ, **ENGLAND**.
(T) 01922 626430 (F) 01922 610163.
Contact/s
Owner: Mr A Foster Ref: YH05400

FOSTER, LOUIS

Mr Louis Foster, 18 Moss Side, Allonby, Maryport, **Cumbria**, CA15 6QW, **ENGLAND**.
(T) 01900 881272.
Profile Supplies. Ref: YH05401

FOSTER, R

Mr R Foster, Darlae Cottage, Udstonhead Farm, Strathaven, **Lanarkshire (South)**, ML10 6SX, **SCOTLAND**.
(T) 01357 522395. Ref: YH05402

FOTHERINGHAY

Fotheringhay Forge & Woodburners, The Old Forge, Fotheringhay, Peterborough, **Cambridgeshire**, PE8 5HZ, **ENGLAND**.
(T) 01832 226323.
Profile Blacksmith. Ref: YH05403

FOTO SPORT

Foto Sport, 41 Tower Hill, Ormskirk, **Lancashire**, L39 2EE, **ENGLAND**.
(T) 01695 574389. Ref: YH05404

FOULDS, ROGER

Mr Roger Foulds, Pinchpools Farm, Manuden, Bishop's Stortford, **Hertfordshire**, CM23 1DX, **ENGLAND**.
(T) 01279 815661 (F) 01279 815661.
Profile Breeder. Ref: YH05405

FOULKES, JUSTIN & CHRISTINE

Justin & Christine Foulkes, Bryn Gwian Farm, Eglwysbach, Colwyn Bay, **Conwy**, LL28 5UN, **WALES**.
(T) 01492 650382.
Profile Stable/Livery. Ref: YH05406

FOUNDATION FOR ANIMAL HEALING

Foundation for Animal Healing, 34 Jackshill Pk, Graveley, Hitchin, **Hertfordshire**, SG4 7EQ, **ENGLAND**.
(T) 01707 661005 (F) 01707 662058.
Profile Medical Support. Ref: YH05407

FOUR LEGGED FRIENDS

Four Legged Friends, Unit 3B Bridge End Ind Est, Egremont, **Cumbria**, CA22 2RD, **ENGLAND**.
(T) 01946 820800.
Profile Saddlery Retailer. Ref: YH05408

FOUR OAKS LIVERY

Four Oaks Livery, Hillwood Rd, Sutton Coldfield, **Midlands (West)**, B75 5QW, **ENGLAND**.
(T) 0121 3087600.
Contact/s
Owner: Mrs R Jordan
Profile Stable/Livery. Ref: YH05409

FOUR SEASONS

Four Seasons (The), Addlestead Farm, Headley Rd, Epsom, **Surrey**, KT18 6ET, **ENGLAND**.
(T) 01372 379102.
Contact/s
Owner: Miss S Cliff
Profile Stable/Livery. Ref: YH05410

FOUR SEASONS FEEDS

Four Seasons Feeds, Station Farm, Allington Rd, Sedgebrook, Grantham, **Lincolnshire**, NG32 2EJ, **ENGLAND**.
(T) 01949 843698.
Profile Feed Merchant. Ref: YH05411

FOUR SEASONS RACING

Four Seasons Racing Ltd, Mabberleys, Front St, East Garston, Hungerford, **Berkshire**, RG17 7EU, **ENGLAND**.
(T) 01488 648180 (F) 01488 648181.
Profile Trainer. Ref: YH05412

FOUR WINDS

Four Winds Equitation Centre, Leaveslake Drove, West Pinchbeck, Spalding, **Lincolnshire**, PE11 3QJ, **ENGLAND**.
(T) 01775 640533 (F) 01775 640533
(E) fourwinds.equitation@virgin.net.
Contact/s
Owner: Mrs P Leverton
Profile Equestrian Centre, Riding School, Stable/Livery. No.Staff: 5 Yr. Est: 1980
C.Size: 15 Acres
Opening Times
Sp: Open 08:00. Closed 20:30.
Su: Open 08:00. Closed 20:30.
Au: Open 08:00. Closed 20:30.
Wn: Open 08:00. Closed 20:30. Ref: YH05413

FOURFIELDS FARM

Fourfields Farm, Ashendene Rd, Bayford, Hertford, **Hertfordshire**, SG13 8PX, **ENGLAND**.
(T) 01992 511331.
Profile Stable/Livery. Ref: YH05414

FOURWAYS STUD

Fourways Stud, Cheese Hill Lane, Norley, Frodsham, **Cheshire**, WA6 8LF, **ENGLAND**.
(T) 01606 882235.
Contact/s
Owner: Mr J Haywood
Profile Breeder. Ref: YH05415

FOWBERRY FARMS

Fowberry Farms, 18-20 Glendale Rd, Wooler, **Northumberland**, NE71 6EU, **ENGLAND**.
(T) 01668 281611 (F) 01668 281113.
Profile Riding School, Stable/Livery. Ref: YH05416

FOWLER, PAT

Mrs Pat Fowler, Lea Cottage, The City, Radnage, High Wycombe, **Buckinghamshire**, HP14 4DW, **ENGLAND**.
(T) 01494 482339 (F) 01844 278333. Ref: YH05417

FOX ELECTRONIC

Fox Electronic Surveillance Systems, 65A High St, Thrapston, **Northamptonshire**, NN14 4JJ, **ENGLAND**.
(T) 01832 734134 (F) 01832 733300. Ref: YH05418

FOX END STABLES

Fox End Stables, King St, Rampton, **Cambridgeshire**, CB4 8QD, **ENGLAND**.
(T) 01954 250772.
Profile Trainer. Ref: YH05419

FOX FEEDS

Fox Feeds Ltd, Beaches Yard, Brent Pelham, Buntingford, **Hertfordshire**, SG9 0HJ, **ENGLAND**.
(T) 01778 341130 (F) 01279 777506
(E) info@foxfeedsltd.co.uk
(W) www.foxfeedsltd.co.uk. Ref: YH05420

FOX FIELD FARM RACING STABLES

Fox Field Farm Racing Stables, The Greenings, Foxfield Farm, Fowlmere Rd, Melbourn, Royston, **Hertfordshire**, SG8 6EZ, **ENGLAND**.
(T) 01763 263166.
Profile Trainer. Ref: YH05421

FOX HILL FARM EQUESTRIAN CTRE

Fox Hill Farm Equestrian Centre, Sywell Rd, Holcot, Northampton, **Northamptonshire**, NN6 9SN, **ENGLAND**.
(T) 01604 781191.
Contact/s
Owner: Miss L Stephenson (Q) BHSI
Profile Riding School, Saddlery Retailer.
Ref: YH05422

FOX HILL RACING

Fox Hill Racing, Stow Rd, Andoversford, Cheltenham, **Gloucestershire**, GL54 5RL, **ENGLAND**.
(T) 01451 850602 (F) 01451 850602.
Contact/s
Owner: Mrs S Marston
Profile Trainer. Ref: YH05423

FOX MANIA

Fox Mania, Mount Farm, Irby Upon Humberside, Grimsby, **Lincolnshire (North East)**, DN37 7JR, **ENGLAND**.
(T) 01472 371356 (F) 01472 371147.
Profile Saddlery Retailer. Ref: YH05424

FOX SADDLERS

Fox Saddlers, Northgates, Wetherby, **Yorkshire (West)**, LS22 6NX, **ENGLAND**.
(T) 01937 586070 (F) 01937 586070
(E) admin@foxsaddlers.co.uk
(W) www.foxsaddlers.co.uk.
Contact/s
Owner: Mr K Whitehouse
Profile Riding Wear Retailer, Saddlery Retailer.
No.Staff: 4 Yr. Est: 1901
Opening Times
Sp: Open Mon - Sat 09:00. Closed Mon - Sat 17:00.
Su: Open Mon - Sat 09:00. Closed Mon - Sat 17:00.
Au: Open Mon - Sat 09:00. Closed Mon - Sat 17:00.
Wn: Open Mon - Sat 09:00. Closed Mon - Sat 17:00.
Ref: YH05425

FOX, C

Mrs C Fox, Kenmal, Hawkenbury, Staplehurst, **Kent**, TN12 0EG, **ENGLAND**.
(T) 01622 842264.
Profile Breeder. Ref: YH05426

FOX, DAVID L

David L Fox DWCF, Spunham Farm, Whicham Valley, Millom, **Cumbria**, LA18 5JP, **ENGLAND**.
(T) 01229 772609.
Profile Farrier. Ref: YH05427

FOX, F A

F A Fox, 35 Tubbs Farm Cl, Lambourn, **Berkshire**, RG17 8PE, **ENGLAND**.
(T) 01935 850838.
Profile Farrier. Ref: YH05428

FOX, GRAHAM P

Graham P Fox BEM RSS BII, 1 Huish, Sydling St Nicholas, Dorchester, **Dorset**, DT2 9NS, **ENGLAND**.
(T) 01300 341867.
Profile Farrier. Ref: YH05429

FOX, J & M

Mr J & Mr M Fox, 28 Hill Rd, Stonehouse, **Lanarkshire (South)**, ML9 3EA, **SCOTLAND**.
(T) 01698 792950.
Contact/s
Partner: Mr J Fox Ref: YH05430

FOXES FARM & RIDING SCHOOL

Foxes Farm & Riding School, Badgers Rake Lane, Ledsham, Ellesmere Port, **Cheshire**, CH66 8PF, **ENGLAND**.
(T) 0151 3396797 (F) 0151 3395926.
Contact/s
Owner: Mrs J Davey
Profile Riding School, Stable/Livery. Ref: YH05431

FOXHAVEN STABLES

Foxhaven Stables, Turnpike Cottage, 26 Westbury Rd, Bratton, Westbury, **Wiltshire**, BA13 4TD, **ENGLAND**.
(T) 01380 830826.
Profile Transport/Horse Boxes. Ref: YH05432

FOXHILL EQUESTRIAN

Foxhill Equestrian Ltd, Foxhill Farm, Eydon, Daventry, **Northamptonshire**, NN11 3QB, **ENGLAND**.
(T) 01295 760230.

Contact/s
Owner: Mr K Smith Ref: YH05433

FOXHILL RACING PROMOTIONS

Foxhill Racing Promotions, Pollardstown, Foxhill, Wanborough, Swindon, **Wiltshire**, SN4 0DR, **ENGLAND**.
(T) 01793 790950 (F) 01793 790871
(E) foxhill@pollardstown.demon.co.uk.
Profile Club/Association. Ref: YH05434

FOXHILLS

Foxhills Leisure Ltd, Foxhills Riding School, Beacon Rd, Barr Beacon, Walsall, **Midlands (West)**, WS9 0QP, **ENGLAND**.
(T) 0121 3609160
(E) info@foxhillsleisure.com
(W) www.foxhillsleisure.com.
Contact/s
General Manager: Mrs J Bull
Profile Arena, Breeder, Riding School, Stable/Livery, Track/Course, Trainer, Transport/Horse Boxes.
No.Staff: 4 Yr. Est: 1955 C.Size: 40 Acres
Opening Times
Sp: Open Tues - Sun 09:00. Closed Tues - Sun 19:00.
Su: Open Tues - Sun 09:00. Closed Tues - Sun 19:00.
Au: Open Tues - Sun 09:00. Closed Tues - Sun 19:00.
Wn: Open Tues - Sun 09:00. Closed Tues - Sun 19:00.
Open until 19:00 where light permitting. Closed on Mondays Ref: YH05435

FOXHOLE LIVERY STABLE

Foxhole Livery Stable, Dulrarich, Foxhole, Kiltarlity, Beauly, **Highlands**, IV4 7HT, **SCOTLAND**.
(T) 01463 741433.
Contact/s
Owner: Ms C Hill
Profile Stable/Livery, Supplies. No.Staff: 1
Yr. Est: 1993 C.Size: 22 Acres Ref: YH05436

FOXHOLM STUD

Foxholm Stud & Livery Yard, Gravel Hole Farm, Norton, Stockton-on-Tees, **Cleveland**, TS20 1PF, **ENGLAND**.
(T) 01642 554578 (F) 01642 554578.
Profile Arena, Breeder, Equestrian Centre, Stable/Livery, Trainer. No.Staff: 3 Yr. Est: 1977
C.Size: 50 Acres Ref: YH05437

FOXHOUNDS RIDING SCHOOL

Foxhounds Riding School, Baker St, Orsett, Grays, **Essex**, RM16 3LJ, **ENGLAND**.
(T) 01375 891367.
Contact/s
Partner: Mrs R Cremer
Profile Riding School, Saddlery Retailer.
Ref: YH05438

FOXLEA HORSE BOXES

Foxlea Horse Boxes, Unit 22 Burton Wood Ind Est, Phipps Lane, Burton Wood, Warrington, **Cheshire**, WA5 4HX, **ENGLAND**.
(T) 01925 222208 (F) 01925 222274
(M) 07850 747694.
Profile Transport/Horse Boxes. Ref: YH05439

FRAME, J & N W

J & N W Frame, Vetnry Clinic, Brunswick Sq, Penrith, **Cumbria**, CA11 7LP, **ENGLAND**.
(T) 01768 862454 (F) 01768 867163.
Profile Medical Support. Ref: YH05440

FRAMPTON

Mr Frampton, Harrow Wood Farm, Bransgore, Christchurch, **Dorset**, BH23 8JE, **ENGLAND**.
(T) 01425 72487.
Profile Breeder. Ref: YH05441

FRAMPTON HSE STABLES

Frampton House Stables, Newbury Rd, East Hendred, **Oxfordshire**, OX12 8LG, **ENGLAND**.
(T) 01235 834537.
Profile Supplies. Ref: YH05442

FRAMPTON ZIEGLER AGRICULTURE

Frampton Ziegler Agriculture, Crow Farm Stores, Crow Lane, Ringwood, **Hampshire**, BH24 3EA, **ENGLAND**.
(T) 01425 472341 (F) 01425 480522.
Profile Supplies. Ref: YH05443

FRANCES ANN BROWN SADDLERY

Frances Ann Brown Saddlery, Belt View Farm, Bednall Head, Cannock Rd, Stafford, **Staffordshire**, ST17 0SH, **ENGLAND**.
(T) 01785 665006 (F) 01785 665006.
Contact/s
Owner: Ms F Brown (Q) BHSAI
Profile Riding Wear Retailer, Saddlery Retailer, Supplies. No.Staff: 4 Yr. Est: 1997
Ref: YH05444

FRANCES ANN BROWN SADDLERY

Frances Ann Brown Saddlery, The Saddlery, Market St, Penkridge, Stafford, **Staffordshire**, ST19 5DH, **ENGLAND**.
(T) 01785 711055 (F) 01785 665006.
Contact/s
Owner: Mrs F Brown Ref: YH05445

FRANCES BULLOCK'S SADDLERY

Frances Bullock's Saddlery, Low Moor Acres Farm, North Moor Rd, Easingwold, **Yorkshire (North)**, YO61 3QD, **ENGLAND**.
(T) 01347 823430.
Contact/s
Owner: Ms F Bullock
Profile Saddlery Retailer. Ref: YH05446

FRANCIS & HERDMAN

Francis & Herdman, Milford Farm, Mill St, Bakewell, **Derbyshire**, DE45 1DX, **ENGLAND**.
(T) 01629 812035.
Profile Medical Support. Ref: YH05447

FRANCIS CUPISS

Francis Cupiss Ltd, The Wilderness, The Entry, Diss, **Norfolk**, IP22 3NT, **ENGLAND**.
(T) 01379 642045 (F) 01379 642045.
Profile Medical Support. Ref: YH05448

FRANCIS WILLEY

Francis Willey (Bromyard), Three Mills, Bromyard, **Herefordshire**, HR7 4HS, **ENGLAND**.
(T) 01885 488205.
Profile Supplies. Ref: YH05449

FRANCIS, K

K Francis, Fox Lane, Holmesfield, Dronfield, **Derbyshire**, S18 7WG, **ENGLAND**.
(T) 0114 2890956.
Contact/s
Partner: Mrs C Shaw
Profile Breeder. Ref: YH05450

FRANCIS, LEE M R

Lee M R Francis DWCF BII, 8 Wollaton Rd, Ferndown, **Dorset**, BH22 8QR, **ENGLAND**.
(T) 01202 895910.
Profile Farrier. Ref: YH05451

FRANCIS, M E D

M E D Francis, Folly Hse, Upper Lambourn Rd, Lambourn, Hungerford, **Berkshire**, RG17 8QG, **ENGLAND**.
(T) 01488 71700 (F) 01488 73208.
Contact/s
Owner: Mr M Francis
Profile Transport/Horse Boxes. Ref: YH05452

FRANCIS, W D

W D Francis, Cliffe Bank, Higher Carden, Tilston, Malpas, **Cheshire**, SY14 7HR, **ENGLAND**.
(T) 01829 250515 (F) 01829 250515.
Contact/s
Partner: Mr R Francis
Profile Transport/Horse Boxes. Ref: YH05453

FRANDHAM KENNELS & TACK SHOP

Frandham Kennels & Tack Shop, Minnis Lane, River, Dover, **Kent**, CT15 7ON, **ENGLAND**.
(T) 01304 823133.
Profile Saddlery Retailer, Stable/Livery.
Ref: YH05454

FRANK BAINES SADDLERY

Frank Baines Saddlery, Northcote St, Walsall, **Midlands (West)**, WS2 8BQ, **ENGLAND**.
(T) 01922 640847. Ref: YH05455

FRANK H DALE

Frank H Dale Ltd, PO Box 2, Leominster, **Herefordshire**, HR6 8EF, **ENGLAND**.
(T) 01568 612212 (F) 01568 619401.
Profile Supplies. Ref: YH05456

FRANK HALL BESPOKE TAILORS

Frank Hall Bespoke Tailors, 30 St Mary's Rd, Market Harborough, **Leicestershire**, LE16 7DU, **ENGLAND**.
(T) 01858 462402.
Contact/s
Owner: Mr C Ripley Ref: YH05457

FRANK HARVEY INT

Frank Harvey International, 24 Tomo Ind Est, Creeting Rd, Stowmarket, **Suffolk**, IP14 5AY, **ENGLAND**.
(T) 01449 612646 (F) 01449 774844.
Profile Supplies. Ref: YH05458

FRANK HILL & SON

Frank Hill & Son, 18 Market Pl, Patrington, **Yorkshire (East)**, HU12 0RB, **ENGLAND**.
(T) 01964 630531 (F) 01964 631203.
Contact/s
Partner: Mr R Ward Ref: YH05459

FRANK MARSHALL

Frank Marshall & Co, Chelford Agricultural Ctre, Chelford, Macclesfield, **Cheshire**, SK11 9AX, **ENGLAND**.
(T) 01625 861122 (F) 01625 860079.
Profile Auctioneer. Ref: YH05460

FRANK STEPHENS & SON

Frank Stephens & Son, Sandy Acres Feeds, Great Saredon, Shareshill, Wolverhampton, **Midlands (West)**, WV10 7LN, **ENGLAND**.
(T) 01922 415390 (F) 01922 415228.
Profile Medical Support. Ref: YH05461

FRANK WARD

Frank Ward Clothing Manufacturing Co Ltd, Ivy Lane, Carrickmacross, **County Monaghan**, **IRELAND**.
(T) 042 9663498 (F) 042 9663498
(E) franktw@eircom.net.
Profile Saddlery Retailer.
Frank Ward specialises in leather and suede
Ref: YH05462

FRANK WRIGHT FEEDS

Frank Wright Feeds Ltd, Blenheim Hse, Blenheim Rd, Ashbourne, **Derbyshire**, DE6 1HA, **ENGLAND**.
(T) 01335 343243 (F) 01335 340016.
Profile Feed Merchant. Ref: YH05463

FRANK, S

Mrs S Frank, Quarry Farm, Ingleby Barwick, **Cleveland**, TS17 0JF, **ENGLAND**.
(T) 01642 760538.
Profile Supplies. Ref: YH05464

FRANKLAND, DEREK S

Derek S Frankland DWCF, The Old Post Office, No 13 Mixbury, Brackley, **Northamptonshire**, NN13 5PR, **ENGLAND**.
(T) 01280 848513.
Profile Farrier. Ref: YH05465

FRANKLAND, FRANK A

Frank A Frankland, The Lodge, Egerton Stud, Cambridge Rd, Newmarket, **Suffolk**, CB8 0PU, **ENGLAND**.
(T) 01638 560440 (F) 01638 561990.
Profile Blood Stock Agency. Ref: YH05466

FRANKLAND, RONALD A

Ronald A Frankland RSS, 6 Crown Hill, Upshire, Waltham Abbey, **Essex**, EN9 3TF, **ENGLAND**.
(T) 01992 764158.
Profile Farrier. Ref: YH05467

FRANKLEY INTERNATIONAL HORSES

Frankley International Horses, Berry Lane, Elmbridge, Droitwich, **Worcestershire**, WR9 0DA, **ENGLAND**.
(T) 01527 869090.
Contact/s
Partner: Mrs J Hamer
Profile Breeder. Ref: YH05468

FRANKLIN, MARK A

Mark A Franklin DWCF, Old Witham Lodge, Ferry Lane, Brothertoft, Boston, **Lincolnshire**, PE20 3SS, **ENGLAND**.
(T) 01205 280590.
Profile Farrier. Ref: YH05469

FRANKLIN, ROYSTON E

Royston E Franklin AFCL Hons, The Poplars, Berrow, Malvern, **Worcestershire**, WR13 6AS, **ENGLAND**.
(T) 01684 833550.
Profile Farrier. Ref: YH05470

FRANKS, MICHAEL R

Michael R Franks DWCF, 1 Bowhouse Farm Cottages, East Wemyss, **Fife**, KY1 4TF, **SCOTLAND**.
(T) 01592 652216.
Profile Farrier. Ref: YH05471

Key: (T) telephone (F) fax (M) mobile (E) E-Mail Address (W) Website Address (Q) Qualifications
Yr. Est: Year Established C.Size: Complex Size Sp: Spring Su: Summer Au: Autumn Wn: Winter

FRASER, J D
J D Fraser, The Smithy, Inshes, Inverness, **Highlands**, IV2 5BA, **SCOTLAND**.
(T) 01463 240875.
Profile Blacksmith. **Ref: YH05472**

FRASER, J L
J L Fraser, Glenalva, Stirling Rd, Drymen, **Stirling**, G63 0AA, **SCOTLAND**.
(T) 01360 660491.
Profile Farrier. **Ref: YH05473**

FRASER, J M
Mrs J M Fraser, Westhide Court Farm, Westhide, **Herefordshire**, HR1 3RN, **ENGLAND**.
(T) 01432 850444.
Profile Supplies. **Ref: YH05474**

FREAK, N R
N R Freak DWCF, Beaulieu Hse, Partway Lane, Hazelbury Bryan, Sturminster Newton, **Dorset**, DT10 2DP, **ENGLAND**.
(T) 01258 817643.
Profile Farrier. **Ref: YH05475**

FRECOL AUTO SVS
Frecol Auto Services, 106 Connaught Rd, Fleet, **Hampshire**, GU13 9QX, **ENGLAND**.
(T) 01252 622451.
Profile Transport/Horse Boxes. **Ref: YH05476**

FRED WADDINGTON & SON
Fred Waddington & Son Ltd, Gatherley Rd, Brompton-on-Swale, Richmond, **Yorkshire (North)**, DL10 7JH, **ENGLAND**.
(T) 01748 812323 **(F)** 01748 812145.
Profile Transport/Horse Boxes. **Ref: YH05477**

FREDERICK J CHANDLER
Frederick J Chandler (Est 1796), 5 Angel Yard, Marlborough, **Wiltshire**, SN8 1AG, **ENGLAND**.
(T) 01672 512633 **(F)** 01672 511662.
Profile Saddlery Retailer. **Ref: YH05478**

FREDERICKS, CLAYTON
Clayton Fredericks (AUS), Elston Stables, Shrewton, Salisbury, **Wiltshire**, SP3 4HQ, **ENGLAND**.
(T) 01980 621288 **(F)** 01980 621367. **Ref: YH05479**

FREE & EASY SADDLE
Free & Easy Saddle Co, Low Selset, Lunedale, Middleton-In-Teesdale, Barnard Castle, **County Durham**, DL12 0PR, **ENGLAND**.
(T) 01833 640887 **(F)** 01833 640620.
Contact/s
Owner: Mr L Spark
Profile Saddlery Retailer. **Ref: YH05480**

FREEDOM FARM
Freedom Farm, Dallinghoo, Woodbridge, **Suffolk**, IP31 0LR, **ENGLAND**.
(T) 01473 37351 **(F)** 01473 37625.
Profile Breeder. **Ref: YH05481**

FREEDOM FARM STUD
Freedom Farm Stud, East Green, Great Bradley, Newmarket, **Suffolk**, CB8 9LU, **ENGLAND**.
(T) 01440 783667 **(F)** 01440 783665.
Contact/s
Manager: Miss L Cooper
Profile Breeder. **Ref: YH05482**

FREELANCE FEATURES
Freelance Features, Leathley Lodge, Leathley, Otley, **Yorkshire (West)**, LS21 2JS, **ENGLAND**.
(T) 0113 2843439 **(F)** 0113 2843439
(M) 07774 460926
(E) stephie@freefeat.freeserve.co.uk.
Profile Supplies. **Ref: YH05483**

FREEMAN, J
Mrs J Freeman, Reeves Green, Wareside, **Hertfordshire**, SG12 7QS, **ENGLAND**.
(T) 01920 463695.
Profile Breeder. **Ref: YH05484**

FREEMAN, KEITH
Keith Freeman, The Old Rectory, The Street, Bergh Apton, Norwich, **Norfolk**, NR15 1BN, **ENGLAND**.
(T) 01508 550280.
Contact/s
Owner: Mr K Freeman
Profile Blood Stock Agency. **Ref: YH05485**

FREEWARREN FARM
Freewarren Farm Livery Competion Yard, Freewarren Farm, Burbage, Marlborough, **Wiltshire**, SN8 3DN, **ENGLAND**.
(T) 01672 851791.
Contact/s
Partner: Mrs G Young
Profile Stable/Livery. **Ref: YH05486**

FREEZEMARK
Freezemark Ltd, Oxbow Farm, Avon Dassett, Southam, **Warwickshire**, CV47 2AQ, **ENGLAND**.
(T) 01295 690090 **(F)** 01295 690080.
Contact/s
General Manager: Claire Howard
Profile Horse Security - Freeze Marking.
Operate a freeze marking security service, introduced into the UK by Mary Awre in 1978.
Opening Times
Sp: Open Mon - Fri 09:00.
Closed Mon - Fri 17:00.
Su: Open Mon - Fri 09:00.
Closed Mon - Fri 17:00.
Au: Open Mon - Fri 09:00.
Closed Mon - Fri 17:00.
Wn: Open Mon - Fri 09:00.
Closed Mon - Fri 17:00.
An answer phone operates 24 hours a day.
Ref: YH05487

FRENCH DAVIS, D
Mr D French Davis, Upper Manor Farm, Letcombe Regis, Wantage, **Oxfordshire**, OX12 9LD, **ENGLAND**.
(T) 01488 72342 **(F)** 01488 72342
(M) 07831 118764.
Profile Trainer. **Ref: YH05488**

FRENCH FURZE STABLES
French Furze Stables, Maddanstown, Curragh, **County Kildare**, **IRELAND**.
(T) 045 441275.
Profile Supplies. **Ref: YH05489**

FRENCH, B & B
B & B French, Forlan Stud, Slaughterford, Chippenham, **Wiltshire**, SN14 8RD, **ENGLAND**.
(T) 01249 782333.
Profile Breeder. **Ref: YH05490**

FRENCH, D
Mrs D French, 68A South Green, Coates, Peterborough, **Cambridgeshire**, PE7 2BL, **ENGLAND**.
(T) 01733 840262.
Profile Breeder. **Ref: YH05491**

FRENCH, J
Mrs J French, 1 Upper Birch Cottage, Shatterford, Bewdley, **Worcestershire**, DY12 1TR, **ENGLAND**.
(T) 01299 861242.
Profile Breeder. **Ref: YH05492**

FRENCH, MARK W
Mark W French DWCF, 26 Ellingham Rd, Adeyfield, Hemel Hempstead, **Hertfordshire**, HP2 5LE, **ENGLAND**.
(T) 07071 880898
(M) 07973 746088.
Profile Farrier. **Ref: YH05493**

FRENCH, S
Mrs S French, Ashmere Farm, Camer Pk Rd, Meopham, Gravesend, **Kent**, DA13 0AL, **ENGLAND**.
(T) 01474 814397.
Profile Supplies. **Ref: YH05494**

FRENCH'S FARM RIDING CTRE
French's Farm Riding Centre, Frenchs Farm, Pond Hall Rd, Hadleigh, Ipswich, **Suffolk**, IP7 5PQ, **ENGLAND**.
(T) 01473 828334.
Profile Riding Club. **Ref: YH05495**

FRENSHAM RIDING CLUB
Frensham Riding Club, Horseshoe Cottage, Shackleford, Godalming, **Surrey**, GU8 6BL, **ENGLAND**.
(T) 01252 702294.
Profile Club/Association, Riding Club. **Ref: YH05496**

FREQUENCY PRECISION
Frequency Precision, Shorts Farm, Northlew, Okehampton, **Devon**, EX20 3NR, **ENGLAND**.
(T) 01837 810590.
Profile Supplies. **Ref: YH05497**

FRERE-SMITH, NICHOLAS P
Nicholas P Frere-Smith, 16 Webster St, Bungay, **Suffolk**, NR35 1DX, **ENGLAND**.
(T) 01986 782489.
Profile Farrier. **Ref: YH05498**

FRESHFIELDS
Freshfields Equestrian Centre, Longford Turning, Market Drayton, **Shropshire**, TF9 3PW, **ENGLAND**.
(T) 01630 652495
Affiliated Bodies BHS.
Contact/s
Owner: Ms R Bailey
Profile Equestrian Centre, Riding School.
No.Staff: 4 Yr. Est: 2001 C.Size: 6 Acres
Ref: YH05499

FRIAR PK EQUESTRIAN SUP
Friar Park Equestrian Supplies, Gravel Hill, Henley-on-Thames, **Oxfordshire**, RG9 2EG, **ENGLAND**.
(T) 01491 575479.
Profile Saddlery Retailer. **Ref: YH05500**

FRIARS HILL STABLES
Friars Hill Stables, Friars Hill, Sinnington, York, **Yorkshire (North)**, YO62 6SL, **ENGLAND**.
(T) 01751 432758
Affiliated Bodies BHS.
Contact/s
Owner: Ms A Brown **(Q)** BHSAI
Profile Arena, Equestrian Centre, Riding School, Stable/Livery, Transport/Horse Boxes. No.Staff: 5
Yr. Est: 1991 C.Size: 20 Acres
Opening Times
Sp: Open 09:00. Closed 17:00.
Su: Open 09:00. Closed 21:00.
Au: Open 09:00. Closed 17:00.
Wn: Open 09:00. Closed 15:00. **Ref: YH05501**

FRIDAY FIELD STABLES
Friday Field Stables, Holywell Lane, Upchurch, Sittingbourne, **Kent**, ME9 7HN, **ENGLAND**.
(T) 01634 386801 **(F)** 01634 386800.
Contact/s
Owner: Ms S Marshall **(Q)** BHSAI, Monty Roberts Cert.
(E) cabodles@dircon.co.uk
Profile Stable/Livery, Trainer.
One of only two recommended associates in Kent, for Kelly Marks - Intelligent Horsemanship. Friday Fields holds the Monty Roberts Preliminary Certificate of Horsemanship, and has trained with Kelly Marks, who is Monty Roberts protégée. No.Staff: 1
Yr. Est: 2000 C.Size: 14 Acres
Opening Times
Telephone for further information **Ref: YH05502**

FRIENDSHIP ESTATES
Friendship Estates Ltd, Old Hse Farm, Stubbs Walden, Doncaster, **Yorkshire (South)**, DN6 9BU, **ENGLAND**.
(T) 01302 700220 **(F)** 01302 700958
(E) info@friendshipestates.co.uk
(W) www.friendshipestates.co.uk.
Profile Supplies. **Ref: YH05503**

FRIESIAN HORSE ASS
Friesian Horse Association Of Great Britian & Ireland, Wingfield Castle, Diss, **Norfolk**, IP21 5RB, **ENGLAND**.
(T) 01379 388088.
Profile Club/Association. **Ref: YH05504**

FRIEZE FARM LIVERIES
Frieze Farm Liveries, Frieze Farm, Crowsley, Henley-on-Thames, **Oxfordshire**, RG9 4JL, **ENGLAND**.
(T) 0118 9724427.
Contact/s
Partner: Miss R Holt
Profile Stable/Livery. **Ref: YH05505**

FRIMBLE OF RIPON
Frimble of Ripon, Pendle Hse, Dallamires Lane, Ripon, **Yorkshire (North)**, HG4 1TT, **ENGLAND**.
(T) 01765 603888 **(F)** 01765 601389.
Profile Supplies. **Ref: YH05506**

FRINGFORD FEEDS
Fringford Feeds, Hall Farm, Fringford, Bicester, **Oxfordshire**, OX6 9DP, **ENGLAND**.
(T) 01869 277301 **(F)** 01869 277060.
Profile Feed Merchant. **Ref: YH05507**

FRISBY FLYERS HORSEBALL CLUB
Frisby Flyers Horseball Club, C/O Ten Steps, Church St, Seagrave, **Leicestershire**, LE12 7LT, **ENGLAND**.
(T) 01509 812806 **(F)** 01509 812334
(E) melaniewilson@compuserve.com.

Profile Club/Association. Ref: YH05508

FRISTON, MARTIN

Martin Friston DWCF, 83 Main St, Cranswick, Driffield, **Yorkshire (East)**, YO25 9QN, **ENGLAND**.
(T) 01377 270817.
Profile Farrier. Ref: YH05509

FRITH MANOR EQUESTRIAN CTRE

Frith Manor Equestrian Centre, Lullington Garth, London, **London (Greater)**, N12 7BP, **ENGLAND**.
(T) 020 83466703.
Contact/s
Manager: Mrs P Rule
Profile Riding School, Stable/Livery. Ref: YH05510

FRITTON LAKE

Fritton Lake Country World, Beccles Rd, Fritton, Great Yarmouth, **Norfolk**, NR31 9HA, **ENGLAND**.
(T) 01493 488208/488288 **(F)** 01493 488355
(W) www.frittonlake.co.uk.
Contact/s
Owner: Mr E Knowles
Profile Stable/Livery.
Heavy horse centre with harnessing displays, pony rides and wagon rides. Other attractions include fishing, golf, falconry centre, a children's farm, gardens and woodland walks. Leisure attraction entry £5.30 for adults and £3.90 for children Yr. Est: 1976
Opening Times
Sp: Open Mon - Sun 10:00. Closed Mon - Sun 17:30.
Su: Open Mon - Sun 10:00. Closed Mon - Sun 17:30.
Au: Open Mon - Sun 10:00. Closed Mon - Sun 17:30.
Open from 1st April - 30th September also weekends and half term during Oct Ref: YH05511

FROGGATT, D M

D M Froggatt AFCL, 37 Chalk Lane, Sidlesham, **Sussex (West)**, PO20 7LW, **ENGLAND**.
(T) 01243 641517.
Profile Farrier. Ref: YH05512

FROGHILL TACK

Froghill Tack, Froghill Farm, Sandford, Ventnor, **Isle of Wight**, PO38 3AN, **ENGLAND**.
(T) 01983 840205.
Contact/s
Owner: Mrs S Richardson Ref: YH05513

FROGMORE STABLES LIVERY YARD

Frogmore Stables Livery Yard, Frogmore Stables, Frogmore Bottom, Kings Walden, Hitchin, **Hertfordshire**, SG4 8NN, **ENGLAND**.
(T) 01438 871733.
Contact/s
Owner: Miss H Lasham Ref: YH05514

FROGPOOL MANOR SADDLERY

Frogpool Manor Farm, Perry St, Chislehurst, **Kent**, BR7 6HA, **ENGLAND**.
(T) 020 83000716 **(F)** 020 83080210
(E) sales@frogpool.com
(W) www.frogpool.com.
Contact/s
General Manager: Ms K Boxall
(E) kate@frogpool.com
Profile Riding Wear Retailer, Saddlery Retailer, Supplies.
Restaurant serving breakfast, lunch and afternoon tea. One of the largest equestrian retailers in the country
No.Staff: 30 Yr. Est: 1979 C.Size: 5 Acres
Opening Times
Sp: Open Mon - Sun 09:30. Closed Mon - Sun 18:00.
Su: Open Mon - Sun 09:30. Closed Mon - Sun 18:00.
Au: Open Mon - Sun 09:30. Closed Mon - Sun 18:00.
Wn: Open Mon - Sun 09:30. Closed Mon - Sun 18:00. Ref: YH05515

FROMUS VETNRY GROUP

Fromus Veterinary Group, Fromus Hse, Street Farm Rd, Saxmundham, **Suffolk**, IP17 1DU, **ENGLAND**.
(T) 01728 602599 **(F)** 01728 603960.
Profile Medical Support. Ref: YH05516

FRONT RUNNER RACE

Front Runner Race Horse Transport, Upper Woods Field Farm, Woodsfield, Madresfield, Malvern, **Worcestershire**, WR13 5BE, **ENGLAND**.
(T) 01905 831161.
Profile Transport/Horse Boxes. Ref: YH05517

FROSBURY FARM FEEDS

Frosbury Farm Feeds, Frosbury Farm, Gravetts Lane, Guildford, **Surrey**, GU3 3JW, **ENGLAND**.
(T) 01483 232294 **(F)** 01483 237037.
Profile Feed Merchant. Ref: YH05518

FROSBURY'S

Frosbury's, Peacock Lane, Bracknell, **Berkshire**, RG12 8SS, **ENGLAND**.
(T) 01344 861130.
Profile Saddlery Retailer. Ref: YH05519

FROST, R G

R G Frost, Hawson Stables, Buckfastleigh, **Devon**, TQ11 0HP, **ENGLAND**.
(T) 01364 642267 **(F)** 01364 643182.
Contact/s
Owner: Mr R Frost
Profile Trainer. Ref: YH05520

FROST, T

T Frost, South Prde, Bawtry, Doncaster, **Yorkshire (South)**, DN10 6JH, **ENGLAND**.
(T) 01302 710309.
Profile Saddlery Retailer. Ref: YH05521

FROST, T J

T J Frost DWCF, Broad Lane Farm, Broad Lane, Brown Edge, Stoke-on-Trent, **Staffordshire**, ST6 8TT, **ENGLAND**.
(T) 01782 503516
(M) 07850 512061.
Profile Farrier. Ref: YH05522

FROSTS ROSETTES

Frosts Rosettes, 365 Totnes Rd, Collaton St Mary, Paignton, **Devon**, TQ4 7DE, **ENGLAND**.
(T) 01803 664848.
Profile Supplies. Ref: YH05523

FROXFIELD TRAINING CTRE

Froxfield Training Centre, Froxfield Stud Farm, Alexanders Lane, Privett, Alton, **Hampshire**, GU34 3PW, **ENGLAND**.
(T) 01730 828426.
Profile Trainer. Ref: YH05524

FRUEHAUF, CRANE

Crane Fruehauf Ltd, Unit 1-9 Thames Rd, Barking, **Essex**, IG11 0HN, **ENGLAND**.
(T) 020 85948831 **(F)** 020 85946187.
Contact/s
Manager: Mr C Bowers
Profile Transport/Horse Boxes. Ref: YH05525

FRY USHER & EDWARDS

Fry Usher & Edwards, Vetnry Surgery, Trevithick Rd, Camborne, **Cornwall**, TR14 8LQ, **ENGLAND**.
(T) 01209 718281.
Profile Medical Support. Ref: YH05526

FRY USHER & EDWARDS

Fry Usher & Edwards, The Vetnry Ctre, Drump Rd, Redruth, **Cornwall**, TR15 1SW, **ENGLAND**.
(T) 01209 214737.
Profile Medical Support. Ref: YH05527

FRYATT, T J

T J Fryatt RSS, Maple Farm, Cudham Lane South, Cudham, Sevenoaks, **Kent**, TN14 7QD, **ENGLAND**.
(T) 01959 572383.
Profile Farrier. Ref: YH05528

FRYER, LEWIS E

Lewis E Fryer, Barn Forge, Milde Drove, Ramsey Heights, Huntingdon, **Cambridgeshire**, PE26 2RG, **ENGLAND**.
(T) 01487 814142.
Profile Breeder, Farrier. Ref: YH05529

FULCHER, J P

J P Fulcher, 8 Gordon Ave, Harrogate, **Yorkshire (North)**, HG1 3DH, **ENGLAND**.
(T) 01423 561009.
Contact/s
Owner: Mr J Fulcher Ref: YH05530

FULLER, C A

C A Fuller, 5 Nant Y Gollen, Felindre, Brecon, **Powys**, LD3 0TB, **WALES**.
(T) 01497 847439.
Profile Farrier. Ref: YH05531

FULLER, D A

D A Fuller, Lower Rd, Castle Rising, King's Lynn, **Norfolk**, PE31 6AD, **ENGLAND**.
(T) 01553 631484.
Contact/s
Owner: Mr D Fuller
Profile Farrier. Ref: YH05532

FULLER, R S

R S Fuller, Riverside Ind Est, Littlehampton, **Sussex (West)**, BN17 7DR, **ENGLAND**.
(T) 01903 726458.
Profile Blacksmith. Ref: YH05533

FULLER, T W

T W Fuller, 9 Marquis Cl, Bishop's Stortford, **Hertfordshire**, CM23 4PH, **ENGLAND**.
(T) 01279 651053.
Profile Farrier. Ref: YH05534

FULLERTON CAR & TRAILER

Fullerton Car & Trailer, 201 Gilford Rd, Portadown, Craigavon, **County Armagh**, BT63 5LG, **NORTHERN IRELAND**.
(T) 028 38831697.
Contact/s
Owner: Mr A Fullerton
Profile Transport/Horse Boxes. Ref: YH05535

FULLING MILL STUD

Fulling Mill Stud, Selsfield Rd, Ardingly, Haywards Heath, **Sussex (West)**, RH17 6TJ, **ENGLAND**.
(T) 01444 892847.
Contact/s
Manager: Mr M Roberts
Profile Breeder. Ref: YH05536

FULWOOD RIDING CTRE

Fulwood Riding Centre, Sandyforth Lane, Lightfoot Green, Preston, **Lancashire**, PR4 0AL, **ENGLAND**.
(T) 01772 864836.
Contact/s
Owner: Mrs N Fawcett
Profile Riding School, Stable/Livery. Ref: YH05537

FUNNELL, JOHN

John Funnell, Little Paddock Farm, Aston-Le-Walls, Daventry, **Northamptonshire**, NN11 6UD, **ENGLAND**.
(T) 01295 660021 **(F)** 01295 660152.
Profile Breeder. Ref: YH05538

FUNNELL, PIPPA

Pippa Funnell (Nee Nolan), Cobbitts Farm, Lyfield Lane, Forrest Green, Dorking, **Surrey**, RH5 5SN, **ENGLAND**.
(T) 01306 621351 **(F)** 01306 621450
(M) 07831 809093. Ref: YH05539

FUNWAY EQUESTRIAN CTRE

Funway Equestrian Centre, Maiden Lane, Hogsthorpe, Skegness, **Lincolnshire**, PE24 5QH, **ENGLAND**.
(T) 01754 872969.
Contact/s
Partner: Mrs J Sessions
Profile Riding School, Stable/Livery. Ref: YH05540

FURLING PRINTS

Furling Prints, Lyvennet, Crosby, Ravensworth, Pendrith, **Cumbria**, CA10 3JP, **ENGLAND**.
(T) 01931 5282. Ref: YH05541

FURLONG EQUESTRIAN SVS

Furlong Equestrian Services, Featherstone Hse, 375 High St, Rochester, **Kent**, ME1 1DQ, **ENGLAND**.
(T) 01634 848886 **(F)** 01634 848887
(M) 07850 958330. Ref: YH05542

FURNACE MILL STUD

Furnace Mill Stud, Wyre Forest, Kidderminster, **Worcestershire**, DY14 8NR, **ENGLAND**.
(T) 01299 266160 **(F)** 01299 266160.
Profile Breeder. Ref: YH05543

FURNASIA

Furnasia Ltd, Kestrels, Burwash, **Sussex (East)**, TN19 7JP, **ENGLAND**.
(T) 01435 8833345 **(F)** 01435 883642
(E) furnasia@dialpipex.com
(W) www.greenguard.co.uk.
Profile Supplies.
Greenguard produce the grazing mask, which restricts the amount of grass that can be eaten. This reduces grass consumption by 33%, enabling longer hours out at grass. Ref: YH05544

FURNESS & S CUMBERLAND SUPPLY

Furness & S Cumberland Supply Ltd, Kepplewray, Broughton-In-Furness, Ulverston, **Cumbria**, LA20 6BH, **ENGLAND**.
(T) 01229 716229.
Profile Supplies. Ref: YH05545

Key: (T) telephone (F) fax (M) mobile (E) E-Mail Address (W) Website Address (Q) Qualifications
Yr. Est: Year Established C.Size: Complex Size Sp: Spring Su: Summer Au: Autumn Wn: Winter

FURNESS FARM CROSS COUNTRY

Furness Farm Cross Country, Ivy Barn Lane, Margaretting, Ingatestone, **Essex**, CM4 0HB, **ENGLAND**.
(T) 01277 354794 (F) 01277 354042.
Profile Track/Course. Ref: YH05546

FURNESS, G A

G A Furness, Pallet Hill, Kirby Knowle, Thirsk, **Yorkshire (North)**, YO7 2JB, **ENGLAND**.
(T) 01845 537209.
Contact/s
Owner: Mrs G Anne-Furness
Profile Breeder. Ref: YH05547

FURNESS, J

Miss J Furness, Thirlestane Castle, Lauder, **Scottish Borders**, TD2 6RU, **SCOTLAND**.
(T) 01578 722542.
Profile Stable/Livery. Ref: YH05548

FURNESS, P M & J J

P M & J J Furness, Oddo Hse Farm, West End, Elton, Matlock, **Derbyshire**, DE4 2BZ, **ENGLAND**.
(T) 01629 650125. Ref: YH05549

FURNESS, ROBIN

Robin Furness, Stanhow Farm, Great Langton, Northallerton, **Yorkshire (North)**, DL7 0TJ, **ENGLAND**.
(T) 01609 748614
Affiliated Bodies EAS.
Contact/s
Owner: Mr R Furness
Profile Commission Artist.
Mr R Furness is President of the Darlington Society of Art and a Member of the Armed Forces Art.
Yr. Est: 1956
Opening Times
By appointment only Ref: YH05550

FURNISS & MORTON

Furniss & Morton, The Veterinary Ctre, Summer Lane North, Worle, Weston-Super-Mare, **Somerset (North)**, BS22 6BE, **ENGLAND**.
(T) 01934 511611 (F) 01934 515976.
Profile Medical Support. Ref: YH05551

FURNIVAL STEEL

Furnival Steel Co Ltd, London Works, 86-88 Bridge St, Sheffield, **Yorkshire (South)**, S3 8NT, **ENGLAND**.
(T) 0114 2720403.
Profile Blacksmith. Ref: YH05552

FURTH, ELIZABETH

Elizabeth Furth, 11 Holdernesse Rd, London, **London (Greater)**, SW17 7RG, **ENGLAND**.
(T) 020 86822684 (F) 020 86823241.
Profile Photographer/Journalist. Ref: YH05553

FURZE HILL FARM & STUD

Furze Hill Farm & Stud, Star Hill, Churt, Farnham, **Surrey**, GU10 2HS, **ENGLAND**.
(T) 01428 714313.
Profile Breeder. Ref: YH05554

FUTURE DISTRIBUTION UK

Future Distribution UK, PO Box 87, Crawley, **Sussex (West)**, RH10 2WU, **ENGLAND**.
(T) 01293 416759 (F) 01293 416759.
Profile Supplies. Ref: YH05555

FYLDE COAST BRIDLEWAY ASS

Fylde Coast Bridleway Association, Old Vicarage Farm, Pk Lane, Preesall, **Lancashire**, FY6 0NQ, **ENGLAND**.
(T) 01253 810068.
Profile Club/Association. Ref: YH05556

FYLDE HORSE CLUB

Fylde Horse Club, 40 Carshalton Rd, Blackpool, **Lancashire**, FY1 2NR, **ENGLAND**.
(T) 01253 23396.
Contact/s
Secretary: Mrs B Thomas
Profile Club/Association. Ref: YH05557

FYNA-LITE

Fyna-Lite, Wixford Lodge, Georges Elm Lane, Bidford-on-Avon, Alcester, **Warwickshire**, B50 4JT, **ENGLAND**.
(T) 01789 773320 (F) 01789 490326.
Contact/s
General Manager: Mr L Fynn
Profile Supplies. Ref: YH05558

FYRNWY EQUINE CLINICS

Fyrnwy Equine Clinics (Llanymynech), Bron Fyrnwy, Llanymynech, **Powys**, SY22 6LG, **WALES**.
(T) 01691 830597.
Profile Medical Support. Ref: YH05559

FYRNWY EQUINE CLINICS

Fyrnwy Equine Clinics (Shrewsbury), Pearhill Stud, Broadoak, Shrewsbury, **Shropshire**, SY4 3AF, **ENGLAND**.
(T) 01939 290638.
Contact/s
Partner: Mr D Jagger
Profile Medical Support. Ref: YH05560

G & A HORSE TRANSPORT

G & A Horse Transport, Lochnager, 15 Harcourt Drive, Harrogate, **Yorkshire (North)**, HG1 5AA, **ENGLAND**.
(T) 01423 504947
(M) 07710 730849.
Profile Transport/Horse Boxes. Ref: YH05561

G & C HORSE TRANSPORT

G & C Horse Transport, Meadowview, East Allington, Totnes, **Devon**, TQ9 7RQ, **ENGLAND**.
(T) 01548 521434.
Contact/s
Partner: Mr G Luscombe
Profile Transport/Horse Boxes. Ref: YH05562

G & K CRADDOCK & SONS

G & K Craddock & Sons, Hill Farm, Agden, Whitchurch, **Shropshire**, SY13 4RB, **ENGLAND**.
(T) 01948 860230 (F) 01948 860230.
Contact/s
Partner: Mrs K Craddock
Profile Stable/Livery. Ref: YH05563

G & K SVS

G & K Services, Sunny Mead Farm, Woodchurch, Ashford, **Kent**, TN26 3QW, **ENGLAND**.
(T) 01233 860863 (F) 01233 860864
(E) gkservices@cwcom.net.
Contact/s
Owner: Mr G Bell
Profile Transport/Horse Boxes. Trailer Repairs.
Ref: YH05564

G & L MNGMT CONSULTANTS

G & L Management Consultants, 92 Castlecatt Rd, Dervock, Ballymoney, **County Antrim**, BT53 8AW, **NORTHERN IRELAND**.
(T) 028 20742221 (F) 028 20741635.
Profile Club/Association. Ref: YH05565

G & L TRAILERS

G & L Trailers, 9 Jellicoe Cl, Willesborough, Ashford, **Kent**, TN24 0UW, **ENGLAND**.
(T) 01233 632139.
Profile Transport/Horse Boxes. Ref: YH05566

G & M PET SUPPLIES

G & M Pet Supplies, 52 High St, Chasetown, Burntwood, **Staffordshire**, WS7 8XF, **ENGLAND**.
(T) 01543 686991 (F) 01543 686991
(M) 07778 841206.
Contact/s
Owner: Mr C Willett
Profile Supplies. Ref: YH05567

G & M RODGER

G & M Rodger Ltd, Unit 7 Block B Whiteside Ind Est, Bathgate, **Lothian (West)**, EH48 2RX, **SCOTLAND**.
(T) 01506 633390 (F) 01506 633390.
Profile Blacksmith. Ref: YH05568

G A COMMERCIALS

G A Commercials, Hankham Hall Farm, Hankham Hall Rd, Hankham, Pevensey, **Sussex (East)**, BN24 5AH, **ENGLAND**.
(T) 01323 763617.
Contact/s
Owner: Mr G Bearcoe
Profile Transport/Horse Boxes.
Buy, sell, and repair horseboxes and trailers.
Ref: YH05569

G B GOMME & SON

G B Gomme & Son Ltd, Longwick Mill, Longwick, Princes Risborough, **Buckinghamshire**, HP27 9SA, **ENGLAND**.
(T) 01844 343143 (F) 01844 274912.
Contact/s
Owner: Mr M Gomme
Profile Saddlery Retailer. Ref: YH05570

G C HAYBALL

G C Hayball Ltd, Norton Hse, Hawkchurch, Axminster, **Devon**, EX13 5XW, **ENGLAND**.
(T) 01297 678410.
Profile Supplies. Ref: YH05571

G C MACINTYRE & PARTNERS

G C MacIntyre & Partners, Veterinary Surgery, Church St, Dingwall, **Highlands**, IV15 9SB, **SCOTLAND**.
(T) 01349 863117.
Profile Medical Support. Ref: YH05572

G C SEARLE & SONS

G C Searle & Sons, Trowlesworthy Farm, Plympton, Plymouth, **Devon**, PL7 5EJ, **ENGLAND**.
(T) 01752 839292.
Profile Equestrian Centre. Pony Trekking Stables.
Ref: YH05573

G COOKE COACHBUILDERS

G Cooke Coachbuilders, 41-43 Quakers Coppice, Crewe Gate Farm Ind Est, Crewe, **Cheshire**, CW1 6FA, **ENGLAND**.
(T) 01270 588598 (F) 01270 583787.
Profile Transport/Horse Boxes. Ref: YH05574

G E BAILEY & SONS

G E Bailey & Sons, Hempsall Farm, Rampton Rd, Willingham, **Cambridgeshire**, CB4 5JG, **ENGLAND**.
(T) 01954 60233.
Profile Breeder. Ref: YH05575

G E HUNT

G E Hunt, Sprink Farm, Dicken's Lane, Poynton, **Cheshire**, SK12 1NU, **ENGLAND**.
(T) 01625 872865.
Profile Medical Support. Ref: YH05576

G FITZSIMMONS & SON

G Fitzsimmons & Son, 25 Thornton Rd, Rosewell, **Lothian (Mid)**, EH24 9DP, **SCOTLAND**.
(T) 0131 4482186 (F) 0131 4482186.
Contact/s
Owner: Mr G Fitzsimmons
Profile Blacksmith. Ref: YH05577

G G H EQUITATION CTRE

G G H Equitation Centre, Ballacallin Beg, Crosby, Marown, **Isle of Man**, IN4 2HD, **ENGLAND**.
(T) 01624 851574.
Profile Breeder, Equestrian Centre, Riding School, Stable/Livery, Trainer. Ref: YH05578

G H BRADSHAW & SONS

G H Bradshaw & Sons Ltd, The Vineyard, Alkington, Whitchurch, **Shropshire**, SY13 3NE, **ENGLAND**.
(T) 01948 663621 (F) 01948 663621.
Profile Transport/Horse Boxes. Ref: YH05579

G H GARDNER & SONS

G H Gardner & Sons, Dibden Hill Farm, Dibden Hill, Chalfont St Giles, **Buckinghamshire**, HP8 4RD, **ENGLAND**.
(T) 01494 871669.
Contact/s
Owner: Mr G Gardner Ref: YH05580

G HARRAWAY & SONS

G Harraway & Sons, Wrington Vale Hse, Wrington Rd, Backwell, Bristol, **Bristol**, BS48 4AE, **ENGLAND**.
(T) 01934 833000 (F) 01934 877330.
Contact/s
Owner: Mr G Harraway
Profile Transport/Horse Boxes. Ref: YH05581

G HOWSAM & SON

G Howsam & Son, The Mill, Chapel Rd, Old Leake, Boston, **Lincolnshire**, PE22 9PW, **ENGLAND**.
(T) 01205 870232.
Profile Supplies. Ref: YH05582

G J & G A DAVIES

G J & G A Davies Ltd, Moor Hall Cottages, Dodds Green Lane, Aston, Nantwich, **Cheshire**, CW5 8DP, **ENGLAND**.
(T) 01270 780645 (F) 01270 780538.
Profile Blacksmith. Ref: YH05583

G J GARNER & SON

G J Garner & Son, Hawkes Farm, Dores Lane, Braishfield, Romsey, **Hampshire**, SO50 0PJ, **ENGLAND**.
(T) 01794 68151. Ref: YH05584

G J L

G J L Animal Feeds, Enterprise Way, Commercial

Pk, Fakenham, **Norfolk**, NR21 8SN, **ENGLAND**.
(T) 01328 851351 (F) 01328 851351
(E) sales@gjlanimalfeeds.co.uk
(W) www.gjlanimalfeeds.co.uk.
Contact/s
Manager: Mr I Gibson
(E) ian@gjlanimal-feeds.co.uk
Profile Feed Merchant. No.Staff: 5
Yr. Est: 1988
Opening Times
Sp: Open Mon - Sat 08:30. Closed Mon - Fri 17:00, Sat 12:00.
Su: Open Mon - Sat 08:30. Closed Mon - Fri 17:00, Sat 12:00.
Au: Open Mon - Sat 08:30. Closed Mon - Fri 17:00, Sat 12:00.
Wn: Open Mon - Sat 08:30. Closed Mon - Fri 17:00, Sat 12:00.
Closed Sundays Ref: YH05585

G J W TITMUSS

G J W Titmuss Ltd, New Mill, Lamer Lane, Wheathampstead, **Hertfordshire**, AL4 8RG, **ENGLAND**.
(T) 01582 833883 (F) 01582 833105.
Profile Supplies. Ref: YH05586

G JONES BROS

G Jones Bros, Fronarth Stud, Frongoy, Pennant, Llanon, **Ceredigion**, ST23 5PD, **WALES**.
(T) 01974 272246.
Profile Breeder. Ref: YH05587

G MAGSON FEEDS

G Magson Feeds, Southgate, Pickering, **Yorkshire (North)**, YO18 8BS, **ENGLAND**.
(T) 01751 472657.
Profile Feed Merchant. Ref: YH05588

G N GOULD & PARTNERS

G N Gould & Partners, 10 & 12 Languard Rd, Southampton, **Hampshire**, SO9 2QT, **ENGLAND**.
(T) 023 80223161.
Profile Medical Support. Ref: YH05589

G P TRAILERS & TOWBARS

G P Trailers & Towbars, 29 Ganton Cl, Southport, **Merseyside**, PR8 6JN, **ENGLAND**.
(T) 01704 540455 (F) 01704 540455.
Contact/s
Owner: Mr G Pearson
Profile Transport/Horse Boxes. Ref: YH05590

G PRUDHOE

G Prudhoe & Co Ltd, Phoenix Hse, Faverdale, **County Durham**, DL3 0QE, **ENGLAND**.
(T) 01325 486641 (F) 01325 382004
(E) prudhoe@compuserve.com.
Profile Club/Association. Ref: YH05591

G R M TRAILERS

G R M Trailers, 76A Ladysmith Ter, Ballymena, **County Antrim**, BT42 2AG, **NORTHERN IRELAND**.
(T) 028 25650900 (F) 028 25650900.
Contact/s
Owner: Mr R McKay
Profile Transport/Horse Boxes. Ref: YH05592

G R S NIXON

Mr G R S Nixon, Oakwood Farm, Ettrickbridge, Selkirk, **Scottish Borders**, TD7 5HJ, **SCOTLAND**.
(T) 01750 52245.
Profile Supplies. Ref: YH05593

G R WADE & SON

G R Wade & Son, 6 Hemingway Cl, Newthorpe, Nottingham, **Nottinghamshire**, NG16 2DJ, **ENGLAND**.
(T) 01773 712966. Ref: YH05594

G RANDALL & SONS

G Randall & Sons, 1 Newstead Rd, Weymouth, **Dorset**, DT4 0AY, **ENGLAND**.
(T) 01305 783455 (F) 01305 783455.
Contact/s
Partner: Mr W Randall
Profile Blacksmith. Ref: YH05595

G REES AGRICULTURAL MERCHANTS

G Rees Agricultural Merchants, North St, Coerwys, Mold, **Flintshire**, CH7 5AW, **WALES**.
(T) 01352 720111.
Profile Supplies. Ref: YH05596

G T TOWING

G T Towing Ltd, 6 Hatfield Rd, Potters Bar, **Hertfordshire**, EN6 1HP, **ENGLAND**.
(T) 01707 658312 (F) 01707 644638.
Contact/s
Manager: Mr A Thurgood
Profile Transport/Horse Boxes.
Trailers for hire/self-drive. Yr. Est: 1976
Opening Times
Sp: Open Mon - Sat 08:45. Closed Mon - Fri 17:30, Sat 16:00.
Su: Open Mon - Sat 08:45. Closed Mon - Fri 17:30, Sat 16:00.
Au: Open Mon - Sat 08:45. Closed Mon - Fri 17:30, Sat 16:00.
Wn: Open Mon - Sat 08:45. Closed Mon - Fri 17:30, Sat 16:00.
Closed Sundays Ref: YH05597

G T TRAILERS

G T Trailers, Main St, Leire, Lutterworth, **Leicestershire**, LE17 5HF, **ENGLAND**.
(T) 01455 202095 (F) 01455 202095.
Contact/s
Owner: Mr G Bundock
Profile Transport/Horse Boxes. Ref: YH05598

G T WARD & SON

G T Ward & Son Ltd, Decoy Farm, Gorefield, Wisbech, **Cambridgeshire**, PE13 4PL, **ENGLAND**.
(T) 01945 870207 (F) 01945 870207.
Profile Breeder. Ref: YH05599

G WESTAWAY & SON

G Westaway & Son, Anvil Hse, 9 Keybury Pk, Newton Abbot, **Devon**, TQ12 1DF, **ENGLAND**.
(T) 01626 356525.
Profile Farrier. Ref: YH05600

GABRIEL POWER

Gabriel Power & Co, Leamore Lane Ind Est, Walsall, **Midlands (West)**, WS2 7NT, **ENGLAND**.
(T) 01922 476330. Ref: YH05601

GABRIELS FARM

Gabriels Farm, Marsh Green Rd, Marsh Green, Edenbridge, **Kent**, TN8 5PP, **ENGLAND**.
(T) 01732 864812 (F) 01732 864812
(M) 07730 066088.
Profile Stable/Livery. Ref: YH05602

GACHE, R

R Gache, Newchapel Rd, Lingfield, **Surrey**, RH7 6BJ, **ENGLAND**.
(T) 01342 832570.
Contact/s
Owner: Mr R Gache
Profile Farrier. Ref: YH05603

GADD, CELIA

Celia Gadd, The Lodge, Shrub Farm, Burton Row, Brent Knoll, **Somerset**, TA9 4BX, **ENGLAND**.
(T) 01278 760787 (F) 01278 760787.
Profile Trainer. Ref: YH05604

GADDESDEN PLACE STABLES

Gaddesden Place Stables, Gaddesden Pl, Great Gaddesden, Hemel Hempstead, **Hertfordshire**, HP2 6EX, **ENGLAND**.
(T) 01442 252446.
Profile Riding School. Ref: YH05605

GAINSBOROUGH STABLES

Gainsborough Stables Limited, Hamilton Rd, Newmarket, **Suffolk**, CB8 0TE, **ENGLAND**.
(T) 01638 661998 (F) 01638 667394
(W) www.edunlop.com
Affiliated Bodies Newmarket Trainers Fed.
Contact/s
General Manager: Mr E Dunlop
(E) edunlop@gainsborough.ndirect.co.uk
Profile Trainer. No.Staff: 70 Yr. Est: 1980
C.Size: 10 Acres Ref: YH05606

GAINSBOROUGH STUD MNGMT

Gainsborough Stud Management Ltd, Woolton Hill, Newbury, **Berkshire**, RG20 9TE, **ENGLAND**.
(T) 01635 253273 (F) 01635 254690.
Contact/s
Manager: Mr P Bowles
Profile Breeder. Ref: YH05607

GALBRAITH, KEEVILL & GLEESON

Galbraith, Keevill & Gleeson, 43 St Johns Rd, Newbury, **Berkshire**, RG14 7PS, **ENGLAND**.
(T) 01635 40565.
Profile Medical Support. Ref: YH05608

GALBRAITH, KEEVILL & GLEESON

Galbraith, Keevill & Gleeson, 55A The Broadway, Thatcham, **Berkshire**, RG13 4HP, **ENGLAND**.
(T) 01635 868047.
Profile Medical Support. Ref: YH05609

GALE & PHILLIPSON

Gale & Phillipson Ltd (Harrogate), Alexandra Hse, 4 Alexandra Rd, Harrogate, **Yorkshire (North)**, HG1 5JS, **ENGLAND**.
(T) 01423 503521 (F) 01423 527631
(E) ridingschools@gale-phillipson-freeserve.co.uk.
Profile Club/Association. Ref: YH05610

GALE & PHILLIPSON

Gale & Phillipson Ltd (Northallerton), 74 High St, Northallerton, **Yorkshire (North)**, DL7 8EG, **ENGLAND**.
(T) 01609 780488 (F) 01609 773272.
Profile Club/Association. Ref: YH05611

GALE, BARBARA

Barbara Gale, 23 Manor Cl, Sherston, Malmesbury, **Wiltshire**, SN16 0NS, **ENGLAND**.
(T) 01666 840527
(M) 07831 835578.
Profile Supplies. Ref: YH05612

GALEA, P C

P C Galea, The Langdales, Brook Lane, Little Hoole, Preston, **Lancashire**, PR4 5JB, **ENGLAND**.
(T) 01772 614169.
Profile Breeder. Ref: YH05613

GALGORM MANOR EQUESTRIAN CTRE

Galgorm Manor Equestrian Centre, 136 Fenaghy Rd, Ballymena, **County Antrim**, BT42 1EA, **NORTHERN IRELAND**.
(T) 028 25881222
Affiliated Bodies BHS.
Profile Riding School, Stable/Livery. Ref: YH05614

GALGORM PARKS RIDING SCHOOL

Galgorm Parks Riding School, 112 Sand Rd, Galgorm, Ballymena, **County Antrim**, BT42 1DN, **NORTHERN IRELAND**.
(T) 028 25880269
Affiliated Bodies BHS.
Contact/s
Owner: Ms S Kyle (Q) BHSAI
Profile Riding School.
30 minute group lesson - £4.00. Yr. Est: 1979
Opening Times
Sp: Open Mon - Sat 09:00. Closed Mon - Sat 21:00.
Su: Open Mon - Sat 09:00. Closed Mon - Sat 21:00.
Au: Open Mon - Sat 09:00. Closed Mon - Sat 21:00.
Wn: Open Mon - Sat 09:00. Closed Mon - Sat 21:00.
Ref: YH05615

GALLACHER, A

A Gallacher, 30 Hillend Rd, Glasgow, **Glasgow (City of)**, G22 6NY, **SCOTLAND**.
(T) 0141 3365149.
Contact/s
Owner: Mr A Gallacher
Profile Blacksmith. Ref: YH05616

GALLAGHER POWER FENCE

Gallagher Power Fence UK Ltd, Curriers Cl, Canley, Coventry, **Midlands (West)**, CV4 8AW, **ENGLAND**.
(T) 024 76470141 (F) 024 76461464
(E) admin@gallagher.co.uk. Ref: YH05617

GALLERY OF SPORTING ART

Gallery of Sporting Art (The), 11 Main St, Grey Abbey, **County Down**, BT22 2NE, **NORTHERN IRELAND**.
(T) 028 9174293. Ref: YH05618

GALLERY, JULIAN M

Julian M Gallery DWCF, 29 Fosseway Court, Seaton, **Devon**, EX12 2LP, **ENGLAND**.
(T) 01297 22151.
Profile Farrier. Ref: YH05619

GALLEY, G

Mr & Mrs G Galley, Greenhouse Farm, Meerbrook, Leek, **Staffordshire**, ST13 8SX, **ENGLAND**.
(T) 01538 300238.
Profile Breeder. Ref: YH05620

GALLIERS, MARK E

Mark E Galliers DWCF, 4 Cae Pentice, Bridgend, **Bridgend**, CF32 0BN, **WALES**.
(T) 01656 746336.
Profile Farrier. Ref: YH05621

GALLOPING JOB SHOP

Galloping Job Shop (The), 52 High St, Westley Waterless, Newmarket, **Suffolk**, CB8 0RQ, **ENGLAND**.
(T) 01638 507451 (F) 01638 507799. Ref: YH05622

GALLOPON

Gallopon, 15 Lower Byfield, Monks Eleigh, Ipswich, **Suffolk**, IP7 7JJ, **ENGLAND**.
(T) 01449 740783 **(F)** 01449 740783.
Contact/s
Owner: Mr T Woodgate
Profile Supplies. **Ref: YH05623**

GALLOPS

Gallops (The), 49 Wilson Marriage Rd, Colchester, **Essex**, CO4 4DF, **ENGLAND**.
(T) 01206 861622.
Profile Supplies. **Ref: YH05624**

GALLOWAY & MACLEOD

Galloway & Macleod Ltd, New Cander Mill, 55 King St, Stonehouse, Larkhall, **Lanarkshire (South)**, ML9 3EH, **SCOTLAND**.
(T) 01698 791919 **(F)** 01698 793079. **Ref: YH05625**

GALLOWAY, SIMON C

Simon C Galloway RSS, 4 Ardenron Cottages, Tandridge Lane, Lingfield, **Surrey**, RH7 6LL, **ENGLAND**.
(T) 01342 833990.
Profile Farrier. **Ref: YH05626**

GALLOWAY, TOM

Tom Galloway, Culnoag Farm, Sorbie, Newton Stewart, **Dumfries and Galloway**, **SCOTLAND**..
Profile Breeder. **Ref: YH05627**

GALTRES VETNRY SURGERY

Galtres Veterinary Surgery, Applegarth, Flawith, Alne, **Yorkshire (North)**, YO61 1SF, **ENGLAND**.
(T) 01347 838888 **(F)** 01347 838877
(E) galtresvet@compuserve.com.
Profile Medical Support. **Ref: YH05628**

GALWAY RACE COMMITTEE

Galway Race Committee, The Race Course, Ballybrit, **County Galway**, **IRELAND**.
(T) 091 753870
(E) galway@iol.ie
(W) www.iol.ie/galway-races.
Profile Club/Association. **Ref: YH05629**

GAMBLE

Mr & Mrs Gamble, Lanes End Garage, Meer End, Kenilworth, **Warwickshire**, CV8 1PT, **ENGLAND**.
(T) 01676 532294.
Profile Breeder. **Ref: YH05630**

GAMBLE, KEN

Ken Gamble, Little Barton, Ashdale Cl, Aldsworth, Cheltenham, **Gloucestershire**, GL54 3QT, **ENGLAND**.
(T) 01451 844716.
Profile Transport/Horse Boxes. **Ref: YH05631**

GAMBLE, SEAN

Sean Gamble DWCF, 1 Well Rd, Waterston, Milford Haven, **Pembrokeshire**, SA73 1DT, **WALES**.
(T) 01646 698713
(M) 07831 472555.
Profile Farrier. **Ref: YH05632**

GAME PLAN DEVELOPMENTS

Game Plan Developments Ltd, Office 4 Unit 5, 30 Sedgley Rd, Penn, **Midlands (West)**, WV4 5LE, **ENGLAND**.
(T) 01902 345200 **(F)** 01902 346200.
Profile Club/Association. **Ref: YH05633**

GAME, DAVID C

David C Game DWCF, 119 Heybridge Rd, Ingatestone, **Essex**, CM4 9AH, **ENGLAND**.
(T) 01277 352468
(M) 07768 310661.
Profile Breeder, Farrier, Stable/Livery. **Ref: YH05634**

GAMIC TRAILERS

Gamic Trailers, Hollybank, Dolfor, Newtown, **Powys**, SY16 4BJ, **WALES**.
(T) 01686 627181.
Contact/s
Partner: Mr M Francis
Profile Transport/Horse Boxes. **Ref: YH05635**

GAMMACK, C A

Charles A Gammack, 83 High St, Aberlour, **Moray**, AB38 9QB, **SCOTLAND**.
(T) 01340 871319
(E) cag@cagmmack.fsnet.co.uk
(W) www.cagammack.fsnet.co.uk.
Contact/s
General Manager: Mrs R Gammack
Profile Saddlery Retailer. Repair Tack and Clean Horse Rugs.
Repair tack and clean horse rugs
Opening Times
Sp: Open 09:00. Closed 17:30.
Su: Open 09:00. Closed 17:30.
Au: Open 09:00. Closed 17:30.
Wn: Open 09:00. Closed 17:30. **Ref: YH05636**

GAMMELL EQUESTRIAN

Gammell Equestrian, Cregane, Rathluirc, **County Limerick**, **IRELAND**.
(T) 063 81619.
Profile Supplies. **Ref: YH05637**

GAMMIE, J W

J W Gammie, Drumforber, Laurencekirk, **Aberdeenshire**, AB30 1RS, **SCOTLAND**.
(T) 01561 377407 **(F)** 01561 377318.
Profile Breeder. **Ref: YH05638**

GANDOLFO, D R

D R Gandolfo, The Downs Stables, Manor Rd, Wantage, **Oxfordshire**, OX12 8NF, **ENGLAND**.
(T) 01235 763242 **(F)** 01235 764149.
Contact/s
Owner: Mr D Gandolfo
Profile Trainer. **Ref: YH05639**

GANE, A R

A R Gane, Lydford Agricultural Store, West Lydford, Somerton, **Somerset**, TA11 7DL, **ENGLAND**.
(T) 01963 240501.
Profile Supplies. **Ref: YH05640**

GANSTEAD EQUESTRIAN CTRE

Ganstead Equestrian Centre, Swine Lane, Ganstead, Hull, **Yorkshire (East)**, HU11 4BE, **ENGLAND**.
(T) 01482 812378.
Profile Farrier. **Ref: YH05641**

GANT, D & E

D & E Gant, 7 Kirkham Ave, Kirkhamgate, Wakefield, **Yorkshire (West)**, WF2 0RY, **ENGLAND**.
(T) 01924 365974.
Profile Breeder. **Ref: YH05642**

GANWICK FODDER STORE

Ganwick Fodder Store, Ganwick Farm, Wagon Rd, Barnet, **Hertfordshire**, EN4 0PL, **ENGLAND**.
(T) 020 84410431.
Contact/s
Owner: Mr A Challk
Profile Feed Merchant. **Ref: YH05643**

GARDEN IMAGES

Garden Images Ltd, Highfield Hse, Wawensmere Rd, Solihull, **Midlands (West)**, B95 6BN, **ENGLAND**.
(T) 01564 794035 **(F)** 01564 794756
(E) info@garden-images.co.uk.
Profile Supplies. **Ref: YH05644**

GARDNER, ANNA

Mrs Anna Gardner, Brownrigg Farm, Alresdon, Frizington, **Cumbria**, CA26 3UW, **ENGLAND**.
(T) 01946 861795.
Profile Breeder. **Ref: YH05645**

GARDNER, C D

C D Gardner, The Hay Cabin, Nethercote, Banbury, **Oxfordshire**, OX17 2BN, **ENGLAND**.
(T) 01295 262028.
Contact/s
Owner: Mr C Gardner **Ref: YH05646**

GARDNER, DEREK T

Derek T Gardner AWCF, Grey Hound Hse, Little Strickland, Penrith, **Cumbria**, CA10 3EG, **ENGLAND**.
(T) 01931 716000.
Profile Farrier. **Ref: YH05647**

GARDNER, R

R Gardner, 50 Desborough Rd, Rothwell, Kettering, **Northamptonshire**, NN14 6JG, **ENGLAND**.
(T) 01536 710599.
Profile Blacksmith. **Ref: YH05648**

GARDNER, R & D M

Messrs R & D M Gardner, Morris Dean Farm, Out Rawcliffe, Preston, **Lancashire**, FY6 0NX, **ENGLAND**.
(T) 01253 700451.
Profile Breeder. **Ref: YH05649**

GARELOCH RIDING CLUB

Gareloch Riding Club, 22A Suffolk St, Helensburgh, **Argyll and Bute**, G84 8YL, **SCOTLAND**.
(T) 01436 671292.
Contact/s
Chairman: Mrs A Fisher
Profile Club/Association, Riding Club. **Ref: YH05650**

GARFORTH LIVERY YARD

Garforth Livery Yard, Whitehouse Farm, Nanny Goat Lane, Garforth, Leeds, **Yorkshire (West)**, LS25 2DQ, **ENGLAND**.
(T) 0113 2862014.
Contact/s
Owner: Miss M Cleamer
Profile Stable/Livery, Transport/Horse Boxes.
Private riding. **Ref: YH05651**

GARLICK S & V, RUSSELL M

S & V Garlick & M Russell, Newhse Welsh Cobs, Charlwood Farm, Camps End, Castle Camps, **Cambridgeshire**, CB1 6TR, **ENGLAND**.
(T) 01799 584320.
Profile Breeder. **Ref: YH05652**

GARLOWBANK SMITHY

Garlowbank Smithy, Kinnordy, Kirriemuir, **Angus**, DD8 4LH, **SCOTLAND**.
(T) 01575 573903.
Contact/s
Owner: Mr G Butler
Profile Blacksmith. **Ref: YH05653**

GARNER, SEBASTIAN

Sebastian Garner, PO Box 119, Knutsford, **Cheshire**, WA16 9FN, **ENGLAND**.
(T) 07050 609110 **(F)** 07070 657517.
Profile Medical Support.
A paging service for equestrian emergencies.
Ref: YH05654

GARRARD, STUART R

Stuart R Garrard DWCF, No 2 Pigutle Cottage, The Street, Bedingfield, Eye, **Suffolk**, IP23 7LQ, **ENGLAND**.
(T) 01728 76720
(M) 07860 779667.
Profile Farrier. **Ref: YH05655**

GARRETT, DAI

Dai Garrett, Ysgwyddgwyn Isaf Farm, Deri, Bargoed, **Caerphilly**, CF8 9NT, **WALES**.
(T) 01443 831632.
Profile Breeder. **Ref: YH05656**

GARROD'S SADDLERY

Garrod's Saddlery, Station Farm, High Rd, Wortwell, Harleston, **Suffolk**, IP20 0EN, **ENGLAND**.
(T) 01986 788288.
Profile Supplies. **Ref: YH05657**

GARSON FARM

Garson Farm Livery Stables & Riding School, Winterdown Rd, Esher, **Surrey**, KT10 8LS, **ENGLAND**.
(T) 01372 462026.
Contact/s
Owner: Miss S Timpson
Profile Riding School, Stable/Livery. **Ref: YH05658**

GARSTON VETNRY GRP

Garston Veterinary Group, Garston Hse, Frome, **Somerset**, BA11 1PZ, **ENGLAND**.
(T) 01373 451115 **(F)** 01373 451005
(E) garstonvets@telinco.co.uk.
Contact/s
Partner: Mr D Francis **(Q)** MRCVS
Profile Medical Support. **Ref: YH05659**

GARTH FOLD VETNRY CTRE

Garth Fold Veterinary Centre, 48 High St, Idle, **Yorkshire (West)**, BD10 8NN, **ENGLAND**.
(T) 01274 618075.
Profile Medical Support. **Ref: YH05660**

GARTH HSE

Garth House Veterinary Surgery (The), Garth Hse, 17 Market Pl, Bridlington, **Yorkshire (East)**, YO16 4QJ, **ENGLAND**.
(T) 01262 674085 **(F)** 01262 671120.
Profile Medical Support. **Ref: YH05661**

GARTH VETNRY GROUP

Garth Veterinary Group, Straight Lane, Beeford, **Yorkshire (East)**, YO25 8BE, **ENGLAND**.
(T) 01262 488323 **(F)** 01262 488770.
Contact/s
Partner: Mr N Kingston **(Q)** MRCVS
Profile Medical Support. **Ref: YH05662**

GARTH-ROBERTS, GORDON

Gordon Garth-Roberts, Dyfnog Stud, Llanrhaeadr, Denbigh, **Denbighshire**, LL16 4NG, **WALES**.
(T) 01745 812921 **(F)** 01745 816404.
Contact/s

Owner: Mr G Garth-Roberts
Profile Saddlery Retailer. Ref: YH05663

GARTMORE RIDING SCHOOL

Gartmore Riding School, Hall Lane, Hammerwich, Burntwood, **Staffordshire**, WS7 0JT, **ENGLAND**.
(T) 01543 686117.
Contact/s
Partner: Mr M Evans
Profile Riding School. Ref: YH05664

GARVEY, ARNOLD

Arnold Garvey, C/O Horse & Hound, Kings Reach Tower, Stamford St, London, **London (Greater)**, SE1 9LS, **ENGLAND**.
(T) 020 72616453 (F) 020 72615429.
Profile Supplies. Ref: YH05665

GARWAY HAFLINGERS

Garway Haflingers, 13 Parkfield, Pucklechurch, Bristol, **Bristol**, BS16 9NR, **ENGLAND**.
(T) 01179 373479
Affiliated Bodies HS GB.
Contact/s
Owner: Ms H Robbins
(E) helen.m.robbins@orange.co.uk
Profile Breeder. Ref: YH05666

GASCOIGNE, R F

R F Gascoigne, 17 Worton Rd, Middle Barton, **Oxfordshire**, OX7 4EE, **ENGLAND**.
(T) 01869 340376.
Profile Farrier. Ref: YH05667

GASCOINES

Gascoines, 1 Church St, Southwell, **Nottinghamshire**, NG25 0HH, **ENGLAND**.
(T) 01636 813245 (F) 01636 815342.
Contact/s
Partner: Mr D Gascoine
Profile Auctioneers. Ref: YH05668

GASELEE, N

N Gaselee, Saxon Cottage, Upper Lambourn, Hungerford, **Berkshire**, RG17 8QN, **ENGLAND**.
(T) 01488 71503.
Contact/s
Owner: Mr N Gaselee
Profile Trainer. Ref: YH05669

GASKELL

Mrs Gaskell, Grove Farm, Yatton Keynell, Chippenham, **Wiltshire**, SN14 7BS, **ENGLAND**.
(T) 01249 782289.
Profile Breeder. Ref: YH05670

GATE INN RIDING CLUB

Gate Inn Riding Club, 70 Coton Rd, Whitacre Heath, Coleshill, **Warwickshire**, B46 2HL, **ENGLAND**.
(T) 01675 464591.
Contact/s
Secretary: Mrs K Lapworth
Profile Club/Association, Riding Club. Ref: YH05671

GATEHOUSE VETNRY HOSPITAL

Gatehouse Veterinary Hospital, Wayside Veterinary Surgery, 2 Long Lane, Hoole, Chester, **Cheshire**, CH2 2PD, **ENGLAND**.
(T) 01244 570364.
Profile Medical Support. Ref: YH05672

GATERLEY MINIATURE HORSE STUD

Gaterley Miniature Horse Stud, High Gaterley Farm, Huttons Ambo, **Yorkshire (North)**, YO60 7HT, **ENGLAND**.
(T) 07000 782077.
Profile Breeder. Ref: YH05673

GATES TO GRATES

Gates To Grates, Five Acres, 41 The Heath, Hevingham, Norwich, **Norfolk**, NR10 5QL, **ENGLAND**.
(T) 01603 754256.
Profile Blacksmith. Ref: YH05674

GATESMAN, NIGEL W

Nigel W Gatesman DWCF, 1 Elm Court, Sonning Common, Reading, **Berkshire**, RG4 9ND, **ENGLAND**.
(T) 0118 9723974.
Profile Farrier. Ref: YH05675

GATEWOOD STABLES

Gatewood Stables, Gatewood, Wilmington, Polegate, **Sussex (East)**, BN26 6RP, **ENGLAND**.
(T) 01323 483709.
Profile Riding School. Ref: YH05676

GATLAND, J

Mr J Gatland, 51 The Crossways, Merstham, **Surrey**, RH1 3NA, **ENGLAND**.
(T) 01737 642366.
Profile Breeder. Ref: YH05677

GAUVAIN, E

Mrs E Gauvain, Jack's Plat, Duddleswell, Ashdown Forest, **Sussex (East)**, TN22 3JR, **ENGLAND**.
(T) 01825 712550.
Profile Breeder. Ref: YH05678

GAWTHORPE SADDLERS

Gawthorpe Saddlers, Chequers Lane, Eversley, Hook, **Hampshire**, RG27 0NT, **ENGLAND**.
(T) 0118 9732293.
Profile Saddlery Retailer. Ref: YH05679

GAY KALLIWAY RACING

Gay Kalliway Racing, Lingfield Pk Racecourse, Racecourse Rd, Lingfield, **Surrey**, RH7 6PQ, **ENGLAND**.
(T) 01342 837100 (F) 01342 837101.
Profile Trainer. Ref: YH05680

GAYDEN PALOMINOS

Gayden Palominos, Worden Farm, Shebbear, Beaworthy, **Devon**, EX21 5TD, **ENGLAND**.
(T) 01409 281839 (F) 01409 281840.
Profile Breeder. Ref: YH05681

GAYNORS SADDLERY

Hound Horse & Rider, 75-79 King St, Dukinfield, **Cheshire**, SK16 4NQ, **ENGLAND**.
(T) 0161 3305798
Affiliated Bodies BETA.
Contact/s
Owner: Ms G Richardson
Profile Riding Wear Retailer, Saddlery Retailer, Supplies.
Specialists in straight cut saddles. Free saddle fitting service on new leather saddles. No.Staff: 4
Yr. Est: 1970
Opening Times
Sp: Open Mon - Sat 09:30. Closed Mon, Wed - Sat 17:30, Tues 13:00.
Su: Open Mon - Sat 09:30. Closed Mon, Wed - Sat 17:30, Tues 13:00.
Au: Open Mon - Sat 09:30. Closed Mon, Wed - Sat 17:30, Tues 13:00.
Wn: Open Mon - Sat 09:30. Closed Mon, Wed - Sat 17:30, Tues 13:00. Ref: YH05682

GAYTON VETNRY GROUP

Gayton Veterinary Group, Gayton Hse, 40 Hatchlands Rd, Redhill, **Surrey**, RH1 6AT, **ENGLAND**.
(T) 01737 760585 (F) 01737 778879.
Profile Medical Support. Ref: YH05683

GAZELEY STUD FARM

Gazeley Stud Farm, Moulton Rd, Gazeley, Newmarket, **Suffolk**, CB8 8RA, **ENGLAND**.
(T) 01638 750260.
Profile Breeder. Ref: YH05684

GB TRUCK & TRAILER RENTAL

GB Truck & Trailer Rental, Unit 10F Goldthorpe Ind Est, Commercial Rd, Goldthorpe, Rotherham, **Yorkshire (South)**, S63 9BL, **ENGLAND**.
(T) 07071 226786 (F) 01709 896556.
Profile Transport/Horse Boxes. Ref: YH05685

GEBBIE VALLEYS

Gebbie Valleys Hanovarian Stud Farm, Ambervale Farm, North Common Lane, Sway, Lymington, **Hampshire**, SO41 8LL, **ENGLAND**.
(T) 07831 101093 (F) 01590 683727.
Profile Breeder, Stable/Livery. Ref: YH05686

GEDDES-BODEN, LESLIE

Leslie Geddes-Boden, Midland Trce, Victoria Rd, London, **London (Greater)**, NW10 6DB, **ENGLAND**.
(T) 020 84531535 (F) 020 84531536
(W) www.lesliegeddesbrown.com.
Contact/s
Owner: Leslie Geddes-Boden
Profile Riding Wear Retailer. Ref: YH05687

GEDDING MILL FORGE

Gedding Mill Forge, Mill Hse, Gedding, Bury St Edmunds, **Suffolk**, IP30 0PZ, **ENGLAND**.
(T) 01449 736301 (F) 01449 736103.
Contact/s
Owner: Mr E Hitchcock
Profile Blacksmith. Ref: YH05688

GEDDIS TRANSPORT

Geddis Transport, 21 Bridge Rd South, Helens Bay, **County Down**, BT19 1JT, **NORTHERN IRELAND**.
(T) 028 91853897 (F) 028 91853666.
Profile Transport/Horse Boxes. Ref: YH05689

GEE GEE'S

Donna Gibson T/A Gee Gee's (Equestrian Outfitters), 13 Bank St, Dumfries, **Dumfries and Galloway**, DG1 2NX, **SCOTLAND**.
(T) 01387 249977
(E) info@geegees-equestrian.co.uk
(W) www.geegees-equestrian.co.uk.
Contact/s
Owner: Miss D Gibson
Profile Riding Wear Retailer, Saddlery Retailer, Supplies. No.Staff: 3 Yr. Est: 1999
Opening Times
Sp: Open 10:00. Closed 17:00.
Su: Open 09:00. Closed 18:00.
Au: Open 10:00. Closed 17:00.
Wn: Open 10:00. Closed 17:00. Ref: YH05690

GEE, M P

Mr M P Gee, Cottage Farm, Water Lane, Carlton In Lindrick, Worksop, **Nottinghamshire**, S81 9EU, **ENGLAND**.
(T) 01909 732602 (F) 01909 731101
(M) 07966 181845.
Profile Breeder. Ref: YH05691

GEE, MICHAEL

Michael Gee, The Croft, 44 Back Lane, Holme upon Spalding Moor, **Yorkshire (East)**, YO43 4AU, **ENGLAND**.
(T) 01430 860346.
Profile Architectural/Property svs. Ref: YH05692

GEEGEES

GeeGees, Coltsfoot, 11 Ebbsgrove, Loughton, Milton Keynes, **Buckinghamshire**, MK5 8BD, **ENGLAND**.
(T) 07010 710647 (F) 07010 710647
(E) sm@geegees.co.uk.
Profile Saddlery Retailer. Ref: YH05693

GEERINGS OF ASHFORD

Geerings of Ashford Ltd, Cobbs Wood Hse, Chart Rd, Ashford, **Kent**, TN23 1EP, **ENGLAND**.
(T) 01233 633366 (F) 01233 665713
(E) print-sales@geerings.co.uk.
Profile Club/Association. Ref: YH05694

GELLER, J S

J S Geller, The Plough, Boxford Rd, Milden, Ipswich, **Suffolk**, IP7 7AN, **ENGLAND**.
(T) 01787 247200.
Profile Breeder. Ref: YH05695

GELLIGAER POINT TO POINT

Gelligaer Point to Point, Pantygwreiddyn Farm, Hollybush, Blackwood, **Caerphilly**, NP12 0SD, **WALES**.
(T) 01495 224925 (F) 01495 224838.
Profile Club/Association. Ref: YH05696

GELLINGS FARM RIDING SCHOOL

Gellings Farm Riding School, School Lane, Knowsley, Prescot, **Merseyside**, L34 9EN, **ENGLAND**.
(T) 0151 5489595 (F) 0151 5471923.
Contact/s
Owner: Mr T McHugh
Profile Riding School. Ref: YH05697

GEMINI FORGE

Gemini Forge, The Old Forge, Barrows Hole Lane, Little Dunham, King's Lynn, **Norfolk**, PE32 2DP, **ENGLAND**.
(T) 01760 721645.
Contact/s
Owner: Mr A Keeble
Profile Blacksmith. Ref: YH05698

GEMMELL, WILLIAM

William Gemmell, North Bankend, Coalburn, Lesmahagow, **Lanarkshire (South)**, **SCOTLAND**..
Profile Breeder. Ref: YH05699

GEMS CLEARWAY

Gems Clearway, Unit 1 Mill Prde, Newport, **Newport**, NP20 2JR, **WALES**.
(T) 01633 222533 (F) 01633 264855.
Contact/s
Owner: Mr G Edmunds
Profile Transport/Horse Boxes. Ref: YH05700

GENERAL ACCIDENT

General Accident Fire & Life Association plc, Pitheavlis, Perth, **Perth and Kinross**, PH2 0NH, **SCOTLAND**.
(T) 01738 621202 (F) 01738 633583.

Key: (T) telephone (F) fax (M) mobile (E) E-Mail Address (W) Website Address (Q) Qualifications
Yr. Est: Year Established C.Size: Complex Size Sp: Spring Su: Summer Au: Autumn Wn: Winter

Contact/s
Press Officer: Mr T Kerfoot
Profile Club/Association. Insurance Company.
Ref: YH05701

GENERAL STORE

General Store Ltd (The), 10 Belfast Rd, Saintfield, Ballynahinch, **County Down**, BT24 7AP, **NORTHERN IRELAND**.
(T) 028 97510782 (F) 028 97511319.
Contact/s
Manager: Mr T Steel
Profile Saddlery Retailer. Ref: YH05702

GENERAL TRAILER ENGINEERING

General Trailer Engineering, Albert Works, Main St, Albert Village, Swadlincote, **Derbyshire**, DE11 8EN, **ENGLAND**.
(T) 01283 210800 (F) 01283 224067.
Contact/s
Owner: Mr D Elton
Profile Transport/Horse Boxes. Ref: YH05703

GENERAL TRAILERS

General Trailers United Kingdom Ltd, Princes Yard, Avonmouth Way, Bristol, **Bristol**, BS11 8DE, **ENGLAND**.
(T) 01179 381760.
Contact/s
Accountant: Nicholas Graham Brien
Profile Transport/Horse Boxes. Ref: YH05704

GENERAL TRAILERS

General Trailers Ltd, East Rd, Oundle, Peterborough, **Cambridgeshire**, PE8 4BZ, **ENGLAND**.
(T) 01832 273663 (F) 01832 274540.
Contact/s
Manager: Mr J Daly
Profile Transport/Horse Boxes. Ref: YH05705

GENERAL TRAILERS

General Trailers Ltd, 655 Antrim Rd, Newtownabbey, **County Antrim**, BT36 4RJ, **NORTHERN IRELAND**.
(T) 028 90844861 (F) 028 90843540.
Profile Transport/Horse Boxes. Ref: YH05706

GENERAL TRAILERS

General Trailers, South Green, Dereham, **Norfolk**, NR19 1JE, **ENGLAND**.
(T) 01362 697011 (F) 01362 698045.
Contact/s
Manager: Mr A Griffin
Profile Transport/Horse Boxes. Ref: YH05707

GENERAL TRAILERS

General Trailers UK Ltd, Longlands Trading Est, Milner Way, Ossett, **Yorkshire (West)**, WF5 9JQ, **ENGLAND**.
(T) 01924 273943 (F) 01924 280415.
Contact/s
Manager: Mr G Beanland
Profile Transport/Horse Boxes. Ref: YH05708

GENESIS EQUESTRIAN CTRE/STUD

Genesis Equestrian Centre & Stud, Leesview, Yearngill, Carlisle, **Cumbria**, CA5 3JX, **ENGLAND**.
(T) 01697 320408.
Profile Breeder, Stable/Livery. Ref: YH05709

GENESIS GREEN STUD

Genesis Green Stud, Wickhambrook, Newmarket, **Suffolk**, CB8 8UX, **ENGLAND**.
(T) 01440 820277.
Profile Breeder, Supplies. Ref: YH05710

GENUS EQUINE

Genus Equine, Malmesbury Rd, Kington Langley, Chippenham, **Wiltshire**, SN15 5PZ, **ENGLAND**.
(T) 01249 758861 (F) 01249 758195
(E) equine@genus-plc.co.uk
(W) www.genusequine.com.
Contact/s
For Bookings: Ms S MacMahon
Profile Breeder. Semen Sales.
Opening Times
Sp: Open 08:00. Closed 17:00.
Su: Open 08:00. Closed 17:00.
Au: Open 08:00. Closed 17:00.
Wn: Open 08:00. Closed 17:00. Ref: YH05711

GEO HEAPHY & SONS

Geo Heaphy & Sons Ltd, 3 William St, Old Town Ctre, Redditch, **Worcestershire**, B97 4AJ, **ENGLAND**.
(T) 01527 62097.
Profile Saddlery Retailer. Ref: YH05712

GEO HOLLOWAY

Geo Holloway Ltd, 16 Old St, Ashton-under-Lyne, **Manchester (Greater)**, OL6 6LB, **ENGLAND**.
(T) 0161 3301482 (F) 0161 3301107
(E) holloways@bt.internet.com.
Profile Saddlery Retailer. Ref: YH05713

GEOFF DEAN SADDLERY

Geoff Dean Saddlery, Kings Prde, 154 Findon Rd, Worthing, **Sussex (West)**, BN14 0EL, **ENGLAND**.
(T) 01903 264066 (F) 01903 264066
(W) www.geoff-dean.com
Affiliated Bodies SMS.
Contact/s
General Manager: Ms S Smith (Q) Saddle Fitter
Profile Riding Wear Retailer, Saddlery Retailer, Supplies.
Harness Maker No.Staff: 4 Yr. Est: 1976
Opening Times
Sp: Open 08:30. Closed 17:30.
Su: Open 08:30. Closed 17:30.
Au: Open 08:30. Closed 17:30.
Wn: Open 08:30. Closed 17:30. Ref: YH05714

GEOFF TINEY

Geoff Tiney (Sculptor), Castle Cottage, Braybrooke, Market Harborough, **Leicestershire**, LE16 8LS, **ENGLAND**.
(T) 01858 464386. Ref: YH05715

GEOFFREY GIBSON SADDLER

Geoffrey Gibson Saddler, Buddles Farm, Guist Rd, Stibbard, **Norfolk**, NR21 0AQ, **ENGLAND**.
(T) 01328 829441.
Contact/s
Owner: Mr G Gibson
Profile Saddlery Retailer. Ref: YH05716

GEOFFREY SALE

Geoffrey Sale, 5 Holland Pk, Cheveley, Newmarket, **Suffolk**, CB8 9DL, **ENGLAND**.
(T) 01638 730269.
Profile Supplies. Ref: YH05717

GEORGE PERKS BROS

George Perks Bros, 47 Gatwick Rd, Crawley, **Sussex (West)**, RH10 2FF, **ENGLAND**.
(T) 01293 427200 (F) 01293 427203.
Profile Architectual/Property Services. Ref: YH05718

GEORGE SMITH HORSEBOXES

George Smith Horseboxes, Elston Hill Farm, Shrewton, Salisbury, **Wiltshire**, SP3 4HR, **ENGLAND**.
(T) 01980 620158 (F) 01980 621164
(E) gsmithhorseboxes@c.s.com
(W) www.georgesmithhorseboxes.com.
Contact/s
Owner: Mr G Smith
Profile Transport/Horse Boxes.
Horseboxes repaired and built to individual specifications. No.Staff: 14 Yr. Est: 1988
Opening Times
Sp: Open Mon - Fri 08:30. Closed Mon - Fri 17:15.
Su: Open Mon - Fri 08:30. Closed Mon - Fri 17:15.
Au: Open Mon - Fri 08:30. Closed Mon - Fri 17:15.
Wn: Open Mon - Fri 08:30. Closed Mon - Fri 17:15.
Weekends by appointment only. Ref: YH05719

GEORGE TUTILL

George Tutill Ltd Est 1837, 9 Higham Rd, Chesham, **Buckinghamshire**, HP5 2AF, **ENGLAND**.
(T) 01494 783938 (F) 01494 791241.
Profile Yr. Est: 1837 Ref: YH05720

GEORGE VETNRY GRP

George Veterinary Group (The), The George Veterinary Hospital, High St, Malmesbury, **Wiltshire**, SN16 9AU, **ENGLAND**.
(T) 01666 826456 (F) 01666 824662.
Profile Medical Support. Ref: YH05721

GEORGE WOODALL & SONS

George Woodall & Sons Ltd, 35/37 Market Pl, Malton, **Yorkshire (North)**, YO17 7LP, **ENGLAND**.
(T) 01653 692086 (F) 01653 692086.
Contact/s
Owner: Mr J Woodall
Profile Saddlery Retailer. Ref: YH05722

GEORGE, B

Mrs B George, 36 Clusterbolts, Stapleford, **Hertfordshire**, SG14 3ND, **ENGLAND**.
(T) 01992 558657.
Profile Breeder. Ref: YH05723

GEORGE, K M

Miss K M George, Hill Hse, Brimmers Rd, Princes Risborough, **Buckinghamshire**, HP27 0LE, **ENGLAND**.
(T) 01844 342008
(M) 07778 422494.
Profile Trainer. Ref: YH05724

GEORGE, SARAH

Sarah George, Upper Wick Stables, Upper Wick, Dursley, **Gloucestershire**, GL11 6DF, **ENGLAND**.
(T) 01453 547049.
Contact/s
Owner: Ms S George
Profile Trainer. Ref: YH05725

GEORGES SADDLERY

Georges Saddlery Ltd, Cliftonwood, Clifton Rd, Newbridge, **Lothian (Mid)**, EH37 5US, **SCOTLAND**.
(T) 0131 3353734.
Profile Saddlery Retailer. Ref: YH05726

GEORGES, D

D Georges, 6 Hundred Acres, Wickham, Fareham, **Hampshire**, PO17 6JB, **ENGLAND**.
(T) 01329 833044 (F) 01329 833044.
Contact/s
Partner: Miss K Gross
Profile Farrier. Ref: YH05727

GEORGIAN STUD

Mrs Gwenda Holmden, Sandhurst Hill, Shamley Green, **Surrey**, GU5 0SP, **ENGLAND**.
(T) 01483 893386.
Contact/s
Owner: Mrs G Holmden
Profile Breeder.
Breed Welsh Section A & B ponies. No.Staff: 1
Yr. Est: 1964 C.Size: 19 Acres
Opening Times
Telephone for an appointment Ref: YH05728

GERALD, ROBINSON

Robinson Gerald, Rath Hse, Stud, Portlaoise, **County Laois**, **IRELAND**.
(T) 050 246771.
Profile Supplies. Ref: YH05729

GERNI SALES & SERVICE

Gerni Sales & Service Ltd, Westernway, Bury St Edmunds, **Suffolk**, IP33 3SP, **ENGLAND**.
(T) 01284 772277 (F) 01284 725125.
Profile Supplies. Ref: YH05730

GERTRUDE RD RIDING STABLES

Gertrude Road Riding Stables, 88 Gertrude Rd, West Bridgford, Nottingham, **Nottinghamshire**, NG2 5DA, **ENGLAND**.
(T) 0115 9813658.
Profile Riding School. Ref: YH05731

GET SMART

Get Smart, Walnut Hill, Barrow-In-Furness, **Cumbria**, LA13 0JX, **ENGLAND**.
(T) 01229 877266 (F) 01229 877266.
Contact/s
Owner: Mr M Smart
Profile Supplies. Ref: YH05732

GETHIN, D

Mr & Mrs D Gethin, Tynbryn, Tregynon, Newtown, **Powys**, SY16 3PJ, **WALES**.
(T) 01686 650227.
Profile Breeder. Ref: YH05733

GETHIN, M

M Gethin, Coulmhor, Loch Flemington, Gollanfield, Inverness, **Highlands**, IV2 7QR, **SCOTLAND**.
(T) 01667 462408.
Profile Breeder. Ref: YH05734

GETHING & BOWDITCH

Gething & Bowditch, 8 The Square, Beaminster, **Dorset**, DT8 3AW, **ENGLAND**.
(T) 01308 862312.
Profile Medical Support. Ref: YH05735

GIAMANDREA, J

Mr J Giamandrea, Mailer's, 96 High St, Auchterarder, **Perth and Kinross**, PH3 1BJ, **SCOTLAND**..
Profile Trainer. Ref: YH05736

GIBBINS, J & C

J & C Gibbins, Lodge Rd, Hollesley, Woodbridge, **Suffolk**, IP12 3RR, **ENGLAND**.
(T) 01394 411195 (F) 01394 410015.
Contact/s
Partner: Mrs C Gibbins
Profile Riding Wear Retailer, Saddlery Retailer.
Ref: YH05737

GIBBINS, JONATHON
Mr Jonathon Gibbins MC AMC MMCA, 17 Alexandra Rd, Malvern, **Worcestershire**, WR14 1HA, **ENGLAND**.
(T) 01684 567480.
Profile Medical Support. **Ref: YH05738**

GIBBON WM A.
Gibbon Wm A., Foulksmills, **County Wexford**, **IRELAND**.
(T) 051 565650 **(F)** 051 565902.
Profile Supplies. **Ref: YH05739**

GIBBONS, P & S
P & S Gibbons, Park Hse, 28 St Andrews Rd, Bedford, **Bedfordshire**, MK40 2LW, **ENGLAND**.
(T) 01234 351740.
Profile Breeder. **Ref: YH05740**

GIBBONS, PAUL M
Paul M Gibbons DWCF, Copse Brook Forge, Union Lane, Kingsclere, Newbury, **Berkshire**, RG20 4ST, **ENGLAND**.
(T) 01635 268313.
Profile Farrier. **Ref: YH05741**

GIBPRINT
Gibprint, 14 Maidstone Ave, Chorlton-cum-Hardy, Manchester, **Manchester (Greater)**, M21 1XJ, **ENGLAND**.
(T) 0161 8607672. **Ref: YH05742**

GIBSON & GIBSON
Gibson & Gibson, Veterinary Clinic, Gala Trce, Galashiels, **Scottish Borders**, TD1 3JY, **SCOTLAND**.
(T) 01896 752156.
Profile Medical Support. **Ref: YH05743**

GIBSON & JONES
Gibson & Jones (Llanelli), Veterinary Surgery, 154C Sandy Rd, Llanelli, **Carmarthenshire**, SA15 4DS, **WALES**.
(T) 01554 773943 **(F)** 01554 749495.
Profile Medical Support. **Ref: YH05744**

GIBSON & JONES
Gibson & Jones (Swansea), 2 Brynymor Rd, Gowerton, Swansea, **Swansea**, SA4 3EZ, **WALES**.
(T) 01792 879822.
Profile Medical Support. **Ref: YH05745**

GIBSON SADDLERS
Gibson Saddlers Ltd, Queensbury Rd, Newmarket, **Suffolk**, CB8 9AX, **ENGLAND**.
(T) 01638 662330 **(F)** 01638 666467
(E) enquiries@gibson-saddlers.com
(W) www.gibsonsaddlers.com.
Contact/s
Owner: Mr K Butcher
Profile Saddlery Retailer, Supplies. No.Staff: 21
Opening Times
Sp: Open Mon - Fri 08:00, Sat 09:00. Closed Mon - Fri 17:30, Sat 17:00.
Su: Open Mon - Fri 08:00, Sat 09:00. Closed Mon - Fri 17:30, Sat 17:00.
Au: Open Mon - Fri 08:00, Sat 09:00. Closed Mon - Fri 17:30, Sat 17:00.
Wn: Open Mon - Fri 08:00, Sat 09:00. Closed Mon - Fri 17:30, Sat 17:00. **Ref: YH05746**

GIBSON, ANNETTE
Mrs Annette Gibson, Appleacre, Crickham, Wedmore, **Somerset**, BS28 4JT, **ENGLAND**.
(T) 01934 713370.
Profile Breeder. **Ref: YH05747**

GIBSON, E
Miss E Gibson, West Town Hse, Nempnett Thrubwell, Blagdon, **Somerset (North)**, BS40 7XE, **ENGLAND**.
(T) 01761 462264.
Profile Breeder. **Ref: YH05748**

GIBSON, FREDERICK
Frederick Gibson RSS, Camelot Forge, 58 Church St, Wales, Dronfield, **Derbyshire**, S18 2LQ, **ENGLAND**.
(T) 01909 771591.
Profile Farrier. **Ref: YH05749**

GIBSON, J P
Mr J P Gibson, Cut Thorn Farm, Gibside, Burnopfield, Newcastle-upon-Tyne, **Tyne and Wear**, NE16 6BG, **ENGLAND**.
(T) 01207 270230.
Profile Breeder. **Ref: YH05750**

GIBSON, L W
L W Gibson BVetMed MRCVS, Little Holland, Church Rd, Great Bookham, **Surrey**, KT23 3JT, **ENGLAND**.
(T) 01372 456381.
Profile Medical Support. **Ref: YH05751**

GIBSON, P L
P L Gibson, 2-3 Park St, Stow On The Wold, Cheltenham, **Gloucestershire**, GL54 1AQ, **ENGLAND**.
(T) 01451 830003 **(F)** 01451 870156.
Contact/s
Owner: Mr P Gibson
Profile Supplies. **Ref: YH05752**

GIBSON, SUSAN
Ms Susan Gibson, 156 Wycombe Lane, Wooburn Green, **Buckinghamshire**, HP10 0HH, **ENGLAND**.
(T) 01628 524637.
Profile Supplies. **Ref: YH05753**

GIBSON, T M
Mrs T M Gibson, Embley, Steel, Hexham, **Northumberland**, NE47 0HW, **ENGLAND**.
(T) 01434 673334.
Profile Supplies. **Ref: YH05754**

GIBSONS OF KENDAL
Gibsons of Kendal, Low Butterbent Barn, New Hutton, Kendal, **Cumbria**, LA8 0AH, **ENGLAND**.
(T) 01539 721721 **(F)** 01539 734898. **Ref: YH05755**

GIBSONS, M W
M W Gibsons MRCVS, Veterinary Hospital, Braunston Rd, Oakham, **Rutland**, LE15 6LD, **ENGLAND**.
(T) 01572 722647 **(F)** 01572 722936.
Contact/s
Vet: Mr M Gibson
Profile Medical Support. **Ref: YH05756**

GIFFORD, J T
J T Gifford, Downstables, Stable Lane, Findon, Worthing, **Sussex (West)**, BN14 0RR, **ENGLAND**.
(T) 01903 872226 **(F)** 01903 877232.
Contact/s
Owner: Mr J Gifford
Profile Trainer. **Ref: YH05757**

GIGANT UK
Gigant UK Ltd, Dale Rd Ind Est, Dale Rd, Shildon, **County Durham**, DL4 2RE, **ENGLAND**.
(T) 01388 777650 **(F)** 01388 777744.
Profile Transport/Horse Boxes. **Ref: YH05758**

GILBERT, J
Mr J Gilbert, Albion Hse, Birds End, Hargrave, Bury St Edmunds, **Suffolk**, IP29 5HE, **ENGLAND**.
(T) 01284 850908
(M) 07702 189086
(W) www.newmarketracehorsetrainers.co.uk
Affiliated Bodies Newmarket Trainers Fed.
Contact/s
Trainer: Mr J Gilbert
Profile Trainer. **Ref: YH05759**

GILBERT, K F
Mrs K F Gilbert, 10 Ballylagan Rd, Straid, Ballyclare, **County Antrim**, BT39 9NF, **NORTHERN IRELAND**.
(T) 028 93322284.
Profile Breeder. **Ref: YH05760**

GILBERTSON, RICHARD D
Richard D Gilbertson DWCF, 15 Cuckoo Lane, Wick, Winterbourne Down, **Gloucestershire (South)**, BS36 1AG, **ENGLAND**.
(T) 01179 565205.
Profile Farrier. **Ref: YH05761**

GILDERS
Gilders, 32 Montagu St, Kettering, **Northamptonshire**, NN16 8RU, **ENGLAND**.
(T) 01536 514509.
Contact/s
Owner: Mr T Davies
Profile Saddlery Retailer. **Ref: YH05762**

GILDERS NORTHAMPTON
Gilders Northampton Ltd, 250-252 Wellingborough Rd, Northampton, **Northamptonshire**, NN1 4EJ, **ENGLAND**.
(T) 01604 636723.
Profile Saddlery Retailer. **Ref: YH05763**

GILES, R
R Giles, Cublands Cottage, London Rd, Ashington, Pulborough, **Sussex (West)**, RH20 3AX, **ENGLAND**.
(T) 01903 892838.
Contact/s
Owner: Mr R Giles
Profile Breeder. **Ref: YH05764**

GILFACH HOLIDAY VILLAGE
Gilfach Holiday Village, Llwyncelyn, Aberaeron, **Ceredigion**, SA46 0HN, **WALES**.
(T) 01545 580288.
Profile Equestrian Centre. **Ref: YH05765**

GILHOOLEY ENGINEERING
Gilhooley Engineering, Unit 11 St. Margarets, Loanhead, **Lothian (Mid)**, EH20 9SS, **SCOTLAND**.
(T) 0131 6604414 **(F)** 0131 6604414.
Contact/s
Owner: Mr S Gilhooley
Profile Blacksmith. **Ref: YH05766**

GILKHORN FARM SADDLERY
Gilkhorn Farm Saddlery, Gilkhorn, Maud, Peterhead, **Aberdeenshire**, AB42 5RR, **SCOTLAND**.
(T) 01771 613328 **(F)** 01771 613328.
Contact/s
Owner: Mrs J Adkin
Profile Saddlery Retailer. **Ref: YH05767**

GILL & PUNTER RACING SUPPLIES
Gill & Punter Racing Supplies, Leonard Hse, Vincent Lane, Dorking, **Surrey**, RH4 3HW, **ENGLAND**.
(T) 01306 742240 **(F)** 01306 742940.
Profile Supplies. **Ref: YH05768**

GILL FOX COUNTRY CLOTHES
Gill Fox Country Clothes, Warren Hse, 67 Main St, Great Gidding, Huntingdon, **Cambridgeshire**, PE17 5NU, **ENGLAND**.
(T) 01832 293360.
Profile Supplies. **Ref: YH05769**

GILL WALKER SADDLERY
Gill Walker Saddlery, The Chase, Ashmead, Cam, Dursley, **Gloucestershire**, GL11 5EN, **ENGLAND**.
(T) 01453 543572.
Profile Supplies. **Ref: YH05770**

GILL, C G & D W
C G & D W Gill, Mill Lane, Aslockton, Nottingham, **Nottinghamshire**, NG13 9AS, **ENGLAND**.
(T) 01949 850651 **(F)** 01949 850651.
Contact/s
Partner: Mr G Gill
Profile Farrier. **Ref: YH05771**

GILL, D
D Gill, Stanton Cottage, Aslockton Rd, Scarrington, Nottingham, **Nottinghamshire**, NG13 9BP, **ENGLAND**.
(T) 01949 850373.
Contact/s
Owner: Mr D Gill
Profile Farrier. **Ref: YH05772**

GILL, J
J Gill, 28 Oughley Rd, Saintfield, Ballynahinch, **County Down**, BT24 7DA, **NORTHERN IRELAND**.
(T) 028 97510415.
Contact/s
Owner: Mr J Gill
Profile Trainer. **Ref: YH05773**

GILL, MR H J
Mr H J Gill, Nut Hill Farm, Aberford, **Yorkshire (West)**, LS25 3AU, **ENGLAND**.
(T) 0113 2813273 **(F)** 0113 2813273.
Profile Breeder. **Ref: YH05774**

GILL, R M
R M Gill, The Copse, Hunger Hill, East Stour, Gillingham, **Dorset**, SP8 5JR, **ENGLAND**.
(T) 01747 823915.
Profile Farrier. **Ref: YH05775**

GILL, S A
Mrs S A Gill, Chastleton, Moreton In Marsh, **Gloucestershire**, GL56 0ST, **ENGLAND**.
(T) 01608 74466.
Profile Supplies. **Ref: YH05776**

GILL, TERRY V
Terry V Gill DWCF, 5 The Malthouses, Ashbury, Swindon, **Wiltshire**, SN6 8NB, **ENGLAND**.
(T) 07710 457786.
Profile Farrier. **Ref: YH05777**

GILLAM HALL STABLES
Gillam Hall Stables, Red Lodge, Bury St Edmunds, **Suffolk**, IP28 8LD, **ENGLAND**.
(T) 01638 750929.

Contact/s
Owner: Mrs P Gordon
Profile Stable/Livery. Ref: YH05778

GILLESPIE, D.F.

Gillespie D.F., Hazelwood Stables Pollardstown, Curragh, **County Kildare**, **IRELAND**.
(T) 045 521048.
Profile Supplies. Ref: YH05779

GILLET COOK

Gillet Cook Ltd, Monks Granary, Standard Quay, Faversham, **Kent**, ME13 7BX, **ENGLAND**.
(T) 01795 532235 (F) 01795 538868.
Contact/s
Owner: Mr D Hover
Profile Supplies. Ref: YH05780

GILLETT, M P

M P Gillett, The Forge, Church Farm, Cole Lane, Ockbrook, Derby, **Derbyshire**, DE72 3RD, **ENGLAND**.
(T) 01332 662805.
Contact/s
Owner: Mr M Gillett
Profile Farrier. Ref: YH05781

GILLHAM HOUSE VETNRY

Gillham House Veterinary Surgery, Wells Rd, Fakenham, **Norfolk**, NR21 9AA, **ENGLAND**.
(T) 01328 862137 (F) 01328 855913.
Profile Medical Support. Ref: YH05782

GILLIAN HARRIS

Gillian Harris (Animal Portraits & Sporting Prints), Morning Flight, Broad Rd, Handbrook, Chichester, **Sussex (West)**, PO18 8RE, **ENGLAND**.
(T) 01243 572781.
Profile Artist. Ref: YH05783

GILLIAN'S RIDING SCHOOL

Gillian's Riding School, Brayside Farm, Clay Hill, Enfield, **London (Greater)**, EN2 9JL, **ENGLAND**.
(T) 020 83665445.
Contact/s
Owner: Mrs G Head
Profile Riding School, Stable/Livery. Ref: YH05784

GILLIGAN, P L

P L Gilligan, Sackville St, Newmarket, **Suffolk**, CB8 8DX, **ENGLAND**.
(T) 01638 669151 (F) 01638 605107
(M) 07802 679437
(E) patrick.gilligan@dtn.ntl.com
(W) www.patrickgilligan.co.uk
Affiliated Bodies Newmarket Trainers Fed.
Contact/s
Trainer: Mr P Gilligan
Profile Trainer. Ref: YH05785

GILLINGS, B G

B G Gillings, Rushbrooke Hse, Cavendish Rd, Clare, **Suffolk**, CO10 8PE, **ENGLAND**.
(T) 01787 277305.
Profile Breeder. Ref: YH05786

GILLS SADDLERY & CANE

Gills Saddlery & Cane, Unit 3, John H Gill & Sons, Leeming, Northallerton, **Yorkshire (North)**, DL7 9AP, **ENGLAND**.
(T) 01677 422844 (F) 01677 424039.
Contact/s
Manager: Mrs K Blanchard
Profile Riding Wear Retailer, Saddlery Retailer, Supplies. Yr. Est: 1912
Opening Times
Sp: Open Mon - Sat 09:00, Sun 10:00. Closed Mon - Sat 17:00, Sun 16:00.
Su: Open Mon - Sat 09:00, Sun 10:00. Closed Mon - Sat 17:00, Sun 16:00.
Au: Open Mon - Sat 09:00, Sun 10:00. Closed Mon - Sat 17:00, Sun 16:00.
Wn: Open Mon - Sat 09:00, Sun 10:00. Closed Mon - Sat 17:00, Sun 16:00. Ref: YH05787

GILLTOWN STUD

Gilltown Stud, Kilcullen, **County Kildare**, **IRELAND**.
(T) 045 481216 (F) 045 481687
(E) gilltownstud@kildarehorse.ie.
Contact/s
Key Contact: Ms P Downes
Profile Breeder. Ref: YH05788

GILMORE, JIM

Jim Gilmore, 70 Foundry Rd, Malmesbury, **Wiltshire**, SN16 0AW, **ENGLAND**.
(T) 01666 823335 (F) 01666 823335.
Profile Supplies. Ref: YH05789

GILMOUR, JOHN

John Gilmour & Co Ltd, Unit 4 Glenburn Rd Ind Est, Prestwick, **Ayrshire (South)**, KA9 2NS, **SCOTLAND**.
(T) 01292 470743.
Profile Blacksmith. Ref: YH05790

GILSTON LIVERY STABLES

Gilston Livery Stables, Pye Corner, Gilston, Harlow, **Essex**, CM20 2RB, **ENGLAND**.
(T) 01279 444165 (F) 01279 444165.
Contact/s
General Manager: Miss Y Buteux
Profile Stable/Livery. No.Staff: 1
Yr. Est: 1983 C.Size: 60 Acres
Opening Times
Sp: Open Mon - Sun 06:00. Closed Mon - Sun 21:00.
Su: Open Mon - Sun 06:00. Closed Mon - Sun 21:00.
Au: Open Mon - Sun 06:00. Closed Mon - Sun 21:00.
Wn: Open Mon - Sun 06:00. Closed Mon - Sun 21:00.
Yard open to owners seven days a week, telephone for further information. Ref: YH05791

GILSTON PK FARM

Gilston Park Farm Equestrian Centre, Pope Hole, Harlow, **Essex**, CM20 2RN, **ENGLAND**.
(T) 01279 444165.
Profile Riding School. Ref: YH05792

GILYHEAD, G M

Mr G M Gilyhead, Ivy Hse, Coneythorpe, Knaresborough, **Yorkshire (North)**, HG5 0RY, **ENGLAND**.
(T) 01423 864643.
Profile Trainer. Ref: YH05793

GIRDLER, K & C

K & C Girdler, Ffrethi Stud, Bryncothi, Abergorlech, Carmarthen, **Carmarthenshire**, SA32 7BH, **WALES**.
(T) 01267 202273.
Profile Breeder. Ref: YH05794

GIRSONFIELD STUD

Girsonfield Stud, Girsonfield, Otterburn, **Tyne and Wear**, NE19 1NT, **ENGLAND**.
(T) 01830 520771 (F) 01830 520771
(W) www.girsonfield.F9.co.uk
Affiliated Bodies TBA.
Profile Breeder, Stable/Livery, Stud Farm.
The Stud Farm usually has a good selection of well bred and youngstock for sale:- yearlings and 2 year olds, both thoroughbred and non thoroughbred, suitable for racing, Point to Point, Eventing, Showing & Show Jumping. No.Staff: 3 Yr. Est: 1998
C.Size: 574 Acres
Opening Times
Telephone for further information Ref: YH05795

GISBORNE, SIMON PATRICK

Simon Patrick Gisborne DWCF, Basketmakers Cottage, Wick Lane, Lower Apperley, **Gloucestershire**, GL19 4DS, **ENGLAND**.
(T) 01452 780300.
Profile Farrier. Ref: YH05796

GISSING, M

M Gissing, Moor Farm, Walesby Lane, Tealby, Market Rasen, **Lincolnshire**, LN8 3UP, **ENGLAND**.
(T) 01673 838090 (F) 01673 838594.
Contact/s
Owner: Mr M Gissing
Profile Transport/Horse Boxes. Ref: YH05797

GITTENS, W R

W R Gittens, Upper Tyn Y Coed, Cyfronydd, Welshpool, **Powys**, SY21 9EE, **WALES**.
(T) 01938 850268.
Contact/s
Owner: Mr W Gittens
Profile Supplies. Ref: YH05798

GITTINS, H W

Mr H W Gittins, Woodseaves Manor Farm, Woodseaves, Market Drayton, **Shropshire**, TF9 2LN, **ENGLAND**.
(T) 01630 654884.
Profile Supplies. Ref: YH05799

GITTINS, STEPHEN

Mr Stephen Gittins, Furlong Farm, Nether Westcote, Chipping Norton, **Oxfordshire**, OX7 6SD, **ENGLAND**.
(T) 01993 831681 (F) 01993 831681.
Profile Breeder. Ref: YH05800

GIVONS, J

J Givons, Bucklands Farm, Brantridge Lane, Balcombe, Haywards Heath, **Sussex (West)**, RH17 6JT, **ENGLAND**.
(T) 01444 400722.
Profile Supplies. Ref: YH05801

GLADWELLS

H G Gladwell & Sons Ltd, Copdock Mill, Copdock, Ipswich, **Suffolk**, IP8 3LA, **ENGLAND**.
(T) 01473 730246 (F) 01473 730875
(E) mark-gladwell@cs.com.
(W) www.copdockmill.co.uk.
Contact/s
Coach: Mrs G Wilden
Profile Feed Merchant, Supplies.
Have five stores across East Anglia, all with retail outlets. Stock a variety of equestrian supplies from feed to shovels. Also stock petfood. Yr. Est: 1912
Opening Times
Sp: Open Mon - Sat 08:00. Closed Mon - Fri 17:00, Sat 12:00.
Su: Open Mon - Sat 08:00. Closed Mon - Fri 17:00, Sat 12:00.
Au: Open Mon - Sat 08:00. Closed Mon - Fri 17:00, Sat 12:00.
Wn: Open Mon - Sat 08:00. Closed Mon - Fri 17:00, Sat 12:00.
Closed Sundays Ref: YH05802

GLAISTER, JAMES

James Glaister, West Gate, Bewaldeth, Cockermouth, **Cumbria**, CA13 NSU, **ENGLAND**.
(T) 01768 776565.
Profile Farrier. Ref: YH05803

GLAN YR AFON HOLIDAYS

Glan Yr Afon Holidays, Foel, Welshpool, **Powys**, SY21 0PD, **WALES**.
(T) 01938 820494 (F) 01938 820494.
Contact/s
Owner: Mrs F Whiffin
Profile Holidays, Horse/Rider Accom, Stable/Livery.
No.Staff: 1 Yr. Est: 1994 C.Size: 6 Acres
Ref: YH05804

GLANFIELD, J

Miss J Glanfield, Seven Hills Rd, Iver, **Buckinghamshire**, SL0 0NY, **ENGLAND**.
(T) 01753 662420.
Profile Breeder. Ref: YH05805

GLANVILLE, DAVID PETER

David Peter Glanville, 34 Southernhay, Winkleigh, **Devon**, EX19 8JH, **ENGLAND**.
(T) 01837 83494.
Profile Farrier. Ref: YH05806

GLASGOW & WEIR

Glasgow & Weir, 5 Ravenscroft St, Edinburgh, **Edinburgh (City of)**, EH17 8QJ, **SCOTLAND**.
(T) 0131 6643001 (F) 0131 6647357.
Contact/s
Owner: Mr D Glasgow
Profile Blacksmith. Ref: YH05807

GLASS, DAVID G

David G Glass, 38 Fairway, Stakeford, Choppington, **Northumberland**, NE62 5LH, **ENGLAND**.
(T) 01670 812595.
Profile Farrier. Ref: YH05808

GLASS, J

J Glass, Wolds Stud, 49 London Lane, Wymeswold, Loughborough, **Leicestershire**, LE12 6UB, **ENGLAND**.
(T) 01509 880261.
Contact/s
Owner: Miss J Glass
Profile Breeder. Ref: YH05809

GLASS, JOHN

John Glass, 90 Moyarget Rd, Ballycastle, **County Antrim**, **NORTHERN IRELAND**.
Profile Breeder. Ref: YH05810

GLAZEBROOK, M S

M S Glazebrook DWCF, 14 St Barnabas, Sutton, **Surrey**, SM1 4NL, **ENGLAND**.
(T) 020 87701297.
Profile Farrier. Ref: YH05811

GLAZELEY STUD

Glazeley Stud, Wadeley Farm, Glazeley, Bridgnorth, **Shropshire**, WV16 6AD, **ENGLAND**.
(T) 01746 789288.
Profile Breeder. Ref: YH05812

GLAZZARD, G

G Glazzard, Blackladies Farm, Kiddemore Green Rd, Brewood, Stafford, **Staffordshire**, ST19 9BQ, **ENGLAND**.
(T) 01902 850919.
Profile Trainer. **Ref: YH05813**

GLEADHILL HOUSE STUD

Gleadhill House Stud Ltd, Dawbers Lane, Euxton, Chorley, **Lancashire**, PR7 6EA, **ENGLAND**.
(T) 01257 265434 **(F)** 01257 231328.
Profile Breeder. **Ref: YH05814**

GLEBE FARM EQUESTRIAN CTRE

Glebe Farm Equestrian Centre, Glebe Farm, Harold Rd, Bozeat, Wellingborough, **Northamptonshire**, NN29 7LB, **ENGLAND**.
(T) 01933 665083.
Contact/s
Owner: Mrs H Reeves
Profile Riding School, Stable/Livery. **Ref: YH05815**

GLEBE FIELD RIDING EST

Glebe Field Riding Establishment, Forecourt Park Rd, Mexborough, **Yorkshire (South)**, S64 9PE, **ENGLAND**.
(T) 01709 583377 **(F)** 01709 571870
(M) 07774 142705.
Profile Riding School, Stable/Livery. **Ref: YH05816**

GLEBE INT ENTERPRISE

Glebe International Enterprise, Glebe Farm, Whitestone, Exeter, **Devon**, EX4 2HP, **ENGLAND**.
(T) 01392 811633.
Contact/s
Owner: Mr A Daems
Profile Stable/Livery, Trainer.
Competition livery is available, details on request. Also offer dressage and competition training. **Ref: YH05817**

GLEBE RIDING STABLES

Glebe Riding Stables, Glebe Farm, Bucknowle, Wareham, **Dorset**, BH20 5NS, **ENGLAND**.
(T) 01929 480280. **Ref: YH05818**

GLEBE STABLES

Glebe Stables, Little Ham, Winsford, Minehead, **Somerset**, TA24 7JH, **ENGLAND**.
(T) 01643 851265.
Profile Trainer. **Ref: YH05819**

GLEBE STUD

Glebe Stud, Glebe Hse, Cheveley, Newmarket, **Suffolk**, CB8 9DG, **ENGLAND**.
(T) 01638 730237 **(F)** 01638 730127.
Contact/s
Stud Groom: Graham Nicklin
Profile Breeder. **Ref: YH05820**

GLEBEDALE

Mrs J Williams, Parsonage Farm, Llanddewi Skirrid, Abergavenny, **Monmouthshire**, NP7 8AG, **WALES**.
(T) 01873 854358 **(F)** 01873 853942
(E) tedwilliams@kolvox.net
(W) www.welshponyandcob.co.uk
Affiliated Bodies NPS, WPCS.
Contact/s
General Manager: Miss K Williams
Profile Breeder.
Breed Suffolk Punch Partbreds. No.Staff: 2
Yr. Est: 1960 C.Size: 100 Acres
Opening Times
Please telephone for an appointment **Ref: YH05821**

GLEDDOCH RIDING SCHOOL

Gleddoch Riding School, Gleddoch Farm, Old Greenock Rd, Langbank, Port Glasgow, **Renfrewshire**, PA14 6YE, **SCOTLAND**.
(T) 01475 540350.
Contact/s
General Manager: Mr L Conn
Profile Riding School, Stable/Livery. **Ref: YH05822**

GLEDSON, J L

Mr J L Gledson, Buteland, Bellingham, Hexham, **Northumberland**, NE48 2EX, **ENGLAND**.
(T) 01434 220218.
Profile Supplies. **Ref: YH05823**

GLEN ANDRED STUD

Glen Andred Stud, Old, Northampton, **Northamptonshire**, NN6 9RJ, **ENGLAND**.
(T) 01604 781266 **(F)** 01604 781232.
Contact/s
Owner: Mr R Percival
Profile Breeder. **Ref: YH05824**

GLEN EAGLES EQUESTRIAN

Glen Eagles Equestrian Centre (The), Auchterarder, **Perth and Kinross**, PH3 1NZ, **SCOTLAND**.
(T) 01764 663507
(W) www.gleneagles.com
Affiliated Bodies BHS.
Contact/s
Coach: Mr E McKecknie **(Q)** BHSI
Profile Arena, Equestrian Centre, Equestrian Centre, Horse/Rider Accom, Riding Club, Riding School, Riding Wear Retailer, Saddlery Retailer, Stable/Livery, Track/Course, Trainer, Transport/Horse Boxes.
Yr. Est: 1988
Opening Times
Sp: Open Mon - Sun 08:00. Closed Mon - Thurs 20:00, Fri - Sun 18:00.
Su: Open Mon - Sun 08:00. Closed Mon - Thurs 20:00, Fri - Sun 18:00.
Au: Open Mon - Sun 08:00. Closed Mon - Thurs 20:00, Fri - Sun 18:00.
Wn: Open Mon - Sun 08:00. Closed Mon - Thurs 20:00, Fri - Sun 18:00. **Ref: YH05825**

GLEN RIVER RIDING SCHOOL

Glen River Riding School, Swinstead Rd, Corby Glen, Grantham, **Lincolnshire**, NG33 4NX, **ENGLAND**.
(T) 01476 550569 **(F)** 01476 550569
Affiliated Bodies BHS.
Contact/s
Partner: Mr G Percival
Profile Riding School, Stable/Livery.
Hacks take place over their own ground. All instructors are BHS qualified. No.Staff: 3 Yr. Est: 1971
Ref: YH05826

GLEN TANAR EQUESTRIAN CTRE

Glen Tanar Equestrian Centre, Glen Tanar, Aboyne, **Aberdeenshire**, AB34 5EU, **SCOTLAND**.
(T) 01339 886448 **(F)** 01339 887391.
Contact/s
Owner: Mrs J Rider
Profile Breeder, Riding School, Stable/Livery.
Ref: YH05827

GLENBRAE RIDING CLUB

Glenbrae Riding Club, 38 Dovecote Rd, Westquarter, **Falkirk**, FK2 9YT, **SCOTLAND**.
(T) 01324 715969
(E) julieballantine@uk.sun.com.
Contact/s
Secretary: Miss J Ballantine
Profile Club/Association, Riding Club. **Ref: YH05828**

GLENBURN VETNRY CLNC

Glenburn Veterinary Clinic, 7 Nutts Corner Rd, Crumlin, **County Antrim**, BT29 4BW, **NORTHERN IRELAND**.
(T) 028 94452226 **(F)** 028 94422838.
Profile Medical Support. **Ref: YH05829**

GLENDALE EQUESTRIAN FEEDS

Glendale Equestrian Feeds, Newbridge Rd, Glen Parva, Leicester, **Leicestershire**, LE2 9TG, **ENGLAND**.
(T) 0116 2783015.
Contact/s
Owner: Mrs M Sturges
Profile Breeder, Stable/Livery, Track/Course.
Ref: YH05830

GLENDEVON YOUTH HOSTEL

Glendevon Youth Hostel, Glendevon, Dollar, **Clackmannanshire**, FK14 7JY, **SCOTLAND**.
(T) 01259 781206.
Profile Equestrian Centre. **Ref: YH05831**

GLENEAGLES

Gleneagles, Allington Lane, West End, Southampton, **Hampshire**, SO30 3HQ, **ENGLAND**.
(T) 023 80473164 **(F)** 023 80473164.
Contact/s
Owner: Mrs D Day
Profile Riding School, Stable/Livery, Trainer. Training Course. **Ref: YH05832**

GLENFALL PONY STUD

Glenfall Pony Stud, Knowle Hill, Badsey, Evesham, **Worcestershire**, WR11 5EN, **ENGLAND**.
(T) 01386 831164.
Profile Breeder. **Ref: YH05833**

GLENFARG RIDING SCHOOL

Glenfarg Riding School, Smiddyhill, Glenfarg, Perth, **Perth and Kinross**, PH2 9NL, **SCOTLAND**.
(T) 01577 830262
Affiliated Bodies BHS, RDA.
Contact/s
Owner: Mrs A Stocks **(Q)** BHSAI
Profile Riding School. No.Staff: 1
Yr. Est: 1973 C.Size: 12 Acres
Opening Times
Sp: Open 10:00. Closed 16:00.
Su: Open 10:00. Closed 16:00.
Au: Open 10:00. Closed 16:00.
Wn: Open 10:00. Closed 16:00. **Ref: YH05834**

GLENFIELDS STUD

T Armstrong, Glenfields Stud, Great Oaks Farm, Chiddingfold, **Surrey**, GU8 4XL, **ENGLAND**.
(T) 01428 682761.
Contact/s
Owner: Mr T Armstrong
Profile Breeder. **Ref: YH05835**

GLENGORSE STABLES

Glengorse Stables, Glengorse Est, Battle, **Sussex (East)**, TN33 0TX, **ENGLAND**.
(T) 01424 775555.
Contact/s
Manager: Mr M Garton
Profile Stable/Livery. **Ref: YH05836**

GLENIFFER STABLES

Gleniffer Stables, 20 Drift Rd, Maidenhead, **Berkshire**, SL6 3ST, **ENGLAND**.
(T) 01628 626615.
Contact/s
Owner: Mr R Pearson
Profile Riding School, Stable/Livery. Horse Dealer.
Ref: YH05837

GLENISLA HOTEL

Glenisla Hotel, Kirkton Of Glenisla, Alyth, **Perth and Kinross**, PH11 8PH, **SCOTLAND**.
(T) 01575 582223 **(F)** 01575 582203.
Profile Equestrian Centre. **Ref: YH05838**

GLEN-JAKES RIDING SCHOOL

Glen-Jakes Riding School, Bean Leach Rd, Stockport, **Cheshire**, SK2 5JE, **ENGLAND**.
(T) 0161 4837063.
Contact/s
Owner: Miss R Homer
Profile Riding School. **Ref: YH05839**

GLENMARKIE

Glenmarkie Guest House, Health Spa and Riding Centre, Glenmarkie Farmhouse, Glenisla, Blairgowrie, **Perth and Kinross**, PH11 8QB, **SCOTLAND**.
(T) 01575 582295
(E) glenmarkie@freedomnames.co.uk
(W) www.glenmarkie.co.uk.
Contact/s
General Manager: Miss S Shepard **(Q)** BHSAI
(T) 01575 582204
Profile Arena, Equestrian Centre, Riding School, Stable/Livery, Trainer. Hacking/Trekking Centre.
There is also a health and beauty spa on site.
Ref: YH05840

GLENROTHES RIDING CTRE

Glenrothes Riding Centre, 1 Balgeddie Farm, Leslie, Glenrothes, **Fife**, KY6 3ET, **SCOTLAND**.
(T) 01592 742428.
Profile Riding School, Stable/Livery. **Ref: YH05841**

GLEN'S RIDING CLUB

Glen's Riding Club, 29 Glenann Rd, Cushendall, Ballymena, **County Antrim**, BT44 0TG, **NORTHERN IRELAND**.
(T) 028 25771019.
Contact/s
Chairman: Mr J Connolly
Profile Club/Association, Riding Club. **Ref: YH05842**

GLENSIDE ORGANICS

Glenside Organics Ltd, Block 2, Unit 4, Bandeath Ind Est, Throsk, **Stirling**, FK7 7XY, **SCOTLAND**.
(T) 01786 816655 **(F)** 01786 816100.
Profile Medical Support. **Ref: YH05843**

GLENTEL TRAILERS

Glentel Trailers, Darley Abbey Mills, Darley Abbey, Derby, **Derbyshire**, DE22 1DZ, **ENGLAND**.
(T) 01332 368394 **(F)** 01332 368394.
Contact/s
Owner: Mr G Starbuck
Profile Transport/Horse Boxes. **Ref: YH05844**

GLENWOOD RIDING

Glenwood Riding, Glenwood Farm, Denwood St, Crundale, Canterbury, **Kent**, CT4 7EF, **ENGLAND**.
(T) 01227 730592.
Contact/s

Owner: Mrs H Rigley
Profile Stable/Livery. Ref: YH05845

GLESSING, J & C

J & C Glessing, Buckwyns Farm, Buckwyns, Billericay, **Essex**, CM12 0TP, **ENGLAND**.
(T) 01277 657878.
Contact/s
General Manager: Mrs C Glessing
Profile Stable/Livery. Yr. Est: 1969 C.Size: 48 Acres Ref: YH05846

GLEVERING HALL FARM

Glevering Hall Farm, Hacheston, Woodbridge, **Suffolk**, IP13 0EX, **ENGLAND**.
(T) 01728 747741.
Contact/s
Owner: Ms D McNab
Profile Stable/Livery. Ref: YH05847

GLOBE ORGANIC SVS

Globe Organic Services, 163A Warwick Rd, Solihull, **Midlands (West)**, B92 7AR, **ENGLAND**.
(T) 0121 7074120 (F) 0121 7074934
(M) 07850 171080.
Profile Supplies. Ref: YH05848

GLOBEPOST TRAVEL

Globepost Travel, 324 Kennington Park Rd, London, **London (Greater)**, SE11 4PD, **ENGLAND**.
(T) 020 75870303. Ref: YH05849

GLOUCESTER FABRICATIONS

Gloucester Fabrications, Unit 1 Mansfield Trading Est, Church Lane, Moreton Valence, Gloucester, **Gloucestershire**, GL2 7NB, **ENGLAND**.
(T) 01452 723060 (F) 01452 720981
(M) 07974 940252
(E) sales@gloucesterfabrications.co.uk
(W) www.gloucesterfabrications.co.uk.
Contact/s
Owner: Mrs E Hopson
Profile Transport/Horse Boxes.
Horsebox repairs, spares, servicing (including MOT), re-sprays and re-vamps. Gloucester Fabrications will also build horseboxes to individual specifications.
Opening Times
Sp: Open Mon - Fri 08:00. Closed Mon - Fri 18:00.
Su: Open Mon - Fri 08:00. Closed Mon - Fri 18:00.
Au: Open Mon - Fri 08:00. Closed Mon - Fri 18:00.
Wn: Open Mon - Fri 08:00. Closed Mon - Fri 18:00.
Weekends by appointment. Ref: YH05850

GLOUCESTER MIXED FEEDS

Gloucester Mixed Feeds Ltd, Droys Court, Witcombe, **Gloucestershire**, GL3 4TN, **ENGLAND**.
(T) 01452 863462.
Profile Supplies. Ref: YH05851

GLOUCESTER ST FORGE

Gloucester St Forge, The Old Forge, 140 Slad Rd, Stroud, **Gloucestershire**, GL5 1RE, **ENGLAND**.
(T) 01453 766542 (F) 01453 757530.
Contact/s
Partner: Mr D Fudge
Profile Blacksmith. Ref: YH05852

GLOUCESTERSHIRE BRIDLEWAYS

Gloucestershire Bridleways, 20 Greenhills Rd, Charlton Kings, Cheltenham, **Gloucestershire**, GL53 9EB, **ENGLAND**.
(T) 01242 516639. Ref: YH05853

GLOVER, H F & J H

H F & J H Glover, Hartley Bottom Farm, Hartley Bottom Rd, Hartley, Longfield, **Kent**, DA3 8LJ, **ENGLAND**.
(T) 01474 872970 (F) 01474 872970.
Contact/s
Manager: Mrs H Glover
Profile Riding Wear Retailer, Supplies. Ref: YH05854

GLOVER, STEVEN

Steven Glover, 34 Wesley Pl, Trecwn, Haverfordwest, **Pembrokeshire**, SA62 5XR, **WALES**.
(T) 01348 840972.
Profile Farrier. Ref: YH05855

GLOVER, STEVEN P

Steven P Glover DWCF, Wayside, Glanrhyd, Cardigan, **Ceredigion**, SA43 3DA, **WALES**.
(T) 01239 86653.
Profile Farrier. Ref: YH05856

GLYN VALLEY HOTEL

Glyn Valley Hotel, Glyn Ceiriog, Llangollen, **Denbighshire**, LL20 7EU, **WALES**.
(T) 01691 718896 (F) 01691 718896.
Profile Equestrian Centre. Ref: YH05857

GLYNHIR LODGE STABLES

Glynhir Lodge Stables, Glynmir Rd, Llandybie, Ammanford, **Carmarthenshire**, SA18 2TB, **WALES**.
(T) 01269 850664.
Profile Riding School. Ref: YH05858

GO 4 IT

Go 4 It Ltd, Berryhill Farm, Newburgh, Cupar, **Fife**, KY14 6HZ, **SCOTLAND**.
(T) 01337 840355 (F) 01337 840412.
Profile Transport/Horse Boxes. Ref: YH05859

GO ENTERTAINMENTS

Go Entertainments, The Arts Exchange, Congleton, **Cheshire**, CW12 1JG, **ENGLAND**.
(T) 01260 276627 (F) 01260 270777
(E) phillipgandey@netcentral.co.uk
(W) www.circus-online.co.uk.
Profile Arena. Ref: YH05860

GO RIDING GRP

South Causey Equestrian Centre, Bearish Burn Rd, Stanley, **County Durham**, DH9 0LS, **ENGLAND**.
(T) 01207 281136 (F) 01207 283098
(E) goridinggroup@hotmail.com
(W) www.goriding.net
Affiliated Bodies BHS.
Contact/s
Owner: Mr P Moiser (Q) BHSAI
Profile Arena, Equestrian Centre, Riding School, Riding Wear Retailer, Stable/Livery, Supplies.
Mr Philip Moiser is a member of the England Horseball Team and Captain of the European Cup Squad. No.Staff: 10 Yr. Est: 1978
C.Size: 110 Acres Ref: YH05861

GO RIDING GRP

Tiley Equestrian Centre, Kirkley Mill, Ponteland, **Tyne and Wear**, NE20 0BQ, **ENGLAND**.
(T) 01661 822073
(W) www.goriding.net
Affiliated Bodies BHS.
Contact/s
Owner: Mr P Moiser (Q) BHSAI
(E) goridinggroup@hotmail.com
Profile Arena, Equestrian Centre, Riding School, Riding Wear Retailer, Stable/Livery, Supplies.
Mr Philip Moiser is a member of the England Horseball Team and Captain of the European Cup Squad. No.Staff: 4 Yr. Est: 2000 C.Size: 20 Acres Ref: YH05862

GODDARD, D F

D F Goddard, 30 Brookdean Rd, Worthing, **Sussex (West)**, BN11 2PB, **ENGLAND**.
(T) 01903 211398.
Profile Farrier. Ref: YH05863

GODDARD, R C

Mr R C Goddard, 1 Priest Thorn, Fifehead Neville, Sturminster Newton, **Dorset**, DT10 2AQ, **ENGLAND**.
(T) 01258 817161.
Profile Breeder. Ref: YH05864

GODFREY, TIMOTHY

Timothy Godfrey DWCF BII, Savona, 24 Folly Hill, Farnham, **Surrey**, GU9 0BD, **ENGLAND**.
(T) 01252 710190.
Profile Farrier. Ref: YH05865

GODFREY, TOM D

Tom D Godfrey DWCF, Brook Cottage Farm, Charney Bassett, Wantage, **Oxfordshire**, OX12 0EN, **ENGLAND**.
(T) 01235 868492.
Profile Farrier. Ref: YH05866

GODINGTON STUD

Godington Farm, Godington, Bicester, **Oxfordshire**, OX27 9AF, **ENGLAND**.
(T) 01869 277562 (F) 01869 277762.
Contact/s
General Manager: Ms R Burnard (Q) BHSAI
Profile Breeder, Stable/Livery, Trainer. No.Staff: 3 Yr. Est: 1998 C.Size: 30 Acres
Opening Times
Sp: Open 10:00. Closed 18:00.
Su: Open 10:00. Closed 18:00.
Au: Open 10:00. Closed 18:00.
Wn: Open 10:00. Closed 18:00. Ref: YH05867

GODLEY STUD RIDING SCHOOL

Godley Stud Riding School, Green Lane, Gee Cross, Hyde, Manchester, **Manchester (Greater)**, SK14 3BD, **ENGLAND**.
(T) 0161 3669103.
Contact/s
Owner: Mrs P Hazelhurst
Profile Riding School, Stable/Livery.
Teach children from the age of six upwards. Group lessons from £6.00. All instructors are BHS qualified.
No.Staff: 4 Yr. Est: 1993
Opening Times
Sp: Open Tues - Sun 10:00. Closed Tues - Sun 18:00.
Su: Open Tues - Sun 10:00. Closed Tues - Sun 18:00.
Au: Open Tues - Sun 10:00. Closed Tues - Sun 18:00.
Wn: Open Tues - Sun 10:00. Closed Tues - Sun 18:00.
Closed on Mondays Ref: YH05868

GODOLPHIN MNGMT

Godolphin Management Co Ltd, White Lodge, Broad Green, Newmarket, **Suffolk**, CB8 9RF, **ENGLAND**.
(T) 01638 730182.
Profile Trainer. Ref: YH05869

GODSON, ALAN RICHARD

Alan Richard Godson DWCF, 6 Gerrard Rd, Alcester, **Warwickshire**, B49 6QC, **ENGLAND**.
(T) 01789 400907.
Profile Farrier. Ref: YH05870

GOESS-SAURAU, (COUNTESS)

Countess Goess-Saurau, Temple Farm, Rockley, Marlborough, **Wiltshire**, SN8 1RU, **ENGLAND**.
(T) 01672 514428 (F) 01672 514116
(M) 07860 851900.
Profile Breeder. Ref: YH05871

GOFF, J

Mrs J Goff, 95 South Ave, Kidlington, Oxford, **Oxfordshire**, OX5 1DQ, **ENGLAND**.
(T) 01867 56286.
Profile Breeder. Ref: YH05872

GOGGIN, F M

F M Goggin, 47 Blaen Dowlais, Dowlais, Merthyr Tydfil, **Glamorgan (Vale of)**, CF48 3RB, **WALES**.
(T) 01685 375116.
Profile Breeder. Ref: YH05873

GOHL, CHRIS

Chris Gohl, Broadway Hse, Chartridge, Chesham, **Buckinghamshire**, HP5 2TT, **ENGLAND**.
(T) 01494 837138.
Profile Riding Wear Retailer, Saddlery Retailer.
Ref: YH05874

GOLBY, B

B Golby RSS, 210 Coventry Rd, Exhall, Coventry, **Warwickshire**, CV7 9BH, **ENGLAND**.
(T) 024 76312997.
Profile Farrier. Ref: YH05875

GOLD CUP FEEDS

Gold Cup Feeds, The Homestead, Braishfield, Romsey, **Hampshire**, SO51 0QE, **ENGLAND**.
(T) 01794 368264 (F) 01794 368264
(M) 07836 663190.
Profile Supplies. Ref: YH05876

GOLDEN CASTLE

Golden Castle Riding & Livery Stables, Llangattock, Crickhowell, **Powys**, NP8 1PY, **WALES**.
(T) 01873 810469/810469 (F) 01873 730987
(E) enquiries@golden-castle.co.uk
(W) www.golden-castle.co.uk
Affiliated Bodies BHS.
Profile Arena, Equestrian Centre, Riding School, Stable/Livery, Trainer, Transport/Horse Boxes.
No.Staff: 4 Yr. Est: 1998 C.Size: 30 Acres
Ref: YH05877

GOLDEN CROSS

Golden Cross Equestrian Centre, Chalvington Rd, Golden Cross, Hailsham, **Sussex (East)**, BN27 3SS, **ENGLAND**.
(T) 01825 873022
(E) goldencross@equestrian.co.uk.
Contact/s
Owner: Mr I Boreham
Profile Equestrian Centre, Stable/Livery. Competition Centre. No.Staff: 6 Yr. Est: 1998 C.Size: 70 Acres Ref: YH05878

GOLDEN FLEECE

Golden Fleece, 12 Walsall Rd, Lichfield, **Staffordshire**, WS13 8AB, **ENGLAND**.
(T) 01543 258448 (F) 01543 418251.
Profile Supplies. Ref: YH05879

GOLDEN VALLEY

Golden Valley Veterinary Hospital, 2 The Vinery,

Harford Sq, Chew Magna, **Bath & Somerset (North East)**, BS18 8RD, **ENGLAND**.
(T) 01275 332442.
Profile Medical Support. **Ref: YH05880**

GOLDEN VALLEY

Golden Valley, Lower Broadmeadow Cottage, Hardwick, Hay On Wye, **Herefordshire**, HR3 5TA, **ENGLAND**.
(T) 01497 821492. **Ref: YH05881**

GOLDENEYE

Goldeneye, Hyde Ecchinswell, Newbury, **Berkshire**, RG20 4UN, **ENGLAND**.
(T) 01285 850892 **(F)** 01285 851110.
Profile Supplies. **Ref: YH05882**

GOLDENEYE

Goldeneye Video, Sunhill Hse, Meysey Hampton, Cirencester, **Gloucestershire**, GL7 5SZ, **ENGLAND**.
(T) 01285 850892 **(F)** 01285 851110
(E) 6@goldeneyevideo.co.uk
(W) www.goldeneyevideo.co.uk.
Profile Video Production.
Promotional material produced.
Opening Times
Telephone for more information **Ref: YH05883**

GOLDENFIELDS STUD

Goldenfields Stud, Badger Farm, Bedale, **Yorkshire (North)**, DL8 2LR, **ENGLAND**.
(T) 01545 5300.
Profile Breeder. **Ref: YH05884**

GOLDENMOOR

Goldenmoor Stud, Denwick, Alnwick, **Northumberland**, NE66 3RB, **ENGLAND**.
(T) 01665 602421.
Contact/s
Owner: Mr J Robson
Profile Breeder, Stud Farm. C.Size: 160 Acres
Opening Times
Telephone for further information **Ref: YH05885**

GOLDER, ROBERT M

Robert M Golder DWCF, 242 Gregson Lane, Hoghton, Preston, **Lancashire**, PR5 0LA, **ENGLAND**.
(T) 01254 853261.
Profile Farrier. **Ref: YH05886**

GOLDIE, DAVID

David Goldie, 4-6 High St, Skipton, **Yorkshire (North)**, BD23 1JZ, **ENGLAND**.
(T) 01756 795939 **(F)** 01756 795939.
Profile Saddlery Retailer. **Ref: YH05887**

GOLDIE, J S

Mr J S Goldie, Libo Hill Farm, Uplawmoor, **Glasgow (City of)**, G78 4BA, **SCOTLAND**.
(T) 01505 850212
(M) 07778 522241.
Profile Trainer. **Ref: YH05888**

GOLDIE, ROBERT H

Mr Robert H Goldie, Harpercroft, Old Loans Rd, Dundonald, Kilmarnock, **Ayrshire (East)**, KA2 9DD, **SCOTLAND**.
(T) 01292 317222 **(F)** 01292 313585
(M) 07801 922552.
Profile Trainer. **Ref: YH05889**

GOLDIE, T

Mr T Goldie, Dorain, Laigh Patterton, Kilwinning, **Ayrshire (North)**, KA13 7RE, **SCOTLAND**.
(T) 01294 385.
Profile Supplies. **Ref: YH05890**

GOLDING & SON

Golding & Son Ltd, 67 High St, Newmarket, **Suffolk**, CB8 8NA, **ENGLAND**.
(T) 01638 664682 **(F)** 01638 666657.
Profile Saddlery Retailer. **Ref: YH05891**

GOLDING, MICHAEL E

Michael E Golding, 37 Fairoaks, Aldershot Rd, Guildford, **Surrey**, GU3 3HG, **ENGLAND**.
(T) 01483 234157.
Profile Farrier. **Ref: YH05892**

GOLDSMITH, G R

G R Goldsmith, Grove Cottages, Wickham Market, Woodbridge, **Suffolk**, IP13 0NG, **ENGLAND**.
(T) 01728 746848.
Profile Farrier. **Ref: YH05893**

GOLDSWORTHY, C

C Goldsworthy, Manor Farm Cottage, Ryme Intrinseca, Sherborne, **Dorset**, DT9 6JX, **ENGLAND**.
(T) 01935 872699 **(F)** 01935 872592.
Profile Farrier. **Ref: YH05894**

GOLDTHORPE, DAVID

David Goldthorpe RSS, 31 Norwood Drive, Birstall, Batley, **Yorkshire (West)**, WF17 0BN, **ENGLAND**.
(T) 01924 475639.
Profile Farrier. **Ref: YH05895**

GOLDTHORPE, K

Mrs K Goldthorpe, The Chapel, Crowedge, Sheffield, **Yorkshire (South)**, S36 4HF, **ENGLAND**.
(T) 01226 766326.
Profile Breeder. **Ref: YH05896**

GOLLINGS, JAYNE

Jayne Gollings, Highfield Hse, Scamblesby, Louth, **Lincolnshire**, LN11 9XT, **ENGLAND**.
(T) 01507 343204 **(F)** 01507 343204
(M) 07860 218910.
Profile Blood Stock Agency. **Ref: YH05897**

GOLLINGS, S

Mr S Gollings, Highfield Hse, Scamblesby, Louth, **Lincolnshire**, LN11 9XT, **ENGLAND**.
(T) 01507 343204 **(F)** 01507 343204
(M) 07860 218910.
Profile Trainer. **Ref: YH05898**

GOOD BIT

Good Bit (The), 16 Lincoln Ave, Clayton, Newcastle-under-Lyme, **Staffordshire**, ST5 3AR, **ENGLAND**.
(T) 01782 256587
(M) 07951 012696
(E) pr@thegoodbit.com. **Ref: YH05899**

GOOD, RAYMOND D

Raymond D Good DWCF, 15 Rochester Rd, Dartford, **Kent**, DA1 1SP, **ENGLAND**.
(T) 01322 224529.
Profile Farrier. **Ref: YH05900**

GOODE, WILLIAM J M

William J M Goode RSS, Hill Hse Farm, Lower Rd, Glemsford, Sudbury, **Suffolk**, CO10 7QU, **ENGLAND**.
(T) 01787 281428.
Profile Breeder, Farrier. **Ref: YH05901**

GOODEY, V

Mrs V Goodey, Marsh Cottage, Marshlands Lane, Heathfield, **Sussex (East)**, TN21 8EX, **ENGLAND**.
(T) 01435 862322.
Profile Breeder. **Ref: YH05902**

GOODFELLOWS

Goodfellows, Penmellow Works, Trenant Ind Est, Wadebridge, **Cornwall**, PL27 6HB, **ENGLAND**.
(T) 01208 812115.
Contact/s
Partner: Mr C Goodfellow
Profile Transport/Horse Boxes. **Ref: YH05903**

GOODMAN HORSE BOX SVS

Goodman Horse Box Services, Stanways Garage, Hooton Rd, Hooton, Ellesmere Port, **Cheshire**, CH66 7NG, **ENGLAND**.
(T) 0151 3247147 **(F)** 0151 3278147.
Contact/s
Owner: Mr M Goodman
Profile Transport/Horse Boxes.
Repair, buy, sell, build and refurbish horseboxes.
Yr. Est: 1998
Opening Times
Sp: Open Mon - Sat 09:00. Closed Mon - Sat 18:00.
Su: Open Mon - Sat 09:00. Closed Mon - Sat 18:00.
Au: Open Mon - Sat 09:00. Closed Mon - Sat 18:00.
Wn: Open Mon - Sat 09:00. Closed Mon - Sat 18:00.
Closed Sundays **Ref: YH05904**

GOODNESTONE CT EQUESTRIAN

Goodnestone Court Equestrian, Goodnestone Court, Goodnestone, Graveney, Faversham, **Kent**, ME13 9BZ, **ENGLAND**.
(T) 01795 535806 **(F)** 01795 534202.
Profile Riding School, Stable/Livery. **Ref: YH05905**

GOODRICK, H

Mr H Goodrick, Bay View, 18 Orchard Rd, Bardsea, Ulverston, **Cumbria**, LA12 9QN, **ENGLAND**.
(T) 01229 869357.
Profile Architectural/ Property Services.
Ref: YH05906

GOODRICKS EQUESTRIAN

Goodricks Equestrian, Outgang Lane, Osbaldwick, **Yorkshire (North)**, YO19 5UP, **ENGLAND**.
(T) 01904 430630 **(F)** 01904 430363
(E) info@goodricks.co.uk.
Profile Transport/Horse Boxes. **Ref: YH05907**

GOODROWES OF CHICHESTER

Goodrowes of Chichester Ltd, 6 The Hornet, Chichester, **Sussex (West)**, PO19 4JQ, **ENGLAND**.
(T) 01243 784411.
Profile Saddlery Retailer. **Ref: YH05908**

GOODTIMES LEISURE

Goodtimes Leisure Ltd, 27 Victoria St, Kettering, **Northamptonshire**, NN16 0BU, **ENGLAND**.
(T) 01536 481071 **(F)** 01536 312424.
Profile Saddlery Retailer. **Ref: YH05909**

GOODWIN, GEOFF

Geoff Goodwin, Willowdale Farm, Leek Rd, Wetley Rocks, Stoke-on-Trent, **Staffordshire**, ST9 0AP, **ENGLAND**.
(T) 01782 550479. **Ref: YH05910**

GOODWIN, MARTIN LEE

Martin Lee Goodwin RSS, Chobham Forge, Burrow Hill Green, Chobham, **Surrey**, GU24 8QP, **ENGLAND**.
(T) 01276 856808.
Profile Farrier. **Ref: YH05911**

GOODWIN, P

Mr P Goodwin, 31 Bar Lane, Midgley, Wakefield, **Yorkshire (West)**, WF4 4JH, **ENGLAND**.
(T) 01924 830381.
Profile Architectural/ Property Services.
Ref: YH05912

GOODWIN, S E V

Mrs S E V Goodwin, The Coach Hse, Spring Lane, Packington, Ashby-De-La-Zouch, **Leicestershire**, LE16 1WU, **ENGLAND**.
(T) 01530 413523.
Profile Breeder. **Ref: YH05913**

GOODWOOD RACECOURSE

Goodwood Racecourse Ltd, Goodwood, Chichester, **Sussex (West)**, PO18 0PX, **ENGLAND**.
(T) 01243 755022 **(F)** 01243 755025
(E) racing@goodwood.co.uk.
Contact/s
Clerk of Course: Mr R Fabricius
Profile Track/Course. **Ref: YH05914**

GOONBELL RIDING CTRE

Goonbell Riding Centre, Goonbell, St Agnes, **Cornwall**, TR5 0PN, **ENGLAND**.
(T) 01872 552063.
Contact/s
Owner: Mr F Daniels
Profile Riding School. **Ref: YH05915**

GOOSEFORD RIDING SCHOOL

Gooseford Riding School, St. Mellion, Saltash, **Cornwall**, PL12 6RT, **ENGLAND**.
(T) 01579 350715.
Profile Riding School. **Ref: YH05916**

GOOSEHAM BARTON STABLES

Gooseham Barton Stables, Gooseham Barton Farm, Gooseham, Bude, **Cornwall**, EX23 9PG, **ENGLAND**.
(T) 01288 331204 **(F)** 01288 331204.
Contact/s
Manager: Ms D Hamilton
Profile Riding School. **Ref: YH05917**

GOOSEMOOR STUD

Goosemoor Stud, Cowthorpe, Wetherby, **Yorkshire (West)**, LS22 5EU, **ENGLAND**.
(T) 01423 359397.
Profile Breeder. **Ref: YH05918**

GOOSEN, G

Mr G Goosen, Ladbrook Hall, Penn Lane, Tanworth-In-Arden, Solihull, **Warwickshire**, B94 5HJ, **ENGLAND**.
(T) 01564 742235 **(F)** 01564 742720. **Ref: YH05919**

GOOSEWELL TREKKING CTRE

Goosewell Trekking Centre, Goosewell Farm, Keswick, **Cumbria**, CA12 4RN, **ENGLAND**.
(T) 05967 2385.
Profile Equestrian Centre. Trekking Centre.
Ref: YH05920

GORDANO VALLEY RIDING CTRE

Gordano Valley Riding Centre, Moor Lane, Clapton In Gordano, Bristol, **Bristol**, BS20 7RF, **ENGLAND**.
(T) 01275 843473.
Profile Riding School. **Ref: YH05921**

GORDIAN TROELLER BLOODSTOCK

Gordian Troeller Bloodstock Ltd, 33 Berry's Rd,

Upper Bucklebury, **Berkshire**, RG7 6QL, **ENGLAND**.
(T) 01635 869370 **(F)** 01635 876246.
Profile Blood Stock Agency. **Ref: YH05922**

GORDON DRESSAGE GROUP

Gordon Dressage Group, 10 Woodland Pk, Durris, Banchory, **Aberdeenshire**, AB31 6BF, **SCOTLAND**.
(T) 01330 811401.
Profile Club/Association. **Ref: YH05923**

GORDON MARTIN & SON

Gordon Martin & Son, The Chalet, Tresarrett, Bodmin, **Cornwall**, PL30 4QF, **ENGLAND**.
(T) 01208 851405 **(F)** 01208 851405.
Contact/s
Owner: Mr G Martin
Profile Transport/Horse Boxes. **Ref: YH05924**

GORDON, LAWRENCE A

Lawrence A Gordon DWCF, 19 Carey Down, Ambleside Ave, Telscombe Cliffs, **Sussex (East)**, BN10 7LF, **ENGLAND**.
(T) 01273 581509.
Profile Farrier. **Ref: YH05925**

GORDON, PAUL T

Paul T Gordon DWCF, Chapel Cottage, 14 Chapel Lane, Moulton, Northwich, **Cheshire**, CW9 8PQ, **ENGLAND**.
(T) 07973 752693.
Profile Farrier. **Ref: YH05926**

GORDON, R

R Gordon, 111 Market St, Musselburgh, **Lothian (East)**, EH21 6PZ, **SCOTLAND**.
(T) 0131 6652124.
Profile Medical Support. **Ref: YH05927**

GORDON-SMITH, F

Mrs F Gordon-Smith, Lordington Pk, Chichester, **Sussex (West)**, PO18 9DX, **ENGLAND**.
(T) 01243 378905.
Contact/s
Owner: Mrs F Gordon-Smith
Profile Breeder. **Ref: YH05928**

GORDON-WATSON BLOODSTOCK

Gordon-Watson Bloodstock, Fairholt Hse, 2 Pont St, London, **London (Greater)**, SW1X 9EL, **ENGLAND**.
(T) 020 78389747 **(F)** 020 78389767.
Profile Blood Stock Agency. **Ref: YH05929**

GORDON-WATSON, CHARLES

Charles Gordon-Watson, 26 Redburn St, London, **London (Greater)**, SW3 4BX, **ENGLAND**.
(T) 020 73515666 **(F)** 020 73517666
(W) www.gordon-watson.com.
Contact/s
Assistant: Miss H Michael
Profile Blood Stock Agency. Yr. Est: 1985
Opening Times
By appointment only **Ref: YH05930**

GORDON-WATSON, M

M Gordon-Watson, East Blagdon Farm, Cranborne, Wimborne, **Dorset**, BH21 5RZ, **ENGLAND**.
(T) 01725 517304.
Profile Breeder. **Ref: YH05931**

GORE, J S

J S Gore, 9 Brookside Gardens, Yockleton, Shrewsbury, **Shropshire**, SY5 9PR, **ENGLAND**.
(T) 01743 821637.
Profile Hay & Straw Merchants. **Ref: YH05932**

GORING & DISTRICT RIDING CLUB

Goring & District Riding Club, 19 Brendon Rd, Worthing, **Sussex (West)**, BN13 2PS, **ENGLAND**.
(T) 01903 265899.
Contact/s
Secretary: Mrs S Baker
Profile Club/Association, Riding Club. **Ref: YH05933**

GORLESTON TACK ROOM

Gorleston Tack Room (The), 84 High St, Gorleston, Great Yarmouth, **Norfolk**, NR31 6RQ, **ENGLAND**.
(T) 01493 601486.
Profile Riding Wear Retailer, Saddlery Retailer.
Ref: YH05934

GORMAN, JIM

Jim Gorman, Brownstown Lodge, The Curragh, **County Kildare**, **IRELAND**.
(T) 045 441404.
Contact/s
Trainer: Mr J Gorman
(E) jimgorman@kildarehorse.ie
Profile Trainer. **Ref: YH05935**

GORRINGE SPORTSWEAR

Gorringe Sportswear Ltd, 2 Short St, Premier Business Pk, Walsall, **Midlands (West)**, WS2 9EB, **ENGLAND**.
(T) 01922 628131 **(F)** 01922 724336.
Profile Riding Wear Retailer. **Ref: YH05936**

GORS WEN FARM

Gors Wen Farm & Riding Stables, Gorswen, Holyhead, **Isle of Anglesey**, LL65 2LY, **WALES**.
(T) 01407 769136 **(F)** 01407 761111.
Contact/s
Owner: Mr K Jones
Profile Riding School, Track/Course. **Ref: YH05937**

GORS WEN RIDING STABLES

Gors Wen Riding Stables, Plas Rd, Holyhead, **Isle of Anglesey**, LL65 1LY, **WALES**.
(T) 01407 762706.
Profile Equestrian Centre. Trekking Centre.
Ref: YH05938

GORSE FARM ARENA

Gorse Farm Arena, Lazy Hill, Stonnall, Aldridge, **Midlands (West)**, WS9 9DS, **ENGLAND**.
(T) 01543 371478 **(F)** 0121 3222123.
Profile Stable/Livery. **Ref: YH05939**

GORSE FARM LIVERY STABLES

Gorse Farm Livery Stables, Gorse Farm, Gorse Drove, Scredington, Sleaford, **Lincolnshire**, NG34 0AL, **ENGLAND**.
(T) 01529 305266 **(F)** 01529 305266.
Profile Stable/Livery. **Ref: YH05940**

GOSDEN, J H M

Mr J H M Gosden, Manton Hse Est, Marlborough, **Wiltshire**, SN8 1PN, **ENGLAND**.
(T) 01672 516426 **(F)** 01672 516428.
Profile Trainer. **Ref: YH05941**

GOSLING, VICKY

Miss Vicky Gosling, Yellow Hammers, Bletchingley Rd, Godstone, **Surrey**, RH9 8NB, **ENGLAND**.
(T) 01883 742459. **Ref: YH05942**

GOSPELS FARM

Gospels Farm, Beacon Rd, Ditchling, Hassocks, **Sussex (West)**, BN6 8UL, **ENGLAND**.
(T) 01273 842503.
Contact/s
Owner: Mr D Kent
Profile Stable/Livery. **Ref: YH05943**

GOSWELL, TREVOR M

Trevor M Goswell RSS, 65 Broad Rd, Lower Willingdon, Eastbourne, **Sussex (East)**, BN20 9QT, **ENGLAND**.
(T) 01323 488198.
Profile Farrier. **Ref: YH05944**

GOTHERSLEY FARM

Gothersley Farm, Greensforge Lane, Stourton, Stourbridge, **Staffordshire**, DY7 5AZ, **ENGLAND**.
(T) 01384 872561.
Profile Saddlery Retailer, Stable/Livery.
Ref: YH05945

GOTTS, A R

A R Gotts, The Old Corn Mill, Mill St, Gimingham, Norwich, **Norfolk**, NR11 8AB, **ENGLAND**.
(T) 01263 720993 **(F)** 01263 720993.
Contact/s
Owner: Mr A Gotts
Profile Transport/Horse Boxes. **Ref: YH05946**

GOTTS, H J

H J Gotts, Cornish Shire Horse Farm & Carriage Museum, Lower Grillis Farm, Treskillard, Redruth, **Cornwall**, TR16 6LA, **ENGLAND**.
(T) 01209 713606.
Profile Breeder. **Ref: YH05947**

GOUDY, RAY

Ray Goudy, 1 Tomo Ind Est, Creeting Rd, Stowmarket, **Suffolk**, IP14 5AY, **ENGLAND**.
(T) 01449 673989 **(F)** 01449 775220.
Profile Transport/Horse Boxes. **Ref: YH05948**

GOUGH, GARRY C

Garry C Gough DWCF, 6 River Lane, Saltney, Chester, **Cheshire**, CH4 8RH, **ENGLAND**.
(T) 01244 682976.
Profile Farrier. **Ref: YH05949**

GOULDING, J

Mr J Goulding, Quarry Bank, Brigham, Cockermouth, **Cumbria**, CA13 0TW, **ENGLAND**.
(T) 01900 825393.
Profile Trainer. **Ref: YH05950**

GOULDING, PHILIP

Philip Goulding DWCF, Rose Cottage, Little Broughton, Cockermouth, **Cumbria**, CA13 0XZ, **ENGLAND**.
(T) 01900 829415.
Profile Farrier. **Ref: YH05951**

GOULDS GREEN

Goulds Green Riding School, The Stables, Goulds Green, Uxbridge, **London (Greater)**, UB8 3DG, **ENGLAND**.
(T) 01895 446256 **(F)** 01895 447561
Affiliated Bodies BHS.
Contact/s
Owner: Mr M Jupp
Profile Riding School, Riding Wear Retailer, Saddlery Retailer, Stable/Livery. Yr. Est: 1965
Opening Times
Sp: Open Mon - Sun 09:00. Closed Mon - Sun 18:00.
Su: Open Mon - Sun 09:00. Closed Mon - Sun 18:00.
Au: Open Mon - Sun 09:00. Closed Mon - Sun 18:00.
Wn: Open Mon - Sun 09:00. Closed Mon - Sun 18:00. **Ref: YH05952**

GOW, D J H

Mrs D J H Gow, Pitscandly, Forfar, **Angus**, DD8 3NZ, **SCOTLAND**.
(T) 01307 462437.
Profile Breeder. **Ref: YH05953**

GOW, ROBIN

Robin Gow Equestrian Services Health & Safety, Appletree Farm, 56 North Rd, Great Abington, **Cambridgeshire**, CB1 6AS, **ENGLAND**.
(T) 01223 894294 **(F)** 01223 894294.
Profile Medical Support, Supplies. **Ref: YH05954**

GOWER RIDING CLUB

Gower Riding Club, Gelli Gwm Isaf, Felindre, Swansea, **Swansea**, SA5 7PP, **WALES**.
(T) 01792 884085 **(F)** 01792 884934.
Profile Club/Association, Riding Club. **Ref: YH05955**

GOWING, STEPHEN PETER

Stephen Peter Gowing AWCF, Infields Farm, Grandford Drove, March, **Cambridgeshire**, PE15 0AB, **ENGLAND**.
(T) 01733 840036.
Profile Farrier. **Ref: YH05956**

GRABELLA STUD

Grabella Stud, Kentford, **Cambridgeshire**, CB4 7QS, **ENGLAND**.
(T) 01638 751888.
Profile Stable/Livery, Supplies. **Ref: YH05957**

GRACELANDS

Gracelands Equestrian Centre, Crutch Lane, Elmbridge, Droitwich, **Worcestershire**, WR9 0BE, **ENGLAND**.
(T) 01527 861476 **(F)** 01527 861476.
Contact/s
Owner: Mr C Napier
Profile Arena, Equestrian Centre, Stable/Livery. Competition Centre.
The livery yard consists of 16 brick and 9 wooden boxes and 4 converted barns. The centre has a warm up area, a grass indoor school and a sand outdoor school. They hold show jumping competitions for BSJA and Dressage. Show jumping is held on a Tuesday - BSJA and unaffiliated, also on Wednesday & Thursday evenings in the indoor school, and at weekends in either the indoor or the outdoor school. In the winter competitions are only held on a Sunday.
Yr. Est: 1986 C.Size: 14 Acres
Opening Times
Telephone for further information, there is an answer phone with details **Ref: YH05958**

GRAFHAM STUD

Grafham Stud, Lower Denham Farm, Quainton, Aylesbury, **Buckinghamshire**, HP22 4AG, **ENGLAND**.
(T) 01296 655727.
Profile Breeder. **Ref: YH05959**

GRAFTON DONKEY STUD

Grafton Donkey Stud, Lovelwood Hse, Lillingstone Lovell, **Buckinghamshire**, MK18 5AZ, **ENGLAND**.
(T) 01280 860279.
Profile Breeder. **Ref: YH05960**

GRAFTON FARM STUD
Grafton Farm Stud, Curtis Mill Green, Stapleford Tawney, Romford, **Essex**, RM4 1RT, **ENGLAND**.
(T) 01708 688372 **(F)** 01708 688578.
Profile Breeder. **Ref: YH05961**

GRAHAM BROWN
Graham Brown Insurance Brokers Ltd, Trevone Hse, Pannells Court, Guildford, **Surrey**, GU1 4EY, **ENGLAND**.
(T) 01483 301355 **(F)** 01483 301869.
Profile Club/Association. **Ref: YH05962**

GRAHAM C S JEANS
Graham C S Jeans, Ramblers, Lanchards Lane, Shillingstone, Blandford Forum, **Dorset**, DT11 0TF, **ENGLAND**.
(T) 01258 860001.
Profile Farrier. **Ref: YH05963**

GRAHAM EDWARDS TRAILERS
Graham Edwards Trailers Ltd, Moor Lane, Stamford Bridge, York, **Yorkshire (North)**, YO41 1HX, **ENGLAND**.
(T) 01759 373062 **(F)** 01759 372929.
Profile Transport/Horse Boxes. **Ref: YH05964**

GRAHAM LODGE STABLES
Graham Lodge Stables, Graham Lodge, Birdcage Walk, Newmarket, **Suffolk**, CB8 0NF, **ENGLAND**.
(T) 01638 668043 **(F)** 01638 668043
(M) 07860 198303
(W) www.newmarketracehorsetrainers.co.uk
Affiliated Bodies Newmarket Trainers Fed.
Contact/s
Trainer: Mr G Margarson
Profile Trainer. **Ref: YH05965**

GRAHAM, FERGUS
Fergus Graham, Cross Pk, Woodland, Newton Abbott, **Devon**, TQ13 7JU, **ENGLAND**.
(T) 01364 653453 **(F)** 01364 653593.
Profile Breeder. **Ref: YH05966**

GRAHAM, H O
Mrs H O Graham, Brundeanlaws Cottage, Camptown, Jedburgh, **Scottish Borders**, TD8 6NW, **SCOTLAND**.
(T) 01835 840354
(M) 07798 755467.
Profile Supplies. **Ref: YH05967**

GRAHAM, HUGH
Mr Hugh Graham, 13 North Cross St, Leadgate, Consett, **County Durham**, DH8 6DT, **ENGLAND**.
(T) 01207 583198.
Profile Supplies. **Ref: YH05968**

GRAHAM, I
Mr & Mrs I Graham, Delf Field Farm, Kebroyd Lane, Triangle, Halifax, **Yorkshire (West)**, HX6 3HT, **ENGLAND**.
(T) 01422 824213.
Profile Breeder. **Ref: YH05969**

GRAHAM, JAMES A
James A Graham DWCF, 14 Pinfold View, Bakewell, **Derbyshire**, DE45 1GR, **ENGLAND**.
(T) 01629 815310.
Profile Farrier. **Ref: YH05970**

GRAHAM, LINDSAY
Lindsay Graham, 105 Boghill Rd, Templepatrick, Ballyclare, **County Antrim**, BT39 0HS, **NORTHERN IRELAND**.
(T) 028 90825280.
Contact/s
Owner: Mr L Graham
Profile Transport/Horse Boxes. **Ref: YH05971**

GRAHAM, N
Mr N Graham, Station Approach, Newmarket, **Suffolk**, CB8 9RF, **ENGLAND**.
(T) 01638 665202 **(F)** 01638 667849
(M) 07770 321571
(W) www.newmarketracehorsetrainers.co.uk
Affiliated Bodies Newmarket Trainers Fed.
Contact/s
Trainer: Mr N Graham
Profile Trainer. **Ref: YH05972**

GRAHAM-ROGERS, C
Ms C Graham-Rogers, Hellyer Way, Bourne End, **Buckinghamshire**, SL8 5XL, **ENGLAND**.
(T) 07768 456216.
Contact/s
Owner: Ms C Graham-Roger
Profile Riding School.
Private riding tuition. **Ref: YH05973**

GRAHAMS
Grahams Equestrian Horse And Rider, Old Hall Rd, Sale, **Cheshire**, M33 2HP, **ENGLAND**.
(T) 0161 9731046 **(F)** 0161 9731046.
Contact/s
Owner: Mr R Graham
Profile Supplies. **Ref: YH05974**

GRAIG FAWR LIVERY YARD
Graig Fawr Livery Yard, Graig Fawr Farm, Caerphilly, **Caerphilly**, CF83 1NF, **WALES**.
(T) 029 20883659.
Contact/s
Owner: Mr D Jones
Profile Stable/Livery. **Ref: YH05975**

GRAIN HARVESTERS
Grain Harvesters Ltd, Old Colliery, Wingham, Canterbury, **Kent**, CT3 1LS, **ENGLAND**.
(T) 01227 720374.
Contact/s
Feed Specialist: Mr C Page
Profile Supplies. **Ref: YH05976**

GRAMPIAN HIGHLAND RIDING
Grampian Highland Riding, Langstrath, Carrbridge, **Highlands**, PH23 3AX, **SCOTLAND**.
(T) 01479 841799.
Profile Equestrian Centre. **Ref: YH05977**

GRAMPS HILL RIDING CTRE
Gramps Hill Riding Centre, Letcombe Bassett, Wantage, **Oxfordshire**, OX12 9LX, **ENGLAND**.
(T) 01235 763536.
Contact/s
Owner: Mrs L Inns
Profile Stable/Livery. **Ref: YH05978**

GRANARY
Granary (The), Woodleys Farm, Bow Brickhill Rd, Woburn Sands, Milton Keynes, **Buckinghamshire**, MK17 8DE, **ENGLAND**.
(T) 01908 281460.
Contact/s
Owner: Mr J Young
Profile Stable/Livery. **Ref: YH05979**

GRANARY
Granary (The), 15 Station Sq, Whitby, **Yorkshire (North)**, YO21 1DU, **ENGLAND**.
(T) 01947 600813.
Contact/s
Partner: Mrs H Varley
Profile Saddlery Retailer. **Ref: YH05980**

GRANARY HORSE FEEDS
Granary Horse Feeds, Hundredsteddle Lane, Birdham, Chichester, **Sussex (West)**, PO20 7BL, **ENGLAND**.
(T) 01243 512108.
Profile Supplies. **Ref: YH05981**

GRANBY STUD
Granby Stud, Field Farm, Northleigh, Witney, **Oxfordshire**, OX8 6PX, **ENGLAND**.
(T) 01993 881207.
Profile Breeder. **Ref: YH05982**

GRAND PLAN CONSULTANCY
Grand Plan Consultancy (The), Yew Tree Studios, Avon Dassett, Southam, **Warwickshire**, CV47 2AY, **ENGLAND**.
(T) 01295 690060 **(F)** 01295 690068
(E) panda@thegpc.prestel.co.uk.
Profile Club/Association. **Ref: YH05983**

GRANDSTAND MEDIA
Grandstand Media Ltd, Elvin Hse, Stadium Way, Wembley, **London (Greater)**, HA9 0EH, **ENGLAND**.
(T) 020 89009282 **(F)** 020 89002660
(E) info@hoys.co.uk.
Profile Club/Association. **Ref: YH05984**

GRANE STUD
Grane Stud, Stubbs Farm, Stubbs Green, Loddon, Norwich, **Norfolk**, NR14 6EA, **ENGLAND**.
(T) 01508 528180 **(F)** 01508 528180.
Contact/s
Owner: Mrs B Kittle
Profile Breeder.
Breed and import dressage horses from Denmark. Recent successes include Mrs. B Harrison-Bland's impressive stallion Wikefield Grane Viking, who this year qualified for Prevac-Pro International Dressage Horse (for the second year running). **Ref: YH05985**

GRANGE EQUESTRIAN
Grange Equestrian, 60 Trench Rd, Hydepark Ind Est, Mallusk, Newtownabbey, **County Antrim**, BT36 4TY, **NORTHERN IRELAND**.
(T) 028 90835177.
Contact/s
General Manager: Mr R Carlisle
Profile Medical Support, Supplies. C.Size: 0.5 Acres
Opening Times
Sp: Open Mon - Fri 08:30. Closed Mon - Fri 17:00.
Su: Open Mon - Fri 08:30. Closed Mon - Fri 17:00.
Au: Open Mon - Fri 08:30. Closed Mon - Fri 17:00.
Wn: Open Mon - Fri 08:30. Closed Mon - Fri 17:00.
Closed weekends **Ref: YH05986**

GRANGE EQUESTRIAN CTRE
Grange Equestrian Centre, Northlew Rd, Inwardleigh, Okehampton, **Devon**, EX20 3DA, **ENGLAND**.
(T) 01837 52303 **(F)** 01837 55392.
Contact/s
Owner: Mrs S Courtney
Profile Riding School, Stable/Livery, Track/Course.
Ref: YH05987

GRANGE FARM EQUESTRIAN CTRE
Grange Farm Equestrian Centre, Wittering Grange, Leicester Rd, Wansford, Peterborough, **Cambridgeshire**, PE8 6NR, **ENGLAND**.
(T) 01780 782459.
Profile Riding School, Saddlery Retailer, Stable/Livery. **Ref: YH05988**

GRANGE FARM LIVERIES
Grange Farm Liveries, Grange Farm, Boon Hill Rd, Bignall End, Stoke-on-Trent, **Staffordshire**, ST7 8LG, **ENGLAND**.
(T) 01782 722232.
Profile Stable/Livery. **Ref: YH05989**

GRANGE FARM LIVERY
Grange Farm Livery, Spixworth, Norwich, **Norfolk**, NR10 3PR, **ENGLAND**.
(T) 01603 898272.
Profile Stable/Livery. **Ref: YH05990**

GRANGE LIVERY STABLES
Grange Livery Stables (The), 17 Station Rd, Goostrey, Crewe, **Cheshire**, CW4 8PJ, **ENGLAND**.
(T) 01477 533249 **(F)** 01477 533249.
Contact/s
Owner: Mr R Wood
Profile Stable/Livery. **Ref: YH05991**

GRANGE METALWORK
Grange Metalwork Co Ltd, 410 Gorgie Rd, Edinburgh, **Edinburgh (City of)**, EH11 2RN, **SCOTLAND**.
(T) 0131 3372889.
Profile Blacksmith. **Ref: YH05992**

GRANGE RIDING CTRE
Grange Riding Centre, West Calder, **Lothian (West)**, EH55 8PS, **SCOTLAND**.
(T) 01506 871219 **(F)** 01506 871219
Affiliated Bodies BHS.
Contact/s
Owner: Mrs E Knight
Profile Riding School. No.Staff: 3
Yr. Est: 1975 C.Size: 50 Acres
Opening Times
Sp: Open Mon - Sat 09:00. Closed Mon - Sat 18:00.
Su: Open Mon - Sat 09:00. Closed Mon - Sat 18:00.
Au: Open Mon - Sat 09:00. Closed Mon - Sat 18:00.
Wn: Open Mon - Sat 09:00. Closed Mon - Sat 18:00.
Ref: YH05993

GRANGE RIDING SCHOOL
Grange Riding School, Riding School Stable, Cross Lane, Wisbech, **Cambridgeshire**, PE13 4TX, **ENGLAND**.
(T) 01945 410160.
Profile Riding School. **Ref: YH05994**

GRANGE SADDLERY
Grange Saddlery, Grange Glebe, Carlanstown, Kells, **County Meath**, **IRELAND**.
(T) 046 46644.
Profile Supplies. **Ref: YH05995**

GRANGE SADDLERY
Grange Saddlery, Grange Riding Ctre, West Calder, **Lothian (West)**, EH55 8PS, **SCOTLAND**.
(T) 01506 873666 **(F)** 01506 873071
(E) sales@grangesaddlery.co.uk
(W) www.grangesaddlery.co.uk
Affiliated Bodies BETA, MSA.

Contact/s
Owner: Mrs E Knight
Profile Riding Wear Retailer, Saddlery Retailer.
Yr. Est: 1995
Opening Times
Sp: Open Mon - Fri 09:00. Closed Mon - Fri 20:00.
Su: Open Mon - Fri 09:00. Closed Mon - Fri 20:00.
Au: Open Mon - Fri 09:00. Closed Mon - Fri 20:00.
Wn: Open Mon - Fri 09:00. Closed Mon - Fri 20:00.
Ref: YH05996

GRANGE SALES

Grange Sales, St Rumbalds Barn, Upper Astrop Rd, Kings Sutton, Banbury, **Oxfordshire**, OX17 3QL, **ENGLAND**.
(T) 01295 811648 **(F)** 01295 811648.
Profile Supplies. Ref: YH05997

GRANGE STABLES

Grange Stables, Violet Lane, Glendon, Kettering, **Northamptonshire**, NN14 1QL, **ENGLAND**.
(T) 01536 414196.
Profile Stable/Livery. Ref: YH05998

GRANGE TREKKING

Grange Trekking, The Grange, Capel-Y-Ffin, Abergavenny, **Monmouthshire**, NP7 7NP, **WALES**.
(T) 01873 890215 **(F)** 01873 890157
Affiliated Bodies WTRA.
Profile Equestrian Centre, Riding School. Trekking Centre. No.Staff: 4 Yr. Est: 1957 C.Size: 65 Acres Ref: YH05999

GRANGEFIELD

Grangefield Childrens Riding School, Grangefield, Bepton, Midhurst, **Sussex (West)**, GU29 0JB, **ENGLAND**.
(T) 01730 813538.
Profile Riding School. Ref: YH06000

GRANGEFIELD STUD

Grangefield Stud, Blackfriars Farm, Rusper, Horsham, **Sussex (West)**, RH12 4QA, **ENGLAND**.
(T) 01293 871294.
Profile Breeder. Ref: YH06001

GRANGEMORE STUD

Grangemore Stud, Pollardstown, The Curragh, **County Kildare**, **IRELAND**.
(T) 045 431970 **(F)** 045 438234
(E) grangemorestud@kildarehorse.ie.
Contact/s
Key Contact: Mr J Colleran
Profile Breeder, Medical Support, Stable/Livery.
The stud is located 1 mile from the Curragh racecourse. They have 26 loose boxes, monitored foaling boxes and a local vet within the immediate vacinity.
Yr. Est: 1980 C.Size: 145 Acres Ref: YH06002

GRANGEWAY STUD

Grangeway Stud, Temple Bar, Felinfach, Lampeter, **Ceredigion**, SA48 7SA, **WALES**.
(T) 01545 570776
(W) www.zenton.co.uk/grangeway.
Contact/s
Owner: Mrs A Coleman
Profile Breeder.
Specialises in Arab horses. Stud fees range from £40.00 - £100.00 Yr. Est: 1980
Opening Times
Open 7 days a week, best time to call is 17:00 - 22:00
Ref: YH06003

GRANNY'S TACK ROOM

Granny's Tack Room, 318 Teignmouth Rd, Torquay, **Devon**, TQ1 4RR, **ENGLAND**.
(T) 01803 315006 **(F)** 01803 315006.
Contact/s
Owner: Mr G Poel
Profile Supplies. Ref: YH06004

GRANSDEN HALL

Gransden Hall, 21 Meadow Rd, Great Gransden, Sandy, **Bedfordshire**, SG19 3BD, **ENGLAND**.
(T) 01767 677366.
Profile Riding School, Stable/Livery, Trainer.
Ref: YH06005

GRANSHA EQUESTRIAN

Gransha Equestrian Riding Club, 7 Glen Annesley Ave, Bangor, **County Down**, BT19 4GR, **NORTHERN IRELAND**.
(T) 028 91273704.
Contact/s
Chairman: Mr D Robinson
Profile Club/Association, Riding Club. Ref: YH06006

GRANSHA EQUESTRIAN CTRE

Gransha Equestrian Centre, 10 Kerrs Rd, Bangor, **County Down**, BT19 7QD, **NORTHERN IRELAND**.
(T) 028 91813313 **(F)** 028 91813313.
Contact/s
Owner: Mrs A Stuart
Profile Equestrian Centre. Competition and Show Centre.
Opening Times
Sp: Open Tues - Sun 09:00. Closed Tues - Sun 19:30.
Su: Open Tues - Sun 09:00. Closed Tues - Sun 19:30.
Au: Open Tues - Sun 09:00. Closed Tues - Sun 19:30.
Wn: Open Tues - Sun 09:00. Closed Tues - Sun 19:30. Ref: YH06007

GRANT & PARTNERS

Grant & Partners, Isle Valley Equine Clinic, Eleighwater, Chard, **Somerset**, TA20 3AF, **ENGLAND**.
(T) 01460 66099 **(F)** 01460 68052.
Profile Medical Support. Ref: YH06008

GRANT BARNES & SON

Grant Barnes & Son, Horsefair, Malmesbury, **Wiltshire**, SN16 0AP, **ENGLAND**.
(T) 01666 822316 **(F)** 01666 822316.
Contact/s
Partner: Mr P Barnes
Profile Saddlery Retailer.
Sells oils and polishes for tack. Yr. Est: 1947
Opening Times
Sp: Open Mon - Sat 08:30. Closed Mon - Fri 17:30, Sat 13:00.
Su: Open Mon - Sat 08:30. Closed Mon - Fri 17:30, Sat 13:00.
Au: Open Mon - Sat 08:30. Closed Mon - Fri 17:30, Sat 13:00.
Wn: Open Mon - Sat 08:30. Closed Mon - Fri 17:30, Sat 13:00.
Closed between 13:00 - 14:00 Mon - Fri
Ref: YH06009

GRANT NORRIE & ALMOND

Grant Norrie & Almond, Oaklands, Park St, Masham, Ripon, **Yorkshire (North)**, HG4 4HN, **ENGLAND**.
(T) 01765 689219 **(F)** 01765 688022.
Profile Medical Support. Ref: YH06010

GRANT, CHRIS

Mr Chris Grant, Low Burntoft Farm, Wolviston, Billingham, Stockton-on-Tees, **Cleveland**, TS22 5PD, **ENGLAND**.
(T) 01740 644054 **(F)** 01740 644054
(M) 07860 577998.
Profile Trainer. Ref: YH06011

GRANT, G B

G B Grant, 16 Forfar Rd, Dundee, **Angus**, DD4 7AS, **SCOTLAND**.
(T) 01382 462191 **(F)** 01382 462191.
Contact/s
Owner: Mr G Grant
Profile Blacksmith. Ref: YH06012

GRANT, LEWIS

Lewis Grant, Picton Country Club, St Clears, Carmarthen, **Carmarthenshire**, SA33 4HJ, **WALES**.
(T) 01994 231332.
Profile Farrier. Ref: YH06013

GRANT, R

R Grant, Bedlam Court Lane, Minster, Ramsgate, **Kent**, CT12 4HQ, **ENGLAND**.
(T) 01843 822312.
Profile Blacksmith. Ref: YH06014

GRANVILLE SADDLERY

Granville Saddlery, 10 Market Pl, Wymondham, **Norfolk**, NR18 0AQ, **ENGLAND**.
(T) 01953 602967 **(F)** 01953 602967.
Contact/s
Owner: Mr R Taylor
Profile Saddlery Retailer. Ref: YH06015

GRANVILLE SADDLERY

Granville Saddlery, 35 Heigham Rd, Norwich, **Norfolk**, NR2 3AU, **ENGLAND**.
(T) 01603 614825 **(F)** 01603 614825.
Contact/s
Owner: Mr R Taylor
Profile Saddlery Retailer. Ref: YH06016

GRAPES VILLA FARM SUPPLIES

Grapes Villa Farm Supplies, 170 Kenilworth Rd, Balsall Common, Coventry, **Warwickshire**, CV7 7EW, **ENGLAND**.
(T) 01676 533536.
Profile Supplies. Ref: YH06017

GRASS ROOTS

Grass Roots (Equine) Ltd, Ash Tree Cottage, Clopton Rd, Thurning, Peterborough, **Cambridgeshire**, PE8 5RE, **ENGLAND**.
(T) 01832 293773 **(F)** 01536 510895
(M) 07889 489330.
Profile Medical Support. Ref: YH06018

GRASSGARTH HORSE FEEDS

Grassgarth Horse Feeds, Grass Garth Farm, Lyth Valley, Kendal, **Cumbria**, LA8 8DG, **ENGLAND**.
(T) 01539 552591 **(F)** 01539 352559.
Profile Supplies. Ref: YH06019

GRASSICK, L P

L P Grassick, Postlip Racing Stables, Winchcombe, Cheltenham, **Gloucestershire**, GL54 5AQ, **ENGLAND**.
(T) 01242 603124.
Contact/s
Owner: Mr L Grassick
Profile Trainer. Ref: YH06020

GRASSICK, MICHAEL

Michael Grassick, Fenpark Stables, Pollardstown, The Curragh, **County Kildare**, **IRELAND**.
(T) 045 434483 **(F)** 045 434483.
Contact/s
Trainer: Mr M Grassick
Profile Trainer.
Michael Grassick trains mainly flat and national hunt horses. There are also railed paddocks and lungeing rings available. No.Staff: 15 C.Size: 22 Acres
Ref: YH06021

GRATTAN

Grattan plc, Anchor Hse, Ingleby Road, **Yorkshire (West)**, BD99 2XG, **ENGLAND**.
(T) 01274 575511.
Profile Supplies. Ref: YH06022

GRAVENHURST

Gravenhurst Ltd, Ion Farms, Gravenhurst, Bedford, **Bedfordshire**, MK45 4HH, **ENGLAND**.
(T) 01525 862868
(M) 07721 384508.
Contact/s
Owner: Mr J Chapman
Profile Medical Support. Ref: YH06023

GRAVENHURST SADDLERY

Gravenhurst Saddlery, Ion Farm, Gravenhurst, Bedford, **Bedfordshire**, MK45 4HH, **ENGLAND**.
(T) 01525 861687.
Contact/s
Owner: Mrs J Chandler
(E) achandlerbeds@genie.co.uk
Profile Saddlery Retailer, Supplies.
Opening Times
Sp: Open 09:00. Closed 17:30.
Su: Open 09:00. Closed 17:30.
Au: Open 09:00. Closed 17:30.
Wn: Open 09:00. Closed 17:30. Ref: YH06024

GRAVETTS LANE STABLES

Gravetts Lane Stables, Gravetts Lane, Guildford, **Surrey**, GU3 3JY, **ENGLAND**.
(T) 01483 232068.
Contact/s
Owner: Miss O Lewis
Profile Stable/Livery. Ref: YH06025

GRAY & ADAMS

Gray & Adams Ltd, South Rd, Fraserburgh, **Aberdeenshire**, AB43 9HU, **SCOTLAND**.
(T) 01346 518001 **(F)** 01346 519175.
Profile Transport/Horse Boxes. Ref: YH06026

GRAY, D

D Gray, Rossendale A, Wayside Rd, Basingstoke, **Hampshire**, RG23 8BH, **ENGLAND**.
(T) 01256 350967.
Contact/s
Owner: Mr D Gray
Profile Transport/Horse Boxes. Ref: YH06027

GRAY, GARY S

Gary S Gray DWCF, White Cottage, Bollowal, St Just, **Cornwall**, TR19 7NP, **ENGLAND**.
(T) 01736 786183.
Profile Farrier. Ref: YH06028

GRAY, GLENN

Glenn Gray DWCF, 67 Abbey Rd, Bourne, **Lincolnshire**, PE10 9EN, **ENGLAND**.
(T) 01778 423718.
Profile Farrier. Ref: YH06029

GRAY, P J

P J Gray, Moorwards Farm, Chandlers Hill, Slough Rd, Iver, **Buckinghamshire**, SL0 0DZ, **ENGLAND**.
(T) 01895 31088.
Profile Breeder. **Ref: YH06030**

GRAY, PHILIP M

Philip M Gray DWCF, C/O Lyne Forge, Lyne Lane, Lyne, Chertsey, **Surrey**, KT16 0AJ, **ENGLAND**.
(T) 01932 874126.
Profile Farrier. **Ref: YH06031**

GRAYLEASE RENTALS

Graylease Rentals Ltd, Claylake, Spalding, **Lincolnshire**, PE12 6BL, **ENGLAND**.
(T) 01775 767621 **(F)** 01775 761610.
Contact/s
Owner: Mr D Sandell
Profile Transport/Horse Boxes. **Ref: YH06032**

GRAYLEASE RENTALS

Graylease Rentals Ltd, Kiln Lane Ind Est, Stallingborough, Grimsby, **Lincolnshire (North East)**, DN41 8DW, **ENGLAND**.
(T) 01469 574599 **(F)** 01469 571549.
Contact/s
Chairman: Mr K Spoor
Profile Transport/Horse Boxes. **Ref: YH06033**

GRAYLING BOOKS

Grayling Books, Lyvennet, Crosby Ravensworth, Penrith, **Cumbria**, CA10 3JP, **ENGLAND**.
(T) 01931 715282.
Profile Supplies. **Ref: YH06034**

GRAYSON STUD

Grayson Stud, 6 Grayson Drive, Pakefield, Lowestoft, **Suffolk**, NR33 7BA, **ENGLAND**.
(T) 01502 574981.
Profile Breeder. **Ref: YH06035**

GRAYSWOOD CARRIAGES

Grayswood Carriages, Lowhill Farm, Portsmouth Rd, Fishers Pond, Eastleigh, **Hampshire**, SO50 7HF, **ENGLAND**.
(T) 01962 777863.
Profile Horse Drawn Vehicles.
Available for hire for all events such as weddings and funerals.
Opening Times
Telephone for further information **Ref: YH06036**

GRAYTHORP FORGE

Graythorp Forge, Graythorp Ind Est, Hartlepool, **Cleveland**, TS25 2DP, **ENGLAND**.
(T) 01429 273268 **(F)** 01429 236553.
Contact/s
Owner: Mr P Kitchen
Profile Blacksmith. **Ref: YH06037**

GREAT CLOTHES

Great Clothes, 4 Berking Ave, Leeds, **Yorkshire (West)**, LS9 9LF, **ENGLAND**.
(T) 0113 2350800 **(F)** 0113 2350668.
Contact/s
Owner: Mr S Reynolds
Profile Riding Wear Retailer, Saddlery Retailer.
Ref: YH06038

GREAT MEADOW STUD

Great Meadow Stud, Castletown, **Isle of Man**, IM99, **ENGLAND**.
(T) 01624 823053 **(F)** 01624 822332.
Profile Breeder. **Ref: YH06039**

GREAT MISSENDEN RIDING CLUB

Great Missenden Riding Club, Hook Cottage, Askett, Princes Risborough, **Buckinghamshire**, HP27 9LT, **ENGLAND**.
(T) 01844 343265.
Contact/s
Secretary: Mrs L Pearl
Profile Club/Association, Riding Club. **Ref: YH06040**

GREAT PAN FARM STABLES

Great Pan Farm Stables, Pan Lane, Newport, **Isle of Wight**, PO30 2PH, **ENGLAND**.
(T) 01983 521870.
Contact/s
Owner: Mr R Booth
Profile Stable/Livery, Trainer. **Ref: YH06041**

GREAT PONTON UK CHASERS

Great Ponton UK Chasers, Heath Farm, Great Ponton, Grantham, **Lincolnshire**, NG33 5DQ, **ENGLAND**.
(T) 01476 530495 **(F)** 01476 530207
Affiliated Bodies UK Chasers&Riders.
Contact/s
General Manager: Granville Thompson
(T) 01476 530495
(E) g.thompson@farming.co.uk
Profile Track/Course. **No.Staff:** 2
Yr. Est: 1996 **C.Size:** 200 Acres
Opening Times
Su: Open 07:00. Closed 20:00.
Wn: Open 09:00. Closed 16:00. **Ref: YH06042**

GREAT WESTERN TACK

Great Western Tack, Garden Cottage, Stoney Lane, Chantry, **Somerset**, BA11 3LH, **ENGLAND**.
(T) 01373 836294 **(F)** 01373 836930
(M) 07774 691581.
Profile Supplies. **Ref: YH06043**

GREAT WESTWOOD

Great Westwood Equestrian Park, The Paddocks, Croft Lane, Chipperfield, **Hertfordshire**, WD4 9DX, **ENGLAND**.
(T) 01923 263650 **(F)** 01923 261237
(E) gwep@pipex.com.
Contact/s
Owner: Mr N Thornton
Profile Track/Course. **Ref: YH06044**

GREAT YARMOUTH RACECOURSE

Great Yarmouth Racecourse, Jellicoe Rd, Great Yarmouth, **Norfolk**, NR30 4AU, **ENGLAND**.
(T) 01493 842527 **(F)** 01493 843254.
Profile Track/Course. **Ref: YH06045**

GREATHEAD, T R

Mr T R Greathead, Chalford Oaks, Oxford Rd, Chipping Norton, **Oxfordshire**, OX7 5QP, **ENGLAND**.
(T) 01608 642954.
Profile Supplies. **Ref: YH06046**

GREAVES SPORTS

Greaves Sports Ltd, 23 Gordon St, Glasgow, **Glasgow (City of)**, G1 3PW, **SCOTLAND**.
(T) 0141 2213322 **(F)** 0141 2219200.
Profile Saddlery Retailer. **Ref: YH06047**

GREEN

Green (Agriculture) Co, Old Station Buildings, Coopies Lane, Morpeth, **Northumberland**, NE61 2SL, **ENGLAND**.
(T) 01670 518474 **(F)** 01670 503113.
Profile Supplies. **Ref: YH06048**

GREEN BANK

Green Bank Farm, Coach Rd, Warton, Carnforth, **Lancashire**, LA5 9PS, **ENGLAND**.
(T) 01524 732643 **(F)** 01524 732643.
Contact/s
For Bookings: Miss S Pennington **(Q)** AI, ISM
Profile Riding School, Stable/Livery. **No.Staff:** 5
Yr. Est: 1986 **C.Size:** 10 Acres
Opening Times
Sp: Open Tues - Thurs, Sat, Sun 09:00. Closed Tues - Thurs 20:00, Sat, Sun 18:00.
Su: Open Tues - Thurs, Sat, Sun 09:00. Closed Tues - Thurs 20:00, Sat, Sun 18:00.
Au: Open Tues - Thurs, Sat, Sun Sun 09:00. Closed Tues - Thurs 20:00, Sat, Sun 18:00.
Wn: Open Tues - Thurs, Sat, Sun 09:00. Closed Tues - Thurs 20:00, Sat, Sun 18:00.
Closed on Mondays and Fridays **Ref: YH06049**

GREEN BANK RACING STABLES

Green Bank Racing Stables, St Peter, **Jersey**, JE3 7AH, **ENGLAND**.
(T) 01534 483800.
Profile Trainer. **Ref: YH06050**

GREEN BROS

Green Bros, Yew Tree Farm, Fiddington, Tewkesbury, **Gloucestershire**, GL20 7BJ, **ENGLAND**.
(T) 01684 296358.
Profile Transport/Horse Boxes. **Ref: YH06051**

GREEN COTTAGE

Green Cottage Riding Centre & Stud, 136 Church Lane, Three Legged Cross, Wimborne, **Dorset**, BH21 6RF, **ENGLAND**.
(T) 01202 823769.
Profile Breeder, Riding School. **Ref: YH06052**

GREEN END FARM

Green End Farm, Green End, Maulden, **Bedfordshire**, MK45 2AB, **ENGLAND**.
(T) 01525 860239
(M) 07702 314137.
Profile Stable/Livery. **Ref: YH06053**

GREEN FARM

Green Farm Livery Centre, The Green, Trebanos, Pontardawe, Swansea, **Swansea**, SA8 4BR, **WALES**.
(T) 01792 862947.
Contact/s
Owner: Mrs Z Llewellyn
Profile Riding School, Stable/Livery.
Specialise in childrens lessons, but adult lessons are also available. **Yr. Est:** 1994
Opening Times
Sp: Open Mon - Sun 09:00. Closed Mon - Sun 18:00.
Su: Open Mon - Sun 09:00. Closed Mon - Sun 18:00.
Au: Open Mon - Sun 09:00. Closed Mon - Sun 18:00.
Wn: Open Mon - Sun 09:00. Closed Mon - Sun 18:00. **Ref: YH06054**

GREEN FARM FEEDS

Baterley Green Farm, Balterley Green Farm, Deans Lane, Balterley, Crewe, **Cheshire**, CW2 5QJ, **ENGLAND**.
(T) 01270 820214.
Contact/s
Owner: Mrs J Hollins
Profile Feed Merchant, Stable/Livery, Supplies.
Delivery available.
Opening Times
Sp: Open Mon - Sun 08:00. Closed Mon - Sun 21:00.
Su: Open Mon - Sun 08:00. Closed Mon - Sun 21:00.
Au: Open Mon - Sun 08:00. Closed Mon - Sun 21:00.
Wn: Open Mon - Sun 08:00. Closed Mon - Sun 21:00. **Ref: YH06055**

GREEN LANE FARM

Green Lane Farm, Green Lane, Shamley Green, Guildford, **Surrey**, GU5 0RD, **ENGLAND**.
(T) 01483 898275 **(F)** 01483 898704.
Contact/s
Owner: Mr P Martin-Dye
Profile Stable/Livery. **Ref: YH06056**

GREEN LANE RIDING SCHOOL

Green Lane Riding School, Green Lane Farm, Green Lane, Chester, **Cheshire**, CH4 8LS, **ENGLAND**.
(T) 01244 671321.
Profile Riding School. **Ref: YH06057**

GREEN LANE STABLES

Green Lane Riding Stables, Green Lane, Off Garth Rd, Morden, **Surrey**, SM4 6SE, **ENGLAND**.
(T) 020 8337 3853 **(F)** 020 8337 8383
(E) enquiries@green-lane.co.uk
(W) www.green-lane.co.uk
Affiliated Bodies BHS.
Contact/s
General Manager: Ms L Bielecki
Profile Club/Association, Riding School. Pony Club.
Hacking, pony days, birthday parties, Pony Club and short rides for 2 year olds are all available at the stables. **C.Size:** 30 Acres
Opening Times
Sp: Open Sat, Sun 08:00, Tues - Fri 09:00. Closed Sat, Sun 17:00, Wed, Fri 18:00, Tues, Thurs 20:00.
Su: Open Sat, Sun 08:00, Tues - Fri 09:00. Closed Sat, Sun 17:00, Wed, Fri 18:00, Tues, Thurs 20:00.
Au: Open Sat, Sun 08:00, Tues - Fri 09:00. Closed Sat, Sun 17:00, Wed, Fri 18:00, Tues, Thurs 20:00.
Wn: Open Sat, Sun 08:00, Tues - Fri 09:00. Closed Sat, Sun 17:00, Wed, Fri 18:00, Tues, Thurs 20:00.
Times may vary bank holidays and school holidays
Ref: YH06058

GREEN RIDGE STABLES

Green Ridge Stables, Hamilton Rd, Newmarket, **Suffolk**, CB8 7JQ, **ENGLAND**.
(T) 01638 666185 **(F)** 01638 666184
(M) 07802 699456
(W) www.newmarketracehorsetrainers.co.uk
Affiliated Bodies Newmarket Trainers Fed.
Contact/s
Trainer: Mr K Mahdi
Profile Trainer. **Ref: YH06059**

GREEN SMITHY

Green Smithy, High Bentham, **Lancashire**, LA2 7DH, **ENGLAND**.
(T) 01524 261353.
Profile Farrier. **Ref: YH06060**

GREEN, CAROL & STOKES, MARIE

Carol Green & Marie Stokes, Higham Farm, Chapel Lane, Guestling, Hastings, **Sussex (East)**, TN35 4HP, **ENGLAND**.
(T) 01424 812636.
Profile Trainer. **Ref: YH06061**

GREEN, CLIFTON

Clifton Green, 1 Edgcumbe Gardens, Newquay, **Cornwall**, TR7 2QD, **ENGLAND**.
(T) 01637 872103.
Profile Medical Support. **Ref: YH06062**

GREEN, DANA

Mrs Dana Green DC AMC MMCA, 26 East St, Olney, **Buckinghamshire**, MK46 4AP, **ENGLAND**.
(T) 01234 712196 **(F)** 01234 712196.
Profile Medical Support. **Ref: YH06063**

GREEN, GREAVES & THOMSON

Green, Greaves & Thomson, Aireworth Veterinary Ctre, Aireworth Rd, Keighley, **Yorkshire (West)**, BD21 4DJ, **ENGLAND**.
(T) 01535 602988 **(F)** 01535 691498.
Profile Medical Support. **Ref: YH06064**

GREEN, HARRY

Harry Green, The Smithy, Dunnington, Alcester, **Warwickshire**, B49 5NN, **ENGLAND**.
(T) 01789 490125.
Profile Blacksmith. **Ref: YH06065**

GREEN, J A H

J A H Green, Ipley Manor Farm, Marchwood, Southampton, **Hampshire**, SO4 4UR, **ENGLAND**.
(T) 023 80841831.
Profile Farrier. **Ref: YH06066**

GREEN, JASON L

Jason L Green DWCF, 63 Leicester Rd, Fleckney, **Leicestershire**, LE8 0BG, **ENGLAND**.
(T) 0116 2402818.
Profile Farrier. **Ref: YH06067**

GREEN, KEVIN J

Kevin J Green AWCF, Anvil Farm, Mill Lane, Syderstone, King's Lynn, **Norfolk**, PE31 8RX, **ENGLAND**.
(T) 01485 578241.
Profile Farrier. **Ref: YH06068**

GREEN, LUCINDA

Lucinda Green (MBE), The Tree Hse, Appleshaw, Andover, **Hampshire**, SP11 9BS, **ENGLAND**.
(T) 01264 771133 **(F)** 01264 773905.
Profile Trainer.
Cross Country Trainer. Travels all over the country.
Ref: YH06069

GREEN, M A

M A Green, Fair Bank, Hay-on-Wye, Hereford, **Herefordshire**, HR3 5HA, **ENGLAND**.
(T) 01497 831531.
Contact/s
Owner: Mr M Green
Profile Breeder, Farrier. **Ref: YH06070**

GREEN, PETER & TONG, MATTHEW

Peter Green & Matthew Tong Veterinary Surgeons, Fellowes Farm Equine Clinic, Abbots Ripton, Huntingdon, **Cambridgeshire**, PE17 2LH, **ENGLAND**.
(T) 01487 773333 **(F)** 01487 773527
(E) pg&mt@pgmt.globalnet.co.uk.
Profile Medical Support. **Ref: YH06071**

GREEN, RICHARD

Richard Green (Fine Paintings), 147 New Bond St, London, **London (Greater)**, W1Y 9FE, **ENGLAND**.
(T) 020 74933939 **(F)** 020 76292609
(E) pictures@rgreen.ftech.co.uk.
Profile Artist. **Ref: YH06072**

GREEN, ROBERT G

Robert G Green, Fort End Ironworks, Haddenham, Aylesbury, **Buckinghamshire**, HP17 8EJ, **ENGLAND**.
(T) 01844 291330 **(F)** 01844 290388.
Contact/s
Partner: Mr R Green
Profile Blacksmith. **Ref: YH06073**

GREEN, STUART E

Stuart E Green DWCF, Rookery Hse Farm, Blackbrook, Chapel-En-Le-Frith, High Peak, **Derbyshire**, SK23 0PU, **ENGLAND**.
(T) 01298 813650
(M) 07970 490158.
Profile Farrier. **Ref: YH06074**

GREENACRES

Greenacres, Tytherley Rd, Winterslow, Salisbury, **Wiltshire**, SP5 1PZ, **ENGLAND**.
(T) 01980 862809.
Contact/s
Owner: Mrs E Peerless **(Q)** AI
Profile Stable/Livery.
There is a large outdoor school which has all weather flooring. Mrs Peerless competes in dressage competitions, and owners also compete from the yard. There is Part and DIY livery available. Telephone for further price information **Yr. Est:** 1992 **C.Size:** 12 Acres
Opening Times
Telephone between 08:00 - 22:00 for further information **Ref: YH06075**

GREENACRES EQUESTRIAN

Greenacres Equestrian, Lower Luton Rd, Harpenden, **Hertfordshire**, AL5 5EG, **ENGLAND**.
(T) 01582 760612 **(F)** 01582 416008.
Contact/s
Manager: Mrs K Tynan
Profile Breeder, Riding School, Stable/Livery.
Ref: YH06076

GREENACRES LIVERY CTRE

Greenacres Livery Centre, Green Farm, Puxley, Towcester, **Northamptonshire**, NN12 7QS, **ENGLAND**.
(T) 01908 566092.
Profile Stable/Livery. **Ref: YH06077**

GREENACRES RIDING SCHOOL

Greenacres Riding School, Ashmore Lane, Leaves Green, Keston, **Kent**, BR2 6DL, **ENGLAND**.
(T) 01959 572008.
Contact/s
Owner: Mrs S Cutts
Profile Riding School, Stable/Livery. **Ref: YH06078**

GREENACRES RIDING SCHOOL

Greenacres Riding School, Gate Hse Lane, North Wootton, King's Lynn, **Norfolk**, PE30 3RJ, **ENGLAND**.
(T) 01553 631339.
Contact/s
Owner: Ms S Cole **(Q)** BHSAI
Profile Equestrian Centre, Riding School, Trainer.
No.Staff: 2 **Yr. Est:** 1997 **C.Size:** 5 Acres
Opening Times
Sp: Open 09:00. Closed 21:00.
Su: Open 09:00. Closed 21:00.
Au: Open 09:00. Closed 21:00.
Wn: Open 09:00. Closed 21:00.
There is an answer phone for further details
Ref: YH06079

GREENACRES STUD

Greenacres Stud, Hollybush Farm, Balsall Common, Coventry, **Warwickshire**, CV7 7EB, **ENGLAND**.
(T) 01676 533589.
Contact/s
Head Girl: Miss B Gallimore **(Q)** BHSII, NPS Dip
Profile Breeder, Horse/Rider Accom, Stable/Livery.
Full, part and DIY Livery available, prices on request.
No.Staff: 2 **Yr. Est:** 1976
Opening Times
Sp: Open Mon - Sun 18:00. Closed Mon - Sun 21:00.
Su: Open Mon - Sun 18:00. Closed Mon - Sun 21:00.
Au: Open Mon - Sun 18:00. Closed Mon - Sun 21:00.
Wn: Open Mon - Sun 18:00. Closed Mon - Sun 21:00. **Ref: YH06080**

GREENFERNS STUD

Greenferns Stud, Little Bishopston, Portlethen, **Aberdeen (City of)**, AB12 4RS, **SCOTLAND**.
(T) 01224 780352.
Profile Breeder. **Ref: YH06081**

GREENFIELD FARM STABLES

Greenfield Farm Stables, Orestan Lane, Effingham, Leatherhead, **Surrey**, KT24 5SJ, **ENGLAND**.
(T) 01372 457262.
Contact/s
Owner: Mrs C Morrison-Jones
Profile Stable/Livery.
Adults only at livery. **No.Staff:** 3 **Yr. Est:** 1995 **C.Size:** 50 Acres
Opening Times
Sp: Open Mon - Sun 08:00. Closed Mon - Sun 20:00.
Su: Open Mon - Sun 08:00. Closed Mon - Sun 20:00.
Au: Open Mon - Sun 08:00. Closed Mon - Sun 20:00.
Wn: Open Mon - Sun 08:00. Closed Mon - Sun 20:00. **Ref: YH06082**

GREENFIELDS

Greenfields, 21 Milford St, Salisbury, **Wiltshire**, SP1 2AP, **ENGLAND**.
(T) 01722 333796 **(F)** 01722 421733.
Profile Saddlery Retailer. **Ref: YH06083**

GREENFIELDS COUNTRY PURSUITS

Greenfields Country Pursuits, 9 High St, Wem, Shrewsbury, **Shropshire**, SY4 5AA, **ENGLAND**.
(T) 01939 233062.
Contact/s
Owner: Mrs M Johnson
Profile Riding Wear Retailer, Supplies. **Ref: YH06084**

GREENFIELDS SADDLERY

Greenfields Saddlery & Country Clothing, Greenfields, Lhanbryde, Elgin, **Moray**, IV30 8LN, **SCOTLAND**.
(T) 01343 842633 **(F)** 01343 842633
(W) www.greenfields-saddlery.co.uk.
Contact/s
Owner: Mr C Roberts
Profile Riding Wear Retailer, Saddlery Retailer, Supplies.
Saddle fitting service. Flair fitting & converting qualified. **No.Staff:** 3 **Yr. Est:** 1990
Opening Times
Sp: Open Mon - Fri 09:00, Sat 10:00. Closed Mon - Sat 17:00.
Su: Open Mon - Fri 09:00, Sat 10:00. Closed Mon - Sat 17:00.
Au: Open Mon - Fri 09:00, Sat 10:00. Closed Mon - Sat 17:00.
Wn: Open Mon - Fri 09:00, Sat 10:00. Closed Mon - Sat 17:00.
Closed on Sundays **Ref: YH06085**

GREENGATES

Greengates, Woodlands St Mary, Hungerford, **Berkshire**, RG17 7SS, **ENGLAND**.
(T) 01488 71742.
Profile Riding School. **Ref: YH06086**

GREENHAM EQUESTRIAN CTRE

Greenham Equestrian Centre, Ridge Farm, Greenham, Wellington, **Somerset**, TA21 0JS, **ENGLAND**.
(T) 01823 673024.
Contact/s
Owner: Miss S Edwards
Profile Equestrian Centre. **Ref: YH06087**

GREENHILL MILLING

Greenhill Milling Ltd (Coalville), Abbots Oak, Warrenhills Rd, Coalville, **Leicestershire**, LE6 3UY, **ENGLAND**.
(T) 01530 32328.
Profile Supplies. **Ref: YH06088**

GREENHILL, A

A Greenhill, Upper Tulloes, Forfar, **Angus**, DD8 2LZ, **SCOTLAND**.
(T) 01307 818204.
Profile Breeder. **Ref: YH06089**

GREENHILLS FARM

Greenhills Farm, Meggett Hill, Alkham, Dover, **Kent**, CT15 7DG, **ENGLAND**.
(T) 01303 892056.
Profile Stable/Livery. **Ref: YH06090**

GREENLAND PARK STUD

Greenland Park Stud, Hockeridge Farm, Chesham Rd, Berkhamsted, **Hertfordshire**, HP4 2SZ, **ENGLAND**.
(T) 01442 863521.
Profile Breeder. **Ref: YH06091**

GREENLANDS LIVERY STABLES

Greenlands Livery Stables, Greenlands, Wreay, Carlisle, **Cumbria**, CA4 0RR, **ENGLAND**.
(T) 01697 473374.
Contact/s
Owner: Mr S Wilson
Profile Stable/Livery. **Ref: YH06092**

GREENLEAF, J R

J R Greenleaf, Brook Hall, Ballast Quay Rd, Fingringhoe, Colchester, **Essex**, CO5 7DB, **ENGLAND**.
(T) 01206 729716.
Contact/s
Partner: Mrs J Greenleaf
Profile Breeder. **Ref: YH06093**

GREENLEAF, P J

P J Greenleaf, Beech Hill, Buckland St Mary, Chard, **Somerset**, TA20 3SP, **ENGLAND**.
(T) 01460 234438.
Profile Breeder. **Ref: YH06094**

GREENLEES

Greenlees, Brecklate, Southend, **Argyll and Bute**, PA28 6PJ, **SCOTLAND**.
(T) 01586 830307.
Profile Supplies. Ref: YH06095

GREENLEY, ALLAN

Allan Greenley RSS, Willow Tree Farm, Kirkland Lane, Gowthorpe, **Yorkshire (North)**, YO41 5QN, **ENGLAND**.
(T) 01759 368176.
Profile Farrier. Ref: YH06096

GREENLEY, BRIAN

Brian Greenley, Treetops, West St, Swinton, Malton, **Yorkshire (North)**, YO17 6SR, **ENGLAND**.
(T) 01653 697454.
Profile Farrier. Ref: YH06097

GREENLOANING EQUINE CARE

Greenloaning Equine Care & Childrens Riding Club, Dam Of Quoigs, Greenloaning, Dunblane, **Perth and Kinross**, FK15 0ND, **SCOTLAND**.
(T) 01786 880278.
Contact/s
Owner: Mrs D MacFarlane
Profile Club/Association, Medical Support.
Ref: YH06098

GREENMEADOW RIDING CTRE

Greenmeadow Riding Centre, Tir Evan Bach Draws Farm, Aberdare, **Rhondda Cynon Taff**, CF44 7PT, **WALES**.
(T) 01685 874961 (F) 01685 874961.
Contact/s
Partner: Mr A Williams
Profile Riding School. Ref: YH06099

GREENSFORGE

Greensforge Stables Horse Feed Supplies, The Paddocks, Mile Flat, Greensforge, Kingswinford, **Midlands (West)**, DY6 0AU, **ENGLAND**.
(T) 01384 292483 (F) 01384 292483.
Profile Supplies. Ref: YH06100

GREENSLADE HORSE TRAILERS

Greenslade Horse Trailers, 12 Sheringham Cl, Staplecross, Robertsbridge, **Sussex (East)**, TN32 5PZ, **ENGLAND**.
(T) 01580 830088 (F) 01580 830088
(E) fgsmith@freezone.co.uk.
Profile Transport/Horse Boxes. Ref: YH06101

GREENWAY FARM

Greenway Farm, Magpie Hill, Newcastle Rd, Astbury, Congleton, **Cheshire**, CW12 4RL, **ENGLAND**.
(T) 01260 299299 (F) 01260 299299.
Contact/s
Owner: Mr D Lamb
Profile Trainer. Horse Dealer. Yr. Est: 1971
C.Size: 80 Acres
Opening Times
Telephone for an appointment Ref: YH06102

GREENWAY, V G

Mr V G Greenway, Higher Vexford Farm, Lydeard St Lawrence, Taunton, **Somerset**, TA4 3QG, **ENGLAND**.
(T) 01984 656548.
Profile Supplies. Ref: YH06103

GREENWAYS

Greenways, 1004 Chester Rd, Erdington, Birmingham, **Midlands (West)**, B24 0LL, **ENGLAND**.
(T) 0121 3730057 (F) 0121 3820045.
Profile Saddlery Retailer. Ref: YH06104

GREENWAYS FARM & STABLES

Greenways Farm & Stables, Lower Eashing, Godalming, **Surrey**, GU7 2QF, **ENGLAND**.
(T) 01483 414741.
Contact/s
Partner: Mrs L Sprake
Profile Riding School, Stable/Livery. Ref: YH06105

GREENWOOD & BROWN

Greenwood & Brown, The Veterinary Surgery, Mill Hill, Pontefract, **Yorkshire (West)**, WF8 4HR, **ENGLAND**.
(T) 01977 702056 (F) 01977 600952.
Contact/s
Vet: Mr N Greenwood
Profile Medical Support. Ref: YH06106

GREENWOOD, ELLIS & PARTNERS

Greenwood, Ellis & Partners, Reynolds Hse, 166 High St, Newmarket, **Suffolk**, CB8 9AQ, **ENGLAND**.
(T) 01638 663004 (F) 01638 663521.
Profile Medical Support. Ref: YH06107

GREENWOOD, K

Ms K Greenwood, Oaken Bank Farm, Trawden, Colne, **Lancashire**, BB18 8PS, **ENGLAND**.
(T) 01282 865161.
Profile Breeder. Ref: YH06108

GREEP, R J

R J Greep, Lower Hele Farm, Cornwood, Ivybridge, **Devon**, PL21 9RE, **ENGLAND**.
(T) 01752 837254.
Profile Farrier. Ref: YH06109

GREER S & SON

Greer S & Son, 7 Poolbeg St, Dublin, **County Dublin**, **IRELAND**.
(T) 01 6774192.
Profile Supplies. Ref: YH06110

GREETHAM, RACHEL

Rachel Greetham BScHons,MCSP,SRP, Mount Pleasant, Llanarmon Rd, Bwlchgwyn, **Wrexham**, LL11 5YP, **WALES**.
(T) 07801 270053.
Profile Medical Support. Ref: YH06111

GREETLAND & DISTRICT TRAD SOC

Greetland & District Trading Society Ltd, Victoria St, West Vale, Greetland, Halifax, **Yorkshire (West)**, HX4 8DF, **ENGLAND**.
(T) 01422 372642.
Profile Supplies. Ref: YH06112

GREGGS RIDING SCHOOL

Greggs Riding School, Placket Lane, West Coker Rd, East Coker, Yeovil, **Somerset**, BA22 9HJ, **ENGLAND**.
(T) 01935 423894.
Profile Riding School. Ref: YH06113

GREGORY ENTERPRISES

Gregory Enterprises, Unit 11 Norman-D-Gate, Bedford Rd, Northampton, **Northamptonshire**, NN1 5NT, **ENGLAND**.
(T) 01604 602734.
Profile Supplies. Ref: YH06114

GREGORY, CHARLES J N M

Charles J N M Gregory DWCF, Erpingham, The Street, Beeston, King's Lynn, **Norfolk**, PE32 2NF, **ENGLAND**.
(T) 01328 700855.
Profile Farrier. Ref: YH06115

GREGORY, J S

J S Gregory, New Forge, Springcroft, Well Hill, Orpington, **Kent**, BR6 7PR, **ENGLAND**.
(T) 01959 534093 (F) 01959 532929.
Contact/s
Owner: Mr J Gregory
Profile Blacksmith. Ref: YH06116

GREGORY, MAXWELL J

Maxwell J Gregory, 20 Longridge Rd, Chipping, Preston, **Lancashire**, PR3 2QD, **ENGLAND**.
(T) 01995 61040.
Profile Farrier. Ref: YH06117

GREGORY, Y

Miss Y Gregory, Furzley, Hazler Rd, Church Stretton, **Shropshire**, SY6 7AQ, **ENGLAND**.
(T) 01694 722203.
Profile Breeder. Ref: YH06118

GREIG, COLIN A R

Colin A R Greig DWCF, Gartverrie Farm, Airdrie, **Lanarkshire (North)**, ML6 0PL, **SCOTLAND**.
(T) 01236 875368.
Profile Farrier. Ref: YH06119

GREIG, D R

Mr D R Greig, Pittance Farm, Smithwood Common, Cranleigh, **Surrey**, GU6 8QY, **ENGLAND**.
(T) 01483 272737.
Profile Supplies. Ref: YH06120

GREIG, JOHN

John Greig, Grassie Hill Farm, Maud, Peterhead, **Aberdeenshire**, AB42 4QR, **SCOTLAND**.
(T) 01771 637431.
Contact/s
Owner: Mr J Greig
Profile Transport/Horse Boxes. Ref: YH06121

GREINAN FARM

Greinan Farm, Tower Hill, Chipperfield, Kings Langley, **Hertfordshire**, WD4 9LU, **ENGLAND**.
(T) 01442 832134.
Contact/s
Owner: Mrs H Mullholland
Profile Saddlery Retailer. Ref: YH06122

GRETA BANK VETNRY CTRE

Greta Bank Veterinary Centre, Brundholme Rd, Keswick, **Cumbria**, CA12 4NS, **ENGLAND**.
(T) 01768 772590.
Profile Medical Support. Ref: YH06123

GREY HORSE RIDING CTRE

Grey Horse Riding Centre (The), Brough, **Cumbria**, CA17 4BH, **ENGLAND**.
(T) 01768 341651.
Profile Equestrian Centre. Ref: YH06124

GREYBROOK RIDING SCHOOL

Greybrook Riding School Ltd, Old Abbey Waterfall, Cork, **County Cork**, **IRELAND**.
(T) 021 4885858.
Profile Riding Club, Riding School, Supplies.
Ref: YH06125

GREYFRIARS RIDING SCHOOL

Greyfriars Riding School, Blantyre Farm Rd Haughhead, Uddingston, Glasgow, **Glasgow (City of)**, G71 7RR, **SCOTLAND**.
(T) 0141 6412843.
Profile Riding School. Ref: YH06126

GRICE, W A

W A Grice, 26 Front St, Staindrop, Darlington, **County Durham**, DL2 3NH, **ENGLAND**.
(T) 01833 660260.
Profile Transport/Horse Boxes. Ref: YH06127

GRIEVE, GEORGE WISHART

George Wishart Grieve, 325 Cluny Pl, Pittenchar, Glenrothes, **Fife**, KY7 4QY, **SCOTLAND**.
(T) 01592 771667.
Profile Farrier. Ref: YH06128

GRIFFIN ENGINEERING

Griffin Engineering, Parsonage Farm, Parsonage Lane, Barnston, Dunmow, **Essex**, CM6 3PB, **ENGLAND**.
(T) 01371 820716 (F) 01371 820768.
Profile Transport/Horse Boxes. Ref: YH06129

GRIFFIN NUU MED

Griffin NUU Med, Pipers Farm, Berhill, Ashcott, Bridgwater, **Somerset**, TA7 9QN, **ENGLAND**.
(T) 01458 210324 (F) 01458 210396.
Contact/s
Owner: Mr I Pocock
Profile Supplies. Ref: YH06130

GRIFFIN, L M

Mrs L M Griffin, Hawthorne Cottage, Thoroton, **Nottinghamshire**, NG13 9DS, **ENGLAND**.
(T) 01949 851426.
Profile Saddlery Retailer. Ref: YH06131

GRIFFIN, M A

Mr M A Griffin, Sportmans Arms Hotel, Lower Clicker Rd, Menheniot, Liskeard, **Cornwall**, PL14 3PJ, **ENGLAND**.
(T) 01503 240249.
Profile Breeder. Ref: YH06132

GRIFFIN, T R

T R Griffin, 29 Cwmgarw Rd, Brynamman, Ammanford, **Carmarthenshire**, SA18 1BY, **WALES**.
(T) 01269 823130.
Profile Farrier. Ref: YH06133

GRIFFITH, W H

W H Griffith, Llys Farm, Brynrefail, Caernarfon, **Gwynedd**, LL55 3BY, **WALES**.
(T) 01286 870332.
Profile Breeder. Ref: YH06134

GRIFFITHS & CLARKE

Griffiths & Clarke Animal & Pet Foods, Greenway Farm, Hawthorns, Drybrook, **Gloucestershire**, GL17 9HW, **ENGLAND**.
(T) 01594 542945 (F) 01594 544857.
Profile Feed Merchant. Ref: YH06135

GRIFFITHS & SIMPSON

Griffiths & Simpson Ltd, Highbury Hse, Great Hales St, Market Drayton, **Shropshire**, TF9 1JW, **ENGLAND**.
(T) 01630 652493.
Profile Supplies. Ref: YH06136

GRIFFITHS & SIMPSON

Griffiths & Simpson Ltd (Newport), Audley Ave

Ind Est, Newport, **Shropshire**, TF10 7BX, **ENGLAND**.
(T) 01952 820104.
Profile Supplies. **Ref: YH06137**

GRIFFITHS, COLIN A

Colin A Griffiths DWCF, 15 Ashtree Bank, Brereton, Rugeley, **Staffordshire**, WS15 1HN, **ENGLAND**.
(T) 01889 574823.
Profile Farrier. **Ref: YH06138**

GRIFFITHS, DAVID

David Griffiths DWCF, C/O Sunnybank Farm, Rudry, **Caerphilly**, CF8 3DT, **WALES**.
(T) 029 20864943.
Profile Farrier. **Ref: YH06139**

GRIFFITHS, DAVID W

David W Griffiths RSS, 182 Lower Farnham Rd, Aldershot, **Hampshire**, GU12 4EN, **ENGLAND**.
(T) 01252 314372.
Profile Farrier. **Ref: YH06140**

GRIFFITHS, HELEN

Helen Grifiths, Yew Tree Cottage, Hornblotton, Shepton Mallet, **Somerset**, BA4 6SF, **ENGLAND**.
(T) 01963 240381
Affiliated Bodies NAAT.
Contact/s
Physiotherapist: Helen Griffiths **(Q)** BHSII
Profile Medical Support.
Physiotherapist for horses & dogs. **Ref: YH06141**

GRIFFITHS, KEVIN

Kevin Griffiths DWCF, 4 Hengoed Rd, Hengoed, **Caerphilly**, CF82 7NW, **WALES**.
(T) 01443 815629.
Profile Farrier. **Ref: YH06142**

GRIFFITHS, S G

Mr S G Griffiths, Rwyth Farm, Nantgaredig, Carmarthen, **Carmarthenshire**, SA32 7LG, **WALES**.
(T) 01267 290321.
Profile Supplies. **Ref: YH06143**

GRIGGS, KEVIN W

Kevin W Griggs DWCF, The Forge, Warkton, Kettering, **Northamptonshire**, NN16 9XF, **ENGLAND**.
(T) 07785 951617.
Profile Farrier. **Ref: YH06144**

GRIMSTON SADDLERY

Grimston Saddlery Co Ltd, Church Lane, Grimston, Melton Mowbray, **Leicestershire**, LE14 3BY, **ENGLAND**.
(T) 01664 812298.
Profile Saddlery Retailer. **Ref: YH06145**

GRISSELL, D M

D M Grissell, Brightling Pk, Brightling, Robertsbridge, **Sussex (East)**, TN32 5HH, **ENGLAND**.
(T) 01424 838241 **(F)** 01424 838378.
Contact/s
Owner: Mr D Grissell
Profile Trainer. **Ref: YH06146**

GROESWEN RIDING STABLES

Groeswen Riding Stables, Ty Canol Farm, White Cross Lane, Caerphilly, **Caerphilly**, CF83 2RL, **WALES**.
(T) 029 20880500.
Contact/s
Owner: Mrs K Jones
Profile Riding School, Stable/Livery. **Ref: YH06147**

GROOBY, NICHOLAS J

Nicholas J Grooby DWCF, The Mill Hse, 1 Easthorpe Rd, Bottesford, **Nottinghamshire**, NG13 0DS, **ENGLAND**.
(T) 01949 844502.
Profile Farrier. **Ref: YH06148**

GROOM HIRE

Groom Hire, 37 Alma Rd, Maesteg, **Bridgend**, CF34 9AN, **WALES**.
(T) 01656 739433. **Ref: YH06149**

GROOM, P A

P A Groom, 27 Elcombe Ave, Wroughton, Swindon, **Wiltshire**, SN4 9EL, **ENGLAND**.
(T) 01793 814185.
Contact/s
Owner: Mr P Groom
Profile Farrier. **Ref: YH06150**

GROOM, PETER JOHN

Peter John Groom RSS, 22 Iffley Rd, Swindon, **Wiltshire**, SN2 1DL, **ENGLAND**.
(T) 01793 644123.
Profile Farrier. **Ref: YH06151**

GROOME, JIMMY

Jimmy Groome, Kilcumney Hse, Kildare, **County Kildare**, **IRELAND**.
(T) 045 521507 **(F)** 045 520050.
Contact/s
Trainer: Mr J Groome
(E) jimmygroome@kildarehorse.ie
Profile Trainer. **Ref: YH06152**

GROOME, M

Mrs M Groome, East Cl, Ditcheat, Shepton Mallet, **Somerset**, BA4 6PS, **ENGLAND**.
(T) 01749 860651.
Profile Breeder. **Ref: YH06153**

GROOMERS

Groomers, 40 Balmoral Rd, Queens Pk, Northampton, **Northamptonshire**, NN2 6JZ, **ENGLAND**.
(T) 01604 720035.
Profile Saddlery Retailer. **Ref: YH06154**

GROOMS LIVESTOCK TRANSPORT

Grooms Livestock Transport, The Lodge, Whaddon Farm, Slapton, Leighton Buzzard, **Bedfordshire**, LU7 0QT, **ENGLAND**.
(T) 01525 852853.
Profile Transport/Horse Boxes. **Ref: YH06155**

GROOMS LIVESTOCK TRANSPORT

Grooms Livestock Transport, 14 Rye Cl, Leighton Buzzard, **Bedfordshire**, LU7 8YD, **ENGLAND**.
(T) 01525 376219.
Profile Transport/Horse Boxes. **Ref: YH06156**

GROSMONT HSE

Grosmont House, Office Row, Grosmont, Whitby, **Yorkshire (North)**, YO22 5PE, **ENGLAND**.
(T) 01947 85539.
Profile Stable/Livery. **Ref: YH06157**

GROSSICK, JOHN

John Grossick, 19 Weymouth Rd, Longniddry, **Lothian (East)**, EH32 0LL, **SCOTLAND**.
(T) 01875 852115
(E) jgrossick@btconnect.com. **Ref: YH06158**

GROUCOTT, W & MORRIS, T A

W Groucott & T A Morris, Hafodyrynys Farm, Crumlin, **Monmouthshire**, NT11 5BE, **WALES**.
(T) 01495 245290.
Profile Breeder.
Breeder of Section C horses. **Ref: YH06159**

GROUP 1 RACING

Group 1 Racing (1994) Ltd, Moorlands Lodge, Bidford On Avon, **Warwickshire**, B50 4AU, **ENGLAND**.
(T) 01789 772981.
Profile Blood Stock Agency. **Ref: YH06160**

GROVE EQUITATION CTRE

Grove Equitation Centre, Lane End Rd, Lane End, High Wycombe, **Buckinghamshire**, HP14 3NR, **ENGLAND**.
(T) 01494 881939.
Profile Riding School, Stable/Livery. **Ref: YH06161**

GROVE FARM

Grove Farm Livery, Grove Farm, Ivinghoe Aston, Leighton Buzzard, **Bedfordshire**, LU7 9DF, **ENGLAND**.
(T) 01525 220160.
Contact/s
Manager: Mr P Pearce
Profile Stable/Livery.
Opening Times
Sp: Open Mon - Sun 24 Hours.
Su: Open Mon - Sun 24 Hours.
Au: Open Mon - Sun 24 Hours.
Wn: Open Mon - Sun 24 Hours. **Ref: YH06162**

GROVE FARM

Grove Farm Racing Stables, Grove Farm, Chastleton, Moreton In Marsh, **Gloucestershire**, GL56 0SZ, **ENGLAND**.
(T) 01608 674492 **(F)** 01608 674326
Affiliated Bodies JC.
Contact/s
Owner: Mr J Gallagher
(E) gallagher.racing@virgin.net
Profile Blood Stock Agency, Trainer, Transport/Horse Boxes.
Grove Farm also sell ex-racehorses, to go into riding, show jumping, eventing, jobs and homes. The farm also has a racing club and 10% shares in racehorses.
No.Staff: 3 Yr. Est: 1999 C.Size: 60 Acres
Ref: YH06163

GROVE FARM

Grove Farm, Warren Lane, Stanmore, **London (Greater)**, HA7 4LE, **ENGLAND**.
(T) 020 89545443 **(F)** 020 89545443.
Contact/s
Owner: Mrs S Clifford
Profile Stable/Livery. Yr. Est: 1980
Opening Times
Sp: Open Mon - Sun 09:00. Closed Mon - Sun 16:00.
Su: Open Mon - Sun 09:00. Closed Mon - Sun 16:00.
Au: Open Mon - Sun 09:00. Closed Mon - Sun 16:00.
Wn: Open Mon - Sun 09:00. Closed Mon - Sun 16:00. **Ref: YH06164**

GROVE FARM

Grove Farm, Llanfoist, Abergavenny, **Monmouthshire**, NP7 9HE, **WALES**.
(T) 01873 852345 **(F)** 01873 852345.
Profile Stable/Livery. **Ref: YH06165**

GROVE FARM DRIVING & LIVERY

Grove Farm Driving & Livery, Worlington, Mildenhall, **Suffolk**, IP28 8RU, **ENGLAND**.
(T) 01638 716096.
Profile Stable/Livery, Trainer. **Ref: YH06166**

GROVE FARM LIVERY STABLES

Grove Farm Livery Stables, Maize Lane, Warfield, Bracknell, **Berkshire**, RG42 6BE, **ENGLAND**.
(T) 01344 423661 **(F)** 01344 457705.
Contact/s
Owner: Mrs L Scruby
Profile Stable/Livery. **Ref: YH06167**

GROVE HOUSE

Grove House Stables, Grovewood Rd, Misterton, Doncaster, **Yorkshire (South)**, DN10 4EF, **ENGLAND**.
(T) 01427 890802 **(F)** 01427 891471
(W) www.grovehousestables.co.uk
Affiliated Bodies ABRS, BHS.
Contact/s
Owner: Mr A Stennett **(Q)** BHS SM
Profile Riding School.
Grove House offers examination training up to BHS stage 4, two lecture rooms, two floodlit arenas, a computer suite, 34 horses and ponies, North Nottinghamshire College Partnership, a restaurant on site, and a Pony Club Centre for 3 years upwards.
No.Staff: 12 Yr. Est: 1991 C.Size: 14 Acres
Opening Times
Sp: Open Mon - Wed, Fri - Sun 08:00. Closed Mon - Wed, Fri 21:00, Sat, Sun 17:00.
Su: Open Mon - Wed, Fri - Sun 08:00. Closed Mon - Wed, Fri 21:00, Sat, Sun 17:00.
Au: Open Mon - Wed, Fri - Sun 08:00. Closed Mon - Wed, Fri 21:00, Sat, Sun 17:00.
Wn: Open Mon - Wed, Fri - Sun 08:00. Closed Mon - Wed, Fri 21:00, Sat, Sun 17:00.
Closed Thursdays **Ref: YH06168**

GROVE HSE RIDING SCHOOL

Grove House Riding School, Grove Hse Farm, Hall Rd, Spexhall, Halesworth, **Suffolk**, IP19 0RR, **ENGLAND**.
(T) 01986 781502.
Profile Riding School. **Ref: YH06169**

GROVE HSE STABLES

Grove House Stables, Grovewood Rd, Misterton, Doncaster, **Yorkshire (South)**, DN10 4EF, **ENGLAND**.
(T) 01427 890802 **(F)** 01427 891471.
Contact/s
Owner: Mr A Stennett
Profile Riding School, Stable/Livery. **Ref: YH06170**

GROVE LIVERY STABLES

Grove Livery Stables (The), Pipers Lane, Harpenden, **Hertfordshire**, AL5 1AJ, **ENGLAND**.
(T) 01582 766999.
Profile Stable/Livery. **Ref: YH06171**

GROVE RIDING CTRE

Grove Riding Centre, Whiterashes, Aberdeen, **Aberdeen (City of)**, AB21 0RB, **SCOTLAND**.
(T) 01651 882263 **(F)** 01651 882263.
Contact/s
Partner: Mr R Taylor
Profile Riding School, Stable/Livery. **Ref: YH06172**

GROVE VETNRY HOSPITAL

Grove Veterinary Hospital, 2 Hibbert St, New Mills, Stockport, **Manchester (Greater)**, SK12 3JJ,

ENGLAND.
(T) 01663 745294.
Profile Medical Support. Ref:YH06173

GROVEBRIDGE LIVERY YARD

Grovebridge Livery Yard, Little London Rd, Cross In Hand, Heathfield, **Sussex (East)**, TN21 0AX, **ENGLAND**.
(T) 01435 862704.
Contact/s
Owner: Miss S Massey
Profile Stable/Livery. Ref:YH06174

GROVELY

Grovely Riding Centre, Water Ditchampton, Wilton, Salisbury, **Wiltshire**, SP2 0JB, **ENGLAND**.
(T) 01722 742288 (F) 01722 743842
Affiliated Bodies BHS, BSJA.
Contact/s
Partner: Miss S Curtis
Profile Riding School, Stable/Livery.
Full, part and DIY livery available, prices on request. Lessons are 45 minutes long and cost £21.50 for children and £23.50 for adults, Tuesdays - Sundays.
No.Staff: 4 Yr. Est: 1975
Opening Times
Sp: Open Tues - Sun 10:00. Closed Tues - Sun 20:00.
Su: Open Tues - Sun 10:00. Closed Tues - Sun 20:00.
Au: Open Tues - Sun 10:00. Closed Tues - Sun 20:00.
Wn: Open Tues - Sun 10:00.
Close earlier in the winter Ref:YH06175

GRO-WELL FEEDS

Gro-Well Feeds Ltd, Hercules Way, Bowerhill Est, Melksham, **Wiltshire**, SN12 6TS, **ENGLAND**.
(T) 01225 708482 (F) 01225 702270
(E) info@equilibra.co.uk
(W) www.equilibra.co.uk.
Profile Supplies. Ref:YH06176

GRUNEWALD, P

P Grunewald, Forge Hse, Jubilee St, Llanharan, Pontyclun, **Rhondda Cynon Taff**, CF72 9RF, **WALES**.
(T) 01443 226131.
Contact/s
Owner: Mr P Grunewald
Profile Farrier. Ref:YH06177

GUARDS POLO CLUB

Guards Polo Club (The), Windsor Great Pk, Englefield Green, Egham, **Surrey**, TW20 0HP, **ENGLAND**.
(T) 01784 434212.
Profile Polo Club. Ref:YH06178

GUBB, TONY

Tony Gubb, 6 Greenfield Cres, Nailsea, **Somerset (North)**, BS48 1HL, **ENGLAND**.
(T) 01275 790459.
Profile Trainer. Ref:YH06179

GUBBY, B

Mr B Gubby, Dukes Wood Stud Farm, Bracknell Rd, Bagshot, **Surrey**, GU19 5HX, **ENGLAND**.
(T) 01276 63282 (F) 01276 34445
(M) 07768 867368.
Profile Breeder. Ref:YH06180

GUELDER ROSE

Guelder Rose Equestrian & Therapeutic Centre (The), Wethersfield Rd, Sible Hedingham, Halstead, **Essex**, CO9 3NA, **ENGLAND**.
(T) 01787 462529.
Profile Equestrian Centre, Medical Support.
Ref:YH06181

GUERNSEY

Guernsey Equestrian & Saddlery Centre, Grandes Capelles, St Sampsons, **Guernsey**, GY2 4UT, **ENGLAND**.
(T) 01481 725257 (F) 01481 716642.
Contact/s
Partner: Mr R Humphries
Profile Equestrian Centre, Saddlery Retailer, Stable/Livery, Transport/Horse Boxes. Ref:YH06182

GUEST, R

Ray Guest's Chestnut Tree Stables, Hamilton Rd, Newmarket, **Suffolk**, CB8 0NY, **ENGLAND**.
(T) 01638 661508 (F) 01638 667317
(W) www.newmarketracehorsetrainers.co.uk
Affiliated Bodies Newmarket Trainers Fed.
Contact/s
Trainer: Mr R Guest
Profile Trainer. Ref:YH06183

GUILD OF MASTER CRAFTSMAN

Guild of Master Craftsman, 166 High St, Lewes, **Sussex (East)**, BN7 1XU, **ENGLAND**.
(T) 01273 477374 (F) 01273 478606.
Profile Club/Association. Ref:YH06184

GUILD ST VETNRY CTRE

Guild Street Veterinary Centre, 14 Guild St, Stratford-upon-Avon, **Warwickshire**, CV37 6RE, **ENGLAND**.
(T) 01789 292753 (F) 01789 299360.
Contact/s
Partner: Mr J Blayney
Profile Medical Support. Ref:YH06185

GUILFOYLE, M

M Guilfoyle, 7 Dawson Rd, Heald Green, Cheadle, **Cheshire**, SK8 3AE, **ENGLAND**.
(T) 0161 4363201.
Profile Farrier. Ref:YH06186

GUISBOROUGH RIDING CLUB

Guisborough Riding Club, 19 Dulverton Way, Guisborough, **Cleveland**, TS14 7BZ, **ENGLAND**.
(T) 01287 635166.
Profile Club/Association, Riding Club. Ref:YH06187

GUIVER, DAVID

David Guiver, 46 Birchwood Ave, Wallington, **Surrey**, SM6 7EN, **ENGLAND**.
(T) 020 86475764. Ref:YH06188

GULLEY, D L

D L Gulley, Cottage Farm, 36 Main St, Thorpe Satchville, Melton Mowbray, **Leicestershire**, LE14 2DQ, **ENGLAND**.
(T) 01664 840528 (F) 01664 840528.
Contact/s
Owner: Mr D Gulley
Profile Farrier. Ref:YH06189

GULLEY, MICHAEL

Michael Gulley AWCF, Ivydene, 2 Church St, Ascott Under Wychwood, Chipping Norton, **Oxfordshire**, OX7 6AZ, **ENGLAND**.
(T) 01295 730135.
Profile Farrier. Ref:YH06190

GUMTREE ENTERPRISES

Gumtree Enterprises, Fallbrook, Plumpton Lane, Plumpton, **Sussex (East)**, BN7 3AH, **ENGLAND**.
(T) 01273 890259 (F) 01273 891010
(E) gumtree@ukonline.co.uk.
Profile Transport/Horse Boxes. Ref:YH06191

GUNSTONE HALL RIDING CTRE

Gunstone Hall Riding Centre, Whitehouse Lane, Codsall, Wolverhampton, **Staffordshire**, WV8 1QQ, **ENGLAND**.
(T) 01902 846693.
Profile Riding School, Stable/Livery. Ref:YH06192

GUNTER, T J

T J Gunter, Northerwood, Over Lane, Rudgeway, Bristol, **Bristol**, BS35 3RS, **ENGLAND**.
(T) 01454 619674.
Profile Farrier. Ref:YH06193

GURDON, MELANIE

Melanie Gurdon, 1 Watership Cottage, Sydmonton, Newbury, **Berkshire**, RG20 9AD, **ENGLAND**.
(T) 01635 299945 (F) 01635 299945
Affiliated Bodies NAAT.
Contact/s
Physiotherapist: Melanie Gurdon
Profile Medical Support. Ref:YH06194

GUTHRIE RIGBY

Guthrie Rigby (Horsebox Manufacturer), Grange Farm, Drain Lane, Holme upon Spalding Moor, **Yorkshire (East)**, YO43 4DG, **ENGLAND**.
(T) 01430 861399 (F) 01430 861410.
Profile Transport/Horse Boxes. Ref:YH06195

GUTIERREZ-INOSTROZA, ABEL R

Abel R Gutierrez-Inostroza DWCF, Key Stone Forge, Taylors Lane Farm, Taylors Lane, Breightmet, Bolton, **Manchester (Greater)**, **ENGLAND**.
(T) 01204 373957.
Profile Farrier. Ref:YH06196

GUY, JOHN

John Guy, The Blacksmiths Shop, Bog Row, Hetton-Le-Hole, **Tyne and Wear**, DH5 9JN, **ENGLAND**.
(T) 07710 942511.
Profile Farrier. Ref:YH06197

GUYHIRN RIDING SCHOOL

Guyhirn Riding School, Drummond Lodge, Spencer Drove, Guyhirn, Wisbech, **Cambridgeshire**, PE13 4EU, **ENGLAND**.
(T) 01945 450255.
Contact/s
Owner: Miss P Gilbert
Profile Riding School, Stable/Livery. Ref:YH06198

GWAUN VETNRY GRP

Gwaun Veterinary Group, 52 High St, Fishguard, Pembroke, **Pembrokeshire**, SA65 9AR, **WALES**.
(T) 01348 873810.
Profile Medical Support. Ref:YH06199

GWENNAP RIDING CLUB

Gwennap Riding Club, Crougy Farm, Ponsanooth, Truro, **Cornwall**, **ENGLAND**.
(T) 01872 864027.
Profile Club/Association, Riding Club. Ref:YH06200

GWENT SADDLERY

Gwent Saddlery Ltd, 219 Cardiff Rd, Newport, **Newport**, NP20 3AG, **WALES**.
(T) 01633 810550.
Profile Saddlery Retailer. Ref:YH06201

GWENT TERTIARY

Gwent Tertiary, The Rhadyr, Usk, **Monmouthshire**, NP15 1XJ, **WALES**.
(T) 01495 333333 (F) 01495 333629.
Profile Riding School. Ref:YH06202

GWERSYLL YR URDD/URDD CAMP

Gwersyll yr Urdd/Urdd Camp (Residents only), Llangrannog, Llandysul, **Carmarthenshire**, SA44 6AE, **WALES**.
(T) 01239 654473 (F) 01239 654912.
Profile Equestrian Centre. Ref:YH06203

GWINEAR & DISTRICT FARMERS

Gwinear & District Farmers Ltd, 20 Cathebedron Rd, Carnhell Green, Camborne, **Cornwall**, TR14 0NB, **ENGLAND**.
(T) 01209 831320 (F) 01209 831582. Ref:YH06204

GWYN LEWIS FARM SUPPLIES

Gwyn Lewis Farm Supplies, The Pet Pl, Rhuddlan Rd, Abergele, **Conwy**, LL22 7HT, **WALES**.
(T) 01745 823188 (F) 01745 823189.
Contact/s
Owner: Mr G Lewis
Profile Supplies. Ref:YH06205

GYPSYVILLE STUD

Gypsyville Stud, Bleakhouse Stables, West Melton, Rotherham, **Yorkshire (South)**, S63 6AH, **ENGLAND**.
(T) 01709 873166.
Contact/s
Owner: Mr T Kersey
Profile Breeder.
Breeds Welsh section B ponies Ref:YH06206

H & C BEART

H & C Beart Ltd, Brighton Mill, Stowbridge, King's Lynn, **Norfolk**, PE34 3PD, **ENGLAND**.
(T) 01366 388151 (F) 01366 382603
(E) bearts@freeuk.com.
Contact/s
Owner: Mr S Brighton
Profile Saddlery Retailer. Ref:YH06207

H & K SIMS

H & K Sims (Devon) Ltd, Mardle Hse, Mardle Way, Buckfastleigh, **Devon**, TQ11 0NR, **ENGLAND**.
(T) 01364 642040 (F) 01364 642044.
Profile Supplies. Ref:YH06208

H & S EUROPEAN TRANSPORT

H & S European Transport, Ballencrieff Cottages, Longniddry, **Lothian (East)**, EH32 0PJ, **SCOTLAND**.
(T) 01875 870217 (F) 01875 870217.
Contact/s
Partner: Miss L Holland
Profile Transport/Horse Boxes. Ref:YH06209

H A C S SHOP

H A C S Shop, Latchmore Bank, Little Hallingbury, Bishop's Stortford, **Essex**, CM22 7PJ, **ENGLAND**.
(T) 01279 713221 (F) 01279 755395.
Profile Saddlery Retailer. Ref:YH06210

H B H FORGINGS

H B H Forgings Ltd, Unit 25 Southgate Ind Est, Cross St, Heywood, **Lancashire**, OL10 1PW, **ENGLAND**.
(T) 01706 691600 (F) 01706 691622.

Profile Blacksmith. **Ref: YH06211**

H B SADDLERY

H B Saddlery, Foxhole Farm, Horseshoe Lane, Beckley, Rye, **Sussex (East)**, TN31 6RZ, **ENGLAND**.
(T) 01797 260749.
Profile Saddlery Retailer. **Ref: YH06212**

H BANHAM

H Banham Ltd, Raynham Rd, Hempton, Fakenham, **Norfolk**, NR21 7LN, **ENGLAND**.
(T) 01328 863741 **(F)** 01328 855731.
Profile Supplies. **Ref: YH06213**

H BLYTH & SON

H Blyth & Son, Honingham, Norwich, **Norfolk**, NR9 5BL, **ENGLAND**.
(T) 01603 880286.
Profile Blacksmith. **Ref: YH06214**

H C S

H C S (Clipping & Shearing) Services, Unit 23D, Oak Rd, West Chirton North Ind Est, North Shields, **Tyne and Wear**, NE29 8SF, **ENGLAND**.
(T) 0191 2596666 **(F)** 0191 2580989
(E) hcsservices@btinternet.com.
Contact/s
Owner: Mr M Tinmouth
Profile Supplies.
Stockists of the following brands; Hamtner, Heiniger, Lister, Ostler, Stewart, Wahl & Wolsley. Also stock dog grooming equipment, shampoos & conditioners. HCS Services supply a wide range of clipping equipment in the UK. **No.Staff:** 6 **Yr. Est:** 1984
C.Size: 0.5 Acres
Opening Times
Open every Sat 09:00 - 12:00, except bank holiday weekends and statutory holidays **Ref: YH06215**

H C STAR METALS

H C Star Metals, North Overgate, Kinghorn, Burntisland, **Fife**, KY3 9XJ, **SCOTLAND**.
(T) 01592 890807 **(F)** 01592 890807.
Contact/s
Owner: Mr A Kelly
Profile Blacksmith. **Ref: YH06216**

H E F MORRIS

H E F Morris & Co, 1 Milsom St, Bath, **Bath & Somerset (North East)**, BA1 1DA, **ENGLAND**.
(T) 01225 424680 **(F)** 01225 481406.
Profile Property Agents. **Ref: YH06217**

H E I

H E I Ltd, P O Box 1090, Pulborough, **Sussex (West)**, RH20 4YY, **ENGLAND**.
(T) 01903 745444 **(F)** 01903 740716.
Profile Trainer. **Ref: YH06218**

H E MILLINGTON & SONS

H E Millington & Sons, St Patricks, 13 Bedhampton Rd, Havant, **Hampshire**, PO9 3ES, **ENGLAND**.
(T) 023 92483216.
Profile Transport/Horse Boxes. **Ref: YH06219**

H E PRINGLE

H E Pringle Ltd, Gills Hill Farm, Bourn, **Cambridgeshire**, CB3 7TS, **ENGLAND**.
(T) 01954 719222.
Profile Supplies. **Ref: YH06220**

H F PUGH & SONS

H F Pugh & Sons, Upper Spoad, Newcastle, Craven Arms, **Shropshire**, SY7 8PB, **ENGLAND**.
(T) 01588 640006 **(F)** 01588 640006.
Contact/s
Owner: Mr J Pugh
Profile Transport/Horse Boxes. **Ref: YH06221**

H F S SUPPLIES

H F S Supplies, 19 Reigate Rd, Hookwood, Horley, **Surrey**, RH6 0HL, **ENGLAND**.
(T) 01293 821428.
Contact/s
Owner: Mr J Chapman
Profile Supplies. **Ref: YH06222**

H G MIDDLETON & SONS

H G Middleton & Sons, Zion Pl, Dartmouth, **Devon**, TQ6 9NR, **ENGLAND**.
(T) 01803 832346.
Contact/s
Owner: Mr T Middleton
Profile Blacksmith. **Ref: YH06223**

H GARNHAM & SON

H Garnham & Son, Corn Merchants, 85 Front St, Sacriston, **County Durham**, DH7 6JW, **ENGLAND**.
(T) 0191 3710373.
Profile Supplies. **Ref: YH06224**

H HUNTSMAN & SONS

H Huntsman & Sons Ltd, 11 Savile Row, London, **London (Greater)**, W1X 2PS, **ENGLAND**.
(T) 020 77347441 **(F)** 020 72872937.
Profile Riding Wear Retailer. **Ref: YH06225**

H J BURT & SON

H J Burt & Son, The Estate Offices, Steyning, **Sussex (West)**, BN44 3RE, **ENGLAND**.
(T) 01903 879488 **(F)** 01903 816461.
Contact/s
Partner: Mr P Hughes
Profile Property Agents. **Ref: YH06226**

H J WEBB & SON

H J Webb & Son, Pear Tree Farm, Great Coxwell, Faringdon, **Oxfordshire**, SN7 7NG, **ENGLAND**.
(T) 01367 240173. **Ref: YH06227**

H M C HOPSFORD MARKETING

H M C Hopsford Marketing Communications, Agricultural, Equestrian & Countryside Marketing, Hopsford Hall, Withybrook Lane, Shilton, Coventry, **Warwickshire**, CV7 9JJ, **ENGLAND**.
(T) 01455 220974 **(F)** 01455 220375.
Profile Club/Association. **Ref: YH06228**

H M P HOLLESLEY BAY COLONY

H M P Hollesley Bay Colony, Hollesley, Woodbridge, **Suffolk**, IP12 3JS, **ENGLAND**.
(T) 01394 411741 **(F)** 01394 411071.
Profile Breeder. **Ref: YH06229**

H M SCARTERFIELD & SONS

H M Scarterfield & Sons, Cedars, Leggatts Farm, Old Park Lane, Fishbourne, Chichester, **Sussex (West)**, PO18 8AP, **ENGLAND**.
(T) 01243 572732 **(F)** 01243 576899
(E) sales-scarterfield@farmersweekly.net
(W) www.scarterfield.co.uk.
Profile Supplies. **Ref: YH06230**

H M THRESHER

H M Thresher (Crediton), 108 High St, Crediton, **Devon**, EX17 3LF, **ENGLAND**.
(T) 01363 772539.
Profile Medical Support. **Ref: YH06231**

H O E

H O E Country Feeds, Church St, Newnham, Daventry, **Northamptonshire**, NN11 3ET, **ENGLAND**.
(T) 01327 300643 **(F)** 01327 310961.
Profile Supplies. **Ref: YH06232**

H P T SADDLERY

H P T Saddlery, Kinloch Cottages, Kinlochlaggan, Newtonmore, **Highlands**, PH20 1BX, **SCOTLAND**.
(T) 01528 544302.
Profile Supplies. **Ref: YH06233**

H PITTAM SADDLERY

H Pittam Saddlery, Ty'r Haul, Rhydlewis, Llandysul, **Carmarthenshire**, SA44 5QT, **WALES**.
(T) 01239 851535.
Profile Saddlery Retailer. **Ref: YH06234**

H R PHILPOT & SON

H R Philpot & Son (Barleylands) Ltd, Barleylands Farm, Barleylands Rd, Billericay, **Essex**, CM11 2UD, **ENGLAND**.
(T) 01268 532253 **(F)** 01268 532032.
Profile Stable/Livery. **Ref: YH06235**

H S E

H S E Ltd, Enterprise Ind Pk, Hunters Rd, Weldon North Ind Est, Corby, **Northamptonshire**, NN17 5JE, **ENGLAND**.
(T) 01536 204233 **(F)** 01536 205594.
Profile Transport/Horse Boxes. **Ref: YH06236**

H S JACKSON & SON

H S Jackson & Son (Fencing) Ltd, New Rock, Chilcompton, Bath, **Bath & Somerset (North East)**, BA3 4JE, **ENGLAND**.
(T) 01761 232666 **(F)** 01761 232647.
Profile Track/Course. **Ref: YH06237**

H S JACKSON & SON

H S Jackson & Son (Fencing) Ltd, Dragon Hall, Whitchurch Rd, Chowley, Tattenhall, **Cheshire**, CH3 9DU, **ENGLAND**.
(T) 01829 770776 **(F)** 01829 770778.
Contact/s
Manager: W Morris
Profile Track/Course. **Ref: YH06238**

H S JACKSON & SON

H S Jackson & Son (Fencing) Ltd (South East), 44 Stowting Common, Ashford, **Kent**, TN25 6BN, **ENGLAND**.
(T) 01233 750393 **(F)** 01233 750403.
Profile Track/Course. **Ref: YH06239**

H SIMPSON & SON

H Simpson & Son Ltd, 25 Burringham Rd, Scunthorpe, **Lincolnshire (North)**, DN17 2BA, **ENGLAND**.
(T) 01724 842502.
Profile Saddlery Retailer. **Ref: YH06240**

H T GREEN & SON

H T Green & Son, Filliams Bungalow, Plaistow Rd, Kirdford, Billingshurst, **Sussex (West)**, RH14 0JS, **ENGLAND**.
(T) 01403 820425.
Contact/s
Senior Partner: Mr H Green
Profile Transport/Horse Boxes. **Ref: YH06241**

H T S EQUESTRIAN

H T S Equestrian, Unit 87 Laurence Leyland Complex, Irthlingborough Rd, Wellingborough, **Northamptonshire**, NN8 1RT, **ENGLAND**.
(T) 01933 277515 **(F)** 01933 271832.
Profile Saddlery Retailer. **Ref: YH06242**

H THOMPSON & SON

H Thompson & Son, 21 Guildford St, Chertsey, **Surrey**, KT16 9BG, **ENGLAND**.
(T) 01932 562314.
Contact/s
Owner: Mr H Thompson
Profile Blacksmith. **Ref: YH06243**

H THORNBER

H Thornber Ltd, Miall St, Halifax, **Yorkshire (West)**, HX1 4AE, **ENGLAND**.
(T) 01422 355581.
Profile Supplies. **Ref: YH06244**

H W DABBS SADDLEMAKERS

H W Dabbs Saddlemakers Ltd, William Hse, Marsh Lane, Walsall, **Midlands (West)**, WS2 9TR, **ENGLAND**.
(T) 01922 612238 **(F)** 01922 647691.
Profile Saddlery Retailer. Saddler. **Ref: YH06245**

H WADDINGTON

H Waddington Ltd, The Stores, Halton West, Hellifield, Skipton, **Yorkshire (North)**, BD23 4LL, **ENGLAND**.
(T) 01729 850206.
Profile Supplies. **Ref: YH06246**

H WOOLLEY & SON

H Woolley & Son, Church Sq, Uttoxeter, **Staffordshire**, ST14 8AP, **ENGLAND**.
(T) 01889 562629.
Profile Riding Wear Retailer, Saddlery Retailer.
Ref: YH06247

HAAG, R

R Haag, High Hse Farm, Birds Lane, Framsden, Stowmarket, **Suffolk**, IP14 6HR, **ENGLAND**.
(T) 01728 685717.
Contact/s
Owner: Mr R Haag
Profile Stable/Livery, Trainer. **Ref: YH06248**

HABGOOD, T

T Habgood, Dairy Farm, Eydon Rd, Woodford Halse, Daventry, **Northamptonshire**, NN11 3RG, **ENGLAND**.
(T) 01327 261850. **Ref: YH06249**

HACKETT, KEITH J

Keith J Hackett RSS, 23 High St, Hail Weston, Huntingdon, **Cambridgeshire**, PE19 4JW, **ENGLAND**.
(T) 01480 475469.
Profile Farrier. **Ref: YH06250**

HACKETT, L

L Hackett, Murcot Farm, Murcot, Broadway, **Worcestershire**, WR12 7HS, **ENGLAND**.
(T) 01386 830341.
Contact/s
Partner: Mr J Hackett
Profile Stable/Livery. **Ref: YH06251**

HACKETTS

Hacketts, 222 Newtownsaville, Eskra, Omagh, **County Tyrone**, BT78 2RW, **NORTHERN IRELAND**.
(T) 028 82568253.

Profile Supplies. **Ref: YH06252**

HACKETTS SADDLERY

Hacketts Saddlery, Unit 7 Sycamore Trading Est Squires Gate Lane, Blackpool, **Lancashire**, FY4 3RL, **ENGLAND**.
(T) 01253 298898.
Contact/s
Owner: Mr B Hackett
Profile Saddlery Retailer. **Ref: YH06253**

HACKING IN THE COUNTRYSIDE

Hacking In The Countryside, Little Vergers, Kirdford, Billingshurst, **Sussex (West)**, RH14 0LT, **ENGLAND**.
(T) 01403 820303.
Profile Equestrian Centre. Hacking Centre.
Ref: YH06254

HACKING WITH A DIFFERENCE

Hacking With A Difference, Painshill Farm, Hascombe Rd, Cranleigh, **Surrey**, GU6 8LF, **ENGLAND**.
(T) 01483 200227.
Profile Equestrian Centre. Hacking Centre.
Ref: YH06255

HACKNESS VILLA STABLES

Hackness Villa Stables, Hackness Villa, Exeter Rd, Newmarket, **Suffolk**, CB8 8LP, **ENGLAND**.
(T) 01638 667959
(W) www.newmarketracehorsetrainers.co.uk
Affiliated Bodies Newmarket Trainers Fed.
Contact/s
Trainer: D Morris
Profile Trainer. **Ref: YH06256**

HACKNEY HORSE SOC

Hackney Horse Society, Fallowfields, Little London, Heytesbury, Warminster, **Wiltshire**, BA12 0ES, **ENGLAND**.
(T) 01985 840717 **(F)** 01985 840616
(E) hackney.horse@talk21.com.
Contact/s
Key Contact: Mrs D Hicketts
Profile Club/Association. **Ref: YH06257**

HACKNEY PK

Mrs Helen Beale, Mount Pleasant, Lymington, **Hampshire**, SO41 8LS, **ENGLAND**.
(T) 01590 682049.
Contact/s
Owner: Ms H Beale
Profile Farrier, Horse/Rider Accom.
Full & DIY Livery available, stabling and grazing, details on request. **Yr. Est:** 1989 **C.Size:** 40 Acres
Opening Times
Accommodation is available all year, farrier as required, telephone for more details **Ref: YH06258**

HAC-TAC

Hac-Tac Ltd, Park Rd, Faringdon, **Oxfordshire**, SN7 8LA, **ENGLAND**.
(T) 01367 242818 /0845 6002701 **(F)** 01367 242819.
Profile Riding Wear Retailer, Saddlery Retailer.
Ref: YH06259

HADDON CRAFT FORGE

Haddon Craft Forge Ltd, Estate Yard, Upper Harlestone, Northampton, **Northamptonshire**, NN7 4EH, **ENGLAND**.
(T) 01604 580559 **(F)** 01604 580541.
Contact/s
Manager: Mr D Bayes
Profile Blacksmith. **Ref: YH06260**

HADDON HSE

C E Mosley, Haddon Hse Riding Stables, Monyash Rd, Over Haddon, Bakewell, **Derbyshire**, DE45 1HZ, **ENGLAND**.
(T) 01629 813723
(E) info@haddonhousestables.co.uk
(W) www.haddonhousestables.co.uk.
Contact/s
General Manager: Mrs C Mosley
Profile Breeder, Riding School.
The homebred horses are schooled and trained on site to ensure they are well mannered and behaved.
Yr. Est: 1991
Opening Times
Sp: Open Mon - Sun 10:30. Closed Mon - Sun 16:30.
Su: Open Mon - Sun 10:30. Closed Mon - Sun 16:30.
Au: Open Mon - Sun 10:30. Closed Mon - Sun 16:30.
Wn: Open Mon - Sun 10:30. Closed Mon - Sun 16:30.
Telephone for further information, open six days but day off varies. Evening rides in summer: **Ref: YH06261**

HADDON ROCKING HORSES

Haddon Rocking Horses Ltd, 5 Telford Rd, Clacton-on-Sea, **Essex**, CO15 4LP, **ENGLAND**.
(T) 01255 424745 **(F)** 01255 475505.
Profile Sculptor. **Ref: YH06262**

HADDON STUD

Haddon Stud, High St, Manton, Marlborough, **Wiltshire**, SN8 4HH, **ENGLAND**.
(T) 01672 516261 **(F)** 01672 516261.
Contact/s
Owner: Mr C Hewlett
Profile Breeder, Stable/Livery, Trainer. **Ref: YH06263**

HADFIELD, G

Mr G Hadfield, Lumb Farm, Lumb Lane, Little Moss, Droylsden, Manchester, **Manchester (Greater)**, M43 7LB, **ENGLAND**.
(T) 0161 3702360.
Profile Trainer. **Ref: YH06264**

HADFIELD, M A

M A Hadfield, 57 Commercial St, Norton, Malton, **Yorkshire (North)**, YO17 9HX, **ENGLAND**.
(T) 01653 694095.
Contact/s
Owner: Mr M Hadfield
Profile Saddlery Retailer. **Ref: YH06265**

HADLEIGH RIDING CTRE

Hadleigh Riding Centre, Benton End Fm, Benton End, Hadleigh, Ipswich, **Suffolk**, IP7 5JR, **ENGLAND**.
(T) 01473 824946.
Profile Equestrian Centre, Riding School.
Ref: YH06266

HADLEY RIDING STABLES

Hadley Riding Stables, Brick Hse Farm, Hadley, Droitwich, **Worcestershire**, WR9 0AS, **ENGLAND**.
(T) 01905 620206.
Contact/s
Owner: Miss T Bradshaw
Profile Riding School, Stable/Livery. **Ref: YH06267**

HADLEY, STEPHEN

Stephen Hadley, Bloxham Barn Farm, Chadshunt, Kineton, **Warwickshire**, CV35 0EL, **ENGLAND**.
(T) 01926 640223 **(F)** 01926 640915.
Profile Trainer. **Ref: YH06268**

HADLOW CLGE

Hadlow College Equestrian Centre, Hadlow College, Hadlow, Tonbridge, **Kent**, TN11 0AL, **ENGLAND**.
(T) 01732 852204.
Profile Equestrian Centre. **Ref: YH06269**

HADNELL SADDLERY

Hadnell Saddlery, 2a Hardwicke Stables, Hadnall, Shrewsbury, **Shropshire**, SY4 4AR, **ENGLAND**.
(T) 01939 210680 **(F)** 01939 210680.
Contact/s
Owner: Mr C Garrett
Profile Saddlery Retailer. **Ref: YH06270**

HADRIAN EQUINE

Hadrian Equine, West Hse Farm, Bishopton, Stockton-on-Tees, **Cleveland**, TS21 1LL, **ENGLAND**.
(T) 01740 630260.
Profile Supplies. **Ref: YH06271**

HADRIAN VETNRY GRP

Hadrian Veterinary Group, Dene Ave, Hexham, **Northumberland**, NE46 1HJ, **ENGLAND**.
(T) 01434 602703.
Contact/s
Practice Manager: Vivien Foster
Profile Medical Support. **Ref: YH06272**

HAFLINGER SOC

Haflinger Society of GB, Wayside Cottage, 2 The Hopground, Finchingfield, **Essex**, CM7 4LU, **ENGLAND**.
(T) 01371 810216
(E) secretary@haflingersgb.com.
Contact/s
Secretary: Mrs S Seel
Profile Club/Association. **Ref: YH06273**

HAFLINGER SOC

Haflinger Society of GB, 25 Hilltop Pk, Rugby Rd, Princethorpe, Warwick, **Warwickshire**, **ENGLAND**.
(T) 01926 632516.
Contact/s
Key Contact: Mrs D Parkinson
Profile Club/Association. **Ref: YH06274**

HAFOD TRAILERS

Hafod Trailers, Hafod Iwan, Caerwedros Rd, Llandysul, **Carmarthenshire**, SA44 6BJ, **WALES**.
(T) 01545 560397 **(F)** 01545 560397.
Contact/s
Owner: Mr G Evans
Profile Transport/Horse Boxes. **Ref: YH06275**

HAGGAS, W

W Haggas, Somerville Lodge, Fordham Rd, Newmarket, **Suffolk**, CB8 7AA, **ENGLAND**.
(T) 01638 667013 **(F)** 01638 660534
(W) www.newmarketracehorsetrainers.co.uk
Affiliated Bodies Newmarket Trainers Fed.
Contact/s
Owner: Mr W Haggas
Profile Trainer. **Ref: YH06276**

HAGGERSTON

Haggerston Castle Riding Stables, Chapel Hse, Haggerston, Berwick-upon-Tweed, **Northumberland**, TD15 2NZ, **ENGLAND**.
(T) 01289 381237.
Profile Riding School, Stable/Livery. **Ref: YH06277**

HAGGIS FARM STABLES

Haggis Farm Stables, Haggis Farm, Cambridge Rd, Barton, Cambridge, **Cambridgeshire**, CB3 7AT, **ENGLAND**.
(T) 01223 460353 **(F)** 01223 460353.
Contact/s
Owner: Mrs J Morris-Lowe
Profile Riding School, Stable/Livery. **Ref: YH06278**

HAIDA DARTMOOR PONY STUD

Haida Dartmoor Pony Stud, Fore Stoke Farm, Holne, Newton Abbot, **Devon**, TQ13 7SS, **ENGLAND**.
(T) 01364 394.
Profile Breeder. **Ref: YH06279**

HAIE FLEURIE

Haie Fleurie Livery Stables & Saddlery Centre, St Martin, Channel Isles, **Jersey**, JE3 6BN, **ENGLAND**.
(T) 01534 852617 **(F)** 01534 857624.
Profile Riding School, Saddlery Retailer, Stable/Livery. **Ref: YH06280**

HAIE FLEURIE CLASSICS

Haie Fleurie Classics, Vent D'ete, Ruede L'etoquet, St John, **Jersey**, JE1, **ENGLAND**.
(T) 01534 62540. **Ref: YH06281**

HAIGHS

C & G Haigh, Fulham Hse Farm, Whitley Bridge, Goole, Doncaster, **Yorkshire (East)**, DN14 0JL, **ENGLAND**.
(T) 01977 661006 **(F)** 01977 662476.
Contact/s
Owner: Mrs K Haigh
Profile Feed Merchant, Supplies. Hay and Straw merchants. **No.Staff:** 3 **Yr. Est:** 1980
Opening Times
Sp: Open Mon - Fri 08:00. Closed Mon - Fri 18:00.
Su: Open Mon - Fri 08:00. Closed Mon - Fri 18:00.
Au: Open Mon - Fri 08:00. Closed Mon - Fri 18:00.
Wn: Open Mon - Fri 08:00. Closed Mon - Fri 18:00.
Open weekends by appointment **Ref: YH06282**

HAILEY EQUITATION CTRE

Hailey Equitation Centre, Poffley End, Hailey, Witney, **Oxfordshire**, OX8 5US, **ENGLAND**.
(T) 01993 702844.
Profile Riding School. **Ref: YH06283**

HAINE, D

Mrs D Haine, Woodland, The Severals, Newmarket, **Suffolk**, CB8 9BS, **ENGLAND**.
(T) 01638 608040
(W) www.newmarketracehorsetrainers.co.uk
Affiliated Bodies Newmarket Trainers Fed.
Contact/s
Trainer: Mrs D Haine
Profile Trainer. **Ref: YH06284**

HAINES ROSETTE

Haines Rosette Co, 42 High St, Addlestone, **Surrey**, KT15 1TR, **ENGLAND**.
(T) 01932 829295 **(F)** 01932 841944.
Profile Supplies. **Ref: YH06285**

HAINES, T J

T J Haines DWCF, Habgood Cottage, 30 Malmesbury Rd, Leigh, **Wiltshire**, SN6 6RH, **ENGLAND**.
(T) 01793 752759.
Profile Farrier. **Ref: YH06286**

HAINSWORTH FORGE
Hainsworth Forge, Hainsworth St, Silsden, Keighley, **Yorkshire (West)**, BD20 0EY, **ENGLAND**.
(T) 01535 652659.
Contact/s
Owner: Mr N Blair
Profile Blacksmith. **Ref: YH06287**

HAIRSINE TRAILER REPAIRS
Hairsine Trailer Repairs, Tower Hse Lane, Saltend, Hull, **Yorkshire (East)**, HU12 8EE, **ENGLAND**.
(T) 01482 899410 **(F)** 01482 891524.
Contact/s
Owner: Mr T Hairsine
Profile Transport/Horse Boxes. **Ref: YH06288**

HALDANE, J S
Mr J S Haldane, The Yard Cottage, Mindrum, **Northumberland**, TD12 4QN, **ENGLAND**.
(T) 01890 850382.
Profile Trainer. **Ref: YH06289**

HALDON RIDING STABLES
Haldon Riding Stables, Home Farm, Dunchideock, Exeter, **Devon**, EX6 7YD, **ENGLAND**.
(T) 01392 832645.
Contact/s
Owner: Ms M Carr
Profile Riding School, Stable/Livery.
Hacking in quiet lanes, tracks and Haldon Forest. Children's morning clubs and school activity weeks a speciality. Yr. Est: 1992 C.Size: 120 Acres
Ref: YH06290

HALE STUD
Hale Stud (The), Hale Farm Hse, Lewes, Chiddingly, **Sussex (East)**, BN8 6HQ, **ENGLAND**.
(T) 01825 872323.
Profile Breeder. **Ref: YH06291**

HALE, ROGER K
Roger K Hale RSS, The Forge, Johnby, Penrith, **Cumbria**, CA11 0UU, **ENGLAND**.
(T) 01876 843564.
Profile Farrier. **Ref: YH06292**

HALES, ALFRED (SNR)
Alfred Hales Snr, 42 Manor Rd, Wales, Sheffield, **Yorkshire (South)**, S26 5PD, **ENGLAND**.
(T) 01909 770476.
Contact/s
Owner: Mr A Hales
Profile Produce Carriage Lamps. **Ref: YH06293**

HALES, S J
Mrs S J Hales Veterinary Services, The Old School Hse, Higher Wych, Malpas, **Cheshire**, SY14 7JT, **ENGLAND**.
(T) 01948 780242 **(F)** 01948 780623.
Profile Medical Support. **Ref: YH06294**

HALF BRED HORSE BREEDERS SOC
Half Bred Horse Breeders Society (The), Forthill Livery, 14 School Rd, Crossnacrevvy, Belfast, **County Antrim**, BT5 7UA, **NORTHERN IRELAND**.
(T) 028 90448814 **(F)** 028 90448814.
Contact/s
Secretary: Ms S White
Profile Club/Association. **Ref: YH06295**

HALF MOON RIDING STABLES
Half Moon Riding Stables, Hill Farm, Wood Drove, Bowdens, Langport, **Somerset**, TA10 0DD, **ENGLAND**.
(T) 01458 250304.
Profile Riding School, Stable/Livery. **Ref: YH06296**

HALFACRE, G W D
G W D Halfacre, 2 Stable Cottages, Kennel Lane, Bracknell, **Berkshire**, RG42 2EX, **ENGLAND**.
(T) 01344 425411.
Profile Farrier. **Ref: YH06297**

HALFORD FORGE
Halford Forge, Queen St, Halford, Shipston-on-Stour, **Warwickshire**, CV36 5BT, **ENGLAND**.
(T) 01789 740026 **(F)** 01789 740223.
Contact/s
Owner: Mr C Harness
Profile Blacksmith. **Ref: YH06298**

HALFORD, MICHAEL
Michael Halford, Pollardstown, Curragh, **County Kildare**, **IRELAND**.
(T) 045 432560 **(F)** 045 432560.
Contact/s
Trainer: Mr M Halford
(E) michaelhalford@kildarehorse.ie
Profile Trainer. **Ref: YH06299**

HALFROD, T K
T K Halfrod, Brook Forge, Hightown Rd, Cleckheaton, **Yorkshire (West)**, BD19 5JS, **ENGLAND**.
(T) 01274 874734 **(F)** 01274 869716.
Profile Blacksmith. **Ref: YH06300**

HALIFAX FARRIER SUPPLIES
Halifax Farrier Supplies, Unit C2 Tenterfields Ind Pk, Luddendenfoot, Halifax, **Yorkshire (West)**, HX2 6EQ, **ENGLAND**.
(T) 01422 886882.
Contact/s
Partner: Mr J Hall
Profile Farrier. **Ref: YH06301**

HALINA TOMBS
Halina Tombs, 2 The Five Hses, School St, Churchover, Rugby, **Warwickshire**, CV23 0EQ, **ENGLAND**.
(T) 01788 833538 **(F)** 01788 833538
Affiliated Bodies NAAT.
Contact/s
Physiotherapist: Halina Tombs
Profile Medical Support. **Ref: YH06302**

HALL & AST
Hall & Associates, Unit 9G Lowesden Works, Lambourn Woodlands, Hungerford, **Berkshire**, RG17 7RU, **ENGLAND**.
(T) 01488 73755 **(F)** 01488 73744
(E) hall.jenny@virgin.net.
Contact/s
Partner: Hattie Lawrence
Profile Blood Stock Agency, Medical Support.
Ref: YH06303

HALL FARM FORAGE
Hall Farm Forage, Grubb St, Happisburgh, **Norfolk**, NR12 0RQ, **ENGLAND**.
(T) 01692 650321.
Profile Transport/Horse Boxes. **Ref: YH06304**

HALL FARM STABLES
Hall Farm Stables, Waltham-on-the-Wolds, Melton Mowbray, **Leicestershire**, LE14 4AJ, **ENGLAND**.
(T) 01664 464711 **(F)** 01664 464492
(M) 07768 996103.
Profile Trainer. **Ref: YH06305**

HALL FARM STUD
Hall Farm Stud, Heronfield Cottage, 2 Bosworth Rd, Snarestone, **Derbyshire**, DE12 7DQ, **ENGLAND**.
(T) 01530 273061.
Profile Breeder, Stable/Livery. **Ref: YH06306**

HALL PLACE EQUESTRIAN CTRE
Hall Place Equestrian Centre, Hall Pl Farm, Little Heath Rd, Tilehurst, Reading, **Berkshire**, RG31 5TX, **ENGLAND**.
(T) 0118 9426938 **(F)** 0118 9425178.
Contact/s
Manageress: Miss S Scanlan
Profile Riding School, Stable/Livery, Track/Course.
Ref: YH06307

HALL PLACE STABLES
Hall Place Stables, Watery Lane, Sparsholt, Wantage, **Oxfordshire**, OX12 9PL, **ENGLAND**.
(T) 01235 751392 **(F)** 01488 648898.
Contact/s
Owner: Mr P Shakespeare
Profile Trainer. **Ref: YH06308**

HALL PLACE VETNRY CTRE
Hall Place Veterinary Centre, Burchetts Green, Maidenhead, **Berkshire**, SL6 6XD, **ENGLAND**.
(T) 01628 829880 **(F)** 01628 829789
(E) tonycollins@cwcom.net.
Profile Medical Support. **Ref: YH06309**

HALL ROBERT
Hall Robert, The Forge, Oaksey, Malmesbury, **Wiltshire**, SN16 9TF, **ENGLAND**.
(T) 01666 577260.
Profile Farrier. **Ref: YH06310**

HALL, ALBERT J
Albert J Hall, Redwood Kiln Rd, Prestwood, Great Missenden, **Buckinghamshire**, HP16 9DH, **ENGLAND**.
(T) 01494 866911.
Profile Farrier. **Ref: YH06311**

HALL, ALEC W G
Alec W G Hall, 64 Market Pl, Driffield, **Yorkshire (East)**, YO25 6AW, **ENGLAND**.
(T) 01377 252136.
Profile Saddlery Retailer. **Ref: YH06312**

HALL, ALFRED
Alfred Hall DWCF, Station Hse, Challow Station, Faringdon, **Oxfordshire**, SN7 8NT, **ENGLAND**.
(T) 01367 710566.
Profile Farrier. **Ref: YH06313**

HALL, D
D Hall, 8 Sandpiper Cl, Quedgeley, Gloucester, **Gloucestershire**, GL2 4LZ, **ENGLAND**.
(T) 01452 722458.
Profile Farrier. **Ref: YH06314**

HALL, DAVID A
David A Hall DWCF Hons, 15 Nene Cl, Quedgeley, **Gloucestershire**, GL2 6LZ, **ENGLAND**.
(T) 01452 722458.
Profile Farrier. **Ref: YH06315**

HALL, LYNN M
Lynn M Hall DWCF, Crosswinds Farm, Higher Bulstone, Branscombe, Seaton, **Devon**, EX12 3BL, **ENGLAND**.
(T) 01297 680217.
Profile Farrier. **Ref: YH06316**

HALL, M J
M J Hall, Ladys Green Farm, Ladys Green, Ousden, Newmarket, **Suffolk**, CB8 8TU, **ENGLAND**.
(T) 01284 850366 **(F)** 01284 753023.
Contact/s
Owner: Mr M Hall
Profile Breeder. **Ref: YH06317**

HALL, MARK LESLIE
Mark Leslie Hall RSS, 4 Homelands Cottages, Bines Rd, Partridge Green, Horsham, **Sussex (West)**, RH13 8EQ, **ENGLAND**.
(T) 01403 710586.
Profile Farrier. **Ref: YH06318**

HALL, TIMOTHY J
Timothy J Hall DWCF, 9 Arthurs Cl, Rossett Acre, Harrogate, **Yorkshire (North)**, HG2 0EF, **ENGLAND**.
(T) 01423 522600.
Profile Farrier. **Ref: YH06319**

HALL, TONY
Tony Hall BSc MSc M.I. Biol, Azevinhos, 154 Bradford Rd, Wakefield, **Yorkshire (West)**, WF1 2AP, **ENGLAND**.
(T) 01924 360369.
Profile Medical Support. **Ref: YH06320**

HALLAGENNA RIDING SCHOOL
Hallagenna Riding School, Hallagenna Farm, St. Breward, Bodmin, **Cornwall**, PL30 4NS, **ENGLAND**.
(T) 01208 851500.
Contact/s
Owner: Mr P Millward
Profile Riding School. **Ref: YH06321**

HALLAGENNA STUD FARM
Hallagenna Stud Farm, Hallagenna Farm, St. Breward, Bodmin, **Cornwall**, PL30 4NS, **ENGLAND**.
(T) 01208 850439.
Profile Breeder, Saddlery Retailer, Stable/Livery.
Ref: YH06322

HALLAM VETNRY CTRE
Hallam Veterinary Centre, 47 Holme Lane, Sheffield, **Yorkshire (South)**, S6 4JP, **ENGLAND**.
(T) 0114 2343013.
Profile Medical Support. **Ref: YH06323**

HALLAM, J B
J B Hallam, The Windmill, Priest Gate, East Markham, Newark, **Nottinghamshire**, NG22 0QT, **ENGLAND**.
(T) 01777 870845.
Contact/s
Owner: Mr J Hallam
Profile Farrier. **Ref: YH06324**

HALLAM, JEREMY
Jeremy Hallam DWCF, Paddock Wood Forge, Rose Cottage, West Stockwith, Doncaster, **Yorkshire (South)**, DN10 4HA, **ENGLAND**.
(T) 01427 890553.
Profile Farrier. **Ref: YH06325**

HALLAMSHIRE RIDING SOC
Hallamshire Riding Society, 22 Bute St, Crookes, Sheffield, **Yorkshire (South)**, S10 1UP, **ENGLAND**.
(T) 0114 2686530.
Contact/s
Secretary: Mrs A Lingard
Profile Club/Association. **Ref: YH06326**

HALLAS LANE LIVERY STABLES
Hallas Lane Livery Stables, Hallas Lane, Cullingworth, Bradford, **Yorkshire (West)**, BD13 5BU, **ENGLAND**.
(T) 01535 275124.
Contact/s
Owner: Mr P Chamberlain
Profile Stable/Livery.
Show jumping and dressage events held during the summer months (May - Aug). **No.Staff:** 2
Yr. Est: 1996 **C.Size:** 22 Acres
Opening Times
Sp: Open Mon - Sun 09:00. Closed Mon - Sun 20:00.
Su: Open Mon - Sun 09:00. Closed Mon - Sun 20:00.
Au: Open Mon - Sun 09:00. Closed Mon - Sun 20:00.
Wn: Open Mon - Sun 09:00. Closed Mon - Sun 20:00. **Ref: YH06327**

HALLEGA STABLES
Hallega Stables, Heath Farm, Church Lane, Headley, Epsom, **Surrey**, KT18 6LD, **ENGLAND**.
(T) 01372 361252.
Contact/s
Owner: Mrs L Scurry
Profile Stable/Livery. **Ref: YH06328**

HALLETT, J P
J P Hallett, The Laurels, The Street, Pettistree, Woodbridge, **Suffolk**, IP13 0HU, **ENGLAND**.
(T) 01728 746210.
Profile Breeder. **Ref: YH06329**

HALLIDAY, J
J Halliday, Druim Farm, Lochloy Rd, Nairn, **Highlands**, IV12 5LF, **SCOTLAND**.
(T) 01667 455493.
Contact/s
Owner: Mr J Halliday
Profile Farrier. **Ref: YH06330**

HALLINGBURY HALL
Hallingbury Hall Equestrian Centre, Little Hallingbury, Bishop's Stortford, **Essex**, CM22 7RP, **ENGLAND**.
(T) 01279 730348 **(F)** 01279 731567.
Contact/s
General Manager: Ms E Hazlewood **(Q)** BHSII
Profile Arena, Breeder, Equestrian Centre, Riding Club, Riding School, Stable/Livery, Supplies, Trainer.
BHS Exam Centre. **No.Staff:** 14 **Yr. Est:** 1985
C.Size: 35 Acres **Ref: YH06331**

HALLINGBURY RIDING CLUB
Hallingbury Riding Club, C/O Tom Chambers, Martinside Stud, Howe Green, Great Hallingbury, Bishop's Stortford, **Essex**, M22 7UE, **ENGLAND**.
(T) 01279 653277
(M) 07831 869990
(E) tom@astrolab.cix.co.uk.
Profile Club/Association, Riding Club. **Ref: YH06332**

HALLOW MILLS
Hallow Mill Equestrian Centre, Hallow Mill, Broadheath Lane, Hallow, Worcester, **Worcestershire**, WR2 6PR, **ENGLAND**.
(T) 01905 640373
Affiliated Bodies BHS.
Contact/s
Owner: Mrs B Johnson **(Q)** BHS 1
Profile Riding School. **Yr. Est:** 1971
C.Size: 17 Acres
Opening Times
Sp: Open Mon - Sun 09:00. Closed Mon - Sun 17:00.
Su: Open Mon - Sun 09:00. Closed Mon - Sun 17:00.
Au: Open Mon - Sun 09:00. Closed Mon - Sun 17:00.
Wn: Open Mon - Sun 09:00. Closed Mon - Sun 17:00. **Ref: YH06333**

HALLS, IAN S
Ian S Halls DWCF, Ten Acres, Woodcote Lane, Bromsgrove, **Worcestershire**, B61 9EE, **ENGLAND**.
(T) 01562 83472.
Profile Farrier. **Ref: YH06334**

HALLUM, DAVID J
David J Hallum DWCF, 5 Brimley Hill, Kingsclere, Newbury, **Berkshire**, RG20 8PN, **ENGLAND**.
(T) 01635 299021.
Profile Farrier. **Ref: YH06335**

HALSALL RIDING & LIVERY CTRE
Halsall Riding & Livery Centre, Terra Nova, Gregory Lane, Halsall, Ormskirk, **Lancashire**, L39 8SP, **ENGLAND**.
(T) 01704 840001.
Contact/s
Owner: Mrs J Beilensohn
Profile Riding School, Stable/Livery. **Ref: YH06336**

HALSDON ARABIANS
Halsdon Arabians, Dolton, Winkleigh, **Devon**, EX19 8RS, **ENGLAND**.
(T) 01805 603635 **(F)** 01805 603639.
Profile Breeder. **Ref: YH06337**

HALWILL ELITE LIVERY SVS
Halwill Elite Livery Services, Isted Hse, Halwill, Beaworthy, **Devon**, EX21 5UJ, **ENGLAND**.
(T) 01409 221343.
Profile Stable/Livery, Trainer. **Ref: YH06338**

HAM FARM LIVERY & STUD
Ham Farm Livery & Stud, Ham Farm/Ham Lane, North End, Yatton, Bristol, **Bristol**, BS49 4QL, **ENGLAND**.
(T) 01934 832154.
Contact/s
Owner: Mr D Crossman
Profile Breeder, Stable/Livery. **Ref: YH06339**

HAM HSE STABLES
Ham House Stables, Ham Hse, Scaynes Hill, Haywards Heath, **Sussex (West)**, RH17 7NP, **ENGLAND**.
(T) 01444 831585.
Profile Stable/Livery. **Ref: YH06340**

HAM POLO CLUB
Ham Polo Club (The), 20 Queens Rd, Thames Ditton, **Surrey**, KT7 0QX, **ENGLAND**.
(T) 020 8334 0000
(E) office@hampoloclub.org.uk.
Contact/s
Secretary: Mrs P Bannister
Profile Polo club. **Ref: YH06341**

HAM, G A
Mr G A Ham, Rose Farm, Rooksbridge, Axbridge, **Somerset**, BS26 2TH, **ENGLAND**.
(T) 01934 750331 **(F)** 01934 750331.
Profile Trainer. **Ref: YH06342**

HAMAR, ROSITA J
Rosita J Hamar, Lagden Farm, Colebatch, Bishops Castle, **Shropshire**, SY9 5JY, **ENGLAND**.
(T) 01588 638252 **(F)** 01588 638794
(W) www.hamarshorses.co.uk.
Contact/s
Owner: Rosita Hamar
(E) rositahamar@lineone.net
Profile Breeder. **No.Staff:** 2 **Yr. Est:** 1987
C.Size: 40 Acres **Ref: YH06343**

HAMBLE VALLEY RIDING CLUB
Hamble Valley Riding Club, Burwood, 37 Chapel Rd, West End, **Hampshire**, SO30 3FG, **ENGLAND**.
(T) 023 80476756.
Contact/s
Secretary: Miss C King
Profile Club/Association, Riding Club. **Ref: YH06344**

HAMER, WAYNE
Wayne Hamer DWCF, 97 Limpsfield Rd, Warlingham, **Surrey**, CR6 9RH, **ENGLAND**.
(T) 01883 622532.
Profile Farrier. **Ref: YH06345**

HAMES SADDLERY
Hames Saddlery, Bank Hse, Market St, Stratton, Bude, **Cornwall**, EX23 9DF, **ENGLAND**.
(T) 01288 356162.
Contact/s
Owner: Mr A Hames
Profile Saddlery Retailer. **Ref: YH06346**

HAMILTON PK RACE COURSE
Hamilton Park Race Course Co Ltd, Hamilton Pk Racecourse, Bothwell Rd, Hamilton, **Lanarkshire (South)**, ML3 0DZ, **SCOTLAND**.
(T) 01698 283806 **(F)** 01698 286621.
Contact/s
Chief Executive: Mrs M Gray
Profile Track/Course. **Ref: YH06347**

HAMILTON RACING
Hamilton Racing, 6 Council Hses, Eastbury, Hungerford, **Berkshire**, RG17 7JG, **ENGLAND**.
(T) 01488 72222.
Profile Trainer. **Ref: YH06348**

HAMILTON SHOW WEAR
Hamilton Show Wear, 7 Mansfield Rd, Urmston, Manchester, **Manchester (Greater)**, M41 6HF, **ENGLAND**.
(T) 0161 7479817 **(F)** 0161 7479817.
Contact/s
Owner: Mrs M Ogden
Profile Riding Wear Retailer. **Ref: YH06349**

HAMILTON STABLES
Hamilton Stables, Hamilton Rd, Newmarket, **Suffolk**, CB8 7JQ, **ENGLAND**.
(T) 01638 660013
(M) 0860 680803
(W) www.newmarketracehorsetrainers.co.uk
Affiliated Bodies Newmarket Trainers Fed.
Contact/s
Trainer: Mr P Mitchell **(T)** 0860 680803
(E) mitchell@hamiltonstables.fsnet.co.uk
Profile Trainer. **Ref: YH06350**

HAMILTON, A
Mrs A Hamilton, Claywalls Farm, Capheaton, Newcastle-upon-Tyne, **Tyne and Wear**, NE19 2BP, **ENGLAND**.
(T) 01830 530219.
Profile Supplies. **Ref: YH06351**

HAMILTON, C
Miss C Hamilton, High Ash Barn, Sandy Lane, Chisworth, Glossop, **Derbyshire**, SK13 5RZ, **ENGLAND**.
(T) 01457 857023.
Profile Breeder. **Ref: YH06352**

HAMILTON, H B
Miss H B Hamilton, Whitehope, Innerleithen, **Scottish Borders**, EH44 6NN, **SCOTLAND**.
(T) 01896 830288.
Profile Breeder. **Ref: YH06353**

HAMILTON-FAIRLEY, A J
Mrs A J Hamilton-Fairley, Moor Pl, Plough Lane, Bramshill, Basingstoke, **Hampshire**, RG25 0RF, **ENGLAND**.
(T) 0118 9326269
(M) 07798 577761.
Profile Supplies. **Ref: YH06354**

HAMISH MACLEAN FARM PRODUCTS
Hamish Maclean Farm Products, Unit 9-10 Auction Mart, Halston Ind Est, Kirkwall, **Orkney Isles**, KW15 1RE, **SCOTLAND**.
(T) 01856 871700.
Profile Feed Merchant. **Ref: YH06355**

HAMLYN-WRIGHT HORSE RUGS
Hamlyn-Wright Horse Rugs, 33 Blundell Lane, Cobham, **Surrey**, KT11 2SU, **ENGLAND**.
(T) 01372 843960.
Profile Supplies. **Ref: YH06356**

HAMMER & TONGS
Hammer & Tongs, Setherwood Yard, Stocks Rd, Aldbury, Tring, **Hertfordshire**, HP23 5RX, **ENGLAND**.
(T) 01442 851007 **(F)** 01442 851007.
Contact/s
Owner: Mr P Elliott
Profile Blacksmith. **Ref: YH06357**

HAMMER 'N' HOE
Hammer 'n' Hoe, Goldmartin Sq, Mawnan Smith, Falmouth, **Cornwall**, TR11 5EP, **ENGLAND**.
(T) 01326 250137 **(F)** 01326 250137.
Profile Supplies. **Ref: YH06358**

HAMMOND LIVERY STABLES
Hammond Livery Stables, Woodstock Lane South, Chessington, **Surrey**, KT9 1UF, **ENGLAND**.
(T) 020 83987855.
Contact/s
Owner: Mrs C Hammond
Profile Stable/Livery. **Ref: YH06359**

HAMMOND, DAVID
David Hammond, 61 Old Mill Rd, Scarva, Craigavon, **County Armagh**, BT63 6NN, **NORTHERN IRELAND**.
(T) 028 38831556.
Profile Transport/Horse Boxes. **Ref: YH06360**

HAMMOND, WILLIAM E
William E Hammond DWCF BII, Wern Isaf, Nant Y Ffrith, Bwlchgwyn, **Wrexham**, LL11 5YR, **WALES**.
(T) 01978 759786.
Profile Farrier. **Ref: YH06361**

HAMMONDS
Hammonds Feeds (Huyton Ltd), Unit 5 Wilsons Business Ctre, Wilson Rd, Huyton, **Merseyside**, L36

A-Z of COMPANIES

6AN, **ENGLAND**.
(T) 0151 4804377 **(F)** 0151 4804021
(E) hammondsfeeds@hotmail.com
(W) www.hammondfeeds.co.uk.
Contact/s
Owner: Mrs J Young
Profile Feed Merchant. Yr. Est: 1977
Ref: **YH06362**

HAMPDEN & SIMONSIDE VETNRY

Hampden & Simonside Veterinary Group (Alnwick), Belvedere Trce, Alnwick, **Northumberland**, NE66 2NX, **ENGLAND**.
(T) 01665 602516 **(F)** 01665 605550.
Profile Medical Support. Ref: **YH06363**

HAMPSHIRE CARRIAGE

Hampshire Carriage Co, 8 Broxhead Trading Est, Broxhead Farm Rd, Lindford, Bordon, **Hampshire**, GU35 0JX, **ENGLAND**.
(T) 01420 478857 **(F)** 01420 478857.
Profile Transport/Horse Boxes. Ref: **YH06364**

HAMPSHIRE CTRY RIDE

Hampshire Country Ride, West Stoke Farm, Stoke Charity, Winchester, **Hampshire**, SO21 3PN, **ENGLAND**.
(T) 01962 760220 **(F)** 01962 760220.
Contact/s
Hon Secretary: G J Rowsell Ref: **YH06365**

HAMPSHIRE RURAL RIDING CLUB

Hampshire Rural Riding Club, Seven Oaks, 39 Abbey Rd, Medstead, Alton, **Hampshire**, GU34 5PB, **ENGLAND**.
(T) 01252 795252.
Contact/s
Chairman: Mrs S Sansom
Profile Club/Association, Riding Club. Ref: **YH06366**

HAMPSHIRE SADDLERY

Hampshire Saddlery, Botley Mills, Botley, Southampton, **Hampshire**, SO30 2GB, **ENGLAND**.
(T) 01489 783616.
Profile Saddlery Retailer. Ref: **YH06367**

HAMPSLEY HOLLOW

Hampsley Hollow Riding Centre, Hempsley Hollow, Heddington, Calne, **Wiltshire**, SN11 0PP, **ENGLAND**.
(T) 01380 850333 **(F)** 01380 850367.
Contact/s
Partner: Miss A Frankes
Profile Holidays, Riding School.
Cross country schooling fences. Residential riding holidays for children aged 8 - 15 years, with or without their own pony. Access to downs but no road riding. The centre has four instructors, all BHS qualified.
No.Staff: 7 Yr. Est: 1971 C.Size: 35 Acres
Opening Times
Sp: Open Mon - Sun 09:00. Closed Mon - Sun 20:00.
Su: Open Mon - Sun 09:00. Closed Mon - Sun 20:00.
Au: Open Mon - Sun 09:00. Closed Mon - Sun 20:00.
Wn: Open Mon - Sun 09:00. Closed Mon - Sun 20:00. Ref: **YH06368**

HAMPSON, P

P Hampson, Clifton Hse, Mill Lane, Lindford, Bordon, **Hampshire**, GU35 0PE, **ENGLAND**.
(T) 01420 473963.
Contact/s
Owner: Mrs H Hampson
Profile Farrier. Ref: **YH06369**

HAMPTON VETNRY GRP

Hampton Veterinary Group, Hampton Heath, Malpas, **Cheshire**, SY14 8JQ, **ENGLAND**.
(T) 01948 820345 **(F)** 01948 820688.
Profile Medical Support. Ref: **YH06370**

HAMSEY RIDING SCHOOL

Hamsey Riding School, Brighton Rd, Lewes, **Sussex (East)**, BN7 3JH, **ENGLAND**.
(T) 01273 477120 **(F)** 01273 477120.
Contact/s
Partner: Mr R Goldstein
Profile Riding School.
Hacking is also available. Yr. Est: 1979
C.Size: 2 Acres
Opening Times
Sp: Open Tues - Sun 10:30. Closed Tues - Sun 17:30.
Su: Open Tues - Sun 10:30. Closed Tues - Sun 17:30.
Au: Open Tues - Sun 10:30. Closed Tues - Sun 17:30.
Wn: Open Tues - Sun 10:30. Closed Tues - Sun 17:30.
Closed Mondays Ref: **YH06371**

HAMSTERLEY RIDING SCHOOL

Hamsterley Riding School & Livery Stable, Hamsterley, Bishop Auckland, **County Durham**, DL13 3NH, **ENGLAND**.
(T) 01388 488328
(W) www.geocities.com/hamsterleyridingschool
Affiliated Bodies ABRS.
Contact/s
Owner: Mrs J Dennis
Profile Horse/Rider Accom, Riding School, Stable/Livery.
Full, part & DIY livery available, prices on request.
No.Staff: 6 Yr. Est: 1970 C.Size: 32.5 Acres
Opening Times
Sp: Open Mon - Sun 08:00. Closed Mon - Sun 20:00.
Su: Open Mon - Sun 08:00. Closed Mon - Sun 20:00.
Au: Open Mon - Sun 08:00. Closed Mon - Sun 20:00.
Wn: Open Mon - Sun 08:00. Closed Mon - Sun 20:00. Ref: **YH06372**

HANBURY PK STUD

Hanbury Park Stud, Anslow Rd, Hanbury, Burton-on-Trent, **Staffordshire**, DE13 8TU, **ENGLAND**.
(T) 01283 820031.
Profile Breeder. Ref: **YH06373**

HANBURY, B

B Hanbury, Hamilton Rd, Newmarket, **Suffolk**, CB8 0PD, **ENGLAND**.
(T) 01638 664799 **(F)** 01638 667209
(W) www.race-horses.com
Affiliated Bodies Newmarket Trainers Fed.
Contact/s
Trainer: Mr B Hanbury
Profile Trainer. Ref: **YH06374**

HANCOCK, J & V

J & V Hancock, Woodhouse Farm, Redhill, Telford, **Shropshire**, TF2 9NZ, **ENGLAND**.
(T) 01952 612822.
Profile Breeder, Stable/Livery. Ref: **YH06375**

HANCOX, J & J

J & J Hancox, The Sunrising Stud, The Butts Farm, South Cerney, Cirencester, **Gloucestershire**, GL7 5QE, **ENGLAND**.
(T) 01285 862205.
Profile Breeder. Ref: **YH06376**

HAND EQUESTRIAN CTRE

Hand Equestrian Centre, Davis Lane, Clevedon, **Somerset (North)**, BS21 6TG, **ENGLAND**.
(T) 01275 874856 **(F)** 01275 878439
Affiliated Bodies BSJA.
Contact/s
General Manager: Ms D Spriggs
Profile Equestrian Centre. Yr. Est: 1985
Ref: **YH06377**

HANDEL, PETER

Peter Handel DWCF, 2 Gaer Lane, Forden, Welshpool, **Powys**, SY21 8NR, **WALES**.
(T) 01686 668821.
Profile Farrier. Ref: **YH06378**

HANDLEY, PETER CHARLES

Peter Charles Handley AFCL Hons, Moreton Wood Forge, Moreton Wood, Market Drayton, **Shropshire**, TF9 3SE, **ENGLAND**.
(T) 01948 890301.
Profile Farrier. Ref: **YH06379**

HANDLING AIDS

Handling Aids Ltd, Crowe Arch Lane, Ringwood, **Hampshire**, BH24 1PB, **ENGLAND**.
(T) 01425 472264 **(F)** 01425 471248.
Profile Transport/Horse Boxes. Ref: **YH06380**

HANDMADE SHOES UK

Handmade Shoes UK Ltd., Croften Rd, Mentmore, Leighton Buzzard, **Bedfordshire**, LU7 0QJ, **ENGLAND**.
(T) 01296 662473 **(F)** 01296 660779.
Contact/s
Owner: Mr B Crothers
Profile Supplies. Horseshoe Manufacturer and Farrier Tool Supplier. Yr. Est: 1996
Opening Times
Sp: Open Mon - Fri 09:00. Closed Mon - Fri 18:00.
Su: Open Mon - Fri 09:00. Closed Mon - Fri 18:00.
Au: Open Mon - Fri 09:00. Closed Mon - Fri 18:00.
Wn: Open Mon - Fri 09:00. Closed Mon - Fri 18:00.
Ref: **YH06381**

HANDSOME HORSES

Handsome Horses, 195A High St, Cottenham, Cambridge, **Cambridgeshire**, CB4 8RX, **ENGLAND**.
(T) 01954 206061 **(F)** 01954 206061.
Contact/s
Owner: Miss E Trezise
Profile Supplies. Ref: **YH06382**

HANDSWORTH RIDING STABLES

Handsworth Riding Stables, Waverley Lane, Handsworth, Sheffield, **Yorkshire (South)**, S13 9AA, **ENGLAND**.
(T) 0114 2440546.
Profile Farrier. Ref: **YH06383**

HANEY, B

B Haney, Unit J3 Doulton Trading Est, Doulton Rd, Rowley Regis, **Midlands (West)**, B65 8JQ, **ENGLAND**.
(T) 01384 257400.
Contact/s
Owner: Mrs B Haney
Profile Blacksmith. Ref: **YH06384**

HANFORD TRAILER SPARES

Hanford Trailer Spares, 152 Stone Rd, Stoke-on-Trent, **Staffordshire**, ST4 8NS, **ENGLAND**.
(T) 01782 658594.
Profile Transport/Horse Boxes. Ref: **YH06385**

HANGLETON FARM

Hangleton Farm Equestrian Centre, Hangleton Lane, Ferring, Worthing, **Sussex (West)**, BN12 6PP, **ENGLAND**.
(T) 01903 240352.
Contact/s
Owner: Mr C Ellis
Profile Riding School, Stable/Livery. Ref: **YH06386**

HANKEY, R P

R P Hankey, Hole Hse Farm, Wash Lane, Allostock, Knutsford, **Cheshire**, WA16 9JS, **ENGLAND**.
(T) 01565 722437.
Profile Stable/Livery. Ref: **YH06387**

HANKIN, WILLIAM D & DAVID M

William D & David M Hankin DWCF, Ashleigh, 116 Moss Lane, Hesketh Bank, Preston, **Lancashire**, PR4 6AD, **ENGLAND**.
(T) 01772 816914.
Profile Farrier. Ref: **YH06388**

HANKINSON, JOHN DEREK

John Derek Hankinson AFCL, 8 Wilford Rd, Hilcott, Pewsey, Marlborough, **Wiltshire**, **ENGLAND**.
(M) 07808219492.
Profile Farrier. Ref: **YH06389**

HANLEY, DAVID

David Hanley, Maddenstown Lodge, Maddenstown, The Curragh, **County Kildare**, **IRELAND**.
(T) 016 288839 **(F)** 016 288873.
Contact/s
Trainer: Mr D Hanley
(E) davidhanley@kildarehorse.ie
Profile Trainer. Ref: **YH06390**

HANN, JAMES S

James S Hann, Beechcroft, Hallworthy, Camelford, **Cornwall**, PL32 9SJ, **ENGLAND**.
(T) 01840 261666.
Profile Farrier. Ref: **YH06391**

HANN, PRISCILLA

Priscilla Hann, Tetstill, Neen Scollars, Cleobury Mortimer, Kidderminster, **Worcestershire**, DY14 9AH, **ENGLAND**.
(T) 01299 270414 **(F)** 01299 271156.
Profile Sculptor. Ref: **YH06392**

HANNA TRAILERS

Hanna Trailers Ltd, 642 Saintfield Rd, Carryduff, Belfast, **County Antrim**, BT8 8BT, **NORTHERN IRELAND**.
(T) 028 90812410 **(F)** 028 90812410.
Contact/s
Owner: Mr R Hanna
Profile Transport/Horse Boxes. Ref: **YH06393**

HANNAH, DAVID

David Hannah DWCF, Summerhill Hse, 51 Springfield Rd, Bigrigg, Egremont, **Cumbria**, CA22 2TQ, **ENGLAND**.
(T) 01946 812581.
Profile Farrier. Ref: **YH06394**

HANNON, R

R Hannon, East Everleigh Stables, Everleigh, Marlborough, **Wiltshire**, SN8 3EY, **ENGLAND**.
(T) 01264 850254 **(F)** 01264 850820.
Profile Trainer. **Ref: YH06395**

HANNS HALL LIVERY

Hanns Hall Livery, Hanns Hall Rd, Willaston, **Cheshire**, L64 2TQ, **ENGLAND**.
(T) 0151 3538080.
Profile Stable/Livery. **Ref: YH06396**

HANSFORDS

Hansfords, 3 High St, Fareham, **Hampshire**, PO16 7AN, **ENGLAND**.
(T) 01329 280213.
Profile Saddlery Retailer. **Ref: YH06397**

HANSON, S

S Hanson, Longhurst Farm, Buxton Rd, Furness Vale, High Peak, **Derbyshire**, SK23 7PH, **ENGLAND**.
(T) 01663 742525.
Contact/s
Owner: Ms S Hanson
Profile Breeder. **Ref: YH06398**

HAPPY HORSE

Happy Horse, Fox Lane, 21 Airyhall Rd, Aberdeen, **Aberdeen (City of)**, AB15 7QT, **SCOTLAND**.
Profile Supplies. **Ref: YH06399**

HAPPY TACK

Happy Tack, 8 Main St, Keyworth, Nottingham, **Nottinghamshire**, NG12 5AD, **ENGLAND**.
(T) 0115 9372227.
Profile Riding Wear Retailer. **Ref: YH06400**

HAPPY VALLEY RIDING STABLES

Happy Valley Riding Stables, Slonk Hill Farm, New Barn Rd, Shoreham By Sea, **Sussex (West)**, BN43 6HL, **ENGLAND**.
(T) 01273 464537.
Contact/s
Owner: Mrs E Turrell
Profile Riding School, Stable/Livery. **Ref: YH06401**

HAPS PET & ANIMAL FEEDS

Haps Pet & Animal Feeds, Hennock Rd, Marsh Barton, Exeter, **Devon**, EX2 8NN, **ENGLAND**.
(T) 01392 424240.
Profile Supplies. **Ref: YH06402**

HARBIT & RYDER

Harbit & Ryder, Mill Surgery, Taybridge Trce, Aberfeldy, **Perth and Kinross**, PH15 2BS, **SCOTLAND**.
(T) 01887 20771.
Profile Medical Support. **Ref: YH06403**

HARBRO FARM SALES

Harbro Farm Sales Ltd, Markethill, Turriff, **Aberdeenshire**, AB53 4PA, **SCOTLAND**.
(T) 01888 545206 **(F)** 01888 563939.
Profile Saddlery Retailer. **Ref: YH06404**

HARBRO FARM SALES

Harbro Farm Sales Ltd, Thainstone Agricultural Ctre, Inverurie, **Aberdeenshire**, AB51 5XZ, **SCOTLAND**.
(T) 01467 623822.
Profile Supplies. **Ref: YH06405**

HARCOURT STUD

Harcourt Stud, Newton Harcourt, Leicester, **Leicestershire**, LE8 9FH, **ENGLAND**.
(T) 0116 2593752.
Contact/s
Owner: Mr P Millington
Profile Breeder. **Ref: YH06406**

HARDAKER, S J

Mr S J Hardaker DWCF, 14 Booth Bridge Lane, Thornton in Craven, Skipton, **Yorkshire (North)**, BD23 3TE, **ENGLAND**.
(T) 07091 001283.
Profile Farrier. **Ref: YH06407**

HARDCASTLE, C

C Hardcastle, 62 Top Lane, Copmanthorpe, **Yorkshire (North)**, YO23 3UJ, **ENGLAND**.
(T) 01904 703726.
Profile Farrier. **Ref: YH06408**

HARDERN YOUNG & OTTY

Hardern Young & Otty, Rosevean Hse, Penzance, **Cornwall**, TR18 3HU, **ENGLAND**.
(T) 01736 362215.
Profile Medical Support. **Ref: YH06409**

HARDHAM, M G

Mrs M G Hardham, Upper Knolls Farm, Frogs Gutter, Stiperstones, Minsterley, **Shropshire**, SY5 0NL, **ENGLAND**.
(T) 01588 650362.
Profile Breeder. **Ref: YH06410**

HARDING, E J

E J Harding RSS, 49 Strathmore Dr, Verwood, Wimborne, **Dorset**, BH31 7BJ, **ENGLAND**.
(T) 01202 827641.
Profile Farrier. **Ref: YH06411**

HARDING, J

J Harding, Chimney St Farm, Hundon, Sudbury, **Suffolk**, CO10 8DX, **ENGLAND**.
(T) 01440 786246.
Profile Breeder. **Ref: YH06412**

HARDINGHAM FARMS

Hardingham Farms Limited, Hardingham Hall, Norwich, **Norfolk**, NR9 4AE, **ENGLAND**.
(T) 01953 851829.
Profile Stable/Livery. **Ref: YH06413**

HARDWEAR CLOTHING

Hardwear Clothing, 78 Hagley Rd, Stourbridge, **Midlands (West)**, DY8 1QU, **ENGLAND**.
(T) 01384 370843 **(F)** 01384 370843.
Profile Riding Wear Retailer. **Ref: YH06414**

HARDWICK STABLES

Hardwick Stables, Horsecroft Rd, Bury St Edmunds, **Suffolk**, IP29 5NY, **ENGLAND**.
(T) 01284 766570.
Contact/s
Owner: Miss H Harris
Profile Stable/Livery. **Ref: YH06415**

HARDWICKE LODGE STABLES

Hardwicke Lodge Stables, Hardwicke Lodge Farm, Forest Rd, Enderby, Leicester, **Leicestershire**, LE9 5LD, **ENGLAND**.
(T) 0116 2863056 **(F)** 0116 2863056
(E) hardwicke.ridingstables@virgin.net
Affiliated Bodies BHS.
Contact/s
General Manager: Mrs J Smith **(Q)** BHSAI
Profile Arena, Riding School, Stable/Livery.
Discipline riding, Pony Club and mounted games. Specialise in teaching children. Yr. Est: 1991
Ref: YH06416

HARDY, R C C

Mr R C C Hardy, Springfield Hse, Gillingham, **Dorset**, SP8 5RD, **ENGLAND**.
(T) 01747 62501.
Profile Supplies. **Ref: YH06417**

HARDY, RUSSELL C

Russell C Hardy DWCF, Knighton Farm Cottage, 160 Netheravon Rd, Durrington, Salisbury, **Wiltshire**, SP4 8AT, **ENGLAND**.
(T) 01980 655537
(M) 07802 354167.
Profile Farrier. **Ref: YH06418**

HARDY, W

Mr W Hardy, Harlow Wood Farm, Park Lane, Lambley, **Nottinghamshire**, NG4 4QA, **ENGLAND**.
(T) 0115 9312519.
Profile Supplies. **Ref: YH06419**

HARELAW EQUESTRIAN CTRE

Harelaw Equestrian Centre, 2 Harelaw Farm Cottages, Longniddry, **Lothian (East)**, EH32 0PH, **SCOTLAND**.
(T) 01875 853559.
Contact/s
Owner: Mr M Bain
Profile Riding School.
Beach rides are also available. Yr. Est: 1989
Opening Times
Sp: Open Mon - Sun 09:00. Closed Mon - Sun 20:00.
Su: Open Mon - Sun 09:00. Closed Mon - Sun 20:00.
Au: Open Mon - Sun 09:00. Closed Mon - Sun 20:00.
Wn: Open Mon - Sun 09:00. Closed Mon - Sun 20:00. **Ref: YH06420**

HAREWOOD LIVERY STABLES

Harewood Livery Stables, New Laithe Farm, Harewood Ave, Harewood, Leeds, **Yorkshire (West)**, LS17 9LB, **ENGLAND**.
(T) 0113 2886621 **(F)** 0113 2886621.
Contact/s
Owner: Mr J Thackary
Profile Stable/Livery. **Ref: YH06421**

HARFORTH, J F

J F Harforth, Stanley Grange Stud, Great Ayton, Middlesbrough, **Cleveland**, TS9 6QD, **ENGLAND**.
(T) 01642 722386.
Contact/s
Secretary: Andrea Charlesworth
Profile Breeder. **Ref: YH06422**

HARGATE EQUESTRIAN

Hargate Equestrian, Egginton Rd, Hilton, Derby, **Derbyshire**, DE65 5FJ, **ENGLAND**.
(T) 01283 730606.
Contact/s
Owner: Ms C Smith
Profile Saddlery Retailer. **Ref: YH06423**

HARGATE HILL

Hargate Hill, Hargate Hill, Glossop, **Derbyshire**, SK13 6JL, **ENGLAND**.
(T) 01457 865518.
Contact/s
Owner: Mr M Tyldesley
Profile Riding School, Stable/Livery. **Ref: YH06424**

HARGREAVE EQUINE SVS

Hargreave Equine Services, Fallodon Mill, Chathill, **Northumberland**, NE67 5ED, **ENGLAND**.
(T) 01665 589273.
Contact/s
Partner: Mrs K Hargreaves
Profile Stable/Livery, Track/Course, Trainer.
Ref: YH06425

HARGREAVES BANNISTER

Hargreaves Bannister Ltd, Corn Mill, Laneshawbridge, Colne, **Lancashire**, BB18 7HX, **ENGLAND**.
(T) 01282 865084.
Profile Supplies. **Ref: YH06426**

HARGREAVES, G

G Hargreaves, 391 Wheatley Lane Rd, Fence, Burnley, **Lancashire**, BB12 9PZ, **ENGLAND**.
(T) 01282 618919.
Profile Transport/Horse Boxes. **Ref: YH06427**

HARGREAVES, PAUL W

Paul W Hargreaves DWCF, Linden Villa, Bordel Lane, Vale, **Guernsey**, GY3 5DB, **ENGLAND**.
(T) 01481 43202.
Profile Farrier. **Ref: YH06428**

HARGREAVES, TERENCE D

Terence D Hargreaves AFCL BI, Highbank Cottage, 8 Birches Lane, Lostock Green, Northwich, **Cheshire**, CW9 7SL, **ENGLAND**.
(T) 01606 40110
(M) 07860 319427.
Profile Farrier. **Ref: YH06429**

HARKAWAY CLUB

Harkaway Club, Farley Farm, Farley Lane, Romsley, Halesowen, **Midlands (West)**, B62 0LN, **ENGLAND**.
(T) 01562 710292.
Profile Club/Association. **Ref: YH06430**

HARKER, G A

Mr G A Harker, Oldhall Cottage, Pepper Arden, East Cowton, Northallerton, **Yorkshire (North)**, DL7 0JF, **ENGLAND**.
(T) 01325 378634.
Profile Supplies. **Ref: YH06431**

HARKER, MICHAEL

Michael Harker, Kirkbys Farm, Nangreaves, Bury, **Lancashire**, BL9 6TB, **ENGLAND**.
(T) 01706 824660.
Profile Blood Stock Agency. **Ref: YH06432**

HARLAND, GARRY

Garry Harland AWCF, 14 Parklands, Spofforth, Harrogate, **Yorkshire (North)**, HG3 1DB, **ENGLAND**.
(T) 01937 590365.
Profile Farrier. **Ref: YH06433**

HARLAND, JOHN W

John W Harland, Green Cross Hse, Plumpton Lane, Plumpton, Lewes, **Sussex (East)**, BN7 3AD, **ENGLAND**.
(T) 01273 891125.
Profile Farrier. **Ref: YH06434**

HARLAND, PHIL

Phil Harland, 24 Drome Rd, Copmanthorpe, York, **Yorkshire (North)**, YO23 3TG, **ENGLAND**.
(T) 01904 708437.

Profile Farrier. Ref:YH06435

HARLEY

Harley Equestrian, 24 Station Rd, Woodford Halse, Daventry, **Northamptonshire**, NN11 3RB, **ENGLAND**.
(T) 01327 260818 (F) 01327 264941.
Contact/s
Owner: Mrs T Habgood
Profile Saddlery Retailer. Ref:YH06436

HARLEY HORSEBOXES

Harley Horseboxes, Visicks Works, Perranwell Station, Truro, **Cornwall**, TR3 7NB, **ENGLAND**.
(T) 01872 870204.
Contact/s
Owner: Mr J Davies
Profile Transport/Horse Boxes. Ref:YH06437

HARLEY, JEREMY

Harley Jeremy, New Rathbride Stables, Rathbride, **County Kildare**, **IRELAND**.
(T) 045 522377.
Profile Supplies. Ref:YH06438

HARLEY, THOMAS H

Thomas H Harley, 41 Boston Rd, East Ham, **London (Greater)**, E6 3NH, **ENGLAND**.
(T) 020 84704994.
Profile Farrier. Ref:YH06439

HARLOW BROTHERS

Harlow Brothers Ltd, Long Whatton, Loughborough, **Leicestershire**, LE12 5DE, **ENGLAND**.
(T) 01509 842561 (F) 01509 843577.
Contact/s
Owner: Mr J Harlow
Profile Transport/Horse Boxes. Ref:YH06440

HARMAN, CHARLES

Charles Harman, 20 Lisburn Rd, Newmarket, **Suffolk**, CB8 8HS, **ENGLAND**.
(T) 01638 662610.
Profile Farrier. Ref:YH06441

HARMAN, M W

M W Harman, 1 Approach Rd, Taplow, Maidenhead, **Berkshire**, SL6 0NP, **ENGLAND**.
(T) 01628 630556.
Profile Farrier. Ref:YH06442

HARMANS

Harmans, 110 Weyhill, Haslemere, **Surrey**, GU27 1HS, **ENGLAND**.
(T) 01428 643501.
Contact/s
Owner: Mr J Harman
Profile Transport/Horse Boxes. Ref:YH06443

HARMANS HAULAGE CONTRACTORS

Harmans Haulage Contractors, Modden Farm, Hollywater Rd, Bordon, **Hampshire**, GU35 0AE, **ENGLAND**.
(T) 01428 751340 (F) 01428 751761.
Contact/s
Owner: Mr J Harman
Profile Transport/Horse Boxes. Ref:YH06444

HARMONY & HEALTH FORMULATIONS

Harmony & Health Formulations, P O Box 6061, London, **London (Greater)**, W2 5WD, **ENGLAND**.
(T) 020 88139959 (F) 020 85715337
(E) info@hhflld.com.
Profile Medical Support. Ref:YH06445

HARMSWORTH FARM

Harmsworth Farm Equestrian Centre Ltd, Curbridge, Botley, Southampton, **Hampshire**, SO30 2HB, **ENGLAND**.
(T) 01489 783869
(E) harmsworth@totalise.co.uk.
Contact/s
Owner: Mrs S Richards (Q) BHSAI
Profile Breeder, Equestrian Centre, Stable/Livery.
Yr. Est: 1994
Opening Times
Telephone for an appointment Ref:YH06446

HARNESS ROOM

Harness Room (The), Rob Roy Cottage, Pilley St, Pilley, Lymington, **Hampshire**, SO41 5QP, **ENGLAND**.
(T) 01590 689259.
Contact/s
Owner: Mrs H Black
Profile Riding Wear Retailer, Saddlery Retailer.
Ref:YH06447

HARNOR STUD

Harnor Stud, Moorside Farm, Onecote, Leek, **Staffordshire**, ST13 7SD, **ENGLAND**.
(T) 01538 304281
(E) sharon@norweign-fjord-horse.co.uk.
Profile Breeder, Stud Farm. Ref:YH06448

HAROLDS PK RIDING CTRE

Harolds Park Riding Centre, Bentland Farm, Harold Pk, Nazeing, Waltham Abbey, **Essex**, EN9 2SF, **ENGLAND**.
(T) 01992 893948 (F) 01992 891109.
Contact/s
Owner: Mr G Mackie
Profile Equestrian Centre, Riding School.
Ref:YH06449

HARPENDENBURY STABLES

Harpendenbury Stables, 2 Ivy Cottages, Harpendenbury, Redbourn, St Albans, **Hertfordshire**, AL3 7PZ, **ENGLAND**.
(T) 01582 792779.
Profile Riding School. Ref:YH06450

HARPER ADAMS

Harper Adams University College, Library Department, Newport, **Shropshire**, TF10 8NB, **ENGLAND**.
(T) 01952 820280 (F) 01952 814783.
Profile Equestrian Centre. Ref:YH06451

HARPER FOLD STABLES

Harper Fold Stables, Harper Fold Farm, Lavender St, Radcliffe, Manchester, **Manchester (Greater)**, M26 3TJ, **ENGLAND**.
(T) 0161 7245827.
Contact/s
Owner: Mrs P Lysak
Profile Stable/Livery.
DIY Livery. Regular worming programme. Fully insured. Yr. Est: 1996 C.Size: 100 Acres
Opening Times
Sp: Open Mon - Sun 06:30. Closed Mon - Sun 21:30.
Su: Open Mon - Sun 06:30. Closed Mon - Sun 21:30.
Au: Open Mon - Sun 06:30. Closed Mon - Sun 21:30.
Wn: Open Mon - Sun 06:30. Closed Mon - Sun 21:30. Ref:YH06452

HARPER, D

D Harper, Shaw Hill Farm, 487 Fox Hill Rd, Sheffield, **Yorkshire (South)**, S6 1BL, **ENGLAND**.
(T) 0114 2311925.
Contact/s
Manager: Ms J Harper Ref:YH06453

HARPER, D & R

D & R Harper, Carn-Ifor Farm, Prince Phillip Ave, Garnlydan, Ebbw Vale, **Blaenau Gwent**, MP23 5DE, **WALES**.
(T) 01495 304877.
Profile Breeder. Ref:YH06454

HARPER, R C

Mr R C Harper, Home Farm, Kings Sutton, Banbury, **Oxfordshire**, OX17 3RY, **ENGLAND**.
(T) 01295 810997.
Profile Supplies. Ref:YH06455

HARPERLAND LIVERY

Harperland Livery, 2B Harperland, Dundonald, Kilmarnock, **Ayrshire (East)**, KA2 9BY, **SCOTLAND**.
(T) 01563 850206.
Contact/s
Owner: Miss A Lauchlan
Profile Stable/Livery.
Full, part, DIY and grass livery available, prices on request. Yr. Est: 2000
Opening Times
Sp: Open Mon - Sun 09:00. Closed Mon - Sun 21:00.
Su: Open Mon - Sun 09:00. Closed Mon - Sun 21:00.
Au: Open Mon - Sun 09:00. Closed Mon - Sun 21:00.
Wn: Open Mon - Sun 09:00. Closed Mon - Sun 21:00. Ref:YH06456

HARRELL, CHRISTOPHER J

Christopher J Harrell AFCL, 15 Linhouse Drive, East Clader, **Lothian (West)**, EH53 0DG, **SCOTLAND**.
(T) 07973 187758.
Profile Farrier. Ref:YH06457

HARRIES, STELLA

Stella Harries, Little Barn, Ascot Rd, Nuptown, Warfield, Bracknell, **Berkshire**, RG42 6HR, **ENGLAND**.
(T) 01344 882064.
Profile Breeder. Ref:YH06458

HARRIET GLEN DESIGN

Harriet Glen Design, Claypits Farm, Winfrith, Dorchester, **Dorset**, DT2 8JX, **ENGLAND**.
(T) 01305 852803 (F) 01305 852740
(E) david.walsh@ukgateway.net
(W) www.hgd.co.uk.
Profile Sculptor.
Designers and manufacturers of equestrian jewellery and sculptures. Ref:YH06459

HARRIMAN, JOHN

John Harriman, Hen-Tafern (Old Britannia), Market St, Tredegar, **Blaenau Gwent**, NP22 3NH, **WALES**.
(T) 01495 723724.
Profile Supplies. Ref:YH06460

HARRINGWORTH MANOR

Harringworth Manor Stables, Wakerley Rd, Harringworth, Corby, **Northamptonshire**, NN17 3AH, **ENGLAND**.
(T) 01572 747400.
Contact/s
Owner: Mrs P Harrison
Profile Riding School, Stable/Livery.
Full, part and DIY livery available, prices on request. Access to two outdoor schools. Western Riding training is also available. Yr. Est: 1986 C.Size: 93 Acres
Opening Times
Sp: Open Mon - Sun 08:00. Closed Mon - Sun 18:00.
Su: Open Mon - Sun 08:00. Closed Mon - Sun 18:00.
Au: Open Mon - Sun 08:00. Closed Mon - Sun 18:00.
Wn: Open Mon - Sun 08:00. Closed Mon - Sun 18:00. Ref:YH06461

HARRIS CROFT RIDING CTRE

Harris Croft Riding Centre, Binknoll, Wootton Bassett, Swindon, **Wiltshire**, SN4 8QS, **ENGLAND**.
(T) 01793 853388.
Contact/s
Owner: Ms C Gates
Profile Riding School, Stable/Livery. Ref:YH06462

HARRIS OF WHEPSTEAD

Harris Of Whepstead, Straight Rd, Whepstead, Bury St Edmunds, **Suffolk**, IP29 4TF, **ENGLAND**.
(T) 01284 735279.
Profile Transport/Horse Boxes. Ref:YH06463

HARRIS, ANDREW

Andrew Harris, 1 Warborne Farm Cottages, Warborne Lane, Pilley, Lymington, **Hampshire**, SO41 5QD, **ENGLAND**.
(T) 01590 678315 (F) 01590 670024.
Profile Blood Stock Agency, Stable/Livery, Track/Course. Ref:YH06464

HARRIS, ANDREW J

Andrew J Harris DWCF, 40 Lester Piggott Way, Newmarket, **Suffolk**, CB8 0BJ, **ENGLAND**.
(T) 01638 668415.
Profile Farrier. Ref:YH06465

HARRIS, C P

C P Harris, 87 Ware Rd, Hertford, **Hertfordshire**, SG13 7EE, **ENGLAND**.
(T) 01992 554436 (F) 01992 501631.
Profile Medical Support. Ref:YH06466

HARRIS, DEAN R

Dean R Harris DWCF, 44 Maldon Rd, Great Baddow, Chelmsford, **Essex**, CM2 7DL, **ENGLAND**.
(T) 01245 471319.
Profile Farrier. Ref:YH06467

HARRIS, G W

G W Harris, 7a Front St, Prudhoe, **Northumberland**, NE41 5HJ, **ENGLAND**.
(T) 01661 36222.
Profile Medical Support. Ref:YH06468

HARRIS, GAVIN T

Gavin T Harris DWCF, 3 Pot Hse Lane, Stocksbridge, Sheffield, **Yorkshire (South)**, S36 1ES, **ENGLAND**.
(T) 0114 2886514.
Profile Farrier. Ref:YH06469

HARRIS, HILL & WARNER

Harris, Hill & Warner (Wiltshire), 28 Haynes Rd, Westbury, **Wiltshire**, BA13 3HD, **ENGLAND**.
(T) 01373 823546.
Contact/s

Partner: Mr N Hill
Profile Medical Support. Ref: YH06470

HARRIS, HILL & WARNER

Harris, Hill & Warner (Bradford-on-Avon), Frome Rd, Bradford-on-Avon, **Wiltshire**, BA15 1LA, **ENGLAND**.
(T) 01225 862656.
Contact/s
Partner: Mr N Hill
Profile Medical Support. Ref: YH06471

HARRIS, HILL & WARNER

Harris, Hill & Warner (Trowbridge), 4 Paxcroft Way, Trowbridge, **Wiltshire**, BA14 7DG, **ENGLAND**.
(T) 01225 760630.
Contact/s
Partner: Mr N Hill
Profile Medical Support. Ref: YH06472

HARRIS, HILL & WARNER

Harris, Hill & Warner (Warminster), 12/13 Silver St, Warminster, **Wiltshire**, BA12 8PS, **ENGLAND**.
(T) 01985 213522.
Profile Medical Support. Ref: YH06473

HARRIS, IAN

Ian Harris DWCF, 26 Lagoon View, West Yelland, Barnstaple, **Devon**, EX31 3LD, **ENGLAND**.
(T) 01271 861322.
Profile Farrier. Ref: YH06474

HARRIS, J

J Harris, 2 Limefield Rd, Polbeth, West Calder, **Lothian (West)**, EH55 8UD, **SCOTLAND**.
(T) 01506 871111.
Contact/s
Partner: Mrs J Harris
Profile Blacksmith. Ref: YH06475

HARRIS, J A

J A Harris, Bridge Farm/Windmill Rd, Gimingham, Norwich, **Norfolk**, NR11 8HL, **ENGLAND**.
(T) 01263 720028.
Profile Holidays, Medical Support, Riding School, Stable/Livery. Ref: YH06476

HARRIS, JOHNNY

Johnny Harris, Froxfield Stud, Alexanders Lane, Privett, Alton, **Hampshire**, GU34 3PW, **ENGLAND**.
(T) 01730 828426. Ref: YH06477

HARRIS, P W

P W Harris, Church Farm, Station Rd, Aldbury, Tring, **Hertfordshire**, HP23 5RS, **ENGLAND**.
(T) 01442 851328 **(F)** 01442 851063.
Contact/s
Owner: Mr P Harris
Profile Trainer. Ref: YH06478

HARRIS, P W

Mr P W Harris, Sallow Copse, Ringshall, Berkhamsted, **Hertfordshire**, HP4 1LZ, **ENGLAND**.
(T) 01442 842480 **(F)** 01442 842521.
Profile Trainer. Ref: YH06479

HARRIS, R

Mr R Harris, Brooklyn Farm, Chaper Lane, Sissinghurst, Cranbrook, **Kent**, TN17 3NU, **ENGLAND**.
(T) 01580 715714.
Profile Breeder. Ref: YH06480

HARRIS, R M

Mrs R M Harris, 45 Harrison Rd, Adlington, **Lancashire**, PR7 4HN, **ENGLAND**.
(T) 01257 482187.
Profile Trainer. Ref: YH06481

HARRIS, SIMON P

Simon P Harris DWCF, 40 Pitsham Wood, Midhirst, **Sussex (West)**, GU29 9QZ, **ENGLAND**.
(T) 01730 812363.
Profile Farrier. Ref: YH06482

HARRISON, L N

Mr L N Harrison, Savick Brook Farm, Blackpool Rd, Clifton, Preston, **Lancashire**, PR4 0XD, **ENGLAND**.
(T) 01772 631167.
Profile Breeder. Ref: YH06483

HARRISON, MALCOLM A

Malcolm A Harrison DWCF, 6 The Square, Prestwick, Newcastle-upon-Tyne, **Tyne and Wear**, NE20 9TY, **ENGLAND**.
(T) 01661 872088.
Profile Farrier. Ref: YH06484

HARRISON, MARK

Mark Harrison DWCF, 2 Millmeece, Eccleshall, **Staffordshire**, ST21 6QT, **ENGLAND**.
(T) 01782 791314.
Profile Farrier. Ref: YH06485

HARRISON, PAM

Pam Harrison, Expo Life, Beck Grange, Warwick Bridge, Carlisle, **Cumbria**, CA4 8RL, **ENGLAND**.
(T) 01228 561957 **(F)** 01228 561957
(E) expo.life@dial.pipex.com.
Profile Supplies. Ref: YH06486

HARRISON, S

Ms S Harrison, Chapel Oak Farm, Irons Cross, Salford Priors, Evesham, **Worcestershire**, WR11 8SH, **ENGLAND**.
(T) 01386 871092.
Profile Breeder. Ref: YH06487

HARRISON, T H

Mr T H Harrison, Thorny Bank, Wet Sleddale, Shap, Penrith, **Cumbria**, CA10 3NE, **ENGLAND**.
(T) 01931 6653.
Profile Breeder. Ref: YH06488

HARRISON, WILLIAM P

William P Harrison DWCF, 2 Cannon Gr, Fetcham, Leatherhead, **Surrey**, KT22 9JZ, **ENGLAND**.
(T) 01372 386937.
Profile Farrier. Ref: YH06489

HARROGATE

Harrogate Riding & Language Centre, Brackenthwaite Lane, Harrogate, **Yorkshire (North)**, HG3 1PW, **ENGLAND**.
(T) 01423 871894 **(F)** 01423 871907.
Contact/s
Manager: Mr D Birtwistle
Profile Riding School, Stable/Livery. Ref: YH06490

HARROGATE BRIDLEWAYS ASS

Harrogate Bridleways Association, Holly Cottage, Main St, Markington, Harrogate, **Yorkshire (North)**, HG3 3NR, **ENGLAND**.
(T) 01765 677810.
Profile Club/Association. Ref: YH06491

HARROW & DISTRICT RIDING CLUB

Harrow & District Riding Club, 39 Mayfield Ave, Kenton, Harrow, **London (Greater)**, HA3 8EX, **ENGLAND**.
(T) 020 89078363.
Contact/s
Chairman: Mr R Doughty
Profile Club/Association, Riding Club. Ref: YH06492

HARROW, S

S Harrow, The Forge/Coxs Farm, Broad Rd, Hambrook, Chichester, **Sussex (West)**, PO18 8RF, **ENGLAND**.
(T) 01243 573090.
Contact/s
Owner: Mr S Harrow
Profile Farrier. Ref: YH06493

HARROW, SIMON P

Simon P Harrow RSS, 20 Bosmere Gardens, Emsworth, **Hampshire**, PO10 7NP, **ENGLAND**.
(T) 01243 371335.
Profile Farrier. Ref: YH06494

HARROWAY HSE RIDING SCHOOL

Harroway House Riding School, Harroway Hse, Penton Mewsey, Andover, **Hampshire**, SP11 0RA, **ENGLAND**.
(T) 01264 772295.
Contact/s
Owner: Mrs E Skelton
Profile Riding School, Trainer. Ref: YH06495

HARROWER, HENRY

Henry Harrower, Luggate Burn, Haddington, **Lothian (East)**, EH41 4QA, **SCOTLAND**.
(T) 01620 860352.
Profile Blacksmith. Ref: YH06496

HARRY, RICHARD J

Richard J Harry, St Nicholas Forge, St. Brides-Super-Ely, Cardiff, **Glamorgan (Vale of)**, CF5 6HA, **WALES**.
(T) 01446 760303.
Profile Blacksmith. Ref: YH06497

HART, ROSEMARY

Rosemary Hart, Gorse Cottage, Gorse Green Lane, Belbroughton, Stourbridge, **Midlands (West)**, DY9 9UH, **ENGLAND**.
(T) 01562 731223.
Contact/s
Owner: Mrs R Hart
Profile Riding School, Stable/Livery. Ref: YH06498

HARTBURY CLGE

Hartbury College Horseball Club, C/O Rathmore, Churchdown Lane, Hucclecote, **Gloucestershire**, GL3 2LR, **ENGLAND**.
(T) 01452 713913.
Profile Club/Association. Ref: YH06499

HARTFORD BLOODSTOCK

Hartford Bloodstock, 145 Handside Lane, Welwyn Garden City, **Hertfordshire**, AL8 6TA, **ENGLAND**.
(T) 01707 325896.
Contact/s
Owner: Mr C Cory
Profile Blood Stock Agency. Ref: YH06500

HARTGROVE, ANDREW JOHN

Andrew John Hartgrove DWCF, 19 Carrs Way, Harpole, **Northamptonshire**, NN7 4BZ, **ENGLAND**.
(T) 01604 831419.
Profile Farrier. Ref: YH06501

HARTGROVE, TIMOTHY G

Timothy G Hartgrove DWCF, Loddington Lodge, Kettering, **Northamptonshire**, NN14 1LH, **ENGLAND**.
(T) 01536 790212.
Profile Farrier. Ref: YH06502

HARTGROVE, TREVOR E

Trevor E Hartgrove RSS Hons, The New Forge, Park Lane, Harpole, **Northamptonshire**, NN7 4BT, **ENGLAND**.
(T) 01604 830805.
Profile Farrier. Ref: YH06503

HARTLAND CARRIAGE SUPPLIES

Hartland Carriage Supplies, Hale Oaks Farm, Loxwood Rd, Rudgwick, **Sussex (West)**, RH12 3BP, **ENGLAND**.
(T) 01403 753194 **(F)** 01403 753360
(M) 07778 423735.
Contact/s
Manager: Mrs J Hartland
Profile Trainer. Ref: YH06504

HARTLEBURY EQUESTRIAN CTRE

Hartlebury Equestrian Centre, Manor lane, Hartlebury, Kidderminster, **Worcestershire**, DY11 7XN, **ENGLAND**.
(T) 01299 250710
Affiliated Bodies ABRS.
Contact/s
Chief Instructor: Mrs S Webb **(Q)** BHSI
Profile Equestrian Centre, Riding School, Stable/Livery.
Training for NVQ and BHS exams is available
Ref: YH06505

HARTLEY WOOD RIDING CTRE

Hartley Wood Riding Centre, King Lane, Clutton Hill, Clutton, Bristol, **Bristol**, BS39 5QQ, **ENGLAND**.
(T) 01761 452063.
Profile Riding School. Ref: YH06506

HARTPURY CLGE

Hartpury College, Hartpury Hse, Gloucester, **Gloucestershire**, GL19 3BE, **ENGLAND**.
(T) 01452 700283 **(F)** 01452 700629.
Profile Breeder, Riding School. Ref: YH06507

HARTS FARM

Harts Farm, 112 Little Bushey Lane, Bushey, Watford, **Hertfordshire**, WD2 3SE, **ENGLAND**.
(T) 020 89503356.
Profile Stable/Livery. Ref: YH06508

HARTWELL RIDING STABLES

Hartwell Riding Stables, Oxford Rd, Stone, Aylesbury, **Buckinghamshire**, HP17 8NP, **ENGLAND**.
(T) 01296 748641.
Contact/s
Owner: Mr H Herring
Profile Riding School, Stable/Livery. Ref: YH06509

HARVEST SVS

Harvest Services, Manor Farm, West Farndon, **Northamptonshire**, NN11 6TU, **ENGLAND**.
(T) 01327 261038 **(F)** 01327 260644
(E) harvests@freenetname.co.uk
(W) www.harvest-services.co.uk.
Profile Mobile stables. Ref: YH06510

HARVESTERS FARM SUPPLIES

Harvesters Farm Supplies, Unit B New St, Bridgend, **Bridgend**, CF31 3UD, **WALES**.
(T) 01656 658772.
Contact/s
Owner: Mr O Gore
Profile Supplies. **Ref: YH06511**

HARVEY, A

Mrs A Harvey, The Cottage, Hele Barton, Bickleigh, Plymouth, **Devon**, PL6 7AQ, **ENGLAND**.
(T) 01755 39577.
Profile Breeder. **Ref: YH06512**

HARVEY, A

A Harvey, Wickham Hall Hadham Rd, Bishop's Stortford, **Hertfordshire**, CM23 1JG, **ENGLAND**.
(T) 01279 461546 (F) 01279 461546.
Contact/s
Owner: Mr A Harvey
Profile Trainer. **Ref: YH06513**

HARVEY, GREIG V

Greig V Harvey DWCF, 17 Weston Cl, Blofield Heath, Norwich, **Norfolk**, NR13 4QN, **ENGLAND**.
(T) 01603 716718.
Profile Farrier. **Ref: YH06514**

HARVEY, JUDY

Mrs Judy Harvey FBHS, 41 Greenway, Great Horwood, Milton Keynes, **Buckinghamshire**, MK17 0QR, **ENGLAND**.
(T) 01296 713224 (F) 01296 712560.
Profile Trainer. **Ref: YH06515**

HARVEY, PAUL B

Paul B Harvey DWCF, Brook Farm, Cookley, Halesworth, **Suffolk**, IP19 0LN, **ENGLAND**.
(T) 01986 85230.
Profile Farrier. **Ref: YH06516**

HARVEY, SIMON F

Simon F Harvey MRCVS, 1 Folly Gardens, Tewkesbury, **Gloucestershire**, GL20 5QP, **ENGLAND**.
(T) 01684 292244 (F) 01684 293399.
Profile Medical Support. **Ref: YH06517**

HARWOOD ARABIAN STUD

Harwood Arabian Stud, Worthing Rd, Horsham, **Sussex (West)**, RH13 7AR, **ENGLAND**.
(T) 01403 730651.
Contact/s
Owner: Mrs M Calvert
Profile Breeder. **Ref: YH06518**

HARWOOD HALL LIVERY

Harwood Hall Livery, West Lodge, Harwood Hall Lane, Upminster, **Essex**, RM14 2YG, **ENGLAND**.
(T) 01708 222587.
Profile Stable/Livery. **Ref: YH06519**

HASGUARD SHETLAND PONY STUD

Hasguard Shetland Pony Stud, Lower Hasguard Farm, Haverfordwest, **Pembrokeshire**, SA62 3DT, **WALES**.
(T) 01437 781238.
Profile Breeder. **Ref: YH06520**

HASKER, GLENN M

Glenn M Hasker, 31 Southampton Rd, Ringwood, **Hampshire**, BH24 1HB, **ENGLAND**.
(T) 01425 476092.
Contact/s
Owner: Mr G Hasker
Profile Saddlery Retailer. **Ref: YH06521**

HASKETT, ISOBEL

Isobel Haskett, Lea Bailey Riding Ctre, Ross-on-Wye, **Herefordshire**, HR9 5TY, **ENGLAND**.
(T) 01989 750360.
Profile Trainer. **Ref: YH06522**

HASLAM, P C

P C Haslam, Castle Stables, West End, Middleham, Leyburn, **Yorkshire (North)**, DL8 4QQ, **ENGLAND**.
(T) 01969 624351 (F) 01969 624463.
Contact/s
Owner: Mr P Haslam
Profile Trainer. **Ref: YH06523**

HASLEM, ROBERT

Robert Haslem, No 3 Stone Cottage's, Blackleach Lane, Catorth, Preston, **Lancashire**, PR4 0JA, **ENGLAND**.
(T) 01772 690235.
Profile Supplies. **Ref: YH06524**

HASLEMERE FORGE

Haslemere Forge, Greenland Farm, Jobsons Lane, Haslemere, **Surrey**, GU27 3BZ, **ENGLAND**.
(T) 01428 707311.
Profile Blacksmith. **Ref: YH06525**

HASTILOW COMPETITION SADDLES

B & H Saddlery, Saddlers Barn, Prestwick Lane, Chiddingfold, Godalming, **Surrey**, GU8 4XP, **ENGLAND**.
(T) 01428 654619 (F) 01428 654619
(W) www.hastilow.co.uk
Affiliated Bodies SMS.
Contact/s
Owner: Mr I Hastilow
(E) ian.hastilow@virgin.net
Profile Riding Wear Retailer, Saddlery Retailer, Supplies.
One of the only true bespoke saddle manufacturers in the south of England. Saddles made on the premises. Supply competition riders and non-competiotion riders alike. Specialise in close contact saddles
No.Staff: 5 Yr. Est: 1981
Opening Times
Sp: Open 09:00. Closed 17:30.
Su: Open 09:00. Closed 17:30.
Au: Open 09:00. Closed 17:30.
Wn: Open 09:00. Closed 17:30. **Ref: YH06526**

HASTING CTRE

Hasting Centre, Queensberry Hse, 129 High St, Newmarket, **Suffolk**, CB8 9BD, **ENGLAND**.
(T) 01638 665722.
Profile Blood Stock Agency. **Ref: YH06527**

HASTOE HILL RIDING SCHOOL

Hastoe Hill Riding School, Hastoe Hill, Hastoe, Tring, **Hertfordshire**, HP23 6LU, **ENGLAND**.
(T) 01442 828909.
Contact/s
Owner: Mr R Jarman
Profile Riding School. **Ref: YH06528**

HASTPACE DATA

Hastpace Data Ltd, Rectory Farm, Lockington, Driffield, **Yorkshire (East)**, YO25 9SQ, **ENGLAND**.
(T) 01430 810202 (F) 01430 810479
(M) 07860 473666
(E) stuart@hastpace.co.uk.
Profile Club/Association. **Ref: YH06529**

HATCH FARM STABLES

Hatch Farm Stables, Chertsey Rd, Addlestone, **Surrey**, KT15 2EH, **ENGLAND**.
(T) 01932 855550 (F) 01932 855550.
Contact/s
Partner: Mrs A Millman (T) 07876 230636
Profile Riding School, Stable/Livery.
Riding lessons for children only. **Ref: YH06530**

HATCHAM

Hatcham Ltd, 67 Hall Barn Rd, Isleham, Ely, **Cambridgeshire**, CB7 5QZ, **ENGLAND**.
(T) 01638 781140 (F) 01638 781141.
Profile Transport/Horse Boxes. **Ref: YH06531**

HATFIELD'S HORSE TRANSPORT

Hatfield's Horse Transport, High Onn Wharf, Church Eaton, Stafford, **Staffordshire**, ST20 0AX, **ENGLAND**.
(T) 01785 823032.
Contact/s
Owner: Mrs B Hatfield
Profile Transport/Horse Boxes. **Ref: YH06532**

HATTON STABLES

Hatton Stables, Pillmoss Farm, Pillmoss Lane, Hatton, Warrington, **Cheshire**, WA4 4DN, **ENGLAND**.
(T) 01925 730322.
Profile Stable/Livery. **Ref: YH06533**

HATTON STUD

Hatton Stud, Woodmill Farm, Platt Lane, Ellerdine, Telford, **Shropshire**, TF6 6RT, **ENGLAND**.
(T) 01952 541759.
Profile Breeder. **Ref: YH06534**

HATTON, IAN R

Ian R Hatton DWCF, 5 Andrew Cl, Stoke Golding, Nuneaton, **Leicestershire**, CV13 6EL, **ENGLAND**.
(T) 01455 212077 (F) 01455 212077
(M) 07850 300441.
Profile Farrier. **Ref: YH06535**

HAULRITE TRAILERS

Haulrite Trailers, C/O Pads & Co, Sully Moors Rd, Sully, Penarth, **Glamorgan (Vale of)**, CF64 5SY, **WALES**.
(T) 01446 747877.
Profile Transport/Horse Boxes. **Ref: YH06536**

HAVANA HORSE UK

Havana Horse UK Ltd, 20 Kinnerton St, London, **London (Greater)**, SW1X 8ES, **ENGLAND**.
(T) 020 72355704 (F) 020 72356389.
Contact/s
Assistant: Miss Z Crawley
Profile Blood Stock Agency. No.Staff: 4
Opening Times
Sp: Open Mon - Fri 09:30. Closed Mon - Fri 18:00.
Su: Open Mon - Fri 09:30. Closed Mon - Fri 18:00.
Au: Open Mon - Fri 09:30. Closed Mon - Fri 18:00.
Wn: Open Mon - Fri 09:30. Closed Mon - Fri 18:00.
Ref: YH06537

HAVEN HOMES

Haven Homes, Bristol Rd, Cam, Dursley, **Gloucestershire**, GL11 5HX, **ENGLAND**.
(T) 01453 890506 (F) 01453 890508.
Profile Supplies. **Ref: YH06538**

HAVEN SADDLERY

Haven Saddlery, 53 Cookstown Rd, Moneymore, Magherafelt, **County Londonderry**, BT45 7QF, **NORTHERN IRELAND**.
(T) 028 86748293 (F) 028 86748878.
Contact/s
Owner: Mrs D Hartley
Profile Riding Wear Retailer, Saddlery Retailer, Supplies. No.Staff: 2 Yr. Est: 1991
Opening Times
Sp: Open Mon - Sat 09:00. Closed Mon - Sat 21:00.
Su: Open Mon - Sat 09:00. Closed Mon - Sat 21:00.
Au: Open Mon - Sat 09:00. Closed Mon - Sat 21:00.
Wn: Open Mon - Sat 09:00. Closed Mon - Sat 21:00.
Ref: YH06539

HAVERING PK RIDING SCHOOL

Havering Park Riding School, Havering Atte-Bower, Romford, **Essex**, RM4 1RJ, **ENGLAND**.
(T) 01708 746246.
Contact/s
Owner: Mr D Smyth
Profile Riding School, Stable/Livery. **Ref: YH06540**

HAW STUD

Haw Stud, Mill Farm, Brighton Cross, Grampound Rd, Truro, **Cornwall**, TR2 4HD, **ENGLAND**.
(T) 01726 882807.
Profile Breeder. **Ref: YH06541**

HAWES, MATTHEW D

Matthew D Hawes AWCF, 2 Rose Cottage, Honing Rd, Dilham, North Walsham, **Norfolk**, NR28 9PR, **ENGLAND**.
(T) 01692 535467.
Profile Farrier. **Ref: YH06542**

HAWES, ROBERT A

Robert A Hawes RSS, 56 Brooklands Ave, Fulwood, Sheffield, **Yorkshire (South)**, S10 4GD, **ENGLAND**.
(T) 0114 2301535.
Profile Farrier. **Ref: YH06543**

HAWKE, N

Mr N Hawke, Blackmore Farm, Woolminstone, **Somerset**, TA18 8QP, **ENGLAND**.
(T) 01460 74478
(M) 07831 415473.
Profile Trainer. **Ref: YH06544**

HAWKES, JACK

Jack Hawkes, Waterhouse Farm, Withypool, Minehead, **Somerset**, TA24 7RD, **ENGLAND**.
(T) 01643 831338 (F) 01643 831338.
Contact/s
Owner: Mr J Hawkes
Profile Breeder. **Ref: YH06545**

HAWKINS FARM RIDING STABLES

Hawkins Farm Riding Stables, Hawkins Farm, Mendlesham Green, Stowmarket, **Suffolk**, IP14 5RB, **ENGLAND**.
(T) 01449 766264.
Contact/s
Owner: Mrs F Harrison
Profile Riding School. **Ref: YH06546**

HAWKINS SADDLERY

Hawkins Saddlery, 106A Little Cottage St, Brierley Hill, **Midlands (West)**, DY5 1RG, **ENGLAND**.
(T) 01384 484815.
Profile Saddlery Retailer. **Ref: YH06547**

HAWKINS, J E

Mrs J E Hawkins, White Horse Farm, Penycaemawr, Usk, **Monmouthshire**, NP15 1LX, **WALES**.

(T) 01291 650415
(M) 07718 197933.
Profile Supplies. Ref: YH06548

HAWKINS, JOANNE

Mrs Joanne Hawkins, Forest Lodge, Maescoed Woods, Rogerstone, **Newport**, NP1 9GN, **WALES**.
(T) 01633 895329.
Profile Supplies. Ref: YH06549

HAWKINS, MARTYN R

Martyn R Hawkins DWCF, Brookland, Prospect Rd, Upton, Didcot, **Oxfordshire**, OX11 9HT, **ENGLAND**.
(T) 01235 850150
(E) martyn@uptoninoxon.freeserve.co.uk.
Profile Farrier. Ref: YH06550

HAWKLANDS STUD

Hawklands Stud, Jacobstow, **Cornwall**, EX23 0BR, **ENGLAND**.
(T) 01840 230602.
Profile Breeder. Ref: YH06551

HAWKSTAVE

Hawkstave Ltd, 1 Nimmings Rd, Halesowen, **Midlands (West)**, B62 9JQ, **ENGLAND**.
(T) 01299 405572 (F) 01299 405571
(E) hawkstave.co.uk.
Profile Club/Association. Ref: YH06552

HAWLEY EQUITATION CTRE

Hawley Equitation Centre, Hawley Pk/Hawley Rd, Hawley, Blackwater, Camberley, **Hampshire**, GU17 9JB, **ENGLAND**.
(T) 01276 31990.
Contact/s
Owner: Mrs S Pullen
Profile Riding School. Ref: YH06553

HAWLING LODGE STABLES

Hawling Lodge Stables, Hawling, Cheltenham, **Gloucestershire**, GL54 5SY, **ENGLAND**.
(T) 01451 850781.
Profile Stable/Livery. Ref: YH06554

HAWSON, C

Mr C Hawson, Lane End Farm, Abney, Hathersage, Hope Valley, **Derbyshire**, S32 1AH, **ENGLAND**.
(T) 01433 650371 (F) 01433 650371
(E) laneendfarm@btinternet.com.
Profile Stable/Livery. Ref: YH06555

HAWTHORN SADDLERY

Hawthorn Saddlery, Sandhurst Lane, Sandhurst, **Gloucestershire**, GL2 9NW, **ENGLAND**.
(T) 01452 730455
(M) 07831 682489.
Profile Saddlery Retailer, Supplies. Ref: YH06556

HAWTHORN VILLAGE

Hawthorn Village Riding School, East Farm, Hawthorn, Seaham, **County Durham**, SR7 8SG, **ENGLAND**.
(T) 0191 5270404.
Profile Riding School. Ref: YH06557

HAY & BRECON FARMERS

Hay & Brecon Farmers (Hay-on-Wye), Newport St, Hay-on-Wye, **Herefordshire**, HR3 5BH, **ENGLAND**.
(T) 01497 820516.
Contact/s
Chief Executive: Mr N Perkins
Profile Supplies. Ref: YH06558

HAY & BRECON FARMERS

Hay & Brecon Farmers, Old Station Yard, Sennybridge, Brecon, **Powys**, LD3 8RF, **WALES**.
(T) 01874 636237.
Profile Supplies. Ref: YH06559

HAY & BRECON FARMERS

Hay & Brecon Farmers (Brecon), Ffrwydgrech Est, Brecon, **Powys**, LD3 4LA, **WALES**.
(T) 01874 624161 (F) 01874 623854.
Profile Supplies. Ref: YH06560

HAY & BRECON FARMERS

Hay & Brecon Farmers (Builth Wells), Unit 1 Garth Rd, Builth Wells, **Powys**, LD2 3ED, **WALES**.
(T) 01982 552210.
Profile Supplies. Ref: YH06561

HAY & BRECON FARMERS

Hay & Brecon Farmers (Llandrindod Wells), Old Station Yard, Pennybont, Llandrindod Wells, **Powys**, LD1 6RE, **WALES**.
(T) 01597 851274.
Profile Supplies. Ref: YH06562

HAY, A M

Mrs A M Hay BHSII (Regd), Blairview, Milnathort, **Perth and Kinross**, KY13 0SF, **SCOTLAND**.
(T) 01577 863284.
Profile Trainer. Ref: YH06563

HAYBRAKE SHETLAND PONY STUD

Haybrake Shetland Pony Stud, Rogerseat, Rothienorman, Inverurie, **Aberdeenshire**, AB51 8YJ, **SCOTLAND**.
(T) 01651 821088.
Profile Breeder. Ref: YH06564

HAYBURN, J

J Hayburn, 16 Gladstone Rd, Spondon, Derby, **Derbyshire**, DE2 7JJ, **ENGLAND**.
(T) 01332 673582.
Profile Farrier. Ref: YH06565

HAYCOCK

Mrs Haycock, Newton Peveril Manor, Wimborne, **Dorset**, BH21 4AN, **ENGLAND**.
(T) 01258 85305.
Profile Breeder. Ref: YH06566

HAYCOCKS LIVERY STABLES

Haycocks Livery Stables, Blue Row, East Mersea Rd, Colchester, **Essex**, CO5 8SH, **ENGLAND**.
(T) 01206 383974.
Profile Stable/Livery. Ref: YH06567

HAYDEN WEBB CARRIAGES

Hayden Webb Carriages, Lambs Farm Business Pk, Basingstoke Rd, Spencers Wood, Reading, **Berkshire**, RG7 1AJ, **ENGLAND**.
(T) 0118 9883334.
Contact/s
Owner: Mr H Webb
Profile Transport/Horse Boxes. Ref: YH06568

HAYDEN, JOHN

John Hayden, Castlemartin Abbey Hse, Kilcullen, **County Kildare**, **IRELAND**.
(T) 045 481598.
Contact/s
Trainer: Mr J Hayden
(E) johnhayden@kildarehorse.ie
Profile Trainer. Ref: YH06569

HAYDEN, RICHARD J

Richard J Hayden DWCF, Sanstone, Yeolmbridge, Launceston, **Cornwall**, PL15 8TL, **ENGLAND**.
(T) 01566 776431.
Profile Farrier. Ref: YH06570

HAYDOCK PK RACECOURSE

Haydock Park Racecourse, Newton-Le-Willows, **Merseyside**, WA12 0HQ, **ENGLAND**.
(T) 01942 725963 (F) 01942 270879
(E) info@haydock-park.com.
Contact/s
Company Secretary: Geoff Proctor
Profile Track/Course. Ref: YH06571

HAYDON

Haydon, Bramble Cottage, Dalton, Hexham, **Northumberland**, NE46 2LB, **ENGLAND**.
(T) 01434 673601. Ref: YH06572

HAYDON VETNRY GRP

Haydon Veterinary Group, Gore Cross Veterinary Clinic, Corbin Way, Bridport, **Dorset**, DT6 3UX, **ENGLAND**.
(T) 01308 456808 (F) 01308 458008.
Profile Medical Support. Ref: YH06573

HAYES FARM FEEDS

Hayes Farm Feeds, Hucknall Rd, Newstead Village, **Nottinghamshire**, NG15 0BD, **ENGLAND**.
(T) 0115 9632755.
Profile Supplies. Ref: YH06574

HAYES J SADDLERY

Hayes J Saddlery, Units 1-2 Oxleaze Farm, Filkins, Lechlade, **Gloucestershire**, GL7 3RB, **ENGLAND**.
(T) 01367 850472.
Profile Saddlery Retailer. Ref: YH06575

HAYESCASTLE FARM

Hayescastle Farm, Distington, Workington, **Cumbria**, CA14 5YB, **ENGLAND**.
(T) 01946 830309.
Profile Stable/Livery, Track/Course. Ref: YH06576

HAYFIELD LIVERY

Hayfield Livery, Hayfield Farm, Bonnybridge, **Falkirk**, FK4 2ET, **SCOTLAND**.
(T) 01324 813987.
Contact/s
Owner: Mrs E Munnoch
Profile Stable/Livery. Ref: YH06577

HAYFIELD RIDING

Hayfield Riding Centre Ltd, Hazlehead Pk, Aberdeen, **Aberdeen (City of)**, AB15 8BB, **SCOTLAND**.
(T) 01224 315703 (F) 01224 313834
(E) info@hayfield.com
(W) www.hayfield.com
Affiliated Bodies ABRS, BHS.
Contact/s
For Bookings: Ms K Glegg (Q) BHSII
Profile Horse/Rider Accom, Riding School.
Yr. Est: 1958 Ref: YH06578

HAYFIELD SADDLERY

Hayfield Saddlery (The), Hazlehead, Aberdeen, **Aberdeen (City of)**, AB15 8BB, **SCOTLAND**.
(T) 01224 209220.
Profile Riding School, Saddlery Retailer, Stable/Livery, Trainer. Ref: YH06579

HAYFIELD SADDLERY REPAIRS

Hayfield Saddlery Repairs, Hayfield Bungalow, Carlton In Lindrick, Worksop, **Nottinghamshire**, S81 9EL, **ENGLAND**.
(T) 01909 730896.
Profile Supplies. Ref: YH06580

HAYGATE VETNRY CTRE

Haygate Veterinary Centre, 78 Haygate Rd, Wellington, Telford, **Shropshire**, TF1 2BJ, **ENGLAND**.
(T) 01952 223122 (F) 01952 243719.
Contact/s
Owner: Mr C Matkin
Profile Medical Support. Ref: YH06581

HAYKIN, M

M Haykin, 18 Strait Lane, Stainton, Middlesbrough, **Cleveland**, TS8 9BB, **ENGLAND**.
(T) 01642 591678.
Contact/s
Farrier: Mr M Haykin
Profile Farrier. Ref: YH06582

HAYLING TRAILER

Hayling Trailer Co Ltd, 254A Havant Rd, Hayling Island, **Hampshire**, PO11 0LW, **ENGLAND**.
(T) 023 92464176 (F) 023 92463069.
Profile Transport/Horse Boxes. Ref: YH06583

HAYLORS

Haylors, Casita, Waverley Ave, Minster On Sea, Sheerness, **Kent**, ME12 2JL, **ENGLAND**.
(T) 01795 872203 (F) 01795 872203.
Contact/s
Partner: Mr R Hayler
Profile Riding School, Stable/Livery. Ref: YH06584

HAYMARK PRODUCTS

Haymark Products, New Barn Farm, Blendworth, Waterlooville, **Hampshire**, PO8 0QG, **ENGLAND**.
(T) 023 92571700.
Profile Blacksmith. Ref: YH06585

HAYMAX

Haymax, Detchant, Belford, **Northumberland**, NE70 7PF, **ENGLAND**.
(T) 01668 213467 (F) 01668 213467.
Profile Supplies. Hay and Straw Merchant.
Ref: YH06586

HAYNE BARN RIDING STABLES

Hayne Barn Riding Stables, Saltwood, Hythe, **Kent**, CT21 4EH, **ENGLAND**.
(T) 01303 260338.
Contact/s
Owner: Mr D Mostato
Profile Riding School. Ref: YH06587

HAYNES, H E

Mr H E Haynes, Red Down Farm, Highworth, Swindon, **Wiltshire**, SN6 7SH, **ENGLAND**.
(T) 01793 762437 (F) 01793 762437.
Profile Trainer. Ref: YH06588

HAYNES, J C

Mr J C Haynes, Moss Lea, Bridge End, Levens, Kendal, **Cumbria**, LA8 8EJ, **ENGLAND**.
(T) 01539 552280
(M) 07771 511471.
Profile Supplies. Ref: YH06589

HAYNES, MICHAEL J

Michael J Haynes, Tattenham Corner Racing Stables, Epsom, **Surrey**, KT18 5PP, **ENGLAND**.
(T) 01737 351140.

Contact/s
Owner: Mr M Haynes
Profile Trainer. Ref: YH06590

HAYNET

Haynet, Chesterfield Bungalow, Ashcroft Lane, Chesterfield, Lichfield, **Staffordshire**, WS14 0EQ, **ENGLAND**.
(T) 0121 3534175.
Profile Supplies. Ref: YH06591

HAYSELDEN

Hayselden Connemara Ponies, Lower Woolwich, Mounts Lane, Rolvenden, Cranbrook, **Kent**, TN17 4NX, **ENGLAND**.
(T) 01580 241200 (F) 01580 713827.
Contact/s
Owner: Mrs A Harries
(E) harries@lowerwoolwich.demon.co.uk
Profile Breeder. Yr. Est: 1979
Opening Times
Telephone for an appointment Ref: YH06592

HAYTER, D J

D J Hayter, Haven View, Wharf Rd, Fobbing, Stanford-Le-Hope, **Essex**, SS17 9JL, **ENGLAND**.
(T) 01375 670545.
Profile Breeder, Farrier. Ref: YH06593

HAYTER, JAMES W

James W Hayter DWCF Hons, 64 Swaines Way, Heathfield, **Sussex (East)**, TN21 0AN, **ENGLAND**.
(T) 01435 867162.
Profile Farrier. Ref: YH06594

HAYTIP

Haytip, Green Farm, Puxley, Towcester, **Northamptonshire**, NN12 7QS, **ENGLAND**.
(T) 01908 569238.
Profile Medical Support. Ref: YH06595

HAYWOOD DESIGN

Haywood Design, Hixon Ind Est, Church Lane, Hixon, Stafford, **Staffordshire**, ST18 0PY, **ENGLAND**.
(T) 01889 270663 (F) 01889 271995.
Contact/s
Owner: Mr G Valler
Profile Transport/Horse Boxes. Ref: YH06596

HAYWOOD, J & G

J & G Haywood, Westwinds, Mere Cres, Oakmere, Northwich, **Cheshire**, **ENGLAND**.
(T) 01606 882235.
Profile Breeder. Ref: YH06597

HAZEL END FARM SHOP

Hazel End Farm Shop, Gypsy Lane, Hazel End, Bishop's Stortford, **Hertfordshire**, CM23 1HA, **ENGLAND**.
(T) 01279 816336.
Profile Supplies. Ref: YH06598

HAZEL FARM

Hazel Farm, St Peters Lane, Bickenhill, Solihull, **Midlands (West)**, B92 0DP, **ENGLAND**.
(T) 01675 442737.
Profile Breeder, Saddlery Retailer, Stable/Livery.
Ref: YH06599

HAZEL SLADE STABLES

Hazel Slade Stables, Rugeley Rd, Hednesford, **Staffordshire**, WS12 5PH, **ENGLAND**.
(T) 01543 879611
(M) 07976 321468.
Profile Trainer. Ref: YH06600

HAZELDEAN RIDING CTRE

Hazeldean Riding Centre, Hazeldean Hse, Hawick, **Scottish Borders**, TD9 8RU, **SCOTLAND**.
(T) 01450 870419.
Profile Riding School. Ref: YH06601

HAZELDEN SADDLERY

Hazelden Saddlery, Hazelden School Of Equitation, Hazelden Rd, Newton Mearns, Glasgow, **Glasgow (City of)**, G77 6RR, **SCOTLAND**.
(T) 0141 6393101 (F) 0141 6399444.
Contact/s
Partner: Miss N Young
Profile Riding School, Saddlery Retailer, Stable/Livery. Ref: YH06602

HAZELTINE, J J

J J Hazeltine, Croft End, Horsham Rd, Wallis Wood, Dorking, **Surrey**, RH5 5QG, **ENGLAND**.
(T) 01306 627325.
Profile Farrier. Ref: YH06603

HAZELWOOD STUD

Hazelwood Stud, Farleigh Court Rd, Warlingham, **Surrey**, CR6 9PX, **ENGLAND**.
(T) 01883 626611.
Contact/s
Owner: Miss D Mathews
Profile Breeder, Stud Farm. Ref: YH06604

HAZLEWOOD TRAILERS

Hazlewood Trailers, Bishampton Rd, Rous Lench, Evesham, **Worcestershire**, WR11 4UN, **ENGLAND**.
(T) 01386 792916 (F) 01386 793320.
Profile Transport/Horse Boxes. Ref: YH06605

HEAD & HEAD

Head & Head, Veterinary Ctre, Water-Ma-Trout, Helston, **Cornwall**, TR13 0LW, **ENGLAND**.
(T) 01326 572216.
Profile Medical Support. Ref: YH06606

HEAD LADS ASS

Head Lads Association, 196 New Cheverley Rd, Newmarket, **Suffolk**, CB8 8BZ, **ENGLAND**.
(T) 01638 662683.
Profile Club/Association. Ref: YH06607

HEAD TO HOOF

Head To Hoof, 25 Stafford St, Market Drayton, **Shropshire**, TF9 1PS, **ENGLAND**.
(T) 01630 661207.
Contact/s
Owner: Mr M Comer
Profile Supplies.
Supplying magnetic therapy rugs. Ref: YH06608

HEAD, MARTIN J

Martin J Head DWCF, The Old Tanyard, Pound Hill, Corsham, **Wiltshire**, SN13 9HT, **ENGLAND**.
(T) 01249 713410.
Profile Farrier. Ref: YH06609

HEAD, SAMUEL C

Samuel C Head DWCF, Haines Farm, Stoke Lane, Great Brickhill, **Buckinghamshire**, MK17 9AQ, **ENGLAND**.
(T) 01525 261417.
Profile Farrier. Ref: YH06610

HEADLEY GR STABLES

Headley Grove Stables, Headley Common Rd, Headley, Epsom, **Surrey**, KT18 6NR, **ENGLAND**.
(T) 01372 376172.
Profile Riding School, Stable/Livery. Ref: YH06611

HEADLEY STUD

Headley Stud, Newbury Rd, Headley, Thatcham, **Berkshire**, RG19 8LB, **ENGLAND**.
(T) 01635 268232 (F) 01635 269158.
Contact/s
Owner: Mrs L Woods
Profile Breeder. Ref: YH06612

HEADS FARM STABLES

Heads Farm Stables, Chaddleworth, Newbury, **Berkshire**, RG20 7EE, **ENGLAND**.
(T) 01488 638771 (F) 01488 638832
(M) 07785 508058.
Contact/s
Owner: Mr C Egerton
Profile Trainer. Ref: YH06613

HEALEY ENGINEERING

Healey Engineering, Melton Rd, Oakham, **Leicestershire**, LE15 6AY, **ENGLAND**.
(T) 01572 723604.
Contact/s
Owner: Mr G Healey
Profile Transport/Horse Boxes. Ref: YH06614

HEARNESBROOK CONNEMARA STUD

Hearnesbrook Connemara Stud, Kimberley Hall, Wymondham, **Norfolk**, NR18 0RT, **ENGLAND**.
(T) 01603 759276 (F) 01603 759276.
Profile Breeder. Ref: YH06615

HEARSAY STUD

Hearsay Stud, West Hill Court, Ottery St Mary, **Devon**, EX11 1JX, **ENGLAND**.
(T) 01404 812066.
Profile Breeder. Ref: YH06616

HEART OF ENGLAND EQUESTRIAN

Heart Of England Equestrian, Spot Acre, Stone, **Staffordshire**, ST15 8RN, **ENGLAND**.
(T) 01889 505048 (F) 01889 505049.
Contact/s
Partner: Mrs E Ballentyne
Profile Stable/Livery. Ref: YH06617

HEART OF ENGLAND TOURIST

Heart of England Tourist Board, Woodside, Larkhill, **Worcestershire**, WR5 2EF, **ENGLAND**.
(T) 01905 761100 (F) 01905 763450.
Profile Club/Association. Ref: YH06618

HEART OF WALES RIDING SCHOOL

Heart of Wales Riding School, Tyddu, Dolau, Llandrindod Wells, **Powys**, LD1 5TB, **WALES**.
(T) 01597 851884 (F) 01597 851647.
Contact/s
Partner: Mrs B Brown
Profile Riding School. Ref: YH06619

HEARTLAND EXTRUSION FORGE

Heartland Extrusion Forge Ltd, Rocky Lane, Nechells, Birmingham, **Midlands (West)**, B7 5EU, **ENGLAND**.
(T) 0121 3596861 (F) 0121 3592972.
Profile Blacksmith. Ref: YH06620

HEATH FARM

Heath Farm, Egerton Rd, Charing Heath, Ashford, **Kent**, TN27 0AX, **ENGLAND**.
(T) 01233 712030.
Profile Breeder. Ref: YH06621

HEATH RACING STABLES

Heath Racing Stables, Newbold Rd, Bishop Burton, Beverley, **Yorkshire (East)**, HU17 8EF, **ENGLAND**.
(T) 01482 882520.
Contact/s
Owner: Mr A Smith
Profile Trainer. Ref: YH06622

HEATH, F W

F W Heath, Kingswood Farm, Lovedean Lane, Waterlooville, **Hampshire**, PO8 0UA, **ENGLAND**.
(T) 02392 592237.
Contact/s
Owner: Mr F Heath
Profile Stable/Livery. Ref: YH06623

HEATH, NICHOLAS J R

Nicholas J R Heath DWCF, Pebbles Cottage, Ilchester Rd, Charton Mackrell, Somerton, **Somerset**, TA11 6AD, **ENGLAND**.
(T) 07976 162256.
Profile Farrier. Ref: YH06624

HEATHER ARABIAN RACING STUD

Heather Arabian Racing Stud, Heather Farm, Heath Rd, Hickling, Norwich, **Norfolk**, NR12 0AX, **ENGLAND**.
(T) 01692 598434.
Profile Breeder, Trainer. Ref: YH06625

HEATHER HALL

Heather Hall, Heather, **Leicestershire**, LE67 2RF, **ENGLAND**.
(T) 01530 260467.
Profile Stable/Livery. Ref: YH06626

HEATHERFIELD RIDING CTRE

Heatherfield Riding Centre, Lochloy Rd, Nairn, **Highlands**, IV12 5LE, **SCOTLAND**.
(T) 01667 456682.
Contact/s
Owner: Mrs A Johnstone
Profile Riding School. Ref: YH06627

HEATHERTON RIDING STABLES

Heatherton Riding Stables, Heatherton Country Sports Pk, Devonshire Dr, Saundersfoot, **Pembrokeshire**, SA69 9EE, **WALES**.
(T) 01646 651025 (F) 01646 651055.
Contact/s
Owner: Mr C Davies
Profile Riding School, Stable/Livery. Ref: YH06628

HEATHERWOLD STUD

Heatherwold Stud, Burghclere, Newbury, **Berkshire**, RG20 9DU, **ENGLAND**.
(T) 01635 278289.
Contact/s
Manager: Mrs A Jenkins
Profile Breeder. Ref: YH06629

HEATHFIELD PK STABLES

Heathfield Park Stables, Reigate Heath, Reigate, **Surrey**, RH2 8QR, **ENGLAND**.
(T) 01737 222034.
Profile Supplies. Ref: YH06630

HEATHFIELD RIDING CLUB

Heathfield Riding Club, Marle Green Farm, Marle Green, Horam, **Sussex (East)**, TN21 9HN, **ENGLAND**.

(T) 01435 32136.
Profile Club/Association. Ref: YH06631

HEATHFIELDS FARM LIVERY

Heathfields Farm Livery, Smarts Heath Rd, Woking, **Surrey**, GU22 0RG, **ENGLAND**.
(T) 01483 236363 (F) 01483 236492.
Contact/s
Owner: Mrs T Gibb
Profile Stable/Livery. Ref: YH06632

HEATHLANDS FARMS

Heathlands Farms, Priory Farm, Blackborough End, King's Lynn, **Norfolk**, PE32 1SQ, **ENGLAND**.
(T) 01553 841282 (F) 01553 841472.
Contact/s
Partner: Mr B Carter
Profile Breeder. Ref: YH06633

HEATHLANDS RIDING CTRE

Heathlands Riding Centre, Heathlands Rd, Wokingham, **Berkshire**, RG40 3AS, **ENGLAND**.
(T) 01344 772453.
Profile Riding School, Stable/Livery. Ref: YH06634

HEAZLE RIDING CTRE

Heazle Riding Centre, Heazle Farm, Clayhidon, Cullompton, **Devon**, EX15 3TH, **ENGLAND**.
(T) 01823 680280.
Profile Riding School. Ref: YH06635

HEBERTSTOWN STUD FARM

Hebertstown Stud Farm, Two Mile Hse, Newbridge, **County Kildare**, **IRELAND**.
(T) 045 481933 (F) 045 481933
(E) equidadt@eircom.
Contact/s
Key Contact: Mr T Watkins
Profile Breeder, Stable/Livery.
The stud has full livery available for breeding, rearing, sales preparation and competitions. They also offer training programmes in equine skills and purchase sport horses and thoroughbreds for clients.
C.Size: 180 Acres Ref: YH06636

HEBRIDEAN TREKKING HOLIDAYS

Hebridean Trekking Holidays, Isle Of Canna, Small Isles, **Highlands**, PH44 4RS, **SCOTLAND**.
(T) 01687 462829.
Profile Equestrian Centre. Trekking Centre.
Ref: YH06637

HECKINGTON SUPPLIES

Heckington Supplies, Unit 8 Hazelwoods Yard, Boston Rd, Heckington, **Lincolnshire**, NG34 9JE, **ENGLAND**.
(T) 01529 460675 (F) 01529 461818.
Profile Saddlery Retailer. Ref: YH06638

HEDDINGTON WICK

Heddington Wick Childrens Riding School, The Common, Heddington, Calne, **Wiltshire**, SN11 0NZ, **ENGLAND**.
(T) 01380 850182.
Contact/s
Owner: Mrs I Gage (Q) BHSAI
Profile Riding School.
Teach children only. Insured for children of two and half years upwards. Yr. Est: 1978 C.Size: 17 Acres
Opening Times
Sp: Open Mon, Wed, Thurs, Sat 09:00, Sun 09:30. Closed Mon, Wed, Thurs, Sat, Sun 17:30.
Su: Open Mon, Wed, Thurs, Sat 09:00, Sun 09:30. Closed Mon, Wed, Thurs, Sat, Sun 17:30.
Au: Open Mon, Wed, Thurs, Sat 09:00, Sun 09:30. Closed Mon, Wed, Thurs, Sat, Sun 17:30.
Wn: Open Mon, Wed, Thurs, Sat 09:00, Sun 09:30. Closed Mon, Wed, Thurs, Sat, Sun 17:30.
Times may vary, telephone for an appointment
Ref: YH06639

HEDGE FARM LIVERIES

Hedge Farm Liveries, Highfield Lane, Thursley, Godalming, **Surrey**, GU8 6QJ, **ENGLAND**.
(T) 01252 702903.
Contact/s
Owner: Mr T Cowan
Profile Stable/Livery. Ref: YH06640

HEDGEHOG EQUESTRIAN

Hedgehog Equestrian, Alton Nether Farm, Tinkerley Lane, Ashbourne, **Derbyshire**, DE6 3LF, **ENGLAND**.
(T) 01335 370270 (F) 01335 370270.
Profile Transport/Horse Boxes. Ref: YH06641

HEDGERS HORSE TRANSPORT

Hedgers Horse Transport, Melcroft, Eastergate Lane, Eastergate, Chichester, **Sussex (West)**, PO20 6SJ, **ENGLAND**.
(T) 01243 543863 (F) 01243 543863.
Contact/s
For Bookings: Mrs L Hedger
Profile Transport/Horse Boxes. Ref: YH06642

HEDGES, ANTONY A

Antony A Hedges DWCF, 15 Wickford Cl, Harold Hill, Romford, **Essex**, RM3 9SD, **ENGLAND**.
(T) 07885 257689.
Profile Farrier. Ref: YH06643

HEDLEY RIDING SCHOOL

Hedley Riding School, Higher Elbut Farm, Elbut Lane, Bury, **Lancashire**, BL9 7TU, **ENGLAND**.
(T) 0161 7646573.
Contact/s
Owner: Mrs B Hedley
Profile Riding School. Ref: YH06644

HEDLEY, K H

K H Hedley, The Forge I.E.C., Invershin, Lairg, **Highlands**, IV27 4ET, **SCOTLAND**.
(T) 01549 421234.
Profile Farrier. Ref: YH06645

HEDLEYS ALARMS/TOWING CTRE

Hedleys Alarms & Towing Centre, 20A Dragonville Ind Pk, Dragon Lane, Durham, **County Durham**, DH1 2XH, **ENGLAND**.
(T) 0191 3863972 (F) 0191 3868886.
Contact/s
Owner: Mr P Hedley
Profile Transport/Horse Boxes. Ref: YH06646

HEDSOR STUD

Hedsor Stud, Harvest Hill, Bourne End, **Buckinghamshire**, SL8 5JS, **ENGLAND**.
(T) 01628 521993
(M) 07836 244973.
Profile Breeder. Ref: YH06647

HEID & BRAZIER

Heid & Brazier Western Performance Horses, Manor Farm, St Johns Rd, Stourport-on-Severn, **Worcestershire**, DY13 9DS, **ENGLAND**.
(T) 07932 690271
(E) heidbrazier@lineone.net
(W) www.heidbrazier.virtualave.net
Alt Contact Address
35 St Johns Rd, Stourport-on-Severn, Worcestershire, DY13 9DS, England.(T) 07932 690271
Contact/s
Owner: Mr A Brazier
Profile Riding School, Trainer.
Western training and lessons. Mrs Terrie Heid-Brazier is CEF and WES certified. Yr. Est: 1999
Opening Times
Varying opening times. Telephone for further information Ref: YH06648

HEIGHTS HSE

Heights House Farm Livery Stables, Inchfield Rd, Todmorden, **Yorkshire (West)**, OL14 7QP, **ENGLAND**.
(T) 01706 818010.
Contact/s
Owner: Mrs K Yearsley
Profile Stable/Livery. Ref: YH06649

HEIGHTS STABLES

Heights Stables, Westerham Hill, Westerham, **Kent**, TN16 2ED, **ENGLAND**.
(T) 01959 571953 (F) 01959 571953.
Contact/s
Owner: Ms M Chapman (Q) BHSAI 6
Profile Equestrian Centre, Stable/Livery.
Yr. Est: 1985 C.Size: 85 Acres Ref: YH06650

HELAWI SHETLAND STUD

Helawi Shetland Stud, Applecroft, 38 Marford Rd, Wheathampstead, **Hertfordshire**, AL4 8AS, **ENGLAND**.
(T) 01582 833867.
Profile Breeder. Ref: YH06651

HELEN J BRAY STUDIO

Helen J Bray Studio, 16-22 Dunford Rd, Holmfirth, Huddersfield, **Yorkshire (West)**, HD7 1DP, **ENGLAND**.
(T) 01484 681978. Ref: YH06652

HELLENS, J A

Mr J A Hellens, Felledge Farm, Walldridge Lane, Chester Moor, Chester Le Street, **County Durham**, DH2 3RX, **ENGLAND**.
(T) 0191 3885403.
Profile Supplies. Ref: YH06653

HELLINGS (LADY)

Lady Hellings, The Leys, Milton Coombe, Yelverton, **Devon**, PL20 6HW, **ENGLAND**.
(T) 01822 853355.
Profile Breeder. Ref: YH06654

HELLMAN, GLENN

Glenn Hellman, Pantrhedyn, Pontrhydfendigaid, Ystrad Meurig, **Ceredigion**, SY25 6EL, **WALES**.
(T) 01974 831294.
Profile Saddlery Retailer. Ref: YH06655

HELSHAW GRANGE STUD

Helshaw Grange Stud, Tern Hill, Market Drayton, **Shropshire**, TF9 2JP, **ENGLAND**.
(T) 01630 638988 (F) 01630 638678.
Profile Breeder. Ref: YH06656

HELSTON SADDLERY

Helston Saddlery, 69A Meneage St, Helston, **Cornwall**, TR13 8RB, **ENGLAND**.
(T) 01326 574448.
Contact/s
General Manager: Mrs R Cannon
Profile Riding Wear Retailer, Saddlery Retailer, Supplies. Freelance Instructor BHS. No.Staff: 3
Yr. Est: 1994
Opening Times
Sp: Open 09:30. Closed 17:00.
Su: Open 09:30. Closed 17:00.
Au: Open 09:30. Closed 17:00.
Wn: Open 09:30. Closed 17:00. Ref: YH06657

HEMBROW, S J R

Mrs S J R Hembrow, Chico, Lipe Lane, Henlade, Taunton, **Somerset**, TA3 5HZ, **ENGLAND**.
(T) 01823 442546.
Profile Supplies. Ref: YH06658

HEMCORE

Hemcore Ltd, Latchmore Bank, Little Hallingbury, Bishop's Stortford, **Essex**, CM22 7PJ, **ENGLAND**.
(T) 01279 504466 (F) 01279 755395.
Profile Supplies. Ref: YH06659

HEMESLEY LIVERY STABLES

Hemesley Livery Stables, Ash Rd, Hartley, Longfield, **Kent**, DA3 8HA, **ENGLAND**.
(T) 01474 709198.
Profile Stable/Livery. Ref: YH06660

HEMMINGS, A W

Mr A W Hemmings, 96 Dallington Rd, Duston, **Northamptonshire**, NN5 7BW, **ENGLAND**.
(T) 01604 54150.
Profile Supplies. Ref: YH06661

HEMPSTEAD STUD

Hempstead Stud, Chittenden Farm, Golford Rd, Benenden, Cranbrook, **Kent**, TN17 4AJ, **ENGLAND**.
(T) 01580 240086 (F) 01580 240086.
Contact/s
Owner: Miss A Austin
Profile Stable/Livery.
DIY livery available, prices on request. Yr. Est: 1999
C.Size: 31.5 Acres
Opening Times
Sp: Open Mon - Sun 07:30. Closed Mon - Sun 20:30.
Su: Open Mon - Sun 07:30. Closed Mon - Sun 20:30.
Au: Open Mon - Sun 07:30. Closed Mon - Sun 20:30.
Wn: Open Mon - Sun 07:30. Closed Mon - Sun 20:30.
Telephone for more information between 09.00 - 17.30
Ref: YH06662

HEN MILL SADDLERY

Hen Mill Saddlery, Hen Mill Farm, 42 Holmgate Rd, Clay Cross, **Derbyshire**, S45 9QD, **ENGLAND**.
(T) 01246 864773.
Profile Saddlery Retailer. Ref: YH06663

HENDEN CASPIAN STUD

Henden Caspian Stud, Sparrow Farm, Lanhill, Chippenham, **Wiltshire**, SN14 6LX, **ENGLAND**.
(T) 01249 782246 (F) 01249 782256
(E) henden@compuserve.com
Affiliated Bodies BAES, BHS, CPR.
Contact/s
Owner: Mrs J Scott
Profile Breeder. No.Staff: 2 Yr. Est: 1978
C.Size: 60 Acres
Opening Times
Telephone for an appointment Ref: YH06664

HENDERSON FABRICATION

Henderson Fabrication, Scooniehill Farm, St Andrews, **Fife**, KY16 8NN, **SCOTLAND**.
(T) 01334 472265.
Profile Blacksmith. **Ref: YH06665**

HENDERSON, FRANCIS

Francis Henderson, Rock Bank Farm, 158 Airdrie Rd, Caldercruix, Airdrie, **Lanarkshire (North)**, ML6 8PA, **SCOTLAND**.
(T) 01236 842329.
Profile Farrier. **Ref: YH06666**

HENDERSON, N J

N J Henderson, Seven Barrows, Lambourn, Hungerford, **Berkshire**, RG17 8UH, **ENGLAND**.
(T) 01488 72300 **(F)** 01488 72596.
Contact/s
Owner: Mr N Henderson
Profile Trainer. **Ref: YH06667**

HENDERSON, PAUL F

Paul F Henderson AFCL BI, River View, Mill Lane, Nursling, Southampton, **Hampshire**, SO16 0YE, **ENGLAND**.
(T) 023 80731785.
Profile Farrier. **Ref: YH06668**

HENDRY, JAMES

James Hendry, Kippen Smiddy, Rennie's Loan, Kippen, Stirling, **Stirling**, FK8 3DX, **SCOTLAND**.
(T) 01786 870100.
Contact/s
Owner: Mr J Hendry
Profile Blacksmith.
Blacksmith, fabrication, modern furniture, made to order. Show jumping stands and sculptors of horses heads are amongst the products, though any request can be made **No.Staff:** 2 **Yr. Est:** 1999
Opening Times
Sp: Open 08:00. Closed 20:00.
Su: Open 08:00. Closed 20:00.
Au: Open 08:00. Closed 20:00.
Wn: Open 08:00. Closed 20:00. **Ref: YH06669**

HENDY EQUESTRIAN

Hendy Equestrian, Hendy, Four Mile Bridge, Holyhead, **Isle of Anglesey**, LL65 2HZ, **WALES**.
(T) 01407 740709 **(F)** 01407 740709.
Profile Breeder. **Ref: YH06670**

HENEAGE, ROBERT

Robert Heneage, Newport Cottage, North Carlton, Lincoln, **Lincolnshire**, LN1 2RR, **ENGLAND**.
(T) 01522 730562 **(F)** 01522 730562. **Ref: YH06671**

HENGEST FARM SHOP

Hengest Farm Shop, Hengust Farm, Woodmansterne Lane, Banstead, **Surrey**, SM7 3EY, **ENGLAND**.
(T) 01737 358926 **(F)** 01737 371461.
Contact/s
Partner: Mrs I Compton
Profile Saddlery Retailer. **Ref: YH06672**

HENLEY IN ARDEN AUCTION SALES

Henley In Arden Auction Sales Ltd, The Estate Office, Warwick Rd, Henley In Arden, Solihull, **Warwickshire**, B95 5BH, **ENGLAND**.
(T) 01564 792154.
Profile Auctioneers. **Ref: YH06673**

HENLEY RIDING SCHOOL

Henley Riding School, White Hse Farm, School Rd, Henley, Ipswich, **Suffolk**, IP6 0SA, **ENGLAND**.
(T) 01473 785055.
Profile Riding School. **Ref: YH06674**

HENLEY TIMBER

Henley Timber, Bear Lane, Off Station Rd, Henley-In-Arden, Solihull, **Warwickshire**, B95 5JJ, **ENGLAND**.
(T) 01564 792714.
Profile Transport/Horse Boxes. **Ref: YH06675**

HENMAN, C

Mrs C Henman, The Old Mill, Islip, Kidlington, **Oxfordshire**, OX5 2SX, **ENGLAND**.
(T) 01865 375454.
Profile Breeder. **Ref: YH06676**

HENNESSEY, M P

Mr & Mrs M P Hennessey, The Grange Farm, Grange Gardens, Ruxbury Rd, Chertsey, **Surrey**, KT16 9EP **ENGLAND**.
(T) 01932 566995.
Profile Breeder. **Ref: YH06677**

HENRIQUES, M R Q

M R Q Henriques, Winson Manor, Winson, Cirencester, **Gloucestershire**, GL7 5ES, **ENGLAND**.
(T) 01285 72304 **(F)** 01285 72614.
Profile Supplies. **Ref: YH06678**

HENRY ADAMS

Henry Adams & Partners, Mulberry Hse, The Sq, Storrington, **Sussex (West)**, RH20 4DJ, **ENGLAND**.
(T) 01903 742291 **(F)** 01903 740671
(E) storrington@henry-adams.co.uk
(W) www.henry-adams.co.uk.
Contact/s
Branch Manager: Mr M Selwood
Profile Property Services.
Opening Times
Sp: Open Mon - Sat 09:00. Closed Mon - Fri 17:30, Sat 16:00.
Su: Open Mon - Sat 09:00. Closed Mon - Fri 17:30, Sat 16:00.
Au: Open Mon - Sat 09:00. Closed Mon - Fri 17:30, Sat 16:00.
Wn: Open Mon - Sat 09:00. Closed Mon - Fri 17:30, Sat 16:00.
Closed Sundays **Ref: YH06679**

HENRY CARRIAGE CARTS

Henry Carriage Carts, The Old Wharf, Madeley Heath, Crewe, **Cheshire**, CW3 9LW, **ENGLAND**.
(T) 01782 751494.
Profile Transport/Horse Boxes. **Ref: YH06680**

HENRY COLE

Henry Cole & Co Ltd, Cotswold Ctre, Purlieus Farm, Ewen, Cirencester, **Gloucestershire**, GL7 6BY, **ENGLAND**.
(T) 01285 770387 **(F)** 01285 770366
(E) info@henrycole.co.uk
(W) www.henrycole.co.uk.
Profile Feed Merchant, Supplies.
Petfood and farm feed stockists with delivery to the South West of England. **Yr. Est:** 1896 **Ref: YH06681**

HENRY FIELDS STUD

Henry Fields Stud (The), Seaford Lane, Naunton Beauchamp, Pershore, **Worcestershire**, WR10 2LN, **ENGLAND**.
(T) 01386 462562 **(F)** 01386 462562
(W) www.henryfieldstud.com.
Contact/s
General Manager: Ms P Merriman
(E) pat@henryfieldstud.com
Profile Breeder.
Opening Times
Telephone for further information. In the evenings use 01905 352536. **Ref: YH06682**

HENRY FINGLETON

Henry Fingleton Horsedrawn Caravans, Kilvahan Timohoe, Portlaoise, **County Laois**, **IRELAND**.
(T) 050 227048 **(F)** 050 227225
(E) kilvahan@eircom.net.
Profile Transport/Horse Boxes. Horsedrawn Caravans. **Ref: YH06683**

HENRY H BLETSOE & SON

Henry H Bletsoe & Son, Oakleigh Hse, 28 High St, Thrapston, Kettering, **Northamptonshire**, NN14 4LJ, **ENGLAND**.
(T) 01832 732241 **(F)** 01832 733807.
Contact/s
Partner: Mr M Bletsoe
Profile Auctioneers & Estate Agents. **Ref: YH06684**

HENRY POOLE

Henry Poole & Co, 15 Savile Row, London, **London (Greater)**, W1X 1AE, **ENGLAND**.
(T) 020 77345985 **(F)** 020 72872161.
Contact/s
Owner: Mr A Cundey
Profile Riding Wear Retailer. **Ref: YH06685**

HENRY, DAVID

David Henry DWCF, Lower Bough Farm, Heathfield Rd, Burwash Common, Etchingham, **Sussex (East)**, TN19 7LQ, **ENGLAND**.
(T) 07889 969342.
Profile Farrier. **Ref: YH06686**

HENSBY, G R

G R Hensby, Denby Hall, Lower Denby, Flockton, Wakefield, **Yorkshire (West)**, **ENGLAND**.
(T) 01924 848770.
Profile Breeder. **Ref: YH06687**

HENSON, A

Mr A Henson, Cotswold Farm Pk, Kineton, Guiting Power, Cheltenham, **Gloucestershire**, GL54 5UG, **ENGLAND**.
(T) 01451 850307 **(F)** 01451 850423.
Profile Breeder. **Ref: YH06688**

HENSON, LUCY

Lucy Henson, The Shootung Lodge, Torksey, Lincoln, **Lincolnshire**, LN1 2ED, **ENGLAND**.
(T) 01427 719031 **(F)** 01427 718108
(M) 07788 185998
(E) lucy@hensonfranklyn.co.uk
(W) www.lucyhenson.co.uk.
Contact/s
International Event Rider: Mrs L Henson
Profile Trainer. **Ref: YH06689**

HENTY, JOHN R

John R Henty RSS, Steel Works, Lower Rd, Eastbourne, **Sussex (East)**, BN21 1QE, **ENGLAND**.
(T) 01323 721938.
Profile Farrier. **Ref: YH06690**

HEPPENSTALL, S R

Mr & Mrs S R Heppenstall, Glynwyn, Gawthorpe Lane, Gawthorpe, Ossett, **Yorkshire (West)**, WF5 9BB, **ENGLAND**.
(T) 01924 260105.
Profile Breeder.
Breeder of Welsh Section C ponies **Ref: YH06691**

HEPPLEWOOD STUD

Hepplewood Stud, Heatherlea Cottage, Edmundbyers, Consett, **County Durham**, DH8 9NN, **ENGLAND**.
(T) 01207 255281.
Profile Breeder. **Ref: YH06692**

HEPWORTH MINERAL & CHEMICALS

Hepworth Mineral & Chemicals Ltd, Brookside Hall, Sandbach, **Cheshire**, CW11 4TF, **ENGLAND**.
(T) 01270 752752 **(F)** 01270 752753.
Contact/s
Sales Manager: Mr T Leadbeter
Profile Supplies. **Ref: YH06693**

HEPWORTH, ROBIN & SHIRLEY

Robin & Shirley Hepworth, 9 Keats Drive, Towcester, **Northamptonshire**, NN12 6LT, **ENGLAND**.
(T) 01327 353077
(E) intergain@intergain.co.uk.
Profile Breeder. **Ref: YH06694**

HERBERT, IVOR

Ivor Herbert, The Old Rectory, Bradenham, High Wycombe, **Buckinghamshire**, HP14 4HD, **ENGLAND**.
(T) 01494 563310 **(F)** 01494 564504.
Profile Supplies. **Ref: YH06695**

HERBERT, JOHN FITZ

John Fitz Herbert, 3 The Green, Frieston, Grantham, **Lincolnshire**, NG32 3BZ, **ENGLAND**.
(T) 01400 273636. **Ref: YH06696**

HERBERT, KARN J

Karn J Herbert DWCF, The Paddocks, Kingwood Common, Henley-on-Thames, **Oxfordshire**, RG9 5NL, **ENGLAND**.
(T) 01491 628806.
Profile Farrier. **Ref: YH06697**

HERBERTSON, B R

Mrs B R Herbertson MC AMC MMCA, Easton Mead, Guyers Rd, Freshwater Bay, **Isle of Wight**, PO40 9QA, **ENGLAND**.
(T) 01983 754175.
Profile Medical Support. **Ref: YH06698**

HERD HSE RIDING SCHOOL

Herd House Riding School, Herd Hse Farm, Halifax Rd, Briercliffe, Burnley, **Lancashire**, BB10 3QZ, **ENGLAND**.
(T) 01282 436091 **(F)** 01282 436091
Affiliated Bodies ABRS.
Contact/s
Owner: Ms C Billington
(E) catherine@herdhousefarm.fsnet.co.uk
Profile Equestrian Centre, Riding School, Saddlery Retailer, Stable/Livery, Supplies.
There are a range of lessons on offer, including horse riding and stable management classes for both adults and children. The school holds shows and organises competitions. It also offers ABRS tests for pupils in both riding and stable management. **Yr. Est:** 1990
C.Size: 50 Acres
Opening Times
Sp: Open Mon - Sun 10:00. Closed Mon - Sun 21:00.
Su: Open Mon - Sun 10:00. Closed Mon - Sun

22:00.
Au: Open Mon - Sun 10:00. Closed Mon - Sun 21:00.
Wn: Open Mon - Sun 10:00. Closed Mon - Sun 21:00. **Ref: YH06699**

HEREFORD & DISTRICT

Hereford & District Riding Club, Castle Nibole Bungalow, Little Birch, **Herefordshire**, HR2 8BB, **ENGLAND**.
(T) 01981 540364.
Profile Club/Association, Riding Club. **Ref: YH06700**

HEREFORD RACECOURSE

Hereford Racecourse Co Ltd, Shepherds Meadow, Eaton Bishop, **Herefordshire**, HR2 9UA, **ENGLAND**.
(T) 01432 273560 **(F)** 01432 352807.
Contact/s
Commercial Manager: Mr S Kershaw
(E) skershaw@hereford-racecourse.co.uk
Profile Track/Course. **Ref: YH06701**

HEREFORD RIDING CTRE

Hereford Riding Centre, Grafton, Hereford, **Herefordshire**, HR2 8BL, **ENGLAND**.
(T) 01432 370240.
Contact/s
Partner: Mrs F Watkins
Profile Equestrian Centre, Riding School.
Ref: YH06702

HERITAGE COAST STUD

Heritage Coast Stud, Sudbourne, Woodbridge, **Suffolk**, IP12 2HD, **ENGLAND**.
(T) 01394 450850 **(F)** 01394 450757
(E) hcs@horseit.com
(W) www.horseit.com.
Contact/s
General Manager: Mr J Skepper
(E) jane@horseit.com
Profile Blood Stock Agency, Breeder, Stable/Livery. Specialise in Youngstock Livery. Small and large bales of hay delivered nationally. No.Staff: 4
Yr. Est: 1975 C.Size: 500 Acres **Ref: YH06703**

HERITAGE COUNTRYWEAR

Heritage Countrywear Ltd, Unit 3F Westfield Hse, Broad Lane, Leeds, **Yorkshire (West)**, LS13 3HA, **ENGLAND**.
(T) 0113 2562424.
Contact/s
Production Manager: Mr V Smith
Profile Riding Wear Retailer. **Ref: YH06704**

HERITAGE FORGE SHOWROOM

Heritage Forge Showroom, Punnetts Town, Heathfield, **Sussex (East)**, TN21 9DL, **ENGLAND**.
(T) 01435 831143.
Contact/s
Owner: Mr S Jones
Profile Blacksmith. **Ref: YH06705**

HERMANN, ANNA

Anna Hermann (SWE), 2 Highbarn Cottages, Highbarn Rd, Effingham, **Surrey**, KT24 5PR, **ENGLAND**.
(T) 01980 621309 **(F)** 01980 621188. **Ref: YH06706**

HERNE BAY

Herne Bay Trailer & Auto Services, Rear Yard/Richmond Hse, 1 Richmond St, Herne Bay, **Kent**, CT6 5LU, **ENGLAND**.
(T) 01227 749739.
Contact/s
Owner: Mr P Brown
Profile Transport/Horse Boxes. **Ref: YH06707**

HERNISS FARM LIVERY YARD

Herniss Farm Livery Yard, Herniss Farm, Longdowns, Penryn, **Cornwall**, TR10 9DS, **ENGLAND**.
(T) 01209 860959.
Profile Stable/Livery. **Ref: YH06708**

HERON BARN SADDLERY

Heron Barn Saddlery, Heron Barn, Arthog, **Gwynedd**, LL39 1BQ, **WALES**.
(T) 01341 250135.
Profile Saddlery Retailer. **Ref: YH06709**

HERON CONVERSIONS

Heron Conversions, 45 Herons Way, Pembury, Tunbridge Wells, **Kent**, TN2 4DW, **ENGLAND**.
(T) 01892 823891.
Profile Transport/Horse Boxes. **Ref: YH06710**

HERON FIELD

Heron Field Riding Stable & Animal Rescue, Warwick Rd, Knowle, Solihull, **Midlands (West)**, B93 0AU, **ENGLAND**.
(T) 01564 773406.
Profile Equestrian Centre, Medical Support.
Ref: YH06711

HERON STREAM STUD

Heron Stream Stud, Meadow Farm, Knodishall, Saxmundham, **Suffolk**, IP17 1TQ, **ENGLAND**.
(T) 01728 604008.
Profile Breeder. **Ref: YH06712**

HERONDEN INT HORSE TRANSPORT

Heronden International Horse Transport, The Mill Hse, Brede, Rye, **Sussex (East)**, TN31 6EA, **ENGLAND**.
(T) 01424 882831 **(F)** 01424 882538
(M) 07768 592088.
Profile Transport/Horse Boxes. **Ref: YH06713**

HERONWOOD STABLES

Heronwood Stables, Heron Wood, Gracious Lane, Sevenoaks, **Kent**, TN13 1TJ, **ENGLAND**.
(T) 01732 452866.
Profile Riding School, Stable/Livery. **Ref: YH06714**

HERRICK HORSEBOXES

Herrick Horseboxes, Folly Farm, Shilton Rd, Kirkby Mallory, **Leicestershire**, LE9 7QL, **ENGLAND**.
(T) 01455 888577.
Profile Transport/Horse Boxes. **Ref: YH06715**

HERRICK, H

Mrs H Herrick, Englands Farm, Croft Lane, Thurlaston, **Leicestershire**, LE9 7TB, **ENGLAND**.
(T) 01455 888224.
Profile Supplies. **Ref: YH06716**

HERRINGSWELL BLOODSTOCK CTRE

Herringswell Bloodstock Centre, Hall Farm, Church Rd, Barrow, Bury St Edmunds, **Suffolk**, IP29 5AX, **ENGLAND**.
(T) 01284 811448.
Contact/s
Owner: Captain C Coldrey **(Q)** MAE, MELA
Profile Trainer.
Break and Pre-Train Racehorses. Yr. Est: 1980
Opening Times
Telephone for further information. **Ref: YH06717**

HERRINGSWELL MANOR STUD

Herringswell Manor Stud, Tuddenham Rd, Herringswell, Bury St Edmunds, **Suffolk**, IP28 6SW, **ENGLAND**.
(T) 01638 552594 **(F)** 01639 552581.
Contact/s
Owner: Mr A Cantillon
Profile Breeder. **Ref: YH06718**

HERSHAM

Hersham Equestrian Centre & Riding School, Field Common Lane, Walton-on-Thames, **Surrey**, KT12 3QD, **ENGLAND**.
(T) 01932 222828 **(F)** 01932 222828.
Contact/s
Owner: Mrs T Underhay
Profile Riding School. **Ref: YH06719**

HERTFORD HORSE CLOTHING

Hertford Horse Clothing, 12 Templefields, Benego, Hertford, **Hertfordshire**, SG14 3LR, **ENGLAND**.
(T) 01992 581911.
Profile Supplies. **Ref: YH06720**

HERTFORDSHIRE TRAILS

Hertfordshire Trails, 12 Templefields, Bengeo, Hertford, **Hertfordshire**, SG14 3LR, **ENGLAND**.
(T) 01992 581911.
Profile Equestrian Centre. **Ref: YH06721**

HESLOP, SIMON

Simon Heslop DWCF, 57 Vindomora Rd, Ebchester, **County Durham**, DH8 0PP, **ENGLAND**.
(T) 01207 561031.
Profile Farrier. **Ref: YH06722**

HESMONDS STUD

Hesmonds Stud Ltd, Annandale Farm, East Hoathly, Lewes, **Sussex (East)**, BN8 6EL, **ENGLAND**.
(T) 01825 840471.
Profile Breeder. **Ref: YH06723**

HESTAR, EDDA

Edda Hestar, Bentleigh Farm, Pitton, Salisbury, **Wiltshire**, SP5 1EG, **ENGLAND**.
(T) 01980 863130 **(F)** 01980 863764. **Ref: YH06724**

HETHERTON, JAMES

James Hetherton, Highfield Stables, Beverley Rd, Norton, Malton, **Yorkshire (North)**, YO17 9PJ, **ENGLAND**.
(T) 01653 696778.
Profile Trainer. **Ref: YH06725**

HEVER CASTLE STUD FARM

Hever Castle Stud Farm, Hever, **Kent**, TN8 7NG, **ENGLAND**.
(T) 01732 70566 **(F)** 01732 70602.
Profile Breeder. **Ref: YH06726**

HEWITT, PAUL W

Paul W Hewitt DWCF, 4 Randall Cl, Erith, **Kent**, DA8 3ER, **ENGLAND**.
(T) 01322 342951.
Profile Farrier. **Ref: YH06727**

HEWITT, STEPHEN N

Stephen N Hewitt DWCF, Thick Penny Farm Bungalow, Red Hse Lane, Moor Monkton, **Yorkshire (North)**, YO26 8JG, **ENGLAND**.
(T) 01904 738508.
Profile Breeder, Farrier. **Ref: YH06728**

HEWITTS RIDING STABLES

Hewitts Riding Stables, Benllech Farm, Benllech Bay, **Isle of Anglesey**, LL74 8SW, **WALES**.
(T) 01248 852345.
Profile Riding School. **Ref: YH06729**

HEWLETT & ALFORD

Hewlett & Alford, 54 North St, Wilton, Salisbury, **Wiltshire**, SP2 0HH, **ENGLAND**.
(T) 01722 744006.
Contact/s
Partner: Mr R Alford
Profile Farrier. **Ref: YH06730**

HEWLETT & ALFORD

Hewlett & Alford, 38 Water Ditchampton, Wilton, Salisbury, **Wiltshire**, SP2 0JB, **ENGLAND**.
(T) 01722 743461.
Contact/s
Partner: Mr M Hewlett
Profile Farrier. **Ref: YH06731**

HEXHAM STEEPLECHASE

Hexham Steeplechase Co Ltd, The Riding, Hexham, **Northumberland**, NE46 4PF, **ENGLAND**.
(T) 01434 606881 **(F)** 01434 605814
(E) hexrace@aol.com.
Contact/s
Owner: Mr C Enderby
Profile Track/Course. **Ref: YH06732**

HEXT BROTHERS

Hext Brothers Ltd, 1-4 Roseberry Pl, Lower Bristol Rd, Bath, **Bath & Somerset (North East)**, BA2 3DS, **ENGLAND**.
(T) 01225 311956.
Profile Supplies. **Ref: YH06733**

HEY, MARTIN G

Martin G Hey DWCF, Highfield Hse, Clough Rd, Flockton, Wakefield, **Yorkshire (West)**, WF4 4AQ, **ENGLAND**.
(T) 01924 840124.
Profile Farrier. **Ref: YH06734**

HEYBROOK EQUESTRIAN CTRE

Heybrook Equestrian Centre, Slag Lane, Lowton, Warrington, **Cheshire**, WA3 1BZ, **ENGLAND**.
(T) 01942 681520.
Profile Riding School. **Ref: YH06735**

HEYLAND, A R M A

A R M A Heyland, Gazeley Gate Stables, Bures, **Suffolk**, CO8 5BW, **ENGLAND**.
(T) 01787 227361.
Contact/s
Manager: Miss J Heyland
Profile Equestrian Centre. **Ref: YH06736**

HEYWOOD

Heywood Equestrian Centre, Church Rd, Heywood, Westbury, **Wiltshire**, BA13 4LP, **ENGLAND**.
(T) 01373 823476 **(F)** 01373 823476
Affiliated Bodies BD, BSJA.
Contact/s
Partner: Mr M Discombe
Profile Arena, Equestrian Centre, Riding School, Stable/Livery, Track/Course. Summer Event Arena. Competition livery available, prices on request. Tuition for competitive and established riders offered. However, as from March 2002 the centre will be more of an event course/arena than a riding school and livery yard. Yr. Est: 1999 C.Size: 12 Acres
Ref: YH06737

HI TECH MAINTENANCE

Hi Tech Maintenance, Bryon Ave, Felixstowe, **Suffolk**, IP11 3HZ, **ENGLAND**.
(T) 01394 679123 **(F)** 01394 679124.
Contact/s
Owner: Mr H Brunt
Profile Transport/Horse Boxes. **Ref: YH06738**

HIATT, P W

Mr P W Hiatt, Six Ash Farm, Hook Norton, Banbury, **Oxfordshire**, OX15 5DB, **ENGLAND**.
(T) 01608 737255 **(F)** 01608 730641
(M) 09757 51115.
Profile Trainer. **Ref: YH06739**

HIBBERD, MICHAEL FRANCIS

Michael Francis Hibberd DWCF, Spittleborough Cottage, 67 Old Swindon Rd, Wooton Bassett, Swindon, **Wiltshire**, SN4 8ET, **ENGLAND**.
(T) 01793 850967.
Profile Farrier. **Ref: YH06740**

HICKLING, L M

Mrs L M Hickling, Ffosyr Ewig, Llandfynydd, Carmarthen, **Carmarthenshire**, SA32 7DD, **WALES**.
(T) 01558 668771 **(F)** 01558 668771.
Profile Supplies. **Ref: YH06741**

HICKMAN, JACKIE A

Jackie A Hickman DWCF, Holbeche Croft, Wolverhampton Rd, Wallheath, Kingswinford, **Midlands (West)**, DY6 7DA, **ENGLAND**.
(T) 01384 287270.
Profile Farrier. **Ref: YH06742**

HICKS COMMON LIVERY STABLES

Hicks Common Livery Stables, Warren Farm, Cloisters Rd, Winterbourne, Bristol, **Bristol**, BS36 1QS, **ENGLAND**.
(T) 01454 772128.
Contact/s
Owner: Mr S Mann
Profile Stable/Livery. **Ref: YH06743**

HICKS, A F

A F Hicks, Welsh End Farm, Welshend, Whixall, Whitchurch, **Shropshire**, SY13 2NU, **ENGLAND**.
(T) 01948 880630.
Profile Breeder. **Ref: YH06744**

HICKS, ANDREW G

Andrew G Hicks DWCF, Bridge Hse, Enstone, **Oxfordshire**, OX7 4NE, **ENGLAND**.
(T) 01608 677611.
Profile Farrier. **Ref: YH06745**

HICKS, C M

Mrs C M Hicks, Hill Farm, Aylworth, Naunton, Cheltenham, **Gloucestershire**, GL54 3AH, **ENGLAND**.
(T) 01451 850981.
Profile Trainer. **Ref: YH06746**

HIDE TO HARNESS

Hide to Harness, Brynglas, Lampeter, Velfrey, Narberth, **Pembrokeshire**, SA67 8TS, **WALES**.
(T) 01834 860534.
Profile Saddlery Retailer. **Ref: YH06747**

HIETT, PETER H

Peter H Hiett DWCF, Glenthorne, 324 Hethersett Cl, Studlands Pk, Newmarket, **Suffolk**, CB8 7BA, **ENGLAND**.
(T) 01638 668975.
Profile Farrier. **Ref: YH06748**

HIGGINS, G B

G B Higgins, Oat Sheaf Hse, Metheringham Fen, Lincoln, **Lincolnshire**, LN4 3AH, **ENGLAND**.
(T) 01526 320799.
Profile Transport/Horse Boxes. **Ref: YH06749**

HIGGS, NIGEL

Nigel Higgs, Windy Way, 76 Stratton Heights, Cirencester, **Gloucestershire**, GL7 2RL, **ENGLAND**.
(T) 01285 658397.
Profile Riding Wear Retailer, Saddlery Retailer.
Ref: YH06750

HIGGS, PHILIP DOUGLAS

Philip Douglas Higgs, 50 Swindon Rd, Horsham, **Sussex (West)**, RH12 2HD, **ENGLAND**.
(T) 01403 240686.
Profile Farrier. **Ref: YH06751**

HIGH ASH CTRY STORE

High Ash Country Store, High Ash Farm, Abbots Bromley, Rugeley, **Staffordshire**, WS15 3DF, **ENGLAND**.
(T) 01283 840267.
Profile Supplies. **Ref: YH06752**

HIGH BANK RIDING SCHOOL

High Bank Riding School, High Bank Cottage, Melford Rd, Sudbury, **Suffolk**, CO10 1XU, **ENGLAND**.
(T) 01787 310654.
Profile Riding School. **Ref: YH06753**

HIGH BEECH RIDING SCHOOL

High Beech Riding School, Packsaddle Farm, Pynest Green Lane, Waltham Abbey, **Essex**, EN9 3QL, **ENGLAND**.
(T) 020 85088866.
Contact/s
Owner: Mr C Taylor
Profile Riding School. **Ref: YH06754**

HIGH BELTHORPE LIVERY

High Belthorpe Livery, Bishop Wilton, **Yorkshire (East)**, YO42 1SB, **ENGLAND**.
(T) 01739 368238.
Profile Stable/Livery. **Ref: YH06755**

HIGH CRUNDALLS STABLES

High Crundalls Stables, Crundalls Lane, Bewdley, **Worcestershire**, DY12 1NB, **ENGLAND**.
(T) 01299 404045.
Profile Stable/Livery. **Ref: YH06756**

HIGH ELMS LIVERY

High Elms Livery, Hicks Forstal Rd, Hoath, Canterbury, **Kent**, CT3 4NA, **ENGLAND**.
(T) 01227 713324.
Profile Stable/Livery. **Ref: YH06757**

HIGH FARM STABLES

High Farm Stables, High Farm, Etton, Beverley, **Yorkshire (East)**, HU17 7PG, **ENGLAND**.
(T) 01430 810278.
Profile Stable/Livery. **Ref: YH06758**

HIGH FLIERS VAULTING GRP

High Fliers Vaulting Group, Flaxland Hse, Carleton Rode, **Norfolk**, NR16 1AD, **ENGLAND**.
(T) 01953 788705.
Profile Club/Association. **Ref: YH06759**

HIGH HERTS FARM RIDING SCHOOL

High Herts Farm Riding School, High Herts Farm, Bedmond Rd, Pimlico, Hemel Hempstead, **Hertfordshire**, HP3 8SJ, **ENGLAND**.
(T) 01923 269265 **(F)** 01923 291081.
Contact/s
Owner: Mr O Couldridge
Profile Riding School, Stable/Livery. **Ref: YH06760**

HIGH HORSES

High Horses, Little Preston, Daventry, **Northamptonshire**, NN11 6TG, **ENGLAND**.
(T) 01327 361509.
Profile Breeder. **Ref: YH06761**

HIGH HSE

High House Livery, High Hse Farm, Mendlesham Green, Stowmarket, **Suffolk**, IP14 5RQ, **ENGLAND**.
(T) 01449 766716.
Contact/s
Owner: Mr D Nunn
Profile Stable/Livery.
This is a family run business. Full, part and DIY livery available, prices on request. Vets and dentists make regular visits. **Yr. Est:** 1997 **C.Size:** 9 Acres
Opening Times
Sp: Open Mon - Sun 05:30. Closed Mon - Sun 21:00.
Su: Open Mon - Sun 05:30. Closed Mon - Sun 21:00.
Au: Open Mon - Sun 05:30. Closed Mon - Sun 21:00.
Wn: Open Mon - Sun 05:30. Closed Mon - Sun 21:00. **Ref: YH06762**

HIGH HSE EVENTING CTRE

High House Eventing Centre, Castle Acre, King's Lynn, **Norfolk**, PE32 2BW, **ENGLAND**.
(T) 01760 755781 **(F)** 01760 755778.
Contact/s
Owner: Miss R McMullan
Profile Trainer. **Ref: YH06763**

HIGH HURLANDS EQUESTRIAN CTRE

High Hurlands Equestrian Centre, High Hurlands Est, High Hurlands, Nr Passfield, Liphook, **Hampshire**, GU30 7RY, **ENGLAND**.
(T) 01428 751202.
Profile Stable/Livery. **Ref: YH06764**

HIGH PEAK TRAILERS

High Peak Trailers, Unit 12, Bridgeholme Mill, Charley Lane, Chinley, High Peak, **Derbyshire**, SK23 6DU, **ENGLAND**.
(T) 01663 750811 **(F)** 01663 750811
(W) www.trailers4sale.co.uk.
Contact/s
Accountant: J Williamson
Profile Transport/Horse Boxes. **Ref: YH06765**

HIGH TOR ARABIAN STUD

High Tor Arabian Stud, Staynall Lane, Hambleton, Blackpool, **Lancashire**, FY6 9DR, **ENGLAND**.
(T) 01253 700438 **(F)** 01253 701806.
Profile Breeder. **Ref: YH06766**

HIGH WYCOMBE RIDING CLUB

High Wycombe Riding Club, 66 Warren Wood Drive, High Wycombe, **Buckinghamshire**, HP11 1EA, **ENGLAND**.
(T) 01494 532261.
Contact/s
Chairman: Mrs J Eedle-Wells
Profile Club/Association, Riding Club. **Ref: YH06767**

HIGHAM FARM

Higham Farm, Chapel Lane, Guestling Green, Hastings, **Sussex (East)**, TN35 4HP, **ENGLAND**.
(T) 01424 812636.
Profile Riding School, Stable/Livery. **Ref: YH06768**

HIGHAM FORGE

Higham Forge, Lower Green, Higham, Bury St Edmunds, **Suffolk**, IP28 6NJ, **ENGLAND**.
(T) 01284 811111 **(F)** 01284 811111.
Contact/s
Owner: Mr A Martin
Profile Blacksmith. **Ref: YH06769**

HIGHAM, B

Mr B Higham, The Stables, Shop Lane, Badminton, **Gloucestershire**, GL9 1DH, **ENGLAND**.
(T) 01454 218324.
Profile Breeder. **Ref: YH06770**

HIGHBARN DARTMOORS

Highbarn Dartmoors, 3 Campbell Lane, Trumpington, **Cambridgeshire**, CB2 2LL, **ENGLAND**.
(T) 01223 840660.
Profile Breeder. **Ref: YH06771**

HIGHBROOK FENCING

Highbrook Fencing Co, Hammingden Lane, Highbrook, Ardingly, **Sussex (West)**, RH16 6SS, **ENGLAND**.
(T) 01444 892646.
Profile Supplies. Architectural. **Ref: YH06772**

HIGHBURN STABLES

Highburn Stables, Lesmahagow, Lanark, **Lanarkshire (South)**, ML11 9PG, **SCOTLAND**.
(T) 01555 895003.
Contact/s
Owner: Mrs J Hall
Profile Stable/Livery. **Ref: YH06773**

HIGHCLARE WOODCHIPS SUPPLIES

Highclare Woodchips Supplies, 319 Derby Rd, Bootle, **Merseyside**, L20 8LQ, **ENGLAND**.
(T) 0151 9226313.
Profile Track/Course. **Ref: YH06774**

HIGHCLERE THOROUGHBRED RACING

Highclere Thoroughbred Racing Ltd, South Gate Lodge, Woolton Hse, Woolton Hill, Newbury, **Berkshire**, RG20 9TZ, **ENGLAND**.
(T) 01635 253281 **(F)** 01635 255066.
Profile Blood Stock Agency. **Ref: YH06775**

HIGHCLIFF VETNRY PRACTICE

Highcliff Veterinary Practice, 96 High St, Hadleigh, Ipswich, **Suffolk**, IP7 5EN, **ENGLAND**.
(T) 01473 822704 **(F)** 01473 824732.
Profile Medical Support. **Ref: YH06776**

HIGHCROFT VETNRY GROUP

Highcroft Veterinary Group, High Croft, 25 London Rd, Hailsham, **Sussex (East)**, BN27 3BN, **ENGLAND**.
(T) 01323 841666 **(F)** 01323 842339.
Profile Medical Support. **Ref: YH06777**

HIGHER COBDEN FARM

Higher Cobden Farm, Cobden, Whimple, Exeter, **Devon**, EX5 2PZ, **ENGLAND**.
(T) 01404 822617.
Profile Equestrian Centre. **Ref: YH06778**

HIGHER PK FARM

Higher Park Farm, Halebourne Lane, Chobham, Woking, **Surrey**, GU24 8SL, **ENGLAND**.
(T) 01276 856335.
Contact/s
Owner: Ms K Matthews
Profile Riding School. **Ref: YH06779**

HIGHER POUND RIDING CTRE

Higher Pound Riding Centre, Higher Pound Farm, Monkton Wyld, Bridport, **Dorset**, DT6 6DD, **ENGLAND**.
(T) 01297 678747 **(F)** 01297 678730.
Contact/s
Manager: Miss C Blackford
Profile Riding School. **Ref: YH06780**

HIGHER WILLYARDS FARM

Higher Willyards Farm, Broadclyst, Exeter, **Devon**, EX5 3DB, **ENGLAND**.
(T) 01404 822423.
Contact/s
Owner: Mrs H Fuller
Profile Equestrian Centre. **Ref: YH06781**

HIGHER WINSFORD FARM STABLES

Higher Winsford Farm Stables, Abbotsham Rd, Bideford, **Devon**, EX39 3QW, **ENGLAND**.
(T) 01237 422543 **(F)** 01237 422702.
Contact/s
Owner: Mr D Patterson
Profile Riding School. **Ref: YH06782**

HIGHET JASPER SADDLER

Highet Jasper Saddler, Bracklesham Cl, Farnborough, **Hampshire**, GU14 8LP, **ENGLAND**.
(T) 01297 553317 **(F)** 01297 553317.
Contact/s
Owner: Mr J Highet
Profile Saddlery Retailer. **Ref: YH06783**

HIGHFIELD EQUESTRIAN CTRE

Highfield Equestrian Centre, Newport Rd, Hemsby, Great Yarmouth, **Norfolk**, NR29 4NN, **ENGLAND**.
(T) 01493 384423
Affiliated Bodies BHS.
Contact/s
Owner: Mr R Brown
Profile Stable/Livery. Yr. Est: 1990 C.Size: 32 Acres
Opening Times
Sp: Open 06:00. Closed 20:00.
Su: Open 06:00. Closed 20:00.
Au: Open 06:00. Closed 20:00.
Wn: Open 06:00. Closed 20:00. **Ref: YH06784**

HIGHFIELD STABLES

Highfield Stables, Highfield Farm, Hangingstone Rd, Ilkley, **Yorkshire (West)**, LS29 8BT, **ENGLAND**.
(T) 01943 609137.
Contact/s
Owner: Miss S Batters **Ref: YH06785**

HIGHGATE FARM

Highgate Farm, Over Rd, Willingham, **Cambridgeshire**, CB4 5EU, **ENGLAND**.
(T) 01954 260798 **(F)** 01954 261997.
Contact/s
Owner: Mr B Papworth
Profile Saddlery Retailer. **Ref: YH06786**

HIGHGATE VETNRY CLNC

Highgate Veterinary Clinic, 173 Highgate, Kendal, **Cumbria**, LA9 4EN, **ENGLAND**.
(T) 01539 721344 **(F)** 01539 720535.
Profile Medical Support. **Ref: YH06787**

HIGHGROVE SCHOOL OF RIDING

Highgrove School Of Riding, Long Lane, Craven Arms, **Shropshire**, SY7 8DU, **ENGLAND**.
(T) 01588 672765.
Contact/s
Owner: Mrs C Roberts
Profile Arena, Equestrian Centre, Riding School, Stable/Livery. No.Staff: 5 Yr. Est: 1995
C.Size: 26 Acres **Ref: YH06788**

HIGHLAND EQUESTRIAN SVS

Highland Equestrian Services, 7 Muir Of Clunes, Kirkhill, Inverness, **Highlands**, IV5 7PN, **SCOTLAND**.
(T) 01463 831755 **(F)** 01463 831755.
Profile Supplies. **Ref: YH06789**

HIGHLAND HORSE BACK

Highland Horse Back, Cairnarget, Longhill, Huntly, **Aberdeenshire**, AB54 4XA, **SCOTLAND**.
(T) 01466 700304.
Contact/s
Owner: Mrs F Hamilton
Profile Riding School. **Ref: YH06790**

HIGHLAND PONY GAZETTE

Highland Pony Gazette, Denmill, Tough, Alford, **Aberdeenshire**, AB33 8EP, **SCOTLAND**.
(T) 01975 562582 **(F)** 01975 562582
(E) gazette@highland-pony.demon.co.uk.
Profile Supplies. **Ref: YH06791**

HIGHLAND PONY SOC

Highland Pony Society, 22 York Pl, Perth, **Perth and Kinross**, PH2 8EH, **SCOTLAND**.
(T) 01738 451861.
Profile Club/Association. **Ref: YH06792**

HIGHLAND RIDING CTRE

Highland Riding Centre, Borlum Farm, Drumnadrochit, Inverness, **Highlands**, IV63 6XN, **SCOTLAND**.
(T) 01456 450220
(E) enquires@borlum.com
(W) www.borlum.com
Affiliated Bodies ABRS, BHS, RDA.
Contact/s
General Manager: Ms P Corker **(Q)** BHS 2, BHSII, RDASI
Profile Equestrian Centre, Riding School, Stable/Livery, Trainer.
Riding through magnificent scenery overlooking Loch Ness. No.Staff: 7 Yr. Est: 1965 C.Size: 300 Acres
Opening Times
Sp: Open 08:00. Closed 18:00.
Su: Open 08:00. Closed 18:00.
Au: Open 08:00. Closed 18:00.
Wn: Open 08:00. Closed 18:00. **Ref: YH06793**

HIGHLANDER EQUINE CTRE

Highlander Equine Centre, Bramble Farm, Old Salts Farm Rd, Lancing, **Sussex (West)**, BN15 8JQ, **ENGLAND**.
(T) 01903 754071.
Profile Stable/Livery. **Ref: YH06794**

HIGHLANDS FARM RACING STABLES

Highlands Farm Racing Stables, Collingbourne Ducis, Marlborough, **Wiltshire**, SN8 3EG, **ENGLAND**.
(T) 01264 850218
(M) 07702 880010.
Profile Trainer. **Ref: YH06795**

HIGHLANDS FARM STABLES

Highlands Farm Stables, Headley Rd, Leatherhead, **Surrey**, KT22 8QE, **ENGLAND**.
(T) 01372 378219.
Profile Stable/Livery. **Ref: YH06796**

HIGHLEA STUD & LIVERY STABLES

Highlea Stud & Livery Stables, Boxhill Rd, Tadworth, **Surrey**, KT20 7PL, **ENGLAND**.
(T) 01737 842673.
Profile Stable/Livery. **Ref: YH06797**

HIGHLING EQUESTRIAN CTRE

Highling Equestrian Centre, Highling Close Farm, Durham Rd, Haswell, Durham, **County Durham**, DH6 2AY, **ENGLAND**.
(T) 0191 5261199 **(F)** 0191 5261199.
Contact/s
Owner: Ms R Reay **(Q)** BHSAI, BSc
Profile Equestrian Centre, Riding School, Stable/Livery. No.Staff: 3 Yr. Est: 1998
C.Size: 50 Acres
Opening Times
Sp: Open 09:00. Closed 20:00.
Su: Open 09:00. Closed 20:00.
Au: Open 09:00. Closed 20:00.
Wn: Open 09:00. Closed 20:00. **Ref: YH06798**

HIGHMOOR RIDING STABLES

Highmoor Riding Stables, Cottage Farm, Thorpe Rd, Southead, Oldham, **Lancashire**, OL4 3SA, **ENGLAND**.
(T) 01457 874386.
Contact/s
Owner: Mrs E Longden
Profile Riding School. **Ref: YH06799**

HIGHSTEAD RIDING CTRE

Highstead Riding Centre, Highstead, Chislet, Canterbury, **Kent**, CT3 4LX, **ENGLAND**.
(T) 01227 860491.
Profile Riding School, Stable/Livery. **Ref: YH06800**

HIGHWAY GALLERY

Highway Gallery (The), 40 Old St, Upton-upon-Severn, **Worcestershire**, WR8 0HW, **ENGLAND**.
(T) 01684 592645 **(F)** 01684 592909.
Profile Artist and Gallery.
Also able to paint commissions, (abstract style.)
Yr. Est: 1971
Opening Times
Telephone for an appointment **Ref: YH06801**

HIGHWELL STUD

Highwell Stud, Houghton Bank, Darlington, **County Durham**, DL2 2UQ, **ENGLAND**.
(T) 01388 775148 **(F)** 01388 775148
(E) stallions@highwelltrakehnerstud.co.uk
(W) www.highwelltrakehnerstud.co.uk
Affiliated Bodies DEFRA
Alt Contact Address
La Betoulie, St Claud, Charente, France, .
Contact/s
Owner: Mr C Horn
Profile Breeder. Stud Semen Collection Centre.
Stallion production and training. No.Staff: 5
Yr. Est: 1984 C.Size: 87 Acres
Opening Times
Sp: Open 09:00. Closed 18:00.
Su: Open 09:00. Closed 18:00.
Au: Open 09:00. Closed 18:00.
Wn: Open 09:00. Closed 18:00. **Ref: YH06802**

HIGHWOOD

Highwood, Unit 1 Warneford Ave, Ossett, **Yorkshire (West)**, WF5 9NJ, **ENGLAND**.
(T) 01924 261154 **(F)** 01924 280310.
Profile Transport/Horse Boxes. **Ref: YH06803**

HIGHWOOD HORSEBOXES

Highwood Horseboxes, Highwood Farm, Off Shay Lane, Walton, Wakefield, **Yorkshire (West)**, WF2 6PR, **ENGLAND**.
(T) 01924 862252 **(F)** 01924 862252.
Contact/s
Owner: Mr C Ellis **(T)** 01924 261154
Profile Transport/Horse Boxes. Horsebox accessories. **Ref: YH06804**

HIGHWOOD STUD

Highwood Stud, Off Shay Lane, Walton, Wakefield, **Yorkshire (West)**, WF2 6PR, **ENGLAND**.
(T) 01924 862252 **(F)** 01924 862252
(W) www.irishdraughthorseuk.com.
Contact/s
Owner: Mrs C Saynor
(E) caroline@highwood34.freeserve.co.uk
Profile Breeder. **Ref: YH06805**

HILBURY SADDLERY

Hilbury Saddlery, Bury Ring Farm, Red Rice Rd, Upper Clatford, Andover, **Hampshire**, SP11 7PS, **ENGLAND**.
(T) 01264 350355.
Profile Saddlery Retailer. **Ref: YH06806**

HILDEN, D

Mr D Hilden, Plot 1, Caravan Site, Beddington Farm Rd, Croydon, **Surrey**, **ENGLAND**..
Profile Trainer. **Ref: YH06807**

HILEY, ROGER

Roger Hiley DWCF BII, 34 Woodcote Rd, Bicester, **Oxfordshire**, OX6 9UB, **ENGLAND**.
(T) 01869 242672.
Profile Farrier. **Ref: YH06808**

HI-LINE HORSEBOXES

Hi-Line Horseboxes, Westview, Broad Lane, Cawood, **Yorkshire (North)**, YO8 3SQ, **ENGLAND**.
(T) 01757 268128 **(F)** 01757 269060.
Profile Transport/Horse Boxes. **Ref: YH06809**

HILL CROFT FARM

Hill Croft Farm & Riding School, Kirkby Lane, Sicklinghall, Wetherby, **Yorkshire (West)**, LS22 4BP, **ENGLAND**.
(T) 01937 582262.
Profile Riding School. **Ref: YH06810**

HILL ENGINEERING

Hill Engineering, Old Briefing Room, 7-11 Learoyd Rd, Hemswell Cliff Ind Est, Gainsborough, **Lincolnshire**, DN21 5TJ, **ENGLAND**.
(T) 01427 668020 **(F)** 01427 668020.
Contact/s
Owner: Mr T Hill
Profile Farrier.
Shoes can be provided, or customers may bring their own shoes, the farrier offers a mobile service as well as on-site shoeing. Yr. Est: 1980
Opening Times
Open by appointment only **Ref: YH06811**

HILL FARM
Hill Farm Equestrian Training Centre, Hill Farm, Pan Lane, East Hanningfield, Chelmsford, **Essex**, CM3 8BJ, **ENGLAND**.
(T) 01245 400115 (F) 01245 400115.
Contact/s
Owner: Mr R Lawrence
Profile Riding School. Ref: YH06812

HILL FARM FEEDS
Hill Farm Feeds, Main Rd, Unstone, Dronfield, **Derbyshire**, S18 4AF, **ENGLAND**.
(T) 01246 412600.
Contact/s
Owner: Mr J Laidler
Profile Feed Merchant. Ref: YH06813

HILL FARM RIDING CTRE
Hill Farm Riding Centre, 47 Altikeeragh Rd, Castlerock, Coleraine, **County Londonderry**, BT51 4SR, **NORTHERN IRELAND**.
(T) 028 70848629
Affiliated Bodies BHS, Pony Club UK.
Contact/s
Owner: Mrs G Doherty
Profile Riding School, Stable/Livery.
Grass livery available, £20.00 a week. No.Staff: 3
Yr. Est: 1981 C.Size: 120 Acres
Opening Times
Sp: Open Mon - Sun 09:00. Closed Mon - Sun 22:00.
Su: Open Mon - Sun 09:00. Closed Mon - Sun 22:00.
Au: Open Mon - Sun 09:00. Closed Mon - Sun 22:00.
Wn: Open Mon - Sun 09:00. Closed Mon - Sun 22:00. Ref: YH06814

HILL FARM RIDING SCHOOL
Hill Farm Riding School, Hill Lane, Freshwater, **Isle of Wight**, PO40 9TQ, **ENGLAND**.
(T) 01983 752502.
Contact/s
Partner: Mr L Osman
Profile Riding School. Ref: YH06815

HILL FARM STABLES
Hill Farm Stables, Nether Wallop, Stockbridge, **Hampshire**, SO20 8ES, **ENGLAND**.
(T) 01264 781140.
Profile Trainer. Ref: YH06816

HILL HIRE
Hill Hire PLC, Colts Holm Rd, Old Wolverton, Milton Keynes, **Buckinghamshire**, MK12 5QD, **ENGLAND**.
(T) 01908 313155 (F) 01908 221798.
Contact/s
Manager: Mr A Thompson
Profile Transport/Horse Boxes. Ref: YH06817

HILL HIRE
Hill Hire PLC, Melford Rd, Righead Ind Est, Bellshill, **Lanarkshire (North)**, ML4 3LR, **SCOTLAND**.
(T) 01698 740900 (F) 01698 749609.
Contact/s
Manager: Mr D Ross
Profile Transport/Horse Boxes. Ref: YH06818

HILL HIRE
Hill Hire PLC, Bankfield Rd, Tyldesley, Manchester, **Manchester (Greater)**, M29 8QH, **ENGLAND**.
(T) 0161 7038287 (F) 0161 7038277.
Contact/s
General Manager: Mr A Morris
Profile Transport/Horse Boxes. Ref: YH06819

HILL HSE
Hill House Nursing Home and Equestrian Centre, Sand Lane, Osgodby, Market Rasen, **Lincolnshire**, LN8 3TE, **ENGLAND**.
(T) 01673 843407 (F) 01673 843357
Affiliated Bodies ABRS, BHS.
Contact/s
General Manager: Mrs S Clargo
Profile Equestrian Centre.
North Lincolnshire College Equestrian Centre is based here Yr. Est: 1986
Opening Times
Sp: Open Mon - Sun 10:00. Closed Mon - Sun 20:00.
Su: Open Mon - Sun 10:00. Closed Mon - Sun 20:00.
Au: Open Mon - Sun 10:00. Closed Mon - Sun 20:00.
Wn: Open Mon - Sun 10:00. Closed Mon - Sun 20:00. Ref: YH06820

HILL HSE STABLES
Hill House Stables, Folly Rd, Lambourn, Hungerford, **Berkshire**, RG17 8QE, **ENGLAND**.
(T) 01488 72005
(M) 07831 635817.
Profile Trainer. Ref: YH06821

HILL TOP FARM LIVERY STABLES
Hill Top Farm Livery Stables, Hill Top Farm, Ridge Rd, Marple, Stockport, **Cheshire**, SK6 7HN, **ENGLAND**.
(T) 0161 4271482.
Profile Stable/Livery. Ref: YH06822

HILL VALLEY RIDING CTRE
Hill Valley Riding Centre, Llangynidr, Crickhowell, **Powys**, NP8 1NU, **WALES**.
(T) 01874 730841.
Profile Equestrian Centre. Cross Country/ Trekking Centre. Ref: YH06823

HILL VIEW RIDING/LIVERY CTRE
Hill View Riding & Livery Centre, Sunnyside Farm, Cathole Bridge Rd, Crewkerne, **Somerset**, TA18 8PA, **ENGLAND**.
(T) 01460 72731.
Contact/s
Owner: Mrs P Congdon Ref: YH06824

HILL, ALAN
Alan Hill, Tally Hse, Stortford Rd, Standon, Ware, **Hertfordshire**, SG11 1ND, **ENGLAND**.
(T) 01920 821451.
Contact/s
Owner: Mr A Hill
Profile Saddlery Retailer. Ref: YH06825

HILL, ALAN
Alan Hill, 3 The Sidings, East Markham, Newark, **Nottinghamshire**, NG22 0RH, **ENGLAND**.
(T) 01777 838748.
Contact/s
Owner: Mr A Hill
Profile Farrier. Ref: YH06826

HILL, C R
C R Hill, 6 Torquay Rd, Kingskerswell, Newton Abbot, **Devon**, TQ12 5EZ, **ENGLAND**.
(T) 01803 872675.
Contact/s
Owner: Mr C Hill
Profile Farrier. Ref: YH06827

HILL, DOUGLAS
Douglas Hill, Pattens Farm, Southend Rd, Howe Green, Chelmsford, **Essex**, CM2 7TD, **ENGLAND**.
(T) 01245 400277 (F) 01245 400871.
Contact/s
Owner: Mr D Hill
Profile Breeder. Ref: YH06828

HILL, E BARBOUR
E Barbour Hill, Tan Y Coed, High St, Penlon, Bangor, **Gwynedd**, LL57 1PX, **WALES**.
(T) 01248 355674.
Profile Medical Support. Ref: YH06829

HILL, GEORGE
George Hill, Harraton Hse, 4 Church Lane, Exning, Newmarket, **Suffolk**, CB8 7HF, **ENGLAND**.
(T) 01638 578001.
Contact/s
Owner: Mr G Hill
Profile Blood Stock Agency. Ref: YH06830

HILL, LINDSAY
Lindsay Hill, 8 Dane Drive, Wimslow, **Cheshire**, SK9 2AH, **ENGLAND**.
(T) 01625 520368.
Profile Atrist. Ref: YH06831

HILL, N & J A
N & J A Hill, The Bothy, Hall Lane, Bitteswell, Lutterworth, **Leicestershire**, LE17 4LN, **ENGLAND**.
(T) 01455 552534 (F) 01455 552647.
Profile Breeder, Stable/Livery. Ref: YH06832

HILL, STEPHEN J H
Stephen J H Hill DWCF, Stable Cottage, Mill Rd, Gt Gidding, Huntingdon, **Cambridgeshire**, PE17 5NT, **ENGLAND**.
(T) 01832 293156
(M) 07966 248593.
Profile Farrier. Ref: YH06833

HILL, T
T Hill RSS, 30 West End, Ingham, **Lincolnshire**, LN1 2XY, **ENGLAND**.
(T) 01427 668020.
Profile Farrier. Ref: YH06834

HILL, TONY
Tony Hill, Great Rapscott Farm, South Molton, **Devon**, EX36 3EL, **ENGLAND**.
(T) 01598 760247 (F) 01598 760334.
Profile Trainer. Ref: YH06835

HILLAM FEEDS
Hillam Feeds, Border Farm, Hillam Lane, Hillam, South Milford, **Yorkshire (West)**, LS25 5HW, **ENGLAND**.
(T) 01977 683369 (F) 01977 683369
(M) 07860 328287
(E) hillamfeeds@freeuk.com.
Contact/s
Owner: Mr A Leach
Profile Feed Merchant, Saddlery Retailer.
Ref: YH06836

HILLAM TRAILERS
J Hillam Trailers Ltd, Brookside Works, Brick St, Westgate, Cleckheaton, **Yorkshire (West)**, BD19 5LD, **ENGLAND**.
(T) 01274 870632 (F) 01274 862815.
Contact/s
General Manager: Mr A Bottomley
Profile Transport/Horse Boxes. Paddock and arena maintenance.
All terrain vehicle equipment and modification of trailers can carry exercise vehicles. Ref: YH06837

HILLCLIFF STUD
Hillcliff Stud, Old Hillcliff Lane, Turnditch, Belper, **Derbyshire**, DE56 2EA, **ENGLAND**.
(T) 01773 550369 (F) 01773 550428.
Contact/s
Owner: Mrs J Woffenden (Q) BHSAI, NPS Dip
Profile Arena, Equestrian Centre, Horse/Rider Accom, Medical Support, Stable/Livery, Trainer.
No.Staff: 2 Yr. Est: 1967 C.Size: 4.5 Acres
Ref: YH06838

HILLCREST & HAVEN FARM
Hillcrest & Haven Farm, Shilton Rd, Withybrook, **Warwickshire**, CV7 9LL, **ENGLAND**.
(T) 01455 220665.
Profile Breeder. Ref: YH06839

HILLCREST FARM RIDING SCHOOL
Hillcrest Farm Riding School, Hillcrest Farm, Handcross Rd, Plummers Plain, Horsham, **Sussex (West)**, RH13 6NX, **ENGLAND**.
(T) 01403 891264.
Profile Riding School. Ref: YH06840

HILLCREST FORGE
Hillcrest Forge, Abson Rd, Pucklechurch, Bristol, **Bristol**, BS16 9SD, **ENGLAND**.
(T) 01179 373383.
Profile Farrier. Ref: YH06841

HILLCREST LIVERY CTRE
Hillcrest Livery Centre, Hillcrest Farm, Filby, Great Yarmouth, **Norfolk**, NR29 3JG, **ENGLAND**.
(T) 01493 730394.
Contact/s
Manager: Mrs J Young
Profile Stable/Livery. Ref: YH06842

HILLCREST STABLES
Hillcrest Stables, Levedale, **Staffordshire**, ST18 9AH, **ENGLAND**.
(T) 01902 892232
(M) 07880 517039.
Profile Supplies. Ref: YH06843

HILLCREST VETNRY CTRE
Hillcrest Veterinary Centre (The), Hillcrest Drive, Plympton, Plymouth, **Devon**, PL7 3DX, **ENGLAND**.
(T) 01752 336644 (F) 01752 342778.
Profile Medical Support. Ref: YH06844

HILLCROFT FARM RIDING STABLES
Hillcroft Farm Riding Stables Sicklinghall, Sicklinghall, Wetherby, **Yorkshire (West)**, LS22 6AD, **ENGLAND**.
(T) 01937 582262.
Profile Riding School, Stable/Livery. Ref: YH06845

HILLHEAD
Hillhead Equestrian Centre, South Hillhead Farm, Braidwood, Carluke, **Lanarkshire (South)**, ML8 5ND, **SCOTLAND**.
(T) 01555 772151 (F) 01555 751256.
Contact/s
Owner: Mrs P Haynes (Q) AI, BHS Int SM, BHSAI
Profile Equestrian Centre, Riding School, Stable/Livery. Yr. Est: 1983 C.Size: 70 Acres
Opening Times

Telephone for further information **Ref: YH06846**

HILLOCKS FARM

Hillocks Farm, Cleobury Mortimer, Kidderminster, **Worcestershire**, DY14 0EB, **ENGLAND**.
(T) 01299 270710 **(F)** 01299 270411.
Profile Stable/Livery, Track/Course. **Ref: YH06847**

HILLS, J W

J W Hills, Upper Lambourn, Hungerford, **Berkshire**, RG17 8QH, **ENGLAND**.
(T) 01488 73144 **(F)** 01488 73099.
Contact/s
Owner: Mr J Hills
Profile Trainer. **Ref: YH06848**

HILLS, JOHN R

John R Hills RSS, Primrose Cottage, Rumford, Wadebridge, **Cornwall**, PL27 7SS, **ENGLAND**.
(T) 01841 540748.
Profile Farrier. **Ref: YH06849**

HILLS, T

Mr T Hills, Burleigh Farm, Charing, Ashford, **Kent**, **ENGLAND**.
(T) 01233 712224.
Profile Supplies. **Ref: YH06850**

HILLSDON, ROGER C

Roger C Hillsdon RSS, 37 Cambridge Rd, Marlow, **Buckinghamshire**, SL7 2NS, **ENGLAND**.
(T) 01628 471738.
Profile Farrier. **Ref: YH06851**

HILLSIDE CLYSDALE STUD

Hillside Clysdale Stud, Middleholm Farm, Lesmahagow, **Lanarkshire (South)**, ML11 0HL, **SCOTLAND**.
(T) 01555 893616
(E) clydehorses@yahoo.co.uk
(W) www.clydehorses.co.uk.
Contact/s
General Manager: John Zawadzki
Profile Breeder. Magazine.
Producers of the Clydesdale International magazine. John Zawadzki has an extensive archive on the history of the Clydesdale breed and he continues to conduct research and writes articles about them. The Clydesdale International magazine is distributed world-wide and only contains information on Clydesdales.
No.Staff: 2 Yr. Est: 1990 C.Size: 7 Acres
Ref: YH06852

HILLSIDE RIDING CTRE

Hillside Riding Centre, Merrivale, Princetown, **Devon**, PL20 6ST, **ENGLAND**..
Profile Equestrian Centre. **Ref: YH06853**

HILLSIDE SADDLERS

Hillside Saddlers, Sutton Bingham, Yeovil, **Somerset**, BA22 9QN, **ENGLAND**.
(T) 01935 862251.
Profile Saddlery Retailer. Saddle Manufacturer.
Ref: YH06854

HILLSIDE STUD

Hillside Stud, Great Shefford, Hungerford, **Berkshire**, RG17 7DL, **ENGLAND**.
(T) 01488 638636 **(F)** 01488 638121
(M) 07887 984127
(E) davidwilliams@davidwilliams.co.uk.
Profile Blood Stock Agency, Breeder, Trainer.
Ref: YH06855

HILLSIDE STUD EQUINE SWIMMING

Hillside Stud Equine Swimming, Training Ctre, Hillside, Chieveley, Newbury, **Berkshire**, RG20 8XG, **ENGLAND**.
(T) 01488 638636.
Profile Medical Support. Swimming centre.
Ref: YH06856

HILLTOP EQUESTRIAN CTRE

Hilltop Equestrian Centre, Hillfoot Lane, Frodsham, **Cheshire**, WA6 6TA, **ENGLAND**.
(T) 01928 788235.
Profile Equestrian Centre. **Ref: YH06857**

HILLTOP RIDING SCHOOL

Hilltop Riding School, Pennsylvania Rd, Exeter, **Devon**, EX4 5BN, **ENGLAND**.
(T) 01392 251370.
Contact/s
Owner: Miss J Portbury
Profile Riding School, Stable/Livery. **Ref: YH06858**

HILLVIEW RIDING STABLES

Hillview Riding Stables, Broughton Rd, Holt, Trowbridge, **Wiltshire**, BA14 6QU, **ENGLAND**.
(T) 01225 783217.
Contact/s
Owner: Mr R Kew
Profile Riding School, Stable/Livery. **Ref: YH06859**

HILLWOOD STUD

Hillwood Stud, Stock Lane, Aldbourne, Marlborough, **Wiltshire**, SN8 2NU, **ENGLAND**.
(T) 01672 540127 **(F)** 01672 540127.
Contact/s
Partner: Miss A Darey
Profile Breeder. **Ref: YH06860**

HILLYER, M

Mr M Hillyer, South Hill Farm, Bleadon, Weston-Super-Mare, **Somerset (North)**, BS24 0BD, **ENGLAND**.
(T) 01934 812834 **(F)** 01934 812834.
Profile Breeder. **Ref: YH06861**

HILLYERS HORSE BOXES

Hillyers Horse Boxes, 82 West End, Street, **Somerset**, BA16 0LP, **ENGLAND**.
(T) 01458 442164 **(F)** 01458 448328.
Contact/s
Owner: Mr A Hillyer
Profile Transport/Horse Boxes.
Supply light weight aluminum horse box ramps and partitions. Also able to convert commercial vehicles to horseboxes. **Ref: YH06862**

HILTON HERBS

Hilton Herbs Ltd, Downclose Farm, North Perrot, Crewkerne, **Somerset**, TA18 7SH, **ENGLAND**.
(T) 01460 78301 **(F)** 01460 78302
(E) helpline@hiltonherbs.com
(W) www.hiltonherbs.com
Affiliated Bodies BETA.
Profile Medical Support, Supplies.
Export worldwide. Also stock products for humans and other animals. Yr. Est: 1990
Opening Times
Sp: Open Mon - Fri 09:00. Closed Mon - Fri 17:00.
Su: Open Mon - Fri 09:00. Closed Mon - Fri 17:00.
Au: Open Mon - Fri 09:00. Closed Mon - Fri 17:00.
Wn: Open Mon - Fri 09:00. Closed Mon - Fri 17:00.
The hotline is manned during the above hours and there is an answer phone for all other times.
Ref: YH06863

HILTON PARK STABLES

Hilton Park Stables, Hilton Lane, Essington, Wolverhampton, **Midlands (West)**, WV11 2AU, **ENGLAND**.
(T) 01922 417003.
Profile Stable/Livery. **Ref: YH06864**

HILTON, JOHN

John Hilton, 121 Lodge Lane, Dukinfield, Tameside, **Cheshire**, SK16 5JF, **ENGLAND**.
(T) 0161 3387257.
Profile Farrier. **Ref: YH06865**

HINCHLIFFE, M

Racehorse Transport, Moor Mill Cottage, Uffington, Faringdon, **Oxfordshire**, SN7 7QD, **ENGLAND**.
(T) 01367 820443 **(F)** 01367 820448.
Contact/s
Owner: Mr M Hinchcliffe
Profile Transport/Horse Boxes. No.Staff: 7
Yr. Est: 1984 **Ref: YH06866**

HINCHLIFFE, M J

M J Hinchliffe, Postdown Farmhouse, Seven Barrows, Lambourn, Hungerford, **Berkshire**, RG17 8UH, **ENGLAND**.
(T) 01488 73224 **(F)** 01488 73328.
Contact/s
Owner: Mr M Hinchliffe
Profile Transport/Horse Boxes. **Ref: YH06867**

HINCKLEY & DISTRICT DRESSAGE

Hinckley & District Dressage Group, 241A Church Lane, Whitwick, **Leicestershire**, LE6 4DP, **ENGLAND**.
(T) 01530 37343.
Profile Club/Association. **Ref: YH06868**

HINCKLEY, K A (DR)

Dr K A Hinckley, Amber Hse, Kelstedge, Ashover, Chesterfield, **Derbyshire**, S45 0EA, **ENGLAND**.
(T) 01246 590304 **(F)** 01246 590019.
Profile Breeder. **Ref: YH06869**

HINDHAUGH, HENRY HALL

Henry Hall Hindhaugh, Burdon Farm, Old Burdon South, **County Durham**, SR7 0NW, **ENGLAND**.
(T) 07774 231296.
Profile Farrier. **Ref: YH06870**

HINDHEAD TRAILER CTRE

Hindhead Trailer Centre, Rake Business Pk, London Rd, Rake, Liss, **Hampshire**, GU33 7PN, **ENGLAND**.
(T) 01730 891377.
Profile Transport/Horse Boxes. **Ref: YH06871**

HINDLIP EQUESTRIAN CTRE

Hindlip Equestrian Centre, Pershore & Hindlip College, Hindlip, **Worcestershire**, WR3 8SS, **ENGLAND**.
(T) 01905 451310 **(F)** 01905 754760.
Profile Equestrian Centre, Trainer. **Ref: YH06872**

HINDON FARM

Hindon Farm, Minehead, **Somerset**, TA24 8SH, **ENGLAND**.
(T) 01643 705244.
Profile Stable/Livery. **Ref: YH06873**

HINKLEY EQUESTRIAN CTRE

Hinkley Equestrian Centre, Marefield Farm, Mill Lane, Earl Shilton, Leicester, **Leicestershire**, LE9 7AX, **ENGLAND**.
(T) 01455 847464.
Contact/s
Owner: Mrs J Clark
Profile Equestrian Centre. **Ref: YH06874**

HINKLEY, T

T Hinkley, 6 Bell Chapel Cl, Kingsnorth, Ashford, **Kent**, TN23 3NN, **ENGLAND**.
(T) 01233 503195.
Contact/s
Manager: Mr T Hinkley
Profile Blacksmith. **Ref: YH06875**

HINTLESHAM RACING

Hintlesham Racing Ltd, Hintlesham Hall, Hintlesham, Ipswich, **Suffolk**, IP8 3NS, **ENGLAND**.
(T) 01473 652700.
Contact/s
Manager: Mr T Sunderland
Profile Trainer. **Ref: YH06876**

HINTON BULL HIRE

Hinton Bull Hire, Knypersley Farm, Stanley Bank, Stanley, Stoke-on-Trent, **Staffordshire**, ST9 9LT, **ENGLAND**.
(T) 01782 504657.
Profile Blood Stock Agency. **Ref: YH06877**

HIPPOMINIMUS STUD

Hippominimus Stud, Stone Cottage, Greatham, Pulborough, **Sussex (West)**, RH20 2ES, **ENGLAND**.
(T) 01403 77576.
Profile Breeder. **Ref: YH06878**

HIPSHOW FARM RIDING STABLES

Hipshow Farm Riding Stables, Patton, Kendal, **Cumbria**, LA8 9DR, **ENGLAND**.
(T) 01539 735689
(E) sales@horseridingholidays.co.uk
(W) www.horseridingholidays.co.uk.
Profile Holidays.
An hour and a half ride costs £14.00, two hour rides cost £20.00. Pub lunch rides are £30.00 and day rides £40.00. Group discounts available. **Ref: YH06879**

HIRCOCK, P CHALIS

P Chalis Hircock, The Smithy, Fore St, Holbeton, Plymouth, **Devon**, PL8 1NA, **ENGLAND**.
(T) 01752 830468.
Profile Farrier. **Ref: YH06880**

HIRD, JAMES C B

James C B Hird DWCF, Model Farm, Rocklands St Peter, Attleborough, **Norfolk**, NR17 1UJ, **ENGLAND**.
(T) 01953 483419.
Profile Farrier. **Ref: YH06881**

HIRE A TRAILER

Hire A Trailer, 54A Arnewood Rd, Bournemouth, **Dorset**, BH6 5DL, **ENGLAND**.
(T) 01202 424770.
Contact/s
Owner: Mr J Viney
Profile Transport/Horse Boxes. **Ref: YH06882**

HIRECO NI

Hireco NI Ltd, Herdman, Channel Rd, Belfast, **County Antrim**, BT3 9DA, **NORTHERN IRELAND**.
(T) 028 90740202 **(F)** 028 90740203.
Profile Transport/Horse Boxes. **Ref: YH06883**

HIRONS, G T

G T Hirons, 15, Wasperton, Warwick, **Warwickshire**, CV35 8EB, **ENGLAND**.

(T) 01295 680371.
Contact/s
Partner: Mrs J Hirons
Profile Transport/Horse Boxes. Ref: YH06884

HISLEY STUD

Hisley Stud, Lower Hisley, Lustleigh, Newton Abbot, **Devon**, TQ13 9SH, **ENGLAND**.
(T) 01647 277389.
Contact/s
Breeding Manager: Miss P Roberts
Profile Breeder. Ref: YH06885

HITCH N LIFT TRAILERS

Hitch N Lift Trailers Ltd, Lower Haven Farm, Trowbridge Rd, Norton St. Philip, Bath, **Bath & Somerset (North East)**, BA3 6NG, **ENGLAND**.
(T) 01225 723215 (F) 01225 722595.
Contact/s
Manager: Mr M Bryant
Profile Transport/Horse Boxes. Ref: YH06886

HITCHINGS, PETER D

Peter D Hitchings, Eulyn Farm, Croydon Barn Lane, South Godstone, Godstone, **Surrey**, RH9 8JP, **ENGLAND**.
(T) 01342 842158 (F) 01342 842158.
Contact/s
Owner: Mr P Hitchins
Profile Breeder. Ref: YH06887

HITCHMOUGH RIDING SCHOOL

Hitchmough Riding School, Monkstown, **County Cork**, **IRELAND**.
(T) 021 4371267 (F) 021 4374842.
Profile Supplies. Ref: YH06888

HJEMDAL

Hjemdal Fjordhorse Stud, Richmond Hill, Netherbrae, Turriff, **Aberdeenshire**, AB53 5SH, **SCOTLAND**.
(T) 01261 851150
(E) hjemdalstud@aol.com.
Contact/s
Owner: Mrs L Bain
Profile Blood Stock Agency, Breeder.
Opening Times
Telephone for an appointment Ref: YH06889

HOAD, R P C

R P C Hoad, Windmill Lodge Stable, Spital Rd, Lewes, **Sussex (East)**, BN7 1LS, **ENGLAND**.
(T) 01273 477124.
Contact/s
Owner: Mr R Hoad
Profile Transport/Horse Boxes. Ref: YH06890

HOARE, NICHOLAS J

Nicholas J Hoare DWCF, 1 Fallows Mead, Holton, Wincanton, **Somerset**, BA9 8AW, **ENGLAND**.
(T) 01963 34031.
Profile Farrier. Ref: YH06891

HOBBLES GREEN ANIMAL FEEDS

Hobbles Green Animal Feeds, Hobbles Green, Cowlinge, Newmarket, **Suffolk**, CB8 9HX, **ENGLAND**.
(T) 01440 783276.
Profile Supplies. Ref: YH06892

HOBBS CROSS EQUESTRIAN CTRE

Hobbs Cross Equestrian Centre, Theydon Garnon, Epping, **Essex**, CM16 7NY, **ENGLAND**.
(T) 01992 812545 (F) 01992 814840.
Contact/s
Administration: Pat Holland
Profile Equestrian Centre, Saddlery Retailer, Stable/Livery, Track/Course. Ref: YH06893

HOBBS PARKER

Hobbs Parker, Rommey Hse, Orbital Pk, Ashford, **Kent**, TN24 0HB, **ENGLAND**.
(T) 01233 502222 (F) 01233 502211
(W) www.hobbsparker.co.uk.
Contact/s
Partner: Mr J Hickman
Profile Riding Wear Retailer, Saddlery Retailer. Chartered Surveyors, Auctioneers, Valuers & Estate Agents. No.Staff: 100 Ref: YH06894

HOBBS, B

B Hobbs, The Forge, Post Office Lane, Minehead, **Somerset**, TA24 5AB, **ENGLAND**.
(T) 01643 702782.
Contact/s
Owner: Mr B Hobbs
Profile Blacksmith. Ref: YH06895

HOBBS, ROBERT

Robert Hobbs, Bath Rd, Burrington, Bristol, **Bristol**, BS40 7AD, **ENGLAND**.
(T) 01934 853258.
Contact/s
Owner: Mr R Hobbs
Profile Blacksmith. Ref: YH06896

HOBBY HORSE

Chase Cross Saddlery Ltd, 236 High Rd, Chadwell Heath, Romford, **Essex**, RM6 6AP, **ENGLAND**.
(T) 020 85993627 (F) 020 85993627.
Contact/s
Owner: Mrs M Dulake
Profile Riding Wear Retailer, Saddlery Retailer.
No.Staff: 2 Yr. Est: 2000
Opening Times
Sp: Open Mon - Fri 10:00, Sat 09:00, Sun 10:00.
Closed Mon - Fri 20:00, Sat 18:00, Sun 16:00.
Su: Open Mon - Fri 10:00, Sat 09:00, Sun 10:00.
Closed Mon - Fri 20:00, Sat 18:00, Sun 16:00.
Au: Open Mon - Fri 10:00, Sat 09:00, Sun 10:00.
Closed Mon - Fri 20:00, Sat 18:00, Sun 16:00.
Wn: Open Mon - Fri 10:00, Sat 09:00, Sun 10:00.
Closed Mon - Fri 20:00, Sat 18:00, Sun 16:00.
Ref: YH06897

HOBDEN, W J

W J Hobden, Yew Tree Cottage, Battle Rd, Dallington, Heathfield, **Sussex (East)**, TN21 9LE, **ENGLAND**.
(T) 01424 838416.
Profile Transport/Horse Boxes. Ref: YH06898

HOBGOBLINS

Mrs Hobgoblins, Westside Hse, Drumnagesk, Aboyne, **Aberdeenshire**, AB34 5BH, **SCOTLAND**.
(T) 01339 884437 (F) 01339 884437
(M) 07801 508072.
Profile Trainer. Ref: YH06899

HOBSON, J H

J H Hobson, Glovershaw Farm, Glovershaw Lane, Bingley, **Yorkshire (West)**, BD16 3AR, **ENGLAND**.
(T) 01274 566925.
Profile Stable/Livery. Ref: YH06900

HOCKENHULL, D

D Hockenhull, Shade Oak Stud, Bagley, Ellesmere, **Shropshire**, SY12 9BY, **ENGLAND**.
(T) 01939 270235 (F) 01939 270516.
Contact/s
Owner: Mr D Hockenhull
Profile Breeder. Ref: YH06901

HOCKLEY EQUESTRIAN CTRE

Hockley Equestrian Centre, Church Rd, Hockley, **Essex**, SS5 6AE, **ENGLAND**.
(T) 01702 207166.
Profile Equestrian Centre. Ref: YH06902

HOCKLEY GREEN RIDING STABLES

Hockley Green Riding Stables, Lordship Farm, Hockley Cl, Shudy Camps, Cambridge, **Cambridgeshire**, CB1 6RB, **ENGLAND**.
(T) 01799 584289.
Contact/s
Owner: Mrs J Haylock
Profile Riding School, Stable/Livery. Ref: YH06903

HOCKLEY HEATH RIDING SUPPLIES

Hockley Heath Riding Supplies, 1A Old Warwick Rd, Lapworth, Solihull, **Warwickshire**, B94 6HH, **ENGLAND**.
(T) 01564 783900.
Contact/s
Owner: Mrs S Curtis
Profile Saddlery Retailer. Ref: YH06904

HOCKLEY HOUSE STUD

Hockley House Stud, Cheriton, Alresford, **Hampshire**, SO24 0NU, **ENGLAND**.
(T) 01962 771489 (F) 01962 771787.
Profile Breeder. Ref: YH06905

HOCKWOLD LODGE

Hockwold Lodge Equestrian Centre, Cowles Drove, Hockwold, Thetford, **Norfolk**, IP26 4JQ, **ENGLAND**.
(T) 01842 828376.
Contact/s
Owner: Mrs P Ladell
Profile Riding School, Stable/Livery. Ref: YH06906

HODGE, H B

Mr H B Hodge, Pentlows, Braughing, Ware, **Hertfordshire**, SG11 2NJ, **ENGLAND**.
(T) 01920 821686 (F) 01920 823859.
Profile Supplies. Ref: YH06907

HODGES, JO

Jo Hodges Cert Ed, ACP, BHS.SM, LCSP(Phys), LSSM(Dip), Maple Pound, Church Farm Barn, Rushden Rd, Newton Bromswold, Rushden, **Northamptonshire**, NN10 0SP, **ENGLAND**.
(T) 01767 626218.
Profile Medical Support. Ref: YH06908

HODGES, R J

R J Hodges, Footsteps/Cedar Lodge, High St, Charlton Adam, Somerton, **Somerset**, TA11 7AR, **ENGLAND**.
(T) 01458 223922 (F) 01458 223969.
Contact/s
Partner: Mrs A Hodges
Profile Trainer. Ref: YH06909

HODGSON & HUNTER

Hodgson & Hunter, Galemire Veterinary Hospital, Cleator Moor, **Cumbria**, CA25 5QX, **ENGLAND**.
(T) 01946 810295.
Profile Medical Support. Ref: YH06910

HODGSON & HUNTER

Hodgson & Hunter, The Veterinary Surgery, Gray St, Workington, **Cumbria**, CA14 2NQ, **ENGLAND**.
(T) 01900 602138.
Profile Medical Support. Ref: YH06911

HODGSON, D C

D C Hodgson RSS, Moorside, 6 Lodge Lane, Danby, Whitby, **Yorkshire (North)**, YO21 2NX, **ENGLAND**.
(T) 01287 660755.
Profile Farrier. Ref: YH06912

HODGSON, J

Mr J Hodgson, Fletcher Hill Farm, High Lands, Bishop Auckland, **County Durham**, DL13 5BH, **ENGLAND**.
(T) 01388 810301.
Profile Breeder. Ref: YH06913

HODGSONS MINIBUS HIRE

Hodgsons Minibus & Private Hire, 8 West Shaw, Oxenhope, Keighley, **Yorkshire (West)**, BD22 9QR, **ENGLAND**.
(T) 01535 642913.
Contact/s
Partner: Mrs J Hodgson
Profile Transport/Horse Boxes. Ref: YH06914

HODSOCK STABLES

Hodsock Stables, Hodsock Priory, Blyth, Worksop, **Nottinghamshire**, S81 0TY, **ENGLAND**.
(T) 01909 591768.
Profile Stable/Livery. Ref: YH06915

HODSTOLL STREET LIVERIES

Hodstoll Street Liveries, Dairy Hse, Rosemary Lane, Hodsoll St, Sevenoaks, **Kent**, TN15 7JX, **ENGLAND**.
(T) 01474 813246.
Contact/s
Owner: Miss E Homewood
Profile Stable/Livery. Ref: YH06916

HOEG-MUDD, CLEA

Clea Hoeg-Mudd, The Rectory, Eyke, Woodbridge, **Suffolk**, IP12 2QW, **ENGLAND**.
(T) 01394 420800 (F) 01473 737387
(M) 07771 544865.
Profile Trainer. Ref: YH06917

HOGAN, M J

M J Hogan RSS, 2 New Cottages, Gallops Farm, Findon, Worthing, **Sussex (West)**, BN14 0RQ, **ENGLAND**.
(T) 01903 873348.
Profile Farrier. Ref: YH06918

HOGBROOK RIDING SCHOOL

Hogbrook Riding School, Alkham, Dover, **Kent**, CT15 7BU, **ENGLAND**.
(T) 01304 827644.
Contact/s
Owner: Mr J Pearson-Smith
Profile Stable/Livery. Ref: YH06919

HOGG, W

W Hogg, Greendykes Farm, Tranent, **Lothian (East)**, EH33 1EB, **SCOTLAND**.
(T) 01875 613038.
Contact/s
Owner: Mr W Hogg
Profile Blacksmith. Ref: YH06920

HOGSTON, W D

W D Hogston, Kirkstone, Mill Rd, Wingham, Canterbury, **Kent**, CT3 1NJ, **ENGLAND**.
(T) 01227 720680.
Profile Farrier. Ref: YH06921

HOLD YOUR HORSES

Hold Your Horses, Newhall Equestrian Ctre, Budlake, Exeter, **Devon**, EX5 3LW, **ENGLAND**.
(T) 01392 460125.
Contact/s
Owner: Ms L McCallum
Profile Supplies. **Ref: YH06922**

HOLDEN, MAUREEN

Mrs Maureen Holden, Tumbleweed Farm, Woodton, Bungay, **Suffolk**, NR35 2NG, **ENGLAND**.
(T) 01508 482301 **(F)** 01508 482301.
Profile Trainer. **Ref: YH06923**

HOLDENBY RIDING SCHOOL

Holdenby Riding School, Holdenby, Northampton, **Northamptonshire**, NN6 8DJ, **ENGLAND**.
(T) 01604 770752.
Profile Riding School. **Ref: YH06924**

HOLDER, MARC P

Marc P Holder DWCF, 12 Fenns Lane, Westend, Woking, **Surrey**, GU24 9QF, **ENGLAND**.
(T) 01483 797698.
Profile Farrier. **Ref: YH06925**

HOLDERNESS-RODDAM, JANE

Jane Holderness-Roddam L.V.O., Church Farm, West Kington, Chippenham, **Wiltshire**, SN14 7JE, **ENGLAND**.
(T) 01249 782050 **(F)** 01249 782940
(E) admin@westkingtonstud.co.uk.
Profile Breeder, Trainer. **Ref: YH06926**

HOLDING FALABELLA

Holding Falabella, Holding Hse, The Barracks, Hook, **Hampshire**, RG27 9NW, **ENGLAND**.
(T) 01256 763425
(E) saffi@netcomuk.co.uk.
Profile Breeder. **Ref: YH06927**

HOLE FARM

Hole Farm, Dodds Bottom, Crackle St, Nutley, Uckfield, **Sussex (East)**, TN22 3LX, **ENGLAND**.
(T) 01825 712714 **(F)** 01825 712714.
Contact/s
Owner: Ms T Fearman **(Q)** BHSAI
Profile Stable/Livery, Instructor.
DIY livery is available, details on request. Tuition is also available in eventing and confidence training.
Yr. Est: 1976 C.Size: 50 Acres
Opening Times
Telephone for an appointment **Ref: YH06928**

HOLE FARM LIVERY STABLES

Hole Farm Livery Stables, Hole Farm, Preston Bagot, Henley-In-Arden, Solihull, **Warwickshire**, B95 5DR, **ENGLAND**.
(T) 01564 795792.
Contact/s
Owner: Mr C Stevens
Profile Stable/Livery. **Ref: YH06929**

HOLE IN THE WALL

Hole In The Wall Riding School, Crook, **County Durham**, DL15 9AG, **ENGLAND**.
(T) 01388 764835.
Contact/s
Owner: Mr T Dawell
Profile Riding School. **Ref: YH06930**

HOLEMOOR HOUSE STABLES

Holemoor House Stables, Coombe St Nicholls, Chard, **Somerset**, TA20 4AE, **ENGLAND**.
(T) 01460 68865 **(F)** 01460 68865
(M) 07831 392638
(E) southcombe@racing.5.freeserve.co.uk.
Profile Trainer. **Ref: YH06931**

HOLGATE, T

Mr T Holgate, Long Gill Farm, Wigglesworth, Skipton, **Yorkshire (North)**, **ENGLAND**.
(T) 01729 840208.
Contact/s
Trainer: Mr I Holgate
Profile Trainer. **Ref: YH06932**

HOLIDAY HOMEWATCH

Holiday Homewatch, Nursery Cottage, Penybont, Llandrindod Wells, **Powys**, LD1 5SP, **WALES**.
(T) 01597 851840. **Ref: YH06933**

HOLISTIC HORSECARE

Holistic Horsecare and Equitation Centre (The), Sunnyside Manor, Hartwell, Northampton, **Nottinghamshire**, NN7 2EY, **ENGLAND**.
(T) 01604 864777
(W) www.cathytindall.com.
Contact/s
For Bookings: Olivia Absolom
(E) info@cathytindall.com
Profile Medical Support, Trainer.
Cathy Tindall is an equine behaviour therapist, she has studied for 2 years, in practical equine behaviour and equine shiatsu bodywork. She has also studied the methods of Monty Roberts. Cathy also gives advice on behavioural problems to horse magazine readers, as she is on the expert panel. Cathy is available for group workshops at your own yard, ring for further details.
No.Staff: 4 C.Size: 8.3 Acres
Opening Times
Sp: Open Mon - Sun 09:00. Closed Mon - Sun 17:00.
Su: Open Mon - Sun 09:00. Closed Mon - Sun 17:00.
Au: Open Mon - Sun 09:00. Closed Mon - Sun 17:00.
Wn: Open Mon - Sun 09:00. Closed Mon - Sun 17:00.
Can be booked by appointment **Ref: YH06934**

HOLISTIC RIDING

Holistic Riding, 11 Churchill Dr, Upper Bruntingthorpe, Lutterworth, **Leicestershire**, LE17 5QX, **ENGLAND**.
(T) 08007 830292 **(F)** 08007 830292
(W) www.holisticriding.com
Affiliated Bodies BRCP, MSEC.
Contact/s
Owner: Miss W Price **(Q)** BHS 1, BHS 2, BHS 3, BHS 4, BHS IT, Dip PM, Reiki II
Profile Medical Support. Holistic Riding Instructor.
Miss Price is a Holistic Riding Instructor, prepared to travel both in the UK and Internationally. Holistic consultation for mind, body & soul of horse & rider, particularly helpful for nervous riders, those with low confidence and low self esteem and problem horses. Advises on holistic care and management of horses. Miss Price's approach to Holistic Riding has been included on Radio 4's 'All in the Mind'.
Yr. Est: 1991
Opening Times
Sp: Open Mon - Sun 10:00. Closed Mon - Sun 17:30.
Su: Open Mon - Sun 10:00. Closed Mon - Sun 17:30.
Au: Open Mon - Sun 10:00. Closed Mon - Sun 17:30.
Wn: Open Mon - Sun 10:00. Closed Mon - Sun 17:30.
Miss Price works six days a week but her day off varies
Ref: YH06935

HOLISTIC VET

Holistic Vet, Top Cart Shed, Chilgrove Farm, Chilgrove, Chichester, **Sussex (West)**, PO18 9HU, **ENGLAND**.
(T) 01243 535494 **(F)** 07092 233930
(W) www.holisticvet.co.uk.
Contact/s
Owner: Mr N Thompson **(Q)** MRCVS
(E) nickthompson@holisticvet.co.uk
Profile Medical Support.
Veterinary Homeopathy, Acupuncture & Nutrition Referrals No.Staff: 2 Yr. Est: 1999
Opening Times
Available 24 hours **Ref: YH06936**

HOLLAND & HOLLAND

Holland & Holland, Ducks Hill Rd, Northwood, **London (Greater)**, HA6 2SS, **ENGLAND**.
(T) 01923 825349 **(F)** 01923 836266.
Profile Saddlery Retailer. **Ref: YH06937**

HOLLAND, J T

J T Holland, 8 Delph St, Whittlesey, Peterborough, **Cambridgeshire**, PE7 2HT, **ENGLAND**.
(T) 01733 840241
(M) 07721 864811.
Profile Breeder. **Ref: YH06938**

HOLLANDS, TERESA

Teresa Hollands BSc (Hons) MSc, Dodson & Horrell Ltd, Spencer St, Ringstead, Kettering, **Northamptonshire**, NN14 4BX, **ENGLAND**.
(T) 01933 624221 **(F)** 01933 625461.
Profile Medical Support. **Ref: YH06939**

HOLLIDAY, N

N Holliday, 7 Little Lane, Ilkley, **Yorkshire (West)**, LS29 8EA, **ENGLAND**.
(T) 01943 609860.
Profile Blacksmith. **Ref: YH06940**

HOLLIES FARM

Hollies Farm, Hollies Lane, Kidderminster, **Worcestershire**, DY11 5RW, **ENGLAND**.
(T) 01562 754075.
Contact/s
Owner: Sally Merritt-Collins
Profile Stable/Livery. **Ref: YH06941**

HOLLIES FARM STABLES

Hollies Farm Stables, Hollies Farm, Spondon Rd, Dale Abbey, Ilkeston, **Derbyshire**, DE7 4PQ, **ENGLAND**.
(T) 01332 280350.
Contact/s
Owner: Mr J Simpkin **Ref: YH06942**

HOLLINGDON GRANGE

Hollingdon Grange, Hollingdon, Leighton Buzzard, **Bedfordshire**, LU7 0DN, **ENGLAND**.
(T) 01525 270717.
Profile Breeder. **Ref: YH06943**

HOLLINGSWORTH, A F

Mr A F Hollingsworth, Lanket Hse, Crofts Lane, Feckenham, Redditch, **Worcestershire**, B96 6PU, **ENGLAND**.
(T) 01527 892054.
Profile Supplies. **Ref: YH06944**

HOLLINGSWORTH, R D

R D Hollingsworth, Arches Hall, Latchford, Standon, Ware, **Hertfordshire**, SG11 1QY, **ENGLAND**.
(T) 01920 821335 **(F)** 01920 822502.
Contact/s
Owner: Mr R Hollingsworth
Profile Breeder.
Full, part and DIY livery available, prices on request. Hacking available. **Ref: YH06945**

HOLLINHALL RIDE & DRIVE

Hollinhall Ride & Drive, Great Fryupdale, Lealholm, Whitby, **Yorkshire (North)**, YO21 2AS, **ENGLAND**.
(T) 01947 897470
(E) hollinequest@hotmail.com.
Contact/s
Owner: Mrs A Carter
Profile Equestrian Centre, Horse/Rider Accom.
Ride & Drive Trips. Pony & Trap drives. Small scale Bed & Breakfast opening Spring 2002. Yr. Est: 1989
C.Size: 17 Acres
Opening Times
Sp: Open Mon - Sun 09:30. Closed Mon - Sun 19:00.
Su: Open Mon - Sun 09:30. Closed Mon - Sun 19:00.
Au: Open Mon - Sun 09:30. Closed Mon - Sun 19:00.
Wn: Open Mon - Sun 09:30. Closed Mon - Sun 19:00.
Best to telephone during evenings **Ref: YH06946**

HOLLINSHEAD, DAWN

Mrs Dawn Hollinshead, Poplar Farm, Wettenhall, Winsford, **Cheshire**, CW7 4DU, **ENGLAND**.
(T) 01270 528351.
Profile Stable/Livery. **Ref: YH06947**

HOLLINSHEAD, R

R Hollinshead, Lodge Farm, Stockings Lane, Rugeley, **Staffordshire**, WS15 1QF, **ENGLAND**.
(T) 01543 490298 **(F)** 01543 490490.
Contact/s
Owner: Mr R Hollinshead
Profile Trainer. **Ref: YH06948**

HOLLIS FARRIERS

Hollis Farriers, 39 Park Rd, Tiverton, **Devon**, EX16 6AY, **ENGLAND**.
(T) 01884 258453.
Profile Farrier. **Ref: YH06949**

HOLLIS HORSE/HOLLIS FARRIERS

Hollis Horse & Hollis Farriers, Kentismoor Farm, Kentisbeare, Cullompton, **Devon**, EX15 2BT, **ENGLAND**.
(T) 01884 266398.
Profile Farrier. **Ref: YH06950**

HOLLIS, PAUL M

Paul M Hollis DWCF, 3 Newbury Cottages, Newbury Lane, Cousley Wood, **Sussex (East)**, TN5 6HB, **ENGLAND**.
(T) 01892 784636.
Profile Farrier. **Ref: YH06951**

HOLLOBONE, J C

J C Hollobone RSS, 32 Adastral Cl, Newmarket, **Suffolk**, CB8 0PX, **ENGLAND**.
(T) 01638 602259.
Profile Farrier. **Ref: YH06952**

HOLLY FARM

Holly Farm Livery Stables, Holly Farm, Cheriton

Bishop, Exeter, **Devon**, EX6 6JD, **ENGLAND**.
(T) 01647 24616 **(F)** 01647 24182.
Contact/s
Owner: Mr G Sears
(E) graham.sears@lineone.net
Profile Stable/Livery. No.Staff: 1
Yr. Est: 1994 C.Size: 50 Acres **Ref: YH06953**

HOLLY HILL RIDING CLUB

Holly Hill Riding Club, Hatfield Lodge, Nyn Pk, Northaw, **Hertfordshire**, EN6 4BW, **ENGLAND**.
(T) 01707 644580.
Profile Club/Association, Riding Club. **Ref: YH06954**

HOLLY HSE

Holly House Veterinary Surgery, 468 St Lane, Moortown, **Yorkshire (West)**, LS17 6HA, **ENGLAND**.
(T) 0113 2369030.
Profile Medical Support. **Ref: YH06955**

HOLLY RIDING SCHOOL

Holly Riding School, Holly Farm, Fellside Rd, Sunniside, Newcastle-upon-Tyne, **Tyne and Wear**, NE16 5LE, **ENGLAND**.
(T) 01207 272202.
Contact/s
Owner: Miss T Bowman
Profile Riding School. **Ref: YH06956**

HOLLY RIDING SCHOOL

Holly Riding School, Holly Cottage, Hurley Common, Hurley, Atherstone, **Warwickshire**, CV9 2LR, **ENGLAND**.
(T) 01827 872205.
Contact/s
Owner: Mrs B Brown
Profile Riding School, Stable/Livery. **Ref: YH06957**

HOLLY TREE RIDING SCHOOL

Holly Tree Riding School, Plumley Moor Rd, Plumley, Knutsford, **Cheshire**, WA16 9RU, **ENGLAND**.
(T) 01565 722188 **(F)** 01565 722188.
Contact/s
Owner: Mrs K Tramontin
Profile Riding School. **Ref: YH06958**

HOLLYWALL FARM & STABLES

Hollywall Farm & Stables, Holly Lane, Stoke-on-Trent, **Staffordshire**, ST6 4QB, **ENGLAND**.
(T) 01782 835066.
Profile Stable/Livery. **Ref: YH06959**

HOLMAN, A

Mrs A Holman, Belt Farm, Aylsham, **Norfolk**, NR11 6HZ, **ENGLAND**.
(T) 01263 733254.
Profile Breeder. **Ref: YH06960**

HOLMAN, A E & A B

A E & A B Holman, Tythe Farm, York Rd, Cliffe, Selby, **Yorkshire (North)**, YO8 6NU, **ENGLAND**.
(T) 01757 638577 **(F)** 01757 630848.
Contact/s
Partner: Mrs A Holman
Profile Hay and Straw Merchants. **Ref: YH06961**

HOLMAN, T J & I M

Messrs T J & I M Holman, Cawsand Dartmoor Pony Stud, Hazelwood, Gidleigh, Chagford, **Devon**, TQ13 8HP, **ENGLAND**.
(T) 01647 433454.
Profile Breeder. **Ref: YH06962**

HOLME FARM EQUESTRIAN CTRE

Holme Farm Equestrian Centre, Sweetholme Farm, Watery Lane, Scropton, Derby, **Derbyshire**, DE65 5PL, **ENGLAND**.
(T) 01283 813284.
Contact/s
Owner: Mrs J Freere
Profile Riding School, Trainer. **Ref: YH06963**

HOLME FARM LIVERY

Holme Farm Livery, Holme Farm, Norwell Rd, Caunton, Newark, **Nottinghamshire**, NG23 6AQ, **ENGLAND**.
(T) 01636 636552.
Contact/s
Owner: Mr K Baugh
Profile Stable/Livery. **Ref: YH06964**

HOLME GROVE FARM

Holme Grove Farm, Holme Court, Biggleswade, **Bedfordshire**, SG18 9ST, **ENGLAND**.
(T) 01767 600333 **(F)** 01767 317945.
Profile Breeder. **Ref: YH06965**

HOLME PK STUD

Messrs P R & S B Attew, Bedford Rd, Northill, Biggleswade, **Bedfordshire**, SG18 9AL, **ENGLAND**.
(T) 01767 600333 **(F)** 01767 317945
(W) www.holmetrakehners.com
Affiliated Bodies TBF.
Contact/s
Owner: Mr P Attew
Profile Breeder. No.Staff: 4 Yr. Est: 1986
C.Size: 86 Acres **Ref: YH06966**

HOLME VALLEY RIDING CLUB

Holme Valley Riding Club, 178 Meltham Rd, Lockwood, Huddersfield, **Yorkshire (West)**, HD4 7BG, **ENGLAND**.
(T) 01484 444707.
Profile Club/Association, Riding Club. **Ref: YH06967**

HOLME VALLEY SPORTS

Holme Valley Sports, 76 Huddersfield Rd, Holmfirth, **Yorkshire (West)**, HD7 1AZ, **ENGLAND**.
(T) 01484 684128.
Profile Saddlery Retailer. **Ref: YH06968**

HOLMEDOWN

Holmedown Highland Ponies, The Elms, Black Torrington, Beaworthy, **Devon**, EX21 5QD, **ENGLAND**.
(T) 01409 231285
(E) wendy.bridges@ntlworld.com
(W) www.wendy.firsedge.btinternet.co.uk.
Contact/s
Owner: Mrs W Bridges
Profile Breeder.
Opening Times
Telephone for an appointment **Ref: YH06969**

HOLMEFIELD VETNRY CTRE

Holmefield Veterinary Centre, Brayton Lane, Brayton, Selby, **Yorkshire (North)**, YO8 9DU, **ENGLAND**.
(T) 01757 705562.
Profile Medical Support. **Ref: YH06970**

HOLMEFIELD VETNRY CTRE

Holmefield Veterinary Centre, The Surgery, 17 Finkle Hill, Sherburn In Elmet, **Yorkshire (West)**, LS25 6EB, **ENGLAND**.
(T) 01977 684952.
Profile Medical Support. **Ref: YH06971**

HOLMES JOINERY

Holmes Joinery Ltd, Lincoln Rd, Wragby, Market Rasen, **Lincolnshire**, LN8 5NE, **ENGLAND**.
(T) 01673 857108 **(F)** 01673 858771.
Profile Transport/Horse Boxes. **Ref: YH06972**

HOLMES RIDING STABLES

Holmes Riding Stables, Blackburn Hse Farm, Redhouse Rd, Bathgate, **Lothian (West)**, EH47 7AQ, **SCOTLAND**.
(T) 01506 636556
Affiliated Bodies RDA, TRSS.
Contact/s
Owner: Mrs K Dennison
Profile Riding School, Stable/Livery. Trekking Centre. Livery available, prices on request, currently a waiting list. Specialise in services for the disabled
No.Staff: 12 Yr. Est: 1985
Opening Times
Sp: Open Mon - Sun 10:00. Closed Mon - Fri 19:00, Sat, Sun 16:00.
Su: Open Mon - Sun 10:00. Closed Mon - Fri 19:00, Sat, Sun 16:00.
Au: Open Mon - Sun 10:00. Closed Mon - Fri 19:00, Sat, Sun 16:00.
Wn: Open Mon - Sun 10:00. Closed Mon - Fri 19:00, Sat, Sun 16:00. **Ref: YH06973**

HOLMES, J W

J W Holmes, Long Acre, Soames Lane, Ropley, Alresford, **Hampshire**, SO24 0ER, **ENGLAND**.
(T) 01962 773191.
Contact/s
Owner: Mr J Holmes
Profile Trainer. **Ref: YH06974**

HOLMES, G

Mr G Holmes, Burlington Hse, Newton Upon Rawcliffe, Pickering, **Yorkshire (North)**, YO18 8QA, **ENGLAND**.
(T) 01751 473446.
Profile Trainer. **Ref: YH06975**

HOLMES, G L

G L Holmes, 55 Hatch Way, Kidlington, **Oxfordshire**, OX5 3JS, **ENGLAND**.
(T) 01869 350641.
Profile Farrier. **Ref: YH06976**

HOLMES, JULIA

Mrs Julia Holmes, South Gardens Cottage, South Harting, Petersfield, **Hampshire**, GU31 5QJ, **ENGLAND**.
(T) 01730 825040.
Profile Horse/Rider Accom. **Ref: YH06977**

HOLMES, M H

M H Holmes, 2 Top Rd, Worlaby, Brigg, **Lincolnshire (North)**, DN20 0NN, **ENGLAND**.
(T) 01652 618778.
Profile Farrier. **Ref: YH06978**

HOLMES, STEPHEN

Stephen Holmes, Badgers End, 214 High St, Cheveley, Newmarket, **Suffolk**, CB8 9RH, **ENGLAND**.
(T) 01638 730789
(M) 07836 264566.
Profile Medical Support. **Ref: YH06979**

HOLMESCALES RIDING CTRE

Holmescales Riding Centre, Holmescales Farm, Old Hutton, Kendal, **Cumbria**, LA8 0NB, **ENGLAND**.
(T) 01539 729388.
Contact/s
Owner: Mrs E Jones
Profile Riding School. **Ref: YH06980**

HOLMESTEAD SADDLERY

Holmestead Saddlery Superstore, Clanmaghery Rd, Downpatrick, **County Down**, BT30 8SU, **NORTHERN IRELAND**.
(T) 028 44851427 **(F)** 028 44851760.
Contact/s
General Manager: Mrs R Holmes
Profile Riding Wear Retailer, Saddlery Retailer, Supplies.
Myler bits from USA, huge range of supplements and herbs, 100's of second hand and new saddles, mobile saddle fitting service. Large and well-appointed superstore, bargain basement and complimentary coffee for all. No.Staff: 6 Yr. Est: 1980 C.Size: 3 Acres
Opening Times
Sp: Open Mon - Sat 09:00. Closed Mon, Tues, Sat 17:30, Wed, Thurs, Fri 21:00.
Su: Open Mon - Sat 09:00. Closed Mon, Tues, Sat 17:30, Wed, Thurs, Fri 21:00.
Au: Open Mon - Sat 09:00. Closed Mon, Tues, Sat 17:30, Wed, Thurs, Fri 21:00.
Wn: Open Mon - Sat 09:00. Closed Mon, Tues, Sat 17:30, Wed, Thurs, Fri 21:00.
Closed Christmas Day, Boxing Day and on the 12th July **Ref: YH06981**

HOLMESTEAD SADDLERY

Holmestead Saddlery, Holmestead Stud Farmervale, Kill, **County Kildare**, **IRELAND**.
(T) 01 4588600 **(F)** 01 4588655.
Profile Supplies. **Ref: YH06982**

HOLMESWOOD STUD

Holmeswood Stud, 104 Chapel Rd, Longton, Preston, **Lancashire**, PR4 4RA, **ENGLAND**.
(T) 01772 617570.
Profile Breeder, Stable/Livery. **Ref: YH06983**

HOLSWORTHY & DISTRICT

Holsworthy & District Riding Club, Lymsworthy Old Farmhouse, Kilkhamptonbrandis Corner, Bude, **Cornwall**, EX23 9RY, **ENGLAND**.
(T) 01288 321454.
Contact/s
Chairman: Mrs P Minchin
Profile Club/Association, Riding Club. **Ref: YH06984**

HOLSWORTHY & STRATTON

Holsworthy & Stratton Agricultural Association, Kivells, Stanhope Hse, Fore St, Holsworthy, **Devon**, EX22 6DT, **ENGLAND**.
(T) 01409 253275.
Contact/s
Joint Secretary: Mrs A Dennis
Profile Club/Association. **Ref: YH06985**

HOLT MANOR FARM

Holt Manor Farm, Hamstead Marshall, Kintbury Holt, Newbury, **Berkshire**, RG20 0HX, **ENGLAND**.
(T) 01488 658790.
Contact/s
Owner: Mr R Fiddler
Profile Breeder. **Ref: YH06986**

HOLT WOOD STABLES

Holt Wood Stables, Orchard Cottage, Holt Wood, Holt, Wimborne, **Dorset**, BH21 7DX, **ENGLAND**.
(T) 01258 840293. **Ref: YH06987**

HOLT, J J

J J Holt, The Veterinary Surgery, Inns Pk, Camelford, **Cornwall**, PL32 9RX, **ENGLAND**.
(T) 01840 212229.
Profile Medical Support. **Ref: YH06988**

HOLT, J R

Mr J R Holt, Hall Farm, Peckleton, **Leicestershire**, LE9 7RA, **ENGLAND**.
(T) 01455 824608.
Contact/s
Owner: Mr J Holt
Profile Trainer. **Ref: YH06989**

HOLTOM, GILES E

Giles E Holtom FWCF, Waunlas, Taliaris, Llandeilo, **Carmarthenshire**, SA19 7DF, **WALES**.
(T) 01558 685576.
Profile Farrier. **Ref: YH06990**

HOLTON, IVOR J

Ivor J Holton, Lower Hse Farm, High Easter, Chelmsford, **Essex**, CM1 4QL, **ENGLAND**.
(T) 01245 231469.
Profile Farrier. **Ref: YH06991**

HOLY OAK HILL

Holy Oak Hill, South Farm, Stanton Fitzwarren, Swindon, **Wiltshire**, SN6 7RZ, **ENGLAND**.
(T) 01793 763094.
Profile Stable/Livery. **Ref: YH06992**

HOLYROOD DARTMOORS

Holyrood Dartmoors, Holyrood Farm, Balne, Goole, **Yorkshire (East)**, DN14 0ED, **ENGLAND**.
(T) 01405 861936.
Profile Breeder. **Ref: YH06993**

HOME FARM

Home Farm (Driving Courses & Holidays), Maryculter, Aberdeen, **Aberdeen (City of)**, AB12 5FR, **SCOTLAND**.
(T) 01224 3732310.
Profile Equestrian Centre. **Ref: YH06994**

HOME FARM

Home Farm Riding School, Langton, Malton, **Yorkshire (North)**, YO17 9QW, **ENGLAND**.
(T) 01653 658207.
Contact/s
Instructor: Ms M Dellar **(Q)** BHSAI
Profile Riding School.
There is a flood lit outdoor school offering training for novice dressage riders and in basic jumping.
No.Staff: 2 Yr. Est: 1993 C.Size: 10 Acres
Opening Times
Sp: Open Tues - Sun 09:00. Closed Tues - Sun 20:00.
Su: Open Tues - Sun 09:00. Closed Tues - Sun 20:00.
Au: Open Tues - Sun 09:00. Closed Tues - Sun 20:00.
Wn: Open Tues - Sun 09:00. Closed Tues - Sun 18:00.
Closed on Mondays **Ref: YH06995**

HOME FARM LIVERY

Home Farm Livery, Home Farm, School Lane, Normanton Le Heath, Coalville, **Leicestershire**, LE67 2TH, **ENGLAND**.
(T) 01530 260289.
Profile Stable/Livery. **Ref: YH06996**

HOME FARM LIVERY STABLES

Home Farm Livery Stables, Bower Hse Tye, Polstead, Colchester, **Essex**, CO6 5DE, **ENGLAND**.
(T) 01787 210188.
Contact/s
Owner: Mrs O Lincoln
Profile Stable/Livery. **Ref: YH06997**

HOME FARM LIVERY YARD

Home Farm Livery Yard, Tack Room/Home Farm, Islip Rd, Bletchingdon, Kidlington, **Oxfordshire**, OX5 3DP, **ENGLAND**.
(T) 01869 350911.
Profile Stable/Livery. **Ref: YH06998**

HOME FARM RIDING STABLES

Home Farm Riding Stables, Home Farm, Langton, Malton, **Yorkshire (North)**, YO17 9QP, **ENGLAND**.
(T) 01653 658226.
Profile Riding School. **Ref: YH06999**

HOME FARM STABLES

Home Farm Stables, Kemnal Rd, Chislehurst, **Kent**, BR7 6LY, **ENGLAND**.
(T) 020 84676016 **(F)** 020 84676016.
Contact/s
Owner: Mrs P Selby
Profile Stable/Livery. **Ref: YH07000**

HOME FIELD FARM

Home Field Farm, Isle Of Wight Lane, Kensworth, Dunstable, **Bedfordshire**, LU6 2PN, **ENGLAND**.
(T) 01582 872884 **(F)** 01582 872884.
Contact/s
Owner: Mr E Maguire
Profile Stable/Livery.
Full, part and DIY livery, prices on request. Capacity of 44 boxes. Regular veterinary visits. Menage.
Yr. Est: 1989 C.Size: 2 Acres
Opening Times
Sp: Open Mon - Sun 08:00. Closed Mon - Sun 18:00.
Su: Open Mon - Sun 08:00. Closed Mon - Sun 18:00.
Au: Open Mon - Sun 08:00. Closed Mon - Sun 18:00.
Wn: Open Mon - Sun 08:00. Closed Mon - Sun 18:00. **Ref: YH07001**

HOME LIVERY & RIDING CTRE

Home Livery & Riding Centre, Home Farm, Walsall Rd, Great Wyrley, Walsall, **Midlands (West)**, WS6 6HX, **ENGLAND**.
(T) 01922 417880.
Contact/s
Owner: Mrs A Holford
Profile Riding School, Stable/Livery. **Ref: YH07002**

HOME OF REST FOR HORSES

Home of Rest for Horses, Westcroft Stables, Speen Farm, Nr Lacey Green, Princes Risborough, **Buckinghamshire**, HP27 0PP, **ENGLAND**.
(T) 01494 488464 **(F)** 01494 488767
(E) homeofrestforhorses@btinternet.com.
Profile Medical Support. **Ref: YH07003**

HOME PARK RIDING CTRE

Home Park Riding Centre, Cynghordy, Llandovery, **Carmarthenshire**, SA20 0LL, **WALES**.
(T) 01550 5204.
Profile Equestrian Centre. **Ref: YH07004**

HOME STUD

Home Stud Ltd, Rectory Hill, West Dean, Salisbury, **Wiltshire**, SP5 1JL, **ENGLAND**.
(T) 01794 341718 **(F)** 01794 341534.
Contact/s
Manager: Mr F Roland
Profile Breeder. **Ref: YH07005**

HOMESTEAD FARM JUMPING CLUB

Homestead Farm Jumping/Gymkhana Club, Homestead Farm, Galley Lane, Barnet, **Hertfordshire**, EN5 4RA, **ENGLAND**.
(T) 020 84493531.
Contact/s
Secretary: Mrs H Shelley
Profile Club/Association. **Ref: YH07006**

HOMEWOOD, J S

Mr J S Homewood, Pett Farm, Charing, Ashford, **Kent**, TN27 0DS, **ENGLAND**.
(T) 01233 713897 **(F)** 01233 714193
(M) 07836 514194.
Profile Supplies. **Ref: YH07007**

HOMFRAY, S

Mrs S Homfray, Church Cotts, Penllyn, Crowbridge, **Glamorgan (Vale of)**, CF7 7RQ, **WALES**.
(T) 01446 772228.
Profile Breeder. **Ref: YH07008**

HOMOEOPATHY FOR HORSES

Homoeopathy for Horses, Manor Cottage, Cedar St, Braunston-In-Rutland, Oakham, **Rutland**, LE15 8QS, **ENGLAND**.
(T) 01572 770220.
Profile Medical Support. **Ref: YH07009**

HONES, MARK A

Mark A Hones DWCF, Lynton, Waterside, Burwell, **Cambridgeshire**, CB5 0BJ, **ENGLAND**.
(T) 01638 741803.
Profile Farrier. **Ref: YH07010**

HONEYBALL, J

Mr J Honeyball, Manor Farm, Waterpitts, Broomfield, Bridgwater, **Somerset**, TA5 1AT, **ENGLAND**.
(T) 01823 451266.
Profile Breeder. **Ref: YH07011**

HONEYBOURNE STABLES

Honeybourne Stables Ltd, 28 Greenhill, Burcot, Bromsgrove, **Worcestershire**, B60 1BJ, **ENGLAND**.
(T) 0121 4454435.
Profile Riding School, Stable/Livery. **Ref: YH07012**

HONEYBROOK STUD

Honeybrook Stud, Bridgnorth Rd, Franche, Kidderminster, **Worcestershire**, DY11 5RP, **ENGLAND**.
(T) 01562 824575.
Profile Breeder. **Ref: YH07013**

HONEYHILL FARM RIDING STABLES

Honeyhill Farm Riding Stables, Honey Hill Farm, Little Saxham, Bury St Edmunds, **Suffolk**, IP29 5LH, **ENGLAND**.
(T) 01284 810793.
Profile Stable/Livery. **Ref: YH07014**

HONEYHILL ROSETTES

Honeyhill Rosettes, 73 Drumnasoo Rd, Portadown, **County Armagh**, BT62 4EX, **NORTHERN IRELAND**.
(T) 028 38334268 **(F)** 028 38334268.
Profile Supplies. **Ref: YH07015**

HONEYPOT

Honeypot Stud, Crossways Farm, Minehead, **Somerset**, TA24 6HQ, **ENGLAND**.
(T) 01984 41312.
Contact/s
Owner: Mrs S Kennedy
Profile Breeder.
Pure British & Irish Thoroughbred Lines for breeding coloured horses for top events. No.Staff: 1
Yr. Est: 1964 C.Size: 33.5 Acres
Opening Times
Telephone for an appointment **Ref: YH07016**

HONEYSUCKLE FARM

Honeysuckle Farm Equestrian Centre, Newton Abbot, **Devon**, TQ12 4SA, **ENGLAND**.
(T) 01626 355944.
Contact/s
Owner: Mrs A McAyaj
Profile Breeder, Riding School, Stable/Livery, Track/Course. **Ref: YH07017**

HONLEY LIVERY STABLES

Honley Livery Stables, Westfield Farm, Wood Nook, Meltham, Huddersfield, **Yorkshire (West)**, HD7 3DU, **ENGLAND**.
(T) 01484 661976.
Contact/s
Owner: Mr P Mellor
Profile Stable/Livery. **Ref: YH07018**

HONNINGTON

Honnington Equestrian Centre, Vauxhall Lane, Tunbridge Wells, **Kent**, TN4 0XD, **ENGLAND**.
(T) 01892 546230.
Contact/s
Instructor: Mr B Cooke **(Q)** BHSII
Profile Equestrian Centre, Riding School, Stable/Livery.
Full, part and DIY livery, prices on request. Training up to BHS AI. No.Staff: 15 Yr. Est: 1981
C.Size: 750 Acres
Opening Times
Sp: Open Mon - Sun 09:00. Closed Mon - Fri 21:00, Sat, Sun 18:00.
Su: Open Mon - Sun 09:00. Closed Mon - Fri 21:00, Sat, Sun 18:00.
Au: Open Mon - Sun 09:00. Closed Mon - Fri 21:00, Sat, Sun 18:00.
Wn: Open Mon - Sun 09:00. Closed Mon - Fri 21:00, Sat, Sun 18:00.
No lessons on Mondays, weekends last lesson at 17:00 **Ref: YH07019**

HOOD, BARBARA

Mrs Barbara Hood, Ivytodd Farm, Ashdon, Saffron Walden, **Essex**, CB10 2NA, **ENGLAND**.
(T) 01799 584445.
Profile Medical Support. **Ref: YH07020**

HOOD, C L

C L Hood RSS, Robin Hill, Chapel Rd, Swanmore, **Hampshire**, SO32 2QA, **ENGLAND**.
(T) 01489 895419.
Profile Farrier. **Ref: YH07021**

HOOD, G

G Hood, Chapelwell Hse, Cupar, **Fife**, KY15 4RH, **SCOTLAND**.
(T) 01334 655848.
Profile Farrier. **Ref: YH07022**

HOOD, J R

J R Hood Ltd, Chesney Farm, Wansford Rd, Driffield, **Yorkshire (East)**, YO25 5NW, **ENGLAND**.

(T) 01377 241619 (F) 01377 252958.
Profile Hay and Straw Merchants. Ref: YH07023

HOOD, J S F

J S F Hood Ltd, The Grange, Grange-De-Lings, **Lincolnshire**, LN2 2NB, **ENGLAND**.
(T) 01522 750602 (F) 01522 595923.
Profile Track/Course. Ref: YH07024

HOOF ALOOF

Hoof Aloof, 29 Oakwood Drive, Ravenshead, Nottingham, **Nottinghamshire**, NG15 9DP, **ENGLAND**.
(T) 01623 795628.
Profile Riding Wear Retailer, Saddlery Retailer, Supplies. Ref: YH07025

HOOF CARE

Hoof Care Ltd, 14 Thorn Lane, Four Marks, Alton, **Hampshire**, GU34 5BT, **ENGLAND**.
(T) 01420 562800 (F) 01420 563728.
Profile Farrier. Ref: YH07026

HOOF PRINTS

Hoof Prints, Pear Tree Cottage, 14 Rosemary Lane, Haddenham, **Buckinghamshire**, HP17 8JS, **ENGLAND**.
(T) 01844 291132 (F) 01844 291132. Ref: YH07027

HOOFBEAT

Hoofbeat, 12 Tolbooth St, Forres, **Moray**, IV36 1PH, **SCOTLAND**.
(T) 01309 676830.
Contact/s
Owner: Mrs L Spence
Profile Riding Wear Retailer, Saddlery Retailer.
Ref: YH07028

HOOFBEATS

Hoofbeats, 66 Old Station Rd, Newmarket, **Suffolk**, CB8 8AA, **ENGLAND**.
(T) 01638 668455. Ref: YH07029

HOOFBEATS & PAWPRINTS

Hoofbeats & Pawprints, Game Lea Farm, Eastmore, Chesterfield, **Derbyshire**, S42 7DB, **ENGLAND**.
(T) 01246 566557 (F) 01246 567878
(E) sales@hoofs&paws.co.uk.
Contact/s
Editor: Mrs E Hill
Profile Supplies. Ref: YH07030

HOOF'N'HOUND

Hoof'n'Hound, 68 Murray St, Hartlepool, **Cleveland**, TS26 8PL, **ENGLAND**.
(T) 01429 266566 (F) 01429 854004
Affiliated Bodies BETA.
Contact/s
Owner: Mr D Hutchinson
Profile Riding Wear Retailer, Saddlery Retailer, Supplies. No.Staff: 5 Yr. Est: 1999
Opening Times
Sp: Open Mon, Wed - Fri 11:00, Sat 10:00. Closed Mon, Wed - Fri 18:00, Sat 17:00.
Su: Open Mon, Wed - Fri 11:00, Sat 10:00. Closed Mon, Wed - Fri 18:00, Sat 17:00.
Au: Open Mon, Wed - Fri 11:00, Sat 10:00. Closed Mon, Wed - Fri 18:00, Sat 17:00.
Wn: Open Mon, Wed - Fri 11:00, Sat 10:00. Closed Mon, Wed - Fri 18:00, Sat 17:00. Ref: YH07031

HOOF'N'HOUND

Hoof'n'Hound, 63 Acklam Rd, Middlesbrough, **Cleveland**, TS5 5HA, **ENGLAND**.
(T) 01642 829158.
Contact/s
Partner: Mrs K Hutchinson
Profile Riding Wear Retailer, Saddlery Retailer, Supplies.
Opening Times
Sp: Open Mon, Wed -Sat 10:00. Closed Mon, Wed - Sat 17:00.
Su: Open Mon, Wed -Sat 10:00. Closed Mon, Wed - Sat 17:00.
Au: Open Mon, Wed -Sat 10:00. Closed Mon, Wed - Sat 17:00.
Wn: Open Mon, Wed -Sat 10:00. Closed Mon, Wed - Sat 17:00. Ref: YH07032

HOOFPRINT

Hoofprint, P O Box 7, Knutsford, **Cheshire**, WA16 7PP, **ENGLAND**.
(T) 01565 872107 (F) 01565 873943.
Profile Supplies. Ref: YH07033

HOOK FARM EQUESTRIAN CTRE

Hook Farm Equestrian Centre, Hook Farm Rd, Bridgnorth, **Shropshire**, WV16 4RD, **ENGLAND**.
(T) 01746 762872.
Contact/s
Owner: Mr G Bennett
Profile Equestrian Centre. Ref: YH07034

HOOK HSE

Hook House, Hook Rd, Wimblington, March, **Cambridgeshire**, PE15 0QL, **ENGLAND**.
(T) 01354 741538 (F) 01453 741182
(E) hook.house@virgin.net.
Contact/s
Owner: Mrs L Wright
Profile Breeder, Riding Wear Retailer, Saddlery Retailer, Stable/Livery, Supplies, Trainer.
Mrs Wright is a riding and road safety examiner, an NVQ assessor and a Ponies UK judge. She trains Exmoor ponies for show production, and has a standing Exmoor stallion. No.Staff: 1 Yr. Est: 2001
C.Size: 4 Acres
Opening Times
Sp: Open Mon - Sun 08:00. Closed Mon - Sun 20:00.
Su: Open Mon - Sun 08:00. Closed Mon - Sun 20:00.
Au: Open Mon - Sun 08:00. Closed Mon - Sun 20:00.
Wn: Open Mon - Sun 08:00. Closed Mon - Sun 20:00. Ref: YH07035

HOOK, ELLIOT W G

Elliot W G Hook DWCF, 7 Union St, Hawick, **Scottish Borders**, TD9 9LR, **SCOTLAND**.
(T) 01450 378118.
Profile Farrier. Ref: YH07036

HOOKE FARM LIVERY STABLES

Hooke Farm Livery Stables, Effingham Common, Effingham, Leatherhead, **Surrey**, KT24 5JE, **ENGLAND**.
(T) 01372 454922.
Profile Stable/Livery. Ref: YH07037

HOOKS & HOOVES

Hooks & Hooves, 15 High St, Ringstead, Kettering, **Northamptonshire**, NN14 4DA, **ENGLAND**.
(T) 01933 461539 (F) 01933 461692.
Contact/s
Owner: Miss S Johnson
Profile Riding Wear Retailer.
Angling & equestrian shop. Yr. Est: 2000
Opening Times
Sp: Open Mon - Sat 09:00, Sun 10:00. Closed Mon, Tues, Wed 17:00, Thurs 18:00, Fri 19:00, Sat 17:00, Sun 14:00.
Su: Open Mon - Sat 09:00, Sun 10:00. Closed Mon, Tues, Wed 17:00, Thurs 18:00, Fri 19:00, Sat 17:00, Sun 14:00.
Au: Open Mon - Sat 09:00, Sun 10:00. Closed Mon, Tues, Wed 17:00, Thurs 18:00, Fri 19:00, Sat 17:00, Sun 14:00.
Wn: Open Mon - Sat 09:00, Sun 10:00. Closed Mon, Tues, Wed 17:00, Thurs 18:00, Fri 19:00, Sat 17:00, Sun 14:00. Ref: YH07038

HOOKS HALL EQUESTRIAN CLUB

Hooks Hall Equestrian Club (Barking), 95 Stanley Rd North, Rainham, **Essex**, RM13 8BA, **ENGLAND**.
(T) 01708 556253.
Contact/s
Chairman: Mrs J Bowerman
Profile Club/Association. Ref: YH07039

HOOLE, J J

J J Hoole, School Farm, Bank Lane, Warton, Preston, **Lancashire**, PR4 1TB, **ENGLAND**.
(T) 01772 679166.
Profile Farrier. Ref: YH07040

HOOLEY, C & A

C & A Hooley, Sheppon Hill Stables, Hoarwithy, Hereford, **Herefordshire**, HR2 6QU, **ENGLAND**.
(T) 01989 730620.
Contact/s
Owner: Mrs A Hooley
Profile Trainer. Ref: YH07041

HOOPER, FRANCES

Frances Hooper, Palmers Cottage, Coneyhurst, Billingshurst, **Sussex (West)**, RH14 9DN, **ENGLAND**.
(T) 01403 782575. Ref: YH07042

HOOPER, K E

K E Hooper, Gelli Ganol Farm, Llwynteg, Llannon, Llanelli, **Carmarthenshire**, SA14 8JP, **WALES**.
(T) 01269 845488.
Contact/s
Owner: Mrs K Hooper
Profile Breeder.
Breeder of Welsh Section B ponies Ref: YH07043

HOOPER, PENNIE

Ms Pennie Hooper, Fruit, Froxfield, Marlborough, **Wiltshire**, SN8 3LD, **ENGLAND**.
(T) 01488 684111 (F) 01488 684111
(M) 07710 380994.
Profile Medical Support. Ref: YH07044

HOOPER'S SADDLERS SHOP

Hooper's Saddlers Shop, 10-12 South St, Walsall, **Midlands (West)**, WS1 4HE, **ENGLAND**.
(T) 01922 633773 (F) 01922 720940.
Profile Saddlery Retailer. Ref: YH07045

HOORAY HENRY'S

Hooray Henry's, 26 High St, Much Wenlock, **Shropshire**, TF13 6AB, **ENGLAND**.
(T) 01952 727042 (F) 01952 727799.
Profile Saddlery Retailer. Ref: YH07046

HOOVES EQUESTRIAN

Hooves Equestrian, Churchill Hall, Whitehall Rd East, Birkenshaw, Bradford, **Yorkshire (West)**, BD11 2NA, **ENGLAND**.
(T) 01274 653533 (F) 01274 653045
(W) www.hooves-equestrian.co.uk.
Contact/s
General Manager: Mr J Lyner
(E) jim@hooves-equestrian.co.uk
Profile Riding Wear Retailer, Saddlery Retailer, Supplies.
Specialise in Western saddles and safety wear.
No.Staff: 4 Yr. Est: 1996
Opening Times
Sp: Open Mon - Sat 10:00. Closed Mon - Sat 17:30.
Su: Open Mon - Sat 10:00. Closed Mon - Sat 17:30.
Au: Open Mon - Sat 10:00. Closed Mon - Sat 17:30.
Wn: Open Mon - Sat 10:00. Closed Mon - Sat 17:30.
Ref: YH07047

HOP GARDEN STABLES

Hop Garden Stables, Tonbridge Rd, Teston, Maidstone, **Kent**, ME18 5BT, **ENGLAND**.
(T) 01622 813907.
Profile Stable/Livery. Ref: YH07048

HOPCROFT TRANSPORT

Hopcroft Transport, 25 Oxford Rd, Oakley, Aylesbury, **Buckinghamshire**, HP18 9RD, **ENGLAND**.
(T) 01844 237553.
Profile Transport/Horse Boxes. Ref: YH07049

HOPE END RACING

Hope End Racing Ltd, Hope End, Ledbury, **Herefordshire**, HR8 1JQ, **ENGLAND**.
(T) 01684 311760 (F) 01684 311960
(M) 07887 558627.
Contact/s
Assistant Trainer: Miss J Tremain
Profile Trainer. Ref: YH07050

HOPE FARM RIDING SCHOOL

Hope Farm Riding School, Hope Farm, Halegate Rd, Widnes, **Cheshire**, WA8 8LZ, **ENGLAND**.
(T) 0151 4253878.
Contact/s
Owner: Mr P Brindle
Profile Riding School. Ref: YH07051

HOPES AUCTION

Hopes Auction Co Ltd, Wigton, **Cumbria**, CA7 9PG, **ENGLAND**.
(T) 01697 342202 (F) 01697 345001.
Profile Auctioneers. Ref: YH07052

HOPKINS, K

Mr & Mrs K Hopkins, The Barn, Portfield Farm, Whalley, Clitheroe, **Lancashire**, BB7 9DP, **ENGLAND**.
(T) 01254 824515.
Profile Breeder. Ref: YH07053

HOPKINS, PAUL T

Paul T Hopkins RSS, Summerhill Hse, Naunton, Cheltenham, **Gloucestershire**, GL54 3AZ, **ENGLAND**.
(T) 01451 850514.
Profile Farrier. Ref: YH07054

HOPKINSON & HURST

Hopkinson & Hurst, 16 Nottingham Rd, Alfreton, **Derbyshire**, DE55 7HL, **ENGLAND**.
(T) 01773 832218.
Profile Medical Support. Ref: YH07055

HOPKINSON, RICHARD

Mr Richard Hopkinson, Common Farm, Thorpe Audlin, Pontefract, **Yorkshire (West)**, WF8 3HE,

ENGLAND.
(T) 01977 621383. Ref: YH07056

HOPKINSON, S R

S R Hopkinson, Poplar Birch, Rowthorne Village, Glapwell, Chesterfield, **Derbyshire**, S44 5QQ, **ENGLAND**.
(T) 01623 810930.
Contact/s
Owner: Mr S Hopkinson
Profile Transport/Horse Boxes. Ref: YH07057

HOPLANDS EQUESTRIAN

Hoplands Equestrian Centre, Kings Somborne, Stockbridge, **Hampshire**, SO20 6QH, **ENGLAND**.
(T) 01794 389085/ 389022 (F) 01794 389020
(W) www.horsefair.co.uk.
Contact/s
Customer Service Manager: Mrs A Porter
(E) abby@horsefair.co.uk
Profile Arena, Equestrian Centre, Saddlery Retailer, Stable/Livery, Supplies, Track/Course, Trainer.
No.Staff: 4 Yr. Est: 1995 C.Size: 70 Acres
Ref: YH07058

HOPPER

Hopper, Home Farm, East End, Adderbury, Banbury, **Oxfordshire**, OX17 3NW, **ENGLAND**.
(T) 01295 810310.
Profile Transport/Horse Boxes. Ref: YH07059

HOPSFORD HALL LIVERY YARD

Hopsford Hall Livery Yard, Withybrook Lane, Shilton, Coventry, **Warwickshire**, CV7 9JJ, **ENGLAND**.
(T) 01455 220974 (F) 01455 220375.
Profile Stable/Livery. Ref: YH07060

HOPTON

Hopton Horse Centre, Mount Pleasant Farm, Jackroyd Lane, Upper Hopton, Mirfield, **Yorkshire (West)**, WF14 8EH, **ENGLAND**.
(T) 01924 492020
Affiliated Bodies BHS.
Contact/s
Owner: Miss J Chambers
Profile Arena, Stable/Livery.
There are three arenas available for hire. There is also a horse shower on site. Yr. Est: 1984 C.Size: 60 Acres
Opening Times
Telephone for further information Ref: YH07061

HOPWOOD, CHRISTOPHER J

Christopher J Hopwood DWCF, Hockmoor Farm, Buckfastleigh, **Devon**, TQ11 0HW, **ENGLAND**.
(T) 01364 642951.
Profile Farrier. Ref: YH07062

HORACE FULLER

Horace Fuller Ltd, Feedex Works, 72 Park St, Horsham, **Sussex (West)**, RH12 1BY, **ENGLAND**.
(T) 01403 265030.
Contact/s
Owner: Mr B Stally
Profile Saddlery Retailer. Ref: YH07063

HORAM MANOR

Horam Manor Riding & Livery Stables, Horam, Heathfield, **Sussex (East)**, TN21 0JD, **ENGLAND**.
(T) 01435 812363.
Profile Riding School. Ref: YH07064

HORAN T & SONS

Horan T & Sons Ltd, 22 Tralee Rd, Castleisland, Kerry, **County Kerry**, **IRELAND**.
(T) 066 7141274.
Profile Supplies. Ref: YH07065

HORGAN, C A

Mr C A Horgan, Codmore Field Hse, Hill Farm Lane, Pulborough, **Sussex (West)**, RH20 1BJ, **ENGLAND**.
(T) 01798 874511 (F) 01798 874221
(M) 07850 365459.
Profile Trainer. Ref: YH07066

HORGAN, TIMOTHY

Horgan Timothy, Glenview Hse, Bandon, **County Cork**, **IRELAND**.
(T) 023 41523.
Profile Supplies. Ref: YH07067

HORIZONT

Horizont UK Ltd, P O Box 167, Gloucester, **Gloucestershire**, GL2 8YS, **ENGLAND**.
(T) 01452 300 450 (F) 01452 308 776
(E) bramley@horizont.com
(W) www.bramley.co.uk.
Profile Supplies.
Produce electric netting, wires, fences, batteries, posts and lamps. Ref: YH07068

HORLER, CAROL J

Carol J Horler, Bowerhill Lodge Farm, Longleaze Lane, Melksham, **Wiltshire**, SN12 6QL, **ENGLAND**.
(T) 01225 707737 (F) 01225 707737
(M) 07712 929829. Ref: YH07069

HORLER, M A

M A Horler (Radford), The Old Malt Hse, Radford, Timsbury, Bath, **Bath & Somerset (North East)**, BA3 1QF, **ENGLAND**.
(T) 01761 470106.
Contact/s
Owner: Mr M Horler
Profile Breeder, Trainer. Ref: YH07070

HORLEY & DISTRICT RIDING CLUB

Horley & District Riding Club, Dowlands Park Farm, Cross Lane, Smallfield, **Surrey**, RH6 9SA, **ENGLAND**.
(T) 01342 843132.
Contact/s
Secretary: Jan Williams
Profile Club/Association, Riding Club. Ref: YH07071

HORN, CAMILLA

Camilla Horn, Upper Woodbatch Farm, Deerfold, Lingen, Bucknell, **Shropshire**, SY7 0EF, **ENGLAND**.
(T) 01568 770425 (F) 01568 770524.
Profile Breeder. Ref: YH07072

HORN, J M

J M Horn, Main Rd, Holland Fen, Lincoln, **Lincolnshire**, LN4 4QH, **ENGLAND**.
(T) 01205 280228.
Contact/s
Owner: Mr J Horn
Profile Blacksmith. Ref: YH07073

HORNBLOWER, S & SEARS, S

S Hornblower & S Sears, Ivycroft Stud, Wall Hill Rd, Corley Moor, Coventry, **Warwickshire**, CV7 8AH, **ENGLAND**.
(T) 01676 540771.
Profile Breeder. Ref: YH07074

HORNBY, W M

Pool House Farm, Moss Lane, Churchtown, Southport, **Merseyside**, PR9 7QS, **ENGLAND**.
(T) 01704 225304.
Profile Stable/Livery. Ref: YH07075

HORNER COMPONENTS

Horner Components, 30 Lough Rd, Ballinderry Upper, Lisburn, **County Antrim**, BT28 2LA, **NORTHERN IRELAND**.
(T) 028 94422207.
Contact/s
Partner: Mr E Turtle
Profile Transport/Horse Boxes. Ref: YH07076

HORNER FARM RIDING STABLES

Horner Farm Riding Stables, Horner, Porlock, Minehead, **Somerset**, TA24 8HY, **ENGLAND**.
(T) 01643 862456.
Profile Riding School. Ref: YH07077

HORNER, ADRIAN J

Adrian J Horner RSS, Holly Cottage, 1 Colton Rd, Marlingford, Norwich, **Norfolk**, NR9 5HS, **ENGLAND**.
(T) 01603 880012.
Profile Farrier. Ref: YH07078

HORNER, JOHN D

John D Horner, 91 Gawston Rd, Aylsham, **Norfolk**, NR11 6NB, **ENGLAND**.
(T) 01263 731220.
Profile Farrier. Ref: YH07079

HORNER, PAUL J

Paul J Horner DWCF, Quinces, Wick-St-Lawrence, Weston-Super-Mare, **Somerset (North)**, BS22 0YL, **ENGLAND**.
(T) 01934 515064.
Profile Farrier. Ref: YH07080

HORNER-HARKER, S

Mrs S Horner-Harker, Saltergill Pk, Low Worsall, Yarm, Stockton-on-Tees, **Cleveland**, TS15 9PG, **ENGLAND**.
(T) 01642 788825
(M) 07767 368706.
Profile Supplies. Ref: YH07081

HORNS FARM

Horns Farm Livery Yard, Horns Rd, Stroud, **Gloucestershire**, GL6 7LF, **ENGLAND**.
(T) 01453 751695.
Contact/s
Owner: Miss H Silverthorne
Profile Stable/Livery.
Full, part and DIY livery available, prices on request.
No.Staff: 1 Yr. Est: 1981
Opening Times
Sp: Open Mon - Sun 08:00. Closed Mon - Sun 20:00.
Su: Open Mon - Sun 08:00. Closed Mon - Sun 20:00.
Au: Open Mon - Sun 08:00. Closed Mon - Sun 20:00.
Wn: Open Mon - Sun 08:00. Closed Mon - Sun 20:00. Ref: YH07082

HORNWALK EQUESTRIAN

Hornwalk Equestrian Ltd, Corke Farm, Cwmcarvan, Monmouth, **Monmouthshire**, NP25 4JP, **WALES**.
(T) 01600 860279.
Contact/s
Owner: Mr M Courtney
Profile Stable/Livery.
Pony hire available. Ref: YH07083

HORSBURGH, THOMAS

Thomas Horsburgh, 243 Willowbrae Rd, Edinburgh, **Edinburgh (City of)**, EH8 7NE, **SCOTLAND**.
(T) 0131 6692079.
Profile Blacksmith. Ref: YH07084

HORSCRAFT, MARIANNE

Mrs Marianne Horscraft, 12 Mill Rd, Steyning, **Sussex (West)**, BN44 3LN, **ENGLAND**.
(T) 01903 812336.
Profile Breeder. Ref: YH07085

HORSE & COUNTRY

Horse & Country, 36 St. Mary St, Newport, **Shropshire**, TF10 7AB, **ENGLAND**.
(T) 01952 814684.
Profile Riding Wear Retailer, Saddlery Retailer.
Ref: YH07086

HORSE & COUNTRY STORE

Horse & Country Store, Egan Complex, Dargle Rd, Bray, **County Wicklow**, **IRELAND**.
(T) 01 2761271 (F) 01 2761273. Ref: YH07087

HORSE & COUNTRY SUPERSTORE

Horse & Country Superstore, Newnham Court Ctre, Bearsted Rd, Weavering, Maidstone, **Kent**, ME14 5LH, **ENGLAND**.
(T) 01622 735537 (F) 01622 631633.
Contact/s
Manageress: Mrs L Adams
Profile Riding Wear Retailer, Supplies. Ref: YH07088

HORSE & GARDEN

Horse & Garden Supplies, The Thoroughfare, Halesworth, **Suffolk**, IP19 8AP, **ENGLAND**.
(T) 01986 873484 (F) 01986 873484.
Contact/s
Owner: Ms D Howlett
Profile Riding Wear Retailer, Supplies.
Also stock electric fencing, stable fittings and country clothing. No.Staff: 6 Yr. Est: 1980
Opening Times
Sp: Open Mon - Sat 09:00. Closed Mon - Sat 17:00.
Su: Open Mon - Sat 09:00. Closed Mon - Sat 17:00.
Au: Open Mon - Sat 09:00. Closed Mon - Sat 17:00.
Wn: Open Mon - Sat 09:00. Closed Mon - Sat 17:00.
The shop is closed between 13:00 - 14:00 and on Sundays Ref: YH07089

HORSE & HOUND

Horse & Hound, Room 2123, Kings Reach Tower, Stamford St, London, **London (Greater)**, SE1 9LS, **ENGLAND**.
(T) 020 72615313 (F) 020 72615202
(E) suzanne_aust@ipc.co.uk.
Contact/s
Editor: Mr M Hedges
Profile Supplies. Ref: YH07090

HORSE & HOUND FEED SUPPLIES

Horse & Hound Feed Supplies, Craigmaddie Rd, Bardowie, Milngavie, **Glasgow (City of)**, G62 6EY, **SCOTLAND**.
(T) 01360 620754 (F) 01360 620754
(E) sales@equi-store.wiz.net.uk.
Profile Supplies. Ref: YH07091

HORSE & HOUNDS

Horse & Hounds (The), Buckland Common, Tring, **Hertfordshire**, HP23 6NQ, **ENGLAND**.
(T) 01494 758336
(M) 07831 309646.
Profile Farrier. Ref: YH07092

HORSE & JOCKEY

Horse & Jockey Ltd, Peterchurch, Hereford, **Herefordshire**, HR2 0RP, **ENGLAND**.
(T) 01981 550467 **(F)** 01981 550432.
Contact/s
Senior Partner: Mrs C Murrin
Profile Riding Wear Retailer, Saddlery Retailer, Supplies.
Manufacturer of hat silks **Ref: YH07093**

HORSE & RIDER

Horse & Rider, 7 Exeter St, Launceston, **Cornwall**, PL15 9EQ, **ENGLAND**.
(T) 01566 774253 **(F)** 01566 774253.
Contact/s
Owner: Mrs J Napper
Profile Riding Wear Retailer, Saddlery Retailer.
Ref: YH07094

HORSE & RIDER

Horse & Rider Insurance Direct, Crown Hse, Augusta Pl, Leamington Spa, **Warwickshire**, CV32 5EL, **ENGLAND**.
(T) 01926 452626 **(F)** 01926 888999.
Profile Club/Association. **Ref: YH07095**

HORSE & RIDER

Horse & Rider, Unit 2, Main St, Hatfield Woodhouse, Doncaster, **Yorkshire (South)**, DN7 6NE, **ENGLAND**.
(T) 01302 845734.
Contact/s
Owner: Miss K Idema
Profile Riding Wear Retailer, Saddlery Retailer.
Repair bridles. Saddler is offsite No.Staff: 2
Yr. Est: 1976
Opening Times
Sp: Open Mon, Wed - Sun 09:00. Closed Mon, Wed - Fri 17:30, Sat, Sun 13:00.
Su: Open Mon, Wed - Sun 09:00. Closed Mon, Wed - Fri 17:30, Sat, Sun 13:00.
Au: Open Mon, Wed - Sun 09:00. Closed Mon, Wed - Fri 17:30, Sat, Sun 13:00.
Wn: Open Mon, Wed - Sun 09:00. Closed Mon, Wed - Fri 17:30, Sat, Sun 13:00.
Closed Tuesdays **Ref: YH07096**

HORSE & RIDER

Horse & Rider, 187 Northfield Rd, Crookes, Sheffield, **Yorkshire (South)**, S10 1QQ, **ENGLAND**.
(T) 0114 2666001 **(F)** 0114 2670355
(W) www.horsenrider.co.uk.
Contact/s
Manageress: Mrs W Lynch
(E) info@horsenrider
Profile Riding Wear Retailer, Saddlery Retailer, Supplies.
Wormers available from sister company Adams Chemist, mail order or in person from nearby chemist.
No.Staff: 10 Yr. Est: 1982
Opening Times
Sp: Open Mon - Sat 09:30. Closed Mon - Wed, Fri, Sat 17:30, Thur 13:00.
Su: Open Mon - Sat 09:30. Closed Mon - Wed, Fri, Sat 17:30, Thur 13:00.
Au: Open Mon - Sat 09:30. Closed Mon - Wed, Fri, Sat 17:30, Thur 13:00.
Wn: Open Mon - Sat 09:30. Closed Mon - Wed, Fri, Sat 17:30, Thur 13:00. **Ref: YH07097**

HORSE & RIDER OUTFITTERS

Horse & Rider Outfitters, 33 Evan St, Stonehaven, **Aberdeenshire**, AB39 2ET, **SCOTLAND**.
(T) 01569 763462 **(F)** 01569 763462.
Profile Saddlery Retailer. **Ref: YH07098**

HORSE & RIDER SUPPLIES

Horse & Rider Supplies, 9 Front St, Annfield Plain, Stanley, **County Durham**, DH9 7SY, **ENGLAND**.
(T) 01207 284574 **(F)** 01207 230482.
Contact/s
Owner: Mr A Jarvis
Profile Saddlery Retailer. **Ref: YH07099**

HORSE & RIDER TACK SHOP

Horse & Rider Tack Shop (The), 64 Station Rd, Sandiacre, Nottingham, **Derbyshire**, NG10 5AP, **ENGLAND**.
(T) 0115 9392259.
Contact/s
Owner: Mrs R Ellis
Profile Riding Wear Retailer, Saddlery Retailer.
Ref: YH07100

HORSE & RIDER TACK SHOP

Horse & Rider Tack Shop, Per Ardua, 109 Inmans Rd, Hedon, Hull, **Yorkshire (East)**, HU12 8HU, **ENGLAND**.
(T) 01482 898921.
Profile Saddlery Retailer. **Ref: YH07101**

HORSE AND PONY PROTECTION

Horse and Pony Protection Association, The Stable, Burnley Wharf, Manchester Rd, Burnley, **Lancashire**, BB11 1JZ, **ENGLAND**.
(T) 01282 455992 **(F)** 01282 451992.
Contact/s
Key Contact: Mrs I Milton-Hall
Profile Club/Association. **Ref: YH07102**

HORSE BEAUTIQUE

Horse Beautique (The), North Rd, Leominster, **Herefordshire**, HR6 0AN, **ENGLAND**.
(T) 01568 708280 **(F)** 01568 708101.
Contact/s
Owner: Mr M Burleigh
Profile Saddlery Retailer. **Ref: YH07103**

HORSE BITS

Horse Bits, 1a Froud Way, Corfe Mullen, Wimborne, **Dorset**, BH21 3UU, **ENGLAND**.
(T) 01202 600550 **(F)** 01202 386841.
Contact/s
Partner: Mr A Ponchaud **Ref: YH07104**

HORSE BITS

Horse Bits, Unit 1 Quaysideindust Est, Woodbridge, **Suffolk**, IP12 1BN, **ENGLAND**.
(T) 01394 610320 **(F)** 01394 610321.
Contact/s
Owner: Ms C Navaratnam
Profile Riding Wear Retailer, Saddlery Retailer.
Ref: YH07105

HORSE BITS SADDLERY

Hilary Hartley T/A Horse Bits Saddlery, 18 Bridge St, Ramsbottom, Bury, **Lancashire**, BL0 9AQ, **ENGLAND**.
(T) 01706 822322
(W) www.horse-bits.co.uk
Affiliated Bodies BETA.
Contact/s
Owner: Ms H Hartley
Profile Saddlery Retailer. No.Staff: 5
Yr. Est: 1991
Opening Times
Sp: Open 10:00. Closed 17:30.
Su: Open 10:00. Closed 17:30.
Au: Open 10:00. Closed 17:30.
Wn: Open 10:00. Closed 17:30. **Ref: YH07106**

HORSE BITZ

Horse Bitz, Gotechnic Hse, 27 Woodthorpe Rd, Ashford, **Surrey**, TW15 2RP, **ENGLAND**.
(T) 01784 880480.
Profile Supplies. **Ref: YH07107**

HORSE BOOKS

Horse Books Ltd, 1 The Paddocks, Loddington Lane, Linton, Maidstone, **Kent**, ME17 4AG, **ENGLAND**.
(T) 01622 741092 **(F)** 01622 741092.
Profile Supplies. **Ref: YH07108**

HORSE BOX

Horse Box (The), 16 Old St, Ashton-under-Lyne, **Manchester (Greater)**, OL6 6LB, **ENGLAND**.
(T) 0161 3301482.
Contact/s
Owner: Mr G Holloway **Ref: YH07109**

HORSE BOX

Horse Box (The), Bridge Hse, Five Oaks Rd, Slinfold, Horsham, **Sussex (West)**, RH13 7QW, **ENGLAND**.
(T) 01403 790003.
Contact/s
Owner: Mr P Guest
Profile Saddlery Retailer. **Ref: YH07110**

HORSE BOX & TRAILER OWNERS

Organisation Of Horse Box & Trailer Owners (The), Whitehill Farm, Hamstead Marshall, Newbury, **Berkshire**, RG20 0HP, **ENGLAND**.
(T) 01488 657651 **(F)** 01488 657652.
Profile Transport/Horse Boxes. Breakdown & Recovery Service. **Ref: YH07111**

HORSE BOX SERVICES

Horse Box Services, Cliffe Common, Cliffe, Selby, **Yorkshire (North)**, YO8 6NU, **ENGLAND**.
(T) 01757 630233.
Profile Transport/Horse Boxes. **Ref: YH07112**

HORSE BOXES WELDING

Horse Boxes Welding, Unit 18 Bunns Bank, Old Buckenham, Attleborough, **Norfolk**, NR17 1QD, **ENGLAND**.
(T) 01953 456647.
Contact/s
Owner: Mr L Christman
Profile Transport/Horse Boxes. **Ref: YH07113**

HORSE CLOTHING

Horse Clothing Co, Unit 1 48 Jubilee Business Ctre, Aston Rd, Waterlooville, **Hampshire**, PO7 7XD, **ENGLAND**.
(T) 023 92266057 **(F)** 023 92266058.
Contact/s
Owner: Miss S Snocken
Profile Riding Wear Retailer, Saddlery Retailer.
Ref: YH07114

HORSE CTRE

Horse Centre (The), Pentre Cwrt, Llandysul, **Carmarthenshire**, SA44 5AT, **WALES**.
(T) 01559 362303.
Profile Saddlery Retailer. **Ref: YH07115**

HORSE CTRE

Horse Centre (The), Unit 1 Beaufort Rd, Plasmarl, Swansea, **Swansea**, SA6 8JG, **WALES**.
(T) 01792 310544.
Contact/s
Partner: Mr M Cumes
Profile Riding Wear Retailer, Saddlery Retailer.
Ref: YH07116

HORSE DRAWN CARRIAGES

Horse Drawn Carriages Ltd, The Coach Hse, Church Lane, Gawsworth, Macclesfield, **Cheshire**, SK11 9RJ, **ENGLAND**.
(T) 01260 223468.
Profile Horse Drawn Vehicles. **Ref: YH07117**

HORSE DRAWN PROMOTIONS

Horse Drawn Promotions, Poultry Farm Cottages, South Harewood, Andover, **Hampshire**, SP11 7AP, **ENGLAND**.
(T) 01264 720200.
Contact/s
Owner: Mr B Hook
Profile Horse Drawn Vehicles. **Ref: YH07118**

HORSE DRAWN WEDDING CARRIAGES

Oxford Carriages, Mill Lane Farm, Kirtlington, Oxford, **Oxfordshire**, OX5 3HW, **ENGLAND**.
(T) 01869 350501
Affiliated Bodies BDS, ODC.
Contact/s
Partner: Mrs J Fanner-Hoskin
Profile Carriage hire.
Horse drawn carriage hire for weddings. No.Staff: 3
Yr. Est: 1985 C.Size: 18 Acres
Opening Times
Sp: Open 09:15. Closed 18:00.
Su: Open 09:15. Closed 18:00.
Au: Open 09:15. Closed 18:00.
Wn: Open 09:15. Closed 18:00. **Ref: YH07119**

HORSE DRIVING TRIALS

Horse Driving Trials Supporters Club, The Pillars, Seacliffe, North Berwick, **Lothian (East)**, EH39 5PP, **SCOTLAND**.
(T) 01620 893744.
Profile Club/Association. **Ref: YH07120**

HORSE HEALTH PRODUCTS

Horse Health Products (UK) Ltd, Broomers Pk, Broomers Hill Lane, Pulborough, **Sussex (West)**, RH20 2HY, **ENGLAND**.
(T) 01798 875337 **(F)** 01798 872202
(E) rholdsworth@horsehealth.co.uk.
Profile Medical Support. **Ref: YH07121**

HORSE HIRE HOLIDAYS

Horse Hire Holidays, Stockdale Hall, Uldale, Wigton, **Cumbria**, CA7 1HL, **ENGLAND**.
(T) 01697 371217
(E) j-irving@lineone.net
(W) www.horsehire.co.uk.
Profile Horse/Rider Accom.
Explore the Lake District on horseback on The Skiddaw Trail. Costs. Prices start from £85.00 per day including B&B accommodation. **Ref: YH07122**

HORSE HOUSE

Horse House (The), Ducks Hill Farm, Ducks Hill Rd, Northwood, **London (Greater)**, HA6 2SP, **ENGLAND**.
(T) 01923 823271 **(F)** 01895 820771.
Profile Breeder, Saddlery Retailer, Trainer.
Ref: YH07123

HORSE HOUSE

Horse House (The), Slyes Farm Equestrian Ctre, Downash, Hailsham, **Sussex (East)**, BN27 2RP, **ENGLAND**.
(T) 01323 848989.
Profile Saddlery Retailer. **Ref: YH07124**

HORSE INDEX

Horse Index (The), 51 West End, Silverstone, **Northamptonshire**, NN12 8UY, **ENGLAND**.
(T) 01327 858100.
Profile Breeder. **Ref: YH07125**

HORSE IT

Horse IT Ltd, Ferry Lane, Sudbourne, Woodbridge, **Suffolk**, IP12 2HD, **ENGLAND**.
(T) 01394 450850 **(F)** 01394 450757.
Contact/s
Manager: Mr P Marson
Profile Supplies. **Ref: YH07126**

HORSE PARAPHENALIA

Horse Paraphenalia, 49 Dunkell Rd, Sheffield, **Yorkshire (South)**, S11 9HN, **ENGLAND**.
(T) 0114 2366077.
Profile Supplies. **Ref: YH07127**

HORSE POWER INTERNATIONAL

Horse Power International, P O Box 1417, Windsor, **Berkshire**, SL4 1FP, **ENGLAND**.
(T) 01753 847900 **(F)** 01753 847901
(E) mail@bcmg.co.uk. **Ref: YH07128**

HORSE POWER TRANSPORT

Horse Power Transport Ltd, Daltons Yard Milford, Milford, **County Carlow**, **IRELAND**.
(T) 050 346111.
Profile Supplies. **Ref: YH07129**

HORSE RACING ABROAD

Horse Racing Abroad, 24 Sussex Rd, Haywards Heath, **Sussex (West)**, RH16 4EA, **ENGLAND**.
(T) 01444 441661 **(F)** 01444 416169. **Ref: YH07130**

HORSE RANGERS ASS

Horse Rangers Association, Royal Mews, Hampton Court Palace, East Molesey, **Surrey**, KT8 9BW, **ENGLAND**.
(T) 020 89794196.
Profile Club/Association. **Ref: YH07131**

HORSE REQUISITES

Horse Requisites Newmarket Ltd, Black Bear Lane, Newmarket, **Suffolk**, CB8 0JT, **ENGLAND**.
(T) 01638 664619 **(F)** 01638 661562.
Profile Riding Wear Retailer, Saddlery Retailer, Supplies.
Stock everything for horse & rider. **Ref: YH07132**

HORSE RESCUE FUND

Horse Rescue Fund, 2 Becks Green Lane, Ilketshall St Andrew, Beccles, **Suffolk**, NR34 8NB, **ENGLAND**.
(T) 01986 781696.
Profile Club/Association. **Ref: YH07133**

HORSE RESOURCE

Horse Resource (The), 1 Marshes Hses, West Sleekburn, Choppington, **Northumberland**, NE62 5XD, **ENGLAND**.
(T) 01670 814507.
Contact/s
Owner: Miss J Lamb **Ref: YH07134**

HORSE RIDING HOLIDAYS

Horse Riding Holidays, Inntravel, Hovingham, **Yorkshire (North)**, YO62 4JZ, **ENGLAND**.
(T) 01653 629003 **(F)** 01653 628741
(E) inntravel@inntravel.co.uk. **Ref: YH07135**

HORSE RUG WASH

Horse Rug Wash Co, Northcliff Farm, Duffryn, St Nicholas, Cardiff, **Glamorgan (Vale of)**, CF5 6SU, **WALES**.
(T) 01446 735791 **(F)** 01446 722273
(W) www.nfs-wales.co.uk.
Contact/s
Owner: Mr D Palmer
Profile Supplies.
Rug re-proofing, made to measure. No.Staff: 3
C.Size: 130 Acres
Opening Times
Sp: Open 09:00. Closed 18:00.
Su: Open 09:00. Closed 18:00.
Au: Open 09:00. Closed 18:00.
Wn: Open 09:00. Closed 18:00. **Ref: YH07136**

HORSE SENSE

Horse Sense, Currarie Farm, Lendalfoot, Girvan, **Ayrshire (South)**, KA26 0JB, **SCOTLAND**.
(T) 01465 891213.
Contact/s
Owner: Mrs M Cartney
Profile Equestrian Centre.
Train Skill Seekers in all areas of horsemanship.
Ref: YH07137

HORSE SHOP

Horse Shop (The), 4b Marlborough Trading Est, Cockshutts Lane, **Midlands (West)**, WV2 3HP, **ENGLAND**.
(T) 01902 454771 **(F)** 01902 454771.
Profile Saddlery Retailer. **Ref: YH07138**

HORSE SHOP

Horse Shop (The), The Bull Ring, Hollybush Rd, Bridgnorth, **Shropshire**, WV16 4AX, **ENGLAND**.
(T) 01952 506699.
Contact/s
Owner: Mrs M Lewis
Profile Riding Wear Retailer, Saddlery Retailer.
Ref: YH07139

HORSE SHOP

Horse Shop (The), Hartfield Hse, Pool Hill Rd, Horsehay, Telford, **Shropshire**, TF4 3AS, **ENGLAND**.
(T) 01952 506699 **(F)** 01952 506699
(E) admin@saddlesuk.com
(W) www.saddlesuk.com
Affiliated Bodies BETA, SMS.
Contact/s
Owner: Ms M Lewis **(Q)** Saddle Fitter
Profile Saddlery Retailer. No.Staff: 1
Yr. Est: 1988 **Ref: YH07140**

HORSE STUFF & RIDERWEAR

Horse Stuff & Riderwear, Lesparrow, Merther Lane, St. Michael Penkivel, Truro, **Cornwall**, TR2 4AQ, **ENGLAND**.
(T) 01872 520644 **(F)** 01872 520644.
Contact/s
Owner: Mrs P Kear
Profile Supplies. **Ref: YH07141**

HORSE TRANSPORT

Horse Transport, 1 Arlary Cottage, Milnathort, **Perth and Kinross**, KY13 9SJ, **SCOTLAND**.
(T) 01577 862551 **(F)** 01577 862551
(M) 07836 377039.
Profile Transport/Horse Boxes. **Ref: YH07142**

HORSE TRIALS SUPPORT GROUP

Horse Trials Support Group, 19 Alexandra Court, Maida Vale, London, **London (Greater)**, W9 1SQ, **ENGLAND**.
(T) 020 72869935.
Contact/s
Secretary: Mrs J Pontifex
Profile Club/Association.
Private association. Raises money to help train promising horses and riders. Yr. Est: 1978
Opening Times
Sp: Open 09:00. Closed 18:00.
Su: Open 09:00. Closed 18:00.
Au: Open 09:00. Closed 18:00.
Wn: Open 09:00. Closed 18:00. **Ref: YH07143**

HORSE TROUGH

Horse Trough (The), Dishley Grange Farm, Derby Rd, Loughborough, **Leicestershire**, LE11 5SF, **ENGLAND**.
(T) 01509 842236.
Contact/s
Owner: Mrs J Gilby
Profile Equestrian Centre, Stable/Livery. Tack Shop.
Have a DIY livery yard, based at Dishley Grange Farm.
Yr. Est: 1994
Opening Times
Sp: Open Mon - Fri 13:00, Sat, Sun 10:00. Closed Mon - Fri 18:00, Sat, Sun 16:00.
Su: Open Mon - Fri 13:00, Sat, Sun 10:00. Closed Mon - Fri 18:00, Sat, Sun 16:00.
Au: Open Mon - Fri 13:00, Sat, Sun 10:00. Closed Mon - Fri 18:00, Sat, Sun 16:00.
Wn: Open Mon - Fri 13:00, Sat, Sun 10:00. Closed Mon - Fri 18:00, Sat, Sun 16:00.
Open October - April for the winter **Ref: YH07144**

HORSE VOGUE

Horse Vogue, Garden Cottage, Bylands, Stratfield Turgis, Basingstoke, **Hampshire**, RG27 0AR, **ENGLAND**.
(T) 01256 881730.
Profile Supplies. **Ref: YH07145**

HORSE WEAR

Horse Wear House, Harborough Rd, Kibworth, Leicester, **Leicestershire**, LE8 0RF, **ENGLAND**.
(T) 0116 2792276 **(F)** 0116 2793415.
Contact/s
Owner: Mr A York **Ref: YH07146**

HORSEAROUND

Horsearound, 54 Westway, Caterham, **Surrey**, CR3 5TP, **ENGLAND**.
(T) 01883 348839.
Contact/s
Owner: Mrs J Burrows **Ref: YH07147**

HORSEBED STABLE SUPPLIES

Horsebed Stable Supplies, Ranaghan, Collooney, **County Sligo**, **IRELAND**.
(T) 071 67968.
Profile Supplies. **Ref: YH07148**

HORSEBOX

Horsebox (The), 17A High St, Upton, Pontefract, **Yorkshire (West)**, WF9 1HR, **ENGLAND**.
(T) 01977 658888.
Profile Saddlery Retailer. **Ref: YH07149**

HORSEBOX BITS

Horsebox Bits, Unit 22 Burton Wood Ind Est, Phipps Lane, Burton Wood, Warrington, **Cheshire**, WA5 4HX, **ENGLAND**.
(T) 01925 222208 **(F)** 01925 222274.
Profile Transport/Horse Boxes. **Ref: YH07150**

HORSEBOX UPHOLSTERY

Horsebox Upholstery, Monarchs Meadow, Hindley Rd, Westhoughton, **Lancashire**, BL5 2DY, **ENGLAND**.
(T) 01942 815611 **(F)** 01942 792934.
Profile Transport/Horse Boxes. **Ref: YH07151**

HORSECOMBE VALE ARABIANS

Horsecombe Vale Arabians, Hill Hse Farm, Kentisbeare, Cullompton, **Devon**, EX15 2EU, **ENGLAND**.
(T) 01884 266232 **(F)** 01884 266778.
Contact/s
Owner: Mrs M Morris
Profile Breeder. **Ref: YH07152**

HORSE-E-THINGS

Horse-E-Things, Ashford Works Ind Est, Fordingbridge, **Hampshire**, SP6 1DA, **ENGLAND**.
(T) 01425 650505.
Contact/s
Owner: Mrs S Andrews
Profile Saddlery Retailer. **Ref: YH07153**

HORSEFEEDSUK

S H Wetherald T/A Webmiller Website Design, 52 St Georges Rd, Harrogate, **Yorkshire (North)**, HG2 9BS, **ENGLAND**.
(T) 01423 503207 **(F)** 0870 0548991
(E) info@horsefeeds.co.uk
(W) www.horsefeeds.co.uk.
Contact/s
Owner: Mrs S Wetherald
(E) simon@horsefeeds.co.uk
Profile Supplies. Internet Portal.
Horsefeed Internet Portal. No.Staff: 1
Yr. Est: 1998
Opening Times
Internet company accessible 24 hours a day, 7 days a week **Ref: YH07154**

HORSEFERRY TRANSPORT

Horseferry Transport Ltd, Carousel, Beechenlea Lane, Swanley, **Kent**, BR8 8DR, **ENGLAND**.
(T) 01322 664848 **(F)** 01322 667355.
Profile Transport/Horse Boxes. **Ref: YH07155**

HORSEFLEX UK

Horseflex UK, Pond Cottage, Wrotham Pk, Wrotham, **Kent**, TN15 7RE, **ENGLAND**.
(T) 01732 886990 **(F)** 01732 886990.
Profile Supplies. **Ref: YH07156**

HORSEGUARDS

Horseguards, 2 High Corner, Pentyrch, Cardiff, **Glamorgan (Vale of)**, CF15 9PW, **WALES**.
(T) 029 20891000 **(F)** 029 20891000.
Contact/s
Partner: Mrs E Parry
Profile Saddlery Retailer. **Ref: YH07157**

HORSELAKE ARABIANS

Horselake Arabians, Horselake Farm, Cheriton Bishop, Exeter, **Devon**, EX6 6HD, **ENGLAND**.
(T) 01647 24220.
Profile Breeder. **Ref: YH07158**

HORSEMANIA

Horsemania, 24 Commercial St, Camborne, **Cornwall**, TR14 8JX, **ENGLAND**.
(T) 01209 612342.
Contact/s
Owner: Mrs G Rowe **Ref: YH07159**

HORSEMAN'S STOP

Horseman's Stop, 7 Troed Y Bryn, Abercrave,

Powys, SA9 1YJ, **WALES**.
(T) 01639 730931 **(F)** 01639 730931
(M) 07974 114585
(E) sandy@horseshop.freeserve.co.uk
Profile Saddlery Retailer. **Ref: YH07160**

HORSEMANSHIP

L & Mr Stanton, Vowley Farm, Bincknoll Lane, Wootton Bassett, **Wiltshire**, SN4 8QR, **ENGLAND**.
(T) 01793 852115
(E) centre@nusoft.demon.co.uk
(W) www.nusoft.demon.co.uk
Affiliated Bodies IBEM.
Contact/s
Owner: Mr M Stanton
Profile Equestrian Centre, Stable/Livery, Trainer.
Specialise in facilitating peoples relationships with horses, getting to know horses by watching and being with them. Horses are ridden in partnership, ideal for those wanting to overcome fear and looking for true harmony No.Staff: 3 Yr. Est: 2000
C.Size: 110 Acres
Opening Times
Open all year **Ref: YH07161**

HORSEMASTER DISTRIBUTION

Horsemaster Distribution Ltd, Ickleford Manor, Ickleford, Hitchin, **Hertfordshire**, SG5 3XE, **ENGLAND**.
(T) 01462 432596 **(F)** 01462 420423. **Ref: YH07162**

HORSEPOWER

Horsepower, The Queens, High St, Selborne, Alton, **Hampshire**, GU34 3JJ, **ENGLAND**.
(T) 01420 511640
(M) 07774 149592.
Profile Trainer. **Ref: YH07163**

HORSEPOWER COVENTRY

Horsepower Coventry, Coombe View, Ansty Lane, Walsgrave On Sowe, Coventry, **Midlands (West)**, CV2 2DT, **ENGLAND**.
(T) 024 76614094.
Profile Breeder. **Ref: YH07164**

HORSERACE BETTING LEVY BOARD

Horserace Betting Levy Board, 52 Grosvenor Gardens, London, **London (Greater)**, SW1W 0AU, **ENGLAND**.
(T) 020 73330043 **(F)** 020 73330041
(W) www.hblb.org.uk.
Contact/s
Administration: Mr A Stone
Profile Club/Association.
The Levy Board is responsible for collection of a levy on off-course betting turnover from bookmakers and the Tote. The funds are then put back into horse racing.
Yr. Est: 1961
Opening Times
Sp: Open Mon - Fri 09:00. Closed Mon - Fri 17:00.
Su: Open Mon - Fri 09:00. Closed Mon - Fri 17:00.
Au: Open Mon - Fri 09:00. Closed Mon - Fri 17:00.
Wn: Open Mon - Fri 09:00. Closed Mon - Fri 17:00.
Ref: YH07165

HORSERACING SPONSORS ASS

Horseracing Sponsors Association, Stirling Way, Borehamwood, **Hertfordshire**, WD7 2AZ, **ENGLAND**.
(T) 020 82074114 **(F)** 01964 551135.
Profile Club/Association. **Ref: YH07166**

HORSES

Horses Etc, Rhos Uchaf, Llanfynydd, Wrexham, **Flintshire**, LL11 5HR, **WALES**.
(T) 01352 771718 **(F)** 01352 771717
(E) horses@sweetitch.com
(W) www.sweetitch.com.
Contact/s
Partner: Dr T Greaves
Profile Supplies.
Main Stockists of the Boett Sweetitch Blanket and also run the Sweetitch Hotline on the number given.
No.Staff: 4 Yr. Est: 1998
Opening Times
Mail order, please ring for a brochure **Ref: YH07167**

HORSES GALORE

Horses Galore, Durfold Farm, Plaistow Rd, Dunsfold, **Surrey**, GU8 4PQ, **ENGLAND**.
(T) 01483 200277
(M) 07860 790940.
Profile Trainer. **Ref: YH07168**

HORSES IN SPORT

Horses In Sport, Leylans, The Heywood, Diss, **Norfolk**, IP22 5TD, **ENGLAND**.
(T) 01379 651647 **(F)** 01379 651647
(M) 07889 126369
(E) horsesinsport@equestrianet.co.uk
(W) www.horsesinsport.co.uk.
Contact/s
Owner: Mr J Harvey
Profile Riding Wear Retailer, Saddlery Retailer, Supplies.
They have a mobile unit and travel to the many events across the country. Visit the website for further information. **Ref: YH07169**

HORSESENSE

Horsesense, Solihull Riding Club, Four Ashes Rd, Dorridge, Solihull, **Midlands (West)**, B93 8QE, **ENGLAND**.
(T) 01564 778899 **(F)** 01564 730236.
Profile Feed Merchant, Riding Wear Retailer, Saddlery Retailer. **Ref: YH07170**

HORSESHOE & FARRIER SUPPLIES

Horseshoe & Farrier Supplies (Midlands) Ltd, Unit 10D Castle Vale Ind Est, Maybrook Rd, Minworth, Sutton Coldfield, **Midlands (West)**, B76 1AL, **ENGLAND**.
(T) 0121 3131719 **(F)** 0121 3131690.
Profile Supplies. **Ref: YH07171**

HORSESHOE CTRE

Horseshoe Centre for Handicapped Riders, Picketts Hill, Headley, Bordon, **Hampshire**, GU35 8TI, **ENGLAND**.
(T) 01428 713858.
Profile Riding School. **Ref: YH07172**

HORSESHOE FARM

Horseshoe Farm Harness Supplies, North Brewham, Bruton, **Somerset**, BA10 0JG, **ENGLAND**.
(T) 01749 850577.
Contact/s
Owner: Mrs J Vandy **Ref: YH07173**

HORSESHOES

Horseshoes Animal Supplies, The Coach Hse, High St, Wrentham, **Suffolk**, NR34 7HB, **ENGLAND**.
(T) 01502 675679 **(F)** 01502 675679
(E) info@horseshoesas.com
(W) www.horseshoesas.com.
Profile Saddlery Retailer, Supplies. Pet Shop.
Ref: YH07174

HORSESHOES RIDING SCHOOL

Horseshoes Riding School, Dean St, East Farleigh, Maidstone, **Kent**, ME15 0PR, **ENGLAND**.
(T) 01622 746161.
Contact/s
Owner: Mr A Hargreaves
Profile Riding School. **Ref: YH07175**

HORSETALK

Horsetalk Saddlery, Fen Lane, Pott Row, King's Lynn, **Norfolk**, PE32 1DA, **ENGLAND**.
(T) 01553 630285.
Contact/s
Owner: Mr T Major
Profile Riding Wear Retailer, Saddlery Retailer, Supplies.
Horsecare products, safety equipment, grooming equipment, tack, bridle spares, advice and riding wear.
No.Staff: 2 Yr. Est: 1968
Opening Times
Sp: Open Tues - Sun 10:00. Closed Tues - Sun 17:00.
Su: Open Tues - Sun 10:00. Closed Tues - Sun 17:00.
Au: Open Tues - Sun 10:00. Closed Tues - Sun 17:00.
Wn: Open Tues - Sun 10:00. Closed Tues - Sun 17:00.
Closed on Mondays **Ref: YH07176**

HORSEWARE

Horseware Ireland Ltd, Quay St, Dundalk, **County Louth**, **IRELAND**.
(T) 042 9335431 **(F)** 042 9337671
(E) info@horseware.com
(W) www.horseware.com.
Contact/s
Owner: Tom McGuinness
Profile Riding Wear Retailer, Supplies. **Ref: YH07177**

HORSEWISE

Horsewise, 6 Lion St, Hay-on-Wye, Hereford, **Herefordshire**, HR3 5AA, **ENGLAND**.
(T) 01497 820240.
Contact/s
Owner: Mrs S Jordan
Profile Riding Wear Retailer, Saddlery Retailer. Book & Gift Shop. **Ref: YH07178**

HORSEWISE CLOTHING

Horsewise Clothing, Brookfield Cottage, Low Hill, Evesham Rd, Egdon, Worcester, **Worcestershire**, WR7 4QR, **ENGLAND**.
(T) 01905 345413
(M) 07721 001995.
Profile Saddlery Retailer. **Ref: YH07179**

HORSE-WORLD

Horse-World, Willow Beds Farm, Lamesley, Gateshead, **Tyne and Wear**, NE11 0EW, **ENGLAND**.
(T) 0191 4821288.
Profile Saddlery Retailer. **Ref: YH07180**

HORSEY HABIT

Horsey Habit, Mill Rd, Thurles, Tipperary, **County Tipperary**, **IRELAND**.
(T) 0504 26703.
Profile Trainer. **Ref: YH07181**

HORSEY HUMOR

Horsey Humor (Cards/Prints), 88 Saltergate, Chesterfield, **Derbyshire**, S40 1LG, **ENGLAND**.
(T) 01246 555484 **(F)** 01246 220478. **Ref: YH07182**

HORSEY STUFF

Horsey Stuff, 61 Grove Rd, Emmer Green, Reading, **Berkshire**, RG4 8LJ, **ENGLAND**.
(T) 0118 9546767. **Ref: YH07183**

HORSEY THINGS

Horsey Things, Eccleshall Animal Health & Food Ctre, The Mill, Stone Rd, Eccleshall, **Staffordshire**, ST21 6DJ, **ENGLAND**.
(T) 01785 850631.
Profile Saddlery Retailer. **Ref: YH07184**

HORSFIELD

Mrs Horsfield, 1 Selangor Ave, Emsworth, **Hampshire**, PO10 7LR, **ENGLAND**.
(T) 01243 430614.
Profile Breeder. **Ref: YH07185**

HORSFORTH RIDING CLUB

Horsforth Riding Club, 24 Gladstone Rd, Rawdon, **Yorkshire (West)**, LS19 6HZ, **ENGLAND**.
(T) 0113 2506679.
Profile Club/Association, Riding Club. **Ref: YH07186**

HORSHAM & DISTRICT

Horsham & District Riding Club, Old Doomsday, Doomsday Green, Horsham, **Sussex (West)**, RH13 6LA, **ENGLAND**.
(T) 01403 252270.
Contact/s
Chairman: Mr D Kear **(Q)** BHSI
Profile Club/Association, Riding Club. **Ref: YH07187**

HORSHAM PET CTRE

Horsham Pet Centre, Brighton Rd, Horsham, **Sussex (West)**, RH13 6QA, **ENGLAND**.
(T) 01403 61049.
Profile Supplies. **Ref: YH07188**

HORSIN' AROUND

Horsin' Around Ltd, High St, Epworth, Doncaster, **Yorkshire (South)**, DN9 1EP, **ENGLAND**.
(T) 01427 875274. **Ref: YH07189**

HORSING AROUND

Horsing Around The Mobile Tack Shop, Oldbury, Sandy Lane, Three Legged Cross, Wimborne, **Dorset**, BH21 6RH, **ENGLAND**.
(T) 01202 820911. **Ref: YH07190**

HORSLEY, ANDREW

Andrew Horsley RSS, 117 Danube Rd, Wold Rd, Hull, **Yorkshire (East)**, HU5 5UU, **ENGLAND**.
(T) 01482 353340.
Profile Farrier. **Ref: YH07191**

HORTICULTURAL/AGRCLTRL SOC

Skelton Horticultural & Agricultural Society, Penrith, **Cumbria**, **ENGLAND**.
(T) 01768 484122.
Contact/s
Secretary: Mrs A Reid
Profile Club/Association. **Ref: YH07192**

HORTONS IRISH HORSES

Hortons Irish Horses, Horton Stables, Cockering Rd, Chartham, Canterbury, **Kent**, CT4 7LG, **ENGLAND**.
(T) 01227 730627.
Contact/s
Owner: Mrs J Marchant
Profile Breeder. **Ref: YH07193**

HOSE SHETLAND PONY STUD

Hose Shetland Pony Stud, Hose, Melton Mowbray, **Leicestershire**, LE14 4JX, **ENGLAND**.

(T) 01949 860275.
Profile Breeder. Ref: **YH07194**

HOSGOOD, P

Mr P Hosgood, Attwell Farm, Nadderwater, Exeter, **Devon**, EX4 2JE, **ENGLAND**.
(T) 01392 498741.
Profile Medical Support. Ref: **YH07195**

HOSKING, J A

J A Hosking, Trembothick Farm, St. Buryan, Penzance, **Cornwall**, TR19 6EA, **ENGLAND**.
(T) 01736 810392.
Profile Transport/Horse Boxes. Ref: **YH07196**

HOSKINS FARM LIVERY STABLES

Hoskins Farm Livery Stables, Hoskins Farm, High Wych, Sawbridgeworth, **Hertfordshire**, CM21 0LD, **ENGLAND**.
(T) 01279 722165 **(F)** 01279 723207.
Contact/s
Owner: Mrs K Backshall
Profile Stable/Livery. Ref: **YH07197**

HOSSNOSH FEEDS

Hossnosh Feeds, Homestead Farm, Croxden, Uttoxeter, **Staffordshire**, ST14 5JD, **ENGLAND**.
(T) 01889 507324 **(F)** 01889 507324
(E) hossnosh@connectfree.co.uk Ref: **YH07198**

HOT METAL DESIGN

Hot Metal Design, Tosca Workshops, Lupton, Carnforth, **Lancashire**, LA6 2QE, **ENGLAND**.
(T) 01524 272949 **(F)** 01524 272949.
Contact/s
Owner: Mr A Kay
Profile Blacksmith. Ref: **YH07199**

HOTHAM, KEVIN

Kevin Hotham AWCF, 19 Norwood Gr, Norwood, Harrogate, **Yorkshire (North)**, HG3 1TQ, **ENGLAND**.
(T) 01423 501190.
Profile Farrier. Ref: **YH07200**

HOUGH FARM

Hough Farm, Hough Lane, Middleton, Manchester, **Manchester (Greater)**, M24 2RS, **ENGLAND**.
(T) 0161 6521106.
Contact/s
Partner: Mr J Tonge
Profile Stable/Livery. Ref: **YH07201**

HOUGHALL STABLES

Houghall Stables, Houghall Farm, Houghall, Durham, **County Durham**, DH1 3SN, **ENGLAND**.
(T) 0191 3830625. Ref: **YH07202**

HOUGHTON TRAILERS

Houghton Trailers, Colliery Lane, Hetton-Le-Hole, Houghton Le Spring, **Tyne and Wear**, DH5 0BG, **ENGLAND**.
(T) 0191 5170154 **(F)** 0191 5170154.
Contact/s
Owner: Mr R Steel
Profile Transport/Horse Boxes. Ref: **YH07203**

HOUGHTON, JASPER ANTHONY

Jasper Anthony Houghton, Highfields, Station Rd, Potterhanworth, **Lincolnshire**, LN4 2DX, **ENGLAND**.
(T) 01522 791247.
Profile Farrier. Ref: **YH07204**

HOUGHTON, R J

R J Houghton, Corcas Farm, Back Lane, Stalmine, Blackpool, **Lancashire**, FY6 0JD, **ENGLAND**.
(T) 01253 811048.
Profile Farrier. Ref: **YH07205**

HOUND & HORSE

Hound & Horse, 215 Station Rd, Wythall, **Midlands (West)**, B47 6ET, **ENGLAND**.
(T) 01564 824848.
Profile Saddlery Retailer. Ref: **YH07206**

HOURIGAN, M L

Hourigan M I, Lisaleen, Patrickswell, **County Limerick**, **IRELAND**.
(T) 061 396603.
Profile Supplies. Ref: **YH07207**

HOUSE OF BRUAR

House of Bruar (The), Blair Atholl, **Perth and Kinross**, PH18 5TW, **SCOTLAND**.
(T) 01796 483236 **(F)** 01796 483218.
Profile Saddlery Retailer. Ref: **YH07208**

HOUSE OF ST WILFIDS

House of St Wilfids, Church Lane, Barrow-on-Trent, **Derbyshire**, DE7 1HB, **ENGLAND**.
(T) 01332 701384.
Profile Supplies. Ref: **YH07209**

HOUSEMAKERS

Housemakers, 1 Mill St, Whitchurch, **Shropshire**, SY13 1PL, **ENGLAND**.
(T) 01948 665353 **(F)** 01948 666103.
Profile Saddlery Retailer. Ref: **YH07210**

HOUSEMAN, S

Mr S Houseman, Blacknest Cottage, Brimpton Common, Reading, **Berkshire**, RG7 4RP, **ENGLAND**.
(T) 0118 9810975 **(F)** 0118 9810770. Ref: **YH07211**

HOUSTON FARM RIDING SCHOOL

Houston Farm Riding School, 1 Houstoun Mains, Uphull, Broxburn, **Lothian (West)**, EH52 6JX, **SCOTLAND**.
(T) 01506 811351 **(F)** 01506 811351/811490
(W) www.hfrs.co.uk
Affiliated Bodies ABRS, BHS.
Contact/s
Owner: Mrs E Comrie **(Q)** AI
Profile Riding School, Stable/Livery.
Competition training centre. No.Staff: 7
Yr. Est: 1972
Opening Times
Sp: Open Mon - Sun 08:30. Closed Mon - Sun 19:30.
Su: Open Mon - Sun 08:30. Closed Mon - Sun 19:30.
Au: Open Mon - Sun 08:30. Closed Mon - Sun 19:30.
Wn: Open Mon - Sun 08:30. Closed Mon - Sun 19:30. Ref: **YH07212**

HOVE TACK ROOM

Hove Tack Room, 424-426 Portland Rd, Hove, **Sussex (East)**, BN3 5SJ, **ENGLAND**.
(T) 01273 410200.
Contact/s
Owner: Miss F Baker-Smith
Profile Riding Wear Retailer. Ref: **YH07213**

HOVINGTON, S

S Hovington, Robins Nest Stables, Post Office Rd, Seisdon, Wolverhampton, **Midlands (West)**, WV5 7HA, **ENGLAND**.
(T) 01902 893438.
Profile Breeder. Ref: **YH07214**

HOWARD ALLEN SEEDS

Howard Allen Seeds, 42 Calverstown Rd, Calvert Complex, Portadown, Craigavon, **County Armagh**, BT63 5NY, **NORTHERN IRELAND**.
(T) 028 38323213 **(F)** 028 38345583.
Profile Medical Support. Ref: **YH07215**

HOWARD, R

R Howard, 16 Copperfield Ave, Hillingdon, **London (Greater)**, **ENGLAND**.
(T) 01895 253293.
Profile Breeder. Ref: **YH07216**

HOWARD-CARTER

Mr & Mrs Howard-Carter, Hale Grange, Kirkby Thore, Penrith, **Cumbria**, CA10 1XS, **ENGLAND**.
(T) 01768 361845
(M) 07885 374428.
Profile Breeder. Ref: **YH07217**

HOWARD-CHAPPELL, A S E

Miss A S E Howard-Chappell, 9 Packs Cl, Harbetonford, Totnes, **Devon**, TQ9 7TL, **ENGLAND**.
(T) 01803 732377
(M) 07989 618246.
Profile Supplies. Ref: **YH07218**

HOWARTH HOUSE RIDING SCHOOL

Howarth House Riding School, Orton, Kettering, **Northamptonshire**, NN14 1LJ, **ENGLAND**.
(T) 01536 710520.
Profile Riding School. Ref: **YH07219**

HOWARTH LODGE RIDING CTRE

Howarth Lodge Riding Centre, Howarth Lane, Whiston, Rotherham, **Yorkshire (South)**, S60 4NB, **ENGLAND**.
(T) 01709 366248.
Profile Breeder, Riding School, Stable/Livery.
Ref: **YH07220**

HOWDEN

Howden & Co, Headswood Mill, Denny, **Stirling**, FK6 6BW, **SCOTLAND**.
(T) 01324 826693 **(F)** 01324 826100.
Contact/s
Owner: Ms L McLochlan
Profile Blacksmith. Ref: **YH07221**

HOWE & STARNES

Howe & Starnes, Fairfield Hse, Uckfield, **Sussex (East)**, TN22 5DE, **ENGLAND**.
(T) 01825 764268 **(F)** 01825 769686.
Profile Medical Support. Ref: **YH07222**

HOWE, B M

Mrs B M Howe, Four Winds, Wharley Farm, Cranfield, **Bedfordshire**, MK43 0AH, **ENGLAND**.
(T) 01234 750260.
Profile Breeder. Ref: **YH07223**

HOWE, DAVID J

David J Howe DWCF, The Maltings, Malting Lane, Isleham, Ely, **Cambridgeshire**, CB7 5RZ, **ENGLAND**.
(T) 01638 780999.
Profile Farrier. Ref: **YH07224**

HOWE, H S

Mr H S Howe, Northside, Oakford, Tiverton, **Devon**, EX16 9EW, **ENGLAND**.
(T) 01398 351224 **(F)** 01398 351224
(M) 07802 506344.
Profile Trainer. Ref: **YH07225**

HOWELL, A J

A J Howell, 65 Water St, Bollington, Macclesfield, **Cheshire**, SK10 5PA, **ENGLAND**.
(T) 01625 575200.
Contact/s
Owner: Mr A Howell
Profile Farrier. Ref: **YH07226**

HOWELL, CASTELL

Castell Howell, Pontshaen, Llandysul, **Carmarthenshire**, SA44 4UA, **WALES**.
(T) 01545 55209.
Profile Trainer. Ref: **YH07227**

HOWELL, DAVID

David Howell, North Barwick, Iddesleigh, Winkleigh, **Devon**, EX19 8BP, **ENGLAND**.
(T) 01837 83902 **(F)** 01837 38399. Ref: **YH07228**

HOWELL, DAVID LEE

David Lee Howell DWCF, 30 Stevens Lane, Claygate, Esher, **Surrey**, KT10 0TE, **ENGLAND**.
(T) 01372 466138.
Profile Farrier. Ref: **YH07229**

HOWES, E A

E A Howes, Home Farm, Ingleden Pk, St. Michaels, Tenterden, **Kent**, TN30 6SL, **ENGLAND**.
(T) 01580 764140.
Contact/s
Partner: Mrs E Howes
Profile Stable/Livery, Trainer. Ref: **YH07230**

HOWES, N

N Howes, Ring-O-Bells Cottage, Hinton, Chippenham, **Wiltshire**, SN14 8HH, **ENGLAND**.
(T) 01179 373664.
Profile Farrier. Ref: **YH07231**

HOWIE, C J

C J Howie, Stripshay, St. Mellion, Saltash, **Cornwall**, PL12 6SH, **ENGLAND**.
(T) 01579 351029.
Contact/s
Owner: Mr C Howie
Profile Farrier. Ref: **YH07232**

HOWITT, GORDON R

Gordon R Howitt DWCF, 21 Bakers Lane, Shutlanger, Towcester, **Northamptonshire**, NN12 7RT, **ENGLAND**.
(T) 01604 863305.
Profile Farrier. Ref: **YH07233**

HOWKINS & HARRISON

Howkins & Harrison, 62 Pall Mall, London, **London (Greater)**, SW1Y 5HZ, **ENGLAND**.
(T) 020 78390888 **(F)** 020 78390444
(E) property@howkinsandharrison
(W) www.howkinsandharrison.co.uk.
Profile Property Services. Ref: **YH07234**

HOWKINS & HARRISON

Howkins & Harrison, 23 Warwick Row, Coventry, **Midlands (West)**, CV1 1EY, **ENGLAND**.
(T) 02476 227384 **(F)** 02476 520030
(E) property@howkinsandharrison.co.uk
(W) www.howkinsandharrison.co.uk.
Profile Property Services. Ref: **YH07235**

HOWKINS & HARRISON

Howkins & Harrison, Drft Marketing Suite, Celtic Way, Derft South, Northampton, **Northamptonshire**,

NN6 7GW, **ENGLAND**.
(T) 01788 824000 **(F)** 01788 822700
(E) property@howkinsandharrison.co.uk
(W) www.howkinsandharrison.co.uk.
Profile Property Services. **Ref: YH07236**

HOWKINS & HARRISON

Howkins & Harrison, 7-11 Albert St, Rugby, **Warwickshire**, CV21 2RX, **ENGLAND**.
(T) 01788 560321 **(F)** 01788 540257
(E) property@howkinsandharrison.co.uk
(W) www.howkinsandharrison.co.uk.
Contact/s
Associate: Mr D Masters
Profile Property Services. **Ref: YH07237**

HOWKINS & HARRISON

Howkins & Harrison, 12 Church St, Atherstone, **Warwickshire**, CV9 1RN, **ENGLAND**.
(T) 01827 718021 **(F)** 01827 718410
(E) property@howkinsandharrison.co.uk
(W) www.howkinsandharrison.co.uk.
Profile Property Services. **Ref: YH07238**

HOWKINS & HARRISON

Howkins & Harrison, 129 High St, Henley-In-Arden, **Warwickshire**, B95 5AT, **ENGLAND**.
(T) 01564 793400 **(F)** 01564 793390
(E) property@howkinsandharrison.co.uk
(W) www.howkinsandharrison.co.uk.
Profile Property Services. **Ref: YH07239**

HOWKINS, T J

T J Howkins, Hunters Lodge, Dores Lane, Braishfield, Romsey, **Hampshire**, SO51 0QJ, **ENGLAND**.
(T) 01794 368330 **(F)** 01794 367879.
Contact/s
Partner: Mrs C Howkins **Ref: YH07240**

HOWLETT, ANDREW

Andrew Howlett, Llwyncelyn Bach, Llanwenog, Llanybydder, **Carmarthenshire**, SA40 9UT, **WALES**.
(T) 01570 480600.
Contact/s
Owner: Mr A Howlett
Profile Blacksmith. **Ref: YH07241**

HOWLETTS HALL EQUESTRIAN CTRE

Howletts Hall Equestrian Centre, Howletts Hall, Chelmsford Rd, Blackmore, Ingatestone, **Essex**, CM4 0QA, **ENGLAND**.
(T) 01277 821495 **(F)** 01277 823487.
Contact/s
Owner: Miss L McClure **Ref: YH07242**

HOWLING, PAUL

Paul Howling, Wellbottom Lodge, Moulton Paddocks, Bury Rd, Newmarket, **Suffolk**, CB8 9XX, **ENGLAND**.
(T) 01638 668503 **(F)** 01638 668503
(W) www.racehorsetrainers.co.uk
Affiliated Bodies Newmarket Trainers Fed.
Contact/s
Owner: Mr P Howling
Profile Trainer. **Ref: YH07243**

HOWS RACESAFE

Hows Racesafe, 9 Carlton Rd, Wilbarston, Market Harborough, **Leicestershire**, LE16 8QD, **ENGLAND**.
(T) 01536 771051 **(F)** 01536 779144.
Contact/s
Owner: Mr T How
Profile Supplies. Racing Equipment. Yr. Est: 1971
Opening Times
Sp: Open Mon - Fri 08:00. Closed Mon - Fri 16:30.
Su: Open Mon - Fri 08:00. Closed Mon - Fri 16:30.
Au: Open Mon - Fri 08:00. Closed Mon - Fri 16:30.
Wn: Open Mon - Fri 08:00. Closed Mon - Fri 16:30.
Closed weekends **Ref: YH07244**

HOWSON, GEOFFREY

Geoffrey Howson, Long Barrow, Farmington, Cheltenham, **Gloucestershire**, GL54 3NQ, **ENGLAND**.
(T) 01451 860428 **(F)** 01451 860166.
Contact/s
Owner: Mr G Howson
Profile Blood Stock Agency. Yr. Est: 1982
Opening Times
Telephone for an appointment **Ref: YH07245**

HOY, RONALD GEORGE

Ronald George Hoy, Moat Hse Farm, Great Bricett, Ipswich, **Suffolk**, IP7 7DB, **ENGLAND**.
(T) 01473 658405.
Profile Farrier. **Ref: YH07246**

HOYLES, C

C Hoyles, Pentre, Ciliau Aeron, Lampeter, **Ceredigion**, SA48 8LE, **WALES**.
(T) 01570 470714.
Profile Breeder. **Ref: YH07247**

HPA

Hurlingham Polo Association (The), Manor Farm, Little Coxwell, Faringdon, **Oxfordshire**, SN7 7LW, **ENGLAND**.
(T) 01367 242828 **(F)** 01367 242829
(E) enquiries@hpa-polo.co.uk
(W) www.hpa-polo.co.uk.
Contact/s
Chief Executive: Mr D Wood
Profile Club/Association. **Ref: YH07248**

HTL

Horse Tranship Logistics, Albion Hse, Birds End, Hargrave, Bury St Edmunds, **Suffolk**, IP29 5HE, **ENGLAND**.
(T) 01284 850908 **(F)** 01284 850908.
Contact/s
General Manager: Mr A Buckley
Profile Transport/Horse Boxes. No.Staff: 4
Yr. Est: 1980 **Ref: YH07249**

HUBBARD, D A

D A Hubbard RSS, Forge Cottage, Palgrave, Diss, **Norfolk**, IP22 1AQ, **ENGLAND**.
(T) 01379 643321.
Profile Farrier. **Ref: YH07250**

HUBBARD, DANIEL S W

Daniel S W Hubbard DWCF, Willow Farm, Puxton Lane, Puxton, **Somerset (North)**, BS24 6TD, **ENGLAND**.
(M) 07831 862408.
Profile Farrier. **Ref: YH07251**

HUBBARD, G A

Mr G A Hubbard, Worlingworth Hall, Worlingworth, Woodbridge, **Suffolk**, IP13 7NS, **ENGLAND**.
(T) 01728 628243.
Profile Trainer. **Ref: YH07252**

HUCKLESBY'S TACK SHOP

Hucklesby's Tack Shop, Pear Tree Farm/Long Rd, Saham Waite, Shipdham, Thetford, **Norfolk**, IP25 7RH, **ENGLAND**.
(T) 01362 820235 **(F)** 01362 821033.
Contact/s
Owner: Mr T Hucklesby **Ref: YH07253**

HUDDS FARM

Hudds Farm Livery Stables, Hudds Farm, Westwood Rd, Bradford-on-Avon, **Wiltshire**, BA15 2AH, **ENGLAND**.
(T) 01225 865040 **(F)** 01225 865040.
Contact/s
Owner: Mr M Long
Profile Stable/Livery.
Full, part and DIY livery available, prices on request. Can take 20 - 30 horses. Yr. Est: 1984
Opening Times
Telephone between 08:00 - 17:00 **Ref: YH07254**

HUDSON, BRIAN

Brian Hudson, Chesham, Rosslyn Aveune, Preesall, **Lancashire**, FY6 0HE, **ENGLAND**.
(T) 01253 810380.
Profile Farrier. **Ref: YH07255**

HUGHES RACEHORSE TRANSPORT

Hughes Racehorse Transport, Cricket Field Rd, Newmarket, **Suffolk**, CB8 8BT, **ENGLAND**.
(T) 01638 663155 **(F)** 01638 560894.
Contact/s
Manager: Mr J Spry
Profile Transport/Horse Boxes. **Ref: YH07256**

HUGHES, A L

A L Hughes, Mayalls Farm, Upper Welland, Malvern, **Worcestershire**, WR14 4JX, **ENGLAND**.
(T) 01684 573917.
Profile Supplies. **Ref: YH07257**

HUGHES, A LANCE

A Lance Hughes, Dulas Hse, Cusop, Hay-on-Wye, Hereford, **Herefordshire**, HR3 5RD, **ENGLAND**.
(T) 01497 820657.
Profile Medical Support. **Ref: YH07258**

HUGHES, AMANDA

Amanda Hughes, 2 Oak St, Gilfach Goch, Porth, **Rhondda Cynon Taff**, CF39 8UG, **WALES**.
(T) 01443 672111.
Contact/s
Owner: Miss A Hughes **(Q)** Dip EDT
Profile Medical Support.
Mobile Equine Dental Technician Yr. Est: 2001
Opening Times
Sp: Open Mon - Sat 09:00. Closed Mon - Fri 21:00, Sat 14:00.
Su: Open Mon - Sat 09:00. Closed Mon - Fri 21:00, Sat 14:00.
Au: Open Mon - Sat 09:00. Closed Mon - Fri 21:00, Sat 14:00.
Wn: Open Mon - Sat 09:00. Closed Mon - Fri 21:00, Sat 14:00. **Ref: YH07259**

HUGHES, B E

B E Hughes, Craignant Bank, Selattyn, Oswestry, **Shropshire**, **ENGLAND**.
(T) 01691 718882.
Profile Breeder. **Ref: YH07260**

HUGHES, BRIAN

Brian Hughes, 10 Alfred St, Gilfach Goch, Porth, **Rhondda Cynon Taff**, CF39 8TL, **WALES**.
(T) 01443 671512 **(F)** 01443 672000
Affiliated Bodies FRC.
Contact/s
Owner: Mr B Hughes **(Q)** RSS
Profile Farrier.
Mobile farrier. Yr. Est: 1977
Opening Times
Telephone for an appointment, there is an answer-phone **Ref: YH07261**

HUGHES, C J

C J Hughes, The New Buildings, Vale View Farm, Worcester, **Worcestershire**, WR1 1UG, **ENGLAND**.
(T) 01386 446915. **Ref: YH07262**

HUGHES, CLINT

Clint Hughes, 66 Linden Gr, Hoole, Chester, **Cheshire**, CH2 3JY, **ENGLAND**.
(T) 01244 314926. **Ref: YH07263**

HUGHES, DESMOND T

Desmond T Hughes, Osborne Lodge, Kildare, **County Kildare**, **IRELAND**.
(T) 045 521490.
Contact/s
Trainer: Desmond T Hughes
Profile Trainer.
Opening Times
Telephone for an appointment **Ref: YH07264**

HUGHES, DESSIE

Dessie Hughes, Osborne Lodge, Kildare, **County Kildare**, **IRELAND**.
(T) 045 521490.
Contact/s
Trainer: Mr D Hughes
(E) dessiehughes@kildarehorse.ie
Profile Trainer. **Ref: YH07265**

HUGHES, G

G Hughes, New Inn Cottage, Tremeirchion, St Asaph, **Denbighshire**, LL17 0UG, **WALES**.
(T) 01745 710431.
Profile Farrier. **Ref: YH07266**

HUGHES, HELEN

Helen Hughes, Black Horse Stables, 60 Blackmoor Lane, Bardsey, Leeds, **Yorkshire (West)**, LS17 9DY, **ENGLAND**.
(T) 01937 573845.
Profile Stable/Livery. **Ref: YH07267**

HUGHES, IAN G

Ian G Hughes DWCF, Smithy Cottage, Village Rd, Nercwys, Mold, **Flintshire**, CH7 4AX, **WALES**.
(T) 01352 758524.
Profile Farrier. **Ref: YH07268**

HUGHES, JOHN W

John W Hughes, Hampton Smithy, Ebnal, Malpas, **Cheshire**, SY14 8JE, **ENGLAND**.
(T) 01948 820587.
Profile Farrier. **Ref: YH07269**

HUGHES, KEVIN G

Kevin G Hughes DWCF, 100 Thomas St, Garden Village, Gilfach Goch, Porthcawl, **Rhondda Cynon Taff**, CF39 8TA, **WALES**.
(T) 01443 672414.
Profile Farrier. **Ref: YH07270**

HUGHES, PATRICK

Patrick Hughes, Fenniscourt Stables, Bagenalstown, **County Carlow**, **IRELAND**.
(T) 0503 21250.
Profile Trainer. **Ref: YH07271**

HUGHES, R L

R L Hughes, New Hse, Hazleton, Cheltenham, **Gloucestershire**, GL54 4EB, **ENGLAND**.

(T) 01451 860561.
Contact/s
Owner: Mr R Hughes
Profile Supplies. Ref: YH07272

HUGHES, S A

S A Hughes, 2 Oak St, Gilfach Goch, Porth, **Rhondda Cynon Taff**, CF39 8UG, **WALES**.
(T) 01443 672111
Affiliated Bodies FRC.
Contact/s
Owner: Mr S Hughes
Profile Farrier. Yr. Est: 1983
Opening Times
Sp: Open Mon - Sun 09:00. Closed Mon - Fri 21:00, Sat, Sun 14:00.
Su: Open Mon - Sun 09:00. Closed Mon - Fri 21:00, Sat, Sun 14:00.
Au: Open Mon - Sun 09:00. Closed Mon - Fri 21:00, Sat, Sun 14:00.
Wn: Open Mon - Sun 09:00. Closed Mon - Fri 21:00, Sat, Sun 14:00. Ref: YH07273

HUGHES-GIBB

Hughes-Gibb & Co Ltd, Ten Trinity Sq, London, **London (Greater)**, EC3P 3AX, **ENGLAND**.
(T) 020 79752161 (F) 020 79752331.
Profile Club/Association. Ref: YH07274

HUGILL, J D

Mr J D Hugill, Raikes Farm, Scugdale, Swainby, Northallerton, **Yorkshire (North)**, DL6 3DT, **ENGLAND**.
(T) 01642 701102.
Profile Supplies. Ref: YH07275

HUGO LASCELLES BLOODSTOCK

Hugo Lascelles Bloodstock, The Old Rectory, Tuddenham, Bury St Edmunds, **Suffolk**, IP28 6SG, **ENGLAND**.
(T) 01638 715144.
Profile Blood Stock Agency. Ref: YH07276

HUISH ENGINEERING

Huish Engineering, East Huish Farm, Tedburn St. Mary, Exeter, **Devon**, EX6 6AF, **ENGLAND**.
(T) 01647 61716 (F) 01647 61716.
Contact/s
Partner: Mr S Anthony
Profile Transport/Horse Boxes. Ref: YH07277

HULA ANIMAL RESCUE

Hula Animal Rescue, Bedford Home For Unwanted & Lost Animal Sanctuary, Glebe Farm, Aspley Guise, Milton Keynes, **Buckinghamshire**, MK17 8HZ, **ENGLAND**.
(T) 01908 584000.
Profile Medical Support. Ref: YH07278

HULBERTS GREEN

Hulberts Green, Hulberts Green Farm, Brinkworth, Chippenham, **Wiltshire**, SN15 5AR, **ENGLAND**.
(T) 01666 510268 (F) 01666 510268.
Contact/s
Owner: Mrs J Aspin
Profile Riding School. Ref: YH07279

HULL, DAVID C

David C Hull, Riverside Farm, Scrooby, Doncaster, **Yorkshire (South)**, DN10 6AD, **ENGLAND**.
(T) 01302 710439.
Profile Farrier. Ref: YH07280

HULLAND EQUESTRIAN

Hulland Equestrian Products, Longcliffe Dale Farm, Longcliffe, Brassington, Matlock, **Derbyshire**, DE4 4HN, **ENGLAND**.
(T) 01629 540343.
Contact/s
Owner: Mrs S Carson
Profile Supplies. Ref: YH07281

HULLAND SADDLERY

Hulland Saddlery, Hulland Ward, Ashbourne, **Derbyshire**, DE6 3EA, **ENGLAND**.
(T) 01335 370858 (F) 01335 370858.
Contact/s
Owner: Mrs N Annabell
Profile Saddlery Retailer. Ref: YH07282

HULLOCK, A

Mr A Hullock, Ghyll View, Dufton, Appleby, **Cumbria**, CA16 6DF, **ENGLAND**.
(T) 01768 351855.
Profile Trainer. Ref: YH07283

HUMBLE ORIGINS INT

Humble Origins Int Ltd, 125 Norton Lane, Sheffield, **Yorkshire (South)**, S8 8GX, **ENGLAND**.
(T) 0114 2352227
(M) 07768 405221.
Profile Supplies. Ref: YH07284

HUMPHREY, MARTIN

Martin Humphrey MRCVS AWCF, 3 Roughdown Villas Rd, Felden, Hemel Hempstead, **Hertfordshire**, HP3 0AX, **ENGLAND**.
(T) 01442 248657.
Profile Farrier. Ref: YH07285

HUMPHREY, P O

P O Humphrey, Paradise Building, Moor Lane, Gotham, Nottingham, **Nottinghamshire**, NG11 0LH, **ENGLAND**.
(T) 0115 9831117.
Contact/s
Partner: Mrs J Humphrey
Profile Farrier. Ref: YH07286

HUNGERFORD PARK EST

Hungerford Park Estate, Stud Groom/1 Templeton Stud Cottage, Templeton Rd, Kintbury, Hungerford, **Berkshire**, RG17 9SG, **ENGLAND**.
(T) 01488 682168.
Contact/s
Secretary: Mr W Scroope
Profile Breeder. Ref: YH07287

HUNGRY HALL CONNEMARA STUD

Hungry Hall Connemara Stud, Hungry Hall, Witham, **Essex**, CM8 1RL, **ENGLAND**.
(T) 01376 83305.
Profile Breeder. Ref: YH07288

HUNGRY HORSE

Hungry Horse (The), The Mitchell Cowre Weeford Rd, Four Oaks, Sutton Coldfield, **Midlands (West)**, B75 6NA, **ENGLAND**.
(T) 0121 3088080.
Contact/s
Owner: Mr R Mitchell
Profile Supplies. Ref: YH07289

HUNKINSON, MARK

Mark Hunkinson, Dembleby Hse, Dembleby, Sleaford, **Lincolnshire**, NG34 0EN, **ENGLAND**.
(T) 01529 455562. Ref: YH07290

HUNNABLE, CHRIS & SAM

Chris & Sam Hunnable, Mill Farm, Mill Lane, Great Maplestead, Halstead, **Essex**, CO9 2RA, **ENGLAND**.
(T) 01787 462232
(M) 07885 967439.
Profile Event Rider. Ref: YH07291

HUNSHELF SADDLERY

Hunshelf Saddlery, 6 Castleview, Green Moor, Wortley, Sheffield, **Yorkshire (South)**, S35 7DQ, **ENGLAND**.
(T) 0114 2885376 (F) 0114 2885376.
Contact/s
Owner: Mrs H Blakemore
Profile Saddlery Retailer.
Mobile saddlery retailer No.Staff: 1
Yr. Est: 2001 Ref: YH07292

HUNSLEY HOUSE STUD

Hunsley House Stud, High Hunsley, Cottingham, **Yorkshire (East)**, HU20 3UR, **ENGLAND**.
(T) 01430 827327 (F) 01430 827327.
Contact/s
Owner: Mr R Urquhart
Profile Breeder. Ref: YH07293

HUNSTRETE RIDING SCHOOL

Hunstrete Riding School, Hunstrete, Pensford, **Bath & Somerset (North East)**, BS39 4NT, **ENGLAND**.
(T) 01761 490645.
Profile Riding School, Stable/Livery, Track/Course, Trainer. Ref: YH07294

HUNT RANGE

Hunt Range (The), Unit 8/Dickens Court, Enterprise Cl, Rochester, **Kent**, ME2 4LY, **ENGLAND**.
(T) 01634 293308 (F) 01634 293308.
Contact/s
Owner: Mrs M Taylor Ref: YH07295

HUNT SERVANTS BENEFIT SOCIETY

Hunt Servants Benefit Society, Parsloes Cottage, Bagendon, Cirencester, **Gloucestershire**, GL7 7DU, **ENGLAND**.
(T) 01285 831470 (F) 01285 831737.
Profile Club/Association. Ref: YH07296

HUNT, LANCE A

Lance A Hunt RSS, Holly Cottage, Chevin Rd, Belper, **Derbyshire**, DE56 2UN, **ENGLAND**.
(T) 07970 111969.
Profile Farrier. Ref: YH07297

HUNT, SHOLTO A

Sholto A Hunt DWCF, 14 Thorn Lane, Four Marks, Alton, **Hampshire**, GU34 5EY, **ENGLAND**.
(T) 01420 562800
(M) 07767 356349.
Profile Farrier. Ref: YH07298

HUNTER CHASERS

Hunter Chasers & Point to Pointers, Chase Publications, Stour Hse, 68 Grove Rd, Wimborne, **Dorset**, BH21 1BW, **ENGLAND**.
(T) 01202 888200 (F) 01202 886090.
Profile Supplies. Ref: YH07299

HUNTER SADDLERY

Hunter Saddlery, Eden Hse, Birchills St, Walsall, **Midlands (West)**, WS2 8NG, **ENGLAND**.
(T) 01922 610956 (F) 01922 726165.
Contact/s
Owner: Mr P Keane
Profile Saddlery Retailer. Ref: YH07300

HUNTERS

Hunters, Beech Cl, Newton, Stocksfield, **Northumberland**, NE43 7UQ, **ENGLAND**.
(T) 01661 842905 (F) 01661 843074.
Contact/s
Owner: Mr M Hunter
Profile Transport/Horse Boxes. Ref: YH07301

HUNTERS LODGE RIDING CTRE

Hunters Lodge Riding Centre, Hunston, Chichester, **Sussex (West)**, PO20 6NR, **ENGLAND**.
(T) 01243 780651. Ref: YH07302

HUNTERSFIELD FARM RIDING CTRE

Huntersfield Farm Riding Centre, Huntersfield Farm, Fairlawn Rd, Banstead, **Surrey**, SM7 3AU, **ENGLAND**.
(T) 02086 431333.
Profile Riding School, Stable/Livery. Ref: YH07303

HUNTINGDON & DISTRICT

Huntingdon & District Riding Club, 9 Elm Drive, Offord Cluny, Huntingdon, **Cambridgeshire**, PE18 9RN, **ENGLAND**.
(T) 01480 811364.
Profile Club/Association, Riding Club. Ref: YH07304

HUNTINGDON STEEPLECHASE

Huntingdon Steeplechase Co Ltd, The Racecourse, Brampton, Huntingdon, **Cambridgeshire**, PE29 4NN, **ENGLAND**.
(T) 01480 453373 (F) 01480 455275.
Profile Track/Course. Ref: YH07305

HUNTLEY SCHOOL OF EQUITATION

Huntley School Of Equitation, Woodend Farm, Huntley, Gloucester, **Gloucestershire**, GL19 3EY, **ENGLAND**.
(T) 01452 830440 (F) 01452 830846.
Contact/s
Owner: Mrs T Freeman
Profile Riding School, Stable/Livery. Ref: YH07306

HUNTON LEGG

Hunton Legg (Running Gear) Ltd, Stonewall Farm, Lower Rd, Hemingstone, Ipswich, **Suffolk**, IP6 9RT, **ENGLAND**.
(T) 01449 760275 (F) 01449 760585.
Profile Transport/Horse Boxes. Ref: YH07307

HUNTS FARM STUD & STABLES

Hunts Farm Stud & Stables, Hunts Farm, Church Rd, Crowle, Worcester, **Worcestershire**, WR7 4AT, **ENGLAND**.
(T) 01905 381808.
Profile Breeder. Ref: YH07308

HUNTSMOOR PARK FARM

Huntsmoor Park Farm, Ford Lane, Iver, **Buckinghamshire**, SL0 9LL, **ENGLAND**.
(T) 01895 846606.
Profile Stable/Livery. Ref: YH07309

HURCOMB, RICHARD I

Richard I Hurcomb DWCF, 21 Fincham Rd, Barton Bendish, King's Lynn, **Norfolk**, PE33 9DN, **ENGLAND**.
(T) 01366 347994.
Profile Farrier. Ref: YH07310

HURDCOTT LIVERY STABLES

Hurdcott Saddlery & Livery Stables, Winterbourne Earls, Salisbury, **Wiltshire**, SP4 6HR,

ENGLAND.
(T) 01980 611276 (F) 01980 611276.
Contact/s
General Manager: Ms J Waters
Profile Riding Wear Retailer, Saddlery Retailer, Stable/Livery. No.Staff: 4 Yr. Est: 1979
C.Size: 14 Acres
Opening Times
Sp: Open 08:00. Closed 17:00.
Su: Open 08:00. Closed 17:00.
Au: Open 08:00. Closed 17:00.
Wn: Open 08:00. Closed 17:00. Ref: YH07311

HURLEY, BRONWEN

Mrs Bronwen Hurley MC AMC MMCA, Kineton Grange Farm, Kineton, **Warwickshire**, CV35 0EE, **ENGLAND**.
(T) 01926 640380 (F) 01926 640380.
Profile Medical Support. Ref: YH07312

HURN BRIDGE CTRE

Hurn Bridge Saddlery and Equestrian Centre, Hurn Bridge Farm, Hurn, Christchurch, **Dorset**, BH23 6AD, **ENGLAND**.
(T) 01202 484920 (F) 01202 483931.
Contact/s
Owner: Mr I Christie (T) 01202 483931
Profile Equestrian Centre, Saddlery Retailer, Supplies. No.Staff: 7 Yr. Est: 1980
Opening Times
Sp: Open Mon - Sun 10:00. Closed Mon, Tues 16:30, Wed - Sun 17:30.
Su: Open Mon - Sun 10:00. Closed Mon, Tues 16:30, Wed - Sun 17:30.
Au: Open Mon - Sun 10:00. Closed Mon, Tues 16:30, Wed - Sun 17:30.
Wn: Open Mon - Sun 10:00. Closed Mon, Tues 16:30, Wed - Sun 17:30. Ref: YH07313

HURST FARM LIVERY STABLES

Hurst Farm Livery Stables, Thorpe Green, Thorpe, Egham, **Surrey**, TW20 8QL, **ENGLAND**.
(T) 01344 843966 (F) 01344 843966.
Contact/s
Owner: Mrs B Turner Ref: YH07314

HURST RIDERS CLUB

Hurst Riders Club, White Rose Cottage, Poplar Lane, Hurst, **Berkshire**, RG10 0DJ, **ENGLAND**.
(T) 0118 9341205.
Profile Club/Association, Riding Club. Ref: YH07315

HURST SADDLERS

Hurst Saddlers, 52 Brabazon Rd, Oadby, Leicester, **Leicestershire**, LE2 5HD, **ENGLAND**.
(T) 0116 2713741
Affiliated Bodies BHS, BSJA.
Contact/s
Owner: Ms S Hurst (Q) Master Saddler, RGN
Profile Breeder, Medical Support, Riding Wear Retailer, Saddlery Retailer, Supplies. No.Staff: 2 Yr. Est: 1978
Opening Times
Sp: Open 11:00. Closed 18:00.
Su: Open 11:00. Closed 18:00.
Au: Open 11:00. Closed 18:00.
Wn: Open 11:00. Closed 18:00. Ref: YH07316

HURST, K B

K B Hurst, The Forge, Swallow Rd, Thorganby, Grimsby, **Lincolnshire (North East)**, DN37 0SU, **ENGLAND**.
(T) 01472 398381 (F) 01472 398631.
Contact/s
Owner: Mr K Hurst
Profile Blacksmith. Ref: YH07317

HURST, PAUL S

Paul S Hurst DWCF, 130 Lovelace Drive, Pyrford, Woking, **Surrey**, GU22 8RZ, **ENGLAND**.
(T) 01932 341660.
Profile Farrier. Ref: YH07318

HURSTFIELD SADDLERY

Hurstfield Saddlery, Longhurst, Northampton Rd, Brackley, **Northamptonshire**, NN13 6LL, **ENGLAND**.
(T) 01280 840592 (F) 01280 706179
(E) mary.astbury@virgin.net.
Profile Saddlery Retailer. Ref: YH07319

HURSTFIELD STABLES

Hurstfield Livery & Riding Stables, Hurstfield, Hurst Rd, Tadworth, **Surrey**, KT20 5BN, **ENGLAND**.
(T) 01737 813750.
Contact/s
Owner: Mrs K Gosling Ref: YH07320

HURSTFIELDS EQUESTRIAN CTRE

Hurstfields Equestrian Centre, Hurst Rd, Walton On The Hill, Tadworth, **Surrey**, KT20 5BD, **ENGLAND**.
(T) 01737 814305.
Profile Stable/Livery, Track/Course. Ref: YH07321

HURTWOOD PARK

Hurtwood Park Polo Club, Horsham Lane, Ewhurst Green, Ewhurst, Cranleigh, **Surrey**, GU6 7SW, **ENGLAND**.
(T) 01483 272828 (F) 01483 272671
(E) hurtwoodparkpolo@btconnect.com.
Contact/s
Assistant Manager: Ms A Fisher
Profile Club/Association. Polo Club.
The club is available for hire for private functions including weddings, seminars, conferences and corporate days. Other activities available include 4 x 4 off roading, archery, golf, shooting and fly fishing.
Ref: YH07322

HURWITZ, STANLEY

Stanley Hurwitz, 8 Bowly Rd, Cirencester, **Gloucestershire**, GL7 1SE, **ENGLAND**.
(T) 01285 652792. Ref: YH07323

HURWORTH HUNT

Hurworth Hunt Pony Club Junior ODE, The Shades, Sutton Under Whitestone, Thirsk, **Yorkshire (North)**, YO7 2PU, **ENGLAND**.
(T) 01845 597457.
Contact/s
Chief Instructor: Mrs P Arrand
Profile Riding Club. Ref: YH07324

HUSBANDS SADDLERY

Husbands Saddlery, Saddlery Only/Walnut Tree Farm, The Street, Ryarsh, West Malling, **Kent**, ME19 5LJ, **ENGLAND**.
(T) 01732 874906 (F) 01732 874906.
Contact/s
Owner: Mr P Husband
Profile Saddlery Retailer. Ref: YH07325

HUSSEY, P & L

P & L Hussey, Henfold Farm, Henfold Lane, Beare Green, Dorking, **Surrey**, RH5 4RW, **ENGLAND**.
(T) 01306 631729.
Profile Breeder. Ref: YH07326

HUSSEY, R D

R D Hussey, Riverside Farm, Burhill Rd, Walton-on-Thames, **Surrey**, KT12 4BG, **ENGLAND**.
(T) 01932 226370.
Contact/s
Owner: Mr R Hussey Ref: YH07327

HUSSEY, TRACY

Tracy Hussey, 34 Woodsage Drive, Gillingham, **Dorset**, SP8 4UF, **ENGLAND**.
(T) 01747 825918.
Contact/s
Owner: Mrs T Hussey Ref: YH07328

HUSSEYS

Husseys, Chartered Surveyors, The Auction Ctre, Matford Park Rd, Exeter, **Devon**, EX2 8FD, **ENGLAND**.
(T) 01392 425481 (F) 01392 250610. Ref: YH07329

HUSTEADS RIDING SCHOOL

Husteads Riding School, Husteads Farm, Dobcross, Saddleworth, Oldham, **Lancashire**, OL3 5RA, **ENGLAND**.
(T) 01457 870904
(W) www.husteads.co.uk.
Contact/s
Owner: Ms J Longden (Q) BHSAI
Profile Riding School, Stable/Livery.
Riding school shows and picnic rides available.
No.Staff: 2 Yr. Est: 1971 C.Size: 40 Acres
Ref: YH07330

HUSTON, D N

Mr D N Huston, 79 Ballylesson Rd, Belfast, **County Antrim**, BT8 8JT, **NORTHERN IRELAND**.
(T) 028 90826349.
Profile Breeder. Ref: YH07331

HUSTON, G S

G S Huston DWCF, 14 Barnes Ave, Chesham, **Buckinghamshire**, HP5 1AP, **ENGLAND**.
(T) 01494 791379.
Profile Farrier. Ref: YH07332

HUTCHESON, TOM

Tom Hutcheson, P O Box 29, Boxall, **Essex**, RM10 8XQ, **ENGLAND**.
(T) 020 89240328.
Profile Trainer. Ref: YH07333

HUTCHINS, L

L Hutchins, Manor Cottage, Stinchcombe, Dursley, **Gloucestershire**, GL11 6BD, **ENGLAND**.
(T) 01453 543533.
Profile Breeder. Ref: YH07334

HUTCHINSON, A

A Hutchinson, 36 Nell Gap Lane, Midlestown, Wakefield, **Yorkshire (West)**, WF4 4PH, **ENGLAND**.
(T) 01924 274742.
Profile Supplies. Ref: YH07335

HUTCHINSON, LYNNE

Lynne Hutchinson, Bristol Evening Post, Stable Cottage, Lower Morton, Thornbury, **Gloucestershire (South)**, BS35 1LF, **ENGLAND**.
(T) 01454 411632 (F) 01454 273545
(M) 07711 952766.
Profile Supplies. Ref: YH07336

HUTCHISON, DUNLOP & BAIRD

Hutchison, Dunlop & Baird, The Veterinary Surgery, Hallfield Lane, Wetherby, **Yorkshire (West)**, LS22 6JU, **ENGLAND**.
(T) 01937 582025.
Profile Medical Support. Ref: YH07337

HUTSBY, G

Mr G Hutsby, Little Hill, Wellesbourne, **Warwickshire**, **ENGLAND**..
Profile Supplies. Ref: YH07338

HUTTON HALL FARM

Hutton Hall Farm, Hutton Conyers, Ripon, **Yorkshire (North)**, HG4 5DU, **ENGLAND**.
(T) 01765 640426.
Profile Stable/Livery. Ref: YH07339

HUTTON, C D

C D Hutton, 10 Greenlees Rd, Cambuslang, Glasgow, **Lanarkshire (South)**, G72 8JH, **SCOTLAND**.
(T) 0141 6461400.
Profile Blacksmith. Ref: YH07340

HUTTON, G

Miss G Hutton, Windyridge, Hillside Rd, Barrhead, Glasgow, **Glasgow (City of)**, G78 1ES, **SCOTLAND**.
(T) 0141 8813710. Ref: YH07341

HUTTON, LEN

Len Hutton, The Forge, Bishopsbourne, Canterbury, **Kent**, CT4 5HT, **ENGLAND**.
(T) 01227 830784.
Profile Blacksmith. Ref: YH07342

HYDE PARK BRANCH

Hyde Park Branch of The Pony Club (The), 8 Bathurst Mews, Hyde Pk, London, **London (Greater)**, W2 2SB, **ENGLAND**.
(T) 020 72623791.
Profile Club/Association. Ref: YH07343

HYDE PARK HORSEMEN'S SUNDAY

Hyde Park Horsemen's Sunday, 8 Bathhurst Mews, London, **London (Greater)**, W2 2SB, **ENGLAND**.
(T) 020 72623791.
Profile Riding Club.
There is a 'Ride out' the first Sunday of the month.
Ref: YH07344

HYDE PARK RIDING WEAR

London Riding Schools Ltd, 63 Bathurst Mews, London, **London (Greater)**, W2 2SB, **ENGLAND**.
(T) 020 77063806 (F) 020 78234512
(E) info@hydeparkstables.com
(W) www.hydeparkstables.com
Affiliated Bodies ABRS, BHS.
Contact/s
Manager: Stephen Ballantyne
Profile Equestrian Centre, Riding Wear Retailer.
Stable management and 'Horse Sense' days are available. No.Staff: 10 Yr. Est: 1835
Opening Times
Sp: Open Tues - Sun 07:15. Closed Tues - Sun 16:30.
Su: Open Tues - Sun 07:15. Closed Tues - Sun 18:00.
Au: Open Tues - Sun 07:15. Closed Tues - Sun 16:30.
Wn: Open Tues - Sun 07:15. Closed Tues - Sun 16:00.
Closed Mondays Ref: YH07345

HYDE PARK STABLES

London Riding Schools Ltd, 63 Bathurst Mews, London, **London (Greater)**, W2 2SB, **ENGLAND**.
(T) 020 77232813 (F) 020 78234512

(E) info@hydeparkstables.com
(W) www.hydeparkstables.com.
Contact/s
Manager: Joanne Mister
Profile Equestrian Centre, Riding School.
Weekdays - 60 minute one-to-one lesson £32.00, course of 10 lessons £250.00. Weekends - course of 10 lessons £270.00. 60 minute group lessons £34.00, course of ten lessons £300.00. Course of 10 children's lessons £260.00. Children are able to join in gymkhanas and day camps and take ABRS and BHS riding tests. Also organises shooting parties.
Opening Times
Sp: Open Tues - Thurs 10:00, Fri 07:00, Sat, Sun 08:30. Closed Tues - Thurs 19:00, Fri - Sun 17:00.
Su: Open Tues - Thurs 10:00, Fri 07:00, Sat, Sun 08:30. Closed Tues - Thurs 19:00, Fri - Sun 17:00.
Au: Open Tues - Thurs 10:00, Fri 07:00, Sat, Sun 08:30. Closed Tues - Fri 17:00, Sat, Sun 16:00.
Wn: Open Tues - Thurs 10:00, Fri 07:00, Sat, Sun 08:30. Closed Tues - Fri 17:00, Sat, Sun 16:00.
Mondays - open for bookings only. Autumn/ Winter closing hours may vary **Ref: YH07346**

HYDE PARK STUD
Hyde Park Stud, Hyde Pk, Killucan, **County Westmeath**, **IRELAND**.
(T) 044 74022.
Profile Supplies. **Ref: YH07347**

HYDE PK BARRACKS
Hyde Park Barracks - Farriers, The Forge, Hyde Pk Barracks, Knightsbridge, London, **London (Greater)**, SW7 1SE, **ENGLAND**.
(T) 020 75849443.
Contact/s
Farrier: Christopher J Carrel **(Q)** DWCF
Profile Farrier. **Ref: YH07348**

HYDE RIDING CTRE
Hyde Riding Centre, Chalford, Stroud, **Gloucestershire**, GL6 8PB, **ENGLAND**.
(T) 01453 882413. **Ref: YH07349**

HYDE STUD FARM
Hyde Stud Farm, Hyde Farm, Hyde Lane, Ecchinswell, Newbury, **Berkshire**, RG20 4UN, **ENGLAND**.
(T) 01635 268083.
Profile Breeder. **Ref: YH07350**

HYDE WOODS RIDING STABLES
Hyde Woods Riding Stables, Hyde, Wareham, **Dorset**, BH20 7NT, **ENGLAND**.
(T) 01929 471087. **Ref: YH07351**

HYDRO AGRI
Hydro Agri (UK) Ltd, Bury Rd, Chedburgh, Bury St Edmunds, **Suffolk**, IP29 4UQ, **ENGLAND**.
(T) 01284 850500 **(F)** 01284 850881.
Profile Supplies. **Ref: YH07352**

HYFIELD STABLES
Hyfield Stables, Crowhurst, Battle, **Sussex (East)**, TN33 9BX, **ENGLAND**.
(T) 01424 830416. **Ref: YH07353**

HYKEHAM ANIMAL FEEDS
Hykeham Animal Feeds, 554 Newark Rd, North Hykeham, Lincoln, **Lincolnshire**, LN6 9NG, **ENGLAND**.
(T) 01522 681410.
Profile Supplies. **Ref: YH07354**

HYKEHAM RIDING STABLES
Hykeham Riding Stables, 140 Mill Lane, North Hykeham, **Lincolnshire**, LN6 9PE, **ENGLAND**.
(T) 01522 691277.
Profile Riding School. **Ref: YH07355**

HYLAND LIVESTOCK CARRYING
Hyland Livestock Carrying, New Morgay Farm, Cripps Corner Rd, Staplecross, Robertsbridge, **Sussex (East)**, TN32 5QR, **ENGLAND**.
(T) 01580 830302.
Contact/s
Owner: Mr K Hyland
Profile Transport/Horse Boxes. **Ref: YH07356**

HYLANDS STABLES
Hylands Stables, 2 Highlands Farm Cottages, Arlington Rd West, Hailsham, **Sussex (East)**, BN27 3RD, **ENGLAND**.
(T) 01323 846797.
Profile Riding School. **Ref: YH07357**

HYLTON LIVERY
Hylton Livery, North Moor Farm, West Boldon, East Boldon, **Tyne and Wear**, NE36 0BB, **ENGLAND**.
(T) 0191 5362734.
Contact/s
Owner: Mr G Johnson
Profile Stable/Livery. **Ref: YH07358**

HYLTON, J H
J H Hylton, 5 Englefields, South St, Tillingham, Southminster, **Essex**, CM0 7AT, **ENGLAND**.
(T) 01621 778555.
Contact/s
Owner: Mr J Hylton
Profile Farrier.
Mobile farrier. **Yr. Est:** 1982
Opening Times
Open by appointment only **Ref: YH07359**

HYND, MIKE
Mike Hynd, Rathmore, Churchdown Lane, Hucclecote, **Gloucestershire**, GL3 2LR, **ENGLAND**.
(T) 01452 713913.
Profile Trainer. **Ref: YH07360**

HYPERION SADDLERY
Hyperion Saddlery, 264 Park View, Gilfach, Bargoed, **Caerphilly**, CF81 8QP, **WALES**.
(T) 01443 832985.
Profile Saddlery Retailer. **Ref: YH07361**

HYSLOP, J F
J F Hyslop, Slateyford Farm, Wolsingham, Bishop Auckland, **County Durham**, DL13 3LZ, **ENGLAND**.
(T) 01388 527410.
Profile Breeder. **Ref: YH07362**

I C S
International Competition Stallions, P O Box 8110, Mauchline, **Ayrshire (South)**, KA5 5YB, **SCOTLAND**.
(T) 01290 552999 **(F)** 01290 552998
(E) ics@sporthorse-breeder.com
(W) www.sporthorse-breeder.com
Affiliated Bodies BSJA.
Profile Breeder.
Opening Times
Sp: Open Mon - Fri 09:00. Closed Mon - Fri 17:00.
Su: Open Mon - Fri 09:00. Closed Mon - Fri 17:00.
Au: Open Mon - Fri 09:00. Closed Mon - Fri 17:00.
Wn: Open Mon - Fri 09:00. Closed Mon - Fri 17:00.
Closed at weekends **Ref: YH07363**

I C S BLOODSTOCK
I C S Bloodstock, P O Box 8110, Mauchline, **Ayrshire (South)**, KA5 5YB, **SCOTLAND**.
(T) 01290 552999 **(F)** 01290 552998
(E) hugh@icsbloodstock.com
(W) www.icsbloodstock.com
Affiliated Bodies BSJA.
Profile Blood Stock Agency.
Opening Times
Sp: Open Mon - Fri 09:00. Closed Mon - Fri 17:00.
Su: Open Mon - Fri 09:00. Closed Mon - Fri 17:00.
Au: Open Mon - Fri 09:00. Closed Mon - Fri 17:00.
Wn: Open Mon - Fri 09:00. Closed Mon - Fri 17:00.
Closed at weekends but the answer phone is on 24 hours a day and checked regularly **Ref: YH07364**

I H A
Intelligent Horsemanship Association, P O Box 2035, Bayden, Marlborough, **Wiltshire**, SN8 2TL, **ENGLAND**.
(T) 01672 541155.
Profile Club/Association. **Ref: YH07365**

I J A ENGINEERING
I J A Engineering, Islebeck, Thirsk, **Yorkshire (North)**, YO7 3AN, **ENGLAND**.
(T) 01845 501601.
Contact/s
Owner: Mr I Atherton
Profile Transport/Horse Boxes. **Ref: YH07366**

I P D COACHBUILDERS
I P D Coachbuilders Ltd, The Watertower Site, Anchor Lane, Abbess Roding, Ongar, **Essex**, CM5 0JR, **ENGLAND**.
(T) 01279 876464 **(F)** 01279 876464.
Profile Transport/Horse Boxes. **Ref: YH07367**

I SINTON & SON
I Sinton & Son, 63 Stratton Heights, Cirencester, **Gloucestershire**, GL7 2RN, **ENGLAND**.
(T) 01285 651219.
Contact/s
Owner: Mr I Sinton
Profile Farrier. **Ref: YH07368**

I T A
I T A, 20 Sandy Lane, Walton-on-Thames, **Surrey**, KT12 2EQ, **ENGLAND**.
(T) 01932 228846.
Contact/s
Owner: Mrs M Ayers
Profile Transport/Horse Boxes. **Ref: YH07369**

IAN DENNIS PARTNERSHIP
Ian Dennis Partnership, The Forge, Llandeilo'r Fan, Brecon, **Powys**, LD3 8UD, **WALES**.
(T) 01874 636535 **(F)** 01874 636535.
Contact/s
Owner: Mr I Dennis
Profile Blacksmith. **Ref: YH07370**

IAN P BRADBURY
Ian P Bradbury RSS, 4 Tarn Mount, Macclesfield, **Cheshire**, SK11 7XX, **ENGLAND**.
(T) 01625 422481.
Profile Farrier. **Ref: YH07371**

IANSON, STEVE (ESQ)
Steve Ianson Esq, 2 Manor Farm Cottage, Branston, Grantham, **Lincolnshire**, **ENGLAND**..
Profile Medical Support. **Ref: YH07372**

IBBOTSON, CHRISTOPHER J
Christopher J Ibbotson RSS, Walton Forge, Walton-on-the-Hill, Tadworth, **Surrey**, KT20 7RO, **ENGLAND**.
(T) 01737 813120.
Profile Farrier. **Ref: YH07373**

IBBOTSON, PAUL T
Paul T Ibbotson AWCF, 23 Walton St, Walton-on-the-Hill, Tadworth, **Surrey**, KT20 7RR, **ENGLAND**.
(T) 01737 813120.
Profile Farrier. **Ref: YH07374**

IBBOTSON, PETER J
Peter J Ibbotson RSS, 7 Meadow Walk, Walton-on-the-Hill, Tadworth, **Surrey**, KT20 7UF, **ENGLAND**.
(T) 01737 813120.
Profile Farrier. **Ref: YH07375**

IBEM
Institute Of Barefoot Equine Mangement, 21 Ivy Rd, Stirchley, Birmingham, **Midlands (West)**, B30 2NU, **ENGLAND**.
(W) www.ibem.org.uk.
Contact/s
Treasurer: Helen Trott
Profile Club/Association. **Ref: YH07376**

IBEX
Ibex Equine Ltd, Charnley Fold Lane, Bamber Bridge, Preston, **Lancashire**, PR5 6BE, **ENGLAND**.
(T) 01772 324444 **(F)** 01772 324455
(W) www.horseshoes.com.
Contact/s
Manager: Mr N Charnley
Profile Farrier.
Supply and use plastic glue on shoes for theraputic purposes **No.Staff:** 3 **Yr. Est:** 1997
Opening Times
Sp: Open Mon - Fri 09:00. Closed Mon - Fri 17:00.
Su: Open Mon - Fri 09:00. Closed Mon - Fri 17:00.
Au: Open Mon - Fri 09:00. Closed Mon - Fri 17:00.
Wn: Open Mon - Fri 09:00. Closed Mon - Fri 17:00.
Ref: YH07377

IBM RIDING CLUB
IBM (South Hants) Riding Club, C/O Ibm Uk Ltd, P O Box 6, Langstone Rd, Havant, **Hampshire**, PO9 1SA, **ENGLAND**.
(T) 023 92486363.
Profile Club/Association, Riding Club. **Ref: YH07378**

ICELANDIC HORSE SOCIETY
Icelandic Horse Society (The), 77 Wagon Rd, Falkirk, **Falkirk**, FK2 0EL, **SCOTLAND**.
(T) 01324 715503
(E) heather@phd.crsnet.co.uk.
Profile Club/Association. **Ref: YH07379**

ICELANDIC HORSE SOCIETY OF GB
Icelandic Horse Society of GB, 22 Smileyknowes Court, North Berwick, **Lothian (East)**, EH39 4RG, **SCOTLAND**.
(T) 01620 893391 **(F)** 01620 893391.
Profile Club/Association. **Ref: YH07380**

ICKE, S M
S M Icke DWCF, Orchard Cottage, Weare St, Ockley, **Surrey**, RH5 5JD, **ENGLAND**.
(T) 01306 712579.
Profile Farrier. **Ref: YH07381**

ICKLEFORD EQUESTRIAN
Ickleford Equestrian Centre, Lower Green Farm, Lower Green, Ickleford, Hitchin, **Hertfordshire**, SG5

3TW, **ENGLAND**.
(T) 01462 459081
Affiliated Bodies ABRS.
Contact/s
Owner: Mrs D Nicholls
Profile Riding Club, Riding School, Stable/Livery.
Evening lectures - NVQ, BHS examinations. Livery - full, part and DIY, prices on request. 30 minutes of one to one coaching £14 before 15:30. Pony Club Centre, ponies provided. Yr. Est: 1965
Opening Times
Telephone between 08:00 - 18:00 Mon - Sun
Ref: YH07382

ICKNIELD VETNRY GROUP

Icknield Veterinary Group, 25-25A Princes St, Dunstable, **Bedfordshire**, LU6 3AS, **ENGLAND**.
(T) 01582 471177 **(F)** 01582 475245.
Profile Medical Support. **Ref: YH07383**

ICKNIELD VETNRY GROUP

Icknield Veterinary Group, 1 Brook St, Luton, **Bedfordshire**, LU3 1DS, **ENGLAND**.
(T) 01582 727571 **(F)** 01582 401984.
Profile Medical Support. **Ref: YH07384**

IDEAL SADDLE

Ideal Saddle Co, The Old School, Hollyhedge Lane, Walsall, **Midlands (West)**, WS2 8PZ, **ENGLAND**.
(T) 01922 620233 **(F)** 01922 623853.
Contact/s
Partner: Mr S Marks **Ref: YH07385**

IDLEBECK PUBLISHING

Idlebeck Publishing & Support Service, Merry Hill Cottage, Long Lane, Colehill, Wimborne, **Dorset**, BH21 7AQ, **ENGLAND**.
(T) 01202 885589 **(F)** 01202 885589.
Profile Club/Association. **Ref: YH07386**

IDOVER HOUSE STABLES

Idover House Stables, Dauntsey, Purton, Swindon, **Wiltshire**, SN5 4HW, **ENGLAND**.
(T) 01249 720255.
Profile Trainer. **Ref: YH07387**

IEDEMA, BARRY

Mr Barry Iedema BHSI, 7 Feltham Cl, Romsey, **Hampshire**, SO51 8PB, **ENGLAND**.
(T) 01794 523610
(M) 07973 711054.
Contact/s
Trainer: Mr B Iedema **(Q)** BHSI
Profile Trainer. **Ref: YH07388**

IFIELD PARK FEED TACK & WEAR

Ifield Park Feed Tack & Wear, Ifield Hse, Bonnetts Lane, Ifield, Crawley, **Sussex (West)**, RH11 0NY, **ENGLAND**.
(T) 01293 511832 **(F)** 01293 531882.
Contact/s
Owner: Mr N Capstick
Profile Saddlery Retailer. **Ref: YH07389**

IFMHS

International Falabella Miniature Horse Society, Holding Hse, The Barracks, Hook, **Hampshire**, RG27 9NW, **ENGLAND**.
(T) 01256 763425
(E) ifmhs@falabella.co.uk
Contact/s
Registrar: Mr M Beer
Profile Club/Association. **Ref: YH07390**

IFOR WILLIAMS

Ifor Williams Trailers Ltd, Cynwyd, Corwen, **Denbighshire**, LL21 0LS, **WALES**.
(T) 01490 412626 **(F)** 01490 412770.
Profile Transport/Horse Boxes. **Ref: YH07391**

IFOR WILLIAMS TRAILERS

Ifor Williams Trailers (Thurso), Keoltag, Reay, Thurso, Caithness, **Highlands**, KW14 7RE, **SCOTLAND**.
(T) 01847 81365.
Profile Transport/Horse Boxes. **Ref: YH07392**

IFOR WILLIAMS TRAILERS

Ifor Williams Trailers Ltd, Unit 14 Blaydon Ind Pk, Blaydon-on-Tyne, **Tyne and Wear**, NE21 5AB, **ENGLAND**.
(T) 0191 4146301.
Profile Transport/Horse Boxes. **Ref: YH07393**

IGER

Institute of Grassland & Enviromental Research, Plas Gogerddan, Aberystwyth, **Ceredigion**, SY23 3EB, **WALES**.
(T) 01970 828255 **(F)** 01970 820212.
Profile Club/Association. **Ref: YH07394**

IHA

Irish Horseracing Authority, Leopardstown Racecourse Foxrock, Dublin, **County Dublin**, **IRELAND**.
(T) 01 2892888 **(F)** 01 2892019
(W) www.iha.ie.
Profile Club/Association. Authority of Racecourses. The IHA is responsible for the development and promotions of horseracing. **Ref: YH07395**

IJO FINE SADDLERY

IJO Fine Saddlery, 46A Bradford Lane, Walsall, **Midlands (West)**, WS1 3LU, **ENGLAND**.
(T) 01922 721669 **(F)** 01922 721669.
Contact/s
Owner: Mr J Gregory **Ref: YH07396**

IKIN, D & D

D & D Ikin, Broomy Farm, Woodville Rd, Hartshorne, Swadlincote, **Derbyshire**, DE11 7EY, **ENGLAND**.
(T) 01283 217761.
Contact/s
Owner: Mr D Ikin
Profile Stable/Livery.
DIY livery available, prices on request.
Opening Times
Telephone for an appointment **Ref: YH07397**

ILDRA

Irish Long Distance Riding Association Ulster Branch, 188 Ballynahinch Rd, Dromore, **County Down**, BT25 1EU, **NORTHERN IRELAND**.
(T) 028 97532061 **(F)** 028 97532061
(W) www.members.tripod.com/~ildra/.
Profile Club/Association. Yr. Est: 1990
Ref: YH07398

ILFRACOMBE & DISTRICT

Ilfracombe & District Riding Club, 2 The Farthings, Chivenor Village, Barnstaple, **Devon**, **ENGLAND**..
Profile Club/Association, Riding Club. **Ref: YH07399**

ILKLEY RIDING CTRE

Ilkley Riding Centre, Wheatley Grange Farm, Ilkley, **Yorkshire (West)**, LS29 8BP, **ENGLAND**.
(T) 01943 607960 **(F)** 01943 607960.
Contact/s
For Bookings: Miss L Lawson
Profile Riding School, Riding Wear Retailer, Stable/Livery. **Ref: YH07400**

ILPH

International League for the Protection of Horses, Anne Colvin Hse, Snetterton, Norwich, **Norfolk**, NR16 2LR, **ENGLAND**.
(T) 01953 498682 **(F)** 01953 498373
(E) ilph@ilph.org
(W) www.ilph.org.
Profile Club/Association.
Prevention of ill treatment to horses - fundraising, adoption schemes, donations. Offer horse loan and horse rehabilitation schemes. Registered charity No 206658. Yr. Est: 1927 **Ref: YH07401**

IMPACT SIGNS

Impact Signs, Fox's Mill, Tonedale, Wellington, **Somerset**, TA21 0AW, **ENGLAND**.
(T) 01823 662006 **(F)** 01823 662006.
Profile Supplies. **Ref: YH07402**

IMPERIAL ARABIAN STUD

Imperial Arabian Stud, Diana Lodge, Collins Lane, Purton, Swindon, **Wiltshire**, SN5 9JR, **ENGLAND**.
(T) 01793 770205.
Profile Breeder. **Ref: YH07403**

IMPEY, LINDA

Mrs Linda Impey, Oak Croft, Priors Green, Hartford End, Chelmsford, **Essex**, CM3 1JR, **ENGLAND**.
(T) 01371 820706 **(F)** 01371 820706.
Contact/s
Owner: Linda Impey
Profile Breeder.
Opening Times
Telephone for an appointment **Ref: YH07404**

IN STEEL

In Steel, Unit 1 Halwin Ind Est, Porkellis, Helston, **Cornwall**, TR13 0LB, **ENGLAND**.
(T) 01326 340044 **(F)** 01326 340044.
Contact/s
Owner: Mr I Nicholls
Profile Blacksmith. **Ref: YH07405**

IN THE SADDLE

In The Saddle Ltd, Baughurst Rd, Ramsdell, Tadley, **Hampshire**, RG26 5SH, **ENGLAND**.
(T) 01256 851665 **(F)** 01256 851667
(E) rides@inthesaddle.com
(W) www.inthesaddle.com.
Profile Holidays, Horse/Rider Accom.
Worldwide riding holidays to places such as Spain, Portugal, Mongolia, Chile and Argentina. Although holidays are not available in England they are on offer in both Northern & Southern Ireland. Yr. Est: 1996
Opening Times
Sp: Open Mon - Fri 09:00. Closed Mon - Fri 17:30.
Su: Open Mon - Fri 09:00. Closed Mon - Fri 17:30.
Au: Open Mon - Fri 09:00. Closed Mon - Fri 17:30.
Wn: Open Mon - Fri 09:00. Closed Mon - Fri 17:30.
Ref: YH07406

INADOWN FARM STABLES

F B Janson T/A Inadown Farm Livery Stables, Newton Valence, Alton, **Hampshire**, GU34 3RR, **ENGLAND**.
(T) 01420 588439 **(F)** 01420 588424
Affiliated Bodies BHS.
Contact/s
General Manager: Ms J Betteley **(Q)** BHSII
(T) 01420 588697
Profile Equestrian Centre, Riding Club, Riding School, Stable/Livery. No.Staff: 5 Yr. Est: 1980
C.Size: 200 Acres **Ref: YH07407**

INCH'S SADDLERY

Inch's Saddlery, Unit 5 Hannington Farm, Hannington, Tadley, **Hampshire**, RG26 5TZ, **ENGLAND**.
(T) 01635 297090 **(F)** 01635 297993.
Contact/s
Owner: Mrs A Gibbs
Profile Saddlery Retailer. **Ref: YH07408**

INCISA, DON ENRICO

Don Enrico Incisa, Thorngill, Coverham, Middleham, Leyburn, **Yorkshire (North)**, DL8 4TJ, **ENGLAND**.
(T) 01969 640653 **(F)** 01969 640694.
Profile Trainer. **Ref: YH07409**

INCUS DESIGNS

Incus Designs, Brechfa, Carmarthen, **Carmarthenshire**, SA32 7RE, **WALES**.
(T) 01267 202727.
Contact/s
Owner: Mrs L Harding
Profile Blacksmith. **Ref: YH07410**

INDESPENSION

Indespension Ltd, 8 Richfield Ave, Reading, **Berkshire**, RG1 8EQ, **ENGLAND**.
(T) 0118 9575004 **(F)** 0118 9567419
(E) reading@indespension.co.uk
(W) www.indespension.com.
Profile Transport/Horse Boxes.
Opening Times
Sp: Open Mon - Sat 08:00. Closed Mon - Fri 17:30, Sat 12:30.
Su: Open Mon - Sat 08:00. Closed Mon - Fri 17:30, Sat 12:30.
Au: Open Mon - Sat 08:00. Closed Mon - Fri 17:30, Sat 12:30.
Wn: Open Mon - Sat 08:00. Closed Mon - Fri 17:30, Sat 12:30. **Ref: YH07411**

INDESPENSION

Indespension Ltd, 214A Manchester Rd, Broadheath, Altrincham, **Cheshire**, WA14 5GR, **ENGLAND**.
(T) 0161 9284740 **(F)** 0161 9269395
(E) altrincham@indespresion.co.uk
(W) www.indespension.com.
Profile Transport/Horse Boxes.
Opening Times
Sp: Open Mon - Sat 08:30. Closed Mon - Fri 17:30, Sat 12:30.
Su: Open Mon - Sat 08:30. Closed Mon - Fri 17:30, Sat 12:30.
Au: Open Mon - Sat 08:30. Closed Mon - Fri 17:30, Sat 12:30.
Wn: Open Mon - Sat 08:30. Closed Mon - Fri 17:30, Sat 12:30. **Ref: YH07412**

INDESPENSION

Indespension Ltd, 2 Cloughmore Rd, Newtownabbey, **County Antrim**, BT36 4WW, **NORTHERN IRELAND**.
(T) 028 90839983 **(F)** 028 90839550
(E) belfast@indespension.co.uk
(W) www.indespension.com.
Profile Transport/Horse Boxes.
Opening Times
Sp: Open Mon - Sat 08:30. Closed Mon - Fri 17:30, Sat 12:30.

Su: Open Mon - Sat 08:30. Closed Mon - Fri 17:30, Sat 12:30.
Au: Open Mon - Sat 09:00. Closed Mon - Fri 17:30, Sat 12:30.
Wn: Open Mon - Sat 08:30. Closed Mon - Fri 17:30, Sat 12:30. **Ref: YH07413**

INDESPENSION

Indespension Ltd, Parrell Trailer & Castor Ctre, Unit D1, Hibernian Ind Est, Tallaght, **County Dublin**, **IRELAND**.
(T) 01 4512588 **(F)** 01 4512622
(E) dublin@indesprension.co.uk
(W) www.indespension.com.
Profile Transport/Horse Boxes.
Opening Times
Sp: Open Mon - Fri 08:30. Closed Mon - Fri 17:30.
Su: Open Mon - Fri 08:30. Closed Mon - Fri 17:30.
Au: Open Mon - Fri 08:30. Closed Mon - Fri 17:30.
Wn: Open Mon - Fri 08:30. Closed Mon - Fri 17:30.
Ref: YH07414

INDESPENSION

Indespension Ltd, Castle Mungret, Dock Rd, Limerick, **County Limerick**, **IRELAND**.
(T) 061 225700 **(F)** 061 225699.
Profile Transport/Horse Boxes.
Opening Times
Sp: Open Mon - Fri 08:30. Closed Mon - Fri 17:30.
Su: Open Mon - Fri 08:30. Closed Mon - Fri 17:30.
Au: Open Mon - Fri 08:30. Closed Mon - Fri 17:30.
Wn: Open Mon - Fri 08:30. Closed Mon - Fri 17:30.
Ref: YH07415

INDESPENSION

Indespension Ltd, Ascot Drive, Derby, **Derbyshire**, DE24 8ST, **ENGLAND**.
(T) 01332 348555 **(F)** 01332 294614
(E) derby@indespension.co.uk
(W) www.indespension.com.
Profile Transport/Horse Boxes.
Opening Times
Sp: Open Mon - Sat 08:30. Closed Mon - Fri 17:30, Sat 12:30.
Su: Open Mon - Sat 08:30. Closed Mon - Fri 17:30, Sat 12:30.
Au: Open Mon - Sat 08:30. Closed Mon - Fri 17:30, Sat 12:30.
Wn: Open Mon - Sat 08:30. Closed Mon - Fri 17:30, Sat 12:30. **Ref: YH07416**

INDESPENSION

Indespension Ltd, 57 London Rd, Edinburgh, **Edinburgh (City of)**, EH7 6AA, **SCOTLAND**.
(T) 0131 6617571 **(F)** 0131 6617576
(E) edinburgh@indespension.co.uk
(W) www.indespension.com.
Profile Transport/Horse Boxes.
Opening Times
Sp: Open Mon - Sat 08:30. Closed Mon - Fri 17:30, Sat 12:30.
Su: Open Mon - Sat 08:30. Closed Mon - Fri 17:30, Sat 12:30.
Au: Open Mon - Sat 08:30. Closed Mon - Fri 17:30, Sat 12:30.
Wn: Open Mon - Sat 08:30. Closed Mon - Fri 17:30, Sat 12:30. **Ref: YH07417**

INDESPENSION

Indespension Ltd, Riverside Grange, Cardiff Rd, Taffs Well, Cardiff, **Glamorgan (Vale of)**, CF4 7RA, **WALES**.
(T) 029 20813311 **(F)** 029 20813855
(E) cardiff@indespension.co.uk
(W) www.indespension.com.
Profile Transport/Horse Boxes.
Opening Times
Sp: Open Mon - Sat 08:30. Closed Mon - Fri 17:30, Sat 12:30.
Su: Open Mon - Sat 08:30. Closed Mon - Fri 17:30, Sat 12:30.
Au: Open Mon - Sat 08:30. Closed Mon - Fri 17:30, Sat 12:30.
Wn: Open Mon - Sat 08:30. Closed Mon - Fri 17:30, Sat 12:30. **Ref: YH07418**

INDESPENSION

Indespension Ltd, 4-6 Riverside, Milngavie, Glasgow, **Glasgow (City of)**, G62 6PQ, **SCOTLAND**.
(T) 0141 9563055 **(F)** 0141 9562385
(E) glasgow@indespension.co.uk
(W) www.indespension.com.
Profile Transport/Horse Boxes.
Opening Times
Sp: Open Mon - Sat 08:30. Closed Mon - Fri 17:30, Sat 12:30.
Su: Open Mon - Sat 08:30. Closed Mon - Fri 17:30, Sat 12:30.
Au: Open Mon - Sat 08:30. Closed Mon - Fri 17:30, Sat 12:30.
Wn: Open Mon - Sat 08:30. Closed Mon - Fri 17:30, Sat 12:30. **Ref: YH07419**

INDESPENSION

Indespension Ltd, 24 Bridge Rd, Park Gate, Southampton, **Hampshire**, SO31 7GE, **ENGLAND**.
(T) 01489 571133 **(F)** 01489 571144
(E) southhampton@indespension.co.uk
(W) www.indespension.com.
Profile Transport/Horse Boxes.
Opening Times
Sp: Open Mon - Sat 08:30. Closed Mon - Fri 17:30, Sat 12:30.
Su: Open Mon - Sat 08:30. Closed Mon - Fri 17:30, Sat 12:30.
Au: Open Mon - Sat 08:30. Closed Mon - Fri 17:30, Sat 12:30.
Wn: Open Mon - Sat 08:30. Closed Mon - Fri 17:30, Sat 12:30. **Ref: YH07420**

INDESPENSION

Indespension Ltd, Stanhill Works, Tennyson Ave, Oswaldtwistle, Blackburn, **Lancashire**, BB5 4QZ, **ENGLAND**.
(T) 01254 390855 **(F)** 01254 388292
(W) www.indespension.com.
Contact/s
Manager: Mr M Deighton
Profile Transport/Horse Boxes. **Ref: YH07421**

INDESPENSION

Indespension Ltd, Warren Rd, Scunthorpe, **Lincolnshire (North)**, DN15 6XH, **ENGLAND**.
(T) 01724 850164 **(F)** 01724 850174
(W) www.indespension.com.
Profile Transport/Horse Boxes. Yr. Est: 1968
Ref: YH07422

INDESPENSION

Indespension Ltd, 12-14 Hertford Rd, London, **London (Greater)**, N1 5SH, **ENGLAND**.
(T) 020 72499905 **(F)** 020 72416745
(E) london@indespension.co.uk
(W) www.indespension.com.
Contact/s
General Manager: Mr P Drayton
Profile Transport/Horse Boxes. Yr. Est: 1965
Opening Times
Sp: Open Mon - Sat 08:30. Closed Mon - Fri 17:30, Sat 12:00.
Su: Open Mon - Sat 08:30. Closed Mon - Fri 17:30, Sat 12:00.
Au: Open Mon - Sat 08:30. Closed Mon - Fri 17:30, Sat 12:00.
Wn: Open Mon - Sat 08:30. Closed Mon - Fri 17:30, Sat 12:00. **Ref: YH07423**

INDESPENSION

Indespension Ltd, Hillfold Mill, Belmont Rd, Bolton, **Manchester (Greater)**, BL1 7AQ, **ENGLAND**.
(T) 01204 458500 **(F)** 01204 458583.
Contact/s
Chairman: Mr T Graham
Profile Transport/Horse Boxes. **Ref: YH07424**

INDESPENSION

Indespension Ltd, 238 Waterloo St, Bolton, **Manchester (Greater)**, BL1 8HU, **ENGLAND**.
(T) 01204 397999 **(F)** 01204 373666
(E) bolton@indespension.co.uk
(W) www.indespension.com.
Profile Transport/Horse Boxes.
Opening Times
Sp: Open Mon - Sat 08:30. Closed Mon - Fri 17:30, Sat 12:30.
Su: Open Mon - Sat 08:30. Closed Mon - Fri 17:30, Sat 12:30.
Au: Open Mon - Sat 08:30. Closed Mon - Fri 17:30, Sat 12:30.
Wn: Open Mon - Sat 08:30. Closed Mon - Fri 17:30, Sat 12:30. **Ref: YH07425**

INDESPENSION

Indespension Ltd, Paragon Business Pk, Chorley New Rd, Harwich, Bolton, **Manchester (Greater)**, BL6 6HG, **ENGLAND**.
(T) 01204 478500 **(F)** 01204 668717
(E) sales@indespension.co.uk
(W) www.indespension.com.
Profile Transport/Horse Boxes. Yr. Est: 1968
Opening Times
Sp: Open Mon - Sat 08:30. Closed Mon - Fri 17:30, Sat 12:30.
Su: Open Mon - Sat 08:30. Closed Mon - Fri 17:30, Sat 12:30.
Au: Open Mon - Sat 08:30. Closed Mon - Fri 17:30, Sat 12:30.
Wn: Open Mon - Sat 08:30. Closed Mon - Fri 17:30, Sat 12:30. **Ref: YH07426**

INDESPENSION

Indespension Ltd, 38A Nimmings Rd, Halesowen, **Midlands (West)**, B62 9JE, **ENGLAND**.
(T) 0121 5615467 **(F)** 0121 5612180
(E) westmidlands@indespension.co.uk
(W) www.indespension.com.
Profile Transport/Horse Boxes.
Opening Times
Sp: Open Mon - Sat 08:30. Closed Mon - Fri 17:30, Sat 12:30.
Su: Open Mon - Sat 08:30. Closed Mon - Fri 17:30, Sat 12:30.
Au: Open Mon - Sat 08:30. Closed Mon - Fri 17:30, Sat 12:30.
Wn: Open Mon - Sat 08:30. Closed Mon - Fri 17:30, Sat 12:30. **Ref: YH07427**

INDESPENSION

Indespension Ltd, 21 Morgan Way, Bowthorpe Employment Area, Norwich, **Norfolk**, NR5 9JJ, **ENGLAND**.
(T) 01603 741666 **(F)** 01603 741561
(E) norwich@indespension.co.uk
(W) www.indespension.com.
Profile Transport/Horse Boxes.
Opening Times
Sp: Open Mon - Sat 08:30. Closed Mon - Fri 17:30, Sat 12:30.
Su: Open Mon - Sat 08:30. Closed Mon - Fri 17:30, Sat 12:30.
Au: Open Mon - Sat 08:30. Closed Mon - Fri 17:30, Sat 12:30.
Wn: Open Mon - Sat 08:30. Closed Mon - Fri 17:30, Sat 12:30. **Ref: YH07428**

INDESPENSION

Indespension Ltd, St Peters Way, Northampton, **Northamptonshire**, NN1 1SZ, **ENGLAND**.
(T) 01604 636700/259221 **(F)** 01604 259223
(E) northhampton@indespension.co.uk
(W) www.indespension.com.
Profile Transport/Horse Boxes.
Opening Times
Sp: Open Mon - Sat 08:30. Closed Mon - Fri 17:30, Sat 12:30.
Su: Open Mon - Sat 08:30. Closed Mon - Fri 17:30, Sat 12:30.
Au: Open Mon - Sat 08:30. Closed Mon - Fri 17:30, Sat 12:30.
Wn: Open Mon - Sat 08:30. Closed Mon - Fri 17:30, Sat 12:30. **Ref: YH07429**

INDESPENSION

Indespension Ltd, 76 Vale Rd, Colwick, Nottingham, **Nottinghamshire**, NG4 2EB, **ENGLAND**.
(T) 0115 9873997 **(F)** 0115 9400844
(E) nottingham@indespension.co.uk
(W) www.indespension.com.
Profile Transport/Horse Boxes.
Opening Times
Sp: Open Mon - Sat 08:30. Closed Mon - Fri 17:30, Sat 12:30.
Su: Open Mon - Sat 08:30. Closed Mon - Fri 17:30, Sat 12:30.
Au: Open Mon - Sat 08:30. Closed Mon - Fri 17:30, Sat 12:30.
Wn: Open Mon - Sat 08:30. Closed Mon - Fri 17:30, Sat 12:30. **Ref: YH07430**

INDESPENSION

Indespension Ltd, Unit 7-9 King St, Fenton, Stoke-on-Trent, **Staffordshire**, ST4 3ER, **ENGLAND**.
(T) 01782 336645 **(F)** 01782 336646
(E) stoke@indespension.co.uk
(W) www.indespension.com.
Profile Transport/Horse Boxes.
Opening Times
Sp: Open Mon -Sat 08:30. Closed Mon - Fri 17:30, Sat 12:30.
Su: Open Mon -Sat 08:30. Closed Mon - Fri 17:30, Sat 12:30.
Au: Open Mon -Sat 08:30. Closed Mon - Fri 17:30, Sat 12:30.
Wn: Open Mon -Sat 08:30. Closed Mon - Fri 17:30, Sat 12:30. **Ref: YH07431**

INDESPENSION

Indespension Ltd, 89 Dales Rd, Ipswich, **Suffolk**, IP1 4JR, **ENGLAND**.
(T) 01473 749922 **(F)** 01473 749920
(E) ipswich@indespension.co.uk
(W) www.indespension.com.
Profile Transport/Horse Boxes.
Opening Times
Sp: Open Mon - Sat 08:30. Closed Mon - Fri 17:30, Sat 12:30.
Su: Open Mon - Sat 08:30. Closed Mon - Fri 17:30, Sat 12:30.
Au: Open Mon - Sat 08:30. Closed Mon - Fri 17:30,

Sat 12:30.
Wn: Open Mon - Sat 08:30. Closed Mon - Fri 17:30, Sat 12:30. **Ref: YH07432**

INDESPENSION

Indespension Ltd, 19 Woodhatch Rd, Redhill, **Surrey**, RH1 5HQ, **ENGLAND**.
(T) 01737 768185 **(F)** 01737 768610
(E) redhill@indespension.co.uk
(W) www.indespension.com.
Profile Transport/Horse Boxes.
Opening Times
Sp: Open Mon - Sat 08:30. Closed Mon - Fri 17:30, Sat 12:30.
Su: Open Mon - Sat 08:30. Closed Mon - Fri 17:30, Sat 12:30.
Au: Open Mon - Sat 08:30. Closed Mon - Fri 17:30, Sat 12:30.
Wn: Open Mon - Sat 08:30. Closed Mon - Fri 17:30, Sat 12:30. **Ref: YH07433**

INDESPENSION

Indespension Ltd, 166 Brinkburn St, Off Walker Rd, Newcastle-upon-Tyne, **Tyne and Wear**, NE6 2AR, **ENGLAND**.
(T) 0191 2761162 **(F)** 0191 2765846
(E) newcastle@indespension.co.uk
(W) www.indespension.com.
Profile Transport/Horse Boxes.
Opening Times
Sp: Open Mon - Sat 08:30. Closed Mon - Fri 17:30, Sat 12:30.
Su: Open Mon - Sat 08:30. Closed Mon - Fri 17:30, Sat 12:30.
Au: Open Mon - Sat 08:30. Closed Mon - Fri 17:30, Sat 12:30.
Wn: Open Mon - Sat 08:30. Closed Mon - Fri 17:30, Sat 12:30. **Ref: YH07434**

INDESPENSION

Indespension Ltd, Hunslet Business Pk, National Rd, Hunslet, Leeds, **Yorkshire (West)**, LS10 1TD, **ENGLAND**.
(T) 0113 2707444 **(F)** 0113 2708282
(E) leeds@indespension.co.uk
(W) www.indespension.com.
Profile Transport/Horse Boxes.
Opening Times
Sp: Open Mon -Sat 08:30. Closed Mon - Fri 17:30, Sat 12:30.
Su: Open Mon -Sat 08:30. Closed Mon - Fri 17:30, Sat 12:30.
Au: Open Mon -Sat 08:30. Closed Mon - Fri 17:30, Sat 12:30.
Wn: Open Mon -Sat 08:30. Closed Mon - Fri 17:30, Sat 12:30. **Ref: YH07435**

INDI POLO & RACING

Indi Polo & Racing, 6 Denne Pk Hse, Horsham, **Sussex (West)**, RH13 7AY, **ENGLAND**.
(T) 01403 270195 **(F)** 01403 270195.
Profile Polo club. **Ref: YH07436**

INDIAN FARM STABLES

Indian Farm Stables, Indian Farm, Effingham Common Rd, Effingham, Leatherhead, **Surrey**, KT24 5JG, **ENGLAND**.
(T) 01372 459956.
Contact/s
Partner: Ms S Rance **Ref: YH07437**

INDOMBA DONKEY STUD

Indomba Donkey Stud, 131 Fleetwood Rd, South Thornton, Blackpool, **Lancashire**, **ENGLAND**.
(T) 01253 856792.
Profile Breeder. **Ref: YH07438**

INDUNA STABLES

Induna Stables, Fordham Rd, Newmarket, **Suffolk**, CB8 7AQ, **ENGLAND**.
(T) 01638 661999 **(F)** 01638 667279.
Contact/s
Trainer: Mr C Wall
Profile Trainer. **Ref: YH07439**

INDUSTRI ART

Industri Art, Unit 8, John Hillhouse Ind Est, 211 Cambuslang Rd, Cambuslang, Glasgow, **Lanarkshire (South)**, G72 7TS, **SCOTLAND**.
(T) 0141 6477960.
Profile Blacksmith. **Ref: YH07440**

INFANTRY SADDLE CLUB

Warminster Saddle Club, Oxendene, Warminster, **Wiltshire**, BA12 0DZ, **ENGLAND**.
(T) 01985 213925 **(F)** 01985 213925
Affiliated Bodies BHS.
Contact/s
Equitation Officer: Mr R Sullivan-Tailyour
(Q) BHSAI **(T)** 01985 840515
(E) rbst@bhs_inter.net
Profile Equestrian Centre, Riding School, Stable/Livery. No.Staff: 11 Yr. Est: 1970
C.Size: 75 Acres
Opening Times
Sp: Open 08:30. Closed 21:00.
Su: Open 08:30. Closed 21:00.
Au: Open 08:30. Closed 21:00.
Wn: Open 08:30. Closed 21:00. **Ref: YH07441**

INGATESTONE SADDLERY

Ingatestone Saddlery Centre, Main Rd, Margaretting, Ingatestone, **Essex**, CM4 0EF, **ENGLAND**.
(T) 01277 353723 **(F)** 01277 355199.
Contact/s
Owner: Mrs L Mortlock
Profile Riding Wear Retailer, Saddlery Retailer.
No.Staff: 12 Yr. Est: 1975
Opening Times
Sp: Open Mon - Sat 09:00, Sun 10:00. Closed Mon - Sat 17:30, Sun 16:00.
Su: Open Mon - Sat 09:00, Sun 10:00. Closed Mon - Sat 17:30, Sun 16:00.
Au: Open Mon - Sat 09:00, Sun 10:00. Closed Mon - Sat 17:30, Sun 16:00.
Wn: Open Mon - Sat 09:00, Sun 10:00. Closed Mon - Sat 17:30, Sun 16:00. **Ref: YH07442**

INGATESTONE/BLACKMORE

Ingatestone & Blackmore Riding Club, 9 Kennel Lane, Billericay, **Essex**, CM12 9RU, **ENGLAND**.
(T) 01277 657238.
Contact/s
Chairman: Mrs E Warr
Profile Club/Association, Riding Club. **Ref: YH07443**

INGENUS

Ingenus, 1 Nene Way, Sutton, Peterborough, **Cambridgeshire**, PE5 7XB, **ENGLAND**.
(T) 01780 784124.
Profile Supplies. **Ref: YH07444**

INGESTRE STABLES

Ingestre Stables, Ingestre, Stafford, **Staffordshire**, ST18 0RE, **ENGLAND**.
(T) 01889 271165.
Profile Riding School, Stable/Livery, Trainer.
Ref: YH07445

INGFIELD HACKNEY STUD

Ingfield Hackney Stud, Law Farm, Law Lane, Southowram, Halifax, **Yorkshire (West)**, HX3 9UG, **ENGLAND**.
(T) 01422 362789 **(F)** 01422 362871.
Profile Breeder. **Ref: YH07446**

INGLEDEN PARK RIDING CTRE

Ingleden Park Riding Centre, Tenterden, **Kent**, TN30 6SL, **ENGLAND**.
(T) 01580 64140.
Profile Stable/Livery. **Ref: YH07447**

INGLEGARTH FELL PONIES

Inglegarth Fell Ponies, Moorgarth Farm, Ingleton, Carnforth, **Lancashire**, LA6 3DP, **ENGLAND**.
(T) 01524 241428 **(F)** 01524 241428.
Profile Breeder. **Ref: YH07448**

INGLENOOK LIVERY STABLES

Inglenook Livery Stables, 59 Moss Lane, Hesketh Bank, Preston, **Lancashire**, PR4 6AA, **ENGLAND**.
(T) 01772 815269. **Ref: YH07449**

INGLESHAM POLO CTRE

Inglesham Polo Centre, Lynt Farm, Inglesham, Swindon, **Wiltshire**, SN6 7QZ, **ENGLAND**.
(T) 01367 253939 **(F)** 01367 253939.
Profile Trainer. **Ref: YH07450**

INGLESIDE RACING STABLES

Ingleside Racing Stables, 4 Downland Cl, Woodingdean, Brighton, **Sussex (East)**, BN2 6DN, **ENGLAND**.
(T) 01273 620405.
Contact/s
Owner: Mr G Moore
Profile Trainer. **Ref: YH07451**

INGLIS, J A

J A Inglis, Ottery Cl, Higher Metcombe, Ottery St Mary, **Devon**, EX11 1SQ, **ENGLAND**.
(T) 01404 815053.
Profile Farrier. **Ref: YH07452**

INGRAM, C & D

C & D Ingram, 11 Chestnut Ave, Walkden, Manchester, **Manchester (Greater)**, M28 7EE, **ENGLAND**.
(T) 0161 9501224.
Profile Breeder. **Ref: YH07453**

INGRAM, PAUL

Paul Ingram BHSI, 5 Lower Chaddesley Corbett, Kidderminster, **Worcestershire**, DY10 4QN, **ENGLAND**.
(T) 01562 777773.
Profile Breeder, Trainer. **Ref: YH07454**

INGRAM, ROGER

Roger Ingram, Burgh Heath Rd, Epsom, **Surrey**, KT17 4LX, **ENGLAND**.
(T) 01372 748505.
Contact/s
Owner: Mr R Ingram
Profile Trainer. **Ref: YH07455**

INHURST FARM STABLES

Inhurst Farm Stables, Baughurst, Tadley, Basingstoke, **Hampshire**, RG26 5JS, **ENGLAND**.
(T) 0118 9814494 **(F)** 0118 9820454
(M) 07831 360970.
Profile Trainer. **Ref: YH07456**

INJURED JOCKEY FUND

Injured Jockey Fund (The), 1 Lynxcourt, Victoria Way, Newmarket, **Suffolk**, CB8 7SH, **ENGLAND**.
(T) 01638 662246 **(F)** 01638 668988.
Contact/s
Chief Executive: Mr J Richardson
Profile Club/Association. **Ref: YH07457**

INJURED RIDERS FUND

Mark Davies Injured Riders Fund, Unit 1 The Street, Ewhurst, Cranleigh, **Surrey**, GU6 7QD, **ENGLAND**.
(T) 01483 274800.
Contact/s
Manager: Mrs M Russell
Profile Riding Wear Retailer, Saddlery Retailer.
Ref: YH07458

INMAN, JENNY

Jenny Inman, Lofthus, Oxenholme Lane, Natland, Kendal, **Cumbria**, LA9 7QH, **ENGLAND**.
(T) 01539 724949 **(F)** 01539 724949.
Profile Supplies. **Ref: YH07459**

INNES, J

J Innes, The Old Smiddy, Wanton Walls Farm, 103 Newcraighall Rd, Musselburgh, **Lothian (Mid)**, EH21 8QU, **SCOTLAND**.
(T) 0131 6653900.
Profile Blacksmith. **Ref: YH07460**

INNS, FRANK

Frank Inns, Gramps Hill Stud, Letcombe Bassett, Wantage, **Oxfordshire**, OX12 9LX, **ENGLAND**.
(T) 01235 763536 **(F)** 01235 763536.
Contact/s
Owner: Mrs L Inns **Ref: YH07461**

INSTITUTE OF GROUNDMANSHIP

Institute of Groundmanship (The), 19-23 Church St, The Agora, Wolverton, Milton Keynes, **Buckinghamshire**, MK12 5LG, **ENGLAND**.
(T) 01908 312511/311856.
Profile Club/Association. **Ref: YH07462**

INSTONE AIR SERVICES

Instone Air Services Ltd, Charity Farm, Pulborough Rd, Cootham, Pulborough, **Sussex (West)**, RH20 4HP, **ENGLAND**.
(T) 01903 740101 **(F)** 01903 740102.
Contact/s
Manager: Mr M Rule
Profile Transport/Horse Boxes. **Ref: YH07463**

INSURANCE OMBUDSMAN

Insurance Ombudsman (The), City Gate One, 135 Park St, London, **London (Greater)**, SE1 9EA, **ENGLAND**.
(T) 020 79287600 **(F)** 020 74018700.
Profile Club/Association. **Ref: YH07464**

INT BLOODSTOCK FINANCE

International Bloodstock Finance Ltd, Kildare Paddocks, Kill, Naas, **County Kildare**, **IRELAND**.
(T) 045 886600 **(F)** 045 877119
(E) sales@goffs.com
(W) www.goffs.com.
Contact/s
Key Contact: Mr P McGrath
Profile Supplies. Equine Insurance. Yr. Est: 1976
Ref: YH07465

INT COUNTRY CLOTHING RETAILER
International Country Clothing Retailer, The School Hse, 16 Church St, Alwalton, Peterborough, **Cambridgeshire**, PE7 3UU, **ENGLAND**.
(T) 01733 391700.
Profile Supplies. **Ref: YH07466**

INT EQUESTRIAN
Int Equestrian Exchange Program Stablemate Staff Mgt (The), The Old Rectory, Belton In Rutland, Oakham, **Rutland**, LE15 9LE, **ENGLAND**.
(T) 01572 717383 **(F)** 01572 717343
(E) ep@stablemate.demon.co.uk.
Profile Club/Association. **Ref: YH07467**

INT EQUINE LOGISTICS
International Equine Logistics, Tyddyn Fadog, Llanfairpwllgwyn, **Isle of Anglesey**, LL66, **WALES**.
(T) 01248 355029 **(F)** 01248 354997.
Profile Club/Association. **Ref: YH07468**

INT MINIATURE HORSE/PONY SOC
International Miniature Horse & Pony Society Ltd, Cilmaren, Caio, Llanwrda, **Carmarthenshire**, SA19 8PN, **WALES**.
(T) 07000 781216 **(F)** 07000 781216.
Profile Club/Association. **Ref: YH07469**

INT PARALYMPIC EQUESTRIAN SP
International Paralympic Equestrian Sports, C/O Blackdown Farm, Leamington Spa, **Warwickshire**, CV32 6QS, **ENGLAND**.
(T) 01926 422522 **(F)** 01926 450996
(W) www.paralympic.org.
Contact/s
Chairman: Mrs J Solt
Profile Club/Association.
A non profit making organisation and worldwide charity. Develops & governs equestrian sport to paralympic standard. **Ref: YH07470**

INT RACECOURSE MNGMT
International Racecourse Management Limited, The Grandstand, Leger Way, Doncaster, **Yorkshire (South)**, DN2 6BB, **ENGLAND**.
(T) 01302 320066 **(F)** 01302 730431.
Contact/s
Chief Executive: John F Sanderson
Profile Supplies. **Ref: YH07471**

INT RACEHORSE TRANSPORT
International Racehorse Transport (UK) Ltd, Harefield Pk, Westley Waterless, Newmarket, **Suffolk**, CB8 0GG, **ENGLAND**.
(T) 01638 508080 **(F)** 01638 507070.
Profile Transport/Horse Boxes. **Ref: YH07472**

INT SPORTS MARKETING
International Sports Marketing, Bales Court, Barrington Rd, Dorking, **Surrey**, RH4 3EJ, **ENGLAND**.
(T) 01306 743322 **(F)** 01306 743007.
Profile Club/Association. **Ref: YH07473**

INT STUDENTS/YOUTH EXCHANGES
International Students & Youth Exchanges, (in Assoc With Markfield Equestrian Ctre), Markfield, Leicester, **Leicestershire**, LE2 1ZE, **ENGLAND**.
(T) 0116 2703351 **(F)** 0116 2703313.
Profile Equestrian Centre. **Ref: YH07474**

INTER PARALYMPIC EQUESTRIAN
International Paralympic Equestrian Committee, Blackdown Farm, Leamington Spa, **Warwickshire**, CW32 6QS, **ENGLAND**.
(T) 01926 422522 **(F)** 01926 450996
(E) jonqhil@solt.demon.co.uk.
Profile Club/Association. **Ref: YH07475**

INTERIOR ART METAL WORKS
Interior Art Metal Works, Cambourne Forge, Trevu Rd, Camborne, **Cornwall**, TR14 8SR, **ENGLAND**.
(T) 01209 719911.
Profile Blacksmith. **Ref: YH07476**

INTERNATIONAL PERFORMANCE
International Performance, Horse Agency, Church Farm, Bishops Wood, Brewde, **Staffordshire**, ST19 9AD, **ENGLAND**.
(T) 01785 840229.
Profile Breeder. **Ref: YH07477**

INTERNATIONAL RACING BUREAU
International Racing Bureau Ltd, Alton Hse, 117 High St, Newmarket, **Suffolk**, CB8 9AG, **ENGLAND**.
(T) 01638 668881 **(F)** 01638 665032.
Profile Supplies. **Ref: YH07478**

INTERNATIONAL RACING MEDIA
International Racing Media Limited, Grandstand, Leger Way, Doncaster, **Yorkshire (South)**, DN2 6BB, **ENGLAND**.
(T) 01302 320066 **(F)** 01302 730431.
Contact/s
Chief Executive: John F Sanderson
Profile Club/Association. **Ref: YH07479**

INTERNATIONAL WARWICK SCHOOL
International Warwick School Of Riding, Guys Cliffe, Coventry Rd, Guys Cliffe, Warwick, **Warwickshire**, CV34 5YD, **ENGLAND**.
(T) 01926 494313 **(F)** 01926 492497.
Contact/s
Owner: Miss J Martinez
Profile Club/Association, Riding School, Stable/Livery, Track/Course. **Ref: YH07480**

INTERNET HORSE
Internet Horse (The), P O Box 523, Stoke-on-Trent, **Staffordshire**, ST10 2QL, **ENGLAND**.
(T) 01538 266113
(M) 07971 383431.
Profile Supplies. **Ref: YH07481**

INTERTRADE ENGINEERING
Intertrade Engineering Ltd, Holden Fold, Holden Fold Lane, Royton, Oldham, **Lancashire**, OL2 5BY, **ENGLAND**.
(T) 0161 6274757 **(F)** 0161 6272016.
Profile Transport/Horse Boxes. **Ref: YH07482**

INTERVET UK
Intervet UK Ltd, Science Pk, Milton Rd, Cambridge, **Cambridgeshire**, CB4 0FP, **ENGLAND**.
(T) 01223 420221 **(F)** 01223 420601.
Profile Medical Support. **Ref: YH07483**

INVICTA POLOCROSSE CLUB
Invicta Polocrosse Club, Brushwood Farm, Cuckfield Rd, Ansty, **Sussex (West)**, RH17 5AL, **ENGLAND**.
(T) 01444 413624.
Contact/s
Chairman: Ms A Feltham
Profile Club/Association. Polocrosse Club.
Ref: YH07484

INVICTA RIDING CLUB
Invicta Riding Club, Sillibourne Farmhouse, Brook, Ashford, **Kent**, TN25 5NY, **ENGLAND**.
(T) 01233 623588.
Profile Club/Association, Riding Club. **Ref: YH07485**

INVICTA RIDING CLUB DRESSAGE
Invicta Riding Club Dressage, Spelders Hill Farm, Brook, Ashford, **Kent**, TN25 5PB, **ENGLAND**.
(T) 01233 812433.
Profile Club/Association. **Ref: YH07486**

IRELAND, D
D Ireland, Unit 6 Weasenham Lane, Wisbech, **Cambridgeshire**, PE13 2RY, **ENGLAND**.
(T) 01945 463161 **(F)** 01945 589170.
Contact/s
Partner: Mrs D Ireland
Profile Transport/Horse Boxes. **Ref: YH07487**

IRELAND, KEITH
Keith Ireland, 19 Hayes Green Rd, Bedworth, Nuneaton, **Warwickshire**, CV12 0BU, **ENGLAND**.
(T) 024 76732468
(M) 07970 910034.
Profile Trainer. **Ref: YH07488**

IRENES
Irenes (Wombourne) Ltd, 12 Windmill Bank, Wombourne, **Midlands (West)**, WV5 9JD, **ENGLAND**.
(T) 01902 892563.
Profile Saddlery Retailer. **Ref: YH07489**

IRISH DRAUGHT HORSE SOCIETY
Irish Draught Horse Society (N Ireland) (The), 12 Grove Rd, Ballymacormick, Dromore, **County Down**, BT25 1QX, **NORTHERN IRELAND**.
(T) 028 97692256.
Contact/s
Chairman: Mr R Butler
Profile Club/Association. **Ref: YH07490**

IRISH DRAUGHT HORSE SOCIETY
Irish Draught Horse Society, Mayo, **County Mayo**, **IRELAND**.
(T) 094 80247 **(F)** 094 80247
(E) s3amus@gofree.indigo.ie.
Contact/s
Chairperson: Mr L Morley
Profile Club/Association. Yr. Est: 1975
Ref: YH07491

IRISH DRAUGHT HORSE SOCIETY
Irish Draught Horse Society of Great Britain, P O Box 1486, Coventry, **Warwickshire**, CV8 3ZP, **ENGLAND**.
(T) 024 76306677 **(F)** 024 76306678.
Contact/s
Society Secretary: Mrs A Hill
Profile Club/Association. **Ref: YH07492**

IRISH EQUESTRIAN PRODUCTS
Chartridge Trading Ltd, Unit U3A, Enterprise Ctre, Melitta Rd, Kildare, **County Kildare**, **IRELAND**.
(T) 045 522999 **(F)** 045 522999
(E) irisheq@eircom.net.
Contact/s
Owner: Mr J Brophy
Profile Supplies. Wholesale/Distribution.
Supply horseshoes and tools for farriers. **Ref: YH07493**

IRISH EQUIMARKET
Irish Equimarket, Ballinbranig Ballyduff, Tralee, **County Kerry**, **IRELAND**.
(T) 066 7131713
(W) www.irishequimarket.com.
Profile Supplies. **Ref: YH07494**

IRISH HORSE SOCIETY
Irish Horse Society, C/O Andrew Roberts, Rushbrooke, Cobh, **County Cork**, **IRELAND**.
(T) 021 4811960
(E) irishhorsesociety@eircom.net.
Profile Club/Association. **Ref: YH07495**

IRISH JOCKEYS RACEWEAR
Irish Jockeys Racewear Ltd, Kilgoran Lodge, Kildare, **County Kildare**, **IRELAND**.
(T) 045 520333. **Ref: YH07496**

IRISH NATIONAL STUD
Irish National Stud Co Ltd, Tully, Kildare, **County Kildare**, **IRELAND**.
(T) 045 521251 **(F)** 045 522129
(E) stud@irish-national-stud.ie
(W) www.irish-national-stud.ie.
Profile Supplies. **Ref: YH07497**

IRISH PIEBALD & SKEWBALD ASS
Irish Piebald & Skewbald Association, 6 O'connell Pl, Fermoy, **County Cork**, **IRELAND**.
(T) 025 31110 **(F)** 025 31110
(E) flyfish@eircom.net.
Contact/s
Key Contact: Mr J O'Sullivan
Profile Club/Association. **Ref: YH07498**

IRISH PONY SOCIETY
Irish Pony Society (Northern Region Committee), Thornleigh Hse, Downpatrick Rd, Ballynahinch, **County Down**, BT24 8SH, **NORTHERN IRELAND**.
(T) 028 97562411.
Profile Club/Association. **Ref: YH07499**

IRISH SPORT HORSE DEVELOPMENT
Irish Sport Horse Development, Castle Irvine Desmesne, Irvinestown, Enniskillen, **County Fermanagh**, BT94 1GG, **NORTHERN IRELAND**.
(T) 028 68621050 **(F)** 028 68628440.
Contact/s
Manager: Mrs S Meadows
Profile Club/Association. **Ref: YH07500**

IRISH THOROUGHBRED
Irish Thoroughbred Breeders Association, 12 Lough Rd, Crossgar, **County Down**, BT30 9LB, **NORTHERN IRELAND**.
(T) 028 44830188 **(F)** 028 44661089.
Profile Club/Association. **Ref: YH07501**

IRISH THOROUGHBRED MARKETING
Irish Thoroughbred Marketing, Leopardstown Racecourse, Dublin, **County Dublin**, **IRELAND**.
(T) 01 2897302 **(F)** 01 2897297
(E) info@itm.ie
(W) www.itm.ie.
Profile Supplies. **Ref: YH07502**

IRON AWE
Iron Awe, Guydenes Farm, Oxford Rd, Garsington, Oxford, **Oxfordshire**, OX44 9AZ, **ENGLAND**.
(T) 01865 368278 **(F)** 01865 368020.
Contact/s
Owner: Mr C Atkinson
Profile Blacksmith. **Ref: YH07503**

IRON FIGHTERS

Iron Fighters, Unit 113A Skillion Ctre, 49 Greenwich High Rd, London, **London (Greater)**, SE10 8JL, **ENGLAND**.
(T) 020 86915255.
Contact/s
Owner: Mr S Capper
Profile Blacksmith. Ref: YH07504

IRONART FABRICATIONS

Ironart Fabrications Ltd, Roadhead Forge, Lochwinnoch, **Renfrewshire**, PA12 4JG, **SCOTLAND**.
(T) 01505 842016.
Profile Blacksmith. Ref: YH07505

IRONHORSE STABLING

Ironhorse Stabling, Unit 1/The Grange Ctre, Hall Rd, Barsham, Beccles, **Suffolk**, NR34 8JN, **ENGLAND**.
(T) 01502 712050 (F) 01502 712080. Ref: YH07506

IRONSTONE FARM

Ironstone Farm, Ironstone Lane, Holwell, **Leicestershire**, LE14 3HX, **ENGLAND**.
(T) 01664 823791.
Profile Riding School. Ref: YH07507

IRRIGATION SYSTEMS & SERVICES

Irrigation Systems & Services, Unit 18, Downton Ind Est, Batten Rd, Downton, Salisbury, **Wiltshire**, SP5 3HU, **ENGLAND**.
(T) 01725 513880 (F) 01725 513003.
Profile Supplies. Ref: YH07508

IRVINE ENGINEERING

Irvine Engineering, 7 Livingstone Pl, St Andrews, **Fife**, KY16 8JH, **SCOTLAND**.
(T) 01334 473787.
Profile Blacksmith. Ref: YH07509

IRVING, HEATHER

Miss Heather Irving, Lodge Barn, Culworth, Banbury, **Oxfordshire**, OX17 2HL, **ENGLAND**.
(T) 01295 768198.
Profile Trainer. Ref: YH07510

ISAAC, C & D

C & D Isaac, 19 Nuttingtons, Leckhampstead, Newbury, **Berkshire**, RG20 8QL, **ENGLAND**.
(T) 01488 638600.
Profile Breeder, Stable/Livery. Ref: YH07511

ISAACS STORES

Isaacs Stores, 119-123 The Homend, Ledbury, **Herefordshire**, HR8 1BP, **ENGLAND**.
(T) 01531 632695.
Contact/s
Partner: Mr A Isaacs
Profile Supplies.
Isaacs specialise in footwear Ref: YH07512

ISABELLE VETS

Isabelle Vets, Route Isabelle, St Peter Port, **Guernsey**, GY1 1QR, **ENGLAND**.
(T) 01481 723863 (F) 01481 700012.
Profile Medical Support. Ref: YH07513

ISCA LIVERY STABLES

Isca Livery Stables, Greigydd/Candwr Rd, Ponthir, Newport, **Newport**, NP18 1HU, **WALES**.
(T) 01633 420293.
Contact/s
Accountant: Owain Cooper Davies Ref: YH07514

ISCOYD RIDING STABLES

Iscoyd Riding Stables, Iscoyd, Whitchurch, **Shropshire**, SY13 3AT, **ENGLAND**.
(T) 01948 780134.
Contact/s
Owner: Ms R Scott (T) 01948 780253
Ref: YH07515

ISHERWOOD, GABRIELLE

Gabrielle Isherwood, Rosemary Cottage, Dark Lane, Henbury, Macclesfield, **Cheshire**, SK11 9PE, **ENGLAND**.
(T) 01625 430280 (F) 01625 425790
Affiliated Bodies NAAT.
Contact/s
Physiotherapist: Gabrielle Isherwood
(Q) BSc(Hons)
Profile Medical Support.
Physiotherapist for horses & dogs. Ref: YH07516

ISHERWOOD, M

M Isherwood, Radcliffe Farm, Chapel Lane, New Longton, Preston, **Lancashire**, PR4 4AB, **ENGLAND**.
(T) 01772 612786. Ref: YH07517

ISLAND CASUALS

Island Casuals, Main St, Ratoath, **County Meath**, **IRELAND**.
(T) 01 8257062.
Contact/s
Owner: Danny Gaughan Ref: YH07518

ISLAND CASUALS

Island Casuals, Drogheda St, Balbriggan Dublin Market St, Trim, **County Meath**, **IRELAND**.
(T) 046 37655.
Contact/s
Owner: Danny Gaughan Ref: YH07519

ISLAND EQUESTRIAN CTRE

Island Equestrian Centre, 49 Ballyrashane Rd, Coleraine, **County Londonderry**, BT52 2NL, **NORTHERN IRELAND**.
(T) 028 70342599.
Contact/s
Owner: Mrs J McCollum (Q) BHSAI, BHSSM
Profile Riding School, Stable/Livery.
Opening Times
Sp: Open Wed - Sat 11:00. Closed Wed - Sat 17:00.
Su: Open Wed - Sat 11:00. Closed Wed - Sat 17:00.
Au: Open Wed - Sat 11:00. Closed Wed - Sat 17:00.
Wn: Open Wed - Sat 11:00. Closed Wed - Sat 17:00.
Telephone for an appointment. Closed Sunday - Tuesday Ref: YH07520

ISLAND FARM RIDING STABLES

Island Farm Riding Stables, Devonshire Drive, Saundersfoot, **Pembrokeshire**, SA69 9EE, **WALES**.
(T) 01834 813263.
Profile Equestrian Centre. Ref: YH07521

ISLAND PET & EQUESTRIAN SUP

Island Pet & Equestrian Supplies, 17 Elm Gr, Hayling Island, **Hampshire**, PO11 9EA, **ENGLAND**.
(T) 023 92466311. Ref: YH07522

ISLAY FARMERS

Islay Farmers Ltd, Bowmore, Isle Of Islay, **Argyll and Bute**, PA43 7LJ, **SCOTLAND**.
(T) 01496 810491.
Contact/s
Branch Manager: Mr H Jackson
Profile Saddlery Retailer. Ref: YH07523

ISLE OF MAN

Isle of Man Home of Rest for Old Horses, Bulrherry Farm, Richmond Hill, Douglas, **Isle of Man**, IM4 1JH, **ENGLAND**.
(T) 01624 674594 (F) 01624 613278.
Profile Medical Support. Ref: YH07524

ISLE OF WIGHT RIDING CLUB

Isle of Wight Riding Club, Greenacres, Chapel Lane, Merstone, **Isle of Wight**, PO30 3DD, **ENGLAND**.
(T) 01983 521192.
Contact/s
Chairman: Mrs S Lightbown
Profile Club/Association, Riding Club. Ref: YH07525

ISSEA

International Saddle Seat Equitation Association - GB, 58 Rosebury Rd, London, **London (Greater)**, SW6 2NG, **ENGLAND**.
(T) 020 77317885
(M) 07956 192722
(E) lyn.jarvis@tvu.ac.uk.
Profile Club/Association. Ref: YH07526

ISSEA - GB

International Saddle Seat Equitation Association of Great Britain, 36 Philpot Sq, Peterborough Rd, London, **London (Greater)**, SW6 3HT, **ENGLAND**.
(T) 020 77317885 (F) 020 82312442.
Contact/s
Coach: Ms C Lockhart (T) 01227 860625
(E) c_lockhart@talk21.com
Profile Club/Association, Trainer.
The ISSEA - GB is the governing body of the sport of saddle seat equitation in the UK. They select the British team to represent the nation at the World Cup. Hold training clinics. Yr. Est: 1997 Ref: YH07527

ISVA

Incorporated Society of Values & Auctioneers, 3 Cadogan Gate, London, **London (Greater)**, SW1X 0AS, **ENGLAND**.
(T) 020 72352282 (F) 020 72354390
(E) hq@isva.co.uk
(W) www.martex.co.uk.
Contact/s
Chief Executive: Clive Evans
Profile Club/Association. Ref: YH07528

ITCHELL HOME FARM

Itchell Home Farm, Crondall, Farnham, **Surrey**, GU10 5PT, **ENGLAND**.
(T) 01252 850769.
Profile Horse/Rider Accom. Ref: YH07529

ITHON SADDLERY

Ithon Saddlery, Middleton St, Llandrindod Wells, **Powys**, LD1 5ET, **WALES**.
(T) 01597 824356 (F) 01597 824356.
Contact/s
Partner: Mr J Mason Ref: YH07530

ITTON COURT STUD

Itton Court Stud & Equestrian Centre, At Eairy Ploydwell, Foxdale Rd, The Braaid, **Isle of Man**, IM4 2HQ, **ENGLAND**.
(T) 01624 852780.
Profile Breeder, Stable/Livery. Ref: YH07531

IVANHOE EQUESTRIAN

Ivanhoe Equestrian, Smisby Rd, Ashby-De-La-Zouch, **Leicestershire**, LE65 2UG, **ENGLAND**.
(T) 01530 413629 (F) 01530 413629
(E) lebutt@ivanhoe-equestrian.freeserve.co.uk
(W) www.ivanhoe-equestrian.freeserve.co.uk
Affiliated Bodies ABRS, BHS.
Contact/s
Owner: Mr J Lebutt
Profile Riding School. No.Staff: 4
Yr. Est: 1990 C.Size: 35 Acres
Opening Times
By appointment only Ref: YH07532

IVANHOE FEEDS

Ivanhoe Feeds Ltd, Countrystore, Ashby Rd, Boundary, Swadlincote, **Derbyshire**, DE11 7BA, **ENGLAND**.
(T) 01283 212300 (F) 01283 221836.
Profile Feed Merchant, Saddlery Retailer.
Ref: YH07533

IVEAGH BRANCH

Iveagh Branch of The Pony Club, 58 Moyallon Rd, Portadown, **County Armagh**, BT63 5JX, **NORTHERN IRELAND**.
(T) 028 38832040.
Contact/s
Dist Comm: Mrs V Campbell
Profile Club/Association. Ref: YH07534

IVERS HOUSE

Ivers House, Ivers Hains Lane, Marnhull, Sturminster Newton, **Dorset**, DT10 1JU, **ENGLAND**.
(T) 01258 820164.
Profile Riding School. Ref: YH07535

IVESLEY EQUESTRIAN CTRE

Ivesley Equestrian Centre, Ivesley, Waterhouses, Durham, **County Durham**, DH7 9HB, **ENGLAND**.
(T) 0191 3734324 (F) 0191 373 4757
(E) ivesley@msn.com
(W) www.ridingholidays-ivesley.co.uk
Affiliated Bodies BHS.
Contact/s
Partner: Mr R Booth
Profile Equestrian Centre, Horse/Rider Accom, Riding School, Stable/Livery.
Offer week stays, mid week and weekend breaks, B&B at reasonable prices. The cost of the riding holidays include food and accomodation, horse hire and instruction. DIY livery is available if you take your own horse. Access to fun hacking and bridleways through woodland and moorlands. The area is ideal for mountain biking and walking, on the edge of the North Pennine Moors. Holidays are for both riders and non riders. Also have BSJA showjumps, schooling fences and expert tuition available in classical dressage and cross country. Quality horses to suit all levels, novice riders welcome. C.Size: 220 Acres Ref: YH07536

IVORY, ERIC JOHN

Eric John Ivory, Lyefield Hse, Ewhurst, **Surrey**, GU6 7SQ, **ENGLAND**.
(T) 01483 275050.
Profile Farrier. Ref: YH07537

IVORY, K T

K T Ivory, Harper Lodge/Harper Lodge Farm, Harper Lane, Radlett, **Hertfordshire**, WD7 7HU, **ENGLAND**.
(T) 01923 855337 (F) 01923 855337.
Contact/s
Owner: Mr K Ivory
Profile Stable/Livery, Supplies, Trainer. Ref: YH07538

IVY FARM EQUESTRIAN CTRE

Ivy Farm Equestrian Centre, C/O 31 Brackenwood, Necton, Swaffham, **Norfolk**, PE37 8EU, **ENGLAND**.
(T) 01760 722125.
Profile Riding School. **Ref: YH07539**

IVY LANE RIDING SCHOOL

Ivy Lane Riding School, Ivy Lane, Coningsby, Lincoln, **Lincolnshire**, LN4 4RY, **ENGLAND**.
(T) 01526 342461 **(F)** 01526 345951.
Contact/s
Owner: Mrs J Dodson
Profile Riding School, Stable/Livery. **Ref: YH07540**

IZAAK WALTON SMITHY

Izaak Walton Smithy, Whitehouse Farm, Norton Bridge, Stone, **Staffordshire**, ST15 0NS, **ENGLAND**.
(T) 01785 761450 **(F)** 01785 761450.
Contact/s
Owner: Mr P Forester
Profile Blacksmith. **Ref: YH07541**

J & A MAIL ORDER

J & A Mail Order, 2A White St, Walsall, **Midlands (West)**, WS1 3PH, **ENGLAND**.
(T) 01922 636429 **(F)** 01922 636429.
Contact/s
Owner: Mr A Fox
Profile Supplies. **Ref: YH07542**

J & A POUNTNEY

J & A Pountney (Walsall) Ltd, 9 Birmingham Rd, Walsall, **Midlands (West)**, WS1 2LY, **ENGLAND**.
(T) 01922 623077 **(F)** 01922 724216. **Ref: YH07543**

J & D WOODS

J & D Woods Traditional Wooden Rocking Horses, 180 Chorley Rd, Westhoughton, Bolton, **Manchester (Greater)**, BL5 3PN, **ENGLAND**.
(T) 01942 816246.
Profile Supplies. **Ref: YH07544**

J & E PETFOODS

J & E Petfoods, New Building, Rope Walk, Coach Rd, Whitehaven, **Cumbria**, CA28 7TE, **ENGLAND**.
(T) 01946 65093.
Profile Supplies. **Ref: YH07545**

J & J FABRICATION

J & J Fabrication, Eagle Mill Complex 18 Victoria St, Dundee, **Angus**, DD4 6EB, **SCOTLAND**.
(T) 01382 229118.
Profile Blacksmith. **Ref: YH07546**

J & J L WATKINSON

J & J L Watkinson, The Veterinary Surgery, Hollin Rigg, Leyburn, **Yorkshire (North)**, DL8 5HD, **ENGLAND**.
(T) 01969 623107 **(F)** 01969 622026.
Profile Medical Support. **Ref: YH07547**

J & J STEWART

J & J Stewart (Blacksmith) Ltd, Elliot Ind Est, Arbroath, **Angus**, DD11 2NJ, **SCOTLAND**.
(T) 01241 873905.
Profile Blacksmith. **Ref: YH07548**

J & K ANIMAL FEEDS

J & K Animal Feeds, The Old Warehouse, 13 Weymouth St, Warminster, **Wiltshire**, BA12 9NR, **ENGLAND**.
(T) 01985 219602.
Contact/s
Owner: Mr J Burton
Profile Supplies. **Ref: YH07549**

J & M ASSOCIATES

J & M Associates, Valley Farm, Stoke, Andover, **Hampshire**, SP11 0NR, **ENGLAND**.
(T) 01264 738318 **(F)** 01264 738777.
Profile Club/Association. **Ref: YH07550**

J & M L HENFREY & SON

J & M L Henfrey & Son, Gull Farm, Deeping High Bank, Deeping St. Nicholas, Spalding, **Lincolnshire**, PE11 3DY, **ENGLAND**.
(T) 01775 630548 **(F)** 01775 630092.
Contact/s
Owner: Mrs J Henfrey **(Q)** NVQ 3
Profile Breeder.
Mr & Mrs Henfrey are council members of the Percheron Horse Society. **Yr. Est:** 1960
Opening Times
By appointment only **Ref: YH07551**

J & W WROUGHT IRONWORK

J & W Ornamental Wrought Ironwork, 17A Greenhill Rd, Paisley, **Renfrewshire**, PA3 1RN, **SCOTLAND**.
(T) 0141 8897973.
Contact/s
Owner: Mr J Barclay
Profile Blacksmith. **Ref: YH07552**

J A B OLD

J A B Old, Upper Herdswick Farm, Hackpen, Burderop, Swindon, **Wiltshire**, SN4 0QH, **ENGLAND**.
(T) 01793 845900.
Profile Trainer. **Ref: YH07553**

J A E TRAILERS

J A E Trailers, Railway Hse, Station Rd, Ilminster, **Somerset**, TA19 9BL, **ENGLAND**.
(T) 01460 259144 **(F)** 01460 259115.
Contact/s
Owner: Mrs J Walters
Profile Transport/Horse Boxes. **Ref: YH07554**

J A HOPKINSON & SON

J A Hopkinson & Son, Oak Tree Farm, Pilsley, Chesterfield, **Derbyshire**, S45 8AN, **ENGLAND**.
(T) 01246 850856 **(F)** 01246 850856.
Contact/s
Partner: Mr R Hopkinson
Profile Transport/Horse Boxes. **Ref: YH07555**

J A IBBOTSON & SONS

J A Ibbotson & Sons, 72 Walton St, Tadworth, **Surrey**, KT20 7RU, **ENGLAND**.
(T) 01737 813120.
Contact/s
Partner: Mr P Ibbotson
Profile Farrier. **Ref: YH07556**

J A, WILSON

A J Wilson, Glenfall Stables, Ham Rd, Charlton Kings, Cheltenham, **Gloucestershire**, GL52 6NH, **ENGLAND**.
(T) 01242 244713.
Contact/s
Owner: Mr A Wilson
Profile Trainer. **Yr. Est:** 1984
Opening Times
Telephone for an appointment, there is an answerphone **Ref: YH07557**

J ALLEN

J Allen (Cambridge & Newmarket), Brunswick, 18 Woodditton Rd, Newmarket, **Suffolk**, CB8 9BQ, **ENGLAND**.
(T) 01638 662507.
Profile Trainer.
J Allen trains polo ponies. **Ref: YH07558**

J B ARENAS

J B Arenas, Rockrose Farm, Clayton Hill, Pyecombe, Brighton, **Sussex (West)**, BN45 7FF, **ENGLAND**.
(T) 01273 844007 **(F)** 01273 844007
(M) 07860 206269.
Profile Supplies. **Ref: YH07559**

J B CORRIE

J B Corrie & Co Ltd (Blairgowrie), Signal Box Rd, Welton Rd Ind Est, Blairgowrie, **Perth and Kinross**, PH10 6NB, **SCOTLAND**.
(T) 01250 873989 **(F)** 01250 875884. **Ref: YH07560**

J B CORRIE & CO

J B Corrie & Co Ltd (Petersfield), Frenchmans Rd, Petersfield, **Hampshire**, GU32 3AP, **ENGLAND**.
(T) 01730 262552 **(F)** 01730 264915. **Ref: YH07561**

J B EQUESTRIAN SVS

J B Equestrian Services, 48 Langton Pk, Newbridge, **County Kildare**, **IRELAND**.
(T) 045 433449 **(F)** 045 438050
(E) 2obriens@gofree.indigo.ie. **Ref: YH07562**

J B FENWICK & SON

J B Fenwick & Son, Lark Hall, Six Mile Bottom, Newmarket, **Suffolk**, CB8 0UT, **ENGLAND**.
(T) 01638 570206 **(F)** 01638 570333.
Contact/s
Owner: Mr R Fenwick
Profile Hay and Straw Merchants. **Ref: YH07563**

J B HORSE SUPPLIES

J B Horse Supplies, 155 Weymouth, Pipe Gate, Market Drayton, **Shropshire**, TF9 4JQ, **ENGLAND**.
(T) 01630 647674 **(F)** 01630 647674.
Profile Supplies. **Ref: YH07564**

J B PET SUPPLIES

J B Pet Supplies, Campbell St, Belper, **Derbyshire**, DE56 1AP, **ENGLAND**.
(T) 01773 828944.
Profile Supplies. **Ref: YH07565**

J B THORNE

J B Thorne Ltd, Church Hill Rd, Thurmaston, **Leicestershire**, LE4 8DH, **ENGLAND**.
(T) 0116 2605757 **(F)** 0116 2640408.
Profile Medical Support. **Ref: YH07566**

J BIBBY AGRICULTURE

J Bibby Agriculture Ltd, Cillefwr Ind Est, Johnstown, Carmarthen, **Carmarthenshire**, SA31 3RB, **WALES**.
(T) 01267 232041.
Profile Supplies. **Ref: YH07567**

J C & N C WARD

J C & N C Ward Ltd, Buckholdhill Farm, Pangbourne, **Berkshire**, RG8 8QE, **ENGLAND**.
(T) 0118 9744388 **(F)** 0118 9744995.
Contact/s
Owner: Mr R Ward
Profile Stable/Livery. **No.Staff:** 1
Yr. Est: 1960 **C.Size:** 65 Acres
Opening Times
Sp: Open Mon - Sun 08:00. Closed Mon - Sun 18:00.
Su: Open Mon - Sun 08:00. Closed Mon - Sun 18:00.
Au: Open Mon - Sun 08:00. Closed Mon - Sun 18:00.
Wn: Open Mon - Sun 08:00. Closed Mon - Sun 18:00. **Ref: YH07568**

J C EDWARDS & ASSOCIATES

J C Edwards & Associates, Moorhedge Surgery, Davids Cross, Ivybridge, **Devon**, PL21 0DP, **ENGLAND**.
(T) 01752 892700.
Profile Medical Support. **Ref: YH07569**

J C HELLENIA

J C Hellenia Ltd, 24 Camphill Cl, Dallamires Lane, Ripon, **Yorkshire (North)**, HG4 1TT, **ENGLAND**.
(T) 01765 603816 **(F)** 01765 607746.
Profile Medical Support. **Ref: YH07570**

J C HUSKISSON & SON

J C Huskisson & Son, 211 Pleck Rd, Walsall, **Midlands (West)**, WS2 9EX, **ENGLAND**.
(T) 01922 611887 **(F)** 01922 611887.
Contact/s
Owner: Mr J Huskisson **Ref: YH07571**

J C M

J C M Metalwork & Trailer Services, 14 Culvain Pl, Falkirk, **Falkirk**, FK1 2QF, **SCOTLAND**.
(T) 07977 659849.
Contact/s
Owner: Mr J Murphy
Profile Transport/Horse Boxes. Trailer Manufacturer.
Make trailers to customer specification **No.Staff:** 1
Yr. Est: 1986
Opening Times
Sp: Open Mon - Sun 09:00. Closed Mon - Sun 18:00.
Su: Open Mon - Sun 09:00. Closed Mon - Sun 18:00.
Au: Open Mon - Sun 09:00. Closed Mon - Sun 18:00.
Wn: Open Mon - Sun 09:00. Closed Mon - Sun 18:00. **Ref: YH07572**

J C PRICE

J C Price, Agricultural & Electrical Sales & Services, Claypits, Eastington, Stonehouse, **Gloucestershire**, GL10 3AH, **ENGLAND**.
(T) 01453 826793 **(F)** 01453 828608. **Ref: YH07573**

J C RIDDIOUGH

J C Riddiough (Trailer Sales & Hire) Ltd, Cottingley Mills, Bradford Old Rd, Bingley, **Yorkshire (West)**, BD16 1PF, **ENGLAND**.
(T) 01274 562202 **(F)** 01274 560619.
Contact/s
Partner: Mr M Elston
Profile Transport/Horse Boxes. **Ref: YH07574**

J C RIDDIOUGH TRAILER SALES

J C Riddiough Trailer Sales & Hire Ltd, Unit 4A B & C/Hillam Court, Hillam Rd, Bradford, **Yorkshire (West)**, BD2 1QN, **ENGLAND**.
(T) 01274 726600 **(F)** 01274 727700.
Contact/s
Manager: Mr T Morgan
Profile Transport/Horse Boxes. **Ref: YH07575**

J C SCHAAY TIMBER BUILDINGS

J C Schaay Timber Buildings, The Timber Yard, Common Rd, Burston, Diss, **Norfolk**, IP22 3TN, **ENGLAND**.

(T) 01692 582956 (F) 01692 582956
(E) kwa9498@aol.com. **Ref: YH07576**

J CROOK & SONS

J Crook & Sons (Engineering) Ltd, London Rd, Ashford, **Surrey**, TW15 3AW, **ENGLAND**.
(T) 01784 253188.
Profile Transport/Horse Boxes. **Ref: YH07577**

J D GOODACRE & SON

J D Goodacre & Son, Saxelby Lodge, Saxelby Pastures, Melton Mowbray, **Leicestershire**, LE14 3NA, **ENGLAND**.
(T) 01664 823718 (F) 01664 823719. **Ref: YH07578**

J D MOULDING

J D Moulding, New Bungalow/Daintree Rd, Ramsey St Marys, Ramsey, Huntingdon, **Cambridgeshire**, PE26 2TF, **ENGLAND**.
(T) 01733 844408.
Contact/s
Owner: Mr J Moulding **Ref: YH07579**

J ELLIS & SONS

J Ellis & Sons (Bordon) Ltd, Headley Mill, Bordon, **Hampshire**, GU35 8RJ, **ENGLAND**.
(T) 01420 472031. **Ref: YH07580**

J EVERITT & SONS

J Everitt & Sons, 10 Primrose Hill, Doddington, March, **Cambridgeshire**, PE15 0SU, **ENGLAND**.
(T) 01354 740524 (F) 01354 741721.
Contact/s
Partner: Mrs J Everitt **Ref: YH07581**

J F SPENCE & SON

J F Spence & Son, Station Rd, Uppingham, Oakham, **Leicestershire**, LE15 9TX, **ENGLAND**.
(T) 01572 822758.
Contact/s
Owner: Mr D Spence
Profile Blacksmith. **Ref: YH07582**

J G & J M JONES

J G & J M Jones, Dunton Hall, Curdworth, Sutton Coldfield, **Midlands (West)**, B76 0BA, **ENGLAND**.
(T) 01675 470322.
Profile Medical Support. **Ref: YH07583**

J G INT EQUINE CONSULTANTS

J G International Equine Consultants, 4 St Giles Rd, Gaydon, **Warwickshire**, CV35 0EN, **ENGLAND**.
(T) 01926 642571.
Profile Club/Association. **Ref: YH07584**

J GRIEVE & ASSOCIATES

J Grieve & Associates, Radnor Courts Veterinary Practice, 89A Cherry Hinton Rd, Cambridge, **Cambridgeshire**, CB1 7BS, **ENGLAND**.
(T) 01223 249331 (F) 01223 210773.
Profile Medical Support. **Ref: YH07585**

J H COMMERCIALS

J H Commercials, West Pk, Arlington, Barnstaple, **Devon**, EX31 4SN, **ENGLAND**.
(T) 01271 850522.
Contact/s
Owner: Mr J House
Profile Transport/Horse Boxes. **Ref: YH07586**

J H KENDALL LIVERY STABLES

J H Kendall Livery Stables, Manor Farm, West Dean, Chichester, **Sussex (West)**, PO18 0QY, **ENGLAND**.
(T) 01243 811227.
Contact/s
Owner: Mr J Kendall **Ref: YH07587**

J HARKNESS & SONS

J Harkness & Sons, Newfieldburn Smithy, Ruthwell, Dumfries, **Dumfries and Galloway**, DG1 4NS, **SCOTLAND**.
(T) 01387 870285 (F) 01387 870285.
Profile Blacksmith. **Ref: YH07588**

J HOGARTH

J Hogarth Ltd, Kelso Mills, Kelso, **Scottish Borders**, TD5 7HR, **SCOTLAND**.
(T) 01573 24224.
Profile Supplies. **Ref: YH07589**

J HOUGHTON & SONS

J Houghton & Sons, 11-13 Bolton Rd, Darwen, **Lancashire**, BB3 1DF, **ENGLAND**.
(T) 01254 702282. **Ref: YH07590**

J J EQUESTRIAN TACK & TURNOUT

J J Equestrian Tack & Turnout, High St, Carlton, Goole, **Yorkshire (East)**, DN14 9LY, **ENGLAND**.
(T) 01405 862951.
Profile Saddlery Retailer. **Ref: YH07591**

J J S PHOTOGRAPHY

J J S Photography, Loanhead, Abernethy, Perth, **Perth and Kinross**, PH2 9LG, **SCOTLAND**.
(T) 01738 850610. **Ref: YH07592**

J JORDAN & SONS

J Jordan & Sons, College Rd, Windermere, **Cumbria**, LA23 1BX, **ENGLAND**.
(T) 01539 443157.
Profile Supplies. **Ref: YH07593**

J L H ENGINEERING

J L H Engineering, Providence St, Stourbridge, **Midlands (West)**, DY9 8HN, **ENGLAND**.
(T) 01384 423122 (F) 01384 893889.
Profile Blacksmith. **Ref: YH07594**

J M BELL & SON

J M Bell & Son, Archard Garth, Bagby, Thirsk, **Yorkshire (North)**, YO7 2PH, **ENGLAND**.
(T) 01845 597205.
Contact/s
Owner: Mr J Bell
Profile Transport/Horse Boxes. **Ref: YH07595**

J M EDMUNDS KENNS FARM

J M Edmunds Kenns Farm, Kenns Farm, Carterton, **Oxfordshire**, OX18 1PE, **ENGLAND**.
(T) 01993 842141.
Contact/s
Owner: Mrs J Edmonds
Profile Stable/Livery. **Ref: YH07596**

J M JONES

J M Jones & Co, Frongoy, Pennant, Llanon, **Ceredigion**, SY23 5PD, **WALES**.
(T) 01974 272246 (F) 01974 272246.
Contact/s
Owner: Mr G Jones
Profile Breeder. **Ref: YH07597**

J M P SADDLERY

J M P Saddlery, 127 Heol Llanishen Fach, Cardiff, **Glamorgan (Vale of)**, CF14 6RE, **WALES**.
(T) 029 20624813 (F) 029 20624813.
Contact/s
Owner: Miss J Pearce
Profile Saddlery Retailer. **Ref: YH07598**

J MANNING & SON

J Manning & Son, Upper Hse Farm, Didley, Hereford, **Herefordshire**, HR2 9DA, **ENGLAND**.
(T) 01981 570212 (F) 01981 570441.
Contact/s
Owner: Mr M Manning
Profile Breeder. **Ref: YH07599**

J MCKIRDLE & SONS

J McKirdle & Sons, Smithy, Shearington, Dumfries, **Dumfries and Galloway**, DG1 4RT, **SCOTLAND**.
(T) 01387 770248.
Profile Blacksmith. **Ref: YH07600**

J MITCHELL

J Mitchell & Co, Mercat Green, Kinrossie, Perth, **Perth and Kinross**, PH2 6HT, **SCOTLAND**.
(T) 01821 650211 (F) 01821 650766.
Contact/s
Partner: Mr J Mitchell
Profile Blacksmith. **Ref: YH07601**

J N B SADDLERS

J N B Saddlers, Unit X Twydall Enterprise Ctre, Lower Twydall Lane, Gillingham, **Kent**, ME8 6XX, **ENGLAND**.
(T) 01634 238736.
Contact/s
Manager: Mr J Stockbridge **Ref: YH07602**

J N PEARCE RACING TRAINERS

J N Pearce Racing Trainers, Wroughton Hse Stables, 37 Old Station Rd, Newmarket, **Suffolk**, CB8 8DT, **ENGLAND**.
(T) 01638 664669
(M) 07887 803100
(W) www.newmarketracehorsetrainers.co.uk
Affiliated Bodies Newmarket Trainers Fed.
Contact/s
Key Contact: Mrs L Pearce
Profile Trainer. **Ref: YH07603**

J ODDY & SONS

J Oddy & Sons, Woodyard, Ingatestone Rd, Highwood, Chelmsford, **Essex**, CM1 3QZ, **ENGLAND**.
(T) 01277 352388 (F) 01277 354665. **Ref: YH07604**

J P WALKER & SON

J P Walker & Son, 19 Mill Rd, Great Gransden, Sandy, **Bedfordshire**, SG19 3AG, **ENGLAND**.
(T) 01767 677374 (F) 01767 677726.
Contact/s
Partner: Mr P Walker **Ref: YH07605**

J PRESTON & SON

J Preston & Son, Pitt St, Widnes, **Cheshire**, WA8 0TG, **ENGLAND**.
(T) 0151 4243718 (F) 0151 4952360.
Contact/s
Partner: Mr J Preston
Profile Farrier. **Ref: YH07606**

J R COUNTRY & PET SUPPLIES

J R Country & Pet Supplies, 7 Horsefair, Wetherby, **Yorkshire (West)**, LS22 4JG, **ENGLAND**.
(T) 01937 585919.
Profile Supplies. **Ref: YH07607**

J R FEEDS

J R Feeds, Chapel Hill Farm, Heanor Rd, Ilkeston, **Derbyshire**, DE7 8LP, **ENGLAND**.
(T) 07973 821891 (F) 0115 9321605.
Profile Supplies. **Ref: YH07608**

J R HORSEWEAR

J R Horsewear, 36 Milestone Drive, West Hagley, Stourbridge, **Midlands (West)**, DY9 0LW, **ENGLAND**.
(T) 01562 885781.
Profile Saddlery Retailer. **Ref: YH07609**

J R SERPELL & SON

J R Serpell & Son (Yealmpton), Blackpool Farm, Yealmpton, Plymouth, **Devon**, PL8 2LF, **ENGLAND**.
(T) 01752 348376. **Ref: YH07610**

J R THOMAS & SON

J R Thomas & Son, 76 Bethesda Rd, Tumble, Llanelli, **Carmarthenshire**, SA14 6LG, **WALES**.
(T) 01269 841612.
Profile Blacksmith. **Ref: YH07611**

J R W SEDGWICK

J R W Sedgwick, The Grand Theatre, Cockermouth, **Cumbria**, CA13 0PZ, **ENGLAND**.
(T) 01900 823187.
Profile Medical Support. **Ref: YH07612**

J ROBERTS SADDLERY

J Roberts Saddlery, Ivy Cottage, Ivy Lane, Romsley, Halesowen, **Midlands (West)**, B62 0NJ, **ENGLAND**.
(T) 01562 710343.
Profile Saddlery Retailer. **Ref: YH07613**

J S EQUINE

J S Equine, P O Box 3004, Gloucester, **Gloucestershire**, GL4 0SX, **ENGLAND**.
(T) 01452 500997 (F) 01452 310170.
Profile Supplies. **Ref: YH07614**

J S FRASER PROPERTIES

J S Fraser Properties Ltd, Oakfield Ind Est, Stanton Harcourt Rd, Eynsham, Witney, **Oxfordshire**, OX8 1JN, **ENGLAND**.
(T) 01865 882471 (F) 01865 883323.
Profile Transport/Horse Boxes. **Ref: YH07615**

J S HUBBUCK

J S Hubbuck Ltd, Unit 1 Hexham Auction Mart, Tyne Green, Hexham, **Northumberland**, NE46 3EG, **ENGLAND**.
(T) 01434 602417.
Contact/s
Owner: Mr J Hubbuck
Profile Feed Merchant. **Ref: YH07616**

J S MAIN & SONS

J S Main & Sons, 87/89 High St, Haddington, **Lothian (East)**, EH41 3ET, **SCOTLAND**.
(T) 01620 822148 (F) 01620 824662
Affiliated Bodies BETA.
Contact/s
Owner: John Main
Profile Riding Wear Retailer, Saddlery Retailer, Supplies. No.Staff: 5 Yr. Est: 1926
Opening Times
Sp: Open 09:30. Closed 17:30.
Su: Open 09:30. Closed 17:30.
Au: Open 09:30. Closed 17:30.
Wn: Open 09:30. Closed 17:30. **Ref: YH07617**

J S R SADDLERY

J S R Saddlery, 91A Hospital St, Nantwich, **Cheshire**, CW5 5RU, **ENGLAND**.
(T) 01270 627457. **Ref: YH07618**

J S W & SON COACHBUILDERS

J S W & Son Coachbuilders Est 1961, 49-51 High St, Northallerton, **Yorkshire (North)**, DL7 8EG, **ENGLAND**.
(T) 01609 772449 (F) 01609 777995.
Profile Transport/Horse Boxes. Ref: YH07619

J SHILLITTO

J Shillitto (Forage) Ltd, Chaworth Farm, Salmon Lane, Kirkby-In-Ashfield, Nottingham, **Nottinghamshire**, NG17 9HB, **ENGLAND**.
(T) 01623 752481 (F) 01623 720481. Ref: YH07620

J T EQUI-SPORT

J T Equi-Sport, 6 Castlemead Rd, Rodborough, Stroud, **Gloucestershire**, GL5 3SF, **ENGLAND**.
(T) 01453 753529.
Profile Supplies. Ref: YH07621

J TODD

J Todd (AFCL) Ltd, The Forge, Great Warley St, Great Warley, Brentwood, **Essex**, CM13 3JF, **ENGLAND**.
(T) 01277 222645 (F) 01277 224522.
Profile Farrier. Ref: YH07622

J VERHOEVEN

J Verhoeven (UK) Ltd, Brick Kiln Lane, Parhouse Ind Est, West Chesterton, Newcastle-under-Lyme, **Staffordshire**, ST5 7AS, **ENGLAND**.
(T) 01782 566054 (F) 01782 564754. Ref: YH07623

J W ATTLEE

J & W Attlee Ltd, Parsonage Mills, Station Rd, Dorking, **Surrey**, RH4 1EL, **ENGLAND**.
(T) 01306 883533 (F) 01306 876595.
Contact/s
Sales: Mrs C Vass
Profile Feed Merchant, Supplies.
Feed is manufactured on site. Also supply agricultural feeds. Ref: YH07624

J W GREEN

J W Green & Co (Cork) Ltd, Po Box 58 Monahan Rd, Cork, **County Cork**, **IRELAND**.
(T) 021 4312755 (F) 021 4963601.
Profile Supplies. Ref: YH07625

J W PIGOTT & SONS

J W Pigott & Sons, Thrales End, Thrales End Lane, Harpenden, **Hertfordshire**, AL5 3NS, **ENGLAND**.
(T) 01582 712844. Ref: YH07626

J W WILKINSON

J W Wilkinson & Co Ltd, New Inn Works, Highgate, Kendal, **Cumbria**, LA9 4AG, **ENGLAND**.
(T) 01539 721347 (F) 01539 729119. Ref: YH07627

J W WILKINSON

J W Wilkinson & Co Ltd, Dockray Hall Rd, Kendal, **Cumbria**, LA9 4QY, **ENGLAND**.
(T) 01539 720013 (F) 01539 729119
(E) sales@kingshead-saddlery.co.uk
(W) www.kingshead-saddlery.co.uk.
Profile Supplies.
Kingshead produce a range of rugs including turnout, stable, day and paddock. Ref: YH07628

J WALLINGTON & SONS

J Wallington & Sons, Boundary Farm, Piddington, Bicester, **Oxfordshire**, OX6 0QN, **ENGLAND**.
(T) 01296 770531.
Contact/s
Owner: Mr N Wallington
Profile Transport/Horse Boxes. Ref: YH07629

J WAREING & SON

J Wareing & Son, Wrea Green, Preston, **Lancashire**, PR4 7NB, **ENGLAND**.
(T) 01772 682159.
Profile Transport/Horse Boxes. Ref: YH07630

J WATTS & SONS

J Watts & Sons, Cowles, Manor Rd, Landkey, Barnstaple, **Devon**, EX32 0JJ, **ENGLAND**.
(T) 01271 830340.
Contact/s
Owner: Mr J Watts
Profile Transport/Horse Boxes. Ref: YH07631

J WATTS & SONS

J Watts & Sons, 44 South St, Braunton, **Devon**, EX33 2AA, **ENGLAND**.
(T) 01271 812014.
Profile Transport/Horse Boxes. Ref: YH07632

J, MILLER

Miller J, The Workshop, North Corston, Coupar Angus, Blairgowrie, **Perth and Kinross**, PH13 9JH, **SCOTLAND**.
(T) 01828 627557.
Profile Blacksmith. Ref: YH07633

J, MORGAN

Morgan J, Portlester Stud, Ballivor, **County Meath**, **IRELAND**.
(T) 040 546006.
Profile Supplies. Ref: YH07634

J.SAVILL INT HORSE TRANSPORT

Janet Savill International Horse Transport, 12 Oxford St, Exning, Newmarket, **Suffolk**, CB8 7EW, **ENGLAND**.
(T) 01638 578150 (F) 01638 577412.
Contact/s
Owner: Mrs J Savill
(E) janet.savill@ntlworld.com
Profile Transport/Horse Boxes.
Import and export documentation. Yr. Est: 1990
Opening Times
Sp: Open Mon - Sun 24 Hours.
Su: Open Mon - Sun 24 Hours.
Au: Open Mon - Sun 24 Hours.
Wn: Open Mon - Sun 24 Hours. Ref: YH07635

JABEZ CLIFF

Jabez Cliff & Co Ltd, Globe Works, Lower Forster St, Walsall, **Midlands (West)**, WS1 1XG, **ENGLAND**.
(T) 01922 621676 (F) 01922 722575. Ref: YH07636

JACK ELLIS BODY PROTECTION

Jack Ellis Body Protection, Marshall Hse, West St, Glenfield, Leicester, **Leicestershire**, LE3 8DT, **ENGLAND**.
(T) 0116 2320022 (F) 0116 2320032
(E) sales@jackellis.co.uk
(W) www.jackellis.co.uk.
Contact/s
Owner: Mr M Riley
(E) mr@jackellis.co.uk
Profile Riding Wear Retailer. Body Protection Manufacturer.
Designer and manufacturer equestrian body protectors for all ages, sizes, disciplines and levels.
Ref: YH07637

JACK LEES

Jack Lees Ltd, Sports Outfitter, 15-19 George St, Halifax, **Yorkshire (West)**, HX1 1HA, **ENGLAND**.
(T) 01422 354039.
Profile Riding Wear Retailer. Ref: YH07638

JACKETS STUD

Jackets Stud, Hurston Pl Farm, Pulborough, **Sussex (West)**, RH20 2EW, **ENGLAND**.
(T) 01403 730126.
Profile Breeder. Ref: YH07639

JACKMAN, DAVID

David Jackman RSS, Farthings, 23 Andor Ave, Kingsteignton, Newton Abbot, **Devon**, TQ12 3EJ, **ENGLAND**.
(T) 01626 368531.
Profile Farrier. Ref: YH07640

JACKSON FRANCIS & SONS

Jackson Francis & Sons, Market Sq, Haltwhistle, **Northumberland**, NE49 0BL, **ENGLAND**.
(T) 01434 320342.
Contact/s
Owner: Mr I Scott
Profile Blacksmith. Ref: YH07641

JACKSON, ADRIAN

Adrian Jackson, Low Wood, Benningholme Lane, Skirlaugh, Hull, **Yorkshire (East)**, HU11 5EA, **ENGLAND**.
(T) 01964 562534 (F) 01964 563389.
Contact/s
Owner: Mr A Jackson
Profile Transport/Horse Boxes. Ref: YH07642

JACKSON, BRIAN FRANK

Brian Frank Jackson, Forge Farm, Clettwr Side, Pontshaen, Llandysul, **Carmarthenshire**, SA44 4UP, **WALES**.
(T) 01545 590237.
Profile Farrier. Ref: YH07643

JACKSON, C F C

Mr C F C Jackson, Whitehouse Farm, Tanhouse Lane, Cradley, Malvern, **Worcestershire**, WR13 5JX, **ENGLAND**.
(T) 01886 880463.
Profile Trainer. Ref: YH07644

JACKSON, CHRIS

Chris Jackson, 40 East View, New Barnet, **Hertfordshire**, EN5 5NG, **ENGLAND**.
(T) 020 84406537.
Profile Trainer. Ref: YH07645

JACKSON, G

Mr G Jackson, Whiteacres, Shard Lane, Hambleton, Poulton-Le-Fylde, **Lancashire**, FY6 9BX, **ENGLAND**.
(T) 01253 700172.
Profile Breeder. Ref: YH07646

JACKSON, I L

I L Jackson RSS, 4 Water Lane Cottages, Water Lane, Ulcombe, Maidstone, **Kent**, ME17 1DL, **ENGLAND**.
(T) 01622 844499.
Contact/s
Owner: Mr I Jackson
Profile Farrier. Ref: YH07647

JACKSON, JOANNA

Joanna Jackson, The Royds, Clitheroe, **Lancashire**, BB7 4LB, **ENGLAND**.
(T) 01200 441271. Ref: YH07648

JACKSON, MATTHEW W

Matthew W Jackson DWCF, 3 Queens Rd, Alnwick, **Northumberland**, NE66 1RB, **ENGLAND**.
(T) 01665 602806.
Profile Farrier. Ref: YH07649

JACKSON, NEIL

Neil Jackson, Gordon Hse Cottage, Esperley Lane, Cockfield, Bishop Auckland, **County Durham**, DL14 5EJ, **ENGLAND**.
(T) 01388 718473.
Profile Farrier. Ref: YH07650

JACKSON, PAUL

Paul Jackson RSS, 22 Skipton Cl, Hazel Gr, Stockport, **Cheshire**, SK7 5NQ, **ENGLAND**.
(T) 07836 633350.
Profile Farrier. Ref: YH07651

JACKSON, R

R Jackson, North Blackhall Farm, Blackhall Colliery, Hartlepool, **Cleveland**, TS27 4AL, **ENGLAND**.
(T) 0191 5872058.
Profile Breeder. Ref: YH07652

JACKSON, ROGER

Mr Roger Jackson, Holme Farm, Gonalston, Nottingham, **Nottinghamshire**, NG14 7JA, **ENGLAND**.
(T) 0115 9663970.
Profile Supplies. Ref: YH07653

JACKSON, SIMON D

Simon D Jackson DWCF, The Villas, Claxton, **Yorkshire (North)**, YO60 7RZ, **ENGLAND**.
(T) 01904 468647.
Profile Farrier. Ref: YH07654

JACKSON, T & E

T & E Jackson, 4 Pye Lane, Broad Town, Swindon, **Wiltshire**, SN4 7RR, **ENGLAND**.
(T) 01793 731662.
Contact/s
Owner: Mr T Jackson Ref: YH07655

JACKSON, TONY

Tony Jackson, The Lowe, Loveridge Lane, Tatworth, Chard, **Somerset**, TA20 2SE, **ENGLAND**.
(T) 01460 220038 (F) 01460 221377.
Profile Supplies. Ref: YH07656

JACKSONS OF SILSDEN

Jacksons of Silsden (1998) Ltd, New Close Garage, Silsden, Keighley, **Yorkshire (West)**, BD20 0ES, **ENGLAND**.
(T) 01535 652376 (F) 01535 653300.
Profile Saddlery Retailer. Ref: YH07657

JACKTON SMIDDY

Jackton Smiddy, 332 Eaglesham Rd, East Kilbride, Glasgow, **Lanarkshire (South)**, G75 8RW, **SCOTLAND**.
(T) 0141 6327353 (F) 01355 302089.
Contact/s
Owner: Mr S Hamilton
Profile Blacksmith. Ref: YH07658

JACOBS, STUART M

Stuart M Jacobs RSS, 32 New Rd, Carhampton, Minehead, **Somerset**, TA24 6LT, **ENGLAND**..
Profile Farrier. Ref: YH07659

JACQUES, RODNEY
Rodney Jacques, Brookfield, Sharnford, **Leicestershire**, LE10 3PB, **ENGLAND**.
(T) 01455 273384.
Profile Supplies. **Ref: YH07660**

JACTAC SADDLERY
Jactac Saddlery, 55 High St, Saxilby, Lincoln, **Lincolnshire**, LN1 2HA, **ENGLAND**.
(T) 01522 703608.
Contact/s
Owner: Mrs J Gorman **Ref: YH07661**

JAKOBSON, TONY
Tony Jakobson, The Brambles, Mildenhall Rd, Worlington, Bury St Edmunds, **Suffolk**, IP28 8RY, **ENGLAND**.
(T) 01638 713121 **(F)** 01638 713121.
Profile Supplies. **Ref: YH07662**

JAMES BURNHILL & SON
James Burnhill & Son, Northgate Mills, Cleckheaton, **Yorkshire (West)**, BD19 3HX, **ENGLAND**.
(T) 01274 872423 **(F)** 01274 861499.
Profile Supplies. **Ref: YH07663**

JAMES COTTERELL & SONS
James Cotterell & Sons Ltd, Bridgeman St, Walsall, **Midlands (West)**, WS2 9LS, **ENGLAND**.
(T) 01922 627331 **(F)** 01922 629232
(E) dewsbury@compuserve.com
(W) www.kangaroobits.com.
Contact/s
Sales: Ms J Harley
Profile Supplies. Saddlery Manufacturers.
Ref: YH07664

JAMES E. JAMES
James E. James Ltd, c/o 4-14 Newton St, Liverpool, **Merseyside**, L3 5RL, **ENGLAND**.
(T) 0151 7088088.
Profile Supplies. **Ref: YH07665**

JAMES GEORGE & SONS
James George & Sons, 22 Cransley Hill, Broughton, Kettering, **Northamptonshire**, NN14 1NB, **ENGLAND**.
(T) 01536 790295.
Profile Blacksmith. **Ref: YH07666**

JAMES GIBB
James Gibb (Animal Feeds) Ltd, Threepwood Farm, Sorn Rd, Galston, **Ayrshire (East)**, KA4 8ND, **SCOTLAND**.
(T) 01563 820233 **(F)** 01563 821413.
Contact/s
Partner: Mr J Gibb
(E) james.gibb@farmline.com
Profile Medical Support.
Opening Times
Sp: Open Mon - Fri 08:00, Sat 09:00, Sun 10:00.
Closed Mon - Fri 17:30, Sat 17:00, Sun 16:00.
Su: Open Mon - Fri 08:00, Sat 09:00, Sun 10:00.
Closed Mon - Fri 17:30, Sat 17:00, Sun 16:00.
Au: Open Mon - Fri 08:00, Sat 09:00, Sun 10:00.
Closed Mon - Fri 17:30, Sat 17:00, Sun 16:00.
Wn: Open Mon - Fri 08:00, Sat 09:00, Sun 10:00.
Closed Mon - Fri 17:30, Sat 17:00, Sun 16:00.
Ref: YH07667

JAMES GIVEN RACING
James Given Racing Ltd, Staffords Yard, Northfield Lane, Willoughton, Gainsborough, **Lincolnshire**, DN21 5RT, **ENGLAND**.
(T) 01427 667618 **(F)** 01427 667734
Affiliated Bodies JC.
Contact/s
Owner: Mr J Given **(Q)** B.V.M, MRCVS
Profile Trainer. No.Staff: 12 Yr. Est: 1998
C.Size: 50 Acres **Ref: YH07668**

JAMES GLOVER & SONS
James Glover & Sons, 74 Drumaghlis Rd, Crossgar, **County Down**, BT30 9JS, **NORTHERN IRELAND**.
(T) 028 44830303.
Profile Supplies. **Ref: YH07669**

JAMES KEYSER
James Keyser Products, Lady Lamb Farm, Cirencester, **Gloucestershire**, GL7 5LH, **ENGLAND**.
(T) 01285 712206 **(F)** 01285 712206
(W) www.hay-ball.com.
Contact/s
For Bookings: Mr J Keyser
Profile Stable/Livery, Supplies. 'Hayball' Manufacturer.
Stable and feeding equipment available. No.Staff: 3
Yr. Est: 1972 C.Size: 210 Acres
Opening Times
Telephone for further information **Ref: YH07670**

JAMES M BARCLAY & SON
James M Barclay & Son, East Brockloch Farm, Maybole, **Ayrshire (South)**, KA19 8DG, **SCOTLAND**.
(T) 01655 883212.
Contact/s
Owner: Mr W Barclay
Profile Blood Stock Agency, Breeder.
Yr. Est: 1971
Opening Times
Telephone for an appointment **Ref: YH07671**

JAMES MACKINTOSH & SON
James Mackintosh & Son, 10 Horne Ter, Edinburgh, **Edinburgh (City of)**, EH11 1JL, **SCOTLAND**.
(T) 0131 2293149 **(F)** 0131 6207200.
Profile Blacksmith. **Ref: YH07672**

JAMES MEADE
James Meade Ltd, 48 Charlton Rd, Andover, **Hampshire**, SP10 3JL, **ENGLAND**.
(T) 01264 387700 **(F)** 01264 363200.
Profile Supplies. **Ref: YH07673**

JAMES NICHOL
James Nichol Racing, St Gatien, All Saints Rd, Newmarket, **Suffolk**, CB8 8HJ, **ENGLAND**.
(T) 01638 560420 **(F)** 01638 662412
(M) 07799 884681
(W) www.newmarketracehorsetrainers.co.uk
Affiliated Bodies Newmarket Trainers Fed.
Contact/s
Owner: Mr J Nichol
Profile Trainer. **Ref: YH07674**

JAMES THE SADDLER
James The Saddler, Redstone Hse, Redstone Rd, Narberth, **Pembrokeshire**, SA67 7ES, **WALES**.
(T) 01834 861898.
Contact/s
Owner: Mr R James **Ref: YH07675**

JAMES, A
A James, Chequers Farm, Scotchey Lane, Stour Provost, Gillingham, **Dorset**, SP8 5LT, **ENGLAND**.
(T) 01747 838705. **Ref: YH07676**

JAMES, A P
A P James, Elliot Hse Farm, Vine Lane, Sutton, Tenbury Wells, **Worcestershire**, WR15 8RL, **ENGLAND**.
(T) 01885 410240.
Profile Trainer. **Ref: YH07677**

JAMES, BRYAN GERALD
Bryan Gerald James DWCF, Sandhampton Cottage, Sandhampton Lane, Astley, Stourport-on-Severn, **Worcestershire**, DY13 0RQ, **ENGLAND**.
(T) 01299 822799.
Profile Farrier. **Ref: YH07678**

JAMES, COLIN I
Colin I James DWCF, 30 Sandhampton, Astley, Stourport-on-Severn, **Worcestershire**, DY13 0RQ, **ENGLAND**.
(T) 01299 828419.
Profile Farrier. **Ref: YH07679**

JAMES, D W
Mr D W James, Penpant Farm, Pontardulais Rd, Tycross, Ammanford, **Carmarthenshire**, **WALES**..
Profile Trainer. **Ref: YH07680**

JAMES, E
E James, Mask Cottage Stables, Front St, East Garston, Hungerford, **Berkshire**, RG17 7EU, **ENGLAND**.
(T) 01488 648077 **(F)** 01488 649781.
Contact/s
Owner: Mr E James
(E) edward@racing9.fsnet.co.uk
Profile Trainer. No.Staff: 8 Yr. Est: 1998
Ref: YH07681

JAMES, K & S
K & S James, 10 Coronation Rd, Beswood Village, Nottingham, **Nottinghamshire**, NG6 8TH, **ENGLAND**.
(T) 0115 9569294.
Contact/s
Partner: Mr S James
Profile Breeder. **Ref: YH07682**

JAMES, MARK A
Mark A James DWCF, Southview, Uphampton Lane, Ombersley, Droitwich, **Worcestershire**, WR9 0JW, **ENGLAND**.
(T) 07771 641405.
Profile Farrier. **Ref: YH07683**

JAMES, MARK ROY
Mark Roy James DWCF, 7 Phillimore Pl, Radlett, **Hertfordshire**, WD7 8NH, **ENGLAND**.
(T) 01923 857052.
Profile Farrier. **Ref: YH07684**

JAMES, NICHOLAS J
Nicholas J James RSS, Pear Tree Farm, Llanfair, Caereinion, **Powys**, SY21 0BH, **WALES**.
(T) 01938 810031.
Profile Farrier. **Ref: YH07685**

JAMES, PAUL ELLIS
Paul Ellis James DWCF, Tyddyn Waen, Waen Wen, Caerhun, Bangor, **Gwynedd**, LL57 4UF, **WALES**.
(T) 01407 810309.
Profile Farrier. **Ref: YH07686**

JAMES, SIMON
Simon James, Patch Park Farm, 156 Ongar Rd, Abridge, Romford, **Essex**, RM4 1AA, **ENGLAND**.
(T) 01708 688087 **(F)** 01708 688087.
Contact/s
Manager: Mr R Donovan
Profile Transport/Horse Boxes. **Ref: YH07687**

JAMES, T H
T H James, Penpontbren, Capel Bangor, Aberystwyth, **Ceredigion**, SY23 3NN, **WALES**.
(T) 01970 880602.
Profile Breeder. **Ref: YH07688**

JAMES, TIMOTHY P
Timothy P James DWCF, 4 The Common, Melbourne, **Derbyshire**, DE73 1DH, **ENGLAND**.
(T) 07836 567932.
Profile Farrier. **Ref: YH07689**

JAMES, W D
Mr W D James, Trefusis Farm, Bradford-on-Tone, Taunton, **Somerset**, **ENGLAND**..
Profile Supplies. **Ref: YH07690**

JAMESON, W E
W E Jameson, Leyburn Rd, Masham, Ripon, **Yorkshire (North)**, HG4 4ER, **ENGLAND**.
(T) 01765 689666 **(F)** 01765 689662.
Profile Supplies. **Ref: YH07691**

JAMIESON, C J
C J Jamieson, Equine Clinic, The Stables, Locko Park, **Derbyshire**, DE21 7BW, **ENGLAND**.
(T) 0115 9329322.
Profile Medical Support. **Ref: YH07692**

JANAWAY, P H
P H Janaway B.Vet.Med.MRCVS, Buryhill Hse, Didmarton, Badminton, **Gloucestershire**, GL9 1DX, **ENGLAND**.
(T) 01454 238565.
Profile Medical Support. **Ref: YH07693**

JANE NEVILLE GALLERY
Jane Neville Gallery (The), Elm Hse, Abbey Lane, Aslockton, **Nottinghamshire**, NG13 9AE, **ENGLAND**.
(T) 01949 850220 **(F)** 01949 851337. **Ref: YH07694**

JANES HANDMADE SADDLERY
Janes Handmade Saddlery, The Paddocks, 82 High St, Waltham On The Wolds, Melton Mowbray, **Leicestershire**, LE14 4AH, **ENGLAND**.
(T) 01664 464829.
Profile Saddlery Retailer. **Ref: YH07695**

JANET JENKINSON CARTOONS
Janet Jenkinson Cartoons, The Poplars, Welbourn Rd, Brant Broughton, **Lincolnshire**, LN5 0SP, **ENGLAND**.
(T) 01522 788542. **Ref: YH07696**

JANICE GORDON
Janice Gordon Studio and Gallery, Church St, Throney, Peterborough, **Cambridgeshire**, PE6 0QB, **ENGLAND**.
(T) 01733 270374
(W) www.chamer-web.co.uk/janicegordonstudio.
Contact/s
Owner: Ms J Gordon **(T)** 01733 270518
Profile Artist. No.Staff: 1 Yr. Est: 1994
Opening Times
By appointment only **Ref: YH07697**

JANSCH, HEATHER
Heather Jansch, The Coach Hse, East St, Ashborne,

Devon, TQ13 7AT, **ENGLAND**.
(T) 01364 653831. **Ref: YH07698**

JANSWEAR

Janswear, 84 Station Rd, Warboys, Huntingdon, **Cambridgeshire**, PE17 2TH, **ENGLAND**.
(T) 01487 822128.
Profile Supplies. **Ref: YH07699**

JANTON STUD

Janton Stud, Rhos-Y-Gilwern, Garth, Llangammarch Wells, **Powys**, LD4 4BG, **WALES**.
(T) 01591 620601.
Contact/s
Owner: Miss T Baldwin
Profile Breeder. **Ref: YH07700**

JARDEN, J

Mrs J Jarden, 9 Ballyhill Lane, Nutts Corner, Crumlin, **County Antrim**, BT29 4YP, **NORTHERN IRELAND**.
(T) 028 90825540.
Profile Medical Support. **Ref: YH07701**

JARMAN, KAREN

Miss Karen Jarman MC AMC MMCA, West Dene, 12 Brackley Rd, Buckingham, **Buckinghamshire**, MK18 1JD, **ENGLAND**.
(T) 01280 824648.
Profile Medical Support. **Ref: YH07702**

JARRETT, EDWIN

Edwin Jarrett AFCL BI, 11 Lunan St, Friockheim, Arbroath, **Angus**, DD11 4TB, **SCOTLAND**.
(T) 01241 828490.
Profile Farrier. **Ref: YH07703**

JARVIE, JAMES

James Jarvie DWCF, 2 Roebank St, Glasgow, **Glasgow (City of)**, G31 3HX, **SCOTLAND**.
(T) 0141 5564728.
Profile Farrier. **Ref: YH07704**

JARVIS, A P

A P Jarvis, Frimley Stables, Aston Upthorpe, Didcot, **Oxfordshire**, OX11 9EE, **ENGLAND**.
(T) 01235 851341.
Profile Trainer. **Ref: YH07705**

JARVIS, M A

M A Jarvis, Kremlin Hse, Fordham Rd, Newmarket, **Suffolk**, CB8 7AQ, **ENGLAND**.
(T) 01638 661702 **(F)** 01638 667018
(W) www.newmarketracehorsetraining.co.uk
Affiliated Bodies Newmarket Trainers Fed.
Contact/s
Owner: Mr M Jarvis
Profile Trainer. **Ref: YH07706**

JARVIS, P

Mr P Jarvis, 73 Woodside Green, Great Hallingbury, Bishop's Stortford, **Essex**, CM22 7UU, **ENGLAND**.
(T) 01279 653711 **(F)** 01279 465960
(M) 07771 823217
(E) paul@pauljarvis.co.uk. **Ref: YH07707**

JARVIS, W

W Jarvis, Phantom Hse Cottage, Fordham Rd, Newmarket, **Suffolk**, CB8 7AA, **ENGLAND**.
(T) 01638 669873 **(F)** 01638 667328
(W) www.newmarketracehorsetrainers.co.uk
Affiliated Bodies Newmarket Trainers Fed.
Contact/s
Owner: Mr W Jarvis
Profile Trainer. **Ref: YH07708**

JAS, DOYLE

Doyle Jas, Glenbane Lr Holycross, Holycross, **County Tipperary**, **IRELAND**.
(T) 050 443251.
Profile Supplies. **Ref: YH07709**

JASPERS

Jaspers, Carewell Farm, St Piers Lane, Lingfield, **Surrey**, RH7 6PN, **ENGLAND**.
(T) 01342 836777.
Profile Supplies. **Ref: YH07710**

JAYBEE EQUESTRIAN

Jaybee Equestrian, 1st Floor/Unit 1/Image Business Pk, East Cannock Rd, Cannock, **Staffordshire**, WS12 5LT, **ENGLAND**.
(T) 01543 426398 **(F)** 01543 425988.
Contact/s
Owner: Mrs J Bird **Ref: YH07711**

JAYCLARE SADDLERY

Jayclare Saddlery, 24 Landsborough Gate, Willen, Milton Keynes, **Buckinghamshire**, MK15 9JT, **ENGLAND**.
(T) 01908 605745.
Profile Supplies. **Ref: YH07712**

JEANS, JOHN H

John H Jeans DWCF, 17 Crouchfield, Rushettes Drive, Goodwinds, Dorking, **Surrey**, RH4 2NE, **ENGLAND**.
(T) 07970 393529.
Profile Farrier. **Ref: YH07713**

JEE, D G

D G Jee, Field Hse, Upper Chalkley, Horton, Chipping Sodbury, **Gloucestershire (South)**, BS37 6QS, **ENGLAND**.
(T) 01454 314390.
Profile Farrier. **Ref: YH07714**

JEFFERIES, NIGEL P

Nigel P Jefferies, Hanscombe End Cottage, Hanscombe End, Shillington, **Hertfordshire**, SG5 3NB, **ENGLAND**.
(T) 01462 711333.
Profile Farrier. **Ref: YH07715**

JEFFERY COMMUNICATIONS

Jeffery Communications, Castle Farm, Exford, Minehead, **Somerset**, TA24 7NL, **ENGLAND**.
(T) 01643 831011 **(F)** 01643 831040
(E) peterjeff@msn.com.
Profile Club/Association. Equestrian PR and Media Consultant. **Ref: YH07716**

JEFFERY, C A

C A Jeffery, Hill Farm, Oxford Rd, Witney, **Oxfordshire**, OX8 6UY, **ENGLAND**.
(T) 01993 705965 **(F)** 01993 709269.
Contact/s
Owner: Mr P Jeffrey
Profile Stable/Livery. **Ref: YH07717**

JEFFERY, JULIET

Juliet Jeffery, The Providence, Compton, Chichester, **Sussex (West)**, PO18 9HD, **ENGLAND**.
(T) 023 92631880. **Ref: YH07718**

JEFFERY, PETER

Peter Jeffery, Cox Corner, Ockley Rd, Ockley, **Surrey**, RH5 5RT, **ENGLAND**.
(T) 01306 621331 **(F)** 01306 621510
(E) peterjeff@msn.com. **Ref: YH07719**

JEFFERY, RICHARD N

Richard N Jeffery DWCF, Belmont, Ashford Rd, Bethersden, **Kent**, TN26 3BD, **ENGLAND**.
(T) 01233 820282.
Profile Farrier. **Ref: YH07720**

JEFFERY, S A

Mrs S A Jeffery, High Hse Farm, Timber Lane, Pilsley, Chesterfield, **Derbyshire**, S45 8AL, **ENGLAND**.
(T) 01246 851520.
Profile Breeder. **Ref: YH07721**

JEFFORD, S

S Jefford, 6 Malthouse Cl, Arundel, **Sussex (West)**, BN18 9JF, **ENGLAND**.
(T) 01903 883676 **(F)** 01903 885399.
Contact/s
Senior Partner: Mr S Jefford
Profile Farrier. **Ref: YH07722**

JEFFREY THOMAS & SON

Jeffrey Thomas & Son, Sunderland Hall Stables, Galashiels, **Scottish Borders**, TD1 3PG, **SCOTLAND**.
(T) 01750 21521.
Profile Farrier. **Ref: YH07723**

JEFFREY, A T

A T Jeffrey, West Mains, Blyth Bridge, West Linton, **Scottish Borders**, EH46 7AH, **SCOTLAND**.
(T) 01721 752687.
Contact/s
Owner: Mr A Jeffrey
Profile Blacksmith. **Ref: YH07724**

JEFFREY, T E

Mr T E Jeffrey, Cold Harbour Farm, Christon Bank, Alnwick, **Northumberland**, NE66 3HB, **ENGLAND**.
(T) 01665 576664.
Profile Breeder. **Ref: YH07725**

JEFFS, H S

Mrs H S Jeffs, Willowbrook, 15 Tinacre Hill, Wightwick, Wolverhampton, **Midlands (West)**, WV6 8DB, **ENGLAND**.
(T) 01902 761049.
Profile Breeder. **Ref: YH07726**

JEHAN, F W

Mr F W Jehan, White Hart Inn, 36 Carmarthan Rd, Llandeilo, **Carmarthenshire**, SA19 6RS, **WALES**.
(T) 01558 823419.
Profile Breeder. **Ref: YH07727**

JEMMESON, JOHN D

John D Jemmeson RSS, Castle Hse, Middleham, **Yorkshire (North)**, DL8 4QP, **ENGLAND**.
(T) 01969 622148.
Profile Farrier. **Ref: YH07728**

JENKINS DUNN FORGINGS

Jenkins Dunn Forgings Ltd, Dudley Central Trading Est, Shaw Rd, Dudley, **Midlands (West)**, DY2 8QX, **ENGLAND**.
(T) 01384 232844 **(F)** 01384 455628.
Profile Blacksmith. **Ref: YH07729**

JENKINS, A & E

A & E Jenkins, Dan-Y-Coed Farm, Llandyfan, Ammanford, **Carmarthenshire**, **WALES**.
(T) 01269 850456.
Profile Breeder. **Ref: YH07730**

JENKINS, G M

G M Jenkins BVSc MRCVS, Llwynteg, Bryncrug, Tywyn, **Gwynedd**, LL36 9NU, **WALES**.
(T) 01654 710416.
Profile Medical Support. **Ref: YH07731**

JENKINS, G M

G M Jenkins BVSc MRCVS, Graigle, Graigfach, Maghynlleth, **Powys**, SY20 8BB, **WALES**.
(T) 01654 702444.
Profile Medical Support. **Ref: YH07732**

JENKINS, J

J Jenkins, Kings Ride Stables, Baldock Rd, Royston, **Hertfordshire**, SG8 9NN, **ENGLAND**.
(T) 01763 241141 **(F)** 01763 248223.
Contact/s
Owner: Mr J Jenkins
Profile Trainer. **Ref: YH07733**

JENKINS, LLOYD P

Lloyd P Jenkins AWCF, 10 Cleves Court, Firs Ave, Windsor, **Berkshire**, SL4 4EF, **ENGLAND**.
(T) 01753 859181.
Profile Farrier. **Ref: YH07734**

JENKINS, P

Mr P Jenkins, Goss Farm, Ashleworth, **Gloucestershire**, GL19 4HU, **ENGLAND**.
(T) 01452 700092
(M) 07768 644548.
Profile Medical Support. **Ref: YH07735**

JENKINS, R

R Jenkins, Units 1-2, Linton Trading Est, Bromyard, **Herefordshire**, HR7 4QT, **ENGLAND**.
(T) 01885 483202 **(F)** 01895 483202.
Contact/s
Owner: Mr R Jenkins **Ref: YH07736**

JENKINS, W J P

W J P Jenkins, Twyn Gwyn, Manmoel, Blackwood, **Caerphilly**, NP12 0RQ, **WALES**.
(T) 01495 226008.
Profile Breeder. **Ref: YH07737**

JENKINSON, T H

T H Jenkinson, New Castle Market, Whiteford Hill, Ayr, **Ayrshire (South)**, KA6 5JW, **SCOTLAND**.
(T) 01292 619193 **(F)** 01292 619190
(W) www.thjenkinson.co.uk.
Contact/s
Partner: Mr T Jenkinson
(E) tom@thjenkinson.co.uk
Profile Transport/Horse Boxes. Distributors for Ifor Williams Trailers.
Sell, repair and service horseboxes, can also deliver if required. Yr. Est: 1995
Opening Times
Sp: Open Mon - Fri 08:00. Closed Mon - Fri 17:00.
Su: Open Mon - Fri 08:00. Closed Mon - Fri 17:00.
Au: Open Mon - Fri 08:00. Closed Mon - Fri 17:00.
Wn: Open Mon - Fri 08:00. Closed Mon - Fri 17:00.
Ref: YH07738

JENKINSON, T H

T H Jenkinson, Greenlaw, Castle Douglas, **Dumfries and Galloway**, DG7 2LH, **SCOTLAND**.
(T) 01556 504133 **(F)** 01556 504190
(W) www.thjenkinson.co.uk.
Contact/s
Partner: Mr T Jenkinson

(E) tom@thjenkinson.co.uk
Profile Transport/Horse Boxes. Distributors for Ifor Williams Trailers.
Sell, repair and service horseboxes, can also deliver if required. **Yr. Est:** 1989
Opening Times
Sp: Open Mon - Fri 08:30. Closed Mon - Fri 17:00.
Su: Open Mon - Fri 08:30. Closed Mon - Fri 17:00.
Au: Open Mon - Fri 08:30. Closed Mon - Fri 17:00.
Wn: Open Mon - Fri 08:30. Closed Mon - Fri 17:00.
Ref: YH07739

JENKINSONS

B Jenkinson & Sons, 5 Wellington Rd, Dewsbury, **Yorkshire (West)**, WF13 1HF, **ENGLAND**.
(T) 01924 469242/454681 **(F)** 01924 458696
(E) info@elico.co.uk
(W) www.elico.co.uk.
Profile Riding Wear Retailer, Supplies.
Export goods worldwide.
Opening Times
Sp: Open Mon - Fri 09:00. Closed Mon - Fri 17:00.
Su: Open Mon - Fri 09:00. Closed Mon - Fri 17:00.
Au: Open Mon - Fri 09:00. Closed Mon - Fri 17:00.
Wn: Open Mon - Fri 09:00. Closed Mon - Fri 17:00.
Closed weekends **Ref: YH07740**

JENKINSONS HUDDERSFIELD

Jenkinsons Huddersfield Towbar Centre, 23A St Johns Rd, Huddersfield, **Yorkshire (West)**, HD1 5BW, **ENGLAND**.
(T) 01484 549512 **(F)** 01484 549516.
Contact/s
Owner: Mr M Jenkinson
Profile Transport/Horse Boxes. **Ref: YH07741**

JENKS, WILLIAM P

Mr William P Jenks, Wadeley Farm, Glazeley, Bridgnorth, **Shropshire**, WV16 6AD, **ENGLAND**.
(T) 01746 789288 **(F)** 01746 789535.
Contact/s
Trainer: William Jenks
Profile Trainer. **Ref: YH07742**

JENNA LIVESTOCK

Jenna Livestock Ltd, Cwm Farm, Rudry, **Caerphilly**, CF24 3DT, **WALES**.
(T) 029 20869191.
Profile Breeder. **Ref: YH07743**

JENNER, B A

B A Jenner, Callis Court Lodge, Sandy Lane, Ryarsh, West Malling, **Kent**, ME19 6TG, **ENGLAND**.
(T) 01732 841188.
Profile Stable/Livery.
DIY Livery **Ref: YH07744**

JENNER, M

Mr M Jenner, Three Gables, Walnut Hill, Meopham, **Kent**, DA13 9HL, **ENGLAND**.
(T) 01474 708664.
Profile Breeder. **Ref: YH07745**

JENNINGS FARM PRODUCE

Jennings Farm Produce, Wheatley Rd, Garsington, **Oxfordshire**, OX44 9DY, **ENGLAND**.
(T) 01865 361247.
Profile Supplies. **Ref: YH07746**

JENNINGS, E

E. Jennings, Bohercuill, Tuam, **County Galway**, **IRELAND**.
(T) 093 55343 **(F)** 093 55348.
Profile Supplies. **Ref: YH07747**

JENNINGS, JOHN R

John R Jennings DWCF, 54 Slade Rd, Stokenchurch, **Buckinghamshire**, HP14 3PX, **ENGLAND**.
(T) 01494 485003.
Profile Farrier. **Ref: YH07748**

JENNISON, A P

A P Jennison, Skerne Rd, Driffield, **Yorkshire (East)**, YO25 6SF, **ENGLAND**.
(T) 01377 252584.
Contact/s
Owner: Mr A Jennison
Profile Transport/Horse Boxes. **Ref: YH07749**

JENNY'S TACK SHOP

Jenny's Tack Shop, Bath Rd, Longwell Green, Bristol, **Bristol**, BS30 6DL, **ENGLAND**.
(T) 01179 608800.
Contact/s
Owner: Mrs J Godwin
Profile Riding Wear Retailer, Saddlery Retailer.
Ref: YH07750

JEPHCOTT, KIM E

Kim E Jephcott RSS, The Nook, Scarfield Hill, Alvechurch, Birmingham, **Midlands (West)**, B48 7DB, **ENGLAND**.
(T) 0121 4456022.
Contact/s
Farrier: Mr K Jephcott
Profile Farrier. **Ref: YH07751**

JEREMY FRANKS TACK REPAIRS

Jeremy Franks Tack Repairs, Piers Cottage, The Hamlet, Slades Hill, Templecombe, **Somerset**, BA8 0HJ, **ENGLAND**.
(T) 01963 371479.
Profile Supplies. **Ref: YH07752**

JEREMY NOSEDA

Jeremy Noseda (Racing) Ltd, Shalfleet Stables, 17 Bury Rd, Newmarket, **Suffolk**, CB8 7BX, **ENGLAND**.
(T) 01638 664010 **(F)** 01636 664100
(W) www.jeremynoseda-racing.com
Affiliated Bodies Newmarket Trainers Fed.
Contact/s
Trainer: Mr J Noseda
Profile Trainer. **Ref: YH07753**

JEROME, E A

E A Jerome B Vet Med MRCVS, The Grange, Braunston, Daventry, **Northamptonshire**, NN11 7JG, **ENGLAND**.
(T) 01788 891260 **(F)** 01788 891811.
Profile Medical Support. **Ref: YH07754**

JERPOINT LIVERY

Jerpoint Livery, Jerpoint W, Thomastown, **County Kilkenny**, **IRELAND**.
(T) 086 2602054.
Profile Supplies. **Ref: YH07755**

JERSEY RIDING CLUB

Jersey Riding Club, Sorrel Stables, Mont Fallu, St Peter, **Jersey**, JE3 8EE, **ENGLAND**.
(T) 01534 490020.
Contact/s
Chairman: Miss V Baal
Profile Club/Association, Riding Club. **Ref: YH07756**

JERUSALEM FARM

Jerusalem Farm, Skipton Old Rd, Colne, **Lancashire**, BB8 7EW, **ENGLAND**.
(T) 01282 869900 **(F)** 01282 869900.
Contact/s
Owner: Mrs L Bowker **Ref: YH07757**

JERVIS, JOHN

John Jervis, Seifton View, Culmington, Ludlow, **Shropshire**, SY8 2DF, **ENGLAND**.
(T) 01584 861328.
Contact/s
Owner: Mr J Jervis
Profile Transport/Horse Boxes. **Ref: YH07758**

JESSIMAN, D C

D C Jessiman, The Veterinary Surgery, Kirkcudbright, **Dumfries and Galloway**, DG6 4HX, **SCOTLAND**.
(T) 01557 30632.
Profile Medical Support. **Ref: YH07759**

JESSOP, A E M

Mr A E M Jessop, Flemings Farm, Warren Rd, South Hanningfield, Chelmsford, **Essex**, CM3 8HU, **ENGLAND**.
(T) 01268 710210.
Profile Supplies. **Ref: YH07760**

JESTERS FORGE

Jesters Forge, Jesters, Cotleigh, Honiton, **Devon**, EX14 9HJ, **ENGLAND**.
(T) 01404 831717 **(F)** 01404 831717.
Contact/s
Owner: Mr M Dingle
Profile Blacksmith. **Ref: YH07761**

JESTIN, F

Mr F Jestin, Hilltop, Brocklebank, Wigton, **Cumbria**, CA7 8DL, **ENGLAND**.
(T) 01697 478439.
Profile Supplies. **Ref: YH07762**

JET SET

Jet Set, Garden Ctre, Boclair Rd, Milngavie, Glasgow, **Glasgow (City of)**, G62 6EP, **SCOTLAND**.
(T) 01360 620666 **(F)** 01360 622815.
Contact/s
Owner: Mrs M Morrison
Profile Riding Wear Retailer, Saddlery Retailer.
Ref: YH07763

JET SET SADDLERY

Jet Set Saddlery, 72 - 74 Main St, Prestwick, **Ayrshire (South)**, KA9 1PA, **SCOTLAND**.
(T) 01292 477419 **(F)** 01292 678494.
Profile Saddlery Retailer. **Ref: YH07764**

JEWELL, L

L Jewell, South Lane, Sutton Valence, Maidstone, **Kent**, ME17 3AZ, **ENGLAND**.
(T) 01622 842788 **(F)** 01622 842788.
Contact/s
Owner: Mrs L Jewell **Ref: YH07765**

JIGGINSTOWN HOUSE STABLES

Jigginstown House Stables, Jigginstown, Naas, **County Kildare**, **IRELAND**.
(T) 045 871040
(E) jigginstownhousestables@kildarehorse.ie.
Contact/s
Key Contact: Mr T McDonald
Profile Breeder. **C.Size:** 100 Acres
Ref: YH07766

JILL LAMB BLOODSTOCK

Jill Lamb Bloodstock, Chapel Lodge, Chapel Row, Ashley, Newmarket, **Suffolk**, CB8 9ED, **ENGLAND**.
(T) 01638 731048 **(F)** 01638 731048
(M) 07774 119478
(E) jill.lamb@virgin.net.
Profile Blood Stock Agency, Breeder. **Ref: YH07767**

JIM MEADS - PHOTOGRAPHER

Jim Meads - Photographer, The Old Vicarage, Carno, Caersws, **Powys**, SY17 5LL, **WALES**.
(T) 01686 420436 **(F)** 01686 420436.
Profile Photographer. **Ref: YH07768**

JJG BLACKSMITHS

JJG Blacksmiths, 79 Portland St, Edinburgh, **Edinburgh (City of)**, EH6 4AY, **SCOTLAND**.
(F) 0131 4673546
(M) 07808 757053.
Contact/s
Partner: Mr J Farquhar
Profile Blacksmith. **Ref: YH07769**

JOBSON R L & SON

Jobson R L & Son, Tower Showrooms, Alnwick, **Northumberland**, NE66 1SX, **ENGLAND**.
(T) 01665 602135.
Contact/s
Owner: Mr C Todd **Ref: YH07770**

JOCKEY CLUB

Jockey Club (The), 42 Portman Sq, London, **London (Greater)**, W1H 0EN, **ENGLAND**.
(T) 020 74864921 **(F)** 020 79358703
(W) www.thejockeyclub.co.uk.
Contact/s
Public Relations Officer: Mr J Mosie
Profile Club/Association.
It is a regulatory body of horseracing. The Jockey Club own and operate 13 racecourses. **Yr. Est:** 1752
Opening Times
Sp: Open Mon - Fri 09:00. Closed Mon - Fri 17:30.
Su: Open Mon - Fri 09:00. Closed Mon - Fri 17:30.
Au: Open Mon - Fri 09:00. Closed Mon - Fri 17:30.
Wn: Open Mon - Fri 09:00. Closed Mon - Fri 17:30.
Ref: YH07771

JOCKEYS ASS OF GREAT BRITAIN

Jockeys Association of Great Britain Ltd, 39B Kingfisher Court, Hambridge Rd, Newbury, **Berkshire**, RG14 5SJ, **ENGLAND**.
(T) 01635 44102 **(F)** 01635 37932
(E) jockeys@jagb.co.uk.
Profile Club/Association. **Ref: YH07772**

JOCKEYS EMPLOYMENT & TRAINING

Jockeys Employment & Training Scheme, Pollardstown, Foxhill, Wanborough, Swindon, **Wiltshire**, SN4 0DR, **ENGLAND**.
(T) 01793 791491
(E) jets@pollardstown.demon.co.uk.
Profile Club/Association. **Ref: YH07773**

JODHPURS

Jodhpurs Riding School, Blind Lane, Tockwith, York, **Yorkshire (North)**, YO5 8QJ, **ENGLAND**.
(T) 01423 358645.
Contact/s
Instructor: Ms E Banks
Profile Riding School.
Has a Western instructor. **No.Staff:** 5
Yr. Est: 1991 **C.Size:** 17 Acres
Opening Times
Sp: Open Mon, Wed - Sun 09:00. Closed Mon, Wed - Fri 19:00, Sat 18:00, Sun 17:30.

Su: Open Mon, Wed - Sun 09:00. Closed Mon, Wed - Fri 19:00, Sat 18:00, Sun 17:30.
Au: Open Mon, Wed - Sun 09:00. Closed Mon, Wed - Fri 19:00, Sat 18:00, Sun 17:30.
Wn: Open Mon, Wed - Sun 09:00. Closed Mon, Wed - Fri 19:00, Sat 18:00, Sun 17:30.
Closed Tuesdays **Ref: YH07774**

JODS GALORE
Jods Galore, 73 Bell St, Henley-on-Thames, **Oxfordshire**, RG9 2BD, **ENGLAND**.
(T) 01491 576125 **(F)** 01491 576125
Affiliated Bodies BETA.
Contact/s
General Manager: Ms J Walford **(Q)** BHS IT
Profile Riding Wear Retailer, Saddlery Retailer, Supplies. **No.Staff:** 3 **Yr. Est:** 1980
Opening Times
Sp: Open 09:30. Closed 17:30.
Su: Open 09:30. Closed 17:30.
Au: Open 09:30. Closed 17:30.
Wn: Open 09:30. Closed 17:30. **Ref: YH07775**

JODS, DOBBIES
Dobbies Jods, 20 Newlands Lane, Ash Green, Coventry, **Warwickshire**, CV7 9BA, **ENGLAND**.
(T) 024 76367107.
Profile Saddlery Retailer. **Ref: YH07776**

JOEL ENTERPRISES
Joel Enterprises, Box 33, 10 Barley Mow Passage, London, **London (Greater)**, W4 4PH, **ENGLAND**.
(T) 01923 285302. **Ref: YH07777**

JOHN ATTWOOLL
John Attwooll & Co (Tents) Ltd, Whitminster, **Gloucestershire**, GL2 7LX, **ENGLAND**.
(T) 01452 740278.
Contact/s
Owner: Mr P Attwooll **Ref: YH07778**

JOHN BARNETT
John Barnett Ltd, City Mills, Padmore St, Worcester, **Worcestershire**, WR1 2PA, **ENGLAND**.
(T) 01905 22351 **(F)** 01905 617221.
Profile Supplies. **Ref: YH07779**

JOHN BELLAMY BLACKSMITHS
John Bellamy Blacksmiths, 2 Eastdon Farm Hse, Starcross, Exeter, **Devon**, EX6 8RJ, **ENGLAND**.
(T) 01626 890503 **(F)** 01626 890503.
Contact/s
Owner: Mr J Bellamy
Profile Blacksmith. **Ref: YH07780**

JOHN BIRON EQUESTRIAN
John Biron Equestrian, Rushford Farm, Three Cups, Heathfield, **Sussex (East)**, TN21 9LR, **ENGLAND**.
(T) 01435 830342 **(F)** 01435 830342.
Profile Breeder, Stable/Livery. **Ref: YH07781**

JOHN BRITTER PHOTOGRAPHY
John Britter Photography, 2 Grange Farm Bungalow, Thornbrough Grounds, Buckingham, **Buckinghamshire**, MK18 2AB, **ENGLAND**.
(T) 01280 824997
(E) john.britter@tesco.net. **Ref: YH07782**

JOHN C ALBOROUGH
John C Alborough Ltd, Battisford Rd, Ringshall, **Suffolk**, IP14 2JA, **ENGLAND**.
(T) 01473 658006 **(F)** 01473 658922. **Ref: YH07783**

JOHN COOK (CORN MERCHANTS)
John Cook (Corn Merchants) Ltd, Rushton Mills, Rushton Spencer, Macclesfield, **Cheshire**, SK11 0RT, **ENGLAND**.
(T) 01260 226233.
Profile Feed Merchant, Supplies. **Ref: YH07784**

JOHN D WOOD TEAM CHASE
John D Wood Team Chase, The Dower Cottage, Ardington, Wantage, **Oxfordshire**, **ENGLAND**..
Profile Club/Association. **Ref: YH07785**

JOHN DICKSON & SON
John Dickson & Son Ltd, 21 Frederick St, Edinburgh, **Edinburgh (City of)**, EH2 2NE, **SCOTLAND**.
(T) 0131 2254218 **(F)** 0131 2253658.
Profile Saddlery Retailer. **Ref: YH07786**

JOHN FERGUSON BLOODSTOCK
John Ferguson Bloodstock, Bloomfields, Cowlinge, Newmarket, **Suffolk**, CB8 9HN, **ENGLAND**.
(T) 01638 500423 **(F)** 01638 500387.
Profile Blood Stock Agency. **Ref: YH07787**

JOHN FINDLATER & SON
John Findlater & Son, Gairloch, Skene, Westhill, **Aberdeenshire**, AB32 6YJ, **SCOTLAND**.
(T) 01224 743214 **(F)** 01224 742878.
Contact/s
Owner: Mr J Findlater
Profile Blacksmith. **Ref: YH07788**

JOHN FOWLER & SON
John Fowler & Son, Unit 2 Abbey Mill, Garden St, Abbey Village, Chorley, **Lancashire**, PR6 8DN, **ENGLAND**.
(T) 01254 831370 **(F)** 01254 832302.
Contact/s
Owner: Mr J Fowler
Profile Blacksmith. **Ref: YH07789**

JOHN FOWLER & SON
John Fowler & Son, 18 Bury Lane, Withnell, Chorley, **Lancashire**, PR6 8RX, **ENGLAND**.
(T) 01254 830396.
Contact/s
Owner: Mr J Fowler
Profile Blacksmith. **Ref: YH07790**

JOHN GIBSON & SONS
John Gibson & Sons, Unit 215 Heathhall Ind Est, Heathhall, Dumfries, **Dumfries and Galloway**, DG1 3PH, **SCOTLAND**.
(T) 01387 254764 **(F)** 01387 266005.
Contact/s
Partner: Mr L Hastings
Profile Blacksmith. **Ref: YH07791**

JOHN HATTON AGRICULTURAL
John Hatton Agricultural, Unit 2, The Auction Mart, Wyresdale Road, **Lancashire**, LA1 3JQ, **ENGLAND**.
(T) 01704 840990
(M) 07833 384082.
Profile Supplies. **Ref: YH07792**

JOHN HESKETH & SON
John Hesketh & Son Ltd, Castlecroft Ironworks, Bury Ground, Bury, **Lancashire**, BL9 0HU, **ENGLAND**.
(T) 0161 7649587.
Profile Blacksmith. **Ref: YH07793**

JOHN HORLOCK & ASSOCIATES
John Horlock & Associates, 40 Etnam St, Leominster, **Herefordshire**, HR6 8AQ, **ENGLAND**.
(T) 01568 612077 **(F)** 01568 616733.
Profile Medical Support. **Ref: YH07794**

JOHN HUDSON
John Hudson Commercial Vehicles, Doncaster Rd, Bawtry, Doncaster, **Yorkshire (South)**, DN10 6NX, **ENGLAND**.
(T) 01302 710711.
Profile Transport/Horse Boxes.
Repair Horseboxes **Ref: YH07795**

JOHN JENKINS & SON
John Jenkins & Son, Unit 7 Redding Ind Est, Redding, Falkirk, **Falkirk**, FK2 9TT, **SCOTLAND**.
(T) 01324 716911.
Profile Blacksmith. **Ref: YH07796**

JOHN JONES
John Jones (Wilmslow) Ltd, Dean Row Smithy, Adlington Rd, Wilmslow, **Cheshire**, SK9 2LN, **ENGLAND**.
(T) 01625 523438.
Profile Blacksmith. **Ref: YH07797**

JOHN LILLY
John Lilly Decorative Ironwork, Manor Stables Craft Workshop, Fulbeck, Grantham, **Lincolnshire**, NG32 3JN, **ENGLAND**.
(T) 01400 273744.
Profile Blacksmith. **Ref: YH07798**

JOHN LOADER
John Loader (Wessex) Ltd, Station Mills, Fordingbridge, **Hampshire**, SP6 1BY, **ENGLAND**.
(T) 01425 652394 **(F)** 01425 652625
(E) simon.freeman@wessex-feeds.co.uk
(W) www.wessex-feeds.co.uk.
Profile Feed Merchant, Supplies. **Ref: YH07799**

JOHN MCDONALD
John McDonald - Collar & Harnessmaker, Clayford, Andrews Hill, Dulverton, **Somerset**, TA22 9RH, **ENGLAND**.
(T) 01398 324040 **(F)** 01398 324040. **Ref: YH07800**

JOHN MCKNIGHT & SON
John Mcknight & Son, The Smiddy, Lochans, Stranraer, **Dumfries and Galloway**, DG9 9AS, **SCOTLAND**.
(T) 01776 820292.
Profile Blacksmith. **Ref: YH07801**

JOHN MOORHOUSE
John Moorhouse Horseboxes, The Whispers, Whinney Hill, Stockton-on-Tees, **Cleveland**, TS21 1BQ, **ENGLAND**.
(T) 01642 582896 **(F)** 01642 582896.
Contact/s
Owner: Mr J Moorhouse
Profile Transport/Horse Boxes.
Manufacturers and suppliers of high quality horseboxes.
Opening Times
Sp: Open Mon - Sun 08:00. Closed Mon - Sun 21:00.
Su: Open Mon - Sun 08:00. Closed Mon - Sun 21:00.
Au: Open Mon - Sun 08:00. Closed Mon - Sun 21:00.
Wn: Open Mon - Sun 08:00. Closed Mon - Sun 21:00. **Ref: YH07802**

JOHN NISBET
John Nisbet DWCF, Ash Villa, Ayton, Eyemouth, **Scottish Borders**, TD14 5QR, **SCOTLAND**.
(T) 07802 444152 **(F)** 01890 752185.
Profile Farrier. **Ref: YH07803**

JOHN PARKER
John Parker Swingletree Stables, Wingfield, Diss, **Norfolk**, IP21 5QZ, **ENGLAND**.
(T) 01379 384496 **(F)** 01379 388314
(E) john@swingletree.co.uk.
Profile Trainer. **Ref: YH07804**

JOHN PARKER INTERNATIONAL
John Parker International Ltd, Little Owl Barn, Pedlinge, Hythe, **Kent**, CT21 4JJ, **ENGLAND**.
(T) 01303 266621 **(F)** 01303 269400.
Contact/s
Partner: Mrs J Parker
Profile Transport/Horse Boxes. **Ref: YH07805**

JOHN PEEL RIDING CLUB
John Peel Riding Club, Croft Hse, Newly East, Wetherall, Carlisle, **Cumbria**, CA4 8QX, **ENGLAND**.
(T) 01228 573439.
Contact/s
Chairman: Mrs A Lawson
Profile Club/Association, Riding Club. **Ref: YH07806**

JOHN REES
John Rees Ltd, 86 Merthyr St, Barry, **Glamorgan (Vale of)**, CF63 4UL, **WALES**.
(T) 01446 733336 **(F)** 01446 .
Profile Saddlery Retailer. **Ref: YH07807**

JOHN REID & SONS
John Reid & Sons (Strucsteel) Ltd, 159-160 Reid St, Christchurch, **Dorset**, BH23 2BT, **ENGLAND**.
(T) 01202 483333.
Profile Transport/Horse Boxes. **Ref: YH07808**

JOHN ROTHERY WHOLESALE
John Rothery Wholesale Co Ltd, Bedford Rd, Petersfield, **Hampshire**, GU32 3AX, **ENGLAND**.
(T) 01730 268011 **(F)** 01730 260074
(E) sales@bisley-uk.com.
Profile Medical Support. **Ref: YH07809**

JOHN ROWING SADDLERY
John Rowing Saddlery, Lower Tadmarton Farm, Tadmarton, Banbury, **Oxfordshire**, OX15 5SZ, **ENGLAND**.
(T) 01295 788375.
Profile Supplies. **Ref: YH07810**

JOHN SCOTT SPORTING BOOKS
John Scott Sporting Books, The Beeches, Wynniatts Way, Abberley, **Worcestershire**, WR6 6BZ, **ENGLAND**.
(T) 01299 896779 **(F)** 01299 896060.
Profile Supplies. **Ref: YH07811**

JOHN SKELTONS
John Skeltons Western Store, 602 High Rd, Benfleet, **Essex**, SS7 5RW, **ENGLAND**.
(T) 01268 792769 **(F)** 01268 566775
(E) john@saddles.freeserve.co.uk.
Contact/s
Owner: Mr J Skelton
Profile Saddlery Retailer.
Importers of high quality leather goods from America.

Handmade goods available as gifts. **Ref: YH07812**

JOHN SNOWDON HARNESS MAKER

John Snowdon Harness Maker, Lark Rise, Hemley, Woodbridge, **Suffolk**, IP12 4QA, **ENGLAND**.
(T) 01473 736364.
Profile Breeder, Trainer. **Ref: YH07813**

JOHN THOMPSON & SONS

John Thompson & Sons Ltd, 35-39 York Rd, Belfast, **County Antrim**, BT15 3GW, **NORTHERN IRELAND**.
(T) 028 90351321 **(F)** 028 90351420.
Profile Supplies. **Ref: YH07814**

JOHN TOOMER

John Toomer Ltd, 27 Moormead Rd, Wroughton, Swindon, **Wiltshire**, SN4 9BS, **ENGLAND**.
(T) 01793 845565 **(F)** 01793 845547.
Profile Feed Merchant, Supplies. **Ref: YH07815**

JOHN WEBBER & PARTNERS

John Webber & Partners, Cropredy Lawn, Cropredy, Banbury, **Oxfordshire**, OX17 1DR, **ENGLAND**.
(T) 01295 750226.
Profile Trainer. **Ref: YH07816**

JOHN WILLIE'S SADDLE ROOM

John Willie's Saddle Room, 2-3 Ringwood Rd, Burley, Ringwood, **Hampshire**, BH24 4AD, **ENGLAND**.
(T) 01425 402386.
Profile Saddlery Retailer. **Ref: YH07817**

JOHN WRIGHT PHOTOGRAPHY

John Wright Photography, Scarbank, Millers Rd, Warwick, **Warwickshire**, CV34 5AN, **ENGLAND**.
(T) 01926 494345 **(F)** 01926 410932.
Contact/s
Photographer: Graham Emery **Ref: YH07818**

JOHN, JOYCE

Joyce John, Garryduff, Claremorris, **County Mayo**, **IRELAND**.
(T) 094 64069.
Profile Supplies. **Ref: YH07819**

JOHN, RYAN

Ryan John, The Bungalow, Holycross, Thurles, **County Tipperary**, **IRELAND**.
(T) 050 443293.
Profile Supplies. **Ref: YH07820**

JOHNSEY, CLAIRE

Claire Johnsey, Devauden Court, Devauden, Chepstow, **Monmouthshire**, NP16 6PL, **WALES**.
(T) 01291 650680.
Contact/s
Owner: Miss C Johnsey
Profile Trainer. **Ref: YH07821**

JOHNSON BROTHERS

Johnson Brothers, Hill Farm, Little Johnson Lane, Aldridge, Walsall, **Midlands (West)**, WS9 0QN, **ENGLAND**.
(T) 01922 453182.
Profile Supplies. **Ref: YH07822**

JOHNSON, ELIZABETH

Miss Elizabeth Johnson, Theakston Hall, Bedale, **Yorkshire (North)**, DL8 2HL, **ENGLAND**.
(T) 01677 422647 **(F)** 01677 422647.
Profile Supplies. **Ref: YH07823**

JOHNSON, GAVIN J

Gavin J Johnson DWCF, Cannonbrook, Ongar Rd, Stondon Massey, Brentwood, **Essex**, CM15 0EQ, **ENGLAND**.
(T) 01277 821693.
Profile Farrier. **Ref: YH07824**

JOHNSON, J

J Johnson, Llandyn Hall Farm, Llangollen, **Denbighshire**, LL20 7UH, **WALES**.
(T) 01978 860783.
Profile Breeder. **Ref: YH07825**

JOHNSON, J H

Mr J H Johnson, White Lea Farm, Crook, **County Durham**, DL15 9QN, **ENGLAND**.
(T) 01388 762113 **(F)** 01388 768278
(M) 07714 691016.
Profile Trainer. **Ref: YH07826**

JOHNSON, M A

Mr M A Johnson, Glebe Hse, Little Hormead, Buntingford, **Hertfordshire**, SG9 0LT, **ENGLAND**.
(T) 01763 89372.
Profile Supplies. **Ref: YH07827**

JOHNSON, MARK E J

Mark E J Johnson DWCF, 11 Kingston Cl, Middleton Cheney, Banbury, **Oxfordshire**, OX17 2LH, **ENGLAND**.
(T) 01295 712276.
Profile Farrier. **Ref: YH07828**

JOHNSON, NIGEL K

Nigel K Johnson RSS, Renwood, 4 Church Pl, Chale, Ventnor, **Isle of Wight**, PO38 2HA, **ENGLAND**.
(T) 01983 731143.
Profile Farrier. **Ref: YH07829**

JOHNSON, NORMAN

Norman Johnson DWCF, Hummlers, 8 Barway Rd, Barway, Ely, **Cambridgeshire**, CB7 5UA, **ENGLAND**.
(M) 07778 268622.
Profile Farrier. **Ref: YH07830**

JOHNSON, P

P Johnson & Co, Ratho Byres Forge, Freelands Rd, Ratho, Newbridge, **Edinburgh (City of)**, EH28 8NW, **SCOTLAND**.
(T) 0131 3331824 **(F)** 0131 3333354.
Contact/s
Owner: Mr P Johnson
Profile Blacksmith. **Ref: YH07831**

JOHNSON, P R

Mr P R Johnson, Pinetrees Farm, Stafford Rd, Huntington, Cannock, **Staffordshire**, WS12 4PQ, **ENGLAND**.
(T) 01543 502962.
Profile Breeder. **Ref: YH07832**

JOHNSON, PAUL

Paul Johnson, 7 Woodland Rise, Rilla Mill, Callington, **Cornwall**, PL17 7NZ, **ENGLAND**.
(T) 01579 362101.
Contact/s
Owner: Mr P Johnson
Profile Farrier. **Ref: YH07833**

JOHNSON, PAUL J

Paul J Johnson RSS, 589 Aylestone Rd, Leicester, **Leicestershire**, LE2 8TD, **ENGLAND**.
(T) 0116 2839081.
Profile Farrier. **Ref: YH07834**

JOHNSON, R C

R C Johnson, Ford Croft Hse, Oak Rd, Denstone, Uttoxeter, **Staffordshire**, ST14 5HT, **ENGLAND**.
(T) 01889 590822.
Profile Breeder. **Ref: YH07835**

JOHNSON, R W

Mr R W Johnson, Grange Farm, Newburn, Newcastle-upon-Tyne, **Tyne and Wear**, NE15 8QA, **ENGLAND**.
(T) 0191 2674464
(M) 07774 131133.
Profile Trainer. **Ref: YH07836**

JOHNSON, RICHARD A

Richard A Johnson DWCF, 19 Victoria St, Wheelton, Chorley, **Lancashire**, PR6 8HG, **ENGLAND**.
(T) 01254 830257.
Profile Farrier. **Ref: YH07837**

JOHNSON, S M

Mrs S M Johnson, Carwardine Farm, Madley, **Herefordshire**, HR2 9JQ, **ENGLAND**.
(T) 01981 250214.
Profile Supplies. **Ref: YH07838**

JOHNSON, SALLY

Mrs Sally Johnson (Saddler), Highmoor Farm, Tickencote Rd, Exton, Oakham, **Rutland**, LE15 8BA, **ENGLAND**.
(T) 01780 460524.
Contact/s
Saddler: Mrs S Johnson
Profile Saddlery Retailer. **Ref: YH07839**

JOHNSON, TREVOR

Trevor Johnson, 32 Woodland Rd, Hertford Heath, **Hertfordshire**, SG13 7QQ, **ENGLAND**.
(T) 01992 587395.
Profile Farrier. **Ref: YH07840**

JOHNSON, TRICIA

Tricia Johnson, Parsons Cl, Aunsby, Sleaford, **Lincolnshire**, NG34 8SX, **ENGLAND**.
(T) 01529 455609 **(F)** 01529 455395.
Profile Breeder. **Ref: YH07841**

JOHNSON-HOUGHTON, R F

R F Johnson-Houghton, Woodway, Blewbury, Didcot, **Oxfordshire**, OX11 9EZ, **ENGLAND**.
(T) 01235 850480 **(F)** 01235 851045.
Contact/s
Manager: Mrs M Spackman
Profile Trainer. **Ref: YH07842**

JOHNSTON

Mr Johnston, Landford Common Farm, Landford, Salisbury, **Wiltshire**, SP5 2GS, **ENGLAND**.
(T) 01794 323305 **(F)** 01794 323654.
Profile Breeder. **Ref: YH07843**

JOHNSTON ENGINEERING

Johnston Engineering Ltd, The Forge, 56A South St, Bridport, **Dorset**, DT6 3NN, **ENGLAND**.
(T) 01308 424415.
Profile Blacksmith. **Ref: YH07844**

JOHNSTON, G J

G J Johnston RSS, 8 Albert Pl, Kelso, **Scottish Borders**, **SCOTLAND**.
(T) 01573 224421.
Profile Farrier. **Ref: YH07845**

JOHNSTON, M

M Johnston, Court Hay Cottage, Farrington, Blandford Forum, **Dorset**, DT11 8RA, **ENGLAND**.
(T) 01747 811226.
Profile Breeder. **Ref: YH07846**

JOHNSTON, PAUL J

Paul J Johnston DWCF, 9 Bowness Court, Workington, **Cumbria**, CA14 3SG, **ENGLAND**.
(T) 01900 68917.
Profile Farrier. **Ref: YH07847**

JOHNSTONE

Johnstone, 12 Highfield Circle, Muir Of Ord, **Highlands**, **SCOTLAND**..
Profile Breeder. **Ref: YH07848**

JOICEY, (LADY)

Lady Joicey, Beech Hse, Etal, Cornhill-on-Tweed, **Northumberland**, TD12 4TL, **ENGLAND**.
(T) 01890 820621 **(F)** 01890 820622.
Profile Trainer. **Ref: YH07849**

JOINT COUNCIL

Joint Council of Heavy Horse Breed Societies, Park Cottage, West Dean, Chichester, **Sussex (West)**, PO18 0RX, **ENGLAND**.
(T) 01243 811364.
Profile Club/Association. **Ref: YH07850**

JOINT MEASUREMENT BOARD

Joint Measurement Board Ltd, Nac Stoneliegh Pk, Kenilworth, **Warwickshire**, CV8 2LR, **ENGLAND**.
(T) 024 76696620 **(F)** 024 76696685.
Contact/s
Key Contact: Mrs P Barnsley
Profile Club/Association. **Ref: YH07851**

JOLLYES

Jollyes (Milton Keynes), Unit B Westcroft District Ctre, Tattenhoe St, Milton Keynes, **Buckinghamshire**, MK4 4DD, **ENGLAND**.
(T) 01908 503744 **(F)** 01908 507917
(E) info@jollyes.co.uk.
Profile Supplies. **Ref: YH07852**

JOLLYES

Jollyes (Ballymena), Unit 2 Albin Retail Pk, Larne Rd Link, Ballymena, **County Antrim**, BT42 3HA, **NORTHERN IRELAND**.
(T) 02825 641975 **(F)** 02825 641992
(E) info@jollyes.co.uk.
Contact/s
Shop Manager: Mr D Coates
Profile Supplies. **Ref: YH07853**

JOLLYES

Jollyes (Glengormley), Unit 11 Clenwell Rd, Glengormley, **County Antrim**, BT36 7RF, **NORTHERN IRELAND**.
(T) 02890 838772 **(F)** 02890 838917
(E) info@jollyes.co.uk.
Contact/s
Shop Manager: Mr J Beggs
Profile Supplies. **Ref: YH07854**

JOLLYES

Jollyes (Lisburn), Unit 2 Blaris Ind Est, Altona Rd, Lisburn, **County Antrim**, BT27 5QR, **NORTHERN IRELAND**.
(T) 028 92644704 **(F)** 028 92604714
(E) info@jollyes.co.uk.

Profile Supplies. **Ref: YH07855**

JOLLYES

Jollyes (Bangor), Unit 2, 1 Faulkner Rd, Bangor, **County Down**, BT20 3JS, **NORTHERN IRELAND**.
(T) 02891 273590 **(F)** 02891 273603
(E) info@jollyes.co.uk.
Contact/s
Shop Manager: Mr M Brand
Profile Supplies. **Ref: YH07856**

JOLLYES

Jollyes (Newry), Old Customs Post, Dublin Rd, Newry, **County Down**, BT35 8QP, **NORTHERN IRELAND**.
(T) 028 30250260 **(F)** 028 30252007
(E) info@jollyes.co.uk.
Profile Supplies. **Ref: YH07857**

JOLLYES

Jollyes (Eniskillen), Wellington Rd, Eniskillen, **County Fermanagh**, BT74 7HL, **NORTHERN IRELAND**.
(T) 028 66320350 **(F)** 028 66320351
(E) info@jollyes.co.uk.
Profile Supplies. **Ref: YH07858**

JOLLYES

Jollyes (Flint), Unit J Flintshire Retail Pk, Flint, **Flintshire**, CH6 5GB, **WALES**.
(T) 01352 730030 **(F)** 01352 761414
(E) info@jollyes.co.uk.
Profile Supplies. **Ref: YH07859**

JOLLYES

Jollyes (Bristol), Aldermoor Way, Longwell Green, **Gloucestershire (South)**, BS15 7DA, **ENGLAND**.
(T) 01179 602960 **(F)** 01179 602980
(E) info@jollyes.co.uk.
Profile Supplies. **Ref: YH07860**

JOLLYES

Jollyes (Waterlooville), Unit 5 Hambledon Pk Retail Pk, Waterlooville, Portsmouth, **Hampshire**, PO7 7UL, **ENGLAND**.
(T) 023 92261441 **(F)** 023 92230846
(E) info@jollyes.co.uk.
Contact/s
Shop Manager: Mr D Hyatt
Profile Supplies. **Ref: YH07861**

JOLLYES

Jollyes (Newport), Units 13-14 River Way Ind Est, Hurstake Rd, Newport, **Isle of Wight**, PO30 5BP, **ENGLAND**.
(T) 01983 533577 **(F)** 01983 533588
(E) info@jollyes.co.uk.
Profile Supplies. **Ref: YH07862**

JOLLYES

Jollyes (Coalville), Unit C2 Whitwick Retail Pk, Coalville, **Leicestershire**, LE67 3SA, **ENGLAND**.
(T) 01530 811667 **(F)** 01530 814943
(E) info@jollyes.co.uk.
Profile Supplies. **Ref: YH07863**

JOLLYES

Jollyes (Fallowfield), Unit F Fallowfield Shopping Ctre, Birchfields Rd, Fallowfield, Manchester, **Manchester (Greater)**, M14 6FS, **ENGLAND**.
(T) 0161 2480401 **(F)** 0161 2489076
(E) info@jollyes.co.uk.
Profile Supplies. **Ref: YH07864**

JOLLYES

Jollyes (Dereham), Yaxham Rd, East Dereham, **Norfolk**, NR19 1HB, **ENGLAND**.
(T) 01362 690802 **(F)** 01362 690803
(E) info@jollyes.co.uk.
Profile Supplies. **Ref: YH07865**

JOLLYES

Jollyes (Kettering), Unit 9 Trafalgar Rd, Kettering, **Northamptonshire**, NN16 8DB, **ENGLAND**.
(T) 01536 415065 **(F)** 01536 416040
(E) info@jollyes.co.uk.
Profile Supplies. **Ref: YH07866**

JOLLYES

Jollyes (Hailsham), Kennedy's Garden Ctre, Lower Dicker, Hailsham, **Sussex (East)**, BN27 2BJ, **ENGLAND**.
(T) 01323 846477 **(F)** 01323 845434
(E) info@jollyes.co.uk.
Profile Supplies. **Ref: YH07867**

JOLLYES

Jollyes (Newcastle), Unit 2A West Denton Retail Pk, West Denton Way, Newcastle-upon-Tyne, **Tyne and Wear**, NE5 2JZ, **ENGLAND**.
(T) 0191 2867589 **(F)** 0191 2867591
(E) info@jollyes.co.uk.
Contact/s
Shop Manager: Mr T Bennett
Profile Supplies. **Ref: YH07868**

JOLLYES

Jollyes (Stratford), Unit F2 Maybird Ctre, Birmingham Rd, Stratford-upon-Avon, **Warwickshire**, CV37 0AZ, **ENGLAND**.
(T) 01789 261889 **(F)** 01789 261887
(E) info@jollyes.co.uk.
Profile Supplies. **Ref: YH07869**

JOLLYES

Jollyes (Chippenham), Unit 2B Hathaway Retail Pk, Foundry Lane, Chippenham, **Wiltshire**, SN15 1JB, **ENGLAND**.
(T) 01249 448620 **(F)** 01249 445742
(E) info@jollyes.co.uk.
Profile Supplies. **Ref: YH07870**

JOLLYES

Jollyes (Doncaster), Wheatley Retail Pk, Wheatley Hall Rd, Doncaster, **Yorkshire (South)**, DN2 4PE, **ENGLAND**.
(T) 01302 340064 **(F)** 01302 340089
(E) info@jollyes.co.uk.
Profile Supplies. **Ref: YH07871**

JON WILLIAM STABLES

Jon William Stables, Netherstreet, Chippenham, **Wiltshire**, SN15 2GS, **ENGLAND**.
(T) 01380 850965.
Profile Transport/Horse Boxes. **Ref: YH07872**

JONES CHARITY SADDLERY

Jones Charity Saddlery & Country Clothing, Guildhall St, Grantham, **Lincolnshire**, NG31 6NJ, **ENGLAND**.
(T) 01476 568434.
Contact/s
Manager: Mr B Pattinson
Profile Riding Wear Retailer.
Also sell shooting and fishing accessories.
Opening Times
Sp: Open 09:00. Closed 17:00.
Su: Open 09:00. Closed 17:00.
Au: Open 09:00. Closed 17:00.
Wn: Open 09:00. Closed 17:00.
Closed Sundays **Ref: YH07873**

JONES STRAUGHAN, & MARSDEN

Jones Straughan, & Marsden, Veterinary Surgeons, 21 Birch Rd, Birkenhead, **Merseyside**, CH43 5UF, **ENGLAND**.
(T) 0151 6523284 **(F)** 0151 6537244.
Profile Medical Support. **Ref: YH07874**

JONES, A & M

A & M Jones, Min-Y-Fordd, Adfa, Newton, **Powys**, SY16 3DB, **WALES**.
(T) 01938 810563.
Contact/s
Owner: Mr M Jones
Profile Breeder. **Ref: YH07875**

JONES, A W

Mr A W Jones, 12 Tir-Y-Coed, Glanamman, Ammanford, **Carmarthenshire**, **WALES**..
Profile Trainer. **Ref: YH07876**

JONES, ALAN

Alan Jones, Fell Briggs Farm, New Marske, Redcar, **Cleveland**, TS11 8ED, **ENGLAND**.
(T) 01642 483014.
Profile Trainer. **Ref: YH07877**

JONES, B

B Jones, 64 The Drive, Whickham, Newcastle-upon-Tyne, **Tyne and Wear**, NE16 4RR, **ENGLAND**.
(T) 0191 4881453.
Profile Farrier. **Ref: YH07878**

JONES, BRIAN

Brian Jones RSS, 2 Glanford, Hanley Swan, Malvern, **Worcestershire**, WR8 0DF, **ENGLAND**.
(T) 01684 310773.
Profile Farrier. **Ref: YH07879**

JONES, C

Mr & Mrs C Jones, Gellihen Farm, Talgarreg, Llandysul, **Carmarthenshire**, SA44 4HE, **WALES**.
(T) 01545 55602.
Profile Breeder. **Ref: YH07880**

JONES, C M

Mrs C M Jones, Friars Parks Farm, Mollington, Chester, **Cheshire**, **ENGLAND**.
(T) 01244 851333.
Profile Breeder. **Ref: YH07881**

JONES, CARL (MAJOR)

Major Carl Jones FWCF, 5 Ingle Court, Woolsthorpe By Colsterworth, Grantham, **Lincolnshire**, NG33 5PB, **ENGLAND**.
(T) 01476 861289.
Profile Farrier. **Ref: YH07882**

JONES, COLIN

Colin Jones, 24 New St, Chase Trce, Burntwood, **Staffordshire**, WS7 8BS, **ENGLAND**.
(T) 01543 300361 **(F)** 01543 300361. **Ref: YH07883**

JONES, D & R

D & R Jones, Gwynfa, Bethania, Llanon, **Ceredigion**, SY23 5NJ, **WALES**.
(T) 01974 272306.
Profile Breeder. **Ref: YH07884**

JONES, D A G

D A G Jones, Star Forge, Uplands, Carmarthen, **Carmarthenshire**, SA32 8EA, **WALES**.
(T) 01267 267841 **(F)** 01267 267313.
Contact/s
Partner: Mr D Jones
Profile Blacksmith. **Ref: YH07885**

JONES, D J

D J Jones, Duckhurst Farm Equestrian Ctre, Clapper Lane, Staplehurst, **Kent**, TN12 0JW, **ENGLAND**.
(T) 01580 891057.
Profile Breeder. **Ref: YH07886**

JONES, D T

Mrs D T Jones, Brynffynnon, Penegoes, Machynlleth, **Powys**, **WALES**.
(T) 01654 702873.
Profile Breeder. **Ref: YH07887**

JONES, DAVID

David Jones, 2 Church Cl, Ashwell, Oakham, **Rutland**, LE15 7LP, **ENGLAND**.
(T) 01572 723558 **(F)** 01572 723558
(M) 07970 405344.
Profile Medical Support. **Ref: YH07888**

JONES, DAVID D

David D Jones, 20 Laity Rd, Troon, Camborne, **Cornwall**, TR14 9EL, **ENGLAND**.
(T) 01209 716611.
Contact/s
Owner: Mr D Jones
Profile Farrier. **Ref: YH07889**

JONES, DAVID H

David H Jones DWCF BII, 28 Hanson Rd, Andover, **Hampshire**, SP10 3HL, **ENGLAND**.
(M) 07785 706098.
Profile Farrier. **Ref: YH07890**

JONES, DAVID THOMAS

David Thomas Jones, The Vardo, Garreg Boeth, Rhydymwyn, Mold, **Flintshire**, CH7 5HP, **WALES**.
(T) 01352 740788.
Profile Farrier. **Ref: YH07891**

JONES, DAWN

Dawn Jones, 2 Ye Olde Hse, Sleapshyde, Smallford, St. Albans, **Hertfordshire**, AL4 0SE, **ENGLAND**.
(T) 01727 824467
Affiliated Bodies NAAT.
Contact/s
Physiotherapist: Dawn Jones **(Q)** BSc
Profile Medical Support.
Physiotherapist for horses & dogs. **Ref: YH07892**

JONES, DEREK H

Derek H Jones, Garth Paddocks, Efail Isaf, Pontypridd, **Rhondda Cynon Taff**, CF38 1SN, **WALES**.
(T) 01443 202515.
Contact/s
Owner: Mr D Jones
Profile Trainer. **Ref: YH07893**

JONES, DYFED W

Dyfed W Jones DWCF, Hendre, Ffordd Eglwyswen, Denbigh, **Conwy**, LL16 4ER, **WALES**.
(T) 01745 813426.
Profile Farrier. **Ref: YH07894**

JONES, E A & C

E A & Mrs C Jones, Bucks Farm Stud, Bucks Farm, Shorewell, Newport, **Isle of Wight**, PO30 3LP, **ENGLAND**.
(T) 01983 551206 **(F)** 01983 551206.

Profile Breeder, Stable/Livery. Ref: YH07895

JONES, EDWARD GLYN

Edward Glyn Jones RSS, Brynafon Bach, Cemaes, Machynlleth, **Powys**, SY20 8LE, **WALES**.
(T) 01650 511218.
Profile Farrier. Ref: YH07896

JONES, EMMA-JANE

Emma-Jane Jones, The Quest, Unstone Lane, Old Whittington, Chesterfield, **Derbyshire**, S41 9QS, **ENGLAND**.
(T) 01246 450528.
Profile Trainer. Ref: YH07897

JONES, ERIC

Mr Eric Jones, Willowbrook, Ashwell, Mere, **Wiltshire**, BA12 6AY, **ENGLAND**.
(T) 01747 860625 (F) 01747 860625. Ref: YH07898

JONES, G C

G C Jones, 9 Chestnut Gardens, Stamford, **Lincolnshire**, PE9 2JY, **ENGLAND**.
(T) 01780 754635.
Contact/s
Owner: Mr G Jones Ref: YH07899

JONES, G E

Mr G E Jones, Lluestnewydd, Bettws, Lampeter, **Ceredigion**, SA48 8PB, **WALES**.
(T) 01570 493261.
Profile Supplies. Ref: YH07900

JONES, G M

G M Jones, Coedygof, Llanddew Brefi, Tregaron, **Ceredigion**, SY25 6PB, **WALES**.
(T) 01570 45245.
Profile Breeder. Ref: YH07901

JONES, G W

Mr & Mrs G W Jones, Nerwyn Rosettes, 1 Bod Hyfryd, Dolwen, Abergele, **Conwy**, LL22 8NY, **WALES**.
(T) 01492 680234 (F) 01492 680234
(E) g.wyn.jones@lineone.net.
Profile Breeder. Ref: YH07902

JONES, H B

H B Jones, The Forge, Lower Machen, **Newport**, NP10 8UU, **WALES**.
(T) 01633 440226.
Profile Farrier. Ref: YH07903

JONES, H G

H G Jones, Blaen-Y-Cwm, Llanbrynmair, **Powys**, SY19 7EA, **WALES**.
(T) 01650 521600.
Profile Breeder. Ref: YH07904

JONES, I G

I G Jones, Pandy Smithy, Bontuchel, Ruthin, **Denbighshire**, LL15 2DG, **WALES**.
(T) 01824 710223.
Profile Farrier. Ref: YH07905

JONES, J

Mr & Mrs J Jones, Hendreforion, L'anllyfni, Penygroes, Caernarfon, **Gwynedd**, **WALES**..
Profile Breeder. Ref: YH07906

JONES, J D

J D Jones, Corner Cottage, Slipton Lane, Slipton, Kettering, **Northamptonshire**, NN14 3AR, **ENGLAND**.
(T) 01832 732532.
Contact/s
Owner: Mrs J Jones
Profile Trainer. Ref: YH07907

JONES, J P

J P Jones, Brynysgawen Farm, Maesycwmmer, Hengoed, **Caerphilly**, CF82 7SN, **WALES**.
(T) 01495 224292.
Contact/s
Owner: Mrs J Jones
Profile Breeder. Yr. Est: 1976 Ref: YH07908

JONES, K M

Mr K M Jones, Bodernog, Llanddeusant, Holyhead, **Isle of Anglesey**, LL65 4AY, **WALES**.
(T) 01407 730210.
Profile Breeder. Ref: YH07909

JONES, KAREN

Karen Jones, Blaenllyn, Llangolman, Clunderwen, **Pembrokeshire**, SA66 7XR, **WALES**.
(T) 01437 532446. Ref: YH07910

JONES, KARL D

Karl D Jones DWCF, 3 Van Gogh Cl, Heathhays, Cannock, **Staffordshire**, WS11 2GP, **ENGLAND**.
(T) 01543 274177.
Profile Farrier. Ref: YH07911

JONES, KENNETH

Kenneth Jones, Tyr Gof, Rydymyuin Rd, Mold, **Flintshire**, CH7 5DE, **WALES**.
(T) 01352 740046.
Profile Farrier. Ref: YH07912

JONES, M

M Jones, Llechen Uchaf, Llechwedd, **Conwy**, LL32 8LX, **WALES**.
(T) 01492 592451.
Contact/s
Owner: Mr M Jones Ref: YH07913

JONES, M A

Mrs M A Jones, Felstead Court, Folly Rd, Lambourn, Hungerford, **Berkshire**, RG17 8QE, **ENGLAND**.
(T) 01488 72409 (F) 01488 72409
(M) 07798 641478.
Profile Trainer. Ref: YH07914

JONES, M P

Mr M P Jones, Hill Farm, Pontrilas, **Herefordshire**, HR2 0BL, **ENGLAND**.
(T) 01981 240406
(M) 07882 5265742.
Profile Farrier. Ref: YH07915

JONES, MARC T

Marc T Jones DWCF Hons, The Forge, 16 Upper Colliers Row, Ynysfach, Merthyr Tydfil, **Glamorgan (Vale of)**, CF48 1UN, **WALES**.
(T) 01685 373618.
Profile Farrier. Ref: YH07916

JONES, MARK A

Mark A Jones DWCF, 1 Oaklands Pl, Dorstone, **Herefordshire**, HR3 6AR, **ENGLAND**.
(T) 01981 550442.
Profile Farrier. Ref: YH07917

JONES, MATTHEW J

Matthew J Jones DWCF, 11 Hergest Rd, Kington, **Herefordshire**, HR5 3EQ, **ENGLAND**.
(T) 01544 230766.
Profile Farrier. Ref: YH07918

JONES, MERRITA

Merrita Jones, Stork Hse, Baydon Rd, Lambourn, Hungerford, **Berkshire**, RG17 8NU, **ENGLAND**.
(T) 01488 72409 (F) 01488 72409.
Contact/s
Partner: Mr L Jones
Profile Trainer. Ref: YH07919

JONES, N A

N A Jones, Conygar, Cusop, Hay-on-Wye, Hereford, **Herefordshire**, HR3 5RD, **ENGLAND**.
(T) 01497 820398.
Profile Breeder. Ref: YH07920

JONES, P J

P J Jones, Homeword Cottage, Vicarage Lane, Clarkes Rd, North Killingholme, **Lincolnshire**, DN40 3JL, **ENGLAND**.
(T) 01469 541458.
Profile Farrier. Ref: YH07921

JONES, P T

P T Jones, Shalimar, Victoria, Roche, St Austell, **Cornwall**, PL26 8LT, **ENGLAND**.
(T) 01726 890342.
Profile Transport/Horse Boxes. Ref: YH07922

JONES, R F

Mr R F Jones DWCF, Towers Farm, Landon Rd North, Poynton, Stockport, **Manchester (Greater)**, SK12 1BY, **ENGLAND**.
(T) 01625 850793
(M) 07831 456002.
Profile Farrier. Ref: YH07923

JONES, R M

R M Jones (Hay-on-Wye), Farmcentre, Oxford Rd, Hay-on-Wye, **Herefordshire**, HR3 5AJ, **ENGLAND**.
(T) 01497 820410 (F) 01497 821282
(E) info@rmjones.com.
Profile Saddlery Retailer. Ref: YH07924

JONES, R M

R M Jones (Hereford), The Farm Ctre, Bay LB12, Cattle Market, **Herefordshire**, HR4 9HX, **ENGLAND**.
(T) 01432 265451 (F) 01432 265451.
Profile Saddlery Retailer. Ref: YH07925

JONES, R M

R M Jones (Abergavenny), Farm Ctre, Cattle Market, Park Rd, Abergavenny, **Monmouthshire**, NP7 5PR, **WALES**.
(T) 01873 858300 (F) 01873 858300.
Profile Saddlery Retailer. Ref: YH07926

JONES, R W

R W Jones, Boyden End, Wickhambrook, Newmarket, **Suffolk**, CB8 8XX, **ENGLAND**.
(T) 01440 820342 (F) 01440 820958.
Contact/s
Owner: Mr B Jones
Profile Trainer. Ref: YH07927

JONES, ROBIN L

Robin L Jones, Thrifts Hall Farm, Thrifts Hill, Theydon Bois, Epping, **Essex**, CM16 7NL, **ENGLAND**.
(T) 01992 813365 (F) 01992 813365.
Contact/s
Owner: Mr R Jones Ref: YH07928

JONES, ROGER M L

Roger M L Jones RSS, The Oaks, Norleywood, Lymington, **Hampshire**, SO41 5RT, **ENGLAND**.
(T) 01590 626256.
Profile Farrier. Ref: YH07929

JONES, S & T

S & T Jones, 25 Hales Rd, Cheltenham, **Gloucestershire**, GL52 6SL, **ENGLAND**.
(T) 01242 573911.
Profile Breeder. Ref: YH07930

JONES, S L

S L Jones, Keepers Lodge, Cilybebyll, Pontardawe, Swansea, **Swansea**, SA8 3JS, **WALES**.
(T) 01792 869763. Ref: YH07931

JONES, SIMON B

Simon B Jones DWCF, Coleham Green Oast, Woodchurch, Ashford, **Kent**, TN26 3PP, **ENGLAND**.
(T) 01233 733079.
Profile Farrier. Ref: YH07932

JONES, SUZANNE

Suzanne Jones, 7 Summerside, Rawnsley, Cannock, **Staffordshire**, WS12 5QG, **ENGLAND**.
(T) 01543 274124 (F) 01543 300361
(M) 07798 605167.
Contact/s
Photographer: Suzanne Jones Ref: YH07933

JONES, T M

Mr T M Jones, Brook Farm, Albury, Guildford, **Surrey**, GU5 9DJ, **ENGLAND**.
(T) 01483 202604 (F) 01483 202604
(E) buck@brookfarmalbury.freeserve.co.uk.
Profile Trainer. Ref: YH07934

JONES, W T

Mr W T Jones, Caerberllan, Llanfihangel-Y-Pennant, Tywyn, **Gwynedd**, LL36 9TW, **WALES**.
(T) 01654 782243.
Profile Breeder. Ref: YH07935

JONES, WATSON

Watson Jones, Dale St, Bilston, **Midlands (West)**, WV14 7LE, **ENGLAND**.
(T) 01902 495662 (F) 01902 354953.
Profile Transport/Horse Boxes. Ref: YH07936

JOPLING SELF TOW HIRE

Jopling Self Tow Hire, Mill Riggs Farm, Mill Riggs, Stokesley, Middlesbrough, **Cleveland**, TS9 5HQ, **ENGLAND**.
(T) 01642 711711.
Contact/s
Owner: Mr T Jopling
Profile Transport/Horse Boxes. Ref: YH07937

JORDAN, FRANK T J

Frank T J Jordan, Gallop View, Risbury, Leominster, **Herefordshire**, HR6 0NQ, **ENGLAND**.
(T) 01568 760281 (F) 01568 760281.
Contact/s
Partner: Mr T Jordan
Profile Trainer. Ref: YH07938

JORDAN, PHILIP

Philip Jordan DWCF, 463 Bury Old Rd, Prestwich, Manchester, **Manchester (Greater)**, M25 5WJ, **ENGLAND**.
(T) 0161 7987831.
Profile Farrier. Ref: YH07939

JORDAN, R & D

R & D Jordan, New Ridgeway Farm, Crown Lane, Wychbold, Droitwich, **Worcestershire**, WR9 0BX, **ENGLAND**.
(T) 01527 861844.
Profile Breeder. **Ref: YH07940**

JOSEPH A GORDON & SON

Joseph A Gordon & Son, 551-553 Lisburn Rd, Belfast, **County Antrim**, BT9 7GQ, **NORTHERN IRELAND**.
(T) 028 90661401 **(F)** 028 90663863.
Contact/s
Manager: Ms J Stewart **Ref: YH07941**

JOSEPH BAILEY & SONS

Joseph Bailey & Sons, Durham Rd, East Rainton, Houghton Le Spring, **Tyne and Wear**, DH5 9QT, **ENGLAND**.
(T) 0191 5842703 **(F)** 0191 5842703.
Profile Transport/Horse Boxes. **Ref: YH07942**

JOSEPH HOWARD & SON

Joseph Howard & Son, Park Hill, Toppings Farm, Cabus, Garstang, Preston, **Lancashire**, **ENGLAND**.
(T) 01524 792094.
Contact/s
Owner: Mr J Howard
Profile Breeder. Yr. Est: 1900 **Ref: YH07943**

JOSEPH MURPHY

Joseph Murphy DWCF, 116 East Lancs Rd, Lowton, Warrington, **Cheshire**, WA3 1LE, **ENGLAND**.
(T) 01942 671656.
Profile Farrier. **Ref: YH07944**

JOSEPH, J

Mr J Joseph, Cherry Tree Farm, Coleshill, Amersham, **Buckinghamshire**, HP7 0LX, **ENGLAND**.
(T) 01494 722239 **(F)** 01494 432992.
Profile Supplies. **Ref: YH07945**

JOSHUA TETLEY

Joshua Tetley Ltd, The Brewery, Hunslet, **Yorkshire (West)**, LS1 1QG, **ENGLAND**.
(T) 0113 2435282.
Profile Breeder. **Ref: YH07946**

JOSLIN, EDWARD JOHN

Edward John Joslin, 18 Dooley Rd, Halstead, **Essex**, CO9 1JW, **ENGLAND**.
(T) 01787 473110.
Profile Farrier. **Ref: YH07947**

JOUSTING & ASSOCIATED SKILLS

International Jousting Association, C/O Post Office Cottage, Cowesby Village, Thirsk, **Yorkshire (North)**, YO7 2JJ, **ENGLAND**.
(T) 01845 537431
Affiliated Bodies BHS.
Contact/s
Coach: Mr F Beattie
Profile Arena, Club/Association, Trainer.
The IJA is a non profit organisation without prejudice to professional or voluntary groups at home and/or overseas. Operates on a self financing basis. Jousting displays and tournaments at home and overseas take place. Competition results authorised. No.Staff: 4
Yr. Est: 1986 C.Size: 5 Acres **Ref: YH07948**

JOUSTING CONSULTANTS

Jousting Consultants, 'Knightschool', Tapeley Pk, Bideford, **Devon**, EX39 4NT, **ENGLAND**.
(T) 01271 861200.
Profile Club/Association. **Ref: YH07949**

JOYCE M A

Joyce M A, Tack-Lynn Hse, Ballinderry, Mullingar, **County Westmeath**, **IRELAND**.
(T) 044 42206.
Profile Supplies. **Ref: YH07950**

JOYCE, CHRISTOPHER G

Christopher G Joyce DWCF, 8 Bainbridge Rd, Wigston, **Leicestershire**, LE18 3YH, **ENGLAND**.
(M) 07702 507595.
Profile Farrier. **Ref: YH07951**

JOYDENS BRIDLEWAY GRP

Joydens Bridleway Group, C/O Vicarage Rd, Bexley, **Kent**, DA5 2AW, **ENGLAND**.
(T) 01322 553508
(E) oldbex@cs.com.
Profile Club/Association. **Ref: YH07952**

JOYDENS RIDING CLUB

Joydens Riding Club, Vicarage Rd, Bexley, **Kent**, DA5 2AW, **ENGLAND**.
(T) 01322 525391.
Profile Club/Association, Riding Club. **Ref: YH07953**

JOYSONS HILL

Joysons Hill, Church Rd, Whyteleafe, **Surrey**, CR3 0AR, **ENGLAND**.
(T) 020 86680294 **(F)** 020 86680294.
Contact/s
Partner: Mrs A Bolton
Profile Stable/Livery. **Ref: YH07954**

J-SIX S C RIDING SCHOOL

J-Six S C Riding School, Thorpe Lane, Tingley, Wakefield, **Yorkshire (West)**, WF3 1QY, **ENGLAND**.
(T) 0113 2520429.
Profile Riding School. **Ref: YH07955**

JUCKES, R T

R T Juckes, Bank Lane, Abberley, Worcester, **Worcestershire**, WR6 6BQ, **ENGLAND**.
(T) 01299 896471.
Profile Trainer. **Ref: YH07956**

JUDDMONTE FARMS

Juddmonte Farms, Warren Row, Wargrave On Thames, **Berkshire**, RG10 8QE, **ENGLAND**.
(T) 01628 826543 **(F)** 01628 823904.
Profile Breeder. **Ref: YH07957**

JUDDPURS SADDLERY

Juddpurs Saddlery, 1-5 Hungate, Beccles, **Suffolk**, NR34 9TT, **ENGLAND**.
(T) 01502 711379 **(F)** 01502 711317.
Contact/s
Owner: Mr R Judd **Ref: YH07958**

JUDE

'Jude' Equestrian Portraits, 74 Kew Green, Richmond, **Surrey**, TW9 3AP, **ENGLAND**.
(T) 020 89403193 **(F)** 00335 45396899.
Contact/s
Owner: Julie 'Jude' Deutsch **(T)** 00335 45396899
Profile Artist.
Opening Times
Telephone for an appointment **Ref: YH07959**

JUGGINS, PHILIP J

Philip J Juggins RSS, 2 Rose Cottage, Naunton, Cheltenham, **Gloucestershire**, GL54 3AF, **ENGLAND**.
(T) 01451 850817.
Profile Farrier. **Ref: YH07960**

JUHL, G

G Juhl, Mutlow Farm Hse, Wendens Ambo, Saffron Walden, **Essex**, CB11 4JZ, **ENGLAND**.
(T) 01799 540434.
Contact/s
Owner: Mrs G Juhl
Profile Riding School.
Opening Times
Opening Times: Mon, Tues, Thurs - Sat 08:00, Closing Times: Mon, Tues, Thurs - Sat 18:00 **Ref: YH07961**

JULIA FIELDEN RACING

Julia Fielden Racing, Chapel St, Exning, Newmarket, **Suffolk**, CB8 7HA, **ENGLAND**.
(T) 01638 577470
(W) www.newmarketracehorsetrainers.co.uk
Affiliated Bodies Newmarket Trainers Fed.
Contact/s
Trainer: Ms J Fielden
Profile Trainer. **Ref: YH07962**

JULIETTE WETTERN SADDLER

Juliette Wettern Saddler & Harness Maker, Woodlands View, Old Lane Gardens, Cobham, **Surrey**, KT11 1NN, **ENGLAND**.
(T) 01483 282310.
Profile Specialise in Driving Harnesses.
Ref: YH07963

JULIP HORSES

Julip Horses Ltd, The Granary, Melbury Osmond, Dorchester, **Dorset**, DT2 0LX, **ENGLAND**.
(T) 01935 873771 **(F)** 01935 873772
(E) annabel@julip.freeserve.co.uk
(W) www.juliphorses.com.
Profile Supplies. **Ref: YH07964**

JUMP FOR JOY SHOWJUMPS

Jump for Joy Showjumps, Hill View, 25 Bridport Rd, Drimpton, Beaminster, **Dorset**, DT8 3RD, **ENGLAND**.
(T) 01308 868123.
Profile Supplies. **Ref: YH07965**

JUMPERS HORSELINE

Jumpers Horseline, Little Pk, Breach Lane, Wootton Bassett, **Wiltshire**, SN4 7QW, **ENGLAND**.
(T) 01793 850508 **(F)** 01793 848580
(E) sales@jumpershorseline.com.
Profile Saddlery Retailer. **Ref: YH07966**

JUMPS

Jumps Equestrian Centre, East Side Farm, Carluke, **Lanarkshire (South)**, ML8 4QY, **SCOTLAND**.
(T) 01555 773206 **(F)** 01555 772392
(E) jumps@compuserve.com.
Contact/s
For Bookings: Mrs J Freeman **(T)** 01555 772392
Profile Equestrian Centre, Riding School, Stable/Livery. RDA and show centre.
7 arenas 2 x 40m x 20m sand x 2 floodlit. 80m x 80m grass, 80m x 60m grass, 30m x 15m sand, show jumping 100m x 90m BSJ jump, indoor school (for hire) 38m x 17m. Full grass, part and DIY livery costs between £20.00 and £60.00 per week. No.Staff: 6
Yr. Est: 1991 C.Size: 40 Acres
Opening Times
Sp: Open Mon - Sun 08:30. Closed Mon - Fri 20:30, Sat, Sun 18:00.
Su: Open Mon - Sun 08:30. Closed Mon - Fri 20:30, Sat, Sun 18:00.
Au: Open Mon - Sun 08:30. Closed Mon - Fri 20:30, Sat, Sun 18:00.
Wn: Open Mon - Sun 08:30. Closed Mon - Fri 20:30, Sat, Sun 18:00. **Ref: YH07967**

JUMPS EQUESTRIAN CTRE

Jumps Equestrian Centre, East Side Farm, Carluke, **Lanarkshire (South)**, ML8 4QY, **SCOTLAND**.
(T) 01555 772392 **(F)** 01555 772392. **Ref: YH07968**

JUMPS FOR JOY

N U Direct, Unit 2, Knowle Fields Ind Est, Alcester Rd, Inkberrow, Worcester, **Worcestershire**, WR7 4HR, **ENGLAND**.
(T) 01386 793339 **(F)** 01386 792030.
Contact/s
Owner: Mr N Underwood
Profile Supplies. Build Jumps. **Ref: YH07969**

JUPP, BARBARA

Barbara Jupp, 5 Beverstone Cl, South Cerney, Cirencester, **Gloucestershire**, GL7 5XT, **ENGLAND**.
(T) 01285 861185.
Contact/s
Instructor: Mrs B Jupp
Profile Trainer. **Ref: YH07970**

JURBY STUD

Jurby Stud, Loughan, Jurby, **Isle of Man**, IM7 3EZ, **ENGLAND**.
(T) 01624 897658.
Profile Breeder. **Ref: YH07971**

JUST AS GOOD

Just As Good, High Cleaves, Sutton, Thirsk, **Yorkshire (North)**, YO7 2QD, **ENGLAND**.
(T) 01845 597612 **(F)** 01845 597612.
Contact/s
Owner: Mrs S Haggas
Profile Supplies. **Ref: YH07972**

JUST DANDY

Just Dandy Horse & Carriage Services, Weddings & Special Occassions, 4A Turks Hall Pl, The Street, Upper Halling, Rochester, **Kent**, ME2 1HU, **ENGLAND**.
(T) 01634 247602
Affiliated Bodies BDS.
Contact/s
Owner: Miss S Port
Profile Horse & Carriage Services .
Horse & carriages available for hire for weddings, funerals and special occasions. Have worked in many different areas, including carnivals, TV promotions, weddings, funerals and London theatre work. Will also dress in costume for themes. No.Staff: 1
Yr. Est: 1999 **Ref: YH07973**

JUST JODS

Just Jods, Rutland Mill, Tootall St, Wakefield, **Yorkshire (West)**, WF1 5JR, **ENGLAND**.
(T) 07000 781326.
Profile Supplies. **Ref: YH07974**

JUST LEATHER

Just Leather, 15 The Hopmarket, Worcester, **Worcestershire**, WR1 1DL, **ENGLAND**.
(T) 01905 612612.

Contact/s
Owner: Mr H Hartwright
Profile Saddlery Retailer. Ref: YH07975

JUST REWARDS

Just Rewards, The Lodge, Stockland, Bridgwater, **Somerset**, TA5 2QB, **ENGLAND**.
(T) 01278 652884.
Contact/s
General Manager: Mrs H Stickley
Profile Supplies. No.Staff: 2 Yr. Est: 2000
Ref: YH07976

JUST THE BIT

Just The Bit, Woodfalls Ind Est, Unit 9 Gravelly Ways, Laddingford, Maidstone, **Kent**, ME18 6DA, **ENGLAND**.
(T) 01622 871949.
Contact/s
Owner: Mrs L Turner
Profile Saddlery Retailer. Ref: YH07977

JUST TOGS

Just Togs Ltd, Birchalls Ind Est, Green Lane, Birchills, Walsall, **Midlands (West)**, WS2 8LE, **ENGLAND**.
(T) 01922 616777 **(F)** 01922 622921.
Profile Riding Wear Wholesaler. Ref: YH07978

K & B TACK SHOPS

K & B Tack Shops, 91 St John St, Bridlington, **Yorkshire (East)**, YO16 4XE, **ENGLAND**.
(T) 01262 673086.
Profile Saddlery Retailer. Ref: YH07979

K & K PET SHOPS

K & K Pet Shops, Market Sq, Toddington, Dunstable, **Bedfordshire**, LU5 6BS, **ENGLAND**.
(T) 01525 872003.
Profile Saddlery Retailer. Ref: YH07980

K & T FOOTWEAR

K & T Footwear, 7 Clifton Gr, Kettering, **Northamptonshire**, NN15 7NB, **ENGLAND**.
(T) 01536 414582.
Profile Riding Wear Retailer.
Mail order, retail and wholesale options. Telephone for further information Yr. Est: 1963 Ref: YH07981

K 9 PET FOODS

K 9 Pet Foods, Station Rd, Framlingham, **Suffolk**, IP13 9EE, **ENGLAND**.
(T) 01728 621054 **(F)** 01728 621122.
Profile Feed Merchant. Ref: YH07982

K B M F AUDIO

K B M F Audio Ltd, Hillside Cottage, Llanvaches, **Newport**, NP26 3AZ, **WALES**.
(T) 01633 400555 **(F)** 01633 400555.
Profile Supplies. Ref: YH07983

K C EQUESTRIAN

K C Equestrian Ltd, Unit 1 Lowmoor Ind Est, Tonedale, Wellington, **Somerset**, TA21 0AZ, **ENGLAND**.
(T) 01823 662800 **(F)** 01823 662800.
Profile Supplies. Ref: YH07984

K D SADDLERY

K D Saddlery, Lodge Rd, Hockley, Birmingham, **Midlands (West)**, B18 5QY, **ENGLAND**.
(T) 0121 5549354 **(F)** 0121 5549354.
Contact/s
Owner: Mrs B Kumari Ref: YH07985

K E S POWER & LIGHT

K E S Power & Light Ltd, Stanton Rd, Regents Park, **Hampshire**, SO15 4HU, **ENGLAND**.
(T) 023 80704703 **(F)** 023 80701430.
Profile Club/Association. Ref: YH07986

K G L C FEEDS

K G L C Feeds, Smart's Ctre, Main Rd (A25), Sundridge, **Kent**, TN14 6ED, **ENGLAND**.
(T) 01959 564165 **(F)** 01959 563796.
Profile Supplies. Ref: YH07987

K LITTLEWORTH & SON

K Littleworth & Son, Red Hse, Belchford, Horncastle, **Lincolnshire**, LN9 6LL, **ENGLAND**.
(T) 01507 533242 **(F)** 01507 533242.
Contact/s
Owner: Mr J Littleworth
Profile Transport/Horse Boxes. Ref: YH07988

K M F QUALITY BRIDLES

K M F Quality Bridles, 4A Ablewell St, Walsall, **Midlands (West)**, WS1 2EQ, **ENGLAND**.
(T) 01922 621773 **(F)** 01922 621773.
Contact/s
Owner: Mr K Foster Ref: YH07989

K P COMMERCIALS

K P Commercials, The Levels, Byngs Heath, Astley, Shrewsbury, **Shropshire**, SY4 4BY, **ENGLAND**.
(T) 01939 251140.
Contact/s
Owner: Mr K Poole
Profile Transport/Horse Boxes. Ref: YH07990

K S CUNDELL & PARTNERS

K S Cundell & Partners, Roden Hse, Wallingford Rd, Compton, Newbury, **Berkshire**, RG20 6QR, **ENGLAND**.
(T) 01635 578267 **(F)** 01635 578267.
Contact/s
Senior Partner: Mr K Cundell
Profile Trainer. Ref: YH07991

K T FORGE

K T Forge Ltd, Unit 14-15 Springfield Cl/Barbot Hall Ind E, Mangham Way, Rotherham, **Yorkshire (South)**, S61 4RL, **ENGLAND**.
(T) 01709 829340.
Profile Blacksmith. Ref: YH07992

K Y P LEATHER

K Y P Leather, 33 Townfield Rd, Mobberley, **Cheshire**, WA16 7HG, **ENGLAND**.
(T) 01565 872971.
Profile Supplies. Ref: YH07993

KADAN STUD

Kadan Stud, 175 Old Rd, Thornton, Bradford, **Yorkshire (West)**, BD13 3DR, **ENGLAND**.
(T) 01294 831800 **(F)** 01274 831800
(E) sundowners@amserve.com.
Contact/s
Owner: Miss S Beaumont
Profile Breeder.
Opening Times
Telephone for further information Ref: YH07994

KANLET

Kanlet Ltd, Slade Barn Farm, Winchcombe, Cheltenham, **Gloucestershire**, GL54 5AX, **ENGLAND**.
(T) 01242 603915.
Profile Trainer. Ref: YH07995

KARL BUTLER BUSINESS

Karl Butler Business, 55 Scarborough Rd, Norton, Malton, **Yorkshire (North)**, YO17 8AA, **ENGLAND**.
(T) 01653 694213.
Profile Supplies. Ref: YH07996

KATANYA PETS

Katanya Pets, Katanya, Magdalene Farm, Woodland, Bishop Auckland, **County Durham**, DL13 5RQ, **ENGLAND**.
(T) 01388 710427.
Contact/s
Owner: Mrs C Wallace
Profile Saddlery Retailer. Ref: YH07997

KATIE WHETREN

Katie Whetren Saddlery Repairs, Calmore Cottage, Paulettes Lane, Calmore, Totton, **Hampshire**, SO40 2RS, **ENGLAND**.
(T) 023 80814394.
Profile Supplies. Ref: YH07998

KAUNTZE MICHAEL

Kauntze Michael, Bullstown, Ashbourne, **County Meath**, **IRELAND**.
(T) 01 8350440 **(F)** 01 8351306.
Profile Supplies. Ref: YH07999

KAVANAGH, JOHN S

John S Kavanagh DWCF, 24 Sandringham Way, Frimley Green, Camberley, **Surrey**, GU16 5XY, **ENGLAND**.
(T) 01252 837602.
Profile Farrier. Ref: YH08000

KAVANAGH, MARY & PETER

Mary & Peter Kavanagh, Neilstown Cottage, Boharmeen, **County Meath**, **IRELAND**.
(T) 046 27259.
Profile Supplies. Ref: YH08001

KAY ENGINEERING

Kay Engineering, Butlerfield Ind Est, Bonnyrigg, **Lothian (Mid)**, EH19 3JQ, **SCOTLAND**.
(T) 01875 822402 **(F)** 01875 820167.
Contact/s
Owner: Mr E Kay
Profile Blacksmith. Ref: YH08002

KAY TRAILERS

Kay Trailers, 27 Stirling Rd, Milnathort, Kinross, **Perth and Kinross**, KY13 9XS, **SCOTLAND**.
(T) 01577 862741.
Profile Transport/Horse Boxes. Ref: YH08003

KAY, D

D Kay, 9 The Square, Bankside Lane, Bacup, **Lancashire**, OL13 8HR, **ENGLAND**.
(T) 01706 876846.
Profile Farrier. Ref: YH08004

KAY, RAYMOND JAMES

Raymond James Kay RSS, Old Chapel Hse Farm, Commons Lane, Balderstone, Blackburn, **Lancashire**, BB2 7LL, **ENGLAND**.
(T) 01254 813095.
Profile Farrier. Ref: YH08005

KAYE, ANTHONY S

Anthony S Kaye, Lower Greenhill Barn, Kelbrook Rd, Salterforth, Barnoldswick, **Lancashire**, BB18 5TG, **ENGLAND**.
(T) 01282 850532.
Profile Farrier. Ref: YH08006

KAYE, GILES

Giles Kaye (Rhinefield), 45 Church Rd, Three Legged Cross, Wimborne, **Dorset**, BH21 6RQ, **ENGLAND**.
(T) 01202 829525.
Profile Trainer. Ref: YH08007

KAYE, HARVEY STUART

Harvey Stuart Kaye, Breworth Fold, Brindle, Chorley, **Lancashire**, PR6 8NZ, **ENGLAND**.
(T) 01254 853891.
Profile Farrier. Ref: YH08008

KAYE, HILARY LOIS

Hilary Lois Kaye DWCF, Cwmcynwal, Llandovery, **Carmarthenshire**, SA19 8BS, **WALES**.
(T) 01558 650358.
Profile Farrier. Ref: YH08009

KAYES ANIMAL FEEDS

Kayes Animal Feeds, Pear Tree Works, Woodside Rd, Wyke, **Yorkshire (West)**, BD12 8HT, **ENGLAND**.
(T) 01274 607848.
Profile Supplies. Ref: YH08010

KAYTE FARM EQUESTRIAN LIVERY

Kayte Farm Equestrian Livery, 4 Kayte Farm, Southam Lane, Southam, Cheltenham, **Gloucestershire**, GL52 3PE, **ENGLAND**.
(T) 01242 677451.
Profile Stable/Livery. Ref: YH08011

KAZMIRA

Kazmira Arabians & Miniature Horses, Park Farm Hse, Tunbeck Rd, Wortwell, Harleston, **Suffolk**, IP20 0HP, **ENGLAND**.
(T) 01986 788459 **(F)** 01986 788459.
Profile Breeder. Ref: YH08012

KBIS

KBIS Ltd, Cullimore Hse, Peasemore, Newbury, **Berkshire**, RG20 7JN, **ENGLAND**.
(T) 01635 247474 **(F)** 01635 248660.
Profile Club/Association. Ref: YH08013

KEABLE, CHRISTOPHER P

Christopher P Keable DWCF, 23 Manor Rd, New Milton, **Hampshire**, BH25 5EW, **ENGLAND**.
(M) 07775 924207.
Profile Farrier. Ref: YH08014

KEANE, ALLAN

Allan Keane, Greenacres Farm, Oakfield Lane, Warsop, Mansfield, **Nottinghamshire**, NG20 0JF, **ENGLAND**.
(T) 01623 842276.
Profile Medical Support. Ref: YH08015

KEAR, BILL

Bill Kear Arenas & Gallops, Beambrook, Field Station, Partridge Lane, Newdigate, Dorking, **Surrey**, RH5 5EE, **ENGLAND**.
(T) 01293 862666 **(F)** 01293 862189.
Contact/s
Administration: Ms S Mann
Profile Arena Construction.
Riding arena & gallop construction.
Opening Times
Sp: Open Mon - Fri 09:00. Closed Mon - Fri 17:00.
Su: Open Mon - Fri 09:00. Closed Mon - Fri 17:00.
Au: Open Mon - Fri 09:00. Closed Mon - Fri 17:00.
Wn: Open Mon - Fri 09:00. Closed Mon - Fri 17:00.

Closed at weekends except by appointment
Ref: YH08016

KEARN, RICHARD A

Richard A Kearn DWCF, 75 Forest St, Shepshed, **Leicestershire**, LE12 9BZ, **ENGLAND**.
(T) 01509 507624.
Profile Farrier. Ref: **YH08017**

KEARNS & REA

Kearns & Rea, Three Counties Equine Hospital, Stratford Bridge, Ripple, Tewkesbury, **Gloucestershire**, GL20 6HE, **ENGLAND**.
(T) 01684 592099 **(F)** 01684 592181
(E) equinehospital@kearnsandrea.freeserve.co.uk.
Profile Medical Support. Ref: **YH08018**

KEATE, CHRIS

Chris Keate, 10 Wykeham Way, Burgess Hill, **Sussex (West)**, RH15 0HF, **ENGLAND**.
(T) 01444 250028
(M) 07836 640582.
Profile Medical Support. Ref: **YH08019**

KEATES, REBEKAH

Rebekah Keates, 16 Cheyne Gardens, Bournemouth, **Dorset**, BH4 8AS, **ENGLAND**.
(T) 01202 757539
Affiliated Bodies NAAT.
Contact/s
Physiotherapist: Rebekah Keates **(Q)** MCSP, SRP
Profile Medical Support.
Physiotherapist for horses & dogs. Ref: **YH08020**

KEBCOTE COUNTRYWEAR

Kebcote Countrywear, Croft Mill, Albert St, Hebden Bridge, **Yorkshire (West)**, HX7 8AH, **ENGLAND**.
(T) 01422 842248.
Profile Saddlery Retailer. Ref: **YH08021**

KEDDIE FARM

Keddie Farm, Hall Rd, Rochford, **Essex**, SS4 1PJ, **ENGLAND**.
(T) 01702 203701.
Contact/s
Owner: Mr D Keddie
Profile Stable/Livery.
Opening Times
Open to owners 24 hours, 7 days a week. Telephone for further information from 09:00 - 18:00
Ref: **YH08022**

KEDDIE T & R

Keddie T & R, Heatherlie Works, Heatherlie Trce, Selkirk, **Scottish Borders**, TD7 5AH, **SCOTLAND**.
(T) 01750 20710 **(F)** 01750 23242.
Contact/s
Partner: Mrs S Scott
Profile Blacksmith. Ref: **YH08023**

KEDWARD, TIMOTHY J

Timothy J Kedward DWCF, 11 Rocklea, Mitchel Troy, Monmouth, **Monmouthshire**, NP25 4JE, **WALES**.
(T) 01600 714029.
Profile Farrier. Ref: **YH08024**

KEE, W R

Mr & Mrs W R Kee, Greenhurst, 34 Curleyhill Rd, Strabane, **County Tyrone**, BT82 8LP, **NORTHERN IRELAND**.
(T) 028 71882210.
Profile Breeder. Ref: **YH08025**

KEEGAN, M W

M W Keegan, The Houndsell Stud, Wadhurst Rd, Mark Cross, Crowborough, **Sussex (East)**, TN6 3PF, **ENGLAND**.
(T) 01892 783523 **(F)** 01892 783177.
Contact/s
Owner: Mr M Keegan
Profile Breeder. Ref: **YH08026**

KEELEY, PAULA

Paula Keeley, SSA Panel Instructor, Coldharbour Pk Farm, Rake, Liss, **Hampshire**, GU33 7JJ, **ENGLAND**.
(T) 01730 893100
(M) 07710 094951.
Contact/s
Instructor: Paula Keeley **(Q)** BHSII
Profile Stable/Livery, Trainer. Ref: **YH08027**

KEELING, F J

F J Keeling RSS, 293 Hursley Rd, Chandlersford, Eastleigh, **Hampshire**, SO50 1PJ, **ENGLAND**.
(T) 023 80253439.
Profile Farrier. Ref: **YH08028**

KEENELAND ASS

Keeneland Association, 9 Black Bear Ct, High St, Newmarket, **Suffolk**, CB8 9AF, **ENGLAND**.
(T) 01638 668026 **(F)** 01638 668036.
Contact/s
Manager: Mr T Preston
Profile Breeder, Club/Association. Ref: **YH08029**

KEENTHORNE SADDLERY

Keenthorne Saddlery, Keenthorne, Nether Stowey, Bridgwater, **Somerset**, TA5 1HZ, **ENGLAND**.
(T) 01278 732767.
Contact/s
Manager: Miss A Gwilliam Ref: **YH08030**

KEEPERS STABLES

Keepers Stables, West Ilsley, Newbury, **Berkshire**, RG20 7AH, **ENGLAND**.
(T) 01635 281622
(M) 07768 658056.
Profile Trainer. Ref: **YH08031**

KEITH BRYAN SADDLERY

Keith Bryan Saddlery Co, 13A Lime St, Walsall, **Midlands (West)**, WS1 2JL, **ENGLAND**.
(T) 01922 628325 **(F)** 01922 628325.
Contact/s
Owner: Mr K Bryan Ref: **YH08032**

KEITH DRAKE

Keith Drake Ltd (Corn & Agricultural Merchants), Honley Mill, Newtown, Honley, Huddersfield, **Yorkshire (West)**, HD7 2PQ, **ENGLAND**.
(T) 01484 663803.
Profile Feed Merchant, Supplies. Ref: **YH08033**

KEITH GARRY FENCING

Keith Garry Fencing, Sundial Walk, Lathrisk, Freuchie, **Fife**, KY15 7HX, **SCOTLAND**.
(T) 01337 831699 **(F)** 01337 857895.
Profile Supplies.
Fencing for arenas, electric fencing, jump poles
Ref: **YH08034**

KEITH GOOCH TRAILERS

Keith Gooch Trailers, The Firs, Long Lane, Bracon Ash, Norwich, **Norfolk**, NR14 8AN, **ENGLAND**.
(T) 01508 570755.
Profile Transport/Horse Boxes. Ref: **YH08035**

KEITH PROWSE HOSPITALITY

Keith Prowse Hospitality, Wembley Conference Ctre, Wembley, **London (Greater)**, HA9 0DT, **ENGLAND**.
(T) 020 87952222.
Profile Club/Association. Ref: **YH08036**

KEITH WARTH & ASSOCIATES

Keith Warth & Associates, Chalk Farm, High St, Babraham, **Cambridgeshire**, CB2 4AG, **ENGLAND**.
(T) 01223 839992 **(F)** 01223 839994
(E) kwa9498@aol.com. Ref: **YH08037**

KELANNE STUD

Kelanne Stud, Kelanne Hse, Hambleton, **Hampshire**, PO7 6RD, **ENGLAND**.
(T) 023 92632574 **(F)** 023 92632589.
Profile Breeder. Ref: **YH08038**

KELBURN COUNTRY CTRE

Kelburn Country Centre, South Offices, Kelburn Est, Fairlie, **Ayrshire (North)**, KA29 0BE, **SCOTLAND**.
(T) 01475 568544.
Profile Riding School, Stable/Livery. Ref: **YH08039**

KELLARD, SARAH

Sarah Kellard, Little Meadows, Choice Hill, Over Norton, **Oxfordshire**, OX7 5PZ, **ENGLAND**.
(T) 01608 642584. Ref: **YH08040**

KELLEHER, NEAL

Kelleher Neal D.W.C.F., Rathcannon, Kilmallock, **County Limerick**, **IRELAND**.
(T) 063 90909.
Profile Supplies. Ref: **YH08041**

KELLEWAY, GAY

Gay Kelleway, Charnwood Stables, Hamilton Rd, Newmarket, **Suffolk**, CB8 7JQ, **ENGLAND**.
(T) 01638 663187
(W) www.newmarketracehorsetrainers.co.uk
Affiliated Bodies Newmarket Trainers Fed.
Contact/s
Trainer: Miss G Kelleway
Profile Trainer. Ref: **YH08042**

KELLOE PK STUD

Kelloe Park Stud, Duns, **Scottish Borders**, TD11 3PT, **SCOTLAND**.
(T) 01890 818446.
Profile Breeder. Ref: **YH08043**

KELLY, G P

Mr G P Kelly, Golden Flatts Farm, Torrington Rd, Sheriff Hutton, **Yorkshire (North)**, YO60 6RS, **ENGLAND**.
(T) 01347 878518
(M) 07718 515805.
Profile Trainer. Ref: **YH08044**

KELLY, MARTIN

Martin Kelly, 25 Loomsway, Wirral, **Merseyside**, CH61 4UD, **ENGLAND**.
(T) 0151 6481000.
Contact/s
Owner: Mr M Kelly
Profile Farrier. Ref: **YH08045**

KELLY, NEIL J

Neil J Kelly DWCF, The Old Vicarage, Tillingham, Southminster, **Essex**, CM0 7TW, **ENGLAND**.
(T) 01621 778064.
Profile Farrier. Ref: **YH08046**

KELLY, R

R Kelly, Low Ash Farm, Park Rd, Thackley, Bradford, **Yorkshire (West)**, BD10 0TJ, **ENGLAND**.
(T) 01274 615407. Ref: **YH08047**

KELLY, SHARON

Sharon Kelly, c/o 157 Killynure Rd, Saintfield, **County Down**, **NORTHERN IRELAND**.
(T) 02897 510965
Affiliated Bodies NAAT.
Contact/s
Physiotherapist: Sharon Kelly
Profile Medical Support.
Physiotherapist for horses & dogs. Ref: **YH08048**

KELLY, SIMON

Simon Kelly, Oakhanger Riding Ctre, Holmshaw Lane, Oakhanger, Crewe, **Cheshire**, CW1 5XE, **ENGLAND**.
(M) 07973 730429.
Profile Equestrian Centre. Ref: **YH08049**

KELMAN ENGINEERING

Kelman Engineering, The Smiddy, Smiddy Lane, Turriff, **Aberdeenshire**, AB53 4FW, **SCOTLAND**.
(T) 01888 562715 **(F)** 01888 562715.
Contact/s
Owner: Mr M Kelman
Profile Blacksmith. Ref: **YH08050**

KELSO RACES

Kelso Races Ltd, R M Landale, 18/20 Glendale Rd, Wooler, **Northumberland**, NE71 6DW, **ENGLAND**.
(T) 01668 281611 **(F)** 01668 281113.
Contact/s
Secretary: Mrs P Punton
Profile Track/Course. Ref: **YH08051**

KEMNAL MANOR

Kemnal Manor, Kemnal Stables, Kemnal Rd, Chislehurst, **Kent**, BR7 6LT, **ENGLAND**.
(T) 020 84676609.
Contact/s
Owner: Mrs B Myers Ref: **YH08052**

KEMP, F

Mrs F Kemp, Hammingden Farm, Highbrook, Ardingly, **Sussex (West)**, RH17 6SS, **ENGLAND**.
(T) 01444 892292.
Profile Breeder. Ref: **YH08053**

KEMP, J T

J T Kemp, Low Leighton Rd, New Mills, High Peak, **Derbyshire**, SK22 4JG, **ENGLAND**.
(T) 01663 743990.
Contact/s
Owner: Mr J Kemp
Profile Transport/Horse Boxes. Ref: **YH08054**

KEMP, W T

Mr W T Kemp, Drake Myre, Grants Hse, Duns, **Scottish Borders**, TD11 3RL, **SCOTLAND**.
(T) 01361 850242.
Profile Trainer. Ref: **YH08055**

KEMPTON PK RACECOURSES

Kempton Park - United Racecourses Ltd, Sunbury-on-Thames, **Surrey**, TW16 5AQ, **ENGLAND**.
(T) 01932 782292 **(F)** 01932 782044.
Contact/s
General Manager: Mr J Thick

Profile Track/Course. Ref: YH08056

KEN JACKSON CARRIAGES

Ken Jackson Carriages, Robsacks, Eynsford, **Kent**, DA4 0HX, **ENGLAND**.
(T) 01322 863424. Ref: YH08057

KEN LANGFORD SADDLERY

Ken Langford Saddlery, Eaton Rd, Appleton, Abingdon, **Oxfordshire**, OX13 5JR, **ENGLAND**.
(T) 01865 863774 **(F)** 01865 863774.
Contact/s
Owner: Mr K Langford
Profile Riding Wear Retailer, Saddlery Retailer.
Ref: YH08058

KENDAL, SARAH

Miss Sarah Kendal MC AMC MMCA, The Blade Mill, Yarde, Williton, **Somerset**, TA4 4HW, **ENGLAND**.
(T) 01984 640270.
Profile Medical Support. Ref: YH08059

KENDALL, R

R Kendall, Grey Horse Stables, Brough, Kirkby Stephen, **Cumbria**, CA17 4DS, **ENGLAND**.
(T) 01768 341651.
Profile Trainer. Ref: YH08060

KENDREW, J

J Kendrew, The Forge, Cole Yard, Ashreigney, Chulmleigh, **Devon**, EX18 7LP, **ENGLAND**.
(T) 01769 520576.
Profile Blacksmith. Ref: YH08061

KENFIG HILL & DISTRICT

Kenfig Hill & District Riding Club, Ogmore Farm, Ewenny, **Bridgend**, **WALES**..
Contact/s
Secretary: Mr C Kerrygan
Profile Club/Association, Riding Club. Ref: YH08062

KENILWORTH EQUESTRIAN CTRE

Kenilworth Equestrian Centre, Dorking Rd, Bookham, Leatherhead, **Surrey**, KT23 4PZ, **ENGLAND**.
(T) 01372 458709.
Profile Stable/Livery. Ref: YH08063

KENLIN TRADING

Kenlin Trading, 75 Fairlawn, Liden, Swindon, **Wiltshire**, SN3 6EU, **ENGLAND**.
(T) 01793 495012 **(F)** 01793 495012
(M) 07860 813612.
Profile Supplies. Ref: YH08064

KENMURE RIDING SCHOOL

Kenmure Riding School, Kenmure Ave, Bishopbriggs, Glasgow, **Glasgow (City of)**, G64 2QN, **SCOTLAND**.
(T) 0141 7723041.
Profile Riding School, Stable/Livery. Ref: YH08065

KENNEDY & CHEETHAM

Kennedy & Cheetham, Market Pl, Forfar, **Angus**, DD8 3BQ, **SCOTLAND**.
(T) 01307 467812.
Profile Blacksmith. Ref: YH08066

KENNEDY, B J

Mr B J Kennedy, Southlands, Bryants Lane, Woodham Mortimer, Maldon, **Essex**, CM9 6TB, **ENGLAND**.
(T) 01245 223187.
Profile Supplies. Ref: YH08067

KENNEDY, R

Mr R Kennedy, 98 Wishaw Rd, Waterloo, Wishaw, **Lanarkshire (North)**, **SCOTLAND**..
Profile Trainer. Ref: YH08068

KENNEDY, R R & K

R R & K Kennedy, Whittlees, Gilsland, Brampton, **Cumbria**, CA8 7EL, **ENGLAND**.
(T) 01697 747240.
Profile Transport/Horse Boxes. Ref: YH08069

KENNEDY, ROBERT M

Robert M Kennedy DWCF, 68 Oakfield Drive, Georgetown, **Dumfries and Galloway**, DG1 4UZ, **SCOTLAND**.
(T) 01387 269853.
Profile Farrier. Ref: YH08070

KENNEDY, VIVIAN

Vivian Kennedy, Robin Hill Stables, Green Rd, The Curragh, **County Kildare**, **IRELAND**.
(T) 045 441511 **(F)** 045 441864.
Contact/s
Trainer: Ms V Kennedy
(E) viviankennedy@kildarehorse.ie
Profile Trainer. Ref: YH08071

KENNET VALE RIDING CLUB

Kennet Vale Riding Club, 7 Hunts Mead, Bromham, Chippenham, **Wiltshire**, SN15 2JP, **ENGLAND**.
(T) 01380 850577.
Contact/s
Chairman: Mr J Collins
Profile Club/Association, Riding Club. Ref: YH08072

KENNET VALLEY THOROUGHBREDS

Kennet Valley Thoroughbreds, Cooper's Farmhouse, Bell Lane, Ellisfield, Basingstoke, **Hampshire**, RG25 2QD, **ENGLAND**.
(T) 01256 381881 **(F)** 01256 381882
(E) dirturf@aol.com.
Profile Blood Stock Agency. Ref: YH08073

KENNET VALLEY THOROUGHBREDS

Kennet Valley Thoroughbreds, 134 Lots Rd, London, **London (Greater)**, SW10 0RJ, **ENGLAND**.
(T) 01380 816777 **(F)** 01380 816778.
Profile Blood Stock Agency. Ref: YH08074

KENNY, SHAUN J

Shaun J Kenny AFCL BI, Coneybury Bungalow, West Amesbury, Salisbury, **Wiltshire**, SP4 7BH, **ENGLAND**.
(T) 01980 626877.
Profile Farrier. Ref: YH08075

KEN'S CORN STORES

Ken's Corn Stores, Fir Covert Rd, Taverham, Norwich, **Norfolk**, NR8 6HT, **ENGLAND**.
(T) 01603 861370 **(F)** 01603 260708.
Profile Supplies. Ref: YH08076

KENSINGTON ARABIAN STUD

Kensington Arabian Stud, Hollywood Villa, Compton Greenfield, Easter Compton, **Gloucestershire (South)**, BS35 5RU, **ENGLAND**.
(T) 01454 632423.
Profile Breeder. Ref: YH08077

KENSINGTON STABLES

London Riding Schools Ltd, 11 Elvaston Mews, London, **London (Greater)**, SW7 5HY, **ENGLAND**.
(T) 020 75892299 **(F)** 020 78234512
(E) info@hydeparkstables.com
(W) www.hydeparkstables.com.
Contact/s
Manager: Catherine Brown
Profile Riding School, Riding Wear Retailer.
Private lessons with a mounted instructor. Course of 10 one-to-one lessons - £450.00. Private group riding lessons - £50.00 per hour. Group lessons are only taken if it's a private group. Course of 10 private children's lessons - £400.00. The school specialises in teaching adults as its sister school at Hyde Park caters for children. The tack shop has everything for horse and rider. Polo equipment and saddles can be specially ordered.
Opening Times
Sp: Open Tues - Fri 07:30, Sat, Sun 08:30. Closed Tues - Thurs 19:00, Fri - Sun 17:00.
Su: Open Tues - Fri 07:30, Sat, Sun 08:30. Closed Tues - Thurs 19:00, Fri - Sun 17:00.
Au: Open Tues - Fri 07:00, Sat, Sun 08:30. Closed Tues - Fri 17:00, Sat, Sun 16:00.
Wn: Open Tues - Fri 07:00, Sat, Sun 08:30. Closed Tues - Fri 17:00, Sat, Sun 16:00.
Mondays - open for bookings only. Autumn/ Winter closing hours may vary Ref: YH08078

KENT BROS

Kent Bros, Unit 16, Coopies Haugh Lane Ind Est, Morpeth, **Northumberland**, NE61 6JN, **ENGLAND**.
(T) 01670 518528.
Profile Transport/Horse Boxes. Ref: YH08079

KENT LIVERIES

Kent Liveries, Pye Corner, Ulcombe, Maidstone, **Kent**, ME17 1ED, **ENGLAND**.
(T) 01622 843231.
Profile Stable/Livery. Ref: YH08080

KENT LIVERIES & RIDING SCHOOL

Kent Liveries & Riding School, Ulcombe, Maidstone, **Kent**, ME17 1DP, **ENGLAND**.
(T) 01622 842909.
Profile Riding School, Stable/Livery. Ref: YH08081

KENT TARGET POLOCROSSE CLUB

Kent Target Polocrosse Club, Risebridge Farm, Ranters Lane, Goudhurst, **Kent**, TN17 1HN, **ENGLAND**.
(T) 01580 211775.
Contact/s
Chairman: Mr R Edmondson
Profile Club/Association. Polocrosse Club.
Ref: YH08082

KENT WOOL GROWERS

Kent Wool Growers Ltd, Brundett Hse, Tannery Lane, Ashford, **Kent**, TN23 1PN, **ENGLAND**.
(T) 01233 622444 **(F)** 01233 611888.
Profile Saddlery Retailer. Ref: YH08083

KENT, A

A Kent, Madams Farm, Kings Drive, Midhurst, **Sussex (West)**, GU29 0BH, **ENGLAND**.
(T) 01730 813943 **(F)** 01730 815787.
Profile Stable/Livery. Polo Centre. Ref: YH08084

KENT, JOHN

John Kent, Coulsdon Area Farm, Lion Green Rd, Coulsdon, **Surrey**, CR5 2NL, **ENGLAND**.
(T) 020 86681294 **(F)** 020 86687347.
Contact/s
Owner: Mr J Kent Ref: YH08085

KENTDALE FARRIERS

Kentdale Farriers, Broadthorn, Patton, Kendal, **Cumbria**, LA8 9DR, **ENGLAND**.
(T) 01539 735292.
Contact/s
Owner: Mr A Wiseman **(Q)** DWCF
(E) wwbroadthorn@aol.com
Profile Farrier. Yr. Est: 1993 Ref: YH08086

KENTISH TOWN CITY FARM

Kentish Town City Farm, 1 Cressfield Cl, Off Grafton Rd, London, **London (Greater)**, NW5 4BN, **ENGLAND**.
(T) 020 79165421.
Profile Riding School. Ref: YH08087

KENTON RIDING SCHOOL

Kenton Riding School, Kenton Lane, Newcastle-upon-Tyne, **Tyne and Wear**, NE3 3EB, **ENGLAND**.
(T) 0191 2869126.
Contact/s
Owner: Mr J Ward Ref: YH08088

KENTON WOOD STABLES

Kenton Wood Stables, Little Brewery Lane, Formby, Liverpool, **Merseyside**, L37 7DY, **ENGLAND**.
(T) 01704 872286.
Contact/s
Owner: Ms A Rimmer Ref: YH08089

KENWARD, ALLISON

Allison Kenward, Sixosix, High St, Paulersbury, Towcester, **Northamptonshire**, NN12 7NA, **ENGLAND**.
(T) 01327 811387.
Profile Trainer. Ref: YH08090

KENWOOD FEEDS

Kenwood Feeds, Kenwood Farm, Harthall Lane, Pimlico, Hemel Hempstead, **Hertfordshire**, HP3 8SD, **ENGLAND**.
(T) 01923 268227. Ref: YH08091

KENWYN VETNRY CTRE

Kenwyn Veterinary Centre, Kenwyn Hill, Truro, **Cornwall**, TR1 3ED, **ENGLAND**.
(T) 01872 225599 **(F)** 01872 264406.
Profile Medical Support. Ref: YH08092

KENYON BROTHERS

Kenyon Brothers, Suttons Farm, Drummersdale Lane, Scarisbrick, Ormskirk, **Lancashire**, L40 1SU, **ENGLAND**.
(T) 01704 880301 **(F)** 01704 889035.
Profile Supplies. Ref: YH08093

KENYON FARM RIDING CTRE

Kenyon Farm Riding Centre, Boarshaw Lane, Middleton, Manchester, **Manchester (Greater)**, M24 2PA, **ENGLAND**.
(T) 0161 6433900 **(F)** 0161 6433901.
Contact/s
Instructor: Ms S Bamford **(Q)** BHSAI
Profile Riding School, Stable/Livery.
Full, part and DIY livery available, prices on request. 45 minutes of one to one coaching costs £17.50.
No.Staff: 5
Opening Times
Sp: Open Mon - Fri 13:00, Sat, Sun 10:00. Closed Mon - Fri 21:00, Sat, Sun 14:00.
Su: Open Mon - Fri 13:00, Sat, Sun 10:00. Closed Mon - Fri 21:00, Sat, Sun 14:00.
Au: Open Mon - Fri 13:00, Sat, Sun 10:00. Closed Mon - Fri 21:00, Sat, Sun 14:00.

Wn: Open Mon - Fri 13:00, Sat, Sun 10:00. Closed Mon - Fri 21:00, Sat, Sun 14:00. **Ref: YH08094**

KENYONS OF MORLEY

Kenyons of Morley Limited, Ackroyd St, Morley, **Yorkshire (West)**, LS27 9PZ, **ENGLAND**.
(T) 0113 2532526.
Profile Saddlery Retailer. **Ref: YH08095**

KERBECK

Kerbeck Fell Ponies, North Fell Dyke, Lamplugh, Workington, **Cumbria**, CA14 4SH, **ENGLAND**.
(T) 01946 862439/861302 **(F)** 01946 861397
(W) www.kerbeck-fell-ponies.co.uk.
Contact/s
Partner: Christine Robinson
(E) christine@kerbcek-fell-ponies.co.uk
Profile Breeder, Stable/Livery.
Also offer a holiday livery, prices on request.
Yr. Est: 1981 C.Size: 23 Acres
Opening Times
Open all year, telephone for an appointment
Ref: YH08096

KERLEY, KEITH

Keith Kerley RSS, Kiddles Farm, Winterbourne Zelston, Blandford Forum, **Dorset**, DT11 9EU, **ENGLAND**.
(T) 01929 45535.
Profile Farrier. **Ref: YH08097**

KER-RAMSAY, ROBERT N

Robert N Ker-Ramsay DWCF, Corsby Lodge, Strathore Rd, Thornton, Kirkcaldy, **Fife**, KY11 4DN, **SCOTLAND**.
(T) 01592 631330.
Profile Farrier. **Ref: YH08098**

KERRIDGE, J

J Kerridge, Martins Farm, Stonham Aspal, Stowmarket, **Suffolk**, IP14 6AX, **ENGLAND**.
(T) 01473 890429 **(F)** 01473 890922.
Contact/s
Owner: Mr J Kerridge **Ref: YH08099**

KERRUISH, CHARLES (SIR)

Sir Charles Kerruish, Ballafayle, Maughold, **Isle of Man**, **ENGLAND**..
Profile Breeder. **Ref: YH08100**

KERRY FARM SUPPLIES

Kerry Farm Supplies Ltd, Farranfore, Tralee, **County Kerry**, **IRELAND**.
(T) 066 9764466.
Profile Supplies. **Ref: YH08101**

KERRY, JOHN

John Kerry, 18 Swallowdale Rd, Melton Mowbray, **Leicestershire**, LE13 0AU, **ENGLAND**.
(T) 01664 566865.
Profile Trainer. **Ref: YH08102**

KERSEY, J

Mrs J Kersey, The Terrace Hse, Holly Hill, Colemans Hatch, **Sussex (East)**, TN7 4EP, **ENGLAND**.
(T) 01342 823328.
Profile Breeder. **Ref: YH08103**

KERSTING, MICHAEL

Michael Kersting DWCF BII, 1 Barnards Trce, London Rd, Gisleham, Lowestoft, **Suffolk**, NR33 7QP, **ENGLAND**.
(T) 01502 512005.
Profile Farrier. **Ref: YH08104**

KESWICK RIDING CTRE

Keswick Riding Centre, High Hill, Keswick, **Cumbria**, CA12 4RA, **ENGLAND**.
(T) 01768 775255 **(F)** 01768 773216
(M) 07711 763019.
Profile Stable/Livery, Track/Course. **Ref: YH08105**

KESWICK RIDING STABLES

Keswick Riding Stables, Bridle Lane, Norwich, **Norfolk**, NR4 6RU, **ENGLAND**.
(T) 01603 451526.
Contact/s
Partner: Mr A Hewitt
Profile Riding School, Stable/Livery.
Adult hacks cost £14.00 for 60 minutes and £7.50 for 30 minutes
Opening Times
Telephone for further information **Ref: YH08106**

KETTERING TRAILER CTRE

Kettering Trailer Centre Ltd, Queen St, Kettering, **Northamptonshire**, NN16 0BY, **ENGLAND**.
(T) 01536 412646 **(F)** 01536 412515.
Profile Transport/Horse Boxes. **Ref: YH08107**

KETTLE, CAROLINE

Mrs Caroline Kettle, 2 Little Bungalow, Woodway Rd, Blewbury, **Oxfordshire**, OX11 9EZ, **ENGLAND**.
(T) 01235 851161.
Profile Trainer. **Ref: YH08108**

KETTLEWELL, S E

S E Kettlewell, Tupgill Pk Stables, Middleham, Leyburn, **Yorkshire (North)**, DL8 4TJ, **ENGLAND**.
(T) 01969 640411 **(F)** 01969 640494.
Profile Trainer. **Ref: YH08109**

KETTON HALL RIDING STABLES

Ketton Hall Riding Stables, Ketton Hall Farm, Brafferton, Darlington, **County Durham**, DL1 3LJ, **ENGLAND**.
(T) 01325 312069.
Contact/s
Owner: Mrs S Price **Ref: YH08110**

KEVINS MENSWEAR

Kevins Menswear, 4 Wessex Business Ctre, Meadow Lane, Westbury, **Wiltshire**, BA13 3EG, **ENGLAND**.
(T) 01373 822150 **(F)** 01373 822150.
Profile Saddlery Retailer. **Ref: YH08111**

KEWAL TRAILER PRODUCTS

Kewal Trailer Products Ltd, Eden Garage/Albert Hill, Dodsworth St, Darlington, **County Durham**, DL1 2NG, **ENGLAND**.
(T) 01325 359789.
Profile Transport/Horse Boxes. **Ref: YH08112**

KEY GREEN SADDLERY

Key Green Saddlery, Spout Hse Farm, Key Green, Congleton, **Cheshire**, CW12 3PT, **ENGLAND**.
(T) 01260 297291.
Profile Saddlery Retailer. **Ref: YH08113**

KEY, J U

J U Key, Lineside Farm, Lineside, Amber Hill, Boston, **Lincolnshire**, PE20 3RA, **ENGLAND**.
(T) 01205 820744 **(F)** 01205 820573.
Contact/s
Owner: Mrs J Key
Profile Riding School, Stable/Livery.
Sell tack to order. Also organises hacks.
C.Size: 1977 Acres
Opening Times
Sp: Open Mon - Sun 08:00. Closed Mon - Sun 20:00.
Su: Open Mon - Sun 08:00. Closed Mon - Sun 20:00.
Au: Open Mon - Sun 08:00. Closed Mon - Sun 20:00.
Wn: Open Mon - Sun 08:00. Closed Mon - Sun 20:00. **Ref: YH08114**

KEYLOCK, CARMEL

Carmel Keylock, Midland Windsurfing Ctre, Edgbaston Reservoir, Icknield Port Rd, Birmingham, **Midlands (West)**, B16 0AA, **ENGLAND**.
(T) 01214 559952/ 01217 451354
Affiliated Bodies NAAT.
Contact/s
Physiotherapist: Carmel Keylock
Profile Medical Support.
Physiotherapist for horses & dogs. **Ref: YH08115**

KEYSLEY HORSE RUGS

Keysley Horse Rugs, Brookway Hse, Fovant, Salisbury, **Wiltshire**, SP3 5JT, **ENGLAND**.
(T) 01722 714687.
Profile Supplies. **Ref: YH08116**

KEYSTONE EQUESTRIAN

Keystone Equestrian, Cedar Stables, Castle St, Medstead, Alton, **Hampshire**, GU34 5LU, **ENGLAND**.
(T) 01420 562881.
Contact/s
Owner: Mr D Mattia
Profile Stable/Livery.
Competition Livery Yard **Ref: YH08117**

K-FEEDS

K-Feeds, Cowsland Farm, Grove Rd, South Leverton, Retford, **Nottinghamshire**, DN22 0EA, **ENGLAND**.
(T) 01427 880914 **(F)** 01427 881221.
Profile Supplies. **Ref: YH08118**

KIDBY INTERNATIONAL

Kidby International, Trundle Cottage, Singleton, **Sussex (West)**, PO18 0HD, **ENGLAND**.
(T) 01243 811265.
Profile Supplies. **Ref: YH08119**

KIDD SADDLERY

Kidd Saddlery, 3 Hill Rd, Ballinaskeagh, Banbridge, **County Down**, BT32 5EH, **NORTHERN IRELAND**.
(T) 028 40651668 **(F)** 028 40651339.
Contact/s
Owner: Mrs G Kidd
Profile Saddlery Retailer. **Ref: YH08120**

KIDD, D

D Kidd, 33 Minor Ave, Lyme Green, Macclesfield, **Cheshire**, SK11 0LQ, **ENGLAND**.
(T) 01260 252248.
Profile Transport/Horse Boxes. **Ref: YH08121**

KIDD, JANE

Jane Kidd, The Barn Hse, Aldsworth, **Gloucestershire**, GL54 3RE, **ENGLAND**.
(T) 01451 844748 **(F)** 01451 844848.
Profile Supplies. **Ref: YH08122**

KIDDY, S M

Mrs S M Kiddy, Yole Farm, Linton Rd, Balsham, **Cambridgeshire**, CB1 6HB, **ENGLAND**.
(T) 01223 893280 **(F)** 01223 892599.
Profile Breeder, Stable/Livery. **Ref: YH08123**

KIDLENDLEE TRAIL RIDING

Kidlendlee Trail Riding, The Cottage, Kidlendlee, Harbottle, Morpeth, **Northumberland**, NE65 7DA, **ENGLAND**.
(T) 01669 650254.
Contact/s
Partner: Mrs E Davison
Profile Equestrian Centre. **Ref: YH08124**

KIERNAN, LYDIA

Lydia Kiernan Equestrian Art, The Old Court Hse, Bell St, Talgarth, Brecon, **Blaenau Gwent**, LD30 0BO, **WALES**.
(T) 01484 687422
(M) 07970 545706
(E) sales@lydiakiernan.co.uk
(W) www.lydiakiernan.co.uk.
Contact/s
Artist: Lydia Kiernan
Profile Artist.
Accepts commissions for originals and trade.
Ref: YH08125

KIFTSGATE COURT

Kiftsgate Court Livery Stables, Stable Cottage, Kiftsgate, Mickleton, Chipping Campden, **Gloucestershire**, GL55 6LN, **ENGLAND**.
(T) 01386 438776.
Contact/s
Owner: Miss K Williams **Ref: YH08126**

KILBYRNE STABLES

Kilbyrne Stables, Kilbyrne, Doneraile, **County Cork**, **IRELAND**.
(T) 022 24205.
Profile Stable/Livery. **Ref: YH08127**

KILCANNON HOUSE TACK SHOP

Kilcannon House Tack Shop & Art Gallery, Cappagh, **County Waterford**, **IRELAND**.
(T) 058 68300.
Profile Supplies. **Ref: YH08128**

KILCONQUHAR RIDING STABLES

Kilconquhar Riding Stables, Kilconquhar, Elie, Leven, **Fife**, KY9 1EZ, **SCOTLAND**.
(T) 01333 340501.
Profile Riding School. **Ref: YH08129**

KILDANGAN STUD

Kildangan Stud, Kildare, **County Kildare**, **IRELAND**.
(T) 045 527600 **(F)** 045 523461
(E) enquiries@kildangan.com.
Contact/s
Key Contact: Mr J Osborne
Profile Breeder. **Ref: YH08130**

KILDARAGH STUD

Kildaragh Stud, Kildangan, **County Kildare**, **IRELAND**.
(T) 045 523637 **(F)** 045 523544
(E) kildaraghstud@aircom.net.
Contact/s
Key Contact: Mr P Kavanagh
(E) kildaraghstud@eircom.net
Profile Breeder. C.Size: 150 Acres
Ref: YH08131

KILDARE HORSE DEVELOPMENT

Kildare Horse Development Co, The Curragh Racehorse, The Curragh, **County Kildare**, **IRELAND**.

Key: **(T)** telephone **(F)** fax **(M)** mobile **(E)** E-Mail Address **(W)** Website Address **(Q)** Qualifications
Yr. Est: Year Established C.Size: Complex Size Sp: Spring Su: Summer Au: Autumn Wn: Winter

(T) 045 442486 **(F)** 045 441442
(E) info@kildarehorse.ie
(W) www.kildarehorse.ie.
Contact/s
Business Development Executive: Ms J Creighton
Profile Club/Association. Equine promotional company.
Organisation designed to promote and market the entire equine industry in Kildare. No.Staff: 2 Yr. Est: 1997 Ref:YH08132

KILEY-WORTHINGTON, M (DR)

Dr M Kiley-Worthington, Little Ash Eco-Farm, Throwleigh, Okehampton, **Devon**, EX20 2QG, **ENGLAND**.
(T) 01647 231394.
Profile Breeder, Trainer. Ref:YH08133

KILFORD

Mrs Kilford, Moorlands Farm, Rossiten Lane, Woodlands, **Hampshire**, SO30 3HD, **ENGLAND**.
(T) 023 80872176.
Profile Breeder. Ref:YH08134

KILGETTY TRAILER HIRE

Kilgetty Trailer Hire Ltd, Mountain Pk, Templebar Rd, Kilgetty, **Pembrokeshire**, SA68 0RD, **WALES**.
(T) 01834 813626.
Contact/s
Owner: Mr J Greenhough
Profile Transport/Horse Boxes. Ref:YH08135

KILGOUR, Y

Ms Y Kilgour, The Kerse Nursery, Kilbirmie Rd, Lochwinnoch, **Renfrewshire**, PA12 4DT, **SCOTLAND**.
(T) 01505 503804.
Profile Farrier. Ref:YH08136

KILIJARO

Kilijaro Ltd, Cooper's Farmhouse, Bell Lane, Ellisfield, Basingstoke, **Hampshire**, RG25 2QD, **ENGLAND**.
(T) 01256 381881 **(F)** 01256 381882
(E) dirturf@aol.com.
Profile Supplies. Ref:YH08137

KILKEA LODGE FARM

Kilkea Lodge Farm, Kilkea Lodge, Castledermot, **County Kildare**, **IRELAND**.
(T) 050 345112 **(F)** 050 345112
(E) kilkealodgefarm@kildarehorse.ie.
Profile Equestrian Centre.
The centre offers advice on the purchasing of Irish bred horses and also offers courses and workshops.
Ref:YH08138

KILKEEL & DISTRICT

Kilkeel & District Riding Club, Beechmount, 76 Greencastle Rd, Kilkeel, Newry, **County Down**, BT34 4JL, **NORTHERN IRELAND**.
(T) 028 41763423.
Contact/s
Chairman: Mr B Boyd
Profile Riding Club. Ref:YH08139

KILL EQUESTRIAN CTRE

Kill Equestrian Centre, Kill, **County Kildare**, **IRELAND**.
(T) 045 877208 **(F)** 045 877704
(E) killequestrian@kildarehorse.ie.
Contact/s
Key Contact: Mr F Flannelly
Profile Equestrian Centre.
The centre organise and run, horse and pony leagues.
Ref:YH08140

KILLARNEY RACE

Killarney Race Co Ltd, Ross Golf Club Ross Rd, Killarney, **County Kerry**, **IRELAND**.
(T) 064 31125 **(F)** 064 31860.
Profile Track/Course. Ref:YH08141

KILLINEY

Killiney Stud, Caely, Penybont, Llandrindod Wells, **Powys**, LD1 5SY, **WALES**.
(T) 01597 851180 **(F)** 01597 851917
(E) killineystud@freeserve.co.uk
(W) www.killineystud.freeserve.co.uk.
Contact/s
Owner: Mrs L Mason
Profile Breeder. No.Staff: 2 Yr. Est: 1992
C.Size: 70 Acres
Opening Times
Telephone for an appointment Ref:YH08142

KILLINGHOLME

Killingholme Animal Feeds, Town St, South Killingholme, Grimsby, **Lincolnshire (North)**, DN40 3DD, **ENGLAND**.
(T) 01469 540793 **(F)** 01469 540793.
Contact/s
General Manager: Mr P Bennett
Profile Feed Merchant, Riding Wear Retailer, Saddlery Retailer. No.Staff: 3 Yr. Est: 1976
Opening Times
Sp: Open Mon - Sat 09:00, Sun 10:00. Closed Mon - Fri 17:30, Sat 16:00, Sun 14:00.
Su: Open Mon - Sat 09:00, Sun 10:00. Closed Mon - Fri 17:30, Sat 16:00, Sun 14:00.
Au: Open Mon - Sat 09:00, Sun 10:00. Closed Mon - Fri 17:30, Sat 16:00, Sun 14:00.
Wn: Open Mon - Sat 09:00, Sun 10:00. Closed Mon - Fri 17:30, Sat 16:00, Sun 14:00. Ref:YH08143

KILLIWORGIE RIDING STABLE

Killiworgie Riding Stable, Black Cross, Newquay, **Cornwall**, TR8 4LU, **ENGLAND**.
(T) 01637 880570.
Contact/s
Owner: Mrs C Carne
Profile Equestrian Centre. Ref:YH08144

KILLOAN RIDING CTRE

Killoan Riding Centre, 40 Killyless Rd, Cullybackey, Ballymena, **County Antrim**, BT42 1HB, **NORTHERN IRELAND**.
(T) 028 25881713.
Profile Riding School. Ref:YH08145

KILLYLESS RIDING CLUB

Killyless Riding Club, 1A Mckeestown Lane, Shankbridge, Ballymena, **County Antrim**, BT42 2LU, **NORTHERN IRELAND**.
(T) 028 25891652.
Contact/s
Chairman: Mr M Gourley
Profile Club/Association, Riding Club. Ref:YH08146

KILMACOLM RIDING CLUB

Kilmacolm Riding Club, 16 Ewing St, Kilbarchan, **Renfrewshire**, PA10 2JA, **SCOTLAND**.
(T) 01505 704398.
Profile Club/Association, Riding Club. Ref:YH08147

KILMAURS FARMERS SOC

Kilmaurs Farmers Society, Langlands Farm, Kilmaurs, **Ayrshire (East)**, KA3 2PJ, **SCOTLAND**.
(T) 01563 38227.
Contact/s
Secretary: Janet Smith
Profile Club/Association. Ref:YH08148

KILN COTTAGE

Kiln Cottage Stables Riding School, Kiln Cottage, Badshot Farm Lane, Badshot Lea, Farnham, **Surrey**, GU9 9HY, **ENGLAND**.
(T) 01252 333200.
Contact/s
Owner: Mrs A Andrew
Profile Riding School. Ref:YH08149

KILN FARM RIDING SCHOOL

Kiln Farm Riding School, Packridge, Rownhams Lane, North Baddesley, Southampton, **Hampshire**, **ENGLAND**.
(T) 023 8073 0463
(M) 07889 116776.
Contact/s
Owner: Mrs W Carter
Profile Riding School. Ref:YH08150

KILN SADDLERY

Kiln Saddlery, Park Hse, Layer Rd, Kingsford, Colchester, **Essex**, CO2 0HT, **ENGLAND**.
(T) 01206 734695 **(F)** 01206 734688.
Contact/s
Owner: Mr D Merrett
Profile Riding Wear Retailer, Saddlery Retailer.
Made to measure saddles. Fitting on site or at home.
No.Staff: 4 Yr. Est: 1970
Opening Times
Sp: Open Mon - Fri 09:00, Sat 09:30. Closed Mon - Fri 18:00, Sat 17:30.
Su: Open Mon - Fri 09:00, Sat 09:30. Closed Mon - Fri 18:00, Sat 17:30.
Au: Open Mon - Fri 09:00, Sat 09:30. Closed Mon - Fri 18:00, Sat 17:30.
Wn: Open Mon - Fri 09:00, Sat 09:30. Closed Mon - Fri 18:00, Sat 17:30. Ref:YH08151

KILNCOPSE STUD

Kilncopse Stud, Warnford, **Hampshire**, SO30 1LH, **ENGLAND**.
(T) 01962 771794.
Profile Breeder. Ref:YH08152

KILNSEY TREKKING CTRE

Kilnsey Trekking Centre, Homestead Farm, Conistone With Kilnsey, Skipton, **Yorkshire (North)**, BD23 5HS, **ENGLAND**.
(T) 01756 752861 **(F)** 01756 752224.
Profile Equestrian Centre. Ref:YH08153

KILROE, R J

Mrs R J Kilroe, The Stables, Sowerby Hall, Sowerby, Preston, **Lancashire**, PR3 0TU, **ENGLAND**.
(T) 01995 679216.
Profile Trainer. Ref:YH08154

KILVAHAN

Kilvahan Horse-Drawn Caravans, Kilvahan, Portlaoise, **County Laois**, **IRELAND**.
(T) 502 27048 **(F)** 502 27225
(E) kilvahan@eircom.net
(W) www.horsedrawncaravans.com.
Contact/s
Owner: Mr H Fingleton
Profile Holidays. Horse Drawn Caravans.
Visitors can travel independently. Kilvahan is a winner of 2 tourism awards, one of which is the Sunday Times 'Worlds Best 101 Holidays' award. No.Staff: 3
Yr. Est: 1993 C.Size: 197 Acres Ref:YH08155

KILVEY TACK

Kilvey Tack, Danybeacon, St. Thomas, Swansea, **Swansea**, SA1 8ED, **WALES**.
(T) 01792 643286.
Contact/s
Partner: Mrs A Kesans
Profile Supplies. Ref:YH08156

KIM SUTTON FINE ART

Kim Sutton Fine Art, The Knoll, Upper Poppleton, **Yorkshire (North)**, YO26 6QB, **ENGLAND**.
(T) 01904 788501 **(F)** 01904 782353. Ref:YH08157

KIMBER, IAN JAMES

Ian James Kimber DWCF, 1 Balmoral Cl, Malvern, **Worcestershire**, WR14 1YB, **ENGLAND**.
(T) 01684 565111.
Profile Farrier. Ref:YH08158

KIMBERS FARM LIVERY CTRE

Kimbers Farm Livery Centre, Oakley Green Rd, Oakley Green, Windsor, **Berkshire**, SL4 4QF, **ENGLAND**.
(T) 01628 771326.
Contact/s
Manager: Mr J Davey Ref:YH08159

KIMBLEWICK FEEDS

Kimblewick Feeds, Unit 3 Ackwell Simmonds, Chapel Croft, Chipperfield, **Hertfordshire**, WD4 9EG, **ENGLAND**.
(T) 01923 291376.
Contact/s
Manager: Mrs J Hern
Profile Feed Merchant. Ref:YH08160

KIMMERSTON RIDING CTRE

Kimmerston Riding Centre, Kimmerston Farm Cottages, Wooler, **Northumberland**, NE71 6JH, **ENGLAND**.
(T) 01668 216283.
Contact/s
Partner: Mrs J Jeffries
Profile Riding School. Ref:YH08161

KIMPTON BROS

Kimpton Bros Ltd, 10-14 Hewett St, London, **London (Greater)**, EC2A 3HA, **ENGLAND**.
(T) 020 72472072 **(F)** 020 72472784
(E) admin@kimpton.co.uk.
Profile Medical Support. Ref:YH08162

KINALDY EQUESTRIAN CTRE

Kinaldy Equestrian Centre, Kinaldy, St Andrews, **Fife**, KY16 8NA, **SCOTLAND**.
(T) 01334 470909.
Contact/s
Owner: Mr G Milne Ref:YH08163

KINANE, MICHAEL F

Michael F Kinane, 20 Rachaels Lake View, Warfield, Bracknell, **Berkshire**, RG12 6XU, **ENGLAND**.
(T) 01344 862950.
Profile Farrier. Ref:YH08164

KINCAID, CLAIRE

Claire Kincaid, 11 Home Farm Cl, Peasedown St John, Bath, **Bath & Somerset (North East)**, BA2 8SE, **ENGLAND**.
(T) 01761 432253
Affiliated Bodies NAAT.

Contact/s
Physiotherapist: Claire Kincaid
Profile Medical Support.
Physiotherapist for horses & dogs. Ref: YH08165

KINCARDINE COUNTY RIDING CLUB

Kincardine County Riding Club, 134 Forest Pk, Stonehaven, **Aberdeenshire**, AB39 2GF, **SCOTLAND**.
(T) 01569 765321.
Profile Club/Association, Riding Club. Ref: YH08166

KING BROS

King Bros, 13 Bannanstown Rd, Castlewellan, **County Down**, BT31 9BG, **NORTHERN IRELAND**.
(T) 028 43778651.
Profile Equestrian Centre. Ref: YH08167

KING FOREST ANIMAL SANCTUARY

King Forest Animal Sanctuary, Suncroft, Forest Moor Drive, Knaresborough, **Yorkshire (North)**, HG5 8JT, **ENGLAND**.
(T) 01423 862501.
Profile Club/Association. Ref: YH08168

KING OF THE ROAD TRAILERS

King Of The Road Trailers, Shire Lane, Sutton Scarsdale, Chesterfield, **Derbyshire**, S44 5SX, **ENGLAND**.
(T) 01246 859991.
Contact/s
Partner: Mr A France
Profile Transport/Horse Boxes. Ref: YH08169

KING TRAILERS

King Trailers Ltd, Riverside, Market Harborough, **Leicestershire**, LE16 7QE, **ENGLAND**.
(T) 01858 467361 (F) 01858 467161.
Profile Transport/Horse Boxes. Ref: YH08170

KING VEAN STUD

King Vean Stud, Fladbury Hill, Bishampton, Pershore, **Worcestershire**, WR10 2NE, **ENGLAND**.
(T) 01386 861099 (F) 01386 860067
(E) kingvean@cwcom.net
(W) www.kingvean.co.uk.
Contact/s
Owner: Mr B Burt
Profile Breeder. No.Staff: 3 Yr. Est: 1987
C.Size: 57 Acres
Opening Times
Telephone for an appointment Ref: YH08171

KING, A

A King, Moor Farm Racing Stable, Wilmcote, Stratford-upon-Avon, **Warwickshire**, CV37 9XG, **ENGLAND**.
(T) 01789 205087 (F) 01789 205087.
Contact/s
Owner: Mrs A King
Profile Trainer. Ref: YH08172

KING, A & L

A & L King, Drill Hall, Montrose Rd, Auchterarder, **Perth and Kinross**, PH3 1BZ, **SCOTLAND**.
(T) 01764 664010.
Contact/s
Owner: Mr R McQuen
Profile Blacksmith. Ref: YH08173

KING, ANN

Ann King, Howton Rd, Newton Abbot, **Devon**, TQ12 6NB, **ENGLAND**.
(T) 01626 334141.
Contact/s
Owner: Miss A King (T) 07932 625101
Profile Stable/Livery. Ref: YH08174

KING, BRUCE M

Bruce M King DWCF, Durhams Farm, Chastleton, Moreton In Marsh, **Gloucestershire**, GL56, **ENGLAND**.
(T) 01608 674052.
Profile Farrier. Ref: YH08175

KING, CHRISTOPHER G

Christopher G King RSS Hons, Willow Cottage, Clarks Green Rd, Capel, Dorking, **Surrey**, RH5 5HH, **ENGLAND**.
(T) 01306 712083.
Profile Farrier. Ref: YH08176

KING, D J

D J King BHSI, 35 Union Rd, Bridge, Canterbury, **Kent**, CT4 5LN, **ENGLAND**.
(T) 01227 830139.
Profile Trainer. Ref: YH08177

KING, D W

Mr D W King, 50 Wheatbottom, Crook, **County Durham**, DL15 9HA, **ENGLAND**.
(T) 01388 766525. Ref: YH08178

KING, E & M J

E & M J King, Peaked Elm Farm, Selsley West, Stroud, **Gloucestershire**, GL5 5LG, **ENGLAND**.
(T) 01453 822901.
Contact/s
Owner: Mrs M King
Profile Transport/Horse Boxes. Ref: YH08179

KING, G W & C E

Mr G W & Mrs C E King, Oakleigh Hse, Mamhead, Kenton, Exeter, **Devon**, EX6 8EX, **ENGLAND**.
(T) 01626 891636.
Profile Breeder. Ref: YH08180

KING, J S & PM

J S & PM King, Elmcross Hse, Broad Hinton, Swindon, **Wiltshire**, SN4 9PF, **ENGLAND**.
(T) 01793 731481 (F) 01793 739001
Affiliated Bodies NTF.
Contact/s
General Manager: Mrs P King
Profile Trainer. Yr. Est: 1981 C.Size: 40 Acres
Ref: YH08181

KING, JAMES D

James D King DWCF, Meadowside Cottage, Oasby, Grantham, **Lincolnshire**, NG32 3NB, **ENGLAND**.
(T) 01529 455615.
Profile Farrier. Ref: YH08182

KING, MARY ELIZABETH

Mrs Mary Elizabeth King, School Hse, Salcombe Regis, Sidmouth, **Devon**, EX10 0JQ, **ENGLAND**.
(T) 01395 514882 (F) 01392 432531. Ref: YH08183

KING, P

P King RSS, Bent Farm, Farley, Matlock, **Derbyshire**, DE4 5LT, **ENGLAND**.
(T) 01629 582792.
Profile Farrier. Ref: YH08184

KING, P

P King, Coombe Valley, Tedburn St Mary, **Devon**, EX6 6BH, **ENGLAND**.
(T) 01647 61573 (F) 01647 61112.
Profile Transport/Horse Boxes. Ref: YH08185

KING, PAUL D

Paul D King DWCF, The Hollies, Leigh Rd, Betchworth, **Surrey**, RH3 7AW, **ENGLAND**.
(T) 01306 611674.
Profile Farrier. Ref: YH08186

KING, R A

R A King RSS, 2 Eastleigh Cottages, Bartons Rd, Havant, **Hampshire**, PO9 5NA, **ENGLAND**.
(T) 023 92480713.
Profile Farrier. Ref: YH08187

KING, STUART L

Stuart L King DWCF, 3 Beales Farm Rd, Hungerford, **Berkshire**, RG17 8PZ, **ENGLAND**.
(T) 01488 73508.
Profile Farrier. Ref: YH08188

KINGARTH TREKKING CTRE

Kingarth Trekking Centre, Kingarth, Isle Of Bute, **Argyll and Bute**, PA20 9NS, **SCOTLAND**.
(T) 01700 831627 (F) 01700 831673.
Profile Riding School. Trekking Centre. Ref: YH08189

KINGDOM PRODUCTS

Kingdom Products Ltd, P O Box 417, Stafford, **Staffordshire**, ST18 9LB, **ENGLAND**.
(T) 01785 780060.
Profile Supplies. Ref: YH08190

KINGFISHER

Kingfisher Paper Products, Bardsea Business Pk, Bardsea, Ulverston, **Cumbria**, LA12 9RA, **ENGLAND**.
(T) 01229 869969 (F) 01229 869969.
Contact/s
Owner: Mr I Marland
Profile Supplies. Bedding Manufacturers.
Kingfisher paper bedding offers the following advantages: it is sterile, therapeutic, a fitness aid, warm, economical, time saving, disposable, manageable and convenient. Ref: YH08191

KINGS

Kings, Monica Hse/Long St, Premier Business Pk, Walsall, **Midlands (West)**, WS2 9DY, **ENGLAND**.
(T) 01922 641391 (F) 01922 647982.
Contact/s
Owner: Mr D Rathbone
Profile Saddlery Retailer. Ref: YH08192

KINGS FARM STABLES

Kings Farm Stables, Upper Lambourne, Hungerford, **Berkshire**, RG17 8QT, **ENGLAND**.
(M) 07785 757090.
Profile Trainer. Ref: YH08193

KINGS LANGLEY RIDING SCHOOL

Kings Langley Riding School, Whippendell Spinney, Chipperfield Rd, Kings Langley, **Hertfordshire**, WD4 9JE, **ENGLAND**.
(T) 01923 270719.
Contact/s
Owner: Mr T McCarthy Ref: YH08194

KINGS LANGLEY TACK SHOP

Kings Langley Tack Shop, 10 High St, Kings Langley, **Hertfordshire**, WD4 8BH, **ENGLAND**.
(T) 01442 831323 (F) 01923 266447.
Contact/s
Owner: Mrs E Potter Ref: YH08195

KINGS OAK EQUESTRIAN CTRE

Kings Oak Equestrian Centre, Kings Oak Riding School/Theobalds Park Rd, Crews Hill, Enfield, **London (Greater)**, EN2 9BL, **ENGLAND**.
(T) 020 83637868.
Contact/s
Partner: Miss G Gill
Profile Riding School, Stable/Livery. Ref: YH08196

KINGS SADDLERY & COUNTRY WARE

Kings Saddlery & Country Ware, Grange Barn, Grundisburgh Rd, Hasketon, Woodbridge, **Suffolk**, IP13 6HN, **ENGLAND**.
(T) 01473 738237 (F) 01473 735148.
Contact/s
Owner: Mrs P Watts Ref: YH08197

KINGS VETNRY SURGERY

Kings Veterinary Surgery, 53 Henver Rd, Newquay, **Cornwall**, TR7 3DQ, **ENGLAND**.
(T) 01637 851122.
Profile Medical Support. Ref: YH08198

KINGSCOTE PARK STUD

Kingscote Park Stud, Coombe Cottage, Charlton, Malmesbury, **Wiltshire**, SN16 9DR, **ENGLAND**.
(T) 01666 823563 (F) 01666 823563.
Contact/s
Owner: Lt Col R Bromley-Gardner
Profile Breeder. Ref: YH08199

KINGSDOWN

Kingsdown, Lower Kingsdown Rd, Kingsdown, Corsham, **Wiltshire**, SN13 8BB, **ENGLAND**.
(T) 01225 743406. Ref: YH08200

KINGSDOWN PICTURES

Kingsdown Pictures, 164 Park Rd, Stapleton, **Bristol**, BS16 1DW, **ENGLAND**.
(T) 01179 651596.
Profile Photographer. Ref: YH08201

KINGSETTLE STUD

Kingsettle Stud, Dolau Cwerchyr, Penrhiwllan, Llandysssul, **Carmarthenshire**, SA44 5NZ, **WALES**.
(T) 01239 851387 (F) 01239 851040.
Profile Breeder. Ref: YH08202

KINGSLAND STABLING

Kingsland Stabling, Kingsland Sawmills, Kingsland, Leominster, **Herefordshire**, HR6 9SF, **ENGLAND**.
(T) 01568 708206 (F) 01568 708258
(M) 07971 887372
(E) info@kingslandstabling.com.
Profile Transport/Horse Boxes. Ref: YH08203

KINGSLEY FORGE

Kingsley Forge, 3 Frognall Cottages, Grove Rd, Wickhambreaux, Canterbury, **Kent**, CT3 1SB, **ENGLAND**.
(T) 01227 721686.
Profile Blacksmith. Ref: YH08204

KINGSMEAD EQUESTRIAN CTRE

Kingsmead Equestrian Centre, Kingswood Lane, Warlingham, **Surrey**, CR6 9AB, **ENGLAND**.
(T) 020 86570832.
Contact/s
Owner: Mrs A Cottier Ref: YH08205

KINGSTON & DISTRICT

Kingston & District Riding Club, 21 Dorking Rd, Great Bookham, **Surrey**, KT23 4PU, **ENGLAND**.
(T) 01372 450179.

Profile Club/Association, Riding Club. **Ref: YH08206**

KINGSTON RIDING CTRE

Kingston Riding Centre, 38 Crescent Rd, Kingston Upon Thames, **London (Greater)**, KT2 7RG, **ENGLAND**.
(T) 020 85466361 **(F)** 020 89745585.
Contact/s
Owner: Mrs L Mastroianni
Profile Riding School, Stable/Livery. **Ref: YH08207**

KINGSWESTON STABLES

Kingsweston Stables, Lime Kiln, Kings Weston Rd, Lawrence Weston, Bristol, **Bristol**, BS11 0UX, **ENGLAND**.
(T) 01179 828929.
Profile Riding School. **Ref: YH08208**

KINGSWOOD AST

Kingswood Associates, Equestrian Press & PR Consultants, The Bungalow, Poppinghole Lane, Robertsbridge, **Sussex (East)**, TN32 5QY, **ENGLAND**.
(T) 01580 830979 **(F)** 01580 830979.
Profile Club/Association. **Ref: YH08209**

KINGSWOOD EQUESTRIAN CTRE

Kingswood Equestrian Centre, Kingswood Lodge, County Lane, Albrighton, Wolverhampton, **Midlands (West)**, WV7 3AH, **ENGLAND**.
(T) 01902 374480
Affiliated Bodies ABRS, BHS, RDA.
Contact/s
Owner: Mr R Lickley
Profile Riding School.
Hacking available. Lesson prices vary fom £12.00 to £14.00.
Opening Times
Sp: Open Mon - Sun 08:00. Closed Mon - Sun 17:00.
Su: Open Mon - Sun 08:00. Closed Mon - Sun 17:00.
Au: Open Mon - Sun 08:00. Closed Mon - Sun 17:00.
Wn: Open Mon - Sun 08:00. Closed Mon - Sun 17:00. **Ref: YH08210**

KINGSWOOD FARM HOUSE

Kingswood Farm House, Dalehouse Lane, Kenilworth, **Warwickshire**, CV8 2JZ, **ENGLAND**.
(T) 024 76418121.
Profile Stable/Livery. **Ref: YH08211**

KINGTON RIDING STABLES

Kington Riding Stables, Fewsters Farm, Thornbury, Bristol, **Bristol**, BS35 1ND, **ENGLAND**.
(T) 01454 416685.
Profile Riding School. **Ref: YH08212**

KINGTON, JOHN

John Kington, The Larches, Four Oaks, Newent, **Gloucestershire**, GL18 1LU, **ENGLAND**.
(T) 01531 890445.
Contact/s
Owner: Mr J Kington
Profile Saddlery Retailer. **Ref: YH08213**

KINGWATER EQUESTRIAN CTRE

Kingwater Equestrian Centre, Burtyinghurst, Walton, Carlisle, **Cumbria**, CA8 2JW, **ENGLAND**.
(T) 01697 72558.
Profile Equestrian Centre. **Ref: YH08214**

KINGWOOD HOUSE STABLES

Kingwood House Stables Ltd, Kingwood Hse, Lambourn Woodlands, Hungerford, **Berkshire**, RG17 7RS, **ENGLAND**.
(T) 01488 73300 **(F)** 01488 71728.
Contact/s
Accountant: Mr C Kennard
Profile Breeder, Trainer. **Ref: YH08215**

KINNARD, D W & A M

D W & A M Kinnard, Blaenoethie, Llanddewi Brefi, Tregaron, **Ceredigion**, **WALES**.
(T) 01974 298821.
Profile Breeder. **Ref: YH08216**

KINNEAR, TERRY

Terry Kinnear, Wester Bandrum, Nr Faline, Saline, Dunfermline, **Fife**, KY12 9HR, **SCOTLAND**.
(T) 01383 851915.
Profile Stable/Livery. **Ref: YH08217**

KINNERSLEY RACING STABLES

Kinnersley Racing Stables, Severn Stoke, **Worcestershire**, WR8 9JR, **ENGLAND**.
(T) 01905 371054 **(F)** 01905 371054.
Profile Trainer. **Ref: YH08218**

KINSEY, T R

Mr T R Kinsey, Peel Hall, Ashton, **Cheshire**, CH3 8AY, **ENGLAND**.
(T) 01829 751230.
Profile Supplies. **Ref: YH08219**

KINSHALDY RIDING STABLES

Kinshaldy Riding Stables, Kinshaldy Farm, Leuchars, St Andrews, **Fife**, KY16 0DR, **SCOTLAND**.
(T) 01334 838527.
Contact/s
Owner: Mr B Collier
Profile Riding School. **Ref: YH08220**

KINSLEY GREEN FARM

Kinsley Green Farm, Kinsley Green, Ackworth, Pontefract, **Yorkshire (West)**, WF7 7BL, **ENGLAND**.
(T) 01977 611906 **(F)** 01977 611906.
Profile Transport/Horse Boxes. **Ref: YH08221**

KIPPAX

Kippax Equestrian & Animal Feed, 87 Oxford Drive, Kippax, Leeds, **Yorkshire (West)**, LS25 7JD, **ENGLAND**.
(T) 0113 2865450 **(F)** 0113 2865450.
Contact/s
Owner: Miss L Crowther
Profile Supplies. **No.Staff:** 1 **Yr. Est:** 1991
Opening Times
Sp: Open Mon - Sat 09:00, Sun 10:00. Closed Mon - Sun 18:00.
Su: Open Mon - Sat 09:00, Sun 10:00. Closed Mon - Sun 18:00.
Au: Open Mon - Sat 09:00, Sun 10:00. Closed Mon - Sun 18:00.
Wn: Open Mon - Sat 09:00, Sun 10:00. Closed Mon - Sun 18:00. **Ref: YH08222**

KIRBY & COOK & PEGG

Kirby & Cook & Pegg, Pype Hayes Vetnry Ctre, Badington, Birmingham, **Midlands (West)**, B24 0SA, **ENGLAND**.
(T) 0121 3502303.
Profile Medical Support. **Ref: YH08223**

KIRBY HSE COTTAGE

Kirby House Cottage Livery Stables, Kirby Hse Cottage, Woolsthorpe, Grantham, **Lincolnshire**, NG32 1NT, **ENGLAND**.
(T) 01476 870889.
Contact/s
Owner: Mrs S Jackson
Profile Stable/Livery. **Ref: YH08224**

KIRBY HSE STUD & RACING

Kirby House Stud & Racing Ltd, Woolsthorpe-By-Belvoir, Grantham, **Lincolnshire**, NG32 INT, **ENGLAND**.
(T) 01476 870177 **(F)** 01476 870382.
Profile Breeder. **Ref: YH08225**

KIRBY, E M

Mrs E M Kirby, Cherry Trees, Llandennis Ave, Cyncoed, Cardiff, **Glamorgan (Vale of)**, CF23 6JG, **WALES**.
(T) 029 20753605.
Profile Breeder. **Ref: YH08226**

KIRBY, F

Mr F Kirby, High Whinholme Farm, Streetlam, Danby Wiske, Northallerton, **Yorkshire (North)**, DL7 0AS, **ENGLAND**.
(T) 01325 378213 **(F)** 01325 378213.
Profile Supplies. **Ref: YH08227**

KIRBY, J

Mr J Kirby, Pewit Farm, Manor Rd, Wantage, **Oxfordshire**, OX12 8LY, **ENGLAND**.
(T) 01235 767987 **(F)** 01235 767987.
Profile Supplies. **Ref: YH08228**

KIRBY, M J

M J Kirby, Vicarage Farm, Cowlinge Rd, Kirtling, Newmarket, **Suffolk**, CB8 9HL, **ENGLAND**.
(T) 01638 730129 **(F)** 01638 730129.
Contact/s
Owner: Mr M Kirby
Profile Breeder. **Ref: YH08229**

KIRK RD SMIDDY

Kirk Road Smiddy, Viewbank Farm, Allanton Rd, Shotts, **Lanarkshire (North)**, ML7 5AQ, **SCOTLAND**.
(T) 01501 821674 **(F)** 01501 821674
(W) www.wroughtiron-scotland.co.uk
Affiliated Bodies FSB.
Contact/s
Owner: Mr R Sneddon **(T)** 01501 821289
(E) kirkroadsmiddy@cw.co.uk.net
Profile Blacksmith. **Ref: YH08230**

KIRK, C

Mr C Kirk, New Bungalow Scar View, Melmerby, Penrith, **Cumbria**, CA10 1HN, **ENGLAND**.
(T) 01768 881387.
Profile Trainer. **Ref: YH08231**

KIRKBY

Kirkby Farriers Ltd, The Fearnall Stud, Tilstone Fearnall, Tarporley, **Cheshire**, CW6 9HS, **ENGLAND**.
(T) 01829 733665
Affiliated Bodies FRC.
Contact/s
Partner: Mr D Thomson **(Q)** DWCF
Profile Farrier.
International Farrier/ Consultant **Yr. Est:** 1975
Opening Times
Telephone for an appointment **Ref: YH08232**

KIRKBY, GEORGE

George Kirkby, Boundway, Boundway Hill, Sway, Lymington, **Hampshire**, SO41 6EN, **ENGLAND**.
(T) 01590 682543.
Contact/s
Owner: Mr G Kirkby
Profile Farrier. **Ref: YH08233**

KIRKFIELD EQUESTRIAN CTRE

Kirkfield Equestrian Centre, Calverton Rd, Lower Blidworth, **Nottinghamshire**, NG21 0NW, **ENGLAND**.
(T) 01623 794831 **(F)** 01623 793411.
Profile Riding School, Stable/Livery. **Ref: YH08234**

KIRKFIELD STABLES

Kirkfield Stables, Calverton Rd, Lower Blidworth, **Nottinghamshire**, NG21 0NW, **ENGLAND**.
(T) 01623 794831 **(F)** 01623 793411.
Profile Trainer. **Ref: YH08235**

KIRKLAND SADDLERY

Kirkland Saddlery, 116 Lichfield Rd, Shelfield, Walsall, **Midlands (West)**, WS4 1PS, **ENGLAND**.
(T) 01922 684103.
Contact/s
Owner: Ms D Kirkland
Profile Riding Wear Retailer, Saddlery Retailer. **Ref: YH08236**

KIRKLEVINGTON RIDING SCHOOL

Kirklevington Riding School, Town End Farm, Kirklevington, Yarm, **Cleveland**, TS15 9LX, **ENGLAND**.
(T) 01642 780756.
Contact/s
Owner: Ms J Brookes
Profile Riding School.
One to one private lessons are avaliable as well as group lessons.
Opening Times
Sp: Open Mon - Sun 09:00. Closed Mon - Sun 17:00.
Su: Open Mon - Sun 09:00. Closed Mon - Sun 17:00.
Au: Open Mon - Sun 09:00. Closed Mon - Sun 17:00.
Wn: Open Mon - Sun 09:00. Closed Mon - Sun 17:00.
Late night lessons avaliable on Wednesdays.
Ref: YH08237

KIRKPATRICK, JOE

Joe Kirkpatrick, Kirkwin, 41 Hollymount, Finaghy, Belfast, **County Antrim**, BT10 0GN, **NORTHERN IRELAND**.
(T) 028 90615345. **Ref: YH08238**

KIRKTON RIDING CTRE

Kirkton Riding Centre, Fisherie, Turriff, **Aberdeenshire**, AB53 5QB, **SCOTLAND**.
(T) 01888 551610 **(F)** 01888 551680.
Contact/s
Owner: Mr K Chisman **Ref: YH08239**

KIRRIEMUIR HORSE SUPPLIES

Kirriemuir Horse Supplies, Pathhead Farm, Forfar Rd, Kirriemuir, **Angus**, DD8 5BY, **SCOTLAND**.
(T) 01575 572173 **(F)** 01575 575272
(W) www.pathhead.com
Affiliated Bodies ABRS.
Contact/s
Owner: Mrs J Collins
(E) joycecollins@pathhead.com
Profile Riding School, Riding Wear Retailer, Stable/Livery, Supplies. **Ref: YH08240**

KIRTLINGTON PARK POLO SCHOOL
Kirtlington Park Polo School, Park Farm Technology Ctre, Akeman St, Kirtlington, Kidlington, **Oxfordshire**, OX5 3JQ, **ENGLAND**.
(T) 01869 350083.
Profile Breeder. **Ref: YH08241**

KIRTLINGTON POLO CLUB
Kirtlington Polo Club (The), Westfield Barn Hse, North Lane, Weston-on-the-Green, Bicester, **Oxfordshire**, OX6 8RG, **ENGLAND**.
(T) 01869 350138 **(F)** 01869 350777.
Profile Polo club. **Ref: YH08242**

KIRTLINGTON STUD
Kirtlington Stud, Kirtlington, Kidlington, **Oxfordshire**, OX5 3EU, **ENGLAND**.
(T) 01869 350101 **(F)** 01869 351199.
Profile Breeder. **Ref: YH08243**

KIT HOUGHTON PHOTOGRAPHY
Kit Houghton Photography, Radlett Cottage, Spaxton, Bridgwater, **Somerset**, TA5 1DE, **ENGLAND**.
(T) 01278 671362 **(F)** 01278 671739
(M) 07836 342847
(E) kit@enterprise.net.
Profile Photographer.
Specialises in photographing horses. **Ref: YH08244**

KIT LAMBERT BLACKSMITHS
Kit Lambert Blacksmiths, The Forge/Jayes Pk, Stane St, Ockley, Dorking, **Surrey**, RH5 5TD, **ENGLAND**.
(T) 01306 621552.
Profile Blacksmith. **Ref: YH08245**

KIT WILSON TRUST
Kit Wilson Trust for Animal Welfare, Animal Rescue Ctre, Stonehurst Lane, Hadlow Down, Uckfield, **Sussex (East)**, TN22 4ED, **ENGLAND**.
(T) 01825 830444 **(F)** 01825 830887.
Profile Medical Support. **Ref: YH08246**

KITCHING & LEES
Kitching & Lees, Fryup Gill Farm, Leaholm, Fryup, Whitby, **Yorkshire (North)**, YO21 2AP, **ENGLAND**.
(T) 01287 660379 **(F)** 01287 660379.
Profile Breeder. **Ref: YH08247**

KLIPONOFF TRAILER HIRE/SALES
Kliponoff Trailer Hire & Sales, Walker Engineering, Works Number 4 Lee Bridge Ind Est, Dean Clough Ind Pk, Halifax, **Yorkshire (West)**, HX3 5AT, **ENGLAND**.
(T) 01422 345568.
Profile Transport/Horse Boxes. **Ref: YH08248**

KNABBHALL EQUESTRIAN CTRE
Knabbhall Equestrian Centre, Hopkin Farm, Tansley, Matlock, **Derbyshire**, DE4 5GD, **ENGLAND**.
(T) 01629 582253.
Profile Riding School. **Ref: YH08249**

KNAPTOFT HOUSE FARM
Knaptoft House Farm, Bruntingthorpe Rd, Nr Shearsby, Lutterworth, **Leicestershire**, LE17 6PR, **ENGLAND**.
(T) 0116 2478388 **(F)** 0116 2478388
(E) info@knaptoft.com
(W) www.knaptoft.com.
Contact/s
General Manager: Mrs A Hutchinson
Profile Horse/Rider Accom. **No.Staff:** 2
Yr. Est: 1973 **C.Size:** 135 Acres
Opening Times
Sp: Open Mon - Sun 09:00. Closed Mon - Sun 21:00.
Su: Open Mon - Sun 09:00. Closed Mon - Sun 21:00.
Au: Open Mon - Sun 09:00. Closed Mon - Sun 21:00.
Wn: Open Mon - Sun 09:00. Closed Mon - Sun 21:00. **Ref: YH08250**

KNAPWELL CHURCH RIDE
Knapwell Church Ride, Manor Farm, Knapwell, **Cambridgeshire**, CB3 8NR, **ENGLAND**.
(T) 01954 7212. **Ref: YH08251**

KNEEN, J E
J E Kneen, Hill Hse, Arbroath, **Angus**, DD11 1AH, **SCOTLAND**.
(T) 01241 873100 **(F)** 01241 872703.
Profile Medical Support. **Ref: YH08252**

KNELLER, DAVID VINCENT
David Vincent Kneller DWCF, 2 Denton Drive, Denton, Newhaven, **Sussex (East)**, BN9 0PT, **ENGLAND**.
(T) 01273 512242.
Profile Farrier. **Ref: YH08253**

KNELLER, R & P
R & P Kneller, Old Vine Cottage, Chalk Lane, Wickham Rd, Fareham, **Hampshire**, PO17 5DP, **ENGLAND**.
(T) 01329 834248.
Contact/s
Owner: Mr R Kneller
Profile Breeder.
Breeder of Welsh Section A and C ponies
Ref: YH08254

KNEPP CASTLE POLO CLUB
Knepp Castle Polo Club, Knepp Castle, West Grinstead, Horsham, **Sussex (West)**, RH13 8LJ, **ENGLAND**.
(T) 01403 741007 **(F)** 01403 741006.
Contact/s
Coach: Alex Parrott
Profile Club/Association. Polo club. **Ref: YH08255**

KNIGHT & BUTLER
Knight & Butler Ltd, Crowhurst Rd, Lingfield, **Surrey**, RH7 6DB, **ENGLAND**.
(T) 01342 832132 **(F)** 01342 834546.
Profile Supplies. **Ref: YH08256**

KNIGHT EQUESTRIAN SUPPLIES
Knight Equestrian Supplies, Garth Crook, Thruscross, Summerbridge, Harrogate, **Yorkshire (North)**, HG3 4AZ, **ENGLAND**.
(T) 01943 880466
(E) knight@harrogate.com.
Profile Supplies. **Ref: YH08257**

KNIGHT, ADAM R
Adam R Knight DWCF, Cygnet Thatch, The Green, Radwell, **Bedfordshire**, MK43 7HT, **ENGLAND**.
(T) 01234 781529.
Profile Farrier. **Ref: YH08258**

KNIGHT, G C & LINDSEY, J E
G C Knight & J E Lindsey, Rockingham Hse Farm, Haugh Rd, Rawmarsh, Rotherham, **Yorkshire (South)**, S62 7DP, **ENGLAND**.
(T) 01709 524045.
Profile Riding School. **Ref: YH08259**

KNIGHT, GEORGE
Mr George Knight, Vincents Farm, West Hatch, Taunton, **Somerset**, TA3 5RJ, **ENGLAND**.
(T) 01823 480320
(M) 07778 549452.
Profile Trainer. **Ref: YH08260**

KNIGHT, HENRIETTA
Miss Henrietta Knight, West Lockinge Farm, Wantage, **Oxfordshire**, OX12 8QF, **ENGLAND**.
(T) 01235 833535 **(F)** 01235 820110
(M) 07860 110153.
Profile Trainer. **Ref: YH08261**

KNIGHT, K J
K J Knight RSS, Forge Cottage, 31 Plough Lane, Wokingham, **Berkshire**, RG11 1RQ, **ENGLAND**.
(T) 01734 772821.
Profile Farrier. **Ref: YH08262**

KNIGHT, P W
P W Knight, Silverdale Pk, Perranwell Station, Truro, **Cornwall**, TR3 7LW, **ENGLAND**.
(T) 01872 862395.
Profile Farrier. **Ref: YH08263**

KNIGHT, R C
R C Knight, 1 Home Farm, Beaulieu, Brockenhurst, **Hampshire**, SO42 7YG, **ENGLAND**.
(T) 01590 612317.
Profile Breeder. **Ref: YH08264**

KNIGHT, RICHARD
Richard Knight, 64 Horsefair St, Charlton Kings, Cheltenham, **Gloucestershire**, GL53 8JH, **ENGLAND**.
(T) 01242 243663.
Contact/s
Owner: Mr R Knight
Profile Farrier. **Ref: YH08265**

KNIGHTBRIDGE, A
A Knightbridge, Mwingo, Green Lane, Blackfield, Southampton, **Hampshire**, SO45 1YG, **ENGLAND**.
(T) 023 80893686.
Profile Farrier. **Ref: YH08266**

KNIGHTONCOMBE EXMOOR
Knightoncombe Exmoor Pony Stud, Knighton, Minehead, **Somerset**, TA24 7RD, **ENGLAND**.
(T) 01643 831210.
Profile Breeder. **Ref: YH08267**

KNIGHTS END FARM
Knights End Farm Training Centre, Knights End Rd, March, **Cambridgeshire**, PE15 0YR, **ENGLAND**.
(T) 01354 650334 **(F)** 01354 650334
(E) kefdressage@onetel.net.uk
(W) www.kefdressage.com
Affiliated Bodies BD, DEFRA.
Contact/s
Partner: Miss A Hessay **(Q)** BHS SM, BHSI(SM), BHSII
Profile Arena, Stable/Livery, Trainer. Dressage Competition.
A 45 minute lesson with Angela is £35.00. Andrea charges £32.50. Livery is also available, details on request.
Opening Times
Visitors are welcome any time between Tuesdays - Sundays, the yard is closed Mondays. Please telephone to ensure either Angela or Andrea will be available. **Ref: YH08268**

KNIGHTS OF ARKLEY
Knights of Arkley (The), Glyn Sylen, Five Roads, Llanelli, **Carmarthenshire**, SA15 5BJ, **WALES**.
(T) 01269 861001 **(F)** 01269 861001. **Ref: YH08269**

KNIGHTS OF THE TOURNAMENT
Knights of the Tournament, 41 Littleworth Rd, Downley, High Wycombe, **Buckinghamshire**, HP13 5XB, **ENGLAND**.
(T) 01494 452635.
Profile Club/Association. **Ref: YH08270**

KNIGHTS, DEREK
Derek Knights, Sedbury East Farm, Gilling West, Richmond, **Yorkshire (North)**, DL10 5ER, **ENGLAND**.
(T) 01748 850089.
Profile Farrier. **Ref: YH08271**

KNIGHTSBRIDGE STABLES
Knightsbridge Stables, South Sway Lane, Sway, **Hampshire**, **ENGLAND**.
(T) 01590 682271.
Profile Stable/Livery. **Ref: YH08272**

KNIPE, R F
R F Knipe, Cobhall Court Stud, Allensmore, Hereford, **Herefordshire**, HR2 9BG, **ENGLAND**.
(T) 01432 277245 **(F)** 01432 341149.
Profile Breeder. **Ref: YH08273**

KNITSLEY MILL STUD
Knitsley Mill Stud, Knitsley, Consett, **County Durham**, DH8 9EL, **ENGLAND**.
(T) 01207 501553 **(F)** 0191 3863955.
Profile Breeder. **Ref: YH08274**

KNOCK SHETLAND PONY STUD
Knock Shetland Pony Stud, White Hse, Knock, Appleby-In-Westmorland, **Cumbria**, CA16 6DN, **ENGLAND**.
(T) 01768 361311.
Profile Breeder. **Ref: YH08275**

KNOLL & OAKTREE FARMS
Knoll & Oaktree Farms, Ladywood Rd, Martin Hussingtree, Worcester, **Worcestershire**, WR3 7SX, **ENGLAND**.
(T) 01905 455565.
Profile Stable/Livery. **Ref: YH08276**

KNOTT HILL FARM
Knott Hill Farm, Knott Hill, Ashton-under-Lyne, **Manchester (Greater)**, OL6 9AG, **ENGLAND**.
(T) 01457 833447.
Contact/s
Owner: Mr I Baugh **Ref: YH08277**

KNOTT, J B & J E
J B & J E Knott, Upper Hookpit Farmhouse, Worthy Down Lane, Kingsworthy, Winchester, **Hampshire**, SO21 2RR, **ENGLAND**.
(T) 01962 884013 **(F)** 01962 883522
(E) john@vet-surgery.demon.co.uk.
Profile Medical Support. **Ref: YH08278**

KNOWLE FARM LIVERIES
Knowle Farm Liveries, Knowle Farm, Old Park Lane, Farnham, **Surrey**, GU9 0AN, **ENGLAND**.
(T) 01252 726503.
Contact/s

A-Z of COMPANIES

Owner: Mr J Ricketts **Ref: YH08279**

KNOWLE HILL EQUESTRIAN

Knowle Hill Equestrian Centre, Knowle Hill Farm, Ingleby Lane, Ticknall, Derby, **Derbyshire**, DE73 1JQ, **ENGLAND**.
(T) 01332 862044
Affiliated Bodies BHS.
Contact/s
Owner: Ms H Stanton
Profile Equestrian Centre, Riding School, Riding Wear Retailer, Saddlery Retailer, Stable/Livery.
Cross Country Course for Hire **Ref: YH08280**

KNOWLE MANOR

Knowle Manor Guest House & Riding Centre, Knowle Manor, Timberscombe, Minehead, **Somerset**, TA24 6TZ, **ENGLAND**.
(T) 01643 841342 **(F)** 01643 841644
(E) knowlemnr@aol.com
(W) www.ridingholidaysuk.com
Affiliated Bodies ABRS, BHS.
Contact/s
Owner: Mr J Lamacraft
Profile Holidays, Riding School.
Quality horses and ponies suitable for all types of rider. Accommodation in large country house with a licenced bar.Trout lake, river fishing, heated outdoor swimming pool and steam train rides. DIY livery for guests own horses. Well behaved dogs welcome.
C.Size: 100 Acres **Ref: YH08281**

KNOWLES BANK STUD

Knowles Bank Stud, Knowles Bank, Half Moon Lane, Tudeley, Tonbridge, **Kent**, TN11 0PU, **ENGLAND**.
(T) 01892 824747 **(F)** 01892 823906.
Contact/s
Owner: Mr B O'Brien
Profile Breeder. **Ref: YH08282**

KNOWLES, A & J

A & J Knowles, Edisford Bridge Farm, Edisford Bridge, Clitheroe, **Lancashire**, BB7 3LJ, **ENGLAND**.
(T) 01200 427868 **(F)** 01200 442023.
Contact/s
Partner: Mrs J Knowles **Ref: YH08283**

KNOWLES, E

Mrs E Knowles, Charnwood, Stoke Hill, Stoke St Michael, Bath, **Bath & Somerset (North East)**, BA3 5JJ, **ENGLAND**.
(T) 01749 840015.
Profile Breeder. **Ref: YH08284**

KNOWLES, S W

S W Knowles, Beechwood Grange Stud, Malton Rd, York, **Yorkshire (North)**, YO32 9TH, **ENGLAND**.
(T) 01904 424573 **(F)** 01904 424573.
Contact/s
Owner: Mrs S Knowles
Profile Breeder. **Ref: YH08285**

KNOWLTON STUD

Knowlton Stud, Knowlton Court, Canterbury, **Kent**, CT3 1PT, **ENGLAND**.
(T) 01304 842402 **(F)** 01304 842403.
Profile Breeder, Horse/Rider Accom. **Ref: YH08286**

KNOX & DEVLIN

Knox & Devlin, 10 Bridge St, Whaley Bridge, High Peak, **Derbyshire**, SK23 7LR, **ENGLAND**.
(T) 01663 732692 **(F)** 01663 732693.
Profile Medical Support. **Ref: YH08287**

KNOX, T K

T K Knox, Southwood Farm, Streetlam, Danby Wiske, North Allerton, **Yorkshire (North)**, DL7 0AS, **ENGLAND**.
(T) 01325 378044.
Profile Breeder. **Ref: YH08288**

KNOX, THOMAS T

Thomas T Knox DWCF, No 2 Blue Hse Cottages, Stirrup St, Laxfield, Woodbridge, **Suffolk**, IP13 8EQ, **ENGLAND**.
(T) 01986 798713.
Profile Farrier. **Ref: YH08289**

KONGSKILDE UK

Kongskilde UK Ltd, Hempstead Rd, Holt, **Norfolk**, NR25 6EE, **ENGLAND**.
(T) 01263 713291.
Profile Supplies. **Ref: YH08290**

KONIG, ANTHONY JOSEPH

Anthony Joseph Konig RSS, 10 Tithe Cl, Codicote, **Hertfordshire**, SG4 8VX, **ENGLAND**.
(T) 01438 820080.
Profile Farrier. **Ref: YH08291**

KOPEL, EDWARD R

Edward R Kopel DWCF, The Flat, Wolds Farm, Fosse Way, Cotgrave, **Nottinghamshire**, NG12 3HG, **ENGLAND**.
(T) 0115 9899491.
Profile Farrier. **Ref: YH08292**

KRAIBURG

Kraiburg Stable Mats Ltd, Po Box 140, Bridgwater, **Somerset**, TA5 1HT, **ENGLAND**.
(T) 01984 667552 **(F)** 01984 618397
(E) kraiburg@dalsouple.com
(W) www.kraiburg.co.uk.
Profile Supplies.
Flooring Specialists. Have five distributors across the UK. See website for further details Yr. Est: 1961
Ref: YH08293

KRIS PARSONS MOBILE

Kris Parsons Mobile, 32 Gribb View, Thorncombe, Chard, **Somerset**, TA20 4ND, **ENGLAND**.
(T) 01460 30890.
Contact/s
Owner: Mr K Parsons
Profile Farrier. **Ref: YH08294**

KRISLAN TRAVEL

Krislan Travel Ltd, 24 Goodge St, London, **London (Greater)**, W1P 1FG, **ENGLAND**.
(T) 020 73231244 **(F)** 020 73235638. **Ref: YH08295**

KRONE COMMERCIAL TRAILERS

Krone Commercial Trailers, 14 Fairview Rd, Hungerford, **Berkshire**, RG17 0BT, **ENGLAND**.
(T) 01488 681374 **(F)** 01488 681392.
Contact/s
Owner: Mr T Hird
Profile Transport/Horse Boxes. **Ref: YH08296**

KRONE COMMERCIAL TRAILERS

Krone Commercial Trailers, Nelthorpe Lodge, Ulceby, **Lincolnshire (North)**, DN39 6FB, **ENGLAND**.
(T) 01469 589353 **(F)** 01469 589354.
Profile Transport/Horse Boxes. **Ref: YH08297**

KRONSBEC RIDING CLUB

Kronsbec Riding Club, 44 Stamford St, Ellesmere Port, **Cheshire**, CH65 8HJ, **ENGLAND**.
(T) 0151 3565909 **(F)** 0151 3565909.
Profile Riding Club. **Ref: YH08298**

KRUUSE

Kruuse Ltd, 14A Moor Lane Ind Est, Sherburn In Elmet, **Yorkshire (West)**, LS25 6ES, **ENGLAND**.
(T) 01977 681523 **(F)** 01977 683537.
Profile Medical Support. **Ref: YH08299**

KUBOTA

Kubota (UK) Ltd, Dormer Rd, Thame, **Oxfordshire**, OX9 3UN, **ENGLAND**.
(T) 01844 214500.
Profile Transport/Horse Boxes. **Ref: YH08300**

K-VEST UK

K-Vest UK, Unit 1 21 Waresley Rd, Gamlingay, Sandy, **Bedfordshire**, SG19 3EJ, **ENGLAND**.
(T) 01767 652172 **(F)** 01767 652145.
Profile Supplies. **Ref: YH08301**

KWIKSPACE

Kwikspace Ltd, Broomham, Laughton, Lewes, **Sussex (East)**, BN8 6JG, **ENGLAND**.
(T) 01825 872000 **(F)** 01825 872999.
Profile Club/Association. **Ref: YH08302**

K-WORKS BLACKSMITHING

K-Works Blacksmithing, Sutton Rd, Langley, Maidstone, **Kent**, ME17 3LY, **ENGLAND**.
(T) 01622 862600.
Contact/s
Owner: Mr C Keay
Profile Blacksmith. **Ref: YH08303**

KYLDANE FIELDSPORTS

Kyldane Fieldsports, Spendlover Corner, Enstone Rd, Charlbury, **Oxfordshire**, OX7 3QR, **ENGLAND**.
(T) 01608 810291.
Profile Saddlery Retailer. **Ref: YH08304**

KYRE EQUESTRIAN CTRE

Kyre Equestrian Centre, Lower Hse Farm, Sutton, Tenbury Wells, **Worcestershire**, WR15 8RL, **ENGLAND**.
(T) 01885 410233.
Contact/s
Owner: Ms A Durston-Smith **(Q)** BHSAI
Profile Arena, Equestrian Centre, Horse/Rider Accom, Riding Club, Stable/Livery, Track/Course, Trainer.
Hacking available. Cross country course available to hire, plus facilities for events, camps and shows. Instruction given for all levels. DIY livery also available, prices on request. No.Staff: 1
Yr. Est: 1960 C.Size: 220 Acres **Ref: YH08305**

L & A HOLIDAY & RIDING CTRE

L & A Holiday & Riding Centre, Goytre, Port Talbot, **Neath Port Talbot**, SA13 2YP, **WALES**.
(T) 01639 885509 **(F)** 01639 885509
Affiliated Bodies BHS, WTRA.
Contact/s
Owner: Mr S Baulch
Profile Holidays.
The centre is set within a conservation area and specialises in riding holidays, hiking holidays and mountain bike holidays. The centre has a outdoor, heated swimming pool.
Opening Times
Sp: Open Mon - Sun 08:00. Closed Mon - Sun 17:00.
Su: Open Mon - Sun 08:00. Closed Mon - Sun 17:00.
Au: Open Mon - Sun 08:00. Closed Mon - Sun 17:00.
Wn: Open Mon - Sun 08:00. Closed Mon - Sun 17:00. **Ref: YH08306**

L & H SADDLERY

L & H Saddlery, 56 High St, Northwood, **London (Greater)**, HA6 1BL, **ENGLAND**.
(T) 01923 840082. **Ref: YH08307**

L & R SADDLES

L & R Saddles Ltd, Clifford Hse, 10-14 Butts Rd, Walsall, **Midlands (West)**, WS4 2AR, **ENGLAND**.
(T) 01922 630740 **(F)** 01922 721149.
Profile Manufacture and wholesalers of saddles.
Ref: YH08308

L A EQUESTRIAN

L A Equestrian, 15 Beeby Rd, Barkby, Leicester, **Leicestershire**, LE7 3QB, **ENGLAND**.
(T) 0116 2602505 **(F)** 0116 2602505
(E) laequestrian91@aol.com.
Contact/s
Owner: Mr A Longstaff
Profile Supplies.
Manufactures horse clothing, rugs etc. All UK based products. Yr. Est: 1991
Opening Times
Sp: Open Mon - Sat 08:00. Closed Mon - Sat 18:00.
Su: Open Mon - Sat 08:00. Closed Mon - Sat 18:00.
Au: Open Mon - Sat 08:00. Closed Mon - Sat 18:00.
Wn: Open Mon - Sat 08:00. Closed Mon - Sat 18:00.
Closed Sundays **Ref: YH08309**

L A EQUESTRIAN

L A Equestrian, 1872 Melton Rd, Rearsby, Leicester, **Leicestershire**, LE7 4YS, **ENGLAND**.
(T) 01664 424230 **(F)** 01664 424230.
Contact/s
Owner: Mr A Longstaff
Profile Supplies. **Ref: YH08310**

L A RICHARDSON & SON

L A Richardson & Son Ltd, 1 Stephendale Rd, Fulham, London, **London (Greater)**, SW6 2LT, **ENGLAND**.
(T) 020 77361566.
Profile Blacksmith. **Ref: YH08311**

L A S TRAILERS

L A S Trailers (Kent) Ltd, Gordon Rd, Canterbury, **Kent**, CT1 3PP, **ENGLAND**.
(T) 01227 463681 **(F)** 01227 766656.
Profile Transport/Horse Boxes. **Ref: YH08312**

L A SADDLERY

L A Saddlery, Norwich Rd, Acle, Great Yarmouth, **Norfolk**, NR13 3BY, **ENGLAND**.
(T) 01493 754029.
Profile Feed Merchant, Riding Wear Retailer, Saddlery Retailer. **Ref: YH08313**

L A SADDLERY

L A Saddlery, Mill View Barn, Low Rd, South Walsham, Norwich, **Norfolk**, NR13 6EQ, **ENGLAND**.
(T) 01603 270011.
Contact/s
Owner: Ms D Holmes **Ref: YH08314**

L A SMITH

L A Smith & Co, Newhall Smithy, Balblair, Dingwall, **Highlands**, IV7 8LQ, **SCOTLAND**.
(T) 01381 610244 **(F)** 01381 610337.

Contact/s
Partner: Mr A Smith
Profile Blacksmith. Ref: YH08315

L CLARK

L Clark Livestock Transport, Pigyn Uchaf, Llanrhystud, **Ceredigion**, SY23 5EL, **WALES**.
(T) 01974 272265
Affiliated Bodies FU, RBA, RHA.
Contact/s
Owner: Miss L Clark (Q) CPC, HGV Nat
Profile Transport/Horse Boxes.
Transportation for horses and other livestock
Yr. Est: 1996
Opening Times
By appointment only Ref: YH08316

L DUNNING SHOW JUMPING

L Dunning Show Jumping, Rose Cottage, Brant Broughton, Lincoln, **Lincolnshire**, LN5 0SL, **ENGLAND**.
(T) 01400 272735.
Profile Trainer. Ref: YH08317

L E SLANEY & SON

L E Slaney & Son, Swilcar Lawn Farm, Marchington Cliff, Uttoxeter, **Staffordshire**, ST14 8ND, **ENGLAND**.
(T) 01283 820306.
Profile Supplies. Ref: YH08318

L F JOLLYES

L F Jollyes (Saddlery Dept), The Granaries, Crews Hill, Enfield, **London (Greater)**, EN2 9BB, **ENGLAND**.
(T) 020 83636980 (F) 020 83675491
(E) kevin@jollyes.co.uk.
Profile Saddlery Retailer. Ref: YH08319

L FOR LEATHER

L For Leather, 61 Liverpool Rd, Irlam, Manchester, **Manchester (Greater)**, M44 6EH, **ENGLAND**.
(T) 0161 7750476
(M) 07831 758690.
Contact/s
Saddler: Mr K Lamb
Profile Saddlery Retailer. Ref: YH08320

L H H ANIMAL FEEDS

L H H Animal Feeds, Sloemans Farm, Whitewebbs Rd, Enfield, **London (Greater)**, EN2 9HW, **ENGLAND**.
(T) 020 83634638 (F) 020 83634638.
Profile Transport/Horse Boxes. Ref: YH08321

L H WOODHOUSE

L H Woodhouse & Co Ltd, Camelot St, Ruddington, **Nottinghamshire**, NG11 6AS, **ENGLAND**.
(T) 0115 9456565 (F) 0115 9843323
(E) info@lhwoodhouse.co.uk.
Contact/s
Owner: Mr R Woodhouse
Profile Transport/Horse Boxes. Ref: YH08322

L J'S EQUESTRIAN

L J's Equestrian, The Forge, Devizes Rd, Wroughton, Swindon, **Wiltshire**, SN4 0RZ, **ENGLAND**.
(T) 01793 815123 (F) 01793 815123.
Contact/s
Owner: Mrs L Ham
Profile Supplies. Ref: YH08323

L K F ANIMAL BEDDING

L K F Animal Bedding, Lime Kiln Farm, Quidenham Rd, Banham, **Norfolk**, NR16 2BT, **ENGLAND**.
(T) 01953 887401.
Profile Supplies. Ref: YH08324

L M COMMERCIALS

L M Commercials, Whitestone Farm Cottages, Main Rd, Birdham, Chichester, **Sussex (West)**, PO20 7HU, **ENGLAND**.
(T) 01243 514582.
Contact/s
Owner: Mr L Messingham
Profile Transport/Horse Boxes. Ref: YH08325

L S K

Lacy Scott & Knight, Market Pl, Stowmarket, **Suffolk**, IP14 1DN, **ENGLAND**.
(T) 01449 612384 (F) 01449 677185
(E) mail@lsk.co.uk
(W) www.lsk.co.uk.
Contact/s
Estate Agent: Mr J Harris
Profile Property Services.
Auctioneers, property surveyors and developers.
Ref: YH08326

L S K

Lacy Scott & Knight, 10 Risbygate St, Bury St Edmunds, **Suffolk**, IP33 3AA, **ENGLAND**.
(T) 01284 748600 (F) 01284 748610
(E) info @lsk.co.uk.
Contact/s
Estate Agent: Jan Jones
Profile Property Services.
Auctioneers, property surveyors and developers.
Ref: YH08327

L S SADDLERY

L S Saddlery, 64 Lynn Rd, Dersingham, King's Lynn, **Norfolk**, PE31 6LA, **ENGLAND**.
(T) 01485 540676.
Profile Supplies. Ref: YH08328

L S SYSTEMS

L S Systems Ltd, 188 Blackgate Lane, Tarleton, Preston, **Lancashire**, PR4 6UU, **ENGLAND**.
(T) 01772 815080 (F) 01772 815417
(E) sales@lssystems.co.uk.
Profile Medical Support. Dust Control.
Installation of Damping Down Equipment.
Ref: YH08329

L W & H B GIBSON & SON

L W & H B Gibson & Son, Springfield Farm, Loads Rd, Holymoorside, Chesterfield, **Derbyshire**, S42 7HW, **ENGLAND**.
(T) 01246 568091.
Profile Supplies. Ref: YH08330

LA CARRIERE

La Carriere Stables & Tack Shop, Baubigny, St Sampson, **Guernsey**, GY2 4EE, **ENGLAND**.
(T) 01481 49998 (F) 01481 41049.
Profile Riding School, Saddlery Retailer, Stable/Livery. Ref: YH08331

LACKHAM CLGE EQUESTRIAN CTRE

Lackham College Equestrian Centre, Lackham Pk, Lacock, Chippenham, **Wiltshire**, SN15 2NY, **ENGLAND**.
(T) 01249 466817 (F) 01249 444474
(E) lackham@wiltscoll.ac.uk & info@wiltscoll.ac.uk
(W) www.wiltscoll.ac.uk.
Contact/s
Manager: Miss S Ord
Profile Equestrian Centre, Horse/Rider Accom.
Unaffiliated Competition Centre Yr. Est: 1986
C.Size: 524 Acres
Opening Times
Sp: Open Mon - Sun 08:00. Closed Mon - Sun 20:00.
Su: Open Mon - Sun 08:00. Closed Mon - Sun 20:00.
Au: Open Mon - Sun 08:00. Closed Mon - Sun 20:00.
Wn: Open Mon - Sun 08:00. Closed Mon - Sun 20:00.
College is closed for most of July and all of August
Ref: YH08332

LACOCK RIDING CTRE

Lacock Riding Centre (The), 23 Bewley Lane, Lacock, Chippenham, **Wiltshire**, SN15 2PH, **ENGLAND**.
(T) 01249 730400.
Profile Riding School. Ref: YH08333

LADDENBROOK STUD

Laddenbrook Stud, Chase Lane, Wickwar, Wotton-under-Edge, **Gloucestershire**, GL12 8JY, **ENGLAND**.
(T) 01454 299737.
Contact/s
Owner: Mr B Buchanan
Profile Breeder. Ref: YH08334

LADY FISHER

Lady Fisher (The), Falabella Miniature Horses, Marklye, Rushlake Green, Heathfield, **Sussex (East)**, TN21 9PN, **ENGLAND**.
(T) 01435 830270 (F) 01435 830767.
Profile Breeder. Ref: YH08335

LADY HERRIES STABLES

Lady Herries Stables, The Tack Room, Angmering Pk, Angmering, Littlehampton, **Sussex (West)**, BN16 4EX, **ENGLAND**.
(T) 01903 871460 (F) 01903 871609.
Profile Trainer. Ref: YH08336

LADY JOCKEY ASSOCIATION

Lady Jockey Association, Ballyduff, Cork, **County Cork**, **IRELAND**.
(T) 021 4657241 (F) 021 4657241.
Contact/s
Key Contact: Ms A Sloa-Lee
Profile Club/Association. Ref: YH08337

LADYMIRE EQUESTRIAN CTRE

Ladymire Equestrian Centre, Ladymires Farm, Ellon, **Aberdeenshire**, AB41 8LH, **SCOTLAND**.
(T) 01358 721075.
Profile Riding School, Stable/Livery, Track/Course.
Ref: YH08338

LADYMOOR GATE

Ladymoor Gate, Brown Edge, Stoke-on-Trent, **Staffordshire**, ST6 8UF, **ENGLAND**.
(T) 01782 502009.
Profile Breeder, Stable/Livery. Ref: YH08339

LADYSMITHS EQUESTRIAN CTRE

Cowley Bros Ltd, Draycot Yard, Ladysmith Rd, Wroughton, Swindon, **Wiltshire**, SN4 0RW, **ENGLAND**.
(T) 01793 741433.
Contact/s
Manager: Mr H Carly
Profile Equestrian Centre, Stable/Livery.
Ref: YH08340

LAFFAK RIDING CLUB

Laffak Riding Club, 38 Tarbock Rd, Speke, Liverpool, **Merseyside**, L24 0SN, **ENGLAND**.
(T) 0151 4865128.
Contact/s
Secretary: Miss L Armstrong
Profile Club/Association, Riding Club. Ref: YH08341

LAGAN VALLEY EQUESTRIAN CTRE

Lagan Valley Equestrian Centre, 170 Upper Malone Rd, Dunmurray, Belfast, **County Antrim**, BT17 9JZ, **NORTHERN IRELAND**.
(T) 028 90614853.
Profile Riding School, Stable/Livery. Ref: YH08342

LAGAN VALLEY RIDING CLUB

Lagan Valley Riding Club, Monte Bre, 136 Upper Malone Rd, Belfast, **County Antrim**, BT9 5PE, **NORTHERN IRELAND**.
(T) 028 90611567 (F) 028 90611567.
Contact/s
Chairman: Miss R Stewart
Profile Club/Association, Riding Club. Ref: YH08343

LAGUS, S E

S E Lagus, Rockwell Reads Lane, Cublington, Leighton Buzzard, **Bedfordshire**, LU7 0LE, **ENGLAND**.
(T) 01296 681806.
Contact/s
Owner: Mrs S Lagus
Profile Saddlery Retailer.
Makes made to measure saddles and bridlewear
Yr. Est: 1984
Opening Times
By appointment only Ref: YH08344

LAIDLAW, G D W

G D W Laidlaw, 6 Sopley, Christchurch, **Dorset**, BH23 7AZ, **ENGLAND**.
(T) 01425 72666.
Profile Farrier. Ref: YH08345

LAIDLAW, L

Mrs L Laidlaw, 232 Stony Lane, Winkston, Christchurch, **Dorset**, BH23 7LB, **ENGLAND**.
(T) 01202 477800.
Profile Breeder. Ref: YH08346

LAIRD, ALEXANDER

Alexander Laird, Stanebent Farm, Torbothie Rd, Shotts, **Lanarkshire (North)**, ML7 5BW, **SCOTLAND**.
(T) 01501 820505.
Contact/s
Trainer: Mr S Laird
Profile Breeder, Trainer. No.Staff: 2
Yr. Est: 1995 C.Size: 40 Acres
Opening Times
View by appointment Ref: YH08347

LAIT, MAURICE H

Mr Maurice H Lait, Coln Rogers, Fossebridge, Cheltenham, **Gloucestershire**, GL54 3LB, **ENGLAND**.
(T) 01285 72246.
Profile Supplies. Ref: YH08348

LAKE DISTRICT TRAIL CTRE

Lake District Trail Riding Centre, Rydal, Ambleside, **Cumbria**, LA22 9LW, **ENGLAND**.
(T) 01539 432765.
Profile Equestrian Centre. Ref: YH08349

A-Z of COMPANIES

LAKE FARM

Lake Farm Equestrian Centre, Lake Farm, Chequers Inn Rd, Rookley, Ventnor, **Isle of Wight**, PO38 3NZ, **ENGLAND**.
(T) 01983 840251.
Contact/s
Partner: Mr L Vanassche
Profile Riding School, Stable/Livery.
Livery available, prices on request. Tack shop on site.
Yr. Est: 1971 C.Size: 89 Acres
Opening Times
Sp: Open Mon - Sun 09:00. Closed Mon - Sun 18:00.
Su: Open Mon - Sun 09:00. Closed Mon - Sun 18:00.
Au: Open Mon - Sun 09:00. Closed Mon - Sun 18:00.
Wn: Open Mon - Sun 09:00. Closed Mon - Sun 18:00. **Ref: YH08350**

LAKEFIELD EQUESTRIAN CTRE

Lakefield Equestrian Centre, Pendavey Farm, Camelford, **Cornwall**, PL32 9TX, **ENGLAND**.
(T) 01840 213279.
Profile Riding School. **Ref: YH08351**

LAKEHEAD PONY STUD

Lakehead Pony Stud, Bellever Hse, Bellever, Postbridge, Yelverton, **Devon**, PL20 6TU, **ENGLAND**.
(T) 01822 880221.
Contact/s
Owner: Mr W Shillibeer
Profile Breeder. **Ref: YH08352**

LAKELAND ARABIANS

Lakeland Arabians, Derwent Hse Farm, Broughton Beck Bridge, Gt Broughton, Cockermouth, **Cumbria**, CA13 0LG, **ENGLAND**.
(T) 01900 827067.
Profile Breeder. **Ref: YH08353**

LAKELAND EQUESTRIAN

Lakeland Equestrian, Wynlass Beck, Windermere, **Cumbria**, LA23 1EU, **ENGLAND**.
(T) 01539 443811 **(F)** 01539 443717
(E) info@lakelandequestrian.co.uk
(W) www.lakelandequestrian.co.uk
Affiliated Bodies ABRS, BHS.
Contact/s
For Bookings: Anthea Kendrick **(T)** 01539 443811
Profile Equestrian Centre, Riding School, Riding Wear Retailer, Saddlery Retailer, Stable/Livery, Trainer.
Ref: YH08354

LAKELAND RIDING CTRE

Lakeland Riding Centre, Lakeland Leisure Pk, Moor Lane, Flookburgh, Grange-Over-Sands, **Cumbria**, LA11 7LT, **ENGLAND**.
(T) 01539 558131.
Profile Riding School. **Ref: YH08355**

LAKES LANE RIDING STABLES

Lakes Lane Riding Stables, Lakes Lane, Newport Pagnell, **Buckinghamshire**, MK16 8EE, **ENGLAND**.
(T) 01908 617199.
Profile Riding School. **Ref: YH08356**

LAKES RIDING CLUB

Lakes Riding Club, Alice Howe Farm, Windermere, **Cumbria**, LA23 1JG, **ENGLAND**.
(T) 01539 443635
(W) www.lakesridingclub.org.uk.
Contact/s
Chairperson: Mr D Moore
Profile Club/Association, Riding Club. **Ref: YH08357**

LAKESIDE PADDOCK STUD

Lakeside Paddock Stud, Lincombe, Lee, Ilfracombe, **Devon**, EX34 8LL, **ENGLAND**.
(T) 01271 862791.
Profile Breeder, Farrier. **Ref: YH08358**

LAKEVIEW HORSE RIDING CTRE

Lakeview Horse Riding Centre, Derryrona Leggs Post Office, Leggs, Enniskillen, **County Fermanagh**, BT93 2AY, **NORTHERN IRELAND**.
(T) 028 68658163.
Profile Riding School. **Ref: YH08359**

LAKIN BLOODSTOCK

Lakin Bloodstock, Whites Farm, New Pound Lane, Wisborough Green, **Sussex (West)**, RH14 0EF, **ENGLAND**.
(T) 01403 700293 **(F)** 01403 700170.
Profile Blood Stock Agency, Breeder. **Ref: YH08360**

LALLEY, A F

A F Lalley RSS, Twyn Hendrance Farm, Earlswood, Chepstow, **Monmouthshire**, NP16 6RD, **WALES**.
(T) 01291 641389.
Profile Farrier. **Ref: YH08361**

LAMB, K M

Mrs K M Lamb, Burnhouse Farm, Seahouses, **Northumberland**, NE68 7UZ, **ENGLAND**.
(T) 01665 720251 **(F)** 01665 720251
(M) 07790 339261.
Profile Supplies. **Ref: YH08362**

LAMB, PETER K

Peter K Lamb, 14 Bankfield Trce, Stacksteads, Bacup, **Lancashire**, OL13 8LP, **ENGLAND**.
(T) 01706 878671.
Profile Farrier. **Ref: YH08363**

LAMBERT, B P

B P Lambert, 2 Jubilee Cottage, Calais St, Boxford, Sudbury, **Suffolk**, CO10 5JA, **ENGLAND**.
(T) 01787 210634.
Contact/s
Partner: Mr B Lambert
Profile Farrier. **Ref: YH08364**

LAMBERTS CASTLE RIDING CLUB

Lamberts Castle Riding Club, Little Oaks, Birchill, Axminster, **Devon**, EX13 7LB, **ENGLAND**.
(T) 01460 220387.
Profile Club/Association, Riding Club. **Ref: YH08365**

LAMBERTS COUNTRY STORE

Lamberts Country Store, Charles Ave, Bideford, **Devon**, EX39 2PH, **ENGLAND**.
(T) 01237 424410 **(F)** 01237 475335.
Contact/s
Owner: Miss K Lambert
Profile Saddlery Retailer. **Ref: YH08366**

LAMBOURN RACEHORSE TRANSPORT

Lambourn Racehorse Transport Ltd, Delamere Paddock, Baydon Rd, Lambourn, Hungerford, **Berkshire**, RG17 8NT, **ENGLAND**.
(T) 01488 71710 **(F)** 01488 73208.
Contact/s
Owner: Mr M Francis
Profile Trainer. **Ref: YH08367**

LAMBOURN RIDING SCHOOL

Lambourn Riding School, 22 Northfields, Lambourn, Hungerford, **Berkshire**, RG17 8YJ, **ENGLAND**.
(T) 01488 71059.
Contact/s
Owner: Miss A Annetts **Ref: YH08368**

LAMBOURN TRAINERS ASSOCIATION

Lambourn Trainers Association, C/O Windsor Hse, Lambourn, Hungerford, **Berkshire**, RG17 8NR, **ENGLAND**.
(T) 01488 71347 **(F)** 01488 72664.
Profile Club/Association. **Ref: YH08369**

LAMBOURNE, JAMES

James Lambourne DWCF, Forge Cottage, 82 Boxford, Newbury, **Berkshire**, RG20 8DP, **ENGLAND**.
(T) 01488 608256
(M) 07771 541532.
Profile Farrier. **Ref: YH08370**

LAMBSKIN MARKETING

Lambskin Marketing Ltd, Unit 15 Canvin Ct, Bancombe Rd, Somerton, **Somerset**, TA11 6SB, **ENGLAND**.
(T) 01458 274799 **(F)** 01458 274151.
Contact/s
Accountant: Mrs K Wright
Profile Supplies. **Ref: YH08371**

LAMINITIS CLINIC

Laminitis Clinic (The), Mead Hse Farm, Dauntsey, Chippenham, **Wiltshire**, SN15 4JA, **ENGLAND**.
(T) 01249 890784 **(F)** 01249 890780
(E) rae@equilife.co.uk.
Profile Medical Support.
The Clinic provides a free helpline for owners whose horses have laminitis, founder and sinking syndrome.
Ref: YH08372

LAMINITIS TRUST

Laminitis Trust (The), Mead Hse Farm, Dauntsey, Chippenham, **Wiltshire**, SN15 4JA, **ENGLAND**.
(T) 01249 890784 **(F)** 01249 890780
(E) info@laminitis.org
(W) www.laminitis.org.
Profile Club/Association. Registered Charity.
The Trust is a registered charity dedicated to raising funds for research into laminitis. **Ref: YH08373**

LAMOND, A

A Lamond, 2 Crowhill Rd, Bishopbriggs, Glasgow, **Glasgow (City of)**, G64 1QR, **SCOTLAND**.
(T) 0141 7721744.
Profile Blacksmith. **Ref: YH08374**

LAMPARD, DI

Di Lampard, Spring Farm, Cold Overton Rd, Oakham, **Rutland**, LE15 8DA, **ENGLAND**.
(T) 01572 755919 **(F)** 01572 771150.
Profile Trainer. **Ref: YH08375**

LAMPERT TRAILERS

Lampert Trailers, Catsgore, Somerton, **Somerset**, TA11 7HY, **ENGLAND**.
(T) 01458 241235.
Contact/s
Owner: Mr M Lampert
Profile Transport/Horse Boxes. **Ref: YH08376**

LAMYMAN, P E L

P E L Lamyman, 168 High St, Newmarket, **Suffolk**, CB8 9AQ, **ENGLAND**.
(T) 01638 561142 **(F)** 01638 561146.
Contact/s
Manageress: Ms A Reeder **Ref: YH08377**

LAMYMAN, S

Mrs S Lamyman, Ruckland Manor, Louth, **Lincolnshire**, LN11 8RQ, **ENGLAND**.
(T) 01507 533260 **(F)** 01507 533715
(M) 07971 969097.
Profile Trainer. **Ref: YH08378**

LAN GARTH STUD

Lan Garth Stud, The Grange, Llanvihangel-Ystern-Llewern, **Monmouthshire**, NP25 5HW, **WALES**.
(T) 01600 780228.
Profile Breeder. **Ref: YH08379**

LANBURN STUD

Lanburn Stud, Claypit Lane, Westhampnett, Chichester, **Sussex (West)**, PO18 0NU, **ENGLAND**.
(T) 01243 786871 **(F)** 01243 786871.
Profile Breeder. **Ref: YH08380**

LANCASTER, P R

P R Lancaster, Scarbarrow Paddock, Leece, Ulverston, **Cumbria**, LA12 0QU, **ENGLAND**.
(T) 01229 834930.
Profile Saddlery Retailer, Stable/Livery.
Ref: YH08381

LANCHESTER COUNTRY STORE

Lanchester Country Store, 7 Station Rd, Lanchester, **County Durham**, DH7 0EX, **ENGLAND**.
(T) 01207 521710 **(F)** 01207 521710.
Profile Feed Merchant, Supplies. **Ref: YH08382**

LANDLORDS FARM

Landlords Farm Riding Centre, Dicconson Lane, Aspull, Wigan, **Lancashire**, WN2 1QD, **ENGLAND**.
(T) 01942 831329.
Contact/s
Owner: Mrs P Hurst
Profile Riding School. **Ref: YH08383**

LANDOWN FARM RIDING STABLES

Landown Farm Riding Stables, Landown Farm, Bakeacre Lane, Findern, Derby, **Derbyshire**, DE65 6BH, **ENGLAND**.
(T) 01332 516465 **(F)** 01332 510136.
Contact/s
Owner: Mrs L Penny
Profile Riding School, Stable/Livery. **Ref: YH08384**

LANDS' END

Lands' End Direct Merchants UK Ltd, Pillings Rd, Oakham, **Rutland**, LE15 6NY, **ENGLAND**.
(T) 08002 20106.
Profile Supplies. **Ref: YH08385**

LANDS END EQUESTRIAN CTRE

Lands End Equestrian Centre, Lands End, Landsend Lane, Twyford, Reading, **Berkshire**, RG10 0UE, **ENGLAND**.
(T) 0118 9341367 **(F)** 0118 9321372.
Contact/s
Owner: Mr I Lucken
Profile Equestrian Centre. **Ref: YH08386**

LANDS END RIDING SCHOOL

Lands End Riding School, Trevescan Farm Hse, Sennen, Penzance, **Cornwall**, TR19 7AQ, **ENGLAND**.
(T) 01736 871989.
Contact/s

Owner: Mr D Hicks
Profile Riding School. Ref:YH08387

LANDSIDE MORGANS/SADDLEBREDS
Landside Morgans & Saddlebreds, Arrowsmith Farm, Hand Lane, Leigh, **Lancashire**, WN7 3RU, **ENGLAND**.
(T) 01942 606006.
Profile Breeder. Ref:YH08388

LANE FARM SHOP
Lane Farm Shop, Bedlington Lane Farm, Bedlington, **Northumberland**, NE22 6AA, **ENGLAND**.
(T) 01670 823042 (F) 01670 823042.
Profile Supplies. Ref:YH08389

LANE, CHARLIE
Charlie Lane MA,Dip Equine Studies, MIMgt,BHSII, The White Hse, Crockerton, Warminster, **Wiltshire**, BA12 8AH, **ENGLAND**.
(T) 01985 212380 (F) 01985 212495
(E) lane-equestrian@cockerton.fsnet.co.uk.
Profile Trainer. Ref:YH08390

LANE, V G
V G Lane, Marlin Chapel Cottage, Berkhamsted, **Hertfordshire**, HP4 3UQ, **ENGLAND**.
(T) 01442 864785.
Contact/s
Owner: Mr V Lane
Profile Farrier. Ref:YH08391

LANEHAM LIVERY STABLE
Laneham Riding Centre, Crow Holts Farm, Main St, Laneham, Retford, **Nottinghamshire**, DN22 0NA, **ENGLAND**.
(T) 01777 228439.
Contact/s
Owner: Ms S Scrini (Q) BHSII, RDAI
Profile Stable/Livery, Trainer. No.Staff: 1
Yr. Est: 1978 C.Size: 12 Acres Ref:YH08392

LANEHOUSE EQUITATION CTRE
Lanehouse Equitation Centre, 537 Chickerell Rd, Chickerell Hill, Weymouth, **Dorset**, DT3 4DL, **ENGLAND**.
(T) 01305 770177
Affiliated Bodies BHS.
Contact/s
Owner: Mr R Addison
Profile Arena, Breeder, Equestrian Centre, Riding School. No.Staff: 2 Yr. Est: 1978
C.Size: 30 Acres Ref:YH08393

LANES FARM D I Y STABLES
Lanes Farm D I Y Stables, Lanes Farm, Marlborough Rd, Wootton Bassett, Swindon, **Wiltshire**, SN4 7SA, **ENGLAND**.
(T) 01793 852539.
Profile Stable/Livery. Ref:YH08394

LANES SADDLERY & ANIMAL FEEDS
Lanes Saddlery & Animal Feeds, Church Lane, Stoke Goldington, Newport Pagnell, **Buckinghamshire**, MK16 8NZ, **ENGLAND**.
(T) 01908 551240.
Profile Feed Merchant, Saddlery Retailer.
Ref:YH08395

LANG, JAMES H
James H Lang DWCF, Windyridge Farm, Lower Predannack, Mullion, **Cornwall**, TR12 7EZ, **ENGLAND**.
(T) 01326 240267.
Profile Farrier. Ref:YH08396

LANGAN, ANNIE
Annie Langan, C/O The Kildare Horse Development Company, The Curragh Racecourse, Curragh, **County Kildare**, **IRELAND**.
(T) 045 442486 (F) 045 441442
(M) 086 2544749.
Contact/s
Key Contact: Ms A Langan
Profile Artist. Ref:YH08397

LANGAR ENGINEERING
Langar Engineering, Langar Ind Est North, Harby Rd, Langar, Nottingham, **Nottinghamshire**, NG13 9HY, **ENGLAND**.
(T) 01949 860786 (F) 01949 860762.
Profile Transport/Horse Boxes. Ref:YH08398

LANGARTH
Langarth Stud, The Grange, Llanvihangel-Ystern-Llewern, Monmouth, **Monmouthshire**, NP25 5HW, **WALES**.
(T) 01600 780228 (F) 01600 780408
(M) 07779 977840
(E) deidr@aol.com
(W) www.langarth-stud.co.uk.
Profile Breeder, Stud Farm.
Langarth Stud has two stallions standing
Yr. Est: 1975 Ref:YH08399

LANGBAURGH BOROUGH COUNCIL
Langbaurgh Borough Council, Tourism & Leisure, P O Box South Bank 20, Middlesbrough Rd, South Bank, **Cleveland**, TS6 6EL, **ENGLAND**.
(T) 01642 231212.
Profile Club/Association. Ref:YH08400

LANGDALE VETNRY CTRE
Langdale Veterinary Centre, 31 Tatton St, Knutsford, **Cheshire**, WA16 6AE, **ENGLAND**.
(T) 01565 632132 (F) 01565 633750.
Profile Medical Support. Ref:YH08401

LANGFIELD STUD
Langfield Stud, Broad Carr Farm, Langfield, Todmorden, **Yorkshire (West)**, OL14 6HW, **ENGLAND**.
(T) 01706 812740.
Profile Breeder. Ref:YH08402

LANGFORD FARM
Langford Farm, Paradise Lane, Woodlands, **Hampshire**, SO40 2GS, **ENGLAND**.
(T) 023 80812932 (F) 023 80814851.
Profile Stable/Livery. Ref:YH08403

LANGFORD LIVERY
Langford Livery Stables, Howells Farm, Maypole Rd, Langford, Maldon, **Essex**, CM9 4SZ, **ENGLAND**.
(T) 01621 854595.
Contact/s
General Manager: Miss A Mead
Profile Stable/Livery. No.Staff: 1
Yr. Est: 1997
Opening Times
Sp: Open Mon - Sun 06:00. Closed Mon - Sun 19:30.
Su: Open Mon - Sun 06:00. Closed Mon - Sun 19:30.
Au: Open Mon - Sun 06:00. Closed Mon - Sun 19:30.
Wn: Open Mon - Sun 06:00. Closed Mon - Sun 19:30. Ref:YH08404

LANGFORD SADDLERY
Langford Saddlery, 10 Coronation Rd, Bestwood Village, Nottingham, **Nottinghamshire**, NG5 7HR, **ENGLAND**.
(T) 0115 9569294
(M) 07770 470722.
Profile Supplies. Ref:YH08405

LANGHAM HALL
Langham Hall Arabian Stud, Langham, Bury St Edmunds, **Suffolk**, IP31 3EG, **ENGLAND**.
(T) 01359 259370 (F) 01359 259370
Affiliated Bodies AHS.
Contact/s
General Manager: Ms L Deymonaz
Profile Stud Farm. Yr. Est: 1993
Opening Times
Open by appointment Ref:YH08406

LANGLEY FORGED PRODUCTS
Langley Forged Products Ltd, Birch Rd, Sheffield, **Yorkshire (South)**, S9 3XL, **ENGLAND**.
(T) 0114 2560914.
Profile Blacksmith. Ref:YH08407

LANGLEY GORSE LIVERY
Langley Gorse Livery, Langley Gorse, Fox Hollies Rd, Sutton Coldfield, **Midlands (West)**, B76 2RU, **ENGLAND**.
(T) 0121 3131586 (F) 0121 3130672.
Contact/s
Owner: Ms Z Morris Ref:YH08408

LANGLEY POND FARM STABLES
Langley Pond Farm Stables, Langley Pond Farm, School Rd, Barkham, Wokingham, **Berkshire**, RG41 4TN, **ENGLAND**.
(T) 0118 9760162. Ref:YH08409

LANGLEY, GRAHAM A
Graham A Langley DWCF, 2 Rowan Cl, Shaftesbury, **Dorset**, SP7 8RG, **ENGLAND**.
(T) 01747 851090.
Profile Farrier. Ref:YH08410

LANGLEY, RODNEY DONALD
Rodney Donald Langley, The Old Stable Hse, 18 Acresford Rd, Overseal, Swadlincote, **Derbyshire**, DE12 6HX, **ENGLAND**.
(T) 01283 761836.
Profile Farrier. Ref:YH08411

LANGRISH, BOB
Bob Langrish, The Old Court Hse, High St, Bisley, Stroud, **Gloucestershire**, GL6 7AA, **ENGLAND**.
(T) 01452 770140 (F) 01452 770146.
Contact/s
Owner: Mr B Langrish
Profile Supplies. Ref:YH08412

LANGROP TRAILERS CTRE
Langrop Trailers Centre Ltd, Cropston Rd, Anstey, Leicester, **Leicestershire**, LE7 7BP, **ENGLAND**.
(T) 0116 2340026 (F) 0116 2354739.
Contact/s
Manager: Mr A Bloom
Profile Transport/Horse Boxes. Ref:YH08413

LANGSHOT EQUESTRIAN CTRE
Langshot Equestrian Centre, Gracious Pond Rd, Chobham, **Surrey**, GU24 8HJ, **ENGLAND**.
(T) 01276 856949.
Profile Riding School, Stable/Livery. Ref:YH08414

LANGSTON & SON
Langston & Son, 42 The Pantiles, Tunbridge Wells, **Kent**, TN2 5TN, **ENGLAND**.
(T) 01892 527742.
Contact/s
Partner: Mr A Langston
Profile Saddlery Retailer. Ref:YH08415

LANGTON HORSE WEAR
Langton Horse Wear, Honeyclose Farm, Great Langton, Northallerton, **Yorkshire (North)**, DL7 0TG, **ENGLAND**.
(T) 01609 748495 (F) 01609 748495
(W) www.langtonhorsewear.co.uk
Affiliated Bodies BETA.
Contact/s
Owner: Ms G Poad (Q) BSc
(E) gill@langtonhorsewear.co.uk
Profile Riding Wear Retailer, Saddlery Retailer.
Opening Times
Sp: Open 09:30. Closed 17:30.
Su: Open 09:30. Closed 17:30.
Au: Open 09:30. Closed 17:30.
Wn: Open 09:30. Closed 17:30. Ref:YH08416

LANGTON STUD
Langton Stud, Langton Long, Blandford Forum, **Dorset**, DT11 9HS, **ENGLAND**.
(T) 01258 451730.
Profile Breeder. Ref:YH08417

LANJETH RIDING SCHOOL
Lanjeth Riding School, Coombe, St Austell, **Cornwall**, PL26 7LQ, **ENGLAND**.
(T) 01726 74633.
Profile Riding School, Stable/Livery. Ref:YH08418

LANNI, JOHN
John Lanni, Willow Tops, Allington Lane, Allington, Grantham, **Lincolnshire**, NG32 2EF, **ENGLAND**.
(T) 01476 591569 (F) 01476 565442.
Profile Trainer. Ref:YH08419

LANNON, BARRY P
Barry P Lannon DWCF, 18 Dawley, Welwyn Garden City, **Hertfordshire**, AL7 1DZ, **ENGLAND**.
(T) 01707 894076.
Profile Farrier. Ref:YH08420

LANSDOWN ACTION RUGS
Lansdown Action Rugs Ltd, 2 Beechwood Cottages, Lansdown, Bath, **Bath & Somerset (North East)**, BA1 9DB, **ENGLAND**.
(T) 01179 324609 (F) 01179 323137.
Profile Supplies. Ref:YH08421

LANSDOWN VETNRY SURGEONS
Lansdown Veterinary Surgeons, The Clockhouse Veterinary Hospital, Wallbridge, Stroud, **Gloucestershire**, GL5 3JD, **ENGLAND**.
(T) 01453 752555 (F) 01453 756065
(E) info@lansdown.vets.co.uk.
Contact/s
Practice Manager: Melvyn Wilkins
Profile Medical Support. Ref:YH08422

LANSDOWNE HORSE & RIDER
Lansdowne Horse & Rider Ltd, 10 Pool Bank, High St, Tarvin, Chester, **Cheshire**, CH3 8JJ, **ENGLAND**.
(T) 01829 741176 (F) 01829 749126.
Contact/s
General Manager: Mr J Ashworth
Profile Riding Wear Retailer, Saddlery Retailer,

Key: (T) telephone (F) fax (M) mobile (E) E-Mail Address (W) Website Address (Q) Qualifications
Yr. Est: Year Established C.Size: Complex Size Sp: Spring Su: Summer Au: Autumn Wn: Winter

Supplies, Transport/Horse Boxes. No.Staff: 2
Yr. Est: 1998 C.Size: 5 Acres
Opening Times
Sp: Open 09:00. Closed 19:30.
Su: Open 09:00. Closed 19:30.
Au: Open 09:00. Closed 19:30.
Wn: Open 09:00. Closed 19:30. Ref: YH08423

LANTWOOD STABLES

Lantwood Stables, Lantwood Hse, Scotland Lane, Horsforth, Leeds, **Yorkshire (West)**, LS18 5HL, **ENGLAND**.
(T) 0113 2586048.
Contact/s
Owner: Mr T O'Hara
Profile Breeder, Stable/Livery. Ref: YH08424

LANTYAN STUD

Lantyan Stud, Perrose, Lostwithiel, **Cornwall**, PL22 0JJ, **ENGLAND**.
(T) 01208 872511.
Profile Breeder. Ref: YH08425

LANWADES STUD

Lanwades Stud, Kennett, Newmarket, **Suffolk**, CB8 8QS, **ENGLAND**.
(T) 01638 750222 **(F)** 01638 751186.
Profile Breeder. Ref: YH08426

LAPIDGE, ANDREW

Andrew Lapidge DWCF, 151 Bottey Rd, North Baddesley, Southampton, **Hampshire**, SO52 9ED, **ENGLAND**.
(T) 023 80731524.
Profile Farrier. Ref: YH08427

LARIOT EQUESTRIAN SUPPLIES

Lariot Equestrian Supplies, Lariot Works, William St, Walsall, **Midlands (West)**, WS4 2AX, **ENGLAND**.
(T) 01922 611113 **(F)** 01922 611115.
Contact/s
Owner: Mr I Rae
Profile Supplies. Ref: YH08428

LARKENSHAW FARM

Larkenshaw Farm & Livery Stables, Stonehill Rd, Chobham, Woking, **Surrey**, GU24 8HW, **ENGLAND**.
(T) 01276 856515 **(F)** 01276 858664.
Contact/s
Owner: Mrs C McAllister
Profile Stable/Livery. Ref: YH08429

LARKFIELD HOUSE STUD

Larkfield House Stud, Welsh East Rd, Southam, Leamington Spa, **Warwickshire**, **ENGLAND**..
Ref: YH08430

LARKHILL H S DRESSAGE

Larkhill H S Dressage, Parsonage Farmhouse, Slipton Bellinger, Tidworth, **Hampshire**, **ENGLAND**.
(T) 01980 842404.
Profile Club/Association. Ref: YH08431

LARKHILL SADDLERY

Larkhill Saddlery, Larkhill Stud, Bellhouse Lane, Burton-on-Trent, **Staffordshire**, DE13 9PA, **ENGLAND**.
(T) 01283 515533.
Contact/s
Owner: Mr J Archer
Profile Riding Wear Retailer, Saddlery Retailer, Supplies.
Made to measure saddlery & harness manufacturers.
No.Staff: 2
Opening Times
Sp: Open 09:00. Closed 17:00.
Su: Open 09:00. Closed 17:00.
Au: Open 09:00. Closed 17:00.
Wn: Open 09:00. Closed 17:00. Ref: YH08432

LARKIN, JOHN

John Larkin, Capranny Stables Kildalkey Rd, Trim, **County Meath**, **IRELAND**.
(T) 046 36178.
Profile Supplies. Ref: YH08433

LARKRIGG RIDING SCHOOL

Larkrigg Riding School, Larkrigg Riding School, Natland, Kendal, **Cumbria**, LA9 7QS, **ENGLAND**.
(T) 01539 560245 **(F)** 01539 561693
Affiliated Bodies ABRS, BHS.
Contact/s
Owner: Ms A Wilson **(Q)** BHSAI
Profile Equestrian Centre, Riding School, Stable/Livery. No.Staff: 2
Opening Times
Sp: Open 10:00. Closed 16:00.
Su: Open 10:00. Closed 18:00.
Au: Open 10:00. Closed 18:00.
Wn: Open 10:00. Closed 16:00. Ref: YH08434

LARTON LIVERY

Larton Livery, The Styles, Wirral, **Merseyside**, CH48 1PL, **ENGLAND**.
(T) 0151 6256477 **(F)** 0151 6256477.
Contact/s
Owner: Mr B Titley
Profile Stable/Livery. Ref: YH08435

LARTON RIDING SCHOOL

Larton Riding School, Frankby Rd, Wirral, **Merseyside**, CH48 1PL, **ENGLAND**.
(T) 0151 6251080.
Profile Riding School. Ref: YH08436

LASAR EUROPE

Lasar Europe Ltd, Rougham Ind Est, Bury St Edmunds, **Suffolk**, IP30 9ND, **ENGLAND**.
(T) 01359 271417 **(F)** 01359 270008
(W) www.lasarcontracts.ltd.uk.
Profile Supplies. Flooring. Ref: YH08437

LASLETT, E E

E E Laslett, Rosedale Farm, Marshborough Rd, Marshborough, Sandwich, **Kent**, CT13 0PF, **ENGLAND**.
(T) 01304 812231.
Profile Stable/Livery. DIY Livery. Ref: YH08438

LASSA

Licensed Animal Slaughterers & Salvage Association, Birch Hse, Birch Vale, High Peak, **Derbyshire**, SK22 1DH, **ENGLAND**.
(T) 01663 744154 **(F)** 01663 750557.
Contact/s
Company Secretary: Ms S Lawton
Profile Club/Association. Animal Slaughterers and Salvages. Ref: YH08439

LASSALE WATCHES

Lassale Watches, Hattori Hse, Vanwall Rd, Maidenhead, **Berkshire**, SL6 4UW, **ENGLAND**.
(T) 01628 770001.
Profile Supplies. Ref: YH08440

LASSELL HOUSE RIDING CTRE

Lassell House Riding Centre, Mossy Lea Rd, Wrightington, Wigan, **Lancashire**, WN6 9RE, **ENGLAND**.
(T) 01257 427319.
Contact/s
Partner: Mr K Gardner
Profile Riding School. Ref: YH08441

LASSETTER, JOHN F

John F Lassetter, 3 Dairy Cottages, Molecomb Stud, Goodwood, Chichester, **Sussex (West)**, PO18 0QD, **ENGLAND**.
(T) 01243 533540 **(F)** 01243 533540.
Profile Stable/Livery, Trainer. Ref: YH08442

LAST EMPIRE STABLES

Last Empire Stables (The), Crews Hill, Suckley, **Worcestershire**, WR6 5HP, **ENGLAND**.
(T) 01886 884144 **(F)** 01886 884144
(M) 07710 450982.
Profile Trainer. Ref: YH08443

LATCHAM, DEAN L

Dean L Latcham BII, 1 Forest Lodge Cottages, Motcome, Shaftesbury, **Dorset**, SP7 9PJ, **ENGLAND**.
(T) 07966 276738.
Profile Farrier. Ref: YH08444

LATHAM FARM

Latham Farm Equinery, Brookside Works, Brick St, Westgate, Cleckheaton, **Yorkshire (West)**, BD19 5LD, **ENGLAND**.
(T) 01274 870632 **(F)** 01274 874939.
Contact/s
General Manager: Mr A Bottomley
Profile Stable/Livery, Transport/Horse Boxes. Exercise Vehicles. Ref: YH08445

LATHERON RIDING CTRE

Latheron Riding Centre, Upper Latheron Farm, Caithness, **Highlands**, KW5 6DT, **SCOTLAND**.
(T) 01593 741224.
Profile Equestrian Centre. Ref: YH08446

LATIMER & CRICK

Latimer & Crick, 2-4 Cattle Market Rd, Northampton, **Northamptonshire**, NN1 1HL, **ENGLAND**.
(T) 01604 36322.
Profile Supplies. Ref: YH08447

LAUGHTON MANOR

Laughton Manor Equestrian Centre, The Manor Farm, Laughton, Sleaford, **Lincolnshire**, NG34 0HB, **ENGLAND**.
(T) 01529 497519.
Contact/s
Secretary: Mrs C Leach
Profile Riding School. Ref: YH08448

LAUGHTON WOOD EQUESTRIAN CTRE

Laughton Wood Equestrian Centre, Laughton Lane, Morton, Gainsborough, **Lincolnshire**, DN21 3ET, **ENGLAND**.
(T) 01427 615554.
Contact/s
Owner: Mr F Brown
Profile Equestrian Centre, Riding School, Stable/Livery. No.Staff: 3 Yr. Est: 1995
Opening Times
Sp: Open Tues - Sun 10:00. Closed Tues - Sun 16:00.
Su: Open Tues - Sun 10:00. Closed Tues - Sun 16:00.
Au: Open Tues - Sun 10:00. Closed Tues - Sun 16:00.
Wn: Open Tues - Sun 10:00. Closed Tues - Sun 16:00.
Closed Mondays Ref: YH08449

LAUNCH PAD

Launch Pad (The), Ramsdale Hse, Mattingley, Hook, **Hampshire**, RG27 8JY, **ENGLAND**.
(T) 0118 9326686 **(F)** 0118 9326194
(M) 07778 528839
(E) nutter@easynet.co.uk.
Profile PR Consultant. Ref: YH08450

LAUND VIEW STABLES

Laund View Stables, Higher Laund Farm, Higham, Burnley, **Lancashire**, BB12 9BX, **ENGLAND**.
(T) 01282 619087.
Contact/s
Owner: Mr P Grindrod
Profile Stable/Livery. Ref: YH08451

LAUNDER, E J

E J Launder, 27 Church Rd, Malvern, **Worcestershire**, WR14 1LT, **ENGLAND**.
(T) 01684 577852.
Profile Breeder. Ref: YH08452

LAUNDER, J W

J W Launder, 2 Castle Rd, Rowland's Castle, **Hampshire**, PO9 6AS, **ENGLAND**.
(T) 023 92412645.
Profile Farrier. Ref: YH08453

LAUNDRY MACHINE

Laundry Machine Ltd, Bannerley Rd, Garretts Green Ind Est, Birmingham, **Midlands (West)**, B33 0SL, **ENGLAND**.
(T) 0121 7899843.
Profile Supplies. Ref: YH08454

LAUNDY, D

D Laundy, Burma Rd, Hurworth Moor, Darlington, **County Durham**, DL2 1QF, **ENGLAND**.
(T) 01325 484355 **(F)** 01325 484355.
Contact/s
Owner: Mrs D Laundy Ref: YH08455

LAUNTON SADDLERY

Launton Saddlery, 18 Blackthorn Rd, Launton, Bicester, **Oxfordshire**, OX6 0DA, **ENGLAND**.
(T) 01869 252317.
Profile Supplies. Ref: YH08456

LAUREL FARM EQUESTRIAN CTRE

Laurel Farm Equestrian Centre, The Coach Hse/Laurel Farm, Long Lane, Haughton, Tarporley, **Cheshire**, CW6 9RN, **ENGLAND**.
(T) 01829 260551.
Profile Stable/Livery.
Facilities for training polo ponies and a complete polo training ground Ref: YH08457

LAUREL STUD

Laurel Star Quarter Horse Stud, Carnhot Farm Stables, Carnhot, Blackwater, Truro, **Cornwall**, TR4 8HB, **ENGLAND**.
(T) 01872 561478
(M) 07970 731533.
Contact/s
Instructor: Mrs L Silvey **(T)** 01872 573726
Profile Breeder, Stable/Livery.
Western training for horse and rider. Advice on tack and equipment. Advice on Quarter Horses and Exmoor Ponies. No.Staff: 3 Yr. Est: 1998 C.Size: 2

Acres **Ref: YH08458**

LAURELS

Laurels Stables, Horringer, Bury St Edmunds, **Suffolk**, IP29 5SN, **ENGLAND**.
(T) 01284 735281.
Contact/s
Owner: Mrs A James
Profile Horse/Rider Accom.
Horses must have current Equine Flu certificates. Wooden boxes for horses, yard large enough for four horse boxes. Accommodation is also available for up to 3 team members. The venue borders on National Parkland and has a lungeing area. **Yr. Est:** 1975
C.Size: 15 Acres
Opening Times
Telephone for bookings **Ref: YH08459**

LAVANT HSE STABLES

Lavant House Stables, Lavant Hse, Lavant, Chichester, **Sussex (West)**, PO18 9AH, **ENGLAND**.
(T) 01243 530460 **(F)** 01243 538129
(W) www.lavanthousestables.co.uk
Affiliated Bodies ABRS, BHS.
Contact/s
Chief Instructor: Mrs M Claxton **(Q)** BHS SM, BHSII (sm)
Profile Arena, Equestrian Centre, Riding Club, Riding School, Stable/Livery, Stable/Livery, Trainer.
Children's activities, competitions and membership schemes for clients are available. **No.Staff:** 6
Yr. Est: 1998 **C.Size:** 50 Acres
Opening Times
Sp: Open 09:00. Closed 17:30.
Su: Open 09:00. Closed 17:30.
Au: Open 09:00. Closed 17:30.
Wn: Open 09:00. Closed 17:30. **Ref: YH08460**

LAVENDER FARM LIVERY STABLES

Lavender Farm Livery Stables, Nursery Lane, Slough, **Berkshire**, SL3 6BY, **ENGLAND**.
(T) 01753 527221.
Contact/s
Owner: Mr B Winterson
Profile Stable/Livery. **Ref: YH08461**

LAVENHAM HALL LIVERIES

Lavenham Hall Liveries, The Hall, Lavenham, **Suffolk**, CO10 9QX, **ENGLAND**.
(T) 01787 247286.
Profile Breeder, Stable/Livery. **Ref: YH08462**

LAVENHAM LEISURE

Lavenham Leisure Ltd, List Hse Works, Hall St, Long Melford, Sudbury, **Suffolk**, CO10 9LL, **ENGLAND**.
(T) 01787 379535 **(F)** 01787 880096.
Contact/s
Manageress: Ms J Nicholls
Profile Manufacturers of country clothing.
Ref: YH08463

LAVERTY LIVESTOCK

Laverty Livestock, 122 Corkey Rd, Loughgiel, Ballymena, **County Antrim**, BT44 9JJ, **NORTHERN IRELAND**.
(T) 028 27641441.
Contact/s
Owner: Mr L Laverty
Profile Transport/Horse Boxes. **Ref: YH08464**

LAVERTY, M

M Laverty, 203 Trew Mount Rd, Dungannon, **County Tyrone**, BT71 7ED, **NORTHERN IRELAND**.
(T) 028 87784608.
Profile Farrier. **Ref: YH08465**

LAVINGTON STUD

Lavington Stud, Lavington Pk, Petworth, **Sussex (West)**, GU28 0NQ, **ENGLAND**.
(T) 01798 867275 **(F)** 01798 867358.
Contact/s
Manager: Mr T Read
Profile Breeder. **Ref: YH08466**

LAVIS, H W

Mr H W Lavis, The Stables, Simpson South Farm, Simpson Cross, Haverfordwest, **Pembrokeshire**, SA62 6ET, **WALES**.
(T) 01437 710531.
Profile Trainer. **Ref: YH08467**

LAW, DEREK

Mr Derek Law, 109 Etherley Lane, Bishop Auckland, **County Durham**, DL14 6UQ, **ENGLAND**.
(T) 01388 661080.
Profile Breeder. **Ref: YH08468**

LAW, GRAHAM

Graham Law, The Quarry, Nether Westcote, Chipping Norton, **Oxfordshire**, OX7 6SD, **ENGLAND**.
(T) 01993 831911.
Contact/s
Owner: Mr G Law
Profile Trainer. **Ref: YH08469**

LAW, LESLIE & HARRIET

Leslie & Harriet Law, 26 Popes Meade, Highnam, **Gloucestershire**, GL2 8LH, **ENGLAND**.
(T) 01452 529719
(M) 07836 727869. **Ref: YH08470**

LAWRENCE, DAVID C

David C Lawrence DWCF, 9 Stibb Cross, Langtree, Torrington, **Devon**, EX38 8LH, **ENGLAND**.
(T) 01805 601541.
Profile Farrier. **Ref: YH08471**

LAWRENCE, E C

E C Lawrence, 8 Church Lane, Frithelstockstone, Torrington, **Devon**, EX38 8JL, **ENGLAND**.
(T) 01805 622198.
Contact/s
Owner: Mrs E Lawrence
Profile Farrier. **Ref: YH08472**

LAWRENCE, R J

R J Lawrence, 1 North Parks, Burrington, Umberleigh, **Devon**, EX37 9JW, **ENGLAND**.
(T) 01769 520412.
Profile Farrier. **Ref: YH08473**

LAWRIE, D

Mr D Lawrie, 10 Cherry Tree Loan, Balerno, **Edinburgh (City of)**, EH14 5AW, **SCOTLAND**.
(T) 0131 5385143 **(F)** 0131 5385143.
Profile Breeder. **Ref: YH08474**

LAWRIE, JOHN

John Lawrie, Rosenun Farm, Horningtops, Liskeard, **Cornwall**, PL14 3QE, **ENGLAND**.
(T) 01579 342408.
Profile Farrier. **Ref: YH08475**

LAWSHIELD UK

Lawshield UK Ltd, St James' Court, Wilderspool Causeway, Warrington, **Cheshire**, WA4 6PS, **ENGLAND**.
(T) 01925 444847 **(F)** 01925 573355
(E) lawshield@compuserve.com.
Profile Club/Association. Insurance Company.
Ref: YH08476

LAWSON, CHARLOTTE

Charlotte Lawson, 30 Goldsboro Rd, London, **London (Greater)**, SW8 4RR, **ENGLAND**.
(T) 01716 226648 **(F)** 01716 226648
(E) c-lawson@msn.com.
Profile Supplies. **Ref: YH08477**

LAWSON, P A

Mr P A Lawson, Cleveland Hse, Hutton Gate, Guisborough, **Cleveland**, TS14 8EG, **ENGLAND**.
(T) 01287 632440.
Profile Breeder. **Ref: YH08478**

LAWSON, SCOTT

Scott Lawson, Nelson Lane, Tayport, **Fife**, DD6 9DL, **SCOTLAND**.
(T) 01382 552244 **(F)** 01382 552244.
Contact/s
Owner: Mr S Lawson
Profile Blacksmith. **Ref: YH08479**

LAWTHER, J R

J R Lawther RSS, 41 Chiltern Rd, Ballinger, Great Missenden, **Buckinghamshire**, HP16 9LJ, **ENGLAND**.
(T) 01494 837294.
Profile Farrier. **Ref: YH08480**

LAWTON, E

E Lawton, 63A Hillary St, Walsall, **Midlands (West)**, WS2 9BP, **ENGLAND**.
(T) 01922 724622.
Contact/s
Owner: Mr E Lawton **Ref: YH08481**

LAXTON, TREVOR

Mr Trevor Laxton, New Page Fold Farm, Waddington, Clitheroe, **Lancashire**, BB7 3JH, **ENGLAND**.
(T) 01200 443566 **(F)** 01200 443566.
Profile Supplies. **Ref: YH08482**

LAYTEM CRAFT

Laytem Craft, 4B Addington St, Ramsgate, **Kent**, CT11 9JL, **ENGLAND**.
(T) 01843 588330 **(F)** 01843 588330.
Contact/s
Owner: Mr J Barrett
Profile Blacksmith. **Ref: YH08483**

LAYTON, T

Miss T Layton BHSI, Willow Tree Farm, Colliers End, Ware, **Hertfordshire**, SG11 1EN, **ENGLAND**.
(T) 01920 821496 **(F)** 01920 821496.
Profile Trainer. **Ref: YH08484**

LAZARO, L

Miss L Lazaro BSc Eq, 5 Lexden Rd, West Bergholt, Colchester, **Essex**, CO6 3BT, **ENGLAND**.
(T) 01206 240203
(M) 07808 141848.
Profile Medical Support. **Ref: YH08485**

LAZYGRAZER

Lazygrazer, 95 Barkham Ride, Wokingham, **Berkshire**, RG11 4HB, **ENGLAND**.
(T) 0118 9733084 **(F)** 0118 9733868.
Profile Medical Support. **Ref: YH08486**

LAZYLAWN

Lazylawn, The Dog Hse, 45A Church St, Oakham, **Leicestershire**, LE15 7JE, **ENGLAND**.
(T) 01572 722923 **(F)** 01572 724386.
Profile Track/Course. **Ref: YH08487**

LE GRICE, T C

Mr T C Le Grice, Trereife Farm, Penzance, **Cornwall**, TR20 8TJ, **ENGLAND**.
(T) 01736 69851.
Profile Breeder, Supplies. **Ref: YH08488**

LE GUP

Le Gup Co, Blakshaw Heys Farm, Breach Hse Lane, Mobberley, **Cheshire**, WA16 7NS, **ENGLAND**.
(T) 01565 873519 **(F)** 01565 873819.
Profile Supplies. **Ref: YH08489**

LE MAISTRE BROS

Le Maistre Bros (Growers) Ltd, Peacock Farm, Rue De La Piece Mauger, Trinity, **Jersey**, JE3 5HW, **ENGLAND**.
(T) 01534 868000 **(F)** 01534.
Contact/s
Owner: Mr R Le Maistre
Profile Feed Merchant, Riding Wear Retailer, Saddlery Retailer, Supplies. **Ref: YH08490**

LE PREVO LEATHERS

Le Prevo Leathers, Black Friars, Stowell St, Newcastle-upon-Tyne, **Tyne and Wear**, NE1 4XN, **ENGLAND**.
(T) 0191 2324179 **(F)** 0191 2617648.
Contact/s
Owner: Mr S Hails
Profile Saddlery Retailer. **Ref: YH08491**

LEA BAILEY RIDING SCHOOL

Lea Bailey Riding School, Ross-on-Wye, **Herefordshire**, HR9 5TY, **ENGLAND**.
(T) 01989 750360.
Profile Riding School, Stable/Livery. **Ref: YH08492**

LEA CASTLE EQUESTRIAN CTRE

Lea Castle Equestrian Centre, Wolverley Rd, Wolverley, Kidderminster, **Worcestershire**, DY10 3QB, **ENGLAND**.
(T) 01562 850088.
Contact/s
Owner: Mrs J Smith
Profile Riding School, Trainer. **Ref: YH08493**

LEA CASTLE SADDLERY

Lea Castle Saddlery Ltd, Lee Castle, Wolverley Rd, Wolverley, Kidderminster, **Worcestershire**, DY10 3QB, **ENGLAND**.
(T) 01562 850611.
Profile Saddlery Retailer. **Ref: YH08494**

LEA, SUE

Sue Lea, Steep Acre Farm, Windlesham Rd, Chobham, **Surrey**, GU24 8SW, **ENGLAND**.
(T) 01276 857174.
Profile Breeder. **Ref: YH08495**

LEACH, S J

S J Leach, 9 Crake Mount, Spark Bridge, Ulverston, **Cumbria**, LA12 7RS, **ENGLAND**.
(T) 01229 861669. **Ref: YH08496**

LEADBETTER, R

R Leadbetter, Maltings Farm Workshop, Malthouse Lane, Burgess Hill, **Sussex (West)**, RH15 9XA, **ENGLAND**.
(T) 01444 243113 **(F)** 01273 832907.
Contact/s
Owner: Mr R Leadbetter
Profile Blacksmith. **Ref: YH08497**

LEADBETTER, S J

S J Leadbetter, Ladykirk Ho Stables, Berwick-upon-Tweed, **Northumberland**, TD15 1SU, **ENGLAND**.
(T) 01289 382519.
Contact/s
Owner: Mr S Leadbetter
Profile Trainer. **Ref: YH08498**

LEADBITTER, P M & F

P M & F Leadbitter, Bwlch Gwyn Farm, Ystradowen, Cowbridge, Cardiff, **Glamorgan (Vale of)**, CF71 7SX, **WALES**.
(T) 01446 773342.
Contact/s
Partner: Miss F Leadbitter
Profile Breeder.
Breeder of Welsh Section B ponies **Ref: YH08499**

LEAHY, P N

Miss P N Leahy, 37 Danes Drive, Glasgow, **Glasgow (City of)**, G14 9HY, **SCOTLAND**.
(T) 0141 9595191.
Profile Breeder. **Ref: YH08500**

LEARY, C W

C W Leary, Barns Farm, Hale Rd, Woodgreen, Fordingbridge, **Hampshire**, SP6 2AJ, **ENGLAND**.
(T) 01725 512246.
Contact/s
Owner: Mr C Leary
Profile Hand made saddles and harnesses.
Ref: YH08501

LEASEY BRIDGE LIVERY STABLES

Leasey Bridge Livery Stables, Leasey Bridge Lane, Wheathampstead, St Albans, **Hertfordshire**, AL4 8EE, **ENGLAND**.
(T) 01582 834343.
Profile Stable/Livery. **Ref: YH08502**

LEATHER LINES SADDLERY

Leather Lines Saddlery, Hague Lane, Wentworth, Rotherham, **Yorkshire (South)**, S62 7TN, **ENGLAND**.
(T) 01226 748548.
Contact/s
Owner: Mr G Wilde
Profile Saddlery Retailer. **Ref: YH08503**

LEATHER SHOP

Leather Shop (The), 37 Stockton Rd, Sunderland, **Tyne and Wear**, SR1 3NR, **ENGLAND**.
(T) 0191 5656402 **(F)** 0191 5656402.
Profile Saddlery Retailer. **Ref: YH08504**

LEATHER WORKSHOP

Leather Workshop (The), Wheatley Grange, Pocombe Bridge, Exeter, **Devon**, EX2 9SX, **ENGLAND**.
(T) 01392 411112.
Profile Saddlery Retailer. **Ref: YH08505**

LEATHER WORKSHOP

Leather Workshop, Oak Bark Bend, Chapel Lane, Burley, Ringwood, **Hampshire**, BH24 4DJ, **ENGLAND**.
(T) 01425 403511.
Profile Supplies. **Ref: YH08506**

LEATHERBARROW, GORDON P

Gordon P Leatherbarrow DWCF, Nuholme, Drigg Rd, Seascale, **Cumbria**, CA20 1NS, **ENGLAND**.
(T) 01946 728557.
Profile Farrier. **Ref: YH08507**

LEATHERDALE, HOWARD M

Howard M Leatherdale DWCF, 1 Cottage, Warrens Cross Farm, Lechlade, **Gloucestershire**, GL7 3DR, **ENGLAND**.
(T) 01367 253019.
Profile Farrier. **Ref: YH08508**

LEAVY, B D

Mr B D Leavy, 366 Uttoxeter Rd, Blythe Bridge, Stoke-on-Trent, **Staffordshire**, ST11 9LY, **ENGLAND**.
(T) 01782 398591 **(F)** 01889 562786
(M) 07711 165198.
Profile Trainer. **Ref: YH08509**

LEAWOOD RIDING CTRE

Leawood Riding Centre, Leawood Hse, Bridestowe, Okehampton, **Devon**, EX20 4ET, **ENGLAND**.
(T) 01837 861203.
Contact/s
Chief Instructor: Ms A Hamlyn
Profile Riding School, Stable/Livery. **Ref: YH08510**

LECALE RIDING CLUB

Lecale Riding Club, 20 Crossgar Rd East, Crossgar, Downpatrick, **County Down**, BT30 9ER, **NORTHERN IRELAND**.
(T) 028 44830824.
Contact/s
Chairman: Mr B Kearney
Profile Riding Club. **Ref: YH08511**

LECKENBY, DAVID

David Leckenby, No 1 Cottage, Broad Oak Farm, Hamsterley Colliery, Newcastle-upon-Tyne, **Tyne and Wear**, NE17 7QD, **ENGLAND**.
(T) 01207 560491.
Profile Farrier. **Ref: YH08512**

LECKHAMPSTEAD WHARF STUD

Leckhampstead Wharf Stud, Leckhampstead Wharf Hse, Leckhampstead, Buckingham, **Buckinghamshire**, MK18 5EZ, **ENGLAND**.
(T) 01280 812230
(W) www.leckhampsteadwharfstud.com.
Contact/s
Owner: Mrs S Mynard
Profile Breeder, Stable/Livery. **Ref: YH08513**

LECKPATRICK AGRCLTRL SVS

Leckpatrick Agricultural Services Ltd, 27 Art Rd, Artigarvan, Strabane, **County Tyrone**, BT82 0HA, **NORTHERN IRELAND**.
(T) 028 71382377.
Profile Supplies. **Ref: YH08514**

LEDGER, R

Mr R Ledger, Sorrento, School Lane, Borden, Sittingbourne, **Kent**, ME9 8JS, **ENGLAND**.
(T) 01795 423360.
Profile Supplies. **Ref: YH08515**

LEE & BRAIN

Lee & Brain, 62 New St, Honiton, **Devon**, EX14 8BZ, **ENGLAND**.
(T) 01404 42750.
Profile Medical Support. **Ref: YH08516**

LEE MARSDEN EQUESTRIAN

Lee Marsden Equestrian, Woodhouse Farm, Church Lane, Lea Marston, Sutton Coldfield, **Midlands (West)**, B76 0BJ, **ENGLAND**.
(T) 01675 470320.
Profile Stable/Livery. **Ref: YH08517**

LEE SADDLERY

Lee Saddlery & Country Clothing, Bridge Hse, Bandon, **County Cork**, **IRELAND**.
(T) 023 41178.
Profile Supplies. **Ref: YH08518**

LEE VALLEY RIDING CTRE

Lee Valley Riding Centre, 71 Lea Bridge Rd, London, **London (Greater)**, E10 7QL, **ENGLAND**.
(T) 020 85562629 **(F)** 020 85589030
(E) leevalley-centre@pcuk.org
(W) www.leevalleypark.org.uk
Affiliated Bodies Pony Club UK.
Contact/s
Owner: Mrs D Corbetts
Profile Riding School, Stable/Livery.
Offer group lessons starting at £13.50 for children and £16.00 for adults. Run 'Have a Go' sessions where adults and children can get a taste of riding and see if they enjoy it. Lecture facilities and classroom to hire.
Opening Times
Sp: Open Mon - Fri 07:00, Sat, Sun 08:00. Closed Mon - Fri 20:30, Sat, Sun 17:30.
Su: Open Mon - Fri 07:00, Sat, Sun 08:00. Closed Mon - Fri 20:30, Sat, Sun 17:30.
Au: Open Mon - Fri 07:00, Sat, Sun 08:00. Closed Mon - Fri 20:30, Sat, Sun 17:30.
Wn: Open Mon - Fri 07:00, Sat, Sun 08:00. Closed Mon - Fri 20:30, Sat, Sun 17:30.
Sat, Sun Closed for lunch between 12:30 and 13:30
Ref: YH08519

LEE VALLEY SADDLERY

Lee Valley Saddlery, Chapel On Leader, Earlston, **Scottish Borders**, TD4 6AW, **SCOTLAND**.
(T) 01896 849586.
Contact/s
Owner: Mr P Howard
Profile Saddlery Retailer.
Specialise in made to measure bridles, saddles and general accessories. **Ref: YH08520**

LEE WOOD HOTEL

Lee Wood Hotel, Manchester Rd, Buxton, **Derbyshire**, SK17 6TQ, **ENGLAND**.
(T) 01298 3002.
Profile Equestrian Centre. **Ref: YH08521**

LEE, C

Mrs C Lee, Home Farm, Bodrhyddan, Rhuddlan, **Denbighshire**, 0018 5SB, **WALES**.
(T) 01745 591193.
Profile Trainer. **Ref: YH08522**

LEE, C F

Mr C F Lee, Coneygre Farm, Hoveringham, **Nottinghamshire**, NG14 7JX, **ENGLAND**.
(T) 01636 830318.
Profile Supplies. **Ref: YH08523**

LEE, GEOFFREY

Geoffrey Lee, The Old Post Office, Barholm, Stamford, **Lincolnshire**, PE9 4RA, **ENGLAND**.
(T) 01778 560362.
Contact/s
Farrier: Geoffrey Lee **(Q)** DWCF
Profile Farrier. **Ref: YH08524**

LEE, P

Mr P Lee, Home Farm, Bodrhyddan, Rhuddlan, Rhyl, **Denbighshire**, LL18 5PE, **WALES**.
(T) 01745 591193.
Profile Breeder, Trainer. **Ref: YH08525**

LEE, RICHARD

Richard Lee, Bell Hse, Byton, Presteigne, **Powys**, LD8 2HS, **WALES**.
(T) 01544 267672 **(F)** 01544 260247.
Contact/s
Owner: Mr R Lee
Profile Trainer. **Ref: YH08526**

LEE, RICHARD A

Mr Richard A Lee RSS, The Bell Hse, Byton, Presteigne, **Powys**, LD8 2US, **WALES**.
(T) 01544 267672 **(F)** 01544 260247
(M) 07836 537145.
Profile Farrier, Trainer. **Ref: YH08527**

LEE, THOMAS H

Thomas H Lee DWCF, 5 The St, Kilmington, Warminster, **Wiltshire**, BA12 6RG, **ENGLAND**.
(T) 01985 844091.
Profile Farrier. **Ref: YH08528**

LEE, WILLIAM P

William P Lee, Fferam Bach, Ty Croes, **Isle of Anglesey**, LL63 5HZ, **WALES**.
(T) 01407 810129.
Profile Farrier. **Ref: YH08529**

LEECH, W A

Mr W A Leech, Shamrock Cottage, Foxcovert Lane, Lower Peover, Knutsford, **Cheshire**, WA16 9QS, **ENGLAND**.
(T) 01565 812384.
Profile Breeder. **Ref: YH08530**

LEEK TRAILERS

Leek Trailers, Gadshill Farm, Lask Edge, Leek, **Staffordshire**, ST13 8QN, **ENGLAND**.
(T) 01782 502544.
Profile Transport/Horse Boxes. **Ref: YH08531**

LEES, T D

Mr T D Lees, Peartree Farm, Fishley Lane, Pelsall, **Staffordshire**, **ENGLAND**..
Profile Trainer. **Ref: YH08532**

LEESE, E

E Leese, 286 Congleton Rd, Scholar Green, Stoke-on-Trent, **Staffordshire**, ST7 3JG, **ENGLAND**.
(T) 01782 783923.
Profile Farrier. **Ref: YH08533**

LEGARD, HILARY

Hilary Legard, 18A Leighton Gardens, Kensal Rise, London, **London (Greater)**, NW10 3PT, **ENGLAND**.
(T) 020 89609247.
Profile Breeder, Medical Support. Freelance Journalist.
Pioneered the Welsh Part Bred Horse Group. Also offers Reiki. **Ref: YH08534**

LEGEND SVS

Legend Services, Rookery Farm, Ashfield Rd, Norton, Bury St Edmunds, **Suffolk**, IP31 3ND,

ENGLAND.
(T) 01359 230049 **(F)** 01359 230049
(M) 07860 826033. **Ref: YH08535**

LEGG, K J

K J Legg, Glenmoor Pk, Pitney, Langport, **Somerset**, TA10 9AU, **ENGLAND**.
(T) 01458 274374.
Profile Farrier. **Ref: YH08536**

LEGG, KEVIN J

Kevin J Legg RSS, Roman Farm, Park, Pitney, Langport, **Somerset**, TA10 9AT, **ENGLAND**.
(T) 01458 274374.
Profile Farrier. **Ref: YH08537**

LEGGA LIVERY & SALES

Legga Livery & Sales, Bodenstown, Naas, **County Kildare**, **IRELAND**.
(T) 086 2053451.
Contact/s
Owner: Billie Jean O'Neill
Profile Stable/Livery. Horse Sales Agency.
Legga specialise in breaking and schooling horses, preparing them for sale. They mainly deal with part-bred Irish Sports horses. No.Staff: 1
Yr. Est: 1998
Opening Times
Telephone for further details **Ref: YH08538**

LEGGATE, J

Leggate J, Leelaw Farm, Lesmahagow, Lanark, **Lanarkshire (South)**, ML11 9QA, **SCOTLAND**.
(T) 01555 892405.
Profile Blacksmith. **Ref: YH08539**

LEGGATE, JENNY

Mrs Jenny Leggate BHSI, Greenlawdean Hse, Greenlaw, **Scottish Borders**, TD10 6XP, **SCOTLAND**.
(T) 01361 810577.
Profile Trainer. Horse & Pony Rescue Centre.
Ref: YH08540

LEGGE, A M

A M Legge DWCF, Yew Tree Cottage, Bredenbury, Bromyard, **Herefordshire**, HR7 4TJ, **ENGLAND**.
(T) 01885 482572.
Profile Farrier. **Ref: YH08541**

LEHEUP, GEOFFREY AVENT

Geoffrey Avent Leheup, Keepers Cottage, Colerne Pk, Chippenham, **Wiltshire**, SN14 8BH, **ENGLAND**.
(T) 01225 743601.
Profile Farrier. **Ref: YH08542**

LEICESTER LIONS

Leicester Lions Horseball Club, C/O Hall Farm, Beeby Rd, Scraptoft, **Leicestershire**, LE7 9SJ, **ENGLAND**.
(T) 0116 2114976.
Profile Club/Association. **Ref: YH08543**

LEICESTER RACECOURSE

Leicester Racecourse Co Ltd, The Racecourse, Oadby, **Leicestershire**, LE2 4AL, **ENGLAND**.
(T) 0116 2716515 **(F)** 0116 2711746
(E) lrc@eggconnect.net.
Contact/s
Hospitality Manager: Maria Szebor
Profile Track/Course.
Corporate days and Race Naming options are also available. **Ref: YH08544**

LEICESTERSHIRE & RUTLAND

Leicestershire & Rutland Bridleways Association, C/O 123 Pk Rd, Loughborough, **Leicestershire**, LE11 2HD, **ENGLAND**.
(T) 01509 215619
Affiliated Bodies BHS, FEMBW Ass.
Contact/s
Chairman: Ms V Allen
Profile Club/Association. **Ref: YH08545**

LEICESTERSHIRE AGRCLTRL SOC

Leicestershire Agricultural Society, Show Office, Dishley Grange Farm, Derby Rd, Loughborough, **Leicestershire**, LE11 5SF, **ENGLAND**.
(T) 01509 646786 **(F)** 01509 646787
(E) leicsag@farming.co.uk
(W) www.leicestershire-county-show.co.uk.
Contact/s
Secretary: Annabel Briggs
Profile Club/Association. **Ref: YH08546**

LEIGH, J

Mr & Mrs J Leigh, Pocket Nook Farm, Lowton St Mary's, Warrington, **Cheshire**, WA3 1AY, **ENGLAND**.
(T) 01942 608585.
Profile Breeder. **Ref: YH08547**

LEISURE VISION

Leisure Vision, Dept Rm, 2 Sandford Cottages, Kingsclere, Newbury, **Berkshire**, RG15 8NZ, **ENGLAND**.
(T) 01635 298231.
Profile Supplies. **Ref: YH08548**

LEJEUNE

Louis Lejeune Ltd, Wilburton, Ely, **Cambridgeshire**, CB6 3RA, **ENGLAND**.
(T) 01353 740444 **(F)** 01353 741599
(E) info@louislejeune.com.
Contact/s
Owner: Sir D Hughes
Profile Trophy Manufacturers.
Bronze and silver ornamental work, car mascots and trophies. **Ref: YH08549**

LEMANS BARN FARM

Lemans Barn Farm, Wykehurst Lane, Ewhurst, Cranleigh, **Surrey**, GU6 7PF, **ENGLAND**.
(T) 01483 277507.
Contact/s
Partner: Miss M Griffin
Profile Stable/Livery. Hacking. **Ref: YH08550**

LENAMORE STABLES

Lenamore Stables, Lenamore Muff, Donegal, **County Donegal**, **IRELAND**.
(T) 077 84022.
Profile Stable/Livery. **Ref: YH08551**

LENRYS ASSOCIATES

Lenrys Associates Ltd, 6 Maurice Gaymer Rd, Attleborough, **Norfolk**, NR17 2QZ, **ENGLAND**.
(T) 01953 457452 **(F)** 01953 457273.
Profile Club/Association, Medical Support.
Ref: YH08552

LEONARD COOMBE

Leonard Coombe, 13 Highweek St, Newton Abbot, **Devon**, TQ12 1TG, **ENGLAND**.
(T) 01626 204099 **(F)** 01626 204045
(W) www.leonardcoombe.co.uk
Affiliated Bodies SMS.
Contact/s
Owner: Ms E Learmonth
(E) leonardcoombe@equesmanet.co.uk
Profile Riding Wear Retailer, Saddlery Retailer, Supplies. No.Staff: 7 Yr. Est: 1800
Opening Times
Sp: Open 09:00. Closed 17:00.
Su: Open 09:00. Closed 17:00.
Au: Open 09:00. Closed 17:00.
Wn: Open 09:00. Closed 17:00. **Ref: YH08553**

LEOPARDSTOWN CLUB

Leopardstown Club Ltd, Foxrock, Dublin, **County Dublin**, **IRELAND**.
(T) 01 2893607 **(F)** 01 2892634
(E) info@leopardstown.com
(W) www.leopardstown.com.
Profile Club/Association. **Ref: YH08554**

LEO'S SADDLERY

Leo's Saddlery, 15C Market Pl, Oundle, Peterborough, **Cambridgeshire**, PE8 4BA, **ENGLAND**.
(T) 01832 275699.
Profile Riding Wear Retailer, Saddlery Retailer.
Ref: YH08555

LES LEY HORSE TRANSPORT

L S V Equestrian Transport, 72 Pillar Ave, Brixham, **Devon**, TQ5 8LB, **ENGLAND**.
(T) 01803 856933.
Contact/s
Owner: Mr L Ley
(E) les@ley.frewwire.co.uk
Profile Transport/Horse Boxes. **Ref: YH08556**

LESLEY RALPH SADDLER

Lesley Ralph Saddler, 2 Culver Rd, Basingstoke, **Hampshire**, RG21 3LS, **ENGLAND**.
(T) 01256 475326 **(F)** 01256 475326.
Contact/s
General Manager: Mr T Ralph
Profile Saddlery Retailer. Saddler and Harness Maker. Yr. Est: 1980 **Ref: YH08557**

LESLIE LANE

Leslie Lane, 18 Hawthorn Rise, Mundesley, **Norfolk**, NR11 8JY, **ENGLAND**.
(T) 01263 721830. **Ref: YH08558**

LESLIE, A C

A C Leslie, Spey Bridge, Newtonmore, **Highlands**, PH20 1BB, **SCOTLAND**.
(T) 01540 3275.
Profile Farrier. **Ref: YH08559**

LESSANS RIDING CLUB

Lessans Riding Club, 79 Saintfield Rd, Ballygowan, **County Down**, BT23 6HN, **NORTHERN IRELAND**.
(T) 028 97521361.
Contact/s
Chairman: Miss R McBride
Profile Riding Club. **Ref: YH08560**

LESSANS RIDING STABLES

Lessans Riding Stables, 126 Monlough Rd, Saintfield, Ballynahinch, **County Down**, BT24 7EU, **NORTHERN IRELAND**.
(T) 028 97510141
Affiliated Bodies BHS.
Contact/s
Instructor: Mr T Watters **(Q)** BHS PTT
Profile Riding School, Stable/Livery.
The prices for livery and lessons may vary depending on individual needs.
Opening Times
Sp: Open Mon - Sun 08:00. Closed Mon - Sun 21:00.
Su: Open Mon - Sun 08:00. Closed Mon - Sun 21:00.
Au: Open Mon - Sun 08:00. Closed Mon - Sun 21:00.
Wn: Open Mon - Sun 08:00. Closed Mon - Sun 21:00. **Ref: YH08561**

LESTER BOWDEN

Lester Bowden (1898) Ltd, The Old Spread Eagle, High St, Epsom, **Surrey**, KT19 8DN, **ENGLAND**.
(T) 01372 747474 **(F)** 01372 743129.
Profile Saddlery Retailer. **Ref: YH08562**

LESTER, MACKINNON & BENSON

Lester, Mackinnon & Benson, 45 Lewis Lane, Cirencester, **Gloucestershire**, GL7 1EA, **ENGLAND**.
(T) 01285 653151.
Profile Medical Support. **Ref: YH08563**

LESTER, P

Miss P Lester, Homefield, Fontley Rd, Titchfield, Fareham, **Hampshire**, PO15 6QZ, **ENGLAND**.
(T) 01329 845740.
Profile Breeder, Stable/Livery. **Ref: YH08564**

LETCHWORTH BALDOCK & DISTRICT

Letchworth Baldock & District Riding Club, 5 The Orchard, Pinnock Lane, Baldock, **Hertfordshire**, SG7 6DE, **ENGLAND**.
(T) 01462 893682.
Profile Club/Association, Riding Club. **Ref: YH08565**

LETHAM, SNELL & HUTCHINSON

Letham, Snell & Hutchinson, 4 Ditton St, Ilminster, **Somerset**, TA19 0BQ, **ENGLAND**.
(T) 01460 52487.
Profile Medical Support. **Ref: YH08566**

LETHAME HOUSE EQUESTRIAN CTRE

Lethame House Equestrian Centre, Lethame Rd, Strathaven, **Lanarkshire (South)**, ML10 6RW, **SCOTLAND**.
(T) 01357 521108.
Contact/s
Owner: Mrs V Nugent
Profile Riding School, Stable/Livery. **Ref: YH08567**

LETHERS OF BROCKHAM

Lethers Of Brockham, 54 Middle St, Brockham, Betchworth, **Surrey**, RH3 7HW, **ENGLAND**.
(T) 01737 842966
Affiliated Bodies SMS.
Contact/s
Partner: Mr F Hughes
Profile Saddlery Retailer.
Bridle repairs are available. Yr. Est: 1972
Opening Times
Sp: Open 09:30. Closed Mon - Fri 17:30, Sat 17:00.
Su: Open 09:30. Closed Mon - Fri 17:30, Sat 17:00.
Au: Open 09:30. Closed Mon - Fri 17:30, Sat 17:00.
Wn: Open 09:30. Closed Mon - Fri 17:30, Sat 17:00.
Closed Sundays **Ref: YH08568**

LETHERS OF MERSTHAM

Lethers Of Merstham, 56 Nutfield Rd, Merstham, Redhill, **Surrey**, RH1 3EP, **ENGLAND**.
(T) 01737 644508
Affiliated Bodies SMS.
Contact/s
Partner: Mr F Hughes
Profile Saddlery Retailer.
Bridle repairs are available. Yr. Est: 1972
Opening Times
Sp: Open 09:30. Closed Mon - Fri 17:30, Sat 17:00.

Su: Open 09:30. Closed Mon - Fri 17:30, Sat 17:00.
Au: Open 09:30. Closed Mon - Fri 17:30, Sat 17:00.
Wn: Open 09:30. Closed Mon - Fri 17:30, Sat 17:00.
Closed Sundays **Ref: YH08569**

LETTERSHUNA RIDING CTRE

Lettershuna Riding Centre, Lettershuna Hse, Appin, **Argyll and Bute**, PA38 4BN, **SCOTLAND**.
(T) 01631 730227 **(F)** 01631 730551
(E) 100523.142@compuserve.com
Affiliated Bodies BHS.
Contact/s
Owner: Mr D Craig **(Q)** BHSII
Profile Horse/Rider Accom, Riding School, Stable/Livery.
DIY Livery, prices on request **Ref: YH08570**

LEVACE HORSEBOXES

Levace Horseboxes, Gloucester Enterprise Workshops, Unit 8-9 Chequers Rd, Gloucester, **Gloucestershire**, GL4 6PN, **ENGLAND**.
(T) 01452 500014.
Contact/s
Owner: Mr J Cleeve
Profile Transport/Horse Boxes. **Ref: YH08571**

LEVADE SYSTEMS

Levade Systems, Lines Farm Est, Parrock Lane, Colemans Hatch, Hartfield, **Sussex (East)**, TN7 4HT, **ENGLAND**.
(T) 01342 824117 **(F)** 01342 824117.
Profile Transport/Horse Boxes. **Ref: YH08572**

LEVEN VALLEY RIDING CLUB

Leven Valley Riding Club, Hillside Cottage, Red Rd, Cardross, Dunbarton, **Dunbartonshire (West)**, G82 5HH, **SCOTLAND**.
(T) 01389 841396.
Contact/s
Chairman: Mrs F Hunter
Profile Riding Club. **Ref: YH08573**

LEVER, J S

J S Lever, Woodlands, School Lane, High Witley, Warrington, **Cheshire**, **ENGLAND**..
Profile Breeder. **Ref: YH08574**

LEVERETT, C J & S

C J & S Leverett, Pant Glas Farm, Tyn-Y-Morfa, Holywell, **Flintshire**, CH8 9JN, **WALES**.
(T) 01745 853381 **(F)** 01745 886728.
Profile Breeder. **Ref: YH08575**

LEVERTON

Leverton & Co, Unit 6 Heapham Rd Ind Est, Gainsborough, **Lincolnshire**, DN21 1RZ, **ENGLAND**.
(T) 01777 860860 **(F)** 01777 860840.
Profile Medical Support. **Ref: YH08576**

LE-WECHNER, NICHOLAS J

Nicholas J Le-Wechner DWCF, 60 Ely Rd, Little Downham, Ely, **Cambridgeshire**, CB6 2SN, **ENGLAND**.
(T) 01353 698228.
Profile Farrier. **Ref: YH08577**

LEWES FORGE

Lewes Forge (The), Fisher St, Lewes, **Sussex (East)**, BN7 2DG, **ENGLAND**.
(T) 01273 473355.
Contact/s
Owner: Mr B Autie
Profile Blacksmith. **Ref: YH08578**

LEWIN, HEATHER

Heather Lewin, 3 Carlisle Trce, St Ives, **Cambridgeshire**, PE27 5PQ, **ENGLAND**.
(T) 01480 301993.
Contact/s
Owner: Ms H Eggert **Ref: YH08579**

LEWINGTON, RICHARD W

Richard W Lewington DWCF, Dixholme, Middleton Tyas, Richmond, **Yorkshire (North)**, DL10 6PS, **ENGLAND**.
(T) 01325 377784.
Profile Farrier. **Ref: YH08580**

LEWIS BROS

Lewis Bros, The Gr, Hollyhurst, Leebotwood, Church Stretton, **Shropshire**, SY6 7JP, **ENGLAND**.
(T) 01694 751212.
Contact/s
Partner: Mr A Lewis **Ref: YH08581**

LEWIS G H & SONS

Lewis G H & Sons, Sandygate Forge, Brewery Rd, Wath-upon-Dearne, Rotherham, **Yorkshire (South)**, S63 7BX, **ENGLAND**.
(T) 01709 872300.
Profile Blacksmith. **Ref: YH08582**

LEWIS JONES & AST

Lewis Jones & Associates, 5 High St, Honiton, **Devon**, EX14 8PR, **ENGLAND**.
(T) 01404 42657 **(F)** 01404 44349.
Profile Medical Support. **Ref: YH08583**

LEWIS, A S

A S Lewis RSS, 12 St Davids Ave, Carmarthen, **Carmarthenshire**, SA31 3DW, **WALES**.
(T) 01267 236901.
Profile Farrier. **Ref: YH08584**

LEWIS, ANNETTE

Annette Lewis, Tutein Farm, Grove Lane, Chigwell Row, Chigwell, **Essex**, IG7 6JQ, **ENGLAND**.
(T) 020 85005040 **(F)** 020 85005040.
Profile Trainer. **Ref: YH08585**

LEWIS, ANTHONY

Anthony Lewis, Tutein Farm, Grove Lane, Chigwell Row, Chigwell, **Essex**, IG7 6JQ, **ENGLAND**.
(T) 020 85005040 **(F)** 020 85005040.
Profile Supplies. **Ref: YH08586**

LEWIS, CLARE

Clare Lewis, Valley Farm, Horstead Keynes, **Sussex (West)**, RH17 7BP, **ENGLAND**.
(T) 01444 790247. **Ref: YH08587**

LEWIS, CLEO

Miss Cleo Lewis, 29 Middle Furlong, Bushey, **Hertfordshire**, WD2 3SZ, **ENGLAND**.
(T) 020 89501696.
Profile Breeder. **Ref: YH08588**

LEWIS, DAVID CHARLES

David Charles Lewis, The Laundry, Walton, **Warwickshire**, CV35 9HX, **ENGLAND**.
(T) 01789 840380.
Profile Farrier. **Ref: YH08589**

LEWIS, DAVID G

David G Lewis AFCL, Fryern Home Farm, Fryern Pk, Storrington, Pulborough, **Sussex (West)**, RN20 4BQ, **ENGLAND**.
(T) 01903 740159.
Profile Farrier. **Ref: YH08590**

LEWIS, G

G Lewis, Thirty Acre Barn, Shepherds Walk, Epsom, **Surrey**, KT18 6BX, **ENGLAND**.
(T) 01372 277662 **(F)** 01372 277366.
Contact/s
Owner: Mr G Lewis
Profile Trainer. **Ref: YH08591**

LEWIS, J E

Mrs J E Lewis BHSAI, 61 Mill Rd, Blofield Heath, Norwich, **Norfolk**, NR13 4QS, **ENGLAND**.
(T) 01603 715850 **(F)** 01603 715850
(E) jelewis@compuserve.com.
Profile Trainer. **Ref: YH08592**

LEWIS, MARTIN J

Martin J Lewis RSS Hons, 10 Willow Drv, Waterbrook Mews, Devizes, **Wiltshire**, SN10 2SN, **ENGLAND**.
(T) 01380 727385.
Profile Farrier. **Ref: YH08593**

LEWIS, MEGAN

Megan Lewis, Cwrtycadno Stud, Ffrwdfal Farm, Pumpsaint, Llanwrda, **Carmarthenshire**, SA19 8TE, **WALES**.
(T) 01558 650582.
Profile Breeder. **Ref: YH08594**

LEWIS, ROBERT I

Robert I Lewis DWCF, 4 Grange Ave, Hulland Ward, Ashbourne, **Derbyshire**, DE6 3FX, **ENGLAND**.
(T) 01335 370511.
Profile Farrier. **Ref: YH08595**

LEWIS, THOMAS HUGH

Thomas Hugh Lewis, 96 Bwllfa Rd, Cwmdare, Aberdare, **Rhondda Cynon Taff**, CF44 8TR, **WALES**.
(T) 01685 872317.
Profile Farrier. **Ref: YH08596**

LEWIS, W D

W D Lewis, Pantycaws, Efailwen, Clynderwen, **Carmarthenshire**, SA66 7XD, **WALES**.
(T) 01994 419272.
Contact/s
Owner: Mr W Lewis
Profile Breeder. **Ref: YH08597**

LEWNEY, E

Mr E Lewney, 6 Silver St, Marton, Ulverston, **Cumbria**, LA12 0NQ, **ENGLAND**.
(T) 01229 62243.
Profile Breeder. **Ref: YH08598**

LEY, CLIVE H

Clive H Ley DWCF, The Oaks, St Brannocks Rd, Ilfracombe, **Devon**, EX34 8EP, **ENGLAND**.
(T) 01271 867548.
Profile Farrier. **Ref: YH08599**

LEYBOURNE GRANGE

Leybourne Grange Riding Centre For The Disabled, Birling Rd, Leybourne, West Malling, **Kent**, ME19 2HZ, **ENGLAND**.
(T) 01732 872844 **(F)** 01732 872844.
Contact/s
Chairman: Mr R Barnes **(T)** 020 86691511
Profile Arena, Equestrian Centre, Riding School, Stable/Livery. No.Staff: 7 Yr. Est: 1992
C.Size: 60 Acres
Opening Times
Sp: Open 09:00. Closed 17:00.
Su: Open 09:00. Closed 17:00.
Au: Open 09:00. Closed 17:00.
Wn: Open 09:00. Closed 17:00. **Ref: YH08600**

LEYLAND COURT

Leyland Court, Northwoods, Winterbourne, Bristol, **Bristol**, BS36 1RY, **ENGLAND**.
(T) 01454 773163.
Contact/s
Owner: Mrs M Irish
Profile Riding School, Saddlery Retailer, Stable/Livery. **Ref: YH08601**

LIBBY'S

Libby's, 57 Farringdon Rd, Plymouth, **Devon**, PL4 9ER, **ENGLAND**.
(T) 01752 341584 **(F)** 01752 255558.
Profile Supplies. **Ref: YH08602**

LIBERTY INTELLECTUAL

Liberty Intellectual Pony Stallion, Meadowview, Forest Rd, Wokingham, **Berkshire**, RG11 5SA, **ENGLAND**.
(T) 01344 867688 **(F)** 01344 867688.
Profile Club/Association. **Ref: YH08603**

LICHFIELD BRIDLE SPECIALISTS

Lichfield Bridle Specialists, 17 Lime St, Walsall, **Midlands (West)**, WS1 2JL, **ENGLAND**.
(T) 01922 646915 **(F)** 01922 646915.
Contact/s
Owner: Mr P Parsons **Ref: YH08604**

LICHFIELD SIDE SADDLE

Lichfield Side Saddle Specialists (The), Huckers Buildings, Long Acre St, Walsall, **Midlands (West)**, WS2 8HP, **ENGLAND**.
(T) 01922 646468 **(F)** 01922 638936.
Contact/s
Owner: Mr B Swaine **Ref: YH08605**

LIDDLE, H T

Mr H T Liddle, 55 Glamis Rd, Forfar, **Angus**, DD8 1DH, **SCOTLAND**.
(T) 01307 462341.
Profile Trainer. **Ref: YH08606**

LIDSTONE FARMS

Lidstone Farms Ltd, All Souls Farm, George Green, Slough, **Buckinghamshire**, SL3 6AN, **ENGLAND**.
(T) 01753 522700.
Profile Supplies. **Ref: YH08607**

LIDUN PET FOODS

Lidun Pet Foods Ltd, Boundary Ind Est, Boundary Rd, Lytham, **Lancashire**, FY8 5HU, **ENGLAND**.
(T) 01253 730888 **(F)** 01253 734505.
Profile Supplies. **Ref: YH08608**

LIEGE MANOR

Liege Manor Equestrian Centre, Liege Manor Farm, Llancarfan Lane, Bonvilston, Cardiff, **Glamorgan (Vale of)**, CF5 6TQ, **WALES**.
(T) 01446 781648.
Contact/s
Groom: Ms L Davies
Profile Riding School, Trainer. Yr. Est: 1987
Opening Times
Sp: Open Tues - Fri 13:00, Sat, Sun 09:00. Closed Tues, Wed, Fri 20:00, Thurs 21:00, Sat, Sun 18:00.
Su: Open Tues - Fri 13:00, Sat, Sun 09:00. Closed Tues, Wed, Fri 20:00, Thurs 21:00, Sat, Sun 18:00.
Au: Open Tues - Fri 13:00, Sat, Sun 09:00. Closed

Tues, Wed, Fri 20:00, Thurs 21:00, Sat, Sun 18:00.
Wn: Open Tues - Fri 13:00, Sat, Sun 09:00. Closed Tues, Wed, Fri 20:00, Thurs 21:00, Sat, Sun 18:00. Closed Mondays, student training in the mornings Tues - Fri. **Ref: YH08609**

LIFE SOURCE SUPPLEMENTS

Life Source Supplements, Camphill Ind Est, Ripon, **Yorkshire (North)**, HG4 1QY, **ENGLAND**.
(T) 01765 692323 **(F)** 01765 607746.
Profile Medical Support. **Ref: YH08610**

LIFELIGHTS

Lifelights U K, Valewood Farm, Smith Lane, Mobberley, **Cheshire**, WA16 7QE, **ENGLAND**.
(T) 01565 873464 **(F)** 01565 615276.
Profile Supplies. **Ref: YH08611**

LIGHT CAVALRY

Light Cavalry, Flemish Farm, Winkfield, Windsor, **Berkshire**, SL4 4UG, **ENGLAND**.
(T) 01753 622291 **(F)** 01753 622291.
Contact/s
Manager: Mr P Alison **Ref: YH08612**

LIGHTFOOT INT

Lightfoot International Ltd, 11 Low March Ind Est, Low March, Daventry, **Northamptonshire**, NN11 4SD, **ENGLAND**.
(T) 01327 311077 **(F)** 01327 311977.
Contact/s
Company Secretary: Mr R Dodd
Profile Supplies. **Ref: YH08613**

LIGHTFOOT, R

R Lightfoot, Cae-Ap-Edward, Llanarmon-Yn-Ial, Mold, **Flintshire**, CH7 4QD, **WALES**.
(T) 01824 780261.
Profile Breeder. **Ref: YH08614**

LIGHTFOOT, R & D M

R & D M Lightfoot, Doxford Dairy Farm, Doxford, Chathill, **Northumberland**, NE67 5DL, **ENGLAND**.
(T) 01665 589463.
Contact/s
Partner: Mrs D Lightfoot **Ref: YH08615**

LIGHTS

Lights Sussex Shavings & Horse Feeds, London Rd, Pyecombe, Brighton, **Sussex (West)**, BN45 7ED, **ENGLAND**.
(T) 01273 844508 **(F)** 01273 844322
(W) www.brendon-pyecombe.co.uk.
Contact/s
Assistant: Ms C Light
Profile Equestrian Centre, Feed Merchant, Saddlery Retailer, Supplies.
Stockists of Easibed, feed balancers, poultry & dog-food. No.Staff: 2 Yr. Est: 1980
Opening Times
Sp: Open Mon - Sat 09:00. Closed Mon - Sat 17:30.
Su: Open Mon - Sat 09:00. Closed Mon - Sat 17:30.
Au: Open Mon - Sat 09:00. Closed Mon - Sat 17:30.
Wn: Open Mon - Sat 09:00. Closed Mon - Sat 17:30.
Open on Show Sundays through the Winter.
Ref: YH08616

LIGHTWOOD SADDLE

Lightwood Saddle Co, Neptune Hall, Neptune Rd, Tywyn, **Gwynedd**, LL36 0DL, **WALES**.
(T) 01654 712314.
Profile Saddle Manufacturer. **Ref: YH08617**

LIGHTWOOD, ROBERT IAN

Robert Ian Lightwood, 1 Bladon Farm Cottage, Bladon Farm, Winshill, Burton-on-Trent, **Staffordshire**, DE15 0RS, **ENGLAND**.
(T) 01283 538797.
Profile Farrier. **Ref: YH08618**

LILAC FARM COURTYARD LIVERY

Lilac Farm Courtyard Livery, Lilac Farm, Jewitt Lane, Collingham, Wetherby, **Yorkshire (West)**, LS22 5BA, **ENGLAND**.
(T) 01937 573162 **(F)** 01937 572084.
Contact/s
Owner: Mrs S Kilby
Profile Horse/Rider Accom, Stable/Livery, Track/Course. **Ref: YH08619**

LILLESHALL EQUESTRIAN CTRE

Lilleshall Equestrian Centre, Child Pits Lane, Lilleshall, Newport, **Shropshire**, TF10 9AR, **ENGLAND**.
(T) 01952 677166.
Contact/s
Owner: Miss S Francis
Profile Breeder, Equestrian Centre, Riding School, Stable/Livery. **Ref: YH08620**

LILLEY RIDING SCHOOL

Lilley Riding School, West St, Lilley, Luton, **Bedfordshire**, LU2 8LH, **ENGLAND**.
(T) 01462 768372.
Profile Riding School. **Ref: YH08621**

LILLEY, M J

M J Lilley, Oaklands Farm, Cordy Lane, Brinsley, Nottingham, **Nottinghamshire**, NG16 5BZ, **ENGLAND**.
(T) 01773 713736.
Contact/s
Owner: Mr M Lilley
Profile Transport/Horse Boxes. **Ref: YH08622**

LILLIDALE ANIMAL HEALTH

Lillidale Animal Health, Badbury View, Wimborne, **Dorset**, BH21 4HU, **ENGLAND**.
(T) 01202 848456 **(F)** 01202 848570.
Profile Medical Support. **Ref: YH08623**

LILLINGSTON BLOODSTOCK

Lillingston Bloodstock, The Dairy, Butlers Lands Farm, Mortimer, Reading, **Berkshire**, RG7 2AG, **ENGLAND**.
(T) 0118 9331944 **(F)** 0118 9331945
(E) lukelillingston@yahoo.com.
Contact/s
Assistant: Rachel Boffey
Profile Blood Stock Agency. **Ref: YH08624**

LIMBURY FARM & STUD

Limbury Farm & Stud, Buttersend Lane, Hartpury, Gloucester, **Gloucestershire**, GL19 3DD, **ENGLAND**.
(T) 01452 700268.
Profile Breeder. **Ref: YH08625**

LIME PARK EQUESTRIAN

Lime Park Equestrian Centre, 5 Lime Kiln Rd, Maghaberry, Moira, Craigavon, **County Armagh**, BT67 0JD, **NORTHERN IRELAND**.
(T) 028 92621139/92621153 **(F)** 028 92621139
(E) info@limeparkequestrian.com
(W) www.limeparkequestrian.com
Affiliated Bodies SJAI.
Contact/s
Partner: Mr D McMillan
Profile Blacksmith, Equestrian Centre, Farrier, Riding School, Stable/Livery.
Group lessons are available at £8.00 for children and £10.00 for adults per hour. Other facilities include floodlit all weather arena, stabling for up to 100 horses, changing rooms, and showers and dormitories (the latter are all under construction). The centre also holds shows, pony camps and day trips to the forest and the beach. Loan a Pony weeks are also on offer.
Yr. Est: 1983
Opening Times
Sp: Open Mon - Sun 09:00. Closed Mon - Sun 21:00.
Su: Open Mon - Sun 09:00. Closed Mon - Sun 21:00.
Au: Open Mon - Sun 09:00. Closed Mon - Sun 21:00.
Wn: Open Mon - Sun 09:00. Closed Mon - Sun 21:00. **Ref: YH08626**

LIME TREE FARM

Lime Tree Farm, Hutts Lane, Grewelthorpe, Ripon, **Yorkshire (North)**, HG4 3DA, **ENGLAND**.
(T) 01765 83450.
Profile Stable/Livery. **Ref: YH08627**

LIMEBROOK

Limebrook Farm Riding School, Limebrook Farm, Wycke Hill, Maldon, **Essex**, CM9 6SH, **ENGLAND**.
(T) 01621 853671.
Contact/s
Owner: Mrs S Lowe
Profile Riding School.
Opening Times
Sp: Open Tues - Thurs, Sat, Sun 09:00. Closed Tues - Thurs 20:00, Sat, Sun 17:00.
Su: Open Tues - Thurs, Sat, Sun 09:00. Closed Tues - Thurs 20:00, Sat, Sun 17:00.
Au: Open Tues - Thurs, Sat, Sun 09:00. Closed Tues - Thurs 20:00, Sat, Sun 17:00.
Wn: Open Tues - Thurs, Sat, Sun 09:00. Closed Tues - Thurs 20:00, Sat, Sun 17:00.
Closed Mondays and Fridays. **Ref: YH08628**

LIMEFITT PK

Limefitt Park Pony Trekking Centre, C/O Wynlass Beck, Windermere, **Cumbria**, LA23 1EU, **ENGLAND**.
(T) 01539 432564.
Profile Equestrian Centre. Trekking Centre.
Ref: YH08629

LIMEPARK RIDING CLUB

Limepark Riding Club, 7 Trummery Rd, Maghaberry, Moira, **County Armagh**, BT67 0JX, **NORTHERN IRELAND**.
(T) 028 92619447.
Contact/s
Chairman: Mr H Edwards
Profile Riding Club. **Ref: YH08630**

LIMERICK RACE

Limerick Race Co Ltd, Racecourse Greenpark, Limerick, **County Limerick**, **IRELAND**.
(T) 061 229377.
Profile Track/Course. **Ref: YH08631**

LIMERICK STUD

Limerick Stud, Potton Rd, Gamlingay, **Bedfordshire**, SG19, **ENGLAND**.
(T) 01767 650797.
Profile Breeder. **Ref: YH08632**

LIMES EQUESTRIAN CTRE

Limes Equestrian Centre (The), Hinkley Rd, Sapcote, **Leicestershire**, LE9 6LG, **ENGLAND**.
(T) 01455 272271.
Profile Riding School, Stable/Livery. **Ref: YH08633**

LIMES FARM

Limes Farm (The), Hough-on-the-Hill, Grantham, **Lincolnshire**, NG32 2BH, **ENGLAND**.
(T) 01400 250203 **(F)** 01400 251199
(M) 07710 873300.
Profile Trainer. **Ref: YH08634**

LIMES FARM EQUESTRIAN

Limes Farm Equestrian Centre, The Limes, Pay St, Hawkinge, Folkestone, **Kent**, CT18 7DZ, **ENGLAND**.
(T) 01303 892335 **(F)** 01303 894020
(E) office@limesfarmequestriancentre.co.uk
(W) www.limesfarmequestriancentre.co.uk.
Contact/s
General Manager: Mrs J Croucher
Profile Equestrian Centre, Riding School, Stable/Livery.
Training courses towards BHS in partnership with South Kent College available There is a clubroom and licensed bar. C.Size: 60 Acres **Ref: YH08635**

LIMES FARM STABLES

Limes Farm Stables, Upper Lambourn, Hungerford, **Berkshire**, RG17 8QP, **ENGLAND**.
(T) 01488 71890.
Profile Trainer. **Ref: YH08636**

LIMESTONE STUD

Limestone Stud, Willoughton, Gainsborough, **Lincolnshire**, DN21 5SP, **ENGLAND**.
(T) 01427 668232 **(F)** 01427 668233
(E) cgm@limestonefarm.v-net.com
Affiliated Bodies TBA.
Contact/s
Manager: Mr W Morgan
Profile Breeder, Trainer. Thoroughbred Stud.
No.Staff: 5 Yr. Est: 1900
Opening Times
Sp: Open Mon - Sun 08:00. Closed Mon - Sun 17:00.
Su: Open Mon - Sun 08:00. Closed Mon - Sun 17:00.
Au: Open Mon - Sun 08:00. Closed Mon - Sun 17:00.
Wn: Open Mon - Sun 08:00. Closed Mon - Sun 17:00. **Ref: YH08637**

LIMPET ANTI-SLIP SADDLE PADS

Happy Horse Ltd, Gosford Farm, Ottery St Mary, **Devon**, EX11 1XX, **ENGLAND**.
(T) 01404 814998 **(F)** 01404 813653
(E) happyhorse@eurobell.co.uk
(W) www.limpetsaddlepad.co.uk.
Contact/s
Owner: Mrs A Holmes
Profile Supplies.
Supply anti-slip saddle pads which have been used for performance, dressage and Grand Prix III & IV. The pad helps to prevent the saddle from slipping and also protects the horse from sores. There is also a noseband buffer to relieve pressure points, and boot mates to help prevent sore shins and windgalls.
Ref: YH08638

LINACRE SHETLAND PONIES

Linacre Shetland Ponies, Shipmans Barn Stud, Saxby Rd, Brentingby, Melton Mowbray, **Leicestershire**, LE14 4RZ, **ENGLAND**.
(T) 01664 565520 **(F)** 01664 482104.
Profile Breeder. **Ref: YH08639**

LINCOLN & DISTRICT

Lincoln & District Riding Club, 140 Newland St West, Lincoln, **Lincolnshire**, LN1 1QE, **ENGLAND**.
(T) 01522 26168.
Profile Club/Association, Riding Club. **Ref: YH08640**

LINCOLNSFIELD RIDING CTRE

Lincolnsfield Riding Centre (The), Bushey Hall Drv, Bushey, Watford, **Hertfordshire**, WD2 2ER, **ENGLAND**.
(T) 01923 240127.
Contact/s
Owner: Mrs D Snell **Ref: YH08641**

LINCOLNSHIRE IRONMASTERS

Lincolnshire Ironmasters, Church Farm, Cold Hanworth, Lincoln, **Lincolnshire**, LN2 3RE, **ENGLAND**.
(T) 01673 861580.
Contact/s
Owner: Mr P Richardson
Profile Blacksmith. **Ref: YH08642**

LINCS RURAL ACTIVITIES

Lincs Rural Activities & Equestrian Centre, Kenwick Hill, Louth, **Lincolnshire**, LN11 8NR, **ENGLAND**.
(T) 01507 608855.
Profile Equestrian Centre, Riding School.
Ref: YH08643

LINDALL HARNESS & SADDLERY

Lindall Harness & Saddlery, 59 Horncastle Rd, Woodhall Spa, **Lincolnshire**, LN10 6UY, **ENGLAND**.
(T) 01526 353174.
Contact/s
Owner: Mr D Tyler **Ref: YH08644**

LINDEN LODGE STABLES

Linden Lodge Stables, Rowley Drv, Newmarket, **Suffolk**, CB8 0NH, **ENGLAND**.
(T) 01638 664348 **(F)** 01638 660338
(M) 07802 204281
(W) www.abcinternetservices.co.uk
Affiliated Bodies Newmarket Trainers Fed.
Profile Trainer. **Ref: YH08645**

LINDER, P J

P J Linder, Rednil Farm Riding Stables, Lincoln Rd, Welton, **Lincolnshire**, LN2 3JA, **ENGLAND**.
(T) 01673 860548.
Profile Farrier. **Ref: YH08646**

LINDLEY, B

B Lindley, 519 Bickershaw Lane, Abram, Wigan, **Lancashire**, WN2, **ENGLAND**.
(T) 01942 512734.
Profile Farrier. **Ref: YH08647**

LINDLEY, BERNARD J

Bernard J Lindley DWCF, C/O C Zinon, The Smithy, Little Bollington, Altrincham, **Cheshire**, WA14 4TD, **ENGLAND**.
(T) 01925 756540.
Profile Farrier. **Ref: YH08648**

LINDLEY, J F

J F Lindley, Elmfield, Speen Lane, Newbury, **Berkshire**, RG14 1RW, **ENGLAND**.
(T) 01635 40834 **(F)** 01635 44556.
Contact/s
Owner: Mr J Lindley
Profile Blood Stock Agency. **Ref: YH08649**

LINDON EQUESTRIAN

Lindon Equestrian, 276 Wragby Rd, Lincoln, **Lincolnshire**, LN2 4PX, **ENGLAND**.
(T) 01522 567737 **(F)** 01522 567737.
Contact/s
Owner: Mrs V Malone **Ref: YH08650**

LINDRIDGE, KEITH P

Keith P Lindridge, Little Forge, Keith, **Moray**, AB55 3QS, **SCOTLAND**.
(T) 01542 882229.
Profile Farrier. **Ref: YH08651**

LINDSAY RUGS

Lindsay Rugs, 99 Ballycraigy Rd, Newtownabbey, **County Antrim**, BT36 4TB, **NORTHERN IRELAND**.
(T) 028 90832993.
Profile Supplies. **Ref: YH08652**

LINDSAY, I

I Lindsay, Two Oaks, The Causeway, Congresbury, Bristol, **Bristol**, BS49 5DJ, **ENGLAND**.
(T) 01934 876798.
Profile Farrier. **Ref: YH08653**

LINDSAY, P M

Miss P M Lindsay, Holmes Farm, Hatherleigh, Okehampton, **Devon**, EX20 3LF, **ENGLAND**.
(T) 01837 810362.
Profile Breeder. **Ref: YH08654**

LINDSEY FARM SVS

Lindsey Farm Services, 14 South St, Horncastle, **Lincolnshire**, LN9 6DX, **ENGLAND**.
(T) 01507 522525 **(F)** 01507 522525.
Contact/s
Assistant Manager: Mrs V Booth
Profile Feed Merchant, Supplies. **Ref: YH08655**

LINE 1

Line 1, Unit 12 8 Haviland Rd, Ferndown Ind Est, Wimborne, **Dorset**, BH21 7RF, **ENGLAND**.
(T) 01202 893855 **(F)** 01202 893844.
Contact/s
General Manager: Mr T Goodison
Profile Transport/Horse Boxes. **Ref: YH08656**

LINESIDE RIDING STABLES

Lineside Riding Stables, Lineside Farm, Amberhill, Boston, **Lincolnshire**, PE20 3RA, **ENGLAND**.
(T) 01205 820744 **(F)** 01205 820574.
Profile Riding School, Stable/Livery. **Ref: YH08657**

LINGE, NOEL A

Noel A Linge, School Farm, Brancaster, Hunstanton, **Norfolk**, PE31 8AY, **ENGLAND**.
(T) 01485 210318.
Profile Breeder. **Ref: YH08658**

LINGFIELD PARK RACECOURSE

Lingfield Park Racecourse, Lingfield, **Surrey**, RH7 6PQ, **ENGLAND**.
(T) 01342 837100 **(F)** 01342 837101
(M) 07974 948768.
Profile Track/Course. **Ref: YH08659**

LINGFIELD TACK

Lingfield Tack, Oldencraig Equestrian Ctre, Tandridge Lane, Lingfield, **Surrey**, RH7 6LL, **ENGLAND**.
(T) 01342 835888
(E) info@lingfield-tack.co.uk
(W) www.lingfield-tack.co.uk.
Contact/s
Owner: Mrs L Dobbie
Profile Supplies. No.Staff: 2 Yr. Est: 2000
Opening Times
Sp: Open Tues, Wed 13:00, Thurs, Fri 10:30, Sat 09:30, Sun 11:00. Closed Tues, Wed 17:30, Thurs 18:00, Fri 17:30, Sat 17:00, Sun 15:00.
Su: Open Tues, Wed 13:00, Thurs, Fri 10:30, Sat 09:30, Sun 11:00. Closed Tues, Wed 17:30, Thurs 18:00, Fri 17:30, Sat 17:00, Sun 15:00.
Au: Open Tues, Wed 13:00, Thurs, Fri 10:30, Sat 09:30, Sun 11:00. Closed Tues, Wed 17:30, Thurs 18:00, Fri 17:30, Sat 17:00, Sun 15:00.
Wn: Open Tues, Wed 13:00, Thurs, Fri 10:30, Sat 09:30, Sun 11:00. Closed Tues, Wed 17:30, Thurs 18:00, Fri 17:30, Sat 17:00, Sun 15:00.
Closed on Mondays **Ref: YH08660**

LINGLIE STABLES

Linglie Stables, Linglie Farm, Linglie Rd, Selkirk, **Scottish Borders**, TD7 5LT, **SCOTLAND**.
(T) 01750 20252.
Contact/s
Owner: Mr A Hogarth **Ref: YH08661**

LINGS LANE RIDING STABLES

Lings Lane Riding Stables, Keyworth, Nottingham, **Nottinghamshire**, NG12 5AF, **ENGLAND**.
(T) 0115 9372527
Affiliated Bodies BHS.
Contact/s
Owner: Mr T Flint **(Q)** BHS IT
Profile Riding School. Yr. Est: 1980
C.Size: 70 Acres **Ref: YH08662**

LINGWOOD SHIRE PROMOTIONS

Lingwood Shire Promotions, Ashwells Rd, Pilgrims Hatch, Brentwood, **Essex**, CM15 9SE, **ENGLAND**.
(T) 01277 372082.
Profile Breeder. **Ref: YH08663**

LINKSLADE STABLES

Linkslade Stables, Wantage Rd, Mile End, Lambourn, Hungerford, **Berkshire**, RG17 8UG, **ENGLAND**.
(T) 01488 73098 **(F)** 01488 73490
(M) 07831 457074.
Contact/s
Trainer: Mr W Muir
Profile Trainer. **Ref: YH08664**

LINKWOOD EQUESTIAN

Linkwood Equestrian Centre, Bury Rd, Bradfield St. George, Bury St Edmunds, **Suffolk**, IP30 0EN, **ENGLAND**.
(T) 01284 386390 **(F)** 01284 386390
(M) 07867 518716
(W) www.linkwoode.c.co.uk.
Contact/s
Owner: Mrs C Cooper
(E) chris@linkwoode.c.co.uk
Profile Arena, Breeder, Equestrian Centre, Riding Wear Retailer, Saddlery Retailer, Stable/Livery, Supplies. Show Centre, Horse Dealer. No.Staff: 4
Yr. Est: 1994 C.Size: 140 Acres **Ref: YH08665**

LINN PARK EQUESTRIAN CTRE

Linn Park Equestrian Centre, Stable Yard, Linn Pk, Glasgow, **Glasgow (City of)**, G44 5TA, **SCOTLAND**.
(T) 0141 6373096 **(F)** 0141 6373096.
Profile Equestrian Centre. **Ref: YH08666**

LINSCOTT & BEST

Linscott & Best (Bedale Office), 1 Market Pl, Bedale, **Yorkshire (North)**, DL8 1ED, **ENGLAND**.
(T) 01677 422432 **(F)** 01677 425998.
Profile Medical Support. **Ref: YH08667**

LINSCOTT & BEST

Linscott & Best (Masham), The Croft, Masham, Ripon, **Yorkshire (North)**, HG4 4EF, **ENGLAND**.
(T) 01765 689422.
Profile Medical Support. **Ref: YH08668**

LINSSNER, C P

C P Linssner, The Farriery, Appleshaw, Andover, **Hampshire**, SP11 9AD, **ENGLAND**.
(T) 01264 772184.
Profile Farrier. **Ref: YH08669**

LINTRAN

Lintran, Brentwood Lodge, 1 Hawthorn Rd, Cherry Willingham, Lincoln, **Lincolnshire**, LN3 4JU, **ENGLAND**.
(T) 01522 595959.
Profile Transport/Horse Boxes. **Ref: YH08670**

LION ROYAL HOTEL

Lion Royal Hotel & Trekking Centre (The), Rhayader, **Powys**, LD6 5AB, **WALES**.
(T) 01597 810202.
Profile Stable/Livery. Trekking Centre. **Ref: YH08671**

LIONHART MORGANS

Lionhart Morgans, The Courtyard, Onslow Green, Great Dunmow, **Essex**, CM6 3PR, **ENGLAND**.
(T) 01371 820798.
Profile Breeder. **Ref: YH08672**

LIONSGATE STABLES

Lionsgate Stables, Lionsgate, Ayr, **Ayrshire (South)**, KA6 6AJ, **SCOTLAND**.
(T) 01292 261556.
Contact/s
Owner: Mrs M Wilson **Ref: YH08673**

LIPHOOK EQUINE HOSPITAL

Liphook Equine Hospital (The), Forest Mere, Liphook, **Hampshire**, GU30 7JG, **ENGLAND**.
(T) 01428 723594 **(F)** 01428 722263
(E) post@liphookequinehosp.co.uk
(W) www.liphookequinehosp.co.uk.
Contact/s
Secretary: Mrs B Thornley
Profile Medical Support. **Ref: YH08674**

LIPIZZANER NATIONAL STUDBOOK

Lipizzaner National Studbook Association of GB (The), Cilyblaidd Manor, Pencarreg, Lampeter, **Carmarthenshire**, SA40 9QL, **WALES**.
(T) 01570 480090 **(F)** 01570 480012
(E) info@lipizzaner.org.uk
(W) www.lipizzaner.org.uk.
Contact/s
Key Contact: Miss L Moran
Profile Club/Association. **Ref: YH08675**

LIPLANDS STABLES

Liplands Stables, Downs Rd, Compton, Newbury, **Berkshire**, RG20 6RE, **ENGLAND**.
(T) 01635 579090 **(F)** 01635 578000.
Profile Trainer. **Ref: YH08676**

LISA HUNT EQUESTRIAN

Lisa Hunt Equestrian, Hartley Farm, Barrow Hill Rd, Copythorne, **Hampshire**, SO40 2PH, **ENGLAND**.
(T) 023 80811020 **(F)** 023 80811020
(M) 07802 670612.

Profile Supplies. Ref: YH08677

LISCOMBE PK RIDING SCHOOL

Liscombe Park Riding School, Liscombe Pk, Soulbury, Leighton Buzzard, **Bedfordshire**, LU7 0JL, **ENGLAND**.
(T) 01296 689090.
Contact/s
Owner: Mrs D Phillips
Profile Riding School, Stable/Livery. Ref: YH08678

LIST, G C

G C List, Chestnut Rise Farm, Kington Lane, Claverdon, Warwick, **Warwickshire**, CV35 8PW, **ENGLAND**.
(T) 01926 842806.
Contact/s
Owner: Mrs G List
Profile Breeder. Ref: YH08679

LISTER SHEARING EQUIPMENT

Lister Shearing Equipment Ltd, Long St, Dursley, **Gloucestershire**, GL11 4HR, **ENGLAND**.
(T) 01453 544832/3 /544831 (F) 01453 544831
(E) info@lister-shearing.co.uk
(W) www.lister-shearing.co.uk.
Profile Supplies. Ref: YH08680

LISTER, M

M Lister BVMS MRCVS, The Vetnry Surgery, Manse Brae, Lochgilphead, **Argyll and Bute**, PA31 8QX, **SCOTLAND**.
(T) 01546 602240 (F) 01546 606016.
Profile Medical Support. Ref: YH08681

LISTOWEL RACE CO RACECOURSE

Listowel Race Co Racecourse, Listowel, **County Kerry**, **IRELAND**.
(T) 068 21172.
Profile Track/Course. Ref: YH08682

LITTLE ASH ECO-FARM & STUD

Little Ash Eco-Farm & Stud, Throwleigh, Okehampton, **Devon**, EX20 2QG, **ENGLAND**.
(T) 01647 231394.
Profile Breeder, Riding School, Stable/Livery.
Ref: YH08683

LITTLE BRIARS STUD

Little Briars Stud, Bleakhouse Stables, West Melton, Rotherham, **Yorkshire (South)**, S63 6AH, **ENGLAND**.
(T) 01709 873166.
Contact/s
Owner: Miss S Kersey
Profile Breeder.
Breeder of Welsh Section A ponies Ref: YH08684

LITTLE BROOK EQUESTRIAN

Little Brook Equestrian, East Pk Lane, Newchapel, Lingfield, **Surrey**, RH7 6HS, **ENGLAND**.
(T) 01342 832360.
Contact/s
Owner: Mrs D Ford
Profile Stable/Livery. Ref: YH08685

LITTLE BURGATE FARM

Little Burgate Farm, Markwick Lane, Loxhill, Godalming, **Surrey**, GU8 4BD, **ENGLAND**.
(T) 01483 208652. Ref: YH08686

LITTLE FORSHAM FARM STABLES

Little Forsham Farm Stables, Wassall Lane, Rolvenden, Cranbrook, **Kent**, TN17 4PP, **ENGLAND**.
(T) 01580 241207.
Profile Stable/Livery. Ref: YH08687

LITTLE HARLE STABLES

Henri Plag Equestrian Training & Services, Kirkwhelpington, Newcastle-upon-Tyne, **Tyne and Wear**, NE19 2PD, **ENGLAND**.
(T) 01830 540334 (F) 01830 540334
(E) littleharle@henriplag.co.uk
(W) www.henriplag.co.uk.
Affiliated Bodies BD, BHS.
Contact/s
Owner: Ms H Plag (Q) BHS SM, BHSII, RDASI
Profile Equestrian Centre, Riding School, Stable/Livery, Trainer.
Specialise in one to one tuition to improve confidence for horse and rider. No.Staff: 2 Yr. Est: 1999
Ref: YH08688

LITTLE KELK RIDING SCHOOL

Little Kelk Riding School, Little Kelk Farm, Little Kelk, Driffield, **Yorkshire (East)**, YO25 8HG, **ENGLAND**.
(T) 01262 490539.
Profile Riding School. Ref: YH08689

LITTLE LONDON HORSES

Little London Horses Ltd, Little London, Church Lane, Waltham, Canterbury, **Kent**, CT4 5SS, **ENGLAND**.
(T) 01227 700282.
Profile Breeder. Ref: YH08690

LITTLE LONDON TACK SHOP

Little London Tack Shop (The), 2 Church Cottages, Silchester Rd, Little London, Tadley, **Hampshire**, RG26 5ES, **ENGLAND**.
(T) 01256 850737 (F) 01256 850518.
Profile Saddlery Retailer. Ref: YH08691

LITTLE MALVERN SADDLE

Little Malvern Saddle Co, The Old Dairy, North Farm, Malvern, **Worcestershire**, WR14 4JN, **ENGLAND**.
(T) 01684 572485.
Profile Saddlery Retailer. Ref: YH08692

LITTLE MANOR FARM

Little Manor Farm Livery Stables Ltd, Manor Lane, Claverdon, Warwick, **Warwickshire**, CV35 8NH, **ENGLAND**.
(T) 01926 843898.
Contact/s
Owner: Ms A Kimberley
Profile Stable/Livery. No.Staff: 6
Yr. Est: 1997 C.Size: 60 Acres Ref: YH08693

LITTLE MEADOWS

Little Meadows Stud Farm, Church Lane, Chalvington, Hailsham, **Sussex (East)**, BN27 3TE, **ENGLAND**.
(T) 01323 811990.
Contact/s
Owner: Mrs T Evans
Profile Breeder, Trainer.
Tamsin Evans (nee Wiggins) began riding at an early age, showing working hunter ponies. She progressed to young riders then to AITS and was ranked number forty two in the senior ranking. Tamsin is available for limited show jumping training. Renowned for breeding and producing youngsters and competition sports horses. There are several top quality horses in the stud, these include; Cor de la Bryere, Lord, Grannus, Jalisco B, Quidam de Reveil, Landgraf, Lady Killer, Goldfalk, Flugel van la Roche and Didi.
Yr. Est: 2000 C.Size: 89 Acres
Opening Times
Telephone for an appointment Ref: YH08694

LITTLE MONTROSE

Little Montrose, Birchwood Rd, Purleigh, Chelmsford, **Essex**, CM3 6PR, **ENGLAND**.
(T) 01621 828231.
Contact/s
Partner: Mr G Mercer
Profile Riding School. Ref: YH08695

LITTLE NEWSHAM FORGE

Little Newsham Forge, Little Newsham, Darlington, **County Durham**, DL2 3QN, **ENGLAND**.
(T) 01833 660547.
Contact/s
Owner: Mr B Russell
Profile Blacksmith. Ref: YH08696

LITTLE OAKS SHOWJUMPS

Little Oaks Showjumps, Little Oaks, 203 Higher Walton Rd, Walton-Le-Dale, Preston, **Lancashire**, PR5 4HS, **ENGLAND**.
(T) 01772 253116
(M) 07710 721126.
Profile Supplies. Ref: YH08697

LITTLE PADDOCK

Little Paddock Livery Yard, Frating Rd, Great Bromley, Colchester, **Essex**, CO7 7JL, **ENGLAND**.
(T) 01206 250921.
Contact/s
Supervisor: Mrs E O'Kane
Profile Stable/Livery.
Nearby facilities for competitions. Full livery, including feeding, grooming, exercising, prices on request.
Yr. Est: 1986 C.Size: 2.5 Acres
Opening Times
Sp: Open Mon - Sun 08:00. Closed Mon - Sun 17:00.
Su: Open Mon - Sun 08:00. Closed Mon - Sun 17:00.
Au: Open Mon - Sun 08:00. Closed Mon - Sun 17:00.
Wn: Open Mon - Sun 08:00. Closed Mon - Sun 17:00. Ref: YH08698

LITTLE PADDOCKS RIDING SCHOOL

Little Paddocks Riding School, Kemishford, Mayford, Woking, **Surrey**, GU22 0RP, **ENGLAND**.
(T) 01483 232766.
Profile Riding School. Ref: YH08699

LITTLE PASTURE TREKKING CTRE

Little Pasture Trekking Centre, Little Pasture, Bar Lane, Knaresborough, **Yorkshire (North)**, HG5 0QG, **ENGLAND**.
(T) 01423 860593.
Profile Equestrian Centre. Ref: YH08700

LITTLE RAHANE

Little Rahane, Rahane, Helensburgh, **Argyll and Bute**, G84 0QW, **SCOTLAND**.
(T) 01436 831214
(W) www.scottish.heartlands.org.
Contact/s
Owner: Ms A Edmondson
Profile Stable/Livery.
Opening Times
Telephone for an appointment Ref: YH08701

LITTLE SPATHAM FARM

Little Spatham Farm Livery Yard, Spatham Lane, Ditchling, Hassocks, **Sussex (West)**, BN6 8XH, **ENGLAND**.
(T) 01273 846370.
Contact/s
Partner: Mr R Philpotts Ref: YH08702

LITTLEBOURNE FARM

Littlebourne Farm Equestrian Centre, Northwood Rd, Uxbridge, **London (Greater)**, UB9 6PT, **ENGLAND**.
(T) 01895 824350 (F) 01895 825625.
Contact/s
Owner: Mrs C Dent
Profile Equestrian Centre, Riding School, Stable/Livery.
Hacking available. Yr. Est: 1981
Opening Times
Sp: Open 08:00. Closed 20:00.
Su: Open 08:00. Closed 20:00.
Au: Open 08:00. Closed 20:00.
Wn: Open 08:00. Closed 20:00. Ref: YH08703

LITTLEBURY HALL LIVERY YARD

Littlebury Hall Livery Yard, Littlebury Hall, Romford Rd, Ongar, **Essex**, CM5 9PE, **ENGLAND**.
(T) 01277 365763.
Contact/s
Owner: Mr H Padfield Ref: YH08704

LITTLECOMBE RIDING CTRE

Littlecombe Riding Centre, Littlecombe, Holne, Newton Abbot, **Devon**, TQ13 7SW, **ENGLAND**.
(T) 01364 631260.
Contact/s
Owner: Mrs E Osbourne Ref: YH08705

LITTLECOMBE SHETLAND STUD

Littlecombe Shetland Stud, Berry Barton, Branscombe, Seaton, **Devon**, EX12 3BD, **ENGLAND**.
(T) 01297 680208 (F) 01297 680108.
Contact/s
Owner: Mrs A White
Profile Breeder. Ref: YH08706

LITTLEDEAN RIDING CTRE

Littledean Riding Centre, Wellingtons Farm, Sutton, Littledean, Cinderford, **Gloucestershire**, GL14 2TU, **ENGLAND**.
(T) 01594 823955 (F) 01594 823955.
Contact/s
Owner: Mrs G Chamberlain
Profile Riding School. Ref: YH08707

LITTLER, MARTIN E

Martin E Littler DWCF, 38 Wallace Ave, Worthing, **Sussex (West)**, BN11 5QX, **ENGLAND**.
(T) 01903 502589.
Profile Farrier. Ref: YH08708

LITTLETON STUD

Littleton Stud, Littleton, Winchester, **Hampshire**, SO22 6QX, **ENGLAND**.
(T) 01962 880210 (F) 01962 882290.
Contact/s
Manager: Mr J Coulter
Profile Breeder. Ref: YH08709

LITTLETON, C E J

C E J Littleton, Bridge Hse, Ponsanooth, Truro, **Cornwall**, TR3 7JB, **ENGLAND**.
(T) 01872 864351.
Profile Medical Support. Ref: YH08710

LITTMODEN, N P

Southgate Stables, Hamilton Rd, Newmarket,

Key: (T) telephone (F) fax (M) mobile (E) E-Mail Address (W) Website Address (Q) Qualifications
Yr. Est: Year Established C.Size: Complex Size Sp: Spring Su: Summer Au: Autumn Wn: Winter

Suffolk, CB8 0NQ, ENGLAND.
(T) 01638 663375 (F) 01638 663375
(M) 07770 964865
Affiliated Bodies Newmarket Trainers Fed.
Contact/s
Trainer: Mr N Littmoden
Profile Trainer. Ref:YH08711

LIVERIES

Liveries, Little Lodge Farm, Santon Downham, Brandon, Suffolk, IP27 0TX, ENGLAND.
(T) 01842 813438.
Contact/s
Partner: Mrs S Hibbs Ref:YH08712

LIVERMORE, R E A

Mr R E A Livermore, Red Hse Farm, Penycaemawr, Usk, Monmouthshire, NP15 1LX, WALES.
(T) 01291 650774 (F) 01291 650469
(M) 07770 953030.
Profile Supplies. Ref:YH08713

LIVERY STABLES

Livery Stables, The Old Hill End Farm, Hill End Lane, Mottram, Hyde, Cheshire, SK14 6JP, ENGLAND.
(T) 01457 765159.
Contact/s
Owner: Ms L Cheetham Ref:YH08714

LIVESTOCK SUPPLIES INTL

Livestock Supplies Intl Ltd, Crosby Lodge, Milnthorpe, Cumbria, LA7 7DQ, ENGLAND.
(T) 01539 562230 (F) 01539 563005.
Profile Supplies. Ref:YH08715

LIVEWIRE GATES & FENCING

Livewire Gates & Fencing, Unit 7 Stainton Gr, Barnard Castle, County Durham, DL12 8UJ, ENGLAND.
(T) 01833 690274 (F) 01833 690053
(M) 07801 834681. Ref:YH08716

LIVING WORLD

Living World, 206 Armley Rd, Leeds, Yorkshire (West), LS12 2LY, ENGLAND.
(T) 0113 2311426.
Contact/s
Manager: Mr T Smethhurst
Profile Saddlery Retailer. Ref:YH08717

LIZARD TRAILER SVS

Lizard Trailer Services, 15 Water-Ma-Trout Ind Est, Wendron, Helston, Cornwall, TR13 0NN, ENGLAND.
(T) 01326 563282.
Profile Transport/Horse Boxes. Ref:YH08718

LLANBEDROG RIDING CTRE

Llanbedrog Riding Centre, Halfway Bungalow, Llanbedrog, Pwllheli, Gwynedd, LL53 7UB, WALES.
(T) 01758 740267.
Contact/s
Owner: Mr A Mills Ref:YH08719

LLANDDONA

Llanddona Riding School, Llanddona, Beaumaris, Isle of Anglesey, LL58 8UB, WALES.
(T) 01248 810183.
Contact/s
General Manager: Miss C Matthews
(Q) BHSAI
Profile Riding School.
Beach rides for experienced riders and a holiday cottage available Yr. Est: 1981 C.Size: 10 Acres
Opening Times
Telephone for further information, there is an answer phone Ref:YH08720

LLANELLI TRAILER CTRE

Llanelli Trailer Centre, Unit 3A Llanelli Workshops, Trostre Ind Est, Llanelli, Carmarthenshire, SA14 9UU, WALES.
(T) 01554 773608.
Profile Transport/Horse Boxes. Ref:YH08721

LLANELWEDD RIDING CLUB

Llanelwedd Riding Club, 6 Creigiau Cottages, Church St, Talgarth, Brecon, Powys, LD3 0DR, WALES.
(T) 01874 711676.
Contact/s
Training Officer: Miss J Wilson
Profile Club/Association, Riding Club. Ref:YH08722

LLANFYLLIN SADDLERY

Llanfyllin Saddlery, Bodyddon Fawr, Llanfyllin, Powys, SY22 5HJ, WALES.
(T) 01691 648916 (F) 01691 648916
(M) 07712 552924
(E) saddlery@equestrianet.co.uk.
Profile Saddlery Retailer. Ref:YH08723

LLANGENNY PONY TREKKING CTRE

Llangenny Pony Trekking Centre, Ty Cerrig, Llangenny, Crickhowell, Powys, NP8 1HA, WALES.
(T) 01873 810175.
Profile Equestrian Centre. Trekking Centre.
Ref:YH08724

LLANGORSE RIDING

Llangorse Riding Centre, Gilfach Farm, Llangorse, Brecon, Powys, LD3 7UH, WALES.
(T) 01874 658584/ 658272 (F) 01874 658280
(W) www.activityuk.com
Affiliated Bodies AALA, BHS, WTRA.
Contact/s
General Manager: Mrs R Thomas
Profile Equestrian Centre.
Mid-week riding holidays for school groups, with over 26 miles of private bridleway. No.Staff: 15
Yr. Est: 1959 C.Size: 500 Acres
Ref:YH08725

LLANNERCH EQUESTRIAN CTRE

Llannerch Equestrian Centre, Upper Denbigh Rd, St Asaph, Denbighshire, LL17 0BD, WALES.
(T) 01745 730199 (F) 01745 730266.
Contact/s
Owner: Ms S Gresley-Jones
Profile Breeder, Equestrian Centre, Medical Support, Riding School, Stable/Livery, Track/Course.
No.Staff: 4 Yr. Est: 1979 Ref:YH08726

LLANWNDA STABLES

Llanwnda Stables, Penrhiw Fach, Llanwnda, Goodwick, Pembrokeshire, SA64 0HS, WALES.
(T) 01348 873595.
Contact/s
Owner: Ms I Evans (Q) BHSAI
Profile Riding School, Stable/Livery. No.Staff: 2
Yr. Est: 1994 C.Size: 20 Acres
Opening Times
Telephone for further information Ref:YH08727

LLETTY MAWR TREKKING

Lletty Mawr Trekking Centre, Lletty Bach, Llangadfan, Welshpool, Powys, SY21 0PS, WALES.
(T) 01938 820646.
Contact/s
General Manager: Miss L Hollinshead
Profile Equestrian Centre, Riding School, Stable/Livery, Trainer.
Cater for all ages and abilities, disabled groups are welcome as are school/youth groups. Horses and ponies to suit all abilities available. Rides are escorted by experienced riders with first aid training. The centre offers breaking and schooling, horses and ponies taken. Every care is taken to make sure the horse has a stress free time, breaking period of about 6-8 weeks. Please telephone for price information. No.Staff: 2
Yr. Est: 1997 C.Size: 17 Acres
Opening Times
Sp: Open Mon - Sun 09:00. Closed Mon - Sun 17:00.
Su: Open Mon - Sun 09:00. Closed Mon - Sun 21:00.
Au: Open Mon - Sun 09:00. Closed Mon - Sun 17:00.
Wn: Open Mon - Sun 09:00. Closed Mon - Sun 16:00. Ref:YH08728

LLETY

Llety Stud, Tyn-Y-Waun, Nantgaredig, Carmarthen, Carmarthenshire, SA32 7NR, WALES.
(T) 01267 290528.
Profile Breeder. Ref:YH08729

LLEWELLYN-JAMES, J

J Llewellyn-James, Blaythorn, Mill Lane, Drakes Broughton, Pershore, Worcestershire, WR10 2AF, ENGLAND.
(T) 01905 840624 (F) 01905 613376.
Profile Breeder. Ref:YH08730

L'LIWETTO RIDING SCHOOL

L'Liwetto Riding School, L'liwetto Kings Stag, King Stag, Sturminster Newton, Dorset, DT10 2BE, ENGLAND.
(T) 01258 817964.
Profile Riding School. Ref:YH08731

LLONG MILL

Llong Mill, Chester Rd, Mold, Flintshire, CH7 4JP, WALES.
(T) 01244 547505 (F) 01352 757688.
Profile Supplies. Ref:YH08732

LLOYD FARM STUD

Lloyd Farm Stud, The Lloyd, Hales, Market Drayton, Shropshire, TF9 2PS, ENGLAND.
(T) 01630 661603 (F) 01630 661604.
Profile Breeder. Ref:YH08733

LLOYD, D G

D G Lloyd, Garthddulwyd Fach, Llanarth, Ceredigion, SA47 0QS, WALES.
(T) 01545 580340.
Contact/s
Owner: Mr D Lloyd Ref:YH08734

LLOYD, D M

Mr D M Lloyd, Avalon, Brynmenyn, Bridgend, CF32 9LF, WALES.
(T) 01656 724654.
Profile Supplies. Ref:YH08735

LLOYD, E

E Lloyd, Hendy Farm, Four Mile Bridge, Holyhead, Isle of Anglesey, LL65 2HZ, WALES.
(T) 01407 740709.
Contact/s
Owner: Mr E Lloyd
Profile Breeder. Ref:YH08736

LLOYD, EVAN JOHN

Evan John Lloyd DWCF, Shetlands, Far End, Sheepscombe, Stroud, Gloucestershire, GL6 7RL, ENGLAND.
(T) 01452 813343.
Profile Farrier. Ref:YH08737

LLOYD, F

Mr F Lloyd, Althrey Woodhouse, Bangor-on-Dee, Wrexham, LL13 0DA, WALES.
(T) 01978 780356 (F) 01978 660152.
Profile Supplies. Ref:YH08738

LLOYD, I J R

Mr & Mrs I J R Lloyd, Derwen, Pennant, Ceredigion, SY23 5JN, WALES.
(T) 01545 570250.
Profile Breeder. Ref:YH08739

LLOYD, KEVIN

Kevin Lloyd, 60 Broad St, Llandovery, Carmarthenshire, SA20 0AY, WALES.
(T) 01550 720830.
Profile Farrier. Ref:YH08740

LLOYD, PAUL R

Paul R Lloyd RSS, 8 Birlingham Cl, Pershore, Worcestershire, WR10 1LZ, ENGLAND.
(T) 01386 556275.
Profile Farrier. Ref:YH08741

LLOYD, S

S Lloyd, Teifi Stud, Temple Bar, Lampeter, Ceredigion, SA48 8BH, WALES.
(T) 01570 470602.
Profile Breeder. Ref:YH08742

LLOYD, STEPHEN DEREK

Stephen Derek Lloyd RSS, The Pippins, Farriers Orchard, Fromes Hill, Ledbury, Herefordshire, HR8 1HY, ENGLAND.
(T) 01531 640062.
Profile Farrier. Ref:YH08743

LLOYDS ANIMAL FEEDS

Lloyds Animal Feeds, Moreton, Oswestry, Shropshire, SY10 8BH, ENGLAND.
(T) 01691 830741.
Profile Supplies. Ref:YH08744

LLOYDS ANIMAL FEEDS

Lloyds Animal Feeds, Weeping Cross Lane, Ludlow, Shropshire, SY8 1JH, ENGLAND.
(T) 01584 872431 (F) 01584 877295.
Profile Saddlery Retailer. Ref:YH08745

LLOYD-WILLIAMS SADDLERY

Lloyd-Williams Saddlery Co Ltd (The), Durlock Hse, Elsley Rd, Tilehurst, Reading, Berkshire, RG31 6RP, ENGLAND.
(T) 0118 9614441 (F) 0118 9452225
(E) rapscallion@sporthorse.co.uk.
Profile Saddlery Retailer. Ref:YH08746

LLUEST HORSE & PONY TRUST

Lluest Horse & Pony Trust, Beili Bedw, Llanddeusant, Llangadog, Carmarthenshire, SA19 9TG, WALES.
(T) 01550 740661.
Contact/s
Manageress: Mrs L Griffiths

Profile Club/Association. **Ref: YH08747**

LLWYNGARTH WELSH COBS

Llwyngarth Welsh Cobs, Ty Canol, Trawscoed Rd, Llysfaen, Colwyn Bay, **Conwy**, LL29 8LQ, **WALES**.
(T) 01492 513260
(E) med@helmem.freeserve.co.uk
Profile Breeder. **Ref: YH08748**

LLWYNON

Llwynon Saddlery, Trecastle, Brecon, **Powys**, LD3 8RG, **WALES**.
(T) 01874 638091 **(F)** 01874 638091
(E) enquiries@llwynonsaddlery.co.uk
(W) www.llwynonsaddlery.co.uk.
Contact/s
Instructor: Ms J Langley **(Q)** BHSAI
Profile Saddlery Retailer. No.Staff: 5
Yr. Est: 1995 C.Size: 14 Acres
Opening Times
Sp: Open Mon - Sat 10:00. Closed Mon - Sat 17:00.
Su: Open Mon - Sat 10:00. Closed Mon - Sat 17:00.
Au: Open Mon - Sat 10:00. Closed Mon - Sat 17:00.
Wn: Open Mon - Sat 10:00. Closed Mon - Sat 17:00.
Ref: YH08749

LOAFERS

Loafers, Matteson Farm, Lower Dunsforth, **Yorkshire (North)**, YO26 9SA, **ENGLAND**.
(T) 01423 322901.
Profile Supplies. **Ref: YH08750**

LOBB STABLES RIDING SCHOOL

Lobb Stables Riding School, The Stables, Halifax Rd, Todmorden, **Yorkshire (West)**, OL14 6BX, **ENGLAND**.
(T) 01706 812698.
Profile Riding School. **Ref: YH08751**

LOCH NESS RIDING

Loch Ness Riding, Drummond Farm, Dores, Inverness, **Highlands**, IV2 6TX, **SCOTLAND**.
(T) 01463 751251 **(F)** 01463 751240.
Contact/s
General Manager: Mrs C Cameron **(Q)** BHS Int SM
(E) candycameron@hotmail.com
Profile Horse/Rider Accom, Trainer.
Endurance trainer No.Staff: 1 Yr. Est: 1975
C.Size: 100 Acres **Ref: YH08752**

LOCH TAY HIGHLAND

Loch Tay Highland Lodges Equestrian Centre, Milton Morenish, Killin, **Perth and Kinross**, FK21 8TX, **SCOTLAND**.
(T) 01567 820736.
Contact/s
Manager: Miss C Lesllie
Profile Riding School, Stable/Livery, Trainer.
Ref: YH08753

LOCH, SYLVIA (LADY)

Lady Sylvia Loch, Eden Hall, Kelso, **Scottish Borders**, TD5 7QD, **SCOTLAND**.
(T) 01890 830380.
Profile Breeder, Trainer. **Ref: YH08754**

LOCHRIE, G K A

Mr G K A Lochrie, 17 North St, Morton, Gainsborough, **Lincolnshire**, DN21 3AS, **ENGLAND**.
(T) 01427 612662.
Profile Medical Support. **Ref: YH08755**

LOCK, JAMES

James Lock & Co Ltd, 6 St James St, London, **London (Greater)**, SW1A 1EF, **ENGLAND**.
(T) 207 9308874/ 9305849 **(F)** 207 9761908
(E) sales@lockhatters.co.uk
(W) www.lockhatters.co.uk.
Profile Supplies. Hat Manufacturer. **Ref: YH08756**

LOCKE & PRESTON VETNRY GRP

Locke & Preston Veterinary Group, The Strand Vetnry Ctre, The Strand, Bude, **Cornwall**, EX23 8QU, **ENGLAND**.
(T) 01288 354796.
Profile Medical Support. **Ref: YH08757**

LOCKE & PRESTON VETNRY GRP

Locke & Preston Veterinary Group, North Rd Vetnry Ctre, North Rd, Bradworthy, **Devon**, EX22 7TJ, **ENGLAND**.
(T) 01409 241539.
Profile Medical Support. **Ref: YH08758**

LOCKINGE PONY STUD

Lockinge Pony Stud, Lockinge Manor, Wantage, **Oxfordshire**, OX12 8QQ, **ENGLAND**.
(T) 01235 833266.
Profile Breeder. **Ref: YH08759**

LOCKNER FARM

Lockner Farm, Dorking Rd, Chilworth, Guildford, **Surrey**, GU4 8RH, **ENGLAND**.
(T) 01483 577127 **(F)** 01483 564104
Affiliated Bodies BHS.
Contact/s
Owner: Mr R Parker
Profile Stable/Livery. No.Staff: 2
Yr. Est: 1949 C.Size: 60 Acres **Ref: YH08760**

LOCKS GARAGE FEEDS

Locks Garage Feeds, Locks Garage, Allensmore, **Herefordshire**, HR2 9AS, **ENGLAND**.
(T) 01981 570206.
Profile Supplies. **Ref: YH08761**

LOCKWOOD, A

Mr A Lockwood, Fleet Cross Farm, Brawby, Malton, **Yorkshire (North)**, YO17 6QA, **ENGLAND**.
(T) 01751 431796 **(F)** 01751 431796
(M) 07747 002535.
Profile Trainer. **Ref: YH08762**

LOCKWOOD, C A

C A Lockwood, 3 Winteringham Lane, West Halton, Scunthorpe, **Lincolnshire (North)**, DN15 9AX, **ENGLAND**.
(T) 01724 733063.
Profile Transport/Horse Boxes. **Ref: YH08763**

LOCKYERS ANIMAL PROVISIONS

Lockyers Animal Provisions, Danelea, Tiptoe Rd, Wooton, New Milton, **Hampshire**, BH25 5SL, **ENGLAND**.
(T) 01425 611527.
Contact/s
Owner: Mrs J Lockyers
Profile Supplies. **Ref: YH08764**

LOCOS SADDLERY

Locos Saddlery Co Ltd, Down Farm, Westonbirt, Tetbury, **Gloucestershire**, GL8 8QW, **ENGLAND**.
(T) 01666 880214 **(F)** 01666 880266.
Profile Saddlery Retailer. **Ref: YH08765**

LODDON

Loddon Limited, Beccles Rd, Loddon, Norwich, **Norfolk**, NR14 6JJ, **ENGLAND**.
(T) 01508 520744 **(F)** 01508 528055.
Profile Transport/Horse Boxes. **Ref: YH08766**

LODGE FARM

Lodge Farm, Chavenage, Tetbury, **Gloucestershire**, GL8 8XW, **ENGLAND**.
(T) 01666 505339
(W) www.lodgefarm.co.uk.
Contact/s
Owner: Mr R Salmon
Profile Horse/Rider Accom.
Opening Times
By appointment only **Ref: YH08767**

LODGE FARM ARABIAN STUD

Lodge Farm Arabian Stud, Stadhampton, Oxford, **Oxfordshire**, OX44 7TZ, **ENGLAND**.
(T) 01865 891718 **(F)** 01865 891547.
Contact/s
Owner: Emma Maxwell
Profile Breeder. **Ref: YH08768**

LODGE FARM LIVERIES

Lodge Farm Liveries, Lodge Farm, Fiveways, Hatton, **Warwickshire**, CV35 7JD, **ENGLAND**.
(T) 01296 484649 **(F)** 01926 485042.
Profile Stable/Livery. **Ref: YH08769**

LODGE FARM STUD

Lodge Farm Stud, Hose Lane, Harby, Melton Mowbray, **Leicestershire**, LE14 4BJ, **ENGLAND**.
(T) 01949 861621 **(F)** 01949 860547.
Contact/s
Owner: Mrs D Turner
Profile Breeder. **Ref: YH08770**

LODGE LIVERIES

Lodge Liveries, Bookham Lodge Stud, Cobham Rd, Stoke D'abernon, Cobham, **Surrey**, KT11 3QJ, **ENGLAND**.
(T) 01932 867420.
Contact/s
Owner: Miss R Stevens
Profile Stable/Livery. **Ref: YH08771**

LODGE RIDING & LIVERY CTRE

Lodge Riding & Livery Centre, Dacres Bridge Lane, Tarbock Green, Prescot, **Merseyside**, L35 1QZ, **ENGLAND**.
(T) 0151 4898886.
Contact/s
Owner: Mrs S Blong **Ref: YH08772**

LODGE, DIANA ROSEMARY

Diana Rosemary Lodge, High Croft, Burnsall, Skipton, **Yorkshire (North)**, BD23 6BP, **ENGLAND**.
(T) 01756 720668.
Profile Artist. **Ref: YH08773**

LODGE, E D

Miss E D Lodge, Fernleigh Forge, The Rowans, Tun Lane, South Hiendley, Barnsley, **Yorkshire (South)**, S72 9BZ, **ENGLAND**.
(T) 01226 711562.
Profile Farrier. **Ref: YH08774**

LOGGIN, C W

Mr C W Loggin, Gaydons, Hinton, Brackley, **Northamptonshire**, **ENGLAND**.
Profile Supplies. **Ref: YH08775**

LOGGIN, MERRICK

Merrick Loggin, Clge Farm, Bicester Hill, Evenley, Brackley, **Northamptonshire**, NN13 5SD, **ENGLAND**.
(T) 01280 702725 **(F)** 01280 702849.
Contact/s
Owner: Mr M Loggin
Profile Transport/Horse Boxes. **Ref: YH08776**

LOGIC ATV EQUIPMENT

Logic ATV Equipment, Foundry Ind Est, Bridge End, Hexham, **Northumberland**, NE46 4JL, **ENGLAND**.
(T) 01434 606661 **(F)** 01434 608143
(M) 07831 361558.
Profile Supplies. **Ref: YH08777**

LOGIE FARM

Logie Farm Riding Centre, Glenferness, Nairn, **Highlands**, IV12 5XA, **SCOTLAND**.
(T) 01309 651226 **(F)** 01309 651226
Affiliated Bodies BHS, TRSS.
Contact/s
General Manager: Mrs C Morton
Profile Equestrian Centre, Holidays, Riding School, Stable/Livery. **Ref: YH08778**

LOMAS, E A

E A Lomas, Frogmill Stables, Black Boy Lane, Hurley, Maidenhead, **Berkshire**, SL6 5NH, **ENGLAND**.
(T) 01628 823442.
Contact/s
Partner: Mr E Lomas
Profile Stable/Livery. **Ref: YH08779**

LOMAX, CHRISTIE

Christie Lomax, 2 The Green, Clipston, Market Harborough, **Leicestershire**, LE16 9RS, **ENGLAND**.
(T) 07702 309547 **(F)** 01858 525295
(W) www.christielomax.co.uk.
Contact/s
International Event Rider: Ms C Lomax
(Q) BET, BHSI
(E) lomaxchristie@hotmail.com
Profile Trainer.
Trains horses to be evented, broken & sold. Based at Rushton Eventing Centre where the facilities include 60+ fence cross country course, a 60m x 25m all weather arena and showjumps. Ms Lomax is also an International Event Rider. **Ref: YH08780**

LOMAX, M & J

M & J Lomax, 560 Radcliffe Rd, Bolton, **Manchester (Greater)**, BL3 1AN, **ENGLAND**.
(T) 01204 528345.
Profile Stable/Livery. **Ref: YH08781**

LOMONDSIDE STUD

Lomondside Stud & Equestrian Centre, Buchanan Home Farm, Drymen, Glasgow, **Stirling**, G63 0HU, **SCOTLAND**.
(T) 01360 660481.
Contact/s
Partner: Mrs P Rennie
Profile Breeder, Riding School, Stable/Livery.
Ref: YH08782

LONDON COMMUNICATIONS

London Communications plc, 134 Gloucester Ave, Regents Park, **London (Greater)**, NW1 8JA, **ENGLAND**.
(T) 020 75869851 **(F)** 020 77220966.
Profile Supplies. **Ref: YH08783**

LONDON EQUESTRIAN CTRE

Bravebyte Ltd, Lullington Garth, London, **London (Greater)**, N12 7BP, **ENGLAND**.
(T) 020 83491345 **(F)** 020 74390555

Affiliated Bodies BHS.
Contact/s
Instructor: Ms S Burgess
Profile Equestrian Centre, Riding School, Stable/Livery.
There is a restaurant on site. Training for examinations up to BHS stage 4 is available. Lessons are on offer for children four years plus, and Tiny Tots is available for children under four. Yr. Est: 1989
Opening Times
Sp: Open Tues - Sun 09:00. Closed Tues - Sun 21:00.
Su: Open Tues - Sun 09:00. Closed Tues - Sun 21:00.
Au: Open Tues - Sun 09:00. Closed Tues - Sun 21:00.
Wn: Open Tues - Sun 09:00. Closed Tues - Sun 21:00.
Closed Mondays Ref: YH08784

LONDON EQUESTRIAN CTRE

London Equestrian Centre, Lullington Garth, Finchley, **London (Greater)**, N12 7BP, **ENGLAND**.
(T) 020 83491345.
Contact/s
Manager: Miss A Ross
Profile Equestrian Centre, Riding School, Stable/Livery.
Training for examinations up to BHS stage 4 is available. Lessons are on offer for children four years plus, and Tiny Tots is available for children under four.
Ref: YH08785

LONDON HARNESS HORSE PARADE

London Harness Horse Parade Society, East Of England Showground, Peterborough, **Cambridgeshire**, PE2 6XE, **ENGLAND**.
(T) 01733 234451 (F) 01733 370038.
Contact/s
Key Contact: Mr A Mercer
Profile Club/Association. Ref: YH08786

LONDON RIDING HORSE PARADE

London Riding Horse Parade, 10A The Pavement, Chapel Rd, London, **London (Greater)**, SE27 0UN, **ENGLAND**.
(T) 020 87615651.
Profile Club/Association. Ref: YH08787

LONDON SCHOOLS HORSE SOC

London Schools Horse Society, Sedgehill School, Sedgehill Rd, London, **London (Greater)**, SW1X 8QB, **ENGLAND**.
(T) 020 86988911.
Profile Club/Association. Ref: YH08788

LONDON STUD

London Stud, 2 Toatwood Bungalow, Blackgate Lane, Pulborough, **Sussex (West)**, RH20 1DD, **ENGLAND**.
(T) 01798 875790 (F) 01798 873928
Affiliated Bodies WPCS.
Contact/s
Owner: Ms S Edwards
Profile Breeder.
Welsh Cob Stud Ref: YH08789

LONDON THOROUGHBRED SVS

London Thoroughbred Services Ltd, Biddlesgate Farm, Cranborne, Wimborne, **Dorset**, BH21 5RS, **ENGLAND**.
(T) 01725 517711 (F) 01725 517833.
Profile Blood Stock Agency. Ref: YH08790

LONDON UNIVERSITY POLO CLUB

London University Polo Club, Ash Farm, Bousley Rise, Ottershaw, Chertsey, **Surrey**, KT16 0LA, **ENGLAND**.
(T) 01932 872521 (F) 01932 872006
(W) www.ulpolo.co.uk.
Contact/s
Owner: Mr P Sweeney
(E) paulsweeney@ashfronts.freeserve.co.uk
Profile Club/Association. Polo Club. Ref: YH08791

LONDON, MOIRA

Moira London BHSAI (Regd), No 1 Rose Cottages, Pitmore Lane, Sway, Lymington, **Hampshire**, SO41 6BX, **ENGLAND**.
(T) 01590 683167 (F) 01590 683828.
Profile Trainer. Ref: YH08792

LONDONDERRY FARRIERS

Londonderry Farriers & Blacksmiths, The Forge, Londonderry, Northallerton, **Yorkshire (North)**, DL7 9NE, **ENGLAND**.
(T) 01677 422587 (F) 01677 426587.
Contact/s
Partner: Mrs J Dyer
Profile Farrier. Ref: YH08793

LONE PINE RIDING CTRE

The Lone Pine Riding Centre, Beattock, Moffat, **Dumfries and Galloway**, DG10 9RF, **SCOTLAND**.
(T) 01683 300396.
Profile Riding School. Ref: YH08794

LONG ACRE FEEDS

Long Acre Feeds, Long Acre Hse, Winchester Rd, Botley, **Hampshire**, SO32 2DH, **ENGLAND**.
(T) 01489 784751.
Contact/s
Owner: Mr A Owton
Profile Supplies. Ref: YH08795

LONG LANE RIDING STABLES

Long Lane Riding Stables, Penselwood, Wincanton, **Somerset**, BA9 8NJ, **ENGLAND**.
(T) 01747 840283.
Profile Riding School, Stable/Livery. Ref: YH08796

LONG LEYS RIDING CTRE

Long Leys Riding Centre, Upper Whitley Farm, Leys Rd, Cumnor, Oxford, **Oxfordshire**, OX2 9QQ, **ENGLAND**.
(T) 01865 864554.
Contact/s
Manager: Mrs C Guy Ref: YH08797

LONG MELFORD

Long Melford Saddlery II, Hill Farm, Castle Camps, Cambridge, **Cambridgeshire**, CB1 6SX, **ENGLAND**.
(T) 01799 584802
(E) info@longmelfordsaddlery.co.uk
(W) www.longmelfordsaddlery.co.uk.
Contact/s
Owner: Mr J May
Profile Saddlery Retailer, Supplies. Yr. Est: 2001
Opening Times
Sp: Open Mon - Sun 09:00. Closed Mon - Sun 17:30.
Su: Open Mon - Sun 09:00. Closed Mon - Sun 17:30.
Au: Open Mon - Sun 09:00. Closed Mon - Sun 17:30.
Wn: Open Mon - Sun 09:00. Closed Mon - Sun 17:30. Ref: YH08798

LONG MELFORD

Long Melford Saddlery I, Hall St, Long Melford, Sudbury, **Suffolk**, CO10 9LQ, **ENGLAND**.
(T) 01787 378734 (F) 01787 378734
(E) info@longmelfordsaddlery.co.uk
(W) www.longmelfordsaddlery.co.uk.
Contact/s
Owner: Mr J May
Profile Saddlery Retailer, Supplies. Yr. Est: 1980
Opening Times
Sp: Open Mon - Sat 09:00. Closed Mon - Sat 17:30.
Su: Open Mon - Sat 09:00. Closed Mon - Sat 17:30.
Au: Open Mon - Sat 09:00. Closed Mon - Sat 17:30.
Wn: Open Mon - Sat 09:00. Closed Mon - Sat 17:30.
Closed Sundays Ref: YH08799

LONG REACH LIVERY STABLES

Long Reach Livery Stables, South End Corner, Long Reach, Ockham, Woking, **Surrey**, GU23 6PF, **ENGLAND**.
(T) 01483 282081.
Contact/s
Owner: Mrs S Price Ref: YH08800

LONG, A D

A D Long, 1 Coopers Croft, Hatton, **Derbyshire**, DE16 5QE, **ENGLAND**.
(T) 01283 815284.
Profile Farrier. Ref: YH08801

LONG, D J

Mr D J Long, 29 Ashby Rd East, Bretby, Burton-on-Trent, **Staffordshire**, DE15 0PS, **ENGLAND**.
(T) 01283 563760.
Profile Breeder. Ref: YH08802

LONG, J E

Mr J E Long, Main Yard, Tillingdowns, Woldingham, Caterham, **Surrey**, CR3 7JA, **ENGLAND**.
(T) 01883 348250
(M) 07931 995541.
Profile Trainer. Ref: YH08803

LONG, MAURICE

Maurice Long, Buscot, Faringdon, **Oxfordshire**, SN7 8BZ, **ENGLAND**.
(T) 01367 252787.
Contact/s
Owner: Mrs V Long
Profile Blacksmith. Ref: YH08804

LONG, S P

S P Long, Primrose Farm, Chasewater, Truro, **Cornwall**, TR4 8QH, **ENGLAND**.
(T) 01872 560014.
Profile Farrier. Ref: YH08805

LONGACRES

Longacres Riding School, Southport Rd, Lydiate, Liverpool, **Merseyside**, L31 4EQ, **ENGLAND**.
(T) 0151 5260327 (F) 0151 5272439
Affiliated Bodies ABRS, BHS.
Contact/s
General Manager: Mrs K Horner (Q) BHSII
Profile Riding School.
Riders are able to hire riding clothes, hats, jodhpurs, gloves etc. Ref: YH08806

LONGBRIDGE ENGINEERING

Longbridge Engineering Co Ltd, 2-6 Stourbridge Rd, Catshill, Bromsgrove, **Worcestershire**, B61 9LF, **ENGLAND**.
(T) 01527 579193 (F) 01527 878200.
Contact/s
Manager: Mr K Beckett
Profile Transport/Horse Boxes. Ref: YH08807

LONGDON STUD

Longdon Stud Ltd, Deva Hse, Bardy Lane, Longdon, Rugeley, **Staffordshire**, WS15 4LJ, **ENGLAND**.
(T) 01543 492656 (F) 01543 493656.
Contact/s
Manager: Mr T Hollinshead
Profile Breeder. Ref: YH08808

LONGDON STUD MATTING

Longdon Stud Matting Ltd, Elms Farm Ind Est, Huncote Rd, Huncote, **Leicestershire**, LE9 6AW, **ENGLAND**.
(T) 0116 2866218 (F) 0116 2751810.
Profile Track/Course. Ref: YH08809

LONGFIELD & APPLEDORE

Longfield Horse Transport & Appledore Stud, Ash Rd, Hartley, Longfield, **Kent**, DA3 8HA, **ENGLAND**.
(T) 01474 703329.
Profile Saddlery Retailer, Transport/Horse Boxes.
Ref: YH08810

LONGFIELD EQUESTRIAN CTRE

Longfield Equestrian Centre, Middle Longfield Farm, Long Hey Lane, Todmorden, **Yorkshire (West)**, OL14 6JN, **ENGLAND**.
(T) 01706 812736.
Contact/s
Owner: Mrs C Farnaby
Profile Breeder, Riding School. Ref: YH08811

LONGHOLES STUD

Longholes Stud, Newmarket Rd, Cheveley, Newmarket, **Suffolk**, CB8 9EJ, **ENGLAND**.
(T) 01638 730321.
Profile Breeder. Ref: YH08812

LONGHORN

Longhorn Western Riding, Longhedge Farm, Longhedge, Corsley, Warminster, **Wiltshire**, BA12 7QZ, **ENGLAND**.
(T) 01373 832422 (F) 01373 832495.
Contact/s
Owner: Miss C Bayman
Profile Equestrian Centre. Trekking Centre.
Trekking takes place around Longleat, lasting about an hour, longer available if required. All treks are mainly off road and have parkland access to 100's of acres.
No.Staff: 9 Yr. Est: 1994
Opening Times
Sp: Open Sat - Thurs 08:45. Closed Sat - Thurs 15:15.
Su: Open Sat - Thurs 08:45. Closed Sat - Thurs 15:15.
Au: Open Sat - Thurs 08:45. Closed Sat - Thurs 15:15.
Wn: Open Sat - Thurs 08:45. Closed Sat - Thurs 15:15.
Closed on Fridays Ref: YH08813

LONGLAND, MICHAEL

Michael Longland, 2 Church Way, Alconbury Weston, Huntingdon, **Cambridgeshire**, PE28 4JB, **ENGLAND**.
(T) 01480 891034 (F) 01480 891034.
Contact/s
Owner: Mr M Longland
Profile Saddlery Retailer. Ref: YH08814

LONGLEY RIDING SCHOOL

Longley Riding School, 203 Longley, Huddersfield, **Yorkshire (West)**, HD4 6PH, **ENGLAND**.
(T) 01484 431520.
Contact/s
Owner: Mrs S First
Profile Riding School. **Ref: YH08815**

LONGSDALE, C L

C L Longsdale, 5 Park Ter, Great Harwood, Blackburn, **Lancashire**, BB6 7SW, **ENGLAND**.
(T) 01254 887744.
Contact/s
Owner: Mrs C Longsdale
Profile Saddlery Retailer. **Ref: YH08816**

LONGSHAW STABLES

Longshaw Stables, Hazelwood Lane, Coulsdon, **Surrey**, CR5 3QU, **ENGLAND**.
(T) 01737 553129.
Profile Stable/Livery. **Ref: YH08817**

LONGSTONES

Longstones, Station Rd, Kennett, Newmarket, **Suffolk**, CB8 7QF, **ENGLAND**.
(T) 01638 750453 **(F)** 01638 750453.
Contact/s
General Manager: Mr B Parry
Profile Trainer. **No.Staff:** 8 **Yr. Est:** 1979
C.Size: 90 Acres **Ref: YH08818**

LONGTON EQUESTRIAN CTRE

Longton Equestrian Centre, 195 Chapel Lane, Longton, Preston, **Lancashire**, PR4 5NA, **ENGLAND**.
(T) 01772 613355 **(F)** 01772 613355.
Contact/s
Owner: Mrs C Kilshaw
Profile Riding School, Saddlery Retailer.
Ref: YH08819

LONGWOOD EQUESTRIAN CTRE

Longwood Equestrian Centre, Dry St, Basildon, **Essex**, SS16 5NG, **ENGLAND**.
(T) 01277 353147
(M) 07850 333620.
Profile Riding School, Stable/Livery. **Ref: YH08820**

LONGWOOD FEED CTRE

Longwood Feed Centre, Malgrave Nurseries, Lower Dunton Rd, Bulphan, Upminster, **Essex**, RM14 3TD, **ENGLAND**.
(T) 01268 541711.
Contact/s
Owner: Mr D Lockyer
Profile Supplies. **Ref: YH08821**

LOOKER, R D

R D Looker, 18 Cornmill, Elmley Castle, Pershore, **Worcestershire**, WR10 3JQ, **ENGLAND**.
(T) 01386 710006.
Profile Farrier. **Ref: YH08822**

LOPHAMS EQUESTRIAN CTRE

Lophams Equestrian Centre, Lophams, Thorn Lane, Goxhill, Barrow-upon-Humber, **Lincolnshire (North)**, DN19 7LY, **ENGLAND**.
(T) 01469 530381.
Profile Riding School. **Ref: YH08823**

LOQUENS GALLERY

Loquens Gallery (The), 3 Montpellier Ave, Cheltenham, **Gloucestershire**, GL50 1SA, **ENGLAND**.
(T) 01242 254313.
Profile Art Gallery. **Ref: YH08824**

LOQUENS GALLERY

Loquens Gallery (The), The Minories, Rother St, Stratford-upon-Avon, **Warwickshire**, CV37 6NE, **ENGLAND**.
(T) 01789 297706.
Profile Art Gallery. **Ref: YH08825**

LORDINGTON LIVERY

Lordington Livery, Lordington Pk, Lordington, Chichester, **Sussex (West)**, PO18 9DX, **ENGLAND**.
(T) 01243 378905.
Contact/s
Partner: Mrs D Rutland
Profile Stable/Livery. **Ref: YH08826**

LORDS HOUSE FARM

Lords House Farm Special Needs Education Centre, Wilpshire Rd, Rishton, Blackburn, **Lancashire**, BB1 4AH, **ENGLAND**.
(T) 01254 876388 **(F)** 01254 877400.
Contact/s
Manager: Mrs M Walker
Profile Riding School. **Ref: YH08827**

LORDSBRIDGE ARENA

Lordsbridge Arena, Wimpole Rd, Barton, Cambridge, **Cambridgeshire**, CB3 7AE, **ENGLAND**.
(T) 01223 262343 **(F)** 01223 262343.
Contact/s
Owner: Mr M Buckingham
Profile Arena. **Ref: YH08828**

LORDSHIP STUD

Lordship Stud, London Rd, Newmarket, **Suffolk**, CB8 0TP, **ENGLAND**.
(T) 01638 560933 **(F)** 01638 561628.
Contact/s
Manager: Mr M Russell
Profile Breeder. **Ref: YH08829**

LORENZEN, P J

Mrs P J Lorenzen, Little Banks, Kingsdown Rd, St Margarets-At-Cliffe, Dover, **Kent**, CT15 6BB, **ENGLAND**.
(T) 01304 852417.
Profile Breeder. **Ref: YH08830**

LORETTA LODGE RACING STABLE

Loretta Lodge Racing Stable, Loretta Lodge, Tilley Lane, Headley, Epsom, **Surrey**, KT18 6EP, **ENGLAND**.
(T) 01372 377209 **(F)** 01372 386578.
Contact/s
Manager: Mr R Ryan
Profile Blood Stock Agency, Trainer. **Ref: YH08831**

LOTHIAN FABRICATIONS

Lothian Fabrications, 3 Greenside Pl, Rosewell, **Lothian (Mid)**, EH24 9AG, **SCOTLAND**.
(T) 0131 4400554.
Profile Blacksmith. **Ref: YH08832**

LOTHIAN TRAILER CTRE

Lothian Trailer Centre, Anfield Farm, Winton Loan, Tranent, **Lothian (East)**, EH33 1EA, **SCOTLAND**.
(T) 01875 610625 **(F)** 01875 614199.
Contact/s
Owner: Mr A Finley
Profile Transport/Horse Boxes.
Sell Bateson trailers **Yr. Est:** 1960
Opening Times
Sp: Open Mon - Sat 09:00. Closed Mon - Sat 17:00.
Su: Open Mon - Sat 09:00. Closed Mon - Sat 17:00.
Au: Open Mon - Sat 09:00. Closed Mon - Sat 17:00.
Wn: Open Mon - Sat 09:00. Closed Mon - Sat 17:00.
Ref: YH08833

LOUELLA STUD

Louella Stud, Bardon Grange, Grange Rd, Hugglescote, Coalville, **Leicestershire**, LE67 2BT, **ENGLAND**.
(T) 01530 813357 **(F)** 01530 242783.
Contact/s
Manager: Miss M Massarella
Profile Breeder. **Ref: YH08834**

LOUELLA STUD

Louella Stud, Stockhill Green, York Rd, Thirkleby, Thirsk, **Yorkshire (North)**, YO7 3AS, **ENGLAND**.
(T) 01845 501319 **(F)** 01845 501319.
Contact/s
Manager: Mr D Chambers
Profile Breeder. **Ref: YH08835**

LOUGH NEAGH EQUESTRIAN CTRE

Lough Neagh Equestrian Centre, 47A Crumlin Rd, Ballinderry Upper, Lisburn, **County Antrim**, BT28 2JZ, **NORTHERN IRELAND**.
(T) 028 94453595.
Contact/s
Owner: Mrs A Thomas
Profile Equestrian Centre. **Ref: YH08836**

LOUGHAVEEMA TREKKING CTRE

Loughaveema Trekking Centre, Watertop Open Farm & Family Activity Ctre, 188 Cushendall Rd, Ballycastle, **County Antrim**, BT54 6RL, **NORTHERN IRELAND**.
(T) 028 20762576 **(F)** 028 20762175.
Profile Equestrian Centre. **Ref: YH08837**

LOUGHBOROUGH STUDENTS UNION

Loughborough Students Union Equestrian Club, C/O Athletic Union, Union Building, Ashby Rd, Loughborough, **Leicestershire**, LE11 3TT, **ENGLAND**.
(T) 01509 217766 **(F)** 01509 632010
(E) lsu.au@lut.ac.uk.
Profile Club/Association. **Ref: YH08838**

LOUGHBROWN STUD

Loughbrown Stud, The Curragh, **County Kildare**, **IRELAND**.
(T) 045 432292 **(F)** 045 435744
(E) loughbrown@kildarehorse.ie.
Contact/s
Key Contact: Mr R Griffin
Profile Breeder.
The Curragh racecourse is in the locality
C.Size: 130 Acres **Ref: YH08839**

LOUGHTON MANOR

Loughton Manor Equestrian Centre, Redland Drv, Loughton, Milton Keynes, **Buckinghamshire**, MK5 8EJ, **ENGLAND**.
(T) 01908 666434.
Contact/s
Partner: Mrs J Mitchell
Profile Riding School, Stable/Livery. **Ref: YH08840**

LOUGHTOWN STUD

Loughtown Stud, Donadea, Naas, **County Kildare**, **IRELAND**.
(T) 045 869115 **(F)** 045 869010
(E) loughtown@indigo.ie.
Contact/s
Key Contact: Mr D Naughton
Profile Breeder. **C.Size:** 240 Acres
Ref: YH08841

LOUGHVIEW STABLES

Loughview Stables, 24 Derrytrasna Rd, Lurgan, **County Armagh**, BT66 6NW, **NORTHERN IRELAND**.
(T) 028 38340152.
Profile Stable/Livery. **Yr. Est:** 1976
Opening Times
Sp: Open Mon - Sun 08:00. Closed Mon - Sun 20:00.
Su: Open Mon - Sun 08:00. Closed Mon - Sun 20:00.
Au: Open Mon - Sun 08:00. Closed Mon - Sun 20:00.
Wn: Open Mon - Sun 08:00. Closed Mon - Sun 20:00. **Ref: YH08842**

LOUISE LEACH

Louise Leach Marketing, Sherburn Enterprise Pk, Spitfire Way, Sherburn In Elmet, **Yorkshire (West)**, LS25 6NB, **ENGLAND**.
(T) 01977 685722 **(F)** 01977 685733.
Profile Club/Association. **Ref: YH08843**

LOVE, ANDREW

Messrs Andrew Love, Bridge Of Aird, Stranraer, **Dumfries and Galloway**, **SCOTLAND**..
Profile Breeder. **Ref: YH08844**

LOVE, GORDON

Gordon Love, 273 Summer Lane, Birmingham, **Midlands (West)**, B19 2PX, **ENGLAND**.
(T) 0121 3596343 **(F)** 0121 3590317.
Contact/s
Manager: Mr N Badger
Profile Transport/Horse Boxes. **Ref: YH08845**

LOVE-JONES & KILLEN

Love-Jones & Killen, Highcroft Vetnry Surgery, 615 Wells Rd, Whitchurch, **Bath & Somerset (North East)**, BS14 9BE, **ENGLAND**.
(T) 01275 832410.
Profile Medical Support. **Ref: YH08846**

LOVE-JONES & KILLEN

Love-Jones & Killen, 4 Smyth Rd, Bedminster, **Bristol**, BS3 2BX, **ENGLAND**.
(T) 01179 832410.
Profile Medical Support. **Ref: YH08847**

LOVEJOY, RICHARD E W

Richard E W Lovejoy DWCF, 2 Chalkdell Cottages, East Meon, Petersfield, **Hampshire**, GU32 1PQ, **ENGLAND**.
(T) 01730 823646.
Profile Farrier. **Ref: YH08848**

LOVELL, MARTYN A

Martyn A Lovell, C/O G Taylor, Moors Farm, Corse Lawn, Gloucester, **Gloucestershire**, GL19 4LY, **ENGLAND**.
(T) 01684 593830.
Contact/s
Farrier: Martyn A Lovell **(Q)** RSS
Profile Farrier. **Ref: YH08849**

LOVELY VIEW STABLES

Lovely View Stables, Lovely View, Shaftenhoe End, Barley, Royston, **Hertfordshire**, SG8 8LB,

ENGLAND.
(T) 01763 848282 (F) 01763 848282.
Contact/s
Owner: Mrs E Fisher
Profile Stable/Livery. Ref: YH08850

LOVESON

Loveson, Station Rd, Irthlingborough, **Northamptonshire**, NN9 5QE, **ENGLAND**.
(T) 01933 652652 (F) 01933 650454
(E) thl@loveson.co.uk
(W) www.loveson.co.uk.
Profile Riding Wear Retailer, Supplies.
Loveson also stock walking equipment Ref: YH08851

LOVETT, I

Mr I Lovett, 134 Forest Pk, Stonehaven, **Aberdeenshire**, AB39 2GF, **SCOTLAND**.
(T) 01569 765321.
Profile Supplies. Ref: YH08852

LOW ASH RIDING CTRE

Low Ash Riding Centre, Low Ash Farm, Worrall, Sheffield, **Yorkshire (South)**, S35 0AP, **ENGLAND**.
(T) 0114 2343577.
Profile Riding School. Ref: YH08853

LOW FALLOWFIELD

Low Fallowfield Livery & Riding School, Low Fallowfield Farm, South Hetton, Durham, **County Durham**, DH6 2TA, **ENGLAND**.
(T) 0191 5173563.
Contact/s
Manager: Mrs G Graham
Profile Riding School, Stable/Livery. Ref: YH08854

LOW FOLD RIDING CTRE

Low Fold Riding Centre, Low Fold Farm, Sunnybrow, Crook, **County Durham**, DL15 0RL, **ENGLAND**.
(T) 01388 747313 (F) 01388 747055.
Contact/s
Owner: Miss M Hedley
Profile Riding School, Stable/Livery, Track/Course.
Ref: YH08855

LOW MEADOWS FARM LIVERY

Low Meadows Farm Livery, Low Meadows Farm, Lanchester, Durham, **County Durham**, DH7 0RE, **ENGLAND**.
(T) 01207 520503.
Contact/s
General Manager: Ms J Speight (T) 01207 529365
Profile Arena, Stable/Livery, Track/Course. Rest and retirement for horses. No.Staff: 2 Yr. Est: 1968
C.Size: 80 Acres Ref: YH08856

LOWBRIDGE STABLES

Lowbridge Stables, Bremhill, Calne, **Wiltshire**, SN11 9HS, **ENGLAND**.
(T) 01249 817661 (F) 01249 814232
(M) 07973 793485.
Profile Breeder. Ref: YH08857

LOWDHAM LODGE

Lowdham Lodge, Pole Hill Rd, Uxbridge, **London (Greater)**, UB10 0QE, **ENGLAND**.
(T) 020 88135800.
Profile Stable/Livery. Ref: YH08858

LOWE, DAVID J

David J Lowe, Peachaven, Clos Du Grande Mielles, Rue De La Ronde Chemines, Castel, **Guernsey**, GY5 7GD, **ENGLAND**.
(T) 01481 52315.
Profile Farrier. Ref: YH08859

LOWE, EDDIE

Eddie Lowe FWCF, 9 Infirmary Rd, Parkgate, Rotherham, **Yorkshire (South)**, S62 6BE, **ENGLAND**.
(T) 01709 522257.
Profile Farrier. Ref: YH08860

LOWE, ROBIN J

Robin J Lowe DWCF, Little Dunwood Farm, Weobley Marsh, **Herefordshire**, HR4 8RR, **ENGLAND**.
(T) 01544 318162.
Profile Farrier. Ref: YH08861

LOWER BELL RIDING SCHOOL

Lower Bell Riding School, Lower Bell, Back Lane, Boughton Monchelsea, Maidstone, **Kent**, ME17 4JR, **ENGLAND**.
(T) 01622 745906.
Contact/s
Partner: Mrs D Harris
Profile Riding School. Ref: YH08862

LOWER FARM

Lower Farm, Berrick Salome, Wallingford, **Oxfordshire**, OX10 6JL, **ENGLAND**.
(T) 01865 891073 (F) 01865 891073.
Contact/s
Owner: Mrs S Clayton
Profile Stable/Livery. Ref: YH08863

LOWER FARM

Lower Farm Riding & Livery Stables, Stoke Rd, Stoke D'abernon, Cobham, **Surrey**, KT11 3PU, **ENGLAND**.
(T) 01932 867545/866997.
Contact/s
Partner: Mrs H Lambourne
Profile Riding School, Stable/Livery. Ref: YH08864

LOWER FARM STABLES

Lower Farm Stables, Castle Rd, Lavendon, Olney, **Buckinghamshire**, MK46 4JG, **ENGLAND**.
(T) 01234 712692.
Profile Riding School. Ref: YH08865

LOWER HALDON

Lower Haldon Private Livery Yard, Kennford, Exeter, **Devon**, EX6 7XY, **ENGLAND**.
(T) 01392 833482 (F) 01392 833482.
Contact/s
Manager: Ms W Gibson
Profile Stable/Livery. Ref: YH08866

LOWER PORTLAND RIDING SCHOOL

Lower Portland Riding School, Lower Portland, Kirkby-In-Ashfield, Nottingham, **Nottinghamshire**, NG17 9LD, **ENGLAND**.
(T) 01623 755505.
Profile Riding School. Ref: YH08867

LOWER PRIORY FARM

Lower Priory Farm Livery Yard, Clamp Hill, Stanmore, **London (Greater)**, HA7 3JJ, **ENGLAND**.
(T) 020 89541864 (F) 020 89549329.
Contact/s
Owner: Mr R Walker
Profile Stable/Livery.
No horses over 16 hands. Yr. Est: 1977
Opening Times
Sp: Open 09:00. Closed 18:00.
Su: Open 09:00. Closed 18:00.
Au: Open 09:00. Closed 18:00.
Wn: Open 09:00. Closed 18:00. Ref: YH08868

LOWER SALDEN STABLES

Lower Salden Stables, Lower Salden Farm, Salden Lane, Little Horwood, Milton Keynes, **Buckinghamshire**, MK17 0PN, **ENGLAND**.
(T) 01296 720678.
Profile Stable/Livery. Ref: YH08869

LOWER SPARR FARM

Lower Sparr Farm Ltd, Skiff Lane, Wisborough Green, Billingshurst, **Sussex (West)**, RH14 0AA, **ENGLAND**.
(T) 01403 820678 (F) 01403 820678
(E) enquiries@surreytreadmills.co.uk
(W) www.surreytreadmills.co.uk.
Contact/s
Owner: Mr C Slater
(E) sclater@lowersparrbb.f9.co.uk
Profile Supplies. No.Staff: 2 Yr. Est: 1979
C.Size: 0.5 Acres
Opening Times
Sp: Open 08:00. Closed 18:00.
Su: Open 08:00. Closed 18:00.
Au: Open 08:00. Closed 18:00.
Wn: Open 08:00. Closed 18:00. Ref: YH08870

LOWER TOWNHEAD FARM

Lower Townhead Farm, Dunford Bridge, Penistone, Sheffield, **Yorkshire (South)**, S30 6PG, **ENGLAND**.
(T) 01226 767314.
Contact/s
Owner: Mrs R Howard
Profile Horse/Rider Accom. Ref: YH08871

LOWES GARAGE SVS

Lowes Garage Services, Unit 3 Weir La Ind Est, Weir Lane, Worcester, **Worcestershire**, WR2 4AY, **ENGLAND**.
(T) 01905 426533.
Profile Transport/Horse Boxes. Ref: YH08872

LOWES, J I

J I Lowes, Forge Hse, Ellerton Upon Swale, Richmond, **Yorkshire (North)**, DL10 6AP, **ENGLAND**.
(T) 01748 811405.
Profile Farrier. Ref: YH08873

LOWFIELD LIVERY STABLES

Lowfield Livery Stables, Low Middlefield Farm, Blakeston Lane, Norton, Stockton-on-Tees, **Cleveland**, TS21 3LE, **ENGLAND**.
(T) 01642 605592
(M) 07798 550052.
Profile Stable/Livery. Ref: YH08874

LOWLEYS NATIVE PONIES

Lowleys Native Ponies, Lowlands, Mainroad, North Mundham, Chichester, **Sussex (West)**, PO20 6EP, **ENGLAND**.
(T) 01243 779284.
Profile Breeder. Ref: YH08875

LOW-MITCHELL, D I

D I Low-Mitchell, Balcormo Stud Farm, Leven, **Fife**, KY8 5QF, **SCOTLAND**.
(T) 01333 360287 (F) 01333 360699
(M) 07715 5445769 / 07715545770.
Contact/s
Owner: Mr D Low-Mitchell
Profile Breeder, Trainer. Artificial Insemination & Frozen Semen. Yr. Est: 1976 C.Size: 135 Acres
Opening Times
Sp: Open Mon - Sun 24 Hours. Closed Mon - Sun 24 Hours.
Su: Open Mon - Sun 24 Hours. Closed Mon - Sun 24 Hours.
Au: Open Mon - Sun 24 Hours. Closed Mon - Sun 24 Hours.
Wn: Open Mon - Sun 24 Hours. Closed Mon - Sun 24 Hours. Ref: YH08876

LOWTHER EQUESTRIAN

Lowther Equestrian, 3 Tower Court, West Tower St, Carlisle, **Cumbria**, CA3 8QS, **ENGLAND**.
(T) 01228 594404 (F) 01228 536872
(W) www.lowtherequestrian.com.
Contact/s
Owner: Mr D Bowman
Profile Riding Wear Retailer, Saddlery Retailer, Supplies. No.Staff: 3 Yr. Est: 1990
Opening Times
Sp: Open 09:30. Closed 17:00.
Su: Open 09:30. Closed 17:00.
Au: Open 09:30. Closed 17:00.
Wn: Open 09:30. Closed 17:00. Ref: YH08877

LOWTON RIDING CTRE

Lowton Riding Centre, 106 Slag Lane, Lowton, Warrington, **Cheshire**, WA3 1BX, **ENGLAND**.
(T) 01942 677164.
Contact/s
Owner: Miss V Woods
Profile Riding School. Ref: YH08878

LOY, JOHN S W

John S W Loy, Croft Cottage, Church Lane, High Hoyland, Barnsley, **Yorkshire (South)**, S75 4BJ, **ENGLAND**.
(T) 01226 382163.
Profile Farrier. Ref: YH08879

LPPS

Lundy Pony Preservation Society, 33 Gregorys Tyning, Paulton, **Bath & Somerset (North East)**, BS39 7PW, **ENGLAND**.
(T) 01761 415073.
Contact/s
Secretary: Mrs D Minall
Profile Club/Association.
Charity for Breeding, Registering & Protection of Lundy Ponies.
Opening Times
Contact for further details Ref: YH08880

LTT IMMINGHAM

LTT Immingham Ltd -Purfleet Division, Purfleet Ind Pk, London Rd, Aveley, South Ockendon, **Essex**, RM15 4YA, **ENGLAND**.
(T) 01708 867040 (F) 01708 865044.
Profile Transport/Horse Boxes. Ref: YH08881

LUBIN, J R B

J R B Lubin, 33 Salisbury Rd, Holland-on-Sea, **Essex**, CO15 5LL, **ENGLAND**.
(T) 01255 814752.
Profile Farrier. Ref: YH08882

LUCAS, J E

J E Lucas, Coleshill Hall Farm, Birmingham Rd, Coleshill, Birmingham, **Warwickshire**, B46 1DP, **ENGLAND**.
(T) 01675 462257.
Contact/s
Partner: Mrs J Lucas
Profile Breeder. Ref: YH08883

LUCAS, R & M
R & M Lucas & Co, Roscoe Hse Farm, Delph Lane, Charnock Richard, Chorley, **Lancashire**, PR7 5LD, **ENGLAND**.
(T) 01257 791392 **(F)** 01257 791392.
Contact/s
Partner: Mrs M Lucas
Profile Trainer. **Ref: YH08884**

LUCEY, P E
Mrs P E Lucey, Gartmorn Hill Farm, Alloa, **Clackmannanshire**, FK10 3AU, **SCOTLAND**.
(T) 01259 50549.
Profile Breeder. **Ref: YH08885**

LUCK, B M
B M Luck RSS, Salden, Beech Lane, Matfield, Tonbridge, **Kent**, TN12 7HG, **ENGLAND**.
(T) 01892 822613.
Profile Farrier. **Ref: YH08886**

LUCKETT, GEOFF
Geoff Luckett, Foxhill, Horley, Banbury, **Oxfordshire**, OX15 6BN, **ENGLAND**.
(T) 01295 670657 **(F)** 01295 670657
(M) 07831 828594.
Profile Trainer. **Ref: YH08887**

LUCKNAM PK EQUESTRIAN CTRE
Lucknam Park Equestrian Centre, Studs Farm, Lucknam Pk, Colerne, Chippenham, **Wiltshire**, SN14 8AZ, **ENGLAND**.
(T) 01225 744753.
Contact/s
Manager: Mrs D Rossiter **Ref: YH08888**

LUCY TURMAINE
Miss Lucy Turmaine (Bridlemaker), Fairways, Patchacott, Beaworthy, **Devon**, EX21 5AR, **ENGLAND**.
(T) 01409 221136
(E) j.a.turmaine@btinternet.com.
Profile Riding Wear Retailer. **Ref: YH08889**

LUDLOW RACECOURSE
Ludlow Racecourse, Bromfield, Ludlow, **Shropshire**, SY8 2BT, **ENGLAND**.
(T) 01584 856221 **(F)** 01981 250192.
Contact/s
Admin: Mrs D Davies
Profile Track/Course. **Ref: YH08890**

LUDLOW-MONK, STEPHEN P
Stephen P Ludlow-Monk DWCF, 49 Nursery Hill, Shamley Green, Guildford, **Surrey**, GU5 0UL, **ENGLAND**.
(T) 01483 893926.
Profile Farrier. **Ref: YH08891**

LUFFENHALL EQUESTRIAN CTRE
Luffenhall Equestrian Centre, The Old Ram & Hurdle, Luffenhall, Walkern, Stevenage, **Hertfordshire**, SG2 7PX, **ENGLAND**.
(T) 07956 408491.
Profile Equestrian Centre. **Ref: YH08892**

LUKE TRAILERS
Luke Trailers, Ladyside Farm, Grindon, Leek, **Staffordshire**, ST13 7TS, **ENGLAND**.
(T) 01538 304275.
Profile Transport/Horse Boxes. **Ref: YH08893**

LUKE, DOYLE
Doyle Luke, Rosbercon, New Ross, **County Wexford**, **IRELAND**.
(T) 051 421517.
Profile Supplies. **Ref: YH08894**

LUKIN, P D
Mr P D Lukin, Manor Farm, Tortington, Arundel, **Sussex (West)**, BN18 0BG, **ENGLAND**.
(T) 01903 882124.
Profile Supplies. **Ref: YH08895**

LULLINGSTONE PK
Lullingstone Park Riding School, Park Gate Farm, Parkgate Rd, Orpington, **Kent**, BR6 7PX, **ENGLAND**.
(T) 01959 534746.
Contact/s
Partner: Mr M Osman
Profile Riding School. **Ref: YH08896**

LULWORTH EQUESTRIAN CTRE
Lulworth Equestrian Centre, Kennel Farm, Coombe Keynes, Wareham, **Dorset**, BH20 5QR, **ENGLAND**.
(T) 01929 400396 **(F)** 01929 400396
Affiliated Bodies BHS.
Contact/s
Assistant: Ms P Elsdon **(Q)** BHSAI
Profile Arena, Equestrian Centre, Riding School, Stable/Livery. **No.Staff:** 5 **C.Size:** 65 Acres
Opening Times
Sp: Open 10:00. Closed 16:00.
Su: Open 10:00. Closed 16:00.
Au: Open 10:00. Closed 16:00.
Wn: Open 10:00. Closed 16:00. **Ref: YH08897**

LUNDY ISLAND
Lundy Island Company (The), Lundy Island, Bristol Channel, Bideford, **Devon**, EX39 2LY, **ENGLAND**.
(T) 01237 431831 **(F)** 01237 431832.
Profile Breeder. **Ref: YH08898**

LUNE VALLEY MARKETING
Lune Valley Marketing, Gatelands, High Biggins, Kirkby Lonsdale, Carnforth, **Lancashire**, LA6 2NP, **ENGLAND**.
(T) 01524 272700 **(F)** 01524 770056. **Ref: YH08899**

LUNGO, L
L Lungo, Hetlandhill Farm, Carrutherstown, Dumfries, **Dumfries and Galloway**, DG1 4JX, **SCOTLAND**.
(T) 01387 840691.
Contact/s
Owner: Mr L Lungo
Profile Trainer. **Ref: YH08900**

LUNNUN, NORMAN
Norman Lunnun, Eaton Croft, Upwoods Rd, Doveridge, Ashbourne, **Derbyshire**, DE6 5LL, **ENGLAND**.
(T) 01889 563383 **(F)** 01889 563383
(M) 07860 826712.
Contact/s
Farrier: Norman Lunnun **(Q)** RSS
Profile Farrier. **Ref: YH08901**

LUSCOMBE ARENA CONSTRUCTION
Luscombe Arena Construction, Charlecombe Cottage, Combeinteignhead, Newton Abbot, **Devon**, TQ12 4RE, **ENGLAND**.
(T) 01626 872780.
Profile Supplies. **Ref: YH08902**

LUSHER, RONALD MICHAEL
Ronald Michael Lusher, Brambling, 1 Station Rd, Leziate, King's Lynn, **Norfolk**, PE32 1EJ, **ENGLAND**.
(T) 0116 2630554.
Profile Farrier. **Ref: YH08903**

LUSITANO BREED SOC
Lusitano Breed Society of Great Britain (The), Greenhouse Farm, Meerbrook, Leek, **Staffordshire**, ST13 8SX, **ENGLAND**.
(T) 01538 300238 **(F)** 01538 300238.
Contact/s
Key Contact: Mrs Z Galley
Profile Club/Association. **Ref: YH08904**

LUSK EQUESTRIAN
Lusk Equestrian, 48 Knockany Rd, Lisburn, **County Antrim**, BT27 6YB, **NORTHERN IRELAND**.
(T) 028 92638407 **(F)** 028 92638981
(E) info@luskhorsesireland.com
(W) www.luskhorsesireland.com.
Contact/s
Owner: Mrs J Lusk
Profile Breeder, Stable/Livery.
Opening Times
Sp: Open Mon - Sun 09:00. Closed Mon - Sun 18:00.
Su: Open Mon - Sun 09:00. Closed Mon - Sun 18:00.
Au: Open Mon - Sun 09:00. Closed Mon - Sun 18:00.
Wn: Open Mon - Sun 09:00. Closed Mon - Sun 18:00. **Ref: YH08905**

LUSK TRANSPORT
Lusk Transport Ltd, 48 Knockany Rd, Lisburn, **County Antrim**, BT27 6YB, **NORTHERN IRELAND**.
(T) 028 92638407/ 92639202 **(F)** 028 92638981
(E) transport@luskhoursesireland.com
(W) www.luskhorsesireland.com.
Contact/s
Owner: Mrs J Lusk
Profile Transport/Horse Boxes.
Transport to the UK and Europe
Opening Times
Sp: Open Mon - Sun 09:00. Closed Mon - Sun 18:00.
Su: Open Mon - Sun 09:00. Closed Mon - Sun 18:00.
Au: Open Mon - Sun 09:00. Closed Mon - Sun 18:00.
Wn: Open Mon - Sun 09:00. Closed Mon - Sun 18:00. **Ref: YH08906**

LUSTED FEEDS
Lusted Feeds, Lusted Farm, Glynleigh Rd, Hankham, **Sussex (East)**, BN24 5GJ, **ENGLAND**.
(T) 01323 768937.
Profile Supplies. **Ref: YH08907**

LUTEY, R A
Mr & Mrs R A Lutey, Trevarth, St Newlyn East, Newquay, **Cornwall**, TR8 5NT, **ENGLAND**.
(T) 01872 510337.
Profile Breeder. **Ref: YH08908**

LUTON, WILLIAM A
William A Luton DWCF, 24 Queen's Drive, Shafton, Barnsley, **Yorkshire (South)**, S72 8PB, **ENGLAND**.
(T) 01226 712287.
Profile Farrier. **Ref: YH08909**

LUXFORD, KEITH
Mr Keith Luxford, Saddlers, 35 Arlington Ave, Goring By Sea, Worthing, **Sussex (West)**, BN12 4SX, **ENGLAND**.
(T) 01903 242223. **Ref: YH08910**

LUXSTOWE VETNRY CTRE
Luxstowe Veterinary Centre, Callington Rd, Luxstowe, Liskeard, **Cornwall**, PL14 3QF, **ENGLAND**.
(T) 01579 342120 **(F)** 01579 340760.
Profile Medical Support. **Ref: YH08911**

LUXTON, MARCUS N
Marcus N Luxton DWCF, East Loosemoor, Oakford, Tiverton, **Devon**, EX16 9JE, **ENGLAND**.
(T) 01398 351565.
Profile Farrier. **Ref: YH08912**

LUXTON, STEVEN
Steven Luxton AWCF, Higher Cholwell Bungalow, Lewdown, Okehampton, **Devon**, EX20 4BX, **ENGLAND**.
(T) 07860 363203.
Profile Farrier. **Ref: YH08913**

LYBURY RIDING CTRE
Lybury Riding Centre, Lybury Lane, Redbourn, St Albans, **Hertfordshire**, AL3 7JH, **ENGLAND**.
(T) 01582 794184.
Contact/s
Partner: Mr T Gear **Ref: YH08914**

LYDE HOUSE LIVERIES
Lyde House Liveries, Greywell Rd, Up Nately, Hook, **Hampshire**, RG27 9PJ, **ENGLAND**.
(T) 01256 762952.
Contact/s
Owner: Mrs S Priddy
Profile Stable/Livery. **Ref: YH08915**

LYDFORD HOUSE RIDING STABLES
Lydford House Riding Stables, Lydford, Okehampton, **Devon**, EX20 4AU, **ENGLAND**.
(T) 01822 820321.
Contact/s
Manager: Miss H Searle **(Q)** BHSII
Profile Riding School, Stable/Livery. **Ref: YH08916**

LYFORDS MEADOW STABLES
Lyfords Meadow Stables, 127 Locks Ride, Ascot, **Berkshire**, SL5 8RX, **ENGLAND**.
(T) 01344 882129.
Profile Stable/Livery. **Ref: YH08917**

LYLE, W
W Lyle, 45 Dalsholm Ave, Glasgow, **Glasgow (City of)**, G20 0TS, **SCOTLAND**.
(T) 0141 9455325.
Profile Blacksmith. **Ref: YH08918**

LYMER, KELVIN A
Kelvin A Lymer DWCF, Sandpit Cottage, Walton Lane, Grimley, **Worcestershire**, WR2 6LR, **ENGLAND**.
(T) 01905 641133 **(F)** 01905 641133.
Profile Farrier. **Ref: YH08919**

LYMER, WENDY
Mrs Wendy Lymer BHSII, Sandpit Cottage, Walton Lane, Grimley, **Worcestershire**, WR2 6LR, **ENGLAND**.
(T) 01905 641133 **(F)** 01905 641133.
Profile Trainer. **Ref: YH08920**

LYNCAR
Lyncar, Briff Lane, Bucklebury, Reading, **Berkshire**, RG7 6SN, **ENGLAND**.
(T) 01635 860066 **(F)** 01635 860066.
Contact/s

Owner: Mr M Slater Ref: YH08921

LYNCH COTTAGE FARM

Lynch Cottage Farm, Totteridge Common, **London (Greater)**, N20 8LU, **ENGLAND**.
(T) 020 89595800.
Profile Stable/Livery. Ref: YH08922

LYNCH FARM EQUESTRIAN CLUB

Lynch Farm Equestrian Club Ltd, Lynch Farm, Orton Wistow, Peterborough, **Cambridgeshire**, PE2 6XA, **ENGLAND**.
(T) 01733 234445.
Profile Riding School. Ref: YH08923

LYNCH, GERRY

Lynch Gerry, Ganty, Craughwell, **County Galway**, **IRELAND**.
(T) 091 846309.
Profile Supplies. Ref: YH08924

LYNCHGATE FARM RIDING SCHOOL

Lynchgate Farm Riding School, Lynchgate Lane, Burbage, Hinckley, **Leicestershire**, LE10 2DS, **ENGLAND**.
(T) 01455 631470.
Contact/s
Partner: Mr T Saunders
Profile Riding School, Stable/Livery.
Only ponies are kept at the stables, hence being ideal for children. Yr. Est: 1990
Opening Times
Sp: Open Sat 08:00, Tues, Wed, Fri 16:00. Closed Sat 13:00, Tues, Wed, Fri 18:00.
Su: Open Sat 08:00, Tues, Wed, Fri 16:00. Closed Sat 13:00, Tues, Wed, Fri 18:00.
Au: Open Sat 08:00, Tues, Wed, Fri 16:00. Closed Sat 13:00, Tues, Wed, Fri 18:00.
Wn: Open Sat 08:00, Tues, Wed, Fri 16:00. Closed Sat 13:00, Tues, Wed, Fri 18:00. Ref: YH08925

LYNDEN FARM

Lynden Farm Riding & Trekking Centre, Rhes-Y-Cae, Holywell, **Flintshire**, CH8 8JT, **WALES**.
(T) 01352 780539.
Profile Riding School, Stable/Livery. Ref: YH08926

LYNDHURST COUNTRY CLOTHING

Lyndhurst Country Clothing, 49 High St, Lyndhurst, **Hampshire**, SO43 7BE, **ENGLAND**.
(T) 023 80283644 (F) 023 80284407.
Profile Saddlery Retailer. Ref: YH08927

LYNDHURST PK HOTEL

Lyndhurst Park Hotel, 78 High St, Lyndhurst, **Hampshire**, SO43 7NL, **ENGLAND**.
(T) 023 80283923 (F) 023 80283019.
Profile Equestrian Centre. Ref: YH08928

LYNDHURST SADDLERY

Lyndhurst Saddlery, Main Rd, A443, Between Hallow & Holt, Worcester, **Worcestershire**, WR2 6LS, **ENGLAND**.
(T) 01905 640092.
Profile Saddlery Retailer. Ref: YH08929

LYNFORDS

Lynfords, Lynfords New Farm, Runwell Rd, Wickford, **Essex**, SS11 7PS, **ENGLAND**.
(T) 01268 562818.
Profile Saddlery Retailer, Stable/Livery.
Ref: YH08930

LYNG COURT LIVERY

Lyng Court Livery, West Lyng, Taunton, **Somerset**, TA3 5AP, **ENGLAND**.
(T) 01823 490510.
Contact/s
Partner: Mr R Loyde-Jones
Profile Stable/Livery. Ref: YH08931

LYNMARI TACK & ACCESSORIES

Lynmari Tack & Accessories, Manor Farm Craft Ctre, Wood Lane, Earlswood, Solihull, **Warwickshire**, B94 5JH, **ENGLAND**.
(T) 01564 700008 (F) 01564 700008.
Contact/s
Partner: Mrs M Pittaway
Profile Saddlery Retailer, Supplies. Ref: YH08932

LYNTON CROSS TRAILER CTRE

Lynton Cross Trailer Centre, Lynton Cross, Ilfracombe, **Devon**, EX34 9RQ, **ENGLAND**.
(T) 01271 862691.
Profile Transport/Horse Boxes. Ref: YH08933

LYNTON TRAILERS

Lynton Trailers, Jubilee Works, Constable St, Manchester, **Manchester (Greater)**, M18 8GJ, **ENGLAND**.
(T) 0161 2310507 (F) 0161 2230933.
Profile Transport/Horse Boxes. Ref: YH08934

LYNTRIDGE FARM RIDING STABLES

Lyntridge Farm Riding Stables, Lyntridge Farm, Bromsberrow Heath, Redmarley, Gloucester, **Gloucestershire**, GL19 3JU, **ENGLAND**.
(T) 01531 650690.
Contact/s
Owner: Mrs H Williams
Profile Riding School. Ref: YH08935

LYNX PK RIDING STABLES

Lynx Park Riding Stables, Lynx Pk, Colliers Green, Cranbrook, **Kent**, TN17 2LR, **ENGLAND**.
(T) 01580 211020.
Contact/s
Owner: Mr A Scott-Prott
Profile Riding School, Stable/Livery. Ref: YH08936

LYON BENNETT & AST

Lyon Bennett & Associates, 3 Victoria St, Chatteris, **Cambridgeshire**, PE16 6AP, **ENGLAND**.
(T) 01354 692309.
Profile Medical Support. Ref: YH08937

LYON BENNETT & AST

Lyon Bennett & Associates, 6 Barr St, Whittlesey, **Cambridgeshire**, PE7 1DA, **ENGLAND**.
(T) 01733 208090.
Profile Medical Support. Ref: YH08938

LYON, BENNETT & AST

Lyon, Bennett & Associates, 3 Upwell Rd, March, **Cambridgeshire**, PE15 9DS, **ENGLAND**.
(T) 01354 653435 (F) 01354 660381.
Profile Medical Support. Ref: YH08939

LYON, POLLY

Polly Lyon, The Stable Flat, Charlton Pk, Malmesbury, **Wiltshire**, SN16 9DG, **ENGLAND**.
(T) 01666 822824.
Profile Trainer. Ref: YH08940

LYTH STABLES

Lyth Stables, Crossroads, Lyth, Wick, **Highlands**, KW1 4UD, **SCOTLAND**.
(T) 01955 641318.
Contact/s
Owner: Mrs L Alexander
Profile Riding School. Ref: YH08941

M & A OUTDOOR CLOTHING

M & A Outdoor Clothing & Tussa International Footwear, Stafford Hse, Bonnetts Lane, Ifield, Crawley, **Sussex (West)**, RH11 0NX, **ENGLAND**.
(T) 01293 520721 (F) 01293 510422
(M) 07860 377797.
Profile Saddlery Retailer. Ref: YH08942

M & B EQUESTRIAN

M & B Equestrian, 30 Thornyhill Rd, Killinchy, **County Down**, BT23 6SL, **NORTHERN IRELAND**.
(T) 028 97542172 (F) 028 97542172.
Profile Saddlery Retailer. Ref: YH08943

M & B RIDING CLUB

M & B Riding Club, 958 Green Lane, Dagenham, **Essex**, RM8 1BU, **ENGLAND**.
(T) 020 85934362.
Profile Club/Association, Riding Club. Ref: YH08944

M & B TRAILER SALES

M & B Trailer Sales Ltd, Day St, Dewsbury, **Yorkshire (West)**, WF13 3LJ, **ENGLAND**.
(T) 01924 498199.
Profile Transport/Horse Boxes. Ref: YH08945

M & G TRAILERS

M & G Trailers Ltd, Hayes Lane, Stourbridge, **Midlands (West)**, DY9 8PA, **ENGLAND**.
(T) 01384 424200.
Profile Transport/Horse Boxes. Ref: YH08946

M & J SADDLERY

M & J Saddlery, Walsall Rd, Pipehill, Lichfield, **Staffordshire**, WS13 8JN, **ENGLAND**.
(T) 01543 255665 (F) 01543 255666.
Contact/s
Manager: Mrs J Round
Profile Saddlery Retailer. Ref: YH08947

M & M OILS

M & M Oils Ltd, Lane End Farm, Lane End, Hopwood, Heywood, **Lancashire**, OL10 2JE, **ENGLAND**.
(T) 01706 369619 (F) 01706 366151.
Contact/s
Owner: Mr M Yates
Profile Supplies. Ref: YH08948

M & M TIMBER

M & M Timber Co Ltd, Hunt Hse Sawmill, Clows Top, Kidderminster, **Worcestershire**, DY14 9HY, **ENGLAND**.
(T) 01299 832611 (F) 01299 832536. Ref: YH08949

M & S HAULIERS

M & S Hauliers Ltd, Trehill Yard, St. Dominick, Saltash, **Cornwall**, PL12 6SQ, **ENGLAND**.
(T) 01579 351007 (F) 01579 350922.
Contact/s
Manager: Mr M Beaver
Profile Transport/Horse Boxes. Ref: YH08950

M & S LIVERY

M & S Livery, Georges Farm, West Buckland, Wellington, **Somerset**, TA21 9LE, **ENGLAND**.
(T) 01823 660760.
Contact/s
Owner: Mrs M Watson Ref: YH08951

M A FABRICATION

M A Fabrication, 112 Outgang Rd, Pickering, **Yorkshire (North)**, YO18 7EL, **ENGLAND**.
(T) 01751 473493 (F) 01751 473493.
Contact/s
Owner: Mr M Agar
Profile Transport/Horse Boxes. Ref: YH08952

M A V SADDLERY & PET STORE

M A V Saddlery & Pet Store, 11 Hope St, Crook, **County Durham**, DL15 9HS, **ENGLAND**.
(T) 01388 765757.
Contact/s
Owner: Mrs M Heatherington
Profile Saddlery Retailer. Ref: YH08953

M ALLEN & SONS

M Allen & Sons, 165 Snydale Rd, Normanton, **Yorkshire (West)**, WF6 1PA, **ENGLAND**.
(T) 01924 893850 (F) 01924 893850.
Contact/s
Owner: Mr J Allen
Profile Blacksmith. Ref: YH08954

M C A TACK

M C A Tack, 18 West Wiltshire Craft Ctre, Storridge Rd, Westbury, **Wiltshire**, BA13 4HU, **ENGLAND**.
(T) 01373 824499.
Contact/s
Owner: Mrs C Morris
Profile Supplies. Ref: YH08955

M C INT HORSE TRANSPORT

M C International Horse Transport, Wits End, Dullingham Ley, Dullingham, Newmarket, **Suffolk**, CB8 9XG, **ENGLAND**.
(T) 01638 507379.
Contact/s
Owner: Mr M Carvalho
Profile Transport/Horse Boxes. Yr. Est: 1986
Opening Times
24 hours, 7 days a week Ref: YH08956

M C WESTERN

M C Western (Show Jumps), Groveside, Gloucester Rd, Hartpury, Gloucester, **Gloucestershire**, GL19 3BG, **ENGLAND**.
(T) 01452 700319.
Profile Supplies. Ref: YH08957

M D F CARRIAGE TUITION

M D F Carriage Driving Tuition, Manor Farm, Church St, Hartshorne, Swadlincote, **Derbyshire**, DE11 7ER, **ENGLAND**.
(T) 01283 215279.
Contact/s
Owner: Miss M Flintham Ref: YH08958

M E FRENCH

M E French & Co (Insurance Brokers), 40A Liverpool Rd, Penwortham, Preston, **Lancashire**, PR1 0DQ, **ENGLAND**.
(T) 01772 745204.
Profile Club/Association. Insurance. Ref: YH08959

M E HOWITT SADDLERS

M E Howitt Saddlers, 2 & 4 Turk St, Alton, **Hampshire**, GU34 1AG, **ENGLAND**.
(T) 01420 83049.
Contact/s
Saddler: Mr M Howitt
Profile Saddlery Retailer. Ref: YH08960

M E L

M E L, 30 Bridge St, Berwick-upon-Tweed,

Northumberland, TD15 1AQ, **ENGLAND**.
(T) 01289 330292 **(F)** 01289 330292.
Profile Saddlery Retailer. Ref: **YH08961**

M F HOWARD & SONS

M F Howard & Sons, Upper Goosehill Farm, Upper Goosehill, Broughton Green, Droitwich, **Worcestershire**, WR9 7ED, **ENGLAND**.
(T) 01905 391270.
Profile Supplies. Ref: **YH08962**

M H COLLEY

M H Colley Ltd, Moor Lane Forge, Moor St, Brierley Hill, **Midlands (West)**, DY5 3SP, **ENGLAND**.
(T) 01384 77278 **(F)** 01384 77278.
Profile Blacksmith. Ref: **YH08963**

M H M BLACKSMITHS

M H M Blacksmiths, 30 Eastmuir St, Glasgow, **Glasgow (City of)**, G32 0HS, **SCOTLAND**.
(T) 0141 7780202 **(F)** 0141 7740303.
Profile Blacksmith. Ref: **YH08964**

M H W S J FRATERNITY

M H W S J Fraternity Ltd, Cilmaren, Caio, Llanwrda, **Carmarthenshire**, SA19 8PN, **WALES**.
(T) 07000 781216 **(F)** 07000 781216.
Profile Breeder, Club/Association. Ref: **YH08965**

M HANCOCK & SON

M Hancock & Son Ltd, Hanover Mills, Mersham, Ashford, **Kent**, TN25 6NU, **ENGLAND**.
(T) 01233 720871 **(F)** 01233 721200.
Profile Saddlery Retailer. Ref: **YH08966**

M J EQUESTRIAN

M J Equestrian, Tregastic Hse, Wide Gates, Looe, **Cornwall**, PL13 1PZ, **ENGLAND**.
(T) 01503 240516.
Contact/s
Owner: Mrs M Hutchins
Profile Stable/Livery. Ref: **YH08967**

M J HALE & SONS

M J Hale & Sons, Woodcroft Farm, Nessacre Lane, Willaston, **Cheshire**, CH64 2TL, **ENGLAND**.
(T) 0151 3274074.
Profile Stable/Livery. Ref: **YH08968**

M J HAYWARD & SONS

M J Hayward & Sons, Green Farm, North Gorley, Fordingbridge, **Hampshire**, SP6 2PB, **ENGLAND**.
(T) 01425 652007.
Profile Supplies. Ref: **YH08969**

M J MAC

M J Mac & Co, The Lodge, Trinity Hse, Trinity St, Leamington Spa, **Warwickshire**, CV32 5YN, **ENGLAND**.
(T) 01926 470777 **(F)** 01926 470818
(M) 07831 470777.
Profile Club/Association. Ref: **YH08970**

M J O'BRIEN SADDLERY

M J O'Brien Saddlery, Edward St, Newbridge, **County Kildare**, **IRELAND**.
(T) 045 432385 **(F)** 045 435236.
Profile Supplies. Ref: **YH08971**

M K M RACING

M K M Racing, Brough Farm, Middleham, Leyburn, **Yorkshire (North)**, DL8 4SG, **ENGLAND**.
(T) 01969 623221.
Profile Stable/Livery. Ref: **YH08972**

M M T SERVICES

M M T Services, Bourne Works, Collingbourne Ducis, Marlborough, **Wiltshire**, SN8 3EH, **ENGLAND**.
(T) 01264 850235.
Profile Supplies. Ref: **YH08973**

M P TRAILERS

M P Trailers, 17 Burnham Business Pk, Springfield Rd, Burnham-on-Crouch, **Essex**, CM0 8TE, **ENGLAND**.
(T) 01621 782254 **(F)** 01621 784220
(E) info@mptrailers.co.uk
(W) www.gotrailers.co.uk.
Profile Transport/Horse Boxes. Yr. Est: 1988
Opening Times
Sp: Open 09:00. Closed 17:00.
Su: Open 09:00. Closed 17:00.
Au: Open 09:00. Closed 17:00.
Wn: Open 09:00. Closed 17:00.
Closed weekends Ref: **YH08974**

M S F EQUINE

M S F Equine, East Barn, Benham Chase, Stockcross, Newbury, **Berkshire**, RG20 8LQ, **ENGLAND**.
(T) 01635 524478
(M) 07776 242865
(W) www.msf-equine.co.uk.
Profile Medical Support. Ref: **YH08975**

M S RACE GEAR

M S Race Gear, Low Esh Farm, Esh, Durham, **County Durham**, DH7 9RB, **ENGLAND**.
(T) 0191 3730881.
Profile Saddlery Retailer. Ref: **YH08976**

M V R PHOTOGRAPHIC

M V R Photographic, 8-10 Whelpley Hill Pk, Chesham, **Buckinghamshire**, HP5 3RH, **ENGLAND**.
(T) 01442 832858 **(F)** 01442 832858.
Contact/s
Owner: Mrs J Ambridge Ref: **YH08977**

M6 TRAILER RENTAL

M6 Trailer Rental Ltd, Airfield Hse, Barley Castle Lane, Appleton, Warrington, **Cheshire**, WA4 4RG, **ENGLAND**.
(T) 01925 213330 **(F)** 01925 213332.
Profile Transport/Horse Boxes. Ref: **YH08978**

MABBETT, JOHN

John Mabbett, Bryn Farm, Penuel, Llanmorlais, Swansea, **Swansea**, SA4 3UQ, **WALES**.
(T) 01792 851377 **(F)** 01792 851377.
Contact/s
Owner: Mr J Mabbett
Profile Supplies. Ref: **YH08979**

MABERS SADDLERY

Mabers Saddlery & Leather Goods, 49 Cheap St, Sherborne, **Dorset**, DT9 3AX, **ENGLAND**.
(T) 01935 812570.
Contact/s
Owner: Mrs M Watts
Profile Saddlery Retailer. Ref: **YH08980**

MACARTHUR, JENNY

Jenny MacArthur, Wood Burcote Court, Towcester, **Northamptonshire**, NN12 7JP, **ENGLAND**.
(T) 01327 350443.
Profile Supplies. Ref: **YH08981**

MACAULAYS TACK SHOP

Macaulays Tack Shop, 29 Priors Gate, Oakdale, Blackwood, **Caerphilly**, NP12 0EL, **WALES**.
(T) 01495 222098.
Profile Saddlery Retailer. Ref: **YH08982**

MACAULEY, N J

Mrs N J Macauley, The Sidings, Saltby Rd, Sproxton, Melton Mowbray, **Leicestershire**, LE14 4RA, **ENGLAND**.
(T) 01476 860090 **(F)** 01476 860611
(M) 07741 004444.
Profile Trainer. Ref: **YH08983**

MACCLESFIELD & DISTRICT

Macclesfield & District Riding Club, Bryer Cottage, 15 Walker Lane, Sutton, Macclesfield, **Cheshire**, SK11 0DZ, **ENGLAND**.
(T) 01260 252404.
Contact/s
Secretary: Jenny Laydock
Profile Club/Association, Riding Club. Ref: **YH08984**

MACCLESFIELD SADDLERY

Macclesfield Saddlery, 39 Sunderland St, Macclesfield, **Cheshire**, SK11 6JL, **ENGLAND**.
(T) 01625 619298.
Profile Saddlery Retailer. Ref: **YH08985**

MACCONNAL-MASON GALLERY

MacConnal-Mason Gallery, 14-17 Duke St, St James's, London, **London (Greater)**, SW1Y 6DB, **ENGLAND**.
(T) 020 78397693/4 **(F)** 020 78396797.
Profile Art Gallery. Ref: **YH08986**

MACDONALD, A R

Mr & Mrs A R MacDonald, Little Garlowbank, Kirriemuir, **Angus**, DD8 4LG, **SCOTLAND**.
(T) 01575 72536.
Profile Breeder, Supplies. Ref: **YH08987**

MACDONALD, D W

Mr D W MacDonald, Bonny Hill Farm, Bridekirk, Cockermouth, **Cumbria**, CA13 0PE, **ENGLAND**.
(T) 01900 826092.
Profile Supplies. Ref: **YH08988**

MACDONALD, PETER

Mr Peter Macdonald, 3 Kilmore, Teangue, Sleat, **Highlands**, IV44 8RG, **SCOTLAND**.
(T) 01471 4272.
Profile Breeder. Ref: **YH08989**

MACDONALD, S

S MacDonald, 115 Church St, Inverness, **Highlands**, IV1 1EY, **SCOTLAND**.
(T) 01463 240875.
Profile Farrier. Ref: **YH08990**

MACDONALD, T P

T P MacDonald, St Clairs Farm, Pensax, Abberley, Worcester, **Worcestershire**, WR6 6AE, **ENGLAND**.
(T) 01299 896488.
Profile Breeder. Ref: **YH08991**

MACDONALD-HALL, ANNI

Mrs Anni MacDonald-Hall, Sopps Farm, Stony Batter, West Tytherley, Salisbury, **Wiltshire**, SP5 1LE, **ENGLAND**.
(T) 01794 341800. Ref: **YH08992**

MACE FARM

Mace Farm, Cudham, Sevenoaks, **Kent**, TN14 7QN, **ENGLAND**.
(T) 01959 572077.
Profile Stable/Livery. Ref: **YH08993**

MACFARLANE GOVAN, A L

A L MacFarlane Govan (Arbroath), 19 Keptie St, Arbroath, **Angus**, DD11 3AE, **SCOTLAND**.
(T) 01241 875789.
Profile Medical Support. Ref: **YH08994**

MACFARLANE GOVAN, A L

A L MacFarlane Govan (Montrose), Golf Vetnry Ctre, East Links, Montrose, **Angus**, DD10 8SW, **SCOTLAND**.
(T) 01674 672358.
Profile Medical Support. Ref: **YH08995**

MACFARLANE, THOMAS W

Thomas W MacFarlane, Addiewell Farm, West Calder, **Lothian (West)**, **SCOTLAND**..
Profile Breeder. Ref: **YH08996**

MACGREGOR, E & I

E & I Macgregor, Pinkerton Stud, Dunbar, **Lothian (East)**, EH42 1RX, **SCOTLAND**.
(T) 01368 840212.
Profile Breeder. Ref: **YH08997**

MACKEAN, P

P Mackean, 51A Loughanmore Rd, Dunadry, Antrim, **County Antrim**, BT41 2HN, **NORTHERN IRELAND**.
(T) 028 94433587 **(F)** 028 94433251.
Contact/s
Owner: Mrs P MacKean
Profile Breeder. Ref: **YH08998**

MACKENZIE BRYSON & MARSHALL

MacKenzie Bryson & Marshall, 21 Hill St, Kilmarnock, **Ayrshire (East)**, KA3 1HF, **SCOTLAND**.
(T) 01563 522701.
Profile Medical Support. Ref: **YH08999**

MACKENZIE, F

Mrs F MacKenzie, Yew Tree Farm Hse, Ford End, Clavening, Saffron Walden, **Essex**, CB11 4PU, **ENGLAND**.
(T) 01799 777230.
Profile Breeder. Ref: **YH09000**

MACKENZIE, G A

G A MacKenzie, St Gilbert St, Dornoch, **Highlands**, IV25 3SL, **SCOTLAND**.
(T) 01862 810341.
Contact/s
Owner: Mr R MacKensie
Profile Blacksmith. Ref: **YH09001**

MACKENZIE, IAIN

Iain Mackenzie, 31 High St, Cheveley, Newmarket, **Suffolk**, CB8 9DQ, **ENGLAND**.
(T) 01638 730361.
Profile Supplies. Ref: **YH09002**

MACKEY EQUESTRIAN WHOLESALE

Mackey Equestrian Wholesale Ltd, Ballinclea Hse, Donard, **County Wicklow**, **IRELAND**.
(T) 045 404620 **(F)** 045 404770
(E) mackey@iol.ie.
Profile Supplies. Ref: **YH09003**

MACKIE & BRECHIN

Mackie & Brechin, 29 Main St, Kirkliston, **Edinburgh (City of)**, EH29 9AE, **SCOTLAND**.
(T) 0131 3333203 **(F)** 0131 3335423.
Contact/s
Vet: Mr R Brechin

Profile Medical Support. Ref: YH09004

MACKIE, HENRI

Mrs Henri Mackie BHSII BHS(SM) RDASI Regd, The Stables, Little Harle, Kirkwhelpington, Newcastle-upon-Tyne, **Tyne and Wear**, NE19 2PD, **ENGLAND**.
(T) 01830 540334 **(F)** 01830 540334
(M) 07885 852003.
Profile Riding School, Stable/Livery, Trainer.
Ref: YH09005

MACKIE, JAMES A

James A Mackie (Agricultural), 3 Braehead, Lornshill Pk, Alloa, **Clackmannanshire**, FK10 2EW, **SCOTLAND**.
(T) 01259 215136 **(F)** 01259 211053.
Profile Supplies. Ref: YH09006

MACKIE, ROSS V

Ross V Mackie DWCF Hons, 1 The Grove, East Keswick, **Yorkshire (West)**, LS17 9EX, **ENGLAND**.
(T) 01937 574763.
Profile Farrier. Ref: YH09007

MACKIE, W J W

Mr W J W Mackie, The Bungalow, Barton Blount, Church Broughton, **Derbyshire**, DE65 5AN, **ENGLAND**.
(T) 01283 585604
(M) 07721 938070.
Profile Trainer. Ref: YH09008

MACKINNON, A

A MacKinnon, Achnalarig, Glencruitten, Oban, **Argyll and Bute**, PA34 4QA, **SCOTLAND**.
(T) 01631 562745.
Contact/s
Owner: Miss A MacKinnon Ref: YH09009

MACLEAN, TINA

Tina Maclean, Hall Farm, Beeby Rd, Scraptoft, **Leicestershire**, LE7 9SJ, **ENGLAND**.
(T) 0116 2416767.
Profile Trainer. Ref: YH09010

MACLEOD/ALLAN/RUSHTON-TAYLOR

MacLeod, Allan & Rushton-Taylor, Ballantraie, La Rue Mahier, St Mary, **Jersey**, JE3 3DT, **ENGLAND**.
(T) 01534 482202 **(F)** 01534 481339.
Profile Medical Support. Ref: YH09011

MACMILLAN, J A

J A MacMillan, Hyde Farm, Hyde Lane, Nash Mills, Hemel Hempstead, **Hertfordshire**, HP3 8SA, **ENGLAND**.
(T) 01923 262375 **(F)** 01923 262375.
Contact/s
Owner: Mr J MacMillan Ref: YH09012

MACMILLAN, WILLIAM G

Mr William G MacMillan, Cumrue, Lockerbie, **Dumfries and Galloway**, DG11 1TL, **SCOTLAND**.
(T) 01387 810335.
Profile Breeder. Ref: YH09013

MACNAUGHTON, DONALD

Donald MacNaughton RSS, 10 Baberton Mains Gardens, Edinburgh, **Edinburgh (City of)**, EH14 3BX, **SCOTLAND**.
(T) 0131 4421461.
Profile Farrier. Ref: YH09014

MACPHERSON T J & SON

MacPherson T J & Son, 4 Barnes St, Barrhead, Glasgow, **Glasgow (City of)**, G78 1QN, **SCOTLAND**.
(T) 0141 8811701.
Profile Blacksmith. Ref: YH09015

MACPHERSON, JOHN

Mr John MacPherson, 8 Darward Pl, Montrose, **Angus**, DD10 8RH, **SCOTLAND**.
(T) 01674 671532 **(F)** 01674 671532
(E) john.macpherson@talk21.com.
Profile Farrier.
Mobile farrier Ref: YH09016

MACTAGGART, A B

Mr A B MacTaggart, Greendale, Hawick, **Scottish Borders**, TD9 7NT, **SCOTLAND**.
(T) 01450 372086 **(F)** 01450 372086
(M) 07712 069245.
Profile Breeder, Trainer. Ref: YH09017

MAD HATTER

Mad Hatter (The), Criftins Hse, 3 Thorpe Rd, Chacombe, Banbury, **Oxfordshire**, OX17 2JW, **ENGLAND**.
(T) 01295 711484 **(F)** 01295 711484.
Contact/s
Manager: Mr P Williams
Profile Saddlery Retailer. Ref: YH09018

MADDEN, NIALL

Niall Madden, 44 Lakelands, Naas, **County Kildare**, **IRELAND**.
(T) 045 879432.
Profile Supplies. Ref: YH09019

MADDOX

Maddox Ltd, Gooseberry Farm, Whinney Hill, Elton, **County Durham**, TS21 1PG, **ENGLAND**.
(T) 01642 588519.
Profile Supplies. Ref: YH09020

MADDRELL, BUXTON & TAYLOR

Maddrell, Buxton & Taylor, Rear of 79 St Helens Rd, Leigh, **Lancashire**, WN7 4HA, **ENGLAND**.
(T) 01942 673777 **(F)** 01942 262691.
Contact/s
Vet: Mr C Northcott
Profile Medical Support. Ref: YH09021

MADDYBENNY RIDING CTRE

Maddybenny Riding Centre, Atlantic Rd, Coleraine, **County Londonderry**, BT52 2PT, **NORTHERN IRELAND**.
(T) 028 70823394
(E) accommodation@maddybenny22.freeserve.co.uk
(W) www.maddybenny.freeserve.co.uk
Affiliated Bodies BHS, DEFRA.
Contact/s
Chief Instructor: Mr P White **(Q)** BHSAI
Profile Horse/Rider Accom, Riding School.
Lessons and hacking cost £10.00 per hour. Liveries and grazing, details on request. Clipping services also available. **No.Staff:** 6 **Yr. Est:** 1976
C.Size: 120 Acres
Opening Times
Sp: Open Mon - Sun 10:00. Closed Mon - Sun 17:30.
Su: Open Mon - Sun 10:00. Closed Mon - Sun 17:30.
Au: Open Mon - Sun 10:00. Closed Mon - Sun 17:30.
Wn: Open Mon - Sun 10:00. Closed Mon - Sun 17:30.
In the evenings telephone 028 7082 3603
Ref: YH09022

MADGWICK, M J

Mr M J Madgwick, Forest Farm, Forest Rd, Denmead, **Hampshire**, PO7 6UA, **ENGLAND**.
(T) 023 92258313.
Profile Trainer. Ref: YH09023

MADGWICK, PHILIP

Philip Madgwick, Vinnells Farm, Froxfield, Petersfield, **Hampshire**, GU32 1DT, **ENGLAND**.
(T) 01730 268949.
Profile Breeder. Ref: YH09024

MADRESFIELD RIDING CTRE

Madresfield Riding Centre, Hayswood Farm, Madresfield Village, Madresfield, Malvern, **Worcestershire**, WR13 5AA, **ENGLAND**.
(T) 01684 567333 **(F)** 01684 567333.
Contact/s
Owner: Mr R Owen Ref: YH09025

MADWAR, ALLAN

Allan Madwar, 41 Oak Drive, Beck Row, Bury St Edmunds, **Suffolk**, IP28 8UA, **ENGLAND**.
(T) 07860 848488.
Profile Farrier. Ref: YH09026

MAELOR RIDING CLUB

Maelor Riding Club, Oakfields Hse, Ellesmere Rd, Bronington, Whitchurch, **Shropshire**, SY13 3HW, **ENGLAND**.
(T) 01948 73287.
Profile Club/Association, Riding Club. Ref: YH09027

MAER LANE RIDING STABLES

Maer Lane Riding Stables, Maer Lane, Bude, **Cornwall**, EX23 9EE, **ENGLAND**.
(T) 01288 354141.
Contact/s
Owner: Mrs A Prideaux
Profile Riding School. Ref: YH09028

MAER STABLES

Maer Stables, Bude, **Cornwall**, EX23 9EG, **ENGLAND**.
(T) 01288 354141.
Profile Equestrian Centre. Ref: YH09029

MAESGLAS MOUNTAIN RIDERS

Maesglas Mountain Riders, Penpomren, Tregaron, **Ceredigion**, SY25 6NG, **WALES**.
(T) 01974 298584.
Profile Equestrian Centre. Ref: YH09030

MAESGWYNNE RIDING STABLES

Maesgwynne Riding Stables, Maesgwynne Farm, Fishguard, **Pembrokeshire**, SA65 9PR, **WALES**.
(T) 01348 872659 **(F)** 01348 872659.
Contact/s
Owner: Mr D Llewllyn
Profile Riding School. Ref: YH09031

MAESMYNACH STUD

Maesmynach Stud, Maesmynach, Cribyn, Lampeter, **Ceredigion**, SA48 7LZ, **WALES**.
(T) 01570 470670
(E) info@maesmynachstud.co.uk
(W) www.maesmynachstud.co.uk.
Profile Stud Farm. Ref: YH09032

MAGGS, P

P Maggs, 10 Tormarton Rd, Marshfield, Chippenham, **Wiltshire**, SN14 8NN, **ENGLAND**.
(T) 01225 892143.
Profile Farrier. Ref: YH09033

MAGHERADARTIN SHETLAND STUD

Magheradartin Shetland Stud Farm, Magheradartin Hse, 57 Magheradartin Rd, Hillsborough, **County Down**, BT26 6LY, **NORTHERN IRELAND**.
(T) 028 92683048
Affiliated Bodies NISPG, SPSBS.
Contact/s
Owner: Catherine Lyttle
(E) cathye_57@yahoo.com
Profile Breeder.
Opening Times
Telephone for further information Ref: YH09034

MAGNA CARTA POLO

Magna Carta Polo Ltd, London Rd, Sunningdale, Ascot, **Berkshire**, SL5 9RY, **ENGLAND**.
(T) 01344 876744. Ref: YH09035

MAHER-BURNS, MATTHEW J

Matthew J Maher-Burns DWCF, 9 Drummond Way, Macclesfield, **Cheshire**, SK10 4XJ, **ENGLAND**.
(T) 01625 827115.
Profile Farrier. Ref: YH09036

MAIDSTONE & DISTRICT

Maidstone & District Riding Club, Anchor Farm, Rochester Rd, Aylesford, **Kent**, ME20 7EA, **ENGLAND**.
(T) 01732 849465.
Contact/s
Secretary: Miss C Rillie
Profile Club/Association, Riding Club. Ref: YH09037

MAIN RING ROSETTES

Main Ring Rosettes, 6 Homestead Rd, Torquay, **Devon**, TQ1 4JL, **ENGLAND**.
(T) 01803 328081.
Contact/s
Owner: Mrs S Greenland
Profile Supplies. Ref: YH09038

MAINS DISTRIBUTION SVS

Mains Distribution Services, Trerose Cottage, Kirdford, **Sussex (West)**, RH14 0LU, **ENGLAND**.
(T) 01403 820600 **(F)** 01403 820641.
Profile Club/Association. Ref: YH09039

MAINS OF BADENSCOTH

Mains of Badenscoth, Badenscoth Stud, Rothienorman, Inverurie, **Aberdeenshire**, AB51 8XR, **SCOTLAND**.
(T) 01651 821223.
Profile Breeder. Ref: YH09040

MAISON DIEU VETNRY CTRE

Maison Dieu Veterinary Centre, 76-77 Maison Dieu Rd, Dover, **Kent**, CT16 1RE, **ENGLAND**.
(T) 01304 201617 **(F)** 01304 210660.
Profile Medical Support. Ref: YH09041

MALACHY, RYAN

Ryan Malachy, Mountain View Clonpet, Tipperary, **County Tipperary**, **IRELAND**.
(T) 062 51875.
Profile Supplies. Ref: YH09042

MALAN GODDARD

Ms Malan Goddard Saddler, Ermine Farm, Bridge St, Whaddon, **Hertfordshire**, SG8 5SP, **ENGLAND**.
(T) 01223 207358 **(F)** 01223 207358.
Contact/s
Saddler: Ms M Goddard

Profile Saddlery Retailer. Ref: YH09043

MALCOLM DUNNING SADDLERY

Malcolm Dunning Saddlery Ltd, The Paddocks, Catherington Lane, Waterlooville, **Hampshire**, PO8 0TD, **ENGLAND**.
(T) 023 92592295 **(F)** 023 92593889.
Contact/s
Owner: Mr M Dunning
Profile Saddlery Retailer. Ref: YH09044

MALCOLM INNES GALLERY

Malcolm Innes Gallery (Edinburgh), 4 Dundas St, Edinburgh, **Edinburgh (City of)**, EH3 6HZ, **SCOTLAND**.
(T) 0131 5589544/5 **(F)** 0131 5589525.
Profile Art Gallery. Ref: YH09045

MALDON TRAILER SVS

Maldon Trailer Services Ltd, New Rd, Rainham, **Essex**, RM13 9PN, **ENGLAND**.
(T) 01708 522391.
Profile Transport/Horse Boxes. Ref: YH09046

MALE, TREVOR

Trevor Male, 2 Lands End Rd, St. Buryan, Penzance, **Cornwall**, TR19 6ES, **ENGLAND**.
(T) 01736 810737.
Profile Farrier. Ref: YH09047

MALEARD, A

Mrs A Maleard, Mon Repos, Grosnez, St Owen, **Jersey**, JE3 2AD, **ENGLAND**.
(T) 01534 483773 **(F)** 01534 483087
(M) 07797 738128.
Profile Trainer. Ref: YH09048

MALIN, MARK R W

Mark R W Malin RSS, Waydown, Timerscombe, Minehead, **Somerset**, TA24 7UE, **ENGLAND**.
(T) 01643 707144.
Profile Farrier. Ref: YH09049

MALLARD HSE

Mallard House Riding Centre, Finkle St, Wortley, Sheffield, **Yorkshire (South)**, S35 7DH, **ENGLAND**.
(T) 0114 2888031.
Contact/s
Owner: Mrs J Hillis
Profile Riding School, Stable/Livery.
Offer full and working livery & three day activities. 'Own a pony' for children during summer holidays. Tiny tots 30 minute lessons. All day picnic rides on Bank Holidays. No.Staff: 4 Yr. Est: 1989
Opening Times
Sp: Open Tues - Sun 09:30. Closed Tues - Fri 19:30, Sat, Sun 16:30.
Su: Open Tues - Sun 09:30. Closed Tues - Fri 19:30, Sat, Sun 16:30.
Au: Open Tues - Sun 09:30. Closed Tues - Fri 19:30, Sat, Sun 16:30.
Wn: Open Tues - Sun 09:30. Closed Tues - Fri 19:30, Sat, Sun 16:30.
Closed Mondays Ref: YH09050

MALLENDER BROS

Mallender Bros, Bryndale, Whitwell Common, Worksop, **Nottinghamshire**, S80 3EH, **ENGLAND**.
(T) 01909 720732.
Contact/s
General Manager: Mr D Mallender **(Q)** AWCF
Profile Blacksmith, Breeder, Farrier, Supplies.
Opening Times
Sp: Open 07:30. Closed 18:00.
Su: Open 07:30. Closed 18:00.
Au: Open 07:30. Closed 18:00.
Wn: Open 07:30. Closed 18:00. Ref: YH09051

MALLOW RACE CO

Mallow Race Co (1939) Ltd, Racecourse, Mallow, **County Cork**, **IRELAND**.
(T) 022 21338.
Profile Supplies. Ref: YH09052

MALMESBURY TRAILERS

Malmesbury Trailers, Westgate, Corston, Malmesbury, **Wiltshire**, SN16 0HD, **ENGLAND**.
(T) 01666 822851.
Profile Transport/Horse Boxes. Ref: YH09053

MALONE, B

B Malone, 23 Shepherds Rd, Winchester, **Hampshire**, SO23 0NR, **ENGLAND**.
(T) 01962 862662.
Profile Farrier. Ref: YH09054

MALT KILN TRAILERS

Malt Kiln Trailers, Stanley St, Sowerby Bridge, **Yorkshire (West)**, HX6 2AH, **ENGLAND**.
(T) 01422 833461 **(F)** 01422 835319.
Contact/s
Partner: Mr P Whitworth
Profile Transport/Horse Boxes. Ref: YH09055

MALTBY-SMITH, RICHARD P

Richard P Maltby-Smith DWCF, The Farrier, 11 Queensway, Kirkby In Ashfield, **Nottinghamshire**, NG17 7GG, **ENGLAND**.
(T) 01623 753917.
Profile Farrier. Ref: YH09056

MALTHOUSE ARABIANS

Malthouse Arabians, Malthouse Farm, Streat, Hassocks, **Sussex (West)**, BN6 8SA, **ENGLAND**.
(T) 01273 890356.
Profile Breeder. Ref: YH09057

MALTHOUSE EQUESTRIAN CTRE

Malthouse Equestrian Centre, Bushton, Swindon, **Wiltshire**, SN4 7PX, **ENGLAND**.
(T) 01793 731342.
Contact/s
Owner: Mrs R Greenway
Profile Arena, Equestrian Centre, Riding School, Stable/Livery, Trainer. Holistic Teacher.
Offer show production and ring craft lessons, also provide a video service of horse and rider in action.
Ref: YH09058

MALTHOUSE TRAINING CTRE

Malthouse Training Centre, Malthouse Stud, Hanney Rd, Steventon, Abingdon, **Oxfordshire**, OX13 6AP, **ENGLAND**.
(T) 01235 831488.
Profile Stable/Livery. Ref: YH09059

MALTON RACING ASS

Malton Racing Association, 4 Whitewall, Norton, Malton, **Yorkshire (North)**, YO17 9EH, **ENGLAND**.
(T) 01653 698725 **(F)** 01653 698725.
Contact/s
Secretary: Mrs R Carter
Profile Club/Association. Ref: YH09060

MALYONS STUD

Malyons Stud, Malyons Farm, Malyons Lane, Hullbridge, **Essex**, SS5 6EN, **ENGLAND**.
(T) 01702 230274.
Profile Breeder. Ref: YH09061

MANACRAFT LEATHER

Manacraft Leather Co, 88 Bruntsfield Pl, Burntsfield, Edinburgh, **Edinburgh (City of)**, EH10 4HG, **SCOTLAND**.
(T) 0131 2281055 **(F)** 0131 2292415.
Profile Saddlery Retailer. Ref: YH09062

MANAGRAKEM, N W F

N W F Managrakem, Unit 6 Spring Valley Ind Est, Braddan, Douglas, **Isle of Man**, IM2 2QR, **ENGLAND**.
(T) 01624 673884 **(F)** 01624 661475.
Profile Supplies. Ref: YH09063

MANAR STUD & RIDING CTRE

Manar Stud & Riding Centre, Manar Stud, Cushnie Hse, Cushnie, Alford, **Aberdeenshire**, AB33 8LA, **SCOTLAND**.
(T) 01975 581321.
Profile Breeder, Equestrian Centre, Trainer.
Ref: YH09064

MANCHESTER EQUESTRIAN CTRE

Manchester Equestrian Centre (The), Torbay Rd, Urmston, Manchester, **Manchester (Greater)**, M41 9LH, **ENGLAND**.
(T) 0161 7484374.
Contact/s
Owner: Mr W Tough
Profile Equestrian Centre. Ref: YH09065

MANCHESTER MANIACS

Manchester Maniacs Horseball Club, C/O New Cross Farm, Torbay Rd, Manchester, **Manchester (Greater)**, M41 9WO, **ENGLAND**.
(T) 0161 7476820.
Contact/s
Partner: Mr B Kilcourse
Profile Club/Association. Ref: YH09066

MANCHESTER PLASTICS

Manchester Plastics Ltd, Units 3-6, Chillington Toolworks, Hickman Ave, Wolverhampton, **Midlands (West)**, WV1 2BT, **ENGLAND**.
(T) 01902 451400 **(F)** 01902 451255.
Profile Track/Course. Ref: YH09067

MANCHESTER TOWBAR/TRAILER

Manchester Towbar & Trailer Centre Ltd, Bond St Ind Est, Mancunian Way, Manchester, **Manchester (Greater)**, M12 6HW, **ENGLAND**.
(T) 0161 2735816 **(F)** 0161 2736678.
Profile Transport/Horse Boxes. Ref: YH09068

MANCHESTER UNITED RACING CLUB

Manchester United Racing Club, Main St, Chaddleworth, Newbury, **Berkshire**, RG20 7EH, **ENGLAND**.
(T) 01488 638098.
Profile Racing Club. Ref: YH09069

MANCHIP, R & M

R & M Manchip, Garreg Goch, Llanharry, **Rhondda Cynon Taff**, **WALES**.
(T) 01443 225127.
Profile Breeder. Ref: YH09070

MANDI'S LIVERIES

Mandi's Liveries, Teeton Lodge, Teeton, Northampton, **Northamptonshire**, NN6 8LP, **ENGLAND**.
(T) 01604 505400 **(F)** 01604 505777
Affiliated Bodies BHS.
Contact/s
Owner: Ms M Gale
Profile Stable/Livery.
Livery prices available on request. Yr. Est: 1996
C.Size: 10 Acres
Opening Times
Sp: Open Mon - Sun 08:00. Closed Mon - Sun 20:00.
Su: Open Mon - Sun 08:00. Closed Mon - Sun 20:00.
Au: Open Mon - Sun 08:00. Closed Mon - Sun 20:00.
Wn: Open Mon - Sun 08:00. Closed Mon - Sun 20:00. Ref: YH09071

MANE BRIDLES

Mane Bridles, Unit 1A Deeleys Trading Est, Leamore Lane, Walsall, **Midlands (West)**, WS2 7BY, **ENGLAND**.
(T) 01922 492888 **(F)** 01922 492888.
Contact/s
Owner: Mr A Milay
Profile Saddlery Retailer. Ref: YH09072

MANE LINE

Mane Line Inc, Roundabouts, The Ridings, Shotover, Oxford, **Oxfordshire**, OX3 8TB, **ENGLAND**.
(T) 07000 765626 **(F)** 01865 308722
(E) tompratt@maneline.co.uk.
Profile Supplies. Ref: YH09073

MANE TO TAIL SUPPLIES

Mane To Tail Supplies, Unit 14 Broadlands, Abbotts Yard, Blean, Canterbury, **Kent**, CT2 9JQ, **ENGLAND**.
(T) 01227 787993 **(F)** 01227 787993
(M) 07860 227735.
Profile Supplies. Ref: YH09074

MANELINE, B G I

B G I Maneline Ltd, Bush Hse, Spaxton, Bridgwater, **Somerset**, TA5 1AH, **ENGLAND**.
(T) 01278 671105 **(F)** 01278 671105
(W) www.bgi-maneline.co.uk.
Contact/s
Owner: Miss V Hawker
(E) venetia@bgi-maneline.co.uk
Profile Supplies.
Mainly a wholesalers but can supply direct. Grooming accessories and sundries
Opening Times
Sp: Open Mon - Sat 09:00. Closed Mon - Sat 17:30.
Su: Open Mon - Sat 09:00. Closed Mon - Sat 17:30.
Au: Open Mon - Sat 09:00. Closed Mon - Sat 17:30.
Wn: Open Mon - Sat 09:00. Closed Mon - Sat 17:30.
Ref: YH09075

MANGAN & WEBB

Mangan & Webb Saddlery, Digbeth St, Stow On The Wold, Cheltenham, **Gloucestershire**, GL54 1BN, **ENGLAND**.
(T) 01451 831245 **(F)** 01451 831245.
Contact/s
Owner: Ms B Webb
Profile Saddlery Retailer.
Racing, Eventing & Dressage Specialists. Can carry out repairs on site. No.Staff: 5 Yr. Est: 1991
Opening Times
Sp: Open Mon - Sat 09:00. Closed Mon - Sat 17:30.
Su: Open Mon - Sat 09:00. Closed Mon - Sat 17:30.
Au: Open Mon - Sat 09:00. Closed Mon - Sat 17:30.
Wn: Open Mon - Sat 09:00. Closed Mon - Sat 17:30.
Closed Sundays Ref: YH09076

MANGER, DAVID A

David A Manger BII, 23 Linton Rise, Byng Rd, Catterick Garrison, **Yorkshire (North)**, DL9 4DN, **ENGLAND**.
(T) 01748 832610.
Profile Farrier. **Ref: YH09077**

MANHIRE

Manhire, Coach Hse Cottage, Little Trewince, Stithians, Truro, **Cornwall**, TR3 7BZ, **ENGLAND**.
(T) 01209 861235.
Profile Horse Drawn Vehicles. **Ref: YH09078**

MANIFOLD, MALCOLM T

Malcolm T Manifold AFCL, The Bunglow, 30A High St, Godley, Hyde, **Cheshire**, SK14 2PU, **ENGLAND**.
(T) 0161 3660842.
Profile Farrier. **Ref: YH09079**

MANLEY, JENNY

Jenny Manley PR, 28 Severn Side South, Bewdley, **Worcestershire**, DY12 2DX, **ENGLAND**.
(T) 01299 401161 **(F)** 01299 401161. **Ref: YH09080**

MANLEY, JOHN

John Manley, 20 Gt Wm O'Brien St, Blackpool, **County Cork**, **IRELAND**.
(T) 021 4508394.
Profile Supplies. **Ref: YH09081**

MANN, JOHN ANTHONY

John Anthony Mann RSS, Long Meadow Farm, Coombe Rd, Ringmore, Shaldon, Teignmouth, **Devon**, TQ14 0EX, **ENGLAND**.
(T) 01626 872732.
Profile Farrier. **Ref: YH09082**

MANN, TIMOTHY A

Timothy A Mann RSS, 45 The Plat, Edenbridge, **Kent**, TN8 5BL, **ENGLAND**.
(T) 01732 867110.
Profile Farrier. **Ref: YH09083**

MANNDELL'S GALLERY

Manndell's Gallery, Elm Hill, Norwich, **Norfolk**, NR3 1HN, **ENGLAND**.
(T) 01603 626892 **(F)** 01630 767271.
Profile Art Gallery. **Ref: YH09084**

MANNERS, ANDREW M

Andrew M Manners DWCF, 51 Rippleside Rd, Clevedon, **Somerset (North)**, BS21 7JX, **ENGLAND**.
(T) 07774 156398.
Profile Farrier. **Ref: YH09085**

MANNERS, JOHN

Mr John Manners, Common Farm, Highworth, Swindon, **Wiltshire**, SN6 7PP, **ENGLAND**.
(T) 01793 762232 **(F)** 01793 861781.
Profile Trainer. **Ref: YH09086**

MANNING, L

Miss L Manning, Blofield Hall, Blofield, Norwich, **Norfolk**, NR13 4DD, **ENGLAND**.
(T) 01603 716428.
Profile Breeder. **Ref: YH09087**

MANNING, PAT

Miss Pat Manning F.B.H.S., Kingsway Hse, Greensward Lane, Arborfield, Reading, **Berkshire**, RG2 9JN, **ENGLAND**.
(T) 0118 9760386.
Profile Trainer. **Ref: YH09088**

MANNINGS LIVERIES

Mannings Liveries, Mannings Farm, Edburton, Henfield, **Sussex (West)**, BN5 9LJ, **ENGLAND**.
(T) 01903 814428.
Profile Stable/Livery, Trainer. **Ref: YH09089**

MANNION, W

Mannion W, Glenamaddy, **County Roscommon**, **IRELAND**.
(T) 090 759004.
Profile Supplies. **Ref: YH09090**

MANNIX STUD

Mannix Stud Equestrian Centre and Childrens Riding Holidays, Nightingale Farm, Whiteacre Lane, Waltham, Canterbury, **Kent**, CT4 5SR, **ENGLAND**.
(T) 01227 700349 **(F)** 01227 700349
(E) mannixstud@euphony.net
(W) www.mannixstud.com
Affiliated Bodies ABRS, BHS.
Contact/s
Owner: Mr T Williams
Profile Equestrian Centre, Holidays, Riding Club, Riding School, Stable/Livery.
Childrens residential riding holiday with a variety of other games & sports available, including trampolining, volleyball, rounders, badminton, a games room, tuck shop and gift shop.
No.Staff: 5 Yr. Est: 1989 C.Size: 50 Acres
Ref: YH09091

MANNOG

Mannog Appaloosas, Garreg Ganol, Whitford, Holywell, **Flintshire**, CH8 8SD, **WALES**.
(T) 01745 561486.
Contact/s
Owner: Mrs A Chamberlain
(E) r.chamberlain@telinco.co.uk
Profile Breeder. No.Staff: 1 Yr. Est: 1997
C.Size: 11 Acres
Opening Times
Telephone for an appointment **Ref: YH09092**

MANOR COURT VETNRY CTRE

Manor Court Veterinary Centre, Brookdale Hse, High St, Tattenhall, **Cheshire**, CH3 9PX, **ENGLAND**.
(T) 01829 770207 **(F)** 01829 741054.
Profile Medical Support. **Ref: YH09093**

MANOR COURT VETNRY CTRE

Manor Court Veterinary Centre, Church St, Tarvin, Chester, **Cheshire**, CH3 8EB, **ENGLAND**.
(T) 01829 740216 **(F)** 01829 741054.
Profile Medical Support. **Ref: YH09094**

MANOR FARM

Manor Farm, Manor Farm, Chilworth Old Village, Chilworth, Southampton, **Hampshire**, SO16 7JP, **ENGLAND**.
(T) 023 80767800.
Contact/s
Owner: Mr W Hay
Profile Stable/Livery.
DIY livery available - grazing and stabling provided.
Yr. Est: 1984
Opening Times
Sp: Open Mon - Sun 10:00. Closed Mon - Sun 17:00.
Su: Open Mon - Sun 10:00. Closed Mon - Sun 17:00.
Au: Open Mon - Sun 10:00. Closed Mon - Sun 17:00.
Wn: Open Mon - Sun 10:00. Closed Mon - Sun 17:00. **Ref: YH09095**

MANOR FARM

Manor Farm, Hampton Poyle, Oxford, **Oxfordshire**, OX5 2QF, **ENGLAND**.
(T) 01865 376812.
Profile Stable/Livery. **Ref: YH09096**

MANOR FARM

Manor Farm, Newton-on-Rawcliffe, Pickering, **Yorkshire (North)**, YO18 8QA, **ENGLAND**.
(T) 01751 472601.
Contact/s
Owner: Lady E Kirk
Profile Stable/Livery. **Ref: YH09097**

MANOR FARM FEEDS

Manor Farm Feeds (North Ockendon), Manor Farm, Ockendon Rd, North Ockendon, Upminster, **Essex**, RM14 2TZ, **ENGLAND**.
(T) 01708 224666 **(F)** 01708 640223.
Profile Supplies. **Ref: YH09098**

MANOR FARM FEEDS

Manor Farm Feeds (Owston), Owston, Oakham, Rutland, **Rutland**, LE15 8DH, **ENGLAND**.
(T) 01664 454256.
Profile Supplies. **Ref: YH09099**

MANOR FARM LIVERY

Manor Farm Livery, The Farmhouse, Manor Farm, Hartshorne, Swadlincote, **Derbyshire**, DE11 7ER, **ENGLAND**.
(T) 01283 215769.
Profile Stable/Livery. **Ref: YH09100**

MANOR FARM LIVERY STABLES

Manor Farm Livery Stables, Petersham Rd, Richmond, **Surrey**, TW10 7AH, **ENGLAND**.
(T) 020 89408511.
Profile Stable/Livery. **Ref: YH09101**

MANOR FARM LIVERY YARD

Manor Farm Livery Yard, Manor Farm, Moor Lane, Gotham, **Nottinghamshire**, NG11 0ZH, **ENGLAND**.
(T) 0115 9830051.
Profile Stable/Livery. **Ref: YH09102**

MANOR FARM RACING STABLES

Manor Farm Racing Stables, Kingston Lisle, Wantage, **Oxfordshire**, OX12 9QL, **ENGLAND**.
(T) 01367 820881 **(F)** 01367 820883
(M) 07831 873531.
Profile Trainer. **Ref: YH09103**

MANOR FARM RIDING CTRE/LIVERY

Manor Farm Riding Centre & Livery Yard, Lydford, Okehampton, **Devon**, EX20 4BL, **ENGLAND**.
(T) 01822 820526.
Contact/s
Owner: Mr J North
Profile Equestrian Centre, Stable/Livery.
Ref: YH09104

MANOR FARM RIDING SCHOOL

Manor Farm Riding School, Manor Farm, Saddington, Leicester, **Leicestershire**, LE8 0QY, **ENGLAND**.
(T) 0116 2403780.
Profile Riding School. **Ref: YH09105**

MANOR FARM RIDING SCHOOL

Manor Farm Riding School, Easton Maudit, Wellingborough, **Northamptonshire**, NN9 7NR, **ENGLAND**.
(T) 01933 663750
(M) 07970 068535
(E) info@manorfarmriding.fsnet.co.uk
(W) www.manorfarmriding.fsnet.co.uk
Affiliated Bodies ABRS, Pony Club UK.
Contact/s
Owner: Mr T Clipstone
Profile Equestrian Centre, Riding Club, Riding School, Transport/Horse Boxes.
Trailer hire available, self tow. No.Staff: 2
Yr. Est: 1968 C.Size: 17 Acres **Ref: YH09106**

MANOR FARM RIDING SCHOOL

Manor Farm Riding School, 2 St Johns Rd, Stourport-on-Severn, **Worcestershire**, DY13 9DS, **ENGLAND**.
(T) 01299 822403.
Profile Riding School, Trainer. **Ref: YH09107**

MANOR FARM STUD

Manor Farm Stud (Royston), Manor Farm, Thriplow, Royston, **Hertfordshire**, SG8 7RE, **ENGLAND**.
(T) 01763 82205.
Profile Breeder. **Ref: YH09108**

MANOR GRANGE STUD SCHOOL

Manor Grange Stud School of Equitation, Cobcroft Lane, Cridling Stubbs, Knottingley, Wakefield, **Yorkshire (West)**, WF11 0AZ, **ENGLAND**.
(T) 01977 679249.
Profile Riding School, Stable/Livery, Trainer.
Ref: YH09109

MANOR HOUSE FARM STUD

Manor House Farm Stud, Lower Icknield Way, Marsworth, Tring, **Hertfordshire**, HP23 4LN, **ENGLAND**.
(T) 01296 668461 **(F)** 01296 668461.
Contact/s
Owner: Mrs J Rawding
Profile Breeder, Supplies. **Ref: YH09110**

MANOR HOUSE STUD

Manor House Stud, Queniborough, **Leicestershire**, LE7 8DB, **ENGLAND**.
(T) 0116 2605703.
Profile Stable/Livery. **Ref: YH09111**

MANOR HOUSE STUD

Manor House Stud, Manor Hse, Middleham, Leyburn, **Yorkshire (North)**, DL8 4QL, **ENGLAND**.
(T) 01969 623291.
Profile Breeder. **Ref: YH09112**

MANOR HSE FARM

Manor House Farm, Sinnington, Pickering, **Yorkshire (North)**, YO62 6SN, **ENGLAND**.
(T) 01751 433296 **(F)** 01751 433296.
Contact/s
Owner: Mr C Wilson **(Q)** BHSAI
(E) charles.wilson@finningtonmanor.ffnet.co.uk
Profile Horse/Rider Accom, Riding School.
No.Staff: 2 Yr. Est: 1992 C.Size: 280 Acres
Opening Times
Sp: Open Mon - Sun 09:00. Closed Mon - Sun 21:00.
Su: Open Mon - Sun 09:00. Closed Mon - Sun 21:00.
Au: Open Mon - Sun 09:00. Closed Mon - Sun 21:00.

Wn: Open Mon - Sun 09:00. Closed Mon - Sun 21:00. Ref: YH09113

MANOR LIVERY

Manor Livery, Manor Rd, Tatsfield, Westerham, **Kent**, TN16 2ND, **ENGLAND**.
(T) 01959 577496.
Contact/s
Owner: Mrs A Miller
Profile Stable/Livery. Ref: YH09114

MANOR PARK EQUESTRIAN CTRE

Manor Park Equestrian Centre, Wychnor Manor, Wychnor Pk, Wychnor, Burton-on-Trent, **Staffordshire**, DE13 8BU, **ENGLAND**.
(T) 01283 791791 **(F)** 01283 791791.
Contact/s
Owner: Ms S Degcille Ref: YH09115

MANOR PK LIVERY STABLES

Manor Park Livery Stables, Lyne Lane, Lyne, Chertsey, **Surrey**, KT16 0AW, **ENGLAND**.
(T) 01932 567460.
Profile Stable/Livery. Ref: YH09116

MANOR SADDLERY

Manor Saddlery, Whipley Manor Farm, Palmers Cross, Bramley, Guildford, **Surrey**, GU5 0LL, **ENGLAND**.
(T) 01483 271416 **(F)** 01483 271416
Affiliated Bodies SMS.
Contact/s
Owner: Mr B Roberts
Profile Saddlery Retailer. Yr. Est: 1984
Opening Times
Sp: Open 09:30. Closed 17:00.
Su: Open 09:30. Closed 17:00.
Au: Open 09:30. Closed 17:00.
Wn: Open 09:30. Closed 17:00.
Wednesday 09:30 - 13:00: Closed Sundays.
Ref: YH09117

MANOR SADDLES

Manor Saddles (The), Hazel Lane, Walsall, **Midlands (West)**, WS6 6AA, **ENGLAND**.
(T) 01922 415215 **(F)** 01922 415215.
Contact/s
Owner: Mr N Somerfield
Profile Saddlery Retailer. Ref: YH09118

MANOR STABLES CRAFT WORKSHOPS

Manor Stables Craft Workshops, Fulbeck, Grantham, **Lincolnshire**, NG32 7JN, **ENGLAND**.
(T) 01400 273711.
Contact/s
Saddler: Mark Bushell
Profile Saddlery Retailer. Ref: YH09119

MANOR TREKKING CTRE

Manor Trekking Centre, Kirkton Manor, Peebles, **Scottish Borders**, EH45 9JN, **SCOTLAND**.
(T) 01721 740250.
Contact/s
Owner: Miss S Mackintosh
Profile Equestrian Centre. Ref: YH09120

MANSBRIDGE, G E

G E Mansbridge, Farringdon Cottage, Lane End, Marchwood, **Hampshire**, SO43 4UJ, **ENGLAND**.
(T) 023 80863292.
Profile Farrier. Ref: YH09121

MANSBRIDGE, M G

M G Mansbridge, Station View Farm, Grateley, Andover, **Hampshire**, SP11 7EG, **ENGLAND**.
(T) 01264 889219.
Contact/s
Senior Partner: Mr S Mansbridge Ref: YH09122

MANSFIELD SAND

Mansfield Sand Co Ltd, Sandhurst Ave, Mansfield, **Nottinghamshire**, NG18 4BE, **ENGLAND**.
(T) 01623 22441 **(F)** 01623 420904
(E) mansfield-sand.co.uk.
Contact/s
General Manager: Dr V Armond
Profile Arena. Ref: YH09123

MANSFIELD, T J

T J Mansfield, Walnut Tree Farm, Church Rd, Smeeth, Ashford, **Kent**, TN25 6SA, **ENGLAND**.
(T) 01303 812794 **(F)** 01303 814401.
Contact/s
Owner: Mr T Mansfield
Profile Supplies. Ref: YH09124

MANSION FARM STUD

Mansion Farm Stud, 41 Main St, Coveney, Ely, **Cambridgeshire**, CB6 2DJ, **ENGLAND**.
(T) 01353 775181 **(F)** 01353 777909.
Contact/s
Owner: Mrs R Fyfe
Profile Breeder. Ref: YH09125

MANSTON RIDING CTRE

Manston Riding Centre, 15 Alland Grange Lane, Manston, Ramsgate, **Kent**, CT12 5BX, **ENGLAND**.
(T) 01843 823622.
Contact/s
Owner: Mrs L Evans
Profile Riding School, Saddlery Retailer, Stable/Livery. Ref: YH09126

MANTON LODGE STABLES

Manton Lodge Stables, Manton Lodge Farm, Oakham, Rutland, **Rutland**, LE15 8SS, **ENGLAND**.
(T) 01572 737269.
Profile Stable/Livery, Track/Course, Trainer.
Ref: YH09127

MANX RIDING SUPPLIES

Manx Riding Supplies, Lower Ballacottier, Onchan, **Isle of Man**, IM4 5BQ, **ENGLAND**.
(T) 01624 675687.
Contact/s
Owner: Mr R Kewley
Profile Saddlery Retailer, Stable/Livery.
Yr. Est: 1979
Opening Times
The longest running equestrian business on the Isle of Man Ref: YH09128

MANX TURF AUTHORITY

Manx Turf Authority, Great Meadow Stud, Castletown, **Isle of Man**, IM9 4EB, **ENGLAND**.
(T) 01624 823053 **(F)** 01624 822332.
Contact/s
Owner: Mrs E Riggall Ref: YH09129

MAPLE ASH LIVERY STABLES

Maple Ash Livery Stables, Bussock Hill Hse, Snelsmore Common, Newbury, **Berkshire**, RG14 3BL, **ENGLAND**.
(T) 01635 247094.
Profile Stable/Livery. Ref: YH09130

MAPLE LEAF QUARTER HORSES

Maple Leaf Quarter Horses, The Maples, Rosneath, **Argyll and Bute**, G84 0RF, **SCOTLAND**.
(T) 01436 831228.
Profile Breeder. Ref: YH09131

MAPLE POLLARD RIDING SCHOOL

Maple Pollard Riding School, Dairy Farm, Little Hallingbury, Bishop's Stortford, **Essex**, CM22 7PX, **ENGLAND**.
(T) 01279 724046.
Contact/s
Owner: Mrs M Marsh
Profile Riding School. Ref: YH09132

MAPLE STUD EQUESTRIAN CTRE

Maple Stud Equestrian Centre, Cranleigh Rd, Ewhurst, Cranleigh, **Surrey**, GU6 7SA, **ENGLAND**.
(T) 01483 278384.
Profile Equestrian Centre. Ref: YH09133

MAPLES LIVERY CTRE

Maples Livery Centre, Streethay Farm, Burton Rd, Streethay, Lichfield, **Staffordshire**, WS13 8RJ, **ENGLAND**.
(T) 01543 418417.
Contact/s
Owner: Mrs E McLardy
Profile Stable/Livery. Ref: YH09134

MARABOUT ANIMAL FEEDS

Marabout Animal Feeds, Unit G1, Marabout Trading Est, Dorchester, **Dorset**, DT1 1YA, **ENGLAND**.
(T) 01305 262080.
Profile Supplies. Ref: YH09135

MARBERDAM RIDING CTRE

Marberdam Riding Centre, Maxted St, Stelling Minnis, Canterbury, **Kent**, CT4 6DJ, **ENGLAND**.
(T) 01233 750308.
Contact/s
Owner: Mrs M Neudeck
Profile Riding School. Ref: YH09136

MARBERDUM

Marberdam Riding Centre, Maxted St, Stelling Minnis, Canterbury, **Kent**, CT4 6DJ, **ENGLAND**.
(T) 01233 750308.
Contact/s
Owner: Mrs M Neudeck
Profile Riding School, Stable/Livery.
Offer hacks. Full, part and DIY livery available, prices on request.
Yr. Est: 1966 C.Size: 12 Acres
Opening Times
Sp: Open Mon - Sat 08:00. Closed Mon - Sat 18:00.
Su: Open Mon - Sat 08:00. Closed Mon - Sat 18:00.
Au: Open Mon - Sat 08:00. Closed Mon - Sat 18:00.
Wn: Open Mon - Sat 08:00. Closed Mon - Sat 18:00.
Ref: YH09137

MARCH EQUESTRIAN

March Equestrian, Kinckhams Barns, Bures Rd, West Bergholt, Colchester, **Essex**, CO6 3DN, **ENGLAND**.
(T) 01206 242240 **(F)** 01206 242241.
Profile Saddlery Retailer. Ref: YH09138

MARCH EQUESTRIAN

March Equestrian, Hunnable Ind Est, Toppesfield Rd, Great Yeldham, Halstead, **Essex**, CO9 4HD, **ENGLAND**.
(T) 01787 238111 **(F)** 01787 238111.
Profile Saddlery Retailer. Ref: YH09139

MARCH EQUESTRIAN FRAMLINGHAM

March Equestrian Framlingham, 21 Earl Soham Business Ctre, The Street, Earl Soham, Woodbridge, **Suffolk**, IP13 7SA, **ENGLAND**.
(T) 01728 685660 **(F)** 01728 685660.
Contact/s
Partner: Mrs M Arbon
Profile Saddlery Retailer. Ref: YH09140

MARCH, BILL

Bill March, 77 Shuttlewood Rd, Bolsover, Chesterfield, **Derbyshire**, S44 6NU, **ENGLAND**.
(T) 01246 826226.
Profile Transport/Horse Boxes. Ref: YH09141

MARCH, ERIC

Eric March DWCF, 30 Grange Court Drive, Bexhill-on-Sea, **Sussex (East)**, TN39 4AU, **ENGLAND**.
(T) 01424 221353.
Profile Farrier. Ref: YH09142

MARCHANT, I R

I R Marchant, The Smithy, 10 West St, Abbotsbury, Weymouth, **Dorset**, DT3 4JT, **ENGLAND**.
(T) 01305 871999.
Profile Farrier. Ref: YH09143

MARCO TRAILERS

Marco Trailers, Railway Rd, Newhaven, **Sussex (East)**, BN9 0AY, **ENGLAND**.
(T) 01273 513718 **(F)** 01273 512132.
Contact/s
Owner: Mr J Marsom
Profile Transport/Horse Boxes. Ref: YH09144

MARDEN GRANGE LIVERY STABLES

Marden Grange Livery Stables, Marden Grange, The Street, Marden, Devizes, **Wiltshire**, SN10 3RQ, **ENGLAND**.
(T) 01380 840010.
Contact/s
Partner: Mr R Carpenter
Profile Stable/Livery. Ref: YH09145

MARDEN SADDLERY

Marden Saddlery, 49-50 New Greenmarket, Newcastle-upon-Tyne, **Tyne and Wear**, NE1 7YB, **ENGLAND**.
(T) 0191 2611406.
Contact/s
Manager: Mr M Simons
Profile Saddlery Retailer. Ref: YH09146

MARFLEET, H E

H E Marfleet, Ancaster Hse, Aby, Alford, **Lincolnshire**, LN13 0DP, **ENGLAND**.
(T) 01507 480649.
Contact/s
Owner: Mr H Marfleet
Profile Blacksmith. Ref: YH09147

MARIE STERNER

Marie Sterner - Imagination on Camera, 15 Warwick Hse, Windsor Way, Brook Green, **London (Greater)**, W14 0UQ, **ENGLAND**.
(T) 020 76104926. Ref: YH09148

MARINE MECHANICAL

Marine Mechanical, Templehill, Troon, **Ayrshire (South)**, KA10 6BE, **SCOTLAND**.
(T) 01292 313400.
Profile Transport/Horse Boxes. Ref: YH09149

MARJORAM, IAN S

Ian S Marjoram DWCF, 51 Carter Rd, Drayton, Norwich, **Norfolk**, NR8 6DY, **ENGLAND**.

(T) 07976 320387.
Profile Farrier. Ref: YH09150

MARK DAVIES

Mark Davies Injured Riders Fund, Little Woolpit, Ewhurst, Cranleigh, **Surrey**, GU6 7NP, **ENGLAND**.
(T) 01483 277344/268632/278494 (F) 01483 277899.
Profile Club/Association. Ref: YH09151

MARK FABRICATION

Mark Fabrication, Unit 11 Angus Works, Tannadice St, Dundee, **Angus**, DD3 7PT, **SCOTLAND**.
(T) 01382 835777 (F) 01382 835777.
Contact/s
Owner: Mr M Smith
Profile Blacksmith. Ref: YH09152

MARK JOHNSTON RACING

Mark Johnston Racing Ltd, Kingsley Hse, Kirkgate, Middleham, Leyburn, **Yorkshire (North)**, DL8 4PH, **ENGLAND**.
(T) 01969 622237.
Contact/s
Owner: Mr M Johnston
Profile Trainer. Ref: YH09153

MARK PITMAN RACING

Mark Pitman Racing Ltd, Weathercock Hse, Upper Lambourn, Hungerford, **Berkshire**, RG17 8QT, **ENGLAND**.
(T) 01488 73311 (F) 01488 71065.
Contact/s
Partner: Mrs N Pitman
Profile Trainer. Ref: YH09154

MARK SLINGSBY

Mark Slingsby Equine Dental Services, 2 Essex Farm Cottages, Marsh Gibbon Rd, Marsh Gibbon, Bicester, **Oxfordshire**, OX27 0AO, **ENGLAND**.
(T) 01869 243595
(M) 07977 076920
(W) www.mps-equine-dental-services.co.uk.
Contact/s
Owner: Mark Slingsby
Profile Medical Support.
Equine dentist
Opening Times
By appointment Ref: YH09155

MARK USHER RACING

Mark Usher Racing, Manor Farm, Kingston Lisle, Wantage, **Oxfordshire**, OX12 9QL, **ENGLAND**.
(T) 01367 820881.
Profile Trainer. Ref: YH09156

MARK WESTAWAY & SON

Mark Westaway & Son, Love Lane Farm, Marldon, Paignton, **Devon**, TQ3 1SP, **ENGLAND**.
(T) 01803 527257 (F) 01803 528010
(E) sales@horsehage.co.uk
(W) www.horsehage.co.uk.
Contact/s
Partner: Mark Westaway
Profile Supplies. HorseHage Manufacturer.
Ref: YH09157

MARKET RACING AGENCY

Market Racing Agency (The), Hillside Hse, Wantage, **Oxfordshire**, OX12 0EX, **ENGLAND**.
(T) 01235 868838 (F) 01235 868762
(E) mra@raceweb.com.
Profile Club/Association. Ref: YH09158

MARKET RASEN RACECOURSE

Market Rasen Racecourse Ltd, The Racecourse, Legsby Rd, Market Rasen, **Lincolnshire**, LN8 3EA, **ENGLAND**.
(T) 01673 843434 (F) 01673 844532
(E) marketrasen@rht.net.
Contact/s
Clerk of Course: Major C Moore
Profile Track/Course. Ref: YH09159

MARKETING & DEVELOPMENT SVS

Marketing & Development Services, 63 Bewdley Rd North, Stourport-on-Severn, **Worcestershire**, DY13 8PT, **ENGLAND**.
(T) 01299 823452 (F) 01299 823452.
Profile Medical Support. Ref: YH09160

MARKFIELD EQUESTRIAN

Markfield Equestrian, Stanton Lane Farm, Stanton Lane, Stanton Under Bardon, Markfield, **Leicestershire**, LE67 9TT, **ENGLAND**.
(T) 01530 242373 (F) 01530 242373.
Contact/s
Partner: Mr J Duffield
Profile Equestrian Centre, Riding School, Stable/Livery. Ref: YH09161

MARKS FABRICATIONS

Marks Fabrications, Unit 3, Peddie St, Dundee, **Angus**, DD1 5LB, **SCOTLAND**.
(T) 01382 642424 (F) 01382 642424.
Contact/s
Owner: Mr M Smith
Profile Blacksmith. Ref: YH09162

MARKS, C F

Miss C F Marks, Quarry Bungalow, Long Burton, Sherborne, **Dorset**, DT9 5NZ, **ENGLAND**.
(T) 01963 210699.
Profile Breeder. Ref: YH09163

MARKS, D

Mr D Marks, Lethornes, Lambourn, Hungerford, **Berkshire**, RG17 8QS, **ENGLAND**.
(T) 01488 71767 (F) 01488 73783
(M) 07778 453997.
Profile Trainer. Ref: YH09164

MARKS, KELLY

Intelligent Horsemanship, Lethornes, Lambourn, Hungerford, **Berkshire**, RG17 8QS, **ENGLAND**.
(T) 01488 71300 (F) 01488 73783
(W) www.intelligenthorsemanship.co.uk.
Contact/s
Owner: Ms K Marks
(E) kelly@montyroberts.co.uk
Profile Trainer.
'I could not recommend a better teacher of my methods anywhere in the world than Kelly Marks.' Monty Roberts. Ref: YH09165

MARKS, SALLY K

Sally K Marks, Dewhurst Farm, Dewhurst Lane, Wadhurst, **Sussex (East)**, TN5 6QE, **ENGLAND**.
(T) 01892 782494.
Profile Farrier. Ref: YH09166

MARL STUD MARL CRIS STUD

Marl Stud Marl Cris Stud, Minfield Farm, Bronllys, Brecon, **Powys**, LD3 0LW, **WALES**.
(T) 01874 754510 (F) 01874 754510.
Contact/s
Owner: Sue Howe (Q) BHSAI
Profile Breeder, Stable/Livery. Ref: YH09167

MARLAND

Mr & Mrs W B Marland, Strawberry Hall Farm, Willisham, Ipswich, **Suffolk**, IP8 4SJ, **ENGLAND**.
(T) 01473 658354.
Profile Breeder. Ref: YH09168

MARLBOROUGH DOWNS

Marlborough Downs Riding Centre, Maisey Farm, Ogbourne Maizey, Marlborough, **Wiltshire**, SN8 1RY, **ENGLAND**.
(T) 01672 511411 (F) 01672 516692.
Contact/s
Owner: Mrs J Carter
Profile Riding School. Yr. Est: 1991
Opening Times
Sp: Open Mon - Sun 09:00. Closed Mon - Sun 19:00.
Su: Open Mon - Sun 09:00. Closed Mon - Sun 19:00.
Au: Open Mon - Sun 09:00. Closed Mon - Sun 19:00.
Wn: Open Mon - Sun 09:00. Closed Mon - Sun 19:00. Ref: YH09169

MARLEY, D H

D H Marley, Stone Hall Farm, High Hurstwood, Uckfield, **Sussex (East)**, TN22 4AN, **ENGLAND**.
(T) 01825 733469.
Profile Farrier. Ref: YH09170

MARLEY, P

P Marley, Little Forest Farm, Boars Head, Crowborough, **Sussex (East)**, TN6 3HD, **ENGLAND**.
(T) 01892 664484.
Profile Farrier. Ref: YH09171

MARNER, FIONA

Fiona Marner, Lambourn Woodlands, Hungerford, **Berkshire**, RG17 7RS, **ENGLAND**.
(T) 01488 72811 (F) 01488 73434.
Contact/s
Owner: Mrs F Marner
Profile Breeder. Ref: YH09172

MARPLES, H W

H W Marples, Rumbling Farm, Far Lane, Barlow, Dronfield, **Derbyshire**, S18 7SE, **ENGLAND**.
(T) 0114 2890317.
Profile Farrier. Ref: YH09173

MARRIOTT, ADRIAN N

Adrian N Marriott DWCF, Mowdales, Twyford Rd, South Croxton, **Leicestershire**, LE7 3RZ, **ENGLAND**.
(T) 01664 840469.
Profile Farrier. Ref: YH09174

MARRIOTT, K

Mrs K Marriott, 311 Devonshire Rd, Blackpool, **Lancashire**, FY2 0TP, **ENGLAND**.
(T) 01253 595781.
Profile Breeder. Ref: YH09175

MARRIOTT, K L

K L Marriott, Lancaster Rd, Out Rawcliffe, Preston, **Lancashire**, PR3 6BN, **ENGLAND**.
(T) 01995 671476.
Profile Breeder. Ref: YH09176

MARROS RIDING CTRE

Marros Riding Centre, Marros Farm, Marros, Pendine, Carmarthen, **Carmarthenshire**, SA33 4PN, **WALES**.
(T) 01994 453238 (F) 01994 453238.
Contact/s
Partner: Mrs M Goodwin
Profile Equestrian Centre. Ref: YH09177

MARROWELL FARM SVS

Marrowell Farm Services, Marrowell Farm, West Haddon, **Northamptonshire**, NN6 7AG, **ENGLAND**.
(T) 01788 510645 (F) 01788 510607.
Profile Supplies. Ref: YH09178

MARRS

Marrs & Co, The Old Coachyard, 21 Vicarage Rd, Foulden, Thetford, **Norfolk**, IP26 5AB, **ENGLAND**.
(T) 01366 328270 (F) 01366 328140.
Contact/s
Owner: Mr A Marrs
Profile Supplies. Ref: YH09179

MARSCOM

Marscom, The Haulage Yard, Wyck Beacon, Upper Rissington, Cheltenham, **Gloucestershire**, GL54 2NE, **ENGLAND**.
(T) 01451 821289 (F) 01451 810423.
Contact/s
Manager: Mr M Gowers
Profile Transport/Horse Boxes. Ref: YH09180

MARSDEN MANOR STUD

Marsden Manor Stud & Farm, Marsden Manor, Cirencester, **Gloucestershire**, GL7 7EU, **ENGLAND**.
(T) 01285 831238.
Contact/s
Owner: Mr R Worsley
Profile Breeder, Horse/Rider Accom.
Breed English sport horses. Yr. Est: 1960
C.Size: 1 Acres
Opening Times
Telephone for an appointment and further information
Ref: YH09181

MARSDEN, A J

A J Marsden, 4 Llys Clwyd, St Asaph, **Denbighshire**, LL17 0UA, **WALES**.
(T) 01745 584353.
Contact/s
Owner: Mr A Marsden
Profile Farrier. Ref: YH09182

MARSDEN, DEBBIE (DR)

Dr Debbie Marsden, P O Box 12981, Dalkeith, **Lothian (Mid)**, EH23 4YF, **SCOTLAND**.
(T) 01875 830526 (F) 01875 830526
Affiliated Bodies RSVS.
Contact/s
Owner: Dr D Marsden (Q) BSc
Profile Medical Support.
Practical solutions to handling and performance problems. Yr. Est: 1990
Opening Times
Has a 24 hour answering service Ref: YH09183

MARSDEN, JOHN

John Marsden, 2 Horse Shoe Cottage, School Lane, Henbury, Macclesfield, **Cheshire**, **ENGLAND**.
(T) 01625 421379. Ref: YH09184

MARSDEN, M A

M A Marsden, Wilderness Lodge, Matching Green, **Essex**, CM17 0PZ, **ENGLAND**.
(T) 01279 731486.
Profile Farrier. Ref: YH09185

MARSH KYFE RIDING SCHOOL

Marsh Kyfe Riding School, 123 Ballyronan Rd, Magherafelt, **County Londonderry**, BT45 6HP,

NORTHERN IRELAND.
(T) 028 79418860
Affiliated Bodies BHS.
Contact/s
Owner: Mr P Evans
Profile Equestrian Centre, Riding School, Track/Course.
Self catering cottage available. Can accommodate upt to 8 people. There are also horse and carriage rides.
No.Staff: 4 Yr. Est: 1986 C.Size: 50 Acres
Opening Times
Sp: Open Tues - Sat 09:00. Closed Tues - Sat 20:00.
Su: Open Tues - Sat 09:00. Closed Tues - Sat 20:00.
Au: Open Tues - Sat 09:00. Closed Tues - Sat 20:00.
Wn: Open Tues - Sat 09:00. Closed Tues - Sat 20:00.
Closed Sundays and Mondays **Ref: YH09186**

MARSH PRIVATE CLIENT SVS

Marsh Private Client Services, Rural Division, Garden Hse, 42 Bancroft, Hitchin, **Hertfordshire**, SG5 1DD, **ENGLAND**.
(T) 01462 428181 **(F)** 01462 428182.
Contact/s
Key Contact: Georgia Jessin
Profile Club/Association. **Ref: YH09187**

MARSH, ANDREW

Andrew Marsh RSS, 84 Wimborne Rd, East End, Corfe Mullen, **Dorset**, BH21 3EA, **ENGLAND**.
(T) 01202 883657.
Profile Farrier. **Ref: YH09188**

MARSH, S

Mr S Marsh, Heath Farm, 18 Deacon Cl, Warrington, **Cheshire**, WA3 7DD, **ENGLAND**.
(T) 01925 763108. **Ref: YH09189**

MARSHALL & TILL

Marshall & Till, 59 Blagreaves Lane, Littleover, **Derbyshire**, DE23 7FN, **ENGLAND**.
(T) 01332 760553.
Profile Medical Support. **Ref: YH09190**

MARSHALL & TILL

Marshall & Till, 134 Osmaston Rd, Derby, **Derbyshire**, DE1 2RF, **ENGLAND**.
(T) 01332 345119.
Profile Medical Support. **Ref: YH09191**

MARSHALL, ANDREW PHILIP

Andrew Philip Marshall, 2 Hatfield Cottages, Oare, Marlborough, **Wiltshire**, SN8 4AA, **ENGLAND**.
(T) 01672 63428.
Profile Farrier. **Ref: YH09192**

MARSHALL, BOB

Bob Marshall, 32A Moss Rd, Southport, **Merseyside**, PR8 4HZ, **ENGLAND**.
(T) 01704 500613.
Profile Farrier. **Ref: YH09193**

MARSHALL, JOHN

John Marshall, Unit 2 Cornton Rd, Stirling, **Stirling**, FK9 5EG, **SCOTLAND**.
(T) 01786 449918 **(F)** 01786 449918.
Contact/s
Owner: Mr J Marshall
Profile Blacksmith. **Ref: YH09194**

MARSHALL, KEITH WILLIAM

Keith William Marshall, Niffany Farm, Skipton, **Yorkshire (North)**, BD23 3AA, **ENGLAND**.
(T) 01756 793765.
Profile Farrier. **Ref: YH09195**

MARSHALL, KENNETH

Kenneth Marshall BII, 14 Beechnut Cl, Solihull, **Midlands (West)**, B91 2NT, **ENGLAND**.
(T) 0121 2445938.
Profile Farrier. **Ref: YH09196**

MARSHALL, L A

Mrs L A Marshall, Togston Hall Farmhouse, North Togston, Amble, Morpeth, **Northumberland**, NE65 0HR, **ENGLAND**.
(T) 01665 712699.
Profile Supplies. **Ref: YH09197**

MARSHALL, LV & JUDY

LV & Judy Marshall, Grove Farm, Little Fenton, Barkston Ash, Tadcaster, **Yorkshire (North)**, **ENGLAND**..
Profile Breeder. **Ref: YH09198**

MARSHALL, M C

M C Marshall, Rochdale Rd East, Heywood, **Lancashire**, OL10 1RL, **ENGLAND**.
(T) 01706 522291.
Contact/s
Manager: Mrs W Crompton
Profile Stable/Livery. **Ref: YH09199**

MARSHALL, MICHELLE

Michelle Marshall BHSAI (Reg), The Willows, 151 Rochdale Rd East, Heywood, **Lancashire**, OL10 1QU, **ENGLAND**.
(T) 01706 522291.
Profile Stable/Livery, Trainer. **Ref: YH09200**

MARSHALL, N

N Marshall, Blacksmith's Shop, 2 Station Rd, Heckington, Sleaford, **Lincolnshire**, NG34 9JJ, **ENGLAND**.
(T) 01529 460008.
Profile Blacksmith. **Ref: YH09201**

MARSHALL, ROBERT

Robert Marshall, 27 Main Rd, Gateside, Beith, **Ayrshire (North)**, KA15 2LF, **SCOTLAND**.
(T) 01505 502101.
Profile Farrier. **Ref: YH09202**

MARSHALL, ROBERT C

Robert C Marshall DWCF, 158 Southbank Rd, Southport, **Merseyside**, PR8 6LY, **ENGLAND**.
(T) 01704 500613.
Profile Farrier. **Ref: YH09203**

MARSHALL, STUART A

Stuart A Marshall DWCF, No 1 Broomhill Cottages, Broomhill Lane, Fakenham Magna, Thetford, **Norfolk**, IP24 2QY, **ENGLAND**.
(T) 01359 269499.
Profile Farrier. **Ref: YH09204**

MARSHALL, VICTORIA

Victoria Marshall, Sherwood Stables, Folly Rd, Lambourn, Hungerford, **Berkshire**, RG17 8QE, **ENGLAND**.
(T) 01488 71632 **(F)** 01488 73859
Affiliated Bodies NAAT.
Contact/s
Physiotherapist: Victoria Marshall
Profile Medical Support. **Ref: YH09205**

MARSHALL, W

W Marshall, Grigorhill, Nairn, **Highlands**, IV12 5HY, **SCOTLAND**.
(T) 01667 455511 **(F)** 01667 455511.
Contact/s
Owner: Mr R Douglas
Profile Blacksmith. **Ref: YH09206**

MARSHALLS

Marshalls (Woodshavings) Ltd, 73 High St, Holme upon Spalding Moor, **Yorkshire (East)**, YO43 4EN, **ENGLAND**.
(T) 01430 860337 **(F)** 01430 861082.
Profile Supplies. **Ref: YH09207**

MARSON, KENNETH S

Kenneth S Marson BII, Church View, Whitmore, Newcastle-under-Lyme, **Staffordshire**, ST5 5HR, **ENGLAND**.
(T) 01782 680594.
Profile Farrier. **Ref: YH09208**

MARSTON STUD

Marston Stud, Marston St Lawrence, Banbury, **Oxfordshire**, OX17 2DA, **ENGLAND**.
(T) 01295 710616 **(F)** 01295 711161.
Profile Breeder. **Ref: YH09209**

MARTEN, D W

D W Marten MRCVS, Gennetts Farm, Pulborough, **Sussex (West)**, RH20 2HN, **ENGLAND**.
(T) 01798 22873.
Profile Medical Support. **Ref: YH09210**

MARTIN BIRD PRODUCTIONS

Martin Bird Productions, Saucelands Barn, Coolham, Horsham, **Sussex (West)**, RH13 8QG, **ENGLAND**.
(T) 01403 741620 **(F)** 01403 741647.
Profile Supplies. **Ref: YH09211**

MARTIN COLLINS ENTERPRISES

Martin Collins Enterprises Ltd, Cuckoo Corpse, Lambourn Woodlands, Hungerford, **Berkshire**, RG17 7TJ, **ENGLAND**.
(T) 01488 71100 **(F)** 01488 73177
(E) glynnie@mceltd.com.
Profile Track/Course. **Ref: YH09212**

MARTIN PICKERING

Martin Pickering Bloodstock Services, 69 Northlands, Potters Bar, **Hertfordshire**, EN6 5JD, **ENGLAND**.
(T) 01707 655269 **(F)** 01707 655269.
Profile Supplies. **Ref: YH09213**

MARTIN WORKS

Martin Works, 271 Lynn Rd, Wisbech, **Cambridgeshire**, PE13 3DZ, **ENGLAND**.
(T) 01945 589005.
Contact/s
Owner: Mr D Patrick
Profile Blacksmith. **Ref: YH09214**

MARTIN, ANDREW J

Andrew J Martin AWCF, Yew Tree Barn, Hook Norton Rd, Swerford, Chipping Norton, **Oxfordshire**, OX7 4BF, **ENGLAND**.
(T) 01608 737479.
Profile Farrier. **Ref: YH09215**

MARTIN, CLAIRE L

Claire L Martin DWCF, Stable Cottage, New Rd, Fundenhall, Norwich, **Norfolk**, NR16 1HG, **ENGLAND**.
(T) 01508 488044
(M) 07930 945655.
Profile Farrier. **Ref: YH09216**

MARTIN, EDWARD

Edward Martin FWCF, Field-End, Closeburn, Thornhill, **Dumfries and Galloway**, DG3 5HU, **SCOTLAND**.
(T) 01848 331267 **(F)** 01848 331780.
Profile Farrier. **Ref: YH09217**

MARTIN, FIONA

Fiona Martin, 33 Rugby Cl, East Farndon Rd, Market Harborough, **Leicestershire**, LE16 9QZ, **ENGLAND**.
(T) 01858 468428
Affiliated Bodies NAAT.
Contact/s
Physiotherapist: Fiona Martin **(Q)** BHSII, BSc(Hons), MSc
Profile Medical Support. **Ref: YH09218**

MARTIN, GARY

Gary Martin AWCF, The Forge, Layndon, Parkwood Lane, Little Totham, Maldon, **Essex**, CM11 2TX, **ENGLAND**.
(T) 07836 213633.
Profile Farrier. **Ref: YH09219**

MARTIN, JULIET

Mrs Juliet Martin, Home Farm, Mount Edgcumbe, Torpoint, **Cornwall**, PL10 1JA, **ENGLAND**.
(T) 01752 822691.
Profile Breeder. **Ref: YH09220**

MARTIN, KEVIN JAMES

Kevin James Martin DWCF, Corner Cottage, 4 Ivy Lane, Stewkley, Leighton Buzzard, **Bedfordshire**, LU7 0XEN, **ENGLAND**.
(T) 01525 240381.
Profile Farrier. **Ref: YH09221**

MARTIN, MICHAEL

Michael Martin, 43 High Cross Ave, Cross Hses, Shrewsbury, **Shropshire**, SY5 6LJ, **ENGLAND**.
(T) 01743 761165
(E) info@michaelmartins.co.uk
(W) www.michaelmartin.co.uk.
Contact/s
Owner: Mr M Martin **(Q)** BHS SM, BHSII
Profile Estate Agent. Yr. Est: 1998 **Ref: YH09222**

MARTIN, MURRAY

Murray Martin RSS, Stables Cottage, Rammerscales, Hightae, Lockerbie, **Dumfries and Galloway**, DG11 1LD, **SCOTLAND**.
(T) 01387 810470.
Profile Farrier. **Ref: YH09223**

MARTIN, PAUL

Paul Martin, Biscovey Forge, Tyward, Par, **Cornwall**, PL24 2RX, **ENGLAND**.
(T) 01726 817998.
Profile Farrier. **Ref: YH09224**

MARTIN, PHILLIP J

Phillip J Martin DWCF, Flat 1 Above France Hse, Digbeth St, Stow-on-the-Wold, **Gloucestershire**, GL54 1BN, **ENGLAND**.
(T) 07974 217334.
Profile Farrier. **Ref: YH09225**

MARTIN, S

Mrs S Martin BHSII, Harnage Hse, Harnage, Shrewsbury, **Shropshire**, SY5 6EJ, **ENGLAND**.
(T) 01743 761165.
Profile Trainer. **Ref: YH09226**

A-Z of COMPANIES

MARTIN, TERRY

Terry Martin, Main St, Newthorpe, Nottingham, **Nottinghamshire**, NG16 2DH, **ENGLAND**.
(T) 01773 713868 **(F)** 01773 713868.
Contact/s
Owner: Mr T Martin
Profile Farrier. **Ref: YH09227**

MARTIN'S SHOWJUMPS

Martin's Showjumps, Wyndrose, Trowell Moor, Trowell, **Nottinghamshire**, NG9 3PQ, **ENGLAND**.
(T) 0115 9285867 **(F)** 0115 9285867. **Ref: YH09228**

MARTINSIDE STUD

Martinside Stud, Howe Green, Great Hallingbury, Bishop's Stortford, **Essex**, CM22 7UE, **ENGLAND**.
(T) 01279 653277
(M) 07771 657110
(E) elaine@astrolab.cix.co.uk.
Profile Breeder. **Ref: YH09229**

MARTLEAVES WELSH COBS

Martleaves Welsh Cobs, Longlands, Martleaves Farm, 39 South Rd, Weymouth, **Dorset**, DT4 9NR, **ENGLAND**.
(T) 01305 785244.
Profile Breeder. **Ref: YH09230**

MARTLEW, J W

J W Martlew, Forge Farm, Furnace Lane, Broad Oak, Rye, **Sussex (East)**, TN31 6ES, **ENGLAND**.
(T) 01424 883083.
Profile Farrier. **Ref: YH09231**

MARTON FORGE

Marton Forge, Rear Of 19 Lomond Ave, Blackpool, **Lancashire**, FY3 9QL, **ENGLAND**.
(T) 01253 764016.
Profile Blacksmith. **Ref: YH09232**

MARVIN, R F

Mr R F Marvin, The Hunter Yard, Southwell Racecourse, Rolleston, Newark, **Nottinghamshire**, NG25 0TS, **ENGLAND**.
(T) 01636 814481
(M) 07808 373151.
Profile Trainer. **Ref: YH09233**

MARWELL ZOOLOGICAL PK

Marwell Zoological Park, Colden Common, Winchester, **Hampshire**, SO21 1JH, **ENGLAND**.
(T) 01962 777407 **(F)** 01962 777511
(W) www.marwell.org.uk.
Profile Breeder.
Marwell Zoological Park is a tourist attraction
Ref: YH09234

MARY ROSE STUD

Mary Rose Stud, 25 Stanton Walk, Warwick, **Warwickshire**, CV34 5UY, **ENGLAND**.
(T) 01926 496417.
Profile Breeder. **Ref: YH09235**

MARYAN, M

Mr M Maryan, Upper Prestwood Farm, Charlwood, **Surrey**, RH6 0DR, **ENGLAND**.
(T) 01306 885883.
Profile Breeder. **Ref: YH09236**

MASKELL, TIM

Tim Maskell DWCF Hons, Meadow Edge, Silver St, Hordle, Lymington, **Hampshire**, SO41 0FN, **ENGLAND**.
(T) 01425 610785.
Profile Farrier. **Ref: YH09237**

MASON, CLAIRE

Claire Mason, 4 Cheeks Farm, Bentley, Farnham, **Surrey**, GU10 5HD, **ENGLAND**.
(T) 01420 23695
(M) 07836 236510. **Ref: YH09238**

MASON, D & M

D & M Mason (Saddlery), 68 Mary St, Scunthorpe, **Lincolnshire (North)**, DN15 6LB, **ENGLAND**.
(T) 01724 864213 **(F)** 01724 864213.
Contact/s
Owner: Mrs M Mason
Profile Riding Wear Retailer, Saddlery Retailer, Supplies. No.Staff: 1 Yr. Est: 1981
Opening Times
Sp: Open 09:30. Closed 17:00.
Su: Open 09:30. Closed 17:00.
Au: Open 09:30. Closed 17:00.
Wn: Open 09:30. Closed 17:00. **Ref: YH09239**

MASON, D A

D A Mason, Gresty Lane Smithy, Gresty Lane, Shavington, Crewe, **Cheshire**, CW2 5DD, **ENGLAND**.
(T) 01270 583371.
Profile Blacksmith. **Ref: YH09240**

MASON, D G

D G Mason, 7 Panworth Farm Cottages, Ashill, Thetford, **Norfolk**, IP25 7BB, **ENGLAND**.
(T) 01760 441660.
Contact/s
Owner: Mr D Mason
Profile Breeder. **Ref: YH09241**

MASON, D W

D W Mason DWCF, 27 Exchange Row, Nether St, Harby, Melton Mowbray, **Leicestershire**, LE14 4BS, **ENGLAND**.
(T) 01949 861086.
Profile Farrier. **Ref: YH09242**

MASON, G

Miss G Mason, Grayswood Farm, Grayswood, Haslemere, **Surrey**, GU27 2DQ, **ENGLAND**.
(T) 01428 3889.
Profile Breeder. **Ref: YH09243**

MASON, G K

G K Mason, 28, Trelawney, Launceston, **Cornwall**, PL15 9BL, **ENGLAND**.
(T) 01566 777392.
Contact/s
Owner: Mr G Mason
Profile Transport/Horse Boxes. **Ref: YH09244**

MASON, J W

J W Mason, The Smithy, 32 Tarbock Rd, Huyton, Liverpool, **Merseyside**, L36 5XW, **ENGLAND**.
(T) 0151 4891664 **(F)** 0151 4490449.
Contact/s
Owner: Mr J Mason
Profile Blacksmith. **Ref: YH09245**

MASON, N B

Mr N B Mason, Brancepeth Manor Farm, Crook, **County Durham**, DL15 9AS, **ENGLAND**.
(T) 0191 3736277 **(F)** 0191 5642089.
Profile Supplies. **Ref: YH09246**

MASON, R J

R J Mason, 125 Fengate, Peterborough, **Cambridgeshire**, PE1 5BA, **ENGLAND**.
(T) 01733 565677.
Profile Farrier. **Ref: YH09247**

MASSARELLA

Massarella, Thurcroft Hall, Brookhouse, Laughton, Sheffield, **Yorkshire (South)**, S25 1YA, **ENGLAND**.
(T) 01909 566429.
Contact/s
Owner: Miss G Liggins
Profile Stable/Livery. **Ref: YH09248**

MASSIE, NIGEL R

Nigel R Massie DWCF, 37 Canal Rd, Strood, Rochester, **Kent**, ME2 4DR, **ENGLAND**.
(T) 01634 710802.
Profile Farrier. **Ref: YH09249**

MASTERS DISPLAYS

Masters Displays, Isfryn, Non Cae Glas, Llanbedr Dc, Ruthin, **Denbighshire**, LL15 1US, **WALES**.
(T) 01824 705176 **(F)** 01824 705176.
Profile Supplies. **Ref: YH09250**

MASTERS OF BASSET HOUNDS ASS

Masters of Basset Hounds Association, Yew Tree Cottage, Hazleton, Cheltenham, **Gloucestershire**, GL54 4DX, **ENGLAND**.
(T) 01451 860500 **(F)** 01451 861200.
Profile Club/Association. **Ref: YH09251**

MASTERS OF DEERHOUNDS ASS

Masters of Deerhounds Association, Bilboa Hse, Dulverton, **Somerset**, TA22 9DW, **ENGLAND**.
(T) 01398 323475.
Profile Club/Association. **Ref: YH09252**

MASTERS OF DRAGHOUNDS

Masters of Draghounds & Bloodhounds Association, Stable Cottage, Wheatsheaf Rd, Henfield, **Sussex (West)**, BN5 9AU, **ENGLAND**.
(T) 01273 495188 **(F)** 01273 495199.
Contact/s
Key Contact: Mr B Stern
Profile Club/Association. **Ref: YH09253**

MASTERS OF FOXHOUNDS ASS

Masters of Foxhounds Association, Parsloes Cottages, Bagendon, Cirencester, **Gloucestershire**, GL7 7DU, **ENGLAND**.
(T) 01285 831470 **(F)** 01285 831737.
Contact/s
Key Contact: Mr A Hart
Profile Club/Association. **Ref: YH09254**

MASTROIANNI, J

Mr J Mastroianni, 35 Fife Rd, East Sheen, **London (Greater)**, SW14 7EJ, **ENGLAND**.
(T) 020 85466361.
Profile Breeder. **Ref: YH09255**

MATCHMAKER HORSE & PONY

Matchmaker Horse & Pony Agency, Pond Head Farm, Oulston, York, **Yorkshire (North)**, YO61 3RD, **ENGLAND**.
(T) 01347 868622.
Profile Trainer. Dealers. **Ref: YH09256**

MATCHMOOR RIDING CTRE

Matchmoor Riding Centre, Matchmoor Lane, Horwich, Bolton, **Manchester (Greater)**, BL6 6AJ, **ENGLAND**.
(T) 01204 693323
Affiliated Bodies ABRS.
Contact/s
Owner: Ms S Ashworth
Profile Breeder, Equestrian Centre, Riding School. Hacking available. **Ref: YH09257**

MATHER, ALISON

Mrs Alison Mather, 60 Southover, Daisy Hill, Bolton, **Manchester (Greater)**, BL5 2HA, **ENGLAND**.
(T) 01942 810466.
Profile Breeder. **Ref: YH09258**

MATHER, F E

Mr F E Mather, 32 Astbury Cres, Bridge Hall, Stockport, **Cheshire**, **ENGLAND**.
Profile Trainer. **Ref: YH09259**

MATHER, ROWLAND J

Rowland J Mather DWCF, 60 Apollo Ave, Sunny Bank Est, Bury, **Lancashire**, BL9 8HG, **ENGLAND**.
(T) 0161 7667225.
Profile Farrier. **Ref: YH09260**

MATHERS ENGINEERS

Mathers Engineers, 82 High St, Tibshelf, Alfreton, **Derbyshire**, DE55 5NX, **ENGLAND**.
(T) 01773 872349 **(F)** 01773 872349.
Contact/s
Partner: Mr R Beckett
Profile Blacksmith. **Ref: YH09261**

MATHEW, ROBIN

Mr Robin Mathew, Church Farm, Little Barrington, Burford, **Oxfordshire**, OX18 4TE, **ENGLAND**.
(T) 01451 844311 **(F)** 01451 844768.
Profile Supplies. **Ref: YH09262**

MATHEWS COMFORT

Mathews Comfort & Co Ltd, Biiba Members, P O Box 37, Tuns Lane, Henley-on-Thames, **Oxfordshire**, RG9 1BR, **ENGLAND**.
(T) 01491 572083 **(F)** 01491 410143.
Profile Club/Association. **Ref: YH09263**

MATHEWS, V

Mrs V Mathews, Hillview Farm, Yetminster, Sherborne, **Dorset**, DT9 6NN, **ENGLAND**.
(T) 01935 872379.
Profile Breeder. **Ref: YH09264**

MATLOCK SADDLERY

Matlock Saddlery, 85-87 Wellington St, Matlock, **Derbyshire**, DE4 3GW, **ENGLAND**.
(T) 01629 583135.
Profile Saddlery Retailer. **Ref: YH09265**

MATRAVERS, DAVID P

David P Matravers BII, 40 Abbey Cl, Curry Rivel, Langport, **Somerset**, TA10 0EL, **ENGLAND**.
(T) 01458 253146.
Profile Farrier. **Ref: YH09266**

MATRAVERS, P J

P J Matravers, Cross Cl, Isle Abbotts, Taunton, **Somerset**, TA3 6RR, **ENGLAND**.
(T) 01460 281239.
Profile Farrier. **Ref: YH09267**

MATTHEWS OF KEYNSHAM

Matthews of Keynsham, Bitton Rd, Keynsham, **Bath & Somerset (North East)**, BS31 2DE, **ENGLAND**.
(T) 01179 864356 **(F)** 01179 867491.
Profile Saddlery Retailer. **Ref: YH09268**

MATTHEWS RIDING CTRE

Matthews Riding Centre, Capstone Farm Country Pk, Capstone Rd, Chatham, **Kent**, ME5 7PA, **ENGLAND**.
(T) 01634 403623.
Profile Riding School. Ref: **YH09269**

MATTHEWS, BRIAN

Brian Matthews, 17 Meadow How, St Ives, Huntingdon, **Cambridgeshire**, PE17 4HZ, **ENGLAND**.
(T) 01480 301940.
Profile Farrier. Ref: **YH09270**

MATTHEWS, D

Mrs D Matthews, Nash St Farm, Lower Dicker, Hailsham, **Sussex (East)**, BN27 4AG, **ENGLAND**.
(T) 01825 872344.
Profile Breeder. Ref: **YH09271**

MATTHEWS, DAVID J

David J Matthews DWCF, The Forge, Dean Lane, Cookham Dean, Maidenhead, **Berkshire**, SL6 9AG, **ENGLAND**.
(T) 01628 483093.
Profile Farrier. Ref: **YH09272**

MATTHEWS, JULIE

Julie Matthews, Bowden Head Cottage, Chapel-En-Le-Frith, High Peak, **Derbyshire**, SK23, **ENGLAND**.
(T) 01298 812542.
Profile Breeder. Ref: **YH09273**

MATTHEWS, K L

Mrs K L Matthews, Grange Farm, Cottam, Retford, **Nottinghamshire**, DN22 0EZ, **ENGLAND**.
(T) 01777 248543.
Profile Breeder. Ref: **YH09274**

MATTHEWS, M P

Mrs M P Matthews, Manor Farm, Guildford Rd, Wotton, Dorking, **Surrey**, RH5 6QF, **ENGLAND**.
(T) 01306 730220. Ref: **YH09275**

MATTHEWS, SALLY

Sally Matthews, The Castle, Rhosgoch, Builth Wells, **Powys**, LD2 3JU, **WALES**.
(T) 01497 851221.
Profile Sculptor. Ref: **YH09276**

MATTHEWS, STAX D

Stax D Matthews DWCF, 55 Five Oaks, Caddington, Luton, **Bedfordshire**, LU1 4JD, **ENGLAND**.
(T) 01582 429803.
Profile Farrier. Ref: **YH09277**

MAUDSLEY COMMERCIAL BODIES

Maudsley Commercial Bodies, Ellesmere Rd, Off Earnsdale Rd, Darwen, **Lancashire**, BB3 1HT, **ENGLAND**.
(T) 01254 701984.
Contact/s
Manager: Mr A Maudsley
Profile Transport/Horse Boxes. Ref: **YH09278**

MAUDSLEY HORSEBOXES

Maudsley Horseboxes, Harwoods Farm, Harwoods Lane, Hoddlesden, Darwen, **Lancashire**, BB3 3LL, **ENGLAND**.
(T) 01254 702978.
Profile Transport/Horse Boxes. Ref: **YH09279**

MAUREEN'S SADDLERY

Maureen's Saddlery, Moss Cottage, Todhills, Blackford, Carlisle, **Cumbria**, CA6 4HB, **ENGLAND**.
(T) 01228 74402.
Profile Supplies. Ref: **YH09280**

MAVITA RIDING SCHOOL

Mavita Riding School, 346-348 Wigan Rd, Westhoughton, Bolton, **Manchester (Greater)**, BL5 2AR, **ENGLAND**.
(T) 01942 813707.
Profile Riding School. Ref: **YH09281**

MAW, J D

Mr J D Maw, 105 The Broadway, Sunderland, **Tyne and Wear**, SR4 8PA, **ENGLAND**.
(T) 0191 5284218.
Profile Trainer. Ref: **YH09282**

MAWERS FARM RIDING CTRE

Mawers Farm Riding Centre, Long Leys Rd, Lincoln, **Lincolnshire**, LN1 1DT, **ENGLAND**.
(T) 01522 545547 **(F)** 01522 545547.
Contact/s
Owner: Mr K Bell Ref: **YH09283**

MAXICROP INTERNATIONAL

Maxicrop International Ltd, Weldon Rd, Corby, **Northamptonshire**, NN17 5US, **ENGLAND**.
(T) 01536 402182 **(F)** 01536 204254.
Profile Medical Support. Ref: **YH09284**

MAXIMILLIAN STUD

Maximillian Stud Ltd, Higher Lowton Farm, Bondleigh, North Tawton, **Devon**, EX20 2AL, **ENGLAND**.
(T) 01837 82070 **(F)** 01837 82452.
Profile Breeder, Supplies. Ref: **YH09285**

MAXY HOUSE FARM LIVERY

Maxy House Farm Livery, Maxy Hse, Sandy Lane, Cottam, Preston, **Lancashire**, PR4 0LE, **ENGLAND**.
(T) 01772 729055.
Profile Stable/Livery. Ref: **YH09286**

MAY ROSE FARM

May Rose Farm, Helstone, Camelford, **Cornwall**, PL32 9RN, **ENGLAND**.
(T) 01840 212017.
Profile Breeder. Ref: **YH09287**

MAY, CLIVE D

Clive D May RSS, 90 Staverton Pk, Staverton, Cheltenham, **Gloucestershire**, GL51 6TD, **ENGLAND**.
(T) 07976 623889.
Profile Farrier. Ref: **YH09288**

MAY, JAMES

James May Saddlery and Leathercraft, Horseshoe Cottage, Basin Rd, Outwell, Wisbech, **Norfolk**, PE14 8TH, **ENGLAND**.
(T) 01945 773873 **(F)** 01945 773873.
Contact/s
Saddle Fitter: Mr J May
(E) jrm.saddlery@virgin.net
Profile Saddlery Retailer.
Makes stock saddles for Polo Crosse. Repairs and makes leathercraft.
No.Staff: 1 Yr. Est: 2000
Opening Times
Sp: Open Mon - Sun 24 Hours. Closed Mon - Sun 24 Hours.
Su: Open Mon - Sun 24 Hours. Closed Mon - Sun 24 Hours.
Au: Open Mon - Sun 24 Hours. Closed Mon - Sun 24 Hours.
Wn: Open Mon - Sun 24 Hours. Closed Mon - Sun 24 Hours.
Ref: **YH09289**

MAY, R S

R S May, Briona, 65 Rectory Rd, Little Oakley, Harwich, **Essex**, CO12 5LA, **ENGLAND**.
(T) 01255 880855.
Profile Farrier. Ref: **YH09291**

MAY, ROBIN PETER

Robin Peter May AWCF, Gleniffer Farm, Sandy Lane, Wokingham, **Berkshire**, RG11 4DD, **ENGLAND**.
(T) 0118 9784334.
Profile Farrier. Ref: **YH09292**

MAYCOCK, ADAM

Adam Maycock, The Elms, Badgeworth Lane, Cheltenham, **Gloucestershire**, GL51 6RQ, **ENGLAND**.
(T) 01452 712725.
Profile Trainer. Ref: **YH09293**

MAYES, NORMAN B

Norman B Mayes RSS, Cliffe Cottage, Rotherham Rd, Monk Bretton, Barnsley, **Yorkshire (South)**, S71 5QX, **ENGLAND**.
(T) 01226 202580.
Profile Farrier. Ref: **YH09294**

MAYES, ROGER W

Roger W Mayes DWCF, 1 Knoll Farm Hse, Off Lydgett Lane, Tankersley, Barnsley, **Yorkshire (South)**, S75 3BS, **ENGLAND**.
(T) 01226 742349.
Profile Farrier. Ref: **YH09295**

MAYFAIR FARM RIDING STABLES

Mayfair Farm Riding Stables, Churt Rd, Churt, Farnham, **Surrey**, GU10 2QS, **ENGLAND**.
(T) 01428 712264.
Contact/s
Owner: Mrs M Peters Ref: **YH09296**

MAYFIELD FORGE

Mayfield Forge, Old Pl Farm, Little Trodgers Lane, Mayfield, **Sussex (East)**, TN20 6PN, **ENGLAND**.
(T) 01435 872085.
Profile Blacksmith. Ref: **YH09297**

MAYHEW, BOB

Wye Oak Quarter Horses, Dumpford Manor Farm, Trotton, Petersfield, **Hampshire**, GU31 5JR, **ENGLAND**.
(T) 01730 812000 **(F)** 01730 813124
Affiliated Bodies BRHA.
Contact/s
Assistant Trainer: Rikke Madson **(Q)** WESI
Profile Breeder, Trainer. Western Stud.
Demonstrations of Western riding and training are given worldwide by Bob Mayhew. There are currently three Western Stallions standing at Wye Oak.
No.Staff: 4 Yr. Est: 1990 C.Size: 17 Acres
Opening Times
Telephone between 09:00 - 17:00 for an appointment
Ref: **YH09298**

MAYHILL STUD FARM

Mayhill Stud Farm, Swanmore Rd, Droxford, Southampton, **Hampshire**, SO32 3PT, **ENGLAND**.
(T) 01489 877511.
Profile Breeder. Ref: **YH09299**

MAYHILL STUD SHOW JUMPING

Mayhill Stud Show Jumping, C/O Mayhill Stud, Swanmore Rd, Droxford, **Hampshire**, SO3 1PT, **ENGLAND**.
(T) 01489 877511. Ref: **YH09300**

MAYLAND, ROBERT P

Robert P Mayland DWCF, 2 The Forks, Lewisburn, Kielder, Hexham, **Northumberland**, NE48 1HR, **ENGLAND**.
(T) 01434 250208.
Profile Farrier. Ref: **YH09301**

MAYPOLE

Maypole Ltd, 54 Kettles Wood Drive, Birmingham, **Midlands (West)**, B32 3DB, **ENGLAND**.
(T) 0121 4233011 **(F)** 0121 4233020.
Profile Transport/Horse Boxes. Ref: **YH09302**

MAYPOLE FARM

Maypole Farm Riding & Livery Centre, Maypole Farm, Knowsley Lane, Knowsley, Prescot, **Merseyside**, L34 9ER, **ENGLAND**.
(T) 0151 5461327.
Profile Riding School, Saddlery Retailer, Stable/Livery. Ref: **YH09303**

MAYPOLE PET & GARDEN CTRE

Maypole Pet & Garden Centre, Maypole Rd, Wickham Bishops, Witham, **Essex**, CM8 3LX, **ENGLAND**.
(T) 01621 892411.
Contact/s
Partner: Mr G Tinker
Profile Feed Merchant. Ref: **YH09304**

MAYS, PHILIP

Philip Mays RSS, 33 Birkdale Rd, Durrington, Worthing, **Sussex (West)**, BN13 2QY, **ENGLAND**.
(T) 01903 267106.
Profile Farrier. Ref: **YH09305**

MAYS-SMITH, ELIZA (LADY)

Lady Eliza Mays-Smith, Chaddleworth Hse, Newbury, **Berkshire**, RG20 7EB, **ENGLAND**.
(T) 01488 638209 **(F)** 01488 638341.
Profile Supplies. Ref: **YH09306**

MAYTREE FARM FEEDS

Maytree Farm Feeds, Cannards Grave, Shepton Mallet, **Somerset**, BA4 4LY, **ENGLAND**.
(T) 01749 342606.
Profile Feed Merchant. Ref: **YH09307**

MAYWAY

Mayway Stables & Stud, Hill Hse, Great Hockham, Thetford, **Norfolk**, IP24 1NX, **ENGLAND**.
(T) 01953 498370.
Contact/s
Owner: Mrs E Mason
Profile Blood Stock Agency, Breeder, Riding School.
No.Staff: 3 Yr. Est: 1965 C.Size: 30 Acres
Opening Times
Telephone for further information Ref: **YH09308**

MAYWOOD STUD

Maywood Promotions, Maywood Stud, Frogs Hole Lane, Woodchurch, Ashford, **Kent**, TN26 3QZ, **ENGLAND**.

(T) 01233 860051 (F) 01233 860103
(W) www.larrigan-equestrian-promotions.com.
Contact/s
Owner: Miss T Larrigan (Q) BHS DST
(E) tanya@tanyalarrigan.co.uk
Profile Breeder, Equestrian Centre, Holidays.
Opening Times
Sp: Open Mon - Sun 09:00. Closed Mon - Sun 17:00.
Su: Open Mon - Sun 09:00. Closed Mon - Sun 17:00.
Au: Open Mon - Sun 09:00. Closed Mon - Sun 17:00.
Wn: Open Mon - Sun 09:00. Closed Mon - Sun 17:00.
By arrangement only, telephone for an appointment
Ref: YH09309

MCALEAR, STUART D

Stuart D McAlear DWCF, 19 St Mary's Meadow, Yapton, Arundel, **Sussex (West)**, BN18 0EE, **ENGLAND**.
(T) 01243 554454.
Profile Farrier. Ref: YH09310

MCARA

Mcara Ltd, Willingham Hall, Market Rasen, **Lincolnshire**, LN8 3RH, **ENGLAND**.
(T) 020 75048598 (F) 020 75048599
(E) mcara@towheads.com.
Profile Transport/Horse Boxes. Ref: YH09311

MCARDLE FABRICATIONS

Mcardle Fabrications, Unit 3 Shilton Ind Est, Bulkington Rd, Coventry, **Midlands (West)**, CV7 9QL, **ENGLAND**.
(T) 024 76612463.
Profile Supplies. Ref: YH09312

MCBANE, SUSAN

Susan McBane, 63 Chaigley Rd, Longridge, **Lancashire**, PR3 3TQ, **ENGLAND**.
(T) 01772 786037 (F) 01772 786037.
Profile Trainer. Ref: YH09313

MCBEAN, W F

McBean, W F, Burnside Smithy, Nairn, **Highlands**, IV12 5QH, **SCOTLAND**.
(T) 01667 453016 (F) 01667 453016.
Contact/s
Owner: Mr W McBean
Profile Blacksmith. Ref: YH09314

MCCABE, JIM

Jim McCabe, 62 Killyleagh Rd, Ballygally, Downpatrick, **County Down**, **NORTHERN IRELAND**..
Profile Breeder. Ref: YH09315

MCCAIN, D

Mr D McCain, Bankhouse, Cholmondeley, **Cheshire**, SY14 8AL, **ENGLAND**.
(T) 01829 720352 (F) 01829 720475
(M) 07970 488756.
Profile Trainer. Ref: YH09316

MCCALL, DAVID

David McCall Ltd, 2 White Causeway, Knaphill, Woking, **Surrey**, GU21 2TU, **ENGLAND**.
(T) 01276 856993 (F) 01814 607908.
Profile Blood Stock Agency. Ref: YH09317

MCCARROLL, KAY

Miss Kay McCarroll MC AMC MMCA, C/O Penna White, 4 Livera St, Evanton, **Highlands**, IV16 9YA, **SCOTLAND**.
(T) 01349 830367.
Profile Medical Support. Ref: YH09318

MCCARROLL, KAY

Miss Kay McCarroll MC AMC MMCA, 12 Golders Rise, Hendon, **London (Greater)**, NW4 2HR, **ENGLAND**.
(T) 020 82029747 (F) 020 82023890.
Profile Medical Support. Ref: YH09319

MCCARROLL, KAY

Miss Kay McCarroll MC AMC MMCA, Orkney Isles, Kirkwall, **Orkney Isles**, **SCOTLAND**.
(T) 0856 831439.
Contact/s
Owner: Miss K McCarroll Ref: YH09320

MCCARTEN, ELAINE

Elaine McCarten, 2 Roper St, Cleator, **Cumbria**, CA23 3EE, **ENGLAND**.
(T) 01946 812431.
Profile Supplies. Ref: YH09321

MCCARTHY, TIM

Mr Tim McCarthy, Nagshall Farm, Oxted Rd, Godstone, **Surrey**, RH9 8DB, **ENGLAND**.
(T) 01883 740379 (F) 01883 740381
(M) 07887 763062.
Profile Trainer. Ref: YH09322

MCCARTIE, R

R McCartie, Little Church Farm, Vicarage Lane, Wilstead, Bedford, **Bedfordshire**, MK45 3EU, **ENGLAND**.
(T) 01234 740859.
Contact/s
Owner: Mr R McCartie
Profile Farrier. Ref: YH09323

MCCARTNEY, LINDA

Mrs Linda McCartney, 1 Soho Sq, London, **London (Greater)**, W1V 6BQ, **ENGLAND**.
(T) 020 74396621.
Profile Breeder. Ref: YH09324

MCCARTON, GERALD

McCarton Gerald, Grangemore, Kilcullen, **County Kildare**, **IRELAND**.
(T) 045 481406.
Profile Supplies. Ref: YH09325

MCCASH'S

McCash's Country Store, 1 Feus Rd, Perth, **Perth and Kinross**, PH1 2AS, **SCOTLAND**.
(T) 01738 623245 (F) 01738 451011
(E) advice@mccash.uk.com
(W) www.mccash.uk.com
Affiliated Bodies BETA.
Contact/s
Owner: Mr A Muirhead
Profile Riding Wear Retailer, Supplies.
No.Staff: 10 Yr. Est: 1746
Opening Times
Sp: Open Mon - Sat 09:00, Sun 10:00. Closed Mon - Sat 17:30, Sun 16:00.
Su: Open Mon - Sat 09:00, Sun 10:00. Closed Mon - Sat 17:30, Sun 16:00.
Au: Open Mon - Sat 09:00, Sun 10:00. Closed Mon - Sat 17:30, Sun 16:00.
Wn: Open Mon - Sat 09:00, Sun 10:00. Closed Mon - Sat 17:30, Sun 16:00. Ref: YH09326

MCCAULEY TRAILERS

Mccauley Trailers, 72 Gloverstown Rd, Toomebridge, Antrim, **County Antrim**, BT41 3RB, **NORTHERN IRELAND**.
(T) 028 79659191 (F) 028 79659195.
Profile Transport/Horse Boxes. Ref: YH09327

MCCOLLUM, JEANNIE

Jeannie McCollum BHSAI BHS SM, The Island, 49 Ballyrashane Rd, Coleraine, **County Londonderry**, BT52 2NL, **NORTHERN IRELAND**.
(T) 028 70342599.
Profile Breeder. Ref: YH09328

MCCONNOCHIE, J

J McConnochie, Racing Stables/2 North Farm Cottage, Snetterton North End, Snetterton, Norwich, **Norfolk**, NR16 2LD, **ENGLAND**.
(T) 01953 498989 (F) 01953 498989.
Contact/s
Owner: Mr J McConnochie
Profile Trainer. Ref: YH09329

MCCONVEY, J

J McConvey, 30 Church Rd, Ardglass, Downpatrick, **County Down**, BT30 7SZ, **NORTHERN IRELAND**.
(T) 028 44841813.
Contact/s
Owner: Mr J McConvey
Profile Breeder. Ref: YH09330

MCCORMACK, JOHN

John McCormack, 3 St Alkeldas Rd, Middleham, Leyburn, **Yorkshire (North)**, DL8 4PW, **ENGLAND**.
(T) 01969 22788.
Profile Farrier. Ref: YH09331

MCCORMICK, MICHAEL G

Michael G McCormick DWCF, The Farriers, Daglingworth, Cirencester, **Gloucestershire**, GL7 7AE, **ENGLAND**.
(T) 01285 652486.
Profile Farrier. Ref: YH09332

MCCOURT RACING

McCourt Racing, Antwicks Stud, Letcombe Regis, Wantage, **Oxfordshire**, OX12 9LH, **ENGLAND**.
(T) 01235 764456 (F) 01235 764456.
Contact/s
Owner: Mr G McCourt
Profile Trainer. Ref: YH09333

MCCOY SADDLERY

McCoy Saddlery & Leathercraft, High St, Porlock, Minehead, **Somerset**, TA24 8QD, **ENGLAND**.
(T) 01643 862518 (F) 01643 863088
(E) info@mccoysaddlery.co.uk
(W) www.mccoysaddlery.co.uk.
Contact/s
Owner: Mr M McCoy
Profile Riding Wear Retailer, Saddlery Retailer, Supplies. No.Staff: 4 Yr. Est: 1972
Opening Times
Sp: Open 09:00. Closed 17:00.
Su: Open 09:00. Closed 17:00.
Au: Open 09:00. Closed 17:00.
Wn: Open 09:00. Closed 17:00. Ref: YH09334

MCCRAE, JOHN & HODGE, C

John McCrae & C Hodge, Muirdyke Farm, Cumnock, **Ayrshire (East)**, KA18 2SG, **SCOTLAND**.
(T) 01290 423021.
Contact/s
Farrier: C Hodge
Profile Farrier. Ref: YH09335

MCCREERY, P D

P D McCreery, Capdoo, Clane, **County Kildare**, **IRELAND**.
(T) 045 868148.
Profile Trainer. Ref: YH09336

MCCREERY, PETER

Peter McCreery, Capdoo, Clane, **County Kildare**, **IRELAND**.
(T) 045 868148.
Contact/s
Trainer: Mr P McCreery
(E) mccreery@indigo.ie
Profile Trainer. Yr. Est: 1971 Ref: YH09337

MCCREERY, R J

R J Mccreery, Stowell Hill, Horsington, Templecombe, **Somerset**, BA8 0DF, **ENGLAND**.
(T) 01963 370212 (F) 01963 371335.
Profile Breeder. Ref: YH09338

MCCULLAM

Mr McCullam, Top End Farm, Little Staughton, **Bedfordshire**, MK44 2BY, **ENGLAND**.
(T) 01234 376426.
Profile Supplies. Ref: YH09339

MCCULLOCH, IAN WALKER

Ian Walker McCulloch, 22 Osterley Dri, Caversham Pk Village, Reading, **Berkshire**, RG4 0XP, **ENGLAND**.
(T) 07885 647054.
Profile Farrier. Ref: YH09340

MCCULLY BROS

McCully Bros & Co (Saddlers) Ltd, 6 Court St, Newtownards, **County Down**, BT23 7NX, **NORTHERN IRELAND**.
(T) 028 91813428.
Profile Saddlery Retailer. Ref: YH09341

MCCUNE, D

Mr D McCune, Springfield Hse, High St, Bishopton, **County Durham**, TS21 1HA, **ENGLAND**.
(T) 01740 30722.
Profile Supplies. Ref: YH09342

MCDONAGH, ANDREW

McDonagh Andrew, Gortigara Gurteen, Boyle, **County Sligo**, **IRELAND**.
(T) 071 82158.
Profile Supplies. Ref: YH09343

MCDONALD, BRIAN

Brian McDonald, Bridge Hse, Murton, Appleby-In-Westmorland, **Cumbria**, CA16 6ND, **ENGLAND**.
(T) 01768 352586.
Profile Farrier. Ref: YH09344

MCDONALD, CLARE

Ms Clare McDonald BSc(Hons) MCSP SRP, Greenlands, Whiccon Down, Okehampton, **Devon**, EX20 2QN, **ENGLAND**.
(T) 01647 231279
(M) 07785 566953
(E) clare.mcdonald@virgin.net.
Profile Medical Support. Ref: YH09345

MCDONALD, LIAM P

Liam P McDonald DWCF, 1 Garbridge Ct, Priory Grange, Appleby, **Cumbria**, CA16 6JE, **ENGLAND**.
(T) 01768 353937.

Profile Farrier. **Ref: YH09346**

MCDOUGALL, A

A McDougall, 469 Gorgie Rd, Edinburgh, **Edinburgh (City of)**, EH11 3AD, **SCOTLAND**.
(T) 0131 4431743.
Profile Blacksmith. **Ref: YH09347**

MCDOUGALL, ERNEST

Ernest McDougall RSS, 13 Green Lane, Stobhill, Morpeth, **Northumberland**, NE61 2HD, **ENGLAND**.
(T) 01670 503861.
Profile Farrier. **Ref: YH09348**

MCELLIGOTT, P

Miss P McElligott, Roseheath Wood Cottage, Bullbeggars Lane, Berkhamsted, **Hertfordshire**, HP4 2RT, **ENGLAND**.
(T) 01442 863651.
Profile Breeder. **Ref: YH09349**

MCEWAN BROS

McEwan Bros (Kirkintilloch) Ltd, The Smithy Hse, Old Duntiblae Rd, Kirkintilloch, Glasgow, **Glasgow (City of)**, G66 3LG, **SCOTLAND**.
(T) 0141 7761880.
Contact/s
Owner: Mr A McEwan
Profile Blacksmith. **Ref: YH09350**

MCEWEN, J C

J C McEwen BVMS, MRCVS, Veterinary Health Ctre, Old Forge Court, 17A Moor St, Chepstow, **Monmouthshire**, NP16 5DB, **WALES**.
(T) 01291 625205 **(F)** 01291 626116.
Contact/s
Partner: Mr D Thompson
Profile Medical Support. **Ref: YH09351**

MCFADZEAN, ROBERT L

Robert L McFadzean AWCF, Gateside Of Broomhill, Forteviot, Dunning, **Perth and Kinross**, PH2 9BU, **SCOTLAND**.
(T) 01764 84415.
Profile Farrier. **Ref: YH09352**

MCGAWN, D

Mrs D McGawn, 33 Castle Hill Rd, Ayr, **Ayrshire (South)**, KA7 2HY, **SCOTLAND**.
(T) 01292 264457.
Profile Trainer. **Ref: YH09353**

MCGEOGH, J & I

J & I McGeogh, The Hse On The Hill, Stranraer, **Dumfries and Galloway**, DG9 8LY, **SCOTLAND**.
(T) 01776 704828 **(F)** 01776 704828.
Contact/s
Partner: Mrs I McGeogh
Profile Breeder. **Ref: YH09354**

MCGETTIGAN & MCGETTIGAN

McGettigan & McGettigan, Lissadell, 106 The Ridgeway, Astwood Bank, Redditch, **Worcestershire**, B98 8BP, **ENGLAND**.
(T) 01527 893016.
Profile Medical Support. **Ref: YH09355**

MCGILL SADDLE FITTING

McGill Saddle Fitting, 5 Speen Rd, North Dean, High Wycombe, **Buckinghamshire**, HP14 4NN, **ENGLAND**.
(T) 01494 562863 **(F)** 01494 562863.
Contact/s
Owner: Mrs S McGill **Ref: YH09356**

MCGILLIVRAY, D & M

Mr D & Mrs M McGillivray, Woodcroft, Polinard, Comrie, **Perth and Kinross**, PH6 2HJ, **SCOTLAND**.
(T) 01764 670626 **(F)** 01764 670626
Affiliated Bodies BHS.
Contact/s
Partner: Mary McGillivray
Profile Breeder.
Braincroft is also affiliated to the Rare Breeds Survival Trust and the Eriskay Pony Society.
Opening Times
Telephone for further information, there is an answer phone. **Ref: YH09357**

MCGINN, J D

J D McGinn, Greenwell Cottage, Kirkby Thore, Penrith, **Cumbria**, CA10 1UP, **ENGLAND**.
(T) 01768 361538 **(F)** 01768 361538.
Contact/s
Owner: Mr J McGinn
Profile Blacksmith. **Ref: YH09358**

MCGOVERN, T P

T P McGovern, Grandstand Stables, The Old Racecourse, Lewes, **Sussex (East)**, BN7 1UR, **ENGLAND**.
(T) 01273 487813.
Profile Trainer. **Ref: YH09359**

MCGRATH TRAILERS

McGrath Trailers, 17-18 Princes Dock St, Belfast, **County Antrim**, BT1 3AA, **NORTHERN IRELAND**.
(T) 028 90352007.
Profile Transport/Horse Boxes. **Ref: YH09360**

MCGRATH, A

Miss A McGrath, Vernons Hill Cottage, Bishops Waltham, **Hampshire**, SO32 1FH, **ENGLAND**.
(T) 01489 892602.
Profile Breeder. **Ref: YH09361**

MCGRATH, CHRIS

Chris McGrath, The Coach Hse, 14 Langley Rd, Merton Park, **London (Greater)**, SW19 3NZ, **ENGLAND**.
(T) 020 85405387 **(F)** 020 85405387
(M) 07767 306697.
Profile Supplies. **Ref: YH09362**

MCGRATH, NEIL S

Neil S McGrath, The, Curragh, **County Kildare**, **IRELAND**.
(T) 045 441303.
Profile Supplies. **Ref: YH09363**

MCGRATH'S SADDLERY

McGrath's Saddlery, Ashline Kilrush Rd, Ennis, **County Clare**, **IRELAND**.
(T) 065 6840566.
Profile Supplies. **Ref: YH09364**

MCGREGOR & PARTNERS

McGregor & Partners (Wick), 5 Saltoun St, Wick, **Highlands**, KW1 5ET, **SCOTLAND**.
(T) 01955 602088 **(F)** 01955 604269.
Profile Medical Support. **Ref: YH09365**

MCGREGOR RACING

McGregor Racing, Ermyn Lodge, Shepherds Walk, Epsom, **Surrey**, KT18 6DF, **ENGLAND**.
(T) 01372 279755.
Profile Trainer. **Ref: YH09366**

MCGREGOR, HUGH SCOTT

Hugh Scott Mcgregor, Ballinton, Thornhill, Stirling, **Stirling**, FK8 3QE, **SCOTLAND**.
(T) 01786 850219.
Profile Breeder. **Ref: YH09367**

MCGUIRE, STEWART

Stewart McGuire, Blue Waters, Hilton, Tain, **Highlands**, IV20 1XR, **SCOTLAND**.
(T) 01862 832661 **(F)** 01862 832661.
Contact/s
Owner: Mr S McGuire
Profile Farrier. **Ref: YH09368**

MCGURK, M

M McGurk, 4 Grange Rd, Magherafelt, **County Londonderry**, BT45 5EL, **NORTHERN IRELAND**.
(T) 028 79632581 **(F)** 028 79301244.
Contact/s
Partner: Mr M McGurk
Profile Transport/Horse Boxes. **Ref: YH09369**

MCHALE, DENISE

Harraton Stables, Harraton Court Stables, Chapel St, Exning, Newmarket, **Suffolk**, CB8 7HA, **ENGLAND**.
(T) 01638 578726
(W) www.newmarketracehorsetrainers.co.uk
Affiliated Bodies Newmarket Trainers Fed.
Contact/s
Owner: Mr H Collingridge
Profile Trainer. **Ref: YH09370**

MCILVEEN, W M

W M McIlveen, 53 Market St, Omagh, **County Tyrone**, BT78 1EL, **NORTHERN IRELAND**.
(T) 028 82242690.
Contact/s
Owner: Mr W McIlveen
Profile Saddlery Retailer. **Ref: YH09371**

MCILWAINE TRAILERS

McIlwaine Trailers, 14 Corcreeny Rd, Hillsborough, **County Down**, BT26 6EH, **NORTHERN IRELAND**.
(T) 028 92689226 **(F)** 028 92689226.
Contact/s
Owner: Mr M McIlwaine
Profile Transport/Horse Boxes. **Ref: YH09372**

MCILWRAITH, A M

Miss A M McIlwraith BHSII (Reg), St Mungo's, Gleneagles, Auchterarder, **Perth and Kinross**, PH3 1PL, **SCOTLAND**.
(T) 01764 82247.
Profile Trainer. **Ref: YH09373**

MCINNES, SKINNER & BROADHEAD

Mesdames McInnes Skinner & Broadhead, Primrose Farm, Wicklewood, Wymondham, **Norfolk**, **ENGLAND**.
(T) 01953 605256.
Profile Breeder. **Ref: YH09374**

MCINNES, WILLIAM

William McInnes, Auchenlaw, West Overland Cottage, Hurlford, Kilmarnock, **Ayrshire (East)**, KA1 5JY, **SCOTLAND**.
(T) 01563 884208.
Profile Breeder. **Ref: YH09375**

MCINTOSH, DUNCAN R

McIntosh Duncan R, Forfar Rd, Brechin, **Angus**, DD9 6RG, **SCOTLAND**.
(T) 01356 624600.
Profile Transport/Horse Boxes. **Ref: YH09376**

MCINTOSH, WILLIAM G

Mr William G McIntosh, Craigneil, Off Old Gamrie Rd, Macduff, **Aberdeenshire**, AB45 3SQ, **SCOTLAND**.
(T) 01261 833534.
Profile Breeder. **Ref: YH09377**

MCIVOR, A

A McIvor, 11 Mullaghdrin Rd, Dromara, Dromore, **County Down**, BT25 2AF, **NORTHERN IRELAND**.
(T) 028 97532624.
Profile Breeder. **Ref: YH09378**

MCKAY, J & S

J & S McKay, 17 Edinbane, Portree, **Highlands**, **SCOTLAND**..
Profile Breeder. **Ref: YH09379**

MCKEAN, LORNE

Miss Lorne McKean FRBS, Lethendry, Polecat Valley, Hindhead, **Surrey**, GU26 6BE, **ENGLAND**.
(T) 01428 605655. **Ref: YH09380**

MCKEAND, B W

B W McKeand, 15 Kirktown Gdns, Tillicoultry, **Clackmannanshire**, FK13 6PG, **SCOTLAND**.
(T) 01259 750462.
Profile Farrier. **Ref: YH09381**

MCKENNA, C

Miss C McKenna, Chester Lane Farm, Chester Rd, Marton, Winsford, **Cheshire**, CW7 2QP, **ENGLAND**.
(T) 01829 760331.
Profile Breeder. **Ref: YH09382**

MCKENZIE AGRICULTURAL

McKenzie Agricultural Merchants, The Dabbins, 5 Nether Locharwoods, Ruthwell, **Dumfries and Galloway**, DG1 4NQ, **SCOTLAND**.
(T) 01387 870229
(M) 07770 826820.
Profile Supplies. **Ref: YH09383**

MCKENZIE-COLES, W G

Mr W G McKenzie-Coles, Bells Cottage, Lydeard St. Lawrence, Taunton, **Somerset**, TA4 3RN, **ENGLAND**.
(T) 01984 667334 **(F)** 01984 667543.
Profile Supplies. **Ref: YH09384**

MCKEOWN, W J

Mr W J McKeown, East Wideopen Farm, Wideopen, Newcastle-upon-Tyne, **Tyne and Wear**, NE13 6DW, **ENGLAND**.
(T) 0191 2367545 **(F)** 0191 2362959.
Profile Trainer. **Ref: YH09385**

MCKIE, V

Mrs V McKie, Twyford Mill, Twyford, **Buckinghamshire**, MK18 4HA, **ENGLAND**.
(T) 01296 730707 **(F)** 01296 730806.
Profile Breeder. **Ref: YH09386**

MCLEAN, H S

H S Mclean, Unit 12, 38 Rochsolloch Rd, Airdrie, **Lanarkshire (North)**, ML6 9BG, **SCOTLAND**.
(T) 01236 751100.
Contact/s
Owner: Mr H McLean
Profile Blacksmith. **Ref: YH09387**

Key: **(T)** telephone **(F)** fax **(M)** mobile **(E)** E-Mail Address **(W)** Website Address **(Q)** Qualifications
Yr. Est: Year Established C.Size: Complex Size Sp: Spring Su: Summer Au: Autumn Wn: Winter

MCLELLAN, B M
B M McLellan, The Forge, The St, Great Hallingbury, Bishop's Stortford, **Essex**, CM22 7TR, **ENGLAND**.
(T) 01279 652683 **(F)** 01279 652683.
Contact/s
Owner: Mr B McLellan
Profile Farrier. **Ref: YH09388**

MCLENNAN, ALEXANDER
Alexander McLennan, 22 Dunedin St, Edinburgh, **Edinburgh (City of)**, EH7 4JG, **SCOTLAND**.
(T) 0131 5564553.
Profile Blacksmith. **Ref: YH09389**

MCLEOD & HUNTER
McLeod & Hunter, 27 Buffies Brae, Dunfermline, **Fife**, KY12 8ED, **SCOTLAND**.
(T) 01383 735515 **(F)** 01383 735515.
Profile Blacksmith. **Ref: YH09390**

MCLERNON, P
P McLernon, 36 Drumballyhugh Rd, Dungannon, **County Tyrone**, BT70 3JA, **NORTHERN IRELAND**.
(T) 028 87758242.
Profile Supplies. **Ref: YH09391**

MCMATH, B J
Mr B J McMath, Docklands Cottage, Stockbridge Stables, Newmarket, **Suffolk**, CB8 9AF, **ENGLAND**.
(T) 01638 665868 **(F)** 01638 665868
(M) 07711 129575.
Profile Trainer. **Ref: YH09392**

MCMORRIS, KATE
Kate McMorris, 3 Grange Cottages, The Green, Shipbourne, Tonbridge, **Kent**, TN11 9PJ, **ENGLAND**.
(T) 01732 811452.
Profile Trainer. **Ref: YH09393**

MCMULLEN, R P
R P McMullen, Mill Cottage, West Acre, King's Lynn, **Norfolk**, PE32 1UE, **ENGLAND**.
(T) 01760 755778 **(F)** 01760 755778.
Contact/s
Owner: Miss R McMullen
Profile Trainer. **Ref: YH09394**

MCMURTY & HARDING
McMurty & Harding, 34 Market Pl, Ashbourne, **Derbyshire**, DE6 1ES, **ENGLAND**.
(T) 01335 342227.
Profile Medical Support. **Ref: YH09395**

MCNAB SADDLERS
McNab Saddlers, 27 High St, Selkirk, **Scottish Borders**, TD7 4BZ, **SCOTLAND**.
(T) 01750 22603 **(F)** 01750 22603
Affiliated Bodies BETA, FSB.
Contact/s
Owner: Mr G Stirrat
Profile Saddlery Retailer. Horse Clothing Manufacturers.
Manufacturers of Eildon horse clothing, also make bespoke bridlework and have a nationwide trade stand in operation. Offer a clipper maintenance service.
No.Staff: 6 Yr. Est: 1964
Opening Times
Sp: Open Mon - Sat 09:00. Closed Mon - Sat 17:00.
Su: Open Mon - Sat 09:00. Closed Mon - Sat 17:00.
Au: Open Mon - Sat 09:00. Closed Mon - Sat 17:00.
Wn: Open Mon - Sat 09:00. Closed Mon - Sat 17:00.
Closed Sundays **Ref: YH09396**

MCNAB SADDLERS
McNab Saddlers, 11 Woodmarket, Kelso, **Scottish Borders**, TD5 7AT, **SCOTLAND**.
(T) 01573 224238.
Contact/s
Owner: Heather Stirrat
Profile Saddlery Retailer.
Manufacturers of Eildon horse clothing, also make bespoke bridlework and have a nationwide trade stand in operation. Offer a clipper maintenance service.
No.Staff: 6 Yr. Est: 1964
Opening Times
Sp: Open Mon - Sat 09:00. Closed Mon - Sat 17:00.
Su: Open Mon - Sat 09:00. Closed Mon - Sat 17:00.
Au: Open Mon - Sat 09:00. Closed Mon - Sat 17:00.
Wn: Open Mon - Sat 09:00. Closed Mon - Sat 17:00.
Closed Sundays **Ref: YH09397**

MCNAMARA, ERIC
Eric McNamara, Beechmount, Rathkeale, **County Limerick**, **IRELAND**.
(T) 069 64795.
Profile Supplies. **Ref: YH09398**

MCNAMARA, MICHAEL F J
Michael F J McNamara, The Bungalow, Broadmoor Farm, Stockton Cross, Saltash, **Cornwall**, PL12 4SA, **ENGLAND**.
(M) 07860 267084.
Profile Farrier. **Ref: YH09399**

MCNAMARA'S
McNamara's, Shinrone, Birr, **County Offaly**, **IRELAND**.
(T) 050 547183.
Profile Supplies. **Ref: YH09400**

MCNEIL, CRAIG
Craig McNeil DWCF, 67 Ridgely Drive, Ponteland, Newcastle-upon-Tyne, **Tyne and Wear**, NE20 9BJ, **ENGLAND**.
(T) 01661 825453.
Profile Farrier. **Ref: YH09401**

MCNEILL, IAN
Ian McNeill, Redhill Farm, Red Hill, Medstead, Alton, **Hampshire**, GU34 5EE, **ENGLAND**.
(T) 01420 562249 **(F)** 01420 563897.
Contact/s
Owner: Mr I McNeill
Profile Saddlery Retailer. **Ref: YH09402**

MCNEILL, P A
Mrs P A McNeill, Corrybracken, Shennanton, Kirkcowan, Newton Stewart, **Dumfries and Galloway**, DG8 0EG, **SCOTLAND**.
(T) 01671 83266.
Profile Supplies. **Ref: YH09403**

MCPHERSON A BLACKSMITHS
McPherson A Blacksmiths Ltd, West Fulton Smithy, Craigends Rd, Houston, Johnstone, **Renfrewshire**, PA6 7EH, **SCOTLAND**.
(T) 01505 321282.
Profile Blacksmith. **Ref: YH09404**

MCROSTIE'S
McRostie's, The Harness Room, Bowfield Mews, Howwood, **Renfrewshire**, PA9 1DB, **SCOTLAND**.
(T) 01505 705030 **(F)** 01505 705010.
Profile Saddlery Retailer. **Ref: YH09405**

MCSWEENEY TRAILERS
McSweeney Trailers, Oliver Plunkett St, Bandon, **County Cork**, **IRELAND**.
(T) 023 41202.
Profile Transport/Horse Boxes. **Ref: YH09406**

MCTIMONEY CHIROPRACTIC ASS
McTimoney Chiropractic Association (The), (formerly Known As The Institute Of Pure Chiroprac, 21 High St, Eynsham, **Oxfordshire**, OX8 1HE, **ENGLAND**.
(T) 01865 880974 **(F)** 01865 880975
(E) admin@mctimoney-chiropractic.org.
Profile Medical Support. **Ref: YH09407**

MCTIMONEY CHIROPRACTIC CLGE
McTimoney Chiropractic College (The), The Clock Hse, 22-26 Ock St, Abingdon, **Oxfordshire**, OX14 5SH, **ENGLAND**.
(T) 01235 523336.
Profile Medical Support. **Ref: YH09408**

MCVICAR, JOHN R
John R McVicar, Blackhill Farm, Airlie, Kirriemuir, **Angus**, DD8 5NX, **SCOTLAND**.
(T) 01575 530207 **(F)** 01575 530207.
Contact/s
Owner: Mr J McVicar **Ref: YH09409**

MCVICKERS, DEREK
Derek McVickers, 23 Front St, Consett, **County Durham**, DH8 5AB, **ENGLAND**.
(T) 01207 592058 **(F)** 01207 591634.
Profile Saddlery Retailer. **Ref: YH09410**

MEAD GOODBODY
Mead Goodbody Ltd, 9 Paddocks Drive, Newmarket, **Suffolk**, CB8 9BE, **ENGLAND**.
(T) 01638 561116 **(F)** 01638 560332.
Profile Blood Stock Agency. **Ref: YH09411**

MEADE, LOUIS
Louis Meade DWCF, 170 Repton Rd, Orpington, **Kent**, BR6 9JA, **ENGLAND**.
(T) 01689 874625.
Profile Farrier. **Ref: YH09412**

MEADE, MARTYN
Martyn Meade, Ladyswood Farm, Ladyswood, Malmesbury, **Wiltshire**, SN16 0LA, **ENGLAND**.
(T) 01666 840880 **(F)** 01666 840073.
Contact/s
Owner: Mr M Meade
Profile Breeder, Trainer. **Ref: YH09413**

MEADE, NOEL
Noel Meade, Tuva Castletown, Kilpatrick, **County Meath**, **IRELAND**.
(T) 046 54197.
Profile Supplies. **Ref: YH09414**

MEADE, RICHARD
Richard Meade OBE, Church Farm, West Littleton, Chippenham, **Wiltshire**, SN14 8JB, **ENGLAND**.
(T) 01225 891226.
Profile Trainer. **Ref: YH09415**

MEADEN, ABIGAIL R L
Abigail R L Meaden DWCF, The Flat, Gorcombe Farm, Thornicombe, Blandford Forum, **Dorset**, DT11 9AG, **ENGLAND**.
(T) 01258 452219.
Profile Farrier. **Ref: YH09416**

MEADOW BANK FARM RIDING CTRE
Meadow Bank Farm Riding Centre, Sugar Lane, Manley, Frodsham, **Cheshire**, WA6 9DZ, **ENGLAND**.
(T) 01928 740370. **Ref: YH09417**

MEADOW FARM EQUESTRIAN CTRE
Meadow Farm Equestrian Centre, Meadow Farm, Meadow Farm Lane, Horsham St. Faith, Norwich, **Norfolk**, NR10 3BY, **ENGLAND**.
(T) 01603 890924.
Contact/s
Owner: Mr T Mallet
Profile Stable/Livery. **Ref: YH09418**

MEADOW FARM STUD
Meadow Farm Stud, Ramsbury, Marlborough, **Wiltshire**, SN8 2PP, **ENGLAND**.
(T) 01672 520265.
Profile Breeder. **Ref: YH09419**

MEADOW FORGE
Meadow Forge, Unit 30 Canal Bridge Enterprise Ctre, Meadow Lane, Ellesmere Port, **Cheshire**, CH65 4EH, **ENGLAND**.
(T) 0151 3563507.
Profile Blacksmith. **Ref: YH09420**

MEADOW PK
Meadow Park Equestrian Centre, Waterlea Farm, Kilmacolm Rd, Houston, Johnstone, **Renfrewshire**, PA6 7DP, **SCOTLAND**.
(T) 01505 612955 **(F)** 01505 612977.
Contact/s
Owner: Ms A Wilson
Profile Equestrian Centre, Riding School, Stable/Livery. No.Staff: 4 Yr. Est: 1999
C.Size: 90 Acres **Ref: YH09421**

MEADOW SCHOOL
Meadow School Of Riding Stanford, The Stables, Main St, Stanford On Soar, Loughborough, **Leicestershire**, LE12 5PY, **ENGLAND**.
(T) 01509 263782.
Contact/s
Partner: Mr D Allenby
Profile Riding School, Stable/Livery. **Ref: YH09422**

MEADOW VIEW EQUESTRIAN CTRE
Meadow View Equestrian Centre, Meadow View Cottage, Warden Rd, Eastchurch, Sheerness, **Kent**, ME12 4EN, **ENGLAND**.
(T) 01795 880016.
Contact/s
Owner: Mrs S Woods **Ref: YH09423**

MEADOW VIEW RIDING CTRE
Meadow View Riding Centre, Newton Rd, Tibshelf, Alfreton, **Derbyshire**, DE55 5PH, **ENGLAND**.
(T) 01773 874790.
Contact/s
Owner: Mr P Revill **Ref: YH09424**

MEADOWBANK EQUESTRIAN CTRE
Meadowbank Equestrian Centre, Thorpemarsh Lane, Downash, Hailsham, **Sussex (East)**, BN27 2RP, **ENGLAND**.
(T) 01323 848777 **(F)** 01323 848542.
Contact/s
Owner: Mrs S Vincent
Profile Riding School. **Ref: YH09425**

MEADOWS RIDING CTRE
Meadows Riding Centre, Kilby Rd, Fleckney, **Leicestershire**, LE8 0BQ, **ENGLAND**.
(T) 0116 2402336.

Profile Riding School, Track/Course. **Ref: YH09426**

MEAKER, MARTYN A
Martyn A Meaker DWCF, Greenacre, Manchester Rd, Sway, Lymington, **Hampshire**, SO41 6AS, **ENGLAND**.
(T) 01590 682802.
Profile Farrier. **Ref: YH09427**

MEARCLOUGH FARM FEEDS
Mearclough Farm Feeds, Mearclough Rd, Sowerby Bridge, Halifax, **Yorkshire (West)**, HX6 3LF, **ENGLAND**.
(T) 01422 834713.
Profile Supplies. **Ref: YH09428**

MEARS, E & S
E & S Mears, Belt View Farm, Cannock Rd, Bednall Head, Stafford, **Staffordshire**, ST17 0QH, **ENGLAND**.
(T) 01785 665806 **(F)** 01785 660243.
Profile Supplies. **Ref: YH09429**

MEARS, IVAN
Ivan Mears, Soulbury Stud, 2 Pound Hill, Great Brickhill, **Buckinghamshire**, MK17 9AS, **ENGLAND**.
(T) 01525 261606.
Profile Breeder. **Ref: YH09430**

MECA RIDING CTRE
Meca Riding Centre, Wooburn Common Rd, Wooburn Green, High Wycombe, **Buckinghamshire**, HP10 0JS, **ENGLAND**.
(T) 01628 529666.
Contact/s
Owner: Mrs P Tickell
Profile Riding School. **Ref: YH09431**

MEDATA EQUESTRIAN
Medata Equestrian, Old Bilsham Farm, Bilsham Lane, Yapton, Arundel, **Sussex (West)**, BN18 0JX, **ENGLAND**.
(T) 01243 587866 **(F)** 01243 587988.
Profile Supplies. **Ref: YH09432**

MEDCROFT, JASON R
Jason R Medcroft DWCF, Rose Cottage, Ross Rd, Kilcot, Newent, **Gloucestershire**, GL18 1NE, **ENGLAND**.
(T) 01531 821318.
Profile Farrier. **Ref: YH09433**

MEDDICKS, J
J Meddicks, Ruthvenfield Pl, Inveralmond Ind Est, Perth, **Perth and Kinross**, PH1 3XU, **SCOTLAND**.
(T) 01738 632671.
Profile Blacksmith. **Ref: YH09434**

MEDICAL EQUESTRIAN ASS
Medical Equestrian Association (N Ireland), Laragh, Ballinamallard, Enniskillen, **County Fermanagh**, BT94 2GS, **NORTHERN IRELAND**.
(T) 028 66324377.
Profile Club/Association, Medical Support.
Ref: YH09435

MEDICAL EQUESTRIAN ASS
Medical Equestrian Association, C/O The Medical Comm Of Accident, Prevention, 35-43 Lincolns Inn Fields, London, **London (Greater)**, WC2A 3PN, **ENGLAND**.
(T) 020 72423176.
Profile Club/Association. **Ref: YH09436**

MEDITRINA
Meditrina, P.O. Box 530, Woldingham, Caterham, **Surrey**, CR3 7YG, **ENGLAND**.
(T) 01883 652483 **(F)** 01883 653492.
Profile Medical Support. **Ref: YH09437**

MEDLAND SANDERS & TWOSE
Medland Sanders & Twose, Edward Cl, Meade Ave, Hounstound Bus Pk, Yeovil, **Somerset**, BA22 8RU, **ENGLAND**.
(T) 01935 478877.
Profile Supplies. **Ref: YH09438**

MEDWAY RIDING CTRE
Medway Riding Centre, Southminster Rd, Althorne, Chelmsford, **Essex**, CM3 6EN, **ENGLAND**.
(T) 01621 740419.
Contact/s
Owner: Mr J Castle
Profile Riding School, Stable/Livery. **Ref: YH09439**

MEE, JOHN S
John S Mee RSS, Pear Tree Farm, Yeldersley Lane, Bradley, Ashbourne, **Derbyshire**, DE6 1PJ, **ENGLAND**.
(T) 01335 60684.
Profile Farrier. **Ref: YH09440**

MEEHAN, BRIAN
Brian Meehan, Newlands Stables, Upper Lambourn, Hungerford, **Berkshire**, RG17 8QX, **ENGLAND**.
(T) 01488 73656 **(F)** 01488 73633.
Contact/s
Owner: Mr B Meehan
Profile Trainer. **Ref: YH09441**

MEEK, MATTHEW R
Matthew R Meek DWCF, The Cottage, Higher St, Bower Hinton, Martock, **Somerset**, TA12 6LT, **ENGLAND**.
(T) 01935 825797.
Profile Farrier. **Ref: YH09442**

MEES, RON
Ron Mees, 9 Swallow Gardens, Hatfield, **Hertfordshire**, AL10 8QR, **ENGLAND**.
(T) 01707 264573.
Profile Trainer. **Ref: YH09443**

MEESON, J
J Meeson, Bodrigan Farm, Tresarrett, Bodmin, **Cornwall**, PL30 4QQ, **ENGLAND**.
(T) 01208 850991 **(F)** 01208 850991.
Contact/s
Owner: Mr J Meeson
Profile Breeder. **Ref: YH09444**

MEGAN, JASON J
Jason J Megan DWCF, 7 Osprey Cl, Whittington, Lichfield, **Staffordshire**, WS14 9HT, **ENGLAND**.
(T) 01543 433461.
Profile Farrier. **Ref: YH09445**

MEIFOD-ISAF
Meifod-Isaf Pony Trekking & Riding Centre, Dyffryn Ardudwy, **Gwynedd**, LL44 2DS, **WALES**.
(T) 01341 247651.
Profile Equestrian Centre. **Ref: YH09446**

MEIKLE WELSH COBS
Meikle Welsh Cobs, Toull Farm, Castle Douglas, **Dumfries and Galloway**, DG7 1PD, **SCOTLAND**.
(T) 01556 610356
(E) meiklecobs@aol.com
(W) www.welshponyandcob.com/meikle
Affiliated Bodies WPCS.
Contact/s
Owner: Mrs C Whitaker
Profile Breeder, Trainer.
'Meike Welsh Cobs' specialise in breeding and producing hardy sports horses. Yr. Est: 1989
Ref: YH09447

MEL FORDHAM
Mel Fordham Racehorse Photography, Herons Ghyll Manor, Herons Ghyll, Uckfield, **Sussex (East)**, TN22 3TX, **ENGLAND**.
(T) 01825 713337. **Ref: YH09448**

MELBOURNE HALL STUD
Melbourne Hall Stud, Melbourne Hall, Melbourne, **Yorkshire (East)**, YO42 4SU, **ENGLAND**.
(T) 01759 318210.
Contact/s
Owner: Cherry Target
Profile Breeder. No.Staff: 3 Yr. Est: 1982
C.Size: 82 Acres **Ref: YH09449**

MELCOURT INDUSTRIES
Melcourt Industries Ltd, Eight Bells Hse, Tetbury, **Gloucestershire**, GL8 8JG, **ENGLAND**.
(T) 01666 502711 **(F)** 01666 504398
(E) mail@melcourt.co.uk.
Profile Track/Course. **Ref: YH09450**

MELDRETH MANOR
Meldreth Manor School Riding Centre, Fenny Lane, Meldreth, Royston, **Hertfordshire**, SG8 6LG, **ENGLAND**.
(T) 01763 268071.
Contact/s
Manager: Mrs R Lewis
Profile Riding School, Stable/Livery. **Ref: YH09451**

MELFORT RIDING CTRE
Melfort Riding Centre (The), Melfort Hse, Kilmelford, Oban, **Argyll and Bute**, PA34 4XD, **SCOTLAND**.
(T) 01852 500257.
Profile Riding School. **Ref: YH09452**

MELINDY STABLES
Melindy Stables, Horsham Rd, Steyning, **Sussex (West)**, BN44 3AA, **ENGLAND**.
(T) 01903 879059.
Contact/s
Owner: Ms K Battleday **Ref: YH09453**

MELLON & BODEN
Mellon & Boden, Unit 1, Church Rd, Tostock, Bury St Edmunds, **Suffolk**, IP30 9PG, **ENGLAND**.
(T) 01359 271180 **(F)** 01359 271180.
Contact/s
Partner: Mr J Bowden
Profile Transport/Horse Boxes. **Ref: YH09454**

MELLOR, CLIVE
Clive Mellor, The Blacksmiths Shop/Railway Stables, Churnet View Rd, Oakamoor, Stoke-on-Trent, **Staffordshire**, ST10 3AE, **ENGLAND**.
(T) 01538 702744.
Profile Farrier. **Ref: YH09455**

MELPLASH AGRICULTURAL SOCIETY
Melplash Agricultural Society, 23 South St, Bridport, **Dorset**, DT6 3NT, **ENGLAND**.
(T) 01308 423337 **(F)** 01308 423337.
Profile Club/Association. **Ref: YH09456**

MELTON MOWBRAY RIDING CLUB
Melton Mowbray Riding Club, Manor Barn Farm, Upper Broughton, Melton Mowbray, **Leicestershire**, LE14 3BH, **ENGLAND**.
(T) 01664 823686 **(F)** 01664 822346.
Contact/s
Chairman: Ian Jalland
Profile Club/Association, Riding Club. **Ref: YH09457**

MENDIP RIDING CTRE
High Action Ltd, Lyncombe Lodge, Churchill, **Somerset (North)**, BS25 5PQ, **ENGLAND**.
(T) 01934 852335 **(F)** 01934 853314
(E) info@highaction.co.uk
(W) www.highaction.co.uk.
Contact/s
Equitation Officer: Ms S Spears **(Q)** BHSII
Profile Arena, Equestrian Centre, Riding School, Track/Course. No.Staff: 80 Yr. Est: 1998
C.Size: 150 Acres
Opening Times
Sp: Open Mon - Sun 09:00. Closed Mon - Sun 19:00.
Su: Open Mon - Sun 09:00. Closed Mon - Sun 21:00.
Au: Open Mon - Sun 09:00. Closed Mon - Sun 19:00.
Wn: Open Mon - Sun 09:00. Closed Mon - Sun 17:00. **Ref: YH09458**

MENDIP WOODSHAVINGS
Mendip Woodshavings, Charterhouse Factory, Charterhouse, Blagdon, **Somerset (North)**, BS40 7SX, **ENGLAND**.
(T) 01761 462996 **(F)** 01761 463171.
Profile Track/Course. **Ref: YH09459**

MEON RIDING CLUB
Meon Riding Club, Wheelers Farm, Froxfield, Petersfield, **Hampshire**, GU32 1DR, **ENGLAND**.
(T) 01730 264178 **(F)** 01730 264178.
Contact/s
Chairman: Mrs B Wood
Profile Club/Association, Riding Club. **Ref: YH09460**

MEPHAM, KIRSTY
Kirsty Mepham, Rockfield, Kiln Lane, Isfield, Uckfield, **Sussex (East)**, TN6 5UE, **ENGLAND**.
(T) 07768 551179. **Ref: YH09461**

MERCER, FRANK
Frank Mercer AFCL, Doddiscombe Cottage, Shillingford, Tiverton, **Devon**, EX16 9BN, **ENGLAND**.
(T) 01398 331856.
Profile Farrier. **Ref: YH09462**

MERCER, I J
I J Mercer, Silver Hope, Middlestoke, Rochester, **Kent**, ME3 9RR, **ENGLAND**.
(T) 01634 270278.
Profile Farrier. **Ref: YH09463**

MERCHANT PET & ANIMAL FEED
Merchant Pet & Animal Feed Ltd, South Hall, Beverley Rd, Cranswick, Driffield, **Yorkshire (East)**, YO25 9PF, **ENGLAND**.
(T) 01377 270684 **(F)** 01377 271591.
Profile Supplies. **Ref: YH09464**

MERCHANT, D
D Merchant, Carlton Mills, Carlton Le Moorland, **Lincolnshire**, LN5 9HJ, **ENGLAND**.
(T) 01522 788231.
Profile Supplies. **Ref: YH09465**

Key: **(T)** telephone **(F)** fax **(M)** mobile **(E)** E-Mail Address **(W)** Website Address **(Q)** Qualifications
Yr. Est: Year Established C.Size: Complex Size Sp: Spring Su: Summer Au: Autumn Wn: Winter

MERCHANT, SIMON

Simon Merchant DWCF, Ashurst Farm, Wood Lane, Shilton, **Warwickshire**, CV7 9LA, **ENGLAND**.
(T) 07836 743254.
Profile Farrier. Ref: YH09466

MERCURY TRAILERS

Mercury Trailers Ltd, Capetown Mill, Pickles St, Burnley, **Lancashire**, BB12 0NJ, **ENGLAND**.
(T) 01282 835405 (F) 01282 416552.
Profile Transport/Horse Boxes. Ref: YH09467

MEREDITH, D & S

D & S Meredith, Dolgun Uchaf, Dolgellau, **Gwynedd**, LL40 2AB, **WALES**.
(T) 01341 422269.
Profile Breeder, Stable/Livery. Ref: YH09468

MEREDITH, D P

D P Meredith, Vaynor Pony Stud, Berthllwyd Farm, Vaynor, Merthyr Tydfil, **Glamorgan (Vale of)**, CF48 2TT, **WALES**.
(T) 01685 384192.
Contact/s
Partner: Mr J Meredith
Profile Breeder. Ref: YH09469

MEREHAM GRANGE

Mereham Grange Equestrian Centre, Mereham Grange, Mareham On The Hill, Horncastle, **Lincolnshire**, **ENGLAND**.
(T) 01507 522944.
Profile Equestrian Centre. Ref: YH09470

MERES FELL STUD

Meres Fell Stud, Meres Farm, Five Ashes, Mayfield, **Sussex (East)**, TN20 6JS, **ENGLAND**.
(T) 01435 872180.
Profile Breeder. Ref: YH09471

MEREWORTH STORES & TACK SHOP

Mereworth Stores & Tack Shop, 93 The Street, Mereworth, **Kent**, ME18 5LU, **ENGLAND**.
(T) 01622 817994 (F) 01622 817529.
Profile Saddlery Retailer. Ref: YH09472

MERGIE LIVERY STABLES

Mergie Livery Stables, Rickarton, Stonehaven, **Aberdeenshire**, AB39 3TH, **SCOTLAND**.
(T) 01569 767505.
Contact/s
Owner: Mrs M Warrender
Profile Stable/Livery. Ref: YH09473

MERIDEN RIDING CLUB

Meriden Riding Club, Hillside, Pickford Green Lane, Allesley, Coventry, **Midlands (West)**, CV5 9AQ, **ENGLAND**.
(T) 01676 522831.
Profile Club/Association, Riding Club. Ref: YH09474

MERIDIAN ENGINEERING SVS

Meridian Engineering Services, Unit 1 41 Mowbray St, Sheffield, **Yorkshire (South)**, S3 8EN, **ENGLAND**.
(T) 0114 2812808 (F) 0114 2812809.
Contact/s
Senior Partner: Mr B Mason
Profile Blacksmith. Ref: YH09475

MERIDIAN RADIONICS

Meridian Radionics, Lanzeague, St Just In Roseland, Truro, **Cornwall**, TR2 5JD, **ENGLAND**.
(T) 01326 270990
(M) 07974 409575.
Profile Medical Support. Ref: YH09476

MERIDIAN TRAILERS

Meridian Trailers, Unit 1A Ellough Ind Est, Ellough, Beccles, **Suffolk**, NR34 7TF, **ENGLAND**.
(T) 01502 712425 (F) 01502 712741.
Profile Transport/Horse Boxes. Ref: YH09477

MERLIN VETS

Merlin Vets, Sydenham Veterinary Health Ctre, Edinburgh Rd, Kelso, **Scottish Borders**, TD5 7EN, **SCOTLAND**.
(T) 01573 224496 (F) 01573 225601.
Contact/s
Vet: Mr R Anderson
Profile Medical Support. Ref: YH09478

MERRETT, D T

D T Merrett BHSI, Layer De La Haye, Colchester, **Essex**, CO2 0HT, **ENGLAND**.
(T) 01206 734695 (F) 01206 734688.
Profile Trainer. Ref: YH09479

MERRIE STUD

Merrie Stud Messrs Sibley, Corhampton Farm, Corhampton, Southampton, **Hampshire**, SO32 3NB, **ENGLAND**.
(T) 01489 877564 (F) 01489 877564.
Contact/s
Owner: Mrs S Shaw
(E) merriestud@netscapeonline.co.uk
Profile Breeder, Riding School. Ref: YH09480

MERRILL, S

Mrs S Merrill, 4 Waterworks Cottages, Stourbridge Rd, Ismere, Kidderminster, **Worcestershire**, DY10 3NX, **ENGLAND**.
(T) 01562 700078 (F) 01562 700078.
Profile Breeder. Ref: YH09481

MERRIST WOOD CLGE

Merrist Wood College Livery Yard, Worplesdon, Guildford, **Surrey**, GU3 3PE, **ENGLAND**.
(T) 01483 234718.
Contact/s
Manager: Mrs E Brady
Profile Track/Course. Ref: YH09482

MERRIVALE TRADING

Merrivale Trading Company, Plungar, Nottingham, **Nottinghamshire**, NG13 0JJ, **ENGLAND**.
(T) 01949 60267.
Profile Supplies. Ref: YH09483

MERRIWORTH TRAILERS

Merriworth Trailers, Darenth Ind Pk, Wallhouse Rd, Erith, **Kent**, DA8 2EW, **ENGLAND**.
(T) 01322 349956.
Profile Transport/Horse Boxes. Ref: YH09484

MERRYBOYS

Merryboys, Cooling St, Cliffe, Rochester, **Kent**, ME3 7UA, **ENGLAND**.
(T) 01634 220276. Ref: YH09485

MERRYBROOK EQUESTRIAN CTRE

Merrybrook Equestrian Centre, Haselor Lane, Hinton-on-the-Green, Evesham, **Worcestershire**, WR11 6QZ, **ENGLAND**.
(T) 01386 861452.
Profile Equestrian Centre. Ref: YH09486

MERRYDOWN STUD

Merrydown Stud, Ardleugh, Colchester, **Essex**, CO7 7SY, **ENGLAND**.
(T) 01206 230707.
Profile Breeder. Ref: YH09487

MERRYLEES, G

G Merrylees, Wyllieland Hill, Wyllieland, Fenwick, Kilmarnock, **Ayrshire (East)**, KA3 6DA, **SCOTLAND**.
(T) 01560 600396.
Contact/s
Owner: Mr G Merrylees
Profile Breeder. Ref: YH09488

MERRYMAN, W & M

W & M Merryman, Moor Farm, Moor Lane, Staines, **Surrey**, **ENGLAND**.
(T) 01784 456817.
Profile Breeder. Ref: YH09489

MERRYWEATHERS

Merryweathers, Chilsham Lane, Bodel St, Herstmonceux, Hailsham, **Sussex (East)**, BN27 4QH, **ENGLAND**.
(T) 01323 832098 (F) 01323 833852.
Contact/s
Owner: Mr P Clarke
Profile Trainer. Ref: YH09490

MERSEYSIDE BHS DRESSAGE

Merseyside BHS Dressage, 8 Redwood Rd, Liverpool, **Merseyside**, L25 2QR, **ENGLAND**.
(T) 0151 4880015.
Profile Club/Association. Ref: YH09491

MERTON STUD

Merton Stud, Merton, Bicester, **Oxfordshire**, OX6 0NF, **ENGLAND**.
(T) 01865 331425.
Contact/s
Partner: Mrs M O'Neill
Profile Breeder. Ref: YH09492

MET ART

Met Art, 9 Newry Rd, Poyntzpass, Newry, **County Down**, BT35 6TH, **NORTHERN IRELAND**.
(T) 028 38318731 (F) 028 38318731.
Contact/s
Owner: Mrs M Hudson
Profile Transport/Horse Boxes. Ref: YH09493

METAL ARTEFACTS

Metal Artefacts, 209A Coldharbour Lane, London, **London (Greater)**, SW9 8RU, **ENGLAND**.
(T) 020 72743091 (F) 020 72743091.
Contact/s
Owner: Mr D Peters
Profile Blacksmith. Ref: YH09494

METAL ARTWORK

Metal Artwork, The Old Blacksmith Shop, The Cross, Bishopstone, Salisbury, **Wiltshire**, SP5 4BW, **ENGLAND**.
(T) 01722 781212 (F) 01722 781191.
Profile Blacksmith. Ref: YH09495

METAL COMPONENT FABRICATORS

Metal Component Fabricators, Unit 2 42-44 East Main St, Blackburn, Bathgate, **Lothian (West)**, EH47 7QU, **SCOTLAND**.
(T) 01506 634178 (F) 01506 634178.
Contact/s
Owner: Mr A Kerr
Profile Blacksmith. Ref: YH09496

METAL MART

Metal Mart, 130A Upper Knockbreda Rd, Belfast, **County Antrim**, BT6 9QB, **NORTHERN IRELAND**.
(T) 028 90793186 (F) 028 90793186.
Contact/s
Owner: Mr T Hannah
Profile Transport/Horse Boxes. Ref: YH09497

METALCRAFT

Metalcraft Ltd, The Forge, Gayton Rd, Grimston, King's Lynn, **Norfolk**, PE32 1BG, **ENGLAND**.
(T) 01485 600387 (F) 01485 600387.
Profile Blacksmith. Ref: YH09498

METCALFE, ANTHONY J

Anthony J Metcalfe DWCF, 2 Manor Farm Cottages, Fullerton, Andover, **Hampshire**, SP11 7LD, **ENGLAND**.
(T) 01264 860138.
Profile Farrier. Ref: YH09499

METCALFE, DAVID

David Metcalfe, 21 Oakwell Cl, Dunstable, **Bedfordshire**, LU6 2PY, **ENGLAND**.
(T) 01582 667206 (F) 01582 477966.
Contact/s
Owner: Mr D Metcalfe
Profile Blood Stock Agency. Ref: YH09500

METCALFE, STUART

Stuart Metcalfe, Steadhall Farm, Woodhead, Burley In Wharfedale, Ilkley, **Yorkshire (West)**, LS29 7BH, **ENGLAND**.
(T) 01943 602086.
Contact/s
Trainer: Stuart Metcalfe (Q) BHSI(SM)
Profile Trainer. Ref: YH09501

METHAM GRANGE STABLES

Metham Grange Stables, Metham Grange/Hive, Gilberdyke, Hive, Brough, **Yorkshire (East)**, HU15 2XR, **ENGLAND**.
(T) 01430 440326.
Contact/s
Owner: Miss H Laverack
Profile Stable/Livery. Ref: YH09502

METTLEWORK

Mettlework Ltd, 95 High St, Sawston, Cambridge, **Cambridgeshire**, CB2 4HJ, **ENGLAND**.
(T) 01223 506112 (F) 01223 506112.
Contact/s
Owner: Mr N Byers
Profile Blacksmith. Ref: YH09503

METWOOD FORGE

Metwood Forge, School Lane, Sudbury, Ashbourne, **Derbyshire**, DE6 5HZ, **ENGLAND**.
(T) 01283 585589.
Contact/s
Owner: Mr T Sendell
Profile Blacksmith. Ref: YH09504

MEU

MEU, Hill Farm Est, Irthlingborough Rd, Little Addington, Kettering, **Northamptonshire**, NN14 4AS, **ENGLAND**.
(T) 01933 653252 (F) 01933 653252.
Contact/s
Partner: Mr B O'Dell
Profile Transport/Horse Boxes. Ref: YH09505

MEWS COTTAGE STABLES

Mews Cottage Stables, Brookfield Lane, Aughton, Ormskirk, **Lancashire**, L39 6SN, **ENGLAND**.
(T) 01695 423182.
Profile Stable/Livery. **Ref: YH09506**

MEYNELL & SOUTH STAFFS

Meynell & South Staffs, Home Farm, School Lane, Hints, Tamworth, **Staffordshire**, B78 3DW, **ENGLAND**.
(T) 01543 480984. **Ref: YH09507**

MEYRICK, R M

R M Meyrick, 31 Coleford Bridge Rd, Mytchett, Camberley, **Surrey**, GU16 6DH, **ENGLAND**.
(T) 01252 673990.
Contact/s
Owner: Mr R Meyrick
Profile Farrier. **Ref: YH09508**

MIALL, T C & J F

T C & J F Miall, Lower Farm, Duns Tew, Bicester, **Oxfordshire**, OX6 4JX, **ENGLAND**.
(T) 01869 338254.
Profile Breeder. **Ref: YH09509**

MICHAEL GULLEY FARRIER

Michael Gulley Farrier, Bayliss's Forge, Banbury, **Oxfordshire**, OX16 1DN, **ENGLAND**.
(T) 01295 730135.
Profile Farrier. **Ref: YH09510**

MICHAEL, KIERNAN

Kiernan Michael, Rathcore Dysart, Mullingar, **County Westmeath**, **IRELAND**.
(T) 044 26314.
Profile Supplies. **Ref: YH09511**

MICHELL, K N

K N Michell, Hooton Farm Cottage, Hooton Rd, Wirral, **Merseyside**, CH66 1QU, **ENGLAND**.
(T) 0151 3275598.
Profile Farrier. **Ref: YH09512**

MICHELLE GILES MARKETING

Michelle Giles Marketing & Market Research, The Porter's Hse, Ludgershall Rd, Brill, **Buckinghamshire**, HP18 9TY, **ENGLAND**.
(T) 01844 237301 **(F)** 01844 238530.
Profile Club/Association. **Ref: YH09513**

MICHIE, ERIC

Eric Michie, 18 Badenoch Drive, Huntly, **Aberdeenshire**, AB54 8HW, **SCOTLAND**.
(T) 01466 793205.
Profile Saddlery Retailer. **Ref: YH09514**

MICHO, MICHAEL

Michael Micho, Leopardstown Rd, Dublin, **County Dublin**, **IRELAND**.
(T) 01 2898856
(E) info@buyandsellhorses.com.
Profile Supplies. **Ref: YH09515**

MICKLEBURGH, ROBERT

Robert Mickleburgh, 86 Walcot St, Bath, **Bath & Somerset (North East)**, BA1 5BD, **ENGLAND**.
(T) 01225 4469972. **Ref: YH09516**

MICKY HAMMOND RACING

Micky Hammond Racing Ltd, Oakwood Stables, East Witton Rd, Middleham, Leyburn, **Yorkshire (North)**, DL8 4PT, **ENGLAND**.
(T) 01969 625224 **(F)** 01969 625224.
Profile Trainer. **Ref: YH09517**

MICROBIAL MANAGEMENT

Microbial Management Ltd, Hilltop, Ashampstead, Reading, **Berkshire**, RG8 8RH, **ENGLAND**.
(T) 01635 578838 **(F)** 01635 578059.
Profile Club/Association. **Ref: YH09518**

MICROM

Microm UK Ltd, 8 Thame Business Pk, Wenman Rd, Thame, **Oxfordshire**, OX9 3XA, **ENGLAND**.
(T) 01844 213645 **(F)** 01844 213644.
Contact/s
Administration: Ms D Howlett
(E) dawn.howlett@imas.co.uk
Profile Medical Support, Supplies.
Opening Times
Sp: Open Mon - Fri 09:00. Closed Mon - Fri 17:30.
Su: Open Mon - Fri 09:00. Closed Mon - Fri 17:30.
Au: Open Mon - Fri 09:00. Closed Mon - Fri 17:30.
Wn: Open Mon - Fri 09:00. Closed Mon - Fri 17:30.
Ref: YH09519

MID & EAST DEVON BRIDLEWAYS

Mid & East Devon Bridleways, Regency Hse, Hemyock, Cullompton, **Devon**, EX15 3RQ, **ENGLAND**.
(T) 01823 680238. **Ref: YH09520**

MID ANTRIM PONY CLUB

Mid Antrim Branch of The Pony Club, 67 Straid Rd, Gracehill, Ballymena, **County Antrim**, BT42 3QF, **NORTHERN IRELAND**.
(T) 028 25871492.
Contact/s
Dist Comm: Mr G Maybin
Profile Club/Association. **Ref: YH09521**

MID CHESHIRE BRIDLEWAYS ASS

Mid Cheshire Bridleways Association, 42 Station Rd, Acton Bridge, Northwich, **Cheshire**, CW8 3PZ, **ENGLAND**.
(T) 01606 851965.
Profile Club/Association. **Ref: YH09522**

MID CHESHIRE RIDING CLUB

Mid Cheshire Riding Club, 20 Shelburne Drive, Haslington, Crewe, **Cheshire**, CW1 5QG, **ENGLAND**.
(T) 01270 584484.
Contact/s
Chairman: Mr M Watson
Profile Club/Association, Riding Club. **Ref: YH09523**

MID DEVON RIDING CLUB

Mid Devon Riding Club, 6 The Old Mill, Mill Rd, Okehampton, **Devon**, EX20 1PR, **ENGLAND**.
(T) 01837 54830.
Contact/s
Chairman: Mr D Cowling
Profile Club/Association, Riding Club. **Ref: YH09524**

MID DEVON RIDING CTRE

Mid Devon Riding Centre, 9 Newcourt Rd, Silverton, Exeter, **Devon**, EX5 4HR, **ENGLAND**.
(T) 01392 860612. **Ref: YH09525**

MID DRUMLOCH

Mid Drumloch Equestrian Centre, Hamilton, **Lanarkshire (South)**, ML3 8RL, **SCOTLAND**.
(T) 01357 300273 **(F)** 01357 300273.
Contact/s
Owner: Miss M Pickering
Profile Riding School, Stable/Livery.
Full, part and DIY livery avaliable, prices on request. Show jumping arena in use only during summer months Yr. Est: 1991 C.Size: 100 Acres
Opening Times
Sp: Open Mon - Sun 09:00. Closed Mon - Sun 18:00.
Su: Open Mon - Sun 09:00. Closed Mon - Sun 18:00.
Au: Open Mon - Sun 09:00. Closed Mon - Sun 18:00.
Wn: Open Mon - Sun 09:00. Closed Mon - Sun 18:00. **Ref: YH09526**

MID GAVIN FARM

Mid Gavin Farm, Mid Gavin, Howwood, Johnstone, **Renfrewshire**, PA9 1DL, **SCOTLAND**.
(T) 01505 842994.
Profile Horse/Rider Accom. **Ref: YH09527**

MID SOMERSET RIDING CLUB

Mid Somerset Riding Club, Annis Hill Farm, Downhead, West Camel, Yeovil, **Somerset**, BA22 7RG, **ENGLAND**.
(T) 01935 850248.
Contact/s
Chairman: Mrs M Peverley
Profile Club/Association, Riding Club. **Ref: YH09528**

MID SURREY FARMERS DRAGHOUNDS

Mid Surrey Farmers Draghounds, Chart Stud Farm, Heverham Rd, Kemsing, Sevenoaks, **Kent**, TN15 6NE, **ENGLAND**.
(T) 01732 761451. **Ref: YH09529**

MID SUSSEX AREA BRIDLEWAYS

Mid Sussex Area Bridleways Group, 1 Hammonds Mill Cottages, London Rd, Hassocks, **Sussex (West)**, BN6 9NB, **ENGLAND**.
(T) 01444 244470.
Contact/s
Secretary: Mrs J Dabbs
Profile Club/Association. **Ref: YH09530**

MID SUSSEX RIDING CLUB

Mid Sussex Riding Club, 17 Church Hill, Patcham, **Sussex (East)**, BN1 8YE, **ENGLAND**.
(T) 01273 563891
(E) joanna_wright@compuserve.com.
Contact/s
Chairman: Mrs K Lawless
Profile Club/Association, Riding Club. **Ref: YH09531**

MID ULSTER SHOWJUMPERS

Mid Ulster Showjumpers, 42 Killagan Rd, Glarryford, Ballymena, **County Antrim**, BT44 9PR, **NORTHERN IRELAND**.
(T) 028 25663792.
Contact/s
Chairman: Mr B Scott
Profile Club/Association. **Ref: YH09532**

MID YORKSHIRE RIDING CLUB

Mid Yorkshire Riding Club, 2 Kentmere Cres, Seacroft, Leeds, **Yorkshire (West)**, LS14 1JS, **ENGLAND**.
(T) 0113 2736376.
Profile Club/Association, Riding Club. **Ref: YH09533**

MIDDLE BAYLES LIVERY

Middle Bayles Livery, Alston, **Cumbria**, CA9 3BS, **ENGLAND**.
(T) 01434 382426.
Contact/s
General Manager: Mr R Munro
Profile Arena, Equestrian Centre, Stable/Livery, Track/Course. No.Staff: 2 Yr. Est: 1999 C.Size: 1000 Acres
Opening Times
Sp: Open 07:30. Closed 20:30.
Su: Open 07:30. Closed 21:30.
Au: Open 07:30. Closed 20:30.
Wn: Open 07:30. Closed 20:30. **Ref: YH09534**

MIDDLE FARM

Middle Farm, Field Aston Lane, Chetwynd Aston, Newport, **Shropshire**, TF10 9LE, **ENGLAND**.
(T) 01952 811618.
Profile Stable/Livery. **Ref: YH09535**

MIDDLE PARK STUD

Middle Park Stud, Unex Hse, Church Lane, Stetchworth, Newmarket, **Suffolk**, CB8 9TN, **ENGLAND**.
(T) 01638 507991 **(F)** 01638 507992.
Contact/s
Manager: Mr M Raynor
Profile Breeder. **Ref: YH09536**

MIDDLEBROOK, SIMON E

Simon E Middlebrook DWCF, Broken Banks, 1 Lowe St, Macclesfield, **Cheshire**, SK11 7NJ, **ENGLAND**.
(T) 01625 435626.
Profile Farrier. **Ref: YH09537**

MIDDLEHAM SWIMMING POOL

Middleham Swimming Pool, Coverham, Leyburn, **Yorkshire (North)**, DL8 4TL, **ENGLAND**.
(T) 01969 624880 **(F)** 01969 624880. **Ref: YH09538**

MIDDLER, C

C Middler, 38 Holdings, Tealing, Dundee, **Angus**, DD4 0QZ, **SCOTLAND**.
(T) 01382 380246.
Contact/s
Owner: Ms C Middler
Profile Stable/Livery. **Ref: YH09539**

MIDDLESTOWN SADDLERY

Middlestown Saddlery, 140 New Rd, Middlestown, Wakefield, **Yorkshire (West)**, WF4 4NU, **ENGLAND**.
(T) 01924 260405
Affiliated Bodies BHS.
Contact/s
Owner: Mrs A Oldroyd
Profile Riding Wear Retailer, Saddlery Retailer, Supplies. No.Staff: 1 Yr. Est: 1985 C.Size: 0.5 Acres
Opening Times
Sp: Open Mon - Fri 14:00, Sat, Sun 10:00. Closed Mon - Sun 19:30.
Su: Open Mon - Fri 14:00, Sat, Sun 10:00. Closed Mon - Sun 19:30.
Au: Open Mon - Fri 14:00, Sat, Sun 10:00. Closed Mon - Sun 19:30.
Wn: Open Mon - Fri 14:00, Sat, Sun 10:00. Closed Mon - Sun 19:30. **Ref: YH09540**

MIDDLETON EQUESTRIAN CTRE

Middleton Equestrian Centre Ltd, Vicarage Hill, Middleton, Tamworth, **Staffordshire**, B78 2AT, **ENGLAND**.
(T) 0121 3111601.
Profile Riding School. **Ref: YH09541**

MIDDLETON PK EQUESTRIAN CTRE

Middleton Park Equestrian Centre, Middleton Gr,

Dewsbury, **Yorkshire (West)**, LS11 5TZ, **ENGLAND**.
(T) 0113 2771962.
Profile Equestrian Centre. **Ref: YH09542**

MIDDLETON POINT TO POINT

Middleton Point to Point, The Old Lodge, Husthwaite, **Yorkshire (North)**, YO61 4PE, **ENGLAND**.
(T) 01347 868513.
Profile Club/Association. **Ref: YH09543**

MIDDLETON STABLES

Middleton Stables, Plantation Cottage, Sadberge Rd, Middleton St. George, Darlington, **County Durham**, DL2 1RJ, **ENGLAND**.
(T) 01325 332685.
Contact/s
Owner: Ms C Dingley **Ref: YH09544**

MIDDLETON, ADRIAN

Adrian Middleton, 27 Bramshill Ave, Balmoral Pk, Kettering, **Northamptonshire**, NN16 9FL, **ENGLAND**.
(T) 01536 483908
(M) 07703 391124
(E) adrian.alison@talk21.com.
Profile Farrier. **Ref: YH09545**

MIDDLETON, LIONEL J P

Lionel J P Middleton AFCL, Moorview, Didworthy, South Brent, **Devon**, TQ10 9EF, **ENGLAND**.
(T) 01364 73491.
Profile Farrier. **Ref: YH09546**

MIDDLEWOOD

Middlewood, Halkyn Old Hall, Afonwen, Mold, **Flintshire**, CH7 5UB, **WALES**.
(T) 01352 721050 **(F)** 01352 720872.
Profile Transport/Horse Boxes. **Ref: YH09547**

MIDDLEWOOD LIVERY STABLES

Middlewood Livery Stables, Middlewood Stables, Lyme Rd, Poynton, Stockport, **Manchester (Greater)**, SK12 1TH, **ENGLAND**.
(T) 01625 859991.
Contact/s
Owner: Miss A Derbyshire
Profile Stable/Livery. **Ref: YH09548**

MIDFORD VALLEY RIDING STABLES

Midford Valley Riding Stables, Midford Valley, Midford, Bath, **Bath & Somerset (North East)**, BA2 7BY, **ENGLAND**.
(T) 01225 837613.
Contact/s
Owner: Mrs J Skegell **Ref: YH09549**

MIDGELAND

Midgeland Indoor Riding School, 460 Midgeland Rd, Blackpool, **Lancashire**, FY4 5EE, **ENGLAND**.
(T) 01253 693312.
Contact/s
Owner: Mrs W Ellis
Profile Riding School. **Ref: YH09550**

MIDGLEY, A D

A D Midgley, Hilltop Farm, Hobberley Lane, **Yorkshire (West)**, LS17 8LX, **ENGLAND**.
(T) 0113 2737017.
Profile Trainer. **Ref: YH09551**

MIDHURST GRANARIES

Midhurst Granaries Ltd, Bepton Rd, Midhurst, **Sussex (West)**, GU29 9LU, **ENGLAND**.
(T) 01730 812334 **(F)** 01730 814662.
Profile Supplies. **Ref: YH09552**

MIDHURST SHOES

Midhurst Shoes, 7 West St, Midhurst, **Sussex (West)**, GU29 9NQ, **ENGLAND**.
(T) 01730 814214.
Profile Saddlery Retailer. **Ref: YH09553**

MIDLAND EQUINE THERAPY

Midland Equine Therapy Ltd, Town Crier Cottage, Fen End Rd, Kenilworth, **Warwickshire**, CV8 1NW, **ENGLAND**.
(T) 01676 532829.
Profile Medical Support. **Ref: YH09554**

MIDLAND MARTS

Midland Marts Ltd, P.O. Box 10, Banbury Stockyard, Banbury, **Oxfordshire**, OX16 8EP, **ENGLAND**.
(T) 01295 50501. **Ref: YH09555**

MIDLAND TRAILER REPAIRS

Midland Trailer Repairs Ltd, 118-122 Charles Henry St, Birmingham, **Midlands (West)**, B12 0SJ, **ENGLAND**.
(T) 0121 6224856 **(F)** 0121 6226798.
Profile Transport/Horse Boxes. **Ref: YH09556**

MIDLANDS AREA CLUB

Midlands Area Club, Quince Cottage, Thorpe, Newark, **Nottinghamshire**, NG23 5PX, **ENGLAND**.
(T) 01636 525221.
Profile Club/Association. **Ref: YH09557**

MIDLANDS EQUITRANS

Midlands Equitrans, Barr Lakes Lane, Aldridge, Walsall, **Midlands (West)**, WS9 0PG, **ENGLAND**.
(T) 0121 3582344.
Contact/s
Owner: Mrs B Ray
Profile Transport/Horse Boxes. **Ref: YH09558**

MIDLANDS HAIRY PONY CLUB

Midlands Hairy Pony Club, Merefield, Oaks Green, Sudbury, Ashbourne, **Derbyshire**, DE6 5HX, **ENGLAND**.
(T) 01283 585358.
Profile Club/Association. **Ref: YH09559**

MIDLOTHIAN'S TOWBAR CTRE

Midlothian's Towbar Centre, 101A High St, Bonnyrigg, **Lothian (Mid)**, EH19 2ET, **SCOTLAND**.
(T) 0131 6630989.
Profile Transport/Horse Boxes. **Ref: YH09560**

MID-NORFOLK CANOPIES/TRAILERS

Mid-Norfolk Canopies & Trailers Of Scarning, The Garage, Scarning, Dereham, **Norfolk**, NR19 2PG, **ENGLAND**.
(T) 01362 687297 **(F)** 01362 687257.
Contact/s
Owner: Mr G Long
Profile Transport/Horse Boxes. **Ref: YH09561**

MIDWAY MANOR

Midway Manor, Bradford-on-Avon, **Wiltshire**, BA15 2AJ, **ENGLAND**.
(T) 01225 868444.
Profile Stable/Livery, Track/Course. **Ref: YH09562**

MIFLIN, WILLIAM

William Miflin, Kennels Cottage, The Old Kennels, Cirencester Pk, Tetbury Rd, Cirencester, **Gloucestershire**, GL7 1UR, **ENGLAND**.
(T) 01285 640335 **(F)** 01285 640335
(M) 07889 448291.
Profile Stable/Livery, Trainer. **Ref: YH09563**

MIKE DANIELL

Mike Daniell Horse Drawn Promotions, Driving Yard, Poplar Pk, Woodbridge, **Suffolk**, IP12 3NA, **ENGLAND**.
(T) 01394 410293 **(F)** 01394 411674
(W) www.mikedaniell.co.uk.
Contact/s
Owner: Mr M Daniell
(E) mike@mikedaniell.co.uk
Profile Horse Drawn Carriages.
Opening Times
Sp: Open Mon - Sun 08:00. Closed Mon - Sun 17:30.
Su: Open Mon - Sun 08:00. Closed Mon - Sun 17:30.
Au: Open Mon - Sun 08:00. Closed Mon - Sun 17:30.
Wn: Open Mon - Sun 08:00. Closed Mon - Sun 17:30. **Ref: YH09564**

MIKE JONES BLACKSMITHS

Mike Jones Blacksmiths, Unit 1 Eastwick Farm, Eastwick, Ellesmere, **Shropshire**, SY12 9DU, **ENGLAND**.
(T) 01691 690394.
Profile Blacksmith. **Ref: YH09565**

MILBOURN EQUINE VET HOSPITAL

Milbourn Equine Vet Hospital, Barrow Hill Hse, Ashford, **Kent**, TN24 8UA, **ENGLAND**.
(T) 01233 623331 **(F)** 01233 639675.
Profile Medical Support. **Ref: YH09566**

MILBY, CHRISTOPHER L

Christopher L Milby DWCF, 138 Park Rd, Swarthmoor, Ulverston, **Cumbria**, LA12 0SD, **ENGLAND**.
(T) 01229 580025.
Profile Farrier. **Ref: YH09567**

MILFEDDYGON BODRWNSIWN

Milfeddygon Bodrwnsiwn Veterinary Group, Bodrwnsiwn, Rhosneigr, **Isle of Anglesey**, LL63, **WALES**.
(T) 01407 810202.
Profile Medical Support. **Ref: YH09568**

MILL END RACING

Mill End Racing, Netherton Lane, Elmley Castle, Pershore, **Worcestershire**, WR10 3JF, **ENGLAND**.
(T) 01386 710772.
Contact/s
Partner: Mr R Brotherton
Profile Trainer. **Ref: YH09569**

MILL FARM CARAVAN & CAMP SITE

Mill Farm Caravan & Camping Site, Fiddington, Bridgwater, **Somerset**, TA5 1JQ, **ENGLAND**.
(T) 01278 732286.
Profile Riding School. **Ref: YH09570**

MILL FARM DIY LIVERY STABLES

Mill Farm DIY Livery Stables, Mill Farm Cottage, Crow Hole, Barlow, Dronfield, **Derbyshire**, S18 7TJ, **ENGLAND**.
(T) 0114 2899309 **(F)** 0114 2899167.
Contact/s
Owner: Mr C Ward
Profile Stable/Livery. **Ref: YH09571**

MILL FARM RIDING CTRE

Mill Farm Riding Centre, Mill Farm, Hughley, Shrewsbury, **Shropshire**, SY5 6NT, **ENGLAND**.
(T) 01746 785645
Affiliated Bodies BHS.
Contact/s
Owner: Mrs E Bosworth **(Q)** BHS 2
Profile Equestrian Centre, Horse/Rider Accom, Stable/Livery.
Hacking a speciality. Full, part and DIY livery avaliable, prices on request. Family riding holidays - children must be accompanied by their parents. No.Staff: 3 Yr. Est: 1976 C.Size: 200 Acres
Opening Times
By appointment only **Ref: YH09572**

MILL FARM RIDING SCHOOL

Mill Farm Riding School, Mill Lane, Credenhill, Hereford, **Herefordshire**, HR4 7EJ, **ENGLAND**.
(T) 01432 761798/760241.
Contact/s
Owner: Mrs C Ballentine
Profile Riding School. **Ref: YH09573**

MILL FARM STABLES

Mill Farm Stables, Mill Farm, Great Witchingham, **Norfolk**, NR9 5PQ, **ENGLAND**.
(T) 01603 870236.
Profile Stable/Livery. **Ref: YH09574**

MILL FORGE

Mill Forge, Caerphilly Rd, Ystrad Mynach, Hengoed, **Caerphilly**, CF82 7EP, **WALES**.
(T) 01443 812827.
Contact/s
Owner: Mr J West
Profile Blacksmith. **Ref: YH09575**

MILL GREEN RIDING SCHOOL

Mill Green Riding School, 3 Waterside Cottages, Mill Green, Hatfield, **Hertfordshire**, AL9 5NY, **ENGLAND**.
(T) 01707 263434.
Profile Riding School. **Ref: YH09576**

MILL HILL FARM

Mill Hill Farm, Chalk St, Rettendon Common, Chelmsford, **Essex**, CM3 8DE, **ENGLAND**.
(T) 01245 400480.
Contact/s
Owner: Mr T Barnes
Profile Stable/Livery. **Ref: YH09577**

MILL HOUSE STUD

Mill House Stud, Acresdyke, 63 Laughton Rd, Lubenham, Market Harborough, **Leicestershire**, LE16 9TE, **ENGLAND**.
(T) 01858 465892 **(F)** 01858 462772
(M) 07802 396964
(E) patorjohn@dyke.tslnet.co.uk.
Profile Breeder. **Ref: YH09578**

MILL LANE

Mill Lane Stables, Mill Lane, Brayton, Selby, **Yorkshire (North)**, YO8 9LB, **ENGLAND**.
(T) 01757 702940
(E) details@milllanestables.co.uk
(W) www.milllanestables.co.uk
Affiliated Bodies ABRS, BHS, RDA.
Contact/s
Owner: Mrs P Wilson **(Q)** NVQ Ass, RDAI
(E) pat@milllanestables.co.uk
Profile Riding School, Stable/Livery.
Home of the Selby & District Riding Club. Full, part and DIY livery avaliable, prices on request. Clinics are

held regularly. **No.Staff:** 5 **Yr. Est:** 1990
C.Size: 14 Acres
Opening Times
Sp: Open Mon - Sat 09:30. Closed Mon - Sat 20:00.
Su: Open Mon - Sat 09:30. Closed Mon - Sat 20:00.
Au: Open Mon - Sat 09:30. Closed Mon - Sat 20:00.
Wn: Open Mon - Sat 09:30. Closed Mon - Sat 20:00.
Competitions on Sundays **Ref: YH09579**

MILL LANE EQUESTRIAN CTRE

Mill Lane Equestrian Centre, Mill Lane, Swindon, **Wiltshire**, SN1 4HG, **ENGLAND**.
(T) 01793 617761.
Contact/s
Manageress: Ms S Holt
Profile Equestrian Centre. **Ref: YH09580**

MILL LANE RIDING SCHOOL

Mill Lane Riding School, Littlebury Hall, Romford Rd, Ongar, **Essex**, CM5 9PE, **ENGLAND**.
(T) 01277 366766.
Contact/s
Owner: Mrs N Maguire
Profile Riding School. **Ref: YH09581**

MILL LODGE EQUESTRIAN CTRE

Mill Lodge Equestrian Centre, Rectory Rd, Outwell, Wisbech, **Cambridgeshire**, PE14 8RD, **ENGLAND**.
(T) 01945 772535.
Profile Equestrian Centre. **Ref: YH09582**

MILL OF URAS EQUESTRIAN

Mill Of Uras Equestrian, Mill Of Uras, Dunnottar, Stonehaven, **Aberdeenshire**, AB39 2TQ, **SCOTLAND**.
(T) 01569 750514 **(F)** 01569 750567.
Contact/s
Owner: Mrs D Masson
Profile Breeder, Saddlery Retailer, Stable/Livery, Supplies. **No.Staff:** 1 **Yr. Est:** 1993
C.Size: 25 Acres
Opening Times
Sp: Open Mon - Sun 10:00. Closed Mon - Sun 18:00.
Su: Open Mon - Sun 10:00. Closed Mon - Sun 18:00.
Au: Open Mon - Sun 10:00. Closed Mon - Sun 18:00.
Wn: Open Mon - Sun 10:00. Closed Mon - Sun 18:00. **Ref: YH09583**

MILL PONY TREKKING CTRE

Mill Pony Trekking Centre (The), Bwlch-Y-Ffridd, Newtown, **Powys**, SY16 3JE, **WALES**.
(T) 01686 688440 **(F)** 01686 688440.
Contact/s
Owner: Mr R Evans
Profile Riding School. **Ref: YH09584**

MILL RIDING CLUB

Mill Riding Club (The), Widford Rd, Much Hadham, **Hertfordshire**, SG10 6EZ, **ENGLAND**.
(T) 01279 841040.
Contact/s
Owner: Mrs J Kennett
Profile Riding School, Stable/Livery. **Ref: YH09585**

MILL RIDING CTRE

Mill Riding Centre (The), Warstone Hill Rd, Pattingham, Wolverhampton, **Midlands (West)**, WV6 7HH, **ENGLAND**.
(T) 01902 700924.
Profile Riding School. **Ref: YH09586**

MILL SADDLERY

Mill Saddlery & Countrywear, Mill St, Stowupland, Stowmarket, **Suffolk**, IP14 5BJ, **ENGLAND**.
(T) 01449 672225.
Contact/s
Owner: Mr P Yeldham
(E) waterford@freenetname
Profile Medical Support, Riding Wear Retailer, Saddlery Retailer, Supplies. **Yr. Est:** 1994
Opening Times
Sp: Open Mon - Sat 09:00. Closed Mon - Sat 17:00.
Su: Open Mon - Sat 09:00. Closed Mon - Sat 17:00.
Au: Open Mon - Sat 09:00. Closed Mon - Sat 17:00.
Wn: Open Mon - Sat 09:00. Closed Mon - Sat 17:00.
Closed Sundays **Ref: YH09587**

MILL VIEW FARM

Mill View Farm, Burton Rd, Heckington, Sleaford, **Lincolnshire**, NG34 9QS, **ENGLAND**.
(T) 01529 461887 **(F)** 01529 461887
(E) 100543.741@compuserve.com
(W) www.millviewfarmridingschool.co.uk.
Contact/s
Owner: Mr D Roberts **(Q)** BHSII
Profile Breeder, Riding School. Classical Buyers. Train classical riding, also have a cafe on-site.
No.Staff: 3 **Yr. Est:** 1996
Opening Times
Sp: Open Wed - Sun 09:00. Closed Wed - Fri 12:00, Sat - Sun 16:30.
Su: Open Wed - Sun 09:00. Closed Wed - Fri 12:00, Sat - Sun 16:30.
Au: Open Wed - Sun 09:00. Closed Wed - Fri 12:00, Sat - Sun 16:30.
Wn: Open Wed - Sun 09:00. Closed Wed - Fri 12:00, Sat - Sun 16:30.
Open Wednesday - Friday evenings 16:00- 19:00. Closed Mondays & Tuesdays **Ref: YH09588**

MILLA LAUQUEN ARABIAN STUD

Milla Lauquen Arabian Stud, Tivetshall St. Margaret, Norwich, **Norfolk**, NR15 2DJ, **ENGLAND**.
(T) 01379 676369.
Contact/s
Owner: Mrs M Popp
Profile Breeder. **Ref: YH09589**

MILLAIS, RAOUL

Raoul Millais, Westcote Manor, Kingham, **Oxfordshire**, OX7 6SF, **ENGLAND**.
(T) 01993 830316. **Ref: YH09590**

MILLAR FEEDS

Millar Feeds, 9 Longmore Rd, Aughafarten, Ballymena, **County Antrim**, BT43 7JR, **NORTHERN IRELAND**..
Profile Supplies. **Ref: YH09591**

MILLARD, SUE

Mrs Sue Millard, Daw Bank, Greenholme, Tebay, **Cumbria**, CA10 3TA, **ENGLAND**.
(T) 01539 624636.
Profile Supplies. **Ref: YH09592**

MILLBRAE SADDLERY

Millbrae Saddlery, Redwood Drive (Peel Park), Thorntonhall, Glasgow, **Lanarkshire (South)**, G74 5BD, **SCOTLAND**.
(T) 01355 573000 **(F)** 01355 573000.
Profile Saddlery Retailer. **Ref: YH09593**

MILLBRIDGE RIDING CTRE

Millbridge Riding Centre, 129 Glen Rd, Comber, Newtownards, **County Down**, BT23 5QT, **NORTHERN IRELAND**.
(T) 028 91872200.
Contact/s
Chairman: Mr D Gillespie
Profile Riding School, Stable/Livery. **Ref: YH09594**

MILLCROFT VETNRY GROUP

Millcroft Veterinary Group, Wakefield Rd, Cockermouth, **Cumbria**, CA13 0HR, **ENGLAND**.
(T) 01900 826666 **(F)** 01900 823737.
Profile Medical Support. **Ref: YH09595**

MILLCROFT VETNRY GROUP

Millcroft Veterinary Group, 18 Curzon St, Maryport, **Cumbria**, CA15 6LN, **ENGLAND**.
(T) 01900 816666 **(F)** 01900 823737.
Profile Medical Support. **Ref: YH09596**

MILLEECA HORSEBOXES

Milleeca Horseboxes, Unit 16D Whitehall Ind Est, Whitehall Rd, Leeds, **Yorkshire (West)**, LS12 5JB, **ENGLAND**.
(T) 0113 2794499 **(F)** 0113 2794499.
Profile Transport/Horse Boxes.
Manufacture and repair horseboxes. **No.Staff:** 7 **Yr. Est:** 1993
Opening Times
Sp: Open Mon - Fri 08:00. Closed Mon - Fri 16:30.
Su: Open Mon - Fri 08:00. Closed Mon - Fri 16:30.
Au: Open Mon - Fri 08:00. Closed Mon - Fri 16:30.
Wn: Open Mon - Fri 08:00. Closed Mon - Fri 16:30.
Closed weekends **Ref: YH09597**

MILLENNIUM ANIMAL BEDDING

Millennium Animal Bedding, 61 Culcheth Hall Drive, Culcheth, Warrington, **Cheshire**, WA3 4PX, **ENGLAND**.
(T) 01925 762580 **(F)** 01925 767692
(M) 07831 811119.
Profile Supplies. **Ref: YH09598**

MILLER & COCHRANE

Miller & Cochrane, 6 Academy St, Stranraer, **Dumfries and Galloway**, DG9 7DR, **SCOTLAND**.
(T) 01776 703131 **(F)** 01776 706896
(E) alan@scotvet.demon.co.uk.
Profile Medical Support. **Ref: YH09599**

MILLER & WHIMSTER

Miller & Whimster, Bridge View, 9 East End, Stokesley, **Cleveland**, TS9 5DP, **ENGLAND**.
(T) 01642 710234.
Profile Medical Support. **Ref: YH09600**

MILLER PLANT

Miller Plant, North Lurg, Midmar, Inverurie, **Aberdeenshire**, AB51 7NB, **SCOTLAND**.
(T) 01330 833462 **(F)** 01330 833478.
Contact/s
Owner: Mrs M Miller
Profile Riding Wear Retailer, Supplies.
Supplies supplements and wormers **Ref: YH09601**

MILLER SADDLERY

Miller Saddlery, 624 Burnley Rd East, Rossendale, **Lancashire**, BB4 9NT, **ENGLAND**.
(T) 01706 226983 **(F)** 01706 217886.
Contact/s
Owner: Mrs M Miller
Profile Saddlery Retailer. **Ref: YH09602**

MILLER TRAILERS

Miller Trailers Ltd, Unit 3 Meadow St, Burnley, **Lancashire**, BB11 1NF, **ENGLAND**.
(T) 01282 411600 **(F)** 01282 457800.
Contact/s
Manager: Mr P Brennand
Profile Transport/Horse Boxes.
Sole UK & Ireland Importers of Bockmann Horseboxes from Germany. **Yr. Est:** 1999
Opening Times
Sp: Open Mon - Sat 09:00. Closed Mon - Sat 17:30.
Su: Open Mon - Sat 09:00. Closed Mon - Sat 17:30.
Au: Open Mon - Sat 09:00. Closed Mon - Sat 17:30.
Wn: Open Mon - Sat 09:00. Closed Mon - Sat 17:30.
Ref: YH09603

MILLER TRAILERS

Miller Trailers Ltd, Unit 56 Cowley Rd, Blackpool, **Lancashire**, FY4 4NE, **ENGLAND**.
(T) 01253 839940 **(F)** 01253 839941.
Contact/s
Owner: Mr C Miller
Profile Transport/Horse Boxes. **Ref: YH09604**

MILLER, EMMA DOUGLAS

Emma Douglas Miller, C/O Hyde Farm, Hyde Lane, Great Missenden, **Buckinghamshire**, HP16 0RF, **ENGLAND**.
(T) 01494 866023. **Ref: YH09605**

MILLER, F V

F V Miller DWCF, 2 Church Lane, Finghall, Leyburn, **Yorkshire (North)**, DL8 5NA, **ENGLAND**.
(T) 01677 50600.
Profile Farrier. **Ref: YH09606**

MILLER, IAN

Mr Ian Miller DC FCC AMC FMCA, 12 Kingswood Cl, Merrow, Guildford, **Surrey**, GU1 2SD, **ENGLAND**.
(T) 01483 304744.
Profile Medical Support. **Ref: YH09607**

MILLER, N A

N A Miller, Honeybrook, Storemore, Dilton Marsh, Westbury, **Wiltshire**, BA13 4BH, **ENGLAND**.
(T) 01373 823040.
Profile Farrier. **Ref: YH09608**

MILLER, P J

P J Miller, The Old Baths, Main Rd, Far Cotton, Northampton, **Northamptonshire**, NN4 8EN, **ENGLAND**.
(T) 01604 767710 **(F)** 01604 767710.
Contact/s
Owner: Mr P Miller
Profile Blacksmith. **Ref: YH09609**

MILLER, R

R Miller, 39 Main St, Dunshalt, Cupar, **Fife**, KY14 7EX, **SCOTLAND**.
(T) 01337 828365.
Contact/s
Partner: Mr D Miller
Profile Blacksmith. **Ref: YH09610**

MILLER, R & DAVIES, M

R Miller & M Davies, Heniarth, Ferryside, **Carmarthenshire**, SA17 5YW, **WALES**.
(T) 01267 267264.
Profile Breeder. **Ref: YH09611**

MILLER, ROY

Roy Miller, 11 Vaughan Ave, Tonbridge, **Kent**, TN10 4EB, **ENGLAND**.
(T) 01732 356874

(E) rmillerart@aol.com. **Ref:YH09612**

MILLER, T F

T F Miller, Flying Horse Farm, Maulden, Bedford, **Bedfordshire**, MK45 2DN, **ENGLAND**.
(T) 01525 280277.
Profile Transport/Horse Boxes. **Ref:YH09613**

MILLER, W & M

W & M Miller, Roadside Cottage, Wester Delnies Farm, Nairn, **Highlands**, IV12 5NU, **SCOTLAND**.
(T) 01667 456324 (F) 01667 456324.
Profile Breeder. **Ref:YH09614**

MILLERS TRADING POST

Millers Trading Post Ltd, Unit 90 The Acorn Ctre, Barry St, Oldham, **Manchester (Greater)**, OL1 3NE, **ENGLAND**.
(T) 0161 6249686 (F) 0161 6268734
(E) tradingpost@flowermill.co.uk
(W) www.flowermill.co.uk/westernwear.
Contact/s
Owner: Miss J Miller
Profile Supplies. **Ref:YH09615**

MILLET

Mrs Millet, The Boot, Kirtling, Newmarket, **Suffolk**, CB8 9PG, **ENGLAND**.
(T) 01638 730275.
Profile Breeder. **Ref:YH09616**

MILLFIELD SCHOOL

Millfield School, Street, **Somerset**, BA16 0YD, **ENGLAND**.
(T) 01458 442297 (F) 01458 447276.
Profile Equestrian Centre. **Ref:YH09617**

MILLFIELDS CONNEMARA

Millfields Connemara Pony Stud, Springfields, North Common, Hepworth, Diss, **Norfolk**, IP22 2PR, **ENGLAND**.
(T) 01359 250019.
Profile Breeder. **Ref:YH09618**

MILLHOLLOW STUD

Millhollow Stud, 10 Lisboy Rd, Downpatrick, **County Down**, BT30 7LE, **NORTHERN IRELAND**.
(T) 028 44619134.
Contact/s
Owner: Miss M McKenna
Profile Breeder. **Ref:YH09619**

MILLHOUSE EQUESTRIAN CTRE

Millhouse Equestrian Centre, Bradford On Tone, Taunton, **Somerset**, TA4 1EP, **ENGLAND**.
(T) 01823 461322.
Contact/s
Owner: Mrs B Venn
Profile Breeder, Riding School, Stable/Livery.
Ref:YH09620

MILLHOUSE RACING

Millhouse Racing, Wixford, Alcester, **Warwickshire**, B49 6DL, **ENGLAND**.
(T) 01789 772808 (F) 01789 772808.
Contact/s
Owner: Mr A Carroll
Profile Trainer. **Ref:YH09621**

MILLHOUSE STABLES

Millhouse Stables, Mill Hse, Bathley Lane, South Muskham, Newark, **Nottinghamshire**, NG23 6DT, **ENGLAND**.
(T) 01636 610550.
Contact/s
Owner: Miss N Coton **Ref:YH09622**

MILLIN INSURANCE SVS

Millin Insurance Services, 1A The Common, Parbold, **Lancashire**, WN8 7DA, **ENGLAND**.
(T) 01257 463161 (F) 01257 463666
(E) wendy@millins.co.uk.
Profile Club/Association. **Ref:YH09623**

MILLINGTON, CHARLES

Mr Charles Millington, Arnesby Lodge, Arnesby, **Leicestershire**, LE8 5WB, **ENGLAND**.
(T) 0116 2478191.
Profile Supplies. **Ref:YH09624**

MILLMAN, B R

Mr B R Millman, The Paddocks, Kentisbeare, Cullompton, **Devon**, EX15 2DX, **ENGLAND**.
(T) 01884 266620 (F) 01884 266620
(M) 07585 168447.
Profile Trainer. **Ref:YH09625**

MILLPARK

Millpark Andalusian Stud, Lutterworth Rd, Arnesby, **Leicestershire**, LE8 3UT, **ENGLAND**.
(T) 0116 2478075 (F) 0116 2478075
Affiliated Bodies BAPSH.
Contact/s
Owner: Miss M Wheatcroft
Profile Breeder. No.Staff: 3 Yr. Est: 1988
C.Size: 40 Acres
Opening Times
Telephone for an appointment, there is an answerphone **Ref:YH09626**

MILLPORT RIDING SCHOOL

Millport Riding School, Golf Rd, Millport, **Ayrshire (North)**, KA28 0BW, **SCOTLAND**.
(T) 01475 530689.
Contact/s
Owner: Christine McCulloch
Profile Riding School. **Ref:YH09627**

MILLS FORGINGS

Mills Forgings Ltd, Charterhouse Rd, Coventry, **Midlands (West)**, CV1 2BJ, **ENGLAND**.
(T) 024 76555559.
Profile Blacksmith. **Ref:YH09628**

MILLS, A M

Mrs A M Mills, Geldridge Farm, Forest Lane, Punnetts Town, Heathfield, **Sussex (East)**, TN21 9JA, **ENGLAND**.
(T) 01435 830284.
Profile Supplies. **Ref:YH09629**

MILLS, ALAN JOHN

Alan John Mills RSS, Halfway Bungalow, Abersoch Rd, Llanbedrog, Pwllheli, **Gwynedd**, LL53 7UB, **WALES**.
(T) 01758 740267.
Profile Farrier. **Ref:YH09630**

MILLS, ANDREW W

Andrew W Mills, The Limes, The Street, Fersfield, Diss, **Norfolk**, IP22 2BL, **ENGLAND**.
(T) 01379 688038.
Profile Farrier. **Ref:YH09631**

MILLS, C D

C D Mills RSS, 12 Guildings Way, Kings Stanley, **Gloucestershire**, GL10 3RF, **ENGLAND**.
(T) 01453 824901.
Profile Farrier. **Ref:YH09632**

MILLS, GLYNIS

Glynis Mills, 41 Wharfedale Cres, Tadcaster, **Yorkshire (North)**, LS24 9JH, **ENGLAND**.
(T) 01937 833008. **Ref:YH09633**

MILLS, J C

J C Mills, Orchard End Farm, Curridge Green, Curridge, Newbury, **Berkshire**, RG16 9GA, **ENGLAND**.
(T) 01635 200694. **Ref:YH09634**

MILLSIDE MANUFACTURING

Millside Manufacturing Co, The Forge/Lock Farm, Spellbrook Lane East, Spellbrook, Bishop's Stortford, **Essex**, CM22 7SE, **ENGLAND**.
(T) 01279 726095.
Contact/s
Owner: Mr R Brown
Profile Blacksmith. **Ref:YH09635**

MILLSLADE FARM STUD

Millslade Farm Stud, Ashcott, Bridgwater, **Somerset**, TA7 9QP, **ENGLAND**.
(T) 01458 210272.
Profile Breeder. **Ref:YH09636**

MILLSTONFORD

Millstonford Farm, West Kilbride, **Ayrshire (North)**, KA23 9PS, **SCOTLAND**.
(T) 01294 822631 (F) 01294 822631
(E) lauchland@cwcom.net.
Contact/s
Owner: Mrs R Lauchland
(E) lauchland@btinternet.com
Profile Stable/Livery. Yr. Est: 1985
Opening Times
Telephone or email for further information
Ref:YH09637

MILLVIEW

Millview Saddlery, 1 Haxby Rd, Misterton, Doncaster, **Yorkshire (South)**, DN10 4AA, **ENGLAND**.
(T) 01427 890509 (F) 01427 890509
(E) mail@millviewsaddlery.com
(W) www.millviewsaddlery.com.
Contact/s
Owner: Mr M Greenwood
Profile Saddlery Retailer.
Has a mobile unit for eventing. Specialists in Eventing Products. No.Staff: 2 Yr. Est: 1981
Opening Times
Sp: Open Mon - Sat 09:00. Closed Mon - Thurs, Sat 18:00, Fri 12:00.
Su: Open Mon - Sat 09:00. Closed Mon - Thurs, Sat 18:00, Fri 12:00.
Au: Open Mon - Sat 09:00. Closed Mon - Thurs, Sat 18:00, Fri 12:00.
Wn: Open Mon - Sat 09:00. Closed Mon - Thurs, Sat 18:00, Fri 12:00.
Closed Sundays **Ref:YH09638**

MILLWARD, GRAHAM N

Graham N Millward DWCF, 17 Grove End, Drayton, Belbroughton, Stourbridge, **Midlands (West)**, DY9 0BW, **ENGLAND**.
(T) 01562 731192.
Profile Farrier. **Ref:YH09639**

MILLWARD, PHILIP E

Philip E Millward DWCF, 2 Ashcroft Cottages, Bagpath, Kingscote, **Gloucestershire**, GL8 8YF, **ENGLAND**.
(T) 01453 861055.
Profile Farrier. **Ref:YH09640**

MILLWHEEL TACK SHOP

Millwheel Tack Shop, Ashleigh, Terrace Rd South, Binfield, Bracknell, **Berkshire**, RG42 4DS, **ENGLAND**.
(T) 01344 486059.
Contact/s
Partner: Mrs S Mills **Ref:YH09641**

MILNER, WAYNE

Wayne Milner DWCF, Rat Hall Farm, Old Brodsworth, Hooton Pagnell, Doncaster, **Yorkshire (South)**, DN5 7DL, **ENGLAND**.
(T) 01302 725185.
Profile Farrier. **Ref:YH09642**

MILNHOLM

Milnholm Riding & Trekking Centre, Milnholm Farm, Polmont, Falkirk, **Falkirk**, FK2 0YD, **SCOTLAND**.
(T) 01324 712847.
Contact/s
Owner: Mr A Buchanan
Profile Riding School. Trekking Centre.
Lessons are mainly given in groups. Yr. Est: 1993
C.Size: 5 Acres
Opening Times
Sp: Open Sat - Sun 11:00. Closed Sat - Sun 15:00.
Su: Open Sat - Sun 11:00. Closed Sat - Sun 15:00.
Au: Open Sat - Sun 11:00. Closed Sat - Sun 15:00.
Wn: Open Sat - Sun 11:00. Closed Sat - Sun 15:00.
Telephone for further information **Ref:YH09643**

MILOJEVIC, NEIL J

Neil J Milojevic DWCF, 18 High St, Woolton, Liverpool, **Merseyside**, L25 7TE, **ENGLAND**.
(T) 0151 4210979.
Profile Farrier. **Ref:YH09644**

MILTON KEYNES EVENTING

Milton Keynes Eventing Centre, Maltmill Farm, Castlethorpe Rd, Hanslope, Milton Keynes, **Buckinghamshire**, MK19 7HQ, **ENGLAND**.
(T) 01908 511329 (F) 01908 510167
(E) ridingclub@mkec.freeserve.co.uk
(W) www.mkec.freeserve.co.uk.
Contact/s
General Manager: Mrs M Trevor-Roper
Profile Equestrian Centre. No.Staff: 7
Yr. Est: 1991 C.Size: 150 Acres
Opening Times
Sp: Open Mon - Sun 09:00. Closed Mon - Sun 17:00.
Su: Open Mon - Sun 09:00. Closed Mon - Sun 17:00.
Au: Open Mon - Sun 09:00. Closed Mon - Sun 17:00.
Wn: Open Mon - Sun 09:00. Closed Mon - Sun 17:00.
Evenings telephone 01908 511964 **Ref:YH09645**

MILWRIGHT, R D P

R D P Milwright, The Veterinary Surgery, 17 Forehill, Ely, **Cambridgeshire**, CB7 4AA, **ENGLAND**.
(T) 01353 665925.
Profile Medical Support. **Ref:YH09646**

MINDHAM, DAVID R

David R Mindham DWCF, 10 The Paddock, Westerham, **Kent**, TN16 1ER, **ENGLAND**.
(T) 01959 563434.
Profile Farrier. **Ref:YH09647**

MINEHEAD HARRIERS
Minehead Harriers, Huntsham Cottage, Wootton Courtenay, Minehead, **Somerset**, TA24 8QZ, **ENGLAND**.
(T) 01643 841376.
Contact/s
Owner: Mr S Weston
Profile Breeder. **Ref: YH09648**

MINEHEAD HARRIERS & FOXHOUNDS
Minehead Harriers & West Somerset Foxhounds, Toomer Farm, Hewstridge, Templecombe, **Somerset**, BA8 0PH, **ENGLAND**.
(T) 01963 250237.
Profile Stable/Livery. **Ref: YH09649**

MINNISMOOR STABLES
Minnismoor Stables, Bankside, Stowting, Ashford, **Kent**, TN25 6AX, **ENGLAND**.
(T) 01303 812688.
Profile Breeder, Riding School, Stable/Livery. **Ref: YH09650**

MINSTER EQUINE VETNRY PRAC
Minster Equine Veterinary Practice (The), Northfield Lane, Upper Poppleton, **Yorkshire (North)**, YO26 6QF, **ENGLAND**.
(T) 01904 788840 **(F)** 01904 788837.
Contact/s
Vet: Mr J Rishworth
Profile Medical Support. **Ref: YH09651**

MINSTER SADDLERY
Minster Saddlery, 79 High St, Minster, Ramsgate, **Kent**, CT12 4AB, **ENGLAND**.
(T) 01843 823923.
Contact/s
Owner: Mr K Jenkin
Profile Saddlery Retailer. **Ref: YH09652**

MINSTER VETNRY CTRE
Minster Veterinary Centre, Orchard Lodge, Newark Rd, Southwell, **Nottinghamshire**, NG25 0ES, **ENGLAND**.
(T) 01636 812133 **(F)** 01636 815362.
Profile Medical Support. **Ref: YH09653**

MINSUPS
Minsups Limited UK, Road One, Ind Est, Winsford, **Cheshire**, CW7 3RG, **ENGLAND**.
(T) 01606 556161 **(F)** 01606 861350.
Profile Medical Support. **Ref: YH09654**

MINTA WINN CARRIAGE DRIVING
Minta Winn Carriage Driving, Wisborough Green, Billingshurst, **Sussex (West)**, RH14 0AB, **ENGLAND**.
(T) 01403 820113.
Profile Trainer. **Ref: YH09655**

MINTY, B
B Minty, Hollybush Farm, The Street, Acton Turville, Badminton, **Gloucestershire**, GL9 1HL, **ENGLAND**.
(T) 01454 218233 **(F)** 01454 218238.
Contact/s
Owner: Mr B Minty
Profile Breeder. **Ref: YH09656**

MINTY, D J
Mr D J Minty, Brooklands, 29 Battleton, Dulverton, **Somerset**, TA22 9HU, **ENGLAND**.
(T) 01398 323838.
Profile Supplies. **Ref: YH09657**

MIRACLE TREES
Miracle Trees, Cott Lane, Burley, Ringwood, **Hampshire**, BH24 4BB, **ENGLAND**.
(T) 01425 403380.
Profile Equestrian Centre. **Ref: YH09658**

MISBOURNE RIDING CTRE
Misbourne Riding Centre, Lower Misbourne Farm, Nutley, Uckfield, **Sussex (East)**, TN22 3LN, **ENGLAND**.
(T) 01825 712516.
Contact/s
Owner: Mr G Osbourne
Profile Equestrian Centre.
Hacking is available. **Yr. Est:** 1967 **C.Size:** 20 Acres
Opening Times
Sp: Open Mon - Sun 09:30. Closed Mon - Sun 20:00.
Su: Open Mon - Sun 09:30. Closed Mon - Sun 20:00.
Au: Open Mon - Sun 09:30. Closed Mon - Sun 20:00.
Wn: Open Mon - Sun 09:30. Closed Mon - Sun 16:00. **Ref: YH09659**

MISSES, B & MILLER, R
B Misses & R Miller (The), Berrywood Hse, Donhead St. Andrew, Shaftesbury, **Dorset**, SP7 9DH, **ENGLAND**.
(T) 01747 828211.
Profile Breeder. **Ref: YH09660**

MISTHAVEN
Misthaven Miniature Horses, Warrant Bungalow, Warrant Rd, Tern Hill, **Shropshire**, TF9 2JA, **ENGLAND**.
(T) 01630 638933 **(F)** 01630 638933.
Contact/s
Owner: Mrs P Hawker
(E) pat@misthaven.freeserve.co.uk
Profile Breeder.
Hobby breeder **Yr. Est:** 1987 **C.Size:** 5 Acres
Opening Times
Sp: Open Mon - Sun 10:00. Closed Mon - Sun 18:00.
Su: Open Mon - Sun 10:00. Closed Mon - Sun 20:00.
Au: Open Mon - Sun 10:00. Closed Mon - Sun 18:00.
Wn: Open Mon - Sun 10:00. Closed Mon - Sun 16:00. **Ref: YH09661**

MISTRAL
Mistral Public Relations, Jericho Farm Barns, Cassington, **Oxfordshire**, OX8 1EB, **ENGLAND**.
(T) 01865 883308 **(F)** 01865 883190
(E) enquiries@mistral-pr.co.uk.
Profile Club/Association. PR Agency.
The business is comprised of specialist equine consultants, including international riders and industry VIP's **Ref: YH09662**

MITCHELL BRIDGES
Mitchell Bridges Ltd, London Rd, Kings Worthy, Winchester, **Hampshire**, SO23 7QN, **ENGLAND**.
(T) 01962 882255.
Contact/s
Manager: Mr C Mitchell
Profile Club/Association. **Ref: YH09663**

MITCHELL, C W
Mr C W Mitchell, White Hse, Buckland Newton, Dorchester, **Dorset**, DT2 7DE, **ENGLAND**.
(T) 01300 345276.
Profile Supplies. **Ref: YH09664**

MITCHELL, DAVID
Mr David Mitchell, The Hideaway, Uffculme, Cullompton, **Devon**, EX15 3DH, **ENGLAND**.
(T) 01884 840762
(M) 07721 623037.
Profile Supplies. **Ref: YH09665**

MITCHELL, DAVID
David Mitchell, South Lodge, Southlands Rd, Crays Hill, **Essex**, CM11 2XB, **ENGLAND**.
(T) 01268 530696.
Profile Farrier. **Ref: YH09666**

MITCHELL, HAMISH
Hamish Mitchell LMPA, Tredegol, Higher Lank, St Breward, Bodmin, **Cornwall**, PL30 4NB, **ENGLAND**.
(T) 01208 851611
(M) 07971 292213. **Ref: YH09667**

MITCHELL, HARVEY STANLEY
Harvey Stanley Mitchell DWCF, Pool Hse Farm, Pool Hse Rd, Higher Poynton, Stockport, **Manchester (Greater)**, SK12 1TY, **ENGLAND**.
(T) 01625 858799.
Profile Farrier. **Ref: YH09668**

MITCHELL, J
J Mitchell, Highsteppers Farm, Glue Hill, Sturminster Newton, **Dorset**, DT10 2DJ, **ENGLAND**.
(T) 01258 472684.
Profile Transport/Horse Boxes. **Ref: YH09669**

MITCHELL, J EDWARD
J Edward Mitchell DWCF, 4 Moorland Drive, Birkenshaw, **Yorkshire (West)**, BD11 2UB, **ENGLAND**.
(T) 01274 683899.
Profile Farrier. **Ref: YH09670**

MITCHELL, JAMES K
James K Mitchell, Brookton, 3 Strathview Pl, Comrie, Crieff, **Perth and Kinross**, PH6 2HG, **SCOTLAND**.
(T) 01764 670754 **(F)** 01764 670754.
Contact/s
Owner: Mr J Mitchell
Profile Transport/Horse Boxes. **Ref: YH09671**

MITCHELL, JEFFREY
Jeffrey Mitchell, Drove End Farm, Alderholt, Fordingbridge, **Hampshire**, SP6 3BH, **ENGLAND**.
(T) 01425 652063.
Profile Breeder. **Ref: YH09672**

MITCHELL, K & K
K & K Mitchell, 9 Wares Rd, Ridgewood, Uckfield, **Sussex (East)**, TN22 5TW, **ENGLAND**.
(T) 01825 764095. **Ref: YH09673**

MITCHELL, K A
K A Mitchell, 68 Causewayhead Rd, Stirling, **Stirling**, FK9 5EZ, **SCOTLAND**.
(T) 01786 445053.
Profile Farrier. **Ref: YH09674**

MITCHELL, N R
N R Mitchell, East Hill Stable, Piddletrenthide, Dorchester, **Dorset**, DT2 7QY, **ENGLAND**.
(T) 01300 348739.
Profile Trainer. **Ref: YH09675**

MITCHELL, P
P Mitchell, Downs Hse, Epsom Downs, Epsom, **Surrey**, KT18 5ND, **ENGLAND**.
(T) 01372 273729.
Contact/s
Owner: Mr P Mitchell
Profile Trainer. **Ref: YH09676**

MITCHELL, TOM
Tom Mitchell, Barnahill, Kilmaurs, Kilmarnock, **Ayrshire (East)**, KA3 2PD, **SCOTLAND**.
(T) 01294 850225.
Profile Breeder. **Ref: YH09677**

MITCHELL, W J
W J Mitchell, Viewpoint, Smithy Lane, Crosthwaite, Kendal, **Cumbria**, LA8 8BW, **ENGLAND**.
(T) 01539 568560.
Profile Farrier. **Ref: YH09678**

MITCHELLS
Mitchells, Egerton Hall, Egerton, Malpas, **Cheshire**, SY14 8AE, **ENGLAND**.
(T) 01829 720428.
Contact/s
Owner: Mr J Mitchell **Ref: YH09679**

MITCO
Mitco (London), Hainault Rd, Little Heath, Romford, **Essex**, RM6 5ST, **ENGLAND**.
(T) 020 85906070 **(F)** 020 85994613. **Ref: YH09680**

MITCO
Mitco (Glasgow), 356 Amulree St, Glasgow, **Glasgow (City of)**, G32 7SL, **SCOTLAND**.
(T) 0141 7785461 **(F)** 0141 7788144. **Ref: YH09681**

MITEL MARKETING
Mitel Marketing, Breedon Hse, 73 Mansfield Rd, Papplewick, **Nottinghamshire**, NG15 8FJ, **ENGLAND**.
(T) 0115 9636679 **(F)** 0115 9636679
(M) 07702 161632.
Contact/s
Owner: Mr M Tellmann
Profile Supplies.
Retailer of water and feeding equipment such as feed and water troughs, hay soakers, and feed mangers. Also sell equestrian luggage such as tack boxes, tack trucks and blanket chests. **Ref: YH09682**

MITRE BRIDLE
Mitre Bridle Co Ltd, 59-61 Wednesbury Rd, Walsall, **Midlands (West)**, WS1 4JL, **ENGLAND**.
(T) 01922 636220 **(F)** 01922 636220. **Ref: YH09683**

MITSON, J E & C
J E & C Mitson, Higher Wanless Farm, Red Lane, Colne, **Lancashire**, BB18 7JP, **ENGLAND**.
(T) 01282 865301.
Profile Breeder. **Ref: YH09684**

MOAT FARM RIDING SCHOOL
Moat Farm Riding School, Moat Farm, Malleson Rd, Gotherington, Cheltenham, **Gloucestershire**, GL52 4ET, **ENGLAND**.
(T) 01242 672055.
Contact/s
Owner: Mrs A Tilley
Profile Riding School. **Ref: YH09685**

MOAT HOUSE STUD
Moat House Stud, Ullenhall, Henley In Arden, **Warwickshire**, B95 5RS, **ENGLAND**.
(T) 01564 792560 **(F)** 01564 793350.

Contact/s
Owner: Mr R Westwood
Profile Breeder, Riding School, Trainer. Ref: YH09686

MOBBERLEY RIDING SCHOOL

Mobberley Riding School, Oak Hse, Newton Hall Lane, Mobberley, Knutsford, **Cheshire**, WA16 7LQ, **ENGLAND**.
(T) 01565 873123.
Profile Riding School, Stable/Livery. Ref: YH09687

MOBBS, F I

F I Mobbs, Keepers Cottage, Broad St Green Rd, Great Totham, Maldon, **Essex**, CM9 8NU, **ENGLAND**.
(T) 01621 891108.
Contact/s
Owner: Mr F Mobbs
Profile Farrier.
Mobile farrier.
Opening Times
Sp: Open Mon - Sat 08:00. Closed Mon - Fri 17:00, Sat 13:00.
Su: Open Mon - Sat 08:00. Closed Mon - Fri 17:00, Sat 13:00.
Au: Open Mon - Sat 08:00. Closed Mon - Fri 17:00, Sat 13:00.
Wn: Open Mon - Sat 08:00. Closed Mon - Fri 17:00, Sat 13:00.
Closed Sundays Ref: YH09688

MOBILE PROMOTIONS COMPANY

Mobile Promotions Company (The), New Brook, Titchmarsh, **Northamptonshire**, NN14 3DG, **ENGLAND**.
(T) 01832 733460 (F) 01832 732737
(E) mobile.promotions@btinternet.com
(W) www.mobilepromotions.com.
Profile Transport/Horse Boxes. Marketing Event Company. Ref: YH09689

MOBILE TACK SHOP

Mobile Tack Shop, Bunkers Hill, Sidcup, **Kent**, DA14 5EX, **ENGLAND**.
(T) 020 83021176.
Contact/s
Owner: Mrs C Remy Ref: YH09690

MOBILE TOWBAR SERVICES

Mobile Towbar Services, 42A West St, Beighton, Sheffield, **Yorkshire (South)**, S20 1EP, **ENGLAND**.
(T) 0114 2486325.
Contact/s
Owner: Mr P Hardy
Profile Transport/Horse Boxes. Ref: YH09691

MOBILE TOWBARS

Mobile Towbars, 28 Longfield Ave, High Halstow, Rochester, **Kent**, ME3 8TD, **ENGLAND**.
(T) 01634 251890.
Profile Transport/Horse Boxes. Ref: YH09692

MOBILE TRANSPORT MAINTENANCE

Mobile Transport Maintenance, 283 Becontree Ave, Dagenham, **Essex**, RM8 2UT, **ENGLAND**.
(T) 020 85970971 (F) 020 85975861.
Contact/s
Owner: Mr A Barden
Profile Transport/Horse Boxes. Ref: YH09693

MOBLEY, HELEN

Mrs Helen Mobley, Homelands Farm, Farthinghoe, Brackley, **Northamptonshire**, NN13 5NU, **ENGLAND**.
(T) 01295 710297 (F) 01295 712066.
Profile Trainer. Ref: YH09694

MODDERSHALL RIDING SCHOOL

Moddershall Riding School, Manor Hse Farm, Moddershall, Stone, **Staffordshire**, ST15 8TG, **ENGLAND**.
(T) 01785 813919.
Profile Riding School. Ref: YH09695

MODEL FARM RIDING CTRE

Model Farm Riding Centre, Kitchenham Rd, Ninfield, Battle, **Sussex (East)**, TN33 9LF, **ENGLAND**.
(T) 01424 773088 (F) 01424 775362.
Contact/s
Partner: Mrs D Barclay-Bernard Ref: YH09696

MODERN SADDLERY WALSALL

Modern Saddlery Walsall, Leamore Lane Ind Est, Walsall, **Midlands (West)**, WS2 7NT, **ENGLAND**.
(T) 01922 476166. Ref: YH09697

MOELFRE LEATHER WORKSHOP

Moelfre Leather Workshop, 89 Ffordd Lligwy, Moelfre, **Isle of Anglesey**, LL72 8LT, **WALES**.
(T) 01248 410929.
Profile Saddlery Retailer. Ref: YH09698

MOELFRYN RIDING CTRE

Moelfryn Riding Centre, Bethania, Aberystwyth, **Ceredigion**, SY23 5NP, **WALES**.
(T) 01974 272228.
Contact/s
Owner: Mrs J Davies (Q) BHS 2
Profile Riding School, Stable/Livery, Stud Farm.
Yr. Est: 1964 C.Size: 80 Acres
Opening Times
Sp: Open Mon - Sun 18:00. Closed Mon - Sun 22:00.
Su: Open Mon - Sun 18:00. Closed Mon - Sun 22:00.
Au: Open Mon - Sun 18:00. Closed Mon - Sun 22:00.
Wn: Open Mon - Sun 18:00. Closed Mon - Sun 22:00. Ref: YH09699

MOFFATT, D

D Moffatt, Pitt Farm Racing Stables, Cartmel, Grange-Over-Sands, **Cumbria**, LA11 6PJ, **ENGLAND**.
(T) 01539 536689 (F) 01539 536236.
Contact/s
Manager: Mr J Moffatt
Profile Trainer. Ref: YH09700

MOFFETT, HEATHER

Heather Moffett, East Leigh Farm, Harberton, Totnes, **Devon**, TQ9 7SS, **ENGLAND**.
(T) 01803 863676.
Profile Trainer. Ref: YH09701

MOIR, DAVID

David Moir, 11-13 Broomhill Rd, Aberdeen, **Aberdeen (City of)**, AB10 6JA, **SCOTLAND**.
(T) 01224 584823.
Profile Blacksmith. Ref: YH09702

MOIR, H & F

H & F Moir, Birchwood Works, Kinellar, Aberdeen, **Aberdeen (City of)**, AB21 0SH, **SCOTLAND**.
(T) 01224 790411 (F) 01224 790534.
Contact/s
Partner: Mrs F Moir
Profile Transport/Horse Boxes. Ref: YH09703

MOIR, JOHN ANDERSON

John Anderson Moir, Lismore, 8 Westerlea Drive, Bridge Of Allan, **Stirling**, FK9 4DQ, **SCOTLAND**.
(T) 01786 832205.
Profile Farrier. Ref: YH09704

MOISER, PHILLIP

Phillip Moiser, Parkhouse Farm, Stanley, **County Durham**, DH9 6RG, **ENGLAND**.
(T) 01207 281136
(M) 07710 804084.
Profile Trainer. Ref: YH09705

MOLD VALLEY SADDLERY

Mold Valley Saddlery, 'Northwood', Mold Rd, Alltami, Mold, **Flintshire**, CH7 6LG, **WALES**.
(T) 01244 545130.
Profile Saddlery Retailer, Supplies. Ref: YH09706

MOLE AVON TRADING

Mole Avon Trading Ltd (Axminster), Station Yard, Axminster, **Devon**, EX13 5PF, **ENGLAND**.
(T) 01297 32441.
Profile Saddlery Retailer. Ref: YH09707

MOLE AVON TRADING

Mole Avon Trading Ltd (Okehampton), Exeter Rd, Okehampton, **Devon**, EX20 1QQ, **ENGLAND**.
(T) 01837 53886.
Contact/s
Branch Manager: Mr R Sampson
Profile Saddlery Retailer. Ref: YH09708

MOLE AVON TRADING

Mole Avon Trading Ltd (Crediton), Mill St, Crediton, **Devon**, EX17 1HL, **ENGLAND**.
(T) 01363 774786 (F) 01363 775071
(E) mole.avon@farmline.com.
Contact/s
Branch Manager: Richard Billson
Profile Saddlery Retailer. Ref: YH09709

MOLE VALLEY FARMERS

Mole Valley Farmers Ltd, Underlane, Holsworthy, **Devon**, EX22 6BL, **ENGLAND**.
(T) 01409 253014 (F) 01409 254510.
Profile Feed Merchant, Supplies. Ref: YH09710

MOLE VALLEY FARMERS

Mole Valley Farmers Ltd (Frome), Standerwick, Frome, **Somerset**, BA11 2PN, **ENGLAND**.
(T) 01373 831114 (F) 01373 831016.
Profile Saddlery Retailer. Ref: YH09711

MOLECOMB STUD

Molecomb Stud, Goodwood, Chichester, **Sussex (West)**, PO18 0QD, **ENGLAND**.
(T) 01243 533540
(M) 07702 810056.
Contact/s
General Manager: Mrs C Lassetter (T) 01243 527244
Profile Equestrian Centre, Stable/Livery, Trainer.
No.Staff: 5 Yr. Est: 1984 C.Size: 20 Acres
Ref: YH09712

MOLYNEAX LIVERY STABLES

Molyneax Livery Stables, Fackley Rd, Teversal, Sutton-In-Ashfield, **Nottinghamshire**, NG17 3HL, **ENGLAND**.
(T) 01623 552763.
Contact/s
Owner: Mr J Keeling Ref: YH09713

MOMBER, F

Mr & Mrs F Momber, Blinkworth, Snailing Lane, Blackmoor, Liss, **Hampshire**, GU33 6HQ, **ENGLAND**.
(T) 01420 538412.
Profile Breeder. Ref: YH09714

MONAGHAN SADDLERY WORKSHOP

Monaghan Saddlery Workshop, Plantation Tce, Monaghan, **County Monaghan**, **IRELAND**.
(T) 047 72356.
Profile Supplies. Ref: YH09715

MONARCH ENGINEERING

Monarch Engineering, 93 Portadown Rd, Armagh, **County Armagh**, BT61 9HJ, **NORTHERN IRELAND**.
(T) 028 37522702.
Contact/s
Owner: Mr D Ryan
Profile Transport/Horse Boxes. Ref: YH09716

MONARCH EQUESTRIAN

Monarch Equestrian, King St, Willenhall, **Midlands (West)**, WV13 1QT, **ENGLAND**.
(T) 01902 605566 (F) 01902 633556
(W) www.monarch-equestrian.co.uk.
Contact/s
Partner: Mr T Holliday
Profile Supplies. Ref: YH09717

MONARCH FARM

Monarch Farm, The Green, Hilton, Huntingdon, **Cambridgeshire**, PE18 9NB, **ENGLAND**.
(T) 01380 830426 (F) 01380 830308.
Profile Riding School. Ref: YH09718

MONARCHS HILL STUD

Monarchs Hill Stud, Monarchs Meadow, Hindley Rd, Daisy Hill, Westhoughton, **Lancashire**, BL5 2DY, **ENGLAND**.
(T) 01942 815611 (F) 01942 792934
(E) bob@monarch.prestel.co.uk.
Profile Breeder. Ref: YH09719

MONCK, S (HON)

Hon Mrs S Monck, Yaverland Manor, Sandown, **Isle of Wight**, PO36 8QW, **ENGLAND**.
(T) 01983 406149.
Profile Breeder. Ref: YH09720

MONCUR, J & M

J & M Moncur, St Lawrence Farm, Waltham Rd, Nazeing, **Essex**, EN9 2LU, **ENGLAND**.
(T) 01992 892139 (F) 01992 892139.
Contact/s
Partner: Mr J Moncur
Profile Supplies. Ref: YH09721

MONIFIETH TRAILERS

Monifieth Trailers, 16 Fotheringham Drive, Monifieth, Dundee, **Angus**, DD5 4SN, **SCOTLAND**.
(T) 01382 534652.
Profile Transport/Horse Boxes. Ref: YH09722

MONK & WILLIAMS

Monk & Williams, 3 Swan St, Leamington Spa, **Warwickshire**, CV32 4SR, **ENGLAND**.
(T) 01926 425515.
Contact/s
Owner: Mr A Cox
Profile Blacksmith. Ref: YH09723

MONKHOUSE, PHILIP J

Philip J Monkhouse DWCF, 25 The Fairway, Midhurst, **Sussex (West)**, GU29 9JD, **ENGLAND**.
(T) 01730 814351.

Profile Farrier. **Ref: YH09724**

MONKHOUSE, TONY

Tony Monkhouse, Heatherview, Hill End, Frosterley, Bishop Auckland, **County Durham**, DL13 2SX, **ENGLAND**.
(T) 01388 528726.
Profile Transport/Horse Boxes. **Ref: YH09725**

MONKLANDS & DISTRICT

Monklands & District Riding Club, 11 Main St, Calderbank, Airdrie, **Lanarkshire (North)**, ML6 9SG, **SCOTLAND**.
(T) 01236 62349.
Profile Club/Association. **Ref: YH09726**

MONKSPATH SADDLERY

Monkspath Saddlery, Blunts Green, Henley In Arden, Solihull, **Warwickshire**, B95 5RE, **ENGLAND**.
(T) 01564 794609.
Profile Saddlery Retailer. **Ref: YH09727**

MONNINGTON

Monnington Morgans, Monnington Court, Monnington-on-Wye, Hereford, **Herefordshire**, HR4 7NL, **ENGLAND**.
(T) 01981 500488 **(F)** 01981 500699
(E) monnington.morgans@which.net
(W) www.monnington-morgans.co.uk.
Contact/s
Manager: Ms T Connolly
Profile Arena, Breeder, Horse/Rider Accom, Stable/Livery, Trainer. **No.Staff:** 8 **Yr. Est:** 1975
C.Size: 50 Acres
Opening Times
Sp: Open Mon - Sun 08:00. Closed Mon - Sun 18:00.
Su: Open Mon - Sun 08:00. Closed Mon - Sun 18:00.
Au: Open Mon - Sun 08:00. Closed Mon - Sun 18:00.
Wn: Open Mon - Sun 08:00. Closed Mon - Sun 18:00.
Yard open to livery owners seven days a week. For arena, breeding & training, telephone for further details
Ref: YH09728

MONTAGUE HARRIS

Montague Harris & Co Auctioneers Offices/Estate Agents, 30 Lion St, Abergavenny, **Monmouthshire**, NP7 5NT, **WALES**.
(T) 01873 853041 **(F)** 01873 850773
(E) jsg@montague.harris.abergaveny.co.uk.
Profile Estate Agents.
Land Auctioneers. **Ref: YH09729**

MONTALTO FARM & FORESTRY

Montalto Farm & Forestry, Spa Rd, Ballynahinch, **County Down**, BT24 8PX, **NORTHERN IRELAND**.
(T) 028 97566110.
Profile Riding School. **Ref: YH09730**

MONTEITH, HELEN

Helen Monteith, Grange Cottage, Low Rd, Barrowby, Grantham, **Lincolnshire**, NG32 1DL, **ENGLAND**.
(T) 01476 76312.
Profile Trainer. **Ref: YH09731**

MONTEITH, PETER

Mr Peter Monteith, Grange Cottage, Low Rd, Grantham, **Lincolnshire**, NG32 1DL, **ENGLAND**.
(E) pmonteith@skynow.net.
Profile Trainer. **Ref: YH09732**

MONTRACON

Montracon (Ireland) Ltd, Mckinney Ind Est, 50 Mallusk Rd, Newtownabbey, **County Antrim**, BT36 4PX, **NORTHERN IRELAND**.
(T) 028 90848274.
Profile Transport/Horse Boxes. **Ref: YH09733**

MONTRACON

Montracon Ltd, Unit 4, Atcost Rd, Barking, **Essex**, IG11 0EQ, **ENGLAND**.
(T) 020 85070230 **(F)** 020 85070250.
Contact/s
Owner: Mr M Chamberlain
Profile Transport/Horse Boxes. **Ref: YH09734**

MONTRACON

Montracon Ltd, Carr Hill, Doncaster, **Yorkshire (South)**, DN4 8DE, **ENGLAND**.
(T) 01302 739292 **(F)** 01302 730660.
Contact/s
Controller: Mrs C Proctor
Profile Transport/Horse Boxes. **Ref: YH09735**

MOODY, A D

Mr A D Moody, Escomb Farm, Escomb, Bishop Auckland, **County Durham**, DL14 7SZ, **ENGLAND**.
(T) 01388 663034.
Profile Breeder. **Ref: YH09736**

MOODY, F

F Moody & Co, Tagmore Nurseries, Rabley Heath Rd, Rabley Heath, Welwyn, **Hertfordshire**, AL6 9UD, **ENGLAND**.
(T) 01438 820105.
Profile Farrier. **Ref: YH09737**

MOODY, GAVIN R

Gavin R Moody DWCF, 17 Lester Piggott Way, Newmarket, **Suffolk**, CB8 0BJ, **ENGLAND**.
(T) 01638 667185.
Profile Farrier. **Ref: YH09738**

MOONSHINE FARM

Moonshine Farm Miniature Spotted Ponies, Hollygate Hse, Ridlington, Oakham, **Rutland**, LE15 9AU, **ENGLAND**.
(T) 01572 821781.
Profile Breeder. **Ref: YH09739**

MOONWIND ARABIANS

Moonwind Arabians, Thorington Hall, Thorington, Saxmundham, **Suffolk**, IP17 3QZ, **ENGLAND**.
(T) 01502 478247 **(F)** 01502 478247.
Profile Breeder. **Ref: YH09740**

MOOR END LIVERY YARD

Moor End Livery Yard, Great Sampford, Saffron Walden, **Essex**, CB10 2RQ, **ENGLAND**.
(T) 01799 586338.
Contact/s
Owner: Mrs S Burton
Profile Stable/Livery. **Ref: YH09741**

MOOR END STABLES

Moor End Stables Equestrian Centre, Moor End Rd, Radwell, Bedford, **Bedfordshire**, MK43 7HY, **ENGLAND**.
(T) 01234 781205.
Contact/s
Owner: Ms F Nicol
Profile Equestrian Centre. **Ref: YH09742**

MOOR FARM

Moor Farm, Throwleigh, Okehampton, **Devon**, EX20 2QE, **ENGLAND**.
(T) 01647 23512.
Profile Horse/Rider Accom. **Ref: YH09743**

MOOR FARM RIDING STABLES

Moor Farm Riding Stables, Troopers Inn, Haverfordwest, **Pembrokeshire**, SA62 4NL, **WALES**.
(T) 01437 890762.
Contact/s
Owner: Mrs J Ridge
Profile Stable/Livery. **Ref: YH09744**

MOOR FARM STABLES

Moor Farm Stables, Wall Hill Rd, Corley, Coventry, **Midlands (West)**, CV7 8AP, **ENGLAND**.
(T) 01676 540594
Affiliated Bodies ABRS.
Contact/s
Owner: Miss L Hassall
Profile Riding School, Stable/Livery.
Training and examination centre for NVQ to level 3, BHS to stage 4 and also ABRS tests. Full livery is available, prices on request. Group lessons for children are £6.50 for half an hour, £10.50 an hour, adults are £7.50 for half hour and £11.50 hour.
Yr. Est: 1966 **C.Size:** 25 Acres
Opening Times
Sp: Open Tues - Sun 09:00. Closed Tues - Fri 21:00, Sat 17:00, Sun 15:00.
Su: Open Tues - Sun 09:00. Closed Tues - Fri 21:00, Sat 17:00, Sun 15:00.
Au: Open Tues - Sun 09:00. Closed Tues - Fri 21:00, Sat 17:00, Sun 15:00.
Wn: Open Tues - Sun 09:00. Closed Tues - Fri 21:00, Sat 17:00, Sun 15:00.
Closed Mondays **Ref: YH09745**

MOORAH STUD

Moorah Stud, Little Totham, Maldon, **Essex**, CM9 8JF, **ENGLAND**.
(T) 01621 891323.
Contact/s
Owner: Mr S Mitchell **(Q)** RSS
Profile Stud Farm. **Ref: YH09746**

MOORBRIDGE RIDING STABLES

Moorbridge Riding Stables, Aston Lane, Chellaston, Derby, **Derbyshire**, DE73 1TT, **ENGLAND**.
(T) 01332 702508 **(F)** 01332 705993
(E) mail@moorbridge.freeserve.co.uk
(W) www.moorbridge.freeserve.co.uk
Affiliated Bodies ABRS.
Contact/s
General Manager: Ms R Marshment
Profile Riding School. **Ref: YH09747**

MOORCROFT CTRE

Moorcroft Racehorse Welfare Centre, (The), Wilton Hse, Catsfield, Battle, **Sussex (East)**, TN33 9DL, **ENGLAND**.
(T) 01424 892266 **(F)** 01424 892266
(E) mrwc@talk21.com
(W) www.mrwc.org.uk.
Contact/s
Chief Executive: Mr G Oldfield
Profile Re-schooling and re-homing of ex-racehorses.
British Horseracing Board approved Rehabilitation Centre for Ex-racehorses. Registered Charity: 1076278. **No.Staff:** 8 **Yr. Est:** 1997
C.Size: 28 Acres **Ref: YH09748**

MOORCROFT EQUESTRIAN

Moorcroft Equestrian Ltd, Willowell, Spring Valley Lane, Ardleigh, Colchester, **Essex**, CO7 7SD, **ENGLAND**.
(T) 01206 230530 **(F)** 01206 230970
(E) sales@moorcroft-equestrian.co.uk
(W) www.stablerugs.co.uk.
Contact/s
Owner: Mrs S Moorcroft
Profile Riding Wear Retailer, Saddlery Retailer, Supplies.
They sell a variety of rugs, including stable, turnout, cooler and anti fly rugs as well as summer sheeting. Travel boots are also available. A mail order catalogue is available. **Yr. Est:** 2000
Opening Times
Sp: Open Mon - Fri 10:00. Closed Mon - Fri 17:00.
Su: Open Mon - Fri 10:00. Closed Mon - Fri 17:00.
Au: Open Mon - Fri 10:00. Closed Mon - Fri 17:00.
Wn: Open Mon - Fri 10:00. Closed Mon - Fri 17:00.
Closed weekends **Ref: YH09749**

MOORE & SONS

Moore & Sons, 26 Christchurch St West, Frome, **Somerset**, BA11 1EB, **ENGLAND**.
(T) 01373 462157.
Profile Supplies. **Ref: YH09750**

MOORE BROS

Moore Bros, 3 Finkle St, Market Weighton, York, **Yorkshire (North)**, YO43 3JL, **ENGLAND**.
(T) 01696 872521.
Contact/s
Owner: Mr N Moore
Profile Farrier. **Ref: YH09751**

MOORE ENGINEERING SERVICES

Moore Engineering Services, Oil Mill Lane, Clyst St. Mary, Exeter, **Devon**, EX5 1AG, **ENGLAND**.
(T) 01392 877603.
Profile Blacksmith. **Ref: YH09752**

MOORE, A J & R A

A J & R A Moore, Marsh Farm, Wood Lane, Fishtoft, Boston, **Lincolnshire**, PE22 0RA, **ENGLAND**.
(T) 01205 363684 **(F)** 01205 363684.
Contact/s
Owner: Mrs R Moore
Profile Breeder. **Yr. Est:** 1986 **C.Size:** 110 Acres
Opening Times
Sp: Open Mon - Sun 09:00. Closed Mon - Sun 17:00.
Su: Open Mon - Sun 09:00. Closed Mon - Sun 17:00.
Au: Open Mon - Sun 09:00. Closed Mon - Sun 17:00.
Wn: Open Mon - Sun 09:00. Closed Mon - Sun 17:00.
Times may vary, please telephone for further information **Ref: YH09753**

MOORE, ANTHONY C

Anthony C Moore DWCF, 13 Brokehall Gardens, Ipswich, **Suffolk**, IP3 8RA, **ENGLAND**.
(T) 01473 726920
(M) 07860 926400.
Profile Farrier. **Ref: YH09754**

MOORE, ARTHUR

Arthur Moore, Dereens Stables, Dereens, Naas, **County Kildare**, **IRELAND**.
(T) 045 876292 **(F)** 045 876292.
Contact/s
Trainer: Mr A Moore
(E) arthurmoore@kildarehorse.ie

Profile Supplies, Trainer.
There are two all weather gallops and a sand gallop.
Ref: YH09755

MOORE, C

C Moore, Drift End Stables, The Drift, Bourn, Cambridge, **Cambridgeshire**, CB3 7TB, **ENGLAND**.
(T) 01954 719565.
Contact/s
Owner: Mr C Moore
Profile Farrier. **Ref: YH09756**

MOORE, C L (MAJ)

Maj C L Moore, Hamilton Hse, Toft Next Newton, Market Rasen, **Lincolnshire**, LN8 3NE, **ENGLAND**.
(T) 01673 878575. **Ref: YH09757**

MOORE, CHRISTINE M

Christine M Moore, 4 Abbey Lane, Healaugh, Tadcaster, **Yorkshire (North)**, LS24 8HN, **ENGLAND**.
(T) 01937 834640. **Ref: YH09758**

MOORE, GEORGE

George Moore, Warwick Lodge, North Rd, Middleham, Leyburn, **Yorkshire (North)**, DL8 4PB, **ENGLAND**.
(T) 01969 623823 **(F)** 01969 623823.
Contact/s
Owner: Mr G Moore
Profile Trainer. **Ref: YH09759**

MOORE, HAZEL

Hazel Moore Artist Blacksmiths, Gate Farm Forge/Langley Gate Farm, Swindon Rd, Kington Langley, Chippenham, **Wiltshire**, SN15 5NB, **ENGLAND**.
(T) 01249 750580.
Contact/s
Partner: Miss H Moore
Profile Blacksmith. **Ref: YH09760**

MOORE, J

J Moore, 4 Manor Fields, Market Weighton, **Yorkshire (East)**, YO43 3JW, **ENGLAND**.
(T) 01430 873817.
Profile Farrier. **Ref: YH09761**

MOORE, K & A E

K & A E Moore, Hollyvag, Lewannick, Launceston, **Cornwall**, PL15 7QH, **ENGLAND**.
(T) 01566 782309 **(F)** 01566 782956.
Profile Track/Course. **Ref: YH09762**

MOORE, M B

M B Moore, The Forge, Fromes Hill, Ledbury, **Herefordshire**, HR8 1HT, **ENGLAND**.
(T) 01531 640301.
Contact/s
Owner: Mr M Moore
Profile Blacksmith. **Ref: YH09763**

MOORE, NICHOLAS J

Nicholas J Moore DWCF, Braeburn, 37 Southgate, Market Weighton, **Yorkshire (East)**, YO43 3BG, **ENGLAND**.
(T) 01430 873316.
Profile Farrier. **Ref: YH09764**

MOORE, SIMON A

Simon A Moore DWCF, 1 New Row, Treskillard, Redruth, **Cornwall**, TR16 6JZ, **ENGLAND**.
(T) 01209 714214
(M) 07768 387918.
Profile Farrier. **Ref: YH09765**

MOORE, STEVE

Steve Moore, Peartree Farm, Padgetts Rd, Christchurch, Wisbech, **Cambridgeshire**, PE14 9PL, **ENGLAND**.
(T) 01354 638291. **Ref: YH09766**

MOORE, T E

T E Moore, Sleepbrook Farm, Alderholt, Fordingbridge, **Hampshire**, SP6 3DF, **ENGLAND**.
(T) 01425 653060 **(F)** 01425 653060.
Profile Medical Support. **Ref: YH09767**

MOORE, W

W Moore, 17 Primrose Hill, Etherley Dene, Bishop Auckland, **County Durham**, DL14 0JS, **ENGLAND**.
(T) 01388 450112.
Profile Farrier. **Ref: YH09768**

MOORE, W

W Moore, 66 Main St, Kelty, **Fife**, **SCOTLAND**..
Profile Breeder. **Ref: YH09769**

MOOREHOUSE HORSEBOXES

Moorehouse Horseboxes, Sunnyfield, Whinney Hill, **County Durham**, TS21 1BJ, **ENGLAND**.
(T) 01642 582792 **(F)** 01642 589440
(M) 07976 280515.
Contact/s
Owner: Mr W Moorehouse
Profile Transport/Horse Boxes. **Ref: YH09770**

MOORES FARM EQUESTRIAN CTRE

Moores Farm Equestrian Centre, Corse Lawn, Gloucester, **Gloucestershire**, GL19 4LY, **ENGLAND**.
(T) 01452 780284.
Contact/s
Key Contact: Ms V Taylor
Profile Equestrian Centre, Riding School.
Ref: YH09771

MOORFIELD RIDING

Moorfield Riding, Moor Rd, Milking Nook, Peterborough, **Cambridgeshire**, PE6 7PQ, **ENGLAND**.
(T) 01733 810444.
Contact/s
Owner: Mr G Bellamy
Profile Riding School. **Ref: YH09772**

MOORFIELD TRAILER & TOWBARS

Moorfield Trailer & Towbars, Moor Rd, Milking Nook, Peterborough, **Cambridgeshire**, PE6 7PQ, **ENGLAND**.
(T) 01733 810444.
Contact/s
Owner: Mr G Bellamy
Profile Riding School. **Ref: YH09773**

MOORHOUSE

Moorhouse Equestrian Centre, Gap Farm, Moorhouse Lane, Moorhouse, Doncaster, **Yorkshire (South)**, DN6 7HA, **ENGLAND**.
(T) 01977 642109 **(F)** 01977 642109.
Contact/s
Owner: Mrs S Hobson-Pratt
Profile Equestrian Centre, Saddlery Retailer, Stable/Livery.
Full livery is available, prices on request.
Showjumping and dressage competitions are held in the two indoor schools from September to April. This is the sister site of Moorhouse Riding School.
Yr. Est: 1989 **C.Size:** 6 Acres
Opening Times
Telephone for an appointment between the times of 08:00 - 20:00 **Ref: YH09774**

MOORHOUSE

Moorhouse Riding School, Gap Farm, Moorhouse Lane, Moorhouse, Doncaster, **Yorkshire (South)**, DN6 7HA, **ENGLAND**.
(T) 01977 642109 **(F)** 01977 642109.
Contact/s
Owner: Mrs D Harris **(Q)** BHS SM, BHSII
Profile Riding School.
Dressage training is given to riders on their own horses. This site is the sister of Moorhouse Equestrian Centre & Saddlery. **Yr. Est:** 1988 **C.Size:** 6 Acres
Opening Times
Telephone for an appointment between the times of 08:00 - 20:00. No lessons on Sundays between October - March. **Ref: YH09775**

MOORHOUSE RIDING CTRE

Moorhouse Riding Centre, Moor Hse, Sutton Rd, Wigginton, York, **Yorkshire (North)**, YO32 2RB, **ENGLAND**.
(T) 01904 769029.
Contact/s
Instructor: Miss P Kemp-Welsh **(Q)** BHS SM, BHSII
Profile Riding School.
Hold monthly dressage trainers clinic open to registered dressage riders with own horses. **Yr. Est:** 1971
C.Size: 9.5 Acres
Opening Times
Sp: Open Mon - Sun 08:00. Closed Mon - Sun 19:00.
Su: Open Mon - Sun 08:00. Closed Mon - Sun 19:00.
Au: Open Mon - Sun 08:00. Closed Mon - Sun 19:00.
Wn: Open Mon - Sun 08:00. Closed Mon - Sun 19:00.
If further information required, please telephone during opening hours **Ref: YH09776**

MOORINGS EQUESTRIAN CTRE

Moorings Equestrian Centre, Lock Lane, Holme upon Spalding Moor, **Yorkshire (East)**, YO43 4DY, **ENGLAND**.
(T) 01430 861178.
Profile Riding School. **Ref: YH09777**

MOORLAND RIDING STABLES

Moorland Riding Stables, Will Farm, Willsworthy, Peter Tavy, Tavistock, **Devon**, PL19 9NB, **ENGLAND**.
(T) 01822 810293. **Ref: YH09778**

MOORLANDS

Moorlands Riding Centre, Hindlip Lane, Hindlip, Worcester, **Worcestershire**, WR3 8SA, **ENGLAND**.
(T) 01905 451487.
Contact/s
Owner: Mr R Tudor
Profile Riding School, Stable/Livery.
Full livery service available **Yr. Est:** 1980
C.Size: 6.5 Acres
Opening Times
Sp: Open Wed - Fri 09:00, Sat 09:30, Sun 10:00. Closed Wed - Fri 18:00, Sat 17:30, Sun 18:00.
Su: Open Wed - Fri 09:00, Sat 09:30, Sun 10:00. Closed Wed - Fri 18:00, Sat 17:30, Sun 18:00.
Au: Open Wed - Fri 09:00, Sat 09:30, Sun 10:00. Closed Wed - Fri 18:00, Sat 17:30, Sun 18:00.
Wn: Open Wed - Fri 09:00, Sat 09:30, Sun 10:00. Closed Wed - Fri 18:00, Sat 17:30, Sun 18:00.
Closed Mondays and Tuesdays **Ref: YH09779**

MOORSIDE EQUESTRIAN

Moorside Equestrian Centre, Moorside Farm, Hawksworth Rd, Baildon, Shipley, **Yorkshire (West)**, BD17 6BJ, **ENGLAND**.
(T) 01274 587849 **(F)** 01274 530192
(W) www.moorsideequestrian.co.uk
Affiliated Bodies BHS.
Contact/s
Owner: Mrs K Metcalfe
(E) kath@moorsideequestrian.co.uk
Profile Stable/Livery. **No.Staff:** 2 **C.Size:** 80 Acres
Opening Times
Sp: Open Mon - Fri 09:00. Closed Mon - Fri 17:00.
Su: Open Mon - Fri 09:00. Closed Mon - Fri 17:00.
Au: Open Mon - Fri 09:00. Closed Mon - Fri 17:00.
Wn: Open Mon - Fri 09:00. Closed Mon - Fri 17:00.
Closed weekends **Ref: YH09780**

MOORTOWN STUD

Moortown Stud, Moortown Farm, Gidleigh, Chagford, **Devon**, **ENGLAND**..
Profile Breeder. **Ref: YH09781**

MOORVIEW

Moorview Equestrian Centre, Roman Rd, Blacksnape, Darwen, **Lancashire**, BB3 3PP, **ENGLAND**.
(T) 01254 701557 **(F)** 01254 701557
(E) general@moorview.co.uk
(W) www.moorview.co.uk.
Contact/s
Owner: Miss U McGuinness **(Q)** BHS INT
Profile Equestrian Centre. **Yr. Est:** 1991
C.Size: 20 Acres
Opening Times
Sp: Open Tues - Sat 11:00. Closed Tues - Sat 20:00.
Su: Open Tues - Sat 11:00. Closed Tues - Sat 20:00.
Au: Open Tues - Sat 11:00. Closed Tues - Sat 20:00.
Wn: Open Tues - Sat 11:00. Closed Tues - Sat 20:00.
Closed Sundays & Mondays **Ref: YH09782**

MOORVIEW MORGANS

Moorview Morgans, Owler Car Farm, Eckington Rd, Coal Aston, Dronfield, **Derbyshire**, S18 3BA, **ENGLAND**.
(T) 01246 413568.
Profile Breeder. **Ref: YH09783**

MOORWOOD STABLES

Moorwood Stables, Moorwood, Woodmancote, Cirencester, **Gloucestershire**, GL7 7EB, **ENGLAND**.
(T) 01285 831787.
Contact/s
Partner: Mrs V Cumbertatch **Ref: YH09784**

MORAN, GRAEME BRYAN

Graeme Bryan Moran DWCF, The Forge, New York, North Shields, **Tyne and Wear**, NE29 8EP, **ENGLAND**.
(T) 0191 2581868.
Profile Farrier. **Ref: YH09785**

MORAY COAST VET GROUP

Moray Coast Vet Group, West Rd, Greshop Est, Forres, **Moray**, IV36 2GN, **SCOTLAND**.
(T) 01309 672243 **(F)** 01309 676710.
Profile Medical Support. **Ref: YH09786**

MORDAX STUDS

Mordax Studs Ltd, Calder Works, Burnley Rd, Simonstone, Burnley, **Lancashire**, BB12 7NL, **ENGLAND**.

(T) 01282 772011 (F) 01282 773600.
Profile Supplies. Ref: YH09787

MORE, W A

Mr W A More, 54 Leander Cres, Dean Park, **Renfrewshire**, PA4 0XB, **SCOTLAND**.
(T) 0141 8851314. Ref: YH09788

MORETON PADDOX STUD

Moreton Paddox Stud, Moreton Paddox, Moreton Morrell, Warwick, **Warwickshire**, CV35 9BU, **ENGLAND**.
(T) 01926 651335.
Profile Breeder. Ref: YH09789

MORETON SADDLERY

Moreton Saddlery Ltd, 3A Oxford St, Moreton In Marsh, **Gloucestershire**, GL56 0LA, **ENGLAND**.
(T) 01608 652222 (F) 01608 652247
(E) enquiries@moretonsaddlery.co.uk
(W) www.moretonsaddlery.co.uk
Affiliated Bodies BETA, SMS.
Contact/s
Saddle Fitter: Mr J Loffet
Profile Riding Wear Retailer, Saddlery Retailer, Supplies.
Country clothing also available. No.Staff: 5
Yr. Est: 1994
Opening Times
Sp: Open Mon - Sat 09:00. Closed Mon - Sat 17:30.
Su: Open Mon - Sat 09:00. Closed Mon - Sat 17:30.
Au: Open Mon - Sat 09:00. Closed Mon - Sat 17:30.
Wn: Open Mon - Sat 09:00. Closed Mon - Sat 17:30.
Closed Sundays and Bank Holidays Ref: YH09790

MORETON WOOD FORGE

Moreton Wood Forge, Moreton Wood Forge, Moreton Wood, Market Drayton, **Shropshire**, TF9 3SF, **ENGLAND**.
(T) 01948 890301 (F) 01948 890639.
Contact/s
Owner: Mr P Handley
Profile Farrier. Ref: YH09791

MORGAN BLACKSMITH

Morgan Blacksmith, Hogg St, Airdrie, **Lanarkshire (North)**, ML6 9JH, **SCOTLAND**.
(T) 01236 764392 (F) 01236 764392.
Contact/s
Owner: Mr G Shanks
Profile Blacksmith. Ref: YH09792

MORGAN BLACKSMITHS

Morgan Blacksmiths Ltd, Chase Forge, Upper Chase Rd, Malvern, **Worcestershire**, WR14 2BT, **ENGLAND**.
(T) 01684 573848 (F) 01684 573848.
Contact/s
Owner: Mr D Morgan
Profile Farrier, Saddlery Retailer. Ref: YH09793

MORGAN EQUINE

Morgan Equine Ltd, Long Hse Farm, Manordeilo, Llandeilo, **Carmarthenshire**, SA19 7BL, **WALES**.
(T) 01550 777775 (F) 01550 777766.
Profile Riding Wear Retailer, Supplies.
Specialise in dressage supplies and accessories.
Ref: YH09794

MORGAN EQUINE STUD

Morgan Equine Stud, Long Hse Farm, Manordeilo, Llandeilo, **Carmarthenshire**, SA19 7BL, **WALES**.
(T) 01550 777990 (F) 01550 777766.
Profile Breeder. Ref: YH09795

MORGAN HORSE ASS

Morgan Horse Association (UK) (The), The Firs, London Rd, Pampisford, **Cambridgeshire**, CB2 4EW, **ENGLAND**.
(T) 01223 833186 (F) 01233 837215.
Profile Club/Association. Ref: YH09796

MORGAN PLATTS

Morgan Platts Ltd, St Annes Rd, Willenhall, **Midlands (West)**, WV13 1DU, **ENGLAND**.
(T) 01902 601141.
Profile Blacksmith. Ref: YH09797

MORGAN, A R

A R Morgan, The Forge, Shutford Rd, North Newington, Banbury, **Oxfordshire**, OX15 6AL, **ENGLAND**.
(T) 01295 730601.
Profile Farrier. Ref: YH09798

MORGAN, B A

B A Morgan RSS, 6 Roundway, Egham, **Surrey**, TW20 8BX, **ENGLAND**.
(T) 01784 459119.
Profile Farrier. Ref: YH09799

MORGAN, B C

B C Morgan, Stoneyford Farm, Stoneyford, Barton Under Needwood, Burton-on-Trent, **Staffordshire**, DE13 8BW, **ENGLAND**.
(T) 01283 575304 (F) 01283 575304.
Contact/s
Owner: Mr B Morgan
Profile Trainer. Ref: YH09800

MORGAN, CLIVE J

Clive J Morgan RSS, Lower Gelli, Pystyll Farm, Tranch, Pontypool, **Torfaen**, NP4 6BP, **WALES**.
(T) 01495 553292.
Profile Farrier. Ref: YH09801

MORGAN, D D P

D D P Morgan, 15 St Martins Rd, Portland, **Dorset**, DT5 1JY, **ENGLAND**.
(T) 01305 820647.
Profile Farrier. Ref: YH09802

MORGAN, DAVID JOHN

David John Morgan, 11 Martin Cl, Soham, Ely, **Cambridgeshire**, CB7 5EJ, **ENGLAND**.
(T) 01353 722624.
Profile Farrier. Ref: YH09803

MORGAN, G W

G W Morgan, 320 Thorpe Rd, Peterborough, **Cambridgeshire**, PE3 6LX, **ENGLAND**.
(T) 01733 264371.
Profile Farrier. Ref: YH09804

MORGAN, GEOFFREY K

Geoffrey K Morgan AFCL, 415 Pickersleigh Rd, Malvern, **Worcestershire**, WR14 2QJ, **ENGLAND**.
(T) 01684 568618.
Profile Farrier. Ref: YH09805

MORGAN, H R

H R Morgan, Garn Hse Yard, Penygarn, Bow Street, **Ceredigion**, SY24 5BQ, **WALES**.
(T) 01970 820474.
Profile Transport/Horse Boxes. Ref: YH09806

MORGAN, JAMES REGINALD

James Reginald Morgan, Ormsaig, Pennyghael, Isle Of Mull, **Argyll and Bute**, PA70 6HF, **SCOTLAND**.
(T) 01681 704230.
Profile Farrier. Ref: YH09807

MORGAN, K A

K A Morgan, 1 Grantham Rd, Waltham On The Wolds, Melton Mowbray, **Leicestershire**, LE14 4AQ, **ENGLAND**.
(T) 01664 464711 (F) 01664 464492.
Contact/s
Trainer: Mr K Morgan
Profile Trainer. National Hunt Trainer. Yr. Est: 1986
Opening Times
Telephone for an appointment Ref: YH09808

MORGAN, LEE P

Lee P Morgan DWCF, 15 Cresswell Cl, Fernhill Heath, **Worcestershire**, WR3 7TP, **ENGLAND**.
(T) 01905 453071.
Profile Farrier. Ref: YH09809

MORGAN, LEE W

Lee W Morgan DWCF, 19 Stepping Stones, Goytre, Pontypool, **Torfaen**, NP4 0BP, **WALES**.
(T) 01873 881024.
Profile Farrier. Ref: YH09810

MORGAN, R

R Morgan, The Forge, Llangybi, Usk, **Monmouthshire**, NP15 1NP, **WALES**.
(T) 01633 450230.
Profile Blacksmith. Ref: YH09811

MORGAN, R W J

R W J Morgan, St. Athan, Barry, **Glamorgan (Vale of)**, CF62 4WA, **WALES**.
(T) 01446 750403.
Contact/s
Owner: Mr R Morgan
Profile Blacksmith. Ref: YH09812

MORGAN, VINCENT E

Vincent E Morgan DWCF, 3 Kingsland Cottages, Benover Rd, Yalding, Maidstone, **Kent**, ME18 6EL, **ENGLAND**.
(T) 01795 890708.
Profile Farrier. Ref: YH09813

MORGANS, FREYJA

Freyja Morgans, Brook Lodge, Isfield, Uckfield, **Sussex (East)**, TN22 5UH, **ENGLAND**.
(T) 01825 750318.
Profile Breeder. Ref: YH09814

MORGANS, O H M

O H M Morgans, Oak Head Caravan Pk, Ayside, Grange-Over-Sands, **Cumbria**, LA11 6JA, **ENGLAND**.
(T) 01539 531475.
Profile Breeder. Ref: YH09815

MORIARTY, KEVIN J D

Kevin J D Moriarty DWCF, Townhead Cottage, Mauchline Rd, Mossblown, **Ayrshire (South)**, KA6 5AR, **SCOTLAND**.
(T) 01292 521002.
Profile Farrier. Ref: YH09816

MORLEY BONNER

Morley Bonner, Ivanmore, Radnor Rd, Redruth, **Cornwall**, TR16 4BQ, **ENGLAND**.
(T) 01209 215303.
Contact/s
Owner: Mrs A Thomas
Profile Transport/Horse Boxes. Ref: YH09817

MORLEY LIVERY YARD

Morley Livery Yard, Lime Lane, Morley, Ilkeston, **Derbyshire**, DE7 6DE, **ENGLAND**.
(T) 01332 831584.
Contact/s
Owner: Mr E Parker
Profile Stable/Livery. Ref: YH09818

MORLEY PARTNERS

Morley Partners, The Animal Health Ctre, 31 Bridge St, Taunton, **Somerset**, TA1 1TQ, **ENGLAND**.
(T) 01823 276959.
Profile Medical Support. Ref: YH09819

MORLEY, P C

P C Morley, Lower Farm, Milden, Ipswich, **Suffolk**, IP7 7AN, **ENGLAND**.
(T) 01787 247332.
Profile Breeder. Ref: YH09820

MORLEY, ROBERT G

Robert G Morley RSS, Sunnyside, Allerston, Pickering, **Yorkshire (North)**, YO18 7PG, **ENGLAND**.
(T) 01723 85680.
Profile Farrier. Ref: YH09821

MORLOCK, C

Mr C Morlock, Raceyard Cottage, Kingston Lisle, Wantage, **Oxfordshire**, OX12 9QH, **ENGLAND**.
(T) 01367 820510 (F) 01367 820510
(M) 07768 923444
(E) morlock@raceyard.co.uk.
Profile Trainer. Ref: YH09822

MORPHETT, S E

Mrs S E Morphett MC AMC MMCA, Tangley Farm Cottages, Milton Under Wychwood, **Oxfordshire**, OX7 6HT, **ENGLAND**.
(T) 01993 830034.
Profile Medical Support. Ref: YH09823

MORPHEUS

Morpheus Designs Co Ltd, The Studio, Mangrove Rd, Cockernhoe, Luton, **Bedfordshire**, LU2 8QD, **ENGLAND**.
(T) 01582 487220
(E) sales@morpheus-designs.com.
Profile Supplies.
Manufacturers of equine accessories in both classic and fun prints. Ref: YH09824

MORRELL ANTHONY & SONS

Morrell Anthony & Sons, Jameston Farm, Maidens, Girvan, **Ayrshire (South)**, KA26 9NF, **SCOTLAND**.
(T) 01655 332010.
Contact/s
Partner: Mrs M Morrell
Profile Blacksmith. Ref: YH09825

MORRIS & NOLAN

Morris & Nolan, Stafford St Business Ctre, 115-120 Stafford St, Walsall, **Midlands (West)**, WS2 8DP, **ENGLAND**.
(T) 01922 637673.
Contact/s
Owner: Mr B Morris Ref: YH09826

MORRIS HOLDINGS

Morris Holdings (UK) Ltd, Holding Hse, 17 Mile Oak, Maesbury Rd, Oswestry, **Shropshire**, SY10 8HA, **ENGLAND**.

A-Z of COMPANIES

(T) 01691 656989 **(F)** 01691 654789.
Profile Club/Association. **Ref: YH09827**

MORRIS, D

D Morris, Neuadd Parc, Capel Bangor, Aberystwyth, **Ceredigion**, **WALES**.
(T) 01970 880260.
Profile Breeder. **Ref: YH09828**

MORRIS, F

F Morris, Timmourie Fell, Skipton Rd, Keighley, **Yorkshire (West)**, BD20 6HJ, **ENGLAND**.
(T) 01535 605999.
Contact/s
Owner: Mr F Morris
Profile Farrier. **Ref: YH09829**

MORRIS, GILES

Giles Morris DWCF, Woodruff, Meeting Hill, Worstead, North Walsham, **Norfolk**, NR28 9LS, **ENGLAND**.
(T) 01692 405704.
Profile Farrier. **Ref: YH09830**

MORRIS, H & H A

H & Mrs H A Morris, Meidrym, Llangeitho, Tregaron, **Ceredigion**, SY25 6GL, **WALES**.
(T) 01974 821234.
Profile Breeder. **Ref: YH09831**

MORRIS, J, C & S

J, C & S Morris, Tyn-Y-Coed Farm, Glan Conwy, Colwyn Bay, **Conwy**, LL28 5TN, **WALES**.
(T) 01492 580689.
Profile Breeder. **Ref: YH09832**

MORRIS, MICHAEL

Michael Morris, Everadsgrange, Fethard, **County Tipperary**, **IRELAND**.
(T) 052 31474.
Contact/s
Trainer: Michael Morris
Profile Trainer. **Ref: YH09833**

MORRIS, NICKY

Nicky Morris, 1 Grenadier Court, Gibson Pl, Stanwell, **Surrey**, TW19 7NW, **ENGLAND**.
(T) 01784 248690.
Profile Trainer. **Ref: YH09834**

MORRIS, S & HUNTON, J

Miss S Morris & J Hunton, Bruntwood, Longhill Lane, Hankelow, Audlem, **Cheshire**, **ENGLAND**.
(T) 01270 811055.
Profile Breeder. **Ref: YH09835**

MORRIS, V

Mrs V Morris, Wood Mill Farm, Ellerdine, Telford, **Shropshire**, **ENGLAND**.
(T) 01952 541759 **(F)** 01952 541976
(E) knmorris@accountant.net.
Profile Breeder. **Ref: YH09836**

MORRISON, H

H Morrison (Racing) Ltd, Summerdown, East Ilsley, Newbury, **Berkshire**, RG20 7LB, **ENGLAND**.
(T) 01635 281678 **(F)** 01635 281746
(M) 07836 687799.
Contact/s
Owner: Mr H Morrison
Profile Trainer. **Ref: YH09837**

MORRISON, LIZ

Liz Morrison BHSI (SM) Regd, Pippins, The Drive, Ifold, Loxwood, Billingshurst, **Sussex (West)**, RH14 0TD, **ENGLAND**.
(T) 07860 637449.
Profile Trainer. **Ref: YH09838**

MORRISON, S J

S J Morrison, Thornhill Rd, Cuminestown, Turriff, **Aberdeenshire**, AB53 5WH, **SCOTLAND**.
(T) 01888 544418 **(F)** 01888 544418.
Contact/s
Owner: Mr S Morrison
Profile Blacksmith. **Ref: YH09839**

MORRISON, WILLIAM G

William G Morrison, Loanhead, Cairnie, Huntly, **Aberdeenshire**, AB54 4TU, **SCOTLAND**.
(T) 01466 760205.
Profile Blacksmith. **Ref: YH09840**

MORRISSEY, JIM

Jim Morrissey, Cappamahone Granagh, Charleville, **County Limerick**, **IRELAND**.
(T) 061 399101.
Profile Supplies. **Ref: YH09841**

MORRISSEY, TIMOTHY P

Timothy P Morrissey DWCF Hons, The Forge, Stainswick, Shrivenham, Swindon, **Wiltshire**, SN6 8LD, **ENGLAND**.
(T) 01793 783581.
Profile Farrier. **Ref: YH09842**

MORRISTOWN LATTIN STUD

Morristown Lattin Stud, Naas, **County Kildare**, **IRELAND**.
(T) 045 897314 **(F)** 045 897708/434200.
Contact/s
Owner: Mr G O'Callaghan
(E) morristownlattinstud@eircom.net
Profile Breeder.
The stud has 2 barns and outdoor yards, with a seperate foaling unit available. Yr. Est: 1989
C.Size: 300 Acres **Ref: YH09843**

MORSTEAD STABLES

Morstead Stables, Morstead, Twyford, Winchester, **Hampshire**, SO20 1JD, **ENGLAND**.
(T) 01962 715915
(M) 07785 390737.
Profile Trainer. **Ref: YH09844**

MORT, LIZ

Liz Mort, Yvans Hall, Hadleigh Heath, Hadleigh, **Suffolk**, IP7 5NX, **ENGLAND**.
(T) 01787 211555 **(F)** 01787 211200.
Profile Supplies. **Ref: YH09845**

MORTIMER RIDING CLUB

Mortimer Riding Club, Holmgarth, Betchworth Ave, Earley, Reading, **Berkshire**, RG6 7RB, **ENGLAND**.
(T) 0118 9265637.
Contact/s
Secretary: Mrs L Bellia
Profile Club/Association, Riding Club. **Ref: YH09846**

MORTIMER, R T

R T Mortimer, Earnshaw Shire Farm, Ulnes Walton Lane, Leyland, **Lancashire**, PR5 3TB, **ENGLAND**.
(T) 01772 423902.
Profile Breeder. **Ref: YH09847**

MORTIMORE, IAN

Ian Mortimore DWCF, Leewood Cottage, Huckworthy Bridge, Sampford Spiney, Yelverton, **Devon**, PL20 6LP, **ENGLAND**.
(T) 01822 854281.
Profile Farrier. **Ref: YH09848**

MORTLOCK, BARRIE J

Barrie J Mortlock, 118A High St, Ingatestone, **Essex**, CM4 0BA, **ENGLAND**.
(T) 01277 353723 **(F)** 01277 355199.
Profile Farrier. **Ref: YH09849**

MORTON MAINS LIVERY

Morton Mains Livery, Morton Mains Farm, 37 Winton Loan, Edinburgh, **Edinburgh (City of)**, EH10 7AW, **SCOTLAND**.
(T) 0131 4451517.
Contact/s
Owner: Mrs L Boswell
Profile Stable/Livery. **Ref: YH09850**

MORTON, GEOFFREY

Geoffrey Morton MBE, Hasholme Carr Farm, Holme upon Spalding Moor, **Yorkshire (East)**, YO43 4BD, **ENGLAND**.
(T) 01430 860393 **(F)** 01430 860057.
Profile Breeder. **Ref: YH09851**

MORTON, LAURIE

Laurie Morton, Snail Hse, River Lane, Fordham, Ely, **Cambridgeshire**, CB7 5PF, **ENGLAND**.
(T) 01638 720846 **(F)** 01638 720846
(E) snailhouse@clara.co.uk. **Ref: YH09852**

MORTON, T

Mr T Morton, Little London, Downwood, Shobdon, Leominster, **Herefordshire**, HR6 9NH, **ENGLAND**.
(T) 01568 708488.
Profile Supplies. **Ref: YH09853**

MORWYN STUD

Morwyn Stud, Bryn Meibion, Clawddnewydd, Ruthin, **Denbighshire**, LL15 2NL, **WALES**.
(T) 01824 750256
Affiliated Bodies WPCS.
Contact/s
Owner: Ms A Weaver
Profile Breeder, Horse/Rider Accom. No.Staff: 1
Yr. Est: 1981 C.Size: 10 Acres
Opening Times
Sp: Open Mon - Sun 09:00. Closed Mon - Sun 21:00.
Su: Open Mon - Sun 09:00. Closed Mon - Sun 21:00.
Au: Open Mon - Sun 09:00. Closed Mon - Sun 21:00.
Wn: Open Mon - Sun 09:00. Closed Mon - Sun 21:00. **Ref: YH09854**

MOSELEY STUD

Moseley Stud, Owston Grange, Bentley, **Yorkshire (South)**, DN5 0LS, **ENGLAND**.
(T) 01302 722586.
Profile Breeder. **Ref: YH09855**

MOSS SIDE RACING STABLES

Moss Side Racing Stables, Moss Side Racing Stables, Crimbles Lane, Cockerham, Lancaster, **Lancashire**, LA2 0ES, **ENGLAND**.
(T) 01524 791179 **(F)** 01524 791958
(M) 07880 553515
(E) info@alanberryracing.com
(W) www.alanberryracing.com.
Contact/s
Owner: Mr A Berry
Profile Trainer. No.Staff: 20 Yr. Est: 1974
C.Size: 100 Acres
Opening Times
By appointment only. Please telephone for further information. **Ref: YH09856**

MOSS, D

D Moss, 71 High St, Thame, **Oxfordshire**, OX9 3AE, **ENGLAND**.
(T) 01844 215979.
Contact/s
Owner: Mr D Moss
Profile Blacksmith. **Ref: YH09857**

MOSS, JANETTE

Janette Moss, 9 Arlingham Mews, Waltham Abbey, **Essex**, EN9 1ED, **ENGLAND**.
(T) 01992 712908 **(F)** 01992 764560
(W) www.janettemoss.co.uk.
Contact/s
Owner: Mrs J Moss
(E) enquiries@janettemoss.co.uk
Profile Riding Wear Retailer, Saddlery Retailer.
No.Staff: 6 Yr. Est: 1988
Opening Times
Sp: Open Mon - Fri 10:00, Sat 09:30. Closed Mon - Sat 17:30.
Su: Open Mon - Fri 10:00, Sat 09:30. Closed Mon - Sat 17:30.
Au: Open Mon - Fri 10:00, Sat 09:30. Closed Mon - Sat 17:30.
Wn: Open Mon - Fri 10:00, Sat 09:30. Closed Mon - Sat 17:30.
Closed Sundays **Ref: YH09858**

MOSS, JOHN

John Moss, 7 Hall Farm Cl, Melton, Woodbridge, **Suffolk**, IP12 1RL, **ENGLAND**.
(T) 01394 380552.
Profile Trainer. **Ref: YH09859**

MOSS, JOHN D

John D Moss DWCF, Hawthorn Farm, Edge View Lane, Knutsford Rd, Alderley Edge, **Cheshire**, SK9 7SU, **ENGLAND**.
(T) 01663 33609.
Profile Farrier. **Ref: YH09860**

MOSS, MICHAEL R

Michael R Moss DWCF, 1 Westfield, Merstone Lane, Merstone, Newport, **Isle of Wight**, PO30 3DE, **ENGLAND**.
(T) 01962 772010.
Profile Farrier. **Ref: YH09861**

MOSS, PHILIP

Philip Moss, Hillmoor Farm, Eaton, Congleton, **Cheshire**, CW12 2NH, **ENGLAND**.
(T) 01260 273487.
Profile Breeder. **Ref: YH09862**

MOSS, R S

R S Moss, The Forge, 75 Froxfield Green, Froxfield, Petersfield, **Hampshire**, GU32 1DQ, **ENGLAND**.
(T) 01730 263536.
Profile Farrier. **Ref: YH09863**

MOSS, T

T Moss, Bookhouse Mill, Dilhorne Rd, Cheadle, **Staffordshire**, ST10 1PR, **ENGLAND**.
(T) 01538 752431.
Profile Supplies. **Ref: YH09864**

MOSSBACK RIDING SCHOOL

Mossback Riding School, Cairn Rd, Cumnock,

Ayrshire (East), KA18 1SL, **SCOTLAND**.
(T) 01290 421422.
Contact/s
Owner: Mrs K Murdoch
Profile Riding School, Stable/Livery. No.Staff: 2
Yr. Est: 1970 C.Size: 60 Acres Ref: YH09865

MOSSBROOK ARENA & STUD

Mossbrook Arena & Stud, Lower Green Lane, Astley, **Manchester (Greater)**, M29 7JZ, **ENGLAND**.
(T) 01942 888287 **(F)** 01942 891861
Affiliated Bodies BSJA.
Contact/s
Owner: Mr A Fazacerley
Profile Equestrian Centre, Stable/Livery.
Mossbrook has a freelance showjumping trainer, and hosts arena BSJA shows.
Opening Times
Sp: Open Mon - Sun 08:00. Closed Mon - Sun 18:00.
Su: Open Mon - Sun 08:00. Closed Mon - Sun 18:00.
Au: Open Mon - Sun 08:00. Closed Mon - Sun 18:00.
Wn: Open Mon - Sun 08:00. Closed Mon - Sun 18:00. Ref: YH09866

MOSSCARR STUD

Mosscarr Stud, Hollinsclough, Longnor, Buxton, **Derbyshire**, SN17 0NQ, **ENGLAND**.
(T) 01298 83247.
Profile Breeder. Ref: YH09867

MOSSMAN COLLECTION

Mossman Collection of Horse Drawn Vehicles (The), Stockwood Pk Craft Museum, Stockwood Country Pk, Farley Hill, Luton, **Bedfordshire**, LU1 5EH, **ENGLAND**.
(T) 01582 738714.
Profile
The Hackney Horse Society Museum is also located here. Ref: YH09868

MOSSOP, J

J Mossop, 2A Preston St, Whitehaven, **Cumbria**, CA28 9DL, **ENGLAND**.
(T) 01946 65878.
Contact/s
Owner: Mr J Mossop
Profile Blacksmith. Ref: YH09869

MOSSVALE BLOODSTOCK SALES

Mossvale Bloodstock Sales, 10 Tullymore Rd, Poyntzpass, Newry, **County Down**, BT35 6QP, **NORTHERN IRELAND**.
(T) 01762 86256 **(F)** 00353 4271315.
Profile Blood Stock Agency. Ref: YH09870

MOSSVALE EQUESTRIAN CTRE

Mossvale Equestrian Centre, 18 Church Rd, Dromara, Dromore, **County Down**, BT25 2NS, **NORTHERN IRELAND**.
(T) 028 97532279.
Profile Equestrian Centre. Ref: YH09871

MOSTYN GALLERIES

Mostyn Galleries, 171 Longwood Gardens, Barkingside, Ilford, **Essex**, IG5 0EN, **ENGLAND**.
(T) 020 85519245.
Contact/s
Owner: Mr D Bresgall
Profile Art Gallery.
Specialise in Dog and Farming Images.
Opening Times
Sp: Open Mon - Sat 09:00. Closed Mon - Sat 17:30.
Su: Open Mon - Sat 09:00. Closed Mon - Sat 17:30.
Au: Open Mon - Sat 09:00. Closed Mon - Sat 17:30.
Wn: Open Mon - Sat 09:00. Closed Mon - Sat 17:30.
Ref: YH09872

MOTEK PORTABLE PRODUCTS

Motek Portable Products Ltd, Unit 4, Sandtoft Ind Est, Belton, Doncaster, **Yorkshire (South)**, DN9 1PN, **ENGLAND**.
(T) 08001 12920 **(F)** 01427 874037.
Profile Club/Association. Ref: YH09873

MOTLEY ENGINEERING

Motley Engineering, Main Rd, East Keal, Spilsby, **Lincolnshire**, PE23 4AS, **ENGLAND**.
(T) 01790 753332.
Contact/s
Owner: Mr G Motley
Profile Blacksmith. Ref: YH09874

MOTORHOME & TRAILER RENTALS

Motorhome & Trailer Rentals Ltd, Lowood Garage, 12 Kings Ave, Clapham, **London (Greater)**, SW4 8BQ, **ENGLAND**.
(T) 020 77206492 **(F)** 020 77206721.
Profile Club/Association. Ref: YH09875

MOTTINGHAM FARM

Mottingham Farm Riding Centre, Mottingham Lane, London, **London (Greater)**, SE9 4RT, **ENGLAND**.
(T) 020 8857 3003.
Contact/s
Groom: Miss S Cooke
Profile Riding School.
Group lessons are only available at weekends.
Yr. Est: 1970
Opening Times
Sp: Open 08:00. Closed 18:00.
Su: Open 08:00. Closed 18:00.
Au: Open 08:00. Closed 18:00.
Wn: Open 08:00. Closed 18:00.
Telephone for further information Ref: YH09876

MOTTRAM & DISTRICT AGRI SOC

Mottram & District Agricultural Society, 10 Gamesley Fold, Glossop, **Derbyshire**, SK13 6JJ, **ENGLAND**.
(T) 01457 867856.
Profile Club/Association. Ref: YH09877

MOTTRAM ST ANDREW

Mottram St Andrew Livery & Horse Transport, Wilmslow Old Rd, Mottram St. Andrew, Macclesfield, **Cheshire**, SK10 4QP, **ENGLAND**.
(T) 01625 584401.
Profile Transport/Horse Boxes. Ref: YH09878

MOUL, PETER L

Peter L Moul DWCF, Eastmede, Off Ternal Mead, Godshill, **Isle of Wight**, PO38 3LJ, **ENGLAND**.
(T) 01983 840094.
Profile Farrier. Ref: YH09879

MOULD, DEAN S

Dean S Mould DWCF, Station Hse, Cox Green, Sunderland, **Tyne and Wear**, SR4 9JR, **ENGLAND**.
(T) 0191 5342104.
Profile Farrier. Ref: YH09880

MOULDRON STUD

Mouldron Stud, Aske, Richmond, **Yorkshire (North)**, DL10 5HD, **ENGLAND**.
(T) 01748 822879.
Profile Breeder. Ref: YH09881

MOULHAM & HORN

Moulham & Horn, Pound Lane, Heacham, King's Lynn, **Norfolk**, PE31 7ET, **ENGLAND**.
(T) 01485 570241.
Profile Supplies. Ref: YH09882

MOULTON CLGE

Moulton College Equestrian Centre, Pitsford Ctre, Pitsford Rd, Moulton, Northampton, **Northamptonshire**, NN3 7RR, **ENGLAND**.
(T) 01604 492653/491131 **(F)** 01604 491127
(W) www.moulton.ac.uk
Affiliated Bodies BHS.
Contact/s
Course Subject Manager: Mr S Maxwell
Profile Equestrian Centre. College.
The College has two outdoor schools, one 60m x 20m, the other 40m x 20m. At College you may attend lectures, demonstrations and equine events and join in competitions. You can work towards National Certificates, BScs and BAs. Yr. Est: 1921
Opening Times
Sp: Open Mon - Fri 09:00. Closed Mon - Fri 17:00.
Su: Open Mon - Fri 09:00. Closed Mon - Fri 17:00.
Au: Open Mon - Fri 09:00. Closed Mon - Fri 17:00.
Wn: Open Mon - Fri 09:00. Closed Mon - Fri 17:00.
Closed at weekends Ref: YH09883

MOULTON PET STORES

Moulton Pet Stores, 90 East Cobgate, Moulton, Spalding, **Lincolnshire**, PE12 6QJ, **ENGLAND**.
(T) 01406 370461.
Contact/s
Owner: Mr N Mynott
Profile Saddlery Retailer. Ref: YH09884

MOULTON POLOCROSSE CLUB

Moulton Polocrosse Club, Moulton Agricultural College, West St Moulton, **Northamptonshire**, NN3 7RR, **ENGLAND**.
(T) 01604 492653.
Contact/s
Chairman: Ms S Edwards
Profile Club/Association. Polocrosse Club.
Ref: YH09885

MOULTON RIDING CTRE

Moulton Riding Centre, 18A Thorpeville, Moulton, Northampton, **Northamptonshire**, NN3 7TR, **ENGLAND**.
(T) 01604 646006 **(F)** 01604 646006.
Contact/s
Owner: Mrs K Meadow Ref: YH09886

MOULTON, A L

A L Moulton, 262 Harrowden Lane, Cardington, **Bedfordshire**, MK44 3ST, **ENGLAND**.
(T) 01234 838430.
Profile Farrier. Ref: YH09887

MOUNT HOUSE STABLES

Mount House Stables, 12 Long Lane, Willoughton, Gainsborough, **Lincolnshire**, DN21 5SQ, **ENGLAND**.
(T) 01427 668210 **(F)** 01427 668233.
Profile Trainer. Ref: YH09888

MOUNT MASCAL RIDING CLUB

Mount Mascal Riding Club, 1 Maylands Drive, Albury Pk, Sidcup, **Kent**, DA14 4SB, **ENGLAND**.
(T) 020 83007400.
Contact/s
Chairman: Miss D Fullilove
Profile Club/Association, Riding Club. Ref: YH09889

MOUNT MASCAL STABLES

Mount Mascal Stables Ltd, Vicarage Rd, Bexley, **Kent**, DA5 2AW, **ENGLAND**.
(T) 020 8300 3947 **(F)** 020 8309 7275
(E) mountmascal.stables@virgin.net
(W) www.mountmascalstables.com
Affiliated Bodies ABRS, BHS.
Contact/s
Chief Instructor: Ms P Dell **(Q)** BHS Int SM
Profile Equestrian Centre. No.Staff: 12
Yr. Est: 1967 C.Size: 25 Acres Ref: YH09890

MOUNT PLEASANT

Mount Pleasant Trekking Centre, 15 Bannonstown Rd, Castlewellan, **County Down**, BT31 9PG, **NORTHERN IRELAND**.
(T) 028 43778651 **(F)** 028 43770030
(E) equestrian.mountpleasant@virgin.net
(W) www.mountpleasantcentre.com
Affiliated Bodies BHS.
Contact/s
General Manager: Mrs M King
Profile Equestrian Centre, Holidays, Horse/Rider Accom.
Horse and pony trekking. Situated within a large forest.
No.Staff: 10 Yr. Est: 1967 C.Size: 2000 Acres
Opening Times
Sp: Open Mon - Sun 09:00. Closed Mon - Sun 21:00.
Su: Open Mon - Sun 09:00. Closed Mon - Sun 21:00.
Au: Open Mon - Sun 09:00. Closed Mon - Sun 16:00.
Wn: Open Mon - Sun 09:00. Closed Mon - Sun 16:00. Ref: YH09891

MOUNT PLEASANT STUD

Mount Pleasant Stud, Mount Pleasant Farm, Blackmoor, Leeds, **Yorkshire (West)**, LS17 9HZ, **ENGLAND**.
(T) 0113 2892304.
Profile Riding School, Stable/Livery. Ref: YH09892

MOUNT ROYAL RIDING SCHOOL

Mount Royal Riding School, The Gables, Lower Wintringham Farm, Croxton, St Neots, **Cambridgeshire**, PE19 4SP, **ENGLAND**.
(T) 01480 880388.
Profile Riding School. Ref: YH09893

MOUNT RULE EQUESTRIAN CTRE

Mount Rule Equestrian Centre Ltd, Braddan, **Isle of Man**, IM4 4HW, **ENGLAND**.
(T) 01624 851922.
Profile Equestrian Centre, Riding School.
Ref: YH09894

MOUNT VETNRY HOSPITAL

Mount Veterinary Hospital, High St, Wellington, **Somerset**, TA21 8QS, **ENGLAND**.
(T) 01823 662286.
Profile Medical Support. Ref: YH09895

MOUNTAIN BREEZE AIR IONISERS

Mountain Breeze Air Ionisers Ltd, C/O Pifco, Failsworth, **Manchester (Greater)**, M35 0HS, **ENGLAND**.
(T) 0161 9473000 **(F)** 0161 6821708.
Profile Medical Support. Ref: YH09896

MOUNTAIN TOP MORGANS
Mountain Top Morgans, Mountain Blow Farm, Haywood, Forth, **Lanarkshire (South)**, ML11 8ES, **SCOTLAND**.
(T) 01555 811462.
Profile Breeder. **Ref: YH09897**

MOUNTAIN, A M
Mrs A M Mountain, Twyford Farm, Horsted Keynes, **Sussex (West)**, RH17 7DJ, **ENGLAND**.
(T) 01825 740313.
Profile Breeder. **Ref: YH09898**

MOUNTALIFAN STABLES
Mountalifan Stables, Long Lane, Newport, **Isle of Wight**, PO30 2NW, **ENGLAND**.
(T) 01983 529833. **Ref: YH09899**

MOUNTED GAMES ASSOCIATION
Mounted Games Association of Great Britain, Europa Trading Est, Parsonage Rd, Stratton St Margaret, Swindon, **Wiltshire**, SN3 4RJ, **ENGLAND**.
(T) 01793 820709 **(F)** 01793 820716
(E) mary@mgagb.co.uk.
Contact/s
Key Contact: Ms M Worth
Profile Club/Association. **Ref: YH09900**

MOUNTFOLD
Mountfold Limited, Mount Bures, Bures, **Suffolk**, CO8 5AZ, **ENGLAND**.
(T) 01787 227573 **(F)** 01787 227333
(E) mountfold.ltd@virgin.net. **Ref: YH09901**

MOUNTIAN, ANTHONY J
Anthony J Mountian DWCF, 57 Castle Gr, Portchester, Fareham, **Hampshire**, PO16 9NY, **ENGLAND**.
(T) 023 92630479.
Profile Farrier. **Ref: YH09902**

MOURNE ROSETTES
Mourne Rosettes, 67 Carnbane Rd, Hillsborough, **County Down**, BT26 6LY, **NORTHERN IRELAND**.
(T) 028 92688049 **(F)** 028 92688049.
Contact/s
Owner: Miss V Walker
Profile Supplies. **Ref: YH09903**

MOURNE TRAIL RIDING CTRE
Mourne Trail Riding Centre, 96 Castlewellan Rd, Newcastle, **County Down**, BT33 0JP, **NORTHERN IRELAND**.
(T) 028 43724351.
Profile Equestrian Centre.
Offer trail rides for the novice to advanced riders, evening rides are also available.
Opening Times
Telephone for further information **Ref: YH09904**

MOW-COP RIDING CTRE
Mow-Cop Riding Centre, Congleton Rd, Mow Cop, Stoke-on-Trent, **Staffordshire**, ST7 3PP, **ENGLAND**.
(T) 01782 514502.
Contact/s
Owner: Mrs J Siddall
Profile Farrier, Riding School. **Ref: YH09905**

MOWSLEY STABLES
Mowsley Stables, High Forge, Theddingworth Rd, Mowsley, Lutterworth, **Leicestershire**, LE17 6NR, **ENGLAND**.
(T) 0116 2402567.
Contact/s
Owner: Miss S Bennett **Ref: YH09906**

MOY RIDING SCHOOL
Moy Riding School, 131 Derrycaw Rd, Dungannon, **County Tyrone**, BT71 6NA, **NORTHERN IRELAND**.
(T) 028 87784440 **(F)** 028 87784440
Affiliated Bodies BHS.
Contact/s
Chairman: Mr P Douglas
Profile Riding School, Stable/Livery, Track/Course.
Opening Times
Sp: Open Mon - Fri 09:00. Closed Mon - Fri 22:00, Sat 17:00.
Su: Open Mon - Fri 09:00. Closed Mon - Fri 22:00, Sat 17:00.
Au: Open Mon - Fri 09:00. Closed Mon - Fri 22:00, Sat 17:00.
Wn: Open Mon - Fri 09:00. Closed Mon - Fri 22:00, Sat 17:00.
Closed on Sundays **Ref: YH09907**

MOYFIELD RIDING SCHOOL
Moyfield Riding School, Shinehill Lane, South Littleton, Evesham, **Worcestershire**, WR11 8TP, **ENGLAND**.
(T) 01386 830207.
Contact/s
Owner: Mrs J Bomford
Profile Riding School.
Side saddle lessons available No.Staff: 5
Yr. Est: 1954 C.Size: 500 Acres
Opening Times
Sp: Open Thurs - Tues 10:00. Closed Mon, Tues, Thurs, Fri 20:00, Sat, Sun 13:00.
Su: Open Thurs - Tues 10:00. Closed Mon, Tues, Thurs, Fri 20:00, Sat, Sun 13:00.
Au: Open Thurs - Tues 10:00. Closed Mon, Tues, Thurs, Fri 20:00, Sat, Sun 13:00.
Wn: Open Thurs - Tues 10:00. Closed Mon, Tues, Thurs, Fri 20:00, Sat, Sun 13:00.
Closed Wednesdays **Ref: YH09908**

MOYGLARE FARM LIVERY STABLES
Moyglare Farm Livery Stables, Moyglare Farm, Stoney Heath, Baughurst, Tadley, **Hampshire**, RG26 5SN, **ENGLAND**.
(T) 01635 299653.
Contact/s
Manager: Mrs M Ravenscroft **Ref: YH09909**

MOYGLARE LIVERY
Moyglare Livery & Training Centre, Moyglare Farm, Stoney Heath, Ramsdell, Tadley, **Hampshire**, RG26 5SN, **ENGLAND**.
(T) 01256 851355.
Contact/s
Owner: Mrs M Ravenscroft
Profile Stable/Livery, Supplies, Trainer.
No.Staff: 1 Yr. Est: 1970 C.Size: 28 Acres
Ref: YH09910

MOYGLARE STUD
Moyglare Stud, Stan Cosgrove, Maynooth, **County Kildare**, **IRELAND**.
(T) 01 6286014 **(F)** 01 6285909
(E) moyglarestud@kildarehorse.ie.
Contact/s
Key Contact: Mr S Cosgrove
Profile Breeder. C.Size: 440 Acres
Ref: YH09911

MOYOLA CANVAS
Moyola Canvas, 42 Tobermore Rd, Maghera, **County Londonderry**, BT46 5DR, **NORTHERN IRELAND**.
(T) 028 79645545 **(F)** 028 79643511.
Contact/s
Manager: Mr G McCready
Profile Supplies. **Ref: YH09912**

MOYOLA STABLES
Moyola Stables, Moyola Pk, Castledawson, Magherafelt, **County Londonderry**, BT45 8ED, **NORTHERN IRELAND**.
(T) 028 79469489.
Contact/s
Owner: Mr L McKee **Ref: YH09913**

MOYSE, ROWENA
Rowena Moyse, Llwynmawr Farm, Penclawdd Rd, Penclawdd, Swansea, **Swansea**, SA4 3RB, **WALES**.
(T) 01792 874299.
Profile Trainer. **Ref: YH09914**

MR ED'S
Mr Ed's Saddlery, Coronation Buildings, Muglet Lane, Maltby, Rotherham, **Yorkshire (South)**, S66 7NA, **ENGLAND**.
(T) 01709 769710.
Contact/s
Manager: Mr A Gisbourne
Profile Riding Wear Retailer, Saddlery Retailer.
No.Staff: 1 Yr. Est: 1999
Opening Times
Sp: Open Mon - Fri 09:00, Sat 10:00. Closed Mon - Fri 16:30, Sat 16:00.
Su: Open Mon - Fri 09:00, Sat 10:00. Closed Mon - Fri 16:30, Sat 16:00.
Au: Open Mon - Fri 09:00, Sat 10:00. Closed Mon - Fri 16:30, Sat 16:00.
Wn: Open Mon - Fri 09:00, Sat 10:00. Closed Mon - Fri 16:30, Sat 16:00.
Closed Sundays **Ref: YH09915**

MR POTTER'S TROTTERS
Mr Potter's Trotters, 12 Saunders Way, Derwen Fawr, Swansea, **Swansea**, SA2 8AY, **WALES**.
(T) 01792 204301.
Profile Supplies. **Ref: YH09916**

MRS HUNT
Mrs Hunt, Maryfield, Terregles, **Dumfries and Galloway**, DG2 9TH, **SCOTLAND**.
(T) 01387 720280.
Profile Breeder. **Ref: YH09917**

MRS R H VAUGHAN
Mrs R H Vaughan, Huntsham Court, Goodrich, Ross-on-Wye, **Herefordshire**, HR9 6JN, **ENGLAND**.
(T) 01600 890296.
Profile Breeder. **Ref: YH09918**

MTS MOBILE TRAILER SERVICES
MTS Mobile Trailer Services, 35 Eastdown, Castleford, **Yorkshire (West)**, WF10 4SG, **ENGLAND**.
(T) 01977 734705 **(F)** 01977 734705.
Contact/s
Owner: Mr M Wardle
Profile Transport/Horse Boxes.
Buy, sell and repair horseboxes. Also supply and fit towbars No.Staff: 3 Yr. Est: 1996
Opening Times
Sp: Open Mon - Sat 08:00. Closed Mon - Fri 17:30, Sat 12:30.
Su: Open Mon - Sat 08:00. Closed Mon - Fri 17:30, Sat 12:30.
Au: Open Mon - Sat 08:00. Closed Mon - Fri 17:30, Sat 12:30.
Wn: Open Mon - Sat 08:00. Closed Mon - Fri 17:30, Sat 12:30. **Ref: YH09919**

MUDCHUTE FARM STABLES
Mudchute Farm Stables, Pier St, London, **London (Greater)**, E14 3HP, **ENGLAND**.
(T) 020 75150749. **Ref: YH09920**

MUIR, WILLIAM R
William R Muir, Wantage Rd, Lambourn, Hungerford, **Berkshire**, RG17 8UG, **ENGLAND**.
(T) 01488 73098 **(F)** 01488 73490.
Contact/s
Owner: Mr W Muir
Profile Trainer. **Ref: YH09921**

MUIRDYKE STUD FARM
Muirdyke Stud Farm, Muirdyke Farm, Cumnock, **Ayrshire (East)**, KA18 2SG, **SCOTLAND**.
(T) 01290 423021.
Contact/s
Owner: Ms A Craig
Profile Breeder, Stable/Livery. **Ref: YH09922**

MUIRHEAD
Muirhead Riding School & Stables, Old Dronley Rd, Muirhead, **Angus**, DD2 5QT, **SCOTLAND**.
(T) 01382 580246.
Profile Equestrian Centre. **Ref: YH09923**

MUIRHEAD BLACKSMITH
Muirhead Blacksmith, Unit 13 Arran Pl, Perth, **Perth and Kinross**, PH1 3DU, **SCOTLAND**.
(T) 01738 643936 **(F)** 01738 643936.
Contact/s
Owner: Mr R Muirhead
Profile Blacksmith. **Ref: YH09924**

MUIRHEAD BLACKSMITHS
Muirhead Blacksmiths, 157 Cumbernauld Rd, Muirhead, Glasgow, **Lanarkshire (North)**, G69 9DY, **SCOTLAND**.
(T) 0141 7794666.
Profile Blacksmith. **Ref: YH09925**

MUIRHEAD STABLES
Muirhead Stables, The Stables, Old Dronley Rd, Backmuir Of Liff, Dundee, **Angus**, DD2 5QT, **SCOTLAND**.
(T) 01382 580246.
Contact/s
Owner: Mr P Gibb
Profile Riding School, Stable/Livery. **Ref: YH09926**

MUIRMILL INTERNATIONAL E C
Muirmill International Equestrian Centre, Muirmill Farm, Symington, Kilmarnock, **Ayrshire (East)**, KA1 5SH, **SCOTLAND**.
(T) 01563 830537
Affiliated Bodies BHS.
Contact/s
Owner: Mrs A Sapwell
Profile Equestrian Centre, Riding School, Stable/Livery.
Centre has cafe on site. Dressage and BSJA shows are held at the centre. The centre also hold clinics and have visiting specialists such as horse whisperers.
Yr. Est: 2001
Opening Times
Sp: Open Mon - Sun 09:00. Closed Mon - Sun 21:00.
Su: Open Mon - Sun 09:00. Closed Mon - Sun 21:00.

Au: Open Mon - Sun 09:00. Closed Mon - Sun 21:00.
Wn: Open Mon - Sun 09:00. Closed Mon - Sun 21:00. Ref: YH09927

MUIRTON STUD

Muirton Stud, Abbey, Madderty, Crieff, **Perth and Kinross**, PH7 3PA, **SCOTLAND**.
(T) 01764 83349.
Profile Breeder. Ref: YH09928

MUIRYHALL STABLES

Muiryhall Stables, Miltonduff, Elgin, **Moray**, IV30 3TG, **SCOTLAND**.
(T) 01343 543478
(M) 07768 636401.
Profile Trainer. Ref: YH09929

MULBERRY BUSH

Mulberry Bush, The Farm, Harvest Hill Lane, Allesley, Coventry, **Midlands (West)**, CV5 9DD, **ENGLAND**.
(T) 024 76403113.
Profile Supplies. Ref: YH09930

MULFRA TREKKING CTRE

Mulfra Trekking Centre, Newmill, Penzance, **Cornwall**, TR20 8XP, **ENGLAND**.
(T) 01736 361601.
Contact/s
Owner: Mrs R Phillips
Profile Equestrian Centre. Ref: YH09931

MULHERN, J E

Mulhern J E, Rathbride Stables, Rathbride, **County Kildare**, **IRELAND**.
(T) 045 521442.
Profile Supplies. Ref: YH09932

MULHOLLAND, T

Mr T Mulholland, Burtree Hse, Hutton Sessay, Thirsk, **Yorkshire (North)**, YO7 3AY, **ENGLAND**.
(T) 07974 359097.
Profile Trainer. Ref: YH09933

MULL OF KINTYRE

Mull of Kintyre Equestrian Centre, Homeston Farm, Campbeltown, **Argyll and Bute**, PA28 6RL, **SCOTLAND**.
(T) 01586 552437.
Profile Equestrian Centre. Ref: YH09934

MULLACOTT EQUESTRIAN

MEC Limited, Honeycleave Farm, Ilfracombe, **Devon**, EX34 8NA, **ENGLAND**.
(T) 01271 866685.
Contact/s
General Manager: Ms H Fennell
Profile Arena, Equestrian Centre, Riding School, Supplies.
Riding holidays and beach rides are also available. No road work is required and the horses, staff and atmosphere are friendly. No.Staff: 4 Yr. Est: 2000
C.Size: 120 Acres
Opening Times
Sp: Open 09:00. Closed 19:30.
Su: Open 09:00. Closed 19:30.
Au: Open 09:00. Closed 17:00.
Wn: Open 09:00. Closed 17:00. Ref: YH09935

MULLACOTT VETNRY HOSPITAL

Mullacott Veterinary Hospital, Sticklepath Veterinary Clinic, Bickington Rd, Barnstaple, **Devon**, EX31 2DB, **ENGLAND**.
(T) 01271 371115.
Profile Medical Support. Ref: YH09936

MULLACOTT VETNRY HOSPITAL GRP

Mullacott Veterinary Hospital Group, Bickenbridge Farm, Ilfracombe, **Devon**, EX34 8NZ, **ENGLAND**.
(T) 01271 866770 **(F)** 01271 866978.
Profile Medical Support. Ref: YH09937

MULLHERN, JOHN

Jonh Mullhern, Meadow Court Stud, Maddenstown, The Curragh, **County Kildare**, **IRELAND**.
(T) 045 521366.
Contact/s
Trainer: Mr J Mullhern
(E) johnmullhern@kildarehorse.ie
Profile Trainer. Ref: YH09938

MULLINEAUX, M

Mr M Mullineaux, Southley Farm, Alpraham, Tarporley, **Cheshire**, CW6 9JD, **ENGLAND**.
(T) 01829 261440 **(F)** 01829 261662
(M) 07801 398570.
Profile Trainer. Ref: YH09939

MULLINS PATK

Mullins Patk, Doninga Goresbridge, **County Carlow**, **IRELAND**.
(T) 050 375121.
Profile Supplies. Ref: YH09940

MULLINS, A

A Mullins, Wateree Gowran, **County Kilkenny**, **IRELAND**.
(T) 056 26377.
Contact/s
Trainer: Mr A Mullins
Profile Trainer. Ref: YH09941

MULLINS, W P

W P Mullins, Closutton, Bagenalstown, **County Carlow**, **IRELAND**.
(T) 050 321786
(E) wpmullins@eircom.net
(W) www.wpmullins.com.
Profile Supplies. Ref: YH09942

MULLIS, ROBERT

Robert Mullis Rocking Horse Maker, 55 Berkeley Rd, Wroughton, Swindon, **Wiltshire**, SN4 9BN, **ENGLAND**.
(T) 01793 813583 **(F)** 01793 813583
(W) www.rockinghorsemaker.com.
Contact/s
Owner: Mr R Mullis
(E) robert@rockinghorses.freeserve.co.uk
Profile Supplies. Rocking Horse Maker.
Restoration service available.
Opening Times
Telephone for an appointment Ref: YH09943

MULTINA RIDING SCHOOL

Multina Riding School, Ville Au Neveu, St Ouen, **Jersey**, JE3 2DU, **ENGLAND**.
(T) 01534 481843.
Profile Riding School. Ref: YH09944

MULTI-SHRED

Multi-Shred (UK) Ltd (Paper Bedding), 3 Brynmawr Rd, Lanesfiels, **Midlands (West)**, WV14 9BU, **ENGLAND**.
(T) 01902 885910.
Profile Supplies. Ref: YH09945

MUMFORD SPECIALIST VEHICLES

Mumford Specialist Vehicles, Gigg Mill, Nailsworth, Stroud, **Gloucestershire**, GL6 0JP, **ENGLAND**.
(T) 01453 832707.
Profile Transport/Horse Boxes. Ref: YH09946

MUMFORD, H S & G R

H S & G R Mumford, Manor Farm, Wellsborough, Nuneaton, **Warwickshire**, CV13 6LP, **ENGLAND**.
(T) 01455 290346.
Profile Supplies. Ref: YH09947

MUNFORD, GEOFFREY F

Geoffrey F Munford Ltd, Stirk Hse, Cross Lanes, Tollerton, York, **Yorkshire (North)**, YO61 1RB, **ENGLAND**.
(T) 01347 838502. Ref: YH09948

MUNNINGS MITCHELL & PEPLOW

Munnings Mitchell & Peplow, Seymour Cottage Veterinary Surgery, Bridgetown, Totnes, **Devon**, TQ9 5BT, **ENGLAND**.
(T) 01803 866283 **(F)** 01803 863309.
Profile Medical Support. Ref: YH09949

MUNRO COMMERCIALS

Munro Commercials Ltd, Ringtail Rd, Burscough Ind Est, Burscough, **Lancashire**, L40 8JB, **ENGLAND**.
(T) 01704 896005.
Profile Transport/Horse Boxes. Ref: YH09950

MURFITT, D G

D G Murfitt, Dairy Ground Cottage, Soham Rd, Stuntney, Ely, **Cambridgeshire**, CB7 5RT, **ENGLAND**.
(T) 01353 662844.
Profile Farrier. Ref: YH09951

MURFITT, TIMOTHY J

Timothy J Murfitt DWCF, 38 Great Fen Rd, Soham, **Cambridgeshire**, CB7 5UQ, **ENGLAND**.
(T) 01353 723674.
Profile Farrier. Ref: YH09952

MURPHY CLIPPING SV

Murphy Clipping Service, Derryhasna, O'Briansbridge, **County Clare**, **IRELAND**.
(T) 061 372024.
Contact/s
Owner: Mr B Murphy
Profile Medical Support. Clipping Blades Service.
Clipping Blades brought back to their original condition by "The Lapping Process" Ref: YH09953

MURPHY EQUESTRIAN

Murphy Equestrian Video Studios, Elphin St, Strokestown, **County Roscommon**, **IRELAND**.
(T) 078 33244.
Contact/s
Owner: Mr J Murphy
(E) jkamurphy@eircom.net
Profile Supplies.
Videos of show jumping horses in competition, including events at Millstreet and Cavan equestrian centres. All horses jumping at these centres are in archives. Yr. Est: 1988 Ref: YH09954

MURPHY HIRE

Murphy Hire Limited, Communications Hse, Vauxhall Rd, Sheffield, **Yorkshire (South)**, S9 1LD, **ENGLAND**.
(T) 0114 2434567 **(F)** 0114 2434127.
Profile Supplies. Ref: YH09955

MURPHY, GENEVIEVE

Genevieve Murphy, 13 Oakley Rd, Warlingham, **Surrey**, CR6 9BE, **ENGLAND**.
(T) 01883 622942.
Profile Supplies. Ref: YH09956

MURPHY, J G

J G Murphy, Crampscastle, Fethard, **County Tipperary**, **IRELAND**.
(T) 052 31347.
Profile Supplies. Ref: YH09957

MURPHY, LARRY

Larry Murphy, Danescastle Bannow, Wexford, **County Wexford**, **IRELAND**.
(T) 051 561480.
Profile Supplies. Ref: YH09958

MURPHY, PETER

Peter Murphy, Thurcroft Hall, Laughton, Brookhouse, Sheffield, **Yorkshire (South)**, S25 1YA, **ENGLAND**.
(T) 01909 564862
(M) 07831 445865. Ref: YH09959

MURPHY, SAM

Sam Murphy, Esker Hill Kildangan, Monasterevin, **County Kildare**, **IRELAND**.
(T) 045 523551.
Profile Supplies. Ref: YH09960

MURPHYS SADDLERY

Murphys Saddlery, The Tack Shop, Pool Farm, Hewish, Weston-Super-Mare, **Somerset (North)**, BS24 6SG, **ENGLAND**.
(T) 01934 833138.
Contact/s
Owner: Mr T Murphy
Profile Saddlery Retailer. Ref: YH09961

MURRAY, ALEXANDER C

Alexander C Murray, Lower Sibster, Wick, **Highlands**, **SCOTLAND**..
Profile Breeder. Ref: YH09962

MURRAY, B W

Mr B W Murray, 60 Parliament St, Norton, Malton, **Yorkshire (North)**, YO17 9HE, **ENGLAND**.
(T) 01653 692879
(M) 07931 974485.
Profile Trainer. Ref: YH09963

MURRAY, BERNARD

Bernard Murray, Cullencastle, Tramore, **County Waterford**, **IRELAND**.
(T) 051 391277.
Profile Supplies. Ref: YH09964

MURRAY, DAVID

David Murray, Unit 50 Suthers St, Oldham, **Lancashire**, OL9 7AH, **ENGLAND**.
(T) 0161 6282649 **(F)** 0161 6282649.
Contact/s
Manager: Mr P Mellor
Profile Transport/Horse Boxes. Ref: YH09965

MURRAY, G

G Murray, 9 Vulcan Hse, Vulcan Rd North, Norwich, **Norfolk**, NR6 6AQ, **ENGLAND**.
(T) 01603 487102.
Contact/s
Owner: Mr G Murray Ref: YH09966

A-Z of COMPANIES

MURRAY, J I

J I Murray, 40 St Cecilia's Rd, Belle Vue, Doncaster, **Yorkshire (South)**, DN4 5EG, **ENGLAND**.
(T) 01302 344681.
Profile Farrier. **Ref: YH09967**

MURRAY, JOHN

John Murray RSS, 18 Belle Vue Ave, Doncaster, **Yorkshire (South)**, DN4 5DX, **ENGLAND**.
(T) 01302 323286.
Profile Farrier. **Ref: YH09968**

MURRAY, SIMON

Simon Murray DWCF, 24 Derbyshire Drive, Westwood, **Nottinghamshire**, NG16 5HQ, **ENGLAND**.
(T) 01773 541243.
Profile Farrier. **Ref: YH09969**

MURT O'BRIEN SADDLERS

Murt O'Brien Saddlers, Naas Rd, Rathcoole, **County Dublin**, **IRELAND**.
(T) 01 4588462.
Profile Saddlery Retailer, Supplies. **Ref: YH09970**

MURTAGH, F P

Mr F P Murtagh, Hurst Farm, Ivegill, Carlisle, **Cumbria**, CA4 0NL, **ENGLAND**.
(T) 01768 484362
(M) 07887 546907.
Profile Trainer. **Ref: YH09971**

MURTON RIDING SCHOOL

Murton Riding School, The Bridle, Murton, Newcastle-upon-Tyne, **Tyne and Wear**, NE27 0QD, **ENGLAND**.
(T) 0191 2571369.
Contact/s
Owner: Mrs J Douglas
Profile Riding School. **Ref: YH09972**

MUSCAT EQUESTRIAN

Muscat Equestrian, Preston Farm Stables, Lower Rd, Fetcham, Leatherhead, **Surrey**, KT22 9EL, **ENGLAND**.
(T) 01372 451914. **Ref: YH09973**

MUSCHAMP STUD

Muschamp Stud, Windmill Rd, Fulmer, Slough, **Berkshire**, SL3 6HG, **ENGLAND**.
(T) 01753 662290 **(F)** 01753 790099.
Contact/s
Owner: Mrs J Lorch
Profile Breeder, Stable/Livery. **Ref: YH09974**

MUSLEY BANK STABLES

Musley Bank Stables, Malton, **Yorkshire (North)**, YO17 9DW, **ENGLAND**.
(T) 01653 696872 **(F)** 01653 696914
(M) 07712 739458.
Profile Breeder, Trainer. **Ref: YH09975**

MUSSON, W J

W J Musson, Saville Hse, St. Marys Sq, Newmarket, **Suffolk**, CB8 9HZ, **ENGLAND**.
(T) 01638 663371 **(F)** 01638 667979
(W) www.newmarketracehorsetrainers.co.uk
Affiliated Bodies Newmarket Trainers Fed.
Contact/s
Trainer: Mr W Musson
Profile Trainer. **Ref: YH09976**

MUTEHILL SMITHY

Mutehill Smithy, Mutehill, Kirkcudbright, **Dumfries and Galloway**, DG6 4XE, **SCOTLAND**.
(T) 01557 330263.
Profile Blacksmith. **Ref: YH09977**

MY BEAUTIFUL HORSES

D J Murphy Publishers Ltd, Haslemere Hse, Lower St, Haslemere, **Surrey**, GU27 2PE, **ENGLAND**.
(T) 01428 651551 **(F)** 01428 653888.
Profile Supplies. **Ref: YH09978**

MYALL, AARON J

Aaron J Myall DWCF, 9 Tylers Green, Bradwell Common, Milton Keynes, **Buckinghamshire**, MK13 8AS, **ENGLAND**.
(T) 07710 445201.
Profile Farrier. **Ref: YH09979**

MYCAWKA, ALEXANDER H

Alexander H Mycawka BII, 39 Empingham Rd, Ketton, Stamford, **Lincolnshire**, PE9 3UP, **ENGLAND**.
(T) 01780 721691.
Profile Farrier. **Ref: YH09980**

MYERS, PETER V

Peter V Myers, 2 Cross Heights, Scholes, Huddersfield, **Yorkshire (West)**, HD7 1BN, **ENGLAND**.
(T) 01484 684166.
Profile Farrier. **Ref: YH09981**

MYERSCOUGH CLGE

Myerscough College, Myerscough Hall, Bilsborrow, Preston, **Lancashire**, PR3 0RY, **ENGLAND**.
(T) 01995 640611 **(F)** 01995 640842
(E) enquiries@myerscough.ac.uk.
Contact/s
Academic Registrar: Christine Hulme
Profile Equestrian Centre. **Ref: YH09982**

MYMMS HALL LIVERY STABLES

Mymms Hall Livery Stables, Warrengate Lane, South Mimms, Potters Bar, **Hertfordshire**, EN6 3NN, **ENGLAND**.
(T) 01707 650067.
Contact/s
Partner: Mrs T Perry
Profile Stable/Livery. **Ref: YH09983**

MYNDERLEY STABLES

Mynderley Stables, High Pk, All Stretton, **Shropshire**, SY6 6LW, **ENGLAND**.
(T) 01694 751277.
Profile Riding School. **Ref: YH09984**

MYOTHILL HSE EQUESTRIAN CTRE

Myothill House Equestrian Centre, Denny, **Stirling**, FK6 5HH, **SCOTLAND**.
(T) 01324 823420.
Profile Breeder, Equestrian Centre, Riding School, Saddlery Retailer, Stable/Livery, Trainer. **Ref: YH09985**

N A S T A

National Stallion Association, Godington Farm, Godington, Bicester, **Oxfordshire**, OX6 9AF, **ENGLAND**.
(T) 01869 277360.
Profile Club/Association. **Ref: YH09986**

N B SANDERS

N B Sanders (Trailers) Ltd, Sandiacre, Werrington Bridge Rd, Milking Nook, Peterborough, **Cambridgeshire**, PE6 7PP, **ENGLAND**.
(T) 01733 810288 **(F)** 01733 810510.
Profile Transport/Horse Boxes. **Ref: YH09987**

N D S ANIMAL FEEDS

N D S Animal Feeds, Unit 15A/B, Balmakeith Ind Est, Nairn, **Highlands**, IV12 5QW, **SCOTLAND**.
(T) 01667 452730 **(F)** 01667 454527.
Profile Supplies. **Ref: YH09988**

N F U COUNTRYSIDE

N F U Countryside, Agriculture Hse, North Gate, Uppingham, **Rutland**, LE15 9PL, **ENGLAND**.
(T) 01572 824220 **(F)** 01572 824201
(E) nfu.membership.services@nfu.org.uk
(W) www.nfucountryside.org.uk.
Profile Club/Association.
Provide practical information, professional advice and legal assistance to people who live and work in the British countryside. **Ref: YH09989**

N F U MUTUAL

N F U Mutual, Tiddington Rd, Stratford-upon-Avon, **Warwickshire**, CV37 7BJ, **ENGLAND**.
(T) 01789 204211 **(F)** 01789 298992.
Profile Club/Association. Insurance Company.
Ref: YH09990

N I S P G

Northern Ireland Shetland Pony Group, 109 Cladymilltown Rd, Mowhan, **County Armagh**, BT60 2EG, **NORTHERN IRELAND**.
(T) 028 37507499 **(F)** 028 37507266.
Contact/s
Chairman: Mr W Kee
Profile Breeder, Club/Association. **Ref: YH09991**

N J CRIDDLE

N J Criddle Ltd, 116 Tregwilyn Rd, Rogerstone, Newport, **Newport**, NP10 9EJ, **WALES**.
(T) 01633 895115.
Profile Saddlery Retailer. **Ref: YH09992**

N P R DATATAG DIVISION

N P R Datatag Division, 1 Marina Court, Castle St, Hull, **Yorkshire (East)**, HU1 1TJ, **ENGLAND**.
(T) 01482 222070 **(F)** 01482 224545
(E) info@identify-europe.co.uk.
Profile Supplies. **Ref: YH09993**

N R OMELL

N R Omell Gallery, 6 Duke St, St James's, London, **London (Greater)**, SW1Y 6BN, **ENGLAND**.
(T) 020 78396223 **(F)** 020 79301625.
Contact/s
Manager: Richard Joslin **Ref: YH09994**

N S R COMMUNICATIONS

N S R Communications Ltd, Stable End, Beesons Yard, Bury Lane, Rickmansworth, **Hertfordshire**, WD3 1DS, **ENGLAND**.
(T) 01923 771693 **(F)** 01923 772128
(E) sales@nsrcommunications.co.uk
(W) www.nsrcommunications.co.uk.
Profile Supplies. **Ref: YH09995**

N S RESEARCH

N S Research, The Priory, Churchyard, Mildenhall, **Suffolk**, IP28 7EE, **ENGLAND**.
(T) 01638 712192 **(F)** 01638 711120
(E) david.l.frape@btinternet.com.
Profile Medical Support. **Ref: YH09996**

N W F COUNTRYSTORE

N W F Countrystore (Melton), 56 Scalford Rd, Melton Mowbray, **Leicestershire**, LE13 1JY, **ENGLAND**.
(T) 01664 480480.
Profile Saddlery Retailer. **Ref: YH09997**

N W F COUNTRYSTORE

N W F Countrystore (Market Drayton), Farm Parts, Adderley Rd Ind Est, Bert Smith Way, Market Drayton, **Shropshire**, TF9 3SN, **ENGLAND**.
(T) 01630 655766 **(F)** 01630 658413
(E) shop@farmparts.freeserve.co.uk.
Profile Saddlery Retailer. **Ref: YH09998**

N W F COUNTRYSTORE

N W F Countrystore (Whitchurch), Station Rd, Whitchurch, **Shropshire**, SY13 9RD, **ENGLAND**.
(T) 01948 662274 **(F)** 01948 665928.
Profile Saddlery Retailer. **Ref: YH09999**

N W F COUNTRYSTORE

N W F Countrystore, The Depot, Station Approach, Mold Rd, Wrexham, **Wrexham**, LL11 2AA, **WALES**.
(T) 01978 361561 **(F)** 01978 361561.
Profile Saddlery Retailer. **Ref: YH10000**

N W F COUNTRYWISE

N W F Countrywise, A51, Wardle, Nantwich, **Cheshire**, CW5 6AQ, **ENGLAND**.
(T) 01829 260980 **(F)** 01829 261335.
Profile Saddlery Retailer. **Ref: YH10001**

N.C.P.A. DERBYSHIRE BRANCH

N.C.P.A. Derbyshire Branch, Hollinhurst Head Farm, New Mills, High Peak, **Derbyshire**, SK22 4QL, **ENGLAND**.
(T) 01663 746126 **(F)** 01663 749302.
Contact/s
Secretary: Mrs P Ashton
Profile Club/Association. **Ref: YH10002**

N.P.S. AREA 11

N.P.S. Area 11 (W Midlands), Court View, Regency Drive, Kings Coughton, Alcester, **Warwickshire**, **ENGLAND**.
(T) 01789 764630.
Profile Club/Association. **Ref: YH10003**

N.P.S. AREA 17

N.P.S. Area 17, Sedges Farm, Nags Head Lane, Great Missenden, **Buckinghamshire**, HP16 0HQ, **ENGLAND**.
(T) 01240 62473.
Profile Club/Association. **Ref: YH10004**

N.P.S. SCOTTISH SHOW KINROSS

N.P.S. Scottish Show Kinross, Broomiebank Hse, Westruther, Gordon, **Scottish Borders**, TD3 6LZ, **SCOTLAND**.
(T) 01578 740200.
Profile Club/Association. **Ref: YH10005**

NAAS RACECOURSE

Naas Race PLC, Tipper Rd, Naas, **County Kildare**, **IRELAND**.
(T) 045 897391 **(F)** 045 879486
(E) goracing@naasracecourse.com
(W) www.naasracecourse.com.
Contact/s
General Manager: Ms M McGlinness
Profile Club/Association, Equestrian Centre, Track/Course, Trainer.
Naas offers a range of options for corporate guests and groups. Naas racecourse is the ideal setting for host-

ing a day out for special friends, companies, organisations and clubs enabling all to enjoy a day at the races. No.Staff: 7 Yr. Est: 1924 Ref: YH10006

NAB BRIDGE RIDING SCHOOL

Nab Bridge Riding School, North Rigton, Huby, Harrogate, **Yorkshire (North)**, OS17 0DR, **ENGLAND**.
(T) 01423 872792.
Contact/s
Owner: Miss A Dorsey
Profile Riding School. Ref: YH10007

NABURN GRANGE RIDING CTRE

Naburn Grange Riding Centre, Naburn, York, **Yorkshire (North)**, YO19 4RU, **ENGLAND**.
(T) 01904 728283 (F) 01904 728958
(E) horses@globalnet.co.uk
(W) www.adveb.co.uk/naburn
Affiliated Bodies BHS.
Contact/s
For Bookings: Mrs D Smith (Q) BHSAI
Profile Equestrian Centre, Riding School, Stable/Livery, Trainer.
Residential holidays - £325.00 for a child, £350.00 for an adult. Also offer a tack security service with the use of Identitack-Electronic chipping. No.Staff: 6
Yr. Est: 1980 C.Size: 25 Acres
Opening Times
Open all year Ref: YH10008

NAG TAGS

Nag Tags, 30 Verbena Way, Sutton Hill, Telford, **Shropshire**, TF7 4DX, **ENGLAND**.
(T) 01952 583471 (F) 01902 743110.
Profile Supplies. Ref: YH10009

NAGWARE

Nagware Ltd, Tobergregan Garristown, Dublin, **County Dublin**, **IRELAND**.
(T) 01 8354270.
Profile Supplies. Ref: YH10010

NAILBOURNE FORGE

Nailbourne Forge Ltd, Nailbourne Forge, Court Hill, Littlebourne, Canterbury, **Kent**, CT3 1TX, **ENGLAND**.
(T) 01227 728336 (F) 01227 728336.
Profile Blacksmith. Ref: YH10011

NAILOR, W C

W C Nailor RSS, Iona, Hussell Lane, Medstead, Alton, **Hampshire**, GU34 5PF, **ENGLAND**.
(T) 01420 564002.
Profile Farrier. Ref: YH10012

NAILSEA PET CTRE

Nailsea Pet Centre, 98 High St, Nailsea, **Somerset (North)**, BS48 1AH, **ENGLAND**.
(T) 01275 859580.
Profile Supplies. Ref: YH10013

NAME PLATES

Name Plates, Northfield Farmhouse, Thornton Curtis, Ulceby, **Lincolnshire (North)**, DN39 6XW, **ENGLAND**.
(T) 01469 530131 (F) 01469 530131.
Contact/s
Owner: Mr D Neville
Profile Supplies.
Supplier and engraver of name plates for stable doors, head collars and saddles etc. Ref: YH10014

NANTEAGUE STABLES

Nanteague Stables, Nanteqgue Stables, Marazanvose, Truro, **Cornwall**, TR4 9DQ, **ENGLAND**.
(T) 01872 540303.
Contact/s
Owner: Mrs M Yeatman Ref: YH10015

NANTGWINAU WELSH COBS

Nantgwinau Welsh Cobs, Pantycelyn Guest Hse, Llanwnnen, Lampeter, **Ceredigion**, SA48 7LW, **WALES**.
(T) 01570 434455 (F) 01570 434455
(E) huwann@pantycelyn.co.uk
(W) www.pantycelyn.co.uk.
Contact/s
Owner: Mr H Jenkins
Profile Breeder, Horse/Rider Accom.
B&B is £20.00 - £22.00 per night. The B&B has stables for overnight stays, but does not have riding facilities. Yr. Est: 1991
Opening Times
Open between Feb - Oct. Best to call beween 12:00 - 14:00 and 19:00 - 22:00 Ref: YH10016

NANTURRIAN STUD FARM

Nanturrian Stud Farm, The Bungalow, Argal Manor, Budock, Falmouth, **Cornwall**, **ENGLAND**..
Profile Breeder, Supplies. Ref: YH10017

NANTWICH RIDING CLUB

Nantwich Riding Club, Mates Farm, Edge Green, Malpas, **Cheshire**, SY14 8LG, **ENGLAND**.
(T) 01948 820625.
Contact/s
Chairman: Mrs J Bailey
Profile Club/Association, Riding Club. Ref: YH10018

NANTWICH VETNRY GROUP

Nantwich Veterinary Group, Nantwich Veterinary Hospital, Crewe Rd End, Nantwich, **Cheshire**, CW5 5SF, **ENGLAND**.
(T) 01270 610349 (F) 01270 628367.
Profile Medical Support. Ref: YH10019

NANTWICH VETNRY GROUP

Nantwich Veterinary Group, Beech St Veterinary Surgery, Beech St, Crewe, **Cheshire**, CW1 2PY, **ENGLAND**.
(T) 01270 211022.
Profile Medical Support. Ref: YH10020

NAPIER, MILES

Miles Napier, Banbury Hse, Great Easton, Market Harborough, **Leicestershire**, LE16 8SF, **ENGLAND**.
(T) 01536 770449.
Profile Supplies. Ref: YH10021

NAPPA STUD

Nappa Stud, Liddel Pk, Penton, Carlisle, **Cumbria**, CA6 5QW, **ENGLAND**.
(T) 01228 577440.
Profile Breeder. Ref: YH10022

NARRAMORE STUD

Narramore Stud, Moretonhampstead, Newton Abbot, **Devon**, TQ13 8QT, **ENGLAND**.
(T) 01647 440455
(W) www.narramorefarm.co.uk.
Contact/s
Owner: Mrs S Horn
(E) narramore@btinternet.com
Profile Breeder, Holidays, Horse/Rider Accom, Stable/Livery.
Horses and dogs are welcome at the holiday cottages.
No.Staff: 2 Yr. Est: 1970 C.Size: 107 Acres
Ref: YH10023

NASEBY HALL

Naseby Hall, Naseby, Rugby, **Warwickshire**, **ENGLAND**..
Profile Riding School. Ref: YH10024

NASH, A

Mrs A Nash, Tyn Y Fron, Llandderfel, Bala, **Gwynedd**, LL23 7RG, **WALES**.
(T) 01678 530334.
Profile Breeder. Ref: YH10025

NASH, J

J Nash (Toulston), Neswick Farm, Bainton, Driffield, **Yorkshire (East)**, YO25 9EG, **ENGLAND**.
(T) 01377 217230.
Profile Trainer. Ref: YH10026

NASH, N

N Nash, Wards Pl Farm, Lateley Common, Glazebury, Warrington, **Cheshire**, WA3 5PA, **ENGLAND**.
(T) 01942 680093.
Contact/s
Owner: Mrs N Nash
Profile Breeder. Ref: YH10027

NASHEND STUD

Nashend Stud, Nashend, Bisley, Stroud, **Gloucestershire**, GL6 7AJ, **ENGLAND**.
(T) 01452 77257.
Profile Breeder. Ref: YH10028

NASSAU, WILLIAM

Mr William Nassau, Murray Cottage, St Johns Rd, Crowborough, **Sussex (East)**, TN6 1SA, **ENGLAND**.
(T) 01892 653873. Ref: YH10029

NAT ASS FARRIERS/BLACKSMITHS

National Association of Farriers & Blacksmiths, 'The Forge', Avenue B, 10th St, N A C, Stoneleigh Park, Kenilworth, **Warwickshire**, CV8 2LG, **ENGLAND**.
(T) 024 76696595 (F) 024 76696708.
Contact/s
Key Contact: Anne Huckvale
Profile Club/Association. Ref: YH10030

NAT INS OF MEDICAL HERBALISTS

National Institute of Medical Herbalists, 56 Longbrook St, Exeter, **Devon**, EX4 6AH, **ENGLAND**.
(T) 01392 426022.
Profile Club/Association. Ref: YH10031

NAT OFFICE OF ANIMAL HEALTH

National Office of Animal Health Ltd, 3 Crossfield Chambers, Gladbeck Way, Enfield, **London (Greater)**, EN2 7HF, **ENGLAND**.
(T) 020 83673131 (F) 020 83631155
(E) noah@noah.co.uk.
Profile Club/Association. Ref: YH10032

NATIONAL AGRICULTURAL CTRE

National Agricultural Centre, Stoneleigh Pk, Kenilworth, **Warwickshire**, CV8 2RP, **ENGLAND**.
(T) 024 76698863 (F) 024 76418429. Ref: YH10033

NATIONAL ANIMAL RESCUE ASS

National Animal Rescue Association, 11 Gorse Gr, Helmshore, Rossendale, **Lancashire**, BB4 43E, **ENGLAND**..
Profile Club/Association. Ref: YH10034

NATIONAL ASS OF BOOKMAKERS

National Association of Bookmakers, 298 Ewell Rd, Surbiton, **Surrey**, KT6 7AQ, **ENGLAND**.
(T) 020 83908222 (F) 020 83399940.
Profile Club/Association. Ref: YH10035

NATIONAL EQUINE WELFARE COUNC

National Equine Welfare Council, Stanton, 10 Wales St, Kings Sutton, Banbury, **Oxfordshire**, OX17 3RR, **ENGLAND**.
(T) 01295 810060 (F) 01295 810060
(E) new@kingssutton.freeserve.co.uk.
Contact/s
Key Contact: Mrs J Cannon
Profile Club/Association. Ref: YH10036

NATIONAL FOALING BANK

National Foaling Bank, Meretown Stud, Meretown, Newport, **Shropshire**, TF10 8BX, **ENGLAND**.
(T) 01952 811234 (F) 01952 811202.
Contact/s
Owner: Mrs J Vardon
Profile Breeder, Supplies. Ref: YH10037

NATIONAL LIGHT HORSE SOC

National Light Horse Breeding Society (The), 96 High St, Edenbridge, **Kent**, TN8 5AR, **ENGLAND**.
(T) 01732 866277.
Profile Club/Association. Ref: YH10038

NATIONAL PONY SOCIETY

National Pony Society (N Ireland), 48 Lisnastrean Rd, Lisburn, **County Antrim**, BT27 5PB, **NORTHERN IRELAND**.
(T) 028 92638525.
Contact/s
Chairman: Mr M Gibson
Profile Club/Association. Ref: YH10039

NATIONAL PONY SOCIETY

National Pony Society (Area 32), 31 Ballywillian Rd, Larne, **County Antrim**, BT40 3LQ, **NORTHERN IRELAND**.
(T) 028 93378850
(E) tony@beltoy.freeserve.co.uk.
Contact/s
Secretary: Mrs M Bell
Profile Club/Association. Ref: YH10040

NATIONAL PONY SOCIETY

National Pony Society, Willingdon Hse, 102 High St, Alton, **Hampshire**, GU34 1EN, **ENGLAND**.
(T) 01420 88333 (F) 01420 80599.
Contact/s
Key Contact: Mrs L Wilkins Maat
Profile Club/Association. Ref: YH10041

NATIONAL REINING HORSE ASS

National Reining Horse Association of GB, Burnt Ash, Sheep St Lane, Etchingham, **Sussex (East)**, TN19 7AY, **ENGLAND**.
(T) 01580 819208.
Profile Club/Association. Ref: YH10042

NATIONAL SADDLE CTRE

National Saddle Centre, Cottage Farm, Potter Lane, Higher Walton, Preston, **Lancashire**, PR5 4EN, **ENGLAND**.
(T) 01772 877245. Ref: YH10043

NATIONAL STALLION ASSOCIATION

National Stallion Association, School Farm, School Lane, Pickmere, Knutsford, **Cheshire**, WA16 0JF, **ENGLAND**.
(T) 01565 733222.
Contact/s
Key Contact: Mr J Keleher

Profile Club/Association. **Ref: YH10044**

NATIONAL STUD

National Stud (The), Stud Grooms Hse, Newmarket, **Suffolk**, CB8 0XE, **ENGLAND**.
(T) 01638 663464 **(F)** 01638 665173.
Contact/s
Key Contact: Emma Rutherford
Profile Club/Association. **Ref: YH10045**

NATIONAL TRUST

National Trust (The), The Home Farm, Wimpole, Arrington, Royston, **Hertfordshire**, SG8 0EW, **ENGLAND**.
(T) 01763 208987.
Profile Club/Association. **Ref: YH10046**

NATIONWIDE EQUESTRIAN

Nationwide Equestrian Development Services, Hillside Cottage, Stather Rd, Burton-upon-Stather, Scunthorpe, **Lincolnshire (North)**, DN15 9DH, **ENGLAND**.
(T) 01724 720544.
Contact/s
Owner: Mrs K Scott
Profile Supplies. **Ref: YH10047**

NATIONWIDE PROP/PET SITTERS

Nationwide Property & Pet Sitters, 33 The Manor Drive, Worcester Park, **Surrey**, KT4 7LG, **ENGLAND**.
(T) 020 83302530.
Profile Transport/Horse Boxes. **Ref: YH10048**

NATIVE PONY ASS OF CORNWALL

Native Pony Association of Cornwall, 3 Polkanuggo Cottage, Hernis, Longdowns, Penryn, **Cornwall**, TR10 9DT, **ENGLAND**.
(T) 01209 861405.
Profile Club/Association. **Ref: YH10049**

NATURAL ANIMAL FEEDS

Natural Animal Feeds Ltd, High Hse, Penrhos, Raglan, **Monmouthshire**, NP15 2DJ, **WALES**.
(T) 01600 780256 **(F)** 01600 780536
(E) naf@nutri.org
(W) www.naf-uk.com.
Profile Medical Support, Supplies.
Manufacturers of equine, canine and human supplements. Freephone 0800 373106. **Ref: YH10050**

NATURAL APPROACH

Natural Approach (The), West Cottage, Cockerstone Farm, Litte Glenshee, Bankfoot, **Perth and Kinross**, PH1 4DN, **SCOTLAND**.
(T) 01738 787539.
Profile Medical Support. **Ref: YH10051**

NATURAL HORSE FOOD

Natural Horse Food Co, Longwick Mill, Longwick, Princes Risborough, **Buckinghamshire**, HP27 9SA, **ENGLAND**.
(T) 01844 343143 **(F)** 01844 343143.
Profile Supplies. **Ref: YH10052**

NATURAL PARTNERSHIP

Natural Partnership Horse & Human, 4 Linarce Rd, London, **London (Greater)**, NW2 5BB, **ENGLAND**.
(T) 020 84510016 **(F)** 020 88304655
Affiliated Bodies IHA.
Contact/s
Owner: Mr D Groder
(E) david@naturalpartnership.co.uk
Profile Trainer.
Trainer for horse and people with special needs or problems. **Ref: YH10053**

NATURAL REMEDIES

Natural Remedies (UK) Ltd, 2 Bate St, Walsall, **Midlands (West)**, WS2 8EL, **ENGLAND**.
(T) 01922 725404 **(F)** 01922 611333
(E) pclusker@compuserve.com.
Profile Medical Support. **Ref: YH10054**

NATURALLY

S G Naturally Ltd, Po Box 17, Towcester, **Northamptonshire**, NN12 8YJ, **ENGLAND**.
(T) 01295 768750
(W) www.susangeorgenaturally.co.uk.
Contact/s
Owner: Mrs S George
Profile Medical Support, Supplies. **Ref: YH10055**

NAUGHTON, A M

A M Naughton, High Gingrfield, Hurgill Rd, Richmond, **Yorkshire (North)**, DL10 4TD, **ENGLAND**.
(T) 01748 822803 **(F)** 01748 822803.
Contact/s
Owner: Mr A Naughton
Profile Trainer. **Ref: YH10056**

NAVAN RACE

Navan Race Co Ltd, The Racecourse Proudstown Pk, Navan, **County Meath**, **IRELAND**.
(T) 046 27967.
Profile Supplies. **Ref: YH10057**

NAYLOR, F K

F K Naylor, The Blacksmiths Shop, Goldthorpe Green, Goldthorpe, Rotherham, **Yorkshire (South)**, S63 9EL, **ENGLAND**.
(T) 01709 880339.
Profile Blacksmith. **Ref: YH10058**

NAYLOR, J R J (DR)

Dr J R J Naylor, The Cleeve, Elston Lane, Shrewton, Salisbury, **Wiltshire**, SP3 4HL, **ENGLAND**.
(T) 01980 620804 **(F)** 01980 621999
(M) 07771 740126.
Profile Breeder, Trainer. **Ref: YH10059**

NAYLORS SADDLERY STORES

Naylors Saddlery Stores, 472 Edenfield Rd, Rochdale, **Lancashire**, OL12 7QL, **ENGLAND**.
(T) 01706 631909.
Contact/s
Owner: Mrs K Naylor **Ref: YH10060**

NEAL, PAMELA

Miss Pamela Neal, Middle Stoke Farm, Holne, Newton Abbott, **Devon**, TQ13 7SS, **ENGLAND**.
(T) 01364 631444.
Profile Stable/Livery. **Ref: YH10061**

NEARDOWN STABLES

Neardown Stables, Upper Lambourn, Hungerford, **Berkshire**, RG17 8QP, **ENGLAND**.
(T) 01488 72324 **(F)** 01488 71477
(M) 07767 861174.
Profile Trainer. **Ref: YH10062**

NEATE BRAKE CONTROLS

Neate Brake Controls Ltd, Hanworth Trading Est, Hampton Rd West, Feltham, **London (Greater)**, TW13 6DN, **ENGLAND**.
(T) 020 88986021 **(F)** 020 88981246.
Profile Transport/Horse Boxes. **Ref: YH10063**

NEATE, DREWEATT

Dreweatt Neate, Donnington Priory, Newbury, **Berkshire**, RG14 2JE, **ENGLAND**.
(T) 01635 553500.
Contact/s
Partner: Mr C Boreham **Ref: YH10064**

NEBO STUD

Nebo Stud, Nebo, Llanon, **Ceredigion**, SY23 5LH, **WALES**.
(T) 01974 272653.
Profile Breeder. **Ref: YH10065**

NECARNE CASTLE

Necarne Castle, Department Of Agriculture & Rural Development, Necarne Castle, Irvinestown, Enniskillen, **County Fermanagh**, BT94 1GG, **NORTHERN IRELAND**.
(T) 028 68621919 **(F)** 028 68628382.
Contact/s
Manager: Mrs L Pottie
Profile Riding School.
Trains to National Diploma, Higher National Diploma and Degree level. **Ref: YH10066**

NEEDHAM, J

J Needham, Limestone Hill Cottage, Limestone Hill, Tickhill, Doncaster, **Yorkshire (South)**, DN11 9PG, **ENGLAND**.
(T) 01302 744957.
Profile Transport/Horse Boxes. **Ref: YH10067**

NEEDHAM, J L

Mr J L Needham, Gorsty Farm, Maryknoll, Ludlow, **Shropshire**, SY8 2HD, **ENGLAND**.
(T) 01584 874826 **(F)** 01584 873256.
Profile Supplies. **Ref: YH10068**

NEEDHAM, P

Mr P Needham, Woolhouse Farm, Marwood, Barnard Castle, **County Durham**, DL12 8RG, **ENGLAND**.
(T) 01833 690155.
Profile Supplies. **Ref: YH10069**

NEILL, IVOR

Ivor Neill, 21 Tartaraghan Rd, Portadown, Craigavon, **County Armagh**, BT62 1RQ, **NORTHERN IRELAND**.
(T) 028 38851457.
Contact/s
Owner: Mr I Neill
Profile Transport/Horse Boxes. **Ref: YH10070**

NELMES CHIROPRACTIC CLINIC

Nelmes Chiropractic Clinic, 25 St Stephen's Lane, Verwood, **Dorset**, BH31 7BQ, **ENGLAND**.
(T) 01202 822126.
Profile Medical Support. **Ref: YH10071**

NELSON PARK RIDING CTRE

Nelson Park Riding Centre, St Margarets Rd, Woodchurch, Birchington, **Kent**, CT7 0HJ, **ENGLAND**.
(T) 01843 822251.
Profile Riding School. **Ref: YH10072**

NELSON VETNRY & EQUINE

Nelson Veterinary & Equine Ltd, No 3 The Elliott Ctre, Elliott Rd, Cirencester, **Gloucestershire**, GL7 1YS, **ENGLAND**.
(T) 01285 655122 **(F)** 01285 655133
(E) nve@nve.co.uk.
Profile Medical Support. **Ref: YH10073**

NELSON, GARRICK S R

Garrick S R Nelson DWCF, Yartleton Farm, Yartleton Lane, Mayhill, Longhope, **Gloucestershire**, GL17 0RF, **ENGLAND**.
(T) 01452 830266.
Profile Farrier. **Ref: YH10074**

NELSON, PETER

Peter Nelson, Malthouse Stud, Malthouse Farm, Cods Hill, Beenham, Reading, **Berkshire**, RG7 5QH, **ENGLAND**.
(T) 0118 9713841 **(F)** 0118 9713953.
Contact/s
Owner: Peter Nelson
Profile Blood Stock Agency. **Ref: YH10075**

NELSON, W M

Mr W M Nelson, Longrigg, Torthorwald, **Dumfries and Galloway**, DG1 3PS, **SCOTLAND**.
(T) 01387 75237.
Profile Supplies. **Ref: YH10076**

NENTHORN STABLES

Nenthorn Stables, Edenside Cottage, Nenthorn, Kelso, **Scottish Borders**, TD5 7RY, **SCOTLAND**.
(T) 01573 224073.
Contact/s
Owner: Mrs A Allen
Profile Riding School, Stable/Livery. **Ref: YH10077**

NEPTUNE TRAILERS

Neptune Trailers, 15 Stanbury Rd, Torquay, **Devon**, TQ2 7LL, **ENGLAND**.
(T) 01803 615157 **(F)** 01803 615157.
Contact/s
Owner: Mr D Ebdon
Profile Transport/Horse Boxes. **Ref: YH10078**

NESBA

North East Somerset Bridleways Association, Lilac Cottage, Upper Vobster, Bath, **Bath & Somerset (North East)**, BA3 5SB, **ENGLAND**.
(T) 01373 813091.
Profile Club/Association. **Ref: YH10079**

NET INFO WORKS

Net Info Works, 134 Church Rd, Hove, **Sussex (East)**, BN3 2DL, **ENGLAND**.
(T) 01273 711000 **(F)** 01273 711100.
Contact/s
Owner: Mr M Jacobs
Profile Supplies. **Ref: YH10080**

NETHER FARM RIDING STABLES

Nether Farm Riding Stables, Nether Farm, 45 Nethergate, Nafferton, Driffield, **Yorkshire (East)**, YO25 4LP, **ENGLAND**.
(T) 01377 254357.
Contact/s
Owner: Miss D Blakeston **Ref: YH10081**

NETHER HALL RIDING SCHOOL

Nether Hall Riding School, 225 Rawthorpe Lane, Huddersfield, **Yorkshire (West)**, HD5 9PD, **ENGLAND**.
(T) 01484 431173.
Contact/s
Owner: Ms A Clayton
Profile Riding School. **Ref: YH10082**

NETHERWOOD FARM

Netherwood Farm Livery Stables, Netherwood Farm, Briercliffe, Burnley, **Lancashire**, BB10 3PZ, **ENGLAND**.
(T) 01282 422672.
Contact/s

Owner: Mr A Phillipson
Profile Stable/Livery. Yr. Est: 1989 C.Size: 98 Acres Ref: YH10083

NET-WEAR

Net-Wear, 250 Higham Lane, Nuneaton, **Warwickshire**, CV11 6AR, **ENGLAND**.
(T) 024 76384087 (F) 01675 467051.
Profile Supplies. Ref: YH10084

NETWORKS

Networks (The), 33 Manor Orchard, Taunton, **Somerset**, TA1 4PR, **ENGLAND**.
(T) 01823 352215 (F) 01823 352215.
Profile Club/Association. Ref: YH10085

NEVILLE BLAKEY FEEDSTUFFS

Neville Blakey Feedstuffs Ltd, Country Store, The Street, Pulham St Mary, **Norfolk**, IP21 4RD, **ENGLAND**.
(T) 01379 608217.
Profile Supplies. Ref: YH10086

NEVILLE GRAHAM

Neville Graham (Engineering) Ltd, 29 Church Rd, Ballynure, Ballyclare, **County Antrim**, BT39 9UF, **NORTHERN IRELAND**.
(T) 028 93342427 (F) 028 93340135.
Contact/s
Owner: Mr N Graham
Profile Transport/Horse Boxes. Ref: YH10087

NEVILLE SYMONDS ASSOCIATES

Neville Symonds Associates, Drakewell, Stoke Lacy, Bromyard, **Herefordshire**, HR7 4HG, **ENGLAND**.
(T) 01885 490267 (F) 01885 490792
(M) 07831 613900.
Profile Club/Association. Ref: YH10088

NEVIN, RICHARD

Richard Nevin, Ballintemple Cashel Rd, Fethard, **County Tipperary**, **IRELAND**.
(T) 052 31424.
Profile Supplies. Ref: YH10089

NEW BARN FARM

New Barn Farm, Chelford Rd, Ollerton, Knutsford, **Cheshire**, WA16 8SZ, **ENGLAND**.
(T) 01565 651122 (F) 01565 651129.
Contact/s
Partner: Mrs S Roberts
Profile Stable/Livery. Ref: YH10090

NEW BARN STUD

New Barn Stud, Lullingstone Lane, Eynsford, **Kent**, DA4 0HY, **ENGLAND**.
(T) 01322 863046.
Profile Breeder, Trainer. Ref: YH10091

NEW ENGLAND STUD FARM

New England Stud Farm Ltd, New England Stud, Newmarket, **Suffolk**, CB8 0XA, **ENGLAND**.
(T) 01223 811249.
Profile Breeder. Ref: YH10092

NEW EQUINE WEAR

New Equine Wear Ltd, P O Box 823, Malmesbury, **Wiltshire**, SN16 0RT, **ENGLAND**.
(T) 01666 577788 (F) 01666 577744
(E) sales@newequinewear.co.uk
(W) www.newequinewear.co.uk
Affiliated Bodies BETA.
Profile Riding Wear Retailer, Supplies.
Manufacturers of leg protection wear for horses. Can ship small orders if there is no local stockist.
No.Staff: 14 Yr. Est: 1995
Opening Times
Sp: Open Mon - Fri 09:00. Closed Mon - Fri 17:30.
Su: Open Mon - Fri 09:00. Closed Mon - Fri 17:30.
Au: Open Mon - Fri 09:00. Closed Mon - Fri 17:30.
Wn: Open Mon - Fri 09:00. Closed Mon - Fri 17:30.
Closed weekends but there is an answer phone
Ref: YH10093

NEW EQUINE WEAR

New Equine Wear, Sevington Farm, Sevington, Grittleton, Chippenham, **Wiltshire**, SN14 7LD, **ENGLAND**.
(T) 01249 783337 (F) 01249 783254.
Contact/s
Owner: Mr R Balfry Ref: YH10094

NEW FARM

New Farm, Coombe Rd, Compton, Newbury, **Berkshire**, RG20 6RQ, **ENGLAND**.
(T) 01635 578863.
Contact/s
Owner: Mrs D Hope
Profile Stable/Livery, Track/Course. Ref: YH10095

NEW FOREST

New Forest Riding Driving & Watersports, Dale Farm, Manor Rd, Applemore, Dibden, **Hampshire**, SO4 5TJ, **ENGLAND**.
(T) 023 80843180
(M) 07836 693966.
Profile Riding School. Ref: YH10096

NEW FOREST AUTOS

New Forest Autos, Ringwood Rd, Woodlands, Southampton, **Hampshire**, SO40 7GX, **ENGLAND**.
(T) 023 80863033 (F) 023 80863033.
Contact/s
Owner: Mr D Burdle
Profile Transport/Horse Boxes. Ref: YH10097

NEW FOREST EQUESTRIAN CTRE

New Forest Equestrian Centre, The Stables/Shirley Holms Farm, Shirley Holms Rd, Lymington, **Hampshire**, SO41 8NH, **ENGLAND**.
(T) 01590 683619.
Contact/s
Partner: Mr C Moore
Profile Riding School. Ref: YH10098

NEW FOREST HORSE BOXES

New Forest Horse Boxes, Peartree Cottage, Arnewood Bridge Rd, Sway, Lymington, **Hampshire**, SO41 6ER, **ENGLAND**.
(T) 01590 682633 (F) 01590 683497.
Contact/s
Owner: Mr M Edwards
Profile Transport/Horse Boxes. Ref: YH10099

NEW FOREST HOUNDS

New Forest Hounds, Barrs Farm, High St, Soberton, **Hampshire**, SO32 3PN, **ENGLAND**.
(T) 01489 878548. Ref: YH10100

NEW FOREST POLO CLUB

New Forest (Rhinefield) Polo Club, Five Oaks, Shobley, Ringwood, **Hampshire**, BH24 3HT, **ENGLAND**.
(T) 01425 473359 (F) 01425 473359.
Profile Club/Association. Polo Club. Ref: YH10101

NEW FOREST PONY

New Forest Pony & Cattle Breeding Society, Beacon Cottage, Burley, Ringwood, **Hampshire**, BH24 4EW, **ENGLAND**.
(T) 01425 402272.
Contact/s
Chairman: Mrs G Lowth
Profile Club/Association. Ref: YH10102

NEW FOREST PONY ENTHUSIASTS

New Forest Pony Enthusiasts Club, Alderholt Mill Farm, Sandleheath Rd, Alderholt, Fordingbridge, **Hampshire**, SP6 3EG, **ENGLAND**.
(T) 01425 655527 (F) 01425 655889.
Contact/s
Chairman: Mrs P Harvey-Richards
Profile Club/Association. Ref: YH10103

NEW FOREST RIDING CLUB

New Forest Riding Club, 9 Tamar Gr, Hythe, **Hampshire**, SO4 5XE, **ENGLAND**.
(T) 023 80842734.
Contact/s
Chairman: Mrs T O'Ryan
Profile Club/Association, Riding Club. Ref: YH10104

NEW FORGE

New Forge, 1 Jedburgh Pl, Perth, **Perth and Kinross**, PH1 1SJ, **SCOTLAND**.
(T) 01738 633543.
Contact/s
Owner: Mr D Hoodles
Profile Blacksmith. Ref: YH10105

NEW HALL FARM

New Hall Farm & Equestrian Centre, Newhall Farm, Killerton, Budlake, Exeter, **Devon**, EX5 3LW, **ENGLAND**.
(T) 01392 462453.
Contact/s
Owner: Mrs J Llewellin
Profile Equestrian Centre. Ref: YH10106

NEW HILL FARM

New Hill Farm & Stud, Manchester Rd, Walkden, Manchester, **Manchester (Greater)**, M28 3NL, **ENGLAND**.
(T) 0161 7902831 (F) 0161 7902831
(E) enquiries@newhillfarmstud.co.uk
(W) www.newhillfarmstud.co.uk.
Contact/s
Owner: Mr M Fitton
Profile Breeder, Stable/Livery. No.Staff: 3
C.Size: 185 Acres
Opening Times
Sp: Open Mon - Sun 08:00. Closed Mon - Sun 20:00.
Su: Open Mon - Sun 08:00. Closed Mon - Sun 20:00.
Au: Open Mon - Sun 08:00. Closed Mon - Sun 20:00.
Wn: Open Mon - Sun 08:00. Closed Mon - Sun 20:00. Ref: YH10107

NEW HOUSE FARM

New House Farm, Gaddesden Turn, Great Billington, Leighton Buzzard, **Bedfordshire**, LU7 9BW, **ENGLAND**.
(T) 01525 373359.
Contact/s
Owner: Mrs P Edwins
Profile Stable/Livery.
DIY Livery available, prices on request. Ref: YH10108

NEW HOUSE LIVERY

New House Livery, New Hse Farm, Hanney Rd, Southmoor, Abingdon, **Oxfordshire**, OX13 5HR, **ENGLAND**.
(T) 01865 821180 (F) 01865 821180
(W) www.newhouselivery.ukhq.co.uk
Affiliated Bodies BHS.
Contact/s
Owner: Ms P Blanchard (Q) BHSAI
(E) blanchard@ukhq.co.uk
Profile Arena, Stable/Livery, Track/Course.
No.Staff: 2 Yr. Est: 1996 C.Size: 400 Acres
Ref: YH10109

NEW IRISH SANT PANCRAZIO

New Irish Sant Pancrazio, Herbertstown, Newbridge, **County Kildare**, **IRELAND**.
(T) 045 434440
(E) newirishsantpancrazio@kildarehorse.ie.
Contact/s
Key Contact: Ms J Norris
Profile Breeder. Ref: YH10110

NEW LODGE FARM LIVERY STABLES

New Lodge Farm Livery Stables, Little Woodcote Lane, Carshalton, **Surrey**, SM5 4BY, **ENGLAND**.
(T) 020 86600599.
Contact/s
Manager: Mr P Naughton
Profile Stable/Livery. Ref: YH10111

NEW LODGE RIDING CTRE

New Lodge Riding Centre, Mottingham Lane, London, **London (Greater)**, SE9 4RW, **ENGLAND**.
(T) 020 88516447.
Contact/s
Manager: Miss H Crawford Ref: YH10112

NEW LODGE SADDLERY

New Lodge Saddlery, Pulchrins Barn, 1 Rysley, Hollybread Lane, Little Baddow, Chelmsford, **Essex**, CN3 4AZ, **ENGLAND**.
(T) 01245 223073.
Profile Stable/Livery. Ref: YH10113

NEW MOORS

New Moors Training & Livery Centre, New Moors Farm, Evenwood Gate, Bishop Auckland, **County Durham**, DL14 9NN, **ENGLAND**.
(T) 01388 833542
Affiliated Bodies BHS.
Profile Breeder, Stable/Livery, Track/Course, Trainer.
Opening Times
Telephone for an appointment. Livery open to horse owners. Ref: YH10114

NEW PARK HOTEL

New Park Hotel Riding Stables, New Park Manor Hotel, Lydhurst Rd, Brokenhurst, New Forest, **Hampshire**, SO42 7QH, **ENGLAND**.
(T) 01590 623346/623919 (F) 01590 622268.
Contact/s
Head Girl: Mrs L Davis
Profile Horse/Rider Accom, Riding School, Stable/Livery.
Forty five minutes private tuition is £16.00.
Opening Times
Sp: Open Mon - Sun 10:00. Closed Mon - Sun 15:00.
Su: Open Mon - Sun 10:00. Closed Mon - Sun 15:00.
Au: Open Mon - Sun 10:00. Closed Mon - Sun 15:00.
Wn: Open Mon - Sun 10:00. Closed Mon - Sun 15:00.
Accommodation available all year. Lessons are

between 10:00 - 11:00 and 14:00 - 15:00, with Thursday as the horses rest day. **Ref:YH10115**

NEW PARK MANOR STABLES

New Park Manor Stables, Lyndhurst Rd, Brockenhurst, **Hampshire**, SO42 7QH, **ENGLAND**.
(T) 01590 623919.
Contact/s
Manager: Ms A Lawson
Profile Riding School, Stable/Livery. **Ref:YH10116**

NEW PARK STUD

New Park Stud, New Pk, Buckfastleigh, **Devon**, TQ11 0HL, **ENGLAND**.
(T) 01364 42260.
Profile Breeder. **Ref:YH10117**

NEW PRIORY STUD

New Priory Stud, Kington St. Michael, Chippenham, **Wiltshire**, SN14 6JP, **ENGLAND**.
(T) 01249 750263 **(F)** 01249 758181.
Profile Breeder. **Ref:YH10118**

NEW RANGE EQUESTRIAN CTRE

New Range Equestrian Centre (The), Hern Rd, Ramsey St. Marys, Ramsey, Huntingdon, **Cambridgeshire**, PE26 2SR, **ENGLAND**.
(T) 01733 844542.
Profile Riding School. **Ref:YH10119**

NEW WOAD LIVERY STABLES

New Woad Livery Stables, New Woad Farm, Northampton Rd, Lathbury, Newport Pagnell, **Buckinghamshire**, MK16 8QZ, **ENGLAND**.
(T) 01908 616688 **(F)** 01908 210063.
Contact/s
Owner: Mr F Lauritzen **Ref:YH10120**

NEWARK SADDLERY

Newark Saddlery, 6 Boar Lane, Newark, **Nottinghamshire**, NG24 1HA, **ENGLAND**.
(T) 01636 679009 **(F)** 01636 679009.
Contact/s
Owner: Mrs D Lloyd
Profile Saddlery Retailer. **Ref:YH10121**

NEWBARN FARM STABLES

Newbarn Farm Stables, Piddington Rd, Ludgershall, Aylesbury, **Buckinghamshire**, HP18 9PH, **ENGLAND**.
(T) 01844 237708.
Profile Stable/Livery. **Ref:YH10122**

NEWBERRY STUD FARM

Newberry Stud Farm, Kildare, **County Kildare**, **IRELAND**.
(T) 045 481248 **(F)** 045 481256.
Contact/s
Key Contact: Ms P Mutagh
Profile Breeder. **Ref:YH10123**

NEWBERT, PAUL F

Paul F Newbert, Pine Croft, Cottam Rd, South Leverton, Retford, **Nottinghamshire**, DN22 0BU, **ENGLAND**.
(T) 01427 884095.
Profile Farrier. **Ref:YH10124**

NEWBOULT & THORP

Newboult & Thorp Ltd, Bridgegate, Retford, **Nottinghamshire**, DN22 7XB, **ENGLAND**.
(T) 01777 703508 **(F)** 01777 703508.
Profile Supplies. **Ref:YH10125**

NEWBURY RACECOURSE

Newbury Racecourse plc, The Racecourse, Newbury, **Berkshire**, RG14 7NZ, **ENGLAND**.
(T) 01635 40015 **(F)** 01635 528354
(E) newbury@raceweb.com.
Contact/s
Managing Director/Clerk of Course: Mark Kershaw
Profile Track/Course. **Ref:YH10126**

NEWCASTLE & DISTRICT

Newcastle & District Riding Club, Croft Cottage, 53 Dundrine Rd, Castlewellan, **County Down**, BT31 9EX, **NORTHERN IRELAND**.
(T) 028 44778965.
Contact/s
Chairperson: Mr D McCombe
Profile Club/Association, Riding Club. **Ref:YH10127**

NEWCASTLE RACES

Newcastle Races, High Gosforth Pk, Newcastle-upon-Tyne, **Tyne and Wear**, NE3 5HP, **ENGLAND**.
(T) 0191 2362020 **(F)** 0191 2367761.
Profile Track/Course. **Ref:YH10128**

NEWCASTLE RIDING CTRE

Newcastle Riding Centre, 35 Carnacaville Rd, Castlewellan, **County Down**, BT31 9HD, **NORTHERN IRELAND**.
(T) 028 43722694
Affiliated Bodies BHS.
Contact/s
Partner: Miss E Martin
Profile Riding School, Stable/Livery.
Offer evening rides, mainly during the school holidays.
Opening Times
Telephone for further information **Ref:YH10129**

NEWCOMB, SALLY

Sally Newcomb, Warham Court, Breinton, Hereford, **Herefordshire**, HR4 7PF, **ENGLAND**.
(T) 01432 268731 **(F)** 01432 273608.
Contact/s
Owner: Ms S Newcomb **(Q)** BHSI
(E) sallynewcomb@hotmail.com
Profile Stable/Livery, Trainer. No.Staff: 2
Yr. Est: 1979 **Ref:YH10130**

NEWCOMBE & EAST

Newcombe & East, Warren Hse Farm, Barracks Lane, Brownhills, **Midlands (West)**, WS8 6LS, **ENGLAND**.
(T) 01543 373033 **(F)** 01543 375852.
Profile Breeder. **Ref:YH10131**

NEWCOMBE, A G

Mr A G Newcombe, Lower Delworthy, Yarnscombe, Barnstaple, **Devon**, EX31 3LT, **ENGLAND**.
(T) 01271 858554 **(F)** 01271 858554
(M) 07785 297210.
Profile Trainer. **Ref:YH10132**

NEWCOMBE, P & A

P & A Newcombe, 40 Raines Ave, Worksop, **Nottinghamshire**, S81 7PB, **ENGLAND**.
(T) 01909 475664.
Contact/s
Partner: Mr A Newcombe **Ref:YH10133**

NEWCOMBES HORSE & DOG SHOP

Newcombes Horse & Dog Shop, 426A Chepstow Rd, Newport, **Newport**, NP19 8JH, **WALES**.
(T) 01633 671500 **(F)** 01633 671501.
Profile Saddlery Retailer. **Ref:YH10134**

NEWCOURT FARM

Newcourt Farm (Mills Bros), Three Cocks, Glasbury, **Powys**, LD3 0SS, **WALES**.
(T) 01497 847285.
Profile Equestrian Centre. **Ref:YH10135**

NEWHALL LIVERY

Newhall Livery, New Hall Farm, Stringers Lane, Higher Kinnerton, Chester, **Cheshire**, CH4 9BR, **ENGLAND**.
(T) 01244 661022.
Contact/s
Partner: Mrs L Morris
Profile Stable/Livery. **Ref:YH10136**

NEWHAM RIDING SCHOOL & ASS

Newham Riding School & Association Ltd, Docklands Equestrian Ctre, 2 Claps Gate Lane, Beckton, **London (Greater)**, E6 4JF, **ENGLAND**.
(T) 020 75113917 **(F)** 020 74734956.
Profile Riding School. **Ref:YH10137**

NEWHAVEN BLACKSMITHS

Newhaven Blacksmiths, Unit 17 North Peffer Pl, Edinburgh, **Edinburgh (City of)**, EH16 4UZ, **SCOTLAND**.
(T) 0131 6522941 **(F)** 0131 6526107.
Contact/s
Partner: Mr D McKeich
Profile Blacksmith. **Ref:YH10138**

NEWHILLS FARM & STABLES

Newhills Farm & Stables, Chilthorne Domer, Yeovil, **Somerset**, BA22 8QY, **ENGLAND**.
(T) 01935 825480. **Ref:YH10139**

NEWHOUSE FARM

Newhouse Farm, Newhouse Farm, East Kilbride, Glasgow, **Lanarkshire (South)**, G75 8RR, **SCOTLAND**.
(T) 01355 303435.
Contact/s
Owner: Mr J Meikle
Profile Stable/Livery. **Ref:YH10140**

NEWLAND HALL EQUESTRIAN CTRE

Newland Hall Equestrian Centre, Bishop Stortford Rd, Roxwell, Chelmsford, **Essex**, CM1 4LH, **ENGLAND**.
(T) 01245 231016
(M) 07980 302174.
Contact/s
Key Contact: Ms L Woolloff
Profile Riding School, Stable/Livery. **Ref:YH10141**

NEWLANDS CORNER RIDING CLUB

Newlands Corner Riding Club, 45 Dartnell Park Rd, West Byfleet, **Surrey**, KT14 6PR, **ENGLAND**.
(T) 01932 346378.
Contact/s
Chairman: Mrs E Alexander
Profile Club/Association, Riding Club. **Ref:YH10142**

NEWLANDS GRANGE LIVERY YARD

Newlands Grange Livery Yard, Newlands Grange, Shotley Bridge, Consett, **County Durham**, DH8 9LH, **ENGLAND**.
(T) 01207 591574/503870.
Contact/s
Manageress: Mrs S Vickery
Profile Stable/Livery. **Ref:YH10143**

NEWLANDS GRANGE MORGANS

Newlands Grange Morgans, Newlands Grange, Shotley Bridge, Consett, **County Durham**, DH8 9LH, **ENGLAND**.
(T) 01207 591574/503870.
Contact/s
Manager: Mrs S Vickery
Profile Breeder. **Ref:YH10144**

NEWLANDS STABLES

Newlands Stables, Upper Lambourn, Hungerford, **Berkshire**, RG17 8QT, **ENGLAND**.
(T) 01488 73656 **(F)** 01488 73633
(M) 07836 754254.
Profile Trainer. **Ref:YH10145**

NEWLANDS VETNRY GROUP

Newlands Veterinary Group, Ludlow Rd, Craven Arms, **Shropshire**, SY7 9QL, **ENGLAND**.
(T) 01588 673354 **(F)** 01588 672096.
Profile Medical Support. **Ref:YH10146**

NEWLEY, K & L

Misses K & L Newley (The), Brooklands Farm, Wootton Lane, Balsall Common, Coventry, **Warwickshire**, CV7 7BS, **ENGLAND**.
(T) 01676 532257.
Profile Stable/Livery. **Ref:YH10147**

NEWMAN, LAURENCE

Laurence Newman RSS, Cross Ash Cottage, Dark Lane, Longdon, Rugeley, **Staffordshire**, WS15 4LP, **ENGLAND**..
Profile Farrier. **Ref:YH10148**

NEWMAN, PHIL

Phil Newman, Farthings, Southlands Lane, West Chiltington, Pulborough, **Sussex (West)**, RH20 2JU, **ENGLAND**.
(T) 01798 813230. **Ref:YH10149**

NEWMAN, R

R Newman, Ryeland Farm, Wilde St, Beck Row, Bury St Edmunds, **Suffolk**, IP28 8BP, **ENGLAND**.
(T) 01842 861573. **Ref:YH10150**

NEWMAN, R & J

R & J Newman, Derehams Farm, Derehams Lane, Loudwater, High Wycombe, **Buckinghamshire**, HP10 9RR, **ENGLAND**.
(T) 01494 520964 **(F)** 01494 520964.
Contact/s
Partner: Mrs J Newman
Profile Transport/Horse Boxes.
Opening Times
By appointment only **Ref:YH10151**

NEWMAN, SOPHIE

Sophie Newman, Blackmoore Farm, Woolminster, Crewkerne, **Somerset**, TA18 8QT, **ENGLAND**.
(T) 01460 74146. **Ref:YH10152**

NEWMAN-TAYLOR, TOBIN R

Tobin R Newman-Taylor DWCF, 7 Highwood Cottages, Ingatestone Rd, Highwood, Brentwood, **Essex**, CM1 3QT, **ENGLAND**..
Profile Farrier. **Ref:YH10153**

NEWMARKET EQUINE SECURITY

Newmarket Equine Security Ltd, 8a Rosemary Hse, Landwade Business Pk, Landwade Kannett, Newmarket, **Suffolk**, CB8 7PW, **ENGLAND**.
(T) 01638 560837 **(F)** 01638 560837. **Ref:YH10154**

NEWMARKET FARRIER SUPPLIES
Newmarket Farrier Supplies, The Forge, Moulton Rd, Newmarket, **Suffolk**, CB8 8DU, **ENGLAND**.
(T) 01638 665895 **(F)** 01638 665895.
Contact/s
Manager: Mr A Dearling
Profile Farrier. **Ref: YH10155**

NEWMARKET PHOTONEWS AGENCY
Newmarket Photonews Agency, Brambles, Mildenhall Rd, Worlington, Bury St Edmunds, **Suffolk**, IP28 8RY, **ENGLAND**.
(T) 01638 713121 **(F)** 01638 713121. **Ref: YH10156**

NEWMARKET RACECOURSES TRUST
Newmarket Racecourses Trust, Westfield Hse, The Links, Cambridge Rd, Newmarket, **Suffolk**, CB8 0TG, **ENGLAND**.
(T) 01638 663482 **(F)** 01638 663044.
Contact/s
Clerk of Course: Capt N Lees
Profile Track/Course. **Ref: YH10157**

NEWNHAM COURT VETNRY GRP
Newnham Court Veterinary Group, Bearsted Rd, Weavering, Maidstone, **Kent**, ME14 5EL, **ENGLAND**.
(T) 01622 734555 **(F)** 01622 736512.
Profile Medical Support. **Ref: YH10158**

NEWNHAM EQUESTRIAN CTRE
Newnham Equestrian Centre, Big Hyde Farm, Hyde Lane, Newnham, **Gloucestershire**, GL14 1HQ, **ENGLAND**.
(T) 01594 516513.
Contact/s
Owner: Mrs J Charles
Profile Riding School. **Ref: YH10159**

NEWNHAM, JEFFREY
Jeffrey Newnham DWCF, Rowan, Beaconsfield Rd, Bexhill-on-Sea, **Sussex (East)**, TN40 2BN, **ENGLAND**.
(T) 01424 210516.
Contact/s
Farrier: Mr J Newnham
Profile Farrier. **Ref: YH10160**

NEWNS, J L
J L Newns, Vetmix, D6 Tamar Pk, Coxpark, Gunnislake, **Cornwall**, PL18 9BD, **ENGLAND**.
(T) 01822 833402
(E) james_newns@compuserve.com.
Profile Medical Support. **Ref: YH10161**

NEWPORT RIDING ACADEMY
Newport Riding Academy, Poplar Farm, Mill Lane, Newport, Brough, **Yorkshire (East)**, HU15 2QE, **ENGLAND**.
(T) 01430 449494 **(F)** 01430 449494.
Contact/s
Owner: Mrs S Carlill **Ref: YH10162**

NEWQUAY RIDING CLUB
Newquay Riding Club, The Old Barn, Cranstock Plains, Cranstock, Newquay, **Cornwall**, **ENGLAND**..
Contact/s
Chairman: Miss C Cleaver
Profile Club/Association, Riding Club. **Ref: YH10163**

NEWSHAM, A L
Miss A L Newsham, Cotton Farm, Middlewich Rd, Holmes Chapel, Crewe, **Cheshire**, CW4 7ET, **ENGLAND**.
(T) 01477 533200. **Ref: YH10164**

NEWSTEAD COTTAGE STABLES
Newstead Cottage Stables, Beverley Rd, Norton, Malton, **Yorkshire (North)**, YO17 9PJ, **ENGLAND**.
(T) 01653 697225 **(F)** 01653 697225
(M) 07710 502044.
Profile Trainer. **Ref: YH10165**

NEWSTEAD RIDING CTRE
Newstead Riding Centre, Snipe Lane, Neasham Rd, Hurworth Moor, Darlington, **County Durham**, DL2 1QB, **ENGLAND**.
(T) 01325 465492 **(F)** 01325 482695.
Contact/s
Owner: Mr M Lee
Profile Stable/Livery.
Indoor school is for hire and surrounding fields are available for use. No.Staff: 2 Yr. Est: 1986
Opening Times
Sp: Open Mon - Sun 09:00. Closed Mon - Sun 17:00.
Su: Open Mon - Sun 09:00. Closed Mon - Sun 17:00.
Au: Open Mon - Sun 09:00. Closed Mon - Sun 17:00.
Wn: Open Mon - Sun 09:00. Closed Mon - Sun 17:00. **Ref: YH10166**

NEWSUM, GILLIAN
Gillian Newsum, Priory Hse, Station Rd, Swavesey, **Cambridgeshire**, CB4 5QJ, **ENGLAND**.
(T) 01954 232084 **(F)** 01954 231362
(M) 07775 992124.
Profile Supplies. **Ref: YH10167**

NEWTON ABBOT RACECOURSE
Newton Abbot Racecourse Co Ltd, The Racecourse, Kingsteignton Rd, Newton Abbot, **Devon**, TQ12 3AF, **ENGLAND**.
(T) 01626 353235 **(F)** 01626 336972.
Contact/s
Chief Executive: Mr P Masterson
Profile Track/Course. **Ref: YH10168**

NEWTON CROFT COUNTRY
Newton Croft Country Schooling Course, Newton Hse Farm, Main St, Newton, Nottingham, **Nottinghamshire**, NG13 8HN, **ENGLAND**.
(T) 01949 20235 **(F)** 01949 20235.
Contact/s
Owner: Mrs C Fisher
Profile Stable/Livery, Track/Course. **Ref: YH10169**

NEWTON FERRERS
Newton Ferrers Equestrian Centre, Newton Ferrers, Plymouth, **Devon**, PL8 1JA, **ENGLAND**.
(T) 01752 872807.
Profile Breeder, Stable/Livery, Trainer. **Ref: YH10170**

NEWTON HALL EQUITATION CTRE
Newton Hall Equitation Centre, Swilland, Ipswich, **Suffolk**, IP6 9LT, **ENGLAND**.
(T) 01473 785616 **(F)** 01473 785617.
Contact/s
Owner: Mrs R Theobald
Profile Riding School, Stable/Livery. **Ref: YH10171**

NEWTON HORSEFEEDS & TRAILER
Newton Horsefeeds & Trailer Centre, Newstead Church Farm, Newton Reigny, Penrith, **Cumbria**, CA11 0AY, **ENGLAND**.
(T) 01768 862985 **(F)** 01768 862985.
Contact/s
Partner: Mr T Blackburn
Profile Transport/Horse Boxes. **Ref: YH10172**

NEWTON RIGG
Newton Rigg College Equestrian Centre, Newton Rigg College, Penrith, **Cumbria**, CA11 0AH, **ENGLAND**.
(T) 01768 863791 **(F)** 01768 867249.
Profile Equestrian Centre. **Ref: YH10173**

NEWTON STUD
Newton Stud, Naas, **County Kildare**, **IRELAND**.
(T) 045 895021 **(F)** 045 895022.
Contact/s
Key Contact: Mr B Grassick
Profile Breeder.
Newtown has stabling facilities for up to 36 horses and has a large indoor arena. C.Size: 120 Acres
Ref: YH10174

NEWTON-SMITH, A M
Miss A M Newton-Smith, Home Farm Barn, Jevington, Polegate, **Sussex (East)**, BN26 5QB, **ENGLAND**.
(T) 01323 488354
(M) 07970 914124.
Profile Trainer. **Ref: YH10175**

NIALL'S STABLE SVS
Niall's Stable Services, Robin Hill Hse, Green Rd, Curragh, **County Kildare**, **IRELAND**.
(T) 045 441338.
Contact/s
Owner: Niall Kennedy
Profile Equestrian Laundry. Yr. Est: 1990
Opening Times
Sp: Open Mon - Sat 09:00. Closed Mon - Sat 17:00.
Su: Open Mon - Sat 09:00. Closed Mon - Sat 17:00.
Au: Open Mon - Sat 09:00. Closed Mon - Sat 17:00.
Wn: Open Mon - Sat 09:00. Closed Mon - Sat 17:00.
Closed Sundays **Ref: YH10176**

NICDA
Northern Ireland Carriage Driving Association, 1 Mandeville Drive, Trandragee, **County Armagh**, BT62 2DQ, **NORTHERN IRELAND**.
(T) 01762 849624.
Profile Club/Association. **Ref: YH10177**

NICHOL, CHARLOTTE
Charlotte Nichol, Hetherington, Wark, Hexham, **Northumberland**, NE48 3DR, **ENGLAND**.
(T) 01434 230260
(M) 07831 307566. **Ref: YH10178**

NICHOL, D W
Mr D W Nichol, 70 Hoxton St, Thornton Rd, Bradford, **Yorkshire (West)**, BD8, **ENGLAND**..
Profile Trainer. **Ref: YH10179**

NICHOL, J
St Gatien, All Saints Rd, Newmarket, **Suffolk**, **ENGLAND**..
Profile Trainer. **Ref: YH10180**

NICHOLLS & SONS
Nicholls & Sons, Bellview Farm, Carnkie, Wendron, Helston, **Cornwall**, TR13 0DY, **ENGLAND**.
(T) 01209 860453.
Contact/s
Owner: Mr D Nicholls
Profile Supplies. **Ref: YH10181**

NICHOLLS, D E
D E Nicholls, Sandwaithe Hse, Ludney, Grainthorpe, Louth, **Lincolnshire**, LN11 7JU, **ENGLAND**.
(T) 01507 358289.
Profile Farrier. **Ref: YH10182**

NICHOLLS, E A
Mrs E A Nicholls, Hillside Cottage, Old London Rd, Wotton-under-Edge, **Gloucestershire**, GL12 7DT, **ENGLAND**.
(T) 01453 843804.
Profile Breeder. **Ref: YH10183**

NICHOLLS, N E
N E Nicholls, 7 The Knoll, South St, Uley, Dursley, **Gloucestershire**, GL11 5SR, **ENGLAND**.
(T) 01453 860090.
Profile Farrier. **Ref: YH10184**

NICHOLLS, RUSSELL KEITH
Russell Keith Nicholls DWCF, 3 Warwick Cl, Branston, Burton-on-Trent, **Staffordshire**, DE14 3JJ, **ENGLAND**.
(T) 01283 531696.
Profile Farrier. **Ref: YH10185**

NICHOLLS, W
W Nicholls (Crickhowell) Ltd, 19 High St, Crickhowell, **Powys**, NP8 1BH, **WALES**.
(T) 01873 810370.
Contact/s
Owner: Mr C Nicholls
Profile Saddlery Retailer. **Ref: YH10186**

NICHOLLS, WESLEY
Wesley Nicholls DWCF, 6 Grist Mill Cl, Arie Farm, Cheltenham, **Gloucestershire**, GL51 0PZ, **ENGLAND**.
(T) 01242 570026.
Profile Farrier. **Ref: YH10187**

NICHOLSON EQUESTRIAN SVS
Nicholson Equestrian Services, Cayton Gill Farm, South Stainley, Harrogate, **Yorkshire (North)**, HG3 3NB, **ENGLAND**.
(T) 01423 770101 **(F)** 01423 770101
(M) 07860 894802.
Profile Supplies. **Ref: YH10188**

NICHOLSON FARM MACHINERY
Nicholson Farm Machinery, 33 Common Lane, Southery, Downham Market, **Norfolk**, PE38 0PB, **ENGLAND**.
(T) 01366 377444 **(F)** 01366 377745.
Profile Supplies. **Ref: YH10189**

NICHOLSON, ANDREW
Andrew Nicholson (NZL), Woodlands Farm, Marston, Devizes, **Wiltshire**, SN10 5SP, **ENGLAND**.
(T) 01370 722102.
Profile Blood Stock Agency, Trainer. **Ref: YH10190**

NICHOLSON, BRIAN
Brian Nicholson, 24A Kesh Rd, Lisburn, **County Antrim**, BT27 5RP, **NORTHERN IRELAND**.
(T) 028 92621699.
Profile Transport/Horse Boxes. **Ref: YH10191**

NICHOLSON, BRIAN
Brian Nicholson, Transporting Horses Only, 28 Tullywest Rd, Nutts Corner, Crumlin, **County Antrim**, BT29 4SP, **NORTHERN IRELAND**.
(T) 028 94422763.
Profile Transport/Horse Boxes. **Ref: YH10192**

Key: (T) telephone (F) fax (M) mobile (E) E-Mail Address (W) Website Address (Q) Qualifications
Yr. Est: Year Established C.Size: Complex Size Sp: Spring Su: Summer Au: Autumn Wn: Winter

NICHOLSON, CHERYL
Cheryl Nicholson, 20 Frederick Rd, New Arley, Coventry, **Warwickshire**, CV7 8GQ, **ENGLAND**.
(T) 01676 541995.
Profile Saddlery Retailer. **Ref: YH10193**

NICHOLSON, MYLES
Myles Nicholson, Cayton Gill Farm, South Stainley, Harrogate, **Yorkshire (North)**, HG3 3NB, **ENGLAND**.
(T) 01423 770101 **(F)** 01423 770101.
Profile Trainer. **Ref: YH10194**

NICK MORRIS PHOTOGRAPHY
Nick Morris Photography, P O Box 28, Alnwick, **Northumberland**, NE66 3YR, **ENGLAND**.
(T) 01665 577151 **(F)** 01665 577151. **Ref: YH10195**

NICOL & PARTNERS
Nicol & Partners, Stocton Cl, Woodbridge Rd, Guildford, **Surrey**, GU1 1HR, **ENGLAND**.
(T) 01483 575155 **(F)** 01483 34674.
Profile Medical Support. **Ref: YH10196**

NICOL, A
A Nicol, Loriston Cottage, Hillside, Portlethen, Aberdeen, **Aberdeen (City of)**, AB12 4RB, **SCOTLAND**.
(T) 01224 780345.
Contact/s
Owner: Mr D Nicol **(Q)** AWCF
Profile Farrier. Surgical Shoes. Yr. Est: 1983
Opening Times
Telephone for an appointment **Ref: YH10197**

NICOL, C
Miss C Nicol, New Barn Farm, Capel Rd, Rusper, Horsham, **Sussex (West)**, RH12 4PZ, **ENGLAND**.
(T) 01293 871463.
Profile Breeder, Stable/Livery. **Ref: YH10198**

NICOLA M HUNT DWCF
Nicola M Hunt DWCF, 21 Lendon Rd, Borough Green, Sevenoaks, **Kent**, TN15 8SE, **ENGLAND**.
(T) 01732 884444.
Profile Farrier. **Ref: YH10199**

NICOLL FARM STABLES
Nicoll Farm Stables, Allum Lane, Elstree, Borehamwood, **Hertfordshire**, WD6 3NP, **ENGLAND**.
(T) 020 82070205.
Contact/s
Owner: Mrs A Robins **Ref: YH10200**

NIDD SMITHY
Nidd Smithy, Joinery Works, Main St, Great Ouseburn, York, **Yorkshire (North)**, YO26 9RQ, **ENGLAND**.
(T) 01423 331674.
Contact/s
Owner: Mr N Saville
Profile Blacksmith. **Ref: YH10201**

NIDD VALLEY RIDING CLUB
Nidd Valley Riding Club, 24 The Robins, Burley-In-Wharfedale, **Yorkshire (West)**, LS29 7PR, **ENGLAND**.
(T) 01937 573415.
Contact/s
Chairman: Mrs M Gibson
Profile Club/Association, Riding Club. **Ref: YH10202**

NIELD, G E
G E Nield, Norbury Common Farm, Norbury Common, Whitchurch, **Shropshire**, SY13 4JD, **ENGLAND**.
(T) 01829 720395.
Contact/s
Owner: Mr G Nield
Profile Breeder. **Ref: YH10203**

NIGHTINGALE RIDING SCHOOL
Nightingale Riding Centre, Epping New Rd, Buckhurst Hill, **Essex**, IG9 5UA, **ENGLAND**.
(T) 020 85046413.
Contact/s
Owner: Miss L Eveleigh
Profile Riding School, Stable/Livery.
Hacking is available. No.Staff: 2 Yr. Est: 1971
Opening Times
Sp: Open Tues - Sun 07:00. Closed Tues - Sun 20:00.
Su: Open Tues - Sun 07:00. Closed Tues - Sun 20:00.
Au: Open Tues - Sun 07:00. Closed Tues - Sun 20:00.
Wn: Open Tues - Sun 07:00. Closed Tues - Sun 20:00.
Closed Mondays **Ref: YH10204**

NIGHTINGALE, STEPHEN A
Stephen A Nightingale DWCF Hons, 5 Squirrels Cl, Huncoat, Accrington, **Lancashire**, BB5 6XL, **ENGLAND**.
(T) 01254 238994.
Profile Farrier. **Ref: YH10205**

NIMMO, J ALASTAIR
J Alastair Nimmo, Highmeadows, Thankerton, Biggar, **Lanarkshire (South)**, ML12 6NF, **SCOTLAND**.
(T) 01899 308180.
Profile Farrier. **Ref: YH10206**

NIMMO, M C
Mrs M C Nimmo, Duntarvie, Winchburgh, Broxburn, **Lothian (West)**, EH52 6QA, **SCOTLAND**.
(T) 01506 834331 **(F)** 01506 834331.
Profile Breeder. **Ref: YH10207**

NIMMO, R W F
Mr R W F Nimmo, 11 Brannock Ave, Newarthill, **Lanarkshire (North)**, ML1 5DS, **SCOTLAND**.
(T) 01698 833815.
Profile Trainer. **Ref: YH10208**

NIMROD SADDLERS
Nimrod Saddlers, 93-95 Canal St, Perth, **Perth and Kinross**, PH2 8HX, **SCOTLAND**.
(T) 01738 620538 **(F)** 01738 620538.
Contact/s
Owner: Mr E Milne **Ref: YH10209**

NINE MILE VETNRY HOSPITAL
Nine Mile Veterinary Hospital, 177 Nine Mile Ride, Finchampstead, Wokingham, **Berkshire**, RG40 4JD, **ENGLAND**.
(T) 0118 9733466 **(F)** 0118 9734213.
Profile Medical Support. **Ref: YH10210**

NINE TOR RIDING CTRE
Nine Tor Riding Centre, North Hill, Launceston, **Cornwall**, PL15 7PE, **ENGLAND**.
(T) 01566 782232.
Profile Riding School. **Ref: YH10211**

NINEHAM, T & YOUNG, J
Miss T Nineham & J Young, Ford Cottage, The Weirs, Brokenhurst, **Hampshire**, SO42 7UQ, **ENGLAND**.
(T) 01590 623043 **(F)** 01590 622515.
Contact/s
Partner: Miss T Nineham
Profile Breeder, Riding School, Stable/Livery.
Ref: YH10212

NIPPERBOUT
Nipperbout, 84 Clonmell Rd, London, **London (Greater)**, N17 6JU, **ENGLAND**.
(T) 020 88010148. **Ref: YH10213**

NIWHA
Northern Ireland Working Hunter Association, 84 Newtownards Rd, Donaghadee, **County Down**, BT21 0PT, **NORTHERN IRELAND**.
(T) 028 91888483.
Profile Club/Association. **Ref: YH10214**

NIXEY, M
Miss M Nixey, Harrington Farm, Great Milton, **Oxfordshire**, OX44 7JE, **ENGLAND**.
(T) 01844 279233.
Profile Breeder. **Ref: YH10215**

NIXON & MARSHALL
Nixon & Marshall, Overton, Maids Moreton, Buckingham, **Buckinghamshire**, MK18 1RE, **ENGLAND**.
(T) 01280 813258 **(F)** 01280 814983
(E) jnixonvet@aol.com.
Profile Medical Support. **Ref: YH10216**

NIXON, G
G Nixon, Hawksley Bungalow, Upton, Retford, **Nottinghamshire**, DN22 0QZ, **ENGLAND**.
(T) 01777 838812.
Contact/s
Farrier: Mr M Nixon
Profile Farrier. **Ref: YH10217**

NOBLE, ANNETTE
Mrs Annette Noble, Peggyslea Farm, Nine Mile Burn, Penicuik, **Lothian (Mid)**, **SCOTLAND**..
Profile Breeder. **Ref: YH10218**

NOBLE, MARK
Mark Noble, 28 Dunsgreen Court, Ponteland, Newcastle Upon Tyne, **Tyne and Wear**, NE20 9EX, **ENGLAND**.
(T) 01661 872383
Affiliated Bodies NAAT.
Contact/s
Physiotherapist: Mark Noble **(Q)** BSc(Hons)
Profile Medical Support. **Ref: YH10219**

NOBLE, R
R Noble, Ayton Mill, Eyemouth, **Scottish Borders**, TD14 5RQ, **SCOTLAND**.
(T) 01890 781600.
Profile Blacksmith. **Ref: YH10220**

NOBLE, W S
W S Noble, High Hse, Butterwick, Askham, Penrith, **Cumbria**, CA10 2QQ, **ENGLAND**.
(T) 01931 713318.
Profile Breeder. **Ref: YH10221**

NOBLET, G V
G V Noblet, 2 Moss Trce, Moss Lane, Whittle-Le-Woods, Chorley, **Lancashire**, PR6 8AB, **ENGLAND**.
(T) 01257 272973.
Profile Transport/Horse Boxes. **Ref: YH10222**

NOBLETT, T
T Noblett, Longfield, Whittingham Rd, Longridge, Preston, **Lancashire**, PR3 2AB, **ENGLAND**.
(T) 01772 784857.
Contact/s
Owner: Mr T Noblett **Ref: YH10223**

NOBOTTLE STUD
Nobottle Stud, Nobottle, **Northamptonshire**, NN7 4HJ, **ENGLAND**.
(T) 07702 220890.
Profile Stud Farm. **Ref: YH10224**

NOCK DEIGHTON AGRICULTURAL
Nock Deighton Agricultural, Bridgnorth Livestock & Auction Ctre, Tasley, Bridgnorth, **Shropshire**, WV16 4QR, **ENGLAND**.
(T) 01746 762666 **(F)** 01746 767475.
Contact/s
Partner: Mr M Walters
Profile Blood Stock Agency. **Ref: YH10225**

NOCK, S
Mrs S Nock, Smenham Farm, Icomb, Stow On The Wold, Cheltenham, **Gloucestershire**, GL54 1JT, **ENGLAND**.
(T) 01451 831688 **(F)** 01451 831404.
Profile Supplies. **Ref: YH10226**

NORBROOK TRAILERS
Norbrook Trailers Ltd, Norcott Brook Garage, Tarporley Rd, Bradley Brook, Warrington, **Cheshire**, WA4 4DS, **ENGLAND**.
(T) 01925 730005 **(F)** 01925 730005.
Profile Transport/Horse Boxes. **Ref: YH10227**

NORCHARD FARM RIDING SCHOOL
Norchard Farm Riding School, Thornhill, Manorbier, Tenby, **Pembrokeshire**, SA70 7SJ, **WALES**.
(T) 01834 871242.
Profile Riding School. **Ref: YH10228**

NORCLIFFE SHIRES
Norcliffe Shires, The Coppice, Smithy Lane, Mottram St Andrew, Macclesfield, **Cheshire**, SK10 4QJ, **ENGLAND**.
(T) 01625 827271 **(F)** 01625 827271.
Contact/s
Owner: Mr J Dale
Profile Breeder. No.Staff: 2 Yr. Est: 1980
C.Size: 12 Acres **Ref: YH10229**

NORCROFT EQUESTRIAN DVLP
Norcroft Equestrian Development, Park Farm Business Ctre, Fornham Pk, Fornham St. Genevieve, Bury St Edmunds, **Suffolk**, IP28 6TS, **ENGLAND**.
(T) 01284 706880 **(F)** 01284 706870.
Contact/s
Owner: Mr R Jermy
Profile Track/Course. **Ref: YH10230**

NORFOLK CLGE
Norfolk College of Arts & Technology, Tennyson Ave, King's Lynn, **Norfolk**, PE30 2QW, **ENGLAND**.
(T) 01553 761144 **(F)** 01553 764902.
Profile Equestrian Centre. **Ref: YH10231**

NORFOLK SHIRE HORSE CTRE
Norfolk Shire Horse Centre, West Runton Riding Stables, Cromer, **Norfolk**, NR27 9QH, **ENGLAND**.
(T) 01263 837339 **(F)** 01263 837132
(M) 07789 226362
(E) bakewell@norfolkshirehorse.fsnet.co.uk

(W) www.norfolk-shirehorse-centre.co.uk.
Contact/s
Key Contact: Ms J Bakewell
Profile Breeder, Riding School. Ref: YH10232

NORFOLK SHOW JUMPING CLUB

Norfolk Show Jumping Club, Old Hall Farm, Harlingwood Lane, Old Buckenham, Attleborough, **Norfolk**, NR17 1PT, **ENGLAND**..
Contact/s
Secretary: Mrs C Arksey
Profile Club/Association. Ref: YH10233

NORLAND EQUESTRIAN CTRE

Norland Equestrian Centre, Hullen Edge Farm, Norland, Halifax, **Yorkshire (West)**, HX6 3QW, **ENGLAND**.
(T) 01422 834290
Affiliated Bodies ABRS.
Contact/s
General Manager: Ms L Emerton (Q) BHS 2, NVQ 2
Profile Riding School. No.Staff: 3
Yr. Est: 1975 C.Size: 37 Acres
Opening Times
Sp: Open Mon - Sun 08:30. Closed Mon, Fri, Sun 12:00, Tues - Thurs 20:30, Sat 16:00.
Su: Open Mon - Sun 08:30. Closed Mon, Fri, Sun 12:00, Tues - Thurs 20:30, Sat 16:00.
Au: Open Mon - Sun 08:30. Closed Mon, Fri, Sun 12:00, Tues - Thurs 20:30, Sat 16:00.
Wn: Open Mon - Sun 08:30. Closed Mon, Fri, Sun 12:00, Tues - Thurs 20:30, Sat 16:00. Ref: YH10234

NORMAN & SPICER

Norman & Spicer (Agriculture) Ltd, Drayton Lodge, Daventry, **Northamptonshire**, NN11 4NL, **ENGLAND**.
(T) 01327 702449 (F) 01327 872110
(M) 07801 455092.
Profile Saddlery Retailer. Ref: YH10235

NORMAN BERRY RACING

Norman Berry Racing, Frenchmans Hse, Upper Lambourn, Hungerford, **Berkshire**, RG17 8QT, **ENGLAND**.
(T) 01488 72817.
Profile Trainer. Ref: YH10236

NORMAN LUNNUN ANIMAL HEALTH

Norman Lunnun Animal Health, Eaton Croft, Upwoods Rd, Doveridge, Ashbourne, **Derbyshire**, DE6 5LL, **ENGLAND**.
(T) 01889 563383 (F) 01889 563383.
Contact/s
Owner: Noman Lunnun
Profile Farrier, Medical Support, Supplies.
Ref: YH10237

NORMAN, JILL

Mrs Jill Norman, Augustus Hse, Ouseburn Rd, Whixley, **Yorkshire (North)**, YO26 8AL, **ENGLAND**.
(T) 01423 330055. Ref: YH10238

NORMANBY PARK RIDING SCHOOL

Normanby Park Riding School, Normanby Pk, Normanby, Scunthorpe, **Lincolnshire (North)**, DN15 9HU, **ENGLAND**.
(T) 01724 720783.
Contact/s
Owner: Mrs E Lawton-Smith Ref: YH10239

NORMANDIE STUD

Normandie Stud, Boxalland Farm, Kirdford, Billingshurst, **Sussex (West)**, RH14 0NN, **ENGLAND**.
(T) 01403 820047 (F) 01403 820083.
Contact/s
Manager: Mr R Brunger
Profile Breeder. Ref: YH10240

NORMANDY HORSE TRAILERS

Normandy Horse Trailers, Foxwell Cottage, Hunts Hill, Normandy, Guildford, **Surrey**, GU3 2AH, **ENGLAND**.
(T) 01483 811628 (F) 01483 811628.
Contact/s
Owner: Mrs A Cory
Profile Transport/Horse Boxes. Ref: YH10241

NORMILE, LUCY

Lucy Normile, Duncrevie, Glenfarg, **Perth and Kinross**, PH2 9PD, **SCOTLAND**.
(T) 01577 830330 (F) 01577 830330
(E) normile@btinternet.com
Affiliated Bodies JC.
Contact/s
General Manager: Mr A Normile
Profile Trainer. No.Staff: 5 Yr. Est: 2000
C.Size: 60 Acres
Opening Times
Telephone for an appointment Ref: YH10242

NORRINGTON

Norrington & Co, 9-15 Shacklewell Lane, London, **London (Greater)**, E8 2DA, **ENGLAND**.
(T) 020 76905866 (F) 020 76908221.
Contact/s
Owner: Mr P Norrington Ref: YH10243

NORRIS & SONS

Norris & Sons, Home Farm, Palace Lane, Beaulieu, Brockenhurst, **Hampshire**, SO42 7YG, **ENGLAND**.
(T) 01590 612215 (F) 01590 612215.
Contact/s
Owner: Mr F Norris
Profile Saddlery Retailer. Ref: YH10244

NORRIS, PAULINE

Brocklebeck Fell Ponies, Llys Gwyn, Cefn Mawr, Newtown, **Powys**, SY16 3LB, **WALES**.
(T) 01686 622217 (F) 01686 621232
(E) pauline@fulmar.demon.co.uk
Affiliated Bodies FPS.
Contact/s
Owner: Mrs P Norris (Q) HND (dist), M Phil ES
(E) pauline@fulmerdemon.co.uk
Profile Breeder, Supplies. Equine Lecturer.
Visiting parties are welcome to attend talks on rare pony breeds. Pauline Norris is a lecturer and researcher, in all aspects of the transportation of horses Yr. Est: 1996
Opening Times
Telephone for an appointment Ref: YH10245

NORTH CHESHIRE

North Cheshire Equestrian Centre, Carrington Lane, Carrington, Manchester, **Manchester (Greater)**, M31 4AE, **ENGLAND**.
(T) 0161 9731672 (F) 0161 9693017.
Contact/s
Owner: Mr T Groos
Profile Riding School. Ref: YH10246

NORTH COAST ADVENTURE HOLS

North Coast Adventure Holidays, Lundies, Tongue-By-Lairg, Sutherland, **Highlands**, IV27 4XF, **SCOTLAND**.
(T) 01847 55256.
Profile Equestrian Centre. Ref: YH10247

NORTH COAST RIDING CLUB

North Coast Riding Club, Brook Cottage, 23 Ardreagh Rd, Aghadowey, **County Londonderry**, BT51 4DN, **NORTHERN IRELAND**.
(T) 028 70353793.
Contact/s
Chairman: Mr L Bradley
Profile Club/Association. Ref: YH10248

NORTH COCKERHAM STABLES

North Cockerham Stables, Hacche Lane, South Molton, **Devon**, EX36 3EH, **ENGLAND**.
(T) 01598 740337. Ref: YH10249

NORTH CORNWALL ARENA

North Cornwall Arena, Davidstow, Camelford, **Cornwall**, PL32 9XR, **ENGLAND**.
(T) 01840 261249.
Profile Arena, Breeder, Stable/Livery. Ref: YH10250

NORTH COTSWOLD STUD

North Cotswold Stud, Coach Hse Farm, Cheltenham Rd, Broadway, **Worcestershire**, WR12 7BY, **ENGLAND**.
(T) 01386 858878 (F) 01386 858878.
Profile Blood Stock Agency, Breeder. Ref: YH10251

NORTH CRAY & SIDCUP

North Cray & Sidcup Riding School, 25 Parsonage Lane, Sidcup, **Kent**, DA14 5EZ, **ENGLAND**.
(T) 020 83001378.
Contact/s
Partner: Mrs S Whiley Ref: YH10252

NORTH DEVON BRIDLEWAYS

North Devon Bridleways, Tidicombe Farm, Arlington, Barnstaple, **Devon**, EX31 4SP, **ENGLAND**.
(T) 01271 850300.
Contact/s
Key Contact: Mrs M Balman Ref: YH10253

NORTH DEVON EQUESTRIAN CTRE

North Devon Equestrian Centre, Shirwell, Barnstaple, **Devon**, EX31 4HR, **ENGLAND**.
(T) 01271 850864.
Profile Riding School. Ref: YH10254

NORTH DEVON RIDING CLUB

North Devon Riding Club, Sunset Cottage, Comyn Hill, West Down, Ilfracombe, **Devon**, EX34 8NE, **ENGLAND**.
(T) 01271 815016.
Contact/s
Chairman: Mrs L Ashford
Profile Club/Association, Riding Club. Ref: YH10255

NORTH DOWN HARRIERS PONY CLUB

North Down Harriers Branch of The Pony Club, 88 Whinney Hill, Craigantlet, Dundonald, Belfast, **County Antrim**, BT16 1UA, **NORTHERN IRELAND**.
(T) 028 90426425.
Contact/s
Dist Comm: Mrs B Lowry
Profile Club/Association. Ref: YH10256

NORTH EAST LANCS RIDING CLUB

North East Lancs Riding Club, 490 Padiham Rd, Burnley, **Lancashire**, BB12 6TF, **ENGLAND**.
(T) 01282 424785.
Contact/s
Secretary: Mrs A Hindle
Profile Club/Association, Riding Club. Ref: YH10257

NORTH EASTERN FARMERS

North Eastern Farmers Ltd (Inverurie), Thainstone Agricultural Ctre, Inverurie, **Aberdeenshire**, AB51 9XY, **SCOTLAND**.
(T) 01467 623844 (F) 01467 626100.
Profile Medical Support, Supplies.
Farm supplies Ref: YH10258

NORTH EASTERN FARMERS

North Eastern Farmers Ltd (Forfar), Queenswell Rd, Forfar, **Angus**, DD8 3JA, **SCOTLAND**.
(T) 01307 463651.
Contact/s
District Shops Manager: Ruth Chalmers
Profile Supplies. Ref: YH10259

NORTH EASTERN POLOCROSSE CLUB

North Eastern Polocrosse Club, High Moor Hse, Shipton-By-Benningborough, York, **Yorkshire (North)**, YO30 1AS, **ENGLAND**.
(T) 01904 470603.
Contact/s
Chairman: Mr J Beckeriegge
Profile Club/Association. Polocrosse Club.
Ref: YH10260

NORTH FARM RACING STABLES

North Farm Racing Stables, Cottage No 2, North Farm, Snetterton, Norwich, **Norfolk**, NR16 2LD, **ENGLAND**.
(T) 01953 498989 (F) 01789 415499
(M) 07801 743783.
Profile Trainer. Ref: YH10261

NORTH FARM RIDING EST

North Farm Riding Establishment, North Farm, Ludlow, **Shropshire**, SY8 2HD, **ENGLAND**.
(T) 01584 872026 (F) 01584 872026
Affiliated Bodies BHS, RDA.
Contact/s
Owner: Mr P Dickin (Q) RDA
Profile Equestrian Centre. No.Staff: 3
Yr. Est: 1968 Ref: YH10262

NORTH HAYE

North Haye, North Bovey, Mortonhampstead, **Devon**, **ENGLAND**..
Profile Riding School. Ref: YH10263

NORTH HUMBERSIDE

North Humberside Riding Centre, Easington, Hull, **Yorkshire (East)**, HU12 0UA, **ENGLAND**.
(T) 01964 650250
Affiliated Bodies BHS.
Contact/s
Owner: Toni Biglin
Profile Equestrian Centre, Riding School, Stable/Livery. No.Staff: 4 Yr. Est: 1965
C.Size: 40 Acres Ref: YH10264

NORTH IVES FARM

North Ives Farm, Brownberrie Drive, Horsforth, **Yorkshire (West)**, LS18 5PR, **ENGLAND**.
(T) 0113 2583093.
Profile Riding School. Ref: YH10265

NORTH LAMMERMUIR RIDING CLUB

North Lammermuir Riding Club, 40 Annfield Court, Macmerry, Tranent, **Lothian (East)**, EH33 1PN, **SCOTLAND**.
(T) 01875 615757.
Contact/s

Chairman: Mrs S Clark
Profile Club/Association, Riding Club. Ref:YH10266

NORTH LANARKSHIRE RIDING CLUB

North Lanarkshire Riding Club, 42 Meadow View, Kildrum, Cumbernauld, **Lanarkshire (North)**, G67 2BZ, **SCOTLAND**.
(T) 01236 726159.
Contact/s
Chairman: Mr I Simpson
Profile Club/Association, Riding Club. Ref:YH10267

NORTH LIGHT

North Light, Yarn Mill, Stringer St, Biddulph, Stoke-on-Trent, **Staffordshire**, ST8 6BQ, **ENGLAND**.
(T) 01782 523050 (F) 01782 523036. Ref:YH10268

NORTH LINCOLNSHIRE

North Lincolnshire Riding Club, The Oban, Grimsby Rd, Laceby, Grimsby, **Lincolnshire (North East)**, DN37 7DU, **ENGLAND**.
(T) 01472 71196.
Contact/s
Secretary: Mrs J Foulds
Profile Club/Association, Riding Club. Ref:YH10269

NORTH LINCOLNSHIRE COLLEGE

North Lincolnshire College, Sport Science & Cultural Studies Division, Monks Rd, Lincoln, **Lincolnshire**, LN2 5HQ, **ENGLAND**.
(T) 01522 876000 (F) 01522 876200.
Profile Equestrian Centre. Ref:YH10270

NORTH LIZARD RIDING SCHOOL

North Lizard Riding School, Lizard Lane, South Shields, **Tyne and Wear**, NE34 7AE, **ENGLAND**.
(T) 0191 5292198.
Contact/s
Partner: Mrs D Tuck
Profile Riding School, Stable/Livery. Ref:YH10271

NORTH MUNSTEAD STUD

North Munstead Stud, North Munstead Lane, Godalming, **Surrey**, GU8 4AX, **ENGLAND**.
(T) 01483 424181 (F) 01483 426043.
Profile Breeder. Ref:YH10272

NORTH MYMMS RIDING CLUB

North Mymms Riding Club, 74 Georges Wood Rd, Brookmans Pk, Hatfield, **Hertfordshire**, AL9 7BU, **ENGLAND**.
(T) 01707 652010.
Contact/s
Chairman: Mrs A Cole
Profile Club/Association, Riding Club. Ref:YH10273

NORTH NORFOLK RIDING CTRE

North Norfolk Riding Centre, Old Wells Rd, Walsingham, **Norfolk**, NR22 6BS, **ENGLAND**.
(T) 01328 820796.
Contact/s
Owner: Mrs S Noakes
Profile Riding School. Ref:YH10274

NORTH NORTHUMBERLAND

North Northumberland Light Horse Breeding Society, Goldenmoor, Denwick, **Northumberland**, NE66 3RB, **ENGLAND**.
(T) 01665 602421.
Contact/s
Manager: Mr J Robson
Profile Breeder, Club/Association, Supplies.
Ref:YH10275

NORTH OF ENGLAND

North of England & Scottish Team Event Association, Catless Farm, Wark, Hexham, **Northumberland**, NE48 3BD, **ENGLAND**.
(T) 01484 681142.
Contact/s
Secretary: Miss E Nixon
Profile Club/Association. Ref:YH10276

NORTH OF ENGLAND SADDLE

North Of England Saddle Co, 27A North End, Bedale, **Yorkshire (North)**, DL8 1AF, **ENGLAND**.
(T) 01677 422213.
Contact/s
Owner: Mr L Broadway Ref:YH10277

NORTH OXFORDSHIRE RIDING CLUB

North Oxfordshire Riding Club, 3 The Close, Great Bourton, Banbury, **Oxfordshire**, **ENGLAND**.
(T) 01295 758172.
Contact/s
Chairman: Mr T Hunter
Profile Club/Association, Riding Club. Ref:YH10278

NORTH PARK VETNRY GROUP

North Park Veterinary Group, 64 Fore St, North Tawton, **Devon**, EX20 2DT, **ENGLAND**.
(T) 01837 82327 (F) 01837 89001.
Profile Medical Support. Ref:YH10279

NORTH RIDING ROSETTES

North Riding Rosettes, Old Mill Hse, Bempton, Bridlington, **Yorkshire (East)**, YO16 6XG, **ENGLAND**.
(T) 01262 401065 (F) 01262 401065
(E) enquiries@rosettesonline.co.uk.
Profile Supplies. Ref:YH10280

NORTH RIDING TRAINING GROUP

North Riding Training Group, 4 Ingleby Gr, Hartburn, **Cleveland**, TS18 5AX, **ENGLAND**.
(T) 01642 570464.
Contact/s
Chairman: Mr B Morris Ref:YH10281

NORTH SHROPSHIRE TRAILER CTRE

North Shropshire Trailer Centre, Newcastle Rd, Market Drayton, **Shropshire**, TF9 1HW, **ENGLAND**.
(T) 01630 652641.
Contact/s
Partner: Mrs M Machin
Profile Transport/Horse Boxes. Ref:YH10282

NORTH TAWTON RIDING CLUB

North Tawton Riding Club, Whitethorn Cottage, Hittisleigh, Exeter, **Devon**, EX6 6LG, **ENGLAND**.
(T) 01647 24323 (F) 01647 24323.
Contact/s
Chairman: Mrs M Weeks
Profile Club/Association, Riding Club. Ref:YH10283

NORTH WALSHAM SADDLERY

North Walsham Saddlery, Heath Farm, 88 High St, Marsham, Norwich, **Norfolk**, NR10 5QG, **ENGLAND**.
(T) 01263 734422 (F) 01263 734422.
Contact/s
Partner: Mrs S Gray
Profile Saddlery Retailer. Ref:YH10284

NORTH WEST KENT PONY CLUB

North West Kent Branch of the Pony Club, Bramley, 67 Goldsel Rd, Swanley, **Kent**, BR8 8HA, **ENGLAND**.
(T) 01322 662233.
Profile Club/Association. Ref:YH10285

NORTH WEST TOURIST BOARD

North West Tourist Board, Swan Hse, Swan Meadow Rd, Wigan, **Lancashire**, WN3 5BB, **ENGLAND**.
(T) 01942 821222 (F) 01942 820002
(E) info@nwtb.u-net.com.
Profile Club/Association. Ref:YH10286

NORTH WORCESTERSHIRE

North Worcestershire Equestrian Centre (The), Inc Silvretta Haflinger Stud, Shangri-La, Woodfield Lane, Halesowen, **Midlands (West)**, B62 0LR, **ENGLAND**.
(T) 01562 710245.
Profile Breeder, Riding School, Stable/Livery.
Ref:YH10287

NORTH YORKSHIRE TRAINING GRP

North Yorkshire Training Group, 12 Sydney Rd, Marton, **Cleveland**, TS7 8HG, **ENGLAND**.
(T) 01642 318223.
Contact/s
Chairman: Mr S Peacock
Profile Club/Association. Ref:YH10288

NORTHALL, S & M

S & M Northall, Hollydene, Brook St, Gornal Wood, Dudley, **Midlands (West)**, DY3 2NB, **ENGLAND**.
(T) 01384 455838
(E) m.f.northall@bham.ac.uk.
Contact/s
Owner: Mr M Northall
Profile Breeder.
Breeder of Welsh Section A, C and D ponies
Ref:YH10289

NORTHALLERTON EQUESTRIAN

Northallerton Equestrian Centre, Yafforth, Northallerton, **Yorkshire (North)**, DL6 0PQ, **ENGLAND**.
(T) 01609 772942 (F) 01609 772942
(E) info@northallertonequestriancentre.co.uk
(W) www.northallertonequestriancentre.co.uk
Affiliated Bodies BD, BSJA.
Contact/s
Administration: Ms J Bentley
Profile Horse/Rider Accom, Riding School.
Holiday accommodation on site and DIY livery also available, making this ideal for riders to bring their own horse on holiday. Lessons from £15.00 per person. Yr. Est: 1986 C.Size: 26 Acres
Opening Times
Sp: Open Mon - Sun 10:00. Closed Mon - Sun 14:00.
Su: Open Mon - Sun 10:00. Closed Mon - Sun 14:00.
Au: Open Mon - Sun 10:00. Closed Mon - Sun 14:00.
Wn: Open Mon - Sun 10:00. Closed Mon - Sun 14:00. Ref:YH10290

NORTHALLERTON RIDING CLUB

Northallerton Riding Club, The Manor Hse, Danby Wiske, Northallerton, **Yorkshire (North)**, DL7 0LZ, **ENGLAND**.
(T) 01609 774662.
Contact/s
Chairman: Mrs A Cawood
Profile Club/Association, Riding Club. Ref:YH10291

NORTHALLETON

Northallerton Equestrian Centre, C/O 9B Ickwell Rd, Northill, Biggleswade, **Bedfordshire**, SG18 9AA, **ENGLAND**.
(T) 01462 752451
(W) www.northallerton-ec.co.uk.
Contact/s
Instructor: Ian Brown (Q) BHSII
Profile Riding School, Stable/Livery.
Arrange affiliated and unaffiliated competitions.
Ref:YH10292

NORTHAMPTONSHIRE AUCTIONS

Northamptonshire Auctions plc, Liliput Rd, Brackmills, **Northamptonshire**, NN4 7BY, **ENGLAND**.
(T) 01604 769990 (F) 01604 763155. Ref:YH10293

NORTHBROOK EQUESTRIAN CTRE

Northbrook Equestrian Centre, New Rd, Offord Cluny, Huntingdon, **Cambridgeshire**, PE18 9RT, **ENGLAND**.
(T) 01480 812654.
Contact/s
For Bookings: Ms K Warren
Profile Equestrian Centre, Riding School, Stable/Livery.
Shows are held every month. No.Staff: 4
Yr. Est: 1992 C.Size: 5 Acres
Opening Times
Sp: Open 09:00. Closed 21:00.
Su: Open 09:00. Closed 21:00.
Au: Open 09:00. Closed 21:00.
Wn: Open 09:00. Closed 21:00. Ref:YH10294

NORTHBROOK FARM

Northbrook Farm, Titnore Rd, Goring, Worthing, **Sussex (West)**, BN12 6NY, **ENGLAND**.
(T) 01903 671854.
Profile Stable/Livery. Ref:YH10295

NORTHCOTE HEAVY HORSE CTRE

Northcote Heavy Horse Centre, Great Steeping, Spilsby, **Lincolnshire**, PE23 5PS, **ENGLAND**.
(T) 01754 830286 (F) 01754 830286
(E) northcote.horses@virgin.net
(W) www.northcote-horses.co.uk.
Profile
Working Sanctuary for retired and handicapped Heavy Horses. Ref:YH10296

NORTH-EAST LANCASHIRE

North-East Lancashire Riding Club, Gibb Field Farm Cottage, Crown Point Rd, Burnley, **Lancashire**, BB11 3RU, **ENGLAND**.
(T) 01282 30378.
Profile Club/Association, Riding Club. Ref:YH10297

NORTHERN BLOODSTOCK

Northern Bloodstock, Highfield Hse, Ings Lane, Scamblesby, Louth, **Lincolnshire**, LN11 9XT, **ENGLAND**.
(T) 01507 343204.
Contact/s
Owner: Mr J Gollings
Profile Blood Stock Agency, Trainer. Ref:YH10298

NORTHERN COUNTIES

Northern Counties Horse Protection Society, Galloping Green Rd, Eighton Banks, Gateshead, **Tyne and Wear**, NE9 7YD, **ENGLAND**.
(T) 0191 4875858.
Profile Club/Association. Ref:YH10299

NORTHERN COUNTIES PONY ASS

Northern Counties Pony Association, 8 Broadfleet Cl, Pilling, Preston, **Lancashire**, PR3 6BT, **ENGLAND**.
(T) 01253 790562 **(F)** 01253 790667.
Profile Club/Association. **Ref: YH10300**

NORTHERN DRESSAGE GROUP

Northern Dressage Group, 66 Nursery Ave, Ormskirk, **Lancashire**, L39 2DZ, **ENGLAND**.
(T) 01695 579619.
Contact/s
Chairman: Mrs B Smith
Profile Club/Association. **Ref: YH10301**

NORTHERN EQUINE SERVICES

Northern Equine Services Ltd, Burgham Farm, Morpeth, **Northumberland**, NE65 8TJ, **ENGLAND**.
(T) 01670 87314.
Profile Blood Stock Agency. **Ref: YH10302**

NORTHERN EQUINE THERAPY CTRE

Northern Equine Therapy Centre (The), Beautry Hse, Rathmell, Settle, **Yorkshire (North)**, BD24 0LA, **ENGLAND**.
(T) 01729 840284.
Profile Medical Support, Stable/Livery. **Ref: YH10303**

NORTHERN IRELAND DRIVING CLUB

Northern Ireland Driving Club (The), 68 Edgewater, Lisburn, **County Antrim**, BT27 5PZ, **NORTHERN IRELAND**.
(T) 028 92665893.
Contact/s
Chairman: Mr E Larkin
Profile Club/Association. **Ref: YH10304**

NORTHERN IRELAND HORSE BOARD

Northern Ireland Horse Board Co-Operative Society Limited, 23 Ballykeigle Rd, Comber, Newtownards, **County Down**, BT23 5SD, **NORTHERN IRELAND**.
(T) 028 97528324 **(F)** 028 97528500
(W) www.nihorseboard.org.
Contact/s
Owner: Mrs C Kirkpatrick
(E) charlotte@nihorseboard.org
Profile Breeder. Registration Organisaton.
Irish Horse Registration for sport horses also run the Irish Stud Book. **Ref: YH10305**

NORTHERN IRELAND SHOWS ASS

Northern Ireland Shows Association, Royal Ulster Agricultural Society, The King's Hall, Balmoral, Belfast, **County Antrim**, BT9 6GW, **NORTHERN IRELAND**.
(T) 028 90665225 **(F)** 028 90661264
(E) general@kingshall.co.uk.
Contact/s
Chief Executive: Mr W Yarr
Profile Club/Association. **Ref: YH10306**

NORTHERN RACING COLLEGE

South Yorkshire Training Trust, The Stables, Rossington Hall, Great North Rd, Doncaster, **Yorkshire (South)**, DN11 0HN, **ENGLAND**.
(T) 01302 861000 **(F)** 01302 84151
(W) www.northernracingcollege.co.uk.
Contact/s
Administration: Mr P Foster
(E) paul@nrcdonc.demon.co.uk
Profile Equestrian Centre. College. No.Staff: 15
Yr. Est: 1984 C.Size: 60 Acres **Ref: YH10307**

NORTHERN RIDING/CARRIAGE

Northern Riding & Carriage Driving Centre, Water Lane, Thornhill Rd, Dewsbury, **Yorkshire (West)**, WF12 9PY, **ENGLAND**.
(T) 01924 439579.
Contact/s
Owner: Mr N Ray **Ref: YH10308**

NORTHERN SHIRE

Northern Shire Horse Centre & Museum, Flower Hill Farm, North Newbald, **Yorkshire (East)**, YO43 4TG, **ENGLAND**.
(T) 01430 827270.
Profile Breeder.
Northern Shire is a tourist attraction **Ref: YH10309**

NORTHERN STANDARDBREDS

Northern Standardbreds, 63 Waterloo Rd, Kelbrook, Barnoldswick, **Lancashire**, BB18 6TY, **ENGLAND**.
(T) 01282 843736 **(F)** 01282 843736.
Profile Medical Support. **Ref: YH10310**

NORTHERN STRAW

Northern Straw Co Ltd, Heck Hall Farm, Goole, **Yorkshire (East)**, DN14 0BL, **ENGLAND**.
(T) 01405 861196 **(F)** 01405 862328.
Contact/s
Administration: Ms C Haigh
Profile Supplies. Yr. Est: 1980
Opening Times
Sp: Open Mon - Sun 08:00. Closed Mon - Sun 17:00.
Su: Open Mon - Sun 08:00. Closed Mon - Sun 17:00.
Au: Open Mon - Sun 08:00. Closed Mon - Sun 17:00.
Wn: Open Mon - Sun 08:00. Closed Mon - Sun 17:00. **Ref: YH10311**

NORTHFIELD FARM

Northfield Farm Riding & Trekking Centre, Northfield Farm, Flash, Buxton, **Derbyshire**, SK17 0SW, **ENGLAND**.
(T) 01298 22543 **(F)** 01298 27849
(E) northfield@btinternet.com
Affiliated Bodies BAPSH, BHS.
Contact/s
Owner: Ms L Andrews **(Q)** BHSAI
Profile Breeder, Horse/Rider Accom, Riding School, Stable/Livery.
LeTrec training and competitions. No.Staff: 4
Yr. Est: 1976 C.Size: 150 Acres **Ref: YH10312**

NORTHFIELD HORSE SUPPLIES

Northfield Horse Supplies, Northfield Hse, Invergordon, **Highlands**, IV18 0LN, **SCOTLAND**.
(T) 01349 853138.
Profile Supplies. **Ref: YH10313**

NORTHFIELD RIDING CTRE

Northfield Riding Centre, Northfield Farm, Gorsey Lane, Bold, St Helens, **Merseyside**, WA9 4SW, **ENGLAND**.
(T) 01744 816075.
Contact/s
Key Contact: Mr T Cotterill
Profile Riding School. **Ref: YH10314**

NORTHLANDS VETNRY HOSPITAL

Northlands Veterinary Hospital, 2 Northampton Rd, Kettering, **Northamptonshire**, NN15 7JU, **ENGLAND**.
(T) 01536 485543 **(F)** 01536 414344
(E) info@northlands-vets.co.uk
(W) www.northlands-vets.co.uk.
Contact/s
Vet: Mr J Hawkins
Profile Medical Support. **Ref: YH10315**

NORTHMORE STUD

Northmore Stud, Northend Rd, Exning, Newmarket, **Suffolk**, CB8 7JR, **ENGLAND**.
(T) 01638 577022 **(F)** 01638 577021.
Profile Breeder. **Ref: YH10316**

NORTHORPE HACKNEY STUD

Northorpe Hackney Stud, Newroyds, 71 Gomersal Lane, Gomersal, Cleckheaton, **Yorkshire (West)**, BD19 4JQ, **ENGLAND**.
(T) 01274 870451.
Profile Breeder. **Ref: YH10317**

NORTHSIDE VERERINARY CTRE

Northside Vererinary Centre, Northside, Vale, **Guernsey**, GY3 5TS, **ENGLAND**.
(T) 01481 248464 **(F)** 01481 243883.
Profile Medical Support. **Ref: YH10318**

NORTHUMBERLAND EQUESTRIAN SVS

Northumberland Equestrian Services, The Stables, Town Foot Farm, Shilbottle, Alnwick, **Northumberland**, NE66 2HG, **ENGLAND**.
(T) 01665 575020. **Ref: YH10319**

NORTHUMBRIA HORSE HOLIDAYS

Snowgain Limited T/A Northumbria Horse Holidays, East Castle, Annfield Plain, Stanley, **County Durham**, DH9 8PH, **ENGLAND**.
(T) 01207 235354
Affiliated Bodies BAHA.
Profile Equestrian Centre, Holidays.
Trail riding & riding weekends. Learn to ride and improve your riding on open moorland in a picturesque area. Yr. Est: 1976 C.Size: 70 Acres
Ref: YH10320

NORTHUMBRIAN SADDLERY

Northumbrian Saddlery, Anick Rd, Fellside, Hexham, **Northumberland**, NE46 1RG, **ENGLAND**.
(T) 01434 604020 **(F)** 01434 604020.
Contact/s
Partner: Mr G Brown
Profile Saddlery Retailer. **Ref: YH10321**

NORTHWILDS RIDING CTRE

Northwilds Riding Centre, Fendom, Tain, **Highlands**, IV19 1PE, **SCOTLAND**.
(T) 01862 892468.
Profile Riding School. **Ref: YH10322**

NORTHWOOD RIDING CLUB

Northwood Riding Club, 9 Conniston Gardens, Pinner, **London (Greater)**, HA5 2JN, **ENGLAND**.
(T) 01895 674730.
Contact/s
Chairman: Mr T Breadmore
Profile Club/Association, Riding Club. **Ref: YH10323**

NORTHWOOD, GLYN

Glyn Northwood AFCL, Elm Cottage, Stretton Baskerville, Hinckley, **Leicestershire**, LE10 3DP, **ENGLAND**.
(T) 01455 234223.
Profile Farrier. **Ref: YH10324**

NORTON

Norton & Co, 21B Stuart Hse, Cromwell Pk, Chipping Norton, **Oxfordshire**, OX7 5SR, **ENGLAND**.
(T) 01608 641500 **(F)** 01608 644666. **Ref: YH10325**

NORTON & NEWBY

Norton & Newby, 11 Windsor End, Beaconsfield, **Buckinghamshire**, HP9 2JJ, **ENGLAND**.
(T) 01494 676583 **(F)** 01494 681173. **Ref: YH10326**

NORTON GROVE STUD

Norton Grove Stud Ltd, Scarborough Rd, Norton, Malton, **Yorkshire (North)**, YO17 8EF, **ENGLAND**.
(T) 01653 693887.
Profile Breeder. **Ref: YH10327**

NORTON HEATH EQUESTRIAN CTRE

Norton Heath Equestrian Centre, Fingrith Hall Lane, Ingatestone, **Essex**, CM4 0JP, **ENGLAND**.
(T) 01277 821848 **(F)** 01277 821008.
Contact/s
Owner: Mr N Everett
Profile Stable/Livery. **Ref: YH10328**

NORTON HEATH EQUITATION

Norton Heath Equitation Products, Norton Heath Equestrian Ctre, Fingrith Hall Lane, Ingatestone, **Essex**, CM4 0JP, **ENGLAND**.
(T) 01277 824035. **Ref: YH10329**

NORTON HIND SADDLERY

Norton Hind Saddlery, 2 Orchard Cres, Arundel Rd, Fontwell, Arundel, **Sussex (West)**, BN18 0SD, **ENGLAND**.
(T) 01243 543191.
Contact/s
Partner: Mr N Hind
Profile Saddlery Retailer.
Leather repairs Yr. Est: 1978
Opening Times
Sp: Open 09:00. Closed 18:00.
Su: Open 09:00. Closed 18:00.
Au: Open 09:00. Closed 18:00.
Wn: Open 09:00. Closed 18:00. **Ref: YH10330**

NORTON, B J

B J Norton, Dunroamin, Gardiners Cl, Basildon, **Essex**, SS14 3AW, **ENGLAND**.
(T) 01268 527080.
Profile Farrier. **Ref: YH10331**

NORTON, J

Mr J Norton, Globe Farm, High Hoyland, Barnsley, **Yorkshire (South)**, S75 4BE, **ENGLAND**.
(T) 01226 387633 **(F)** 01226 387633
(M) 07970 212707.
Profile Trainer. **Ref: YH10332**

NORVITE

Norvite Feed Supplements, Wardhouse, Insch, **Aberdeenshire**, AB52 6YD, **SCOTLAND**.
(T) 01464 831261 **(F)** 01464 831400
(W) www.norvite.com.
Contact/s
General Manager: Mr A Pirie
Profile Feed Merchant. No.Staff: 30
Yr. Est: 1974
Opening Times
Sp: Open Mon - Fri 08:00. Closed Mon - Fri 17:00.
Su: Open Mon - Fri 08:00. Closed Mon - Fri 17:00.
Au: Open Mon - Fri 08:00. Closed Mon - Fri 17:00.
Wn: Open Mon - Fri 08:00. Closed Mon - Fri 17:00.
Closed at weekends **Ref: YH10333**

NORWICH TRAILER CTRE

Norwich Trailer Centre, 12 Roundtree Cl, Norwich, **Norfolk**, NR7 8SX, **ENGLAND**.
(T) 01603 424566.
Profile Transport/Horse Boxes. **Ref: YH10334**

NORWOOD EQUESTRIAN CTRE

Norwood Equestrian Centre, Norwood Lane, Graffham, Petworth, **Sussex (West)**, GU28 0QG, **ENGLAND**.
(T) 01798 867693
Affiliated Bodies BHS.
Contact/s
Owner: Ms R Jenner **(Q)** AI
Profile Equestrian Centre, Stable/Livery.
Hacking is available. Yr. Est: 1992 C.Size: 30 Acres
Opening Times
Sp: Open 07:30. Closed 17:30.
Su: Open 07:30. Closed 17:30.
Au: Open 07:30. Closed 17:30.
Wn: Open 07:30. Closed 17:30. **Ref: YH10335**

NORWOOD VETNRY GROUP

Norwood Veterinary Group, 28 Norwood, Beverley, **Yorkshire (East)**, HU17 9HB, **ENGLAND**.
(T) 01482 882613 **(F)** 01482 872858.
Profile Medical Support. **Ref: YH10336**

NOTEHOME

Notehome Ltd, 31 Cobden St, Salford, **Lancashire**, M6 6WF, **ENGLAND**.
(T) 0161 7378474 **(F)** 0161 7361014.
Profile Transport/Horse Boxes. **Ref: YH10337**

NOTT, J

J Nott, The Forge, Little Saredon, Wolverhampton, **Midlands (West)**, WV10 7LJ, **ENGLAND**.
(T) 01922 412614.
Profile Farrier. **Ref: YH10338**

NOTT, PHILIP GEOFFREY

Philip Geoffrey Nott RSS, 45 Green Lane, Rugeley, **Staffordshire**, WS15 2PH, **ENGLAND**.
(T) 01922 412614.
Profile Breeder, Farrier. **Ref: YH10339**

NOTTINGHAM HORSE TRANSPORT

Nottingham Horse Transport, Bottom Hse Farm, Mansfield Rd, Arnold, Nottingham, **Nottinghamshire**, NG5 8PH, **ENGLAND**.
(T) 0115 9207844.
Profile Transport/Horse Boxes. **Ref: YH10340**

NOTTINGHAM HORSEBALL CLUB

Nottingham Horseball Club, C/O Arkenfield Stables, Lowdham Rd, Gunthorpe, **Nottinghamshire**, NG14 7ER, **ENGLAND**.
(T) 0115 9664574.
Profile Club/Association. **Ref: YH10341**

NOTTINGHAM JOUSTING ASS

Nottingham Jousting Association, Bunny Hill Top, Costock, Loughborough, **Leicestershire**, LE12 6XE, **ENGLAND**.
(T) 01509 852366 **(F)** 01509 856067.
Profile Club/Association. **Ref: YH10342**

NOTTINGHAM JUNIOR

Nottingham Junior Horseball Team, C/O 40 King St, Beeston, Nottingham, **Nottinghamshire**, NG9 2DL, **ENGLAND**.
(T) 0115 9227917.
Profile Club/Association. **Ref: YH10343**

NOTTINGHAM RACECOURSE

Nottingham Racecourse Co Ltd, Colwick Pk, Nottingham, **Nottinghamshire**, NG2 4BE, **ENGLAND**.
(T) 0115 9580620 **(F)** 0115 9584515.
Profile Track/Course. **Ref: YH10344**

NOTTINGHAM TRAILER SPARES

Nottingham Trailer Spares, County Business Pk, Clarke Rd, Nottingham, **Nottinghamshire**, NG2 3JW, **ENGLAND**.
(T) 0115 9868420 **(F)** 0115 9861204.
Contact/s
Owner: Mr S Chappell
Profile Transport/Horse Boxes. No.Staff: 4
Yr. Est: 1979
Opening Times
Sp: Open 08:30. Closed 17:30.
Su: Open 08:30. Closed 18:00.
Au: Open 08:30. Closed 17:30.
Wn: Open 08:30. Closed 17:30. **Ref: YH10345**

NOVA ENGINEERING

Nova Engineering, Unit 1, Gale Saw Mills, Chagford, Newton Abbot, **Devon**, TQ13 8AP, **ENGLAND**.
(T) 01647 441189 **(F)** 01647 441189.
Contact/s
Partner: Mr N Chamberlain
Profile Transport/Horse Boxes. **Ref: YH10346**

NOVA TRAILERS

Nova Trailers, Southwood Piggery, Bridford, Exeter, **Devon**, EX6 7LQ, **ENGLAND**.
(T) 01647 253020 **(F)** 01647 253020.
Contact/s
Partner: Mr N Chamberlain
Profile Transport/Horse Boxes. **Ref: YH10347**

NRC

Naval Riding Centre, H M S Dryad, Southwick, Fareham, **Hampshire**, PO17 6EJ, **ENGLAND**.
(T) 023 92259748 **(F)** 023 92259748
Affiliated Bodies ABRS, BHS, BSJA.
Contact/s
Chief Instructor: Mr A Nodrdjyk **(Q)** BHSI
Profile Arena, Equestrian Centre, Riding Club, Riding School, Stable/Livery. No.Staff: 25
Yr. Est: 1982 C.Size: 20 Acres
Ref: YH10348

NSBA

North Staffordshire Bridleways Association, Smithy Hse, Highway Lane, Keele, **Staffordshire**, ST5 5AN, **ENGLAND**.
(T) 01782 627243.
Profile Club/Association. **Ref: YH10349**

NTF

National Trainers Federation, 9 High St, Lambourn, Hungerford, **Berkshire**, RG17 8XN, **ENGLAND**.
(T) 01488 71719 **(F)** 01488 73005
(E) ntf@martex.co.uk.
Contact/s
Assistant: Harriet Smulders
Profile Club/Association. **Ref: YH10350**

NU-CO FORGE & WELDING

Nu-Co Forge & Welding, The Bungalow, Bull Hill, Lymington, **Hampshire**, SO41 8BA, **ENGLAND**.
(T) 01590 674928.
Profile Blacksmith. **Ref: YH10351**

NUGENT TRAILERS

Nugent Trailers, 122 Aghnagar Rd, Galbally, Dungannon, **County Tyrone**, BT70 2PP, **NORTHERN IRELAND**.
(T) 028 87759400.
Contact/s
Owner: Mr J Nugent
Profile Transport/Horse Boxes. **Ref: YH10352**

NUNEATON & NORTH WARWICKSHIRE

Nuneaton & North Warwickshire Equestrian Centre, Valley Rd, Galley Common, Nuneaton, **Warwickshire**, CV10 9NJ, **ENGLAND**.
(T) 024 76392397.
Profile Equestrian Centre. **Ref: YH10353**

NUNN, ERIC J

Eric J Nunn DWCF, 68 Hamsterley Cres, Wrekenton, Gateshead, **Tyne and Wear**, NE9 7LB, **ENGLAND**.
(T) 0191 4915380.
Profile Farrier. **Ref: YH10354**

NUNN, JONATHAN

Jonathan Nunn DWCF, 11 Audmore Rd, Gnosall, **Staffordshire**, ST20 0HA, **ENGLAND**.
(T) 01785 824078.
Profile Farrier. **Ref: YH10355**

NUTE, G & P J

G & Mrs P J Nute, The Veterinary Surgery, Higher Trenant, Wadebridge, **Cornwall**, PL27 6HB, **ENGLAND**.
(T) 01208 813258 **(F)** 01208 815301.
Profile Medical Support. **Ref: YH10356**

NUTEC

NuTec Ltd, Eastern Ave, Lichfield, **Staffordshire**, WS13 7SE, **ENGLAND**.
(T) 01543 306306 **(F)** 01543 306307
(E) marionc@nutec.ltd.uk.
Profile Medical Support. **Ref: YH10357**

NUTLAND, J

Mrs J Nutland, Newmans Farm, Newmans Lane, West Moors, Wimborne, **Dorset**, BH22 0LD, **ENGLAND**.
(T) 01202 897469.
Profile Breeder. **Ref: YH10358**

NUTRI-MECH UK

Nutri-Mech UK Ltd, Lower Moss Farm, Malpas, **Cheshire**, SY14 7JJ, **ENGLAND**.
(T) 01948 860175 **(F)** 01948 860176
(M) 07802 396733.
Profile Supplies. **Ref: YH10359**

NUTSHELL

Nutshell (The), 9c Whitburn St, Bridgnorth, **Shropshire**, WV16 4QN, **ENGLAND**.
(T) 01746 768343.
Profile Saddlery Retailer. **Ref: YH10360**

NUTTALL, JOHN

John Nuttall, Foundry Yard,Treales, Treales, Preston, **Lancashire**, PR4 3SD, **ENGLAND**.
(T) 01772 673184.
Profile Transport/Horse Boxes. **Ref: YH10361**

NYTACK EQUESTRIAN

Nytack Equestrian, Underwood Business Pk, Wookey Hole Rd, Wells, **Somerset**, BA5 1AF, **ENGLAND**.
(T) 01749 676702 **(F)** 01749 676702.
Contact/s
Partner: Miss N Careless
Profile Supplies. **Ref: YH10362**

O A CURTIS & SONS

O A Curtis & Sons, Moulton Rd, Newmarket, **Suffolk**, CB8 8DU, **ENGLAND**.
(T) 01638 665761.
Profile Farrier. **Ref: YH10363**

O F A H SADDLERY

O F A H Saddlery, Greenleas Farm, London Rd, Billericay, **Essex**, CM12 9HP, **ENGLAND**.
(T) 01277 626584
(M) 07703 582128.
Contact/s
Partner: Mr F Collier-Brown
Profile Supplies. **Ref: YH10364**

O M C HORSEBOX REPAIRS

O M C Horsebox Repairs, Hartley Mauditt Rd, Oakhanger, Bordon, **Hampshire**, GU35 9JR, **ENGLAND**.
(T) 01420 488691 **(F)** 01420 479919.
Contact/s
Owner: Mr O Clutterbuck
Profile Transport/Horse Boxes. **Ref: YH10365**

O SHEPHERD & SON

O Shepherd & Son, Unit 8 Riding Court, Riding Rd, Buckingham Rd Ind Est, Brackley, **Northamptonshire**, NN13 7BH, **ENGLAND**.
(T) 01280 702224 **(F)** 01280 700223
Affiliated Bodies BETA.
Contact/s
Owner: Mr R Shepherd
Profile Saddlery Retailer.
Manufacturers of racing and eventing equipment.
Yr. Est: 1913
Opening Times
Sp: Open Mon - Fri 08:15. Closed Mon - Fri 17:30.
Su: Open Mon - Fri 08:15. Closed Mon - Fri 17:30.
Au: Open Mon - Fri 08:15. Closed Mon - Fri 17:30.
Wn: Open Mon - Fri 08:15. Closed Mon - Fri 17:30.
Ref: YH10366

O V WEBSTER & SON

O V Webster & Son, Scaddows Farm, Ticknall, **Derbyshire**, DE7 1JP, **ENGLAND**.
(T) 01332 864369.
Profile Breeder, Supplies. **Ref: YH10367**

O WARNER, KEITH

Keith O Warner, Meadow View Cottage, The Pavement, Brewood, **Staffordshire**, ST19 9BZ, **ENGLAND**.
(T) 01902 850814.
Contact/s
Owner: Mr K O Warner
Profile Supplies. **Ref: YH10368**

O Y C

O Y C Arabians, Mead End, Mead Rd, Corfe Castle, Wareham, **Dorset**, BH20 5EW, **ENGLAND**.
(T) 01929 480531 **(F)** 01929 480499.
Contact/s
For Bookings: Ms H Gilmore-Andrews
Profile Breeder, Feed Merchant, Supplies, Trainer.
Forage, Feedstuffs & Bedding Agents. No.Staff: 2
Yr. Est: 1983 C.Size: 62 Acres
Opening Times
Telephone for an appointment **Ref: YH10369**

OAK LODGE LIVERIES
Oak Lodge Liveries, Oak Lodge, Thompson Hill, High Green, Sheffield, **Yorkshire (South)**, S35 4JT, **ENGLAND**.
(T) 0114 2869091.
Profile Stable/Livery. **Ref: YH10370**

OAK TREE RIDING CTRE
Oak Tree Riding Centre, Common Lane, Marton, Winsford, **Cheshire**, CW7 2QF, **ENGLAND**.
(T) 01606 888543.
Contact/s
Chairman: Mr C Dewitt **Ref: YH10371**

OAKAGE RIDING CTRE
Oakage Riding Centre, The Tankerville, Hope, Minsterley, Shrewsbury, **Shropshire**, SY5 0JB, **ENGLAND**.
(T) 01743 791418.
Profile Riding School. **Ref: YH10372**

OAKDEN, JAMES
James Oakden, The Lodge, Wynlass Beck, Windermere, **Cumbria**, LA23 1EU, **ENGLAND**.
(T) 01539 446154 **(F)** 01539 448717
(M) 07778 928115.
Profile Trainer. **Ref: YH10373**

OAKDENE SADDLERY
Oakdene Saddlery, Oakdene, Pookbourne Lane, Sayers Common, Hassocks, **Sussex (West)**, BN6 9HD, **ENGLAND**.
(T) 01273 835130 **(F)** 01273 833924.
Profile Saddlery Retailer. **Ref: YH10374**

OAKEN LAWN RIDING SCHOOL
Oaken Lawn Riding School, Kingswood, Albrighton, Wolverhampton, **Midlands (West)**, WV7 3AL, **ENGLAND**.
(T) 01902 842551.
Contact/s
Owner: Mr M Budd
Profile Riding School. **Ref: YH10375**

OAKES, D G
D G Oakes DWCF, 45A Corner Hse, Watling St, Brewood, **Staffordshire**, ST19 9LL, **ENGLAND**.
(T) 01902 850387.
Profile Farrier. **Ref: YH10376**

OAKES, IRENE
Irene Oakes, Rosemore Lodge, Aughaloora, Castlewarden, Stroud, **County Kildare**, **IRELAND**.
(T) 045 861620.
Contact/s
Trainer: Ms I Oakes
(E) ireneoakes@kildarehorse.ie
Profile Trainer. **Ref: YH10377**

OAKFIELD ICELANDIC HORSES
Oakfield Icelandic Horses, Oakfield Farm, Horton Way, Verwood, **Dorset**, BH31 6JJ, **ENGLAND**.
(T) 01202 822882.
Profile Breeder. **Ref: YH10378**

OAKFIELD RIDING SCHOOL
Oakfield Riding School, Stanifield Lane, Farington, Preston, **Lancashire**, PR5 2UA, **ENGLAND**.
(T) 01772 421352.
Contact/s
Owner: Mrs S Prescot
Profile Riding School. **Ref: YH10379**

OAKFIELD RIDING SCHOOL
Oakfield Riding School, Great Coxwell, Faringdon, **Oxfordshire**, SN7 7LU, **ENGLAND**.
(T) 01367 240126.
Profile Riding School. **Ref: YH10380**

OAKFIELD SADDLERY
Oakfield Saddlery, Oakfield Riding Stables, Stanifield Lane, Farington, Preston, **Lancashire**, PR25 4UA, **ENGLAND**.
(T) 01772 622346 **(F)** 01772 421999.
Contact/s
Partner: Mr N Leadbeater **Ref: YH10381**

OAKFIELD VETNRY GROUP
Oakfield Veterinary Group, 713/715 Chester Rd, Bacons End, Castle Bromwich, Birmingham, **Midlands (West)**, B36 0LN, **ENGLAND**.
(T) 0121 7704966.
Profile Medical Support. **Ref: YH10382**

OAKHANGER RIDING CTRE
Oakhanger Riding Centre, Holmshaw Lane, Oakhanger, Crewe, **Cheshire**, CW1 5XE, **ENGLAND**.
(T) 01270 876311. **Ref: YH10383**

OAKHILL RIDING SCHOOL
Oakhill Riding School, Daisy Nook Farm, Daisy Nook, Failsworth, Manchester, **Manchester (Greater)**, M35 9WJ, **ENGLAND**.
(T) 0161 3307273.
Contact/s
Owner: Mrs A Parker
Profile Riding School, Stable/Livery.
Livery prices range from £48.00 for hay and £58.00 for a box per month. Yr. Est: 1965
Opening Times
Sp: Open 09:00. Closed 20:00.
Su: Open 09:00. Closed 20:00.
Au: Open 09:00. Closed 20:00.
Wn: Open 09:00. Closed 20:00. **Ref: YH10384**

OAKHILL VETNRY GRP
Oakhill Veterinary Group, Sycamore Cottage, 1 Church St, Ambleside, **Cumbria**, LA22 0BU, **ENGLAND**.
(T) 01539 432631 **(F)** 01539 432631.
Profile Medical Support. **Ref: YH10385**

OAKINGTON RIDING SCHOOL
Oakington Riding School, High St, Oakington, **Cambridgeshire**, CB45 5AG, **ENGLAND**.
(T) 01223 233929.
Profile Riding School. **Ref: YH10386**

OAKLAND CARRIAGES
Oakland Carriages, Little Laches Farm, Laches Lane, Coven, Wolverhampton, **Midlands (West)**, WV10 7PA, **ENGLAND**.
(T) 01902 790107. **Ref: YH10387**

OAKLAND HORSEBOXES
Oakland Horseboxes, Unit 3, KDO Business Pk, Little Witley, **Worcestershire**, WR6 6LR, **ENGLAND**.
(T) 01299 896754 **(F)** 01299 896885.
Profile Transport/Horse Boxes. **Ref: YH10388**

OAKLANDS CLGE
Oaklands College, Hatfield Rd, St Albans, **Hertfordshire**, AL4 0JA, **ENGLAND**.
(T) 01727 850651 **(F)** 01727 847987.
Profile Stable/Livery. **Ref: YH10389**

OAKLANDS LIVERY STABLES
Oaklands Livery Stables, Rayleigh Downs Rd, Rayleigh, **Essex**, SS6 7LP, **ENGLAND**.
(T) 01702 510224.
Contact/s
Owner: Ms C Hobbs
Profile Stable/Livery. **Ref: YH10390**

OAKLANDS RIDING SCHOOL
Oaklands Riding School, The Rosary, Balls Farm Rd, Exeter, **Devon**, EX2 9JA, **ENGLAND**.
(T) 01392 272105.
Contact/s
Owner: Mrs J Newbury
Profile Riding School. **Ref: YH10391**

OAKLANDS RIDING SCHOOL
Oaklands Riding School, Shipston Rd, Upper Tysoe, Warwick, **Warwickshire**, CV35 0TR, **ENGLAND**.
(T) 01295 688045.
Contact/s
Owner: Mrs J Tye
Profile Riding School. **Ref: YH10392**

OAKLANDS VETNRY CTRE
Oaklands Veterinary Centre (The), High Leven, Yarm, **Tyne and Wear**, TS15 9JT, **ENGLAND**.
(T) 01642 760313 **(F)** 01642 762370.
Profile Medical Support. **Ref: YH10393**

OAKLAWN STUD
Oaklawn Stud, Friarstown, Kildare, **County Kildare**, **IRELAND**.
(T) 045 521508 **(F)** 045 522365
(E) oaklawn@indigo.ie.
Contact/s
Key Contact: Ms C McStay
Profile Breeder. C.Size: 40 Acres **Ref: YH10394**

OAKLEA LIVERY STABLES
Oaklea Livery Stables, Oaklea Rd, Roanhead, Barrow-In-Furness, **Cumbria**, LA14 4QW, **ENGLAND**.
(T) 01229 830342.
Profile Stable/Livery. **Ref: YH10395**

OAKLEIGH FARM
Oakleigh Farm, 83 Codicote Rd, Welwyn, **Hertfordshire**, AL6 9TT, **ENGLAND**.
(T) 01438 821065.
Contact/s
Owner: Mr M Telehone
Profile Stud Farm. **Ref: YH10396**

OAKLEIGH STUD FARM
Oakleigh Stud Farm, Oakleigh Hse, Hall Lane, Longton, Preston, **Lancashire**, PR4 5ZD, **ENGLAND**.
(T) 01772 611594.
Profile Blood Stock Agency, Breeder. **Ref: YH10397**

OAKLEY COACHBUILDERS
Oakley Coachbuilders, High Cross, Ware, **Hertfordshire**, SG11 1AD, **ENGLAND**.
(T) 01920 466781 **(F)** 01920 467895.
Contact/s
Owner: Mr B Oakley
Profile Transport/Horse Boxes. **Ref: YH10398**

OAKLEY, N W
N W Oakley, Rede Hall Farm Pk, Rede, Bury St Edmunds, **Suffolk**, IP29 4UG, **ENGLAND**.
(T) 01284 850695 **(F)** 01284 850345.
Profile Breeder. **Ref: YH10399**

OAKLEY'S HORSE & ANIMAL FEED
Oakley's Horse & Animal Feed, Oakley Rd, Bencewell Granaries, Bromley Common, **Kent**, BR2 8HG, **ENGLAND**.
(T) 020 84621140 **(F)** 020 84620152
(E) carterinc@compuserve.com.
Profile Supplies. **Ref: YH10400**

OAKLODGE STUD
Oaklodge Stud, Naas, **County Kildare**, **IRELAND**.
(T) 045 897316/879620 **(F)** 045 879253
(E) oaklodgestud@eircom.net.
Contact/s
Manager: Mr A Sharry
Profile Blood Stock Agency, Breeder, Stud Farm.
C.Size: 400 Acres **Ref: YH10401**

OAKS PK RIDING SCHOOL
Oaks Park Riding School, Carshalton Rd, Woodmansterne, Banstead, **Surrey**, SM7 3HZ, **ENGLAND**.
(T) 01737 353278.
Contact/s
Partner: Mr G Poynter **(Q)** BHSAI
Profile Riding School.
Specialise in nervous riders. Yr. Est: 1972
C.Size: 3 Acres
Opening Times
Weekends 09:00 - 14:00: Contact for opening times during the week. **Ref: YH10402**

OAKS RIDING SCHOOL
Oaks Riding School, 59 Wythenshawe Rd, Sale, **Cheshire**, M33 2JR, **ENGLAND**.
(T) 0161 9734583.
Contact/s
Owner: Mrs R Meehan
Profile Riding School. **Ref: YH10403**

OAKSEY, (LORD)
Lord Oaksey, Hill Farm, Oaksey, Malmesbury, **Wiltshire**, **ENGLAND**.
(T) 01666 577303 **(F)** 01666 577962. **Ref: YH10404**

OAKSFORD & BIRCH
Oaksford & Birch, The Exchange, High St, Yetminster, Sherborne, **Dorset**, DT9 6LF, **ENGLAND**.
(T) 01935 873432.
Profile Medical Support. **Ref: YH10405**

OAKTREE FARM
Oaktree Farm, Buckholt Lane, Bexhill-on-Sea, **Sussex (East)**, TN39 5AX, **ENGLAND**.
(T) 01424 219485.
Contact/s
Owner: Mrs M Plimmer
Profile Breeder. **Ref: YH10406**

OAKTREE STABLES
Oaktree Stables, Moorgreen Farm, Burnetts Lane, West End, Southampton, **Hampshire**, SO30 2HH, **ENGLAND**.
(T) 023 80470407.
Contact/s
Manager: Miss J Shotten **Ref: YH10407**

OAKWOOD EQUESTRIAN
Oakwood Equestrian, The Paddocks, Padbury, Buckingham, **Buckinghamshire**, MK18 2AU, **ENGLAND**.
(T) 01280 824174 **(F)** 01280 821875.
Contact/s
Owner: Mrs K Ettery
Profile Supplies. **Ref: YH10408**

OAKWOOD FARM STUD/RIDING CTRE

Oakwood Farm Stud & Riding Centre, Ideford, Chudleigh, Newton Abbot, **Devon**, TQ13 0BQ, **ENGLAND**.
(T) 01626 853226. **Ref:YH10409**

OAKWOOD RIDING SERVICES

Oakwood Riding Services, Chapel Gate, Whaplode Drove, Spalding, **Lincolnshire**, PE12 0TR, **ENGLAND**.
(T) 01406 330602.
Profile Stable/Livery, Trainer. **Ref:YH10410**

OAKWOOD VETNRY GRP

Oakwood Veterinary Group, Oakwood Hse, Fuller Rd, Harleston, **Suffolk**, IP20 9EA, **ENGLAND**.
(T) 01379 852146 **(F)** 01379 854293.
Contact/s
Vet: Mr I Dennis
Profile Medical Support. **Ref:YH10411**

OASIS PARK EQUESTRIAN CTRE

Oasis Park Equestrian Centre, Martletwy, Narberth, **Pembrokeshire**, SA67 8AD, **WALES**.
(T) 01834 891300
(W) www.oasisp.f9.co.uk.
Contact/s
General Manager: Mr J Brass
(E) john@oasisp.f9.co.uk.
Profile Arena, Equestrian Centre, Riding School, Trainer.
One hour group lessons and hacks from £8.00. A whole day's fun with horses from £11.00. Tea rooms and gift shop on site. No.Staff: 7 Yr. Est: 1992
C.Size: 23 Acres
Opening Times
Sp: Open Mon - Sun 10:00. Closed Mon - Sun 18:00.
Su: Open Mon - Sun 10:00. Closed Mon - Sun 18:00.
Au: Open Mon - Sun 10:00. Closed Mon - Sun 18:00.
Wn: Open Mon - Sun 10:00. Closed Mon - Sun 18:00.
Evenings by appointment **Ref:YH10412**

OASIS RIDING CTRE

Oasis Riding Centre, Beech Cottage, Pylands Lane, Bursledon, Southampton, **Hampshire**, SO31 1BH, **ENGLAND**.
(T) 023 80403480.
Contact/s
Owner: Mrs S Tiley
Profile Riding School. **Ref:YH10413**

OASIS TRAILER CTRE

Oasis Trailer Centre, Exeter Rd, Braunton, **Devon**, EX33 2BH, **ENGLAND**.
(T) 01271 816866.
Profile Transport/Horse Boxes. **Ref:YH10414**

OATHILL FARM RIDING CTRE

Oathill Farm Riding Centre, Pound Lane, Molash, Canterbury, **Kent**, CT4 8HQ, **ENGLAND**.
(T) 01233 740573.
Profile Riding School, Stable/Livery. **Ref:YH10415**

OATHILL FARM SUPPLIES

Oathill Farm Supplies, Cropredy, Banbury, **Oxfordshire**, OX17 1QA, **ENGLAND**.
(T) 01295 750301.
Profile Supplies. **Ref:YH10416**

OATRIDGE

Oatridge Agricultural College, Ecclesmachen, Broxburn, **Lothian (West)**, EH52 6NH, **SCOTLAND**.
(T) 01506 854387 **(F)** 01506 853373
(E) info@oatridge.ac.uk
(W) www.oatridge.ac.uk.
Contact/s
Enquiries: Cathi Wotherspoon
Profile Equestrian Centre. College.
The college offers full time courses in National Certificate/ Diploma in Horse Management, also part time and short courses in BHS qualifications.
Yr. Est: 1975
Opening Times
Sp: Open Mon -Fri 09:00. Closed Mon - Fri 17:00.
Su: Open Mon -Fri 09:00. Closed Mon - Fri 17:00.
Au: Open Mon -Fri 09:00. Closed Mon - Fri 17:00.
Wn: Open Mon -Fri 09:00. Closed Mon - Fri 17:00.
Ref:YH10417

OBERON SADDLERY

Oberon Saddlery, 68 West Church St, Buckie, **Moray**, AB56 1HP, **SCOTLAND**.
(T) 01542 835254.
Contact/s
Owner: Mrs M Haire
Profile Saddlery Retailer. **Ref:YH10418**

O'BRIEN, CHARLES

Charles O'Brien, Ridge Manor Stables Rathfield, Curragh, **County Kildare**, **IRELAND**.
(T) 045 522607.
Profile Supplies. **Ref:YH10419**

O'BRIEN, H H

Mr H H O'Brien, Lynholm Cottage, Laundry Lane, Off Cumbernauld Rd, Stepps, **Lanarkshire (North)**, T33 6LT, **SCOTLAND**.
(T) 0141 7792694.
Profile Trainer. **Ref:YH10420**

O'BRIEN, JIMMY

Jimmy O'Brien Dip WCF, High Rd, Ballyduff, **County Waterford**, **IRELAND**.
(T) 058 60386.
Profile Supplies. **Ref:YH10421**

O'BRIEN, MICHAEL

Michael O'Brien, Beechcourt Hse, Newlands, Naas, **County Kildare**, **IRELAND**.
(T) 045 879008.
Profile Supplies. **Ref:YH10422**

O'BRIEN, VAL

Val O'Brien, Mount Prague Grange, Athenry, **County Galway**, **IRELAND**.
(T) 091 797119.
Profile Supplies. **Ref:YH10423**

O'BRIEN'S

O'Brien's Saddlery & Country Clothing, 10 South Main St, Bandon, **County Cork**, **IRELAND**.
(T) 023 43237
(E) obriensaddlery@eircom.net.
Profile Supplies. **Ref:YH10424**

O'CALLAGHAN, JAS

Jas O'Callaghan, Main St, Mohill, **County Leitrim**, **IRELAND**.
(T) 078 31028.
Profile Supplies. **Ref:YH10425**

OCKENDON-DAY, R F

Miss R F Ockendon-Day, Prince Halfyards, Stebbing Rd, Felsted, Dunmow, **Essex**, CM6 3LG, **ENGLAND**.
(T) 01371 820392 **(F)** 01371 821280.
Profile Breeder. **Ref:YH10426**

OCKNELL HSE EQUESTRIAN CTRE

Ocknell House Equestrian Centre, Ocknell Hse, Stoney Cross, Lyndhurst, **Hampshire**, SO43 7GN, **ENGLAND**.
(T) 023 80814083.
Profile Riding School. **Ref:YH10427**

O'CONNELL, JAMES

James O'Connell, 46 William St, Limerick, **County Limerick**, **IRELAND**.
(T) 061 410225.
Profile Supplies. **Ref:YH10428**

O'CONNELL, PATRICK

Patrick O'Connell, Main St, Bansha, **County Tipperary**, **IRELAND**.
(T) 062 54114.
Profile Farrier. **Ref:YH10429**

O'CONNELL, PATRICK

Patrick O'Connell, Main St, Bansha, **County Tipperary**, **IRELAND**.
(T) 062 54114.
Profile Farrier. **Ref:YH10430**

ODELL, S M

Mrs S M Odell, Little Brook Hse, Little Tew, Chipping Norton, **Oxfordshire**, OX7 4JJ, **ENGLAND**.
(T) 01608 683249 **(F)** 01608 683249.
Profile Supplies. **Ref:YH10431**

O'DONNELL, E O

Mrs E O O'Donnell, 42 Foliat Drive, Wantage, **Oxfordshire**, OX12 7AL, **ENGLAND**.
(T) 01235 760460 **(F)** 01235 760460.
Profile Medical Support. **Ref:YH10432**

O'DONOVAN, RICHARD

Richard O'Donovan, Beech Lawn Stables, Kildare, **County Kildare**, **IRELAND**.
(T) 045 521743.
Profile Supplies. **Ref:YH10433**

ODYSSEY

Odyssey, Knott Hall Farm, Lowgill, Kendal, **Cumbria**, LA8 9DG, **ENGLAND**.
(T) 01539 824086.
Profile Breeder. **Ref:YH10434**

OFFEN, MALCOLM J

Malcolm J Offen DWCF, Heather Cottage, The Street, Culford, Bury St Edmunds, **Suffolk**, IP28 6DP, **ENGLAND**.
(T) 01284 728082.
Profile Farrier. **Ref:YH10435**

OFFLEY BROOK LIVERY STABLES

Offley Brook Livery Stables, Heath Hse, Offley Brook, Eccleshall, **Staffordshire**, ST21 6HA, **ENGLAND**.
(T) 01785 280318.
Profile Stable/Livery, Track/Course, Trainer.
Ref:YH10436

OGLE, M B

Mr M B Ogle, Skerraton, Buckfastleigh, **Devon**, TQ11 0NS, **ENGLAND**.
(T) 01364 642232 **(F)** 01364 644282.
Profile Supplies. **Ref:YH10437**

O'GORMAN, SLATER & MAIN

O'Gorman, Slater & Main (Newbury), Donnington Grove Veterinary Surgery, Oxford Rd, Newbury, **Berkshire**, RG14 2JB, **ENGLAND**.
(T) 01635 37800 **(F)** 01635 37400
(E) ogsm@donningtongrove.u-net.com.
Profile Medical Support. **Ref:YH10438**

O'GORMAN, SLATER & MAIN

O'Gorman, Slater & Main, 10 London Rd, Thatcham, **Berkshire**, RG13 1JX, **ENGLAND**.
(T) 01635 868382.
Profile Medical Support. **Ref:YH10439**

O'GORMAN, W

W O'Gorman, Seven Springs, Hamilton Rd, Newmarket, **Suffolk**, CB8 7JQ, **ENGLAND**.
(T) 01638 663330 **(F)** 01638 713900
(W) www.newmarketracehorsetrainers.co.uk
Affiliated Bodies Newmarket Trainers Fed.
Contact/s
Trainer: Mr W O'Gorman
Profile Trainer. **Ref:YH10440**

O'GRADY, EDWARD J

Edward J O'Grady, Killeens, Ballynonty, Thurles, **County Tipperary**, **IRELAND**.
(T) 052 56156.
Profile Trainer. Yr. Est: 1971
Opening Times
Telephone for further information **Ref:YH10441**

O'HARA, JOHNNIE

Johnnie O'Hara, 4 Grinsdale Ave, Carlisle, **Cumbria**, CA2 7LX, **ENGLAND**.
(T) 01228 530875.
Contact/s
Owner: Mr J O'Hara
Profile Supplies. **Ref:YH10442**

O'HARE, BROMLEY

Bromley O'Hare, Pembridge, Leominster, **Herefordshire**, HR6 9JE, **ENGLAND**.
(T) 01544 388645.
Profile Blacksmith. **Ref:YH10443**

O'HARES

O'Hares Ltd, 26-32 Dublin Rd, Burrenbridge, Castlewellan, **County Down**, BT31 9AQ, **NORTHERN IRELAND**.
(T) 028 43778288.
Profile Supplies. **Ref:YH10444**

OKEDEN STUD

Okeden Stud, Appledene, North Ferriby, **Yorkshire (East)**, HU14 3AN, **ENGLAND**.
(T) 01482 632184 **(F)** 01482 632184
(E) juno@appledene.karoo.co.uk.
Profile Breeder. **Ref:YH10445**

OKEFORD VETNRY CTRE

Okeford Veterinary Centre, The Veterinary Clnc, School Way, **Devon**, EX20 1EU, **ENGLAND**.
(T) 01837 52148 **(F)** 01837 53992.
Profile Medical Support. **Ref:YH10446**

OKELEAT STUD

Okeleat Stud, Niases, Jacobstowe, Okehampton, **Devon**, EX20 3RJ, **ENGLAND**.
(T) 01837 851308.
Profile Breeder. **Ref:YH10447**

OLD BARN SADDLERY

Old Barn Saddlery, 110 Ware Rd, Hoddesdon,

Hertfordshire, EN11 9ET, **ENGLAND**.
(T) 01992 448303.
Profile Saddlery Retailer. **Ref: YH10448**

OLD BARN STABLES

Old Barn Stables, Waffrons Farm, Woodstock Lane South, Chessington, **Surrey**, KT9 1UF, **ENGLAND**.
(T) 020 83980822 **(F)** 020 83987553.
Contact/s
Owner: Mrs J Best **Ref: YH10449**

OLD BASING SADDLERY

Old Basing Saddlery, 69 The Street, Old Basing, Basingstoke, **Hampshire**, RG24 7BW, **ENGLAND**.
(T) 01256 323510 **(F)** 01256 323510.
Contact/s
Partner: Mr M Douglas
Profile Saddlery Retailer. **Ref: YH10450**

OLD BEXLEY EQUESTRIAN

Old Bexley Equestrian Training Centre, Stable Lane, Vicarage Rd, Bexley, **Kent**, DA5 2AW, **ENGLAND**.
(T) 01322 553508 **(F)** 01322 553508
(E) oldbex@cs.com
(W) www.oldbexley.co.uk
Affiliated Bodies BHSETC, C & G.
Contact/s
Owner: Ms W Bradfield
Profile Equestrian Centre, Riding Club, Riding School, Stable/Livery. Training Centre.
NVQ Examination Centre also offers GCSE PE Horse Riding as an option. No.Staff: 3 Yr. Est: 1980
C.Size: 30 Acres
Opening Times
Open seven days a week. Tuition is available Tuesday, Thursday & Saturday between 09:30 - 14:30.
Ref: YH10451

OLD BREWERY WORKSHOP

Old Brewery Workshop, Fitzalan Rd, Arundel, **Sussex (West)**, BN18 9JP, **ENGLAND**.
(T) 01903 884204 **(F)** 01903 884205.
Contact/s
Owner: Mr T Dove
Profile Blacksmith. **Ref: YH10452**

OLD BUCKENHAM STUD

Old Buckenham Stud Ltd, Old Buckenham, Attleborough, **Norfolk**, NR17 1RS, **ENGLAND**.
(T) 01953 860612 **(F)** 01953 860945.
Contact/s
Manager: Mr D Miles
Profile Breeder. **Ref: YH10453**

OLD DAIRY SADDLERY LTD

Old Dairy Saddlery Limited, Greenway Farm, Tockenham, Swindon, **Wiltshire**, SN4 7PP, **ENGLAND**.
(T) 01793 849284 **(F)** 01793 849284.
Profile Saddlery Retailer. **Ref: YH10454**

OLD FARM

Old Farm, Bridgend, Ockham, Ripley, **Surrey**, GU23 6NU, **ENGLAND**.
(T) 01483 225257 **(F)** 01483 225995.
Profile Stable/Livery. **Ref: YH10455**

OLD FARM STABLES

Old Farm Stables, Oak Ave, Hampton, **London (Greater)**, TW12 3QD, **ENGLAND**.
(T) 020 89799470.
Contact/s
Manager: Mrs L Johns
Profile Stable/Livery. **Ref: YH10456**

OLD FORGE

Old Forge (St Albans) (The), Lye Lane, Bricket Wood, St Albans, **Hertfordshire**, AL2 3TJ, **ENGLAND**.
(T) 01923 678411.
Profile Stable/Livery. **Ref: YH10457**

OLD FORGE

Old Forge (Reigate) (The), High Rd, Upper Gratton, Reigate, **Surrey**, RH2 0TY, **ENGLAND**.
(T) 01737 42341.
Profile Stable/Livery. **Ref: YH10458**

OLD GOLFHOUSE VETNRY GRP

Old Golfhouse Veterinary Group (Thetford) (The), The Old Golfhouse, Brandon Rd, Thetford, **Norfolk**, IP24 3ND, **ENGLAND**.
(T) 01842 764244 **(F)** 01842 763717.
Profile Medical Support. **Ref: YH10459**

OLD HALL MILL RIDING SCHOOL

Old Hall Mill Riding School, Old Hall Mill Lane, Atherton, **Lancashire**, N46 0RG, **ENGLAND**.
(T) 01942 677052.
Profile Riding School. **Ref: YH10460**

OLD MANOR HSE

Old Manor House, North Hinksey Lane, Oxford, **Oxfordshire**, OX2 0LX, **ENGLAND**.
(T) 01865 242274.
Contact/s
Owner: Miss P Halliday
Profile Arena, Riding School, Stable/Livery.
Ref: YH10461

OLD MANOR MILL

Old Manor Mill, Mill St, Newtownards, **County Down**, BT23 4LN, **NORTHERN IRELAND**.
(T) 028 91813186.
Profile Supplies. **Ref: YH10462**

OLD MANOR STABLES

Old Manor Stables, Letcombe Bassett, Wantage, **Oxfordshire**, OX12 9LP, **ENGLAND**.
(T) 01235 760780 **(F)** 01235 760754
(E) mark.bradstock@btinternet.com.
Profile Trainer. **Ref: YH10463**

OLD MEADOW STUD

Old Meadow Stud, Donadea, Naas, **County Kildare**, **IRELAND**.
(T) 045 869125 **(F)** 045 869383
(E) oldmeadowstud@kildarehorse.ie.
Contact/s
Key Contact: Mr D Weld
Profile Breeder. **Ref: YH10464**

OLD MILL

Old Mill Saddlery, 110 Larne Rd, Ballycarry, Carrickfergus, **County Antrim**, BT38 9JN, **NORTHERN IRELAND**.
(T) 028 93353268 **(F)** 028 93353111
(E) sales@oldmillsaddlery.co.uk
Affiliated Bodies SMS.
Contact/s
Sales: Ms B McElnea
Profile Riding Wear Retailer, Saddlery Retailer.
Yr. Est: 1985
Opening Times
Sp: Open Mon - Sat 09:00. Closed Mon, Tues, Thurs, Sat 17:30, Wed, Fri, 20:30.
Su: Open Mon - Sat 09:00. Closed Mon, Tues, Thurs, Sat 17:30, Wed, Fri, 20:30:.
Au: Open Mon - Sat 09:00. Closed Mon, Tues, Thurs, Sat 17:30, Wed, Fri, 20:30:.
Wn: Open Mon - Sat 09:00. Closed Mon, Tues, Thurs, Sat 17:30, Wed, Fri, 20:30:. **Ref: YH10465**

OLD MILL ANIMAL FEEDS

Old Mill Animal Feeds, Units 8 & 9, Block 6, Old Mill Pk, Mansfield Woodhouse, **Nottinghamshire**, NG19 9BG, **ENGLAND**.
(T) 01623 420316.
Profile Supplies. **Ref: YH10466**

OLD MILL EQUESTRIAN CTRE

Old Mill Equestrian Centre, Clement St, Swanley, **Kent**, BR8 7PQ, **ENGLAND**.
(T) 01322 666699.
Contact/s
Owner: Mr M Washer
Profile Saddlery Retailer. **Ref: YH10467**

OLD MILL SADDLERY

Old Mill Saddlery, 57 Lower Forster St, Walsall, **Midlands (West)**, WS1 1XB, **ENGLAND**.
(T) 01922 646646 **(F)** 01922 723146.
Contact/s
Owner: Mr L Hewitt **Ref: YH10468**

OLD MILL STABLES

Old Mill Stables, Lelant Downs, Hayle, **Cornwall**, TR27 6LN, **ENGLAND**.
(T) 01736 753045.
Contact/s
Partner: Miss M Scotting
Profile Riding School. **Ref: YH10469**

OLD MILL STUD

Old Mill Stud, Chippenham, Ely, **Cambridgeshire**, CB7 5PR, **ENGLAND**.
(T) 01638 720946 **(F)** 01638 721384.
Contact/s
Partner: Mr D Shekells
Profile Breeder. **Ref: YH10470**

OLD MILL WHIPS

Old Mill Whips, Unit 9 C.E.A, 9 Meadowbank Rd, Carrickfergus, **County Antrim**, BT38 8YF, **NORTHERN IRELAND**.
(T) 028 93368599 **(F)** 028 93353111
(E) info@ridingwhips.com
(W) www.ridingwhips.com.
Contact/s
Manager: Mrs J Bright
Profile Supplies. Riding Whip Manufacturer and Wholesaler. Yr. Est: 1997
Opening Times
Sp: Open Mon - Fri 07:30. Closed Mon - Thurs 16:30, Fri 14:30.
Su: Open Mon - Fri 07:30. Closed Mon - Thurs 16:30, Fri 14:30.
Au: Open Mon - Fri 07:30. Closed Mon - Thurs 16:30, Fri 14:30.
Wn: Open Mon - Fri 07:30. Closed Mon - Thurs 16:30, Fri 14:30. **Ref: YH10471**

OLD PK STABLES

Old Park Stables, Old Pk Lane, Farnham, **Surrey**, GU9 0AN, **ENGLAND**.
(T) 01252 715492.
Contact/s
Owner: Mr J Rickets
Profile Riding School, Stable/Livery. **Ref: YH10472**

OLD PORTWAY FARM

Old Portway Farm, Old Portway Farm, Portway Hill, Rowley Regis, **Midlands (West)**, B65 9DJ, **ENGLAND**.
(T) 01384 232115. **Ref: YH10473**

OLD RECTORY

Old Rectory (The), Belton In Rutland, Oakham, **Rutland**, LE15 9LE, **ENGLAND**.
(T) 01572 717279 **(F)** 01572 717343
(E) bb@stablemate.demon.co.uk
(W) www.rutnet.co.uk/orb.
Contact/s
Owner: Mr R Peach
Profile Horse/Rider Accom.
Stable relief service No.Staff: 1 Yr. Est: 1986
Opening Times
Sp: Open Mon - Sun 09:00. Closed Mon - Sun 21:00.
Su: Open Mon - Sun 09:00. Closed Mon - Sun 21:00.
Au: Open Mon - Sun 09:00. Closed Mon - Sun 21:00.
Wn: Open Mon - Sun 09:00. Closed Mon - Sun 21:00. **Ref: YH10474**

OLD RUNNEL FARM

Old Runnel Farm, East Bank Ave, Marton Moss, Blackpool, **Lancashire**, FY4 5BF, **ENGLAND**.
(T) 01253 695670.
Profile Saddlery Retailer. **Ref: YH10475**

OLD STABLES

Old Stables, Ousby, Penrith, **Cumbria**, CA10 1QA, **ENGLAND**.
Profile Supplies. **Ref: YH10476**

OLD STABLES

Old Stables (The), Godden Green, Godden Green, Sevenoaks, **Kent**, TN15 0JJ, **ENGLAND**.
(T) 01732 762618.
Contact/s
Owner: Beryl Fellows
Profile Stable/Livery. **Ref: YH10477**

OLD SUFFOLK STUD

Old Suffolk Stud, Bears Farm, Valley Wash, Hundon, Sudbury, **Suffolk**, CO10 8EJ, **ENGLAND**.
(T) 01440 786604 **(F)** 01440 786969.
Contact/s
Owner: Mr H Ormesher
Profile Breeder. **Ref: YH10478**

OLD TIGER STABLES

Old Tiger Stables, 22A Northfield Rd, Soham, Ely, **Cambridgeshire**, CB7 5UF, **ENGLAND**.
(T) 01353 720125
Affiliated Bodies ABRS.
Contact/s
General Manager: Ms K Griggs
Profile Breeder, Riding School, Stable/Livery.
No.Staff: 6 Yr. Est: 1987 C.Size: 16 Acres
Opening Times
Sp: Open Tues - Sun 09:00. Closed Tues - Sun 20:00.
Su: Open Tues - Sun 09:00. Closed Tues - Sun 20:00.
Au: Open Tues - Sun 09:00. Closed Tues - Sun 20:00.
Wn: Open Tues - Sun 09:00. Closed Tues - Sun 20:00.
Closed on Mondays **Ref: YH10479**

OLD TWELVE STABLES

Old Twelve Stables (The), Moulton Paddocks, Newmarket, **Suffolk**, CB8 8QJ, **ENGLAND**.

(T) 01638 660048
(M) 07711 108612.
Profile Trainer. Ref:YH10480

OLD WOOD STABLES

Old Wood Stables, Old Wood, Skellingthorpe, Lincoln, **Lincolnshire**, LN6 5UA, **ENGLAND**.
(T) 01522 693644.
Contact/s
Owner: Mr R Barnett Ref:YH10481

OLDBURY COMPONENTS

Oldbury Components Ltd, Bull Lane, Wednesbury, **Midlands (West)**, WS10 8RW, **ENGLAND**.
(T) 0121 5021411 (F) 0121 5567025.
Contact/s
Manager: Mr J Pearson
Profile Transport/Horse Boxes. Ref:YH10482

OLDBURY RIDING SCHOOL

Oldbury Riding School, Pill Hse, Church Rd, Oldbury-on-Severn, Bristol, **Bristol**, BS35 1QA, **ENGLAND**.
(T) 01454 411545. Ref:YH10483

OLDENCRAIG EQUESTRIAN CTRE

Oldencraig Equestrian Centre, Tandridge Lane, Lingfield, **Surrey**, RH7 6LL, **ENGLAND**.
(T) 01342 833317
(E) info@oldencraig.com
(W) www.oldencraig.com.
Profile Breeder, Stable/Livery. Ref:YH10484

OLDERNEY STUD

Olderney Stud (The), Quarry Farm, Empshott Green, Empshott, Liss, **Hampshire**, GU33 6HU, **ENGLAND**.
(T) 01730 827564 (F) 01730 827564.
Contact/s
Owner: Mr E Grenville-Hill
Profile Breeder. Ref:YH10485

OLDFIELD, D T

Mr D T Oldfield, The Coachouse, Bryn Hyfryd Park, **Conwy**, LL32 8PF, **WALES**.
(T) 01492 592350.
Profile Breeder. Ref:YH10486

OLDFIELD, JOHN

John Oldfield, 42 Morton St, Leamington Spa, **Warwickshire**, CV32 5SY, **ENGLAND**.
(T) 01926 425263 (F) 01926 426382.
Contact/s
Owner: Mr S Harrold
Profile Transport/Horse Boxes. Ref:YH10487

OLDFOLD STABLES

Oldfold Stables, Milltimber, **Aberdeenshire**, AB13 0HQ, **SCOTLAND**.
(T) 01224 867226 (F) 01224 867226.
Contact/s
Owner: Mr G Scott Ref:YH10488

OLDGATE SADDLERS

Oldgate Saddlers, 35A Oldgate, Morpeth, **Northumberland**, NE61 1QF, **ENGLAND**.
(T) 01670 513231 (F) 01670 513231.
Contact/s
Owner: Mr B Richardson Ref:YH10489

OLDHAM & DISTRICT RIDING CLUB

Oldham & District Riding Club, 218 Long Lane, Chadderton, Oldham, **Lancashire**, OL9 8AY, **ENGLAND**.
(T) 0161 6810734.
Contact/s
Chairman: Ms V Leech
Profile Club/Association, Riding Club. Ref:YH10490

OLDHAMS WOOD LIVERY

Oldhams Wood Livery, Finlow Hill Lane, Over Alderley, Macclesfield, **Cheshire**, SK10 4UG, **ENGLAND**.
(T) 01625 585888.
Contact/s
Manageress: Ms K Mottram
Profile Stable/Livery. Ref:YH10491

OLDKNOW, P L

P L Oldknow, 121 Alfreton Rd, Little Eaton, Derby, **Derbyshire**, DE21 5DF, **ENGLAND**.
(T) 01332 833449.
Profile Farrier. Ref:YH10492

OLDMAN, PETER D

Peter D Oldman DWCF, Bungalow Farm, Woodborough, Pewsey, **Wiltshire**, SN9 5PL, **ENGLAND**.
(T) 01672 851275
(M) 07774 160661.
Profile Farrier. Ref:YH10493

OLDMELDRUM LIVERY YARD

Oldmeldrum Livery Yard, Ardmedden Farm, Oldmeldrum, Inverurie, **Aberdeenshire**, AB51 0AG, **SCOTLAND**.
(T) 01651 872261. Ref:YH10494

OLDWICK SADDLERY

Oldwick Saddlery, Oldwick Farm, West Stoke Rd, West Lavant, Chichester, **Sussex (West)**, PO18 9AA, **ENGLAND**.
(T) 01243 527415 (F) 01243 771438.
Profile Saddlery Retailer. Ref:YH10495

OLIVE, DAVID W

David W Olive DWCF, The Post Hse, Wilmington, Honiton, **Devon**, EX14 9JQ, **ENGLAND**.
(T) 01404 831201.
Profile Farrier. Ref:YH10496

OLIVER, IAN R J

Ian R J Oliver DWCF, Hill Farm, Cradley, Malvern, **Worcestershire**, WR13 5JT, **ENGLAND**.
(T) 01531 86339.
Profile Farrier. Ref:YH10497

OLIVER, MARK S

Mark S Oliver DWCF, 72A Ensbury Park Rd, Ensbury Pk, Bournemouth, **Dorset**, BH9 2SL, **ENGLAND**.
(T) 07768 657469.
Profile Farrier. Ref:YH10498

OLIVER, R N

R N Oliver, Upper Hse Farm, Upleadon, Newent, **Gloucestershire**, GL18 1HL, **ENGLAND**.
(T) 01452 790265 (F) 01452 790265.
Contact/s
Owner: Mr R Oliver
Profile Trainer. Ref:YH10499

OLIVER, RHONA

Mrs Rhona Oliver, Hassendean Bank, Hawick, **Scottish Borders**, TD9 8RX, **SCOTLAND**.
(T) 01450 870216 (F) 01450 870357
(M) 07774 426017.
Profile Breeder, Trainer. Ref:YH10500

OLIVERS FARM CLEAN/REPAIR SVS

Olivers Farm Horse Rug Clean & Repair Service, West Yoke, Ash, Sevenoaks, **Kent**, TN15 7HT, **ENGLAND**.
(T) 01474 879393.
Contact/s
Owner: Mrs V Godfrey Ref:YH10501

OLNEY SADDLERY

Olney Saddlery, 33 Market Pl, Olney, **Buckinghamshire**, MK46 4AJ, **ENGLAND**.
(T) 01234 712157 (F) 01234 241309.
Contact/s
Partner: Mr R Gordon Ref:YH10502

OLYMPIC BLOODSTOCK

Olympic Bloodstock Ltd, Batsford Stud, Moreton In Marsh, **Gloucestershire**, GL56 9QF, **ENGLAND**.
(T) 01608 650210 (F) 01608 651809.
Profile Blood Stock Agency. Ref:YH10503

OLYMPIC BLOODSTOCK

Olympic Bloodstock Ltd, 6 Rouse Rd, Newmarket, **Suffolk**, CB8 8DL, **ENGLAND**.
(T) 01638 663121 (F) 01638 661404.
Contact/s
Owner: Mr R Morgan-Jones
Profile Blood Stock Agency. Ref:YH10504

OLYMPIC COACHBUILDERS

Olympic Coachbuilders Ltd, 154C Milton Pk, Milton, Abingdon, **Oxfordshire**, OX14 4SD, **ENGLAND**.
(T) 01235 861177 (F) 01235 862277.
Profile Transport/Horse Boxes. Ref:YH10505

OMAGH

Omagh Equestrian & Countrywear, 14 Gillygooley Rd, Omagh, **County Tyrone**, BT78 5PN, **NORTHERN IRELAND**.
(T) 028 82244567 (F) 028 82247614.
Contact/s
Manager: Mr T Patterson
Profile Saddlery Retailer. Ref:YH10506

O'MARA, THOMOND

O'Mara Thomond, Garden Ctge, Lismacue, Bansha, **County Tipperary**, **IRELAND**.
(T) 062 54522.
Profile Supplies. Ref:YH10507

OMEGA BLACKSMITHS

Omega Blacksmiths, 104 Iona Way, Kirkintilloch, Glasgow, **Glasgow (City of)**, G66 3PT, **SCOTLAND**.
(T) 0141 7776313.
Profile Blacksmith. Ref:YH10508

OMEGA TRAILERS

Omega Trailers, Warrington Central Trading Est, Bewsey Rd, Warrington, **Cheshire**, WA2 7LS, **ENGLAND**.
(T) 01925 638008 (F) 01925 638660.
Contact/s
Manager: Mr C Wordsworth
Profile Transport/Horse Boxes. Ref:YH10509

ON THE HOOF

On The Hoof, Beresford Cottage, 9 Raymend Rd, Victoria Park, **Bristol**, BS3 4QR, **ENGLAND**.
(T) 01179 147989
(M) 07775 946504.
Profile Supplies. Ref:YH10510

ONE JUMP AHEAD

One Jump Ahead, The Old Farm Hse, Bucks Alley, Little Berkhamsted, Hertford, **Hertfordshire**, SG13 8LT, **ENGLAND**.
(T) 01992 511563 (F) 01992 511563.
Contact/s
Owner: Mrs S Cookson Ref:YH10511

ONE STOP

One Stop Equine Services, Tedfold Stud Farm, Okehurst Rd, Billingshurst, **Sussex (West)**, RH14 9HU, **ENGLAND**.
(T) 01403 785862
(E) enquiries@one-stop-equine-services.co.uk.
Contact/s
Owner: Mrs J Merrin
Profile Supplies. Laundry Service. Waterproofing of rugs. Ref:YH10512

ONE STOP TACK SHOP

One Stop Tack Shop, 64 Walton Rd, East Molesey, **Surrey**, KT8 0DL, **ENGLAND**.
(T) 020 88731352.
Contact/s
Owner: Mrs S Hibberd
Profile Supplies. Yr. Est: 1996
Opening Times
Sp: Open Mon - Fri 10:00. Closed Mon - Fri 17:30.
Su: Open Mon - Fri 10:00. Closed Mon - Fri 17:30.
Au: Open Mon - Fri 10:00. Closed Mon - Fri 17:30.
Wn: Open Mon - Fri 10:00. Closed Mon - Fri 17:30.
Saturday 09:00 - 17:30 Ref:YH10513

O'NEIL, HUGH

Hugh O'Neil, 4 Glebe Cres, Ayr, **Ayrshire (South)**, **SCOTLAND**..
Profile Breeder. Ref:YH10514

O'NEILL, E

Mr E O'Neill, Machell Pl, Old Station Rd, Newmarket, **Suffolk**, CB8 8DW, **ENGLAND**.
(T) 01638 669569
(M) 07931 704392
(E) ejo'n.trainer@virgin.net
(W) www.newmarketracehorsetrainers.co.uk
Affiliated Bodies Newmarket Trainers Fed.
Contact/s
Trainer: Mr E O'Neill
Profile Trainer. Ref:YH10515

O'NEILL, EAMONN

Eamonn O'Neill, 80 Windsor Ave, Hillingdon, **London (Greater)**, UB10 9AY, **ENGLAND**.
(T) 01895 258232.
Contact/s
Owner: Mr E O'Neill (Q) DWCF
(E) heleamoneill@aol.com
Profile Farrier. Ref:YH10516

O'NEILL, J G

Mr J G O'Neill, Willows Farmhouse, Stratton Audley, Bicester, **Oxfordshire**, OX6 9BA, **ENGLAND**.
(T) 01869 277202 (F) 01869 277202.
Profile Supplies. Ref:YH10517

O'NEILL, J J

Mr J J O'Neill, Ivy Hse, Skelton Wood End, Penrith, **Cumbria**, CA11 9UB, **ENGLAND**.
(T) 01768 484555 (F) 01768 484559
(M) 07831 399500
(E) jonjo@jonjooneill.demon.co.uk.
Profile Trainer. Ref:YH10518

O'NEILL, OWEN

Owen O'Neill, Cleeve Lodge, Cleeve Hill, Cheltenham, **Gloucestershire**, GL52 3PW,

ENGLAND.
(T) 01242 673275 (F) 01242 673275.
Contact/s
Owner: Mr O O'Neill
Profile Trainer. Ref: YH10519

O'NEIL-MORAN, BRIAN R

Brian R O'Neil-Moran DWCF, The Forge, New York, North Shields, **Tyne and Wear**, NE29 8EU, **ENGLAND**.
(T) 0191 2581868.
Profile Farrier. Ref: YH10520

ONIONS, MARTIN F

Martin F Onions DWCF, Roselands Lodge, Rugeley Rd, Armitage, **Staffordshire**, WS15 4AU, **ENGLAND**.
(T) 01543 307125.
Profile Farrier. Ref: YH10521

ONLY FOALS & HORSES

Only Foals & Horses, Upper Jincox Farm, Popes Lane, Oxted, **Surrey**, RH8 9PL, **ENGLAND**.
(T) 01883 714003.
Contact/s
Partner: Ms D Johnson
Profile Equestrian Centre, Riding School.
Ref: YH10522

OPEN CLGE OF EQUINE STUDIES

Open College of Equine Studies (The), The Old Mill, West Stow Rd, Flempton, Bury St Edmunds, **Suffolk**, IP28 6EN, **ENGLAND**.
(T) 01284 728867 (F) 01284 728830
(E) enquiries@equinestudies.co.uk
(W) www.equinestudies.co.uk.
Profile Equestrian Centre. College. Ref: YH10523

OPEN COUNTRY

Open Country, Golden Sq, Petworth, **Sussex (West)**, GU28 0AP, **ENGLAND**.
(T) 01798 342108.
Profile Saddlery Retailer. Ref: YH10524

OPPENHEIMER, S L

S L Oppenheimer, The Old Stable/Headmoor Farm, Headmoor Lane, Four Marks, Alton, **Hampshire**, GU34 3ES, **ENGLAND**.
(T) 01420 588211. Ref: YH10525

ORAM, S

Mrs S Oram, Parklands Farm, Sleight, Devizes, **Wiltshire**, SN10 3HW, **ENGLAND**.
(T) 01380 723561.
Profile Breeder. Ref: YH10526

ORCHARD COTTAGE

Orchard Cottage Riding Stables, Babylon Lane, Lower Kingswood, Wickham Market, **Surrey**, KT20 6XA, **ENGLAND**.
(T) 01737 241311
(E) ocrs@dial.pipex.com
(W) http://ds.dial.pipex.com/ocrs
Affiliated Bodies ABRS, BHS.
Contact/s
General Manager: Miss A Vickery
Profile Riding School.
Access to hacking on the North Downs. No.Staff: 8
Yr. Est: 1926 C.Size: 15 Acres
Opening Times
Sp: Open Mon - Wed 08:00. Closed Mon - Wed 22:00.
Su: Open Mon - Wed 08:00. Closed Mon - Wed 22:00.
Au: Open Mon - Wed 08:00. Closed Mon - Wed 22:00.
Wn: Open Mon - Wed 08:00. Closed Mon - Wed 22:00.
Fri 08:00 - 21:00, Sat, Sun 07:30 - 18:00
Ref: YH10527

ORCHARD END LIVERIES

Orchard End Liveries, Inkerman Hill, Hazlemere, High Wycombe, **Buckinghamshire**, HP15 7JH, **ENGLAND**.
(T) 01494 711293.
Contact/s
Owner: Mrs C Percvial
Profile Riding School. Ref: YH10528

ORCHARD FARM EQUESTRIAN

Orchard Farm Equestrian Centre, Orchard Farm, West End, Hogsthorpe, Skegness, **Lincolnshire**, PE24 5PA, **ENGLAND**.
(T) 01754 872319.
Contact/s
Owner: Mrs M Blanchard
Profile Equestrian Centre, Riding School, Stable/Livery.
Holiday facilities for caravans also livery, ideal for taking horses on holiday with their owners. Forty minute lesson of one to one coaching £8.50. Yr. Est: 1986
Opening Times
Sp: Open Mon - Sun 09:00. Closed Mon - Sun 19:30.
Su: Open Mon - Sun 09:00. Closed Mon - Sun 19:30.
Au: Open Mon - Sun 09:00. Closed Mon - Sun 19:30.
Wn: Open Mon - Sun 09:00. Closed Mon - Sun 19:30. Ref: YH10529

ORCHARD FARM FEEDS

Orchard Farm Feeds, Holtye Rd, East Grinstead, **Sussex (West)**, RH19 3PP, **ENGLAND**.
(T) 01342 321411.
Profile Supplies. Ref: YH10530

ORCHARD FARM STABLES

Orchard Farm Stables, Southfields Rd, Woldingham, Caterham, **Surrey**, CR3 7BG, **ENGLAND**.
(T) 01883 653034 (F) 01883 653519.
Contact/s
Partner: Mr G Miller Ref: YH10531

ORCHARD FARM STUD

Orchard Farm Stud, Hanney Rd, Steventon, Abingdon, **Oxfordshire**, OX13 6AP, **ENGLAND**.
(T) 01235 832629.
Contact/s
Owner: Mrs M Jones
Profile Breeder. Ref: YH10532

ORCHARD FIELD LIVERY STABLES

Orchard Field Livery Stables, 29 Boggs Holdings, Pencaitland, Tranent, **Lothian (East)**, EH34 5BA, **SCOTLAND**.
(T) 01875 340774.
Contact/s
Owner: Miss F McDonald
Profile Stable/Livery. Yr. Est: 1995
Opening Times
Sp: Open Mon - Sun 09:00. Closed Mon - Sun 18:00.
Su: Open Mon - Sun 09:00. Closed Mon - Sun 18:00.
Au: Open Mon - Sun 09:00. Closed Mon - Sun 18:00.
Wn: Open Mon - Sun 09:00. Closed Mon - Sun 18:00. Ref: YH10533

ORCHARD HSE

Orchard House, South Thorpe, Barnard Castle, **County Durham**, DL12 9DU, **ENGLAND**.
(T) 01833 627369.
Contact/s
Owner: Miss C Scrope
Profile Horse/Rider Accom. No.Staff: 1
Opening Times
Sp: Open Mon - Sun 09:00. Closed Mon - Sun 21:00.
Su: Open Mon - Sun 09:00. Closed Mon - Sun 21:00.
Au: Open Mon - Sun 09:00. Closed Mon - Sun 21:00.
Wn: Open Mon - Sun 09:00. Closed Mon - Sun 21:00. Ref: YH10534

ORCHARD POYLE

Orchard Poyle Horse Drawn Carriage Hire, Southgates, Wick Lane, Englefield Green, Egham, **Surrey**, TW20 0XA, **ENGLAND**.
(T) 01784 435983.
Contact/s
Owner: Mr J Seear Ref: YH10535

ORCHARD STABLES

Orchard Stables, Lanercost Pk, Cramlington, **Northumberland**, NE23 6RU, **ENGLAND**.
(T) 01670 715174. Ref: YH10536

ORCHARDS LIVERY STABLES

Orchards Livery Stables (The), Upper Hill Farm, Frankley Hill Lane, Birmingham, **Midlands (West)**, B32 4BE, **ENGLAND**.
(T) 0121 4601385 (F) 0121 4578635.
Contact/s
Owner: Mrs J Hamer
Profile Farrier. Ref: YH10537

ORCHID RIDING CTRE

Orchid Riding Centre, Walshes Rd, Crowborough, **Sussex (East)**, TN6 3RE, **ENGLAND**.
(T) 01892 652020.
Profile Riding School. Ref: YH10538

ORDE-POWLETT, H

Mr H Orde-Powlett, Wensley Hall, Wensley, Leyburn, **Yorkshire (North)**, DL8 4HN, **ENGLAND**.
(T) 01969 623674.
Profile Supplies. Ref: YH10539

O'REARDON, M

M O'Reardon, 12 Albion Rd, Sileby, Loughborough, **Leicestershire**, LE12 7RA, **ENGLAND**.
(T) 01509 814568.
Profile Farrier. Ref: YH10540

ORGANICS LAB

Organics Lab Of Forge Metalwork (The), Colston Rd, Buckfastleigh, **Devon**, TQ11 0LW, **ENGLAND**.
(T) 01364 643808.
Contact/s
Owner: Mr S Larkham
Profile Blacksmith. Ref: YH10541

ORIGINALS

Originals, 17 Scarthingwell Cres, Saxton, Tadcaster, **Yorkshire (North)**, LS24 9QE, **ENGLAND**.
(T) 01937 817513. Ref: YH10542

ORION STUD

Orion Stud (The), Kents Farm, Malthouse Lane, Hurstpierpoint, Hassocks, **Sussex (West)**, BN6 9JZ, **ENGLAND**.
(T) 01273 833030.
Contact/s
Owner: Mrs A Wear
Profile Breeder. Ref: YH10543

O'RIORDAN RIDING CTRE

O'Riordan Riding Centre, Sixmilewater, Whitechurch, **County Cork**, **IRELAND**.
(T) 021 4886666.
Profile Supplies. Ref: YH10544

O'RIORDAN, MICHAEL J

Michael J O'Riordan DWCF, Flat 152 Grovener Yard, Newmarket, **Suffolk**, CB8 8DL, **ENGLAND**.
(T) 07768 871594.
Profile Farrier. Ref: YH10545

ORKNEY RIDING CLUB

Orkney Riding Club, Shenavall, East Hill, Kirkwall, **Orkney Isles**, KW15 1LY, **SCOTLAND**.
(T) 01856 3456.
Contact/s
Chairman: Capt W Spence
Profile Club/Association, Riding Club. Ref: YH10546

ORLESTONE RIDING CTRE

Orlestone Riding Centre, Church Lane, Shadoxhurst, Ashford, **Kent**, TN26 1LY, **ENGLAND**.
(T) 01233 732423.
Contact/s
Owner: Mrs M Smith Ref: YH10547

ORMEROD, GILES

Giles Ormerod, Druids Lodge Stables, Druids Lodge, Salisbury, **Wiltshire**, SP3 4QN, **ENGLAND**.
(T) 01722 782577.
Profile Stable/Livery, Trainer. Ref: YH10548

ORMISTON, EWAN C

Ewan C Ormiston, The Birches, Boa Vista Rd, Kingussie, **Highlands**, PH21 1LE, **SCOTLAND**.
(T) 01540 661705.
Profile Breeder. Ref: YH10549

ORMSTON, J M

Mr J M Ormston, Rokeby Cl, Hutton Magna, Richmond, **Yorkshire (North)**, DL11 7HF, **ENGLAND**.
(T) 01833 27378.
Profile Supplies. Ref: YH10550

O'ROURKE, SHAUN

Shaun O'Rourke DWCF, 11 Sharon Rd, West End, Southampton, **Hampshire**, SO30 3AP, **ENGLAND**.
(T) 023 80476777.
Profile Farrier. Ref: YH10551

ORR, CHRISTOPHER J

Christopher J Orr DWCF, 8 Alton Holdings, Milton Of Campsie, **Glasgow (City of)**, G66 8AD, **SCOTLAND**.
(T) 0141 7762509.
Profile Farrier. Ref: YH10552

ORSETT HORSEBOX REPAIRERS

Orsett Horsebox Repairers, Dollymans Farm, Doublegate Lane, Rawreth, Wickford, **Essex**, SS11 8UD, **ENGLAND**.
(T) 01268 735333.
Contact/s
Owner: Mr T Binks

Profile Transport/Horse Boxes. **No.Staff:** 2
Yr. Est: 1991
Opening Times
Sp: Open Mon - Fri 09:00. Closed Mon - Fri 17:00.
Su: Open Mon - Fri 09:00. Closed Mon - Fri 17:00.
Au: Open Mon - Fri 09:00. Closed Mon - Fri 17:00.
Wn: Open Mon - Fri 09:00. Closed Mon - Fri 17:00.
Closed weekends **Ref: YH10553**

ORTON EQUINE SWIMMING CTRE
Orton Equine Swimming Centre, Clarks Farm, Orton-on-the-Hill, Atherstone, **Warwickshire**, CV9 3NP, **ENGLAND**.
(T) 01827 880387.
Profile Medical Support. Swimming centre.
Ref: YH10554

ORVIS CO INC
Orvis Co Inc, Vermont Hse, Unit 30A North Way, Andover, **Hampshire**, SP10 5RW, **ENGLAND**.
(T) 01264 349538 **(F)** 01264 349507.
Profile Supplies. **Ref: YH10555**

ORWELL ARENA
Orwell Arena Bridge Farm, Bridge Farm Cottage, Levington, Ipswich, **Suffolk**, IP10 0LJ, **ENGLAND**.
(T) 01473 659446.
Contact/s
For Bookings: Mrs S McGuires
Profile Arena, Breeder, Equestrian Centre, Riding School, Stable/Livery, Supplies, Trainer, Transport/Horse Boxes. Competition Centre.
Ref: YH10556

OSBALDESTON RIDING CTRE
Ross Farms Lancs Ltd, Osbaldeston, Blackburn, **Lancashire**, BB2 7LZ, **ENGLAND**.
(T) 01254 813159 **(F)** 01254 813159.
Contact/s
Livery Manager: Ms J Bargh **(Q)** BHS 2
Profile Arena, Equestrian Centre, Riding Club, Stable/Livery, Track/Course. **No.Staff:** 4
Yr. Est: 1964 **C.Size:** 100 Acres **Ref: YH10557**

OSBERTOWN RIDING CTRE
Osbertown Riding Centre, Enoville Hse, Osbertown, Naas, **County Kildare**, **IRELAND**.
(T) 045 879074 **(F)** 045 879074
(M) 087 6880762
(E) osberstown@kildarehorse.ie.
Contact/s
Key Contact: Mr L Gaffney
Profile Equestrian Centre. **C.Size:** 25 Acres
Ref: YH10558

OSBORNE PK
Osborne Park, Craddockstown Hse, Naas, **County Kildare**, **IRELAND**.
(T) 045 876205.
Profile Supplies. **Ref: YH10559**

OSBORNE, ROBERT
Robert Osborne, Craddockstown Hse, Naas, **County Kildare**, **IRELAND**.
(T) 045 876205.
Contact/s
Trainer: Robert Osbourne
Profile Trainer. **Ref: YH10560**

OSBOURNE STUDIO GALLERY
Osbourne Studio Gallery, 6 Alexandra Ave, Battersea, **London (Greater)**, SW11 4DZ, **ENGLAND**.
(T) 020 749980486. **Ref: YH10561**

OSBOURNE, J
Mr J Osbourne, Kingsdown, Upper Lambourn, Hungerford, **Berkshire**, RG17 8QX, **ENGLAND**.
(T) 01488 73139 **(F)** 01488 73084.
Contact/s
Owner: Mr J Osbourne
Profile Trainer. **Ref: YH10562**

OSBOURNES
Osbournes, Crookford Hill, Elkesley, Retford, **Nottinghamshire**, DN22 8BT, **ENGLAND**.
(T) 01777 838670. **Ref: YH10563**

OSCARS PET & EQUINE SUPPLIES
Oscars Pet & Equine Supplies, 13 Elizabeth Court, Collingham, Wetherby, **Yorkshire (West)**, LS22 5JL, **ENGLAND**.
(T) 01937 574838.
Profile Supplies. **Ref: YH10564**

OSGILIATH FEEDS
Osgiliath Feeds, 17 Clearwood, Dilton Marsh, Westbury, **Wiltshire**, BA13 4BD, **ENGLAND**.
(T) 01373 864544 **(F)** 01373 824513
(E) mkimmins@easynet.co.uk.
Contact/s
Owner: Mr M Kimmins
Profile Feed Merchant, Supplies. **Ref: YH10565**

O'SHEA, JOHN
O'Shea John, Kiltalaghan, Callan, **County Kilkenny**, **IRELAND**.
(T) 051 647092.
Profile Supplies. **Ref: YH10566**

O'SHEA, THOMAS J
Thomas J O'Shea BII, 10 Siskin Cl, Bushey, **Hertfordshire**, WD2 2HN, **ENGLAND**.
(T) 07770 764277.
Profile Farrier. **Ref: YH10567**

OSMAN, BRIAN
Brian Osman, Jacobs, Langham Rd, Boxted, Colchester, **Essex**, CO4 5HT, **ENGLAND**.
(T) 01206 272534
(M) 07770 883672
(E) brian@osbox.freeserve.com.
Profile Supplies. **Ref: YH10568**

OSMINGTON MILLS
Osmington Mills Riding Stables, Weymouth, **Dorset**, DT3 6HB, **ENGLAND**.
(T) 01305 833578.
Contact/s
Manager: Mrs J Hintze
Profile Riding School. **Ref: YH10569**

OSMOND, T P
T P Osmond RSS BII, 451 New Inn Lane, Trenthem, Stoke-on-Trent, **Staffordshire**, ST4 8BN, **ENGLAND**.
(T) 01782 658385.
Profile Farrier. **Ref: YH10570**

OSMONDS
Osmonds, Ferriby High Rd, North Ferriby, **Yorkshire (East)**, HU14 3LE, **ENGLAND**.
(T) 01482 665783 **(F)** 01482 665782
(E) sales@osmonds.co.uk.
Profile Medical Support. **Ref: YH10571**

OSS-I-CHAFF
Oss-i-Chaff Limited, Highland Farm, Ossington, Newark, **Nottinghamshire**, NG23 6LJ, **ENGLAND**.
(T) 01636 821255 **(F)** 01636 822082.
Contact/s
Owner: Mr D Lambert **Ref: YH10572**

OSTERLEY BOOKSHOP
Osterley Bookshop, 168A Thornbury Rd, Osterley, **London (Greater)**, TW7 4QE, **ENGLAND**.
(T) 020 85606206.
Profile Supplies. **Ref: YH10573**

OSTOY, VALERIE
Valerie Ostoya SEA, 20 Pembridge Villas, London, **London (Greater)**, W11 2SU, **ENGLAND**.
(T) 020 77270411. **Ref: YH10574**

OSWALDTWISTLE ANIMAL FEEDS
Oswaldtwistle Animal Feeds, Waterside Farm, Pothouse Lane, Oswaldtwistle, **Lancashire**, BB5 3RU, **ENGLAND**.
(T) 01254 234383.
Contact/s
Owner: Mrs M Procter
Profile Feed Merchant, Saddlery Retailer.
Ref: YH10575

OSWESTRY EQUEST CTRE
Oswestry Equestrian Centre, Carreg Y Big, Oswestry, **Shropshire**, SY10 7HX, **ENGLAND**.
(T) 01691 654754 **(F)** 01691 654792.
Contact/s
Assistant Instructor: Ms K Evans **(Q)** NVQ 1
Profile Arena, Equestrian Centre, Riding School, Stable/Livery, Trainer. **No.Staff:** 5 **C.Size:** 24 Acres **Ref: YH10576**

OTLEY CLGE
Otley College, Otley, Ipswich, **Suffolk**, IP6 9EY, **ENGLAND**.
(T) 01473 785543 **(F)** 01473 785353
(E) otley@mail.anglianet.co.uk.
Contact/s
Marketing Manager: Richard Robinson
Profile Equestrian Centre. **Ref: YH10577**

O'TOOLE, ANN F
O'Toole Ann F, Carnew Stud, Carnew, Wicklow, **County Wexford**, **IRELAND**.
(T) 055 26111.
Profile Supplies. **Ref: YH10578**

O'TOOLE, M L
M I O'Toole, Maddenstown, **County Kildare**, **IRELAND**.
(T) 045 441317.
Profile Supplies. **Ref: YH10579**

OTTERBOURNE RIDING CTRE
Otterbourne Riding Centre, Rue De Planel, Torteval, **Guernsey**, GY8 0LX, **ENGLAND**.
(T) 01481 63085.
Profile Riding School. **Ref: YH10580**

OTTERSWICK
Otterswick Marketing, P O Box 8110, Mauchine, **Ayrshire (South)**, KA5 5YB, **SCOTLAND**.
(T) 01290 552999 **(F)** 01290 552998
(E) otterswick@sporthorsebreeder.com
(W) www.sporthorse-breeder.com
Affiliated Bodies BSJA.
Contact/s
General Manager: Mr H McMahon
(E) hugh@sporthorse-breeder.com
Profile Medical Support, Supplies.
Opening Times
Sp: Open Mon - Fri 09:00. Closed Mon - Fri 17:00.
Su: Open Mon - Fri 09:00. Closed Mon - Fri 17:00.
Au: Open Mon - Fri 09:00. Closed Mon - Fri 17:00.
Wn: Open Mon - Fri 09:00. Closed Mon - Fri 17:00.
There is a 24 hour Answer Phone in operation over the weekends which is regularly checked. **Ref: YH10581**

OTTERY INSURANCE SVS
Ottery Insurance Services, 62 Mill St, Ottery St Mary, **Devon**, EX11 1AF, **ENGLAND**.
(T) 01404 813495 **(F)** 01404 814277
(E) ois@cpages.co.uk.
Profile Club/Association. **Ref: YH10582**

OUGHTON, A
A Oughton, Hill Top, Deerfold, Birtley, Bucknell, **Shropshire**, SY7 0EF, **ENGLAND**.
(T) 01568 770605.
Contact/s
Owner: Mrs A Oughton
Profile Trainer. **Ref: YH10583**

OUSBEY CARRIAGES
Ousbey Carriages, Ormond Lodge, Newbold-on-Stour, Statford-on-Avon, **Warwickshire**, CV37 8TS, **ENGLAND**.
(T) 01789 450351 **(F)** 01789 450351
(M) 07788 673153. **Ref: YH10584**

OUSBEY'S HARNESS ROOM
Ousbey's Harness Room, Manor Farm, Ratcliffe Culey, Atherstone, **Warwickshire**, CV9 3NY, **ENGLAND**.
(T) 01827 716947. **Ref: YH10585**

OUSE VALLEY RIDING CLUB
Ouse Valley Riding Club, 138 South Rd, Peacehaven, **Sussex (East)**, BN10 8ER, **ENGLAND**.
(T) 01273 582101.
Contact/s
Chairman: Mr G Moore
Profile Club/Association, Riding Club. **Ref: YH10586**

OUTBACK TRADING
Outback Trading Co, 51 The Ridgeway, Sanderstead, South Croydon, **Surrey**, CR2 0LJ, **ENGLAND**.
(T) 020 86573039 **(F)** 020 86571477.
Profile Supplies. **Ref: YH10587**

OUTDOORS - SCOUT SHOPS
Outdoors - Scout Shops Ltd, Lancing Business Pk, Lancing, **Sussex (West)**, BN15 8UG, **ENGLAND**.
(T) 01903 755352 **(F)** 01903 750993.
Contact/s
Manager: Ms J McLaren
Profile Saddlery Retailer. **Ref: YH10588**

OUTWEAR
Outwear, The Old Post Office, Alvescot, Oxford, **Oxfordshire**, OX18 2PU, **ENGLAND**.
(T) 01993 842225.
Profile Saddlery Retailer. **Ref: YH10589**

OVER WHITLAW STABLES
Over Whitlaw Stables, Over Whitlaw Farm, Selkirk, **Scottish Borders**, TD7 4QN, **SCOTLAND**.
(T) 01750 21281.
Contact/s
Owner: Mrs F Walling **(Q)** BSc(Hons)
Profile Breeder, Stable/Livery, Trainer.
Breeds and sells Black Arabians of English/Egyptian Bloodlines. Hunter liveries available **Yr. Est:** 1980
C.Size: 500 Acres **Ref: YH10590**

OVERDALE VETNRY CTRE

Overdale Veterinary Centre, New Market St, Buxton, **Derbyshire**, SK17 6LP, **ENGLAND**.
(T) 01298 23499 **(F)** 01298 70623.
Profile Medical Support. **Ref: YH10591**

OVERHILL LIVERY STABLES

Overhill Livery Stables, Sandy Lane, Tilford, Farnham, **Surrey**, GU10 2ET, **ENGLAND**.
(T) 01252 792476.
Contact/s
Owner: Ms H Clarke
Profile Stable/Livery. **Ref: YH10592**

OVERIDER

Overider, Hopsford Hall, Withybrook Lane, Shilton, Coventry, **Midlands (West)**, CV7 9HY, **ENGLAND**.
(T) 01455 220974 **(F)** 01455 221403
(E) admin@overider.com
(W) www.overider.com
Affiliated Bodies BETA, BHS.
Contact/s
Administration: Ms E James
Profile Riding Wear Retailer, Saddlery Retailer, Supplies. No.Staff: 5 Yr. Est: 1993
Ref: YH10593

OVERLAND PONY TREK

Overland Pony Trek, Dyffryn Farm, Rhayader Rd, Llanwrthwl, Llandrindod Wells, **Powys**, LD6 5PE, **WALES**.
(T) 01597 810402.
Profile Riding School. **Ref: YH10594**

OVERTON HORSE DEALER

Overton Horse Dealer, 185 Robin Hood Rd, Coventry, **Midlands (West)**, CV3 3AL, **ENGLAND**.
(T) 024 76306022.
Contact/s
Owner: Mr R Overton
Profile Breeder. **Ref: YH10595**

OWEN BROWN

Owen Brown Ltd, Station Rd, Castle Donington, **Derbyshire**, DE74 2NL, **ENGLAND**.
(T) 01332 850000 **(F)** 01332 850005
(E) enq@owen-brown.co.uk. **Ref: YH10596**

OWEN FARMING TRANSPORT

Owen Farming Transport Ltd, Peddars Way, School Rd, Rattlesden, Bury St Edmunds, **Suffolk**, IP30 0SE, **ENGLAND**.
(T) 01449 737194.
Contact/s
Transport Manager: Mr R Owen
Profile Transport/Horse Boxes. **Ref: YH10597**

OWEN MILLS HAULAGE

Owen Mills Haulage Ltd, Hoppin/Barrow Hill Rd, Copythorne, Cadnam, Southampton, **Hampshire**, SO40 2NW, **ENGLAND**.
(T) 023 80812167.
Profile Transport/Horse Boxes. **Ref: YH10598**

OWEN, E HOLLISTER

Mr E Hollister Owen, Y Wern, Llandyrnog, Denbigh, **Conwy**, LL16 4HW, **WALES**.
(T) 01824 790264.
Profile Supplies. **Ref: YH10599**

OWEN, F M

Mrs F M Owen, Brick Kiln Farm, Hood Lane, Armitage, Rugeley, **Staffordshire**, WS15 4AG, **ENGLAND**.
(T) 01543 490320.
Profile Supplies. **Ref: YH10600**

OWEN, GARETH J

Gareth J Owen DWCF, 18 Brookside, Ashton, Chester, **Cheshire**, CH3 8BZ, **ENGLAND**.
(T) 01829 751327.
Profile Farrier. **Ref: YH10601**

OWEN, J R

J R Owen, Hoofield Rd, Huxley, Chester, **Cheshire**, CH3 9BR, **ENGLAND**.
(T) 01829 781391.
Profile Farrier. **Ref: YH10602**

OWEN, J R

J R Owen, Milldene, Uffington, Shrewsbury, **Shropshire**, SY4 4SE, **ENGLAND**.
(T) 01743 369904. **Ref: YH10603**

OWEN, JOHN

John Owen, Hollybush Farm, Acton Turville, Badminton, **Gloucestershire**, GL9 1HL, **ENGLAND**.
(T) 01454 218753 **(F)** 01454 218753.
Profile Medical Support. **Ref: YH10604**

OWEN, JONATHAN

Jonathan Owen, Torwood, 5 Louvain Rd, Derby, **Derbyshire**, DE23 6DA, **ENGLAND**.
(T) 01332 382323 **(F)** 01332 382353.
Contact/s
Owner: Mr J Owen
Profile Blacksmith. **Ref: YH10605**

OWEN, TUFFY

Tuffy Owen, Tyn-Y-Coed, Cefn Meiriadog, St Asaph, **Denbighshire**, LL17 0HH, **WALES**.
(T) 01745 584393. **Ref: YH10606**

OWENS, P M

P M Owens - Cascob Stud, Woodhouse Farm, Shobdon, Leominster, **Herefordshire**, HR6 9NL, **ENGLAND**.
(T) 01568 708615.
Profile Breeder. **Ref: YH10607**

OWENS, R

Mr & Mrs R Owens, Bryn Coch, Star, Gaerwen, **Isle of Anglesey**, LL60 6AS, **WALES**.
(T) 01248 714687.
Profile Breeder. **Ref: YH10608**

OWENS, R M L

Mr R M L Owens, Caerwys Hall, Caerwys, Mold, **Flintshire**, **WALES**..
Profile Trainer. **Ref: YH10609**

OWENSTOWN STUD

Owenstown Stud, Maynooth, **County Kildare**, **IRELAND**.
(T) 01 6289197
(E) owenstownstud@kildarehorse.ie.
Contact/s
Key Contact: Mr J Tuthill
Profile Breeder. **Ref: YH10610**

OWL HSE STABLES

Owl House Stables, 12 St Radigunds Rd, Dover, **Kent**, CT17 0JX, **ENGLAND**.
(T) 01304 207722. **Ref: YH10611**

OWL LEATHERCRAFT

Owl Leathercraft, Teignbridge Level Crossing, Higher Sandygate, Newton Abbot, **Devon**, TQ12 3QJ, **ENGLAND**.
(T) 01626 336966.
Contact/s
Owner: Mrs J Oliver
Profile Supplies. **Ref: YH10612**

OWLET FARM LIVERY STABLES

Owlet Farm Livery Stables, Scotland Lane, Horsforth, Leeds, **Yorkshire (West)**, LS18 5HW, **ENGLAND**.
(T) 0113 2583859.
Contact/s
Owner: Mrs J Totty
Profile Stable/Livery.
DIY livery available, details on request. No.Staff: 1
Yr. Est: 1971
Opening Times
Sp: Open Mon - Sun 09:00. Closed Mon - Sun 21:00.
Su: Open Mon - Sun 09:00. Closed Mon - Sun 21:00.
Au: Open Mon - Sun 09:00. Closed Mon - Sun 21:00.
Wn: Open Mon - Sun 09:00. Closed Mon - Sun 21:00. **Ref: YH10613**

OXBUTTS FARM & STABLE SVS

Oxbutts Farm & Stable Services (Cheltenham), Station Rd, Woodmancote, Cheltenham, **Gloucestershire**, GL52 4HN, **ENGLAND**.
(T) 01242 675726.
Contact/s
Owner: Mr J Rees
Profile Feed Merchant. **Ref: YH10614**

OXENDALE

Oxendale Shetland Pony Stud, Calf Hse Farm, Abbott Brow, Mellor, Blackburn, **Lancashire**, BB2 7HU, **ENGLAND**.
(T) 01254 812354 **(F)** 01254 813209.
Contact/s
Owner: Mr J Kay
(E) jdkay@calfhouse.freeserve.co.uk
Profile Breeder.
Opening Times
Telephone for an appointment **Ref: YH10615**

OXFORD BOOTSTORE

Oxford Bootstore, Ave 1 Covered Market, Oxford, **Oxfordshire**, OX1 3OX, **ENGLAND**.
(T) 01865 251940 **(F)** 01235 770178.
Profile Saddlery Retailer. **Ref: YH10616**

OXFORD BROOKES UNI

Oxford Brookes University, Gipsy Campus, Headington, Oxford, **Oxfordshire**, OX3 0BP, **ENGLAND**.
(T) 01865 483240 **(F)** 01865 483242.
Profile Equestrian Centre. **Ref: YH10617**

OXFORD HILL RUGS

Oxford Hill Rugs, 28 Oxford Hill, Witney, **Oxfordshire**, OX8 6JR, **ENGLAND**.
(T) 01993 705597 **(F)** 01993 705597.
Contact/s
Owner: Miss M Fowler
Profile Saddlery Retailer. **Ref: YH10618**

OXFORD MCTIMONEY CHIROPRACTIC

Oxford McTimoney Chiropractic Clinic, 40 North Hinksey Lane, Botley, **Oxfordshire**, OX2 0LY, **ENGLAND**.
(T) 01865 200489 **(F)** 01865 200838.
Profile Medical Support. **Ref: YH10619**

OXFORD RIDING CLUB

Oxford Riding Club, The Old Rectory, Steeple Barton, **Oxfordshire**, OX7 3QP, **ENGLAND**.
(T) 01869 340019.
Profile Club/Association, Riding Club. **Ref: YH10620**

OXFORD RIDING SCHOOL

Oxford Riding School, Watlington Rd, Garsington, Oxford, **Oxfordshire**, OX44 9DP, **ENGLAND**.
(T) 01865 361383.
Profile Riding School. **Ref: YH10621**

OXFORD UNI POLO CLUB

Oxford University Polo Club, Oxford University Student Union, 28, Little Clarendon St, Oxford, **Oxfordshire**, OX1 2HU, **ENGLAND**.
(T) 01865 270777.
Contact/s
Secretary: Alexandra Hento
(E) alexandra.hento@chch.ox.ac.uk
Profile Club/Association. Polo Club. **Ref: YH10622**

OXLEY FARM STUD

Oxley Farm Stud, Oxley Farm, D'arcy Rd, Tiptree, Colchester, **Essex**, CO5 0RT, **ENGLAND**.
(T) 01621 818660 **(F)** 01621 818660.
Contact/s
Manager: Mr O Smith
Profile Breeder. **Ref: YH10623**

OXNEAD HAFLINGER STUD

Oxnead Haflinger Stud, Oxnead Hse, Oxnead, Norwich, **Norfolk**, NR10 5HP, **ENGLAND**.
(T) 01603 279205.
Profile Breeder. **Ref: YH10624**

OXSTALLS FARM STUD

Oxstalls Farm Stud, Warwick Rd, Stratford-upon-Avon, **Warwickshire**, CV37 3NS, **ENGLAND**.
(T) 01789 205277.
Profile Breeder. **Ref: YH10625**

OXTED VETNRY CLNC

Oxted Veterinary Clinic, 89 High St, Edenbridge, **Kent**, TN8 5AU, **ENGLAND**.
(T) 01732 863287 **(F)** 01883 730430.
Profile Medical Support. **Ref: YH10626**

OXTED VETNRY CLNC

Oxted Veterinary Clinic, 1 Barrow Green Rd, Oxted, **Surrey**, RH8 0RA, **ENGLAND**.
(T) 01883 712206 **(F)** 01883 730430.
Profile Medical Support. **Ref: YH10627**

OXX, JOHN

John Oxx, Currabeg Stables, Creeve, Currabeg, Kildare, **County Kildare**, **IRELAND**..
Contact/s
Trainer: Mr J Oxx
(E) johnoxx@kildarehorse.ie
Profile Trainer. No.Staff: 55 Yr. Est: 1979
Ref: YH10628

P & G FARM SUPPLIES

P & G Farm Supplies, Long Lane, Newport, **Isle of Wight**, PO32 2NW, **ENGLAND**.
(T) 01983 523073.
Profile Supplies. **Ref: YH10629**

P & G STABLES

P & G Stables, Three Turns Lane, South Croxton, Leicester, **Leicestershire**, LE7 9BY, **ENGLAND**.
(T) 01664 840195 **(F)** 01664 840195.

Contact/s
Partner: Mr P Seymour
Profile Riding School, Stable/Livery.
DIY livery available, prices on request. Yr. Est: 1996
C.Size: 20 Acres
Opening Times
Sp: Open Mon - Sun 09:00. Closed Mon - Sun 20:00.
Su: Open Mon - Sun 09:00. Closed Mon - Sun 20:00.
Au: Open Mon - Sun 09:00. Closed Mon - Sun 16:00.
Wn: Open Mon - Sun 09:00. Closed Mon - Sun 16:00. Ref: YH10630

P & L LUCK HORSE TRANSPORT

P & L Luck Horse Transport, Durban Cottage, Merrymeet, Liskeard, **Cornwall**, PL14 3LP, **ENGLAND**.
(T) 01579 345151 (F) 01579 345151
(M) 07774 814160.
Profile Transport/Horse Boxes. Ref: YH10631

P & N LAMERS

Miss P & N Lamers, 9 Gun Meadow Ave, Knebworth, **Hertfordshire**, SG3 6BS, **ENGLAND**.
(T) 01438 812117.
Profile Breeder. Ref: YH10632

P ADAMS & SONS

P Adams & Sons (Farms) Ltd, Laurel Farm, Felixstowe, **Suffolk**, IP11 9RN, **ENGLAND**.
(T) 01394 282460.
Profile Breeder. Ref: YH10633

P BOX - WORKING SADDLER

Mrs P Box - Working Saddler, Spring Ducks, Horton Rd, Ashley Heath, Ringwood, **Hampshire**, BH24 2EU, **ENGLAND**.
(T) 01425 472177.
Profile Supplies. Ref: YH10634

P D LEVI & SON

P D Levi & Son, Brine Pits Cottage, Wychbold, Droitwich, **Worcestershire**, WR9 0BY, **ENGLAND**.
(T) 01527 861580.
Contact/s
Partner: Mrs S Levi
Profile Transport/Horse Boxes. Ref: YH10635

P E P PHILLIPS

P E P Phillips Equestrian Promotions, Preston Hse, Preston Capes, Daventry, **Northamptonshire**, NN11 3TB, **ENGLAND**.
(T) 01327 361232 (F) 01327 361556.
Profile Club/Association. Ref: YH10636

P F & B NICHOLLS RACING

P F & B Nicholls Racing Ltd, Manor Farm Stables, Ditcheat, Shepton Mallet, **Somerset**, BA4 6RD, **ENGLAND**.
(T) 01749 860656 (F) 01749 860523.
Contact/s
Owner: Mr P Nicholls
Profile Trainer. Ref: YH10637

P F I COLE

P F I Cole, Whatcombe Hse, Whatcombe, Wantage, **Oxfordshire**, OX12 9NW, **ENGLAND**.
(T) 01488 638433 (F) 01488 638609.
Profile Trainer. Ref: YH10638

P FROUD & SON

P Froud & Son, Pond Farm, High St, Childrey, Wantage, **Oxfordshire**, OX12 9UA, **ENGLAND**.
(T) 01235 751529 (F) 01235 751331.
Contact/s
Owner: Mrs L Froud
Profile Transport/Horse Boxes. Ref: YH10639

P G L TRAVEL

P G L Travel Ltd, Alton Court, Penyard Lane, Ross-on-Wye, **Herefordshire**, HR9 5NR, **ENGLAND**.
(T) 01989 764211 (F) 01989 766306
(E) holidays@pgl.co.uk
(W) www.pgl.co.uk
Affiliated Bodies BHS
Alt Contact Address
Boreatton Pk, Baschurch, Shrewsbury, Shropshire, SY4 2EZ, England.(T) 01939 260551
Contact/s
Owner: Mr P Laurence (T) 01989 764211
Profile Equestrian Centre, Holidays.
Activity holidays for 6 - 18 year olds. Schools and youth groups are welcome. Holidays are available throughout the UK, France and Spain. The park is ABTA approved. No.Staff: 250 Yr. Est: 1979
C.Size: 250 Acres
Opening Times
Open between 1st March and the end of October
Ref: YH10640

P G L YOUNG ADVENTURE CTRE

P G L Young Adventure Centre, Boreatton Pk, Baschurch, Shrewsbury, **Shropshire**, SY4 2EZ, **ENGLAND**.
(T) 01939 260551 (F) 01939 261179.
Profile Breeder, Riding School. Ref: YH10641

P H PHOTOGRAPHY

P H Photography, 15 Fen Lane, Pott Row, Kings Lynn, **Norfolk**, PE32 1DA, **ENGLAND**.
(T) 01553 630582 (F) 01553 630582
(M) 07889 379260. Ref: YH10642

P H SADDLERS

P H Saddlers, Park Farm, Winkleigh, **Devon**, EX19 8LE, **ENGLAND**.
(T) 01837 83757.
Profile Saddlery Retailer. Ref: YH10643

P HANDLEY & SONS

P Handley & Sons, The Smithy, Smithy Lane, Knighton, Market Drayton, **Shropshire**, TF9 4HP, **ENGLAND**.
(T) 01630 647268.
Profile Farrier. Ref: YH10644

P J & F CARRIAGES

P J & F Carriages, Gannaway Farm Hse, Gannaway, Norton Lindsey, Warwick, **Warwickshire**, CV35 8JT, **ENGLAND**.
(T) 01926 842330.
Contact/s
Partner: Mr P Jones Ref: YH10645

P J A POND

P J A Pond, Home Farm, Padworth, Reading, **Berkshire**, RG7 4NP, **ENGLAND**.
(T) 0118 9833251.
Contact/s
Owner: Mr P Pond Ref: YH10646

P J COYNE

P J Coyne Bridle Manufacturers, 52 Short Acre St, Walsall, **Midlands (West)**, WS2 8HW, **ENGLAND**.
(T) 01922 646511 (F) 01922 639544
(E) pjbridles@hotmail.com.
Contact/s
Owner: Mr P Coyne
Profile Supplies. Ref: YH10647

P J N

P J N, Unit 6, Fiddington Hse Farm, Fiddington, Tewkesbury, **Gloucestershire**, GL20 7BJ, **ENGLAND**.
(T) 01684 275700.
Profile Transport/Horse Boxes. Ref: YH10648

P J SMALL

P J Small Wheelwright, The Forge, Whisby Rd, Doddington, Lincoln, **Lincolnshire**, LN6 4RT, **ENGLAND**.
(T) 01522 500323.
Contact/s
Owner: Mr P Small
Profile Horse drawn carriage building and repair.
Yr. Est: 1976
Opening Times
By appointment only Ref: YH10649

P K ENGINEERING

P K Engineering, Samlesbury Mill, Samlesbury Bottoms, Preston, **Lancashire**, PR5 0RN, **ENGLAND**.
(T) 01254 853824 (F) 01254 853824.
Contact/s
Owner: Mr P Jewes
Profile Blacksmith. Ref: YH10650

P LAVELLE & SONS

P Lavelle & Sons Ltd, 80 New Rd, Silver Bridge, Newry, **County Down**, BT35 9LR, **NORTHERN IRELAND**.
(T) 028 30288216.
Profile Supplies. Ref: YH10651

P M H SVS

P M H Services Ltd, Fiveways, New Rd, Nafferton, Driffield, **Yorkshire (East)**, YO25 4JP, **ENGLAND**.
(T) 01377 254727 (F) 01377 241262.
Profile Club/Association. Ref: YH10652

P MONKHOUSE HAULAGE

P Monkhouse Haulage, Durham Rd, Wolsingham, Bishop Auckland, **County Durham**, DL13 3JB, **ENGLAND**.
(T) 01388 528814 (F) 01388 527213.
Contact/s
Owner: Mr P Monkhouse
Profile Transport/Horse Boxes. Ref: YH10653

P R B HORSE BOXES

P R B Horse Boxes, Unit 1 Amtex Building, Southern Ave, Leominster, **Herefordshire**, HR6 0QF, **ENGLAND**.
(T) 01568 614638.
Profile Transport/Horse Boxes. Ref: YH10654

P R J ENGINEERING

P R J Engineering, Newton Farm, Lewannick, Launceston, **Cornwall**, PL15 7QH, **ENGLAND**.
(T) 01566 782794 (F) 01566 782101.
Contact/s
Owner: Mr P Jasper
Profile Transport/Horse Boxes. Ref: YH10655

P S A EQUESTRIAN SVS

P S A Equestrian Services, Foxhollows Farm, Rectory Lane, Shenley, **Hertfordshire**, WD7 9AW, **ENGLAND**.
(T) 01707 644507 (F) 01707 662636.
Profile Supplies. Ref: YH10656

P S B ANIMAL HEALTH

P S B Animal Health, Unit D Hampton St Ind Est, Hampton St, Tetbury, **Gloucestershire**, GL8 8LD, **ENGLAND**.
(T) 01666 502366.
Profile Supplies. Ref: YH10657

P SLAMAKER LIVERY

P Slamaker Livery, Fontley Hse Farm, Iron Mill Lane, Titchfield, Fareham, **Hampshire**, PO15 6QT, **ENGLAND**.
(T) 01329 842532.
Contact/s
Owner: Mrs P Slamaker Ref: YH10658

P W HARDING & MICHAEL NG

P W Harding & Michael NG, 83 Hockcliffe Rd, Leighton Buzzard, **Bedfordshire**, LU7 8JR, **ENGLAND**.
(T) 01525 377105.
Profile Medical Support. Ref: YH10659

PACEMAKER & THOROUGHBRED

Pacemaker & Thoroughbred Breeder, 38-42 Hampton Rd, Teddington, **London (Greater)**, TW11 0JE, **ENGLAND**.
(T) 020 89435083 (F) 020 89435011.
Profile Supplies. Ref: YH10660

PACHESHAM EQUESTRIAN CTRE

Pachesham Equestrian Centre, Randalls Rd, Leatherhead, **Surrey**, KT22 0AL, **ENGLAND**.
(T) 01372 377888 (F) 01372 360226.
Profile Stable/Livery. Ref: YH10661

PACK, COLIN D

Colin D Pack AWCF, 43 Ilkley Rd, Otley, **Yorkshire (West)**, LS21 3JP, **ENGLAND**.
(T) 01943 467097
(M) 07831 442789.
Profile Farrier. Ref: YH10662

PACKER, C S

C S Packer, Tyddu Farm, Itton, Chepstow, **Monmouthshire**, NP16 6BZ, **WALES**.
(T) 01291 641236.
Contact/s
Owner: Mr C Packer
Profile Farrier. Ref: YH10663

PACKHAM, STUART G

Stuart G Packham DWCF, Flint Cottage, Muntham Farm, Northend, Findon, Worthing, **Sussex (West)**, BN14 0RQ, **ENGLAND**.
(T) 01903 877051.
Profile Farrier. Ref: YH10664

PADD FARM SHOP

Padd Farm Shop, Padd Farm, Hurst Lane, Egham, **Surrey**, TW20 8QJ, **ENGLAND**.
(T) 01784 453168.
Profile Supplies. Ref: YH10665

PADDOCK

Paddock (The), 247 Woolton Rd, Childwall, Liverpool, **Merseyside**, L16 8NA, **ENGLAND**.
(T) 0151 7224626.
Contact/s
Owner: Miss P Thomas Ref: YH10666

PADDOCK LINES

Paddock Lines, Unit 7 Stainton Gr, Barnard Castle, **County Durham**, DL12 8UJ, **ENGLAND**.
(T) 01833 690274 (F) 01833 690053

(M) 07801 834681. Ref: YH10667

PADDOCK LODGE STABLES
Paddock Lodge Stables, Paddock Lodge, Ashtead Woods Rd, Ashtead, **Surrey**, KT21 2ET, **ENGLAND**.
(T) 01372 278739.
Contact/s
Owner: Miss J Callow Ref: YH10668

PADDOCK MAINTENANCE COMPANY
Paddock Maintenance Company, Aldham Gate, Aldham, Ipswich, **Suffolk**, IP7 6XR, **ENGLAND**.
(T) 01473 827391 (F) 01473 824402
(M) 07860 712510.
Profile Supplies. Ref: YH10669

PADDOCK RIDING
Paddock Riding Equipment & Repairs, Summerland Sq, Yellow Rd, Waterford, **County Waterford**, **IRELAND**.
(T) 051 358353.
Profile Supplies. Ref: YH10670

PADDOCK STORES
Paddock Stores, 27 Plants Hollow, Brierley Hill, **Midlands (West)**, DY5 2BZ, **ENGLAND**.
(T) 01384 830457.
Profile Saddlery Retailer. Ref: YH10671

PADDOCKS
Paddocks (The), Bankfoot, Inverkip, Greenock, **Inverclyde**, PA16 0DT, **SCOTLAND**.
(T) 01475 522662 (F) 01475 522662.
Contact/s
Owner: Mrs J Kennedy Ref: YH10672

PADDOCKS
Paddocks (The), 971 Loughborough Rd, Rothley, **Leicestershire**, LE7 7NJ, **ENGLAND**.
(T) 0116 2374431.
Profile Stable/Livery. Ref: YH10673

PADDOCKS RIDING CTRE
Paddocks Riding Centre, Woodside Rd, Sandyford, **County Dublin**, **IRELAND**.
(T) 01 2954278.
Profile Riding School. Ref: YH10674

PADDOCKS RIDING CTRE
Paddocks Riding Centre (The), Hough Lodge, Hough-on-the-Hill, Grantham, **Lincolnshire**, NG32 2BE, **ENGLAND**.
(T) 01400 250228
Affiliated Bodies RDA.
Contact/s
Owner: Mrs K Thompson (Q) BHSII, RDASI
(T) 01476 565638
Profile Riding School. No.Staff: 2
Yr. Est: 1988 C.Size: 9 Acres Ref: YH10675

PADFIELD, M G B
Mr M G B Padfield, Ovington Grange, Clare, Sudbury, **Suffolk**, CO10 8JX, **ENGLAND**.
(T) 01787 278600.
Profile Breeder. Ref: YH10676

PAGE FARM STUD LIVERY STABLES
Page Farm Stud Livery Stables, Dagger Lane, Elstree, Borehamwood, **Hertfordshire**, WD6 3AU, **ENGLAND**.
(T) 020 89534150.
Contact/s
Owner: Miss N Simpson
Profile Breeder. Ref: YH10677

PAGE TRAILERS
Page Trailers, Unit 4 Fenner Business Ctre, Fenner Rd, Great Yarmouth, **Norfolk**, NR30 3PS, **ENGLAND**.
(T) 01493 854187 (F) 01493 854187.
Contact/s
Partner: Mr A Nicholls
Profile Transport/Horse Boxes. Ref: YH10678

PAGE, ALEC
Alec Page, The Forge, Barley Mow, Lampeter, **Carmarthenshire**, SA48 7BY, **WALES**.
(T) 01570 423955.
Profile Blacksmith. Ref: YH10679

PAGE, CLIVE
Clive Page, Deri Fach, 14 Main Rd, Cilfrew, **Glamorgan (Vale of)**, SA10 8LP, **WALES**.
(T) 01639 639300.
Profile Farrier. Ref: YH10680

PAGE, JOHN
John Page, Tenterden Rd, Biddenden, Ashford, **Kent**, TN27 8BH, **ENGLAND**.
(T) 01580 291088 (F) 01580 291211.
Contact/s
Owner: Mr J Page
Profile Transport/Horse Boxes. Ref: YH10681

PAGE, R G
R G Page, Oakmead Farm, Lime Kiln Rd, Yate, Bristol, **Bristol**, BS37 7QB, **ENGLAND**.
(T) 01454 228168.
Profile Transport/Horse Boxes. Ref: YH10682

PAGE, S
Mrs S Page, Shoelands, Grayswood, Haslemere, **Surrey**, GU27, **ENGLAND**.
(T) 01428 653900.
Profile Breeder. Ref: YH10683

PAGET, EDWARD
Edward Paget, 3 Oldfield Rd, Hampton, **London (Greater)**, TW12 2AD, **ENGLAND**.
(T) 020 89414312 (F) 020 89794341. Ref: YH10684

PAGLESHAM SCHOOL
Paglesham School of Equitation, Ingulfs, Paglesham, Rochford, **Essex**, SS4 2DG, **ENGLAND**.
(T) 01702 258285.
Profile Riding School, Stable/Livery. Ref: YH10685

PAISLEY, R
Mr R Paisley, Hallcrofts, Langholm, **Dumfries and Galloway**, DG13 0LP, **SCOTLAND**.
(T) 01387 380698.
Profile Supplies. Ref: YH10686

PAKEFIELD RIDING SCHOOL
Pakefield Riding School, Carlton Rd, Lowestoft, **Suffolk**, NR33 0ND, **ENGLAND**.
(T) 01502 572257
Affiliated Bodies ABRS, BHS, Ponies Ass UK, RDA.
Contact/s
Instructor: Miss A Harding (Q) BHS SM, BHSAI
Profile Riding School.
Other attractions include 'Own a Pony', beach and country rides, pony parties, picnics and pub rides. Road Safety tests can also be arranged. The school is the headquarters of the Lowestoft Riding for the Disabled Association Group. Yr. Est: 1946
C.Size: 5 Acres
Opening Times
Sp: Open Mon - Sun 07:30. Closed Mon - Sun 22:00.
Su: Open Mon - Sun 07:30. Closed Mon - Sun 22:00.
Au: Open Mon - Sun 07:30. Closed Mon - Sun 22:00.
Wn: Open Mon - Sun 07:30. Closed Mon - Sun 22:00. Ref: YH10687

PALBOURNE STUD
Palbourne Stud, Crow Trees Farm, Bradley, Ashbourne, **Derbyshire**, DE6 1PG, **ENGLAND**.
(T) 01335 262.
Profile Breeder. Ref: YH10688

PALLING, BRYN
Bryn Palling, Ty Wyth Newydd, Tredodridge, Cowbridge, **Glamorgan (Vale of)**, CF71 7UL, **WALES**.
(T) 01446 760122 (F) 01446 760067.
Contact/s
Owner: Mr B Palling
Profile Trainer. No.Staff: 14 Yr. Est: 1976
Ref: YH10689

PALLINSBURN STABLES
Pallinsburn Stables, Cornhill-on-Tweed, **Northumberland**, TD12 4SG, **ENGLAND**.
(T) 01890 820581
(M) 07768 850014.
Profile Trainer. Ref: YH10690

PALMER, D W
Mr D W Palmer, Northcliffe Farm, St Nicholas, **Glamorgan (Vale of)**, CF5 6SU, **WALES**.
(T) 01466 735791.
Profile Breeder. Ref: YH10691

PALMERS
George A Palmer Ltd, Amenity Hse, 1 Maizefield, Hinkley Fields Ind Est, Hinckley, **Leicestershire**, LE10 1YF, **ENGLAND**.
(T) 01455 639600 (F) 01455 234714.
Contact/s
Owner: Mr R Palmer
Profile Supplies.
Produce organic based fertiliser and small fertiliser spreaders. Ref: YH10692

PALMERS RIDING STABLES
Palmers Riding Stables, Rosehill Farm Cottages, Peppard Rd, Emmer Green, Reading, **Berkshire**, RG4 8XD, **ENGLAND**.
(T) 0118 9483449.
Contact/s
Owner: Mrs K Challis Ref: YH10693

PALS
P A L S, Woodhead Bauds, Cullen, **Moray**, AB56 4DY, **SCOTLAND**.
(T) 01542 841226.
Contact/s
Commercial Manager: Mr B Bream
Profile Saddlery Retailer. Ref: YH10694

PANAMA SPORT HORSES
Panama Sport Horses Ltd, Gisburn Pk Stables, Gisburn Pk Est, Gisburn, Clitheroe, **Lancashire**, BB7 4HU, **ENGLAND**.
(T) 01200 445687 (F) 01200 445687
(E) info@panamasporthorses.co.uk
(W) www.panamasporthorses.co.uk.
Contact/s
Manager: Mr N Saville
Profile Equestrian Centre, Stable/Livery, Trainer.
Train up to International Level No.Staff: 5
Yr. Est: 1991 C.Size: 10 Acres
Opening Times
Telephone for an appointment Ref: YH10695

PANAYIOTOU, E
Mr & Mrs E Panayiotou, North Lodge, Lower Rd, Chalfont St. Peter, Gerrards Cross, **Buckinghamshire**, SL9 8LA, **ENGLAND**.
(T) 01753 892401.
Profile Breeder. Ref: YH10696

PANCEUTICS
Panceutics Ltd, P O Box 1358, Swindon, **Wiltshire**, SN3 4GP, **ENGLAND**.
(T) 01793 822275 (F) 01793 822275.
Profile Medical Support. Ref: YH10697

PANKHURST, W R
W R Pankhurst, The Forge, Oakridge Lynch, Stroud, **Gloucestershire**, GL6 7NS, **ENGLAND**.
(T) 01285 760236.
Contact/s
Owner: Mr W Pankhurst
Profile Blacksmith. Ref: YH10698

PANNETT
Pannett, 25 The Rise, Sevenoaks, **Kent**, TN13 1RQ, **ENGLAND**.
(T) 01732 450925.
Profile Trainer. Ref: YH10699

PANT GLAS MAWR
Pant Glas Mawr School of Equitation, Axton, Holywell, **Flintshire**, CH8 9DH, **WALES**.
(T) 01745 571400.
Profile Riding School. Ref: YH10700

PANT RHYN TREKKING CTRE
Pant Rhyn Trekking Centre, Cwmtydu, New Quay, **Ceredigion**, SA44 6LH, **WALES**.
(T) 01545 560494.
Contact/s
Owner: Mr R Rees
Profile Equestrian Centre. Ref: YH10701

PANTOMIME HORSE
Pantomime Horse, Slack Trce Farm, Cumberworth, Huddersfield, **Yorkshire (West)**, HD8 8YE, **ENGLAND**.
(T) 01484 681423 (F) 01484 689979.
Contact/s
Owner: Mrs J Hinchliffe
Profile Saddlery Retailer. Ref: YH10702

PANT-Y-SAIS
Pant-Y-Sais Riding & Trekking Stables, Jersey Marine, Neath Port Talbot, **Neath Port Talbot**, SA10 6JS, **WALES**.
(T) 01792 813213.
Profile Riding School. Ref: YH10703

PANT-Y-SAIS RIDING STABLES
Pant-Y-Sais Riding Stables, Jersey Marine, Neath, **Glamorgan (Vale of)**, SA10 6JF, **WALES**.
(T) 01792 816439.
Contact/s
Manageress: Mrs J Gorvett Ref: YH10704

PANVERT, J F
Mr J F Panvert, Alexander Coach Hse, Vines Lane, Hildenborough, Tonbridge, **Kent**, TN11 9LT,

A-Z of COMPANIES

ENGLAND.
(T) 01732 838395 **(F)** 01732 838395.
Profile Supplies. **Ref: YH10705**

PAPE, R ROBIN

R Robin Pape, Lower Farley, Beauly, **Highlands**, IV4 7EY, **SCOTLAND**.
(T) 01463 782297.
Profile Farrier. **Ref: YH10706**

PAPER BEDDING SUPPLIES

Paper Bedding Supplies, Springwood Farm, Drinsey Nook Lane, Thorney, Newark, **Nottinghamshire**, NG23 7BY, **ENGLAND**.
(T) 01522 704344 **(F)** 01522 704344
(M) 0771 3358115.
Contact/s
Owner: Mr G Moulds
Profile Supplies. No.Staff: 2 Yr. Est: 1993
Opening Times
Sp: Open 07:30. Closed 17:00.
Su: Open 07:30. Closed 17:00.
Au: Open 07:30. Closed 17:00.
Wn: Open 07:30. Closed 17:00. **Ref: YH10707**

PAPERSHRED

Papershred Ltd, P O Box 56, Cwmbran, **Torfaen**, NP44 6YL, **WALES**.
(T) 01633 876656 **(F)** 01633 876656.
Profile Supplies. **Ref: YH10708**

PAPPLEWICK EQUESTRIAN CTRE

Papplewick Equestrian Centre, 151 Mansfield Rd, Papplewick, Nottingham, **Nottinghamshire**, NG15 8FL, **ENGLAND**.
(T) 0115 9636917. **Ref: YH10709**

PAPWORTH, H L

H L Papworth, Shuttleworth Ctre, Old Warden Pk, Biggleswade, **Bedfordshire**, SG18 9EA, **ENGLAND**.
(T) 01767 627317 **(F)** 01767 627764
(E) helen_vet@compuserve.com.
Profile Medical Support. **Ref: YH10710**

PARADISE RIDING CTRE

Paradise Riding Centre, Witchford Rd, Ely, **Cambridgeshire**, CB6 3NN, **ENGLAND**.
(T) 01353 662453.
Contact/s
Manager: Mr G Bedford
Profile Riding School. **Ref: YH10711**

PARC - STUD

S.D. Morgan & Sons Penparc Farm, Penparc, Lampeter, **Ceredigion**, SA48 8NU, **WALES**.
(T) 01570 493338
(W) www.parc-stud.co.uk
Affiliated Bodies WPCS.
Contact/s
General Manager: Daniel Morgan
Profile Breeder. **Ref: YH10712**

PARDOE, CHRISTOPHER H

Christopher H Pardoe BSc (Hons) AWCF, 10 Kingsley Lane, Thundersley, Benfleet, **Essex**, SS7 3TU, **ENGLAND**.
(T) 01268 741370
(M) 07836 676470.
Profile Farrier. **Ref: YH10713**

PARDOE, R C

R C Pardoe, Hill Farm, Putley, Ledbury, **Herefordshire**, HR8 2RF, **ENGLAND**.
(T) 01531 670552 **(F)** 01531 670552.
Contact/s
Owner: Mr R Pardoe **Ref: YH10714**

PARGETER, J

J Pargeter, Longmans Barn Farm, Avening, Tetbury, **Gloucestershire**, GL8 8NH, **ENGLAND**.
(T) 01453 832125.
Contact/s
Partner: Mrs J Pargeter **Ref: YH10715**

PARK CORNER FARM

Park Corner Farm, Duntisbourne Rouse, Cirencester, **Gloucestershire**, GL7 6LS, **ENGLAND**.
(T) 01285 760210 **(F)** 01285 760850.
Contact/s
General Manager: Ms S Taylor
Profile Stable/Livery. No.Staff: 1
Yr. Est: 1989 C.Size: 900 Acres **Ref: YH10716**

PARK FARM

Park Farm Riding School, Park Farm, Westwood Pk Rd, West Bergholt, Colchester, **Essex**, CO6 3DJ, **ENGLAND**.
(T) 01206 271535 **(F)** 01206 271535.
Contact/s
Owner: Mrs S Hollingsworth **(Q)** BHSI
Profile Riding School.
Offer childrens mini camps and school holiday activity days. Yr. Est: 1971 C.Size: 40 Acres
Opening Times
Sp: Open Mon - Sun 08:00. Closed Mon - Sun 17:00.
Su: Open Mon - Sun 08:00. Closed Mon - Sun 17:00.
Au: Open Mon - Sun 08:00. Closed Mon - Sun 17:00.
Wn: Open Mon - Sun 08:00. Closed Mon - Sun 17:00. **Ref: YH10717**

PARK FARM

Park Farm Riding and Livery Stables, Tunbeck Rd, Wortwell, Harleston, **Suffolk**, IP20 0HP, **ENGLAND**.
(T) 01986 86459 **(F)** 01986 86459.
Profile Riding School, Stable/Livery. **Ref: YH10718**

PARK FARM EQUESTRIAN CTRE

Park Farm Equestrian Centre, Northaw Rd West, Northaw, Potters Bar, **Hertfordshire**, EN6 4NT, **ENGLAND**.
(T) 01707 665552.
Contact/s
Owner: Miss B Venn **Ref: YH10719**

PARK FARM LIVERY

Park Farm Livery, 281 Park Rd, Kingston Upon Thames, **London (Greater)**, KT2 5LW, **ENGLAND**.
(T) 020 85468437 **(F)** 020 85468437.
Contact/s
Manager: Mr S Thompson **Ref: YH10720**

PARK FARM LIVERY YARD

Park Farm Livery Yard, Park Farm, Aldercar Lane, Langley Mill, Nottingham, **Nottinghamshire**, NG16 4HJ, **ENGLAND**.
(T) 01773 768427.
Contact/s
Owner: Mrs J Yorston **Ref: YH10721**

PARK FARM RIDING CTRE

Park Farm Riding Centre, Snettisham, King's Lynn, **Norfolk**, PE31 7NQ, **ENGLAND**.
(T) 01485 543815.
Contact/s
Owner: Mrs M Neporadnyj **Ref: YH10722**

PARK FARM SADDLERY

Park Farm Saddlery, Park Farm Riding School, Station Rd, Oakley, Basingstoke, **Hampshire**, RG23 7EH, **ENGLAND**.
(T) 01256 780375 **(F)** 01256 780375.
Contact/s
Owner: Mrs S Small
Profile Riding School, Saddlery Retailer.
Ref: YH10723

PARK FARM STABLES

Park Farm Stables, Park Farm, Ousden, Newmarket, **Suffolk**, CB8 8TN, **ENGLAND**.
(T) 01638 667189 **(F)** 01638 667189
(M) 07785 528293.
Profile Stable/Livery. **Ref: YH10724**

PARK FOOT TREKKING CTRE

Park Foot Trekking Centre, Park Foot Farm, Howtown, Penrith, **Cumbria**, CA10 2NA, **ENGLAND**.
(T) 01768 486696.
Contact/s
Owner: Mr A Hale
Profile Equestrian Centre. **Ref: YH10725**

PARK HALL FARM EQUEST CTRE

Park Hall Farm Equestrian Centre, Park Hall Farm, Mapperley, Ilkeston, **Derbyshire**, DE7 6DA, **ENGLAND**.
(T) 0115 9301581.
Profile Stable/Livery. **Ref: YH10726**

PARK HALL STABLES

Park Hall Stables, Off Park Hall Rd, Mansfield Woodhouse, **Nottinghamshire**, NG19 8QX, **ENGLAND**.
(T) 01623 620784 **(F)** 01623 620615.
Profile Medical Support. **Ref: YH10727**

PARK HSE STABLES

Park House Stables, Winchester Rd, Kingsclere, Newbury, **Berkshire**, RG20 5PY, **ENGLAND**.
(T) 01635 298244
(W) www.kingsclere.com.
Profile Trainer. **Ref: YH10728**

PARK LANE CLGE

Park Lane College, Park Lane, Leeds, **Yorkshire (West)**, LS3 1AA, **ENGLAND**.
(T) 0113 2443011 **(F)** 0113 2446372.
Profile Equestrian Centre. **Ref: YH10729**

PARK LANE LIVERIES

Park Lane Liveries & Riding Centre, Park Lane, Wirral, **Merseyside**, CH47 8XT, **ENGLAND**.
(T) 0151 6320839.
Contact/s
Instructor: Miss J Billington
Profile Riding School, Stable/Livery.
Training for disabled is available by arrangement. Full livery, prices on request. Offer organised hacks and day rides on grass or beach. The centre is mainly a hacking centre. Yr. Est: 1991
Opening Times
Sp: Open Thurs - Tues 09:00. Closed Thurs - Tues 20:00.
Su: Open Thurs - Tues 09:00. Closed Thurs - Tues 20:00.
Au: Open Thurs - Tues 09:00. Closed Thurs - Tues 20:00.
Wn: Open Thurs - Tues 09:00. Closed Thurs - Tues 20:00.
Closed on Wednesdays **Ref: YH10730**

PARK LANE RIDING SCHOOL

Park Lane Riding School Livery Stables, Park Lane, Ramsden Heath, Billericay, **Essex**, CM11 1NN, **ENGLAND**.
(T) 01268 710145.
Profile Riding School, Stable/Livery. **Ref: YH10731**

PARK LANE STABLES

Park Lane Stables, Park Lane, Teddington, **London (Greater)**, TW11 0HY, **ENGLAND**.
(T) 020 89774951.
Contact/s
Owner: Mr M Dailly
Profile Riding School. **Ref: YH10732**

PARK MANOR FARM RIDING CTRE

Park Manor Farm Riding Centre, Whaddon Rd, Newton Longville, Milton Keynes, **Buckinghamshire**, MK17 0AU, **ENGLAND**.
(T) 01908 372148 **(F)** 01908 616279.
Contact/s
Partner: Mrs C Relph **Ref: YH10733**

PARK PETS

Park Pets, 6 Park Ave, Deal, **Kent**, CT14 9AL, **ENGLAND**.
(T) 01304 375790.
Profile Saddlery Retailer. **Ref: YH10734**

PARK RIDING SCHOOL

Park Riding School, Newland St West, Lincoln, **Lincolnshire**, LN1 1QE, **ENGLAND**.
(T) 01522 526168.
Contact/s
Owner: Mr A Baker
Profile Equestrian Centre, Riding Club, Riding School. Blood hounding, Fox hunting. Yr. Est: 1930
Opening Times
Sp: Open Mon - Sun 09:00. Closed Mon - Sun 16:30.
Su: Open Mon - Sun 09:00. Closed Mon - Sun 16:30.
Au: Open Mon - Sun 09:00. Closed Mon - Sun 16:30.
Wn: Open Mon - Sun 09:00. Closed Mon - Sun 16:30.
Wednesday evenings during the summer the school opens for the riding club. **Ref: YH10735**

PARK STABLES

Park Stables, Bounstead Rd, Blackheath, Colchester, **Essex**, CO2 0DF, **ENGLAND**.
(T) 01206 576707.
Contact/s
Owner: Miss L Matthews **Ref: YH10736**

PARK STABLES

Park Stables, Parkhurst, Abinger Common, Dorking, **Surrey**, RH5 6LW, **ENGLAND**.
(T) 01306 730783.
Profile Stable/Livery. **Ref: YH10737**

PARK TONKS

Park Tonks Limited, 48 North Rd, Great Abington, **Cambridgeshire**, CB1 6AS, **ENGLAND**.
(T) 01223 891721 **(F)** 01223 893571.
Profile Medical Support. **Ref: YH10738**

PARK VETNRY CTRE

Park Veterinary Centre (The), 256 Cassiobury Drive, Watford, **Hertfordshire**, WD1 3AP, **ENGLAND**.
(T) 01923 223321 **(F)** 01923 218023.
Profile Medical Support. **Ref: YH10739**

PARK VETNRY GRP

Park Veterinary Group (Cardiff) (The), 186 Landowne Rd, Cardiff, **Glamorgan (Vale of)**, CF5 1JT, **WALES**.
(T) 029 20382211 **(F)** 029 20891494
(E) hcrobinson@email.com.
Profile Medical Support. **Ref: YH10740**

PARK VIEW RIDING CTRE

Park View Riding Centre, Park View, Chimney Lane, Lepton, Huddersfield, **Yorkshire (West)**, HD8 0NL, **ENGLAND**.
(T) 01484 425333.
Profile Riding School. **Ref: YH10741**

PARK, ADRIAN JOHN

Adrian John Park DWCF, Moor Farmhouse, Moor Lane, Charlton, Malmesbury, **Wiltshire**, SN16 9DS, **ENGLAND**.
(T) 01666 823817.
Profile Farrier. **Ref: YH10742**

PARK, I

Mr I Park, 2 Willow Bank, Durham Lane, Eaglescliffe, **Cleveland**, TS16 0PY, **ENGLAND**.
(T) 01642 580263.
Profile Supplies. **Ref: YH10743**

PARKER BROTHERS

Parker Brothers Ltd, Lark Mill, Mill St, Mildenhall, Bury St Edmunds, **Suffolk**, IP28 7DP, **ENGLAND**.
(T) 01638 713920 **(F)** 01638 711002.
Profile Supplies. **Ref: YH10744**

PARKER HANNIFIN

Parker Hannifin PLC, Woods Lane, Cradley Heath, **Midlands (West)**, B64 7AS, **ENGLAND**.
(T) 01384 566603 **(F)** 01384 567275.
Contact/s
Manager: Mr J Tillsey
Profile Blacksmith. **Ref: YH10745**

PARKER MERCHANTING

Parker Merchanting Ltd, John O'Gaunts Ind Est, Leeds Rd, Rothwell, **Yorkshire (West)**, LS26 0DU, **ENGLAND**.
(T) 0113 2822933 **(F)** 0113 2822620.
Profile Transport/Horse Boxes. **Ref: YH10746**

PARKER, C

C Parker, Douglas Hall Farm, Lockerbie, **Dumfries and Galloway**, DG11 1AD, **SCOTLAND**.
(T) 01576 510232.
Contact/s
Owner: Mr C Parker
Profile Trainer. **Ref: YH10747**

PARKER, D

Mr D Parker, The Shires, Top Of The Bank, Thurstonland, Huddersfield, **Yorkshire (West)**, HD4 6XZ, **ENGLAND**.
(T) 01484 663541 **(F)** 01484 662759.
Profile Breeder. **Ref: YH10748**

PARKER, GILL

Gill Parker SEA ARBS Sculptress, 18 Tibbs Meadow, Upper Chute, Andover, **Hampshire**, SP11 9HG, **ENGLAND**.
(T) 01264 730702 **(F)** 01264 730702
(M) 07885 273309
(E) bronze@gillparker.co.uk. **Ref: YH10749**

PARKER, KATIE

Katie Parker, Keyford Farmhouse, Frome, **Somerset**, BA11 5BG, **ENGLAND**.
(T) 01373 463842. **Ref: YH10750**

PARKER, N

N Parker, Saddlery Workshop, Chapel Farm, Hanslope Rd, Hartwell, Northampton, **Northamptonshire**, NN7 2EU, **ENGLAND**.
(T) 01908 511594.
Contact/s
Owner: Mr N Parker
Profile Saddlery Retailer. Yr. Est: 1973
Ref: YH10751

PARKER, R D

Mr R D Parker, The Croft, Swalesmoor Rd, Halifax, **Yorkshire (West)**, **ENGLAND**.
(T) 01274 882621.
Profile Breeder. **Ref: YH10752**

PARKERS

Parkers, Po Box 83, Horsham, **Sussex (West)**, RH13 7YW, **ENGLAND**.
(T) 01403 711947 **(F)** 01403 711947.
Contact/s
Owner: Mr A Parker
Profile Saddlery Retailer.
Supply a great range of saddles and bridlework. Can supply saddles for children, for general purpose and show saddles. Racing, competition and pony saddles can also be supplied. All saddles are made of the finest quality, built on a conventional English Tree. Goods are dispatched anywhere in the world.
Yr. Est: 1851
Opening Times
Sp: Open 09:00. Closed 17:00.
Su: Open 09:00. Closed 17:00.
Au: Open 09:00. Closed 17:00.
Wn: Open 09:00. Closed 17:00. **Ref: YH10753**

PARKES

Parkes, Ingersoll Hse, 7 Kingsway, London, **London (Greater)**, WC2B 6XF, **ENGLAND**.
(T) 020 73791233.
Contact/s
Manager: Mr S Henrick **Ref: YH10754**

PARKES INT TRANSPORT

Parkes International Transport Ltd, Oxford Rd, Chieveley, Newbury, **Berkshire**, RG20 8RU, **ENGLAND**.
(T) 01635 247742 **(F)** 01635 247114.
Contact/s
Owner: Mr H Parkes
Profile Transport/Horse Boxes. **Ref: YH10755**

PARKES INT TRANSPORT

Parkes International Transport Ltd, Queensberry Rd, Newmarket, **Suffolk**, CB8 9AU, **ENGLAND**.
(T) 01638 665660 **(F)** 01638 665660.
Profile Transport/Horse Boxes. **Ref: YH10756**

PARKES, J E

Mr J E Parkes, Common Farm Hse, Common Farm, Upper Helmsley, **Yorkshire (North)**, YO41 1JX, **ENGLAND**.
(T) 01759 373354.
Profile Trainer. **Ref: YH10757**

PARKES, STUART J

Stuart J Parkes AFCL, 15 Conyers Rd, Doncaster, **Yorkshire (South)**, DN5 9SD, **ENGLAND**.
(T) 01302 785656.
Profile Farrier. **Ref: YH10758**

PARKFOOT TREKKING CTRE

Parkfoot Trekking Centre, Parkfoot Caravan Pk, Howtown Rd, Pooley Bridge, Ullswater, **Cumbria**, CA10 2NA, **ENGLAND**.
(T) 01768 486696. **Ref: YH10759**

PARKGATE SADDLERY

Parkgate Saddlery, 77 Grange Rd, Parkgate, Ballyclare, **County Antrim**, BT39 0DH, **NORTHERN IRELAND**.
(T) 028 94433285 **(F)** 028 94433285.
Contact/s
Owner: Mrs D Alexander **Ref: YH10760**

PARKHEAD WELDING

Parkhead Welding Co Ltd, 20 Quarryknowe St, Glasgow, **Glasgow (City of)**, G31 5LS, **SCOTLAND**.
(T) 0141 5565485.
Profile Blacksmith. **Ref: YH10761**

PARKHOUSE STABLES

Parkhouse Stables, 91 High St, Harston, Cambridge, **Cambridgeshire**, CB2 5PZ, **ENGLAND**.
(T) 01223 870075.
Profile Riding School, Stable/Livery. **Ref: YH10762**

PARKIN, BERNARD

Bernard Parkin, Beldon Hse, Bushcombe Lane, Woodmancote, Cheltenham, **Gloucestershire**, GL52 4QQ, **ENGLAND**.
(T) 01242 672784. **Ref: YH10763**

PARKIN, KEITH JOHN

Keith John Parkin DWCF, Swallow Cottage, Stowford, Bratton Fleming, Barnstaple, **Devon**, EX31 4SG, **ENGLAND**.
(T) 01598 763545.
Profile Farrier. **Ref: YH10764**

PARKIN, M

Mrs M Parkin, UpperHse, North Lane, Cawthorne, Barnsley, **Yorkshire (South)**, S75 4AF, **ENGLAND**.
(T) 01226 790218.
Profile Breeder. **Ref: YH10765**

PARKINS, WENDY

Wendy Parkins, 9 Boxwell Pk, Bodmin, **Cornwall**, PL31 2BB, **ENGLAND**.
(T) 01208 76204.
Profile Trainer. **Ref: YH10766**

PARKINSON, R N & V

R N & V Parkinson, Pulpit Lane, Oving, Aylesbury, **Buckinghamshire**, HP22 4EZ, **ENGLAND**.
(T) 01296 641603.
Contact/s
Owner: Miss G Parkinson **Ref: YH10767**

PARKLAND SADDLEBREDS

Parkland Saddlebreds, 33 Croft St, Ipswich, **Suffolk**, IP2 8EF, **ENGLAND**.
(T) 01473 604185.
Profile Breeder. **Ref: YH10768**

PARKLANDS FARM LIVERY

Parklands Farm Livery, The Stables, Lower Green, Galleywood, Chelmsford, **Essex**, CM2 8QS, **ENGLAND**.
(T) 01245 475758.
Profile Riding School, Stable/Livery. **Ref: YH10769**

PARKLANDS RIDING SCHOOL

Parklands Riding School, Worksop Rd, Aston, Sheffield, **Yorkshire (South)**, S26 2AD, **ENGLAND**.
(T) 0114 2875278.
Contact/s
Owner: Mr R Sampson
Profile Riding School, Saddlery Retailer, Stable/Livery. **Ref: YH10770**

PARKLANDS STABLES

Parklands Stables, Loughborough Rd, Ruddington, Nottingham, **Nottinghamshire**, NG11 6AB, **ENGLAND**.
(T) 0115 9846674.
Contact/s
Owner: Mr G Atkinson **Ref: YH10771**

PARKS, DAVID

David Parks, 3 Reaskmore Rd, Dungannon, **County Tyrone**, BT70 1RR, **NORTHERN IRELAND**.
(T) 028 87761398.
Contact/s
Owner: Mr D Parks
Profile Transport/Horse Boxes. **Ref: YH10772**

PARKSIDE RIDING STABLES

Parkside Riding Stables, Wingfield Rd, Alfreton, **Derbyshire**, DE55 7AP, **ENGLAND**.
(T) 01773 835193. **Ref: YH10773**

PARKSTONE TRAILER HIRE

Parkstone Trailer Hire, 552 Ringwood Rd, Poole, **Dorset**, BH12 4LY, **ENGLAND**.
(T) 01202 722167.
Contact/s
Owner: Mr P Ainsworth
Profile Transport/Horse Boxes. **Ref: YH10774**

PARKSWOOD ANGLO-ARAB STUD

Parkswood Anglo-Arab Stud, Meadowbrook, Weeton, **Yorkshire (West)**, LS17 0AY, **ENGLAND**.
(T) 01423 734339.
Profile Breeder, Stable/Livery. **Ref: YH10775**

PARKVIEW ANDALUSIANS

Parkview Andalusians, Parkview Stables, Maidenhead Rd, Billingbear, Wokingham, **Berkshire**, RG11 5RR, **ENGLAND**.
(T) 01344 424531 **(F)** 01344 360548
(M) 07836 317460.
Profile Breeder. **Ref: YH10776**

PARKVIEW RIDING SCHOOL

Parkview Riding School, Parkview, Anstey Lane, Thurcaston, Leicester, **Leicestershire**, LE7 7JB, **ENGLAND**.
(T) 0116 2364858.
Contact/s
Owner: Mr J McDonald
Profile Riding School. **Ref: YH10777**

PARKVIEW VETNRY GRP

Parkview Veterinary Group, 70 Railway Rd, Strabane, **County Tyrone**, BT82 8EQ, **NORTHERN IRELAND**.
(T) 028 71382636.
Profile Medical Support. **Ref: YH10778**

PARKWAY

Parkway (UK) Ltd, Coppards Lane Ind Est, Northiam, **Sussex (East)**, TN31 6QR, **ENGLAND**.
(T) 01797 253900 **(F)** 01797 253811
(E) parkway.uk@virgin.net
(W) www.parkwayuk.co.uk.
Contact/s
Owner: Mr G Lewis
Profile Supplies.

Make all weather synthetic sufaces for polo, racing, showjumping, dressage, carriage driving, lungeing or general use. Yr. Est: 1977 Ref: YH10779

PARKWAY

Parkway (UK) Ltd, Paines Corner, Swife Lane, Broad Oak, Heathfield, **Sussex (East)**, TN21 8UT, **ENGLAND**.
(T) 01435 883553 (F) 01435 883770.
Profile Track/Course. Ref: YH10780

PARKWOOD FEEDS & SADDLERY

Parkwood Feeds & Saddlery, Byers Lane, South Godstone, Godstone, **Surrey**, RH9 8JQ, **ENGLAND**.
(T) 01342 893264 (F) 01342 893883. Ref: YH10781

PARKWOOD VETNRY GRP

Parkwood Veterinary Group, 62 Hensington Rd, Woodstock, **Oxfordshire**, OX7 1JL, **ENGLAND**.
(T) 01993 811355.
Profile Medical Support. Ref: YH10782

PARKYN, SHAUN & SALLY

Shaun & Sally Parkyn, Hodge Nichols Farm, Chelmarsh, Bridgnorth, **Shropshire**, WV16 6QA, **ENGLAND**.
(T) 01746 861223 (F) 01746 861223
(M) 07971 465258
(E) parkyn@eventhorse.co.uk
(W) www.eventhorses.co.uk.
Contact/s
General Manager: Mrs S Parkyn
Profile Blood Stock Agency.
Event Horse Dealer. Yr. Est: 1976
Opening Times
Telephone for an appointment. Accommodation can be arrranged nearby. Ref: YH10783

PARNHAM LANDSCAPES

Parnham Landscapes Ltd, Spear Fir Nurseries, Leeds, **Yorkshire (West)**, LS17 9EA, **ENGLAND**.
(T) 01937 574319.
Profile Track/Course. Ref: YH10784

PARR, IAN T

Ian T Parr, 12 Sterling Ave, Crosby, Liverpool, **Merseyside**, L23 0QR, **ENGLAND**.
(T) 0151 9281723.
Profile Farrier. Ref: YH10785

PARRINGTON, M C

Miss M C Parrington, Lane Side Farm, Wigglesworth, Skipton, **Yorkshire (North)**, **ENGLAND**..
Profile Trainer. Ref: YH10786

PARRIS, STEPHEN M

Stephen M Parris, 81 Wentworth Drive, Bedford, **Bedfordshire**, MK41 8QD, **ENGLAND**.
(T) 01234 346785. Ref: YH10787

PARROTT, RICHARD M

Richard M Parrott DWCF, Woodlands, Newick Lane, Heathfield, **Sussex (East)**, TN21 8PY, **ENGLAND**.
(T) 01435 863338.
Profile Farrier. Ref: YH10788

PARRY, ANDREW C

Andrew C Parry DWCF, 58 Lindley St, Norwich, **Norfolk**, NR1 2HF, **ENGLAND**.
(T) 01603 621701.
Profile Farrier. Ref: YH10789

PARRY, ERIC

Eric Parry, Pen Y Bryn, Bodffordd, Llangefni, **Isle of Anglesey**, LL77 7PJ, **WALES**.
(T) 01248 722924 (F) 01248 722924.
Contact/s
Owner: Mr E Parry Ref: YH10790

PARRY, G & M

G & M Parry, Cae Isaf, Llanddeusant, Holyhead, **Isle of Anglesey**, LL65 4AA, **WALES**.
(T) 01407 730120.
Profile Breeder. Ref: YH10791

PARRY, JOHN LLOYD (DR)

Dr John Lloyd Parry, Hon Medical Advisor, The British Horse Society, Widbrook Cottage, Cookham, **Berkshire**, SL6 9RB, **ENGLAND**.
(T) 01628 851199 (F) 01628 851105.
Profile Medical Support. Ref: YH10792

PARRY, K G

K G Parry, Green Farm, Buttington, Welshpool, **Powys**, SY21 8SX, **WALES**.
(T) 01938 570237.
Profile Supplies. Ref: YH10793

PARRY-JONES, A W

A W Parry-Jones, Graig Fawr Riding Stables, Pontypridd, **Rhondda Cynon Taff**, CF38 1NF, **WALES**.
(T) 029 20883659.
Profile Farrier. Ref: YH10794

PARSLOW, JONATHAN D

Jonathan D Parslow DWCF, 2 Stanchester Cottage, Old Church Way, Stanchester, Curry Rivel, **Somerset**, TA10 0EB, **ENGLAND**.
(T) 01458 250585.
Profile Farrier. Ref: YH10795

PARSLOW, PHILLIP J

Phillip J Parslow DWCF, 8 Fifth Row, Linton, Morpeth, **Northumberland**, NE61 5SL, **ENGLAND**.
(T) 01670 861580.
Profile Farrier. Ref: YH10796

PARSONAGE FARM RACING STABLES

Parsonage Farm Racing Stables, Newbury Rd, East Garston, Hungerford, **Berkshire**, RG17 7ER, **ENGLAND**.
(T) 01488 648822 (F) 01488 648185
(M) 07860 811127.
Profile Trainer. Ref: YH10797

PARSONAGE, GARY

Gary Parsonage, 16 Folville St, Ashby Folville, Melton Mowbray, **Leicestershire**, LE14 2TE, **ENGLAND**.
(T) 01664 77330.
Profile Trainer. Ref: YH10798

PARSONS, G R

Mrs G R Parsons M Rad A, Westering, Hillbrow, Liss, **Hampshire**, GU33 7QE, **ENGLAND**.
(T) 01730 893858.
Profile Medical Support. Ref: YH10799

PARSONS, KRIS

Kris Parsons, The Old Dairy, Wyld Court, Hawkchurch, Axminster, **Devon**, EX13 5TZ, **ENGLAND**.
(T) 01297 678674 (F) 01297 678674.
Contact/s
Owner: Mr K Parsons
Profile Blacksmith. Ref: YH10800

PARSONS, ROYSTON J

Royston J Parsons, Tynewydd Hse, Llanwenarth Citra, Abergavenny, **Monmouthshire**, NP7 7ET, **WALES**.
(T) 01873 811798.
Profile Farrier. Ref: YH10801

PARTIS, COLIN

Colin Partis, 33 The Drive, Gil Fach, Bargoed, **Caerphilly**, CF8 8JX, **WALES**.
(T) 01443 832021.
Profile Farrier. Ref: YH10802

PARTNERS PET SUPERMARKET

Partners Pet Supermarket (Bedford), 35-37 Ampthill Rd, Bedford, **Bedfordshire**, MK42 9JP, **ENGLAND**.
(T) 01234 211611 (F) 01234 219963.
Profile Supplies. Ref: YH10803

PARTNERS PET SUPERMARKET

Partners Pet Supermarket, 27 Heddon Court Prde, Cockfosters, Barnet, **Hertfordshire**, EN4 0DB, **ENGLAND**.
(T) 020 84499345.
Profile Supplies. Ref: YH10804

PARTNERS PET SUPERMARKET

Partners Pet Supermarket (St Albans), North Orbital Rd, London Colney, St Albans, **Hertfordshire**, AL2 1DL, **ENGLAND**.
(T) 01727 827500 (F) 01727 827400
(E) sales@partnerspets.com.
Profile Supplies. Ref: YH10805

PARTRIDGE CLOSE STUD

Partridge Close Stud, Lanchester, **County Durham**, DH7 0SZ, **ENGLAND**.
(T) 01207 520066 (F) 01207 520066.
Profile Breeder. Ref: YH10806

PARTRIDGE, M A

M A Partridge, 3 Hembury Pk, Buckfast, Buckfastleigh, **Devon**, TQ11 0ES, **ENGLAND**.
(T) 01364 643040.
Profile Farrier. Ref: YH10807

PARTRIDGE, NICHOLAS S

Nicholas S Partridge DWCF, Yew Tree Cottage, The Quarry, Brockhampton, Cheltenham, **Gloucestershire**, GL54 5XL, **ENGLAND**.
(T) 01242 870585
(M) 07785 905139.
Profile Farrier. Ref: YH10808

PASCOE, A L

A L Pascoe, 19A Hayle Rd, Fraddam, Hayle, **Cornwall**, TR27 6EH, **ENGLAND**.
(T) 01736 850708.
Contact/s
Owner: Mr A Pascoe
Profile Breeder. Ref: YH10809

PASSFORD HSE HOTEL

Passford House Hotel, Lymington, **Hampshire**, SO41 8LS, **ENGLAND**.
(T) 01590 682398 (F) 01590 683494.
Profile Equestrian Centre. Ref: YH10810

PASSMORE, M J

M J Passmore, Burrow Cottage, Brook St, Timberscombe, Minehead, **Somerset**, TA24 7TG, **ENGLAND**.
(T) 01643 841185.
Profile Transport/Horse Boxes. Ref: YH10811

PASSMORES PORTABLE BUILDINGS

Passmores Portable Buildings Ltd, High St & Canal Rd, Strood, Rochester, **Kent**, ME2 4DR, **ENGLAND**.
(T) 01634 290033 (F) 01634 290084
(E) buildings@passmores.co.uk.
Contact/s
Sales: Mr S Slaughter
Profile Transport/Horse Boxes. Ref: YH10812

PASTURES CLEAN

Pastures Clean, Murcot Farm, Murcot, Broadway, **Worcestershire**, WR12 7HS, **ENGLAND**.
(T) 01386 830341.
Profile Supplies.
Offer a Paddock Vacuum hire service. Ref: YH10813

PATCHES

Patches, 3 Mews Cottages, Cryers Hill, High Wycombe, **Buckinghamshire**, HP15 6JT, **ENGLAND**.
(T) 01494 712129.
Profile Supplies. Ref: YH10814

PATCHETTS

Patchetts Equestrian Centre, Hilfield Lane, Aldenham, Watford, **Hertfordshire**, WD2 8DP, **ENGLAND**.
(T) 01923 855776/852255 (F) 01923 859289
(W) www.patchetts.co.uk.
Contact/s
Livery Manager: Miss L Tuke
Profile Riding Wear Retailer, Saddlery Retailer, Stable/Livery, Supplies. Show Centre.
There are two indoor schools, one 20m x 60m, one 20m x 50m. The outdoor school is 20m x 60m, the jumping arena is 60m x 80m and outdoor. Livery is available, prices on request. The site is used to hold British Show Jumping, and British Dressage shows.
Opening Times
Sp: Open Mon - Sun 07:30. Closed Mon - Sun 21:30.
Su: Open Mon - Sun 07:30. Closed Mon - Sun 21:30.
Au: Open Mon - Sun 07:30. Closed Mon - Sun 21:30.
Wn: Open Mon - Sun 07:30. Closed Mon - Sun 21:30. Ref: YH10815

PATCHING LIVERY YARD

Patching Livery Yard, Dairy Lane, Patching, Worthing, **Sussex (West)**, BN13 3XL, **ENGLAND**.
(T) 01903 871255.
Profile Stable/Livery. Ref: YH10816

PATCHWORK

Patchwork-Mobile Rug and Tack Repairs, Wester Mosshat, West Calder, **Lothian (West)**, EH55 8LL, **SCOTLAND**.
(T) 01501 785220.
Contact/s
Owner: Ms J Horberry
Profile Rug and Tack Repairs.
Mobile repair service. Yr. Est: 1991 Ref: YH10817

PATEMAN, C W

C W Pateman, North End Hse, Luckington, Chippenham, **Wiltshire**, SN14 6PN, **ENGLAND**.
(T) 01666 840287.

Profile Farrier. Ref: YH10818

PATERSON, ALEXANDER MILLER

Alexander Miller Paterson, Parkhead Farm, Braehead Forth, **Lanarkshire (South)**, ML11 8HA, **SCOTLAND**.
(T) 01555 811049.
Profile Farrier. Ref: YH10819

PATEY

Patey (London) Ltd, 1 Amelia St, London, **London (Greater)**, SE17 3PY, **ENGLAND**.
(T) 020 77036528.
Profile Supplies. Hat Manufacturer. Ref: YH10820

PATHHEAD STABLES

Pathhead Stables, Forfar Rd, Kirriemuir, **Angus**, DD8 5BY, **SCOTLAND**.
(T) 01575 572173 **(F)** 01575 575272
(W) www.pathhead.com
Affiliated Bodies ABRS.
Contact/s
Owner: Mrs J Collins
(E) joycecollins@pathhead.com
Profile Riding School, Riding Wear Retailer, Stable/Livery, Supplies. No.Staff: 5
Yr. Est: 1995 C.Size: 80 Acres
Opening Times
Sp: Open Tues - Sun 09:00. Closed Tues - Sun 17:00.
Su: Open Tues - Sun 09:00. Closed Tues - Sun 17:00.
Au: Open Tues - Sun 09:00. Closed Tues - Sun 17:00.
Wn: Open Tues - Sun 09:00. Closed Tues - Sun 17:00.
Closed on Mondays Ref: YH10821

PATHLOW RIDING CTRE

Pathlow Riding Centre, Featherbed Lane, Pathlow, Stratford-upon-Avon, **Warwickshire**, CV37 0ER, **ENGLAND**.
(T) 01789 299984. Ref: YH10822

PATON-SMITH, JASON C

Jason C Paton-Smith DWCF, 1 Brenley Bridge Cottages, Brenley Lane, Boughton, **Kent**, ME13 9LZ, **ENGLAND**.
(T) 01227 750681.
Profile Farrier. Ref: YH10823

PATRICK PINKER

Patrick Pinker (Game Farm) Ltd, Saddlery Shop, Latteridge Lane, Iron Acton, Bristol, **Bristol**, BS37 9TY, **ENGLAND**.
(T) 01454 228109.
Contact/s
Owner: Mr P Pinker
Profile Saddlery Retailer. Ref: YH10824

PATRICK WILKINSON

Patrick Wilkinson (Saddlers Ltd), 108 Walkergate, Beverley, **Yorkshire (East)**, HU17 9BT, **ENGLAND**.
(T) 01482 870800 **(F)** 01482 883376
(W) www.onlinesaddlery.co.uk
Affiliated Bodies SMS.
Contact/s
Owner: Mr P Wilkinson
(E) patrick@onlinesaddlery.co.uk
Profile Riding Wear Retailer, Saddlery Retailer, Supplies. No.Staff: 4 Yr. Est: 1988
Opening Times
Sp: Open 09:00. Closed 17:30.
Su: Open 09:00. Closed 17:30.
Au: Open 09:00. Closed 17:30.
Wn: Open 09:00. Closed 17:30. Ref: YH10825

PATS VIGORS PHOTOGRAPHY

Pats Vigors Photography, Great Chalfield Manor, Melksham, **Wiltshire**, SN12 8NJ, **ENGLAND**.
(T) 01225 782239. Ref: YH10826

PATTEN, D

D Patten, Knowsley Lane Farm, Knowsley Lane, Knowsley, Prescot, **Merseyside**, L34 4AH, **ENGLAND**.
(T) 0151 4893498.
Contact/s
Owner: Mrs D Patten
Profile Stable/Livery.
DIY livery available. Ref: YH10827

PATTENDEN, KEVIN J

Kevin J Pattenden, 56 Pollards Drive, Horsham, **Sussex (West)**, RH13 5HH, **ENGLAND**.
(T) 01403 261563.
Profile Farrier. Ref: YH10828

PATTERSON, W

W Patterson, Bennybeg Smithy, Crieff, **Perth and Kinross**, PH7 4HN, **SCOTLAND**.
(T) 01764 654993 **(F)** 01764 654993.
Contact/s
Owner: Mr W Patterson
Profile Blacksmith. Ref: YH10829

PATTIES OF DUMFRIES

Patties of Dumfries, 109 Queensbury St, Dumfries, **Dumfries and Galloway**, DG1 1BH, **SCOTLAND**.
(T) 01387 252891.
Profile Saddlery Retailer. Ref: YH10830

PATTULLO & PARTNERS

Pattullo & Partners Ltd, Sevenoaks Cattle Market, 154 London Rd, Sevenoaks, **Kent**, TN13 1DJ, **ENGLAND**.
(T) 01732 452329 **(F)** 01732 742448. Ref: YH10831

PAUL HUTCHINSON

Paul Hutchinson Saddlery Repairs, Holborn Stables, 70A Holborn Hill, Ormskirk, **Lancashire**, L39 3LJ, **ENGLAND**.
(T) 01695 570761.
Profile Saddlery Retailer, Supplies. Ref: YH10832

PAUL, G W

Mr G W Paul, Bluegates, Wherstead, Ipswich, **Suffolk**, IP9 2AU, **ENGLAND**.
(T) 01473 730274 **(F)** 01473 730136.
Profile Breeder. Ref: YH10833

PAUL, NIGEL

Nigel Paul Blacksmith, Unit 2, Body Repair Ctre, Yeovil Rd, Crewkerne, **Somerset**, TA18 7NS, **ENGLAND**.
(T) 01460 73144.
Contact/s
Owner: Mr N Paul
Profile Blacksmith. Ref: YH10834

PAULDARY STUD

Pauldary Stud, Barefoot Farm Buildings, Wheatham Rd, Liss, **Hampshire**, GU33 6JR, **ENGLAND**.
(T) 01730 827044.
Contact/s
Partner: Ms P Filer
Profile Breeder. Ref: YH10835

PAULINE ROBSON LIVERY

Pauline Robson Livery, Kidlaw Farm, Capheaton, Newcastle-upon-Tyne, **Tyne and Wear**, NE19 2AW, **ENGLAND**.
(T) 01830 530241.
Profile Stable/Livery. Ref: YH10836

PAULL, C W

C W Paull, The Forge, 4 Cheddon Fitzpaine, Taunton, **Somerset**, TA2 8JU, **ENGLAND**.
(T) 01823 412282.
Profile Farrier. Ref: YH10837

PAVESCO UK

Pavesco UK Ltd, 116 High Rd, Needham, Harleston, **Suffolk**, IP20 9LG, **ENGLAND**.
(T) 01379 852885 **(F)** 01379 854178.
Profile Medical Support. Ref: YH10838

PAVORD, MARCY

Marcy Pavord, Lower Pen-Y-Graig Farm, Llanfoist, Abergavenny, **Monmouthshire**, NP7 9LE, **WALES**.
(T) 01873 859207 **(F)** 01873 858186. Ref: YH10839

PAWLEY, ZARA

Miss Zara Pawley, Croft Hse, North St, Kings Lynn, **Norfolk**, PE32 2LR, **ENGLAND**.
(T) 01328 701587.
Profile Trainer. Ref: YH10840

PAWS & HOOFS

Paws & Hoofs, 10 Jordon Way, Aldridge, **Midlands (West)**, WS9 8SB, **ENGLAND**.
(M) 07974 020786
(E) michelle@hoof.demon.co.uk.
Profile Medical Support. Ref: YH10841

PAWSON, R E

R E Pawson, 26 Abbey Rd, Ulceby, **Lincolnshire (North)**, DN39 6TJ, **ENGLAND**.
(T) 01469 588332.
Contact/s
Owner: Mrs I Pawson Ref: YH10842

PAXTON & CLARK

Paxton & Clark Ltd, Waverley Trce, Bonnyrigg, **Lothian (Mid)**, EH19 3BD, **SCOTLAND**.
(T) 0131 6639206.
Profile Blacksmith. Ref: YH10843

PAXWELD

Paxweld, Unit 3 Station Rd, Bourton-on-the-Water, Cheltenham, **Gloucestershire**, GL54 2ER, **ENGLAND**.
(T) 01451 821877 **(F)** 01451 822872.
Contact/s
Owner: Mr T King
Profile Blacksmith. Ref: YH10844

PAY, RICHARD

Richard Pay DWCF, Fays Harvest, Mill Lane, Fobbing, **Essex**, SS17 9HP, **ENGLAND**.
(T) 01375 361073.
Profile Farrier. Ref: YH10845

PAYNE BROS

Payne Bros (East Anglia) Ltd, Helhoughton Rd, Hempton, Fakenham, **Norfolk**, NR21 7DY, **ENGLAND**.
(T) 01328 864864 **(F)** 01328 856900.
Profile Transport/Horse Boxes. Ref: YH10846

PAYNE STEEPLECHASE FENCES

Payne Steeplechase Fences, Pensarn Hse, Cwm Lane, Highcross, **Newport**, NP1 9GQ, **WALES**.
(T) 01633 892175.
Profile Trainer. Ref: YH10847

PAYNE, J R

Mr J R Payne, Lower Holworthy Farm, Brompton Regis, Dulverton, **Somerset**, TA22 9NY, **ENGLAND**.
(T) 01398 327244.
Profile Supplies. Ref: YH10848

PAYNE, J W

J W Payne, Frankland Lodge, Hamilton Rd, Newmarket, **Suffolk**, CB8 7JQ, **ENGLAND**.
(T) 01638 668675
(M) 07850 133116
(W) www.newmarketracehorsetrainers.co.uk
Affiliated Bodies Newmarket Trainers Fed.
Contact/s
Trainer: Mr J Payne
Profile Trainer. Ref: YH10849

PAYNE, MARK A

Mark A Payne DWCF, 7 Bridge Trce, Michaelston-Y-Fedw, Cardiff, **Glamorgan (Vale of)**, CF3 6YZ, **WALES**.
(T) 01589 226564.
Profile Farrier. Ref: YH10850

PAYNE, MATTHEW

Matthew Payne, 29 New Rd, Okehampton, **Devon**, EX20 1JE, **ENGLAND**.
(T) 01837 55967.
Profile Saddlery Retailer. Ref: YH10851

PAYNE, NIKKI

Nikki Payne, 2 Water Villas, Rock Hill Rd, Pleasant Valley, Egerton, **Kent**, TN27 9ED, **ENGLAND**.
(T) 01233 756447
(M) 07721 336232.
Profile Supplies. Ref: YH10852

PAYNE, SAMUEL M

Samuel M Payne DWCF, 13 Wanstead Rd, Dundonald, **County Down**, BT16 0EJ, **NORTHERN IRELAND**.
(T) 028 90484781.
Profile Farrier. Ref: YH10853

PEACE COLLECTION

Peace Collection (The), Thornes Farm, Icomb Lane, Stow-on-the-Wold, **Gloucestershire**, GL54 1JQ, **ENGLAND**.
(T) 01451 830459 **(F)** 01451 830259. Ref: YH10854

PEACE SEEDS

Peace Seeds, Rupert's Hse, Bowers Hill, Evesham, **Worcestershire**, WR11 5HG, **ENGLAND**.
(T) 01386 830262 **(F)** 01386 833295.
Profile Medical Support. Ref: YH10855

PEACEHAVEN RIDING CTRE

Peacehaven Riding Centre, Terrace Lane, Penyffordd, Chester, **Cheshire**, CH4 0HB, **ENGLAND**.
(T) 01244 546819.
Contact/s
Owner: Mrs V Williams
Profile Riding School, Saddlery Retailer.
Ref: YH10856

PEACHEY, H E

Mr H E Peachey, Woodlands, 2 Ridgway, Stratford-upon-Avon, **Warwickshire**, CV37 9JL, **ENGLAND**.
(T) 01789 294520.
Profile Supplies. Ref: YH10857

Key: **(T)** telephone **(F)** fax **(M)** mobile **(E)** E-Mail Address **(W)** Website Address **(Q)** Qualifications
Yr. Est: Year Established C.Size: Complex Size Sp: Spring Su: Summer Au: Autumn Wn: Winter

PEACHEY, KA

Kevin and Samson's Equine Services, 43 Windrush Way, Maidenhead, **Berkshire**, SL6 8AR, **ENGLAND**.
(T) 01628 621308.
Contact/s
Owner: Mr K Peachey **(Q)** BHS-Driving
Profile Trainer. Equine services.
Heavy Horse driving, instruction, harnessing and demonstrations, available No.Staff: 2
Yr. Est: 2001 **Ref: YH10858**

PEACOCK FARMS

Peacock Farms, Waterloo Farm, Morley, Wymondham, **Norfolk**, NR18 9TE, **ENGLAND**.
(T) 01953 601561 **(F)** 01953 600678.
Profile Breeder. **Ref: YH10859**

PEACOCK, C J

C J Peacock, Nash Vineyard, Horsham Rd, Steyning, **Sussex (West)**, BN44 3AA, **ENGLAND**.
(T) 01903 813445.
Profile Farrier. **Ref: YH10860**

PEACOCK, R

R Peacock, 8 Turvers Lane, Ramsey, Huntingdon, **Cambridgeshire**, PE17 1ES, **ENGLAND**.
(T) 01487 812490.
Profile Breeder. **Ref: YH10861**

PEACOCK, R E

R E Peacock, Oliver Hse Stud, Chedglow, Malmesbury, **Wiltshire**, SN16 9EZ, **ENGLAND**.
(T) 01666 577238.
Contact/s
Owner: Mr C Peacock
Profile Trainer. **Ref: YH10862**

PEACOCK, RAYMOND JAMES

Raymond James Peacock DWCF, 168 Cramptons Rd, Sevenoaks, **Kent**, TN14 5DZ, **ENGLAND**.
(T) 01732 465425.
Profile Farrier. **Ref: YH10863**

PEAK SECURITY SVS

Peak Security Services, Peak Security Building, Waterswallows Rd, Buxton, **Derbyshire**, SK17 7JR, **ENGLAND**.
(T) 01298 24012 **(F)** 01298 79913
(M) 07836 541597. **Ref: YH10864**

PEAK TRAILERS

Peak Trailers Ltd, Waterloo Ind Est, Waterloo Rd, Bidford-on-Avon, Alcester, **Warwickshire**, B50 4JH, **ENGLAND**.
(T) 01789 773111 **(F)** 01789 490331.
Profile Transport/Horse Boxes. **Ref: YH10865**

PEAKDALE SADDLERY

Peakdale Saddlery, Hallsteads Ind Est, Dove Holes, Buxton, **Derbyshire**, SK17 8BP, **ENGLAND**.
(T) 01298 814040
Affiliated Bodies BETA.
Contact/s
Owner: Jack Richardson
Profile Feed Merchant, Riding Wear Retailer, Saddlery Retailer, Supplies.
Specialists in straight cut saddles, including dressage, show, show hunter and working hunter. No.Staff: 1
Yr. Est: 1996
Opening Times
Sp: Open 09:30. Closed 17:30.
Su: Open 09:30. Closed 17:30.
Au: Open 09:30. Closed 17:30.
Wn: Open 09:30. Closed 17:30. **Ref: YH10866**

PEAR TREE LAKE

Pear Tree Lake Equestrian Centre, Balterley Green Rd, Balterley, Crewe, **Cheshire**, CW2 5QE, **ENGLAND**.
(T) 01270 820307 **(F)** 01270 820868.
Contact/s
Owner: Mr D Doulgas **Ref: YH10867**

PEARCE, A W

A W Pearce, Myrtle Farm, Oldbury Naite, Oldbury-on-Severn, Bristol, **Bristol**, BS35 1RU, **ENGLAND**.
(T) 01454 412056.
Contact/s
Owner: Mr A Pearce
Profile Transport/Horse Boxes. **Ref: YH10868**

PEARCE, ANTHONY P

Anthony P Pearce RSS, Court Hill, Bardfield Rd, Finchingfield, Braintree, **Essex**, CM7 4LX, **ENGLAND**.
(T) 01371 811328.
Profile Farrier. **Ref: YH10869**

PEARCE, B A

Mr B A Pearce, Sheridan Farm, West Park Rd, Newchapel, Lingfield, **Surrey**, RH7 6HT, **ENGLAND**.
(T) 01342 713437
(M) 07889 189564.
Profile Trainer. **Ref: YH10870**

PEARCE, H & C

H & C Pearce Ltd, Aylesbury Rd, Thame, **Oxfordshire**, OX9 3AS, **ENGLAND**.
(T) 01844 212034 **(F)** 01844 261358.
Contact/s
Manager: Mr R Gronmark
Profile Supplies. **Ref: YH10871**

PEARCE, J & A

J & A Pearce, Penllyne Court, Glyncoch, Trapp, St Clears, Carmarthen, **Carmarthenshire**, **WALES**.
(T) 01994 230871.
Profile Breeder. **Ref: YH10872**

PEARCE, K R

Mr K R Pearce, The Brambles, Mapsland Rd, Laugharne, **Carmarthenshire**, SA33 4QP, **WALES**.
(T) 01267 232360 **(F)** 01267 237083
(E) sandra.pearce@talk21.com.
Profile Supplies. **Ref: YH10873**

PEARCE, MICHAEL

Michael Pearce, Badgers Lodge, Badgers Cross, Gulval, Penzance, **Cornwall**, TR20 8XE, **ENGLAND**.
(T) 01736 350270 **(F)** 01736 350270.
Contact/s
Owner: Mr M Pearce
Profile Blacksmith. **Ref: YH10874**

PEARCE, P

Mrs P Pearce, 26 Stafford St, St George, Telford, **Shropshire**, TF2 9JQ, **ENGLAND**.
(T) 01952 615088.
Profile Breeder. **Ref: YH10875**

PEARS, ROBERT A

Robert A Pears DWCF, Forge Cottage, Main Rd, Raithby, Spilsby, **Lincolnshire**, PE23 4DS, **ENGLAND**.
(T) 01790 752121.
Profile Farrier. **Ref: YH10876**

PEARSON, A

Mr A Pearson, 1 Princess Plantation, Firbeck, Worksop, **Nottinghamshire**, S81 8LB, **ENGLAND**.
(T) 01709 812341. **Ref: YH10877**

PEARSON, D

Mr D Pearson, 1 Birchtree Pl, Thorton, **Fife**, KY1 4AU, **SCOTLAND**.
(T) 01592 774589.
Profile Trainer. **Ref: YH10878**

PEARSON, D

D Pearson, Ringehay Farm, Basford, Leek, **Staffordshire**, ST13 7ET, **ENGLAND**.
(T) 01538 360251.
Contact/s
Owner: Mr P Pearson
Profile Farrier. **Ref: YH10879**

PEARSON, H

H Pearson, Blue Hse Point Rd, Portrack Ind Est, Stockton-on-Tees, **Cleveland**, TS18 2PQ, **ENGLAND**.
(T) 01642 676490.
Profile Blacksmith. **Ref: YH10880**

PEARSON, MICHAEL

Michael Pearson, Whitegates, Button End, Harston, **Cambridgeshire**, CB2 5NX, **ENGLAND**.
(T) 01223 871072.
Profile Supplies. **Ref: YH10881**

PEARSON, S R

Mrs S R Pearson, The Stables, Great Wacton, Bredenbury, Bromyard, **Herefordshire**, HR7 4TG, **ENGLAND**.
(T) 01885 482418.
Profile Stable/Livery. **Ref: YH10882**

PEASEBROOK

Peasebrook Racing, Cheltenham Rd, Broadway, **Worcestershire**, WR12 7LX, **ENGLAND**.
(T) 01386 858980 **(F)** 01386 858943.
Contact/s
Owner: Mr B Doran
(E) racer@netline.uk
Profile Trainer.
Mr Doran is an ex-Jump Jockey.
Opening Times
Telephone for an appointment, there is an answer-phone. **Ref: YH10883**

PEASRIDGE, S S

Peasridge S S Limited, Stonelink, Stubb Lane, Brede, Rye, **Sussex (East)**, TN31 6BL, **ENGLAND**.
(T) 01424 882900 **(F)** 01424 882926.
Profile Supplies. **Ref: YH10884**

PEATE, JEFFREY

Jeffrey Peate, Manor Farm Stud, Bells Yew Green, Tunbridge Wells, **Kent**, TN3 9BH, **ENGLAND**.
(T) 01892 750288 **(F)** 01892 750061.
Contact/s
Partner: Mrs P Peate
Profile Stable/Livery.
Livery yard for resting race horses, mares and foals.
Opening Times
Sp: Open Mon - Sun 07:45. Closed Mon - Sun 17:00.
Su: Open Mon - Sun 07:45. Closed Mon - Sun 17:00.
Au: Open Mon - Sun 07:45. Closed Mon - Sun 17:00.
Wn: Open Mon - Sun 07:45. Closed Mon - Sun 17:00. **Ref: YH10885**

PEATLING

Peatling Saddlery & Country Clothing, Kibworth Rd, Wistow, Leicester, **Leicestershire**, LE8 0QF, **ENGLAND**.
(T) 0116 2590000 **(F)** 0116 2590000.
Contact/s
Partner: Mrs M Wood **Ref: YH10886**

PEATLING SADDLERY

Peatling Saddlery, White Hse Farm, Main St, Bruntingthorpe, Lutterworth, **Leicestershire**, LE17 5QF, **ENGLAND**.
(T) 0116 2478000 **(F)** 0116 2478000.
Contact/s
Partner: Miss A Wood
Profile Saddlery Retailer. **Ref: YH10887**

PEBSHAM RIDING SCHOOL

Pebsham Riding School, Pebsham Lane, Bexhill-on-Sea, **Sussex (East)**, TN40 2RZ, **ENGLAND**.
(T) 01424 732637.
Contact/s
Owner: Mrs A Rodrijuez
Profile Riding School. **Ref: YH10888**

PEBWORTH VALE

Pebworth Vale, Moat Farm, Pebworth, Stratford-upon-Avon, **Warwickshire**, CV37 8AW, **ENGLAND**.
(T) 01789 720900 **(F)** 01789 720900.
Contact/s
Owner: Mrs K Boulton **Ref: YH10889**

PEBWORTH VALE SADDLERY

Pebworth Vale Saddlery & Equestrian Centre, Moat Farm, Dorsington, Stratford-upon-Avon, **Warwickshire**, CV37 8AN, **ENGLAND**.
(T) 01789 720900.
Profile Riding School, Saddlery Retailer, Stable/Livery. **Ref: YH10890**

PEDEN BLOODSTOCK

Peden Bloodstock Limited, Borough Court, Hartley Wintney, Hook, **Hampshire**, RG27 8JA, **ENGLAND**.
(T) 01252 844042 **(F)** 01252 844043
(E) shipping@peden.co.uk.
Profile Transport/Horse Boxes. **Ref: YH10891**

PEDEN, D W

D W Peden, Bakersfield/Bullscross Farm, Bulls Cross Ride, Waltham Cross, **Hertfordshire**, EN7 5HS, **ENGLAND**.
(T) 01992 788512.
Contact/s
Owner: Mr D Peden
Profile Stable/Livery. **Ref: YH10892**

PEDLEY, JOHN D C

John D C Pedley DWCF, 1 Beaker Cottage, Pannal Rd, Follifoot, Harrogate, **Yorkshire (North)**, HG3 1DN, **ENGLAND**.
(T) 01423 870912
(M) 07836 739371.
Profile Farrier. **Ref: YH10893**

PEDRICK, R

R Pedrick, 17 Cooks Cl, Ashburton, Newton Abbot, **Devon**, TQ13 7AN, **ENGLAND**.
(T) 01364 652023.
Contact/s
Owner: Mr R Pedrick
Profile Farrier. **Ref: YH10894**

PEEBLES & DISTRICT
Peebles & District Riding Club, 5a Rosetta Rd, Peebles, **Scottish Borders**, EH45 8JU, **SCOTLAND**.
(T) 01721 720085.
Contact/s
Chairman: Mr D Parker
Profile Club/Association, Riding Club. **Ref: YH10895**

PEEBLES HYDRO STABLES
Peebles Hydro Stables, Innerleithen Rd, Peebles, **Scottish Borders**, EH45 8BQ, **SCOTLAND**.
(T) 01721 721325.
Profile Farrier, Riding School. **Ref: YH10896**

PEEKE, ALBERT
Albert Peeke AFCL BI, 92 St Michaels Rd, Sheerwater, Woking, **Surrey**, GU21 5TZ, **ENGLAND**.
(T) 01276 858416.
Profile Farrier. **Ref: YH10897**

PEEKS THE EVENT MAKERS
Peeks the Event Makers, Reid St, Christchurch, **Dorset**, BH23 2BT, **ENGLAND**.
(T) 01202 489489 **(F)** 01202 489400. **Ref: YH10898**

PEEL VETNRY GRP
Peel Veterinary Group (The), Peel Pl, North Bar Without, Beverley, **Yorkshire (East)**, HU17 7AH, **ENGLAND**.
(T) 01482 882377.
Profile Medical Support. **Ref: YH10899**

PEERS, PETER S
Peter S Peers DWCF, Little Rhode Farm, Green Lane, Rhodes Minnis, Canterbury, **Kent**, CT4 6XU, **ENGLAND**.
(T) 01303 863835.
Profile Farrier. **Ref: YH10900**

PEGASUS
Pegasus Quality Show Jumps, Lansdowne, Kings Arms Lane, Polebrook, Peterborough, **Cambridgeshire**, PE8 5LW, **ENGLAND**.
(T) 01832 273919
(E) sales@pegasus-sj.co.uk
(W) www.pegasus-sj.co.uk.
Profile Supplies. Manufacturers of Show Jumps.
Manufacturers of show jumps and portable cross country fences. They offer three ranges of fences, the BSJA range, standard range and the paddock range. Deliveries are available. Telephone for further information Yr. Est: 1980 **Ref: YH10901**

PEGASUS
Pegasus, 43 Cartlett, Haverfordwest, **Pembrokeshire**, SA61 2LH, **WALES**.
(T) 01437 765711 **(F)** 01437 765711.
Contact/s
Manager: Mrs M Butcher
Profile Saddlery Retailer, Supplies. **Ref: YH10902**

PEGASUS
Pegasus, 7-8 St. James St, Taunton, **Somerset**, TA1 1JH, **ENGLAND**.
(T) 01823 284613.
Contact/s
Owner: Mr C Robinson
Profile Riding Wear Retailer. **Ref: YH10903**

PEGASUS HOLDINGS
Pegasus Holdings, Frogmore Hse, The Forest, Hatfield Broad Oak, Bishop's Stortford, **Essex**, CM22 7BT, **ENGLAND**.
(T) 01279 718191 **(F)** 01279 718914.
Profile Medical Support. **Ref: YH10904**

PEGASUS HORSESHOES
Pegasus Horseshoes, Pledgers Yard, West St, Stamford, **Lincolnshire**, PE9 2JD, **ENGLAND**.
(T) 01780 54531.
Profile Farrier. **Ref: YH10905**

PEGASUS PONY TREKKING CTRE
Pegasus Pony Trekking Centre, Coed Farm, Patrishaw, Abergavenny, **Monmouthshire**, NP7 7LY, **WALES**.
(T) 01873 890425.
Profile Equestrian Centre. **Ref: YH10906**

PEGASUS SADDLERY
Pegasus Saddlery, Elliot St, Newcastle, **Staffordshire**, ST5 1JL, **ENGLAND**.
(T) 01782 740123.
Contact/s
Owner: Mr R Fairbrother
Profile Saddlery Retailer. **Ref: YH10907**

PEGASUS TRAILERS
Pegasus Trailers (UK) Ltd, Elms Farm, Watling St, Hinckley, **Leicestershire**, LE10 3EE, **ENGLAND**.
(T) 01455 616199 **(F)** 01455 632211.
Profile Transport/Horse Boxes. **Ref: YH10908**

PELHAMS
Pelhams, The Old Barn, Mares Pond Farm, Loxhill, Godalming, **Surrey**, GU8 4BD, **ENGLAND**.
(T) 01483 208060 **(F)** 01483 208030
(E) info@pelhams.co.uk
(W) www.pelhams.co.uk.
Contact/s
Administration: Muriel Bullard
Profile Property Agents.
Equestrian and country property agents for property across the South and South East of England.
No.Staff: 7
Opening Times
Sp: Open Mon - Fri 09:00. Closed Mon - Fri 17:00.
Su: Open Mon - Fri 09:00. Closed Mon - Fri 17:00.
Au: Open Mon - Fri 09:00. Closed Mon - Fri 17:00.
Wn: Open Mon - Fri 09:00. Closed Mon - Fri 17:00.
Weekends by appointment. **Ref: YH10909**

PELL, DAVID
David Pell, 62 Mason Rd, Ilkeston, **Derbyshire**, DE7 9JP, **ENGLAND**.
(T) 0115 9320203.
Profile Trainer. **Ref: YH10910**

PELL, MARK A
Mark A Pell RSS, Tweenways, Hall Rd, Barton Turf, Norwich, **Norfolk**, NR12 8AS, **ENGLAND**.
(T) 01692 536325.
Profile Farrier. **Ref: YH10911**

PELL, NATALIE
Natalie Pell, 10 St Mary's Cres, Ruddington, **Nottinghamshire**, NG11 6FQ, **ENGLAND**.
(T) 0115 9844522.
Profile Trainer. **Ref: YH10912**

PELYN VETNRY GRP
Pelyn Veterinary Group, Edgcumbe Rd, Nomansland, Lostwithiel, **Cornwall**, PL22 0DZ, **ENGLAND**.
(T) 01208 872254.
Profile Medical Support. **Ref: YH10913**

PEMBREY EQUESTRIAN
Pembrey Equestrian, Hir Aros, Pinged, Burry Port, **Carmarthenshire**, SA16 0JR, **WALES**.
(T) 01554 890361.
Contact/s
Owner: Miss L Buckley
Profile Stable/Livery. **Ref: YH10914**

PEMBREY PARK EQUEST CTRE
Pembrey Park Equestrian Centre, Pembrey Country Pk, Pembrey, Burry Port, Llanelli, **Carmarthenshire**, SA16 0EJ, **WALES**.
(T) 01554 832160.
Contact/s
Secretary: Miss L Buckley
Profile Equestrian Centre. **Ref: YH10915**

PEMBRIDGE PERFORMANCE HORSES
Pembridge Performance Horses, Newton Farm, Welsh Newton, Monmouth, **Monmouthshire**, NP25 5RN, **WALES**.
(T) 01989 770419.
Profile Breeder. **Ref: YH10916**

PEMBROKE FARM FEEDS
Pembroke Farm Feeds, Tilshead, Salisbury, **Wiltshire**, SP3 4RX, **ENGLAND**.
(T) 01980 621081.
Profile Supplies. **Ref: YH10917**

PEMBROKESHIRE CLGE
Pembrokeshire College, Pembrokeshire College, Haverfordwest, **Pembrokeshire**, SA61 1SZ, **WALES**.
(T) 01437 765247 **(F)** 01437 767279
(W) www.pembrokeshire.ac.uk.
Profile Equestrian Centre. **Ref: YH10918**

PEMBROKESHIRE EQUESTRIAN
Pembrokeshire Equestrian Supplies Ltd, 43 Cartlett, Haverfordwest, **Pembrokeshire**, SA61 2LH, **WALES**.
(T) 01437 765711 **(F)** 01437 765711
Affiliated Bodies BETA.
Contact/s
Owner: Mr I Lewis
Profile Saddlery Retailer. No.Staff: 4
Yr. Est: 2001
Opening Times
Sp: Open Mon - Sat 09:30. Closed Mon - Sat 17:30.
Su: Open Mon - Sat 09:30. Closed Mon - Sat 17:30.
Au: Open Mon - Sat 09:30. Closed Mon - Sat 17:30.
Wn: Open Mon - Sat 09:30. Closed Mon - Sat 17:30.
Ref: YH10919

PEMBROKESHIRE RIDING CTRE
Pembrokeshire Riding Centre, Pennybridge Farm, Hundleton, Pembroke, **Pembrokeshire**, SA71 5RD, **WALES**.
(T) 01646 682513 **(F)** 01646 682513
(W) www.just-riding.co.uk.
Contact/s
Instructor: Ms A Philipps **(Q)** BHSII
Profile Horse/Rider Accom, Riding School, Saddlery Retailer, Stable/Livery.
Opening Times
Accommodation by appointment. **Ref: YH10920**

PEN & PADDOCK
Pen & Paddock, Tamsin Hse, Field End, Crendon Ind Est, Long Crendon, **Buckinghamshire**, HP18 9EJ, **ENGLAND**.
(M) 07702 606131.
Profile Transport/Horse Boxes. **Ref: YH10921**

PEN ISAR FARM
Pen Isar Farm, Guest House and Riding School, Pen Isar Llan, Bala, **Gwynedd**, LL23 7DW, **WALES**.
(T) 01678 520507.
Profile Riding School, Stable/Livery. **Ref: YH10922**

PENARTH STUD
Penarth Stud, Farnham Rd, Odiham, Hook, **Hampshire**, RG29 1HR, **ENGLAND**.
(T) 01256 703663.
Contact/s
Owner: Mr R Jenner
Profile Breeder. **Ref: YH10923**

PENBAULLT ROSETTES
Penbaullt Rosettes, Yr Hen Ysgol, Llangammarch Wells, **Powys**, LD4 4DH, **WALES**.
(T) 01591 620343 **(F)** 01591 620343.
Profile Supplies. **Ref: YH10924**

PENBODE VETNRY GRP
Penbode Veterinary Group, Horizon View, Hillhead, Stratton, Bude, **Cornwall**, EX23 9AB, **ENGLAND**.
(T) 01288 353766 **(F)** 01288 356823.
Contact/s
Key Contact: Mr J Boundy
Profile Medical Support. **Ref: YH10925**

PENBODE VETNRY GRP
Penbode Veterinary Group, Ashleigh Hse, Bradworthy, Holsworthy, **Devon**, EX22 7SZ, **ENGLAND**.
(T) 01409 241241 **(F)** 01409 241972.
Profile Medical Support. **Ref: YH10926**

PENBODE VETNRY GRP
Penbode Veterinary Group, North Rd, Holsworthy, **Devon**, EX22 6HB, **ENGLAND**.
(T) 01409 253418 **(F)** 01409 254732.
Profile Medical Support. **Ref: YH10927**

PENCADER STUD
Pencader Stud, Pencader, New Inn, Pencader, **Carmarthenshire**, SA39 9BE, **WALES**.
(T) 01559 384734 **(F)** 01559 384734.
Contact/s
Owner: Mr R Heggerty
Profile Breeder, Stable/Livery, Supplies, Trainer.
No.Staff: 2 Yr. Est: 1997 C.Size: 28 Acres
Ref: YH10928

PENCARN FORGE
Pencarn Forge, Canonstown, Hayle, **Cornwall**, TR27 6NA, **ENGLAND**.
(T) 01736 740586.
Profile Farrier. **Ref: YH10929**

PENCOED CLGE
Pencoed College, Pencoed, **Glamorgan (Vale of)**, CF35 5LG, **WALES**.
(T) 01656 860202.
Profile Track/Course. **Ref: YH10930**

PENDARVES, C
C Pendarves, Clover Hill, Steart, Charlton Adam, Somerton, **Somerset**, TA11 7BD, **ENGLAND**.
(T) 01458 223128.
Contact/s
Owner: Ms P Scholes
Profile Farrier. **Ref: YH10931**

PENDLESIDE BRIDLEWAYS ASS
Pendleside Bridleways Association, 138 Harrison Drive, Colne, **Lancashire**, BB8 9SF, **ENGLAND**.
(T) 01282 871255.
Profile Club/Association. **Ref: YH10932**

PENDOCK WELSH PONY STUD
Pendock Welsh Pony Stud, Barlands, Pendock, Malvern, **Worcestershire**, WR13 6JW, **ENGLAND**.
(T) 01684 833537.
Contact/s
Owner: Miss R Philipson-Stow
Profile Breeder. **Ref: YH10933**

PENFOLD & SONS
Penfold & Sons, Old Talbot Hse, High St, Cuckfield, Haywards Heath, **Sussex (West)**, RH17 5JX, **ENGLAND**.
(T) 01444 454164 **(F)** 01444 454164.
Contact/s
General Manager: Ms L Dines
Profile Riding Wear Retailer, Saddlery Retailer, Supplies.
Shoe repairs
Opening Times
Sp: Open Mon - Sat 09:00. Closed Mon - Sat 17:30.
Su: Open Mon - Sat 09:00. Closed Mon - Sat 17:30.
Au: Open Mon - Sat 09:00. Closed Mon - Sat 17:30.
Wn: Open Mon - Sat 09:00. Closed Mon - Sat 17:30.
Closed Sundays **Ref: YH10934**

PENFOLDS OF CUCKFIELD
Penfolds of Cuckfield, 1 Bank Buildings, Cuckfield, Haywards Heath, **Sussex (West)**, RH17 5JU, **ENGLAND**.
(T) 01444 454164.
Profile Saddlery Retailer. **Ref: YH10935**

PENGELLY, DAVID
David Pengelly, Croyle Farm, Kentisbeare, Cullompton, **Devon**, EX15 2AP, **ENGLAND**.
(T) 01884 266322 **(F)** 01884 266626.
Contact/s
Owner: Mr D Pengelly
Profile Transport/Horse Boxes. **Ref: YH10936**

PENGELLY, PENGELLY & MIZEN
Pengelly, Pengelly & Mizen, 89-93 Park Rd, Peterborough, **Cambridgeshire**, PE1 2TR, **ENGLAND**.
(T) 01733 554953.
Profile Medical Support. **Ref: YH10937**

PENGWERN MILL DRIVING STABLES
Pengwern Mill Driving Stables, Pengwern Valley, Llangollen, **Denbighshire**, LL20 8AR, **WALES**.
(T) 01978 860435 **(F)** 01978 860435.
Contact/s
General Manager: Mrs S Marriott
Profile Horse/Rider Accom. **Ref: YH10938**

PENHALWYN
Penhalwyn Trekking Centre & School, Goonmine Mellyn, Halsetown, St Ives, **Cornwall**, TR26 3NA, **ENGLAND**.
(T) 01736 796113.
Contact/s
Owner: Mr R Bennett
Profile Riding School. **Ref: YH10939**

PENINSULA EQUESTRIAN ACADEMY
Peninsula Equestrian Academy, 4 Cardy Rd, Grey Abbey, Newtownards, **County Down**, BT22 2LS, **NORTHERN IRELAND**.
(T) 028 91788681.
Profile Riding School, Stable/Livery. **Ref: YH10940**

PENISTONE & DISTRICT
Penistone & District Riding Club, Tanyard Farm, Roughbirchworth, Oxspring, Sheffield, **Yorkshire (South)**, S36 8YP, **ENGLAND**.
(T) 01226 765919.
Profile Club/Association, Riding Club. **Ref: YH10941**

PENKRIDGE & DISTRICT
Penkridge & District Riding Club, 5 Hearn Court, Rising Brook, Stafford, **Staffordshire**, ST17 9QN, **ENGLAND**.
(T) 01785 46889.
Contact/s
Show Secretary: Mrs P Clay
Profile Club/Association, Riding Club. **Ref: YH10942**

PEN-LLEYN RIDING CTRE
Pen-Lleyn Riding Centre, Llaniestyn, Pwllheli, **Gwynedd**, LL53 8SL, **WALES**.
(T) 01758 730741.
Contact/s
Partner: Miss J Pendelbury
Profile Breeder, Riding School, Trainer. **Ref: YH10943**

PEN-MAEN LIVERY YARD
Pen-Maen Livery Yard, St. Mary Church, Cowbridge, **Glamorgan (Vale of)**, CF71 7LT, **WALES**.
(T) 01446 750382.
Contact/s
Owner: Mrs S Bater **(Q)** BHSI
Profile Riding School, Stable/Livery, Trainer.
Ref: YH10944

PENMELLYN VETNRY GRP
Penmellyn Veterinary Group, Penmellyn Veterinary Ctre, Lower East St, St Columb, **Cornwall**, TR9 6AX, **ENGLAND**.
(T) 01637 880307 **(F)** 01637 880825.
Profile Medical Support. **Ref: YH10945**

PENMELLYN VETNRY GRP
Penmellyn Veterinary Group, Riviera Surgery, St Merryn, Padstow, **Cornwall**, PL28 8NR, **ENGLAND**.
(T) 01841 520647.
Profile Medical Support. **Ref: YH10946**

PENN HOUSE PUBLISHING
Penn House Publishing Ltd, Hoofprint, P O Box 7, Knutsford, **Cheshire**, WA16 7PP, **ENGLAND**.
(T) 01565 872107.
Profile Club/Association. **Ref: YH10947**

PENN TACK & FEED CTRE
Penn Tack & Feed Centre, Killiney, Hammersley Lane, Penn, High Wycombe, **Buckinghamshire**, HP10 8HF, **ENGLAND**.
(T) 01494 812261 **(F)** 01494 812183.
Contact/s
Owner: Mr J Mason **Ref: YH10948**

PENNBRETTI STUD
Pennbretti Stud, 50 Highview, Vigo Village, Meopham, **Kent**, DA13 0TG, **ENGLAND**.
(T) 01732 823297.
Profile Breeder. **Ref: YH10949**

PENNIES STUD
Pennies Stud, Greenways, Off Crown Rd, Christchurch, Wisbech, **Cambridgeshire**, PE14 9NA, **ENGLAND**.
(T) 01354 638459.
Profile Breeder. **Ref: YH10950**

PENNINE FARM SVS
Pennine Farm Services, Kitchen Fold, Kiln Hill, Slaithwaite, Huddersfield, **Yorkshire (West)**, HD7 5JS, **ENGLAND**.
(T) 01484 847606
(M) 07831 849126.
Contact/s
Owner: Mr M Ratcliffe
Profile Saddlery Retailer.
Animal health suppliers including vaccines.
Ref: YH10951

PENNINE LEISURE PRODUCTS
Pennine Leisure Products Ltd, Unit 4 Chester St, Accrington, **Lancashire**, BB5 0SD, **ENGLAND**.
(T) 01254 385991 **(F)** 01254 386111.
Profile Transport/Horse Boxes. **Ref: YH10952**

PENNINE POLOCROSSE CLUB
Pennine Polocrosse Club, 84 Barnsley Rd, Flockton, Wakefield, **Yorkshire (West)**, WF4 4DH, **ENGLAND**.
(T) 01924 840038.
Contact/s
Chairman: Mr D Wigglesworth
Profile Club/Association. Polocrosse Club.
Ref: YH10953

PENNINE RIDING CLUB
Pennine Riding Club, 2 Woodlands Ave, Todmorden, **Yorkshire (West)**, OL14 5LT, **ENGLAND**.
(T) 01706 813841.
Contact/s
Secretary: Theresa Sowerby
Profile Club/Association, Riding Club. **Ref: YH10954**

PENNINGTON'S LIVERY STABLES
Pennington's Livery Stables & Equestrian Centre, Dairyground Farm, Seal Rd, Bramhall, Stockport, **Cheshire**, SK7 2JX, **ENGLAND**.
(T) 0161 4394895. **Ref: YH10955**

PENNIWELLS RIDING GRP
Penniwells Riding Group For The Disabled, Penniwells Farm, Edgwarebury Lane, Elstree, Borehamwood, **Hertfordshire**, WD6 3RG, **ENGLAND**.
(T) 020 82074525.
Contact/s
Manager: Mrs S Healing
Profile Riding Club. **Ref: YH10956**

PENORCHARDS FARM
Penorchards Farm, Penorchard, Hagley Wood Lane, Romsley, Halesowen, **Midlands (West)**, B62 0NL, **ENGLAND**.
(T) 01562 710425.
Contact/s
Owner: Mrs M Harrison
Profile Breeder. **Ref: YH10957**

PENRYHN STUD FARM
Penryhn Stud Farm, Penrhyn Farm, Llanrug, Caernarfon, **Gwynedd**, LL55 4BP, **WALES**.
(T) 01248 670298.
Profile Breeder. **Ref: YH10958**

PENSHAW HILL RIDING SCHOOL
Penshaw Hill Riding School, Penshaw Village, Old Penshaw, Houghton Le Spring, **Tyne and Wear**, DH4 7ER, **ENGLAND**.
(T) 0191 5844828.
Contact/s
Key Contact: Miss J Roseberry
Profile Riding School. **Ref: YH10959**

PENTATALE
Pentatale Ltd, Corner Farm, Broad Oak, Heathfield, **Sussex (East)**, TN21 8UT, **ENGLAND**.
(T) 01435 882977.
Profile Supplies. **Ref: YH10960**

PENTLAND HILLS ICELANDICS
Pentland Hills Icelandics, Windy Gowl Farm, Carlops, Penicuik, **Lothian (Mid)**, EH26 9NL, **SCOTLAND**.
(T) 01968 661095 **(F)** 01968 661095
(W) www.phicelandics.co.uk
Affiliated Bodies SIHA, TRSS.
Contact/s
Owner: Miss J Noble
(E) jnoble@phicelandics.co.uk
Profile Breeder, Equestrian Centre, Riding Club, Stable/Livery.
Run specialist courses for learning to ride Icelandic horses, as Icelandics have 2 extra gaits. Hacking is also available. Livery is on offer for Icelandic horses at £80.00 per month. **No.Staff:** 4 **Yr. Est:** 1988
Opening Times
Sp: Open Mon - Sun 08:00. Closed Mon - Sun 20:00.
Su: Open Mon - Sun 08:00. Closed Mon - Sun 20:00.
Au: Open Mon - Sun 08:00. Closed Mon - Sun 20:00.
Wn: Open Mon - Sun 08:00. Closed Mon - Sun 20:00. **Ref: YH10961**

PENTRE RIDING STABLES
Pentre Riding Stables, Pen-Y-Cae, Ystradgynlais, Swansea, **Swansea**, SA9 1JR, **WALES**.
(T) 01639 730639.
Contact/s
Owner: Miss K Williams
Profile Riding School, Stable/Livery.
Pony trekking holidays **Yr. Est:** 1971
Opening Times
Sp: Open Mon - Sun 09:00. Closed Mon - Sun 17:00.
Su: Open Mon - Sun 09:00. Closed Mon - Sun 17:00.
Au: Open Mon - Sun 09:00. Closed Mon - Sun 17:00.
Wn: Open Mon - Sun 09:00. Closed Mon - Sun 17:00. **Ref: YH10962**

PENTREFELIN STUD
Pentrefelin Stud, Farfield Farm, Cricklade, Swindon, **Wiltshire**, SN6 6HZ, **ENGLAND**.
(T) 01793 750301.
Profile Breeder. **Ref: YH10963**

PEN-Y-BINC FARM
Pen-Y-Binc Farm, Old Highway, Colwyn Bay, **Conwy**, LL28 5YF, **WALES**.
(T) 01492 545309.
Contact/s
Owner: Mr J Smith-Jones
Profile Saddlery Retailer. **Ref: YH10964**

PEN-Y-BRYN RIDING CTRE
Pen-Y-Bryn Riding Centre, High St, Pentre Broughton, Wrexham, **Wrexham**, LL11 6AW, **WALES**.
(T) 01978 752909.

Contact/s
Owner: Mrs L Williams **Ref: YH10965**

PENYCOED RIDING STABLES

Penycoed Riding Stables, Llynclys Hill, Pant, Oswestry, **Shropshire**, SY10 8LG, **ENGLAND**.
(T) 01691 830608
(W) www.penycoedholidays.co.uk.
Contact/s
Owner: Mrs P Hanson
Profile Holidays, Horse/Rider Accom. **Ref: YH10966**

PEN-Y-FEDW RIDING CTRE

Pen-Y-Fedw Riding Centre, Penyfedw Farm, Rhydypandy Rd, Pantlasau, Morriston, Swansea, **Swansea**, SA6 6NX, **WALES**.
(T) 01792 842303.
Profile Equestrian Centre. **Ref: YH10967**

PEPER HAROW HORSE TRAILERS

Peper Harow Horse Trailers, Chephurst Farm, Havem Rd, Bucks Green, Horsham, **Sussex (West)**, RH12 3JH, **ENGLAND**.
(T) 01483 416555 **(F)** 01483 429998
(W) www.phht.co.uk.
Contact/s
Owner: Ms J McNeill
(E) julie@phht.co.uk
Profile Transport/Horse Boxes.
Horse Box Sales and Repairs **No.Staff:** 10
Yr. Est: 1994 **Ref: YH10968**

PEPPARD, JOHN S J

John S J Peppard, 18 Green St, Ston Easton, Bath, **Bath & Somerset (North East)**, BA3 4DB, **ENGLAND**.
(T) 01761 241511.
Profile Farrier. **Ref: YH10969**

PEPPERCORN DONKEY STUD

Peppercorn Donkey Stud, Peppercorn Hse, Langley, **Kent**, ME17 3JN, **ENGLAND**.
(T) 01622 843149 **(F)** 01691 648168.
Profile Breeder. **Ref: YH10970**

PERCIVAL, ALEXANDER J

Alexander J Percival DWCF, Paddocks Farm, Woodford Halse, Daventry, **Northamptonshire**, NN11 6RE, **ENGLAND**.
(T) 01327 261721.
Profile Farrier. **Ref: YH10971**

PERCIVAL, MARK F B

Mark F B Percival DWCF, 67 Fern Cl, Okehampton, **Devon**, EX20 1PD, **ENGLAND**.
(T) 01837 55179.
Profile Farrier. **Ref: YH10972**

PERCIVAL, R G

R G Percival, Spring Cottage, Chapel Lane, Old, Northampton, **Northamptonshire**, NN6 9RD, **ENGLAND**.
(T) 01604 781529.
Contact/s
Owner: Mr R Percival
Profile Breeder. **Ref: YH10973**

PERCY STONE

Percy Stone Ltd, 4-10 Reading Rd, Pangbourne, **Berkshire**, RG8 7LY, **ENGLAND**.
(T) 0118 9842111.
Profile Supplies. **Ref: YH10974**

PERISI, J S

Miss J S Perisi, Kimbers Lane Farm, Oakley Green Rd, Windsor, **Berkshire**, **ENGLAND**..
Profile Trainer. **Ref: YH10975**

PERITON PK RIDING STABLES

Periton Park Riding Stables, Periton Rd, Middlecombe, Minehead, **Somerset**, TA24 8SN, **ENGLAND**.
(T) 01643 705970 **(F)** 01643 705970
(E) peritonparkcourt@btinternet.com
Affiliated Bodies BHS.
Contact/s
Owner: Mr J Borland
Profile Horse/Rider Accom.
Hacking on Exmoor for all levels of ability
No.Staff: 2 **Yr. Est:** 1987
Opening Times
Sp: Open Mon - Sun 08:00. Closed Mon - Sun 21:00.
Su: Open Mon - Sun 08:00. Closed Mon - Sun 21:00.
Au: Open Mon - Sun 08:00. Closed Mon - Sun 21:00.
Wn: Open Mon - Sun 08:00. Closed Mon - Sun 21:00. **Ref: YH10976**

PERKINS, P

P Perkins, West Flatts Farm, High St, Slingsby, York, **Yorkshire (North)**, YO62 4AE, **ENGLAND**.
(T) 01653 628347 **(F)** 01653 628347.
Contact/s
Owner: Mrs P Perkins
Profile Breeder. **Ref: YH10977**

PERKINS, STEPHEN

Stephen Perkins DWCF, Thatched Cottage, Cherry Orchard Lane, Bonnington, Ashford, **Kent**, TN25 7AZ, **ENGLAND**.
(T) 01233 720691.
Profile Farrier. **Ref: YH10978**

PERKIS, BARRY A

Barry A Perkis RSS, Shamsah, 38 Station Ave, Sandown, **Isle of Wight**, **ENGLAND**.
(T) 01983 406284.
Profile Farrier. **Ref: YH10979**

PERMIT TRAINERS ASS

Permit Trainers Association, Drewitts, Warninglid, Haywards Heath, **Sussex (West)**, RH17 5TB, **ENGLAND**.
(T) 01444 461235 **(F)** 01444 461485.
Profile Club/Association. **Ref: YH10980**

PERPOP STUD

Perpop Stud, Perpop, Roslin, **Lothian (Mid)**, EH25 9QJ, **SCOTLAND**.
(T) 01968 675664
(M) 07850 880271.
Profile Breeder. **Ref: YH10981**

PERRAN SANDS

Perran Sands Riding & Trekking Centre, 2 Lower Hillcrest, Perranporth, **Cornwall**, TR6 0JZ, **ENGLAND**.
(T) 01872 573884.
Contact/s
Owner: Ms L Martin **Ref: YH10982**

PERRETT, A C J

Mr A C J Perrett, Yew Tree, Shipton Oliffe, Cheltenham, **Gloucestershire**, GL54 4JE, **ENGLAND**.
(T) 01242 820244.
Profile Supplies. **Ref: YH10983**

PERRETTS STUD

Perretts Stud, Knights Farm, Smithers Hill, Shipley, Horsham, **Sussex (West)**, RH13 8PP, **ENGLAND**.
(T) 01403 741299 **(F)** 01403 741388.
Contact/s
Owner: Mr M Richardson
Profile Breeder. **Ref: YH10984**

PERRINS, S & J

S & J Perrins, Grove Farm, Kirkgate, Hanging Heaton, Batley, **Yorkshire (West)**, **ENGLAND**.
(T) 01924 462200.
Profile Breeder. **Ref: YH10985**

PERROTT, NIGEL R

Nigel R Perrott DWCF Hons, School Hse Farm, Stoke Trister, Wincanton, **Somerset**, BA9 9PE, **ENGLAND**.
(T) 07966 209540.
Profile Farrier. **Ref: YH10986**

PERRY, M A C

M A C Perry, Swinford Rd, Walcote, Lutterworth, **Leicestershire**, LE17 4JZ, **ENGLAND**.
(T) 01455 554206.
Contact/s
Partner: Mr M Perry
Profile Riding School.
Lessons for children only. **Yr. Est:** 1975
Opening Times
Sp: Open Thurs 15:30, Sat, Sun 09:00. Closed Thurs 18:00, Sat 17:00, Sun 13:00.
Su: Open Thurs 15:30, Sat, Sun 09:00. Closed Thurs 18:00, Sat 17:00, Sun 13:00.
Au: Open Thurs 15:30, Sat, Sun 09:00. Closed Thurs 18:00, Sat 17:00, Sun 13:00.
Wn: Open Thurs 15:30, Sat, Sun 09:00. Closed Thurs 18:00, Sat 17:00, Sun 13:00. **Ref: YH10987**

PERRY, MICHELLE

Michelle Perry, Windrush, Rushbrook Lane, Tanworth-In-Arden, **Warwickshire**, B94 5HP, **ENGLAND**.
(T) 01564 742809
(M) 07958 670509. **Ref: YH10988**

PERRY, R L

R L Perry RSS BII, 19 West St, Enderby, **Leicestershire**, LE9 5LT, **ENGLAND**.
(T) 0116 2861249.
Profile Farrier. **Ref: YH10989**

PERRYMAN, PHILLIP D

Phillip D Perryman AWCF, Breach Hse, Marston, Devizes, **Wiltshire**, SN10 5SP, **ENGLAND**.
(T) 01380 720373.
Profile Farrier. **Ref: YH10990**

PERRYS EQUESTRIAN SVS

Perrys Equestrian Services, Stable Cottage, Brookfield Farm, Warfield, Bracknell, **Berkshire**, RG42 6BH, **ENGLAND**.
(T) 01344 890055 **(F)** 01344 890055.
Contact/s
Owner: Mr J Perry
Profile Stable/Livery. **Ref: YH10991**

PERRYS PLACE

Perrys Place Farm, Perry's Pl, Burley Rd, Brokenhurst, **Hampshire**, SO42 7TB, **ENGLAND**.
(T) 01590 623769.
Contact/s
General Manager: Mrs A Perry
Profile Breeder.
Offer full/part livery, also have a B&B across the road from the yard, perfect for weekend breaks. Have access to 90,000 acres of land. **No.Staff:** 3
Yr. Est: 1995
Opening Times
Telephone for an appointment **Ref: YH10992**

PERSHORE & HINDLIP CLGE

Pershore & Hindlip College, Hindlip Campus, Hindlip, **Worcestershire**, WR3 8SS, **ENGLAND**.
(T) 01905 451310 **(F)** 01905 754760.
Profile Stable/Livery, Track/Course, Trainer.
Ref: YH10993

PERSHORE TRANSPORT

Pershore Transport Ltd, Willows Farm, Lenchwick, Evesham, **Worcestershire**, WR11 4TG, **ENGLAND**.
(T) 01386 871011.
Contact/s
Owner: Mr D Ricketts
Profile Transport/Horse Boxes. **Ref: YH10994**

PERSIAN BLOODSTOCK

Persian Bloodstock, 29 Letchworth Ave, Feltham, **London (Greater)**, TW14 9RZ, **ENGLAND**.
(T) 020 88901503 **(F)** 020 88901503.
Profile Blood Stock Agency, Breeder. **Ref: YH10995**

PERSSE, BURTON S H

Burton S H Persse DWCF, Cider Barn, Court Barton, Kentisbeare, Cullompton, **Devon**, EX15 2BG, **ENGLAND**.
(T) 01884 266599.
Profile Farrier. **Ref: YH10996**

PERTH HUNT

Perth Hunt (Perth Racecourse) (The), Scone Palace Pk, Perth, **Perth and Kinross**, PH2 6BB, **SCOTLAND**.
(T) 01738 551597 **(F)** 01738 553021.
Contact/s
General Manager: Mr S Morshead
Profile Track/Course. **Ref: YH10997**

PERUZZI, R S N

R S N Peruzzi RSS, 3 Cherry Tree Cl, Mattishall, Dereham, **Norfolk**, NR20 3PR, **ENGLAND**.
(T) 01362 850043
(M) 07860 789448.
Profile Farrier. **Ref: YH10998**

PESTELL, S

Mrs S Pestell, Highbury Farm, Colby Rd, Banningham, Norwich, **Norfolk**, NR11 7DY, **ENGLAND**.
(T) 01263 732985.
Profile Breeder. **Ref: YH10999**

PET & EQUINE SUPPLIES

Pet & Equine Supplies, 46 Red Lion Yard, Okehampton, **Devon**, EX20 1AW, **ENGLAND**.
(T) 01837 55403 **(F)** 01837 55403
(E) g4fiv@teco.net.
Contact/s
Owner: Mrs J Morley
Profile Riding Wear Retailer, Saddlery Retailer.
Ref: YH11000

PET CABS

Pet Cabs, 183A Whitehorse Rd, Croydon, **Surrey**, CR0 2LJ, **ENGLAND**.
(T) 020 86832252.
Contact/s

Owner: Mrs E Howarth
Profile Transport/Horse Boxes. Ref:YH11001

PET CARRIER SVS

Pet Carrier Services, 3 Kingsley Green, Havant, **Hampshire**, PO9 5DU, **ENGLAND**.
(T) 023 92453477.
Contact/s
Owner: Mr R Fewings
Profile Transport/Horse Boxes. Ref:YH11002

PET FOOD & HORSE SUPPLIES

Pet Food & Horse Supplies, 70 Moss Lane, Macclesfield, **Cheshire**, SK11 7TT, **ENGLAND**.
(T) 01625 424071.
Contact/s
Owner: Mr L Astbury
Profile Supplies. Ref:YH11003

PET FOOD DISCOUNT CTRE

Pet Food Discount Centre, Brookfold Farm, Gooley, Hyde, **Cheshire**, SK14 3BG, **ENGLAND**.
(T) 0161 3688147.
Contact/s
Owner: William Tym
Profile Supplies. Ref:YH11004

PET LOVE SUPPLIES

Pet Love Supplies, 17 High St, Daventry, **Northamptonshire**, NN11 4BG, **ENGLAND**.
(T) 01327 705918.
Profile Saddlery Retailer. Ref:YH11005

PET PLAN

Pet Plan Ltd, Computer Hse, Gt West Rd, Brentford, **London (Greater)**, TW8 9DX, **ENGLAND**.
(T) 0800 7837777 (F) 020 85808183
(E) equineservice@petplan.co.uk
(W) www.petplanequine.co.uk.
Profile Insurance Services.
Opening Times
Sp: Open Mon - Fri 08:00, Sat 09:00. Closed Mon - Fri 20:00, Sat 13:00.
Su: Open Mon - Fri 08:00, Sat 09:00. Closed Mon - Fri 20:00, Sat 13:00.
Au: Open Mon - Fri 08:00, Sat 09:00. Closed Mon - Fri 20:00, Sat 13:00.
Wn: Open Mon - Fri 08:00, Sat 09:00. Closed Mon - Fri 20:00, Sat 13:00.
Closed on Sundays. Ref:YH11006

PETASFIELD STABLES

Petasfield Stables, Mangrove Rd, Hertford, **Hertfordshire**, SG13 8AJ, **ENGLAND**.
(T) 01992 587989.
Contact/s
Owner: Miss C Dudley Ref:YH11007

PETCARE ANIMAL SITTING SVS

Petcare Animal Sitting Services, 6 Belvidere Rd, Crosby, Liverpool, **Merseyside**, L23 0SR, **ENGLAND**.
(T) 0151 9209442.
Contact/s
Owner: Mr D Guidera
Profile Transport/Horse Boxes. Ref:YH11008

PETER BECK TRAILERS

Peter Beck Trailers, Polton Farm, Polton Rd, Lasswade, **Lothian (Mid)**, EH18 1BS, **SCOTLAND**.
(T) 0131 6631558.
Profile Transport/Horse Boxes. Ref:YH11009

PETER HUNTER

Hunter, Peter, Keepers Cottage, Oulton, Tarporley, **Cheshire**, CW6 9BL, **ENGLAND**.
(T) 01829 760397 (F) 01829 760526.
Profile Supplies. Ref:YH11010

PETER MCKENZIE & SON

Peter McKenzie & Son, 35 Polmaise Rd, Stirling, **Stirling**, FK7 9JH, **SCOTLAND**.
(T) 01786 474711.
Profile Transport/Horse Boxes. Ref:YH11011

PETER MCKENZIE & SON

Peter Mckenzie & Son, Level Crossing, Cornton, Blairdrummond, Stirling, **Stirling**, FK9 4XF, **SCOTLAND**.
(T) 01786 833424 (F) 01786 833368.
Contact/s
Owner: Mr P McKenzie
Profile Transport/Horse Boxes. Ref:YH11012

PETER ORR PHOTOGRAPHY

Peter Orr Photography, West End Hse, Main Rd, Hagworthingham, Spilsby, **Lincolnshire**, PE23 4LT, **ENGLAND**.
(T) 01507 588412 (F) 01507 588412. Ref:YH11013

PETER PITTS

Peter Pitts Management, 6 South Prde, Headingley, **Yorkshire (West)**, LS6 3LF, **ENGLAND**.
(T) 0113 2789789 (F) 0113 2745745
(M) 07831 358979. Ref:YH11014

PETER SMITH SADDLERY

Peter Smith Saddlery, Glen Almond, Simons Lane, Shipton-under-Wychwood, Chipping Norton, **Oxfordshire**, OX7 6DH, **ENGLAND**.
(T) 01993 831306.
Profile Saddlery Retailer. Ref:YH11015

PETER STUNT COUNTRY PURSUITS

Peter Stunt Country Pursuits, 29A Bridge St, Taunton, **Somerset**, TA1 1TQ, **ENGLAND**.
(T) 01823 336123 (F) 01823 413848
(M) 07768 570135.
Profile Supplies. Ref:YH11016

PETER WEBSTER DESIGN

Peter Webster Design, The Birches, Costock Rd, Wysall, **Nottinghamshire**, NG12 5QT, **ENGLAND**.
(T) 01509 881140 (F) 01509 881140. Ref:YH11017

PETERBOROUGH REGIONAL CLGE

Peterborough Regional College, Park Cres, Peterborough, **Cambridgeshire**, PE1 4DZ, **ENGLAND**.
(T) 01733 767366.
Profile Equestrian Centre. Ref:YH11018

PETERLEA TOWING & TRAILER

Peterlea Towing & Trailer Spares, Peterlea Works, Shaw Rd South, Stockport, **Cheshire**, SK3 8JG, **ENGLAND**.
(T) 0161 4802377 (F) 0161 4804104.
Profile Transport/Horse Boxes. Ref:YH11019

PETERS & PARTNERS

Peters & Partners, Fenton Veterinary Practice, 21 Portfield, Haverfordwest, **Pembrokeshire**, SA61 1BN, **WALES**.
(T) 01437 762806.
Profile Medical Support. Ref:YH11020

PETERS FRASER & DUNLOPS

Agents Peters Fraser & Dunlops Grp Ltd, 5th Floor The Chambers, Chelsea Harbour, Lots Rd, London, **London (Greater)**, SW10 0XF, **ENGLAND**.
(T) 020 73527356.
Profile Supplies. Ref:YH11021

PETERSFIELD SADDLERY

Petersfield Saddlery, 25-27 Chapel St, Petersfield, **Hampshire**, GU32 3DY, **ENGLAND**.
(T) 01730 266816.
Profile Saddlery Retailer. Ref:YH11022

PETERSHAM FARM

Petersham Farm, Petersham Rd, Richmond, **Surrey**, TW10 7AH, **ENGLAND**.
(T) 020 83322563.
Profile Stable/Livery. Ref:YH11023

PETE'S BLACKSMITHS WORKSHOP

Pete's Blacksmiths Workshop, The Forge, Rear Of 38 Osborne Rd, Access Via Clifton Rd, Southsea, **Hampshire**, PO5 3LT, **ENGLAND**.
(T) 023 92753562.
Profile Blacksmith. Ref:YH11024

PETE'S TACK

Pete's Tack, Bank Bottom Cottage, Sandy Banks, Harden, Bingley, **Yorkshire (West)**, BD16 1BG, **ENGLAND**.
(T) 01535 275050.
Profile Supplies. Ref:YH11025

PETFOOD EXPRESS

Petfood Express, 36 Maypole Rd, Taplow, Maidenhead, **Berkshire**, SL6 0NB, **ENGLAND**.
(T) 01628 662834.
Profile Supplies. Ref:YH11026

PETIT, S G & A

Mr S G & Miss A Petit, Maple Bank, Henley Ave, Rawdon, **Yorkshire (West)**, LS19 6NZ, **ENGLAND**.
(T) 0113 2501387.
Contact/s
Partner: Miss A Petit
Profile Breeder. Ref:YH11027

PETMEALS

Petmeals, 24 East View, North Rd, Boldon Colliery, **Tyne and Wear**, NE35 9AU, **ENGLAND**.
(T) 0191 5366600 (F) 0191 5366600.
Profile Saddlery Retailer. Ref:YH11028

PETS & PONIES

Pets & Ponies, 192 Oldham Rd, Ashton-under-Lyne, **Manchester (Greater)**, OL7 9AN, **ENGLAND**.
(T) 0161 3396240.
Contact/s
Partner: Mr D Keevil Ref:YH11029

PETS ON PARADE

Pets on Parade, 35 The Parade, Claygate, **Surrey**, KT10 0PD, **ENGLAND**.
(T) 01372 467773.
Profile Saddlery Retailer. Ref:YH11030

PETS TO VETS

Pets To Vets, Flat 1/Warren Edge Court, 15 Warren Edge Rd, Bournemouth, **Dorset**, BH6 4AX, **ENGLAND**.
(T) 01202 417011.
Contact/s
Owner: Mr A Applin
Profile Transport/Horse Boxes. Ref:YH11031

PETS TO VETS

Pets To Vets, 14 St Anns Rd, Southsea, **Hampshire**, PO4 9AT, **ENGLAND**.
(T) 023 92730343.
Profile Transport/Horse Boxes. Ref:YH11032

PETSTOP

Petstop, Kwik Save, Llantarnum Rd, Cwmbran, **Torfaen**, NP4 4OX, **WALES**.
(T) 01633 484804.
Profile Supplies. Ref:YH11033

PETTS, KATHRINE

Kathrine Petts BSc (Hons) MCSP, SRP, Cliff Lodge, Town End, Crick, Matlock, **Derbyshire**, DE4 5DP, **ENGLAND**.
(T) 07979 755267.
Profile Medical Support. Ref:YH11034

PEVLINGS FARM

Pevlings Farm Riding & Livery Stables, Cabbage Lane, Horsington, Templecombe, **Somerset**, BA8 0DA, **ENGLAND**.
(T) 01963 370990
Affiliated Bodies ABRS, Pony Club UK.
Contact/s
Owner: Ms A Tytheridge
Profile Riding School, Stable/Livery. Yr. Est: 1985
C.Size: 18 Acres Ref:YH11035

PEVSNER, DANIEL

Daniel Pevsner FBHS MSTAT, Letchmore Farm, Rush Green, Hitchin, **Hertfordshire**, SG4 7PJ, **ENGLAND**.
(T) 01438 355470.
Profile Trainer. Ref:YH11036

PEWSEY VALE

Pewsey Vale Riding Centre, Church Farm, Stanton St. Bernard, Marlborough, **Wiltshire**, SN8 4LJ, **ENGLAND**.
(T) 01672 851400/851237 (F) 01672 851473
(W) www.pewseyvaleridingcentre.com
Affiliated Bodies ABRS, BHS.
Contact/s
General Manager: Ms L Ainley
Profile Riding School, Stable/Livery.
Situated in the heart of rural Wiltshire the area is steeped with historical landscapes and monuments and is truly a fabulous place to ride. The centre caters for all ages and abilities and has an excellent variety of horses and ponies. This, together with friendly qualified staff, provides an excellent place to ride/train. Also offer an extensive range of livery services, all of which are supported by a professional team of staff.
Yr. Est: 1986 Ref:YH11037

PG SHOE

PG Shoe, Newchapel Rd, Lingfield, **Surrey**, RH7 6BJ, **ENGLAND**.
(T) 01342 832570.
Profile Farrier.
Imports horseshoes from Sweden. Ref:YH11038

PH GREENHILL

PH Greenhill Ltd, 152 Windmill Lane, Norwood Green, **London (Greater)**, UB2 4NF, **ENGLAND**.
(T) 020 85746915 (F) 020 85715916.
Profile Club/Association. Ref:YH11039

PHARO COMMUNICATIONS

Pharo Communications, 10Th St, National Agricultural Ctre, Stoneleigh, **Warwickshire**, CV8 2LG, **ENGLAND**.
(T) 024 76696721 (F) 024 76696737
(E) joes@pharo-comms.demon.co.uk.

Contact/s
Accounts Manager: Miss J Smith Ref: YH11040

PHIL TURNER SADDLERY

Phil Turner Saddlery, Ollys Cottage, Bronley, Hoarwithy, **Herefordshire**, HR2 6QN, **ENGLAND**.
(T) 01432 840403.
Profile Breeder, Saddlery Retailer. Ref: YH11041

PHILIP BATE DISPLAY

Philip Bate Display, Unit 1A, The Mill Ind Est, Stoke Canon, Exeter, **Devon**, EX5 4RJ, **ENGLAND**.
(T) 01392 841808 **(F)** 01392 841504. Ref: YH11042

PHILIP DAY

Philip Day Farrier Services, 2 Drift Cottages, Edmondthorpe, Melton Mowbray, **Leicestershire**, LE14 2JY, **ENGLAND**.
(T) 01572 787468
(M) 07774 152731.
Contact/s
Owner: Mr P Day **(Q)** DWCF
(E) philthefarrier@aol.com
Profile Farrier. Ref: YH11043

PHILIP MCENTEE RACING

Philip McEntee Racing, Southfield Stables, Hamilton Rd, Newmarket, **Suffolk**, CB8 0PD, **ENGLAND**.
(T) 01638 662092
(M) 07802 663256
(W) www.newmarketracehorsetrainers.co.uk
Affiliated Bodies Newmarket Trainers Fed.
Contact/s
Trainer: Mr P McEntee
Profile Trainer. Ref: YH11044

PHILIP MORRIS & SON

Philip Morris & Son, 21/23 Widemarsh St, Hereford, **Herefordshire**, HR4 9EE, **ENGLAND**.
(T) 01432 269501 **(F)** 01432 353448.
Contact/s
Partner: Mr M Jones
Profile Saddlery Retailer. Ref: YH11045

PHILIPSON, (MAJOR)

Major Philipson, Lofts Hall, Wenden Lofts, Saffron Walden, **Essex**, CB11 4UN, **ENGLAND**.
(T) 01763 838200 **(F)** 01763 837044.
Contact/s
Partner: Major C Philipson
Profile Breeder. Ref: YH11046

PHILLIPS BROS

Phillips Bros, Lillingstone Hse, Lillingstone Dayrell, Buckingham, **Buckinghamshire**, MK18 5AG, **ENGLAND**.
(T) 01280 860334.
Profile Farrier. Ref: YH11047

PHILLIPS BROS

Phillips Bros (Woodshavings) Ltd, 49-51 Southampton Way, Camberwell, **London (Greater)**, SE5 7SW, **ENGLAND**.
(T) 020 77019747.
Profile Supplies. Ref: YH11048

PHILLIPS IN SCOTLAND

Phillips in Scotland, 65 George St, Edinburgh, **Edinburgh (City of)**, EH2 2JL, **SCOTLAND**.
(T) 0131 225226. Ref: YH11049

PHILLIPS STRUCTURES

Phillips Structures Ltd, Red Barn Drive, Westfields Trading Est, Hereford, **Herefordshire**, HR4 9NU, **ENGLAND**.
(T) 01432 267661 **(F)** 01432 352693.
Profile Supplies. Ref: YH11050

PHILLIPS, A K

Mrs A K Phillips, 11 Chester Cl, Ashford, **Kent**, **ENGLAND**..
Profile Trainer. Ref: YH11051

PHILLIPS, C E

Miss C E Phillips, Priory Farm, Clifford, **Herefordshire**, HR3 5EZ, **ENGLAND**.
(T) 01497 831204.
Profile Supplies. Ref: YH11052

PHILLIPS, C M

Mr C M Phillips, Waun Mary Gunter Farm, Garn-Yr-Erw, Blaenavon, **Torfaen**, NP4 9SJ, **WALES**.
(T) 01495 790525.
Profile Breeder. Ref: YH11053

PHILLIPS, D J

Mr & Mrs D J Phillips, Penrose Farm, Cilibon, Gower, Swansea, **Swansea**, SA3 1EB, **WALES**.
(T) 01792 390133.
Profile Breeder. Ref: YH11054

PHILLIPS, E R

Mr E R Phillips, High Gate, New Radnor, Presteigne, **Powys**, **WALES**..
Profile Trainer. Ref: YH11055

PHILLIPS, F S L

F S L Phillips, Clicketts Heath, Twycross, Saundersfoot, **Pembrokeshire**, SA69 9DJ, **WALES**.
(T) 01834 813401.
Profile Breeder. Ref: YH11056

PHILLIPS, J G

J G Phillips, Kilkenny Stables/Kilkenny Farm, Kilkenny, Bibury, Cirencester, **Gloucestershire**, GL7 5PD, **ENGLAND**.
(T) 01451 844671.
Profile Trainer. Ref: YH11057

PHILLIPS, J G

Mrs J G Phillips, Kentwell Hall, Long Melford, Sudbury, **Suffolk**, CO10 9BA, **ENGLAND**.
(T) 01787 310207.
Profile Breeder. Ref: YH11058

PHILLIPS, LESLIE M

Leslie M Phillips RSS, 17 West Mills Rd, Dorchester, **Dorset**, DT1 1SP, **ENGLAND**.
(T) 01305 264030.
Profile Farrier. Ref: YH11059

PHILLIPS, MARK J

Mark J Phillips DWCF, 15 Forest Cl, Waltham Chase, **Hampshire**, SO3 2ND, **ENGLAND**.
(T) 07836 754298.
Profile Farrier. Ref: YH11060

PHILLIPS, MICHAEL J

Michael J Phillips DWCF, 25 Hick's Court, Towcester, **Northamptonshire**, NN12 6EJ, **ENGLAND**.
(T) 01327 353660.
Profile Farrier. Ref: YH11061

PHILLIPS, NIGEL

Nigel Phillips DWCF BII, Sutton Pl, Langport Rd, Long Sutton, Langport, **Somerset**, TA10 9NQ, **ENGLAND**.
(T) 01458 241057.
Profile Farrier. Ref: YH11062

PHILLIPS, R

Mr R Phillips, Jackdaws Castle, Temple Guiting, Cheltenham, **Gloucestershire**, GL54 5XU, **ENGLAND**.
(T) 01386 584209 **(F)** 01386 584218
(M) 07774 832715.
Profile Trainer. Ref: YH11063

PHILLIPS, RICHARD J

Richard J Phillips DWCF, 14 Alpha Cl, Balsall Heath, Birmingham, **Midlands (West)**, B12 9HF, **ENGLAND**.
(T) 0121 4404876.
Profile Farrier. Ref: YH11064

PHILLIPS, T S R

T S R Phillips DWCF, 3 Chartwell Cl, Beacon Heights, Seaford, **Sussex (East)**, BN25 2XQ, **ENGLAND**.
(T) 01323 890242.
Profile Farrier. Ref: YH11065

PHILLIPS, TERENCE J

Terence J Phillips BA RSS, The Gas Hse, Lillingstone Dayrell, **Buckinghamshire**, MK18 5AN, **ENGLAND**.
(T) 01280 860334.
Profile Farrier. Ref: YH11066

PHILLIPS, W E

Mr W E Phillips, Shire Farm, Ruskington Fen, Billinghay, **Lincolnshire**, LN4 4DS, **ENGLAND**.
(T) 01526 832269.
Profile Breeder. Ref: YH11067

PHIPPS, A

Mrs A Phipps, Manor Farm, Kerso, Pershore, **Worcestershire**, WR10 3JD, **ENGLAND**.
(T) 01386 710254 **(F)** 01386 710410
(E) 106311.1572@compuserve.com.
Contact/s
Owner: Mrs A Phipps
Profile Medical Support.
Independent distributer of 'Forever Living' nutritional products for horses and humans. Ref: YH11068

PHOENIX

Phoenix, Unit 1, Rear of 115/120 Stafford St, Walsall, **Midlands (West)**, WS2 8DX, **ENGLAND**.
(T) 01922 628800 **(F)** 01922 636138
(W) www.phoenixsaddlery.co.uk.
Contact/s
Partner: Mr W Pountney
Profile Saddlery Retailer.
Manufacturers and retailers of a wide range of saddles including show saddles, dressage saddles and made to measure. Saddles can also be made to design.
Ref: YH11069

PHOENIX CLGE OF RADIONICS

Phoenix College of Radionics, 62 Alexandra Rd, Hemel Hempstead, **Hertfordshire**, HP2 4AQ, **ENGLAND**.
(T) 01442 243333.
Profile Medical Support. Ref: YH11070

PHOENIX EQUESTRIAN CTRE

Phoenix Equestrian Centre, Ledston Hall Stables, Hall Lane, Ledston, Castleford, **Yorkshire (West)**, WF10 2BB, **ENGLAND**.
(T) 01977 513544.
Contact/s
Owner: Mr D Constance
Profile Riding School. Ref: YH11071

PHOENIX EVENTS SECURITY

Phoenix Events Security, Phoenix Hse, 8 Penrose Cl, Coventry, **Midlands (West)**, CV4 8DR, **ENGLAND**.
(T) 024 76421377. Ref: YH11072

PHOENIX FORGE

Phoenix Forge, Unit 2E Heathlands Ind Est, Liskeard, **Cornwall**, PL14 4DH, **ENGLAND**.
(T) 01579 342343 **(F)** 01579 342345.
Profile Blacksmith. Ref: YH11073

PHOENIX FORGE UK

Phoenix Forge UK Ltd, 460 Rathgar Rd, London, **London (Greater)**, SW9 7EP, **ENGLAND**.
(T) 020 72744534 **(F)** 020 72742853.
Profile Blacksmith. Ref: YH11074

PHOENIX PK RACECOURSE

Phoenix Park Racecourse, Dublin Ltd, Phoenix Pk, Dublin, **County Dublin**, **IRELAND**.
(T) 01 8381317.
Profile Supplies. Ref: YH11075

PHOENIX RIDING WEAR

Phoenix Riding Wear, 2 Selborne St, Walsall, **Midlands (West)**, WS1 2JN, **ENGLAND**.
(T) 01922 620000 **(F)** 01922 724848. Ref: YH11076

PHOSYN

Phosyn, Manor Pl, The Airfield, Wellington Rd, Pocklington, York, **Yorkshire (North)**, YO42 1NR, **ENGLAND**.
(T) 01759 302545 **(F)** 01759 303650.
Profile Medical Support. Ref: YH11077

PHOTO SOURCE

Photo Source (The), Unit C1, Enterprise Business Est, 2 Mill Harbour, London, **London (Greater)**, E14 9TE, **ENGLAND**.
(T) 020 79871212.
Contact/s
Photographer: Roy Moreton Ref: YH11078

PHYLISS HARVEY

Phyllis Harvey Horse & Donkey Trust (The), Tethers End, The Ring Rd, Weetwood, **Yorkshire (West)**, LS16 5PH, **ENGLAND**.
(T) 0113 2676122.
Profile Club/Association. Ref: YH11079

PICKARD, ROBERT D

Robert D Pickard RSS, 6 Tram Lane, Kirkby Lonsdale, Carnforth, **Lancashire**, **ENGLAND**.
(T) 01524 271086.
Profile Farrier. Ref: YH11080

PICKERING & DAWSON

Pickering & Dawson, Unit 5 Royce Court, Billingham, **Cleveland**, TS23 4DE, **ENGLAND**.
(T) 01642 562107.
Profile Blacksmith. Ref: YH11081

PICKERING, GEOFF

Geoff Pickering, Little Pockthorpe Farm, Kilham, Driffield, **Yorkshire (East)**, YO25 4SY, **ENGLAND**.
(T) 01377 257115.
Contact/s
Owner: Mr G Pickering

Profile Breeder. **Ref: YH11082**

PICKERING, J A

Mr J A Pickering, Cottage Farm, Wigston Parva, Sharnford, Hinckley, **Leicestershire**, LE10 3AP, **ENGLAND**.
(T) 01455 220535.
Profile Trainer. **Ref: YH11083**

PICKERING, JOHN T

John T Pickering, 15 Castle Court, Helmsley, **Yorkshire (North)**, YO62 5AZ, **ENGLAND**.
(T) 01439 770931.
Profile Supplies. **Ref: YH11084**

PICKERSTON STUD

Pickerston Stud, Flemingston Court, Flemington, Barry, **Glamorgan (Vale of)**, CF62 4QJ, **WALES**.
(T) 01446 750216 **(F)** 01446 750216
(E) flemingstoncourt@aol.com.
Contact/s
Owner: Mr J Thomas
Profile Breeder, Stable/Livery. **Ref: YH11085**

PICKLES, A C

A C Pickles, Rayne Farm, Gaisgill, Penrith, **Cumbria**, CA10 3UD, **ENGLAND**.
(T) 01539 624096.
Profile Medical Support. **Ref: YH11086**

PICKMERE

Pickmere Stud & Feed, School Farm, School Lane, Pickmere, Knutsford, **Cheshire**, WA16 0JF, **ENGLAND**.
(T) 01565 733259 **(F)** 01565 733222
(E) pickmerestud@lineone.net.
Profile Breeder.
Have a champion pony stallion and a hacking stallion.
Ref: YH11087

PIDGEON, G

Mrs G Pidgeon, Astwell Castle Farm, Helmdon, Brackley, **Northamptonshire**, NN13 5QU, **ENGLAND**.
(T) 01295 768237 **(F)** 01295 768237.
Profile Supplies. **Ref: YH11088**

PIDGEON, STEVEN G

Steven G Pidgeon DWCF, 16 Bowring Mead, Moretonhampstead, **Devon**, TQ13 8NP, **ENGLAND**.
(T) 01647 440660.
Profile Farrier. **Ref: YH11089**

PIER HSE STUD

Pier House Stud, Martinstown, The Curragh, **County Kildare**, **IRELAND**.
(E) pierhousestud@kildarehorse.ie.
Contact/s
Key Contact: Mr B Morrin
Profile Breeder. **Ref: YH11090**

PIERSON STEWART & PARTNERS

Pierson Stewart & Partners, (Cranbrook), Brooksden, Cranbrook, **Kent**, TN17 3DT, **ENGLAND**.
(T) 01580 713381.
Contact/s
Partner: Mr G Ross
Profile Medical Support. **Ref: YH11091**

PIERSON STEWART & PARTNERS,

Pierson Stewart & Partners, (Marden), South Lodge, Marden, **Kent**, TN12 9HS, **ENGLAND**.
(T) 01622 831357.
Profile Medical Support. **Ref: YH11092**

PIG & WHISTLE ROCKING HORSES

Pig & Whistle Rocking Horses, Grove Cottage, Church End, North Somercotes, **Lincolnshire**, LN11 7PZ, **ENGLAND**.
(T) 01507 358648.
Profile Supplies. **Ref: YH11093**

PIGEON HOUSE STABLES

Pigeon House Stables, 33 Roosevelt Rd, Long Hanborough, Witney, **Oxfordshire**, OX8 8JG, **ENGLAND**.
(T) 01993 881628 **(F)** 01993 880310.
Profile Riding School. **Ref: YH11094**

PIGEON HOUSE STABLES

Pigeon House Stables, Pigeon Hse Lane, Church Hanborough, Witney, **Oxfordshire**, OX29 8AH, **ENGLAND**.
(T) 01993 881628
(W) www.horse-rides.co.uk
Affiliated Bodies BHS.
Contact/s
Owner: Ms A Smart
Profile Equestrian Centre, Riding School, Stable/Livery. No.Staff: 4 C.Size: 72 Acres
Opening Times
Sp: Open Tues - Sat 08:30. Closed Tues - Sat 18:00.
Su: Open Tues - Sat 08:30. Closed Tues - Sat 20:00.
Au: Open Tues - Sat 08:30. Closed Tues - Sat 17:00.
Wn: Open Tues - Sat 08:30. Closed Tues - Sat 16:00.
Closed on Mondays **Ref: YH11095**

PIGGOTT & ARNOLD

Piggott & Arnold, 21 Fore St, Bovey Tracey, **Devon**, TQ13 9AD, **ENGLAND**.
(T) 01626 833023.
Profile Medical Support. **Ref: YH11096**

PIGGOTT BROS

Piggott Bros & Co Ltd, Stanford Rivers, Ongar, **Essex**, CM5 9PJ, **ENGLAND**.
(T) 01277 363262 **(F)** 01277 365162.
Profile Club/Association. **Ref: YH11097**

PIGGOTT, R L

R L Piggott, Cherrytree Cottage Farm, Rectory Rd, Bacton, Stowmarket, **Suffolk**, IP14 4LE, **ENGLAND**.
(T) 01449 781216.
Profile Breeder. **Ref: YH11098**

PIGS BOTTOM LANE

Pigs Bottom Lane Riding School, Hurstvale Cottage, Grange Rd, Biddulph, Stoke-on-Trent, **Staffordshire**, ST8 7RZ, **ENGLAND**.
(T) 01782 519619. **Ref: YH11099**

PIKE, B J

Mr B J Pike, Middleton Barton, Clayhidon, Cullompton, **Devon**, EX15 3QF, **ENGLAND**.
(T) 01823 601208.
Profile Breeder. **Ref: YH11100**

PIKE, NIGEL S

Nigel S Pike RSS, Trindle Well, North Perrott, Crewkerne, **Somerset**, TA18 7SX, **ENGLAND**.
(T) 01460 74673 **(F)** 01460 74673
Affiliated Bodies WCF.
Profile Farrier. **Ref: YH11101**

PIKE, S L

Mr S L Pike, Synderborough Farm, Sidbury, Sidmouth, **Devon**, EX10 0QJ, **ENGLAND**.
(T) 01395 597485.
Profile Supplies. **Ref: YH11102**

PIKE, STAN

Stan Pike, Waylands Forge, Ayle, Alston, **Cumbria**, CA9 3NH, **ENGLAND**.
(T) 01434 381587.
Contact/s
Owner: Mr S Pike
Profile Blacksmith. **Ref: YH11103**

PILBROW, KENNETH

Kenneth Pilbrow, 58 The Rank, Maiden Bradley, Warminster, **Wiltshire**, BA12 7JF, **ENGLAND**.
(T) 01985 422.
Profile Farrier. **Ref: YH11104**

PILGRIM STUD

Pilgrim Stud, 3 Culand Cottages, Pilgrims Way, Burham, Rochester, **Kent**, ME1 3SN, **ENGLAND**.
(T) 01634 666287.
Profile Breeder. **Ref: YH11105**

PILKINGTON, J

Mr J Pilkington, The Leys, Birt St, Birtsmorton, Malvern, **Worcestershire**, WR13 6AW, **ENGLAND**.
(T) 01684 833580.
Profile Supplies. **Ref: YH11106**

PILKINGTON, T D

Mrs T D Pilkington, Hyde Mill, Stow-on-the-Wold, Cheltenham, **Gloucestershire**, GL54 1LA, **ENGLAND**.
(T) 01451 830641.
Profile Breeder. **Ref: YH11107**

PILKINGTON, TIMOTHY

Timothy Pilkington BII, Melaine, Fairfield Rd, New Romney, **Kent**, TN28 8HW, **ENGLAND**.
(T) 01797 366120.
Profile Farrier. **Ref: YH11108**

PILL FARM

Pill Farm, Pill Farm, Middle Pill, Saltash, **Cornwall**, PL12 6LQ, **ENGLAND**.
(T) 01752 842322.
Contact/s
Owner: Mr D Batten
Profile Stable/Livery. **Ref: YH11109**

PILOT HIRE

Pilot Hire Limited, British Rail Est, Church St, Luton, **Bedfordshire**, LU1 3JG, **ENGLAND**.
(T) 020 85743882 **(F)** 020 85713515. **Ref: YH11110**

PIMBLEY, ALEX T

Alex T Pimbley DWCF, Lower Hudsons Farm, Chapel Lane, Outrawcliffe, Preston, **Lancashire**, PR3 6TB, **ENGLAND**.
(T) 01253 701014 **(F)** 01253 701014.
Profile Farrier. **Ref: YH11111**

PIMLOTT, C & N

C & N Pimlott, Lacys Cottage, Scrayingham, York, **Yorkshire (North)**, YO41 1JD, **ENGLAND**.
(T) 01759 371586.
Profile Riding School, Stable/Livery. **Ref: YH11112**

PIMLOTT, L K

L K Pimlott, The Smithy, Westwood Heat Rd, Tilehill, Coventry, **Midlands (West)**, CV4 8GP, **ENGLAND**.
(T) 024 76504062.
Profile Farrier. **Ref: YH11113**

PIMM, J

J Pimm, 32 Brighton Rd, Lower Beeding, Horsham, **Sussex (West)**, RH13 6NH, **ENGLAND**.
(T) 01403 891686.
Contact/s
Owner: Mr J Pimm
Profile Farrier. **Ref: YH11114**

PIMM, JAMES V

James V Pimm RSS, 32 Crabtree Cottages, Brighton Rd, Lower Beeding, Horsham, **Sussex (West)**, RH13 6PT, **ENGLAND**.
(T) 01403 76686.
Profile Farrier. **Ref: YH11115**

PINCOMBE, R W

Mr R W Pincombe, Town Living Farm, Mariansleigh, South Molton, **Devon**, EX36 4LN, **ENGLAND**.
(T) 01769 7331.
Profile Supplies. **Ref: YH11116**

PINDER, P J

P J Pinder, Summer Villa, Penmaenmawr Rd, Llanfairfechan, **Gwynedd**, LL33 0NY, **WALES**.
(T) 01248 680037.
Profile Medical Support. **Ref: YH11117**

PINE LODGE

Pine Lodge Livery Yard, Springfield Farm, Lippitts Hill, Loughton, **Essex**, IG10 4AL, **ENGLAND**.
(T) 020 85087070.
Contact/s
Owner: Mrs S Jeapes-Quin
Profile Stable/Livery. Yr. Est: 1976 C.Size: 8 Acres **Ref: YH11118**

PINE LODGE RIDING HOLIDAY

Pine Lodge Riding Holiday, Higher Chilcott Farm, Dulverton, **Somerset**, TA22 9QQ, **ENGLAND**.
(T) 01398 323559.
Profile Riding School. **Ref: YH11119**

PINE RIDGE

Pine Ridge, Pound Lane, Knockholt, Sevenoaks, **Kent**, TN14 7NE, **ENGLAND**.
(T) 01959 533161.
Contact/s
Owner: Miss T Dyson
Profile Riding School. Yr. Est: 1981 C.Size: 4 Acres
Opening Times
Sp: Open Tues - Sun 10:00. Closed Tues - Sun 17:00.
Su: Open Tues - Sun 10:00. Closed Tues - Sun 17:00.
Au: Open Tues - Sun 10:00. Closed Tues - Sun 17:00.
Wn: Open Tues - Sun 10:00. Closed Tues - Sun 17:00.
Closed Mondays **Ref: YH11120**

PINE RIDGE FARM

Pine Ridge Farm Ltd, Forest Rd, Colgate, Horsham, **Sussex (West)**, RH12 4TB, **ENGLAND**.
(T) 01293 851600 **(F)** 01293 851600.
Contact/s
Owner: Mr B Stevens
Profile Breeder. **Ref: YH11121**

PINE TREE LIVERY

Pine Tree Stud, Horse Hill, Goadby, Leicester, **Leicestershire**, LE7 9EE, **ENGLAND**.
(T) 0116 2598257 **(F)** 0116 2330551.
Contact/s

Owner: Mr G Marshall
Profile Stable/Livery.
Full, part and DIY livery available, prices on request.
Yr. Est: 1997 C.Size: 26 Acres
Opening Times
Sp: Open Mon - Sun 07:00. Closed Mon - Sun 22:00.
Su: Open Mon - Sun 07:00. Closed Mon - Sun 22:00.
Au: Open Mon - Sun 07:00. Closed Mon - Sun 22:00.
Wn: Open Mon - Sun 07:00. Closed Mon - Sun 22:00.
Times given are for enquiries. Clients are able to use facilities during daylight hours and in the winter at the owners discretion. Ref: YH11122

PINE WOOD STUD

Pine Wood Stud, Hamilton Rd, Newmarket, **Suffolk**, CB8 8JQ, **ENGLAND**.
(T) 01638 665025 (F) 01638 661538
(M) 07850 725105.
Profile Breeder. Ref: YH11123

PINEFIELD TACK SHOP

Pinefield Tack Shop, Pinefield, Lund Lane, Killinghall, Harrogate, **Yorkshire (North)**, HG3 2BQ, **ENGLAND**.
(T) 01423 506367.
Contact/s
Owner: Mrs D Bentley Ref: YH11124

PINEGROVE STABLES

Pinegrove Stables, Pinegrove, Whites Cross, Cork, **County Cork**, **IRELAND**.
(T) 021 4303857.
Contact/s
Owner: Mr C Hennessy
Profile Trainer. No.Staff: 2 Yr. Est: 1994
C.Size: 40 Acres
Opening Times
Telephone for an appointment Ref: YH11125

PINEWOOD STABLES

Pinewood Stables, Sychnant Pass Rd, Llechwedd, **Conwy**, LL32 8BZ, **WALES**.
(T) 01492 592256.
Contact/s
Owner: Mrs P Jones
Profile Riding School. Ref: YH11126

PINEWOOD STABLES

Pinewood Stables, Carburton, Worksop, **Nottinghamshire**, S80 3BT, **ENGLAND**.
(T) 01909 475425.
Profile Trainer. Ref: YH11127

PINEWOOD STABLES

Pinewood Stables, Mill Lane, Branton, Doncaster, **Yorkshire (South)**, DN3 3NX, **ENGLAND**.
(T) 01302 535221. Ref: YH11128

PINEWOOD VETNRY PRACTICE

Pinewood Veterinary Practice, 23 Crown St, Chorley, **Lancashire**, PR7 1DX, **ENGLAND**.
(T) 01257 276517 (F) 01257 279577.
Profile Medical Support. Ref: YH11129

PINFOLD STABLES

Pinfold Stables, Pinfold Lane, Marthall, Knutsford, **Cheshire**, WA16 7SN, **ENGLAND**.
(T) 01565 873190. Ref: YH11130

PINGLE NOOK FORGE

Pingle Nook Forge, Hollin Edge, Denby Dale, Huddersfield, **Yorkshire (West)**, HD8 8YW, **ENGLAND**.
(T) 01484 866081.
Profile Farrier. Ref: YH11131

PINHOE RIDING CTRE

Pinhoe Riding Centre, Church Hill, Pinhoe, Exeter, **Devon**, EX4 9JG, **ENGLAND**.
(T) 01392 468683. Ref: YH11132

PININA STUD

Pinina Stud (The), Pinfold Lane, Moss, Doncaster, **Yorkshire (South)**, DN6 0ED, **ENGLAND**.
(T) 01302 700535.
Contact/s
Owner: Mrs N Clayton
Profile Breeder. Ref: YH11133

PINNER, TERRY

T F Pinner, Pringle Farm, Little Stukeley, Huntingdon, **Cambridgeshire**, PE28 4BH, **ENGLAND**.
(T) 01480 455471 (F) 01480 455471.
Contact/s
Owner: Mr T Pinner
(E) teryle@lineone.net
Profile Equestrian Centre, Stable/Livery, Trainer.
Horses schooled and reschooled. No.Staff: 2
Yr. Est: 1954 C.Size: 50 Acres
Opening Times
Sp: Open 08:00. Closed 17:00.
Su: Open 08:00. Closed 17:00.
Au: Open 08:30. Closed 16:30.
Wn: Open 09:00. Closed 16:30. Ref: YH11134

PINNERWOOD & DISTRICT

Pinnerwood & District Riding Club, 22 Farm Way, Bushey, **Hertfordshire**, WD2 3SS, **ENGLAND**.
(T) 01707 52270.
Contact/s
Chairman: Mrs C Lynn
Profile Club/Association, Riding Club. Ref: YH11135

PINNERWOOD ARABIAN STUD

Pinnerwood Arabian Stud, Pinnerwood Farm, Hatch End, **London (Greater)**, HA5 4UA, **ENGLAND**.
(T) 020 84282530 (F) 020 84280313
(W) www.pinnerwood.com.
Contact/s
Owner: Mr D Angold (Q) Dip Ag
(E) david.angold@which.net
Profile Breeder, Stable/Livery. Yr. Est: 1960
C.Size: 120 Acres
Opening Times
Sp: Open 07:00. Closed 22:00.
Su: Open 07:00. Closed 22:00.
Au: Open 07:00. Closed 22:00.
Wn: Open 07:00. Closed 22:00. Ref: YH11136

PINNERWOOD FARM

Pinnerwood Farm, Hatch End, Pinner, **London (Greater)**, HA5 4UA, **ENGLAND**.
(T) 020 84282530. Ref: YH11137

PINNEY, WILLIAM G M

William G M Pinney DWCF, 36 Newark Rd, Windlesham, **Surrey**, GU20 6NE, **ENGLAND**.
(T) 07966 388873.
Profile Farrier. Ref: YH11138

PINNOCKS WOOD EQUESTRIAN CTRE

Pinnocks Wood Equestrian Centre, Burchetts Green Lane, Burchetts Green, Maidenhead, **Berkshire**, SL6 3QP, **ENGLAND**.
(T) 01628 822031 (F) 01628 820143.
Contact/s
Owner: Mr D Isles
Profile Stable/Livery. Ref: YH11139

PINTOFIELDS

PintoFields, Booth Hall, Kingsley, Stoke-on-Trent, **Staffordshire**, ST10 2EG, **ENGLAND**.
(T) 01538 750939
(E) nskilpatrick@pintofields.ndirect.co.uk
(W) www.pintofields.ndirect.co.uk.
Contact/s
Owner: Dr M Kilpatrick
Profile Breeder.
Breed Coloured Sports Horses. Yr. Est: 1984
Opening Times
Telephone for an appointment Ref: YH11140

PIONEER ANIMAL FEEDS

Pioneer Animal Feeds, Units 8 & 9, Dymock Rd Trading Est, Ledbury, **Herefordshire**, HR8 2HT, **ENGLAND**.
(T) 01531 635272.
Profile Supplies. Ref: YH11141

PIONEER ANIMAL FEEDS

Pioneer Animal Feeds, Crome Nurseries, Upton-upon-Severn, **Worcestershire**, WR8 9DA, **ENGLAND**.
(T) 01684 594441.
Profile Supplies. Ref: YH11142

PIONEER STUD

Pioneer Stud, 185 New St, Biddulph Moor, Stoke-on-Trent, **Staffordshire**, ST8 7NY, **ENGLAND**.
(T) 01782 517610.
Profile Breeder. Ref: YH11143

PIPE, K

K Pipe, Benshayne Farm, Culmstock, Cullompton, **Devon**, EX15 3HW, **ENGLAND**.
(T) 01884 840713.
Contact/s
Owner: Mr K Pipe
Profile Trainer. Ref: YH11144

PIPE, M C

Mr M C Pipe, Pond Hse, Nicholashayne, Wellington, **Somerset**, TA21 9QY, **ENGLAND**.
(T) 01884 840715 (F) 01884 841343.
Profile Trainer. Ref: YH11145

PIPER, JUDI

Judi Piper, Starnash Farmhouse, Upper Dicker, Hailsham, **Sussex (East)**, BN27 3PY, **ENGLAND**.
(T) 01323 440041 (F) 01323 442041.
Profile Breeder, Trainer. Ref: YH11146

PIPERS FARM LIVERY YARD

Pipers Farm Livery Yard, Lippitts Hill, Loughton, **Essex**, IG10 4AL, **ENGLAND**.
(T) 020 85086081 (F) 020 85023560.
Contact/s
Partner: Mr E Bovis Ref: YH11147

PIPERS FORGE

Pipers Forge, Victoria St, Kirkpatrick Durham, Castle Douglas, **Dumfries and Galloway**, DG7 3HQ, **SCOTLAND**.
(T) 01556 650513.
Profile Blacksmith. Ref: YH11148

PIPERS STUD

Pipers Stud, Pipers Lane, Harpenden, **Hertfordshire**, AL5 1AF, **ENGLAND**.
(T) 01582 832576.
Contact/s
Manageress: Mrs H Wesley
Profile Breeder. Ref: YH11149

PIROUET, TIMOTHY RYAN

Timothy Ryan Pirouet, 11 Croft Rd, Newbury, **Berkshire**, RG14 7AL, **ENGLAND**.
(T) 01635 30015.
Profile Farrier. Ref: YH11150

PITCHER, MARK S

Mark S Pitcher DWCF, 97 Glendower Cres, Orpington, **Kent**, BR6 7RR, **ENGLAND**.
(T) 01689 829749.
Profile Farrier. Ref: YH11151

PITMAN, TERRY R

Terry R Pitman DWCF, 61 Valley Rd, Codicote, Hitchin, **Hertfordshire**, SG4 8YW, **ENGLAND**.
(T) 01438 820633.
Profile Farrier. Ref: YH11152

PITMEDDEN STUD

Pitmedden Stud, Rogerseat, Rothienorman, Inverurie, **Aberdeenshire**, AB51 8YJ, **SCOTLAND**.
(T) 01651 821088.
Profile Breeder. Ref: YH11153

PITTENDRIGH, P I

P I Pittendrigh, Bradley Hall Farm, Wylam, **Northumberland**, NE41 8JP, **ENGLAND**.
(T) 01661 852676.
Profile Trainer. Ref: YH11154

PITTERN HILL

Pittern Hill, Pittern Hill, Kineton, Warwick, **Warwickshire**, CV35 0JF, **ENGLAND**.
(T) 01926 640370.
Contact/s
Owner: Mr R Philpot
Profile Riding School, Saddlery Retailer.
Ref: YH11155

PITTHAM & BODILY

Pittham & Bodily, Hill Crest, Hellidon Rd, Priors Marston, Southam, **Warwickshire**, CV47 7RX, **ENGLAND**.
(T) 01327 260392.
Contact/s
Partner: Mrs B Bodily
Profile Transport/Horse Boxes. Ref: YH11156

PITTON CROSS TREKKING CTRE

Pitton Cross Trekking Centre, Pitton Cross, Rhossili, Swansea, **Swansea**, SA3 1PH, **WALES**.
(T) 01792 390554.
Contact/s
Owner: Mr W Tucker
Profile Equestrian Centre. Ref: YH11157

PITTS FARM STUD

Pitts Farm Stud, Newlands Lane, Glanvilles Wootton, Sherborne, **Dorset**, DT9 5QG, **ENGLAND**.
(T) 01300 345274 (F) 01300 345495.
Contact/s
Owner: Mr C Wilson
Profile Breeder. Ref: YH11158

PIX FARM FEED STORE

Pix Farm Feed Store, Pix Farm, Bourne End, Hemel Hempstead, **Hertfordshire**, HP1 2RY, **ENGLAND**.
(T) 01442 864652 (F) 01442 864652

Key: (T) telephone (F) fax (M) mobile (E) E-Mail Address (W) Website Address (Q) Qualifications
Yr. Est: Year Established C.Size: Complex Size Sp: Spring Su: Summer Au: Autumn Wn: Winter

(E) pixfarm@equestrianet.co.uk
(W) www.pixfarm.co.uk.
Profile Saddlery Retailer. **Ref:YH11159**

PIZER, GEOFFREY R

Geoffrey R Pizer RSS, The Old Post Office, 29 Main St, Goadby Marwood, Melton Mowbray, **Leicestershire**, LE14 4LN, **ENGLAND**.
(T) 01664 464470.
Profile Farrier. **Ref:YH11160**

PLANT, JANET

Ms Janet Plant BHSI, Rose Cottage, Broom Bank, Knightley, Woodseaves, **Staffordshire**, ST20 0JW, **ENGLAND**.
(T) 01785 284632
(M) 07836 579810.
Profile Trainer. **Ref:YH11161**

PLANT, MICHAEL J

Michael J Plant RSS, 5 Mill Lane, Great Ponton, Grantham, **Lincolnshire**, NG33 5DT, **ENGLAND**.
(T) 01476 83229.
Profile Farrier. **Ref:YH11162**

PLANTATION STUD

Plantation Stud, Snailwell, Newmarket, **Suffolk**, CB8 7LJ, **ENGLAND**.
(T) 01638 577341 **(F)** 01638 578474.
Contact/s
Manager: Mr A Harrison
Profile Breeder. **Ref:YH11163**

PLAS EQUESTRIAN

Plas Equestrian, Plas-Y-Mista, Rhydargaeau, Carmarthen, **Carmarthenshire**, SA32 7JJ, **WALES**.
(T) 01267 253251 **(F)** 01267 253251
(E) info@plasequestrian.co.uk
(W) www.plasequestrian.co.uk.
Contact/s
Owner: Ms G Green
Profile Saddlery Retailer, Supplies. Specialist Harness Manufacturers.
Credit cards will be accepted from 2002.
No.Staff: 14 Yr. Est: 1993 CREDIT
Opening Times
Mainly mail order, viewing by appointment
Ref:YH11164

PLAS-Y-CELYN

Plas-Y-Celyn Trekking & Riding Centre, Ceunant, Nr Waunfawr, Caernarfon, **Gwynedd**, LL55 4SA, **WALES**.
(T) 01286 85642.
Profile Riding School. **Ref:YH11165**

PLAS-Y-MAES

Plas-y-Maes Saddlery & Repair Centre, Morfa Farm, Trimsaran Rd, Kidwelly, Llanelli, **Carmarthenshire**, SA17 4ED, **WALES**.
(T) 01554 890248
(M) 07967 860537.
Profile Supplies. **Ref:YH11166**

PLATT MILL LIVERY STABLES

Platt Mill Livery Stables, Birch Park Farm, Stanwardine Rd, Baschurch, Shrewsbury, **Shropshire**, SY4 2ES, **ENGLAND**.
(T) 01939 260109.
Contact/s
Owner: Miss K Webster **Ref:YH11167**

PLATT, ANGELA D

Angela D Platt DWCF, 100 Townfield Rd, Flitwick, **Bedfordshire**, MK45 1JG, **ENGLAND**.
(T) 01525 715891.
Profile Farrier. **Ref:YH11168**

PLAYBARN

Playbarn (The), R W Kidner (Farms) Ltd, West Green Farm, Shotesham Rd, Poringland, **Norfolk**, NR14 7LP, **ENGLAND**.
(T) 01508 494150 **(F)** 01508 494420.
Profile Riding School, Saddlery Retailer.
Ref:YH11169

PLAYLE, J

J Playle, Mains Of Bodychell, Fraserburgh, **Aberdeenshire**, AB43 7DB, **SCOTLAND**.
(T) 01346 541449
(M) 07831 790942
Affiliated Bodies FRC.
Contact/s
Owner: Mr J Playle **(Q)** Reg Farrier
Profile Farrier.
Mobile service available or can work from own site. Can provide and make shoes. No.Staff: 1
Yr. Est: 1995
Opening Times
Sp: Open Mon - Sat 08:00. Closed Mon - Sat 19:00.
Su: Open Mon - Sat 08:00. Closed Mon - Sat 19:00.
Au: Open Mon - Sat 08:00. Closed Mon - Sat 19:00.
Wn: Open Mon - Sat 08:00. Closed Mon - Sat 19:00.
Ref:YH11170

PLAYLE, KENNETH R

Kenneth R Playle, Wester Chalder, Keith, **Aberdeenshire**, AB55 5QD, **SCOTLAND**.
(T) 01542 810338.
Contact/s
Owner: Mr K Playle
Profile Farrier. **Ref:YH11171**

PLAYMATE CHILDRENS

Playmate Childrens Riding School (The), Hardwicke Mews, Elmstone Hardwicke, Cheltenham, **Gloucestershire**, GL51 9TD, **ENGLAND**.
(T) 01242 680888.
Profile Riding School. **Ref:YH11172**

PLC DESIGNS

P L C Designs Computer Software, Mythe Villa, The Mythe, Tewkesbury, **Gloucestershire**, GL20 6EB, **ENGLAND**.
(T) 01684 293765 **(F)** 01684 293765
(E) crosspl@aol.com. **Ref:YH11173**

PLEASLEY PARK LIVERY

Pleasley Park Livery, Wood Lane, Pleasley Vale, Mansfield, **Nottinghamshire**, NG19 8RY, **ENGLAND**.
(T) 01623 748494.
Contact/s
Owner: Mrs D Welch
Profile Stable/Livery. **Ref:YH11174**

PLEASURE PRINTS

Pleasure Prints, Po Box 171, Walton-on-Thames, **Surrey**, KT12 4NL, **ENGLAND**.
(T) 01932 254500 **(F)** 01932 254500
(E) pleasureprints@aol.com. **Ref:YH11175**

PLEASURE PRINTS AREA C

Pleasure Prints Area C, Coombe Hse, Crookham Common, Newbury, **Berkshire**, RG15 8DG, **ENGLAND**.
(T) 01635 863063. **Ref:YH11176**

PLEASURE PRINTS AREA D

Pleasure Prints Area D, Dark Orchard, Pumpsaint, Llanwrda, **Carmarthenshire**, SA19 8DJ, **WALES**.
(T) 01558 650111 **(F)** 01558 650780
(E) ccook@aol.com.
Contact/s
Partner: Mr C Cook **Ref:YH11177**

PLOVER HILL RIDING SCHOOL

Plover Hill Riding School & Trekking Centre, By Dipton Mill Inn, Hexham, **Northumberland**, NE46 1YA, **ENGLAND**.
(T) 01434 607196.
Profile Riding School. **Ref:YH11178**

PLOVERS DARTMOORS

Plovers Dartmoors, Garden Cottage, Glebe Hse, Bucknowle, Wareham, **Dorset**, BH20 5NS, **ENGLAND**.
(T) 01929 480384 **(F)** 01929 480671.
Profile Breeder. **Ref:YH11179**

PLOWRIGHT, G S

Mrs G S Plowright, 252 Lingwell Gate Lane, Lofthouse, Wakefield, **Yorkshire (West)**, WF3 3JU, **ENGLAND**.
(T) 01924 870240.
Profile Supplies. **Ref:YH11180**

PLUESS, KERENSA

Kerensa Pluess, Trevoutlter, Poundstock, Bude, **Cornwall**, EX23 0DH, **ENGLAND**.
(T) 01288 361368 **(F)** 01288 361361.
Contact/s
Owner: Mr G Pluess
Profile Trainer. **Ref:YH11181**

PLUM PUDDING EQUESTRIAN CTRE

Plum Pudding Equestrian Centre, Plum Pudding Island, Birchington, **Kent**, CT7 9QS, **ENGLAND**.
(T) 01843 847142. **Ref:YH11182**

PLUMPTON CLGE

Plumpton College, Plumpton, Lewes, **Sussex (East)**, BN7 3AE, **ENGLAND**.
(T) 01273 890454 **(F)** 01273 890071.
Profile Equestrian Centre. **Ref:YH11183**

PLUMPTON RACECOURSE

Plumpton Racecourse Ltd, Plumpton Racecourse, Plumpton, **Sussex (East)**, BN7 3AL, **ENGLAND**.
(T) 01273 890383 **(F)** 01273 891557.
Contact/s
Chief Executive: Patrick Davies
Profile Track/Course. **Ref:YH11184**

PLUMSTONE TREKKING CTRE

Plumstone Trekking Centre, Precelly Viewfarm, Camrose, Haverfordwest, **Pembrokeshire**, SA62 6JP, **WALES**.
(T) 01437 741536.
Contact/s
Partner: Mrs W Border
Profile Equestrian Centre. **Ref:YH11185**

PLUMTREE, R T J

Mr R T J Plumtree, 20 Hollington Cres, New Malden, **Surrey**, KT3 6RP, **ENGLAND**.
(T) 020 89425673.
Profile Breeder. **Ref:YH11186**

PLYMPTON TACK

Plympton Tack, 11 Underwood Rd, Plymouth, **Devon**, PL7 1SY, **ENGLAND**.
(T) 01752 343384 **(F)** 01752 343373.
Contact/s
Owner: Mrs S Hingston **Ref:YH11187**

POCOCK, R E

Mr R E Pocock, Stringston Farm, Holford, Bridgwater, **Somerset**, TA5 1SX, **ENGLAND**.
(T) 01278 741236 **(F)** 01278 741240.
Profile Breeder. **Ref:YH11188**

POGSON, CHARLES

Mr Charles Pogson, Allamoor Farm, Farnsfield, Newark, **Nottinghamshire**, NG22 8HZ, **ENGLAND**.
(T) 01623 882275.
Profile Supplies. **Ref:YH11189**

POINT TO POINT

Point to Point Owners & Riders Association, Horton Court, Westbere Lane, Westbere, Canterbury, **Kent**, CT2 0HH, **ENGLAND**.
(T) 01227 713080.
Contact/s
Hon Secretary: Jeanette Dawson
Profile Club/Association. **Ref:YH11190**

POINT TO POINT

Point to Point Secretaries Association, 42 Portman Sq, London, **London (Greater)**, W1H 0EN, **ENGLAND**.
(T) 020 74864921 **(F)** 020 79358703.
Profile Club/Association. **Ref:YH11191**

POINT TO POINT & HUNTER CHASE

Point to Point & Hunter Chase, Poundbury Publishing Ltd, Agriculture Hse, Acland Rd, Dorchester, **Dorset**, DT1 1EF, **ENGLAND**.
(T) 01305 266360 **(F)** 01305 262760
(E) poundbury@wdi.co.uk.
Contact/s
Editor: Brian Elliott
Profile Supplies. **Ref:YH11192**

POINTER

Pointer (The), 68 Eagle Brow, Lymm, **Cheshire**, WA13 0LZ, **ENGLAND**.
(T) 01925 753097.
Contact/s
Owner: Mr D Coulton
Profile Supplies. **Ref:YH11193**

POINTING SADDLERY

Pointing Saddlery, Blathwayt Stables, Lansdown, Bath, **Bath & Somerset (North East)**, BA1 9BT, **ENGLAND**.
(T) 01225 462136 **(F)** 01225 483983.
Contact/s
Owner: Mr P Lewis **Ref:YH11194**

POIRRIER, BILL

Bill Poirrier, Riverden Forge, Roadwater, Watchet, **Somerset**, TA23 0QH, **ENGLAND**.
(T) 01984 640648.
Contact/s
Owner: Mr B Poirrier
Profile Blacksmith. **Ref:YH11195**

POLAK GALLERY

Polak Gallery, 21 King St, St James's, London, **London (Greater)**, SW1Y 6QY, **ENGLAND**.
(T) 020 78392671 **(F)** 020 79303467. **Ref:YH11196**

POLDEN LEA STABLES

Polden Lea Stables, Catcott, Bridgwater, **Somerset**, TA7 9HJ, **ENGLAND**.
(T) 01823 662660.
Profile Supplies. **Ref:YH11197**

POLEGATE SADDLERY
Polegate Saddlery, 3 Millfields, Station Rd, Polegate, **Sussex (East)**, BN26 6AS, **ENGLAND**.
(T) 01323 483382 **(F)** 01323 484575.
Contact/s
Partner: Mr R Streeter
Profile Saddlery Retailer. **Ref: YH11198**

POLESBURN VETNRY CTRE
Polesburn Veterinary Centre, Polesburn, Methlick, Ellon, **Aberdeenshire**, AB41 0DU, **SCOTLAND**.
(T) 01651 806212 **(F)** 01651 806404.
Contact/s
Vet: Mr R Loggie
Profile Medical Support. **Ref: YH11199**

POLGLASE, MARK
Mark Polglase, Training Barn, Southwell Racecourse, Southwell, **Nottinghamshire**, NG25 0TS, **ENGLAND**.
(T) 01636 816717 **(F)** 01636 816517.
Contact/s
Owner: Mr M Polglase
Profile Trainer. **Ref: YH11200**

POLGODA LIVERY YARD
Polgoda Livery Yard, Zelah, Truro, **Cornwall**, TR4 9HA, **ENGLAND**.
(T) 01872 540434.
Contact/s
Owner: Miss J Simmons **Ref: YH11201**

POLHILL RIDING CTRE
Polhill Riding Centre, Otford Lane, Halstead, Sevenoaks, **Kent**, TN14 7EA, **ENGLAND**.
(T) 01959 532530.
Profile Riding School. **Ref: YH11202**

POLKEY, FREDERICK C
Frederick C Polkey DWCF BII, 135 Baker St, Alvaston, **Derbyshire**, DE2 8SE, **ENGLAND**.
(T) 01332 571935.
Profile Farrier. **Ref: YH11203**

POLLARD, G S
Mrs G S Pollard, 19 Blackburn Rd, Whittle-Le-Woods, Chorley, **Lancashire**, PR6 8LD, **ENGLAND**.
(T) 01257 267883. **Ref: YH11204**

POLLARD, ROBERT
Robert Pollard DWCF, Cloverdale, Willow Rd, Little Mongeham, Deal, **Kent**, CT14 7QS, **ENGLAND**.
(T) 01304 372393.
Profile Farrier. **Ref: YH11205**

POLLARD, V
Mrs V Pollard, Alton Nether Farm, Tinkerley Lane, Kirk Ireton, Ashbourne, **Derbyshire**, DE6 3LF, **ENGLAND**.
(T) 01335 370270 **(F)** 01335 370270.
Profile Trainer. **Ref: YH11206**

POLLY FLINDERS
Polly Flinders, 23 Bull Ring, Ludlow, **Shropshire**, SY8 1AA, **ENGLAND**.
(T) 01584 875124.
Profile Saddlery Retailer. **Ref: YH11207**

POLLY LUNN PET & AQUATICS
Polly Lunn Pet & Aquatics, Quencwell Rd, Carnon Downs, Truro, **Cornwall**, TR3 6LN, **ENGLAND**.
(T) 01872 862277.
Contact/s
Owner: Mr M Hassle
Profile Riding Wear Retailer, Saddlery Retailer, Supplies. **Ref: YH11208**

POLLY PRODUCTS
Polly Products Ltd, Phoenix Works, South St, Horncastle, **Lincolnshire**, LN9 6DT, **ENGLAND**.
(T) 01507 522326 **(F)** 01507 522326
(E) tfrost@btconnect.com
(W) www.t-frost-bawtry.co.uk.
Contact/s
Owner: Mr B Hunter
Profile Saddlery Retailer, Supplies. Manufacturer horse clothing. **Yr. Est:** 1985
Opening Times
Sp: Open Mon - Sat 08:00. Closed Mon - Sat 16:30.
Su: Open Mon - Sat 08:00. Closed Mon - Sat 16:30.
Au: Open Mon - Sat 08:00. Closed Mon - Sat 16:30.
Wn: Open Mon - Sat 08:00. Closed Mon - Sat 16:30.
Closed Sundays **Ref: YH11209**

POLNOON CASTLE RIDERS ASS
Polnoon Castle Riders Association, Ardochrig Farm, Auldhouse, East Kilbride, **Lanarkshire (South)**, G75 0QN, **SCOTLAND**.
(T) 01355 246352
(E) polnoon@sedona.co.uk.
Profile Club/Association. **Ref: YH11210**

POLO PONY WELFARE COMMITTEE
Polo Pony Welfare Committee, B M F, Burton Pk Rd, Petworth, **Sussex (West)**, GU28 0JR, **ENGLAND**.
(T) 01798 869496 **(F)** 01798 869497.
Profile Club/Association. **Ref: YH11211**

POLPEVER RIDING STABLES
Polpever Riding Stables, Duloe, Liskeard, **Cornwall**, PL14 4PS, **ENGLAND**.
(T) 01503 263010.
Profile Riding School, Stable/Livery. **Ref: YH11212**

POLY PROP
Poly Prop (Wales), Llain, Llwyndafydd, Llandysul, **Carmarthenshire**, SA44 6BY, **WALES**.
(T) 01545 560602 **(F)** 01545 561076.
Profile Supplies. **Ref: YH11213**

POLYMER RECLAMATION
Polymer Reclamation Ltd, Unit 44 Ind Est, Harbour Rd, Lydney, **Gloucestershire**, GL15 4EJ, **ENGLAND**.
(T) 01594 841925 **(F)** 01594 841925. **Ref: YH11214**

POLYTECHNIC OF NORTH LONDON
Polytechnic of North London Riding Club, Nl Sports Liason Officer, Polytechnic Of North London, Holloway Road, **London (Greater)**, N7 8DB, **ENGLAND**.
(T) 020 83403315.
Profile Club/Association, Riding Club. **Ref: YH11215**

POMFRET, J B
J B Pomfret, 34 Pant Glas, Cardiff, **Glamorgan (Vale of)**, CF23 7EU, **WALES**.
(T) 029 20736504.
Profile Farrier. **Ref: YH11216**

POND FARM
Pond Farm, Bakers Lane, Black Notley, Braintree, **Essex**, CM7 8JU, **ENGLAND**.
(T) 01376 328033.
Contact/s
Partner: Mr T Ridler
Profile Saddlery Retailer. **Ref: YH11217**

POND, STEPHEN
Stephen Pond, The Brake, Ledbury Rd, Staunton, **Gloucestershire**, GL19 3QX, **ENGLAND**.
(T) 01452 840731. **Ref: YH11218**

PONDEROSA EQUESTRIAN CTRE
Ponderosa Equestrian Centre, Newport Rd, New Inn, Pontypool, **Monmouthshire**, NP4 0TP, **WALES**.
(T) 01495 762660.
Profile Riding School, Stable/Livery. **Ref: YH11219**

PONDEROSA RIDING ACADEMY
Ponderosa Riding Academy, Nr Astley Green Lights, East Lancs Rd, Astley, Tyldesley, **Manchester (Greater)**, M29 7QQ, **ENGLAND**.
(T) 01942 883102.
Contact/s
Owner: Mrs W Terry
Profile Riding School. **Ref: YH11220**

PONDS FARM LIVERY STABLES
Ponds Farm Livery Stables, Ponds Farm, Ponds Lane, Shere, Guildford, **Surrey**, GU5 9JL, **ENGLAND**.
(T) 01483 203608. **Ref: YH11221**

PONDWOOD LIVERY STABLES
Pondwood Livery Stables, Pondwood Lane, White Waltham, Maidenhead, **Berkshire**, SL6 3SS, **ENGLAND**.
(T) 0118 9321031 **(F)** 0118 9340012.
Contact/s
Owner: Mr M Holdaway **Ref: YH11222**

PONIES ASSOCIATION
Ponies Association (Uk), Chesham Hse, 56 Green End Rd, Sawtry, Huntingdon, **Cambridgeshire**, PE17 5UY, **ENGLAND**.
(T) 01487 830278 **(F)** 01487 832086
(E) info@poniesuk.org.
Contact/s
Key Contact: Mrs D Whiteman
Profile Club/Association. **Ref: YH11223**

PONSBOURNE RIDING CTRE
Ponsbourne Riding Centre, Newgate St Village, Hertford, **Hertfordshire**, SG13 8QR, **ENGLAND**.
(T) 01707 874777.
Contact/s
Owner: Mrs S Fitzgerald
Profile Riding School, Saddlery Retailer, Stable/Livery. **Ref: YH11224**

PONTEFRACT PK RACE
Pontefract Park Race Co Ltd, 33 Ropergate, Pontefract, **Yorkshire (West)**, WF8 1LE, **ENGLAND**.
(T) 01977 703224 **(F)** 01977 600577.
Contact/s
Assistant Manager: Mrs N Kawood
Profile Track/Course. **Ref: YH11225**

PONTERWYD TREKING CTRE
Ponterwyd Treking Centre, Anslow Lodge, Ponterwyd, Aberystwyth, **Ceredigion**, SY23 3JY, **WALES**.
(T) 01970 890683.
Profile Equestrian Centre. **Ref: YH11226**

PONTING, M F
M F Ponting, The Veterinary Surgery, Sheep St, Cirencester, **Gloucestershire**, GL7 1QW, **ENGLAND**.
(T) 01285 643146
(M) 07831 414516.
Profile Medical Support. **Ref: YH11227**

PONY CLUB
Pony Club (Area 14 - Bath), Norton Hse, Norton St. Phillip, Bath, **Bath & Somerset (North East)**, BA2 7LW, **ENGLAND**.
(T) 01373 834239
(E) area14@pcuk.org
(W) www.pony-club.org.uk.
Contact/s
Area Representative: Mrs S Wardle
Profile Club/Association.
The centre offers Pony Club membership to children without a pony. This is a charitable organisation promoting high standards of horsemanship, training, events and competitions. There are 24 branches within this area. **Ref: YH11228**

PONY CLUB
Pony Club (Area 13 - South), Lockram Hse, Goodards Green, Mortimer, Reading, **Berkshire**, RG7 3AR, **ENGLAND**.
(T) 0118 9832218 **(F)** 0118 9831944
(E) area13@pcuk.org
(W) www.pony-club.org.uk.
Profile Club/Association.
The centre offers Pony Club membership to children without a pony. This is a charitable organisation promoting high standards of horsemanship, training, events and competitions. There are 20 branches within this area. **Ref: YH11229**

PONY CLUB
Pony Club (Area 18 - W Wales), Bryn Hyfryd, Maesquarre Rd, Ammanford, **Carmarthenshire**, SA18 2HQ, **WALES**.
(T) 01269 592962
(E) area18@pcuk.org
(W) www.pony-club.org.uk.
Contact/s
Area Representative: Mrs M Panes
Profile Club/Association.
The centre offers Pony Club membership to children without a pony. This is a charitable organisation promoting high standards of horsemanship, training, events and competitions. There are 20 branches within this area. **Ref: YH11230**

PONY CLUB
Pony Club (Area 5 - Cheshire), Fennywood Farm, Woodford Lane, Winsford, **Cheshire**, CW7 4EG, **ENGLAND**.
(T) 01829 760573 **(F)** 01829 760573
(E) area5@pcuk.org
(W) www.pony-club.org.co.uk.
Contact/s
Area Representative: Mrs G Summers
Profile Club/Association.
The centre offers Pony Club membership to children without a pony. This is a charitable organisation promoting high standards of horsemanship, training, events and competitions. There are 14 branches within this area. **Ref: YH11231**

PONY CLUB
Pony Club (Area 16 - Cornwall/Devon), Higher Miltown, Lostwithiel, **Cornwall**, PL22 0JN, **ENGLAND**.
(T) 01208 872605
(E) area16@pcuk.org
(W) www.pony-club.org.uk.
Contact/s
Area Representative: Mrs R Cook
Profile Club/Association.
The centre offers Pony Club membership to children without a pony. This is a charitable organisation promoting high standards of horsemanship, training,

events and competitions. There are 17 branches within this area. **Ref: YH11232**

PONY CLUB

Pony Club (Area 17 - N Ireland), Ruth Mount, 64 Hillhead Rd, Carrickfergus, **County Antrim**, BT38 9JF, **NORTHERN IRELAND**.
(T) 028 93373386 **(F)** 028 93373386
(E) area17@pcuk.org
(W) www.pony-club.org.uk.
Contact/s
Area Representative: Mrs M Andrews
Profile Club/Association.
The centre offers Pony Club membership to children without a pony. This is a charitable organisation promoting high standards of horsemanship, training, events and competitions. There are 12 branches within this area. **Ref: YH11233**

PONY CLUB

Pony Club (Area 15 - West), Vale Hse, Burnt Oak, Sidmouth, **Devon**, EX10 0RB, **ENGLAND**.
(T) 01395 597484
(E) area15@pcuk.org
(W) www.pony-club.org.uk.
Contact/s
Area Representative: Mr G Edmunds (Esq)
Profile Club/Association.
The centre offers Pony Club membership to children without a pony. This is a charitable organisation promoting high standards of horsemanship, training, events and competitions. There are 16 branches within this area. **Ref: YH11234**

PONY CLUB

Pony Club (Area 19 - Southern Scotland), Airntully, Kirkcudbright, **Dumfries and Galloway**, DG6 4NF, **SCOTLAND**.
(T) 01557 331257 **(F)** 024 76696836
(E) area19@pcuk.org
(W) www.pony-club.org.uk.
Contact/s
Area Representative: Mrs M Jessiman
Profile Club/Association.
The centre offers Pony Club membership to children without a pony. This is a charitable organisation promoting high standards of horsemanship, training, events and competitions. There are 20 branches within this area. **Ref: YH11235**

PONY CLUB

Pony Club (Area 8 - East Anglia), Homeview, Warren Rd, Rettendon, Chelmsford, **Essex**, CM3 8DF, **ENGLAND**.
(T) 01245 400401
(E) area8@pcuk.org
(W) www.pony-club.org.uk.
Contact/s
Area Representative: Mrs P Coster
(E) coster@warrenrd.fsnet.co.uk
Profile Club/Association.
The centre offers Pony Club membership to children without a pony. This is a charitable organisation promoting high standards of horsemanship, training, events and competitions. There are 22 branches within this area. **Ref: YH11236**

PONY CLUB

Pony Club (Area 9 - W Central), Stable Cottage, Hentland, Ross On Wye, **Herefordshire**, HR9 6PL, **ENGLAND**.
(T) 01989 730324
(E) area9@pcuk.org
(W) www.pony-club.org.uk.
Contact/s
Area Representative: Mrs C Wasdell
Profile Club/Association.
The centre offers Pony Club membership to children without a pony. This is a charitable organisation promoting high standards of horsemanship, training, events and competitions. There are 20 branches within this area. **Ref: YH11237**

PONY CLUB

Pony Club (Area 12 - Northern Home Counties), Friars Cottage, Rushden, Buntingford, **Hertfordshire**, SG9 0TF, **ENGLAND**.
(T) 01494 881777.
Profile Club/Association. **Ref: YH11238**

PONY CLUB

Pony Club (Area 4 - N West), Woodnook Farm, Roach Rd, Samlesbury, Preston, **Lancashire**, PR5 0RB, **ENGLAND**.
(T) 01254 852560
(E) area4@pcuk.org
(W) www.pony-club.org.co.uk.
Contact/s
Area Representative: Mrs E Slinger
Profile Club/Association.
The centre offers Pony Club membership to children without a pony. This is a charitable organisation promoting high standards of horsemanship, training, events and competitions. There are 17 branches within this area. **Ref: YH11239**

PONY CLUB

Pony Club (Area 6 - Lincs), Easton Farm, Easton, Grantham, **Lincolnshire**, NG33 5AR, **ENGLAND**.
(T) 01476 530297
(E) area6@pcuk.org
(W) www.pony-club.org.co.uk.
Contact/s
Area Representative: Mrs R Skelton
Profile Club/Association.
The centre offers Pony Club membership to children without a pony. This is a charitable organisation promoting high standards of horsemanship, training, events and competitions. There are 19 branches within this area. **Ref: YH11240**

PONY CLUB

Pony Club (Area 1 - N Scotland), Dalvey, Forres, **Moray**, IV36 2SP, **SCOTLAND**.
(T) 01309 672481
(E) area1@pcuk.org
(W) www.pony-club.org.uk.
Contact/s
Area Representative: Mrs R MacLeod
Profile Club/Association.
The centre offers Pony Club membership to children without a pony. This is a charitable organisation promoting high standards of horsemanship, training, events and competitions. There are 22 branches within this area. **Ref: YH11241**

PONY CLUB

Pony Club (Area 2 - Northern England), Howick Hall, Howick, Alnwick, **Northumberland**, NE66 3LB, **ENGLAND**.
(T) 01665 577624 **(F)** 01665 577285
(E) area2@pcuk.org
(W) www.ponyclub.org.uk.
Profile Club/Association.
The centre offers Pony Club membership to children without a pony. This is a charitable organisation promoting high standards of horsemanship, training, events and competitions. There are 16 branches within this area. **Ref: YH11242**

PONY CLUB

Pony Club (Area 10 - Wales), The Old Vicarage, Brecon, Llangorse, **Powys**, LD3 7UB, **WALES**.
(T) 01874 658639
(E) area10@pcuk.org
(W) www.pony-club.org.uk.
Contact/s
Area Representative: Mrs M Anderson
Profile Club/Association.
The centre offers Pony Club membership to children without a pony. This is a charitable organisation promoting high standards of horsemanship, training, events and competitions. There are 18 branches within this area. **Ref: YH11243**

PONY CLUB

Pony Club (Area 7 - Midlands), Orchard Croft, Fradley, Lichfield, **Staffordshire**, WS13 8PA, **ENGLAND**.
(T) 01283 790336
(E) area7@pcuk.org
(W) www.pony-club.org.uk.
Contact/s
Area Representative: Mr D Cashmore
Profile Club/Association.
The centre offers Pony Club membership to children without a pony. This is a charitable organisation promoting high standards of horsemanship, training, events and competitions. There are 17 branches within this area. **Ref: YH11244**

PONY CLUB

Pony Club (Area 11 - London), The Moat Farm, Robertsbridge, **Sussex (East)**, TN32 5PR, **ENGLAND**.
(T) 01580 882179
(E) area11@pcuk.prg
(W) www.pony-club.org.uk.
Contact/s
Area Representative: Mrs C Michell
Profile Club/Association.
The centre offers Pony Club membership to children without a pony. This is a charitable organisation promoting high standards of horsemanship, training, events and competitions. There are 24 branches within this area. **Ref: YH11245**

PONY CLUB

Pony Club (The), The National Agricultural Ctre, Stoneleigh Pk, Kenilworth, **Warwickshire**, CV8 2RW, **ENGLAND**.
(T) 024 76698300 **(F)** 024 76696836
(W) www.pony-club.org.uk.
Contact/s
Manager: Mr D Robb
(E) duncan@pcuk.org
Profile Club/Association.
Head office of The Pony Club Association.
Ref: YH11246

PONY CLUB

Pony Club (Area 14 - Wessex Area), The River Bank, Park Lane, Heytesbury, Warminster, **Wiltshire**, BA12 0HE, **ENGLAND**.
(T) 01985 840695 **(F)** 01985 840695.
Profile Club/Association. **Ref: YH11247**

PONY CLUB

Pony Club (Area 3 - Yorks), Hill Crest, Kirk Deighton, Wetherby, **Yorkshire (North)**, LS22 4EB, **ENGLAND**.
(T) 01937 581777
(E) area3@pcuk.org
(W) www.pony-club.org.uk.
Contact/s
Area Representative: Mrs P Alpin
Profile Club/Association.
The centre offers Pony Club membership to children without a pony. This is a charitable organisation promoting high standards of horsemanship, training, events and competitions. There are 18 branches within this area. **Ref: YH11248**

PONY CLUB FIXTURES

Blackmore & Sparkford Vale Pony Club Fixtures, Golden Hill Cottage, Stourton Caundle, Sturminster Newton, **Dorset**, DT10 2JW, **ENGLAND**.
(T) 01963 62109.
Profile Club/Association. **Ref: YH11249**

PONY KIDS

Pony Kids, Upperwood, Pottery Lane, Inkpen, Hungerford, **Berkshire**, RG17 9QA, **ENGLAND**.
(T) 01488 668627.
Contact/s
Owner: Mrs J Beale
Profile Stable/Livery. **Ref: YH11250**

PONY PIT-STOP

Pony Pit-Stop (The), 34 Westwood Ave, Bradford, **Yorkshire (West)**, BD2 2NJ, **ENGLAND**.
(T) 01274 633275 **(F)** 01274 633275
(M) 07970 690837.
Profile Supplies. **Ref: YH11251**

PONY RIDERS' ASS

Pony Riders' Association of GB, 28 Hazelwood, Great Linford, Milton Keynes, **Buckinghamshire**, MK14 5DU, **ENGLAND**.
(T) 01908 677791.
Contact/s
Key Contact: Mrs N Parsler
Profile Club/Association. **Ref: YH11252**

PONY RIDING

Pony Riding For Disabled Trust, Grange Farm, High Rd, Chigwell, **Essex**, IG7 6DP, **ENGLAND**.
(T) 020 85006051.
Profile Club/Association. **Ref: YH11253**

PONY SADDLE

Pony Saddle Co Ltd (The), 3 Lariot Works, William St, Walsall, **Midlands (West)**, WS4 2AX, **ENGLAND**.
(T) 01922 611660.
Profile Supplies. **Ref: YH11254**

PONY TREKKING CTRE

Pony Trekking Centre (The), Cwmyoy, Abergavenny, **Monmouthshire**, NP7 7NE, **WALES**.
(T) 01873 890241.
Contact/s
Owner: Mr W Wheeler
Profile Equestrian Centre. **Ref: YH11255**

PONY WORLD

Pony World, Crimdon Pk, Crimdon Dene, **Cleveland**, TS27 4BQ, **ENGLAND**.
(T) 01429 267635.
Profile Riding School. **Ref: YH11256**

PONYMANIA MAIL ORDER

Ponymania Mail Order, 69 Burrell Rd, Compton, Newbury, **Berkshire**, RG20 6QX, **ENGLAND**.
(T) 01635 579179.
Profile Supplies. **Ref: YH11257**

PONYTEL

Ponytel, Sutton Lodge Farm, Twyford, Banbury,

Oxfordshire, OX17 3JR, **ENGLAND**.
(T) 01295 812149 **(F)** 01295 811228.
Profile Stable/Livery. **Ref: YH11258**

POOK LANE RIDING STABLES

Pook Lane Riding Stables, Rectory Cottage, Pook Lane, Havant, **Hampshire**, PO9 2TJ, **ENGLAND**.
(T) 023 92479222.
Contact/s
Owner: Mrs D Hann
Profile Riding School, Stable/Livery. **Ref: YH11259**

POOL BANK FARM STABLES

Pool Bank Farm Stables, Pool Bank Farm, Bow Lane, Bowdon, Altrincham, **Cheshire**, WA14 3BY, **ENGLAND**.
(T) 0161 9284760.
Profile Stable/Livery. **Ref: YH11260**

POOL FARM VETNRY SURGERY

Pool Farm Veterinary Surgery, Pool Farm, Poolside, Madeley, **Cheshire**, CW3 9AB, **ENGLAND**.
(T) 01782 750075.
Profile Medical Support. **Ref: YH11261**

POOL HSE VETNRY HOS

Pool House Veterinary Hospital, Pool Hse, Dam St, Lichfield, **Staffordshire**, WS13 6AA, **ENGLAND**.
(T) 01543 262464 **(F)** 01543 254680.
Profile Medical Support. **Ref: YH11262**

POOLE FARM HORSE/ANIMAL FEED

Poole Farm Horse & Animal Feed, Poole Farm, Great Yeldham, **Essex**, CO9 4HP, **ENGLAND**.
(T) 01787 237542.
Profile Supplies. **Ref: YH11263**

POOLE, ANTHONY E

Anthony E Poole, 10 Gunns Farm, Liphook, **Hampshire**, GU30 7HL, **ENGLAND**.
(T) 01428 727056.
Profile Farrier. **Ref: YH11264**

POOLE, JOHN

John Poole, Alcott Farm, Weatheroak, Alvechurch, **Midlands (West)**, B48 7EH, **ENGLAND**.
(T) 01564 824051 **(F)** 01564 824051.
Profile Breeder, Trainer. **Ref: YH11265**

POPE, DAVID J

David J Pope DWCF, 1 Blenheim Rd, Barnet, **Hertfordshire**, EN5 4NF, **ENGLAND**..
Profile Farrier. **Ref: YH11266**

POPHAM, C L

C L Popham, Bagborough, Taunton, **Somerset**, TA4 3EF, **ENGLAND**.
(T) 01823 432769 **(F)** 01823 432769.
Contact/s
Owner: Mrs S Popham
Profile Trainer. **Ref: YH11267**

POPHAMS

Pophams, Trevenna, Harp Rd, Mark, Highbridge, **Somerset**, TA9 4QL, **ENGLAND**.
(T) 01278 641202.
Contact/s
Owner: Mrs L Seabourne
Profile Saddlery Retailer. **Ref: YH11268**

POPLAR FARM RIDING SCHOOL

Poplar Farm Riding School, Poplar Farm, Duckmanton, Chesterfield, **Derbyshire**, S44 5EF, **ENGLAND**.
(T) 01246 826424.
Contact/s
Owner: Mr D Wilkinson **Ref: YH11269**

POPLAR FARM RIDING STABLES

Poplar Farm Riding Stables, Poplar Farm, Brockley Green, Hundon, **Suffolk**, CO10 8DS, **ENGLAND**.
(T) 01440 786595.
Profile Riding School. **Ref: YH11270**

POPLAR PK

Poplar Park Equestrian Training Centre, Heath Rd, Hollesley, Woodbridge, **Suffolk**, IP12 3NA, **ENGLAND**.
(T) 01394 411023 **(F)** 01394 411023.
Contact/s
Head Girl: Miss L Dorman-O'gowan
Profile Horse/Rider Accom, Riding School, Stable/Livery, Track/Course.
Cross Country & Show Jumping events held regularly. Full, working and half livery available, details and prices on request.
Opening Times
Sp: Open Tues - Sun 09:00. Closed Tues - Fri 20:00, Sat, Sun 16:30.
Su: Open Tues - Sun 09:00. Closed Tues - Fri 20:00, Sat, Sun 16:30.
Au: Open Tues - Sun 09:00. Closed Tues - Fri 20:00, Sat, Sun 16:30.
Wn: Open Tues - Sun 09:00. Closed Tues - Fri 20:00, Sat, Sun 16:30.
Closed Mondays **Ref: YH11271**

POPLARS ARABIAN STUD

Poplars Arabian Stud (The), The Poplars, Rothersthorpe, **Northamptonshire**, NN7 3JE, **ENGLAND**.
(T) 01604 830282.
Profile Breeder. **Ref: YH11272**

POPLARS FARM RIDING SCHOOL

Poplars Farm Riding School, The Poplars Farm/Hilderstone Rd, Meir Heath, Stoke-on-Trent, **Staffordshire**, ST3 7NY, **ENGLAND**.
(T) 01782 394686.
Contact/s
Owner: Mrs M Smith
Profile Riding School. **Ref: YH11273**

POPLARS PONY TREKKING

Poplars Pony Trekking, South Ewster, West Butterwick, Scunthorpe, **Lincolnshire (North)**, DN17 3JX, **ENGLAND**.
(T) 01427 728279.
Profile Riding School. **Ref: YH11274**

POPPYFIELDS

Poppyfields Equestrian, Branston Rd, Heighington, Lincoln, **Lincolnshire**, LN4 1QQ, **ENGLAND**.
(T) 01522 871788 **(F)** 07980 709261.
Contact/s
For Bookings: Ms K Breeton **(Q)** BHSAI 4
Profile Arena, Equestrian Centre, Riding School, Stable/Livery, Trainer.
Has a small cross country course which is ideal for small children. Holiday livery available from £35.00 per week. There is also a professional for breaking, schooling and producing of competition ponies/horses (12.0 - 17hh). No.Staff: 3 Yr. Est: 1998
C.Size: 22 Acres **Ref: YH11275**

POPSTERS

Popsters, Wyncolls Farm, Lumbars Lane, Elton, Newnham, **Gloucestershire**, GL14 1LH, **ENGLAND**.
(T) 01452 760923 **(F)** 01452 760870.
Contact/s
Manager: Mr J Davies
Profile Breeder. **Ref: YH11276**

PORCHES FARM STABLES

Porches Farm Stables, Porches Farm, Birch Gr, Horsted Keynes, Haywards Heath, **Sussex (West)**, RH17 7BU, **ENGLAND**.
(T) 01825 740644.
Contact/s
Owner: Mrs F Parker **Ref: YH11277**

PORLOCK VALE HSE/RIDING CTRE

Porlock Vale House & Riding Centre, Porlock Weir, **Somerset**, TA24 8NY, **ENGLAND**.
(T) 01643 862338 **(F)** 01643 863338
(E) info@porlockvale.co.
Profile Riding School, Stable/Livery. **Ref: YH11278**

PORT SUNLIGHT TRAILER

Port Sunlight Trailer Co Ltd, 103 New Chester Rd, Wirral, **Merseyside**, CH62 4RA, **ENGLAND**.
(T) 0151 6454735.
Profile Transport/Horse Boxes. **Ref: YH11279**

PORTABLE FLOORMAKERS

Portable Floormakers Ltd, Redhill Marina, Ratcliffe-on-Soar, **Nottinghamshire**, NG11 0EB, **ENGLAND**.
(T) 01509 673753 **(F)** 01509 674749
(E) floormakers@compuserve.com. **Ref: YH11280**

PORTER, A

A Porter, The Byeways, Birchwood Rd, Suckley, Worcester, **Worcestershire**, WR6 5DT, **ENGLAND**.
(T) 01886 884504.
Contact/s
Owner: Mr A Porter **Ref: YH11281**

PORTER, JOHN

John Porter, Berkeley Hse Stables, Upper Lambourn, Hungerford, **Berkshire**, RG17 8QP, **ENGLAND**.
(T) 01488 73381 **(F)** 01488 73381.
Contact/s
Owner: Mr J Porter
Profile Trainer.
Buys three year old hunters, trains them and then sells them on. Yr. Est: 1971
Opening Times
Telephone for an appointment **Ref: YH11282**

PORTER, K B

K B Porter RSS Hons, 93 Barrow Rd, Quorn, **Leicestershire**, LE12 8DH, **ENGLAND**.
(T) 01509 412364.
Profile Farrier. **Ref: YH11283**

PORTER, LESLIE

Leslie Porter, Liberty Farm Forge, Liberty Farm, New Pitsligo, **Aberdeenshire**, AB43 6PR, **SCOTLAND**.
(T) 01771 653133.
Profile Farrier. **Ref: YH11284**

PORTER, NOEL

Noel Porter, Roes Hall, Laurencetown, Guildford, **County Down**, **NORTHERN IRELAND**..
Profile Breeder. **Ref: YH11285**

PORTERFIELD IRON WORKS

Porterfield Iron Works, Wolds Village, Manor Farm, Bainton, Driffield, **Yorkshire (East)**, YO25 9EF, **ENGLAND**.
(T) 01377 217707 **(F)** 01377 217707.
Contact/s
Owner: Mr S Porter
Profile Blacksmith. **Ref: YH11286**

PORTERS

Porters, 76 Church Rd, Winterbourne, **Gloucestershire (South)**, BS36 1BY, **ENGLAND**.
(T) 01454 773391 **(F)** 01454 773391.
Profile Saddlery Retailer. **Ref: YH11287**

PORTER'S SADDLERY

Porter's Saddlery, Tullabog Tullaherin, Dungarvan, **County Kilkenny**, **IRELAND**.
(T) 056 24664.
Profile Supplies. **Ref: YH11288**

PORTHCAWL HORSE & PONY GRP

Porthcawl Horse & Pony Group, 1 George St, Porthcawl, **Bridgend**, CF36 3EL, **WALES**.
(T) 01656 771646.
Profile Club/Association. **Ref: YH11289**

PORTHCAWL HORSE SHOW SOC

Porthcawl Horse Show Society, 14 Hall Drive, North Cornelly, **Bridgend**, CF33 4HS, **WALES**.
(T) 01656 742895.
Profile Club/Association. **Ref: YH11290**

PORTH-Y-POST RIDING STABLES

Porth-y-Post Riding Stables, Porth-y-Post, Lon Isallt, Trearddur Bay, Holyhead, **Isle of Anglesey**, LL65 2UP, **WALES**.
(T) 01407 861358.
Contact/s
Owner: Mrs S Roberts **(T)** 01407 860601
Ref: YH11291

PORTLAND TOWING CTRE

Portland Towing Centre, 39 Chieftain Way, Tritton Rd Trading Est, Lincoln, **Lincolnshire**, LN6 7RY, **ENGLAND**.
(T) 01522 545473 **(F)** 01522 545473.
Profile Transport/Horse Boxes. **Ref: YH11292**

PORTLANDS STUD

Portlands Stud, Crossmere Farm, Davenport Lane, Brereton Heath, Congleton, **Cheshire**, CW12 4SU, **ENGLAND**.
(T) 01477 537822.
Profile Breeder, Trainer. **Ref: YH11293**

PORTMANS FARM

Portmans Farm, Newbridge Green, Upton-upon-Severn, **Worcestershire**, WR8 0QP, **ENGLAND**.
(T) 01684 592873.
Contact/s
Partner: Mr P Challens
Profile Riding School. **Ref: YH11294**

PORTRAITS

Portraits, Fearglas Hse, Granard Bridge, Castleknock, Dublin, **County Dublin**, **IRELAND**.
(T) 01 8221586.
Contact/s
Artist: Matt Grogan
Profile Artist.
Paints by commission
Opening Times
Telephone for further information **Ref: YH11295**

PORTREE RIDING/TREKKING CTRE

Portree Riding & Trekking Centre, Garalapin, Portree, **Highlands**, IV51 9LN, **SCOTLAND**.
(T) 01478 612945.

Profile Riding School. Ref:YH11296

POSH PONIES

Posh Ponies, Ladymoor Gate Farm, Brown Edge, Stoke-on-Trent, **Staffordshire**, ST6 8UE, **ENGLAND**.
(T) 01782 502009.
Profile Saddlery Retailer. Ref:YH11297

POSNETT, A J

A J Posnett, The Home Farm, Norley, Warrington, **Cheshire**, **ENGLAND**..
Profile Breeder. Ref:YH11298

POTTER, LAWRENCE J

Lawrence J Potter, Cappards Farm, Bishop, Sutton, **Bath & Somerset (North East)**, BS39 5XD, **ENGLAND**.
(T) 01275 332235 (F) 01275 332640. Ref:YH11299

POTTER, W S

Mr W S Potter, Stoneygill Farm, Shap, **Cumbria**, **ENGLAND**.
(T) 01931 716267.
Profile Breeder. Ref:YH11300

POTTERS TYE

Potters Tye Livery Yard & Stud, Newmans Green, Acton, Sudbury, **Suffolk**, CO10 0AD, **ENGLAND**.
(T) 01787 375540 (F) 01787 375540.
Profile Stable/Livery. Ref:YH11301

POTTIE, A D

A D Pottie, Castletown, 18 Carnalea Rd, Fintona, **County Tyrone**, BT78 2HP, **NORTHERN IRELAND**.
(T) 028 82841302 (F) 028 82841558.
Profile Medical Support. Ref:YH11302

POULTER, D M

Mrs D M Poulter, The Croft, Trellack, Monmouth, **Monmouthshire**, NP25 4PN, **WALES**.
(T) 01600 860681.
Profile Breeder. Ref:YH11303

POULTON, J C

Mr J C Poulton, Balmer Farm, Brighton Rd, Lewes, **Sussex (East)**, BN7 3JN, **ENGLAND**.
(T) 01273 603824 (F) 01273 673866
(M) 07711 491993.
Profile Trainer. Ref:YH11304

POULTON, J R

Mr J R Poulton, White Cottage, Stud Farm, Telscombe Village, Lewes, **Sussex (East)**, BN7 3HZ, **ENGLAND**.
(T) 01273 302486 (F) 01273 302486
(M) 07980 161731.
Profile Trainer. Ref:YH11305

POUND CLOSE STABLES

Pound Close Stables, Madjeston, Gillingham, **Staffordshire**, ST8 5JH, **ENGLAND**.
(T) 01747 823189.
Profile Equestrian Centre. Ref:YH11306

POUND COTTAGE RIDING CTRE

Pound Cottage Riding Centre, East Luccombe Farm, Milton Abbas, Blandford Forum, **Dorset**, DT11 0BD, **ENGLAND**.
(T) 01258 880057
Affiliated Bodies ABRS, BHS.
Contact/s
Admin: Sarah Lockyear
Profile Arena, Equestrian Centre, Horse/Rider Accom, Riding School, Stable/Livery, Trainer.
Full, part and DIY livery available, prices on request. Specialise in nervous riders and can provide sports psychology riding instruction. Can provide BHS/NVQ training for full or part time students. No.Staff: 6
Opening Times
By appointment only Ref:YH11307

POUND FARM FEEDS

Pound Farm Feeds, Hollybush Lane, Datchworth, **Hertfordshire**, SG3 6RE, **ENGLAND**.
(T) 01438 811720 (F) 01438 814415.
Contact/s
Owner: Mr P Piper Ref:YH11308

POUND FARM LIVERIES STABLE

Pound Farm Liveries Stable, Pound Farm, Old Lane, Cobham, **Surrey**, KT11 1NH, **ENGLAND**.
(T) 01932 588756.
Contact/s
Partner: Mr C Reynolds Ref:YH11309

POUND FARM RIDING CTRE

Pound Farm Riding Centre, Pound Farm, Old Lane, Cobham, **Surrey**, KT11 1NH, **ENGLAND**.
(T) 01932 868652. Ref:YH11310

POUNDER, W C & GREEN, B A

W C Pounder & Mrs B A Green, 3 Hilltop Cottages, Pencoedcae, Pontypridd, **Rhondda Cynon Taff**, CF37 1PP, **WALES**.
(T) 01443 402994.
Contact/s
Partner: Mr W Pounder
Profile Breeder. Ref:YH11311

POVEY, A L

A L Povey, The Forge, Owslebury Bottom, Winchester, **Hampshire**, SO21 1LY, **ENGLAND**.
(T) 01962 777473.
Profile Farrier. Ref:YH11312

POVEY, RAYMOND J

Raymond J Povey, Brick Hse Farm, Brickhouse Hill, Eversley, Hook, **Hampshire**, RG27 0PY, **ENGLAND**.
(T) 0118 9732127.
Contact/s
Owner: Mr R Povey Ref:YH11313

POWELL, BROUGHTON

Broughton Powell, 1 Sadler Rd, Lincoln, **Lincolnshire**, LN6 3RS, **ENGLAND**.
(T) 01522 874141 (F) 01522 874144.
Profile Blacksmith. Ref:YH11314

POWELL, BRYNLEY

Brynley Powell, Marsh Farm, Bowling Alley Lane, Crondall, Farnham, **Surrey**, GU10 5RJ, **ENGLAND**.
(T) 01252 850628 (F) 01252 850628
(M) 07768 837976.
Contact/s
Owner: Mr B Powell
Profile Trainer.
Trainer for 3 Day Event. Ref:YH11315

POWELL, DUPE

Dupe Powell, Kiln Hse, Truncheaunts Lane, East Worldham, Alton, **Hampshire**, GU34 3AA, **ENGLAND**.
(T) 01420 82306 (F) 01420 549899. Ref:YH11316

POWELL, G J

Mr G J Powell, Tan Hse Farm, Abbeydore, **Herefordshire**, HR2 0AA, **ENGLAND**.
(T) 01981 240204.
Profile Supplies. Ref:YH11317

POWELL, J

J Powell, Hogshaw Horse Hire, Lower Farm, Hogshaw, Buckingham, **Buckinghamshire**, MK18 3LB, **ENGLAND**.
(T) 01296 670236.
Contact/s
Partner: Mrs J Powell Ref:YH11318

POWELL, JOHN C

Mr John C Powell, Mill Farm, Llanthony, Abergavenny, **Monmouthshire**, NP7 7NN, **WALES**.
(T) 01873 890434.
Profile Breeder. Ref:YH11319

POWELL, R A

R A Powell, Justa Farm, Little Heath Lane, Potten End, Berkhamsted, **Hertfordshire**, HP4 2RY, **ENGLAND**.
(T) 01442 864061.
Contact/s
Owner: Mr R Powell Ref:YH11320

POWELL, RODNEY

Rodney Powell, Manor Farm, Bishop Stone, Swindon, **Wiltshire**, SN6 8PT, **ENGLAND**.
(T) 01793 790028. Ref:YH11321

POWELL, T E

Mr T E Powell, Nutwood Farm, Gatton Park Rd, Reigate, **Surrey**, RH2 0SX, **ENGLAND**.
(T) 01737 765612.
Profile Trainer. Ref:YH11322

POWELLS OF COOLHAM

Powells of Coolham Ltd, The Mill, Coolham, Horsham, **Sussex (West)**, RH13 7JR, **ENGLAND**.
(T) 01403 741226 (F) 01403 741784.
Profile Supplies. Ref:YH11323

POWER PLASTICS

Power Plastics Ltd, Station Rd, Thirsk, **Yorkshire (North)**, YO7 1PZ, **ENGLAND**.
(T) 01845 525503 (F) 01845 525485. Ref:YH11324

POWER, DURGA

Mr Durga Power, 7 Pixholme Court, Pixholme Lane, Dorking, **Surrey**, RH4 1PG, **ENGLAND**.
(T) 01306 742698.
Profile Breeder. Ref:YH11325

POWER, GARY

Gary Power DWCF, Calflands Farm, Tomkyns Lane, Upminster Common, Upminster, **Essex**, RM14 1TP, **ENGLAND**.
(T) 01708 375259.
Profile Farrier. Ref:YH11326

POWER, J C

J C Power, Strawberry Gardens Riding School, Reskadinnick, Camborne, **Cornwall**, TR14 0BH, **ENGLAND**.
(T) 01209 713661. Ref:YH11327

POWERLINE PRODUCTIONS

Powerline Productions, Unit 23 Winston Cl, Romford, **Essex**, RM7 8LL, **ENGLAND**.
(T) 01708 724544 (F) 01708 744166
(E) peter@powerlineproductions.com. Ref:YH11328

POYNDERS END FARM

Poynders End Farm Ltd, Poynders Farm, Preston, Hitchin, **Hertfordshire**, SG4 7RX, **ENGLAND**.
(T) 01462 458085.
Contact/s
Partner: Mr M Doonan
Profile Stable/Livery. Ref:YH11329

POYNTERS

Poynters Riding Centre, Ockham Lane, Cobham, **Surrey**, KT11 1LJ, **ENGLAND**.
(T) 01932 865951.
Contact/s
For Bookings: Mr J Hill
Profile Breeder, Equestrian Centre, Riding School, Stable/Livery.
Childrens Riding Specialist. Also available Showjump Training and hacking for all abilities. No.Staff: 1
Yr. Est: 1984
Opening Times
Sp: Open Tues - Sun 09:00. Closed Tues - Sun 18:00.
Su: Open Tues - Sun 09:00. Closed Tues - Sun 18:00.
Au: Open Tues - Sun 09:00. Closed Tues - Sun 18:00.
Wn: Open Tues - Sun 09:00. Closed Tues - Sun 18:00.
Closed Mondays Ref:YH11330

POYNTON, ANDREW PAUL

Andrew Paul Poynton AWCF, 60 High St, Malmesbury, **Wiltshire**, SN16 9AT, **ENGLAND**.
(T) 01666 822953.
Profile Farrier. Ref:YH11331

PPSA AREA CHAIRMAN

PPSA Area Chairman (Taunton), W H Batten Esq, Church Hse, Yeovil, **Somerset**, BA20 1HB, **ENGLAND**.
(T) 01935 23685.
Profile Club/Association. Ref:YH11332

PPSA AREA SECRETARY

PPSA Area Secretary (Welsh Border Counties), J R Pike Esq, The Priory, Kilpeck, **Herefordshire**, HR2 9DN, **ENGLAND**.
(T) 01981 570366 (F) 01981 570778.
Profile Club/Association. Ref:YH11333

PPSA AREA SECRETARY

PPSA Area Secretary (West Wales), Mrs C Higgon, Newton Hall, Crundale, Haverfordwest, **Pembrokeshire**, SA62 4EB, **WALES**.
(T) 01437 731239.
Profile Club/Association. Ref:YH11334

PPSA AREA SECRETARY

PPSA Area Secretary (Northern), Mosshouses, Galashiels, **Scottish Borders**, TD1 2PG, **SCOTLAND**.
(T) 01896 860242 (F) 01896 860295.
Profile Club/Association. Ref:YH11335

PR PROFESSIONAL SERVICES

PR Professional Services, Delves Lane, Consett, **County Durham**, DH8 7LH, **ENGLAND**.
(T) 01207 500883.
Contact/s
Partner: Mr P Raisbeck
Profile Transport/Horse Boxes. Ref:YH11336

PR+

PR+, The Barn, May Farm, Pendock Rd, Redmarley, **Gloucestershire**, GL19 3LG, **ENGLAND**.
(T) 01531 650103 (F) 01531 650105. Ref:YH11337

PRATT, IAN

Ian Pratt, Greenacres, 2 Stillington Rd, Sutton-on-Forest, **Yorkshire (North)**, YO61 1EQ, **ENGLAND**.
(T) 01347 810179. **Ref: YH11338**

PRATT, JEFFERY A

Jeffery A Pratt NDA, Hunton, Kings Lane, Chipperfield, **Hertfordshire**, WD4 9EN, **ENGLAND**.
(T) 01923 263877.
Contact/s
Owner: Mr J Pratt
Profile Medical Support. **Ref: YH11339**

PREECE, JOHN L

John L Preece RSS, The Grove, Upper Longwood, Eaton Constantine, Shrewsbury, **Shropshire**, SY5 6SB, **ENGLAND**.
(T) 01952 740264.
Profile Farrier. **Ref: YH11340**

PREECE, MARK

Mark Preece AWCF, Penlee, Towerhill, St Giles-on-the-Heath, Launceston, **Cornwall**, PL15 9RT, **ENGLAND**.
(T) 01566 772692.
Profile Farrier. **Ref: YH11341**

PREECE, W G

W G Preece, The Smithy, Uppington, Telford, **Shropshire**, TF6 5HN, **ENGLAND**.
(T) 01952 740249.
Contact/s
Owner: Mr W Preece
Profile Trainer. **Ref: YH11342**

PREECE, WAYNE

Wayne Preece DWCF Hons, 6 Kirkgate, Settle, **Yorkshire (North)**, BD24 9DZ, **ENGLAND**.
(T) 01729 823303.
Profile Farrier. **Ref: YH11343**

PREETHA BALSE

Preetha Balse, Crofton Manor Equestrian Ctre, 213 Titchfield Rd, Stubbington, Fareham, **Hampshire**, PO14 3EW, **ENGLAND**.
(T) 01329 668855. **Ref: YH11344**

PREMIER BADGES

Premier Badges Limited, Adams Hse, 219 North St, Romford, **Essex**, RM1 4QA, **ENGLAND**.
(T) 01708 767844 **(F)** 01708 733815. **Ref: YH11345**

PREMIER GIRTHS MANUFACTURING

Premier Girths Manufacturing, Unit 8 Acorn Small Firms Units, Ablewell St, Walsall, **Midlands (West)**, WS1 2EG, **ENGLAND**.
(T) 01922 647427 **(F)** 01922 647427.
Contact/s
Owner: Mr D Nicholas
Profile Supplies. **Ref: YH11346**

PREMIER MOLASSES

Premier Molasses Co Ltd, Harbour Rd, Foynes, **County Limerick**, **IRELAND**.
(T) 069 65311 **(F)** 069 65537.
Profile Supplies. **Ref: YH11347**

PREMIER NUTRITION PRODUCTS

Premier Nutrition Products Ltd, The Levels, Rugeley, **Staffordshire**, WS15 1RD, **ENGLAND**.
(T) 01889 577027 **(F)** 01889 577074.
Profile Medical Support. **Ref: YH11348**

PREMIER SADDLERY

Premier Saddlery, 11 Ballyscandal Rd, Armagh, **County Armagh**, BT61 8BL, **NORTHERN IRELAND**.
(T) 028 37525492 **(F)** 028 37525492
(W) www.premiersaddlery.com.
Contact/s
Owner: Mr L Murtagh
Profile Riding Wear Retailer, Saddlery Retailer.
Yr. Est: 1997
Opening Times
Sp: Open Mon - Sat 09:00. Closed Mon, Wed, Fri 20:00, Tues, Thurs, Sat 18:00.
Su: Open Mon - Sat 09:00. Closed Mon, Wed, Fri 20:00, Tues, Thurs, Sat 18:00.
Au: Open Mon - Sat 09:00. Closed Mon, Wed, Fri 20:00, Tues, Thurs, Sat 18:00.
Wn: Open Mon - Sat 09:00. Closed Mon, Wed, Fri 20:00, Tues, Thurs, Sat 18:00. **Ref: YH11349**

PREMIER SHOW JUMPS

Premier Show Jumps, Triddles Farm, Plough Rd, Smallfield, Horley, **Surrey**, RH6 9JN, **ENGLAND**.
(T) 01342 842454 **(F)** 01342 844241.
Contact/s
Manager: Mr A Pollock
Profile Supplies. **Ref: YH11350**

PREMIER TRAILERS

Premier Trailers, Busgrove Lane, Stoke Row, Henley-on-Thames, **Oxfordshire**, RG9 5QB, **ENGLAND**.
(T) 01491 680052 **(F)** 01491 681415.
Contact/s
Owner: Mr R Thorp
Profile Transport/Horse Boxes. **Ref: YH11351**

PREMIERE ROSETTE COMPANY

Premiere Rosette Company (The), Premiere Hse, P O Box 405, Harpenden, **Hertfordshire**, AL5 5EN, **ENGLAND**.
(T) 01582 467746.
Profile Supplies. **Ref: YH11352**

PRENDERGAST, KEVIN

Kevin Prendergast, Erindale, Friarstown, Kildare, **County Kildare**, **IRELAND**.
(T) 045 521387.
Contact/s
Trainer: Mr K Prendergast
(E) kevinprendergast@kildarehorse.ie
Profile Trainer. **Ref: YH11353**

PRENDERGAST, MICHAEL E

Michael E Prendergast DWCF, 18 Woodruff Ave, Burpham, Guildford, **Surrey**, GU1 1XS, **ENGLAND**.
(T) 01483 826157.
Profile Farrier. **Ref: YH11354**

PRENDERGAST, P J

Prendergast P J, Melitta Lodge, Kildare, **County Kildare**, **IRELAND**.
(T) 045 521288 **(F)** 045 521875.
Profile Supplies. **Ref: YH11355**

PRESCOTT RIDING CTRE

Prescott Riding Centre, Baschurch, Shrewsbury, **Shropshire**, SY4 2DR, **ENGLAND**.
(T) 01939 260712 **(F)** 01939 261452.
Contact/s
Owner: Mrs J Haydon
Profile Riding School, Stable/Livery. **Ref: YH11356**

PRESCOTT, J & W

J & W Prescott, Lesser Marsh Farm, Station Rd, Little Hoole, Preston, **Lancashire**, PR4 5LH, **ENGLAND**.
(T) 01772 613688 **(F)** 01772 613688.
Contact/s
Partner: Mr W Prescott
Profile Transport/Horse Boxes. **Ref: YH11357**

PRESCOTT, MARK (SIR)

Sit Mark Prescott, Heath Hse, Moulton Rd, Newmarket, **Suffolk**, CB8 8DU, **ENGLAND**.
(T) 01638 662117 **(F)** 01638 666572
(W) www.newmarketracehorsetrainers.co.uk
Affiliated Bodies Newmarket Trainers Fed.
Contact/s
Trainer: Sir M Prescott
Profile Trainer. **Ref: YH11358**

PRESS ASSOCIATION SPORT

Press Association Sport Ltd (The), London Hse, Central Pk, New Lane, Leeds, **Yorkshire (West)**, LS11 5DZ, **ENGLAND**.
(T) 0113 2344411 **(F)** 0113 2440758.
Profile Club/Association. **Ref: YH11359**

PRESTBURY PK EQUINE SUPPLIES

Prestbury Park Equine Supplies, Cheltenham Racecourse, Cheltenham, **Gloucestershire**, GL50 4SH, **ENGLAND**.
(T) 01242 578150 **(F)** 01242 580250.
Profile Saddlery Retailer. **Ref: YH11360**

PRESTBURY RIDING SCHOOL

Prestbury Riding School, Park Hse Farm, Butley Lanes, Prestbury, Macclesfield, **Cheshire**, SK10 4DS, **ENGLAND**.
(T) 01625 829675. **Ref: YH11361**

PRESTIGE

Prestige, Unit 3 The Sawmill, Somerley, Ringwood, **Hampshire**, BH24 3PW, **ENGLAND**.
(T) 01425 472562 **(F)** 01425 472716.
Contact/s
Owner: Mr J Cambell
Profile Transport/Horse Boxes. **Ref: YH11362**

PRESTIGE PRESENTATIONS

Prestige Presentations, Springfield Stables, Sitwell Grange Lane, Pilsley, Chesterfield, **Derbyshire**, S45 8EN, **ENGLAND**.
(T) 01773 872548.
Profile Supplies. **Ref: YH11363**

PRESTIGE RACING CLUB

Prestige Racing Club, Robson Hse, 6b East St, Epsom, **Surrey**, KT17 1HH, **ENGLAND**.
(T) 01372 729860.
Profile Club/Association, Riding Club. **Ref: YH11364**

PRESTIGE SPORTS SERVICES

Prestige Sports Services, Moor Croft, Lismore Rd, Buxton, **Derbyshire**, SK17 9AP, **ENGLAND**.
(T) 01298 013740 **(F)** 01298 213677
(E) topsport@tarmac.co.uk.
Profile Track/Course. **Ref: YH11365**

PRESTON & BRAMLEY

Preston & Bramley, The Veterinary Surgery, 14 Long Lane, Sedbergh, **Cumbria**, LA10 5AH, **ENGLAND**.
(T) 01539 620335.
Profile Medical Support. **Ref: YH11366**

PRESTON FARM STABLES

Preston Farm Stables, Lower Rd, Fetcham, Leatherhead, **Surrey**, KT22 9EL, **ENGLAND**.
(T) 01372 456486.
Contact/s
Owner: Mrs J Knight **Ref: YH11367**

PRESTON SADDLERY

Preston Saddlery, Boyes Farm, Durton Lane, Broughton, Preston, **Lancashire**, PR3 5LE, **ENGLAND**.
(T) 01772 863130. **Ref: YH11368**

PRESTWICH, ISOBEL

Isobel Prestwich, Daisy Cottage, Lower Main St, Glapthorne, Oundle, Peterborough, **Cambridgeshire**, PE8 5BE, **ENGLAND**.
(T) 01832 274376
(M) 07957 424451.
Profile Medical Support. **Ref: YH11369**

PRESTWICK FARM

Prestwick Farm, Prestwick Lane, Chiddingfold, Godalming, **Surrey**, GU8 4XP, **ENGLAND**.
(T) 01428 654695. **Ref: YH11370**

PRETTY OAK FARM

Pretty Oak Farm, Chard, **Somerset**, TA20 3PT, **ENGLAND**.
(T) 01460 64653.
Profile Breeder. **Ref: YH11371**

PRETTY PONIES

Pretty Ponies Ltd, Unit 9, The Sidings Ind Est, Station Rd, Clitheroe, **Lancashire**, BB7 9SE, **ENGLAND**.
(T) 01254 822044 **(F)** 01254 822034
(W) www.prettyponies.co.uk.
Contact/s
Owner: Miss C Francis
(E) clfranc@aol.com
Profile Riding Wear Retailer, Supplies.
Showing accessories and gifts. Online catalogue and ordering. No.Staff: 18 Yr. Est: 1991
Opening Times
Sp: Open Mon - Fri 09:00. Closed Mon - Fri 17:00.
Su: Open Mon - Fri 09:00. Closed Mon - Fri 17:00.
Au: Open Mon - Fri 09:00. Closed Mon - Fri 17:00.
Wn: Open Mon - Fri 09:00. Closed Mon - Fri 17:00.
Ref: YH11372

PRICE, A

Mrs A Price, The Meeting Hse, Norton, Presteigne, **Powys**, LD8 2HA, **WALES**.
(T) 01544 267221.
Profile Supplies. **Ref: YH11373**

PRICE, A C

A C Price, 1 Crown Cottage, Crown Lane, Parkend, Lydney, **Gloucestershire**, GL15 4JE, **ENGLAND**.
(T) 01594 564469.
Profile Farrier. **Ref: YH11374**

PRICE, C G

Mr C G Price, Willow Croft, Hay-on-Wye, **Herefordshire**, HR3 5PN, **ENGLAND**.
(T) 01497 820819 **(F)** 01497 820776.
Profile Supplies. **Ref: YH11375**

PRICE, C J

Mr C J Price, Brockmanton Hall, Brockmanton, Leominster, **Herefordshire**, HR6 0QU, **ENGLAND**.
(T) 01568 760695.
Profile Trainer. **Ref: YH11376**

PRICE, D A

D A Price, Cambrian Forge, Builth Rd, Builth Wells,

Powys, LD2 3RG, **WALES**.
(T) 01982 552466.
Contact/s
Owner: Mr D Price
Profile Blacksmith. Ref:YH11377

PRICE, G

G Price, Wernished, Llandeffale, Brecon, **Powys**, LD3 0NW, **WALES**.
(T) 01874 754405.
Contact/s
Owner: Mr G Price
Profile Breeder.
Breeder of Welsh Section A ponies. Ref:YH11378

PRICE, G M

Mr G M Price, Drostre, Llanwern, Brecon, **Powys**, LD3 0RP, **WALES**.
(T) 01874 658212.
Profile Supplies. Ref:YH11379

PRICE, J J E

Mrs J J E Price, Chapel Farm, Llandevaud, **Newport**, NP18 2AF, **WALES**.
(T) 01633 400575.
Profile Supplies. Ref:YH11380

PRICE, J K

Mr J K Price, 41 Beaufort Trce, Ebbw Vale, **Blaenau Gwent**, NP3 5NW, **WALES**.
(T) 01495 306113.
Profile Supplies. Ref:YH11381

PRICE, M & G

M & G Price, Seagulls, St Brides, Wentloog, **Newport**, NP1 9SR, **WALES**.
(T) 01633 680836.
Profile Breeder. Ref:YH11382

PRICE, M A

M A Price, Bird Cottage, Melton Rd, Keyworth, Nottingham, **Nottinghamshire**, NG12 5QH, **ENGLAND**.
(T) 01949 81262.
Profile Farrier. Ref:YH11383

PRICE, MATTHEW R

Matthew R Price DWCF, Pool Mill Cottage, Bridstow, Ross-on-Wye, **Herefordshire**, HR9 6QE, **ENGLAND**.
(T) 01989 566876.
Profile Farrier. Ref:YH11384

PRICE, N

N Price, Fleetmead Stud, Langsmead Bungalow, Blindley Heath, Lingfield, **Surrey**, RH7 6JX, **ENGLAND**.
(T) 01342 832796.
Contact/s
Owner: Miss N Price
Profile Supplies. Ref:YH11385

PRICE, P E

P E Price, Mount Pleasant, Buckland Lane, Staple, Canterbury, **Kent**, CT3 1LA, **ENGLAND**.
(T) 01303 892339.
Contact/s
Owner: Mr P Price
Profile Transport/Horse Boxes. Ref:YH11386

PRICE, RICHARD

Mr Richard Price, Criftige Farm, Ullingswick, Hereford, **Herefordshire**, HR1 1JG, **ENGLAND**.
(T) 01432 820263.
Profile Trainer. Ref:YH11387

PRICE, ROGER J

Roger J Price DWCF, Brickyard Cottage, Hernhill, Lugwardine, **Herefordshire**, HR1 4AQ, **ENGLAND**.
(T) 01432 850725.
Profile Farrier. Ref:YH11388

PRICE, T J

Mr T J Price, Bradbury Farm, Crick, Chepstow, **Newport**, NP26 5UW, **WALES**.
(T) 01291 421596.
Profile Supplies. Ref:YH11389

PRICE, W

Mr W Price, Cholstrey Court, Leominster, **Herefordshire**, HR6 9AP, **ENGLAND**.
(T) 01568 708439.
Profile Supplies. Ref:YH11390

PRICES

Prices Riding School & Livery Stables, Meadowhall Rd, Rotherham, **Yorkshire (South)**, S61 2JD, **ENGLAND**.
(T) 01709 554302.
Contact/s
Owner: Mrs V Goldsborough
Profile Riding School, Stable/Livery.
Hacking. Schooling/Show production. Bi-annual shows. Full Livery - prices start at £30 per week. Veterinary services provided by the same vet for last 17 years. Farrier services - 18 years of experience.
Yr. Est: 1977 C.Size: 6 Acres
Opening Times
Sp: Open Mon - Sun 09:00. Closed Mon - Sun 17:00.
Su: Open Mon - Sun 09:00. Closed Mon - Sun 17:00.
Au: Open Mon - Sun 09:00. Closed Mon - Sun 17:00.
Wn: Open Mon - Sun 09:00. Closed Mon - Sun 17:00.
Answer phone service outside these hours
Ref:YH11391

PRICHARD, D, J & T

D, J & T Prichard, Castellau Fawr Farm, Llantrisant, **Rhondda Cynon Taff**, CF72 8LP, **WALES**.
(T) 01443 224253.
Profile Breeder. Ref:YH11392

PRIDDLE, KEITH

Keith Priddle, 2 Muccleshell Cottage, Throop Rd, Throop, Bournemouth, **Dorset**, BH8 0DH, **ENGLAND**.
(T) 01202 526218 (F) 01202 526218.
Contact/s
Owner: Mr K Priddle
Profile Transport/Horse Boxes. Ref:YH11393

PRIDDY

Mrs Priddy, Molehouse Farm, Clive Back Lane, Clive, Winsford, **Cheshire**, CW7 3NX, **ENGLAND**.
(T) 01606 556288.
Profile Breeder. Ref:YH11394

PRIESTWOOD STUD

Priestwood Stud, Beulah, Further Quarter, High Halden, Ashford, **Kent**, TN26 3HN, **ENGLAND**.
(T) 01233 850376.
Profile Breeder. Ref:YH11395

PRIMMORE FARM HORSES

Primmore Farm Horses, Hedging, North Newton, Bridgwater, **Somerset**, TA7 0DF, **ENGLAND**.
(T) 01278 662896 (F) 01278 662896
(M) 07774 256635.
Profile Trainer. Ref:YH11396

PRINCE & DOYLE

Prince & Doyle Ltd, Unit 12A, Ludlow Business Pk, Ludlow, **Shropshire**, SY8 1ME, **ENGLAND**.
(T) 01584 872134 (F) 01584 873135.
Profile Saddlery Retailer. Ref:YH11397

PRINT GALLERY

Print Gallery Ltd (The), Old Surrenden Manor, Bethersden, Ashford, **Kent**, TN26 3DL, **ENGLAND**.
(T) 01233 82544. Ref:YH11398

PRIOR ROYD FARM

Prior Royd Farm Riding Stables, Prior Royd Farm, Top Side, Grenoside, Sheffield, **Yorkshire (South)**, S35 8RD, **ENGLAND**.
(T) 0114 2468449.
Contact/s
Owner: Mrs S Huntingdon
Profile Riding Stables.
Full and DIY livery available, prices on request. Woodland treks - 30 minutes, 1 hour and occasionally 2 hour treks on offer. No.Staff: 2 Yr. Est: 1990
C.Size: 23 Acres
Opening Times
Telephone between 08:00 - 18:00 daily Ref:YH11399

PRIORY EQUESTRIAN CTRE

Priory Equestrian Centre, Millbridge, Frensham, Farnham, **Surrey**, GU10 3DP, **ENGLAND**.
(T) 01252 794161.
Contact/s
Partner: Miss M Fogg Ref:YH11400

PRIORY HORSEWEAR

Priory Horsewear, 7 Hunters Rise, Kirby Bellars, Melton Mowbray, **Leicestershire**, LE14 2DT, **ENGLAND**.
(T) 01664 812210.
Contact/s
Owner: Ms D Startin Ref:YH11401

PRIORY SADDLERY

Priory Saddlery, 25-29 Church St, Guisborough, **Cleveland**, TS14 6HG, **ENGLAND**.
(T) 01287 633439. Ref:YH11402

PRIORY SADDLERY

Priory Saddlery, Old Hse Lane, Boxted, Colchester, **Essex**, CO4 5RF, **ENGLAND**.
(T) 01206 273730 (F) 01206 273730.
Contact/s
Owner: Mr D Smith
Profile Riding Wear Retailer, Saddlery Retailer.
No.Staff: 2 Yr. Est: 1986
Opening Times
Sp: Open Mon - Sat 08:00, Sun 10:00. Closed Mon - Sat 18:00, Sun 12:15.
Su: Open Mon - Sat 08:00, Sun 10:00. Closed Mon - Sat 18:00, Sun 12:15.
Au: Open Mon - Sat 08:00, Sun 10:00. Closed Mon - Sat 18:00, Sun 12:15.
Wn: Open Mon - Sat 08:00, Sun 10:00. Closed Mon - Sat 18:00, Sun 12:15. Ref:YH11403

PRIORY STABLES

Priory Stables, Church Rd, Old Windsor, Windsor, **Berkshire**, SL4 2JW, **ENGLAND**.
(T) 01753 850796. Ref:YH11404

PRIORY STABLES

Priory Stables, Coed Saeson Farm, Pentre Rd, Grovesend, Swansea, **Swansea**, SA4 1DD, **WALES**.
(T) 01792 895087
Affiliated Bodies BHS.
Contact/s
General Manager: Mrs J Rees (T) 01792 897732
Profile Stable/Livery. No.Staff: 3
Yr. Est: 2000 C.Size: 15 Acres
Opening Times
Sp: Open 08:00. Closed 19:00.
Su: Open 08:00. Closed 20:00.
Au: Open 08:00. Closed 18:00.
Wn: Open 08:00. Closed 18:00. Ref:YH11405

PRIORY STUD

Priory Stud, Meadowside, Littlefield Green, White Waltham, **Berkshire**, SL6 3JP, **ENGLAND**.
(T) 0118 9343450.
Profile Breeder. Ref:YH11406

PRIORY VETNRY GRP

Priory Veterinary Group, 59 Purewell, Christchurch, **Dorset**, BH23 1EN, **ENGLAND**.
(T) 01202 484466 (F) 01202 470141.
Profile Medical Support. Ref:YH11407

PRIORY VETNRY SURGERY

Priory Veterinary Surgery, 27 High St, Banstead, **Surrey**, SM7 2NE, **ENGLAND**.
(T) 01737 356655.
Profile Medical Support. Ref:YH11408

PRIORY VETNRY SURGERY

Priory Veterinary Surgery, 139 Brighton Rd, Redhill, **Surrey**, RH1 6PP, **ENGLAND**.
(T) 01737 765353.
Profile Medical Support. Ref:YH11409

PRIORY VETNRY SURGERY

Priory Veterinary Surgery, North Lodge, 11 High St, Tadworth, **Surrey**, KT20 5SD, **ENGLAND**.
(T) 01737 812496.
Profile Medical Support. Ref:YH11410

PRIORY VETNRY SURGERY

Priory Veterinary Surgery, 10 Evesham Rd, Reigate, **Surrey**, RH2 9DF, **ENGLAND**.
(T) 01737 242190 (F) 01737 222474.
Profile Medical Support. Ref:YH11411

PRITCHARD, E

E Pritchard, Felinrhyd Bach, Maentwrog, Blaenau Ffestiniog, **Gwynedd**, LL41 4HY, **WALES**.
(T) 01766 590231.
Profile Track/Course. Ref:YH11412

PRITCHARD, F

F Pritchard, Hillgates, Hillgates, Hereford, **Herefordshire**, HR2 8JG, **ENGLAND**.
(T) 01981 540465.
Contact/s
Partner: Mr A Pritchard Ref:YH11413

PRITCHARD, FIONA

Miss Fiona Pritchard, 8 Westbourne Drive, Garforth, **Yorkshire (West)**, LS25 1BT, **ENGLAND**.
(T) 0113 2872387.
Profile Breeder. Ref:YH11414

PRITCHARD, GEORGE B

George B Pritchard, Waen Wen, Crickheath, Oswestry, **Shropshire**, SY10 8BT, **ENGLAND**.
(T) 01691 830513.

Profile Farrier. Ref:YH11415

PRITCHARD, H G

H G Pritchard, Glasfryn, Llandwrog, Caernarfon, **Gwynedd**, LL54 5TE, **WALES**.
(T) 01286 830774.
Profile Farrier. Ref:YH11416

PRITCHARD, K V

K V Pritchard, Eilian Hse, High St, Bryngwran, Holyhead, **Isle of Anglesey**, LL65 3PP, **WALES**.
(T) 01407 720415 (F) 01407 720415.
Contact/s
Owner: Mr K Pritchard
Profile Trainer. Ref:YH11417

PRITCHARD, M W T

M W T Pritchard, Yew Tree Cottage, Hillgates, Hereford, **Herefordshire**, HR2 8JG, **ENGLAND**.
(T) 01981 540828. Ref:YH11418

PRITCHARD, P A

Mr P A Pritchard, The Gate Hse, Whatcote, Shipston-on-Stour, **Warwickshire**, CV36 5EF, **ENGLAND**.
(T) 01295 680689.
Profile Trainer. Ref:YH11419

PRITCHARD, P L J (DR)

Dr P L J Pritchard, Timber Pond Hse, Purton, Berkeley, **Gloucestershire**, GL13 9HY, **ENGLAND**.
(T) 01453 811989
(M) 07741 013359
(E) 101655.157@compuserve.com.
Profile Trainer. Ref:YH11420

PRITCHARD, P M

P M Pritchard, Heather View, Asterton, Lydbury North, **Shropshire**, SY7 8BH, **ENGLAND**.
(T) 01588 650687.
Contact/s
Owner: Mr J Pritchard Ref:YH11421

PRITCHARD, RUSSELL J

Russell J Pritchard DWCF BII, Trebettyn Fach, Trebettyn, Llansannor, Cowbridge, **Glamorgan (Vale of)**, CF71 7RX, **WALES**.
(T) 01446 775215.
Profile Farrier. Ref:YH11422

PRITCHARD, S

Miss S Pritchard, Foel Isaf, Bylchau, Denbigh, **Conwy**, LL16 5SL, **WALES**.
(T) 01745 550384.
Profile Breeder. Ref:YH11423

PRITCHARD, TERESA

Mrs Teresa Pritchard MC AMC MMCA, Scrumpy Cottage, Purton, Berkeley, **Gloucestershire**, GL13 9HY, **ENGLAND**.
(T) 01453 811881.
Profile Medical Support. Ref:YH11424

PRITCHARDS

Pritchards, Old Wheelwright Yard, Newbridge Rd, Llantrisant, Pontyclun, **Rhondda Cynon Taff**, CF72 8EX, **WALES**.
(T) 01443 224370 (F) 01443 224370.
Contact/s
Owner: Mr K Pritchard Ref:YH11425

PRITCHETT, MICHAEL J

Michael J Pritchett DWCF HONS, 58 Wyatts Lane, Northwood, Cowes, **Isle of Wight**, PO31 8QA, **ENGLAND**.
(T) 01983 200414.
Profile Farrier. Ref:YH11426

PRODDROMOW, GEORGE

Mr George Proddromow, Georges Farm, Bryants Bridge, East Harling, **Norfolk**, NR16 2JR, **ENGLAND**.
(T) 01953 717224.
Profile Trainer. Ref:YH11427

PROFESSIONAL EVENT RIDERS ASS

Professional Event Riders Association (Pera) (The), St Martins Hse, Ockham Rd South, East Horsley, **Surrey**, KT24 6RX, **ENGLAND**.
(T) 01483 282745 (F) 01483 281180
(E) peraworld@compuserve.com.
Contact/s
President: Mark Todd (MBE)
Profile Club/Association. Ref:YH11428

PROFESSIONAL SECRETARIAL SVS

Professional Secretarial Services, The Lodge, Staunton Grange, Staunton In The Vale, **Nottinghamshire**, NG13 9PE, **ENGLAND**.
(T) 01400 282404 (F) 01400 282355
(E) metw.pss@mcmail.com.
Profile Club/Association. Ref:YH11429

PROFESSIONAL SPORTS TURF

Professional Sports Turf Design Ltd, 42 Garstang Rd, Preston, **Lancashire**, PR1 1NA, **ENGLAND**.
(T) 01772 884450 (F) 01772 884445. Ref:YH11430

PROFFITT, N J

N J Proffitt, Kingscroft, Den Lane, Wrinehill, Crewe, **Cheshire**, CW3 9BT, **ENGLAND**.
(T) 01270 820450.
Contact/s
Owner: Mr N Proffitt
Profile Breeder. Ref:YH11431

PROLITE

Prolite Ltd, The Saddlery, Fryers Rd, Bloxwich, Walsall, **Midlands (West)**, WS3 2XJ, **ENGLAND**.
(T) 01922 711676 (F) 01922 711654
(E) enquiries@prolitepads.com
(W) www.prolite-equestrian.com.
Profile Supplies. Ref:YH11432

PROLITE

ProLite, P O Box 1090, Pulborough, **Sussex (West)**, RH20 4YY, **ENGLAND**.
(T) 01903 745444 (F) 01903 740716.
Profile Supplies. Ref:YH11433

PROP FARM

Prop Farm Ltd, Grange Farm, Elmton, Worksop, **Nottinghamshire**, S80 4LX, **ENGLAND**.
(T) 01909 723100.
Contact/s
Owner: Mr L Powell Ref:YH11434

PROSPECT FARM

Prospect Farm, Marton-cum-Grafton, **Yorkshire (North)**, YO51 9QJ, **ENGLAND**.
(T) 01423 322045.
Profile Riding School. Ref:YH11435

PROSPECT FARM LIVERY STABLES

Prospect Farm Livery Stables, Prospect Farm, Cattistock, Dorchester, **Dorset**, DT2 0JB, **ENGLAND**.
(T) 01300 320820.
Contact/s
Owner: Mrs G Makey-Harfield
Profile Stable/Livery, Trainer. Ref:YH11436

PROSPECT STUD

Prospect Stud, The Garner Cottages, Grantchester, **Cambridgeshire**, CB3 9NB, **ENGLAND**.
(T) 01223 840225 (F) 01223 840450.
Profile Breeder. Ref:YH11437

PROTAC

Protac, Charlcote Cresent, East Boldon, **Tyne and Wear**, NE36 0DT, **ENGLAND**.
(T) 0191 5192759.
Profile Supplies. Ref:YH11438

PROTEAN FORGE

Protean Forge (The), Bicester Rd, Westcott, Aylesbury, **Buckinghamshire**, HP18 0QD, **ENGLAND**.
(T) 01296 658855 (F) 01296 658855.
Contact/s
Owner: Mr P Warner
Profile Blacksmith. Ref:YH11439

PROUDLOVE, D A

D A Proudlove, Whitegate Farm, St Helens Rd, Bolton, **Manchester (Greater)**, BL5 1AD, **ENGLAND**.
(T) 01204 63219.
Contact/s
Owner: Mr D Proudlove Ref:YH11440

PROUSE, H W

Mr & Mrs H W Prouse, Creedy Barton, Shobrooke, Crediton, **Devon**, EX17 1AQ, **ENGLAND**.
(T) 01395 232567.
Profile Breeder. Ref:YH11441

PRUST, K R

K R Prust, Orchard Cottage, Holt Wood, Holt, Wimborne, **Dorset**, BH21 7DX, **ENGLAND**.
(T) 01258 840293.
Profile Farrier. Ref:YH11442

PRYCE, A L

A L Pryce, New Hse, Aberhafesp, Newtown, **Powys**, SY16 3HH, **WALES**.
(T) 01686 688425. Ref:YH11443

PRYCE, DAVID J

David J Pryce DWCF, Le Vieux Magasin, Rue De La Bouterie, Trinity, **Jersey**, JE3 5HQ, **ENGLAND**.
(T) 01534 865984
(M) 07860 768924.
Profile Farrier. Ref:YH11444

PRYCE, DOUGLAS F

Douglas F Pryce DWCF, Victoria Stores, Victoria Village, Trinity, **Jersey**, JE3 5HQ, **ENGLAND**.
(T) 01534 861901.
Profile Farrier. Ref:YH11445

PUBLICITY DIRECT

Publicity Direct, Lea Farm, Farnham Rd, Ewshot, **Surrey**, GU10 5AY, **ENGLAND**.
(T) 01252 851186 (F) 01252 851074. Ref:YH11446

PUDDLEDUB STUD

Fiona Reed, Bankhead, Auchtertool, Kirkcaldy, **Fife**, KY2 5XA, **SCOTLAND**.
(T) 01592 872717 (F) 01592 872717.
Contact/s
Owner: Ms F Reed
Profile Breeder, Stable/Livery, Stud Farm.
Stud standing Thoroughbred Stallion. No.Staff: 1
Yr. Est: 1991 C.Size: 55 Acres
Opening Times
Ms Reed is contactable 24 hours a day Ref:YH11447

PUDSEY & DISTRICT RIDING CLUB

Pudsey & District Riding Club, 32 Highgate, Heaton, Bradford, **Yorkshire (West)**, BD9 4BB, **ENGLAND**.
(T) 01274 44688.
Contact/s
Secretary: Miss A Bell
Profile Club/Association, Riding Club. Ref:YH11448

PUDSEY AGRICULTURAL SVS

Pudsey Agricultural Services, Crossfield Farm, Woodhall Rd, Calverley, Pudsey, **Yorkshire (West)**, LS28 5QX, **ENGLAND**.
(T) 0113 2570719.
Contact/s
Partner: Mr T Illingworth
Profile Supplies. Ref:YH11449

PUGH & SON

Pugh & Son, 5 Adam And Eve St, Market Harborough, **Leicestershire**, LE16 7LT, **ENGLAND**.
(T) 01858 462200.
Contact/s
Owner: Mr P Pugh Ref:YH11450

PUGH, L

L Pugh, Wolston Fields Farm, Wolston Lane, Wolston, Coventry, **Midlands (West)**, CV8 3FQ, **ENGLAND**.
(T) 024 76542131.
Profile Breeder. Ref:YH11451

PUGH, P

Mr & Mrs P Pugh, Pantycelyn, Adfa, Newtown, **Powys**, **WALES**.
(T) 01938 810771.
Profile Breeder. Ref:YH11452

PUGH, S M

Mrs S M Pugh, The Lodge, Tilstone Paddocks, Tilstone, Fearnall, Tarporley, **Cheshire**, CW6 9HU, **ENGLAND**.
(T) 01829 733002.
Profile Breeder. Ref:YH11453

PUGHE, J S

Pughe, J S, Ivy Hse, Glyn Ceiriog, Llangollen, **Denbighshire**, LL20 7EE, **WALES**.
(T) 01691 718333.
Profile Farrier. Ref:YH11454

PULFORDS

Pulfords Of Dunmow, 19 High St, Great Dunmow, **Essex**, CM6 1AB, **ENGLAND**.
(T) 01371 872829 (F) 01799 542092.
Profile Feed Merchant, Supplies. Ref:YH11455

PUMP HSE FARM STABLES

Pump House Farm Stables, Chance Hall Lane, Scholar Green, Stoke-on-Trent, **Staffordshire**, ST7 3ST, **ENGLAND**.
(T) 01270 873072.
Profile Riding School. Ref:YH11456

PUMPHILL DARTMOORS

Pumphill Dartmoors, Becca Farm, Aberford, **Yorkshire (West)**, LS25 3AH, **ENGLAND**.
(T) 0113 2813440.
Profile Breeder. Ref:YH11457

PUNCHESTOWN NATIONAL CTRE

Punchestown National Centre for Equestrian &

A-Z of COMPANIES

Field Sports, Punchestown, Naas, **County Kildare**, **IRELAND**.
(T) 045 876800 **(F)** 045 876466
(E) info@punchestown.com
(W) www.punchestown.com.
Contact/s
Key Contact: Ms M Edgill
Profile Equestrian Centre. **C.Size:** 500 Acres
Ref: YH11458

PUNNETT, L

Mr L Punnett, Gelli Gwm Isaf Farm, Felindre, Swansea, **Swansea**, SA5 7PP, **WALES**.
(T) 01792 884085 **(F)** 01792 884934
(E) bustimes@aol.com. **Ref: YH11459**

PURBECK & DISTRICT

Purbeck & District Riding Club, Long Coppice, Bindon Lane, East Stoke, Wareham, **Dorset**, BH20 6AS, **ENGLAND**.
(T) 01929 463123.
Profile Club/Association, Riding Club. **Ref: YH11460**

PURBECK HORSE BOXES

Purbeck Horse Boxes, 15 Fincarn Rd, Drumahoe, Londonderry, **County Londonderry**, BT47 3LD, **NORTHERN IRELAND**.
(T) 028 71301118 **(F)** 028 71301118.
Contact/s
Owner: Mr A Eastwood
Profile Transport/Horse Boxes. **Ref: YH11461**

PURBECK PETS & EQUESTRIAN

Purbeck Pets & Equestrian, 8 West St, Wareham, **Dorset**, BH20 4JU, **ENGLAND**.
(T) 01929 552568 **(F)** 01929 554904.
Contact/s
Owner: Ms A Elliot
Profile Saddlery Retailer. **Ref: YH11462**

PURBRICK, LIZZIE

Lizzie Purbrick, Chestnut Farm, Braunston, Oakham, **Rutland**, LE15 8QZ, **ENGLAND**.
(T) 01572 723317 **(F)** 01572 724936.
Profile Stable/Livery, Trainer. **Ref: YH11463**

PURCELL JAMES

Purcell James, 76 O'Connell St, Limerick, **County Limerick**, **IRELAND**.
(T) 061 314312.
Profile Supplies. **Ref: YH11464**

PURCELL, MALCOLM G

Malcolm G Purcell, Blackwater Mill Farm, Blackwater, Newport, **Isle of Wight**, PO30 3BJ, **ENGLAND**.
(T) 01983 523394.
Contact/s
Owner: Mr M Purcell
Profile Farrier. **Ref: YH11465**

PURDIE, GARRY R

Garry R Purdie DWCF BII, 2 Summer Bank Cottage, Lower Dicker, Hailsham, **Sussex (East)**, BN27 4BT, **ENGLAND**.
(T) 01323 845624.
Profile Farrier. **Ref: YH11466**

PURKIS, IAN B

Ian B Purkis, Crossfield Cottage, Ellesmere Lane, Ellesmere, **Shropshire**, SY12 0NG, **ENGLAND**.
(T) 01691 623624. **Ref: YH11467**

PUTLANDS VETNRY SURGERY

Putlands Veterinary Surgery, Maidstone Rd, Paddock Wood, Tonbridge, **Kent**, TN12 6DZ, **ENGLAND**.
(T) 01892 835456 **(F)** 01892 838164.
Profile Medical Support. **Ref: YH11468**

PYE, E

E Pye, Cowall Moor Farm, Cowall Moor Lane, Lask Edge, Leek, **Staffordshire**, ST13 8QN, **ENGLAND**.
(T) 01782 502230.
Contact/s
Owner: Mr E Pye
Profile Transport/Horse Boxes. **Ref: YH11469**

PYE, W & J

W & J Pye Ltd, Fleet Sq, Lancaster, **Lancashire**, LA1 1HA, **ENGLAND**.
(T) 01524 597200 **(F)** 01524 844832.
Profile Supplies. **Ref: YH11470**

PYRAH, MALCOLM

Malcolm Pyrah, Keyworths Farm Hse, Old Forge Lane, Granby, Nottingham, **Nottinghamshire**, NG13 9PS, **ENGLAND**.
(T) 01949 850599.
Profile Trainer. **Ref: YH11471**

PYTCHLEY HUNT STABLES

Pytchley Hunt Stables, Station Rd, Brixworth, Northampton, **Northamptonshire**, NN6 9BP, **ENGLAND**.
(T) 01604 880610.
Contact/s
Manager: Mr P Jones **Ref: YH11472**

Q E CLASSIC

Q E Classic, Thorpe Underwood Hall, Great Ouseburn, **Yorkshire (North)**, YO7 9SZ, **ENGLAND**.
(T) 01423 331444 **(F)** 01423 331308. **Ref: YH11473**

QUACKERIES

Quackeries - Remedial Health Products, Lamberts Barn, Cropredy, Banbury, **Oxfordshire**, OX17 1QA, **ENGLAND**.
(T) 01295 750758 **(F)** 01295 750039.
Contact/s
Owner: Dr R Elwell
(E) relwell@bigfoot.com
Profile Medical Support. **Ref: YH11474**

QUADRANGLE

Quadrangle (The), Shoreham Rd, Shoreham, Sevenoaks, **Kent**, TN14 7RP, **ENGLAND**.
(T) 01959 525136.
Contact/s
Owner: Ms K Plowman
Profile Stable/Livery. **C.Size:** 15 Acres
Ref: YH11475

QUALITY IRRIGATION

Quality Irrigation, 309 Vale Rd, Ash Vale, Aldershot, **Hampshire**, GU12 5LN, **ENGLAND**.
(T) 01252 328017 **(F)** 01252 328017
(E) xqn95@dial.pipex.com.
Profile Supplies. **Ref: YH11476**

QUALTEX

Qualtex Horse Clothing Manufacturers, Bonds St Works, Off Hanging Royd Lane, Hebden Bridge, **Yorkshire (West)**, HX7 7DE, **ENGLAND**.
(T) 01422 844347 **(F)** 01422 845663
(E) sales@qualtex.co.uk
(W) www.qualtex.co.uk.
Contact/s
Partner: Mr G Foster
Profile Supplies. Horse Clothing Manufacturer.
Manufacturers of Horse Clothing for trade only.
No.Staff: 12 Yr. Est: 1978
Opening Times
Sp: Open Mon - Fri 09:00. Closed Mon - Thurs 17:00, Fri 15:00.
Su: Open Mon - Fri 09:00. Closed Mon - Thurs 17:00, Fri 15:00.
Au: Open Mon - Fri 09:00. Closed Mon - Thurs 17:00, Fri 15:00.
Wn: Open Mon - Fri 09:00. Closed Mon - Thurs 17:00, Fri 15:00.
Closed at weekends **Ref: YH11477**

QUANTOCK RIDING CLUB

Quantock Riding Club, Belf Farm, Rhode, Bridgwater, **Somerset**, TA5 2AB, **ENGLAND**.
(T) 01278 662289.
Contact/s
Secretary: Mrs S Jones
Profile Club/Association, Riding Club. **Ref: YH11478**

QUANTOCK STAGHOUNDS

Quantock Staghounds, Fire Beacon, Little Quantock, Crowcombe, Taunton, **Somerset**, TA4 4AP, **ENGLAND**.
(T) 01984 618605. **Ref: YH11479**

QUARLEY RIDING

Quarley Riding, The Priory, Wherwell, Andover, **Hampshire**, SP11 7JH, **ENGLAND**.
(T) 01264 860814.
Contact/s
Owner: Miss A Poulton **Ref: YH11480**

QUARNHILL SCHOOL

Quarnhill School of Equitation, Addcrofts Farm, Kirk Ireton, **Derbyshire**, DE4 4LG, **ENGLAND**.
(T) 01335 70335.
Profile Riding School. **Ref: YH11481**

QUARRY HSE VETNRY CTRE

Quarry House Veterinary Centre, 148 Teignmouth Rd, Torquay, **Devon**, TQ1 4RY, **ENGLAND**.
(T) 01803 324341 **(F)** 01803 311378.
Profile Medical Support. **Ref: YH11482**

QUARRY PARK STABLES

Quarry Park Livery Stables, Wardley Lane, Gateshead, **Tyne and Wear**, NE10 8AA, **ENGLAND**.
(T) 0191 4385367.
Contact/s
Owner: Mr G Lamb
Profile Riding Club, Riding School, Stable/Livery, Transport/Horse Boxes. Horse Dealer.
Buys, sells and leases horses and ponies to other riding schools and private clients. Teach a large number of nervous pupils both adults and children.
No.Staff: 4 Yr. Est: 1987 C.Size: 74 Acres
Opening Times
Sp: Open 09:00. Closed 19:00.
Su: Open 09:00. Closed 19:00.
Au: Open 09:00. Closed 18:00.
Wn: Open 09:00. Closed 18:00. **Ref: YH11483**

QUARTERMAN, GARETH J

Gareth J Quarterman DWCF, Horseshoe Lodge, Clock Tower Stables, Brighton Rd, Tadworth, **Surrey**, KT20 6QZ, **ENGLAND**.
(T) 01737 832362.
Profile Farrier. **Ref: YH11484**

QUAY EQUESTRIAN

Quay Equestrian Ltd, St George's Quay, Lancaster, **Lancashire**, LA1 5QJ, **ENGLAND**.
(T) 01524 381821 **(F)** 01524 32080
(E) horses@quayeqestrian.com
(W) www.quayequestrian.com.
Contact/s
Marketing Manager: Hazel Hubble
Profile Supplies.
Produce Carr and Day and Martin leather care, hoof care, coat care and natural products, as well as Day Son and Hewitt feed supplements and equestrian equipment.
Opening Times
Sp: Open Mon - Fri 09:00. Closed Mon - Fri 17:00.
Su: Open Mon - Fri 09:00. Closed Mon - Fri 17:00.
Au: Open Mon - Fri 09:00. Closed Mon - Fri 17:00.
Wn: Open Mon - Fri 09:00. Closed Mon - Fri 17:00.
Ref: YH11485

QUAYSIDE CARRIAGES

Quayside Carriages, Fell View, High Seaton, Workington, **Cumbria**, CA14 2NP, **ENGLAND**.
(T) 01900 66056. **Ref: YH11486**

QUEALLY, JOHN

Queally John, Coolagh, Dungarvan, **County Waterford**, **IRELAND**.
(T) 058 42487.
Profile Supplies. **Ref: YH11487**

QUEEN ELIZABETH RIDING SCHOOL

Queen Elizabeth Riding School, 94 Forest Side, Chingford, **London (Greater)**, E4 6BA, **ENGLAND**.
(T) 020 85291223.
Contact/s
Groom: Miss L Marner
Profile Riding School, Stable/Livery.
Hacking in Epping forest No.Staff: 3
Opening Times
Sp: Open Tues - Thurs 11:30, Sat 09:00, Sun 09:45. Closed Tues - Thurs 16:30, Sat, Sun 14:30.
Su: Open Tues - Thurs 11:30, Sat, Sun 09:45. Closed Tues - Thurs 16:30, Sat, Sun 14:30.
Au: Open Tues - Thurs 11:30, Sat, Sun 09:45. Closed Tues - Thurs 16:30, Sat, Sun 14:30.
Wn: Open Tues - Thurs 11:30, Sat, Sun 09:45. Closed Tues - Thurs 16:30, Sat, Sun 14:30.
Ref: YH11488

QUEEN ETHELBURGA'S CLGE

Queen Ethelburga's Collage, Thorpe Underwood Hall, Quseburn, York, **Yorkshire (North)**, YO26 9SZ, **ENGLAND**.
(T) 01423 330859 **(F)** 01423 331007.
Profile Riding School, Stable/Livery. **Ref: YH11489**

QUEEN MARGARETS RIDING SCHOOL

Queen Margarets Riding School, Escrick Pk, Escrick, York, **Yorkshire (North)**, YO19 6EA, **ENGLAND**.
(T) 01904 728632.
Profile Riding School. **Ref: YH11490**

QUEENHOLME BLOODSTOCK STABLES

Queenholme Bloodstock Stables, Willingham Fen, Willingham, Cambridge, **Cambridgeshire**, CB4 5JN, **ENGLAND**.
(T) 01954 261458 **(F)** 01954 260611.
Profile Stable/Livery. **Ref: YH11491**

QUEENSFERRY METALS

Queensferry Metals, Port Edgar Marina, Port Edgar, South Queensferry, **Lothian (West)**, EH30 9SQ, **SCOTLAND**.
(T) 0131 3311791 **(F)** 0131 3314603.

Profile Blacksmith. Ref:YH11492

QUENBY HALL STUD & STABLES
Quenby Hall Stud & Stables, Hungarton Rd, Hungarton, **Leicestershire**, LE7 9JF, **ENGLAND**.
(T) 0116 2595278
(M) 07702 311749.
Profile Breeder. Ref:YH11493

QUEST HORSE CLOTHING
Quest Horse Clothing, Springhill Cottage, Newton Rd, Innellan, **Argyll and Bute**, PA23 7SY, **SCOTLAND**.
(T) 01369 830248.
Profile Supplies. Ref:YH11494

QUEST WHOLESALERS
Quest Wholesalers, Pinfold Ind Est, Field Cl, Bloxwich, Walsall, **Midlands (West)**, WS3 3JS, **ENGLAND**.
(T) 01922 493888 **(F)** 01922 493777.
Contact/s
Owner: Mr G Baines
Profile Supplies. Ref:YH11495

QUICKWAY BUILDINGS
Quickway Buildings Ltd, Unit 8, Building 2, Sandwich Ind Est, Sandwich, **Kent**, CT13 9LY, **ENGLAND**.
(T) 01304 612284 **(F)** 01304 620012.
Profile Club/Association. Ref:YH11496

QUIGLEY, H D
H D Quigley, Burnfoot Stores, 297 Drumane Rd, Dungiven, **County Londonderry**, BT47 4NL, **NORTHERN IRELAND**.
(T) 028 77741658.
Profile Supplies. Ref:YH11497

QUINLAN, F W
F W Quinlan, 12 Jackson St, Mottram, Hyde, **Cheshire**, SK14 6JF, **ENGLAND**.
(T) 01457 764563.
Contact/s
Owner: Mr F Quinlan
Profile Transport/Horse Boxes. Ref:YH11498

QUINLAN, NICHOLAS D
Nicholas D Quinlan DWCF, Horsham Hall, Helions Bumpstead, Haverhill, **Suffolk**, CB9 7AB, **ENGLAND**.
(T) 01440 702077.
Profile Farrier. Ref:YH11499

QUINLAN, PETER G
Peter G Quinlan DWCF, 80 Chase Ave, Potters Bar, **Hertfordshire**, EN6 5NL, **ENGLAND**.
(T) 07958 532556.
Profile Farrier. Ref:YH11500

QUITS EQUESTRIAN
Quits Equestrian, Boulston Manor, Haverfordwest, **Pembrokeshire**, SA62 4AO, **WALES**.
(T) 01437 769338. Ref:YH11501

QUOB STABLES
Quob Stables, Durley Brook Rd, Durley, Southampton, **Hampshire**, SO32 2AR, **ENGLAND**.
(T) 023 80694657.
Contact/s
Owner: Mrs B Davis Ref:YH11502

QUORN
Quorn, The Limes, 22 Main Rd, Asforby Valley, Melton Mowbray, **Leicestershire**, LE14 3SP, **ENGLAND**.
(T) 01664 812639.
Profile Track/Course. Ref:YH11503

R & D BLACKSMITHS
R & D Blacksmiths, 325 Orbiston St, Motherwell, **Lanarkshire (North)**, ML1 1QN, **SCOTLAND**.
(T) 01698 275689.
Contact/s
Owner: Mr R Orr
Profile Blacksmith. Ref:YH11504

R & E BAMFORD
R & E Bamford Ltd, Globe Mill, Midge Hall Lane, Midge Hall, Leyland, **Lancashire**, PR5 3TN, **ENGLAND**.
(T) 01772 456300 **(F)** 01772 456302. Ref:YH11505

R & P FEEDERS
R & P Feeders Ltd, Athol Hse, 19 Charles St, Sheffield, **Yorkshire (South)**, S1 2HS, **ENGLAND**.
(T) 0114 272471 **(F)** 0114 2750526.
Profile Supplies. Ref:YH11506

R & R COUNTRY
R & R Falkingham, Hull Rd, Hemingbrough, Selby, **Yorkshire (North)**, YO8 6QJ, **ENGLAND**.
(T) 01757 638555 **(F)** 01757 630770
(W) www.randrcountry.co.uk
Affiliated Bodies BETA, GMC, SMS.
Contact/s
General Manager: Mr S Moxon
Profile Riding Wear Retailer, Saddlery Retailer, Supplies.
There is also a licensed tearoom on-site.
No.Staff: 17
Opening Times
Sp: Open Mon 10:00, Tues - Sat 09:00, Sun 11:00. Closed Mon - Wed, Fri, Sat 18:00, Thurs 20:00, Sun 19:00.
Su: Open Mon 10:00, Tues - Sat 09:00, Sun 11:00. Closed Mon - Wed, Fri, Sat 18:00, Thurs 20:00, Sun 17:00.
Au: Open Mon 10:00, Tues - Sat 09:00, Sun 11:00. Closed Mon - Wed, Fri, Sat 18:00, Thurs 20:00, Sun 17:00.
Wn: Open Mon 10:00, Tues - Sat 09:00, Sun 11:00. Closed Mon -Wed, Fri, Sat 18:00, Thurs 20:00, Sun 17:00. Ref:YH11507

R & S PRICE
R & S Price Ltd, Warren Farm, Warren Rd, Little Horwood, Milton Keynes, **Buckinghamshire**, MK17 0PT, **ENGLAND**.
(T) 01296 715700 **(F)** 01296 715900.
Profile Supplies. Ref:YH11508

R A BENEVOLENT INSTITUTION
Royal Agricultural Benevolent Institution, Shaw Hse, 27 West Way, Oxford, **Oxfordshire**, OX2 0QH, **ENGLAND**.
(T) 01865 724931 **(F)** 01865 202025
(E) rabi@btinternet.com.
Contact/s
Chief Executive: Mr T McMahon
Profile Club/Association. Ref:YH11509

R A BUSBY & SON
R A Busby & Son, Harland Hse, Marrick, Richmond, **Yorkshire (North)**, DL11 7LQ, **ENGLAND**.
(T) 01748 884261.
Contact/s
Owner: Mr R Busby
Profile Transport/Horse Boxes. Ref:YH11510

R A C E
R A C E, 2 Raleigh Cl, Churchdown, **Gloucestershire**, GL3 1NT, **ENGLAND**.
(T) 01452 714707 **(F)** 01242 252622.
Profile Medical Support. Ref:YH11511

R A F HALTON SADDLE CLUB
R A F Halton Saddle Club, Royal Air Force, Halton, Aylesbury, **Buckinghamshire**, HP22 5PG, **ENGLAND**.
(T) 01296 623535ext6197
(E) pope@connect-2.co.uk.
Contact/s
Stable Manager: Mrs S Pope **(Q)** BHSII, BHSSM
Profile Club/Association. Ref:YH11512

R A OWEN & SONS
R A Owen & Sons, Coal & Agricultural Merchants, Minafon, Llandinam, **Powys**, SY17 5DG, **WALES**.
(T) 01686 688271 **(F)** 01686 688057.
Profile Supplies. Ref:YH11513

R B EQUESTRIAN
R B Equestrian, Dollar Farm, Soulbury, Leighton Buzzard, **Bedfordshire**, LU7 0JH, **ENGLAND**.
(T) 01525 270780.
Profile Saddlery Retailer. Ref:YH11514

R B I BLOODSTOCK
R B I Bloodstock Ltd, 11A & 26 Bute St, South Kensington, **London (Greater)**, SW7 3EY, **ENGLAND**.
(T) 020 75814916 **(F)** 020 75894213
(M) 07836 507343
(E) rbi@dialin.net.
Profile Blood Stock Agency. Ref:YH11515

R B I PROMOTIONS
R B I Promotions Ltd, 26 Bute St, South Kensington, **London (Greater)**, SW7 3EX, **ENGLAND**.
(T) 020 75811111 **(F)** 020 75894213
(M) 07771 790231
(E) rbi@dialin.net.
Profile Club/Association. Ref:YH11516

R C BLAND
R C Bland Ltd, Scarah Mill, Ripley, Harrogate, **Yorkshire (North)**, HG3 3EB, **ENGLAND**.
(T) 01423 770115 **(F)** 01423 770294.
Profile Saddlery Retailer. Ref:YH11517

R C GOWING
R C Gowing, The Forge, Twentypence Rd, Cottenham, Cambridge, **Cambridgeshire**, CB4 8PS, **ENGLAND**.
(T) 01954 252462.
Contact/s
Owner: Mr M Overall
Profile Blacksmith. Ref:YH11518

R C GOWING
R C Gowing, The Forge, Red Lion Sq, Soham, Ely, **Cambridgeshire**, CB7 5HQ, **ENGLAND**.
(T) 01353 721041.
Contact/s
Owner: Mr M Overall
Profile Farrier. Ref:YH11519

R C LARKIN BLACKSMITHS
R C Larkin Blacksmiths, The Forge, Tandridge Lane, Oxted, **Surrey**, RH8 9NJ, **ENGLAND**.
(T) 01883 713466 **(F)** 01883 713466.
Contact/s
Owner: Mr S Larkin
Profile Blacksmith. Ref:YH11520

R COOKE & SONS
R Cooke & Sons, Manor Farm, Oby, Nr Fleggburgh, Great Yarmouth, **Norfolk**, NR29 3BW, **ENGLAND**.
(T) 01493 369325.
Profile Breeder. Ref:YH11521

R D A SOUTH DOWNS
R D A South Downs, Newbrook Farm, Upper Beeding, Steyning, **Sussex (West)**, BN44 3HP, **ENGLAND**.
(T) 01903 815924.
Profile Club/Association. Ref:YH11522

R D A SOUTH REGION
R D A South Region, Mill Hse Farm, Frame Wood Rd, Fulmer, **Buckinghamshire**, SL3 6JR, **ENGLAND**.
(T) 01753 662211 **(F)** 01753 663873.
Profile Club/Association. Ref:YH11523

R D A SPONSORED RIDE
R D A Sponsored Ride, The Poplars, School Lane, Milton, Abingdon, **Oxfordshire**, OX14 4EH, **ENGLAND**.
(T) 01235 834744.
Profile Club/Association. Ref:YH11524

R D A STABLES
R D A Stables (The), Digswell Pl, Welwyn Garden City, **Hertfordshire**, AL8 7SU, **ENGLAND**.
(T) 01707 332159.
Contact/s
Manager: Ms S Jenkins Ref:YH11525

R D A WAVERLEY DRIVING GROUP
R D A Waverley Driving Group, 74 Georges Wood Rd, Brookmans Pk, Hatfield, **Hertfordshire**, AL9 7BU, **ENGLAND**.
(T) 01707 652010.
Contact/s
Chairman: Mrs A Cole
Profile Club/Association. Ref:YH11526

R D DAVIES & SON
R D Davies & Son, Lower Park Rd, Tenby, **Pembrokeshire**, SA70 8ES, **WALES**.
(T) 01834 842921 **(F)** 01834 842921.
Contact/s
Owner: Mr M Davies
Profile Blacksmith. Ref:YH11527

R DAVIDSON & SONS
R Davidson & Sons, South Pk, Lochfoot, Dumfries, **Dumfries and Galloway**, DG2 8NH, **SCOTLAND**.
(T) 01387 730308 **(F)** 01387 730308.
Contact/s
Partner: Mr W Davidson
Profile Transport/Horse Boxes. Ref:YH11528

R DAYCOCK & SON
R Daycock & Son, 15 Commercial Rd, Talbach, **Neath Port Talbot**, SA13 1LN, **WALES**.
(T) 01639 882713.
Profile Saddlery Retailer. Ref:YH11529

R E & P KETTLE
R E & P Kettle Ltd, 11 Ruston Rd, Grantham, **Lincolnshire**, NG31 9SW, **ENGLAND**.

(T) 01476 563473 (F) 01476 570900.
Contact/s
Owner: Mr R Kettle
Profile Blacksmith. Ref: YH11530

R E D ROSETTES

R E D Rosettes, Unit 1 Gardners Nursery, Brent Rd, Cossington, Bridgwater, **Somerset**, TA7 8LF, **ENGLAND**.
(T) 01278 722553.
Profile Supplies. Ref: YH11531

R E F N A

R E F N A, 2 Mildred's Farm Barn, Preston, Cirencester, **Gloucestershire**, GL7 5PR, **ENGLAND**.
(T) 01285 659918. Ref: YH11532

R E FARMS

R E Farms, 26-33 Cattle Market, West Meadows Ind Est, Derby, **Derbyshire**, DE21 6EP, **ENGLAND**.
(T) 01332 381060.
Profile Saddlery Retailer. Ref: YH11533

R E FARMS

R E Farms (Hulland), Stydd Farm, Dog Lane, Hulland, Ashbourne, **Derbyshire**, DE6 3EH, **ENGLAND**.
(T) 01335 370198.
Profile Supplies. Ref: YH11534

R E TRICKERS

R E Trickers Ltd, St Michaels Rd, Northampton, **Northamptonshire**, NN1 3JX, **ENGLAND**.
(T) 01604 30595 (F) 01604 24978. Ref: YH11535

R G EQUESTRIAN

R G Equestrian Enterprise, Cottagers Plot, Laceby, Grimsby, **Lincolnshire (North East)**, DN37 7DX, **ENGLAND**.
(T) 01472 276427
Affiliated Bodies ABRS.
Contact/s
General Manager: Ms M Taylor
Profile Equestrian Centre, Riding Club, Riding School, Stable/Livery, Trainer. No.Staff: 5
Yr. Est: 1987 C.Size: 3.5 Acres
Opening Times
Sp: Open Mon - Sun 07:00. Closed Mon, Wed - Fri 20:00, Tues, Sat, Sun 17:30.
Su: Open Mon - Sun 07:00. Closed Mon , Wed - Fri 20:00, Tues, Sat, Sun 17:30.
Au: Open Mon - Sun 07:00. Closed Mon, Wed - Fri 20:00, Tues, Sat, Sun 17:30.
Wn: Open Mon - Sun 07:00. Closed Mon, Wed - Fri 20:00, Tues, Sat, Sun 17:30. Ref: YH11536

R GREGORY & SON

R Gregory & Son, Tivoli Forge, 2 Hollington Old Lane, St Leonards-on-Sea, **Sussex (East)**, TN38 9DT, **ENGLAND**.
(T) 01424 436256.
Contact/s
Owner: Mr R Gregory
Profile Blacksmith. Ref: YH11537

R H A FORGE

R H A Forge (The), Kings Troop R H A, St John's Wood Barracks, Ordnance Hill, London, **London (Greater)**, NW8 6PT, **ENGLAND**.
(T) 020 74144621.
Contact/s
Farrier: Brendan L Murray (Q) AWCF
Profile Farrier. Ref: YH11538

R H HANGERSLEY HEIGHT

R H Hangersley Height, Hangersley, Ringwood, **Hampshire**, BH24 3JS, **ENGLAND**.
(T) 01425 43186.
Profile Riding School. Ref: YH11539

R H MEARS

R H Mears Ltd, 10 Harrison St, Walsall, **Midlands (West)**, WS3 3HP, **ENGLAND**.
(T) 01922 476930 (F) 01922 710519. Ref: YH11540

R H MILLER

R H Miller Agricultural Ltd, Fordel, Lauder Rd, Dalkeith, **Lothian (Mid)**, EH22 2PH, **SCOTLAND**.
(T) 0131 6542638 (F) 0131 6638891
(E) enquiries@rhmiller.co.uk
(W) www.rhmiller.co.uk
Affiliated Bodies SMS.
Contact/s
Manager: Mrs J Barr
Profile Riding Wear Retailer, Saddlery Retailer, Supplies. No.Staff: 8 Yr. Est: 1978
Opening Times
Sp: Open Mon - Sat 09:00, Sun 11:00. Closed Mon - Fri 18:00, Sat 16:00, Sun 15:00.
Su: Open Mon - Sat 09:00, Sun 11:00. Closed Mon - Fri 18:00, Sat 16:00, Sun 15:00.
Au: Open Mon - Sat 09:00, Sun 11:00. Closed Mon - Fri 18:00, Sat 16:00, Sun 15:00.
Wn: Open Mon - Sat 09:00, Sun 11:00. Closed Mon - Fri 18:00, Sat 16:00, Sun 15:00. Ref: YH11541

R H MILLER

R H Miller Agricultural Ltd, 64 - 66 Old Town, Peebles, **Scottish Borders**, EH45 8JE, **SCOTLAND**.
(T) 01721 720711 (F) 01721 729968
(W) www.rhmiller.co.uk.
Contact/s
General Manager: Mr J Clark
Profile Supplies.
The company has sales representatives covering Fife, Lothians, Lanarks and the Scottish Borders. Deliveries can be arranged or a self collect warehouse at Fordel, Dalkeith is available. This has a public weigh bridge.
Yr. Est: 1978
Opening Times
Sp: Open Mon - Fri 08:00, Sat 08:30. Closed Mon - Fri 17:30, Sat 17:00.
Su: Open Mon - Fri 08:00, Sat 08:30. Closed Mon - Fri 17:30, Sat 17:00.
Au: Open Mon - Fri 08:00, Sat 08:30. Closed Mon - Fri 17:30, Sat 17:00.
Wn: Open Mon - Fri 08:00, Sat 08:30. Closed Mon - Fri 17:30, Sat 17:00. Ref: YH11542

R H MILLER AGRICULTURAL

R H Miller Agricultural, 10 Commercial Rd, Hawick, **Scottish Borders**, TD9 7AQ, **SCOTLAND**.
(T) 01450 370050.
Profile Saddlery Retailer. Ref: YH11543

R HACKWORTH ANIMAL FEEDS

R Hackworth Animal Feeds, Burnedge Mill, Broad Lane, Burnedge, Rochdale, **Lancashire**, OL16 4PU, **ENGLAND**.
(T) 01706 355044 (F) 01706 355044.
Profile Saddlery Retailer. Ref: YH11544

R HUNT

R Hunt, Bottom Farm, Brecon Hill, Penn, **Buckinghamshire**, HP10 8NJ, **ENGLAND**.
(T) 01494 813867 (F) 01494 816469.
Profile Breeder. Ref: YH11545

R HUTT & PARTNERS

R Hutt & Partners, Lee Farm, Lee Lane, Maidenhead, **Berkshire**, SL6 6PE, **ENGLAND**.
(T) 01628 632229.
Contact/s
Owner: Mr R Hutt
Profile Feed Merchant, Stable/Livery. Ref: YH11546

R J & I WELLS

R J & I Wells Ltd, New Hollins Garage, Brock Rd, Great Eccleston, Preston, **Lancashire**, PR3 0XE, **ENGLAND**.
(T) 01995 670343 (F) 01995 671385.
Contact/s
Owner: Mr R Wells
Profile Transport/Horse Boxes. Ref: YH11547

R J A ROBSON & SON

R J A Robson & Son, 25-27 Scarborough Rd, Bridlington, **Yorkshire (East)**, YO16 7PJ, **ENGLAND**.
(T) 01262 602597.
Contact/s
Owner: Mr D Robson
Profile Blacksmith.
Horsebox repair Yr. Est: 1800
Opening Times
Sp: Open Mon - Fri 08:00, Sat 08:30. Closed Mon - Fri 21:00, Sat 17:00.
Su: Open Mon - Fri 08:00, Sat 08:30. Closed Mon - Fri 21:00, Sat 17:00.
Au: Open Mon - Fri 08:00, Sat 08:30. Closed Mon - Fri 21:00, Sat 17:00.
Wn: Open Mon - Fri 08:00, Sat 08:30. Closed Mon - Fri 21:00, Sat 17:00. Ref: YH11548

R J B SADDLERY

R J B Saddlery, Unit 7 Grove Court, North Rd, Bridgend Ind Est, Bridgend, **Bridgend**, CF31 3TP, **WALES**.
(T) 01656 664019.
Contact/s
Owner: Miss R Bushell Ref: YH11549

R J HUNTER

R J Hunter, Manor Farm, Pitchcott, Aylesbury, **Buckinghamshire**, HP22 4HT, **ENGLAND**.
(T) 01296 641387.
Contact/s
Owner: Mr R Hunter Ref: YH11550

R JONES

R Jones & Co, The Forge/Manor Farm, Hinckley Rd, Burton Hastings, Nuneaton, **Warwickshire**, CV11 6RG, **ENGLAND**.
(T) 01455 221087.
Contact/s
Owner: Mr R Jones
Profile Blacksmith. Ref: YH11551

R L JOBSON & SON

R L Jobson & Son, 8-10 Marygate, Berwick-upon-Tweed, **Northumberland**, TD15 1AT, **ENGLAND**.
(T) 01289 306163.
Profile Saddlery Retailer. Ref: YH11552

R L JOBSON & SON

R L Jobson & Son (Kelso), Tower Showrooms, Bondgate Within, Alnwick, **Northumberland**, NE66 1SX, **ENGLAND**.
(T) 01665 602135.
Profile Saddlery Retailer. Ref: YH11553

R L PROUDLOCK & SONS

R L Proudlock & Sons, The Cottage, East Farm, Great Bavington, Newcastle-upon-Tyne, **Tyne and Wear**, NE19 2BJ, **ENGLAND**.
(T) 01830 530277.
Contact/s
Owner: Mrs M Proudlock
Profile Transport/Horse Boxes. Ref: YH11554

R M ADDY & SONS

R M Addy & Sons, Cranmore Barn Farm, Station Rd, Deeping St. James, Peterborough, **Cambridgeshire**, PE6 8RQ, **ENGLAND**.
(T) 01778 343314.
Contact/s
Owner: Mr C Addy Ref: YH11555

R M TRAILERS

R M Trailers Ltd, Prospect Rd, Alresford, **Hampshire**, SO24 9QF, **ENGLAND**.
(T) 01962 732560 (F) 01962 734027.
Profile Transport/Horse Boxes. Ref: YH11556

R MILES SADDLER & HARNESS

R Miles Saddler & Harness Maker, Bracken Farm, Tunstall, Woodbridge, **Suffolk**, IP12 2HH, **ENGLAND**.
(T) 01728 688272.
Profile Saddlery Retailer. Ref: YH11557

R MILLER BLACKSMITH

R Miller Blacksmith Ltd, Barton Hall Works, Overtown Rd, Waterloo, Wishaw, **Lanarkshire (North)**, ML2 8EW, **SCOTLAND**.
(T) 01698 373770 (F) 01698 373711.
Profile Blacksmith. Ref: YH11558

R P LOVATT INSURANCE

R P Lovatt Insurance, 35 Market Pl, Brackley, **Northamptonshire**, NN13 7AB, **ENGLAND**.
(T) 01280 703476 (F) 01280 704681
(E) lovinsure2@aol.com.
Profile Club/Association. Ref: YH11559

R PARKIN & SON

R Parkin & Son, 42 Wear St, Sunderland, **Tyne and Wear**, SR5 2BH, **ENGLAND**.
(T) 0191 5480255.
Profile Blacksmith. Ref: YH11560

R PLANT & SON

R Plant & Son, The Forge, Great Ponton, Grantham, **Lincolnshire**, NG33 5DP, **ENGLAND**.
(T) 01476 530325.
Profile Farrier. Ref: YH11561

R S ASSEMBLIES

R S Assemblies Ltd, Home Farm, Merton, Bicester, **Oxfordshire**, OX6 0ND, **ENGLAND**.
(T) 01869 240628 (F) 01869 321241. Ref: YH11562

R SHIELD & SON

R Shield & Son, Wheathall Farm Livery Yard, Mill Lane, Sunderland, **Tyne and Wear**, SR6 7EU, **ENGLAND**.
(T) 0191 5293559 (F) 0191 5295550.
Contact/s
Owner: Mr R Shield Ref: YH11563

R T ANIMAL FEEDS

R T Animal Feeds, Kings Arms Yard, Bromyard, Hereford, **Herefordshire**, HR7 4TU, **ENGLAND**.
(T) 01885 482682.
Profile Supplies. Ref: YH11564

R T NELSON & SON

R T Nelson & Son Ltd, 1 Kingston Drive, Beccles, **Suffolk**, NR34 9RP, **ENGLAND**.
(T) 01502 712423 **(F)** 01502 711353.
Contact/s
Owner: Mr R Nelson
Profile Transport/Horse Boxes. **Ref: YH11565**

R THOMPSON

R Thompson & Co, 12 Manderston St, Edinburgh, **Edinburgh (City of)**, EH6 8LY, **SCOTLAND**.
(T) 0131 5546501.
Contact/s
Owner: Mr C Montgomery
Profile Blacksmith. **Ref: YH11566**

R T'S SADDLERY

R T's Saddlery, Stable Cottage, Calder Pk, Hamilton Rd, Newmarket, **Suffolk**, CB8 0UY, **ENGLAND**.
(T) 01638 663469.
Profile Supplies. **Ref: YH11567**

R W TAYLOR ANIMAL FEEDS

R W Taylor Animal Feeds, Fullers Yard, Withersfield Rd, Haverhill, **Suffolk**, CB9 9HH, **ENGLAND**.
(T) 01440 706067.
Profile Supplies. **Ref: YH11568**

R W TOASE

R W Toase Ltd, 13-14 Merchants Quay, Newry, **County Down**, BT35 6AH, **NORTHERN IRELAND**.
(T) 028 30262354 **(F)** 028 30262354.
Contact/s
Sales: Mr D Blakley
Profile Supplies. **Ref: YH11569**

R.C.V.S

Royal College of Veterinary Surgeons, Belgravia Hse, 62-69 Horseferry Rd, London, **London (Greater)**, SW1P 2AF, **ENGLAND**.
(T) 020 72222001 **(F)** 020 72222004
(E) admin@rcvs.org.uk
(W) www.rcvs.org.uk.
Contact/s
Registrar: Miss J Hern
Profile Club/Association.
The RCVS is a body for veterinary surgeons. They deal with professional conduct, standards and keep a register of all veterinary surgeons in the UK.
Yr. Est: 1844
Opening Times
Sp: Open Mon - Fri 09:15. Closed Mon - Fri 17:00.
Su: Open Mon - Fri 09:15. Closed Mon - Fri 17:00.
Au: Open Mon - Fri 09:15. Closed Mon - Fri 17:00.
Wn: Open Mon - Fri 09:15. Closed Mon - Fri 17:00.
Closed Saturdays and Sundays **Ref: YH11570**

RABY HOUSE STABLES

Raby House Stables, Benty Heath Lane, Willaston, Neston, **Merseyside**, CH64 1SB, **ENGLAND**.
(T) 0151 3281108
(E) rabyhorsestables@btopenworld.com.
Contact/s
Owner: Mr M Cinch
Profile Stable/Livery. Yr. Est: 1999
Opening Times
Sp: Open 09:00. Closed 20:00.
Su: Open 09:00. Closed 20:00.
Au: Open 09:00. Closed 20:00.
Wn: Open 09:00. Closed 20:00. **Ref: YH11571**

RACE HORSE TRAINER

Race Horse Trainer, Eastbury Cottage Stables, Eastbury, Lambourn, Hungerford, **Berkshire**, RG17 8XZ, **ENGLAND**.
(T) 01488 72637.
Profile Trainer. **Ref: YH11572**

RACECOURSE & COVERTSIDE

Racecourse & Covertside, 14 Clinton Ave, Hampton Magna, **Warwickshire**, CV35 8TX, **ENGLAND**.
(T) 01926 495712.
Profile Supplies. **Ref: YH11573**

RACECOURSE ASSOCIATION

Racecourse Association Ltd (The), Winkfield Rd, Ascot, **Berkshire**, SL5 7HX, **ENGLAND**.
(T) 01344 873536 **(F)** 01344 627233
(E) info@rcarcl.co.uk.
Profile Club/Association. **Ref: YH11574**

RACECOURSE FARM

Racecourse Farm Racing Stables, Portbury, **Somerset (North)**, BS20 7SN, **ENGLAND**.
(T) 01275 373581 **(F)** 01275 375053
(M) 07831 410409.
Profile Trainer. **Ref: YH11575**

RACEDAY EVENTS

Raceday Events Ltd, U1 Marangoni Hse, Oldenway Busi Ballybrit, Ballybrit, **County Galway**, **IRELAND**.
(T) 091 773933.
Profile Supplies. **Ref: YH11576**

RACEHORSE OWNERS' ASS

Racehorse Owners' Association, 42 Portman Sq, London, **London (Greater)**, W1H 0EQ, **ENGLAND**.
(T) 020 74866977.
Contact/s
Key Contact: Mr M Harris
Profile Club/Association. **Ref: YH11577**

RACEHORSE OWNERS ASSOCIATION

Racehorse Owners Association, Fifth Floor, 60 St James's St, London, **London (Greater)**, SW1W 1LE, **ENGLAND**.
(T) 020 74080903 **(F)** 020 74081662
(W) www.racehorseowners.net.
Contact/s
Assistant: Miss S Evans
Profile Club/Association.
The Racehorse Owners Association provides information and advice on all aspects of ownership. Members receive benefits such as free entry to race meetings and a magazine. Yr. Est: 1945
Opening Times
Sp: Open Mon - Fri 09:00. Closed Mon - Fri 17:00.
Su: Open Mon - Fri 09:00. Closed Mon - Fri 17:00.
Au: Open Mon - Fri 09:00. Closed Mon - Fri 17:00.
Wn: Open Mon - Fri 09:00. Closed Mon - Fri 17:00.
Ref: YH11578

RACEHORSE TRANSPORTERS ASS

Racehorse Transporters Association Ltd, New Barn Farm, Bucklebury Village, Reading, **Berkshire**, RG7 6EF, **ENGLAND**.
(T) 0118 9714714 **(F)** 0118 9714800.
Profile Club/Association. **Ref: YH11579**

RACETECH

RaceTech, Racecourse Technical Services Ltd, 88 Bushey Rd, Raynes Park, **London (Greater)**, SW20 0JH, **ENGLAND**.
(T) 020 89473333 **(F)** 020 88797354. **Ref: YH11580**

RACEWOOD

Racewood Ltd, The Mount, 17 Park Rd, Tarporley, **Cheshire**, CW6 0AN, **ENGLAND**.
(T) 01829 732006 **(F)** 01829 733667
(M) 07774 249330
(E) racewood.ltd@virgin.net
(W) www.racewood.com.
Profile Trainer. Racehorse Simulators.
Yr. Est: 1980 **Ref: YH11581**

RACING & FOOTBALL OUTLOOK

Racing & Football Outlook, High St, Compton, Newbury, **Berkshire**, RG20 6NL, **ENGLAND**.
(T) 01635 578080 **(F)** 01635 578101.
Profile Supplies. **Ref: YH11582**

RACING ANCILLARY SERVICES

Racing Ancillary Services Ltd, 2 School Hse, Gittisham, Honiton, **Devon**, EX14 0AH, **ENGLAND**.
(T) 01404 851171 **(F)** 01404 851171.
Profile Supplies. **Ref: YH11583**

RACING CALENDAR

Racing Calendar (The), BHB Publications, Weatherbys Group Ltd, Sanders Rd, Wellingborough, **Northamptonshire**, NN8 4BX, **ENGLAND**.
(T) 01933 440077 **(F)** 01933 270300.
Contact/s
Advertising: Steve Gibbon
Profile Supplies. **Ref: YH11584**

RACING POST

Racing Post, 1 Canada Sq, Canary Wharf, **London (Greater)**, E14 5AP, **ENGLAND**.
(T) 020 72933000 **(F)** 020 72933758.
Contact/s
Editor: Alan Byrne
Profile Supplies. **Ref: YH11585**

RACING REVIEW

Racing Review, 22-24 Swan St, Kingsclere, Newbury, **Berkshire**, RG20 5PJ, **ENGLAND**.
(T) 01635 299992 **(F)** 01635 299991.
Profile Supplies. **Ref: YH11586**

RACING TIMES

Racing Times (The), 15-16 Douglas Bader Cl, Lyngate Ind Est, North Walsham, **Norfolk**, NR28 0TZ, **ENGLAND**.
(T) 01692 500555 **(F)** 01692 500502.
Profile Supplies. **Ref: YH11587**

RACING WELFARE

Racing Welfare, 20B Park Lane, Newmarket, **Suffolk**, CB8 8AX, **ENGLAND**.
(T) 01638 560763 **(F)** 01638 560831.
Profile Club/Association. **Ref: YH11588**

RACK, FRANCIS

Francis Rack, 16 Leaze, South Cerney, Cirencester, **Gloucestershire**, GL7 5UL, **ENGLAND**.
(T) 01285 862190.
Profile Farrier. **Ref: YH11589**

RACK, W

W Rack, 56 Berkeley Cl, South Cerney, Cirencester, **Gloucestershire**, GL7 5UW, **ENGLAND**.
(T) 01285 860624.
Profile Farrier. **Ref: YH11590**

RACKENFORD EQUESTIAN CTRE

Rackenford Equestian Centre, Blindwell Farm, Rackenford, Tiverton, **Devon**, EX16 8ER, **ENGLAND**.
(T) 01884 881444. **Ref: YH11591**

RACKHAM, E R & R T

E R & R T Rackham, Deben Mills, Wickham Market, Woodbridge, **Suffolk**, IP13 0RG, **ENGLAND**.
(T) 01728 746207.
Profile Supplies. **Ref: YH11592**

RADDERY EQUINE

Raddery Equine Ltd, Raddery Pk, Raddery, Fortrose, **Highlands**, IV10 8SN, **SCOTLAND**.
(T) 01381 620615 **(F)** 01381 620615
(E) info@raddery.co.uk
(W) www.raddery.com
Affiliated Bodies BERA.
Contact/s
Owner: Mr B Smith
Profile Riding Wear Retailer, Saddlery Retailer, Supplies.
Everything for the Endurance Rider. Sell riding tights and heart rate monitors. Mail order only.
No.Staff: 4 Yr. Est: 1991 **Ref: YH11593**

RADICAL FORGING IRONWORK

Radical Forging Ironwork, Walker Hse/Sovereign Enterprise Pk, King William St, Salford, **Manchester (Greater)**, M5 2UP, **ENGLAND**.
(T) 0161 8487005 **(F)** 0161 8487005.
Contact/s
Owner: Mr D Lamberton
Profile Blacksmith. **Ref: YH11594**

RADIO LINKS COMMUNICATIONS

Radio Links Communications Ltd, Eaton Hse, Gt North Rd, Eaton Socon, St Neots, **Cambridgeshire**, PE19 3EG, **ENGLAND**.
(T) 01480 217220 **(F)** 01480 406667.
Contact/s
Marketing Pr Executive: Mrs K MacKenzie
Profile Club/Association. **Ref: YH11595**

RADIONIC & RADIESTHESIC

Confederation of Radionic & Radiesthesic Organ (The), Maperton Stud, Wincanton, **Somerset**, BA9 8EH, **ENGLAND**.
(T) 01963 32651 **(F)** 01963 32626.
Profile Club/Association. **Ref: YH11596**

RADIONIC ASSOCIATION

Radionic Association (The), Baerlein Hse, Goose Green, Deddington, Banbury, **Oxfordshire**, OX15 0SZ, **ENGLAND**.
(T) 01869 338852 **(F)** 01869 338852
(E) radionics@association.freeserve.co.uk.
Profile Medical Support. **Ref: YH11597**

RADMORE LANE FARM

Radmore Lane Farm, Radmore Lane, Gnosall, **Staffordshire**, ST20 0EG, **ENGLAND**.
(T) 01785 822328.
Contact/s
Owner: Mr J Salter
Profile Breeder. **Ref: YH11598**

RADNAGE HOUSE

Radnage House Stables, Radnage Hse, Green End Rd, Radnage, High Wycombe, **Buckinghamshire**, HP14 4BZ, **ENGLAND**.
(T) 01494 483268.
Contact/s
Owner: Ms C Williams
Profile Stable/Livery. No.Staff: 2
Yr. Est: 2001 C.Size: 14 Acres **Ref: YH11599**

RADWAY RIDING SCHOOL

Radway Riding School, Great Grounds Farm,

Radway, Warwick, **Warwickshire**, CV35 0UQ, **ENGLAND**.
(T) 01295 670265.
Contact/s
Owner: Mr J Boswell
Profile Riding School. Ref: YH11600

RADWINTER SADDLERY

Radwinter Saddlery, Brook Farm, Radwinter, Saffron Walden, **Essex**, CB10 2TH, **ENGLAND**.
(T) 01799 599262.
Profile Saddlery Retailer. Ref: YH11601

RAE BEAN & PARTNERS

Rae Bean & Partners, Veterinary Surgery, New Row, Boroughbridge, **Yorkshire (North)**, YO51 9AX, **ENGLAND**.
(T) 01423 322316 (F) 01423 324141.
Profile Medical Support. Ref: YH11602

RAFFERTY NEWMAN

Rafferty Newman, Specialist Machinery Div, Unit 4 Bedford Rd, Petersfield, **Hampshire**, GU32 3LJ, **ENGLAND**.
(T) 01730 264484 (F) 01730 264625.
Profile Transport/Horse Boxes. Ref: YH11603

RAFFIN STUD

Raffin Stud, West Soley, Chilton Foliat, Hungerford, **Berkshire**, RG17 0TL, **ENGLAND**.
(T) 01488 686953 (F) 01488 686117.
Contact/s
Owner: Mr S Kelly
Profile Breeder. Ref: YH11604

RAFIQUE, M

M Rafique, Garden Hse, Kingston Cross, Sturminster Newton, **Dorset**, DT10 2AR, **ENGLAND**.
(T) 01258 817018.
Profile Blood Stock Agency. Ref: YH11605

RAGLAN HOUSE ANDALUSIAN STUD

Raglan House Andalusian Stud, 107 Aylesbury Rd, Aston Clinton, **Buckinghamshire**, HP22 5AJ, **ENGLAND**.
(T) 01296 630326.
Profile Breeder. Ref: YH11606

RAGLAN, C A

C A Raglan, Somerford Pk Farm, Holmes Chapel Rd, Somerford, Congleton, **Cheshire**, CW12 4SW, **ENGLAND**.
(T) 01260 280858. Ref: YH11607

RAGUS SUGARS

Ragus Sugars Ltd, 193 Bedford Ave, Trading Est, Slough, **Buckinghamshire**, SL1 4RT, **ENGLAND**.
(T) 01753 75353 (F) 01753 691514.
Profile Medical Support. Ref: YH11608

RAGWOOD RIDING CTRE

Ragwood Riding Centre, 154 Daws Heath Rd, Benfleet, **Essex**, SS7 2TB, **ENGLAND**.
(T) 01702 556520.
Contact/s
General Manager: Mrs C Lazell (Q) PCB Test
Profile Riding School. No.Staff: 5
Yr. Est: 1981
Opening Times
Sp: Open Mon, Tues, Thurs, Fri, Sat 10:00, Sun 09:00. Closed Mon, Tues, Thurs, Fri, Sat 19:00, Sun 13:00.
Su: Open Mon, Tues, Thurs, Fri, Sat 10:00, Sun 09:00. Closed Mon, Tues, Thurs, Fri, Sat 19:00, Sun 13:00.
Au: Open Mon, Tues, Thurs, Fri, Sat 10:00, Sun 09:00. Closed Mon, Tues, Thurs, Fri, Sat 19:00, Sun 13:00.
Wn: Open Mon, Tues, Thurs, Fri, Sat 10:00, Sun 09:00. Closed Mon, Tues, Thurs, Fri, Sat 19:00, Sun 13:00.
Closed Wednesdays Ref: YH11609

RAHMATALLAH, S

Mrs S Rahmatallah, El Bustan, The Drive, Ifold, Billingshurst, **Sussex (West)**, RH14 0TD, **ENGLAND**.
(T) 01403 753445.
Profile Breeder. Ref: YH11610

RAIL, P A

P A Rail, Maespwll, Talgarreg, Llandysul, **Carmarthenshire**, SA44 4HB, **WALES**.
(T) 01545 590385.
Contact/s
Owner: Mr P Rail
Profile Farrier. Ref: YH11611

RAILTON, JAMIE

Jamie Railton, Tanglin Farm, Brinkworth, Chippenham, **Wiltshire**, SN15 5AU, **ENGLAND**.
(T) 01666 860067 (F) 01666 860881
(M) 07774 149336.
Profile Blood Stock Agency. Ref: YH11612

RAINBOW ARENA'S

Rainbow Arena's, Low Barn, Summerbridge, Harrogate, **Yorkshire (North)**, HG3 4JS, **ENGLAND**.
(T) 01423 780825 (F) 01423 781563.
Profile Track/Course. Ref: YH11613

RAINBOW EQUESTRIAN CTRE

Rainbow Equestrian Centre (The), 26 Hollow Rd, Islandmagee, Larne, **County Antrim**, BT40 3RL, **NORTHERN IRELAND**.
(T) 028 93382929
Affiliated Bodies BHS.
Profile Riding School. Ref: YH11614

RAINBOW EQUINE CLINIC

Rainbow Equine Clinic, Rainbow Farm, Old Malton, Malton, **Yorkshire (North)**, YO17 6SG, **ENGLAND**.
(T) 01653 695743 (F) 01653 600319
(E) rainbow_equine_clinic@compuserve.com.
Profile Medical Support. Ref: YH11615

RAINBOW HALL RIDING STABLES

Rainbow Hall Riding Stables, Rainbow Hall Farm, Old Watling St, Markyate, St Albans, **Hertfordshire**, AL3 8LS, **ENGLAND**.
(T) 01582 840204.
Contact/s
Owner: Mr C Waddington Ref: YH11616

RAINGER, CLIVE M

Clive M Rainger RSS BII, 2 Eden Villas, Mill Hill, Edenbridge, **Kent**, TN8 5DG, **ENGLAND**.
(T) 01732 865458.
Profile Farrier. Ref: YH11617

RAKE 'N' LIFT

Rake 'n' Lift & Co- The Nottingham Tack Rakes, 33 Firs Rd, Edwalton, **Nottinghamshire**, NG12 4BY, **ENGLAND**.
(T) 0115 9233166.
Contact/s
Owner: Mr M Garton-Smith (T) 0115 9233166
Profile Supplies.
Rake specialists. Manufacturers of magnetic safety rakes for collecting nails and tacks in the stable yard. Also manufacturers of tack and menage rakes.
Ref: YH11618

RAMSAY, R M & M F

R M & M F Ramsay, Woodlands Park Farm, Ashford Hill, Thatcham, **Berkshire**, RG19 8AY, **ENGLAND**.
(T) 01635 268098.
Contact/s
Partner: Mr R Ramsay Ref: YH11619

RAMSBOTTOM, J

J Ramsbottom, Craigton Farm, Kinbuck, Dunblane, **Perth and Kinross**, FK15 0NN, **SCOTLAND**.
(T) 01786 823331.
Contact/s
Owner: Mr J Ramsbottom
Profile Stable/Livery. Ref: YH11620

RAMSEY, J

J Ramsey, Ratheane Hse, 85 Mountsandel Rd, Coleraine, **County Londonderry**, BT52 1JF, **NORTHERN IRELAND**.
(T) 028 70342785 (F) 028 70342785.
Profile Medical Support. Ref: YH11621

RAMSEY, K

Mr K Ramsey, Larch How, Old Knebworth, **Hertfordshire**, SG3 6PS, **ENGLAND**.
(T) 01438 811021.
Profile Breeder. Ref: YH11622

RAMSHAW, JOHN

John Ramshaw DWCF, 10 Blackboy Rd, Chilton Moor, Houghton Le Spring, **Tyne and Wear**, DH4 6LX, **ENGLAND**.
(T) 0191 3854874.
Profile Farrier. Ref: YH11623

RAMSHAW, T

Mr T Ramshaw, 1 Tweed Rd, Spennymoor, **County Durham**, DL16 6SS, **ENGLAND**.
(T) 01388 811453.
Profile Breeder. Ref: YH11624

RANCH HOUSE STABLES

Ranch House Stables (The), East Farm, Osmington, Weymouth, **Dorset**, DT3 6EX, **ENGLAND**.
(T) 01305 833578.
Contact/s
Owner: Mrs M Green Ref: YH11625

RANCH HSE WESTERN WARE INT

Ranch House Western Ware Int, The Ranch Hse, 58 Halesowen Rd, Netherton, Dudley, **Midlands (West)**, DY2 9QA, **ENGLAND**.
(T) 01384 234142 (F) 01384 236054.
Profile Supplies. Ref: YH11626

RANCH TRUCKS & TRAILERS

Ranch Trucks & Trailers Ltd, Normanton Lane Ind Est, Bottesford, Nottingham, **Nottinghamshire**, NG13 0EL, **ENGLAND**.
(T) 01949 842038 (F) 01949 842421.
Profile Transport/Horse Boxes. Ref: YH11627

RANDALL, MONICA

Monica Randall, 48 Alton Rd, Fleet, **Hampshire**, GU13 9HW, **ENGLAND**.
(T) 01252 674796.
Profile Saddlery Retailer. Ref: YH11628

RANDLE, M J

M J Randle, Brynbank Stud, Brawlings Lane, Chalfont St. Peter, Gerrards Cross, **Buckinghamshire**, SL9 0RE, **ENGLAND**.
(T) 01494 875226.
Contact/s
Owner: Mr M Randle
Profile Breeder. Ref: YH11629

RANDLE, TIM

Tim Randle, Gardeners Cottage, The Short Yard, Wolverley, Kidderminster, **Worcestershire**, DY11 5XF, **ENGLAND**.
(T) 01179 289620 (F) 01179 289622
(M) 07970 917086. Ref: YH11630

RANDLES, JOHN M

John M Randles AFCL, 67 Avon Drive, Congleton, **Cheshire**, CW12 3RG, **ENGLAND**.
(T) 01260 298416.
Profile Farrier. Ref: YH11631

RANELAGH FARM LIVERY STABLES

Ranelagh Farm Livery Stables, Ranelagh Farm, Crouch Lane, Winkfield, Windsor, **Berkshire**, SL4 4TN, **ENGLAND**.
(T) 01344 891191 (F) 01344 891381.
Contact/s
Owner: Mrs D Lake Ref: YH11632

RANGE FARM DIY LIVERY YARD

Range Farm DIY Livery Yard, Range Farm, Upton Lane, Brookthorpe, Gloucester, **Gloucestershire**, GL4 0UT, **ENGLAND**.
(T) 01452 813722.
Contact/s
Partner: Mrs M Carlisle Ref: YH11633

RANGE RIDES

Range Rides, Blaen Y Cwm Farm, Llanwrthwl, Llandrindod Wells, **Powys**, LD1 6NU, **WALES**.
(T) 01597 810627.
Profile Equestrian Centre. Ref: YH11634

RANKIN, JULIA

Miss Julia Rankin, 32 Smiths Way, Alcester, **Warwickshire**, B49 6BL, **ENGLAND**.
(T) 01789 764135.
Profile Trainer. Ref: YH11635

RANSFORDS

Ransfords, Station St, Bishops Castle, **Shropshire**, SY9 5AQ, **ENGLAND**.
(T) 01588 638331.
Profile Track/Course. Ref: YH11636

RANSLEY, J & J

J & J Ransley, Golden Wood Farm, Brisley Lane, Ruckinge, Ashford, **Kent**, TN26 2PW, **ENGLAND**.
(T) 01233 731001 (F) 01233 731002.
Contact/s
Partner: Mrs D Ransley Ref: YH11637

RANSOME BODY PROTECTORS

Ransome Body Protectors, Bickington, Newton Abbot, **Devon**, TQ12 6JZ, **ENGLAND**.
(T) 01626 821789 (F) 01626 821044.
Contact/s
Partner: Mr R Mills Ref: YH11638

RAPER-ZULLIG

Raper-Zullig Translations & Photography, Christmas Cottage, Wilderness Rd, Woodhurst Pk, Oxted, **Surrey**, RH8 9HS, **ENGLAND**.
(T) 07146 00356 (F) 07146 00357
(E) isabella@raper-zullig.com. Ref: YH11639

RAPIDO HORSE SERVICES

Rapido Horse Services (UK) Ltd, Old Station Yard, Green Rd, Newmarket, **Suffolk**, CB8 9BA, **ENGLAND**.
(T) 01638 665145 **(F)** 01638 660848.
Contact/s
Manager: Mr A Branchini
Profile Transport/Horse Boxes. **Ref: YH11640**

RAPKYNS

Rapkyns, Rapkyns Cottage, Guildford Rd, Broadbridge Heath, Horsham, **Sussex (West)**, RH12 3PQ, **ENGLAND**.
(T) 01403 240939.
Profile Breeder. **Ref: YH11641**

RARE BREEDS & WATERFOWL PARK

Isle of Wight Rare Breeds & Waterfowl Park, Lisle Combe, Ventnor, **Isle of Wight**, PO38 1UW, **ENGLAND**.
(T) 01983 852582.
Profile Breeder. **Ref: YH11642**

RARE BREEDS SURVIVAL TRUST

Rare Breeds Survival Trust Ltd, Avenue Q, National Agricultural Ctre, Stoneleigh Pk, Kenilworth, **Warwickshire**, CV8 2LG, **ENGLAND**.
(T) 024 76696551 **(F)** 024 76696706.
Profile Club/Association. **Ref: YH11643**

RASCALS OF WARWICK

Rascals of Warwick, 1 Coten End, Warwick, **Warwickshire**, CV34 4NT, **ENGLAND**.
(T) 01926 497879.
Profile Saddlery Retailer. **Ref: YH11644**

RASE VETNRY CTRE

Rase Veterinary Centre (Market Rasen), Gallamore Lane, Market Rasen, **Lincolnshire**, LN8 3RX, **ENGLAND**.
(T) 01673 842448 **(F)** 01673 844430.
Profile Medical Support. **Ref: YH11645**

RASE VETNRY CTRE

Rase Veterinary Centre (Grimsby), 455 Laceby Rd, Grimsby, **Lincolnshire (North East)**, DN34 5NX, **ENGLAND**.
(T) 01472 751802.
Contact/s
Manager: Mr D Grantham
Profile Medical Support. **Ref: YH11646**

RATCATCHER

Ratcatcher, 1 Hillside Ave, Guiseley, **Yorkshire (West)**, LS20 9DH, **ENGLAND**.
(T) 01943 876712
(M) 07831 327657.
Profile Supplies. **Ref: YH11647**

RATCLIFF, A E

Mrs A E Ratcliff, South Yarde Farm, Rose Ash, South Molton, **Devon**, EX16 4PP, **ENGLAND**.
(T) 01769 550409
(E) stormhill.stud@btinternet.com.
Profile Breeder, Stable/Livery. **Ref: YH11648**

RATCLIFFE, J M

J M Ratcliffe, High St, Chippenham, Ely, **Cambridgeshire**, CB7 5PR, **ENGLAND**.
(T) 01638 720036 **(F)** 01638 721310.
Contact/s
Owner: Mr J Ratcliffe
Profile Transport/Horse Boxes. **Ref: YH11649**

RATCLIFFE, J W

J W Ratcliffe, 37 Granville St, Woodville, Burton-on-Trent, **Staffordshire**, DE11 7JQ, **ENGLAND**.
(T) 01283 213663.
Profile Farrier. **Ref: YH11650**

RATCLIFFE, L J

Mrs L J Ratcliffe, Brotheridge Farm, Cranham, **Gloucestershire**, GL4 8HD, **ENGLAND**.
(T) 01452 864145 **(F)** 01452 864145.
Profile Supplies. **Ref: YH11651**

RATCLIFFE, P

P Ratcliffe, The Hawthornes, Earlsway, Waterhouses, Stoke-on-Trent, **Staffordshire**, ST10 3EG, **ENGLAND**.
(T) 01538 308403.
Contact/s
Owner: Mr P Ratcliffe
Profile Farrier. **Ref: YH11652**

RATHASKER STUD

Rathasker Stud, Kilcullen Rd, Naas, **County Kildare**, **IRELAND**.
(T) 045 876940 **(F)** 045 897410
(E) info@rathasker.iol.ie
(W) www.rathasker-horse-farm.ie.
Contact/s
Key Contact: Mr M Burns
Profile Breeder. **Ref: YH11653**

RATHBONE, K

Mrs K Rathbone, Sharley Cop, Ravensthorpe, **Northamptonshire**, NN6 8EU, **ENGLAND**.
(T) 01788 510259.
Profile Breeder, Stable/Livery. **Ref: YH11654**

RATHFARNHAN EQUESTRIAN CTRE

Rathfarnhan Equestrian Centre, Ballycullen Rd, Knocklyon, Dublin, **County Dublin**, **IRELAND**.
(T) 01 4945415 **(F)** 01 4945415.
Contact/s
Owner: Bernadette Brooks
Profile Riding School, Stable/Livery.
This centre offers mountain trekking with instructions for children and beginners. Full livery is available, details on request.
Opening Times
Sp: Open Mon - Sun 10:00. Closed Mon - Thur 21:00, Fri - Sun 18:00.
Su: Open Mon - Sun 10:00. Closed Mon - Thur 21:00, Fri - Sun 18:00.
Au: Open Mon - Sun 10:00. Closed Mon - Thur 21:00, Fri - Sun 18:00.
Wn: Open Mon - Sun 10:00. Closed Mon - Thur 21:00, Fri - Sun 18:00. **Ref: YH11655**

RAVEL FARM

Ravel Farm, Brynberian, Crymych, **Pembrokeshire**, SA41 3TO, **WALES**.
(T) 01239 891316.
Profile Equestrian Centre. **Ref: YH11656**

RAVEN ROYD LIVERY FARM

Raven Royd Livery Farm, Raven Royd Farm, Marley, Bingley, **Yorkshire (West)**, BD16 2DL, **ENGLAND**.
(T) 01274 510520.
Contact/s
Owner: Mr P Patchett **Ref: YH11657**

RAVENSCROFT, JAMES C

James C Ravenscroft DWCF, Yew Farm, Canada Rd, West Wellow, Romsey, **Hampshire**, SO51 6DD, **ENGLAND**.
(T) 01794 22580.
Profile Farrier. **Ref: YH11658**

RAVENSHEAR, J

Mr J Ravenshear, Heatheryfield, Cairnie, Huntly, **Aberdeenshire**, AB54 4UE, **SCOTLAND**.
(T) 01466 760318.
Profile Breeder. **Ref: YH11659**

RAVENSHILL RIDING CTRE

Ravenshill Riding Centre, Ravenshill, Kielder, Hexham, **Northumberland**, NE48 1EL, **ENGLAND**.
(T) 01434 250251.
Profile Riding School. **Ref: YH11660**

RAW, W

Mr W Raw, Uckerby Mill, Scorton, Richmond, **Yorkshire (North)**, DL10 6DA, **ENGLAND**.
(T) 01748 818371.
Profile Breeder. **Ref: YH11661**

RAWDING, J & S M

J & S M Rawding, Church Farm Stud, Gr, Leighton Buzzard, **Bedfordshire**, LU7 0QU, **ENGLAND**.
(T) 01525 851044.
Profile Breeder, Stable/Livery. **Ref: YH11662**

RAWLE & SON

Rawle & Son Ltd, 424-428 Garratt Lane, London, **London (Greater)**, SW18 4HN, **ENGLAND**.
(T) 020 89471747.
Profile Saddlery Retailer. **Ref: YH11663**

RAWLEY PLANT

Rawley Plant Ltd, Ivy Mill Lane, Godstone, **Surrey**, RH9 8NR, **ENGLAND**.
(T) 01883 744022.
Profile Club/Association. **Ref: YH11664**

RAWLINGS, M A

Mr M A Rawlings, Ardra Grena, Wield Rd, Medstead, Alton, **Hampshire**, GU34 5LY, **ENGLAND**.
(T) 01420 62010.
Profile Supplies. **Ref: YH11665**

RAWLINGS, P S

P S Rawlings, Avon Lodge, London Rd West, Bath, **Bath & Somerset (North East)**, BA1 7DD, **ENGLAND**.
(T) 01225 858533.
Contact/s
Owner: Mr S Rawlings
Profile Transport/Horse Boxes. **Ref: YH11666**

RAWLINS FARM

Rawlins Farm Competition Horses, Rawlins Farm, Charter Alley, Tadley, **Hampshire**, RG26 5PU, **ENGLAND**.
(T) 01256 851326 **(F)** 01256 850272
Affiliated Bodies BE.
Contact/s
Owner: Mr M Corbett
Profile Trainer.
Purely training for 3 day eventing. There is access to gallops and jumps. **No.Staff:** 4 **Yr. Est:** 1989
Opening Times
Telephone for an appointment **Ref: YH11667**

RAWLSBURY FARM

Rawlsbury Farm, Higher Ansty, Dorchester, **Dorset**, DT2 7PT, **ENGLAND**.
(T) 01258 881744 **(F)** 01258 881744.
Contact/s
Owner: Mr S Rayner
Profile Breeder. **Ref: YH11668**

RAWRETH EQUESTRIAN CTRE

Rawreth Equestrian Centre, Old Burrells, Church Rd, Rawreth, Wickford, **Essex**, SS11 8SH, **ENGLAND**.
(T) 01268 733008.
Profile Riding School, Stable/Livery. **Ref: YH11669**

RAWSTRONS

Rawstrons, Cefn Foelallt Isaf, Llanfair Clydogau, Lampeter, **Carmarthenshire**, SA48 8NE, **WALES**.
(T) 01570 493258.
Contact/s
Owner: Mr P Rawstrons **Ref: YH11670**

RAXTER MOTOR ENGINEERING

Raxter Motor Engineering, Hanbury Garage, Droitwich Rd, Hanbury, Bromsgrove, **Worcestershire**, B60 4DB, **ENGLAND**.
(T) 01527 821408 **(F)** 01527 821551.
Contact/s
Owner: Mr R Raxter
Profile Transport/Horse Boxes. **Ref: YH11671**

RAYGILL

Raygill Riding Centre, Raygill Farm, Lartington, Barnard Castle, **County Durham**, DL12 9DG, **ENGLAND**.
(T) 01833 690118 **(F)** 01833 690988
Affiliated Bodies BHS.
Profile Breeder, Riding School, Stable/Livery, Track/Course.
Opening Times
Telephone for further information, there is an answer phone **Ref: YH11672**

RAYLEIGH SADDLERY

Rayleigh Saddlery, 1007 London Rd, Leigh-on-Sea, **Essex**, SS9 3JY, **ENGLAND**.
(T) 01702 480022 **(F)** 01702 480022.
Contact/s
Owner: Mrs M Fuller **Ref: YH11673**

RAYMARK TRAILERS

Raymark Trailers, Curdridge Lane, Curdridge, Southampton, **Hampshire**, SO32 2BH, **ENGLAND**.
(T) 01489 890930.
Contact/s
Owner: Mr M Stanner
Profile Transport/Horse Boxes. **Ref: YH11674**

RAYMOND POSKITT

Raymond Poskitt Ltd, Thorpe Grange Farm, Newark Rd, Aubourn, Lincoln, **Lincolnshire**, LN5 9EJ, **ENGLAND**.
(T) 01522 680159 **(F)** 01522 500022. **Ref: YH11675**

RAYNE RIDING CTRE

Rayne Riding Centre, Fairy Hall Lane, Rayne, Braintree, **Essex**, CM7 8SZ, **ENGLAND**.
(T) 01376 322231 **(F)** 01376 349803.
Contact/s
Owner: Mr B Pewter
Profile Riding School, Saddlery Retailer, Stable/Livery. **No.Staff:** 12 **Yr. Est:** 1981
Opening Times
Sp: Open 06:00. Closed 20:00.
Su: Open 06:00. Closed 20:00.
Au: Open 06:00. Closed 20:00.
Wn: Open 06:00. Closed 20:00. **Ref: YH11676**

RAY'S SADDLESHOP

Ray's Custom Western Saddleshop, Botley Mills, Botley, Southampton, **Hampshire**, SO30 2GB,

ENGLAND.
(T) 01489 797767 **(F)** 023 80473870
(W) www.rayssaddleshop.co.uk.
Contact/s
Owner: Mr R Cooper
(E) saddlemaker@msn.com
Profile Saddlery Retailer. Western Saddle Maker.
Western tack and custom Western saddles.
No.Staff: 2 Yr. Est: 1994
Opening Times
Sp: Open Mon - Fri 09:00, Sat 09:30. Closed Mon - Thurs 17:00, Fri 16:00, Sat 13:00.
Su: Open Mon - Fri 09:00, Sat 09:30. Closed Mon - Thurs 17:00, Fri 16:00, Sat 13:00.
Au: Open Mon - Fri 09:00, Sat 09:30. Closed Mon - Thurs 17:00, Fri 16:00, Sat 13:00.
Wn: Open Mon - Fri 09:00, Sat 09:30. Closed Mon - Thurs 17:00, Fri 16:00, Sat 13:00. **Ref: YH11677**

READ, ANNE
Anne Read, 163 Fairway, Waltham, Grimsby, **Lincolnshire (North East)**, DN37 0PY, **ENGLAND**.
(T) 01472 506150. **Ref: YH11678**

READ, G A
G A Read, Beech Tree Farm, Main St, Cantley, Doncaster, **Yorkshire (South)**, DN3 3QH, **ENGLAND**.
(T) 01302 536276.
Profile Breeder. **Ref: YH11679**

READ, T J G
T J G Read, The Flint Hse, Pook Lane, East Lavant, Chichester, **Sussex (West)**, PO18 0AS, **ENGLAND**.
(T) 01243 773482.
Contact/s
Owner: Mr T Read
Profile Breeder. **Ref: YH11680**

READ, TERENCE J
Terence J Read AWCF, Bluebell Cottage, Campsheath, Oulton, Lowestoft, **Suffolk**, NR32 5DW, **ENGLAND**.
(T) 01502 584452.
Profile Farrier. **Ref: YH11681**

READING, R H
R H Reading, Yarty Welsh Cobs (C&D), Ty'r Efail, Llanarthne, Carmarthen, **Carmarthenshire**, SA32 8LD, **WALES**.
(T) 01558 668708.
Profile Breeder. **Ref: YH11682**

READMAN, MICHAEL
Michael Readman, Anvilla, Beck Lane, Cloughton, Scarborough, **Yorkshire (North)**, YO13 0AQ, **ENGLAND**.
(T) 01723 870376.
Profile Farrier. **Ref: YH11683**

READWOOD
Readwood, Back Lane, Read, Burnley, **Lancashire**, BB12 7RZ, **ENGLAND**.
(T) 01282 771716 **(F)** 01282 777129.
Contact/s
Owner: Mr R Atkinson
Profile Saddlery Retailer. **Ref: YH11684**

REAL TIME IMAGING
Real Time Imaging, 1 Winslade Cl, Tunstall Village, Sunderland, **Tyne and Wear**, SR3 1EG, **ENGLAND**.
(T) 0191 5212991 **(F)** 0191 5212991
(M) 07768 210979. **Ref: YH11685**

REALITIES
Realities (UK), Flat 5, 9 Westgate Trce, London, **London (Greater)**, SW10 9BT, **ENGLAND**.
(T) 020 73705923. **Ref: YH11686**

REARSBY LODGE FEEDS
Rearsby Lodge Feeds, Rearsby Lodge Farm, Melton Rd, Rearsby, Leicester, **Leicestershire**, LE7 4YQ, **ENGLAND**.
(T) 0116 2606835.
Profile Saddlery Retailer. **Ref: YH11687**

REARSBY LODGE RIDING CLUB
Rearsby Lodge Riding Club, 124 Colby Drive, Thurmaston, **Leicestershire**, LE4 8LB, **ENGLAND**.
(T) 0116 2696876 **(F)** 0116 2696876.
Contact/s
Chairman: Mr R Andrews
Profile Club/Association, Riding Club. **Ref: YH11688**

REASEHEATH CLGE
Reaseheath College, Reaseheath, Nantwich, **Cheshire**, CW5 6DF, **ENGLAND**.
(T) 01270 625131 **(F)** 01270 625665.
Profile Equestrian Centre. **Ref: YH11689**

RECORD, NICHOLAS J
Nicholas J Record DWCF, Finch Cottage, Finch Lane, London Rd East, Amersham, **Buckinghamshire**, HP7 9DS, **ENGLAND**.
(T) 07836 573204.
Profile Farrier. **Ref: YH11690**

RECTORY FARM
Rectory Farm, Graveley, Huntingdon, **Cambridgeshire**, PE18 9PP, **ENGLAND**.
(T) 01480 830336.
Contact/s
Owner: Mr R Pembroke
Profile Stable/Livery. **Ref: YH11691**

RECTORY RIDING STABLES
Rectory Riding Stables, The Old Rectory Farm, Waterside, Peartree Bridge, Milton Keynes, **Buckinghamshire**, MK6 3EJ, **ENGLAND**.
(T) 01908 230081. **Ref: YH11692**

RECTORY ROAD RIDING SCHOOL
Rectory Road Riding School, Old Rectory, Suffield, Norwich, **Norfolk**, NR11 7ER, **ENGLAND**.
(T) 01263 761367.
Profile Riding School, Stable/Livery. **Ref: YH11693**

RED ALERT
Red Alert, Monument Way, Orbital Pk, Ashford, **Kent**, TN24 0HB, **ENGLAND**.
(T) 01233 501999 **(F)** 01233 501888. **Ref: YH11694**

RED CASTLE RIDING CTRE
Red Castle Riding Centre, Selattyn, Oswestry, **Shropshire**, SY10 7LL, **ENGLAND**.
(T) 01691 659704.
Profile Riding School. **Ref: YH11695**

RED HSE FARM LIVERY STABLES
Red House Farm Livery Stables, Black Lane, Leamington Spa, **Warwickshire**, CV32 7UA, **ENGLAND**.
(T) 01926 882883.
Contact/s
Owner: Mr H Johnson
Profile Riding School, Saddlery Retailer, Stable/Livery, Track/Course. **Ref: YH11696**

RED HSE FARM STABLES
Red House Farm Stables, Top Yard, Campion Hills, Leamington Spa, **Warwickshire**, CV32 4UX, **ENGLAND**.
(T) 01926 832714.
Contact/s
Owner: Mr N Dutton **Ref: YH11697**

RED HSE STABLES
Red House Stables (The), Carriage Museum, Old Rd, Darley Dale, Matlock, **Derbyshire**, DE4 2ER, **ENGLAND**.
(T) 01629 733583 **(F)** 01629 733583.
Profile Riding School, Stable/Livery, Trainer.
Ref: YH11698

RED HSE STABLES
Red House Stables, Red Hse, Hamilton Rd, Newmarket, **Suffolk**, CB8 0TE, **ENGLAND**.
(T) 01638 663254 **(F)** 01638 667767
(M) 07785 350705
Affiliated Bodies Newmarket Trainers Fed.
Contact/s
Trainer: Dr J Scargill
Profile Trainer. **Ref: YH11699**

RED HSE STUD
Red House Stud, Red Hse Stud, Landwade, Newmarket, **Suffolk**, CB8 7NE, **ENGLAND**.
(T) 01638 577491.
Contact/s
Owner: Mr T Warner
Profile Breeder. **Ref: YH11700**

RED MOSS CLYDEDALES
Red Moss Clydedales, Isobel Cottage, Parkhill, Newmachar, Aberdeen, **Aberdeen (City of)**, AB21 7XA, **SCOTLAND**.
(T) 01224 723897.
Contact/s
Owner: Mr G Walker **Ref: YH11701**

RED POST FEEDS
Red Post Feeds, Lillisford Stud, Littlehempston, Totnes, **Devon**, TQ9 6NG, **ENGLAND**.
(T) 01803 812040 **(F)** 01803 812040.
Profile Saddlery Retailer. **Ref: YH11702**

RED POST SHOW JUMPING CLUB
Red Post Show Jumping Club, Red Post Feeds, Lillisford Stud, Littlehempston, Totnes, **Devon**, TQ9 6NG, **ENGLAND**.
(T) 01803 812040 **(F)** 01803 812040.
Profile Club/Association. **Ref: YH11703**

RED RAE SADDLERY CTRE
Red Rae Saddlery Centre, 25 Amwell End, Ware, **Hertfordshire**, SG12 9HP, **ENGLAND**.
(T) 01920 463170 **(F)** 01920 463170.
Contact/s
Owner: Mr R Howitt
Profile Saddlery Retailer. **Ref: YH11704**

RED ROSETTE PET PRODUCTS
Red Rosette Pet Products, Whinrigg Farm, Stirling Rd, Riggend, Airdrie, **Lanarkshire (North)**, ML6 7SS, **SCOTLAND**.
(T) 01236 83655.
Profile Supplies. **Ref: YH11705**

RED STABLES FARM
Red Stables Farm Riding & Livery Stables, Warren Lane, Doddinghurst, Brentwood, **Essex**, CM15 0JD, **ENGLAND**.
(T) 01277 372336.
Profile Riding School, Stable/Livery. **Ref: YH11706**

REDCAR RACECOURSE
Redcar Racecourse Ltd, The Racecourse, Redcar, **Cleveland**, TS10 2BY, **ENGLAND**.
(T) 01642 484068 **(F)** 01642 488272.
Profile Track/Course. **Ref: YH11707**

REDENHAM PK STUD
Redenham Park Stud, Redenham Park Stud, Redenham Pk, Andover, **Hampshire**, SP11 9AJ, **ENGLAND**.
(T) 01264 772990.
Contact/s
Owner: Mr M Humby
Profile Blood Stock Agency, Breeder.
Stabling available for yearlings, foals and brood mares.
No.Staff: 2 Yr. Est: 1971 C.Size: 30 Acres
Opening Times
Telephone for an appointment **Ref: YH11708**

REDESDALE RESEARCH COMPANY
Redesdale Research Company, 29 Clarendon Rd, London, **London (Greater)**, W5 1AA, **ENGLAND**.
(T) 020 88106908 **(F)** 020 88106908.
Profile Supplies. **Ref: YH11709**

REDESDALE RIDING CTRE
Redesdale Riding and Carriage Driving Centre, Soppit Farm, Elsdon, Otterburn, **Northumberland**, NE19 1AF, **ENGLAND**.
(T) 01830 520276
(W) www.redesdale-riding.co.uk
Affiliated Bodies ABRS.
Contact/s
Owner: Mr W Rowe
Profile Equestrian Centre. No.Staff: 3
Yr. Est: 1989 C.Size: 25 Acres **Ref: YH11710**

REDGRAVE, CAROLE
Carole Redgrave, Foxholme Stables, Moor Lane, Wilmslow, **Cheshire**, SK9 6DN, **ENGLAND**.
(T) 01625 548553.
Contact/s
Owner: Carole Redgrave
(E) caroleredgrave@lineone.net
Profile Stable/Livery, Transport/Horse Boxes. Saddler (Non-Retail). Yr. Est: 1992 C.Size: 5 Acres
Opening Times
Sp: Open Mon - Sat 09:00. Closed Mon - Sat 17:00.
Su: Open Mon - Sat 09:00. Closed Mon - Sat 17:00.
Au: Open Mon - Sat 09:00. Closed Mon - Sat 17:00.
Wn: Open Mon - Sat 09:00. Closed Mon - Sat 17:00.
Ref: YH11711

REDHALL RIDING CLUB
Redhall Riding Club, 145 Beltoy Rd, Ballycarry, Carrickfergus, **County Antrim**, BT38 9LB, **NORTHERN IRELAND**.
(T) 028 93372235.
Contact/s
Secretary: Mrs W Adrain
Profile Club/Association, Riding Club. **Ref: YH11712**

REDHILLS EQUESTRIAN
Redhills Equestrian Ltd, Redhills, **County Cavan**, **IRELAND**.
(T) 047 55042 **(F)** 047 55056.
Contact/s
Manager: Helen Fossey
Profile Horse/Rider Accom, Riding School, Stable/Livery.
The RDA use the centre on Thursday mornings. 'Redhills' offers training to BHS level. Full, part and

DIY livery is also available.
Opening Times
Sp: Open Tues - Sun 09:00. Closed Tues - Sun 20:00.
Su: Open Tues - Sun 09:00. Closed Tues - Sun 20:00.
Au: Open Tues - Sun 09:00. Closed Tues - Sun 20:00.
Wn: Open Tues - Sun 09:00. Closed Tues - Sun 20:00.
Closed Mondays **Ref: YH11713**

REDMAYNE THE TAILORS

Redmayne The Tailors, 30 High St, Wigton, **Cumbria**, CA7 9NJ, **ENGLAND**.
(T) 01697 342221 **(F)** 01697 344587
(M) 07831 488189. **Ref: YH11714**

REDMIRE STABLES & BUILDINGS

Redmire Stables & Buildings Ltd, Coneymore, The Plantation, Storrington, **Sussex (West)**, RH20 4JG, **ENGLAND**.
(T) 01403 785508 **(F)** 01403 785333
(E) enquiries@redmire.co.uk
(W) www.redmire.co.uk.
Profile Stable/Livery. **Ref: YH11715**

REDNIL EQUESTRIAN CTRE

Rednil Equestrian Centre, Lincoln Rd, Welton, Lincoln, **Lincolnshire**, LN2 3JE, **ENGLAND**.
(T) 01673 860548
Affiliated Bodies ABRS, BHS.
Contact/s
Owner: Mr P Linder
Profile Arena, Equestrian Centre, Farrier, Riding Club, Riding School, Saddlery Retailer, Stable/Livery, Transport/Horse Boxes.
Rednil specialises in picinc and pleasure hacks. Children's day courses are available during the holidays. Plus side-saddle lessons and lessons for the disabled. Rednil also offer DIY livery, shoeing, clipping, transport and training. No.Staff: 7
Yr. Est: 1962 C.Size: 65 Acres
Opening Times
Sp: Open Mon - Sun 07:30. Closed Mon - Sun 21:00.
Su: Open Mon - Sun 07:30. Closed Mon - Sun 21:00.
Au: Open Mon - Sun 07:30. Closed Mon - Sun 21:00.
Wn: Open Mon - Sun 07:30. Closed Mon - Sun 21:00.
Closed from 13:00-14:00 **Ref: YH11716**

REDWING RIDING SCHOOL

Redwing Riding School, Maryculter, Aberdeen, **Aberdeen (City of)**, AB12 5FS, **SCOTLAND**.
(T) 01224 732952.
Profile Riding School, Stable/Livery. **Ref: YH11717**

REDWINGS HORSE SANCTUARY

Redwings Horse Sanctuary, Hapton Hall Farm, Hapton, Norwich, **Norfolk**, NR15 1SP, **ENGLAND**.
(T) 01508 481000
(E) info@redwings.co.uk
(W) www.redwings.co.uk.
Contact/s
Chief Executive: Mr J Archibald **(T)** 01508 481001
(E) jarchibald@redwings.co.uk
Profile Club/Association. **Ref: YH11718**

REED, ANGELA

Mrs Angela Reed, Lloegr, Llanfihangelnant-Bran, Pontfaen, Brecon, **Powys**, LD3 9ND, **WALES**.
(T) 01874 89288.
Profile Breeder. **Ref: YH11719**

REED, J M

J M Reed, Longhouse, Wiston, Haverfordwest, **Pembrokeshire**, SA62 4PS, **WALES**.
(T) 01437 731323.
Contact/s
Owner: Miss J Reed
Profile Breeder. **Ref: YH11720**

REED, MARTIN C

Martin C Reed DWCF, 2 St George's Cres, Banbury, **Oxfordshire**, OX16 9HN, **ENGLAND**.
(T) 01295 266982.
Profile Farrier. **Ref: YH11721**

REED, W G

Mr W G Reed, Pens Cl, Stamfordham, Hexham, Newcastle-upon-Tyne, **Tyne and Wear**, NE18 0NE, **ENGLAND**.
(T) 01661 886683
(M) 07885 9343463.
Profile Trainer. **Ref: YH11722**

REED, W J

Mr W J Reed, Stowford Farm, East Stowford, Chittlehampton, Umberleigh, **Devon**, EX37 9RU, **ENGLAND**.
(T) 01769 540292.
Profile Supplies. **Ref: YH11723**

REEDER, PENNY

Penny Reeder BHSII, Alice Ford Farm, Sourton Down, Okehampton, **Devon**, EX20 4HR, **ENGLAND**.
(T) 01837 861293.
Profile Trainer. **Ref: YH11724**

REEDER'S OF WORLINGTON

Reeder's Of Worlington, 10 The Street, Worlington, Bury St Edmunds, **Suffolk**, IP28 8RU, **ENGLAND**.
(T) 01638 712182. **Ref: YH11725**

REEL THING

Reel Thing (Classic Vintage Hunting Books) (The), 17 Royal Opera Arcade, Pall Mall, London, **London (Greater)**, SW1Y 4UY, **ENGLAND**.
(T) 020 79761830.
Profile Supplies. **Ref: YH11726**

REEN MANOR RIDING STABLES

Reen Manor Riding Stables, Reen Manor Farm, Perranporth, **Cornwall**, TR6 0AJ, **ENGLAND**.
(T) 01872 573064.
Contact/s
Owner: Mrs C Opie **Ref: YH11727**

REES, D W

D W Rees, 87 Wenallt Forge, Wenallt Rd, Tonna, Neath, **Neath Port Talbot**, SA11 3QH, **WALES**.
(T) 01639 637682.
Profile Farrier. **Ref: YH11728**

REES, G

G Rees, 12 Harford St, Sirhowy, Tredegar, **Monmouthshire**, NP22 4QE, **WALES**.
(T) 01495 717997.
Profile Breeder. **Ref: YH11729**

REES, GERALDINE

Mrs Geraldine Rees, Moor Farm, Sollom, Tarleton, Preston, **Lancashire**, PR4 6US, **ENGLAND**.
(T) 01772 812780 **(F)** 01772 812799
(M) 07973 710403.
Profile Trainer. **Ref: YH11730**

REES, K M & W P

K M & W P Rees, Tynewydd, Llandefalle, Brecon, **Powys**, **WALES**.
(T) 01874 754253.
Profile Breeder. **Ref: YH11731**

REES, M Q

M Q Rees, Village Farm, Bilton In Ainsty, **Yorkshire (North)**, **ENGLAND**.
(T) 01423 358503.
Profile Breeder. **Ref: YH11732**

REES, S R

S R Rees, Pantrhyn, Llwyndafydd, Llandysul, **Carmarthenshire**, SA44 6LH, **WALES**.
(T) 01545 560494.
Contact/s
Owner: Mr S Rees
Profile Equestrian Centre. **Ref: YH11733**

REESTACK

ReesTack, The Stables, Coppings Farm, Leigh, Tonbridge, **Kent**, TN11 8PN, **ENGLAND**.
(T) 01732 460180.
Contact/s
Owner: Mrs S Rees
Profile Supplies. **Ref: YH11734**

REEVE SMITH, J R M

J R M Reeve Smith, Crouchfield, Chapmore End, Ware, **Hertfordshire**, SG12 0EX, **ENGLAND**.
(T) 07889 598308.
Contact/s
Owner: Mr R Smith
Profile Farrier. **Ref: YH11735**

REEVE, S C

S C Reeve, 113 Church St, Matlock, **Derbyshire**, DE4 3BZ, **ENGLAND**.
(T) 01629 582844.
Profile Medical Support. **Ref: YH11736**

REEVES, MARK

Mark Reeves, Ottery, St Mary, **Devon**, EX14 1LE, **ENGLAND**.
(T) 01404 822173.
Profile Transport/Horse Boxes. **Ref: YH11737**

REEVES, PAUL R

Paul R Reeves DWCF, Thorne Bungalow, Heathend Rd, Baughurst, **Hampshire**, RG26 5ND, **ENGLAND**.
(T) 01734 814529.
Profile Farrier. **Ref: YH11738**

REGAN, T A

T A Regan, Moores Bdge The, Curragh, **County Kildare**, **IRELAND**.
(T) 045 521673.
Profile Supplies. **Ref: YH11739**

REGENCY CARRIAGES

Regency Carriages, Old Green End Farm, Common Rd, Kensworth, Dunstable, **Bedfordshire**, LU6 2PW, **ENGLAND**.
(T) 01582 872676 **(F)** 01582 873942.
Contact/s
Owner: Mr J Dick **Ref: YH11740**

REGENT VETNRY GROUP

Regent Veterinary Group (The), Upper York St, Coventry, **Midlands (West)**, CV1 3GP, **ENGLAND**.
(T) 024 76225101 **(F)** 024 76225751.
Contact/s
Vet: Mr G Nicholson
Profile Medical Support. **Ref: YH11741**

REGISTRY OFFICE TURF CLUB

Registry Office Of The Turf Club, The, Curragh, **County Kildare**, **IRELAND**.
(T) 045 445600 **(F)** 045 445699
(E) sales@curragh.ie
(W) www.turfclub.ie.
Profile Supplies. **Ref: YH11742**

REID, JOHN R

John R Reid DWCF, 83 Garvine Rd, Coylton, **Ayrshire (South)**, KA6 6SG, **SCOTLAND**.
(T) 01292 570443.
Profile Farrier. **Ref: YH11743**

REID, NOEL A

Noel A Reid DWCF, Lower Flat, Wormstall, Wickham, Newbury, **Berkshire**, RG16 8HB, **ENGLAND**.
(T) 01488 608656.
Profile Farrier. **Ref: YH11744**

REIGATE & DISTRICT

Reigate & District Riding Club, 10 Springcopse Rd, Reigate, **Surrey**, RH2 7HH, **ENGLAND**.
(T) 01737 243487 **(F)** 01737 642341.
Contact/s
Chairman: Mrs J Allard
Profile Club/Association, Riding Club. **Ref: YH11745**

REILLY, J

J Reilly, Chichester Rd, Midhurst, **Sussex (West)**, GU29 9PF, **ENGLAND**.
(T) 01730 813501.
Contact/s
Owner: Mr J Reilley **Ref: YH11746**

REILLY, VINCENT

Vincent Reilly RSS, 31 Fielden Court, Kingsclere, Newbury, **Berkshire**, RG15 8PG, **ENGLAND**.
(T) 01635 298758.
Profile Farrier. **Ref: YH11747**

REINBOW EQUESTRIAN PRODUCTS

Reinbow Equestrian Products, 68 Milton Hill, Worlebury, Weston-Super-Mare, **Somerset (North)**, BS22 9RF, **ENGLAND**.
(T) 01934 632343.
Profile Medical Support. **Ref: YH11748**

REIS, VICKY

Vicky Reis, 147 Lower Weybourne Lane, Badshot Lea, Farnham, **Surrey**, GU9 9LL, **ENGLAND**.
(T) 01252 310457 **(F)** 01483 811300
Affiliated Bodies NAAT.
Contact/s
Physiotherapist: Vicky Reis
Profile Medical Support. **Ref: YH11749**

REIVER ANDALUSIANS

Reiver Andalusians, Fenwick Stead, Belford, **Northumberland**, NE70 7PL, **ENGLAND**.
(T) 01289 381363 **(F)** 01289 381363
Affiliated Bodies BHS.
Contact/s
Owner: Mrs R Hutchinson
Profile Breeder, Horse/Rider Accom. No.Staff: 1
Yr. Est: 1971
Opening Times
By appointment only, telephone for further information.
Ref: YH11750

A-Z of COMPANIES

REMPSTONE STABLES
Rempstone Stables, Rempstone, Corfe Castle, Wareham, **Dorset**, BH20 5JQ, **ENGLAND**.
(T) 01929 480490.
Contact/s
Owner: Mr P Nemitz **(Q)** BHS 4, BHSAI
Profile Equestrian Centre, Riding School, Stable/Livery.
Teaches children from 2 years and upwards.
No.Staff: 4 **Yr. Est:** 1995 **C.Size:** 20 Acres
Opening Times
Sp: Open Mon - Sun 08:00. Closed Mon - Sun 17:00.
Su: Open Mon - Sun 08:00. Closed Mon - Sun 18:00.
Au: Open Mon - Sun 08:00. Closed Mon - Sun 17:00.
Wn: Open Mon - Sun 08:00. Closed Mon - Sun 17:00. **Ref: YH11751**

REMUS EQUESTRIAN
Remus Equestrian, South Dundonald, Cardenden, Lochgelly, **Fife**, KY5 0AL, **SCOTLAND**.
(T) 01592 721727.
Contact/s
Owner: Ms B Harrison
Profile Stable/Livery. **No.Staff:** 1
Yr. Est: 1992 **C.Size:** 14 Acres **Ref: YH11752**

RENARD RIDING CTRE
Renard Livery Stables, Neds Lane, Stalmine, Poulton-Le-Fylde, **Lancashire**, FY6 0LW, **ENGLAND**.
(T) 01253 700313
(W) www.renards.co.uk.
Contact/s
Owner: Mrs N Smith
Profile Equestrian Centre, Medical Support, Riding School, Stable/Livery.
Teach nervous novices, complete beginners of all ages and people who ride for pleasure. Also have a horse bed and breakfast. **Yr. Est:** 1989 **C.Size:** 5 Acres
Opening Times
Closed on Christmas Day. **Ref: YH11753**

RENDALL, K
Mr K Rendall, West End Farm, Lawhill Rd, Law, Carluke, **Lanarkshire (South)**, ML8 5JA, **SCOTLAND**.
(T) 01555 71573. **Ref: YH11754**

RENDELL, PHILIP
Philip Rendell DWCF, Raxters Farm, Five Ash Lane, Sutton Vey, Warminster, **Wiltshire**, BA12 7BH, **ENGLAND**.
(T) 01985 40248.
Profile Farrier. **Ref: YH11755**

RENDENE STUD
Rendene Stud, 172 Hammond St Rd, Cheshunt, **Hertfordshire**, EN7 6NY, **ENGLAND**.
(T) 01992 443122.
Profile Breeder. **Ref: YH11756**

RENE, P
Miss P Rene, The Barns, Southwick Farm, Nomansland, Thelbridge, Tiverton, **Devon**, EX16 8NW, **ENGLAND**.
(T) 01884 860143.
Profile Breeder. **Ref: YH11757**

RENFREW, W G
W G Renfrew, 112 Cross Arthurlie St, Barrhead, Glasgow, **Glasgow (City of)**, G78 1EB, **SCOTLAND**.
(T) 0141 8811481.
Profile Blacksmith. **Ref: YH11758**

RENFREWSHIRE RIDING CLUB
Renfrewshire Riding Club, Glengarnock Lodge, Milton Rd, Kilbirnie, **Ayrshire (North)**, **SCOTLAND**.
(T) 01505 682339.
Contact/s
Secretary: Dr E Knox
Profile Club/Association, Riding Club. **Ref: YH11759**

RENOUARD, STEPHEN G
Stephen G Renouard, 1 Tadburn Cottages, Botley Rd, Romsey, **Hampshire**, S051 5AT, **ENGLAND**.
(T) 01794 502947 **(F)** 01794 502947
(M) 07802 363305
(E) stephen.renouard@ntlworld.com. **Ref: YH11760**

RENOUF, PAUL
Paul Renouf, Laundry Rd, Lairg, **Highlands**, IV27 4DE, **SCOTLAND**.
(T) 01549 402722 **(F)** 01549 402722.
Contact/s
Owner: Mr P Renouf
Profile Blacksmith. **Ref: YH11761**

RENSON, MICHAEL D
Michael D Renson DWCF BII, The Gables, Stonebyres, Kirkfieldbank, Lanark, **Lanarkshire (South)**, ML11 9UW, **SCOTLAND**.
(T) 01555 661413.
Profile Farrier. **Ref: YH11762**

RENTOKIL INTITAL
Rentokil Intital Plc, Felcourt, East Grinstead, **Sussex (West)**, RH19 2JY, **ENGLAND**.
(T) 01342 833022 **(F)** 01342 833029
(E) pr@rentokil-initial.com. **Ref: YH11763**

RENTON SWAN & PARTNERS
Renton Swan & Partners, 112 High St, Coldstream, **Northumberland**, TD12 4AG, **ENGLAND**.
(T) 01890 882322.
Contact/s
Partner: Mr S Renton
Profile Medical Support. **Ref: YH11764**

RENTOUL, ROBIN
Robin Rentoul, Station Rd, Thornton, Kirkcaldy, **Fife**, KY1 4AY, **SCOTLAND**.
(T) 01592 775515 **(F)** 01592 775469.
Contact/s
Owner: Mr R Rentoul
Profile Blacksmith. **Ref: YH11765**

RENVARG STUD & RIDING CTRE
Renvarg Stud & Riding Centre, Hillylaid Rd, Thornton-Cleveleys, **Lancashire**, FY5 4EG, **ENGLAND**.
(T) 01253 859019.
Contact/s
Owner: Mrs D Gravner **Ref: YH11766**

RENWICK
Lady Renwick, Whalton Hse, Whalton, Morpeth, **Northumberland**, NE61 3UZ, **ENGLAND**.
(T) 01670 75383.
Profile Supplies. **Ref: YH11767**

RETFORD SADDLERY SERVICES
Retford Saddlery Services, Bramble Hse, London Rd, Retford, **Nottinghamshire**, DN22 7JG, **ENGLAND**.
(T) 01777 701707 **(F)** 01777 701707.
Contact/s
Manageress: Miss K McGowan **Ref: YH11768**

REVELEY, C
M C Reveley, Groundhill Farm, Lingdale, Saltburn-by-the-Sea, **Cleveland**, TS12 3HD, **ENGLAND**.
(T) 01287 650456.
Profile Trainer. **Ref: YH11769**

REVINGTON, H & SPARKES, S
Ms Helen Revington & Mr Stephen Sparkes, 15 Kitesnest Lane, Lightpill, Stroud, **Gloucestershire**, GL5 3PQ, **ENGLAND**.
(T) 01453 758685 **(F)** 01453 758685.
Profile Supplies. **Ref: YH11770**

REWCASTLE, K
K Rewcastle, The Warren, Brack Lane, North Cave, **Yorkshire (East)**, HU15 2PF, **ENGLAND**.
(T) 01430 423957.
Profile Track/Course. **Ref: YH11771**

REX AGRICULTURE
Rex Agriculture, Shirwell Mill, Loxhore, Barnstaple, **Devon**, EX31 4SZ, **ENGLAND**.
(T) 01271 850521.
Profile Supplies. **Ref: YH11772**

REXON STUD
Rexon Stud, Broadmoorhead Farm, Stowford, Lewdown, **Devon**, EX24 4DE, **ENGLAND**.
(T) 01566 783406.
Profile Breeder. **Ref: YH11773**

REYNOLDS D & SONS
Reynolds D & Sons, Barns Green, Horsham, **Sussex (West)**, RH13 7PS, **ENGLAND**.
(T) 01403 730809.
Contact/s
Partner: Mr D Reynolds
Profile Blacksmith. **Ref: YH11774**

REYNOLDS MOTORS
Reynolds Motors (Cromer), Bridge Farm, Northrepps, Cromer, **Norfolk**, NR27 0LQ, **ENGLAND**.
(T) 01263 833286.
Contact/s
Owner: Mr B Reynolds
Profile Transport/Horse Boxes. **Ref: YH11775**

REYNOLDS, ANTHONY
Mr Anthony Reynolds, Point Farm, The Common, Botesdale, Diss, **Norfolk**, IP22 1LH, **ENGLAND**.
(T) 01379 898514
(M) 07885 374437. **Ref: YH11776**

REYNOLDS, BRIAN
Brian Reynolds, The Forge, Mundesley Rd, Paston, North Walsham, **Norfolk**, NR28 9TE, **ENGLAND**.
(T) 01263 721871.
Contact/s
Owner: Mr B Reynolds
Profile Blacksmith. **Ref: YH11777**

REYNOLDS, GERRY
Gerry Reynolds, The Tack Room, Rowley Drive, Newmarket, **Suffolk**, CB8 0JL, **ENGLAND**.
(T) 01638 668837 **(F)** 01638 668837.
Contact/s
Owner: Mr G Reynolds
Profile Saddlery Retailer. Engravers.
25 years experience **No.Staff:** 3 **Yr. Est:** 1995
Opening Times
Sp: Open Mon - Sat 09:00. Closed Mon - Fri 17:00, Sat 12:00.
Su: Open Mon - Sat 09:00. Closed Mon - Fri 17:00, Sat 12:00.
Au: Open Mon - Sat 09:00. Closed Mon - Fri 17:00, Sat 12:00.
Wn: Open Mon - Sat 09:00. Closed Mon - Fri 17:00, Sat 12:00. **Ref: YH11778**

REYNOLDS, M H
M H Reynolds, Folly, Newcastle, Craven Arms, **Shropshire**, SY7 8QY, **ENGLAND**.
(T) 01588 640396.
Contact/s
Owner: Mr M Reynolds
Profile Transport/Horse Boxes. **Ref: YH11779**

REYNOLDS, SIMON
Simon Reynolds, 98 Park Drive, Sittingbourne, **Kent**, ME10 1RL, **ENGLAND**.
(T) 01795 428998.
Profile Trainer. **Ref: YH11780**

RFC BED-DOWN
Robin Foster-Clarke, Cherry Tree Farm, The Common, Metfield, Harleston, **Norfolk**, IP20 0LP, **ENGLAND**.
(T) 01986 785278 **(F)** 01986 785507
(E) info@bed-down.co.uk
(W) www.bed-down.co.uk.
Contact/s
For Bookings: Ms S Flux **(Q)** BSc(Hons)
Profile Medical Support, Supplies. **No.Staff:** 25
Yr. Est: 1960 **Ref: YH11781**

RHAM, TRICIA
Miss Tricia Rham DC AMC MMCA, 2 Castlegate, Cockermouth, **Cumbria**, CA13 9EU, **ENGLAND**.
(T) 01900 825332.
Profile Medical Support. **Ref: YH11782**

RHAYADER PONY TREKKING ASS
Rhayader Pony Trekking Association, Nantserth Hse, Rhayader, **Powys**, LD6 5LT, **WALES**.
(T) 01597 810298.
Profile Equestrian Centre. **Ref: YH11783**

RHEIDOL RIDING CTRE
Rheidol Riding Centre, Capel Bangor, Aberystwyth, **Ceredigion**, SY23 4EL, **WALES**.
(T) 01970 880863 **(F)** 01970 832398
Affiliated Bodies BHS.
Contact/s
General Manager: Ms I Evans **(Q)** BHSAI, BHSII
(E) brina@btinternet.com
Profile Arena, Equestrian Centre, Riding School, Stable/Livery, Trainer, Transport/Horse Boxes.
No.Staff: 7 **Yr. Est:** 1991 **C.Size:** 36 Acres
Opening Times
Sp: Open Mon - Sun 10:00. Closed Mon - Sun 19:00.
Su: Open Mon - Sun 10:00. Closed Mon - Sun 19:00.
Au: Open Mon - Sun 10:00. Closed Mon - Sun 19:00.
Wn: Open Mon - Sun 10:00. Closed Mon - Sun 19:00. **Ref: YH11784**

RHINESTONE SADDLERY
Rhinestone Saddlery & Country Clothing, Mount Usher, Ashford, **County Wicklow**, **IRELAND**.
(T) 0404 40521.
Contact/s
Owner: Lillia McGuire **Ref: YH11785**

RHINO BODIES

Rhino Bodies Ltd, Lowes La Ind Est, Lowes Lane, Wellesbourne, Warwick, **Warwickshire**, CV35 9RB, **ENGLAND**.
(T) 01789 470611 **(F)** 01789 470099.
Profile Transport/Horse Boxes. **Ref: YH11786**

RHINO TRAILER HIRE

Rhino Trailer Hire, Willow Cottage, Choseley Rd, Knowl Hill, Reading, **Berkshire**, RG10 9YT, **ENGLAND**.
(T) 01628 829982 **(F)** 01628 829982.
Contact/s
Owner: Mr M Fisher
Profile Transport/Horse Boxes. **Ref: YH11787**

RHIWIAU RIDING CTRE

Rhiwiau Riding Centre, Llanfairfechan, **Gwynedd**, LL33 0EH, **WALES**.
(T) 01248 680094 **(F)** 01248 681143
(E) rhiwiau@aol.com
(W) www.rhiwiau.co.uk
Affiliated Bodies ABRS, BHS, WTRA.
Contact/s
Owner: Mrs R Hill **(Q)** BHSAI
Profile Equestrian Centre, Holidays, Riding Club, Riding School. **No.Staff:** 5 **Yr. Est:** 1972
C.Size: 20 Acres
Opening Times
Sp: Open Mon -Sun 09:30. Closed Mon - Sun 17:30.
Su: Open Mon -Sun 09:30. Closed Mon - Sun 17:30.
Au: Open Mon -Sun 09:30. Closed Mon - Sun 17:30.
Wn: Open Mon -Sun 09:30. Closed Mon - Sun 17:30. **Ref: YH11788**

RHODES, KATH

Kath Rhodes, Equine Marketing Ltd, Ledgemoor, Weobley, **Herefordshire**, HR4 8QH, **ENGLAND**.
(T) 01544 318196 **(F)** 01544 318770
(M) 07850 384772
(E) equinem1@wildnet.co.uk. **Ref: YH11789**

RHONDDA RIDING CLUB

Rhondda Riding Club, Maindy Hall, The Parade, Ton Pentre, Rhondda, **Rhondda Cynon Taff**, CF41 7EX, **WALES**.
(T) 01443 432000.
Profile Club/Association, Riding Club. **Ref: YH11790**

RHOSYN GWYN EQUESTRIAN CTRE

Rhosyn Gwyn Equestrian Centre, Ddol Helyg Farm, Cwm-Y-Glo, Caernarfon, **Gwynedd**, LL55 4DA, **WALES**.
(T) 01286 871931.
Profile Riding School, Stable/Livery, Track/Course.
Ref: YH11791

RHYDHIR STUD

Rhydhir Stud, Bryn Iwan, Conwyl Elfed, Carmarthen, **Carmarthenshire**, SA33 6TG, **WALES**.
(T) 01994 484529.
Profile Breeder. **Ref: YH11792**

RIBBLE VALLEY RIDING CLUB

Ribble Valley Riding Club, 7 Barons Cl, Lower Darwen, **Lancashire**, BB3 0RQ, **ENGLAND**.
(T) 01254 663979.
Contact/s
Secretary: Carla Dixon
Profile Club/Association, Riding Club. **Ref: YH11793**

RIBBLESDALE PARK

Ribblesdale Park, Buckhurst Hill, Ascot, **Berkshire**, SL5 7RL, **ENGLAND**.
(T) 01344 624838.
Contact/s
Owner: Mr F Thompson
Profile Trainer. **Ref: YH11794**

RIBBY HALL

Ribby Hall Equestrian Centre, Ribby Rd, Wrea Green, Preston, **Lancashire**, PR4 2PA, **ENGLAND**.
(T) 01772 687829
(W) www.ribbyhall.co.uk.
Contact/s
Assistant Manager: Miss N Gould
Profile Equestrian Centre, Riding School.
Hacks are offered from £12.00. Lessons for groups of 4 from £32.00. Indoor school is for hire. Children on a lead rein from £6.00, 'loan-a-pony' from £20.00 per session, £60.00 for five sessions. **No.Staff:** 6
Yr. Est: 1995 **C.Size:** 106 Acres
Opening Times
Sp: Open Mon - Sun 10:00. Closed Mon, Fri 17:00, Tues - Thurs 21:00, Sat, Sun 18:00.
Su: Open Mon - Sun 10:00. Closed Mon, Fri 17:00, Tues - Thurs 21:00, Sat, Sun 18:00.
Au: Open Mon - Sun 10:00. Closed Mon, Fri 17:00, Tues - Thurs 21:00, Sat, Sun 18:00.
Wn: Open Mon - Sun 10:00. Closed Mon, Fri 17:00, Tues - Thurs 21:00, Sat, Sun 18:00. **Ref: YH11795**

RICCHI, REGALI

Regali Ricchi, Crown Hse, Crown St, Clowne, Chesterfield, **Derbyshire**, S43 4DN, **ENGLAND**.
(T) 01246 570777 **(F)** 01246 570888.
Contact/s
Owner: Mrs S Taylor
Profile Supplies. **Ref: YH11796**

RICE BROS

Rice Bros, 6 West St, Midhurst, **Sussex (West)**, GU29 9NF, **ENGLAND**.
(T) 01730 813395.
Contact/s
Owner: Mr V Finn **Ref: YH11797**

RICH & SON

Rich & Son, 55 Fore St, North Petherton, Bridgwater, **Somerset**, TA6 6PY, **ENGLAND**.
(T) 01278 662574.
Contact/s
Owner: Mr A Rich
Profile Saddlery Retailer. **Ref: YH11798**

RICH, B

B Rich, The Elms, Church Lane, Thorpe Satchville, Melton Mowbray, **Leicestershire**, LE14 2DF, **ENGLAND**.
(T) 01664 840240.
Contact/s
Owner: Mrs B Rich
Profile Breeder. **Ref: YH11799**

RICH, BARBARA

Mrs Barbara Rich, The Elms Cottage, Church Lane, Thorpe Satchville, Melton Mowbray, **Leicestershire**, **ENGLAND**.
(T) 01664 840240.
Contact/s
Owner: Mrs B Rich
Profile Breeder, Stable/Livery. **Ref: YH11800**

RICH, P

Mr P Rich, Llangwendr Farm, Llangovan, Usk, **Monmouthshire**, NP25 4BT, **WALES**.
(T) 01291 690864 **(F)** 01633 262791
(M) 07971 218286
(E) paul@m-rich.freeserve.co.uk.
Profile Trainer. **Ref: YH11801**

RICHARD BATTERSBY

Richard Battersby (Corn Merchant) Ltd, 88/92 York St, Heywood, **Lancashire**, OL10 4NS, **ENGLAND**.
(T) 01706 360572 **(F)** 01706 625040
(E) enquiries@horseandpetfeeds.com
(W) www.horseandpetfeeds.com.
Contact/s
Owner: Mr R Purser
Profile Feed Merchant, Supplies. **No.Staff:** 5
Yr. Est: 1830
Opening Times
Sp: Open Mon - Sat 08:00, Sun 10:00. Closed Mon - Fri 17:30, Sat, Sun 12:00.
Su: Open Mon - Sat 08:00, Sun 10:00. Closed Mon - Fri 17:30, Sat, Sun 12:00.
Au: Open Mon - Sat 08:00, Sun 10:00. Closed Mon - Fri 17:30, Sat, Sun 12:00.
Wn: Open Mon - Sat 08:00, Sun 10:00. Closed Mon - Fri 17:30, Sat, Sun 12:00. **Ref: YH11802**

RICHARD GRICE TRAILERS

Richard Grice Trailers, Folly Farm, North Kelsey Moor, Market Rasen, **Lincolnshire**, LN7 6HE, **ENGLAND**.
(T) 01652 678726.
Contact/s
Owner: Mr R Grice
Profile Transport/Horse Boxes.
New and second hand trailers. **Yr. Est:** 1986
Ref: YH11803

RICHARD O'GORMAN BLOODSTOCK

Richard O'Gorman Bloodstock Ltd, Peel Hse, 1 Cheveley Rd, Newmarket, **Suffolk**, CB8 8AD, **ENGLAND**.
(T) 01638 664787.
Profile Blood Stock Agency. **Ref: YH11804**

RICHARD PITMAN BLOODSTOCK

Richard Pitman Bloodstock Ltd, Curlew Meadow, Denchurch, Wantage, **Oxfordshire**, OX12 0EA, **ENGLAND**.
(T) 01235 868244 **(F)** 01235 868051.
Profile Blood Stock Agency. **Ref: YH11805**

RICHARDS, CHRISTOPHER D

Christopher D Richards DWCF, Hillside Hse, Victoria Rd, Abersychan, **Torfaen**, NP4 8PT, **WALES**.
(T) 01495 774586.
Profile Farrier. **Ref: YH11806**

RICHARDS, D C

D C Richards, 9 Mount Pleasant, Fairford, **Gloucestershire**, GL7 4BA, **ENGLAND**.
(T) 01285 711025.
Contact/s
Owner: Mr D Richards
Profile Farrier. **Ref: YH11807**

RICHARDS, GRAHAM

Mr Graham Richards, 1 Tynewydd Cottage, Llanfabon, Cilfynydd, **Rhondda Cynon Taff**, CF37 4HP, **WALES**.
(T) 01443 453189 **(F)** 01443 453189.
Profile Blood Stock Agency. **Ref: YH11808**

RICHARDS, GRAHAM J

Graham J Richards DWCF, 3 Old Hop Gardens, Peasmarsh, Rye, **Sussex (East)**, TN31 6NB, **ENGLAND**.
(T) 01797 230045.
Profile Farrier. **Ref: YH11809**

RICHARDS, L

Mrs L Richards, Lynch Farm, Funtington, Chichester, **Sussex (West)**, PO18 9LG, **ENGLAND**.
(T) 01243 574379 **(F)** 01243 574882
(M) 07803 199061.
Profile Breeder, Trainer. **Ref: YH11810**

RICHARDS, N G

Mr N G Richards, The Old Rectory, Greystoke, Penrith, **Cumbria**, CA11 0UJ, **ENGLAND**.
(T) 01768 483392 **(F)** 01768 483933
(M) 07771 906609.
Profile Trainer. **Ref: YH11811**

RICHARDS, PETER

Peter Richards, Little Huxham Farm, Huxham Lane, East Pennard, Shepton Mallet, **Somerset**, BA4 6RP, **ENGLAND**.
(T) 01749 860366.
Profile Transport/Horse Boxes. **Ref: YH11812**

RICHARDSON RICE

Richardson Rice Trailers, Main St, Shipton By Beningbrough, York, **Yorkshire (North)**, YO30 1AB, **ENGLAND**.
(T) 01904 470282/470315 **(F)** 01904 470486
(E) info@trailers-uk.com
(W) www.trailers-uk.com.
Profile Transport/Horse Boxes.
Make Richardson & Rice trailers - doubles and trebles. Fully galvanised and all front and rear unload. Tack tidies, breast bars and wheel clamps. Largest stockist of Rice parts. **No.Staff:** 25 **Yr. Est:** 1949
Opening Times
Sp: Open Mon - Fri 09:00, Sat 08:00. Closed Mon - Fri 17:00, Sat 12:00.
Su: Open Mon - Fri 09:00, Sat 08:00. Closed Mon - Fri 17:00, Sat 12:00.
Au: Open Mon - Fri 09:00, Sat 08:00. Closed Mon - Fri 17:00, Sat 12:00.
Wn: Open Mon - Fri 09:00, Sat 08:00. Closed Mon - Fri 17:00, Sat 12:00. **Ref: YH11813**

RICHARDSON STABLES

Richardson Stables, The Stables, Main St, Lambley, Nottingham, **Nottinghamshire**, NG4 4PN, **ENGLAND**.
(T) 0115 9313550.
Profile Stable/Livery. **Ref: YH11814**

RICHARDSON, A M

A M Richardson RSS, 16 Brookfield Ave, Lunsford Pk, Larkfield, Maidstone, **Kent**, ME20 6RT, **ENGLAND**.
(T) 01622 790326.
Profile Farrier. **Ref: YH11815**

RICHARDSON, CLIVE

Mr Clive Richardson, 19 Dragley Beck, Ulverston, **Cumbria**, LA12 0HD, **ENGLAND**.
(T) 01229 582742.
Profile Breeder. **Ref: YH11816**

RICHARDSON, DEBBIE

Debbie Richardson PR, 1 East Garth Cottages, Catterton, Tadcaster, **Yorkshire (North)**, LS24 8DH, **ENGLAND**.
(T) 01937 832490 **(F)** 01937 832490
(E) m03gs100@cwcom.net. **Ref: YH11817**

RICHARDSON, F W O
Mr F W O Richardson, Bewholme Hall, Bewholme, Driffield, **Yorkshire (East)**, YO25 8ED, **ENGLAND**.
(T) 01964 533737.
Profile Breeder. **Ref: YH11818**

RICHARDSON, M F
M F Richardson, Park Farm, Kirton Rd, Bucklesham, Ipswich, **Suffolk**, IP10 0BT, **ENGLAND**.
(T) 01473 659894.
Contact/s
Owner: Mr M Richardson **Ref: YH11819**

RICHARDSON, ROBBIE
Robbie Richardson RSS, Greatcombe, Holne, Newton Abbott, **Devon**, TQ13 7SP, **ENGLAND**.
(T) 01364 631227
(M) 07836 746188.
Profile Farrier. **Ref: YH11820**

RICHARDSON, S
Miss S Richardson, Stone Cottage, Priors Marston, Rugby, **Warwickshire**, CV23 8RL, **ENGLAND**.
(T) 01327 260555.
Profile Breeder. **Ref: YH11821**

RICHARDSON, S L
Mrs S L Richardson, Owdeswall Manor, Andoversford, Cheltenham, **Gloucestershire**, GL54 4LD, **ENGLAND**.
(T) 01242 820297.
Profile Supplies. **Ref: YH11822**

RICHARDSON, S P
S P Richardson, Gale Lodge Stables, Oldlake Rd, Ambleside, **Cumbria**, LA22 0DN, **ENGLAND**.
(T) 01539 433565.
Profile Medical Support. **Ref: YH11823**

RICHARDSONS DESIGNS
Richardsons Designs, Whiteside Farm, Holmside, Burnhope, **County Durham**, DH7 0DR, **ENGLAND**.
(T) 0191 3711591 **(F)** 0191 3711831.
Profile Supplies. **Ref: YH11824**

RICHHILL EQUESTRIAN CTRE
Richhill Equestrian Centre, 38 Annareagh Rd, Richhill, **County Armagh**, BT61 9JT, **NORTHERN IRELAND**.
(T) 028 28871258.
Profile Riding School, Stable/Livery, Track/Course.
Ref: YH11825

RICHINGS, M V
M V Richings, Wharf Bungalow, Uffington, Faringdon, **Oxfordshire**, SN7 7PS, **ENGLAND**.
(T) 01367 820253.
Profile Farrier. **Ref: YH11826**

RICHMOND EQUESTRIAN CTRE
Richmond Equestrian Centre, Breckenbrough Farm, Brough Pk, Richmond, **Yorkshire (North)**, DL10 7PL, **ENGLAND**.
(T) 01748 811629 **(F)** 01748 818019.
Profile Riding School, Stable/Livery. **Ref: YH11827**

RICHMOND FARM STABLES
Richmond Farm Stables, Rye Farm Lane, Barns Green, Horsham, **Sussex (West)**, RH13 7QB, **ENGLAND**.
(T) 01403 732355 **(F)** 01403 732355.
Contact/s
Owner: Mr R Huber **Ref: YH11828**

RICHMOND, DAVID GEORGE
David George Richmond RSS, Northwood Farm, Northwood Lane, Bewdley, **Worcestershire**, DY12 1AP, **ENGLAND**.
(T) 01299 404460.
Profile Farrier. **Ref: YH11829**

RICHMOND, PETER
Peter Richmond, New Stud Farm, Sicklinghall, Wetherby, **Yorkshire (West)**, LS22 4BD, **ENGLAND**.
(T) 01937 582315.
Profile Blood Stock Agency, Breeder, Stable/Livery.
Ref: YH11830

RICHMONDS HORSE TRANSPORT
Richmonds Horse Transport Ltd, New Marsh Farm, Horsley Rd, Cobham, **Kent**, KT11 3JX, **ENGLAND**.
(T) 01932 864007.
Contact/s
Owner: Mr M Stegeman
Profile Transport/Horse Boxes. No.Staff: 11
Ref: YH11831

RICKARD, T R
T R Rickard, Cornminnow, Lanjeth, St Austell, **Cornwall**, PL26 7TE, **ENGLAND**.
(T) 01726 72675.
Profile Supplies. **Ref: YH11832**

RICKELSFORD, DAVID E
David E Rickelsford DWCF, Little Covenhope, Aymestrey, Leominster, **Herefordshire**, HR6 9SY, **ENGLAND**.
(T) 01568 709126
(M) 07970 325933.
Profile Farrier. **Ref: YH11833**

RICKERBY
Rickerby Ltd, Cornhill-on-Tweed, **Northumberland**, TD12 4UG, **ENGLAND**.
(T) 01890 883322 **(F)** 01890 883677.
Profile Saddlery Retailer. **Ref: YH11834**

RICKETTS, A G
A G Ricketts, 42 Oakfield Rd, Blackwater, Camberley, **Hampshire**, GU17 9EA, **ENGLAND**.
(T) 01276 513266.
Contact/s
Owner: Mr A Ricketts
Profile Transport/Horse Boxes. **Ref: YH11835**

RICKETTS, TINA
Tina Ricketts ITEC Dip, 3 St Georges Cottages, Brinkers Lane, Wadhurst, **Sussex (East)**, TN5 6LT, **ENGLAND**.
(T) 01892 785717
(M) 07976 320194.
Profile Medical Support. **Ref: YH11836**

RICKMAN, L
Mrs L Rickman, Fieldgate, Middle Rd, Tiptoe, Lymington, **Hampshire**, SO41 6FX, **ENGLAND**.
(T) 01590 683025.
Profile Breeder. **Ref: YH11837**

RICKNALL GRANGE
Ricknall Grange Livery, Ricknall Grange, Ricknall Lane, Aycliffe, Newton Aycliffe, **County Durham**, DL5 6JQ, **ENGLAND**.
(T) 01325 313128 **(F)** 01325 313317
(W) www.ricknallrugs.co.uk.
Contact/s
Owner: Mr C Walker
(E) chris@ricknall.sagepost.co.uk
Profile Stable/Livery.
Bed & Breakfast for horses - £20 per night. Part livery available, prices on request. Access to numerous bridleways. Rug and tack repairs on site. No.Staff: 3
Yr. Est: 1998 C.Size: 400 Acres
Opening Times
Sp: Open Mon - Sun 08:00. Closed Mon - Sun 20:00.
Su: Open Mon - Sun 08:00. Closed Mon - Sun 20:00.
Au: Open Mon - Sun 08:00. Closed Mon - Sun 20:00.
Wn: Open Mon - Sun 08:00. Closed Mon - Sun 20:00. **Ref: YH11838**

RICKNALL RUGS
Ricknall Rugs, Ricknall Grange, Aycliffe, Darlington, **County Durham**, DL5 6JQ, **ENGLAND**.
(T) 01325 317300 **(F)** 01325 313317
(E) rugs@ricknall.sagepost.co.uk
(W) www.ricknallrugs.co.uk.
Profile Stable/Livery. Rug Repair & Cleaning.
Also repairs tack, tents and awnings. Livery available, prices on request. No.Staff: 3 Yr. Est: 1998
Opening Times
Sp: Open Mon - Sat 08:00. Closed Mon - Sat 18:00.
Su: Open Mon - Sat 08:00. Closed Mon - Sat 18:00.
Au: Open Mon - Sat 08:00. Closed Mon - Sat 18:00.
Wn: Open Mon - Sat 08:00. Closed Mon - Sat 18:00.
Closed Sundays **Ref: YH11839**

RIDDLE RIDING CTRE
Riddle Riding Centre, Eyton, Leominster, **Herefordshire**, HR6 0BZ, **ENGLAND**.
(T) 01568 615166.
Profile Riding School. **Ref: YH11840**

RIDDLE SADDLERY
Riddle Saddlery, The Riddle, Eyton, Leominster, **Herefordshire**, HR6 0BZ, **ENGLAND**.
(T) 01568 615166.
Profile Saddlery Retailer. **Ref: YH11841**

RIDE & DRIVE
Ride & Drive, Greenwood, Smallfield Rd, Horne, **Surrey**, RH6 9JP, **ENGLAND**.
(T) 01342 844452 **(F)** 01342 844452
(E) enquiries@rideanddrive.co.uk
(W) www.rideanddrive.co.uk.
Profile Saddlery Retailer.
Made to measure harnesses and bits for riding and driving. Yr. Est: 1988
Opening Times
Telephone for an appointment **Ref: YH11842**

RIDE & DRIVE SUPPLIES
Ride & Drive Supplies, Croft-An-Carne, Higher Lane, Ashton, Helston, **Cornwall**, TR13 9RZ, **ENGLAND**.
(T) 01736 763849
Affiliated Bodies WCW.
Contact/s
Owner: Terry Ansell
Profile Wheelwright & Carriage Builder.
Ref: YH11843

RIDE & GROOM
Ride & Groom Ltd, Loanwath Rd, Gretna, **Dumfries and Galloway**, DG16 5ES, **SCOTLAND**.
(T) 01461 337290 **(F)** 01461 337594.
Contact/s
General Manager: Mr N Brayton
Profile Supplies. **Ref: YH11844**

RIDE & GROOM
Ride & Groom, Burn Lane, Hexham, **Northumberland**, NE46 3HJ, **ENGLAND**.
(T) 01434 605136 **(F)** 01434 600265.
Contact/s
Manager: Mr D Walton **Ref: YH11845**

RIDE AWAY SADDLERY
Ride Away Saddlery, Cockfield Hall Lane, Westerfield, Ipswich, **Suffolk**, IP6 9AL, **ENGLAND**.
(T) 01473 257096.
Contact/s
Owner: Mr F Coleman
Profile Riding Wear Retailer, Saddlery Retailer, Supplies. No.Staff: 2 Yr. Est: 1976
Opening Times
Sp: Open Mon - Sat 09:00. Closed Mon - Sat 17:00.
Su: Open Mon - Sat 09:00. Closed Mon - Sat 17:00.
Au: Open Mon - Sat 09:00. Closed Mon - Sat 17:00.
Wn: Open Mon - Sat 09:00. Closed Mon - Sat 17:00.
Ref: YH11846

RIDE IN STYLE
Ride In Style Saddlery, 36 Front St, Cleadon Village, Sunderland, **Tyne and Wear**, SR6 7PG, **ENGLAND**.
(T) 0191 5192476 **(F)** 0191 5192476
(W) www.rideinstyle.co.uk.
Contact/s
Owner: Mr S Hardy
Profile Supplies. Yr. Est: 1995
Opening Times
Sp: Open Mon - Fri 10:00, Sat 09:00, Sun 10:00. Closed Mon - Fri 18:00, Sat 17:00, Sun 16:00.
Su: Open Mon - Fri 10:00, Sat 09:00, Sun 10:00. Closed Mon - Fri 18:00, Sat 17:00, Sun 16:00.
Au: Open Mon - Fri 10:00, Sat 09:00, Sun 10:00. Closed Mon - Fri 18:00, Sat 17:00, Sun 16:00.
Wn: Open Mon - Fri 10:00, Sat 09:00, Sun 10:00. Closed Mon - Fri 18:00, Sat 17:00, Sun 16:00.
Ref: YH11847

RIDE 'N' DRIVE EQUESTRIAN SUP
Ride 'N' Drive Equestrian Supplies, Tinkers Lane, Henstead, Beccles, **Suffolk**, NR34 7LB, **ENGLAND**.
(T) 01502 740771 **(F)** 01502 740331.
Profile Saddlery Retailer. **Ref: YH11848**

RIDE OUT
Ride Out, 8 The Maltings, Thaxted, Dunmow, **Essex**, CM6 2NB, **ENGLAND**.
(T) 01371 830118 **(F)** 01371 830118.
Contact/s
Partner: Mrs K Wallis
Profile Supplies. **Ref: YH11849**

RIDE-AWAY
S B & A Clark Ltd T/A Ride-Away, Stillington Rd, Sutton-on-the-Forest, York, **Yorkshire (North)**, YO61 1EH, **ENGLAND**.
(T) 01347 810443 **(F)** 01347 810746
(E) info@rideaway.co.uk
(W) www.rideaway.co.uk.
Contact/s
Owner: Mr S Clark
(E) info@rideaway.co.uk
Profile Saddlery Retailer.
Also stock country wear. No.Staff: 17
Yr. Est: 1980 C.Size: 1 Acres **Ref: YH11850**

RIDE-A-WAY
Ride-A-Way, 3 Sparrows Herne, Bushey, Watford,

Hertfordshire, WD2 1AD, ENGLAND.
(T) 020 89504363.
Contact/s
Owner: Mrs C Bolt Ref: YH11851

RIDEMOOR

Ridemoor (Animal Aids Ltd), Alfreds Way, Wincanton Business Pk, Wincanton, **Somerset**, BA9 9RU, **ENGLAND**.
(T) 01963 33083 (F) 01963 33193
Affiliated Bodies BETA, SMS.
Contact/s
General Manager: Mr M Hoskins
Profile Riding Wear Retailer, Saddlery Retailer, Supplies.
Opening Times
Sp: Open Mon - Sat 09:00. Closed Mon - Fri 17:30, Sat 16:30.
Su: Open Mon - Sat 09:00. Closed Mon - Fri 17:30, Sat 16:30.
Au: Open Mon - Sat 09:00. Closed Mon - Fri 17:30, Sat 16:30.
Wn: Open Mon - Sat 09:00. Closed Mon - Fri 17:30, Sat 16:30. Ref: YH11852

RIDEOUT, NIGEL

Nigel Rideout, Middle Ditchford, Moreton In Marsh, **Gloucestershire**, GL56 9QR, **ENGLAND**.
(T) 01386 78369.
Profile Supplies. Ref: YH11853

RIDERS

Riders, 27 Nile St, North Shields, **Tyne and Wear**, NE29 0AZ, **ENGLAND**.
(T) 0191 2966707 (F) 0191 2966706
(W) www.equiworld.net/ukweb/riders/.
Contact/s
Manager: Mr M Cranston
Profile Riding Wear Retailer, Saddlery Retailer, Supplies. No.Staff: 3 Yr. Est: 1998
Opening Times
Sp: Open 09:00. Closed 17:00.
Su: Open 09:00. Closed 17:00.
Au: Open 09:00. Closed 17:00.
Wn: Open 09:00. Closed 17:00. Ref: YH11854

RIDERS & SQUIRES

Riders & Squires Of Kensington Co Ltd, 8 Thackeray St, London, **London (Greater)**, W8 5ET, **ENGLAND**.
(T) 020 79374377 (F) 020 79372123.
Contact/s
Owner: Mr P Bossard
Profile Riding Wear Retailer, Saddlery Retailer. No.Staff: 3 Yr. Est: 1990
Opening Times
Sp: Open Mon - Sat 09:00. Closed Mon - Fri 19:00, Sat 17:00.
Su: Open Mon - Sat 09:00. Closed Mon - Fri 19:00, Sat 17:00.
Au: Open Mon - Sat 09:00. Closed Mon - Fri 19:00, Sat 17:00.
Wn: Open Mon - Sat 09:00. Closed Mon - Fri 19:00, Sat 17:00. Ref: YH11855

RIDERS INT

Riders International, 86 Mallows Drive, Raunds, **Northamptonshire**, NN9 6SF, **ENGLAND**.
(T) 01933 626855 (F) 01933 626300
(M) 07970 176272.
Profile Saddlery Retailer. Ref: YH11856

RIDERS JOURNAL

Riders Journal (The), Romar, Birgham, Coldstream, **Northumberland**, TD12 4NF, **ENGLAND**.
(T) 01890 830377 (F) 01890 830377
(E) cppub@aol.com.
Profile Supplies. Ref: YH11857

RIDERS LEGAL LINE

Riders Legal Line, Fishergate Chambers, 89 Fishergate Hill, Preston, **Lancashire**, PR1 8JD, **ENGLAND**.
(T) 08003 87815.
Profile Club/Association. Ref: YH11858

RIDERS REPAIRS

Riders Repairs, 18 Follygreen, Woodcote, Reading, **Berkshire**, RG8 0ND, **ENGLAND**.
(T) 01491 681143.
Profile Supplies. Ref: YH11859

RIDERS SADDLERY

Riders Saddlery, Saddlers Farm, Cublington Rd, Aston Abbotts, Aylesbury, **Buckinghamshire**, HP22 4ND, **ENGLAND**.
(T) 01296 681413. Ref: YH11860

RIDERS SADDLERY

Riders Saddlery, 5 Maynard Pl, Cuffley, Potters Bar, **Hertfordshire**, EN6 4JA, **ENGLAND**. (F) 01707 875515.
Contact/s
Manager: Mr M Hull Ref: YH11861

RIDGE HILL STUD & RIDING CTRE

Ridge Hill Stud & Riding Centre, Rectory Lane, Ridge Hill, Shenley, Radlett, **Hertfordshire**, WD7 9BG, **ENGLAND**.
(T) 01707 643377.
Contact/s
Owner: Mr J Noonan Ref: YH11862

RIDGE MANOR STABLES

Ridge Manor Stables, Milltown, **County Kildare**, **IRELAND**.
(T) 045 521498.
Profile Supplies. Ref: YH11863

RIDGEWAY LEATHER

Ridgeway Leather, Unit 10 Townhead Trading Ctre, Main St, Addingham, **Yorkshire (West)**, LS29 0PD, **ENGLAND**.
(T) 01943 830088 (F) 01943 830075.
Profile Supplies. Ref: YH11864

RIDGEWAY RIDING SCHOOL

Ridgeway Riding School, Sloade Lane, Ridgeway, Sheffield, **Yorkshire (South)**, S12 3YA, **ENGLAND**.
(T) 01246 431200. Ref: YH11865

RIDGEWAY SCIENCE

Ridgeway Science Ltd, Research Services, Rodmore Mill Farm, Alvington, **Gloucestershire**, GL15 6AH, **ENGLAND**.
(T) 01594 530204 (F) 01594 516024.
Profile Medical Support. Ref: YH11866

RIDGEWAY VETNRY GROUP

Ridgeway Veterinary Group, 4 Baydon Rd, Lambourn, **Berkshire**, RG17 8NY, **ENGLAND**.
(T) 01488 71002 (F) 01488 71184.
Profile Medical Support. Ref: YH11867

RIDGEWOOD EQUESTRIAN CTRE

Ridgewood Equestrian Centre, Higg Lane, Alderwasley, **Derbyshire**, DE56 2AB, **ENGLAND**.
(T) 01629 825954.
Profile Riding School. Ref: YH11868

RIDGEWOOD RIDING CTRE

Ridgewood Riding Centre, Irons Bottom Rd, Sidlow, Reigate, **Surrey**, RH2 8QG, **ENGLAND**.
(T) 01293 862216 (F) 01293 862281.
Profile Stable/Livery. Ref: YH11869

RIDGWAY STABLES

Dalerises Limited T/A Ridgway Stables, 93 Ridgway, Wimbledon, London, **London (Greater)**, SW19 4SU, **ENGLAND**.
(T) 020 89467400 (F) 020 89448055.
Contact/s
Owner: Mr J Hardy (Q) BHSAI
Profile Riding School, Riding Wear Retailer, Stable/Livery.
Hacking ranges from £18.00 - £25.00. Saturday club £27.00, and 'own a pony' days are £48.00 per day at weekends. All riding lessons can be paid for in a course of six, all courses must be used within 6 months of purchase and are non-refundable.
Ref: YH11870

RIDGWAY, I W

I W Ridgway, The Forge, Aylmerton, Norwich, **Norfolk**, NR11 8PT, **ENGLAND**.
(T) 01263 837658 (F) 01263 837658.
Contact/s
Owner: Mr I Ridgway
Profile Blacksmith. Ref: YH11871

RIDGWAY, SHARON

Sharon Ridgway (AUS), C/O Iron Pear Tree Cottage, Appleshaw, Andover, **Hampshire**, SP11 9BE, **ENGLAND**.
(T) 01264 773894 (F) 01264 773905
(M) 07785 365237. Ref: YH11872

RIDING CTRE

Riding Centre, (The), 13 Upper Old Park Lane, Farnham, **Surrey**, GU9 0AT, **ENGLAND**.
(T) 01252 714917.
Contact/s
Owner: Mrs V Markall (Q) BHSAI
Profile Equestrian Centre, Riding School.
No.Staff: 2 Yr. Est: 1985 C.Size: 12 Acres
Opening Times
Sp: Open 08:30. Closed 18:00.
Su: Open 08:30. Closed 18:00.
Au: Open 08:30. Closed 18:00.
Wn: Open 08:30. Closed 16:00. Ref: YH11873

RIDING CTRE

Riding Centre, (The), Cliff Farm, Fellbeck, Harrogate, **Yorkshire (North)**, HG3 5EH, **ENGLAND**.
(T) 01423 711005
(W) www.nidderdale.co.uk.
Contact/s
Owner: Ms J Butts
Profile Riding School, Stable/Livery.
10% discounts are offered to anyone booking 4 lessons. Groups consists of no more than 6 people. Yorkshire Riding Centre recommend this Centre for hacking, which is all off road. Livery and riding holidays are available, details on request. Monthly shows are held in Winter. No.Staff: 6 Yr. Est: 1994
C.Size: 17 Acres
Opening Times
Sp: Open Mon - Sat 09:00. Closed Mon - Thurs 20:30, Fri, Sat 17:00.
Su: Open Mon - Sat 09:00. Closed Mon - Thurs 20:30, Fri, Sat 17:00.
Au: Open Mon - Sat 09:00. Closed Mon - Thurs 20:30, Fri, Sat 17:00.
Wn: Open Mon - Sat 09:00. Closed Mon - Thurs 20:30, Fri, Sat 17:00.
Closed Sundays Ref: YH11874

RIDING FARM EQUESTRIAN CTRES

Riding Farm Equestrian Centres, Riding Lane, Hildenborough, Tonbridge, **Kent**, TN11 9LN, **ENGLAND**.
(T) 01732 838717 (F) 01732 838717.
Contact/s
Partner: Mr J Gosling
Profile Riding School. Ref: YH11875

RIDING FOR THE DISABLED ASS

Riding for the Disabled Association (N Ireland), 15 Hill Rd, Dromara, **County Down**, BT25 2AH, **NORTHERN IRELAND**.
(T) 028 97532678.
Contact/s
Secretary: Mrs R Watts
Profile Club/Association. Ref: YH11876

RIDING FOR THE DISABLED ASS

Riding for the Disabled Association Glasgow Group, Sandyflat Stables, Caldercuilt Rd, Glasgow, **Glasgow (City of)**, G23 5NA, **SCOTLAND**.
(T) 0141 9451369 (F) 0141 9451369.
Contact/s
Chairman: Mrs A Meakin Ref: YH11877

RIDING FOR THE DISABLED ASS

Riding for the Disabled Association, Prestbury Park Racecourse, Bishops Cleeve, Cheltenham, **Gloucestershire**, GL52 4LZ, **ENGLAND**.
(T) 01242 584420.
Contact/s
Manager: Mrs C Derrett
Profile Club/Association. Ref: YH11878

RIDING FOR THE DISABLED ASS

Riding for the Disabled Association, Epsom Group/St. Ebbas Farm, Hook Rd, Epsom, **Surrey**, KT19 8QW, **ENGLAND**.
(T) 01372 743690.
Profile Club/Association. Ref: YH11879

RIDING FOR THE DISABLED ASS

Riding for the Disabled Association, Lavinia Norfolk Hse, Avenue R National Agricultural Ctre, Stoneleigh Pk, Kenilworth, **Warwickshire**, CV8 2LY, **ENGLAND**.
(T) 024 76696510 (F) 024 76696532.
Profile Club/Association. Ref: YH11880

RIDING HABIT/COUNTRY CLASSICS

Riding Habit & Country Classics, High St, Eastry, Sandwich, **Kent**, CT13 0HE, **ENGLAND**.
(T) 01304 611295.
Contact/s
Partner: Mrs L Emmerson Ref: YH11881

RIDING HIGH

Riding High, 90 Watling St, Towcester, **Northamptonshire**, NN12 7BT, **ENGLAND**.
(T) 01327 350469 (F) 01327 350249.
Profile Saddlery Retailer. Ref: YH11882

RIDING STABLES

Lochore Meadows Riding Stables, Chapel Farm Rd, Lochore, Lochgelly, **Fife**, KY5 8LY, **SCOTLAND**.
(T) 01592 861596 (F) 01592 861899.
Contact/s

Owner: Dr F Anstey
Profile Riding School.
Riding for special needs based groups, there are 24 horses & ponies. Tack shop on-site, free tea & coffee available. Tack can be ordered. Training for novice jumps. Lesson prices range from £13.50 for under 16's and £15.00 for adults. **No.Staff:** 5
Yr. Est: 1981 **C.Size:** 40 Acres
Opening Times
Sp: Open Mon, Wed, Thurs, Fri 11:00, Sat, Sun 10:00. Closed Wed - Mon 18:15.
Su: Open Mon, Wed, Thurs, Fri 11:00, Sat, Sun 10:00. Closed Wed - Mon 18:15.
Au: Open Mon, Wed, Thurs, Fri 11:00, Sat, Sun 10:00. Closed Wed - Mon 18:15.
Wn: Open Mon, Wed, Thurs, Fri 11:00, Sat, Sun 10:00. Closed Wed - Mon 18:15.
Closed on Tuesdays **Ref: YH11883**

RIDING STOCK

Riding Stock, Bryary Hse, 262 Malton Rd, York, **Yorkshire (North)**, YO32 9TE, **ENGLAND**.
(T) 01904 438723 **(F)** 01904 430012.
Contact/s
Partner: Mr M Malarkey
Profile Supplies. **Ref: YH11884**

RIDINGHILL STUD

Ridinghill Stud, Upper Ridinghill Farm, Fraserburgh, **Aberdeenshire**, AB43 8QD, **SCOTLAND**.
(T) 01346 532321 **(F)** 01346 532321.
Contact/s
Owner: Mr N Mercer
Profile Arena, Breeder, Equestrian Centre.
Yr. Est: 1988 **C.Size:** 90 Acres
Opening Times
Sp: Open Mon - Sun 07:00. Closed Mon - Sun 21:00.
Su: Open Mon - Sun 07:00. Closed Mon - Sun 21:00.
Au: Open Mon - Sun 07:00. Closed Mon - Sun 21:00.
Wn: Open Mon - Sun 07:00. Closed Mon - Sun 21:00. **Ref: YH11885**

RIDLEY, B

B Ridley RSS, Hedgerows, Highlands Ave, Ridgewood, Uckfield, **Sussex (East)**, TN22 1PE, **ENGLAND**.
(T) 01825 765915.
Profile Farrier. **Ref: YH11886**

RIDLEY, GEORGE E

George E Ridley, 10 Spring Cl, Annfield Plain, Stanley, **County Durham**, DH9 7XL, **ENGLAND**.
(T) 01207 299174.
Profile Farrier. **Ref: YH11887**

RI-DRY

GPA Ri-Dry Ltd, The Bushloe Office, High St, North Kilworth, Lutterworth, **Leicestershire**, LE17 6ET, **ENGLAND**.
(T) 01858 880771 **(F)** 01858 880776
(E) gparidry@yahoo.com
(W) www.ri-dry.com.
Contact/s
General Manager: Ms C Potter
Profile Supplies.
Rubber stable flooring **Ref: YH11888**

RIETVELD, M

Mrs M Rietveld, Chapel Hse Farm, Okewood Hill, Dorking, **Surrey**, RH5 5PT, **ENGLAND**.
(T) 01306 627492.
Profile Breeder. **Ref: YH11889**

RIGBY, A C

A C Rigby, Low Dykes Cottage, Dykes Lane, Yealand Conyers, Carnforth, **Lancashire**, LA5 9SN, **ENGLAND**.
(T) 01524 720805.
Profile Breeder. **Ref: YH11890**

RIGBY, ROBERT D E

Robert D E Rigby DWCF, 244 Mossy Lea Rd, Wrightington, Wigan, **Lancashire**, WN6 9RL, **ENGLAND**.
(T) 01257 424798.
Profile Farrier. **Ref: YH11891**

RIGBY'S STABLES

Rigby's Stables, Woodside Farm, Huck Lane, Lytham St. Annes, **Lancashire**, FY8 5RU, **ENGLAND**.
(T) 01253 734006. **Ref: YH11892**

RIGTON CARR FARM

Rigton Carr Farm, Wike Lane, Bardsey, **Yorkshire (West)**, LS17 9EB, **ENGLAND**.
(T) 01937 573293
(M) 07860 126940.
Profile Stable/Livery. **Ref: YH11893**

RILEY HILL FARM HOLIDAYS

Riley Hill Farm Holidays, Greenhill, Cradley, **Worcestershire**, WR13 5JE, **ENGLAND**.
(T) 01886 880527.
Profile Riding School. **Ref: YH11894**

RILEY VETNRY CLINICS

Riley Veterinary Clinics, 61 Horse St, Chipping Sodbury, **Gloucestershire (South)**, BS37 6DA, **ENGLAND**.
(T) 01454 312636.
Profile Medical Support. **Ref: YH11895**

RIMELL

Rimell, 1 West St, Shipston-on-Stour, **Warwickshire**, CV36 4AL, **ENGLAND**.
(T) 01608 662000 **(F)** 01608 662000.
Contact/s
Owner: Mr R Wilson
Profile Saddlery Retailer. **Ref: YH11896**

RIMMER, E & S

E & S Rimmer, Bentley Mill Farm, Mill Gate, Bentley, Doncaster, **Yorkshire (South)**, DN5 0DH, **ENGLAND**.
(T) 01302 874212.
Profile Breeder. **Ref: YH11897**

RIMMER, M

Mrs M Rimmer, Sheilhill Farm, Braco, Dunblane, **Perth and Kinross**, FK15 9LH, **SCOTLAND**.
(T) 01786 880250.
Profile Breeder. **Ref: YH11898**

RINGCROFT FARM RIDING SCHOOL

Ringcroft Farm Riding School, Cranfield Rd, North Crawley, Newport Pagnell, **Buckinghamshire**, MK16 9HP, **ENGLAND**.
(T) 01234 751200 **(F)** 01234 751369.
Contact/s
Partner: Mr A Lovell **Ref: YH11899**

RINGER VILLA EQUESTRIAN CTRE

Ringer Villa Equestrian Centre, Ringer Villa Farm, Ringer Lane, Clowne, Chesterfield, **Derbyshire**, S43 4BX, **ENGLAND**.
(T) 01246 810456 **(F)** 01246 810092
Affiliated Bodies ABRS, BHS.
Contact/s
Instructor: Mrs K Clark **(Q)** BHSII
Profile Horse/Rider Accom, Riding School, Stable/Livery.
Full and part livery available, prices on request. Specialises in training people with disabilities and learning difficulties. **No.Staff:** 5
Opening Times
By appointment only **Ref: YH11900**

RINGER, D S

D S Ringer, Saffron Hse, Hamilton Rd, Newmarket, **Suffolk**, CB8 0NY, **ENGLAND**.
(T) 01638 662653.
Profile Trainer. **Ref: YH11901**

RINGWOOD & DISTRICT

Ringwood & District Riding Club, Staddle Stones, New Danehurst Rd, Sway, **Hampshire**, **ENGLAND**..
Contact/s
Chairman: Mrs J Broomfield
Profile Club/Association, Riding Club. **Ref: YH11902**

RINGWOOD ARENAS

Ringwood Arenas, Home Farm, Willington, Tarporley, **Cheshire**, CW6 0NB, **ENGLAND**.
(T) 01829 51281.
Profile Track/Course. **Ref: YH11903**

RINGWOOD FENCING

Ringwood Fencing, Landsdowne Rd, Stamford Bridge, Tarvin, Chester, **Cheshire**, CH3 8EL, **ENGLAND**.
(T) 01829 740136 **(F)** 01829 740248. **Ref: YH11904**

RIPLEY, TYRONE T

Tyrone T Ripley DWCF, 112 Wilson Ave, Rochester, **Kent**, ME1 2SH, **ENGLAND**.
(T) 01634 400806.
Profile Farrier. **Ref: YH11905**

RIPMAN, BARBARA

Barbara Ripman BHSI, Bryn Gwanws, Idole, Carmarthen, **Carmarthenshire**, SA32 8DH, **WALES**.
(T) 01267 236160.
Profile Breeder, Trainer. **Ref: YH11906**

RIPON RACE

Ripon Race Co Ltd, 77 North St, Ripon, **Yorkshire (North)**, HG4 1DS, **ENGLAND**.
(T) 01765 602156 **(F)** 01765 690018.
Contact/s
Clerk of Course: Mr J Hutchinson
Profile Track/Course. **Ref: YH11907**

RISCOMBE FARM

Riscombe Farm Holiday Cottages and Stabling, Exford, Minehead, **Somerset**, TA24 7NH, **ENGLAND**.
(T) 01643 831480 **(F)** 01643 831480
(E) info@riscombe.co.uk
(W) www.riscombe.co.uk.
Contact/s
Owner: Mr L Martin
Profile Horse/Rider Accom, Stable/Livery.
Quality holiday accommodation with excellent stabling in the centre of the National Park. Superb riding with routes and guides provided. **No.Staff:** 2
Yr. Est: 1995 **C.Size:** 12 Acres **Ref: YH11908**

RISING BRIDGE CORN

Rising Bridge Corn, Northfield Rd, Rising Bridge, Accrington, **Lancashire**, BB5 2SF, **ENGLAND**.
(T) 01706 226010.
Profile Supplies. **Ref: YH11909**

RISINGHOE CASTLE STUD

Risinghoe Castle Stud, Risinghoe, Castle Mill, Goldington, **Bedfordshire**, MK41 0HY, **ENGLAND**.
(T) 01234 267739.
Profile Breeder. **Ref: YH11910**

RISLEY SADDLERY

Risley Saddlery, Risley, Draycott, **Derbyshire**, DE7 3SY, **ENGLAND**.
(T) 0115 9392516
(M) 07966 375380
(E) info@risleysaddlery.co.uk
(W) www.risleysaddlery.co.uk.
Contact/s
Owner: Mrs S Matthews
Profile Saddlery Retailer. **Ref: YH11911**

RISSIK, DAVID

David Rissik (RSA), 39 New St, Tiddington, Stratford-upon-Avon, **Warwickshire**, CV37 7DA, **ENGLAND**.
(T) 01789 299744. **Ref: YH11912**

RISTON WHINS LIVERY YARD

Riston Whins Livery Yard, Riston Whins, Whins Lane, Catwick, Beverley, **Yorkshire (East)**, HU17 5PN, **ENGLAND**.
(T) 01964 543854.
Contact/s
Owner: Mr C Lawson
Profile Stable/Livery. **Yr. Est:** 1991
Opening Times
Sp: Open Mon - Sun 06:00. Closed Mon - Sun 22:00.
Su: Open Mon - Sun 06:00. Closed Mon - Sun 22:00.
Au: Open Mon - Sun 06:00. Closed Mon - Sun 22:00.
Wn: Open Mon - Sun 06:00. Closed Mon - Sun 22:00. **Ref: YH11913**

RITCHENS, P C

P C Ritchens, Hill Farm, Bent St, Nether Wallop, Stockbridge, **Hampshire**, SO20 8EJ, **ENGLAND**.
(T) 01264 781140.
Contact/s
Owner: Mr P Ritchens
Profile Trainer. **Ref: YH11914**

RITCHIE, CLIVE G

Clive G Ritchie DWCF, Bowbeer Farm, Spreyton, Crediton, **Devon**, EX17 5AE, **ENGLAND**.
(T) 01363 82356.
Profile Farrier. **Ref: YH11915**

RITCHIE, IAIN BURNS

Iain Burns Ritchie DWCF, Begbie Farm, Haddington, **Lothian (East)**, EH41 4HQ, **SCOTLAND**.
(T) 01620 823391.
Profile Farrier. **Ref: YH11916**

RIVERBANK LIVERY STABLES

Riverbank Livery Stables, Fackley Rd, Stanton Hill, Sutton-In-Ashfield, **Nottinghamshire**, NG17 3HG, **ENGLAND**.
(T) 01623 440800.
Contact/s
Manageress: Ms A Tomlinson **Ref: YH11917**

RIVERBANK POULTRY

Riverbank Poultry, Torr Rd, Bridge Of Weir, **Renfrewshire**, PA11 3BE, **SCOTLAND**.
(T) 01505 613411.
Profile Supplies. **Ref: YH11918**

RIVERBANK RIDING SCHOOL

Riverbank Riding School, Hall Lane, Wincham, Northwich, **Cheshire**, CW9 6DG, **ENGLAND**.
(T) 01606 47955.
Contact/s
Owner: Miss L Whieldon **Ref: YH11919**

RIVERDALE

Riverdale Equine Services, Little Cinders, 3 Whitelands Rd, Thatcham, **Berkshire**, RG18 3AR, **ENGLAND**.
(T) 01635 863199.
Contact/s
Owner: Mr R Dykes **(Q)** SMS
Profile Saddlery Retailer. No.Staff: 2
Yr. Est: 1991
Opening Times
Sp: Open Mon - Sat 09:00. Closed Mon - Fri 18:00, Sat 13:00.
Su: Open Mon - Sat 09:00. Closed Mon - Fri 18:00, Sat 13:00.
Au: Open Mon - Sat 09:00. Closed Mon - Fri 18:00, Sat 13:00.
Wn: Open Mon - Sat 09:00. Closed Mon - Fri 18:00, Sat 13:00.
Closed Sundays **Ref: YH11920**

RIVERDALE HALL HOTEL

Riverdale Hall Hotel, Bellingham, Hexham, **Northumberland**, NE48 2JT, **ENGLAND**.
(T) 01434 220254 **(F)** 01434 220457.
Profile Equestrian Centre. **Ref: YH11921**

RIVERMEAD INSURANCE

Rivermead Insurance, Kestrel Hse, High St, Lechlade, **Gloucestershire**, GL7 3AE, **ENGLAND**.
(T) 01367 253136 **(F)** 01367 252212.
Profile Club/Association. **Ref: YH11922**

RIVERSDALE

Riversdale Stud, Cwmcrwth, Broad Oak, Carmarthen, **Carmarthenshire**, SA32 8QP, **WALES**.
(T) 01558 668484/668121 **(F)** 01558 668121
(E) riversdale@fsnet.co.uk
(W) www.riversdalestud.fsnet.co.uk.
Profile Breeder, Horse/Rider Accom.
Horse Transport Emergency Breakdown Recovery - will take horse home (if nearby) or stable it until collection can be arranged. Covers South Wales. Breeders of Connemara Thoroughbred Crosses. Yr. Est: 1979
C.Size: 90 Acres
Opening Times
Sp: Open Mon - Sun 08:00. Closed Mon - Sun 19:00.
Su: Open Mon - Sun 08:00. Closed Mon - Sun 19:00.
Au: Open Mon - Sun 08:00. Closed Mon - Sun 19:00.
Wn: Open Mon - Sun 08:00. Closed Mon - Sun 19:00. **Ref: YH11923**

RIVERSIDE EQUESTRIAN CTRE

Riverside Equestrian Centre, Old Salts Farm Rd, Lancing, **Sussex (West)**, BN15 8JG, **ENGLAND**.
(T) 01903 762544.
Contact/s
Owner: Ms C Dollemore
Profile Stable/Livery. Yr. Est: 1993
Opening Times
Sp: Open Mon - Sun 08:00. Closed Mon - Sun 17:30.
Su: Open Mon - Sun 08:00. Closed Mon - Sun 17:30.
Au: Open Mon - Sun 08:00. Closed Mon - Sun 17:30.
Wn: Open Mon - Sun 08:00. Closed Mon - Sun 17:30. **Ref: YH11924**

RIVERSIDE RACING STABLES

Riverside Racing Stables, 227A Bonkle Rd, Newmains, Wishaw, **Lanarkshire (North)**, ML2 9QQ, **SCOTLAND**.
(T) 01698 383850 **(F)** 01698 383850.
Profile Trainer. **Ref: YH11925**

RIVERSIDE RIDING CTRE

Riverside Riding Centre, Riverside Rd, Melton Mowbray, **Leicestershire**, LE13 0JF, **ENGLAND**.
(T) 01664 561233.
Contact/s
Owner: Mrs R Simpson **Ref: YH11926**

RIVERSIDE RIDING CTRE

Riverside Riding Centre, Llwyncytrych, Glangrwyney, Crickhowell, **Powys**, NP8 1EE, **WALES**.
(T) 01873 810328
Affiliated Bodies BHS.
Contact/s
Owner: Miss L Nicklin
Profile Riding School, Stable/Livery. No.Staff: 4
Yr. Est: 1995 C.Size: 30 Acres **Ref: YH11927**

RIVERSIDE RIDING CTRE

Riverside Riding Centre, Low Barmston Farm, Washington, **Tyne and Wear**, NE38 8LF, **ENGLAND**.
(T) 0191 4150414. **Ref: YH11928**

RIVERSIDE VETNRY SURGERY

Riverside Veterinary Surgery, Scotter Rd, Bishopstoke, Eastleigh, **Hampshire**, SO50 6AJ, **ENGLAND**.
(T) 023 80620607 **(F)** 023 80614725.
Profile Medical Support. **Ref: YH11929**

RIVERSMEET STABLES

Riversmeet Stables, Sherington Rd, Newport Pagnell, **Buckinghamshire**, MK16 8NL, **ENGLAND**.
(T) 01908 618423.
Contact/s
Key Contact: Mr J Parry
Profile Riding School, Stable/Livery. **Ref: YH11930**

ROB, EVANS

Evans Rob, Kilpedder, Greystones, **County Wicklow**, **IRELAND**.
(T) 01 2819388.
Profile Supplies. **Ref: YH11931**

ROBB & SON

S Robb & Son, New Rd, St Ives, **Cambridgeshire**, PE27 5BG, **ENGLAND**.
(T) 01480 462150 **(F)** 01480 493309.
Contact/s
Owner: Mr R Whitby
Profile Supplies.
Robb & Son supply rope halters, lead reins & haynets.
No.Staff: 3 Yr. Est: 1814
Opening Times
Sp: Open Mon - Sat 08:30. Closed Mon - Fri 17:00, Sat 11:30.
Su: Open Mon - Sat 08:30. Closed Mon - Fri 17:00, Sat 11:30.
Au: Open Mon - Sat 08:30. Closed Mon - Fri 17:00, Sat 11:30.
Wn: Open Mon - Sat 08:30. Closed Mon - Fri 17:00, Sat 11:30.
Closed Sundays **Ref: YH11932**

ROBB, C A

C A Robb, Ladyfield, Glenaray, Inveraray, **Argyll and Bute**, PA32 8XJ, **SCOTLAND**.
(T) 01499 2396.
Profile Farrier. **Ref: YH11933**

ROBB, RUARAIDH C

Ruaraidh C Robb AWCF, Sherrifhall Mains, Millerhill, Dalkeith, **Edinburgh (City of)**, EH22 1RX, **SCOTLAND**.
(T) 0131 6542376.
Profile Farrier. **Ref: YH11934**

ROBBERTS, B A

B A Robberts, The Chalet, 8 Middleton Rd, Ringwood, **Hampshire**, BH24 1RN, **ENGLAND**.
(T) 01425 474869.
Profile Farrier. **Ref: YH11935**

ROBBINS, M A

Mrs M A Robbins, Queens Head, Whielden Gate, Amersham, **Buckinghamshire**, HP7 0NE, **ENGLAND**.
(T) 01494 725240 **(F)** 01494 725240.
Profile Trainer. **Ref: YH11936**

ROBDALE CAR TRAILERS

Robdale Car Trailers, 25 Laburnham Drive, Barnstaple, **Devon**, EX32 8PX, **ENGLAND**.
(T) 01271 377807.
Profile Transport/Horse Boxes. **Ref: YH11937**

ROBERT BELL

Robert Bell & Co, Old Bank Chambers, Auctioneers, Horncastle, **Lincolnshire**, LN9 5HY, **ENGLAND**.
(T) 01507 522222 **(F)** 01507 524444. **Ref: YH11938**

ROBERT BREWSTER & SON

Robert Brewster & Son, Broom Farm, Causewayhead, **Stirling**, FK9 5PL, **SCOTLAND**.
(T) 01786 74329.
Profile Breeder. **Ref: YH11939**

ROBERT LEECH

Robert Leech & Partners - Equestrian Estate Agents, 72 Station Rd East, Oxted, **Surrey**, RH8 0PG, **ENGLAND**.
(T) 01883 717272 **(F)** 01883 730898
(E) oxted@robertleech.com
(W) www.robertleech.com.
Contact/s
Consultant: Mr P Dixon
Profile Estate agents and consultant surveyors.
'Robert Leech & Partners' offer a wide range of services including land and development, commercial, equestrian and letting and management. **Ref: YH11940**

ROBERT LEECH

Robert Leech & Partners, 10 Godstone Rd, Purley, **Surrey**, CR8 2DA, **ENGLAND**.
(T) 020 86685344 **(F)** 020 87639060
(E) purley@robertleech.com
(W) www.robertleech.com.
Contact/s
Consultant: Mr J Youll
Profile Estate agents and consultant surveyors.
'Robert Leech & Partners' offer a wide range of services including land and development, commercial, equestrian and letting and management. **Ref: YH11941**

ROBERT LEECH

Robert Leech & Partners, 312 High St, Croydon, **Surrey**, CR0 1NG, **ENGLAND**.
(T) 020 86881001 **(F)** 020 86882050
(E) croydon@robertleech.com
(W) www.robertleech.com.
Contact/s
Assistant: Ms P Wright
Profile Estate agents and consultant surveyors.
'Robert Leech & Partners' offer a wide range of services including land and development, commercial, equestrian and letting and management. **Ref: YH11942**

ROBERT STEVENS

Robert Stevens Equestrian Contractor, Standon Hse Stables, Standon Lane, Ockley, Dorking, **Surrey**, RH5 5QR, **ENGLAND**.
(T) 01306 627163.
Contact/s
Owner: Miss K Sweet
Profile Supplies. **Ref: YH11943**

ROBERT THORNE

Robert Thorne Estate Supplies, 1-6 The Green, Eastriggs, Annan, **Dumfries and Galloway**, DG12 6NH, **SCOTLAND**.
(T) 01461 40965 **(F)** 01461 700120
(E) robertthorne@robertthorne.co.uk
(W) www.robertthorne.co.uk.
Contact/s
Assistant Manager: Mr M Hunter
Profile Supplies. No.Staff: 4 Yr. Est: 1989
C.Size: 1.5 Acres
Opening Times
Sp: Open Mon - Sat 09:00, Sun 10:00. Closed Mon - Sat 17:00, Sun 16:00.
Su: Open Mon - Sat 09:00, Sun 10:00. Closed Mon - Sat 17:00, Sun 16:00.
Au: Open Mon - Sat 09:00, Sun 10:00. Closed Mon - Sat 17:00, Sun 16:00.
Wn: Open Mon - Sat 09:00, Sun 10:00. Closed Mon - Sat 17:00, Sun 16:00. **Ref: YH11944**

ROBERTS

Roberts, Rear Of 147 Wellington Rd, Rhyl, **Denbighshire**, LL18 1LE, **WALES**.
(T) 01745 338273 **(F)** 01745 337141. **Ref: YH11945**

ROBERTS, ALWYN

Alwyn Roberts DWCF, 45 Irvine Drive, Cove, Farnborough, **Hampshire**, GU14 9HF, **ENGLAND**.
(T) 01276 31855.
Profile Farrier. **Ref: YH11946**

ROBERTS, D A

D A Roberts, 27 White Post Hill, Redhill, **Surrey**, RH1 6DA, **ENGLAND**.
(T) 01737 768821.
Profile Trainer. **Ref: YH11947**

ROBERTS, E N

E N Roberts, Rose Farm, Long Green, Great Barrow, Chester, **Cheshire**, CH3 7JU, **ENGLAND**.
(T) 01244 300322.
Profile Farrier. **Ref: YH11948**

ROBERTS, E P

E P Roberts DWCF, Arosfa, Glydwr Rd, Gwernymynydd, Mold, **Flintshire**, CH7 5LW, **WALES**.
(T) 01352 759637.
Profile Farrier. **Ref: YH11949**

ROBERTS, E W

Mr E W Roberts, Tal-Y-Llyn, Ty Croes, **Isle of Anglesey**, LL63 5TQ, **WALES**.
(T) 01407 720225.
Profile Breeder. Ref: YH11950

ROBERTS, EDWIN

Edwin Roberts, Bryn Herrmon, Rhosgadfan, Caernarfon, **Gwynedd**, LL54 7LB, **WALES**.
(T) 01286 831145.
Profile Farrier. Ref: YH11951

ROBERTS, GORDON

Gordon Roberts, Darklass Hse, Dyke, Forres, **Moray**, IV36 2TL, **SCOTLAND**.
(T) 01309 641657.
Profile Farrier. Ref: YH11952

ROBERTS, JOHN

Mr John Roberts, Poplar Farm, Wakefield Rd, Ackworth, Pontefract, **Yorkshire (West)**, WF7 7AG, **ENGLAND**.
(T) 01977 611193.
Profile Breeder. Ref: YH11953

ROBERTS, L

Miss L Roberts, Furze Farm, Main Rd, Hagworthingham, Spilsby, **Lincolnshire**, PE23 4LE, **ENGLAND**.
(T) 01507 588263.
Contact/s
Owner: Miss L Roberts
Profile Breeder. Ref: YH11954

ROBERTS, M & MARKS, K

Monty Roberts & Kelly Marks, "Iethornes", Upper Lambourn, Hungerford, **Berkshire**, RG17 8QS, **ENGLAND**.
(T) 01488 71300 (F) 01488 73783
(E) kelly@montyroberts.co.uk.
Profile Stable/Livery. Ref: YH11955

ROBERTS, M D

Mr & Mrs M D Roberts, Penrhiwgwaith Farm, Hollybush, Blackwood, **Caerphilly**, NP12 0ST, **WALES**.
(T) 01495 225778.
Profile Breeder. Ref: YH11956

ROBERTS, M J

Mr M J Roberts, Summertree Farm, Bodle St Green, Hailsham, **Sussex (East)**, BN27 4QT, **ENGLAND**.
(T) 01435 830231 (F) 01435 830887.
Profile Trainer. Ref: YH11957

ROBERTS, M T

M T Roberts RSS, 6 Hillcrest, Thickwood Est, Colorne, Chippenham, **Wiltshire**, SN14 8BP, **ENGLAND**.
(T) 01225 743103.
Profile Farrier. Ref: YH11958

ROBERTS, R

R Roberts, Brynmanalog, Parcyrhos, Cwmann, Lampeter, **Ceredigion**, SA48 7LP, **WALES**.
(T) 01570 422445.
Profile Breeder. Ref: YH11959

ROBERTS, R F

R F Roberts, Birch Hse Farm, Selattyn, Oswestry, **Shropshire**, SY10 7DY, **ENGLAND**.
(T) 01691 659716 (F) 01691 650129.
Contact/s
Owner: Mr R Roberts Ref: YH11960

ROBERTS, SHELAGH

Mrs Shelagh Roberts, Cefn-Y-Fedw, Penbryn, Penycae, **Wrexham**, LL14 1UA, **WALES**.
(T) 01978 823403.
Profile Stable/Livery.
Breeds Sport, Section A, and Section D horses
Ref: YH11961

ROBERTS, STUART

Mr Stuart Roberts, 46 Derrington Ave, Crewe, **Cheshire**, CW2 7JB, **ENGLAND**.
(T) 01270 215792.
Profile Trainer. Ref: YH11962

ROBERTS, TYRONE R

Tyrone R Roberts, 16 Greenfields Rd, Dereham, **Norfolk**, NR20 3TE, **ENGLAND**.
(T) 01362 691267 (F) 01362 691267
(M) 07702 642362
(E) tyroneroberts@yahoo.co.uk. Ref: YH11963

ROBERTS, V C

Miss V C Roberts, Poplar Farm, Wakefield Rd, Ackworth, Pontefract, **Yorkshire (West)**, WF7 7AG, **ENGLAND**.
(T) 01977 611193.
Profile Trainer. Ref: YH11964

ROBERTS, V J W

Mrs V J W Roberts, Mossdlae, Coniston With Kilnsey, Skipton, **Yorkshire (North)**, BD23 5HS, **ENGLAND**.
(T) 01756 752320 (F) 01756 752224.
Profile Equestrian Centre. Ref: YH11965

ROBERTSON, A

Mr A Robertson, 16 Douglas St, Strathaven, **Lanarkshire (South)**, ML10 6BU, **SCOTLAND**.
(T) 01357 521424. Ref: YH11966

ROBERTSON, DAVID

Mr David Robertson, Gateside Farm, Craigie, Kilmarnock, **Ayrshire (East)**, KA1 5LR, **SCOTLAND**.
(T) 01563 860201.
Profile Supplies. Ref: YH11967

ROBERTSON, E C

Mrs E C Robertson, Grieves Cottage, Home Farm, Dalkeith, **Edinburgh (City of)**, EH22 1RX, **SCOTLAND**.
(T) 0131 6542563.
Profile Breeder, Stable/Livery. Ref: YH11968

ROBERTSON, G

G Robertson, North Auchray Farm, Strathmartine, Dundee, **Angus**, DD3 0PP, **SCOTLAND**.
(T) 01382 580078.
Contact/s
Partner: Mrs M Robertson
Profile Stable/Livery. Ref: YH11969

ROBERTSON, J P

J P Robertson, Retreat Farm, Main St, Allexton, Oakham, **Leicestershire**, LE15 9AB, **ENGLAND**.
(T) 01572 717347 (F) 01572 718723.
Contact/s
Owner: Mrs J Robertson
Profile Breeder. Ref: YH11970

ROBERTSON, J P

J P Robertson, Cow Close Farm, Burley, Oakham, **Leicestershire**, LE15 7TA, **ENGLAND**.
(T) 01572 757324.
Profile Breeder. Ref: YH11971

ROBERTSON, JASON A

Jason A Robertson DWCF, 16 Maple St, Romford, **Essex**, RM7 7JX, **ENGLAND**.
(T) 07768 077935.
Profile Farrier. Ref: YH11972

ROBERTSON, NEIL

Neil Robertson, Kilfinnan Farm, Spean Bridge, **Highlands**, PH34 4EB, **SCOTLAND**.
(T) 01809 501272.
Profile Transport/Horse Boxes. Ref: YH11973

ROBERTSON, R A M

R A M Robertson RSS, 5 Elms Gr, Loughborough, **Leicestershire**, LE11 1RG, **ENGLAND**.
(T) 01509 263356.
Profile Farrier. Ref: YH11974

ROBERTSON, S A S

Miss S A S Robertson (BHSAI), Wild Duck Hall, Bolton-Le-Sands, Carnforth, **Lancashire**, LA5 8ER, **ENGLAND**.
(T) 01524 733058.
Profile Stable/Livery. Ref: YH11975

ROBERTSON-TIERNEY, ROBERT H

Robert H Robertson Tierney DWCF, Woodlands Farm, Snaiton, Scarborough, **Yorkshire (North)**, YO13 9BA, **ENGLAND**.
(T) 01723 859327.
Profile Farrier. Ref: YH11976

ROBESON, P

Mrs P Robeson, Fences Farm, Tyringham, Newport Pagnell, **Buckinghamshire**, MK16 9EN, **ENGLAND**.
(T) 01908 611255 (F) 01908 611255.
Profile Trainer. Ref: YH11977

ROBIN HOOD LIVERY STABLES

Robin Hood Livery Stables, Cronkshaw Fold Farm, Alden Rd, Rossendale, **Lancashire**, BB4 4AQ, **ENGLAND**.
(T) 01706 218614 (F) 01706 215143.
Contact/s
Owner: Mrs J Macarthy Ref: YH11978

ROBIN HUGHES-PARRY & AST

Robin Hughes-Parry & Associates (Longstanton), 34 High St, Longstanton, **Cambridgeshire**, CB4 5BS, **ENGLAND**.
(T) 01954 780027 (F) 01954 780225.
Profile Medical Support. Ref: YH11979

ROBIN HUGHES-PARRY ASSOCIATES

Robin Hughes-Parry Associates (Cottenham), 66 High St, Cottenham, **Cambridgeshire**, CB4 5SA, **ENGLAND**.
(T) 01954 252122.
Profile Medical Support. Ref: YH11980

ROBIN POST STABLES

Robin Post Stables, Arlington Rd West, Hailsham, **Sussex (East)**, BN27 3RE, **ENGLAND**.
(T) 01323 442500.
Contact/s
Owner: Ms S Champney-Warrener
Profile Stable/Livery. Ref: YH11981

ROBIN STORKEY

Robin Storkey Equine Dentist, 216 Goring Rd, Worthing, **Sussex (West)**, BN12 4PQ, **ENGLAND**.
(T) 01903 700123.
Contact/s
Owner: Mr R Storkey (T) 01903 700125
Profile Medical Support. Equine Dentist.
On-call Dentist, travels to patient. No.Staff: 1
Yr. Est: 1988 Ref: YH11982

ROBINS NEST STABLES

Robins Nest Stables, Post Office Rd, Seisdon, Wolverhampton, **Midlands (West)**, WV5 7HA, **ENGLAND**.
(T) 01902 893438.
Profile Trainer. Ref: YH11983

ROBINS, ADRIAN J

Adrian J Robins, Solcum Farm, Blakeshall, Wolverley, Kidderminster, **Worcestershire**, DY11 5XN, **ENGLAND**.
(T) 01562 851489.
Profile Supplies. Ref: YH11984

ROBINSON

Robinson & Co, 64 Wheelgate, Malton, **Yorkshire (North)**, YO17 7HP, **ENGLAND**.
(T) 01653 697442 (F) 01653 690133
(E) saddles1@aol.com
(W) www.robinsonsequestrian.co.uk.
Contact/s
Owner: Mr J Marshall
Profile Riding Wear Retailer, Saddlery Retailer.
Gifts No.Staff: 7 Yr. Est: 1971
Opening Times
Sp: Open Mon - Sat 09:00. Closed Mon - Sat 17:30.
Su: Open Mon - Sat 09:00. Closed Mon - Sat 17:30.
Au: Open Mon - Sat 09:00. Closed Mon - Sat 17:30.
Wn: Open Mon - Sat 09:00. Closed Mon - Sat 17:30.
Ref: YH11985

ROBINSON, DEIRDRE

Miss Deirdre Robinson, Langsmead Bungalow, Blindley Heath, Lingfield, **Surrey**, RH7 6JX, **ENGLAND**.
(T) 01342 832796.
Profile Trainer. Ref: YH11986

ROBINSON, G

Mr G Robinson, Hockerwood Farm, Upton, Newark, **Nottinghamshire**, NG23 5TA, **ENGLAND**.
(T) 01636 812854 (F) 01636 812854.
Profile Breeder. Ref: YH11987

ROBINSON, J D

J D Robinson, 34 Newgate St Village, Hertford, **Hertfordshire**, SG13 8RB, **ENGLAND**.
(T) 01707 874274.
Profile Breeder. Ref: YH11988

ROBINSON, JOSEPH

Mr Joseph Robinson, Distillery Hse, Annan, **Dumfries and Galloway**, DG12 5LL, **SCOTLAND**..
Profile Supplies. Ref: YH11989

ROBINSON, KIRSTI

Kirsti Robinson, The Mill, Little Broughton, Stokesley, **Cleveland**, TS9 5JR, **ENGLAND**.
(T) 01642 710710. Ref: YH11990

ROBINSON, LISA

Lisa Robinson, Folly Foot, 190 Melton Rd, Stanton-on-the-Wolds, Keyworth, Nottingham, **Nottinghamshire**, NG12 5BQ, **ENGLAND**.
(T) 0115 9376115.
Profile Trainer. Ref: YH11991

ROBINSON, P

Mr P Robinson, 1 Boundary Cottage, Stalybridge, **Cheshire**, SK15 3QA, **ENGLAND**.
(T) 01457 833084.
Profile Trainer. **Ref: YH11992**

ROBINSON, PAUL

Paul Robinson DWCF, The Hill Farm, Galston, **Ayrshire (East)**, KA4 8PH, **SCOTLAND**.
(T) 01560 700234.
Profile Farrier. **Ref: YH11993**

ROBINSON, R & V

R & V Robinson, Ty'r Eos Stud, Gwehelog, Usk, **Monmouthshire**, NP15 1RD, **WALES**.
(T) 01291 672097.
Profile Breeder.
Breeder of Welsh Section C Ponies **Ref: YH11994**

ROBINSON, S J

Mr S J Robinson, Ketton Garage, Durham Rd, Coatham Mundeville, **County Durham**, DL1 3LZ, **ENGLAND**.
(T) 01325 311232 **(F)** 01325 317952.
Profile Supplies. **Ref: YH11995**

ROBINSON, STEVEN D

Steven D Robinson DWCF, 34 Newgate St Village, Hertford, **Hertfordshire**, SG13 8RB, **ENGLAND**.
(T) 01707 874274.
Profile Farrier. **Ref: YH11996**

ROBINSON, T & C

T & C Robinson, 11 Queen St, Louth, **Lincolnshire**, LN11 9AU, **ENGLAND**.
(T) 01507 604596 **(F)** 01507 604596.
Contact/s
Manager: Mrs J Eshelby **Ref: YH11997**

ROBINSON, T & C

T & C Robinson, 40 Clasketgate, Lincoln, **Lincolnshire**, LN2 1JZ, **ENGLAND**.
(T) 01522 541860.
Contact/s
Manageress: Ms B Stubbs **Ref: YH11998**

ROBINSON, T & C

T & C Robinson, Tattershall Rd, Billinghay, Lincoln, **Lincolnshire**, LN4 4BN, **ENGLAND**.
(T) 01526 860436 **(F)** 01526 861352.
Contact/s
Partner: Mr J Robinson **Ref: YH11999**

ROBINSON, T & C

T & C Robinson, 4 St Marys St, Stamford, **Lincolnshire**, PE9 2DE, **ENGLAND**.
(T) 01780 755378 **(F)** 01780 755378.
Contact/s
Manageress: Mrs M Wells **Ref: YH12000**

ROBINSON, W R

Mr W R Robinson, Charm Pk, Wykeham, Scarborough, **Yorkshire (North)**, YO13 9QU, **ENGLAND**.
(T) 01723 862162.
Profile Breeder. **Ref: YH12001**

ROBINSONS

Robinsons Construction, Wincanton Cl, Ascot Drive Ind Est, Derby, **Derbyshire**, DE24 8NJ, **ENGLAND**.
(T) 01332 574711 **(F)** 01332 861401
(E) admin@robinsons.com
(W) www.robinsons.com.
Profile Supplies. Construction Engineers.
Build farms, barns, offices, shops and show stands worldwide. No.Staff: 150 Yr. Est: 1964
Opening Times
Telephone for further information **Ref: YH12002**

ROBINSONS

Robinson Animal Healthcare, Waterside, Walton, Chesterfield, **Derbyshire**, S40 1YF, **ENGLAND**.
(T) 01246 505383 **(F)** 01246 204098
(E) hannahs@r1son.co.uk
(W) www.robinson.uk.com/animal.html.
Profile Medical Support, Supplies.
Manufacturers of medical products for animals.
Ref: YH12003

ROBINSONS COUNTRY LEISURE

Robinsons Country Leisure Ltd (Retail), 71-77 Warrington Rd, Ashton-In-Makerfield, Wigan, **Lancashire**, WN4 9PJ, **ENGLAND**.
(T) 01942 712555.
Profile Saddlery Retailer.
Opening Times
Sp: Open Mon - Fri 10:00, Sat 09:00, Sun 11:00. Closed Mon - Wed, Sat 17:30, Thur, Fri 20:00, Sun 17:00.
Su: Open Mon - Fri 10:00, Sat 09:00, Sun 11:00. Closed Mon - Wed, Sat 17:30, Thur, Fri 20:00, Sun 17:00.
Au: Open Mon - Fri 10:00, Sat 09:00, Sun 11:00. Closed Mon - Wed, Sat 17:30, Thur, Fri 20:00, Sun 17:00.
Wn: Open Mon - Fri 10:00, Sat 09:00, Sun 11:00. Closed Mon - Wed, Sat 17:30, Thur, Fri 20:00, Sun 17:00. **Ref: YH12004**

ROBINSONS COUNTRY LEISURE

Robinsons Country Leisure Ltd (Mail Order), P.O. Box 8, St Helens, **Merseyside**, WA11 8FR, **ENGLAND**.
(T) 01744 887000 **(F)** 01744 887001
(E) export.orders@robcl.co.uk.
Contact/s
Manager: Mr J Bentham
Profile Saddlery Retailer. **Ref: YH12005**

ROBINSON'S RUG WASH

Robinson's Rug Wash, Redside Farm, Carrington, **Lothian (Mid)**, EH23 4LT, **SCOTLAND**.
(T) 01875 830210.
Profile Supplies. **Ref: YH12006**

ROBJENT'S

Robjent's, Halfway Hse, High St, Stockbridge, **Hampshire**, SO20 6EX, **ENGLAND**.
(T) 01264 810829 **(F)** 01264 810829
(W) www.robjents.co.uk.
Contact/s
Owner: Mr R Robjent
Profile Saddlery Retailer. **Ref: YH12007**

ROBLEY, RACHEL

Rachel Robley, The Elms, Haccups Lane, Michelmersh, Romsey, **Hampshire**, SO51 0NS, **ENGLAND**.
(T) 01794 368446
(M) 07860 191375. **Ref: YH12008**

ROBOROUGH, (LORD)

Roborough Lord, Blackdown Stud, Ford St, Wellington, **Somerset**, TA21 9NY, **ENGLAND**.
(T) 01823 661730.
Profile Breeder. **Ref: YH12009**

ROBSCOTT EQUITATION

Robscott Equitation, Wild Duck Hall, Bolton Le Sands, Carnforth, **Lancashire**, LA5 8ER, **ENGLAND**.
(T) 01524 733058 **(F)** 01524 733058
(E) wild-duck@supanet.com.
Contact/s
Manager: Miss S Robertson **(Q)** BHSAI, NVQ Ass
Profile Equestrian Centre, Stable/Livery, Trainer. NVQ and BHS Training Centre. No.Staff: 2
Yr. Est: 1984 C.Size: 30 Acres **Ref: YH12010**

ROBSON & COWAN

Robson & Cowan, Main St, Scots Gap, Morpeth, **Northumberland**, NE61 4DT, **ENGLAND**.
(T) 01670 774205 **(F)** 01670 774319.
Profile Supplies. **Ref: YH12011**

ROBSON & PARTNERS

Robson & Partners, The Robson Veterinary Hospital, Laurencekirk Business Pk, Aberdeen Rd, Laurencekirk, **Aberdeenshire**, AB30 1EY, **SCOTLAND**.
(T) 01561 377314 **(F)** 01561 378083.
Contact/s
Vet: Mr I Anderson
Profile Medical Support. **Ref: YH12012**

ROBSON & PRESCOTT

Robson & Prescott, The Veterinary Ctre, 44 Staithes Lane, Morpeth, **Northumberland**, NE61 1TD, **ENGLAND**.
(T) 01670 512275 **(F)** 01670 518975.
Profile Medical Support. **Ref: YH12013**

ROBSON, E H

Mr E H Robson, East Shaftoe, Middleton, Morpeth, **Northumberland**, NE61 4EA, **ENGLAND**.
(T) 01830 30207.
Profile Supplies. **Ref: YH12014**

ROBSON, JAMES

James Robson, Durham Rd, Wolsingham, **County Durham**, DL13 3HU, **ENGLAND**.
(T) 01388 527242 **(F)** 01388 528494
(E) jr@robsons.demon.co.uk. **Ref: YH12015**

ROBSON, T L A

Mr T L A Robson, Appletree Cottage, Edlingham, Alnwick, **Northumberland**, NE66 2BL, **ENGLAND**.
(T) 01665 74307.
Profile Supplies. **Ref: YH12016**

ROCHDALE & DISTRICT

Rochdale & District Riding Club, The Bungalow, Rushey Fields, Royton, Oldham, **Lancashire**, OL2 7DS, **ENGLAND**.
(T) 01706 843154.
Contact/s
Chairman: Mr D Heather
Profile Club/Association, Riding Club. **Ref: YH12017**

ROCHE, CHRISTY

Christy Roche, Curragh View Hse, Kildare, **County Kildare**, **IRELAND**.
(T) 045 521464.
Contact/s
Owner: Mr C Roche
Profile Trainer.
Christy Roche is a trainer of racehorses, jumping horses. **Ref: YH12018**

ROCHE, SEAN

Sean Roche DWCF, 6 Westdene Meadows, Elmbridge Rd, Cranleigh, **Surrey**, GU6 8UJ, **ENGLAND**.
(T) 01483 278097
(M) 07774 862776.
Profile Farrier. **Ref: YH12019**

ROCHELLES PONY STUD

Rochelles Pony Stud, Lower Rd, Hockley, **Essex**, SS5 5LE, **ENGLAND**.
(T) 01702 201777.
Profile Breeder. **Ref: YH12020**

ROCHEVALLEY

Rochevalley, Boneheys Farm, Newhey, Rochdale, **Lancashire**, OL16 3SZ, **ENGLAND**.
(T) 01706 847554.
Profile Breeder. **Ref: YH12021**

ROCHFORD & BARBER

Rochford & Barber plc, Riverside Garden Ctre, Lower Hatfield Rd, Hertford, **Hertfordshire**, SG13 8XX, **ENGLAND**.
(T) 01992 501502 **(F)** 01992 586596.
Profile Saddlery Retailer. **Ref: YH12022**

ROCHIN TRAILERS

Rochin Trailers, The Old Dairy, Icknield Way, Tring, **Hertfordshire**, HP23 4JU, **ENGLAND**.
(T) 01442 826848 **(F)** 01442 828397.
Contact/s
Partner: Mr J Rouse
Profile Transport/Horse Boxes. **Ref: YH12023**

ROCK INN

Rock Inn, Haytor Vale, Newton Abbot, **Devon**, TQ13 9XT, **ENGLAND**.
(T) 01364 661305 **(F)** 01364 661242.
Profile Equestrian Centre. **Ref: YH12024**

ROCK LANE

Rock Lane, Worsham Farm Hse, Worsham Lane, Bexhill-on-Sea, **Sussex (East)**, TN40 2QP, **ENGLAND**.
(T) 01424 224835.
Profile Stable/Livery. **Ref: YH12025**

ROCK SEMEN CTRE

Rock Semen Centre, 82 Dreen Rd, Cullybackey, Ballymena, **County Antrim**, BT42 1EE, **NORTHERN IRELAND**.
(T) 028 25880668.
Contact/s
Owner: Mr W Rock
Profile Trainer. **Ref: YH12026**

ROCK VALLEY HORSEBALL CLUB

Rock Valley Horseball Club, C/O Folly Foot, 190 Melton Rd, Stanton-on-the-Wolds, Keyworth, Nottingham, **Nottinghamshire**, NG12 5BQ, **ENGLAND**.
(T) 0115 9376114.
Profile Club/Association. **Ref: YH12027**

ROCKBOURNE

Rockbourne Ride, Tenantry Farms, Rockbourne, Fordingbridge, **Hampshire**, SP6 3PB, **ENGLAND**.
(T) 01725 518297 **(F)** 01725 518735.
Contact/s
Owner: Mr R McLeod
Profile Horse/Rider Accom.
Opening Times
Telephone for further information **Ref: YH12028**

ROCKFIELD EQUESTRIAN CTRE

Rockfield Equestrian Centre, 18 Drumhirk Rd, Comber, Newtownards, **County Down**, BT23 5LY, **NORTHERN IRELAND**.
(T) 028 91872548
Affiliated Bodies BHS.
Profile Riding School. **Ref:YH12029**

ROCKHAMPTON EQUESTRIAN CTRE

Rockhampton Equestrian Centre, Rockhampton, Berkeley, **Gloucestershire**, GL13 9DT, **ENGLAND**.
(T) 01454 260963. **Ref:YH12030**

ROCKHILL FARM

Rockhill Farm, Ardbrecknish, Ardbrecknish, Dalmally, **Argyll and Bute**, PA33 1BH, **SCOTLAND**.
(T) 01866 833218 **(F)** 01866 833218.
Contact/s
Owner: Mrs H Wharley
Profile Breeder. **Ref:YH12031**

ROCKHILL HANOVERIAN STUD

Rockhill Hanoverian Stud, Ardbrecknish, Dalmally, **Argyll and Bute**, PA33 1BH, **SCOTLAND**.
(T) 01866 833218 **(F)** 01866 833218
(W) www.rockhillhanoverianstud.co.uk.
Contact/s
Owner: Mr B Whalley
Profile Breeder, Stud Farm.
Rockhill offers a range of accommodation, from the guest house to self catering cottages and bungalows. There is also free trout fishing available.
C.Size: 124 Acres **Ref:YH12032**

ROCKING HORSE CLOTHING

Rocking Horse Clothing, 12 Moat Lane, Wickersley, Rotherham, **Yorkshire (South)**, S66 1DZ, **ENGLAND**.
(T) 01709 541979 **(F)** 01709 701843.
Profile Supplies. **Ref:YH12033**

ROCKING HORSE SHOP

Rocking Horse Shop (The), Fangfoss, Pocklington, **Yorkshire (North)**, YO41 5JH, **ENGLAND**.
(T) 01759 368737 **(F)** 01759 368194
(E) info@rockinghorse.co.uk.
Profile Supplies. **Ref:YH12034**

ROCKINGHAM LANDROVERS

Rockingham Landrovers, Main St, Rockingham, Market Harborough, **Leicestershire**, LE16 8TG, **ENGLAND**.
(T) 01536 770109.
Contact/s
Manageress: Mrs R Links
Profile Transport/Horse Boxes. **Ref:YH12035**

ROCKLANE RIDING CTRE

Rocklane Riding Centre, Orchard Farm, Ivinghoe Aston, Leighton Buzzard, **Bedfordshire**, LU7 9DL, **ENGLAND**.
(T) 01525 222402.
Contact/s
Key Contact: Mrs J Joyce
Profile Riding School. **Ref:YH12036**

ROCKMOUNT RIDING CTRE

Rockmount Riding Centre, Claregalway, **County Galway**, **IRELAND**.
(T) 091 798147.
Contact/s
Owner: David Moore
Profile Riding School.
Hacking, trekking and fieldwork are all available.
Opening Times
Closed on Sundays. Telephone for further information regarding opening times. **Ref:YH12037**

ROCKSIDE FARM TREKKING CTRE

Rockside Farm Trekking Centre, Rockside Farm, Bruichladdich, Isle Of Islay, **Argyll and Bute**, PA49 7UT, **SCOTLAND**.
(T) 01496 850231 **(F)** 01496 850231.
Profile Equestrian Centre. **Ref:YH12038**

ROCKWOOD RIDING CTRE

Rockwood Riding Centre, Craig-Yr-Allt, Caerphilly, **Caerphilly**, CF83 1NF, **WALES**.
(T) 029 20866281
Affiliated Bodies BHS.
Contact/s
Owner: Ms A Dascombe **(Q)** BHSII
Profile Riding School, Stable/Livery. Yr. Est: 1980
C.Size: 300 Acres **Ref:YH12039**

RODBASTON

Rodbaston Stables, Staffordshire College Of Agriculture, Rodbaston, Penkridge, **Staffordshire**, ST19 5PH, **ENGLAND**.
(T) 01785 716801 **(F)** 01785 715701.
Profile Equestrian Centre. College.
Accommodation for students, and their horses, taking courses at the college.
Opening Times
Open during term time only **Ref:YH12040**

RODBASTON CLGE

Rodbaston College, Rodbaston, Penkridge, **Staffordshire**, ST19 5PH, **ENGLAND**.
(T) 01785 712209 **(F)** 01785 715701
(W) www.rodbaston.ac.uk
Contact/s
Head of Equine Department: Mr M Clinton
(E) marcus.clinton@rodbaston.ac.uk
Profile Equestrian Centre, Riding School, Stable/Livery. College.
College for equine qualifications. **Ref:YH12041**

RODD, STUART PAUL

Stuart Paul Rodd DWCF Hons, Meadowcroft, The Causeway, Hitcham, Ipswich, **Suffolk**, IP7 7LJ, **ENGLAND**.
(T) 01449 741558.
Profile Farrier. **Ref:YH12042**

RODDICK, P E & C

P E & C Roddick, Picks Farm, Sewardstone Rd, London, **London (Greater)**, E4 7RA, **ENGLAND**.
(T) 020 85291371.
Contact/s
Partner: Mrs C Roddick **Ref:YH12043**

RODEO DAVE

Rodeo Dave Western Trick Riding, 19 Temple Rd, Croydon, **Surrey**, CR0 1HU, **ENGLAND**.
(T) 020 86810998 **(F)** 020 87761508.
Contact/s
Partner: Mr D Charnley **Ref:YH12044**

RODFORD, P

P Rodford, Lavenoak Hse, Burrough St, Ash, Martock, **Somerset**, TA12 6NZ, **ENGLAND**.
(T) 01935 823459.
Contact/s
Owner: Mr P Rodford
Profile Trainer. **Ref:YH12045**

RODGER, J & T

J & T Rodger, Millers & Grain Merchants, Burnside Mill, Cupar, **Fife**, KY15 1DQ, **SCOTLAND**.
(T) 01334 52912.
Profile Supplies. **Ref:YH12046**

RODGERS, S E

S E Rodgers (Liss), Moor Edge, Forest Rd, Liss, **Hampshire**, GU33 7BX, **ENGLAND**.
(T) 01730 892273.
Profile Medical Support. **Ref:YH12047**

RODGROVE STUD EQUESTRIAN CTRE

Rodgrove Stud Equestrian Centre, Moor Lane, Wincanton, **Somerset**, BA9 9QU, **ENGLAND**.
(T) 01963 371323 **(F)** 01963 371323.
Profile Breeder, Equestrian Centre, Riding School, Stable/Livery. **Ref:YH12048**

ROE RICHARDSON

Roe Richardson Co Ltd, D1/Old Forge Yard, Swanley Village Rd, Swanley, **Kent**, BR8 7NF, **ENGLAND**.
(T) 01322 668838 **(F)** 01322 666517. **Ref:YH12049**

ROE, G

Mr G Roe, Hyde Pk Farm, Lower Hyde, Chalford, Stroud, **Gloucestershire**, GL6 8NZ, **ENGLAND**.
(T) 01453 885487 **(F)** 01453 885204.
Profile Breeder, Trainer. **Ref:YH12050**

ROE, G L

Mr G L Roe, Belliver Farm, Hoo Meavy, Yelverton, **Devon**, PL20 6PZ, **ENGLAND**.
(T) 01822 855244.
Profile Supplies. **Ref:YH12051**

ROE, M A

M A Roe, Braydon Manor Farm, Braydon, Swindon, **Wiltshire**, SN5 0AG, **ENGLAND**.
(T) 01666 860830 **(F)** 01666 860792.
Profile Breeder. **Ref:YH12052**

ROEHAMPTON GATE

Roehampton Gate Equestrian Centre, Priory Lane, London, **London (Greater)**, SW15 5JR, **ENGLAND**.
(T) 020 88767089.
Contact/s
Groom: Ms A Marchesani
Profile Equestrian Centre, Stable/Livery.
The centre has an all weather, flood lit paddock. Clinics are also held for people with their own horses. The centre has now got new facilities, which were completed, February 2001. Yr. Est: 2001
Opening Times
Sp: Open Mon - Sun 07:30. Closed Mon - Fri 21:00, Sat, Sun 18:00.
Su: Open Mon - Sun 07:30. Closed Mon - Fri 21:00, Sat, Sun 18:00.
Au: Open Mon - Sun 07:30. Closed Mon - Fri 21:00, Sat, Sun 18:00.
Wn: Open Mon - Sun 07:30. Closed Mon - Fri 21:00, Sat, Sun 18:00. **Ref:YH12053**

ROGER HEATON

Roger Heaton (Animal Portraits), 2 Park Cottages, Lenton, Grantham, **Lincolnshire**, NG33 4HQ, **ENGLAND**.
(T) 01476 585467
(W) www.rogerheaton.co.uk.
Contact/s
Owner: Mr R Heaton
(E) rogerheaton@lineone.net
Profile Artist. No.Staff: 2 Yr. Est: 1969
C.Size: 0.75 Acres
Opening Times
Sp: Open 09:00. Closed 18:00.
Su: Open 09:00. Closed 18:00.
Au: Open 09:00. Closed 18:00.
Wn: Open 09:00. Closed 18:00. **Ref:YH12054**

ROGERS & BROCK VETNRY

Rogers & Brock Veterinary Surgeons, 1 Watt Pl, Cheadle, Stoke-on-Trent, **Staffordshire**, ST10 1NY, **ENGLAND**.
(T) 01538 753127.
Profile Medical Support. **Ref:YH12055**

ROGERS & TAYLOR

Rogers & Taylor, Agricultural Supplies, Bow St, Aberystwyth, **Ceredigion**, SY24 5BH, **WALES**.
(T) 01970 828680 **(F)** 01970 828680
(E) allanrogers@ukonline.co.uk
(W) www.rogersandtaylor.co.uk.
Profile Riding Wear Retailer, Saddlery Retailer, Supplies. **Ref:YH12056**

ROGERS EQUESTRIAN SERVICES

Rogers Equestrian Services, Kennels Farm, Tylers Causeway, Newgate Street, **Hertfordshire**, SG13 8QN, **ENGLAND**.
(T) 020 77304600. **Ref:YH12057**

ROGERS FARM

Rogers Farm, Rogers Farm, Rogers Lane, Findon, Worthing, **Sussex (West)**, BN14 0RE, **ENGLAND**.
(T) 01903 872576
(E) andrewthefarmer@hotmail.com.
Contact/s
Owner: Mr A Farquharson
Profile Stable/Livery.
DIY Livery and grazing available **Ref:YH12058**

ROGERS, A

A Rogers, Pandy Cottage, Afonwen, Mold, **Flintshire**, CH7 5UB, **WALES**.
(T) 01352 720962.
Profile Farrier. **Ref:YH12059**

ROGERS, ANNE

Anne Rogers, Yeomans, Bedgebury Rd, Goudhurst, **Kent**, TN17 2QU, **ENGLAND**.
(T) 01580 212282 **(F)** 01580 212662
(M) 07801 834080.
Profile Medical Support. **Ref:YH12060**

ROGERSON & PARTNERS

Rogerson & Partners (Galashiels), 120 Gala Pk, Galashiels, **Scottish Borders**, TD1 1EZ, **SCOTLAND**.
(T) 01896 753759 **(F)** 01896 750564.
Profile Medical Support. **Ref:YH12061**

ROGERSON, J

J Rogerson, The Forge, Sherfield Rd, Bramley, Tadley, **Hampshire**, RG26 5AG, **ENGLAND**.
(T) 01256 881526.
Profile Farrier. **Ref:YH12062**

ROGUES GALLERY

Rogues Gallery, 121 Prince Charles Ave, Mackworth, **Derbyshire**, DE3 4BG, **ENGLAND**.
(T) 01332 43426. **Ref:YH12063**

ROKER'S TACK SHOP

Roker's Tack Shop, Fairlands Farm, Holly Lane, Worplesdon, Guildford, **Surrey**, GU3 3PB, **ENGLAND**.
(T) 01483 235355 **(F)** 01483 232324.

Contact/s
Partner: Mrs C Tegg
Profile Supplies. **No.Staff:** 4 **Yr. Est:** 1986
Opening Times
Sp: Open 09:00. Closed 17:30.
Su: Open 09:00. Closed 17:30.
Au: Open 09:00. Closed 17:30.
Wn: Open 09:00. Closed 17:30.
Sunday 09:00 - 13:00. Closed Mondays **Ref: YH12064**

ROLEYSTONE STUD

Roleystone Stud, 21 Wrose Gr, Bradford, **Yorkshire (West)**, BD2 1PQ, **ENGLAND**.
(T) 01274 614087.
Profile Breeder. **Ref: YH12065**

ROLFE, JOHN

John Rolfe, Ivy Cottage, Church View, Rockhampton, Berkeley, **Gloucestershire**, GL13 9DX, **ENGLAND**.
(T) 01454 261069.
Profile Supplies. **Ref: YH12066**

ROLFE, R

R Rolfe, The Green, West Row, Bury St Edmunds, **Suffolk**, **ENGLAND**.
(T) 01638 715925.
Profile Breeder. **Ref: YH12067**

ROLLS LIVESTOCK HAULAGE

Rolls Livestock Haulage Ltd, Homelea, Ragged Appleshaw, Andover, **Hampshire**, SP11 9HR, **ENGLAND**.
(T) 01264 773272 **(F)** 01264 772500.
Contact/s
Owner: Mrs L Rolls
Profile Transport/Horse Boxes. **Ref: YH12068**

ROMANY MUSEUM

Gordon Boswell Romany Museum, Hawthorns Claylake, Claylake, Spalding, **Lincolnshire**, PE12 6BL, **ENGLAND**.
(T) 01775 710599
(W) www.boswell-romany-museum.com.
Contact/s
Owner: Mr G Boswell
Profile Horse Drawn Carriages & Museum.
A member of the East Yorkshire tourist board. Romany Museum has a gift shop, disabled access, and offer days out 'Romany style' which includes a meal.
Yr. Est: 1976
Opening Times
Sp: Open Wed - Sun 10:30. Closed Wed - Sun 17:00.
Su: Open Wed - Sun 10:30. Closed Wed - Sun 17:00.
Au: Open Wed - Sun 10:30. Closed Wed - Sun 17:00.
Wn: Open Wed - Sun 10:30. Closed Wed - Sun 17:00.
Closed on Monday, Tuesday. Open Bank Holidays.
Coach parties by appointment only. **Ref: YH12069**

ROMANY RIDING STABLES

Romany Riding Stables, Whitehouse Rd, Porchfield, Newport, **Isle of Wight**, PO30 4LH, **ENGLAND**.
(T) 01983 525467
Affiliated Bodies BHS.
Contact/s
Owner: Mrs F Dore
Profile Riding School. **Yr. Est:** 1986
C.Size: 16 Acres
Opening Times
Sp: Open Mon - Sun 10:00. Closed Mon - Sun 20:00.
Su: Open Mon - Sun 10:00. Closed Mon - Sun 20:00.
Au: Open Mon - Sun 10:30. Closed Mon - Sun 16:00.
Wn: Open Mon - Sun 10:30. Closed Mon - Sun 16:00. **Ref: YH12070**

ROMANY STUD

Romany Stud, Kirkley West Thorn, Newcastle-upon-Tyne, **Tyne and Wear**, NE20 0AG, **ENGLAND**.
(T) 01661 825439.
Profile Breeder. **Ref: YH12071**

ROMANY WALKS

Romany Walks Riding Stables, Ludgvan, Penzance, **Cornwall**, TR20 8EJ, **ENGLAND**.
(T) 01736 740838
Affiliated Bodies BHS.
Contact/s
Owner: Miss A Richards **(Q)** BHS IT
Profile Holidays, Riding School, Stable/Livery.
No.Staff: 3 **Yr. Est:** 1997 **C.Size:** 33 Acres
Opening Times
Sp: Open Mon - Sun 09:00. Closed Mon - Sun 17:30.
Su: Open Mon - Sun 09:00. Closed Mon - Sun 17:30.
Au: Open Mon - Sun 09:00. Closed Mon - Sun 17:30.
Wn: Open Mon - Sun 09:00. Closed Mon - Sun 17:30. **Ref: YH12072**

RONAN GRASSICK BLOODSTOCK

Ronan Grassick Bloodstock Transport, 24 Ashgrove Dr, Naas, **County Kildare**, **IRELAND**.
(T) 045 866985.
Profile Transport/Horse Boxes. **Ref: YH12073**

ROOKIN HOUSE

Rookin House Farm, Troutbeck, Penrith, **Cumbria**, CA11 0SS, **ENGLAND**.
(T) 01768 483561 **(F)** 01768 483276
Affiliated Bodies ABRS.
Contact/s
Owner: Mr A Hogg
Profile Riding School. **No.Staff:** 4
Yr. Est: 1980 **C.Size:** 240 Acres
Opening Times
Sp: Open Mon - Sun 09:00. Closed Mon - Sun 18:00.
Su: Open Mon - Sun 09:00. Closed Mon - Sun 18:00.
Au: Open Mon - Sun 09:00. Closed Mon - Sun 18:00.
Wn: Open Mon - Sun 09:00. Closed Mon - Sun 18:00. **Ref: YH12074**

ROOKMORE RIDING

Rookmore Riding & Driving School, West Ashling Rd, Hambrook, Chichester, **Sussex (West)**, PO18 8UD, **ENGLAND**.
(T) 01243 573036. **Ref: YH12075**

ROOKS, GORDON

Gordon Rooks, 39 Redcar Rd, Guisborough, **Cleveland**, TS14 6HR, **ENGLAND**.
(T) 01287 638546.
Profile Farrier. **Ref: YH12076**

ROONEY, KEVIN BARRY

Kevin Barry Rooney RSS, 23 Main St, Bishopstone, Aylesbury, **Buckinghamshire**, HP17 8SF, **ENGLAND**.
(T) 01296 748233.
Profile Farrier. **Ref: YH12077**

ROONEY, STEPHEN P

Stephen P Rooney DWCF, 152 Heritage Pk, St Mellons, Cardiff, **Glamorgan (Vale of)**, CF3 0DS, **WALES**.
(T) 029 20793854.
Profile Farrier. **Ref: YH12078**

ROONEY, T P

T P Rooney, St Mellons Rd, Marshfield, Cardiff, **Glamorgan (Vale of)**, CF3 2TX, **WALES**.
(T) 01633 680228.
Profile Farrier. **Ref: YH12079**

ROOS FEEDS

Roos Feeds, Cowley Hill Farm, Hamstall Ridware, Rugeley, **Staffordshire**, WS15 3QQ, **ENGLAND**.
(T) 01889 504288 **(F)** 01889 504453.
Profile Supplies. **Ref: YH12080**

ROOS FEEDS NORTH

Roos Feeds North, Horsley Hse, Kirby Misperton, Malton, **Yorkshire (North)**, YO17 6UU, **ENGLAND**.
(T) 01653 668555.
Profile Supplies. **Ref: YH12081**

ROOTING STREET FARM

Rooting Street Farm Riding Centre, Rooting St, Little Chart, Ashford, **Kent**, TN27 0PX, **ENGLAND**.
(T) 01233 840434.
Contact/s
Owner: Mrs J Rogers
Profile Riding School, Stable/Livery. **Ref: YH12082**

ROPER SERVICES

Roper Services Ltd, Garveston, Norwich, **Norfolk**, NR9 4QT, **ENGLAND**.
(T) 01362 850205.
Profile Transport/Horse Boxes. **Ref: YH12083**

ROPER, J H

Mr J H Roper, Lower Hse, Suckley, **Worcestershire**, WR6 5DQ, **ENGLAND**.
(T) 01886 884368. **Ref: YH12084**

ROPER, MARK

Mark Roper, The Curragh, **County Kildare**, **IRELAND**.
(T) 045 441798 **(F)** 045 441442
(E) markroper@kildarehorse.ie.
Contact/s
Trainer: Mr M Roper
(E) markroper@kildarehorse.ie
Profile Trainer. **Ref: YH12085**

ROPER, W M

Roper W M, Melitta Rd, Clifden, **County Kildare**, **IRELAND**.
(T) 045 520266.
Profile Supplies. **Ref: YH12086**

ROSACH STUD

Rosach Stud, Mill Lane, Leverington, Wisbech, **Cambridgeshire**, PE13 5JP, **ENGLAND**.
(T) 01945 410334.
Profile Breeder, Trainer. **Ref: YH12087**

ROSE & CROWN

Rose & Crown, Palmers Lodge, Calverleigh, Tiverton, **Devon**, EX16 8BA, **ENGLAND**.
(T) 01884 252060.
Contact/s
Owner: Mrs G Tucker
Profile Riding School, Stable/Livery. **Ref: YH12088**

ROSE BANK STORES & SADDLERY

Rose Bank Stores & Saddlery, Middle Lane, Kings Norton, Birmingham, **Midlands (West)**, B38 0DX, **ENGLAND**.
(T) 01564 822112.
Contact/s
Partner: Mrs J Turner
Profile Saddlery Retailer. **Ref: YH12089**

ROSE COTTAGE

Rose Cottage, Long Lane, Southport, **Merseyside**, PR9 8EX, **ENGLAND**.
(T) 01704 232415.
Contact/s
Owner: Miss T McKay
Profile Riding School, Stable/Livery. **Ref: YH12090**

ROSE COTTAGE FARM

Rose Cottage Farm, Moor Lane, Haxby, York, **Yorkshire (North)**, YO32 2QN, **ENGLAND**.
(T) 01904 769758 **(F)** 01904 767931
(W) www.rosecottagefarmkennels.co.uk.
Contact/s
Owner: Mrs D Curtis
(E) dawn@rosecottagefarmkennels.co.uk
Profile Stable/Livery.
Full, part and DIY livery is available, as are shows and hacking. Rose Farm also offers a kennel and cattery service. **C.Size:** 12 Acres
Opening Times
Sp: Open Mon - Sat 09:00, Sun 17:00. Closed Mon - Sat 10:30, Sun 18:00.
Su: Open Mon - Sat 09:00, Sun 17:00. Closed Mon - Sat 10:30, Sun 18:00.
Au: Open Mon - Sat 09:00, Sun 17:00. Closed Mon - Sat 10:30, Sun 18:00.
Wn: Open Mon - Sat 09:00, Sun 17:00. Closed Mon - Sat 10:30, Sun 18:00. **Ref: YH12091**

ROSE COTTAGE VETNRY CTRE

Rose Cottage Veterinary Centre, Chester Rd, Sutton Weaver, Runcorn, **Cheshire**, WA7 3EQ, **ENGLAND**.
(T) 01928 717581.
Profile Medical Support. **Ref: YH12092**

ROSE HALL RIDING STABLES

Rose Hall Riding Stables, Rose Hall Farm, Sarratt, **Hertfordshire**, WD3 4PA, **ENGLAND**.
(T) 01442 833269
Affiliated Bodies BHS.
Contact/s
Manager: Ms M Coleman
Profile Riding School, Stable/Livery.
Hunting yard. **Ref: YH12093**

ROSE MILL FEEDS

Rose Mill Feeds, Unit 3, Rose Mill Ind Est, Ilminster, **Somerset**, TA19 9QA, **ENGLAND**.
(T) 01460 55200.
Contact/s
Owner: Mr S Bridges
(E) equities@lineone.net
Profile Riding Wear Retailer, Saddlery Retailer, Supplies.
Ample free parking. A Reiki Master & Bach Flower Therapist available on-site.
Opening Times
Sp: Open 09:00. Closed 17:30.
Su: Open 09:00. Closed 17:30.
Au: Open 09:00. Closed 17:30.
Wn: Open 09:00. Closed 17:30. **Ref: YH12094**

ROSE, C A

C A Rose, Whitelands, Longrose Lane, Kniveton, Ashbourne, **Derbyshire**, DE6 1JL, **ENGLAND**.
(T) 01335 343297.
Profile Stable/Livery. Ref:YH12095

ROSE, C J

C J Rose, White Hse Farm, Higham, Rochester, **Kent**, ME3 7JJ, **ENGLAND**.
(T) 01634 717122.
Profile Supplies. Ref:YH12096

ROSE, DARREN M

Darren M Rose DWCF, 35 St Peters Ave, Moulton, Newmarket, **Suffolk**, CB8 8SE, **ENGLAND**.
(T) 01638 750480.
Profile Farrier. Ref:YH12097

ROSE, MARK T

Mark T Rose AWCF, Cromwell Cottage, Warren Rd, Kennet, Newmarket, **Suffolk**, CB8 7QP, **ENGLAND**.
(T) 01638 751493.
Profile Farrier. Ref:YH12098

ROSE-ACRE RIDING STABLES

Rose-Acre Riding Stables, Back Mundesley Rd, Mundesley, **Norfolk**, NR11 8HN, **ENGLAND**.
(T) 01263 720671.
Profile Riding School, Stable/Livery. Ref:YH12099

ROSEBANK HORSE & PONY CTRE

Rosebank Horse & Pony Centre, Rosebank Farm, Bankend Rd, Dumfries, **Dumfries and Galloway**, DG1 4TN, **SCOTLAND**.
(T) 01387 55088.
Profile Riding School. Ref:YH12100

ROSEBANK STABLES

Rosebank Stables, Off Factory Rd, Cowdenbeath, **Fife**, KY4 9SQ, **SCOTLAND**.
(T) 01383 511762.
Profile Trainer. Ref:YH12101

ROSEDALE STUD

Rosedale Stud, Gelli Farm, Henllys, Cwmbran, **Torfaen**, NP44 7AT, **WALES**.
(T) 01633 482365.
Profile Breeder. Ref:YH12102

ROSEGARTH STUD

Rosegarth Stud, The Flintstones, Westbury Rd, Little Cheverell, Devizes, **Wiltshire**, SN10 4JP, **ENGLAND**.
(T) 01380 812219 (F) 01380 813638.
Contact/s
Owner: Mr A Harley
Profile Breeder. Ref:YH12103

ROSEMEAD SCHOOL OF EQUITATION

Rosemead School Of Equitation, 25 St James Rd, Hillsborough, **County Down**, BT26 6JT, **NORTHERN IRELAND**.
(T) 028 92621523.
Contact/s
Owner: Mrs Y Morton Ref:YH12104

ROSEMOUNT RIDING SVS

Rosemount Riding Services, Cottage 1, Rosemount, Monkton, Prestwick, **Ayrshire (South)**, KA9 2QZ, **SCOTLAND**.
(T) 01292 474867.
Contact/s
Owner: Mrs E Geddes (Q) AI, SM 4
Profile Riding School, Stable/Livery. Yr. Est: 1985
C.Size: 90 Acres
Opening Times
Sp: Open 08:30. Closed 22:00.
Su: Open 08:30. Closed 22:00.
Au: Open 08:30. Closed 22:00.
Wn: Open 08:30. Closed 22:00. Ref:YH12105

ROSEMULLION

Rosemullion Veterinary Practice, The Veterinary Ctre, 66 Melvill Rd, Falmouth, **Cornwall**, TR11 4DD, **ENGLAND**.
(T) 01326 313991 (F) 01326 318793.
Profile Medical Support. Ref:YH12106

ROSEMULLION VETNRY

Rosemullion Veterinary Practice, The Veterinary Ctre, Angel Ctre, Tyacke Rd, Helston, **Cornwall**, TR13 8RR, **ENGLAND**.
(T) 01326 572596.
Profile Medical Support. Ref:YH12107

ROSET HILL FARM

Roset Hill Farm, Scorton Rd, Brompton-on-Swale, Richmond, **Yorkshire (North)**, DL10 7EQ, **ENGLAND**.
(T) 01748 811392.
Contact/s
Owner: Ms S Lemon
Profile Horse/Rider Accom. Ref:YH12108

ROSETTE COMPANY

Rosette Company (The), 25A Station Rd, Darton, Barnsley, **Yorkshire (South)**, S75 5HT, **ENGLAND**.
(T) 01226 385005 (F) 01226 385005. Ref:YH12109

ROSETTES DIRECT

Rosettes Direct, The Old Chapel, York St, Accrington, **Lancashire**, BB5 3NU, **ENGLAND**.
(T) 01254 397880 (F) 01254 394839.
Profile Supplies. Ref:YH12110

ROSEVIDNEY ARABIANS

Rosevidney Arabians, Rosevidney Barton, Ludgvan, Penzance, **Cornwall**, TR20 9AZ, **ENGLAND**.
(T) 01736 740223 (F) 01736 741332.
Contact/s
Owner: Mr K Hosking
Profile Breeder, Horse/Rider Accom.
Breeders of Arab Horses. Are able to ride along Marazion Beach. No.Staff: 1 Yr. Est: 1988
C.Size: 200 Acres Ref:YH12111

ROSHAUNA RIDING SCHOOL

Roshauna Riding School, 100 Down End Rd, Fareham, **Hampshire**, PO16 8TS, **ENGLAND**.
(T) 01329 823969.
Contact/s
Partner: Miss L Armstrong
Profile Riding School, Stable/Livery. Ref:YH12112

ROSS & BICKERTON

Ross & Bickerton, Brackenbrae Vet Clinic, 2 Duncryne Pl, Bishopbriggs, Glasgow, **Glasgow (City of)**, G64 2DP, **SCOTLAND**.
(T) 0141 7721019 (F) 0141 7728455
(E) brackenbrae.vet@btinternet.com.
Profile Medical Support. Ref:YH12113

ROSS FEED

Ross Feed Ltd, 7 Alton Rd Ind Est, Ross-on-Wye, **Herefordshire**, HR9 5ND, **ENGLAND**.
(T) 01989 768394 (F) 01989 567042.
Profile Saddlery Retailer. Ref:YH12114

ROSS FEED

Ross Feed Ltd, 2 Wonastow Ind Est, Monmouth, **Monmouthshire**, NP25 5JA, **WALES**.
(T) 01600 715448 (F) 01600 715448.
Profile Feed Merchant, Supplies. Ref:YH12115

ROSS HARRIERS

Ross Harriers, Chantry Farm, Perrystone, Ross-on-Wye, **Herefordshire**, HR9 7QU, **ENGLAND**.
(T) 01989 780255. Ref:YH12116

ROSS LODGE SADDLERY

Ross Lodge Saddlery, 2 Ross Pk, Ballee, Ballymena, **County Antrim**, BT42 2JZ, **NORTHERN IRELAND**.
(T) 028 25645731 (F) 028 25645731.
Contact/s
Owner: Mr T Dunlop
Profile Saddlery Retailer. Ref:YH12117

ROSS NYE RIDING STABLES

Ross Nye Riding Stables, 8 Bathurst Mews, London, **London (Greater)**, W2 2SB, **ENGLAND**.
(T) 020 72623791.
Profile Riding School. Ref:YH12118

ROSS, J B

J B Ross, 130 Ballycraigy Rd, Newtownabbey, **County Antrim**, BT36 4TB, **NORTHERN IRELAND**.
(T) 028 90832870 (F) 028 90832870.
Contact/s
Owner: Mrs J Ross
Profile Trainer. Ref:YH12119

ROSS, ROBERT J

Robert J Ross AWCF BI, 135 Tudor Walk, Watford, **Hertfordshire**, WD2 4NZ, **ENGLAND**.
(T) 01923 251348.
Profile Farrier. Ref:YH12120

ROSS, RUSSELL A

Russell A Ross DWCF, Rock Cottage Farm, Iveston, Leadgate, Consett, **County Durham**, DH8 7TB, **ENGLAND**.
(T) 01207 503614.
Profile Farrier. Ref:YH12121

ROSSDALE & PARTNERS

Rossdale & Partners, Beaufort Cottage Stables, High St, Newmarket, **Suffolk**, CB8 8JS, **ENGLAND**.
(T) 01638 663150 (F) 01638 660157.
Contact/s
Partner: Mr S Ricketts
Profile Medical Support. Ref:YH12122

ROSSENDALE & HYNDBURN EC

Rossendale & Hyndburn Equestrain Centre, Croft Top Farm, Stone Fold Village, Rising Bridge, Accrington, **Lancashire**, BB5 2DP, **ENGLAND**.
(T) 01706 213635
(E) elizabeth@crofttop.freeserve.co.uk.
Contact/s
Owner: Mr K Holden
Profile Equestrian Centre, Stable/Livery.
Yr. Est: 1990 C.Size: 200 Acres Ref:YH12123

ROSSENDALE VALLEY RIDING CLUB

Rossendale Valley Riding Club, Flowers Farm, Todmorden Rd, Bacup, Rossendale, **Lancashire**, **ENGLAND**.
(T) 01706 874214.
Profile Club/Association. Ref:YH12124

ROSS-SHIRE HORSE TALK

Ross-Shire Horse Talk, 4-6 King St, Tain, **Highlands**, IV19 1AS, **SCOTLAND**.
(T) 01862 894445.
Contact/s
Owner: Mr I Campbell
Profile Saddlery Retailer. Ref:YH12125

ROSS-THOMSON, C Y

Mrs C Y Ross-Thomson, Underwoods Farm, Borders Lane, Etchingham, **Sussex (East)**, TN19 7AE, **ENGLAND**.
(T) 01580 81229.
Profile Breeder. Ref:YH12126

ROTARY CLUB

Rotary Club of Southport Game & Country Fayre, 25A Sefton St, Southport, **Merseyside**, **ENGLAND**..
Profile Club/Association. Ref:YH12127

ROTHER VALLEY RIDING CLUB

Rother Valley Riding Club, Grandturzel Farm, Fontridge Lane, Etchingham, **Sussex (East)**, TN19 7DE, **ENGLAND**.
(T) 01424 773983.
Contact/s
Chairman: Lesley Martin
Profile Club/Association, Riding Club. Ref:YH12128

ROTHERAM, G

G Rotheram DWCF, Gelli-Unig, Main Rd, Dorton, Aylesbury, **Buckinghamshire**, HP18 9NH, **ENGLAND**.
(T) 01844 237648.
Contact/s
Owner: Mr G Rotheram
Profile Farrier. Ref:YH12129

ROTHERAM, H

H Rotheram, 1 Lee Rd, Quainton, Aylesbury, **Buckinghamshire**, HP22 4BH, **ENGLAND**.
(T) 01296 655589.
Contact/s
Owner: Mr H Rotheram
Profile Farrier. Ref:YH12130

ROTHERDALE STUD

Rotherdale Stud, Cydiad-Y-Ddwysir, Llanwenarth, Abergavenny, **Monmouthshire**, NP8 1EP, **WALES**.
(T) 01873 810377.
Contact/s
Partner: Mrs L Ferris
Profile Breeder. Ref:YH12131

ROTHERHAM SADDLERY

Rotherham Saddlery, 263 Wickersley Rd, Rotherham, **Yorkshire (South)**, S60 4JS, **ENGLAND**.
(T) 01709 700507.
Contact/s
Owner: Mrs B Naylor
Profile Saddlery Retailer. Ref:YH12132

ROTHERWOOD STUD

Rotherwood Stud & Farm, Nook Farm, Nook Lane, Ashby-De-La-Zouch, **Leicestershire**, LE65 2QG, **ENGLAND**.
(T) 01530 412095 (F) 01530 413046
Affiliated Bodies NPS.
Contact/s
Owner: Mrs M Mansfield
Profile Breeder. No.Staff: 2 Yr. Est: 1965
C.Size: 70 Acres Ref:YH12133

ROTHESAY RIDING CTRE

Rothesay Riding Centre, Ardbrannan Farm, Canada

Hill, Rothesay, **Argyll and Bute**, PA20 9EN, **SCOTLAND**.
(T) 01700 504971.
Profile Riding School. **Ref: YH12134**

ROTHIEMAY DARTMOORS

Rothiemay Dartmoors, North Pk, Ashwater, Beaworthy, **Devon**, EX21 5UR, **ENGLAND**.
(T) 01409 221457.
Profile Breeder. **Ref: YH12135**

ROTHWELL PARK EQUESTRIAN CTRE

Rothwell Park Equestrian Centre, Lydiate Farm, Lydiate Lane, Liverpool, **Merseyside**, L23 1TW, **ENGLAND**.
(T) 0151 9244055.
Contact/s
Owner: Mrs G Ellison-Smith **Ref: YH12136**

ROTHWELL, B

Mr B Rothwell, Honeysuckle Cottage, Musley Bank, Malton, **Yorkshire (North)**, YO17 6TD, **ENGLAND**.
(T) 01653 696384 **(F)** 01653 696384
(M) 07711 474904
(E) rothwellb@freeuk.com.
Profile Trainer. **Ref: YH12137**

ROTHWELL, DAVE

Dave Rothwell DWCF BII, Woodbrow Farm, Oldham Rd, Denshaw, Oldham, **Lancashire**, OL3 5SP, **ENGLAND**.
(T) 01457 871337.
Profile Farrier. **Ref: YH12138**

ROTTINGDEAN

Rottingdean Riding School & Livery Yard, Chailey Ave, Rottingdean, Brighton, **Sussex (East)**, BN2 7GH, **ENGLAND**.
(T) 01273 302155 **(F)** 01273 271409.
Contact/s
Owner: Miss J Pope **Ref: YH12139**

ROUCH WILMOT

Rouch Wilmot Thoroughbred Library, 2 Vogan's Mill Wharf, 17 Mill St, London, **London (Greater)**, SE1 2BZ, **ENGLAND**.
(T) 020 72314899 **(F)** 020 72312363. **Ref: YH12140**

ROUNDGREY

Roundgrey Ltd, Highfields Stables, Blakesley Rd, Maidford, Towcester, **Northamptonshire**, NN12 8HN, **ENGLAND**.
(T) 01327 860043 **(F)** 01327 860238.
Contact/s
Manager: Mr J Upson
Profile Trainer. **Ref: YH12141**

ROUNDHILLS STUD

Roundhills Stud, Tusmore, Bicester, **Oxfordshire**, OX6 9SJ, **ENGLAND**.
(T) 01869 345271.
Profile Breeder. **Ref: YH12142**

ROUNDKNOWE FARM

Roundknowe Farm, Roundknowe Rd, Uddingston, Glasgow, **Glasgow (City of)**, G71 7TS, **SCOTLAND**.
(T) 01698 813690.
Contact/s
Groom: Mrs L Adams
Profile Riding School. Yr. Est: 1989
Opening Times
Sp: Open Mon - Sun 09:00. Closed Mon - Fri 21:30, Sat, Sun 17:00.
Su: Open Mon - Sun 09:00. Closed Mon - Fri 21:30, Sat, Sun 17:00.
Au: Open Mon - Sun 09:00. Closed Mon - Fri 21:30, Sat, Sun 17:00.
Wn: Open Mon - Sun 09:00. Closed Mon - Fri 21:30, Sat, Sun 17:00. **Ref: YH12143**

ROUNDMEADOWS RACING STABLES

Roundmeadows Racing Stables, Rownall Rd, Wetley Rocks, Stoke-on-Trent, **Staffordshire**, ST9 0BP, **ENGLAND**.
(T) 01782 550861.
Profile Trainer. **Ref: YH12144**

ROUSE, ANTONY

Mr Antony Rouse, Rouses Fold, Pennyshaw Lane, Sykehouse, Goole, **Yorkshire (East)**, DN14 9AY, **ENGLAND**.
(T) 01405 785379.
Profile Breeder. **Ref: YH12145**

ROUSE, DAVID MICHAEL

David Michael Rouse DWCF, Chalkdells, Dane Bridge Rd, Much Hadham, **Hertfordshire**, SG10 6EJ, **ENGLAND**.
(T) 01279 842343.
Profile Farrier. **Ref: YH12146**

ROUSE, SARAH

Sarah Rouse, 28 Elmleigh, Midhurst, **Sussex (West)**, GU29 9EZ, **ENGLAND**.
(T) 01730 817206 **(F)** 01730 817206
(M) 07778 934362. **Ref: YH12147**

ROUTE HUNT BRANCH

Route Hunt Branch of The Pony Club, 34 Gills Lane, Curragh Rd, Coleraine, **County Londonderry**, BT51 3SD, **NORTHERN IRELAND**.
(T) 028 70868433.
Profile Club/Association. **Ref: YH12148**

ROUTLEDGE, K

Mr K Routledge, Catlow Fold Farm, Burnley, **Lancashire**, BB10 3RN, **ENGLAND**.
(T) 01282 698476. **Ref: YH12149**

ROVERTOW

Rovertow, Batts Farm, Tithepit Shaw Lane, Warlingham, **Surrey**, CR6 9AN, **ENGLAND**.
(T) 01883 625444 **(F)** 01883 623849.
Contact/s
Owner: Mr G Groom
Profile Transport/Horse Boxes. **Ref: YH12150**

ROW BROW FARM

Row Brow Farm, Off Lady Edith's Drive, Scarborough, **Yorkshire (North)**, YO12 5RJ, **ENGLAND**.
(T) 01723 374935.
Profile Riding School, Trainer. **Ref: YH12151**

ROWALLAN ACTIVITY CTRE

Rowallan Activity Centre, Meikle Mosside Farm, Fenwick, Kilmarnock, **Ayrshire (East)**, KA3 6AY, **SCOTLAND**.
(T) 01560 600769 **(F)** 01560 600335
Affiliated Bodies ABRS.
Contact/s
Owner: Lady C Rowallan
Profile Arena, Equestrian Centre, Horse/Rider Accom, Riding Club, Riding School, Stable/Livery, Track/Course. Activity Centre.
Centre has access to paint-balling, fishing, gym and wall climbing as well as shows and music festivals.
No.Staff: 9 Yr. Est: 1989 C.Size: 600 Acres
Opening Times
Sp: Open Mon - Sun 08:00. Closed Mon - Sun 23:00.
Su: Open Mon - Sun 08:00. Closed Mon - Sun 23:00.
Au: Open Mon - Sun 08:00. Closed Mon - Sun 23:00.
Wn: Open Mon - Sun 08:00. Closed Mon - Sun 23:00. **Ref: YH12152**

ROWAN LEA RIDING SCHOOL

Rowan Lea Riding School Ltd, Westcotside, Barry, Carnoustie, **Angus**, DD7 7SA, **SCOTLAND**.
(T) 01382 532536.
Profile Riding School, Stable/Livery. **Ref: YH12153**

ROWAN LODGE

Rowan Lodge Dressage Centre, Rowan Lodge, Fildyke Rd, Meppershall, Shefford, **Bedfordshire**, SG17 5LF, **ENGLAND**.
(T) 01462 812151 **(F)** 01462 851717.
Contact/s
Owner: Mrs J Hurst
Profile Trainer.
Mobile Classical and competition trainer.
Yr. Est: 1986
Opening Times
By appointment only **Ref: YH12154**

ROWAN RIDING WEAR

Rowan Riding Wear, 2 Creevy Rd, Lisburn, **County Antrim**, BT27 6UX, **NORTHERN IRELAND**.
(T) 028 92638329.
Profile Saddlery Retailer. **Ref: YH12155**

ROWAN, J

Mrs J Rowan, Bowdlers Hse, Woolstaston, Church Stretton, **Shropshire**, SY6 6NN, **ENGLAND**.
(T) 01386 584404.
Profile Stable/Livery. **Ref: YH12156**

ROWBERTON STUD

Rowberton Stud, East Cliston Farm, Roborough, Winkleigh, **Devon**, EX19 8TE, **ENGLAND**.
(T) 01769 560117.
Profile Breeder. **Ref: YH12157**

ROWCHESTER ARABIANS

Rowchester Arabians, Rowchester Farm, Greenlaw, Duns, **Scottish Borders**, TD10 6UN, **SCOTLAND**.
(T) 01361 810360.
Profile Breeder. **Ref: YH12158**

ROWCLIFFE HSE VETNRY

Rowcliffe House Veterinary Partnership, Rowcliffe Hse Veterinary Hospital, Crown Sq, Penrith, **Cumbria**, CA11 7AB, **ENGLAND**.
(T) 01768 865661 **(F)** 01768 899760.
Profile Medical Support. **Ref: YH12159**

ROWE VETNRY GROUP

Rowe Veterinary Group (Patchway) (The), 164 Gloucester Rd, Patchway, **Gloucestershire (South)**, BS12 5BG, **ENGLAND**.
(T) 01179 312231.
Profile Medical Support. **Ref: YH12160**

ROWE VETNRY GROUP

Rowe Veterinary Group (Thornbury) (The), 3 Pullins Green, Thornbury, **Gloucestershire (South)**, BS35 2AX, **ENGLAND**.
(T) 01454 415478.
Profile Medical Support. **Ref: YH12161**

ROWE VETNRY GROUP

Rowe Veterinary Group (Yate) (The), 9 Station Rd, Yate, **Gloucestershire (South)**, BS37 5HT, **ENGLAND**.
(T) 01454 318016.
Profile Medical Support. **Ref: YH12162**

ROWE, JOSEPH ROBERT

Joseph Robert Rowe RSS, Fairfields Farm, Nutburn Rd, North Baddesley, **Hampshire**, SO52 9BG, **ENGLAND**.
(T) 023 80732274.
Profile Farrier. **Ref: YH12163**

ROWE, L J

L J Rowe, The Bungalow Farm, Venus Hill, Bovingdon, **Hertfordshire**, HP3 0PG, **ENGLAND**.
(T) 01442 832611
(M) 07860 845375.
Profile Transport/Horse Boxes. **Ref: YH12164**

ROWE, R

R Rowe, Ashleigh Hse, Sullington Lane, Storrington, Pulborough, **Sussex (West)**, RH20 4AE, **ENGLAND**.
(T) 01903 742871 **(F)** 01903 742871.
Contact/s
Owner: Mr R Rowe
Profile Trainer. **Ref: YH12165**

ROWE, ROB

Rob Rowe, Treburgett, St. Teath, Bodmin, **Cornwall**, PL30 3LJ, **ENGLAND**.
(T) 01208 850730.
Profile Transport/Horse Boxes. **Ref: YH12166**

ROWEN-BARBARY HORSE FEEDS

Rowen-Barbary Horse Feeds, Wood Farm, Coppice Lane, Coton, Whitchurch, **Shropshire**, SY13 3LT, **ENGLAND**.
(T) 01948 880598 **(F)** 01948 880730.
Profile Medical Support. **Ref: YH12167**

ROWLAND, M E

Miss M E Rowland, Kirkfields, Calverton Rd, Lower Blidworth, **Nottinghamshire**, NG21 0NW, **ENGLAND**.
(T) 01623 794831 **(F)** 01623 793411
(M) 07768 224666.
Profile Trainer. **Ref: YH12168**

ROWLER FARM LIVERY STABLES

Rowler Farm Livery Stables, Rowler, Brackley, **Northamptonshire**, NN13 5LN, **ENGLAND**.
(T) 01869 810423. **Ref: YH12169**

ROWLEY MANOR STABLES

Rowley Manor Stables, Rowley Manor, Little Weighton, **Yorkshire (East)**, HU20 3XR, **ENGLAND**.
(T) 01482 841498.
Profile Riding School, Stable/Livery. **Ref: YH12170**

ROWLEY, CHARLES

Charles Rowley, Allington Lane, Fair Oak, Eastleigh, **Hampshire**, SO50 7DD, **ENGLAND**.
(T) 023 80692229.
Profile Supplies. **Ref: YH12171**

ROWLEY, G

Mr G Rowley, 44 Stamford St, Ellesmere Port, **Cheshire**, CH65 8HJ, **ENGLAND**.
(T) 0151 3565909 **(F)** 0151 3565909.
Profile Breeder. **Ref: YH12172**

ROWLING, W W

W W Rowling, Glebe Farm, Cow Lane, Womersley,

Doncaster, **Yorkshire (South)**, DN6 9BD, **ENGLAND**.
(T) 01977 620223.
Profile Transport/Horse Boxes. **Ref: YH12173**

ROWLINSON, M

M Rowlinson RSS, Dawn Chorus, Sandy Lane, Off School Rd, Marton, Blackpool, **Lancashire**, FY4 5EQ, **ENGLAND**.
(T) 01253 697556.
Contact/s
Owner: Mr M Rowlinson
Profile Farrier. **Ref: YH12174**

ROXANA HORSE & PET SUPPLIES

Roxana Horse & Pet Supplies, 132 Beacon Rd, Great Barr, Birmingham, **Midlands (West)**, B43 7BN, **ENGLAND**.
(T) 0121 3251170.
Contact/s
Owner: Miss C Catel
Profile Supplies. **Ref: YH12175**

ROXTON

Roxton Sporting Ltd, River Ground Stables, Cowdray Pk, Midhurst, **Sussex (West)**, GU29 9AL, **ENGLAND**.
(T) 01730 815500 **(F)** 01730 815588.
Contact/s
Manager: Mr S Simonds
Profile Saddlery Retailer. **Ref: YH12176**

ROXTON SPORTING

Roxton Sporting Ltd (Cirencester), 3/5 West Market Pl, Cirencester, **Gloucestershire**, GL7 2NH, **ENGLAND**.
(T) 01285 659033 **(F)** 01285 657474.
Profile Saddlery Retailer. **Ref: YH12177**

ROXTON SPORTING

Roxton Sporting Ltd (Midhurst), 6 West St, Midhurst, **Sussex (West)**, GU29 9NF, **ENGLAND**.
(T) 01730 817755 **(F)** 01730 815343.
Profile Saddlery Retailer. **Ref: YH12178**

ROY PARKER PHOTOGRAPHY

Roy Parker Photography, The Old Byre, Dale End, Hutton Buscel, Scarborough, **Yorkshire (North)**, YO13 9LR, **ENGLAND**.
(T) 01723 862094. **Ref: YH12179**

ROYAL AGRICULTURAL CLGE

Royal Agricultural College Cirencester, Stroud Rd, Cirencester, **Gloucestershire**, GL7 6JS, **ENGLAND**.
(T) 01285 652531
(E) admissions@royagcol.ac.uk
(W) www.royagcol.ac.uk.
Profile College.
Offers a range of courses including BSc Equine and Agricultural Business Management, MSc Equine Business Management and MSc Applied Equine Science. **Ref: YH12180**

ROYAL AGRICULTURAL COLLEGE

Royal Agricultural College Polocrosse Club, The Rac, Cirencester, **Gloucestershire**, GL7 6JS, **ENGLAND**.
(T) 01285 652531.
Profile Club/Association. Polocrosse Club.
Ref: YH12181

ROYAL AGRICULTURAL SOCIETY

Royal Agricultural Society of England, National Agricultural Ctre, Stoneleigh Pk, Stoneleigh, **Warwickshire**, CV8 2LZ, **ENGLAND**.
(T) 024 76696969 **(F)** 024 76696900.
Contact/s
Key Contact: Miss E Binions
(E) emilyb@rase.org.uk
Profile Club/Association. **Ref: YH12182**

ROYAL ALEXANDRA/ALBERT SCHOOL

Royal Alexandra & Albert School (The), Gatton Pk, Reigate, **Surrey**, RH2 0TW, **ENGLAND**.
(T) 01737 642818.
Profile Riding School. **Ref: YH12183**

ROYAL ARTILLERY

Royal Artillery, Hook Cottage, Easton Royal, Pewsey, **Wiltshire**, SN9 5LY, **ENGLAND**.
(T) 01672 810275 **(F)** 01672 810275
(M) 07889 144862.
Profile Club/Association. **Ref: YH12184**

ROYAL BATH & WEST OF ENGLAND

Royal Bath & West of England Society, The Showground, Shepton Mallet, **Somerset**, BA4 6QN, **ENGLAND**.
(T) 01749 822200 **(F)** 01749 823169.
Profile Club/Association. **Ref: YH12185**

ROYAL COUNTY OF BERKSHIRE

Royal County of Berkshire Polo Club, North St, Winkfield, Windsor, **Berkshire**, SL4 4TH, **ENGLAND**.
(T) 01344 890060 **(F)** 01344 890385
(E) info@rcbpoloclub.com
(W) www.rcbpoloclub.com.
Contact/s
Chairperson: Mr B Morrison
Profile Club/Association. Polo club. **Ref: YH12186**

ROYAL MEWS

Royal Mews (The), Buckingham Palace, London, **London (Greater)**, SW1W 0QH, **ENGLAND**.
(T) 020 7930 4832
(E) buckinghampalace@royalcollection.org.uk
(W) www.royalresidences.com/royalmews.htm.
Profile Supplies. Tourist Attraction.
The Royal Mews is a working stable. It provides an opportunity to view the State vehicles and the horses which play a role in the Queens official and ceremonial duties. Ticket prices are £4.60 for adults and £2.60 for children.
Opening Times
Sp: Open Mon - Thurs 12:00. Closed Mon - Thurs 16:00.
Su: Open Mon - Thurs 12:00. Closed Mon - Thurs 16:00.
Au: Open Mon - Thurs 12:00. Closed Mon - Thurs 16:00.
Wn: Open Mon - Thurs 12:00. Closed Mon - Thurs 16:00.
Closed 26 - 27 November, 25 - 26 December
Ref: YH12187

ROYAL NAVAL EQUESTRIAN ASS

Royal Naval Equestrian Association, Glebe Hse, Patching, Worthing, **Sussex (West)**, BN13 3XF, **ENGLAND**.
(T) 01903 871589.
Profile Club/Association. **Ref: YH12188**

ROYAL OAK INN

Royal Oak Inn, Withypool, **Somerset**, TA24 7QP, **ENGLAND**.
(T) 01643 831506 **(F)** 01643 831659.
Profile Equestrian Centre. **Ref: YH12189**

ROYAL OAK RIDING CLUB

Royal Oak Riding Club, The Lees, Lower Lees, Old Wives Lees, Canterbury, **Kent**, CT4 8AU, **ENGLAND**.
(T) 01227 730032.
Contact/s
Chairman: Mrs R Cleverdon
Profile Club/Association, Riding Club. **Ref: YH12190**

ROYAL PHARMACEUTICAL SOCIETY

Royal Pharmaceutical Society, 1 Lambeth High St, London, **London (Greater)**, SE1 7JN, **ENGLAND**.
(T) 020 77359141 **(F)** 020 77357629.
Profile Club/Association. **Ref: YH12191**

ROYAL SCHOOL

Royal (Dick) School of Veterinary Studies, Pony Trekking Section, Glendevon Youth Hostel, Glendevon, Dollar, **Clackmannanshire**, FK14 7JY, **SCOTLAND**.
(T) 01259 781206.
Profile Equestrian Centre. **Ref: YH12192**

ROYAL SCHOOL

Royal (Dick) School of Veterinary Studies-R (D)SVS, Easter Bush, Roslin, **Lothian (Mid)**, EH25 9RG, **SCOTLAND**.
(T) 0131 4452001.
Profile Equestrian Centre. University.
University of Edinburgh's Faculty of Veterinary Medicine **Ref: YH12193**

ROYAL SCHOOL

Royal School (The), Farnham Lane, Haslemere, **Surrey**, GU27 1HQ, **ENGLAND**.
(T) 01428 605415 **(F)** 01428 607977.
Profile Equestrian Centre. **Ref: YH12194**

ROYAL STUDS

Royal Studs (The), Sandringham, **Norfolk**, PE35 6EF, **ENGLAND**.
(T) 01485 540588 **(F)** 01485 543372.
Profile Breeder. **Ref: YH12195**

ROYAL ULSTER AGRICULTURAL SOC

Royal Ulster Agricultural Society, The King's Hall, Balmoral, Belfast, **County Antrim**, BT9 6GW, **NORTHERN IRELAND**.
(T) 028 90665225 **(F)** 028 90661264
(E) general@kingshall.co.uk.
Contact/s
Director of Agricultural: T L Rea
Profile Club/Association. **Ref: YH12196**

ROYAL VETERINARY CLGE

Royal Veterinary College Animal Care Trust, Hawkshead Lane, North Mymms, Hatfield, **Hertfordshire**, AL9 7TA, **ENGLAND**.
(T) 01707 666237 **(F)** 01707 652090
(E) act@rvc.ac.uk.
Contact/s
Head of PR/Funding: Midge Blake
Profile Club/Association. **Ref: YH12197**

ROYAL VETERINARY CLGE

Royal Veterinary College Riding Club, Royal Veterinary College, Royal College St, London, **London (Greater)**, NW1 0TU, **ENGLAND**.
(T) 020 74685000 **(F)** 020 73882342.
Profile Club/Association. **Ref: YH12198**

ROYDS HALL RIDING SCHOOL

Royds Hall Riding School, Woodlesford, Oulton, Leeds, **Yorkshire (West)**, LS26 8HD, **ENGLAND**.
(T) 0113 2823466.
Contact/s
Owner: Mrs L Watts
Profile Riding School, Stable/Livery. **Ref: YH12199**

ROYLANDS RIDING STABLES

Roylands Riding Stables, Higher Roylands, Moor Lane, Croyde, Braunton, **Devon**, EX33 1NU, **ENGLAND**.
(T) 01271 890898.
Profile Riding School. **Ref: YH12200**

ROYS RIDING SCHOOL

Roys Riding School, Curload Cottage, Curload, Stoke St. Gregory, Taunton, **Somerset**, TA3 6JE, **ENGLAND**.
(T) 01823 698507.
Contact/s
Owner: Mr R Champion
Profile Riding School.
Hacking is available. Yr. Est: 1972
Opening Times
Sp: Open Mon - Sun 09:00. Closed Mon - Sun 22:00.
Su: Open Mon - Sun 09:00. Closed Mon - Sun 22:00.
Au: Open Mon - Sun 09:00. Closed Mon - Sun 22:00.
Wn: Open Mon - Sun 09:00. Closed Mon - Sun 22:00.
There is a answer phone service if there is no one available. **Ref: YH12201**

ROYSTON PONY CLUB

Royston Horse & Pony Club, 26 Lee Lane, Royston, Barnsley, **Yorkshire (South)**, S71 4RT, **ENGLAND**.
(T) 01226 722449.
Contact/s
General Manager: Mrs D Thomson
Profile Riding Club.
The Horse & Pony Club is a non profit making organisation dedicated to providing fun and competition for all ages and abilities. Children compete against adults and horses against ponies. Training is freely given.
Ref: YH12202

ROYSTONS TRAINING YARD

Roystons Training Yard, Royston, Chapmans Lane, West Mersea, Colchester, **Essex**, CO5 8SG, **ENGLAND**.
(T) 01206 386663.
Contact/s
Owner: Mrs S Meanley
Profile Trainer. **Ref: YH12203**

RSPCA

RSPCA, The Causeway, Horsham, **Sussex (West)**, RH12 1HG, **ENGLAND**.
(T) 01403 264181 **(F)** 01403 241048.
Contact/s
Key Contact: Dr M Potter **(Q)** MRCVS
Profile Club/Association. **Ref: YH12204**

RUDD, A J

A J Rudd RSS, Hillside Farm, Boustead Hill, Burgh By Sands, Carlisle, **Cumbria**, CA5 6AA, **ENGLAND**.
(T) 01228 576398.
Profile Farrier. **Ref: YH12205**

RUDDICK, MARK A

Mark A Ruddick DWCF, No 18 The Terrace, Sudbrook, **Newport**, NP26 5SS, **WALES**.
(T) 01291 422475.
Profile Farrier. **Ref: YH12206**

RUDGE, KEITH D

Keith D Rudge, 2 Hollybush Cottages, Hollybush Lane, Denham, Uxbridge, **London (Greater)**, UB9 4HQ, **ENGLAND**.
(T) 07850 496034.
Profile Farrier. Ref: **YH12207**

RUDGEWAY

Rudgeway Stud, The Mill Hse, Blaisdon, Longhope, **Gloucestershire**, GL17 0AH, **ENGLAND**.
(T) 01452 830541.
Profile Breeder.
Breeds Connemaras and Welsh Section B Ponies.
Yr. Est: 1956
Opening Times
Telephone for an appointment Ref: **YH12208**

RUDGWICK & DISTRICT

Rudgwick & District Riding Club, Windmill Hill, Watersfield, Pulborough, **Sussex (West)**, RH20 1NH, **ENGLAND**.
(T) 01798 831800.
Contact/s
Chairman: Mr S Malia
Profile Club/Association, Riding Club. Ref: **YH12209**

RUDRAM, N

N Rudram, Priory Cl Vetnry Surgery, 17 Canon St, Taunton, **Somerset**, TA1 1SW, **ENGLAND**.
(T) 01823 271042.
Profile Medical Support. Ref: **YH12210**

RUDRY RIDING STABLES

Rudry Riding Stables, Haven Hill, Rudry, Caerphilly, **Caerphilly**, CF83 3EB, **WALES**.
(T) 029 20882217.
Profile Riding School. Ref: **YH12211**

RUFFLES ROSETTES

Ruffles Rosettes, 19 High St, Great Billing, Northampton, **Northamptonshire**, NN3 9DT, **ENGLAND**.
(T) 01604 416436
(E) ronnie@euphony.net.
Profile Supplies. Ref: **YH12212**

RUFFORD PARK TRAINING CTRE

Rufford Park Training Centre, The Old Kennels, Rufford Pk, Ollerton, **Nottinghamshire**, NG22 9DF, **ENGLAND**.
(T) 01623 822826 **(F)** 01623 824369.
Profile Equestrian Centre. Ref: **YH12213**

RUFFORD PONY CLUB

Rufford Pony Club, 6 Wands Close, Southwell, **Nottinghamshire**, NG25 0JT, **ENGLAND**.
(T) 01638 815912
(E) rufford@pcuk.org.
Contact/s
Secretary: Mrs D Shepherd
Profile Club/Association. Ref: **YH12214**

RUG LAUDRY

Rug Laudry (The), Unit 2 Buckholt Business Ctre, Warndon, Worcester, **Worcestershire**, WR4 9ND, **ENGLAND**.
(T) 01905 756066 **(F)** 01905 756066
(E) paul@pcerri.freeserve.co.uk.
Profile Supplies. Ref: **YH12215**

RUG OSTLER

Rug Ostler (The), Blandings, Croesau Bach, Oswestry, **Shropshire**, SY10 9AY, **ENGLAND**.
(T) 07000 678537 **(F)** 01691 659464.
Contact/s
Owner: Mrs L Ling
Profile Supplies. Ref: **YH12216**

RUGBY LIVESTOCK SALES

Rugby Livestock Sales Ltd, Cattle Market, Craven Rd, Rugby, **Warwickshire**, CV21 3HX, **ENGLAND**.
(T) 01788 565233. Ref: **YH12217**

RUGBY RIDING CLUB

Rugby Riding Club, Hazeldene, Main St, Willoughby, Rugby, **Warwickshire**, CV23 8BH, **ENGLAND**.
(T) 01788 890843.
Contact/s
Chairman: Mr N Malka
Profile Club/Association, Riding Club. Ref: **YH12218**

RUGBY TRAILER CTRE

Rugby Trailer Centre, 21 Paradise St, Rugby, **Warwickshire**, CV21 3SZ, **ENGLAND**.
(T) 01788 565561.
Profile Transport/Horse Boxes. Ref: **YH12219**

RUGGED

Rugged, Sandpit Hall Rd, Chobham, Woking, **Surrey**, GU24 8HA, **ENGLAND**.
(T) 01276 855916.
Contact/s
Owner: Ms C Lane
Profile Supplies. Ref: **YH12220**

RUGGERY

Ruggery (The), Patch Pk Farm, Unit 12 Ongar Rd, Abridge, Romford, **Essex**, RM4 1AA, **ENGLAND**.
(T) 01708 688170
(W) www.theruggery.com.
Contact/s
Owner: Mrs A Springett
Profile Saddlery Retailer. Laundry Service.
Laundry service for rugs. Also offer a service to personalise your equine equipment. Yr. Est: 1941
Opening Times
Sp: Open Mon - Sun 10:00. Closed Mon - Sat 18:00, Sun 16:00.
Su: Open Mon - Sun 10:00. Closed Mon - Sat 18:00, Sun 16:00.
Au: Open Mon - Sun 10:00. Closed Mon - Sat 18:00, Sun 16:00.
Wn: Open Mon - Sun 10:00. Closed Mon - Sat 18:00, Sun 16:00. Ref: **YH12221**

RUGGIT

Ruggit, Cannamore Hse, Avonwick, South Brent, **Devon**, TQ10 9HA, **ENGLAND**.
(T) 01364 73873.
Profile Supplies. Ref: **YH12222**

RUG-RITE

Rug-Rite, 2 Churn Court, Cheltenham Rd, Cirencester, **Gloucestershire**, GL7 2JF, **ENGLAND**.
(T) 01285 657781.
Profile Supplies. Ref: **YH12223**

RUGWASH 2000

Rugwash 2000, Bromson Hill Court, Ashorne, Warwick, **Warwickshire**, CV35 9AD, **ENGLAND**.
(T) 01926 651286 **(F)** 01926 651286.
Contact/s
Partner: Ms J Stuart
Profile Saddlery Retailer. Ref: **YH12224**

RUGZ

Rugz, 112 Witton St, Northwich, **Cheshire**, CW9 5DY, **ENGLAND**.
(T) 01829 782581 **(F)** 01829 782334.
Profile Supplies. Ref: **YH12225**

RULER, JOHN

John Ruler, 24 Hilldown Rd, Hayes, Bromley, **Kent**, BR2 7HX, **ENGLAND**.
(T) 020 84623542 **(F)** 020 84623542
(E) rulered@btinternet.com. Ref: **YH12226**

RUMENCO - MAIN RING

Rumenco - Main Ring, Stretton Hse, Derby Rd, Stretton, Burton-on-Trent, **Staffordshire**, DE13 0DW, **ENGLAND**.
(T) 01283 524296 **(F)** 01283 511013.
Profile Medical Support. Ref: **YH12227**

RUMENS, A E

A E Rumens, Upper Crowbourne, Blind Lane, Goudhurst, Cranbrook, **Kent**, TN17 1JD, **ENGLAND**.
(T) 01580 211413.
Contact/s
Partner: Mrs P Rumens
Profile Transport/Horse Boxes. Ref: **YH12228**

RUMER FARM STUD & STABLES

Rumer Farm Stud & Stables, Long Marston Rd, Welford-on-Avon, **Warwickshire**, CV37 8AF, **ENGLAND**.
(T) 01789 750786
(M) 07787 516723.
Profile Breeder, Trainer. Ref: **YH12229**

RUMFORD BOND & BALDWIN

Rumford Bond & Baldwin, 11 Fore St, Bovey Tracey, **Devon**, TQ13 9AD, **ENGLAND**.
(T) 01626 833303.
Profile Medical Support. Ref: **YH12230**

RUMSEY, A J

Mr A J Rumsey, Upper Whittimere Farm, Bobbington, Stourbridge, **Staffordshire**, DY7 5EP, **ENGLAND**.
(T) 01384 88269.
Profile Supplies. Ref: **YH12231**

RUMSEY, WAYNE P

Wayne P Rumsey DWCF, 77 Tironderoga Gardens, Woolston, Southampton, **Hampshire**, SO19 9NG, **ENGLAND**.
(T) 023 80420593.
Profile Farrier. Ref: **YH12232**

RUNCTON HALL

Runcton Hall Equestrian Centre, The Green, North Runcton, King's Lynn, **Norfolk**, PE33 0RB, **ENGLAND**.
(T) 01553 840676
Affiliated Bodies BHS.
Contact/s
General Manager: Miss D Kill **(Q)** AI
Profile Arena, Equestrian Centre, Riding Club, Riding School, Stable/Livery, Trainer. No.Staff: 5
Yr. Est: 1998 C.Size: 33 Acres
Opening Times
Sp: Open 09:00. Closed 20:00.
Su: Open 09:00. Closed 20:00.
Au: Open 09:00. Closed 20:00.
Wn: Open 09:00. Closed 20:00. Ref: **YH12233**

RUNNING JUMP DESIGN CONSULT

Running Jump Design Consultants, Davenport Hse, Glossop Rd, Marple Bridge, Stockport, **Cheshire**, SK6 5EL, **ENGLAND**.
(T) 0161 4497654 **(F)** 0161 4497655.
Profile Club/Association. Ref: **YH12234**

RUNNINGWELL STABLES

Runningwell Stables, Pope Lane, Oxted, **Surrey**, RH8 9PL, **ENGLAND**.
(T) 01883 716939 **(F)** 01883 716939.
Profile Stable/Livery. Ref: **YH12235**

RUNNINGWELL STUD

Runningwell Stud, Warren Rd, South Woodham Ferrers, Chelmsford, **Essex**, CM3 5DG, **ENGLAND**.
(T) 01268 711221.
Contact/s
Owner: Mr I Dowie
Profile Breeder, Riding School, Stable/Livery, Trainer.
Ref: **YH12236**

RURAL CRAFTS ASSOCIATION

Rural Crafts Association, Heights Cottage, Brook Rd, Wormley, Godalming, **Surrey**, GU8 5UA, **ENGLAND**.
(T) 01428 682292 **(F)** 01428 685969.
Profile Club/Association. Ref: **YH12237**

RURAL SCENE

Rural Scene, Est Office, High St, Collingbourne Ducis, Marlborough, **Wiltshire**, SN8 3EH, **ENGLAND**.
(T) 01264 850700 **(F)** 01264 850447
(E) enquiries@ruralscene.demon.co.uk
(W) www.ruralscene.co.uk.
Profile Property Services. Ref: **YH12238**

RUSH, R G

R G Rush, 46 Shuttlewood Rd, Bolsover, Chesterfield, **Derbyshire**, S44 6NU, **ENGLAND**.
(T) 01246 240211.
Contact/s
Owner: Mr R Rush
Profile Farrier. Ref: **YH12239**

RUSH, ROBERT G

Robert G Rush FWCF, 67 Selwyn St, Hillstown, Chesterfield, **Derbyshire**, S44 6LR, **ENGLAND**.
(T) 01246 240211.
Profile Farrier. Ref: **YH12240**

RUSH, ROBERT G

Robert G Rush AWCF, Sunway, Snowhill, Clare, Sudbury, **Suffolk**, CO10 8QE, **ENGLAND**.
(T) 01787 278247.
Profile Farrier. Ref: **YH12241**

RUSHALL PARK RIDING STABLES

Rushall Park Riding Stables, Rushall Lane, Corfe Mullen, Wimborne, **Dorset**, BH21 3RT, **ENGLAND**.
(T) 01202 691988.
Contact/s
Owner: Mr R Dixon Ref: **YH12242**

RUSHMERE FARM CARRIAGES

Rushmere Farm Carriages, Rushmere Farm, Crossways, Coleford, **Gloucestershire**, GL16 8QP, **ENGLAND**.
(T) 01594 835319.
Profile Transport/Horse Boxes. Horse drawn vehicles.
Ref: **YH12243**

RUSHTON & BROWNE

Rushton & Browne, East View, Church St, Broughton In Furness, **Cumbria**, LA20 6DU, **ENGLAND**.
(T) 01229 716230.

Profile Medical Support. **Ref: YH12244**

RUSHTON & BROWNE

Rushton & Browne, 1 Mainsgate Rd, Millom, **Cumbria**, LA18 4JZ, **ENGLAND**.
(T) 01229 716230.
Profile Medical Support. **Ref: YH12245**

RUSHTON HALL FARM

Rushton Hall Farm, Desbrough Rd, Rushton, Kettering, **Northamptonshire**, NN14 1RG, **ENGLAND**.
(T) 01536 712211.
Contact/s
Owner: Mr D Pain
Profile Track/Course. **Ref: YH12246**

RUSHTON, PAUL

Paul Rushton DWCF, Farfield Farm, Bolton Rd, Addingham, Ilkley, **Yorkshire (West)**, LS29 0RQ, **ENGLAND**.
(T) 07930 803795.
Profile Farrier. **Ref: YH12247**

RUSHTON, TIMOTHY D

Timothy D Rushton AWCF, Silver St Farm Hse, Silver St, Withersfield, Haverhill, **Suffolk**, CB9 7SN, **ENGLAND**.
(T) 01440 702685.
Profile Farrier. **Ref: YH12248**

RUSHWORTH, MARTIN D

Martin D Rushworth DWCF, 9 Cornlands, Norton, Malton, **Yorkshire (North)**, YO17 9EN, **ENGLAND**.
(T) 01653 694965.
Profile Farrier. **Ref: YH12249**

RUSKIN HORSE DRAWN CARRIAGES

Ruskin Horse Drawn Carriages, The Stables, Tingley Mill, Bridge St, Morley, Leeds, **Yorkshire (West)**, LS27 0HE, **ENGLAND**.
(T) 0113 2536309 **(F)** 0113 2597437.
Contact/s
Partner: Mr N Brown
Profile Transport/Horse Boxes. **Ref: YH12250**

RUSSELL & WOOD

Russell & Wood, The Vetnry Surgery, Rannes St, Insch, **Aberdeenshire**, AB52 6JJ, **SCOTLAND**.
(T) 01464 820235 **(F)** 01464 821087.
Profile Medical Support. **Ref: YH12251**

RUSSELL EQUESTRIAN CTRE

Russell Equestrian Centre, New Pl, Allington Lane, West End, Southampton, **Hampshire**, SO18 3HT, **ENGLAND**.
(T) 023 80473693.
Profile Equestrian Centre. **Ref: YH12252**

RUSSELL EQUITATION CTRE

Russell Equitation Centre, Black Farm, Gaters Hill, West End, Southampton, **Hampshire**, SO30 3HT, **ENGLAND**.
(T) 023 80473693.
Profile Riding School, Stable/Livery. **Ref: YH12253**

RUSSELL LUSITANO STUD

Russell Lusitano Stud (The), Winchpit, Dyffryn Lane, St Nicholas, **Glamorgan (Vale of)**, CF5 6SH, **WALES**.
(T) 01446 761014 **(F)** 01446 761014.
Profile Breeder. **Ref: YH12254**

RUSSELL, A

Mrs A Russell, Craiglinscheoch Farm, Off High Greenock Rd, Kilmacolm, **Inverclyde**, PA13 4TG, **SCOTLAND**.
(T) 01505 872479 **(F)** 01505 873060.
Profile Supplies. **Ref: YH12255**

RUSSELL, ALEC

Alec Russell, Low Farm Cottage, Huttons Ambo, **Yorkshire (North)**, YO60 7JB, **ENGLAND**.
(T) 01653 693989 **(F)** 01653 693989
(M) 07778 983350.
Contact/s
Photographer: Alec Russell **Ref: YH12256**

RUSSELL, G T

G T Russell, Rillington Manor Equestrian Ctre, Sands Lane, Rillington, Malton, **Yorkshire (North)**, YO17 8LL, **ENGLAND**.
(T) 01944 758246.
Profile Stable/Livery, Track/Course. **Ref: YH12257**

RUSSELL, GILLIAN A

Gillian A Russell, Fouldford Farm, Hightown Hill, Ringwood, **Hampshire**, BH24 3HQ, **ENGLAND**.
(T) 01425 480628 **(F)** 01425 482664.
Contact/s
Owner: Miss G Russell
Profile Horse/Rider Accom, Stable/Livery.
B&B accommodation **Yr. Est:** 1991 **C.Size:** 28 Acres
Opening Times
Open April - October **Ref: YH12258**

RUSSELL, J

J Russell, Shim, 13 Bolton Ave, Richmond, **Yorkshire (North)**, DL10 4BG, **ENGLAND**.
(T) 01748 824805.
Profile Farrier. **Ref: YH12259**

RUSSELL, LUCINDA V

Miss Lucinda V Russell, Arlary Hse, Milnathort, Kinross, **Perth and Kinross**, KY13 9SJ, **SCOTLAND**.
(T) 01577 862482 **(F)** 01577 861171
(M) 07970 645261
(E) lucinda@arlary.fsnet.co.uk.
Profile Trainer. **Ref: YH12260**

RUSSELL, MARK ROBSON

Mark Robson Russell AWCF, 23 Hope Pk, Haddington, **Lothian (East)**, EH41 3ES, **SCOTLAND**.
(T) 01620 823501.
Profile Farrier. **Ref: YH12261**

RUSSELL, P A

Mrs P A Russell, Walker Hse, Claxton, **Yorkshire (North)**, YO60 7SD, **ENGLAND**.
(T) 01904 468425.
Profile Supplies. **Ref: YH12262**

RUSSELL, S

Mrs S Russell, Westlandhill Of Rora, Longside, Peterhead, **Aberdeenshire**, AB42 4UB, **SCOTLAND**.
(T) 01779 82397.
Profile Breeder. **Ref: YH12263**

RUSSELL, S

Mrs S Russell, Bridge Farm, Euximoor, Christchurch, Wisbech, **Cambridgeshire**, PE14 9LP, **ENGLAND**.
(T) 01354 638279.
Profile Breeder. **Ref: YH12264**

RUSSELL, S C

S C Russell, Crown Yard, Heathfield, **Sussex (East)**, TN21 8QZ, **ENGLAND**.
(T) 01435 22966. **Ref: YH12265**

RUSSELL, SUZANNE

Suzanne Russell, 14 Harrow Cottages, Hinton On The Green, Evesham, **Worcestershire**, WR11 6QY, **ENGLAND**.
(T) 01386 765139. **Ref: YH12266**

RUSSIAN HORSE SOCIETY

Russian Horse Society (The), Priam Lodge Stables, Burgh Heath Rd, Epsom, **Surrey**, KT17 4NN, **ENGLAND**.
(T) 01372 722080 **(F)** 01372 749676.
Contact/s
Key Contact: Ron Meddes
Profile Club/Association. **Ref: YH12267**

RUST, STEVEN P

Steven P Rust AWCF, Rosemere, 30 The Glebe, Levenham, Sudbury, **Suffolk**, CO10 9SN, **ENGLAND**.
(T) 01787 247727.
Profile Farrier. **Ref: YH12268**

RUSTICS

Rustics, Long Acres Farm, New Chapel Rd, Lingfield, **Surrey**, RH7 6LE, **ENGLAND**.
(T) 01342 834307.
Profile Supplies. **Ref: YH12269**

RUSTY SPUR

Rusty Spur, 182 Victoria Rd, Kirkby-In-Ashfield, Nottingham, **Nottinghamshire**, NG17 8AT, **ENGLAND**.
(T) 01623 453005 **(F)** 01623 453005.
Contact/s
Owner: Mrs J Fluster **Ref: YH12270**

RUTH HICKMAN SPORTING PRINTS

Ruth Hickman Sporting Prints, Fieldgate, Church Rd, W Hanningfield, Chelmsford, **Essex**, CM2 8UL, **ENGLAND**.
(T) 01245 400075.
Contact/s
Owner: Mrs R Hickman
Profile Art Dealer.
Specialise in Hunting & Polo prints. **Yr. Est:** 1986
Opening Times
Open by appointment only **Ref: YH12271**

RUTH LEE RIDING SERVICES

Ruth Lee Riding Services, 1 Sycamore Court, Moor St, Spondon, Derby, **Derbyshire**, DE21 7EA, **ENGLAND**.
(T) 01332 281578.
Profile Supplies. **Ref: YH12272**

RUTHERFORD, E

Mrs E Rutherford, Cae Rhyd Ar Wea, Cwmdu, Llandeilo, **Carmarthenshire**, SA19 7ED, **WALES**.
(T) 01558 685693
(W) www.glen-horses.co.uk.
Contact/s
Owner: Mrs E Rutherford **(Q)** M Phil
(E) edith.rutherford@btinternet.com
Profile Breeder.
Mrs Rutherford provides sporthorse foals and rare breed ponies. She breeds foals from internationally famous bloodlines, from both sires and dams
No.Staff: 1 **Yr. Est:** 1992 **C.Size:** 26 Acres
Opening Times
Telephone for an appointment, there is an answer-phone **Ref: YH12273**

RUTHERFORD, R W

R W Rutherford, Cloptons, 30 High St, Ashley, Newmarket, **Suffolk**, CB8 9DX, **ENGLAND**.
(T) 01638 730091.
Profile Farrier. **Ref: YH12274**

RUTHIN FARMERS AUCTION

Ruthin Farmers Auction Company Ltd, Market St, Ruthin, **Denbighshire**, LL15 1AU, **WALES**.
(T) 01824 702025. **Ref: YH12275**

RUTHIN RIDING

Ruthin Riding Centre, Cae Coch Farm, Ruthin, **Denbighshire**, LL15 2YE, **WALES**.
(T) 01824 703470
Affiliated Bodies Pony Club UK.
Contact/s
Owner: Ms D Dewhurst **(Q)** BHSII
Profile Riding School. **Ref: YH12276**

RUTLAND POLO CLUB

Rutland Polo Club (The), Axholme Lodge, Newton Way, Woolsthorpe By Colsterworth, Grantham, **Lincolnshire**, NG33 5NP, **ENGLAND**.
(T) 01476 860146 **(F)** 01476 860451.
Profile Polo club. **Ref: YH12277**

RUTLAND RIDING CLUB

Rutland Riding Club, 5 Spring Cl, Market Overton, Oakham, **Rutland**, LE15 7PT, **ENGLAND**.
(T) 01572 767626.
Contact/s
Chairman: Miss R David
Profile Club/Association, Riding Club. **Ref: YH12278**

RUTLAND SADDLERY

Rutland Saddlery, 21 Northgate, Oakham, **Leicestershire**, LE15 6QR, **ENGLAND**.
(T) 01572 756223 **(F)** 01572 756223.
Contact/s
Owner: Ms I Mottram **Ref: YH12279**

RUTLAND STUD

Rutland Stud, Saxon St, Saxon St, Newmarket, **Suffolk**, CB8 9RS, **ENGLAND**.
(T) 01638 730217.
Profile Breeder. **Ref: YH12280**

RUTLAND, SEAN D

Sean D Rutland DWCF, Flat 4, Wheathills Farm, Brum Lane, Mackworth, **Derbyshire**, DE22 4NE, **ENGLAND**.
(T) 01332 824710.
Profile Farrier. **Ref: YH12281**

RUTTER, F G

Mr F G Rutter, Swanmore Barn Farm, Upper Swanmore, **Hampshire**, SO3 2QQ, **ENGLAND**.
(T) 01489 877582.
Profile Breeder. **Ref: YH12282**

RYALL, B J M

Mr B J M Ryall, Higher Farm, Rimpton, Yeovil, **Somerset**, BA22 8AD, **ENGLAND**.
(T) 01935 850222.
Profile Trainer. **Ref: YH12283**

RYAN, KEVIN

Kevin Ryan, Hambleton Lodge, Hambleton, Thirsk, **Yorkshire (North)**, YO7 2HA, **ENGLAND**.
(T) 01845 597622 **(F)** 01845 597622.
Contact/s
Owner: Mr K Ryan
Profile Trainer. **Ref: YH12284**

A-Z of COMPANIES

RYAN, M J

M J Ryan, Cadland Hse Stable, 35 Old Station Rd, Newmarket, **Suffolk**, CB8 8DT, **ENGLAND**.
(T) 01638 664172 **(F)** 01638 560248
(W) www.newmarketracehorsetrainers.co.uk
Affiliated Bodies Newmarket Trainers Fed.
Contact/s
Trainer: Mr M Ryan
Profile Trainer. Ref: **YH12285**

RYAN, MATT

Matt Ryan (AUS), 1 Kitsford Cottage, East Lockinge, Wantage, **Oxfordshire**, OX12 8QN, **ENGLAND**.
(T) 01235 831471. Ref: **YH12286**

RYAN, THOMAS P

Thomas P Ryan FWCF, The Cottage, Pertenhall Rd, Brookend, Keysoe, **Bedfordshire**, MK44 2HR, **ENGLAND**.
(T) 01234 708845.
Profile Farrier. Ref: **YH12287**

RYAN-BELL, CAROLYNE

Carolyne Ryan-Bell, Wickhamford Manor, Evesham, **Worcestershire**, WR11 6SA, **ENGLAND**.
(T) 01386 830296 **(F)** 01386 830296. Ref: **YH12288**

RYARSH EQUESTRIAN CTRE

Ryarsh Equestrian Centre, Old Pl Farm, Birling Rd, Ryarsh, West Malling, **Kent**, ME19 5JS, **ENGLAND**.
(T) 01732 847322.
Contact/s
Owner: Ms J Dyson Ref: **YH12289**

RYCOTE FARMS

Rycote Farms, Milton Common, Oxford, **Oxfordshire**, OX9 2PE, **ENGLAND**.
(T) 01844 339360 **(F)** 01844 339361.
Profile Track/Course. Ref: **YH12290**

RYCROFT SCHOOL OF EQUITATION

Rycroft School Of Equitation, New Mill Lane, Eversley, Hook, **Hampshire**, RG27 0RA, **ENGLAND**.
(T) 0118 9732761 **(F)** 0118 9730549
(W) www.rycroft-equitation.co.uk
Affiliated Bodies BHS.
Contact/s
Partner: Mr W Hundley
Profile Riding School.
Clothing shop available on-site, mail orders are welcome. The centre offers carriage driving, cross country, hacking, for all standards of riders. Hosts BHS exams. No.Staff: 10 Yr. Est: 1975
C.Size: 25 Acres
Opening Times
Sp: Open Tues - Sun 08:00. Closed Tues - Sun 20:00.
Su: Open Tues - Sun 08:00. Closed Tues - Sun 20:00.
Au: Open Tues - Sun 08:00. Closed Tues - Sun 20:00.
Wn: Open Tues - Sun 08:00. Closed Tues - Sun 20:00. Ref: **YH12291**

RYDAL MOUNT

Rydal Mount Stables, Baker St, Potters Bar, **Hertfordshire**, EN6 2BS, **ENGLAND**.
(T) 01707 664665.
Contact/s
Owner: Mrs M Staniscia-Singa **(Q)** BHS 1, BHS 2, BHS 3
Profile Stable/Livery.
Full and part livery available, prices on request.
No.Staff: 4 Yr. Est: 1994
Opening Times
Sp: Open Mon - Sun 08:00. Closed Mon 18:30, Tues - Sun 20:00.
Su: Open Mon - Sun 08:00. Closed Mon 18:30, Tues - Sun 20:00.
Au: Open Mon - Sun 08:00. Closed Mon 18:30, Tues - Sun 20:00.
Wn: Open Mon - Sun 08:00. Closed Mon 18:30, Tues - Sun 20:00. Ref: **YH12292**

RYDAL MOUNT LIVERY STABLES

Rydal Mount Livery Stables, Rydal Mount, Gilcrux, Wigton, **Cumbria**, CA7 2QD, **ENGLAND**.
(T) 01697 322889.
Contact/s
Owner: Mr P Carter
Profile Riding School, Stable/Livery. Ref: **YH12293**

RYDER TOWING EQUIPMENT

Ryder Towing Equipment Ltd, Bond St Ind Est, Mancunian Way, Manchester, **Manchester (Greater)**, M12 6HW, **ENGLAND**.
(T) 0161 2735619 **(F)** 0161 2735641.
Profile Transport/Horse Boxes. Ref: **YH12294**

RYDER, JUSTINE

Justine Ryder, Manor Farm, Newton-By-Castleacre, King's Lynn, **Norfolk**, PE32 2BX, **ENGLAND**.
(T) 01760 755248 **(F)** 01760 755248. Ref: **YH12295**

RYDERS

Ryders, North Hse, St Marys St, Brecon, **Powys**, LD3 7AA, **WALES**.
(T) 01874 623383.
Contact/s
Owner: Mr R Durise Ref: **YH12296**

RYDERS FARM

Philip & Lesley Reading T/A Ryders Farm, Manchester Rd, Kearsley, Bolton, **Manchester (Greater)**, BL4 8RU, **ENGLAND**.
(T) 0161 7941446 **(F)** 0161 7941446
(W) www.rydersfarm.co.uk
Affiliated Bodies BHS.
Contact/s
Assistant Manager: Ms C Brown **(Q)** BHSAI
(T) 0161 7940058
Profile Arena, Equestrian Centre, Riding Club, Riding School, Stable/Livery, Transport/Horse Boxes.
No.Staff: 5 Yr. Est: 1994 C.Size: 26 Acres
Opening Times
Sp: Open 09:00. Closed 20:00.
Su: Open 09:00. Closed 20:00.
Au: Open 09:00. Closed 20:00.
Wn: Open 09:00. Closed 20:00. Ref: **YH12297**

RYDERS INTERNATIONAL

Ryders International, Winch Division, Knowsley Rd, Bootle, Liverpool, **Merseyside**, L20 4NW, **ENGLAND**.
(T) 0151 9227585 **(F)** 0151 9441424.
Contact/s
Division Manager: Mr C Pinchen
Profile Transport/Horse Boxes. Ref: **YH12298**

RYDER'S ROSETTES

Ryder's Rosettes, 117 Hullbridge Rd, South Woodham Ferrers, **Essex**, CM3 5LL, **ENGLAND**.
(T) 01245 323949.
Profile Supplies. Ref: **YH12299**

RYEBECK STUD

Ryebeck Stud, 17 Holker Rd, Buxton, **Derbyshire**, SK17 6QN, **ENGLAND**.
(T) 01298 71229.
Profile Breeder. Ref: **YH12300**

RYEHILL

Ryehill House Farm Stud, Ryehill Hse Farm, Ryehill, Hull, **Yorkshire (East)**, HU12 9NH, **ENGLAND**.
(T) 01964 626102.
Contact/s
Owner: Mr D Habblett
Profile Breeder, Stable/Livery.
Livery yard for resting racehorses and bloodstock with prices from £35.00 + VAT per week.
Opening Times
Telephone for an appointment and directions
Ref: **YH12301**

RYKNILD LIVERY STABLES

Ryknild Livery Stables, Forge Lane, Footherley, Lichfield, **Staffordshire**, WS14 0HX, **ENGLAND**.
(T) 0121 3534967.
Contact/s
Owner: Ms A Filho Ref: **YH12302**

RYKNILD SADDLERY

Ryknild Saddlery, 310 Clarence Rd, Sutton Coldfield, **Midlands (West)**, B74 4LU, **ENGLAND**.
(T) 0121 3520494 **(F)** 0121 3520494.
Contact/s
Owner: Mr P Hill Ref: **YH12303**

RYKNILD SADDLERY

Ryknild Saddlery, Hoar Park Cross, Ansley, Nuneaton, **Warwickshire**, CV10 0QU, **ENGLAND**.
(T) 024 76397331.
Contact/s
Manager: Mr B Pugh Ref: **YH12304**

RYLAND SADDLERS

Ryland Saddlers & Co, 5 Ashley Rd, Cheveley, Newmarket, **Suffolk**, CB8 9DP, **ENGLAND**.
(T) 01638 730113.
Contact/s
Owner: Mr D Stevens
Profile Saddlery Retailer.
Sell bridlewear, veterinary products and stable equipment. Yr. Est: 1976
Opening Times
By appointment only Ref: **YH12305**

RYMANS FORGE

Rymans Forge, Dellquay Lane, Appledram Lane South, Chichester, **Sussex (West)**, PO20 7EF, **ENGLAND**.
(T) 01243 773504 **(F)** 01243 773504.
Contact/s
Owner: Mr R Clark
Profile Blacksmith. Ref: **YH12306**

RYOVAN ARABIAN STUD

Ryovan Arabian Stud, Heath Farm, Whitestripes Rd, Parkhill, Dyce, **Aberdeen (City of)**, AB21 7AP, **SCOTLAND**.
(T) 01224 724012
(E) kbrady7665@aol.com
(W) www.ryovanarabianstud.freeserve.co.uk.
Profile Breeder. Ref: **YH12307**

RYTON LIVESTOCK

Ryton Livestock, The Ponderosa, Freeboard Lane, Ryton On Dunsmore, Coventry, **Midlands (West)**, CV8 3ET, **ENGLAND**.
(T) 024 76302730.
Profile Horse/Rider Accom. Ref: **YH12308**

S & B STABLES

S & B Stables, Nutmeg, Main Rd, Withern, Alford, **Lincolnshire**, LN13 0NB, **ENGLAND**.
(T) 01507 450032.
Contact/s
Owner: Mrs S Brown **(Q)** BHS 1, BHS 2, BHS 3
Profile Riding School, Stable/Livery.
'Own a pony for a day'. Yr. Est: 1989
Opening Times
Sp: Open 09:00. Closed 20:00.
Su: Open 09:00. Closed 20:00.
Au: Open 09:00. Closed 18:00.
Wn: Open 09:00. Closed 18:00. Ref: **YH12309**

S & E JOHNSON

S & E Johnson Ltd, Old Rd Mills, Darley Dale, Matlock, **Derbyshire**, DE4 2ES, **ENGLAND**.
(T) 01629 733342 **(F)** 01629 733918.
Profile Supplies. Ref: **YH12310**

S & J DISTRIBUTORS

S & J Distributors, Unit 6, Bassett Down Workshop, Swindon, **Wiltshire**, SN4 9QP, **ENGLAND**.
(T) 01793 815077 **(F)** 01793 815293
(M) 07850 818590.
Profile Supplies. Ref: **YH12311**

S & J SADDLERY

S & J Saddlery, 7 Kings Rd, Long Clawson, Melton Mowbray, **Leicestershire**, LE14 4NP, **ENGLAND**.
(T) 01664 823080.
Profile Saddlery Retailer. Ref: **YH12312**

S & S SADDLERY

S & S Saddlery, The Bungalow, Nr White Hse Farm, Newcastle Rd, Sunderland, **Tyne and Wear**, SR5 1RS, **ENGLAND**.
(T) 0191 5160332 **(F)** 0191 5496366.
Contact/s
Owner: Ms S Brown
Profile Riding Wear Retailer, Saddlery Retailer, Supplies.
The company has a mobile tack shop and attends agricultural shows. No.Staff: 1 Yr. Est: 1999
Opening Times
Sp: Open Mon - Sun 09:00. Closed Mon - Sun 20:00.
Su: Open Mon - Sun 09:00. Closed Mon - Sun 20:00.
Au: Open Mon - Sun 09:00. Closed Mon - Sun 20:00.
Wn: Open Mon - Sun 09:00. Closed Mon - Sun 20:00. Ref: **YH12313**

S A S

S A S (Bristol) Ltd, Harbour Rd Trading Est, Portishead, **Somerset (North)**, BS20 7BL, **ENGLAND**.
(T) 01275 843403 **(F)** 01275 846260
(M) 07836 310302.
Profile Club/Association. Ref: **YH12314**

S A S TRAILERS

S A S Trailers, Bone Home Lane, Pickhill, Thirsk, **Yorkshire (North)**, YO7 4JG, **ENGLAND**.
(T) 01845 567637.
Contact/s
Owner: Mr J Charlton
Profile Transport/Horse Boxes. Ref: **YH12315**

S B S

S B S Ltd, Woden Rd, Wolverhampton, **Midlands**

(West), WV10 0AS, ENGLAND.
(T) 01902 455655.
Profile Transport/Horse Boxes. Ref: YH12316

S C A SADDLERY

S C A Saddlery, 11C Vicarage Pl, Walsall, **Midlands (West)**, WS1 3NA, **ENGLAND**.
(T) 01922 724795 (F) 01922 724795.
Contact/s
Owner: Mr S Armitage Ref: YH12317

S C S TRAILER SERVICES

S C S Trailer Services, Unit 14F Manywells Ind Est, Manywells Brow, Cullingworth, Bradford, **Yorkshire (West)**, BD13 5DX, **ENGLAND**.
(T) 01535 273568 (F) 01535 273568.
Contact/s
Partner: Mr K Steele
Profile Transport/Horse Boxes.
Trailer and horsebox repair No.Staff: 6
Yr. Est: 1986
Opening Times
Sp: Open Mon - Fri 08:00. Closed Mon - Fri 17:00.
Su: Open Mon - Fri 08:00. Closed Mon - Fri 17:00.
Au: Open Mon - Fri 08:00. Closed Mon - Fri 17:00.
Wn: Open Mon - Fri 08:00. Closed Mon - Fri 17:00.
Closed weekends Ref: YH12318

S D C TRAILERS

S D C Trailers, 116 Deer Park Rd, Toomebridge, Antrim, **County Antrim**, BT41 3SS, **NORTHERN IRELAND**.
(T) 028 79650765.
Profile Transport/Horse Boxes. Ref: YH12319

S D C TRAILERS

S D C Trailers Ltd, 11 Watt Gr, Mayfield, Dalkeith, **Lothian (Mid)**, EH22 5TT, **SCOTLAND**.
(T) 01875 823767.
Profile Transport/Horse Boxes. Ref: YH12320

S D H COACHWORKS

S D H Coachworks, Unit 3 Lodge Works, Great Ashfield, Bury St Edmunds, **Suffolk**, IP31 3HA, **ENGLAND**.
(T) 01359 258504.
Contact/s
Owner: Mr S Howard
Profile Transport/Horse Boxes. Ref: YH12321

S E B INTERNATIONAL

S E B International Ltd, Unity Rd, Lowmoor Ind Est, Kirkby-In-Ashfield, Nottingham, **Nottinghamshire**, NG17 7LE, **ENGLAND**.
(T) 01623 754490 (F) 01623 753477.
Profile Transport/Horse Boxes. Ref: YH12322

S E BURNELL

S E Burnell International Horse Transport, Pear Tree Farm, Ludgershall, Aylesbury, **Buckinghamshire**, HP18 9PD, **ENGLAND**.
(T) 01844 238246.
Profile Transport/Horse Boxes. Ref: YH12323

S F ROBERTSON WHOLESALE

S F Robertson Wholesale Ltd, Bittern Rd, Sowton Ind Est, Exeter, **Devon**, EX2 7LP, **ENGLAND**.
(T) 01392 201644 (F) 01392 431252. Ref: YH12324

S G ANIMAL FEEDS

S G Animal Feeds, Unit 20 Albert Mill, Lower Darwen, Blackburn, **Lancashire**, BB3 0QE, **ENGLAND**.
(T) 01254 261866.
Profile Supplies. Ref: YH12325

S G PRESCOTT & SONS

S G Prescott & Sons, Vicarage Farm, Lund, Driffield, **Yorkshire (East)**, YO25 9TW, **ENGLAND**.
(T) 01377 217300.
Contact/s
Senior Partner: Mr S Prescott Ref: YH12326

S G TRAILER REPAIRS

S G Trailer Repairs, 27 Upper St Helens Rd, Hedge End, Southampton, **Hampshire**, SO30 0LG, **ENGLAND**. (F) 01489 784049
(M) 07721 942844.
Contact/s
Owner: Mr S Griffiths
Profile Transport/Horse Boxes. Ref: YH12327

S J B SADDLERY

S J B Saddlery, 53-55 Neath Rd, Briton Ferry, Neath, **Glamorgan (Vale of)**, SA11 2DX, **WALES**.
(T) 01639 769006.
Contact/s
Owner: Mr S Bushell
Profile Saddlery Retailer. Ref: YH12328

S L B SUPPLIES

S L B Supplies (Animal Feeds), Wiggs Farm, Wood Rd, Ellistown, Coalville, **Leicestershire**, LE67 1GE, **ENGLAND**.
(T) 01530 230377 (F) 01530 231180
(E) slbsupplies@aol.com.
Contact/s
Owner: Sarah L Bailey
Profile Breeder, Medical Support, Supplies.
Ref: YH12329

S MILNER & SON

S Milner & Son, 4 Station Rd, John O' Gaunt, Melton Mowbray, **Leicestershire**, LE14 2RE, **ENGLAND**.
(T) 01664 454839 (F) 01664 454744.
Contact/s
Owner: Mr A Milner
Profile Saddlery Retailer. Ref: YH12330

S O S SADDLERY

S O S Saddlery, Little Pengelly Farm, Lower Sticker, St Austell, **Cornwall**, PL26 7JJ, **ENGLAND**.
(T) 01726 65022.
Contact/s
Partner: Mrs E Hoskin Ref: YH12331

S R OSBORN & SON

S R Osborn & Son, The Bungalow, North Crawley Rd, Newport Pagnell, **Buckinghamshire**, MK16 9HG, **ENGLAND**.
(T) 01908 616564 (F) 01908 216683. Ref: YH12332

S R S

Sunbury Riding School, Off Fordbridge Rd, Sunbury-on-Thames, **Surrey**, TW16 6AS, **ENGLAND**.
(T) 01932 789792 (F) 01932 789792
(W) www.sunburyridingschool.co.uk
Affiliated Bodies BHS.
Contact/s
General Manager: Ms K Taylor (Q) AI
Profile Equestrian Centre, Riding Club, Riding School, Stable/Livery, Transport/Horse Boxes. Aloe Vera Distributors.
Retrain ex-flat and ex-steeplechase horses. Livery is also available, at £381.33 per month for part, and £450.00 per month for full. No.Staff: 5
Yr. Est: 2000 C.Size: 29 Acres
Opening Times
Sp: Open Tues - Sun 09:00. Closed Tues - Sun 17:00.
Su: Open Tues - Sun 09:00. Closed Tues - Sun 17:00.
Au: Open Tues - Sun 09:00. Closed Tues - Sun 17:00.
Wn: Open Tues - Sun 09:00. Closed Tues - Sun 17:00.
Closed on Mondays Ref: YH12333

S RANSLEY & SONS

S Ransley & Sons, Elite, Hornash Lane, Shadoxhurst, Ashford, **Kent**, TN26 1HU, **ENGLAND**.
(T) 01233 732392 (F) 01233 732921.
Contact/s
Partner: Mr S Ransley Ref: YH12334

S S EQUESTRIAN VIDEO

S S Equestrian Video, Locksley Farm Hse, Podimore, Yeovil, **Somerset**, BA22 8JE, **ENGLAND**.
(T) 01935 840235.
Profile Supplies. Ref: YH12335

S T S WHOLESALE

S T S Wholesale, Unit G1-G3 Hilton Pk, East Wittering, Chichester, **Sussex (West)**, PO20 8RL, **ENGLAND**.
(T) 01243 672323 (F) 01243 672424.
Contact/s
Company Secretary: Mr J Cooper
Ref: YH12336

S TWEDDALL & SON

S Tweddall & Son, Forge Hse, Eppleby, Richmond, **Yorkshire (North)**, DL11 7AT, **ENGLAND**.
(T) 01325 718379.
Contact/s
Partner: Mrs S Tweddall
Profile Farrier. Ref: YH12337

S W TRAILER HIRE

S W Trailer Hire, Unit B Mapplewell Business Pk, Blacker Rd, Mapplewell, Barnsley, **Yorkshire (South)**, S75 6BS, **ENGLAND**.
(T) 01226 380091 (F) 01226 380091.
Contact/s
Partner: Mr S Wright
Profile Transport/Horse Boxes. Ref: YH12338

SABRE LEATHER

Sabre Leather Co Ltd, 19-21 Sandwell St, Walsall, **Midlands (West)**, WS1 3DR, **ENGLAND**.
(T) 01922 629925 (F) 01922 723463.
Profile Saddlery Retailer. Ref: YH12339

SADDLE & BRIDLE

Saddle & Bridle, 12 Alms Hse, Wednesbury Rd, Walsall, **Midlands (West)**, WS1 3RP, **ENGLAND**.
(T) 01922 746667.
Profile Supplies. Ref: YH12340

SADDLE & SPUR

Saddle & Spur, Walesby Garden Ctre, Brake Rd, Walesby, Newark, **Nottinghamshire**, NG22 9NQ, **ENGLAND**.
(T) 0115 9939442.
Contact/s
Owner: Mrs J Hemmings Ref: YH12341

SADDLE BOUTIQUE

Saddle Boutique, 16-17 Bevan St West, Lowestoft, **Suffolk**, NR32 2AB, **ENGLAND**.
(T) 01502 561903.
Contact/s
Owner: Mrs E Kemplay Ref: YH12342

SADDLE BOX

Saddle Box, Knagan Croft Blair, Fintray, Aberdeen, **Aberdeen (City of)**, AB21 0JL, **SCOTLAND**.
(T) 01651 882772. Ref: YH12343

SADDLE CTRE

Saddle Centre (The), 10 Church Farm, Marksbury, Bath, **Bath & Somerset (North East)**, BA2 9HQ, **ENGLAND**.
(T) 01761 472158. Ref: YH12344

SADDLE RACK

Saddle Rack (The), 93 Canterbury Rd, Hawkinge, Folkestone, **Kent**, CT18 7BS, **ENGLAND**.
(T) 01303 893659 (F) 01303 893659.
Contact/s
Owner: Miss S Bottomley
Profile Saddlery Retailer. Ref: YH12345

SADDLE RACK

Saddle Rack (The), Common Farm, Common Lane, Watnall, Nottingham, **Nottinghamshire**, NG16 1HD, **ENGLAND**.
(T) 0115 9458818
Affiliated Bodies BETA.
Contact/s
Owner: Ms Y Vohra
Profile Riding Wear Retailer, Saddlery Retailer, Stable/Livery, Supplies. No.Staff: 3
Yr. Est: 1999 C.Size: 2.5 Acres
Opening Times
Sp: Open 11:00. Closed 18:00.
Su: Open 11:00. Closed 18:00.
Au: Open 11:00. Closed 18:00.
Wn: Open 11:00. Closed 18:00. Ref: YH12346

SADDLE SEAT SOCIETY

Saddle Seat Society, Rookery, Gaston St, East Bergholt, Colchester, **Essex**, CO7 6SF, **ENGLAND**.
(T) 01206 298334.
Contact/s
Key Contact: Mrs B Horrocks
Profile Club/Association. Ref: YH12347

SADDLE SENSE

Saddle Sense, Botany Farmhouse, Baldersdale, Barnard Castle, **County Durham**, DL12 9UU, **ENGLAND**.
(T) 01833 650069.
Profile Saddlery Retailer.
Made to measure bridles and saddle accessories. Also makes belts, dog collars and leads. Enquiries welcome. Ref: YH12348

SADDLE SHOP

Saddle Shop, 61 Notte St, Plymouth, **Devon**, PL1 2AG, **ENGLAND**.
(T) 01752 672914 (F) 01752 672914.
Contact/s
Owner: Ms C Norman (T) 01752 202149
Ref: YH12349

SADDLE SHOP

Saddle Shop (The), 357 Old Durham Rd, Gateshead, **Tyne and Wear**, NE9 5LA, **ENGLAND**.
(T) 0191 4774630.
Contact/s
Owner: Mrs C Johnson
Profile Riding Wear Retailer, Saddlery Retailer.
Opening Times
Sp: Open Mon - Fri 09:30, Sat 09:00, Sun 11:00.

Closed Mon - Fri 18:00, Sat 17:00, Sun 16:00.
Su: Open Mon - Fri 09:30, Sat 09:00, Sun 11:00.
Closed Mon - Fri 18:00, Sat 17:00, Sun 16:00.
Au: Open Mon - Fri 09:30, Sat 09:00, Sun 11:00.
Closed Mon - Fri 18:00, Sat 17:00, Sun 16:00.
Wn: Open Mon - Fri 09:30, Sat 09:00, Sun 11:00.
Closed Mon - Fri 18:00, Sat 17:00, Sun 16:00.
Ref: **YH12350**

SADDLE UP

Saddle Up, 110 Botchergate, Carlisle, **Cumbria**, CA1 1SN, **ENGLAND**.
(T) 01228 810822 (F) 01228 810822.
Contact/s
Owner: Mrs J Porter Ref: **YH12351**

SADDLE UP FOR THE FUTURE

Saddle Up For The Future, 34 Duthie Trce, Aberdeen, **Aberdeen (City of)**, AB10 7PQ, **SCOTLAND**.
(T) 01224 313076 (F) 01224 312278. Ref: **YH12352**

SADDLE WORLD

Saddle World Ltd, Leadgate Saddlery, 1a Harpington St, Consett, **County Durham**, DH8 6AA, **ENGLAND**.
(T) 01207 580001.
Contact/s
Owner: Mr H Graham Ref: **YH12353**

SADDLEBROOK CHASE

Saddlebrook Chase Riding School, Jaywick Lane, Clacton-on-Sea, **Essex**, CO16 7BD, **ENGLAND**.
(T) 01255 474554.
Contact/s
Manager: Mrs J Driscall Ref: **YH12354**

SADDLECRAFT

Saddlecraft Equestrian, 3 Cropwell Rd, Radcliffe-on-Trent, Nottingham, **Nottinghamshire**, NG12 2FJ, **ENGLAND**.
(T) 0115 9332800 (F) 0115 9332800
(E) enquiry@saddlecraft.co.uk
(W) www.saddlecraft.co.uk
Affiliated Bodies BETA.
Contact/s
Owner: Ms H Didcock
(E) helen@saddlecraft.co.uk
Profile Riding Wear Retailer, Saddlery Retailer, Supplies.
Saddlecraft also stock children's clothes - Colt Combi, and many other products for both the horse and rider.
No.Staff: 2 Yr. Est: 1972
Opening Times
Sp: Open 09:30. Closed 16:30.
Su: Open 09:30. Closed 16:30.
Au: Open 09:30. Closed 16:30.
Wn: Open 09:30. Closed 16:30. Ref: **YH12355**

SADDLERS

Saddlers (The), 15 Little Dockray, Penrith, **Cumbria**, CA11 7HL, **ENGLAND**.
(T) 01768 862363 (F) 01768 862363.
Contact/s
Partner: Mr J Armstrong Ref: **YH12356**

SADDLERS APPRENTICE

Saddlers Apprentice (The), Larton Livery Stables, The Styles, Wirral, **Merseyside**, CH48 1PL, **ENGLAND**.
(T) 0151 6252551.
Contact/s
Partner: Mrs S Connor Ref: **YH12357**

SADDLERS COMPANY

Saddlers Company (The), Saddlers Hall, 40 Gutter Lane, London, **London (Greater)**, EC2V 6BR, **ENGLAND**.
(T) 020 72268661 (F) 020 76000386
(E) clerk@saddlersco.co.uk
(W) www.saddlersco.co.uk.
Contact/s
Assistant: Ms K Yiangopoylos
Profile Club/Association.
There is a hall for hire
Opening Times
Sp: Open Mon - Fri 09:00. Closed Mon - Fri 17:00.
Su: Open Mon - Fri 09:00. Closed Mon - Fri 17:00.
Au: Open Mon - Fri 09:00. Closed Mon - Fri 17:00.
Wn: Open Mon - Fri 09:00. Closed Mon - Fri 17:00.
Ref: **YH12358**

SADDLERS DEN

Saddlers Den, 60 Norwood Ave, Southport, **Merseyside**, PR9 7EQ, **ENGLAND**.
(T) 01704 228370 (F) 01704 228370.
Contact/s
Owner: Mr C Taylor Ref: **YH12359**

SADDLERS RIDING CLUB

Saddlers Riding Club, 60 Street Lane, Cheslyn Hay, Walsall, **Midlands (West)**, **ENGLAND**..
Contact/s
Secretary: Mrs A Cooper
Profile Club/Association, Riding Club. Ref: **YH12360**

SADDLERS SHOP

Saddlers Shop (The), The Kings Troop R H A, St John's Wood Barracks, Ordnance Hill, London, **London (Greater)**, NW8 6PT, **ENGLAND**.
(T) 020 74144631 (F) 020 74144631.
Profile Saddlery Retailer. Ref: **YH12361**

SADDLERS WORKSHOP

Saddlers Workshop (The), Iron Hill, Hollycombe, Liphook, **Hampshire**, GU30 7LP, **ENGLAND**.
(T) 01428 723085.
Profile Saddlery Retailer. Ref: **YH12362**

SADDLERY

Barn Shop (The), Red Lion Yard, Old North Rd, Kneesworth, Royston, **Hertfordshire**, SG8 5JL, **ENGLAND**.
(T) 01763 249875 (F) 01763 249875.
Contact/s
Owner: Mr S Carter
Profile Riding Wear Retailer, Saddlery Retailer, Supplies. No.Staff: 4 Yr. Est: 1986
C.Size: 0.5 Acres
Opening Times
Sp: Open 09:00. Closed 18:00.
Su: Open 09:00. Closed 18:00.
Au: Open 09:00. Closed 18:00.
Wn: Open 09:00. Closed 18:00. Ref: **YH12363**

SADDLERY

Saddlery (The), 49 High St, Highworth, Swindon, **Wiltshire**, SN6 7AQ, **ENGLAND**.
(T) 01793 766660 (F) 01793 766660
(E) the@saddlery.fslife.co.uk
(W) www.thesaddleryathighworth.co.uk.
Contact/s
Owner: Mr J Webb
Profile Riding Wear Retailer, Saddlery Retailer.
Family run business. Yr. Est: 1994
Opening Times
Sp: Open Mon - Sat 09:00. Closed Mon - Sat 17:15.
Su: Open Mon - Sat 09:00. Closed Mon - Sat 17:15.
Au: Open Mon - Sat 09:00. Closed Mon - Sat 17:15.
Wn: Open Mon - Sat 09:00. Closed Mon - Sat 17:15.
Closed on Sundays Ref: **YH12364**

SADDLERY & GUN ROOM

Saddlery & Gun Room (The), 368 Main Rd, Westerham Hill, Westerham, **Kent**, TN16 2HN, **ENGLAND**.
(T) 01959 573089 (F) 01959 575590
(W) www.saddleryandgunroom.com
Affiliated Bodies BETA, SMS.
Contact/s
General Manager: Mr J Stone
Profile Riding Wear Retailer, Saddlery Retailer, Supplies.
Saddle inspection and fitting specialist.
No.Staff: 10 Yr. Est: 1970 C.Size: 7 Acres
Opening Times
Sp: Open Mon - Sat 09:00, Sun 10:00. Closed Mon - Sat 17:30, Sun 16:00.
Su: Open Mon - Sat 09:00, Sun 10:00. Closed Mon - Sat 17:30, Sun 16:00.
Au: Open Mon - Sat 09:00, Sun 10:00. Closed Mon - Sat 17:30, Sun 16:00.
Wn: Open Mon - Sat 09:00, Sun 10:00. Closed Mon - Sat 17:30, Sun 16:00. Ref: **YH12365**

SADDLERY BALDWINS GATE

Saddlery Baldwins Gate, The Old Booking Office, Keele, Newcastle, **Staffordshire**, ST5 5BS, **ENGLAND**.
(T) 01782 680688. Ref: **YH12366**

SADDLERY SHOP

Saddlery Shop (Stratford), Pebworth Vale Equest Ctre, Stratford, **Warwickshire**, CV37 8XP, **ENGLAND**.
(T) 01789 720505.
Profile Saddlery Retailer. Ref: **YH12367**

SADDLERY TRADE SERVICES

Saddlery Trade Services, Long St, Premier Business Pk, Walsall, **Midlands (West)**, WS2 9DY, **ENGLAND**.
(T) 01922 630013 (F) 01922 724355.
Contact/s
Owner: Mr H Bayliss Ref: **YH12368**

SADDLERY TRADING CO

Saddlery Trading Co (UK) Ltd, 108 Bath St, Walsall, **Midlands (West)**, WS1 3DE, **ENGLAND**.
(T) 01922 644266 (F) 01922 623745. Ref: **YH12369**

SADDLERY WORKSHOP

Saddlery Workshop (The), Higher Stoodley Cottage, Lee Bottom Rd, Todmorden, **Yorkshire (West)**, OL14 6HD, **ENGLAND**.
(T) 01706 812488.
Profile Saddlery Retailer. Ref: **YH12370**

SADDLES, SADDLES, SADDLES

Saddles, Saddles, Saddles, Tudor Tack Shop, Purbrook Common, Purbrook, Portsmouth, **Hampshire**, PO7 5RX, **ENGLAND**.
(T) 023 92259119 (F) 023 92259606.
Contact/s
Saddle Fitter: Mrs A Daniels
Profile Saddlery Retailer.
Saddle fitter No.Staff: 6 Yr. Est: 2000
C.Size: 4 Acres
Opening Times
Sp: Open By Appointment only.
Su: Open By Appointment only.
Au: Open By Appointment only.
Wn: Open By Appointment only. Ref: **YH12371**

SADDLEWORTH PONY CLUB

Saddleworth & District Pony Club, Earnshaw Head Farm, Platting Rd, Lydgate, Oldham, **Lancashire**, OL4 4JP, **ENGLAND**.
(T) 01457 874120.
Contact/s
Secretary: Kathy Scott
Profile Club/Association. Ref: **YH12372**

SADIK, A M

Mr A M Sadik, Wolverley Court, Wolverley, Kidderminster, **Worcestershire**, DY10 3RP, **ENGLAND**.
(T) 07803 040344.
Profile Supplies. Ref: **YH12373**

SADLER, LINDA

Linda Sadler, 3 Manor Farm Barns, Chippenham, Ely, **Cambridgeshire**, CB7 5PR, **ENGLAND**.
(T) 01638 721713 (F) 01638 721713
(M) 07711 905949
(E) linda.sadler@menta.org.uk.
Profile Blood Stock Agency, Breeder. Ref: **YH12374**

SADLERS FARM FEEDS

Sadlers Farm Feeds, London Rd, Bowers Gifford, **Essex**, SS13 2HL, **ENGLAND**.
(T) 01268 792114.
Profile Supplies. Ref: **YH12375**

SAFE & SECURE PRODUCTS

Safe & Secure Products, Chestnut Hse, Chesley Hill, Wick, **Gloucestershire (South)**, BS13 5NE, **ENGLAND**.
(T) 01179 374494 (F) 01179 374642. Ref: **YH12376**

SAFE RIDER

Safe Rider, Bayliss Orchard, Horley, Banbury, **Oxfordshire**, OX15 6BL, **ENGLAND**.
(T) 01295 730844. Ref: **YH12377**

SAFERIDE SADDLERY PRODUCTS

Saferide Saddlery Products, 2 Newfield Cl, Walsall, **Midlands (West)**, WS2 7PB, **ENGLAND**.
(T) 01922 646512. Ref: **YH12378**

SAFETY SYSTEMS

Safety Systems, The Hse On The Hill, Stranraer, **Dumfries and Galloway**, DG9 8LY, **SCOTLAND**.
(T) 01776 704828 (F) 01776 704828.
Contact/s
Partner: Mrs I McGeogh Ref: **YH12379**

SAFFRON HOUSE STABLES

Saffron House Stables, Hamilton Rd, Newmarket, **Suffolk**, CB8 0NY, **ENGLAND**.
(T) 01638 669693
(W) www.newmarketracehorsetrainers.co.uk
Affiliated Bodies Newmarket Trainers Fed.
Contact/s
Trainer: Mr M Quinlan
Profile Trainer. Ref: **YH12380**

SAFFRON WALDEN & DISTRICT

Saffron Walden & District Riding Club, Green Farm, Little Sampford, Saffron Walden, **Essex**, CB10 2QL, **ENGLAND**.
(T) 01799 586498.
Contact/s
Chairman: Mrs G Farrant
Profile Club/Association, Riding Club. Ref: **YH12381**

SAGITTARIUS BLOODSTOCK AGENCY

Sagittarius Bloodstock Agency, The Manor Hse, Church Lane, Sproxton, Melton Mowbray, **Leicestershire**, LE14 4PZ, **ENGLAND**.
(T) 01476 861968 **(F)** 01476 861969.
Contact/s
Partner: Mr W Cameron
Profile Blood Stock Agency, Breeder, Supplies.
Ref: **YH12382**

SAGITTARIUS POLOCROSSE CLUB

Sagittarius Polocrosse Club, 25 Chelford Rd, Somerfield, Congleton, **Cheshire**, CW12 4QD, **ENGLAND**.
(T) 01260 272122.
Contact/s
Chairman: Mr G Bell
Profile Club/Association. Polocrosse Club.
Ref: **YH12383**

SAGROTT, J E & M P G

J E & M P G Sagrott, Tamarin Farm, Littleworth, Warwick, **Warwickshire**, CV35 8HD, **ENGLAND**.
(T) 01926 499421 **(F)** 01926 499421.
Contact/s
Owner: Mrs J Sagrott Ref: **YH12384**

SALAMAN, M

Mr M Salaman, 3 Russley Park Stables, Baydon, Marlborough, **Wiltshire**, SN8 2JY, **ENGLAND**.
(T) 01672 541048 **(F)** 01672 541048.
Profile Trainer. Ref: **YH12385**

SALES OF SANDON

Sales of Sandon, The Mill, Sandon, Buntingford, **Hertfordshire**, SG9 0QQ, **ENGLAND**.
(T) 01763 288206 **(F)** 01763 288422.
Profile Saddlery Retailer. Ref: **YH12386**

SALHOUSE EQUESTRIAN CTRE

Salhouse Equestrian Centre, Lower St, Salhouse, Norwich, **Norfolk**, NR13 6RW, **ENGLAND**.
(T) 01603 720921.
Contact/s
Accountant: Mr R Fielder
Profile Riding School. Ref: **YH12387**

SALISBURY RACECOURSE

Salisbury Racecourse, The Bibury Club, Salisbury Racecourse, Netherhampton, Salisbury, **Wiltshire**, SP2 8PN, **ENGLAND**.
(T) 01722 326461 **(F)** 01722 412710.
Profile Track/Course. Ref: **YH12388**

SALLY ARNUP

Sally Arnup Sculptor ARCA FRBS, Sculpture Studio & Gallery, Panman Lane, Holtby, York, **Yorkshire (North)**, YO1 5UA, **ENGLAND**.
(T) 01904 489377
(W) www.sallyarnup.com.
Contact/s
Owner: Ms S Arnup
Profile Sculptor.
The character and nature of the individual creatures is captured in the sculptures by working directly from the live animal.
Opening Times
Sp: Open Mon - Sun 09:00. Closed Mon - Sun 18:00.
Su: Open Mon - Sun 09:00. Closed Mon - Sun 18:00.
Au: Open Mon - Sun 09:00. Closed Mon - Sun 18:00.
Wn: Open Mon - Sun 09:00. Closed Mon - Sun 18:00. Ref: **YH12389**

SALLY MITCHELL FINE ARTS

Sally Mitchell Fine Arts, Thorniea, Newark, **Nottinghamshire**, NG22 0RN, **ENGLAND**.
(T) 01777 838234 **(F)** 01777 828198. Ref: **YH12390**

SALSA STUD

Salsa Stud, 6 Great North Rd, Chawston, **Bedfordshire**, MK44 3BD, **ENGLAND**.
(T) 01480 214864 **(F)** 01480 214864.
Contact/s
Owner: Mr D Wattiez
Profile Breeder. No.Staff: 2 Yr. Est: 1990
C.Size: 4 Acres
Opening Times
Telephone for an appointment Ref: **YH12391**

SALT, EDWARD M

Edward M Salt DWCF, 25 Church Hill Drive, Tarporley, **Cheshire**, CW6 0BY, **ENGLAND**.
(T) 01829 732941.
Profile Farrier. Ref: **YH12392**

SALTBURN RIDING SCHOOL

Saltburn Riding School (The), Marske Rd, Saltburn-by-the-Sea, **Cleveland**, TS12 1NR, **ENGLAND**.
(T) 01287 622157.
Contact/s
Secretary: Mrs J Hill
Profile Riding School. Ref: **YH12393**

SALTIRE STABLES

Saltire Stables, Kedlock, Cupar, **Fife**, KY15 4PY, **SCOTLAND**.
(T) 01334 654974 **(F)** 01334 653749
(E) info@saltirestables.co.uk.
Profile Track/Course. Ref: **YH12394**

SAM TURNER & SONS

Sam Turner & Sons Ltd, Darlington Rd, Northallerton, **Yorkshire (North)**, DL6 2XB, **ENGLAND**.
(T) 01609 772422 **(F)** 01609 770653.
Profile Saddlery Retailer. Ref: **YH12395**

SAMBOURNE

Sambourne Hall Farm & Livery, Sambourne Hall Farm, Sambourne, Redditch, **Worcestershire**, B96 6NZ, **ENGLAND**.
(T) 01527 852151.
Contact/s
Owner: Mrs J Hammersley
Profile Horse/Rider Accom, Stable/Livery.
B&B, DIY livery - prices and details available on request. Yr. Est: 1981
Opening Times
The B & B is open all year round, the Livery Yard is open to owners all year. Ref: **YH12396**

SAMPLE, H

H Sample, South View, Great Smeaton, Northallerton, **Yorkshire (North)**, DL6 2ET, **ENGLAND**.
(T) 01609 881303.
Contact/s
Owner: Mr J Sample Ref: **YH12397**

SAMPSON, EDWARD

Edward Sampson, Harbridge Farm Cottage, Ringwood, **Hampshire**, BH24 3PW, **ENGLAND**.
(T) 01425 470273.
Profile Breeder, Farrier. Ref: **YH12398**

SAMPSON, LESLEY

Lesley Sampson, 5 London Rd Cottages, Newmarket, **Suffolk**, CB8 0TW, **ENGLAND**.
(T) 01638 661256. Ref: **YH12399**

SAMPSONS

G K E Sampson & Sons, 39 Howard Rd, Newbury, **Berkshire**, RG14 7QD, **ENGLAND**.
(T) 01635 43204
Affiliated Bodies WCF.
Contact/s
Owner: Mr J Sampson **(Q)** FWCF
Profile Farrier.
Opening Times
Telephone to arrange an appointment Ref: **YH12400**

SAMRO TRAILER UK

Samro Trailer UK, 1 Riverford Rd, Rutherglen, Glasgow, **Lanarkshire (South)**, G73 1AT, **SCOTLAND**.
(T) 07002 020200 **(F)** 0141 6130355.
Contact/s
Partner: Mrs M Gilmour
Profile Transport/Horse Boxes. Ref: **YH12401**

SAMWAYS

Samways Stud Farm, Alvediston, Salisbury, **Wiltshire**, SP5 5LQ, **ENGLAND**.
(T) 01722 780286 **(F)** 01722 780286.
Contact/s
Owner: Mrs C Farrow
Profile Breeder, Holidays, Horse/Rider Accom, Stable/Livery.
Self Catering or B & B holidays, available with your own horse. Telephone for further information
No.Staff: 4 Yr. Est: 1911 C.Size: 216 Acres
Opening Times
Telephone for further information Ref: **YH12402**

SANDALL BEAT STABLES

Sandall Beat Stables, Armthorpe Rd, Doncaster, **Yorkshire (South)**, DN2 5QB, **ENGLAND**.
(T) 01302 831322
(W) www.sandallbeat.plus.com.
Contact/s
Manager: Miss S Hudson-Giddings
Profile Stable/Livery.
Full and DIY livery available. Stabling for 26-28. All weather, floodlit outdoor school. No.Staff: 2
Yr. Est: 1998 C.Size: 15 Acres
Opening Times
Sp: Open Mon - Sun 08:00. Closed Mon - Sun 18:00.
Su: Open Mon - Sun 08:00. Closed Mon - Sun 18:00.
Au: Open Mon - Sun 08:00. Closed Mon - Sun 18:00.
Wn: Open Mon - Sun 08:00. Closed Mon - Sun 18:00.
Telephone between the above hours. Ref: **YH12403**

SANDERS, BROOKE

Brooke Sanders, Chalk Pit Stables, Headley Rd, Epsom, **Surrey**, KT18 6BW, **ENGLAND**.
(T) 01372 278453 **(F)** 01372 276137.
Contact/s
Owner: Miss B Sanders
Profile Trainer. Ref: **YH12404**

SANDERS, DAVID

David Sanders DWCF, 58 Church Green, Staplehurst, Tonbridge, **Kent**, TN12 0RJ, **ENGLAND**.
(T) 01580 892928.
Profile Farrier. Ref: **YH12405**

SANDERS, M V

M V Sanders, The Paddocks, Morleigh, Totnes, **Devon**, **ENGLAND**.
Profile Breeder. Ref: **YH12406**

SANDERSON, BRIAN

Brian Sanderson, Halfacres, Carr Lane, Lathom, Ormskirk, **Lancashire**, L40 4BT, **ENGLAND**.
(T) 01704 894632.
Contact/s
Owner: Mrs B Sanderson
Profile Farrier. Ref: **YH12407**

SANDERSONS T C M

Sandersons T C M, Unit 5 Wallace Court, Winsford Ind Est, Winsford, **Cheshire**, CW7 3PD, **ENGLAND**.
(T) 01606 550668. Ref: **YH12408**

SANDFORD ANIMAL FEEDS

Sandford Animal Feeds, Hill Rd, Sandford, **Somerset (North)**, BS25 5RJ, **ENGLAND**.
(T) 01934 820339.
Profile Supplies. Ref: **YH12409**

SANDFORD PARK STABLES

Sandford Park Stables, Organford Rd, Holton Heath, Poole, **Dorset**, BH16 6JZ, **ENGLAND**.
(T) 01202 621782.
Contact/s
Owner: Miss T Kearley
Profile Riding School. Ref: **YH12410**

SANDHILL FARM STABLES

Sandhill Farm Stables, Sandhill Lane, Eridge, Tunbridge Wells, **Kent**, TN3 9LP, **ENGLAND**.
(T) 01892 662294.
Profile Stable/Livery, Trainer. Ref: **YH12411**

SANDHILL RACING STABLES

Sandhill Racing Stables, Bilbrook, Minehead, **Somerset**, TA24 6HA, **ENGLAND**.
(T) 01984 640366 **(F)** 01984 641124
(M) 07860 729795
(E) racing@pjhobbs.freeserve.co.uk.
Profile Trainer. Ref: **YH12412**

SANDILANDS

Sandilands Equestrian Centre, Sandilands Farm, Rogate, Petersfield, **Hampshire**, GU31 5HU, **ENGLAND**.
(T) 01730 821173.
Contact/s
Owner: Mrs D Potter
Profile Breeder, Equestrian Centre, Stable/Livery.
Breeds Thoroughbred Cross Horses No.Staff: 1
Yr. Est: 1995
Opening Times
Sp: Open Mon - Sun 08:00. Closed Mon - Sun 20:00.
Su: Open Mon - Sun 08:00. Closed Mon - Sun 20:00.
Au: Open Mon - Sun 08:00. Closed Mon - Sun 20:00.
Wn: Open Mon - Sun 08:00. Closed Mon - Sun 20:00. Ref: **YH12413**

SANDILANDS FARM FEEDS

Sandilands Farm Feeds, Dangstein Farm, Rogate, Petersfield, **Hampshire**, GU31 5BZ, **ENGLAND**.
(T) 01730 821553 **(F)** 01730 821553.
Profile Saddlery Retailer. Ref: **YH12414**

SANDON SADDLERY
Sandon Saddlery Co, Rushden Rd, Sandon, Buntingford, **Hertfordshire**, SG9 0QW, **ENGLAND**.
(T) 01763 287247 **(F)** 01763 287249.
Contact/s
Owner: Miss D Dodd-Noble
Profile Saddlery Retailer. **Ref: YH12415**

SANDONS THE SADDLERY
Sandons The Saddlery, Powleys Yard, Bintree Rd, Foulsham, Dereham, **Norfolk**, NR20 5RL, **ENGLAND**.
(T) 01362 683383 **(F)** 01362 683383.
Profile Saddlery Retailer. **Ref: YH12416**

SANDOWN PARK RACECOURSE
Sandown Park Racecourse, Esher, **Surrey**, KT10 9AJ, **ENGLAND**.
(T) 01372 463072 **(F)** 01372 465205.
Contact/s
Clerk of Course: Andrew Cooper
Profile Track/Course. **Ref: YH12417**

SANDRA'S RIDING SCHOOL
Sandra's Riding School, Dairy Hse Farm Bungalow, Mason's Bridge Rd, Redhill, **Surrey**, RH1 5JU, **ENGLAND**.
(T) 01737 765096. **Ref: YH12418**

SANDRIDGEBURY
Sandridgebury Livery and Riding Stables, Sandridgebury Farm, Sandridgebury Lane, Sandridge, St Albans, **Hertfordshire**, AL3 6JB, **ENGLAND**.
(T) 01727 854977.
Contact/s
Owner: Mrs C Burrows
Profile Stable/Livery. **Ref: YH12419**

SANDS FARM EQUITATION CTRE
Sands Farm Equitation Centre, Sands Farm, Northlands Rd, Warnham, Horsham, **Sussex (West)**, RH12 3SQ, **ENGLAND**.
(T) 01403 252238 **(F)** 01903 893433.
Contact/s
Secretary: Mrs L Wayman
Profile Riding School. **Ref: YH12420**

SANDWELL VALLEY RIDING CTRE
Sandwell Valley Riding Centre, Wigmore Farm, Wigmore Lane, West Bromwich, **Midlands (West)**, B71 3SU, **ENGLAND**.
(T) 0121 5882103 **(F)** 0121 5882103.
Contact/s
Owner: Mr T Lewis
Profile Riding School, Saddlery Retailer, Stable/Livery. **Ref: YH12421**

SANDWICH ANIMAL FEEDS
Sandwich Animal Feeds, White Mill, Ash Rd, Sandwich, **Kent**, CT13 9JB, **ENGLAND**.
(T) 01304 613402.
Contact/s
Owner: Mrs M Lewington-Turnbull
Profile Saddlery Retailer. **Ref: YH12422**

SANDY BAY TRECKING CTRE
Sandy Bay Trecking Centre, North Seaton, Ashington, **Northumberland**, NE63 9YD, **ENGLAND**.
(T) 01670 523733.
Contact/s
Owner: Mr M Harvey
Profile Equestrian Centre. **Ref: YH12423**

SANDY BROW RACING STABLES
Sandy Brow Racing Stables, Sandybrow, Forest Rd, Cotebrook, Tarporley, **Cheshire**, CW6 9EG, **ENGLAND**.
(T) 01829 760762.
Profile Trainer. **Ref: YH12424**

SANDY LANE RIDING SCHOOL
Sandy Lane Riding School, Mount Pleasant Farm, Sandy Lane, Allerton, Bradford, **Yorkshire (West)**, BD15 9JU, **ENGLAND**.
(T) 01274 543853. **Ref: YH12425**

SANDY'S SADDLERY
Sandy's Saddlery, Northfield Rd, Soham, Ely, **Cambridgeshire**, CB7 5UF, **ENGLAND**.
(T) 01353 721769 **(F)** 01353 720664.
Contact/s
Owner: Ms S Wells
Profile Saddlery Retailer. **Ref: YH12426**

SANSOM & DODWELL
Sansom & Dodwell, Oakhill Veterinary Ctre, Lake Rd, Windermere, **Cumbria**, LA23 2EQ, **ENGLAND**.
(T) 01539 488555 **(F)** 01539 442859.
Profile Medical Support. **Ref: YH12427**

SANSOM, B P A
B P A Sansom, 4 Orchard Cl, Wilmington, Honiton, **Devon**, EX14 9JH, **ENGLAND**.
(T) 01404 831511.
Profile Farrier. **Ref: YH12428**

SANSOMS SADDLERY
Sansoms Saddlery, 11B The High St, Eynsham, Witney, **Oxfordshire**, OX29 4HA, **ENGLAND**.
(T) 01865 884466 **(F)** 01865 884466
(M) 07771 596563
(E) sansoms@aol.com
(W) www.sansomssaddlery.co.uk.
Contact/s
Owner: Mr K McArdle
Profile Riding Wear Retailer, Saddlery Retailer. Repairs to leather goods can be made on site.
Yr. Est: 1996
Opening Times
Sp: Open Mon - Sat 09:30. Closed Mon - Sat 17:30.
Su: Open Mon - Sat 09:30. Closed Mon - Sat 17:30.
Au: Open Mon - Sat 09:30. Closed Mon - Sat 17:30.
Wn: Open Mon - Sat 09:30. Closed Mon - Sat 17:30.
Closed Sundays **Ref: YH12429**

SANT, C J
C J Sant, Lancaster Hse, Whitmore Rd, Newcastle, **Staffordshire**, ST5 4DG, **ENGLAND**.
(T) 01782 658369.
Profile Stable/Livery. **Ref: YH12430**

SAPPERTON STUD & SADDLERY
Sapperton Stud & Saddlery, Chestnuts Farm, Sapperton, Sleaford, **Lincolnshire**, NG34 0TB, **ENGLAND**.
(T) 01476 585241.
Profile Breeder, Saddlery Retailer. **Ref: YH12431**

SARACEN FEEDS
Saracen Horse Feeds, Bradleys Mill, Speldhurst, Tunbridge Wells, **Kent**, TN3 0NG, **ENGLAND**.
(T) 01892 863236 **(F)** 01892 863478
(E) info@saracen-horse-feeds.co.uk
(W) www.saracen-horse-feeds.co.uk.
Contact/s
Marketing Manager: Mr J Scott
Profile Feed Merchant.
Visit the website for more details on the range of feeds available. **Ref: YH12432**

SARAH ANHOLT
Sarah Anholt Saddler, Primmore Farm, Hedging, North Newton, Bridgwater, **Somerset**, TA7 0DF, **ENGLAND**.
(T) 01278 662896.
Profile Saddlery Retailer. **Ref: YH12433**

SARAH'S ROSETTES
Sarah's Rosettes, 5 Murray Ave, Traves, Ellon, **Aberdeenshire**, AB41 7LZ, **SCOTLAND**.
(T) 01651 851381 **(F)** 01651 851381.
Contact/s
Owner: Ms S Pumfrett
(E) sarahsrosettes@quista.net
Profile Supplies.
Open all year for local, national and international orders. In addition to the full standard range, we can supply exceptional rosettes with engraved centres for very special occasions. **Ref: YH12434**

SARA'S
Sara's, 17 Albert Rd, Barnoldswick, **Lancashire**, BB18 5AA, **ENGLAND**.
(T) 01282 817600.
Contact/s
Owner: Mr S Bower **Ref: YH12435**

SARGEANT, C R
C R Sargeant, 17 Rollestons, Writtle, Chelmsford, **Essex**, CM1 3JT, **ENGLAND**.
(T) 01245 422636.
Profile Farrier. **Ref: YH12436**

SARGENT & SONS
Sargent & Sons, Tipton Mills, Sidmouth, **Devon**, EX10 0JX, **ENGLAND**.
(T) 01404 812120.
Profile Supplies. **Ref: YH12437**

SARGENT, C B
C B Sargent, Unit 2, Croxstalls Pl, Walsall, **Midlands (West)**, WS3 2PP, **ENGLAND**.
(T) 01922 496677 **(F)** 01922 494000.
Contact/s
Owner: Mr C Sargent
Profile Supplies. **Ref: YH12438**

SARIAH ARABIAN STUD
Sariah Arabian Stud, Triple Bar Riding Ctre, Abinger Common, Broadmoor, Dorking, **Surrey**, RH5 6JY, **ENGLAND**.
(T) 01306 730959
(E) sariah-arabians@lineone.net
(W) http://website.lineone.net/~sariah-arabians/.
Contact/s
Owner: Mrs S Morgan
Profile Horse/Rider Accom. Yr. Est: 1981
C.Size: 600 Acres
Opening Times
Sp: Open Mon - Sun 08:00. Closed Mon - Sun 12:00.
Su: Open Mon - Sun 08:00. Closed Mon - Sun 12:00.
Au: Open Mon - Sun 08:00. Closed Mon - Sun 12:00.
Wn: Open Mon - Sun 08:00. Closed Mon - Sun 12:00. **Ref: YH12439**

SATCHELL, DOMINIC M
Dominic M Satchell DWCF, Flat 1 229A Worcester Rd, Malvern, **Worcestershire**, WR14 1SU, **ENGLAND**.
(T) 01684 572551.
Profile Farrier. **Ref: YH12440**

SATELLITE INFORMATION SVS
Satellite Information Services Ltd, Satellite Hse, 17 Corsham St, London, **London (Greater)**, N1 6DR, **ENGLAND**.
(T) 020 72532232 **(F)** 020 72513737.
Contact/s
Chief Executive: Jeremy Bridge **Ref: YH12441**

SAUCHENHALL RIDING SCHOOL
Sauchenhall Riding School, Sauchenhall Stables, Gartshore Rd, Kirkintilloch, **Glasgow (City of)**, G66 3TF, **SCOTLAND**.
(T) 0141 7761359.
Profile Riding School. **Ref: YH12442**

SAUNDERS SADDLERY
Saunders Saddlery Ltd, Units 9B Chadwick Ind Est, Stourport-on-Severn, **Worcestershire**, DY13 9QW, **ENGLAND**.
(T) 01299 251500 **(F)** 01299 251045.
Profile Saddlery Retailer. **Ref: YH12443**

SAUNDERS, ANDREW M
Andrew M Saunders DWCF, 2 The Cottages, Honeymead, Simonsbath, Minehead, **Somerset**, TA24 7JX, **ENGLAND**.
(T) 01643 831697.
Profile Farrier. **Ref: YH12444**

SAUNDERS, BRIAN J
Brian J Saunders DWCF, 24 Grosvenor Gardens, Biggleswade, **Bedfordshire**, SG18 0NF, **ENGLAND**.
(T) 01767 600332.
Profile Farrier. **Ref: YH12445**

SAUNDERS, E
E Saunders, 16 Bran End Fields, Stebbing, Dunmow, **Essex**, CM6 3RN, **ENGLAND**.
(T) 01371 856646.
Contact/s
Owner: Mr E Saunders
Profile Farrier. **Ref: YH12446**

SAUNDERS, H W
H W Saunders, 81 High St, Worthing, **Sussex (West)**, BN11 1DN, **ENGLAND**.
(T) 01903 236377.
Profile Blacksmith. **Ref: YH12447**

SAUNDERS, HAROLD DUNCAN
Harold Duncan Saunders, Leyland Hse, 22 Botts Lane, Appleby Magna, Swadlincote, **Derbyshire**, DE12 7AL, **ENGLAND**.
(T) 01530 270253.
Profile Farrier. **Ref: YH12448**

SAUNDERS, J & S
J & S Saunders, 13 Hill Rd, Portchester, Fareham, **Hampshire**, **ENGLAND**.
(T) 023 9232 6526.
Profile Breeder. **Ref: YH12449**

SAUNDERS, MICHAEL
Michael Saunders, 19 Station Rd, Pontrhydyfen, **Neath Port Talbot**, SA12 9SE, **WALES**.
(T) 01639 884577.
Profile Farrier. **Ref: YH12450**

SAUNDERS, NEIL J
Neil J Saunders DWCF, 76 Dunstable Rd,

Totternhoe, Dunstable, **Bedfordshire**, LU6 1QP, **ENGLAND**.
(T) 01582 666888.
Profile Farrier. **Ref: YH12451**

SAUNDERSON, NOEL

Noel Saunderson DWCF; Noel, 6 Red Lane, Meltham, Huddersfield, **Yorkshire (West)**, HD7 3LG, **ENGLAND**.
(T) 01484 851218.
Profile Farrier. **Ref: YH12452**

SAVAGE, E A

Mr E A Savage, The Homestead, Daffy Green, Shipdham, Thetford, **Norfolk**, IP25 7QQ, **ENGLAND**.
(T) 01362 821445.
Profile Supplies. **Ref: YH12453**

SAVAGE, P H

P H Savage, Downings, Norton Rd, Teynham, Sittingbourne, **Kent**, ME9 9JU, **ENGLAND**.
(T) 01795 522089.
Contact/s
Owner: Mrs N Savage
Profile Farrier. **Ref: YH12454**

SAVILL, ROBBIE

Robbie Savill, The Forge, Hockens Hse, St. Cleer, Liskeard, **Cornwall**, PL14 6EF, **ENGLAND**.
(T) 01579 347777.
Contact/s
Owner: Mr R Saville
Profile Blacksmith. **Ref: YH12455**

SAVILLE, LOUISE

Louise Saville, Syerston, Newark, **Nottinghamshire**, NG23 5NE, **ENGLAND**.
(T) 01636 525341 **(F)** 01636 525341.
Profile Trainer. **Ref: YH12456**

SAVOIR FARE

Savoir Fare, 28 Ashby Rd, Woodville, Burton-on-Trent, **Staffordshire**, DE11 7BY, **ENGLAND**.
(T) 01283 212353 **(F)** 01283 213023. **Ref: YH12457**

SAVORY, KEITH

Mr Keith Savory, Hailey Lodge, Coates, Cirencester, **Gloucestershire**, GL7 6LA, **ENGLAND**.
(T) 01285 640067 **(F)** 01285 640067.
Profile Supplies. **Ref: YH12458**

SAWDYE & HARRIS

Messrs Sawdye & Harris, Auctioneers & Valuers, Land Estate Office, West St, Ashburton, **Devon**, TQ13 7DT, **ENGLAND**.
(T) 01364 652304 **(F)** 01364 652762. **Ref: YH12459**

SAWER, NEIL G

Neil G Sawer DWCF, Brigadoon, Tattershall Rd, Boston, **Lincolnshire**, PE21 9NL, **ENGLAND**.
(T) 01205 362234.
Profile Farrier. **Ref: YH12460**

SAWNEY, J

Miss J Sawney, Boy Hill Farm, Seamer, Stokesley, Middlesbrough, **Cleveland**, TS9 5LY, **ENGLAND**.
(T) 01642 590514.
Profile Supplies. **Ref: YH12461**

SAWSTON FARM FEEDS

Sawston Farm Feeds, 12A London Rd Ind Est, Pampisford, **Cambridgeshire**, CB2 4EE, **ENGLAND**.
(T) 01223 837977 **(F)** 01223 834666.
Profile Supplies. **Ref: YH12462**

SAWSTON RIDING SCHOOL

Sawston Riding School, Common Lane, Sawston, Cambridge, **Cambridgeshire**, CB2 4HW, **ENGLAND**.
(T) 01223 835198. **Ref: YH12463**

SAWYERS HALL RIDING ESTAB

Sawyers Hall Riding Estab, Sawyer's Hall Lane, Brentwood, **Essex**, CM15 9BZ, **ENGLAND**.
(T) 01277 220477.
Profile Riding School. **Ref: YH12464**

SAXBY, ALAN K

Alan K Saxby, Hallikeld Hse, Brompton, Northallerton, **Yorkshire (North)**, DL6 2UE, **ENGLAND**.
(T) 01609 773613 **(F)** 01609 770262.
Contact/s
Owner: Mr A Saxby
Profile Stable/Livery, Trainer. **Ref: YH12465**

SAXILBY RIDING SCHOOL

Saxilby Riding School, 40 High St, Saxilby, Lincoln, **Lincolnshire**, LN1 2HA, **ENGLAND**.
(T) 01522 702240.
Contact/s
Owner: Mr M Scott
Profile Riding School, Stable/Livery. **Ref: YH12466**

SAXLEBY STABLES

Saxleby Stables, Saxelby Rd, Asfordby, Melton Mowbray, **Leicestershire**, LE14 3TU, **ENGLAND**.
(T) 01664 813663. **Ref: YH12467**

SAXON GATE STABLES

Saxon Gate Stables, Lambourn, Hungerford, **Berkshire**, RG17 8QH, **ENGLAND**.
(T) 01488 72383
(M) 07836 276464.
Contact/s
Owner: Mr D Arbuthnot
Profile Trainer. **Ref: YH12468**

SAXON HSE STABLES

Saxon House Stables, Upper Lambourn, Hungerford, **Berkshire**, RG17 8QL, **ENGLAND**.
(T) 01488 73436 **(F)** 01488 73436
(M) 07785 300168.
Profile Trainer. **Ref: YH12469**

SAXON SADDLERY

Saxon Saddlery, 5a Kings Rd, Bury St Edmunds, **Suffolk**, IP33 3DJ, **ENGLAND**.
(T) 01284 702323.
Contact/s
Owner: Mr K Birs **Ref: YH12470**

SAXON TACK & TAILS

Saxon Tack & Tails, Lil Bourne Rd, Clifton, Rugby, **Warwickshire**, CV23 0BB, **ENGLAND**.
(T) 01788 546111 **(F)** 01788 562555.
Profile Saddlery Retailer. **Ref: YH12471**

SAXTEAD BOTTOM

Saxtead Bottom Equestrian Centre, Saxtead Bottom Farm, Saxtead Bottoms, Saxtead, Woodbridge, **Suffolk**, IP13 9QS, **ENGLAND**.
(T) 01728 621016. **Ref: YH12472**

SAXTON RIDING CTRE

Saxton Riding Centre, Coldhill Lane, Saxton, Tadcaster, **Yorkshire (North)**, LS24 9TA, **ENGLAND**.
(T) 01937 557436. **Ref: YH12473**

SAYER, H D

Mrs H D Sayer, Town End Farm, Hackthorpe, Penrith, **Cumbria**, CA10 2HX, **ENGLAND**.
(T) 01931 712245
(M) 07889 832347.
Profile Trainer. **Ref: YH12474**

SAYER'S

Sayer's, 66 High St, Yarm, **Cleveland**, TS15 9AH, **ENGLAND**.
(T) 01642 785423 **(F)** 01642 788611.
Contact/s
Owner: Mr D Sayer **Ref: YH12475**

SAYERS, J

J Sayers, Perrybridge Farm, Wokingham Rd, Sandhurst, Camberley, **Hampshire**, GU17 8JB, **ENGLAND**.
(T) 01252 870170.
Profile Breeder. **Ref: YH12476**

SAYERS, MARK

Mark Sayers DWCF, 158 College Rd, College Town, Camberley, **Surrey**, GU15 4RQ, **ENGLAND**.
(T) 01276 600600.
Profile Farrier. **Ref: YH12477**

SAYERS, RICHARD S

Richard S Sayers DWCF, 21 Tesimond Drive, Yateley, **Hampshire**, GU46 6FE, **ENGLAND**.
(T) 01252 651961
(M) 07770 902245.
Profile Farrier. **Ref: YH12478**

SAYWELL, M J

M J Saywell, Grange Farm, Cottam, Retford, **Nottinghamshire**, DN22 0EZ, **ENGLAND**.
(T) 01777 248543.
Profile Breeder. **Ref: YH12479**

SCAIFE, ANDREW

Andrew Scaife DWCF, Crossing Keepers Cottage, Whiley Hill, Coatham Mundeville, **County Durham**, DL3 0XN, **ENGLAND**.
(T) 01325 313721.
Profile Farrier. **Ref: YH12480**

SCALING TRAILERS

Scaling Trailers, The Garth, Terrington, York, **Yorkshire (North)**, YO60 6QB, **ENGLAND**.
(T) 01653 648236.
Contact/s
Owner: Mr P Scaling
Profile Transport/Horse Boxes. **Ref: YH12481**

SCAMELLS SHETLAND STUD

Scamells Shetland Stud, Old Tanyard Farm, Wisborough Green, Billingshurst, **Sussex (West)**, RH14 0BH, **ENGLAND**.
(T) 01403 700277.
Profile Breeder. **Ref: YH12482**

SCAN FIRE + SECURITY SERVICES

Scan Fire + Security Services, 2 Trent Villa, Trent Lane, Colwick, **Nottinghamshire**, N92 4DS, **ENGLAND**.
(T) 0115 9503050 **(F)** 0115 9503050
(W) www.scanfire-security-services.co.uk.
Profile Supplies. **Ref: YH12483**

SCANA EUROSTEEL

Scana Eurosteel Ltd, Ajax Works, Whitehill St, Stockport, **Cheshire**, SK4 1NT, **ENGLAND**.
(T) 0161 4776556 **(F)** 0161 4779339.
Contact/s
Manager: Mr A Pickavanve
Profile Blacksmith. **Ref: YH12484**

SCARBARROW PADDOCK SADDLERY

Scarbarrow Paddock Saddlery, Hardknott Lane, Leece, Ulverston, **Cumbria**, LE12 0QU, **ENGLAND**.
(T) 01229 834930.
Contact/s
Owner: Mr P Lancaster
Profile Saddlery Retailer. **Ref: YH12485**

SCARBOROUGH & DISTRICT

Scarborough & District Riding Club, 59 North St, Scalby, Scarborough, **Yorkshire (North)**, YO13 0RP, **ENGLAND**.
(T) 01723 362953.
Profile Club/Association, Riding Club. **Ref: YH12486**

SCARCROFT HALL LIVERIES

Scarcroft Hall Liveries, Scarcroft Hall Farm, Thorner Lane, Scarcroft, Leeds, **Yorkshire (West)**, LS14 3AQ, **ENGLAND**.
(T) 0113 2893095. **Ref: YH12487**

SCARLETT RIBBONS

Scarlett Ribbons, Scarlett Hse, Wellington St West, Halifax, **Yorkshire (West)**, HX1 2TQ, **ENGLAND**.
(T) 01422 342020 **(F)** 01422 341220.
Contact/s
Owner: Mr A Douglas
Profile Supplies. **Ref: YH12488**

SCARSDALE VETNRY HOSPITAL

Scarsdale Veterinary Hospital, Farm & Equine Branch, Markeaton Lane, Markeaton, **Derbyshire**, DE22 4NH, **ENGLAND**.
(T) 01332 294929 **(F)** 01332 347216.
Profile Medical Support. **Ref: YH12489**

SCARSDALE VETNRY HOSPITAL

Scarsdale Veterinary Hospital, 45-47 Kedleston Rd, Derby, **Derbyshire**, DE22 1FN, **ENGLAND**.
(T) 01332 345191 **(F)** 01332 298152.
Profile Medical Support. **Ref: YH12490**

SCATS

Scats (Hampshire), Capital Hse, 48-52 Andover Rd, Winchester, **Hampshire**, SO23 7XB, **ENGLAND**.
(T) 01962 875200 **(F)** 01962 841760.
Profile Saddlery Retailer. **Ref: YH12491**

SCATS

Scats (Isle of Wight), Southbank, Blackwater Rd, Newport, **Isle of Wight**, PO30 3BG, **ENGLAND**.
(T) 01983 522241 **(F)** 01983 527977.
Profile Supplies. **Ref: YH12492**

SCATS COUNTRYSTORE

Scats Countrystore (Newbury), Kiln Rd, Shaw, Newbury, **Berkshire**, RG13 2HH, **ENGLAND**.
(T) 01635 43436 **(F)** 01635 581296
(E) newbury.countrystore@scats.co.uk
(W) www.scatscountrystores.co.uk.
Profile Riding Wear Retailer, Supplies.
Opening Times
Sp: Open Mon - Sat 08:30, Sun 10:00. Closed Mon - Sat 17:30, Sun 16:00.
Su: Open Mon - Sat 08:30, Sun 10:00. Closed Mon - Sat 17:30, Sun 16:00.
Au: Open Mon - Sat 08:30, Sun 10:00. Closed Mon - Sat 17:30, Sun 16:00.
Wn: Open Mon - Sat 08:30, Sun 10:00. Closed Mon - Sat 17:30, Sun 16:00.
Open Bank Holidays 10:00 - 16:00 **Ref: YH12493**

SCATS COUNTRYSTORE

Scats Countrystore (Dorchester), Grove Trading Est, Dorchester, **Dorset**, DT1 1ST, **ENGLAND**.
(T) 01305 262141 **(F)** 01305 251037
(E) dorchester.countrystore@scats.co.uk
(W) www.scatscountrystores.co.uk.
Profile Riding Wear Retailer, Supplies.
Opening Times
Sp: Open Mon - Sat 08:30. Closed Mon - Sat 17:30.
Su: Open Mon - Sat 08:30. Closed Mon - Sat 17:30.
Au: Open Mon - Sat 08:30. Closed Mon - Sat 17:30.
Wn: Open Mon - Sat 08:30. Closed Mon - Sat 17:30.
Closed Bank Holidays **Ref: YH12494**

SCATS COUNTRYSTORE

Scats Countrystore (Gillingham), Old Market Ctre, Station Rd, Gillingham, **Dorset**, SP8 4QQ, **ENGLAND**.
(T) 01747 824933 **(F)** 01747 826100
(E) gillingham.countrystore@scats.co.uk
(W) www.scatscountrystores.co.uk.
Profile Riding Wear Retailer, Supplies.
Opening Times
Sp: Open Mon - Sat 08:30, Sun 10:00. Closed Mon - Sat 17:30, Sun 16:00.
Su: Open Mon - Sat 08:30, Sun 10:00. Closed Mon - Sat 17:30, Sun 16:00.
Au: Open Mon - Sat 08:30, Sun 10:00. Closed Mon - Sat 17:30, Sun 16:00.
Wn: Open Mon - Sat 08:30, Sun 10:00. Closed Mon - Sat 17:30, Sun 16:00.
Open Bank Holidays 10:00 - 16:00 **Ref: YH12495**

SCATS COUNTRYSTORE

Scats Countrystore (Winterborne Kingston), Winterbourne Kingston, Blandford, **Dorset**, DT11 9AZ, **ENGLAND**.
(T) 01929 471789 **(F)** 01929 472202
(E) winterbourne.countrystore@scats.co.uk
(W) www.scatscountrystores.co.uk.
Profile Riding Wear Retailer, Supplies.
Opening Times
Sp: Open Mon - Fri 08:00, Sat 08:30. Closed Mon - Fri 17:30, Sat 17:00.
Su: Open Mon - Fri 08:00, Sat 08:30. Closed Mon - Fri 17:30, Sat 17:00.
Au: Open Mon - Fri 08:00, Sat 08:30. Closed Mon - Fri 17:30, Sat 17:00.
Wn: Open Mon - Fri 08:00, Sat 08:30. Closed Mon - Fri 17:30, Sat 17:00.
Closed Bank Holidays **Ref: YH12496**

SCATS COUNTRYSTORE

Scats Countrystore (Romsey), Station Rd, Romsey, **Hampshire**, SO5 8DP, **ENGLAND**.
(T) 01794 514426 **(F)** 01794 518416
(E) romsey.countrystore@scats.co.uk
(W) www.scatscountrystores.co.uk.
Profile Riding Wear Retailer, Supplies.
Opening Times
Sp: Open Mon - Sat 08:30, Sun 10:00. Closed Mon - Sat 17:30, Sun 16:00.
Su: Open Mon - Sat 08:30, Sun 10:00. Closed Mon - Sat 17:30, Sun 16:00.
Au: Open Mon - Sat 08:30, Sun 10:00. Closed Mon - Sat 17:30, Sun 16:00.
Wn: Open Mon - Sat 08:30, Sun 10:00. Closed Mon - Sat 17:30, Sun 16:00.
Open Bank Holidays 10:00 - 16:00 **Ref: YH12497**

SCATS COUNTRYSTORE

Scats Countrystore (Winchester), Easton Lane, Winnall, Winchester, **Hampshire**, SO23 7RU, **ENGLAND**.
(T) 01962 863007 **(F)** 01962 843761
(E) winchester.countrystore@scats.co.uk
(W) www.scatscountrystores.co.uk.
Profile Riding Wear Retailer, Supplies.
Opening Times
Sp: Open Mon - Sat 08:30, Sun 16:00. Closed Mon - Sat 17:30, Sun 16:00.
Su: Open Mon - Sat 08:30, Sun 16:00. Closed Mon - Sat 17:30, Sun 16:00.
Au: Open Mon - Sat 08:30, Sun 16:00. Closed Mon - Sat 17:30, Sun 16:00.
Wn: Open Mon - Sat 08:30, Sun 16:00. Closed Mon - Sat 17:30, Sun 16:00.
Open Bank Holidays 10:00 - 16:00 **Ref: YH12498**

SCATS COUNTRYSTORE

Scats Countrystore (Alton), Inhams Rd, Holybourne, Alton, **Hampshire**, GU34 4EX, **ENGLAND**.
(T) 01420 83511 **(F)** 01420 541612
(E) alton.countrystore@scats.co.uk.
Profile Riding Wear Retailer, Supplies.
Opening Times
Sp: Open Mon - Sat 08:00. Closed Mon - Sat 17:00.
Su: Open Mon - Sat 08:00. Closed Mon - Sat 17:00.
Au: Open Mon - Sat 08:00. Closed Mon - Sat 17:00.
Wn: Open Mon - Sat 08:00. Closed Mon - Sat 17:00.
Closed on Bank Holidays **Ref: YH12499**

SCATS COUNTRYSTORE

Scats Countrystore (Andover), 134 Weyhill Rd, Andover, **Hampshire**, SP10 3BH, **ENGLAND**.
(T) 01264 323482 **(F)** 01264 365002
(E) andover.countrystore@scats.co.uk
(W) www.scatscountrystores.co.uk.
Profile Riding Wear Retailer, Supplies.
Opening Times
Sp: Open Mon - Sat 08:30, Sun 10:00. Closed Mon - Sat 17:30, Sun 16:00.
Su: Open Mon - Sat 08:30, Sun 10:00. Closed Mon - Sat 17:30, Sun 16:00.
Au: Open Mon - Sat 08:30, Sun 10:00. Closed Mon - Sat 17:30, Sun 16:00.
Wn: Open Mon - Sat 08:30, Sun 10:00. Closed Mon - Sat 17:30, Sun 16:00.
Open Bank Holidays 10:00 - 16:00 **Ref: YH12500**

SCATS COUNTRYSTORE

Scats Countrystore (Basingstoke), Wildmoor Lane, Sherfield-On-Loddon, Basingstoke, **Hampshire**, RG27 0HA, **ENGLAND**.
(T) 01256 882776 **(F)** 01256 883785
(E) basingstoke.countrystore@scats.co.uk
(W) www.scatscountrystores.co.uk.
Profile Riding Wear Retailer, Supplies.
Opening Times
Sp: Open Mon - Sat 08:30, Sun 10:00. Closed Mon - Sat 17:30, Sun 16:00.
Su: Open Mon - Sat 08:30, Sun 10:00. Closed Mon - Sat 17:30, Sun 16:00.
Au: Open Mon - Sat 08:30, Sun 10:00. Closed Mon - Sat 17:30, Sun 16:00.
Wn: Open Mon - Sat 08:30, Sun 10:00. Closed Mon - Sat 17:30, Sun 16:00.
Open on Bank Holidays 10:00 - 16:00 **Ref: YH12501**

SCATS COUNTRYSTORE

Scats Countrystore (Lymington), Mount Pleasant Lane, Sway Rd, Lymington, **Hampshire**, SO41 9ZS, **ENGLAND**.
(T) 01590 676633 **(F)** 01590 610198
(E) lymington.countrystore@scats.co.uk
(W) www.scatscountrystores.co.uk.
Profile Riding Wear Retailer, Supplies.
Opening Times
Sp: Open Mon - Sat 08:30, Sun 10:00. Closed Mon - Sat 17:30, Sun 16:00.
Su: Open Mon - Sat 08:30, Sun 10:00. Closed Mon - Sat 17:30, Sun 16:00.
Au: Open Mon - Sat 08:30, Sun 10:00. Closed Mon - Sat 17:30, Sun 16:00.
Wn: Open Mon - Sat 08:30, Sun 10:00. Closed Mon - Sat 17:30, Sun 16:00.
Open Bank Holidays 10:00 - 16:00 **Ref: YH12502**

SCATS COUNTRYSTORE

Scats Countrystore (Newport), Southbank, Blackwater Road, Newport, **Isle of Wight**, PO30 5GB, **ENGLAND**.
(T) 01983 524352 **(F)** 01983 525682
(E) newport.countrystore@scats.co.uk
(W) www.scatscountrystores.co.uk.
Profile Riding Wear Retailer, Supplies.
Opening Times
Sp: Open Mon - Sat 08:00, Sun 10:00. Closed Mon - Sat 17:00, Sun 16:00.
Su: Open Mon - Sat 08:00, Sun 10:00. Closed Mon - Sat 17:00, Sun 16:00.
Au: Open Mon - Sat 08:00, Sun 10:00. Closed Mon - Sat 17:00, Sun 16:00.
Wn: Open Mon - Sat 08:00, Sun 10:00. Closed Mon - Sat 17:00, Sun 16:00.
Open Bank Holidays 10:00 - 16:00 **Ref: YH12503**

SCATS COUNTRYSTORE

Scats Countrystore (Canterbury), Maynard Rd, Wincheap Ind Est, Canterbury, **Kent**, CT1 3RH, **ENGLAND**.
(T) 01227 781398 **(F)** 01227 785134
(E) canterbury.countrystore@scats.co.uk
(W) www.scatscountrystores.co.uk.
Profile Riding Wear Retailer, Supplies.
Opening Times
Sp: Open Mon - Sat 08:30. Closed Mon - Sat 17:30.
Su: Open Mon - Sat 08:30. Closed Mon - Sat 17:30.
Au: Open Mon - Sat 08:30. Closed Mon - Sat 17:30.
Wn: Open Mon - Sat 08:30. Closed Mon - Sat 17:30.
Closed Bank Holidays **Ref: YH12504**

SCATS COUNTRYSTORE

Scats Countrystore (Marden), Pattenden Lane, Marden, **Kent**, TN12 9QS, **ENGLAND**.
(T) 01622 831685 **(F)** 01622 832204
(E) marden.countrystore@scats.co.uk
(W) www.scatscountrystores.co.uk.
Profile Riding Wear Retailer, Supplies.
Opening Times
Sp: Open Mon - Sat 08:00. Closed Mon - Sat 17:00.
Su: Open Mon - Sat 08:00. Closed Mon - Sat 17:00.
Au: Open Mon - Sat 08:00. Closed Mon - Sat 17:00.
Wn: Open Mon - Sat 08:00. Closed Mon - Sat 17:00.
Closed Bank Holidays **Ref: YH12505**

SCATS COUNTRYSTORE

Scats Countrystore (Faringdon), The Old Railway Station, Park Rd, Faringdon, **Oxfordshire**, SN7 7BP, **ENGLAND**.
(T) 01367 241768 **(F)** 01367 243962
(E) faringdon.countrystore@scats.co.uk
(W) www.scatscountrystores.co.uk.
Contact/s
Manager: Mrs S Cook
Profile Riding Wear Retailer, Supplies.
Opening Times
Sp: Open Mon - Sat 08:30. Closed Mon - Sat 17:30.
Su: Open Mon - Sat 08:30. Closed Mon - Sat 17:30.
Au: Open Mon - Sat 08:30. Closed Mon - Sat 17:30.
Wn: Open Mon - Sat 08:30. Closed Mon - Sat 17:30.
Closed Bank Holidays **Ref: YH12506**

SCATS COUNTRYSTORE

Scats Countrystore (Godalming), Brighton Rd, Godalming, **Surrey**, GU37 1NS, **ENGLAND**.
(T) 01483 415101 **(F)** 01483 423581
(E) godalming.countrystore@scats.co.uk
(W) www.scatscountrystores.co.uk.
Profile Riding Wear Retailer, Supplies.
Opening Times
Sp: Open Mon - Sat 08:30, Sun 10:00. Closed Mon - Sat 17:30, Sun 16:00.
Su: Open Mon - Sat 08:30, Sun 10:00. Closed Mon - Sat 17:30, Sun 16:00.
Au: Open Mon - Sat 08:30, Sun 10:00. Closed Mon - Sat 17:30, Sun 16:00.
Wn: Open Mon - Sat 08:30, Sun 10:00. Closed Mon - Sat 17:30, Sun 16:00.
Open Bank Holidays 10:00 - 16:00 **Ref: YH12507**

SCATS COUNTRYSTORE

Scats Countrystore (Redhill), Kingsmill Lane, South Nutfield, Redhill, **Surrey**, RH1 5NB, **ENGLAND**.
(T) 01737 823205 **(F)** 01737 822845
(E) redhill.countrystores@scats.co.uk
(W) www.scatscountrystores.co.uk.
Profile Riding Wear Retailer, Supplies.
Opening Times
Sp: Open Mon - Sat 08:30. Closed Mon - Sat 17:30.
Su: Open Mon - Sat 08:30. Closed Mon - Sat 17:30.
Au: Open Mon - Sat 08:30. Closed Mon - Sat 17:30.
Wn: Open Mon - Sat 08:30. Closed Mon - Sat 17:30.
Closed Bank Holidays **Ref: YH12508**

SCATS COUNTRYSTORE

Scats Countrystore (Heathfield), Station Rd, Heathfield, **Sussex (East)**, TN21 8DJ, **ENGLAND**.
(T) 01435 866938 **(F)** 01435 860710
(E) heathfield.countrystore@scats.co.uk
(W) www.scatscountrystores.co.uk.
Profile Riding Wear Retailer, Supplies.
Opening Times
Sp: Open Mon - Sat 08:30. Closed Mon - Fri 17:30, Sat 17:00.
Su: Open Mon - Sat 08:30. Closed Mon - Fri 17:30, Sat 17:00.
Au: Open Mon - Sat 08:30. Closed Mon - Fri 17:30, Sat 17:00.
Wn: Open Mon - Sat 08:30. Closed Mon - Fri 17:30, Sat 17:00.
Closed Bank Holidays **Ref: YH12509**

SCATS COUNTRYSTORE

Scats Countrystore (Billingshurst), Frenches Corner, Billingshurst, **Sussex (West)**, RH14 9LR, **ENGLAND**.
(T) 01403 782031 **(F)** 01403 785033
(E) billinghurst.countrystore@scats.co.uk
(W) www.scatscountrystores.co.uk.
Profile Riding Wear Retailer, Supplies.
Opening Times
Sp: Open Mon - Sat 08:00. Closed Mon - Sat 17:00.
Su: Open Mon - Sat 08:00. Closed Mon - Sat 17:00.
Au: Open Mon - Sat 08:00. Closed Mon - Sat 17:00.
Wn: Open Mon - Sat 08:00. Closed Mon - Sat 17:00.
Closed Bank Holidays **Ref: YH12510**

SCATS COUNTRYSTORE

Scats Countrystore (Salisbury), Churchfields Rd, Salisbury, **Wiltshire**, SP2 7PP, **ENGLAND**.
(T) 01722 336886 **(F)** 01772 338096
(E) salisbury.countrystore@scats.co.uk
(W) www.scatscountrystores.co.uk.
Profile Riding Wear Retailer, Supplies.
Opening Times
Sp: Open Mon - Sat 08:30, Sun 10:00. Closed Mon - Sat 17:30, Sun 16:00.
Su: Open Mon - Sat 08:30, Sun 10:00. Closed Mon -

Sat 17:30, Sun 16:00.
Au: Open Mon - Sat 08:30, Sun 10:00. Closed Mon - Sat 17:30, Sun 16:00.
Wn: Open Mon - Sat 08:30, Sun 10:00. Closed Mon - Sat 17:30, Sun 16:00.
Open Bank Holidays 10:00 - 16:00 **Ref: YH12511**

SCATS COUNTRYSTORE

Scats Countrystore (Devizes), Nursteed Trading Est, Mill Rd, Devizes, **Wiltshire**, SN10 3DY, **ENGLAND**.
(T) 01380 721594 **(F)** 01380 730193
(E) devizes.countrystore@scats.co.uk
(W) www.scatscountrystores.co.uk.
Profile Riding Wear Retailer, Supplies.
Opening Times
Sp: Open Mon - Sat 08:30. Closed Mon - Sat 17:30.
Su: Open Mon - Sat 08:30. Closed Mon - Sat 17:30.
Au: Open Mon - Sat 08:30. Closed Mon - Sat 17:30.
Wn: Open Mon - Sat 08:30. Closed Mon - Sat 17:30.
Closed Bank Holidays **Ref: YH12512**

SCE

Stanway Commercial Engineering Ltd, Gatherley Rd Ind Est, Brompton On Swale, Richmond, **Yorkshire (North)**, DL10 7JQ, **ENGLAND**.
(T) 01748 812336 **(F)** 01748 812338.
Profile Transport/Horse Boxes. **Ref: YH12513**

SCHMITT, H & U

H & U Schmitt, Castell, Ffostrasol, Llandysul, **Carmarthenshire**, SA44 5JS, **WALES**.
(T) 01239 851584.
Profile Breeder. **Ref: YH12514**

SCHNIEDER RIDING BOOT

Schnieder Riding Boot Co, 16 Clifford St, London, **London (Greater)**, W1X 1RG, **ENGLAND**.
(T) 020 74376775.
Contact/s
Owner: Mr R Schnieder
Profile Saddlery Retailer. **Ref: YH12515**

SCHNIEDER RIDING BOOT

Schnieder Riding Boot Co, 62 St Michaels Rd, Northampton, **Northamptonshire**, NN1 3JU, **ENGLAND**.
(T) 01604 639121 **(F)** 01604 627682.
Contact/s
Manager: Mr V Barker
Profile Saddlery Retailer. **Ref: YH12516**

SCHONBRUNN HORSES

Schonbrunn Horses, Schonbrunn Manor, Blunsdon Hill, Blunsdon, Swindon, **Wiltshire**, SN26 8BZ, **ENGLAND**.
(T) 01793 702169 **(F)** 01793 702169.
Profile Breeder. **Ref: YH12517**

SCHOOL FARM EQUESTRIAN

School Farm Equestrian Ltd, 1 Canefield Cottages, Romsey Rd, Lockerley, Romsey, **Hampshire**, SO51 0JA, **ENGLAND**.
(T) 01794 341196. **Ref: YH12518**

SCHOOL FARM PETS & SUPPLIES

School Farm Pets & Supplies, School Farm, Mill Rd, Shelfield, Walsall, **Midlands (West)**, WS4 1BT, **ENGLAND**.
(T) 01922 682335.
Profile Supplies. **Ref: YH12519**

SCHOOL FARM TRAINING CTRE

School Farm Training Centre, School Farm, 1 Canefield Cottage, Romsey Rd, Lockerley, Romsey, **Hampshire**, SO51 0JA, **ENGLAND**.
(T) 01794 341196.
Profile Stable/Livery. **Ref: YH12520**

SCHOOL OF NATIONAL EQUITATION

School Of National Equitation, Bunny Hill Top, Costock, Loughborough, **Leicestershire**, LE12 6XE, **ENGLAND**.
(T) 01509 852366 **(F)** 01509 856067
(E) info@bunny-hill.co.uk
(W) www.bunny-hill.co.uk.
Contact/s
Instructor: Ms J Dwerryhose **(Q)** BHSII
Profile Riding School, Riding Wear Retailer, Saddlery Retailer, Stable/Livery, Supplies.
Unaffiliated showjumping and dressage. Train Pony Club teams. The tack shop also offers horse clothing and accessories. **No.Staff:** 6 **Yr. Est:** 1971
C.Size: 40 Acres
Opening Times
Sp: Open 09:00. Closed 18:00.
Su: Open 09:00. Closed 18:00.
Au: Open 09:00. Closed 18:00.
Wn: Open 09:00. Closed 18:00. **Ref: YH12521**

SCHOOL OF ST MARY & ST ANNE

School of St Mary & St Anne, Lichfield, **Staffordshire**, WS15 3BW, **ENGLAND**.
(T) 01283 840232 **(F)** 01283 840988
(E) abgirls@compuserve.com.
Profile Equestrian Centre. **Ref: YH12522**

SCHOOLS & UNIVERSITIES POLO

Schools & Universities Polo Association, Bolebrook Wood Farm, Edenbridge Rd, Hartfield, **Sussex (East)**, TN7 4JJ, **ENGLAND**.
(T) 01892 770591 **(F)** 01892 770899.
Profile Club/Association. **Ref: YH12523**

SCHUMACHER, GEORGE

George Schumacher, Unit 1 R A C Est, Faringdon, **Oxfordshire**, SN7 8LA, **ENGLAND**.
(T) 01367 244697 **(F)** 01367 242819.
Profile Supplies. **Ref: YH12524**

SCIMGEOUR, ANNABEL

Annabel Scimgeour, 5 Jefferies Cl, College Fields, Marlborough, **Wiltshire**, SN8 1UB, **ENGLAND**.
(T) 01672 514276 **(F)** 01672 514276
(M) 07785 931765.
Profile Trainer. **Ref: YH12525**

SCOBELL, STEVEN CRAIG

Steven Craig Scobell DWCF, Oyster Hill Forge, Clay Hill Lane, Headley, **Surrey**, KT18 6JX, **ENGLAND**.
(T) 01293 775623.
Profile Farrier. **Ref: YH12526**

SCORPION SECURITY

Scorpion Security, 1 The Gate Hse, 90A Bartholemew St, Newbury, **Berkshire**, RG14 2EE, **ENGLAND**.
(T) 01635 43699 **(F)** 01635 43699. **Ref: YH12527**

SCORRAIG EXMOOR PONIES

Scorraig Exmoor Ponies, Scorraig, Dundonnell, Garve, **Highlands**, IV23 2RE, **SCOTLAND**.
(T) 01854 633397
Affiliated Bodies EPS.
Contact/s
Owner: Deborah Davy
Profile Breeder.
Hill Pony Breeder. **Yr. Est:** 1982 **Ref: YH12528**

SCOT, J & A

J & A Scot, Ashby Cottage, Midlem, Selkirk, **Scottish Borders**, TD7 4QD, **SCOTLAND**.
(T) 01835 870244.
Contact/s
Partner: Mr A Scot
Profile Farrier. **Ref: YH12529**

SCOTHORSE

Scothorse, Backmains, Altries, Maryculter, **Aberdeenshire**, **SCOTLAND**.
(T) 01224 732005.
Profile Breeder. **Ref: YH12530**

SCOTT DUNN, ANN

Ann Scott Dunn, Straight Mile Farm, Carters Hill, Billingsbear, Wokingham, **Berkshire**, RG40 5RP, **ENGLAND**.
(T) 01344 51884
Affiliated Bodies NAAT.
Contact/s
Physiotherapist: Ann Scott Dunn
Profile Medical Support. **Ref: YH12531**

SCOTT HALLEYS

Scott Halleys Ltd, Glasgow Rd, Milngavie, **Glasgow (City of)**, G62 6JP, **SCOTLAND**.
(T) 0141 9561126.
Profile Transport/Horse Boxes. **Ref: YH12532**

SCOTT TRAILERS

Scott Trailers, 33 West End, Walcott, Lincoln, **Lincolnshire**, LN4 3ST, **ENGLAND**.
(T) 01526 860741 **(F)** 01526 861357
(E) offfice@scott-trailers.co.uk
(W) www.scott-trailers.co.uk.
Contact/s
Owner: Mr K Scarborough
Profile Transport/Horse Boxes.
Sales, service and repair of road trailers.
No.Staff: 7 **Yr. Est:** 1960
Opening Times
Sp: Open Mon - Thurs, Fri 08:00, Sat 09:00. Closed Mon - Thurs, Fri 17:00, Sat 12:00.
Su: Open Mon - Thurs, Fri 08:00, Sat 09:00. Closed Mon - Thurs, Fri 17:00, Sat 12:00.
Au: Open Mon - Thurs, Fri 08:00, Sat 09:00. Closed Mon - Thurs, Fri 17:00, Sat 12:00.
Wn: Open Mon - Thurs, Fri 08:00, Sat 09:00. Closed Mon - Thurs, Fri 17:00, Sat 12:00. **Ref: YH12533**

SCOTT VETNRY CLINIC

Scott Veterinary Clinic, 405 Goldington Rd, Bedford, **Bedfordshire**, MK41 0DS, **ENGLAND**.
(T) 01234 261622 **(F)** 01234 245601.
Profile Medical Support. **Ref: YH12534**

SCOTT WILSON RESOURCE CONSULT

Scott Wilson Resource Consultants, Avalon Hse, Marcham Rd, Abingdon, **Oxfordshire**, OX14 1UG, **ENGLAND**.
(T) 01235 555535 **(F)** 01235 553203.
Profile Club/Association. **Ref: YH12535**

SCOTT, ALEX

Alex Scott, The Stables Cottage, Home Farm South, Newliston Est, Kinkliston, **Edinburgh (City of)**, EH29 9EB, **SCOTLAND**.
(T) 0131 3334715.
Profile Medical Support. **Ref: YH12536**

SCOTT, ANDY

Mr Andy Scott, Soppitt Farm, Elsdon, Newcastle-upon-Tyne, **Tyne and Wear**, NE19 1AF, **ENGLAND**.
(T) 01830 520038.
Profile Trainer. **Ref: YH12537**

SCOTT, B G

Scott B G, Daddy Barn Farm, Langott Lane, Eccleshall, Stafford, **Staffordshire**, ST21 6PP, **ENGLAND**.
(T) 01630 620681.
Profile Breeder, Riding School, Stable/Livery.
Ref: YH12538

SCOTT, C

C Scott, East Middle Farm Cottage, Hawick, **Scottish Borders**, TD9 8LW, **SCOTLAND**.
(T) 01450 870511.
Profile Breeder. **Ref: YH12539**

SCOTT, D D

Mr D D Scott, East Lynch, Minehead, **Somerset**, TA24 8SS, **ENGLAND**.
(T) 01643 702430.
Profile Breeder. **Ref: YH12540**

SCOTT, D W

Mr D W Scott, Westburnhope, Steel, Hexham, **Northumberland**, NE47 0HT, **ENGLAND**.
(T) 01434 73599.
Profile Supplies. **Ref: YH12541**

SCOTT, E

Mrs E Scott, Home Farm, Nettlecombe, Williton, Taunton, **Somerset**, TA4 4HS, **ENGLAND**.
(T) 01984 640354.
Profile Supplies. **Ref: YH12542**

SCOTT, E B

Mrs E B Scott, Moorland Farm, Axbridge, **Somerset**, BS26 2BA, **ENGLAND**.
(T) 01934 733341.
Profile Supplies. **Ref: YH12543**

SCOTT, HOMER

Homer Scott, Lisheen Stud, Castledermot, **County Kildare**, **IRELAND**.
(T) 050 345110.
Contact/s
Trainer: Mr H Scott
(E) homerscott@kildarehorse.ie
Profile Trainer. **Ref: YH12544**

SCOTT, LESLIE

Leslie Scott, Steelgate, Ivegill, Carlisle, **Cumbria**, CA4 0QF, **ENGLAND**.
(T) 01699 6223.
Profile Farrier. **Ref: YH12545**

SCOTT, R J

R J Scott, Oakfield Farm, Blind Lane, Little Burstead, Billericay, **Essex**, **ENGLAND**..
Profile Breeder. **Ref: YH12546**

SCOTT, S

Mrs S Scott, Upper Blackgrove Farm, Quainton, Aylesbury, **Buckinghamshire**, HP22 4AD, **ENGLAND**.
(T) 01296 655228.
Profile Breeder. **Ref: YH12547**

SCOT-TACK

Scot-Tack, Townend Cottage, Stonehouse, Larkhall, **Lanarkshire (South)**, ML9 3PE, **SCOTLAND**.
(T) 01357 522924.
Profile Supplies. **Ref: YH12548**

SCOTTISH ANIMAL PHYSIOTHERAPY

Scottish Animal Physiotherapy Centre, Gamekeepers Cottage, Glentarkie, Strathmiglo, **Fife**, KY14 7RU, **SCOTLAND**.
(T) 01337 860512.
Contact/s
Physiotherapist: Abbey Smythe **(Q)** BSc, MCSP, SRP
Profile Medical Support. Yr. Est: 1987
Opening Times
Telephone for further information **Ref: YH12549**

SCOTTISH BLOODSTOCK AGENCY

Scottish Bloodstock Agency, Ruecastle, Lanton, Jedburgh, **Scottish Borders**, TD8 6ST, **SCOTLAND**.
(T) 01835 862293 **(F)** 01835 862293
(M) 07774 286786.
Profile Blood Stock Agency. **Ref: YH12550**

SCOTTISH DRESSAGE GROUP

Scottish Dressage Group, Bavelaw Castle, Balerno, **Edinburgh (City of)**, EH14 7JS, **SCOTLAND**.
(T) 0131 4493972 **(F)** 0131 4496228.
Profile Club/Association. **Ref: YH12551**

SCOTTISH ENDURANCE RIDING

Scottish Endurance Riding Club, 9 Eillot Rd, Jedburgh, Borders, **Scottish Borders**, TD8 6HN, **SCOTLAND**.
(T) 01835 863823 **(F)** 01835 864504
(E) lindsayswilson@compuserve.com.
Contact/s
Key Contact: Ms L Wilson
Profile Club/Association, Riding Club. **Ref: YH12552**

SCOTTISH EQUESTRIAN

Scottish Equestrian (The), Ascurry Mill Cottage, Letham, Forfar, **Angus**, DD8 2QQ, **SCOTLAND**.
(T) 01307 818919 **(F)** 01307 818919
(E) horses@marketer.demon.co.uk.
Contact/s
Editor: Ms H Crighton
Profile Supplies. **Ref: YH12553**

SCOTTISH EQUESTRIAN ASS

Scottish Equestrian Association, C/O The Old Manse, Keir Mill, Thornhill, **Dumfries and Galloway**, DG3 4DF, **SCOTLAND**.
(T) 01848 330815 **(F)** 01848 330600.
Profile Club/Association. **Ref: YH12554**

SCOTTISH EQUESTRIAN COMPLEX

Scottish Equestrian Complex, Race Course Stables, Lanark, **Lanarkshire (South)**, ML11 9TA, **SCOTLAND**.
(T) 01555 661853.
Profile Riding School, Stable/Livery. **Ref: YH12555**

SCOTTISH FARMER

Scottish Farmer (The), Caledonian Magazines, 195 Albion St, Glasgow, **Glasgow (City of)**, G1 1QQ, **SCOTLAND**.
(T) 0141 3027700 **(F)** 0141 3027799
(E) farmer@calmags.co.uk.
Profile Supplies. **Ref: YH12556**

SCOTTISH FARRIER

Scottish Farrier Training Centre, Royal Dick Vet Field Station, Easter Bush, Roslin, **Lothian (Mid)**, EH25 9RG, **SCOTLAND**.
(T) 0131 4452001.
Profile Equestrian Centre. **Ref: YH12557**

SCOTTISH SIDE SADDLES

Scottish Side Saddles, , South Thorn, Aiket Rd, Dunlop, **Ayrshire (South)**, KA3 4BP, **SCOTLAND**.
(T) 01560 484916 **(F)** 01560 484916.
Profile Saddlery Retailer. **Ref: YH12558**

SCOTTISH TEXTILE ASSOCIATION

Scottish Textile Association (The), High Sunderland, Galashiels, **Scottish Borders**, TD1 3PL, **SCOTLAND**.
(T) 01750 22312.
Profile Club/Association. **Ref: YH12559**

SCOTTOW FARMS

Scottow Farms Ltd, Scottow Hall, Norwich, **Norfolk**, NR0 5DF, **ENGLAND**.
(T) 01692 538601.
Profile Breeder. **Ref: YH12560**

SCOTTS OF THRAPSTON

Scotts of Thrapston, Bridge St, Thrapston, Kettering, **Northamptonshire**, NN14 4LR, **ENGLAND**.
(T) 01832 732366 **(F)** 01832 733703
(E) equestrian@scottsofthrapston.co.uk.
Profile Transport/Horse Boxes. **Ref: YH12561**

SCOTTS RIDING STABLES

Scotts Riding Stables, 3 St Mary St, Nether Stowey, Bridgwater, **Somerset**, TA5 1LJ, **ENGLAND**.
(T) 01278 732422.
Contact/s
Owner: Mrs C Parsons
Profile Stable/Livery. **Ref: YH12562**

SCOTTSWAY STUD

Scottsway Stud, Castle Camps, **Cambridgeshire**, CB1 6SN, **ENGLAND**.
(T) 01799 584267
(M) 07860 891985.
Profile Breeder. **Ref: YH12563**

SCREATON, M

M Screaton, Embla Farm, Nancledra, Penzance, **Cornwall**, TR20 8LL, **ENGLAND**.
(T) 01736 796965.
Contact/s
Owner: Mr M Screaton
Profile Farrier. **Ref: YH12564**

SCREENCO

Screenco Ltd, Communications Hse, Tower Lane, Eastleigh, **Hampshire**, SO50 6NZ, **ENGLAND**.
(T) 023 80618118 **(F)** 023 80618119.
Profile Club/Association. **Ref: YH12565**

SCRIVEN, B

Mr B Scriven, Cogload Farm, Durston, Taunton, **Somerset**, TA3 5AW, **ENGLAND**.
(T) 01823 490208.
Profile Supplies. **Ref: YH12566**

SCRIVENS, J

Mrs J Scrivens, Little Ball Cottage, Bathealton, Shillingford, Taunton, **Somerset**, TA4 2AR, **ENGLAND**.
(T) 01984 624668
(M) 07850 733683.
Profile Supplies. **Ref: YH12567**

SCROLL FACTORY

Scroll Factory (The), Halley Drive, Glasgow, **Glasgow (City of)**, G13 4DL, **SCOTLAND**.
(T) 0141 9514666 **(F)** 0141 9514666.
Contact/s
Partner: Mr S Ferguson
Profile Blacksmith. **Ref: YH12568**

SCROPTON

East Midlands Riding Association For The Handicapped, The Riding Ctre, Watery Lane, Scropton, Burton-on-Trent, **Staffordshire**, DE65 5PL, **ENGLAND**.
(T) 01283 812753
(E) scroptonrda@aol.com
Affiliated Bodies ABRS, BDS, BHDTA, BHS, RDA.
Contact/s
General Manager: Mr S Roberts **(Q)** BHS 1
Profile Arena, Club/Association, Equestrian Centre, Riding School, Stable/Livery, Trainer. No.Staff: 5
Yr. Est: 1980 C.Size: 13 Acres **Ref: YH12569**

SCRUTON, CHRISTOPHER

Christopher Scruton BII, 19 Beech Ave, Melksham, **Wiltshire**, SN12 6JP, **ENGLAND**.
(T) 01225 790979.
Profile Farrier. **Ref: YH12570**

SCRUTTON, I F

I F Scrutton, The Limes, Garden City, Lawford, Manningtree, **Essex**, CO11 2JS, **ENGLAND**.
(T) 01206 396694.
Profile Farrier. **Ref: YH12571**

SCS

Scottish Communication Systems, Arran Hse, Arran Rd, Perth, **Perth and Kinross**, PH1 3DZ, **SCOTLAND**.
(T) 01738 639885.
Profile Club/Association. **Ref: YH12572**

SCUDIMORE, PETER

Peter Scudimore, Grange Hill Farm, Naunton, Cheltenham, **Gloucestershire**, GL54 3AY, **ENGLAND**.
(T) 01451 850741 **(F)** 01451 850995.
Contact/s
Owner: Mr P Scudimore
Profile Trainer. **Ref: YH12573**

SCULPTURE TO WEAR

Sculpture to Wear, P O Box 24, Leyburn, **Yorkshire (North)**, DL8 4YP, **ENGLAND**.
(T) 01969 624949 **(F)** 01969 623326
(M) 07711 022428.
Profile Supplies. **Ref: YH12574**

SCULPTURE TO WEAR

Sculpture To Wear, PO Box 24, Leyburn, **Yorkshire (North)**, DL8 4YP, **ENGLAND**.
(T) 01969 624949 **(F)** 01969 623326
(W) www.sculpture-to-wear.co.uk.
Profile Sculptor. Yr. Est: 1990 **Ref: YH12575**

SCURRELL, M D

M D Scurrell, 4 Birdbush Pk, Ludwell, Shaftesbury, **Dorset**, SP7 9HH, **ENGLAND**.
(T) 01747 828037.
Profile Breeder. **Ref: YH12576**

SCURRELL, S

Miss S Scurrell, 2 Giles Cross, Bradford Peverell, Dorchester, **Dorset**, DT2 9SJ, **ENGLAND**.
(T) 01305 267763.
Profile Breeder. **Ref: YH12577**

SCURRY DRIVING ASSOCIATION

Scurry Driving Association (The), Hollygate Hse, Hollygate Rd, Ridlington, Oakham, **Rutland**, LE15 9AR, **ENGLAND**.
(T) 01572 821781 **(F)** 01572 821781
Affiliated Bodies BHDTA.
Contact/s
Chairperson: Mr D Matthews **(T)** 01628 483093
Profile Club/Association.
The governing body for competitors, course builders and judges. Performances are held at County Shows and lessons are available from committee members.
Opening Times
Open all year **Ref: YH12578**

SEABORN, J

Miss J Seaborn, Upper Mitchell Farm, Eastnor, Ledbury, **Herefordshire**, HR8 IJF, **ENGLAND**.
(T) 01531 2660.
Profile Stable/Livery. **Ref: YH12579**

SEABROOK FEEDS

Seabrook Feeds, Westgate Farm, Red Lane, Gospel End Rd, Sedgley, **Staffordshire**, DY3 4AN, **ENGLAND**.
(T) 01902 664948.
Profile Saddlery Retailer. **Ref: YH12580**

SEACOMBE RIDING HOLIDAYS

Seacombe Riding Holidays, 54 High St, Langton Matravers, Swanage, **Dorset**, BH19 3HB, **ENGLAND**.
(T) 01929 426066 **(F)** 01929 426006
(E) stella@utal.demon.co.uk
(W) www.langtonia.org.uk.
Contact/s
Owner: Mr B Coe
Profile Holidays.
Seacombe offers riding holidays for experienced adult riders. There is a combination of excellent and varied terrain for riding, with spectacular scenery and plenty of opportunities for long gallops and canters.
Opening Times
Sp: Open Mon - Sun 09:00. Closed Mon - Sun 21:00.
Su: Open Mon - Sun 09:00. Closed Mon - Sun 21:00.
Au: Open Mon - Sun 09:00. Closed Mon - Sun 21:00.
Wn: Open Mon - Sun 09:00. Closed Mon - Sun 21:00. **Ref: YH12581**

SEADOWN VETNRY GROUP

Seadown Veterinary Group, Seadown Veterinary Hospital, Frost Lane, Hythe, **Hampshire**, SO4 6NG, **ENGLAND**.
(T) 023 80842237 **(F)** 023 80842026.
Profile Medical Support. **Ref: YH12582**

SEAFIELD RIDING CTRE

Seafield Riding Centre, Seafield Farm, Forres, **Moray**, IV36 2TN, **SCOTLAND**.
(T) 01309 672253.
Profile Riding School. **Ref: YH12583**

SEAFIELDS RIDING SCHOOL

Seafields Riding School, First Ave, Eastchurch, Sheerness, **Kent**, ME12 4JN, **ENGLAND**.
(T) 01795 880303.
Contact/s
Owner: Mrs K Handybow **Ref: YH12584**

SEAFORTH RIDING CTRE

Seaforth Riding Centre, Dunglass Farm, Brahan Est, Maryburgh, Dingwall, **Highlands**, IV7 8EQ, **SCOTLAND**.
(T) 01349 865495.

Profile Riding School. **Ref: YH12585**

SEAFORTH SADDLERS

Seaforth Saddlers, 32 Waterloo Pl, Inverness, **Highlands**, IV1 1NB, **SCOTLAND**.
(T) 01463 223803 **(F)** 01463 223803
(W) www.seaforthsaddlers.co.uk.
Contact/s
Owner: Lesley Common
(E) lesley@seaforthsaddlers.fsnet.co.uk
Profile Riding Wear Retailer, Saddlery Retailer, Supplies. **No.Staff:** 1
Opening Times
Sp: Open 09:30. Closed 17:30.
Su: Open 09:30. Closed 17:30.
Au: Open 09:30. Closed 17:30.
Wn: Open 09:30. Closed 17:30. **Ref: YH12586**

SEAGOLD CENTURION

Seagold Centurion Equestrian Centre (The), Birtley Lane, Hunwick Village, Crook, **County Durham**, DL15 0SG, **ENGLAND**.
(T) 01388 606347 **(F)** 0191 5672020
Affiliated Bodies Ponies Ass UK, UK Chasers&Riders.
Contact/s
Owner: Mr D Emerson
Profile Arena, Equestrian Centre, Medical Support, Riding School, Riding Wear Retailer. **No.Staff:** 5
Yr. Est: 1996 **C.Size:** 25 Acres
Opening Times
Sp: Open 08:30. Closed 17:30.
Su: Open 08:30. Closed 17:30.
Au: Open 08:30. Closed 17:30.
Wn: Open 08:30. Closed 17:30. **Ref: YH12587**

SEAGRAVE COTTAGE STABLES

Seagrave Cottage Stables, Shipcote Lane, Bishops Waltham, **Hampshire**, SO32 1FH, **ENGLAND**.
(T) 01489 893914.
Profile Breeder, Farrier. **Ref: YH12588**

SEALS FODDER

Seals Fodder Room Ltd, The Mill, High St, Swanwick, Alfreton, **Derbyshire**, DE55 1AA, **ENGLAND**.
(T) 01773 602466 **(F)** 01773 540116
(E) orders@sealsfodder.co.uk
(W) www.sealsfodder.co.uk.
Contact/s
Partner: Mr A Cooper
Profile Feed Merchant, Supplies. **Yr. Est:** 1987
Opening Times
Sp: Open Mon - Sat 08:30. Closed Mon - Sat 17:15, Sat 12:15.
Su: Open Mon - Sat 08:30. Closed Mon - Sat 17:15, Sat 12:15.
Au: Open Mon - Sat 08:30. Closed Mon - Sat 17:15, Sat 12:15.
Wn: Open Mon - Sat 08:30. Closed Mon - Sat 17:15, Sat 12:15.
Half day Saturday, closed on Sunday **Ref: YH12589**

SEALYHAM ACTIVITY CTRE

Sealyham Activity Centre, Wolfscastle, Haverfordwest, **Pembrokeshire**, FA62 5NF, **WALES**.
(T) 01348 840763.
Profile Riding School. **Ref: YH12590**

SEAMAN, JULIAN

Julian Seaman, 41 Gastein Rd, London, **London (Greater)**, W6 8LT, **ENGLAND**.
(T) 020 73869820.
Profile Supplies. **Ref: YH12591**

SEAN WOODS RACING

Sean Woods Racing, La Grange Stables, Snailwell Rd, Newmarket, **Suffolk**, CB8 7DP, **ENGLAND**.
(T) 01638 561844
(W) www.newmarketracehorsetraining.co.uk
Affiliated Bodies Newmarket Trainers Fed.
Contact/s
Trainer: Mr S Woods
Profile Trainer. **Ref: YH12592**

SEARL, RICHARD MICHAEL

Richard Michael Searl DWCF, Castle Stores, 2 Mill Rd, Tongwynlais, Cardiff, **Glamorgan (Vale of)**, CF15 7JP, **WALES**.
(T) 029 20810547.
Profile Farrier. **Ref: YH12593**

SEAVIEW RIDING SCHOOL

Seaview Riding School, Biggar Village, Walney, Barrow-In-Furness, **Cumbria**, LA14 3YG, **ENGLAND**.
(T) 01229 474251.
Contact/s
Owner: Miss J Hayton **Ref: YH12594**

SEAVILL, C A S

C A S Seavill, 1 Chithurst Farm Cottage, Chithurst, Petersfield, **Hampshire**, GU31 5EU, **ENGLAND**.
(T) 01730 813862 **(F)** 01730 821152
(M) 07721 512056
(E) cspolo@aol.com.
Profile Breeder, Trainer. **Ref: YH12595**

SECKINGTON FORGE

Seckington Forge, Seckington Cross Ind Est, Winkleigh, **Devon**, EX19 8EY, **ENGLAND**.
(T) 01837 83671.
Profile Farrier. **Ref: YH12596**

SECOND TIME ROUND

Second Time Round, 83, Hartfield, **Sussex (East)**, TN7 4LB, **ENGLAND**.
(T) 01342 850482. **Ref: YH12597**

SECOND TURNOUT

Second Turnout, Field Hse, Ham Hall Lane, Scruton, Northallerton, **Yorkshire (North)**, DL7 0RJ, **ENGLAND**.
(T) 01677 425317.
Contact/s
Owner: Mrs J Iveson
Profile Riding Wear Retailer.
Supply used equestrian wear **No.Staff:** 1
Yr. Est: 2001
Opening Times
By appointment only **Ref: YH12598**

SECRETT FARM SHOP

Secrett Farm Shop (The), Hurst Farm, Chapel Lane, Milford, Godalming, **Surrey**, GU8 5HU, **ENGLAND**.
(T) 01486 822751.
Profile Supplies. **Ref: YH12599**

SEDBURYS FARM

Sedburys Farm Livery, Sedbury East Farm, Gilling West, Richmond, **Yorkshire (North)**, DL10 5ER, **ENGLAND**.
(T) 01748 822758 **(F)** 01748 822758.
Contact/s
Owner: Mr A Haigh
Profile Stable/Livery.
Opening Times
Telephone for an appointment **Ref: YH12600**

SEDERHOLM, LARS

Lars Sederholm, South Hse, Burley On The Hill, Oakham, **Rutland**, LE15 7SU, **ENGLAND**.
(T) 01572 755430
(M) 07831 699755.
Profile Trainer. **Ref: YH12601**

SEDGECROFT STUD

Sedgecroft Stud, Sedgecroft, Hawkchurch, Axminster, **Devon**, EX13 5XB, **ENGLAND**.
(T) 01297 678267.
Contact/s
Physiotherapist: Mrs D Du Feu
Profile Breeder, Medical Support. **No.Staff:** 2
Yr. Est: 1995 **C.Size:** 10 Acres **Ref: YH12602**

SEDGEFIELD STEEPLECHASES

Sedgefield Steeplechases Ltd, The Bungalow, Sedgefield Racecourse, Stockton-on-Tees, **Cleveland**, TS21 2HW, **ENGLAND**.
(T) 01740 621925 **(F)** 01740 620663.
Profile Track/Course. **Ref: YH12603**

SEDGEHILL SHETLAND PONY STUD

Sedgehill Shetland Pony Stud, Woodlands, 76 Botley Rd, Chesham, **Buckinghamshire**, HP5 1XG, **ENGLAND**.
(T) 01494 785223.
Profile Breeder. **Ref: YH12604**

SEDGWICK, J R W

J R W Sedgwick, 66A Main St, Egremont, **Cumbria**, CA22 2DB, **ENGLAND**.
(T) 01946 820513.
Profile Medical Support. **Ref: YH12605**

SEDGWICK, J R W

J R W Sedgwick, Barclays Bank Chambers, Market Sq, Keswick, **Cumbria**, CA12 5BJ, **ENGLAND**.
(T) 01900 823187.
Profile Medical Support. **Ref: YH12606**

SEECHEM EQUESTRIAN CTRE

Seechem Equestrian Centre, Rowney Green Lane, Alvechurch, Birmingham, **Midlands (West)**, B48 7EL, **ENGLAND**.
(T) 0121 4452333.
Contact/s
Owner: Mrs J Willetts
Profile Breeder, Riding School, Stable/Livery.
Ref: YH12607

SEEDEE PET FOODS

Seedee Pet Foods, 1 Middleton Rd, Sudbury, **Suffolk**, CO10 2DB, **ENGLAND**.
(T) 01787 311122.
Profile Supplies. **Ref: YH12608**

SEEIN RIDING CLUB

Seein Riding Club, Peacock Bank Stud, 89 Peacock Rd, Sion Mills, **County Tyrone**, BT82 9NP, **NORTHERN IRELAND**.
(T) 028 82658255.
Profile Club/Association, Riding Club. **Ref: YH12609**

SEENEY'S ANIMAL & PET FOODS

Seeney's Animal & Pet Foods, The Grain Silos, Water Eaton, **Oxfordshire**, OX2 8HA, **ENGLAND**.
(T) 01865 559750.
Contact/s
Owner: Mr A Seeney
Profile Supplies. **Ref: YH12610**

SEG

S E Gear Ltd, 19 Wenhill Heights, Calne, **Wiltshire**, SN11 0JZ, **ENGLAND**.
(T) 01249 811000 **(F)** 01249 811000.
Profile Saddlery Retailer.
Stockists of SEG gloves. **Ref: YH12611**

SEGGIE, A

A Seggie, Prestonmill Smithy, Preston Mill, Kirkbean, Dumfries, **Dumfries and Galloway**, DG2 8AE, **SCOTLAND**.
(T) 01387 880291.
Contact/s
Owner: Mr A Seggie
Profile Blacksmith. **Ref: YH12612**

SEIS

Scottish Equestrian Insurance Services, Barclay Curle Hse, 739 South St, Glasgow, **Glasgow (City of)**, G14 0AH, **SCOTLAND**.
(T) 0141 9549445.
Profile Club/Association. **Ref: YH12613**

SELBY & DISTRICT RIDING CLUB

Selby & District Riding Club, South Lodge, Bolton Lane, Wilberfoss, **Yorkshire (North)**, YO41 5NZ, **ENGLAND**.
(T) 01759 380643 **(F)** 01759 388869.
Contact/s
Chairman: Mrs H Burley
Profile Club/Association, Riding Club. **Ref: YH12614**

SELBY, J

J Selby, The Smithy, Crosswell, Crymych, **Pembrokeshire**, SA41 3TF, **WALES**.
(T) 01239 891362.
Contact/s
Owner: Mr J Selby
Profile Farrier. **Ref: YH12615**

SELBY, P

P Selby, 3 Ivanhoe Rd, Thurcroft, Rotherham, **Yorkshire (South)**, S66 9EF, **ENGLAND**.
(T) 01246 240907.
Contact/s
Owner: Mr P Selby
Profile Farrier. **Ref: YH12616**

SELBY, PAUL

Paul Selby DWCF, 95 Bentinck Rd, Shuttlewood, Chesterfield, **Derbyshire**, S44 6RG, **ENGLAND**.
(M) 07970 728770.
Profile Farrier. **Ref: YH12617**

SELBY, TERRY

Terry Selby, The Chase, Hinton Martel, Wimborne, **Dorset**, BH21 7HE, **ENGLAND**.
(T) 01258 840650 **(F)** 01258 840243.
Profile Supplies. **Ref: YH12618**

SELBY, TIMOTHY JOHN

Timothy John Selby DWCF, Stoke Fields Farm, Hinckley Rd, Stoke Golding, Nuneaton, **Leicestershire**, CV13 6HR, **ENGLAND**.
(T) 01455 212036.
Profile Farrier. **Ref: YH12619**

SELECT FEEDS & SEED

Select Feeds & Seed, High Gr, Flaxley Rd, Westbury-on-Severn, **Gloucestershire**, GL14 1JW, **ENGLAND**.
(T) 01452 760511.
Profile Supplies. **Ref: YH12620**

SELFE, MADELINE
Mrs Madeline Selfe, The Nether Hse, Poulton, Cirencester, **Gloucestershire**, GL7 5LN, **ENGLAND**.
(T) 01285 85209. **Ref: YH12621**

SELLARS, R
R Sellars, Blacksmiths Shop, Back Lane, Ebberston, Scarborough, **Yorkshire (North)**, YO13 9NS, **ENGLAND**.
(T) 01723 859570.
Contact/s
Owner: Mr R Sellars
Profile Blacksmith. **Ref: YH12622**

SELLERS, F H & D D
F H & D D Sellers, 9 Kensington Cl, Greenmount, Bury, **Lancashire**, BL8 4DG, **ENGLAND**.
(T) 01204 884861.
Profile Supplies. **Ref: YH12623**

SELLERS, F N
F N Sellers, Old Green Farm, Greenmount, Bury, **Lancashire**, BL8 4DP, **ENGLAND**.
(T) 01204 882324. **Ref: YH12624**

SELSEY RIDING CTRE
Selsey Riding Centre, Golf Links Lane, Selsey, **Sussex (West)**, PO20 9DP, **ENGLAND**.
(T) 01243 603050.
Profile Stable/Livery. **Ref: YH12625**

SELSTON EQUESTRIAN CTRE
Selston Equestrian Centre, Hill Bank Farm, Commonside, Selston, Nottingham, **Nottinghamshire**, NG16 6FJ, **ENGLAND**.
(T) 01773 813817.
Contact/s
Owner: Mr E Burr
Profile Riding School. **Ref: YH12626**

SELWAY, K D
K D Selway, Luckington Manor Farm, Newbury, Frome, **Somerset**, BA11 3RQ, **ENGLAND**.
(T) 01373 812217 **(F)** 01373 812217.
Contact/s
Partner: Mrs C Selway
Profile Transport/Horse Boxes. **Ref: YH12627**

SELWOOD SPACEMASTER
Selwood Spacemaster, Bournemouth Rd, Chandler's Ford, Eastleigh, **Hampshire**, SO53 3ZL, **ENGLAND**.
(T) 023 80266311 **(F)** 023 80260906. **Ref: YH12628**

SELWYN, CHRISTOPHER
Christopher Selwyn, 5 Franklin Cl, Chalgrove, Oxford, **Oxfordshire**, OX44 7RG, **ENGLAND**.
(T) 01865 890581.
Profile Farrier. **Ref: YH12629**

SELWYN, GEORGE
George Selwyn, 119 Torriano Ave, London, **London (Greater)**, NW5 2RX, **ENGLAND**.
(T) 020 72676929 **(F)** 020 72844231. **Ref: YH12630**

SEMEX
Semex (UK Sales) Ltd, Maple Pk, Monkton, Prestwick, **Ayrshire (South)**, KA9 2RJ, **SCOTLAND**.
(T) 01292 671525 **(F)** 01292 671418.
Profile Blood Stock Agency. **Ref: YH12631**

SENAPVIEW STUD
Senapview Stud, Bleakhouse Stables, West Melton, Rotherham, **Yorkshire (South)**, S63 6AH, **ENGLAND**.
(T) 01709 873166.
Contact/s
Owner: Miss D Kersey
Profile Breeder. **Ref: YH12632**

SEND BARNS STABLE
Send Barns Stable, Woodhill, Send, Woking, **Surrey**, GU23 7JR, **ENGLAND**.
(T) 01483 223337.
Contact/s
Owner: Mrs L Toms **Ref: YH12633**

SENIOR, A
Mr A Senior, The Stables, Oak Lane, Kerridge, Macclesfield, **Cheshire**, SK10 5AP, **ENGLAND**.
(T) 01625 575735
(M) 07979 335715.
Profile Trainer. **Ref: YH12634**

SENRUF STUD
Senruf Stud, Cockerdale Farm, Oldstead, **Yorkshire (North)**, YO61 4BN, **ENGLAND**.
(T) 01347 868250 **(F)** 01347 868228.
Profile Breeder. **Ref: YH12635**

SEROLOGICALS
Serologicals Ltd, Kings Buildings, West Mains Rd, Edinburgh, **Edinburgh (City of)**, EH9 3JF, **SCOTLAND**.
(T) 0131 6688000 **(F)** 0131 6624279.
Contact/s
Manager: Mr D Lowe
Profile Blood Stock Agency. **Ref: YH12636**

SESSNIE EQUESTRIAN
Sessnie Equestrian, East Torryleith, Newmachar, Aberdeen, **Aberdeen (City of)**, AB21 0QE, **SCOTLAND**.
(T) 01651 862247.
Profile Riding School, Saddlery Retailer, Stable/Livery. **Ref: YH12637**

SEVEN LOWES STABLES
Seven Lowes Stables, Middlewich Rd, Cotebrook, Tarporley, **Cheshire**, CW6 9EH, **ENGLAND**.
(T) 01829 760763. **Ref: YH12638**

SEVEN SAINTS RARE BREEDS
St Clair Shetlands, Severalls Lane, Colchester, **Essex**, CO4 5JB, **ENGLAND**.
(T) 01206 272736 **(F)** 01206 273241.
Contact/s
Owner: Ms T St Clair-Pearce
(E) sspseven@aol.com
Profile Breeder.
Specialists on all types of Shetland. Yr. Est: 2001
C.Size: 34 Acres **Ref: YH12639**

SEVEN SEAS VETNRY DIVISION
Seven Seas Veterinary Division Ltd, Hedon Rd, Marfleet, Hull, **Yorkshire (East)**, HU9 5NJ, **ENGLAND**.
(T) 01482 375234 **(F)** 01482 787865.
Profile Medical Support. **Ref: YH12640**

SEVENACRES RIDING SCHOOL
Sevenacres Riding School, Ham Green, Lower Harcourt Rd, Mathon, Malvern, **Worcestershire**, WR13 5PQ, **ENGLAND**.
(T) 01684 541130. **Ref: YH12641**

SEVENOAKS RIDING CLUB
Sevenoaks Riding Club, Manor Farm Cottage, Dryhill Lane, Sundridge, Tonbridge, **Kent**, TN14 6AA, **ENGLAND**.
(T) 01732 750568.
Profile Club/Association, Riding Club. **Ref: YH12642**

SEVERN IRONWORKS
Severn Ironworks, 179A Easton Rd, Bristol, **Bristol**, BS5 0HQ, **ENGLAND**.
(T) 0117 9399946.
Profile Blacksmith. **Ref: YH12643**

SEVERN QUARTER HORSES
Severn Quarter Horses, Brynfedw Farm, Ystradowen, Cowbridge, **Glamorgan (Vale of)**, CF71 7SZ, **WALES**.
(T) 01446 772534.
Contact/s
Owner: Mrs E Goodliffe
Profile Breeder, Trainer. **Ref: YH12644**

SEVERN VALLEY LIVERY CTRE
Severn Valley Livery Centre, Bewdley Rd North, Stourport-on-Severn, **Worcestershire**, DY13 8PX, **ENGLAND**.
(T) 01299 879269.
Contact/s
Owner: Miss S Ketley **(Q)** BHSAI
Profile Breeder, Stable/Livery. Yr. Est: 1968
C.Size: 15 Acres **Ref: YH12645**

SEVERNVALE EQUESTRIAN CTRE
Severnvale Equestrian Centre, Severnvale, Tidenham, Chepstow, **Monmouthshire**, NP16 7LL, **WALES**.
(T) 01291 623412.
Profile Riding School, Stable/Livery, Track/Course.
Ref: YH12646

SEVERS, MALCOLM
Malcolm Severs, 1 Underriver Hse Cottages, Underriver, Sevenoaks, **Kent**, TN15 0SJ, **ENGLAND**.
(T) 01732 838994.
Profile Supplies. **Ref: YH12647**

SEWARD, ANN
Ann Seward, 11 Coppice Hill, Avon, Bradford-on-Avon, **Wiltshire**, BA15 1JT, **ENGLAND**.
(T) 01225 863344 **(F)** 01225 863344. **Ref: YH12648**

SEWELL, ERNEST CHARLES TREVOR
Ernest Charles Trevor Sewell, Hillcrest, Mill Lane, Fobbing, **Essex**, SS17 9HP, **ENGLAND**.
(T) 01375 672379.
Profile Farrier. **Ref: YH12649**

SEXTON, JOHN
John Sexton, Raventhorpe Cottage, Bygot Lane, Cherry Burton, Beverley, **Yorkshire (East)**, HU17 7RB, **ENGLAND**.
(T) 01964 551135.
Profile Supplies. **Ref: YH12650**

SEYMOUR BLOODSTOCK
Seymour Bloodstock (UK) Ltd, Home Farm Cottage, Burrough Green, Newmarket, **Suffolk**, CB8 9LY, **ENGLAND**.
(T) 01638 507395 **(F)** 01638 508333
(E) alison.wilson1@virgin.net.
Profile Blood Stock Agency. **Ref: YH12651**

SEYMOUR FARM LIVERY YARD
Seymour Farm Livery Yard, Stretcholt, Bridgwater, **Somerset**, TA6 4SR, **ENGLAND**.
(T) 01278 683367.
Contact/s
Owner: Ms C Reason **Ref: YH12652**

SEYMOUR SADDLERY
Seymour Saddlery, Dacre Hse, Ripley, Harrogate, **Yorkshire (North)**, HG3 3AY, **ENGLAND**.
(T) 01423 770772 **(F)** 01423 770772.
Contact/s
Owner: Mr T Seymour **Ref: YH12653**

SEYMOUR, A J C (COLONEL)
Colonel & Mrs A J C Seymour, Wantsley Pony Stud, Broadwindsor, Beaminster, **Dorset**, DT8 3PT, **ENGLAND**.
(T) 01308 868462.
Profile Breeder. **Ref: YH12654**

SHADOWFAX STABLE
Shadowfax Stable, Hamilton Rd, Newmarket, **Suffolk**, CB8 7JQ, **ENGLAND**.
(T) 01638 667870 **(F)** 01638 668005.
Contact/s
Manager: Mr C Allan
Profile Blood Stock Agency, Trainer. **Ref: YH12655**

SHADWELL ESTATE
Shadwell Estate Co Ltd, Nunnery Stud, Thetford, **Norfolk**, IP24 2QE, **ENGLAND**.
(T) 01842 755913 **(F)** 01842 755189
(E) enquiries@shadwellstud.co.uk
(W) www.shadwellandracing.co.uk.
Contact/s
Manager: Mr A Gold
Profile Breeder. **Ref: YH12656**

SHAFTESBURY TRAILER
Shaftesbury Trailer, Unit 11 Station Rd, Semley, Shaftesbury, **Dorset**, SP7 9AN, **ENGLAND**.
(T) 01747 853156 **(F)** 01747 853156.
Contact/s
Owner: Mr N Loxton
Profile Transport/Horse Boxes. **Ref: YH12657**

SHAFTO'S FARM SHOP
Shafto's Farm Shop, South Causey Farm, Stanley, **County Durham**, DH9 0LS, **ENGLAND**.
(T) 01207 290983.
Contact/s
Owner: Mrs M Burrell
Profile Supplies. **Ref: YH12658**

SHAHZADA
Shahzada Stud & Stables, Duck St, Little Easton, Dunmow, **Essex**, CM6 2JE, **ENGLAND**.
(T) 01371 870962 **(F)** 01371 870962
Affiliated Bodies BHS.
Contact/s
Owner: Mrs E Good
Profile Blood Stock Agency, Breeder, Riding School.
Breeds Arab Cross Horses.
Opening Times
Sp: Open Tues, Thurs 10:00, Wed, Fri, Sat, Sun 09:30. Closed Tues, Thurs 20:00, Wed, Fri - Sun 18:30.
Su: Open Tues, Thurs 10:00, Wed, Fri, Sat, Sun 09:30. Closed Tues, Thurs 20:00, Wed, Fri - Sun 18:30.
Au: Open Tues, Thurs 10:00, Sat - Sun 09:30. Closed Tues, Thurs 20:00: Sat - Sun 18:30.
Wn: Open Tues, Thurs 10:00, Sat - Sun 09:30. Closed Tues, Thurs 20:00: Sat - Sun 18:30.
Ref: YH12659

A-Z of COMPANIES

SHAKESHAFT, R K

R K Shakeshaft, Lower Penddaulwyn, Capel Dewi, Carmarthen, **Carmarthenshire**, SA32 8AG, **WALES**.
(T) 01267 290627.
Contact/s
Owner: Mr R Shakeshaft **Ref: YH12660**

SHAKESPEARE, B

B Shakespeare, 219 Commonside, Brierley Hill, **Midlands (West)**, DY5 4AD, **ENGLAND**.
(T) 01384 77275.
Contact/s
Owner: Mr B Shakespeare
Profile Breeder. **Ref: YH12661**

SHALLY, LAURA

Miss Laura Shally, Burley Hill Farm, Burley Hill, Allestree, **Derbyshire**, DE22 2ET, **ENGLAND**.
(T) 01332 840441.
Profile Supplies. **Ref: YH12662**

SHAMLEY SADDLERY

Shamley Saddlery, Shire Horse Ctre, Bath Rd, Littlewick Green, Maidenhead, **Berkshire**, SL6 3QA, **ENGLAND**.
(T) 01628 828380
Affiliated Bodies SMS.
Contact/s
Owner: Ms T Linden **(Q)** Saddle Fitter, SMS
Profile Saddlery Retailer.
Bespoke bridle maker No.Staff: 3 Yr. Est: 1994
Opening Times
Sp: Open 09:00. Closed 17:30.
Su: Open 09:00. Closed 17:30.
Au: Open 09:00. Closed 17:30.
Wn: Open 09:00. Closed 17:30. **Ref: YH12663**

SHAMROCK HORSEBOXES

Shamrock Horseboxes Ltd, 5 Soham Rd, Fordham, Ely, **Cambridgeshire**, CB7 5LB, **ENGLAND**.
(T) 01638 723050 **(F)** 01638 723051.
Contact/s
Owner: Mr M MacKinnon
Profile Transport/Horse Boxes. **Ref: YH12664**

SHAMROCK STABLES RIDING CLUB

Shamrock Stables Riding Club, Lynch Lane, Westbury Sub Mendip, Wells, **Somerset**, BA5 1HW, **ENGLAND**.
(T) 01749 870696 **(F)** 01749 870134.
Contact/s
Owner: Miss R Peacock **Ref: YH12665**

SHANA RIDING SCHOOL

Shana Riding School, New Rd, Walters Ash, High Wycombe, **Buckinghamshire**, HP14 4UZ, **ENGLAND**.
(T) 01494 562200.
Contact/s
Manager: Mrs J Huggard
Profile Riding School. **Ref: YH12666**

SHANA SADDLE SHOP

Shana Saddle Shop Ltd, New Rd, Walters Ash, High Wycombe, **Buckinghamshire**, HP14 4UZ, **ENGLAND**.
(T) 01494 564238 **(F)** 01494 563449.
Contact/s
Owner: Mrs J Haggard **Ref: YH12667**

SHANDON SCHOOL OF EQUITATION

Shandon School of Equitation (Campersdown), Campersdown Pk, Dundee, **Angus**, DD2 4TF, **SCOTLAND**.
(T) 01382 622024.
Profile Riding School. **Ref: YH12668**

SHANKS & MCEWAN PAPER BEDDING

Shanks & McEwan Paper Bedding, Waste Disposal Site, Bury Mead Rd, Hitchin, **Hertfordshire**, SG5 1RT, **ENGLAND**.
(T) 01462 459037 **(F)** 01462 422219.
Profile Medical Support. **Ref: YH12669**

SHANKS & MCLEAN

Shanks & McLean, Aberlour Veterinary Ctre, Aberlour, **Moray**, AB38 9NR, **SCOTLAND**.
(T) 01340 871385.
Profile Medical Support. **Ref: YH12670**

SHANNON-LEIGH STABLES

Shannon-Leigh Stables, Vicarage Rd, Bexley, **Kent**, DA5 2AW, **ENGLAND**.
(T) 020 83007092. **Ref: YH12671**

SHANTER RIDING CTRE

Shanter Riding Centre, Shanter Farm, Maidens, Girvan, **Ayrshire (South)**, KA26 9NQ, **SCOTLAND**.
(T) 01655 331636
Affiliated Bodies ABRS.
Contact/s
Owner: Ms H Young **(Q)** BHSII
Profile Riding School, Stable/Livery.
Run hacks onto the beach, about 15 minutes away, and are also near to the Culzean Country Park.
Yr. Est: 1986
Opening Times
Sp: Open 10:00. Closed 17:30.
Su: Open 10:00. Closed 17:30.
Au: Open 10:00. Closed 17:30.
Wn: Open 10:00. Closed 17:30. **Ref: YH12672**

SHANTER SADDLERY

Shanter Saddlery, 31 Main St, Stewarton, Kilmarnock, **Ayrshire (East)**, KA3 5BS, **SCOTLAND**.
(T) 01560 482489. **Ref: YH12673**

SHAPLEY RANCH EQUINE ACCESS

Shapley Ranch Equine Access, Shapley Ranch, London Rd, Phoenix Green, Hartley Wintney, **Hampshire**, RG27 8HY, **ENGLAND**.
(T) 01252 843414 **(F)** 01252 843414.
Profile Saddlery Retailer. **Ref: YH12674**

SHARIQUE ARABIANS

Sharique Arabians, 333 Rochester Rd, Burham, Rochester, **Kent**, **ENGLAND**.
(T) 01795 844484.
Profile Breeder. **Ref: YH12675**

SHARNFORD LODGE FEEDS/TACK

Sharnford Lodge Feeds and Tack Centre, Sharnford Lodge Farm, Bumble Bee Lane, Sharnford, Hinckley, **Leicestershire**, LE10 3AE, **ENGLAND**.
(T) 01455 209302 **(F)** 01455 202856.
Contact/s
Owner: Mr G Higginbotham
Profile Feed Merchant, Saddlery Retailer.
Ref: YH12676

SHARON TONG

Sharon Tong Animal Portraits, The Studio, 12 Windmill Cl, Upper Beeding, Steyning, **Sussex (West)**, BN44 3JP, **ENGLAND**.
(T) 01903 814643
(E) sharontongart@aol.com
(W) www.sharontongart.co.uk.
Contact/s
Owner: Sharon Tong
Profile Artist.
Also print onto mugs and T-shirts. No.Staff: 1
Yr. Est: 1985
Opening Times
By commission, please telephone for further information **Ref: YH12677**

SHARP, ELIZABETH

Elizabeth Sharp S.Eq.A., S.W.A., Stanton Ct, Casthorpe Rd, Denton, Grantham, **Lincolnshire**, NG32 1JT, **ENGLAND**.
(T) 01476 870362 **(F)** 01476 870362
(M) 07836 567357
(E) esharp@aol.com.
Profile Breeder. **Ref: YH12678**

SHARPE, TIMOTHY S

Timothy S Sharpe DWCF, Lofthouse Grange, Bugthorpe, **Yorkshire (North)**, YO41 2AE, **ENGLAND**.
(T) 01759 368758.
Profile Farrier. **Ref: YH12679**

SHAUN MEASURES BII

Shaun Measures BII, The Briars, 9 College Ride, Camberley, **Surrey**, GU15 4JP, **ENGLAND**.
(T) 01276 500404.
Profile Farrier. **Ref: YH12680**

SHAW, GARRY A

Garry A Shaw DWCF, 11 Cottingham Ct, Darlington, **County Durham**, DL3 0BW, **ENGLAND**.
(T) 01325 259545.
Profile Farrier. **Ref: YH12681**

SHAW, L & D

L & D Shaw, Crofters Cottage, Little Heath, Dunston, **Staffordshire**, ST18 9AJ, **ENGLAND**.
(T) 01785 780584.
Contact/s
Owner: Mr H Shaw
Profile Breeder.
Breeder of Welsh Section D ponies **Ref: YH12682**

SHAW, MARGARET

Margaret Shaw, 18 Lockett St, Latchford, Warrington, **Cheshire**, WA4 1LL, **ENGLAND**.
(T) 01925 572833 **(F)** 01925 572833
(M) 07721 630204.
Profile Supplies. **Ref: YH12683**

SHAW, WALTER H

Walter H Shaw, Creechan, Drummore, Stranraer, **Dumfries and Galloway**, DG9 9RB, **SCOTLAND**.
(T) 01776 840307/840323.
Profile Breeder. **Ref: YH12684**

SHAY GATE RIDING SCHOOL

Shay Gate Riding School, Shay Lane, Wilsden, Bradford, **Yorkshire (West)**, BD15 0DJ, **ENGLAND**.
(T) 01535 274875. **Ref: YH12685**

SHAY LANE STABLES

Shay Lane Stables, 155 Shay Lane, Halifax, **Yorkshire (West)**, HX3 6RR, **ENGLAND**.
(T) 01422 363069.
Profile Riding School, Stable/Livery. **Ref: YH12686**

SHAYLER SADDLERY

Shayler Saddlery, 29 Newhall St, Walsall, **Midlands (West)**, WS1 3DZ, **ENGLAND**.
(T) 01922 631926. **Ref: YH12687**

SHEAR EASE

Shear Ease, Cae Uchaf, Rhosybol, Amlwch, **Isle of Anglesey**, LL68 9TF, **WALES**.
(T) 01407 832800 **(F)** 01407 832272.
Contact/s
Owner: Mrs S Rudolph
Profile Supplies. Mail Order.
Mail order blade sales & sharpening. No.Staff: 4
Yr. Est: 1994
Opening Times
Mail order company **Ref: YH12688**

SHEARER & MORRIS

Shearer & Morris, 12 Short Bridge St, Newtown, **Powys**, SY16 1AA, **WALES**.
(T) 01686 625762. **Ref: YH12689**

SHEARING, WENDY

Mrs Wendy Shearing, 78 Hatherley Cres, Porchester, Fareham, **Hampshire**, PO16 9TG, **ENGLAND**.
(T) 01329 237084.
Profile Breeder. **Ref: YH12690**

SHEARWATER CORPORATE SVS

Shearwater Corporate Services Ltd, Hyde Hse, The Hyde, Edgeware Rd, Colindale, **London (Greater)**, NW9 6LH, **ENGLAND**.
(T) 0870 0718666 **(F)** 020 82000043
(M) 07831 807323
(E) info@shearwater-insurance.com
(W) www.shearwater-insuance.co.uk.
Profile Club/Association. **Ref: YH12691**

SHEARWATER INSURANCE SVS

Shearwater Insurance Services Ltd, Shearwater Hse, 8 Regent Gate, High St, Waltham Cross, **Hertfordshire**, EN8 7AF, **ENGLAND**.
(T) 0870 0718666 **(F)** 0870 0750043
(E) enquiries@shearwater-insurance.co.uk.
Profile Club/Association. **Ref: YH12692**

SHEDFIELD EQUESTRIAN NURSERY

Shedfield Equestrian Nursery, Botley Rd, Shedfield, Southampton, **Hampshire**, SO32 2HN, **ENGLAND**.
(T) 01329 835115.
Contact/s
Manager: Mrs J Marsh
Profile Supplies. **Ref: YH12693**

SHEEDY, W R

Mr W R Sheedy, New Village Farm, Penhow, Newport, **Newport**, NP26 3AD, **WALES**.
(T) 01633 400165.
Profile Supplies. **Ref: YH12694**

SHEEPCOTE EQUESTRIAN

Sheepcote Equestrian Services, Sheepcote Indoor Arena, Bartestree, Hereford, **Herefordshire**, HR1 4DE, **ENGLAND**.
(T) 01432 850396 **(F)** 01432 851249
(E) dspin@hereford.fsbusiness.co.uk
(W) www.egniweb.co.uk/sheepcote.
Contact/s
Trainer: Mr D Pincus **(Q)** BHSI
Profile Arena, Breeder, Equestrian Centre, Medical Support, Riding Wear Retailer, Saddlery Retailer, Supplies, Trainer.
Watering system for dust control. No.Staff: 7
Yr. Est: 1980 C.Size: 50 Acres **Ref: YH12695**

SHEEPGATE EQUESTRIAN

Sheepgate Equestrian, Sheepgate Nursery, Leverton, Boston, **Lincolnshire**, PE22 0AS, **ENGLAND**.
(T) 01205 870236 **(F)** 01205 871221
(E) info@sheepgate.co.uk
(W) www.sheepgate.co.uk
Affiliated Bodies BHS.
Contact/s
Administration: Mrs J Duggan
Profile Equestrian Centre, Riding School, Riding Wear Retailer.
Pony days available throughout the school holidays. Cafe open on showdays.
Opening Times
Sp: Open 09:00. Closed 21:00.
Su: Open 09:00. Closed 21:00.
Au: Open 09:00. Closed 21:00.
Wn: Open 09:00. Closed 21:00. **Ref: YH12696**

SHEEPGATE TACK & TOGS

Sheepgate Tack & Togs, Sheepgate Nursery, Leverton, Boston, **Lincolnshire**, PE22 0AS, **ENGLAND**.
(T) 01205 870236/871710 **(F)** 01205 871221
(E) info@sheepgate.co.uk
(W) www.sheepgate.co.uk
Affiliated Bodies BHS.
Contact/s
Owner: Mrs S Payne **(Q)** BHSAI, BHSI, BHSII
(E) sarah@sheepgate.co.uk
Profile Equestrian Centre, Riding School, Saddlery Retailer.
Competitions are run on a regular basis from "Have -a-go- shows". Dressage tuition for all ages and abilities is available and clinics by appointment. Stable management lessons, horse owner certificates and training for BHS exams. Also hold 'own a pony' days during the school holidays. No.Staff: 6
Opening Times
Sp: Open Tues - Fri 10:00, Sat 09:00. Closed Tues - Thurs 18:00, Fri, Sat 17:00.
Su: Open Tues - Fri 10:00, Sat 09:00. Closed Tues - Thurs 18:00, Fri, Sat 17:00.
Au: Open Tues - Fri 10:00, Sat 09:00. Closed Tues - Thurs 18:00, Fri, Sat 17:00.
Wn: Open Tues - Fri 10:00, Sat 09:00. Closed Tues - Thurs 18:00, Fri, Sat 17:00.
Sundays are competiton days only. **Ref: YH12697**

SHEEPHOUSE STUD

Sheephouse Stud, Reading Rd, Henley-on-Thames, **Oxfordshire**, RG9 4HF, **ENGLAND**.
(T) 01491 413322.
Contact/s
Owner: Mrs C Starkey
Profile Breeder. **Ref: YH12698**

SHEFFIELD, JOHN-PAUL

John-Paul Sheffield, C/O S Leics Riding Establishment, Leire, Lutterworth, **Leicestershire**, LE17 5HP, **ENGLAND**.
(T) 01455 209407. **Ref: YH12699**

SHEKLETON, ALAN

Alan Shekleton, Ballyhoe, Carrickmacross, **County Meath**, **IRELAND**.
(T) 041 6854166.
Contact/s
Owner: Alan Shekleton
Profile Breeder.
Opening Times
Telephone for an appointment **Ref: YH12700**

SHELDON EQUESTRIAN CTRE

Sheldon Equestrian Centre, Higher Northcott Farm, Blackborough, Cullompton, **Devon**, EX15 2JF, **ENGLAND**.
(T) 01823 681118.
Contact/s
Owner: Mrs M Matthews **Ref: YH12701**

SHELDON TRAILER HIRE & SALES

Sheldon Trailer Hire & Sales, 771 Old Lode Lane, Solihull, **Midlands (West)**, B92 8JE, **ENGLAND**.
(T) 0121 7429259 **(F)** 0121 7429259.
Contact/s
Owner: Mr R Coombes
Profile Transport/Horse Boxes. **Ref: YH12702**

SHELLY STUD

Shelly Stud, East Week, South Zeal, Okehampton, **Devon**, EX20 2QB, **ENGLAND**.
(T) 01647 231270.
Profile Breeder. **Ref: YH12703**

SHELTON FARM

Shelton Farm Carriage Driving Centre, Tidmarsh, Reading, **Berkshire**, RG8 8ER, **ENGLAND**.
(T) 0118 9842619 **(F)** 0870 1611280
(W) www.sheltonfarmcarriages.co.uk.
Contact/s
General Manager: Mr C Pawson **(Q)** LHHI
Profile Carriage Driving Centre.
Horse Drawn Carriages for Funerals and Weddings.
Yr. Est: 1993
Opening Times
Sp: Open 10:30. Closed 16:30.
Su: Open 10:30. Closed 16:30.
Au: Open 10:30. Closed 16:00.
Wn: Open 10:30. Closed 16:00. **Ref: YH12704**

SHELTON HSE SADDLERY

Shelton House Saddlery, Shelton Hse, Shelton, Newark, **Nottinghamshire**, NG23 5JQ, **ENGLAND**.
(T) 01949 850056 **(F)** 01949 876478.
Contact/s
Owner: Miss B Edwards
Profile Saddlery Retailer. **Ref: YH12705**

SHENLEY STUD

Shenley Stud, Rectory Farm, Rectory Lane, Shenley, Radlett, **Hertfordshire**, WD7 9AN, **ENGLAND**.
(T) 01923 857774.
Contact/s
Manageress: Mrs D Hugh
Profile Breeder. **Ref: YH12706**

SHENTON, C W

C W Shenton, Bridge Farm, Handforth, Wilmslow, **Cheshire**, SK9 3EN, **ENGLAND**.
(T) 01625 522917.
Profile Supplies. **Ref: YH12707**

SHENTON, MAXINE

Maxine Shenton MSTAT BHSAI, Church End Cottage, Great Hormead, Buntingford, **Hertfordshire**, SG9 0NH, **ENGLAND**.
(T) 01763 289235.
Profile Medical Support. **Ref: YH12708**

SHENVAL FARM

Shenval Farm Equestrian Centre, Shenval Farm, Glenlivet, Ballindalloch, **Moray**, AB37 9DP, **SCOTLAND**.
(T) 01807 590212 **(F)** 01807 590212
(E) shenval@glenlivet1.freeserve.co.uk
(W) www.glenlivet1.freeserve.co.uk.
Contact/s
Owner: Ms R McLeod
Profile Breeder, Equestrian Centre, Stable/Livery.
The only breeders of the American Bashkir Curly Horse in the UK, with a stallion standing at stud. Also produce hypoallergenic coats which may suit people with allergies to horse hair. No.Staff: 3 C.Size: 175 Acres **Ref: YH12709**

SHEPCO

Shepco, Riverside Rd, Gorleston, Great Yarmouth, **Norfolk**, NR31 6PX, **ENGLAND**.
(T) 01493 658457 **(F)** 01493 442705.
Profile Supplies. **Ref: YH12710**

SHEPHERD, A

A Shepherd, Foxdenton Farm, Foxdenton Lane, Middleton, Manchester, **Manchester (Greater)**, M24 1QN, **ENGLAND**.
(T) 0161 6245120. **Ref: YH12711**

SHEPHERD, N

N Shepherd, Green Lane, Markyate, St Albans, **Hertfordshire**, AL3 8LR, **ENGLAND**.
(T) 01582 840515.
Profile Breeder. **Ref: YH12712**

SHEPLEY FORGE

Shepley Forge, Appleton Quarries, Holmfirth Rd, Shepley, Huddersfield, **Yorkshire (West)**, HD8 8BB, **ENGLAND**.
(T) 01484 609124 **(F)** 01422 310724.
Contact/s
Owner: Mr R Street
Profile Blacksmith. **Ref: YH12713**

SHEPPARD, CAWOOD & KINCAID

Sheppard, Cawood & Kincaid (Midsomer Norton), Silva Hse, Silver St, Midsomer Norton, **Bath & Somerset (North East)**, BA3 2ET, **ENGLAND**.
(T) 01761 412223.
Profile Medical Support. **Ref: YH12714**

SHEPPARD, M I

Mr M I Sheppard, Home Farm Cottage, Eastnor, Ledbury, **Herefordshire**, HR8 1RD, **ENGLAND**.
(T) 01531 634846
(M) 07770 625061.
Profile Trainer. **Ref: YH12715**

SHEPPARD, MICHAEL W

Michael W Sheppard DWCF, West Lane Farm, West Lane, Aughton, Sheffield, **Yorkshire (South)**, S26 3XS, **ENGLAND**.
(T) 07973 933610.
Profile Farrier. **Ref: YH12716**

SHEPPARD, P J

P J Sheppard, The Old Stables, Trefeinon Farm, Llangorse, Brecon, **Powys**, LD3 0PS, **WALES**.
(T) 01874 658607.
Profile Breeder. **Ref: YH12717**

SHERBERTON STUD

Sherberton Stud, Great Sherberton, Princetown, Yelverton, **Devon**, PL20 6SF, **ENGLAND**.
(T) 01364 631276.
Profile Breeder. **Ref: YH12718**

SHERBOURNE TACK

Sherbourne Tack, Sherbourne Farm, Nash, Ludlow, **Shropshire**, SY8 3AN, **ENGLAND**.
(T) 01584 890317 **(F)** 01584 890317.
Profile Saddlery Retailer. **Ref: YH12719**

SHERBOURNE TACK

Sherbourne Tack, 38 Teme St, Tenbury Wells, **Worcestershire**, WR15 8AA, **ENGLAND**.
(T) 01584 811566 **(F)** 01584 811566.
Contact/s
Owner: Mrs N Roberts **Ref: YH12720**

SHERECROFT FARM EQUESTRIAN

Sherecroft Farm Equestrian, Mill Hill, Botley, Southampton, **Hampshire**, SO30 2GY, **ENGLAND**.
(T) 01489 783087 **(F)** 01489 782469.
Contact/s
Owner: Mrs S King **Ref: YH12721**

SHERGOLD

Shergold, West End Nursery, Burnetts Lane, West End, Southampton, **Hampshire**, SO30 2HH, **ENGLAND**.
(T) 023 80462162.
Profile Supplies. **Ref: YH12722**

SHERIDAN, FELIX

Mr Felix Sheridan, Shakespeare Hall, Rowington, **Warwickshire**, CV35 7DB, **ENGLAND**.
(T) 01564 32011.
Profile Supplies. **Ref: YH12723**

SHERLOCK, E A

Mrs E A Sherlock, Birch Farm, Station Road, Mouldsworth, **Cheshire**, **ENGLAND**.
(T) 01928 740231.
Profile Breeder. **Ref: YH12724**

SHERMANDELL MORGANS

Shermandell Morgans, Penrhiw, Llansawel, Llandeilo, **Carmarthenshire**, SA19 7JZ, **WALES**.
(T) 01558 685278.
Contact/s
Owner: Ms Y Storkey
Profile Breeder.
A visit to Morgan Farms is recommended to see the breeds first hand. This is the best way to appreciate the horses friendliness and charisma. Yr. Est: 1991
C.Size: 52 Acres
Opening Times
Telephone for an appointment **Ref: YH12725**

SHERMANDELL MORGANS

Shermandell Morgans, 2 Barrack Cottages, Brighton Rd, Shermanbury, **Sussex (West)**, RH13 8HQ, **ENGLAND**.
(T) 01403 711368.
Profile Breeder. **Ref: YH12726**

SHERPA FEEDS

Sherpa Feeds, Church Farm, Church Rd, Dunstable, **Bedfordshire**, LU6 1RE, **ENGLAND**.
(T) 01582 661128.
Profile Supplies. **Ref: YH12727**

SHERRATT FARM SUPPLIES

Sherratt Farm Supplies, Minton Hse, 17 New St, Wem, **Shropshire**, SY4 5AE, **ENGLAND**.
(T) 01939 232468 **(F)** 01939 232165.
Profile Feed Merchant, Riding Wear Retailer.
Ref: YH12728

SHERRATT, GUY

Guy Sherratt, 135 East St, South Molton, **Devon**, EX36 3BU, **ENGLAND**.
(T) 01769 572227 **(F)** 01769 574331
(E) info@guysherratt.co.uk
(W) www.guysherratt.co.uk.

Profile Equestrian/Rural Property Agents.
Ref: YH12729

SHERRING, JAMES R

James R Sherring DWCF, No 8 Bush Rd, Spaxton, Bridgwater, **Somerset**, TA5 1BX, **ENGLAND**.
(T) 01278 671498.
Profile Farrier. Ref: YH12730

SHERRING, MATTHEW J

Matthew J Sherring DWCF, 42 Higher St, West Chinnock, Crewkerne, **Somerset**, TA18 7QA, **ENGLAND**.
(T) 01935 881108.
Profile Farrier. Ref: YH12731

SHERWOOD STABLES

Sherwood Stables, Folly Rd, Lambourn, Hungerford, **Berkshire**, RG17 8QE, **ENGLAND**.
(T) 01488 71632 **(F)** 01488 73859
(M) 07966 374363.
Profile Trainer. Ref: YH12732

SHERWOOD, O M C

O M C Sherwood, Rhonehurst Cottage, Upper Lambourn, Hungerford, **Berkshire**, RG17 8RG, **ENGLAND**.
(T) 01488 71411 **(F)** 01488 72786.
Contact/s
Owner: Mr O Sherwood
Profile Trainer. Ref: YH12733

SHERWOOD, S E H

S E H Sherwood, Uplands, Upper Lambourn, Hungerford, **Berkshire**, RG17 8QH, **ENGLAND**.
(T) 01488 72077 **(F)** 01488 71206.
Profile Trainer. Ref: YH12734

SHETLAND MARTS CO-OPERATIVE

Shetland Marts Co-Operative Ltd, Staneyhill, Lerwick, Shetlands, **Shetland Islands**, ZE1 0AN, **SCOTLAND**.
(T) 01595 692030 **(F)** 01595 696305. Ref: YH12735

SHETLAND PONY STUD BOOK SOC

Shetland Pony Stud Book Society, 22 York Pl, Perth, **Perth and Kinross**, PH2 8EH, **SCOTLAND**.
(T) 01738 623471 **(F)** 01738 442274
(W) www.shetlandponystudbooksociety.co.uk.
Contact/s
Company Secretary: Mrs E Ward
(E) elaineward@shetlandponystudbooksociety.co.uk
Profile Club/Association. No.Staff: 4
Yr. Est: 1890
Opening Times
Sp: Open 09:00. Closed 17:00.
Su: Open 09:00. Closed 17:00.
Au: Open 09:00. Closed 17:00.
Wn: Open 09:00. Closed 17:00. Ref: YH12736

SHEYCOPSE RIDING CTRE

Sheycopse Riding Centre, Old Woking Rd, Woking, **Surrey**, GU22 8UA, **ENGLAND**.
(T) 01483 770022.
Contact/s
Owner: Mr C Barnes
Profile Riding School. Ref: YH12737

SHIBDEN DALE RIDING CLUB

Shibden Dale Riding Club, 158 Ovenden Rd, Halifax, **Yorkshire (West)**, HX3 5PN, **ENGLAND**.
(T) 01422 204551.
Contact/s
Chairman: Mr N Grogan
Profile Club/Association, Riding Club. Ref: YH12738

SHIE NEWTON TRAILERS

Shie Newton Trailers, Green Lane Farm, Lower Eggleton, Ledbury, **Herefordshire**, HR8 2UQ, **ENGLAND**.
(T) 01531 670522.
Profile Transport/Horse Boxes. Ref: YH12739

SHIELDBANK

Shieldbank Riding & Vaulting Club, North Rd, Saline, Dunfermline, **Fife**, KY12 9LN, **SCOTLAND**.
(T) 01383 852874 **(F)** 01383 852306.
Contact/s
General Manager: Mrs M Beasley
Profile Horse/Rider Accom, Riding Club.
Ref: YH12740

SHIELDS, J GILLIES

J Gillies Shields, Walton Hse, Isley Walton, Castle Donington, **Leicestershire**, DE74 2RL, **ENGLAND**.
(T) 01332 810347.
Profile Stable/Livery. Ref: YH12741

SHIELDS, THOMAS

Thomas Shields, 112 Carrginagh Rd, Kilkeel, Newry, **County Down**, BT34 4QA, **NORTHERN IRELAND**.
(T) 028 30262568.
Profile Supplies. Ref: YH12742

SHIELS, R

Mr R Shiels, Parklands, Tedburgh, **Scottish Borders**, TD8 6LS, **SCOTLAND**.
(T) 01835 864060
(M) 07790 295645.
Profile Supplies. Ref: YH12743

SHILLAM, H G

H G Shillam, 14 Dol Wen, Pencoed, Bridgend, **Bridgend**, CF35 6RS, **WALES**.
(T) 01656 861746.
Contact/s
Owner: Mr H Shillam
Profile Farrier. Ref: YH12744

SHILLINGSTONE & DISTRICT

Shillingstone & District Riding Club, Everetts Lane, Shillingstone, Blandford, **Dorset**, DT11 0SJ, **ENGLAND**.
(T) 01258 860783.
Contact/s
Chairman: Mrs J Little
Profile Club/Association, Riding Club. Ref: YH12745

SHILSTONE ROCKS

Shilstone Rocks Riding Centre, Chittleford Farm, Widecombe-In-The-Moor, Newton Abbot, **Devon**, TQ13 7TF, **ENGLAND**.
(T) 01364 621281 **(F)** 01364 621281
(W) www.shilstonerocks.freeserve.co.uk
Affiliated Bodies ABRS, BHS.
Contact/s
General Manager: Mrs J Penfold **(Q)** BHS 3
Profile Breeder, Riding School, Stable/Livery.
No.Staff: 6 Yr. Est: 1959 C.Size: 140 Acres
Ref: YH12746

SHINERS FORGE

Shiners Forge, Fox Bros Ind Est, Tonedale, Wellington, **Somerset**, TA21 0AW, **ENGLAND**.
(T) 01823 662900.
Contact/s
Owner: Mr C Golding
Profile Blacksmith. Ref: YH12747

SHIPHAM RIDING HOLIDAYS

Shipham Riding Holidays, Broadway, Shipham, Winscombe, **Somerset (North)**, BS25 1UE, **ENGLAND**.
(T) 01934 843522.
Profile Holidays. Ref: YH12748

SHIPLEY, ANTHONY RAYMOND

Anthony Raymond Shipley, Derwent Valley Forge, Greengates Lane, South Duffield, Selby, **Yorkshire (North)**, YO8 6EQ, **ENGLAND**.
(T) 01757 288341.
Profile Farrier. Ref: YH12749

SHIPPY'S JOCKEY AGENCY

Shippy's Jockey Agency, 6 Cardigan St, Newmarket, **Suffolk**, CB8 8HZ, **ENGLAND**.
(T) 01638 668484.
Profile Trainer. Ref: YH12750

SHIPSTON MILL

Shipston Mill, 20 Mill St, Shipston-on-Stour, **Warwickshire**, CV36 4AW, **ENGLAND**.
(T) 01608 661411 **(F)** 01608 663020
(E) shipstonmill1@compuserve.com.
Profile Medical Support. Ref: YH12751

SHIPTON CONNEMARA PONY STUD

Shipton Connemara Pony Stud, Ullenwood Manor Farm, Ullenwood, Cheltenham, **Gloucestershire**, GL53 9QT, **ENGLAND**.
(T) 01242 512982.
Contact/s
Owner: Mrs E Beckett
Profile Breeder. Ref: YH12752

SHIPTON RIDING CLUB

Shipton Riding Club, Dowerfield, Long Bredy, Dorchester, **Dorset**, DT2 9AA, **ENGLAND**.
(T) 01308 482258.
Profile Club/Association, Riding Club. Ref: YH12753

SHIRE HORSE SOC

Shire Horse Society, East of England Showground, Peterborough, **Cambridgeshire**, PE2 6XE, **ENGLAND**.
(T) 01733 234451 **(F)** 01733 370038.
Contact/s
Secretary: Ms T Gibson
Profile Club/Association. Ref: YH12754

SHIRES EQUESTRIAN

Shires Equestrian Products, 15 Southern Ave, Leominster, **Herefordshire**, HR6 0QF, **ENGLAND**.
(T) 01568 613600 **(F)** 01568 613599
(E) sales@shires-equestrian.co.uk
(W) www.shires-equestrian.co.uk.
Profile Riding Wear Retailer, Saddlery Retailer, Supplies. Ref: YH12755

SHONE, NEIL J

Neil J Shone DWCF, Northfield Farm, Gorsey Lane, Bold, St Helens, **Merseyside**, WA9 4SW, **ENGLAND**.
(T) 01744 812204.
Profile Farrier. Ref: YH12756

SHOOTER TOWBARS & TRAILERS

Shooter Towbars & Trailers, 189 Weyhill Rd, Andover, **Hampshire**, SP10 3LJ, **ENGLAND**.
(T) 01264 363380.
Contact/s
Owner: Mr J Shooter
Profile Transport/Horse Boxes. Ref: YH12757

SHOPLAND HALL EQUESTRIAN

Shopland Hall Equestrian Centre, Shopland Rd, Rochford, **Essex**, SS4 1LT, **ENGLAND**.
(T) 01702 543377 **(F)** 01702 530600
(E) info@shoplandhall.co.uk
(W) www.shoplandhall.co.uk
Affiliated Bodies BHS.
Contact/s
General Manager: Ms A Murrell
(E) amanda@shoplandhall.co.uk
Profile Equestrian Centre, Riding Club, Riding School, Riding Wear Retailer, Saddlery Retailer, Stable/Livery, Supplies.
Holds BHS progressive riding test for weekly riders. Hacking is available on private tracks. Specialises in Jumping (Show and Cross Country) Training students to NVQ3 and BHSAI level. No.Staff: 22
Yr. Est: 1991 C.Size: 75 Acres
Ref: YH12758

SHORESIDE STABLES

Shoreside Stables, Shoreside Farm, Prestolee Rd, Radcliffe, Manchester, **Manchester (Greater)**, M26 1HJ, **ENGLAND**.
(T) 0161 7232269.
Contact/s
Owner: Mr D Bent
Profile Stable/Livery.
Lessons given on own horses. Yr. Est: 1996
Opening Times
Sp: Open Mon - Sun 09:00. Closed Mon - Sun 18:00.
Su: Open Mon - Sun 09:00. Closed Mon - Sun 18:00.
Au: Open Mon - Sun 09:00. Closed Mon - Sun 18:00.
Wn: Open Mon - Sun 09:00. Closed Mon - Sun 18:00. Ref: YH12759

SHORT, JAMES H

James H Short, Highfield Lodge Farm, Riding Barn Hill, Wick, Bristol, **Bristol**, BS30 5QZ, **ENGLAND**.
(T) 01179 374270 **(F)** 01179 374270.
Contact/s
Owner: Mr J Short
Profile Transport/Horse Boxes. Ref: YH12760

SHORT, JOHN A

John A Short AWCB, Meadowview, 1 Haggonfields Farm Cottage, Rhodesia, Worksop, **Nottinghamshire**, S80 3HW, **ENGLAND**.
(T) 01909 478101.
Profile Farrier. Ref: YH12761

SHORTIS, VICKI

Mrs Vicki Shortis, Costessey Hse, Old Costessey, **Norfolk**, NR8 5DG, **ENGLAND**.
(T) 01603 742012.
Profile Breeder. Ref: YH12762

SHOVELSTRODE RACING

Shovelstrode Racing, Homstall Dutton, Shovelstrode Lane, Ashurst Wood, East Grinstead, **Sussex (West)**, RH19 3PL, **ENGLAND**.
(T) 01342 323153
(W) www.shovelstrode-racing.co.uk.
Contact/s
Assistant Trainer: Mr A Irvine
Profile Trainer. Ref: YH12763

SHOW JUMPERS

Show Jumpers, Meadow Crest Cottage, Burdrop,

Sibford Gower, Banbury, **Oxfordshire**, OX15 5RQ, **ENGLAND**.
(T) 01295 788235 **(F)** 01295 788235.
Profile Supplies. **Ref: YH12764**

SHOW WINNER PRODUCTS

Show Winner Products, 8 Vicarage Cl, Collingham, Newark, **Nottinghamshire**, NG23 7PQ, **ENGLAND**.
(T) 01636 892054.
Profile Supplies. **Ref: YH12765**

SHOWJUMP INT

Showjump International, Snape Hill Works, Snape Hill Rd, Darfield, Barnsley, **Yorkshire (South)**, S73 9LP, **ENGLAND**.
(T) 01226 755057 **(F)** 01226 755057
(W) www.showjumps.net.
Contact/s
Owner: Mr M Wright
(E) showjumpint@hotmail.com
Profile Supplies. No.Staff: 6 **Ref: YH12766**

SHOWTIME ROSETTES

Showtime Rosettes, Bluebells Spinney, The Street, Thorpe Abbotts, **Norfolk**, IP21 5JB, **ENGLAND**.
(T) 07850 716968.
Profile Club/Association. **Ref: YH12767**

SHREWSBURY & DISTRICT

Shrewsbury & District Riding Club, 6 Hatton Common, Hinstock, Market Drayton, **Shropshire**, TF9 2TS, **ENGLAND**.
(T) 01952 78431.
Contact/s
Chairman: Miss B Evans
Profile Club/Association, Riding Club. **Ref: YH12768**

SHRIGLEY-PENNA, JOHN

Mr John Shrigley-Penna, 29 Lauds Rd, Crick, **Northamptonshire**, NN6 7TJ, **ENGLAND**.
(T) 01788 822056.
Profile Breeder. **Ref: YH12769**

SHROPSHIRE SOUTH RIDING CLUB

Shropshire South Riding Club, Lowe Farm, Stockton On Teme, **Worcestershire**, WR6 6UA, **ENGLAND**.
(T) 01584 881242.
Contact/s
Chairman: Mrs J Bargman
Profile Club/Association, Riding Club. **Ref: YH12770**

SHRUB FARM LIVERY YARD

Shrub Farm Livery Yard, Shrub Farm, Burton Row, Brent Knoll, **Somerset**, TA9 4BX, **ENGLAND**.
(T) 01278 760787 **(F)** 01278 760787.
Profile Stable/Livery. **Ref: YH12771**

SHUCKBURGH HSE RIDING CTRE

Shuckburgh House Riding Centre, Shuckburgh Hse, Naseby, **Northamptonshire**, NN6 7DA, **ENGLAND**.
(T) 01604 740481.
Profile Breeder, Equestrian Centre, Trainer.
Ref: YH12772

SHUFFLEBOTTOM

Shufflebottom Ltd, Cross Hands Business Pk, Cross Hands, **Carmarthenshire**, SA14 6RB, **WALES**.
(T) 01269 831831 **(F)** 01269 831031.
Profile Supplies. **Ref: YH12773**

SHUTFORD STUD

Shutford Stud, Banbury, **Oxfordshire**, OX15 6PL, **ENGLAND**.
(T) 01295 78266 **(F)** 01295 78417.
Profile Breeder. **Ref: YH12774**

SHUTLEWORTH, A

Mr A Shutleworth, Barbon Fell Hse, Barbon, Carnforth, **Lancashire**, LA8 2LQ, **ENGLAND**.
(T) 01524 276240.
Profile Breeder. **Ref: YH12775**

SHUTTLEWORTH, ANDREW J

Andrew J Shuttleworth DWCF, 64 Glendale Drive, Mellor, Blackburn, **Lancashire**, BB2 7HD, **ENGLAND**.
(T) 01254 812951.
Profile Farrier. **Ref: YH12776**

SIAN SADDLERY

Sian Saddlery, Vulcan Hse Farm, Coopers Green, Uckfield, **Sussex (East)**, TN22 4AT, **ENGLAND**.
(T) 01825 732636 **(F)** 01825 732636.
Contact/s
Manager: Ms S Mitchell
Profile Saddlery Retailer. **Ref: YH12777**

SIANWOOD STUD

Sianwood Stud, Coedcae Farm, Llandovery, **Carmarthenshire**, **WALES**.
(T) 01550 720849.
Profile Breeder. **Ref: YH12778**

SIBBALD, ROBERT

Robert Sibbald, Thorn Farm, Dollar, **Clackmannanshire**, **SCOTLAND**..
Profile Breeder. **Ref: YH12779**

SID & OTTER VALLEY

Sid & Otter Valley Riding Club, Salt Box Cottage, Awliscombe, Honiton, **Devon**, EX14 0PY, **ENGLAND**.
(T) 01404 841686.
Contact/s
Chairman: Mrs M Moore
Profile Club/Association, Riding Club. **Ref: YH12780**

SID WILSON

Sid Wilson (Leicester) Ltd, 9 Waldron Drive, Leicester, **Leicestershire**, LE2 4PL, **ENGLAND**.
(T) 0116 2712190
(M) 07850 037139.
Profile Supplies. **Ref: YH12781**

SIDDALL, J K & J

J K & J Siddall, Fence Farm, Fence, Woodhouse Mill, Sheffield, **Yorkshire (South)**, S13 9ZB, **ENGLAND**.
(T) 0114 2692772 **(F)** 0114 2692772.
Contact/s
Owner: Mr K Siddall
Profile Stable/Livery.
Stable and grazing livery, prices on request. Can take 10 horses. Yr. Est: 1971 C.Size: 20 Acres
Opening Times
By appointment only **Ref: YH12782**

SIDDALL, L C

Miss L C Siddall, Stonebridge Farm, Colton, Tadcaster, **Yorkshire (North)**, LS24 8EP, **ENGLAND**.
(T) 01904 744291 **(F)** 01904 744291
(M) 07778 216694.
Profile Trainer. **Ref: YH12783**

SIDE HILL STUD

Side Hill Stud, Stanley Rd, Newmarket, **Suffolk**, CB8 8AF, **ENGLAND**.
(T) 01638 662401 **(F)** 01638 666465.
Contact/s
Manager: Mr J Warren
Profile Blood Stock Agency, Breeder. **Ref: YH12784**

SIDE SADDLE ASSOCIATION

Side Saddle Association (The), Highbury Hse, 19 High St, Welford, **Northamptonshire**, NN6 6HT, **ENGLAND**.
(T) 01858 575300 **(F)** 01858 575051
(E) 100600.1531@compuserve.com.
Contact/s
Key Contact: Mrs M James
Profile Club/Association. **Ref: YH12785**

SIDE SADDLE LADY

Side Saddle Lady, 60 Argyll Rd, Pennsylvania, Exeter, **Devon**, EX4 4RY, **ENGLAND**.
(T) 01392 271080
(E) sidesaddlelady@tinyworld.co.uk
(W) www.sidesaddlelady.co.uk.
Contact/s
Owner: Mrs P Housden
Profile Supplies.
Wide range of modern and original designs for riding habits, also embroidered items and gifts. Gift and Craft Shop, specialising in side saddle products, available
Ref: YH12786

SIDE SADDLES

Side Saddles, 2 Mill St, Corfe Mullen, Wimborne, **Dorset**, BH21 3RQ, **ENGLAND**.
(T) 01258 857821
(E) vickyspooner.sidesaddles@virgin.net
(W) www.sidesaddles.co.uk.
Contact/s
Assistant: Mrs P Spooner
Profile Riding Wear Retailer, Saddlery Retailer.
Saddles are made to measure off site. Both new and second hand goods are stocked. Yr. Est: 1986
Opening Times
Sp: Open Mon - Fri 09:00. Closed Mon - Fri 17:00.
Su: Open Mon - Fri 09:00. Closed Mon - Fri 17:00.
Au: Open Mon - Fri 09:00. Closed Mon - Fri 17:00.
Wn: Open Mon - Fri 09:00. Closed Mon - Fri 17:00.
Open weekends by appointment **Ref: YH12787**

SIDEBOTTOM, J

Mrs J Sidebottom, Rhydlewis Grange, Rhydlewis, Llandysul, **Carmarthenshire**, SA44 5PE, **WALES**.
(T) 01239 851455.
Profile Supplies. **Ref: YH12788**

SIDE-SADDLE ASS

Side-Saddle Association (N Ireland) (The), 23 Ballyalton Rd, Comber, **County Down**, BT23 6JX, **NORTHERN IRELAND**.
(T) 028 91874383.
Profile Club/Association. **Ref: YH12789**

SIDWELL, PAUL ALAN

Paul Alan Sidwell RSS, 131 Windsor Rd, Bray, Maidenhead, **Berkshire**, SL6 2DP, **ENGLAND**.
(T) 01628 635024.
Profile Farrier. **Ref: YH12790**

SIER, JOHN

John Sier, Ponies Reach, Hill Lane, Bransgore, Christchurch, **Dorset**, BH23 8BL, **ENGLAND**.
(T) 01425 72746. **Ref: YH12791**

SIERRA SADDLE

Sierra Saddle Co, 602 High Rd, Benfleet, **Essex**, SS7 5RW, **ENGLAND**.
(T) 01268 792769 **(F)** 01268 566775
(W) www.escortgunleather.com.
Contact/s
Owner: Mr J Skelton
(E) john@saddles.freeserve.co.uk
Profile Saddlery Retailer, Supplies.
Western Saddlery (maker and importer).
Yr. Est: 1969 **Ref: YH12792**

SIFTSTAR

Siftstar Ltd, Smithy, Barthomley, Crewe, **Cheshire**, CW2 5PE, **ENGLAND**.
(T) 01270 874502 **(F)** 01270 874502.
Profile Blacksmith. **Ref: YH12793**

SIGNFORD

Signford Ltd, Manor Farm, Warter Rd, Etton, Beverley, **Yorkshire (East)**, HU17 7PQ, **ENGLAND**.
(T) 01430 810244 **(F)** 01430 810777
(M) 07932 163778
(E) signford@farmline.com.
Profile Supplies. **Ref: YH12794**

SIGSWORTH, L C & A E

L C & A E Sigsworth, West Moor Stud, Raskelf, York, **Yorkshire (North)**, YO61 3LR, **ENGLAND**.
(T) 01347 821187.
Profile Breeder. **Ref: YH12795**

SILFIELD BLOODSTOCK

Silfield Bloodstock, Manor Fm, Southburgh, Thetford, **Norfolk**, IP25 7TJ, **ENGLAND**.
(T) 01953 851303.
Profile Blood Stock Agency. **Ref: YH12796**

SILHOUETTE SADDLERY

Silhouette Saddlery, Unit 1 Deeleys Trading Est, Leamore Lane, Walsall, **Midlands (West)**, WS2 7BY, **ENGLAND**.
(T) 01922 400890.
Contact/s
Owner: Mr M Poole **Ref: YH12797**

SILK & STEM

Silk & Stem, Kingston Hse, Kingston Blount, Oxford, **Oxfordshire**, OX9 4SH, **ENGLAND**.
(T) 01844 351216 **(F)** 01844 353103. **Ref: YH12798**

SILK, J

Miss J Silk, Brook Farm, Stapleford Rd, Stapleford Abbots, Romford, **Essex**, RM4 1EJ, **ENGLAND**.
(T) 01708 688284.
Profile Breeder. **Ref: YH12799**

SILKSTONE EQUESTRIAN CTRE

Silkstone Equestrian Centre, Throstle Nest, Moor End Lane, Silkstone Common, Barnsley, **Yorkshire (South)**, S75 4QX, **ENGLAND**.
(T) 01226 790422.
Contact/s
Owner: Ms S Baxter
Profile Riding School. Yr. Est: 1977
C.Size: 27 Acres
Opening Times
Sp: Open Tues - Sun 08:30. Closed Tues - Sun 18:00.
Su: Open Tues - Sun 08:30. Closed Tues - Sun 18:00.
Au: Open Tues - Sun 08:30. Closed Tues - Sun 18:00.
Wn: Open Tues - Sun 08:30. Closed Tues - Sun 18:00.
Closed Monday **Ref: YH12800**

SILLARS, A L

A L Sillars, 18 Watson St, Glasgow, **Glasgow (City of)**, G1 5AF, **SCOTLAND**.
(T) 0141 5523391 **(F)** 0141 5525180.
Contact/s
Owner: Mr A Sillars
Profile Blacksmith. **Ref: YH12801**

SILLARS, BELINDA

Belinda Sillars, Loudham, Brenley, Faversham, **Kent**, ME13 9LX, **ENGLAND**.
(T) 01795 531276. **Ref: YH12802**

SILVER BIRCH STABLES

Silver Birch Stables, Langley Lane, Birch, Heywood, **Lancashire**, OL10 2QJ, **ENGLAND**.
(T) 0161 6436863.
Profile Stable/Livery. **Ref: YH12803**

SILVER FOX EQUESTRIAN

Silver Fox Equestrian Ltd, Wormald St, Liversedge, **Yorkshire (West)**, WF15 6BE, **ENGLAND**.
(T) 01924 520890 **(F)** 01924 411368.
Profile Supplies. **Ref: YH12804**

SILVER HORSESHOE

Silver Horseshoe Riding Stables, High Bullen Farm, Ilkerton, Lynton, **Devon**, **ENGLAND**..
Profile Equestrian Centre. **Ref: YH12805**

SILVER HORSESHOE

Silver Horseshoe Stables & Wayland Stud, Forest Green, Hale, Fordingbridge, **Hampshire**, SP6 2NR, **ENGLAND**.
(T) 01725 510678.
Contact/s
Owner: Ms M Bryant
Profile Breeder, Riding School, Stable/Livery.
Ref: YH12806

SILVER HORSESHOE RIDING CLUB

Silver Horseshoe Riding Club, Hill Farm, Norwell, Newark, **Nottinghamshire**, NG23 6JN, **ENGLAND**.
(T) 01636 636210.
Contact/s
Chairman: Mr D Hall
Profile Club/Association, Riding Club. **Ref: YH12807**

SILVER KNOWES RIDING SCHOOL

Silver Knowes Riding School, 10 Muirhouse Parkway, Edinburgh, **Edinburgh (City of)**, EH4 5EU, **SCOTLAND**.
(T) 0131 3152777. **Ref: YH12808**

SILVER LEY POLOCROSSE CLUB

Silver Ley Polocrosse Club, Duntons Farm, Bridge St Rd, Lavenham, **Suffolk**, CO10 9SL, **ENGLAND**.
(T) 01787 247265.
Profile Club/Association. Polocrosse Club.
Ref: YH12809

SILVER LEYS POLO CLUB

Silver Leys Polo Club, 3 Garden Ave, Hatfield, **Hertfordshire**, **ENGLAND**.
(T) 01707 886563.
Contact/s
Secretary: Ron Mees
Profile Club/Association. Polo Club. **Ref: YH12810**

SILVER MILL RIDING CTRE

Silver Mill Riding Centre, Silver Mill Hill, Otley, **Yorkshire (West)**, LS21 3BJ, **ENGLAND**.
(T) 01943 464019 **(F)** 0113 2886471.
Contact/s
Owner: Mrs S Nutter **Ref: YH12811**

SILVER SHOE RIDING STABLES

Silver Shoe Riding Stables, Back Of, 71 Sea View St, Cleethorpes, **Lincolnshire (North East)**, DN35 8HY, **ENGLAND**.
(T) 01472 200477. **Ref: YH12812**

SILVERDALE ARABIAN STUD

Silverdale Arabian Stud, Northlands Farm, Bodiam, Robertsbridge, **Sussex (East)**, TN32 5UX, **ENGLAND**.
(T) 01580 830789 **(F)** 01580 830789.
Profile Breeder. **Ref: YH12813**

SILVERDALE TRANSPORT

Silverdale Transport, Northlands Farm, Bodiam, Robertsbridge, **Sussex (East)**, TN32 5UX, **ENGLAND**.
(T) 01580 830789
(M) 07785 511099.
Profile Transport/Horse Boxes. **Ref: YH12814**

SILVERDOWN

Silverdown, Reading Rd, Harwell, Didcot, **Oxfordshire**, OX11 0LU, **ENGLAND**.
(T) 01235 835377.
Contact/s
Owner: Mrs V Schuddeboom
Profile Riding School, Stable/Livery. **Ref: YH12815**

SILVERMERE EQUESTRIAN CTRE

Silvermere Equestrian Centre, Redhill Rd, Cobham, **Surrey**, KT11 1EQ, **ENGLAND**.
(T) 01932 865858.
Contact/s
Owner: Ms E Anstis **Ref: YH12816**

SILVERMERE EQUESTRIAN CTRE

Silvermere Equestrian Centre, Bramley Hedge Farm, Redhill Rd, Cobham, **Surrey**, KT11 1EQ, **ENGLAND**.
(T) 01932 863464 **(F)** 01932 863180. **Ref: YH12817**

SIMCOCK, R

R Simcock, Delight Farm, Barkisland, Halifax, **Yorkshire (West)**, HX4 0DZ, **ENGLAND**.
(T) 01422 822260 **(F)** 01422 824564.
Contact/s
Owner: Mr R Simcock
Profile Supplies. Hay & Straw Merchants.
No.Staff: 2 Yr. Est: 1986
Opening Times
Sp: Open Mon - Sun 09:00. Closed Mon - Sun 22:00.
Su: Open Mon - Sun 09:00. Closed Mon - Sun 22:00.
Au: Open Mon - Sun 09:00. Closed Mon - Sun 22:00.
Wn: Open Mon - Sun 09:00. Closed Mon - Sun 22:00. **Ref: YH12818**

SIMES & SON

Simes & Son (Saddlers) Ltd, 27 Wellington St, Aldershot, **Hampshire**, GU11 1DX, **ENGLAND**.
(T) 01252 320111.
Profile Saddlery Retailer. **Ref: YH12819**

SIMMONDS & SAMPSON

Simmonds & Sampson, 5 West St, Wimborne, **Dorset**, BH21 1JN, **ENGLAND**.
(T) 01202 882103.
Profile Chartered Surveyors. **Ref: YH12820**

SIMMONDS, LOUE

Loue Simmonds, 206 Dovercourt Rd, Horefield, Bristol, **Bristol**, BS7 9SL, **ENGLAND**.
(T) 01179 756623
Affiliated Bodies NAAT.
Contact/s
Physiotherapist: Loue Simmonds
Profile Medical Support.
Physiotherapist for horses & dogs. **Ref: YH12821**

SIMMONS

Simmons & Sons, 1 High St, Marlow, **Buckinghamshire**, SL7 1AX, **ENGLAND**.
(T) 01628 484353/891111 **(F)** 01628 898233
(E) marlow@simmonsandsons.com
(W) www.simmonsandsons.com.
Contact/s
Enquiries: Ms C Cope
Profile Chartered Surveyors.
Fine Art Auctioneers & Valuers. Wide range of properties available, from country estates to commercial developments. Yr. Est: 1802
Opening Times
Sp: Open Mon - Sat 09:00. Closed Mon - Fri 17:45, Sat 16:00.
Su: Open Mon - Sat 09:00. Closed Mon - Fri 17:45, Sat 16:00.
Au: Open Mon - Sat 09:00. Closed Mon - Fri 17:45, Sat 16:00.
Wn: Open Mon - Sat 09:00. Closed Mon - Fri 17:45, Sat 16:00.
Closed Sundays **Ref: YH12822**

SIMMONS

Simmons & Sons, 12 Wote St, Basingstoke, **Hampshire**, RG21 7NN, **ENGLAND**.
(T) 01256 840077 **(F)** 01256 320604
(E) basingstoke@simmonsandsons.com
(W) www.simmonsandsons.com.
Contact/s
Enquiries: Ms W Smith
Profile Chartered Surveyors.
Fine Art Auctioneers & Valuers. Wide range of properties available, from country estates to commercial developments. **Ref: YH12823**

SIMMONS

Simmons & Sons, 32 Bell St, Henley-on-Thames, **Oxfordshire**, RG9 2BH, **ENGLAND**.
(T) 01491 571111 **(F)** 01491 579833
(E) henley@simmonsandssons.com
(W) www.simmonsandsons.com.
Contact/s
Enquiries: Ms S Clarke
Profile Chartered Surveyors.
Fine Art Auctioneers & Valuers. Wide range of properties available, from country estates to commercial developments. Yr. Est: 1802
Opening Times
Sp: Open Mon - Sat 09:00. Closed Mon - Fri 17:45, Sat 16:00.
Su: Open Mon - Sat 09:00. Closed Mon - Fri 17:45, Sat 16:00.
Au: Open Mon - Sat 09:00. Closed Mon - Fri 17:45, Sat 16:00.
Wn: Open Mon - Sat 09:00. Closed Mon - Fri 17:45, Sat 16:00.
Closed Sundays **Ref: YH12824**

SIMMONS

Simmons & Sons, The Est Office, Pepr Harlow, Godalming, **Surrey**, GU8 6BQ, **ENGLAND**.
(T) 01483 418151 **(F)** 01483 418171
(E) info@simmonsandsons.com
(W) www.simmonsandsons.com.
Contact/s
Partner: Mr R Fuller
Profile Chartered Surveyors.
Fine Art Auctioneers & Valuers. Wide range of properties available, from country estates to commercial developments. Yr. Est: 1802
Opening Times
Sp: Open Mon - Sat 09:00. Closed Mon - Fri 17:45, Sat 16:00.
Su: Open Mon - Sat 09:00. Closed Mon - Fri 17:45, Sat 16:00.
Au: Open Mon - Sat 09:00. Closed Mon - Fri 17:45, Sat 16:00.
Wn: Open Mon - Sat 09:00. Closed Mon - Fri 17:45, Sat 16:00.
Closed Sundays **Ref: YH12825**

SIMMONS, AVRIL

Avril Simmons, East Lodge, Castleton, Muckhart, Dollar, **Clackmannanshire**, FK14 7PJ, **SCOTLAND**.
(T) 01259 781497.
Profile Stable/Livery. **Ref: YH12826**

SIMMONS, BRYNLY A

Brynly A Simmons DWCF, Villamoura, Westmorland Drive, Warfield, Bracknell, **Berkshire**, RG42 3QP, **ENGLAND**.
(T) 01344 304038.
Profile Farrier. **Ref: YH12827**

SIMMONS, J C

Mr J C Simmons, Countisbury, Abridge Rd, Abridge, **Essex**, RM4 1TX, **ENGLAND**.
(T) 01992 812440 **(F)** 01992 812622.
Profile Supplies. **Ref: YH12828**

SIMMONS, W H & K A

W H & K A Simmons, Mayo Farm, Brazenhill, Haughton, Stafford, **Staffordshire**, ST18 9JP, **ENGLAND**.
(T) 01785 780304.
Contact/s
Partner: Mrs K Simmons
Profile Stable/Livery. **Ref: YH12829**

SIMON HUNTER

Simon Hunter, Windrush, The Camp, Stroud, **Gloucestershire**, GL6 7EZ, **ENGLAND**.
(T) 01285 821231.
Contact/s
Owner: Mr S Hunter
Profile Blacksmith. **Ref: YH12830**

SIMON, (CPT), TOMLINSON C

Captain Simon & Mrs Claire Tomlinson, Down Farm, Westonbirt, Tetbury, **Gloucestershire**, GL8 8QW, **ENGLAND**.
(T) 01666 880214 **(F)** 01666 880266.
Contact/s
Trainer: Captain S Tomlinson
Profile Breeder, Trainer. **Ref: YH12831**

SIMONS, M A P

M A P Simons MRCVS, 5 Orchard Cl, Fetcham, **Surrey**, KT22 9LS, **ENGLAND**.
(T) 01372 379635 **(F)** 01372 374572.
Profile Medical Support. **Ref: YH12832**

SIMONSIDE VETNRY CTRE

Simonside Veterinary Centre, High St, Rothbury, **Northumberland**, NE65 7UG, **ENGLAND**.
(T) 01669 620638 **(F)** 01669 621634

(E) enquiries@simonside.freeserve.co.uk.
Profile Medical Support. Ref: YH12833

SIMPLY BY DESIGN

Simply by Design, Leadon Lodge, Gloucester, **Gloucestershire**, GL19 3HZ, **ENGLAND**.
(T) 01531 822888 (F) 01531 822888.
Profile Supplies. Ref: YH12834

SIMPLY ROSETTES

Simply Rosettes, Craighead Farm, Fauldhouse, **Lothian (West)**, EH47 9AB, **SCOTLAND**.
(T) 01501 771679 (F) 01501 771579.
Profile Club/Association. Ref: YH12835

SIMPSON

Mrs Simpson, Highfield, North Berwick, **Lothian (East)**, EH39 5JG, **SCOTLAND**.
(T) 01620 2150.
Profile Breeder. Ref: YH12836

SIMPSON, ANDREW W

Andrew W Simpson, Wester Coxton Farm, By Lhanbryde, Elgin, **Moray**, IV30 8QS, **SCOTLAND**.
(T) 01343 843324.
Profile Farrier. Ref: YH12837

SIMPSON, G

G Simpson, Woodcroft, The Hills, Bradwell, Sheffield, **Yorkshire (South)**, S33 9HZ, **ENGLAND**.
(T) 01433 621171.
Contact/s
Owner: Mrs G Simpson
Profile Breeder. Ref: YH12838

SIMPSON, JONATHAN

Jonathan Simpson, Little Acre, Newtown, Leominster, **Herefordshire**, HR6 8QD, **ENGLAND**.
(T) 01568 614596.
Contact/s
Owner: Mr J Simpson (Q) DWCF
Profile Blacksmith, Farrier. Yr. Est: 1989
Ref: YH12839

SIMPSON, P B

Duval Stud, Littleacre, Newtown Lane, Leominster, **Herefordshire**, HR6 8QD, **ENGLAND**.
(T) 01568 614596.
Contact/s
Owner: Julia Simpson
Profile Breeder.
The stud farm is small, (semi retired). The Arab horses available for breeding are related to the winners of endurance, racing, jumping etc. Yr. Est: 1964
C.Size: 18 Acres Ref: YH12840

SIMPSON, PETER D

Peter D Simpson, 7 High Mowthorpe, Duggleby, Malton, **Yorkshire (North)**, YO17 8BW, **ENGLAND**.
(T) 01944 3497. Ref: YH12841

SIMPSON, SANDRA

Mrs Sandra Simpson, 28 Church Cl, Plummers Plain, Lower Beeding, Horsham, **Sussex (West)**, RH13 6NS, **ENGLAND**.
(T) 01403 891678.
Profile Breeder. Ref: YH12842

SIMPSONS MANU

Simpsons (Langley) Manufacturing Co, Froize End Works, 2 Froize End, Haddenham, Ely, **Cambridgeshire**, CB6 3UQ, **ENGLAND**.
(T) 01353 740085.
Profile Supplies. Ref: YH12843

SIMS & PARTNERS

Sims & Partners, 16 West Rd, Congleton, **Cheshire**, CW12 4ER, **ENGLAND**.
(T) 01260 273449.
Profile Medical Support. Ref: YH12844

SIMS COTTAGE STABLES

Sims Cottage Stables, Sims Cottage, Wilverley Rd, New Milton, **Hampshire**, BH25 5TX, **ENGLAND**.
(T) 01425 612961.
Contact/s
Owner: Mrs C Sparks Ref: YH12845

SIMS, L

Mrs L Sims, The Malthouse, Penton Mewsey, Andover, **Hampshire**, SP1 6RB, **ENGLAND**.
(T) 01264 773500.
Profile Breeder, Stable/Livery. Ref: YH12846

SINAH WARREN RIDING STABLES

Sinah Warren Riding Stables, Sinah Warren Classic Resort, Ferry Rd, Hayling Island, **Hampshire**, PO11 0BZ, **ENGLAND**.
(T) 023 92464845.
Contact/s
Manageress: Mrs J Bowden Ref: YH12847

SINCLAIR FEEDS

Sinclair Feeds, Foulden, West Newton, Berwick-upon-Tweed, **Northumberland**, TD15 1UL, **ENGLAND**.
(T) 01289 386388.
Profile Supplies. Ref: YH12848

SINCLAIR RIDING WEAR

Sinclair Riding Wear, 177 Pinshill Rd, Cookridge, Leeds, **Yorkshire (West)**, LS16 7LD, **ENGLAND**.
(T) 0113 2673646.
Contact/s
Owner: Mrs I Sinclair
Profile Riding Wear Retailer. No.Staff: 1
Yr. Est: 1996
Opening Times
By appointment only Ref: YH12849

SINDERHOPE PONY TREKKING CTRE

Sinderhope Pony Trekking Centre, High Sinderhope, Sinderhope, Hexham, **Northumberland**, NE47 9SH, **ENGLAND**.
(T) 01434 685266.
Contact/s
Instructor: Ms L Philipson
Profile Pony Trekking Centre. No.Staff: 3
Yr. Est: 1970 C.Size: 150 Acres Ref: YH12850

SINDOLAR

Sindolar Riding & Livery Stables, Manor Rd, Tatsfield, Westerham, **Kent**, **ENGLAND**.
Profile Riding School. Ref: YH12851

SINGH KHAKHIAN, GARY

Gary Singh Khakhian M/EQD AWCF, Brooklands, Bells Hill Rd, Vange, Basildon, **Essex**, SS16 5JT, **ENGLAND**.
(T) 01268 555411
(M) 07831 127537.
Profile Farrier. Ref: YH12852

SINGH, ANITA

Miss Anita Singh, Pondfield Hse, Bellingdon, Chesham, **Buckinghamshire**, HP5 2XL, **ENGLAND**.
(T) 01494 772174.
Profile Breeder. Ref: YH12853

SINGH, PETER G

Peter G Singh DWCF, 82 Pattiswick Sq, Basildon, **Essex**, SS14 2RD, **ENGLAND**.
(T) 01268 525733.
Profile Farrier. Ref: YH12854

SINNINGTON MANOR

Sinnington Manor, Sinnington Manor, York, **Yorkshire (North)**, YO62 6SN, **ENGLAND**.
(T) 01751 433296 (F) 01751 433296.
Contact/s
Owner: Mr C Wilson (Q) BHSAI
(E) charles.wilson@sinningtonmanor.fsnet.co.uk
Profile Riding School. Natural Horsemanship.
Natural horsemanship means a better level of communication between horse and rider. Lessons can vary from one hour to full day sessions. Workshops and displays can be provided at other venues.
Ref: YH12855

SINSTADT, M C W

M C W Sinstadt RSS, 8 Station Rd, Worleston, Nantwich, **Cheshire**, CW5 5SP, **ENGLAND**.
(T) 01270 626276.
Profile Farrier. Ref: YH12856

SIR ALFRED MUNNINGS

Sir Alfred Munnings Art Museum (The), Castle Hse, Dedham, Colchester, **Essex**, CO7 6AZ, **ENGLAND**.
(T) 01206 322127 (F) 01206 322127.
Contact/s
Manager: Mrs C Woodage
Profile Gallery.
The museum has equine art on display.
Opening Times
Sp: Open Wed, Sun 14:00. Closed Wed, Sun 17:00.
Su: Open Wed, Sun 14:00. Closed Wed, Sun 17:00.
Au: Open Wed, Sun 14:00. Closed Wed, Sun 17:00.
Open from Easter Sunday until the first Sunday in October. Office hours are 09:00 - 12:30 Mon -Fri, group openings by appointment only. In August additional openings on Thurs, Sat 14:00 - 17:00.
Ref: YH12857

SIR JOHN HILL FARM

Sir John Hill Farm, Laugharne, **Carmarthenshire**, SA33 4TD, **WALES**.
(T) 01994 427667.
Profile Equestrian Centre. Ref: YH12858

SIRETT, R T

R T Sirett, Selden Lane, Patching, Worthing, **Sussex (West)**, BN13 3UL, **ENGLAND**.
(T) 01903 871590.
Contact/s
Owner: Miss R Sirett
Profile Stable/Livery. Ref: YH12859

SITA

Society of International Thoroughbred Auctioneers, Tattersalls Ltd, Terrace Hse, Newmarket, **Suffolk**, CB8 9BT, **ENGLAND**.
(T) 01638 665931 (F) 01638 660850
(E) sales@tattersalls.com
(W) www.tattersalls.com.
Contact/s
Key Contact: Martin Mitchells
Profile Club/Association. Ref: YH12860

SIX ASHES RIDING CTRE

Six Ashes Riding Centre, Cleobury Mortimer, Kidderminster, **Worcestershire**, DY14 8HJ, **ENGLAND**.
(T) 01299 270417.
Profile Riding School. Ref: YH12861

SIXWAYS RIDING ESTB

Sixways Riding Establishment, Six Ways Farm, Goosedale Lane, Bestwood Village, Nottingham, **Nottinghamshire**, NG6 8UJ, **ENGLAND**.
(T) 0115 9633418. Ref: YH12862

SJAI

Show Jumping Association of Ireland (N Ireland), 78A Carsontown Rd, Saintfield, **County Down**, BT24 7EB, **NORTHERN IRELAND**.
(T) 028 97519229 (F) 028 97519229.
Contact/s
Secretary: Mrs M Peak
Profile Club/Association. Ref: YH12863

S-J'S TACK ROOM

S-J's Tack Room, Rose Cottage, Enniscaven, Roche, **Cornwall**, PL26 8LJ, **ENGLAND**.
(T) 01726 822540.
Contact/s
Owner: Mrs S Eva
Profile Saddlery Retailer, Stable/Livery.
Ref: YH12864

SKAIGH STABLES

Skaigh Stables, Skaigh Garden Cottage, Belstone, Okehampton, **Devon**, EX20 1RD, **ENGLAND**.
(T) 01837 840429 (F) 01837 840917
(E) skaigh@hotmail.co.uk
(W) www.skaighstables.co.uk.
Contact/s
Owner: Mrs R Hooley
Profile Holidays.
Fully inclusive week £500 or day rates available at £95, £80 booking fee per person. Half day ride £25, full day ride £45. The horses and ponies are of all sizes, well mannered and accustomed to cross country. Guests can expect about 27 hours of riding per week and stay at either Tawside House in Sticklepath or Barton Guest House in Belstone, both within easy walking distance of the stables. Yr. Est: 1964
Opening Times
Open Easter - October: Telephone for an appointment
Ref: YH12865

SKELTON, J

Mr J Skelton, Kennels Cottage, Gledstone, Skipton, **Yorkshire (North)**, BD23 3JR, **ENGLAND**.
(T) 01282 842503.
Profile Supplies. Ref: YH12866

SKELTON, NICK

Nick Skelton, Sandall Farm, Narrow Lane, Lowsonford, Henley In Arden, **Warwickshire**, B95 5HN, **ENGLAND**.
(T) 01926 843419. Ref: YH12867

SKER RIDING CLUB

Sker Riding Club, 69 Heol-Las, North Cornelly, **Bridgend**, CF33 4BA, **WALES**.
(T) 01656 743549.
Profile Club/Association, Riding Club. Ref: YH12868

SKERNE LEYS FARM

Skerne Leys Farm, Driffield, **Yorkshire (East)**, YO25 9HN, **ENGLAND**.
(T) 01377 253102 (F) 01377 253102.
Profile Breeder, Stable/Livery. Ref: YH12869

SKERRATON STUD

Skerraton Stud, Skerraton, Buckfastleigh, **Devon**,

TQ11 0NB, **ENGLAND**.
(T) 01364 42232.
Contact/s
Owner: Mr M Ogle
Profile Breeder. **Ref: YH12870**

SKEVANISH EQUESTRIAN

Skevanish Equestrian, Skevanish Innishannon, Cork, **County Cork**, **IRELAND**.
(T) 021 4775476.
Profile Supplies. **Ref: YH12871**

SKEWPIE COTTAGE STUD

Skewpie Cottage Stud, New Barn Farm Cottage, Watlington Rd, Stadhampton, **Oxfordshire**, OX44 7RR, **ENGLAND**.
(T) 01865 400447
(M) 07860 907402.
Profile Breeder. **Ref: YH12872**

SKIDBY LIVERY YARD

Skidby Livery Yard, Middle Farm, Main St, Skidby, Cottingham, **Yorkshire (East)**, HU16 5TG, **ENGLAND**.
(T) 01482 875141.
Contact/s
Owner: Mrs M Watson **Ref: YH12873**

SKINNER, C MCINNES

Mrs C McInnes Skinner, John O'Gaunt Hse, Melton Mowbray, **Leicestershire**, LE14 2RE, **ENGLAND**.
(T) 01664 454327
(M) 07885 215956.
Profile Supplies. **Ref: YH12874**

SKINNER, GEORGE M

George M Skinner, Strathorn Farm, Pitcaple, Inverurie, **Aberdeenshire**, AB51 5EJ, **SCOTLAND**.
(T) 01464 851204 **(F)** 01464 851588.
Profile Breeder, Riding School, Stable/Livery, Trainer.
Ref: YH12875

SKINNER, J L & B

J L & B Skinner, Crockers Hele, Meeth, Okehampton, **Devon**, EX20 3QN, **ENGLAND**.
(T) 01837 810417.
Contact/s
Partner: Mrs B Skinner
Profile Breeder. **Ref: YH12876**

SKINNER, ROGER M

Roger M Skinner RSS, San Michele, Maurys Lane, West Wellow, Romsey, **Hampshire**, SO51 6DA, **ENGLAND**.
(M) 07711 165485.
Profile Farrier. **Ref: YH12877**

SKINNER, ROSS

Mrs H J C Ross Skinner, Warmwell Hse, Dorchester, **Dorset**, DT2 8HS, **ENGLAND**.
(T) 01305 852269.
Contact/s
Stud Groom: Miss K Powell
Profile Breeder, Stable/Livery, Track/Course.
Ref: YH12878

SKIPPON, GUY A

Guy A Skippon RSS, Sky Farm, Cade St, Heathfield, **Sussex (East)**, TN21 9DB, **ENGLAND**.
(T) 01435 862807.
Profile Farrier. **Ref: YH12879**

SKIPPON, M A

M A Skippon, 1 Norman Villas, Cranbrook Rd, Hawkhurst, Cranbrook, **Kent**, TN18 4AU, **ENGLAND**.
(T) 01580 752052.
Contact/s
Owner: Mr M Skippon
Profile Farrier. **Ref: YH12880**

SKYE RIDING CTRE

Skye Riding Centre, 2 Syledale, Portree, **Isle of Skye**, IV51 9PA, **SCOTLAND**.
(T) 01470 582419 **(F)** 01470 532282
(W) www.skye-riding.co.uk
Affiliated Bodies ABRS, TRSS.
Contact/s
General Manager: Ms T MacLeod **(Q)** SVQ II
Profile Arena, Breeder, Equestrian Centre, Riding Club, Riding School, Stable/Livery, Trainer.
Ref: YH12881

SKYMASTER AIRCARGO

Skymaster Aircargo Ltd, Room 15/Building 305, World Freight Terminal, Manchester Airport, Manchester, **Manchester (Greater)**, M90 5PY, **ENGLAND**.
(T) 0161 4362190.
Profile Transport/Horse Boxes. **Ref: YH12882**

SLACK, EVELYN

Mrs Evelyn Slack, Stoneriggs, Hilton, Appleby, **Cumbria**, CA16 6LS, **ENGLAND**.
(T) 01768 351354.
Profile Breeder. **Ref: YH12883**

SLACK'S

Slack's, The Paddock, Gilwilly Trading Est, Gilwilly Ind Est, Penrith, **Cumbria**, CA11 9BN, **ENGLAND**.
(T) 01768 890079 **(F)** 01768 892294.
Contact/s
Owner: Mrs P Slack
Profile Saddlery Retailer. **Ref: YH12884**

SLADD BARN RIDING SCHOOL

Sladd Barn Riding School, Gypsy Lane, Wolverley, Kidderminster, **Worcestershire**, DY11 5XT, **ENGLAND**.
(T) 01562 852774.
Contact/s
Partner: Miss J Owens **Ref: YH12885**

SLADE, BRENT EDBROOK

Brent Edbrook Slade RSS, The Forge, 20 Drivers Mead, Lingfield Village, Lingfield, **Surrey**, RH7 6EU, **ENGLAND**.
(T) 01342 835669
(M) 07860 236291.
Profile Farrier. **Ref: YH12886**

SLADES COUNTRYWISE

Slades Countrywise, Turks Head Corner, Exeter Rd, Honiton, **Devon**, EX14 8AZ, **ENGLAND**.
(T) 01404 45966.
Profile Supplies. **Ref: YH12887**

SLADES LIVERY STABLE

Slades Livery Stable, Vicarage Rd, Bexley, **Kent**, DA5 2AW, **ENGLAND**.
(T) 01322 525219.
Contact/s
Owner: Ms L Purvis **Ref: YH12888**

SLADMORE GALLERY

Sladmore Gallery (The), 32 Bruton Pl, Berkerley Sq, London, **London (Greater)**, W1X 7AA, **ENGLAND**.
(T) 020 74990365 **(F)** 020 74091381
(E) enquiry@sladmore.com
(W) www.sladmore.com.
Contact/s
Owner: Mr E Horswell
Profile Art Gallery.
Specialist in animal sculptures. Yr. Est: 1850
Opening Times
Sp: Open 09:30. Closed 18:00.
Su: Open 09:30. Closed 18:00.
Au: Open 09:30. Closed 18:00.
Wn: Open 09:30. Closed 18:00.
Closed weekends **Ref: YH12889**

SLATE HALL RIDING CTRE

Slate Hall Riding Centre, Main St, North Sunderland, Seahouses, **Northumberland**, NE68 7UA, **ENGLAND**.
(T) 01665 720320.
Contact/s
Owner: Mrs M Nicholls **Ref: YH12890**

SLATER, M

M Slater, Aston Manor, Aston, Market Drayton, **Shropshire**, TF9 4JB, **ENGLAND**.
(T) 01630 647264.
Profile Supplies. **Ref: YH12891**

SLEDMERE STUD

Sledmere Stud, Estate Office, Sledmere, Driffield, **Yorkshire (East)**, YO25 3XQ, **ENGLAND**.
(T) 01377 236525.
Contact/s
Manager: Mr W Macauley
Profile Breeder. **Ref: YH12892**

SLEE, C

Miss C Slee, Lane Cottage, Coverham, **Yorkshire (North)**, DL8 4TG, **ENGLAND**.
(T) 01969 640543.
Profile Trainer. **Ref: YH12893**

SLEEMAN-HISCOCK, ANTHONY IVOR

Anthony Ivor Sleeman-Hiscock, Hazelmead, Churchfoot Lane, Hazelmead Bryan, Sturminster Newton, **Dorset**, DT10 2DS, **ENGLAND**.
(T) 01258 817742.
Profile Farrier. **Ref: YH12894**

SLIEVENAMON SADDLERY

Slievenamon Saddlery, Westgate, Clonmel, **County Tipperary**, **IRELAND**.
(T) 052 28700.
Profile Supplies. **Ref: YH12895**

SLIGHT, ERNEST G

Ernest G Slight RSS, 4 Farthing Cl, Dartford, **Kent**, DA1 5JJ, **ENGLAND**.
(T) 01322 229003.
Profile Farrier. **Ref: YH12896**

SLIGHT, K

Mrs K Slight, Airhouse, Oxton, Lauder, **Scottish Borders**, TD2 6PX, **SCOTLAND**.
(T) 01578 750225.
Profile Breeder. **Ref: YH12897**

SLINFOLD TRAILERS

Slinfold Trailers, Millbay, Rowhook, Horsham, **Sussex (West)**, RH12 3PZ, **ENGLAND**.
(T) 01403 790675.
Profile Transport/Horse Boxes. **Ref: YH12898**

SLIVERICKS

Slivericks Farm, Ashburnham, Battle, **Sussex (East)**, TN33 9PE, **ENGLAND**.
(T) 01435 830571 **(F)** 01435 830591.
Contact/s
Owner: Mrs S Faulker-Wheeler
Profile Horse/Rider Accom. **Ref: YH12899**

SLONE, JOHN

John Slone, Piel View Bungalow, Biggar Village, Barrow-In-Furness, **Dumfries and Galloway**, LA14 3YG, **SCOTLAND**..
Profile Farrier. **Ref: YH12900**

SLOUGH FORT EQUESTRIAN CTRE

Slough Fort Equestrian Centre, Avery Way, Allhallows, Rochester, **Kent**, ME3 9QF, **ENGLAND**.
(T) 01634 271110.
Contact/s
Owner: Mrs L Guyett **Ref: YH12901**

SLUGGETT, S J

S J Sluggett, The Elms, Milton Damerel, Holsworthy, **Devon**, EX22 7DW, **ENGLAND**.
(T) 01409 261457 **(F)** 01409 261364.
Contact/s
Owner: Mr S Sluggett
Profile Transport/Horse Boxes. **Ref: YH12902**

SLY, P M

Mrs P M Sly, Singlecote, Thorney, Peterborough, **Cambridgeshire**, PE6 0PB, **ENGLAND**.
(T) 01733 270212
(M) 07850 511267.
Profile Trainer. **Ref: YH12903**

SLYES FARM

Slyes Farm, Downash, Hailsham, **Sussex (East)**, BN27 2RP, **ENGLAND**.
(T) 01323 848989.
Profile Stable/Livery. **Ref: YH12904**

SMALL WORLD

Small World Stud, 23 Johns Cl, Studley, **Warwickshire**, B80 7EQ, **ENGLAND**.
(M) 07976 367006/07050 606249
(E) michelleodone@compuserve.com.
Contact/s
Owner: Miss M Odone
Profile Breeder. **Ref: YH12905**

SMALL, K W

K W Small, Nordrach Lodge, Charterhouse-on-Mendip, Blagdon, Bristol, **Bristol**, BS40 7XW, **ENGLAND**.
(T) 01761 462659.
Profile Transport/Horse Boxes. **Ref: YH12906**

SMALL, L G

Mr L G Small, East Farm, Charlton Adam, Somerton, **Somerset**, TA11 7AT, **ENGLAND**.
(T) 01458 22213.
Profile Supplies. **Ref: YH12907**

SMALL, M E

Mrs M E Small, 39 Southbridge Rd, Croydon, **Surrey**, CR0 1AG, **ENGLAND**.
(T) 020 86800852.
Profile Stable/Livery. **Ref: YH12908**

SMALL, ROSALIND

Rosalind Small, Wigborough Farm, South Petherton, **Somerset**, TA13 5LP, **ENGLAND**.
(T) 01460 40490.
Profile Trainer. **Ref: YH12909**

SMALLAGE FARM

Smallage Farm, West Lane, Aughton, Sheffield, **Yorkshire (South)**, S31 0XS, **ENGLAND**.
(T) 0114 2693300.
Profile Farrier. **Ref: YH12910**

SMALLEY & BLAXLAND

Smalley & Blaxland, White Mill Veterinary Ctre, Ash Rd, Sandwich, **Kent**, CT13 9JB, **ENGLAND**.
(T) 01304 611999 **(F)** 01304 611998.
Contact/s
Vet: Mr M Smalley
Profile Medical Support. **Ref: YH12911**

SMALL-LAND PONY STUD

Small-land Pony Stud, Meidrim, Carmarthen, **Carmarthenshire**, SA33 5NX, **WALES**.
(T) 01994 230260.
Profile Breeder. **Ref: YH12912**

SMALLPEICE, ALAN

Alan Smallpeice RSS, 77 Green Lane, Godalming, **Surrey**, GU7 3TB, **ENGLAND**.
(T) 07836 634345.
Profile Farrier. **Ref: YH12913**

SMALLRIDGE, ROGER

Roger Smallridge, Lewhill Barn, Ashford, Kingsbridge, **Devon**, TQ7 4NB, **ENGLAND**.
(T) 01548 550100 **(F)** 01548 550100.
Contact/s
Owner: Mr R Smallridge **Ref: YH12914**

SMALLWOOD LIVERY CTRE

Smallwood Livery Centre, Brookhouse Farm, Brookhouse Green, Smallwood, Sandbach, **Cheshire**, CW11 2XE, **ENGLAND**.
(T) 01477 500605 **(F)** 01477 500291.
Contact/s
Partner: Mr I Morris **Ref: YH12915**

SMARDEN EQUESTRIAN SERVICES

Smarden Equestrian Services, Bulland, Smarden, Ashford, **Kent**, TN27 8RQ, **ENGLAND**.
(T) 01233 770394 **(F)** 01233 770105.
Contact/s
Owner: Mrs S Povey
Profile Supplies. **Ref: YH12916**

SMART HORSEBOXES

Smart Horseboxes, Elborough Farm, Banwell Rd, Locking, Weston-Super-Mare, **Somerset (North)**, BS24 8PB, **ENGLAND**.
(T) 01934 823503 **(F)** 01934 820900.
Contact/s
Owner: Mr D Smart
Profile Transport/Horse Boxes. **Ref: YH12917**

SMART HORSEBOXES

Smart Horseboxes, The Coach Hse, Roughmoor, Banwell, **Somerset (North)**, BS29 6HU, **ENGLAND**.
(T) 01934 820900 **(F)** 01934 820900.
Contact/s
Owner: Mr D Smart
Profile Transport/Horse Boxes. **Ref: YH12918**

SMART PR

Smart PR, 146 Paston Lane, Peterborough, **Cambridgeshire**, PE4 6EU, **ENGLAND**.
(T) 01733 571271 **(F)** 01733 571271. **Ref: YH12919**

SMART R'S

Smart R's, 2 Eynon Villas, Ludchurch, Narberth, **Pembrokeshire**, SA67 8JF, **WALES**.
(T) 01834 831542.
Profile Supplies. **Ref: YH12920**

SMART, BRYAN

Bryan Smart, Sherwood, Folly Rd, Lambourn, Hungerford, **Berkshire**, RG17 8QE, **ENGLAND**.
(T) 01488 71632 **(F)** 01488 73859.
Contact/s
Owner: Mr B Smart
Profile Trainer. **Ref: YH12921**

SMART, JAYNE

Mrs Jayne Smart, The Coach Hse, Roughmoor, Knightcott, Banwell, **Somerset (North)**, BS29 6HU, **ENGLAND**.
(T) 01934 820900 **(F)** 01934 820900.
Profile Stable/Livery, Trainer. **Ref: YH12922**

SMART, JOHN

John Smart, The Cottage, Whitehouse Farm, Duddleswell, Uckfield, **Sussex (East)**, TN22 3JA, **ENGLAND**.
(T) 01825 713391.
Profile Trainer. **Ref: YH12923**

SMEDLEY, GILL

Mrs Gill Smedley, 111 Creakavose Pk, St Stephen, St Austell, **Cornwall**, PL26 7NB, **ENGLAND**.
(T) 01726 822112. **Ref: YH12924**

SMEETH SADDLERY

Smeeth Saddlery, The Brindles, 165 Salts Rd, Walton Highway, Wisbech, **Cambridgeshire**, PE14 7EB, **ENGLAND**.
(T) 01945 585998.
Contact/s
Owner: Ms S Jackson
Profile Medical Support, Riding Wear Retailer, Saddlery Retailer, Supplies. Saddle Repairs.
No.Staff: 1 Yr. Est: 1995
Opening Times
Sp: Open Mon - Sat 09:00. Closed Mon - Fri 18:00, Sat 16:00.
Su: Open Mon - Sat 09:00. Closed Mon - Fri 18:00, Sat 16:00.
Au: Open Mon - Sat 09:00. Closed Mon - Fri 18:00, Sat 16:00.
Wn: Open Mon - Sat 09:00. Closed Mon - Fri 18:00, Sat 16:00.
Closed on Sundays and Bank Holidays. **Ref: YH12925**

SMELLY RUG

Smelly Rug Co (The), Millmount Farm, Melrose, **Scottish Borders**, TD6 9BZ, **SCOTLAND**.
(T) 01896 822467.
Contact/s
Owner: Mrs J Kerr **Ref: YH12926**

SMELTINGS FARM RIDING CTRE

Smeltings Farm Riding Centre, Ringinglow Rd, Sheffield, **Yorkshire (South)**, S11 7TD, **ENGLAND**.
(T) 0114 2307661.
Profile Riding School, Saddlery Retailer, Stable/Livery. **Ref: YH12927**

SMIDDY, FYVIE

Fyvie Smiddy, Mill Of Crichie, Fyvie, Turriff, **Aberdeenshire**, AB53 8QL, **SCOTLAND**.
(T) 01651 891563 **(F)** 01651 891563.
Contact/s
Owner: Mr I Patterson
Profile Blacksmith. **Ref: YH12928**

SMILEY, ERIC

Eric Smiley FBHS (Regd) (IRL), Fir Tree Farm, Blacks Lane, Ballynahinch, **County Down**, BT24 8UT, **NORTHERN IRELAND**.
(T) 028 97562742 **(F)** 028 97562742.
Profile Trainer. **Ref: YH12929**

SMILHAN, PETER

Peter Smilhan, Springfield Farm, Lang Gate, Saltfleetby St, St Peter, Louth, **Lincolnshire**, LN11 7SZ, **ENGLAND**.
(T) 01507 338948.
Profile Saddlery Retailer. **Ref: YH12930**

SMITH & JONES

Smith & Jones, 40 Meadoway, The Coppice, Aylesbury, **Buckinghamshire**, HP20 1XS, **ENGLAND**.
(T) 01296 432174.
Profile Breeder. **Ref: YH12931**

SMITH & MORRIS

Smith & Morris Ltd, Four Oaks Farm, Aston Juxta Mondrum, Nantwich, **Cheshire**, CW5 6DT, **ENGLAND**.
(T) 01270 522577 **(F)** 01270 522588
(E) smithand morris@mcmail.com.
Profile Saddlery Retailer, Stable/Livery.
Ref: YH12932

SMITH & MORRIS COUNTRY STORE

Smith & Morris Country Store, Stone Rd, Blackbrook, Newcastle, **Staffordshire**, ST5 5EG, **ENGLAND**.
(T) 01782 680068.
Contact/s
Manager: Miss S Leese
Profile Saddlery Retailer, Stable/Livery.
Ref: YH12933

SMITH & PARTNERS

Smith & Partners, 9 George St, Bridgwater, **Somerset**, TA6 3NA, **ENGLAND**.
(T) 01278 451592 **(F)** 01278 451591.
Profile Medical Support. **Ref: YH12934**

SMITH & RAPPOLD

Smith & Rappold, 6 Haven St, London, **London (Greater)**, NW1 8QX, **ENGLAND**.
(T) 020 74850298.
Profile Blacksmith. **Ref: YH12935**

SMITH GREEN SMITHY

Smith Green Smithy, Stoney Lane, Galgate, Lancaster, **Lancashire**, LA2 0PX, **ENGLAND**.
(T) 01995 600423.
Profile Farrier. **Ref: YH12936**

SMITH RYDER DAVIES & HILLIARD

Smith Ryder Davies & Hilliard, 18 Grundisburgh Rd, Woodbridge, **Suffolk**, IP12 4HG, **ENGLAND**.
(T) 01394 380083 **(F)** 01394 382310.
Contact/s
Vet: Mr R Ryder-Davies
Profile Medical Support. **Ref: YH12937**

SMITH, A G

A G Smith, Hill St, Dufftown, Keith, **Aberdeenshire**, AB55 4AW, **SCOTLAND**.
(T) 01340 820358.
Profile Blacksmith. **Ref: YH12938**

SMITH, ALAN

Alan Smith, Foundry Hse, Clanfield, **Oxfordshire**, OX18 2SP, **ENGLAND**.
(T) 01367 810245 **(F)** 01367 810245
(E) smithequi@aol.com.
Profile Supplies. **Ref: YH12939**

SMITH, ANDREW B

Andrew B Smith DWCF, 41 Hazel Ave, Evesham, **Worcestershire**, WR11 6XT, **ENGLAND**.
(M) 07970 667804.
Profile Farrier. **Ref: YH12940**

SMITH, ANDREW C

Andrew C Smith AFCL, Craigland Hse, Tilston, Malpas, **Cheshire**, SY14 7DW, **ENGLAND**.
(T) 01829 250367.
Profile Farrier. **Ref: YH12941**

SMITH, B J

B J Smith Inc, Tendring Rd, Thorpe-Le-Soken, Clacton-on-Sea, **Essex**, CO16 0AA, **ENGLAND**.
(T) 01255 862411 **(F)** 01255 862340.
Contact/s
Partner: Mr B Smith
Profile Transport/Horse Boxes. **Ref: YH12942**

SMITH, C

Mr C Smith, Thompsons Bottom Farm, Temple Bruer, Wellingore, **Lincolnshire**, LN5 0DE, **ENGLAND**.
(T) 01526 833245 **(F)** 01526 833245
(M) 07778 149188.
Profile Trainer. **Ref: YH12943**

SMITH, C B

C B Smith, Whitford Mill, Whitford Rd, Bromsgrove, **Worcestershire**, B61 7ED, **ENGLAND**.
(T) 01527 874702.
Contact/s
Owner: Mr C Smith
Profile Farrier. **Ref: YH12944**

SMITH, C W

Mr C W Smith, 68 West St, Drighlington, Bradford, **Yorkshire (West)**, **ENGLAND**.
Profile Breeder. **Ref: YH12945**

SMITH, COLIN JOHN

Colin John Smith FWCF Hons, The Paddock, Cutty Lane, North Cadbury, Yeovil, **Somerset**, BA22 7DG, **ENGLAND**.
(T) 01963 440237.
Profile Farrier. **Ref: YH12946**

SMITH, D

Mr D Smith, Holdforth Farm, Bishop Auckland, **County Durham**, DL14 6DJ, **ENGLAND**.
(T) 01388 603317 **(F)** 01388 606180.
Profile Trainer. **Ref: YH12947**

SMITH, D

Mr D Smith, 23 Moulton Rd, Gazeley, Newmarket, **Suffolk**, CB8 8RA, **ENGLAND**.
(T) 01638 751812.
Profile Breeder. **Ref: YH12948**

SMITH, D MURRAY

Mr D Murray Smith, The Old Rectory, Gumley, Market Harborough, **Leicestershire**, LE16 7RX, **ENGLAND**.
(T) 0116 2792201 **(F)** 0116 2796039
(M) 07785 920352
(E) wilder1234@aol.com.
Profile Trainer. **Ref: YH12949**

SMITH, DANIEL A

Daniel A Smith BII, 7 Linces Way, Welwyn Garden

City, **Hertfordshire**, AL7 3JN, **ENGLAND**.
(T) 01707 376858
(M) 07831 839776.
Profile Farrier. **Ref: YH12950**

SMITH, DAVID H
David H Smith DWCF, 73 St James Rd, Cannock, **Staffordshire**, WS11 1SX, **ENGLAND**.
(T) 01543 579559.
Profile Farrier. **Ref: YH12951**

SMITH, DAVID P
David P Smith AWCF, Little Meadows, Choice Hill, Over Norton, **Oxfordshire**, OX7 5PZ, **ENGLAND**.
(T) 01608 642584.
Profile Farrier. **Ref: YH12952**

SMITH, DEAN C
Dean C Smith DWCF, The Round Hse, Hall Rd, Belchamp Walter, Sudbury, **Suffolk**, CO10 7AS, **ENGLAND**.
(T) 01787 282082.
Profile Farrier. **Ref: YH12953**

SMITH, DIANA
Miss Diana Smith, Glebe Farm, Ludborough, Grimsby, **Lincolnshire (North East)**, DN36 5SQ, **ENGLAND**.
(T) 01472 840276.
Profile Supplies. **Ref: YH12954**

SMITH, DINA
Mrs Dina Smith, Hillside Fruit Farm, Bury, Pulborough, **Sussex (West)**, RH20 1NR, **ENGLAND**.
(T) 01798 831206.
Profile Trainer. **Ref: YH12955**

SMITH, DUNCAN R
Duncan R Smith DWCF, 4 West Lane, Cloughton, Scarborough, **Yorkshire (North)**, YO13 0AL, **ENGLAND**.
(T) 01723 870963.
Profile Farrier. **Ref: YH12956**

SMITH, FREDRICK T
Fredrick T Smith DWCF BII, C/O Lane Hse, Higher Bockhampton, Dorchester, **Dorset**, DT2 8QH, **ENGLAND**.
(T) 01305 264651.
Profile Farrier. **Ref: YH12957**

SMITH, G R
Mr G R Smith, Sellack Hse, Ross-on-Wye, **Herefordshire**, HR9 6QP, **ENGLAND**.
(T) 01989 562461 **(F)** 01989 562447.
Profile Supplies. **Ref: YH12958**

SMITH, GRAHAM J
Graham J Smith DWCF, Fox Covert Farm, Narrow Lane, Wymeswold, Loughborough, **Leicestershire**, LE12 6SD, **ENGLAND**.
(T) 01509 881250
(M) 07831 531765.
Profile Farrier. **Ref: YH12959**

SMITH, HARVEY
Harvey Smith, Craiglands Farm, High Eldwick, Bingley, **Yorkshire (West)**, BD16 3BE, **ENGLAND**.
(T) 01274 564930 **(F)** 01274 560626.
Profile Breeder. **Ref: YH12960**

SMITH, I R
I R Smith, Light Ash Cottage, Light Ash Cul De Sac, Coven, Wolverhampton, **Staffordshire**, WV9 5AF, **ENGLAND**.
(T) 01902 790145.
Contact/s
Owner: Mr I Smith
Profile Farrier. **Ref: YH12961**

SMITH, J
J Smith, 10 Belgrave Rd, Bingley, **Yorkshire (West)**, BD16 4NB, **ENGLAND**.
(T) 01274 563830.
Profile Farrier. **Ref: YH12962**

SMITH, J R M
J R M Smith, 3 Waterside Cottages, Mill Green, Hatfield, **Hertfordshire**, AL9 5NY, **ENGLAND**.
(T) 01707 263434.
Profile Farrier. **Ref: YH12963**

SMITH, J S
J S Smith, Hammerdown Farm, Bath Rd, Old Sodbury, Bristol, **Bristol**, BS37 6RR, **ENGLAND**.
(T) 01454 323776.
Contact/s
Owner: Mr J Smith
Profile Farrier. **Ref: YH12964**

SMITH, J S
Mr J S Smith, Tirley Court, Tirley, **Gloucestershire**, GL19 4HA, **ENGLAND**.
(T) 01452 780208 **(F)** 01452 780461.
Profile Trainer. **Ref: YH12965**

SMITH, JAMES HARRY
James Harry Smith, 1 Abbotts Ave, Kilwinning, **Ayrshire (North)**, KA13 6BZ, **SCOTLAND**.
(T) 01294 51509.
Profile Breeder, Farrier. **Ref: YH12966**

SMITH, JEREMY R C
Jeremy R C Smith DWCF, 1 Rawlings Cl, South Marston, Swindon, **Wiltshire**, SN3 4XA, **ENGLAND**.
(T) 01793 828344.
Profile Farrier. **Ref: YH12967**

SMITH, JOHN
Mr & Mrs John Smith, Stoneleigh, Main St, Bielby, **Yorkshire (East)**, YO42 4JW, **ENGLAND**.
(T) 01759 318325.
Profile Breeder. **Ref: YH12968**

SMITH, JOHN (JNR)
John Smith Jnr, South Clutag, Whauphill, Newton Stewart, **Dumfries and Galloway**, **SCOTLAND**..
Profile Breeder. **Ref: YH12969**

SMITH, JOHN R
John R Smith DWCF, Beck Cottage, Amen Corner, Caunton, Newark, **Nottinghamshire**, NG23 6AP, **ENGLAND**.
(T) 01636 636326.
Profile Farrier. **Ref: YH12970**

SMITH, JONATHAN C
Jonathan C Smith DWCF, Gable Cross Farm, Tilston, Malpas, **Cheshire**, SY14 7DW, **ENGLAND**.
(T) 01829 250990.
Profile Farrier. **Ref: YH12971**

SMITH, K
Mrs K Smith, 44 Kingsway, Gillingham, **Kent**, **ENGLAND**.
(T) 01634 854162.
Profile Breeder. **Ref: YH12972**

SMITH, M
M Smith, Waddesdon Stud, Upper Winchendon, Aylesbury, **Buckinghamshire**, HP18 0ER, **ENGLAND**.
(T) 01296 651306 **(F)** 01296 658054.
Contact/s
Manager: Mr M Smith
Profile Breeder. **Ref: YH12973**

SMITH, M J
Mr M J Smith, Northover Farm, Meres Lane, Cross-In-Hand, Heathfield, **Sussex (East)**, TN21 0UA, **ENGLAND**.
(T) 01435 873261.
Profile Supplies. **Ref: YH12974**

SMITH, M M
Mrs M M Smith, Treburland Farm, Lewannick, Launceston, **Cornwall**, PL15 7QU, **ENGLAND**.
(T) 01566 86221.
Profile Supplies. **Ref: YH12975**

SMITH, MATTHEW K
Matthew K Smith AWCF, Chestnut Farm Cottage, Mays Hill, Frampton Cotterell, **Gloucestershire (South)**, BS36 2NS, **ENGLAND**.
(T) 01454 250822.
Profile Farrier. **Ref: YH12976**

SMITH, MICHAEL B
Michael B Smith DWCF, 4 Wayside, Pyles Thorne Rd, Wellington, **Somerset**, TA21 8DZ, **ENGLAND**.
(M) 07798 500909.
Profile Farrier. **Ref: YH12977**

SMITH, N
Miss N Smith, Worthy End Farm, Hornes End Rd, Flitwick, **Bedfordshire**, MK45 1JL, **ENGLAND**.
(T) 01525 712546.
Profile Breeder. **Ref: YH12978**

SMITH, N A
N A Smith, The Barn, Lower Cowsden Farm, Upton Snodsbury, Worcester, **Worcestershire**, WR7 4NY, **ENGLAND**.
(T) 01905 381077 **(F)** 01905 381077.
Profile Trainer. **Ref: YH12979**

SMITH, N H
N H Smith, Glebe Hse, Little Saredon, Wolverhampton, **Midlands (West)**, WV10 7LQ, **ENGLAND**.
(T) 01922 414636.
Contact/s
Owner: Mr N Smith
Profile Farrier. **Ref: YH12980**

SMITH, NORMAN M
Norman M Smith, West Cliff Cottage, Cliff Rd, Saxby, Market Rasen, **Lincolnshire**, LN8 2DJ, **ENGLAND**.
(T) 01673 878458
Affiliated Bodies FRC.
Contact/s
Owner: Mr N Smith
Profile Farrier. Yr. Est: 1975
Opening Times
Visits by appointment only. **Ref: YH12981**

SMITH, O
Mr O Smith, Seven Acres, Barnhall Rd, Tolleshunt Knights, Maldon, **Essex**, CM9 8HD, **ENGLAND**.
(T) 01621 815412.
Profile Breeder. **Ref: YH12982**

SMITH, P & B
P & B Smith, Locksbit Hall Farm, Smithy Fen, Cottenham, **Cambridgeshire**, CB4 8PT, **ENGLAND**.
(T) 01954 252578.
Profile Breeder. **Ref: YH12983**

SMITH, P J
P J Smith, 8 Westlands Ave, Tetney, Grimsby, **Lincolnshire (North East)**, DN36 5LP, **ENGLAND**.
(T) 01472 210002.
Profile Farrier. **Ref: YH12984**

SMITH, PAUL G
Paul G Smith DWCF, Medina Hse, Highfield Hall, Mold, **Flintshire**, CH7 6AX, **WALES**.
(T) 01352 840782.
Profile Farrier. **Ref: YH12985**

SMITH, PETER F
Peter F Smith, 27 Eleventh Row, Ashington, **Northumberland**, NE63 8QQ, **ENGLAND**.
(T) 01670 853036
(M) 07860 704597.
Profile Farrier. **Ref: YH12986**

SMITH, PETER JOHN
Peter John Smith BII, 2 East Town Cottages, West Ashton, Trowbridge, **Wiltshire**, BA14 6BF, **ENGLAND**.
(T) 01380 870907.
Profile Farrier. **Ref: YH12987**

SMITH, R H
R H Smith, Smithy Hse, Airntully, Stanley, Perth, **Perth and Kinross**, PH1 4PH, **SCOTLAND**.
(T) 01738 828374.
Contact/s
Owner: Mr R Smith
Profile Blacksmith. **Ref: YH12988**

SMITH, R I
R I Smith, The Orchard, Old Stafford Rd, Cross Green, Wolverhampton, **Midlands (West)**, WV10 7PL, **ENGLAND**.
(T) 01902 790191.
Contact/s
Owner: Mr R Smith
Profile Farrier. **Ref: YH12989**

SMITH, R J
R J Smith, Tanyard Cottage, Stockwood Vale, Keynsham, Bristol, **Bristol**, BS31 1AL, **ENGLAND**.
(T) 01179 863821.
Contact/s
Owner: Mr R Smith **Ref: YH12990**

SMITH, R J
R J Smith, Brockhill, Naunton, Cheltenham, **Gloucestershire**, GL54 3AF, **ENGLAND**.
(T) 01451 850988.
Contact/s
Partner: Mr R Smith
Profile Trainer. **Ref: YH12991**

SMITH, R J
Mr R J Smith, 1 Sunnybank, Naunton, **Gloucestershire**, GL54 3AS, **ENGLAND**.
(T) 01451 850180.
Profile Trainer. **Ref: YH12992**

SMITH, RAY
Ray Smith, 11 Burn Est, Huntington, York, **Yorkshire (North)**, YO32 9PZ, **ENGLAND**.
(T) 01904 760918.

Contact/s
Owner: Mr R Smith Ref: YH12993

SMITH, RICHARD J

Mr Richard J Smith, New Hse Farm, Badminton, **Gloucestershire**, GL9 1HB, **ENGLAND**.
(T) 01454 218275.
Profile Supplies. Ref: YH12994

SMITH, ROBERT

Robert Smith, The Forge, Gosport Rd, Lower Farringdon, Alton, **Hampshire**, GU34 3DL, **ENGLAND**.
(T) 01420 587233 **(F)** 01420 587233.
Contact/s
Owner: Mr R Smith
Profile Blacksmith. Ref: YH12995

SMITH, ROBIN ABEL

Robin Abel Smith M/Eq D, Barleythorpe, Oakham, Rutland, **Rutland**, LE15 7EQ, **ENGLAND**.
(T) 01664 454160 **(F)** 01664 474613
(M) 07836 637704.
Profile Medical Support. Ref: YH12996

SMITH, ROY J

Mr Roy J Smith, Fox Covert Farm, Narrow Lane, Wymeswold, Loughborough, **Leicestershire**, LE12 6SD, **ENGLAND**.
(T) 01509 881250.
Profile Supplies. Ref: YH12997

SMITH, S C

S C Smith, 15 Mant Rd, Petworth, **Sussex (West)**, GU28 0EH, **ENGLAND**.
(T) 01798 342330.
Contact/s
Owner: Mr S Smith
Profile Farrier. Ref: YH12998

SMITH, S J

Mr S J Smith, Adstone Lodge, Adstone, Towcester, **Northamptonshire**, NN12 8DZ, **ENGLAND**.
(T) 01327 860301.
Profile Breeder. Ref: YH12999

SMITH, S J

Mrs S J Smith, Craiglands Farm, High Eldwick, Bingley, **Yorkshire (West)**, BD16 3BE, **ENGLAND**.
(T) 01274 564930 **(F)** 01274 560626.
Profile Trainer. Ref: YH13000

SMITH, STEVEN P L

Steven P L Smith DWCF, Woodlands Farm, Thornton Common Rd, Thornton Hough, **Merseyside**, CH63 4JU, **ENGLAND**.
(T) 0151 3343091.
Profile Farrier. Ref: YH13001

SMITH, THOMAS

Mr Thomas Smith, Newland Farm, Milton Rd, Banbury, **Oxfordshire**, OX15 4HD, **ENGLAND**.
(T) 01295 720286.
Profile Breeder. Ref: YH13002

SMITH, W

W Smith, 23 Watcombe Rd, Watlington, **Oxfordshire**, OX9 5QJ, **ENGLAND**.
(T) 01491 612872.
Contact/s
Owner: Mr W Smith
Profile Farrier. Ref: YH13003

SMITH, WILLIAM J

Mr William J Smith, Belle Isle, Hurgill Rd, Richmond, **Yorkshire (North)**, DL10 4TA, **ENGLAND**.
(T) 01748 822629.
Profile Supplies. Ref: YH13004

SMITH-MAXWELL, A L

A L Smith-Maxwell, Welland Lodge Farm, Upton-upon-Severn, **Worcestershire**, WR8 0SS, **ENGLAND**.
(T) 01684 592161 **(F)** 01684 592161.
Contact/s
Owner: Mr A Smith-Maxwell
Profile Breeder.
Advise on where to select your trainer. Mr Smith-Maxwell buys and selects foals and yearlings, in association with Luke Lillingston.
Opening Times
Telephone for an appointment Ref: YH13005

SMITHS ANIMAL & PET SUPPLIES

Smiths Animal & Pet Supplies, 72 Castle Rd, Cottingham, **Yorkshire (East)**, HU16 5JG, **ENGLAND**.
(T) 01482 843631.
Contact/s
Manager: Mr M Blyth
Profile Feed Merchant, Saddlery Retailer.
Ref: YH13006

SMITHS GREEN RIDING CTRE

Smiths Green Riding Centre, Smiths Green Farm, Smiths Green, Barthomley, Crewe, **Cheshire**, CW2 5NU, **ENGLAND**.
(T) 01270 582464 **(F)** 01270 215352.
Contact/s
Owner: Mrs S Nield Ref: YH13007

SMITHS INDUSTRIES WATCH

Smiths Industries Watch Co, Gornos Works, Ystradgynlais, **Powys**, SA9 1FX, **WALES**.
(T) 01639 843661.
Profile Supplies. Ref: YH13008

SMITHSON, B H

B H Smithson, The Bungalow, Elwick, **Cleveland**, TS27 3EF, **ENGLAND**.
(T) 01429 71647.
Profile Farrier. Ref: YH13009

SMITHY

Smithy (The), Trenear, Helston, **Cornwall**, TR13 0ER, **ENGLAND**.
(T) 01326 563287.
Contact/s
Owner: Mr I Mullino
Profile Blacksmith. Ref: YH13010

SMITHY

Smithy (The), 2 Queen St, Westhoughton, Bolton, **Manchester (Greater)**, BL5 3BH, **ENGLAND**.
(T) 01942 816886
Affiliated Bodies BETA.
Contact/s
Owner: Mrs J Smethurst
Profile Riding Wear Retailer, Saddlery Retailer.
Repairs tack **No.Staff:** 1 **Yr. Est:** 1999
Opening Times
Sp: Open Mon - Sun 10:00. Closed Mon, Tues, Thurs, Fri, Sat 17:30, Wed and Sun 14:00.
Su: Open Mon - Sun 10:00. Closed Mon, Tues, Thurs, Fri, Sat 17:30, Wed and Sun 14:00.
Au: Open Mon - Sun 10:00. Closed Mon, Tues, Thurs, Fri, Sat 17:30, Wed and Sun 14:00.
Wn: Open Mon - Sun 10:00. Closed Mon, Tues, Thurs, Fri, Sat 17:30, Wed and Sun 14:00.
Ref: YH13011

SMITHY

Smithy, 82 Newtown Rd, Bedworth, **Warwickshire**, CV12 8QS, **ENGLAND**.
(T) 024 76317608.
Contact/s
Owner: Mr L Pimlott
Profile Farrier. Ref: YH13012

SMITHY

David Athey, The Smithy, Main St, Garton-on-the-Wolds, Driffield, **Yorkshire (East)**, YO25 3EU, **ENGLAND**.
(T) 01377 241723 **(F)** 01377 255700.
Contact/s
Owner: Mr D Athey
Profile Blacksmith, Supplies.
Make horse equipment on request including specialist bits, stirrups and training aids. Telephone for further information.
Opening Times
Sp: Open Mon - Fri 08:00. Closed Mon - Fri 17:00.
Su: Open Mon - Fri 08:00. Closed Mon - Fri 17:00.
Au: Open Mon - Fri 08:00. Closed Mon - Fri 17:00.
Wn: Open Mon - Fri 08:00. Closed Mon - Fri 17:00.
Ref: YH13013

SMITHY WORKSHOP

Smithy Workshop, Seymour Pl, Totnes, **Devon**, TQ9 5AY, **ENGLAND**.
(T) 01803 865714.
Contact/s
Owner: Mr R Latham
Profile Blacksmith. Ref: YH13014

SMITHY, LINDEAN

Lindean Smithy, Galashiels, **Scottish Borders**, TD1 3PG, **SCOTLAND**.
(T) 01750 21521.
Profile Farrier. Ref: YH13015

SMYTH-OSBOURNE, J

J Smyth-Osbourne, Highfields Stables, Adstone, Towcester, **Northamptonshire**, NN12 8DS, **ENGLAND**.
(T) 01327 860840 **(F)** 01327 860810.
Contact/s
Owner: Mr J Smyth-Osbourne
Profile Trainer. Ref: YH13016

SMYTHS

Smyths Tack Box, 6-9 Kildare St, Newry, **County Down**, BT34 1DQ, **NORTHERN IRELAND**.
(T) 028 30269229 **(F)** 028 30265054.
Contact/s
Owner: Mr J Smyth
Profile Saddlery Retailer.
Sports Shop. Ref: YH13017

SMYTHSON

Smythson Limited, 40 New Bond St, London, **London (Greater)**, W1Y 0DE, **ENGLAND**.
(T) 020 76298558 **(F)** 020 74956111. Ref: YH13018

SNAFFLES

Snaffles, 4 The Street, Upchurch, Sittingbourne, **Kent**, ME9 7AJ, **ENGLAND**.
(T) 01634 230761.
Contact/s
Owner: Mrs S Godden Ref: YH13019

SNAFFLES

Snaffles, 47 Halifax Rd, Todmorden, Halifax, **Lancashire**, OL14 5BB, **ENGLAND**.
(T) 01706 818616
(E) snaffles@freeuk.com
(W) www.snaffles.freeuk.com.
Contact/s
Owner: Mrs J Barker
Profile Riding Wear Retailer, Saddlery Retailer, Supplies.
Good quality new and used tack and riding wear always in stock. Waterproofs and outdoor wear. Clothing for children from 2 years of age
No.Staff: 1 **Yr. Est:** 1999
Opening Times
Sp: Open Wed - Sat 10:00, Sun 12:00. Closed Wed - Sat 17:00, Sun 15:00.
Su: Open Wed - Sat 10:00, Sun 12:00. Closed Wed - Sat 17:00, Sun 15:00.
Au: Open Wed - Sat 10:00, Sun 12:00. Closed Wed - Sat 17:00, Sun 15:00.
Wn: Open Wed - Sat 10:00, Sun 12:00. Closed Wed - Sat 17:00, Sun 15:00.
Closed on Mondays & Tuesdays Ref: YH13020

SNAFFLES EQUESTRIAN

Snaffles Equestrian, Dean End, Lea, Ross On Wye, **Herefordshire**, HR9 7LN, **ENGLAND**.
(T) 01989 750412 **(F)** 01989 750412.
Profile Supplies. Ref: YH13021

SNAFFLES HORSE COUTURE

Snaffles Horse Couture Ltd, Unit 6/Wrights Yard, Top Rd, Wimbish, Saffron Walden, **Essex**, CB10 2XJ, **ENGLAND**.
(T) 01799 599173 **(F)** 01799 599174. Ref: YH13022

SNAFFLES SADDLERY

Snaffles Saddlery (Reading), 14 Sawtry Cl, Lower Earley, Reading, **Berkshire**, RG6 3AA, **ENGLAND**.
(T) 0118 9667205.
Profile Supplies. Ref: YH13023

SNAFFLES SADDLERY

Snaffles Saddlery, Rear Of 20 The Square, Holsworthy, **Devon**, EX22 6AN, **ENGLAND**.
(T) 01409 254490 **(F)** 01409 254490.
Contact/s
Owner: Mr K Beckhurst Ref: YH13024

SNAFFLES SADDLERY

Snaffles Saddlery (Devon), Unit 1E, Enterprise Ctre, Langdon Rd, Bradworthy, **Devon**, EX22 7SF, **ENGLAND**.
(T) 01409 241528 **(F)** 01409 241528.
Profile Saddlery Retailer. Ref: YH13025

SNAFFLES SADDLERY

Snaffles Saddlery, 5 Westgate, Cowbridge, **Glamorgan (Vale of)**, CF71 7AQ, **WALES**.
(T) 01446 773051 **(F)** 01446 773051.
Contact/s
Owner: Mr J Hopkins
Profile Saddlery Retailer. Ref: YH13026

SNAILWELL STUD

Snailwell Stud Co Ltd (The), Short Rd, Snailwell, Newmarket, **Suffolk**, CB8 7LJ, **ENGLAND**.
(T) 01638 577271 **(F)** 01638 577025.
Contact/s
Company Secretary: Miss A Ludlow
Profile Breeder. Ref: YH13027

SNAINTON RIDING CTRE

Snainton Riding Centre, Station Rd, Snainton,

Scarborough, **Yorkshire (North)**, YO13 9AP, **ENGLAND**.
(T) 01723 859218.
Contact/s
Owner: Mr A Lyall **(Q)** BHSI
Profile Riding School, Stable/Livery, Trainer.
Ref: YH13028

SNELL, C F & J E
C F & J E Snell, Furringdons Farm, Broadshard, Crewkerne, **Somerset**, TA18 7NJ, **ENGLAND**.
(T) 01460 73613.
Profile Supplies. **Ref: YH13029**

SNELL, GEOFFREY
Geoffrey Snell, 45 Green Lane, Radnage, High Wycombe, **Buckinghamshire**, HP14 4BY, **ENGLAND**.
(T) 01494 483057. **Ref: YH13030**

SNIPE TRAILERS
Snipe Trailers, Watling St, Cannock, **Staffordshire**, WS11 3NB, **ENGLAND**.
(T) 01543 363717 **(F)** 01543 454110.
Contact/s
General Manager: Mr D Humphries
Profile Transport/Horse Boxes. **Ref: YH13031**

SNIPPERSGATE EQUESTRIAN CTRE
Snippersgate Equestrian Centre, Snippersgate Farm, South Hetton, Durham, **County Durham**, DH6 2UQ, **ENGLAND**.
(T) 0191 5265888. **Ref: YH13032**

SNODGRASS EDEN & TRETHEWEY
Snodgrass Eden & Trethewey, 111 Botley Rd, Oxford, **Oxfordshire**, OX2 0LF, **ENGLAND**.
(T) 01865 243225.
Profile Medical Support. **Ref: YH13033**

SNOOK, L A
Mr L A Snook, Lower Ridge Farm, Kings Stag, Sturminster Newton, **Dorset**, DT10 2AU, **ENGLAND**.
(T) 01258 817364 **(F)** 01258 817771.
Profile Breeder. **Ref: YH13034**

SNOOTY FOX COUNTRY STORE
Snooty Fox Country Store (The), Northchapel, Petworth, **Sussex (West)**, GU28 9HL, **ENGLAND**.
(T) 01428 707111.
Profile Saddlery Retailer. **Ref: YH13035**

SNOW, S J
S J Snow, Field Hse, Birch Cross, Marchington, Uttoxeter, **Staffordshire**, ST14 8NX, **ENGLAND**.
(T) 01283 820310.
Contact/s
Owner: Miss S Snow
Profile Riding School. **Ref: YH13036**

SNOWBALL FARM EQUESTRIAN CTRE
Snowball Farm Equestrian Centre, Snowball Farm, Dorneywood Rd, Burnham, Slough, **Berkshire**, SL1 8EH, **ENGLAND**.
(T) 01628 666222.
Contact/s
Organiser: Mrs S Western-Kaye
Profile Riding School, Saddlery Retailer, Stable/Livery. **Ref: YH13037**

SNOWBALL, BART J
Bart J Snowball, Impton Studios, 319 Boxley Rd, Penenden Heath, Maidstone, **Kent**, ME14 2HN, **ENGLAND**.
(T) 01622 768666.
Profile Saddlery Retailer. **Ref: YH13038**

SNOWDEN, D S
D S Snowden, 1 Alveston Pl, Oxford St, Leamington Spa, **Warwickshire**, CV32 4RA, **ENGLAND**.
(T) 01926 314056 **(F)** 01926 311327. **Ref: YH13039**

SNOWDON FARM RIDING SCHOOL
Snowdon Farm Riding School, Snowden Lane, Marsh Lane, Sheffield, **Yorkshire (South)**, S21 5RT, **ENGLAND**.
(T) 01246 417172.
Contact/s
Owner: Mr G Jones
Profile Riding School, Saddlery Retailer, Stable/Livery, Track/Course. **Ref: YH13040**

SNOWDONIA RIDING STABLES
Snowdonia Riding Stables, Waunfawr, Caernarfon, **Gwynedd**, LL55 4PQ, **WALES**.
(T) 01286 650342
(W) www.snowdonia2000.fsnet.co.uk
Affiliated Bodies ABRS.
Contact/s
General Manager: Sian Thomas **(Q)** BHSI
Profile Equestrian Centre, Riding School, Stable/Livery. Trekking Centre.
Take working pupils for examination training and have an exceptionally high pass rate. Offer training for BHS exams and NVQs.
Opening Times
Sp: Open 10:00. Closed 16:00.
Su: Open 10:00. Closed 18:00.
Au: Open 10:00. Closed 18:00.
Wn: Open 10:30. Closed 16:00. **Ref: YH13041**

SNOWFLAKE WOODSHAVING
Snowflake Woodshaving Co Ltd, Marsh Lane, Riverside Ind Est, Boston, **Lincolnshire**, PE21 7ST, **ENGLAND**.
(T) 01205 311332 **(F)** 01205 310298
(E) sales@snowflake-group.demon.co.uk.
Profile Supplies. **Ref: YH13042**

SNOWFORD HILL FARM
Snowford Hill Farm, Long Itchington, Rugby, **Warwickshire**, CV47 9QF, **ENGLAND**.
(T) 01926 813985.
Profile Breeder, Stable/Livery. **Ref: YH13043**

SNOWHILL SADDLERY
Snowhill Saddlery & Country Clothing, 15-17 The Parade, East Wittering, Chichester, **Sussex (West)**, PO20 8BN, **ENGLAND**.
(T) 01243 672023 **(F)** 01243 672424.
Contact/s
General Manager: Ms J Buckley
Profile Riding Wear Retailer, Saddlery Retailer, Supplies. **No.Staff:** 5
Opening Times
Sp: Open Mon - Fri 09:00, Sun 10:00. Closed Mon - Fri 17:30, Sun 14:00.
Su: Open Mon - Fri 09:00, Sun 10:00. Closed Mon - Fri 17:30, Sun 14:00.
Au: Open Mon - Fri 09:00, Sun 10:00. Closed Mon - Fri 17:30, Sun 14:00.
Wn: Open Mon - Fri 09:00, Sun 10:00. Closed Mon - Fri 17:30, Sun 14:00.
Closed on Saturdays **Ref: YH13044**

SNOWLAND RIDING CTRE
Snowland Riding Centre, Par Farm, Par, **Cornwall**, PL24 2AE, **ENGLAND**.
(T) 01726 814846
(W) www.snowland-group.co.uk.
Contact/s
Owner: Mrs A Bolam
Profile Riding School, Stable/Livery.
The centre has 25 horses, which are used for hacks, beach rides, forest and picnic rides. **Yr. Est:** 1990
Opening Times
Sp: Open Mon - Sun 08:00. Closed Mon, Tues, Thurs - Sun 17:00, Wed 21:00.
Su: Open Mon - Sun 08:00. Closed Mon, Tues, Thurs - Sun 17:00, Wed 21:00.
Au: Open Mon - Sun 08:00. Closed Mon, Tues, Thurs - Sun 17:00, Wed 21:00.
Wn: Open Mon - Sun 08:00. Closed Mon, Tues, Thurs - Sun 17:00, Wed 21:00. **Ref: YH13045**

SOC FOR THE WELFARE OF HORSES
Society for the Welfare of Horses & Ponies (The), Coxstone, St Maughans, Monmouth, **Monmouthshire**, NP25 3QF, **WALES**.
(T) 01600 750233 **(F)** 01600 750468.
Contact/s
Key Contact: Mrs J MacGregor
Profile Club/Association. **Ref: YH13046**

SOCIETY OF EQUESTRIAN ARTISTS
Society of Equestrian Artists (The), 63 Gordon Cl, Knowle Green, Staines, **Surrey**, TW18 1AP, **ENGLAND**.
(T) 01784 889669.
Profile Club/Association. **Ref: YH13047**

SOCIETY OF MASTERS SADDLERS
Society of Masters Saddlers, Kettles Farm, Mickfield, Stowmarket, **Suffolk**, IP14 6BY, **ENGLAND**.
(T) 01449 711642 **(F)** 01449 711642
(E) enquiries@mastersaddlers.co.uk
(W) www.mastersaddlers.co.uk.
Contact/s
President: Mr D Dyer
Profile Club/Association. **Yr. Est:** 1966
Ref: YH13048

SOCK
Sock Co (The), New Hse Farm, Norton Wood, Hereford, **Herefordshire**, HR4 7BP, **ENGLAND**.
(T) 07850 372893.
Profile Supplies. **Ref: YH13049**

SOCKBRIDGE PONY TREKKING CTRE
Sockbridge Pony Trekking Centre, The Cottage, Sockbridge, Penrith, **Cumbria**, CA10 2JT, **ENGLAND**.
(T) 01768 863468 **(F)** 01768 892698
(W) www.sockbridgeponytrekking.co.uk.
Contact/s
General Manager: Miss J Strong **(Q)** BHS 1, BHS 2
Profile Equestrian Centre. Pony Trekking.
Sockbridge Pony Trekking Centre is a member of the Cumbrian Tourist Board. **Yr. Est:** 1973 **C.Size:** 3 Acres
Opening Times
Sp: Open 10:00. Closed 17:00.
Su: Open 10:00. Closed 18:00.
Au: Open 17:00. Closed 10:00.
Wn: Open 15:30.
Closed for 3 months during the winter, telephone for an appointment **Ref: YH13050**

SODBURY VALE EQUESTRIAN SUP
Sodbury Vale Equestrian Supplies, 68 Hambrook Lane, Stoke Gifford, **Gloucestershire (South)**, BS34 8QF, **ENGLAND**.
(T) 01179 694391.
Contact/s
Partner: Mr J Betts
Profile Saddlery Retailer. **Ref: YH13051**

SOLCUM STUD & STABLES
Solcum Stud & Stables, Solcum Farm, Solcum Lane, Wolverley, Kidderminster, **Worcestershire**, DY11 5XN, **ENGLAND**.
(T) 01562 850009 **(F)** 01562 850009.
Contact/s
Owner: Mr N Bernhard
Profile Breeder, Stable/Livery, Trainer. **Ref: YH13052**

SOLE, DARREN B
Darren B Sole DWCF, C/O 5 Beaconsfield Rd, Preston Circus, Brighton, **Sussex (East)**, BN1 4QH, **ENGLAND**.
(T) 076 25348484.
Profile Farrier. **Ref: YH13053**

SOLENT
Solent Saddlery, Mill Hill, Botley, Southampton, **Hampshire**, SO30 2GY, **ENGLAND**.
(T) 01489 787837 **(F)** 01489 786663.
Contact/s
Owner: Mr J Norris
Profile Saddlery Retailer. **Ref: YH13054**

SOLENT RIDING CLUB
Solent Riding Club, 25 Monarch Cl, Locksheath, **Hampshire**, SO3 6UG, **ENGLAND**.
(T) 01489 885379.
Profile Club/Association, Riding Club. **Ref: YH13055**

SOLEY FARM STUD
Soley Farm Stud, Chilton Foliat, Hungerford, **Berkshire**, RG17 0TW, **ENGLAND**.
(T) 01488 683321 **(F)** 01488 681065.
Profile Club/Association. **Ref: YH13056**

SOLID STAMPINGS
Solid Stampings Ltd, Porters Field Rd, Cradley Heath, **Midlands (West)**, B64 7BL, **ENGLAND**.
(T) 01384 636421.
Profile Blacksmith. **Ref: YH13057**

SOLIHULL RIDING CLUB
Solihull Riding Club, Four Ashes Rd, Dorridge, Solihull, **Midlands (West)**, B93 8QE, **ENGLAND**.
(T) 01564 770180 **(F)** 01564 774121
(E) solihullridingclub@lineone.net
(W) www.solihullridingclub.co.uk.
Contact/s
Chairman: Mr S Scott **(T)** 01564 778624
Profile Club/Association, Riding Club. **Ref: YH13058**

SOLOCOMB
SoloComb Ltd, 50 Masefield Cres, Abingdon, **Oxfordshire**, OX14 5PJ, **ENGLAND**.
(T) 01235 524257 **(F)** 01235 537550.
Profile Supplies. **Ref: YH13059**

SOMERBY EQUESTRIAN CTRE
Somerby Equestrian Centre Ltd, Newbold Lane, Somerby, Melton Mowbray, **Leicestershire**, LE14 2PP, **ENGLAND**.
(T) 01664 454838 **(F)** 01664 454167
(E) secretary@somerbyequestrian.fsnet.co.uk
(W) www.somerbyequestrian.fsnet.co.uk.
Contact/s
For Bookings: Mr S Dempsey
Profile Equestrian Centre, Horse/Rider Accom, Riding School, Stable/Livery.

Livery - full and part-time available. DIY livery £12 per night. No.Staff: 5 Yr. Est: 1990 C.Size: 40 Acres
Opening Times
Sp: Open 08:00. Closed 20:00.
Su: Open 08:00. Closed 20:00.
Au: Open 08:00. Closed 20:00.
Wn: Open 08:00. Closed 20:00. Ref: YH13060

SOMERLAP FOREST PRODUCTS
Somerlap Forest Products, Ubley Sawmill Ltd, Cleeve Hill, Compton Martin, **Bath & Somerset (North East)**, BS40 6PE, **ENGLAND**.
(T) 01761 462446 (F) 01761 462688. Ref: YH13061

SOMERS, R
R Somers, Three Horse Shoes Farm Bungalow, Branscombe, Seaton, **Devon**, EX12 3BR, **ENGLAND**.
(T) 01297 680269.
Contact/s
Owner: Mr R Somers
Profile Farrier. Ref: YH13062

SOMERSET BRIDLEWAYS
Somerset Bridleways, Wambrook Hse, Chard, **Somerset**, TA20 3DF, **ENGLAND**.
(T) 01460 63225.
Profile Club/Association. Ref: YH13063

SOMERSET SMITHY OF FROME
Somerset Smithy Of Frome, Christchurch St West, Frome, **Somerset**, BA11 1EQ, **ENGLAND**.
(T) 01373 462609.
Profile Blacksmith. Ref: YH13064

SOMERTON LIVERY STABLES
Somerton Livery Stables, Midney Farm, Somerton, **Somerset**, TA11 7HT, **ENGLAND**.
(T) 01458 273240. Ref: YH13065

SOMERVILLE, J & M
J & M Somerville, Syke Feeds, Kilmarnock, **Ayrshire (East)**, KA1 5PD, **SCOTLAND**.
(T) 01563 830233 (F) 01563 830600.
Contact/s
Owner: Mr J Somerville
Profile Supplies. Ref: YH13066

SOMERVILLE, JASON P
Jason P Somerville DWCF, 51 Springfield Ave, Shirehampton, **Bristol**, BS11 9TG, **ENGLAND**.
(T) 07802 317480.
Profile Farrier. Ref: YH13067

SOMETHING DIFFERENT
Something Different, Units 3-4 The Village Works, 4 London Rd, East Hoathly, Uckfield, **Sussex (East)**, BN8 6QA, **ENGLAND**.
(T) 01825 840086.
Contact/s
Owner: Ms L Smith (Q) BHSAI
(E) tackshopsd@netscapeonline.co.uk
Profile Riding Wear Retailer, Saddlery Retailer, Supplies. No.Staff: 5 Yr. Est: 1994
Opening Times
Sp: Open 10:00. Closed 17:00.
Su: Open 10:00. Closed 17:00.
Au: Open 10:00. Closed 17:00.
Wn: Open 10:00. Closed 17:00. Ref: YH13068

SOMMERFIELD FLEXABOARD
Sommerfield Flexaboard Ltd, Doseley Ind Est, Frame Lane, Telford, **Shropshire**, TF4 3BT, **ENGLAND**.
(T) 01952 503737 (F) 01952 630132.
Profile Track/Course. Ref: YH13069

SORLEY TUNNEL
Sorley Tunnel Riding School & Restaurant, Sorley Tunnel Adventure Farm Leisure Ctre, Kingsbridge, **Devon**, TQ7 4BP, **ENGLAND**.
(T) 01548 856662.
Contact/s
Owner: Mr S Bennett Ref: YH13070

SORREL SADDLERY
Sorrel Saddlery, Le Mont Fallu, St Peter, **Jersey**, JE3 7EF, **ENGLAND**.
(T) 01534 42009.
Profile Saddlery Retailer, Stable/Livery.
Ref: YH13071

SOUCH, A
Mr A Souch, Parkham Ash, Parkham, Bideford, **Devon**, **ENGLAND**..
Profile Supplies. Ref: YH13072

SOUGH FARM
Sough Farm, 19 Cranberry Cl, Darwen, **Lancashire**, BB3 2HR, **ENGLAND**.
(T) 01254 775062.
Contact/s
Owner: Mrs M Howarth
Profile Stable/Livery, Stud Farm. Ref: YH13073

SOUTH & WEST STRAW
South & West Straw, Longbridge Meadow, Cullompton, **Devon**, EX15 1BT, **ENGLAND**.
(T) 01884 34843 (F) 01884 33505.
Contact/s
Manager: Mr C Donaldson Ref: YH13074

SOUTH AMERICAN TRADE SERVICES
South American Trade Services, Sandpool Hse, Tarlton, Cirencester, **Gloucestershire**, GL7 6PB, **ENGLAND**.
(T) 01285 841542 (F) 01285 841546
(E) sats@lineone.net
(W) www.satsfaction.com.
Contact/s
Partner: Mr T Emerson
Profile Supplies. Polo Equipment Stockists. Polo holidays. Yr. Est: 1989
Opening Times
Sp: Open 08:00. Closed 19:00.
Su: Open 08:00. Closed 19:00.
Au: Open 08:00. Closed 19:00.
Wn: Open 08:00. Closed 19:00.
Closed Sundays Ref: YH13075

SOUTH ARMAGH FARMING
South Armagh Farming Enterprises, 8 Newry Rd, Camlough, Newry, **County Down**, BT35 7JP, **NORTHERN IRELAND**.
(T) 028 30230691.
Profile Supplies. Ref: YH13076

SOUTH BANK STABLES
South Bank Stables, Lambourn, Hungerford, **Berkshire**, RG17 9TP, **ENGLAND**.
(T) 01488 71548 (F) 01488 72823.
Profile Trainer. Ref: YH13077

SOUTH BRENT RIDING CLUB
South Brent Riding Club, Heather Cott, Holsome Lane, Diptford, Totnes, **Devon**, TQ9 7NU, **ENGLAND**.
(T) 01548 821348.
Contact/s
Chairman: Mrs S Franklin
Profile Club/Association, Riding Club. Ref: YH13078

SOUTH BUCKS ESTATES
South Bucks Estates, The Est Yard, Pyebush Lane, Beaconsfield, **Buckinghamshire**, HP9 2RX, **ENGLAND**.
(T) 01494 671921 (F) 01494 670399
(E) sbe@globalnet.co.uk. Ref: YH13079

SOUTH CAUSEY EQUESTRIAN CTRE
South Causey Equestrian Centre, Beamish Burn Rd, Stanley, **County Durham**, DH9 0LS, **ENGLAND**.
(T) 01207 235555 (F) 01207 230137.
Contact/s
Owner: Mrs J Gibson
Profile Riding School. Ref: YH13080

SOUTH CERNEY RIDING SCHOOL
South Cerney Riding School, Cerney Wick, Cirencester, **Gloucestershire**, GL7 5QH, **ENGLAND**.
(T) 01793 750151.
Contact/s
Owner: Miss H Dorling Ref: YH13081

SOUTH DEVON EQUESTRIAN SUP
South Devon Equestrian Supplies, Wild Woods Farm, Marldon, Paignton, **Devon**, TQ3 1RS, **ENGLAND**.
(T) 01803 556253.
Profile Saddlery Retailer. Ref: YH13082

SOUTH DEVON RIDING CLUB
South Devon Riding Club, 92 Marldon Rd, Torquay, **Devon**, TQ2 7EH, **ENGLAND**.
(T) 01803 614852.
Profile Club/Association, Riding Club. Ref: YH13083

SOUTH DOWNS HARNESS CLUB
South Downs Harness Club, Chesham Cottage, Hambledon Rd, Denmead, **Hampshire**, PO7 6JB, **ENGLAND**.
(W) www.sdhc.co.uk.
Profile Club/Association. Ref: YH13084

SOUTH DURHAM SADDLE CLUB
South Durham Saddle Club, 26 Southbrooke Ave, Hartlepool, **Cleveland**, TS25 5JB, **ENGLAND**.
(T) 01429 274881.
Profile Club/Association. Ref: YH13085

SOUTH EAST EQUESTRIAN
South East Equestrian, 23 Henrietta St, Wexford, **County Wexford**, **IRELAND**.
(T) 053 24388.
Profile Supplies. Ref: YH13086

SOUTH EAST SHAVINGS
South East Shavings, Huntshill Farm, Aveley Rd, Upminster, **Essex**, RM14 2TG, **ENGLAND**.
(T) 01708 861325 (F) 01708 861325.
Contact/s
Owner: Mr P Moorley
Profile Supplies. Shavings supplier.
Supply to trade No.Staff: 6 Yr. Est: 1994
Opening Times
Sp: Open Mon - Fri 09:00. Closed Mon - Fri 17:00.
Su: Open Mon - Fri 09:00. Closed Mon - Fri 17:00.
Au: Open Mon - Fri 09:00. Closed Mon - Fri 17:00.
Wn: Open Mon - Fri 09:00. Closed Mon - Fri 17:00.
Ref: YH13087

SOUTH EAST TOURIST BOARD
South East England Tourist Board, The Old Brew Hse, Warwick Pk, Tunbridge Wells, **Kent**, TN2 5TU, **ENGLAND**.
(T) 01892 540766 (F) 01892 511008.
Profile Equestrian Centre. Ref: YH13088

SOUTH EASTERN EQUESTRIAN SVS
South Eastern Equestrian Services Ltd, Oatridges, Best Beech, Wadhurst, **Sussex (East)**, TN5 6JL, **ENGLAND**.
(T) 01892 783227
(M) 07885 160030. Ref: YH13089

SOUTH ESSEX FEED CTRE
South Essex Feed Centre, Hovells Farm, Vange Park Rd, Vange, Basildon, **Essex**, SS16 5LA, **ENGLAND**.
(T) 01268 583733 (F) 01268 450097.
Profile Supplies. Ref: YH13090

SOUTH ESSEX INSURANCE
South Essex Insurance Brokers Limited, South Essex Hse, North Rd, South Ockendon, **Essex**, RM15 5BE, **ENGLAND**.
(T) 01708 850000 (F) 01708 851520.
Profile Club/Association. Ref: YH13091

SOUTH FARM LIVERY YARD
South Farm Livery Yard, 59 Draycott Rd, Chiseldon, Swindon, **Wiltshire**, SN4 0LT, **ENGLAND**.
(T) 01793 740032.
Contact/s
Owner: Mrs S McMurray
Profile Stable/Livery. Ref: YH13092

SOUTH FARM RIDING STABLES
South Farm Riding Stables, Beagle Cottage/South Farm Lane, South Farm, Langton Green, Tunbridge Wells, **Kent**, TN3 9JN, **ENGLAND**.
(T) 01892 864807. Ref: YH13093

SOUTH HAMS BRIDLEWAYS
South Hams Bridleways, The Laurels, North Huish, South Brent, **Devon**, TQ10 9NH, **ENGLAND**.
(T) 01548 821454.
Profile Club/Association. Ref: YH13094

SOUTH HATCH STABLES
South Hatch Stables, 44 Burgh Heath Rd, Epsom, **Surrey**, KT17 4LX, **ENGLAND**.
(T) 01372 748800 (F) 01372 739410
(M) 07880 715292.
Profile Trainer. Ref: YH13095

SOUTH HOUGHTON EQUESTRIAN CTRE
South Houghton Equestrian Centre, South Houghton, Heddon-on-the-Wall, Newcastle-upon-Tyne, **Tyne and Wear**, NE15 0EZ, **ENGLAND**.
(T) 01661 852475 (F) 01661 853110.
Contact/s
Partner: Mrs D Whiting Ref: YH13096

SOUTH KESTEVEN & DISTRICT
South Kesteven & District Riding Club, 29 High Dyke, Harrowby, Grantham, **Lincolnshire**, NG31 9ER, **ENGLAND**.
(T) 01476 72849.
Profile Club/Association, Riding Club. Ref: YH13097

SOUTH LAMMERMUIR RIDING CLUB
South Lammermuir Riding Club, Hillside, Teindhillgreen, Duns, **Scottish Borders**, TD11 3DX, **SCOTLAND**.
(T) 01361 883795.
Contact/s
Chairman: Miss D Calder

Profile Club/Association, Riding Club. Ref: YH13098

SOUTH LEICESTERSHIRE

South Leicestershire Riding Establishment, Frowlesworth Rd, Leire, Lutterworth, **Leicestershire**, LE17 5HP, **ENGLAND**.
(T) 01455 209407.
Profile Riding School. Ref: YH13099

SOUTH LODGE

South Lodge Riding School, South Lodge, Castle Hill, Rotherfield, **Sussex (East)**, TN6 3RR, **ENGLAND**.
(T) 01892 852886 (F) 01892 852886
(E) southlodge@aol.com.
Contact/s
For Bookings: Sylvia Stacey
Profile Riding School, Stable/Livery. Trophy Suppliers.
Telephone for a trophy brochure. Yr. Est: 1990
C.Size: 24 Acres
Opening Times
Sp: Open Wed - Mon 09:00. Closed Wed - Mon 17:00.
Su: Open Wed - Mon 09:00. Closed Wed - Mon 17:00.
Au: Open Wed - Mon 09:00. Closed Wed - Mon 17:00.
Wn: Open Wed - Mon 09:00. Closed Wed - Mon 17:00.
Closed Tuesdays, although this is flexible.
Ref: YH13100

SOUTH MEDBURN

South Medburn Equestrian Centre, Watling St, Elstree, Borehamwood, **Hertfordshire**, WD6 3AA, **ENGLAND**.
(T) 020 82074714 (F) 020 82076118.
Contact/s
Owner: Mrs M Rose
Profile Equestrian Centre, Riding School, Stable/Livery.
Training given to NVQ and AI level. Full livery available, prices on request.
Opening Times
Sp: Open Tues - Sun 08:30. Closed Tues - Sun 16:30.
Su: Open Tues - Sun 08:30. Closed Tues - Sun 16:30.
Au: Open Tues - Sun 08:30. Closed Tues - Sun 16:30.
Wn: Open Tues - Sun 08:30. Closed Tues - Sun 16:30.
Closed Mondays Ref: YH13101

SOUTH NORFOLK EQUESTRIAN CTRE

South Norfolk Equestrian Centre Ltd, Lenrys Lodge, Suton St, Suton, Wymondham, **Norfolk**, NR18 9JQ, **ENGLAND**.
(T) 01953 601066.
Profile Equestrian Centre. Ref: YH13102

SOUTH OF ENGLAND AGRCLTRL SOC

South of England Agricultural Society Riding Club, Ardingly, Haywards Heath, **Sussex (West)**, RH17 6TL, **ENGLAND**.
(T) 01444 892700 (F) 01444 892888.
Profile Club/Association. Ref: YH13103

SOUTH PENNIE PACKHORSE

South Pennie Packhorse Trials Trust, Bell Farm, Laughton, Lewes, **Sussex (East)**, BN8 6BX, **ENGLAND**.
(T) 01825 840306.
Profile Club/Association. Ref: YH13104

SOUTH STAFFORDSHIRE SADDLERY

South Staffordshire Saddlery, 200 Stafford St, Walsall, **Midlands (West)**, WS2 8ED, **ENGLAND**.
(T) 01922 440077.
Profile Saddlery Retailer. Ref: YH13105

SOUTH SWAY FARM

South Sway Farm, South Sway Lane, Sway, Lymington, **Hampshire**, SO41 6DL, **ENGLAND**.
(T) 01590 682649.
Profile Stable/Livery. Ref: YH13106

SOUTH VIEW EQUESTRIAN CTRE

South View Equestrian Centre, South View Manor, Winsford Rd, Wettenhall, Winsford, **Cheshire**, CW7 4DL, **ENGLAND**.
(T) 01270 528684 (F) 01270 528407.
Contact/s
Owner: Mr J Maguire
Profile Equestrian Centre, Riding School.
Ref: YH13107

SOUTH VIEW FARM EQUESTRIAN

South View Farm Equestrian, Bathley Lane, Little Carlton, Newark, **Nottinghamshire**, NG23 6BY, **ENGLAND**.
(T) 01636 708840.
Profile Riding School. Ref: YH13108

SOUTH VIEW RIDING SCHOOL

South View Riding School, South View, Marsh Foot Rd, Chadwell St Mary, Grays, **Essex**, RM16 4LU, **ENGLAND**.
(T) 01375 842698.
Contact/s
Owner: Mrs J Peachey
Profile Riding School. Ref: YH13109

SOUTH VIEW SADDLERY/PET FOOD

South View Saddlery & Pet Food Supplies, South View, Marsh Foot Rd, Chadwell St Mary, Grays, **Essex**, RM16 4LU, **ENGLAND**.
(T) 01375 842698.
Contact/s
Owner: Mr B Peachey
Profile Saddlery Retailer. Ref: YH13110

SOUTH WALES CARRIAGE DRIVING

South Wales Carriage Driving Centre, Llwyn Mawr Farm, Penclawdd Rd, Gowerton, Swansea, **Swansea**, SA4 3RB, **WALES**.
(T) 01792 874299
(W) www.rowena-moyse.com
Affiliated Bodies BDS.
Contact/s
Owner: Miss R Moyse (Q) BHSAI, ISM, LHHI
(E) info@rowena-moyse.com
Profile Equestrian Centre, Stable/Livery, Trainer. Carriage Driving Centre. Yr. Est: 1980
Ref: YH13111

SOUTH WALES EQUESTRIAN CTRE

South Wales Equestrian Centre, Rhiwceiliog Pencoed, Bridgend, **Bridgend**, CF35 6NH, **WALES**.
(T) 01656 862959 (F) 01656 862858.
Contact/s
Office Manager: Mrs D Barnes
Profile Riding School, Stable/Livery. Ref: YH13112

SOUTH WALSHAM HALL

South Walsham Hall Park Riding Centre, Ranworth Rd, South Walsham, Norwich, **Norfolk**, NR13 6DH, **ENGLAND**.
(T) 01603 270260.
Contact/s
Owner: Mr R Fielder Ref: YH13113

SOUTH WARWICKSHIRE

South Warwickshire Riding Club, The Grange, Welton Rd, Braunston, Daventry, **Northamptonshire**, NN11 7JG, **ENGLAND**.
(T) 01788 891260.
Contact/s
Chairman: Mrs F Scott
Profile Club/Association, Riding Club. Ref: YH13114

SOUTH WEST HORSE

South West Horse, Quayside Publishing, Quayside Hse, Barrington St, Tiverton, **Devon**, EX16 6PT, **ENGLAND**.
(T) 01884 243474 (F) 01884 258810.
Profile Supplies. Ref: YH13115

SOUTH WEST LANCASHIRE FARMERS

South West Lancashire Farmers Ltd, Blaguegate Lane, Lathom, Skelmersdale, **Lancashire**, WN8 8TZ, **ENGLAND**.
(T) 01695 724331 (F) 01695 50807.
Profile Supplies. Ref: YH13116

SOUTH WEST REGIONAL

South West Regional Group of The Arab Horse Society, Bentwitchen Cottage, Bentwitchen, North Molton, **Devon**, EX36 3HA, **ENGLAND**.
(T) 01598 740455.
Profile Breeder, Club/Association. Ref: YH13117

SOUTH WEST SCOTLAND

South West Scotland Riding Club, Dalton Burn, Dalton, Lockerbie, **Dumfries and Galloway**, DG11 1DT, **SCOTLAND**.
(T) 01387 840371.
Profile Club/Association, Riding Club. Ref: YH13118

SOUTH WEST TRAILERS

South West Trailers, Hillgate Hse, Bridgwater Rd, Bleadon, Weston-Super-Mare, **Somerset (North)**, BS24 0BA, **ENGLAND**.
(T) 01934 811800.
Contact/s
Owner: Mr C Nelson
Profile Transport/Horse Boxes. Ref: YH13119

SOUTH WESTERN DRESSAGE GROUP

South Western Dressage Group, Wincanton Riding, Rodgrove Copse, Wincanton, **Somerset**, BA9 9QU, **ENGLAND**.
(T) 01963 70142.
Contact/s
Chairman: Mrs J Bagnall
Profile Club/Association. Ref: YH13120

SOUTH WESTERN GARMENTS

South Western Garments (Style Products), Highfield Hse, 101 Badminton Rd, Coalpit Heath, Bristol, **Bristol**, BS36 2TD, **ENGLAND**.
(T) 01454 775505 (F) 01454 775505.
Contact/s
Owner: Mr P Baber Ref: YH13121

SOUTH WESTERN SHOW

South Western Show Jumping Club, Stonelea Cottage, Wilmington, Newton St Loe, Bath, **Bath & Somerset (North East)**, BA2 9JB, **ENGLAND**.
(T) 01225 873687 (F) 01225 874963
(M) 07885 647090.
Profile Club/Association. Ref: YH13122

SOUTH WEYLANDS EQUESTRIAN

South Weylands Equestrian Centre, South Weylands Farm, Esher Rd, Walton-on-Thames, **Surrey**, KT12 4LJ, **ENGLAND**.
(T) 01372 463010.
Contact/s
Owner: Mrs P Bushnell
Profile Riding School. Ref: YH13123

SOUTH WILTSHIRE RIDING CLUB

South Wiltshire Riding Club, Fallowfields, Little London, Heytesbury, Warminster, **Wiltshire**, BA12 0ES, **ENGLAND**.
(T) 01985 840717 (F) 01985 840616.
Contact/s
Chairman: Mrs D Hicketts
Profile Club/Association, Riding Club. Ref: YH13124

SOUTH YARDE FARM

South Yarde Farm, Bishops Nympton, South Molton, **Devon**, EX36 4PP, **ENGLAND**.
(T) 01769 550409.
Contact/s
Owner: Mr G Ratcliff
Profile Breeder. Ref: YH13125

SOUTHALL, J

Miss J Southall, Church Farm, Bratton Seymour, Wincanton, **Somerset**, BA9 8BY, **ENGLAND**.
(T) 01963 32179.
Profile Supplies. Ref: YH13126

SOUTHAMPTON UNI POLO CLUB

Southampton University Polo Club, Athletic Union, Highfield, **Hampshire**, SO17 1BJ, **ENGLAND**.
(T) 023 80553710.
Profile Club/Association. Polo Club. Ref: YH13127

SOUTHBOROUGH LANE STABLES

Southborough Lane Stables, 321A Southborough Lane, Bromley, **Kent**, BR2 8BG, **ENGLAND**.
(T) 020 84675236.
Profile Riding School, Stable/Livery. Ref: YH13128

SOUTHBROOK STUD

Southbrook Stud, Higher Loveham Farm, High Bickington, Umberleigh, **Devon**, EX37 9AU, **ENGLAND**.
(T) 01769 60322.
Profile Breeder. Ref: YH13129

SOUTHBROOKE RIDING SCHOOL

Southbrooke Riding School, Southbrooke Farm, Cactote Road, **Cleveland**, TS25 4EZ, **ENGLAND**.
(T) 01429 420560.
Profile Riding School. Ref: YH13130

SOUTHCOURT STUD

Southcourt Stud, Linslade, Leighton Buzzard, **Bedfordshire**, LU7 7PS, **ENGLAND**.
(T) 01525 373107.
Profile Breeder. Ref: YH13131

SOUTHDOWN & ERIDGE

Southdown & Eridge, The Willows, Brook, Ashford, **Kent**, TN25 5PD, **ENGLAND**.
(T) 01233 812613 (F) 01233 812613. Ref: YH13132

SOUTHDOWN EQUESTRIAN CTRE

Southdown Equestrian Centre, Newbrook Farm, Pound Lane, Upper Beeding, Steyning, **Sussex**

(West), BN44 3JD, **ENGLAND**.
(T) 01903 815924
(E) n.goody@btinternet.com
(W) www.sd/equis.co.uk.
Contact/s
Manager: Mrs J Blake **(Q)** BHSAI
Profile Equestrian Centre, Riding School.
The centre offers livery, Alexander Technique and Linguistic Programming. Yr. Est: 1976
C.Size: 15 Acres
Opening Times
Sp: Open 08:30. Closed 18:00.
Su: Open 08:30. Closed 18:00.
Au: Open 08:30. Closed 18:00.
Wn: Open 08:30. Closed 18:00. Ref: **YH13133**

SOUTHDOWN FARM RIDING STABLES

Southdown Farm Riding Stables, Southdown Farm, Brixham, **Devon**, TQ5 0AJ, **ENGLAND**.
(T) 01803 857991 **(F)** 01803 857991.
Profile Riding School, Stable/Livery. Ref: **YH13134**

SOUTHDOWN FEEDS

Southdown Feeds, 5 Banbridge Rd, Rathfriland, **County Down**, BT34 5PE, **NORTHERN IRELAND**.
(T) 028 40630501.
Profile Supplies. Ref: **YH13135**

SOUTHERN COUNTIES AUCTIONEERS

Southern Counties Auctioneers, The Livestock Market, Christys Lane, Shaftesbury, **Dorset**, SP7 8PH, **ENGLAND**.
(T) 01722 321215 **(F)** 01722 421553. Ref: **YH13136**

SOUTHERN COUNTIES HEAVY HORSE

Southern Counties Heavy Horse Association, Flat 4 Glen Ashton, 44 Rowlands Hill, Wimborne, **Dorset**, BH21 2QH, **ENGLAND**.
(T) 01202 848377.
Profile Club/Association. Ref: **YH13137**

SOUTHERN COUNTIES RIDING CLUB

Southern Counties Riding Club, 6 Moorland Way, Upton, Poole, **Dorset**, BH16 5JT, **ENGLAND**.
(T) 01202 779494.
Profile Club/Association, Riding Club. Ref: **YH13138**

SOUTHERN COUNTIES ROSETTES

Southern Counties Rosettes, Matchbox, Riding Lane, Hildenborough, Tonbridge, **Kent**, TN11 9LL, **ENGLAND**.
(T) 01732 834116 **(F)** 01732 832273.
Profile Supplies. Ref: **YH13139**

SOUTHERN HAY COACH BUILDERS

Southern Hay Coach Builders, Collage Farm, Park Rd, Westoning, Bedford, **Bedfordshire**, MK45 5LA, **ENGLAND**.
(T) 01525 720130 **(F)** 01525 720140.
Contact/s
Partner: Mr B Ring
Profile Transport/Horse Boxes. Ref: **YH13140**

SOUTHERN MOBILE

Southern Mobile, 53 School Lane, Bushey, **Hertfordshire**, WD2 1BY, **ENGLAND**.
(T) 020 89505051 **(F)** 020 89504911.
Profile Transport/Horse Boxes. Ref: **YH13141**

SOUTHERN SHOWS GROUP

Southern Shows Group, 14 St Georges Ave, London, **London (Greater)**, W5 5JF, **ENGLAND**.
(T) 020 85665262. Ref: **YH13142**

SOUTHERN STRAW SERVICES

Southern Straw Services Ltd, Hill Farm, Sutton Scotney, Winchester, **Hampshire**, SO21 3NT, **ENGLAND**.
(T) 01962 760707 **(F)** 01962 886938.
Contact/s
Owner: Mr C Trower Ref: **YH13143**

SOUTHERN TOURIST BOARD

Southern Tourist Board, 40 Chamberlayne Rd, Eastleigh, **Hampshire**, SO50 5JH, **ENGLAND**.
(T) 023 80620006 **(F)** 023 80620010.
Profile Equestrian Centre. Ref: **YH13144**

SOUTHERN TRAILER SYSTEMS

Southern Trailer Systems Ltd, Coach St, Cork, **County Cork**, **IRELAND**.
(T) 021 4270104 **(F)** 021 4274670.
Profile Supplies. Ref: **YH13145**

SOUTHERN TRAILERS

Southern Trailers, Units 3 & 4 Lymington Farm, Lymington Bottom Rd, Medstead, Alton, **Hampshire**, GU34 5EW, **ENGLAND**.
(T) 01420 564191.
Profile Transport/Horse Boxes. Ref: **YH13146**

SOUTHERN, JOHN

John Southern, 373 Hulton Lane, Bolton, **Manchester (Greater)**, BL3 4LH, **ENGLAND**.
(T) 01204 657154.
Profile Farrier. Ref: **YH13147**

SOUTHERN, R

Mrs R Southern, Thomas Farm, Chorton By Backford, Chester, **Cheshire**, CH2 4DD, **ENGLAND**.
(T) 01244 55340.
Profile Breeder. Ref: **YH13148**

SOUTHFIELD EQUESTRIAN CTRE

Southfield Equestrian Centre, Southfields Farm, Whitchurch, **Hampshire**, RG28 7JL, **ENGLAND**.
(T) 01256 896859 **(F)** 01256 896859.
Contact/s
Owner: Mr W Crosbie-Dawson
(E) william@crosbiedawson.junglelink.co.uk
Profile Arena, Equestrian Centre, Stable/Livery, Track/Course, Trainer. Sells and Trains Horses.
Sell and train horses imported from Eire.
No.Staff: 4 Yr. Est: 1994 C.Size: 50 Acres
Opening Times
Sp: Open 07:00. Closed 21:00.
Su: Open 07:00. Closed 21:00.
Au: Open 07:00. Closed 19:00.
Wn: Open 07:00. Closed 19:00. Ref: **YH13149**

SOUTHFIELD FARM RIDING SCHOOL

Southfield Farm Riding School, Southfield Farm, Backwell, **Somerset (North)**, BS48 3PE, **ENGLAND**.
(T) 01275 463807.
Profile Riding School, Stable/Livery. Ref: **YH13150**

SOUTHFIELD STABLES

Southfield Stables, South Lane, Sutton Valence, Maidstone, **Kent**, ME17 3AZ, **ENGLAND**.
(T) 01622 842788
(M) 07714 239100.
Profile Trainer. Ref: **YH13151**

SOUTHFIELD VETNRY CTRE

Southfield Veterinary Centre, Southfield Veterinary Ctre, South Walks, Dorchester, **Dorset**, DT1 IDU, **ENGLAND**.
(T) 01305 262913 **(F)** 01305 250485.
Contact/s
Vet: Mr N Tucker
Profile Medical Support. Ref: **YH13152**

SOUTHFIELDS FARM

Southfields Farm, Stryt Isa, Pen-Y-Ffordd, **Cheshire**, CH4 0JY, **ENGLAND**.
(T) 01978 760496.
Profile Riding School, Stable/Livery. Ref: **YH13153**

SOUTHILL LIVERY & RIDING CTRE

Southill Livery & Riding Centre, Low Cocken Farm, Plawsworth, Chester Le Street, **County Durham**, DH3 4EN, **ENGLAND**.
(T) 0191 3881139. Ref: **YH13154**

SOUTHILL STABLES

Southill Stables, Marlborough Rd, Aldbourne, Marlborough, **Wiltshire**, SN8 2DP, **ENGLAND**.
(T) 01672 540110. Ref: **YH13155**

SOUTHILL VETNRY GROUP

Southill Veterinary Group, The Surgery, Balsam Fields, Wincanton, **Somerset**, BA9 9HE, **ENGLAND**.
(T) 01963 33226 **(F)** 01963 31995.
Contact/s
Vet: Mr J Collyor
Profile Medical Support. Ref: **YH13156**

SOUTHLANDS EQUESTRIAN CTRE

Southlands Equestrian Centre, Chinthurst Lane, Bramley, Guildford, **Surrey**, GU5 0DR, **ENGLAND**.
(T) 01483 898586. Ref: **YH13157**

SOUTHMOOR RIDING CTRE

Southmoor Riding Centre, Beggars Lane, Longworth, Abingdon, **Oxfordshire**, OX13 5BL, **ENGLAND**.
(T) 01865 820443.
Contact/s
Owner: Mrs I Sowden Ref: **YH13158**

SOUTHREY RIDING STABLES

Southrey Riding Stables, Lowthorpe, Southrey, **Lincolnshire**, LN3 5TD, **ENGLAND**.
(T) 01526 398637.
Profile Riding School. Ref: **YH13159**

SOUTHVIEW FARM

Southview Riding Centre, Southview Farm, Bradford-on-Avon, **Wiltshire**, BA15 1UH, **ENGLAND**.
(T) 01225 863361.
Contact/s
Owner: Mr R Fry
Profile Riding School.
Teaches children over six years old. Yr. Est: 1971
C.Size: 60 Acres
Opening Times
Sp: Open Sat - Sun 09:30. Closed Sat - Sun 14:00.
Su: Open Sat - Sun 09:30. Closed Sat - Sun 14:00.
Au: Open Sat - Sun 09:30. Closed Sat - Sun 14:00.
Wn: Open Sat - Sun 09:30. Closed Sat - Sun 14:00.
Telephone for further Information Ref: **YH13160**

SOUTHWELL RACE COURSE

Southwell Race Course, The Racecourse, Rolleston, Newark, **Nottinghamshire**, NG25 0TS, **ENGLAND**.
(T) 01636 814481 **(F)** 01636 812271.
Profile Track/Course. Ref: **YH13161**

SOUTHWEST BLOODSTOCK

Southwest Bloodstock Ltd, 4 Aylesfield Cottage, Froyle Rd, Shalden, Alton, **Hampshire**, GU34 4BY, **ENGLAND**.
(T) 01420 541050 **(F)** 01420 541047.
Profile Blood Stock Agency. Ref: **YH13162**

SOUTHWICK FARM

Southwick Farm, Southwick Farm, Gloucester Rd, Tewkesbury, **Gloucestershire**, GL20 7DG, **ENGLAND**.
(T) 01684 292206 **(F)** 01684 292204.
Contact/s
Partner: Mr J Warner
(E) warners@southwickfarm.freeserve.co.uk
Profile Supplies, Transport/Horse Boxes.
Haylage - hay in plastic. Hay analysis, (including starch analysis, moisture content etc) is available to the buyer. Yr. Est: 1963
Opening Times
Sp: Open 08:00. Closed 20:00.
Su: Open 08:00. Closed 20:00.
Au: Open 08:00. Closed 20:00.
Wn: Open 08:00. Closed 20:00.
Telephone for further information Ref: **YH13163**

SOVERIGN QUARTER HORSES

Soverign Quarter Horses, Lesmond Hse, Creek Fen, March, **Cambridgeshire**, PE15 0BU, **ENGLAND**.
(T) 01354 651944 **(F)** 01354 663163.
Contact/s
Owner: Mrs S Hall
Profile Breeder. Ref: **YH13164**

SOWERBY, G

Mr G Sowerby, Terrys Farm, Ormside, Appleby, **Cumbria**, CA16 6EJ, **ENGLAND**.
(T) 01768 351576.
Profile Trainer. Ref: **YH13165**

SOWERBY, W T

Mr W T Sowerby, Haybanks Farm, Orybeck, Appleby, **Cumbria**, CA16 6TF, **ENGLAND**.
(T) 01768 351112.
Profile Trainer. Ref: **YH13166**

SOWERBYS OF STOURBRIDGE

Sowerbys of Stourbridge, 30 Lower High St, Stourbridge, **Midlands (West)**, DY8 1TA, **ENGLAND**.
(T) 01384 394326
(E) jsow482169@aol.com.
Profile Saddlery Retailer. Ref: **YH13167**

SOWERSBY, M E

Mr M E Sowersby, Southwold Farm, Goodmanham, **Yorkshire (East)**, YO43 3LZ, **ENGLAND**.
(T) 01430 810534
(M) 07809 059756.
Profile Trainer. Ref: **YH13168**

SOXLINE

Soxline Ltd, Soxline Dromahair, Leitrim, **County Leitrim**, **IRELAND**.
(T) 071 64583.
Profile Supplies. Ref: **YH13169**

SPALDING & DISTRICT

Spalding & District Riding Club, New Hse, West End, Swaton, Sleaford, **Lincolnshire**, NG34 0JL, **ENGLAND**.
(T) 01529 421566 **(F)** 01529 421780.
Profile Club/Association, Riding Club. Ref: **YH13170**

SPALDING, C M

C M Spalding, Cliffords Farm, Ovington, Richmond, **Yorkshire (North)**, DL11 7DD, **ENGLAND**.

(T) 01833 627210.
Profile Blood Stock Agency, Breeder, Stable/Livery, Trainer. **Ref: YH13171**

SPALDING, VICTORIA

Ms Victoria Spalding, 24 Elmete Walk, Roundhay, **Yorkshire (West)**, LS8 2LB, **ENGLAND**.
(T) 0113 2174343
(M) 07976 854577.
Profile Medical Support. **Ref: YH13172**

SPANISH BIT RIDING SCHOOL

Spanish Bit Riding School, Elm Farm, Boveney Rd, Dorney, Windsor, **Berkshire**, SL4 6QD, **ENGLAND**.
(T) 01628 661275.
Profile Riding School, Stable/Livery. **Ref: YH13173**

SPARE MOMENTS

Spare Moments, Hasty Brow Rd, Slyne, Lancaster, **Lancashire**, LA2 6AG, **ENGLAND**.
(T) 01524 410575 **(F)** 01524 410575.
Contact/s
Partner: Mr D Nelson **Ref: YH13174**

SPARKES, A J

A J Sparkes, Luke St, Berwick St. John, Shaftesbury, **Dorset**, SP7 0HQ, **ENGLAND**.
(T) 01747 828496.
Contact/s
Partner: Mr A Sparkes
Profile Farrier. **Ref: YH13175**

SPARKES, PAUL J

Paul J Sparkes DWCF, The Forge, Berwick St John, Shaftesbury, **Dorset**, SP7 0HA, **ENGLAND**.
(T) 01747 828900.
Profile Farrier. **Ref: YH13176**

SPARKFORD SAWMILLS

Sparkford Sawmills Ltd (Yeovil), Sparkford, Yeovil, **Somerset**, BA22 7LH, **ENGLAND**.
(T) 01963 440414 **(F)** 01963 440982
(E) info@sparkfords.co.uk
(W) www.sparkford.com.
Profile Stable/Livery, Transport/Horse Boxes.
Ref: YH13177

SPARKLING STUDS

Sparkling Studs, 8 Upper Lane Rd, Eglinton, Londonderry, **County Londonderry**, BT47 3BN, **NORTHERN IRELAND**.
(T) 028 71810331.
Contact/s
Owner: Miss A Roulston
Profile Breeder. No.Staff: 4 Yr. Est: 1991
C.Size: 20 Acres
Opening Times
Sp: Open Mon - Sun 09:00. Closed Mon - Sun 20:00.
Su: Open Mon - Sun 09:00. Closed Mon - Sun 20:00.
Au: Open Mon - Sun 09:00. Closed Mon - Sun 20:00.
Wn: Open Mon - Sun 09:00. Closed Mon - Sun 20:00. **Ref: YH13178**

SPARREY, LIONEL

Lionel Sparrey AFCL, Church Farm Villa, Elmbridge, Droitwich, **Worcestershire**, WR9 0DA, **ENGLAND**.
(T) 01299 23601.
Profile Farrier. **Ref: YH13179**

SPARROW, KEVIN

Kevin Sparrow, 184 Tarlton, Cirencester, **Gloucestershire**, GL7 6PA, **ENGLAND**.
(T) 01285 770623. **Ref: YH13180**

SPARROWHAWK, J A

J A Sparrowhawk, Flat 3, Penny Royal, 130/134 Stafford Rd, Wallington, **Surrey**, SM6 9BW, **ENGLAND**.
(T) 020 86477586.
Profile Farrier. **Ref: YH13181**

SPARROWS HILL LIVERY

Sparrows Hill Livery, Sparrows End, Newport, Saffron Walden, **Essex**, CB11 3TU, **ENGLAND**.
(T) 01799 542504 **(F)** 01799 542244. **Ref: YH13182**

SPARSHOLT COLLEGE

Sparsholt College, Sparsholt, Winchester, **Hampshire**, SO21 2NF, **ENGLAND**.
(T) 01962 776441 **(F)** 01962 776587
(E) enquiry@sparsholt.ac.uk
(W) www.sparsholt.ac.uk.
Profile Stable/Livery. **Ref: YH13183**

SPARTAN RIDING CLUB

Spartan Riding Club, Woodlands, Wenlock Rd, Simonside, South Shields, **Tyne and Wear**, NE34 9AL, **ENGLAND**.
(T) 0191 4554892.
Profile Club/Association, Riding Club. **Ref: YH13184**

SPARTAN STUD

Spartan Stud, Hewletts, North Rd, Havering Atte Bower, Romford, **Essex**, RM4 1PX, **ENGLAND**.
(T) 01708 733820.
Profile Breeder. **Ref: YH13185**

SPEARFIELD STUD

Spearfield Stud, Long Furlong Farm, Long Furlong, Clapham, Worthing, **Sussex (West)**, BN13 3XN, **ENGLAND**.
(T) 01903 871272.
Contact/s
Owner: Mrs C McIntosh
Profile Breeder. **Ref: YH13186**

SPECIAL OCCASIONS

Special Occasions, Shootlands, Abinger Common, Dorking, **Surrey**, RH5 6JX, **ENGLAND**.
(T) 01306 730373.
Contact/s
Partner: Mrs L Mead **Ref: YH13187**

SPECK, A W

A W Speck, The Red Hse, 18 Back Lane, Stonesby, Melton Mowbray, **Leicestershire**, LE14 4PT, **ENGLAND**.
(T) 01664 464751.
Contact/s
Owner: Mr A Speck
Profile Farrier. **Ref: YH13188**

SPECTRUM AGENCY

Spectrum Agency, 119 George V Ave, Worthing, **Sussex (West)**, BN11 5SA, **ENGLAND**.
(T) 01903 506127.
Contact/s
Office Manager: Mrs J Davey
Profile Club/Association. Equestrian Employment Agency. **Ref: YH13189**

SPEEDFIT

Speedfit, Unit 2 Enterprise Ctre/Moniton Trading Est, Worting Rd, Basingstoke, **Hampshire**, RG22 6NQ, **ENGLAND**.
(T) 01256 469618.
Profile Transport/Horse Boxes. **Ref: YH13190**

SPEEDGATE FARM

Speedgate Farm Feeds & Saddlery, Speedgate Farm, Fawkham, Longfield, **Kent**, DA3 8NJ, **ENGLAND**.
(T) 01474 872313 **(F)** 01474 872544.
Contact/s
Manager: Ms J Weavers
Profile Saddlery Retailer, Stable/Livery.
Ref: YH13191

SPEER, EMMA

Emma Speer, Fair Stanton, Bindon Lane, East Stoke, Wareham, **Dorset**, BH20 6AS, **ENGLAND**.
(T) 01929 462797. **Ref: YH13192**

SPELLBOUND SADDLEBREDS

Spellbound Saddlebreds, Abbey Leigh, Abbey Rd, Wingfield, Diss, **Norfolk**, IP21 5QS, **ENGLAND**.
(T) 01379 586704.
Profile Breeder. **Ref: YH13193**

SPELLER, A

A Speller, 17 Thackeray End, Aylesbury, **Buckinghamshire**, HP19 8JE, **ENGLAND**.
(T) 01296 393896.
Profile Farrier. **Ref: YH13194**

SPELLER, ANDREW E

Andrew E Speller DWCF HONS, 17 Thakeray End, Haydon Hill, Aylesbury, **Buckinghamshire**, HP19 3JE, **ENGLAND**.
(T) 01296 393896.
Profile Farrier. **Ref: YH13195**

SPENCER LAVERY AST

Spencer Lavery Associates, 203 Ashley Rd, Hale, **Cheshire**, WA15 9SQ, **ENGLAND**.
(T) 0161 9299130 **(F)** 0161 9299089.
Profile Club/Association. **Ref: YH13196**

SPENCER, D

D Spencer, 209 Coppice Rd, Poynton, Stockport, **Cheshire**, SK12 1SW, **ENGLAND**.
(T) 01625 874617.
Contact/s
Owner: Mr D Spencer
Profile Farrier. **Ref: YH13197**

SPENCER, ERIC

Eric Spencer, 15/17 Church St, Ilkley, **Yorkshire (West)**, LS29 9DR, **ENGLAND**.
(T) 01943 601405.
Profile Saddlery Retailer. **Ref: YH13198**

SPENCER, G

G Spencer, Marlbrook Farm, Castlemorton Common, Welland, Malvern, **Worcestershire**, WR13 6LE, **ENGLAND**.
(T) 01684 310189 **(F)** 01684 310036.
Contact/s
Owner: Mr G Spencer
Profile Transport/Horse Boxes. **Ref: YH13199**

SPENCER, J E

Miss J E Spencer, Coe End Farm, 252 Southport Rd, Scarisbrick, Southport, **Merseyside**, PR8 5LF, **ENGLAND**.
(T) 01704 880911 **(F)** 01704 880911.
Profile Breeder. **Ref: YH13200**

SPENCER, WALTER

Walter Spencer, 63-65 Ladywell Ave, Edinburgh, **Edinburgh (City of)**, EH12 7LL, **SCOTLAND**.
(T) 0131 3340688.
Profile Blacksmith. **Ref: YH13201**

SPICER, R C

Mr R C Spicer, The Gallops, Dozens Bank, West Pinchbeck, Spalding, **Lincolnshire**, PE11 3ND, **ENGLAND**.
(T) 01775 640068
(M) 07957 770343.
Profile Breeder, Trainer. **Ref: YH13202**

SPIGOT LODGE

Spigot Lodge, Middleham, Leyburn, **Yorkshire (North)**, DL8 4TL, **ENGLAND**.
(T) 01969 623350 **(F)** 01969 624374.
Contact/s
Manager: Mr C Thornton
Profile Trainer. **Ref: YH13203**

SPIKINGS, N D

N D Spikings, Church End, Wrangle, Boston, **Lincolnshire**, PE22 9EH, **ENGLAND**.
(T) 01205 870195.
Contact/s
Owner: Mr N Spikings
Profile Blacksmith. **Ref: YH13204**

SPILLER, GRAHAM

Graham Spiller, The Haven, Union Rd, Bradfield, Reading, **Berkshire**, RG7 6AE, **ENGLAND**.
(T) 0118 9744427.
Contact/s
Owner: Mr G Spiller
Profile Farrier. **Ref: YH13205**

SPILLERS SPECIALITY FEEDS

Spillers Speciality Feeds Ltd, Customer Services Dept, Old Wolverton Rd, Old Wolverton, Milton Keynes, **Buckinghamshire**, MK12 5PZ, **ENGLAND**.
(T) 01908 222888 **(F)** 01908 222800
(E) helpline@spillers-feeds.com
(W) www.spillers-feeds.com.
Profile Feed Merchant. **Ref: YH13206**

SPILMAN, THOMASINA

Miss Thomasina Spilman MC AMC MMCA, 78 High St, Yelvertoft, **Northamptonshire**, NN6 6LQ, **ENGLAND**.
(T) 01788 823867.
Profile Medical Support. **Ref: YH13207**

SPINAL INJURIES ASSOCIATION

Spinal Injuries Association, 76 St James Lane, London, **London (Greater)**, N10 3DF, **ENGLAND**.
(T) 020 84442121 **(F)** 020 84443761
(W) www.spinal.co.uk.
Profile Club/Association.
National organisation who work with those with spinal cord injuries Yr. Est: 1974
Opening Times
Sp: Open Mon - Fri 09:30. Closed Mon - Fri 17:30.
Su: Open Mon - Fri 09:30. Closed Mon - Fri 17:30.
Au: Open Mon - Fri 09:30. Closed Mon - Fri 17:30.
Wn: Open Mon - Fri 09:30. Closed Mon - Fri 17:30.
Closed for lunch 13:00 - 14:00 **Ref: YH13208**

SPINNEY LODGE VETNRY HOSP

Spinney Lodge Veterinary Hospital, 491 Kettering Rd, Northampton, **Northamptonshire**, NN3 6QW, **ENGLAND**.
(T) 01604 648221 **(F)** 01604 647913.
Profile Medical Support. **Ref: YH13209**

SPINWAY STUD
Spinway Stud, Buttermilk Farm, Leafield, **Oxfordshire**, OX8 5PL, **ENGLAND**.
(T) 01993 878426 **(F)** 01993 878426.
Profile Breeder. **Ref: YH13210**

SPIRE VETNRY GROUP
Spire Veterinary Group, 161-163 St Johns Rd, Newbold, Chesterfield, **Derbyshire**, S41 8PE, **ENGLAND**.
(T) 01246 455333.
Profile Medical Support. **Ref: YH13211**

SPONDON TACK AGENCY
Spondon Tack Agency, 117 Dale Rd, Spondon, Derby, **Derbyshire**, DE21 7DJ, **ENGLAND**.
(T) 01332 665203.
Contact/s
Manager: Mrs J Farry **Ref: YH13212**

SPONSATROVE
Sponsatrove, Burneston Hall, Bedale, **Yorkshire (North)**, DL8 2JE, **ENGLAND**.
(T) 01677 426340 **(F)** 01677 426340. **Ref: YH13213**

SPOOR, DAVID RUSSELL
David Russell Spoor, The Villa, Green Lane, Bangor Isycoed, Wrexham, **Wrexham**, LL13 0BE, **WALES**.
(T) 01978 780054.
Profile Farrier. **Ref: YH13214**

SPORBORG, C H
Mr C H Sporborg, Brooms Farm, Upwick Green, Albury, Ware, **Hertfordshire**, SG11 2JX, **ENGLAND**.
(T) 01279 771444.
Profile Supplies. **Ref: YH13215**

SPORT & GENERAL PRESS AGENCY
Sport & General Press Agency Ltd, 68 Exmouth Market, London, **London (Greater)**, EC1R 4RA, **ENGLAND**.
(T) 020 72781223 **(F)** 020 72788480.
Contact/s
Chief Librarian: Paul Kurton
Profile Club/Association. **Ref: YH13216**

SPORT & LEISURE
Sport & Leisure, 36 High St, Malmesbury, **Wiltshire**, SN16 9AU, **ENGLAND**.
(T) 01666 822965.
Contact/s
Partner: Mr I Stafford
Profile Saddlery Retailer. **Ref: YH13217**

SPORT HORSE BREEDING
Sport Horse Breeding of Great Britain, 96 High St, Edenbridge, **Kent**, TN8 5AR, **ENGLAND**.
(T) 01732 866277 **(F)** 01732 867464
(E) office@sporthorsegb.co.uk.
Contact/s
Secretary: Mrs K Hall
Profile Club/Association. **Ref: YH13218**

SPORT HORSE TRAINING CTRE
Sport Horse Training Centre (The), The Wolds, The Green, Snitterfield, Stratford-upon-Avon, **Warwickshire**, CV37 0JE, **ENGLAND**.
(T) 01789 730222.
Contact/s
Owner: Mrs J Bird
Profile Equestrian Centre. **Ref: YH13219**

SPORT LEISURE & TRAILERS
Sport Leisure & Commercial Trailers, Cockmannings Farm, Cockmannings Lane, Orpington, **Kent**, BR5 4HF, **ENGLAND**.
(T) 01689 891408.
Contact/s
Owner: Mr T Turner
Profile Transport/Horse Boxes. **Ref: YH13220**

SPORT OF KINGS
Sport Of Kings, Teviotdale Mill, Commercial Rd, Hawick, **Scottish Borders**, TD9 7AQ, **SCOTLAND**.
(T) 01450 379999 **(F)** 01450 376082.
Contact/s
Senior Partner: Mr D Whillans
Profile Saddlery Retailer. **Ref: YH13221**

SPORTABAC
Sportabac, Llanddewi Rhydderch, Abergavenny, **Monmouthshire**, NP7 9UY, **WALES**.
(T) 01873 840004 **(F)** 01873 840004
(E) sales@sportabac.co.uk
(W) www.sportabac.co.uk.
Contact/s
Owner: Mrs L Ticehurst
Profile Medical Support.
Supply trade only No.Staff: 5 Yr. Est: 1990
Ref: YH13222

SPORTACK
Sportack, Damside Of Glenskinno, Montrose, **Angus**, DD10 9LG, **SCOTLAND**.
(T) 01674 830001 **(F)** 01674 830001.
Contact/s
Owner: Ms D Govan **Ref: YH13223**

SPORTING CHOICE
Sporting Choice, Main St, Dunsby, **Lincolnshire**, PE10 0UB, **ENGLAND**.
(T) 01778 440721.
Profile Saddlery Retailer. **Ref: YH13224**

SPORTING COLOURS
Sporting Colours, 2 Drivers End, Codicote, Hitchin, **Hertfordshire**, SG4 8TR, **ENGLAND**.
(T) 01438 820400. **Ref: YH13225**

SPORTING FINE ART
Sporting Fine Art, 88 Gloucester Cresent, Rushden, **Northamptonshire**, NN10 0BN, **ENGLAND**.
(T) 01933 355248 **(F)** 01933 417930. **Ref: YH13226**

SPORTING HEIGHTS
Sporting Heights, Clay Farm, Clows Top, Kidderminster, **Worcestershire**, DY14 9NN, **ENGLAND**.
(T) 01299 832421 **(F)** 01299 832421.
Profile Saddlery Retailer. **Ref: YH13227**

SPORTING LIFE
Sporting Life (The), 19Th Floor, 1 Canada Sq, London, **London (Greater)**, E14 5AP, **ENGLAND**.
(T) 020 72933473 **(F)** 020 72933320.
Profile Supplies. **Ref: YH13228**

SPORTING LIFE WEEKENDER
Sporting Life Weekender, One Canada Sq, Canary Wharf, **London (Greater)**, E14 5AP, **ENGLAND**.
(T) 020 72933291 **(F)** 020 72933758.
Profile Supplies. **Ref: YH13229**

SPORTING PAINTINGS
Sporting Paintings, Carlton Curlieu Manor, Carlton Curlieu, Leicester, **Leicestershire**, LE8 0PB, **ENGLAND**.. **Ref: YH13230**

SPORTING PICTURES
Sporting Pictures (UK) Ltd, 7a Lambs Conduit Passage, Holborn, **London (Greater)**, WC1R 4RG, **ENGLAND**.
(T) 020 74054500 **(F)** 020 78317991. **Ref: YH13231**

SPORTING TWENTY-PAGER
Sporting Twenty-Pager (The), The Studio, 49 Causton St, London, **London (Greater)**, SW1P 4BR, **ENGLAND**.
(T) 020 79765555.
Profile Supplies. **Ref: YH13232**

SPORTS
Sports (Wexford) Ltd, Bettyville, **County Wexford**, **IRELAND**.
(T) 053 42307
(E) info@wexfordraces.ie
(W) www.wexfordraces.ie.
Profile Supplies. **Ref: YH13233**

SPORTS INDUSTRIES FEDERATION
Sports Industries Federation (The), Federation Hse, Stoneleigh Park Pavillion, National Agricultural Centre, Stoneleigh, **Warwickshire**, CV8 2RF, **ENGLAND**.
(T) 024 76414999 **(F)** 024 76414990.
Profile Club/Association. **Ref: YH13234**

SPORTS MARKETING SURVEYS
Sports Marketing Surveys, Byfleet Business Ctre, Chertsey Rd, Byfleet, **Fife**, KY14 7AW, **SCOTLAND**.
(T) 01932 350600 **(F)** 01932 350375.
Profile Club/Association. **Ref: YH13235**

SPORTSMARK
Sportsmark By Signam, Harris Rd, Warwick, **Warwickshire**, CV34 5FY, **ENGLAND**.
(T) 01926 417300 **(F)** 01926 417333
(E) sales@sportmark.co.uk.
Profile Supplies. Arena accessories. **Ref: YH13236**

SPORTSPAGES
Sportspages, Caxton Walk, 94-96 Charing Cross Rd, London, **London (Greater)**, WC2H 0JG, **ENGLAND**.
(T) 020 72409604 **(F)** 020 78360104.
Profile Supplies. **Ref: YH13237**

SPORTSPAGES
Sportspages, Barton Sq, St Ann's Sq, Manchester, **Manchester (Greater)**, M2 7HA, **ENGLAND**.
(T) 0161 8328530 **(F)** 0161 8329391.
Profile Supplies. **Ref: YH13238**

SPORTY TRAILERS
Sporty Trailers, Unit 33/Corringham Ind Est, Corringham Rd, Gainsborough, **Lincolnshire**, DN21 1QB, **ENGLAND**.
(T) 01427 811116 **(F)** 01427 811078.
Profile Transport/Horse Boxes. **Ref: YH13239**

SPOTTED HORSE & PONY SOCIETY
Spotted Horse & Pony Society, 17 School Lane, Dronfield, **Derbyshire**, S18 1RY, **ENGLAND**.
(T) 01246 413201.
Profile Club/Association. **Ref: YH13240**

SPOTTED PONY BREED SOCIETY
Spotted Pony Breed Society (GB) Breed Show, Hollygate Hse, Ridlington, Oakham, **Rutland**, LE15 9AU, **ENGLAND**.
(T) 01572 821781 **(F)** 01572 821781.
Contact/s
Key Contact: Ms J Allen
Profile Club/Association. **Ref: YH13241**

SPOTTISWOOD, P
Mr P Spottiswood, The Cottages, Greenhaugh, Tarset, Hexham, **Northumberland**, NE48 1PP, **ENGLAND**.
(T) 01434 240472
(M) 07803 433403.
Profile Supplies. **Ref: YH13242**

SPPTT
South Pennine Packhorse Trails Trust, The Barn, Mankinholes, **Yorkshire (West)**, OL14 6HR, **ENGLAND**.
(T) 01706 815598 **(F)** 01706 815598
(W) www.rightsofway.org.uk.
Contact/s
Enquiries: Ms S Hogg
(E) suehgg@globalnet.co.uk
Profile Club/Association.
Members pay to fund the opening of bridleways and gain lists of bridleways in their area **Ref: YH13243**

SPRING BANK STABLES
Spring Bank Stables, Slad, Stroud, **Gloucestershire**, GL6 7QE, **ENGLAND**.
(T) 01452 814267 **(F)** 01452 814246
(M) 07860 487426.
Profile Trainer. **Ref: YH13244**

SPRING COTTAGE STABLES
Spring Cottage Stables, Langton Rd, Norton, Melton, **Yorkshire (North)**, YO17 9PY, **ENGLAND**.
(T) 01653 69004
(M) 07785 747426.
Profile Trainer. **Ref: YH13245**

SPRING PADDOCK RIDING SCHOOL
Spring Paddock Riding School, Marple Rd, Charlesworth, Glossop, **Derbyshire**, SK13 5DA, **ENGLAND**.
(T) 01457 853175. **Ref: YH13246**

SPRING WOOD FARM
Spring Wood Farm Livery Stables & Arab Stud, Wharf Rd, Stanton Hill, Sutton-In-Ashfield, **Nottinghamshire**, NG17 3GT, **ENGLAND**.
(T) 01623 554337.
Profile Breeder. **Ref: YH13247**

SPRING, JEREMY
Jeremy Spring, Shuttleworth Grange, Shuttleworth Lane, Cosby, **Leicestershire**, LE9 5RF, **ENGLAND**.
(T) 01455 202078 **(F)** 01455 209455.
Profile Stable/Livery, Trainer. **Ref: YH13248**

SPRINGBANK STUD
Springbank Stud, Green Wickerlie, Besford, **Worcestershire**, WR8 9AP, **ENGLAND**.
(T) 01386 556626.
Profile Breeder. **Ref: YH13249**

SPRINGBOURNE & BLANCHE WELSH
Springbourne & Blanche Welsh Mountain Ponies, Springbourne Stud Farm, Ecchinswell, Newbury, **Berkshire**, RG20 4UJ, **ENGLAND**.
(T) 01635 268428
(E) welcome@springbourne-blanche.com.
Profile Breeder. **Ref: YH13250**

SPRINGDAWN RIDING SCHOOL
Springdawn Riding School, Sheepwash Bank,

Choppington, **Northumberland**, NE62 5NA, **ENGLAND**.
(T) 01670 822568.
Contact/s
Owner: Mrs A Ziegler **Ref: YH13251**

SPRINGFIELD

Springfield Rubber Flooring, Arden Holding, Jasmine Lane, Claverham, **Somerset (North)**, BS49 4PY, **ENGLAND**.
(T) 01934 832759 **(F)** 01934 835550
(M) 07836 350377
(E) mikehobbs@springfield-sr.demon.co.uk.
Profile Supplies, Transport/Horse Boxes.
Rubber flooring and matting specialists. **Ref: YH13252**

SPRINGFIELD FARM

Springfield Farm, Springfield Farm Stables, Benniworth, Market Rasen, **Lincolnshire**, LN8 6JN, **ENGLAND**.
(T) 01507 313234.
Contact/s
Owner: Mrs M Pinney
Profile Horse/Rider Accom, Trainer.
Trains racehorses No.Staff: 1 Yr. Est: 1991
Opening Times
Sp: Open Mon - Sun 09:00. Closed Mon - Sun 21:00.
Su: Open Mon - Sun 09:00. Closed Mon - Sun 21:00.
Au: Open Mon - Sun 09:00. Closed Mon - Sun 21:00.
Wn: Open Mon - Sun 09:00. Closed Mon - Sun 21:00. **Ref: YH13253**

SPRINGFIELD LIVERY

Springfield Livery, Springfield Farm, Flappit, Keighley, **Yorkshire (West)**, BD21 5PT, **ENGLAND**.
(T) 01535 643181.
Contact/s
Owner: Mr J Poole
Profile Stable/Livery. **Ref: YH13254**

SPRINGFIELD LIVERY SVS

Springfield Livery Services, Ashwell Rd, Oakham, **Leicestershire**, LE15 7QH, **ENGLAND**.
(T) 01572 756489.
Contact/s
Owner: Mrs L Matthews **Ref: YH13255**

SPRINGFIELD RIDING STABLES

Springfield Riding Stables, Springfield Hse, St Brides, Wentloog, **Newport**, NP1 9SR, **WALES**.
(T) 01633 680610
Affiliated Bodies BHS.
Contact/s
Partner: Miss C Turner
Profile Riding School.
Springfield teach people of all abilities, from beginners to advanced. Children between 5 - 18 years old are taught in groups.
Opening Times
Sp: Open Tues - Sat 09:00. Closed Tues - Sat 19:00.
Su: Open Tues - Sat 09:00. Closed Tues - Sat 19:00.
Au: Open Tues - Sat 09:00. Closed Tues - Sat 19:00.
Wn: Open Tues - Sat 09:00. Closed Tues - Sat 19:00.
Closed Sundays and Mondays **Ref: YH13256**

SPRINGFIELD SMITHY

Springfield Smithy, Springfield Rd, Grimsby, **Lincolnshire (North East)**, DN33 3JE, **ENGLAND**.
(T) 01472 873638.
Contact/s
Owner: Mr D Weatherhall
Profile Blacksmith. **Ref: YH13257**

SPRINGFIELD STABLES

Springfield Stables, Bridge Of Marnock, Huntly, **Aberdeenshire**, AB54 7QY, **SCOTLAND**.
(T) 01466 86244.
Profile Stable/Livery. **Ref: YH13258**

SPRINGFIELDS

Springfields, 49 Hatchet Lane, Stonely, Huntingdon, **Cambridgeshire**, PE18 0EG, **ENGLAND**.
(T) 01480 860692.
Contact/s
Owner: Mrs M Stubbins **Ref: YH13259**

SPRINGTIME DARTMOORS

Springtime Dartmoors, 31 Plemont Rd, Liverpool, **Merseyside**, L13 6RT, **ENGLAND**.
(T) 0151 2207089.
Profile Breeder. **Ref: YH13260**

SPRINGTIRE

Springtire, Caradoc, Sellack, Ross-on-Wye, **Herefordshire**, HR9 6LS, **ENGLAND**.
(T) 01989 730540 **(F)** 01989 730541.
Contact/s
Owner: Mr P Darling
Profile Breeder. **Ref: YH13261**

SPRINGVALE CARRIAGES

Springvale Carriages, Bradway Grange Farm, Rod Moor Rd, Dronfield Woodhouse, Sheffield, **Yorkshire (South)**, S18 8VL, **ENGLAND**.
(T) 0114 2621249.
Profile Transport/Horse Boxes. Horse drawn vehicles. Horse drawn vehicles are available for hire for special occassions. **Ref: YH13262**

SPRINGWATER STUD

Springwater Stud, Studley Hse, Baddiley, Nantwich, **Cheshire**, CW5 8PY, **ENGLAND**.
(T) 01270 624095 **(F)** 01270 629911.
Contact/s
Owner: Mrs N Tyler
Profile Breeder.
Opening Times
Telephone for an appointment **Ref: YH13263**

SPRINGWELL VETNRY CLINIC

Springwell Veterinary Clinic, Noahs Ark Vet Clinic, 54 High St South, Dunstable, **Bedfordshire**, LU6 3HD, **ENGLAND**.
(T) 01582 606466.
Profile Medical Support. **Ref: YH13264**

SPRINGWOOD STABLES

Springwood Stables, Rainstorth Jumble Lane, Ecclesfield, Sheffield, **Yorkshire (South)**, S35 9XJ, **ENGLAND**.
(T) 0114 2465183 **(F)** 0114 2465183.
Contact/s
Owner: Miss M Wilson **Ref: YH13265**

SPRINGWOOD VETNRY GROUP

Springwood Veterinary Group, 90 Spring Trce Rd, Burton-on-Trent, **Staffordshire**, DE15 9DX, **ENGLAND**.
(T) 01283 568162 **(F)** 01283 517646.
Profile Medical Support. **Ref: YH13266**

SPRY, RUSSELL K

Russell K Spry DWCF, Rideout, Lake Lane, Yelverton, Plymouth, **Devon**, PL20 6NH, **ENGLAND**.
(T) 07885 665144.
Profile Farrier. **Ref: YH13267**

SQUIRES, A W

A W Squires, Squires Farm, 2 Chorley Old Rd, Whittle-Le-Woods, Chorley, **Lancashire**, PR6 7LB, **ENGLAND**.
(T) 01257 262427.
Contact/s
Manageress: Mrs A Squires **Ref: YH13268**

SQUIRREL FARM/LIVERY STABLES

Squirrel Farm & Livery Stables, Risborough Rd, Stoke Mandeville, Aylesbury, **Buckinghamshire**, HP22 5UT, **ENGLAND**.
(T) 01296 612998.
Contact/s
Owner: Mrs S Skier **Ref: YH13269**

ST ANDREW STUD

St Andrew Stud, Stable Cottage, Duck End, Cranford, Kettering, **Northamptonshire**, NN14 4AD, **ENGLAND**.
(T) 01536 330599.
Contact/s
Owner: Mr R Langley
Profile Breeder. **Ref: YH13270**

ST ANNES VETNRY GROUP

St Annes Veterinary Group, 6 St Annes Rd, Eastbourne, **Sussex (East)**, BN21 2DJ, **ENGLAND**.
(T) 01323 640011 **(F)** 01323 738060
(M) 07712 439289.
Profile Medical Support. **Ref: YH13271**

ST BRIDGETS VETNRY CTRE

St Bridgets Veterinary Centre, St Bridgets Lane, Egremont, **Cumbria**, CA22 2BB, **ENGLAND**.
(T) 01946 820312.
Profile Medical Support. **Ref: YH13272**

ST BRIDGETS VETNRY CTRE

St Bridgets Veterinary Centre, Preston St Veterinary Ctre, Preston St, Whitehaven, **Cumbria**, CA28 9DL, **ENGLAND**.
(T) 01946 693303.
Profile Medical Support. **Ref: YH13273**

ST CLEMENTS LODGE

St Clements Lodge Equestrian, Woods Lane, Calverton, Nottingham, **Nottinghamshire**, NG14 6FF, **ENGLAND**.
(T) 0115 9652524 **(F)** 0115 9655994
(W) www.scle.co.uk
Affiliated Bodies ABRS, BHS.
Contact/s
Owner: Mr N Burrows **(Q)** BHSII
Profile Arena, Equestrian Centre, Riding School, Riding Wear Retailer, Saddlery Retailer, Stable/Livery, Supplies.
There are regular dressage clinics held by Andrew Day.
Ref: YH13274

ST EDMUNDS RIDING CLUB

St Edmunds Riding Club, Vine Cottage, Gents Lane, Shimpling, Bury St Edmunds, **Suffolk**, IP29 4HP, **ENGLAND**.
(T) 01284 828035.
Profile Club/Association, Riding Club. **Ref: YH13275**

ST GEORGE'S VETNRY CLINIC

St George's Veterinary Clinic (Wolverhampton), 8 St George's Prde, Wolverhampton, **Midlands (West)**, WV2 1BD, **ENGLAND**.
(T) 01902 425262 **(F)** 01902 714137.
Profile Medical Support. **Ref: YH13276**

ST IVES LIVERY

St Ives Livery, Butcherfield Lane, Hartfield, **Sussex (East)**, TN7 4JX, **ENGLAND**.
(T) 01892 770589.
Profile Stable/Livery. **Ref: YH13277**

ST LEONARDS EQUESTRIAN CTRE

St Leonards Equestrian Centre, The Cyder Hse, Launceston, **Cornwall**, PL15 9QR, **ENGLAND**.
(T) 01566 775543 **(F)** 01566 774926.
Contact/s
Owner: Mr A Reeve
Profile Breeder, Riding School, Stable/Livery, Track/Course, Trainer. **Ref: YH13278**

ST LEONARD'S RIDING SCHOOL

St Leonard's Riding School, Nottingham Rd, Beeston, Nottingham, **Nottinghamshire**, NG9 6EG, **ENGLAND**.
(T) 0115 9732753.
Contact/s
Owner: Mrs S Carnelley
Profile Riding School. **Ref: YH13279**

ST MARGARETS RIDING SCHOOL

St Margarets Riding School, Mobile Home/St Margarets Farm, Botney Hill, Little Burstead, Billericay, **Essex**, CM12 9SJ, **ENGLAND**.
(T) 01277 632438.
Profile Riding School. **Ref: YH13280**

ST MARGRETS STUD

St Margrets Stud, Church Rd, Wereham, King's Lynn, **Norfolk**, PE33 9AP, **ENGLAND**.
(T) 01366 500023.
Profile Breeder. **Ref: YH13281**

ST MERRYN RIDING SCHOOL

St Merryn Riding School, Padstow, **Cornwall**, **ENGLAND**..
Profile Riding School. **Ref: YH13282**

ST NICHOLAS FORGE

St Nicholas Forge, The Forge, The Street, St. Nicholas At Wade, Birchington, **Kent**, CT7 0NR, **ENGLAND**.
(T) 01843 847435.
Profile Farrier. **Ref: YH13283**

ST SIMONS STUD

St Simons Stud, Kennett, Newmarket, **Suffolk**, CB8 8QS, **ENGLAND**.
(T) 01638 750222 **(F)** 01638 751186.
Profile Breeder. **Ref: YH13284**

ST VEEP RIDING STABLES

St Veep Riding Stables, Little Hadley, St. Veep, Lostwithiel, **Cornwall**, PL22 0PA, **ENGLAND**.
(T) 01208 873521.
Contact/s
Owner: Mrs E Baron
Profile Riding School. **Ref: YH13285**

STABLE

Stable (The), 6 Pound Farm Prde, Snape Drive, Lowestoft, **Suffolk**, NR32 4SF, **ENGLAND**.
(T) 01502 531700 **(F)** 01502 568043.
Contact/s
Owner: Miss D Pearson **Ref: YH13286**

STABLE

Stable Banks Green Farm (The), Stable Banks

Green Farm, Banks Green, Upper Bentley, Redditch, **Worcestershire**, B97 5SU, **ENGLAND**.
(T) 01527 542047.
Contact/s
Owner: Mrs A Gibbs
Profile Stable/Livery.
DIY livery available. **Yr. Est:** 1981 **Ref: YH13287**

STABLE CARE KINGSWOOD
Stable Care Kingswood Ltd, The Stables, Bonsor Drive, Tadworth, **Surrey**, KT20 6AY, **ENGLAND**.
(T) 01737 379377.
Contact/s
Partner: Mrs A Cole **Ref: YH13288**

STABLE COLOURS
Stable Colours, Tewin Hill Farm, Tewin Hill, Tewin, Welwyn, **Hertfordshire**, AL6 0LL, **ENGLAND**.
(T) 01707 895964 **(F)** 01923 818337
(E) info@stablecolours.co.uk
(W) www.stablecolours.co.uk.
Profile Saddlery Retailer. **Ref: YH13289**

STABLE CORNER
Stable Corner (The), Victoria Stores, Market Sq, Newcastle Emlyn, **Carmarthenshire**, SA38 9AA, **WALES**.
(T) 01239 711350. **Ref: YH13290**

STABLE DOOR
Stable Door, Brookhouse Farm, Sulhamstead Rd, Burghfield, Reading, **Berkshire**, RG30 3SD, **ENGLAND**.
(T) 0118 9831838 **(F)** 0118 9831838.
Contact/s
Owner: Mrs S Jones
Profile Saddlery Retailer. **Ref: YH13291**

STABLE DOOR TRADING
Stable Door Trading, Hillcroft, Rock Hill, Wrantage, **Somerset**, TA3 6DW, **ENGLAND**.
(T) 01823 490980 **(F)** 01823 490980
(M) 07831 243705.
Profile Saddlery Retailer. **Ref: YH13292**

STABLE EXPRESS
Stable Express, 90 Station Rd, Oakham, **Rutland**, LE15 6QU, **ENGLAND**.
(T) 01572 722615 **(F)** 01572 755211.
Profile Supplies. **Ref: YH13293**

STABLE GEAR
Stable Gear, Church Cottage, Church Lane, Berrick Salome, **Oxfordshire**, OX10 9JP, **ENGLAND**.
(T) 01865 890984 **(F)** 01491 826420.
Profile Saddlery Retailer. **Ref: YH13294**

STABLE LADS ASS
Stable Lads Association, 4 Dunsmore Way, Midway, Swadlincote, **Derbyshire**, DE11 7LA, **ENGLAND**.
(T) 01283 211522 **(F)** 01283 211522.
Profile Club/Association. **Ref: YH13295**

STABLE LOFT SADDLERY
Stable Loft Saddlery, Greenburns Farm, Kettins, Blairgowrie, **Perth and Kinross**, PH13 9HA, **SCOTLAND**.
(T) 01828 627015. **Ref: YH13296**

STABLE MINDS
Stable Minds Ltd, 2 Princess Court, Princess Rd, Ferndown, **Dorset**, BH22 9JG, **ENGLAND**.
(T) 01590 641496
Affiliated Bodies NPSSA.
Contact/s
Owner: Mrs L Pritchard **(Q)** BA(Hons), BHS HM, MSc
Profile Breeder. Sport Psychologist. **Ref: YH13297**

STABLE RELIEF SVS
Stable Relief Services (Est 1974), The Old Rectory, Belton In Rutland, Oakham, **Rutland**, LE15 9LE, **ENGLAND**.
(T) 01572 717381 **(F)** 01572 717343
(E) srs@stablemate.demon.co.uk. **Ref: YH13298**

STABLE ROOM
Stable Room (The), 10 Coronation Buildings, Brougham Rd, Worthing, **Sussex (West)**, BN11 2NW, **ENGLAND**.
(T) 01903 537251. **Ref: YH13299**

STABLECARE
Stablecare, Main St, Bruntingthorpe, Lutterworth, **Leicestershire**, LE17 5QF, **ENGLAND**.
(T) 0116 2478838 **(F)** 0116 2478838
(E) info@stablecare.co.uk.
Profile Supplies. **Ref: YH13300**

STABLECARE
Stablecare, 11 Craven Way, Newmarket, **Suffolk**, CB8 0BW, **ENGLAND**.
(T) 01638 665279.
Contact/s
General Manager: Mr P Erridge
Profile Supplies.
Clean stable rubbers **No.Staff:** 3 **Yr. Est:** 1982
Opening Times
Sp: Open Mon - Sat 08:00. Closed Mon - Sat 18:00.
Su: Open Mon - Sat 08:00. Closed Mon - Sat 18:00.
Au: Open Mon - Sat 08:00. Closed Mon - Sat 18:00.
Wn: Open Mon - Sat 08:00. Closed Mon - Sat 18:00.
Ref: YH13301

STABLE-DRY & EQUIBALE
Jackson Carter Wood Management, Little Grove Farm, Stubbs Walden, Doncaster, **Yorkshire (South)**, DN6 9BT, **ENGLAND**.
(T) 01977 621065 **(F)** 07970 945814
(M) 07966 135777.
Contact/s
Owner: Mr P Jackson
Profile Supplies.
Unique bedding material made from 100% soft wood product specifically designed for the equestrian trade. 100% biodegradable, unique absorbancy and less waste. Manufacturers of Stable-Dry & Equibale.
No.Staff: 7 **Yr. Est:** 2000 **C.Size:** 4 Acres
Opening Times
Sp: Open Mon - Sat 08:00. Closed Mon - Fri 18:00, Sat 16:00.
Su: Open Mon - Sat 08:00. Closed Mon - Fri 18:00, Sat 16:00.
Au: Open Mon - Sat 08:00. Closed Mon - Fri 18:00, Sat 16:00.
Wn: Open Mon - Sat 08:00. Closed Mon - Fri 18:00, Sat 16:00.
Closed Sundays **Ref: YH13302**

STABLEITE
Stableite, Vernon - Dale, Lower Hartlip Rd, Hartlip, Sittingbourne, **Kent**, ME9 7PB, **ENGLAND**.
(T) 01795 842110 **(F)** 01795 842110
(W) www.stableite.co.uk.
Contact/s
Owner: Mrs J Cockerton
Profile Supplies. **Ref: YH13303**

STABLEMATES
StableMates, 463 Blackburn Rd, Bolton, **Manchester (Greater)**, BL1 8NN, **ENGLAND**.
(T) 01204 301230 **(F)** 01204 301230
(E) sales@stablemates.co.uk
(W) www.stablemates.co.uk.
Contact/s
Partner: Mrs J Garth
Profile Supplies.
Feed can be delivered. **No.Staff:** 2
Yr. Est: 2000
Opening Times
Sp: Open Mon - Sat 10:00, Sun 12:00. Closed Mon, Tues 18:00, Wed, Thurs 15:30, Fri, Sat 17:00, Sun 16:00.
Su: Open Mon - Sat 10:00, Sun 12:00. Closed Mon, Tues 18:00, Wed, Thurs 15:30, Fri, Sat 17:00, Sun 16:00.
Au: Open Mon - Sat 10:00, Sun 12:00. Closed Mon, Tues 18:00, Wed, Thurs 15:30, Fri, Sat 17:00, Sun 16:00.
Wn: Open Mon - Sat 10:00, Sun 12:00. Closed Mon, Tues 18:00, Wed, Thurs 15:30, Fri, Sat 17:00, Sun 16:00. **Ref: YH13304**

STABLES
Stables (The), Lippitts Hill, Loughton, **Essex**, IG10 4AL, **ENGLAND**.
(T) 020 85083456.
Contact/s
Owner: Mrs S Budd
Profile Stable/Livery.
Provides high quality livery, details and prices on request. The Stables are two minutes from Epping Forest with access to hacking.
Opening Times
Sp: Open Mon - Sun 08:00. Closed Mon - Sun 17:00.
Su: Open Mon - Sun 08:00. Closed Mon - Sun 17:00.
Au: Open Mon - Sun 08:00. Closed Mon - Sun 17:00.
Wn: Open Mon - Sun 08:00. Closed Mon - Sun 17:00.
Private livery, telephone for an appointment
Ref: YH13305

STABLES
Stables (The), Paslow Hall, King St, High Ongar, **Essex**, CM5 9NT, **ENGLAND**.
(T) 01277 363190.
Profile Breeder, Stable/Livery. **Ref: YH13306**

STABLES
Stables (Hinckley) (The), Sketchley Old Village, Burbage, Hinckley, **Leicestershire**, LE10 3HT, **ENGLAND**.
(T) 01455 230949 **(F)** 01455 230949.
Profile Saddlery Retailer. **Ref: YH13307**

STABLES
Stables (The), Tower Farm, Barby Rd, Rugby, **Warwickshire**, CV22 5QB, **ENGLAND**.
(T) 01788 543644.
Contact/s
Manager: Mrs A Smith
Profile Farrier. **Ref: YH13308**

STABLES EQUESTRIAN CTRE
Stables Equestrian Centre (The), 148 Cotton End Rd, Wilstead, Bedford, **Bedfordshire**, MK45 3DP, **ENGLAND**.
(T) 01234 743287.
Contact/s
Partner: Mrs P Connelly **Ref: YH13309**

STABLES FLAT
Stables Flat, Sansaw Hall, Clive, Shrewsbury, **Shropshire**, SY4 3JP, **ENGLAND**.
(T) 01939 220411
(M) 07860 670184.
Profile Medical Support. **Ref: YH13310**

STABLES HOTEL
Stables Hotel (The), Neuadd Farm, Llangattock, Crickhowell, **Powys**, NP8 1LE, **WALES**.
(T) 01873 810244.
Profile Equestrian Centre. **Ref: YH13311**

STABLES RIDING SCHOOL
Stables Riding School (The), Sketchley Lane, Hinckley, **Leicestershire**, LE10 2NG, **ENGLAND**.
(T) 01455 230949 **(F)** 01455 616333.
Contact/s
Partner: Mrs C Lowe
Profile Riding School. **Ref: YH13312**

STABLES SADDLERY & FEED SHOP
Stables Saddlery & Feed Shop (The), Albrightlee, Shrewsbury, **Shropshire**, SY4 4EE, **ENGLAND**.
(T) 01743 444670.
Contact/s
Owner: Mrs C Johnson
Profile Saddlery Retailer. **Ref: YH13313**

STABLEWARE
Stableware (Marlborough), Rockley Stables, Rockley, Marlborough, **Wiltshire**, SN8 1RT, **ENGLAND**.
(T) 01672 512382.
Contact/s
Owner: Miss J Penn
Profile Saddlery Retailer. **Ref: YH13314**

STACEY, DONALD A
Donald A Stacey DWCF, 11 Harveys Nurseries, Peppard Rd, Caversham, Reading, **Berkshire**, RG4 8JD, **ENGLAND**.
(T) 0118 9479307.
Profile Farrier. **Ref: YH13315**

STACEY, P A
Mr P A Stacey, 1 Dale St, St Helens Auckland, Bishop Auckland, **County Durham**, DL14 9BJ, **ENGLAND**.
(T) 01388 662246 **(F)** 01388 662246.
Profile Breeder. **Ref: YH13316**

STACK, GERARD
Gerard Stack, Hare Field, Milltown, Droichead Nua, Kildare, **County Kildare**, **IRELAND**.
(T) 045 433515.
Profile Supplies. **Ref: YH13317**

STACK, TOMMY
Tommy Stack, Thomastown, Golden, **County Tipperary**, **IRELAND**.
(T) 062 54129 **(F)** 062 54399.
Profile Supplies. **Ref: YH13318**

STADDON HEIGHTS FARM
Staddon Heights Farm, Staddon Heights, Plymstock, Plymouth, **Devon**, PL9 9SP, **ENGLAND**.
(T) 01752 481631.
Profile Stable/Livery. **Ref: YH13319**

STAFF CLGE/SANDHURST HUNTS
Staff College & Sandhurst Hunts Branch of the Pony Club, 1 Springwood, Longdown Lodge,

A-Z of COMPANIES

Sandhurst, **Hampshire**, GU17 8PU, **ENGLAND**.
(T) 01344 777470.
Profile Club/Association. **Ref: YH13320**

STAFFORD SADDLERY SWOP SHOP

Stafford Saddlery Swop Shop (The), Woodings Yard, Bailey St, Stafford, **Staffordshire**, ST17 4BG, **ENGLAND**.
(T) 01785 249911 **(F)** 01785 250021. **Ref: YH13321**

STAFFORD, RICHARD JOHN

Richard John Stafford, Tally Ho Farm Hse, Guiting Power, Cheltenham, **Gloucestershire**, GL54 5UB, **ENGLAND**.
(T) 01451 850637.
Profile Farrier. **Ref: YH13322**

STAFFORD-CHARLES, R N

R N Stafford-Charles, Little Bowlish, Whitestone, Exeter, **Devon**, EX4 2HS, **ENGLAND**.
(T) 01647 61786.
Profile Breeder. **Ref: YH13323**

STAFFORDSHIRE HORSE WORLD

Staffordshire Horse World, P O Box 523, Stoke-on-Trent, **Staffordshire**, ST10 2QL, **ENGLAND**.
(T) 01538 266113 **(F)** 01538 266113
(M) 07971 383431
(E) janeh@staff77.freeserve.co.uk.
Profile Supplies. **Ref: YH13324**

STAFFORDSHIRE TRAILERS

Staffordshire Trailers, Streethay Farm, Burton Rd, Streethay, Lichfield, **Staffordshire**, WS13 8RJ, **ENGLAND**.
(T) 01543 262007.
Profile Transport/Horse Boxes. **Ref: YH13325**

STAG LODGE STABLES

Stag Lodge Stables, Stag Lodge, Kingston Vale, London, **London (Greater)**, SW15 3RS, **ENGLAND**.
(T) 020 89746066 **(F)** 020 85494086.
Contact/s
Owner: Mrs J Gatt
Profile Riding School, Stable/Livery. **Ref: YH13326**

STAG TRAILERS

Stag Trailers, Stag Works, 84 John St, Sheffield, **Yorkshire (South)**, S2 4QU, **ENGLAND**.
(T) 0114 2724886 **(F)** 0114 2759177.
Contact/s
Owner: Mr D Briggs
Profile Transport/Horse Boxes. **Ref: YH13327**

STAGG, W C

W C Stagg, 24 Babs Field, Bentley, Farnham, **Surrey**, GU10 5LS, **ENGLAND**.
(T) 01420 23214.
Profile Farrier. **Ref: YH13328**

STAGS

Stags Estate Agents, Kensey Hse, 18 Western Rd, Launceston, **Cornwall**, PL15 7AS, **ENGLAND**.
(T) 01566 774999 **(F)** 01566 777378
(E) launceston@stags.co.uk
(W) www.stags.co.uk.
Contact/s
Estate Agent: Mr D Robinson
Profile Property Services.
Chartered Surveyors, Land Agents & Auctioneers.
Ref: YH13329

STAGS

Stags Estate Agents, 61 Lemon St, Truro, **Cornwall**, TR1 2PE, **ENGLAND**.
(T) 01872 264488 **(F)** 01872 241777
(E) truro@stags.co.uk
(W) www.stags.co.uk.
Contact/s
Estate Agent: Mr I Osborne
Profile Property Services.
Chartered Surveyors, Land Agents & Auctioneers.
Ref: YH13330

STAGS

Stags Estate Agents, 21 Southernhay West, Exeter, **Devon**, EX1 1PR, **ENGLAND**.
(T) 01392 255202 **(F)** 01392 426183
(E) exeter@stags.co.uk
(W) www.stags.co.uk.
Contact/s
Estate Agent: Mr D Fursdon
Profile Property Services.
Chartered Surveyors, Land Agents & Auctioneers.
Ref: YH13331

STAGS

Stags Estate Agents, 19 Bampton St, Tiverton, **Devon**, EX16 6AA, **ENGLAND**.
(T) 01884 256331 **(F)** 01884 258401
(E) tiverton@stags.co.uk
(W) www.stags.co.uk.
Contact/s
Estate Agent: Mr B Tancock
Profile Property Services.
Chartered Surveyors, Land Agents & Auctioneers.
Ref: YH13332

STAGS

Stags Estate Agents, 30 Boutport St, Barnstaple, **Devon**, EX31 1RP, **ENGLAND**.
(T) 01271 322833 **(F)** 01271 325081
(E) barnstaple@stags.co.uk
(W) www.stags.co.uk.
Contact/s
Estate Agent: Mr A Trump
Profile Property Services.
Chartered Surveyors, Land Agents & Auctioneers.
Ref: YH13333

STAGS

Stags Estate Agents, 29 The Sq, South Molton, **Devon**, EX36 3AQ, **ENGLAND**.
(T) 01769 572263 **(F)** 01769 573985
(E) south-molton@stags.co.uk
(W) www.stags.co.uk.
Contact/s
Estate Agent: Alex Rew
Profile Property Services.
Chartered Surveyors, Land Agents & Auctioneers.
Ref: YH13334

STAGS

Stags Estate Agents, 63 Fore St, Totnes, **Devon**, TQ9 5NJ, **ENGLAND**.
(T) 01803 865454 **(F)** 01803 864227
(E) totnes@stags.co.uk
(W) www.stags.co.uk.
Contact/s
Estate Agent: Mr C Shaw
Profile Property Services.
Chartered Surveyors, Land Agents & Auctioneers.
Ref: YH13335

STAGS

Stags Estate Agents, Bank Hse, 66 High St, Honiton, **Devon**, EX14 8PD, **ENGLAND**.
(T) 01404 45885 **(F)** 01404 41652
(E) honiton@stags.co.uk
(W) www.stags.co.uk.
Contact/s
Estate Agent: Mr A Luxton
Profile Property Services.
Chartered Surveyors, Land Agents & Auctioneers.
Ref: YH13336

STAGS

Stags Estate Agents, 83 Fore St, Kingsbridge, **Devon**, TQ7 1AB, **ENGLAND**.
(T) 01548 853131 **(F)** 01548 854030
(E) kingsbridge@stags.co.uk
(W) www.stags.co.uk.
Contact/s
Estate Agent: Mr R Harwood-Penn
Profile Property Services.
Chartered Surveyors, Land Agents & Auctioneers.
Ref: YH13337

STAGS

Stags Estate Agents, 34-36 North Hill, Plymouth, **Devon**, PL4 8ET, **ENGLAND**.
(T) 01752 223933 **(F)** 01752 26777
(E) plymouth@stags.co.uk
(W) www.stags.co.uk.
Contact/s
Estate Agent: Mr R Punch
Profile Property Services.
Chartered Surveyors, Land Agents & Auctioneers.
Ref: YH13338

STAGS

Stags Estate Agents, 62 Pall Mall, London, **London (Greater)**, SW1Y 5HZ, **ENGLAND**.
(T) 020 78390888 **(F)** 020 78390444.
Contact/s
Estate Agent: Mr B Bickersteth
Profile Property Services.
Chartered Surveyors, Land Agents & Auctioneers.
Ref: YH13339

STAGS

Stags Estate Agents, 13 Fore St, Dulverton, **Somerset**, TA22 9EX, **ENGLAND**.
(T) 01398 323174 **(F)** 01398 323372
(E) dulverton@stags.co.uk
(W) www.stags.co.uk.
Contact/s
Estate Agent: Mr J Green
Profile Property Services.
Chartered Surveyors, Land Agents & Auctioneers.
Ref: YH13340

STAGS

Stags Estate Agents, 7 High St, Wellington, **Somerset**, TA21 8QW, **ENGLAND**.
(T) 01823 662822 **(F)** 01823 666709
(E) wellington@stags.co.uk
(W) www.stags.co.uk.
Contact/s
Estate Agent: Mr A Greed
Profile Property Services.
Chartered Surveyors, Land Agents & Auctioneers.
Ref: YH13341

STAGS END

Stags End Equestrian Centre, Gaddesden Lane, Hemel Hempstead, **Hertfordshire**, HP2 6HN, **ENGLAND**.
(T) 01582 794901.
Contact/s
Manager: Mr G Roberts
Profile Riding School, Stable/Livery. **Ref: YH13342**

STAGSDEN HAFLINGERS

Stagsden Haflingers, Manor Farm, Stagsden, **Bedfordshire**, MK43 8SQ, **ENGLAND**.
(T) 01234 823289 **(F)** 01234 823289
(E) lesleybrown@haflingersgb.com.
Profile Breeder. **Ref: YH13343**

STAINER, D E

D E Stainer, Silver Lea, Derritt Lane, Bransgore, Christchurch, **Dorset**, BH23 8AR, **ENGLAND**.
(T) 01425 672538 **(F)** 01425 672538.
Contact/s
Owner: Mr D Stainer
Profile Breeder. **Ref: YH13344**

STAINMORE STUD

Stainmore Cleveland Bay Horses, Long Crag Hse, North Stainmore, Kirkby Stephen, **Cumbria**, CA17 4DZ, **ENGLAND**.
(T) 01768 341826.
Contact/s
Owner: Mrs B Martindale
Profile Breeder. **Yr. Est:** 1981
Opening Times
Telephone for an appointment **Ref: YH13345**

STAINSBY GRANGE RIDING CTRE

Stainsby Grange Riding Centre, Stainsby Grange Farm, Thornaby, Stockton-on-Tees, **Cleveland**, TS17 9AB, **ENGLAND**.
(T) 01642 762233.
Contact/s
Secretary: Mrs P Allen
Profile Riding School, Stable/Livery. **Ref: YH13346**

STAINSBY GRANGE STUD

Stainsby Grange Stud, Stainsby Grange Farm, Thornaby, Stockton-on-Tees, **Cleveland**, TS17 9AB, **ENGLAND**.
(T) 01642 765040.
Contact/s
Owner: Ms J Tanfield
Profile Breeder. **Ref: YH13347**

STAINTONDALE PONY CLUB

Staintondale Pony Club, Scarborough, **Yorkshire (North)**, **ENGLAND**.
(T) 01723 365558.
Profile Club/Association. **Ref: YH13348**

STAITE, M G

M G Staite, 22 Greenacre Rd, Bristol, **Bristol**, BS14 0HL, **ENGLAND**.
(T) 01275 832248.
Contact/s
Owner: Mr M Staite
Profile Farrier. **Ref: YH13349**

STALLION BOOK

Stallion Book (The), Publications Dept, Weatherbys Group Ltd, Sanders Rd, Wellingborough, **Northamptonshire**, NN8 4BX, **ENGLAND**.
(T) 01933 440077 **(F)** 01933 270300
(E) pubsdept@weatherbys-group.com.
Contact/s
Advertising of Stallions: Steve Cheney
Profile Supplies. **Ref: YH13350**

STALLIONS AT TACKEXCHANGE

Stallions at Tackexchange, Blaenau Isaf, Pentwyn Rd, Crosshands, Llanelli, **Carmarthenshire**, SA14 6DD, **WALES**.
(T) 01269 845660 **(F)** 01269 831089
(E) tackexchange1@aol.com

(W) www.tack4exchange.com.
Contact/s
Owner: Mr K Richards
Profile Breeder, Riding Wear Retailer, Saddlery Retailer, Stable/Livery, Supplies.
Supply new and used equestrian equipment.
No.Staff: 3 Yr. Est: 1997 C.Size: 35 Acres
Opening Times
Sp: Open Mon - Sat 10:00. Closed Mon - Fri 15:00, Sat 17:00.
Su: Open Mon - Sat 10:00. Closed Mon - Fri 15:00, Sat 17:00.
Au: Open Mon - Sat 10:00. Closed Mon - Fri 15:00, Sat 17:00.
Wn: Open Mon - Sat 10:00. Closed Mon - Fri 15:00, Sat 17:00.
Sundays by appointment Ref: YH13351

STAMBROOK STUD
Stambrook Stud, Birdbrook Hall, The Street, Birdbrook, Halstead, **Essex**, CO9 4BJ, **ENGLAND**.
(T) 01440 785253.
Profile Breeder, Stable/Livery. Ref: YH13352

STAMFORD ANIMAL & PET SUP
Stamford Animal & Pet Supplies, 21/27 Melton Rd, Oakham, **Rutland**, LE15 6AX, **ENGLAND**.
(T) 01572 755099.
Profile Supplies. Ref: YH13353

STAMFORD RIDING STABLES
Stamford Riding Stables, 67 Stamford St, Mossley, **Manchester (Greater)**, OL5 0LR, **ENGLAND**.
(T) 01457 837698
(E) tvefstamford@aol.com.
Contact/s
For Bookings: Ms D Marland (Q) BHSAI
Profile Riding School. No.Staff: 3
Yr. Est: 1996 C.Size: 1 Acres
Opening Times
Sp: Closed 18:00.
Su: Closed 18:00.
Au: Closed 18:00.
Wn: Closed 18:00. Ref: YH13354

STAMP, P G
P G Stamp, Binsted, Alton, **Hampshire**, GU34 4PQ, **ENGLAND**.
(T) 01420 22394.
Contact/s
Partner: Mrs D Stamp
Profile Breeder. Ref: YH13355

STAN CHEADLE CLIPPER SVS
Stan Cheadle Clipper Services, 79 Greenacres, Ludlow, **Shropshire**, SY8 1LZ, **ENGLAND**.
(T) 01584 872463.
Contact/s
Owner: Mr S Cheadle
Profile Supplies. Yr. Est: 1991
Opening Times
Sp: Open Mon - Fri 10:00. Closed Mon - Fri 20:00.
Su: Open Mon - Fri 10:00. Closed Mon - Fri 20:00.
Au: Open Mon - Fri 10:00. Closed Mon - Fri 20:00.
Wn: Open Mon - Fri 10:00. Closed Mon - Fri 20:00.
Closed weekends Ref: YH13356

STAN MOORE RACING STABLES
Stan Moore Racing Stables, Parsonage Farm Stables, Newbury Rd, East Garston, Hungerford, **Berkshire**, RG17 7ER, **ENGLAND**.
(T) 01488 648822. Ref: YH13357

STANAH HORSE FEEDS
Stanah Horse Feeds, Stanah Rd, Thornton-Cleveleys, **Lancashire**, FY5 5LW, **ENGLAND**.
(T) 01253 823231.
Contact/s
Owner: Mr C Adams
Profile Supplies. Ref: YH13358

STANDEN CONNEMARAS
Standen Pure and Part-Bred Connemaras, Springhill Farm, Standen St, Benenden, Cranbrook, **Kent**, TN17 4LA, **ENGLAND**.
(T) 01580 240674.
Contact/s
Owner: Mrs V Pollard
Profile Breeder. Yr. Est: 1986 Ref: YH13359

STANDFIELD, M J
M J Standfield, Redbridge Lane, Crossways, Dorchester, **Dorset**, DT2 8DU, **ENGLAND**.
(T) 01305 852132.
Profile Transport/Horse Boxes. Ref: YH13360

STANDHOUSE FARM STABLES
Standhouse Farm Stables, Spencers Lane, Orrell, Wigan, **Lancashire**, WN5 8RB, **ENGLAND**.
(T) 01695 622075.
Contact/s
Partner: Mrs E Sumner Ref: YH13361

STANDLAKE EQUESTRIAN CTRE
Standlake Equestrian Centre and Ranch Retreat, Downs Rd, Standlake, Witney, **Oxfordshire**, OX29 7UH, **ENGLAND**.
(T) 01865 300099
Affiliated Bodies ABRS.
Contact/s
Owner: Ms S Pillans (Q) Prins Dip
(E) wpillans@aol.com
Profile Arena, Equestrian Centre, Riding Club, Riding School, Stable/Livery.
Holiday retreat ranch. No.Staff: 2 Yr. Est: 1996
C.Size: 20 Acres Ref: YH13362

STANFORD EVENTING HORSES
Stanford Eventing Horses at Trefor, The Old Rectory, Trefor, Holyhead, **Isle of Anglesey**, LL65 4TA, **WALES**.
(T) 01407 720395.
Profile Breeder, Trainer. Ref: YH13363

STANFORD STUD HIGHLAND PONIES
Stanford Stud of Highland Ponies, The Stables, Stanford-on-Soar, Loughborough, **Leicestershire**, LE12 5PY, **ENGLAND**.
(T) 01509 263782.
Profile Breeder. Ref: YH13364

STANGRAVE HALL STABLES
Stangrave Hall Stables, Bletchingley Rd, Godstone, **Surrey**, RH9 8NB, **ENGLAND**.
(T) 01883 742263.
Profile Riding School, Stable/Livery. Ref: YH13365

STANIORUM STABLES
Staniorum Stables, Berwick Lane, Hallen, Bristol, **Bristol**, BS10 7RS, **ENGLAND**.
(T) 01454 632928.
Profile Stable/Livery. Ref: YH13366

STANLEY BROS
Stanley Bros, Long St, Premier Business Pk, Walsall, **Midlands (West)**, WS2 9DX, **ENGLAND**.
(T) 01922 621788 (F) 01922 723560. Ref: YH13367

STANLEY ESTATE & STUD
Stanley Estate & Stud Co, Woodland Stud, Snailwell Rd, Newmarket, **Suffolk**, CB8 7DJ, **ENGLAND**.
(T) 01638 663081.
Profile Breeder. Ref: YH13368

STANLEY HOUSE STABLES
Stanley House Stables Ltd, Bury Rd, Newmarket, **Suffolk**, CB8 7DF, **ENGLAND**.
(T) 01638 669944 (F) 01638 669922
(W) www.newmarketracehorsetrainers.co.uk
Affiliated Bodies Newmarket Trainers Fed.
Contact/s
Accountant: David Joseph Tyndall
Profile Trainer. Ref: YH13369

STANLEY HOUSE VETNRY SURGEONS
Stanley House Veterinary Surgeons, 20 Albert Rd, Colne, **Lancashire**, BB18 0AA, **ENGLAND**.
(T) 01282 863892.
Profile Medical Support. Ref: YH13370

STANLEY HUNTER
Stanley Hunter, Tubrid Lr Woodsgift, Freshford, **County Kilkenny**, **IRELAND**.
(T) 056 35163.
Profile Supplies. Ref: YH13371

STANLEY TOWBAR CTRE
Stanley Towbar Centre, Unit 2 Station Rd, Chester Le Street, **County Durham**, DH3 3DY, **ENGLAND**.
(T) 0191 3871422.
Profile Transport/Horse Boxes. Ref: YH13372

STANLEY, ANDREA
Andrea Stanley, The Barley Mow, Clothall, Baldock, **Hertfordshire**, SG7 6RF, **ENGLAND**.
(T) 01462 790542.
Profile Trainer. Ref: YH13373

STANLEY, JOHN
John Stanley DWCF Hons, Ivy Cottage, Brompton, Northallerton, **Yorkshire (North)**, DL6 2PF, **ENGLAND**.
(T) 01609 761102.
Profile Farrier. Ref: YH13374

STANLEY, K J & J
K J & J Stanley, Yew Tree Farm, The Ridgeway, Bloxham, Banbury, **Oxfordshire**, OX15 4EL, **ENGLAND**.
(T) 01295 721133.
Contact/s
Owner: Mrs J Stanley Ref: YH13375

STANLEY-RICKETTS, JOY
Joy Stanley-Ricketts, Woodcroft, Weston, Honiton, **Devon**, EX14 3NY, **ENGLAND**.
(T) 01404 42258 (F) 01404 44514.
Contact/s
Artist: Joy Stanley Ricketts
Profile Artist. Ref: YH13376

STANMORE EQUESTRIAN CTRE
Stanmore Equestrian Centre, Stanmore Stables, Lanark, **Lanarkshire (South)**, ML11 7RR, **SCOTLAND**.
(T) 01555 660150 (F) 01555 660150.
Contact/s
Manager: Mrs L White Ref: YH13377

STANNEY LANDS LIVERY
Stanney Lands Livery, Stanneylands Stud, Stanneylands Rd, Wilmslow, **Cheshire**, SK9 4ER, **ENGLAND**.
(T) 01625 533250 (F) 01625 530589.
Contact/s
Owner: Mr P Moore (T) 01625 530589
Profile Breeder, Stable/Livery. Racehorse Livery.
No.Staff: 2 Yr. Est: 1998 C.Size: 50 Acres
Ref: YH13378

STANTON LIVERY STABLES
Stanton Livery Stables, 170 Woodland Rd, Stanton, Burton-on-Trent, **Staffordshire**, DE15 9TJ, **ENGLAND**.
(T) 01283 544207.
Contact/s
Owner: Mr J Hirons Ref: YH13379

STANTON VIEW RIDING SCHOOL
Stanton View Riding School, Hepworth Rd, Stanton, Bury St Edmunds, **Suffolk**, IP31 2UA, **ENGLAND**.
(T) 01359 251745 (F) 01359 252254.
Profile Riding School. Ref: YH13380

STANTON, ROBERT
Robert Stanton, 12 Alne Bank Rd, Alcester, **Warwickshire**, B49 6QU, **ENGLAND**.
(T) 01789 763742.
Contact/s
Owner: Mr R Stanton
Profile Farrier. Ref: YH13381

STANTONS METSA PRIMA
Stantons Metsa Prima, 46A Berth, Tilbury Docks, Tilbury, **Essex**, RM18 7HS, **ENGLAND**.
(T) 03453 38866 (F) 01375 859594
(E) jackie.penniket@metsaprima.com.
Profile Supplies. Ref: YH13382

STANWELL TRAILERS
Stanwell Trailers, 3 Bedfont Rd, Stanwell, Staines, **Surrey**, TW19 7LR, **ENGLAND**.
(T) 01784 252145 (F) 01784 244217.
Contact/s
Owner: Mr M Chinchen
Profile Transport/Horse Boxes. Ref: YH13383

STANWELLS COUNTRY
Stanwells Country, 28 Brookley Rd, Brockenhurst, **Hampshire**, SO42 7RR, **ENGLAND**.
(T) 01590 622200.
Contact/s
Owner: Mrs J McIntyre
Profile Saddlery Retailer. Ref: YH13384

STAPELFIELD RIDING CTRE
Stapelfield Riding Centre, The Forge, Cuckfield Rd, Staplefield, Haywards Heath, **Sussex (West)**, RH17 6ET, **ENGLAND**.
(T) 01444 400581.
Contact/s
Owner: Mr F Dixon Ref: YH13385

STAPLEFORD HACKNEY STUD
Stapleford Hackney Stud, Stapleford Aerodrome, Stapleford, **Essex**, RM4 1SJ, **ENGLAND**.
(T) 01708 688557.
Contact/s
Key Contact: Mr J Chicken
Profile Breeder. Ref: YH13386

STAPLEFORD MILL FARM STUD
Stapleford Mill Farm Stud, Stapleford Mill Farm, Soulbury, Leighton Buzzard, **Bedfordshire**, LU7 0DS, **ENGLAND**.

A-Z of COMPANIES

(T) 01525 270246.
Profile Breeder. Ref: YH13387

STAPLES, LESLIE R

Leslie R Staples RSS, 16 Oakwood, Twerne Minster, Blandford, **Dorset**, DT11 8QT, **ENGLAND**.
(T) 01747 852470.
Profile Farrier. Ref: YH13388

STAPLES, MATTHEW

Matthew Staples DWCF, 11 Stoneycroft Walk, Ifield, Crawley, **Sussex (West)**, RH11 0SP, **ENGLAND**.
(T) 01293 427489
(M) 07976 273790.
Profile Farrier. Ref: YH13389

STAPLETON SADDLERY

Stapleton Saddlery, 4 Howden Rd, Silsden, **Yorkshire (West)**, BD20 0HA, **ENGLAND**.
(T) 01535 654684.
Profile Saddlery Retailer. Ref: YH13390

STAR BLACKSMITH

Star Blacksmith, 77 Colvend St, Glasgow, **Glasgow (City of)**, G40 4DU, **SCOTLAND**.
(T) 0141 5549559 (F) 0141 5549559.
Contact/s
Manager: Mr B Clint
Profile Blacksmith. Ref: YH13391

STAR COMFORT RUBBER MATTING

Star Comfort Rubber Matting, 77 Stoke Road, Guildford, **Surrey**, GU1 4HT, **ENGLAND**.
(T) 01483 503555 (F) 01483 571162
(M) 07973 361792
(E) star@blueantgroup.com
(W) www.blueantgroup.com/star.
Contact/s
Owner: Mr A Scott
Profile Supplies. Ref: YH13392

STAR INN TREKKING CTRE

Star Inn Trekking Centre, Dylife, Staylittle, Llanbrynmair, **Powys**, SY19 7BW, **WALES**.
(T) 01650 3345.
Profile Equestrian Centre. Ref: YH13393

STARK, IAN

Ian Stark MBE, Haughhead, Ashkirk, Selkirk, **Scottish Borders**, TD7 4NS, **SCOTLAND**.
(T) 01750 32238 (F) 01750 32293
(M) 07831 355674.
Profile Stable/Livery, Trainer. Ref: YH13394

STARKEY, JANE

Jane Starkey, Knights Farm, Avon Dassett, Leamington Spa, **Warwickshire**, CV33 0AS, **ENGLAND**.
(T) 01295 89465.
Profile Breeder, Trainer. Ref: YH13395

STARLIGHT RIDING CTRE

Starlight Riding Centre, Cefnhir, Penrherber, Newcastle Emlyn, **Carmarthenshire**, SA38 9RL, **WALES**.
(T) 01239 710261.
Contact/s
Owner: Miss N Howell
Profile Riding School.
Teaches side saddle to both children and adults.
Opening Times
Sp: Open Mon - Sun 09:00. Closed Mon - Sun 17:00.
Su: Open Mon - Sun 09:00. Closed Mon - Sun 17:00.
Au: Open Mon - Sun 09:00. Closed Mon - Sun 17:00.
Wn: Open Mon - Sun 09:00. Closed Mon - Sun 17:00. Ref: YH13396

STARLINE HORSE BOXES

Starline Horse Boxes, Starline Farm, Starborough Rd, Marsh Green, Edenbridge, **Kent**, TN8 5RB, **ENGLAND**.
(T) 01732 864970 (F) 01732 862498.
Profile Transport/Horse Boxes. Ref: YH13397

STARROCK STUD

Starrock Stud, Ludwell, Shaftesbury, **Dorset**, SP7 0PW, **ENGLAND**.
(T) 01747 828639 (F) 01747 852102
(W) www.lipizzaner.co.uk.
Contact/s
Owner: Mrs U Harley
(E) una@lipizzaner.co.uk
Profile Breeder. Ref: YH13398

STARSHAW STABLES

Starshaw Stables, Woodplace Lane, Coulsdon, **Surrey**, CR5 1NE, **ENGLAND**.
(T) 01737 554515.
Contact/s
General Manager: Ms A Wajih
Profile Riding School, Stable/Livery.
Lessons for children and adults, ranging from £7.50 - £15.00. Ref: YH13399

START & TREMAYNE

Start & Tremayne, 178 High St, Burton-on-Trent, **Staffordshire**, DE14 1HN, **ENGLAND**.
(T) 01283 563650. Ref: YH13400

STATHAM LODGE RIDING CTRE

Statham Lodge Riding Centre, Glebe Farm, 77 Warrington Rd, Lymm, **Cheshire**, WA13 9BU, **ENGLAND**.
(T) 01925 753576. Ref: YH13401

STATION HSE VETNRY CTRE

Station House Veterinary Centre, 157 Ashley Rd, Hale, Altrincham, **Cheshire**, WA14 2UZ, **ENGLAND**.
(T) 0161 9411584 (F) 0161 9298874.
Profile Medical Support. Ref: YH13402

STATION RD VETNRY CLINIC

Station Road Veterinary Clinic, 15A/B Station Rd, Lower Weston, Bath, **Bath & Somerset (North East)**, BA1 3DX, **ENGLAND**.
(T) 01225 428921.
Profile Medical Support. Ref: YH13403

STAUGHTON RIDING SCHOOL

Staughton Riding School, Hawthorn Lodge, The Town, Gt Staughton, Huntingdon, **Cambridgeshire**, **ENGLAND**.
(T) 01480 860409.
Profile Riding School. Ref: YH13404

STAVELEY PEDIGREE LIMOUSINS

Staveley Pedigree Limousins, Neuadd Isaf, Penybont, Llandrindod Wells, **Powys**, LD1 5SW, **WALES**.
(T) 07774 783247 (F) 01597 851908
(E) william@staveleylim.com.
Profile Supplies. Ref: YH13405

STAX SADDLERY

RHH Mfrs Agents Limited T/A Stax (Saddlery, Pet Supply and Angling Centre), South St, Townsend, Montacute, **Somerset**, TA15 6XH, **ENGLAND**.
(T) 01935 822645 (F) 01935 822645.
Contact/s
General Manager: Miss L Hann
Profile Feed Merchant, Riding Wear Retailer, Saddlery Retailer, Supplies. No.Staff: 3
Yr. Est: 1985 C.Size: 1 Acres
Opening Times
Sp: Open 8:30. Closed 18:00.
Su: Open 8:30. Closed 18:00.
Au: Open 8:30. Closed 17:30.
Wn: Open 8:30. Closed 17:30. Ref: YH13406

STEAD, PAUL A

Paul A Stead RSS BII, 13 Ashton Ave, Knott End-on-Sea, Poulton-Le-Fylde, Blackpool, **Lancashire**, FY6 0BU, **ENGLAND**.
(T) 01253 812841.
Profile Farrier. Ref: YH13407

STEADING

Steading (The), Acomb, Hexham, **Northumberland**, NE46 4RH, **ENGLAND**.
(T) 01434 602232.
Contact/s
Owner: Mrs S Dalglish
(E) jane-dalg@ukonline.co.uk
Profile Horse/Rider Accom.
DIY Livery available
Opening Times
Sp: Open Mon - Sun 09:00. Closed Mon - Sun 19:00.
Su: Open Mon - Sun 09:00. Closed Mon - Sun 19:00.
Au: Open Mon - Sun 09:00. Closed Mon - Sun 19:00.
Wn: Open Mon - Sun 09:00. Closed Mon - Sun 19:00. Ref: YH13408

STEADMAN'S MEAD STABLES

Steadman's Mead Stables, 30 Wood St Green, Wood St Village, Guildford, **Surrey**, GU3 3EU, **ENGLAND**.
(T) 01483 236144. Ref: YH13409

STEANSON, DANIEL

Daniel Steanson, 3A Red Lion Cottage, Eighton Banks, Gateshead, **Tyne and Wear**, NE9 7YH, **ENGLAND**.
(T) 0191 4820119.
Profile Farrier. Ref: YH13410

STEART HOUSE RACING STABLES

Steart House Racing Stables, Stoodleigh, Tiverton, **Devon**, EX16 9QA, **ENGLAND**.
(T) 01398 351317.
Profile Trainer. Ref: YH13411

STEBBING, V

V Stebbing, Twinstead Riding School, Pebmarsh Rd, Twinstead, Sudbury, **Suffolk**, CO10 7ND, **ENGLAND**.
(T) 01787 269283. Ref: YH13412

STEEDSMAN

Steedsman Ltd, Blake Hse, Bath St, Walsall, **Midlands (West)**, WS1 3BX, **ENGLAND**.
(T) 01922 630707 (F) 01922 627927.
Contact/s
Manager: Mrs C Sargeant
Profile Supplies. Ref: YH13413

STEEL FABRICATIONS

Steel Fabrications Ltd, East Mill, Currie, **Edinburgh (City of)**, EH14 6AD, **SCOTLAND**.
(T) 0131 4494513 (F) 0131 4515413.
Profile Blacksmith. Ref: YH13414

STEEL TO LIVE

Steel To Live, 25 Winthorpe Rd, London, **London (Greater)**, SW15 2LW, **ENGLAND**.
(T) 020 87892020.
Contact/s
Owner: Mr S Lukic
Profile Blacksmith. Ref: YH13415

STEEL, A & E

A & E Steel, West Hookhead Farm, Strathaven, **Lanarkshire (South)**, **SCOTLAND**..
Profile Breeder. Ref: YH13416

STEEL, R M

R M Steel, Ground Floor Flat, 3 Sea Cliff Rd, South Cliff, Scarborough, **Yorkshire (North)**, YO11 2XU, **ENGLAND**.
(T) 01723 368052. Ref: YH13417

STEEL, RICHARD J

Messrs Richard J Steel, The Cattle Market, High St, Southall, **London (Greater)**, UB1 3DG, **ENGLAND**.
(T) 020 85741611 (F) 020 85746970. Ref: YH13418

STEELE, J A

J A Steele, Glenmidge Smithy, Auldgirth, Dumfries, **Dumfries and Galloway**, DG2 0SW, **SCOTLAND**.
(T) 01387 740328.
Contact/s
Owner: Mr J Steele
Profile Blacksmith. Ref: YH13419

STEER, R G

R G Steer, 83 The Barrows, Looking Castle, Worle, Weston-Super-Mare, **Somerset (North)**, BS22 8PB, **ENGLAND**.
(T) 01934 643314.
Profile Farrier. Ref: YH13420

STENNETT, J & H

J & H Stennett, Gulpher Rd, Felixstowe, **Suffolk**, IP11 9RD, **ENGLAND**.
(T) 01394 286780.
Contact/s
Owner: Miss H Stennett Ref: YH13421

STEPHANIE MEADOWS

Stephanie Meadows of Owen Moore, Rectory Cottage, Salford, Chipping Norton, **Oxfordshire**, OX7 5YL, **ENGLAND**.
(T) 07808 728470
(E) jncollins@lineone.net
(W) www.owen-moore-eventing.co.uk.
Profile Trainer. Ref: YH13422

STEPHENS, ARLO R

Arlo R Stephens DWCF, Little Rose Cottage, Main St, Charlton, Banbury, **Oxfordshire**, OX17 3DR, **ENGLAND**..
Profile Farrier. Ref: YH13423

STEPHENS, V A

Miss V A Stephens, Rock Farm, Tolland, Lydeard St Lawrence, Taunton, **Somerset**, TA4 3PP, **ENGLAND**.
(T) 01984 667427.

Profile Supplies. **Ref: YH13424**

STEPHENSON & SON

Stephenson & Son (York Horse Sales), York Livestock Ctre, Murton, York, **Yorkshire (North)**, YO19 5UF, **ENGLAND**.
(T) 01904 489731 **(F)** 01904 489782. **Ref: YH13425**

STEPHENSON, J F & J M

J F & J M Stephenson, The Great Barn, Howsham, **Yorkshire (North)**, YO60 7PJ, **ENGLAND**.
(T) 01653 618673.
Profile Breeder. **Ref: YH13426**

STEPHENSONS ANIMAL FEEDS

Stephensons Animal Feeds, Riley St Mill, Burnley Rd, Todmorden, **Yorkshire (West)**, OL14 7DH, **ENGLAND**.
(T) 01706 816873.
Profile Supplies. **Ref: YH13427**

STEPLEY STUD

Stepley Stud, Lower Henlade, Taunton, **Somerset**, TA3 5LY, **ENGLAND**.
(T) 01823 443064
(M) 07860 380288.
Profile Breeder. **Ref: YH13428**

STEPNEY BANK STABLES

Stepney Bank Stables, Stepney Bank, Newcastle-upon-Tyne, **Tyne and Wear**, NE1 2PW, **ENGLAND**.
(T) 0191 2332046.
Profile Riding School. **Ref: YH13429**

STERLING QUARTERHORSES

Sterling Quarterhorses, Court Lodge Oast, Bodiam, Robertsbridge, **Sussex (East)**, TN32 5UJ, **ENGLAND**.
(T) 01580 830710 **(F)** 01580 830671.
Contact/s
Owner: Mrs R Sternberg
Profile Breeder. **Ref: YH13430**

STERLING SADDLERY

Sterling Saddlery, Court Lodge Farm, Bodiam, Robertsbridge, **Sussex (East)**, TN32 5UJ, **ENGLAND**.
(T) 01580 830710 **(F)** 01580 830671
(E) mailto:sterlingqh@aol.com
(W) www.sterlingquarterhorses.com.
Contact/s
Owner: Ms F Sternberg
Profile Saddlery Retailer. **Ref: YH13431**

STERLING SPORTS SUPPLIES

Sterling Sports Supplies, Carrington Business Pk, Manchester Rd, Carrington, Manchester, **Manchester (Greater)**, M31 4QW, **ENGLAND**.
(T) 0161 7764408.
Contact/s
Owner: Mrs C Culliney
Profile Saddlery Retailer. **Ref: YH13432**

STERN, CLIVE CHARLES

Clive Charles Stern RSS, 1 Walton Cottages, Goudhurst, Cranbrook, **Kent**, TN17 2NX, **ENGLAND**.
(T) 01580 211765.
Profile Farrier. **Ref: YH13433**

STERN, EDGAR P J

Edgar P J Stern, The Forge, High St, Yalding, Maidstone, **Kent**, ME18 6HX, **ENGLAND**.
(T) 01622 814331.
Contact/s
Farrier: Edgar J Stern **(Q)** FWCF
Profile Farrier. **Ref: YH13434**

STERN, P J

P J Stern, The New Forge, Swan St, Wittersham, Tenterden, **Kent**, TN30 7PH, **ENGLAND**.
(T) 01797 270485.
Contact/s
Owner: Mr P Stern
Profile Farrier. **Ref: YH13435**

STERN, P M

P M Stern, 2 Markham Cottages, Charlton Lane, West Farleigh, Maidstone, **Kent**, ME15 0NL, **ENGLAND**.
(T) 01622 813433.
Profile Farrier. **Ref: YH13436**

STETCHWORTH PARK STUD

Stetchworth Park Stud, Unex Hse, Church Lane, Stetchworth, Newmarket, **Suffolk**, CB8 9TN, **ENGLAND**.
(T) 01638 508144 **(F)** 01638 507449
Affiliated Bodies ROA, TBA.
Contact/s
Owner: Mr W Gredley
Profile Breeder. **C.Size:** 850 Acres
Opening Times
Telephone for an appointment **Ref: YH13437**

STEVE NEWMAN PHOTOGRAPHY

Steve Newman Photography, The Old Bakery, High St, Belford, **Northumberland**, NE70 7NH, **ENGLAND**.
(T) 01668 213042 **(F)** 01668 213555.
Profile Photographer. **Ref: YH13438**

STEVENAGE & DISTRICT

Stevenage & District Riding Club, 54 Lincoln Rd, Stevenage, **Hertfordshire**, SG1 4PL, **ENGLAND**.
(T) 01438 364832.
Contact/s
Chairman: Mrs S Hayes
Profile Club/Association, Riding Club. **Ref: YH13439**

STEVENS

Mr & Mrs Stevens, Meadow Of Tornaveen, Torphins, Banchory, **Aberdeenshire**, AB31 4PJ, **SCOTLAND**.
(T) 01339 883289.
Profile Breeder. **Ref: YH13440**

STEVENS

Mrs Stevens, Trelan Gate, Coverack, Helston, **Cornwall**, TR12 6RP, **ENGLAND**.
(T) 01326 280113.
Profile Blood Stock Agency, Breeder. **Ref: YH13441**

STEVENS STUD

Stevens Stud, By Passage, Compton, Guildford, **Surrey**, GU3 1DT, **ENGLAND**.
(T) 01483 811212 **(F)** 01483 810963.
Contact/s
Owner: Mr J Stevens
Profile Breeder. **Ref: YH13442**

STEVENS, BARRY G

Barry G Stevens, 28 Ely Rd, St Albans, **Hertfordshire**, AL2 1NA, **ENGLAND**.
(T) 07775 784655.
Profile Farrier. **Ref: YH13443**

STEVENS, GUY NICHOLAS

Guy Nicholas Stevens DWCF, Millfield Lodge, High St, Amotherby, Malton, **Yorkshire (North)**, YO17 6TL, **ENGLAND**.
(T) 01653 692081.
Profile Farrier. **Ref: YH13444**

STEVENS, LEONARD

Leonard Stevens, 16 Crown St, Eastbourne, **Sussex (East)**, BN21 1NX, **ENGLAND**.
(T) 01323 734496.
Contact/s
Owner: Leonard Stevens **(Q)** Master Saddler
Profile Riding Wear Retailer, Saddlery Retailer, Supplies. Master Saddler.
Saddles made to measure for all ages and abilities
Yr. Est: 1863
Opening Times
Sp: Open Mon, Tues, Thur - Sat 09:00. Closed Mon, Tues, Thur - Sat 17:30.
Su: Open Mon, Tues, Thur - Sat 09:00. Closed Mon, Tues, Thur - Sat 17:30.
Au: Open Mon, Tues, Thur - Sat 09:00. Closed Mon, Tues, Thur - Sat 17:30.
Wn: Open Mon, Tues, Thur - Sat 09:00. Closed Mon, Tues, Thur - Sat 17:30.
Closed between 13:00 - 14:00 and on Sundays and Wednesdays **Ref: YH13445**

STEVENS, M A

M A Stevens, 2 Kynance Trce, The Lizard, Helston, **Cornwall**, TR12 7NH, **ENGLAND**.
(T) 01326 290807.
Contact/s
Owner: Mr M Stevens
Profile Farrier. **Ref: YH13446**

STEVENS, R

Mr & Mrs R Stevens, Trevaughan, Bolgoed Stud, Sarnau, Llandysul, **Carmarthenshire**, SA44 6QZ, **WALES**.
(T) 01239 810370.
Profile Breeder. **Ref: YH13447**

STEVENS, ROBERT

Robert Stevens, Mid Trees, Lythe Hill Est, Petworth Rd, Hazlemere, **Surrey**, GU27 6EX, **ENGLAND**.
(M) 07774 155889. **Ref: YH13448**

STEVENSON BROS

Stevenson Brothers, The Workshop, Ashford Rd, Bethersden, Ashford, **Kent**, TN26 3AP, **ENGLAND**.
(T) 01233 820363 **(F)** 01233 820580. **Ref: YH13449**

STEVENSON, DONALD E

Donald E Stevenson DWCF, Dunstans Farm, Moreton Rd, Fyfield, Ongar, **Essex**, CM5 0HU, **ENGLAND**.
(T) 01277 899530.
Profile Farrier. **Ref: YH13450**

STEVENSON, J M

Miss J M Stevenson, Glenvale, 46 Glencregagh Rd, Belfast, **County Antrim**, BT8 4FZ, **NORTHERN IRELAND**.
(T) 028 90793014.
Profile Breeder. **Ref: YH13451**

STEVE'S TRAILERS

Steve's Trailers, Mart Rd, Minehead, **Somerset**, TA24 5BJ, **ENGLAND**.
(T) 01643 707575 **(F)** 01643 707575.
Contact/s
Owner: Mr S Chilcott
Profile Transport/Horse Boxes. **Ref: YH13452**

STEWARDS FARM RIDING CTRE

Stewards Farm Riding Centre, Stewards Farm, Commonside Rd, Harlow, **Essex**, CM18 7HZ, **ENGLAND**.
(T) 01279 413805.
Profile Riding School, Stable/Livery. **Ref: YH13453**

STEWART CHRISTIE

Stewart Christie & Co Ltd, 63 Queen St, Edinburgh, **Edinburgh (City of)**, EH2 4NA, **SCOTLAND**.
(T) 0131 2256639 **(F)** 0131 2202397.
Profile Saddlery Retailer. **Ref: YH13454**

STEWART GREENWOOD & HODGSON

Stewart Greenwood & Hodgson, The Veterinary Surgery, 4 Sagar St, Castleford, **Yorkshire (West)**, WF10 1AF, **ENGLAND**.
(T) 01977 554191.
Profile Medical Support. **Ref: YH13455**

STEWART ROBINSON

Stewart Robinson Ltd, 11 Broighter Rd, Limavady, **County Londonderry**, BT49 9BU, **NORTHERN IRELAND**.
(T) 028 77764907.
Profile Supplies. **Ref: YH13456**

STEWART, J

Mr J Stewart, 22 Hope Rd, Kirkmuirhill, **Lanarkshire (South)**, ML11 9QY, **SCOTLAND**.
(T) 01555 895144.
Profile Breeder. **Ref: YH13457**

STEWART, L

L Stewart, 140 Botchergate, Carlisle, **Cumbria**, CA1 1SH, **ENGLAND**.
(T) 01228 541427.
Contact/s
Owner: Mr L Stewart
Profile Saddlery Retailer. **Ref: YH13458**

STEWART, L

Mr L Stewart, Hillhead Poultry Farm, Lizard Lane, Whitburn, **Tyne and Wear**, SR6 7NN, **ENGLAND**.
(T) 0191 5292244.
Profile Breeder. **Ref: YH13459**

STEWART, W

W Stewart, Hoodshill Farm, Lesmahagow, Lanark, **Lanarkshire (South)**, ML11 9PG, **SCOTLAND**.
(T) 01555 893131 **(F)** 01555 893131.
Contact/s
Owner: Mr W Stewart
Profile Breeder. **Ref: YH13460**

STEWARTON & DUNLOP A A

Stewarton & Dunlop A A, Capringstone Farm, Dreghorn, **Ayrshire (North)**, KA11 3DA, **SCOTLAND**.
(T) 01294 211112.
Contact/s
Secretary: Mrs J Smith **Ref: YH13461**

STEWARTSON, WALTER E

Walter E Stewartson AFCL BI, 10 Lower Sandfields, Send, Woking, **Surrey**, GU23 7AX, **ENGLAND**.
(T) 01483 223242.
Profile Farrier. **Ref: YH13462**

STICKLAND, G W

Mr G W Stickland, Triangle Farm, Stalbridge, Sturminster Newton, **Dorset**, DT10 2RT, **ENGLAND**.
(T) 01963 62492.
Profile Supplies. **Ref: YH13463**

STICKLEBALL HILL FARM
Stickleball Hill Farm, Sticklynch, West Pennard, Glastonbury, **Somerset**, BA6 8NA, **ENGLAND**.
(T) 01749 890122.
Contact/s
Owner: Miss J West
Profile Trainer.
Opening Times
Telephone for an appointment **Ref: YH13464**

STIDOLPH'S LIVERY
Stidolph's Livery, Egg Pie Lane, Weald, Sevenoaks, **Kent**, TN14 6NP, **ENGLAND**.
(T) 01732 458996.
Profile Stable/Livery. **Ref: YH13465**

STIDSTON EQUESTRIAN
Stidston Equestrian, Brook Cottage, South Brent, **Devon**, TQ10 9JT, **ENGLAND**.
(T) 01364 73135.
Contact/s
Owner: Mrs G Wonnacott
Profile Stable/Livery. **Ref: YH13466**

STILLMEADOW TACK SHOP
Stillmeadow Tack Shop, Thirtleby, Hull, **Yorkshire (East)**, HU11 4LL, **ENGLAND**.
(T) 01482 811363.
Profile Saddlery Retailer. **Ref: YH13467**

STILLWELL, R L M
R L M Stillwell, Hand Post Farm, School Rd, Barkham, Wokingham, **Berkshire**, RG41 4TN, **ENGLAND**.
(T) 0118 9760267.
Profile Trainer. **Ref: YH13468**

STILWELL, ELAINE
Mrs Elaine Stilwell, Townsend, Dilwyn, **Herefordshire**, HR4 8HL, **ENGLAND**.
(T) 01544 318528 **(F)** 01544 318528
(M) 07774 112077.
Profile Trainer. **Ref: YH13469**

STINSON, J D
J D Stinson, 20 Thomas St, Armagh, **County Armagh**, BT61 7PX, **NORTHERN IRELAND**.
(T) 028 37523339 **(F)** 028 37523339.
Contact/s
Owner: Mr J Stinson
Profile Saddlery Retailer.
Also sell guns and fishing tackle. Yr. Est: 1950
Opening Times
Sp: Open Mon - Sat 09:00. Closed Mon - Sat 17:30.
Su: Open Mon - Sat 09:00. Closed Mon - Sat 17:30.
Au: Open Mon - Sat 09:00. Closed Mon - Sat 17:30.
Wn: Open Mon - Sat 09:00. Closed Mon - Sat 17:30.
Ref: YH13470

STIPETIC, ROBERT A
Robert A Stipetic RSS, Farriers, Middle St, Nafferton, Driffield, **Yorkshire (East)**, YO25 4JS, **ENGLAND**.
(T) 01377 254581.
Profile Farrier. **Ref: YH13471**

STIRK & HAIZELDEN
Stirk & Haizelden, The Grange, Sutton Grange, Ripon, **Yorkshire (North)**, HG4 3JZ, **ENGLAND**.
(T) 01765 690245 **(F)** 01765 690128.
Profile Medical Support. **Ref: YH13472**

STIRLING, J
J Stirling, 1 Main Rd, Parkgate, Templepatrick, Ballyclare, **County Antrim**, BT39 0DJ, **NORTHERN IRELAND**.
(T) 028 9443 2311.
Profile Riding School. **Ref: YH13473**

STIRLINGSHIRE SADDLERY
Stirlingshire Saddlery Co Ltd, 232 Morrison St, Edinburgh, **Edinburgh (City of)**, EH3 8EA, **SCOTLAND**.
(T) 0131 2298179 **(F)** 0131 2283751.
Contact/s
Partner: Miss A Telfer **(Q)** Saddle Fitter, SMS
Profile Riding Wear Retailer, Saddlery Retailer, Supplies. No.Staff: 10 Yr. Est: 1979
Opening Times
Sp: Open Mon - Sat 09:30. Closed Mon - Fri 18:30, Sat 17:00.
Su: Open Mon - Sat 09:30. Closed Mon - Fri 18:30, Sat 17:00.
Au: Open Mon - Sat 09:30. Closed Mon - Fri 18:30, Sat 17:00.
Wn: Open Mon - Sat 09:30. Closed Mon - Fri 18:30, Sat 17:00.
Closed on Sundays **Ref: YH13474**

STIRLINGSHIRE SADDLERY
Stirlingshire Saddlery Co Ltd, Perth Agricultural Ctre, Perth, **Perth and Kinross**, PH1 3JJ, **SCOTLAND**.
(T) 01738 623222.
Contact/s
Manager: Ms J Gairnes **Ref: YH13475**

STIRLINGSHIRE SADDLERY
Stirlingshire Saddlery Co Ltd (The), Linden Ave, Stirling, **Stirling**, FK7 7PG, **SCOTLAND**.
(T) 01786 475033 **(F)** 01786 475033.
Contact/s
Partner: Miss L Smith **Ref: YH13476**

STIRRUP CUP
Stirrup Cup (The), Nursery Farm, Woodborough, Pewsey, **Wiltshire**, SN9 5PF, **ENGLAND**.
(T) 01672 851555.
Contact/s
Partner: Mr A Mellor **Ref: YH13477**

STIRRUPS
Stirrups (Crewe), 145 Richmond Rd, Crewe, **Cheshire**, CW1 4AX, **ENGLAND**.
(T) 01270 585168
(M) 07970 355702.
Profile Supplies. **Ref: YH13478**

STIRRUPS
Stirrups, 40 High St, Godalming, **Surrey**, GU7 1DY, **ENGLAND**.
(T) 01483 422900 **(F)** 01483 422900.
Contact/s
Owner: Mrs A Tipper **Ref: YH13479**

STIRRUPS
Stirrups, 164A Roberttown Lane, Liversedge, **Yorkshire (West)**, WF15 7LT, **ENGLAND**.
(T) 01924 401966.
Contact/s
Owner: Mrs J Wood
Profile Saddlery Retailer. **Ref: YH13480**

STIRRUPS SADDLERY
Stirrups Saddlery, Greystone Cottage, Maw Lane, Haslington, Crewe, **Cheshire**, CW1 5SH, **ENGLAND**.
(T) 01270 584229. **Ref: YH13481**

STIRRUPS TACK SHOP
Stirrups Tack Shop, 202 Main Rd, Sutton At Hone, Dartford, **Kent**, DA4 9HP, **ENGLAND**.
(T) 01322 866261.
Contact/s
Owner: Mr J Cahalane **Ref: YH13482**

STOBART, D T
D T Stobart, Cracrop Farm, Brampton, **Cumbria**, CA8 2BW, **ENGLAND**.
(T) 01697 748245.
Profile Transport/Horse Boxes. **Ref: YH13483**

STOCK FARM EQUITATION
Stock Farm Equitation, Potash Rd, Matching Green, Harlow, **Essex**, CM17 0RN, **ENGLAND**.
(T) 01279 731518.
Contact/s
Owner: Mrs N Darkin **Ref: YH13484**

STOCKACLOSE
Stockaclose Shetland Pony Stud, Stock-A-Close Farm, Cottingley, Bingley, **Yorkshire (West)**, BD16 1UQ, **ENGLAND**.
(T) 01274 480811.
Profile Breeder. **Ref: YH13485**

STOCKBRIDGE
Stockbridge Riding School & Livery Service, Stockbridge Downs, Stockbridge, **Hampshire**, SO20 6HN, **ENGLAND**.
(T) 01264 810727.
Contact/s
Owner: Mr J Rayton
Profile Farrier, Riding School, Stable/Livery.
Ref: YH13486

STOCKBRIDGE HOUSE STABLES
Stockbridge House Stables, High St, Newmarket, **Suffolk**, SB8 9AP, **ENGLAND**.
(T) 07977 802063
(W) www.newmarketracehorsetrainers.co.uk
Affiliated Bodies Newmarket Trainers Fed.
Contact/s
Trainer: Mr D Mullarkey
Profile Trainer. **Ref: YH13487**

STOCKCARE
Stockcare Ltd, 83 West St, Leven, Beverley, **Yorkshire (East)**, HU17 5LR, **ENGLAND**.
(T) 01964 543924 **(F)** 01964 542750
(E) info@goldlabeluk.com
(W) http://freespace.virgin.net/gold.label/.
Contact/s
Partner: Mr T Stockill
Profile Medical Support. **Ref: YH13488**

STOCKDALE STABLES
Stockdale Stables, The Stables, Oakenshaw Lane, Walton, Wakefield, **Yorkshire (West)**, WF2 6NJ, **ENGLAND**.
(T) 01924 254125. **Ref: YH13489**

STOCKDALE, TIM
Tim Stockdale, Dovecote Farm, Hyde Rd, Roade, **Northamptonshire**, NN7 2LX, **ENGLAND**.
(T) 01604 862936.
Profile Trainer. **Ref: YH13490**

STOCKFARM EQUESTRIAN SUPPLIES
Stockfarm Equestrian Supplies, 38 Upton Lane, Upton, Chester, **Cheshire**, CH2 1EE, **ENGLAND**.
(T) 01244 381976.
Contact/s
Owner: Mr J Newton
Profile Saddlery Retailer, Supplies. **Ref: YH13491**

STOCKHAM, G J
G J Stockham, Honeysuckle Cottage, Church Lane, Govilon, Abergavenny, **Monmouthshire**, NP7 9RP, **WALES**.
(T) 01873 830062.
Profile Farrier. **Ref: YH13492**

STOCKLAND LOVELL
Stockland Lovell, Coultings, Fiddington, Bridgwater, **Somerset**, TA5 1JJ, **ENGLAND**.
(T) 01278 652224 **(F)** 01278 603801
(E) info@stocklandlovell.fsnet.co.uk
(W) www.stocklandlovell.com.
Contact/s
General Manager: Mr A Guilding
Profile Equestrian Centre, Horse/Rider Accom, Track/Course.
Cross country schooling, events and residential camps. Arena and show jumps can be hired throughout the year. Group rates on accommodation for horse and rider. No.Staff: 5 Yr. Est: 1990
C.Size: 500 Acres
Opening Times
Sp: Open Mon - Sun 09:00. Closed Mon - Sun 17:00.
Su: Open Mon - Sun 09:00. Closed Mon - Sun 17:00.
Au: Open Mon - Sun 09:00. Closed Mon - Sun 17:00.
Wn: Open Mon - Sun 09:00. Closed Mon - Sun 17:00.
Lessons can be arranged outside above times by telephone. Cross country course open February - November. **Ref: YH13493**

STOCKLEY FARM
Stockley Farm, Stockley Lane, Stretton, Warrington, **Cheshire**, WA4 4PQ, **ENGLAND**.
(T) 01925 730447.
Contact/s
General Manager: Mr S Mason
Profile Breeder, Stable/Livery.
All showing livery catered for from in-hand to ridden. Problem horses considered. Producer of horses and ponies for show the ring. No.Staff: 4
Yr. Est: 1992 C.Size: 20 Acres **Ref: YH13494**

STOCKLEY TRADING
Stockley Trading, Unit N11 Riverside Ind Est, Littlehampton, **Sussex (West)**, BN17 5DF, **ENGLAND**.
(T) 01903 732392.
Contact/s
Owner: Mr J MacGregor
Profile Saddlery Retailer. **Ref: YH13495**

STOCKSHOP WOLSELEY
Stockshop (Livestock Equipment) Ltd, Lodge Trading Est, Broadclyst, Exeter, **Devon**, EX5 3BS, **ENGLAND**.
(T) 01392 460077 **(F)** 01392 460966
(E) sales@stockshop.co.uk
(W) www.stockshop.co.uk.
Profile Supplies. Toy makers.
Produce wooden toys, based on an equestrian theme
No.Staff: 30 Yr. Est: 1983
Opening Times
Sp: Open Mon - Fri 09:00. Closed Mon - Fri 17:00.
Su: Open Mon - Fri 09:00. Closed Mon - Fri 17:00.

Au: Open Mon - Fri 09:00. Closed Mon - Fri 17:00.
Wn: Open Mon - Fri 09:00. Closed Mon - Fri 17:00.
Closed weekends Ref: YH13496

STOCKWELL STUD LIVERY STABLES

Stockwell Stud Livery Stables, Kirkby Wharfe, Tadcaster, **Yorkshire (North)**, LS24 9DE, **ENGLAND**.
(T) 01937 833551 **(F)** 01937 530057
(E) deboraheasterby@kirkbygrange.co.uk.
Profile Breeder, Stable/Livery, Track/Course.
Ref: YH13497

STOCKWOOD PARK

Stockwood Park Stable Complex, Stockwood Pk, Luton, **Bedfordshire**, LU1 4BH, **ENGLAND**.
(T) 01582 720766.
Contact/s
Manager: Ms R Evans
Profile Equestrian Centre, Riding School.
Hacking is available, jumps can be set up. Pony rides for children under 7 years of age. Lessons from 7 years upwards. Examination training for BHS stage 1 & 2. £1.00 per hour discount to Luton Council Advantage card holders. No.Staff: 5 Yr. Est: 1991
Opening Times
Sp: Open Tues - Sun 09:00. Closed Tues - Sun 17:00.
Su: Open Tues - Sun 09:00. Closed Tues - Sun 17:00.
Au: Open Tues - Sun 09:00. Closed Tues - Sun 17:00.
Wn: Open Tues - Sun 09:00. Closed Tues - Sun 17:00.
Training sessions Tues & Wed until 20:00. Closed on Mondays Ref: YH13498

STOCKWOOD STABLES

Stockwood Stables, Stockwood Park Craft Museum, Stockwood Country Pk, Farley Hill, Luton, **Bedfordshire**, LU1 5EH, **ENGLAND**.
(T) 01582 30131.
Profile Riding School. Ref: YH13499

STOCKWOOD VALLEY RIDING CTRE

Stockwood Valley Riding Centre, Bifield Rd, Bristol, **Bristol**, BS14 8TH, **ENGLAND**.
(T) 01275 830002.
Contact/s
Manager: Mrs D Burler Ref: YH13500

STOKE BY CLARE EQUESTRIAN CTRE

Stoke By Clare Equestrian Centre, The Street, Stoke By Clare, Sudbury, **Suffolk**, CO10 8HP, **ENGLAND**.
(T) 01787 277866 **(F)** 01787 278822.
Contact/s
For Bookings: Mrs S Tenwick
Profile Arena, Blood Stock Agency, Equestrian Centre, Riding School, Riding Wear Retailer, Saddlery Retailer, Stable/Livery, Supplies, Trainer.
The specific training of horses to go forward, straight and correct with firmness, kindness and understanding of the horses mental and physical ability. Psychology and racehorse rehabilitation is also provided.
No.Staff: 5 Yr. Est: 1996 C.Size: 20 Acres
Opening Times
Sp: Open 09:00. Closed 19:00.
Su: Open 09:00. Closed 20:00.
Au: Open 09:00. Closed 19:00.
Wn: Open 09:00. Closed 19:00. Ref: YH13501

STOKE LIVERIES

Stoke Liveries, Stoke Rd, Stoke D'abernon, Cobham, **Surrey**, KT11 3QG, **ENGLAND**.
(T) 01932 865122. Ref: YH13502

STOKEHILL LIVERY YARD

Stokehill Livery Yard, Stoke Hill Lane, Crapstone, Yelverton, **Devon**, PL20 7PP, **ENGLAND**.
(T) 01822 852666.
Contact/s
Owner: Mrs B Kublin Ref: YH13503

STOKES OF ENGLAND

Stokes Of England, Bank Top Ind Est, St. Martins, Oswestry, **Shropshire**, SY10 7HB, **ENGLAND**.
(T) 01691 773963 **(F)** 01691 773963.
Contact/s
Partner: Mr C Stokes
Profile Blacksmith. Ref: YH13504

STOKES, PAULA

Miss Paula Stokes DC AMC MMCA, The Stables, Black Lake Lane, Upper Bentley, Redditch, **Worcestershire**, B97 5WD, **ENGLAND**.
(T) 01527 540223.
Profile Medical Support. Ref: YH13505

STOKES, R & S

R & S Stokes, Lower Wyburns Farm, Daws Heath Rd, Rayleigh, **Essex**, SS6 7NP, **ENGLAND**.
(T) 01268 743378 **(F)** 01268 743378
(M) 07850 481867.
Profile Supplies. Ref: YH13506

STONAR SCHOOL

Stonar School, Cottles Pk, Alworth, Melksham, **Wiltshire**, SN12 8NT, **ENGLAND**.
(T) 01225 790422 **(F)** 01225 790830
(E) office@stonar.wilts.sch.uk.
Contact/s
Key Contact: Miss J Storey **(Q)** BHSI
Profile Horse/Rider Accom, Stable/Livery, Track/Course, Trainer. Ref: YH13507

STONE ACRE

Stone Acre Junior Competition Riding School, Stoneacre, Main St, Little Brington, Northampton, **Northamptonshire**, NN7 4HS, **ENGLAND**.
(T) 01604 771111.
Contact/s
Owner: Mrs C Shelton Ref: YH13508

STONE HSE FARM

Stone House Farm Riding School & Livery, Stone Hse Farm, Off Harvers Hill Lane, Arley, Coventry, **Midlands (West)**, CV7 8GB, **ENGLAND**.
(T) 01676 523243. Ref: YH13509

STONE HSE STABLE

Stone House Stable Preston Wynne, Stone Hse, Preston Wynne, Hereford, **Herefordshire**, HR1 3PB, **ENGLAND**.
(T) 01432 820604 **(F)** 01432 820604.
Contact/s
Owner: Mrs P Ford
Profile Trainer. Ref: YH13510

STONE LANE VETNRY CLINIC

Stone Lane Veterinary Clinic, Stone Lane, Meldreth, Royston, **Hertfordshire**, SG8 6NZ, **ENGLAND**.
(T) 01763 261457.
Profile Medical Support. Ref: YH13511

STONE LODGE EQUESTRIAN

Stone Lodge Equestrian Ltd, Stone Lodge Farm, Launde Rd, Tilton On The Hill, Leicester, **Leicestershire**, LE7 9DF, **ENGLAND**.
(T) 0116 2597379 **(F)** 0116 2597379. Ref: YH13512

STONEHAVEN ICELANDICS

Stonehaven Icelandics, Millsburn, Rickarton, Stonehaven, **Aberdeenshire**, AB39 3TE, **SCOTLAND**.
(T) 01569 764166 **(F)** 01569 764966
(E) cphillip@netcomuk.co.uk.
Profile Breeder. Ref: YH13513

STONEHAVEN TREKKING CTRE

Stonehaven Trekking Centre, Cowton, Rickarton, Stonehaven, **Aberdeenshire**, AB39 3SY, **SCOTLAND**.
(T) 01569 63360.
Profile Equestrian Centre. Ref: YH13514

STONEHEWER, GRAHAM

Graham Stonehewer RSS BII, Brick Hse Forge, Luston, Leominster, **Herefordshire**, HR6 0EB, **ENGLAND**.
(T) 01568 613305.
Profile Farrier. Ref: YH13515

STONEHILL RIDING SCHOOL

Stonehill Riding School, Stonehill Farm, Stonehill, Drayton, Abingdon, **Oxfordshire**, OX14 4AA, **ENGLAND**.
(T) 01235 529915.
Contact/s
Owner: Mrs B Webb Ref: YH13516

STONEHOUSE SADDLERY/PET CTRE

Stonehouse Saddlery & Pet Centre, 38 New St, Stonehouse, **Lanarkshire (South)**, ML9 3LT, **SCOTLAND**.
(T) 01698 791670.
Profile Saddlery Retailer. Ref: YH13517

STONELEIGH RIDING CLUB

Stoneleigh Riding Club, Jubilee Cottage, London Rd, Ryton-on-Dunsmore, **Warwickshire**, CV8 3ER, **ENGLAND**.
(T) 024 76307898.
Contact/s
Chairman: Mrs A Bell
Profile Club/Association, Riding Club. Ref: YH13518

STONELEIGH STABLES

Stoneleigh Stables, The Colonels Cottage, Stoneleigh Abbey, Kenilworth, **Warwickshire**, CV8 2LF, **ENGLAND**.
(T) 01926 851996 **(F)** 01926 851997
(E) stables@stoneleighpark.co.uk
(W) www.stoneleighpark.co.uk.
Contact/s
Owner: Honourable D Pritchard Johnson
Profile Arena, Equestrian Centre, Horse/Rider Accom, Riding School, Track/Course.
Can use your own horses or those stabled at the yard
Opening Times
Sp: Open Mon - Sun 09:00. Closed Mon - Sun 17:00.
Su: Open Mon - Sun 09:00. Closed Mon - Sun 17:00.
Au: Open Mon - Sun 09:00. Closed Mon - Sun 17:00.
Wn: Open Mon - Sun 09:00. Closed Mon - Sun 17:00. Ref: YH13519

STONERIGG RIDING CTRE

Stonerigg Riding Centre, Great Orton, Carlisle, **Cumbria**, CA5 6NA, **ENGLAND**.
(T) 01228 576232.
Profile Riding School. Ref: YH13520

STONEWAYS INSURANCE

Stoneways Insurance, 22 Church St, Godalming, **Surrey**, GU7 1EW, **ENGLAND**.
(T) 01483 426966 **(F)** 01483 418834.
Profile Club/Association. Ref: YH13521

STOP GAP

Stop Gap (The), Barkers Field, Shepton Montague, Wincanton, **Somerset**, BA9 8JA, **ENGLAND**.
(T) 01963 33783.
Profile Medical Support. Ref: YH13522

STOREY, ANTHONY J

Anthony J Storey AWCF BI, 106 Moorsfield, Houghton Le Spring, **Tyne and Wear**, DH4 5PG, **ENGLAND**.
(T) 07802 696618.
Profile Farrier. Ref: YH13523

STOREY, F S

Mr F S Storey, Low Dubwath, Kirklinton, Carlisle, **Cumbria**, CA6 6EF, **ENGLAND**.
(T) 01228 75331.
Profile Supplies. Ref: YH13524

STOREY, MARTIN J

Martin J Storey, Goddard Rd, Whitehouse Ind Est, Ipswich, **Suffolk**, IP1 5NP, **ENGLAND**.
(T) 01473 216981.
Profile Supplies. Ref: YH13525

STOREY, W L

W L Storey, Grange Farm, Muggleswick, Consett, **County Durham**, DH8 9DW, **ENGLAND**.
(T) 01207 255259.
Contact/s
Owner: Mr W Storey
Profile Trainer. Ref: YH13526

STORRAR PRACTICE

Storrar Practice (The), Park Cottage, 39 Duke St, Chester, **Cheshire**, CH1 1RP, **ENGLAND**.
(T) 01244 311106.
Profile Medical Support. Ref: YH13527

STOTFOLD CREST STABLES

Stotfold Crest Stables, Elwick, **Cleveland**, TS27 3HQ, **ENGLAND**.
(T) 01740 644040.
Profile Riding School. Ref: YH13528

STOUR VALLEY RIDING CLUB

Stour Valley Riding Club, Pensbury Cl, Motcombe Rd, Shaftesbury, **Dorset**, SP7 0JY, **ENGLAND**.
(T) 01747 811835 **(F)** 01747 811837.
Contact/s
Chairman: Dr A Weir
Profile Club/Association, Riding Club. Ref: YH13529

STOURPORT RIDING CTRE

Stourport Riding Centre Ltd, Upper Poolands Farm, Hartlebury Rd, Stourport-on-Severn, **Worcestershire**, DY13 9JD, **ENGLAND**.
(T) 01299 251125. Ref: YH13530

STOURPORT TIGERS

Stourport Tigers Horseball Club, C/O Manor Farm Riding School, 2 St Johns Rd, Stourport-on-Severn, **Worcestershire**, DY13 9DS, **ENGLAND**.
(T) 01299 822403.

Profile Club/Association. Ref: YH13531

STOURTON HILL STABLES

Stourton Hill Stables, Bridgnorth Rd, Stourton, Stourbridge, **Staffordshire**, DY7 5BQ, **ENGLAND**.
(T) 01384 872865.
Contact/s
Manager: Mrs H Lord
Profile Riding School. Ref: YH13532

STOURTON STUD

Stourton Stud, Stourton Leaze Farm, Holnest, Sherborne, **Dorset**, DT9 6HX, **ENGLAND**.
(T) 01963 210210.
Profile Breeder. Ref: YH13533

STOUTE, MICHAEL (SIR)

Sir Michael Stoute, Bury Rd, Newmarket, **Suffolk**, CB8 7BY, **ENGLAND**.
(T) 01638 663801 (F) 01638 667276
(W) www.newmarketracehorsetrainers.co.uk
Affiliated Bodies Newmarket Trainers Fed.
Contact/s
Owner: Sir M Stoute
Profile Trainer. Ref: YH13534

STOVAR LONG LANE

Stovar Long Lane Riding Stables, Stovar Long Lane, Beer, Seaton, **Devon**, EX12 3LD, **ENGLAND**.
(T) 01297 24278.
Contact/s
Owner: Ms A Cawley Ref: YH13535

STOW FEEDS

Stow Feeds, Pound Farm Buildings, Church Rd, Old Newton, Stowmarket, **Suffolk**, IP14 4ED, **ENGLAND**.
(T) 01449 673806 (F) 01449 673806. Ref: YH13536

STOWE ANIMAL HEALTH

Stowe Animal Health, 54B Bury Rd, Stowmarket, **Suffolk**, IP14 1JF, **ENGLAND**.
(T) 01449 776200 (F) 01449 771362
(E) mail@stowevet.demon.co.uk.
Contact/s
Key Contact: Angela Whiting
Profile Supplies.
There is a wide range of products for all domestic species. Telephone for a free 32 page catalogue.
Opening Times
There is a 24 hour answering phone. Ref: YH13537

STOWE RIDINGS

Stowe Ridings, Blackpit Farm, Silverstone Rd, Stowe, Buckingham, **Buckinghamshire**, MK18 5LJ, **ENGLAND**.
(T) 01280 812363.
Contact/s
Manager: Mrs L Smith
Profile Riding School, Stable/Livery. Ref: YH13538

STOWE VETNRY GROUP

Stowe Veterinary Group (Ipswich), The Mustard Pot, Coddenham Rd, Needham Market, Ipswich, **Suffolk**, IP6 8NU, **ENGLAND**.
(T) 01449 722198.
Profile Medical Support. Ref: YH13539

STOWE VETNRY GROUP

Stowe Veterinary Group (Stowmarket), 54 Bury Rd, Stowmarket, **Suffolk**, IP14 1JF, **ENGLAND**.
(T) 01449 613130 (F) 01449 616033
(E) info@stowevet.demon.co.uk.
Profile Medical Support. Ref: YH13540

STOWER VALLEY HORSEBOXES

Stower Valley Horseboxes & Commercials, Gannetts Quarry, Todber, Sturminster Newton, **Dorset**, DT10 1HS, **ENGLAND**.
(T) 01258 821351.
Contact/s
Owner: Mr M Rendle
Profile Transport/Horse Boxes. Ref: YH13541

STRACHAN & WIGNALL

Strachan & Wignall, Tyddyn St Vetnry Surgery, Tyddyn St, Mold, **Flintshire**, CH7 1DX, **WALES**.
(T) 01352 700087.
Contact/s
Vet: Mr R Wignall
Profile Medical Support. Ref: YH13542

STRACHAN, ARTHUR E

Arthur E Strachan, Lochton Smithy, Durris, Banchory, **Aberdeenshire**, AB31 6DD, **SCOTLAND**.
(T) 01330 844761 (F) 01330 844761.
Contact/s
Owner: Mr A Strachan
Profile Blacksmith. Ref: YH13543

STRACHAN, TYSON & HAMILTON

Strachan, Tyson & Hamilton MRCVS, 36 Heaton Rd, Newcastle-upon-Tyne, **Tyne and Wear**, NE6 1SD, **ENGLAND**.
(T) 0191 2653998 (F) 0191 2764620.
Profile Medical Support. Ref: YH13544

STRAGGLETHORPE ROCKER

Stragglethorpe Rocker, Stragglethorpe Grange, Brant Broughton, **Lincolnshire**, LN5 0RA, **ENGLAND**.
(T) 01636 626309.
Profile Supplies. Ref: YH13545

STRAMONGATE VETNRY CTRE

Stramongate Veterinary Centre, 52 Stramongate, Kendal, **Cumbria**, LA9 4BD, **ENGLAND**.
(T) 01539 722692 (F) 01539 724379
(E) stramonvet@aol.com.
Profile Medical Support. Ref: YH13546

STRANGE, ALF

Alf Strange, The Brow, Ellesmere, **Shropshire**, SY12 9HW, **ENGLAND**.
(T) 01691 623249.
Contact/s
Owner: Mr A Strange
Profile Blacksmith. Ref: YH13547

STRANGEWAYS & DISTRICT

Strangeways & District Riding Club, 24 Crocus Field, Dollis Valley, Barnet, **Hertfordshire**, EN5 2UA, **ENGLAND**.
(T) 020 84410712.
Profile Club/Association. Ref: YH13548

STRANGEWAYS FEEDS

Strangeways Feeds, Strange Farm, Borehamwood, **Hertfordshire**, WD6 5PF, **ENGLAND**.
(T) 020 89536530.
Contact/s
Partner: Miss M Hall
Profile Supplies. Ref: YH13549

STRANRAER & DISTRICT

Stranraer & District Riding Club, The Clavering, Larg Ave, Stanraer, **Dumfries and Galloway**, DG9 0JP, **SCOTLAND**.
(T) 01776 704518.
Profile Club/Association, Riding Club. Ref: YH13550

STRATFORD SHIRE HORSE CTRE

Stratford Shire Horse Centre, Clifford Rd, Stratford-upon-Avon, **Warwickshire**, CV37 8HW, **ENGLAND**.
(T) 01789 266276.
Profile Club/Association. Ref: YH13551

STRATFORD YARD FORGE

Stratford Yard Forge, Cleve Rd, Middle Littleton, Evesham, **Worcestershire**, WR11 5JR, **ENGLAND**.
(T) 01386 833100.
Profile Blacksmith. Ref: YH13552

STRATFORD-ON-AVON RACECOURSE

Stratford-on-Avon Racecourse, Luddington Rd, Stratford-upon-Avon, **Warwickshire**, CV37 9SE, **ENGLAND**.
(T) 01789 267949 (F) 01789 415850.
Contact/s
Secretary/Manager: Mr S Lambert
Profile Track/Course. Ref: YH13553

STRATH ISLA RIDING CLUB

Strath Isla Riding Club, Heatheryfield, Cairnie, Huntly, **Aberdeenshire**, AB54 4UE, **SCOTLAND**.
(T) 01466 760318.
Contact/s
Chairman: Mr J Ravenshear
Profile Club/Association, Riding Club. Ref: YH13554

STRATHBOGIE VETNRY CTRE

Strathbogie Veterinary Centre, 39 Gordon St, Huntly, **Aberdeenshire**, AB54 8EQ, **SCOTLAND**.
(T) 01466 792627 (F) 01466 794962.
Contact/s
Vet: Miss J Andrew
Profile Medical Support. Ref: YH13555

STRATHEARN RIDING CLUB

Strathearn Riding Club, Kilchoan, Kinnaird, Pitlochry, **Perth and Kinross**, PH16 5JL, **SCOTLAND**.
(T) 01796 472035.
Profile Club/Association, Riding Club. Ref: YH13556

STRATHENDRICK RIDING CLUB

Strathendrick Riding Club, Hill Of Arnmore, Kippen, **Stirling**, FK8 3EW, **SCOTLAND**.
(T) 01786 870225.
Contact/s
Secretary: Mrs S Adam
Profile Club/Association, Riding Club. Ref: YH13557

STRATHERN FODDER

Strathern Fodder, Ballochargie Sawmill, Crieff, **Perth and Kinross**, PH7 4HY, **SCOTLAND**.
(T) 01764 655988.
Contact/s
Owner: Mrs M Matthew Ref: YH13558

STRATHISLA RIDING CLUB

Strathisla Riding Club, Holuhill, Station Rd, Keith, **Moray**, AB55 5DR, **SCOTLAND**.
(T) 01261 842276.
Profile Club/Association, Riding Club. Ref: YH13559

STRATHKELVIN RIDING CLUB

Strathkelvin Riding Club, 77 Langmuirhead Rd, Auchinloch, Glasgow, **Glasgow (City of)**, G66 5DJ, **SCOTLAND**.
(T) 0141 7764075 (F) 0141 7799530.
Contact/s
Secretary: Miss J Morrison
Profile Club/Association, Riding Club. Ref: YH13560

STRATHMORE

Strathmore Farm, 21 Rowantree Ave, Baildon, Shipley, **Yorkshire (West)**, BD17 5LQ, **ENGLAND**.
(T) 01274 597500.
Contact/s
Owner: Mrs J Luscombe
Profile Riding School. Ref: YH13561

STRATHMORE & DISTRICT

Strathmore & District Riding Club, 45 Queen St, Woodside, Newport On Tay, **Fife**, DD6 8BD, **SCOTLAND**.
(T) 01382 541521.
Contact/s
Chairman: Mr A Clark
Profile Club/Association, Riding Club. Ref: YH13562

STRATHORN FARM

Strathorn Farm, Pitcaple, Inverurie, **Aberdeenshire**, AB51 5EJ, **SCOTLAND**.
(T) 01464 851204 (F) 01464 851588.
Contact/s
Owner: Mr G Skinner
Profile Horse/Rider Accom. Ref: YH13563

STRATHPEFFER HIGHLAND

Strathpeffer Highland Gathering, Glenesk, Stratheffer, **Highlands**, IV14 9AT, **SCOTLAND**.
(T) 01997 421348.
Profile Club/Association. Ref: YH13564

STRATHSPEY HIGHLAND PONY CTRE

Strathspey Highland Pony Centre, Rowanlea, Faebuie, Cromdale, Grantown-on-Spey, **Moray**, PH26 3PF, **SCOTLAND**.
(T) 01479 873073.
Profile Equestrian Centre. Ref: YH13565

STRATUS DEVELOPMENTS

Stratus Developments, 6 Forval Cl, Wandle Way, Mitcham, **Surrey**, CR4 4NE, **ENGLAND**.
(T) 020 86462222 (F) 020 86461955.
Profile Supplies. Ref: YH13566

STRAW, ALAN BARRETT

Alan Barrett Straw, Link Farm, Wiggonholt, Pulborough, **Sussex (West)**, RH20 2EL, **ENGLAND**.
(T) 01798 874448.
Contact/s
Owner: Mr A Barrett Ref: YH13567

STRAWBERRY STEEL

Strawberry Steel, Tickenham Forge, Stone-Edge Batch, Tickenham, Clevedon, **Somerset (North)**, BS21 6SF, **ENGLAND**.
(T) 01275 854004.
Contact/s
Owner: Mr C Comrie
Profile Blacksmith. Ref: YH13568

STRAWSON, VIRGINIA

Virginia Strawson, Home Farm, Aylesbury, Grimsby, **Lincolnshire (North East)**, **ENGLAND**.
(T) 01472 72663.
Profile Trainer. Ref: YH13569

STREATHER HAYWARD FARMS

Streather Hayward Farms Ltd, Radwell Dene, Radwell, Baldock, **Hertfordshire**, SG7 5ES, **ENGLAND**.
(T) 01462 730478.
Profile Supplies. Ref: YH13570

STREATHER-HAYWARD FARMS

Streather-Hayward Farms Ltd, The Caravan, Bostraze, Praa Sands, Penzance, **Cornwall**, TR20 9TG, **ENGLAND**.
(T) 01736 763359. Ref: **YH13571**

STREET FARM

Street Farm, Beeston, King's Lynn, **Norfolk**, PE32 2NF, **ENGLAND**.
(T) 01328 701286.
Profile Riding School, Stable/Livery. Ref: **YH13572**

STREETER, A

Mr A Streeter, Basford Grange, Basford, Cheddleton, Leek, **Staffordshire**, ST13 7ET, **ENGLAND**.
(T) 01538 360324 (F) 01538 361643
(M) 07976 386227.
Profile Trainer. Ref: **YH13573**

STRETTON RIDING/TRAINING CTRE

Stretton Riding & Training Centre, Manor Bungalow Farm, Manor Rd, Stretton, Oakham, **Leicestershire**, LE15 7QZ, **ENGLAND**.
(T) 01780 410323.
Contact/s
Manager: Mr S Dolbey
Profile Riding School. Ref: **YH13574**

STRETTON-DOWNES, C

Mrs C Stretton-Downes, Lower Hill Farm, Lamerton, Tavistock, **Devon**, PL19 8RR, **ENGLAND**.
(T) 01822 612475.
Profile Stable/Livery. Ref: **YH13575**

STRICK, J

Mrs J Strick, Bryn Awelon, Uwchmynydd, Aberdaron, Pwllheli, **Gwynedd**, LL53 8DD, **WALES**.
(T) 01758 760252.
Profile Breeder. Ref: **YH13576**

STRIDE, DAVID P

David P Stride, Nettles, The Sinnocks, West Chiltington, **Sussex (West)**, RH20 2JX, **ENGLAND**.
(T) 01798 812894.
Profile Farrier. Ref: **YH13577**

STRINES FARM STUD

Strines Farm Stud, Strinesdale, Oldham, **Lancashire**, OL4 3RB, **ENGLAND**.
(T) 0161 6335994.
Profile Breeder. Ref: **YH13578**

STROMSHOLM

Stromsholm, 8 James Way, Bletchley, Milton Keynes, **Buckinghamshire**, MK1 1SU, **ENGLAND**.
(T) 01525 237477.
Contact/s
Partner: Mrs B Thompson
Profile Farrier. Ref: **YH13579**

STRONACH, JOHN

John Stronach, East Bowershall, Dunfermline, **Fife**, KY12 0RZ, **SCOTLAND**.
(T) 01383 722993.
Profile Farrier. Ref: **YH13580**

STRONG, A R

A R Strong, 13 Meadow Prospect, Wolvercote, **Oxfordshire**, OX2 8PP, **ENGLAND**.
(T) 01865 59326.
Profile Farrier. Ref: **YH13581**

STRONG, ALEXANDER G

Alexander G Strong DWCF, Haregrove, Brimpsfield, **Gloucestershire**, GL4 8LL, **ENGLAND**.
(T) 07973 318086.
Profile Farrier. Ref: **YH13582**

STRONG, M G

M G Strong, Castle Hse, Newcastle Emlyn, **Carmarthenshire**, SA38 9AF, **WALES**.
(T) 01239 710187.
Profile Medical Support. Ref: **YH13583**

STRONG, PETER

Peter Strong, North Lodge, Lea Castle Farm, Wolverley, **Worcestershire**, DY10 3RB, **ENGLAND**.
(T) 01562 850145.
Profile Supplies. Ref: **YH13584**

STRONGE, R M

Mr R M Stronge, Woods Folly, Beedon Common, Newbury, **Berkshire**, RG16 8TT, **ENGLAND**.
(T) 01635 248710 (F) 01635 248710.
Profile Trainer. Ref: **YH13585**

STROUD FARM SERVICES

Stroud Farm Services, Unit 4 Chalford Ind Est, London Rd, Chalford, Stroud, **Gloucestershire**, GL6 8NT, **ENGLAND**.
(T) 01453 886189 (F) 01453 886189.
Profile Saddlery Retailer. Ref: **YH13586**

STROUD PONY CLUB

Stroud Pony Club, Windrush, Hay Lane, Horsley, Nailsworth, **Gloucestershire**, GL6 0QD, **ENGLAND**.
(T) 01453 832964.
Contact/s
Key Contact: Mrs S Rind
Profile Club/Association. Ref: **YH13587**

STROUD SADDLERY

Stroud Saddlery, The Cross, Nelson St, Stroud, **Gloucestershire**, GL5 2HL, **ENGLAND**.
(T) 01453 759866 (F) 01453 766487
Affiliated Bodies BETA, SMS.
Contact/s
Owner: Mr L Pearman (Q) Master Saddler, Saddle Fitter, SMS
Profile Riding Wear Retailer, Saddlery Retailer, Supplies. Repair Workshop. No.Staff: 5
Opening Times
Sp: Open 08:30. Closed 17:30.
Su: Open 08:30. Closed 17:30.
Au: Open 08:30. Closed 17:30.
Wn: Open 08:30. Closed 17:30. Ref: **YH13588**

STROUTS, J M (DR)

Dr J M Strouts, 40 Ash Hayes Drive, Nailsea, **Somerset (North)**, BS48 2LQ, **ENGLAND**.
(T) 01275 854941
(M) 07949 282513
(E) drjohnstrouts@talk21.com
(W) www.stroutscarriageanddriving.co.uk. Ref: **YH13589**

STRUAN MOTORS

Struan Motors Limited, 102 Scott St, Perth, **Perth and Kinross**, PH2 8LU, **SCOTLAND**.
(T) 01738 633441.
Profile Transport/Horse Boxes. Ref: **YH13590**

STRUMPSHAW HALL

Strumpshaw Hall Livery Stables, Hall Farm, Strumpshaw, Norwich, **Norfolk**, NR13 4HR, **ENGLAND**.
(T) 01603 715274.
Contact/s
Manageress: Mrs V Sayer
Profile Stable/Livery. Ref: **YH13591**

STRUMPSHAW RIDING CTRE

Strumpshaw Riding Centre, Buckenham Rd, Strumpshaw, Norwich, **Norfolk**, NR13 4NP, **ENGLAND**.
(T) 01603 712815 (F) 01603 712815.
Contact/s
Manager: Mrs W Murray
Profile Riding School, Stable/Livery. Ref: **YH13592**

STS AUTOELECTRICS

STS Autoelectrics, 435 Old Walsall Rd, Birmingham, **Midlands (West)**, B42 1HX, **ENGLAND**.
(T) 0121 3578390.
Profile Transport/Horse Boxes. Ref: **YH13593**

STUART, FIONA

Fiona Stuart, Tullochan, Gartocharn, Alexandria, **Argyll and Bute**, G83 8ND, **SCOTLAND**.
(T) 01389 830205 (F) 01389 830653.
Profile Trainer. Ref: **YH13594**

STUART, G

G Stuart, 8 Thorne Cottages, Ottery St Mary, **Devon**, EX11 1QZ, **ENGLAND**.
(T) 01404 813667.
Profile Farrier. Ref: **YH13595**

STUART, L G

L G Stuart, Tempion, Main St, Longside, Peterhead, **Aberdeenshire**, AB42 4XJ, **SCOTLAND**.
(T) 01779 821269 (F) 01779 821766.
Contact/s
Owner: Mr L Stuart
Profile Blacksmith. Ref: **YH13596**

STUART, PAUL A

Paul A Stuart DWCF, 12 Warrick Cl, Feniton, **Devon**, EX14 0DT, **ENGLAND**.
(T) 01404 850539.
Profile Farrier. Ref: **YH13597**

STUARTS FARRIER SERVICE

Stuarts Farrier Service, 8 Barrack Rd, Ottery St Mary, **Devon**, EX11 1RD, **ENGLAND**.
(T) 01404 813667.
Profile Farrier. Ref: **YH13598**

STUBBEN

Stubben (Ireland) Ltd, Lahinch Rd, Ennistymon, **County Clare**, **IRELAND**.
(T) 065 7071073.
Profile Supplies. Ref: **YH13599**

STUBBEN

Stubben UK, 1-3 Oakley Hay Lodge, Great Fold Rd, Corby, **Northamptonshire**, NN18 9AS, **ENGLAND**.
(T) 01536 744554 (F) 01536 744664.
Contact/s
Owner: Mr A McCune
Profile Saddlery Retailer. Wholesalers. Ref: **YH13600**

STUBBINGTON TRAILERS

Stubbington Trailers, Nursery Workshop, Stubbington Lane, Fareham, **Hampshire**, PO14 2NF, **ENGLAND**.
(T) 01329 667535.
Profile Transport/Horse Boxes. Ref: **YH13601**

STUBBS, A

A Stubbs DWCF, 49 Hemsby Way, Westbury Pk, Clayton, Newcastle, **Staffordshire**, ST5 4QX, **ENGLAND**.
(T) 01782 625444.
Profile Farrier. Ref: **YH13602**

STUBBS, LINDA

Linda Stubbs, Hamilton Rd, Newmarket, **Suffolk**, CB8 7JQ, **ENGLAND**.
(T) 01638 661461 (F) 01638 666238
(M) 07931 954977
(W) www.newmarketracehorsetrainers.co.uk
Affiliated Bodies Newmarket Trainers Fed.
Contact/s
Trainer: Ms L Stubbs
Profile Trainer. Ref: **YH13603**

STUBLEY HOLLOW RIDING CTRE

Stubley Hollow Riding Centre, Stubley Farm, 84 Stubley Hollow, Dronfield, Sheffield, **Yorkshire (South)**, S18 6PA, **ENGLAND**.
(T) 01246 419207.
Contact/s
Owner: Mrs P Day Ref: **YH13604**

STUD & STABLE PHOTOGRAPHY

Stud & Stable Photography, 304-306 Hollins Lane, Hollins, Unsworth, **Lancashire**, BL9 8AY, **ENGLAND**.
(T) 0161 7967448.
Profile Photographer. Ref: **YH13605**

STUD FARM

Bradley Grange Stud, Woodstock Lodge, Shipton Lane, Wigginton, York, **Yorkshire (North)**, YO32 2RQ, **ENGLAND**.
(T) 01904 471247 (F) 01904 471249.
Contact/s
Owner: Mrs S Harrison
Profile Breeder. No.Staff: 2 Yr. Est: 1981
C.Size: 20 Acres Ref: **YH13606**

STUDIO 21

Studio 21, Rivendell, 4 Goodacre Orton, Goldhay, Peterborough, **Cambridgeshire**, PE2 0NZ, **ENGLAND**.
(T) 01733 370339. Ref: **YH13607**

STUDIO FORGE

Studio Forge, Offham, Lewes, **Sussex (East)**, BN7 3QD, **ENGLAND**.
(T) 01273 474173 (F) 01273 474173.
Contact/s
Owner: Mr R Heanley
Profile Blacksmith. Ref: **YH13608**

STUDIO PRINTS

Studio Prints, 23 Westway, Frome, **Somerset**, BA11 1BS, **ENGLAND**.
(T) 01373 464528 (F) 01373 451025.
Contact/s
Key Contact: Mr A Price Ref: **YH13609**

STUDLAND RIDING STABLES

Studland Riding Stables, Ferry Rd, Studland, Swanage, **Dorset**, BH19 3AQ, **ENGLAND**.
(T) 01929 450273.
Contact/s
Owner: Mr R Wheeler Ref: **YH13610**

STUDLAND SERVICES

Studland Services, Kimberley, Upper Benefield, Oundle, **Cambridgeshire**, PE8 5AN, **ENGLAND**.
(T) 01832 205116.
Profile Supplies. Ref: **YH13611**

STURDY, CONAN

Conan Sturdy, 28 Ladbroke Gr, London, **London (Greater)**, W11 3BQ, **ENGLAND**.
(T) 020 77276167 **(F)** 020 77929866.
Contact/s
Owner: Mr C Study **(Q)** BA
(E) conansturdy@ekno.com
Profile Blacksmith. Sculptor.
Horse sculptures, horse box repairs, welding and other metal work are available on request. Telephone for further information. Yr. Est: 1999
Opening Times
Sp: Open 09:00. Closed 18:00.
Su: Open 09:00. Closed 18:00.
Au: Open 09:00. Closed 18:00.
Wn: Open 09:00. Closed 18:00. **Ref: YH13612**

STURGE TRAILERS

Sturge (Brass) Trailers, Unit 1 Speedwell Rd, Parkhouse Ind Est, Parkhouse Ind Est Ea, Newcastle, **Staffordshire**, ST5 7RG, **ENGLAND**.
(T) 01782 562000 **(F)** 01782 561284.
Profile Transport/Horse Boxes. **Ref: YH13613**

STURGES, A M

Mrs A M Sturges, Downlands, Pilgrims Way, Kemsing, Sevenoaks, **Kent**, TN15 6XB, **ENGLAND**.
(T) 01732 763222.
Profile Breeder. **Ref: YH13614**

STURGESS SADDLERY

Sturgess Saddlery, Unit 1, 52 Short Acre St, Walsall, **Midlands (West)**, WS2 8HW, **ENGLAND**.
(T) 01922 620827 **(F)** 01922 620827.
Contact/s
Owner: Mr S Sturgess **Ref: YH13615**

STURGESS, NICHOLAS J

Nicholas J Sturgess DWCF, Wangfield Farm, Wangfield Lane, Curdridge, **Hampshire**, SO32 2DA, **ENGLAND**.
(T) 01489 782437.
Profile Farrier. **Ref: YH13616**

STURMAN, JOHN

John Sturman, Victoria Cornmills, Park St, Rowley Regis, Warley, **Midlands (West)**, B65 0LU, **ENGLAND**.
(T) 0121 5591175.
Profile Supplies. **Ref: YH13617**

STYLE PRODUCTS

Style Products, Aberdeen Nurseries, Dibden Lane, Mangotsfield, **Gloucestershire (South)**, BS16 7AG, **ENGLAND**.
(T) 01179 571253 **(F)** 01179 571253.
Profile Saddlery Retailer. **Ref: YH13618**

STYLES, JAMES

James Styles, 11 Binfield Hse, Binfield, Bracknell, **Berkshire**, RG42 5JG, **ENGLAND**.
(T) 01344 421559.
Profile Farrier. **Ref: YH13619**

STYLO MATCHMAKERS INT

Stylo Matchmakers International Ltd, Pk View Rd, Wibsey Pk Ave, Wibsey, Bradford, **Yorkshire (West)**, BD9 4PL, **ENGLAND**.
(T) 01274 711101 **(F)** 01274 711030
(W) www.masta.co.uku.
Profile Supplies. **Ref: YH13620**

SUDBURY STABLES

Sudbury Stables, Sudbury Rd, Downham, Billericay, **Essex**, CM11 1LB, **ENGLAND**.
(T) 01268 710410.
Profile Stable/Livery, Track/Course. **Ref: YH13621**

SUE ADAMS RIDING SCHOOL

Sue Adams Riding School, The Ox Hse, Shobdon, Leominster, **Herefordshire**, HR6 9LT, **ENGLAND**.
(T) 01568 708973 **(F)** 01544 388193
Affiliated Bodies BHS.
Contact/s
For Bookings: Ms B Webb **(Q)** BHSAI
Profile Equestrian Centre, Riding School, Trainer.
No.Staff: 5 Yr. Est: 1989 **Ref: YH13622**

SUFFOLK ANIMAL FEED

Suffolk Animal Feed & Equipment, North Lodge, Chedburgh Rd, Whepstead, Bury St Edmunds, **Suffolk**, IP29 4UB, **ENGLAND**.
(T) 01284 735220 **(F)** 01284 735220.
Profile Supplies. **Ref: YH13623**

SUFFOLK HORSE SOCIETY

Suffolk Horse Society, The Market Hill, Woodbridge, **Surrey**, IP12 4LU, **ENGLAND**.
(T) 01394 380643.
Contact/s
Key Contact: Mr P Ryder-Davies
Profile Club/Association. **Ref: YH13624**

SUFFOLK RIDING CLUB

Suffolk Riding Club, Stanstead Hall, Hitcham, Ipswich, **Suffolk**, IP7 7NY, **ENGLAND**.
(T) 01499 740270.
Contact/s
Chairman: Mr K Johnson
Profile Club/Association, Riding Club. **Ref: YH13625**

SUFFOLK SADDLES

Suffolk Saddles, The Covey, Chattisham Rd, Washbrook, Ipswich, **Suffolk**, IP8 3HB, **ENGLAND**.
(T) 01473 652563.
Contact/s
Owner: Mrs D Goldstone
Profile Saddlery Retailer, Supplies. No.Staff: 2
Yr. Est: 1986
Opening Times
Sp: Open Mon - Sat 09:00. Closed Mon - Sat 17:00.
Su: Open Mon - Sat 09:00. Closed Mon - Sat 17:00.
Au: Open Mon - Sat 09:00. Closed Mon - Sat 17:00.
Wn: Open Mon - Sat 09:00. Closed Mon - Sat 17:00.
Closed Sundays **Ref: YH13626**

SUGAR BROOK FARM FEEDS

Sugar Brook Farm Feeds, Ashley, Altrincham, **Cheshire**, WA14 3QB, **ENGLAND**.
(T) 0161 9268677.
Profile Supplies. **Ref: YH13627**

SULBY HALL

Sulby Hall Stud, Sulby Hall, Sulby, Northampton, **Northamptonshire**, NN6 6EZ, **ENGLAND**.
(T) 01858 880777 **(F)** 01858 880777.
Contact/s
Owner: Ms A Walton
Profile Breeder, Trainer. Yr. Est: 1980
Opening Times
Telephone for an appointment or further information, there is an answerphone **Ref: YH13628**

SUMMER FRESH

Summer Fresh, Tollgate Farm, Tollgate Rd, Colney Heath, **Hertfordshire**, AL4 0NY, **ENGLAND**.
(T) 01727 827096.
Profile Supplies. **Ref: YH13629**

SUMMERFIELDS SADDLERY

Summerfields Saddlery, 5 Chiltern Court, Back St, Wendover, Aylesbury, **Buckinghamshire**, HP22 6EB, **ENGLAND**.
(T) 01296 622081.
Profile Saddlery Retailer. **Ref: YH13630**

SUMMERHILL STUD

Summerhill Stud, Carnwath Mill, Carnwath, Lanark, **Lanarkshire (South)**, ML11 8LY, **SCOTLAND**.
(T) 01555 840150.
Profile Breeder. **Ref: YH13631**

SUMMERHOUSE

Summerhouse Equitation Centre, Brooklyn, Bath Rd, Hardwicke, Gloucester, **Gloucestershire**, GL2 4RG, **ENGLAND**.
(T) 01452 720288 **(F)** 01452 723688.
Contact/s
Owner: Mrs H Gallop
Profile Equestrian Centre, Riding School, Stable/Livery, Track/Course.
Training can be given to NVQ level. **Ref: YH13632**

SUMMERHOUSE FARM

Summerhouse Farm, Mimety, Malmesbury, **Wiltshire**, **ENGLAND**.
(T) 01666 860249.
Profile Riding School. **Ref: YH13633**

SUMMERHOUSE FARM RIDING CTRE

Summerhouse Farm Riding Centre, Summerhouse Farm, Minety, Malmesbury, **Wiltshire**, SN16 9RP, **ENGLAND**.
(T) 01666 860249.
Contact/s
Owner: Mr M Wood **Ref: YH13634**

SUMMERLEAZE VETNRY GROUP

Summerleaze Veterinary Group, The Veterinary Surgery, Summerleaze Rd, Maidenhead, **Berkshire**, SL6 8EW, **ENGLAND**.
(T) 01628 628121 **(F)** 01628 623462
(E) vets@summerleaze.demon.co.uk.
Profile Medical Support. **Ref: YH13635**

SUMMERS, J V

J V Summers, Green Farm, Twyford, Barrow-on-Trent, **Derbyshire**, DE7 1HJ, **ENGLAND**.
(T) 01283 704003.
Profile Farrier. **Ref: YH13636**

SUMMERS, PAUL

Paul Summers DWCF, 7 Freme Cl, West Derby, Liverpool, **Merseyside**, L11 9AA, **ENGLAND**.
(T) 0151 5464704.
Profile Farrier. **Ref: YH13637**

SUMNER, NICHOLAS J

Nicholas J Sumner DWCF, 7 Church Croft, Fownhope, **Herefordshire**, HR1 4PL, **ENGLAND**.
(T) 01432 860443.
Profile Farrier. **Ref: YH13638**

SUN ALLIANCE

Sun Alliance & London Insurance plc, 1 Bartholomew Lane, London, **London (Greater)**, EC2N 2AB, **ENGLAND**.
(T) 020 75882345 **(F)** 020 78261159.
Profile Club/Association. Insurance Company.
Ref: YH13639

SUN HILL FARM

Sun Hill Farm, Stonestile Rd, Headcorn, Ashford, **Kent**, TN27 9PG, **ENGLAND**.
(T) 01622 890698.
Contact/s
Owner: Mrs N Cook **Ref: YH13640**

SUNBEAM HACKNEY STUD

Sunbeam Hackney Stud, 15 Hedge Hill, Enfield, **London (Greater)**, EN2 8RU, **ENGLAND**.
(T) 020 89833547.
Profile Breeder. **Ref: YH13641**

SUNDERLAND TRAILER & TOWING

Sunderland Trailer & Towing Centre, Old School, Simpson St, Sunderland, **Tyne and Wear**, SR4 6DR, **ENGLAND**.
(T) 0191 5676427 **(F)** 0191 5676427.
Contact/s
Partner: Mr A Johnson
Profile Transport/Horse Boxes. **Ref: YH13642**

SUNDOWN STRAW

Sundown Straw Products Ltd, The Old Station, Tilbrook, Kimbolton, Huntingdon, **Cambridgeshire**, PE28 0JY, **ENGLAND**.
(T) 01480 860745 **(F)** 01480 860781
(E) sundownequine@hotmail.com
Affiliated Bodies BETA.
Contact/s
General Manager: Brian Porter
Profile Supplies.
Sundown Red is used at top racehorse stables.
No.Staff: 15
Opening Times
Sp: Open Mon - Fri 09:00. Closed Mon - Fri 17:00.
Su: Open Mon - Fri 09:00. Closed Mon - Fri 17:00.
Au: Open Mon - Fri 09:00. Closed Mon - Fri 17:00.
Wn: Open Mon - Fri 09:00. Closed Mon - Fri 17:00.
Closed weekends **Ref: YH13643**

SUNNYBANK STUD

Sunnybank Stud, Sunnybank Farm, Accrington Rd, Hapton, Burnley, **Lancashire**, BB11 5QG, **ENGLAND**.
(T) 01282 455820.
Contact/s
Owner: Mrs A Grogan
Profile Breeder. **Ref: YH13644**

SUNNYBRAE FEEDS

Sunnybrae Feeds, Sunnybrae, Kirkwall, **Orkney Isles**, KW15 1TP, **SCOTLAND**.
(T) 01856 874594 **(F)** 01856 876239.
Profile Saddlery Retailer. **Ref: YH13645**

SUNNYHILL STUD

Sunnyhill Stud, Kildare, **County Kildare**, **IRELAND**.
(T) 045 481201 **(F)** 045 481310
(E) sunnyhillstud@kildarehorse.ie.
Contact/s
Key Contact: Mr M Hickey
Profile Breeder. **Ref: YH13646**

SUNNYMEAD FARM

Sunnymead Farm, Codrington Rd, Westerleigh, Bristol, **Bristol**, BS37 8RG, **ENGLAND**.
(T) 01454 312334.
Profile Stable/Livery. **Ref: YH13647**

SUNNYMEADE COUNTRY HOTEL

Sunnymeade Country Hotel, Ilfracombe, **Devon**, EX34 8NT, **ENGLAND**.
(T) 01271 863668 **(F)** 01271 863668.
Profile Stable/Livery. **Ref: YH13648**

SUNNYSIDE

Sunnyside Livery Stables & Carriage Driving Centre, Sunnyside Stables, Cults, Aberdeen, **Aberdeen (City of)**, AB15 9QJ, **SCOTLAND**.
(T) 01224 867262.
Contact/s
Owner: Mrs L McRonald
Profile Stable/Livery, Trainer.
Hacking is available with no road work. Livery is also on offer, details on request. **Ref: YH13649**

SUNNYSIDE HOTEL

Sunnyside Hotel, Camelford, **Cornwall**, PL32 9XB, **ENGLAND**.
(T) 01840 22250.
Profile Equestrian Centre. **Ref: YH13650**

SUNRAY STUD

Sunray Stud, Barr Lakes Lane, Aldridge, Walsall, **Midlands (West)**, WS9 0PG, **ENGLAND**.
(T) 0121 3582344.
Contact/s
Owner: Mr T Ray
Profile Breeder. **Ref: YH13651**

SUNSHINE RIDING SCHOOL

Sunshine Riding School, Warden Hill Rd, Luton, **Bedfordshire**, LU2 7AE, **ENGLAND**.
(T) 01582 505040.
Contact/s
General Manager: Ms L Moule
Profile Riding School.
Hacking is available.
Opening Times
Sp: Open Mon - Sun 09:00. Closed Mon - Sun 17:00.
Su: Open Mon - Sun 09:00. Closed Mon - Sun 17:00.
Au: Open Mon - Sun 09:00. Closed Mon - Sun 17:00.
Wn: Open Mon - Sun 09:00. Closed Mon - Sun 17:00. **Ref: YH13652**

SUPERIOR PORTRAITS

Superior Portraits, 51 New St John's Rd, St Hellier, **Jersey**, JE2, **ENGLAND**.
(T) 01534 22339. **Ref: YH13653**

SUPERPET THE HORSE SHOP

Superpet The Horse Shop, 223 Firtree Rd, Epsom Downs, Epsom, **Surrey**, KT17 3LB, **ENGLAND**.
(T) 01737 371137
(W) www.superpethorseshop.co.uk.
Contact/s
Owner: Ms A Brown
Profile Supplies.
Medical supplies. Stable equipment
Opening Times
Sp: Open Mon - Fri 09:00. Closed Mon - Fri 17:30.
Su: Open Mon - Fri 09:00. Closed Mon - Fri 17:30.
Au: Open Mon - Fri 09:00. Closed Mon - Fri 17:30.
Wn: Open Mon - Fri 09:00. Closed Mon - Fri 17:30.
Ref: YH13654

SUPERPET THE HORSE SHOP

Superpet The Horse Shop, 1 Mogador Rd, Tadworth, **Surrey**, KT20 7EW, **ENGLAND**.
(T) 01737 221722
(W) www.superpethorseshop.co.uk.
Contact/s
Owner: Ms A Brown
Profile Supplies.
Medical Supplies. Stable equipment
Opening Times
Sp: Open Mon - Fri 09:30. Closed Mon - Fri 17:30.
Su: Open Mon - Fri 09:30. Closed Mon - Fri 17:30.
Au: Open Mon - Fri 09:30. Closed Mon - Fri 17:30.
Wn: Open Mon - Fri 09:30. Closed Mon - Fri 17:30.
Ref: YH13655

SUPERPET THE HORSE SHOP

Superpet The Horse Shop, 6 Eastgate, Banstead, **Surrey**, SM7 1AG, **ENGLAND**.
(T) 01737 357060
(W) www.superpethorseshop.co.uk.
Contact/s
Owner: Ms A Brown
Profile Supplies.
Medical supplies. Stable equipment
Opening Times
Sp: Open Mon - Fri 08:30. Closed Mon - Fri 17:30.
Su: Open Mon - Fri 08:30. Closed Mon - Fri 17:30.
Au: Open Mon - Fri 08:30. Closed Mon - Fri 17:30.
Wn: Open Mon - Fri 08:30. Closed Mon - Fri 17:30.
Ref: YH13656

SUPPLE, K R

Mr K R Supple, 1 Park Farm Cottage, Park Farm, Wrotham, **Kent**, TN15 7RE, **ENGLAND**.
(T) 01732 885237.
Profile Supplies. **Ref: YH13657**

SURREY HACKING & RIDING CTRE

Surrey Hacking & Riding Centre, Brook Farm, Brook, Albury, Guildford, **Surrey**, GU5 9DJ, **ENGLAND**.
(T) 01483 202604 (F) 01483 202604.
Contact/s
Owner: Mr T Jones
Profile Riding School. **Ref: YH13658**

SUSEX FARM STABLES

Susex Farm Stables, Sussex Farm, Brancaster, King's Lynn, **Norfolk**, PE31 8AJ, **ENGLAND**.
(T) 01328 730159. **Ref: YH13659**

SUSSEX EQUESTRIAN CLUB

Sussex Equestrian Club, West Wolves Farm, Billingshurst Rd, Ashington, Pulborough, **Sussex (West)**, RH20 3AY, **ENGLAND**.
(T) 01903 892798.
Contact/s
Owner: Mrs Y Ellis **Ref: YH13660**

SUSSEX FARM STABLES

Sussex Farm Stables, Sussex Farm, Burnham Market, King's Lynn, **Norfolk**, PE31 8JY, **ENGLAND**.
(T) 01328 730159.
Profile Stable/Livery. **Ref: YH13661**

SUSSEX STUD

Sussex Stud (The), Park Farm, West Grinstead, Horsham, **Sussex (West)**, RH13 8LP, **ENGLAND**.
(T) 01403 864223 (F) 01403 864092.
Contact/s
Manager: Paul Buckfield
Profile Breeder. **Ref: YH13662**

SUSSEX TOWING BRACKETS

Sussex Towing Brackets, 56 Teville Rd, Worthing, **Sussex (West)**, BN11 1UY, **ENGLAND**.
(T) 01903 216215 (F) 01903 216215.
Contact/s
Owner: Mr R Martin
Profile Transport/Horse Boxes. **Ref: YH13663**

SUTCLIFFE ELECTRONICS

Sutcliffe Electronics, 15 West St, Hothfield, Ashford, **Kent**, TN26 1ET, **ENGLAND**.
(T) 01233 634191 (F) 01233 639269
(E) sales@sutcliffe-electronics.co.uk.
Profile Supplies. **Ref: YH13664**

SUTCLIFFE, ANTHONY W

Anthony W Sutcliffe AFCL, Rose Cottage & Forge, Hilfield, Dorchester, **Dorset**, DT2 7BD, **ENGLAND**.
(T) 01963 210552.
Profile Farrier. **Ref: YH13665**

SUTCLIFFE, R

Mr & Mrs R Sutcliffe, Higher Coney Farm, Off Granville Rd, Darwen, **Lancashire**, BB3 2UB, **ENGLAND**.
(T) 01253 776389.
Profile Breeder. **Ref: YH13666**

SUTHERLAND, G

G Sutherland, Unit 3 Dumbryden Ind Est, 20 Dumbryden Rd, Edinburgh, **Edinburgh (City of)**, EH14 2AB, **SCOTLAND**.
(T) 0131 4585442 (F) 0131 4585442.
Contact/s
Partner: Mr G Sutherland
Profile Blacksmith. **Ref: YH13667**

SUTTON ARABIAN STUD

Sutton Arabian Stud, Sutton Hall, Stalham, Norwich, **Norfolk**, NR12 9RZ, **ENGLAND**.
(T) 01692 580934.
Profile Breeder. **Ref: YH13668**

SUTTON BONINGTON RIDING CLUB

Sutton Bonington Riding Club, Old Plough Cottage, 20 Main St, Sutton Bonington, Loughborough, **Leicestershire**, LE12 5NE, **ENGLAND**.
(T) 01509 672507.
Contact/s
Chairman: Mr C Tom
Profile Club/Association, Riding Club. **Ref: YH13669**

SUTTON COLDFIELD & DISTRICT

Sutton Coldfield & District Riding Club, 36 Clarendon Rd, Four Oaks, Sutton Coldfield, **Midlands (West)**, B75 5JY, **ENGLAND**.
(T) 0121 3086784.
Profile Club/Association, Riding Club. **Ref: YH13670**

SUTTON COURT FARM

Sutton Court Farm, Easthampstead Rd, Wokingham, **Berkshire**, RG40 3BS, **ENGLAND**.
(T) 0118 9783980.
Profile Stable/Livery. **Ref: YH13671**

SUTTON FIELDS FARM

Sutton Fields Farm, Chester Rd, Sutton Weaver, Runcorn, **Cheshire**, WA7 3EY, **ENGLAND**.
(T) 01928 701236.
Profile Stable/Livery. **Ref: YH13672**

SUTTON MANOR FARM

Sutton Manor Farm, Sutton-Cum-Lound, Retford, **Nottinghamshire**, DN22 8PJ, **ENGLAND**.
(T) 01777 705995
Affiliated Bodies ABRS.
Contact/s
Owner: Mrs M Dunn
Profile Riding School, Stable/Livery.
DIY livery is available, and there is an on site ABRS examiner. Lessons are given on own ponies/horses. Telephone for further information Yr. Est: 1968
Opening Times
Private lessons by appointment **Ref: YH13673**

SUTTON MILL RIDING & SADDLERY

Sutton Mill Riding & Saddlery Centre, Sutton Mill, Sutton Lane, Middlewich, **Cheshire**, CW10 0ES, **ENGLAND**.
(T) 01606 832364.
Contact/s
Owner: Mrs M Broad
Profile Riding School. **Ref: YH13674**

SUTTON OAKS

Sutton Oaks Transport, Fyne Court Farm, Broomfield, Bridgwater, **Somerset**, TA5 2EQ, **ENGLAND**.
(T) 01823 451632
Affiliated Bodies NTF.
Contact/s
Owner: Mr P Purdy (T) 07860 392786
Profile Breeder, Trainer, Transport/Horse Boxes.
Opening Times
Telephone for further information **Ref: YH13675**

SUTTON SADDLERY

Sutton Saddlery, Hillwood Rd, Sutton Coldfield, **Midlands (West)**, B75 5QN, **ENGLAND**.
(T) 07774 829274. **Ref: YH13676**

SUTTON, GRAHAM T

Graham T Sutton FWCF, 24 Audley Cres, Hereford, **Herefordshire**, HR1 1BW, **ENGLAND**.
(T) 01432 274701.
Profile Farrier. **Ref: YH13677**

SUTTON, PAUL

Paul Sutton, Middlewood Farm, Threapwood, Malpas, **Cheshire**, SY14 7AW, **ENGLAND**.
(T) 01948 770462 (F) 01948 770466. **Ref: YH13678**

SUZANNE'S RIDING SCHOOL

Suzanne's Riding School, Brookshill Farm, Brookshill Drive, Harrow, **London (Greater)**, HA3 6SB, **ENGLAND**.
(T) 020 89543618 (F) 020 84206461
Affiliated Bodies ABRS, BHS.
Contact/s
Administration: Ms C Mills
Profile Riding School, Stable/Livery. Yr. Est: 1940
C.Size: 300 Acres
Opening Times
Sp: Open Tues - Sun 09:00. Closed Tues - Sun 18:00.
Su: Open Tues - Sun 09:00. Closed Tues - Sun 18:00.
Au: Open Tues - Sun 09:00. Closed Tues - Sun 18:00.
Wn: Open Tues - Sun 09:00. Closed Tues - Sun 18:00.
Closed Mondays **Ref: YH13679**

SVENSSON, MARK ANDREW

Mark Andrew Svensson RSS, Harepath Cottage, Whiddon Down, Okehampton, **Devon**, EX20 2PW, **ENGLAND**.
(T) 07860 590302.
Profile Farrier. **Ref: YH13680**

SWAFFHAM STABLES

Swaffham Stables, Pedlars Hse, Norwich Rd, Swaffham, **Norfolk**, PE37 8DG, **ENGLAND**.
(T) 01760 720133. **Ref: YH13681**

SWAFIELD RIDING

Swafield Riding, Swafield Hse, Swafield, North

Walsham, **Norfolk**, NR28 0QT, **ENGLAND**.
(T) 01692 402348.
Contact/s
Owner: Miss A Slack
Profile Riding School, Stable/Livery. Ref: YH13682

SWAINES HILL STUD

Swaines Hill Stud, South Warnborough, Hook, **Hampshire**, RG29 1SA, **ENGLAND**.
(T) 01256 862245 (F) 01256 862236.
Profile Breeder. Ref: YH13683

SWALE VETNRY SURGERY

Swale Veterinary Surgery, Fairfield Way, Gallowfields Trading Est, Richmond, **Yorkshire (North)**, DL10 4TB, **ENGLAND**.
(T) 01748 822389 (F) 01748 850195.
Contact/s
Vet: Mr R Phillips
Profile Medical Support. Ref: YH13684

SWALLOW SADDLERY

Swallow Saddlery, Coombe Farm, Wilsthorpe, Stamford, **Lincolnshire**, PE9 4PD, **ENGLAND**.
(T) 01778 560574 (F) 01778 561562.
Contact/s
Owner: Mr H Knipe
Profile Saddlery Retailer. Yr. Est: 1993
Opening Times
Sp: Open Mon - Sat 09:00. Closed Mon - Sat 17:00.
Su: Open Mon - Sat 09:00. Closed Mon - Sat 17:00.
Au: Open Mon - Sat 09:00. Closed Mon - Sat 17:00.
Wn: Open Mon - Sat 09:00. Closed Mon - Sat 17:00.
Closed Sundays Ref: YH13685

SWALLOWFIELD EQUESTRIAN

Swallowfield Equestrian Ltd, Rising Lane, Lapworth, Solihull, **Warwickshire**, B94 6JD, **ENGLAND**.
(T) 01564 784475 (F) 01564 784475
(E) jo.swain@swallowfield.net
(W) www.swallowfield.net.
Profile Arena, Equestrian Centre, Riding School, Stable/Livery. Ref: YH13686

SWALLOWFIELD STABLES

Swallowfield Stables, Ford Lane, Edlesborough, Dunstable, **Bedfordshire**, LU6 2JE, **ENGLAND**.
(T) 01525 220398.
Contact/s
Owner: Mrs C Planton
Profile Stable/Livery.
Full, part and DIY livery available, prices on request.
Yr. Est: 1974 C.Size: 14 Acres
Opening Times
Telephone between 09:00 - 19:00 Ref: YH13687

SWAN GALLERY

Swan Gallery, 51 Cheap St, Sherborne, **Dorset**, DT9 3AX, **ENGLAND**.
(T) 01935 814465 (F) 01308 868195. Ref: YH13688

SWAN LODGE

Swan Lodge Ltd, Manor Barn Farm, Station Rd, Upper Broughton, Melton Mowbray, **Leicestershire**, LE14 3BH, **ENGLAND**.
(T) 01664 823686 (F) 01664 822832
(E) swanlodge@btconnect.com
(W) www.mmrc.co.uk
Affiliated Bodies BHS.
Contact/s
Owner: Miss A Jalland (Q) BHSAI
Profile Horse/Rider Accom, Riding Club, Stable/Livery.
Full, part & DIY livery are available, details on request.
No.Staff: 5 Yr. Est: 1988 C.Size: 120 Acres
Opening Times
Telephone for further details Ref: YH13689

SWAN, CECIL T

Cecil T Swan, Johnsons Yard, Overbury, Tewkesbury, **Gloucestershire**, GL20 7NT, **ENGLAND**.
(T) 01386 725245 (F) 01386 725245.
Contact/s
Owner: Mr C Swan
Profile Farrier. Ref: YH13690

SWAN, CECIL T

Cecil T Swan, Unit 1/2/Redwood Hse, Orchard Ind Est, Toddington, Cheltenham, **Gloucestershire**, GL54 5EB, **ENGLAND**.
(T) 01242 621590 (F) 01242 621591.
Contact/s
Owner: Mr C Swan
Profile Farrier. Ref: YH13691

SWANKEY, KASPAR

Kaspar Swankey, The Forge, Kew Bridge Steam Museum, Green Dragon Lane, Brentford, **London (Greater)**, TW8 0EN, **ENGLAND**.
(T) 020 85684459.
Contact/s
Owner: Mr K Swankey
Profile Blacksmith. Ref: YH13692

SWANLAND EQUESTRIAN CTRE

Swanland Equestrian Centre, Westfield Lane, Swanland, North Ferriby, **Yorkshire (East)**, HU14 3PG, **ENGLAND**.
(T) 01482 631485.
Contact/s
Owner: Mr M McCallum
Profile Saddlery Retailer, Stable/Livery.
Ref: YH13693

SWANSCOTT, ROBERT L

Robert L Swanscott DWCF, 158 Bull Lane, Eccles, Aylesford, **Kent**, ME20 7HW, **ENGLAND**.
(T) 01622 715880.
Profile Farrier. Ref: YH13694

SWANSEA & DISTRICT PC

Swansea & District Branch of the Pony Club, 53 Headland Rd, Bishopston, Swansea, **Swansea**, SA3 3HD, **WALES**.
(T) 01792 232665. Ref: YH13695

SWANSTON STABLES

Swanston Stables, Swanston Rd, Edinburgh, **Edinburgh (City of)**, EH10 7DS, **SCOTLAND**.
(T) 0131 4453152.
Contact/s
Owner: Mrs P Stephenson Ref: YH13696

SWANWICK, KIM R

Kim R Swanwick AFCL BI, 99 Baldocks Lane, Melton Mowbray, **Leicestershire**, LE13 1EP, **ENGLAND**.
(T) 01664 61078.
Profile Farrier. Ref: YH13697

SWATHWICK FARM LIVERIES

Swathwick Farm Liveries, Swathwick Farm, Swathwick Lane, Wingerworth, Chesterfield, **Derbyshire**, S42 6QP, **ENGLAND**.
(T) 01246 231468.
Profile Stable/Livery. Ref: YH13698

SWAYNE & PARTNERS

Swayne & Partners (Bury St Edmunds), 34 Southgate St, Bury St Edmunds, **Suffolk**, IP33 2AZ, **ENGLAND**.
(T) 01284 701444 (F) 01284 724365.
Profile Medical Support. Ref: YH13699

SWAYNE & PARTNERS

Swayne & Partners (Newmarket), The Maltings, Fordham Rd, Newmarket, **Suffolk**, CB8 7AA, **ENGLAND**.
(T) 01638 662253.
Profile Medical Support. Ref: YH13700

SWAYNE & PARTNERS

Swayne & Partners (Sudbury), Little St Mary's, Long Melford, Sudbury, **Suffolk**, CO10 9HY, **ENGLAND**.
(T) 01787 370773 (F) 01787 313925.
Profile Medical Support. Ref: YH13701

SWEDISH COTTAGE ANIMAL FEEDS

Swedish Cottage Animal Feeds, The Turnpike, Leicester Rd, Earl Shilton, **Leicestershire**, LE9 7TJ, **ENGLAND**.
(T) 01455 842526.
Contact/s
Owner: Mr B Littlehales
Profile Supplies. Ref: YH13702

SWEET, PETER & MARILYN

Peter & Marilyn Sweet, Lochinver, 21 Lymbridge Drive, Blackrod, Bolton, **Manchester (Greater)**, BL6 5TH, **ENGLAND**.
(T) 01204 695793 (F) 01204 695793
(M) 07885 719178
(E) prsweet@aol.com. Ref: YH13703

SWETTENHAM STUD

Swettenham Stud, Manton Hse Est, Marlborough, **Wiltshire**, SN8 1PN, **ENGLAND**.
(T) 01672 514901 (F) 01672 516806.
Contact/s
Owner: Mr H Sarsfield
Profile Breeder. Ref: YH13704

SWIERS, J E

Mr J E Swiers, Norton Hse, Norton-Le-Clay, Helperby, **Yorkshire (North)**, YO61 2RS, **ENGLAND**.
(T) 01423 322153.
Profile Supplies. Ref: YH13705

SWIFT MANOR FARM

Swift Manor Farm, Preston St. Mary, Sudbury, **Suffolk**, CO10 9NL, **ENGLAND**.
(T) 01449 740862.
Profile Riding School. Ref: YH13706

SWILLINGTON TRAILER CTRE

Swillington Trailer Centre, Goody Cross Lane, Swillington, Leeds, **Yorkshire (West)**, LS26 8UU, **ENGLAND**.
(T) 0113 2871463.
Contact/s
Owner: Mr G Wagstaff
Profile Transport/Horse Boxes. Ref: YH13707

SWINBANK, ALAN

Alan Swinbank (Bloodstock), Thorndale Farms, Melsonby, Richmond, **Yorkshire (North)**, DL10 5NJ, **ENGLAND**.
(T) 01325 377318 (F) 01325 377796
(M) 07860 368365.
Profile Blood Stock Agency. Ref: YH13708

SWINDIN, S J

S J Swindin, Deans Farm, Main St, Mattersey, Doncaster, **Yorkshire (South)**, DN10 5DY, **ENGLAND**.
(T) 01777 817695.
Contact/s
Owner: Mr S Swindin
Profile Farrier. Ref: YH13709

SWINDLEHURST, D G

Mr D G Swindlehurst, Lynefoot, Westlinton, Carlisle, **Cumbria**, CA6 6AJ, **ENGLAND**.
(T) 01228 74376.
Profile Supplies. Ref: YH13710

SWINDON VOLVO TRAILER HIRE

Swindon Volvo Spares Trailer Hire, 4 Beckett Stables, Northford, Shrivenham, Swindon, **Wiltshire**, SN6 8EY, **ENGLAND**.
(T) 01793 784313 (F) 01793 784313.
Contact/s
Owner: Mr C Haynes
Profile Transport/Horse Boxes. Ref: YH13711

SWINFORD PADDOCK STUD

Swinford Paddock Stud, Six Mile Bottom, Newmarket, **Suffolk**, CB8 0UE, **ENGLAND**.
(T) 01638 570232.
Contact/s
Owner: Mr P Bottomly
Profile Breeder. Ref: YH13712

SWINTON PARK

Swinton Park Limited, Masham, Ripon, **Yorkshire (North)**, HG4 4JH, **ENGLAND**.
(T) 01765 680900 (F) 01765 680901
(E) office@swintonpark.com
(W) www.swintonpark.co.uk.
Contact/s
Owner: Mr M Cunliffe-Lister (T) 01765 680945
(E) mark@swintonpark.com
Profile Horse/Rider Accom, Track/Course.
No.Staff: 21 Yr. Est: 2001 C.Size: 200 Acres
Opening Times
Sp: Open Mon - Sun 24 Hours.
Su: Open Mon - Sun 24 Hours.
Au: Open Mon - Sun 24 Hours.
Wn: Open Mon - Sun 24 Hours. Ref: YH13713

SWINTON RIDING/TREKKING CTRE

Swinton Riding & Trekking Centre, Home Farm, Masham, Ripon, **Yorkshire (North)**, HG4 4NS, **ENGLAND**.
(T) 01765 689636.
Profile Breeder, Riding School. Ref: YH13714

SWISH

Swish Limited, P O Box 107, Potters Bar, **Hertfordshire**, EN6 1ZG, **ENGLAND**.
(T) 01707 644066 (F) 01707 653107
(E) info@swish.ltd.uk. Ref: YH13715

SWISS COTTAGE STABLES

Swiss Cottage Stables, School Rd, Marshland St. James, Wisbech, **Cambridgeshire**, PE14 8EZ, **ENGLAND**.
(T) 01945 430315.
Contact/s
Owner: Mrs K Whitby
Profile Riding School. Ref: YH13716

SWISS VALLEY EQUESTRIAN CTRE

Swiss Valley Equestrian Centre, Norton's Wood

Lane, Clevedon, **Somerset (North)**, BS21 7AF, **ENGLAND**.
(T) 01179 340170.
Profile Riding School. **Ref: YH13717**

SWORDHILL EQUESTRIAN

Swordhill Equestrian Training Centre, The Grange, Stalmine, Blackpool, **Lancashire**, FY6 0JR, **ENGLAND**.
(T) 01253 700216.
Profile Riding School. **Ref: YH13718**

SYCAMORE HOUSE FARM

Sycamore House Farm, 2 Denison Trce, North Rigton, Leeds, **Yorkshire (West)**, LS17 0DJ, **ENGLAND**.
(T) 01423 734482.
Contact/s
Owner: Mr C McGram
Profile Stable/Livery, Trainer. **Ref: YH13719**

SYDDALL, G

Mr G Syddall, Lower Giles Farm, Knowsley Lane, Edgeworth, Turton, Bolton, **Manchester (Greater)**, **ENGLAND**.
(T) 01204 852333.
Profile Breeder. **Ref: YH13720**

SYDNEY FREE

Sydney Free (Saddlers) Ltd, 54 Querns Lane, Cirencester, **Gloucestershire**, GL7 1RH, **ENGLAND**.
(T) 01285 655384.
Contact/s
Manager: Ms H Ormonde
Profile Saddlery Retailer. **Ref: YH13721**

SYDNEY INGRAM & SON

Sydney Ingram & Son, 44 Catherine St, Salisbury, **Wiltshire**, SP1 2DD, **ENGLAND**.
(T) 01722 333802.
Contact/s
Partner: Mr C Ingram
Profile Riding Wear Retailer, Saddlery Retailer.
Family based Company. **Yr. Est:** 1921
Opening Times
Sp: Open Mon - Sun 09:00. Closed Mon - Sat 17:30, Wed 17:00.
Su: Open Mon - Sat 09:00. Closed Mon - Sat 17:30, Wed 17:00.
Au: Open Mon - Sat 09:00. Closed Mon - Sat 17:30, Wed 17:00.
Wn: Open Mon - Sat 09:00. Closed Mon - Sat 17:30, Wed 17:00. **Ref: YH13722**

SYKEHOUSE ARENA

Sykehouse Arena, Holmpton Farm, Broad Lane, Sykehouse, Doncaster, **Yorkshire (South)**, DN14 9AX, **ENGLAND**.
(T) 01405 785231.
Contact/s
Owner: Miss K McNicolas
Profile Arena, Stable/Livery. **Yr. Est:** 1995
Opening Times
Sp: Open Mon - Sun 08:00. Closed Mon - Sun 20:00.
Su: Open Mon - Sun 08:00. Closed Mon - Sun 20:00.
Au: Open Mon - Sun 08:00. Closed Mon - Sun 20:00.
Wn: Open Mon - Sun 08:00. Closed Mon - Sun 20:00. **Ref: YH13723**

SYKES, SCOTT S

Scott S Sykes DWCF, Beck Cottage, 10 Dunholme Rd, Welton, **Lincolnshire**, LN2 3RS, **ENGLAND**.
(T) 01673 860452.
Profile Farrier. **Ref: YH13724**

SYMONDS SADDLERY

Symonds Saddlery, 7a Birmingham Rd, Walsall, **Midlands (West)**, WS1 2LT, **ENGLAND**.
(T) 01922 639821 **(F)** 01922 639821.
Contact/s
Owner: Mr R Symonds
Profile Saddlery Retailer. **Ref: YH13725**

SYMONDSBURY STUD

Symondsbury Stud, Yew Tree Farm, Nash Lane, Scaynes Hill, Haywards Heath, **Sussex (West)**, RH17 7NJ, **ENGLAND**.
(T) 01444 831236 **(F)** 01444 831236.
Contact/s
General Manager: Mrs L Company
(E) jaulyn@aol.com
Profile Breeder, Stable/Livery. **No.Staff:** 5
Yr. Est: 1975 **C.Size:** 500 Acres
Opening Times
Telephone for an appointment **Ref: YH13726**

T & A TRAILERS

T & A Trailers, Shrubbery Farm, Daniels Lane, Walsall, **Midlands (West)**, WS9 0RS, **ENGLAND**.
(T) 01922 452456 **(F)** 01922 458153.
Contact/s
Owner: Mr T Neachell
Profile Transport/Horse Boxes. **Ref: YH13727**

T A HULME & SONS

T A Hulme & Sons, Abners, Winchester Rd, Upham, Southampton, **Hampshire**, SO32 1HH, **ENGLAND**.
(T) 01489 860324 **(F)** 01489 860324.
Contact/s
Owner: Mr G Hulme
Profile Transport/Horse Boxes. **Ref: YH13728**

T A T SERVICES

T A T Services Ltd, 4 Heathcote Pl, Old Station Rd, Newmarket, **Suffolk**, CB8 8GB, **ENGLAND**.
(T) 01638 668958 **(F)** 01638 668962.
Contact/s
Manager: Mrs B Fitzgerald
Profile Supplies. **Ref: YH13729**

T ASCROFT & SON

T Ascroft & Son, Mere Brow, Tarleton, Preston, **Lancashire**, PR4 6JT, **ENGLAND**.
(T) 01772 812256.
Profile Supplies. **Ref: YH13730**

T B BARFI

T B Barfi Ltd, Woodcote Stud, Wilmerhatch Lane, Epsom, **Surrey**, KT18 7EH, **ENGLAND**.
(T) 01372 722633.
Profile Blood Stock Agency. **Ref: YH13731**

T C FEEDS

T C Feeds, Dove Hse Lane, Kensworth, Dunstable, **Bedfordshire**, LU6 2PQ, **ENGLAND**.
(T) 01582 872333 **(F)** 01582 872511.
Contact/s
Manager: David A Smith
Profile Feed Merchant. **Ref: YH13732**

T C TACK & THINGS

T C Tack & Things, 3 Valebridge Rd, Burgess Hill, **Sussex (West)**, RH15 0RA, **ENGLAND**.
(T) 01444 230709 **(F)** 01444 230709
(M) 07801 295783.
Profile Saddlery Retailer. **Ref: YH13733**

T C TRAILER

T C Trailer & Tow-Bar Service, Well Head Farm, Lothersdale Rd, Glusburn, Keighley, **Yorkshire (West)**, BD20 8JD, **ENGLAND**.
(T) 01535 633509 **(F)** 01535 633509.
Contact/s
Owner: Mr T Critchley
Profile Transport/Horse Boxes.
Supply and fit towbars. Servicing and repair of trailers, towbars and horseboxes **No.Staff:** 2
Yr. Est: 1981
Opening Times
Sp: Open Mon - Fri 08:30, Sat, 09:00. Closed Mon - Fri 17:30, Sat 12:00.
Su: Open Mon - Fri 08:30, Sat, 09:00. Closed Mon - Fri 17:30, Sat 12:00.
Au: Open Mon - Fri 08:30, Sat, 09:00. Closed Mon - Fri 17:30, Sat 12:00.
Wn: Open Mon - Fri 08:30, Sat, 09:00. Closed Mon - Fri 17:30, Sat 12:00. **Ref: YH13734**

T CONNOLLY & SONS

T Connolly & Sons, 3 Phibsboro Rd, Dublin, **County Dublin**, **IRELAND**.
(T) 01 8301874.
Profile Supplies. **Ref: YH13735**

T E FRASER & SON

T E Fraser & Son, North St, Midhurst, **Sussex (West)**, GU29 9DW, **ENGLAND**.
(T) 01730 813122.
Profile Saddlery Retailer. **Ref: YH13736**

T EBENEZER & SON

T Ebenezer & Son, Felinfach Hse, Llangeitho, Tregaron, **Ceredigion**, SY25 6QQ, **WALES**.
(T) 01974 821211.
Contact/s
Partner: Mrs A Ebenezer
Profile Transport/Horse Boxes. **Ref: YH13737**

T F R C

T F R C, The Kerse Nursery, Kilbirnie Rd, Lochwinnoch, **Renfrewshire**, PA12 4DT, **SCOTLAND**.
(T) 01505 53804.
Profile Supplies. **Ref: YH13738**

T F S

T F S Country Store, Liverpool Rd, Buckley, **Flintshire**, CH7 3LJ, **WALES**.
(T) 01244 548901 **(F)** 01244 548901.
Contact/s
Owner: Mrs W Thompson
Profile Riding Wear Retailer, Supplies. **No.Staff:** 5
Yr. Est: 1985
Opening Times
Sp: Open Mon - Sat 08:30, Sun 09:00. Closed Mon - Fri 17:30, Sat 17:00, Sun 16:00.
Su: Open Mon - Sat 08:30, Sun 09:00. Closed Mon - Fri 17:30, Sat 17:00, Sun 16:00.
Au: Open Mon - Sat 08:30, Sun 09:00. Closed Mon - Fri 17:30, Sat 17:00, Sun 16:00.
Wn: Open Mon - Sat 08:30, Sun 09:00. Closed Mon - Fri 17:30, Sat 17:00, Sun 16:00. **Ref: YH13739**

T G FOOT LONGLANE STABLES

T G Foot Longlane Stables, Pen Selwood, Wincanton, **Somerset**, BA9 8NJ, **ENGLAND**.
(T) 01747 840283.
Contact/s
Partner: Mrs H Foot **Ref: YH13740**

T G JEARY

T G Jeary Ltd, Agricentre, Station Rd, Calne, **Wiltshire**, SN11 0JS, **ENGLAND**.
(T) 01249 814700 **(F)** 01249 821529.
Profile Saddlery Retailer. **Ref: YH13741**

T H BLETSOE & SON

T H Bletsoe & Son, Oakleigh Hse, 28 High St, Thrapston, Kettering, **Northamptonshire**, NN14 4LJ, **ENGLAND**.
(T) 01832 732206 **(F)** 01832 733807.
Profile Breeder. **Ref: YH13742**

T H R ENGINEERING

T H R Engineering, Bostock Green, Bostock, Middlewich, **Cheshire**, CW10 9JP, **ENGLAND**.
(T) 01606 863456.
Contact/s
Owner: Mr T Rowland
Profile Blacksmith. **Ref: YH13743**

T H SKINNER

T H Skinner (Services) Ltd, Drayton, Belbroughton, Stourbridge, **Midlands (West)**, DY9 0BN, **ENGLAND**.
(T) 01562 730027 **(F)** 01562 730425.
Contact/s
Owner: Mr D Cooper
Profile Blacksmith. **Ref: YH13744**

T H WHITE

T H White Ltd (Tetbury), Sherston Works, Knockdown, Tetbury, **Gloucestershire**, GL8 8QY, **ENGLAND**.
(T) 01454 238181.
Profile Supplies. **Ref: YH13745**

T H WHITE

T H White Ltd, London Rd, Marlborough, **Wiltshire**, SN8 2RN, **ENGLAND**.
(T) 01672 512328.
Profile Supplies. **Ref: YH13746**

T I P

T I P, Oxney Rd, Peterborough, **Cambridgeshire**, PE1 5YW, **ENGLAND**.
(T) 01733 313931 **(F)** 01733 553993.
Contact/s
Branch Manager: Mr R Gregory
Profile Transport/Horse Boxes. **Ref: YH13747**

T I P C T R

T I P C T R, Griff Clara Ind Est, Griff Lane, Griff, Nuneaton, **Warwickshire**, CV10 7PP, **ENGLAND**.
(T) 024 76322500 **(F)** 024 76322494.
Profile Transport/Horse Boxes. **Ref: YH13748**

T I P C T R TRAILER RENTAL

T I P C T R Trailer Rental, Old Hall Rd, Sale, **Cheshire**, M33 2HG, **ENGLAND**.
(T) 0161 9055752 **(F)** 0161 9055750.
Profile Transport/Horse Boxes. **Ref: YH13749**

T I P EUROPE

T I P Europe Ltd, 5 Hodgkinson Rd, Felixstowe, **Suffolk**, IP11 3QT, **ENGLAND**.
(T) 01394 675833 **(F)** 01394 673392.
Contact/s
Branch Manager: Mr P Grant
Profile Transport/Horse Boxes. **Ref: YH13750**

T I P TRAILER RENTAL

T I P Trailer Rental, Carrington Works, Isherwood

Rd, Carrington, Manchester, **Manchester (Greater)**, M31 4QZ, **ENGLAND**.
(T) 0161 7776789 **(F)** 0161 7776767.
Contact/s
Manager: Mr M Preedy
Profile Transport/Horse Boxes. **Ref: YH13751**

T I R PRINCE RACEWAY

T I R Prince Raceway, Towyn Rd, Towyn, Abergele, **Conwy**, LL22 9NW, **WALES**.
(T) 01745 345123 **(F)** 01745 331829.
Profile Track/Course. **Ref: YH13752**

T J BISHOP

T J Bishop (Bloodstock) Ltd, 20A Jewry St, Winchester, **Hampshire**, SO23 8RZ, **ENGLAND**.
(T) 01962 861888 **(F)** 01962 861888.
Profile Blood Stock Agency. **Ref: YH13753**

T J STUD & LIVERY STABLE

T J Stud & Livery Stable, Newbridge Farm, Newbridge, Cadnam, Southampton, **Hampshire**, SO40 2NW, **ENGLAND**.
(T) 023 80812922.
Profile Stable/Livery, Stud Farm. **Ref: YH13754**

T JONES & SON

T Jones & Son, 27 Leg St, Oswestry, **Shropshire**, SY11 2NN, **ENGLAND**.
(T) 01691 652822.
Contact/s
Partner: Mr D Jones
Profile Saddlery Retailer. **Ref: YH13755**

T K S

T K S Ltd, 38A Woodgreen Rd, Shankbridge, Ballymena, **County Antrim**, BT42 3DR, **NORTHERN IRELAND**.
(T) 028 25892485 **(F)** 028 25892485.
Profile Supplies. **Ref: YH13756**

T L C EQUESTRIAN

T L C Equestrian, Orchard Farm Stables, Horninghold, Market Harborough, **Leicestershire**, LE16 8DH, **ENGLAND**.
(T) 01858 555240 **(F)** 01858 555778.
Profile Supplies. **Ref: YH13757**

T L TRAILER SERVICES

T L Trailer Services Ltd, Po Box 337, Sandhurst, **Berkshire**, GU47 0ZJ, **ENGLAND**.
(T) 01276 609034 **(F)** 01276 609034.
Contact/s
General Manager: Mr R Roberts
Profile Transport/Horse Boxes. **Ref: YH13758**

T M F ANIMAL FEEDS & SADDLERS

T M F Animal Feeds & Saddlers, Minyos Lodge, Oaklands Pk, Horncastle Rd, Woodhall Spa, **Lincolnshire**, LN10 6UU, **ENGLAND**.
(T) 01526 354549.
Profile Saddlery Retailer. **Ref: YH13759**

T MILES & SON

T Miles & Son, The Forge, High St, Henfield, **Sussex (West)**, BN5 9DD, **ENGLAND**.
(T) 01273 492921 **(F)** 01273 492921.
Contact/s
Owner: Mr A Miles
Profile Blacksmith. **Ref: YH13760**

T N T INT AVIATION SVS

T N T International Aviation Services, Felsted Hse, 2-6 Frances Rd, Windsor, **Berkshire**, SL4 3AA, **ENGLAND**.
(T) 01753 842168 **(F)** 01753 858172.
Profile Transport/Horse Boxes. **Ref: YH13761**

T P TRAILERS

T P Trailers, Askern Rd Garage, Askern Rd, Bentley, Doncaster, **Yorkshire (South)**, DN5 0EP, **ENGLAND**.
(T) 01302 872333.
Profile Transport/Horse Boxes. **Ref: YH13762**

T S RIDING CLUB

T S Riding Club, 2 Muller Pk, Polmont, **Falkirk**, FK2 0UJ, **SCOTLAND**.
(T) 01324 712665.
Profile Club/Association, Riding Club. **Ref: YH13763**

T S S

T S S Ltd, Stalleys Barn, High St, Newport, **Essex**, CB11 3PQ, **ENGLAND**.
(T) 01799 540202 **(F)** 01799 542092.
Profile Saddlery Retailer. **Ref: YH13764**

T SPIERS & SONS

T Spiers & Sons Ltd, Reddinghurst, Langley Rd, Claverdon, Warwick, **Warwickshire**, CV35 8PJ, **ENGLAND**.
(T) 01926 842347.
Contact/s
Partner: Mr D Spiers
Profile Transport/Horse Boxes. **Ref: YH13765**

T TYHURST & SON

T Tyhurst & Son, Glynde Forge, Glynde, Lewes, **Sussex (East)**, BN8 6SU, **ENGLAND**.
(T) 01273 858191.
Contact/s
Owner: Mr D Tyhurst
Profile Blacksmith. **Ref: YH13766**

T W RELPH & SONS

T W Relph & Sons Ltd, Moor Hse, Yanwath, Penrith, **Cumbria**, CA10 2LA, **ENGLAND**.
(T) 01768 864308.
Contact/s
Owner: Mr J Relph
Profile Saddlery Retailer. **Ref: YH13767**

T WILSON & SON

T Wilson & Son, 34 Little Barn Lane, Mansfield, **Nottinghamshire**, NG18 3JE, **ENGLAND**.
(T) 01623 623889.
Contact/s
Owner: Mr W Wilson
Profile Transport/Horse Boxes. **Ref: YH13768**

T.T.T

Training the Teachers of Tomorrow Trust, East Whipley Farm, Shamley Green, Guildford, **Surrey**, GU5 0TE, **ENGLAND**.
(T) 01483 272445 **(F)** 01483 268371
(E) tomeswell@tttrust.freeserve.co.uk
(W) www.tttrust.freeserve.co.uk.
Contact/s
Secretary: Mrs J Sewell
Profile Equestrian Centre, Trainer.
Train up and coming teachers and trainers. One to one tutition is between £20.00 and £40.00 per half hour.
Yr. Est: 1987 **C.Size:** 6 Acres
Opening Times
Between February and mid December, the Event Season, the Trust is open between 09:00 - 17:00 with lectures held in evenings between 19:00 - 21:00
Ref: YH13769

TAAFFE, TOM

Tom Taaffe, Portree Stables, Boston, Straffan, **County Kildare**, **IRELAND**.
(T) 01 6273604 **(F)** 01 6274231.
Contact/s
Trainer: Mr T Taaffe
(E) tomtaaffe@kildarehorse.ie
Profile Trainer. **Ref: YH13770**

TABOR, M J & N J

M J & N J Tabor, Lybrook, Snowshill Rd, Broadway, **Worcestershire**, WR12 7JS, **ENGLAND**.
(T) 01386 858961.
Contact/s
Partner: Mr N Tabor
Profile Equestrian Centre, Track/Course.
Opening Times
Sp: Open Mon - Sun 24 Hours.
Su: Open Mon - Sun 24 Hours.
Au: Open Mon - Sun 24 Hours.
Wn: Open Mon - Sun 24 Hours.
Telephone for an appointment and further information.
Ref: YH13771

TABRE RIDING

Tabre Riding, Wagon Wheels Stables, Wagon Wheels Holiday Parc, Winkleigh, **Devon**, EXL9 8DP, **ENGLAND**.
(T) 01837 83616.
Profile Holidays, Riding School. **Ref: YH13772**

TAC & TOGS

Tac & Togs, Tivybank, Crymych, **Pembrokeshire**, SA41 3RN, **WALES**.
(T) 01239 831819.
Contact/s
Owner: Mrs S Lowe **Ref: YH13773**

TAC-A-MAC

Tac-A-Mac, Unit 2 Great Easton Mill, Harborough Rd, Kibworth, Leicester, **Leicestershire**, LE8 0RB, **ENGLAND**.
(T) 0116 2792318 **(F)** 0116 2796553.
Contact/s
Owner: Mr C Hall **Ref: YH13774**

TACK & COUNTRY

Tack & Country, 9 The Hollows, Elburton, Plymouth, **Devon**, PL0 8TX, **ENGLAND**.
(T) 01752 407194
(M) 07885 219164.
Profile Supplies. **Ref: YH13775**

TACK & FEED SUPPLIES

Tack & Feed Supplies, Lower Cross Farm, East Hagbourne, Didcot, **Oxfordshire**, OX11 9ND, **ENGLAND**.
(T) 01235 813124.
Contact/s
Owner: Mr C Drewe
Profile Saddlery Retailer. **Ref: YH13776**

TACK & STITCH SADDLERY

Tack & Stitch Saddlery, Rhedynog, Isaf, Chwilog, Pwllheli, **Gwynedd**, LL53 6LQ, **WALES**.
(T) 01766 810387.
Profile Saddlery Retailer. **Ref: YH13777**

TACK & TOGS

Tack & Togs, Knotting Rd, Melchbourne, Bedford, **Bedfordshire**, MK44 1BG, **ENGLAND**.
(T) 01234 709970 **(F)** 01234 709970.
Contact/s
Partner: Mr C Kelly **Ref: YH13778**

TACK & TOGS

Tack & Togs, 21A High St, Wolviston, Billingham, **Cleveland**, TS22 5JY, **ENGLAND**.
(T) 01740 644565 **(F)** 01642 565523. **Ref: YH13779**

TACK & TURNOUT EQUESTRIAN

Tack & Turnout Equestrian Supplies, Unit 33, Colne Valley Business Pk, Linthwaite, Huddersfield, **Yorkshire (West)**, HD7 5QG, **ENGLAND**.
(T) 01484 846273.
Contact/s
Owner: Mrs J Armitage
Profile Medical Support, Riding Wear Retailer, Saddlery Retailer, Supplies. **No.Staff:** 3
Yr. Est: 1998
Opening Times
Sp: Open Mon - Fri 12:00, Sat, Sun 10:00. Closed Mon - Fri 18:00, Sat 17:00, Sun 16:00.
Su: Open Mon - Fri 12:00, Sat, Sun 10:00. Closed Mon - Fri 18:00, Sat 17:00, Sun 16:00.
Au: Open Mon - Fri 12:00, Sat, Sun 10:00. Closed Mon - Fri 18:00, Sat 17:00, Sun 16:00.
Wn: Open Mon - Fri 12:00, Sat, Sun 10:00. Closed Mon - Fri 18:00, Sat 17:00, Sun 16:00. **Ref: YH13780**

TACK A ROUND SADDLERY

Tack A Round Saddlery Ltd, 41A High St, Billingshurst, **Sussex (West)**, RH14 9PP, **ENGLAND**.
(T) 01403 783862
Affiliated Bodies SMS.
Contact/s
Owner: Ms A Sturrock
Profile Saddlery Retailer.
Opening Times
Sp: Open Mon - Sat 09:00. Closed Mon - Sat 17:30.
Su: Open Mon - Sat 09:00. Closed Mon - Sat 17:30.
Au: Open Mon - Sat 09:00. Closed Mon - Sat 17:30.
Wn: Open Mon - Sat 09:00. Closed Mon - Sat 17:30.
Closed Sundays **Ref: YH13781**

TACK BARN

Tack Barn (The), Sandpit Lane, Gimingham, Norwich, **Norfolk**, NR11 8HH, **ENGLAND**.
(T) 01263 726006 **(F)** 01263 726001.
Contact/s
Owner: Mrs S MacKenzie
Profile Saddlery Retailer. **Ref: YH13782**

TACK BOX

Tack Box (The), Northfield Rd, Soham, Ely, **Cambridgeshire**, CB7 5UF, **ENGLAND**.
(T) 01353 723226. **Ref: YH13783**

TACK BOX

Tack Box (The), Torver, Coniston, **Cumbria**, LA21 8BP, **ENGLAND**.
(T) 01539 441088.
Contact/s
Owner: Mrs C Barr **Ref: YH13784**

TACK BOX

Tack Box (The), Unit 2, 7 Dixon Way, Lincoln, **Lincolnshire**, LN6 7XN, **ENGLAND**.
(T) 01522 533822 **(F)** 01522 533822
(W) www.thetackbox.co.uk.
Contact/s
Owner: Miss L Hancock **(Q)** BHSAI
Profile Riding Wear Retailer, Saddlery Retailer, Supplies.
Veterinary products are also available. **No.Staff:** 2
Yr. Est: 1992
Opening Times
Sp: Open 09:00. Closed 17:30.
Su: Open 09:00. Closed 17:30.

Au: Open 09:00. Closed 17:30.
Wn: Open 09:00. Closed 17:30.
09:00 - 16:00 Saturday **Ref:YH13785**

TACK DOCTOR

Tack Doctor (The), Old Bridge Country Clothing, 9 Main St, Tweedmouth, Berwick-upon-Tweed, **Northumberland**, TD15 2AA, **ENGLAND**.
(T) 01289 308475
(M) 07702 914525.
Profile Saddlery Retailer. **Ref:YH13786**

TACK EXCHANGE

Tack Exchange, Blaenau Isaf, Pentwyn Rd, Crosshands, Llanelli, **Carmarthenshire**, SA14 6DD, **WALES**.
(T) 01269 845660 **(F)** 01269 831089
(E) tackexchange1@aol.com
(W) www.tack4exchange.com.
Contact/s
Owner: Mr K Richards
Profile Breeder, Riding Wear Retailer, Saddlery Retailer, Supplies.
Tack Exchange stock over 200 saddles, new and second hand. Many equestrian goods bought from the public or accepted in part exchange. No.Staff: 3
Yr. Est: 1988 C.Size: 55 Acres
Opening Times
Sp: Open Mon - Sat 10:00. Closed Mon - Fri 15:00, Sat 17:00.
Su: Open Mon - Sat 10:00. Closed Mon - Fri 15:00, Sat 17:00.
Au: Open Mon - Sat 10:00. Closed Mon - Fri 15:00, Sat 17:00.
Wn: Open Mon - Sat 10:00. Closed Mon - Fri 15:00, Sat 17:00.
Sundays by appointment **Ref:YH13787**

TACK EXCHANGE

Tack Exchange (The), 104 Elm Rd, Leigh-on-Sea, **Essex**, SS9 1SQ, **ENGLAND**.
(T) 01702 719971.
Contact/s
Owner: Mrs J Webb
Profile Riding Wear Retailer, Saddlery Retailer, Supplies. No.Staff: 2 Yr. Est: 1997
Opening Times
Sp: Open Mon, Tues, Thurs - Sun 10:00. Closed Mon, Tues, Thurs - Sun 17:00.
Su: Open Mon, Tues, Thurs - Sun 10:00. Closed Mon, Tues, Thurs - Sun 17:00.
Au: Open Mon, Tues, Thurs - Sun 10:00. Closed Mon, Tues, Thurs - Sun 17:00.
Wn: Open Mon, Tues, Thurs - Sun 10:00. Closed Mon, Tues, Thurs - Sun 17:00.
Closed Wednesdays **Ref:YH13788**

TACK EXCHANGE

Tack Exchange (The), 2c St Johns Rd, Wallasey, **Merseyside**, CH45 3LU, **ENGLAND**.
(T) 0151 6911766. **Ref:YH13789**

TACK HAVEN

Tack Haven (The), Dove Hse Farm, Dove Hse Lane, Kensworth, Dunstable, **Bedfordshire**, LU6 2PQ, **ENGLAND**.
(T) 01582 872333 **(F)** 01582 872511.
Profile Saddlery Retailer. **Ref:YH13790**

TACK 'N' TOGS

Tack 'N' Togs, Fairview, Pampisford Rd, Hildersham, Cambridge, **Cambridgeshire**, CB1 6AY, **ENGLAND**.
(T) 01223 894995 **(F)** 01223 890933.
Contact/s
Owner: Mrs M Hoskin
Profile Saddlery Retailer. **Ref:YH13791**

TACK RACK

Tack Rack (The), Torphichen Mains Farm, Torphichen, Bathgate, **Lothian (West)**, EH48 4LZ, **SCOTLAND**.
(T) 01506 655678.
Profile Saddlery Retailer. **Ref:YH13792**

TACK ROOM

Tack Room (The), 31 London Rd, Thatcham, **Berkshire**, RG18 4GE, **ENGLAND**.
(T) 01635 865421.
Contact/s
Owner: Mrs K Holland **Ref:YH13793**

TACK ROOM

Tack Room (The), 7 Beaufort Mews, Horse St, Portishead, Bristol, **Bristol**, BS20 6DA, **ENGLAND**.
(T) 01454 326116 **(F)** 01454 326116.
Contact/s
Owner: Mr J Fryer **Ref:YH13794**

TACK ROOM

Tack Room (The), Cerbynau, Brechfa, Carmarthen, **Carmarthenshire**, SA32 7QW, **WALES**.
(T) 01267 202275 **(F)** 01267 202275.
Contact/s
Owner: Mr C Doughty **Ref:YH13795**

TACK ROOM

Tack Room Ltd, Unit 3 Academy St, Cork, **County Cork**, **IRELAND**.
(T) 021 4272704.
Profile Supplies. **Ref:YH13796**

TACK ROOM

Tack Room, 120 The Quay, Waterford, **County Waterford**, **IRELAND**.
(T) 051 870577.
Profile Supplies. **Ref:YH13797**

TACK ROOM

Tack Room (The), Elm Tree Cottage, Oak Rd, Crays Hill, Billericay, **Essex**, CM11 2YL, **ENGLAND**.
(T) 01268 521040.
Profile Stable/Livery. **Ref:YH13798**

TACK ROOM

Tack Room (Chipping Sodbury) (The), 7 Horse St, Chipping Sodbury, **Gloucestershire (South)**, BS37 6DA, **ENGLAND**.
(T) 01454 326116 **(F)** 01454 326116
(E) kickon@cix.co.uk.
Profile Saddlery Retailer, Stable/Livery, Track/Course.
Ref:YH13799

TACK ROOM

Tack Room (Southampton) (The), 71 Swift Rd, Woolston, Southampton, **Hampshire**, SO19 9FP, **ENGLAND**.
(T) 023 80433404. **Ref:YH13800**

TACK ROOM

Tack Room Ltd (The), Tillyochie Hse, Kinross, **Perth and Kinross**, KY13 0NL, **SCOTLAND**.
(T) 01577 861921.
Contact/s
Partner: Mrs G Keith **Ref:YH13801**

TACK ROOM

Tack Room (The), Johns Cross, Robertsbridge, **Sussex (East)**, TN32 5JJ, **ENGLAND**.
(T) 01580 882255 **(F)** 01580 880181.
Contact/s
Owner: Mrs A Pyecroft
Profile Saddlery Retailer. **Ref:YH13802**

TACK SHACK

Tack Shack, 83 East Dundry Rd, Bristol, **Bristol**, BS14 0LN, **ENGLAND**.
(T) 01275 835712.
Contact/s
Owner: Miss D Welch **Ref:YH13803**

TACK SHACK

Tack Shack (The), 89 Aghanloo Rd, Limavady, **County Londonderry**, BT49 0HY, **NORTHERN IRELAND**.
(T) 028 77767393.
Contact/s
Owner: Mr K Corr **Ref:YH13804**

TACK SHACK

Tack Shack (The), Willow Farm, Church Broughton, Derby, **Derbyshire**, DE65 5AY, **ENGLAND**.
(T) 01283 585131.
Profile Saddlery Retailer. **Ref:YH13805**

TACK SHACK

Tack Shack New Ridings Supplies Centre, Beecroft Nursery, Queen Anne Drive, Wimborne, **Dorset**, BH21 3BA, **ENGLAND**.
(T) 01202 884558. **Ref:YH13806**

TACK SHACK

Tack Shack, Woodchurch, Ashford, **Kent**, TN26 3TL, **ENGLAND**.
(T) 01233 860438 **(F)** 01233 860890.
Contact/s
Owner: Mrs V Vidal **Ref:YH13807**

TACK SHACK

Tack Shack (The), 26 Field St, Shepshed, Loughborough, **Leicestershire**, LE12 9AL, **ENGLAND**.
(T) 01509 505893.
Contact/s
Owner: Ms L Brown
Profile Supplies. **Ref:YH13808**

TACK SHACK

Tack Shack (The), 47F Broad St, Banbury, **Oxfordshire**, OX16 5BT, **ENGLAND**.
(T) 01295 269505. **Ref:YH13809**

TACK SHOP

Tack Shop (Mill of Strachan) (The), Mill Of Strachan, Strachan, Banchory, **Aberdeenshire**, AB31 6NS, **SCOTLAND**.
(T) 01330 850663
(E) scotsportuk@compuserve.com.
Profile Saddlery Retailer, Track/Course.
Ref:YH13810

TACK SHOP

Tack Shop (The), Hilfield Lane, Aldenham, Watford, **Hertfordshire**, WD2 8DP, **ENGLAND**.
(T) 01923 856287 **(F)** 01923 859289.
Contact/s
Manageress: Mrs L Cheek **Ref:YH13811**

TACK SHOP

Tack Shop (The), 16A Oak Lane, Kingswinford, **Midlands (West)**, DY6 7JS, **ENGLAND**.
(T) 01384 294151. **Ref:YH13812**

TACK SHOP

Tack Shop (The), Shilton Rd Filling Station, Carterton, **Oxfordshire**, OX18 1EH, **ENGLAND**.
(T) 01993 842060 **(F)** 01993 842060
(E) enquiries@cartertontack.co.uk
(W) www.cartertontack.co.uk.
Contact/s
General Manager: Ms J Lewington
Profile Supplies. **Ref:YH13813**

TACK SHOP

Tack Shop (The), 2a Mill St, Armthorpe, Doncaster, **Yorkshire (South)**, DN3 3DL, **ENGLAND**.
(T) 01302 832080.
Contact/s
Owner: Mr P Atkin **Ref:YH13814**

TACK STORE

Tack Store (The), The Bridge, Umberleigh, **Devon**, EX37 9AB, **ENGLAND**.
(T) 01769 560920 **(F)** 01769 560920.
Contact/s
Owner: Mrs S Murch **Ref:YH13815**

TACK TRACK

Tack Track, 2 Chapel Court, Brigg, **Lincolnshire (North)**, DN20 8JZ, **ENGLAND**.
(T) 01652 651122.
Contact/s
Owner: Mrs L Green **Ref:YH13816**

TACK UP

Tack Up, 9 Galgate, Barnard Castle, **County Durham**, DL12 8EQ, **ENGLAND**.
(T) 01833 631934.
Profile Saddlery Retailer. **Ref:YH13817**

TACKLE & TACK

Tackle & Tack, 2/4 Soroba Rd, Oban, **Argyll and Bute**, PA34 4HU, **SCOTLAND**.
(T) 01631 570080.
Contact/s
Owner: Mrs M Simmonds
Profile Feed Merchant, Medical Support, Riding Wear Retailer, Saddlery Retailer, Supplies.
Offer a range of products, from animal feed through to ancillary items. Also supply various pet feeds.
Yr. Est: 1998
Opening Times
Sp: Open 09:30. Closed 17:00.
Su: Open 09:30. Closed 17:00.
Au: Open 09:30. Closed 17:00.
Wn: Open 09:30. Closed 17:00. **Ref:YH13818**

TACK-STITCH

Tack-Stitch, 150 London Rd, Southborough, Tunbridge Wells, **Kent**, TN4 0PJ, **ENGLAND**.
(T) 01892 526559.
Contact/s
Owner: Miss M Newing
Profile Saddlery Retailer. **Ref:YH13819**

TAFFS, PHILIPPA

Philippa Taffs, Homestead Farm, Elmstone Hardwicke, Cheltenham, **Gloucestershire**, GL51 9TH, **ENGLAND**.
(T) 01242 680538.
Profile Trainer. **Ref:YH13820**

TAILWAGGERS

Tailwaggers, 3 Town St, Chapel Allerton, **Yorkshire (West)**, LS7 4NB, **ENGLAND**.

(T) 0113 2370118 **(F)** 0113 2738270.
Contact/s
Partner: Angela Lowrie
Profile Saddlery Retailer. **Ref: YH13821**

TAINSH, W

W Tainsh, Drummondernoch Farm, Cromrie, **Perth and Kinross**, PH6 2JB, **SCOTLAND**.
(T) 01764 670337.
Profile Supplies. **Ref: YH13822**

TAIT, BLYTH

Blyth Tait MBE (NZL), Little Barn, Farmington, Northleach, Cheltenham, **Gloucestershire**, GL54 3NL, **ENGLAND**.
(T) 01451 861098 **(F)** 01451 861098
(M) 07774 883388. **Ref: YH13823**

TAIT, M

Mr M Tait, Botton Gr, Danby Head, Whitby, **Yorkshire (North)**, YO21 2NH, **ENGLAND**.
(T) 01287 640284.
Profile Breeder. **Ref: YH13824**

TAIT, T A

T A Tait, New Smiddy, Maitland Pl, Finstown, Orkney, **Orkney Isles**, KW17 2EQ, **SCOTLAND**.
(T) 01856 761566.
Profile Blacksmith. **Ref: YH13825**

TAIT, THOMAS A

Thomas A Tait DWCF, Hewin-Ho, Stenness, Stromness, **Orkney Isles**, KW16 3HG, **SCOTLAND**..
Profile Farrier. **Ref: YH13826**

TAKEL, FRANCES

Frances Takel, 8 Jury Rd, Dulverton, **Somerset**, TA22 9DU, **ENGLAND**.
(T) 01398 324147.
Profile Supplies. **Ref: YH13827**

TAKTIX

Taktix, Prospect Works, Rear Of 46 Luton Rd, Silsoe, Bedford, **Bedfordshire**, MK45 4EX, **ENGLAND**.
(T) 01234 742822 **(F)** 01234 742822. **Ref: YH13828**

TAL Y FOEL RIDING CTRE

Tal Y Foel Stud Farm and Riding Centre Ltd, Dwyran, Anglesey, **Isle of Anglesey**, LL61 6LQ, **WALES**.
(T) 01248 430377 **(F)** 01248 430977
(E) riding@talyfoel.u-net.com
(W) www.tal-y-foel.co.uk.
Contact/s
General Manager: Ms K Lloyd Hughes **(Q)** AI
Profile Arena, Breeder, Equestrian Centre, Riding School, Stable/Livery. No.Staff: 6 Yr. Est: 1995
C.Size: 50 Acres
Opening Times
Sp: Open 09:00. Closed 18:00.
Su: Open 09:00. Closed 18:00.
Au: Open 09:00. Closed 18:00.
Wn: Open 09:00. Closed 18:00. **Ref: YH13829**

TALAWATER QUARTER HORSES

Talawater Quarter Horses, Whitsam Farm, Bere Alston, Yelverton, **Devon**, PL20 7BN, **ENGLAND**.
(T) 01822 841074.
Contact/s
Owner: Mrs J Collie
Profile Breeder, Trainer. **Ref: YH13830**

TALL TREES

Tall Trees Arena, Davidstow, Camelford, **Cornwall**, PL32 9XR, **ENGLAND**.
(T) 01840 261249 **(F)** 01840 261249
Affiliated Bodies BD, BHS, BSJA.
Contact/s
Owner: Mrs J Deithrick **(T)** 01840 770342
Profile Arena, Breeder. Competition Centre.
No.Staff: 4 Yr. Est: 2001 C.Size: 11 Acres
Opening Times
Available for hire all year, shows are run weekends and occasionally midweek **Ref: YH13831**

TALL TREES RIDING SCHOOL

Tall Trees Riding School, Tall Trees, Church Rd, Herstmonceux, Hailsham, **Sussex (East)**, BN27 1RL, **ENGLAND**.
(T) 01323 832105.
Contact/s
Owner: Mrs J Stripp **Ref: YH13832**

TALLAND SCHOOL OF EQUITATION

Talland School Of Equitation (The), Church Farm, Siddington, Cirencester, **Gloucestershire**, GL7 6EZ, **ENGLAND**.
(T) 01285 652318 **(F)** 01285 659409.
Contact/s
Owner: Mrs P Hutton
Profile Trainer. **Ref: YH13833**

TALLENTIRE & SONS

Tallentire & Sons, 44 Copeland Rd, West Auckland, Bishop Auckland, **County Durham**, DL14 9JL, **ENGLAND**.
(T) 01388 833614.
Profile Farrier. **Ref: YH13834**

TALLENTIRE, M L

M L Tallentire, 39 Pinfold Lane, Butterknowle, Bishop Auckland, **County Durham**, DL13 5NU, **ENGLAND**.
(T) 01388 718282.
Profile Supplies. **Ref: YH13835**

TALLENTS STUD

Tallents Stud (The), 85 Fishers Field, Buckingham, **Buckinghamshire**, MK18 1SF, **ENGLAND**.
(T) 01280 812281 **(F)** 01280 824451
(E) celia@cwath.demon.co.uk.
Profile Breeder. **Ref: YH13836**

TALLY HO

Tally Ho, Beamish Pk, Beamish, **County Durham**, DH9 0RQ, **ENGLAND**.
(T) 01207 232993 **(F)** 01207 232993.
Profile Saddlery Retailer. **Ref: YH13837**

TALLY HO

Tally Ho Ltd, Wineport, Glasson, Athlone, **County Westmeath**, **IRELAND**.
(T) 0902 85201 **(F)** 0902 85201
(E) tallyho@iol.ie
(W) www.tallyho.ie.
Profile Riding Wear Retailer. Riding Wear Wholesaler.
Wholesalers of quality Equestrian Clothing. The company aims to provide clothing you can be comfortable in while getting on with the job in hand. Contact for your nearest stockist. **Ref: YH13838**

TALLY HO

Tally Ho (UK) Ltd, 15 Kingsley Park, Whitchurch, **Hampshire**, RG28 7HA, **ENGLAND**.
(T) 01256 892815 **(F)** 01256 892815
(E) tallyho@aol.com
(W) www.tallyho.ie.
Profile Riding Wear Retailer. **Ref: YH13839**

TALLY HO FARM

Tally Ho Farm, Crouch Lane, Winkfield, Windsor, **Berkshire**, SL4 4RZ, **ENGLAND**.
(T) 01344 885373 **(F)** 01344 891482.
Contact/s
Owner: Mr J Thomas
Profile Feed Merchant, Saddlery Retailer.
Ref: YH13840

TALLY HO FARM

Tally Ho Farm, Troopers Inn, Haverfordwest, Pembroke, **Pembrokeshire**, SA62 4NN, **WALES**.
(T) 01437 891052.
Profile Breeder, Stable/Livery. **Ref: YH13841**

TALLY HO STABLES

Tally Ho Stables, Crouch Lane, Winkfield, Windsor, **Berkshire**, SL4 4RZ, **ENGLAND**.
(T) 01344 893700.
Contact/s
Owner: Mr A Gilbert
Profile Stable/Livery. **Ref: YH13842**

TALLY HO STUD

Tally Ho Stud, Chevington, Bury St Edmunds, **Suffolk**, IP29 5QT, **ENGLAND**.
(T) 01284 850059.
Profile Breeder. **Ref: YH13843**

TALLY-HO RIDING SCHOOL

Tally-Ho Riding School Limited, Biggin Lane, Chadwell-St-Mary, Grays, **Essex**, RM16 4LT, **ENGLAND**.
(T) 01375 858038 **(F)** 01375 891149.
Contact/s
General Manager: Miss C Smith **(Q)** BHS 1, BHS 2, BHS 3 **(T)** 01375 891159
Profile Arena, Riding School, Riding Wear Retailer, Saddlery Retailer, Stable/Livery, Trainer. No.Staff: 5
Yr. Est: 2000 C.Size: 4 Acres **Ref: YH13844**

TALLY-HO TRAILERS

Tally-Ho Trailers, Manor Farm, Ramsey Rd, Kings Ripton, Huntingdon, **Cambridgeshire**, PE28 2NW, **ENGLAND**.
(T) 01487 773030 **(F)** 01487 773354.
Contact/s
Owner: Mr D Collett
Profile Transport/Horse Boxes. **Ref: YH13845**

TALYGARN

Talygarn Equestrian Centre, Talygarn, Pontyclun, **Rhondda Cynon Taff**, CF72 9JT, **WALES**.
(T) 01443 225107 **(F)** 01443 225107.
Contact/s
Owner: Mrs C Rodgers
Profile Equestrian Centre, Riding School.
Talygarn Pony Club Centre. Indoor school is under construction and due for completion April 2002. Childrens lessons given from age 3 years.
Yr. Est: 1995
Opening Times
Sp: Open Mon -Sun 09:00. Closed Mon - Fri 21:00, Sat, Sun 18:00.
Su: Open Mon -Sun 09:00. Closed Mon - Fri 21:00, Sat, Sun 18:00.
Au: Open Mon -Sun 09:00. Closed Mon - Fri 21:00, Sat, Sun 18:00.
Wn: Open Mon -Sun 09:00. Closed Mon - Fri 21:00, Sat, Sun 18:00. **Ref: YH13846**

TAMAR LAKE PRODUCTS

Tamar Lake Products, Tamar Lake View, Holsworthy, **Devon**, EX22 7LB, **ENGLAND**.
(T) 01288 82352.
Profile Supplies. **Ref: YH13847**

TAMAR TRAILER CTRE

Tamar Trailer Centre Ltd, Sugarmill Ind Est, Billacombe Rd, Plymouth, **Devon**, PL9 7HT, **ENGLAND**.
(T) 01752 492020 **(F)** 01752 493368.
Profile Transport/Horse Boxes. **Ref: YH13848**

TAMAR VALLEY TRANSPORT

Tamar Valley Transport, Llawnroc, Harrowbarrow, Callington, **Cornwall**, PL17 8JG, **ENGLAND**.
(T) 01579 350525 **(F)** 01579 351350.
Contact/s
Owner: Mr B Pridham
Profile Transport/Horse Boxes. **Ref: YH13849**

TAMBOUR SUPPLIES

Tambour Supplies, Unit 4A Penbeagle Ind Est, St Ives, **Cornwall**, TR26 1ND, **ENGLAND**.
(T) 01736 793305 **(F)** 01736 794411.
Contact/s
Owner: Mr A Sugrue **Ref: YH13850**

TAME, GRAEME C

Graeme C Tame DWCF Hons, Carylls Lea Farm, Faygate, Horsham, **Sussex (West)**, RH12 4SJ, **ENGLAND**.
(T) 01293 851448.
Profile Farrier. **Ref: YH13851**

TANDLEVIEW STABLES

Tandleview Stables, Tandleview, Beith, **Ayrshire (North)**, KA15 1HU, **SCOTLAND**.
(T) 01505 502137.
Contact/s
Owner: Miss D Rodwell
Profile Riding School, Stable/Livery.
Livery - full available. Bring your own horses for lessons. Yr. Est: 1992
Opening Times
Sp: Open 08:00. Closed 19:00.
Su: Open 08:00. Closed 19:00.
Au: Open 08:00. Closed 19:00.
Wn: Open 08:00. Closed 19:00. **Ref: YH13852**

TANDRIDGE PRIORY

Tandridge Priory Riding Centre, Barrow Green Rd, Oxted, **Surrey**, RH8 9NE, **ENGLAND**.
(T) 01883 712863
Affiliated Bodies Pony Club UK.
Contact/s
Partner: Miss T Worrall **(Q)** AI
Profile Riding School.
Opening Times
Sp: Open 09:00. Closed 17:00.
Su: Open 09:00. Closed 17:00.
Au: Open 09:00. Closed 17:00.
Wn: Open 09:00. Closed 17:00.
Open 09:00 - 16:00 at weekends **Ref: YH13853**

TANGLEWOOD EQUESTRIAN CTRE

Tanglewood Equestrian Centre, Boyers Lane, Colden Common, Winchester, **Hampshire**, SO21 1TA, **ENGLAND**.
(T) 01962 711788. **Ref: YH13854**

TANGYE, JOHN

John Tangye, Littlefield Manor Farm, Littlefield Common, Guildford, **Surrey**, GU3 3HJ, **ENGLAND**.
(T) 01483 233068.
Profile Stable/Livery, Track/Course. **Ref: YH13855**

TANKEY LAKE LIVERY

D M Miller, Tankey Lake Livery, Llangennith, Swansea, **Swansea**, SA3 1DT, **WALES**.
(T) 01792 386383.
Contact/s
For Bookings: Mr V Miller
Profile Arena, Stable/Livery.
Grass, DIY, full livery available, prices on request.
No.Staff: 3 Yr. Est: 1995 C.Size: 31 Acres
Ref: **YH13856**

TANNER, R

R Tanner, Boghead Laithers, Fortrie, Turriff, **Aberdeenshire**, AB53 4HL, **SCOTLAND**.
(T) 01888 563198.
Contact/s
Owner: Mr R Tanner
Profile Farrier. Ref: **YH13857**

TANNER, STEPHEN M

Stephen M Tanner DWCF, 5 Wallow Green, Horsley, **Gloucestershire**, GL6 0PB, **ENGLAND**.
(T) 01453 833363.
Profile Farrier. Ref: **YH13858**

TANNOCK STABLES

Tannock Stables, Palacerigg, Cumbernauld, **Lanarkshire (North)**, G67 3HU, **SCOTLAND**.
(T) 01236 733424.
Profile Riding School, Stable/Livery. Ref: **YH13859**

TANT, RAY

Mr Ray Tant MC AMC MMCA, 34 Manor Rd, Wheathampstead, **Hertfordshire**, AL4 8JD, **ENGLAND**.
(T) 01582 768247.
Profile Medical Support. Ref: **YH13860**

TANTON-BROWN, JULIAN

Julian Tanton-Brown DWCF, Conifers, The Street, Borden, Sittingbourne, **Kent**, ME9 8JN, **ENGLAND**.
(T) 01795 479758.
Profile Farrier. Ref: **YH13861**

TANWOOD STUD

Tanwood Stud (The), Chaddesly, Corbett, Kidderminster, **Worcestershire**, DY10 4NX, **ENGLAND**.
(T) 01562 777296.
Profile Supplies. Ref: **YH13862**

TANYFOEL MORGANS

Tanyfoel Morgans, Rhydlewis, Llandysul, **Carmarthenshire**, SA44 5SO, **WALES**.
(T) 01239 851446.
Profile Breeder. Ref: **YH13863**

TAPITLAW RIDING SCHOOL

Tapitlaw Riding School, Tapitlaw Farm, Comrie, Dunfermline, **Fife**, KY12 9HE, **SCOTLAND**.
(T) 01383 850302. Ref: **YH13864**

TAPLIN, E J

Mrs E J Taplin, Huntscott Cottage Farm, Wootton Courtenay, Minehead, **Somerset**, TA24 8BR, **ENGLAND**.
(T) 01643 841258.
Profile Supplies. Ref: **YH13865**

TAPLOW HORSE SHOW CLUB

Taplow Horse Show Club, Marshmead, Taplow, **Berkshire**, SL6 0DE, **ENGLAND**.
(T) 01628 603179.
Contact/s
Chairman: Mrs E Law
Profile Club/Association. Ref: **YH13866**

TAPSONS

Tapsons Ltd, Unit 36 Second Ave, Westfield Trading Est, Midsomer Norton, **Bath & Somerset (North East)**, BA3 4BH, **ENGLAND**.
(T) 01761 414566.
Profile Supplies. Ref: **YH13867**

TARA EQUESTRIAN

Tara Equestrian, Unit 19A Armagh Business Ctre, Loughgall Rd, Armagh, **County Armagh**, BT61 7DH, **NORTHERN IRELAND**.
(T) 028 37518099.
Contact/s
Owner: Mr E Reid Ref: **YH13868**

TARBOCK GREEN RIDING SCHOOL

Tarbock Green Riding School, The Cottage, Water Lane, Tarbock Green, Prescot, **Merseyside**, L35 1RD, **ENGLAND**.
(T) 0151 4878821 **(F)** 0151 4878821.
Contact/s
Instructor: Ms L Gavan **(Q)** BHSAI
Profile Riding School, Stable/Livery.
Floodlit outdoor school. 3 day courses available during school holidays.Training for NVQ examinations
Yr. Est: 1970
Opening Times
Sp: Open Mon - Sun 09:00. Closed Mon - Sun 19:00.
Su: Open Mon - Sun 09:00. Closed Mon - Sun 19:00.
Au: Open Mon - Sun 09:00. Closed Mon - Sun 19:00.
Wn: Open Mon - Sun 09:00. Closed Mon - Sun 19:00. Ref: **YH13869**

TARDEN FARM STABLES

Tarden Farm Stables, 100 Gibb Lane, Mellor, Stockport, **Cheshire**, SK6 5LZ, **ENGLAND**.
(T) 0161 4273322.
Profile Riding School. Ref: **YH13870**

TARRINGTON TRAILERS

Tarrington Trailers Ltd, Wayside, Sandy Lane, Wildmoor, Bromsgrove, **Worcestershire**, B61 0QW, **ENGLAND**.
(T) 0121 4533120.
Profile Transport/Horse Boxes. Ref: **YH13871**

TATE, J

J Tate, Village Farm, West Tytherley, Salisbury, **Wiltshire**, SP5 1NF, **ENGLAND**.
(T) 01794 341684.
Contact/s
Owner: Mr J Tate
Profile Transport/Horse Boxes. Ref: **YH13872**

TATE, MARTIN

Mr Martin Tate, Winterfold Farm, Chaddesley Corbett, Kidderminster, **Worcestershire**, DY10 4PL, **ENGLAND**.
(T) 01562 777243.
Profile Trainer. Ref: **YH13873**

TATE, RICHARD H

Richard H Tate DWCF, 3 Hillway, Tranmere Pk, Guiseley, **Yorkshire (West)**, LS20 8HU, **ENGLAND**.
(T) 01943 876031.
Profile Farrier. Ref: **YH13874**

TATE, ROBIN

Mr Robin Tate, Hesketh Grange, Boltby, Thirsk, **Yorkshire (North)**, YO7 2HU, **ENGLAND**.
(T) 01845 537375.
Profile Trainer. Ref: **YH13875**

TATE, S E

S E Tate, Southampton Rd, Clarendon, Salisbury, **Wiltshire**, SP5 3DG, **ENGLAND**.
(T) 01722 710844.
Contact/s
Owner: Mrs S Tate
Profile Stable/Livery. Ref: **YH13876**

TATE, TOM

Mr Tom Tate, Castle Farm, Hazlewood, Tadcaster, **Yorkshire (North)**, LS24 9NJ, **ENGLAND**.
(T) 01937 836036 **(F)** 01937 530011
(M) 07970 122818.
Profile Trainer. Ref: **YH13877**

TATLOW, D J

D J Tatlow, Pebbly Hill Stud, Icomb Rd, Bledington, Chipping Norton, **Oxfordshire**, OX7 6XJ, **ENGLAND**.
(T) 01608 659332.
Profile Trainer. Ref: **YH13878**

TATTERSALLS

Tattersalls Ltd, Terrace Hse, Newmarket, **Suffolk**, CB8 9BT, **ENGLAND**.
(T) 01638 665931 **(F)** 01638 660850
(E) sales@tattersalls.com. Ref: **YH13879**

TATTERSALLS COMMITTEE

Tattersalls Committee, P O Box13, 19 Wilwyne Cl, Caversham, Reading, **Berkshire**, RG4 0XZ, **ENGLAND**.
(T) 0118 9461757.
Profile Club/Association. Ref: **YH13880**

TATTONDALE STABLES

Tattondale Stables, Tatton Dale, Knutsford, **Cheshire**, WA16 6QJ, **ENGLAND**.
(T) 01565 650618 **(F)** 01565 650618.
Contact/s
Owner: Mrs S Gager-Tomkinson Ref: **YH13881**

TAUNTON & DISTRICT

Taunton & District Riding Club, Rockhill Farm, Wrantage, Taunton, **Somerset**, TA3 6DL, **ENGLAND**.
(T) 01460 54727.
Contact/s
Chairman: Mrs S Rowe
Profile Club/Association, Riding Club. Ref: **YH13882**

TAUNTON RACECOURSE

Taunton Racecourse Co Ltd, Orchard Portman, Taunton, **Somerset**, TA3 7BL, **ENGLAND**.
(T) 01823 337172 **(F)** 01823 325881.
Profile Track/Course. Ref: **YH13883**

TAUNTON VALE FOXHOUNDS

Taunton Vale Foxhounds, Hayfield Farm, Forest Drove North, Bickenhall, Taunton, **Somerset**, TA3 6UE, **ENGLAND**.
(T) 01823 480732. Ref: **YH13884**

TAVERNER, NIGEL S

Nigel S Taverner RSS Hons, Weirside, Avenue Rd, Dobbs Weir, Hoddesdon, **Hertfordshire**, EN11 0BA, **ENGLAND**.
(T) 01992 447261.
Profile Farrier. Ref: **YH13885**

TAVISTOCK SADDLERY

Tavistock Saddlery, 10 Brook St, Tavistock, **Devon**, PL19 0HD, **ENGLAND**.
(T) 01822 617322.
Contact/s
Partner: Mrs R Townsend
Profile Saddlery Retailer. Ref: **YH13886**

TAVY VALLEY RIDING CLUB

Tavy Valley Riding Club, Penwarden Cottage, Golberdon, Callington, **Cornwall**, PL17 9NF, **ENGLAND**.
(T) 01579 383034.
Contact/s
Chairman: Mr R Hill
Profile Club/Association, Riding Club. Ref: **YH13887**

TAWBITTS EXMOORS

Tawbitts Exmoors, Bulls Eye, Luckwell Bridge, Wheddon Cross, Minehead, **Somerset**, TA24 7EQ, **ENGLAND**.
(T) 01643 841330 **(F)** 01643 841330
Affiliated Bodies EPS.
Contact/s
General Manager: Ms G Langdon
Profile Breeder.
Tawbitts' stock is part broken before it is sold, leaving the youngstock ready to be broken in. Tawbitts also offer their stallions for leasing.
Opening Times
Telephone for further Information Ref: **YH13888**

TAWMARSH STUD

Tawmarsh Stud, Lower Pen-Y-Graig Farm, Llanfoist, Abergavenny, **Monmouthshire**, NP7 9LE, **WALES**.
(T) 01873 859207 **(F)** 01873 858186.
Profile Breeder. Ref: **YH13889**

TAWSE, JAMES E

James E Tawse, Bourtreebush Smithy, Newtonhill, Stonehaven, **Aberdeenshire**, AB39 3PA, **SCOTLAND**.
(T) 01224 780271.
Profile Blacksmith. Ref: **YH13890**

TAYBANK RIDING CLUB

Taybank Riding Club, Hillview Cottage, Collace, **Perth and Kinross**, PH2 6JB, **SCOTLAND**.
(T) 01821 650469.
Contact/s
Chairman: Mr J Cassie
Profile Club/Association, Riding Club. Ref: **YH13891**

TAYINLOAN TREKKING CTRE

Tayinloan Trekking Centre, Calfour Farm, Tarbert, **Argyll and Bute**, PA38 4BN, **SCOTLAND**.
(T) 01583 4259.
Profile Equestrian Centre. Trekking Centre.
Ref: **YH13892**

TAYLER & FLETCHER

Tayler & Fletcher, The Square, Stow-on-the-Wold, **Gloucestershire**, GL54 1BL, **ENGLAND**.
(T) 01451 830383 **(F)** 01451 831791
(W) www.taylerfletcher.com.
Contact/s
Enquiries: Mr D Hovard
Profile Estate Agents, Auctioneers & Valuers.
Sell fine art and some equine stock. Yr. Est: 1801
Opening Times
Sp: Open Mon - Sat 09:00. Closed Mon - Fri 17:00, Sat 12:30.
Su: Open Mon - Sat 09:00. Closed Mon - Fri 17:00, Sat 12:30.
Au: Open Mon - Sat 09:00. Closed Mon - Fri 17:00,

Sat 12:30.
Wn: Open Mon - Sat 09:00. Closed Mon - Fri 17:00, Sat 12:30. **Ref: YH13893**

TAYLOR & LEES

Taylor & Lees, Ardmore, 57 Cornard Rd, Sudbury, **Suffolk**, CO10 2XB, **ENGLAND**.
(T) 01787 372588 **(F)** 01787 373246.
Profile Medical Support. **Ref: YH13894**

TAYLOR, A J

Mr A J Taylor, Deans Farm, Streat Hassocks, **Sussex (West)**, BN6 8SB, **ENGLAND**.
(T) 01273 890318.
Profile Supplies. **Ref: YH13895**

TAYLOR, B W

B W Taylor DWCF, Carabella, Manor Rd, Lambourne End, Romford, **Essex**, RM4 1NB, **ENGLAND**.
(T) 020 85003913 **(F)** 020 85003913.
Profile Farrier. **Ref: YH13896**

TAYLOR, BOB

Mr Bob Taylor, 22 Charlemont Rd, Walsall, **Midlands (West)**, WS5 3NG, **ENGLAND**.
(T) 01922 433333 **(F)** 01922 433343. **Ref: YH13897**

TAYLOR, C

C Taylor RSS, 88 Hitchin Rd, Arlesey, **Bedfordshire**, SG15 6SA, **ENGLAND**.
(T) 01462 733839.
Profile Farrier. **Ref: YH13898**

TAYLOR, D J W

D J W Taylor, 92 Main Rd, Hockley, Southend, **Essex**, SS5 4RL, **ENGLAND**.
(T) 01702 200300 **(F)** 01702 206245
(E) the_vet@compuserve.com.
Contact/s
Owner: Mr D Taylor
Profile Trainer. **Ref: YH13899**

TAYLOR, DAVID

David Taylor, Lockwoods Farm, Green Common Lane, Wooburn Green, High Wycombe, **Buckinghamshire**, HP10 0LD, **ENGLAND**.
(T) 01628 521107 **(F)** 01628 521107.
Contact/s
Owner: Mr D Taylor
Profile Transport/Horse Boxes. **Ref: YH13900**

TAYLOR, F

Mr F Taylor, Micklow Hill, Aldbrough St John, Richmond, **Yorkshire (North)**, DL11 7TS, **ENGLAND**.
(T) 01325 374394.
Profile Supplies. **Ref: YH13901**

TAYLOR, GEORGE S

George S Taylor RSS, 6 Home Cl, Kibworth, **Leicestershire**, LE8 0JY, **ENGLAND**.
(T) 07860 959620.
Profile Farrier. **Ref: YH13902**

TAYLOR, JAMES

James Taylor, Tan Hse, Gadlas, Ellesmere, **Shropshire**, SY12 9DY, **ENGLAND**.
(T) 01691 690370.
Profile Farrier. **Ref: YH13903**

TAYLOR, JEREMY N

Jeremy N Taylor DWCF, 44 Main Rd, Wybunbury, Nantwich, **Cheshire**, CW5 7LY, **ENGLAND**.
(T) 01270 841851.
Profile Farrier. **Ref: YH13904**

TAYLOR, JOHN S

John S Taylor, Arnloss, Slamannan, **Falkirk**, **SCOTLAND**..
Profile Breeder. **Ref: YH13905**

TAYLOR, M

M Taylor, Hilltop, Beacon Hill Rd, Hindhead, **Surrey**, GU26 6QD, **ENGLAND**.
(T) 01428 605746.
Contact/s
Owner: Mr M Taylor
Profile Farrier. **Ref: YH13906**

TAYLOR, NIGEL & ANN

Nigel & Ann Taylor, Washbrook Farm, Aston-Le-Walls, Daventry, **Northamptonshire**, NN11 6RT, **ENGLAND**.
(T) 01327 262256 **(F)** 01327 260805
(E) taylors@flying-changes.com
(W) www.washbrook-farm.co.uk.
Profile Trainer. **Ref: YH13907**

TAYLOR, OWEN

Owen Taylor, 28 Lindon Hse, The Austerby, Bourne, **Lincolnshire**, PE10 9JG, **ENGLAND**.
(T) 01778 422964.
Profile Breeder. **Ref: YH13908**

TAYLOR, P D

P D Taylor, 12 Station Rd, Shepreth, Royston, **Hertfordshire**, SG8 6PZ, **ENGLAND**.
(T) 01763 261061.
Profile Farrier. **Ref: YH13909**

TAYLOR, S F C

S F C Taylor, 44 The Grove, Bicknacre, Danbury, **Essex**, CM3 4XB, **ENGLAND**.
(T) 01245 225696.
Profile Farrier. **Ref: YH13910**

TAYLOR, SARAH

Sarah Taylor, Windy Ridge, Beech Lane, Colesbourne, Cheltenham, **Gloucestershire**, GL53 9NS, **ENGLAND**.
(T) 01242 870287
(M) 07885 413961.
Profile Trainer. **Ref: YH13911**

TAYLOR, T

T Taylor, Ealees Stables, Littleborough, **Lancashire**, OL15 0HJ, **ENGLAND**.
(T) 01706 376283.
Profile Farrier. **Ref: YH13912**

TAYLOR, TREVOR

Trevor Taylor, Hillside, Clifford, Hereford, **Herefordshire**, HR3 5HG, **ENGLAND**.
(T) 01497 831466
(M) 07774 478106. **Ref: YH13913**

TAYLOR, W J D

W J D Taylor, Heavy Horse Ctre, Cricket Pk Ltd, Cricket St Thomas, Chard, **Somerset**, TA20 4DD, **ENGLAND**.
(T) 01460 30755 **(F)** 01460 30668.
Profile Breeder. **Ref: YH13914**

TAYLORED HIRE

Taylored Hire Ltd, 11 Paddock Rd, Skelmersdale, **Lancashire**, WN8 9PL, **ENGLAND**.
(T) 01695 733738 **(F)** 01695 733739.
Contact/s
Manager: Mr A Bate
Profile Transport/Horse Boxes. **Ref: YH13915**

TAYLORS EQUESTRIAN

Taylors Equestrian, 18-20 Sandygate, Burnley, **Lancashire**, BB11 1RW, **ENGLAND**.
(T) 01282 422044 **(F)** 01282 422044.
Contact/s
Owner: Miss W Taylor
Profile Saddlery Retailer. **Ref: YH13916**

TAYLORS OF SOUTH WINGFIELD

Taylors of South Wingfield Ltd, South Wingfield Mill, South Wingfield, **Derbyshire**, DE55 7NJ, **ENGLAND**.
(T) 01773 832631.
Profile Supplies. **Ref: YH13917**

TAYLORS SADDLERY

Taylors Saddlery, 8 New Rd, Belton In Rutland, Oakham, **Rutland**, LE15 9LE, **ENGLAND**.
(T) 01572 718720 **(F)** 01572 717294.
Contact/s
Owner: Mr D Taylor **Ref: YH13918**

TAYLORS TRAILERS

Taylors Trailers, Cellars Clough Business Pk, Marsden, Huddersfield, **Yorkshire (West)**, HD7 6LY, **ENGLAND**.
(T) 01484 840011 **(F)** 01484 840022.
Contact/s
Owner: Mrs G Taylor
Profile Transport/Horse Boxes. **Ref: YH13919**

TDS

TDS, Lymington Barn, Lymington Bottom Rd, Medstead, Alton, **Hampshire**, GU34 5EW, **ENGLAND**.
(T) 01420 562758 **(F)** 01420 563981.
Contact/s
Owner: Mr T Day **Ref: YH13920**

TEAGLE MACHINERY

Teagle Machinery Ltd, Blackwater, Truro, **Cornwall**, TR4 8HQ, **ENGLAND**.
(T) 01872 560592 **(F)** 01872 561166.
Profile Supplies. **Ref: YH13921**

TEAL COTTAGE STUD

Teal Cottage Stud, Welburn, **Yorkshire (North)**, YO60 7EJ, **ENGLAND**.
(T) 01653 618884 **(F)** 01653 618884.
Contact/s
Owner: Mr I Ratcliffe **(Q)** BHSAI
Profile Stable/Livery.
Broodmares & Young Stock Livery No.Staff: 1
Yr. Est: 1991 C.Size: 30 Acres
Opening Times
Sp: Open Mon - Sun 07:30. Closed Mon - Sun 19:30.
Su: Open Mon - Sun 07:30. Closed Mon - Sun 19:30.
Au: Open Mon - Sun 07:30. Closed Mon - Sun 19:30.
Wn: Open Mon - Sun 07:30. Closed Mon - Sun 19:30.
Open the above hours to owners. Telephone for an appointment. **Ref: YH13922**

TEAL, V J

Mrs V J Teal, Little Burrows, Laugharne, St Clears, **Carmarthenshire**, SA33 4RS, **WALES**.
(T) 01994 427396.
Profile Supplies. **Ref: YH13923**

TEAM CHASER

Team Chaser & Amateur Jockey Magazine, 50A Warwick St, Leamington Spa, **Warwickshire**, CV32 5JS, **ENGLAND**.
(T) 01926 451943 **(F)** 0926 .
Profile Supplies. **Ref: YH13924**

TEAM GROUP

Team Group (The), Burton Mill Farmhse, Burton Pk Rd, Petworth, **Sussex (West)**, GU28 0JR, **ENGLAND**.
(T) 01798 869496 **(F)** 01798 869497.
Contact/s
Partner: Mr D Morley
Profile Supplies. **Ref: YH13925**

TEASDALE, D

Mr D Teasdale, 2 Gaunless Trce, Copley, Bishop Auckland, **County Durham**, **ENGLAND**..
Profile Trainer. **Ref: YH13926**

TEBBUTT, N F & A C F

N F & A C F Tebbutt, Hollow Farm Stud, Winwick, Huntingdon, **Cambridgeshire**, PE17 5PU, **ENGLAND**.
(T) 01832 293206.
Profile Breeder. **Ref: YH13927**

TEBBUTT, NORMAN & ALASDAIR

Norman & Alasdair Tebbutt, Church Hse, Brook St, St Neots, **Cambridgeshire**, PE19 2BP, **ENGLAND**.
(T) 01832 293206 **(F)** 01832 293649.
Profile Medical Support. **Ref: YH13928**

TECNOTILE

Tecnotile, 4-5 Gough Sq, London, **London (Greater)**, EC4A 3DE, **ENGLAND**.
(T) 020 75831881 **(F)** 020 75831882.
Contact/s
Sales Manager: Mr P Figg **Ref: YH13929**

TED EDGAR

Ted Edgar Ltd, Rio Grande, Hill Wootton Road, Leek Wootton, Warwick, **Warwickshire**, CV35 7PN, **ENGLAND**.
(T) 01926 855631 **(F)** 01926 864034.
Contact/s
Partner: Ted Edgar
Profile Trainer. **Ref: YH13930**

TEDFOULD FARM MNGMT SVS

Tedfould Farm Management Services Ltd, Okehurst Lane, Billingshurst, **Sussex (West)**, RH14 9HU, **ENGLAND**.
(T) 01403 783524.
Profile Supplies. **Ref: YH13931**

TEDMAN HARNESS

Tedman Harness, P O Box 27, Wheatley, **Oxfordshire**, OX33 1FS, **ENGLAND**.
(T) 01865 876463 **(F)** 01865 876006.
Profile Saddlery Retailer, Trainer. **Ref: YH13932**

TEE JAY EQUESTRIAN

Tee Jay Equestrian, Kimpton Bottom Nursery, Kimpton Bottom, Kimpton, Hitchin, **Hertfordshire**, SG4 8ET, **ENGLAND**.
(T) 01438 832921
(M) 07778 550999.
Profile Saddlery Retailer. **Ref: YH13933**

TEE, B

Mrs B Tee, Gorse Meadow, Sway Rd, Lymington, **Hampshire**, SO41 8LR, **ENGLAND**.
(T) 01590 673354 (F) 01590 673336.
Contact/s
Owner: Mr J Hillman
Profile Breeder. Ref: YH13934

TEEN RANCH SCOTLAND

Teen Ranch Scotland, Ballindean Hse, Inchture, **Perth and Kinross**, PH14 9SF, **SCOTLAND**.
(T) 01828 686227.
Profile Riding School. Ref: YH13935

TEIGNBRIDGE BRIDLEWAYS

Teignbridge Bridleways, Knapps Cottage, Ashcombe, Dawlish, **Devon**, EX7 0QD, **ENGLAND**.
(T) 01626 866655.
Profile Club/Association. Ref: YH13936

TEIZERS EQUESTRIAN CTRE

Teizers Equestrian Centre, Antlands Lane West, Burstow, **Surrey**, RH6 9TE, **ENGLAND**.
(T) 01293 784662 (F) 01293 784662
(M) 07721 521168
(E) brian4fd@aol.com.
Profile Riding School, Stable/Livery. Ref: YH13937

TELFER, J

J Telfer, 37 Park Ave, Bilston, Roslin, **Lothian (Mid)**, EH25 9SE, **SCOTLAND**.
(T) 0131 4403568.
Profile Farrier. Ref: YH13938

TELFER, JOHN

John Telfer, Unit 5 Mansfield Gardens Ind Est, Hawick, **Scottish Borders**, TD9 8AN, **SCOTLAND**.
(T) 01450 372608.
Profile Blacksmith. Ref: YH13939

TELFER, THOMAS

Thomas Telfer DWCF, The Stables, Auchengray, Carnwath, **Lanarkshire (South)**, ML11 8LW, **SCOTLAND**.
(T) 01501 785387
(M) 07831 582229.
Profile Farrier. Ref: YH13940

TELFORD EQUESTRIAN CTRE

Telford Equestrian Centre, Lodge Bank Farm, Donnington Wood, Telford, **Shropshire**, TF2 8AS, **ENGLAND**.
(T) 01952 619825. Ref: YH13941

TELFORD SADDLERY

Telford Saddlery, Wellington Rd, Muxton, Telford, **Shropshire**, TF2 8NN, **ENGLAND**.
(T) 01952 677300 (F) 01952 677775.
Contact/s
Manageress: Mrs S Warren Ref: YH13942

TELFORD, R

R Telford, Stables Cottage, Ayton Castle, Eyemouth, **Scottish Borders**, TD14 5RD, **SCOTLAND**.
(T) 01890 781519
(M) 07885 058451.
Contact/s
Owner: Mr R Telford
Profile Trainer. Trains Show Horses and Event Horses.
R Telford trains Show Horses and Event Horses
Opening Times
Sp: Open Mon - Sun 07:00. Closed Mon - Sun 18:00.
Su: Open Mon - Sun 07:00. Closed Mon - Sun 18:00.
Au: Open Mon - Sun 07:00. Closed Mon - Sun 18:00.
Wn: Open Mon - Sun 07:00. Closed Mon - Sun 18:00. Ref: YH13943

TEME TRAILERS

Teme Trailers, Warwick Hse, Leintwardine, Craven Arms, **Shropshire**, SY7 0NL, **ENGLAND**.
(T) 01547 540322.
Contact/s
Owner: Mr H Edwards
Profile Transport/Horse Boxes. Ref: YH13944

TEME VETNRY PRACTICE

Teme Veterinary Practice (Ludlow), The Casemill, Temeside, Ludlow, **Shropshire**, SY8 1JW, **ENGLAND**.
(T) 01584 872147 (F) 01584 874523.
Profile Medical Support. Ref: YH13945

TEME VETNRY PRACTICE

Teme Veterinary Practice (Tenbury Wells), 2 Cross St, Tenbury Wells, **Worcestershire**, WR15 8EE, **ENGLAND**.
(T) 01584 810227.
Profile Medical Support. Ref: YH13946

TEMPLE FARM STABLES

Temple Farm Stables, Temple Farm, Gorebridge, **Lothian (Mid)**, EH23 4SE, **SCOTLAND**.
(T) 01875 830599.
Contact/s
Manager: Ms G McKeen Ref: YH13947

TEMPLE TRINE STUD

Temple Trine Stud, Hill Hse Farm, Ferry Lane, Brothertoft, Boston, **Lincolnshire**, PE20 3SS, **ENGLAND**.
(T) 01205 280338.
Contact/s
Owner: Mr D Meeds
Profile Breeder. Yr. Est: 1950
Opening Times
Telephone between 08:00 - 10:00 or 18:00 - 21:00.
Telephone for an appointment Ref: YH13948

TEMPLE, B M

Mr B M Temple, Skeeting Farm, Driffield, **Yorkshire (East)**, YO25 5UX, **ENGLAND**.
(T) 01377 252321.
Profile Supplies. Ref: YH13949

TEMPLE, BRIAN ROBERT

Brian Robert Temple, Plum Pk Farm, Watling St, Paulerspury, Towcester, **Northamptonshire**, NN12 6LQ, **ENGLAND**.
(T) 01327 811350.
Profile Farrier. Ref: YH13950

TEMPLEMAN COMPUTER SYSTEMS

Templeman Computer Systems, Clifford Chambers, Stratford-upon-Avon, **Warwickshire**, CV37 8LB, **ENGLAND**.
(T) 01789 266237
(E) tricks@ibm.net. Ref: YH13951

TENACRE EQUESTRIAN CTRE

Tenacre Equestrian Centre, Drainside North, Kirton, Boston, **Lincolnshire**, PE20 1PE, **ENGLAND**.
(T) 01205 724352.
Contact/s
Owner: Mrs M Love Ref: YH13952

TENDRING HUNDRED FARMERS

Tendring Hundred Farmers Club, 9 Oaklands Ave, Colchester, **Essex**, CO3 5ER, **ENGLAND**.
(T) 01206 571517 (F) 01206 571517
(E) anne@tendringshow.demon.co.uk.
Contact/s
Secretary: Mrs A Taylor
Profile Club/Association.
Annual Agricultural Show, held on the second Saturday in July, includes a wide range of equestrian events. Ref: YH13953

TENDRING HUNDRED RIDING CLUB

Tendring Hundred Riding Club, Hill Hse Farm, Thorpe-Le-Soken, Clacton-on-Sea, **Essex**, CO16 0AG, **ENGLAND**.
(T) 01255 830431.
Contact/s
Chairman: Mrs H Lush
Profile Club/Association, Riding Club. Ref: YH13954

TERRA-VAC

Vulcan Engineers Ltd, Vulcan Engineers Ltd, Unit 2 Melbourne Bridge, Withersfield, Haverhill, **Suffolk**, CB9 7RR, **ENGLAND**.
(T) 01440 712171 (F) 01440 714109
(E) sales@terra-vac.com
(W) www.terra-vac.com.
Contact/s
For Bookings: Ms S Barham
Profile Supplies.
Terra-vac supply paddock and stable cleaners.
Yr. Est: 1993
Opening Times
Telephone or email for further details Ref: YH13955

TERRIS, J & D G

J & D G Terris, Market Rd, Grantown-on-Spey, **Moray**, PH26 3HP, **SCOTLAND**.
(T) 01479 872805.
Contact/s
Owner: Mr J Reid
Profile Blacksmith. Ref: YH13956

TERRY DAVIS

Terry Davis Harness & Horse Collar Maker, Bridle Cottage, Leamoor Common, Craven Arms, **Shropshire**, SY7 8DN, **ENGLAND**.
(T) 01694 781206.
Profile Harness Maker.
Harness & Horse Collar Maker. Ref: YH13957

TERRY, GREGORY FRANCIS

Gregory Francis Terry RSS, The Forge, Shantock Lane, Bovingdon, **Hertfordshire**, HP3 0NN, **ENGLAND**.
(T) 01442 833274.
Profile Farrier. Ref: YH13958

TERRY, JOSEPH G

Joseph G Terry DWCF, Rose Cottage, Lycrome Rd, Chesham, **Buckinghamshire**, HP5 3LD, **ENGLAND**.
(T) 01494 775078
(M) 07976 742283.
Profile Farrier. Ref: YH13959

TERTOWIE CTRE

Tertowie Centre, Kinellar, **Aberdeenshire**, AB21 0TN, **SCOTLAND**.
(T) 01224 640366.
Profile Riding School. Ref: YH13960

TEST VALLEY GARAGE

Test Valley Garage, Romsey Rd, Kings Somborne, Stockbridge, **Hampshire**, SO20 6PW, **ENGLAND**.
(T) 01794 388384.
Contact/s
Senior Partner: Mr M Ellis
Profile Transport/Horse Boxes. Ref: YH13961

TETBURY

Tetbury Agricultural Merchants, Grain Hse Farm, Chaceley, **Gloucestershire**, GL19 4EA, **ENGLAND**.
(T) 01452 780499 (F) 01452 780161.
Profile Supplies. Ref: YH13962

TETCHWICK FEED SUPPLIES

Tetchwick Feed Supplies, Panshill Cottage, Murcott, Kidlington, **Oxfordshire**, OX5 2RG, **ENGLAND**.
(T) 01869 241018
(M) 07831 520330.
Profile Supplies. Ref: YH13963

TETTENHALL HORSE SANCTUARY

Tettenhall Horse Sanctuary, South Perton Farm, Jenny Walker's Lane, Old Perton, **Midlands (West)**, WV6 7HB, **ENGLAND**.
(T) 01902 764422 (F) 01902 380370. Ref: YH13964

TEVERSAL SADDLERY

Teversal Saddlery, Doe Hill Hse Farm, Blackwell Lane, Stonebroom, Alfreton, **Derbyshire**, DE55 6JQ, **ENGLAND**.
(T) 01773 872506 (F) 01773 872506.
Contact/s
Owner: Mrs K Barnard
Profile Saddlery Retailer. Ref: YH13965

TEVIOT HORSEWEAR DIRECT

Teviot Horsewear Direct, Glebehead Farm, Roberton, Hawick, **Scottish Borders**, TD9 7LT, **SCOTLAND**.
(T) 01450 880254.
Contact/s
Owner: Mrs J Hendry
Profile Supplies. Ref: YH13966

TEVIOT TOWN & COUNTRY

Teviot Town & Country Supplies, 22 Oliver Cres, Hawick, **Scottish Borders**, TD9 9BQ, **SCOTLAND**.
(T) 01450 371699 (F) 01450 371699.
Contact/s
Owner: Mr C Hamilton
Profile Supplies. Ref: YH13967

TEWIN HILL SADDLERY

Tewin Hill Saddlery, Tewin Hill Farm, Tewin Hill, Tewin, Welwyn, **Hertfordshire**, AL6 0LL, **ENGLAND**.
(T) 01438 715070.
Contact/s
Owner: Mr R Pettitt
Profile Riding School. Ref: YH13968

TEWKESBURY SADDLERY

Pegasus Av Eq, Tolsey Lane, Tewkesbury, **Gloucestershire**, GL20 5AE, **ENGLAND**.
(T) 01684 291357 (F) 01684 293344.
Contact/s
General Manager: Ms C Spencer
Profile Riding Wear Retailer, Saddlery Retailer, Supplies. No.Staff: 2 Yr. Est: 1994
Opening Times
Sp: Open 09:30. Closed 16:00.
Su: Open 09:30. Closed 16:00.
Au: Open 09:30. Closed 16:00.
Wn: Open 09:30. Closed 16:00. Ref: YH13969

A-Z of COMPANIES

TEXAS RODEO BULL

Texas Rodeo Bull, 8 East St, Nettleham, Lincoln, **Lincolnshire**, LN2 2SL, **ENGLAND**.
(T) 01522 754431. Ref: YH13970

TFP

Total Foot Protection Ltd, Bridge Hse Equestrian Ctre, Five Oaks Rd, Slinfold, Horsham, **Sussex (West)**, RH13 7QW, **ENGLAND**.
(T) 01403 791000 (F) 01403 791008
(W) www.tfp.uk.com.
Contact/s
Farrier: Mr D Nicholls
(E) david@tfp.uk.com
Profile Farrier, Medical Support, Supplies.
Opening Times
Sp: Open 08:00. Closed 17:30.
Su: Open 08:00. Closed 17:30.
Au: Open 08:00. Closed 17:30.
Wn: Open 08:00. Closed 17:30. Ref: YH13971

THACKER, GRAHAM

Graham Thacker, 43 Malvern Rd, Grays, **Essex**, RM17 5TH, **ENGLAND**.
(T) 01375 381888.
Profile Farrier. Ref: YH13972

THAMES VALLEY

Thames Valley Equestrian Construction, Orchard Cottage, Cuxham, Oxford, **Oxfordshire**, OX49 5NH, **ENGLAND**.
(T) 01491 613900 (F) 01491 613900.
Contact/s
Owner: Mr H Daly
(E) dalyhugh@hotmail.com Ref: YH13973

THAMES VALLEY CLUB

Thames Valley Club, East Lodge, Wokefield Pk, Reading, **Berkshire**, RG7 3AH, **ENGLAND**.
(T) 0118 9332535.
Profile Club/Association. Ref: YH13974

THAMES VALLEY FENCING

Thames Valley Fencing & Construction, Hillside Cottage, Chiselhampton, **Oxfordshire**, OX44 7XQ, **ENGLAND**.
(T) 01865 400778.
Profile Track/Course. Ref: YH13975

THAMES VALLEY RIDING CLUB

Thames Valley Riding Club, 96 Springfield Pk, Holyport Rd, Maidenhead, **Berkshire**, SL6 2YU, **ENGLAND**.
(T) 01628 672873.
Contact/s
Chairman: Mrs T Taylor
Profile Club/Association, Riding Club. Ref: YH13976

THAMES VALLEY TREKKING

Thames Valley Trekking, Rosehill, Henley-on-Thames, **Oxfordshire**, RG9 3EB, **ENGLAND**.
(T) 01928 824260.
Profile Equestrian Centre. Ref: YH13977

THANET SHOW JUMPS

Thanet Show Jumps, Chestnuts, Woolpack Corner, Biddenden, Ashford, **Kent**, TN27 8BN, **ENGLAND**.
(T) 01580 291932
(E) thanet.showjumps@virgin.net
(W) www.thanetshowjumps.co.uk.
Contact/s
Enquiries: Mrs D Hawker
Profile Supplies. Show Jump Manufacturer.
Producers of wooden and plastic jumps. BSJA range, standard ranges, plastic range, complete fences, walls and poles are all available. Yr. Est: 1977
Opening Times
Please telephone for an appointment Ref: YH13978

THATCHER, G

G Thatcher, 9 Flowerstone, Binegar, Bath, **Bath & Somerset (North East)**, BA3 4UQ, **ENGLAND**.
(T) 01749 840234.
Contact/s
Owner: Mr G Thatcher
Profile Farrier. Ref: YH13979

THEAKSTON STUD

Theakston Stud, Theakston, Bedale, **Yorkshire (North)**, DL8 2HL, **ENGLAND**.
(T) 01677 422647 (F) 01677 422647.
Contact/s
Manager: John McIntyre
Profile Breeder. Ref: YH13980

THELWALL, P A

Mr P A Thelwall, 28 Fen Rd, Bassingbourn, Royston, **Hertfordshire**, SG8 5PQ, **ENGLAND**.
(T) 01763 242019. Ref: YH13981

THEOBALD, CARON

Caron Theobald, 24 Providence St, Greenhithe, **Kent**, DA9 9AA, **ENGLAND**.
(T) 01322 385599/ 01634 815555.
Contact/s
Physiotherapist: Caron Theobald
Profile Medical Support. Ref: YH13982

THEOBALD, L & N

L & N Theobald, 5-6 Park St, Stafford, **Staffordshire**, ST17 4AL, **ENGLAND**.
(T) 01785 252846.
Profile Medical Support. Ref: YH13983

THEOBALDS STUD

Theobalds Stud, Gunsite Farm Cottages, Old Park Ride, Waltham Cross, **Hertfordshire**, EN7 5HZ, **ENGLAND**.
(T) 01992 626747 (F) 01992 624554.
Contact/s
Owner: Mr K Panos
Profile Breeder. Ref: YH13984

THERAPY SYSTEMS

Therapy Systems, Woodend Hse, Carron, Aberlour, **Moray**, AB38 7QP, **SCOTLAND**.
(T) 01340 810549.
Profile Supplies.
Therapy Equipment Stockist Ref: YH13985

THERMATEX

Thermatex Ltd, 27-30 Pentood Ind Est, Station Rd, Cardigan, **Carmarthenshire**, SA43 3AD, **WALES**.
(T) 01239 614648 (F) 01239 621234.
Contact/s
Admin: Vanessa Roberts
Profile Supplies.
Manufacturer and retailer of horse rugs, horse head and neck covers, dog accessories and country clothing. Yr. Est: 1986
Opening Times
Sp: Open Mon - Sun 09:00. Closed Mon - Sun 17:00.
Su: Open Mon - Sun 09:00. Closed Mon - Sun 17:00.
Au: Open Mon - Sun 09:00. Closed Mon - Sun 17:00.
Wn: Open Mon - Sun 09:00. Closed Mon - Sun 17:00. Ref: YH13986

THEW, ARNOTT

Thew, Arnott & Co Ltd, Fodden Works, 270 London Rd, Wallington, **Surrey**, SM6 7DJ, **ENGLAND**.
(T) 020 86699680.
Profile Supplies. Ref: YH13987

THICK, N K

Mr N K Thick, Frog's Hall, Leddington, Dymock, **Gloucestershire**, GL18 2EG, **ENGLAND**.
(T) 01531 890453.
Profile Supplies. Ref: YH13988

THICKETT, MATTHEW C

Matthew C Thickett DWCF, 30 Elgitha Drive, Thurcroft, Rotherham, **Yorkshire (South)**, S66 9PD, **ENGLAND**.
(T) 01709 549374.
Profile Farrier. Ref: YH13989

THIEFBEATERS

Thiefbeaters Ltd Bernard Humphries, Po Box 5789, Towcester, **Northamptonshire**, NN12 5ZJ, **ENGLAND**.
(T) 0870 6064725 (F) 01327 860341
(E) info@thiefbeaters.co.uk
(W) www.thiefbeaters.co.uk.
Profile Security.
Security codes are stamped, etched and engraved into products several times as well as 'non-destruct' labels, electronic tags and micro dots which can be tracked and located. Ref: YH13990

THIMBLEBY & SHORTLAND

Thimbleby & Shortland, Market Hse, 31 Great Knollys St, Reading, **Berkshire**, RG1 7HU, **ENGLAND**.
(T) 0118 9508611 (F) 0118 9505896
(E) sjn@thimbley.demon.co.uk.
Profile Auctioneers. Ref: YH13991

THIMBLEBY FARM STABLES

Thimbleby Farm Stables, Thimbleby Hill, Stanhope, Bishop Auckland, **County Durham**, DL13 2PN, **ENGLAND**.
(T) 01388 526380.
Contact/s
Owner: Mr A Norman Ref: YH13992

THIMBLEBY SADDLERY

Thimbleby Saddlery, Hallgarth Farm, Thimbleby, Horncastle, **Lincolnshire**, LN9 5RE, **ENGLAND**.
(T) 01507 526653.
Contact/s
Manageress: Miss P Heath Ref: YH13993

THINFORD SADDLERY

Thinford Saddlery, Thinford, Durham, **County Durham**, DH6 5JZ, **ENGLAND**.
(T) 01388 814391 (F) 01388 814391.
Contact/s
Partner: Mr J Thompson Ref: YH13994

THINK EQUUS

Think Equus, Ambergate Barn, P O Box 230, Kidlington, **Oxfordshire**, OX5 2TU, **ENGLAND**.
(T) 01865 842806 (F) 01865 842806
(E) michael@thinkequus.com
(W) www.thinkequus.com.
Contact/s
General Manager: Ms S Peace
Profile Trainer. Behaviour Courses. No.Staff: 5
Yr. Est: 1996 C.Size: 9 Acres
Opening Times
Sp: Open 09:00. Closed 17:00.
Su: Open 09:00. Closed 17:00.
Au: Open 09:00. Closed 17:00.
Wn: Open 09:00. Closed 17:00. Ref: YH13995

THINKING HORSES

Thinking Horses, Shirwell, Muddiford, Barnstaple, **Devon**, EX31 4HR, **ENGLAND**.
(T) 01271 850864. Ref: YH13996

THIRLBY, R J & V E

R J & V E Thirlby, Upton Pk, Nuneaton, **Warwickshire**, CVB 6BN, **ENGLAND**.
(T) 01455 213218.
Contact/s
Owner: Mr R Thirlby
Profile Breeder.
Breeder of Welsh Section A ponies Ref: YH13997

THIRLESTANE CASTLE

Thirlestane Castle Scottish Champ H T (Lauder - Borders), Mosshouses, Galashiels, **Scottish Borders**, TD1 2PG, **SCOTLAND**.
(T) 01896 860242 (F) 01896 860295. Ref: YH13998

THIRSK RACECOURSE

Thirsk Racecourse Ltd, The Racecourse, Station Rd, Thirsk, **Yorkshire (North)**, YO7 1QL, **ENGLAND**.
(T) 01845 522276 (F) 01845 525353.
Profile Track/Course. Ref: YH13999

THISTLE VETNRY CTRE

Thistle Veterinary Health Centre, 1 Alcorn Rigg, Clovenstone Drive, Edinburgh, **Edinburgh (City of)**, EH14 3BF, **SCOTLAND**.
(T) 0131 4536699.
Profile Medical Support. Ref: YH14000

THISTLETON FARM SADDLERY

Thistleton Farm Saddlery, Thistleton Farm, Common Lane, Knottingley, **Yorkshire (West)**, WF11 8BN, **ENGLAND**.
(T) 01977 672298.
Profile Saddlery Retailer, Stable/Livery.
Ref: YH14001

THODY, M & P

M & P Thody, Wood View Farm, Toseland Rd, Graveley, Huntingdon, **Cambridgeshire**, PE18 9PS, **ENGLAND**.
(T) 01480 830233.
Profile Supplies. Ref: YH14002

THOM, ALISON

Alison Thom, 40 St. Philips Rd, Newmarket, **Suffolk**, CB8 0EN, **ENGLAND**.
(T) 01638 669843.
Contact/s
Owner: Mr D Thom
Profile Transport/Horse Boxes. Ref: YH14003

THOM, ALLAN

Allan Thom, Milton Of Balhary Farm, Alyth, Blairgowrie, **Perth and Kinross**, PH11 8LS, **SCOTLAND**.
(T) 01828 632562.
Contact/s
Owner: Mr A Thom
Profile Blacksmith. Ref: YH14004

THOM, J G

Mr J G Thom, Hall Farm, Drongon, Ayr, **Ayrshire (South)**, KA6 7EE, **SCOTLAND**.

(T) 01292 570329
(M) 07778 740208.
Profile Breeder. Ref: YH14005

THOMAS & PERCY

Thomas & Percy (Llandeilo), 6 King St, Llandeilo, **Carmarthenshire**, SA19 6BA, **WALES**.
(T) 01558 823377.
Contact/s
Vet: Mr I Percy (Q) BVET, MRCVS
Profile Medical Support. Ref: YH14006

THOMAS IRVING

Thomas Irving 1998, Dunston Rd, Sheepbridge, Chesterfield, **Derbyshire**, S41 9QD, **ENGLAND**.
(T) 01246 260336 (F) 01246 268815.
Profile Supplies. Ref: YH14007

THOMAS JONES

Thomas Jones & Co, Hafron Surgery, Llanidloes Rd, Newtown, **Powys**, SY16 1HA, **WALES**.
(T) 01686 84245.
Profile Medical Support. Ref: YH14008

THOMAS LEATHBRIDGE

Thomas Leathbridge Ltd, 24 Stechworth Rd, Woodditton, Newmarket, **Suffolk**, CB8 9SJ, **ENGLAND**.
(T) 01638 730611. Ref: YH14009

THOMAS PETTIFER

Thomas Pettifer & Company Limited, Newchurch, Romney Marsh, **Kent**, TN29 0DZ, **ENGLAND**.
(T) 01303 874455 (F) 01303 874801.
Profile Medical Support. Ref: YH14010

THOMAS SHOW TEAM

Llanddarog Equestrian Centre, Llanddarog Rd, Llanddarog, Carmarthen, **Carmarthenshire**, SA32 8AN, **WALES**.
(T) 01267 275328 (F) 01267 275228
(E) thomasshowteam@aol.com
(W) www.thomasshowteam.co.uk
Affiliated Bodies BSPS.
Contact/s
For Bookings: Mr P Thomas
Profile Equestrian Centre. Show Horse and Pony Producers.
The leading suppliers of top Wembley Show Ponies in the UK. No.Staff: 3 Yr. Est: 1989
C.Size: 25 Acres Ref: YH14011

THOMAS, A

A Thomas RSS, 11 Heol Treventy, Cefneithin, Llanelli, **Carmarthenshire**, SA14 7DF, **WALES**.
(T) 01269 843015.
Profile Farrier. Ref: YH14012

THOMAS, B

B Thomas, Lodor Fach, Maenclochog, Clynderwen, **Pembrokeshire**, **WALES**.
(T) 01437 532277
(M) 07974 790510.
Profile Breeder. Ref: YH14013

THOMAS, D

Mrs D Thomas, Pen-Y-Lan, Aberkenfig, **Bridgend**, CF32 9AN, **WALES**.
(T) 01656 720254 (F) 01656 721418.
Profile Supplies. Ref: YH14014

THOMAS, D

Mr & Mrs D Thomas, 9 Summerfield Trce, Fleur-De-Lys, Blackwood, **Monmouthshire**, NP12 3US, **WALES**.
(T) 01443 820837.
Contact/s
Owner: Mr D Thomas
Profile Breeder.
Breeder of Welsh Section A ponies. Ref: YH14015

THOMAS, D

Mrs D Thomas, The Revel, Talgarth, **Powys**, **WALES**.
(T) 01874 730117.
Profile Breeder. Ref: YH14016

THOMAS, D G B

Mr D G B Thomas, Glyn Hebog, St Clears Rd, Carmarthen, **Carmarthenshire**, SA33 5DX, **WALES**.
(T) 01267 211227.
Profile Breeder. Ref: YH14017

THOMAS, D J

D J Thomas, Llwynbustach, Llangendeirne, Kidwelly, **Carmarthenshire**, SE17 5DF, **WALES**.
(T) 01269 870381.
Profile Breeder. Ref: YH14018

THOMAS, D J M

D J M Thomas DWCF, Llys-Neuadd, Llanybydder, **Carmarthenshire**, SA40 9TX, **WALES**.
(T) 01570 480832.
Profile Farrier. Ref: YH14019

THOMAS, DAVID

David Thomas, Waen Isa Farm, Waen Isa Lane, Babell, Holywell, **Flintshire**, CH8 8QB, **WALES**.
(T) 01352 720252.
Contact/s
Owner: Mr D Thomas Ref: YH14020

THOMAS, H T

Mr H T Thomas, Panty-Fallen, Waringron Rd, Betws, Ammanford, **Carmarthenshire**, **WALES**.
Profile Trainer. Ref: YH14021

THOMAS, HUW R

Huw R Thomas, 35 Commercial St, Kenfig Hill, Bridgend, **Bridgend**, CF33 6DH, **WALES**.
(T) 01656 740391.
Contact/s
Owner: Mr H Thomas
Profile Saddlery Retailer. Ref: YH14022

THOMAS, J E

J E Thomas, Smithfield, Dinas Cross, Newport, **Pembrokeshire**, SA42 0UY, **WALES**.
(T) 01348 811221.
Profile Blacksmith. Ref: YH14023

THOMAS, J T

J T Thomas, Slade Paddocks, Llanmaes, Llantwit Major, **Glamorgan (Vale of)**, CF61 2XR, **WALES**.
(T) 01446 793317.
Contact/s
Owner: Mrs K Thomas
Profile Breeder. Ref: YH14024

THOMAS, JILL

Mrs Jill Thomas, 1 Cape Trce, St Just, Penzance, **Cornwall**, TR19 7JF, **ENGLAND**.
(T) 01736 787245. Ref: YH14025

THOMAS, MICHAEL JAMES

Michael James Thomas AWCF, Forge Cottage, Eastington, Cheltenham, **Gloucestershire**, GL54 3PL, **ENGLAND**.
(T) 01451 860695.
Profile Farrier. Ref: YH14026

THOMAS, PHILIP J

Philip J Thomas DWCF BII, 5 Haywards Farm Cl, Verwood, **Dorset**, BH31 6XW, **ENGLAND**.
(T) 01202 813890.
Profile Farrier. Ref: YH14027

THOMAS, SHELLEY

Shelley Thomas, The Forge/Kew Bridge Steam Museum, Green Dragon Lane, Brentford, **London (Greater)**, TW8 0EN, **ENGLAND**.
(T) 020 8569 7386.
Profile Blacksmith. Ref: YH14028

THOMAS, V & M

V & M Thomas, Pengraig, Llanfairynghornwy, Holyhead, **Isle of Anglesey**, LL65 4LS, **WALES**.
(T) 01407 730396.
Profile Breeder. Ref: YH14029

THOMPSON BRANCASTER FARMS

Thompson Brancaster Farms & Holiday Homes, Field Hse, Brancaster, King's Lynn, **Norfolk**, PE31 8AG, **ENGLAND**.
(T) 07885 269538 (F) 01485 210261.
Profile Stable/Livery. Ref: YH14030

THOMPSON, A

A Thompson, 220 Main Rd, Sutton At Hone, Dartford, **Kent**, DA4 9HJ, **ENGLAND**.
(T) 01322 863263.
Profile Supplies. Ref: YH14031

THOMPSON, ALAN

Alan Thompson, Southways, Dock Acres, Carnforth, **Lancashire**, LA6 1HP, **ENGLAND**.
(T) 01524 732992 (F) 01524 732073.
Contact/s
Owner: Mr A Thompson
Profile Transport/Horse Boxes. Ref: YH14032

THOMPSON, ARTHUR RICHARD

Arthur Richard Thompson, Woodlands, Thornberry Gardens, Ludchurch, Narberth, **Pembrokeshire**, SA67 8JQ, **WALES**.
(T) 01834 831579.
Profile Farrier. Ref: YH14033

THOMPSON, C

C Thompson, Knowsley Farm, Shawforth, Rochdale, **Lancashire**, OL12 8XE, **ENGLAND**.
(T) 01706 853884.
Profile Farrier. Ref: YH14034

THOMPSON, EMILY

Emily Thompson, Sussex Farm Stables, Burnham Market, King's Lynn, **Norfolk**, PE31 8JY, **ENGLAND**.
(T) 01328 730159.
Profile Trainer. Ref: YH14035

THOMPSON, GEORGE BERNARD

George Bernard Thompson, The Laurels, 277 Bedford Rd, Rushden, **Northamptonshire**, NN10 0SQ, **ENGLAND**.
(T) 01933 357457.
Profile Farrier. Ref: YH14036

THOMPSON, J A

J A Thompson, Vine Hse Farm, Darkinson Lane, Lea Town, Preston, **Lancashire**, PR4 0RJ, **ENGLAND**.
(T) 01772 736240.
Contact/s
Owner: Mrs J Thompson Ref: YH14037

THOMPSON, LUKE P

Luke P Thompson DWCF, Berry Croft, Red Fen Rd, Little Thetford, Ely, **Cambridgeshire**, CB6 3HW, **ENGLAND**.
(T) 01353 649366.
Profile Farrier. Ref: YH14038

THOMPSON, MARGOT

Margot Thompson, Heronfield Cottage, 2 Bosworth Rd, Snarestone, **Derbyshire**, DE12 7DQ, **ENGLAND**.
(T) 01530 273061.
Profile Supplies. Ref: YH14039

THOMPSON, R

R Thompson, Haggs Wood Riding Stables, Stainforth, Doncaster, **Yorkshire (South)**, DN7 5PS, **ENGLAND**.
(T) 01302 845904 (F) 01302 845904.
Profile Trainer. Ref: YH14040

THOMPSON, RONALD

Ronald Thompson RSS BII, Nimmer Farm, Nimmer Mills, Chard, **Somerset**, TA20 3AD, **ENGLAND**.
(T) 01460 62515.
Profile Farrier. Ref: YH14041

THOMPSON, S

Mr S Thompson, 1 Fen Bank, Isleham, Ely, **Cambridgeshire**, CB7 5SL, **ENGLAND**.
(T) 01638 780431.
Profile Breeder. Ref: YH14042

THOMPSON, STEFANIE

Stefanie Thompson, Ridgeway Farm, Ashlawn Rd, Rugby, **Warwickshire**, CV22 5QH, **ENGLAND**.
(T) 01494 866023
(M) 07850 485915. Ref: YH14043

THOMPSON, T C

Mr T C Thompson, High Drybarrows, Bampton, Penrith, **Cumbria**, CA10 2RA, **ENGLAND**.
(T) 01931 713209.
Profile Breeder. Ref: YH14044

THOMPSON, V

Mr V Thompson, Link Hse, Newton-By-The-Sea, Alnwick, **Northumberland**, NE66 3ED, **ENGLAND**.
(T) 01665 576272.
Profile Trainer. Ref: YH14045

THOMSON & JOSEPH

Thomson & Joseph Ltd, T & J Hse, 119 Plumstead Rd, Norwich, **Norfolk**, NR1 4JT, **ENGLAND**.
(T) 01603 4390511 (F) 01603 700243
(E) enquiries@tandj.co.uk
(W) www.tandj.co.uk.
Profile Medical Support. Ref: YH14046

THOMSON CRAFT SADDLERY

Thomson Craft Saddlery, 15 Hamilton St, Carluke, **Lanarkshire (South)**, ML8 4HA, **SCOTLAND**.
(T) 01555 770435.
Profile Saddlery Retailer. Ref: YH14047

THOMSON W. A

Thomson W.A. & Co, 1A Lyon Rd, Linwood, Paisley, **Renfrewshire**, PA3 3BQ, **SCOTLAND**.
(T) 01505 329016.
Profile Blacksmith. Ref: YH14048

THOMSON, A J

A J Thomson, 16 Main St, Lockerbie, **Dumfries and**

Galloway, DG11 2DQ, **SCOTLAND**.
(T) 01576 22653.
Profile Farrier. **Ref:YH14049**

THOMSON, A M

Mr A M Thomson, Lambden Burn, Greenlaw, Duns, **Scottish Borders**, TD10 6UN, **SCOTLAND**.
(T) 01361 810514 **(F)** 01361 810211.
Profile Supplies. **Ref:YH14050**

THOMSON, D W

D W Thomson, Lynedoch Ind Est, Pitcairngreen, Perth, **Perth and Kinross**, PH1 3LX, **SCOTLAND**.
(T) 01738 583608.
Profile Blacksmith. **Ref:YH14051**

THOMSON, J L

J L Thomson, Ingleston Mains, Moniaive, Thornhill, **Dumfries and Galloway**, **SCOTLAND**..
Profile Breeder. **Ref:YH14052**

THOMSON, N B

Mr N B Thomson, Duncliffe Home Farm, Stour Row, Shaftesbury, **Dorset**, SP7 0QW, **ENGLAND**.
(T) 01747 838262.
Profile Trainer. **Ref:YH14053**

THOMSON, R W

Mr R W Thomson, Millcourt, Cavers, Hawick, **Scottish Borders**, TD9 8LN, **SCOTLAND**.
(T) 01450 372668.
Profile Supplies. **Ref:YH14054**

THORBURN, ELSPETH

Mrs Elspeth Thorburn, 22 Smileyknowes Court, North Berwick, **Lothian (East)**, EH39 4RG, **SCOTLAND**.
(T) 01620 893391 **(F)** 01620 893391.
Profile Breeder. **Ref:YH14055**

THORDALE

Thordale Equestrian & Trekking Centre, Mid Walls, Walls, Shetlands, **Shetland Islands**, ZE2 9PE, **SCOTLAND**.
(T) 01595 809799. **Ref:YH14056**

THORN MOWER FARRIER SUP

Thorn Mower Farrier Supplies, Yeat Farm, Lifton, **Devon**, PL16 0EB, **ENGLAND**.
(T) 01566 784622 **(F)** 01566 784743.
Contact/s
Owner: Mrs S Luxton
Profile Farrier. **Ref:YH14057**

THORNBERRY ANIMAL SANCTUARY

Thornberry Animal Sanctuary, C/O 26 Mill Fields, Todwick, Sheffield, **Yorkshire (South)**, S26 1JS, **ENGLAND**.
(T) 01909 564399.
Profile Animal Sanctuary. **Ref:YH14058**

THORNBURY VETNRY GROUP

Thornbury Veterinary Group (The), 744 Bradford Rd, Birkenshaw, **Yorkshire (West)**, BD11 2AE, **ENGLAND**.
(T) 01274 651115.
Profile Medical Support. **Ref:YH14059**

THORNBURY VETNRY GRP

Thornbury Veterinary Group (The), 515 Bradford Rd, Thornbury, Bradford, **Yorkshire (West)**, BD3 7BA, **ENGLAND**.
(T) 01274 663301.
Profile Medical Support. **Ref:YH14060**

THORNDALE FARM STABLES

Thorndale Farm Stables, Melsonby, Richmond, **Yorkshire (North)**, DL10 5NJ, **ENGLAND**.
(T) 01748 818006 **(F)** 01325 377796
(M) 07860 368365.
Profile Trainer. **Ref:YH14061**

THORNE, B

B Thorne, Trafalgar Cottage, Stainland, Halifax, **Yorkshire (West)**, HX4 9LF, **ENGLAND**.
(T) 01422 372279.
Profile Farrier. **Ref:YH14062**

THORNER, GRAHAM

Graham Thorner, Upper Manor Farm, Warborough Rd, Letcombe Regis, Wantage, **Oxfordshire**, OX12 9LD, **ENGLAND**.
(T) 01235 763003 **(F)** 01235 763003.
Contact/s
Owner: Mr G Thorner
Profile Trainer. **Ref:YH14063**

THORNESS BAY RIDING SCHOOL

Thorness Bay Riding School, Thorness Lane, Cowes, **Isle of Wight**, PO31 8NQ, **ENGLAND**.
(T) 01983 298896.
Contact/s
Partner: Mrs E Malcomson **Ref:YH14064**

THORNET WOOD STABLES

Thornet Wood Stables, Effingham Common Rd, Effingham, Leatherhead, **Surrey**, KT24 5JG, **ENGLAND**.
(T) 01372 456387.
Contact/s
Owner: Miss H Wright **Ref:YH14065**

THORNEY COPSE

Thorney Copse Saddlery, Thorney Copse Farm, Charlton Musgrove, Wincanton, **Somerset**, BA9 8EU, **ENGLAND**.
(T) 01963 32690 **(F)** 01963 32690
(E) info@.thorneycopse.co.uk
(W) www.thorneycopse-saddlery.co.uk.
Contact/s
Assistant: Ms S Bennett
Profile Medical Support, Riding Wear Retailer, Saddlery Retailer, Supplies. No.Staff: 3
Yr. Est: 1988
Opening Times
Sp: Open Mon, Wed, Thurs, Fri, Sat 09:00. Closed Mon, Wed, Fri, Sat 17:00, Thurs 20:00.
Su: Open Mon, Wed, Thurs, Fri, Sat 09:00. Closed Mon, Wed, Fri, Sat 17:00, Thurs 20:00.
Au: Open Mon, Wed, Thurs, Fri, Sat 09:00. Closed Mon, Wed, Fri, Sat 17:00, Thurs 20:00.
Wn: Open Mon, Wed, Thurs, Fri, Sat 09:00. Closed Mon, Wed, Fri, Sat 17:00, Thurs 20:00. **Ref:YH14066**

THORNFIELD STUD

Thornfield Stud, 103 Spencer Rd, Emsworth, **Hampshire**, PO10 7XS, **ENGLAND**.
(T) 01243 374718.
Profile Breeder. **Ref:YH14067**

THORNGILL BREEDING

Thorngill Breeding Ltd, Middleham, Leyburn, **Yorkshire (North)**, DL8 4TJ, **ENGLAND**.
(T) 01969 640653 **(F)** 01969 640694.
Profile Breeder. **Ref:YH14068**

THORNHILL STUD

Thornhill Stud, Walcote, Lutterworth, **Leicestershire**, LE17 4JZ, **ENGLAND**.
(T) 01455 554206.
Profile Breeder, Riding School. **Ref:YH14069**

THORNLEY GATE LIVERIES

Thornley Gate Liveries, Thornley Gate, Allendale, Hexham, **Northumberland**, NE47 9EF, **ENGLAND**.
(T) 01434 683378.
Profile Stable/Livery. **Ref:YH14070**

THORNLEY, MARTIN

Martin Thornley, 12A High St, Waltham, Grimsby, **Lincolnshire (North East)**, DN37 0LL, **ENGLAND**.
(T) 01472 827019 **(F)** 01472 827019.
Contact/s
Owner: Mr M Thornley
Profile Saddlery Retailer. **Ref:YH14071**

THORNTON EQUESTRIAN CTRE

Thornton Equestrian Centre, Raikes Rd, Thornton-Cleveleys, **Lancashire**, FY5 5LS, **ENGLAND**.
(T) 01253 820235.
Contact/s
Owner: Mrs S Bowling **Ref:YH14072**

THORNTON FARM LIVERY

Thornton Farm Livery, Raby Rd, Wirral, **Merseyside**, CH63 4JS, **ENGLAND**.
(T) 0151 3363620 **(F)** 0151 3363620.
Contact/s
Owner: Mr R Lyons
Profile Saddlery Retailer, Stable/Livery.
Ref:YH14073

THORNTON PARK

Thornton Park Equestrian Centre, Kilsallaghan, The Ward, Dublin, **County Dublin**, **IRELAND**.
(T) 01 8351164/ 8352448 **(F)** 01 8352725
Affiliated Bodies AIRE.
Contact/s
Owner: Suanne Archer-Murphy
Profile Riding School.
Training to BHSAI level is available. Pony camps and beginners' tuition, is also available C.Size: 30 Acres
Opening Times
Sp: Open Mon - Sun 09:00. Closed Mon - Fri 21:00, Sat, Sun 18:00.
Su: Open Mon - Sun 09:00. Closed Mon - Fri 21:00, Sat, Sun 18:00.
Au: Open Mon - Sun 09:00. Closed Mon - Fri 21:00, Sat, Sun 18:00.
Wn: Open Mon - Sun 09:00. Closed Mon - Fri 21:00, Sat, Sun 18:00. **Ref:YH14074**

THORNTON STABLES

Thornton Stables, Thornton Farm, Berwick-upon-Tweed, **Northumberland**, TD15 2LP, **ENGLAND**.
(T) 01289 382223.
Profile Riding School. **Ref:YH14075**

THORNTON STUD

Thornton Stud, Thornton Pk, Thirsk, **Yorkshire (North)**, YO7 4DW, **ENGLAND**.
(T) 01845 524365 **(F)** 01845 522533.
Profile Breeder. **Ref:YH14076**

THORNTON TACK & RIDING WEAR

Thornton Tack & Riding Wear, 99 Chapel St, Ibstock, **Leicestershire**, LE67 6HF, **ENGLAND**.
(T) 01530 264400 **(F)** 01530 263148.
Contact/s
Owner: Mr T Marsden **Ref:YH14077**

THORNTON, EMMA

Emma Thornton, 133 Brownhills Green Rd, Coventry, **Warwickshire**, CV6 2AR, **ENGLAND**.
(T) 02476 272833
Affiliated Bodies NAAT.
Contact/s
Physiotherapist: Emma Thornton
Profile Medical Support. **Ref:YH14078**

THOROGOODS DIRECT

Thorogoods Direct, Skeggs Farm, Chelmsford Rd, Writtle, Chelmsford, **Essex**, CM1 3ET, **ENGLAND**.
(T) 01245 423002 **(F)** 01245 421767.
Contact/s
Manager: Mr J Thorogood
Profile Feed Merchant. **Ref:YH14079**

THOROUGHBRED ADVERTISING

Thoroughbred Advertising, 2 Vogan's Mill Wharf, 17 Mill St, London, **London (Greater)**, SE1 2BZ, **ENGLAND**.
(T) 020 72314899 **(F)** 020 72312363.
Profile Club/Association. **Ref:YH14080**

THOROUGHBRED BREEDERS ASS

Thoroughbred Breeders Association, Stanstead Hse, The Avenue, Newmarket, **Suffolk**, CB8 9AA, **ENGLAND**.
(T) 01638 661321 **(F)** 01638 665621
(E) tba@dial.pipex.com.
Contact/s
Chief Executive: Louise Kemble
Profile Club/Association. **Ref:YH14081**

THOROUGHBRED BUSINESS GUIDE

Thoroughbred Business Guide, 2 Vogan's Mill Wharf, 17 Mill St, London, **London (Greater)**, SE1 2BZ, **ENGLAND**.
(T) 020 72314899 **(F)** 020 72312363.
Profile Supplies. **Ref:YH14082**

THOROUGHBRED CLOTHING

Thoroughbred Clothing Co Ltd (The), Kinsford Hse, Simonsbath, **Somerset**, TA24 7LE, **ENGLAND**.
(T) 01643 831661 **(F)** 01643 831542
(M) 07831 694777.
Profile Supplies. **Ref:YH14083**

THOROUGHBRED COACHBUILDERS

Thoroughbred Coachbuilders, Barcham Farm, Barcham Rd, Soham, Ely, **Cambridgeshire**, CB7 5TU, **ENGLAND**.
(T) 01353 624784 **(F)** 01353 624784.
Contact/s
Partner: Mr D Poultney
Profile Transport/Horse Boxes. **Ref:YH14084**

THOROUGHBRED COMMUNICATIONS

Thoroughbred Communications, 35 Blunts Wood Rd, Haywards Heath, **Sussex (West)**, RH16 1ND, **ENGLAND**.
(T) 01444 456358.
Profile Club/Association. **Ref:YH14085**

THOROUGHBRED FINE ART

Thoroughbred Fine Art Co, Kents Stud Farm, Kents Lane, North Weald, **Essex**, **ENGLAND**.. **Ref:YH14086**

THOROUGHBRED INFORMATION SVS

Thoroughbred Information Services, 62 Orchard Cl, Tichborne, Down Rd, Alresford, **Hampshire**, SO24 9PY, **ENGLAND**.
(T) 01962 734479 **(F)** 01962 734479.
Profile Supplies. **Ref:YH14087**

THOROUGHBRED REHABILITATION

Thoroughbred Rehabilitation Centre (The), Poplar Grove Farm, Humblescough Lane, Nateby, Preston, **Lancashire**, PR3 0LL, **ENGLAND**.
(T) 01995 605007 **(F)** 01995 605006.
Profile Club/Association. **Ref: YH14088**

THOROWGOOD

Thorowgood Ltd, The Saddlery, Fryers Rd, Walsall, **Midlands (West)**, WS2 7LZ, **ENGLAND**.
(T) 01922 711676
(E) enquiries@thorowgood.co.uk
(W) www.thorowgood.com.
Profile Supplies. Saddle Manufacturers.
Ref: YH14089

THORP, SIMON P

Simon P Thorp DWCF, Ablemarle, Pasture Rd, Hornsea, **Yorkshire (East)**, HU18 1QB, **ENGLAND**.
(T) 01964 534266.
Profile Farrier. **Ref: YH14090**

THORPE GRANGE EQUESTRIAN CTRE

Thorpe Grange Equestrian Centre, Thorpe Grange Farm, Newark Rd, Aubourn, **Lincolnshire**, LN5 9EJ, **ENGLAND**.
(T) 01522 680159.
Profile Riding School. **Ref: YH14091**

THORPE HORSE BOXES

Thorpe Horse Boxes, Tendring Rd, Thorpe-Le-Soken, Clacton-on-Sea, **Essex**, CO16 0AA, **ENGLAND**.
(T) 01255 830650.
Contact/s
Owner: Mr D Smith
Profile Transport/Horse Boxes. **Ref: YH14092**

THORPE MALSOR STUD

Thorpe Malsor Stud, Thorpe Malsor Hall, Church Way, Thorpe Malsor, Kettering, **Northamptonshire**, NN14 1JS, **ENGLAND**.
(T) 01536 3016.
Profile Breeder. **Ref: YH14093**

THORPE SADDLERY

Thorpe Saddlery, 22 Church Way, Thorpe Malsor, Kettering, **Northamptonshire**, NN14 1JS, **ENGLAND**.
(T) 01536 416747.
Contact/s
Owner: Ms C Honnywill
(E) celia.honnywill@btconnect.com
Profile Medical Support, Saddlery Retailer.
No.Staff: 1 Yr. Est: 1997 **Ref: YH14094**

THORPE TACK ROOM

Thorpe Tack Room, High St, Thorpe-Le-Soken, Clacton-on-Sea, **Essex**, CO16 0EA, **ENGLAND**.
(T) 01255 861583.
Contact/s
Owner: Miss C Fletton
Profile Riding Wear Retailer, Saddlery Retailer.
No.Staff: 2 Yr. Est: 1977
Opening Times
Sp: Open Mon - Sat 09:00. Closed Mon 17:00, Tues - Sat 17:30.
Su: Open Mon - Sat 09:00. Closed Mon 17:00, Tues - Sat 17:30.
Au: Open Mon - Sat 09:00. Closed Mon 17:00, Tues - Sat 17:30.
Wn: Open Mon - Sat 09:00. Closed Mon 17:00, Tues - Sat 17:30.
Closed each day 13:00 - 14:00 **Ref: YH14095**

THORPE, MERVYN

Mervyn Thorpe, Burghley Hse, Burghley Pk, Stamford, **Lincolnshire**, PE9 3JY, **ENGLAND**.
(T) 01780 482756.
Contact/s
Owner: Mr M Thorpe
Profile Blacksmith.
Can make horse troughs and jumps etc on request.
No.Staff: 1 Yr. Est: 1994
Opening Times
Sp: Open 08:00. Closed 17:00.
Su: Open 08:00. Closed 17:00.
Au: Open 08:00. Closed 17:00.
Wn: Open 08:00. Closed 17:00. **Ref: YH14096**

THORPES

Thorpes, Court Farm, Littledean, Cinderford, **Gloucestershire**, GL14 3JT, **ENGLAND**.
(T) 01594 823694.
Contact/s
Owner: Mr F Thorpe **Ref: YH14097**

THOS MITCHELL & SON

Thos Mitchell & Son, Hall Of Caldwell, Uplawmoor, **Renfrewshire**, **SCOTLAND**..
Profile Breeder. **Ref: YH14098**

THREAD BEAR

Thread Bear, The Charisworth Workshop, Charisworth, Charlton Marshall, Blandford, **Dorset**, DT11 9AL, **ENGLAND**.
(T) 01258 459304 **(F)** 01258 459304. **Ref: YH14099**

THREADGALL, FRANCIS JOHN

Mr Francis John Threadgall, Cambridge Smiddy, Lauder, **Scottish Borders**, TD2 6SH, **SCOTLAND**.
(T) 01578 722311.
Profile Farrier. **Ref: YH14100**

THREE ACRES LIVERY STABLES

Three Acres Livery Stables, Gildersome Lane, Leeds, **Yorkshire (West)**, LS12 6JJ, **ENGLAND**.
(T) 0113 2854877.
Contact/s
Owner: Mrs J Roberts
Profile Stable/Livery. No.Staff: 1
Yr. Est: 1985 C.Size: 16 Acres
Opening Times
Sp: Open Mon - Sun 09:00. Closed Mon - Sun 21:00.
Su: Open Mon - Sun 09:00. Closed Mon - Sun 21:00.
Au: Open Mon - Sun 09:00. Closed Mon - Sun 21:00.
Wn: Open Mon - Sun 09:00. Closed Mon - Sun 21:00. **Ref: YH14101**

THREE COUNTIES DRESSAGE GROUP

Three Counties Dressage Group, Crowels Ash, Winslow, Bromyard, **Herefordshire**, HR7 4SW, **ENGLAND**.
(T) 01885 400320.
Contact/s
Chairman: Mrs P Nash
Profile Club/Association. **Ref: YH14102**

THREE GATES EQUESTRIAN CTRE

Three Gates Equestrian Centre, Three Gates Hse, Fosse Way, Moreton Morrell, **Warwickshire**, CV35 9DE, **ENGLAND**.
(T) 01926 651946.
Profile Riding School. **Ref: YH14103**

THREE GREYS RIDING SCHOOL

Three Greys Riding School (The), Rock Rose Farm, Clayton Hill, Pyecombe, Brighton, **Sussex (West)**, BN45 7FF, **ENGLAND**.
(T) 01273 843536.
Contact/s
Owner: Mrs S Boyce **Ref: YH14104**

THREE LEGGED CROSS SADDLERY

Three Legged Cross Saddlery, Rafina, Ringwood Rd, Three Legged Cross, **Dorset**, BH21 6QZ, **ENGLAND**.
(T) 01202 826149.
Contact/s
Owner: Mrs M Shearing
Profile Supplies. **Ref: YH14105**

THREE RIVERS VETNRY GROUP

Three Rivers Veterinary Group, The Veterinary Clinic, London Rd, Beccles, **Suffolk**, NR34 9YU, **ENGLAND**.
(T) 01502 712169 **(F)** 01502 712694.
Profile Medical Support. **Ref: YH14106**

THREE SHIRES LIVERY CTRE

Three Shires Livery Centre, Ell Piece, Airfield Rd, Podington, Wellingborough, **Northamptonshire**, NN29 7XA, **ENGLAND**.
(T) 01234 782808.
Contact/s
General Manager: Ms C Talbot **(Q)** HND Equine
(E) tabletclaire@hotmail.com
Profile Stable/Livery.
All year grazing. Off road hacking. No.Staff: 2
Ref: YH14107

THREE SHIRES RIDING CLUB

Three Shires Riding Club, 10 Kelson Ave, Buxton, **Derbyshire**, SK17 9RS, **ENGLAND**.
(T) 01298 77466.
Contact/s
Chairman: Miss L Stott
Profile Club/Association, Riding Club. **Ref: YH14108**

THREEWATERS RIDING CLUB

Threewaters Riding Club, Penrose, Helston, **Cornwall**, TR13 0RD, **ENGLAND**.
(T) 01326 562223.
Profile Club/Association, Riding Club. **Ref: YH14109**

THRESHER, H M

H M Thresher (Tiverton), 4 Bridge St, Westexe, Tiverton, **Devon**, EX16 5LY, **ENGLAND**.
(T) 01884 257864.
Profile Medical Support. **Ref: YH14110**

THRESHERS BARN

Threshers Barn, Lower Henwick Farm, Turnpike Rd, Donnington, Newbury, **Berkshire**, RG14 3AP, **ENGLAND**.
(T) 01635 874374.
Contact/s
Owner: Mrs V Bonner-Davies
Profile Saddlery Retailer. **Ref: YH14111**

THROCKMORTON COURT STUD

Throckmorton Court Stud, Throckmorton, Pershore, **Worcestershire**, WR10 2JX, **ENGLAND**.
(T) 01386 462559 **(F)** 01386 462559.
Contact/s
Partner: Mrs W Balding
Profile Breeder. **Ref: YH14112**

THROSTLE NEST RIDING SCHOOL

Throstle Nest Riding School, Throstle Nest Farm, Fagley Lane, Bradford, **Yorkshire (West)**, BD2 3NU, **ENGLAND**.
(T) 01274 639390
Affiliated Bodies ABRS, BHS, RDA.
Contact/s
Owner: Mrs J Wheeler
Profile Riding School.
Train to NVQ level. DIY Livery is £70 per month.
No.Staff: 4 Yr. Est: 1976 C.Size: 30 Acres
Opening Times
Sp: Open Mon, Wed - Sun 09:00. Closed Mon, Wed - Sun 17:00.
Su: Open Mon, Wed - Sun 09:00. Closed Mon, Wed - Sun 17:00.
Au: Open Mon, Wed - Sun 09:00. Closed Mon, Wed - Sun 17:00.
Wn: Open Mon, Wed - Sun 09:00. Closed Mon, Wed - Sun 17:00.
Closed Tuesdays **Ref: YH14113**

THROSTLE NEST SADDLERY

Throstle Nest Saddlery, Moor End Lane, Silkstone Common, Barnsley, **Yorkshire (South)**, S75 4QX, **ENGLAND**.
(T) 01226 790497 **(F)** 01226 791604
(W) www.throstlenestsaddlery.co.uk.
Contact/s
Owner: Mr D Baxter
Profile Riding Wear Retailer, Saddlery Retailer, Supplies. No.Staff: 6 Yr. Est: 1980
Opening Times
Sp: Open Mon - Fri 09:00, Sat, Sun 10:00. Closed Mon - Wed, Fri 19:00, Thurs 20:30, Sat, Sun 18:00.
Su: Open Mon - Fri 09:00, Sat, Sun 10:00. Closed Mon - Wed, Fri 19:00, Thurs 20:30, Sat, Sun 18:00.
Au: Open Mon - Fri 09:00, Sat, Sun 10:00. Closed Mon - Wed, Fri 19:00, Thurs 20:30, Sat, Sun 18:00.
Wn: Open Mon - Fri 09:00, Sat, Sun 10:00. Closed Mon - Wed, Fri 19:00, Thurs 20:30, Sat, Sun 18:00.
Ref: YH14114

THROUGHBRED SURFACES

Throughbred Surfaces, Salwick Bridge Farm, Treales Rd, Salwick, Preston, **Lancashire**, PR4 0SA, **ENGLAND**.
(T) 01772 690966 **(F)** 01772 690966.
Contact/s
Partner: Mr J Knowles
Profile Track/Course. **Ref: YH14115**

THRUMS VETNRY GROUP

Thrums Veterinary Group, 1 Morrison St, Kirriemuir, **Angus**, DD8 5DB, **SCOTLAND**.
(T) 01575 572643 **(F)** 01575 574099.
Contact/s
Vet: Mr A Mollison
Profile Medical Support. **Ref: YH14116**

THUNDRY COMPETITION HORSES

Thundry Competition Horses, Thundry Farm, Farnham Rd, Elstead, Godalming, **Surrey**, GU8 6LE, **ENGLAND**.
(T) 01252 702552.
Profile Trainer. **Ref: YH14117**

THURLES RACE

Thurles Race Co Ltd, Racecourse, Thurles, **County Tipperary**, **IRELAND**.
(T) 050 423245.
Profile Supplies. **Ref: YH14118**

Key: **(T)** telephone **(F)** fax **(M)** mobile **(E)** E-Mail Address **(W)** Website Address **(Q)** Qualifications
Yr. Est: Year Established C.Size: Complex Size Sp: Spring Su: Summer Au: Autumn Wn: Winter

THURLOE, J

J Thurloe, Oulston, York, **Yorkshire (North)**, YO61 3RD, **ENGLAND**.
(T) 01347 868622 (F) 01347 868622.
Contact/s
Owner: Mrs J Thurloe
Profile Breeder. Ref: YH14119

THURLOW NUNN STANDEN

Thurlow Nunn Standen, Kennett, Newmarket, **Suffolk**, CB8 8QT, **ENGLAND**.
(T) 01638 750322 (F) 01638 552477.
Profile Supplies. Ref: YH14120

THURROCK RIDING CLUB

Thurrock Riding Club, Nada, Meesons Lane, Grays, **Essex**, RM17 5HR, **ENGLAND**.
(T) 01375 375568.
Contact/s
Chairman: Mrs J Lane
Profile Club/Association, Riding Club. Ref: YH14121

THURSO COLLEGE

Thurso College, Ormlie Rd, Thurso, **Highlands**, KW14 7EE, **SCOTLAND**.
(T) 01847 66161 (F) 01847 63872.
Profile Equestrian Centre. Ref: YH14122

THURSTASTON HALL FARM

Thurstaston Hall Farm, Station Rd, Thurstaston, Wirral, **Merseyside**, CH61 0HL, **ENGLAND**.
(T) 0151 6481727.
Profile Stable/Livery. Ref: YH14123

THWAITES, R G

R G Thwaites, Taranaki, Morland, Penrith, **Cumbria**, **ENGLAND**..
Profile Transport/Horse Boxes. Ref: YH14124

TICEHURST, G J

G J Ticehurst, Balklands Farm, Five Ashes, Mayfield, **Sussex (East)**, TN20 6JJ, **ENGLAND**.
(T) 01825 830239 (F) 01825 830239.
Contact/s
Owner: Mr G Ticehurst
Profile Transport/Horse Boxes. Ref: YH14125

TICEHURST, LESLEY J

Miss Lesley J Ticehurst, Little Tresaison Farm, Llanddewi Rhydderch, Abergavenny, **Monmouthshire**, NP7 9UY, **WALES**.
(T) 01873 840544.
Profile Breeder. Ref: YH14126

TICKHILL RIDING CLUB

Tickhill Riding Club, 3 Ashton Ave, Scawthorpe, Doncaster, **Yorkshire (South)**, DN5 9DA, **ENGLAND**.
(T) 01302 781000.
Contact/s
Chairman: Mr A Pearson
Profile Club/Association, Riding Club. Ref: YH14127

TICKLERTON STUD

Ticklerton Stud, Ticklerton Stud, Church Stretton, **Shropshire**, SY6 7DN, **ENGLAND**.
(T) 01694 722419.
Profile Breeder. Ref: YH14128

TICKNER, JOSEPH

Joseph Tickner, Banwen Farm, Pen Y Rhedyn, Swansea, **Swansea**, SA6 5SP, **WALES**.
(T) 01792 842315.
Contact/s
Owner: Ms T Tickner Ref: YH14129

TICQUET, DAVID A

David A Ticquet DWCF, 44 Cloverfields, Thurston, Bury St Edmunds, **Suffolk**, IP31 3TJ, **ENGLAND**.
(T) 07710 426598.
Profile Farrier. Ref: YH14130

TIDBALL, F G

F G Tidball, Danesford, Church Hill, Wroughton, Swindon, **Wiltshire**, SN4 9JR, **ENGLAND**.
(T) 01793 812153.
Contact/s
Owner: Mr F Tidball
Profile Stable/Livery. Ref: YH14131

TIDDIECROSS STABLES

Tiddiecross Stables, Charlton Lane, Wrockwardine, **Shropshire**, TF6 5EY, **ENGLAND**.
(T) 01952 740289
(E) tiddiecross@pcuk.org.
Contact/s
Owner: Mrs S Ward
Profile Riding School. Ref: YH14132

TIDENHAN SADDLERY

Tidenhan Saddlery & Horse Feed, Stroat Farm, Stroat, Chepstow, **Monmouthshire**, NP16 7LR, **WALES**.
(T) 01594 529226. Ref: YH14133

TIDMARSH STUD

Tidmarsh Stud (The), Maiden Hatch, Pangbourne, Reading, **Berkshire**, RG8 8HP, **ENGLAND**.
(T) 0118 9744840
Affiliated Bodies BHS.
Contact/s
Owner: Mr J Harter (Q) BHSI
Profile Stable/Livery, Trainer.
Trains competition horses for dressage and eventing. Livery is available, prices and details on request.
Yr. Est: 1987 C.Size: 40 Acres
Opening Times
Sp: Open Mon - Sun 07:00. Closed Mon - Sun 18:00.
Su: Open Mon - Sun 07:00. Closed Mon - Sun 18:00.
Au: Open Mon - Sun 07:00. Closed Mon - Sun 18:00.
Wn: Open Mon - Sun 07:00. Closed Mon - Sun 18:00. Ref: YH14134

TIDMARSH, B L

B L Tidmarsh, Ye Olde Forge, Tetbury Lane, Crudwell, Malmesbury, **Wiltshire**, SN16 9HB, **ENGLAND**.
(T) 01666 577665.
Profile Farrier. Ref: YH14135

TIDWORTH POLO CLUB

Tidworth Polo Club, Arcot Rd, Tedworth Pk, Tidworth, **Wiltshire**, SP9 7AH, **ENGLAND**.
(T) 01980 846705 (F) 01980 842558.
Contact/s
Manager: Brig John Wright
Profile Club/Association. Polo club. Ref: YH14136

TIDY-TACK

Tidy-Tack, Leys Hill Farm, Leys Hill, Ross-on-Wye, **Herefordshire**, HR9 5QU, **ENGLAND**.
(T) 01600 890863.
Profile Supplies. Ref: YH14137

TIERNEY, N J ROBERTSON

N J Robertson Tierney, C/O Woodlands Farm, Snainton, Scarborough, **Yorkshire (North)**, YO13 9BA, **ENGLAND**.
(T) 01723 859327.
Profile Farrier. Ref: YH14138

TIFLEX

Tiflex Ltd, Treburgie Water, Liskeard, **Cornwall**, PL14 4NB, **ENGLAND**.
(T) 01579 320808 (F) 01579 320802. Ref: YH14139

TIFT, J

J Tift, Westview, Little Billington, Leighton Buzzard, **Bedfordshire**, LU7 9BP, **ENGLAND**.
(T) 01525 373759.
Profile Farrier. Ref: YH14140

TIGGA'S SADDLERY

Tigga's Saddlery, Harburn Head, Harburn Est, Wester Calder, **Lothian (West)**, EH55 8RL, **SCOTLAND**.
(T) 01506 873888.
Profile Saddlery Retailer. Ref: YH14141

TIGNABRUAICH

Tignabruaich Trekking & Riding Centre, The Shieling, Tighnabruaich, **Argyll and Bute**, PA21 2BB, **SCOTLAND**.
(T) 01700 811449.
Profile Riding School. Ref: YH14142

TILEHURST FARM RIDING CTRE

Tilehurst Farm Riding Centre, Hempstead Lane, Hailsham, **Sussex (East)**, BN27 3PR, **ENGLAND**.
(T) 01323 840294.
Profile Riding School. Ref: YH14143

TILFORD HOUSE FARM

Tilford House Farm, Tilford Rd, Tilford, Farnham, **Surrey**, GU10 2BX, **ENGLAND**.
(T) 01252 795167.
Contact/s
Owner: Mr T Holgate
Profile Stable/Livery. Ref: YH14144

TILHILL ECONOMIC FORESTRY

Tilhill Economic Forestry Ltd, Surrey & Hampshire District, Grange Rd, Tilford, Farnham, **Surrey**, GU10 2DY, **ENGLAND**.
(T) 01252 794771 (F) 01252 794977. Ref: YH14145

TILI FARM LIVERIES

Tili Farm Liveries, Lusted Hall Lane, Tatsfield, **Kent**, TN16 2BH, **ENGLAND**.
(T) 01959 570610.
Profile Stable/Livery. Ref: YH14146

TILITA ROSETTES

Tilita Rosettes, 267 Hillbury Rd, Warlingham, **Surrey**, CR6 9TL, **ENGLAND**.
(T) 01883 622121 (F) 01883 622124
(E) info@tilita.co.uk
(W) www.tilita.com.
Profile Supplies. Ref: YH14147

TILL, J A

Mr J A Till, 106 Station Rd, Glenfield, **Leicestershire**, LE3 8BR, **ENGLAND**.
(T) 0116 2331938.
Profile Trainer. Ref: YH14148

TILLBROOK FEEDS

Tillbrook Feeds, Harvel Hill Farm, Harvel St, Meopham, **Kent**, DA13 0DE, **ENGLAND**.
(T) 01474 813350.
Profile Supplies. Ref: YH14149

TILLEY, A & T

A & T Tilley, 12 Woodhouse Way, Cambridge, **Cambridgeshire**, CB4 2NH, **ENGLAND**.
(T) 01223 424060.
Contact/s
Owner: Mr T Tilley
Profile Breeder.
Breeder of Welsh Section A ponies Ref: YH14150

TILLEY, ASHLEY MARK E

Ashley Mark E Tilley DWCF BII, 1 Stonelea Rd, Sywell, Northampton, **Northamptonshire**, NN6 0AZ, **ENGLAND**.
(T) 01604 643034.
Profile Farrier. Ref: YH14151

TILLEY, PAT

Mrs Pat Tilley, Moor Lane Farm, Moor Lane, Woking, **Surrey**, GU22 9RB, **ENGLAND**.
(T) 01483 773544.
Profile Breeder. Ref: YH14152

TILLS HORSE TRANSPORT

Tills Horse Transport, Meadowside, Chartway St, Kingswood, Maidstone, **Kent**, ME17 3QA, **ENGLAND**.
(T) 01622 843675.
Contact/s
Owner: Mr M Till
Profile Transport/Horse Boxes. Ref: YH14153

TILLYER, J

Ms J Tillyer, Ower Batch, Bus Drove, Calshot, **Hampshire**, SO45 1BG, **ENGLAND**.
(T) 023 80891591.
Profile Breeder. Ref: YH14154

TILLYRIE RACING

Dorothy Thomson, Tillyrie Stables, Tillyrie, Milnathort, Kinross, **Perth and Kinross**, KY13 0RW, **SCOTLAND**.
(T) 01577 863418 (F) 01577 863418
(E) dorothythomson@aol.co.uk
(W) www.dorothythomsonracing.co.uk
Affiliated Bodies JC.
Contact/s
Trainer: Mrs D Thomas
Profile Breeder, Trainer. No.Staff: 4
Yr. Est: 1993 C.Size: 880 Acres
Opening Times
Open all year, telephone for an appointment
Ref: YH14155

TILSEY FARM STABLES

Tilsey Farm Stables, Horsham Rd (A281), Palmers Cross, Wonersh, Guildford, **Surrey**, GU5 0RA, **ENGLAND**.
(T) 07850 985165. Ref: YH14156

TILSWORTH RIDERS CHARITY GRP

Tilsworth Riders Charity Group, Chesnut Cottage, 36A Station Rd, Stanbridge, Leighton Buzzard, **Bedfordshire**, LU7 9JG, **ENGLAND**.
(T) 01525 210464.
Profile Club/Association. Ref: YH14157

TILTON HOUSE STABLES

Tilton House Stables, West Barns, Dunbar, **Lothian (East)**, EH42 1UW, **SCOTLAND**.
(T) 01368 864944 (F) 01368 865850.
Contact/s
Owner: Mrs J Dickens

Profile Trainer. Ref: YH14158

TIM BLAKE SADDLERY

Tim Blake Saddlery, 14 Haycroft Drive, St Leonards Pk, Gloucester, **Gloucestershire**, GL4 6XX, **ENGLAND**.
(T) 01452 558996.
Profile Supplies. Ref: YH14159

TIM VIGORS BLOODSTOCK

Tim Vigors Bloodstock Ltd, 48 Lowther St, Newmarket, **Suffolk**, CB8 0JS, **ENGLAND**.
(T) 01638 667441.
Profile Blood Stock Agency. Ref: YH14160

TIMBERDOWN RIDING SCHOOL

Timberdown Riding School, Lidwell Hse, Lidwell, Callington, **Cornwall**, PL17 8LJ, **ENGLAND**.
(T) 01579 370577.
Contact/s
Owner: Mr A Dorouf
Profile Riding School. Ref: YH14161

TIMBERTOPS EQUESTRIAN CTRE

Timbertops Equestrian Centre, Jacksons Lane, Wentbridge, Pontefract, **Yorkshire (West)**, WF8 3HZ, **ENGLAND**.
(T) 01977 620374 (F) 01977 621039
Affiliated Bodies BHS.
Contact/s
Owner: Mrs S Clark
Profile Arena, Equestrian Centre, Riding School.
No.Staff: 6 Yr. Est: 1981
Opening Times
Sp: Open Mon - Sun 09:00. Closed Mon - Sun 17:00.
Su: Open Mon - Sun 09:00. Closed Mon - Sun 17:00.
Au: Open Mon - Sun 09:00. Closed Mon - Sun 17:00.
Wn: Open Mon - Sun 09:00. Closed Mon - Sun 17:00. Ref: YH14162

TIMBERTOPS RIDING CTRE

Timbertops Riding Centre, 160A Curragh Rd, Aghadowey, Coleraine, **County Londonderry**, BT51 4BU, **NORTHERN IRELAND**.
(T) 028 70868788.
Profile Riding School. Ref: YH14163

TIMEFORM ORGANISATION

Timeform Organisation (The), Timeform Hse, Northgate, Halifax, **Yorkshire (West)**, HX1 1XE, **ENGLAND**.
(T) 01422 330330 (F) 01422 398017
(E) timeform@timeform.com.
Profile Supplies. Ref: YH14164

TIMMINS, K

Mr K Timmins, The Cottage, Tillbridge Lane, Sturton, Sturton By Stow, **Lincolnshire**, LN1 2BP, **ENGLAND**.
(T) 01427 788009.
Contact/s
Owner: Mr K Timmons
Profile Breeder. Ref: YH14165

TIMMIS, M

Mrs M Timmis, The Foresters Arms, Kirdford, **Sussex (West)**, RH14 0ND, **ENGLAND**.
(T) 01403 820205.
Profile Breeder. Ref: YH14166

TIMMS, R G

R G Timms, 76 Aylesbury Rd, Thame, **Oxfordshire**, OX9 3AY, **ENGLAND**.
(T) 01844 214853.
Profile Farrier. Ref: YH14167

TIMSBURY INTERNATIONAL

Timsbury International, The Grange, Wansford, Driffield, **Yorkshire (East)**, YO25 8JN, **ENGLAND**.
(T) 01377 240414 (F) 01377 240414.
Contact/s
Partner: Mr J Butler
Profile Supplies. Ref: YH14168

TIN PARK RIDING STABLES

Tin Park Riding Stables, Tin Park Farm, Cornwood, Ivybridge, **Devon**, PL21 9PW, **ENGLAND**.
(T) 01752 837262.
Contact/s
Owner: Mrs M Rendall Ref: YH14169

TINA'S TACK & FEEDS

Tina's Tack & Feeds, 79-80 High St, Hirwaun, Aberdare, **Rhondda Cynon Taff**, CF44 9SN, **WALES**.
(T) 01685 814577.
Contact/s
Owner: Ms T Pedro Ref: YH14170

TINDALLS BOOKSHOP

Tindalls Bookshop, 54/56 High St, Newmarket, **Suffolk**, CB8 8LE, **ENGLAND**.
(T) 01638 561760 (F) 01638 561782
(E) tindalbook@aol.com.
Profile Supplies. Ref: YH14171

TINKLER, C H

C H Tinkler, The Mews Hse, Musley Bank, Malton, **Yorkshire (North)**, YO17 6TD, **ENGLAND**.
(T) 01653 695981 (F) 01653 600241.
Contact/s
Owner: Mr C Tinkler
Profile Breeder. Ref: YH14172

TINKLER, NIGEL

Nigel Tinkler, Woodland Stables, Langton, Malton, **Yorkshire (North)**, YO17 9QR, **ENGLAND**.
(T) 01653 658245 (F) 01653 658542.
Contact/s
Owner: Mr N Tinkler
Profile Trainer. Ref: YH14173

TINNING, BILL

Mr Bill Tinning, High St Farm, Thornton-Le-Clay, **Yorkshire (North)**, YO60 7TE, **ENGLAND**.
(T) 01653 618996.
Profile Trainer. Ref: YH14174

TINSLEY TRAILERS

Tinsley Trailers, Whessoe Rd, Darlington, **County Durham**, DL3 0RG, **ENGLAND**.
(T) 01325 382382 (F) 01325 360028.
Contact/s
General Manager: Mr D Parry
Profile Transport/Horse Boxes. Ref: YH14175

TINSLEYS RIDING CLUB

Tinsleys Riding Club, 2 Lovell Rd, Oakley, **Bedfordshire**, MK43 7RZ, **ENGLAND**.
(T) 01234 823577.
Profile Club/Association, Riding Club. Ref: YH14176

TINSLEYS RIDING SCHOOL

Tinsleys Riding School, Green Lane, Clapham, Bedford, **Bedfordshire**, MK41 6ET, **ENGLAND**.
(T) 01234 268556.
Profile Riding School, Stable/Livery. Ref: YH14177

TIP TRAILER RENTAL

TIP Trailer Rental, Cross St, Wolverhampton, **Midlands (West)**, WV1 2HS, **ENGLAND**.
(T) 01902 457009.
Profile Transport/Horse Boxes. Ref: YH14178

TIP TRAILER RENTAL

TIP Trailer Rental, Pontefract Rd, Knottingley, **Yorkshire (West)**, WF11 8SP, **ENGLAND**.
(T) 01977 675421 (F) 01977 607015.
Contact/s
Branch Manager: Mr M Randall
Profile Transport/Horse Boxes. Ref: YH14179

TIP-CTR EUROPE

TIP-CTR Europe Ltd, Parker Ave, Felixstowe, **Suffolk**, IP11 4HF, **ENGLAND**.
(T) 01394 613336.
Contact/s
Manageress: Ms A Ranson
Profile Transport/Horse Boxes. Ref: YH14180

TIPPERARY RACE COURSE

Tipperary Race Course, Limerick Junction Racecourse, Tipperary, **County Tipperary**, **IRELAND**.
(T) 062 51357 (F) 062 51303.
Profile Supplies. Ref: YH14181

TIPPERARY TACK

Tipperary Tack Co, The Square, Fethard, **County Tipperary**, **IRELAND**.
(T) 052 31765 (F) 052 31078.
Profile Supplies. Ref: YH14182

TIPTON HALL

Tipton Hall Riding School, Cherry Fields, Tedstone Delamere, Bromyard, **Herefordshire**, HR7 4PR, **ENGLAND**.
(T) 01885 488791.
Contact/s
Owner: Mr R Benbow (Q) AI
Profile Breeder, Riding School.
Breed Irish Draught Thoroughbred Cross Horses
Yr. Est: 1991
Opening Times
Sp: Open Mon - Sun 09:00. Closed Mon - Sun 18:00.
Su: Open Mon - Sun 09:00. Closed Mon - Sun 18:00.
Au: Open Mon - Sun 09:00. Closed Mon - Sun 18:00.
Wn: Open Mon - Sun 09:00. Closed Mon - Sun 18:00. Ref: YH14183

TIPTREE EQUESTRIAN CTRE

Tiptree Equestrian Centre, Simpsons Lane, Tiptree, Colchester, **Essex**, CO5 0PP, **ENGLAND**.
(T) 01621 815552
Affiliated Bodies BHS.
Contact/s
Owner: Miss M Dicks (Q) AI
Profile Riding School, Stable/Livery.
Group lessons are no larger than 3 people. Lessons for children over 5 years of age. Livery is offered as full, part and DIY. Yr. Est: 1995
Opening Times
Sp: Open Mon, Wed, Thurs 10:00, Sat, Sun 09:00. Closed Mon, Wed, Thurs 21:00, Sat, Sun 17:30.
Su: Open Mon, Wed, Thurs 10:00, Sat, Sun 09:00. Closed Mon, Wed, Thurs 21:00, Sat, Sun 17:30.
Au: Open Mon, Wed, Thurs 10:00, Sat, Sun 09:00. Closed Mon, Wed, Thurs 21:00, Sat, Sun 17:30.
Wn: Open Mon, Wed, Thurs 10:00, Sat, Sun 09:00. Closed Mon, Wed, Thurs 21:00, Sat, Sun 17:30.
Friday morning - staff training Ref: YH14184

TIRUS EQUESTRIAN PRODUCTS

Tirus Equestrian Products, P O Box 440, Norwich, **Norfolk**, NR4 7EP, **ENGLAND**.
(T) 01603 720148 (F) 01603 720148
(E) mail@tirus.org.
Profile Transport/Horse Boxes. Ref: YH14185

TISDALE, DEREK

Derek Tisdale, The Old Manor Hse, Town Hill, Yoxhall, **Staffordshire**, DE13 8NN, **ENGLAND**.
(T) 01543 473146 (F) 01543 472448.
Profile Breeder. Ref: YH14186

TITAN TRAILERS

Titan Trailers Ltd, Normanby Rd Business Pk, Normanby Rd, Scunthorpe, **Lincolnshire (North)**, DN15 8QZ, **ENGLAND**.
(T) 01724 270870 (F) 01724 278288.
Contact/s
Manager: Mr J Paradine
Profile Transport/Horse Boxes. Ref: YH14187

TITHE BARN VETNRY CTRE

Tithe Barn Veterinary Centre, Kendal Rd, Kirkby Lonsdale, **Cumbria**, LA6 2HH, **ENGLAND**.
(T) 01524 271221 (F) 01524 272963
(E) lakesvet@fsbdial.co.uk.
Profile Medical Support. Ref: YH14188

TITHEBARN

Tithebarn Ltd, P O Box 20, Tithebarn Hse, Weld Rd, Southport, **Merseyside**, PR8 2LY, **ENGLAND**.
(T) 01704 560606 (F) 01704 562469.
Profile Medical Support. Ref: YH14189

TIVENDALE, D A

D A Tivendale, 31 Westfield Ave, Cupar, **Fife**, KY15 5AA, **SCOTLAND**.
(T) 01334 654499. Ref: YH14190

TIVERTON FOXHOUNDS

Tiverton Foxhounds, Grange Lodge, Broadhembury, Honiton, **Devon**, EX14 0LS, **ENGLAND**.
(T) 01404 841223.
Profile Club/Association. Ref: YH14191

TIVERTON STAGHOUNDS

Tiverton Staghounds, Bircham Farm, Burrington, Umberleigh, **Devon**, EX37 9JW, **ENGLAND**.
(T) 01769 520203.
Profile Club/Association. Ref: YH14192

TIVYSIDE RIDING CLUB

Tivyside Riding Club, Can-Y-Wylan, Gwbert, Cardigan, **Ceredigion**, SA43 1PR, **WALES**.
(T) 01239 881232.
Contact/s
Rally Secretary: Ms M Gill
Profile Club/Association, Riding Club. Ref: YH14193

TIZZARD, C

Mr C Tizzard, Venn Farm, Milborne Port, Sherborne, **Dorset**, DT9 5RA, **ENGLAND**.
(T) 01963 250598.
Profile Trainer. Ref: YH14194

TL TRAILER SERVICES

TL Trailer Services Ltd, Unit 27 Cowpen Lane Ind Est, Bentley Ave, Billingham, **Cleveland**, TS23 4BU, **ENGLAND**.

(T) 01642 561143 (F) 01642 564845.
Profile Transport/Horse Boxes. Ref:YH14195

TM INT SCHOOL OF HORSEMANSHIP

T M International School Of Horsemanship, Sunrising Riding School, Henwood, Liskeard, **Cornwall**, PL14 5BP, **ENGLAND**.
(T) 01579 362895 (F) 01579 363646
(E) equiries@tminternational.co.uk
(W) www.tminternational.co.uk
Affiliated Bodies BHS.
Contact/s
General Manager: Ms K Tyrrell
Profile Equestrian Centre, Riding Club, Riding School, Stable/Livery. No.Staff: 5 Yr. Est: 1988
C.Size: 30 Acres
Opening Times
Sp: Open 10:00. Closed 17:00.
Su: Open 10:00. Closed 20:00.
Au: Open 10:00. Closed 17:00.
Wn: Open 10:00. Closed 16:00. Ref:YH14196

TOCKWITH TRAILER HIRE

Tockwith Trailer Hire, Unit 4A Centre Pk, Marston Moor Business Pk, Tockwith, York, **Yorkshire (North)**, YO26 7QF, **ENGLAND**.
(T) 01423 358034 (F) 01423 358034.
Contact/s
Owner: Mr R Frendt
Profile Transport/Horse Boxes. Ref:YH14197

TODD

Mrs Todd, Caecoed Farm, Pontfadog, Llangollen, **Denbighshire**, LL20 7AU, **WALES**.
(T) 01691 718371. Ref:YH14198

TODDBROOK VETNRY CTRE

Toddbrook Veterinary Centre (Cheshunt), Branch Surgery, 217A Turner's Hill, Cheshunt, **Hertfordshire**, EN8 9DG, **ENGLAND**.
(T) 01992 637966 (F) 01992 892519.
Contact/s
Vet: Mr G Oliver
Profile Medical Support. Ref:YH14199

TODDBROOK VETNRY CTRE

Toddbrook Veterinary Centre (Hoddesdon), Branch Surgery, 44 Ware Rd, Hoddesdon, **Hertfordshire**, EN11 9DU, **ENGLAND**.
(T) 01992 460053 (F) 01992 892519.
Contact/s
Vet: Mr G Oliver
Profile Medical Support. Ref:YH14200

TODHAM STABLES

Todham Stables, Great Todham Farm Hse, Little Todham, Ambersham, Midhurst, **Sussex (West)**, GU29 0BU, **ENGLAND**.
(T) 01730 812832.
Contact/s
Manager: Miss M Turner Ref:YH14201

TODHUNTER, MARTIN

Mr Martin Todhunter, The North Lodge, Priory Rd, Ulverston, **Cumbria**, LA12 9RX, **ENGLAND**.
(T) 01229 580529 (F) 01229 583510
(M) 07976 440082.
Profile Trainer. Ref:YH14202

TOFT & STUBBS

Toft & Stubbs, 125 Nantwich Rd, Audley, Stoke-on-Trent, **Staffordshire**, ST7 8DL, **ENGLAND**.
(T) 01782 721375.
Profile Farrier. Ref:YH14203

TOKENBOW STUD

Tokenbow Stud, Duffryn Farm, Llantrisant, Usk, **Monmouthshire**, NP15 1LR, **WALES**.
(T) 01633 450324.
Profile Breeder. Ref:YH14204

TOKENBURY SADDLERY

Tokenbury Saddlery, Lower Tokenbury Farm, Caradon Town, Liskeard, **Cornwall**, PL14 5AR, **ENGLAND**.
(T) 01579 362747.
Profile Saddlery Retailer. Ref:YH14205

TOLLADAY, ANDREW D

Andrew D Tolladay AWCF, Lavender Lodge, Fontwell Ave, Eastergate, Chichester, **Sussex (West)**, PO20 6RZ, **ENGLAND**.
(T) 01243 545100.
Profile Farrier. Ref:YH14206

TOLLARD PARK EQUESTRIAN CTRE

Tollard Park Equestrian Centre, Tollard Royal, Salisbury, **Wiltshire**, SP5 5PU, **ENGLAND**.
(T) 01725 516249.
Contact/s
Owner: Miss K Allen
Profile Breeder, Stable/Livery. Ref:YH14207

TOLLEMACHE, M H

M H Tollemache, Tollemache Hall, Offton, Ipswich, **Suffolk**, IP8 4RT, **ENGLAND**.
(T) 01473 658460.
Profile Breeder. Ref:YH14208

TOLLER TRAILERS

R & T Masters T/A Toller Trailers, The Pottery, Toller Porcorum, Dorchester, **Dorset**, DT2 0DQ, **ENGLAND**.
(T) 01300 320476 (F) 01300 320080
(E) toller@trailers.fsb.co.uk.
Contact/s
General Manager: Mr R Gunning (Q) NVQ 3 (Agric Eng)
Profile Transport/Horse Boxes. No.Staff: 4
Yr. Est: 1971 C.Size: 180 Acres
Opening Times
Sp: Open Mon - Sun 08:00. Closed Mon - Sun 20:00.
Su: Open Mon - Sun 08:00. Closed Mon - Sun 20:00.
Au: Open Mon - Sun 08:00. Closed Mon - Sun 20:00.
Wn: Open Mon - Sun 08:00. Closed Mon - Sun 20:00. Ref:YH14209

TOLLER, J A R

J A R Toller, Hamilton Rd, Newmarket, **Suffolk**, CB8 0NY, **ENGLAND**.
(T) 01638 668918 (F) 01638 669384
(W) www.newmarketracehorsetrainers.co.uk
Affiliated Bodies Newmarket Trainers Fed.
Contact/s
Owner: Mr J Toller
Profile Trainer. Ref:YH14210

TOLLGATE LIVERY CTRE

Tollgate Livery Centre, 397 High St, Felixstowe, **Suffolk**, IP11 9QR, **ENGLAND**.
(T) 01394 285147.
Profile Riding School, Stable/Livery. Ref:YH14211

TOLLIDAY, ERIC S

Eric S Tolliday, Blacksmiths Shop, Lynn Rd, Tilney All Saints, King's Lynn, **Norfolk**, PE34 4RT, **ENGLAND**.
(T) 01553 828533.
Contact/s
Owner: Mr E Tolliday
Profile Blacksmith. Ref:YH14212

TOLPUDDLE HALL

Tolpuddle Hall, Main Rd, Tolpuddle, Dorchester, **Dorset**, DT2 7EW, **ENGLAND**.
(T) 01305 848986
(M) 07702 580648.
Profile Equestrian Centre. Ref:YH14213

TOM HOOPER FENCING

Tom Hooper Fencing, Upper Inkford Farm, Wythall, Birmingham, **Midlands (West)**, B47 6DJ, **ENGLAND**.
(T) 01564 823363
(M) 07970 369101.
Profile Fencing specialist. Ref:YH14214

TOM WALLACE SADDLERS

Tom Wallace Saddlers, 76 O'Connell St, Limerick, **County Limerick**, **IRELAND**.
(T) 061 314312.
Profile Supplies. Ref:YH14215

TOM WILLCOCKS

Tom Willcocks (Corn Merchant), Colebrook, Plympton, Plymouth, **Devon**, PL7 4AA, **ENGLAND**.
(T) 01752 337334.
Profile Supplies. Ref:YH14216

TOM WILLIAMS

Tom Williams & Co, Underfall Yard, Cumberland Rd, Bristol, **Bristol**, BS1 6XG, **ENGLAND**.
(T) 01179 077498 (F) 01179 077498.
Contact/s
Owner: Mr T Williams
Profile Blacksmith. Ref:YH14217

TOMATIN SMITHY

Tomatin Smithy, Tomatin, Inverness, **Highlands**, IV13 7YP, **SCOTLAND**.
(T) 01808 511261 (F) 01808 511261.
Contact/s
Owner: Mr M Crummy
Profile Blacksmith. Ref:YH14218

TOMBS, A & C

A & C Tombs, Old Farm, Sturminster Marshall, Wimborne, **Dorset**, BH21 3RR, **ENGLAND**.
(T) 01258 857501.
Profile Breeder. Ref:YH14219

TOMICK TRAILERS

Tomick Trailers, Unit 341, Rushock Trading Est, Rushock, Droitwich, **Worcestershire**, WR9 0NR, **ENGLAND**.
(T) 01299 253529 (F) 01299 253529.
Contact/s
Partner: Mr T Gardener
Profile Transport/Horse Boxes. Ref:YH14220

TOMINTOUL RIDING CTRE

Tomintoul Riding Centre, St Bridget Farm, Tomintoul, Ballindalloch, **Aberdeenshire**, AB37 9HS, **SCOTLAND**.
(T) 01807 580210 (F) 01807 580210.
Profile Breeder. Ref:YH14221

TOMKINSON, A

Mrs A Tomkinson, The Ranch, Catton Lane, Yapham Rd, Pocklington, **Yorkshire (East)**, YO42 1TN, **ENGLAND**.
(T) 01759 302268.
Profile Supplies. Ref:YH14222

TOMPKINS, M H

M H Tompkins, Flint Cottage Stables, Rayes Lane, Newmarket, **Suffolk**, CB8 7AB, **ENGLAND**.
(T) 01638 661434 (F) 01638 668107
(W) www.marktompkins.co.uk
Affiliated Bodies Newmarket Trainers Fed.
Contact/s
Trainer: Mr M Tompkins
Profile Trainer. Ref:YH14223

TOMPKINS, R J

R J Tompkins (Forage), Parsons Barn Farm, Sibford Gower, Brailes, Banbury, **Oxfordshire**, OX15 5AD, **ENGLAND**.
(T) 01295 780541
(M) 07850 250784. Ref:YH14224

TONDO, UMBERTO R

Umberto R Tondo, Fairview, Jenners Lane, Hastings, **Sussex (East)**, TN35 4LH, **ENGLAND**.
(T) 01424 812411.
Profile Farrier. Ref:YH14225

TONG END LIVERY STABLES

Tong End Livery Stables, Tong End, Whitworth, Rochdale, **Lancashire**, OL12 8BJ, **ENGLAND**.
(T) 01706 852308.
Contact/s
Owner: Mr J Fallon
Profile Stable/Livery. Ref:YH14226

TONG RIDING CTRE

Tong Riding Centre Ltd, Tong, Shifnal, **Shropshire**, TF11 8PW, **ENGLAND**.
(T) 01902 372352 (F) 01952 680175.
Contact/s
General Manager: Mrs D Russell (Q) BHSII
Profile Horse/Rider Accom, Riding School.
No.Staff: 2 Yr. Est: 1971 C.Size: 50 Acres
Opening Times
Sp: Open Mon - Sun 09:00. Closed Mon - Sun 20:00.
Su: Open Mon - Sun 09:00. Closed Mon - Sun 20:00.
Au: Open Mon - Sun 09:00. Closed Mon - Sun 20:00.
Wn: Open Mon - Sun 09:00. Closed Mon - Sun 20:00. Ref:YH14227

TONKS, IAN

Ian Tonks DWCF, 4 Blacksmith Lane, Hockley Heath, Solihull, **Warwickshire**, B94 6QP, **ENGLAND**.
(T) 07831 464454.
Profile Farrier. Ref:YH14228

TONY GOODWIN & SONS

Tony Goodwin & Sons, Main St, Mulhuddart, Dublin, **County Dublin**, **IRELAND**.
(T) 01 8213047 (F) 01 8202843
(E) goodwinsaddlers@eircom.net.
Profile Supplies. Ref:YH14229

TONY SMART ACTION HORSES

Tony Smart Special Action Horses, Parkview Stables, Maidenhead Rd, Billingbear, Wokingham, **Berkshire**, RG11 5RR, **ENGLAND**.
(T) 01344 424531 (F) 01344 360548. Ref:YH14230

TOOGOOD, D A P

D A P Toogood, Garden Reach, Holford Combe, Holford, **Somerset**, TA5 1RZ, **ENGLAND**.
(T) 01278 741447.
Profile Farrier. Ref: YH14231

TOOLE, JUDITH

Judith Toole, Radnall Farm, Elmbridge, Droitwich, **Worcestershire**, WR9 0DA, **ENGLAND**.
(T) 01527 861429.
Profile Breeder. Ref: YH14232

TOORACURRAGH HARNESS SHOP

Tooracurragh Harness Shop, Tooracurragh, Ballymacarbry, **County Tipperary**, **IRELAND**.
(T) 052 36304.
Profile Supplies. Ref: YH14233

TOP CROP ORGANICS

Top Crop Organics, 2 Anstruther Court, Law, **Lanarkshire (South)**, ML8 5JG, **SCOTLAND**.
(T) 01698 373606.
Profile Medical Support. Ref: YH14234

TOP FARM

Top Farm, 10 High St, Great Doddington, Wellingborough, **Northamptonshire**, NN29 7TQ, **ENGLAND**.
(T) 01933 227263.
Contact/s
Owner: Miss G Thompson
Profile Stable/Livery. Ref: YH14235

TOP FARM EQUESTRIAN CTRE

Top Farm Equestrian Centre, Field Rd, Weston Longville, Norwich, **Norfolk**, NR9 5JN, **ENGLAND**.
(T) 01603 872247.
Profile Riding School, Stable/Livery. Ref: YH14236

TOP FLIGHT HORSE BOXES

Top Flight Horse Boxes, Rozel Forge, Stapleford Lane, Durley, Southampton, **Hampshire**, SO32 2BU, **ENGLAND**.
(T) 023 80692519 (F) 023 80694941.
Contact/s
Owner: Mr P Dunning
Profile Transport/Horse Boxes. Ref: YH14237

TOP TAK

Top Tak, The Stables, East Winch Rd, Blackborough End, King's Lynn, **Norfolk**, PE32 1SF, **ENGLAND**.
(T) 01553 841212
(E) sales@beec.slix.co.uk
(W) www.beec.slix.co.uk.
Contact/s
Owner: Mr C Nash
Profile Saddlery Retailer. Ref: YH14238

TOPP, C D

C D Topp, Lyndhurst, Carlton Husthwaite, Thirsk, **Yorkshire (North)**, YO7 2BJ, **ENGLAND**.
(T) 01845 501415 (F) 01845 501072.
Contact/s
Owner: Mr C Topp
Profile Blacksmith. Ref: YH14239

TOPS RIDING CTRE

Tops Riding Centre (The), Blackshawhead, Hebden Bridge, **Yorkshire (West)**, HX7 7JQ, **ENGLAND**.
(T) 01422 843138.
Profile Riding School. Ref: YH14240

TOPSPEC

Topspec Equine Ltd, Studley Hse, Baddiley, Nantwich, **Cheshire**, CW5 8PY, **ENGLAND**.
(T) 01270 624095 (F) 01270 629911
Affiliated Bodies BETA.
Contact/s
Owner: Mr P Tyler (Q) BSc(Hons)
Profile Supplies. Equine Nutritionists.
Manufacturers of feed balances and supplements.
No.Staff: 10 Yr. Est: 1975
Opening Times
Sp: Open Mon - Sat 09:00. Closed Mon - Sat 20:00.
Su: Open Mon - Sat 09:00. Closed Mon - Sat 20:00.
Au: Open Mon - Sat 09:00. Closed Mon - Sat 20:00.
Wn: Open Mon - Sat 09:00. Closed Mon - Sat 20:00.
Ref: YH14241

TORBAY TRAILER & TOWBARS

Torbay Trailer & Towbars, Unit 2 Oak Tree Yard, Upper Manor Rd, Paignton, **Devon**, TQ3 2TP, **ENGLAND**.
(T) 01803 553015 (F) 01803 553015.
Contact/s
Owner: Mr B Dillon
Profile Transport/Horse Boxes. Ref: YH14242

TORBRIDGE VETNRY CTRE

Torbridge Veterinary Centre, 7 Cadsdown Ind Pk, Clovelly Rd, Bideford, **Devon**, EX39 3HN, **ENGLAND**.
(T) 01237 472075 (F) 01237 425976.
Profile Medical Support. Ref: YH14243

TORIC TROPHIES

Toric Trophies, Unit 2 Ryehill, Town St, South Killingholme, Immingham, **Lincolnshire (North)**, DN40 3DD, **ENGLAND**.
(T) 01469 541327.
Profile Supplies. Ref: YH14244

TORLUNDY RIDING CTRE

Torlundy Riding Centre (The), Tomacharich, Fort William, **Highlands**, PH30 6SN, **SCOTLAND**.
(T) 01397 3015.
Profile Riding School. Ref: YH14245

TORNADO WIRE

Tornado Wire Ltd (Crieff), Muthill Rd, Crieff, **Perth and Kinross**, PH7 4HQ, **SCOTLAND**.
(T) 01764 655648 (F) 01764 655649. Ref: YH14246

TORTON BODIES

Torton Bodies Ltd, Pilot Works, Hollyhead Rd, Oakengates, Telford, **Shropshire**, TF2 6BB, **ENGLAND**.
(T) 01952 612648 (F) 01952 620373.
Profile Club/Association. Ref: YH14247

TOR-Y-MYNYDD STUD

Tor-Y-Mynydd Stud, Middle Causwell Farm, Poundstock, Bude, **Cornwall**, EX23 0DW, **ENGLAND**.
(T) 01288 361321 (F) 01288 361871.
Profile Horse/Rider Accom. Ref: YH14248

TOTAL QUALITY EQUINE CLOTHING

Total Quality Equine Clothing, Charnwood, Studley Drive, Swarland, Morpeth, **Northumberland**, NE65 9JT, **ENGLAND**.
(T) 01670 787768.
Profile Riding Wear Retailer. Ref: YH14249

TOTE ACCOUNT

Tote Account, Leopardstown Racecourse, Foxrock, Dublin, **County Dublin**, **IRELAND**.
(T) 01 2895000 (F) 01 2892019
(E) info@tote.ie
(W) www.tote.ie.
Profile Supplies. Ref: YH14250

TOTTERIDGE RIDING SCHOOL

Totteridge Riding School, 32 Totteridge Common, London, **London (Greater)**, N20 8NE, **ENGLAND**.
(T) 020 89597290.
Profile Riding School. Ref: YH14251

TOTTERIDGE STABLES

Totteridge Stables, 62 Redcliffe Gardens, Fulham, **London (Greater)**, SW10 9HD, **ENGLAND**.
(T) 020 73738480.
Profile Breeder. Ref: YH14252

TOUCHDOWN LIVERIES

Touchdown Liveries, Furze Farm, Prees Heath, Whitchurch, **Shropshire**, SY13 3JY, **ENGLAND**.
(T) 01948 841486
Affiliated Bodies BHS.
Contact/s
Owner: Ms F Oerlemans
Profile Equestrian Centre, Medical Support, Stable/Livery, Supplies.
Totally dust free environment. There is an indoor school, menage & round pen. 24 hour care with holistic approach, private, secure setting, owners are on-site. Fully alarmed which includes perimeter CCTV & central monitoring. No.Staff: 3 Yr. Est: 1999
C.Size: 5 Acres Ref: YH14253

TOULSON, V

V Toulson, Gartree Stud, 20 Melton Rd, Burton Lazars, Melton Mowbray, **Leicestershire**, LE14 2UR, **ENGLAND**.
(T) 01664 563670.
Contact/s
Partner: Mrs V Toulson
Profile Breeder. No.Staff: 1 Yr. Est: 1991
C.Size: 60 Acres
Opening Times
Telephone for an appointment Ref: YH14254

TOULSTON POLO CLUB

Toulston Polo Club, Bowers Hall, Barkisland, Halifax, **Yorkshire (West)**, HX4 0BG, **ENGLAND**.
(T) 01422 372529.
Profile Club/Association. Polo Club. Ref: YH14255

TOVEY, JAY D

Jay D Tovey DWCF, Grooms Cottage, Hoo Lane, Great Offley, **Hertfordshire**, SG5 3EB, **ENGLAND**.
(T) 07702 025466.
Profile Farrier. Ref: YH14256

TOW & TRAIL

Tow & Trail, East Warren Stables, Main Rd, Sundridge, Sevenoaks, **Kent**, TN14 6EE, **ENGLAND**.
(T) 01959 564166.
Profile Transport/Horse Boxes. Ref: YH14257

TOW BAR & TRAILER CTRE

Tow Bar & Trailer Centre (The), Tranker Cottage, Tranker Lane, Shireoaks, Worksop, **Nottinghamshire**, S81 8AQ, **ENGLAND**.
(T) 01909 483777.
Profile Transport/Horse Boxes. Ref: YH14258

TOW BAR & TRAILER EQUIPMENT

Tow Bar & Trailer Equipment, 44 Camp Rd, Farnborough, **Hampshire**, GU14 6EP, **ENGLAND**.
(T) 01252 540319.
Contact/s
Owner: Mr P Edminson
Profile Transport/Horse Boxes. Ref: YH14259

TOW BAR SERVICES

Tow Bar Services, 62 Medway Drive, Kearsley, Bolton, **Manchester (Greater)**, BL4 8PJ, **ENGLAND**.
(T) 01204 706317 (F) 01204 706317.
Contact/s
Owner: Mr K Harrison
Profile Transport/Horse Boxes. Ref: YH14260

TOWABILITY TRAILERS

Towability Trailers, Nene Court, 27-31 The Embankment, Wellingborough, **Northamptonshire**, NN8 1LD, **ENGLAND**.
(T) 01933 229025 (F) 01933 227049.
Profile Transport/Horse Boxes. Ref: YH14261

TOWBAR

Mr Towbar, 21 Mallard Rd, Bournemouth, **Dorset**, BH8 9PP, **ENGLAND**.
(T) 01202 535018.
Contact/s
Owner: Mr D Young
Profile Transport/Horse Boxes. Ref: YH14262

TOWBAR CTRE

Towbar Centre (The), 1 Ynys Y Gerwyn Ave, Aberdulais, Neath, **Neath Port Talbot**, SA10 8HH, **WALES**.
(T) 01639 641166.
Profile Transport/Horse Boxes. Ref: YH14263

TOWBARS & TRAILERS

Towbars & Trailers, 12 Athole Gr, Southport, **Merseyside**, PR9 7DE, **ENGLAND**.
(T) 01704 213190.
Contact/s
Owner: Mr D Chapman
Profile Transport/Horse Boxes. Ref: YH14264

TOWBARS NORTH WEST

Towbars North West, Winwick Rd, Warrington, **Cheshire**, WA2 7DQ, **ENGLAND**.
(T) 01925 444515.
Profile Transport/Horse Boxes. Ref: YH14265

TOWBARS SERVICES

Towbars Services (Wakefield) Ltd, Vicarage St, Wakefield, **Yorkshire (West)**, WF1 1QX, **ENGLAND**.
(T) 01924 371204.
Profile Transport/Horse Boxes. Ref: YH14266

TOWCESTER OASIS

Towcester Oasis Horseball Club, C/O The Hse, Oasis Service Station, Watling St, Paulserpury, Towcester, **Northamptonshire**, NN12 6LQ, **ENGLAND**.
(T) 01327 811870.
Profile Club/Association. Ref: YH14267

TOWCESTER RACECOURSE

Towcester Racecourse, Easton Neston, Towcester, **Northamptonshire**, NN12 7HS, **ENGLAND**.
(T) 01327 353414 (F) 01327 358534.
Contact/s
Chief Executive: Mr C Curran
Profile Track/Course. Ref: YH14268

TOWCRAFT

Towcraft, 20-22 Birmingham Rd, Rowley Regis, **Midlands (West)**, B65 9BL, **ENGLAND**.
(T) 0121 5613351 (F) 0121 5591398.

Contact/s
Partner: Mr D Guest
Profile Transport/Horse Boxes. Ref:YH14269

TOWELL, MICHAEL JAMES

Michael James Towell DWCF, Falkland Cottage, 40 Baydon Rd, Lambourn, **Berkshire**, RG16 7NT, **ENGLAND**.
Profile Farrier. Ref:YH14270

TOWER FARM

Tower Farm Riding Stables, 85 Liberton Drive, Edinburgh, **Edinburgh (City of)**, EH16 6NS, **SCOTLAND**.
(T) 0131 6643375 (F) 0131 6661765.
Contact/s
For Bookings: Debbie Henderson
Profile Arena, Equestrian Centre, Riding School, Stable/Livery. No.Staff: 10 Yr. Est: 1970
Opening Times
Sp: Open Mon - Sun 08:00. Closed Mon - Fri 21:00, Sat, Sun 17:00.
Su: Open Mon - Sun 08:00. Closed Mon - Fri 21:00, Sat, Sun 17:00.
Au: Open Mon - Sun 08:00. Closed Mon - Fri 21:00, Sat, Sun 17:00.
Wn: Open Mon - Sun 08:00. Closed Mon - Fri 21:00, Sat, Sun 17:00. Ref:YH14271

TOWER FARM DIY LIVERY

Tower Farm DIY Livery, Tower Farm, Little Downham, Ely, **Cambridgeshire**, CB6 2TD, **ENGLAND**.
(T) 01353 699765.
Profile Stable/Livery. Ref:YH14272

TOWER FARM SADDLERS

Tower Farm Saddlers, 3 King St, Earls Barton, Northampton, **Northamptonshire**, NN6 0LQ, **ENGLAND**.
(T) 01604 811056.
Contact/s
Manager: Mrs A Bragg
Profile Saddlery Retailer. Ref:YH14273

TOWER FARM SADDLERS

Tower Farm Saddlers, Barby Lane, Barby, Rugby, **Warwickshire**, CV23 8UX, **ENGLAND**.
(T) 01788 572929.
Profile Saddlery Retailer. Ref:YH14274

TOWER FARM TRAILERS

Tower Farm Trailers, Tower Rd Farm, South Brewham, Bruton, **Somerset**, BA10 0LA, **ENGLAND**.
(T) 01749 813294.
Profile Transport/Horse Boxes. Ref:YH14275

TOWER SOUND & COMMUNICATIONS

Tower Sound & Communications, 146 Brighton Rd, Horsham, **Sussex (West)**, RH13 6EY, **ENGLAND**.
(T) 01403 271122
(M) 07860 400640.
Contact/s
Owner: Mr C Spurr
Profile Supplies. Ref:YH14276

TOWER WOOD VETNRY GROUP

Tower Wood Veterinary Group, Complementary Animal Therapies, 27 Tinshill Rd, Cookridge, Leeds, **Yorkshire (West)**, LS16 7DR, **ENGLAND**.
(T) 0113 2678419.
Profile Medical Support. Ref:YH14277

TOWERLANDS EQUESTRIAN CTRE

Towerlands Equestrian Centre, Panfield Rd, Braintree, **Essex**, CM7 5BJ, **ENGLAND**.
(T) 01376 326802 (F) 01376 552487.
Profile Riding School, Saddlery Retailer, Stable/Livery. Ref:YH14278

TOWERWOOD ARABIANS

Towerwood Arabians, Tremayna Farm, St Gennys, **Cornwall**, EX23 0NR, **ENGLAND**.
(T) 01840 230389.
Profile Breeder. Ref:YH14279

TOWING LOGISTICS

Towing Logistics Ltd, Trailer Hse, West Quay Rd, Southampton, **Hampshire**, SO15 1GZ, **ENGLAND**.
(T) 023 80333111 (F) 023 80333600.
Profile Transport/Horse Boxes. Ref:YH14280

TOWING SHOP

Towing Shop (The), 173 Walsall Rd, Great Wyrley, Walsall, **Midlands (West)**, WS6 6NL, **ENGLAND**.
(T) 01922 414214.
Contact/s
Partner: Mr M Ghent
Profile Transport/Horse Boxes. Ref:YH14281

TOWING, D C

D C Towing, 7 Radstock Ave, Harrow, **London (Greater)**, HA3 8PE, **ENGLAND**.
(T) 020 89076875.
Profile Transport/Horse Boxes. Ref:YH14282

TOWN & COUNTRY

Town & Country, 33 Washington Lane, Euxton, Chorley, **Lancashire**, PR7 6DF, **ENGLAND**.
(T) 01257 277711.
Profile Supplies. Ref:YH14283

TOWN & COUNTRY PR

Town & Country PR, Cornerstone Hse, Stafford Park 13, Telford, **Shropshire**, TF3 3AZ, **ENGLAND**.
(T) 01952 291911 (F) 01952 291941.
Profile PR Agency. Ref:YH14284

TOWN & COUNTRY PRODUCTIONS

Town & Country Productions Ltd, Parrys Lodge, Threapwood, Malpas, **Cheshire**, SY14 7AW, **ENGLAND**.
(T) 01948 770309 (F) 01948 770452.
Profile Club/Association. Ref:YH14285

TOWN & COUNTRY SUP

Town & Country Supplies (Broadclyst), Old Barns, Crannaford, Broadclyst, Exeter, **Devon**, EX5 3BD, **ENGLAND**.
(T) 01392 461420 (F) 01392 468161.
Profile Riding Wear Retailer, Saddlery Retailer, Supplies.
Opening Times
Sp: Open Mon - Fri 08:30, Sat 09:00, Sun 11:00. Closed Mon - Fri 17:30, Sat 17:00, Sun 16:00.
Su: Open Mon - Fri 08:30, Sat 09:00, Sun 11:00. Closed Mon - Fri 17:30, Sat 17:00, Sun 16:00.
Au: Open Mon - Fri 08:30, Sat 09:00, Sun 11:00. Closed Mon - Fri 17:30, Sat 17:00, Sun 16:00.
Wn: Open Mon - Fri 08:30, Sat 09:00, Sun 11:00. Closed Mon - Fri 17:30, Sat 17:00, Sun 16:00.
Ref:YH14286

TOWN & COUNTRY SUPPLIES

Town & Country Supplies (Ashbourne), King Edward St, Ashbourne, **Derbyshire**, DE6 1BW, **ENGLAND**.
(T) 01335 300589.
Profile Supplies. Ref:YH14287

TOWN & COUNTRY SUPPLIES

Town & Country Supplies (Wrexham), Whitchurch Rd, Bangor-on-Dee, **Wrexham**, LL13 0PL, **WALES**.
(T) 01978 780691.
Profile Saddlery Retailer. Ref:YH14288

TOWN & COUNTRY VETNRY

Town & Country Veterinary Group (Aberdeen), 5 Rubislaw Park Rd, Aberdeen, **Aberdeen (City of)**, AB15 8BX, **SCOTLAND**.
(T) 01224 311555.
Profile Medical Support. Ref:YH14289

TOWN & COUNTRY VETNRY

Town & Country Veterinary Group (Skene), Westhill Drive, Westhill, **Aberdeenshire**, AB32 6FY, **SCOTLAND**.
(T) 01224 741685.
Profile Medical Support. Ref:YH14290

TOWN & COUNTRY VETNRY GROUP

Town & Country Veterinary Group, Kingswells Village Ctre, Kingswells, **Aberdeen (City of)**, AB15 8TG, **SCOTLAND**.
(T) 01224 749191.
Profile Medical Support. Ref:YH14291

TOWN & COUNTRY VETNRY GRP

Town & Country Veterinary Group, 91 North Deeside Rd, Bieldside, Aberdeen, **Aberdeen (City of)**, AB15 9DS, **SCOTLAND**.
(T) 01224 861161.
Profile Medical Support. Ref:YH14292

TOWN & COUNTRY VETNRY GRP

Town & Country Veterinary Group (Banchory), 14A Bridge St, Banchory, **Aberdeenshire**, AB31 5SX, **SCOTLAND**.
(T) 01330 822648 (F) 01330 822648.
Profile Medical Support. Ref:YH14293

TOWN & COUNTY SPORTS SHOP

Town & County Sports Shop, 82 High St, Kilkenny, **County Kilkenny**, **IRELAND**.
(T) 056 21517 (F) 056 67922.
Profile Supplies. Ref:YH14294

TOWN END FARM RIDING CTRE

Town End Farm Riding Centre, Town End Farm, Warton, Carnforth, **Lancashire**, LA5 9NY, **ENGLAND**.
(T) 01524 735917.
Profile Riding School, Stable/Livery. Ref:YH14295

TOWNFIELD SADDLERS

Townfield Saddlers, Butt Lane, Allesley, Coventry, **Midlands (West)**, CV5 9FE, **ENGLAND**.
(T) 024 76402474.
Contact/s
Partner: Adrian Charley
Profile Saddlery Retailer. Ref:YH14296

TOWNS & CARNIE

Towns & Carnie, Thainstone Agricultural Ctre, Inverurie, **Aberdeenshire**, AB51 9XY, **SCOTLAND**.
(T) 01467 623824.
Profile Supplies. Ref:YH14297

TOWNS, I

I Towns, Bay Yard, Level Mare Lane, Eastergate, Chichester, **Sussex (West)**, PO20 6SA, **ENGLAND**.
(T) 01243 542572.
Contact/s
Owner: Mr I Towns
Profile Stable/Livery. Ref:YH14298

TOWNSEND, K

Mrs K Townsend, 3 Glebe Cottages, Chastleton, Moreton In Marsh, **Gloucestershire**, GL56 0SZ, **ENGLAND**.
(T) 01608 74347.
Profile Trainer. Ref:YH14299

TOWNSLEY, P LAXTON

Mrs P Laxton Townsley, Mendips, The Common, Dunsfold, Godalming, **Surrey**, GU8 4LA, **ENGLAND**.
(T) 01483 200849 (F) 01483 200055
(M) 07887 726363.
Profile Trainer. Ref:YH14300

TOWRITE

Towrite, 304 St Marys Lane, Upminster, **Essex**, RM14 3HL, **ENGLAND**.
(T) 01708 223316 (F) 01708 223316.
Contact/s
Partner: Mr A Nicholls
Profile Transport/Horse Boxes. Tow Bar Fitters. Can fit tow bars to horse boxes. Ref:YH14301

TOWRITE FABRICATIONS

Towrite Fabrications Limited, Albert Rd, Market Harborough, **Leicestershire**, LE16 7LU, **ENGLAND**.
(T) 01858 433548 (F) 01858 434209
(E) sales@towrite.co.uk
(W) www.towrite.co.uk.
Contact/s
Owner: Mr N Arthurs
Profile Transport/Horse Boxes.
Towrite manufacture tack room equipment and electric vehicles. Ref:YH14302

TOW-SAFE TRAILER HIRE & SALES

Tow-Safe Trailer Hire & Sales, 36 Fletcher Rd, Ottershaw, Chertsey, **Surrey**, KT16 0JZ, **ENGLAND**.
(T) 01932 873269.
Profile Transport/Horse Boxes. Ref:YH14303

TOW-WIN EQUIPMENT

Tow-Win Equipment, 21 - 23 Page Rd, Sweet Briar Rd Ind Est, Norwich, **Norfolk**, NR3 2BX, **ENGLAND**.
(T) 01603 424424 (F) 01603 414424.
Contact/s
Owner: Mr J Walker
Profile Transport/Horse Boxes. Ref:YH14304

TOWY VALLEY PONY STUD

Towy Valley Pony Stud, Rhandirmwyn, Llandovery, **Carmarthenshire**, **WALES**..
Profile Breeder. Ref:YH14305

TOYHORSE INTERNATIONAL

Toyhorse International, Howick Farm, The Haven, Billingshurst, **Sussex (West)**, RH14 9BQ, **ENGLAND**.
(T) 01403 822639.
Profile Medical Support.
Members of the BHS Horse & Pony Breeds Committee. Offer advice on the upkeep of Toyhorses and also sell Toyhorses. Ref:YH14306

TRACK & FIELD

Track & Field, 11 Nelson Pl, Dereham, **Norfolk**, NR19 1EA, **ENGLAND**.
(T) 01362 698490.
Profile Saddlery Retailer. Ref:YH14307

TRACK RIGHT

Track Right, Three Gables, Brighton Rd, Hassocks, **Sussex (West)**, BN6 9LY, **ENGLAND**.
(T) 01273 841844 **(F)** 01273 841844
(W) www.trackright.co.uk.
Contact/s
Owner: Ms S Bartlett
(E) sandra@trackright.co.uk
Profile Supplies.
Leatherwork. Yr. Est: 1996 Ref: **YH14308**

TRADEWINDS

Tradewinds, Unit E5, Broad Oak Enterprise Village, Sittingbourne, **Kent**, ME9 8AQ, **ENGLAND**.
(T) 01795 599600 **(F)** 01795 599598
(E) gavin@globalnet.co.uk.
Profile Supplies. Ref: **YH14309**

TRADITIONAL ENGLISH SADDLERY

Traditional English Saddlery, Unit 6 May Ave Ind Est, May Ave, Northfleet, Gravesend, **Kent**, DA11 8RU, **ENGLAND**.
(T) 01474 560484. Ref: **YH14310**

TRAGO MILLS

Trago Mills Ltd (Newton Abbott), Staplehill, Liverton, Newton Abbott, **Devon**, TQ12 6JD, **ENGLAND**.
(T) 01626 821111.
Profile Saddlery Retailer. Ref: **YH14311**

TRAIL RIDERS

Trail Riders, Watchcombe Nest, Shute, Axminster, **Devon**, EX13 7QN, **ENGLAND**.
(T) 01297 553999 **(F)** 01297 551299. Ref: **YH14312**

TRAIL WEST

Trail West, 3-4 Mill Lane, Oban, **Argyll and Bute**, PA34 4HA, **SCOTLAND**.
(T) 01631 563638.
Profile Transport/Horse Boxes. Ref: **YH14313**

TRAIL-A-BRAKE SYSTEMS

Trail-a-Brake Systems, Dilltown Hlds Ltd, 3 The Martins Drive, Leighton Buzzard, **Bedfordshire**, LU7 7TQ, **ENGLAND**.
(T) 01525 373765 **(F)** 01525 373765
(E) nw50.hodges@tesco.net.
Profile Transport/Horse Boxes. Ref: **YH14314**

TRAILAMANSYSTEMS

Trailamansystems, The Old Workshop, Blundells Rd, Tiverton, **Devon**, EX16 4BZ, **ENGLAND**.
(T) 01884 256247 **(F)** 01884 259555.
Profile Transport/Horse Boxes. Ref: **YH14315**

TRAIL-A-WAY

Trail-A-Way, Unit 8 City Ind Est, Haven Rd, Exeter, **Devon**, EX2 8DD, **ENGLAND**.
(T) 01392 496866 **(F)** 01392 496866.
Contact/s
Owner: Mr S Brown
Profile Transport/Horse Boxes. Ref: **YH14316**

TRAILER CARE

Trailer Care, Unit 7A Barton Pk, Chickenhall Lane, Eastleigh, **Hampshire**, SO50 6RR, **ENGLAND**.
(T) 023 80613808 **(F)** 023 80613984.
Contact/s
Owner: Mr D Lush
Profile Transport/Horse Boxes. Ref: **YH14317**

TRAILER CTRE

Trailer Centre (The), 72 Shirley Rd, Croydon, **Surrey**, CR0 7EP, **ENGLAND**.
(T) 020 86563499 **(F)** 020 86563106.
Contact/s
Owner: Mr M Hoggan
Profile Transport/Horse Boxes. Ref: **YH14318**

TRAILER CTRE

Trailer Centre (The), 24A Deerbarn Rd, Guildford, **Surrey**, GU2 8AT, **ENGLAND**.
(T) 01483 564988 **(F)** 01483 452440.
Contact/s
Partner: Mr J Trask
Profile Transport/Horse Boxes. Ref: **YH14319**

TRAILER ENGINEERING

Trailer Engineering, Central Ave, Cradley Heath, **Midlands (West)**, B64 7BY, **ENGLAND**.
(T) 01384 564765 **(F)** 01384 410782.
Profile Transport/Horse Boxes. Ref: **YH14320**

TRAILER EXPRESS

Trailer Express Ltd, 5-9 Park St, Birkenhead, **Merseyside**, CH41 1ET, **ENGLAND**.
(T) 0151 6470101 **(F)** 0151 6470708.
Profile Transport/Horse Boxes. Ref: **YH14321**

TRAILER HIRE

Trailer Hire, Robin Croft, Pett Level Rd, Fairlight, Hastings, **Sussex (East)**, TN35 4EA, **ENGLAND**.
(T) 01424 812343.
Contact/s
Owner: Mr P Humphreys
Profile Transport/Horse Boxes. Ref: **YH14322**

TRAILER LAND

Trailer Land, Flerswell, Trehunist, Liskeard, **Cornwall**, PL14 3SD, **ENGLAND**.
(T) 01579 345587 **(F)** 01579 345878.
Contact/s
Owner: Mr A Stoneman
Profile Transport/Horse Boxes. Ref: **YH14323**

TRAILER MEN

Trailer Men (The), 955 Sheffield Rd, Chesterfield, **Derbyshire**, S41 9EJ, **ENGLAND**.
(T) 01246 452606 **(F)** 01246 452606.
Contact/s
Owner: Mr J Richmond
Profile Transport/Horse Boxes. Ref: **YH14324**

TRAILER PRODUCTION

Trailer Production Co The Ltd, Doncaster Rd, Whitley, Goole, **Yorkshire (East)**, DN14 0JW, **ENGLAND**.
(T) 01302 707755 **(F)** 01302 707799.
Contact/s
Manager: Mr M McDonald
Profile Transport/Horse Boxes. Ref: **YH14325**

TRAILER REFURB

Trailer Refurb, Unit 15 M90 Lathalmond, Dunfermline, **Fife**, KY12 0SJ, **SCOTLAND**.
(T) 01383 621994 **(F)** 01383 624984.
Profile Transport/Horse Boxes. Ref: **YH14326**

TRAILER RESOURCES

Trailer Resources Ltd, Grovebury Rd, Leighton Buzzard, **Bedfordshire**, LU7 8SW, **ENGLAND**.
(T) 01525 851022 **(F)** 01525 851033.
Contact/s
Owner: Mr E Edwards
Profile Transport/Horse Boxes. Ref: **YH14327**

TRAILER SERVICES

Trailer Services, Rear Of 8-16 Palace Gates Rd, London, **London (Greater)**, N22 7BN, **ENGLAND**.
(T) 020 88894242.
Contact/s
Owner: Mr P Powell
Profile Transport/Horse Boxes. Ref: **YH14328**

TRAILER SERVICES BANGOR

Trailer Services Bangor, Wern Farm, Pentraeth Rd, Menai Bridge, **Isle of Anglesey**, LL59 5RR, **WALES**.
(T) 01248 716948 **(F)** 01248 716948.
Contact/s
Owner: Mr P Brayshaw
Profile Transport/Horse Boxes. Ref: **YH14329**

TRAILER SUPPLIES

Trailer Supplies, Clayfield Ind Est, Tickhill Rd, Doncaster, **Yorkshire (South)**, DN4 8QG, **ENGLAND**.
(T) 01302 310113.
Contact/s
Partner: Mr J West
Profile Transport/Horse Boxes. Ref: **YH14330**

TRAILER YARD

Trailer Yard (The), Five Oaks Lane, Chigwell, **Essex**, IG7 4QP, **ENGLAND**.
(T) 020 85012441.
Contact/s
Owner: Mr M Walker
Profile Transport/Horse Boxes. Ref: **YH14331**

TRAILERCARE

Trailercare, P O Box 24, Leyland, Preston, **Lancashire**, PR5 1YP, **ENGLAND**.
(T) 01772 432520 **(F)** 01772 432520.
Contact/s
Partner: Mr G Gow
Profile Transport/Horse Boxes. Ref: **YH14332**

TRAILERCARE

Trailercare, Boothen Old Rd, Stoke-on-Trent, **Staffordshire**, ST4 4EE, **ENGLAND**.
(T) 01782 749111 **(F)** 01782 749191.
Contact/s
Operations Manager: Mr R Merrison
Profile Transport/Horse Boxes. Ref: **YH14333**

TRAILERCO

Trailerco, Unit 5, Philadelphia Complex, Philadelphia, Houghton Le Spring, **Tyne and Wear**, DH4 4TG, **ENGLAND**.
(T) 0191 5120355 **(F)** 0191 5120355.
Profile Transport/Horse Boxes. Ref: **YH14334**

TRAILERMATE PRODUCTS

Trailermate Products, 13 Trinity Sq, Llandudno, **Conwy**, LL30 2RB, **WALES**.
(T) 01492 875119 **(F)** 01492 875126.
Contact/s
Partner: Mr D Ricketts
Profile Transport/Horse Boxes. Ref: **YH14335**

TRAILERS & COMPONENTS

Trailers & Components Ltd, Stoneacre, Shrewsbury Rd, Craven Arms, **Shropshire**, SY7 8BX, **ENGLAND**.
(T) 01588 673345 **(F)** 01588 673345.
Contact/s
Owner: Mr N Hughes
Profile Transport/Horse Boxes. Ref: **YH14336**

TRAILERWAY

Trailerway, Unit 2 Pandy Garage Complex, Chester Rd, Oakenholt, Flint, **Flintshire**, CH6 5SD, **WALES**.
(T) 01352 762266 **(F)** 01352 762266.
Contact/s
Owner: Mr K Still
Profile Transport/Horse Boxes. Ref: **YH14337**

TRAILHOLME FARMHOUSE

Trailholme Farmhouse, Trailholme Lane, Overton, Morecambe, **Lancashire**, LA3 3HW, **ENGLAND**.
(T) 01524 71258.
Contact/s
Owner: Ms S Graves
Profile Horse/Rider Accom. Ref: **YH14338**

TRAILOAD TRAILERS

Traiload Trailers Ltd, 5 Brunel Court, Earlstrees Ind Est, Corby, **Northamptonshire**, NN17 4UB, **ENGLAND**.
(T) 01536 403140 **(F)** 01536 403203.
Profile Transport/Horse Boxes. Ref: **YH14339**

TRAIL-O-WAY

Trail-O-Way, 24 Homefield Rd, Walton-on-Thames, **Surrey**, KT12 3RD, **ENGLAND**.
(T) 01932 246413 **(F)** 01932 880677.
Contact/s
Owner: Mr D McGivern
Profile Transport/Horse Boxes. Ref: **YH14340**

TRAILRIDERS

Trailriders, 3, Kingstone, Uttoxeter, **Staffordshire**, ST14 8QH, **ENGLAND**.
(T) 01889 500479 **(F)** 01889 500656.
Contact/s
Owner: Mr B Woolley Ref: **YH14341**

TRAINING & LIVERY CTRE

Training & Livery Centre (The), Warden Lodge Farm, Hertford Rd, Welwyn, **Hertfordshire**, AL6 0BS, **ENGLAND**.
(T) 01707 331263.
Contact/s
Partner: Mrs J Stafford
Profile Stable/Livery, Trainer. Ref: **YH14342**

TRAINING BARN 7

Training Barn 7, Southwell Racecourse, Rolleston, Newark, **Nottinghamshire**, NG25 0TS, **ENGLAND**.
(T) 01636 812252 **(F)** 01636 816484
(M) 07801 553779.
Profile Trainer. Ref: **YH14343**

TRAKEHNER BREEDERS

Trakehner Breeders Fraternity (The), Godington Farm, Godington, Bicester, **Oxfordshire**, OX16 9AF, **ENGLAND**.
(T) 01869 277562 **(F)** 01869 277762.
Profile Club/Association. Ref: **YH14344**

TRAKEHNER BREEDERS FRATERNITY

Trakehner Breeders Fraternity (The), Holme Court Farm, Biggleswade, **Bedfordshire**, SG18 9ST, **ENGLAND**.
(T) 01767 600333 **(F)** 01767 317945
(E) susanattew@watkiss.com.
Contact/s
Chairman: Mrs B Watkiss
Profile Club/Association. Ref: **YH14345**

TRANENT RIDING CTRE

Tranent Riding Centre, Sandee Stables, Elphinstone Rd, Tranent, **Lothian (East)**, EH33 2LG, **SCOTLAND**.
(T) 01875 612641.
Contact/s

Groom: Miss L Kerr
Profile Stable/Livery. No.Staff: 2
Yr. Est: 1986
Opening Times
Sp: Open 09:00. Closed 18:00.
Su: Open 09:00. Closed 18:00.
Au: Open 09:00. Closed 18:00.
Wn: Open 09:00. Closed 18:00. Ref: YH14346

TRANS ATLANTIC FILMS

Trans Atlantic Films, Studio 1, 3 Brackenbury Rd, London, **London (Greater)**, W6 0BE, **ENGLAND**.
(T) 020 87350505 (F) 020 87350605
(E) 106131.1530@compuserve.com.
Contact/s
Owner: Mrs R Guest
Profile Supplies. Ref: YH14347

TRANS-PET

Trans-Pet, 57 Rougemont Ave, Morden, **Surrey**, SM4 5PY, **ENGLAND**.
(T) 020 86407778.
Contact/s
Owner: Mr P Billingham
Profile Transport/Horse Boxes. Ref: YH14348

TRANSPORT & GENERAL

Transport & General Workers Union, Transport Hse, Smith Sq, Westminster, **London (Greater)**, SW1P 3JB, **ENGLAND**.
(T) 020 78287788 (F) 020 76305861.
Profile Club/Association. Ref: YH14349

TRANSPORT ENGINEERING SVS

Transport Engineering Services Ltd, Unit 15 Readmans Yard, Station Rd, East Tilbury, Tilbury, **Essex**, RM18 8QR, **ENGLAND**.
(T) 01375 859908 (F) 01375 859908.
Contact/s
Chairman: Mr E Fennell
Profile Blacksmith. Ref: YH14350

TRANSPORTAPET

Transportapet, Vaila, Torgormack, Beauly, **Highlands**, IV4 7AQ, **SCOTLAND**.
(T) 01463 782742.
Contact/s
Owner: Ms J Bull
Profile Transport/Horse Boxes. Ref: YH14351

TRANSRENT

Transrent PLC, Manchester Rd, Carrington, Manchester, **Manchester (Greater)**, M31 4AG, **ENGLAND**.
(T) 0161 7762197.
Contact/s
Branch Manager: Mr C Ryan
Profile Transport/Horse Boxes. Ref: YH14352

TRANS-WALES TRAILS

Trans-Wales Trails, Cwmfforest Riding Ctre, Pengenffordd, Talgarth, Brecon, **Powys**, LD3 0EU, **WALES**.
(T) 01874 711398 (F) 01874 711122
(E) riding@transwales.demon.co.uk.
Profile Riding School, Stable/Livery. Ref: YH14353

TRANSY SHETLAND PONY STUD

Transy Shetland Pony Stud, Devonshaw, Powmill, Dollar, **Clackmannanshire**, FK14 7NH, **SCOTLAND**.
(T) 01577 840335 (F) 01577 840335.
Profile Breeder. Ref: YH14354

TRAPP, J W

Mr J W Trapp, Roberts End Farm, Long Green, Forthampton, **Gloucestershire**, GL19 4QH, **ENGLAND**.
(T) 01684 833209.
Profile Supplies. Ref: YH14355

TRAVIS, P

P Travis, 41B Dobcross New Rd, Dobcross, Saddleworth, Oldham, **Lancashire**, OL3 5AY, **ENGLAND**.
(T) 01457 874525.
Profile Farrier. Ref: YH14356

TREASURE SEEKERS

Treasure Seekers Ltd, 4 Stetchworth Rd, Woodditton, Newmarket, **Suffolk**, CB8 9SP, **ENGLAND**.
(T) 01638 730920 (F) 01638 731030.
Contact/s
Owner: Mr D Green
Profile Transport/Horse Boxes. Ref: YH14357

TREDOLE

Tredole Trekking & Riding Stables, Tredole Farm, Trevalga, Boscastle, **Cornwall**, PL35 0ED, **ENGLAND**.
(T) 01840 250495.
Contact/s
Owner: Miss K Nixon
Profile Riding School. Trekking Centre. Ref: YH14358

TREE TOPS PARTNERSHIP

Tree Tops Partnership (The), Treetops, Bishops Lane, Warfield, Bracknell, **Berkshire**, RG42 6HY, **ENGLAND**.
(T) 01344 886515.
Contact/s
Owner: Mr J Gibbons
Profile Stable/Livery. Horse Dealer. Ref: YH14359

TREEHOUSE

Treehouse, Rushock, Droitwich, **Worcestershire**, WR9 0NR, **ENGLAND**.
(T) 01299 851625 (F) 01299 851581
(M) 07971 179623.
Profile Saddlery Retailer. Ref: YH14360

TREETEC

Treetec Ltd, Unit 18/Spartan Ind Ctre, Brickhouse Lane, West Bromwich, **Midlands (West)**, B70 0DH, **ENGLAND**.
(T) 0121 5201001 (F) 0121 5579776.
Contact/s
Company Secretary: Mrs L Johnson
Ref: YH14361

TREFACH RIDING CTRE

Trefach Riding Centre, Trefach, Mynachlogddu, Clynderwen, **Carmarthenshire**, SA66 7RU, **WALES**.
(T) 01994 419457.
Contact/s
Partner: Mr D Smith
Profile Riding School, Stable/Livery. Ref: YH14362

TREFOEL STUD

Trefoel Stud, Velindre, Crymych, **Pembrokeshire**, SA41 3XN, **WALES**.
(T) 01239 820392.
Profile Breeder. Ref: YH14363

TREGARON PONY TREKKING ASS

Tregaron Pony Trekking Association, Tan Y Bryn, Tregaron, **Ceredigion**, SY23 3NA, **WALES**.
(T) 01974 298364.
Profile Club/Association. Ref: YH14364

TREGAVETHAN MANOR STUD

Tregavethan Manor Stud, Kenwyn, Truro, **Cornwall**, TR4 9EL, **ENGLAND**.
(T) 01872 560278.
Profile Breeder. Ref: YH14365

TREGO, JOANNE

Ms Joanne Trego, 33 Byron Rd, Locking Village, Weston-Super-Mare, **Somerset (North)**, BS24 8AG, **ENGLAND**.
(T) 01934 823552. Ref: YH14366

TREGOYD MOUNTAIN RIDERS

Tregoyd Mountain Riding Holidays, Tregoyd Riding Ctre, Three Cocks, Brecon, **Powys**, LD3 0SP, **WALES**.
(T) 01497 847351 (F) 01497 847680
(E) info@tregoydriding.co.uk
(W) www.tregoydriding.co.uk
Affiliated Bodies AALA, WTRA.
Contact/s
Owner: Mr H Jones
Profile Equestrian Centre, Holidays, Riding School. Pony Trekking. No.Staff: 9 Yr. Est: 1958
C.Size: 800 Acres Ref: YH14367

TREGURTHA DOWNS

Tregurtha Downs, Plain-An-Gwarry, Goldsithney, Penzance, **Cornwall**, TR20 9LD, **ENGLAND**.
(T) 01736 711422.
Contact/s
Owner: Mrs J Richards
Profile Breeder, Riding School. Ref: YH14368

TREKKING AND RIDING SOCIETY

Trekking And Riding Society For Scotland, Bruaich-Na-H'abhainne, Maragowan, Killin, **Perth and Kinross**, FK21 8TN, **SCOTLAND**.
(T) 01567 820909.
Profile Club/Association. Ref: YH14369

TREMAINES RIDING STABLES

Tremaines Riding Stables, Treemans Rd, Lewes Rd, Horsted Keynes, Haywards Heath, **Sussex (West)**, RH17 7EA, **ENGLAND**.
(T) 01825 790501.
Contact/s
Owner: Mrs F Parker
Profile Riding School, Stable/Livery. Ref: YH14370

TREMLOWS HALL STUD

R L Matson & Son, Twemlows Hall, Whitchurch, **Shropshire**, SY13 2EZ, **ENGLAND**.
(T) 01948 663239 (F) 01948 663836.
Contact/s
Owner: Mr R Matson
Profile Breeder. Ref: YH14371

TRENANCE RIDING STABLES

Trenance Riding Stables, Trenance Lane, Newquay, **Cornwall**, TR7 2HU, **ENGLAND**.
(T) 01637 872699
Affiliated Bodies ABRS, BHS.
Contact/s
General Manager: Miss J Simpson (Q) BHSII
Profile Horse/Rider Accom, Stable/Livery.
Ref: YH14372

TRENAWIN STABLES

Trenawin Stables, Connor Downs, Hayle, **Cornwall**, TR27 5JG, **ENGLAND**.
(T) 01736 759297 (F) 01736 759294.
Profile Stable/Livery. Ref: YH14373

TRENCH VILLA STABLES

Trench Villa Stables, Trench Villa, The Trench, Ellesmere, **Shropshire**, SY12 0LR, **ENGLAND**.
(T) 01691 623950.
Profile Riding School, Stable/Livery. Ref: YH14374

TRENISSICK RIDING STABLES

Trenissick Riding Stables, Trenissick Cottage, Cubert, Newquay, **Cornwall**, TR8 5PJ, **ENGLAND**.
(T) 01637 830413 (F) 01637 830413.
Contact/s
Owner: Mrs S Yeo
Profile Riding School. Ref: YH14375

TRENOUTH, REX H

Rex H Trenouth, Tresallyn Farm, St. Merryn, Padstow, **Cornwall**, PL28 8JZ, **ENGLAND**.
(T) 01841 520454.
Contact/s
Manager: Mrs E Coley Ref: YH14376

TRENSADORE

Trensadore, Unit 16 Welch Hill St, Off Twist Lane, Leigh, **Lancashire**, WN7 4DU, **ENGLAND**.
(T) 01942 676434. Ref: YH14377

TRENT PARK EQUESTRIAN CTRE

Trent Park Equestrian Centre, Bramley Rd, London, **London (Greater)**, N14 4UW, **ENGLAND**.
(T) 020 83639005.
Profile Riding School, Stable/Livery. Ref: YH14378

TRENT POTTERY

Trent Pottery, Regent St Ind Est, Narborough, **Leicestershire**, LE9 5DS, **ENGLAND**.
(T) 0116 2864911 (F) 0116 2867286. Ref: YH14379

TRENT VALLEY HORSEBALL CLUB

Trent Valley Horseball Club, C/O Wolds Farm, Fosse Way, Cotgrave, **Nottinghamshire**, NG12 3HG, **ENGLAND**.
(T) 0115 9899717.
Profile Club/Association. Ref: YH14380

TRENT VALLEY STABLES

Trent Valley Stables, Syndre Farm, Occupation Lane, Fiskerton, Southwell, **Nottinghamshire**, NG25 0TR, **ENGLAND**.
(T) 01636 813588.
Profile Riding School, Stable/Livery. Ref: YH14381

TRENTER, JOHN F

John F Trenter RSS, Neepawa Cottage, Ely Hill, Caple St Andrew, Woodbridge, **Suffolk**, IP12 3NH, **ENGLAND**.
(T) 01394 450148.
Profile Farrier. Ref: YH14382

TRENTSIDE SADDLERY

Trentside Saddlery, 21 Lea Rd, Gainsborough, **Lincolnshire**, DN21 1LL, **ENGLAND**.
(T) 01427 677431 (F) 01427 677431.
Contact/s
Owner: Mr R Robinson Ref: YH14383

TRESALLYN

Tresallyn Riding Stables, Tresallyn Farm, St Merryn, Padstow, **Cornwall**, PL28 8JZ, **ENGLAND**.
(T) 01841 520454.
Contact/s
General Manager: Mrs E Coley
Profile Riding School, Stable/Livery. No.Staff: 5
Yr. Est: 1977 C.Size: 110 Acres
Opening Times

Please telephone for a booking Ref: YH14384

TRESIDDER, ROGER M

Roger M Tresidder RSS, 2 Kinmount Cottages, Kinmount Est, Annan, **Dumfries and Galloway**, DG12 5RH, **SCOTLAND**.
(T) 01461 7298.
Profile Farrier. Ref: YH14385

TREVENA STUD

Trevena Stud, St Madryn, Castle View, Tintagel, **Cornwall**, PL34 0DH, **ENGLAND**.
(T) 01840 770348.
Profile Breeder. Ref: YH14386

TREVILLETT STABLES

Trevillett Stables, Trevillett, Tintagel, **Cornwall**, PL34 0HL, **ENGLAND**.
(T) 01840 770342 **(F)** 01840 770621.
Profile Riding School. Ref: YH14387

TREWINT

Trewint Farm Stables, Trewint Farm, Gills Green, Hawkhurst, Cranbrook, **Kent**, TN18 5AD, **ENGLAND**.
(T) 01580 752272.
Contact/s
Owner: Mrs S Barboun **(Q)** BHSII
Profile Club/Association, Riding School, Stable/Livery, Trainer. Pony Club Centre.
Yr. Est: 1989
Opening Times
Sp: Open Tues - Sun 09:00. Closed Tues - Sat 18:00, Sun 13:00.
Su: Open Tues - Sun 09:00. Closed Tues - Sat 18:00, Sun 13:00.
Au: Open Tues - Sun 09:00. Closed Tues - Sat 18:00, Sun 13:00.
Wn: Open Tues - Sun 09:00. Closed Tues - Sat 18:00, Sun 13:00.
Closed Mondays Ref: YH14388

TREWITHIAN STUD

Trewithian Stud, Little Trewithian, Sticker, St Austell, **Cornwall**, PL26 7EH, **ENGLAND**.
(T) 01726 72114.
Profile Breeder. Ref: YH14389

TRI TRAILER RENTALS

Tri Trailer Rentals, Lock St, Dewsbury, **Yorkshire (West)**, WF12 9BZ, **ENGLAND**.
(T) 01924 456924.
Profile Transport/Horse Boxes. Ref: YH14390

TRIBE, MALCOLM

Malcolm Tribe, Rock Lea, Exeter Rd, Moretonhampstead, Newton Abbot, **Devon**, TQ13 8NW, **ENGLAND**.
(T) 01647 440858.
Contact/s
Owner: Mr M Tribe
Profile Farrier. Ref: YH14391

TRICKLEDOWN STUD

Trickledown Stud, South Rd, Broughton, Stockbridge, **Hampshire**, SO20 8BE, **ENGLAND**.
(T) 01794 301085 **(F)** 01794 301505.
Profile Blood Stock Agency, Breeder. Ref: YH14392

TRIDENT TRAILERS

Trident Trailers Ltd, The Towing Ctre, Gordon Rd, Canterbury, **Kent**, CT1 3PP, **ENGLAND**.
(T) 01227 456534/463681 **(F)** 01227 766656
(W) www.tridenttrailers.com.
Contact/s
General Manager: Mr S Vinten
Profile Transport/Horse Boxes.
Hire out horse boxes for overseas transport.
No.Staff: 7 Yr. Est: 2001
Opening Times
Sp: Open Mon - Sat 08:30. Closed Mon - Fri 17:30, Sat 13:00.
Su: Open Mon - Sat 08:30. Closed Mon - Fri 17:30, Sat 13:00.
Au: Open Mon - Sat 08:30. Closed Mon - Fri 17:30, Sat 13:00.
Wn: Open Mon - Sat 08:30. Closed Mon - Fri 17:30, Sat 13:00. Ref: YH14393

TRIDENT TRAILERS

Trident Trailers Ltd, Medway Rd, Off Quarry Rd, Tunbridge Wells, **Kent**, TN1 2EZ, **ENGLAND**.
(T) 01892 542536 **(F)** 01892 514074
Affiliated Bodies NTTA.
Contact/s
Owner: Mr M Guntrip
Profile Transport/Horse Boxes.
Trailer supplies and repairs, towbar supplies and fitting service. Ref: YH14394

TRIDENT TRAILERS

Trident Trailers Ltd, 45-47 Staplehurst Rd, Sittingbourne, **Kent**, ME10 2NY, **ENGLAND**.
(T) 01795 427551
(W) www.tridenttrailers.com.
Profile Transport/Horse Boxes. Ref: YH14395

TRIDENT TRAILERS

Trident Trailers Ltd, 27A Upper Fant Rd, Maidstone, **Kent**, ME16 8BP, **ENGLAND**.
(T) 01622 678811 **(F)** 01622 678262
(W) www.tridenttrailers.com.
Contact/s
Office Manager: Mr S Vinten
Profile Transport/Horse Boxes. Ref: YH14396

TRILANCO

Trilanco, Bracewell Ave Ind Est, Poulton-Le-Fylde, **Lancashire**, FY6 8JF, **ENGLAND**.
(T) 01253 891697 **(F)** 01253 891249
(E) sales@trilanco.com
(W) www.trilanco.com.
Contact/s
Partner: Martin Balmer
Profile Medical Support.
Suppliers of animal healthcare products.
Yr. Est: 1979 Ref: YH14397

TRILL FARM

Trill Farm, Polmear Hill, Par, **Cornwall**, PL24 2TJ, **ENGLAND**.
(T) 01726 812071.
Contact/s
Owner: Mr P Mitchell
Profile Equestrian Centre. Trekking centre.
Ref: YH14398

TRINITY CONSULTANTS

Trinity Consultants, Church Lane, Barnham, Bognor Regis, **Sussex (West)**, PO22 0BP, **ENGLAND**.
(T) 01243 551766 **(F)** 01243 552622.
Profile Medical Support. Ref: YH14399

TRIPLE BAR RIDING CTRE

Triple Bar Riding Centre Home Of Sariah Arabians, Home Farm Cottage, Broadmoor, Abinger Common, Dorking, **Surrey**, RH5 6JY, **ENGLAND**.
(T) 01306 730959.
Contact/s
Owner: Sheila Morgan
Profile Breeder, Riding School, Stable/Livery.
Ref: YH14400

TRIPLE CROWN

Triple Crown Ltd, 16 Mill St, Oakham, **Rutland**, LE15 6EA, **ENGLAND**.
(T) 01572 756091 **(F)** 01572 756021.
Profile Medical Support. Ref: YH14401

TRIPLE CROWN ASSOCIATES

Triple Crown Associates, 12 West End, Witney, **Oxfordshire**, OX8 6ND, **ENGLAND**.
(T) 01993 778575 **(F)** 01993 778575.
Profile Club/Association. Ref: YH14402

TRIPLE CROWN FENCE

Europro Ltd, Europro Ltd, Horn Hatch Farm, Shalford, Guildford, **Surrey**, GU4 8HS, **ENGLAND**.
(T) 01483 450011 **(F)** 01483 569567
(E) europroltd@aol.com.
Contact/s
Manager: Miss S Roshanazamir
Profile Supplies, Track/Course. Ref: YH14403

TRISCOMBE STABLES

Triscombe Stables, Triscombe, Bishops Lydeard, Taunton, **Somerset**, TA4 3HG, **ENGLAND**.
(T) 01984 618270 **(F)** 01984 618270.
Profile Supplies. Ref: YH14404

TROJAN EQUESTRIAN

Trojan Equestrian, Newton-of-Conmay, Fraserburgh, **Aberdeenshire**, AB43 8UU, **SCOTLAND**.
(T) 01346 532971 **(F)** 01346 532961
(E) trojan@globalnet.co.uk
(W) www.users.globalnet.co.uk/~trojaneq/index.html.
Profile Supplies. Ref: YH14405

TROTTER, D J

Mr D J Trotter, Chapel Hse, Tebay, Penrith, **Cumbria**, CA10 3XB, **ENGLAND**.
(T) 01539 624277.
Profile Breeder. Ref: YH14406

TROTTERS

Chris Trotter Animal Feeds, East Lodge Farm, Westways, Bedhampton, Havant, **Hampshire**, PO9 3LN, **ENGLAND**.
(T) 023 92475804.
Contact/s
Owner: Mr C Trotter
Profile Supplies. Ref: YH14407

TROTTERS

Trotters Saddlery & Riding Wear, High Whittaker, Northtown, Burnley, **Lancashire**, BB12 8TZ, **ENGLAND**.
(T) 01282 771524.
Profile Saddlery Retailer. Ref: YH14408

TROTTERS

Trotters Ltd, 56 High St, Northwood, **London (Greater)**, HA6 1BL, **ENGLAND**.
(T) 01923 840082. Ref: YH14409

TROTTERS EQUESTRIAN SUPPLIES

Trotters Equestrian Supplies, Rear Of Gambles Garage, Birmingham Rd, Kenilworth, **Warwickshire**, CV8 1PT, **ENGLAND**.
(T) 01676 535656 **(F)** 01676 535656.
Contact/s
Partner: Mrs E Algar
Profile Supplies. Ref: YH14410

TROTTERS INDEPENDENT SADDLERY

Trotters Independent Mobile Saddlery, Gwelfryn, Kirkham Rd, Horndon-on-The Hill, **Essex**, SS17 8QE, **ENGLAND**.
(T) 01268 543016 **(F)** 01268 543016.
Profile Supplies. Ref: YH14411

TROTTERS RIDING STABLES

Trotters Riding Stables, Ashey Rd, Ryde, **Isle of Wight**, PO33 2XE, **ENGLAND**.
(T) 01983 568701.
Contact/s
Partner: Mrs C Blackman Ref: YH14412

TROTTS EQUESTRIAN CTRE

Trotts Equestrian Centre, Cowton, Rickarton, Stonehaven, **Aberdeenshire**, AB39 3SY, **SCOTLAND**.
(T) 01569 763360.
Profile Riding School. Ref: YH14413

TROWBRIDGE, B J

B J Trowbridge, The Forge, Semley, Shaftesbury, **Dorset**, SP7 9AS, **ENGLAND**.
(T) 01747 830414.
Contact/s
Owner: Mr A Trowbridge
Profile Farrier. Ref: YH14414

TRSS

Trekking & Riding Society of Scotland (The), Boreland, Fearnan, Aberfeldy, **Perth and Kinross**, PH15 2PG, **SCOTLAND**.
(T) 01887 830212 **(F)** 01887 830212.
Contact/s
Secretary: Mrs L Menzies
Profile Club/Association. Ref: YH14415

TRUCK & TRAILER EQUIPMENT

Truck & Trailer Equipment (Ludlow) Ltd, Shrewsbury Rd, Craven Arms, **Shropshire**, SY7 9QH, **ENGLAND**.
(T) 01588 672283.
Profile Transport/Horse Boxes. Ref: YH14416

TRUCKS 'N' TRAILERS

Trucks 'n' Trailers, 6 Woodhill Rise, Norwich, **Norfolk**, NR5 0DD, **ENGLAND**.
(T) 01603 743090 **(F)** 01603 743090.
Contact/s
Owner: Mr J Matthews
Profile Transport/Horse Boxes. Ref: YH14417

TRUCKS 'N' TRAILERS

Trucks 'n' Trailers, 321 Fakenham Rd, Taverham, Norwich, **Norfolk**, NR8 6LF, **ENGLAND**.
(T) 01603 868745.
Profile Transport/Horse Boxes. Ref: YH14418

TRUCK-TEK

Truck-Tek, 3A Shay Lane Ind Est, Shay Lane, Longridge, Preston, **Lancashire**, PR3 3BT, **ENGLAND**.
(T) 01772 786824 **(F)** 01772 785591.
Profile Transport/Horse Boxes. Ref: YH14419

TRUEMANS HEATH

Truemans Heath Riding School, Truemans Heath Lane, Shirley, Solihull, **Midlands (West)**, B90 1PQ, **ENGLAND**.
(T) 0121 4307974.
Contact/s

Assistant Groom: Ms G Weir (Q) ABRS ST 1, NVQ 1
Profile Riding School. Ref: YH14420

TRUEWELL HALL FARM

Truewell Hall Farm, Holme Hse Lane, Keighley, **Yorkshire (West)**, BD22 0QX, **ENGLAND**.
(T) 01535 603292
Affiliated Bodies BHS.
Contact/s
Owner: Mrs A Pickles
Profile Holidays.
Self-catering cottages. Riding, training, trekking and hacking holidays available. No.Staff: 3
Yr. Est: 1976 C.Size: 25 Acres
Opening Times
Sp: Open Mon - Sun 09:00. Closed Mon - Sun 17:00.
Su: Open Mon - Sun 09:00. Closed Mon - Sun 17:00.
Au: Open Mon - Sun 09:00. Closed Mon - Sun 17:00.
Wn: Open Mon - Sun 09:00. Closed Mon - Sun 17:00. Ref: YH14421

TRUMOR FEEDS

Trumor Feeds, Parkwater Farm, Forest Rd, Newport, **Isle of Wight**, PO30 4LY, **ENGLAND**.
(T) 01983 521690.
Profile Supplies. Ref: YH14422

TRUXFORD RIDING CTRE

Truxford Riding Centre, Thursley Rd, Elstead, Godalming, **Surrey**, GU8 6LW, **ENGLAND**.
(T) 01252 702086
(E) truxford@msn.com.
Contact/s
Owner: Mr T Forest
Profile Stable/Livery.
Full livery available, prices by arrangement.
No.Staff: 2 Yr. Est: 1999
Opening Times
Sp: Open Mon - Sun 09:00. Closed Mon - Sun 21:00.
Su: Open Mon - Sun 09:00. Closed Mon - Sun 21:00.
Au: Open Mon - Sun 09:00. Closed Mon - Sun 21:00.
Wn: Open Mon - Sun 09:00. Closed Mon - Sun 21:00. Ref: YH14423

TRYON & SWAN GALLERY

Tryon & Swan Gallery, 23/24 Cork St, London, **London (Greater)**, W1X 1HB, **ENGLAND**.
(T) 020 77342256 (F) 020 72872480. Ref: YH14424

TRYON GALLERY

Tryon Gallery, 7 Bury St, St James's, London, **London (Greater)**, SW1Y 6AL, **ENGLAND**.
(T) 020 7839 8083/4 (F) 020 78398085
(W) www.cinoa.org.
Contact/s
Owner: Mr O Swann
Profile Art Dealers. Ref: YH14425

TT.E.A.M TRAINING GB

TT.E.A.M Training Great Britain, 20 Heathmount Drive, Crowthorne, **Berkshire**, RG11 6HN, **ENGLAND**.
(T) 01344 751337 (F) 01344 773185.
Profile Club/Association. Ref: YH14426

T-TENTS

T-Tents Ltd, North Waltham Business Ctre, North Waltham, Basingstoke, **Hampshire**, RG25 2DJ, **ENGLAND**.
(T) 01256 397551 (F) 01256 397082.
Profile Club/Association. Ref: YH14427

TUATALLA STUD

Tuatalla Stud, Home Farm, Longcot Rd, Shrivenham, Swindon, **Wiltshire**, SN6 8HF, **ENGLAND**.
(T) 01793 782491 (F) 01793 782491.
Contact/s
Owner: Mr I Aspland
Profile Breeder. Ref: YH14428

TUBBY-BOXES INTERNAL STABLING

Tubby-Boxes Internal Stabling, Cuckoos Hill Farm, Castlethorpe Rd, Hanslope, Milton Keynes, **Buckinghamshire**, MK19 7HQ, **ENGLAND**.
(T) 01908 510748.
Profile Supplies. Supplier of internal stabling.
Ref: YH14429

TUBULAR BARRIERS

Tubular Barriers Ltd, Minster Hse, Plough Lane, London, **London (Greater)**, SW17 0AZ, **ENGLAND**.
(T) 020 88798807 (F) 020 88798808.
Profile Club/Association. Ref: YH14430

TUCK, J C

Mr J C Tuck, Manor Farm, Oldbury-on-the-Hill, Didmarton, **Gloucestershire**, GL9 1EA, **ENGLAND**.
(T) 01454 238236 (F) 01454 238488.
Profile Trainer. Ref: YH14431

TUCKER, ANGELA

Angela Tucker, Church Farm, Long Newnton, Tetbury, **Gloucestershire**, GL8 8RS, **ENGLAND**.
(T) 01666 502352 (F) 01666 504803
(M) 07771 874070.
Profile Trainer. Ref: YH14432

TUCKER, EDWARD W

Edward W Tucker, 1 Brookfield, Bideford, **Devon**, EX39 3DP, **ENGLAND**.
(T) 01237 473091.
Contact/s
Owner: Mr E Tucker
Profile Farrier. Ref: YH14433

TUCKER, F G

Mr F G Tucker, Mudgley Hill Farm, Mudgley, Wedmore, **Somerset**, BS28 4TZ, **ENGLAND**.
(T) 01934 712684.
Profile Supplies. Ref: YH14434

TUCKER, MICHAEL

Mr Michael Tucker, Church Farm, Long Newnton, Tetbury, **Gloucestershire**, GL8 8RS, **ENGLAND**.
(T) 01666 502352 (F) 01666 504803
(M) 07860 533325.
Profile Event Commentator. Ref: YH14435

TUCKER, R

R Tucker, Blakes Cottage, Sandy Lane, Haslemere, **Surrey**, GU27 1QE, **ENGLAND**.
(T) 01428 607935.
Profile Farrier. Ref: YH14436

TUCKETT, GRAHAME J

Grahame J Tuckett DWCF, Trerice, Sancreed, Penzance, **Cornwall**, TR20 8RL, **ENGLAND**.
(T) 01736 810332.
Profile Farrier. Ref: YH14437

TUDOR & LAWSON

Tudor & Lawson, Bala Rd, Dolgellau, **Gwynedd**, LL40 2YF, **WALES**.
(T) 01341 422212.
Profile Medical Support. Ref: YH14438

TUDOR FARM LIVERY STABLES

Tudor Farm Livery Stables, Bristol Rd, Frampton Cotterell, **Gloucestershire (South)**, BS36 2AU, **ENGLAND**.
(T) 01454 778860.
Profile Stable/Livery. Ref: YH14439

TUDOR FARM STABLES

Tudor Farm Stables, Tudor Farm, Church Lane, Broxbourne, **Hertfordshire**, EN10 7QQ, **ENGLAND**.
(T) 01992 460670.
Contact/s
Owner: Mrs S Decoux Ref: YH14440

TUDOR PHOTOGRAPHY

Tudor Photography, Unit 21 Beaumont Court, Beaumont Cl, Banbury, **Oxfordshire**, OX16 7RG, **ENGLAND**.
(T) 01295 270681 (F) 01295 270287
(E) tudorphoto@cwcom.net. Ref: YH14441

TUDOR RACING STABLES

Tudor Racing Stables, Elton Rd, Elton, Newnham, **Gloucestershire**, GL14 1JN, **ENGLAND**.
(T) 01452 760835 (F) 01452 760835.
Contact/s
Owner: Mr J Oshea
Profile Trainer. Ref: YH14442

TUDOR RIDING STABLES

Tudor Riding Stables, Bristol Rd, Iron Acton, Bristol, **Bristol**, BS37 9UP, **ENGLAND**.
(T) 01454 778860. Ref: YH14443

TUDOR STUD FARM

Tudor Stud Farm & Equestrian Centre, Chinnor Rd, Bledlow Ridge, High Wycombe, **Buckinghamshire**, HP14 4AE, **ENGLAND**.
(T) 01494 481685 (F) 01494 481093.
Contact/s
Owner: Ms S Barr
Profile Riding School. Ref: YH14444

TUDOR, J W

Mr J W Tudor, Dolwerdd, Coychurch Rd, Pencoed, **Glamorgan (Vale of)**, CF35 5LP, **WALES**.
(T) 01656 861076
(M) 07768 737513.
Profile Supplies. Ref: YH14445

TUER, E W

Mr E W Tuer, Home Farm, Great Smeaton, Northallerton, **Yorkshire (North)**, DL6 2EP, **ENGLAND**.
(T) 01609 881214
(M) 07808 330306.
Profile Supplies. Ref: YH14446

TUFTERS

Tufters (The), Winsford, **Somerset**, TA24 7HX, **ENGLAND**.
(T) 01643 85318.
Profile Equestrian Centre. Ref: YH14447

TUGGYS

Tuggys Products, Orchard Cottage, Bulstone, Branscombe, **Devon**, EX12 3BL, **ENGLAND**.
(T) 01297 680308 (F) 01297 680308
(E) tuggys@talk21.com.
Profile Trainer. Ref: YH14448

TUKE, DIANA R

Miss Diana R Tuke, Gallery Hse, Duddenhoe End, Saffron Walden, **Essex**, CB11 4UU, **ENGLAND**.
(T) 01763 838614.
Contact/s
Author: Miss D Tuke
Profile Supplies. Author.
Miss Diana Tuke is a writer of technical books based on care of horse & rider. She also writes novels and has been a freelance journalist for nearly 35 years.
Ref: YH14449

TULLAMORE STUD

Tullamore Stud, Elmhurst Farm, Elmhurst Lane, Slinfold, Horsham, **Sussex (West)**, RH13 7RJ, **ENGLAND**.
(T) 01403 790148.
Contact/s
Partner: Mrs T Pendle
Profile Breeder. Ref: YH14450

TULLOCHVILLE LIVERY YARD

Tullochville Livery Yard, Coshieville, Aberfeldy, **Perth and Kinross**, PH15 2LE, **SCOTLAND**.
(T) 01887 830559.
Profile Stable/Livery. Ref: YH14451

TULLY, GRAHAM J

Graham J Tully DWCF, Higher Dunscombe Farm, Chudleigh, **Devon**, TQ13 0BS, **ENGLAND**.
(T) 01626 853149.
Profile Farrier. Ref: YH14452

TULLYLAGAN

Tullylagan Driving Association, 14 Derrygonigan Rd, Cookstown, **County Tyrone**, BT80 8SU, **NORTHERN IRELAND**.
(T) 028 86762239.
Contact/s
Chairman: Mr R Sloan
Profile Club/Association. Ref: YH14453

TULLYLAGAN PONY CLUB

Tullylagan Branch of The Pony Club, 8 Killyneedan Rd, Sandholes, Cookstown, **County Tyrone**, BT80 9BR, **NORTHERN IRELAND**.
(T) 028 86765756.
Contact/s
Dist Comm: Mrs H Pearson
Profile Club/Association. Ref: YH14454

TULLYMURRY EQUESTRIAN CTRE

Tullymurry Equestrian Centre, 145 Ballydugan Rd, Downpatrick, **County Down**, BT30 8HH, **NORTHERN IRELAND**.
(T) 028 44811880.
Profile Riding School. Ref: YH14455

TULLYNEWBANK STABLES

Tullynewbank Stables, 25 Tullynewbank Rd, Glenavy, **County Antrim**, BT29 4PQ, **NORTHERN IRELAND**.
(T) 028 94454657
Affiliated Bodies BHS.
Profile Stable/Livery. Ref: YH14456

TULLYROE STUD

N & C Moore, Tullyroe, 41 Tullywest Rd, Crumlin, **County Antrim**, BT29 4SP, **NORTHERN IRELAND**.
(T) 028 94422585 (F) 028 94422585

(E) tullyroe@nireland.com
(W) www.nireland.com/tullyroe.
Contact/s
Owner: Mr N Moore
Profile Breeder. Yr. Est: 1981
Opening Times
Telephone for an appointment Ref: YH14457

TULLYWHISKER RIDING SCHOOL
Tullywhisker Riding School, 51 Brocklis Rd, Sion Mills, Strabane, **County Tyrone**, BT82 9LZ, **NORTHERN IRELAND**.
(T) 028 81658267.
Contact/s
Owner: Mrs R Boyd (Q) BHSAI
Profile Riding School. Yr. Est: 1986
Opening Times
Sp: Open Mon - Sun 09:00. Closed Mon - Sun 22:00.
Su: Open Mon - Sun 09:00. Closed Mon - Sun 22:00.
Au: Open Mon - Sun 09:00. Closed Mon - Sun 22:00.
Wn: Open Mon - Sun 09:00. Closed Mon - Sun 22:00. Ref: YH14458

TUNBRIDGE WELLS RIDING CLUB
Tunbridge Wells Riding Club, 44 Maidstone Rd, Pembury, **Kent**, TN2 4DE, **ENGLAND**.
(T) 01892 822499.
Profile Club/Association, Riding Club. Ref: YH14459

TUNBRIDGE WELLS TACK ROOM
Tunbridge Wells Tack Room (The), 15 Bayhall Rd, Tunbridge Wells, **Kent**, TN2 4UG, **ENGLAND**.
(T) 01892 530780 (F) 01892 531716.
Contact/s
Owner: Mrs T Nestle
Profile Saddlery Retailer. Ref: YH14460

TUNLEY EQUESTRIAN CTRE
Tunley Equestrian Centre, Tunley Farm, Tunley, Bath, **Bath & Somerset (North East)**, BA3 1DL, **ENGLAND**.
(T) 01761 479143.
Contact/s
Owner: Miss J Clarke Ref: YH14461

TUNSTALL
Tunstall Riding Centre Nunthorpe, Tunstall Farm, Tunstall Lane, Nunthorpe, Middlesbrough, **Cleveland**, TS7 0NU, **ENGLAND**.
(T) 01642 710992.
Contact/s
Owner: Mrs L Horsman Ref: YH14462

TUNWORTH DOWN STABLES
Tunworth Down Stables, Tunworth, Basingstoke, **Hampshire**, RG25 2LE, **ENGLAND**.
(T) 01256 463376 (F) 01256 332968
(M) 07973 178311
(E) mcampion.winners100@freeserve.com.
Profile Trainer. Ref: YH14463

TUPGILL PARK STABLES
Tupgill Park Stables, Middleham, Leyburn, **Yorkshire (North)**, DL8 4TJ, **ENGLAND**.
(T) 01969 640207.
Profile Trainer. Ref: YH14464

TURBLES
Turbles (The), Druggers End, Castlemorton, Malvern, **Worcestershire**, WR13 6JD, **ENGLAND**.
(T) 01684 833773.
Profile Trainer. Ref: YH14465

TURF & TRAVEL
Turf & Travel Saddlery & Equestrian Fashion, The Old Bakery, Wexham St, Wexham, Slough, **Berkshire**, SL3 6NX, **ENGLAND**.
(T) 01753 730099 (F) 01753 790099.
Profile Saddlery Retailer. Ref: YH14466

TURF PICTURES
Turf Pictures (Durham), Briarwood, Penshaw, Houghton Le Spring, **Tyne and Wear**, DH4 7JX, **ENGLAND**.
(T) 0191 3852888 (F) 0191 3857177. Ref: YH14467

TURF VETNRY SUPPLIES
Turf Veterinary Supplies Ltd, Firs Lodge, Green Lane, Boston Spa, Wetherby, **Yorkshire (West)**, LS23 6AZ, **ENGLAND**.
(T) 01937 849997 (F) 01937 841071.
Profile Medical Support. Ref: YH14468

TURKS SADDLERY
Turks Saddlery, 1 Prossers Trce, Cymmer, Port Talbot, **Neath Port Talbot**, SA13 3LD, **WALES**.
(T) 01639 850450.
Contact/s
Owner: Mrs S Phillips Ref: YH14469

TURNBULL TRAILERS
Turnbull Trailers, 80 Clark St, Paisley, **Renfrewshire**, PA3 1RB, **SCOTLAND**.
(T) 0141 8490892.
Profile Transport/Horse Boxes. Ref: YH14470

TURNBULL, T M
Mr T M Turnbull, The Newburn Hotel, Station Rd, Newburn, Newcastle-upon-Tyne, **Tyne and Wear**, NE15 8LS, **ENGLAND**.
(T) 0191 2674813.
Profile Breeder. Ref: YH14471

TURNELL, ALAN J
Alan J Turnell DWCF, Centre Walk, 38 High St, Manton, Marlborough, **Wiltshire**, SN8 4HW, **ENGLAND**.
(T) 07768 535271.
Profile Farrier. Ref: YH14472

TURNELL, ANDY
Mr Andy Turnell, Breckenbrough Hse, Breckenbrough, Sand Hutton, Thirsk, **Yorkshire (North)**, YO7 4EL, **ENGLAND**.
(T) 01845 587226 (F) 01845 587443
(M) 07802 468400.
Profile Trainer. Ref: YH14473

TURNER, A
A Turner, Coldharbour Farm, 189 Queens Rd, Bisley, Woking, **Surrey**, GU24 9AX, **ENGLAND**.
(T) 01483 473151.
Profile Transport/Horse Boxes. Ref: YH14474

TURNER, ANDREW
Andrew Turner, 8 Eastfield Drive, Penicuik, **Lothian (Mid)**, EH26 8BA, **SCOTLAND**.
(T) 01968 673032 (F) 01968 679544.
Contact/s
Owner: Mr G Turner
Profile Blacksmith. Ref: YH14475

TURNER, CORINNA
Mrs Corinna Turner, Knowle Rock, Shepton Montague, Wincanton, **Somerset**, BA9 8JA, **ENGLAND**.
(T) 01963 32138 (F) 01963 32138.
Profile Breeder. Ref: YH14476

TURNER, D C
Mr D C Turner, Higher Collard Farm, Wotter, Plymouth, **Devon**, PL7 5HU, **ENGLAND**.
(T) 01752 839231.
Profile Supplies. Ref: YH14477

TURNER, DAVID
David Turner, Oak Bark Bend, Chapel Lane, Burley, Ringwood, **Hampshire**, BH24 4DJ, **ENGLAND**.
(T) 01425 403511.
Profile Trainer. Ref: YH14478

TURNER, F W
F W Turner DWCF, 2 Turnpike Rd, Red Lodge, Freckenham, Bury St Edmunds, **Suffolk**, IP28 8JZ, **ENGLAND**.
(T) 01638 750163.
Profile Farrier. Ref: YH14479

TURNER, GORDON GEORGE
Gordon George Turner, Mill Drove, Southery, Downham Market, **Norfolk**, PE38 0PJ, **ENGLAND**.
(T) 01366 377489.
Profile Farrier. Ref: YH14480

TURNER, IAN
Ian Turner, 6 Binstead Hill, Ryde, **Isle of Wight**, PO33 3RR, **ENGLAND**.
(T) 01983 568860 (F) 01983 568860.
Contact/s
Owner: Mr I Turner
Profile Farrier. Ref: YH14481

TURNER, J R
Mr J R Turner, Mayfield, Norton-Le-Clay, Helperby, **Yorkshire (North)**, YO61 2RS, **ENGLAND**.
(T) 01423 322239.
Profile Trainer. Ref: YH14482

TURNER, J S E
J S E Turner, Heath Paddocks, Prees Heath, Whitchurch, **Hampshire**, **ENGLAND**.
(T) 01948 663527 (F) 01948 667227. Ref: YH14483

TURNER, JACKY
Jacky Turner, 32 Honeydew Rd, North Cray, Sidcup, **Kent**, DA14 5LX, **ENGLAND**.
(T) 020 83022139.
Profile Trainer. Ref: YH14484

TURNER, M
Mrs M Turner, Ryersh Hse, Ryersh Lane, Capel, Dorking, **Surrey**, RH5 5LJ, **ENGLAND**.
(T) 01306 711069.
Profile Breeder. Ref: YH14485

TURNER, MIKE
Mike Turner, 32 Honeydew Rd, North Cray, Sidcup, **Kent**, DA14 5LX, **ENGLAND**.
(T) 020 83022139.
Profile Trainer. Ref: YH14486

TURNER, N W
N W Turner RSS, Red Roofs, King Row, Shipham, Thetford, Norwich, **Norfolk**, IP25 7RW, **ENGLAND**.
(T) 01362 821029.
Profile Farrier. Ref: YH14487

TURNER, NICK
Nick Turner, Home Farm Hse, Old Warden Pk, Biggleswade, **Bedfordshire**, SG18 9DU, **ENGLAND**.
(T) 01767 627772 (F) 01767 627772.
Profile Trainer. Ref: YH14488

TURNER, NIGEL D
Nigel D Turner DWCF, 5 Mill Rd, Stanbridge, **Bedfordshire**, LU7 9HX, **ENGLAND**.
(T) 01525 211592.
Profile Farrier. Ref: YH14489

TURNER, S J
Miss S J Turner, The Farm, Skelton-on-Ure, Ripon, **Yorkshire (North)**, HG4 5AJ, **ENGLAND**.
(T) 01423 324096.
Profile Supplies. Ref: YH14490

TURNER, W G M
W G M Turner, Sigwells Farm, Sigwells, Sherborne, **Dorset**, DT9 4LN, **ENGLAND**.
(T) 01963 220523 (F) 01963 220046.
Contact/s
Owner: Mr W Turner
Profile Trainer. Ref: YH14491

TURNERS
J & P Turner, Arrow Mills, Kington, **Herefordshire**, HR5 3DU, **ENGLAND**.
(T) 01544 230536 (F) 01544 239109.
Contact/s
Partner: Mr M Turner
Profile Supplies. No.Staff: 3 Yr. Est: 1801
Opening Times
Sp: Open Mon - Sat 08:30. Closed Mon - Fri 17:30, Sat 12:00.
Su: Open Mon - Sat 08:30. Closed Mon - Fri 17:30, Sat 12:00.
Au: Open Mon - Sat 08:30. Closed Mon - Fri 17:30, Sat 12:00.
Wn: Open Mon - Sat 08:30. Closed Mon - Fri 17:30, Sat 12:00.
Closed Sundays and weekdays between 13:00 - 14:00
Ref: YH14492

TURNWELL, G M
G M Turnwell, Curteis Farm, Stone, Tenterden, **Kent**, TN30 7JJ, **ENGLAND**.
(T) 01233 758101.
Profile Farrier. Ref: YH14493

TURPINS LODGE
Turpins Lodge Riding Centre, Turpins Lodge, Tadmarton Heath Rd, Hook Norton, Banbury, **Oxfordshire**, OX15 5DQ, **ENGLAND**.
(T) 01608 737033 (F) 01608 737080
(W) www.turpinslodge.co.uk
Affiliated Bodies ABRS.
Contact/s
Owner: J Romer
Profile Equestrian Centre, Riding School, Stable/Livery. Yr. Est: 1988 C.Size: 30 Acres
Opening Times
Sp: Open 08:30. Closed 19:30.
Su: Open 08:00. Closed 17:00.
Au: Open 08:00. Closed 17:00.
Wn: Open 08:00. Closed 17:00. Ref: YH14494

TURTON, S F
Mr S F Turton, Oakhill Farm, Worston, Yealmpton, Plymouth, **Devon**, PL8 2LN, **ENGLAND**.
(T) 01752 880105.
Profile Supplies. Ref: YH14495

TURTONS SADDLERS & HARNESS
Turtons Saddlers & Harness Makers, Upton

Farm, Berwick St John, Shaftesbury, **Dorset**, SP7 0HP, **ENGLAND**.
(T) 01747 828898 **(F)** 01747 828008.
Profile Saddlery Retailer. **Ref: YH14496**

TURVEY, F C

F C Turvey, May Cottage, 107A Park St, Kidderminster, **Worcestershire**, DY11 6TR, **ENGLAND**.
(T) 01562 745614.
Profile Breeder. **Ref: YH14497**

TURVILL, R.G

Mr & Mrs R.G Turvill, Crest Hill Farm, Lower Froyle, Alton, **Hampshire**, GU34 4LP, **ENGLAND**.
(T) 01420 22201.
Contact/s
Owner: Mrs R Turvill
Profile Breeder. **Ref: YH14498**

TURVILLE VALLEY

Turville Valley Stud Riding School, Turville, Henley-on-Thames, **Oxfordshire**, RG9 6QU, **ENGLAND**.
(T) 01491 638338 **(F)** 01491 613406.
Profile Breeder, Riding School, Trainer. **Ref: YH14499**

TURWESTON HILL FARM SUP

Turweston Hill Farm Supplies, Turweston, Brackley, **Northamptonshire**, NN13 5JB, **ENGLAND**.
(T) 01280 700560.
Profile Supplies. **Ref: YH14500**

TUSCANI STUD

Tuscani Stud, Miners Farm, Miners Lane, Hallen, **Gloucestershire (South)**, BS10 7SF, **ENGLAND**.
(T) 01179 822139.
Profile Breeder. **Ref: YH14501**

TUSHINGHAM STABLE HIRE

Tushingham Stable Hire, Alken, Middlewood Farm, Threapwood, Malpas, **Cheshire**, SY14 7AW, **ENGLAND**.
(T) 01948 664408 **(F)** 01948 666079. **Ref: YH14502**

TUSHINGHAM STABLE HIRE

Tushingham Stable Hire, Rosemary Lane, Whitchurch, **Shropshire**, SY13 1EG, **ENGLAND**.
(T) 01948 664408 **(F)** 01948 666079. **Ref: YH14503**

TUSON, PETER

Peter Tuson, 60 Dorchester Rd, Lytchett Minster, Poole, **Dorset**, BH16 6JF, **ENGLAND**.
(T) 01202 622588.
Contact/s
Owner: Mr P Tuson
Profile Farrier. **Ref: YH14504**

TWEDDELL, BRYAN W

Bryan W Tweddell DWCF, The Forge, Eppleby, Richmond, **Yorkshire (North)**, DL11 7AY, **ENGLAND**.
(T) 01325 710067.
Profile Farrier. **Ref: YH14505**

TWEED HSE VETNRY SURGERY

Tweed House Veterinary Surgery, Harper Lane, Yeadon, Leeds, **Yorkshire (West)**, LS19 7RP, **ENGLAND**.
(T) 0113 2505522.
Contact/s
Owner: Miss G Averis **(Q)** MRCVS
Profile Medical Support. **Ref: YH14506**

TWEEDIE, THOMAS

Thomas Tweedie, 34 Chain Trce, Creetown, Newton Stewart, **Dumfries and Galloway**, DG8 7HP, **SCOTLAND**.
(T) 01671 820485.
Profile Farrier. **Ref: YH14507**

TWEENHILLS FARM & STUD

Tweenhills Farm & Stud, Gloucester Rd, Hartpury, Gloucester, **Gloucestershire**, GL19 3BG, **ENGLAND**.
(T) 01452 700177 **(F)** 01452 700002.
Profile Blood Stock Agency, Breeder. **Ref: YH14508**

TWELVE ACRE LIVERY YARD

Twelve Acre Livery Yard, The Stables/Twelve Acre Farm, Chilbridge Rd, Eynsham, Witney, **Oxfordshire**, OX8 1BH, **ENGLAND**.
(T) 01865 883363. **Ref: YH14509**

TWESELDOWN CLUB

Tweseldown Club, Bottom Hse, Bix, Henley-on-Thames, **Oxfordshire**, RG9 6DF, **ENGLAND**.
(T) 0118 9874311.
Profile Club/Association. **Ref: YH14510**

TWIBELL, J

Mr J Twibell, Hall Farm, Dinnington, Sheffield, **Yorkshire (South)**, S25 2PQ, **ENGLAND**.
(T) 01909 562338.
Profile Supplies. **Ref: YH14511**

TWICKENHAM FORGE

Twickenham Forge, Arlington Works, 23-25 Arlington Rd, Twickenham, **London (Greater)**, TW1 2AZ, **ENGLAND**.
(T) 020 88920201.
Contact/s
Partner: Mr T Saunders
Profile Blacksmith. **Ref: YH14512**

TWIN TREES EQUESTRIAN CTRE

Twin Trees Equestrian Centre, Thorncote Rd, Northill, Biggleswade, **Bedfordshire**, SG18 9AQ, **ENGLAND**.
(T) 01767 627414 **(F)** 01767 627444.
Contact/s
Owner: Mr P Jackson **Ref: YH14513**

TWINSTEAD RIDING SCHOOL

Twinstead Riding School, Pebmarsh Rd, Twinstead, Sudbury, **Suffolk**, CO10 7ND, **ENGLAND**.
(T) 01787 269283.
Profile Riding School. **Ref: YH14514**

TWISTON-DAVIES, N A

Mr N A Twiston-Davies, Grange Hill Farm, Naunton, Cheltenham, **Gloucestershire**, GL54 3AY, **ENGLAND**.
(T) 01451 850278 **(F)** 01451 850101.
Profile Trainer. **Ref: YH14515**

TWYFORD FARM SUPPLIES

Twyford Farm Supplies, 15/16 Mountbatten Rd, Tiverton, **Devon**, EX16 6SW, **ENGLAND**.
(T) 01884 253232 **(F)** 01884 253232.
Profile Riding Wear Retailer, Saddlery Retailer, Supplies. **Ref: YH14516**

TY COCH FARM & TREKKING CTRE

Ty Coch Farm & Trekking Centre, Penmachno, Betws-Y-Coed, **Gwynedd**, LL25 0HJ, **WALES**.
(T) 01690 760248 **(F)** 01690 760266
(E) tycoch@amserve.net
(W) www.a1tourism.com/uk/tycoch.html.
Contact/s
General Manager: Mrs G Morris
Profile Horse/Rider Accom.
Tarriffs - Single £17.00 - £19.00, Double/Twin - £34.00 - £38.00. Children and dogs welcome
No.Staff: 3 Yr. Est: 1973 C.Size: 250 Acres
Opening Times
Sp: Open Mon - Sun 09:00. Closed Mon - Sun 21:00.
Su: Open Mon - Sun 09:00. Closed Mon - Sun 21:00.
Au: Open Mon - Sun 09:00. Closed Mon - Sun 21:00.
Wn: Open Mon - Sun 09:00. Closed Mon - Sun 21:00. **Ref: YH14517**

TYAN CONNEMARA STUD

Tyan Connemara Stud, Bracken Farm, East Grinstead, Salisbury, **Wiltshire**, SP5 3RY, **ENGLAND**.
(T) 01722 712514.
Contact/s
Owner: Ms A Halfpenny
Profile Breeder, Stable/Livery.
Foaling service **Ref: YH14518**

TYLANDS ARABIAN STUD

Tylands Arabian Stud, Tregoodwell, Camelford, **Cornwall**, PL32 9PT, **ENGLAND**.
(T) 01840 213146 **(F)** 01840 213146.
Contact/s
Owner: Mrs M Ainscoe
Profile Breeder. **Ref: YH14519**

TYLER ANIMAL SYSTEMS

Tyler Animal Systems, The Limes Farm, Hough-on-the-Hill, Grantham, **Lincolnshire**, NG32 2BH, **ENGLAND**.
(T) 01400 250203 **(F)** 01400 251199
(M) 07710 873300.
Profile Supplies. **Ref: YH14520**

TYLER, DEREK P

Derek P Tyler AFCL, 7 Geneva Cres, Crowle, **Worcestershire**, WR7 4AW, **ENGLAND**.
(T) 01905 381366
(M) 07860 720804.
Profile Farrier. **Ref: YH14521**

TYLER, S J

S J Tyler, 135 Heathfield Rd, Redditch, **Worcestershire**, B97 5RG, **ENGLAND**.
(T) 01527 403009.
Contact/s
Owner: Mr S Tyler
Profile Farrier. **Ref: YH14522**

TYLERS HALL

Tylers Hall, Nags Head Lane, Upminster, **Essex**, RM14 1TS, **ENGLAND**.
(T) 01708 347071 **(F)** 01708 347071.
Contact/s
Owner: Mrs B Lane
Profile Stable/Livery. **Ref: YH14523**

TY-LLYN TACK

Ty-Llyn Tack, Cwmrheidol, Aberystwyth, **Ceredigion**, SY23 3NB, **WALES**.
(T) 01970 880474.
Profile Supplies. **Ref: YH14524**

TYNDALE FARM SERVICES

Tyndale Farm Services, Holmrook, **Cumbria**, CA19 1UH, **ENGLAND**.
(T) 01946 724112.
Profile Saddlery Retailer. **Ref: YH14525**

TYNE VALLEY SADDLERS

Tyne Valley Saddlers, Woodbine Cottage, Holeyn Hall Rd, Wylam, **Northumberland**, NE41 8BB, **ENGLAND**.
(T) 01661 853285
(M) 07778 424700.
Profile Saddlery Retailer. **Ref: YH14526**

TYNINGS RIDING SCHOOL

Tynings Riding School, Charterhouse, Ubley, Bristol, **Bristol**, BS40 6PT, **ENGLAND**.
(T) 01934 742501.
Contact/s
Owner: Ms L Jones
Profile Riding School, Stable/Livery. **Ref: YH14527**

TYNLLWYN RIDING SCHOOL

Tynllwyn Riding School, Tynllwyn Farm, Bryn-Y-Maen, Colwyn Bay, **Conwy**, LL28 5ER, **WALES**.
(T) 01492 580224
Affiliated Bodies BHS.
Contact/s
Owner: Mr W Lewis
Profile Riding School.
Opening Times
Sp: Open Tues - Sun 09:00. Closed Tues - Sun 21:00.
Su: Open Tues - Sun 09:00. Closed Tues - Sun 21:00.
Au: Open Tues - Sun 09:00. Closed Tues - Sun 21:00.
Wn: Open Tues - Sun 09:00. Closed Tues - Sun 21:00.
Telephone for further information. **Ref: YH14528**

TYN-MORFA RIDING CTRE

Tyn-Morfa Riding Centre, Rhosneigr, **Isle of Anglesey**, LL64 5QX, **WALES**.
(T) 01407 810072 **(F)** 01407 810072.
Contact/s
General Manager: Mr C Carnall
Profile Equestrian Centre, Saddlery Retailer, Stable/Livery, Transport/Horse Boxes.
Stabling facilities for Port of Holyhead. Caravan and camping available. No.Staff: 3 Yr. Est: 1925
C.Size: 3 Acres **Ref: YH14529**

TYRLEY CASTLE STUD

Tyrley Castle Stud, Market Drayton, **Shropshire**, TF9 2AA, **ENGLAND**.
(T) 01630 652435.
Profile Breeder. **Ref: YH14530**

TYRONE SNELL TRAILERS

Tyrone Snell Trailers, Longdowns, Penryn, **Cornwall**, TR10 9DL, **ENGLAND**.
(T) 01209 860945.
Contact/s
Owner: Mr T Snell
Profile Transport/Horse Boxes. **Ref: YH14531**

TYROS SHETLAND PONY STUD

Tyros Shetland Pony Stud, Flat 2, Richmond Court, 63 Richmond Rd, Freemantle, **Hampshire**, SO15 3RW, **ENGLAND**.
(T) 023 80340404.
Profile Breeder. **Ref: YH14532**

TYSOE, JASON R

Jason R Tysoe DWCF, 5 Main St, Mollington,

Banbury, **Oxfordshire**, OX17 1BD, **ENGLAND**.
(T) 01295 758655.
Profile Farrier. **Ref: YH14533**

TYSUL VETNRY GROUP

Tysul Veterinary Group, Pencader Rd, Pontwelly, Llandysul, **Carmarthenshire**, SA44 4AG, **WALES**.
(T) 01559 363318 **(F)** 01559 362881.
Profile Medical Support. **Ref: YH14534**

TY-WYTH-NEWYDD STABLES

Ty-wyth-Newydd Stables, Tredodridge, Cowbridge, **Glamorgan (Vale of)**, CF7 7UL, **WALES**.
(T) 01446 760122 **(F)** 01446 760067.
Profile Trainer. **Ref: YH14535**

U E F

U E F Ltd, P O Box 22, Lincoln, **Lincolnshire**, LN2 5DT, **ENGLAND**.
(T) 01522 525492 **(F)** 01522 521701.
Profile Blacksmith. **Ref: YH14536**

U PULL TRAILERS

U Pull Trailers, Bath Rd, Bridgeyate, Bristol, **Bristol**, BS30 5JW, **ENGLAND**.
(T) 01179 612317.
Contact/s
Owner: Mr R Edwards
Profile Transport/Horse Boxes. **Ref: YH14537**

UDALL, DAVID GEOFFREY

David Geoffrey Udall RSS, Portley Rise, Worston Lane, Little Bridgeford, **Staffordshire**, ST18 9QA, **ENGLAND**.
(T) 01785 282287.
Profile Farrier. **Ref: YH14538**

UFAC

Ufac (UK) Ltd, Waterwitch Hse, Exeter Rd, Newmarket, **Suffolk**, CB8 8LR, **ENGLAND**.
(T) 01638 665923 **(F)** 01638 667756.
Profile Medical Support. **Ref: YH14539**

UFFINGTON RIDING STABLES

Uffington Riding Stables, Essendine Rd, Uffington, Stamford, **Lincolnshire**, PE9 4SR, **ENGLAND**.
(T) 01780 754044.
Contact/s
Owner: Mrs J Musgrove **(Q)** BHS IT
Profile Riding School.
Hold fun days for children during the holidays.
No.Staff: 3 Yr. Est: 1985
Opening Times
Sp: Open Mon - Fri 16:00, Sat 08:00. Closed Mon - Fri 19:30, Sat 18:00.
Su: Open 09:00. Closed 18:00.
Au: Open Mon - Fri 16:00, Sat 08:00. Closed Mon - Fri 19:30, Sat 18:00.
Wn: Open Mon - Fri 16:00, Sat 08:00. Closed Mon - Fri 19:30, Sat 18:00.
Contact for information as times may vary during the holiday season **Ref: YH14540**

UGGLESHALL

Uggeshall Equestrian Centre, Manor Farm, Uggeshall, Beccles, **Suffolk**, NR34 8BD, **ENGLAND**.
(T) 01502 578546.
Profile Riding School, Stable/Livery, Track/Course, Trainer.
Opening Times
Sp: Open Mon - Sun 09:00. Closed Mon - Sun 18:00.
Su: Open Mon - Sun 09:00. Closed Mon - Sun 18:00.
Au: Open Mon - Sun 09:00. Closed Mon - Sun 18:00.
Wn: Open Mon - Sun 09:00. Closed Mon - Sun 18:00. **Ref: YH14541**

UK AST OF HOLISTIC NUTRITION

British Association of Holstic Nutrition & Medicine, Borough Court, Hartley Whitney, Hook, **Hampshire**, RG27 8JA, **ENGLAND**.
(T) 01252 843282 **(F)** 01252 845750.
Contact/s
Secretary: Mrs M Bullen
Profile Club/Association. **Ref: YH14542**

UK CHASERS

UK Chasers Ltd, 1 St Tinivers Cottage, High St, Beckley, Oxford, **Oxfordshire**, OX3 9UU, **ENGLAND**.
(T) 01865 351688 **(F)** 01865 351233.
Profile Equestrian Centre. **Ref: YH14543**

UK CHASERS

UK Chasers Ltd, Otmoor Lane, Beckley, Oxford, **Oxfordshire**, OX3 9TD, **ENGLAND**.
(T) 01865 351688 **(F)** 01865 351233.
Contact/s
Key Contact: Mr D Talbot
Profile Club/Association. **Ref: YH14544**

UK CHASERS & RIDERS

UK Chasers Ltd, Coventry Rd, Cubbington, Leamington Spa, **Warwickshire**, CU32 7UJ, **ENGLAND**.
(T) 01926 450049 **(F)** 01926 422849
(W) www.ukchasers.com.
Contact/s
For Bookings: Ms J Tweedie
(E) info@ukchasers.com
Profile
An organisation that provides safe off-road riding and an affordable national competition series.
Opening Times
Sp: Open 09:00. Closed 17:00.
Su: Open 09:00. Closed 17:00.
Au: Open 09:00. Closed 17:00.
Wn: Open 09:00. Closed 17:00. **Ref: YH14545**

UK PAINT HORSE ASS

UK Paint Horse Association, Linnfall Cottage, Waterheads, Peebles, **Scottish Borders**, EH45 8QX, **SCOTLAND**.. **Ref: YH14546**

UK POLOCROSSE ASSOCIATION

UK Polocrosse Association, 18 Little London, Silverstone, **Warwickshire**, CV8 2LF, **ENGLAND**.
(T) 01327 857720.
Contact/s
Chairman: Mrs P Chapple
Profile Club/Association. **Ref: YH14547**

UK RACING

UK Racing, 79 Byfield Rd, Woodford Halse, Daventry, **Northamptonshire**, NN11 3QS, **ENGLAND**.
(T) 01327 261512 **(F)** 01327 261138.
Contact/s
Owner: Mr J Draper
Profile Saddlery Retailer. **Ref: YH14548**

UK RIDERS

UK Riders, Sandy Lane Farm, Old Milverton Lane, Blackdown, Leamington Spa, **Warwickshire**, CV32 6RW, **ENGLAND**.
(T) 01926 886889 **(F)** 01926 886226.
Profile Club/Association. **Ref: YH14549**

UK SADDLES

UK Saddles, 30 Navigation St, Walsall, **Midlands (West)**, W52 9LT, **ENGLAND**.
(T) 01922 615015 **(F)** 01922 615015.
Contact/s
Owner: Mr A Ellis
Profile Saddlery Retailer. Manufacturers of Reacter Panel Saddles. Yr. Est: 2000
Opening Times
Sp: Open Mon - Fri 08:00, Sat 09:00. Closed Mon - Fri 17:00, Sat 13:00.
Su: Open Mon - Fri 08:00, Sat 09:00. Closed Mon - Fri 17:00, Sat 13:00.
Au: Open Mon - Fri 08:00, Sat 09:00. Closed Mon - Fri 17:00, Sat 13:00.
Wn: Open Mon - Fri 08:00, Sat 09:00. Closed Mon - Fri 17:00, Sat 13:00. **Ref: YH14550**

UK TRAILER PARTS

UK Trailer Parts, Fletchers Yard, Wellowgate, Grimsby, **Lincolnshire (North East)**, DN32 0RG, **ENGLAND**.
(T) 01472 342503.
Profile Transport/Horse Boxes. **Ref: YH14551**

ULCEBY VALE STUD

Ulceby Vale Stud, Vale Farm, Ulceby, **Lincolnshire (North)**, DN39 6TF, **ENGLAND**.
(T) 01469 588210 **(F)** 01469 588324.
Profile Breeder. **Ref: YH14552**

ULLENWOOD COURT RIDING CTRE

Ullenwood Court Riding Centre, Ullenwood Court, Ullenwood, Cheltenham, **Gloucestershire**, GL53 9QS, **ENGLAND**.
(T) 01242 575020.
Contact/s
Owner: Mrs M Pitt **Ref: YH14553**

ULLSWATER PONY SPORTS CLUB

Ullswater Pony Sports Club, White Stone, Newby, Penrith, **Cumbria**, CA10 3HQ, **ENGLAND**.
(T) 01931 714375.
Contact/s
Secretary: Mrs P Slack
Profile Club/Association. **Ref: YH14554**

ULLYOTT, P G

P G Ullyott, Aldham Mill, Barnsley Rd, Wombwell, Barnsley, **Yorkshire (South)**, S73 8EG, **ENGLAND**.
(T) 01226 752204.
Contact/s
Owner: Mrs P Ullyott **Ref: YH14555**

ULSTER PONY SOCIETY

Ulster Pony Society, Rowan Lodge, Creevy Rd, Lisburn, **County Antrim**, **NORTHERN IRELAND**.
(T) 028 638329
(W) www.equiworld.net/gb/directory/bindex.htm.
Contact/s
Chairman: Mr D Stewart
Profile Club/Association. **Ref: YH14556**

ULVERSCROFT SHETLAND PONIES

Ulverscroft Shetland Ponies, Priory Lane, Ulverscroft, **Leicestershire**, LE6 0PH, **ENGLAND**.
(T) 01530 242396.
Profile Breeder. **Ref: YH14557**

UMBERSLADE EQUESTRIAN CTRE

Umberslade Equestrian Centre, Blunts Green Farm, Blunts Green, Henley-In-Arden, Solihull, **Warwickshire**, B95 5RE, **ENGLAND**.
(T) 01564 794609 **(F)** 01564 795985.
Contact/s
Owner: Mr P Pettitt
Profile Riding School. **Ref: YH14558**

UMM QARN MANAGEMENT

Umm Qarn Management Co Ltd, Old Lodge Farm, Moon Lane, Dormansland, Lingfield, **Surrey**, RH7 6PD, **ENGLAND**.
(T) 01342 870217 **(F)** 01342 870215
(W) www.ummqarn.com.
Profile Breeder. **Ref: YH14559**

UNDERHILL RIDING STABLES

Underhill Riding Stables, Underhill Farm, Dolau, Llandrindod Wells, **Powys**, LD1 5TL, **WALES**.
(T) 01597 851890 **(F)** 01597 851161
Affiliated Bodies Pony Club UK.
Contact/s
Owner: Mrs K Bufton
Profile Riding School, Track/Course.
Equestrian Outreach Programme (NVQ for adults, approved by the Yale College in Wrexham). The centre is also a Pony club and works with young horses.
Opening Times
Sp: Open Tues - Sun 10:00. Closed Tues - Sun 16:00.
Su: Open Tues - Sun 10:00. Closed Tues - Sun 16:00.
Au: Open Tues - Sun 10:00. Closed Tues - Sun 16:00.
Wn: Open Tues - Sun 10:00. Closed Tues - Sun 16:00. **Ref: YH14560**

UNDERHILL, DAVID J

David J Underhill AWCF, Rose Cottage, Combeinteignhead, Newton Abbot, **Devon**, TQ12 4RE, **ENGLAND**.
(T) 01626 872343
(M) 07831 856114.
Profile Farrier. **Ref: YH14561**

UNDERWOOD & CROXSON

Underwood & Croxson (Guildford), Greyfriars Farm, Large Animal Ctre, Puttenham, Guildford, **Surrey**, GU3 1AQ, **ENGLAND**.
(T) 01483 811088 **(F)** 01483 811074
(E) greyfriars.farm@virgin.net.
Profile Medical Support. **Ref: YH14562**

UNDERWOOD & CROXSON EQUINE

Underwood & Croxson Equine Unit, Greyfairers, Puttenham, Guildford, **Surrey**, GU3 1AG, **ENGLAND**.
(T) 01483 811088.
Profile Medical Support. **Ref: YH14563**

UNDERWOOD, C M

C M Underwood DWCF, 369 Main Rd, Southbourne, Emsworth, **Hampshire**, PO10 8JH, **ENGLAND**.
(T) 01243 371678.
Profile Farrier. **Ref: YH14564**

UNDERWOOD, R F

R F Underwood DWCF, Slaughter Castle, Kimbolton, Leominster, **Herefordshire**, HR6 0ET, **ENGLAND**.
(T) 01568 612388.
Profile Farrier. **Ref: YH14565**

UNICORN LEATHER SADDLERY

Unicorn Leather Saddlery, 62 Spencer Rd, Caterham, **Surrey**, CR3 5LA, **ENGLAND**.
(T) 01883 347333.
Contact/s
Owner: Mr A Back

A-Z of COMPANIES

Key: **(T)** telephone **(F)** fax **(M)** mobile **(E)** E-Mail Address **(W)** Website Address **(Q)** Qualifications
Yr. Est: Year Established C.Size: Complex Size Sp: Spring Su: Summer Au: Autumn Wn: Winter

Profile Saddlery Retailer. **Ref: YH14566**

UNICORN RDA CTRE

Unicorn RDA Centre, Stainton Way, Hemlington, Middlesbrough, **Cleveland**, TS8 9LX, **ENGLAND**.
(T) 01642 576222 **(F)** 01642 576254.
Contact/s
Manager: Mr C Jones
Profile Riding School. **Ref: YH14567**

UNICORN SADDLERY

Unicorn Saddlery (Reading), Goring Heath Poultry Farm, Goring Heath, Reading, **Berkshire**, RG8 7SB, **ENGLAND**.
(T) 0118 9724427.
Profile Supplies. **Ref: YH14568**

UNICORN SADDLERY

Unicorn Saddlery, Netherclay Farm, Thurlbear, Taunton, **Somerset**, TA3 5AX, **ENGLAND**.
(T) 01823 321753 **(F)** 01823 321753.
Contact/s
Owner: Mr P Ireland
Profile Saddlery Retailer. **Ref: YH14569**

UNION HALL

Union Hall, Brasside, Durham, **County Durham**, DH1 5SG, **ENGLAND**.
(T) 0191 3861308 **(F)** 0191 3868291.
Contact/s
Owner: Mrs H Calzini
Profile Stable/Livery. **Ref: YH14570**

UNION OF COUNTRY SPORTS

Union of Country Sports Workers, P O Box 43, Towcester, **Northamptonshire**, NN12 7ZB, **ENGLAND**.
(T) 01327 811066 **(F)** 01327 811066
(E) office@ucsw.org
(W) www.ucsw.org.
Profile Club/Association. **Yr. Est:** 1997
Ref: YH14571

UNIQUE CARRIAGES

Unique Carriages, 46 Therlow Rd, Plymouth, **Devon**, PL3 6NZ, **ENGLAND**.
(T) 01752 770948.
Contact/s
Partner: Mrs S Watts **Ref: YH14572**

UNITED PACK

United Pack, The Old Byre, Brompton, Church Stoke, Montgomery, **Powys**, SY15 6SP, **WALES**.
(T) 01588 620237. **Ref: YH14573**

UNITED SADDLEBRED ASS

United Saddlebred Association UK, Appledore Stud, Birchwood Forge, Storridge, Malvern, **Worcestershire**, WR13 5EZ, **ENGLAND**.
(T) 01886 884285.
Contact/s
Key Contact: Mrs A Farman
Profile Club/Association. **Ref: YH14574**

UNITED SERVICES

United Services, Westdown Camp, Tilshead, Salisbury, **Wiltshire**, SP3 4RS, **ENGLAND**.
(T) 01980 674740. **Ref: YH14575**

UNIVERSAL ROOFING SYSTEMS

Universal Roofing Systems Ltd, 4 Fourlands Hse, Low Bentham, **Lancashire**, LA2 7EX, **ENGLAND**.
(T) 01524 262533
(M) 07836 511188.
Profile Supplies. **Ref: YH14576**

UNIVERSAL TRAILERS

Universal Trailers, 557 Piercetown Droichead Nua, Newbridge, **County Kildare**, **IRELAND**.
(T) 045 434418.
Profile Supplies. **Ref: YH14577**

UNIVERSAL TRAILERS

Universal Trailers, 28 Stratford Rd, Ipswich, **Suffolk**, IP1 6EF, **ENGLAND**.
(T) 01473 747394.
Profile Transport/Horse Boxes. **Ref: YH14578**

UNIVERSAL TRAILERS

Universal Trailers, Coneyhurst, Billingshurst, **Sussex (West)**, RH14 9DG, **ENGLAND**.
(T) 01403 782862 **(F)** 01403 783528.
Profile Transport/Horse Boxes. **Ref: YH14579**

UNIVERSITY DIAGNOSTICS

University Diagnostics Ltd, LGC Building, Queens Rd, Teddington, **London (Greater)**, TW11 0NJ, **ENGLAND**.
(T) 020 89438400 **(F)** 020 89438401
(E) udl@lgc.co.uk.
Profile Supplies. **Ref: YH14580**

UNIVERSITY OF ABERDEEN

University of Aberdeen, 60 Devonshire Rd, Aberdeen, **Aberdeen (City of)**, AB10 6XQ, **SCOTLAND**.
(T) 01224 322780.
Contact/s
Secretary: Hazel McKnight
Profile Club/Association. **Ref: YH14581**

UNIVERSITY OF BRADFORD

University of Bradford Riding Club, University Of Bradford, Great Horton, **Yorkshire (West)**, BD7 1DP, **ENGLAND**.
(T) 01274 733466.
Profile Club/Association, Riding Club. **Ref: YH14582**

UNIVERSITY OF BRISTOL

University of Bristol, Equine Sports Medicine Ctre, Langford, **Somerset**, BS40 7DU, **ENGLAND**.
(T) 01934 853223 **(F)** 01934 853223.
Profile Medical Support. **Ref: YH14583**

UNIVERSITY OF CAMBRIDGE

University of Cambridge Veterinary School Trust (CAMVET), Cambridge University Vet School, Cambridge, **Cambridgeshire**, CB3 0ES, **ENGLAND**.
(T) 01223 337630 **(F)** 01223 337610
(E) spg1002@cam.ac.uk.
Profile Equestrian Centre. **Ref: YH14584**

UNIVERSITY OF DURHAM

University of Durham Riding Club, D U A U, Dunelm Hse, New Elvet, Durham, **County Durham**, DH1 3AN, **ENGLAND**.
(T) 0191 3742199.
Profile Club/Association, Riding Club. **Ref: YH14585**

UNIVERSITY OF EXETER

University of Exeter Riding Club, Cornwall Hse, St German's Rd, Exeter, **Devon**, EX4 6TG, **ENGLAND**.
(T) 01392 263505 **(F)** 01392 263599
(E) au@ex.ac.uk.
Profile Club/Association, Riding Club. **Ref: YH14586**

UNIVERSITY OF KEELE

University of Keele Riding Club, C/O Students Union, University Of Keele, Keele, **Staffordshire**, ST5 5BJ, **ENGLAND**.
(T) 01782 625411.
Profile Club/Association, Riding Club. **Ref: YH14587**

UNIVERSITY OF LANCASTER

University of Lancaster Riding Club, University Athletic Union, Bailrigg, **Lancashire**, LA1 4YW, **ENGLAND**.
(T) 01524 63735.
Contact/s
President: Miss A Lee-Uff
Profile Club/Association, Riding Club. **Ref: YH14588**

UNIVERSITY OF LEICESTER

University of Leicester Riding Club, The Riding Club, The Sports Ass, Leicester University Students' Union, Leicester, **Leicestershire**, LE1 7RH, **ENGLAND**.
(T) 0116 2553860 **(F)** 0116 2554483.
Profile Club/Association, Riding Club. **Ref: YH14589**

UNIVERSITY OF LIVERPOOL

University of Liverpool, Philip Leverhulme Large Animal Hospital, Dept Vetnry Clinical Science, Leahurst, Neston, South Wirral, **Cheshire**, CH64 7TE, **ENGLAND**.
(T) 0151 7946041 **(F)** 0151 7946034.
Profile Medical Support. **Ref: YH14590**

UNIVERSITY OF MANCHESTER

University of Manchester Riding Club, B22 Westbourne Gr, Withington, Manchester, **Manchester (Greater)**, M20 8JA, **ENGLAND**.
(T) 0161 4348134.
Profile Club/Association, Riding Club. **Ref: YH14591**

UNIVERSITY OF NEWCASTLE

University of Newcastle Riding Club, Union Building, Kings Walk, University Of Newcastle-upon-Tyne, Newcastle-upon-Tyne, **Tyne and Wear**, NE1 8QB, **ENGLAND**.
(T) 0191 2393900.
Profile Club/Association, Riding Club. **Ref: YH14592**

UNIVERSITY OF SURREY

University of Surrey Riding Club, University Of Surrey Union, University Of Surrey, Guildford, **Surrey**, GU2 5XH, **ENGLAND**.
(T) 01483 67785.
Profile Club/Association, Riding Club. **Ref: YH14593**

UNIVERSITY OF SUSSEX

University of Sussex Riding Club, Sports Federation, Falmer Hse, University Of Sussex, Brighton, **Sussex (East)**, BN1 9RJ, **ENGLAND**.
(T) 01273 878322.
Contact/s
Co-ordinator: Ms S Goddard
Profile Club/Association, Riding Club. **Ref: YH14594**

UNIVERSITY OF SWANSEA RIDING CLUB

University College of Swansea Riding Club, C/O Athletic Union, Union Hse, University College Of Swansea, Singleton Park, Swansea, **Swansea**, SA2 8PP, **WALES**.
(T) 01792 295704 **(F)** 01792 206029.
Profile Club/Association, Riding Club. **Ref: YH14595**

UNIVERSITY OF ULSTER

University of Ulster Riding Club (Jordanstown), C/O U U J Students Union, Shore Rd, Newtownabbey, **County Antrim**, BT37 0QB, **NORTHERN IRELAND**.
(T) 028 90365121 **(F)** 028 90366817.
Contact/s
President: Ms F Crunden
Profile Club/Association. **Ref: YH14596**

UNIVERSITY OF ULSTER

University of Ulster Riding Club (Coleraine), C/O University Of Ulster, Coleraine Campus, Coleraine, **County Londonderry**, BT52 1SA, **NORTHERN IRELAND**.
(T) 028 70344141.
Contact/s
Secretary: Miss A Rea
Profile Club/Association. **Ref: YH14597**

UNSWORTH, HARRY W

Harry W Unsworth DWCF, 27 Nightingale Cl, Farndon, **Cheshire**, CH3 6RA, **ENGLAND**.
(T) 01829 270805.
Profile Farrier. **Ref: YH14598**

UPCOTE CROSS COUNTRY COURSE

JRR and SM Platt, Upcote Farm, Withington, Cheltenham, **Gloucestershire**, GL54 4BL, **ENGLAND**.
(T) 01242 890250.
Contact/s
Owner: Mrs S Platt
Profile Equestrian Centre, Track/Course.
Ref: YH14599

UPHILL WELSH COBS

Uphill Welsh Cobs, Cross Roads Farm, Cross Roads, Lewdown, Okehampton, **Devon**, EX20 4DP, **ENGLAND**.
(T) 01566 783326.
Contact/s
Owner: Mr D Pearce
Profile Breeder, Stable/Livery. **Ref: YH14600**

UPLANDS STUD

Uplands Stud, Brook, Godalming, **Surrey**, GU8 6NW, **ENGLAND**.
(T) 01428 682081 **(F)** 01428 685613.
Profile Breeder, Trainer. **Ref: YH14601**

UPLANDS WELSH COBS

Uplands Welsh Cobs, Scotland Farm, Hawkley, Liss, **Hampshire**, GU33 6NH, **ENGLAND**.
(T) 01730 827521 **(F)** 01730 827520.
Profile Breeder. **Ref: YH14602**

UPMINSTER RIDING CLUB

Upminster Riding Club, 12 Arnhem Ave, Aveley, **Essex**, RM15 4AP, **ENGLAND**..
Contact/s
Secretary: Mrs B Satterley
Profile Club/Association, Riding Club. **Ref: YH14603**

UPMINSTER SADDLERY

Upminster Saddlery, 117 Corbets Tey Rd, Upminster, **Essex**, RM14 2AA, **ENGLAND**.
(T) 01708 229797
(W) www.upminstersaddlery.co.uk.
Contact/s
Owner: Mrs D Brooker
(E) diane@upminstersaddlery.com
Profile Riding Wear Retailer, Saddlery Retailer.
10% discount offered to RDA (Riding for the Disabled Association) riders. Do not accept American Express
No.Staff: 4 Yr. Est: 1981
Opening Times
Sp: Open Mon - Sat 09:00, Sun 10:00. Closed Mon - Sat 17:30, Sun 14:00.
Su: Open Mon - Sat 09:00, Sun 10:00. Closed Mon - Sat 17:30, Sun 14:00.

Au: Open Mon - Sat 09:00, Sun 10:00. Closed Mon - Sat 17:30, Sun 14:00.
Wn: Open Mon - Sat 09:00, Sun 10:00. Closed Mon - Sat 17:30, Sun 14:00. **Ref: YH14604**

UPPACOTT STUD DARTMOOR
Uppacott Stud Dartmoor, Uppacott Mill, Moretonhampstead, Newton Abbot, **Devon**, TQ13 8PT, **ENGLAND**.
(T) 01647 433259 **(F)** 01647 433173.
Contact/s
Owner: Mr T Ward
Profile Breeder. **Ref: YH14605**

UPPER HENDRE CLASSICAL RIDING
Upper Hendre Classical Riding, Glewstone, Ross-on-Wye, **Herefordshire**, HR9 6AX, **ENGLAND**.
(T) 01989 770188.
Profile Riding School. **Ref: YH14606**

UPPER RIDGEWAY FARM
Upper Ridgeway Farm, Thursley, Godalming, **Surrey**, GU8 6QR, **ENGLAND**.
(T) 01428 604508.
Profile Stable/Livery. **Ref: YH14607**

UPPER THRUXTED FARM
Upper Thruxted Farm, Pennypott Lane, Waltham, Canterbury, **Kent**, CT4 7HA, **ENGLAND**.
(T) 01227 730276.
Profile Equestrian Centre. **Ref: YH14608**

UPPERWOOD FARM STUD
Harvey Currie & Parsons, Gaddesden Row, Hemel Hempstead, **Hertfordshire**, HP2 6HQ, **ENGLAND**.
(T) 01442 253479 **(F)** 01442 259234.
Contact/s
Owner: Mr G Parson
(E) gparsons@btinternet.com
Profile Blood Stock Agency, Breeder, Horse/Rider Accom, Medical Support, Stable/Livery, Stud Farm, Transport/Horse Boxes.
Accommodation for Riders available off site. Full livery offered. No.Staff: 5 Yr. Est: 1986
C.Size: 100 Acres
Opening Times
Telephone for an appointment **Ref: YH14609**

UPPINGHAM DRESS AGENCY
Uppingham Dress Agency (The), 2-6 Orange St, Uppingham, **Rutland**, LE15 9SQ, **ENGLAND**.
(T) 01572 823276 **(F)** 01572 823815.
Profile Saddlery Retailer. **Ref: YH14610**

UPPINGTON SMITHY
Uppington Smithy, The Grove, Lower Longwood, Eaton Constantine, Shrewsbury, **Shropshire**, SY5 6RB, **ENGLAND**.
(T) 01952 740264.
Profile Farrier. **Ref: YH14611**

UPSHIRE FARM STABLES
Upshire Farm Stables, Hungerford Hill, Lambourn, **Berkshire**, RG17 7NV, **ENGLAND**.
(T) 01488 73483 **(F)** 01488 73483
(M) 07774 465583.
Profile Trainer. **Ref: YH14612**

UPSON, ANNE & PETER
Anne & Peter Upson, Newbarn Cottage, Loughborough, Lyminge, Folkestone, **Kent**, CT18 8DG, **ENGLAND**.
(T) 01303 862776
Affiliated Bodies NAAT.
Contact/s
Physiotherapist: Anne Upson
Profile Medical Support. **Ref: YH14613**

UPSON, J R
Mr J R Upson, Glebe Hse, Blakesley Heath, Maidstone, Towcester, **Northamptonshire**, NN12 8HN, **ENGLAND**.
(T) 01327 860043 **(F)** 01327 860238.
Profile Trainer. **Ref: YH14614**

UPSON, T B
T B Upson, Priory Farm, Braxted Rd, Tiptree, Colchester, **Essex**, CO5 0QB, **ENGLAND**.
(T) 01621 818311 **(F)** 01621 818311.
Contact/s
Owner: Mr T Upson
Profile Transport/Horse Boxes. **Ref: YH14615**

UPTON RIDING STABLES
Upton Riding Stables, Newnham Rd, Ryde, **Isle of Wight**, PO33 3TH, **ENGLAND**.
(T) 01983 615116 **(F)** 01983 562649.
Contact/s
Owner: Mr P Legge **Ref: YH14616**

UPTON, WAYNE E
Wayne E Upton AFCL, Walstead Forge, Snowflake Lane, Walstead, Haywards Heath, **Sussex (West)**, RH16 2QE, **ENGLAND**.
(T) 01444 482992.
Profile Farrier. **Ref: YH14617**

URCH, DAVID L
David L Urch, The Vetnry Ctre, Glebe Hse, Station Rd, Wrington, **Somerset (North)**, BS18 7LL, **ENGLAND**.
(T) 01934 862497.
Profile Medical Support. **Ref: YH14618**

URCH, GARY
Gary Urch DWCF, Fairview Farm, White St, Easterton, Devizes, **Wiltshire**, SN10 4PA, **ENGLAND**.
(T) 01380 813343.
Profile Farrier. **Ref: YH14619**

URCHINWOOD MANOR EQUITATION
Urchinwood Manor Equitation Centre, Urchinwood Lane, Congresbury, Bristol, **Bristol**, BS49 5AP, **ENGLAND**.
(T) 01934 833248 **(F)** 01934 834683
Affiliated Bodies BHS.
Contact/s
Owner: Captain P Hall
Profile Horse/Rider Accom, Riding School, Stable/Livery. No.Staff: 5
Opening Times
By appointment only **Ref: YH14620**

URMSTON & DISTRICT
Urmston & District Riding Club, 1 Aylesbury Ave, Davyhulme, Manchester, **Manchester (Greater)**, M41 0SB, **ENGLAND**.
(T) 0161 7488996.
Contact/s
Secretary: Mrs J Oakes
Profile Club/Association, Riding Club. **Ref: YH14621**

USA PRO JOCKEYS APPAREL
USA Pro Jockeys Apparel, 21 Villier St, Uxbridge, **London (Greater)**, UB8 2PU, **ENGLAND**.
(T) 01895 814933 **(F)** 01895 814933
(M) 07885 476462.
Profile Supplies. **Ref: YH14622**

USPCA
Ulster Society for the Prevention of Cruelty to Animals, 11 Drumview Rd, Lisburn, **County Antrim**, BT27 6YF, **NORTHERN IRELAND**.
(T) 028 92813178 **(F)** 028 92812260.
Profile Club/Association. **Ref: YH14623**

UTILITY INTERNATIONAL
Utility International Ltd, Trailer Yard, Yafforth Rd, Northallerton, **Yorkshire (North)**, DL7 8UD, **ENGLAND**.
(T) 01609 773155 **(F)** 01609 780053.
Profile Transport/Horse Boxes. **Ref: YH14624**

UTOPIA FORGE
Utopia Forge, Midleton Ind Est, Guildford, **Surrey**, GU2 8XW, **ENGLAND**.
(T) 01483 536634 **(F)** 01483 536634.
Contact/s
Owner: Mr A Quirk
Profile Blacksmith. **Ref: YH14625**

UTTOXETER RACECOURSE
Uttoxeter Racecourse, Wood Lane, Uttoxeter, **Staffordshire**, ST14 8BD, **ENGLAND**.
(T) 01889 562561 **(F)** 01889 562786
(E) info@uttoxeterracecourse.co.uk.
Profile Track/Course. **Ref: YH14626**

V E BEER & SONS
V E Beer & Sons, Tan Lane, Exeter, **Devon**, EX2 8EG, **ENGLAND**.
(T) 01392 254871.
Contact/s
Owner: Mr V Beer
Profile Blacksmith. **Ref: YH14627**

V I P EXHIBITIONS
V I P Exhibitions Ltd, Nunn Brook Rd, County Est, Sulton In Ashfield, **Nottinghamshire**, NG17 2HU, **ENGLAND**.
(T) 01623 441114 **(F)** 01623 441454.
Profile Club/Association. **Ref: YH14628**

V J WEBB
V J Webb & Co, 28 Queens Drive, Wavertree, Liverpool, **Merseyside**, L15 7NE, **ENGLAND**.
(T) 0151 7227146 **(F)** 0151 7227146.
Contact/s
Owner: Mr V Webb
Profile Blacksmith. **Ref: YH14629**

VACLAVEK, V (DR)
Dr V Vaclavek, 28 Winkfield Court, Boltro Rd, Haywards Heath, **Sussex (West)**, RH16 1BH, **ENGLAND**.
(T) 01444 440334 **(F)** 01444 440334.
Profile Medical Support. **Ref: YH14630**

VALE AUTOBUILD
Vale Autobuild, Unit 6 Pershore Trading Est, Pershore, **Worcestershire**, WR10 2DD, **ENGLAND**.
(T) 01386 561304 **(F)** 01386 561304.
Contact/s
Owner: Mr M Styzaker
Profile Transport/Horse Boxes. **Ref: YH14631**

VALE BROTHERS
Vale Brothers Limited, Long St, Walsall, **Midlands (West)**, WS2 9QG, **ENGLAND**.
(T) 01922 624363 **(F)** 01922 720994
(W) www.valebrothers.co.uk.
Profile Supplies. Grooming Brushes Manufacturers.
Ref: YH14632

VALE FARM RIDING SCHOOL
Vale Farm Riding School, Mays Lane, Barnet, **Hertfordshire**, EN5 2AQ, **ENGLAND**.
(T) 020 84408866.
Contact/s
Manageress: Mrs S Gourpinar **Ref: YH14633**

VALE FORGE
Vale Forge, Charlton Barn, Charlton, Chichester, **Sussex (West)**, PO18 0HX, **ENGLAND**.
(T) 01243 811434.
Profile Blacksmith. **Ref: YH14634**

VALE LODGE STABLES
Vale Lodge Stables, Downs Lane, Leatherhead, **Surrey**, KT22 8JG, **ENGLAND**.
(T) 01372 373184.
Contact/s
Owner: Miss J Cooper
Profile Riding School, Stable/Livery. **Ref: YH14635**

VALE OF AERON RIDING CLUB
Vale of Aeron Riding Club, Penlan Ganol, Cribyn, Lampeter, **Ceredigion**, SA48 7ND, **WALES**.
(T) 01570 470223 **(F)** 01570 423007.
Contact/s
Chairman: Mrs S Fowden
Profile Club/Association, Riding Club. **Ref: YH14636**

VALE OF ARROW RIDING CLUB
Vale of Arrow Riding Club, Eccles Alley, Woonton, **Herefordshire**, HR3 6QL, **ENGLAND**.
(T) 01544 8560.
Contact/s
Chairman: Mrs P Bishop
Profile Club/Association, Riding Club. **Ref: YH14637**

VALE OF BELVOIR LEATHERS
Vale Of Belvoir Leathers, Unit 4B Rural Ind Est, John O' Gaunt, Melton Mowbray, **Leicestershire**, LE14 2RE, **ENGLAND**.
(T) 01664 454932 **(F)** 01664 454968
(E) info@belvoir-leathers.co.uk
(W) www.belvoir-leathers.co.uk.
Contact/s
Owner: Ms S Seed
Profile Riding Wear Retailer.
Made to measure chaps. **Ref: YH14638**

VALE OF LUNE HARRIERS
Vale of Lune Harriers, Kays Barn, Fleet St Lane, Ribchester, Preston, **Lancashire**, PR3 3XE, **ENGLAND**.
(T) 01254 878049.
Profile Club/Association. **Ref: YH14639**

VALE OF USK RIDING CLUB
Vale of Usk Riding Club, Forge Hse, Llanvetherine, Abergavenny, **Monmouthshire**, NP7 8NL, **WALES**.
(T) 01873 821388.
Contact/s
Chairman: Mrs D Jones
Profile Club/Association, Riding Club. **Ref: YH14640**

VALE OF YORK PONY CLUB
Vale of York Pony Club, 3 White Hse Gr, Elvington, **Yorkshire (North)**, YO41 5AL, **ENGLAND**.
(T) 01904 608247.
Profile Club/Association. **Ref: YH14641**

VALE STUD RIDING SCHOOL
Vale Stud Riding School, Vale Farm, Dorking Rd, Kingsfold, Horsham, **Sussex (West)**, RH12 3SA,

ENGLAND.
(T) 01306 627023.
Contact/s
Owner: Mr L Fly **Ref: YH14642**

VALE VETNRY GROUP

Vale Veterinary Group (The), Areley Kings, Stourport-on-Severn, **Worcestershire**, DY13 0TH, **ENGLAND**.
(T) 01299 822423.
Contact/s
Vet: Mr W Rosie
Profile Medical Support. **Ref: YH14643**

VALESMOOR FARM

Valesmoor Farm, Holmsley Rd, New Milton, **Hampshire**, BH25 5TW, **ENGLAND**.
(T) 01425 614487.
Contact/s
Owner: Mr R Marshallsay
Profile Stable/Livery. **Ref: YH14644**

VALIANTS EQUESTRIAN CTRE

Valiants Equestrian Centre, Valiants Farm, Lancaster Rd, Out Rawcliffe, Preston, **Lancashire**, PR3 6BL, **ENGLAND**.
(T) 01995 671033.
Profile Farrier, Riding School, Stable/Livery.
Ref: YH14645

VALIENT SADDLERY

Valient Saddlery, 10 Pentood Est, Cardigan, **Ceredigion**, SA43 3AG, **WALES**.
(T) 01239 615526 **(F)** 01239 615526.
Contact/s
Owner: Ms J Davies
Profile Riding Wear Retailer, Saddlery Retailer.
Yr. Est: 1991
Opening Times
Sp: Open Mon - Sat 09:30. Closed Mon, Tues, Thurs - Sat 17:00, Wed 13:00.
Su: Open Mon - Sat 09:30. Closed Mon, Tues, Thurs - Sat 17:00, Wed 13:00.
Au: Open Mon - Sat 09:30. Closed Mon, Tues, Thurs - Sat 17:00, Wed 13:00.
Wn: Open Mon - Sat 09:30. Closed Mon, Tues, Thurs - Sat 17:00, Wed 13:00.
Closed Sundays **Ref: YH14646**

VALLANTS EQUESTRIAN CTRE

Vallants Equestrian Centre, Morris Dene Farm, Out Rawcliffe, Preston, **Lancashire**, PR3 6TD, **ENGLAND**.
(T) 01253 700451.
Profile Arena. **Ref: YH14647**

VALLEY EQUINE

Valley Equine Ltd, Unit 5, Lewis Ind Court, Great Shefford, Hungerford, **Berkshire**, RG17 7EL, **ENGLAND**.
(T) 01488 648844 **(F)** 01488 648844
(W) www.blue-horseshoe.co.uk
Alt Contact Address
Unit 4, 109 Fordham Rd, Snailwell, Newmarket, Suffolk, CB8 7NB, England. **(T)** 01638 724000
Contact/s
Assistant Manager: Ms E Cope
Profile Medical Support, Supplies.
Farrier supplies and general equine healthcare products. No.Staff: 3 Yr. Est: 1995
Opening Times
Sp: Open 08:30. Closed 13:30.
Su: Open 08:30. Closed 13:30.
Au: Open 08:30. Closed 13:30.
Wn: Open 08:30. Closed 13:30. **Ref: YH14648**

VALLEY EQUINE HOSPITAL

Valley Equine Hospital, Upper Lambourn Rd, Lambourn, Hungerford, **Berkshire**, RG17 8QG, **ENGLAND**.
(T) 01488 71999 **(F)** 01488 71842.
Profile Medical Support. **Ref: YH14649**

VALLEY FARM

Valley Farm, Moor Lane, Sarratt, Rickmansworth, **Hertfordshire**, WD3 6BZ, **ENGLAND**.
(T) 01923 266405.
Contact/s
Owner: Mr T Shields
Profile Stable/Livery. **Ref: YH14650**

VALLEY FARM

Valley Farm Riding & Driving Centre, Valley Farm, Wickham Market, Woodbridge, **Suffolk**, IP13 0ND, **ENGLAND**.
(T) 01728 746916 **(F)** 01728 746916
(W) www.valleyfarmonline.co.uk.
Contact/s
General Manager: Ms A Ling **(Q)** BSc(Hons)
(E) amanda@valleyfarmonline.co.uk
Profile Breeder, Equestrian Centre, Riding Club, Riding School, Stable/Livery, Trainer. Western Centre. Driving taught to British Driving Society test standard. Day rides can be arranged. Also offer Polocrosse - Vaulting (International), Horseball, Carriage Driving.
No.Staff: 15 Yr. Est: 1976 C.Size: 200 Acres
Ref: YH14651

VALLEY FARM

Valley Farm, Valley Farm Stables, Martineau Lane, Hastings, **Sussex (East)**, TN35 5DR, **ENGLAND**.
(T) 01424 812445.
Contact/s
Owner: Mrs A Constable **Ref: YH14652**

VALLEY FARM EQUESTRIAN CTRE

Valley Farm Equestrian Centre, Valley Farm, Shotteswell, Banbury, **Oxfordshire**, OX17 1HZ, **ENGLAND**.
(T) 01295 730576.
Contact/s
Owner: Mrs D Faulkner
Profile Riding School, Stable/Livery. **Ref: YH14653**

VALLEY FARM LIVERY STABLES

Valley Farm Livery Stables, Monks Hill, Emsworth, **Hampshire**, PO10 8SX, **ENGLAND**.
(T) 01243 372315. **Ref: YH14654**

VALLEY FEEDS

Valley Feeds, Unit A5 Enterprise Ctre, Merthyr Ind Est, Pentrebach, Merthyr Tydfil, **Glamorgan (Vale of)**, CF48 4DR, **WALES**.
(T) 01443 693452.
Profile Supplies. **Ref: YH14655**

VALLEY PADDOCKS RACING

Valley Paddocks Racing Ltd, P O Box 40, Sabden, Clitheroe, **Lancashire**, BB7 9GA, **ENGLAND**.
(T) 01254 822330.
Profile Trainer. **Ref: YH14656**

VALLEY RIDING/LIVERY STABLES

Valley Riding & Livery Stables, Monks & Barrows Farm, Mapletree Lane, Ingatestone, **Essex**, CM4 0PR, **ENGLAND**.
(T) 01277 353491.
Contact/s
General Manager: Mrs L Hunt **(Q)** AI
Profile Riding School, Stable/Livery.
Vet on site. 24 hour supervision. Full Livery - stabling for 39, prices dependent upon horse. Two flat schools for flat work, dressage and teaching No.Staff: 3
Yr. Est: 1966 C.Size: 54 Acres
Opening Times
Sp: Open Mon - Sun 07:30. Closed Mon - Sun 20:00.
Su: Open Mon - Sun 07:30. Closed Mon - Sun 20:00.
Au: Open Mon - Sun 07:30. Closed Mon - Sun 20:00.
Wn: Open Mon - Sun 07:30. Closed Mon - Sun 20:00.
Lessons are avaliable Mon - Sat 09:00 - 16:00
Ref: YH14657

VALLEY STABLES

Valley Stables, Pig Lane, Bishop's Stortford, **Essex**, CM22 7PA, **ENGLAND**.
(T) 01279 657153.
Profile Stable/Livery. **Ref: YH14658**

VALLEY VETNRY GROUP

Valley Veterinary Group, The Vetnry Surgery, Horseshoe Rd, Pangbourne, Reading, **Berkshire**, RG8 7JQ, **ENGLAND**.
(T) 01734 843221.
Profile Medical Support. **Ref: YH14659**

VANSTONE, B

B Vanstone, Pengari, Woolley, Bude, **Cornwall**, EX23 9PW, **ENGLAND**.
(T) 01288 331460.
Profile Transport/Horse Boxes. **Ref: YH14660**

VANTAK SADDLERY

Vantak Saddlery, 35 Crocus St, Kirkby-In-Ashfield, Nottingham, **Nottinghamshire**, NG17 7DY, **ENGLAND**.
(T) 01623 759797.
Contact/s
Owner: Mrs V Willetts **Ref: YH14661**

VARNAM, C

C Varnam, 31 Kingsway North, Braunstone, **Leicestershire**, LE3 3BD, **ENGLAND**.
(T) 0116 2898902.
Profile Farrier. **Ref: YH14662**

VARNAM, PAUL A

Paul A Varnam DWCF, 72 Danvers Rd, Leicester, **Leicestershire**, LE3 2AE, **ENGLAND**.
(T) 0116 22334356.
Profile Farrier. **Ref: YH14663**

VAS

VAS (Kent) Ltd, Vauxhall Pl, Lowfield St, Dartford, **Kent**, DA1 1HU, **ENGLAND**.
(T) 01322 222835 **(F)** 01322 288352.
Contact/s
Manager: Mr D White
Profile Transport/Horse Boxes. **Ref: YH14664**

VASTINGS MEADOW

Vastings Meadow Livery Stables, Vastings Meadow, Sidmouth Rd, Rousdon, Lyme Regis, **Dorset**, DT7 3RD, **ENGLAND**.
(T) 01297 21582.
Contact/s
Partner: Mrs C Hay **Ref: YH14665**

VAUGHAN, P

P Vaughan, 17 Victoria Ave, Llanidloes, **Powys**, SY18 6AS, **WALES**.
(T) 01686 412271.
Contact/s
Manager: Mr J Vaughn
Profile Breeder. **Ref: YH14666**

VAUGHANS HOPE WORKS

Vaughans Hope Works, The Hayes, Stourbridge, **Midlands (West)**, DY9 8RS, **ENGLAND**.
(T) 01384 424232 **(F)** 01384 893171.
Contact/s
Manager: Mr G Cattell
Profile Blacksmith. **Ref: YH14667**

VAUGHANS OF LEICESTER

Vaughans of Leicester Ltd, Aylestone Mill, Disraeli St, Old Aylestone, **Leicestershire**, LE2 8LX, **ENGLAND**.
(T) 0116 2440142 **(F)** 0116 2440309. **Ref: YH14668**

VAUTERHILL STUD

Vauterhill Stud, Vauterhill, High Bickington, Umberleigh, **Devon**, EX37 9BT, **ENGLAND**.
(T) 01769 560414.
Contact/s
Owner: Mr G Heal
Profile Breeder, Supplies. **Ref: YH14669**

VAUX BROS

Vaux Bros Ltd, Robinson St, Pontefract, **Yorkshire (West)**, WF8 1QU, **ENGLAND**.
(T) 01977 703156.
Profile Supplies. **Ref: YH14670**

VEAN STUD

Vean Stud, Hackpen Barton, Ashill, Cullompton, **Devon**, EX15 3LU, **ENGLAND**.
(T) 01884 840255.
Profile Breeder. **Ref: YH14671**

VECTIS EQUESTRIAN CLUB

Vectis Equestrian Club, Squirrels Wood, Cranmore Ave, Yarmouth, **Isle of Wight**, PO41 0XS, **ENGLAND**.
(T) 01983 760650.
Profile Club/Association. **Ref: YH14672**

VEHICLE WINDOW CTRE

Vehicle Window Centre, Unit 2-3 Ashley Est, Carr Wood Rd, Castleford, **Yorkshire (West)**, WF10 4SR, **ENGLAND**.
(T) 01977 604977 **(F)** 01977 603466
(E) sales@horsebox.co.uk
(W) www.horsebox.co.uk.
Contact/s
For Bookings: Mrs L Hambleton
Profile Transport/Horse Boxes.
Manufacture and repair horsebox windows, doors and accessories. Supply and fit accessories.
No.Staff: 12 Yr. Est: 1991
Opening Times
Sp: Open Mon - Fri 08:00. Closed Mon - Thurs 17:00, Fri 16:00.
Su: Open Mon - Fri 08:00. Closed Mon - Thurs 17:00, Fri 16:00.
Au: Open Mon - Fri 08:00. Closed Mon - Thurs 17:00, Fri 16:00.
Wn: Open Mon - Fri 08:00. Closed Mon - Thurs 17:00, Fri 16:00. **Ref: YH14673**

VELCLEAN BRUSH

Velclean Brush (The), 70 Ravenscroft, Holmes Chapel, Crewe, **Cheshire**, CW4 7HJ, **ENGLAND**.
(T) 01477 533892.

Profile Supplies. **Ref: YH14674**

VELVET PATH TREKKING CTRE

Velvet Path Trekking Centre, Rowan Hse, Innellan, Dunoon, **Argyll and Bute**, PA23 7SL, **SCOTLAND**.
(T) 01369 830580.
Profile Equestrian Centre. **Ref: YH14675**

VENFIELD, CHRISTINE

Mrs Christine Venfield, 21 Pound Field, Wootton Wawen, Solihull, **Warwickshire**, B95 6AY, **ENGLAND**.
(T) 01564 792180.
Profile Medical Support. **Ref: YH14676**

VENN, OLIVER J

Oliver J Venn DWCF, Tor Hse, Hartwell Hill, Whitchurch, Aylesbury, **Buckinghamshire**, HP22 4EL, **ENGLAND**.
(T) 01296 641672.
Profile Farrier. **Ref: YH14677**

VENTURE COACHWORKS

Venture Coachworks Ltd, Old Green End Farm, Common Rd, Kensworth, Dunstable, **Bedfordshire**, LU6 2PW, **ENGLAND**.
(T) 01582 872676.
Contact/s
Owner: Mr J Dick
Profile Transport/Horse Boxes. **Ref: YH14678**

VENTURENEED

Ventureneed Ltd, 72 High St, Wallingford, **Oxfordshire**, OX10 0BX, **ENGLAND**.
(T) 01491 833683 **(F)** 01491 825108.
Profile Breeder. **Ref: YH14679**

VENTURENEED

Ventureneed Ltd, 62 St Marys St, Wallingford, **Oxfordshire**, OX10 0EL, **ENGLAND**.
(T) 01491 825035 **(F)** 01491 825108.
Contact/s
Partner: Miss J Hutchins
Profile Transport/Horse Boxes. **Ref: YH14680**

VERE PHILLIPPS

Futurerate Ltd T/A Vere Phillipps, Grange Farm, 1B Wysall Lane, Rempstone, Loughborough, **Leicestershire**, LE12 6RW, **ENGLAND**.
(T) 01509 880678 **(F)** 01509 880678
(M) 07768 687043.
Profile Breeder. **Ref: YH14681**

VERMUYDEN VETNRY PRACTICE

Vermuyden Veterinary Practice, 162 Boothferry Rd, Goole, **Yorkshire (East)**, DN14 6AH, **ENGLAND**.
(T) 01405 763058.
Contact/s
Vet: Mr R Graham
Profile Medical Support. **Ref: YH14682**

VERO, FELICITY

Miss Felicity Vero, Bosworth Mill, Barton Rd, Carlton, Nuneaton, **Warwickshire**, CV13 0DA, **ENGLAND**.
(T) 01455 290438 **(F)** 01455 290712.
Contact/s
Owner: Miss F Vero
Profile Stable/Livery. **Ref: YH14683**

VERRALL, VERNON

Vernon Verrall, The Common, Sissinghurst, Cranbrook, **Kent**, TN17 2AF, **ENGLAND**.
(T) 01580 714141 **(F)** 01580 714398.
Profile Transport/Horse Boxes. **Ref: YH14684**

VERSTER, MICHAEL J

Michael J Verster DWCF, 123 Vincent Rd, Sheffield, **Yorkshire (South)**, S7 1BY, **ENGLAND**.
(T) 0114 2582115.
Profile Farrier. **Ref: YH14685**

VERYAN RIDING CTRE

Veryan Riding Centre (The), Veryan, The Roseland, Truro, **Cornwall**, TR2 5PH, **ENGLAND**.
(T) 01872 501574
Affiliated Bodies ABRS, BHS, RDA.
Contact/s
General Manager: Miss R Trethowan **(Q)** NVQ 2
Profile Riding Club, Riding School, Stable/Livery, Trainer. **No.Staff:** 4 **Yr. Est:** 1973
C.Size: 30 Acres
Opening Times
Sp: Open 09:30. Closed 18:30.
Su: Open 09:30. Closed 18:30.
Au: Open 09:30. Closed 18:30.
Wn: Open 09:30. Closed 18:30. **Ref: YH14686**

VESTEY, P E

Mrs P E Vestey, Manor Hse Farm, Old Park Rd, Bishops Sutton, Alresford, **Hampshire**, SO24 0BA, **ENGLAND**.
(T) 01962 732174.
Profile Breeder. **Ref: YH14687**

VETCARE CTRES

Vetcare Centres (The), Puffins, Eros Hse, St Martins, **Guernsey**, GY4 6LQ, **ENGLAND**.
(T) 01481 238300 **(F)** 01481 238603.
Profile Medical Support. **Ref: YH14688**

VETCARE CTRES

Vetcare Centres (The), Le Val, St Anne's, Alderney, **Guernsey**, GY9 3UL, **ENGLAND**.
(T) 01481 822610 **(F)** 01481 822310.
Profile Medical Support. **Ref: YH14689**

VETCARE CTRES

Vetcare Centres (The), Rue Des Eturs, Castel, **Guernsey**, GY5 7DT, **ENGLAND**.
(T) 01481 257708 **(F)** 01481 251150.
Profile Medical Support. **Ref: YH14690**

VETNRY ACUPUNCTURE REFERRAL

Veterinary Acupuncture Referral Service, East Park Cottage, Handcross, Haywards Heath, **Sussex (West)**, RH17 6BD, **ENGLAND**.
(T) 01444 400213.
Profile Medical Support. **Ref: YH14691**

VETNRY CLINIC

Veterinary Clinic, Grahams Rd, Falkirk, **Falkirk**, FK2 7DJ, **SCOTLAND**.
(T) 01324 23163.
Profile Medical Support. **Ref: YH14692**

VETNRY CTRE

Veterinary Centre (The), 23 Hurst Rd, Twyford, **Berkshire**, RG10 0AG, **ENGLAND**.
(T) 0118 9340259.
Profile Medical Support. **Ref: YH14693**

VETNRY CTRE

Veterinary Centre (The), Albany Rd, Invergordon, **Highlands**, IV18 0HA, **SCOTLAND**.
(T) 01349 852204
(E) john@vetcentre.freeserve.co.uk.
Contact/s
Owner: Mr J Simpson
Profile Medical Support. **Ref: YH14694**

VETNRY CTRE

Veterinary Centre (The), 124A High St, Nailsea, **Somerset (North)**, BS19 1AH, **ENGLAND**.
(T) 01275 858628.
Profile Medical Support. **Ref: YH14695**

VETNRY CTRE

Veterinary Centre (The), 14 Bond End, Yoxall, Burton-on-Trent, **Staffordshire**, DE13 8NH, **ENGLAND**.
(T) 01543 472249.
Profile Medical Support. **Ref: YH14696**

VETNRY HOSPITAL

Veterinary Hospital (The), 1 Riseholme Rd, Lincoln, **Lincolnshire**, LN1 3SN, **ENGLAND**.
(T) 01522 24812 **(F)** 01522 560367.
Profile Medical Support. **Ref: YH14697**

VETNRY HOSPITAL

Veterinary Hospital (Usk) (The), Porthycarne St, Usk, **Monmouthshire**, NP15 1RZ, **WALES**.
(T) 01291 672637 **(F)** 01291 673940.
Profile Medical Support. **Ref: YH14698**

VETNRY SURGERY

Veterinary Surgery (The), 45 High St, Marske By The Sea, Redcar, **Cleveland**, TS11 6JQ, **ENGLAND**.
(T) 01642 488777.
Profile Medical Support. **Ref: YH14699**

VETNRY SURGERY

Veterinary Surgery (The), Sondes Rd, Deal, **Kent**, CT14 7BW, **ENGLAND**.
(T) 01304 373042.
Profile Medical Support. **Ref: YH14700**

VETNRY SURGERY

Veterinary Surgery (The), Unit 5 Station Rd, Southwater, Horsham, **Sussex (West)**, RH13 7HQ, **ENGLAND**.
(T) 01403 732219 **(F)** 01403 732799.
Profile Medical Support. **Ref: YH14701**

VETREPHARM

Vetrepharm Ltd, Unit 15, Sandleheath Ind Est, Fordingbridge, **Hampshire**, SP6 1PA, **ENGLAND**.
(T) 01425 656081 **(F)** 01425 655309.
Profile Medical Support. **Ref: YH14702**

VETSEARCH EQUINE SUPPLIES UK

Vetsearch Equine Supplies UK, Lagden Farm, Colebatch, Bishops Castle, **Shropshire**, SY9 5JY, **ENGLAND**.
(T) 01588 638252 **(F)** 01588 638794.
Contact/s
Partner: Mr B Adams
Profile Medical Support. **Ref: YH14703**

VIBERT, ALYSON

Ms Alyson Vibert, Grosnez Farm, St Ouen, **Jersey**, JE3 2AD, **ENGLAND**.
(T) 01534 483773
(M) 07797 7738128.
Profile Trainer. **Ref: YH14704**

VICARAGE FARM COMPETITIONS

Vicarage Farm Competitions, Vicarage Farm, Halliford Rd, Sunbury-on-Thames, **Surrey**, TW16 6DW, **ENGLAND**.
(T) 01932 765145 **(F)** 01932 765145.
Profile Club/Association. **Ref: YH14705**

VICKERY, L H & R A

L H & R A Vickery, Knowle End, South Barrow, Yeovil, **Somerset**, BA22 7LN, **ENGLAND**.
(T) 01963 440043 **(F)** 01963 440119.
Contact/s
Partner: Mrs R Vickery **Ref: YH14706**

VICKERY, MICHAEL

Michael Vickery DWCF, Farriers, Pinesfield Lane, Trottiscliffe, West Malling, **Kent**, ME19 5EN, **ENGLAND**.
(T) 01732 824368.
Profile Farrier. **Ref: YH14707**

VICTORIA FARM

Victoria Farm, Brunswick Rd, Knaphill, Woking, **Surrey**, GU24 0AQ, **ENGLAND**.
(T) 01483 475470 **(F)** 01483 486886
Alt Contact Address
15 Biknham Rd, Knaphill, Woking, Surrey, GU21 2AE, England.**(T)** 01483 475470
Contact/s
Owner: Mr D Wetherall
Profile Stable/Livery, Trainer. **No.Staff:** 2
Yr. Est: 1998 **C.Size:** 8 Acres
Opening Times
Sp: Open 06:30. Closed 21:00.
Su: Open 06:30. Closed 21:00.
Au: Open 06:30. Closed 21:00.
Wn: Open 06:30. Closed 21:00. **Ref: YH14708**

VICTORIA ROSETTES

Victoria Rosettes, Unit 3, 25 Ladywell Ave, Grangestone Ind Est, Girvan, **Ayrshire (South)**, KA26 9PL, **SCOTLAND**.
(T) 01465 713701 **(F)** 01465 713183.
Profile Supplies. **Ref: YH14709**

VICTORIAN CARRIAGES

Victorian Carriages, Main St, Newark, **Nottinghamshire**, NG22 9LP, **ENGLAND**.
(T) 01623 836291.
Profile Riding School, Stable/Livery, Trainer.
Ref: YH14710

VICTORIAN SADDLES

Victorian Saddles, 117 Halifax Rd, Rochdale, **Lancashire**, OL12 9BA, **ENGLAND**.
(T) 01706 644490.
Contact/s
Owner: Ms V Radcliffe **Ref: YH14711**

VICTOR-SMITH, C I

C I Victor-Smith, Country Ways, Darkwood Farms, Park Corner, Nettlebed, Henley-on-Thames, **Oxfordshire**, RG9 5BJ, **ENGLAND**.
(T) 01491 641324.
Profile Breeder. **Ref: YH14712**

VIDEO CLASSIFIED

Video Classified, 19 Moat Rise, Rayleigh, **Essex**, SS6 7RP, **ENGLAND**.
(T) 01268 773477.
Contact/s
Owner: Mrs Y Dunn
Profile Supplies. **Ref: YH14713**

VIETOR, BERND

Bernd Vietor (GER), Home Farm, School Lane,

A-Z of COMPANIES

Henbury, Macclesfield, **Cheshire**, SK11 9PH, **ENGLAND**.
(T) 01625 422511 **(F)** 01625 511102
(M) 07831 428860. **Ref: YH14714**

VIGORS, J

Mrs J Vigors, Pool Pk, St Tudy, Bodmin, **Cornwall**, PL30 3PS, **ENGLAND**.
(T) 01208 851512.
Profile Breeder. **Ref: YH14715**

VIKING CARRIAGES

Viking Carriages, Plough Hill, Potterhanworth Booths, **Lincolnshire**, LN4 2AU, **ENGLAND**.
(T) 01522 793877. **Ref: YH14716**

VIKING TRAILERS

Viking Trailers Ltd, Taylor Holme Ind Est, Atherton Way, Bacup, **Lancashire**, OL13 0LE, **ENGLAND**.
(T) 01706 875139 **(F)** 01706 875277.
Profile Transport/Horse Boxes. **Ref: YH14717**

VIKKIS STABLES

Vikkis Stables, 1 Longwood Cottages, Aldridge Rd, Walsall, **Midlands (West)**, WS4 2JP, **ENGLAND**.
(T) 01922 630784.
Contact/s
Owner: Mr M Wilding
Profile Riding School. **Ref: YH14718**

VILLAGE FORGE & SHOWROOM

Village Forge & Showroom, Unit 1C Station Rd, Tenterden, **Kent**, TN30 6HN, **ENGLAND**.
(T) 01580 764875 **(F)** 01580 764875.
Contact/s
Owner: Mr T Lewis
Profile Blacksmith. **Ref: YH14719**

VILLAGE SADDLERY

Village Saddlery, 182 Chester Rd, Warrington, **Cheshire**, WA4 6AR, **ENGLAND**.
(T) 01925 629629 **(F)** 01925 629628.
Contact/s
Owner: Mr D Ashton **Ref: YH14720**

VILLAGE STORES

Village Stores (The), Trelleck, Monmouth, **Monmouthshire**, NP25 4PA, **WALES**.
(T) 01600 860362.
Profile Saddlery Retailer. **Ref: YH14721**

VILMORAY LODGE STUD

Vilmoray Lodge Stud, South Brewham, Bruton, **Somerset**, BA10 0JZ, **ENGLAND**.
(T) 01749 850212.
Contact/s
Owner: Mr R Thorman
Profile Breeder. **Ref: YH14722**

VINCENT TRAILERS

Vincent Trailers, Blissetts Farm, Holdrop Hill, Headley, Thatcham, **Berkshire**, RG19 8LJ, **ENGLAND**.
(T) 01635 268446.
Contact/s
Owner: Mr W Vincent
Profile Transport/Horse Boxes. **Ref: YH14723**

VINCENT, JOHN

John Vincent, Colcerrow Farm, Par, **Cornwall**, PL24 2RZ, **ENGLAND**.
(T) 01208 872450.
Profile Farrier. **Ref: YH14724**

VINCENT, JOHN F

John F Vincent, Hill Farm, Charlton, Malmesbury, **Wiltshire**, SN16 9DT, **ENGLAND**.
(T) 01666 860278. **Ref: YH14725**

VINCENT, PETER J

Peter J Vincent DWCF, 54 Bauntons Orchard, Milborne Port, Sherborne, **Dorset**, DT9 5BP, **ENGLAND**.
(T) 01963 250546.
Profile Farrier. **Ref: YH14726**

VINCENTS OF YEOVIL

Vincents of Yeovil, Market St, Yeovil, **Somerset**, BA20 1HJ, **ENGLAND**.
(T) 01935 75242.
Profile Transport/Horse Boxes. **Ref: YH14727**

VINDOMORE EQUESTRIAN CTRE

Vindomore Equestrian Centre, Derwentcote Farm, Hamsterley Colliery, Newcastle-upon-Tyne, **Tyne and Wear**, NE17 7RR, **ENGLAND**.
(T) 01207 562089.
Contact/s
Manager: Mr B Winn **Ref: YH14728**

VINE HERBAL PRODUCTS

Vine Herbal Products, The Vine, Stanton, Broadway, **Worcestershire**, WR12 7NE, **ENGLAND**.
(T) 01386 584250 **(F)** 01386 584385.
Profile Medical Support. **Ref: YH14729**

VINE, IAN DAVID

Ian David Vine, Lye Farm, West Tytherley, Salisbury, **Wiltshire**, SP5 1LA, **ENGLAND**.
(T) 01794 341667.
Profile Farrier. **Ref: YH14730**

VINE, W E

W E Vine, Ersham Farm, Hailsham, **Sussex (East)**, BN27 3LJ, **ENGLAND**.
(T) 01323 841641. **Ref: YH14731**

VIRBAC

Virbac Ltd, Woolpit Business Pk, Windmill Ave, Woolpit, Bury St Edmunds, **Suffolk**, IP30 9UP, **ENGLAND**.
(T) 01359 243243 **(F)** 01359 243200
(E) enquiries@virbac.co.uk.
Profile Medical Support. Produce worming tablets.
Ref: YH14732

VISCORIDE

Graham Potter Associates & Ri-Dry Limited, The Bushloe Office, High St, North Kilworth, Lutterworth, **Leicestershire**, LE17 6ET, **ENGLAND**.
(T) 01858 880771 **(F)** 01858 880776
(E) gparidry@yahoo.com
(W) www.viscoride.com
Affiliated Bodies BHS
Alt Contact Address
Viscoride Direct, Int Marketing Ctre, Stamford, Leicestershire, PE9 2ZS, England. **(T)** 01780 766863
Profile Arena, Track/Course. All Weather Riding Surfaces. **Ref: YH14733**

VITACOLL EQUINE

Vitacoll Equine, 61 Culcheth Hall Drive, Culcheth, Warrington, **Cheshire**, WA3 4PX, **ENGLAND**.
(T) 01925 762580 **(F)** 01925 767692.
Profile Medical Support. **Ref: YH14734**

VITAL MAX

Vital Max, Mountain Blow Farm, Haywood, Forth, **Lanarkshire (South)**, M11 8ES, **SCOTLAND**.
(T) 01555 811462.
Profile Medical Support. **Ref: YH14735**

VITALIN EQUINE FEEDS

Vitalin Equine Feeds, Dallamires Lane, Ripon, **Yorkshire (North)**, HG4 1TT, **ENGLAND**.
(T) 01765 605156 **(F)** 01765 690408. **Ref: YH14736**

VIVIAN PRATT

Vivian Pratt (Bloodstock Consultant), 6 Cobbold Rd, Felixstowe, **Suffolk**, IP11 7HQ, **ENGLAND**.
(T) 01394 276686 **(F)** 01394 283976.
Profile Blood Stock Agency, Breeder. **Ref: YH14737**

VLACQ STUD

VLACQ Stud, Tryddyn Cottage, Treuddyn, Mold, **Flintshire**, CH7 4NS, **WALES**.
(T) 01352 770238.
Contact/s
Partner: Mr D Pyke
(E) david@vlacqfreeserve.co.uk
Profile Breeder. **No.Staff:** 2 **Yr. Est:** 1974
C.Size: 50 Acres **Ref: YH14738**

VOISE

Voise Equestrian Gifts & Incentives, Design Studios, Halcyon Hse, Park Rd, Allington, **Lincolnshire**, NG32 2EB, **ENGLAND**.
(T) 01400 281883 **(F)** 01400 281104.
Profile Saddlery Retailer. **Ref: YH14739**

VOLVO BUS

Volvo Bus (GB) Ltd, Kilwinning Rd, Irvine, **Ayrshire (North)**, KA12 8TB, **SCOTLAND**.
(T) 01294 74120.
Profile Transport/Horse Boxes. **Ref: YH14740**

VOS, A

Miss A Vos, Kenwards Farm, Lindfield, **Sussex (West)**, RH16 1XX, **ENGLAND**.
(T) 01444 414626.
Profile Breeder. **Ref: YH14741**

VOSPER, M

M Vosper, Collytown Forge, Bere Alston, Yelverton, **Devon**, SN7 7PS, **ENGLAND**.
(T) 01822 840481.
Profile Farrier. **Ref: YH14742**

VOWDEN, T R

T R Vowden, The Forge, Middle Rixdale, Luton, Chudleigh, Newton Abbot, **Devon**, TQ13 0BW, **ENGLAND**.
(T) 01626 865484.
Profile Farrier. **Ref: YH14743**

VOWLES RIDING STABLES

Vowles Riding Stables, 33 Sandford Rd, Weston-Super-Mare, **Somerset (North)**, BS23 3EX, **ENGLAND**.
(T) 01934 622395.
Contact/s
Partner: Mrs K Vowles
Profile Riding School, Saddlery Retailer, Stable/Livery. **Ref: YH14744**

VULCAN TOWING CTRE

Vulcan Towing Centre, 338 Leagrave Rd, Luton, **Bedfordshire**, LU3 1RE, **ENGLAND**.
(T) 01582 584088 **(F)** 01582 584088
(W) www.vulcantowing.co.uk.
Contact/s
Owner: Mr B Lust
Profile Transport/Horse Boxes.
Trailer repairs **No.Staff:** 3 **Yr. Est:** 1979
Opening Times
Sp: Open Mon - Sat 08:30. Closed Mon - Fri 17:30, Sat 13:00.
Su: Open Mon - Sat 08:30. Closed Mon - Fri 17:30, Sat 13:00.
Au: Open Mon - Sat 08:30. Closed Mon - Fri 17:30, Sat 13:00.
Wn: Open Mon - Sat 08:30. Closed Mon - Fri 17:30, Sat 13:00. **Ref: YH14745**

VYRNWY VALLEY RIDING CLUB

Vyrnwy Valley Riding Club, Brickfield Cottage, Ardleen, Llanymynech, **Powys**, SY22 6RX, **WALES**.
(T) 01938 75484.
Contact/s
Chairman: Mrs Y Tucker
Profile Club/Association, Riding Club. **Ref: YH14746**

W & G SERVICES

W & G Services, Parker Ave, Felixstowe, **Suffolk**, IP11 4HF, **ENGLAND**.
(T) 01394 676682.
Profile Transport/Horse Boxes. **Ref: YH14747**

W & T GIBSON

W & T Gibson Ltd, Kingsley Mill, Kingsley, Frodsham, **Cheshire**, WA6 8JA, **ENGLAND**.
(T) 01928 788210 **(F)** 01928 788924.
Profile Saddlery Retailer. **Ref: YH14748**

W A ANNETTS & SON

W A Annetts & Son, Tytherley Rd, Winterslow, Salisbury, **Wiltshire**, SP5 1PZ, **ENGLAND**.
(T) 01980 862210.
Profile Transport/Horse Boxes. **Ref: YH14749**

W A THOMSON PLANT HIRE

W A Thomson Plant Hire, Coshieville, Aberfeldy, **Perth and Kinross**, PH15 2LE, **SCOTLAND**.
(T) 01887 830559.
Profile Supplies. **Ref: YH14750**

W B STUBBS

W B Stubbs (Hawksworth) Ltd, Progress Works, Hawksworth, Nottingham, **Nottinghamshire**, NG13 9DF, **ENGLAND**.
(T) 01949 850218 **(F)** 01949 851255.
Contact/s
Owner: Mr C Bradwell **Ref: YH14751**

W BARKER & SONS

W Barker & Sons, Broughton Nook, School Hse Lane, Abbots Bromley, Rugeley, **Staffordshire**, WS15 3BT, **ENGLAND**.
(T) 01283 840266.
Profile Transport/Horse Boxes. **Ref: YH14752**

W BRYAN HORSE SERVICES

W Bryan Horse Services, Worthen Hall, Worthen, Shrewsbury, **Shropshire**, SY5 9HN, **ENGLAND**.
(T) 01743 891212 **(F)** 01743 891817.
Contact/s
For Bookings: Mrs M Bryan
Profile Stable/Livery, Trainer. Horse Breaker. Trainer of problem Horses **No.Staff:** 3
Yr. Est: 1990 **C.Size:** 200 Acres **Ref: YH14753**

W C F COUNTRY CTRE

W C F Country Centre (Castle Douglas), Ride & Groom, Newmarket St, Castle Douglas, **Dumfries and Galloway**, DG7 1HY, **SCOTLAND**.
(T) 01556 504004 **(F)** 01556 502912.

Profile Saddlery Retailer. **Ref: YH14754**

W C F COUNTRY CTRE

W C F Country Centre (Stirling), Ride & Groom, Unit 13-15, Kildean Market, Kildean, **Stirling**, FK9 4AA, **SCOTLAND**.
(T) 01786 462323.
Profile Saddlery Retailer. **Ref: YH14755**

W C F COUNTRY CTRE

W C F Country Centre (Otley), Ride & Groom, Auction Mart, Bridge End, Otley, **Yorkshire (West)**, LS21 2JW, **ENGLAND**.
(T) 01943 465726.
Profile Saddlery Retailer. **Ref: YH14756**

W C F COUNTRY CTRES

W C F Country Centres, Retail Division, Old Jam Works, Station Rd, Wigton, **Cumbria**, CA7 9AX, **ENGLAND**.
(T) 01697 341005 **(F)** 01697 341020.
Contact/s
General Manager: Mr N Brayton
Profile Saddlery Retailer. **Ref: YH14757**

W C SERVICES

W C Services, Longthorn Farm, Millerhill, Dalkeith, Edinburgh, **Edinburgh (City of)**, EH22 1RZ, **SCOTLAND**.
(T) 0131 6601876.
Profile Club/Association. **Ref: YH14758**

W D LEWIS & SON

W D Lewis & Son, Mark Lane Mill, Lampeter, **Ceredigion**, SA48 7AB, **WALES**.
(T) 01570 422540 **(F)** 01570 423644.
Profile Supplies. **Ref: YH14759**

W D MACRAE

W D Macrae & Co, Blackpark Farm, Blackpark, Inverness, **Highlands**, IV3 8PW, **SCOTLAND**.
(T) 01463 241831 **(F)** 01463 241885.
Contact/s
Owner: Mr W Macrae
Profile Transport/Horse Boxes. **Ref: YH14760**

W E HOWDEN

W E Howden - Animal Health Services, 61 High St, Coldstream, **Northumberland**, TD12 4DL, **ENGLAND**.
(T) 01890 882357.
Contact/s
Owner: Mr R Smith
Profile Medical Support. **Ref: YH14761**

W E J KYNASTON & SONS

W E J Kynaston & Sons, Stonehill Farm, 32 Stonehill, Bristol, **Bristol**, BS15 3HW, **ENGLAND**.
(T) 01179 674013.
Profile Stable/Livery.
DIY Livery available, prices on request. **Ref: YH14762**

W E LEWIS & SON

W E Lewis & Son, Cambrian Forge, Mill St, Aberystwyth, **Ceredigion**, SY23 1HZ, **WALES**.
(T) 01970 612531 **(F)** 01970 612531.
Contact/s
Owner: Mr G Lewis
Profile Blacksmith. **Ref: YH14763**

W E STURGESS & SONS

W E Sturgess & Sons Ltd, Almond Rd, Leicester, **Leicestershire**, LE2 7LP, **ENGLAND**.
(T) 0116 2549191.
Profile Transport/Horse Boxes. **Ref: YH14764**

W F EQUESTRIAN SURFACES

W F Equestrian Surfaces Ltd, Old Quarry Works, Fosse Cross, Cheltenham, **Gloucestershire**, GL54 4NW, **ENGLAND**.
(T) 01285 720769.
Profile Track/Course. **Ref: YH14765**

W F S COUNTRY

W F S Country Shop Ltd, Burford Rd, Minster Lovell, Witney, **Oxfordshire**, OX8 5RB, **ENGLAND**.
(T) 01993 704263 **(F)** 01993 771057.
Profile Riding Wear Retailer, Saddlery Retailer, Supplies. **Ref: YH14766**

W G TODD & SONS

W G Todd & Sons, Crescent Green, Kendal, **Cumbria**, LA9 6DR, **ENGLAND**.
(T) 01539 724311 **(F)** 01539 720277.
Contact/s
Partner: Mr J Todd
Profile Saddlery Retailer. **Ref: YH14767**

W H B GRAHAM

W H B Graham (Forage) Ltd, Darwins Farm, Hillside, Odiham, Hook, **Hampshire**, RG29 1HX, **ENGLAND**.
(T) 01256 702296.
Profile Straw Merchant. **Ref: YH14768**

W H EVANS

W H Evans, Melin Llecheiddior, Garndolbenmaen, **Gwynedd**, LL51 9EZ, **WALES**.
(T) 01766 530635 **(F)** 01766 530635.
Profile Supplies. **Ref: YH14769**

W H GIDDEN

W H Gidden Ltd, 16 Clifford St, London, **London (Greater)**, W1S 3RQ, **ENGLAND**.
(T) 020 74376775.
Profile Riding Wear Retailer, Saddlery Retailer.
Ref: YH14770

W H HORSEBOXES

W H Horseboxes, Morton Retreat, Morton Carr Lane, Nunthorpe, **Cleveland**, TS7 0JU, **ENGLAND**.
(T) 01642 300670 **(F)** 01642 318420
(E) clare@whhorseboxes.freeserve.co.uk
(W) www.whhorseboxes.co.uk.
Contact/s
Owner: Mrs C Walker-Hansell
Profile Transport/Horse Boxes.
Build horseboxes to personal specifications.
Ref: YH14771

W H OTTLEY

W H Ottley Ltd, The Old Maltings, Blyth Rd, Ranskill, Retford, **Nottinghamshire**, DN22 8LR, **ENGLAND**.
(T) 01777 818621.
Profile Supplies. **Ref: YH14772**

W H PATTERSON FINE ARTS

W H Patterson Fine Arts Ltd, 19 Albemarle St, London, **London (Greater)**, W1X 4LA, **ENGLAND**.
(T) 020 76294119. **Ref: YH14773**

W H PONSONBY

W H Ponsonby Shefford Blood Stock, Rosemeirion, Chaddleworth, Newbury, **Berkshire**, RG20 7EH, **ENGLAND**.
(T) 01488 638718 **(F)** 01488 638925.
Contact/s
Owner: Mr W Ponsonby
Profile Blood Stock Agency. **Ref: YH14774**

W H SUTTON & SONS

W H Sutton & Sons, The Old Brickyard, Oreton, Cleobury Mortimer, Kidderminster, **Worcestershire**, DY14 0TJ, **ENGLAND**.
(T) 01746 32475.
Profile Supplies. **Ref: YH14775**

W J BEVAN & SON

W J Bevan & Son, Unit 20 Sycamore Trading Est, Squires Gate Lane, Blackpool, **Lancashire**, FY4 3RL, **ENGLAND**.
(T) 01253 343177 **(F)** 01253 341095.
Contact/s
Partner: Mr P Bevan
Profile Blacksmith. **Ref: YH14776**

W J PARDEY & SON

W J Pardey & Son, Gorse Farm, Blissford, Fordingbridge, **Hampshire**, SP6 2JH, **ENGLAND**.
(T) 01425 653250.
Profile Supplies. **Ref: YH14777**

W JORDANS

W Jordon (Cereals) Ltd, Holme Mills, Biggleswade, **Bedfordshire**, SG18 9JX, **ENGLAND**.
(T) 01767 312001 **(F)** 01767 601023
(E) wjordan@animalfeed.fsnet.co.uk.
Contact/s
Sales Manager: Guy Bartlett **(T)** 01462 895336
Profile Feed Merchant, Supplies.
Quality feed manufacturers. **No.Staff:** 30
Yr. Est: 1855
Opening Times
Sp: Open Mon - Sat 08:30. Closed Mon - Fri 17:00, Sat 12:00.
Su: Open Mon - Sat 08:30. Closed Mon - Fri 17:00, Sat 12:00.
Au: Open Mon - Sat 08:30. Closed Mon - Fri 17:00, Sat 12:00.
Wn: Open Mon - Sat 08:30. Closed Mon - Fri 17:00, Sat 12:00.
Closed Sundays and weekdays between 13:00 - 14:00
Ref: YH14778

W KING & SONS

W King & Sons, The Forge, Horsehill, Horley, **Surrey**, RH6 0HN, **ENGLAND**.
(T) 01293 782657 **(F)** 01293 782657.
Contact/s
Owner: Mr W King
Profile Blacksmith. **Ref: YH14779**

W M MCIVOR & SON

W M McIvor & Son, Garmondsway, Bishop Middleham, Ferry Hill, **County Durham**, DL17 9AX, **ENGLAND**.
(T) 0191 3771001 **(F)** 0191 3771002.
Profile Supplies. **Ref: YH14780**

W M THOMPSON

W M Thompson (York) Ltd, Jubilee Mill, Murton, **Yorkshire (North)**, YO19 5UT, **ENGLAND**.
(T) 01904 488388 **(F)** 01904 488517.
Profile Supplies. **Ref: YH14781**

W MARTIN & SON

W Martin & Son, Row Green, Bakers Lane, Black Notley, Braintree, **Essex**, CM7 8QS, **ENGLAND**.
(T) 01376 331136 **(F)** 01376 343711.
Contact/s
Partner: Mr G Martin
Profile Transport/Horse Boxes. Abattoir.
Livestock transportation. Also have an incinerator on site. **Yr. Est:** 1901
Opening Times
Sp: Open Mon - Sat 08:00. Closed Mon - Fri 17:00, Sat 12:30.
Su: Open Mon - Sat 08:00. Closed Mon - Fri 17:00, Sat 12:30.
Au: Open Mon - Sat 08:00. Closed Mon - Fri 17:00, Sat 12:30.
Wn: Open Mon - Sat 08:00. Closed Mon - Fri 17:00, Sat 12:30. **Ref: YH14782**

W MOSS & SONS

W Moss & Sons, Lords Farm, Long Lane, Aston End, Stevenage, **Hertfordshire**, SG2 7HF, **ENGLAND**.
(T) 01438 880247.
Profile Supplies. **Ref: YH14783**

W N SHRIVE & SON

W N Shrive & Son, The Mill, Addlethorpe, Skegness, **Lincolnshire**, PE24 4TB, **ENGLAND**.
(T) 01754 763295.
Profile Saddlery Retailer. **Ref: YH14784**

W O LEWIS

W O Lewis (Badges) Ltd, 39 Howard St, Birmingham, **Midlands (West)**, BI9 3HP, **ENGLAND**.
(T) 0121 2360789 **(F)** 0121 2333057.
Profile Club/Association. **Ref: YH14785**

W PAGE & SON

W Page & Son (Cole Green), Cole Green Garden & Equestrian Ctre, Birchall Lane, Cole Green, **Hertfordshire**, SG14 2NR, **ENGLAND**.
(T) 01707 336928 **(F)** 01707 330201.
Profile Saddlery Retailer. **Ref: YH14786**

W R & J COLLINS

W R & J Collins Ltd, 453 Church Rd, Yardley, Birmingham, **Midlands (West)**, B33 8NY, **ENGLAND**.
(T) 0121 7832742.
Profile Blacksmith. **Ref: YH14787**

W R C FARMS

W R C Farms Ltd, Four Winds, Storrage Lane, Alvechurch, **Midlands (West)**, B48 7EP, **ENGLAND**.
(T) 01527 591533 **(F)** 01527 768757.
Profile Club/Association. **Ref: YH14788**

W R ELGAR & SONS

W R Elgar & Sons, Barville Farm, Barville Rd, Waldershare, Dover, **Kent**, CT15 5BQ, **ENGLAND**.
(T) 01304 830458.
Contact/s
Owner: Mr R Elgar **Ref: YH14789**

W R HALL & SONS

W R Hall & Sons, The Forge, Great Barrington, Burford, **Oxfordshire**, OX18 4UR, **ENGLAND**.
(T) 01451 844319.
Contact/s
Owner: Mr B Hall
Profile Blacksmith. **Ref: YH14790**

W R WILLIAMS & SON

W R Williams & Son, Refail Newydd, Caergeiliog, Holyhead, **Isle of Anglesey**, LL65 3DX, **WALES**.
(T) 01407 740398 **(F)** 01407 740398.
Contact/s

Owner: Mr M Williams
Profile Blacksmith. Ref:YH14791

W REDLAND & SON

W Redland & Son, The Smithy, Sandwick, Stromness, **Orkney Isles**, KW16 3HZ, **SCOTLAND**.
(T) 01856 841888.
Profile Blacksmith. Ref:YH14792

W RICHARDS & SON

W Richards & Son, Trencarsse, Sweethouse, Bodmin, **Cornwall**, PL30 5AW, **ENGLAND**.
(T) 01208 873288.
Profile Supplies. Ref:YH14793

W S HODGSON

W S Hodgson & Co Ltd, Cotherstone, Barnard Castle, **County Durham**, DL12 9PS, **ENGLAND**.
(T) 01833 650274 **(F)** 01833 650737.
Profile Transport/Horse Boxes. Ref:YH14794

W S SHEARING & SONS

W S Shearing & Sons, Southfield Holdings, Amesbury Rd, Weyhill, Andover, **Hampshire**, SP11 8ED, **ENGLAND**.
(T) 01264 772974.
Contact/s
Owner: Mr W Shearing Ref:YH14795

W S WALTON & SONS

W S Walton & Sons, New Rd Farm, New Rd, Swindon, Dudley, **Midlands (West)**, DY3 4PP, **ENGLAND**.
(T) 01902 892207.
Contact/s
Partner: Mr W Walton
Profile Stable/Livery. Ref:YH14796

W SHARPE & SON

W Sharpe & Son, Nook Bungalow, Nook Lane, Antrobus, Northwich, **Cheshire**, CW9 6LA, **ENGLAND**.
(T) 01565 777342.
Contact/s
Owner: Mr F Sharpe Ref:YH14797

W SPENCE & SON

W Spence & Son (Blacksmiths) Ltd, Bolton Hse, 37 Bolton Lane, Hose, Melton Mowbray, **Leicestershire**, LE14 4JE, **ENGLAND**.
(T) 01949 860321.
Contact/s
Owner: Mr S Spence
Profile Farrier. Ref:YH14798

W T ROBINSON & SON

W T Robinson & Son, Ovington Grange, Ovington, Richmond, **Yorkshire (North)**, DL11 7BL, **ENGLAND**.
(T) 01325 730289.
Contact/s
Senior Partner: Mr W Robinson Ref:YH14799

W T WAITE & SONS

W T Waite & Sons, 6 Trummery Lane, Moira, Craigavon, **County Armagh**, BT67 0JN, **NORTHERN IRELAND**.
(T) 028 92611457.
Contact/s
Partner: Mr G Waite
Profile Transport/Horse Boxes. Ref:YH14800

W W SCOTT & SONS

W W Scott & Sons, 49 Market Pl, Thirsk, **Yorkshire (North)**, YO7 1HA, **ENGLAND**.
(T) 01845 522048. Ref:YH14801

W, WATSON

Watson W, 66 Hamilton St, Carluke, **Lanarkshire (South)**, ML8 4HA, **SCOTLAND**.
(T) 01555 750914.
Profile Farrier. Ref:YH14802

W.E.S GARRETT MASTER SADDLERS

WE & SE Garrett Master Saddler, South View, Back Lane, Draycott, Cheddar, **Somerset**, BS27 3TH, **ENGLAND**.
(T) 01934 742367.
Contact/s
General Manager: Ms J Garrett **(Q)** QS
Profile Riding Wear Retailer, Saddlery Retailer, Supplies. Master Saddlers Manufacturer.
Opening Times
Sp: Open 09:00. Closed 17:30.
Su: Open 09:00. Closed 17:30.
Au: Open 09:00. Closed 17:30.
Wn: Open 09:00. Closed 17:30. Ref:YH14803

WACKLEY LODGE FARM

Wackley Lodge Farm, Burlton, Shrewsbury, **Shropshire**, SY4 5TD, **ENGLAND**.
(T) 01939 270565.
Profile Breeder. Ref:YH14804

WADACRE WARMBLOOD STUD

Wadacre Warmblood Stud, Wadacre Farm, Melling, **Merseyside**, L31 1DZ, **ENGLAND**.
(T) 0151 5472293.
Profile Breeder. Ref:YH14805

WADDESDON STUD

Waddesdon Stud, Queen St, Waddesden, Aylesbury, **Buckinghamshire**, HP18 0JW, **ENGLAND**.
(T) 01296 651341 **(F)** 01296 658054.
Profile Breeder. Ref:YH14806

WADDINGTON FARM

Waddington Farm, Brokenstone Rd, Darwen, **Lancashire**, BB3 0LL, **ENGLAND**.
(T) 01254 664767.
Contact/s
Owner: Mrs H Clarkson
Profile Riding School, Saddlery Retailer, Stable/Livery. Ref:YH14807

WADDINGTON, CHRISTOPHER

Mr Christopher Waddington, Rainbow Hall Farm, Old Watling St, Flamstead, **Hertfordshire**, AL3 8HL, **ENGLAND**.
(T) 01582 840204.
Profile Breeder. Ref:YH14808

WADDINGTONS

C A Wadington Saddlery, Watling St, Hockliffe, Leighton Buzzard, **Bedfordshire**, LU7 9LP, **ENGLAND**.
(T) 01525 210212.
Contact/s
Partner: Mr C Waddington
Profile Riding Wear Retailer, Saddlery Retailer.
Yr. Est: 1993
Opening Times
Sp: Open Mon, Tue, Thurs - Sun 09:30. Closed Mon, Tue, Thurs - Sun 17:00.
Su: Open Mon, Tue, Thurs - Sun 09:30. Closed Mon, Tue, Thurs - Sun 17:00.
Au: Open Mon, Tue, Thurs - Sun 09:30. Closed Mon, Tue, Thurs - Sun 17:00.
Wn: Open Mon, Tue, Thurs - Sun 09:30. Closed Mon, Tue, Thurs - Sun 17:00.
Closed Wednesdays Ref:YH14809

WADE, A J

A J Wade, Rose Cottage, Hogpits Bottom, Flaunden, **Hertfordshire**, HP3 0PX, **ENGLAND**.
(T) 01442 833348.
Profile Farrier. Ref:YH14810

WADE, IAN

Ian Wade, Flat 1-2 72 Main St, Barrhead, **Glasgow (City of)**, G78 1SB, **SCOTLAND**.
(T) 0141 8818136.
Profile Farrier. Ref:YH14811

WADE, J

Mr J Wade, Howe Hills, Mordon, Sedgefield, Stockton-on-Tees, **Cleveland**, TS21 2HF, **ENGLAND**.
(T) 01325 313129 **(F)** 01325 320660.
Profile Supplies. Ref:YH14812

WADE, J & A

J & A Wade, Cowdray Park Polo Club, Cowdray Est Office, Midhurst, **Sussex (West)**, GU29 0AQ, **ENGLAND**.
(T) 01730 812423 **(F)** 01730 816335.
Profile Trainer. Ref:YH14813

WADE, JONNY

Jonny Wade, Little Crowshole Farm, Iping Common, Midhurst, **Sussex (West)**, GU29 0JW, **ENGLAND**.
(T) 01730 816335 **(F)** 01730 816335
(E) 100720.2751@compuserve.com.
Profile Breeder, Trainer. Ref:YH14814

WADE, SAM

Sam Wade DWCF, 5 Micklefield Green Cottages, Sarratt Rd, Sarratt, **Hertfordshire**, WD3 6AH, **ENGLAND**.
(T) 07768 394668.
Profile Farrier. Ref:YH14815

WADHAM

Mrs Wadham, The Trainer's Hse, Moulton Paddocks, Newmarket, **Suffolk**, CB8 7PJ, **ENGLAND**.
(T) 01638 662411 **(F)** 01638 668821
(W) www.newmarketracehorsetrainers.co.uk
Affiliated Bodies Newmarket Trainers Fed.
Profile Trainer. Ref:YH14816

WADLANDS HALL EQUESTRIAN CTRE

Wadlands Hall Equestrian Centre, Priesthorpe Rd, Farsley, Pudsey, **Yorkshire (West)**, LS28 5RD, **ENGLAND**.
(T) 0113 2570840
(E) wadlands@pcuk.org
Affiliated Bodies BHS, Pony Club UK.
Contact/s
Owner: Mrs K Driver
Profile Horse/Rider Accom. Ref:YH14817

WADLEY MANOR STABLES

Wadley Manor Stables, Stable Cottage, Faringdon, **Oxfordshire**, SN7 8PN, **ENGLAND**.
(T) 01367 244413 **(F)** 01367 244413.
Contact/s
Owner: Mr F Soloman
Profile Breeder. Ref:YH14818

WADSWICK

Wadswick Country Store Ltd, Manor Farm, Wadswick, Box, Corsham, **Wiltshire**, SN13 8JB, **ENGLAND**.
(T) 01225 810700 **(F)** 01225 810307
(E) barns@wadswick.co.uk
(W) www.shop.
Contact/s
Partner: Mr T Barton
Profile Riding Wear Retailer.
Saddle fitters and repairers. No.Staff: 12
Yr. Est: 1993
Opening Times
Sp: Open Mon - Sat 09:00, Sun 11:00. Closed Mon - Sat 17:00, Sun 15:00.
Su: Open Mon - Sat 09:00, Sun 11:00. Closed Mon - Sat 17:00, Sun 15:00.
Au: Open Mon - Sat 09:00, Sun 11:00. Closed Mon - Sat 17:00, Sun 15:00.
Wn: Open Mon - Sat 09:00, Sun 11:00. Closed Mon - Sat 17:00, Sun 15:00. Ref:YH14819

WAFFRONS SCHOOL OF RIDING

Waffrons School of Riding (The), Off Woodstock Lane South, Chessington, **Surrey**, KT9 1UF, **ENGLAND**.
(T) 020 83987668.
Profile Riding School, Stable/Livery. Ref:YH14820

WAGER, D

D Wager, Saltcote Hall, Goldhanger Rd, Maldon, **Essex**, CM9 7QX, **ENGLAND**.
(T) 01621 853252.
Profile Breeder. Ref:YH14821

WAGG, R G

R G Wagg, Tynewydd, Bangor Teifi, Llandysul, **Carmarthenshire**, SA44 5BQ, **WALES**.
(T) 01559 362705.
Profile Farrier. Ref:YH14822

WAGG, RAYMOND GEORGE

Raymond George Wagg, Tynewydd, Bangor Teifi, Llandysul, **Carmarthenshire**, SA44 4BQ, **WALES**.
(T) 01559 362705.
Profile Farrier. Ref:YH14823

WAGGONWORKS TRAILERS

Waggonworks Trailers, 1 White Cottage, Marshside, Canterbury, **Kent**, CT3 4EJ, **ENGLAND**.
(T) 01227 860650.
Contact/s
Owner: Mr T Quick
Profile Transport/Horse Boxes. Ref:YH14824

WAGGOTT, N

Mr N Waggott, Ingledene, Vyners Cl, Merrington Lane, Spennymoor, **County Durham**, DL16 7HB, **ENGLAND**.
(T) 01388 819012.
Profile Supplies. Ref:YH14825

WAGON WHEEL SADDLERY

Wagon Wheel Saddlery, 29 Queen St, Redcar, **Cleveland**, TS10 1AB, **ENGLAND**.
(T) 01642 470777. Ref:YH14826

WAINWRIGHT, IAN

Ian Wainwright DWCF, 9 Wheelwright Cl, Sutton Upon Derwent, York, **Yorkshire (North)**, YO41 4JZ, **ENGLAND**.
(T) 01904 607180.
Profile Farrier. Ref:YH14827

WAINWRIGHT, J C

Mrs J C Wainwright, Lockgate Farm, Wood Lanes, Adlington, Macclesfield, **Cheshire**, SK10 4PH, **ENGLAND**.

(T) 01625 572356.
Profile Breeder. Ref: YH14828

WAINWRIGHT, J S

J S Wainwright, Hanging Hill Farm, Kennythorpe, Malton, **Yorkshire (North)**, YO17 9LA, **ENGLAND**.
(T) 01653 658537 (F) 01653 658658.
Contact/s
Owner: Mr J Wainwright
Profile Trainer. Ref: YH14829

WAITE, COLIN

Colin Waite DWCF, 7 Quantock View, Kilve, Bridgwater, **Somerset**, TA5 1EE, **ENGLAND**.
(T) 01278 741653.
Profile Farrier. Ref: YH14830

WAKEFIELD LODGE ESTATE

Wakefield Lodge Estate, Wakefield Stud, Potterspury, Towcester, **Northamptonshire**, NN12 7QX, **ENGLAND**.
(T) 01327 811468.
Profile Breeder. Ref: YH14831

WAKEFIELD, G A

G A Wakefield, Shaw Common, Oxenhall, Newent, **Gloucestershire**, GL18 1RW, **ENGLAND**.
(T) 01989 720263.
Contact/s
Owner: Mr G Wakefield
Profile Farrier. Ref: YH14832

WAKEFIELD, HILARY

Hilary Wakefield, North Barn, Slyne Hall Heights, Slyne, Lancaster, **Lancashire**, LA2 6EH, **ENGLAND**.
(T) 01524 824851 (F) 01524 824919.
Contact/s
Owner: Ms H Wakefield (Q) BHSI
Profile Trainer. Private/mobile instructor.
Yr. Est: 1976
Opening Times
By appointment only Ref: YH14833

WAKEFIELD, JASON T

Jason T Wakefield DWCF, Laurel Cottage, Chirk Green, Chirk, **Denbighshire**, LL14 5PY, **WALES**.
(T) 01691 778491.
Profile Farrier. Ref: YH14834

WAKELY, JAN I

Jan I Wakely DWCF, 14 Juniper Cl, Heathfield, Honiton, **Devon**, EX14 8XL, **ENGLAND**.
(T) 01404 46706.
Profile Farrier. Ref: YH14835

WALCIS FARM STUD

Walcis Farm Stud, Lenwade, Norwich, **Norfolk**, NR9 5QR, **ENGLAND**.
(T) 01603 872289 (F) 01603 871267.
Profile Breeder. Ref: YH14836

WALE, R

R Wale, Broom Close Stables, Church Lane, Selston, Nottingham, **Nottinghamshire**, NG16 6FB, **ENGLAND**.
(T) 01773 810442.
Contact/s
Owner: Mr R Wale Ref: YH14837

WALES & THE WEST HARNESS

Wales & The West Harness Racing Association, 36 Mill St, Aberystwyth, **Ceredigion**, SY23 1JB, **WALES**.
(T) 01970 615616.
Profile Track/Course. Ref: YH14838

WALES, H F

Mr H F Wales, Lownthwaite, Milburn, Penrith, **Cumbria**, CA11 1TP, **ENGLAND**.
(T) 01768 361388.
Profile Breeder. Ref: YH14839

WALEY-COHEN, ROBERT B

Mr Robert B Waley-Cohen, Upton Viva, Banbury, **Oxfordshire**, OX15 6HT, **ENGLAND**.
(T) 020 72446022 (F) 020 73702269.
Profile Supplies. Ref: YH14840

WALFORD

Mrs Walford, Scalpay Hse, Broadford, **Highlands**, IV49 9BS, **SCOTLAND**.
(T) 01471 822720.
Profile Breeder. Ref: YH14841

WALFORD COLLEGE

Walford College, Walford, Baschurch, Shrewsbury, **Shropshire**, SY4 2HL, **ENGLAND**.
(T) 01939 262100 (F) 01939 261112
(E) info@walford-college.ac.uk.
Profile Track/Course. Ref: YH14842

WALFORD RIDING & LIVERY EST

Walford Riding & Livery Establishment, Walford Gardens Farm, West Monkton, Taunton, **Somerset**, TA2 8QW, **ENGLAND**.
(T) 01823 41226.
Profile Riding School. Ref: YH14843

WALKE, L

L Walke, Stidston Farm, South Brent, **Devon**, TQ10 9JT, **ENGLAND**.
(T) 01364 73191.
Profile Transport/Horse Boxes. Ref: YH14844

WALKER & TEMPLETON

Walker & Templeton Ltd, Seed & Grain Merchants, 11-15 Old Rivine Rd, Kilmarnock, **Ayrshire (East)**, KA1 2BJ, **SCOTLAND**.
(T) 01563 522494.
Profile Supplies. Ref: YH14845

WALKER, ALAN YUILL

Mr Alan Yuill Walker, Neville Hse, Kintbury, **Berkshire**, RG17 9TJ, **ENGLAND**.
(T) 01488 608717 (F) 01488 608788.
Profile Supplies. Ref: YH14846

WALKER, C

Mrs C Walker, 21 Wilkes Ave, Hucclecote, **Gloucestershire**, GL3 3LN, **ENGLAND**.
(T) 01452 615651.
Profile Breeder. Ref: YH14847

WALKER, D A & C S

D A & C S Walker, Ricknall Grange, Aycliffe, Newton Aycliffe, **County Durham**, DL5 6JQ, **ENGLAND**.
(T) 01325 313128 (F) 01325 313317
(M) 07976 313128
(W) www.ricknallrugs.co.uk.
Contact/s
Owner: Mr C Walker
Profile Stable/Livery. Ref: YH14848

WALKER, GLANVILL & RICHARDS

Walker, Glanvill & Richards, The Vetnry Surgery, Sibford Rd, Hook Norton, **Oxfordshire**, OX15 5JZ, **ENGLAND**.
(T) 01608 730085 (F) 01608 730439.
Contact/s
Partner: Mr J Walker
Profile Medical Support. Ref: YH14849

WALKER, IAN

Ian Walker, 58 Ettington Cl, Wellesbourne, Warwick, **Warwickshire**, CV35 9RJ, **ENGLAND**.
(T) 01789 840341 (F) 01789 840341.
Contact/s
Owner: Mr I Walker
Profile Transport/Horse Boxes. Ref: YH14850

WALKER, J B & V D

J B & V D Walker, Ravendale Top Farm, West Ravendale, Grimsby, **Lincolnshire (North East)**, DN37 0RY, **ENGLAND**.
(T) 01472 823021.
Profile Breeder. Ref: YH14851

WALKER, JIMMY

Jimmy Walker, Belfast Telegraph, 124-144 Royal Aveune, Belfast, **County Antrim**, BT1 1EB, **NORTHERN IRELAND**.
(T) 028 94828744.
Profile Supplies. Ref: YH14852

WALKER, L

Mr L Walker, East High Wood, Langleydale, Barnard Castle, **County Durham**, DL12 8R2, **ENGLAND**.
(T) 01388 718277.
Profile Trainer. Ref: YH14853

WALKER, R

R Walker, St. Austell, Hatton, Warwick, **Warwickshire**, CV35 8XD, **ENGLAND**.
(T) 01926 842090.
Contact/s
Owner: Mr R Walker
Profile Farrier. Ref: YH14854

WALKER, RALPH I

Ralph I Walker DWCF, Bet-Luck, 5 Venus St, Congresbury, **Somerset (North)**, BS19 5HA, **ENGLAND**.
(T) 01934 833561.
Profile Farrier. Ref: YH14855

WALKER, RICHARD

Richard Walker, Point Farm, Stathern, Melton Mowbray, **Leicestershire**, LE14 4HW, **ENGLAND**.
(T) 01949 860637 (F) 01949 861294.
Profile Trainer. Ref: YH14856

WALKER, RICHARD HERBERT

Richard Herbert Walker DWCF, Wellcroft Cottages, Nomansheath, Malpas, **Hertfordshire**, SG14 8DY, **ENGLAND**.
(T) 01948 820737.
Profile Farrier. Ref: YH14857

WALKER, W

W Walker, 14 Bonfield Rd, Strathkinness, St Andrews, **Fife**, KY16 9RP, **SCOTLAND**.
(T) 01334 850622.
Contact/s
Owner: Mr W Walker
Profile Transport/Horse Boxes. Ref: YH14858

WALKERS OF WORCESTERSHIRE

Walkers of Worcestershire Ltd, 28 Snowdon Cl, Kidderminster, **Worcestershire**, DY11 5JH, **ENGLAND**.
(T) 01562 861416 (F) 01562 861416.
Profile Transport/Horse Boxes. Ref: YH14859

WALL, A E

A E Wall, Norgate Hse, Rogart, Sutherland, **Highlands**, IV28 3UA, **SCOTLAND**.
(T) 01408 4352.
Profile Medical Support. Ref: YH14860

WALL, T R

T R Wall, Harton Manor, Harton, Church Stretton, **Shropshire**, SY6 7DL, **ENGLAND**.
(T) 01694 724144.
Profile Trainer. Ref: YH14861

WALL, Y L

Mrs Y L Wall, Home Farm, Munderfield Harold, Bromyard, **Herefordshire**, HR7 4SZ, **ENGLAND**.
(T) 01885 482062.
Profile Breeder. Ref: YH14862

WALLACE RIDING CLUB

Wallace Riding Club, 47 Greycraigs, Cairneyhill, **Fife**, KY12 8XN, **SCOTLAND**.
(T) 01383 880812.
Contact/s
Chairman: Miss A Dunsmore
Profile Club/Association, Riding Club. Ref: YH14863

WALLACE, JANE

Jane Wallace, Fishponds Farm, Stoke Albany, Market Harborough, **Leicestershire**, LE16 8PZ, **ENGLAND**.
(T) 01858 85250 (F) 01858 85499.
Profile Trainer. Ref: YH14864

WALLACE, W T

W T Wallace, Shatton Hall, Lorton, Cockermouth, **Cumbria**, CA13 9TL, **ENGLAND**.
(T) 01900 825633.
Profile Breeder. Ref: YH14865

WALLING, R H

R H Walling, Strickland Tenement, Crosthwaite, Kendal, **Cumbria**, LA8 8BU, **ENGLAND**.
(T) 01539 568214.
Contact/s
Owner: Mr R Walling
Profile Transport/Horse Boxes. Ref: YH14866

WALLINGWELLS EQUESTRIAN CTRE

Wallingwells Equestrian Centre Ltd, Wallingwells Lane, Wallingwells, Worksop, **Nottinghamshire**, S81 8BX, **ENGLAND**.
(T) 01909 730638. Ref: YH14867

WALMSLEY, J W

Mr J W Walmsley, East Garth Farm, Catterton, Tadcaster, **Yorkshire (North)**, LS24 8DH, **ENGLAND**.
(T) 01937 833380.
Profile Supplies. Ref: YH14868

WALMSLEY, KAREN

Karen Walmsley, Yeomans Well, Risplith, Ripon, **Yorkshire (North)**, HG4 3EP, **ENGLAND**.
(T) 01765 620378.
Contact/s
Partner: Mr K Walmsley Ref: YH14869

WALNUT STABLES

Walnut Stables, Blackmore Rd, Malvern, **Worcestershire**, WR14 1QX, **ENGLAND**.
(T) 01684 564824
(W) www.walnutridingstables.com.
Contact/s
Owner: Mrs J Jones (Q) BHS 3
Profile Riding School. No.Staff: 4

Yr. Est: 1986 C.Size: 22 Acres
Opening Times
Sp: Open Mon - Sun 09:00. Closed Mon - Sun 18:00.
Su: Open Mon - Sun 09:00. Closed Mon - Sun 18:00.
Au: Open Mon - Sun 09:00. Closed Mon - Sun 18:00.
Wn: Open Mon - Sun 09:00. Closed Mon - Sun 18:00. Ref:YH14870

WALROND, SALLIE

Mrs Sallie Walrond LHHI, Thorne Lodge, Cockfield, Bury St Edmunds, **Suffolk**, IP30 0JN, **ENGLAND**.
(T) 01284 828296.
Profile Trainer. Ref:YH14871

WALSALL EQUESTRIAN SOCIETY

Walsall Equestrian Society, P O Box 1478, Walsall, **Midlands (West)**, WS1 2GJ, **ENGLAND**.
(T) 01922 720966 **(F)** 01922 720966.
Contact/s
Chairman: Mrs J Pountley
Profile Club/Association. Ref:YH14872

WALSALL RIDING SADDLE

Walsall Riding Saddle Co Ltd, Crosby Hse, Garden St, Walsall, **Midlands (West)**, WS2 8EF, **ENGLAND**.
(T) 01922 624768 **(F)** 01922 641438. Ref:YH14873

WALSGRAVE AMATEUR RIDING CLUB

Walsgrave Amateur Riding Club, 73 Brinklow Rd, Binley, Coventry, **Midlands (West)**, CV3 2JB, **ENGLAND**.
(T) 024 76458155.
Contact/s
Secretary: Mrs J Hinds
Profile Club/Association, Riding Club. Ref:YH14874

WALSH & CO

Walsh & Co, 66 Brookley Rd, Brockenhurst, **Hampshire**, SO42 7RA, **ENGLAND**.
(T) 01590 622138 **(F)** 01590 623422
(W) www.walshandco.co.uk.
Contact/s
Partner: Mr R Bogaerde
(E) rupert@walshandco.co.uk
Profile Planning Consultants.
Planning consultants and property developers.
Yr. Est: 1971
Opening Times
Sp: Open Mon - Fri 09:00. Closed Mon - Fri 17:30.
Su: Open Mon - Fri 09:00. Closed Mon - Fri 17:30.
Au: Open Mon - Fri 09:00. Closed Mon - Fri 17:30.
Wn: Open Mon - Fri 09:00. Closed Mon - Fri 17:30.
Closed weekends Ref:YH14875

WALSH EMMETT FARM SUPPLIES

Walsh Emmett Farm Supplies, Roscore Blueball, Tullamore, **County Offaly**, **IRELAND**.
(T) 050 655844.
Profile Supplies. Ref:YH14876

WALSH, DAVID

David Walsh, Greenrath, Tipperary Town, **County Tipperary**, **IRELAND**.
(T) 062 51259.
Profile Supplies. Ref:YH14877

WALSH, KATHLEEN

Miss Kathleen Walsh, Mill Hse, Cerney Wick, Cirencester, **Gloucestershire**, GL7 5QT, **ENGLAND**.
(T) 01793 751642.
Profile Breeder. Ref:YH14878

WALSH, P

Mrs P Walsh, Highclere Farm, Highclere, Newbury, **Hampshire**, RG20 9PY, **ENGLAND**.
(T) 01635 255013.
Profile Stable/Livery. Ref:YH14879

WALSH, TED

Ted Walsh, Greenhills, Kill, **County Kildare**, **IRELAND**.
(T) 045 877818.
Contact/s
Trainer: Mr T Walsh
(E) tedwalsh@kildarehorse.ie
Profile Trainer. Ref:YH14880

WALTER ALLEN & SONS

Walter Allen & Sons, 12-14 High St, Great Glen, Leicester, **Leicestershire**, LE8 9FJ, **ENGLAND**.
(T) 0116 2592225.
Contact/s
Owner: Mr D Walter
Profile Blacksmith. Ref:YH14881

WALTER BAILEY

Walter Bailey (Parr) Ltd, St Andrews Rd, Parr, St Austell, **Cornwall**, PL24 2LX, **ENGLAND**.
(T) 01726 812245 **(F)** 01726 812246.
Profile Supplies. Ref:YH14882

WALTER HARRISON & SONS

Walter Harrison & Sons, The Crescent, Radcliffe-on-Trent, **Nottinghamshire**, NG12 2GS, **ENGLAND**.
(T) 0115 9332901 **(F)** 0115 9334775.
Contact/s
Manager: Mr G Harrison
Profile Supplies. Ref:YH14883

WALTER, ALAN

Alan Walter, Stones Tenement, Croford, Wiveliscombe, Taunton, **Somerset**, TA4 2TS, **ENGLAND**.
(T) 01984 623624.
Contact/s
Owner: Mr A Walter
Profile Transport/Horse Boxes. Ref:YH14884

WALTERS PET & GARDEN STORES

Walters Pet & Garden Stores, 14 Cowbridge Rd, Bridgend, **Bridgend**, CF31 3DA, **WALES**.
(T) 01656 653124.
Profile Supplies. Ref:YH14885

WALTERS, ALICE

Alice Walters, 22 Streton Ave, Newport, **Shropshire**, TF10 7FF, **ENGLAND**.
(T) 01952 814203. Ref:YH14886

WALTERS, J K & M S

J K & M S Walters, 66 Kimberley Villas, Tredegar, **Blaenau Gwent**, NP22 3LD, **WALES**.
(T) 01495 726055.
Profile Breeder. Ref:YH14887

WALTHAM CTRE

Waltham Centre, Freeby Lane, Waltham On The Wolds, Melton Mowbray, **Leicestershire**, LE14 4RT, **ENGLAND**.
(T) 01664 415400 **(F)** 01644 414933
(E) pat.harris@eu.effem.com.
Contact/s
Equestrian Manager: Dr P Harris
Profile Medical Support. Ref:YH14888

WALTON FIELDS STUD

Walton Fields Stud, Church Lane, Grimston, Melton Mowbray, **Leicestershire**, LE14 3BY, **ENGLAND**.
(T) 01664 812298
(M) 07860 432790.
Profile Breeder. Ref:YH14889

WALTON, A J

A J Walton, Bradeley Hall Farm, Bradeley Hall Rd, Haslington, Crewe, **Cheshire**, CW1 5QN, **ENGLAND**.
(T) 01270 581610.
Contact/s
Partner: Mrs M Walton Ref:YH14890

WALTON, HELEN L

Mrs Helen L Walton, The Dairy, Laughtons Farm, Brandon Rd, Hougham, Grantham, **Lincolnshire**, NG32 2AG, **ENGLAND**.
(T) 01400 251152
(M) 07889 609654.
Profile Trainer. Ref:YH14891

WALTON, J B

Mr J B Walton, Flotterton Hall, Thropton, Morpeth, **Northumberland**, NE65 7LF, **ENGLAND**.
(T) 01669 640253.
Profile Supplies. Ref:YH14892

WALTON, KATE

Mrs Kate Walton, Sharp Hill Farm, Middleham, Leyburn, **Yorkshire (North)**, DL8 4QY, **ENGLAND**.
(T) 01969 622250
(M) 07710 812143.
Profile Supplies. Ref:YH14893

WANLESS, MARY

Mary Wanless BSc, BHSI, Chapel Plaister's Cottage, Wadswick Lane, Box, **Wiltshire**, SN13 8HZ, **ENGLAND**.
(T) 01225 811945.
Profile Trainer. Ref:YH14894

WAPLEY STABLES

Wapley Stables, Wapley Hill, Yate, Bristol, **Bristol**, BS37 4BP, **ENGLAND**.
(T) 01454 324732.
Contact/s
Owner: Mrs T Spargo
Profile Riding School, Stable/Livery. Ref:YH14895

WAPLINGTON MANOR STABLES

Waplington Manor Stables, Waplington Manor, Waplington, York, **Yorkshire (North)**, YO42 4RS, **ENGLAND**.
(T) 01759 305678.
Contact/s
Owner: Mr S Willis
Profile Breeder. Ref:YH14896

WARD SADDLERY

Ward Saddlery, 140 Carmyle Ave, Glasgow, **Glasgow (City of)**, G32 8DL, **SCOTLAND**.
(T) 0141 6419650.
Profile Riding Wear Retailer, Saddlery Retailer.
Ref:YH14897

WARD, ANTHONY

Mr Anthony Ward, The Chestnuts Farm, Priors Marston, Moreton Morrell, **Warwickshire**, CV35 9BL, **ENGLAND**.
(T) 01327 260739.
Profile Riding School, Stable/Livery. Ref:YH14898

WARD, BARRY P

Barry P Ward DWCF, 6 Miler Court, Minster, Sheppey, **Kent**, ME12 3NN, **ENGLAND**.
(T) 01795 875374.
Profile Farrier. Ref:YH14899

WARD, DEAN

Dean Ward, 17 Kingsmere Rd, Wimbledon, **London (Greater)**, SW19 6PY, **ENGLAND**.
(T) 020 87889074.
Profile Breeder. Ref:YH14900

WARD, JONATHAN M

Jonathan M Ward DWCF, 1 The Lodge, Main St, Con St Aldwyns, Cirencester, **Gloucestershire**, GL7 5AJ, **ENGLAND**.
(T) 01285 750711.
Profile Farrier. Ref:YH14901

WARD, K A

K A Ward AFCL, 61 Culverden Pk, Tunbridge Wells, **Kent**, TN4 9QU, **ENGLAND**.
(T) 01892 545400.
Profile Farrier. Ref:YH14902

WARD, M & W

M & W Ward, Rectory Farm, Station Rd, Sutton, Ely, **Cambridgeshire**, CB6 2RL, **ENGLAND**.
(T) 01353 778094 **(F)** 01353 778094.
Contact/s
Partner: Mrs W Ward
Profile Breeder. Ref:YH14903

WARD, MICHAEL J

Michael J Ward, The Jays Forge, Bagbeare Cross, Thornbury, Holsworthy, **Devon**, EX22 6DQ, **ENGLAND**.
(T) 01409 261550.
Profile Breeder, Farrier, Stable/Livery, Trainer.
Ref:YH14904

WARD, R & S

R & S Ward, Lower Ton-Y-Felin Farm, Croespenmaen, Crumlin, Newport, **Blaenau Gwent**, NP11 3BE, **WALES**.
(T) 01495 243016.
Profile Supplies. Ref:YH14905

WARD, R KEITH

R Keith Ward B.V.Sc., M.R.C.V.S., Hillside Vetnry Ctre, 146 Crewe Rd, Nantwich, **Cheshire**, CW5 6NB, **ENGLAND**.
(T) 01270 625310 **(F)** 01270 610999.
Profile Medical Support. Ref:YH14906

WARD, S

Mr S Ward, Ermine Farms, Waddingham Grange, Waddingham, Gainsborough, **Lincolnshire**, DN21 4TB, **ENGLAND**.
(T) 01673 81310.
Profile Breeder. Ref:YH14907

WARD, S A

Mrs S A Ward, High Park Hse, Winton, Northallerton, **Yorkshire (North)**, DL6 2TB, **ENGLAND**.
(T) 01609 82293.
Profile Supplies. Ref:YH14908

WARD, STANLEY A

Stanley A Ward, Oak Cottage, The Common, St Brivels, **Gloucestershire**, GL15 6SJ, **ENGLAND**.
(T) 01594 530440.
Profile Farrier. Ref:YH14909

WARD, STUART J I

Stuart J I Ward DWCF, 2 Carr Lane, Rainton, Thirsk, **Yorkshire (North)**, YO7 3PS, **ENGLAND**.
(T) 01845 578909.
Profile Farrier. **Ref: YH14910**

WARD, V C

Mrs V C Ward, Aisby Hse, Aisby, Grantham, **Lincolnshire**, NG32 3NF, **ENGLAND**.
(T) 01529 455260
(M) 07831 604530.
Profile Trainer. **Ref: YH14911**

WARDALL BLOODSTOCK SHIPPING

Wardall Bloodstock Shipping Ltd, Manor Farm Stud, Alvediston, Salisbury, **Wiltshire**, SP5 5JY, **ENGLAND**.
(T) 01722 780777 **(F)** 01722 780069.
Contact/s
Owner: Mr A Wardell
Profile Transport/Horse Boxes. **Ref: YH14912**

WARDINGTON STUD FARM

Wardington Stud Farm (The), Banbury, **Oxfordshire**, OX17 18P, **ENGLAND**..
Profile Breeder. **Ref: YH14913**

WARE, RONALD

Ronald Ware FWCF, 16 Fairhaven Way, Newmarket, **Suffolk**, CB8 0DQ, **ENGLAND**.
(T) 01638 664084.
Profile Farrier. **Ref: YH14914**

WAREHAM, TONY

Tony Wareham, Sunnyside Farm, Lower St, Winterborne Whitechurch, Blandford Forum, **Dorset**, DT11 9AP, **ENGLAND**.
(T) 01929 471632.
Contact/s
Owner: Mr T Wareham
Profile Transport/Horse Boxes. **Ref: YH14915**

WAREHILL EQUESTRIAN CTRE

Warehill Equestrian Centre, Doolittle Lane, Totternhoe, Dunstable, **Bedfordshire**, LU6 1QX, **ENGLAND**.
(T) 01525 222024 **(F)** 01525 220727.
Contact/s
Owner: Mr T Kemp **Ref: YH14916**

WARESLEY MANOR STABLES

Waresley Manor Stables, Manor Lane, Hartlebury, Kidderminster, **Worcestershire**, DY11 7XN, **ENGLAND**.
(T) 01299 250710.
Profile Riding School. **Ref: YH14917**

WARLINGHAM PONY CLUB

Warlingham Pony Club Supporters Open Fixtures, Windy Ridge, Maesmaur Rd, Tatsfield, Westerham, **Kent**, TN16 2LD, **ENGLAND**.
(T) 01959 577593.
Profile Club/Association. **Ref: YH14918**

WARMAN, JANICE

Ms Janice Warman, Home Farm Cottage, Warren Rd, Crowborough, **Sussex (East)**, TN6 1TX, **ENGLAND**.
(T) 01892 663906 **(F)** 01892 669200.
Profile Supplies. **Ref: YH14919**

WARMAN, STEWART M

Stewart M Warman DWCF, Robin Hill, 1 Spring St, Slaithwaite, Huddersfield, **Yorkshire (West)**, HD7 5HN, **ENGLAND**.
(T) 07860 752814.
Profile Farrier. **Ref: YH14920**

WARMBLOOD FACT FILES

Warmblood Fact Files, 85 Fishers Field, Buckingham, **Buckinghamshire**, MK18 1FF, **ENGLAND**.
(T) 01280 824451.
Profile Breeder. **Ref: YH14921**

WARMINSTER METAL WORKERS

Warminster Metal Workers Ltd, 17 Deverill Rd Trading Est, Deverill Rd, Sutton Veny, Warminster, **Wiltshire**, BA12 7BZ, **ENGLAND**.
(T) 01985 840502 **(F)** 01985 840550.
Profile Blacksmith. **Ref: YH14922**

WARMINSTER SADDLERY

Warminster Saddlery, 10 Chinns Court, Market Pl, Warminster, **Wiltshire**, BA12 9AN, **ENGLAND**.
(T) 01985 214284 **(F)** 01985 216865.
Contact/s
Owner: Mrs S Mologhney
Profile Riding Wear Retailer, Saddlery Retailer.
No.Staff: 5 Yr. Est: 1996
Opening Times
Sp: Open Mon - Fri 09:15, Sat 09:00. Closed Mon - Fri 17:30, Sat 17:00.
Su: Open Mon - Fri 09:15, Sat 09:00. Closed Mon - Fri 17:30, Sat 17:00.
Au: Open Mon - Fri 09:15, Sat 09:00. Closed Mon - Fri 17:30, Sat 17:00.
Wn: Open Mon - Fri 09:15, Sat 09:00. Closed Mon - Fri 17:30, Sat 17:00. **Ref: YH14923**

WARMWELL STUD

Warmwell Stud, C/O 2 Church Cottages, Warmwell, Dorchester, **Dorset**, DT2 8HQ, **ENGLAND**.
(T) 01305 852254 **(F)** 01305 852254.
Contact/s
General Manager: Mrs H Nelmes
Profile Breeder, Stable/Livery.
Warmwell Stud is responsible for resting, recuperation, medical nursing, weaning, stabling for the night and mares taken to foal and wean. No.Staff: 3
Yr. Est: 1971 C.Size: 110 Acres **Ref: YH14924**

WARNER SHEPPARD & WADE

Warner Sheppard & Wade, Mayfield Hse, Chapel Lane, Souldrop, **Bedfordshire**, MK44 1HG, **ENGLAND**.
(T) 01234 782929 **(F)** 01234 782232. **Ref: YH14925**

WARNER, M V

M V Warner DWCF, 11 Arun Vale, Coldwaltham, Pulborough, **Sussex (West)**, RH20 1LP, **ENGLAND**.
(T) 01798 872266.
Profile Farrier. **Ref: YH14926**

WARNER, RONALD V

Ronald V Warner FWCF, 11 Arun Vale, Coldwaltham, Pulborough, **Sussex (West)**, RH20 1LP, **ENGLAND**.
(T) 01798 872266.
Profile Farrier. **Ref: YH14927**

WARR, S

Mrs S Warr, May Day Farm, Castle Hill, Tonbridge, **Kent**, TN11 0QG, **ENGLAND**.
(T) 01732 369569.
Profile Supplies. **Ref: YH14928**

WARR, TONY

Tony Warr, May Day Farm, Castle Hill, Tonbridge, **Kent**, TW11 0QG, **ENGLAND**.
(T) 01892 835456
(M) 07850 333192
(E) tonywarr@bigfoot.com
Affiliated Bodies BEVA.
Contact/s
Owner: Mr T Warr **(Q)** B.V.M, BSc, MRCVS
Profile Medical Support. **Ref: YH14929**

WARREN FARM STABLES

Warren Farm Stables, Southport Old Rd, Formby, Liverpool, **Merseyside**, L37 0AN, **ENGLAND**.
(T) 01704 873820 **(F)** 01704 873820.
Contact/s
Owner: Mrs S Greenwood
Profile Stable/Livery. **Ref: YH14930**

WARREN HALL FARM

Warren Hall Farm Riding Stables, Warrens Hall Farm, 218 Oakham Rd, Tividale, Oldbury, **Midlands (West)**, B69 1PY, **ENGLAND**.
(T) 01384 455473.
Contact/s
Manager: Mrs M Jones **Ref: YH14931**

WARREN HILL STABLING

Warren Hill Stabling, Warren Hill, Skeete Rd, Lyminge, Folkestone, **Kent**, CT18 8DS, **ENGLAND**.
(T) 01303 862061 **(F)** 01303 862061.
Contact/s
Owner: Mrs A Tighe **Ref: YH14932**

WARREN PARK STUD

Warren Park Stud, Moulton Rd, Newmarket, **Suffolk**, CB8 8QL, **ENGLAND**.
(T) 01638 730102 **(F)** 01638 731125.
Profile Breeder. **Ref: YH14933**

WARREN STABLES

Warren Stables, Warren Farm, The Street, Badwell Ash, Bury St Edmunds, **Suffolk**, IP31 3DP, **ENGLAND**.
(T) 01359 258552.
Contact/s
Manager: Mrs H Alderson **Ref: YH14934**

WARREN, A H

A H Warren, Downclose Stud, Downclose Lane, North Perrott, Crewkerne, **Somerset**, TA18 7SH, **ENGLAND**.
(T) 01460 74280.
Profile Breeder. **Ref: YH14935**

WARREN, P

P Warren, Hardacre, Parc Erissey, Redruth, **Cornwall**, TR16 4HW, **ENGLAND**.
(T) 01209 313559.
Profile Breeder. **Ref: YH14936**

WARREN, WILLIAM J

William J Warren RSS, 32 Acacia Ave, Verwood, **Dorset**, BH13 6XG, **ENGLAND**.
(T) 01202 824479.
Profile Farrier. **Ref: YH14937**

WARRENPOINT RIDING CLUB

Warrenpoint Riding Club, 49 Ballydesland Rd, Warrenpoint, **County Down**, BT34 3QB, **NORTHERN IRELAND**.
(T) 028 30772325.
Contact/s
Chairman: Mr J Cunningham
Profile Club/Association, Riding Club. **Ref: YH14938**

WARRENS RIDING CTRE

Warrens Riding Centre, 5 Garsden Ave, Blackburn, **Lancashire**, BB1 2DZ, **ENGLAND**.
(T) 01254 57683.
Contact/s
Owner: Mr M Warren **Ref: YH14939**

WARREN'S TACK

Warren's Tack & Country Clothing, Shellaford Hse, Lydford, Okehampton, **Devon**, EX20 4BE, **ENGLAND**.
(T) 01822 820369.
Profile Supplies. **Ref: YH14940**

WARRIGAL FARM LIVERY STABLES

Warrigal Farm Livery Stables, Sandbanks Hill, Green St, Bean, Dartford, **Kent**, DA2 8EH, **ENGLAND**.
(T) 01474 704093.
Profile Stable/Livery. **Ref: YH14941**

WARRINGTON TRAILER CTRE

Warrington Trailer Centre, Winwick St, Warrington, **Cheshire**, WA2 7DF, **ENGLAND**.
(T) 01925 655513.
Profile Transport/Horse Boxes. **Ref: YH14942**

WARRINGTON, S

Mrs S Warrington BHSISM, East Gr, Little Witley, **Worcestershire**, WR6 6LQ, **ENGLAND**.
(T) 01299 896200 **(F)** 01299 896494.
Contact/s
Owner: Mrs S Warrington **(Q)** BHSI(SM)
Profile Stable/Livery, Trainer.
Small training yard specialising in teenagers and training pupils for the BHS exam system. Preparation of horse and ponies for BHS/Pony Club Horse Trials a speciality. No.Staff: 3 Yr. Est: 1967
C.Size: 200 Acres
Opening Times
Telephone for an appointment **Ref: YH14943**

WARWICK BROS

Warwick Bros (Alresford) Ltd, The Dean, Alresford, **Hampshire**, SO24 9BN, **ENGLAND**.
(T) 01962 732681 **(F)** 01962 735385.
Contact/s
Manager: Mr M Bryant
Profile Transport/Horse Boxes. **Ref: YH14944**

WARWICK BUILDINGS

Warwick Buildings, Southam Rd, Long Itchington, Rugby, **Warwickshire**, CV23 8QL, **ENGLAND**.
(T) 01926 815757 **(F)** 01926 815162.
Profile Transport/Horse Boxes. **Ref: YH14945**

WARWICK RACECOURSE COMPANY

Warwick Racecourse Company Ltd, Hampton St, Warwick, **Warwickshire**, CV34 6HN, **ENGLAND**.
(T) 01926 491553 **(F)** 01926 403223.
Contact/s
Clerk of Course/Manager: Christian Leech
Profile Track/Course. **Ref: YH14946**

WARWICK WARRIORS

Warwick Warriors Horseball Team, C/O Green Belt Bungalow, Nutts Lane, Leicester, **Leicestershire**, LE10 3EG, **ENGLAND**.
(T) 01455 634476.
Profile Club/Association. **Ref: YH14947**

WARWICK, JOHN T

John T Warwick, Monkredding Stables, Kilwinning, **Ayrshire (North)**, KA13 7QA, **SCOTLAND**.
(T) 01294 552466 **(F)** 01294 551962

A-Z of COMPANIES

Key: **(T)** telephone **(F)** fax **(M)** mobile **(E)** E-Mail Address **(W)** Website Address **(Q)** Qualifications
Yr. Est: Year Established C.Size: Complex Size Sp: Spring Su: Summer Au: Autumn Wn: Winter

Affiliated Bodies NAAT.
Contact/s
Physiotherapist: John T Warwick
Profile Medical Support.
Physiotherapist for horses & dogs. Ref:YH14948

WARWICK, S J

S J Warwick, 11 Heather Cresent, Breaston, Derby, **Derbyshire**, DE72 3AR, **ENGLAND**.
(T) 01332 873431.
Contact/s
Owner: Mr S Warwick
Profile Farrier. Ref:YH14949

WARWICK, SIMON J

Simon J Warwick DWCF, 11 Heather Cres, Breaston, **Derbyshire**, DE7 3AR, **ENGLAND**.
(T) 01332 873431.
Profile Farrier. Ref:YH14950

WARWICKSHIRE CLGE HORSE UNIT

Warwickshire College, Moreton Hall, Moreton Morrell, Warwick, **Warwickshire**, CV35 9BL, **ENGLAND**.
(T) 01926 318318 (F) 01926 318300
(E) enquires@warkscol.ac.uk
(W) www.warwickequine.ac.uk.
Contact/s
Equine Team Leader: Phillipa Francis
Profile Breeder, Stable/Livery.
Equine Studies features equine distance learning flexibility, ongoing research programmes, farriery training and the best equine studies library in the UK. Full-time, part-time and home study delivery is available.
Ref: YH14951

WARWICKSHIRE EQUITATION CTRE

Warwickshire Equitation Centre, Kenilworth Rd, Balsall Common, Coventry, **Warwickshire**, CV7 7HD, **ENGLAND**.
(T) 01676 32804.
Profile Club/Association, Riding School.
Ref:YH14952

WARWICKSHIRE TRAILERS

Warwickshire Trailers Ltd, Blunts Green, Henley-In-Arden, Solihull, **Warwickshire**, B95 5RE, **ENGLAND**.
(T) 01564 794579
(W) www.warwickshiretrailers.co.uk.
Contact/s
General Manager: Mr J Rulon-Miller
Profile Transport/Horse Boxes.
Supply spare parts for old Rice trailers. No.Staff: 2
Yr. Est: 1990
Opening Times
Sp: Open 08:30. Closed 17:30.
Su: Open 08:30. Closed 17:30.
Au: Open 08:30. Closed 17:30.
Wn: Open 08:30. Closed 17:30. Ref:YH14953

WASH FARM

Wash Farm, Halstead Rd, Fordham, Colchester, **Essex**, CO6 3LL, **ENGLAND**.
(T) 01206 240235 (F) 01206 241131
(W) www.washfarm.co.uk.
Contact/s
Owner: Miss D Maffingham
Profile Stable/Livery.
Livery - full and D.I.Y. 20 stables with 24 hour security and midnight stable checks. Can offer holiday stabling for horses. Yr. Est: 1995 C.Size: 30 Acres
Opening Times
Sp: Open Mon - Sun 08:00. Closed Mon - Sun 21:00.
Su: Open Mon - Sun 08:00. Closed Mon - Sun 21:00.
Au: Open Mon - Sun 08:00. Closed Mon - Sun 21:00.
Wn: Open Mon - Sun 08:00. Closed Mon - Sun 21:00.
Telephone between these hours before visiting
Ref:YH14954

WASHBROOK FARM

Washbrook Farm, Aston Le Walls, Daventry, **Northamptonshire**, NN11 6RT, **ENGLAND**.
(T) 01327 262256 (F) 01327 260805
(E) taylors@flying-changes.com
(W) www.washbrook-farm.co.uk.
Profile Track/Course. Ref:YH14955

WASON, J C

J C Wason, Lower Tredenham, Lanivet, Bodmin, **Cornwall**, PL30 5HL, **ENGLAND**.
(T) 01208 831956 (F) 01208 831956.
Contact/s
Owner: Mrs S Wason
Profile Breeder. Ref:YH14956

WASON, J K

J K Wason, South Lane Farm, South Lane, Woodmancote, Emsworth, **Hampshire**, PO10 8PT, **ENGLAND**.
(T) 01243 372080 (F) 01243 372080.
Contact/s
Owner: Mr J Wason Ref:YH14957

WASON, S E

S E Wason, Little Trenawin, Trenawin Lane, Connor Downs, Hayle, **Cornwall**, TR27 5JG, **ENGLAND**.
(T) 01736 752330.
Profile Breeder. Ref:YH14958

WASS, A J

Mr A J Wass, The Shires, Stone Rd, Rough Cl, Stoke-on-Trent, **Staffordshire**, ST3 7NQ, **ENGLAND**.
(T) 01782 392467.
Profile Breeder. Ref:YH14959

WASTE WARRIOR PRODUCTS

Waste Warrior Products, 48 Benwick Rd, Doddington, March, **Cambridgeshire**, PE15 0TG, **ENGLAND**.
(T) 01354 741349 (F) 01354 741349.
Contact/s
Owner: Mr C Aveling
Profile Supplies. Ref:YH14960

WATCHGATE FORGE

Watchgate Forge, Selside, Kendal, **Cumbria**, LA8 9JX, **ENGLAND**.
(T) 01539 828236.
Contact/s
Owner: Mr M Tallon
Profile Blacksmith. Ref:YH14961

WATCHORN, KELLY

Ms Kelly Watchorn, Simdor, Melton Spinney Rd, Thorpe Arnold, Melton Mowbray, **Leicestershire**, LE14 4SB, **ENGLAND**.
(T) 01664 444678.
Profile Supplies. Ref:YH14962

WATER FARM STUD

Water Farm Stud, Water Farm, Raydon, Ipswich, **Suffolk**, IP7 5LW, **ENGLAND**.
(T) 01473 310407 (F) 01473 311206
(M) 07770692094
(E) marybancroft@waterfarmarabians.freeserve.co.uk.
Contact/s
Owner: Dr M Bancroft
Profile Breeder. Ref:YH14963

WATER ORTON LIVERY STABLES

Water Orton Livery Stables, The Mount, Coleshill Rd, Curdworth, Sutton Coldfield, **Midlands (West)**, B76 9HP, **ENGLAND**.
(T) 01675 470725.
Contact/s
Owner: Mrs N Coton Ref:YH14964

WATERBECK

Waterbeck Livery & Riding Stables, Waterbeck, Great Busby, Middlesbrough, **Cleveland**, TS9 7AS, **ENGLAND**.
(T) 01642 710868.
Contact/s
Owner: Mr P Dawson Ref:YH14965

WATERDENE VETNRY PRACTICE

Waterdene Veterinary Practice (Caterham), 4 Timberhill Rd, Caterham, **Surrey**, CR3 6LD, **ENGLAND**.
(T) 01883 345277.
Profile Medical Support. Ref:YH14966

WATERDENE VETNRY PRACTICE

Waterdene Veterinary Practice (Purley), 102 Brighton Rd, Purley, **Surrey**, CR2 4DB, **ENGLAND**.
(T) 020 86608184 (F) 01883 349142.
Profile Medical Support. Ref:YH14967

WATERLOO HOUSE VETNRY SURGERY

Waterloo House Veterinary Surgery, 49 West St, Swadlincote, **Derbyshire**, DE11 9DN, **ENGLAND**.
(T) 01283 213707 (F) 01283 221172.
Profile Medical Support. Ref:YH14968

WATERLOO HOUSE VETNRY SURGERY

Waterloo House Veterinary Surgery, Castle Farm, Castle St, Melbourne, **Derbyshire**, DE73 1DY, **ENGLAND**.
(T) 01332 863732.
Profile Medical Support. Ref:YH14969

WATERMAN, M & A

M & A Waterman, Bolham Rd, Tiverton, **Devon**, EX16 6SG, **ENGLAND**.
(T) 01884 257706.
Profile Saddlery Retailer. Ref:YH14970

WATERMAN, S

Miss S Waterman, Melbury Bubb Cottage, Nr Evershot, Dorchester, **Dorset**, DT2 0NQ, **ENGLAND**.
(T) 01935 83394.
Profile Supplies. Ref:YH14971

WATERSHIP DOWN STUD

Watership Down Stud, Sydmonton Hse, Burghclere, Newbury, **Berkshire**, RG20 9NJ, **ENGLAND**.
(T) 01635 278600 (F) 01635 278600.
Contact/s
Manager: Mr T Doherty
Profile Breeder. Ref:YH14972

WATERSTOCK HSE TRAINING CTRE

Waterstock House Training Centre, Wheatley, Oxford, **Oxfordshire**, OX33 1JS, **ENGLAND**.
(T) 01844 339460 (F) 01844 338512.
Contact/s
Owner: Mr J Walker
Profile Equestrian Centre. Ref:YH14973

WATERSTOCK HSE TRAINING CTRE

Waterstock House Training Centre, Waterstock, **Oxfordshire**, OX33 1JT, **ENGLAND**.
(T) 01844 339616 (F) 01844 338147.
Profile Club/Association. Ref:YH14974

WATES, A T A

Mr A T A Wates, Henfold Hse, Beare Green, Dorking, **Surrey**, RH5 4RW, **ENGLAND**.
(T) 01306 631324 (F) 01306 631794.
Profile Supplies. Ref:YH14975

WATFORD EQUESTRIAN CTRE

Watford Equestrian Centre, 37 Bucks Ave, Watford, **Hertfordshire**, WD1 4AR, **ENGLAND**.
(T) 01923 212670.
Profile Riding School, Saddlery Retailer.
Ref:YH14976

WATKINS VETNRY SURGERY

Watkins Veterinary Surgery, 2a Chescombe Rd, Yatton, **Somerset (North)**, BS19 4EQ, **ENGLAND**.
(T) 01934 833685.
Profile Medical Support. Ref:YH14977

WATKINS, GLYNN SYLVESTER

Glynn Sylvester Watkins DWCF, Worsleys Farm, Back Lane, Charnock Richard, Chorley, Preston, **Lancashire**, PR7 5JY, **ENGLAND**.
(T) 01257 452069.
Profile Farrier. Ref:YH14978

WATKINS, MICHAEL GEORGE

Michael George Watkins RSS, 7 Rock Hill, Chipping Norton, **Oxfordshire**, OX7 5BA, **ENGLAND**.
(T) 01608 642897.
Profile Farrier. Ref:YH14979

WATKINS, SIMON D

Simon D Watkins DWCF, Holly Tree Cottage, 11 Malmesbury Rd, Leigh, **Wiltshire**, SN6 6RH, **ENGLAND**.
(T) 01793 750003.
Profile Farrier. Ref:YH14980

WATKINSON, MATTHEW

Matthew Watkinson, 54 Balmoral Rd, Borrowash, Derby, **Derbyshire**, DE72 3FZ, **ENGLAND**.
(T) 01332 665272.
Contact/s
Owner: Mr M Watkinson
Profile Farrier. Ref:YH14981

WATSON TRAILERS

Watson Trailers, Hilltop Garage, 77A Gelderd Rd, Birstall, Batley, **Yorkshire (West)**, WF17 9LX, **ENGLAND**.
(T) 01924 472015 (F) 01924 472015.
Contact/s
Partner: Mr D Watson
Profile Transport/Horse Boxes. Ref:YH14982

WATSON, ERICA

Erica Watson, Tower Cl, Snowshill, Broadway, **Worcestershire**, WR12 7JU, **ENGLAND**.
(T) 01386 852410. Ref:YH14983

WATSON, EUAN MCINTOSH

Euan McIntosh Watson DWCF, 57 Oxford Rd, Linthorpe, Middlesbrough, **Cleveland**, TS5 5DZ, **ENGLAND**.
(T) 01642 813864.
Profile Farrier. Ref: YH14984

WATSON, F

Mr F Watson, Beacon Hill Farm, Sedgefield, Durham, **County Durham**, TS21 3HN, **ENGLAND**.
(T) 01740 620582.
Profile Trainer. Ref: YH14985

WATSON, GILLIAN

Gillian Watson, Hyde Farm West, Hyde Lane, Hyde End, Great Missenden, **Buckinghamshire**, HP16 0RF, **ENGLAND**.
(T) 01494 866023 (F) 01494 863758.
Contact/s
Owner: Ms G Watson
Profile Trainer. Ref: YH14986

WATSON, J A

J A Watson, Horse Pool Rd, Laugharne, Carmarthen, **Carmarthenshire**, SA33 4QL, **WALES**.
(T) 01994 427375. Ref: YH14987

WATSON, JOHN M

John M Watson DWCF, Lower Farm, Halse, Brackley, **Northamptonshire**, NN13 6DY, **ENGLAND**.
(T) 01280 702982.
Profile Farrier. Ref: YH14988

WATSON, KEITH R A

Keith R A Watson AWCF BI, Falconers Farm, Sincox Lane, Shipley, Horsham, **Sussex (West)**, RH13 8PT, **ENGLAND**.
(T) 01403 741446.
Profile Farrier. Ref: YH14989

WATSON, R J

R J Watson, Bridge Mills, Bradford Rd, Dewsbury, **Yorkshire (West)**, WF13 2HD, **ENGLAND**.
(T) 01924 466152.
Profile Transport/Horse Boxes. Ref: YH14990

WATSON, R W D & P

R W D & P Watson, Brynhafod Farm, Llanddewi Velfrey, Narberth, **Pembrokeshire**, SA67 7EG, **WALES**.
(T) 01834 860504 (F) 01834 860504.
Contact/s
Partner: Mrs P Watson
Profile Breeder. Ref: YH14991

WATSON, SIMON

Simon Watson DWCF, 26 Schofield Lane, Atherton, Manchester, **Manchester (Greater)**, M46 0QB, **ENGLAND**.
(T) 01942 876390.
Profile Farrier. Ref: YH14992

WATSON, T R

Mr T R Watson, Slade Barn Farm, Pinnock, Winchcombe, **Gloucestershire**, GL54 5AX, **ENGLAND**.
(T) 01242 603915 (F) 01242 604781
(M) 07774 188824
(E) kanlett.freeserve.co.uk.
Profile Trainer. Ref: YH14993

WATSON, W

W Watson, 9 Hillfoot Cres, Wishaw, **Lanarkshire (North)**, ML2 8TL, **SCOTLAND**.
(T) 01698 381568.
Profile Farrier. Ref: YH14994

WATSONIAN SQUIRE

Watsonian Squire Ltd, Unit 70 Northwick Business Ctre, Northwick Pk, Blockley, Moreton In Marsh, **Gloucestershire**, GL56 9RF, **ENGLAND**.
(T) 01386 701162 (F) 01386 700738.
Contact/s
Manager: Mr T Cox
Profile Transport/Horse Boxes. Ref: YH14995

WATSONS FARM FEEDS

Watsons Farm Feeds, 5 The Square, Clough, Downpatrick, **County Down**, BT30 8RR, **NORTHERN IRELAND**.
(T) 028 44811268.
Profile Supplies. Ref: YH14996

WATT FENCES

Watt Fences, Loos Rd, Catterick Garrison, **Yorkshire (North)**, DL9 4LQ, **ENGLAND**.
(T) 01748 835061.
Contact/s
Owner: Mr E Watt
Profile Supplies. Manufacturers of Jumps & Fences.
Ref: YH14997

WATT TO WEAR

Watt to Wear Ltd, Greenacres, Broomers Corner, Shipley, Horsham, **Sussex (West)**, RH13 8PX, **ENGLAND**.
(T) 01403 741205 (F) 01403 741405.
Profile Supplies. Ref: YH14998

WATT, C

C Watt, West Nerston Farm, Nerston Rd, East Kilbride, Glasgow, **Lanarkshire (South)**, G74 4NZ, **SCOTLAND**.
(T) 01355 224452.
Contact/s
Partner: Mr R Watt
Profile Stable/Livery. Ref: YH14999

WATT, R

R Watt, Benmore Lodge, By Lairg, Sutherland, **Highlands**, **SCOTLAND**.
(T) 01854 666316.
Profile Breeder. Ref: YH15000

WATTERS, R J

R J Watters, 24A Rakeeran Rd, Dromore, Omagh, **County Tyrone**, BT78 3HW, **NORTHERN IRELAND**.
(T) 028 82898483.
Contact/s
Owner: Mr R Watters
Profile Breeder. Ref: YH15001

WATTLEFIELD FARM STUD

Wattlefield Farm Stud, Wattlefield Hall, Wymondham, **Norfolk**, NR18 9JZ, **ENGLAND**.
(T) 01953 605738.
Profile Breeder. Ref: YH15002

WATTS & WATTS SADDLERY

Watts & Watts Saddlery, The Stable Yard, Holdenby Hse, Holdenby, Northampton, **Northamptonshire**, NN6 8DJ, **ENGLAND**.
(T) 01604 770799 (F) 01604 770799.
Contact/s
Owner: Mr S Watts (Q) BA(Hons)
Profile Riding Wear Retailer, Saddlery Retailer, Supplies. No.Staff: 2 Yr. Est: 1998
Opening Times
Sp: Open Mon - Sun 09:30. Closed Mon - Fri 17:00, Sun 16:00.
Su: Open Mon - Sun 09:30. Closed Mon - Fri 17:00, Sun 16:00.
Au: Open Mon - Sun 09:30. Closed Mon - Fri 17:00, Sun 16:00.
Wn: Open Mon - Sun 09:30. Closed Mon - Fri 17:00, Sun 16:00. Ref: YH15003

WATTS, ADAM

Adam Watts DWCF, 1 Lukes Lea, Marsworth, Tring, **Hertfordshire**, HP23 4NH, **ENGLAND**.
(T) 01296 662713.
Profile Farrier. Ref: YH15004

WATTS, GARY

Gary Watts DWCF, 4 St Marys Ave, Northchurch, **Hertfordshire**, HP4 3RW, **ENGLAND**.
(T) 07702 965937.
Profile Farrier. Ref: YH15005

WATTS, NEIL D

Neil D Watts BII, Broomhill Cottage, Rapisham, Evershot, **Dorset**, DT2 0PU, **ENGLAND**.
(T) 01935 83402.
Profile Farrier. Ref: YH15006

WATTS, S

S Watts, 54 Victoria Rd, Barking, **Essex**, IG11 8PY, **ENGLAND**.
(T) 020 82200038.
Profile Breeder. Ref: YH15007

WATTS, S E

S E Watts, Higher Spreacombe, Woolacombe, **Devon**, EX34 7HN, **ENGLAND**.
(T) 01271 870102.
Profile Stable/Livery. Ref: YH15008

WAUN FAWR FARM

Waun Fawr Farm, Rhos, Pontardawe, **Neath Port Talbot**, SA8 3HQ, **WALES**.
(T) 01792 830273.
Profile Stable/Livery. Ref: YH15009

WAUN FAWR FARM

Waun Fawr Farm, Primrose Lane, Rhos, Pontardawe, Swansea, **Swansea**, SA8 3EU, **WALES**.
(T) 01792 830273.
Contact/s
Owner: Miss F Davies
Profile Stable/Livery. Ref: YH15010

WAVERLEY EQUESTRIAN CTRE

Waverley Equestrian Centre, Coventry Rd, Cubbington, Leamington Spa, **Warwickshire**, CV32 7UJ, **ENGLAND**.
(T) 01926 422876 (F) 01926 422849
Affiliated Bodies HPA.
Contact/s
For Bookings: Ms J Tweedie
(E) foxhunting@stoneleighpark.co.uk
Profile Arena, Equestrian Centre, Riding School, Riding Wear Retailer, Saddlery Retailer, Supplies. Polo School. Ref: YH15011

WAXWING STUD

Waxwing Stud, Waxwing Farm, Balgonar, Saline, **Fife**, KY12 9TA, **SCOTLAND**.
(T) 01383 851732.
Contact/s
Owner: Mr D Blair
Profile Breeder. Ref: YH15012

WAY, LAURA

Laura Way, 31 Cable St, Formby, Liverpool, **Merseyside**, L37 3LU, **ENGLAND**.
(T) 01704 834488.
Contact/s
Owner: Mrs L Way
Profile Trainer. Ref: YH15013

WAY, R E & G B

R E & G B Way, Brettons, Burrough Green, Newmarket, **Suffolk**, CB8 9NA, **ENGLAND**.
(T) 01638 507217 (F) 01638 508058
(E) waybks@msn.com.
Profile Supplies. Ref: YH15014

WAYLAND BLOOD STOCK

Wayland Blood Stock, Malthouse Farm, Cods Hill, Beenham, Reading, **Berkshire**, RG7 5QH, **ENGLAND**.
(T) 0118 9713377 (F) 0118 9323237.
Profile Blood Stock Agency. Ref: YH15015

WAYLANDS EQUESTRIAN CTRE

Waylands Equestrian Centre, Rawlings Lane, Seer Green, Beaconsfield, **Buckinghamshire**, HP9 2RQ, **ENGLAND**.
(T) 01494 872301.
Profile Riding School, Stable/Livery. Ref: YH15016

WAYSIDE RIDING STABLES

Wayside Riding Stables, Fifield Rd, Fifield, Maidenhead, **Berkshire**, SL6 2PG, **ENGLAND**.
(T) 01628 777735.
Contact/s
Manager: Mrs P Grimster Ref: YH15017

WEALDEN COLLEGE

Wealden College, 2 Quarry View, Whitehill Rd, Crowborough, **Sussex (East)**, TN6 1JT, **ENGLAND**.
(T) 01892 655195.
Profile Equestrian Centre. Ref: YH15018

WEALDEN IRON CRAFTS

Wealden Iron Crafts, The Forge, High St, Burwash, Etchingham, **Sussex (East)**, TN19 7EP, **ENGLAND**.
(T) 01435 883422 (F) 01435 883422.
Contact/s
Owner: Mr D Hedges
Profile Blacksmith. Ref: YH15019

WEALDEN SADDLERY

Wealden Saddlery, The Saddlery Stores, High St, Staplehurst, Tonbridge, **Kent**, TN12 0AB, **ENGLAND**.
(T) 01580 891423 (F) 01580 891423
Affiliated Bodies SMS.
Contact/s
Owner: Mr J Lloyd (Q) Master Saddler, Saddle Fitter
Profile Riding Wear Retailer, Saddlery Retailer, Supplies. No.Staff: 3 Yr. Est: 1970
Ref: YH15020

WEALDOWN FINE ARTS PRINTS

Wealdown Fine Arts Prints Ltd, Mayflower Hse, Alfriston, Polegate, **Sussex (East)**, BN26 5QT, **ENGLAND**.
(T) 01323 870343
(E) wealdon@aol.com. Ref: YH15021

WEATHERALL SURFACES

Weatherall Surfaces Ltd, Beechgrove Hall, Park Lane, Manby, Louth, **Lincolnshire**, LN11 8UF, **ENGLAND**.
(T) 01507 828991. Ref: YH15022

WEATHERBEETA

Weatherbeeta Ltd, 7 Riverside, Tramway Est, Banbury, **Oxfordshire**, OX16 5RL, **ENGLAND**.
(T) 01295 268123 **(F)** 01295 269036
(E) sales@weatherbeeta.com
(W) www.weatherbeeta.com.
Contact/s
Sales Manager: Michael Mullavey
Profile Supplies. Wholesalers. **Ref: YH15023**

WEATHERBYS

Weatherbys Group Ltd, Sanders Rd, Finedon Rd Ind Est, Wellingborough, **Northamptonshire**, NN8 4BX, **ENGLAND**.
(T) 01933 440077 **(F)** 01933 440807
(W) www.weatherbys-group.com
Affiliated Bodies BHRB.
Contact/s
Chairman: Mr J Weatherby
Profile Club/Association.
Weatherbys has been an integral part of British racing since 1770. Today, they administer racing under contract to the British Horseracing Board and have for over 200 years published the General Stud Book. They are a registered Bank and provide a variety of financial and insurance services. Yr. Est: 1770
Opening Times
Sp: Open Mon - Fri 09:00. Closed Mon - Fri 17:00.
Su: Open Mon - Fri 09:00. Closed Mon - Fri 17:00.
Au: Open Mon - Fri 09:00. Closed Mon - Fri 17:00.
Wn: Open Mon - Fri 09:00. Closed Mon - Fri 17:00.
Closed weekends **Ref: YH15024**

WEATHERBYS IRELAND

Weatherbys Ireland, Tara Court, Dublin Rd, Naas, **County Kildare**, **IRELAND**.
(T) 045 879979 **(F)** 045 879691
(E) weatherbysire@eircom.net
(W) www.weatherbys-group.com.
Profile Club/Association.
Stud book authority for Ireland (thoroughbreds) and a range of other bloodstock related services.
Ref: YH15025

WEATHERILL, P S

Mr P S Weatherill, 7 Heywood Rd, Harrogate, **Yorkshire (North)**, HG2 0LU, **ENGLAND**.
(T) 01423 509801.
Profile Trainer. **Ref: YH15026**

WEAVER BROS

Weaver Bros, P O Box 188, Redhill, **Surrey**, RH1 5FX, **ENGLAND**.
(T) 01293 775885 **(F)** 01293 822386.
Profile Club/Association. **Ref: YH15027**

WEBB WEAR

Webb Wear, Annebille Gaybrook, Mullingar, **County Westmeath**, **IRELAND**.
(T) 044 49153.
Profile Supplies. **Ref: YH15028**

WEBB, PHILIP JAMES

Philip James Webb DWCF, 31 Wharf Rd, Kilnhurst, Mexborough, **Yorkshire (South)**, S64 5SY, **ENGLAND**.
(T) 01709 587248.
Profile Farrier. **Ref: YH15029**

WEBB, STEPHEN EDWARD

Stephen Edward Webb RSS, Wren Cottage, 17 Caunsall Rd, Cookley, Kidderminster, **Worcestershire**, DY11 5YB, **ENGLAND**.
(T) 01562 851193.
Profile Farrier. **Ref: YH15030**

WEBB, T M

T M Webb, Tanyard Farm, Hadlow Rd, Tonbridge, **Kent**, TN9 1PD, **ENGLAND**.
(T) 01732 358999.
Profile Supplies. **Ref: YH15031**

WEBB, TREVOR MARK

Trevor Mark Webb DWCF, 50 Blenheim Gardens, Gr, Wantage, **Oxfordshire**, OX12 0NP, **ENGLAND**.
(T) 01235 765307.
Profile Farrier. **Ref: YH15032**

WEBBER BROS

Webber Bros, The Forge, Morchard Bishop, Crediton, **Devon**, EX17 6SE, **ENGLAND**.
(T) 01363 877525.
Contact/s
Partner: Mr M Webber
Profile Blacksmith. **Ref: YH15033**

WEBBER, BRIAN

Brian Webber, Lanjeth Farm, High St, St Austell, **Cornwall**, PL26 7TN, **ENGLAND**.
(T) 01726 68438.
Profile Farrier. **Ref: YH15034**

WEBBS HILL RIDING SCHOOL

Webbs Hill Riding School, Webbs Hill Farm, Egford Lane, Frome, **Somerset**, BA11 3JL, **ENGLAND**.
(T) 01373 473429.
Profile Riding School. **Ref: YH15035**

WEBBWEAR

Webbwear/Lakeview Stables, Lakeview Stables, Lackan, Multyfarnham, **County Westmeath**, **IRELAND**.
(T) 044 71970
(E) webbwear@oceanfree.net.
Contact/s
General Manager: Ms M Johnston
Profile Saddlery Retailer, Stable/Livery, Supplies.
Tack repair service No.Staff: 2 Yr. Est: 1990
Opening Times
Telephone for further information **Ref: YH15036**

WEBS RIDING STABLES

Webs Riding Stables, Brookview, Hurst Lane, Egham, **Surrey**, TW20 8QJ, **ENGLAND**.
(T) 01344 842011.
Contact/s
Owner: Mrs W Baker **Ref: YH15037**

WEBSTER, J

J Webster, New Hse, Clockhouse Lane, Nutley, Uckfield, **Sussex (East)**, TN22 3NU, **ENGLAND**.
(T) 01825 712500.
Profile Farrier, Trainer. **Ref: YH15038**

WEBSTER, J & M

J & M Webster, The Anchor Farm, Anchor, Newcastle On Clun, Craven Arms, **Shropshire**, SY7 8PR, **ENGLAND**.
(T) 01686 670932.
Profile Breeder. **Ref: YH15039**

WEBSTER, J R

J R Webster, 2 Hailsham Ave, Newcastle-upon-Tyne, **Tyne and Wear**, NE12 8HJ, **ENGLAND**.
(T) 0191 2663080.
Contact/s
Owner: Mr B Webster
Profile Riding Wear Retailer, Saddlery Retailer.
Ref: YH15040

WEBSTER, MICHAEL H

Michael H Webster RSS, The Old Pinfold Cottage, Corkhill Lane, Normanton, Southwell, **Nottinghamshire**, NG25 0PR, **ENGLAND**.
(T) 01636 814872.
Profile Farrier. **Ref: YH15041**

WEBSTER, SHEUMAIS A

Sheumais A Webster DWCF, Court Cottage, North Bovey, Newton Abbott, **Devon**, TQ13 8RA, **ENGLAND**.
(T) 01647 440098.
Profile Farrier. **Ref: YH15042**

WEDDING CARRIAGE HIRE

Wedding Carriage Hire, Fairways, 2 Charlton, Charlton, Telford, **Shropshire**, TF6 5EU, **ENGLAND**.
(T) 01952 740270.
Contact/s
Owner: Mrs A Stanford **Ref: YH15043**

WEDDING CARRIAGES

Wedding Carriages, Thorpe Lane, Crow Pk, South Hykeham, Lincoln, **Lincolnshire**, LN6 9NN, **ENGLAND**.
(T) 01522 697616 **(F)** 01522 697616.
Contact/s
Owner: Mr D Harbord **Ref: YH15044**

WEEDON, C

Mr C Weedon, Coombelands, Coombelands Lane, Pulborough, **Sussex (West)**, RH20 1BP, **ENGLAND**.
(T) 01428 683344
(M) 07831 115009.
Profile Trainer. **Ref: YH15045**

WEEDON, M J

M J Weedon, North Bank Farm, Highfield, Fleet Rd, Fleet, Weymouth, **Dorset**, DT3 4EB, **ENGLAND**.
(T) 01305 776822.
Contact/s
Owner: Mr M Weedon
Profile Trainer. **Ref: YH15046**

WEEFORD STABLES

Weeford Stables, Off Dog Lane, Weeford, Lichfield, **Staffordshire**, WS14 0PP, **ENGLAND**.
(T) 01543 480292. **Ref: YH15047**

WEELSBY PARK RIDING SCHOOL

Weelsby Park Riding School, Weelsby Rd, Grimsby, **Lincolnshire (North East)**, DN32 8PL, **ENGLAND**.
(T) 01472 355562 **(F)** 01472 344627.
Contact/s
Owner: Mrs G Woodhead **Ref: YH15048**

WEHRLE, MARCUS E

Marcus E Wehrle DWCF, Killarney Cottage, Westharting, **Hampshire**, GU31 5PF, **ENGLAND**.
(T) 07785 551192.
Profile Farrier. **Ref: YH15049**

WEIGHT MASTER TRAILERS

Weight Master Trailers, Nessfield Garage, Adlingfleet Rd, Garthorpe, Scunthorpe, **Lincolnshire (North)**, DN17 4SB, **ENGLAND**.
(T) 01724 798320 **(F)** 01724 798320.
Contact/s
Partner: Mr C Wilkinson
Profile Transport/Horse Boxes. **Ref: YH15050**

WEIR

Weir & Co, 34-38 Dromore St, Ballynahinch, **County Down**, BT24 8AS, **NORTHERN IRELAND**.
(T) 028 97562223.
Contact/s
Owner: Geoffrey Weir
Profile Supplies.
Miller & General Merchants.
Opening Times
Sp: Open Mon - Sat 09:00. Closed Mon - Fri 17:30, Sat 12:00.
Su: Open Mon - Sat 09:00. Closed Mon - Fri 17:30, Sat 12:00.
Au: Open Mon - Sat 09:00. Closed Mon - Fri 17:30, Sat 12:00.
Wn: Open Mon - Sat 09:00. Closed Mon - Fri 17:30, Sat 12:00.
Closed Sundays **Ref: YH15051**

WEIR, D

Mr D Weir, Hillhouse, Sandilands, **Lanarkshire (South)**, ML11 9TX, **SCOTLAND**.
(T) 01555 88661.
Profile Breeder. **Ref: YH15052**

WEIR, J

J Weir, The Smiddy, 332 Eaglesham Rd, Jackton, East Kilbride, **Lanarkshire (South)**, G75 8RW, **SCOTLAND**.
(T) 01355 302771.
Profile Farrier. **Ref: YH15053**

WEIR, J C (HON)

Hon Mrs J C Weir, Kilmany, Cupar, **Fife**, KY15 4QW, **SCOTLAND**.
(T) 01826 24753.
Profile Supplies. **Ref: YH15054**

WEIR, M

M Weir, Monksmoor Farm, Bittaford, Ivybridge, **Devon**, PL21 0HE, **ENGLAND**.
(T) 01752 892478.
Profile Farrier. **Ref: YH15055**

WEIR, W S

W S Weir, Gibson Pl, Peebles, **Scottish Borders**, EH45 8JY, **SCOTLAND**.
(T) 01721 720198.
Profile Blacksmith. **Ref: YH15056**

WELBAC CHIROPRACTIC CLINIC

Welbac Chiropractic Clinic, 46 Lymington Rd, New Milton, **Hampshire**, BH25 6PY, **ENGLAND**.
(T) 01425 620177.
Profile Medical Support. **Ref: YH15057**

WELCH, ANDY

Andy Welch, 112 Annesley Rd, Hucknall, Nottingham, **Nottinghamshire**, NG15 7DD, **ENGLAND**.
(T) 0115 9640412.
Contact/s
Owner: Mr A Welch
Profile Farrier. **Ref: YH15058**

WELCH, D G

Mr D G Welch, 16 Kingsley Rd, Harrogate, **Yorkshire (North)**, HG1 4RA, **ENGLAND**.
(T) 01423 886242.
Profile Breeder. **Ref: YH15059**

WELCH, FRED

Mr Fred Welch, Ellis Farm, Sherfield-on-Loddon, Hook, **Hampshire**, RG27 0HF, **ENGLAND**.

(T) 01256 882255 **(F)** 01256 880031.
Profile Breeder. **Ref: YH15060**

WELD, D K
D K Weld, Rosewell Hse, Curragh, **County Kildare**, **IRELAND**.
(T) 045 441273 **(F)** 045 441119.
Contact/s
Trainer: Mr D Weld
(E) dkweld@kildarehorse.ie
Profile Trainer. **Ref: YH15061**

WELDING, A M
A M Welding, Unit K6 Clyde Workshops, Fullarton Rd, Glasgow East Investment Pk, Glasgow, **Glasgow (City of)**, G32 8YL, **SCOTLAND**.
(T) 0141 6410854.
Profile Blacksmith. **Ref: YH15062**

WELDING, P C
P C Welding, Unit 5, South Parks Ind Est, Peebles, **Scottish Borders**, EH45 9ED, **SCOTLAND**.
(T) 01721 724689 **(F)** 01721 724689.
Contact/s
Owner: Mr B Pichlmayer
Profile Blacksmith. **Ref: YH15063**

WELDMECH SERVICES
Weldmech Services, Dungrianach, Taynuilt, **Argyll and Bute**, PA35 1HW, **SCOTLAND**.
(T) 01866 822433.
Profile Blacksmith. **Ref: YH15064**

WELLCROFT STUD
Wellcroft Stud, Sallyfield Lane, Stanton, Ashbourne, **Derbyshire**, DE6 2DA, **ENGLAND**.
(T) 01335 324594.
Contact/s
Stud Groom: Mrs V Brown
Profile Breeder, Stable/Livery. **Ref: YH15065**

WELLEP EQUESTRIAN INT
Wellep Equestrian International (UK) Ltd, Church Farm, Oborne, Sherborne, **Dorset**, DT9 4LA, **ENGLAND**.
(T) 01935 816767. **Ref: YH15066**

WELLER, S F
S F Weller, 2 Worthing Rd, Dial Post, Horsham, **Sussex (West)**, RH13 8NQ, **ENGLAND**.
(T) 01403 710168.
Contact/s
Owner: Mr S Weller
Profile Farrier. **Ref: YH15067**

WELLFAIR, M
M Wellfair DWCF, Orchard Farm, Bentham, Cheltenham, **Gloucestershire**, GL51 5TZ, **ENGLAND**.
(T) 01452 864571
(M) 07836 593753.
Profile Farrier. **Ref: YH15068**

WELLFIELD TREKKING CTRE
Wellfield Trekking Centre, Hillside Farm, Staintondale, Scarborough, **Yorkshire (North)**, YO13 0AY, **ENGLAND**.
(T) 01723 870182.
Contact/s
Owner: Mr M Stafford
Profile Riding School. **Ref: YH15069**

WELLGATE SADDLERY
Wellgate Saddlery, 22 Wellgate, Lanark, **Lanarkshire (South)**, ML11 9DT, **SCOTLAND**.
(T) 01555 664733.
Contact/s
Owner: Ms E Miatchell
Profile Saddlery Retailer. **Ref: YH15070**

WELLGROVE FARM STABLES
Wellgrove Farm Stables, Wellgrove Stables, Kings Toll Rd, Pembury, Tunbridge Wells, **Kent**, TN2 4BE, **ENGLAND**.
(T) 01892 822881 **(F)** 01892 723494.
Contact/s
Owner: Mrs S Whittaker **Ref: YH15071**

WELLING, JASON M
Jason M Welling DWCF, 12 Highfield Cl, Foulsham, Dereham, **Norfolk**, NR20 5SW, **ENGLAND**.
(T) 01362 684227
(M) 07778 780064.
Profile Farrier. **Ref: YH15072**

WELLINGTON CARRIAGE
Wellington Carriage Co, Long Lane, Telford, **Shropshire**, TF6 6HD, **ENGLAND**.
(T) 01952 242495.
Contact/s
Owner: Mr P Holder **Ref: YH15073**

WELLINGTON PET GARDEN
Wellington Pet Garden & Farm Store, 10 High St, Wellington, **Somerset**, TA21 8RA, **ENGLAND**.
(T) 01823 662914 **(F)** 01823 662914.
Profile Supplies. **Ref: YH15074**

WELLINGTON RIDING
Wellington Riding Ltd, Basingstoke Rd, Heckfield, Hook, **Hampshire**, RG27 0LJ, **ENGLAND**.
(T) 0118 9326308 **(F)** 0118 9326661
(E) welly@riding.demon.co.uk
(W) www.wellington-riding.co.uk
Affiliated Bodies ABRS, BHS.
Contact/s
Chief Instructor: Ms P Meir **(Q)** BHS 1
Profile Equestrian Centre, Holidays, Riding Club, Riding School, Riding Wear Retailer, Saddlery Retailer, Stable/Livery, Trainer. No.Staff: 50
Yr. Est: 1973 C.Size: 400 Acres
Opening Times
Sp: Open 09:00. Closed 21:00.
Su: Open 09:00. Closed 21:00.
Au: Open 09:00. Closed 21:00.
Wn: Open 09:00. Closed 21:00. **Ref: YH15075**

WELLMAN, M
Miss M Wellman, Flat 9 The Haughs, School Lane, Upton-upon-Severn, **Worcestershire**, WR8 0LE, **ENGLAND**.
(T) 01684 592140 **(F)** 01684 592140.
Profile Trainer. **Ref: YH15076**

WELLOW PK
Wellow Park Stables & Saddlery, Rufford Lane, Wellow, Newark, **Nottinghamshire**, NG22 0EQ, **ENGLAND**.
(T) 01623 861040 **(F)** 01623 835292.
Contact/s
Owner: Mrs M Willett
Profile Riding School, Saddlery Retailer, Stable/Livery, Track/Course, Trainer. **Ref: YH15077**

WELLOW TREKKING CTRE
Wellow Trekking Centre, Little Horse Croft Farm, Wellow, Bath, **Bath & Somerset (North East)**, BA2 8QE, **ENGLAND**.
(T) 01225 834376 **(F)** 01225 833282.
Contact/s
Owner: Mr F Shellerd
Profile Stable/Livery. **Ref: YH15078**

WELLS AGRICULTURAL
Wells Agricultural Ltd, Granary Hse, Melton Rd, Edwalton, **Nottinghamshire**, NG12 4DR, **ENGLAND**.
(T) 0115 9231822.
Profile Supplies. **Ref: YH15079**

WELLS PARK FARM
Wells Park Farm, Shelford Rd, Whittlesford, **Cambridgeshire**, CB2 4PG, **ENGLAND**.
(T) 01223 833186.
Profile Breeder. **Ref: YH15080**

WELLS, A H MACTAGGART
Mr A H MacTaggart Wells, Denholm, Hawick, **Scottish Borders**, TD9 8TD, **SCOTLAND**.
(T) 01450 870060.
Profile Supplies. **Ref: YH15081**

WELLS, E
Mr E Wells, 17 Lennox Gardens, Linlithgow, **Lothian (West)**, EH49 7PZ, **SCOTLAND**.
(T) 01506 848122. **Ref: YH15082**

WELLS, F & H
F & H Wells, Nether Blainslie, Galashiels, **Scottish Borders**, TD1 2PR, **SCOTLAND**.
(T) 01896 86265.
Profile Supplies. **Ref: YH15083**

WELLS, G D
G D Wells AWCF, Westland Cottage, Fittleworth Lane, Bedham, Wisborough Green, **Sussex (West)**, RH14 0HD, **ENGLAND**.
(T) 01403 700317.
Profile Farrier. **Ref: YH15084**

WELLS, J R
J R Wells, Hookhouse Farm, Outwood, Redhill, **Surrey**, RH1 5PW, **ENGLAND**.
(T) 01342 842168.
Contact/s
Partner: Mrs J Wells
Profile Blacksmith. **Ref: YH15085**

WELLS, L
L Wells, Pallingham Manor Farm, Wisborough Green, Billingshurst, **Sussex (West)**, RH14 0EZ, **ENGLAND**.
(T) 01403 700119 **(F)** 01403 700899.
Contact/s
Owner: Mrs C Zetter-Wales
Profile Trainer. **Ref: YH15086**

WELLSFIELD FARM & LIVERY
Wellsfield Farm & Livery, Wellsfield Farm, Denny, **Stirling**, FK6 6QZ, **SCOTLAND**.
(T) 01324 825044.
Contact/s
Owner: Mr H Harris **Ref: YH15087**

WELLSMAN, DAVID W
David W Wellsman DWCF, 4 Austin Cl, Sittingbourne, **Kent**, ME10 2RU, **ENGLAND**.
(T) 01795 420835.
Profile Farrier. **Ref: YH15088**

WELLWOOD RIDING CTRE
Wellwood Riding Centre, 6 Harperland, Dundonald, Kilmarnock, **Ayrshire (East)**, KA2 9BY, **SCOTLAND**.
(T) 01563 850481. **Ref: YH15089**

WELSH COLLEGE OF HORTICULTURE
Welsh College of Horticulture (The), Northop, Mold, **Flintshire**, CH7 6AA, **WALES**.
(T) 01352 841000 **(F)** 01352 841031.
Profile College. **Ref: YH15090**

WELSH EQUITATION CTRE
Welsh Equitation Centre (The), Pantyrathro Manor, Llangain, Carmarthen, **Carmarthenshire**, SA33 5AJ, **WALES**.
(T) 01267 241226 **(F)** 01267 241630.
Contact/s
Owner: Delyth Morgan
Profile Riding School, Stable/Livery. **Ref: YH15091**

WELSH INS OF RURAL STUDIES
Welsh Institute of Rural Studies, Llanbadarn Fawr, Aberystwyth, **Ceredigion**, SY23 3AL, **WALES**.
(T) 01970 624471 **(F)** 01970 611264.
Profile Equestrian Centre. **Ref: YH15092**

WELSH LONG DISTANCE
Welsh Long Distance Riding Centre, The Pine Lodge Stables, Rhydargaeau, Carmarthen, **Carmarthenshire**, SA32 7JL, **WALES**.
(T) 01267 2533250.
Contact/s
Owner: Mrs J Lloyd-Rogers
Profile Horse/Rider Accom. **Ref: YH15093**

WELSH PART-BRED
Welsh Part-Bred Horse Group, Bromsden Farm Stud, Henley-on-Thames, **Oxfordshire**, RG9 4RG, **ENGLAND**.
(T) 01491 628785 **(F)** 01491 628785
(E) welshpartbredhorse@btinternet.com
(W) www.welshpartbredhorse.org.uk.
Contact/s
Secretary: Mrs L Vintcent
(E) hon-secretary@welshpartbredhorses.org.uk
Profile Club/Association. **Ref: YH15094**

WELSH PONY AND COB SOCIETY
Welsh Pony and Cob Society, 6 Chalybeate St, Aberystwyth, **Ceredigion**, SW13 1HP, **WALES**.
(T) 01970 617501 **(F)** 01970 625401
(W) www.wpcs.uk.com.
Contact/s
Secretary: Mrs L Spenser
(E) secretary@wpcs.uk.com
Profile Club/Association.
Officially registers Welsh Ponies and Welsh Cobs.
Yr. Est: 1901
Opening Times
Sp: Open Mon - Fri 09:00. Closed Mon - Fri 17:00.
Su: Open Mon - Fri 09:00. Closed Mon - Fri 17:00.
Au: Open Mon - Fri 09:00. Closed Mon - Fri 17:00.
Wn: Open Mon - Fri 09:00. Closed Mon - Fri 17:00.
Ref: YH15095

WELSH RIDING & TREKKING ASS
Welsh Riding & Trekking Association, 118 Beacons Pk, Brecon, **Powys**, CF14 5GG, **WALES**.
(T) 01874 622321.
Profile Club/Association. **Ref: YH15096**

WELSH RIDING COAT
Welsh Riding Coat Co, G W Bonser Distribution Ltd, Field Hse, Black Rock, Abergavenny, **Monmouthshire**, NP7 0LW, **WALES**.
(T) 01873 830031 **(F)** 01873 831748.
Profile Supplies. **Ref: YH15097**

A-Z of COMPANIES

WELSH, JOSEPH
Joseph Welsh RSS, 56 Chestnut Drive, Congleton, **Cheshire**, CW12 4UB, **ENGLAND**.
(T) 01260 277139.
Profile Farrier. **Ref: YH15098**

WELTON & DISTRICT RIDING CLUB
Welton & District Riding Club, Hilltop Bungalow, Fillingham, Gainsborough, **Lincolnshire**, DN21 5BU, **ENGLAND**.
(T) 01427 668419.
Contact/s
Chairman: Mrs G Farmery
Profile Club/Association, Riding Club. **Ref: YH15099**

WELTON NORTHSEN
Welton Northsen, 3 Schneider Cl, Felixstowe, **Suffolk**, IP11 3SS, **ENGLAND**.
(T) 01394 613288.
Contact/s
Manageress: Ms A Ranson
Profile Transport/Horse Boxes. **Ref: YH15100**

WELWYN EQUESTRIAN
Welwyn Equestrian Centre, Pottersheath Rd, Welwyn, **Hertfordshire**, AL6 9SZ, **ENGLAND**.
(T) 01438 815491 **(F)** 01438 813821
Affiliated Bodies BSJA.
Contact/s
Assistant: Miss T Ivory **(Q)** BHSAI
Profile Riding School, Stable/Livery.
Childrens Riding School. Part and DIY livery available, prices and details on request. No.Staff: 8
Yr. Est: 1971 C.Size: 60 Acres
Opening Times
Telephone for further information, there is an answer phone **Ref: YH15101**

WEMBLEY RIDING CLUB
Wembley Riding Club, 4 Greenhill Court, Beechfield Rd, Hemel Hempstead, **Hertfordshire**, HP1 1PJ, **ENGLAND**.
(T) 01442 49437.
Profile Club/Association, Riding Club. **Ref: YH15102**

WEMBURY BAY RIDING SCHOOL
Wembury Bay Riding School & Livery Centre, 83 Church Rd, Wembury, Plymouth, **Devon**, PL9 0JW, **ENGLAND**.
(T) 01752 862676
Affiliated Bodies ABRS.
Profile Equestrian Centre, Riding School, Stable/Livery. No.Staff: 5 Yr. Est: 1973
C.Size: 32 Acres
Opening Times
Sp: Open 08:30. Closed 16:00.
Su: Open 08:30. Closed 17:00.
Au: Open 08:30. Closed 16:00.
Wn: Open 08:30. Closed 16:00. **Ref: YH15103**

WENDALS HERBS
Wendals Herbs Ltd, Westfield Hse, Terrington St Clement, King's Lynn, **Norfolk**, PE34 4EX, **ENGLAND**.
(T) 01945 780880
(E) info@wendals.com.
Contact/s
Owner: Mr T Jennings
Profile Medical Support. **Ref: YH15104**

WENDLEBURY GATE STABLES
Wendlebury Gate Stables, Merton Grounds, Merton, Bicester, **Oxfordshire**, OX6 0NS, **ENGLAND**.
(T) 01869 252224 **(F)** 01869 320620.
Contact/s
Owner: Miss H Offord **Ref: YH15105**

WENDOVER STABLES
Wendover Stables, Burgh Heath Rd, Epsom, **Surrey**, KT17 4LX, **ENGLAND**.
(T) 01372 748505 **(F)** 01372 740530
(M) 07710 363210.
Profile Trainer. **Ref: YH15106**

WENDRON RAM BUCK FAIR
Wendron Ram Buck Fair, South Boderwennack, Wendron, Helston, **Cornwall**, TR13 0LT, **ENGLAND**.
(T) 01326 563767
(E) ian_munday@compuserve.com.
Contact/s
Hon Secretary: Lt Cdr I Munday
Profile Club/Association. **Ref: YH15107**

WENSLEY, D C
D C Wensley, The Cary Chambers, Palk St, Torquay, **Devon**, TQ2 5EL, **ENGLAND**.
(T) 01803 214410 **(F)** 01803 214410.
Contact/s
Owner: Mr D Wensley **Ref: YH15108**

WENSUM VALLEY VETNRY SURG
Wensum Valley Veterinary Surgery, The Old Doctors Surgery, 14 Queens Rd, Fakenham, **Norfolk**, NR21 8DB, **ENGLAND**.
(T) 01328 864444.
Profile Medical Support. **Ref: YH15109**

WENTLOOG, PETERSTONE
Peterstone Wentloog, Glanyr Afon, Peterstone, Wentloog, Rumney, Cardiff, **Glamorgan (Vale of)**, CF3 2TN, **WALES**.
(T) 01633 680535.
Contact/s
Secretary: Mrs G Stokes **Ref: YH15110**

WENTWORTH FORGE
Wentworth Forge, Old Building Yard, Cortworth Lane, Wentworth, Rotherham, **Yorkshire (South)**, S62 7SB, **ENGLAND**.
(T) 01226 749234.
Contact/s
Partner: Mrs J Gregory
Profile Blacksmith. **Ref: YH15111**

WERN EQUESTRIAN SERVICES
Wern Equestrian Services, Gilfachrheda, New Quay, **Ceredigion**, SA45 9ST, **WALES**.
(T) 01545 580961.
Contact/s
Owner: Miss H Cook
Profile Supplies. **Ref: YH15112**

WERN FRANK STUD
Wern Frank Stud, East Lockinge, Wantage, **Oxfordshire**, OX12 8QY, **ENGLAND**.
(T) 01235 821064.
Profile Breeder. **Ref: YH15113**

WERN RIDING CTRE
Wern Riding Centre, Hillside, Llangattock, Crickhowell, **Powys**, NP8 1LG, **WALES**.
(T) 01873 810899. **Ref: YH15114**

WERNETH LOW RIDING CLUB
Werneth Low Riding Club, Bowlacre Farm, Bowlacre Rd, Gee Cross, Hyde, **Cheshire**, SK14 5ES, **ENGLAND**.
(T) 0161 3688903.
Profile Club/Association, Riding Club. **Ref: YH15115**

WESCOMB SADDLERY
Wescomb Saddlery, Fields Hse, The Lane, Lower Strensham, **Worcestershire**, WR8 9LN, **ENGLAND**.
(T) 01386 750900 **(F)** 01386 750900.
Profile Saddlery Retailer. **Ref: YH15116**

WESLEY, SOPHIE
Sophie Wesley, Blackmires Farm, Silverstone, Towcester, **Northamptonshire**, NN12 8UZ, **ENGLAND**.
(T) 01327 857280.
Profile Trainer. **Ref: YH15117**

WESSEX FARM & EQUI-PRODUCTS
Wessex Farm & Equi-Products Ltd, Unit A1/Ringwood Trading Est, New St, Ringwood, **Hampshire**, BH24 3BA, **ENGLAND**.
(T) 01425 474455 **(F)** 01425 474446.
Profile Saddlery Retailer. **Ref: YH15118**

WESSEX MACHINERY
Wessex Machinery, Trading Est, Oakhanger Rd, Bordon, **Hampshire**, GU35 9HH, **ENGLAND**.
(T) 01420 478111.
Contact/s
Partner: Mr S James
Profile Supplies. **Ref: YH15119**

WESSEX RIDING CLUB
Wessex Riding Club, Lilac Hse, Old Church Rd, Axbridge, **Somerset**, BS26 2BE, **ENGLAND**.
(T) 01934 732562.
Contact/s
Chairman: Ms G Leahy
Profile Club/Association, Riding Club. **Ref: YH15120**

WESSEX SADDLERY
Wessex Saddlery, Manor Farm, Downhead, Shepton Mallet, **Somerset**, BA4 4LG, **ENGLAND**.
(T) 01749 880446.
Contact/s
Owner: Mrs C Yeomans **Ref: YH15121**

WESSEX TRAILERS
Wessex Trailers, Waddock Cross Garage, Tincleton, Dorchester, **Dorset**, DT2 8QR, **ENGLAND**.
(T) 01929 462534.
Profile Transport/Horse Boxes. **Ref: YH15122**

WEST ANGLIA CLGE
College of West Anglia (The), Landbeach Rd, Milton, **Cambridgeshire**, CB4 6DB, **ENGLAND**.
(T) 01223 860701 **(F)** 01223 860262
(E) enquiries@col-westanglia.ac.uk
(W) www.col-westanglia.ac.uk.
Contact/s
For Bookings: Ms K Dean
Profile Riding School, Stable/Livery.
Training to BTEC level and BHS Riding & Road Safety available. No.Staff: 10 Yr. Est: 1986
C.Size: 5 Acres
Opening Times
Sp: Open Mon - Fri 09:00. Closed Mon - Fri 17:00.
Au: Open Mon - Fri 09:00. Closed Mon - Fri 17:00.
Wn: Open Mon - Fri 09:00. Closed Mon - Fri 17:00.
Closed weekends and through the summer
Ref: YH15123

WEST ANSTEY FARM EXMOOR
West Anstey Farm Exmoor, Waddicombe, Dulverton, **Somerset**, TA22 9RY, **ENGLAND**.
(T) 01398 341354.
Contact/s
Owner: Mrs D Bassett
Profile Farrier. **Ref: YH15124**

WEST ASHTON STUD
West Ashton Stud, Bratton Rd, West Ashton, Trowbridge, **Wiltshire**, BA14 6AX, **ENGLAND**.
(T) 01225 753080 **(F)** 01225 754607.
Profile Breeder. **Ref: YH15125**

WEST AUCKLAND COUNTRY STORE
West Auckland Country Store, 4-6 Staindrop Rd, West Auckland, Bishop Auckland, **County Durham**, DL14 9JX, **ENGLAND**.
(T) 01388 833333.
Profile Riding Wear Retailer, Saddlery Retailer.
Ref: YH15126

WEST BELFAST
West Belfast Harness Driving Club, 83 Colin Glen Rd, Belfast, **County Antrim**, BT17 0LW, **NORTHERN IRELAND**.
(T) 028 90624520.
Contact/s
Secretary: Mr D Douglas
Profile Club/Association. **Ref: YH15127**

WEST BLAGDON STUD
West Blagdon Stud, West Blagdon, Cranborne, **Dorset**, BH21 5RY, **ENGLAND**.
(T) 01725 517212.
Profile Breeder. **Ref: YH15128**

WEST BOWERS
West Bowers, West Bowers Farm, Woodham Walter, Maldon, **Essex**, CM9 6RZ, **ENGLAND**.
(T) 01245 222819.
Profile Stable/Livery. **Ref: YH15129**

WEST BULTHY EQUESTRIAN
West Bulthy Equestrian, Middletown, Welshpool, **Powys**, SY21 8ER, **WALES**.
(T) 01743 884765.
Profile Supplies. **Ref: YH15130**

WEST CHESHIRE TRAINING GROUP
West Cheshire Combined Training Group, Rock Hse, 2 Mill Lane, Greasby, **Merseyside**, CH49 3NN, **ENGLAND**.
(T) 0151 6784948.
Profile Club/Association. **Ref: YH15131**

WEST CLARE SADDLERY
West Clare Saddlery, Lahinch Rd, Ennistymon, **County Clare**, **IRELAND**.
(T) 065 7071249.
Profile Supplies. **Ref: YH15132**

WEST COAST WELDING
West Coast Welding & Engineering Ltd, Kilmory, Lochgilphead, **Argyll and Bute**, PA31 8RR, **SCOTLAND**.
(T) 01546 602021 **(F)** 01546 606020.
Profile Blacksmith. **Ref: YH15133**

WEST COUNTRY FEEDS
West Country Feeds Ltd, Unit 36, Taunton Trading Est, Norton Fitzwarren, Taunton, **Somerset**, TA2 6QF, **ENGLAND**.
(T) 01823 275057 **(F)** 01823 336923.
Profile Supplies. **Ref: YH15134**

WEST COUNTRY POLOCROSSE CLUB
West Country Polocrosse Club (The), April

Green, Old Common, Minchinhampton, Stroud, **Gloucestershire**, GL6 9EH, **ENGLAND**.
(T) 01453 731512.
Contact/s
Secretary: Mr J Duwig
Profile Riding Club. **Ref: YH15135**

WEST COUNTRY ROSETTES

West Country Rosettes, 16 Sandiland Cl, East Stour, Gillingham, **Dorset**, SP8 5LG, **ENGLAND**.
(T) 01747 838157.
Profile Club/Association. **Ref: YH15136**

WEST COUNTRY SHIRE HORSE

West Country Shire Horse Trust, Dunstan, Yealmpton, Plymouth, **Devon**, PL8 2EL, **ENGLAND**.
(T) 01752 880268.
Profile Club/Association. **Ref: YH15137**

WEST COUNTRY VIDEOS

West Country Videos, 24 Hooe Rd, Hooe, Plymouth, **Devon**, PL9 9RG, **ENGLAND**.
(T) 01752 406746 **(F)** 01752 406746.
Profile Supplies. **Ref: YH15138**

WEST DEVON & NORTH CORNWALL

West Devon & North Cornwall Farmers, Under Lane, Holsworthy, **Devon**, EX22 6EE, **ENGLAND**.
(T) 01409 253407 **(F)** 01409 253050.
Profile Saddlery Retailer. **Ref: YH15139**

WEST DOWN RACING STABLES

West Down Racing Stables, Whitechapel, South Molton, **Devon**, EX36 3EQ, **ENGLAND**.
(T) 01769 550373 **(F)** 01769 550839
(M) 07778 700191
(E) westdown@zetnet.co.uk.
Profile Trainer. **Ref: YH15140**

WEST END LIVERIES SUPPLIES

West End Liveries Supplies, West End Fan Units, West End, Warfield, **Berkshire**, RG42 5RH, **ENGLAND**.
(T) 01344 482399.
Profile Stable/Livery. **Ref: YH15141**

WEST END RIDING CLUB

West End Riding Club, 72 Valebridge Rd, Burgess Hill, **Sussex (West)**, RH15 0RP, **ENGLAND**.
(T) 01444 235592.
Contact/s
Chairman: Mr G Cook
Profile Club/Association, Riding Club. **Ref: YH15142**

WEST ESSEX & KERNOW SADDLERY

West Essex & Kernow Saddlery, 113 Station Rd, Chingford, **London (Greater)**, E4 7BU, **ENGLAND**.
(T) 020 85242537.
Profile Saddlery Retailer. **Ref: YH15143**

WEST FARM STABLES

West Farm Stables, Stenson, Barrow-on-Trent, Derby, **Derbyshire**, DE73 1HL, **ENGLAND**.
(T) 01283 703998. **Ref: YH15144**

WEST FENTON LIVERY

West Fenton Livery, West Fenton, North Berwick, **Lothian (East)**, EH39 5AL, **SCOTLAND**.
(T) 01620 842154 **(F)** 01620 842052.
Contact/s
Owner: Mrs G Morrison
Profile Stable/Livery.
Outside Livery - £100 per month, including morning and night feeding. Also offer stabling and DIY Livery, prices vary.
Opening Times
Sp: Open Mon - Sun 09:00. Closed Mon - Sun 19:00.
Su: Open Mon - Sun 09:00. Closed Mon - Sun 19:00.
Au: Open Mon - Sun 09:00. Closed Mon - Sun 19:00.
Wn: Open Mon - Sun 09:00. Closed Mon - Sun 19:00.
Person on site 24 hours **Ref: YH15145**

WEST HALL STUD

West Hall Stud, Longfield Farm, Middleton Tyas, Richmond, **Yorkshire (North)**, DL10 6QZ, **ENGLAND**.
(T) 01325 377265 **(F)** 01325 377012.
Profile Breeder. **Ref: YH15146**

WEST HAMILTON STABLES

West Hamilton Stables, Compton, Newbury, **Berkshire**, RG20 0QR, **ENGLAND**.
(T) 01635 578031 **(F)** 01635 579323
(M) 07798 824513
(E) portman@hamiltonstables@virgin.net.
Profile Trainer. **Ref: YH15147**

WEST HERRINGTON RIDING SCHOOL

West Herrington Riding School, West Herrington, Houghton Le Spring, **Tyne and Wear**, DH4 4ND, **ENGLAND**.
(T) 0191 5841018.
Profile Riding School. **Ref: YH15148**

WEST HOPPYLAND TREKKING CTRE

West Hoppyland Trekking Centre, Hamsterley, Bishop Auckland, **County Durham**, DL13 3NP, **ENGLAND**.
(T) 01388 767419.
Profile Riding School. **Ref: YH15149**

WEST ILKERTON FARM

West Ilkerton Farm Horsedrawn Tours, West Ilkerton Farm, Lynton, **Devon**, EX35 6QA, **ENGLAND**.
(T) 01598 752310 **(F)** 01598 752310
(W) www.westilkerton.co.uk
Affiliated Bodies WCHHS.
Contact/s
Partner: Mr C Eveleigh
(E) eveleigh@westilkerton.co.uk
Profile Holidays, Horse/Rider Accom. Shire Horse Centre.
West Ilkerton Farm offers holiday accommodation and driving holidays. Travelling across farmland and open moorland in a purpose built wagon pulled by Shire horses. Ideal for all the family, all ages and abilities welcome, access for wheelchairs. Also offer birthday and picnic rides.
Opening Times
Telephone for bookings **Ref: YH15150**

WEST KINGTON STUD

T.D & J Holderness-Roddam, Church Farm, West Kington, Chippenham, **Wiltshire**, SN14 7JE, **ENGLAND**.
(T) 01249 782050 **(F)** 01249 782940
(E) admin@westkingtonstud.co.uk
(W) www.westkingtonstud.co.uk.
Contact/s
Manager: Tessa Clarke
(E) tessaclarke50@hotmail.com
Profile Blood Stock Agency, Breeder, Trainer. Stallion Centre.
Semen from British-based Stallions is collected, frozen and distributed throughout the world, from this site. **No.Staff:** 6 **Yr. Est:** 1995 **C.Size:** 800 Acres
Opening Times
Telephone for an appointment **Ref: YH15151**

WEST LANCASHIRE RIDING CLUB

West Lancashire Riding Club, 11 Mawdsley Cl, Formby, Liverpool, **Merseyside**, L37 8DJ, **ENGLAND**.
(T) 01704 831803.
Profile Club/Association, Riding Club. **Ref: YH15152**

WEST LAVINGTON EQUESTRIAN

West Lavington Equestrian Centre, High St, West Lavington, Devizes, **Wiltshire**, SN10 4JB, **ENGLAND**.
(T) 01380 813734.
Contact/s
Manager: Mrs B Chatfield
Profile Equestrian Centre. **Ref: YH15153**

WEST LINCOLN RIDING CLUB

West Lincoln Riding Club, 54 Long Leys Rd, Lincoln, **Lincolnshire**, LN1 1DR, **ENGLAND**.
(T) 01522 538455.
Contact/s
Chairman: Mrs J Storr
Profile Club/Association, Riding Club. **Ref: YH15154**

WEST LOTHIAN BRIDLEWAYS ASS

West Lothian Bridleways Association, Garden Cottage, Champfleurie, Linlithgow, **Lothian (West)**, EH49 6NB, **SCOTLAND**.
(T) 01506 845998.
Profile Club/Association. **Ref: YH15155**

WEST MIDLAND HORSE BOX CTRE

West Midland Horse Box Centre Ltd, Baddymarsh Farm, Lower Eggleton, Ledbury, **Herefordshire**, HR8 2UH, **ENGLAND**.
(T) 01531 670642 **(F)** 01531 670642.
Contact/s
Owner: Mr R Breese
Profile Transport/Horse Boxes. **Ref: YH15156**

WEST NORFOLK FOXHOUNDS

West Norfolk Foxhounds, 19 Back St, Harpley, King's Lynn, **Norfolk**, PE31 6TU, **ENGLAND**.
(T) 01485 520079.
Profile Club/Association. **Ref: YH15157**

WEST OXFORDSHIRE COLLEGE

West Oxfordshire College, Holloway Rd, Witney, **Oxfordshire**, OX8 7EE, **ENGLAND**.
(T) 01993 703464 **(F)** 01993 703006.
Profile Equestrian Centre. **Ref: YH15158**

WEST PITCORTHI STABLES

West Pitcorthi Stables, West Pitcorthi, Anstruther, **Fife**, KY10 3JZ, **SCOTLAND**.
(T) 01333 310271.
Profile Stable/Livery. **Ref: YH15159**

WEST RIDGE VETNRY PRAC

West Ridge Veterinary Practice, 5 Chapple Rd, Witheridge, Tiverton, **Devon**, EX16 8AS, **ENGLAND**.
(T) 01884 860236.
Profile Medical Support. **Ref: YH15160**

WEST RIDING SUPPLIES

West Riding Supplies, 15 Stony Lane, Bradford, **Yorkshire (West)**, BD2 2HL, **ENGLAND**.
(T) 01274 770733.
Profile Riding Wear Retailer, Supplies. **Ref: YH15161**

WEST RUNTON RIDING STABLES

West Runton Riding Stables, West Runton, Cromer, **Norfolk**, NR27 9QH, **ENGLAND**.
(T) 01263 837339.
Contact/s
Partner: Mr D Bakewell
Profile Riding School. **Ref: YH15162**

WEST SOMERSET POLO CLUB

West Somerset Polo Club, Carnarvon Arms Hotel, Brushford, Dulverton, **Somerset**, TA22 9AF, **ENGLAND**.
(T) 01598 710245 **(F)** 01598 710878
(E) rgpeek@sosi.net.
Contact/s
Secretary: Richard Peek
Profile Club/Association. Polo Club. **Ref: YH15163**

WEST SOMERSET RIDING CTRE

West Somerset Riding Centre (The), Moor Rd, North Hill, Minehead, **Somerset**, TA24 5RT, **ENGLAND**.
(T) 01643 705406.
Profile Riding School. **Ref: YH15164**

WEST SURREY RIDING CLUB

West Surrey Riding Club, Black Cottage, Newlands Corner, Guildford, **Surrey**, GU4 8SE, **ENGLAND**.
(T) 01483 422810.
Profile Club/Association, Riding Club. **Ref: YH15165**

WEST TACK

West Tack (Equestrian Supplies), 7 Frizinghall Rd, Bradford, **Yorkshire (West)**, BD9 4LA, **ENGLAND**.
(T) 01274 484827
(M) 07973 839354.
Profile Saddlery Retailer. **Ref: YH15166**

WEST TARF ICELANDIC HORSES

West Tarf Icelandic Horses, West Tarf Hse, West Linton, **Scottish Borders**, EH46 7AA, **SCOTLAND**.
(T) 01968 660873 **(F)** 01968 660055.
Profile Breeder. **Ref: YH15167**

WEST WALES FOODS

West Wales Foods Ltd, Samlet Rd, Llansamlett, Swansea, **Swansea**, SA7 9AH, **WALES**.
(T) 01792 771464.
Profile Supplies. **Ref: YH15168**

WEST WEYLANDS FARM

West Weylands Farm, Esher Rd, Walton-on-Thames, **Surrey**, KT12 4LJ, **ENGLAND**.
(T) 01372 465594.
Contact/s
Owner: Mrs J Harper
Profile Stable/Livery. **Ref: YH15169**

WEST WILTS

West Wilts Equestrian Centre, Melksham Rd, Holt, Trowbridge, **Wiltshire**, BA14 6QT, **ENGLAND**.
(T) 01225 783220 **(F)** 01225 783110
(E) info@westwilts.com
(W) www.westwilts.com.
Contact/s
Manageress: Miss L Rodwell
Profile Arena, Track/Course. Competition Centre.
Have a loose schooling pen, and are an unaffiliated and affiliated dressage and jumping centre, also have a hunter trail. **No.Staff:** 6 **Yr. Est:** 1990
C.Size: 80 Acres
Opening Times
Sp: Open Mon - Fri 14:00. Closed Mon - Fri 17:00.

Su: Open Mon - Fri 14:00. Closed Mon - Fri 17:00.
Au: Open Mon - Fri 14:00. Closed Mon - Fri 17:00.
Wn: Open Mon - Fri 14:00. Closed Mon - Fri 17:00.
Office open all year round **Ref: YH15170**

WEST WIRRAL RIDING SCHOOL

West Wirral Riding School, Fender Farm, Fender Lane, Wirral, **Merseyside**, CH46 9PA, **ENGLAND**.
(T) 0151 6775282.
Contact/s
Owner: Mrs V Catton
Profile Riding School. **Ref: YH15171**

WEST WOLVES RIDING CTRE

West Wolves Riding Centre, Ashington, Pulborough, **Sussex (West)**, RH20 3AY, **ENGLAND**.
(T) 01903 892798.
Profile Riding School.
Opening Times
Closed Monday and Thursday **Ref: YH15172**

WEST WYCOMBE PARK POLO CLUB

West Wycombe Park Polo Club, West Wycombe Pk, West Wycombe, **Buckinghamshire**, HP14 3AJ, **ENGLAND**.
(T) 01494 449187 **(F)** 01494 538316.
Profile Club/Association. **Ref: YH15173**

WEST, E C

E C West DWCF, C/O 21 Bushy Hill Rd, Westbere, Canterbury, **Kent**, CT2 0HE, **ENGLAND**.
(T) 01227 711137.
Profile Farrier. **Ref: YH15174**

WEST, GEORGE

George West, 2 Viewlands, Aberuthven, Auchterarder, **Perth and Kinross**, PH3 1HQ, **SCOTLAND**.
(T) 01764 663029.
Profile Farrier. **Ref: YH15175**

WEST, N J

N J West, Thornton Nurseries, Brownwich Lane, Fareham, **Hampshire**, PO14 4NY, **ENGLAND**.
(T) 01329 844404. **Ref: YH15176**

WEST, RODNEY A

Rodney A West AFCL, Kings Hse, Abinger Hammer, Dorking, **Surrey**, RH5 6RX, **ENGLAND**.
(T) 01306 730651.
Profile Farrier. **Ref: YH15177**

WEST, S D

S D West, Lower Pensworth Farm, Redlynch, Salisbury, **Wiltshire**, SP5 2JU, **ENGLAND**.
(T) 01725 510322 **(F)** 01752 510325.
Contact/s
Owner: Mr S West **Ref: YH15178**

WEST, TIMOTHY J

Timothy J West DWCF, Northbrook, Brook Hse, Brook, **Isle of Wight**, PO30 4EJ, **ENGLAND**.
(T) 01983 741131.
Profile Farrier. **Ref: YH15179**

WESTACOTT RIDING CTRE

Westacott Riding Centre, Westacott Grange, Westacott, Goodleigh, Barnstaple, **Devon**, EX32 7NF, **ENGLAND**.
(T) 01271 372965 **(F)** 01271 372965. **Ref: YH15180**

WESTACRE STABLES

Westacre Stables, Wellhead Drove, Westbury, **Wiltshire**, BA13 3RD, **ENGLAND**.
(T) 01373 823161. **Ref: YH15181**

WESTAWAY MOTORS

Westaway Motors Ltd, Main Rd, Maidwell, **Northamptonshire**, NN6 9JA, **ENGLAND**.
(T) 01604 686311.
Contact/s
Owner: Mr D Westaway
Profile Transport/Horse Boxes. **Ref: YH15182**

WESTBOURNE ANIMAL FEEDS

Westbourne Animal Feeds, Church Rd, Westbourne, **Hampshire**, PO10 8UA, **ENGLAND**.
(T) 01243 370889.
Profile Supplies. **Ref: YH15183**

WESTBRINK FARMS

G F Edge T/A Westbrink Farms, Westley Waterless, Newmarket, **Suffolk**, CB8 0RL, **ENGLAND**.
(T) 01638 507714 **(F)** 01638 508393.
Contact/s
For Bookings: Ms L Brackenbury
Profile Supplies. **Ref: YH15184**

WESTBROOK AGRICULTURAL SUP

Westbrook Agricultural Supplies, Brookside Farm, Rudgwick, **Sussex (West)**, RH12 2AL, **ENGLAND**.
(T) 01403 823401.
Profile Supplies. **Ref: YH15185**

WESTCOATS VETNRY CLINIC

Westcoats Veterinary Clinic, Stanhill, Charlwood, **Surrey**, RH6 0ES, **ENGLAND**.
(T) 01293 862880 **(F)** 01293 863366
(E) hcrobinson@email.com.
Profile Medical Support. **Ref: YH15186**

WESTCOTT WEATHERVANES

Westcott Weathervanes, 32B Forest Rd, Branksome, Poole, **Dorset**, BH13 6DH, **ENGLAND**.
(T) 01202 746408.
Profile Supplies. **Ref: YH15187**

WESTCOTT, W M

W M Westcott DWCF, 14 Lakelands Cl, Witheridge, Tiverton, **Devon**, EX16 8DD, **ENGLAND**.
(T) 01884 860744.
Profile Farrier. **Ref: YH15188**

WESTCOURT

Equine Management Solutions Ltd, Westcourt Stables, Burbage, Marlborough, **Wiltshire**, SN8 3BW, **ENGLAND**.
(T) 01672 811423 **(F)** 01672 811416.
Contact/s
Manager: Ms S Walker
Profile Medical Support. Equine behaviourist.
Opening Times
Sp: Open Mon - Sat 10:00. Closed Mon - Sat 16:00.
Su: Open Mon - Sat 10:00. Closed Mon - Sat 16:00.
Au: Open Mon - Sat 10:00. Closed Mon - Sat 16:00.
Wn: Open Mon - Sat 10:00. Closed Mon - Sat 16:00.
Telephone for an appointment with Gary **Ref: YH15189**

WESTCROFT STABLES

Westcroft Stables & Livery Yard, 147 Havant Rd, Hayling Island, **Hampshire**, PO11 0LF, **ENGLAND**.
(T) 023 92465512. **Ref: YH15190**

WESTER WOODSIDE FARM FEEDS

Wester Woodside Farm Feeds, Linlithgow, **Lothian (West)**, EH49 6QE, **SCOTLAND**.
(T) 01506 652830 **(F)** 01506 652830.
Profile Supplies. **Ref: YH15191**

WESTERKIRK SADDLERY

Westerkirk Saddlery, 6 Sandbed, Hawick, **Scottish Borders**, TD9 0HE, **SCOTLAND**.
(T) 01450 372871.
Contact/s
Partner: Mrs F Blackey **Ref: YH15192**

WESTERKIRK SADDLERY

Westerkirk Saddlery, 48 North Hermitage St, Newcastleton, **Scottish Borders**, TD9 0RA, **SCOTLAND**.
(T) 01387 375655.
Contact/s
Partner: Mrs S Blackey
Profile Saddlery Retailer. **Ref: YH15193**

WESTERLANDS STUD

Westerlands Stud, Graffham, Petworth, **Sussex (West)**, GU28 0QL, **ENGLAND**.
(T) 01798 867273.
Profile Breeder. **Ref: YH15194**

WESTERLEIGH LIVERY STABLES

Westerleigh Livery Stables, Westerleigh, Bristol, **Bristol**, BS37 8QU, **ENGLAND**.
(T) 01454 318458.
Contact/s
Owner: Ms P Hendy **Ref: YH15195**

WESTERMAN, BARRY

Barry Westerman, The Granary, 49A Main St, Riccall, **Yorkshire (North)**, YO8 6QE, **ENGLAND**.
(T) 01757 249368
(M) 07970 177347.
Profile Supplies. **Ref: YH15196**

WESTERN DEPARTMENT

Western Department (The), Rookery Farm, Marsh Rd, Shabbington, Aylesbury, **Buckinghamshire**, HP18 9HF, **ENGLAND**.
(T) 01844 201656 **(F)** 01844 201656.
Contact/s
Owner: Mrs J Weston **Ref: YH15197**

WESTERN EQUESTRIAN SOCIETY

Western Equestrian Society, 20 Newlands Cl, Yateley, **Hampshire**, GU46 6HE, **ENGLAND**.
(T) 01252 875896.
Contact/s
Key Contact: Mr D Lloyd
Profile Club/Association. **Ref: YH15198**

WESTERN EQUESTRIAN SOCIETY

Western Equestrian Society (The), Stable End, Avenue Riding Ctre, Havern, **Worcestershire**, WR14 4PH, **ENGLAND**.
(T) 01252 875896
(M) 07831 251148.
Profile Club/Association. **Ref: YH15199**

WESTERN HORSE SUPPLIES

Western Horse Supplies, Ringwood Rd, Three Legged Cross, Wimborne, **Dorset**, BH21 6RE, **ENGLAND**.
(T) 01202 855977 **(F)** 01202 855977.
Contact/s
Owner: Mr M Owens
Profile Supplies. **Ref: YH15200**

WESTERN HORSE SUPPLIES

Western Horse Supplies, 32 Ashurst Rd, West Moors, **Dorset**, BH22 0LS, **ENGLAND**.
(T) 01202 855977 **(F)** 01202 855977
(E) enquiries@westernhorse.co.uk.
Profile Supplies. **Ref: YH15201**

WESTERN HORSEMAN'S ASS OF GB

Western Horseman's Association of GB, Llmedos, The Clumps, Ashford, **Surrey**, TW15 1AT, **ENGLAND**.
(T) 020 8831 9689.
Profile Club/Association. **Ref: YH15202**

WESTERN HORSEMEN'S ASS OF GB

Western Horsemen's Association of GB, 3 Poplar Cl, Highcross, Ware, **Hertfordshire**, SG11 1AY, **ENGLAND**.
(T) 01920 486182.
Contact/s
Secretary: Mrs J Williams
Profile Club/Association. **Ref: YH15203**

WESTERN RIDING

Western Riding Books and Videos, Old Home Farm, Leamington Hastings, Rugby, **Warwickshire**, CV23 8DZ, **ENGLAND**.
(T) 01926 632916.
Contact/s
Owner: Ms J Creswell
(E) r-jcresswell@msn.com
Profile Western Riding Mail Order. No.Staff: 1
Yr. Est: 1992 **Ref: YH15204**

WESTERN RIDING ASS OF IRELAND

Western Riding Association of Ireland, Cochise Stud, Moystown, Demene, Shannon, **County Offaly**, **IRELAND**.
(T) 086 8373049
(E) info@wrai.net.
Contact/s
President: Mr D O'Bryne
Profile Club/Association. **Ref: YH15205**

WESTERN TOWING

Western Towing, Unit A1, Kingsteignton Ind Est, Kingsteignton, Newton Abbot, **Devon**, TQ12 3BN, **ENGLAND**.
(T) 01626 355115 **(F)** 01626 363111.
Profile Transport/Horse Boxes. **Ref: YH15206**

WESTERN TOWING ATTACHMENTS

Western Towing Attachments, B L Saxton & Sons, 189 Pinhoe Rd, Polsloe Bridge, Exeter, **Devon**, EX4 8AB, **ENGLAND**.
(T) 01392 216226 **(F)** 01392 430415.
Profile Transport/Horse Boxes. **Ref: YH15207**

WESTERN TRAILERS

Western Trailers, 22 The Green, Stoke Gifford, Bristol, **Bristol**, BS34 8PD, **ENGLAND**.
(T) 01179 694273.
Profile Transport/Horse Boxes. **Ref: YH15208**

WESTERN, J

Mr J Western, West Hawkwell Farm, Wheddon Cross, Minehead, **Somerset**, TA24 7EF, **ENGLAND**.
(T) 01643 841210.
Profile Breeder. **Ref: YH15209**

WESTERTON BOXES

Westerton Boxes, Blair Smiddy Croft, Old Meldrum, **Aberdeenshire**, AB51 0BP, **SCOTLAND**.
(T) 01651 872254 **(F)** 01651 872254.
Profile Transport/Horse Boxes. **Ref: YH15210**

WESTERTON RIDING CTRE
Westerton Riding Centre, Westerton Farm, Huntly, **Aberdeenshire**, AB54 4TD, **SCOTLAND**.
(T) 01466 730294.
Profile Riding School. Ref: YH15211

WESTERTOUN
Westertoun Riding Centre, Westruther, Gordon, **Scottish Borders**, TD3 6NE, **SCOTLAND**.
(T) 01578 740270
Affiliated Bodies BE.
Contact/s
For Bookings: Ms M Proctor (Q) BHSAI
Profile Equestrian Centre, Riding School, Stable/Livery, Trainer. No.Staff: 3 Yr. Est: 1999
C.Size: 10 Acres
Opening Times
Sp: Open Mon - Sun 09:00. Closed Mon - Sun 20:00.
Su: Open Mon - Sun 09:00. Closed Mon - Sun 20:00.
Au: Open Mon - Sun 09:00. Closed Mon - Sun 20:00.
Wn: Open Mon - Sun 09:00. Closed Mon - Sun 20:00. Ref: YH15212

WESTFIELD SADDLERY
Westfield Saddlery, Westfield Farm, Churchill Rd, Chipping Norton, **Oxfordshire**, OX7 5UP, **ENGLAND**.
(T) 01608 642518.
Contact/s
Owner: Mrs M Woodcock
Profile Saddlery Retailer, Stable/Livery.
Ref: YH15213

WESTGATE GROUP
Westgate Group Ltd, Newchurch, Romney Marsh, **Kent**, TN29 0DZ, **ENGLAND**.
(T) 01303 874455 (F) 01303 874801. Ref: YH15214

WESTHIDE TRUST
Westhide Trust, Westhide, Hereford, **Herefordshire**, HR1 3RQ, **ENGLAND**.
(T) 01432 850058 (F) 01432 850058.
Contact/s
Owner: Mr D Probitt
Profile Supplies. Ref: YH15215

WESTHILLS EQUINE SUPPLIES
Westhills Equine Supplies, Westhills Farm, Winster, Matlock, **Derbyshire**, DE4 2DD, **ENGLAND**.
(T) 01629 650360 (F) 01629 732195.
Profile Supplies. Ref: YH15216

WESTHOUGHTON RIDING CLUB
Westhoughton Riding Club, Lands Farm, Hindley Rd, Daisy Hill, Wigan, **Lancashire**, WN2 4EX, **ENGLAND**.
(T) 01942 879873.
Contact/s
Chairman: Capt R Harrison
Profile Club/Association, Riding Club. Ref: YH15217

WESTLANDS
Westlands, Russ Hill, Charlwood, Horley, **Surrey**, RH6 0EL, **ENGLAND**.
(T) 01293 862470.
Contact/s
Owner: Mr J Dowsett
Profile Transport/Horse Boxes. Ref: YH15218

WESTLEY HOUSE LIVERY
Westley House Livery, Westley Hse, Ivetsey Rd, Wheaton Aston, Stafford, **Staffordshire**, ST19 9QW, **ENGLAND**.
(T) 01785 840165. Ref: YH15219

WESTMACOTT, SAM
Sam Westmacott, 15 Marina Approach, Willow Tree Marina, Yeading, **London (Greater)**, UB4 9TB, **ENGLAND**.
(T) 020 88410932
(E) samwestmacott@mooring.fsnet.co.uk.
Profile Supplies. Ref: YH15220

WESTMUIR RIDING CTRE
Westmuir Riding Centre, Totley Wells Grange, Winchburgh, Broxburn, **Lothian (West)**, EH52 6QJ, **SCOTLAND**.
(T) 0131 3312990.
Profile Stable/Livery. Ref: YH15221

WESTON & BANWELL HARRIERS
Weston & Banwell Harriers, Manor Farm, Southwick, Mark, Highbridge, **Somerset**, TA9 4LH, **ENGLAND**.
(T) 01278 783261.
Profile Club/Association. Ref: YH15222

WESTON COUNTRY STORES
Weston Country Stores, Weston Barns, Hitchin Rd, Weston, Hitchin, **Hertfordshire**, SG4 7AX, **ENGLAND**.
(T) 01462 790079 (F) 01462 790079.
Contact/s
Partner: Mr C Green Ref: YH15223

WESTON PARK EQUESTRIAN CTRE
Weston Park Equestrian Centre, Morton Lane, Weston Longville, Norwich, **Norfolk**, NR9 5JL, **ENGLAND**.
(T) 01603 872247 (F) 01603 873040
(E) equestrian@weston-park.co.uk
Affiliated Bodies ABRS, BHS.
Contact/s
Assistant Manager: Ms A Webb
Profile Arena, Equestrian Centre, Riding Club, Riding School, Stable/Livery, Track/Course.
Also has polocrosse pitches and a polocrosse club.
No.Staff: 8 Yr. Est: 1986 C.Size: 100 Acres
Opening Times
Sp: Open 08:00. Closed 21:00.
Su: Open 08:00. Closed 21:00.
Au: Open 08:00. Closed 21:00.
Wn: Open 08:00. Closed 21:00. Ref: YH15224

WESTON WAGONS
Weston Wagons, 44 Mallock Rd, Torquay, **Devon**, TQ2 6AD, **ENGLAND**.
(T) 01803 690153.
Profile Club/Association. Ref: YH15225

WESTON, ALAN A
Alan A Weston, 1 Applesore Cottages, Milton Hill, Abingdon, **Oxfordshire**, OX14 4DP, **ENGLAND**.
(T) 01235 820431.
Profile Farrier. Ref: YH15226

WESTON, M H
Mr M H Weston, Offerton Farm, Hindlip, **Worcestershire**, WR3 8SX, **ENGLAND**.
(T) 01905 52361.
Profile Supplies. Ref: YH15227

WESTON, V J
V J Weston, The Ranch, Bridge Hill Rd, Newborough, Peterborough, **Cambridgeshire**, PE6 7SD, **ENGLAND**.
(T) 01733 810280.
Profile Transport/Horse Boxes. Ref: YH15228

WESTOVER VETNRY CTRE
Westover Veterinary Centre, 40 Yarmouth Rd, North Walsham, **Norfolk**, NR28 9AT, **ENGLAND**.
(T) 01692 407040 (F) 01692 500264.
Profile Medical Support. Ref: YH15229

WESTPARK SHETLAND PONY STUD
Westpark Shetland Pony Stud, Fyvie, Turriff, **Aberdeenshire**, **SCOTLAND**..
Profile Breeder. Ref: YH15230

WESTRA DONKEY STUD
Westra Donkey Stud, Gelliaraul Farm, Llangan, Bridgend, **Bridgend**, CF35 5DN, **WALES**.
(T) 01656 860313 (F) 01656 860313.
Profile Breeder. Ref: YH15231

WESTVIEW STUD
Westview Stud, Nortons, Bridgerule, Holsworthy, **Devon**, EX22 7EL, **ENGLAND**.
(T) 01288 381374 (F) 01288 381477.
Contact/s
Owner: Mrs S Nokes
Profile Breeder. Ref: YH15232

WESTWAY SADDLERY
Westway Saddlery, Dottery, Bridport, **Dorset**, DT6 5HR, **ENGLAND**.
(T) 01308 425651 (F) 01308 425651.
Profile Saddlery Retailer, Stable/Livery.
Ref: YH15233

WESTWAY STABLES
Westway Stables, 20 Stable Way, London, **London (Greater)**, W10 6QX, **ENGLAND**.
(T) 020 89642140.
Contact/s
Owner: Ms S Tuvey Ref: YH15234

WESTWAYS
Westways, Green Lane, Hounslow, **London (Greater)**, TW4 6DH, **ENGLAND**.
(T) 020 85701653.
Contact/s
Owner: Mrs J Radford-Howes
Profile Riding School. Ref: YH15235

WESTWAYS RIDING SCHOOL
Westways Riding School, The Homestead, Carr Lane, Thorner, Leeds, **Yorkshire (West)**, LS14 3HD, **ENGLAND**.
(T) 0113 2892598
Affiliated Bodies ABRS, BHS.
Contact/s
Owner: Miss Y Beaumont
Profile Riding School.
Lessons for beginners are £11 children, £11.50 adults. Hats £0.50 to hire. No.Staff: 14 Yr. Est: 1954
C.Size: 15 Acres
Opening Times
Sp: Open Mon - Sun 09:00. Closed Mon - Sun 18:00.
Su: Open Mon - Sun 09:00. Closed Mon - Sun 18:00.
Au: Open Mon - Sun 09:00. Closed Mon - Sun 18:00.
Wn: Open Mon - Sun 09:00. Closed Mon - Sun 18:00. Ref: YH15236

WESTWICK EQUESTRIAN SERVICES
Westwick Equestrian Services, Cocked Hat Croft, Topcliffe Rd, Sowerby, Thirsk, **Yorkshire (North)**, YO7 3HF, **ENGLAND**.
(T) 01845 523473.
Profile Supplies. Ref: YH15237

WESTWOOD FARM
Westwood Farm, Peakley Hill, Barlow, Dronfield, **Derbyshire**, S18 7SU, **ENGLAND**.
(T) 0114 2891207.
Profile Riding School. Ref: YH15238

WESTWOOD HALL FARM
Westwood Hall Farm, Westwood Park Drive, Leek, **Staffordshire**, ST13 8NW, **ENGLAND**.
(T) 01538 384367.
Contact/s
Owner: Mr R Plant
Profile Riding School. Ref: YH15239

WESTWOOD HORSE BOXES
Westwood Horse Boxes, 3 Charles St, Heywood, **Lancashire**, OL10 2HR, **ENGLAND**.
(T) 01706 620444 (F) 01706 620444.
Contact/s
Owner: Mr L Harris
Profile Transport/Horse Boxes. Ref: YH15240

WESTWOOD VETNRY SURGERY
Westwood Veterinary Surgery, Westwood Hse, 106 High St, Boston Spa, **Yorkshire (West)**, LS23 6DR, **ENGLAND**.
(T) 01937 842210.
Contact/s
Vet: Mr K Hughes
Profile Medical Support. Ref: YH15241

WESTWOOD, IFOR WILLIAMS
Ifor Williams Westwood, Kilcullen Rd, Naas, **County Kildare**, **IRELAND**.
(T) 045 879422
(E) info@westwoodtrailers.com
(W) www.westwoodtrailers.com.
Profile Supplies. Ref: YH15242

WETHERBY AGRICULTURAL SOCIETY
Wetherby Agricultural Society, Moor Farm, Catterton, Tadcaster, **Yorkshire (North)**, LS24 8DJ, **ENGLAND**.
(T) 01937 833299.
Profile Club/Association. Ref: YH15243

WETHERBY STEEPLECHASE
Wetherby Steeplechase Committee Limited, The Racecourse, York Rd, Wetherby, **Yorkshire (West)**, LS22 5EJ, **ENGLAND**.
(T) 01937 582035 (F) 01937 588021.
Contact/s
Sales/Marketing: Ms M Green
Profile Track/Course. Ref: YH15244

WETHERILL, N & A
N & A Wetherill, Abbey View, Coxwold, York, **Yorkshire (North)**, YO61 4AD, **ENGLAND**.
(T) 01347 868320. Ref: YH15245

WETHERSFIELD RIDING STABLES
Wethersfield Riding Stables, Hedingham Rd, Wethersfield, Braintree, **Essex**, CM7 4EQ, **ENGLAND**.
(T) 01371 851089.
Contact/s
Owner: Mr S Parker (Q) BHSAI
Profile Riding School, Stable/Livery, Trainer.
No.Staff: 1 Yr. Est: 1986 C.Size: 8 Acres
Ref: YH15246

WEXFORD COUNTRY STORE
Wexford Country Store, Donovans Wharf Cres, Wexford, **County Wexford**, **IRELAND**.
(T) 053 45402.
Profile Supplies. **Ref: YH15247**

WEXHAM & DISTRICT BRIDLEWAYS
Wexham & District Bridleways Association, Ffordd Las, Llanbedr, Ruthin, **Denbighshire**, LL15 1SR, **WALES**.
(T) 01824 705660 (F) 01824 705889.
Profile Club/Association. **Ref: YH15248**

WEY VALLEY RIDING CLUB
Wey Valley Riding Club, Newton Cottage, Newton Valence, Alton, **Hampshire**, GU34 3RR, **ENGLAND**.
(T) 01420 587430 (F) 01420 587430.
Contact/s
Chairman: Mrs C Streather
Profile Club/Association, Riding Club. **Ref: YH15249**

WEYBRIDGE EQUESTRIAN CTRE
Weybridge Equestrian Centre, Broadwater Farmhouse, Grenside Rd, Weybridge, **Surrey**, KT13 8QB, **ENGLAND**.
(T) 01932 248544 (F) 01932 248544.
Contact/s
Owner: Mrs B Firth
Profile Riding School. **Ref: YH15250**

WEYHILL HORSE TRANSPORT
Weyhill Horse Transport Ltd, Fyfield Hse, Fyfield, Andover, **Hampshire**, SP11 8EW, **ENGLAND**.
(T) 01264 773033 (F) 01264 771303.
Contact/s
Owner: Mr J Gordon
Profile Transport/Horse Boxes. **Ref: YH15251**

WEYLODE
Weylode, Tetbury Rd, Old Sodbury, **Gloucestershire (South)**, BS37 6RJ, **ENGLAND**.
(T) 01454 313305 (F) 01454 273054
(M) 07889 660818.
Contact/s
Assistant: Mrs J Wilkie
Profile Supplies. **Ref: YH15252**

WEYMOUTH & DISTRICT
Weymouth & District Riding Club, 15 Cromwell Rd, Weymouth, **Dorset**, DT4 0JQ, **ENGLAND**.
(T) 01305 773524.
Contact/s
Chairman: Mr I Smith
Profile Club/Association, Riding Club. **Ref: YH15253**

WEYMOUTH RIDING CTRE
Weymouth Riding Centre, School Hill, Chickerell, Weymouth, **Dorset**, DT3 4BA, **ENGLAND**.
(T) 01305 771760. **Ref: YH15254**

WHALEY BRIDGE SMITHY
Whaley Bridge Smithy, 36A Old Rd, Whaley Bridge, High Peak, **Derbyshire**, SK23 7HR, **ENGLAND**.
(T) 01663 719179.
Profile Blacksmith. **Ref: YH15255**

WHALEY, J H
J H Whaley, Reedy Loch, Briery Hill, Duns, **Scottish Borders**, TD11 3PS, **SCOTLAND**.
(T) 01361 883533.
Profile Farrier. **Ref: YH15256**

WHALEY, MELISSA
Melissa Whaley, 3 Cowlinge Corner, Lidgate, Newmarket, **Suffolk**, CB8 9DN, **ENGLAND**.
(T) 01638 500687
Affiliated Bodies NAAT.
Contact/s
Physiotherapist: Melissa Whaley
Profile Medical Support.
Physiotherapist for horses & dogs. **Ref: YH15257**

WHALLEY CORN MILLS
Whalley Corn Mills Ltd, Brook Hse Farm, Mitton Rd, Whalley, Blackburn, **Lancashire**, BB6 9PF, **ENGLAND**.
(T) 01254 824643.
Profile Supplies. **Ref: YH15258**

WHALLEY WELSH PONIES & COBS
Whalley Welsh Ponies & Cobs, Sough Farm, Cranberry Lane, Darwen, **Lancashire**, BB3 2HL, **ENGLAND**.
(T) 01254 704378.
Profile Breeder. **Ref: YH15259**

WHALLEY, K R
K R Whalley, Haldon, London Rd, Westerham, **Kent**, TN16 1DP, **ENGLAND**.
(T) 01959 563086.
Contact/s
Owner: Mr K Whalley
Profile Farrier. **Ref: YH15260**

WHALLEY'S LIVESTOCK
Whalley's Livestock Ltd, The Old Cottage, Middleton Lane, Middleton, Tamworth, **Staffordshire**, B78 2BN, **ENGLAND**.
(T) 0121 3292265.
Profile Transport/Horse Boxes. **Ref: YH15261**

WHALTON STUD
Whalton Stud, Park Hse Farm, Spofforth, Harrogate, **Yorkshire (North)**, HG3 1BY, **ENGLAND**.
(T) 01937 590342 (F) 01937 590237.
Profile Breeder, Stable/Livery. **Ref: YH15262**

WHARTON ELECTRONICS
Wharton Electronics, Unit 15 Thame Park Business Ctre, Wenman Rd, Thame, **Oxfordshire**, OX9 3XA, **ENGLAND**.
(T) 01844 260567 (F) 01844 218855
(E) info@wharton.co.uk.
Profile Supplies. **Ref: YH15263**

WHARTON TRAINING STABLES
Wharton Training Stables, Race Course Farm, Bescaby Lane, Waltham On The Wolds, Melton Mowbray, **Leicestershire**, LE14 4AB, **ENGLAND**.
(T) 01664 464334.
Profile Trainer. **Ref: YH15264**

WHARTON, J R H
Mr J R H Wharton, Shipmans Barn Stud Cottage, Saxby Rd, Melton Mowbray, **Leicestershire**, LE14 4RZ, **ENGLAND**.
(T) 01664 464334 (F) 01476 870092
(M) 07770 893092.
Profile Trainer. **Ref: YH15265**

WHAT EVERY HORSE WANTS
What Every Horse Wants, Mambeg Farm, Rahane, Helensburgh, **Argyll and Bute**, G84 0QW, **SCOTLAND**.
(T) 01436 810608 (F) 01436 810861
(W) www.what-every-horse-wants.co.uk
Affiliated Bodies BETA.
Contact/s
Owner: Ms T Rickerby (Q) BHSAI
Profile Riding Wear Retailer, Saddlery Retailer, Supplies. No.Staff: 3 Yr. Est: 1994
Ref: YH15266

WHATTON MANOR STUD
Whatton Manor Stud, Whatton In The Vale, Notts, **Nottinghamshire**, NG13 9EX, **ENGLAND**.
(T) 01949 50221 (F) 01949 50221.
Profile Breeder. **Ref: YH15267**

WHEATHILL RIDING CTRE
Wheathill Riding Centre, Naylors Rd, Liverpool, **Merseyside**, L27 2YA, **ENGLAND**.
(T) 0151 4878515.
Contact/s
Partner: Mrs J Danner
Profile Club/Association, Riding School, Stable/Livery. **Ref: YH15268**

WHEATON TRUCK & TRAILER SALES
Wheaton Truck & Trailer Sales Ltd, West Rd, Barnsley, **Yorkshire (South)**, S75 2DR, **ENGLAND**.
(T) 01226 243736 (F) 01226 284791.
Contact/s
Owner: Mr H Whitehead
Profile Transport/Horse Boxes. **Ref: YH15269**

WHEELER, DEREK
Derek Wheeler RSS, 37 Grimsdyke Cres, Arkley, Barnet, **Hertfordshire**, EN4 9DJ, **ENGLAND**.
(T) 020 84406597.
Profile Farrier. **Ref: YH15270**

WHEELER, GARY M
Gary M Wheeler DWCF, 33 Beltinge Rd, Herne Bay, **Kent**, CT6 6DA, **ENGLAND**.
(T) 01227 361946.
Profile Farrier. **Ref: YH15271**

WHEELER, R
R Wheeler, Manor Farm Stud, Chisbury, Marlborough, **Wiltshire**, SN8 3JA, **ENGLAND**.
(T) 01672 870554.
Contact/s
Owner: Mr R Wheeler
Profile Breeder. **Ref: YH15272**

WHEELER, SIMON C T
Simon C T Wheeler DWCF BII, 1 Lower Bagborough Cottages, Pylle, Shepton Mallet, **Somerset**, BA4 6QP, **ENGLAND**.
(T) 01749 830709.
Profile Farrier. **Ref: YH15273**

WHEELER, T C
T C Wheeler DWCF, 1 Crossway Cottage, Otterhampton, Bridgwater, **Somerset**, TA5 2PT, **ENGLAND**.
(T) 01278 653178.
Profile Farrier. **Ref: YH15274**

WHEELERS PONY STUD
Wheelers Pony Stud, Watermill Farm, Middleton, Saxmundham, **Suffolk**, IP17 3LW, **ENGLAND**.
(T) 01728 648236.
Profile Breeder. **Ref: YH15275**

WHEELERSLAND STUD
Wheelersland Stud, Ashford Hill, Thatcham, **Berkshire**, RG19 8BN, **ENGLAND**.
(T) 01635 298351.
Profile Breeder. **Ref: YH15276**

WHELAN, J G
J G Whelan Blacksmith, College Rd, Whitchurch, Cardiff, **Glamorgan (Vale of)**, CF14 2NW, **WALES**.
(T) 029 20521550.
Contact/s
Owner: Mr J Whelan
Profile Blacksmith. **Ref: YH15277**

WHERRETT, PETER A
Peter A Wherrett DWCF BII, 11 Dallaway, Thrupp, **Gloucestershire**, GL5 2EB, **ENGLAND**.
(T) 01453 886030.
Profile Farrier. **Ref: YH15278**

WHIELDON, P G
P G Whieldon, 22 Main St, Hemington, Derby, **Derbyshire**, DE74 2RB, **ENGLAND**.
(T) 01332 850766 (F) 01332 850766.
Contact/s
Owner: Mr P Whieldon
Profile Blacksmith. **Ref: YH15279**

WHILLANS, A C
Mr A C Whillans, Esker Hse, Newmill-on-Slitrig, Hawick, **Scottish Borders**, TD9 9UQ, **SCOTLAND**.
(T) 01450 376642
(M) 07771 550555.
Profile Trainer. **Ref: YH15280**

WHILLANS, D
Mr D Whillans, Haughhead Farm, Hawick, **Scottish Borders**, TD9 8LF, **SCOTLAND**.
(T) 01450 379810 (F) 01450 376082.
Profile Trainer. **Ref: YH15281**

WHINBERRY DARTMOORS
Whinberry Dartmoors, Millfield Cottage, Wetherby Rd, Long Marston, **Yorkshire (North)**, YO26 7NG, **ENGLAND**.
(T) 01904 738159.
Profile Breeder. **Ref: YH15282**

WHIPPS, TONY
Tony Whipps, Nook Farm, Orestan Lane, Effingham, **Surrey**, KT24 5SN, **ENGLAND**.
(T) 01372 458470. **Ref: YH15283**

WHIRLEDGE & NOTT
Whirledge & Nott - Chartered Surveyors & Valuers, The Estate Office, White Hall, Margaret Roding, Great Dunmow, **Essex**, CM6 1QL, **ENGLAND**.
(T) 01245 231123 (F) 01245 231167.
Profile Club/Association. **Ref: YH15284**

WHISGILLS RIDING CTRE
Whisgills Riding Centre, Whisgills Hse, Newcastleton, **Scottish Borders**, TD9 0TQ, **SCOTLAND**.
(T) 01387 375675 (F) 01387 375675.
Profile Horse/Rider Accom, Riding School, Stable/Livery. **Ref: YH15285**

WHISTLEY FORGE SADDLERY
Whistley Forge Saddlery, Whistley Rd, Pottern, Devizes, **Wiltshire**, SN10 5TD, **ENGLAND**.
(T) 01380 722238.
Profile Saddlery Retailer. **Ref: YH15286**

WHITAKER, A S
A S Whitaker, Adams Farm, Paythorne, Guisburn, Clitheroe, **Lancashire**, BB7 4JD, **ENGLAND**.
(T) 01200 445350 (F) 01200 445350. **Ref: YH15287**

WHITAKER, J A

J A Whitaker, Folgate, Folgate Lane, Walpole St. Andrew, Wisbech, **Cambridgeshire**, PE14 7HY, **ENGLAND**.
(T) 01945 780456.
Contact/s
Owner: Mr J Whitaker **Ref: YH15288**

WHITAKER, JOHN

John Whitaker MBE, Heyside Farm, Cumberworth, Huddersfield, **Yorkshire (West)**, HD8 8YD, **ENGLAND**.
(T) 01484 606789.. **Ref: YH15289**

WHITAKER, MICHAEL

Michael Whitaker, Whatton Fields Farm, Conery Lane, Whatton, **Nottinghamshire**, NG13 9FJ, **ENGLAND**.
(T) 01949 850825. **Ref: YH15290**

WHITAKER, R M

R M Whitaker, Hellwood Stud Farm, Hellwood Lane, Scarcroft, Leeds, **Yorkshire (West)**, LS14 3BP, **ENGLAND**.
(T) 0113 2892265 **(F)** 0113 2893680.
Contact/s
Owner: Mrs R Whitaker
Profile Breeder, Trainer. **Ref: YH15291**

WHITAKERS

Whitakers Equestrian Services Ltd, West Lane, Bledlow, Princes Risborough, **Buckinghamshire**, HP27 9PF, **ENGLAND**.
(T) 01844 342109 **(F)** 01844 347836
(E) jbass@qudos.com.
Profile Trainer.
Whitakers train to showjumping level and retrain problem or difficult horses. **Ref: YH15292**

WHITAKERS EQUESTRIAN

Whitakers Equestrian Services Ltd, 3 Hikers Way, Drakes Drive, Long Crendon, Aylesbury, **Buckinghamshire**, HP18 9RW, **ENGLAND**.
(T) 01844 202151 **(F)** 01844 202152
(E) mandy@pollyjumps.com
(W) www.polyjumps.com.
Profile Supplies. **Ref: YH15293**

WHITBREAD HOP FARM

Whitbread Hop Farm & Shire Horses, Beltring, Paddock Wood, Tonbridge, **Kent**, TN12 6PY, **ENGLAND**.
(T) 01622 872068 **(F)** 01622 872630.
Profile Breeder. **Ref: YH15294**

WHITBY & DISTRICT RIDING CLUB

Whitby & District Riding Club, 2 The Esplanade, Robin Hoods Bay, Whitby, **Yorkshire (North)**, YO22 4RS, **ENGLAND**.
(T) 01947 880330.
Contact/s
Chairman: Mr R Pearson
Profile Club/Association, Riding Club. **Ref: YH15295**

WHITBY, ALEXANDER J

Alexander J Whitby DWCF, 341 St Leonards Rd, Windsor, **Berkshire**, SL4 3DS, **ENGLAND**.
(T) 07000 262253.
Profile Farrier. **Ref: YH15296**

WHITCOMBE, SUSIE

Susie Whitcombe, Redwood Cottage, West Meon, **Hampshire**, GU32 1JU, **ENGLAND**.
(T) 01730 828235
(M) 07774 279080. **Ref: YH15297**

WHITCOOMBE HOUSE STABLES

Whitcoombe House Stables, Upper Lambourn, Hungerford, **Berkshire**, RG17 8RA, **ENGLAND**.
(T) 01488 71717 **(F)** 01488 73223
(M) 07721 888333
(E) charlie.mann@virgin.net.
Profile Trainer. **Ref: YH15298**

WHITE & BISHOP

White & Bishop Ltd, Riding Department, 13-17 Bridge St, Northampton, **Northamptonshire**, NN1 1NL, **ENGLAND**.
(T) 01604 230901 **(F)** 01604 630492.
Contact/s
Retail Manager: Mr S Mosley
Profile Saddlery Retailer. **Ref: YH15299**

WHITE BRIDGE FORGE

White Bridge Forge, Grasmere, Ambleside, **Cumbria**, LA22 9RQ, **ENGLAND**.
(T) 01539 435414.
Profile Blacksmith. **Ref: YH15300**

WHITE CAT STABLES

White Cat Stables, Howsmoor Lane, Emersons Green, Bristol, **Bristol**, BS16 7AQ, **ENGLAND**.
(T) 01179 564370.
Profile Riding School, Stable/Livery. **Ref: YH15301**

WHITE COTTAGE FARM

White Cottage Farm, White Cottage, Lucas Green Rd, West End, Woking, **Surrey**, GU24 9LZ, **ENGLAND**.
(T) 01483 473473. **Ref: YH15302**

WHITE CROSS VET HOSPITAL

White Cross Vet Hospital, 8 Bradford Rd, Guiseley, **Yorkshire (West)**, LS20 8NH, **ENGLAND**.
(T) 01943 873147.
Profile Medical Support. **Ref: YH15303**

WHITE HALL LIVERY STABLES

White Hall Livery Stables (The), The White Hall Est, Little Budworth, **Cheshire**, CW6 9EL, **ENGLAND**.
(T) 01829 760393.
Contact/s
Owner: H Taylor
Profile Breeder, Stable/Livery.
Full, part and DIY livery avaliable, details on request.
Ref: YH15304

WHITE HART STABLES

White Hart Stables, Childrens School of Riding, 47 Main St, Gt Gidding, Huntingdon, **Cambridgeshire**, PE17 5NU, **ENGLAND**.
(T) 01832 293277.
Profile Riding School. **Ref: YH15305**

WHITE HORSE ANIMAL FEEDS

White Horse Animal Feeds, Pond Farm, Childrey, Wantage, **Oxfordshire**, OX12 9UA, **ENGLAND**.
(T) 01235 751529 **(F)** 01235 751331
(W) www.white-horse-animal-feeds.co.uk.
Profile Supplies. **Ref: YH15306**

WHITE HORSE COUNTRY WEAR

White Horse Country Wear, 19B Market Pl, Faringdon, **Oxfordshire**, SN7 7HP, **ENGLAND**.
(T) 01367 242727 **(F)** 01367 820431.
Profile Saddlery Retailer. **Ref: YH15307**

WHITE HORSE EQUESTRIAN CTRE

White Horse Equestrian Centre, Long River Farm, Newtown, Westbury, **Wiltshire**, BA13 3HQ, **ENGLAND**.
(T) 01373 822057 **(F)** 01225 760359
(W) www.whitehorsecentre.co.uk.
Contact/s
Owner: Mrs L Miles
Profile Horse/Rider Accom, Riding School, Stable/Livery, Trekking Centre.
The centre runs all day pub hacks and BBQ rides, the hacks are priced at £10.00 per hour, and there is an option to stay a day, at the price of £18.00 a day. The centre also has livery available with 24 hour security. There is also an opportunity to loan a pony.
No.Staff: 2 Yr. Est: 1992 C.Size: 100 Acres
Opening Times
Open Tues - Sun, telephone between 10:00 - 16:00
Ref: YH15308

WHITE HORSE MOTORS

White Horse Motors, Tedburn Rd, Whitestone, Exeter, **Devon**, EX4 2HF, **ENGLAND**.
(T) 01392 811581 **(F)** 01392 811722
(E) whitehorsemotors@btconnect.com.
Contact/s
Admin: Ms S Bennet
Profile Transport/Horse Boxes.
Specialists in four wheel drive vehicles. Also sell horse boxes and lifestock trailers. **Ref: YH15309**

WHITE HORSE RESCUE STABLES

White Horse Rescue Stables, Worsham Farm Hse, Worsham Lane, Bexhill-on-Sea, **Sussex (East)**, TN40 2QP, **ENGLAND**.
(T) 01424 224835 **(F)** 01424 775362.
Contact/s
Partner: Mrs D Barclay-Bernard **Ref: YH15310**

WHITE HORSE RIDING STABLES

White Horse Riding Stables, Goosey Glebe Smallholding, Goosey, Wantage, **Oxfordshire**, SN7 8PA, **ENGLAND**.
(T) 01367 718806.
Profile Riding School. **Ref: YH15311**

WHITE HORSE SADDLERY

White Horse Saddlery, 12 Fallow Rd, South Shields, **Tyne and Wear**, NE34 7AG, **ENGLAND**.
(T) 0191 4546635.
Contact/s
Owner: Mrs D Geach **Ref: YH15312**

WHITE HORSE SADDLERY

White Horse Saddlery, Rainbows End, Stockbridge Rd, Lopcombe Corner, Salisbury, **Wiltshire**, SP5 1BW, **ENGLAND**.
(T) 01980 863697 **(F)** 01980 863697
(E) whsaddlery@aol.com.
Profile Saddlery Retailer. **Ref: YH15313**

WHITE HORSE STABLES

White Horse Stables, Goosey Glebe Small Holdings, Goosey, Faringdon, **Oxfordshire**, SN7 8PA, **ENGLAND**.
(T) 01367 718806.
Profile Stable/Livery. **Ref: YH15314**

WHITE HORSE VETNRY CLINIC

White Horse Veterinary Clinic, 15 Curzon St, Calne, **Wiltshire**, SN11 0DB, **ENGLAND**.
(T) 01249 812715 **(F)** 01249 813850.
Profile Medical Support. **Ref: YH15315**

WHITE HORSE VETNRY CLINIC

White Horse Veterinary Clinic, The Veterinary Surgery, Chippenham Rd, Lyneham, **Wiltshire**, SN15, **ENGLAND**.
(T) 01249 890358 **(F)** 01249 813850.
Profile Medical Support. **Ref: YH15316**

WHITE HORSES

White Horses, The Old Exchange, Mill Lane, Welwyn, **Hertfordshire**, AL6 9EU, **ENGLAND**.
(T) 01438 715819.
Profile Supplies. **Ref: YH15317**

WHITE HSE FARM

White House Farm Equestrian Centre, St James Rd, Goffs Oak, Waltham Cross, **Hertfordshire**, EN7 6TR, **ENGLAND**.
(T) 01707 872877. **Ref: YH15318**

WHITE HSE STABLES

White House Stables, Theobald Park Rd, Enfield, **London (Greater)**, EN2 9BW, **ENGLAND**.
(T) 020 83670605.
Contact/s
Owner: Mr S Stillwell
Profile Stable/Livery. **Ref: YH15319**

WHITE LODGE SADDLERY

White Lodge Saddlery, White Lodge, Middle Rd, Tiptoe, Lymington, **Hampshire**, SO41 6FX, **ENGLAND**.
(T) 01590 681717 **(F)** 01590 681717.
Contact/s
Owner: Mr A Davis **Ref: YH15320**

WHITE LODGE STABLES

White Lodge Stables, White Lodge, Wood Lane, Iver, **Buckinghamshire**, SL0 0LE, **ENGLAND**.
(T) 01753 653000. **Ref: YH15321**

WHITE ROCKS FARM STUD

White Rocks Farm Stud, Underriver, Sevenoaks, **Kent**, TN15 0SL, **ENGLAND**.
(T) 01732 762913 **(F)** 01732 763767.
Profile Breeder. **Ref: YH15322**

WHITE ROSE RIDING CLUB

White Rose Riding Club, 1 Redgates, Walkington, Beverley, **Yorkshire (East)**, HU17 8TS, **ENGLAND**.
(T) 01482 867677.
Contact/s
Chairman: Mrs J Banks
Profile Club/Association, Riding Club. **Ref: YH15323**

WHITE ROSE SADDLERY

White Rose Saddlery, 62-64 Castlegate, Malton, **Yorkshire (North)**, YO17 7DZ, **ENGLAND**.
(T) 01653 697440 **(F)** 01653 697440.
Contact/s
Owner: Mr C Hoggard
Profile Saddlery Retailer.
Racing specialists No.Staff: 3 Yr. Est: 1984
Opening Times
Sp: Open Mon - Sat 09:00. Closed Mon - Sat 17:30.
Su: Open Mon - Sat 09:00. Closed Mon - Sat 17:30.
Au: Open Mon - Sat 09:00. Closed Mon - Sat 17:30.
Wn: Open Mon - Sat 09:00. Closed Mon - Sat 17:30.
Ref: YH15324

WHITE TOR

White Tor Stables, Broadmoor Farm, Peter Tavy, Tavistock, **Devon**, PL19 9LZ, **ENGLAND**.
(T) 01822 810760
(E) mail@whitetor.co.uk

(W) www.whitetor.co.uk.
Contact/s
Owner: Mr D Turner
(E) enquiries@whitetor.co.uk
Profile Holidays, Horse/Rider Accom.
Parelli Natural Horsemanship and Trail Riding available. Western riding holidays. No.Staff: 4
Yr. Est: 1999 C.Size: 30 Acres
Opening Times
Accommodation is available all year Ref: YH15325

WHITE, A

A White, Knowles Farm, Fox Lane, Holmesfield, Dronfield, **Derbyshire**, S18 7WG, **ENGLAND**.
(T) 0114 2890688.
Profile Farrier. Ref: YH15326

WHITE, BENJAMIN J

Benjamin J White DWCF, No 2 Liddimore Farm Cottages, Watchet, **Somerset**, TA23 0UA, **ENGLAND**.
(T) 01984 632126.
Profile Farrier. Ref: YH15327

WHITE, CHRISTINA

Christina White, Wych Elm, Nottington, Weymouth, **Dorset**, DT3 4BN, **ENGLAND**.
(T) 01305 813430 (F) 01305 813430
Affiliated Bodies BHS, BSJA.
Contact/s
Owner: Christina White
(E) tinawhite@mail.com
Profile Breeder, Supplies, Photographer.
Emergency supplier of artificial foal milk Ref: YH15328

WHITE, F B

Mr F B White, Fernleigh Farm, Teversham, **Cambridgeshire**, CB1 5AN, **ENGLAND**.
(T) 01223 880235.
Profile Breeder. Ref: YH15329

WHITE, F E

Mrs F E White, The Lodge, Nipsells Farm, Nipsells Chase, Mayland, Mayland, Chelmsford, **Essex**, CM3 6EJ, **ENGLAND**.
(T) 01621 742161 (F) 01621 742161
(M) 07850 209368.
Profile Supplies. Ref: YH15330

WHITE, G F

Mr G F White, School Hse, Rennington, Alnwick, **Northumberland**, NE66 3RR, **ENGLAND**.
(T) 01665 603231 (F) 01665 510872.
Profile Supplies. Ref: YH15331

WHITE, K B

K B White, The Forge, Caynham, Ludlow, **Shropshire**, SY8 3BJ, **ENGLAND**.
(T) 01584 877444.
Profile Transport/Horse Boxes. Ref: YH15332

WHITE, KEVIN

Kevin White AWCF, 20 Furzeland Way, Sayers Common, Hassocks, **Sussex (West)**, BN6 9JB, **ENGLAND**.
(T) 01273 834225.
Profile Farrier. Ref: YH15333

WHITE, MARK W

Mark W White DWCF, Meadow View, Days Lane, Pilgrims Hatch, Brentwood, **Essex**, CM15 9SJ, **ENGLAND**.
(T) 01277 375955.
Profile Farrier. Ref: YH15334

WHITE, STEVEN G C

Steven G C White DWCF, 83 Blakefield Rd, St Johns, **Worcestershire**, WR2 5DP, **ENGLAND**.
(T) 01905 749236
(M) 07778 847156.
Profile Farrier. Ref: YH15335

WHITEFIELD, IAN

Ian Whitefield, Barrington Hill Forge, Broadway, Ilminster, **Somerset**, TA19 9LW, **ENGLAND**.
(T) 01823 480340.
Contact/s
Owner: Mr I Whitefield
Profile Blacksmith. Ref: YH15336

WHITEGATE

Whitegate Riding School & Livery Yard, Vale Royal Drive, Whitegate, Northwich, **Cheshire**, CW8 2BA, **ENGLAND**.
(T) 01606 889233.
Profile Riding School, Stable/Livery. Ref: YH15337

WHITEGATE FARM

Whitegate Farm Riding School, Whitegate Farm, Tunstead, Bacup, **Lancashire**, OL13 8NL, **ENGLAND**.
(T) 01706 873555
Affiliated Bodies Pony Club UK.
Contact/s
Owner: Ms E Kay (Q) BHSAI
Profile Arena, Equestrian Centre, Riding School, Stable/Livery, Trainer.
Pony fun days, stable management, gymkhanas. Ponies available on loan. No.Staff: 4
Yr. Est: 1994 C.Size: 50 Acres
Opening Times
Sp: Open 08:00. Closed 17:00.
Su: Open 08:00. Closed 20:00.
Au: Open 08:00. Closed 17:00.
Wn: Open 08:00. Closed 17:00. Ref: YH15338

WHITEGATE STUD

Whitegate Stables, 3 Plans Of Thornton, Glamis, Forfar, **Angus**, DD8 1UA, **SCOTLAND**.
(T) 01307 840654 (F) 01307 840654.
Contact/s
Owner: Mrs L Lindsay
Profile Breeder. Ref: YH15339

WHITEHALL TRAILERS

Whitehall Trailers, Top Tomlow Farm, Tomlow Rd, Stockton-on-Tees, **Cleveland**, CV47 8HX, **ENGLAND**.
(T) 01926 812088 (F) 01926 812915
(W) www.iwt.co.uk.
Profile Transport/Horse Boxes. No.Staff: 3
Yr. Est: 1985 C.Size: 17 Acres
Opening Times
Sp: Open 08:30. Closed 18:00.
Su: Open 08:30. Closed 18:00.
Au: Open 08:30. Closed 18:00.
Wn: Open 08:30. Closed 18:00. Ref: YH15340

WHITEHALL, G

G Whitehall, The Homestead, Broadwell, Rugby, **Warwickshire**, CV23 8HF, **ENGLAND**.
(T) 01926 812088 (F) 01926 812915.
Contact/s
Owner: Mr G Whitehall
Profile Transport/Horse Boxes. Ref: YH15341

WHITEHEAD, P (DR)

Dr P Whitehead, Pegmore, Church Lane, Prior's Norton, **Gloucestershire**, GL2 9LS, **ENGLAND**.
(T) 01452 730352 (F) 01452 714726.
Profile Medical Support. Ref: YH15342

WHITEHILL FORGE & WORKS

Whitehill Forge & Works, Carnethie St, Rosewell, **Lothian (Mid)**, EH24 9DS, **SCOTLAND**.
(T) 0131 4402715.
Contact/s
Owner: Mr D Jack
Profile Blacksmith. Ref: YH15343

WHITEHOUSE FARM

Whitehouse Farm, Birchwood Lane, South Normanton, Alfreton, **Derbyshire**, DE55 3DD, **ENGLAND**.
(T) 01773 811220.
Contact/s
Owner: Mr R Webster
Profile Stable/Livery. Ref: YH15344

WHITEHOUSE RIDING SCHOOL

Whitehouse Riding School, Cornhill Hse, Cornhill-on-Tweed, **Northumberland**, TD12 4UD, **ENGLAND**.
(T) 01890 882422.
Contact/s
Owner: Mrs S Smith
Profile Riding School. Ref: YH15345

WHITEHURST, A E A

A E A Whitehurst, Rose Croft, Lower Frankton, Oswestry, **Shropshire**, SY11 4PB, **ENGLAND**.
(T) 01691 622139.
Profile Farrier. Ref: YH15346

WHITELEAF RIDING CTRE

Whiteleaf Riding Centre, Lower Rd, Teynham, Sittingbourne, **Kent**, ME9 9BY, **ENGLAND**.
(T) 01795 522512
Affiliated Bodies BHS.
Contact/s
Owner: Mrs L Martin (Q) BHSAI
Profile Equestrian Centre, Riding School, Stable/Livery. No.Staff: 4 C.Size: 25 Acres
Opening Times
Sp: Open 08:00. Closed 21:00.
Su: Open 08:00. Closed 21:00.
Au: Open 08:00. Closed 20:30.
Wn: Open 08:00. Closed 20:30. Ref: YH15347

WHITELEY, M

M Whiteley, Stock-A-Close Farm, Cottingley, Bingley, **Yorkshire (West)**, BD16 1RD, **ENGLAND**.
(T) 01274 480811.
Profile Breeder. Ref: YH15348

WHITELOCH FARM STABLES

Whiteloch Farm Stables, Macmerry, Tranent, **Lothian (East)**, EH33 1PQ, **SCOTLAND**.
(T) 01875 613662.
Profile Riding School. Ref: YH15349

WHITELOCKS FARM RIDING SCHOOL

Whitelocks Farm Riding School, Garsons Lane, Warfield, Bracknell, **Berkshire**, RG42 6JA, **ENGLAND**.
(T) 01344 890522.
Profile Riding School, Stable/Livery. Ref: YH15350

WHITEMOOR RIDING CTRE

Whitemoor Riding Centre, Whitemoor Bottom Farm, Whitemoor Rd, Foulridge, Colne, **Lancashire**, BB8 7LX, **ENGLAND**.
(T) 01282 861890.
Contact/s
Partner: Mrs R Stanworth
Profile Riding School, Stable/Livery. Ref: YH15351

WHITEMYRES STUD

Whitemyres Stud (Youngstock), Whitemyres, Lang Stracht, Aberdeen, **Aberdeen (City of)**, AB12 2JW, **SCOTLAND**.
(T) 01224 317154.
Profile Stable/Livery. Ref: YH15352

WHITEMYRES STUD LIVERY YARD

Whitemyres Stud Livery Yard, 8 Small Holdings, Kingswells, Aberdeen, **Aberdeen (City of)**, AB15 8PS, **SCOTLAND**.
(T) 01224 317154.
Contact/s
Owner: Mr D Pocock
Profile Breeder, Stable/Livery. Ref: YH15353

WHITEOAK & SONS

Whiteoak & Sons, 12 Mullion Cl, Manchester, **Manchester (Greater)**, M19 3ZF, **ENGLAND**.
(T) 0161 2488300 (F) 0161 2488300.
Contact/s
Owner: Mr G Whitehall
Profile Blacksmith. Ref: YH15354

WHITES

Whites, Forge Lane, Little Aston, Sutton Coldfield, **Midlands (West)**, B74 3BE, **ENGLAND**.
(T) 01543 677535.
Contact/s
Owner: Mrs L Mullen
Profile Transport/Horse Boxes. Ref: YH15355

WHITES FARM STUD

Whites Farm Stud, Brickyard Lane, Corfe Mullen, Wimborne, **Dorset**, BH21 3RJ, **ENGLAND**.
(T) 01258 857444 (F) 01258 857946.
Contact/s
Owner: Mr I White
Profile Breeder. Ref: YH15356

WHITESHOOT STABLES

Whiteshoot Stables, Woodway Rd, Blewbury, **Oxfordshire**, OX11 9EZ, **ENGLAND**.
(T) 01235 851161
(M) 07711 321813.
Profile Trainer. Ref: YH15357

WHITESIDE TRAILERS

Whiteside Trailers, Airntully, Stanley, Perth, **Perth and Kinross**, PH1 4PH, **SCOTLAND**.
(T) 01738 828716.
Contact/s
Owner: Mr E Whiteside
Profile Transport/Horse Boxes. Ref: YH15358

WHITEWOOD HSE FARM

Whitewood House Farm, Horne, Horley, **Surrey**, RH6 9JZ, **ENGLAND**.
(T) 01342 842059.
Profile Stable/Livery. Ref: YH15359

WHITFIELD, PAUL A

Paul A Whitfield DWCF, 4 Wulphere Cl, Dunkeswell, Honiton, **Devon**, EX14 0UU, **ENGLAND**..
Profile Farrier. Ref: YH15360

WHITFORD RIDING STABLE

Whitford Riding Stable, Whitford Bridge Rd, Stoke Prior, Bromsgrove, **Worcestershire**, B60 4HE, **ENGLAND**.
(T) 01527 832005.
Contact/s
Owner: Mrs S Hedges
Profile Riding School, Stable/Livery. Ref: YH15361

WHITFORD RIDING STABLES

Whitford Riding Stables, Stoke Pound Lane, Stoke Prior, Bromsgrove, **Worcestershire**, B60 4LE, **ENGLAND**.
(T) 01527 832005. **Ref: YH15362**

WHITLEY EQUITATION CTRE

Whitley Equitation Centre, Whitley Rd, Whitley, Dewsbury, **Yorkshire (West)**, WF12 0LY, **ENGLAND**.
(T) 01924 496441 **(F)** 01924 499833.
Contact/s
General Manager: Mrs C Voyce **(Q)** BHS SM, BHSII
Profile Equestrian Centre, Riding Club, Riding School.
Teach people the art of classical riding. Specialise in treasure hunts **No.Staff:** 6 **Yr. Est:** 1983
C.Size: 80 Acres
Opening Times
Sp: Open Mon - Sun 09:00. Closed Mon, Fri - Sun 18:00, Tues - Thurs 21:30.
Su: Open Mon - Sun 09:00. Closed Mon, Fri - Sun 18:00, Tues - Thurs 21:30.
Au: Open Mon - Sun 09:00. Closed Mon, Fri - Sun 18:00, Tues - Thurs 21:30.
Wn: Open Mon - Sun 09:00. Closed Mon, Fri - Sun 18:00, Tues - Thurs 21:30. **Ref: YH15363**

WHITMARSH, R A

R A Whitmarsh, Hill View Farm, East Stoke, Wareham, **Dorset**, BH20 6AW, **ENGLAND**.
(T) 01929 462098.
Profile Farrier. **Ref: YH15364**

WHITMORE RIDING SCHOOL

Whitmore Riding School, Shut Lane Head, Butterton, Newcastle, **Staffordshire**, ST5 4DS, **ENGLAND**.
(T) 01782 680368.
Contact/s
Owner: Mr B Jones
Profile Riding School. **Ref: YH15365**

WHITMORE, B C

B C Whitmore, 1 Hope St, Walsall, **Midlands (West)**, WS1 3RG, **ENGLAND**.
(T) 01922 646212 **(F)** 01922 646212.
Contact/s
Owner: Mr B Whitmore **Ref: YH15366**

WHITMORE, S

Miss S Whitmore, Hilders Farmhouse, Edenbridge, **Kent**, TN8 6LE, **ENGLAND**.
(T) 01732 862679 **(F)** 01732 862268.
Profile Trainer. **Ref: YH15367**

WHITMORE, SUE

Mrs Sue Whitmore, 2 Andrews Way, Raunds, Wellingborough, **Northamptonshire**, NN9 6RD, **ENGLAND**.
(T) 01933 460715.
Profile Trainer. **Ref: YH15368**

WHITNEY, A

A Whitney, 25 Dulais Rd, Seven Sisters, Neath, **Glamorgan (Vale of)**, SA10 9EL, **WALES**.
(T) 01639 701015 **(F)** 01639 701015.
Contact/s
Owner: Mr A Whitney
Profile Farrier. **Ref: YH15369**

WHITSBURY MANOR

Whitsbury Manor Racing Stables, Whitsbury, Fordingbridge, **Hampshire**, SP6 3QQ, **ENGLAND**.
(T) 01725 518889 **(F)** 01725 518747
(M) 07771 804828.
Profile Trainer. **Ref: YH15370**

WHITSBURY MANOR STUD

Whitsbury Manor Stud, Whitsbury, Fordingbridge, **Hampshire**, SP6 3QP, **ENGLAND**.
(T) 01725 518283 **(F)** 01725 518503.
Profile Breeder. **Ref: YH15371**

WHITTABOROUGH

Whittaborough, Shaugh Priory, Plympton, **Devon**, PL7 5ES, **ENGLAND**.
(T) 01752 839762.
Profile Breeder, Stable/Livery. **Ref: YH15372**

WHITTAKER HORSE BOXES

Whittaker Horse Boxes, Agromony Hse, Gamston Airfield, Retford, **Nottinghamshire**, DN22 0QL, **ENGLAND**.
(T) 01777 839086 **(F)** 01777 839170.
Profile Transport/Horse Boxes. **Ref: YH15373**

WHITTAKER, O C

Mr O C Whittaker, Church Farm, Tabley, Knutsford, **Cheshire**, WA16 0PR, **ENGLAND**.
(T) 01565 632367.
Profile Breeder. **Ref: YH15374**

WHITTINGTON, T J

T J Whittington DWCF, 5 Church Down Cl, Crabbs Cross, Redditch, **Worcestershire**, B97 5ND, **ENGLAND**.
(T) 01527 402511.
Profile Farrier. **Ref: YH15375**

WHITTON FARM HSE HOTEL

Whitton Farm House Hotel, Whitton, Rothbury, **Northumberland**, NE65 7RL, **ENGLAND**.
(T) 01669 620811 **(F)** 01669 620811.
Profile Equestrian Centre. **Ref: YH15376**

WHITWAM, EDWARD J

Edward J Whitwam DWCF, C/O Sowerby Croft Farm, Norland, Halifax, **Yorkshire (West)**, HX6 3QS, **ENGLAND**.
(T) 07788 421252.
Profile Farrier. **Ref: YH15377**

WHITWORTH BROS

Whitworth Bros Ltd (Peterborough), Fletton Mills, East Station Rd, Peterborough, **Cambridgeshire**, PE2 8AD, **ENGLAND**.
(T) 01733 343434.
Profile Supplies. **Ref: YH15378**

WHYATT, D J

D J Whyatt BII, Appleslade Cottage, Linwood, Ringwood, **Hampshire**, BH24 3QT, **ENGLAND**.
(T) 01425 473817.
Profile Farrier. **Ref: YH15379**

WHYDOWN PLACE EQUESTRIAN CTRE

Whydown Place Equestrian Centre, Whydown Pl, Whydown Rd, Bexhill-on-Sea, **Sussex (East)**, TN39 4RA, **ENGLAND**.
(T) 01424 848169.
Profile Riding School. **Ref: YH15380**

WHYTE, J W

Mr J W Whyte, Becks Green Farm, Becks Green Lane, Ilketshall St Andrew, Beccles, **Suffolk**, NR34 8NB, **ENGLAND**.
(T) 01986 781221 **(F)** 01986 781406.
Profile Supplies. **Ref: YH15381**

WICKFIELD STUD

Wickfield Stud, Wickfield Lane, Cleeve Hill, Cheltenham, **Gloucestershire**, GL52 3PW, **ENGLAND**.
(T) 01242 675037.
Contact/s
Key Contact: Mr N Brookes
Profile Supplies. **Ref: YH15382**

WICKHAM STABLES

Wickham Stables, The White Hse, Wickham Common, Fareham, **Hampshire**, PO17 6JQ, **ENGLAND**.
(T) 01329 832035.
Contact/s
Owner: Mr R Schofield
Profile Breeder, Stable/Livery. **Ref: YH15383**

WICKHAM TRAILER HIRE

Wickham Trailer Hire, New Barn Cottage, Shinehill Lane, South Littleton, Evesham, **Worcestershire**, WR11 5TR, **ENGLAND**.
(T) 01386 830794 **(F)** 01386 830794.
Contact/s
Owner: Mr J Beasley
Profile Transport/Horse Boxes. **Ref: YH15384**

WICKRIDGE

Wickridge Farm, Folly Lane, Stroud, **Gloucestershire**, GL6 7JT, **ENGLAND**.
(T) 01453 764357.
Contact/s
Partner: Gloria Watkins
Profile Stable/Livery.
DIY livery, details on request. **Yr. Est:** 1987
C.Size: 250 Acres
Opening Times
Sp: Open Mon - Sun 08:00. Closed Mon - Sun 18:00.
Su: Open Mon - Sun 08:00. Closed Mon - Sun 18:00.
Au: Open Mon - Sun 08:00. Closed Mon - Sun 18:00.
Wn: Open Mon - Sun 08:00. Closed Mon - Sun 18:00. **Ref: YH15385**

WICKS, E J

E J Wicks, Newbury St, Lambourn, Hungerford, **Berkshire**, RG17 8PB, **ENGLAND**.
(T) 01488 71766 **(F)** 01488 71707.
Contact/s
Owner: Mr M Bentick **Ref: YH15386**

WICKSTEAD FARM

Wickstead Farm Equestrian Centre, Wickstead Farm, Highworth, Swindon, **Wiltshire**, SN6 7PP, **ENGLAND**.
(T) 01793 762265.
Profile Riding School, Stable/Livery. **Ref: YH15387**

WIDBROOK ARABIAN STUD

Widbrook Arabian Stud & Equestrian Centre, Trowbridge Rd, Widbrook, Bradford-on-Avon, **Wiltshire**, BA15 1UD, **ENGLAND**.
(T) 01225 862608 **(F)** 01225 864562.
Contact/s
General Manager: Ms K Griggs **(Q)** BHSAI
Profile Breeder, Equestrian Centre, Riding School, Stable/Livery.
Polocrosse Lessons and Club, BHS Pony Club Centre, Client Courses and Competitions **No.Staff:** 5
Yr. Est: 1978 **C.Size:** 70 Acres
Opening Times
Sp: Open 09:00. Closed 20:00.
Su: Open 09:00. Closed 20:00.
Au: Open 09:00. Closed 20:00.
Wn: Open 09:00. Closed 20:00. **Ref: YH15388**

WIDDAS, A

A Widdas, 15 Esperley Lane, Cockfield, Bishop Auckland, **County Durham**, DL13 5AN, **ENGLAND**.
(T) 01388 718250.
Contact/s
Owner: Mr A Widdas
Profile Transport/Horse Boxes. **Ref: YH15389**

WIDDAS, TONY

Tony Widdas, 15 Esperley Lane, Cockfield, **County Durham**, DL14 5AN, **ENGLAND**.
(T) 01388 718250.
Profile Transport/Horse Boxes. **Ref: YH15390**

WIDESERVE

Wideserve Ltd, The Ctre, Codicote Rd, Welwyn, **Hertfordshire**, AL6 9TU, **ENGLAND**.
(T) 01438 716873 **(F)** 01438 717535
(E) drtm@aol.com.
Profile Saddlery Retailer. **Ref: YH15391**

WIDMER EQUESTRIAN CTRE

Widmer Equestrian Centre, Widmer Farm, Pink Rd, Lacey Green, Princes Risborough, **Buckinghamshire**, HP27 0PG, **ENGLAND**.
(T) 01844 275139.
Contact/s
Owner: Mrs C Davies
Profile Riding School. **Ref: YH15392**

WIDMER FEEDS

Widmer Feeds Ltd, Pink Rd, Lacey Green, Princes Risborough, **Buckinghamshire**, HP27 0PQ, **ENGLAND**.
(T) 01844 347170 **(F)** 01844 347446.
Profile Feed Merchant. **Ref: YH15393**

WIEGERSMA, HENDRIK J

Hendrik J Wiegersma, Tregembo, Relubbus, Penzance, **Cornwall**, TR20 9EW, **ENGLAND**.
(T) 01736 762445.
Profile Breeder. **Ref: YH15394**

WIERSMA, HAITZE

Haitze Wiersma DWCF, 6 Amberley Drive, Twyford, **Berkshire**, RG10 9BZ, **ENGLAND**.
(T) 0118 9344058.
Profile Farrier. **Ref: YH15395**

WIGGETT-COOPER, J

Mrs J Wiggett-Cooper, 46 Frost Rd, Kinson, **Dorset**, BH11 8HR, **ENGLAND**.
(T) 01202 578987.
Profile Breeder. **Ref: YH15396**

WIGGINS, CELIA

Celia Wiggins, 1 Newlands Farm Cottages, Snoad St, Throwley, Faversham, **Kent**, ME13 0JW, **ENGLAND**.
(T) 01233 712321
(M) 07703 653726.
Profile Trainer. **Ref: YH15397**

WIGGINS, CHRISTOPHER A

Christopher A Wiggins DWCF, 2 Yew Tree Cottage, Upper St, Leeds, Maidstone, **Kent**, ME17 1RU,

ENGLAND.
(T) 01622 816868.
Profile Farrier. **Ref: YH15398**

WIGGINS, R J

R J Wiggins, The Forge, Wolverton, Basingstoke, **Hampshire**, RG26 5SU, **ENGLAND**.
(T) 01635 298994.
Profile Farrier. **Ref: YH15399**

WIGHAM, M

M Wigham, Pond Hse, Church Lane, Exning, Newmarket, **Suffolk**, **ENGLAND**.
(T) 01638 578578
(M) 07831 456426
(W) www.newmarketracehorsetrainers.co.uk.
Contact/s
Trainer: Mr M Wigham
Profile Trainer. **Ref: YH15400**

WIGHT, A J

Mr A J Wight, Ecclaw, Cockburnspath, **Scottish Borders**, TD13 5YJ, **SCOTLAND**.
(T) 01368 3219.
Profile Supplies. **Ref: YH15401**

WIKEFIELD FARM LIVERIES

Wikefield Farm Liveries, Harrogate Rd, Harewood, Leeds, **Yorkshire (West)**, LS17 9JZ, **ENGLAND**.
(T) 0113 2886315 **(F)** 0113 2886315.
Contact/s
Farm Manager: Mr R Harrison
Profile Stable/Livery, Track/Course. **Ref: YH15402**

WILBY DARTMOOR PONIES

Wilby Dartmoor Ponies, The Old Rectory Hse, Wilby, Wellingborough, **Northamptonshire**, NN8 2UQ, **ENGLAND**.
(T) 01933 229394.
Profile Breeder. **Ref: YH15403**

WILCOX COACH WORKS

Wilcox Coach Works, Denbigh Rd, Afonwen, Mold, **Flintshire**, CH7 5UB, **WALES**.
(T) 01352 720955 **(F)** 01352 720872.
Profile Transport/Horse Boxes. **Ref: YH15404**

WILD TRAILER SERVICES

Wild Trailer Services, Unit 2 United Trading Est, Manchester, **Manchester (Greater)**, M16 0RJ, **ENGLAND**.
(T) 0161 8737866.
Profile Transport/Horse Boxes. **Ref: YH15405**

WILD, THOMAS C

Thomas C Wild, Vulcan Works, Tinsley Park Rd, Sheffield, **Yorkshire (South)**, S9 5DP, **ENGLAND**.
(T) 0114 2442471 **(F)** 0114 2442052.
Profile Blacksmith. **Ref: YH15406**

WILDERNESS VENTURES

Wilderness Ventures, 96 Katrina Gr, Purston, Featherstone, **Yorkshire (West)**, WF7 5NU, **ENGLAND**.
(T) 01977 799167 **(F)** 01977 799167.
Profile Saddlery Retailer. **Ref: YH15407**

WILDGOOSE GALLERY

Wildgoose Gallery (The), Silver St, Fairburn, Knottingley, **Yorkshire (West)**, WF11 9JA, **ENGLAND**.
(T) 01977 85089. **Ref: YH15408**

WILDING, R J

Mr R J Wilding, Ragdon Farm, Church Stretton, **Shropshire**, SY6 7EZ, **ENGLAND**.
(T) 01694 781232.
Profile Horse/Rider Accom. **Ref: YH15409**

WILDSMITH SADDLERY

Wildsmith Saddlery, Chapel Drive, Doncaster, **Yorkshire (South)**, DN1 2RF, **ENGLAND**.
(T) 01302 321478.
Profile Saddlery Retailer. **Ref: YH15410**

WILDSMITH, M

M Wildsmith, Hardwick Lane, Aston, Sheffield, **Yorkshire (South)**, S26 2BE, **ENGLAND**.
(T) 0114 2872711.
Contact/s
Partner: Mr A Wildsmith **Ref: YH15411**

WILDSMITHS

Wildsmiths, Church St, Doncaster, **Yorkshire (South)**, DN1 1RD, **ENGLAND**.
(T) 01302 321478 **(F)** 01302 321478/360096.
Contact/s
Owner: Miss A Wildsmith
Profile Riding Wear Retailer, Saddlery Retailer.
No.Staff: 3 Yr. Est: 1975
Opening Times
Sp: Open Mon - Sat 09:00. Closed Mon - Sat 17:30.
Su: Open Mon - Sat 09:00. Closed Mon - Sat 17:30.
Au: Open Mon - Sat 09:00. Closed Mon - Sat 17:30.
Wn: Open Mon - Sat 09:00. Closed Mon - Sat 17:30.
Before Christmas open Sundays 11:00 - 16:30
Ref: **YH15412**

WILDWOODS

Wildwoods Riding Centre, Ebbisham Lane, Tadworth, **Surrey**, KT20 5BH, **ENGLAND**.
(T) 01737 812146
(M) 07956 390398
(E) info@wildwoodsriding.co.uk
(W) www.wildwoodsriding.co.uk
Affiliated Bodies ABRS, BHS.
Contact/s
Owner: Ms A Chambers **(Q)** BHS SM, BHSII, MNCF
Profile Riding Club, Riding School.
Training to BHSAI standard. BHS 1 and 2 examinations. Beach rides and pub rides are available. Wildwoods arranges hacks, showjumping, dressage and childrens days and have 20 well schooled, quality horses. Seventeen miles from London at the foot of the Epsom Downs. Yr. Est: 1976 C.Size: 20 Acres
Opening Times
Sp: Open Mon - Sun 08:00. Closed Mon - Sun 20:00.
Su: Open Mon - Sun 08:00. Closed Mon - Sun 20:00.
Au: Open Mon - Sun 08:00. Closed Mon - Sun 20:00.
Wn: Open Mon - Sun 08:00. Closed Mon - Sun 20:00.
Close at 18:00 at weekends **Ref: YH15413**

WILESMITH, M S

Mr M S Wilesmith, Bellamys Farm, Dymock, **Gloucestershire**, GL18 2DX, **ENGLAND**.
(T) 01531 890410 **(F)** 01684 893428.
Profile Supplies. **Ref: YH15414**

WILKES, MARTIN

Martin Wilkes RSS, Moat Farm, Berrow Hill, Feckenham, Redditch, **Worcestershire**, B96 6QS, **ENGLAND**.
(T) 01527 84345.
Profile Farrier. **Ref: YH15415**

WILKIN, KEITH M

Keith M Wilkin DWCF, 9 Passmore Cl, Blackwater, Truro, **Cornwall**, TR4 8JL, **ENGLAND**.
(T) 01872 561417.
Profile Farrier. **Ref: YH15416**

WILKINSON BROS

Wilkinson Bros, Bustlers Farm, St Peters St, Duxford, Cambridge, **Cambridgeshire**, CB2 4RP, **ENGLAND**.
(T) 01223 833292.
Contact/s
Owner: Mr G Wilkinson
Profile Transport/Horse Boxes. **Ref: YH15417**

WILKINSON, DONALD W

Donald W Wilkinson AFCL BI, The Forge, Funtington, Chichester, **Sussex (West)**, PO18 9LL, **ENGLAND**.
(T) 01243 575577.
Profile Farrier. **Ref: YH15418**

WILKINSON, H B

Mrs H B Wilkinson, 38 Cliff Gardens, Telscombe Cliffs, **Sussex (East)**, BN10 7BX, **ENGLAND**.
(T) 01273 585548.
Profile Breeder. **Ref: YH15419**

WILKINSON, J

J Wilkinson, Babeny, Poundsgate, Newton Abbot, **Devon**, TQ13 7PS, **ENGLAND**.
(T) 01364 631296.
Contact/s
Owner: Mr J Wilkinson **Ref: YH15420**

WILKINSON, J V

Mrs J V Wilkinson, Wrekin Hse, Ibberton, Blandford Forum, **Dorset**, DT11 0EN, **ENGLAND**.
(T) 01258 817719.
Profile Supplies. **Ref: YH15421**

WILKINSON, M J

Mr M J Wilkinson, Trafford Bridge, Edgcote, Banbury, **Oxfordshire**, OX17 1AG, **ENGLAND**.
(T) 01295 660713 **(F)** 01257 660767
(M) 07768 793445
(E) mark@markwilkinsonracing.co.uk.
Profile Trainer. **Ref: YH15422**

WILKINSON, MARTIN

Martin Wilkinson, 78 High St, Redbourn, St Albans, **Hertfordshire**, AL3 7LN, **ENGLAND**.
(T) 01582 793228 **(F)** 01582 793698.
Contact/s
Manager: Miss A Parsons
Profile Saddlery Retailer. **Ref: YH15423**

WILKINSON, S

S Wilkinson, The Stables, Down Hatherley Lane, Down Hatherley, Gloucester, **Gloucestershire**, GL2 9QB, **ENGLAND**.
(T) 01452 731365.
Contact/s
Owner: Ms S Wilkinson
Profile Stable/Livery. **Ref: YH15424**

WILL EDMEADES BLOODSTOCK

Will Edmeades Bloodstock, Fair Winter Farm, Singleborough, Great Horwood, **Buckinghamshire**, MK17 0RB, **ENGLAND**.
(T) 01296 714120
(M) 07802 451372.
Contact/s
Owner: Mr W Edmeades
Profile Blood Stock Agency. **Ref: YH15425**

WILLAIMS, G & R

G & R Willaims, Windle Way Stud, Little London, Llandinam, **Powys**, SY17 5AF, **WALES**.
(T) 01686 688981.
Contact/s
Owner: Mr G Williams
Profile Breeder.
Breeder of Welsh Section A ponies **Ref: YH15426**

WILLAIMS, R A

Mrs R A Willaims, Top Flat/Hill Hse, Tywardreath, Par, **Cornwall**, PL24 2QQ, **ENGLAND**.
(T) 01726 812060.
Contact/s
Owner: Mrs R Williams **Ref: YH15427**

WILLARD, KEVIN J

Kevin J Willard AWCF, 132 Maidstone Rd, Borough Green, Sevenoaks, **Kent**, TN15 8HQ, **ENGLAND**.
(T) 01732 883137
(M) 07860 779807.
Profile Farrier. **Ref: YH15428**

WILLERSEY STABLES

Willersey Stables, Willersey Rd Farm, Willersey Fields, Badsey, Evesham, **Worcestershire**, WR11 5HF, **ENGLAND**.
(T) 01386 858189 **(F)** 01386 858189.
Contact/s
Owner: Miss R Ingles **Ref: YH15429**

WILLESLEY EQUINE CLINIC

Willesley Equine Clinic, Byams Farm, Wilesley, Tetbury, **Gloucestershire**, GL8 8QU, **ENGLAND**.
(T) 01666 880501 **(F)** 01666 880302.
Profile Breeder. **Ref: YH15430**

WILLETT, PETER

Peter Willett, Paddock Hse, Rotherwick, Basingstoke, **Hampshire**, RG27 9BG, **ENGLAND**.
(T) 01256 762488 **(F)** 01256 765088.
Profile Breeder. **Ref: YH15431**

WILLETTS, J

J Willetts, Carriage Works, Trebedw, Henllan, Llandysul, **Carmarthenshire**, SA44 5TJ, **WALES**.
(T) 01559 370631. **Ref: YH15432**

WILLEY, DAVID

David Willey, 1 Lane End Cottage, Denwick, Alnwick, **Northumberland**, NE66 3RG, **ENGLAND**..
Profile Farrier. **Ref: YH15433**

WILLIAM BAILEY AGRICULTURAL

William Bailey Agricultural Merchant, 112 High St, Collingham, Newark, **Nottinghamshire**, NG23 7NG, **ENGLAND**.
(T) 01636 892240.
Profile Supplies. **Ref: YH15434**

WILLIAM MAIN SADDLER

William Main Saddler, 9 West Port, Dunbar, **Lothian (East)**, EH42 1BT, **SCOTLAND**.
(T) 01368 863258 **(F)** 01368 865336.
Contact/s
Owner: Mr W Main
Profile Riding Wear Retailer, Saddlery Retailer, Supplies. **Ref: YH15435**

WILLIAM POWELL & SON

William Powell & Son Ltd, 35-37 Carrs Lane,

Birmingham, **Midlands (West)**, B4 7SX, **ENGLAND**.
(T) 0121 6430689 **(F)** 0121 6313504
(E) sales@william-powell.co.uk.
Profile Saddlery Retailer. **Ref: YH15436**

WILLIAM PUDDY WHITE HORSE

William Puddy White Horse Trekking Centre, Hillside, Codford, Warminster, **Wiltshire**, BA12 0JZ, **ENGLAND**.
(T) 01985 850395 **(F)** 01985 850395.
Contact/s
Owner: Mr W Puddy
Profile Riding School. **Ref: YH15437**

WILLIAM WALTON

William Walton (Sheffield) Ltd, 32 Garden St, Sheffield, **Yorkshire (South)**, S1 4BJ, **ENGLAND**.
(T) 0114 2490740 **(F)** 0114 2493894.
Profile Blacksmith. **Ref: YH15438**

WILLIAM WILLIAMS

William Williams Ltd, 81 High St, Bridgnorth, **Shropshire**, WV16 4DT, **ENGLAND**.
(T) 01746 767878 **(F)** 01746 765611.
Profile Saddlery Retailer. **Ref: YH15439**

WILLIAMS & EVANS

Williams & Evans, 2-4 Queen St, Bridgend, **Bridgend**, CF31 1HX, **WALES**.
(T) 01656 652072.
Profile Saddlery Retailer. **Ref: YH15440**

WILLIAMS & LINGE

Williams & Linge, Homeleigh, Redstone Rd, Narberth, **Pembrokeshire**, SA67 7ES, **WALES**.
(T) 01834 860378
(E) phillinge@enterprise.net.
Profile Medical Support. **Ref: YH15441**

WILLIAMS ENDURANCE

Williams Endurance, Wheal Dunsley, Uskard, **Cornwall**, PL14 5BL, **ENGLAND**.
(T) 01579 362003 **(F)** 01579 362003.
Profile Trainer.
Endurance Specialist. **Ref: YH15442**

WILLIAMS HORSE DRAWN CARRIAGE

Williams Horse Drawn Carriage Co, Working Heavy Horse Ctre, Meadow Lane, Syston, Leicester, **Leicestershire**, LE7 1NR, **ENGLAND**.
(T) 0116 2602666. **Ref: YH15443**

WILLIAMS, A J

Mr A J Williams, Hendrew Farm, Llandevaud, **Newport**, NP18 2AB, **WALES**.
(T) 01633 400188.
Profile Breeder. **Ref: YH15444**

WILLIAMS, A K

A K Williams RSS, Poolspringe, Much Birch, **Herefordshire**, HR2 8JJ, **ENGLAND**.
(T) 01981 540330.
Profile Farrier. **Ref: YH15445**

WILLIAMS, A R

Mr A R Williams, Brandish St Farm, Allerford, Minehead, **Somerset**, TA24 8HR, **ENGLAND**.
(T) 01643 862383.
Profile Breeder. **Ref: YH15446**

WILLIAMS, B

B Williams, The Stables Saddlery, Booths Lane, Lymm, **Cheshire**, WA13 0PF, **ENGLAND**.
(T) 01925 752762.
Contact/s
Owner: Mrs B Williams
Profile Saddlery Retailer. **Ref: YH15447**

WILLIAMS, B

B Williams, 27 Pen Y Bryn, Old Colwyn, Colwyn Bay, **Conwy**, LL29 9UU, **WALES**.
(T) 01492 514099.
Profile Blacksmith. **Ref: YH15448**

WILLIAMS, B

B Williams, 3 Heol Gam, Pentyrch, Cardiff, **Glamorgan (Vale of)**, CF15 9QA, **WALES**.
(T) 029 20890174.
Profile Breeder. **Ref: YH15449**

WILLIAMS, B & K

B & K Williams, Aldingbourne Pk Farm, Halnaker Barn Lane, Eartham, Chichester, **Sussex (West)**, PO18 0LJ, **ENGLAND**.
(T) 01243 773227 **(F)** 01243 774199.
Contact/s
Partner: Mrs E Williams **Ref: YH15450**

WILLIAMS, C M

Mrs C M Williams, Felstead, 6 Hamilton Rd, Newmarket, **Suffolk**, CB8 0NY, **ENGLAND**.
(T) 01638 665819 **(F)** 01638 665819
(M) 07712 649553
(E) clarewilliams@lineone.net. **Ref: YH15451**

WILLIAMS, C P

C P Williams, 72 Argyle St, Birkenhead, **Merseyside**, CH63 5QF, **ENGLAND**.
(T) 0151 6476237.
Profile Medical Support. **Ref: YH15452**

WILLIAMS, CHARLOTTE

Charlotte Williams, 7 South View, Droxford, **Hampshire**, SO32 3QJ, **ENGLAND**.
(T) 01489 877750
Affiliated Bodies NAAT.
Contact/s
Physiotherapist: Charlotte Williams
(Q) BA(Hons)
Profile Medical Support. **Ref: YH15453**

WILLIAMS, DAMIAN D

Damian D Williams DWCF, 1 Main St, Fleckney, **Leicestershire**, LE8 8AP, **ENGLAND**.
(T) 0116 2402407.
Profile Farrier. **Ref: YH15454**

WILLIAMS, E R

Mr E R Williams, Moorfield Hse, Shore Rd, Littleborough, **Lancashire**, OL15 9LG, **ENGLAND**.
(T) 01706 378761 **(F)** 01706 642585.
Profile Breeder. **Ref: YH15455**

WILLIAMS, F

F Williams, Cefnllidiart, Capel Bangor, Aberystwyth, **Ceredigion**, SY23 3LL, **WALES**.
(T) 01970 890639.
Profile Breeder. **Ref: YH15456**

WILLIAMS, G H

G H Williams, Whitegate Farm, Common Wood, Holt, **Wrexham**, LL13 9JB, **WALES**.
(T) 01829 270346.
Profile Farrier. **Ref: YH15457**

WILLIAMS, G L C & R

G L C & R Williams, Cherrington Lane Forge, Tetbury, **Gloucestershire**, GL8 8SE, **ENGLAND**.
(T) 01666 505040 **(F)** 01666 505040.
Contact/s
Partner: Mr A Williams
Profile Blacksmith. **Ref: YH15458**

WILLIAMS, HUMPHREY

Humphrey Williams, Y Ddol, Llaniestyn, Pwllheli, **Gwynedd**, LL53 8SG, **WALES**.
(T) 01758 730662.
Contact/s
Owner: Mr H Williams
Profile Transport/Horse Boxes. **Ref: YH15459**

WILLIAMS, J B

J B Williams, Higher Cargarwen, Praze, Camborne, **Cornwall**, TR14 9PA, **ENGLAND**.
(T) 01209 83387.
Profile Farrier. **Ref: YH15460**

WILLIAMS, J M

J M Williams, 11 Austhorpe Gr, Cottesmore, Oakham, **Leicestershire**, LE15 7BY, **ENGLAND**.
(T) 01572 812427.
Contact/s
Owner: Mr J Williams
Profile Farrier. **Ref: YH15461**

WILLIAMS, KARL

Karl Williams DWCF, Lodge Farm, 5 Ways, Hatton, **Warwickshire**, CV35 7JD, **ENGLAND**.
(T) 01926 484649.
Profile Farrier. **Ref: YH15462**

WILLIAMS, L J

Mr L J Williams, Upper Grange, St Brides Netherwent, Magor, **Newport**, NP26 3AT, **WALES**.
(T) 01633 880605.
Profile Breeder. **Ref: YH15463**

WILLIAMS, M

M Williams, Woodlands Stables, Bassaleg, **Newport**, **WALES**..
Profile Breeder. **Ref: YH15464**

WILLIAMS, M R

M R Williams, Horner Farm, Horner, Minehead, **Somerset**, TA24 8HY, **ENGLAND**.
(T) 01643 862456. **Ref: YH15465**

WILLIAMS, MICHAEL

Michael Williams RSS BII, 2 St Stephens Cottages, Chalk Lane, Harlow, **Essex**, CM17 0PQ, **ENGLAND**.
(T) 01279 438074.
Profile Farrier. **Ref: YH15466**

WILLIAMS, MICHAEL

Michael Williams, 60 Roxeth Hill, Harrow-on-the-Hill, **London (Greater)**, HA2 0JW, **ENGLAND**.
(T) 020 84223116.
Profile Supplies. **Ref: YH15467**

WILLIAMS, NICK

Mr Nick Williams, Merryfield Hse, Georgenympton, South Molton, **Devon**, EX36 4JE, **ENGLAND**.
(T) 01769 574174 **(F)** 01769 573661.
Profile Supplies. **Ref: YH15468**

WILLIAMS, PAUL D

Paul D Williams DWCF, 81 Beverley Rd, Tilehurst, Reading, **Berkshire**, RG31 5PU, **ENGLAND**.
(T) 07831 821991.
Profile Farrier. **Ref: YH15469**

WILLIAMS, R

R Williams, Stable Cottage, Cheeseburn Grange, Newcastle-upon-Tyne, **Tyne and Wear**, NE18 0PT, **ENGLAND**.
(T) 01661 886453.
Profile Equestrian Centre, Stable/Livery.
Ref: YH15470

WILLIAMS, R E

R E Williams, Westwell Farm, Chesterblade, Shepton Mallet, **Somerset**, BA4 4QX, **ENGLAND**.
(T) 01749 880338.
Profile Medical Support. **Ref: YH15471**

WILLIAMS, R P

R P Williams, Scorrier Hse, Scorrier, Redruth, **Cornwall**, TR16 5AU, **ENGLAND**.
(T) 01209 820264 **(F)** 01209 820677.
Contact/s
Owner: Mr R Williams
Profile Breeder. **Ref: YH15472**

WILLIAMS, RICHARD H

Richard H Williams AFCL, Mid Aeron Hse, Talsarn, Lampeter, **Ceredigion**, SA48, **WALES**.
(T) 01570 470346.
Profile Farrier. **Ref: YH15473**

WILLIAMS, RICHARD JOHN

Richard John Williams DWCF, Grove Cottage, Whiteley Rd, Catbrook, Chepstow, **Monmouthshire**, NP16 6NQ, **WALES**.
(T) 01600 860974.
Profile Farrier. **Ref: YH15474**

WILLIAMS, ROBERT C

Robert C Williams DWCF, 29 Park Trce, Burry Port, **Carmarthenshire**, SA16 0BW, **WALES**.
(T) 01548 32623.
Profile Farrier. **Ref: YH15475**

WILLIAMS, ROBIN

Robin Williams DWCF, 1 Penrhiw, Croesyceiliog, Carmarthen, **Carmarthenshire**, SA32 8DS, **WALES**.
(T) 01267 235684.
Profile Farrier. **Ref: YH15476**

WILLIAMS, S C

S C Williams, Trillium Pl, Birdcage Walk, Newmarket, **Suffolk**, CB8 0NE, **ENGLAND**.
(T) 01638 663984
(W) www.newmarketracehorsetrainers.co.uk
Affiliated Bodies Newmarket Trainers Fed.
Contact/s
Trainer: Mr S Williams
Profile Trainer. **Ref: YH15477**

WILLIAMS, S D

Mrs S D Williams, Hilltown, Mariansleigh, South Molton, **Devon**, EX36 4NS, **ENGLAND**.
(T) 01769 550291 **(F)** 01769 550291
(E) sarah.williams@euphony.net.
Profile Trainer. **Ref: YH15478**

WILLIAMS, TED

Ted Williams, Tyr Sais Stables, Argoed, Blackwood, **Caerphilly**, NP2 0JA, **WALES**.
(T) 01495 224297. **Ref: YH15479**

WILLIAMS, TOM

Tom Williams, Felton Hse Farm, Felton, Bristol, **Bristol**, BS40 9YA, **ENGLAND**.
(T) 01275 472025.

Contact/s
Owner: Mr R Fear Ref: YH15480

WILLIAMS, W R

W R Williams, Lower Horrels, Longdown, Exeter, **Devon**, EX6 7BL, **ENGLAND**.
(T) 01392 811558.
Contact/s
Owner: Mr W Williams
Profile Transport/Horse Boxes. **Ref: YH15481**

WILLIAMSON, D J

Mr D J Williamson, Hollyhouse Farm, Pentney, King's Lynn, **Norfolk**, PE32 1JW, **ENGLAND**.
(T) 01760 337234.
Profile Breeder. **Ref: YH15482**

WILLIAMSON, G

Mrs G Williamson, Suilven, 11 Mearness Drive, Ulverston, **Cumbria**, LA12 9PE, **ENGLAND**.
(T) 01229 581002.
Profile Breeder. **Ref: YH15483**

WILLIAMSON, GORDON FERRIER

Gordon Ferrier Williamson, Wilbram, Justinhaugh, Forfar, **Angus**, DD8 3SD, **SCOTLAND**.
(T) 01307 860263.
Profile Farrier. **Ref: YH15484**

WILLIAMSON, LISA

Mrs Lisa Williamson, Heathcroft Farm, Saighton, Chester, **Cheshire**, CH3 6EE, **ENGLAND**.
(T) 01244 314254
(M) 07970 437679.
Profile Trainer. **Ref: YH15485**

WILLIAMSON, TOM

Tom Williamson, Chelmick Forge, Chelmick, Church Stretton, **Shropshire**, SY6 7HA, **ENGLAND**.
(T) 01694 722767.
Profile Farrier. **Ref: YH15486**

WILLIE DALY RIDING SCHOOL

Willie Daly Riding School, Ballingaddy, Ennistymon, **County Clare**, **IRELAND**.
(T) 065 7071385
(W) www.williedaly.com.
Contact/s
Owner: Willie Daly
(E) williedaly@tinet.ie
Profile Equestrian Centre, Holidays.
Between Easter and November six day trail rides, the 'Trail of Love', are available. Beach and farm rides are also on offer as are hourly, half day and full day treks.
Opening Times
Open daily, telephone for further information.
Ref: YH15487

WILLINGCOTT FARM SUPPLIES

Willingcott Farm Supplies, Higher Willingcott Farm, Woolacombe, **Devon**, EX34 7HN, **ENGLAND**.
(T) 01271 870135.
Profile Saddlery Retailer. **Ref: YH15488**

WILLINGHAM HSE STUD

Willingham House Stud, Willingham Green, Brinkley, Newmarket, **Suffolk**, CB8 0SW, **ENGLAND**.
(T) 01638 507530.
Profile Breeder. **Ref: YH15489**

WILLINGTON HALL

Willington Hall Riding Centre & Livery, Willington Hall, Willington, Tarporley, **Cheshire**, CW6 0NB, **ENGLAND**.
(T) 01829 751920.
Profile Riding School. **Ref: YH15490**

WILLIS BROS

Willis Bros, 52 White Lion Pk, Malmesbury, **Wiltshire**, SN16 0QP, **ENGLAND**.
(T) 01666 822117.
Contact/s
Partner: Mr B Willis **Ref: YH15491**

WILLIS WALKER

Willis Walker Ltd, 105-109 Cavendish St, Keighley, **Yorkshire (West)**, BD21 3DG, **ENGLAND**.
(T) 01535 602928.
Profile Saddlery Retailer. **Ref: YH15492**

WILLONYX RACING

Willonyx Racing Ltd, Coombe Pk Stud, Coombe Pk Est, Whitchurch On Thames, Reading, **Berkshire**, RG8 7QT, **ENGLAND**.
(T) 0118 9841317.
Profile Trainer. **Ref: YH15493**

WILLOW END EQUESTRIAN CTRE

Willow End Equestrian Centre, Kemps Corner, Pulham St Mary, Diss, **Norfolk**, IP21 4YH, **ENGLAND**.
(T) 01379 608296.
Profile Riding School. **Ref: YH15494**

WILLOW FARM

Willow Farm, Tylers Green Rd, Swanley, **Kent**, BR8 8LG, **ENGLAND**.
(T) 01322 663389.
Contact/s
Owner: Mr A Scott-Inglis
Profile Stable/Livery. **Ref: YH15495**

WILLOW FARM

Willow Farm, Tyland Lane, Sandling, Maidstone, **Kent**, ME14 3BL, **ENGLAND**.
(T) 01622 695637.
Contact/s
Owner: Mr M Nuttall
Profile Farrier. **Ref: YH15496**

WILLOW FARM

Willow Farm Saddlery, Hansletts Lane, Ospringe, Faversham, **Kent**, ME13 0RS, **ENGLAND**.
(T) 01795 533669 **(F)** 01795 537155
(W) www.willowfarm.org.uk.
Contact/s
Owner: Ms M Openshaw
Profile Arena, Equestrian Centre, Riding Wear Retailer, Saddlery Retailer, Stable/Livery, Supplies.
No.Staff: 5 Yr. Est: 1986 C.Size: 21 Acres
Opening Times
Sp: Open 09:00. Closed 17:00.
Su: Open 09:00. Closed 17:00.
Au: Open 09:00. Closed 17:00.
Wn: Open 09:00. Closed 17:00. **Ref: YH15497**

WILLOW FARM

Willow Farm, Holme Hall, Holme, Scunthorpe, **Lincolnshire (North)**, DN16 3RE, **ENGLAND**.
(T) 01724 840142.
Contact/s
Owner: Ms P Robinson
Profile Riding School, Stable/Livery. **Ref: YH15498**

WILLOW FARM COTTAGE

Willow Farm Cottage Riding Stables, 4 Willow Farm Cottage, Happisburgh Common, Norwich, **Norfolk**, NR12 0BE, **ENGLAND**.
(T) 01692 650879.
Profile Riding School. **Ref: YH15499**

WILLOW FARM RIDING SCHOOL

Willow Farm Riding School, Ormesby St Margaret, Great Yarmouth, **Norfolk**, NR29 3QE, **ENGLAND**.
(T) 01493 730297.
Profile Riding School, Stable/Livery. **Ref: YH15500**

WILLOW FARM STABLES

Willow Farm Stables, Kings Newnham Lane, Bretford, Rugby, **Warwickshire**, CV23 0JU, **ENGLAND**.
(T) 024 76542141.
Contact/s
Owner: Mrs K Wilson **Ref: YH15501**

WILLOW ROYD STABLES

Willow Royd Stables, Luddendenfoot, Halifax, **Yorkshire (West)**, HX2 6LG, **ENGLAND**.
(T) 01422 884095.
Contact/s
Owner: Mrs J Ambler
Profile Stable/Livery.
30 stables. Full Livery only - prices negotiable depending on customers requirements No.Staff: 5
Yr. Est: 1961
Opening Times
Sp: Open Mon - Sun 07:00. Closed Mon - Sun 23:00.
Su: Open Mon - Sun 07:00. Closed Mon - Sun 23:00.
Au: Open Mon - Sun 07:00. Closed Mon - Sun 23:00.
Wn: Open Mon - Sun 07:00. Closed Mon - Sun 23:00. **Ref: YH15502**

WILLOW STUD

Willow Stud, Windmore Farm, Petham, Canterbury, **Kent**, CT4 5QE, **ENGLAND**.
(T) 01227 700264 **(F)** 01227 700264
(E) info@willowstud.co.uk
(W) www.willowstud.co.uk.
Contact/s
Owner: Mrs P Joiner
Profile Breeder, Horse/Rider Accom, Stable/Livery.
No.Staff: 1 Yr. Est: 1971 C.Size: 35 Acres
Ref: YH15503

WILLOW TREE RIDING

Willow Tree Riding Establishment, Ronver Rd, London, **London (Greater)**, SE12 0NL, **ENGLAND**.
(T) 020 88576438
Affiliated Bodies ABRS, BHS.
Profile Riding School.
Specialise in teaching people with special needs.
C.Size: 1960 Acres
Opening Times
Sp: Open 09:00. Closed 17:00.
Su: Open 09:00. Closed 17:00.
Au: Open 09:00. Closed 17:00.
Wn: Open 09:00. Closed 17:00. **Ref: YH15504**

WILLOW WEAR

Willow Wear, 21 Battle Hill, Hexham, **Northumberland**, NE46 1BA, **ENGLAND**.
(T) 01434 600922.
Contact/s
General Manager: Ms A Edwards
Profile Riding Wear Retailer, Saddlery Retailer, Supplies. No.Staff: 4 Yr. Est: 1992
Opening Times
Sp: Open 10:00. Closed 17:00.
Su: Open 10:00. Closed 17:00.
Au: Open 10:00. Closed 17:00.
Wn: Open 10:00. Closed 17:00. **Ref: YH15505**

WILLOWAY STUD

Willoway Stud, Wedge Hill Farm, Woodlands, Wimborne, **Dorset**, BH21 8LX, **ENGLAND**.
(T) 01202 822588.
Profile Breeder. **Ref: YH15506**

WILLOWBROOK FARM FEED & TACK

Willowbrook Farm Feed & Tack Superstore, Bushmead Rd, Whitchurch, Aylesbury, **Buckinghamshire**, HP22 4LG, **ENGLAND**.
(T) 01296 681888 **(F)** 01296 681888.
Profile Saddlery Retailer. **Ref: YH15507**

WILLOWBROOK RIDING CTRE

Willowbrook Riding Centre, Hambrook Hill (South), Hambrook, Chichester, **Sussex (West)**, PO18 8UJ, **ENGLAND**.
(T) 01243 572683
(W) www.willowbrook-riding.co.uk.
Contact/s
General Manager: Ms K Reed
Profile Arena, Equestrian Centre, Horse/Rider Accom, Riding School, Stable/Livery.
Bed and Breakfast on site. No.Staff: 2
Yr. Est: 1979 C.Size: 14 Acres
Ref: YH15508

WILLOWS SHOW JUMPING CLUB

Willows Show Jumping Club, Pin Hi, Lippitts Hill, High Beech, Loughton, **Essex**, IG10 4AL, **ENGLAND**.
(T) 020 85024384
(M) 07860 945694.
Profile Club/Association, Track/Course.
Ref: YH15509

WILLOWS VETNRY GRP

Willows Veterinary Group, Holly Hse, Mobberley, Knutsford, **Cheshire**, WA16 8HT, **ENGLAND**.
(T) 01565 632253.
Profile Medical Support. **Ref: YH15510**

WILLOWS VETNRY GRP

Willows Veterinary Group, 10 Booths Hill Rd, Lymm, **Cheshire**, WA13 0DL, **ENGLAND**.
(T) 01925 752721.
Profile Medical Support. **Ref: YH15511**

WILLOWS VETNRY GRP

Willows Veterinary Group, 39 Newton Heath, Middlewich, **Cheshire**, CW10 9HL, **ENGLAND**.
(T) 01606 843731.
Profile Medical Support. **Ref: YH15512**

WILLOWS VETNRY GRP

Willows Veterinary Group, Willows Veterinary Hospital, 267 Chester Rd, Hartford, Northwich, **Cheshire**, CW8 1LP, **ENGLAND**.
(T) 01606 76498 **(F)** 01606 783496.
Profile Medical Support. **Ref: YH15513**

WILLOWS VETNRY GRP

Willows Veterinary Group, Beech Hse Clinic, Wilderspool Causeway, Warrington, **Cheshire**, WA4 6QP, **ENGLAND**.
(T) 01925 445500.
Profile Medical Support. **Ref: YH15514**

WILLOWS VETNRY GRP

Willows Veterinary Group, 70 High St, Winsford, **Cheshire**, CW7 2AP, **ENGLAND**.

(T) 01606 592714.
Profile Medical Support. Ref: YH15515

WILLOWSIDE STUD
Willowside Stud, Picks Farm, Sewardstone Rd, London, **London (Greater)**, E4 7RA, **ENGLAND**.
(T) 020 85291371.
Profile Breeder. Ref: YH15516

WILLOWTREE RIDING CLUB
Willowtree Riding Club, 5 Wyatt Hse, Wemyss Rd, Blackheath, **London (Greater)**, SE3 0TE, **ENGLAND**.
(T) 020 84630132.
Contact/s
Chairman: Miss M Hawley
Profile Club/Association, Riding Club. Ref: YH15517

WILLS, G J
Mr & Mrs G J Wills, Moelfryn, Bancydarren, Aberystwyth, **Ceredigion**, SY23 3JE, **WALES**.
(T) 01970 828763.
Profile Breeder. Ref: YH15518

WILLS, R J
R J Wills, 27 Mandrake Rd, Alphington, Exeter, **Devon**, EX2 8SQ, **ENGLAND**.
(T) 01392 494707.
Profile Farrier. Ref: YH15519

WILLS, S
S Wills DWCF Hons, Thornleigh, Sinns Croft, Radnor, Redruth, **Cornwall**, TR16 4BJ, **ENGLAND**.
(T) 01209 890953.
Profile Farrier. Ref: YH15520

WILMOT, GUY
Guy Wilmot, The Green, Shalbourne, Marlborough, **Wiltshire**, SN8 3PT, **ENGLAND**.
(T) 01672 870593. Ref: YH15521

WILMOT, S
Mrs S Wilmot, 1 Withinlee Cottages, Withinlee Rd, Prestbury, Macclesfield, **Cheshire**, SK10 4AT, **ENGLAND**.
(T) 01625 829883.
Profile Breeder. Ref: YH15522

WILMOTTS PET/SADDLERY STORES
Wilmotts Pet & Saddlery Stores, 61 Annesley Rd, Hucknall, Nottingham, **Nottinghamshire**, NG15 7DR, **ENGLAND**.
(T) 0115 9632573 (F) 0115 9632573.
Contact/s
Partner: Ms J Wilmott
Profile Saddlery Retailer. Ref: YH15523

WILMSLOW RIDING CLUB
Wilmslow Riding Club, 14 St Marks Ave, Altrincham, **Cheshire**, WA14 4JB, **ENGLAND**.
(T) 0161 9287585.
Contact/s
Chairman: Mr J Berry
Profile Club/Association, Riding Club. Ref: YH15524

WILPSHIRE RIDING CLUB
Wilpshire Riding Club, 6 Duchy Ave, Fulwood, Preston, **Lancashire**, PR2 8DH, **ENGLAND**.
(T) 01772 700283.
Contact/s
Secretary: Janet Zaldats
Profile Club/Association, Riding Club. Ref: YH15525

WILSFORD STABLES
Wilsford Stables, Wilsford-Cum-Lake, Amesbury, Salisbury, **Wiltshire**, SP4 7BP, **ENGLAND**.
(T) 01980 626344 (F) 01980 626344
(M) 07702 559634.
Profile Trainer. Ref: YH15526

WILSON FEEDS
Wilson Feeds, Middlecroft, Thorpe-In-Balne, Doncaster, **Yorkshire (South)**, DN6 0DZ, **ENGLAND**.
(T) 01302 882279.
Profile Supplies. Ref: YH15527

WILSON HORSEWEAR
Wilson Horsewear, Badger Hill Farm, Gwennap, Redruth, **Cornwall**, TR16 6BW, **ENGLAND**.
(T) 01209 861315.
Profile Supplies. Ref: YH15528

WILSON, ANTHONY
Anthony Wilson AWCF, Primrose Cottage, Templefields, Heapey, Chorley, **Lancashire**, PR6 9AS, **ENGLAND**.
(T) 07850 602949.
Profile Farrier. Ref: YH15529

WILSON, B
Mr & Mrs B Wilson, Watergate, Linford, Ringwood, **Hampshire**, BH24 3HX, **ENGLAND**.
(T) 01425 480138.
Profile Breeder. Ref: YH15530

WILSON, C
Mr C Wilson, Manor Hse Farm, Sinnington, Pickering, **Yorkshire (North)**, YO62 6SN, **ENGLAND**.
(T) 01751 433296.
Profile Breeder, Stable/Livery. Ref: YH15531

WILSON, D M
Mrs D M Wilson, Outer Priddacombe, Bolventor, Launceston, **Cornwall**, PL15 7TY, **ENGLAND**.
(T) 01566 86412.
Contact/s
Owner: Ms D Wilson
Profile Horse/Rider Accom. Ref: YH15532

WILSON, DAVID
David Wilson BEM AWCB FWCF, Smithy Hse, Ballmullo, **Fife**, KY16 0BG, **SCOTLAND**.
(T) 01334 870306.
Profile Farrier. Ref: YH15533

WILSON, DAVID G
David G Wilson AWCF, 7 Kirk Brae, Ceres, **Fife**, KY15 5ND, **SCOTLAND**.
(T) 01334 828956.
Profile Farrier. Ref: YH15534

WILSON, E M
Mr E M Wilson, Town End, Haltcliffe, Hesket-New-Market, Wigton, **Cumbria**, CA7 8JT, **ENGLAND**.
(T) 01697 478638.
Profile Breeder. Ref: YH15535

WILSON, G
G Wilson RSS, Blacksmith's Shop, South Rd, Alnwick, **Northumberland**, NE66 2PQ, **ENGLAND**.
(T) 01665 602707.
Profile Farrier. Ref: YH15536

WILSON, GORDON
Gordon Wilson, Blacksmith Shop, South Rd, Longhorsley, Morpeth, **Northumberland**, NE65 8UW, **ENGLAND**.
(T) 01665 604313.
Profile Farrier. Ref: YH15537

WILSON, GORDON
Gordon Wilson, 46 Royal Oak Gardens, Alnwick, **Northumberland**, NE66 2DA, **ENGLAND**.
(T) 01665 602707.
Contact/s
Owner: Mr G Wilson
Profile Farrier. Ref: YH15538

WILSON, J H
J H Wilson, Moor Farm, Liverpool Old Rd, Tarleton, Preston, **Lancashire**, PR4 6HR, **ENGLAND**.
(T) 01772 812780 (F) 01772 812799.
Contact/s
Owner: Mr G Wilson
Profile Trainer. Ref: YH15539

WILSON, LENNOX
Mrs Lennox Wilson, Priestwells, Main St, Greenham, Rutland, **Leicestershire**, LE15 7NU, **ENGLAND**.
(T) 01572 812660.
Profile Stable/Livery. Ref: YH15540

WILSON, M
Mrs M Wilson, Tara Lea, Burnhope, **County Durham**, DH7 0DP, **ENGLAND**.
(T) 01207 529296.
Profile Breeder. Ref: YH15541

WILSON, MELANIE
Melanie Wilson, Ten Steps, Church St, Seagrave, **Leicestershire**, LE12 7LT, **ENGLAND**.
(T) 01509 812806.
Profile Trainer. Ref: YH15542

WILSON, N
Mr N Wilson, Beech Farm, Painsthorpe, Kirby Underdale, **Yorkshire (North)**, YO4 1RG, **ENGLAND**.
(T) 01759 368249.
Profile Trainer. Ref: YH15543

WILSON, PAUL
Paul Wilson, 14 Jerome Way, Shipton-on-Cherwell, Kidlington, **Oxfordshire**, OX5 1JT, **ENGLAND**.
(T) 01865 376890 (F) 01865 376890.
Contact/s
Owner: Mr P Wilson
Profile Farrier. Ref: YH15544

WILSON, R C
R C Wilson, Hill Green Farm, Hill Green Lane, Wigginton, Tring, **Hertfordshire**, HP23 6HD, **ENGLAND**.
(T) 01442 823275 (F) 01442 891555.
Contact/s
Partner: Mr R Wilson
Profile Equestrian Centre. Ref: YH15545

WILSON, T
T Wilson, 10 Glenhead Cres, Hardgate, Clydebank, Glasgow, **Glasgow (City of)**, G81 6LW, **SCOTLAND**.
(T) 01389 74792. Ref: YH15546

WILSON, T M
T M Wilson, Beck Side Farm, Staindrop Rd, High Coniscliffe, Darlington, **County Durham**, DL2 2ND, **ENGLAND**.
(T) 01325 469438. Ref: YH15547

WILSON, WALKER & BARNBY
Wilson, Walker & Barnby, 95 New Rd, Rubery, Rednal, Birmingham, **Midlands (West)**, B45 9JR, **ENGLAND**.
(T) 0121 4535828.
Profile Medical Support. Ref: YH15548

WILSON, WALKER & BARNBY
Wilson, Walker & Barnby, 168 Birmingham Rd, Bromsgrove, **Worcestershire**, B61 0HB, **ENGLAND**.
(T) 01527 831616 (F) 01527 574062.
Profile Medical Support. Ref: YH15549

WILSON, WALKER & BARNBY
Wilson, Walker & Barnby, 2 North St, Droitwich, **Worcestershire**, WR9 8JB, **ENGLAND**.
(T) 01905 772002.
Profile Medical Support. Ref: YH15550

WILSONS PET & ANIMAL CTRE
Wilsons Pet & Animal Centre, 20 Market St, Bromsgrove, **Worcestershire**, B61 8DA, **ENGLAND**.
(T) 01527 871449 (F) 01527 574091.
Profile Supplies. Ref: YH15551

WILSONS SADDLERY
Wilsons Saddlery, Greenmeadows Farm, Castle Hill, Mottram St. Andrew, Macclesfield, **Cheshire**, SK10 4AX, **ENGLAND**.
(T) 01625 829256.
Profile Saddlery Retailer. Ref: YH15552

WILSONS TIMBER SHAVINGS
Wilsons Timber Shavings, 146 Trafalgar St, Burnley, **Lancashire**, BB11 1RA, **ENGLAND**.
(T) 01282 831007.
Profile Supplies. Ref: YH15553

WILSTEAD SADDLERY
Wilstead Saddlery, Montrose Seasons Garden Ctre, Bedford Rd, Wilstead, Bedford, **Bedfordshire**, MK45 3HU, **ENGLAND**.
(T) 01234 743707 (F) 01234 743711.
Contact/s
Owner: Mrs G Norman
Profile Saddlery Retailer. Ref: YH15554

WILTON HSE VETNRY CTRE
Wilton House Veterinary Centre, Wilton Lane, Guisborough, **Cleveland**, TS14 6JA, **ENGLAND**.
(T) 01287 637470.
Profile Medical Support. Ref: YH15555

WILTSHIRE BHS BRIDLEWAYS
Wiltshire BHS Bridleways Officer, 35 Highfield Rise, Shrewton, Salisbury, **Wiltshire**, SP3 4DZ, **ENGLAND**.
(T) 01980 621167 (F) 01980 621167.
Profile Club/Association. Ref: YH15556

WIMBLEDON VILLAGE STABLES
Wimbledon Village Stables, 24A-B High St, Wimbledon, London, **London (Greater)**, SW19 5DX, **ENGLAND**.
(T) 020 89468579 (F) 020 88790213
(E) admin@wvstables.com
(W) www.wvstables.com
Affiliated Bodies BHS.
Contact/s
General Manager: Ms C Stevenson (Q) BHS 1
Profile Riding Club, Riding School, Stable/Livery.
Wimbledon Village Stables offers a unique membership club to benefit the committed equestrians
No.Staff: 8 Yr. Est: 1980
Opening Times
Sp: Open 08:00. Closed 18:00.
Su: Open 08:00. Closed 20:00.

Au: Open 08:00. Closed 18:00.
Wn: Open 08:00. Closed 17:00. **Ref: YH15557**

WIMBORNE & DISTRICT

Wimborne & District Riding Club, 24 Whitchuch Ave, Broadstone, **Dorset**, BH18 8LP, **ENGLAND**.
(T) 01202 600744.
Contact/s
Secretary: Mrs L Houlgrave
Profile Club/Association, Riding Club. **Ref: YH15558**

WIMBOURNE EQUESTRIAN CTRE

Wimbourne Equestrian Centre, Bambers Lane, Blackpool, **Lancashire**, FY4 5LH, **ENGLAND**.
(T) 01253 699005.
Profile Equestrian Centre. **Ref: YH15559**

WINCANTON RACES

Wincanton Races Co Ltd, Wincanton Racecourse, Wincanton, **Somerset**, BA9 8BJ, **ENGLAND**.
(T) 01963 32344 **(F)** 01963 34668.
Contact/s
Assistant Manager: Miss M Bridger
Profile Track/Course. **Ref: YH15560**

WINDACRES FARM

Windacres Farm, Russ Hill, Charlwood, Horley, **Surrey**, RH6 0EL, **ENGLAND**.
(T) 01293 862092
(M) 07775 560472
(E) windacresfarm@btinternet.com.
Profile Stable/Livery, Track/Course. **Ref: YH15561**

WINDER, A

A Winder, Hawthorn Bank, Greenside Lane, Ravenstonedale, Kirkby Stephen, **Cumbria**, CA17 4LU, **ENGLAND**.
(T) 01539 623279 **(F)** 01539 623279.
Contact/s
Owner: Mr A Winder **Ref: YH15562**

WINDMILL FARM RIDING SCHOOL

Windmill Farm Riding School, Fish Lane, Holmeswood, Ormskirk, **Lancashire**, L40 1UQ, **ENGLAND**.
(T) 01704 892282.
Profile Riding School. **Ref: YH15563**

WINDMILL FARM SUPPLIES

Windmill Farm Supplies, Windmill Farm, Upton Cross, Ryde, **Isle of Wight**, PO33 3LA, **ENGLAND**.
(T) 01983 812951.
Profile Supplies. **Ref: YH15564**

WINDMILL FEEDS & SADDLERY

Windmill Feeds & Saddlery, Mill Lane Lewes Rd, Cross In Hand, Heathfield, **Sussex (East)**, TN21 0TA, **ENGLAND**.
(T) 01435 864383 **(F)** 01435 864383.
Contact/s
Partner: Mr J Howitt
Profile Feed Merchant, Saddlery Retailer.
Ref: YH15565

WINDMILL HILL EQUESTRIAN CTRE

Windmill Hill Equestrian Centre, Windmill Hill, Ashill, Ilminster, **Somerset**, TA19 9NT, **ENGLAND**.
(T) 01823 480788.
Profile Stable/Livery, Track/Course, Trainer.
Ref: YH15566

WINDMILL LODGE STABLES

Windmill Lodge Stables, Spital Rd, Lewes, **Sussex (East)**, BN7 1LS, **ENGLAND**.
(T) 01273 477124
(M) 07885 252783.
Profile Trainer. **Ref: YH15567**

WINDMILL STABLES

Windmill Stables, Weston St, Portland, **Dorset**, DT5 2JH, **ENGLAND**.
(T) 01305 823719.
Contact/s
Owner: Ms S Lees
Profile Stable/Livery. **Ref: YH15568**

WINDRIDGE STORES

Windridge Stores, Old Hall Farm, Meriden Rd, Fillongley, Coventry, **Warwickshire**, CV7 8DX, **ENGLAND**.
(T) 01676 40333.
Profile Supplies. **Ref: YH15569**

WINDRUSH SADDLERY

Windrush Saddlery, Windrush, Northlands, Sibsey, Boston, **Lincolnshire**, PE22 0UG, **ENGLAND**.
(T) 01205 750707.
Contact/s
Owner: Mr S Chilvers
Profile Saddlery Retailer. **Ref: YH15570**

WINDRUSH STABLES

Windrush Stables, Munthan Farm, Findon, **Sussex (West)**, BN14 0RQ, **ENGLAND**.
(T) 01903 750244.
Profile Trainer. **Ref: YH15571**

WINDSOR BRIDLES

Windsor Bridles, Unit 1 William St, Walsall, **Midlands (West)**, WS4 2AX, **ENGLAND**.
(T) 01922 648033. **Ref: YH15572**

WINDSOR CLIVE INT

Windsor Clive International, Balak Est Office, Ramsbury, Marlborough, **Wiltshire**, SN8 2HG, **ENGLAND**.
(T) 01672 521155 **(F)** 01672 521313
(E) info@windsorclive.co.uk.
Profile Club/Association. **Ref: YH15573**

WINDSOR GT PK

Windsor Gt Park Country Fair & National Horse Driving Chmps, The Royal Mews, Windsor, **Berkshire**, SL4 1NG, **ENGLAND**.
(T) 01753 860633 **(F)** 01753 831074.
Profile Club/Association. **Ref: YH15574**

WINDSOR INSURANCE BROKERS

Windsor Insurance Brokers, 160-166 Borough High St, London, **London (Greater)**, SE1 1JR, **ENGLAND**.
(T) 020 77395646.
Profile Club/Association. **Ref: YH15575**

WINDSOR PK EQUESTRIAN CLUB

Windsor Park Equestrian Club, 17 Captain Cook Cl, Chalfont St Giles, **Buckinghamshire**, HP8 4DS, **ENGLAND**.
(T) 01494 874724.
Contact/s
Secretary: Mrs M Wilson
Profile Club/Association. **Ref: YH15576**

WINDSOR RACING

Windsor Racing Ltd, The Racecourse, Windsor, **Berkshire**, SL4 5JJ, **ENGLAND**.
(T) 01753 865234 **(F)** 01753 830156.
Contact/s
Clerk of Course: Fraser Garrity
Profile Track/Course. **Ref: YH15577**

WINDSOR, M

Mr M Windsor MC AMC MMCA, Newton Farm, Berwick, Shrewsbury, **Shropshire**, SY4 3JB, **ENGLAND**.
(T) 01743 236650
(M) 07973 710396.
Profile Medical Support. **Ref: YH15578**

WINDUSS HORSEBOXES

Winduss Horseboxes, The Paddocks, Western Lea, Crediton, **Devon**, EX17 3JQ, **ENGLAND**.
(T) 01363 772483.
Contact/s
Sales: Steven Winduss
Profile Transport/Horse Boxes. **Ref: YH15579**

WINDY EDGE STABLES

Windy Edge Stables, Alnmouth Rd, Alnwick, **Northumberland**, NE66 2QB, **ENGLAND**.
(T) 01665 602284.
Contact/s
Owner: Miss E White
Profile Stable/Livery. **Ref: YH15580**

WINDY GAIL STABLES

Windy Gail Stables, Maes Y Deri, Llwyncoed Rd, Blaenannerch, **Ceredigion**, SA43 1DR, **WALES**.
(T) 01239 810026.
Profile Riding School, Stable/Livery. **Ref: YH15581**

WINERGY

Winergy Sales, Suite 404, Springfield Hse, Springfield Business Pk, Grantham, **Lincolnshire**, NG31 7BG, **ENGLAND**.
(T) 01476 514655 **(F)** 01476 514653
(E) sales@gunbyequestrian.co.uk
(W) www.gunbyequestrian.co.uk.
Profile Supplies. Yr. Est: 1997 **Ref: YH15582**

WING DRESSAGE GROUP

Wing Dressage Group, 49 Amy Lane, Chesham, **Buckinghamshire**, HP5 1NA, **ENGLAND**.
(T) 01494 773506.
Contact/s
Chairman: Mrs E Young
Profile Club/Association. **Ref: YH15583**

WINGFIELD STUD

Wingfield Stud, Ebbisham Lane, Walton-on-the-Hill, Tadworth, **Surrey**, KT20 5BS, **ENGLAND**.
(T) 01737 813717.
Profile Breeder. **Ref: YH15584**

WINGFIELD, W M R

W M R Wingfield, Lodge Farm, Wingfield, Diss, **Norfolk**, IP21 5RF, **ENGLAND**.
(T) 01379 75287.
Profile Breeder. **Ref: YH15585**

WINKERS FARM

Winkers Farm Riding & Livery Stables, Denham Lane, Chalfont St Peter, **Buckinghamshire**, SL9 0QJ, **ENGLAND**.
(T) 01753 888704.
Profile Riding School. **Ref: YH15586**

WINKWORTH, P

Mr P Winkworth, Robins Farm, Fisher Lane, Chiddingfold, **Surrey**, GU8 4TB, **ENGLAND**.
(T) 01428 685020.
Profile Trainer. **Ref: YH15587**

WINNERS ANIMAL PET SHOP

Winners Animal Pet Shop, Pyle Rd, Pyle, **Bridgend**, CF33 6PG, **WALES**.
(T) 01656 741690.
Profile Supplies. **Ref: YH15588**

WINNERS OF PETERBOROUGH

Winners of Peterborough, Little Orchard, Elton Rd, Fotheringhay, Peterborough, **Cambridgeshire**, PE8 5JE, **ENGLAND**.
(T) 01832 280384 **(F)** 01832 280384
(M) 07768 288646.
Profile Supplies. **Ref: YH15589**

WINNERS OF WALES

Winners of Wales, 76 Bridgend Rd, Llanharan, Pontyclun, **Rhondda Cynon Taff**, CF72 9RB, **WALES**.
(T) 01443 226517.
Profile Supplies. **Ref: YH15590**

WINNING FARE TACK

Winning Fare Tack, Slieveardagh, Killenaule, **County Tipperary**, **IRELAND**.
(T) 052 56563.
Profile Supplies. **Ref: YH15591**

WINPENNY PHOTOGRAPHY

Winpenny Photography LBIPP LMPA, 3 Wesley St, Otley, **Yorkshire (West)**, LS21 1AZ, **ENGLAND**.
(T) 01943 462597 **(F)** 01943 850861.
Profile Club/Association. **Ref: YH15592**

WINTER, ERIC

Eric Winter, Pill Hse Farm, Tidenham, Chepstow, **Monmouthshire**, NP16 7LL, **WALES**.
(T) 01291 623412.
Profile Trainer. **Ref: YH15593**

WINTER, LINDA

Miss Linda Winter, The Meadows, Off High St, Newchapel, Stoke-on-Trent, **Staffordshire**, ST7 4PT, **ENGLAND**.
(T) 01782 784586.
Profile Breeder. **Ref: YH15594**

WINTER, MICHAEL

Michael Winter, Journey's End, 196 Fairview Rd, Stevenage, **Hertfordshire**, SG1 2NA, **ENGLAND**.
(T) 01438 317630. **Ref: YH15595**

WINTERBOTTOM, S A

Miss S A Winterbottom, Closewood Farm, Boggard Lane, Charlesworth, Broadbottom, Glossop, **Cheshire**, **ENGLAND**.. **Ref: YH15596**

WINTERBOURNE VETNRY CLINIC

Winterbourne Veterinary Clinic, 72A Bradley Ave, Winterbourne, **Gloucestershire (South)**, BS36 1HS, **ENGLAND**.
(T) 01454 776501 **(F)** 01454 776840.
Profile Medical Support. **Ref: YH15597**

WINTERINGHAM FARM LIVERY CTRE

Winteringham Farm Livery Centre, Winteringham Hse, Thorpe In Balne, Doncaster, **Yorkshire (South)**, DN6 0EA, **ENGLAND**.
(T) 01302 882290.
Contact/s
Owner: Mrs M Allison
Profile Stable/Livery. **Ref: YH15598**

WINTLE, D J
Mr D J Wintle, Fox Hill, Stow Rd, Andoversford, Cheltenham, **Gloucestershire**, GL54 5RC, **ENGLAND**.
(T) 01451 850893 **(F)** 01451 850602
(M) 07774 785690.
Profile Trainer. **Ref: YH15599**

WINTON STREET FARM STABLES
Winton Street Farm Stables, Winton St, Alfriston, Polegate, **Sussex (East)**, BN26 5UH, **ENGLAND**.
(T) 01323 870089.
Contact/s
Owner: Mrs H Clark
Profile Riding School, Stable/Livery. **Ref: YH15600**

WINTON, A I
A I Winton, Moss Bridge Farm, Parkers Rd, Crewe, **Cheshire**, CW1 4RZ, **ENGLAND**.
(T) 01270 584323.
Contact/s
Owner: Mr A Winton **Ref: YH15601**

WIRRAL EQUESTRIAN CLUB
Wirral Equestrian Club, 6 Holmwood Ave, Barnston, Wirral, **Merseyside**, CH61 1AX, **ENGLAND**.
(T) 0151 6481016.
Contact/s
Secretary: Mrs J Barnes
Profile Club/Association. **Ref: YH15602**

WIRRAL RIDING CTRE
Wirral Riding Centre, Haddon Lane, Ness, Neston, **Merseyside**, CH64 8TA, **ENGLAND**.
(T) 0151 3363638 **(F)** 0151 3531312.
Contact/s
Manager: Mr T Jenkins
Profile Riding School. **Ref: YH15603**

WIRRALL TRAILERS
Wirrall Trailers, 17A Seymour St, Birkenhead, **Merseyside**, CH42 5LG, **ENGLAND**.
(T) 0151 6479020 **(F)** 0151 6479020.
Contact/s
Partner: Mr D Baker
Profile Transport/Horse Boxes. **Ref: YH15604**

WISBOROUGH GREEN FORGE
Wisborough Green Forge, Unit 3 Ansells Yard, Kirdford Rd, Wisborough Green, Billingshurst, **Sussex (West)**, RH14 0DD, **ENGLAND**.
(T) 01403 700680.
Profile Blacksmith. **Ref: YH15605**

WISCOMBE HAYLAGE
Wiscombe Haylage, Wiscombe Grange, Southleigh, Colyton, **Devon**, EX24 6JF, **ENGLAND**.
(T) 01404 871535 **(F)** 01404 871579.
Contact/s
Owner: Mr J Fowler **Ref: YH15606**

WISE
Mrs Wise, Kelmscott Farm, Horsham, Alfold, **Surrey**, GU6 8JE, **ENGLAND**.
(T) 01403 753094.
Profile Breeder. **Ref: YH15607**

WISE, J W
J W Wise, Wheats Farm, Livery Yard, Mortimer, Reading, **Berkshire**, RG7 3PS, **ENGLAND**.
(T) 0118 9332955.
Contact/s
Owner: Mr J Wise **Ref: YH15608**

WISEMAN, ANGUS W
Angus W Wiseman DWCF, Broadthorn, Patton, Kendal, **Cumbria**, LA8 9DR, **ENGLAND**.
(T) 01539 735292.
Profile Farrier. **Ref: YH15609**

WISEMAN, PAUL
Paul Wiseman DWCF, 2 Nunfield Cottages, Bull Lane, Newington, **Kent**, ME9 7SL, **ENGLAND**.
(T) 01795 842451.
Profile Farrier. **Ref: YH15610**

WISEWEAR
Wisewear, Unit 15 Havenbury Est, Station Rd, Dorking, **Surrey**, RH4 1ES, **ENGLAND**.
(T) 01306 876767 **(F)** 01306 887479.
Profile Supplies. **Ref: YH15611**

WISHANGER EQUESTRIAN CTRE
Wishanger Equestrian Centre, Frensham Lane, Churt, Farnham, **Surrey**, GU10 2QG, **ENGLAND**.
(T) 01252 792604 **(F)** 01252 792604.
Contact/s
Owner: Mrs J Norkett
Profile Stable/Livery. **Ref: YH15612**

WISHANGER LIVERIES
Wishanger Liveries, Frensham Lane, Churt, Farnham, **Surrey**, GU10 2QG, **ENGLAND**.
(T) 01252 793826 **(F)** 01252 793826.
Contact/s
Owner: Mrs J Norkett
Profile Stable/Livery. **Ref: YH15613**

WISHAW RIDING CTRE
Wishaw Riding Centre, Bulls Lane, Wishaw, Sutton Coldfield, **Midlands (West)**, B76 9QW, **ENGLAND**.
(T) 0121 3131663.
Contact/s
Owner: Mrs M Bevan
Profile Riding School, Stable/Livery. **Ref: YH15614**

WISTMAN'S DARTMOOR STUD
Wistman's Dartmoor Stud, 2 Ridgnor, North Bovey, Dartmoor, **Devon**, TQ13 8QX, **ENGLAND**.
(T) 01647 221245.
Profile Breeder. **Ref: YH15615**

WITCHAM EQUESTRIAN CTRE
Witcham Equestrian Centre, Mepal Rd, Witcham, Ely, **Cambridgeshire**, CB6 2LD, **ENGLAND**.
(T) 01353 777588.
Profile Riding School, Saddlery Retailer.
Ref: YH15616

WITCHAM HSE FARM STUD
Witcham House Farm Stud, Witcham, Ely, **Cambridgeshire**, CB6 2LH, **ENGLAND**.
(T) 01353 777078 **(F)** 01353 777078
(E) whfarm@ntlworld.com
Affiliated Bodies BD, BHHS.
Contact/s
Owner: Mrs H Vale
Profile Breeder, Stable/Livery, Trainer. No.Staff: 3
C.Size: 35 Acres **Ref: YH15617**

WITHAM SADDLERY
Witham Saddlery, 63B Newland St, Witham, **Essex**, CM8 1AA, **ENGLAND**.
(T) 01376 501225.
Contact/s
Owner: Mr P Hill
Profile Saddlery Retailer. No.Staff: 2
Yr. Est: 1996
Opening Times
Sp: Open Mon - Sat 09:30. Closed Mon - Sat 17:30.
Su: Open Mon - Sat 09:30. Closed Mon - Sat 17:30.
Au: Open Mon - Sat 09:30. Closed Mon - Sat 17:30.
Wn: Open Mon - Sat 09:30. Closed Mon - Sat 17:30.
Ref: YH15618

WITHAM VALE CONTRACTORS
Witham Vale Contractors, Henshallbrook Farm, High St, Queen Camel, Yeovil, **Somerset**, BA22 7NF, **ENGLAND**.
(T) 01935 850804 **(F)** 01935 850804.
Profile Track/Course. **Ref: YH15619**

WITHAM VILLA RIDING CTRE
Witham Villa Ltd, Cosby Rd, Broughton Astley, Leicester, **Leicestershire**, LE9 6PA, **ENGLAND**.
(T) 01455 282694.
Contact/s
For Bookings: Ms J Tomlinson
Profile Arena, Riding Club, Riding School, Stable/Livery, Trainer.
They have 4 Intermediate Instructors and are a BSJA course builder. No.Staff: 15 Yr. Est: 1991
C.Size: 30 Acres
Opening Times
Sp: Open 08:00. Closed 22:00.
Su: Open 08:00. Closed 22:00.
Au: Open 08:00. Closed 22:00.
Wn: Open 08:00. Closed 22:00. **Ref: YH15620**

WITHAM, JIM
Jim Witham, Gairletter Farm Cottage, Blairmore, Dunoon, **Argyll and Bute**, PA23 8TP, **SCOTLAND**.
(T) 01369 810300.
Profile Farrier. **Ref: YH15621**

WITHERIDGE & DISTRICT RIDING
Witheridge & District Riding Club, Hilltown Farm, Rackenford, Tiverton, **Devon**, EX16 8DX, **ENGLAND**.
(T) 01884 881265.
Contact/s
Chairman: Mrs S Sawyer
Profile Club/Association, Riding Club. **Ref: YH15622**

WITHERIDGE, WILLIAM GEORGE
William George Witheridge AFCL, Middle Stoodleigh, West Buckland, Barnstaple, **Devon**, EX32 0SN, **ENGLAND**.
(T) 01598 710512.
Profile Farrier. **Ref: YH15623**

WITHERSLACK HALL
Witherslack Hall Equestrian Centre, Witherslack Hall Farm, Witherslack, Grange-Over-Sands, **Cumbria**, LA11 6SD, **ENGLAND**.
(T) 01539 552244 **(F)** 01539 552244.
Contact/s
Partner: Mrs L Garrett
Profile Riding School. **Ref: YH15624**

WITHERSTONE, W A
Mr W A Witherstone, The Stables, Warleyside, Great Warley, Brentwood, **Essex**, CM13 3JE, **ENGLAND**.
(T) 01277 230706
(M) 07836 635836.
Profile Medical Support. **Ref: YH15625**

WITHINGTON HILL STABLES
Withington Hill Stables, Unit 1 Hawthorn Ind Est, Albion Rd, Newmills, High Peak, **Derbyshire**, SK22 3EY, **ENGLAND**.
(T) 01663 747742
(E) stables@withingtonhill.freeserve.co.uk.
Contact/s
Owner: Mr P Sutton
Profile Transport/Horse Boxes. **Ref: YH15626**

WITHINGTON, CAROLYN
Carolyn Withington, Halebourne Farm, Bagshot Rd, West End, Chobham, **Surrey**, GU24 9QR, **ENGLAND**.
(T) 01276 6327.
Contact/s
Agent: David Wilson **Ref: YH15627**

WITHNELL BARN FARM
Withnell Barn Farm, Chorley Rd, Withnell, Chorley, **Lancashire**, PR6 8BG, **ENGLAND**.
(T) 01254 832408 **(F)** 01254 832408.
Contact/s
Owner: Mrs A Boden
Profile Breeder. **Ref: YH15628**

WITHYBROOK STABLES
Withybrook Stables, Grange Farm, Featherbed Lane, Withybrook, Coventry, **Midlands (West)**, CV7 9LY, **ENGLAND**.
(T) 01455 220198.
Contact/s
Owner: Mr D Dearden
Profile Riding School, Stable/Livery.
Offer NVQ training for examinations. Yr. Est: 1995
Opening Times
Sp: Open 08:00. Closed 22:00.
Su: Open 08:00. Closed 22:00.
Au: Open 08:00. Closed 22:00.
Wn: Open 08:00. Closed 22:00. **Ref: YH15629**

WITNEY RUG COMPANY
Witney Rug Company, Lower White Flood Farm, Baybridge, Owlesbury, Winchester, **Hampshire**, SO21 1JM, **ENGLAND**.
(T) 01962 777007.
Profile Supplies. **Ref: YH15630**

WITNEY SHOW SERVICES
Witney Show Services, 22 Northfields, Lambourn, Hungerford, **Berkshire**, RG17 8YJ, **ENGLAND**.
(T) 01488 72604.
Profile Supplies. **Ref: YH15631**

WITNEY STUD
Witney Stud (Isle of Man) Ltd (The), Hope Lodge, 6 Albany Rd, Peel, Douglas, **Isle of Man**, IM5 1JR, **ENGLAND**.
(T) 01624 672354.
Profile Breeder. **Ref: YH15632**

WITNEY UK
Witney UK, London Rd, Fairford, **Gloucestershire**, GL7 4DS, **ENGLAND**.
(T) 01285 713370 **(F)** 01285 712257.
Profile Club/Association. **Ref: YH15633**

WITS END STABLES
Wits End Stables, Wits End, Broomhall, Worcester, **Worcestershire**, WR5 2NZ, **ENGLAND**.
(T) 01905 821686 **(F)** 01905 769080.
Contact/s
General Manager: Mr S Larkin
Profile Arena, Stable/Livery.
Full and DIY Livery available. Prices on request
Yr. Est: 1989 C.Size: 3 Acres
Opening Times
Sp: Open Mon - Sun 08:00. Closed Mon - Sun 17:00.

Su: Open Mon - Sun 08:00. Closed Mon - Sun 17:00.
Au: Open Mon - Sun 08:00. Closed Mon - Sun 17:00.
Wn: Open Mon - Sun 08:00. Closed Mon - Sun 17:00. **Ref: YH15634**

WITTON CASTLE RACEWAY

Witton Castle Raceway, 5 Raby Moor, Cickfield, Bishop Auckland, **County Durham**, DL13 5HG, **ENGLAND**.
(T) 0191 2322000.
Profile Track/Course. **Ref: YH15635**

WIX EQUESTRIAN CTRE

Wix Equestrian Centre, Clay Hall, Clacton Rd, Wix, Manningtree, **Essex**, CO11 2RU, **ENGLAND**.
(T) 01255 870744.
Contact/s
General Manager: Mrs J Hall
Profile Equestrian Centre.
Run unaffiliated dressage and showjumping events. Outdoor showjumping course and cross country course for hire. Hold unaffiliated outdoor events. Bring your own horses. Feed shop on site. Emergency tack. Cafeteria No.Staff: 4 Yr. Est: 1987
Opening Times
Sp: Open Mon - Sun 08:30. Closed Mon - Sun 17:00.
Su: Open Mon - Sun 08:30. Closed Mon - Sun 17:00.
Au: Open Mon - Sun 08:30. Closed Mon - Sun 17:00.
Wn: Open Mon - Sun 08:30. Closed Mon - Sun 17:00. **Ref: YH15636**

WIX HILL RIDING STABLES

Wix Hill Riding Stables, Wix Hill, West Horsley, Leatherhead, **Surrey**, KT24 6ED, **ENGLAND**.
(T) 01483 223100.
Profile Riding School. **Ref: YH15637**

WM ALEXANDER & SON

Wm Alexander & Son, Dripps Mill, Waterfoot Row, Clarkston, Glasgow, **Glasgow (City of)**, G76 8RL, **SCOTLAND**.
(T) 0141 6442558 **(F)** 0141 6442558.
Profile Supplies. **Ref: YH15638**

WM EYRE & SONS

Wm Eyre & Sons, Brough Corn Mill, Bradwell, Hope Valley, **Derbyshire**, S33 9NG, **ENGLAND**.
(T) 01433 620353 **(F)** 01433 620430.
Profile Supplies. **Ref: YH15639**

WM LILLICO & SON

WM Lillico & Son Ltd (Lambourn), The Old Bank, Market Pl, Lambourn, Hungerford, **Berkshire**, RG17 8XU, **ENGLAND**.
(T) 01488 73456 **(F)** 01488 73600
(M) 07973 802210.
Profile Supplies. **Ref: YH15640**

WM LILLICO & SONS

Wm Lillico & Sons Ltd (Maidstone), The Forstal,, Beddow Way, Aylesford, Maidstone, **Kent**, ME20 7BT, **ENGLAND**.
(T) 01622 718062 **(F)** 01622 790321.
Profile Saddlery Retailer. **Ref: YH15641**

WM MURRAY FARMCARE

Wm Murray Farmcare, 35 Galloway St, Dumfries, **Dumfries and Galloway**, DG2 7TN, **SCOTLAND**.
(T) 01387 267414 **(F)** 01387 269327
(E) equine@murrayfarmcare.co.uk.
Profile Saddlery Retailer. **Ref: YH15642**

WOFFORD INT HORSE TRANSPORT

Wofford International Horse Transport Ltd, Abnalls Farm, Cross In Hand Lane, Lichfield, **Staffordshire**, WS13 8DZ, **ENGLAND**.
(T) 01543 417225.
Contact/s
Transport Manager: Mr W Wofford
Profile Transport/Horse Boxes. **Ref: YH15643**

WOKINGHAM EQUESTRIAN CTRE

Wokingham Equestrian Centre, Chapel Green Hse, Wokingham, **Berkshire**, RG40 3ER, **ENGLAND**.
(T) 0118 9775549
(E) eventing@wecentre.freeserve.co.uk
(W) www.wokinghamequestriancentre.co.uk.
Contact/s
General Manager: Mr R Algar **(Q)** BHSII
(E) training@rossalgar.com
Profile Stable/Livery. Competition Centre.
One-two day horse trails, Combined Training, Schooling with our British Blyth Tait **Ref: YH15644**

WOKINGHAM RIDING CLUB

Wokingham Riding Club, 36 Liverpool Rd, Reading, **Berkshire**, RG1 3PQ, **ENGLAND**.
(T) 0118 9262764.
Contact/s
Chairman: Mr L Langston
Profile Club/Association, Riding Club. **Ref: YH15645**

WOLDGATE TREKKING

Woldgate Trekking & Riding Centre, 14 Woldgate, Bridlington, **Yorkshire (East)**, YO16 4XE, **ENGLAND**.
(T) 01262 673086
Affiliated Bodies ABRS.
Contact/s
Owner: P W Pickering
(E) woldgate@trekking.fsnet.co.uk
Profile Riding School, Stable/Livery. No.Staff: 3
Yr. Est: 1980 C.Size: 3 Acres
Opening Times
Sp: Open 09:00. Closed 20:00.
Su: Open 09:00. Closed 20:00.
Au: Open 09:00. Closed 19:30.
Wn: Open 09:00. Closed 19:30. **Ref: YH15646**

WOLDINGHAM SADDLERS

Woldingham Saddlers, 10 The Crescent, Station Rd, Woldingham, Caterham, **Surrey**, CR3 7DB, **ENGLAND**.
(T) 01883 652255
Affiliated Bodies SMS.
Contact/s
General Manager: Ms J Birch
Profile Saddlery Retailer. Yr. Est: 1989
Opening Times
Sp: Open 09:00. Closed 17:30.
Su: Open 09:00. Closed 17:30.
Au: Open 09:00. Closed 17:30.
Wn: Open 09:00. Closed 17:30.
Closed Sundays **Ref: YH15647**

WOLFENDEN, SIMON

Simon Wolfenden DWCF, 14 Carlton Drive, Baildon, Shipley, **Yorkshire (West)**, BD17 5NP, **ENGLAND**.
(T) 01274 589905.
Profile Farrier. **Ref: YH15648**

WOLFERTON STUD

Wolferton Stud, Wolferton, King's Lynn, **Norfolk**, PE31 6HA, **ENGLAND**.
(T) 01485 540544 **(F)** 01485 544383.
Profile Breeder. **Ref: YH15649**

WOLVERHAMPTON RACECOURSE

Wolverhampton Racecourse, Gorsebrook Rd, Wolverhampton, **Midlands (West)**, WV6 0PE, **ENGLAND**.
(T) 07930 161792.
Contact/s
Clerk of Course: Mr M Prosser
Profile Track/Course, Trainer. **Ref: YH15650**

WOLVISTON ANIMAL FEEDS

Wolviston Animal Feeds, 99 Thames Rd, Billingham, **Cleveland**, TS22 5EU, **ENGLAND**.
(T) 01642 557147 **(F)** 01642 565523.
Profile Supplies. **Ref: YH15651**

WOLVISTON RIDING STABLES

Wolviston Livery & Riding Stables, Bradley Hse Farm, Durham Rd, Wolviston, Billingham, **Cleveland**, TS22 5LP, **ENGLAND**.
(T) 01740 644692 **(F)** 0870 1208470
Affiliated Bodies ABRS.
Contact/s
Owner: Mr I Cross
(E) wolvrid@aol.com
Profile Riding School, Stable/Livery. No.Staff: 2
Yr. Est: 1982 C.Size: 12 Acres
Opening Times
Sp: Open 08:00. Closed 20:30.
Su: Open 08:00. Closed 20:30.
Au: Open 08:00. Closed 20:30.
Wn: Open 08:00. Closed 20:30. **Ref: YH15652**

WONNACOTT, DAVID J

David J Wonnacott, Zeaston Farmhouse, South Brent, **Devon**, TQ10 9EP, **ENGLAND**.
(T) 01364 72928.
Profile Farrier. **Ref: YH15653**

WONNACOTT, ERIC W J

Eric W J Wonnacott, Beechtree Cottage, Dippertown, Lewdown, **Devon**, EX20 4PT, **ENGLAND**.
(T) 01566 783124.
Profile Farrier. **Ref: YH15654**

WONNACOTT, L J

Miss L J Wonnacott, Kellybeare, Lifton, **Devon**, PL16 0HQ, **ENGLAND**.
(T) 01566 784278.
Profile Supplies. **Ref: YH15655**

WOOD FARM STUD

Wood Farm Stud, Sampford Courtenay, Okehampton, **Devon**, EX20 2RT, **ENGLAND**.
(T) 01837 52868
(M) 07831 427090.
Profile Stable/Livery, Trainer. **Ref: YH15656**

WOOD FARM STUD

Wood Farm Stud, Ellerdine, Wellington, **Shropshire**, TF6 6RS, **ENGLAND**.
(T) 01952 541243 **(F)** 01952 541242.
Profile Breeder, Stable/Livery. **Ref: YH15657**

WOOD HALL STUD

Wood Hall Stud, Wood Hall Lane, Shenley, **London (Greater)**, HA7 3DP, **ENGLAND**..
Profile Breeder, Trainer. **Ref: YH15658**

WOOD LODGE STABLES

Wood Lodge Stables, 7 Drumbuck Rd, Castlewellan, **County Down**, BT31 9NB, **NORTHERN IRELAND**.
(T) 028 43778947.
Contact/s
Manager: Mr D Lavery
Profile Stable/Livery, Trainer.
Trains horses for point to point eventing. **Ref: YH15659**

WOOD 'N' HORSE

Wood 'n' Horse, 7a Albany Business Ctre, Wickham Rd, Fareham, **Hampshire**, PO17 5BD, **ENGLAND**.
(T) 01329 234666 **(F)** 01329 234666.
Contact/s
Owner: Mr T Rose **Ref: YH15660**

WOOD, D

Mrs D Wood, Elm Cottage, Knowle Lane, Wyke, **Yorkshire (West)**, BD12 9EE, **ENGLAND**.
(T) 01274 679800
(E) cjwdbw@aol.com.
Profile Breeder.
Breeder of Welsh Section D ponies **Ref: YH15661**

WOOD, H O

H O Wood, 22 Wollaton Rd, Beeston, Nottingham, **Nottinghamshire**, NG9 2NR, **ENGLAND**.
(T) 0115 9256404.
Profile Blacksmith. **Ref: YH15662**

WOOD, J G P

J G P Wood, Moorcroft, Reepham, Norwich, **Norfolk**, NR10 4NL, **ENGLAND**.
(T) 01603 872220.
Profile Medical Support. **Ref: YH15663**

WOOD, JONATHAN

Jonathan Wood, 32 East St, Crediton, **Devon**, EX17 2EP, **ENGLAND**.
(T) 01363 772319.
Profile Medical Support. **Ref: YH15664**

WOOD, MERVYN

Mervyn Wood, Glebe Farm, Wood Stanway, Cheltenham, **Gloucestershire**, GL54 5PG, **ENGLAND**.
(T) 01386 584404.
Profile Farrier. **Ref: YH15665**

WOOD, PERRY

Perry Wood, 2 Oak Cottages, Perry Wood, Selling, Faversham, **Kent**, ME13 9SE, **ENGLAND**.
(T) 01227 751645 **(F)** 01227 751645.
Contact/s
Owner: Mr S Haggart **Ref: YH15666**

WOOD, R S

Mr R S Wood, Manor Farm, Nawton, **Yorkshire (North)**, YO62 5RD, **ENGLAND**.
(T) 01439 771627.
Profile Supplies. **Ref: YH15667**

WOOD, RICHARD WILLIAM

Richard William Wood RSS, The Gardens, Behind Hayes Lane, South Cheriton, Templecombe, **Somerset**, BA8 0BP, **ENGLAND**.
(T) 01963 370268.
Profile Farrier. **Ref: YH15668**

WOOD, T C

Mr T C Wood, New Farm, Lochgelly, **Fife**, KY5 9HP, **SCOTLAND**.
(T) 01592 780215.

Profile Trainer. **Ref: YH15669**

WOOD, TIMOTHY

Timothy Wood DWCF, 11 Oakdene Ave, Porthill, Newcastle-under-Lyme, **Staffordshire**, ST5 8HQ, **ENGLAND**.
(T) 07961 933582.
Profile Farrier. **Ref: YH15670**

WOOD, V S

V S Wood, 19 Engine Lane, Shafton, Barnsley, **Yorkshire (South)**, S72 8QY, **ENGLAND**.
(T) 01226 780606.
Profile Farrier. **Ref: YH15671**

WOODALL, PAUL

Paul Woodall AWCF, Mount Pleasant, Belan School Lane, Welshpool, **Powys**, SY21 8SJ, **WALES**.
(T) 01938 554864.
Profile Farrier. **Ref: YH15672**

WOODBASTWICK FORGE

Woodbastwick Forge, The Forge, Woodbastwick, Norwich, **Norfolk**, NR13 6AG, **ENGLAND**.
(T) 01603 721677.
Contact/s
Owner: Mr M Harvey
Profile Blacksmith. **Ref: YH15673**

WOODBINE RIDING STABLES

Woodbine Riding Stables, Grandborough Fields, Rugby, **Warwickshire**, CV23 8BA, **ENGLAND**.
(T) 01788 810349.
Profile Riding School. **Ref: YH15674**

WOODBINE STABLES

Woodbine Stables, Woodbine Farm, Grandborough Fields, Rugby, **Warwickshire**, CV23 8BA, **ENGLAND**.
(T) 01788 810349.
Contact/s
Owner: Ms S Ward **(Q)** AI
Profile Riding School, Stable/Livery. **Ref: YH15675**

WOODCOATE STUD

Woodcoate Stud, 2 Rosemary Lane, Abbotsbury, Weymouth, **Dorset**, DT3 4JN, **ENGLAND**.
(T) 01305 871363.
Profile Breeder. **Ref: YH15676**

WOODCOTE & DISTRICT

Woodcote & District Riding Club, 16 Manor Cl, Worcester Park, **Surrey**, KT4 7PJ, **ENGLAND**.
(T) 020 83305843.
Contact/s
Chairman: Mrs J Luxon
Profile Club/Association, Riding Club. **Ref: YH15677**

WOODCOTE FARM

Woodcote Farm, Shere Rd, West Horsley, **Surrey**, KT24 6ET, **ENGLAND**.
(T) 01483 283916
(M) 07831 394750.
Profile Breeder, Stable/Livery. **Ref: YH15678**

WOODCOTE STUD

Woodcote Stud, Wilmerhatch Lane, Epsom, **Surrey**, KT18 7EH, **ENGLAND**.
(T) 01372 725723.
Profile Breeder. **Ref: YH15679**

WOODCRAY FEEDS

Woodcray Feeds Ltd, Woods Farm, Easthampstead Rd, Wokingham, **Berkshire**, RG40 3AE, **ENGLAND**.
(T) 0118 9782690 **(F)** 0118 9796131
(E) info@tackshop.co.uk.
Profile Supplies. **Ref: YH15680**

WOODCROFT SADDLERS

Woodcroft Saddlers, Woodcroft, Stone Rd, Fradswell, Stafford, **Staffordshire**, ST18 0HA, **ENGLAND**.
(T) 01889 502347.
Contact/s
Owner: Mrs C Priest
Profile Saddlery Retailer. **Ref: YH15681**

WOODDITTON STUD

Woodditton Stud Ltd, Ditton Green, Woodditton, Newmarket, **Suffolk**, CB8 9SH, **ENGLAND**.
(T) 01638 730881 **(F)** 01638 730869.
Contact/s
Manager: Mr N Angus-Smith
Profile Breeder. **Ref: YH15682**

WOODEND

Woodend Farm, Hallglen Rd, Falkirk, **Falkirk**, FK1 2AT, **SCOTLAND**.
(T) 01324 625626.
Contact/s
Owner: Mrs J Sharp
Profile Stable/Livery.
Livery available. Prices and details on request. Access to 250 acres of forest. **Yr. Est:** 1972 **C.Size:** 60 Acres
Opening Times
Sp: Open Mon - Sun 09:00. Closed Mon - Sun 18:00.
Su: Open Mon - Sun 09:00. Closed Mon - Sun 18:00.
Au: Open Mon - Sun 09:00. Closed Mon - Sun 18:00.
Wn: Open Mon - Sun 09:00. Closed Mon - Sun 18:00. **Ref: YH15683**

WOODEND

Woodend Equestrian Colzium Livery Stable, Woodend Farm, Kilsyth, Glasgow, **Glasgow (City of)**, G65 0PZ, **SCOTLAND**.
(T) 01236 822201.
Contact/s
Owner: Mr R Chalmers
Profile Riding School, Stable/Livery.
DIY livery is available, prices on request.
Yr. Est: 2000 **C.Size:** 200 Acres
Opening Times
Sp: Open Mon - Fri 09:30, Sat - Sun 10:00. Closed Mon - Fri 21:00, Sat, Sun 18:00.
Su: Open Mon - Fri 09:30, Sat - Sun 10:00. Closed Mon - Fri 21:00, Sat, Sun 18:00.
Au: Open Mon - Fri 09:30, Sat - Sun 10:00. Closed Mon - Fri 21:00, Sat, Sun 18:00.
Wn: Open Mon - Fri 09:30, Sat - Sun 10:00. Closed Mon - Fri 21:00, Sat, Sun 18:00.
Last lesson is an hour before closing **Ref: YH15684**

WOODER MANOR

Wooder Manor Self-Catering Cottages, Widecombe-In-The-Moor, Newton Abbot, **Devon**, TQ13 7TR, **ENGLAND**.
(T) 01364 621391 **(F)** 01364 621391.
Contact/s
Owner: Mrs A Bell
Profile Horse/Rider Accom. **Ref: YH15685**

WOODFLAKES OF DAVENTRY

Woodflakes of Daventry, Michaelmas Hse, Royal Oak Way North, Daventry, **Northamptonshire**, NN11 5PQ, **ENGLAND**.
(T) 01327 879086 **(F)** 01327 300003.
Contact/s
Owner: Mr P Pruden **Ref: YH15686**

WOODFORD CARRIAGES

Woodford Carriages, Woodford Gardens, Church Lane, Woodford, Stockport, **Cheshire**, SK7 1PQ, **ENGLAND**.
(T) 0161 4396932. **Ref: YH15687**

WOODFORD TRAILERS

Woodford Trailers, West Gate, Bridle Rd, Woodford, Stockport, **Cheshire**, SK7 1QN, **ENGLAND**.
(T) 0161 4395696.
Profile Transport/Horse Boxes. **Ref: YH15688**

WOODFORD, MICHAEL O

Michael O Woodford AFCL, Castle View Forge, Goadby Rd, Hallaton, **Leicestershire**, LE16 8UZ, **ENGLAND**.
(T) 01858 555792.
Profile Farrier. **Ref: YH15689**

WOODGREEN ANIMAL SHELTERS

Woodgreen Animal Shelters, Kings Bush Farm, London Rd, Godmanchester, **Cambridgeshire**, CB4 5BZ, **ENGLAND**.
(T) 01480 832808 **(F)** 01480 830566.
Profile Club/Association. **Ref: YH15690**

WOODGREEN ANIMAL SHELTERS

Woodgreen Animal Shelters, Highway Cottage, Chishill Rd, Heydon, Royston, **Hertfordshire**, SG8 8PN, **ENGLAND**.
(T) 01480 830757.
Profile Club/Association. **Ref: YH15691**

WOODGREEN FARM

Woodgreen Farm, Silver St, Goffs Oak, Waltham Cross, **Hertfordshire**, EN7 5JD, **ENGLAND**.
(T) 01707 872319.
Contact/s
Partner: Mrs V Taylor
Profile Stable/Livery.
DIY livery available, prices on request. **Ref: YH15692**

WOODHAVEN STUD

Woodhaven Stud, East Woodhay, East Woodhay, Newbury, **Berkshire**, RG20 0NF, **ENGLAND**.
(T) 01635 254475.
Contact/s
Owner: Miss J Reed
Profile Breeder, Stable/Livery. **Ref: YH15693**

WOODHEAD, J

J Woodhead RSS BII, 607 Hunsworth Lane, East Bierley, **Yorkshire (West)**, BD4 6PU, **ENGLAND**..
Profile Farrier. **Ref: YH15694**

WOODHOUSE STABLES

Woodhouse Stables, Woodhouse Farm, Fauld, Tutbury, Burton-on-Trent, **Staffordshire**, DE13 9HR, **ENGLAND**.
(T) 01283 812185.
Contact/s
Owner: Ms P Guest
Profile Stable/Livery. **Ref: YH15695**

WOODHOUSE, R D E

R D E Woodhouse, Teal Hse, Chestnut Ave, Welburn, York, **Yorkshire (North)**, YO60 7EH, **ENGLAND**.
(T) 01653 618637 **(F)** 01653 618637.
Contact/s
Owner: Mr R Woodhouse
Profile Trainer. **Ref: YH15696**

WOODHURST

Woodhurst Riding & Livery Stables, South St, Woodhurst, Huntingdon, **Cambridgeshire**, PE17 3BW, **ENGLAND**.
(T) 01487 822331.
Profile Riding School, Stable/Livery. **Ref: YH15697**

WOODHURST FARM LIVERY STABLES

Woodhurst Farm Livery Stables, Woodhurst, Cattlegate Rd, Enfield, **London (Greater)**, EN2 8AU, **ENGLAND**.
(T) 01707 873123.
Contact/s
Manager: Mr T Wall **Ref: YH15698**

WOODHURST LIVERY STABLES

Woodhurst Livery Stables, Pennyfarthing Cottage, South St, Woodhurst, Huntingdon, **Cambridgeshire**, PE28 3BW, **ENGLAND**.
(T) 01487 822331 **(F)** 01487 822331.
Contact/s
Owner: Mrs M Keenan **Ref: YH15699**

WOODING, SIMON A

Simon A Wooding DWCF, March Hare, Kuggar, Ruan Minor, Helston, **Cornwall**, TR12 7LY, **ENGLAND**.
(T) 01326 290687.
Profile Farrier. **Ref: YH15700**

WOODINGTON FEEDS

Woodington Feeds, Mill Farm, East Wellow, Romsey, **Hampshire**, CO51 6DQ, **ENGLAND**.
(T) 01794 323440.
Profile Supplies. **Ref: YH15701**

WOODLAND

Woodland Riding Stables, Glebe Farm, Wood Stanway, Cheltenham, **Gloucestershire**, GL54 5PG, **ENGLAND**.
(T) 01386 584404
(W) www.woodstanway.co.uk.
Contact/s
Owner: Mrs A Pratley
Profile Horse/Rider Accom, Riding School, Stable/Livery, Track/Course.
Livery available, details on request. Access to hacking with very little roadwork. Accommodation is available on both a weekly and B&B basis. Pub, picnic and fun rides are organsied through the summer. Prices for lessons are available on request. **No.Staff:** 2
Yr. Est: 1991 **C.Size:** 400 Acres
Opening Times
Sp: Open Mon - Sun 08:00. Closed Mon - Sun 18:00.
Su: Open Mon - Sun 08:00. Closed Mon - Sun 18:00.
Au: Open Mon - Sun 08:00. Closed Mon - Sun 18:00.
Wn: Open Mon - Sun 08:00. Closed Mon - Sun 18:00.
Accommodation is available all year **Ref: YH15702**

WOODLAND STABLES

Woodland Stables, Slades Lane, Meltham, Huddersfield, **Yorkshire (West)**, HD7 3RW, **ENGLAND**.
(T) 01484 852445.
Contact/s
Owner: Miss D Taylor **(Q)** BHS 1
Profile Stable/Livery.
DIY Livery only **No.Staff:** 1 **Yr. Est:** 2000

Opening Times
Sp: Open Mon - Sun 08:30. Closed Mon - Sun 17:30.
Su: Open Mon - Sun 08:30. Closed Mon - Sun 17:30.
Au: Open Mon - Sun 08:30. Closed Mon - Sun 17:30.
Wn: Open Mon - Sun 08:30. Closed Mon - Sun 17:30. **Ref: YH15703**

WOODLANDER STUD

Woodlander Stud, Coed-Y-Gelli, Llanarth, Raglan, **Monmouthshire**, SP15 2NA, **WALES**.
(T) 01873 840521 **(F)** 01873 840556.
Contact/s
Owner: Mrs L Crowden
Profile Breeder, Trainer. No.Staff: 4
Yr. Est: 1981
Opening Times
Sp: Open Mon - Sun 09:00. Closed Mon - Sun 18:00.
Su: Open Mon - Sun 09:00. Closed Mon - Sun 18:00.
Au: Open Mon - Sun 09:00. Closed Mon - Sun 18:00.
Wn: Open Mon - Sun 09:00. Closed Mon - Sun 18:00. **Ref: YH15704**

WOODLANDS

Woodlands Enterprises, Unit 4 Northfield Farm Ind Est, Wantage Rd, Great Shefford, Hungerford, **Berkshire**, RG17 7DQ, **ENGLAND**.
(T) 01488 648820 **(F)** 01488 648755
Affiliated Bodies BETA.
Contact/s
General Manager: Mrs C Morris
Profile Arena, Blacksmith, Blood Stock Agency, Breeder, Equestrian Centre, Farrier, Riding Club, Riding School, Riding Wear Retailer, Saddlery Retailer, Stable/Livery, Supplies, Track/Course, Trainer, Transport/Horse Boxes.
Leading N.H and Flat Trainers, Jockeys. No.Staff: 8
Yr. Est: 2000
Opening Times
Sp: Open 08:30. Closed 17:30.
Su: Open 08:30. Closed 17:30.
Au: Open 08:30. Closed 17:30.
Wn: Open 08:30. Closed 17:30. **Ref: YH15705**

WOODLANDS

Woodlands Equestrian Centre, Cotmans/Ash Lane, Woodlands, Kemsing, Sevenoaks, **Kent**, TN15 6XD, **ENGLAND**.
(T) 01959 524278 **(F)** 01959 525755
Affiliated Bodies BD, BHS.
Contact/s
Partner: Mr C Lewington
Profile Breeder, Equestrian Centre, Stable/Livery.
Full, part and DIY livery available, prices on request.
No.Staff: 3 Yr. Est: 1998
Opening Times
Open all day every day **Ref: YH15706**

WOODLANDS

Woodlands Stables, Holywell Row, Mildenhall, Bury St Edmunds, **Suffolk**, IP28 8NB, **ENGLAND**.
(T) 01638 713825 **(F)** 01638 713825
(W) www.eque-train.co.uk.
Contact/s
Owner: Mrs D Johnstone
(E) boss@eque-train.co.uk
Profile Riding School, Stable/Livery, Trainer. Internet Instructor.
Internet riding training available, for more information visit the website.
Opening Times
Lessons given over the Internet **Ref: YH15707**

WOODLANDS EQUINE VETNRY GRP

Woodlands Equine Veterinary Group, 5, Westfield Cl, Laverstock, Salisbury, **Wiltshire**, SP1 1SG, **ENGLAND**.
(T) 01722 341351.
Contact/s
Partner: Miss R Hamilton-Fletcher
Profile Medical Support. **Ref: YH15708**

WOODLANDS LEISUREWEAR

Woodlands Leisurewear, Unit 1A Northfield Farm Ind Est, Wantage Rd, Great Shefford, Hungerford, **Berkshire**, RG1 7DQ, **ENGLAND**.
(T) 01488 648820 **(F)** 01488 648755
(E) bill_woodlands@compuserve.com.
Profile Saddlery Retailer. **Ref: YH15709**

WOODLANDS RIDING SCHOOL

Woodlands Riding School, Vennaway Lane, Parkmill, Swansea, **Swansea**, SA3 2EA, **WALES**.
(T) 01792 232704.
Profile Riding School. **Ref: YH15710**

WOODLANDS STABLES

Woodlands Stables, Woodlands Lane, Market Rasen, **Lincolnshire**, LN8 3RE, **ENGLAND**.
(T) 01673 843663.
Contact/s
Owner: Mr M Chapman
Profile Blood Stock Agency, Trainer, Transport/Horse Boxes. No.Staff: 10 Yr. Est: 1987
C.Size: 40 Acres **Ref: YH15711**

WOODLANDS STABLES

Woodlands Stables Ltd, Sewardstone Rd, London, **London (Greater)**, E4 7RE, **ENGLAND**.
(T) 020 85292532. **Ref: YH15712**

WOODLANDS STABLES

Woodlands Stables, Titnore Rd, Patching, Worthing, **Sussex (West)**, BN13 3UG, **ENGLAND**.
(T) 01903 871339. **Ref: YH15713**

WOODLANDS STABLES

Woodlands Stables, School Lane, Bearley, Stratford-upon-Avon, **Warwickshire**, CV37 0SQ, **ENGLAND**.
(T) 01789 731774.
Contact/s
Owner: Mr G Batching **Ref: YH15714**

WOODLANDS VETNRY CTRE

Woodlands Veterinary Centre, Cornwood Rd, Ivybridge, **Devon**, PL21 9TX, **ENGLAND**.
(T) 01752 690999.
Profile Medical Support. **Ref: YH15715**

WOODLAY

Woodlay Arabian Stud, Woodlay Farm, Herodsfoot, Liskeard, **Cornwall**, PL14 4RB, **ENGLAND**.
(T) 01503 220221 **(F)** 01503 220802.
Contact/s
Owner: Mrs A Hawke
Profile Breeder. **Ref: YH15716**

WOODLEY RIDING STABLES

Woodley Riding Stables, Marchmont Farm, Piccotts End Lane, Hemel Hempstead, **Hertfordshire**, HP2 6JH, **ENGLAND**.
(T) 01442 231640.
Contact/s
Owner: Ms K Glynn **Ref: YH15717**

WOODLEY, CHRISTINE

Christine Woodley, The Orchard Cottage, Warkton, Kettering, **Northamptonshire**, NN16 9XL, **ENGLAND**.
(T) 01356 515177. **Ref: YH15718**

WOODLEY, G

Mrs G Woodley, Neuadd Farm, Penderyn, Aberdare, **Rhondda Cynon Taff**, CF44 9QA, **WALES**.
(T) 01685 812488.
Profile Breeder. **Ref: YH15719**

WOODMAN, C

C Woodman, Forge, Dilly Lane, Hartley Wintney, Hook, **Hampshire**, RG27 8HE, **ENGLAND**.
(T) 01252 845023.
Contact/s
Owner: Mr C Woodman
Profile Farrier. **Ref: YH15720**

WOODMAN, CHRISTOPHER M

Christopher M Woodman DWCF, 16 Phillips Cres, Headley, Bordon, **Hampshire**, GU35 8NU, **ENGLAND**.
(T) 01428 712841.
Profile Farrier. **Ref: YH15721**

WOODMAN, S

S Woodman, Parkers Stables, Pook Lane, East Lavant, Chichester, **Sussex (West)**, PO18 0AU, **ENGLAND**.
(T) 01243 527136 **(F)** 01243 527136.
Contact/s
Owner: Mr S Woodman
Profile Trainer. **Ref: YH15722**

WOODMANS STABLES

Woodmans Stables, London Rd, Ashington, **Sussex (West)**, RH20 3AU, **ENGLAND**.
(T) 01903 893031
(M) 07710 495951.
Profile Trainer. **Ref: YH15723**

WOODMANTON GALLERY

Woodmanton Gallery, Woodman Manor, Clifton-on-Terne, **Worcestershire**, WR6 6DS, **ENGLAND**.
(T) 01886 812295 **(F)** 01886 812240. **Ref: YH15724**

WOODMINTON FARM

Woodminton Farm, Bowerchalke, Salisbury, **Wiltshire**, SP5 5DD, **ENGLAND**.
(T) 01722 780356.
Profile Breeder. **Ref: YH15725**

WOODNOOK ARENA

Woodnook Arena, Westfield Farm, Meltham, Huddersfield, **Yorkshire (West)**, HD7 3DU, **ENGLAND**.
(T) 01484 661976.
Contact/s
Secretary: Mr P Mellor
Profile Club/Association. **Ref: YH15726**

WOODPECKER PRODUCTS

Woodpecker Products Limited, Rose Wharf, Ropery Rd, Gainsborough, **Lincolnshire**, DN21 2QB, **ENGLAND**.
(T) 01427 810231 **(F)** 01427 810837
(M) 07831 115125.
Profile Supplies. **Ref: YH15727**

WOODREDON RIDING SCHOOL

Woodredon Riding School, Woodredon Farm Lane, Waltham Abbey, **Essex**, EN9 3SX, **ENGLAND**.
(T) 01992 714312.
Profile Riding School, Stable/Livery. **Ref: YH15728**

WOODREDON RIDING SCHOOL

Woodredon Riding School, Woodredon Farm Lane, Waltham Abbey, **Essex**, EN9 3SX, **ENGLAND**.
(T) 01992 711144.
Profile Riding School. **Ref: YH15729**

WOODROW, A

Mrs A Woodrow, Crookswood Stud Farm, Horsleys Green, High Wycombe, **Buckinghamshire**, HP14 3XB, **ENGLAND**.
(T) 01494 482557.
Profile Supplies. **Ref: YH15730**

WOODRUFF EQUESTRIAN

Woodruff Equestrian, Sanway Rd, Byfleet, West Byfleet, **Surrey**, KT14 7SF, **ENGLAND**.
(T) 01932 401592
(W) www.woodruffequestrian.co.uk.
Contact/s
Partner: Mrs J Tugwell
Profile Riding School, Stable/Livery. **Ref: YH15731**

WOODRUFF, RAY

Ray Woodruff, 1 Roberts Cottages, Robin Hood Lane, Warnham, Horsham, **Sussex (West)**, RH12 3RR, **ENGLAND**.
(T) 01403 211134 **(F)** 01403 211134.
Contact/s
Owner: Mr R Woodruff
Profile Transport/Horse Boxes. **Ref: YH15732**

WOODS SADDLERY STORES

Woods Saddlery Stores, Bushey Close Farm, Gowthorpe Lane, Kirkhamgate, Wakefield, **Yorkshire (West)**, WF2 0SR, **ENGLAND**.
(T) 01924 379477
(M) 07831 229385.
Profile Saddlery Retailer. **Ref: YH15733**

WOODS SHOW JUMPS

Woods Show Jumps, Kiddles Farm, Wintringham, Malton, **Yorkshire (North)**, YO17 8HX, **ENGLAND**.
(T) 01944 758474.
Profile Supplies. **Ref: YH15734**

WOODS, A J

A J Woods, Woodsway Stud, Tuddenham, Bury St Edmunds, **Suffolk**, IP28 6TH, **ENGLAND**.
(T) 01638 714495.
Profile Blood Stock Agency. **Ref: YH15735**

WOODS, B D

B D Woods, Whitegates, High Moor, Oldham, **Lancashire**, OL4 3AB, **ENGLAND**.
(T) 01457 874310.
Profile Blacksmith. **Ref: YH15736**

WOODS, J

J Woods, Bates Green Farm, Dickets Lane, Skelmersdale, **Lancashire**, WN8 8UH, **ENGLAND**.
(T) 01695 722351.
Contact/s
Owner: Mr J Woods
Profile Breeder. **Ref: YH15737**

WOODS, L

L Woods, 85 Donaghedy Rd, Bready, Strabane, **County Tyrone**, BT82 0LH, **NORTHERN IRELAND**.
(T) 028 71398665.

Profile Trainer. **Ref: YH15738**

WOODSIDE EQUESTRIAN

Woodside Equestrian, Manor Cottage, Fossebridge, Cheltenham, **Gloucestershire**, GL54 3JN, **ENGLAND**.
(T) 01285 720719.
Profile Supplies. **Ref: YH15739**

WOODSIDE FARM RIDING SCHOOL

Woodside Farm Riding School, Woodside Farm, Forest Rd, Colgate, Horsham, **Sussex (West)**, RH12 4TF, **ENGLAND**.
(T) 01293 851229.
Profile Riding School. **Ref: YH15740**

WOODSIDE FARM STABLES

Woodside Farm Stables, Helmsley Rd, Rainworth, Mansfield, **Nottinghamshire**, NG21 0DG, **ENGLAND**.
(T) 01623 792382.
Profile Stable/Livery. **Ref: YH15741**

WOODSIDE FORGE

Woodside Forge, Woodside Forge, Yealmpton, Plymouth, **Devon**, PL8 2EQ, **ENGLAND**.
(T) 01752 881869.
Contact/s
Owner: Mr C Meheux
Profile Blacksmith. **Ref: YH15742**

WOODSIDE LIVERY STABLES

Woodside Livery Stables, Bestwood Country Pk, Arnold, Nottingham, **Nottinghamshire**, NG5 8NE, **ENGLAND**.
(T) 0115 9265147.
Contact/s
Owner: Mr B Cross
Profile Stable/Livery. **Ref: YH15743**

WOODSIDE RACING STABLES

Woodside Racing Stables, Knoxs Grave Lane, Hopwas, Tamworth, **Staffordshire**, B78 3AR, **ENGLAND**.
(T) 01827 62901 **(F)** 01827 68361.
Contact/s
Partner: Mr B McMahon
Profile Trainer. **Ref: YH15744**

WOODSIDE STABLES

Woodside Stables, Haynes West End, Haynes, Bedford, **Bedfordshire**, MK45 3QU, **ENGLAND**.
(T) 01234 742374.
Profile Stable/Livery. **Ref: YH15745**

WOODSIDE STABLES

Woodside Stables, Lower Ham Lane, Elstead, Godalming, **Surrey**, GU8 6HQ, **ENGLAND**.
(T) 01252 703687.
Profile Stable/Livery. **Ref: YH15746**

WOODSIDE VETNRY GRP

Woodside Veterinary Group, Woodside Rd, Torphins, **Aberdeenshire**, AB31 4JR, **SCOTLAND**.
(T) 01339 882556 **(F)** 01339 882609.
Profile Medical Support. **Ref: YH15747**

WOODSIDE VILLA

Woodside Villa, Woodside Farm, Forresfield, Caldercruix, Airdrie, **Lanarkshire (North)**, ML6 7RY, **SCOTLAND**.
(T) 01236 842921.
Contact/s
Owner: Mrs J Beattie
Profile Horse/Rider Accom. **Ref: YH15748**

WOODSPRING BRIDLEWAYS ASS

Woodspring Bridleways Association, Longbottom Farm, Shipham, Winscombe, **Somerset (North)**, BS25 1RW, **ENGLAND**.
(T) 01934 743166.
Profile Club/Association. **Ref: YH15749**

WOODSTOCK QUARTER HORSES

Woodstock Quarter Horses, Granby Lodge, Uppingham Rd, Bisbrooke, **Rutland**, LE15 9ES, **ENGLAND**.
(T) 01572 822006.
Profile Breeder. **Ref: YH15750**

WOODSTOCK SOUTH STABLES

Woodstock South Stables, Woodstock Lane South, Chessington, **Surrey**, KT9 1UF, **ENGLAND**.
(T) 020 83989008.
Contact/s
Dressage Trainer: Mr J Davis **(T)** 020 83989439
(E) april.whalley@talk21.com
Profile Arena, Farrier, Medical Support, Stable/Livery, Trainer, Transport/Horse Boxes.
Offers equine essential oil therapy, reiki, chakra work and meridian testing. Also, remedial lungeing/training, and referals from vets and physio's. **No.Staff:** 4
Yr. Est: 1980 **C.Size:** 15 Acres
Opening Times
Sp: Open 06:00. Closed 21:30.
Su: Open 06:00. Closed 21:30.
Au: Open 06:00. Closed 21:30.
Wn: Open 06:00. Closed 21:30. **Ref: YH15751**

WOODVILLE

Woodville, Raby Rd, Wirral, **Merseyside**, CH63 4JR, **ENGLAND**.
(T) 0151 3364800 **(F)** 0151 3364800.
Contact/s
Owner: Mrs M Walton
Profile Riding School. **Ref: YH15752**

WOODVILLE FARM SADDLERY

Woodville Farm Saddlery, Dragons Lane, Moston, Sandbach, **Cheshire**, CW11 3QH, **ENGLAND**.
(T) 01270 526460 **(F)** 01270 526460.
Contact/s
Partner: Mr D Wright
Profile Saddlery Retailer. **Ref: YH15753**

WOODWARD, BRIAN A

Brian A Woodward, Rose Cottage, Valley Farm Drive, Sproughton, Ipswich, **Suffolk**, IP8 3EL, **ENGLAND**.
(T) 01473 652272.
Profile Farrier. **Ref: YH15754**

WOODWARD, CAROLINE A

Caroline A Woodward DWCF, Head Hse Farm, Mapperley, Ilkeston, **Derbyshire**, DE7 6BX, **ENGLAND**.
(T) 0115 9324706.
Profile Farrier. **Ref: YH15755**

WOODWARD, G A

G A Woodward, White Hall, Old Newton, Stowmarket, **Suffolk**, IP14 4PF, **ENGLAND**.
(T) 01449 673335.
Profile Breeder. **Ref: YH15756**

WOODWARD, GARRY

Mr Garry Woodward, The Stables, Osberton Hall, Worksop, **Nottinghamshire**, S81 0UF, **ENGLAND**.
(T) 01909 472124.
Profile Trainer. **Ref: YH15757**

WOODWARD, MALCOLM K

Malcolm K Woodward DWCF, 29 Station Rd, Chinnor, **Oxfordshire**, OX9 4PU, **ENGLAND**.
(T) 07831 616654.
Profile Farrier. **Ref: YH15758**

WOODWARD, R S

R S Woodward, Median Farm, Meadows Rd, Cross Hands, Llanelli, **Carmarthenshire**, SA14 6SF, **WALES**.
(T) 01269 844109.
Contact/s
Owner: Mr R Woodward
Profile Farrier. **Ref: YH15759**

WOODYATT, ALAN TERENCE

Alan Terence Woodyatt AWCF, 3 Oakleigh, Lighthorne, Warwick, **Warwickshire**, CV35 0DB, **ENGLAND**.
(T) 01296 642549
(M) 07798 754396.
Profile Farrier. **Ref: YH15760**

WOOF, PHILIP JOHN

Philip John Woof DWCF, Moorfield, 39 Whalley Rd, Gt Harwood, Blackburn, **Lancashire**, BB6 7TE, **ENGLAND**.
(T) 01254 889732.
Profile Farrier. **Ref: YH15761**

WOOFWARE

Woofware, Callywith Gate Ind Est, Launceston Rd, Bodmin, **Cornwall**, PL31 2RQ, **ENGLAND**.
(T) 01208 78100 **(F)** 01208 72349.
Profile Riding Wear Retailer, Supplies.
Retailer of horse protection wear, and equine luggage.
Ref: YH15762

WOOLACOMBE RIDING STABLES

Woolacombe Riding Stables, Beach Rd, Woolacombe, **Devon**, EX34 7AE, **ENGLAND**.
(T) 01271 870260.
Contact/s
Owner: Mr J Middleton
Profile Riding School. **Ref: YH15763**

WOOLBEDING RIDING SCHOOL

Woolbeding Riding School, Woolbeding, Midhurst, **Sussex (West)**, GU29 0QB, **ENGLAND**.
(T) 01730 813303.
Contact/s
Owner: Mrs J Liverton
Profile Riding School. **Ref: YH15764**

WOOLCOTTS FARM

Woolcotts Farm, Brompton Regis, Dulverton, **Somerset**, TA22 9NX, **ENGLAND**.
(T) 01398 371206.
Profile Equestrian Centre. **Ref: YH15765**

WOOLDRIDGE, MICHAEL G

Michael G Wooldridge, 21 Shirley Rd, Acocks Green, Birmingham, **Midlands (West)**, B27 7XU, **ENGLAND**.
(T) 0121 7062259 **(F)** 0121 7069512. **Ref: YH15766**

WOOLFORDS FARM LIVERY STABLES

Woolfords Farm Livery Stables, Woolfords Farm, Woolford Lane, Elstead, Godalming, **Surrey**, GU8 6LL, **ENGLAND**.
(T) 01252 703706.
Profile Stable/Livery. **Ref: YH15767**

WOOLMER COTTAGE STABLES

Woolmer Cottage Stables, Willingham Green, Brinkley, Newmarket, **Suffolk**, CB8 0SW, **ENGLAND**.
(T) 01638 507275 **(F)** 01638 507931.
Profile Stable/Livery. **Ref: YH15768**

WOOLNOUGH, B & S

B & S Woolnough, Rowan, Gorgate Rd, Hoe, Dereham, **Norfolk**, NR20 4BG, **ENGLAND**.
(T) 01362 860953.
Profile Transport/Horse Boxes. **Ref: YH15769**

WOOPERTON

Wooperton Riding & Livery Stables, Eildon Cottage, Wooperton, Alnwick, **Northumberland**, NE66 4XS, **ENGLAND**.
(T) 01668 217241.
Contact/s
Owner: Miss S Stanton **(Q)** BHSI
(E) sstanton@supanet.com
Profile Stable/Livery, Track/Course, Trainer.
No.Staff: 3 **Yr. Est:** 1971 **C.Size:** 300 Acres
Opening Times
Open to livery owners 7 days a week. Telephone during evenings for further information **Ref: YH15770**

WOOTTON COURT FARM

Wootton Court Farm, Leek Wootton, Warwick, **Warwickshire**, CV35 7QU, **ENGLAND**.
(T) 01926 53891.
Profile Stable/Livery. **Ref: YH15771**

WOOTTON GRANGE EQUESTRIAN

Wootton Grange Equestrian, Wootton Grange Farm, Hill Wootton, Warwick, **Warwickshire**, CV35 7PP, **ENGLAND**.
(T) 01926 511811 **(F)** 01926 511015.
Contact/s
Owner: Miss E Bjorkman
(E) emelie-b@talk21.com
Profile Breeder, Equestrian Centre, Trainer.
Show Jumping Horses trained, bred and sold.
No.Staff: 3 **Yr. Est:** 1998 **C.Size:** 66 Acres
Opening Times
Sp: Open 09:00. Closed 16:30.
Su: Open 09:00. Closed 16:30.
Au: Open 09:00. Closed 16:30.
Wn: Open 09:00. Closed 16:30. **Ref: YH15772**

WORCESTER & DISTRICT

Worcester & District Riding Club, Shakespeare Hotel, Angel St, Worcester, **Worcestershire**, WR1 3QT, **ENGLAND**.
(T) 01905 453278.
Contact/s
Chairman: Miss D Budd
Profile Club/Association, Riding Club. **Ref: YH15773**

WORCESTER RACECOURSE

Worcester Racecourse, The Manager, Worcester Racecourse, Pitchcroft, Worcester, **Worcestershire**, WR1 2EY, **ENGLAND**.
(T) 01905 25364 **(F)** 01905 617563.
Contact/s
General Manager: John Baker
Profile Track/Course. **Ref: YH15774**

WORDINGHAM, L

Mr L Wordingham, Foxburrow Farm, Binham, Fakenham, **Norfolk**, NR21 0DH, **ENGLAND**.
(T) 01328 830343.

Profile Supplies. **Ref: YH15775**

WORDSLEY SADDLERY

Wordsley Saddlery, Junction Rd, Wordsley, Stourbridge, **Midlands (West)**, DY8 4YJ, **ENGLAND**.
(T) 01384 440883 **(F)** 01384 395278.
Profile Saddlery Retailer. **Ref: YH15776**

WORK SHOP

Work Shop (The), Wheel Cottage, Waldron, Heathfield, **Sussex (East)**, TN21 0QS, **ENGLAND**.
(T) 01435 812917.
Profile Saddlery Retailer. **Ref: YH15777**

WORKHORSE CONSULTANCY

Workhorse Consultancy (The), 9 Norelands Drive, Burnham, **Buckinghamshire**, SL1 8AZ, **ENGLAND**.
(T) 01628 668463 **(F)** 01628 602785.
Profile Club/Association. **Ref: YH15778**

WORKHORSE SERVICES

Workhorse Services, Blenheim Cottage, Millers Lane, Hornton, **Oxfordshire**, OX15 6BS, **ENGLAND**.
(T) 01295 670639 **(F)** 01295 670639.
Profile Supplies. **Ref: YH15779**

WORKING HORSE TRUST

Working Horse Trust (The), Forge Wood Farm, C/O Estate Office, Sham Farm, Eridge Green, Tunbridge Wells, **Kent**, TN3 9JA, **ENGLAND**.
(T) 01892 750105.
Contact/s
Trustee: Mr R Branscombe
Profile Club/Association. **Ref: YH15780**

WORKING TOGETHER FOR EQUINES

Working Together for Equines UK, Dept Of Clinical Studies, Veterinary Field Station, Easter Bush, Roslin, **Lothian (Mid)**, EH25 9RG, **SCOTLAND**.
(T) 0131 4455539 **(F)** 0131 4455539
(E) wtfeuk@msn.com.
Profile Club/Association. **Ref: YH15781**

WORKSOP MANOR STUD

Worksop Manor Stud, Worksop Manor, Worksop, **Nottinghamshire**, S80 3DQ, **ENGLAND**.
(T) 01909 472025.
Profile Breeder. **Ref: YH15782**

WORLD ARABIAN HORSE ORG

World Arabian Horse Organization, North Farm, 2 Trenchard Rd, Stanton Fitzwarren, Swindon, **Wiltshire**, SN6 7RZ, **ENGLAND**.
(T) 01793 766877 **(F)** 01793 766711
(E) waho@compuserve.com.
Contact/s
Key Contact: Ms K Murray
Profile Club/Association. **Ref: YH15783**

WORLD BETA EQUESTRIAN

World Beta Equestrian Ltd, Soake Rd, Waterlooville, **Hampshire**, PO7 6JA, **ENGLAND**.
(T) 023 92253850.
Profile Riding Wear Retailer, Saddlery Retailer.
Ref: YH15784

WORLD OF EXPERIENCE

World of Experience, 52 Kingston Deverill, Warminster, **Wiltshire**, BA12 7HF, **ENGLAND**.
(T) 01985 844102 **(F)** 01985 844102.
Profile Club/Association. **Ref: YH15785**

WORLD OF HORSES I T L

World of Horses I T L, Itl Hse, School Lane, Layland, **Lancashire**, PR5 1TU, **ENGLAND**.
(T) 01772 621909 **(F)** 01772 622628.
Contact/s
Owner: Mr S Forshaw
(E) steve@itlnet.com
Profile Club/Association. Insurance Company.
Ref: YH15786

WORLDWIDE ANIMAL TRAVEL

Worldwide Animal Travel, 43 London Rd, Brentwood, **Essex**, CM14 4NN, **ENGLAND**.
(T) 01277 231611 **(F)** 01277 262726.
Contact/s
Partner: Mrs B Bromage
Profile Transport/Horse Boxes. **Ref: YH15787**

WORLDWIDE EQUESTRIAN

Worldwide Equestrian Ltd, 10 Ablewell St, Walsall, **Midlands (West)**, WS1 2EQ, **ENGLAND**.
(T) 01922 637070 **(F)** 01922 637070.
Contact/s
Owner: Mr W Price
Profile Riding Wear Retailer, Saddlery Retailer.
Ref: YH15788

WORLE, DEREK A

Derek A Worle, 28 Greensay, Appleshaw, Andover, **Hampshire**, SP11 9HY, **ENGLAND**.
(T) 01264 772978.
Profile Farrier. **Ref: YH15789**

WORLEBURY LIVERY CTRE

Worlebury Livery Centre, Worlebury Hill Rd, Weston-Super-Mare, **Somerset (North)**, BS22 9TG, **ENGLAND**.
(T) 01934 631446.
Contact/s
Partner: Mrs H Tompkins
Profile Riding School. **Ref: YH15790**

WORLINGTON RIDING CLUB

Worlington Riding Club, Needham Hall, Gazeley, Newmarket, **Suffolk**, CB8 8RR, **ENGLAND**.
(T) 01638 750275.
Contact/s
Chairman: Mr J Hiner
Profile Club/Association, Riding Club. **Ref: YH15791**

WORMALL, JILL

Miss Jill Wormall, Ibstock Grange, Ibstock, **Leicestershire**, LE67 6LN, **ENGLAND**.
(T) 01530 260224
(M) 07808 523353.
Profile Supplies. **Ref: YH15792**

WORMWOOD SCRUBS PONY CTRE

Wormwood Scrubs Pony Centre, 30 Sunningdale Ave, East Acton, **London (Greater)**, W3 7NS, **ENGLAND**.
(T) 020 87400573.
Profile Riding School. **Ref: YH15793**

WORRALL, ANDREW G

Andrew G Worrall DWCF, 16 Agbrigg Rd, Sandal, Wakefield, **Yorkshire (West)**, WF1 6AF, **ENGLAND**.
(T) 01924 259501.
Profile Farrier. **Ref: YH15794**

WORSHIPFUL CO COACHMAKERS

Worshipful Company of Coachmakers & Coach Harness, 8 Chandlers Court, Burwell, **Cambridgeshire**, CB5 0AZ, **ENGLAND**.
(T) 01223 373566.
Profile Club/Association. **Ref: YH15795**

WORSHIPFUL CO OF FARRIERS

Worshipful Company of Farriers, 19 Queen St, Chipperfield, Kings Langley, **Hertfordshire**, WD4 9BT, **ENGLAND**.
(T) 01923 260747 **(F)** 01923 261677
(E) theclerk@wcf.org.uk.
Contact/s
Key Contact: Mrs C Clifford **(Q)** BA
Profile Club/Association. **Ref: YH15796**

WORSHIPFUL CO OF LORINERS

Worshipful Company of Loriners, 9 Rayne Rd, Braintree, **Essex**, CM7 2QA, **ENGLAND**.
(T) 01376 320328.
Contact/s
Secretary: Dr J White
Profile Club/Association. **Ref: YH15797**

WORSHIPFUL CO OF LORINERS

Worshipful Company of Loriners, 8 Portland Sq, London, **London (Greater)**, E1W 9QR, **ENGLAND**.
(T) 020 77090222.
Profile Club/Association. **Ref: YH15798**

WORSHIPFUL CO OF SADDLERS

Worshipful Company of Saddlers, Saddlers' Hall, 40 Gutter Lane, Cheapside, London, **London (Greater)**, EC2V 6BR, **ENGLAND**.
(T) 020 77268661/6 **(F)** 020 76000386.
Contact/s
Key Contact: Mr W Brereton Martin
Profile Club/Association. **Ref: YH15799**

WORSLEY RACING STABLES

Worsley Racing Stables, Bank Lane, Abberley, Worcester, **Worcestershire**, WR6 6BQ, **ENGLAND**.
(T) 01299 896522.
Contact/s
Manager: Mr A Juckes
Profile Trainer. **Ref: YH15800**

WORSLEY, R

Mr R Worsley, Marsden Manor Stud & Farm, Cirencester, **Gloucestershire**, GL7 7EU, **ENGLAND**.
(T) 01285 831238.
Profile Medical Support. **Ref: YH15801**

WORSTON FARM STABLES

Worston Farm Stables, Worston Lane, Little Bridgeford, Stafford, **Staffordshire**, ST18 9QA, **ENGLAND**.
(T) 01785 282752.
Contact/s
Owner: Mrs P McGregor **Ref: YH15802**

WORTH ARABIAN STUD

Worth Arabian Stud, East Lodge, Old Hollow, Crawley, **Sussex (West)**, RH10 4SZ, **ENGLAND**.
(T) 01293 883943.
Contact/s
Partner: Mr M Reed
Profile Stud Farm. **Ref: YH15803**

WORTHING TRAILERS & TOWBARS

Worthing Trailers & Towbars, H D Steele & Son, Goring Way, Goring-By-Sea, Worthing, **Sussex (West)**, BN12 4TY, **ENGLAND**.
(T) 01903 700046.
Profile Transport/Horse Boxes. **Ref: YH15804**

WORTHINGTON, ALLAN W

Allan W Worthington AFCL, 81 Hall Rd, Scarisbrick, Ormskirk, **Lancashire**, L40 9QB, **ENGLAND**.
(T) 01704 889049.
Profile Farrier. **Ref: YH15805**

WORTHINGTON, D

Mr D Worthington, Walton Stud Farm, Welsh Row, Nether Alderley, Macclesfield, **Cheshire**, SK10 4TY, **ENGLAND**.
(T) 01625 582393.
Profile Breeder. **Ref: YH15806**

WOTHERSOME GRANGE STUD

Wothersome Grange Stud, Bramham, Wetherby, **Yorkshire (West)**, LS23 6LY, **ENGLAND**.
(T) 0113 2892164
(E) emcbeta@emc.u-net.com.
Profile Breeder. **Ref: YH15807**

WRAGG, G

G Wragg, Abbington Pl, Bury Rd, Newmarket, **Suffolk**, CB8 7BT, **ENGLAND**.
(T) 01638 662328 **(F)** 01638 663576
(W) www.newmarketracehorsetrainers.co.uk
Affiliated Bodies Newmarket Trainers Fed.
Contact/s
Owner: Mr G Wragg
Profile Trainer. **Ref: YH15808**

WRAGG, PETER

Peter Wragg, Glebe Hse, Moulton Rd, Newmarket, **Suffolk**, CB8 8QN, **ENGLAND**.
(T) 01638 664080 **(F)** 01638 664804.
Contact/s
Owner: Mr P Wragg
Profile Blood Stock Agency. **Ref: YH15809**

WRANTAGE MILLS

Wrantage Mills Limited, Wrantage, Taunton, **Somerset**, TA3 6DG, **ENGLAND**.
(T) 01823 480484.
Profile Supplies. **Ref: YH15810**

WRATHALL, J G G

Mr J G G Wrathall, East Haddon Lodge, Northampton, **Northamptonshire**, NN6 8BU, **ENGLAND**.
(T) 01604 711421.
Profile Supplies. **Ref: YH15811**

WRATTEN, SARAH

Sarah Wratten, Woodhay, West Beer, Cheriton Bishop, **Devon**, EX6 6HF, **ENGLAND**.
(T) 01647 24700.
Profile Supplies. **Ref: YH15812**

WRAY, FREDERICK W

Frederick W Wray, Jalna, School Rd, Saxon St, Newmarket, **Suffolk**, CB8 9RX, **ENGLAND**.
(T) 01638 731247.
Profile Farrier. **Ref: YH15813**

WRB RACING

Wetherby Racing Bureau, Po Box Mt 91, Leeds, **Yorkshire (West)**, LS17 9XG, **ENGLAND**.
(T) 01937 574782
(W) www.wrbracing.com.
Contact/s
Owner: Mr A Bates
(E) andy@wrbracing.com
Profile Trainer. Racehorse Syndicates.
Yr. Est: 1988
Opening Times

Contact for further details **Ref: YH15814**

WREA GREEN EQUITATION CTRE

Wrea Green Equitation Centre, Bryning Lane, Wrea Green, Preston, **Lancashire**, PR4 2WJ, **ENGLAND**.
(T) 01772 686576. **Ref: YH15815**

WREA GREEN EQUITATION CTRE

Wrea Green Equitation Centre, Bryning Lane, Wrea Green, Kirkham, **Lancashire**, PR4 1TN, **ENGLAND**.
(T) 01772 686576.
Profile Equestrian Centre, Riding School.
Ref: YH15816

WREKIN FARMERS GARDEN CTRE

Wrekin Farmers Garden Centre Ltd, Bridge Rd, Wellington, Telford, **Shropshire**, TF1 1RU, **ENGLAND**.
(T) 01952 641342.
Profile Feed Merchant, Riding Wear Retailer, Supplies. **Ref: YH15817**

WREKIN NORTH BRIDLEWAYS ASS

Wrekin North Bridleways Association, Six Acres, Arleston Hill, Telford, **Shropshire**, TF1 2JY, **ENGLAND**.
(T) 01952 502433.
Profile Club/Association. **Ref: YH15818**

WREKIN NORTH RIDING CLUB

Wrekin North Riding Club, Six Acres, Arleston Hill, Telford, **Shropshire**, TF1 2JY, **ENGLAND**.
(T) 01952 502433.
Contact/s
Chairman: Mr D Waldron
Profile Club/Association, Riding Club. **Ref: YH15819**

WREN, T E

Mr T E Wren, Low Tranmire, Ugthorpe, Whitby, **Yorkshire (North)**, **ENGLAND**.
(T) 01947 840578.
Profile Breeder. **Ref: YH15820**

WRENCH VETNRY GRP

Wrench Veterinary Group, 4 Beaufort East, London Rd, Bath, **Bath & Somerset (North East)**, BA1 6QD, **ENGLAND**.
(T) 01225 312061.
Profile Medical Support. **Ref: YH15821**

WRENCH VETNRY GRP

Wrench Veterinary Group, 4 Third Ave, Oldfield Pk, Bath, **Bath & Somerset (North East)**, BA2 3NY, **ENGLAND**.
(T) 01225 423652.
Profile Medical Support. **Ref: YH15822**

WRENINGHAM TROTTING RACEWAY

Wreningham Trotting Raceway, South Norfolk Caterers, The Jolly Farmers, Forncett St Peter, Norwich, **Norfolk**, NR16 1LA, **ENGLAND**.
(T) 01953 788197 **(F)** 01953 788033.
Profile Track/Course. **Ref: YH15823**

WRENN'S ANIMAL FEEDS

Wrenn's Animal Feeds, Long Reach Farm, Brightling, Robertsbridge, **Sussex (East)**, TN32 4HJ, **ENGLAND**.
(T) 01424 838574 **(F)** 01424 838574.
Profile Supplies. **Ref: YH15824**

WRETHAM STUD

Wretham Stud, Wretham Hse, West Wretham, Thetford, **Norfolk**, IP24 1RH, **ENGLAND**.
(T) 01953 498411 **(F)** 01953 498887.
Profile Breeder. **Ref: YH15825**

WRIGHT & MORTEN

Wright & Morten, 18 Moody St, Congleton, **Cheshire**, CW12 4AP, **ENGLAND**.
(T) 01260 273222.
Profile Medical Support. **Ref: YH15826**

WRIGHT & MORTEN

Wright & Morten, 36-38 Cumberland St, Macclesfield, **Cheshire**, SK10 1BZ, **ENGLAND**.
(T) 01625 433321 **(F)** 01625 612240.
Profile Medical Support. **Ref: YH15827**

WRIGHT & MORTEN

Wright & Morten, Thorndale Veterinary Surgery, 19 Hawthorn Lane, Wilmslow, **Cheshire**, SK9 5DD, **ENGLAND**.
(T) 01625 524422.
Profile Medical Support. **Ref: YH15828**

WRIGHT BROS

Wright Bros, Beech Tree Farm, Highgate, Leverton, Boston, **Lincolnshire**, PE22 0AW, **ENGLAND**.
(T) 01205 870577.
Profile Breeder. **Ref: YH15829**

WRIGHT TRAILER

Wright Trailer (The), Unit 4 Emmerson Ind Est, Norwich Rd, Lenwade, Norwich, **Norfolk**, NR9 5SH, **ENGLAND**.
(T) 01603 873257 **(F)** 01603 873257.
Contact/s
Partner: Mrs H Wright
Profile Transport/Horse Boxes. **Ref: YH15830**

WRIGHT, A W

Mr A W Wright, Whitley Hall, Whitley, Warrington, **Cheshire**, WA4 4ES, **ENGLAND**.
(T) 01606 891280.
Profile Breeder. **Ref: YH15831**

WRIGHT, ALBERT

Albert Wright, 6 Patricks Cl, Liss, Petersfield, **Hampshire**, GU33 7ER, **ENGLAND**.
(T) 01730 892708.
Profile Farrier. **Ref: YH15832**

WRIGHT, C

C Wright, Stratford Pl Stud, Coln Rogers, Cheltenham, **Gloucestershire**, GL54 3LA, **ENGLAND**.
(T) 01285 720203 **(F)** 01285 720203.
Contact/s
Owner: Mr C Wright
Profile Breeder. **Ref: YH15833**

WRIGHT, D G

D G Wright, 373 London Rd, Hazel Gr, Stockport, **Cheshire**, SK7 6AA, **ENGLAND**.
(T) 0161 4831794.
Profile Medical Support. **Ref: YH15834**

WRIGHT, D G

D G Wright, Carnival Hse, Thornbrook Rd, Chapel-En-Le-Frith, **Cheshire**, SK12 6LX, **ENGLAND**.
(T) 01298 812066.
Profile Medical Support. **Ref: YH15835**

WRIGHT, E

Miss E Wright, Yew Tree Cottage, Crow, Ringwood, **Hampshire**, BH24 3EA, **ENGLAND**.
(T) 01425 478697.
Profile Breeder. **Ref: YH15836**

WRIGHT, L C

L C Wright, 395 Burton Rd, Midway, Swadlincote, **Derbyshire**, DE11 7NB, **ENGLAND**.
(T) 01283 218550.
Contact/s
Owner: Mr L Wright
Profile Saddlery Retailer. **Ref: YH15837**

WRIGHT, M

M Wright, The Forge, Creech St. Michael, Taunton, **Somerset**, TA3 5DP, **ENGLAND**.
(T) 01823 443444 **(F)** 01823 443444.
Contact/s
Owner: Mr M Wright
Profile Blacksmith. **Ref: YH15838**

WRIGHT, R G

R G Wright, 64 Town St, Lound, Retford, **Nottinghamshire**, DN22 8RJ, **ENGLAND**.
(T) 01777 818421.
Profile Breeder. **Ref: YH15839**

WRIGHT, RAY

Ray Wright, 39 Links Rd, West Wickham, **Kent**, BR4 0QN, **ENGLAND**.
(T) 020 87778194. **Ref: YH15840**

WRIGHT, SIMON D

Simon D Wright DWCF, Farriers Cottage, Tilford Rd, Rushmoor, Farnham, **Surrey**, GU10 2EP, **ENGLAND**.
(T) 01252 793799
(M) 07831 373418.
Profile Farrier. **Ref: YH15841**

WRIGHT, W G

W G Wright, Eagle Farm, Erpingham, Norwich, **Norfolk**, NR11 7QA, **ENGLAND**.
(T) 01263 761229.
Profile Transport/Horse Boxes. **Ref: YH15842**

WRIGHTINGTON EQUESTRIAN CTRE

Wrightington Equestrian Centre, Mossy Lea Rd, Wrightington, Wigan, **Lancashire**, WN6 9RE, **ENGLAND**.
(T) 01257 427319.
Profile Riding School. **Ref: YH15843**

WRIGHT-MANLEY AUCTIONEERS

Wright-Manley Auctioneers (Tarporley), Beeston Livestock Ctre, Beeston, Tarporley, **Cheshire**, CW6 9NJ, **ENGLAND**.
(T) 01829 260318 **(F)** 01829 261208.
Contact/s
Marketing Manager: Mr P Narloch
Ref: YH15844

WRIGHT'S OF HUNTLY

Wright's Of Huntly, 37 Gordon St, Huntly, **Aberdeenshire**, AB54 8EQ, **SCOTLAND**.
(T) 01466 792782 **(F)** 01466 792782.
Contact/s
Owner: Ms K Yates **Ref: YH15845**

WRIGHTS OF ROMSEY

Wrights Of Romsey, Hilliers Garden Ctre, Botley Rd, Romsey, **Hampshire**, SO51 5AG, **ENGLAND**.
(T) 01794 518738.
Contact/s
Manager: Claire McManus
Profile Saddlery Retailer. **Ref: YH15846**

WRITERS & PHOTOGRAPHERS

Horserace Writers & Photographers Association, Raventhorpe Cottage, Bygot Lane, Cherry Burton, Berverley, **Yorkshire (East)**, HU17 7RB, **ENGLAND**.
(T) 01964 551135.
Profile Club/Association. **Ref: YH15847**

WRITTLE CLGE

Writtle College, Lordship Rd, Writtle, Chelmsford, **Essex**, CM1 3RR, **ENGLAND**.
(T) 01245 420705 **(F)** 01245 420456
(E) postmaster@writtle.ac.uk.
Profile Riding School. **Ref: YH15848**

WROTHAM PARK STUD

Wrotham Park Stud, Wrotham Pk, Barnet, **Hertfordshire**, EN5 4SB, **ENGLAND**.
(T) 020 84409125 **(F)** 020 84499359.
Profile Breeder. **Ref: YH15849**

WROXHAM SADDLERY

Wroxham Saddlery, Church Rd, Hoveton, Norwich, **Norfolk**, NR12 8UG, **ENGLAND**.
(T) 01603 783995 **(F)** 01603 782103.
Profile Saddlery Retailer. **Ref: YH15850**

WULFSTAN

Wulfstan Stud, Stanley Hse, Silt Drove, Tips End, Welney, **Cambridgeshire**, PE14 9SL, **ENGLAND**.
(T) 01354 638226.
Contact/s
Partner: Ms L Lodge
Profile Breeder.
Opening Times
Telephone for an appointment **Ref: YH15851**

W'UNDERWEAR

W'underwear UK - R W A, 9 Station Rd, Morcott, Oakham, **Rutland**, LE15 9DX, **ENGLAND**.
(T) 01572 747595 **(F)** 01572 747595
(E) roger@wunderwear.co.uk
(W) www.wunderwear.co.uk.
Profile Supplies.
Produce designer underwear for horses. The underwear is designed to protect the shoulder area from blanket rub. **Ref: YH15852**

WYATT, C R & R K

C G & R K Wyatt, Huntscott Hse, Huntscott, Wootton Courtenay, Minehead, **Somerset**, TA24 8RR, **ENGLAND**.
(T) 01643 841272.
Contact/s
Owner: Mrs R Wyatt
Profile Equestrian Centre.
Organised hacking with own horse. £23.00 for 2 hours on Exmoor, Dumkrey Beacon Range. Must be aged 13 years and upwards. Yr. Est: 1963
Opening Times
Sp: Open Mon - Sun 08:00. Closed Mon - Sun 21:00.
Su: Open Mon - Sun 08:00. Closed Mon - Sun 21:00.
Au: Open Mon - Sun 08:00. Closed Mon - Sun 21:00.
Wn: Open Mon - Sun 08:00. Closed Mon - Sun 21:00. **Ref: YH15853**

WYATT, N J S

N J S Wyatt, Compton Graze, Little Compton, Moreton In Marsh, **Gloucestershire**, GL56 0RT,

A-Z of COMPANIES

ENGLAND.
(T) 01608 674102 (F) 01608 674014. Ref: YH15854

WYCHANGER BARTON SADDLERY
N & EA Underwood T/A Wychanger Barton Saddlery, The Haywain, Burlescombe, Tiverton, Devon, EX16 7JY, ENGLAND.
(T) 01823 672071 (F) 01823 672071
(W) www.wychanger.com.
Contact/s
Owner: Mr N Underwood (Q) Master Saddler
Profile Arena, Riding Wear Retailer, Saddlery Retailer, Supplies. No.Staff: 7 Yr. Est: 1984
C.Size: 4.5 Acres
Opening Times
Sp: Open 09:00. Closed 17:30.
Su: Open 09:00. Closed 17:30.
Au: Open 09:00. Closed 17:30.
Wn: Open 09:00. Closed 17:30. Ref: YH15855

WYCHERLEYS OF MALPAS
Wycherleys Of Malpas, Church St, Malpas, Cheshire, SY14 8NU, ENGLAND.
(T) 01948 860316. Ref: YH15856

WYCHWOOD STUD
Wychwood Stud (The), Mursley, Buckinghamshire, MK17 0HX, ENGLAND.
(T) 01296 720854 (F) 01296 720855
(E) gerardnaprous@thedevilshorsemen.freeserve.co.uk.
Profile Breeder. Ref: YH15857

WYCHWOOD STUD
Wychwood Stud, North Four Shires Stone Farm, Moreton In Marsh, Gloucestershire, GL56 0PF, ENGLAND.
(T) 01608 650165.
Profile Breeder. Ref: YH15858

WYCK HALL STUD
Wyck Hall Stud Ltd, Dullingham Rd, Newmarket, Suffolk, CB8 9JT, ENGLAND.
(T) 01638 662181 (F) 01638 662181.
Contact/s
Manager: Mr J Scallam
Profile Breeder. Ref: YH15859

WYE COLLEGE
Wye College, University Of London, Wye, Ashford, Kent, TN25 5AH, ENGLAND.
(T) 01233 812401 (F) 01233 813320
(E) c.jovanovic@wye.ac.uk.
Profile Equestrian Centre. Ref: YH15860

WYE VALLEY RIDING CLUB
Wye Valley Riding Club, The Garstons, Rosemary Lane, Stroat, Chepstow, Monmouthshire, NP16 7LX, WALES.
(T) 01594 529355 (F) 01594 529355.
Contact/s
Chairman: Mrs H Matthews
Profile Club/Association, Riding Club. Ref: YH15861

WYKE EQUESTRIAN CTRE
Wyke Equestrian Centre, The Wyke, Shifnal, Shropshire, TF11 9PP, ENGLAND.
(T) 01952 460560. Ref: YH15862

WYKE OF SHIFNAL
Wyke Of Shifnal, The Wyke, Shifnal, Shropshire, TF11 9PP, ENGLAND.
(T) 01952 460560.
Profile Riding School, Saddlery Retailer, Stable/Livery, Supplies, Track/Course. Ref: YH15863

WYLDER, DEBORAH
Deborah Wylder, Blackwater Cottage, Daggons Rd, Alderholt, Hampshire, SP6 3DP, ENGLAND.
(T) 01425 654093. Ref: YH15864

WYLES, S
S Wyles DWCF, The Forge, Marlpit Hse, Boggy Lane, Heath Top, Church Broughton, Derbyshire, DE65 5AR, ENGLAND.
(T) 01283 585767.
Profile Farrier. Ref: YH15865

WYLYE STUD
Wylye Stud, Orchard Cottage, Stapleford, Salisbury, Wiltshire, SP3 4LP, ENGLAND.
(T) 01722 790248.
Contact/s
Owner: Mrs P Brake
Profile Breeder, Trainer. Eventing yard. Ref: YH15866

WYLYE VALLEY HORSE
Wylye Valley Horse, 124 High St, Codford, Wiltshire, BA12 0NH, ENGLAND.
(T) 01985 850910 (F) 01985 851067
(E) wylehorse@aol.com.
Profile Saddlery Retailer. Ref: YH15867

WYMAN-GORDON
Wyman-Gordon Ltd, Houstoun Rd, Houstoun Ind Est, Livingston, Lothian (West), EH54 5BZ, SCOTLAND.
(T) 01506 446200.
Profile Blacksmith. Ref: YH15868

WYMONDHAM PET & GARDEN
Wymondham Pet & Garden Supplies, 52 Back Lane, Wymondham, Norfolk, NR18 1QT, ENGLAND.
(T) 01953 604932.
Profile Supplies. Ref: YH15869

WYNBURY STABLES
Wynbury Stables, West Witton, Leyburn, Yorkshire (North), DL8 4LR, ENGLAND.
(T) 01969 622289 (F) 01969 625278
(M) 07703 444398.
Profile Trainer. Ref: YH15870

WYNN, JOHN
John Wynn, Rivers Farm Cottage, Copyhold Lane, Haywards Heath, Sussex (West), RH16 1XU, ENGLAND.
(T) 01444 413149. Ref: YH15871

WYNNE, M G
Mr M G Wynne, The Coach Hse, Laurel Farm Equestrian Ctre, Long Lane, Haughton, Tarporley, Cheshire, CW6 9RN, ENGLAND.
(T) 01829 260551 (F) 01829 260551.
Contact/s
Owner: Mr M Wynne
Profile Stable/Livery, Trainer. Ref: YH15872

WYNNS, W W (SIR)
Sir W W Wynn's, Hill View, Church St, Tarvin, Chester, Cheshire, CH3 8NA, ENGLAND.
(T) 01829 741315. Ref: YH15873

WYNNSTAY & CLWYD FARMERS
Wynnstay & Clwyd Farmers, Unit 1, Green Ind Est, The Roe, St Asaph, Denbighshire, LL17 0LB, WALES.
(T) 01745 582527.
Profile Riding Wear Retailer, Supplies. Ref: YH15874

WYNNSTAY & CLWYD FARMERS
Wynnstay & Clwyd Farmers, Eagle Hse, Llansanffraid, Powys, SY22 6AQ, WALES.
(T) 01691 828512.
Profile Riding Wear Retailer, Supplies. Ref: YH15875

WYNNSTAY & CLWYD FARMERS
Wynnstay & Clwyd Farmers, Unit 1 Mile Oak Ind Est, Maesbury Rd, Oswestry, Shropshire, SY10 8JA, ENGLAND.
(T) 01691 659251.
Profile Riding Wear Retailer, Supplies. Ref: YH15876

WYTON TACK SHOP
Wyton Tack Shop, Ivy Cottage, Main Rd, Wyton, Hull, Yorkshire (East), HU11 4DJ, ENGLAND.
(T) 01482 814383.
Profile Saddlery Retailer. Ref: YH15877

WYVENHOE EQUESTRIAN CLUB
Wyvenhoe Equestrian Club, Guildford Rd, Bookham, Leatherhead, Surrey, KT23 4HB, ENGLAND.
(T) 01372 454339.
Contact/s
Owner: Mrs L Campbell Ref: YH15878

WYVERN SMITHY
Wyvern Smithy, 40 Oakwood, Partridge Green, Horsham, Sussex (West), RH13 8JQ, ENGLAND.
(T) 01403 711792.
Profile Blacksmith. Ref: YH15879

YACOMINE, P J
P J Yacomine RSS, Russell Farm Cottage, Cobblers Hill, Wendover, Aylesbury, Buckinghamshire, HP22 6QD, ENGLAND.
(T) 01296 623549.
Profile Farrier. Ref: YH15880

YALE COLLEGE
Yale College, Grove Park Rd, Wrexham, Wrexham, LL12 7AA, WALES.
(T) 01978 311794 (F) 01978 291569.
Profile Equestrian Centre. Ref: YH15881

YARBOROUGH, RACHEL
Rachel Yarborough, 36 Dale Ave, Edgware, London (Greater), HA8 6AE, ENGLAND.
(T) 020 89523741.
Profile Transport/Horse Boxes. Ref: YH15882

YARDLEY, G H
G H Yardley, Upper Woods Field Farm, Woodsfield, Madresfield, Malvern, Worcestershire, WR13 5BE, ENGLAND.
(T) 01905 830245.
Contact/s
Owner: Mr G Yardley
Profile Trainer. Ref: YH15883

YARDLEY, GEORGE HENRY
Mr George Henry Yardley, Upper Woodsfield, Madresfield, Malvern, Worcestershire, WR13 5AQ, ENGLAND.
(T) 01905 830245.
Profile Trainer. Ref: YH15884

YARHAM, A
Mr A Yarham, 31 Winifred Rd, Cobholm, Great Yarmouth, Norfolk, ENGLAND..
Profile Trainer. Ref: YH15885

YARM & DISTRICT RIDING CLUB
Yarm & District Riding Club, Rosedene, Green Lane, Yarm, Stockton-on-Tees, Cleveland, TS15 9EH, ENGLAND.
(T) 01642 788424.
Contact/s
Chairman: Ms D Walker
Profile Club/Association, Riding Club. Ref: YH15886

YAROFF, W
W Yaroff DWCF, C/O Chobham Forge, Burrow Hill Green, Chobham, Surrey, GU24 8QP, ENGLAND.
(T) 01344 482478.
Profile Farrier. Ref: YH15887

YATELEY RIDING ESTABLISHMENT
Yateley Riding Establishment, Firgrove Manor Stable, Firgrove Rd, Eversley, Hook, Hampshire, RG27 0PE, ENGLAND.
(T) 01252 873467.
Profile Riding School. Ref: YH15888

YATES, DAVID
David Yates, 9 Coniston Rd, Blackrod, Bolton, Manchester (Greater), BL6 5DW, ENGLAND.
(T) 01204 697296.
Profile Farrier. Ref: YH15889

YATES, PETER G
Peter G Yates RSS BII, 55 Court Cl, Bradpole, Bridport, Dorset, DT6 3EL, ENGLAND.
(T) 01308 425477.
Profile Farrier. Ref: YH15890

YATES, T J
Mr T J Yates, Farnah Hse Farm, Duffield, Belper, Derbyshire, DE56 4AQ, ENGLAND.
(T) 01332 840625. Ref: YH15891

YAXLEY RIDING CTRE
Yaxley Riding Centre, 99 Main St, Yaxley, Peterborough, Cambridgeshire, PE7 3LP, ENGLAND.
(T) 01733 245783.
Contact/s
Owner: Miss C Thorne
Profile Riding School. Ref: YH15892

YCHRC
Yorkshire Coloured Horse Riding Club, 16 The Village, Earswick, York, Yorkshire (North), YO32 9SL, ENGLAND.
(T) 01904 760514.
Contact/s
Chairman: Mrs J Wilson
Profile Club/Association, Riding Club. Ref: YH15893

YE OLDE FORGE
Ye Olde Forge Saddlery, Sadlers Hall Farm, London Rd, Basildon, Essex, SS13 2HD, ENGLAND.
(T) 01268 753050.
Contact/s
Owner: Mrs S Jennings (Q) NVQ 3 Adv
Profile Riding Wear Retailer, Saddlery Retailer.
Made to measure saddles and bridles including side saddle. No.Staff: 1 Yr. Est: 1999
Opening Times
Sp: Open Tues - Thurs, Sat, Sun 09:00, Mon, Fri 12:00. Closed Mon - Sun 17:00.
Su: Open Tues - Thurs, Sat, Sun 09:00, Mon, Fri 12:00. Closed Mon - Sun 17:00.
Au: Open Tues - Thurs, Sat, Sun 09:00, Mon, Fri 12:00. Closed Mon - Sun 17:00.
Wn: Open Tues - Thurs, Sat, Sun 09:00, Mon, Fri 12:00. Closed Mon, Wed, Fri - Sun 17:00, Tues, Thurs 15:00. Ref: YH15894

A-Z of COMPANIES

YEALAND STUD

Yealand Stud (The), Storrs Barn, Yealand Redmayne, **Lancashire**, LA5 9TD, **ENGLAND**.
(T) 01524 781200.
Profile Breeder. **Ref: YH15895**

YEANDLE, ERIC

Eric Yeandle BII, 11 Mere Rd, Waltham On The Wolds, Melton Mowbray, **Leicestershire**, LE14 4AL, **ENGLAND**.
(T) 01664 464801.
Profile Farrier. **Ref: YH15896**

YEATS, J

J Yeats, Dallance Farm, Galley Hill, Waltham Abbey, **Essex**, EN9 2AQ, **ENGLAND**.
(T) 01992 713349.
Profile Supplies. **Ref: YH15897**

YEGUADA IBERICA

Yeguada Iberica, Manor Farm Hse, Knotting, **Bedfordshire**, MK44 1AE, **ENGLAND**.
(T) 01234 782801 **(F)** 01234 781062.
Profile Breeder. **Ref: YH15898**

YELD BANK ARABIAN STUD

Yeld Bank Arabian Stud, Birch Tree Farm, Knightley, **Staffordshire**, ST20 0JN, **ENGLAND**.
(T) 01785 284279.
Profile Breeder. **Ref: YH15899**

YELVERTOFT EQUESTRIAN CTRE

Yelvertoft Equestrian Centre, Brookside Farm, Ashwells Lane, Yelvertoft, **Northamptonshire**, NN6 7LW, **ENGLAND**.
(T) 01788 823456.
Profile Stable/Livery. **Ref: YH15900**

YEO PAULL

Yeo Paull Ltd (Marquee Hire), North St, Martock, **Somerset**, TA12 6DJ, **ENGLAND**.
(T) 01935 824391.
Profile Club/Association. **Ref: YH15901**

YEO, JANCIS

Jancis Yeo, Street Farm, Cleverton, Chippenham, **Wiltshire**, SN15 5BS, **ENGLAND**.
(T) 01666 823292. **Ref: YH15902**

YEOFORD TRAILERS

Yeoford Trailers, Holwell Barton, Neopardy, Crediton, **Devon**, EX17 5EP, **ENGLAND**.
(T) 01363 773918.
Contact/s
Owner: Mr J Stevens
Profile Transport/Horse Boxes. **Ref: YH15903**

YEOLAND STUD

Yeoland Stud, Holdscroft Farm, Marshwood, Bridport, **Dorset**, DT6 5QL, **ENGLAND**.
(T) 01297 678525.
Profile Breeder. **Ref: YH15904**

YEOMANSTOWN STUD

Yeomanstown Stud, Naas, **County Kildare**, **IRELAND**.
(T) 045 897314 **(F)** 045 897708
(E) yeomanstownstud@eircom.net.
Contact/s
Key Contact: Mr G O'Callaghan
Profile Breeder, Stable/Livery.
The stud has an all weather gallop, individual all weather paddocks, and offers a range of services from boarding to sales preperation and training.
Yr. Est: 1923 C.Size: 300 Acres **Ref: YH15905**

YEOVIL TRAILERS

Yeovil Trailers, 22B Oxford Rd, Pen Mill Trading Est, Yeovil, **Somerset**, BA21 5HR, **ENGLAND**.
(T) 01935 412203 **(F)** 01935 412203.
Profile Transport/Horse Boxes. **Ref: YH15906**

YEOWARD, R

Yeoward R, Wood Farm, Orleton, Ludlow, **Shropshire**, SY8 4JJ, **ENGLAND**.
(T) 01584 831429.
Profile Transport/Horse Boxes. **Ref: YH15907**

YEW TREE FARM EQUESTRIAN CTRE

Yew Tree Farm Equestrian Centre, Budworth Rd, Great Budworth, **Cheshire**, CW9 6LT, **ENGLAND**.
(T) 01565 733233.
Profile Stable/Livery. **Ref: YH15908**

YEW TREE FARM LIVERY STABLES

Yew Tree Farm Livery Stables, Yew Tree Farm, Ringwood Rd, Stoney Cross, Lyndhurst, **Hampshire**, SO43 7GN, **ENGLAND**.
(T) 023 80812526.
Contact/s
Owner: Mr J Partridge **Ref: YH15909**

YEW TREE FARM STABLES

Yew Tree Farm Stables, Yew Tree Farm, Hazelwood, Belper, **Derbyshire**, DE56 4AE, **ENGLAND**.
(T) 01332 841364.
Contact/s
Owner: Mr H Lester
Profile Riding School, Stable/Livery.
Import Irish horses **Ref: YH15910**

YEW TREE STABLES

Yew Tree Stables, 51 Abingdon Rd, Standlake, Witney, **Oxfordshire**, OX8 7QH, **ENGLAND**.
(T) 01865 300082.
Contact/s
Manager: Mrs M Booth
Profile Stable/Livery. **Ref: YH15911**

YNYSCRUG STUD

Ynyscrug Stud, Pant Y Brad, Tonyrefail, **Rhondda Cynon Taff**, CF39 8HX, **WALES**.
(T) 07767 264899.
Profile Stable/Livery. **Ref: YH15912**

YOKEHURST FARM

Yokehurst Farm, South Chailey, Lewes, **Sussex (East)**, BN8 4PY, **ENGLAND**.
(T) 01273 890245.
Profile Breeder. **Ref: YH15913**

YORK & AINSTY SOUTH PONY CLUB

York & Ainsty South Pony Club, Crankley Grange, Low Crankley, Easingwold, **Yorkshire (North)**, YO61 3NZ, **ENGLAND**.
(T) 01347 822935.
Profile Club/Association. **Ref: YH15914**

YORK & DISTRICT RIDING CLUB

York & District Riding Club, Standerton, Wetherby Rd, Long Marston, York, **Yorkshire (North)**, YO26 7NE, **ENGLAND**.
(T) 01904 738323
(E) amdal@euphony.net.
Profile Club/Association, Riding Club. **Ref: YH15915**

YORK RACE COMMITTEE

York Race Committee, The Racecourse, York, **Yorkshire (North)**, YO23 1EX, **ENGLAND**.
(T) 01904 620911 **(F)** 01904 611071
(E) info@yorkracecourse.co.uk.
Contact/s
Manager: Mr J Smith
Profile Track/Course. **Ref: YH15916**

YORK RIDING SCHOOL

York Riding School (The), Wigginton Rd, Wigginton, York, **Yorkshire (North)**, YO32 2RH, **ENGLAND**.
(T) 01904 763686.
Profile Riding School, Stable/Livery. **Ref: YH15917**

YORK, RAY

Ray York, Newmarsh Farm, Horsley Rd, Cobham, **Surrey**, KT11 3JY, **ENGLAND**.
(T) 01932 863594 **(F)** 01932 860703.
Profile Breeder, Farrier. Gallops. **Ref: YH15918**

YORKSHIRE DALES

Yorkshire Dales Trekking Centre, Holme Farm, Malham, Skipton, **Yorkshire (North)**, BD23 4DA, **ENGLAND**.
(T) 01729 830352
(E) info@ydtc.net
(W) www.ydtc.net.
Contact/s
Partner: Miss Z Jackson **(Q)** BET
(E) zana@ydtc.net
Profile Breeder, Holidays, Riding Club, Riding School.
Offer trekking & trail riding holidays. No.Staff: 4
Yr. Est: 1997 C.Size: 25 Acres **Ref: YH15919**

YORKSHIRE EQUESTRIAN FLOORING

Yorkshire Equestrian Flooring, 4 Town St, Farsley, Leeds, **Yorkshire (West)**, LS28 5DB, **ENGLAND**.
(T) 0113 2570845
(M) 07967 789743.
Profile Transport/Horse Boxes. **Ref: YH15920**

YORKSHIRE EQUINE CREMATORIUM

Yorkshire Equine Crematorium, The Bungalow, Near Bank, Shelley, Huddersfield, **Yorkshire (West)**, HD8 8LT, **ENGLAND**.
(T) 01484 604599.
Contact/s
Owner: Stephanie Crowther
Profile Equine Crematorium.
Opening Times
Sp: Open Mon - Sun 24 Hours. Closed Mon - Sun 24 Hours.
Su: Open Mon - Sun 24 Hours. Closed Mon - Sun 24 Hours.
Au: Open Mon - Sun 24 Hours. Closed Mon - Sun 24 Hours.
Wn: Open Mon - Sun 24 Hours. Closed Mon - Sun 24 Hours. **Ref: YH15921**

YORKSHIRE RIDING CTRE

Yorkshire Riding Centre Ltd, Markington, Harrogate, **Yorkshire (North)**, HG3 3PD, **ENGLAND**.
(T) 01765 677207 **(F)** 01765 677065
(E) info@yrc.co.uk
(W) www.yrc.co.uk
Affiliated Bodies BHS.
Contact/s
For Bookings: Miss L Habgood
Profile Arena, Equestrian Centre, Holidays, Riding School, Stable/Livery, Trainer. Show Centre.
Show Centre, lectures, demos and clinics held. No lessons on Sundays. Career and competition training. Summer camps. No.Staff: 15 Yr. Est: 1963
C.Size: 25 Acres
Opening Times
Sp: Open Mon - Sun 09:00. Closed Mon - Fri 19:30, Sat 16:00, Sun 17:00.
Su: Open Mon - Sun 09:00. Closed Mon - Fri 19:30, Sat 16:00, Sun 17:00.
Au: Open Mon - Sun 09:00. Closed Mon - Fri 19:30, Sat 16:00, Sun 17:00.
Wn: Open Mon - Sun 09:00. Closed Mon - Fri 19:30, Sat 16:00, Sun 17:00.
On Mondays only the office is open, on Sundays the office is closed but the centre is open for lessons and shows. Mon - Sat closed 13:00 - 14:00 **Ref: YH15922**

YORKSHIRE RIDING SUPPLIES

Yorkshire Riding Supplies, The Old Saddlers, 3 High St, Boroughbridge, York, **Yorkshire (North)**, YO51 9AW, **ENGLAND**.
(T) 01423 323594
(E) admin@foxsaddlers.co.uk
(W) www.foxsaddlers.co.uk.
Contact/s
Manager: Mrs M Chandler
Profile Riding Wear Retailer, Saddlery Retailer.
Yr. Est: 1901
Opening Times
Sp: Open Mon - Sat 10:00. Closed Mon - Sat 17:00.
Su: Open Mon - Sat 10:00. Closed Mon - Sat 17:00.
Au: Open Mon - Sat 10:00. Closed Mon - Sat 17:00.
Wn: Open Mon - Sat 10:00. Closed Mon - Sat 17:00.
Ref: YH15923

YOUNG

Young & Co, Unit 4B Charles Holland St, Willenhall, **Midlands (West)**, WV13 1NQ, **ENGLAND**.
(T) 01902 602338 **(F)** 01902 631745.
Contact/s
Owner: Mr R Young **Ref: YH15924**

YOUNG ERIC

Young Eric, Lower Hse Farm, Ticklerton, Church Stretton, **Shropshire**, SY6 7DN, **ENGLAND**.
(T) 01694 722419 **(F)** 01694 722419.
Contact/s
Owner: Mr E Young
Profile Breeder. **Ref: YH15925**

YOUNG, ADAM

Adam Young DWCF, Stable Cottage, Howberrywood Farm, Newham Hill, Nettlebed, Henley-on-Thames, **Oxfordshire**, RG9 5DE, **ENGLAND**.
(T) 01491 642148.
Profile Farrier. **Ref: YH15926**

YOUNG, D A

D A Young, Town Head, Midlem, Selkirk, **Scottish Borders**, TD7 4QD, **SCOTLAND**.
(T) 07885 647969.
Profile Farrier. **Ref: YH15927**

YOUNG, D M

D M Young, 42 Rosemount Drive, Uphall, Broxburn, **Lothian (West)**, EH52 6DE, **SCOTLAND**.
(T) 01506 853092.
Contact/s
Owner: Mr D Young
Profile Blacksmith. **Ref: YH15928**

YOUNG, GORDON

Gordon Young DWCF, The Aiket, Ruthwell, Dumfries, **Dumfries and Galloway**, DG1 2NP, **SCOTLAND**.
(T) 01387 870365
(M) 07860 506210.

Profile Farrier. Ref:YH15929

YOUNG, IAN

Ian Young, The Den, Fochabers, **Moray**, IV32 7PQ, **SCOTLAND**.
(T) 01343 820997.
Profile Breeder. Ref:YH15930

YOUNG, J E

Mr J E Young, Corringham Hall Farm, Stanford-Le-Hope, **Essex**, **ENGLAND**..
Profile Breeder. Ref:YH15931

YOUNG, J R A

Mr J R A Young, Brook Hse, Hambleton Rd, Egleton, Oakham, **Rutland**, LE15 8AE, **ENGLAND**.
(T) 01572 770060 **(F)** 01572 770051.
Profile Supplies. Ref:YH15932

YOUNG, J W

J W Young, Fairnington, Kelso, **Scottish Borders**, TD5 8NT, **SCOTLAND**.
(T) 01835 823983 **(F)** 01835 823481.
Contact/s
Owner: Mr J Young
Profile Breeder. Ref:YH15933

YOUNG, JAMES W

James W Young, Hall Farm, Drongan, Ayr, **Ayrshire (South)**, KA6 7EE, **SCOTLAND**.
(T) 01292 570329 **(F)** 01292 570912.
Contact/s
Owner: Mr J Young
Profile Breeder. Yr. Est: 1990
Opening Times
Telephone for an appointment Ref:YH15934

YOUNG, JUDY

Mrs Judy Young, Lower Bupton Hse, Bupton, Hilmarton, Calne, **Wiltshire**, SN11 8SZ, **ENGLAND**.
(T) 01249 760538 **(F)** 01249 760540
(M) 07747 610998.
Contact/s
Owner: Mrs J Young
Profile Breeder, Trainer.
Opening Times
Telephone for an appointment Ref:YH15935

YOUNG, M D

M D Young, Fern Cottage, Leigh St, Leigh Upon Mendip, Bath, **Bath & Somerset (North East)**, BA3 5QQ, **ENGLAND**.
(T) 01373 812846.
Contact/s
Owner: Mr M Young
Profile Farrier. Ref:YH15936

YOUNG, PROCTOR & WAINWRIGHT

Young, Proctor & Wainwright, Bearl Farm Veterinary Clinic, Bearl Farm, Bywell, Stocksfield, **Northumberland**, NE43 7AJ, **ENGLAND**.
(T) 01661 842542 **(F)** 01661 844332.
Profile Medical Support. Ref:YH15937

YOUNG, R

R Young, Townhead Farm, Iveston Village, Consett, **County Durham**, DH8 7TB, **ENGLAND**.
(T) 01207 500200.
Contact/s
Owner: Mr R Young
Profile Breeder. Ref:YH15938

YOUNG, S C

Mrs S C Young, 30 Kennedy Cl, Purbrook, Waterlooville, **Hampshire**, PO7 5NZ, **ENGLAND**.
(T) 023 92264872.
Profile Breeder. Ref:YH15939

YOUNG, SIMON

Simon Young, Green Acres, New Rd, Landford, Salisbury, **Wiltshire**, SP5 2AZ, **ENGLAND**.
(T) 01794 322821.
Contact/s
Owner: Mr S Young
Profile Breeder, Farrier. Ref:YH15940

YOUNG, V P

Mr V P Young, 37A Saxon St, Hastings, **Sussex (East)**, TN35 5HJ, **ENGLAND**.
(T) 01424 438425.
Profile Supplies. Ref:YH15941

YOUNG, W G

Mr W G Young, Overton Farm, Crossford, Carluke, **Lanarkshire (South)**, ML8 5QF, **SCOTLAND**.
(T) 01555 860226
(M) 07889 442584.
Profile Supplies. Ref:YH15942

YOUNGMAN, NICHOLAS EDWARD

Nicholas Edward Youngman DWCF, Llethri Mawr Farm, Llethri Rd, Felinfoel, Llanelli, **Carmarthenshire**, SA14 8QD, **WALES**.
(T) 01554 746455.
Profile Farrier. Ref:YH15943

YOUNGS

Youngs Animal Feeds, Bracken Barn, Holmes Chapel Rd, Somerford, Congleton, **Cheshire**, CW12 4SN, **ENGLAND**.
(T) 01260 272623 **(F)** 01260 299322.
Profile Feed Merchant. Ref:YH15944

YOUNGSON, FRASER W

Fraser W Youngson DWCF Hons, Coed Lyn, **Conwy**, LL32 8YL, **WALES**.
(T) 01993 830674.
Profile Farrier. Ref:YH15945

YOUR CARRIAGE AWAITS

Your Carriage Awaits, Firs Cottage, 74 Queen St, Weedon, Northampton, **Northamptonshire**, NN7 4RA, **ENGLAND**.
(T) 01327 342121.
Contact/s
Owner: Ms C Russell
Profile Horse Drawn Carriages.
Horse Drawn Carriages available for hire, for weddings and special occasions Yr. Est: 1991
Opening Times
Telephone for an appointment Ref:YH15946

YOUR HORSE MAGAZINE

Your Horse Magazine, Apex Hse, Oundle Rd, Peterborough, **Cambridgeshire**, PE2 9NP, **ENGLAND**.
(T) 01733 898100 **(F)** 01733 465711.
Contact/s
Editor: Amanda Stevenson
Profile Supplies. Ref:YH15947

YOUTH HOSTELS ASSOCIATION

Youth Hostels Association (England & Wales), Trevelyan Hse, 8 St Stephen's Hill, St Albans, **Hertfordshire**, AL1 2DY, **ENGLAND**.
(T) 01727 855215 **(F)** 01727 844126.
Profile Club/Association. Ref:YH15948

YSWAIN WELSH COBS

Yswain Stallion & Stud Services, Oak Hollow, Watling St, Hatherton, Cannock, **Staffordshire**, WS11 1RY, **ENGLAND**.
(T) 01543 579021
Affiliated Bodies DEFRA.
Contact/s
Owner: Mr B Squires
(E) w.squires@virgin.net
Profile Breeder.
Semen is collected, frozen and distributed throughout the world, from this site. 'Yswain Stallion Stud Services' is approved by the DEFRA No.Staff: 3
Yr. Est: 1983 C.Size: 15 Acres
Opening Times
Telephone for an appointment Ref:YH15949

ZALKIND

Zalkind, Low Close Farm Stables, Tirril, Penrith, **Cumbria**, CA10 2LG, **ENGLAND**.
(T) 01768 866115.
Profile Stable/Livery, Trainer. Ref:YH15950

ZARA STUD

Zara Stud & Training Centre Ltd, Highleigh Rd, Sidlesham, Chichester, **Sussex (West)**, PO20 7NR, **ENGLAND**.
(T) 01243 641662.
Contact/s
Owner: Ms P Brown **(Q)** WHAI
Profile Arena, Breeder, Equestrian Centre, Horse/Rider Accom, Riding School, Saddlery Retailer, Stable/Livery, Trainer.
Western Specialist. Ms Pam Brown is a National Performance Western Champion and has over 37 years experience. Western training, showing, instruction and holidays. Livery - £60 per week. No.Staff: 2
Yr. Est: 1966 C.Size: 3 Acres
Opening Times
Open all year Ref:YH15951

ZARAFSHAN ARABIAN STUD

Zarafshan Arabian Stud, West Lodge Tiltwood, Hophurst Lane, Crawley Down, Crawley, **Sussex (West)**, RH10 4LL, **ENGLAND**.
(T) 01342 712940.
Contact/s
Owner: Mrs P Horwell
Profile Breeder. Ref:YH15952

ZEBRA

Zebra Products Ltd, 2b Penketh Pl, Skelmersdale, **Lancashire**, WN8 9QX, **ENGLAND**.
(T) 01695 550357 **(F)** 01695 555513.
Profile Riding Wear Retailer, Supplies.
Distributors of Lucinda Green and Kentucky clothing.
Yr. Est: 2000
Opening Times
Sp: Open Mon - Fri 09:00. Closed Mon - Fri 17:30.
Su: Open Mon - Fri 09:00. Closed Mon - Fri 17:30.
Au: Open Mon - Fri 09:00. Closed Mon - Fri 17:30.
Wn: Open Mon - Fri 09:00. Closed Mon - Fri 17:30.
Ref:YH15953

ZEBULON MARKETING SERVICES

Zebulon Marketing Services, Edmonds Drive, Ketton, Stamford, **Lincolnshire**, PE9 3TH, **ENGLAND**.
(T) 01780 720371 **(F)** 01780 721576.
Profile Club/Association. Ref:YH15954

ZEPHYR FLAGS & BANNERS

Zephyr Flags & Banners, Midland Rd, Thrapston, **Northamptonshire**, NN14 4LX, **ENGLAND**.
(T) 01832 734484 **(F)** 01832 733064
(E) sales@zephyrflags.com.
Profile Club/Association. Ref:YH15955

ZINON, CHRISTOPHER

Christopher Zinon RSS, The Smithy, Lymm Rd, Little Bollington, Altrincham, **Cheshire**, WA14 4TD, **ENGLAND**.
(T) 01925 756540.
Profile Farrier. Ref:YH15956

ZOAR HORSE & COUNTRY CTRE

Zoar Horse & Country Centre, Bridge St, Neath Port Talbot, **Neath Port Talbot**, SA11 1RU, **WALES**.
(T) 01639 642180 **(F)** 01639 645250.
Profile Saddlery Retailer. Ref:YH15957

SECTION 2

By Business Type, By County

This section lists companies alphabetically by Country, by Business Type, by County.

e.g. **England,**
Equestrian Centre,
Cheshire:
Barrow Equestrian,
Chester

Once you have located a business using this section you can then refer to the company's detailed profile in Section 1.

ARENAS

BEDFORDSHIRE
- **CLGE EQUESTRIAN CTRE**, Bedford **Ref:**YH03025

BERKSHIRE
- **COURTLANDS**, Wokingham **Ref:**YH03506
- **EAST SOLEY E C 2000**, Hungerford **Ref:**YH04486
- **WOODLANDS**, Hungerford **Ref:**YH15705

BUCKINGHAMSHIRE
- **ADDINGTON MANOR**, Buckingham **Ref:**YH00179
- **EQUESTRIAN CTRE**, Amersham **Ref:**YH04696
- **EQUS HEALTH**, Aylesbury **Ref:**YH04835

CAMBRIDGESHIRE
- **KNIGHTS END FARM**, March **Ref:**YH08268
- **LORDSBRIDGE ARENA**, Cambridge **Ref:**YH08828

CHESHIRE
- **BARROW EQUESTRIAN CTRE**, Chester **Ref:**YH01027
- **BOLD HEATH EQUESTRIAN**, Widnes **Ref:**YH01602
- **EQUIPORT**, Northwich **Ref:**YH04815
- **GO ENTERTAINMENTS**, Congleton **Ref:**YH05860

CLEVELAND
- **FOXHOLM STUD**, Stockton-on-Tees **Ref:**YH05437

CORNWALL
- **NORTH CORNWALL ARENA**, Camelford **Ref:**YH10250
- **TALL TREES**, Camelford **Ref:**YH13831

COUNTY DURHAM
- **BOWES MANOR EQUESTRIAN CTRE**, Chester Le Street **Ref:**YH01709
- **DENE HEAD LIVERY**, Darlington **Ref:**YH04042
- **GO RIDING GRP**, Stanley **Ref:**YH05861
- **LOW MEADOWS FARM LIVERY**, Durham **Ref:**YH08856
- **SEAGOLD CENTURION**, Crook **Ref:**YH12587

CUMBRIA
- **ALLONBY RIDING SCHOOL**, Wigton **Ref:**YH00323
- **MIDDLE BAYLES LIVERY**, Alston **Ref:**YH09534

DERBYSHIRE
- **BARLEYFIELDS**, Derby **Ref:**YH00952
- **CHESTERFIELD**, Chesterfield **Ref:**YH02833
- **HILLCLIFF STUD**, Belper **Ref:**YH06838

DEVON
- **MULLACOTT EQUESTRIAN**, Ilfracombe **Ref:**YH09935
- **WYCHANGER BARTON SADDLERY**, Tiverton **Ref:**YH15855

DORSET
- **LANEHOUSE EQUITATION CTRE**, Weymouth **Ref:**YH08393
- **LULWORTH EQUESTRIAN CTRE**, Wareham **Ref:**YH08897
- **POUND COTTAGE RIDING CTRE**, Blandford Forum **Ref:**YH11307

ESSEX
- **COACH HSE**, Epping **Ref:**YH03102
- **E T A**, West Thurrock **Ref:**YH04427
- **HALLINGBURY HALL**, Bishop's Stortford **Ref:**YH06331
- **TALLY-HO RIDING SCHOOL**, Grays **Ref:**YH13844

HAMPSHIRE
- **FOREST FARM**, Milford On Sea **Ref:**YH05335
- **HOPLANDS EQUESTRIAN**, Stockbridge **Ref:**YH07058
- **NRC**, Fareham **Ref:**YH10348
- **SOUTHFIELD EQUESTRIAN CTRE**, Whitchurch **Ref:**YH13149

HEREFORDSHIRE
- **COUNTY COMPETITION STUD**, Bromyard **Ref:**YH03486
- **MONNINGTON**, Hereford **Ref:**YH09728
- **SHEEPCOTE EQUESTRIAN**, Hereford **Ref:**YH12695

KENT
- **FOREST VIEW**, Sidcup **Ref:**YH05353
- **LEYBOURNE GRANGE**, West Malling **Ref:**YH08600
- **WILLOW FARM**, Faversham **Ref:**YH15497

LANCASHIRE
- **ABRAM HALL RIDING CTRE**, Wigan **Ref:**YH00134
- **ARKENFIELD EQUESTRIAN CTRE**, Chorley **Ref:**YH00530
- **ASOKA**, Worsley **Ref:**YH00625
- **CHORLEY EQUESTRIAN CTRE**, Chorley **Ref:**YH02880
- **OSBALDESTON RIDING CTRE**, Blackburn **Ref:**YH10557
- **VALLANTS EQUESTRIAN CTRE**, Preston **Ref:**YH14647
- **WHITEGATE FARM**, Bacup **Ref:**YH15338

LEICESTERSHIRE
- **HARDWICKE LODGE STABLES**, Leicester **Ref:**YH06416
- **VISCORIDE**, Lutterworth **Ref:**YH14733
- **WITHAM VILLA RIDING CTRE**, Leicester **Ref:**YH15620

LINCOLNSHIRE
- **POPPYFIELDS**, Lincoln **Ref:**YH11275
- **REDNIL EQUESTRIAN CTRE**, Lincoln **Ref:**YH11716

MANCHESTER (GREATER)
- **CARRINGTON RIDING**, Manchester **Ref:**YH02589
- **RYDERS FARM**, Bolton **Ref:**YH12297

MIDLANDS (WEST)
- **BEARLEY CROSS STABLES**, Solihull **Ref:**YH01121
- **FOXHILLS**, Walsall **Ref:**YH05435

NORFOLK
- **CROFT FARM RIDING CTRE**, Great Yarmouth **Ref:**YH03615
- **RUNCTON HALL**, King's Lynn **Ref:**YH12233
- **WESTON PARK EQUESTRIAN CTRE**, Norwich **Ref:**YH15224

NOTTINGHAMSHIRE
- **CLGE FARM**, Newark **Ref:**YH03026
- **MANSFIELD SAND**, Mansfield **Ref:**YH09123
- **ST CLEMENTS LODGE**, Nottingham **Ref:**YH13274

OXFORDSHIRE
- **ASTI STUD & SADDLERY**, Faringdon **Ref:**YH00633
- **NEW HOUSE LIVERY**, Abingdon **Ref:**YH10109
- **OLD MANOR HSE**, Oxford **Ref:**YH10461
- **STANDLAKE EQUESTRIAN CTRE**, Witney **Ref:**YH13362

RUTLAND
- **BARROW STABLES**, Oakham **Ref:**YH01030

SHROPSHIRE
- **CHARLES BRITTON CONSTRUCTION**, Ellesmere **Ref:**YH02754
- **HIGHGROVE SCHOOL OF RIDING**, Craven Arms **Ref:**YH06788
- **OSWESTRY EQUEST CTRE**, Oswestry **Ref:**YH10576

SOMERSET (NORTH)
- **MENDIP RIDING CTRE**, Churchill **Ref:**YH09458

STAFFORDSHIRE
- **SCROPTON**, Burton-on-Trent **Ref:**YH12569

SUFFOLK
- **LINKWOOD EQUESTIAN**, Bury St Edmunds **Ref:**YH08665
- **ORWELL ARENA**, Ipswich **Ref:**YH10556
- **STOKE BY CLARE EQUESTRIAN CTRE**, Sudbury **Ref:**YH13501

SURREY
- **ASCOT PARK**, Woking **Ref:**YH00583
- **CHASE FARM**, Hindhead **Ref:**YH02780
- **WOODSTOCK SOUTH STABLES**, Chessington **Ref:**YH15751

SUSSEX (WEST)
- **ALL ENGLAND JUMPING COURSE**, Haywards Heath **Ref:**YH00284
- **LAVANT HSE STABLES**, Chichester **Ref:**YH08460
- **WILLOWBROOK RIDING CTRE**, Chichester **Ref:**YH15508
- **ZARA STUD**, Chichester **Ref:**YH15951

TYNE AND WEAR
- **GO RIDING GRP**, Ponteland **Ref:**YH05862

WARWICKSHIRE
- **STONELEIGH STABLES**, Kenilworth **Ref:**YH13519
- **SWALLOWFIELD EQUESTRIAN**, Solihull **Ref:**YH13686
- **WAVERLEY EQUESTRIAN CTRE**, Leamington Spa **Ref:**YH15011

WILTSHIRE
- **HEYWOOD**, Westbury **Ref:**YH06737
- **MALTHOUSE EQUESTRIAN CTRE**, Swindon **Ref:**YH09058
- **WEST WILTS**, Trowbridge **Ref:**YH15170

WORCESTERSHIRE
- **GRACELANDS**, Droitwich **Ref:**YH05958
- **KYRE EQUESTRIAN CTRE**, Tenbury Wells **Ref:**YH08305
- **WITS END STABLES**, Worcester **Ref:**YH15634

YORKSHIRE (NORTH)
- **FOLLIFOOT PK**, Harrogate **Ref:**YH05300
- **FRIARS HILL STABLES**, York **Ref:**YH05501
- **JOUSTING & ASSOCIATED SKILLS**, Thirsk **Ref:**YH07948
- **YORKSHIRE RIDING CTRE**, Harrogate **Ref:**YH15922

YORKSHIRE (SOUTH)
- **SYKEHOUSE ARENA**, Doncaster **Ref:**YH13723

YORKSHIRE (WEST)
- **BLACUP TRAINING GRP**, Halifax **Ref:**YH01504
- **HOPTON**, Mirfield **Ref:**YH07061
- **TIMBERTOPS EQUESTRIAN CTRE**, Pontefract **Ref:**YH14162

BLACKSMITHS

BERKSHIRE
- **ARK WROUGHT IRON WORK**, Slough **Ref:**YH00529
- **COUNTRY METALCRAFT**, Reading **Ref:**YH03418
- **WOODLANDS**, Hungerford **Ref:**YH15705

BRISTOL
- **BOUGOURD, W R**, Bristol **Ref:**YH01670
- **BRODNAX, FRED**, Bristol **Ref:**YH02018
- **BUTCHER, ROGER**, Bristol **Ref:**YH02317
- **HOBBS, ROBERT**, Bristol **Ref:**YH06896
- **SEVERN IRONWORKS**, Bristol **Ref:**YH12643
- **TOM WILLIAMS**, Bristol **Ref:**YH14217

BUCKINGHAMSHIRE
- **A HILLSDON & SON**, Marlow **Ref:**YH00036
- **GREEN, ROBERT G**, Aylesbury **Ref:**YH06073
- **PROTEAN FORGE**, Aylesbury **Ref:**YH11439

CAMBRIDGESHIRE

- **BEVAN, G W**, Huntingdon **Ref:**YH01338
- **DOWNING, J**, Peterborough **Ref:**YH04232
- **FOTHERINGHAY**, Peterborough **Ref:**YH05403
- **MARTIN WORKS**, Wisbech **Ref:**YH09214
- **METTLEWORK**, Cambridge **Ref:**YH09503
- **R C GOWING**, Cambridge **Ref:**YH11518

CHESHIRE

- **AINSCOUGH F & J**, Warrington **Ref:**YH00214
- **ARTISTIC METAL DESIGN**, Chester **Ref:**YH00576
- **BAILEY, N E**, Macclesfield **Ref:**YH00804
- **CHURCH FARM SMITHY**, Macclesfield **Ref:**YH02900
- **COOKE, PETER**, Sandbach **Ref:**YH03263
- **G J & G A DAVIES**, Nantwich **Ref:**YH05583
- **JOHN JONES**, Wilmslow **Ref:**YH07797
- **MASON, D A**, Crewe **Ref:**YH09240
- **MEADOW FORGE**, Ellesmere Port **Ref:**YH09420
- **SCANA EUROSTEEL**, Stockport **Ref:**YH12484
- **SIFTSTAR**, Crewe **Ref:**YH12793
- **T H R ENGINEERING**, Middlewich **Ref:**YH13743

CLEVELAND

- **F BRUNTON & SONS**, Guisborough **Ref:**YH04986
- **GRAYTHORP FORGE**, Hartlepool **Ref:**YH06037
- **PEARSON, H**, Stockton-on-Tees **Ref:**YH10880
- **PICKERING & DAWSON**, Billingham **Ref:**YH11081

CORNWALL

- **BARCELONA FORGE**, Looe **Ref:**YH00923
- **C & N ENGINEERING**, Gunnislake **Ref:**YH02358
- **FARRIER SVS**, St Ives **Ref:**YH05088
- **FORD, ROBIN**, Helston **Ref:**YH05326
- **IN STEEL**, Helston **Ref:**YH07405
- **INTERIOR ART METAL WORKS**, Camborne **Ref:**YH07476
- **PEARCE, MICHAEL**, Penzance **Ref:**YH10874
- **PHOENIX FORGE**, Liskeard **Ref:**YH11073
- **SAVILL, ROBBIE**, Liskeard **Ref:**YH12455
- **SMITHY**, Helston **Ref:**YH13010

COUNTY DURHAM

- **DENE HEAD LIVERY**, Darlington **Ref:**YH04042
- **DROVERS FORGE**, Consett **Ref:**YH04279
- **LITTLE NEWSHAM FORGE**, Darlington **Ref:**YH08696

CUMBRIA

- **BLAND BLACKSMITH**, Windermere **Ref:**YH01523
- **BRAMMALL, C A**, Ulverston **Ref:**YH01793
- **DIXONS FORGE**, Barrow-In-Furness **Ref:**YH04146
- **MCGINN, J D**, Penrith **Ref:**YH09358
- **MOSSOP, J**, Whitehaven **Ref:**YH09869
- **PIKE, STAN**, Alston **Ref:**YH11103
- **WATCHGATE FORGE**, Kendal **Ref:**YH14961
- **WHITE BRIDGE FORGE**, Ambleside **Ref:**YH15300

DERBYSHIRE

- **A E C ENGINEERING**, Derby **Ref:**YH00029
- **ARTHUR COTTAM**, Chesterfield **Ref:**YH00565
- **BLACKSMITH**, Matlock **Ref:**YH01495
- **BOWLER, A**, Belper **Ref:**YH01714
- **CRANE FORGE**, Hope Valley **Ref:**YH03559
- **ENDEAVOUR TOOLS**, Chesterfield **Ref:**YH04665
- **FIRTH RIXSON FORGINGS**, Matlock **Ref:**YH05231
- **MATHERS ENGINEERS**, Alfreton **Ref:**YH09261
- **METWOOD FORGE**, Ashbourne **Ref:**YH09504
- **OWEN, JONATHAN**, Derby **Ref:**YH10605
- **WHALEY BRIDGE SMITHY**, High Peak **Ref:**YH15255
- **WHIELDON, P G**, Derby **Ref:**YH15279

DEVON

- **CHURCHILL, J**, Dartmouth **Ref:**YH02914
- **DRIVER, P R**, Seaton **Ref:**YH04278
- **E ADAMS & SON**, Cullompton **Ref:**YH04397
- **FIRE ART**, Exeter **Ref:**YH05223
- **H G MIDDLETON & SONS**, Dartmouth **Ref:**YH06223
- **JESTERS FORGE**, Honiton **Ref:**YH07761
- **JOHN BELLAMY BLACKSMITHS**, Exeter **Ref:**YH07780
- **KENDREW, J**, Chulmleigh **Ref:**YH08061
- **MOORE ENGINEERING SERVICES**, Exeter **Ref:**YH09752
- **ORGANICS LAB**, Buckfastleigh **Ref:**YH10541
- **PARSONS, KRIS**, Axminster **Ref:**YH10800
- **SMITHY WORKSHOP**, Totnes **Ref:**YH13014
- **V E BEER & SONS**, Exeter **Ref:**YH14627
- **WEBBER BROS**, Crediton **Ref:**YH15033
- **WOODSIDE FORGE**, Plymouth **Ref:**YH15742

DORSET

- **ABBOTT STREET FORGE**, Wimborne **Ref:**YH00114
- **APPLEWOOD & PERRY**, Wimborne **Ref:**YH00483
- **BLACKMORE VALEFORGE**, Sturminster Newton **Ref:**YH01488
- **BUCKLEY'S IRONWORKS**, Blandford Forum **Ref:**YH02200
- **CASTLE FORGE**, Sherborne **Ref:**YH02624
- **FORGED AFFAIRS**, Dorchester **Ref:**YH05366
- **G RANDALL & SONS**, Weymouth **Ref:**YH05595
- **JOHNSTON ENGINEERING**, Bridport **Ref:**YH07844

ESSEX

- **BELCHER, A D**, Colchester **Ref:**YH01204
- **ELLIS ENGINEERING**, Billericay **Ref:**YH04622
- **MILLSIDE MANUFACTURING**, Bishop's Stortford **Ref:**YH09635
- **TRANSPORT ENGINEERING SVS**, Tilbury **Ref:**YH14350

GLOUCESTERSHIRE

- **C W LEE & SON**, Tetbury **Ref:**YH02407
- **DISTINCTIVE IRON WORK**, Cheltenham **Ref:**YH04133
- **FIRECRAFT**, Stroud **Ref:**YH05224
- **FLATCHLEY FORGE**, Newnham **Ref:**YH05262
- **GLOUCESTER ST FORGE**, Stroud **Ref:**YH05852
- **PANKHURST, W R**, Stroud **Ref:**YH10698
- **PAXWELD**, Cheltenham **Ref:**YH10844
- **SIMON HUNTER**, Stroud **Ref:**YH12830
- **WILLIAMS, G L C & R**, Tetbury **Ref:**YH15458

HAMPSHIRE

- **A L FRY & SON**, Petersfield **Ref:**YH00046
- **BENT, R**, Romsey **Ref:**YH01283
- **COLLETT, T W**, Waterlooville **Ref:**YH03176
- **COX, DAVE**, Fareham **Ref:**YH03529
- **HAYMARK PRODUCTS**, Waterlooville **Ref:**YH06585
- **NU-CO FORGE & WELDING**, Lymington **Ref:**YH10351
- **PETE'S BLACKSMITHS WORKSHOP**, Southsea **Ref:**YH11024
- **SMITH, ROBERT**, Alton **Ref:**YH12995

HEREFORDSHIRE

- **CADWALLENDER FORGE**, Hereford **Ref:**YH02412
- **CAPLE CRAFT**, Hereford **Ref:**YH02522
- **MOORE, M B**, Ledbury **Ref:**YH09763
- **O'HARE, BROMLEY**, Leominster **Ref:**YH10443
- **SIMPSON, JONATHAN**, Leominster **Ref:**YH12839

HERTFORDSHIRE

- **HAMMER & TONGS**, Tring **Ref:**YH06357

ISLE OF WIGHT

- **B P SVS**, Newport **Ref:**YH00745

KENT

- **BLACK FORGE ART**, Tenterden **Ref:**YH01462
- **DARENTH VALLEY FORGE**, Dartford **Ref:**YH03884
- **EMERY**, Maidstone **Ref:**YH04652
- **GRANT, R**, Ramsgate **Ref:**YH06014
- **GREGORY, J S**, Orpington **Ref:**YH06116
- **HINKLEY, T**, Ashford **Ref:**YH06875
- **HUTTON, LEN**, Canterbury **Ref:**YH07342
- **KINGSLEY FORGE**, Canterbury **Ref:**YH08204
- **K-WORKS BLACKSMITHING**, Maidstone **Ref:**YH08303
- **LAYTEM CRAFT**, Ramsgate **Ref:**YH08483
- **NAILBOURNE FORGE**, Canterbury **Ref:**YH10011
- **VILLAGE FORGE & SHOWROOM**, Tenterden **Ref:**YH14719

LANCASHIRE

- **BLACKBOAR FORGE**, Clitheroe **Ref:**YH01476
- **F & A DUNBAR**, Rochdale **Ref:**YH04979
- **H B H FORGINGS**, Heywood **Ref:**YH06211
- **HOT METAL DESIGN**, Carnforth **Ref:**YH07199
- **JOHN FOWLER & SON**, Chorley **Ref:**YH07790
- **JOHN FOWLER & SON**, Chorley **Ref:**YH07789
- **JOHN HESKETH & SON**, Bury **Ref:**YH07793
- **MARTON FORGE**, Blackpool **Ref:**YH09232
- **P K ENGINEERING**, Preston **Ref:**YH10650
- **W J BEVAN & SON**, Blackpool **Ref:**YH14776
- **WOODS, B D**, Oldham **Ref:**YH15736

LEICESTERSHIRE

- **BUDWORTH, G L**, Ashby-De-La-Zouch **Ref:**YH02209
- **J F SPENCE & SON**, Oakham **Ref:**YH07582
- **WALTER ALLEN & SONS**, Leicester **Ref:**YH14881

LINCOLNSHIRE

- **ALVINGHAM FORGE**, Louth **Ref:**YH00351
- **C CARTER & SON**, Spalding **Ref:**YH02365
- **CAPES & SON**, Lincoln **Ref:**YH02520
- **HORN, J M**, Lincoln **Ref:**YH07073
- **JOHN LILLY**, Grantham **Ref:**YH07798
- **LINCOLNSHIRE IRONMASTERS**, Lincoln **Ref:**YH08642
- **MARFLEET, H E**, Alford **Ref:**YH09147
- **MARSHALL, N**, Sleaford **Ref:**YH09201
- **MOTLEY ENGINEERING**, Spilsby **Ref:**YH09874
- **POWELL, BROUGHTON**, Lincoln **Ref:**YH11314
- **R E & P KETTLE**, Grantham **Ref:**YH11530
- **SPIKINGS, N D**, Boston **Ref:**YH13204
- **THORPE, MERVYN**, Stamford **Ref:**YH14096
- **U E F**, Lincoln **Ref:**YH14536

LINCOLNSHIRE (NORTH EAST)

- **HURST, K B**, Grimsby **Ref:**YH07317
- **SPRINGFIELD SMITHY**, Grimsby **Ref:**YH13257

LINCOLNSHIRE (NORTH)

- **BATCHELOR, B**, Scunthorpe **Ref:**YH01063

LONDON (GREATER)

- **ADAMS, JAMES**, London **Ref:**YH00168
- **BOYS, KEVIN**, London **Ref:**YH01734
- **CLARKE IRON**, Twickenham **Ref:**YH02970
- **IRON FIGHTERS**, London **Ref:**YH07504
- **L A RICHARDSON & SON**, London **Ref:**YH08311
- **METAL ARTEFACTS**, London **Ref:**YH09494
- **PHOENIX FORGE UK**, London **Ref:**YH11074
- **SMITH & RAPPOLD**, London **Ref:**YH12935
- **STEEL TO LIVE**, London **Ref:**YH13415
- **STURDY, CONAN**, London **Ref:**YH13612
- **SWANKEY, KASPAR**, Brentford **Ref:**YH13692

- **THOMAS, SHELLEY**, Brentford **Ref:**YH14028
- **TWICKENHAM FORGE**, Twickenham **Ref:**YH14512

MANCHESTER (GREATER)

- **DICKIE'S FORGE**, Bolton **Ref:**YH04112
- **RADICAL FORGING IRONWORK**, Salford **Ref:**YH11594
- **WHITEOAK & SONS**, Manchester **Ref:**YH15354

MERSEYSIDE

- **MASON, J W**, Liverpool **Ref:**YH09245
- **V J WEBB**, Liverpool **Ref:**YH14629

MIDLANDS (WEST)

- **B B PRICE**, Cradley Heath **Ref:**YH00718
- **BEACONSFIELD PRODUCTS**, Cradley Heath **Ref:**YH01110
- **BENJAMIN BAKER**, Stourbridge **Ref:**YH01268
- **BERKSWELL FORGE WORKS**, Coventry **Ref:**YH01308
- **BLACK, ARTHUR**, Oldbury **Ref:**YH01469
- **BREAKWELL, RON**, Sutton Coldfield **Ref:**YH01827
- **CAUSER, W H**, Birmingham **Ref:**YH02661
- **DUDLEY DIE FORGINGS**, Dudley **Ref:**YH04308
- **FORGEWELD**, Sutton Coldfield **Ref:**YH05369
- **FORGING AHEAD**, Stourbridge **Ref:**YH05370
- **HANEY, B**, Rowley Regis **Ref:**YH06384
- **HEARTLAND EXTRUSION FORGE**, Birmingham **Ref:**YH06620
- **J L H ENGINEERING**, Stourbridge **Ref:**YH07594
- **JENKINS DUNN FORGINGS**, Dudley **Ref:**YH07729
- **M H COLLEY**, Brierley Hill **Ref:**YH08963
- **MILLS FORGINGS**, Coventry **Ref:**YH09628
- **MORGAN PLATTS**, Willenhall **Ref:**YH09797
- **PARKER HANNIFIN**, Cradley Heath **Ref:**YH10745
- **SOLID STAMPINGS**, Cradley Heath **Ref:**YH13057
- **T H SKINNER**, Stourbridge **Ref:**YH13744
- **VAUGHANS HOPE WORKS**, Stourbridge **Ref:**YH14667
- **W R & J COLLINS**, Birmingham **Ref:**YH14787

NORFOLK

- **BUREVALLEY FORGE**, Norwich **Ref:**YH02238
- **BUTLER, D J**, Diss **Ref:**YH02324
- **FITT, MICHAEL**, Norwich **Ref:**YH05245
- **GATES TO GRATES**, Norwich **Ref:**YH05674
- **GEMINI FORGE**, King's Lynn **Ref:**YH05698
- **H BLYTH & SON**, Norwich **Ref:**YH06214
- **METALCRAFT**, King's Lynn **Ref:**YH09498
- **REYNOLDS, BRIAN**, North Walsham **Ref:**YH11777
- **RIDGWAY, I W**, Norwich **Ref:**YH11871
- **TOLLIDAY, ERIC S**, King's Lynn **Ref:**YH14212
- **WOODBASTWICK FORGE**, Norwich **Ref:**YH15673

NORTHAMPTONSHIRE

- **A M C S**, Kettering **Ref:**YH00048
- **BY HAMMER & HAND**, Northampton **Ref:**YH02342
- **GARDNER, R**, Kettering **Ref:**YH05648
- **HADDON CRAFT FORGE**, Northampton **Ref:**YH06260
- **JAMES GEORGE & SONS**, Kettering **Ref:**YH07666
- **MILLER, P J**, Northampton **Ref:**YH09609

NORTHUMBERLAND

- **BALDASERA, P**, Morpeth **Ref:**YH00835
- **DOWNIE, R**, Morpeth **Ref:**YH04231
- **ERROL HUT SMITHY**, Cornhill-on-Tweed **Ref:**YH04855
- **JACKSON FRANCIS & SONS**, Haltwhistle **Ref:**YH07641

NOTTINGHAMSHIRE

- **MALLENDER BROS**, Worksop **Ref:**YH09051
- **WOOD, H O**, Nottingham **Ref:**YH15662

OXFORDSHIRE

- **A & M TURNPIKE FORGE**, Abingdon **Ref:**YH00016
- **CURTIS, P**, Banbury **Ref:**YH03753
- **F C HARRISS & SONS**, Burford **Ref:**YH04987
- **IRON AWE**, Oxford **Ref:**YH07503
- **LONG, MAURICE**, Faringdon **Ref:**YH08804
- **MOSS, D**, Thame **Ref:**YH09857
- **W R HALL & SONS**, Burford **Ref:**YH14790

SHROPSHIRE

- **ANVILCRAFT**, Telford **Ref:**YH00470
- **C J BLACKSMITHS**, Shrewsbury **Ref:**YH02375
- **DICKIE'S FORGE**, Newport **Ref:**YH04113
- **MIKE JONES BLACKSMITHS**, Ellesmere **Ref:**YH09565
- **STOKES OF ENGLAND**, Oswestry **Ref:**YH13504
- **STRANGE, ALF**, Ellesmere **Ref:**YH13547

SOMERSET

- **ASH, RICHARD W J**, Somerton **Ref:**YH00589
- **CHEDDON FITZPAINE FORGE**, Taunton **Ref:**YH02798
- **COOKSLEY, BUZZ**, Minehead **Ref:**YH03266
- **HOBBS, B**, Minehead **Ref:**YH06895
- **PAUL, NIGEL**, Crewkerne **Ref:**YH10834
- **POIRRIER, BILL**, Watchet **Ref:**YH11195
- **SHINERS FORGE**, Wellington **Ref:**YH12747
- **SOMERSET SMITHY OF FROME**, Frome **Ref:**YH13064
- **WHITEFIELD, IAN**, Ilminster **Ref:**YH15336
- **WRIGHT, M**, Taunton **Ref:**YH15838

SOMERSET (NORTH)

- **STRAWBERRY STEEL**, Clevedon **Ref:**YH13568

STAFFORDSHIRE

- **ANVIL FORGE**, Stoke-on-Trent **Ref:**YH00468
- **ARMSTRONG BLACKSMITHS**, Tamworth **Ref:**YH00542
- **ASHMORE BLACKSMITHS**, Burton-on-Trent **Ref:**YH00608
- **BROOKSIDE FORGE**, Stafford **Ref:**YH02069
- **E F SVEIKUTIS BLACKSMITH**, Stoke-on-Trent **Ref:**YH04404
- **E J A FROST**, Stafford **Ref:**YH04408
- **FALCON FORGE**, Burntwood **Ref:**YH05039
- **IZAAK WALTON SMITHY**, Stone **Ref:**YH07541

SUFFOLK

- **E M JACOBS & SONS**, Ipswich **Ref:**YH04416
- **GEDDING MILL FORGE**, Bury St Edmunds **Ref:**YH05688
- **HIGHAM FORGE**, Bury St Edmunds **Ref:**YH06769

SURREY

- **BETCHWORTH FORGE**, Betchworth **Ref:**YH01331
- **BUBEAR & JONES**, Epsom **Ref:**YH02183
- **BURNS, G E**, Staines **Ref:**YH02272
- **BURROWS LEA FORGE**, Guildford **Ref:**YH02284
- **C PILLOW & SON**, Leatherhead **Ref:**YH02385
- **H THOMPSON & SON**, Chertsey **Ref:**YH06243
- **HASLEMERE FORGE**, Haslemere **Ref:**YH06525
- **KIT LAMBERT BLACKSMITHS**, Dorking **Ref:**YH08245
- **R C LARKIN BLACKSMITHS**, Oxted **Ref:**YH11520
- **UTOPIA FORGE**, Guildford **Ref:**YH14625
- **W KING & SONS**, Horley **Ref:**YH14779
- **WELLS, J R**, Redhill **Ref:**YH15085

SUSSEX (EAST)

- **C DEAN & SON**, Lewes **Ref:**YH02366
- **CASTLE FORGE**, Wadhurst **Ref:**YH02625
- **HERITAGE FORGE SHOWROOM**, Heathfield **Ref:**YH06705
- **LEWES FORGE**, Lewes **Ref:**YH08578
- **MAYFIELD FORGE**, Mayfield **Ref:**YH09297
- **R GREGORY & SON**, St Leonards-on-Sea **Ref:**YH11537
- **STUDIO FORGE**, Lewes **Ref:**YH13608
- **T TYHURST & SON**, Lewes **Ref:**YH13766
- **WEALDEN IRON CRAFTS**, Etchingham **Ref:**YH15019

SUSSEX (WEST)

- **ANGMERING FORGE**, Worthing **Ref:**YH00420
- **ANVILS BLACKSMITH**, East Grinstead **Ref:**YH00471
- **ARUNDEL RACING FARRIERS**, Arundel **Ref:**YH00578
- **BRADSHAW, R J W**, Haywards Heath **Ref:**YH01762
- **FULLER, R S**, Littlehampton **Ref:**YH05533
- **LEADBETTER, R**, Burgess Hill **Ref:**YH08497
- **OLD BREWERY WORKSHOP**, Arundel **Ref:**YH10452
- **REYNOLDS D & SONS**, Horsham **Ref:**YH11774
- **RYMANS FORGE**, Chichester **Ref:**YH12306
- **SAUNDERS, H W**, Worthing **Ref:**YH12447
- **T MILES & SON**, Henfield **Ref:**YH13760
- **VALE FORGE**, Chichester **Ref:**YH14634
- **WISBOROUGH GREEN FORGE**, Billingshurst **Ref:**YH15605
- **WYVERN SMITHY**, Horsham **Ref:**YH15879

TYNE AND WEAR

- **CRADLEWELL FORGE**, Newcastle-upon-Tyne **Ref:**YH03540
- **FORMET**, Newcastle-upon-Tyne **Ref:**YH05375
- **R PARKIN & SON**, Sunderland **Ref:**YH11560

WARWICKSHIRE

- **GREEN, HARRY**, Alcester **Ref:**YH06065
- **HALFORD FORGE**, Shipston-on-Stour **Ref:**YH06298
- **MONK & WILLIAMS**, Leamington Spa **Ref:**YH09723
- **R JONES**, Nuneaton **Ref:**YH11551

WILTSHIRE

- **COLE, ARTHUR**, Chippenham **Ref:**YH03150
- **COLE, MELISSA**, Chippenham **Ref:**YH03159
- **DEAN, MARTYN**, Salisbury **Ref:**YH03993
- **DEVICES WALKS & TALKS**, Devizes **Ref:**YH04089
- **FORGE**, Bradford-on-Avon **Ref:**YH05360
- **METAL ARTWORK**, Salisbury **Ref:**YH09495
- **MOORE, HAZEL**, Chippenham **Ref:**YH09760
- **WARMINSTER METAL WORKERS**, Warminster **Ref:**YH14922

WORCESTERSHIRE

- **STRATFORD YARD FORGE**, Evesham **Ref:**YH13552

YORKSHIRE (EAST)

- **CARLTON FORGE**, Hull **Ref:**YH02543
- **PORTERFIELD IRON WORKS**, Driffield **Ref:**YH11286
- **R J A ROBSON & SON**, Bridlington **Ref:**YH11548
- **SMITHY**, Driffield **Ref:**YH13013

YORKSHIRE (NORTH)

- **BROCKWELL, P**, York **Ref:**YH02015
- **CLEMENTS, D & R**, Settle **Ref:**YH03017
- **DESIGN SVS**, Skipton **Ref:**YH04083
- **NIDD SMITHY**, York **Ref:**YH10201
- **SELLARS, R**, Scarborough **Ref:**YH12622
- **TOPP, C D**, Thirsk **Ref:**YH14239

YORKSHIRE (SOUTH)

- **CHURCHILL SMITHY**, Doncaster **Ref:**YH02913
- **FURNIVAL STEEL**, Sheffield **Ref:**YH05552
- **K T FORGE**, Rotherham **Ref:**YH07992
- **LANGLEY FORGED PRODUCTS**, Sheffield **Ref:**YH08407

- **LEWIS G H & SONS**, Rotherham Ref:YH08582
- **MERIDIAN ENGINEERING SVS**, Sheffield Ref:YH09475
- **NAYLOR, F K**, Rotherham Ref:YH10058
- **WENTWORTH FORGE**, Rotherham Ref:YH15111
- **WILD, THOMAS C**, Sheffield Ref:YH15406
- **WILLIAM WALTON**, Sheffield Ref:YH15438

YORKSHIRE (WEST)

- **ALLEN HOLLINGWORTH & SON**, Huddersfield Ref:YH00292
- **CASTLE SMITHY**, Pontefract Ref:YH02634
- **FIRTH, ARTHUR**, Dewsbury Ref:YH05233
- **HAINSWORTH FORGE**, Keighley Ref:YH06287
- **HALFROD, T K**, Cleckheaton Ref:YH06300
- **HOLLIDAY, N**, Ilkley Ref:YH06940
- **M ALLEN & SONS**, Normanton Ref:YH08954
- **SHEPLEY FORGE**, Huddersfield Ref:YH12713

BLOOD STOCK AGENCIES

BEDFORDSHIRE

- **METCALFE, DAVID**, Dunstable Ref:YH09500

BERKSHIRE

- **BERESFORD BLOODSTOCK SERVICES**, Binfield Ref:YH01293
- **BLOODHORSE INT**, Hungerford Ref:YH01547
- **BRITISH BLOODSTOCK AGENCY**, Hungerford Ref:YH01928
- **CHARLES EGERTON BLOODSTOCK**, Newbury Ref:YH02755
- **CLB**, Newbury Ref:YH03007
- **GORDIAN TROELLER BLOODSTOCK**, Upper Bucklebury Ref:YH05922
- **HALL & AST**, Hungerford Ref:YH06303
- **HIGHCLERE THOROUGHBRED RACING**, Newbury Ref:YH06775
- **HILLSIDE STUD**, Hungerford Ref:YH06855
- **LILLINGSTON BLOODSTOCK**, Reading Ref:YH08624
- **LINDLEY, J F**, Newbury Ref:YH08649
- **NELSON, PETER**, Reading Ref:YH10075
- **W H PONSONBY**, Newbury Ref:YH14774
- **WAYLAND BLOOD STOCK**, Reading Ref:YH15015
- **WOODLANDS**, Hungerford Ref:YH15705

BUCKINGHAMSHIRE

- **CHERRY TREE FARM**, Amersham Ref:YH02815
- **WILL EDMEADES BLOODSTOCK**, Great Horwood Ref:YH15425

CAMBRIDGESHIRE

- **ANGLIA BLOODSTOCK**, Ely Ref:YH00412
- **FLUOROCARBON BLOODSTOCK**, Ely Ref:YH05290
- **SADLER, LINDA**, Ely Ref:YH12374

CORNWALL

- **STEVENS**, Helston Ref:YH13441

DERBYSHIRE

- **C E S**, Ashbourne Ref:YH02370

DEVON

- **BARONS, D H**, Kingsbridge Ref:YH00995
- **BARWELL, C R**, Tiverton Ref:YH01052

DORSET

- **LONDON THOROUGHBRED SVS**, Wimborne Ref:YH08790
- **RAFIQUE, M**, Sturminster Newton Ref:YH11605

ESSEX

- **SHAHZADA**, Dunmow Ref:YH12659

GLOUCESTERSHIRE

- **GROVE FARM**, Moreton In Marsh Ref:YH06163
- **HOWSON, GEOFFREY**, Cheltenham Ref:YH07245
- **OLYMPIC BLOODSTOCK**, Moreton In Marsh Ref:YH10503
- **TWEENHILLS FARM & STUD**, Gloucester Ref:YH14508

HAMPSHIRE

- **HARRIS, ANDREW**, Lymington Ref:YH06464
- **KENNET VALLEY THOROUGHBREDS**, Basingstoke Ref:YH08073
- **REDENHAM PK STUD**, Andover Ref:YH11708
- **SOUTHWEST BLOODSTOCK**, Alton Ref:YH13162
- **T J BISHOP**, Winchester Ref:YH13753
- **TRICKLEDOWN STUD**, Stockbridge Ref:YH14392

HEREFORDSHIRE

- **BRIGHTWELLS BLOODSTOCK**, Hereford Ref:YH01910
- **DAVID SMYLY**, Dorstone Ref:YH03923
- **ECKLEY, R J**, Kington Ref:YH04536

HERTFORDSHIRE

- **BRITISH LIVESTOCK**, Buntingford Ref:YH01959
- **HARTFORD BLOODSTOCK**, Welwyn Garden City Ref:YH06500
- **UPPERWOOD FARM STUD**, Hemel Hempstead Ref:YH14609

KENT

- **ELMHURST BLOODSTOCK**, Tonbridge Ref:YH04637

LANCASHIRE

- **BROOKFIELDS**, Ormskirk Ref:YH02051
- **END HSE**, Clitheroe Ref:YH04664
- **HARKER, MICHAEL**, Bury Ref:YH06432
- **OAKLEIGH STUD FARM**, Preston Ref:YH10397

LEICESTERSHIRE

- **CRANSWICK**, Melton Mowbray Ref:YH03570
- **SAGITTARIUS BLOODSTOCK AGENCY**, Melton Mowbray Ref:YH12382

LINCOLNSHIRE

- **BEST/THOROUGHBRED RACING GB**, Louth Ref:YH01327
- **GOLLINGS, JAYNE**, Louth Ref:YH05897
- **NORTHERN BLOODSTOCK**, Louth Ref:YH10298
- **WOODLANDS STABLES**, Market Rasen Ref:YH15711

LONDON (GREATER)

- **CENTAUR BLOODSTOCK**, Kingston Upon Thames Ref:YH02682
- **GORDON-WATSON BLOODSTOCK**, London Ref:YH05929
- **GORDON-WATSON, CHARLES**, London Ref:YH05930
- **HAVANA HORSE UK**, London Ref:YH06537
- **KENNET VALLEY THOROUGHBREDS**, London Ref:YH08074
- **PERSIAN BLOODSTOCK**, Feltham Ref:YH10995
- **R B I BLOODSTOCK**, South Kensington Ref:YH11515

MIDLANDS (WEST)

- **BRITISH ARABIAN BLOODSTOCK**, Birmingham Ref:YH01926

NORFOLK

- **BERGH APTON STUD**, Norwich Ref:YH01297
- **FREEMAN, KEITH**, Norwich Ref:YH05485
- **MAYWAY**, Thetford Ref:YH09308
- **SILFIELD BLOODSTOCK**, Thetford Ref:YH12796

NORTHAMPTONSHIRE

- **EQUINE SVS**, Wellingborough Ref:YH04803

NORTHUMBERLAND

- **NORTHERN EQUINE SERVICES**, Morpeth Ref:YH10302

OXFORDSHIRE

- **BRAIN INTERNATIONAL**, Woodstock Ref:YH01778
- **RICHARD PITMAN BLOODSTOCK**, Wantage Ref:YH11805

SHROPSHIRE

- **NOCK DEIGHTON AGRICULTURAL**, Bridgnorth Ref:YH10225
- **PARKYN, SHAUN & SALLY**, Bridgnorth Ref:YH10783

STAFFORDSHIRE

- **HINTON BULL HIRE**, Stoke-on-Trent Ref:YH06877

SUFFOLK

- **ANDREW SIME**, Newmarket Ref:YH00393
- **ARABIAN BLOODSTOCK AGENCY**, Raydon Ref:YH00491
- **BARNES, RAYMOND**, Newmarket Ref:YH00980
- **BRITISH BLOODSTOCK AGENCY**, Newmarket Ref:YH01929
- **BULWER-LONG, T**, Newmarket Ref:YH02220
- **CHERRY-DOWNS BLOODSTOCK**, Newmarket Ref:YH02820
- **CORMAC MCCORMACK BLOODSTOCK**, Newmarket Ref:YH03319
- **CURRAGH BLOODSTOCK AGENCY**, Newmarket Ref:YH03734
- **DELTA BLOOD STOCK MNGMT**, Newmarket Ref:YH04035
- **ECLIPSE MNGMT**, Newmarket Ref:YH04538
- **EUROPEAN BREEDERS FUND**, Newmarket Ref:YH04906
- **FAIRFIELD BLOODSTOCK**, Woodbridge Ref:YH05017
- **FBA**, Newmarket Ref:YH05113
- **FOSTER BLOODSTOCK**, Bury St Edmunds Ref:YH05399
- **FRANKLAND, FRANK A**, Newmarket Ref:YH05466
- **HASTING CTRE**, Newmarket Ref:YH06527
- **HERITAGE COAST STUD**, Woodbridge Ref:YH06703
- **HILL, GEORGE**, Newmarket Ref:YH06830
- **HUGO LASCELLES BLOODSTOCK**, Bury St Edmunds Ref:YH07276
- **JILL LAMB BLOODSTOCK**, Newmarket Ref:YH07767
- **JOHN FERGUSON BLOODSTOCK**, Newmarket Ref:YH07787
- **MEAD GOODBODY**, Newmarket Ref:YH09411
- **OLYMPIC BLOODSTOCK**, Newmarket Ref:YH10504
- **RICHARD O'GORMAN BLOODSTOCK**, Newmarket Ref:YH11804
- **SEYMOUR BLOODSTOCK**, Newmarket Ref:YH12651
- **SHADOWFAX STABLE**, Newmarket Ref:YH12655
- **SIDE HILL STUD**, Newmarket Ref:YH12784
- **STOKE BY CLARE EQUESTRIAN CTRE**, Sudbury Ref:YH13501
- **TIM VIGORS BLOODSTOCK**, Newmarket Ref:YH14160
- **VIVIAN PRATT**, Felixstowe Ref:YH14737
- **WOODS, A J**, Bury St Edmunds Ref:YH15735
- **WRAGG, PETER**, Newmarket Ref:YH15809

SURREY

- **ALLAN BLOODLINES**, West Byfleet Ref:YH00287
- **BEECHWOOD BLOODSTOCK**, Weybridge Ref:YH01177
- **BURROUGH BLOODSTOCK**, Redhill Ref:YH02281
- **CLAYGATE SPORTS HORSES**, Esher Ref:YH03000
- **LORETTA LODGE RACING STABLE**, Epsom Ref:YH08831
- **MCCALL, DAVID**, Woking Ref:YH09317
- **T B BARFI**, Epsom Ref:YH13731

SUSSEX (WEST)

- **LAKIN BLOODSTOCK**, Wisborough Green Ref:YH08360

WARWICKSHIRE

GROUP 1 RACING, Bidford On Avon **Ref:**YH06160

WILTSHIRE

BRITISH RACING SERVICES, Malmesbury **Ref:**YH01968

NICHOLSON, ANDREW, Devizes **Ref:**YH10190

RAILTON, JAMIE, Chippenham **Ref:**YH11612

WEST KINGTON STUD, Chippenham **Ref:**YH15151

WORCESTERSHIRE

NORTH COTSWOLD STUD, Broadway **Ref:**YH10251

YORKSHIRE (EAST)

ASS BLOOD STOCK CONS, Bridlington **Ref:**YH00629

YORKSHIRE (NORTH)

BARRACA BLOODSTOCK, Thirsk **Ref:**YH01002

DELAHOOKE, JAMES STUART, Richmond **Ref:**YH04027

SPALDING, C M, Richmond **Ref:**YH13171

SWINBANK, ALAN, Richmond **Ref:**YH13708

YORKSHIRE (SOUTH)

BRITISH BLOODSTOCK AGENCY, Doncaster **Ref:**YH01930

YORKSHIRE (WEST)

RICHMOND, PETER, Wetherby **Ref:**YH11830

BREEDERS

BATH & SOMERSET (NORTH EAST)

CONKWELL GRANGE STUD, Bath **Ref:**YH03232

HORLER, M A, Bath **Ref:**YH07070

KNOWLES, E, Bath **Ref:**YH08284

BEDFORDSHIRE

BARKER, E, Harrold **Ref:**YH00942

BLOOMSBURY STUD, Woburn **Ref:**YH01555

COURTENAY, A L, Toddington **Ref:**YH03503

DEONE HART, Bedford **Ref:**YH04070

DIJON STUD, Colmworth **Ref:**YH04120

EVERKERRY, Leighton Buzzard **Ref:**YH04955

GIBBONS, P & S, Bedford **Ref:**YH05740

HOLLINGDON GRANGE, Leighton Buzzard **Ref:**YH06943

HOLME GROVE FARM, Biggleswade **Ref:**YH06965

HOLME PK STUD, Biggleswade **Ref:**YH06966

HOWE, B M, Cranfield **Ref:**YH07223

LIMERICK STUD, Gamlingay **Ref:**YH08632

RAWDING, J & S M, Leighton Buzzard **Ref:**YH11662

RISINGHOE CASTLE STUD, Goldington **Ref:**YH11910

SALSA STUD, Chawston **Ref:**YH12391

SMITH, N, Flitwick **Ref:**YH12978

SOUTHCOURT STUD, Leighton Buzzard **Ref:**YH13131

STAGSDEN HAFLINGERS, Stagsden **Ref:**YH13343

STAPLEFORD MILL FARM STUD, Leighton Buzzard **Ref:**YH13387

YEGUADA IBERICA, Knotting **Ref:**YH15898

BERKSHIRE

BERRYMAN-HORNE, A, Slough **Ref:**YH01319

BOARD-JONES, S, Windsor **Ref:**YH01584

BOOTH, A, Reading **Ref:**YH01633

BROXDOWN STUD, Maidenhead **Ref:**YH02151

BURLEY LODGE STUD, Reading **Ref:**YH02258

CHIEVELEY MANOR STUD, Newbury **Ref:**YH02850

CLEVELANDS STUD, Windsor **Ref:**YH03023

CLIVEDEN STUD, Maidenhead **Ref:**YH03051

DENTON, ROGER C, Hungerford **Ref:**YH04068

EQUICENTRE, Waltham St Lawrence **Ref:**YH04737

EWAR STUD FARM, Wokingham **Ref:**YH04960

FISHER, J T, Reading **Ref:**YH05240

GAINSBOROUGH STUD MNGMT, Newbury **Ref:**YH05607

HARRIES, STELLA, Bracknell **Ref:**YH06458

HEADLEY STUD, Thatcham **Ref:**YH06612

HEATHERWOLD STUD, Newbury **Ref:**YH06629

HILLSIDE STUD, Hungerford **Ref:**YH06855

HOLT MANOR FARM, Newbury **Ref:**YH06986

HUNGERFORD PARK EST, Hungerford **Ref:**YH07287

HYDE STUD FARM, Newbury **Ref:**YH07350

ISAAC, C & D, Newbury **Ref:**YH07511

JUDDMONTE FARMS, Wargrave On Thames **Ref:**YH07957

KINGWOOD HOUSE STABLES, Hungerford **Ref:**YH08215

MARNER, FIONA, Hungerford **Ref:**YH09172

MUSCHAMP STUD, Slough **Ref:**YH09974

PARKVIEW ANDALUSIANS, Wokingham **Ref:**YH10776

PRIORY STUD, White Waltham **Ref:**YH11406

RAFFIN STUD, Hungerford **Ref:**YH11604

SPRINGBOURNE & BLANCHE WELSH, Newbury **Ref:**YH13250

WATERSHIP DOWN STUD, Newbury **Ref:**YH14972

WHEELERSLAND STUD, Thatcham **Ref:**YH15276

WOODHAVEN STUD, Newbury **Ref:**YH15693

WOODLANDS, Hungerford **Ref:**YH15705

BRISTOL

GARWAY HAFLINGERS, Bristol **Ref:**YH05666

HAM FARM LIVERY & STUD, Bristol **Ref:**YH06339

BUCKINGHAMSHIRE

ALLEN, W S, Beaconsfield **Ref:**YH00306

APPLEACRE DARTMOORS, Wendover **Ref:**YH00479

BARKER, K J, Burnham **Ref:**YH00944

BARRETT, R J, Milton Keynes **Ref:**YH01014

BARRETTSTOWN EST STUD FARM, Aylesbury **Ref:**YH01017

CHERRY TREE STABLES, Amersham **Ref:**YH02818

CLARKE, CELIA, Buckingham **Ref:**YH02972

CLARKE, D, Marlow **Ref:**YH02974

COLQUHOUN, ELIZABETH, Buckingham **Ref:**YH03200

DEEPMILL STUD, Great Missenden **Ref:**YH04022

DEVILS HORSEMEN, Milton Keynes **Ref:**YH04090

FAIR WINTER, Milton Keynes **Ref:**YH05013

GLANFIELD, J, Iver **Ref:**YH05805

GRAFHAM STUD, Aylesbury **Ref:**YH05959

GRAFTON DONKEY STUD, Lillingstone Lovell **Ref:**YH05960

GRAY, P J, Iver **Ref:**YH06030

HEDSOR STUD, Bourne End **Ref:**YH06647

LECKHAMPSTEAD WHARF STUD, Buckingham **Ref:**YH08513

MCKIE, V, Twyford **Ref:**YH09386

MEARS, IVAN, Great Brickhill **Ref:**YH09430

PANAYIOTOU, E, Gerrards Cross **Ref:**YH10696

R HUNT, Penn **Ref:**YH11545

RAGLAN HOUSE ANDALUSIAN STUD, Aston Clinton **Ref:**YH11606

RANDLE, M J, Gerrards Cross **Ref:**YH11629

SCOTT, S, Aylesbury **Ref:**YH12547

SEDGEHILL SHETLAND PONY STUD, Chesham **Ref:**YH12604

SINGH, ANITA, Chesham **Ref:**YH12853

SMITH & JONES, Aylesbury **Ref:**YH12931

SMITH, M, Aylesbury **Ref:**YH12973

TALLENTS STUD, Buckingham **Ref:**YH13836

WADDESDON STUD, Aylesbury **Ref:**YH14806

WARMBLOOD FACT FILES, Buckingham **Ref:**YH14921

WYCHWOOD STUD, Mursley **Ref:**YH15857

CAMBRIDGESHIRE

A S JOHNSON & SON, Wisbech **Ref:**YH00058

APPALOOSAS, RODEGA, Histon **Ref:**YH00477

BARRETT, R, Chatteris **Ref:**YH01013

BRADLEY, JOHN, Ely **Ref:**YH01755

BRADLEY, N, Soham **Ref:**YH01758

BRAND, J, Witchford **Ref:**YH01795

BRIDGEHILL PONY STUD, Peterborough **Ref:**YH01881

BRITISH SKEWBALD/PIEBALD ASS, Ely **Ref:**YH01975

BROOKFIELD SHIRES, Huntingdon **Ref:**YH02049

COLE AMBROSE, Ely **Ref:**YH03148

DAYTON, KYM, Wisbech **Ref:**YH03972

FENGATE DARTMOORS, Warboys **Ref:**YH05140

FLUOROCARBON BLOODSTOCK, Ely **Ref:**YH05290

FRENCH, D, Peterborough **Ref:**YH05491

FRYER, LEWIS E, Huntingdon **Ref:**YH05529

G E BAILEY & SONS, Willingham **Ref:**YH05575

G T WARD & SON, Wisbech **Ref:**YH05599

GARLICK S & V, RUSSELL M, Castle Camps **Ref:**YH05652

HIGHBARN DARTMOORS, Trumpington **Ref:**YH06771

HOLLAND, J T, Peterborough **Ref:**YH06938

HOOK HSE, March **Ref:**YH07035

KIDDY, S M, Balsham **Ref:**YH08123

MANSION FARM STUD, Ely **Ref:**YH09125

OLD MILL STUD, Ely **Ref:**YH10470

OLD TIGER STABLES, Ely **Ref:**YH10479

PEACOCK, R, Huntingdon **Ref:**YH10861

PENNIES STUD, Wisbech **Ref:**YH10950

PROSPECT STUD, Grantchester **Ref:**YH11437

ROSACH STUD, Wisbech **Ref:**YH12087

RUSSELL, S, Wisbech **Ref:**YH12264

SADLER, LINDA, Ely **Ref:**YH12374

SCOTTSWAY STUD, Castle Camps **Ref:**YH12563

SMITH, P & B, Cottenham **Ref:**YH12983

SOVERIGN QUARTER HORSES, March **Ref:**YH13164

TEBBUTT, N F & A C F, Huntingdon **Ref:**YH13927

THOMPSON, S, Ely **Ref:**YH14042

TILLEY, A & T, Cambridge **Ref:**YH14150

WARD, M & W, Ely **Ref:**YH14903

WELLS PARK FARM, Whittlesford **Ref:**YH15080

WHITE, F B, Teversham **Ref:**YH15329

WITCHAM HSE FARM STUD, Ely **Ref:**YH15617

WULFSTAN, Welney **Ref:**YH15851

CHESHIRE

A MEALOR & SONS, Chester **Ref:**YH00052

ALLMAN, RAY & MARK, Crewe **Ref:**YH00322

ASTON, R K, Malpas **Ref:**YH00639

BENNETT, R, Heatley **Ref:**YH01272

BROOKHOUSE FARM BUILDINGS, Congleton **Ref:**YH02055

BROOMHILL STUD, Chester **Ref:**YH02081

BRYAN, R, Warrington **Ref:**YH02166

BULL, A, Sandbach **Ref:**YH02213

C H CURBISHLEY FARMS, Congleton **Ref:**YH02373

CALLWOOD, H S & A, Knutsford **Ref:**YH02453

CARLTON STUD, Malpas **Ref:**YH02544

DENSEM, R G, Macclesfield **Ref:**YH04064

DOVE STYLE, Chester **Ref:**YH04217

DUTTON, Holmes Chapel **Ref:**YH04377

E T M, Warrington **Ref:**YH04429

EARDLEY, ANGELA, Hough **Ref:**YH04448

- **ESTATE SUPPLIES & SVS**, Altrincham **Ref:**YH04875
- **F WILLIAMSON & SONS**, Macclesfield **Ref:**YH05005
- **FAIRVIEW ARABIAN STUD**, Wilmslow **Ref:**YH05030
- **FEARNALL**, Tarporley **Ref:**YH05116
- **FOURWAYS STUD**, Frodsham **Ref:**YH05415
- **HAYWOOD, J & G**, Northwich **Ref:**YH06597
- **JONES, C M**, Chester **Ref:**YH07881
- **LEECH, W A**, Knutsford **Ref:**YH08530
- **LEIGH, J**, Warrington **Ref:**YH08547
- **LEVER, J S**, Warrington **Ref:**YH08574
- **MCKENNA, C**, Winsford **Ref:**YH09382
- **MORRIS, S & HUNTON, J**, Audlem **Ref:**YH09835
- **MOSS, PHILIP**, Congleton **Ref:**YH09862
- **NASH, N**, Warrington **Ref:**YH10027
- **NORCLIFFE SHIRES**, Macclesfield **Ref:**YH10229
- **PICKMERE**, Knutsford **Ref:**YH11087
- **PORTLANDS STUD**, Congleton **Ref:**YH11293
- **POSNETT, A J**, Warrington **Ref:**YH11298
- **PRIDDY**, Winsford **Ref:**YH11394
- **PROFFITT, N J**, Crewe **Ref:**YH11431
- **PUGH, S M**, Tarporley **Ref:**YH11453
- **ROWLEY, G**, Ellesmere Port **Ref:**YH12172
- **SHERLOCK, E A**, Mouldsworth **Ref:**YH12724
- **SOUTHERN, R**, Chester **Ref:**YH13148
- **SPRINGWATER STUD**, Nantwich **Ref:**YH13263
- **STANNEY LANDS LIVERY**, Wilmslow **Ref:**YH13378
- **STOCKLEY FARM**, Warrington **Ref:**YH13494
- **WAINWRIGHT, J C**, Macclesfield **Ref:**YH14828
- **WHITE HALL LIVERY STABLES**, Little Budworth **Ref:**YH15304
- **WHITTAKER, O C**, Knutsford **Ref:**YH15374
- **WILMOT, S**, Macclesfield **Ref:**YH15522
- **WORTHINGTON, D**, Macclesfield **Ref:**YH15806
- **WRIGHT, A W**, Warrington **Ref:**YH15831

CLEVELAND

- **AISLABY GRANGE**, Stockton-on-Tees **Ref:**YH00227
- **C & S SWALWELL**, Saltburn-by-the-Sea **Ref:**YH02359
- **CUMBOR, E S**, Middlesbrough **Ref:**YH03714
- **FOXHOLM STUD**, Stockton-on-Tees **Ref:**YH05437
- **HARFORTH, J F**, Middlesbrough **Ref:**YH06422
- **JACKSON, R**, Hartlepool **Ref:**YH07652
- **LAWSON, P A**, Guisborough **Ref:**YH08478
- **STAINSBY GRANGE STUD**, Stockton-on-Tees **Ref:**YH13347

CORNWALL

- **BARRACLOUGH, A & S**, Launceston **Ref:**YH01003
- **BEDFORD, LINDSEY**, St Austell **Ref:**YH01153
- **BURGESS, JOHN**, Callington **Ref:**YH02245
- **CANN, ELIZABETH**, Bude **Ref:**YH02499
- **CHADWICK, R**, Truro **Ref:**YH02703
- **COLE, J J**, Camelford **Ref:**YH03157
- **CORNISH SHIRE HORSE CTRE**, Wadebridge **Ref:**YH03328
- **GOTTS, H J**, Redruth **Ref:**YH05947
- **GRIFFIN, M A**, Liskeard **Ref:**YH06132
- **HALLAGENNA STUD FARM**, Bodmin **Ref:**YH06322
- **HAW STUD**, Truro **Ref:**YH06541
- **HAWKLANDS STUD**, Jacobstow **Ref:**YH06551
- **LANTYAN STUD**, Lostwithiel **Ref:**YH08425
- **LAUREL STUD**, Truro **Ref:**YH08458
- **LE GRICE, T C**, Penzance **Ref:**YH08488
- **LUTEY, R A**, Newquay **Ref:**YH08908
- **MARTIN, JULIET**, Torpoint **Ref:**YH09220
- **MAY ROSE FARM**, Camelford **Ref:**YH09287
- **MEESON, J**, Bodmin **Ref:**YH09444
- **NANTURRIAN STUD FARM**, Falmouth **Ref:**YH10017
- **NORTH CORNWALL ARENA**, Camelford **Ref:**YH10250
- **PASCOE, A L**, Hayle **Ref:**YH10809
- **ROSEVIDNEY ARABIANS**, Penzance **Ref:**YH12111
- **ST LEONARDS EQUESTRIAN CTRE**, Launceston **Ref:**YH13278
- **STEVENS**, Helston **Ref:**YH13441
- **TALL TREES**, Camelford **Ref:**YH13831
- **TOWERWOOD ARABIANS**, St Gennys **Ref:**YH14279
- **TREGAVETHAN MANOR STUD**, Truro **Ref:**YH14365
- **TREGURTHA DOWNS**, Penzance **Ref:**YH14368
- **TREVENA STUD**, Tintagel **Ref:**YH14386
- **TREWITHIAN STUD**, St Austell **Ref:**YH14389
- **TYLANDS ARABIAN STUD**, Camelford **Ref:**YH14519
- **VIGORS, J**, Bodmin **Ref:**YH14715
- **WARREN, P**, Redruth **Ref:**YH14936
- **WASON, J C**, Bodmin **Ref:**YH14956
- **WASON, S E**, Hayle **Ref:**YH14958
- **WIEGERSMA, HENDRIK J**, Penzance **Ref:**YH15394
- **WILLIAMS, R P**, Redruth **Ref:**YH15472
- **WOODLAY**, Liskeard **Ref:**YH15716

COUNTY DURHAM

- **ACRUM LODGE STUD**, Bishop Auckland **Ref:**YH00160
- **BROOM HALL LIVERY YARD**, Durham **Ref:**YH02072
- **CADMAN, S T**, Durham **Ref:**YH02411
- **HEPPLEWOOD STUD**, Consett **Ref:**YH06692
- **HIGHWELL STUD**, Darlington **Ref:**YH06802
- **HODGSON, J**, Bishop Auckland **Ref:**YH06913
- **HYSLOP, J F**, Bishop Auckland **Ref:**YH07362
- **KNITSLEY MILL STUD**, Consett **Ref:**YH08274
- **LAW, DEREK**, Bishop Auckland **Ref:**YH08468
- **MOODY, A D**, Bishop Auckland **Ref:**YH09736
- **NEW MOORS**, Bishop Auckland **Ref:**YH10114
- **NEWLANDS GRANGE MORGANS**, Consett **Ref:**YH10144
- **PARTRIDGE CLOSE STUD**, Lanchester **Ref:**YH10806
- **RAMSHAW, T**, Spennymoor **Ref:**YH11624
- **RAYGILL**, Barnard Castle **Ref:**YH11672
- **STACEY, P A**, Bishop Auckland **Ref:**YH13316
- **WILSON, M**, Burnhope **Ref:**YH15541
- **YOUNG, R**, Consett **Ref:**YH15938

CUMBRIA

- **BARLOW, E**, Workington **Ref:**YH00957
- **BEATTIE, T P**, Carlisle **Ref:**YH01124
- **BEATY, R N**, Kirkby Stephen **Ref:**YH01125
- **BELL, J**, Wigton **Ref:**YH01221
- **BLACK, WENDY**, Windermere **Ref:**YH01473
- **BLAYLOCK, J A**, Brampton **Ref:**YH01529
- **BOUSFIELD, BRYAN**, Kirkby Stephen **Ref:**YH01691
- **BOUSFIELD, C J & J**, Appleby-In-Westmorland **Ref:**YH01692
- **BREED EX EQUINE STUD**, Penrith **Ref:**YH01832
- **BRIERY CLOSE ARABIAN**, Windermere **Ref:**YH01904
- **BRIERY CLOSE ARABIAN STUD**, Windermere **Ref:**YH01905
- **BROWN, J**, Egremont **Ref:**YH02112
- **CRACKENTHORPESTUD**, Appleby-In-Westmorland **Ref:**YH03538
- **CRAYSTON, R**, Egremont **Ref:**YH03581
- **DARGUE, J S**, Appleby-In-Westmorland **Ref:**YH03885
- **DEAN, P**, Brampton **Ref:**YH03994
- **DIXON, JOHN**, Carlisle **Ref:**YH04141
- **EUBANK, A**, Wigton **Ref:**YH04891
- **FELL PONY SOC**, Penrith **Ref:**YH05129
- **FELL PONY SOC**, Penrith **Ref:**YH05130
- **GARDNER, ANNA**, Frizington **Ref:**YH05645
- **GENESIS EQUESTRIAN CTRE/STUD**, Carlisle **Ref:**YH05709
- **HARRISON, T H**, Penrith **Ref:**YH06488
- **HOWARD-CARTER**, Penrith **Ref:**YH07217
- **KERBECK**, Workington **Ref:**YH08096
- **KNOCK SHETLAND PONY STUD**, Appleby-In-Westmorland **Ref:**YH08275
- **LAKELAND ARABIANS**, Cockermouth **Ref:**YH08353
- **LEWNEY, E**, Ulverston **Ref:**YH08598
- **MORGANS, O H M**, Grange-Over-Sands **Ref:**YH09815
- **NAPPA STUD**, Carlisle **Ref:**YH10022
- **NOBLE, W S**, Penrith **Ref:**YH10221
- **ODYSSEY**, Kendal **Ref:**YH10434
- **POTTER, W S**, Shap **Ref:**YH11300
- **RICHARDSON, CLIVE**, Ulverston **Ref:**YH11816
- **SLACK, EVELYN**, Appleby **Ref:**YH12883
- **STAINMORE STUD**, Kirkby Stephen **Ref:**YH13345
- **THOMPSON, T C**, Penrith **Ref:**YH14044
- **TROTTER, D J**, Penrith **Ref:**YH14406
- **WALES, H F**, Penrith **Ref:**YH14839
- **WALLACE, W T**, Cockermouth **Ref:**YH14865
- **WILLIAMSON, G**, Ulverston **Ref:**YH15483
- **WILSON, E M**, Wigton **Ref:**YH15535

DERBYSHIRE

- **ALLEN, D G**, Smalley **Ref:**YH00294
- **ALTON RIDING SCHOOL**, Chesterfield **Ref:**YH00344
- **BERESFORD, H B**, Brackenfield **Ref:**YH01294
- **BROUDEIN STUD FARM**, Swadlincote **Ref:**YH02086
- **BURLEY HILL STUD**, Allestree **Ref:**YH02257
- **C E S**, Ashbourne **Ref:**YH02370
- **CAMM, J A**, Chesterfield **Ref:**YH02482
- **CROOKBANK STUD**, Buxton **Ref:**YH03637
- **DEAN, J G**, Idridgehay **Ref:**YH03992
- **ETCHES, C C**, Ashbourne **Ref:**YH04878
- **FLINT, K M**, Weston Underwood **Ref:**YH05286
- **FRANCIS, K**, Dronfield **Ref:**YH05450
- **HADDON HSE**, Bakewell **Ref:**YH06261
- **HALL FARM STUD**, Snarestone **Ref:**YH06306
- **HAMILTON, C**, Glossop **Ref:**YH06352
- **HANSON, S**, High Peak **Ref:**YH06398
- **HINCKLEY, K A (DR)**, Chesterfield **Ref:**YH06869
- **JEFFERY, S A**, Chesterfield **Ref:**YH07721
- **MATTHEWS, JULIE**, High Peak **Ref:**YH09273
- **MOORVIEW MORGANS**, Dronfield **Ref:**YH09783
- **MOSSCARR STUD**, Buxton **Ref:**YH09867
- **NORTHFIELD FARM**, Buxton **Ref:**YH10312
- **O V WEBSTER & SON**, Ticknall **Ref:**YH10367
- **PALBOURNE STUD**, Ashbourne **Ref:**YH10688
- **RYEBECK STUD**, Buxton **Ref:**YH12300
- **WELLCROFT STUD**, Ashbourne **Ref:**YH15065

DEVON

- **A B B A S STUD**, Ottery St Mary **Ref:**YH00018
- **ANIMAL BEHAVIOUR CONSULTANTS**, Okehampton **Ref:**YH00428
- **ATREE, A L**, Totnes **Ref:**YH00655
- **BARRIBAL**, Okehampton **Ref:**YH01020
- **BECK, M**, Ilfracombe **Ref:**YH01146
- **BLEEKMAN, E & C**, Cullompton **Ref:**YH01533
- **BLOCK, P A**, North Molton **Ref:**YH01543
- **BROOKS, E M**, Bideford **Ref:**YH02064
- **BROWN, YVETTE DU-LANEY**, South Molton **Ref:**YH02133
- **BUDLEIGH SALTERTON**, Budleigh Salterton **Ref:**YH02208
- **C J HORSE TRANSPORT**, Tavistock **Ref:**YH02377
- **CARTER, J**, Dawlish **Ref:**YH02607
- **CHANIN, D**, Exeter **Ref:**YH02733
- **CHICHESTER, T A S**, Colyton **Ref:**YH02848
- **COL, (LT) & STANFORD, E I**, Honiton **Ref:**YH03141

- **COLTON, D W & J K**, Yelverton **Ref:**YH03203
- **COMBE STUD**, Honiton **Ref:**YH03209
- **COSDON DARTMOORS**, Okehampton **Ref:**YH03348
- **CRANLEIGH STUD**, Tiverton **Ref:**YH03566
- **CROSS PK STUD**, Newton Abbott **Ref:**YH03652
- **CROSSWINDS MORGANS**, Branscombe **Ref:**YH03670
- **DIPTFORD STUD**, Totnes **Ref:**YH04126
- **DOWNE FARM**, Tiverton **Ref:**YH04225
- **DUCKHAVEN STUD**, Bideford **Ref:**YH04306
- **DURAL FARM ENTERPRISES**, Holsworthy **Ref:**YH04363
- **EQUITOPIA**, Lynton **Ref:**YH04831
- **FEU, DIANA DU**, Axminster **Ref:**YH05174
- **FIRSEDGE**, Beaworthy **Ref:**YH05228
- **FORKE FARM & STUD**, Tiverton **Ref:**YH05371
- **GAYDEN PALOMINOS**, Beaworthy **Ref:**YH05681
- **GRAHAM, FERGUS**, Newton Abbott **Ref:**YH05966
- **HAIDA DARTMOOR PONY STUD**, Newton Abbot **Ref:**YH06279
- **HALSDON ARABIANS**, Winkleigh **Ref:**YH06337
- **HARVEY, A**, Plymouth **Ref:**YH06512
- **HEARSAY STUD**, Ottery St Mary **Ref:**YH06616
- **HELLINGS (LADY)**, Yelverton **Ref:**YH06654
- **HISLEY STUD**, Newton Abbot **Ref:**YH06885
- **HOLMAN, T J & I M**, Chagford **Ref:**YH06962
- **HOLMEDOWN**, Beaworthy **Ref:**YH06969
- **HONEYSUCKLE FARM**, Newton Abbot **Ref:**YH07017
- **HORSECOMBE VALE ARABIANS**, Cullompton **Ref:**YH07152
- **HORSELAKE ARABIANS**, Exeter **Ref:**YH07158
- **KILEY-WORTHINGTON, M (DR)**, Okehampton **Ref:**YH08133
- **KING, G W & C E**, Exeter **Ref:**YH08180
- **LAKEHEAD PONY STUD**, Yelverton **Ref:**YH08352
- **LAKESIDE PADDOCK STUD**, Ilfracombe **Ref:**YH08358
- **LINDSAY, P M**, Okehampton **Ref:**YH08654
- **LITTLE ASH ECO-FARM & STUD**, Okehampton **Ref:**YH08683
- **LITTLECOMBE SHETLAND STUD**, Seaton **Ref:**YH08706
- **LUNDY ISLAND**, Bideford **Ref:**YH08898
- **MAXIMILLIAN STUD**, North Tawton **Ref:**YH09285
- **MOORTOWN STUD**, Chagford **Ref:**YH09781
- **NARRAMORE STUD**, Newton Abbot **Ref:**YH10023
- **NEW PARK STUD**, Buckfastleigh **Ref:**YH10117
- **NEWTON FERRERS**, Plymouth **Ref:**YH10170
- **OKELEAT STUD**, Okehampton **Ref:**YH10447
- **PIKE, B J**, Cullompton **Ref:**YH11100
- **PROUSE, H W**, Crediton **Ref:**YH11441
- **RATCLIFF, A E**, South Molton **Ref:**YH11648
- **RENE, P**, Tiverton **Ref:**YH11757
- **REXON STUD**, Lewdown **Ref:**YH11773
- **ROTHIEMAY DARTMOORS**, Beaworthy **Ref:**YH12135
- **ROWBERTON STUD**, Winkleigh **Ref:**YH12157
- **SANDERS, M V**, Totnes **Ref:**YH12406
- **SEDGECROFT STUD**, Axminster **Ref:**YH12602
- **SHELLY STUD**, Okehampton **Ref:**YH12703
- **SHERBERTON STUD**, Yelverton **Ref:**YH12718
- **SHILSTONE ROCKS**, Newton Abbot **Ref:**YH12746
- **SKERRATON STUD**, Buckfastleigh **Ref:**YH12870
- **SKINNER, J L & B**, Okehampton **Ref:**YH12876
- **SOUTH WEST REGIONAL**, North Molton **Ref:**YH13117
- **SOUTH YARDE FARM**, South Molton **Ref:**YH13125
- **SOUTHBROOK STUD**, Umberleigh **Ref:**YH13129
- **STAFFORD-CHARLES, R N**, Exeter **Ref:**YH13323
- **TALAWATER QUARTER HORSES**, Yelverton **Ref:**YH13830
- **UPHILL WELSH COBS**, Okehampton **Ref:**YH14600
- **UPPACOTT STUD DARTMOOR**, Newton Abbot **Ref:**YH14605
- **VAUTERHILL STUD**, Umberleigh **Ref:**YH14669
- **VEAN STUD**, Cullompton **Ref:**YH14671
- **WARD, MICHAEL J**, Holsworthy **Ref:**YH14904
- **WESTVIEW STUD**, Holsworthy **Ref:**YH15232
- **WHITTABOROUGH**, Plympton **Ref:**YH15372
- **WISTMAN'S DARTMOOR STUD**, Dartmoor **Ref:**YH15615

DORSET

- **BARBER, R**, Beaminster **Ref:**YH00922
- **BLACKMORE VALE STUD**, Gillingham **Ref:**YH01487
- **CHESNEY, DAVID (DR)**, Dorchester **Ref:**YH02829
- **COLMER STUD**, Bridport **Ref:**YH03193
- **COOMBE, M J**, Weymouth **Ref:**YH03278
- **CRUMPLER, J G**, Beaminster **Ref:**YH03691
- **DORSET HEAVY HORSE CTRE**, Wimborne **Ref:**YH04206
- **DORSET RARE BREEDS CTRE**, Gillingham **Ref:**YH04207
- **EUROPEAN & INT PEDIGREE**, Bridport **Ref:**YH04905
- **FIVE HORSES**, Gillingham **Ref:**YH05252
- **FRAMPTON**, Christchurch **Ref:**YH05441
- **GODDARD, R C**, Sturminster Newton **Ref:**YH05864
- **GORDON-WATSON, M**, Wimborne **Ref:**YH05931
- **GREEN COTTAGE**, Wimborne **Ref:**YH06052
- **HAYCOCK**, Wimborne **Ref:**YH06566
- **JOHNSTON, M**, Blandford Forum **Ref:**YH07846
- **LAIDLAW, L**, Christchurch **Ref:**YH08346
- **LANEHOUSE EQUITATION CTRE**, Weymouth **Ref:**YH08393
- **LANGTON STUD**, Blandford Forum **Ref:**YH08417
- **MARKS, C F**, Sherborne **Ref:**YH09163
- **MARTLEAVES WELSH COBS**, Weymouth **Ref:**YH09230
- **MATHEWS, V**, Sherborne **Ref:**YH09264
- **MISSES, B & MILLER, R**, Shaftesbury **Ref:**YH09660
- **NUTLAND, J**, Wimborne **Ref:**YH10358
- **O Y C**, Wareham **Ref:**YH10369
- **OAKFIELD ICELANDIC HORSES**, Verwood **Ref:**YH10378
- **PITTS FARM STUD**, Sherborne **Ref:**YH11158
- **PLOVERS DARTMOORS**, Wareham **Ref:**YH11179
- **RAWLSBURY FARM**, Dorchester **Ref:**YH11668
- **SCURRELL, M D**, Shaftesbury **Ref:**YH12576
- **SCURRELL, S**, Dorchester **Ref:**YH12577
- **SEYMOUR, A J C (COLONEL)**, Beaminster **Ref:**YH12654
- **SKINNER, ROSS**, Dorchester **Ref:**YH12878
- **SNOOK, L A**, Sturminster Newton **Ref:**YH13034
- **STABLE MINDS**, Ferndown **Ref:**YH13297
- **STAINER, D E**, Christchurch **Ref:**YH13344
- **STARROCK STUD**, Shaftesbury **Ref:**YH13398
- **STOURTON STUD**, Sherborne **Ref:**YH13533
- **TOMBS, A & C**, Wimborne **Ref:**YH14219
- **WARMWELL STUD**, Dorchester **Ref:**YH14924
- **WEST BLAGDON STUD**, Cranborne **Ref:**YH15128
- **WHITE, CHRISTINA**, Weymouth **Ref:**YH15328
- **WHITES FARM STUD**, Wimborne **Ref:**YH15356
- **WIGGETT-COOPER, J**, Kinson **Ref:**YH15396
- **WILLOWAY STUD**, Wimborne **Ref:**YH15506
- **WOODCOATE STUD**, Weymouth **Ref:**YH15676
- **YEOLAND STUD**, Bridport **Ref:**YH15904

ESSEX

- **ACCESS TRAVEL**, Hornchurch **Ref:**YH00139
- **AHMET, M**, Romford **Ref:**YH00205
- **BACKHOUSE, J L & M C**, Frinton-on-Sea **Ref:**YH00769
- **BANKS, P A & C R**, Great Dunmow **Ref:**YH00902
- **BENSON STUD**, Colchester **Ref:**YH01278
- **BRUNDELL, M**, Halstead **Ref:**YH02157
- **CHADWELL FARM**, Halstead **Ref:**YH02702
- **CHAPMAN, K**, Dunmow **Ref:**YH02746
- **COLEMANS FARM STABLES**, Epping **Ref:**YH03165
- **CROFT STUD**, Colchester **Ref:**YH03618
- **D'ARCY STUD**, Maldon **Ref:**YH03881
- **DUDLEY, G (ESQ)**, Brentwood **Ref:**YH04309
- **ELSENHAM STUD**, Bishop's Stortford **Ref:**YH04642
- **GAME, DAVID C**, Ingatestone **Ref:**YH05634
- **GRAFTON FARM STUD**, Romford **Ref:**YH05961
- **GREENLEAF, J R**, Colchester **Ref:**YH06093
- **HALLINGBURY HALL**, Bishop's Stortford **Ref:**YH06331
- **HAYTER, D J**, Stanford-Le-Hope **Ref:**YH06593
- **HILL, DOUGLAS**, Chelmsford **Ref:**YH06828
- **HUNGRY HALL CONNEMARA STUD**, Witham **Ref:**YH07288
- **IMPEY, LINDA**, Chelmsford **Ref:**YH07404
- **LINGWOOD SHIRE PROMOTIONS**, Brentwood **Ref:**YH08663
- **LIONHART MORGANS**, Great Dunmow **Ref:**YH08672
- **MACKENZIE, F**, Saffron Walden **Ref:**YH09000
- **MALYONS STUD**, Hullbridge **Ref:**YH09061
- **MARTINSIDE STUD**, Bishop's Stortford **Ref:**YH09229
- **MERRYDOWN STUD**, Colchester **Ref:**YH09487
- **OCKENDON-DAY, R F**, Dunmow **Ref:**YH10426
- **OXLEY FARM STUD**, Colchester **Ref:**YH10623
- **PHILIPSON, (MAJOR)**, Saffron Walden **Ref:**YH11046
- **ROCHELLES PONY STUD**, Hockley **Ref:**YH12020
- **RUNNINGWELL STUD**, Chelmsford **Ref:**YH12236
- **SCOTT, R J**, Billericay **Ref:**YH12546
- **SEVEN SAINTS RARE BREEDS**, Colchester **Ref:**YH12639
- **SHAHZADA**, Dunmow **Ref:**YH12659
- **SILK, J**, Romford **Ref:**YH12799
- **SMITH, O**, Maldon **Ref:**YH12982
- **SPARTAN STUD**, Romford **Ref:**YH13185
- **STABLES**, High Ongar **Ref:**YH13306
- **STAMBROOK STUD**, Halstead **Ref:**YH13352
- **STAPLEFORD HACKNEY STUD**, Stapleford **Ref:**YH13386
- **WAGER, D**, Maldon **Ref:**YH14821
- **WATTS, S**, Barking **Ref:**YH15007
- **YOUNG, J E**, Stanford-Le-Hope **Ref:**YH15931

GLOUCESTERSHIRE

- **A C BRIDDLECOMBE & SONS**, Newent **Ref:**YH00020
- **ARDMAIR STUD SHETLAND PONIES**, Cheltenham **Ref:**YH00508
- **BARTLETT, W**, Stroud **Ref:**YH01042
- **BEAULIEU PARK STUD**, Coleford **Ref:**YH01129
- **BOLD VENTURE STUD**, Staunton **Ref:**YH01605
- **CHAPLIN, J**, Berkeley **Ref:**YH02742
- **CHARLTON DOWN STUD**, Tetbury **Ref:**YH02765
- **COLLIER, A M**, Lydney **Ref:**YH03179
- **COTSWOLD STUD**, Cheltenham **Ref:**YH03367
- **COTSWOLD STUD**, Moreton In Marsh **Ref:**YH03366

- DALY, PAT, Berkley Ref:YH03852
- DAVIES, W D, Dymock Ref:YH03950
- DAYLESFORD STUD, Moreton-in-Marsh Ref:YH03970
- DENNY, L, Moreton-in-Marsh Ref:YH04063
- DORE, S, Lechlade Ref:YH04199
- ELSON, H & M, Chipping Campden Ref:YH04643
- HANCOX, J & J, Cirencester Ref:YH06376
- HARTPURY CLGE, Gloucester Ref:YH06507
- HENSON, A, Cheltenham Ref:YH06688
- HIGHAM, B, Badminton Ref:YH06770
- HUTCHINS, L, Dursley Ref:YH07334
- JONES, S & T, Cheltenham Ref:YH07930
- LADDENBROOK STUD, Wotton-under-Edge Ref:YH08334
- LIMBURY FARM & STUD, Gloucester Ref:YH08625
- MARSDEN MANOR STUD, Cirencester Ref:YH09181
- MINTY, B, Badminton Ref:YH09656
- NASHEND STUD, Stroud Ref:YH10028
- NICHOLLS, E A, Wotton-under-Edge Ref:YH10183
- PILKINGTON, T D, Cheltenham Ref:YH11107
- POPSTERS, Newnham Ref:YH11276
- ROE, G, Stroud Ref:YH12050
- RUDGEWAY, Longhope Ref:YH12208
- SHIPTON CONNEMARA PONY STUD, Cheltenham Ref:YH12752
- SIMON, (CPT), TOMLINSON C, Tetbury Ref:YH12831
- TWEENHILLS FARM & STUD, Gloucester Ref:YH14508
- WALKER, C, Hucclecote Ref:YH14847
- WALSH, KATHLEEN, Cirencester Ref:YH14878
- WILLESLEY EQUINE CLINIC, Tetbury Ref:YH15430
- WRIGHT, C, Cheltenham Ref:YH15833
- WYCHWOOD STUD, Moreton In Marsh Ref:YH15858

GLOUCESTERSHIRE (SOUTH)

- ARTIFICIAL INSEMINATION CTRE, Kingswood Ref:YH00575
- KENSINGTON ARABIAN STUD, Easter Compton Ref:YH08077
- TUSCANI STUD, Hallen Ref:YH14501

HAMPSHIRE

- ACORN PALOMINO SHETLAND, Lymington Ref:YH00149
- ARNOLD, MATTHEW, Southampton Ref:YH00558
- BAPSH, New Milton Ref:YH00917
- BEALES, K G, Dibden Ref:YH01115
- BIDDESDEN STUD, Andover Ref:YH01396
- BISHOP'S DOWN FARM, Southampton Ref:YH01450
- BLACK, Lymington Ref:YH01460
- BLAKE, M, Petersfield Ref:YH01518
- CHARLES, P, Alton Ref:YH02760
- CLANVILLE STUD, Andover Ref:YH02944
- CLAPHAM, JENNIFER, Hook Ref:YH02946
- CORBETT OVINGTON STUD, Alresford Ref:YH03305
- CORBETT, MARK, Tadley Ref:YH03306
- COURTNEY, S & WALLACE, D, Holbury Ref:YH03510
- CURTIS, J A, Wickham Ref:YH03748
- DANIELS, ALISON, Fareham Ref:YH03872
- DARNTON, A, Lymington Ref:YH03898
- DEANE, A B, Southampton Ref:YH04000
- DEWLAND SHETLAND PONY STUD, Ropley Ref:YH04098
- DIBDIN, W O, Fordingbridge Ref:YH04108
- DOYLE, KEITH, Eversley Ref:YH04248
- DRAPER, M, Lymington Ref:YH04259
- DRURY STUD FARM, Alton Ref:YH04295
- EAST LODGE DONKEY STUD, Waterlooville Ref:YH04478
- ELEDA STABLES, Ringwood Ref:YH04603
- EXTON STUD, Southampton Ref:YH04974
- F NEWMAN & SONS, Alton Ref:YH04997
- FLEETWATER STUD, Lyndhurst Ref:YH05269
- GEBBIE VALLEYS, Lymington Ref:YH05686
- HARMSWORTH FARM, Southampton Ref:YH06446
- HOCKLEY HOUSE STUD, Alresford Ref:YH06905
- HOLDING FALABELLA, Hook Ref:YH06927
- HORSFIELD, Emsworth Ref:YH07185
- KELANNE STUD, Hambleton Ref:YH08038
- KILFORD, Woodlands Ref:YH08134
- KILNCOPSE STUD, Warnford Ref:YH08152
- KNELLER, R & P, Fareham Ref:YH08254
- KNIGHT, R C, Brockenhurst Ref:YH08264
- LESTER, P, Fareham Ref:YH08564
- LITTLETON STUD, Winchester Ref:YH08709
- MADGWICK, PHILIP, Petersfield Ref:YH09024
- MARWELL ZOOLOGICAL PK, Winchester Ref:YH09234
- MAYHEW, BOB, Petersfield Ref:YH09298
- MAYHILL STUD FARM, Southampton Ref:YH09299
- MCGRATH, A, Bishops Waltham Ref:YH09361
- MERRIE STUD, Southampton Ref:YH09480
- MITCHELL, JEFFREY, Fordingbridge Ref:YH09672
- MOMBER, F, Liss Ref:YH09714
- NINEHAM, T & YOUNG, J, Brokenhurst Ref:YH10212
- OLDERNEY STUD, Liss Ref:YH10485
- PAULDARY STUD, Liss Ref:YH10835
- PENARTH STUD, Hook Ref:YH10923
- PERRYS PLACE, Brokenhurst Ref:YH10992
- REDENHAM PK STUD, Andover Ref:YH11708
- RICKMAN, L, Lymington Ref:YH11837
- RUTTER, F G, Upper Swanmore Ref:YH12282
- SAMPSON, EDWARD, Ringwood Ref:YH12398
- SANDILANDS, Petersfield Ref:YH12413
- SAUNDERS, J & S, Fareham Ref:YH12449
- SAYERS, J, Camberley Ref:YH12476
- SEAGRAVE COTTAGE STABLES, Bishops Waltham Ref:YH12588
- SEAVILL, C A S, Petersfield Ref:YH12595
- SHEARING, WENDY, Fareham Ref:YH12690
- SILVER HORSESHOE, Fordingbridge Ref:YH12806
- SIMS, L, Andover Ref:YH12846
- STAMP, P G, Alton Ref:YH13355
- SWAINES HILL STUD, Hook Ref:YH13683
- TEE, B, Lymington Ref:YH13934
- THORNFIELD STUD, Emsworth Ref:YH14067
- TILLYER, J, Calshot Ref:YH14154
- TRICKLEDOWN STUD, Stockbridge Ref:YH14392
- TURVILL, R.G, Alton Ref:YH14498
- TYROS SHETLAND PONY STUD, Freemantle Ref:YH14532
- UPLANDS WELSH COBS, Liss Ref:YH14602
- VESTEY, P E, Alresford Ref:YH14687
- WELCH, FRED, Hook Ref:YH15060
- WHITSBURY MANOR STUD, Fordingbridge Ref:YH15371
- WICKHAM STABLES, Fareham Ref:YH15383
- WILLETT, PETER, Basingstoke Ref:YH15431
- WILSON, B, Ringwood Ref:YH15530
- WRIGHT, E, Ringwood Ref:YH15836
- YOUNG, S C, Waterlooville Ref:YH15939

HEREFORDSHIRE

- BENGOUGH, PIERS (LT COL SIR), Canon Pyon Ref:YH01266
- COUNTY COMPETITION STUD, Bromyard Ref:YH03486
- GREEN, M A, Hereford Ref:YH06070
- J MANNING & SON, Hereford Ref:YH07599
- JONES, N A, Hereford Ref:YH07920
- KNIPE, R F, Hereford Ref:YH08273
- MONNINGTON, Hereford Ref:YH09728
- MRS R H VAUGHAN, Ross-on-Wye Ref:YH09918
- OWENS, P M, Leominster Ref:YH10607
- PHIL TURNER SADDLERY, Hoarwithy Ref:YH11041
- SHEEPCOTE EQUESTRIAN, Hereford Ref:YH12695
- SIMPSON, P B, Leominster Ref:YH12840
- SPRINGTIRE, Ross-on-Wye Ref:YH13261
- TIPTON HALL, Bromyard Ref:YH14183
- WALL, Y L, Bromyard Ref:YH14862

HERTFORDSHIRE

- ALLEN, P A, Ware Ref:YH00300
- ATTEW, P R & S B, Baldock Ref:YH00656
- AYRES, OLIVIA, Hatfield Ref:YH00703
- BARKING STUD, Royston Ref:YH00946
- BARKWAY EQUESTRIAN CTRE, Royston Ref:YH00948
- BEAUMONT AGRCLTRL & STUD FARM, Broxbourne Ref:YH01130
- BEAUMONT STUD, Broxbourne Ref:YH01134
- BIGLEY, L, Eascley Ref:YH01405
- BRIARS STUD, Stevenage Ref:YH01863
- CHILDWICK BURY STUD, St Albans Ref:YH02853
- CONTESSA, Ware Ref:YH03246
- CORMACK, ALEXANDER, Caithness Ref:YH03320
- CROMER STUD, Stevenage Ref:YH03629
- CROUCHFIELD, Ware Ref:YH03674
- DANES ANDALUSIAN STUD, Hertford Ref:YH03867
- DULIEU, B R, Harpenden Ref:YH04325
- FARES STABLES, Royston Ref:YH05051
- FOULDS, ROGER, Bishop's Stortford Ref:YH05405
- FREEMAN, J, Wareside Ref:YH05484
- GEORGE, B, Stapleford Ref:YH05723
- GREENACRES EQUESTRIAN, Harpenden Ref:YH06076
- GREENLAND PARK STUD, Berkhamsted Ref:YH06091
- HELAWI SHETLAND STUD, Wheathampstead Ref:YH06651
- HOLLINGSWORTH, R D, Ware Ref:YH06945
- LEWIS, CLEO, Bushey Ref:YH08588
- MANOR FARM STUD, Royston Ref:YH09108
- MANOR HOUSE FARM STUD, Tring Ref:YH09110
- MCELLIGOTT, P, Berkhamsted Ref:YH09349
- P & N LAMERS, Knebworth Ref:YH10632
- PAGE FARM STUD LIVERY STABLES, Borehamwood Ref:YH10677
- PIPERS STUD, Harpenden Ref:YH11149
- RAMSEY, K, Old Knebworth Ref:YH11622
- RENDENE STUD, Cheshunt Ref:YH11756
- ROBINSON, J D, Hertford Ref:YH11988
- SHENLEY STUD, Radlett Ref:YH12706
- SHEPHERD, N, St Albans Ref:YH12712
- THEOBALDS STUD, Waltham Cross Ref:YH13984
- UPPERWOOD FARM STUD, Hemel Hempstead Ref:YH14609
- WADDINGTON, CHRISTOPHER, Flamstead Ref:YH14808
- WROTHAM PARK STUD, Barnet Ref:YH15849

ISLE OF MAN

- G G H EQUITATION CTRE, Marown Ref:YH05578
- GREAT MEADOW STUD, Castletown Ref:YH06039
- ITTON COURT STUD, The Braaid Ref:YH07531
- JURBY STUD, Jurby Ref:YH07971
- KERRUISH, CHARLES (SIR), Maughold Ref:YH08100
- WITNEY STUD, Douglas Ref:YH15632

ISLE OF WIGHT

- DELYSIA STUD STABLES, Sandown Ref:YH04038
- JONES, E A & C, Newport Ref:YH07895
- MONCK, S (HON), Sandown Ref:YH09720
- RARE BREEDS & WATERFOWL PARK, Ventnor Ref:YH11642

KENT

- **ANGLEY STUD**, Cranbrook **Ref:**YH00411
- **ARDENNES HORSE SOCIETY OF GB**, Sissinghurst **Ref:**YH00505
- **BROOKS, B R**, Sevenoaks **Ref:**YH02063
- **BROSTER, R J**, Dartford **Ref:**YH02085
- **CARRYON QUARTER HORSES**, Ashford **Ref:**YH02603
- **CHESTFIELD MORGANS STABLES**, Whitstable **Ref:**YH02836
- **COATS, A**, New Romney **Ref:**YH03109
- **COBHAMBURY FARM STUD**, Edenbridge **Ref:**YH03115
- **CRUACHAN STUD**, Tonbridge **Ref:**YH03687
- **DANISH HORSES**, Folkestone **Ref:**YH03873
- **EGERDEN FARM STUD**, Ashford **Ref:**YH04591
- **EQUINE SPORT THERAPY**, Edenbridge **Ref:**YH04800
- **EQUINES LIVERIES**, Maidstone **Ref:**YH04809
- **FIRWOOD COURT STUD**, Herne Bay **Ref:**YH05235
- **FIVE OAK GREEN STUD**, Tonbridge **Ref:**YH05253
- **FOX, C**, Staplehurst **Ref:**YH05426
- **HARRIS, R**, Cranbrook **Ref:**YH06480
- **HAYSELDEN**, Cranbrook **Ref:**YH06592
- **HEATH FARM**, Ashford **Ref:**YH06621
- **HEVER CASTLE STUD FARM**, Hever **Ref:**YH06726
- **HORTONS IRISH HORSES**, Canterbury **Ref:**YH07193
- **JENNER, M**, Meopham **Ref:**YH07745
- **JONES, D J**, Staplehurst **Ref:**YH07886
- **KNOWLES BANK STUD**, Tonbridge **Ref:**YH08282
- **KNOWLTON STUD**, Canterbury **Ref:**YH08286
- **LITTLE LONDON HORSES**, Canterbury **Ref:**YH08690
- **LORENZEN, P J**, Dover **Ref:**YH08830
- **MAYWOOD STUD**, Ashford **Ref:**YH09309
- **MINNISMOOR STABLES**, Ashford **Ref:**YH09650
- **NEW BARN STUD**, Eynsford **Ref:**YH10091
- **PENNBRETTI STUD**, Meopham **Ref:**YH10949
- **PEPPERCORN DONKEY STUD**, Langley **Ref:**YH10970
- **PILGRIM STUD**, Rochester **Ref:**YH11105
- **PRIESTWOOD STUD**, Ashford **Ref:**YH11395
- **SHARIQUE ARABIANS**, Rochester **Ref:**YH12675
- **SMITH, K**, Gillingham **Ref:**YH12972
- **STANDEN CONNEMARAS**, Cranbrook **Ref:**YH13359
- **STURGES, A M**, Sevenoaks **Ref:**YH13614
- **WHITBREAD HOP FARM**, Tonbridge **Ref:**YH15294
- **WHITE ROCKS FARM STUD**, Sevenoaks **Ref:**YH15322
- **WILLOW STUD**, Canterbury **Ref:**YH15503
- **WOODLANDS**, Sevenoaks **Ref:**YH15706

LANCASHIRE

- **ABRAM HALL RIDING CTRE**, Wigan **Ref:**YH00134
- **ASOKA**, Worsley **Ref:**YH00625
- **AVERY, S R**, Preston **Ref:**YH00684
- **B1' BRIDGE STUD**, Chorley **Ref:**YH00757
- **BARTON EQUESTRIAN CTRE**, Preston **Ref:**YH01044
- **BOLTON, A**, Chorley **Ref:**YH01611
- **BOUNDARY FARM CARRIAGES**, Wigan **Ref:**YH01677
- **BRANDON, E E (MRS)**, Wigan **Ref:**YH01798
- **BROOKFIELDS**, Ormskirk **Ref:**YH02051
- **BURNT HSE**, Poulton-Le-Fylde **Ref:**YH02275
- **CORNFIELD FARM**, Burnley **Ref:**YH03323
- **DALTON, B**, Ormskirk **Ref:**YH03845
- **DANIEL THWAITES**, Blackburn **Ref:**YH03871
- **DRESSAGE HORSE INT**, Preston **Ref:**YH04266
- **E P ISLES**, Preston **Ref:**YH04420
- **END HSE**, Clitheroe **Ref:**YH04664
- **FLIGHT VIEW**, Poulton-Le-Fylde **Ref:**YH05283
- **GALEA, P C**, Preston **Ref:**YH05613
- **GARDNER, R & D M**, Preston **Ref:**YH05649
- **GLEADHILL HOUSE STUD**, Chorley **Ref:**YH05814
- **GREENWOOD, K**, Colne **Ref:**YH06108
- **HARRISON, L N**, Preston **Ref:**YH06483
- **HIGH TOR ARABIAN STUD**, Blackpool **Ref:**YH06766
- **HOLMESWOOD STUD**, Preston **Ref:**YH06983
- **HOPKINS, K**, Clitheroe **Ref:**YH07053
- **INDOMBA DONKEY STUD**, Blackpool **Ref:**YH07438
- **INGLEGARTH FELL PONIES**, Carnforth **Ref:**YH07448
- **JACKSON, G**, Poulton-Le-Fylde **Ref:**YH07646
- **JOSEPH HOWARD & SON**, Preston **Ref:**YH07943
- **LANDSIDE MORGANS/SADDLEBREDS**, Leigh **Ref:**YH08388
- **MARRIOTT, K**, Blackpool **Ref:**YH09175
- **MARRIOTT, K L**, Preston **Ref:**YH09176
- **MITSON, J E & C**, Colne **Ref:**YH09684
- **MONARCHS HILL STUD**, Westhoughton **Ref:**YH09719
- **MORTIMER, R T**, Leyland **Ref:**YH09847
- **OAKLEIGH STUD FARM**, Preston **Ref:**YH10397
- **OXENDALE**, Blackburn **Ref:**YH10615
- **RIGBY, A C**, Carnforth **Ref:**YH11890
- **ROCHEVALLEY**, Rochdale **Ref:**YH12021
- **SHUTLEWORTH, A**, Carnforth **Ref:**YH12775
- **STRINES FARM STUD**, Oldham **Ref:**YH13578
- **SUNNYBANK STUD**, Burnley **Ref:**YH13644
- **SUTCLIFFE, R**, Darwen **Ref:**YH13666
- **WHALLEY WELSH PONIES & COBS**, Darwen **Ref:**YH15259
- **WILLIAMS, E R**, Littleborough **Ref:**YH15455
- **WITHNELL BARN FARM**, Chorley **Ref:**YH15628
- **WOODS, J**, Skelmersdale **Ref:**YH15737
- **YEALAND STUD**, Yealand Redmayne **Ref:**YH15895

LEICESTERSHIRE

- **AB KETTLEBY STUD**, Melton Mowbray **Ref:**YH00072
- **ALLONBY, D**, Loughborough **Ref:**YH00324
- **BARLEYTHORPE**, Oakham **Ref:**YH00954
- **BROOKSBY EQUESTRIAN CTRE**, Melton Mowbray **Ref:**YH02067
- **CAVELLO PK FARM**, Linford **Ref:**YH02665
- **CENTAUR APPALOOSA STUD**, Leicester **Ref:**YH02681
- **CHARMWOOD ARABIANS**, Leicester **Ref:**YH02771
- **COOMBE, G A**, Melton Mowbray **Ref:**YH03277
- **CRANSWICK**, Melton Mowbray **Ref:**YH03570
- **DAUNT, A N**, Melton Mowbray **Ref:**YH03906
- **DAY, S**, Oakham **Ref:**YH03969
- **GLASS, J**, Loughborough **Ref:**YH05809
- **GLENDALE EQUESTRIAN FEEDS**, Leicester **Ref:**YH05830
- **GOODWIN, S E V**, Ashby-De-La-Zouch **Ref:**YH05913
- **HARCOURT STUD**, Leicester **Ref:**YH06406
- **HILL, N & J A**, Lutterworth **Ref:**YH06832
- **HOSE SHETLAND PONY STUD**, Melton Mowbray **Ref:**YH07194
- **HURST SADDLERS**, Leicester **Ref:**YH07316
- **LINACRE SHETLAND PONIES**, Melton Mowbray **Ref:**YH08639
- **LODGE FARM STUD**, Melton Mowbray **Ref:**YH08770
- **LOUELLA STUD**, Coalville **Ref:**YH08834
- **MILL HOUSE STUD**, Market Harborough **Ref:**YH09578
- **MILLPARK**, Arnesby **Ref:**YH09626
- **QUENBY HALL STUD & STABLES**, Hungarton **Ref:**YH11493
- **RICH, B**, Melton Mowbray **Ref:**YH11799
- **RICH, BARBARA**, Melton Mowbray **Ref:**YH11800
- **ROBERTSON, J P**, Oakham **Ref:**YH11971
- **ROBERTSON, J P**, Oakham **Ref:**YH11970
- **ROTHERWOOD STUD**, Ashby-De-La-Zouch **Ref:**YH12133
- **S L B SUPPLIES**, Coalville **Ref:**YH12329
- **SAGITTARIUS BLOODSTOCK AGENCY**, Melton Mowbray **Ref:**YH12382
- **STANFORD STUD HIGHLAND PONIES**, Loughborough **Ref:**YH13364
- **THORNHILL STUD**, Lutterworth **Ref:**YH14069
- **TOULSON, V**, Melton Mowbray **Ref:**YH14254
- **ULVERSCROFT SHETLAND PONIES**, Ulverscroft **Ref:**YH14557
- **VERE PHILLIPPS**, Loughborough **Ref:**YH14681
- **WALTON FIELDS STUD**, Melton Mowbray **Ref:**YH14889

LINCOLNSHIRE

- **BEECHGROVE STUD**, Louth **Ref:**YH01173
- **BELCHFORD STUD**, Horncastle **Ref:**YH01208
- **BEST/THOROUGHBRED RACING GB**, Louth **Ref:**YH01327
- **BYTHAN CASPIAN STUD**, Grantham **Ref:**YH02352
- **CARR, RENEE**, Scunthorpe **Ref:**YH02573
- **CIRCUS HARLEQUIN**, Spilsby **Ref:**YH02925
- **COLE, B**, Market Rasen **Ref:**YH03151
- **COSGROVE & SON**, Market Rasen **Ref:**YH03350
- **FENBOURNE RIDING SCHOOL**, Bourne **Ref:**YH05137
- **FENJAY STUD**, Boston **Ref:**YH05142
- **FITZSIMMONS, S & G**, Boston **Ref:**YH05250
- **J & M L HENFREY & SON**, Spalding **Ref:**YH07551
- **JOHNSON, TRICIA**, Sleaford **Ref:**YH07841
- **KIRBY HSE STUD & RACING**, Grantham **Ref:**YH08225
- **LIMESTONE STUD**, Gainsborough **Ref:**YH08637
- **MILL VIEW FARM**, Sleaford **Ref:**YH09588
- **MOORE, A J & R A**, Boston **Ref:**YH09753
- **PHILLIPS, W E**, Billinghay **Ref:**YH11067
- **ROBERTS, L**, Spilsby **Ref:**YH11954
- **SAPPERTON STUD & SADDLERY**, Sleaford **Ref:**YH12431
- **SHARP, ELIZABETH**, Grantham **Ref:**YH12678
- **SPICER, R C**, Spalding **Ref:**YH13202
- **TAYLOR, OWEN**, Bourne **Ref:**YH13908
- **TEMPLE TRINE STUD**, Boston **Ref:**YH13948
- **TIMMINS, K**, Sturton By Stow **Ref:**YH14165
- **WARD, S**, Gainsborough **Ref:**YH14907
- **WRIGHT BROS**, Boston **Ref:**YH15829

LINCOLNSHIRE (NORTH EAST)

- **WALKER, J B & V D**, Grimsby **Ref:**YH14851

LINCOLNSHIRE (NORTH)

- **ULCEBY VALE STUD**, Ulceby **Ref:**YH14552

LONDON (GREATER)

- **AAGUS, D**, Chingford **Ref:**YH00069
- **BURR, C A**, Enfield **Ref:**YH02276
- **CENTAUR BLOODSTOCK**, Kingston Upon Thames **Ref:**YH02682
- **COPSEM STUD**, Chessington **Ref:**YH03304
- **DRUMAWHEY**, Uxbridge **Ref:**YH04285
- **HORSE HOUSE**, Northwood **Ref:**YH07123
- **HOWARD, R**, Hillingdon **Ref:**YH07216
- **LEGARD, HILARY**, London **Ref:**YH08534
- **MASTROIANNI, J**, East Sheen **Ref:**YH09255
- **MCCARTNEY, LINDA**, London **Ref:**YH09324
- **PERSIAN BLOODSTOCK**, Feltham **Ref:**YH10995
- **PINNERWOOD ARABIAN STUD**, Hatch End **Ref:**YH11136
- **SUNBEAM HACKNEY STUD**, Enfield **Ref:**YH13641
- **TOTTERIDGE STABLES**, Fulham **Ref:**YH14252
- **WARD, DEAN**, Wimbledon **Ref:**YH14900
- **WILLOWSIDE STUD**, London **Ref:**YH15516

- **WOOD HALL STUD**, Shenley **Ref:**YH15658

MANCHESTER (GREATER)

- **EQUITACK**, Bolton **Ref:**YH04823
- **INGRAM, C & D**, Manchester **Ref:**YH07453
- **MATCHMOOR RIDING CTRE**, Bolton **Ref:**YH09257
- **MATHER, ALISON**, Bolton **Ref:**YH09258
- **NEW HILL FARM**, Manchester **Ref:**YH10107
- **SYDDALL, G**, Bolton **Ref:**YH13720

MERSEYSIDE

- **SPENCER, J E**, Southport **Ref:**YH13200
- **SPRINGTIME DARTMOORS**, Liverpool **Ref:**YH13260
- **WADACRE WARMBLOOD STUD**, Melling **Ref:**YH14805

MIDLANDS (WEST)

- **BEAMAN, J**, Brierley Hill **Ref:**YH01116
- **COLLIER, KATHY**, Romsley **Ref:**YH03180
- **COTTERILL, B, C & A**, Sutton Coldfield **Ref:**YH03383
- **EARLSDON STUD**, Coventry **Ref:**YH04453
- **FOXHILLS**, Walsall **Ref:**YH05435
- **HAZEL FARM**, Solihull **Ref:**YH06599
- **HORSEPOWER COVENTRY**, Coventry **Ref:**YH07164
- **HOVINGTON, S**, Wolverhampton **Ref:**YH07214
- **JEFFS, H S**, Wolverhampton **Ref:**YH07726
- **NEWCOMBE & EAST**, Brownhills **Ref:**YH10131
- **NORTH WORCESTERSHIRE**, Halesowen **Ref:**YH10287
- **NORTHALL, S & M**, Dudley **Ref:**YH10289
- **OVERTON HORSE DEALER**, Coventry **Ref:**YH10595
- **PENORCHARDS FARM**, Halesowen **Ref:**YH10957
- **POOLE, JOHN**, Alvechurch **Ref:**YH11265
- **PUGH, L**, Coventry **Ref:**YH11451
- **SEECHEM EQUESTRIAN CTRE**, Birmingham **Ref:**YH12607
- **SHAKESPEARE, B**, Brierley Hill **Ref:**YH12661
- **SUNRAY STUD**, Walsall **Ref:**YH13651

NORFOLK

- **AL MANZA STUD**, King's Lynn **Ref:**YH00233
- **BANHAM, B D**, Norwich **Ref:**YH00884
- **BATES, D A**, King's Lynn **Ref:**YH01067
- **BERGH APTON STUD**, Norwich **Ref:**YH01297
- **BLOOM, M J**, Wymondham **Ref:**YH01552
- **BROWN ARABIANS**, Norwich **Ref:**YH02091
- **CHURCH FARM STUD**, Wymondham **Ref:**YH02901
- **COUSINS, MAURICE C**, King's Lynn **Ref:**YH03513
- **CULLINGHURST ARABIAN STUD**, Attleborough **Ref:**YH03706
- **DALTON, R**, Dereham **Ref:**YH03849
- **GRANE STUD**, Norwich **Ref:**YH05985
- **HEARNESBROOK CONNEMARA STUD**, Wymondham **Ref:**YH06615
- **HEATHER ARABIAN RACING STUD**, Norwich **Ref:**YH06625
- **HEATHLANDS FARMS**, King's Lynn **Ref:**YH06633
- **HOLMAN, A**, Aylsham **Ref:**YH06960
- **LINGE, NOEL A**, Hunstanton **Ref:**YH08658
- **MANNING, L**, Norwich **Ref:**YH09087
- **MASON, D G**, Thetford **Ref:**YH09241
- **MAYWAY**, Thetford **Ref:**YH09308
- **MCINNES, SKINNER & BROADHEAD**, Wymondham **Ref:**YH09374
- **MILLA LAUQUEN ARABIAN STUD**, Norwich **Ref:**YH09589
- **MILLFIELDS CONNEMARA**, Diss **Ref:**YH09618
- **NORFOLK SHIRE HORSE CTRE**, Cromer **Ref:**YH10232
- **OLD BUCKENHAM STUD**, Attleborough **Ref:**YH10453
- **OXNEAD HAFLINGER STUD**, Norwich **Ref:**YH10624
- **PEACOCK FARMS**, Wymondham **Ref:**YH10859
- **PESTELL, S**, Norwich **Ref:**YH10999
- **R COOKE & SONS**, Great Yarmouth **Ref:**YH11521
- **ROYAL STUDS**, Sandringham **Ref:**YH12195
- **SCOTTOW FARMS**, Norwich **Ref:**YH12560
- **SHADWELL ESTATE**, Thetford **Ref:**YH12656
- **SHORTIS, VICKI**, Old Costessey **Ref:**YH12762
- **SPELLBOUND SADDLEBREDS**, Diss **Ref:**YH13193
- **ST MARGRETS STUD**, King's Lynn **Ref:**YH13281
- **SUTTON ARABIAN STUD**, Norwich **Ref:**YH13668
- **WALCIS FARM STUD**, Norwich **Ref:**YH14836
- **WATTLEFIELD FARM STUD**, Wymondham **Ref:**YH15002
- **WILLIAMSON, D J**, King's Lynn **Ref:**YH15482
- **WINGFIELD, W M R**, Diss **Ref:**YH15585
- **WOLFERTON STUD**, King's Lynn **Ref:**YH15649
- **WRETHAM STUD**, Thetford **Ref:**YH15825

NORTHAMPTONSHIRE

- **ADAMS, VAL**, Corby **Ref:**YH00173
- **ADSTONE LODGE STUD**, Towcester **Ref:**YH00190
- **BOWERS, RICHARD**, Northampton **Ref:**YH01708
- **BRITISH HANOVERIAN HORSE SOC**, Sywell **Ref:**YH01944
- **CLARK, G**, Kettering **Ref:**YH02963
- **CRANFORD HALL STUD**, Kettering **Ref:**YH03563
- **ELMS STUD**, Northampton **Ref:**YH04639
- **EYDON HALL FARM**, Daventry **Ref:**YH04975
- **FUNNELL, JOHN**, Daventry **Ref:**YH05538
- **GLEN ANDRED STUD**, Northampton **Ref:**YH05824
- **HEPWORTH, ROBIN & SHIRLEY**, Towcester **Ref:**YH06694
- **HIGH HORSES**, Daventry **Ref:**YH06761
- **HORSE INDEX**, Silverstone **Ref:**YH07125
- **PERCIVAL, R G**, Northampton **Ref:**YH10973
- **POPLARS ARABIAN STUD**, Rothersthorpe **Ref:**YH11272
- **RATHBONE, K**, Ravensthorpe **Ref:**YH11654
- **SHRIGLEY-PENNA, JOHN**, Crick **Ref:**YH12769
- **SHUCKBURGH HSE RIDING CTRE**, Naseby **Ref:**YH12772
- **SMITH, S J**, Towcester **Ref:**YH12999
- **ST ANDREW STUD**, Kettering **Ref:**YH13270
- **SULBY HALL**, Northampton **Ref:**YH13628
- **T H BLETSOE & SON**, Kettering **Ref:**YH13742
- **THORPE MALSOR STUD**, Kettering **Ref:**YH14093
- **WAKEFIELD LODGE ESTATE**, Towcester **Ref:**YH14831
- **WILBY DARTMOOR PONIES**, Wellingborough **Ref:**YH15403

NORTHUMBERLAND

- **BRATTON STUD**, Alnwick **Ref:**YH01817
- **BREWIS, RHONA**, Belford **Ref:**YH01854
- **CHARLES, D C**, Stocksfield **Ref:**YH02759
- **CHARLTON, R B**, Hexham **Ref:**YH02766
- **EASTON, N**, Blyth **Ref:**YH04515
- **EQUILINK**, Alnwick **Ref:**YH04751
- **FELL PONY SOC**, Morpeth **Ref:**YH05131
- **GOLDENMOOR**, Alnwick **Ref:**YH05885
- **JEFFREY, T E**, Alnwick **Ref:**YH07725
- **NORTH NORTHUMBERLAND**, Denwick **Ref:**YH10275
- **REIVER ANDALUSIANS**, Belford **Ref:**YH11750

NOTTINGHAMSHIRE

- **ASHLEY, J**, Teversal **Ref:**YH00607
- **BROOMSIDE STUD**, Calverton **Ref:**YH02082
- **BRUNT, B**, Newark **Ref:**YH02160
- **EARL, C L**, Cropwell Butler **Ref:**YH04451
- **FAIRBURN, E J C**, Woodthorpe **Ref:**YH05016
- **GEE, M P**, Worksop **Ref:**YH05691
- **JAMES, K & S**, Nottingham **Ref:**YH07682
- **MALLENDER BROS**, Worksop **Ref:**YH09051
- **MATTHEWS, K L**, Retford **Ref:**YH09274
- **ROBINSON, G**, Newark **Ref:**YH11987
- **SAYWELL, M J**, Retford **Ref:**YH12479
- **SPRING WOOD FARM**, Sutton-In-Ashfield **Ref:**YH13247
- **WHATTON MANOR STUD**, Notts **Ref:**YH15267
- **WORKSOP MANOR STUD**, Worksop **Ref:**YH15782
- **WRIGHT, R G**, Retford **Ref:**YH15839

OXFORDSHIRE

- **ALVESCOT STUD**, Carterton **Ref:**YH00349
- **ASTON HSE STUD**, Watlington **Ref:**YH00638
- **ATTINGTON STUD**, Thame **Ref:**YH00657
- **BELLENIE, NICKI**, Woodstock **Ref:**YH01236
- **BLACKER, P & S**, Bampton **Ref:**YH01482
- **BLENHEIM STUD**, Postcombe **Ref:**YH01537
- **BRACKENHILL STUD**, Henley-on-Thames **Ref:**YH01739
- **BRICKELL FARMS**, Witney **Ref:**YH01865
- **BROADSTONE STUD**, Banbury **Ref:**YH02002
- **CONDUIT FARM STUD**, Chipping Norton **Ref:**YH03226
- **DARLEY STUD MNGMT**, Didcot **Ref:**YH03889
- **DECKER, P**, Henley-on-Thames **Ref:**YH04011
- **DURFEE WARM BLOOD STUD**, Witney **Ref:**YH04369
- **FAWLEY STUD**, Wantage **Ref:**YH05110
- **GITTINS, STEPHEN**, Chipping Norton **Ref:**YH05800
- **GODINGTON STUD**, Bicester **Ref:**YH05867
- **GOFF, J**, Oxford **Ref:**YH05872
- **GRANBY STUD**, Witney **Ref:**YH05982
- **HENMAN, C**, Kidlington **Ref:**YH06676
- **KIRTLINGTON PARK POLO SCHOOL**, Kidlington **Ref:**YH08241
- **KIRTLINGTON STUD**, Kidlington **Ref:**YH08243
- **LOCKINGE PONY STUD**, Wantage **Ref:**YH08759
- **LODGE FARM ARABIAN STUD**, Oxford **Ref:**YH08768
- **MARSTON STUD**, Banbury **Ref:**YH09209
- **MERTON STUD**, Bicester **Ref:**YH09492
- **MIALL, T C & J F**, Bicester **Ref:**YH09509
- **NIXEY, M**, Great Milton **Ref:**YH10215
- **ORCHARD FARM STUD**, Abingdon **Ref:**YH10532
- **ROUNDHILLS STUD**, Bicester **Ref:**YH12142
- **SHEEPHOUSE STUD**, Henley-on-Thames **Ref:**YH12698
- **SHUTFORD STUD**, Banbury **Ref:**YH12774
- **SKEWPIE COTTAGE STUD**, Stadhampton **Ref:**YH12872
- **SMITH, THOMAS**, Banbury **Ref:**YH13002
- **SPINWAY STUD**, Leafield **Ref:**YH13210
- **TURVILLE VALLEY**, Henley-on-Thames **Ref:**YH14499
- **VENTURENEED**, Wallingford **Ref:**YH14679
- **VICTOR-SMITH, C I**, Henley-on-Thames **Ref:**YH14712
- **WADLEY MANOR STABLES**, Faringdon **Ref:**YH14818
- **WARDINGTON STUD FARM**, Banbury **Ref:**YH14913
- **WERN FRANK STUD**, Wantage **Ref:**YH15113

RUTLAND

- **ALLEXTON EQUESTRIAN**, Oakham **Ref:**YH00311
- **BARROW STABLES**, Oakham **Ref:**YH01030
- **MOONSHINE FARM**, Oakham **Ref:**YH09739
- **WOODSTOCK QUARTER HORSES**, Bisbrooke **Ref:**YH15750

SHROPSHIRE

- **BARRATT, L J**, Oswestry **Ref:**YH01009
- **BEARSTONE STUD**, Market Drayton **Ref:**YH01122
- **BLAKELEY STUD FARM**, Shrewsbury **Ref:**YH01519

- **BOTTOMLEY, E**, Shrewsbury **Ref:**YH01668
- **BROWNING, R P**, Minsterley **Ref:**YH02140
- **CAMPBELL-DIXON, D F A**, Church Stretton **Ref:**YH02489
- **CAPITALL STUD**, Oswestry **Ref:**YH02521
- **CENTENNIAL ASIL ARABIAN STUD**, Shrewsbury **Ref:**YH02686
- **CRANN, P F**, Bridgnorth **Ref:**YH03568
- **ELLIS, N**, Ellesmere **Ref:**YH04627
- **EQUEST**, Market Drayton **Ref:**YH04688
- **FARRALL, C A**, Ellesmere **Ref:**YH05084
- **GLAZELEY STUD**, Bridgnorth **Ref:**YH05812
- **GREGORY, Y**, Church Stretton **Ref:**YH06118
- **HAMAR, ROSITA J**, Bishops Castle **Ref:**YH06343
- **HANCOCK, J & V**, Telford **Ref:**YH06375
- **HARDHAM, M G**, Minsterley **Ref:**YH06410
- **HATTON STUD**, Telford **Ref:**YH06534
- **HELSHAW GRANGE STUD**, Market Drayton **Ref:**YH06656
- **HICKS, A F**, Whitchurch **Ref:**YH06744
- **HOCKENHULL, D**, Ellesmere **Ref:**YH06901
- **HORN, CAMILLA**, Bucknell **Ref:**YH07072
- **HUGHES, B E**, Oswestry **Ref:**YH07260
- **LILLESHALL EQUESTRIAN CTRE**, Newport **Ref:**YH08620
- **LLOYD FARM STUD**, Market Drayton **Ref:**YH08733
- **MISTHAVEN**, Tern Hill **Ref:**YH09661
- **MORRIS, V**, Telford **Ref:**YH09836
- **NATIONAL FOALING BANK**, Newport **Ref:**YH10037
- **NIELD, G E**, Whitchurch **Ref:**YH10203
- **P G L YOUNG ADVENTURE CTRE**, Shrewsbury **Ref:**YH10641
- **PEARCE, P**, Telford **Ref:**YH10875
- **TICKLERTON STUD**, Church Stretton **Ref:**YH14128
- **TREMLOWS HALL STUD**, Whitchurch **Ref:**YH14371
- **TYRLEY CASTLE STUD**, Market Drayton **Ref:**YH14530
- **WACKLEY LODGE FARM**, Shrewsbury **Ref:**YH14804
- **WEBSTER, J & M**, Craven Arms **Ref:**YH15039
- **WOOD FARM STUD**, Wellington **Ref:**YH15657
- **YOUNG ERIC**, Church Stretton **Ref:**YH15925

SOMERSET

- **ANDREWS, R T**, Dulverton **Ref:**YH00402
- **BANWELL, D**, Highbridge **Ref:**YH00914
- **BARFORD PK RACING STABLES**, Bridgwater **Ref:**YH00932
- **BEECH TREE STUD & FARM**, Shepton Mallet **Ref:**YH01166
- **BINCOMBE STUD**, Bridgwater **Ref:**YH01419
- **BRAKE, J R**, Chard **Ref:**YH01782
- **BRAKE, V**, Ilminster **Ref:**YH01784
- **BRENDON HILL**, Watchet **Ref:**YH01836
- **BRITTON HOUSE STUD**, Crewkerne **Ref:**YH01983
- **BRYER, J**, Yeovil **Ref:**YH02170
- **BURRINGTON, A W**, Minehead **Ref:**YH02280
- **CARR-EVANS, JEANETTE**, Wincanton **Ref:**YH02579
- **DUNKERY**, Minehead **Ref:**YH04343
- **EIGER SHETLANDS**, Yeovil **Ref:**YH04597
- **ENGLISH CONNEMARA PONY SOC**, Dulverton **Ref:**YH04674
- **EXMOOR NATIONAL PK AUTHORITY**, Dulverton **Ref:**YH04968
- **FILLINGHAM, T & P**, Dulverton **Ref:**YH05203
- **GIBSON, ANNETTE**, Wedmore **Ref:**YH05747
- **GREENLEAF, P J**, Chard **Ref:**YH06094
- **GROOME, M**, Shepton Mallet **Ref:**YH06153
- **HAWKES, JACK**, Minehead **Ref:**YH06545
- **HONEYBALL, J**, Bridgwater **Ref:**YH07011
- **HONEYPOT**, Minehead **Ref:**YH07016
- **KNIGHTONCOMBE EXMOOR**, Minehead **Ref:**YH08267
- **MCCREERY, R J**, Templecombe **Ref:**YH09338
- **MILLHOUSE EQUESTRIAN CTRE**, Taunton **Ref:**YH09620
- **MILLSLADE FARM STUD**, Bridgwater **Ref:**YH09636
- **MINEHEAD HARRIERS**, Minehead **Ref:**YH09648
- **POCOCK, R E**, Bridgwater **Ref:**YH11188
- **PRETTY OAK FARM**, Chard **Ref:**YH11371
- **ROBOROUGH, (LORD)**, Wellington **Ref:**YH12009
- **RODGROVE STUD EQUESTRIAN CTRE**, Wincanton **Ref:**YH12048
- **SCOTT, D D**, Minehead **Ref:**YH12540
- **STEPLEY STUD**, Taunton **Ref:**YH13428
- **SUTTON OAKS**, Bridgwater **Ref:**YH13675
- **TAWBITTS EXMOORS**, Minehead **Ref:**YH13888
- **TAYLOR, W J D**, Chard **Ref:**YH13914
- **TURNER, CORINNA**, Wincanton **Ref:**YH14476
- **VILMORAY LODGE STUD**, Bruton **Ref:**YH14722
- **WARREN, A H**, Crewkerne **Ref:**YH14935
- **WESTERN, J**, Minehead **Ref:**YH15209
- **WILLIAMS, A R**, Minehead **Ref:**YH15446

SOMERSET (NORTH)

- **CTRE RIDING SCHOOL**, Weston-Super-Mare **Ref:**YH03696
- **CTRE RIDING SCHOOL**, Weston-Super-Mare **Ref:**YH03695
- **DISNEY, SUE**, Banwell **Ref:**YH04131
- **GIBSON, E**, Blagdon **Ref:**YH05748
- **HILLYER, M**, Weston-Super-Mare **Ref:**YH06861

STAFFORDSHIRE

- **ABBEYFIELD SHETLAND STUD**, Milford **Ref:**YH00094
- **ALSOP, D N**, Burton-on-Trent **Ref:**YH00338
- **BASKEYFIELD, K & A**, Stoke-on-Trent **Ref:**YH01055
- **BOHEMIAN ARABIAN STUD**, Stoke-on-Trent **Ref:**YH01599
- **BORLAND, J S**, Lichfield **Ref:**YH01650
- **BOWDLER, T**, Stafford **Ref:**YH01697
- **BROOKES, JOSEPHINE**, Stafford **Ref:**YH02045
- **DOBBINS DINER**, Tamworth **Ref:**YH04151
- **EMBLA STUD**, Gnosall **Ref:**YH04649
- **FAIRLEY STUD**, Lichfield **Ref:**YH05025
- **FARLEY HALL STUD**, Stoke-on-Trent **Ref:**YH05054
- **FIELD, L E**, Tean **Ref:**YH05187
- **GALLEY, G**, Leek **Ref:**YH05620
- **HANBURY PK STUD**, Burton-on-Trent **Ref:**YH06373
- **HARNOR STUD**, Leek **Ref:**YH06448
- **INTERNATIONAL PERFORMANCE**, Brewde **Ref:**YH07477
- **JOHNSON, P R**, Cannock **Ref:**YH07832
- **JOHNSON, R C**, Uttoxeter **Ref:**YH07835
- **LADYMOOR GATE**, Stoke-on-Trent **Ref:**YH08339
- **LONG, D J**, Burton-on-Trent **Ref:**YH08802
- **LONGDON STUD**, Rugeley **Ref:**YH08808
- **NOTT, PHILIP GEOFFREY**, Rugeley **Ref:**YH10339
- **PINTOFIELDS**, Stoke-on-Trent **Ref:**YH11140
- **PIONEER STUD**, Stoke-on-Trent **Ref:**YH11143
- **RADMORE LANE FARM**, Gnosall **Ref:**YH11598
- **SCOTT, B G**, Stafford **Ref:**YH12538
- **SHAW, L & D**, Dunston **Ref:**YH12682
- **TISDALE, DEREK**, Yoxhall **Ref:**YH14186
- **WASS, A J**, Stoke-on-Trent **Ref:**YH14959
- **WINTER, LINDA**, Stoke-on-Trent **Ref:**YH15594
- **YELD BANK ARABIAN STUD**, Knightley **Ref:**YH15899
- **YSWAIN WELSH COBS**, Cannock **Ref:**YH15949

SUFFOLK

- **ADAM, N**, Newmarket **Ref:**YH00164
- **ALBINS, D J**, Ipswich **Ref:**YH00246
- **ARBON, D W**, Woodbridge **Ref:**YH00495
- **ATKIN, BARRY**, Chevington **Ref:**YH00646
- **BALLYMORE CONNEMARA STUD**, New Market **Ref:**YH00871
- **BANSTEAD MANOR STUD**, Newmarket **Ref:**YH00909
- **BARTON STUD**, Bury St Edmunds **Ref:**YH01046
- **BEECH HOUSE STUD**, Newmarket **Ref:**YH01164
- **BLACKSMITHS SHOP**, Woodbridge **Ref:**YH01496
- **BOTTISHAM HEATH STUD**, Newmarket **Ref:**YH01667
- **BOXTED HALL STUD**, Bury St Edmunds **Ref:**YH01728
- **BRINKLEY STUD**, Newmarket **Ref:**YH01916
- **BROOK STUD**, Newmarket **Ref:**YH02039
- **CARRALEIGH DARTMOORS**, Stowmarket **Ref:**YH02576
- **CARRIAGEWAY STABLES**, Newmarket **Ref:**YH02584
- **CEDAR TREE STUD**, Newmarket **Ref:**YH02675
- **CHERRY-DOWNS BLOODSTOCK**, Newmarket **Ref:**YH02820
- **CHEVELEY PK**, Newmarket **Ref:**YH02842
- **CHEVELEY PK STUD**, Newmarket **Ref:**YH02843
- **CHEVINGTON STUD**, Bury St Edmunds **Ref:**YH02844
- **CLARK, ROGER J**, Ipswich **Ref:**YH02966
- **COWELL, ROBERT**, Newmarket **Ref:**YH03524
- **DARLEY STUD MNGMT**, Newmarket **Ref:**YH03890
- **DELTA BLOOD STOCK MNGMT**, Newmarket **Ref:**YH04035
- **DUKES STUD**, Newmarket **Ref:**YH04324
- **DUNCHURCH LODGE STUD**, Newmarket **Ref:**YH04335
- **EALSDON FARMS**, Newmarket **Ref:**YH04445
- **EGERTON STUD FARM**, Newmarket **Ref:**YH04592
- **ETHERIDGE, A G**, Saxmundham **Ref:**YH04881
- **EXECUTIVE STUD**, Newmarket **Ref:**YH04964
- **FAIRFIELD BLOODSTOCK**, Woodbridge **Ref:**YH05017
- **FARMERS HILL STUD**, Newmarket **Ref:**YH05062
- **FITTOCKS STUD**, Newmarket **Ref:**YH05246
- **FLEMING, J W**, Woodbridge **Ref:**YH05271
- **FREEDOM FARM**, Woodbridge **Ref:**YH05481
- **FREEDOM FARM STUD**, Newmarket **Ref:**YH05482
- **GAZELEY STUD FARM**, Newmarket **Ref:**YH05684
- **GELLER, J S**, Ipswich **Ref:**YH05695
- **GENESIS GREEN STUD**, Newmarket **Ref:**YH05710
- **GILLINGS, B G**, Clare **Ref:**YH05786
- **GLEBE STUD**, Newmarket **Ref:**YH05820
- **GOODE, WILLIAM J M**, Sudbury **Ref:**YH05901
- **GRAYSON STUD**, Lowestoft **Ref:**YH06035
- **H M P HOLLESLEY BAY COLONY**, Woodbridge **Ref:**YH06229
- **HALL, M J**, Newmarket **Ref:**YH06317
- **HALLETT, J P**, Woodbridge **Ref:**YH06329
- **HARDING, J**, Sudbury **Ref:**YH06412
- **HERITAGE COAST STUD**, Woodbridge **Ref:**YH06703
- **HERON STREAM STUD**, Saxmundham **Ref:**YH06712
- **HERRINGSWELL MANOR STUD**, Bury St Edmunds **Ref:**YH06718
- **JILL LAMB BLOODSTOCK**, Newmarket **Ref:**YH07767
- **JOHN SNOWDON HARNESS MAKER**, Woodbridge **Ref:**YH07813
- **KAZMIRA**, Harleston **Ref:**YH08012
- **KEENELAND ASS**, Newmarket **Ref:**YH08029
- **KIRBY, M J**, Newmarket **Ref:**YH08229
- **LANWADES STUD**, Newmarket **Ref:**YH08426
- **LAVENHAM HALL LIVERIES**, Lavenham **Ref:**YH08462

LINKWOOD EQUESTIAN, Bury St Edmunds Ref:YH08665
LONGHOLES STUD, Newmarket Ref:YH08812
LORDSHIP STUD, Newmarket Ref:YH08829
MARLAND, Ipswich Ref:YH09168
MIDDLE PARK STUD, Newmarket Ref:YH09536
MILLET, Newmarket Ref:YH09616
MOONWIND ARABIANS, Saxmundham Ref:YH09740
MORLEY, P C, Ipswich Ref:YH09820
NEW ENGLAND STUD FARM, Newmarket Ref:YH10092
NORTHMORE STUD, Newmarket Ref:YH10316
OAKLEY, N W, Bury St Edmunds Ref:YH10399
OLD SUFFOLK STUD, Sudbury Ref:YH10478
ORWELL ARENA, Ipswich Ref:YH10556
P ADAMS & SONS, Felixstowe Ref:YH10633
PADFIELD, M G B, Sudbury Ref:YH10676
PARKLAND SADDLEBREDS, Ipswich Ref:YH10768
PAUL, G W, Ipswich Ref:YH10833
PHILLIPS, J G, Sudbury Ref:YH11058
PIGGOTT, R L, Stowmarket Ref:YH11098
PINE WOOD STUD, Newmarket Ref:YH11123
PLANTATION STUD, Newmarket Ref:YH11163
RED HSE STUD, Newmarket Ref:YH11700
ROLFE, R, Bury St Edmunds Ref:YH12067
RUTLAND STUD, Newmarket Ref:YH12280
SIDE HILL STUD, Newmarket Ref:YH12784
SMITH, D, Newmarket Ref:YH12948
SNAILWELL STUD, Newmarket Ref:YH13027
ST SIMONS STUD, Newmarket Ref:YH13284
STANLEY ESTATE & STUD, Newmarket Ref:YH13368
STETCHWORTH PARK STUD, Newmarket Ref:YH13437
SWINFORD PADDOCK STUD, Newmarket Ref:YH13712
TALLY HO STUD, Bury St Edmunds Ref:YH13843
TOLLEMACHE, M H, Ipswich Ref:YH14208
VALLEY FARM, Woodbridge Ref:YH14651
VIVIAN PRATT, Felixstowe Ref:YH14737
WARREN PARK STUD, Newmarket Ref:YH14933
WATER FARM STUD, Ipswich Ref:YH14963
WHEELERS PONY STUD, Saxmundham Ref:YH15275
WILLINGHAM HSE STUD, Newmarket Ref:YH15489
WOODDITTON STUD, Newmarket Ref:YH15682
WOODWARD, G A, Stowmarket Ref:YH15756
WYCK HALL STUD, Newmarket Ref:YH15859

SURREY

AL WAHA ARABIAN STUD, Haslemere Ref:YH00234
AL WAHA ARABIAN STUD, Haslemere Ref:YH00235
BACHMAN, T E, Farnham Ref:YH00767
BADEN POWELL STUD, Guildford Ref:YH00775
BOYD & PARTNERS, Staines Ref:YH01731
BUNTING, STANLEY G, Lingfield Ref:YH02228
BURNINGFOLD MANOR STUD FARM, Godalming Ref:YH02266
CASPIAN HORSE, Virginia Water Ref:YH02618
COCUM STUD, Godalming Ref:YH03130
COE, NICOLA, Dorking Ref:YH03133
CROSS FOXES STUD, Cobham Ref:YH03645
DE GRAAFF TRAILERS, Woking Ref:YH03977
EQUARIUS, New Malden Ref:YH04686
FARROW, G M, Richmond Ref:YH05097
FLEETMEAD STUD, Lingfield Ref:YH05268
FURZE HILL FARM & STUD, Farnham Ref:YH05554
GATLAND, J, Merstham Ref:YH05677
GEORGIAN STUD, Shamley Green Ref:YH05728
GLENFIELDS STUD, Chiddingfold Ref:YH05835
GUBBY, B, Bagshot Ref:YH06180
HAZELWOOD STUD, Warlingham Ref:YH06604
HENNESSEY, M P, Chertsey Ref:YH06677
HITCHINGS, PETER D, Godstone Ref:YH06887
HUSSEY, P & L, Dorking Ref:YH07326
LEA, SUE, Chobham Ref:YH08495
MARYAN, M, Charlwood Ref:YH09236
MASON, G, Haslemere Ref:YH09243
MERRYMAN, W & M, Staines Ref:YH09489
NORTH MUNSTEAD STUD, Godalming Ref:YH10272
OLDENCRAIG EQUESTRIAN CTRE, Lingfield Ref:YH10484
PAGE, S, Haslemere Ref:YH10683
PLUMTREE, R T J, New Malden Ref:YH11186
POWER, DURGA, Dorking Ref:YH11325
POYNTERS, Cobham Ref:YH11330
RIETVELD, M, Dorking Ref:YH11889
STEVENS STUD, Guildford Ref:YH13442
TILLEY, PAT, Woking Ref:YH14152
TRIPLE BAR RIDING CTRE, Dorking Ref:YH14400
TURNER, M, Dorking Ref:YH14485
UMM QARN MANAGEMENT, Lingfield Ref:YH14559
UPLANDS STUD, Godalming Ref:YH14601
WINGFIELD STUD, Tadworth Ref:YH15584
WISE, Alfold Ref:YH15607
WOODCOTE FARM, West Horsley Ref:YH15678
WOODCOTE STUD, Epsom Ref:YH15679
YORK, RAY, Cobham Ref:YH15918

SUSSEX (EAST)

AKEHURST STUD, Bexhill-on-Sea Ref:YH00231
ASA OF GB, Alfriston Ref:YH00580
BOLTWOOD STUD, Lewes Ref:YH01614
BROAD REED MORGANS, Mayfield Ref:YH01989
BROWNBREAD STUD, Battle Ref:YH02135
BURT, S, Hartfield Ref:YH02288
CHURCH FARM & STUD, Lewes Ref:YH02896
EQUUS ELITE, Wadhurst Ref:YH04838
ERIMUS STUD, Robertsbridge Ref:YH04848
ESCHEATLANDS STUD, Rye Ref:YH04858
FIELDWICK, T A, Hailsham Ref:YH05197
GAUVAIN, E, Ashdown Forest Ref:YH05678
GOODEY, V, Heathfield Ref:YH05902
HALE STUD, Chiddingly Ref:YH06291
HESMONDS STUD, Lewes Ref:YH06723
JOHN BIRON EQUESTRIAN, Heathfield Ref:YH07781
KEEGAN, M W, Crowborough Ref:YH08026
KERSEY, J, Colemans Hatch Ref:YH08103
LADY FISHER, Heathfield Ref:YH08335
LITTLE MEADOWS, Hailsham Ref:YH08694
MATTHEWS, D, Hailsham Ref:YH09271
MERES FELL STUD, Mayfield Ref:YH09471
MORGANS, FREYJA, Uckfield Ref:YH09814
OAKTREE FARM, Bexhill-on-Sea Ref:YH10406
PIPER, JUDI, Hailsham Ref:YH11146
ROSS-THOMSON, C Y, Etchingham Ref:YH12126
SILVERDALE ARABIAN STUD, Robertsbridge Ref:YH12813
STERLING QUARTERHORSES, Robertsbridge Ref:YH13430
WILKINSON, H B, Telscombe Cliffs Ref:YH15419
YOKEHURST FARM, Lewes Ref:YH15913

SUSSEX (WEST)

AASEN, MORTEN, Horsham Ref:YH00071
BARKFOLD MANOR STUD, Kirdford Ref:YH00945
BARNET, R, Billingshurst Ref:YH00982
BOOTH, D C, Pulborough Ref:YH01635
BRENDON, Brighton Ref:YH01835
BRENDON HORSE & RIDER, Brighton Ref:YH01837
BURCHELL-SMALL & SHEMILT, East Grinstead Ref:YH02231
CASTLE STABLES, Arundel Ref:YH02636
COBB, I, Pulborough Ref:YH03110
CRIMBOURNE STUD, Billingshurst Ref:YH03599
DEACON, P J & K J, Chichester Ref:YH03984
DRAGON STUD, Horsham Ref:YH04251
EDWARDS & TYLER, Pulborough Ref:YH04570
FULLING MILL STUD, Haywards Heath Ref:YH05536
GILES, R, Pulborough Ref:YH05764
GORDON-SMITH, F, Chichester Ref:YH05928
GRANGEFIELD STUD, Horsham Ref:YH06001
HARWOOD ARABIAN STUD, Horsham Ref:YH06518
HIPPOMINIMUS STUD, Pulborough Ref:YH06878
HORSCRAFT, MARIANNE, Steyning Ref:YH07085
JACKETS STUD, Pulborough Ref:YH07639
KEMP, F, Ardingly Ref:YH08053
LAKIN BLOODSTOCK, Wisborough Green Ref:YH08360
LANBURN STUD, Chichester Ref:YH08380
LAVINGTON STUD, Petworth Ref:YH08466
LONDON STUD, Pulborough Ref:YH08789
LOWLEYS NATIVE PONIES, Chichester Ref:YH08875
MALTHOUSE ARABIANS, Hassocks Ref:YH09057
MOUNTAIN, A M, Horsted Keynes Ref:YH09898
NICOL, C, Horsham Ref:YH10198
NORMANDIE STUD, Billingshurst Ref:YH10240
ORION STUD, Hassocks Ref:YH10543
PERRETTS STUD, Horsham Ref:YH10984
PINE RIDGE FARM, Horsham Ref:YH11121
RAHMATALLAH, S, Billingshurst Ref:YH11610
RAPKYNS, Horsham Ref:YH11641
READ, T J G, Chichester Ref:YH11680
RICHARDS, L, Chichester Ref:YH11810
SCAMELLS SHETLAND STUD, Billingshurst Ref:YH12482
SHERMANDELL MORGANS, Shermanbury Ref:YH12726
SIMPSON, SANDRA, Horsham Ref:YH12842
SPEARFIELD STUD, Worthing Ref:YH13186
SUSSEX STUD, Horsham Ref:YH13662
SYMONDSBURY STUD, Haywards Heath Ref:YH13726
TIMMIS, M, Kirdford Ref:YH14166
TULLAMORE STUD, Horsham Ref:YH14450
VOS, A, Lindfield Ref:YH14741
WADE, JONNY, Midhurst Ref:YH14814
WESTERLANDS STUD, Petworth Ref:YH15194
ZARA STUD, Chichester Ref:YH15951
ZARAFSHAN ARABIAN STUD, Crawley Ref:YH15952

TYNE AND WEAR

BRENKLEY STABLES, Newcastle-upon-Tyne Ref:YH01840
DENE STUD, Great Whittington Ref:YH04043
DOBINSON, A W & A B, Whitley Bay Ref:YH04153
FLETCHER, H, Newcastle-upon-Tyne Ref:YH05278
GIBSON, J P, Newcastle-upon-Tyne Ref:YH05750
GIRSONFIELD STUD, Otterburn Ref:YH05795

ROMANY STUD, Newcastle-upon-Tyne **Ref:**YH12071
STEWART, L, Whitburn **Ref:**YH13459
TURNBULL, T M, Newcastle-upon-Tyne **Ref:**YH14471

WARWICKSHIRE

ACCIMASSU, Studley **Ref:**YH00140
BRICK KILN STUD, Stratford-upon-Avon **Ref:**YH01864
CLAVERDON, Warwick **Ref:**YH02992
COCKRAM, R A, Radway **Ref:**YH03127
COLEBRIDGE STUD, Coleshill **Ref:**YH03161
EVANS, R R, Stratford-upon-Avon **Ref:**YH04930
FAR WESTFIELD STUD, Moreton Morrell **Ref:**YH05049
FAYRELANDS, Kenilworth **Ref:**YH05111
GAMBLE, Kenilworth **Ref:**YH05630
GREENACRES STUD, Coventry **Ref:**YH06080
HILLCREST & HAVEN FARM, Withybrook **Ref:**YH06839
HORNBLOWER, S & SEARS, S, Coventry **Ref:**YH07074
LIST, G C, Warwick **Ref:**YH08679
LUCAS, J E, Birmingham **Ref:**YH08883
MARY ROSE STUD, Warwick **Ref:**YH09235
MOAT HOUSE STUD, Henley In Arden **Ref:**YH09686
MORETON PADDOX STUD, Warwick **Ref:**YH09789
OXSTALLS FARM STUD, Stratford-upon-Avon **Ref:**YH10625
RICHARDSON, S, Rugby **Ref:**YH11821
RUMER FARM STUD & STABLES, Welford-on-Avon **Ref:**YH12229
SMALL WORLD, Studley **Ref:**YH12905
SNOWFORD HILL FARM, Rugby **Ref:**YH13043
STARKEY, JANE, Leamington Spa **Ref:**YH13395
THIRLBY, R J & V E, Nuneaton **Ref:**YH13997
WARWICKSHIRE CLGE HORSE UNIT, Warwick **Ref:**YH14951
WOOTTON GRANGE EQUESTRIAN, Warwick **Ref:**YH15772

WILTSHIRE

ANDALUSIANS, Trowbridge **Ref:**YH00378
BENHAM STUD, Marlborough **Ref:**YH01267
BIDDESTONE STUD, Chippenham **Ref:**YH01397
BOWYER, D C, Calne **Ref:**YH01725
BUSH, N, Chippenham **Ref:**YH02308
CATRIDGE FARM STUD, Chippenham **Ref:**YH02654
CHARLESLAND STUD, Salisbury **Ref:**YH02762
CHIDDOCK PONY STUD, Salisbury **Ref:**YH02849
CHURCH FARM STUD, Warminster **Ref:**YH02902
CLARENDON PK STUD, Salisbury **Ref:**YH02953
CONTI, D & D, Salisbury **Ref:**YH03247
COUNTESS OF ROTHES, Salisbury **Ref:**YH03393
DAN Y LAN STUD, Salisbury **Ref:**YH03859
EDMUNDS, H, Salisbury **Ref:**YH04566
FONTHILL STUD, Salisbury **Ref:**YH05308
FORLAN STUD, Chippenham **Ref:**YH05372
FRENCH, B & B, Chippenham **Ref:**YH05490
GASKELL, Chippenham **Ref:**YH05670
GENUS EQUINE, Chippenham **Ref:**YH05711
GOESS-SAURAU, (COUNTESS), Marlborough **Ref:**YH05871
HADDON STUD, Marlborough **Ref:**YH06263
HENDEN CASPIAN STUD, Chippenham **Ref:**YH06664
HILLWOOD STUD, Marlborough **Ref:**YH06860
HOLDERNESS-RODDAM, JANE, Chippenham **Ref:**YH06926
HOME STUD, Salisbury **Ref:**YH07005
IMPERIAL ARABIAN STUD, Swindon **Ref:**YH07403
JOHNSTON, Salisbury **Ref:**YH07843
KINGSCOTE PARK STUD, Malmesbury **Ref:**YH08199
LOWBRIDGE STABLES, Calne **Ref:**YH08857
MEADE, MARTYN, Malmesbury **Ref:**YH09413
MEADOW FARM STUD, Marlborough **Ref:**YH09419
NAYLOR, J R J (DR), Salisbury **Ref:**YH10059
NEW PRIORY STUD, Chippenham **Ref:**YH10118
ORAM, S, Devizes **Ref:**YH10526
PENTREFELIN STUD, Swindon **Ref:**YH10963
ROE, M A, Swindon **Ref:**YH12052
ROSEGARTH STUD, Devizes **Ref:**YH12103
SAMWAYS, Salisbury **Ref:**YH12402
SCHONBRUNN HORSES, Swindon **Ref:**YH12517
SWETTENHAM STUD, Marlborough **Ref:**YH13704
TOLLARD PARK EQUESTRIAN CTRE, Salisbury **Ref:**YH14207
TUATALLA STUD, Swindon **Ref:**YH14428
TYAN CONNEMARA STUD, Salisbury **Ref:**YH14518
WEST ASHTON STUD, Trowbridge **Ref:**YH15125
WEST KINGTON STUD, Chippenham **Ref:**YH15151
WHEELER, R, Marlborough **Ref:**YH15272
WIDBROOK ARABIAN STUD, Bradford-on-Avon **Ref:**YH15388
WOODMINTON FARM, Salisbury **Ref:**YH15725
WYLYE STUD, Salisbury **Ref:**YH15866
YOUNG, JUDY, Calne **Ref:**YH15935
YOUNG, SIMON, Salisbury **Ref:**YH15940

WORCESTERSHIRE

BROCKENCOTE SHETLAND, Great Witley **Ref:**YH02008
COLLINGS, M A, Droitwich **Ref:**YH03185
DITCHAM, JANET, Kidderminster **Ref:**YH04134
EASTERN CASPIAN STUD, Redditch **Ref:**YH04496
EQUINE RESOURCES, Malvern **Ref:**YH04796
EVANS, SALLYANN & LISA, Bromsgrove **Ref:**YH04932
EYRE, M G, Kidderminster **Ref:**YH04977
FRANKLEY INTERNATIONAL HORSES, Droitwich **Ref:**YH05468
FRENCH, J, Bewdley **Ref:**YH05492
FURNACE MILL STUD, Kidderminster **Ref:**YH05543
GLENFALL PONY STUD, Evesham **Ref:**YH05833
HARRISON, S, Evesham **Ref:**YH06487
HENRY FIELDS STUD, Pershore **Ref:**YH06682
HONEYBROOK STUD, Kidderminster **Ref:**YH07013
HUNTS FARM STUD & STABLES, Worcester **Ref:**YH07308
INGRAM, PAUL, Kidderminster **Ref:**YH07454
JORDAN, R & D, Droitwich **Ref:**YH07940
KING VEAN STUD, Pershore **Ref:**YH08171
LAUNDER, E J, Malvern **Ref:**YH08452
LLEWELLYN-JAMES, J, Pershore **Ref:**YH08730
MACDONALD, T P, Worcester **Ref:**YH08991
MERRILL, S, Kidderminster **Ref:**YH09481
NORTH COTSWOLD STUD, Broadway **Ref:**YH10251
PENDOCK WELSH PONY STUD, Malvern **Ref:**YH10933
SEVERN VALLEY LIVERY CTRE, Stourport-on-Severn **Ref:**YH12645
SMITH-MAXWELL, A L, Upton-upon-Severn **Ref:**YH13005
SOLCUM STUD & STABLES, Kidderminster **Ref:**YH13052
SPRINGBANK STUD, Besford **Ref:**YH13249
THROCKMORTON COURT STUD, Pershore **Ref:**YH14112
TOOLE, JUDITH, Droitwich **Ref:**YH14232
TURVEY, F C, Kidderminster **Ref:**YH14497

YORKSHIRE (EAST)

AIKENFIELD, Driffield **Ref:**YH00209
ATKIN, M, Driffield **Ref:**YH00647
BANKS, R T, Beverley **Ref:**YH00903
BELL, J F & C R (ESQ), Howden **Ref:**YH01222
BURTON AGNES STUD FARM, Driffield **Ref:**YH02290
BURTON CONSTABLE RIDING CTRE, Hull **Ref:**YH02291
CAVEWOOD GRANGE ARABIANS, Brough **Ref:**YH02666
CHAMBERS, W H, North Ferriby **Ref:**YH02723
DEARING, R, Driffield **Ref:**YH04001
FISHER, E P, Sancton **Ref:**YH05239
HOLYROOD DARTMOORS, Goole **Ref:**YH06993
HUNSLEY HOUSE STUD, Cottingham **Ref:**YH07293
MELBOURNE HALL STUD, Melbourne **Ref:**YH09449
MORTON, GEOFFREY, Holme upon Spalding Moor **Ref:**YH09851
NORTHERN SHIRE, North Newbald **Ref:**YH10309
OKEDEN STUD, North Ferriby **Ref:**YH10445
PICKERING, GEOFF, Driffield **Ref:**YH11082
RICHARDSON, F W O, Driffield **Ref:**YH11818
ROUSE, ANTONY, Goole **Ref:**YH12145
RYEHILL, Hull **Ref:**YH12301
SKERNE LEYS FARM, Driffield **Ref:**YH12869
SLEDMERE STUD, Driffield **Ref:**YH12892
SMITH, JOHN, Bielby **Ref:**YH12968

YORKSHIRE (NORTH)

ABRAM, T M, York **Ref:**YH00136
ACONLEY, P & V, York **Ref:**YH00145
ANDERSON, D S, Harrogate **Ref:**YH00379
BARFOOT, ROBERT L, Londonderry **Ref:**YH00931
BAXTER, ANN, Boroughbridge **Ref:**YH01085
BEDFORD, P & W, York **Ref:**YH01154
BELMONT LIVERY STABLE, Harrogate **Ref:**YH01247
BOAK, D & J, Malton **Ref:**YH01583
BRAMLEY, H, York **Ref:**YH01792
BREWSTER, J S, Northallerton **Ref:**YH01855
BRITTAIN, M, York **Ref:**YH01982
CARLTON BANK STUD, Stokesley **Ref:**YH02541
CAYBERRY STUD, Ripon **Ref:**YH02670
CHEQUER HALL FARM, York **Ref:**YH02811
CLARETON STUD, Northallerton **Ref:**YH02957
CLIFF STUD, York **Ref:**YH03033
COPE, D M, Harrogate **Ref:**YH03293
COPGROVE HALL STUD, Harrogate **Ref:**YH03296
COUNTESS OF SWINTON, Ripon **Ref:**YH03394
DIMMOCK, Scarborough **Ref:**YH04123
DOUTHWAITE, J D, Leyburn **Ref:**YH04216
EASTERBY, M H, Malton **Ref:**YH04492
EASTHORPE HALL STUD, Malton **Ref:**YH04504
EMMERSON, S A, York **Ref:**YH04654
ETCHINGHAM STUD, Slingsby **Ref:**YH04879
FENWICK, S H, Skipton **Ref:**YH05155
FURNESS, G A, Thirsk **Ref:**YH05547
GATERLEY MINIATURE HORSE STUD, Huttons Ambo **Ref:**YH05673
GOLDENFIELDS STUD, Bedale **Ref:**YH05884
HEWITT, STEPHEN N, Moor Monkton **Ref:**YH06728
KITCHING & LEES, Whitby **Ref:**YH08247
KNOWLES, S W, York **Ref:**YH08285
KNOX, T K, North Allerton **Ref:**YH08288
LOUELLA STUD, Thirsk **Ref:**YH08835
MANOR HOUSE STUD, Leyburn **Ref:**YH09112
MARSHALL, LV & JUDY, Tadcaster **Ref:**YH09198

- **MOULDRON STUD**, Richmond **Ref:**YH09881
- **MUSLEY BANK STABLES**, Malton **Ref:**YH09975
- **NORTON GROVE STUD**, Malton **Ref:**YH10327
- **PERKINS, P**, York **Ref:**YH10977
- **RAW, W**, Richmond **Ref:**YH11661
- **REES, M Q**, Bilton In Ainsty **Ref:**YH11732
- **ROBINSON, W R**, Scarborough **Ref:**YH12001
- **SENRUF STUD**, Oldstead **Ref:**YH12635
- **SIGSWORTH, L C & A E**, York **Ref:**YH12795
- **SPALDING, C M**, Richmond **Ref:**YH13171
- **STEPHENSON, J F & J M**, Howsham **Ref:**YH13426
- **STOCKWELL STUD LIVERY STABLES**, Tadcaster **Ref:**YH13497
- **STUD FARM**, York **Ref:**YH13606
- **SWINTON RIDING/TREKKING CTRE**, Ripon **Ref:**YH13714
- **TAIT, M**, Whitby **Ref:**YH13824
- **THEAKSTON STUD**, Bedale **Ref:**YH13980
- **THORNGILL BREEDING**, Leyburn **Ref:**YH14068
- **THORNTON STUD**, Thirsk **Ref:**YH14076
- **THURLOE, J**, York **Ref:**YH14119
- **TINKLER, C H**, Malton **Ref:**YH14172
- **WAPLINGTON MANOR STABLES**, York **Ref:**YH14896
- **WELCH, D G**, Harrogate **Ref:**YH15059
- **WEST HALL STUD**, Richmond **Ref:**YH15146
- **WHALTON STUD**, Harrogate **Ref:**YH15262
- **WHINBERRY DARTMOORS**, Long Marston **Ref:**YH15282
- **WILSON, C**, Pickering **Ref:**YH15531
- **WREN, T E**, Whitby **Ref:**YH15820
- **YORKSHIRE DALES**, Skipton **Ref:**YH15919

YORKSHIRE (SOUTH)

- **AESTHETE**, Doncaster **Ref:**YH00197
- **BROOK BARN QUARTER HORSES**, Sheffield **Ref:**YH02031
- **BUTTERFIELD, A**, Barnsley **Ref:**YH02330
- **DARKHORSE TINYTACK**, Barnsley **Ref:**YH03888
- **DOYLE, JACK T**, Doncaster **Ref:**YH04246
- **ELDBERRY STUD**, Rotherham **Ref:**YH04601
- **FISHER, ANNA**, Sheffield **Ref:**YH05238
- **GOLDTHORPE, K**, Sheffield **Ref:**YH05896
- **GYPSYVILLE STUD**, Rotherham **Ref:**YH06206
- **HOWARTH LODGE RIDING CTRE**, Rotherham **Ref:**YH07220
- **LITTLE BRIARS STUD**, Rotherham **Ref:**YH08684
- **MOSELEY STUD**, Bentley **Ref:**YH09855
- **PARKIN, M**, Barnsley **Ref:**YH10765
- **PININA STUD**, Doncaster **Ref:**YH11133
- **READ, G A**, Doncaster **Ref:**YH11679
- **RIMMER, E & S**, Doncaster **Ref:**YH11897
- **SENAPVIEW STUD**, Rotherham **Ref:**YH12632
- **SIMPSON, G**, Sheffield **Ref:**YH12838

YORKSHIRE (WEST)

- **ANTHONY WAKEHAM CONSULTING**, Wetherby **Ref:**YH00463
- **ASTLEY RIDING CTRE**, Leeds **Ref:**YH00635
- **BAMFORTH, D**, Huddersfield **Ref:**YH00877
- **BANKSIDE SHIRE STUD**, Huddersfield **Ref:**YH00904
- **BARKER, C**, Batley **Ref:**YH00940
- **BARLOW, B S**, Halifax **Ref:**YH00956
- **BLOCKLEY, E**, Bradford **Ref:**YH01544
- **BRADLEY, M**, Huddersfield **Ref:**YH01757
- **BRADMAN, N**, Pontefract **Ref:**YH01761
- **BROCKADALE ARABIANS**, Pontefract **Ref:**YH02006
- **BUTTERWORTH**, Hebden Bridge **Ref:**YH02333
- **CARR, W**, Halifax **Ref:**YH02575
- **EASTWOOD, M**, Huddersfield **Ref:**YH04520
- **EMMOTT, G H**, Keighley **Ref:**YH04657
- **FEARNLEY, A**, Ilkley **Ref:**YH05118
- **GANT, D & E**, Wakefield **Ref:**YH05642
- **GILL, MR H J**, Aberford **Ref:**YH05774
- **GOOSEMOOR STUD**, Wetherby **Ref:**YH05918
- **GRAHAM, I**, Halifax **Ref:**YH05969
- **HENSBY, G R**, Wakefield **Ref:**YH06687
- **HEPPENSTALL, S R**, Ossett **Ref:**YH06691
- **HIGHWOOD STUD**, Wakefield **Ref:**YH06805
- **INGFIELD HACKNEY STUD**, Halifax **Ref:**YH07446
- **JOSHUA TETLEY**, Hunslet **Ref:**YH07946
- **KADAN STUD**, Bradford **Ref:**YH07994
- **LANGFIELD STUD**, Todmorden **Ref:**YH08402
- **LANTWOOD STABLES**, Leeds **Ref:**YH08424
- **LONGFIELD EQUESTRIAN CTRE**, Todmorden **Ref:**YH08811
- **NORTHORPE HACKNEY STUD**, Cleckheaton **Ref:**YH10317
- **PARKER, D**, Huddersfield **Ref:**YH10748
- **PARKER, R D**, Halifax **Ref:**YH10752
- **PARKSWOOD ANGLO-ARAB STUD**, Weeton **Ref:**YH10775
- **PERRINS, S & J**, Batley **Ref:**YH10985
- **PETIT, S G & A**, Rawdon **Ref:**YH11027
- **PRITCHARD, FIONA**, Garforth **Ref:**YH11414
- **PUMPHILL DARTMOORS**, Aberford **Ref:**YH11457
- **RICHMOND, PETER**, Wetherby **Ref:**YH11830
- **ROBERTS, JOHN**, Pontefract **Ref:**YH11953
- **ROLEYSTONE STUD**, Bradford **Ref:**YH12065
- **SMITH, C W**, Bradford **Ref:**YH12945
- **SMITH, HARVEY**, Bingley **Ref:**YH12960
- **STOCKACLOSE**, Bingley **Ref:**YH13485
- **WHITAKER, R M**, Leeds **Ref:**YH15291
- **WHITELEY, M**, Bingley **Ref:**YH15348
- **WOOD, D**, Wyke **Ref:**YH15661
- **WOTHERSOME GRANGE STUD**, Wetherby **Ref:**YH15807

CLUBS/ASSOCIATIONS

BATH & SOMERSET (NORTH EAST)

- **BATH RIDING CLUB**, Bath **Ref:**YH01073
- **FBHS HORSEWORLD**, Whitchurch **Ref:**YH05114
- **LPPS**, Paulton **Ref:**YH08880
- **NESBA**, Bath **Ref:**YH10079
- **PONY CLUB**, Bath **Ref:**YH11228
- **SOUTH WESTERN SHOW**, Bath **Ref:**YH13122

BEDFORDSHIRE

- **AGRCLTRL SHOW EXHIBITORS AST**, Romford **Ref:**YH00200
- **AIRBORNE SPORTS**, Biggleswade **Ref:**YH00219
- **COUNTRY GENTLEMEN'S ASS**, Biggleswade **Ref:**YH03409
- **TILSWORTH RIDERS CHARITY GRP**, Leighton Buzzard **Ref:**YH14157
- **TINSLEYS RIDING CLUB**, Oakley **Ref:**YH14176
- **TRAKEHNER BREEDERS FRATERNITY**, Biggleswade **Ref:**YH14345

BERKSHIRE

- **AMHB**, Newbury **Ref:**YH00367
- **BHS INSURANCE HUNTER TRIALS**, Newbury **Ref:**YH01378
- **BHS INSURANCE HUNTER TRIALS**, Newbury **Ref:**YH01379
- **CHILTERN RIDING CLUB**, Reading **Ref:**YH02860
- **CONNEMARA PONY SOC**, Hungerford **Ref:**YH03238
- **CRAVEN BRANCH**, Hungerford **Ref:**YH03571
- **DECAL FORM**, Maidenhead **Ref:**YH04007
- **HURST RIDERS CLUB**, Hurst **Ref:**YH07315
- **JOCKEYS ASS OF GREAT BRITAIN**, Newbury **Ref:**YH07772
- **KBIS**, Newbury **Ref:**YH08013
- **LAMBOURN TRAINERS ASSOCIATION**, Hungerford **Ref:**YH08369
- **LIBERTY INTELLECTUAL**, Wokingham **Ref:**YH08603
- **MICROBIAL MANAGEMENT**, Reading **Ref:**YH09518
- **MORTIMER RIDING CLUB**, Reading **Ref:**YH09846
- **NTF**, Hungerford **Ref:**YH10350
- **PONY CLUB**, Reading **Ref:**YH11229
- **RACECOURSE ASSOCIATION**, Ascot **Ref:**YH11574
- **RACEHORSE TRANSPORTERS ASS**, Reading **Ref:**YH11579
- **ROYAL COUNTY OF BERKSHIRE**, Windsor **Ref:**YH12186
- **SOLEY FARM STUD**, Hungerford **Ref:**YH13056
- **TAPLOW HORSE SHOW CLUB**, Taplow **Ref:**YH13866
- **TATTERSALLS COMMITTEE**, Reading **Ref:**YH13880
- **THAMES VALLEY CLUB**, Reading **Ref:**YH13974
- **THAMES VALLEY RIDING CLUB**, Maidenhead **Ref:**YH13976
- **TT.E.A.M TRAINING GB**, Crowthorne **Ref:**YH14426
- **WINDSOR GT PK**, Windsor **Ref:**YH15574
- **WOKINGHAM RIDING CLUB**, Reading **Ref:**YH15645

BUCKINGHAMSHIRE

- **AYLESBURY VALE RIDING CLUB**, Aylesbury **Ref:**YH00696
- **BANKERS EQUINE DIRECT**, High Wycombe **Ref:**YH00893
- **BHS INSURANCE HUNTER TRIALS**, Burnham **Ref:**YH01380
- **BHS INSURANCE HUNTER TRIALS**, Great Missenden **Ref:**YH01381
- **BLUE ASSOCIATES**, Aylesbury **Ref:**YH01562
- **CHALFONT HEIGHTS RIDING CLUB**, Seer Green **Ref:**YH02709
- **GREAT MISSENDEN RIDING CLUB**, Princes Risborough **Ref:**YH06040
- **HIGH WYCOMBE RIDING CLUB**, High Wycombe **Ref:**YH06767
- **INSTITUTE OF GROUNDMANSHIP**, Milton Keynes **Ref:**YH07462
- **KNIGHTS OF THE TOURNAMENT**, High Wycombe **Ref:**YH08270
- **MICHELLE GILES MARKETING**, Brill **Ref:**YH09513
- **N.P.S. AREA 17**, Great Missenden **Ref:**YH10004
- **PONY RIDERS' ASS**, Milton Keynes **Ref:**YH11252
- **R A F HALTON SADDLE CLUB**, Aylesbury **Ref:**YH11512
- **R D A SOUTH REGION**, Fulmer **Ref:**YH11523
- **WEST WYCOMBE PARK POLO CLUB**, West Wycombe **Ref:**YH15173
- **WINDSOR PK EQUESTRIAN CLUB**, Chalfont St Giles **Ref:**YH15576
- **WING DRESSAGE GROUP**, Chesham **Ref:**YH15583
- **WORKHORSE CONSULTANCY**, Burnham **Ref:**YH15778

CAMBRIDGESHIRE

- **BRITISH EQUESTRIAN WRITERS**, Swavesey **Ref:**YH01941
- **BRITISH HORSE FOUNDATION**, Peterborough **Ref:**YH01950
- **BRITISH SKEWBALD/PIEBALD ASS**, Ely **Ref:**YH01975
- **BSPS**, Huntingdon **Ref:**YH02179
- **CAMBRIDGE & DISTRICT**, Histon **Ref:**YH02468
- **CAMBRIDGE & NEWMARKET POLO**, Cambridge **Ref:**YH02469
- **CAMBRIDGE UNIVERSITY**, Cambridge **Ref:**YH02472
- **CONNECTIONS PR**, Sawtry **Ref:**YH03234
- **EAST ENGLAND AGRCLTRL SOC**, Peterborough **Ref:**YH04475
- **EASTERN WELSH PONY & COB ASS**, Peterborough **Ref:**YH04498
- **EQUESTRIAN SVS THORNEY**, Peterborough **Ref:**YH04717
- **FARRIERS REGISTRATION COUNCIL**, Peterborough **Ref:**YH05091
- **HUNTINGDON & DISTRICT**, Huntingdon **Ref:**YH07304
- **LONDON HARNESS HORSE PARADE**, Peterborough **Ref:**YH08786

- **MORGAN HORSE ASS**, Pampisford **Ref:**YH09796
- **PONIES ASSOCIATION**, Huntingdon **Ref:**YH11223
- **RADIO LINKS COMMUNICATIONS**, St Neots **Ref:**YH11595
- **SHIRE HORSE SOC**, Peterborough **Ref:**YH12754
- **WOODGREEN ANIMAL SHELTERS**, Godmanchester **Ref:**YH15690
- **WORSHIPFUL CO COACHMAKERS**, Burwell **Ref:**YH15795

CHESHIRE

- **B.R.A.T.S. RIDING CLUB**, Knutsford **Ref:**YH00756
- **BORDER BRIDLEWAYS ASSOCIATION**, Congleton **Ref:**YH01642
- **CHESHIRE POLO CLUB**, Tarporley **Ref:**YH02827
- **COMBINED TRAINING DRESSAGE**, Tarporley **Ref:**YH03210
- **COMBINED TRAINING GRP**, Sandbach **Ref:**YH03211
- **LAWSHIELD UK**, Warrington **Ref:**YH08476
- **MACCLESFIELD & DISTRICT**, Macclesfield **Ref:**YH08984
- **MID CHESHIRE BRIDLEWAYS ASS**, Northwich **Ref:**YH09522
- **MID CHESHIRE RIDING CLUB**, Crewe **Ref:**YH09523
- **NANTWICH RIDING CLUB**, Malpas **Ref:**YH10018
- **NATIONAL STALLION ASSOCIATION**, Knutsford **Ref:**YH10044
- **PENN HOUSE PUBLISHING**, Knutsford **Ref:**YH10947
- **PONY CLUB**, Winsford **Ref:**YH11231
- **RUNNING JUMP DESIGN CONSULT**, Stockport **Ref:**YH12234
- **SAGITTARIUS POLOCROSSE CLUB**, Congleton **Ref:**YH12383
- **SPENCER LAVERY AST**, Hale **Ref:**YH13196
- **TOWN & COUNTRY PRODUCTIONS**, Malpas **Ref:**YH14285
- **WERNETH LOW RIDING CLUB**, Hyde **Ref:**YH15115
- **WILMSLOW RIDING CLUB**, Altrincham **Ref:**YH15524

CLEVELAND

- **GUISBOROUGH RIDING CLUB**, Guisborough **Ref:**YH06187
- **LANGBAURGH BOROUGH COUNCIL**, South Bank **Ref:**YH08400
- **NORTH YORKSHIRE TRAINING GRP**, Marton **Ref:**YH10288
- **SOUTH DURHAM SADDLE CLUB**, Hartlepool **Ref:**YH13085
- **YARM & DISTRICT RIDING CLUB**, Stockton-on-Tees **Ref:**YH15886

CORNWALL

- **ABRS**, Penzance **Ref:**YH00137
- **AKAL-TEKE SOCIETY**, Wadebridge **Ref:**YH00229
- **CAMEL VALLEY RIDING CLUB**, Cardinham **Ref:**YH02475
- **CORNISH EQUINE REGISTER**, Falmouth **Ref:**YH03326
- **EAST CORNWALL RIDING CLUB**, Liskeard **Ref:**YH04469
- **ENGLISH CHINA CLAYS**, St Austell **Ref:**YH04673
- **GWENNAP RIDING CLUB**, Truro **Ref:**YH06200
- **HOLSWORTHY & DISTRICT**, Bude **Ref:**YH06984
- **NATIVE PONY ASS OF CORNWALL**, Penryn **Ref:**YH10049
- **NEWQUAY RIDING CLUB**, Newquay **Ref:**YH10163
- **PONY CLUB**, Lostwithiel **Ref:**YH11232
- **TAVY VALLEY RIDING CLUB**, Callington **Ref:**YH13887
- **THREEWATERS RIDING CLUB**, Helston **Ref:**YH14109
- **WENDRON RAM BUCK FAIR**, Helston **Ref:**YH15107

COUNTY DURHAM

- **BEDALE COMBINED TRAINING GRP**, Durham **Ref:**YH01151
- **BISHOPS RIDING CLUB**, Durham **Ref:**YH01451
- **DARLINGTON & DISTRICT**, Staindrop **Ref:**YH03891
- **EQUINE PRODUCT MARKETING**, Barnard Castle **Ref:**YH04793
- **G PRUDHOE**, Faverdale **Ref:**YH05591
- **UNIVERSITY OF DURHAM**, Durham **Ref:**YH14585

CUMBRIA

- **CENTRAL COMMITTE FELL PACKS**, Holmrook **Ref:**YH02687
- **CUMBERLAND FARMERS**, Carlisle **Ref:**YH03713
- **CUMBRIA TOURIST BOARD**, Windermere **Ref:**YH03716
- **EDEN VALLEY TROTTING ASS**, Kirkby Stephen **Ref:**YH04549
- **EXPO LIFE**, Carlisle **Ref:**YH04972
- **FELL PONY SOC**, Penrith **Ref:**YH05129
- **FELL PONY SOC**, Penrith **Ref:**YH05130
- **HORTICULTURAL/AGRCLTRL SOC**, Penrith **Ref:**YH07192
- **JOHN PEEL RIDING CLUB**, Carlisle **Ref:**YH07806
- **LAKES RIDING CLUB**, Windermere **Ref:**YH08357
- **ULLSWATER PONY SPORTS CLUB**, Penrith **Ref:**YH14554

DERBYSHIRE

- **ATHERSTONE & DISTRICT**, Swadlincote **Ref:**YH00643
- **BRITISH MULE SOCIETY**, Ashbourne **Ref:**YH01962
- **BUSINESS ADMIN SVS**, Bakewell **Ref:**YH02314
- **F B MARKETING**, Ashbourne **Ref:**YH04983
- **LASSA**, High Peak **Ref:**YH08439
- **MIDLANDS HAIRY PONY CLUB**, Ashbourne **Ref:**YH09559
- **MOTTRAM & DISTRICT AGRI SOC**, Glossop **Ref:**YH09877
- **N.C.P.A. DERBYSHIRE BRANCH**, High Peak **Ref:**YH10002
- **SPOTTED HORSE & PONY SOCIETY**, Dronfield **Ref:**YH13240
- **STABLE LADS ASS**, Swadlincote **Ref:**YH13295
- **THREE SHIRES RIDING CLUB**, Buxton **Ref:**YH14108

DEVON

- **ANGLO & PART-BRED ARAB ASS**, Ottery St Mary **Ref:**YH00418
- **B H S COUNTY BRIDLEWAYS**, Exeter **Ref:**YH00725
- **BRIDESTOWE & DISTRICT**, Yelverton **Ref:**YH01869
- **DALES PONY SOC**, Bakewell **Ref:**YH03829
- **DARTMOOR HUNT SUPPORTERS**, Kingsbridge **Ref:**YH03902
- **DARTMOOR LIVESTOCK PROTECTION**, Tavistock **Ref:**YH03903
- **DARTMOOR PONY SOC**, Ivybridge **Ref:**YH03904
- **EXETER & DISTRICT**, Newton Abbot **Ref:**YH04965
- **HOLSWORTHY & STRATTON**, Holsworthy **Ref:**YH06985
- **ILFRACOMBE & DISTRICT**, Barnstaple **Ref:**YH07399
- **JOUSTING CONSULTANTS**, Bideford **Ref:**YH07949
- **LAMBERTS CASTLE RIDING CLUB**, Axminster **Ref:**YH08365
- **MID DEVON RIDING CLUB**, Okehampton **Ref:**YH09524
- **NAT INS OF MEDICAL HERBALISTS**, Exeter **Ref:**YH10031
- **NORTH DEVON RIDING CLUB**, Ilfracombe **Ref:**YH10255
- **NORTH TAWTON RIDING CLUB**, Exeter **Ref:**YH10283
- **OTTERY INSURANCE SVS**, Ottery St Mary **Ref:**YH10582
- **PONY CLUB**, Sidmouth **Ref:**YH11234
- **RED POST SHOW JUMPING CLUB**, Totnes **Ref:**YH11703
- **SID & OTTER VALLEY**, Honiton **Ref:**YH12780
- **SOUTH BRENT RIDING CLUB**, Totnes **Ref:**YH13078
- **SOUTH DEVON RIDING CLUB**, Torquay **Ref:**YH13083
- **SOUTH HAMS BRIDLEWAYS**, South Brent **Ref:**YH13094
- **SOUTH WEST REGIONAL**, North Molton **Ref:**YH13117
- **TEIGNBRIDGE BRIDLEWAYS**, Dawlish **Ref:**YH13936
- **TIVERTON FOXHOUNDS**, Honiton **Ref:**YH14191
- **TIVERTON STAGHOUNDS**, Umberleigh **Ref:**YH14192
- **UNIVERSITY OF EXETER**, Exeter **Ref:**YH14586
- **WEST COUNTRY SHIRE HORSE**, Plymouth **Ref:**YH15137
- **WESTON WAGONS**, Torquay **Ref:**YH15225
- **WITHERIDGE & DISTRICT RIDING**, Tiverton **Ref:**YH15622

DORSET

- **B M C PUBLIC RELATIONS**, Poole **Ref:**YH00737
- **BOURNEMOUTH BRONCOS**, Southbourne **Ref:**YH01686
- **BRIERLEY BUSINESS SERVICES**, Dorchester **Ref:**YH01903
- **CENTRAL PREFIX REGISTER**, Shaftesbury **Ref:**YH02689
- **CORSCOMBE & HALSTOCK**, Dorchester **Ref:**YH03345
- **DORSET BRIDLEWAYS**, Wimborne **Ref:**YH04204
- **ENDURANCE HORSE AND PONY**, Wareham **Ref:**YH04668
- **ESS**, Dorchester **Ref:**YH04863
- **EUROPEAN & INT PEDIGREE**, Bridport **Ref:**YH04905
- **IDLEBECK PUBLISHING**, Wimborne **Ref:**YH07386
- **MELPLASH AGRICULTURAL SOCIETY**, Bridport **Ref:**YH09456
- **PONY CLUB FIXTURES**, Sturminster Newton **Ref:**YH11249
- **PURBECK & DISTRICT**, Wareham **Ref:**YH11460
- **SHILLINGSTONE & DISTRICT**, Blandford **Ref:**YH12745
- **SHIPTON RIDING CLUB**, Dorchester **Ref:**YH12753
- **SOUTHERN COUNTIES HEAVY HORSE**, Wimborne **Ref:**YH13137
- **SOUTHERN COUNTIES RIDING CLUB**, Poole **Ref:**YH13138
- **STOUR VALLEY RIDING CLUB**, Shaftesbury **Ref:**YH13529
- **WEST COUNTRY ROSETTES**, Gillingham **Ref:**YH15136
- **WEYMOUTH & DISTRICT**, Weymouth **Ref:**YH15253
- **WIMBORNE & DISTRICT**, Broadstone **Ref:**YH15558

ESSEX

- **APPLEWELL INSURANCE BROKERS**, Braintree **Ref:**YH00482
- **BASILDON EQUESTRIAN CLUB**, Billericay **Ref:**YH01053
- **BELMONT COMMUNICATIONS**, Ilford **Ref:**YH01245
- **BILLERICAY & DISTRICT**, Billericay **Ref:**YH01409
- **BILLERICAY & DISTRICT**, Billericay **Ref:**YH01410
- **BRITISH DRESSAGE SUPPORTERS**, Bishop's Stortford **Ref:**YH01936
- **C A MARKETING**, Sible Hedingham **Ref:**YH02363
- **ESSEX COUNTY SHOWGROUND**, Chelmsford **Ref:**YH04867

- **ESSEX FARMERS & UNION**, Colchester **Ref:**YH04868
- **ESSEX FARMERS & UNION**, Colchester **Ref:**YH04869
- **FORESTERS RIDING CLUB**, Waltham Abbey **Ref:**YH05356
- **HAFLINGER SOC**, Finchingfield **Ref:**YH06273
- **HALLINGBURY RIDING CLUB**, Bishop's Stortford **Ref:**YH06332
- **HOOKS HALL EQUESTRIAN CLUB**, Rainham **Ref:**YH07039
- **INGATESTONE/BLACKMORE**, Billericay **Ref:**YH07443
- **M & B RIDING CLUB**, Dagenham **Ref:**YH08944
- **PIGGOTT BROS**, Ongar **Ref:**YH11097
- **PONY CLUB**, Chelmsford **Ref:**YH11236
- **PONY RIDING**, Chigwell **Ref:**YH11253
- **SADDLE SEAT SOCIETY**, Colchester **Ref:**YH12347
- **SAFFRON WALDEN & DISTRICT**, Saffron Walden **Ref:**YH12381
- **SOUTH ESSEX INSURANCE**, South Ockendon **Ref:**YH13091
- **TENDRING HUNDRED FARMERS**, Colchester **Ref:**YH13953
- **TENDRING HUNDRED RIDING CLUB**, Clacton-on-Sea **Ref:**YH13954
- **THURROCK RIDING CLUB**, Grays **Ref:**YH14121
- **UPMINSTER RIDING CLUB**, Aveley **Ref:**YH14603
- **WHIRLEDGE & NOTT**, Great Dunmow **Ref:**YH15284
- **WILLOWS SHOW JUMPING CLUB**, Loughton **Ref:**YH15509
- **WORSHIPFUL CO OF LORINERS**, Braintree **Ref:**YH15797

GLOUCESTERSHIRE

- **C H A O S**, Cheltenham **Ref:**YH02372
- **CHELTENHAM & DISTRICT**, Cheltenham **Ref:**YH02803
- **CIRENCESTER PK POLO CLUB**, Cirencester Park **Ref:**YH02927
- **COTSWOLD VALE**, Cheltenham **Ref:**YH03371
- **EARL OF TYRONE**, Cirencester Park **Ref:**YH04450
- **EDGEWORTH POLO CLUB**, Stroud **Ref:**YH04556
- **ENDURANCE RIDING SUPPORTERS**, Coleford **Ref:**YH04669
- **EQUINE SPORTS MASSAGE ASS**, Cirencester **Ref:**YH04801
- **EQUINE SPORTS MASSAGE ASS**, Dursley **Ref:**YH04802
- **EVENLODE RIDING CLUB**, Winchcombe **Ref:**YH04936
- **HARTBURY CLGE**, Hucclecote **Ref:**YH06499
- **HUNT SERVANTS BENEFIT SOCIETY**, Cirencester **Ref:**YH07296
- **MASTERS OF BASSET HOUNDS ASS**, Cheltenham **Ref:**YH09251
- **MASTERS OF FOXHOUNDS ASS**, Cirencester **Ref:**YH09254
- **RIDING FOR THE DISABLED ASS**, Cheltenham **Ref:**YH11878
- **RIVERMEAD INSURANCE**, Lechlade **Ref:**YH11922
- **ROYAL AGRICULTURAL COLLEGE**, Cirencester **Ref:**YH12181
- **STROUD PONY CLUB**, Nailsworth **Ref:**YH13587
- **WITNEY UK**, Fairford **Ref:**YH15633

GLOUCESTERSHIRE (SOUTH)

- **DANCO INT**, Coalpit Heath **Ref:**YH03862

HAMPSHIRE

- **ACP**, Winchester **Ref:**YH00155
- **BAPSH**, New Milton **Ref:**YH00917
- **BHS INSURANCE HUNTER TRIALS**, Petersfield **Ref:**YH01382
- **BREAKSPEAR RIDING CLUB**, Bordon **Ref:**YH01825
- **ESSO RIDING CLUB**, Fawley **Ref:**YH04874
- **HAMBLE VALLEY RIDING CLUB**, West End **Ref:**YH06344
- **HAMPSHIRE RURAL RIDING CLUB**, Alton **Ref:**YH06366
- **IBM RIDING CLUB**, Havant **Ref:**YH07378
- **IFMHS**, Hook **Ref:**YH07390
- **J & M ASSOCIATES**, Andover **Ref:**YH07550
- **K E S POWER & LIGHT**, Regents Park **Ref:**YH07986
- **LARKHILL H S DRESSAGE**, Tidworth **Ref:**YH08431
- **MEON RIDING CLUB**, Petersfield **Ref:**YH09460
- **MITCHELL BRIDGES**, Winchester **Ref:**YH09663
- **NATIONAL PONY SOCIETY**, Alton **Ref:**YH10041
- **NEW FOREST POLO CLUB**, Ringwood **Ref:**YH10101
- **NEW FOREST PONY**, Ringwood **Ref:**YH10102
- **NEW FOREST PONY ENTHUSIASTS**, Fordingbridge **Ref:**YH10103
- **NEW FOREST RIDING CLUB**, Hythe **Ref:**YH10104
- **RINGWOOD & DISTRICT**, Sway **Ref:**YH11902
- **SCREENCO**, Eastleigh **Ref:**YH12565
- **SOLENT RIDING CLUB**, Locksheath **Ref:**YH13055
- **SOUTH DOWNS HARNESS CLUB**, Denmead **Ref:**YH13084
- **SOUTHAMPTON UNI POLO CLUB**, Highfield **Ref:**YH13127
- **STAFF CLGE/SANDHURST HUNTS**, Sandhurst **Ref:**YH13320
- **T-TENTS**, Basingstoke **Ref:**YH14427
- **UK AST OF HOLISTIC NUTRITION**, Hook **Ref:**YH14542
- **WESTERN EQUESTRIAN SOCIETY**, Yateley **Ref:**YH15198
- **WEY VALLEY RIDING CLUB**, Alton **Ref:**YH15249

HEREFORDSHIRE

- **BROMYARD & DISTRICT**, Bromyard **Ref:**YH02028
- **DUN HORSE & PONY SOC**, Ledbury **Ref:**YH04329
- **EQUINE AROMATHERAPY ASS**, Hereford **Ref:**YH04763
- **HEREFORD & DISTRICT**, Little Birch **Ref:**YH06700
- **NEVILLE SYMONDS ASSOCIATES**, Bromyard **Ref:**YH10088
- **PONY CLUB**, Ross On Wye **Ref:**YH11237
- **PPSA AREA SECRETARY**, Kilpeck **Ref:**YH11333
- **THREE COUNTIES DRESSAGE GROUP**, Bromyard **Ref:**YH14102
- **VALE OF ARROW RIDING CLUB**, Woonton **Ref:**YH14637

HERTFORDSHIRE

- **B S I**, Hemel Hempstead **Ref:**YH00748
- **BRITISH APPALOOSA SOCIETY**, Hertford **Ref:**YH01924
- **BRITISH HAY & STRAW MERCHANTS**, Old Hatfield **Ref:**YH01946
- **BRITISH HORSEBALL ASSOCIATION**, New Barnet **Ref:**YH01954
- **BRITISH HORSEBALL ASSOCIATION**, New Barnet **Ref:**YH01955
- **CHANDLERS CROSS RIDING CLUB**, Kings Langley **Ref:**YH02731
- **CROFT WP & DESIGN**, Chipperfield **Ref:**YH03622
- **EQUINE INDEX**, Knebworth **Ref:**YH04780
- **ESSENDON & DISTRICT**, Buntingford **Ref:**YH04864
- **HOLLY HILL RIDING CLUB**, Northaw **Ref:**YH06954
- **HOMESTEAD FARM JUMPING CLUB**, Barnet **Ref:**YH07006
- **HORSERACING SPONSORS ASS**, Borehamwood **Ref:**YH07166
- **LETCHWORTH BALDOCK & DISTRICT**, Baldock **Ref:**YH08565
- **MARSH PRIVATE CLIENT SVS**, Hitchin **Ref:**YH09187
- **NATIONAL TRUST**, Royston **Ref:**YH10046
- **NORTH MYMMS RIDING CLUB**, Hatfield **Ref:**YH10273
- **PINNERWOOD & DISTRICT**, Bushey **Ref:**YH11135
- **PONY CLUB**, Buntingford **Ref:**YH11238
- **R D A WAVERLEY DRIVING GROUP**, Hatfield **Ref:**YH11526
- **ROYAL VETERINARY CLGE**, Hatfield **Ref:**YH12197
- **SHEARWATER INSURANCE SVS**, Waltham Cross **Ref:**YH12692
- **SILVER LEYS POLO CLUB**, Hatfield **Ref:**YH12810
- **STEVENAGE & DISTRICT**, Stevenage **Ref:**YH13439
- **STRANGEWAYS & DISTRICT**, Barnet **Ref:**YH13548
- **WEMBLEY RIDING CLUB**, Hemel Hempstead **Ref:**YH15102
- **WESTERN HORSEMEN'S ASS OF GB**, Ware **Ref:**YH15203
- **WOODGREEN ANIMAL SHELTERS**, Royston **Ref:**YH15691
- **WORSHIPFUL CO OF FARRIERS**, Kings Langley **Ref:**YH15796
- **YOUTH HOSTELS ASSOCIATION**, St Albans **Ref:**YH15948

ISLE OF WIGHT

- **ISLE OF WIGHT RIDING CLUB**, Merstone **Ref:**YH07525
- **VECTIS EQUESTRIAN CLUB**, Yarmouth **Ref:**YH14672

JERSEY

- **JERSEY RIDING CLUB**, St Peter **Ref:**YH07756

KENT

- **AQHA**, Ashford **Ref:**YH00487
- **ARDENNES HORSE SOCIETY OF GB**, Sissinghurst **Ref:**YH00505
- **BA GREEN CROP DRIERS**, Hythe **Ref:**YH00758
- **BA GREEN CROP DRIERS**, Tunbridge Wells **Ref:**YH00759
- **BHS**, Sidcup **Ref:**YH01357
- **BRADBOURNE RIDING CLUB**, Brenchley **Ref:**YH01744
- **BRITISH EQUESTRIAN BROKERS**, Tonbridge **Ref:**YH01937
- **CANTERBURY RIDING CLUB**, Dover **Ref:**YH02509
- **COBHAM MANOR**, Sittingbourne **Ref:**YH03114
- **CRAWFORD MESSENGER PUBLICITY**, Nettlestead **Ref:**YH03573
- **DONKEY BREED SOC**, Edenbridge **Ref:**YH04183
- **EQUUS INSURANCE**, Orpington **Ref:**YH04842
- **FAVERSHAM & DISTRICT**, Faversham **Ref:**YH05106
- **FAVERSHAM RIDING CLUB**, Sheerness **Ref:**YH05107
- **GEERINGS OF ASHFORD**, Ashford **Ref:**YH05694
- **INVICTA RIDING CLUB**, Ashford **Ref:**YH07485
- **INVICTA RIDING CLUB DRESSAGE**, Ashford **Ref:**YH07486
- **JOYDENS BRIDLEWAY GRP**, Bexley **Ref:**YH07952
- **JOYDENS RIDING CLUB**, Bexley **Ref:**YH07953
- **KENT TARGET POLOCROSSE CLUB**, Goudhurst **Ref:**YH08082
- **MAIDSTONE & DISTRICT**, Aylesford **Ref:**YH09037
- **MOUNT MASCAL RIDING CLUB**, Sidcup **Ref:**YH09889
- **NATIONAL LIGHT HORSE SOC**, Edenbridge **Ref:**YH10038
- **NORTH WEST KENT PONY CLUB**, Swanley **Ref:**YH10285
- **POINT TO POINT**, Canterbury **Ref:**YH11190
- **QUICKWAY BUILDINGS**, Sandwich **Ref:**YH11496

- **ROYAL OAK RIDING CLUB**, Canterbury **Ref:**YH12190
- **SEVENOAKS RIDING CLUB**, Tonbridge **Ref:**YH12642
- **SPORT HORSE BREEDING**, Edenbridge **Ref:**YH13218
- **TREWINT**, Cranbrook **Ref:**YH14388
- **TUNBRIDGE WELLS RIDING CLUB**, Pembury **Ref:**YH14459
- **WARLINGHAM PONY CLUB**, Westerham **Ref:**YH14918
- **WORKING HORSE TRUST**, Tunbridge Wells **Ref:**YH15780

LANCASHIRE

- **BACUP & DISTRICT RIDING CLUB**, Bacup **Ref:**YH00773
- **BHS**, Preston **Ref:**YH01359
- **CHORLEY EQUESTRIAN CTRE**, Chorley **Ref:**YH02880
- **COLNE & DISTRICT RIDING CLUB**, Colne **Ref:**YH03194
- **FYLDE COAST BRIDLEWAY ASS**, Preesall **Ref:**YH05556
- **FYLDE HORSE CLUB**, Blackpool **Ref:**YH05557
- **HORSE AND PONY PROTECTION**, Burnley **Ref:**YH07102
- **M E FRENCH**, Preston **Ref:**YH08959
- **MILLIN INSURANCE SVS**, Parbold **Ref:**YH09623
- **NATIONAL ANIMAL RESCUE ASS**, Rossendale **Ref:**YH10034
- **NORTH EAST LANCS RIDING CLUB**, Burnley **Ref:**YH10257
- **NORTH WEST TOURIST BOARD**, Wigan **Ref:**YH10286
- **NORTH-EAST LANCASHIRE**, Burnley **Ref:**YH10297
- **NORTHERN COUNTIES PONY ASS**, Preston **Ref:**YH10300
- **NORTHERN DRESSAGE GROUP**, Ormskirk **Ref:**YH10301
- **OLDHAM & DISTRICT RIDING CLUB**, Oldham **Ref:**YH10490
- **PENDLESIDE BRIDLEWAYS ASS**, Colne **Ref:**YH10932
- **PONY CLUB**, Preston **Ref:**YH11239
- **RIBBLE VALLEY RIDING CLUB**, Lower Darwen **Ref:**YH11793
- **RIDERS LEGAL LINE**, Preston **Ref:**YH11858
- **ROCHDALE & DISTRICT**, Oldham **Ref:**YH12017
- **ROSSENDALE VALLEY RIDING CLUB**, Rossendale **Ref:**YH12124
- **SADDLEWORTH PONY CLUB**, Oldham **Ref:**YH12372
- **THOROUGHBRED REHABILITATION**, Preston **Ref:**YH14088
- **UNIVERSITY OF LANCASTER**, Bailrigg **Ref:**YH14588
- **VALE OF LUNE HARRIERS**, Preston **Ref:**YH14639
- **WESTHOUGHTON RIDING CLUB**, Wigan **Ref:**YH15217
- **WILPSHIRE RIDING CLUB**, Preston **Ref:**YH15525
- **WORLD OF HORSES I T L**, Layland **Ref:**YH15786

LEICESTERSHIRE

- **BA OF EQUINE SOC**, Markfield **Ref:**YH00760
- **BRITISH CENTRAL PREFIX**, Markfield **Ref:**YH01933
- **FRISBY FLYERS HORSEBALL CLUB**, Seagrave **Ref:**YH05508
- **HINCKLEY & DISTRICT DRESSAGE**, Whitwick **Ref:**YH06868
- **LEICESTER LIONS**, Scraptoft **Ref:**YH08543
- **LEICESTERSHIRE & RUTLAND**, Loughborough **Ref:**YH08545
- **LEICESTERSHIRE AGRCLTRL SOC**, Loughborough **Ref:**YH08546
- **LOUGHBOROUGH STUDENTS UNION**, Loughborough **Ref:**YH08838
- **MELTON MOWBRAY RIDING CLUB**, Melton Mowbray **Ref:**YH09457
- **NOTTINGHAM JOUSTING ASS**, Loughborough **Ref:**YH10342
- **REARSBY LODGE RIDING CLUB**, Thurmaston **Ref:**YH11688
- **SUTTON BONINGTON RIDING CLUB**, Loughborough **Ref:**YH13669
- **UNIVERSITY OF LEICESTER**, Leicester **Ref:**YH14589
- **WARWICK WARRIORS**, Leicester **Ref:**YH14947

LINCOLNSHIRE

- **BASTON & DISTRICT**, Bourne **Ref:**YH01059
- **BASTON & DISTRICT RIDING CLUB**, Bourne **Ref:**YH01060
- **BHS**, Navenby **Ref:**YH01360
- **LINCOLN & DISTRICT**, Lincoln **Ref:**YH08640
- **PONY CLUB**, Grantham **Ref:**YH11240
- **SOUTH KESTEVEN & DISTRICT**, Grantham **Ref:**YH13097
- **SPALDING & DISTRICT**, Sleaford **Ref:**YH13170
- **WELTON & DISTRICT RIDING CLUB**, Gainsborough **Ref:**YH15099
- **WEST LINCOLN RIDING CLUB**, Lincoln **Ref:**YH15154
- **ZEBULON MARKETING SERVICES**, Stamford **Ref:**YH15954

LINCOLNSHIRE (NORTH EAST)

- **NORTH LINCOLNSHIRE**, Grimsby **Ref:**YH10269

LINCOLNSHIRE (NORTH)

- **EQUINE LAWYERS ASS**, Brigg **Ref:**YH04784

LONDON (GREATER)

- **ALEXANDER TECHNIQUE**, London **Ref:**YH00266
- **AMATEUR RIDERS ASS OF GB**, London **Ref:**YH00355
- **B B C RIDING CLUB**, London **Ref:**YH00716
- **B.E.V. A**, London **Ref:**YH00755
- **BETTING OFFICE LICENSEES**, London **Ref:**YH01335
- **BLENHEIM RIDING CLUB**, London **Ref:**YH01536
- **BLOODLINES**, London **Ref:**YH01548
- **BOSTON MANOR RIDING CLUB**, Hanwell **Ref:**YH01660
- **BRITISH APPAREL & TEXTILE**, London **Ref:**YH01925
- **BRITISH HORSERACING BOARD**, London **Ref:**YH01957
- **BRITISH HORSERACING BOARD**, London **Ref:**YH01956
- **BRITISH OAT & BARLEY ASS**, London **Ref:**YH01963
- **BRITISH VETNRY ASS**, London **Ref:**YH01979
- **BRUNEL UNIVERSITY RIDING CLUB**, Uxbridge **Ref:**YH02158
- **CHISLEHURST & DISTRICT**, Penge **Ref:**YH02869
- **CITY & GUILDS**, London **Ref:**YH02930
- **CLARION EVENTS**, London **Ref:**YH02959
- **COUNTRY LANDOWNERS ASS**, London **Ref:**YH03412
- **COUNTRYSIDE ALLIANCE**, London **Ref:**YH03440
- **CREDIT & FINANCIAL SVS**, London **Ref:**YH03585
- **DEFRA**, London **Ref:**YH04025
- **DORCHESTER RACING CLUB**, Islington **Ref:**YH04197
- **EMERGENCY RELIEF**, London **Ref:**YH04651
- **EQUESTRIAN TRAVELLERS CLUB**, London **Ref:**YH04719
- **FINANCIAL OMBUDSMAN SV**, London **Ref:**YH05206
- **FIRST ARTIST CORPORATION**, Wembley **Ref:**YH05229
- **FIRST EQUINE FINANCE**, London **Ref:**YH05230
- **GRANDSTAND MEDIA**, Wembley **Ref:**YH05984
- **HARROW & DISTRICT RIDING CLUB**, Harrow **Ref:**YH06492
- **HORSE TRIALS SUPPORT GROUP**, London **Ref:**YH07143
- **HORSERACE BETTING LEVY BOARD**, London **Ref:**YH07165
- **HUGHES-GIBB**, London **Ref:**YH07274
- **HYDE PARK BRANCH**, London **Ref:**YH07343
- **INSURANCE OMBUDSMAN**, London **Ref:**YH07464
- **ISSEA**, London **Ref:**YH07526
- **ISSEA - GB**, London **Ref:**YH07527
- **ISVA**, London **Ref:**YH07528
- **JOCKEY CLUB**, London **Ref:**YH07771
- **KEITH PROWSE HOSPITALITY**, Wembley **Ref:**YH08036
- **LONDON RIDING HORSE PARADE**, London **Ref:**YH08787
- **LONDON SCHOOLS HORSE SOC**, London **Ref:**YH08788
- **MEDICAL EQUESTRIAN ASS**, London **Ref:**YH09436
- **MOTORHOME & TRAILER RENTALS**, Clapham **Ref:**YH09875
- **NAT OFFICE OF ANIMAL HEALTH**, Enfield **Ref:**YH10032
- **NORTHWOOD RIDING CLUB**, Pinner **Ref:**YH10323
- **PH GREENHILL**, Norwood Green **Ref:**YH11039
- **POINT TO POINT**, London **Ref:**YH11191
- **POLYTECHNIC OF NORTH LONDON**, Holloway Road **Ref:**YH11215
- **R B I PROMOTIONS**, South Kensington **Ref:**YH11516
- **R.C.V.S**, London **Ref:**YH11570
- **RACEHORSE OWNERS' ASS**, London **Ref:**YH11577
- **RACEHORSE OWNERS ASSOCIATION**, London **Ref:**YH11578
- **ROYAL PHARMACEUTICAL SOCIETY**, London **Ref:**YH12191
- **ROYAL VETERINARY CLGE**, London **Ref:**YH12198
- **SADDLERS COMPANY**, London **Ref:**YH12358
- **SHEARWATER CORPORATE SVS**, Colindale **Ref:**YH12691
- **SPINAL INJURIES ASSOCIATION**, London **Ref:**YH13208
- **SPORT & GENERAL PRESS AGENCY**, London **Ref:**YH13216
- **SUN ALLIANCE**, London **Ref:**YH13639
- **THOROUGHBRED ADVERTISING**, London **Ref:**YH14080
- **TRANSPORT & GENERAL**, Westminster **Ref:**YH14349
- **TUBULAR BARRIERS**, London **Ref:**YH14430
- **WILLOWTREE RIDING CLUB**, Blackheath **Ref:**YH15517
- **WINDSOR INSURANCE BROKERS**, London **Ref:**YH15575
- **WORSHIPFUL CO OF LORINERS**, London **Ref:**YH15798
- **WORSHIPFUL CO OF SADDLERS**, London **Ref:**YH15799

MANCHESTER (GREATER)

- **B R ROUND**, Stockport **Ref:**YH00747
- **BOLTON RIDING CLUB**, Bolton **Ref:**YH01610
- **MANCHESTER MANIACS**, Manchester **Ref:**YH09066
- **UNIVERSITY OF MANCHESTER**, Manchester **Ref:**YH14591
- **URMSTON & DISTRICT**, Manchester **Ref:**YH14621

MERSEYSIDE

- **LAFFAK RIDING CLUB**, Liverpool **Ref:**YH08341
- **MERSEYSIDE BHS DRESSAGE**, Liverpool **Ref:**YH09491
- **ROTARY CLUB**, Southport **Ref:**YH12127
- **WEST CHESHIRE TRAINING GROUP**, Greasby **Ref:**YH15131
- **WEST LANCASHIRE RIDING CLUB**, Liverpool **Ref:**YH15152
- **WHEATHILL RIDING CTRE**, Liverpool **Ref:**YH15268
- **WIRRAL EQUESTRIAN CLUB**, Wirral **Ref:**YH15602

MIDLANDS (WEST)

- **BRITISH LUGGAGE/LEATHERGOODS**, Birmingham **Ref:**YH01960
- **BRITISH SPORTS HORSE REGISTER**, Warley Town **Ref:**YH01977
- **BRITISH WARMBLOOD SOCIETY**, Warley **Ref:**YH01980
- **EAST SHROPSHIRE RIDING CLUB**, Tettenhall Wood **Ref:**YH04485
- **GAME PLAN DEVELOPMENTS**, Penn **Ref:**YH05633
- **HARKAWAY CLUB**, Halesowen **Ref:**YH06430
- **HAWKSTAVE**, Halesowen **Ref:**YH06552
- **IBEM**, Birmingham **Ref:**YH07376
- **MERIDEN RIDING CLUB**, Coventry **Ref:**YH09474
- **SADDLERS RIDING CLUB**, Walsall **Ref:**YH12360
- **SOLIHULL RIDING CLUB**, Solihull **Ref:**YH13058
- **SUTTON COLDFIELD & DISTRICT**, Sutton Coldfield **Ref:**YH13670
- **W O LEWIS**, Birmingham **Ref:**YH14785
- **W R C FARMS**, Alvechurch **Ref:**YH14788
- **WALSALL EQUESTRIAN SOCIETY**, Walsall **Ref:**YH14872
- **WALSGRAVE AMATEUR RIDING CLUB**, Coventry **Ref:**YH14874

NORFOLK

- **BHS**, Norwich **Ref:**YH01363
- **BUCKENHAM HORSE GROUP RDA**, Thurton **Ref:**YH02188
- **EAST ANGLIAN RIDING CLUB**, Attleborough **Ref:**YH04464
- **FRIESIAN HORSE ASS**, Diss **Ref:**YH05504
- **HIGH FLIERS VAULTING GRP**, Carleton Rode **Ref:**YH06759
- **ILPH**, Norwich **Ref:**YH07401
- **LENRYS ASSOCIATES**, Attleborough **Ref:**YH08552
- **NORFOLK SHOW JUMPING CLUB**, Attleborough **Ref:**YH10233
- **REDWINGS HORSE SANCTUARY**, Norwich **Ref:**YH11718
- **SHOWTIME ROSETTES**, Thorpe Abbotts **Ref:**YH12767
- **WEST NORFOLK FOXHOUNDS**, King's Lynn **Ref:**YH15157

NORTHAMPTONSHIRE

- **BRITISH HANOVERIAN HORSE SOC**, Sywell **Ref:**YH01944
- **BUCKINGHAM RIDING CLUB**, Daventry **Ref:**YH02192
- **CHERWELL VALLEY RIDING CLUB**, Daventry **Ref:**YH02822
- **EVENTS MNGMT**, Moulton Park **Ref:**YH04947
- **FELLOWS & INSTRUCTORS**, Northampton **Ref:**YH05134
- **MOULTON POLOCROSSE CLUB**, West St Moulton **Ref:**YH09885
- **P E P PHILLIPS**, Daventry **Ref:**YH10636
- **R P LOVATT INSURANCE**, Brackley **Ref:**YH11559
- **SIDE SADDLE ASSOCIATION**, Welford **Ref:**YH12785
- **SOUTH WARWICKSHIRE**, Daventry **Ref:**YH13114
- **TOWCESTER OASIS**, Towcester **Ref:**YH14267
- **UNION OF COUNTRY SPORTS**, Towcester **Ref:**YH14571
- **WEATHERBYS**, Wellingborough **Ref:**YH15024
- **ZEPHYR FLAGS & BANNERS**, Thrapston **Ref:**YH15955

NORTHUMBERLAND

- **BEDLINGTON BLYTH & DISTRICT**, Bedlington **Ref:**YH01156
- **BHS**, Hexham **Ref:**YH01364
- **CORBRIDGE & DISTRICT**, Corbridge **Ref:**YH03308
- **DRURIDGE RIDING CLUB**, Newbiggin **Ref:**YH04293
- **FELL PONY SOC**, Morpeth **Ref:**YH05131
- **NORTH NORTHUMBERLAND**, Denwick **Ref:**YH10275
- **NORTH OF ENGLAND**, Hexham **Ref:**YH10276
- **PONY CLUB**, Alnwick **Ref:**YH11242

NOTTINGHAMSHIRE

- **A N A AST**, Newark **Ref:**YH00053
- **BELVOIR VALE HORSEBALL CLUB**, Ruddington **Ref:**YH01260
- **BRACKENHURST CLGE**, Newark **Ref:**YH01740
- **CALVERTON HORSE & PONY CLUB**, Nottingham **Ref:**YH02458
- **COLLINGHAM & DISTRICT SADDLE**, Retford **Ref:**YH03183
- **EVE TRAKWAY**, Sutton-In-Ashfield **Ref:**YH04935
- **MIDLANDS AREA CLUB**, Newark **Ref:**YH09557
- **NOTTINGHAM HORSEBALL CLUB**, Gunthorpe **Ref:**YH10341
- **NOTTINGHAM JUNIOR**, Nottingham **Ref:**YH10343
- **PROFESSIONAL SECRETARIAL SVS**, Staunton In The Vale **Ref:**YH11429
- **ROCK VALLEY HORSEBALL CLUB**, Nottingham **Ref:**YH12027
- **RUFFORD PONY CLUB**, Southwell **Ref:**YH12214
- **SILVER HORSESHOE RIDING CLUB**, Newark **Ref:**YH12807
- **TRENT VALLEY HORSEBALL CLUB**, Cotgrave **Ref:**YH14380
- **V I P EXHIBITIONS**, Sutton In Ashfield **Ref:**YH14628

OXFORDSHIRE

- **BAHVS**, Faringdon **Ref:**YH00792
- **BERKSHIRE DOWNS RIDING CLUB**, Letcombe Regis **Ref:**YH01305
- **BHS**, Chipping Norton **Ref:**YH01365
- **BHS INSURANCE HUNTER TRIALS**, Ascott Under Wychwood **Ref:**YH01383
- **BHS INSURANCE HUNTER TRIALS**, Henley-on-Thames **Ref:**YH01384
- **BINFIELD HEATH POLO CLUB**, Henley-on-Thames **Ref:**YH01420
- **BLUE CROSS ANIMAL**, Burford **Ref:**YH01566
- **BLUE ZEBRA PR**, Ardington **Ref:**YH01572
- **BUCKINGHAM RIDING CLUB**, Banbury **Ref:**YH02193
- **COSFPS**, Henley-on-Thames **Ref:**YH03349
- **HPA**, Faringdon **Ref:**YH07248
- **JOHN D WOOD TEAM CHASE**, Wantage **Ref:**YH07785
- **MARKET RACING AGENCY**, Wantage **Ref:**YH09158
- **MATHEWS COMFORT**, Henley-on-Thames **Ref:**YH09263
- **MISTRAL**, Cassington **Ref:**YH09662
- **N A S T A**, Bicester **Ref:**YH09986
- **NATIONAL EQUINE WELFARE COUNC**, Banbury **Ref:**YH10036
- **NORTH OXFORDSHIRE RIDING CLUB**, Banbury **Ref:**YH10278
- **OXFORD RIDING CLUB**, Steeple Barton **Ref:**YH10620
- **OXFORD UNI POLO CLUB**, Oxford **Ref:**YH10622
- **R A BENEVOLENT INSTITUTION**, Oxford **Ref:**YH11509
- **R D A SPONSORED RIDE**, Abingdon **Ref:**YH11524
- **SCOTT WILSON RESOURCE CONSULT**, Abingdon **Ref:**YH12535
- **TRAKEHNER BREEDERS**, Bicester **Ref:**YH14344
- **TRIPLE CROWN ASSOCIATES**, Witney **Ref:**YH14402
- **TWESELDOWN CLUB**, Henley-on-Thames **Ref:**YH14510
- **UK CHASERS**, Oxford **Ref:**YH14544
- **WATERSTOCK HSE TRAINING CTRE**, Waterstock **Ref:**YH14974
- **WELSH PART-BRED**, Henley-on-Thames **Ref:**YH15094

RUTLAND

- **BUCKMINSTER & DISTRICT**, Rutland **Ref:**YH02202
- **INT EQUESTRIAN**, Oakham **Ref:**YH07467
- **N F U COUNTRYSIDE**, Uppingham **Ref:**YH09989
- **RUTLAND RIDING CLUB**, Oakham **Ref:**YH12278
- **SCURRY DRIVING ASSOCIATION**, Oakham **Ref:**YH12578
- **SPOTTED PONY BREED SOCIETY**, Oakham **Ref:**YH13241

SHROPSHIRE

- **BRITISH EQUESTRIAN TRADE**, Whitchurch **Ref:**YH01939
- **MAELOR RIDING CLUB**, Whitchurch **Ref:**YH09027
- **MORRIS HOLDINGS**, Oswestry **Ref:**YH09827
- **SHREWSBURY & DISTRICT**, Market Drayton **Ref:**YH12768
- **TORTON BODIES**, Telford **Ref:**YH14247
- **WREKIN NORTH BRIDLEWAYS ASS**, Telford **Ref:**YH15818
- **WREKIN NORTH RIDING CLUB**, Telford **Ref:**YH15819

SOMERSET

- **ASS OF SHOW & AGRICULTURAL**, Shepton Mallet **Ref:**YH00631
- **BRENT & BERROW RIDING CLUB**, Brent Knoll **Ref:**YH01847
- **BRENT KNOLL RIDING CLUB**, Axbridge **Ref:**YH01848
- **DEVON & SOMERSET STAGHOUNDS**, Taunton **Ref:**YH04093
- **ENGLISH CONNEMARA PONY SOC**, Dulverton **Ref:**YH04674
- **EUROPEAN CONFERENCE**, Wincanton **Ref:**YH04907
- **EXMOOR NATIONAL PK AUTHORITY**, Dulverton **Ref:**YH04968
- **EXMOOR PONY SOC**, Dulverton **Ref:**YH04969
- **JEFFERY COMMUNICATIONS**, Minehead **Ref:**YH07716
- **MASTERS OF DEERHOUNDS ASS**, Dulverton **Ref:**YH09252
- **MID SOMERSET RIDING CLUB**, Yeovil **Ref:**YH09528
- **NETWORKS**, Taunton **Ref:**YH10085
- **PPSA AREA CHAIRMAN**, Yeovil **Ref:**YH11332
- **QUANTOCK RIDING CLUB**, Bridgwater **Ref:**YH11478
- **RADIONIC & RADIESTHESIC**, Wincanton **Ref:**YH11596
- **ROYAL BATH & WEST OF ENGLAND**, Shepton Mallet **Ref:**YH12185
- **SOMERSET BRIDLEWAYS**, Chard **Ref:**YH13063
- **SOUTH WESTERN DRESSAGE GROUP**, Wincanton **Ref:**YH13120
- **TAUNTON & DISTRICT**, Taunton **Ref:**YH13882
- **WESSEX RIDING CLUB**, Axbridge **Ref:**YH15120
- **WEST SOMERSET POLO CLUB**, Dulverton **Ref:**YH15163
- **WESTON & BANWELL HARRIERS**, Highbridge **Ref:**YH15222
- **YEO PAULL**, Martock **Ref:**YH15901

SOMERSET (NORTH)

- **BLACKDOWN RIDING CLUB**, Wrington **Ref:**YH01480
- **S A S**, Portishead **Ref:**YH12314
- **WOODSPRING BRIDLEWAYS ASS**, Winscombe **Ref:**YH15749

STAFFORDSHIRE

- **B I S**, Stoke-on-Trent **Ref:**YH00731
- **BALLANTYNE, TONI**, Eccleshall **Ref:**YH00854
- **FOREST OF NEEDWOOD**, Burton-on-Trent **Ref:**YH05347
- **LUSITANO BREED SOC**, Leek **Ref:**YH08904
- **NSBA**, Keele **Ref:**YH10349

PENKRIDGE & DISTRICT, Stafford Ref:YH10942
PONY CLUB, Lichfield Ref:YH11244
SCROPTON, Burton-on-Trent Ref:YH12569
UNIVERSITY OF KEELE, Keele Ref:YH14587

SUFFOLK

ANIMAL HEALTH, Woodbridge Ref:YH00434
ANIMAL HEALTH TRUST, Newmarket Ref:YH00439
ANIMAL MEDICINES, Woodbridge Ref:YH00441
B G I BLOODSTOCK/INSURANCE, Newmarket Ref:YH00721
BRADSTOCK HAMILTON & PARTNERS, Newmarket Ref:YH01763
BRITISH BLOODSTOCK AGENCY, Newmarket Ref:YH01929
BRITISH CAMARGUE HORSE SOC, Woodbridge Ref:YH01932
BRITISH HONOVERIAN HORSE REG, Newmarket Ref:YH01947
BRITISH HORSERACING TRAINING, Newmarket Ref:YH01958
CAMBRIDGE UNIVERSITY, Newmarket Ref:YH02473
COLORLABS INT, Newmarket Ref:YH03198
EAST ANGLIAN BLOODHOUNDS, Ipswich Ref:YH04462
EAST ANGLIAN TRAILS, Stowmarket Ref:YH04465
EQUINE BEHAVIOUR FORUM, Newmarket Ref:YH04767
FBA, Newmarket Ref:YH05113
FINN VALLEY RIDING CLUB, Ipswich Ref:YH05215
HEAD LADS ASS, Newmarket Ref:YH06607
HORSE RESCUE FUND, Beccles Ref:YH07133
INJURED JOCKEY FUND, Newmarket Ref:YH07457
KEENELAND ASS, Newmarket Ref:YH08029
NATIONAL STUD, Newmarket Ref:YH10045
RACING WELFARE, Newmarket Ref:YH11588
SILVER LEY POLOCROSSE CLUB, Lavenham Ref:YH12809
SITA, Newmarket Ref:YH12860
SOCIETY OF MASTERS SADDLERS, Stowmarket Ref:YH13048
ST EDMUNDS RIDING CLUB, Bury St Edmunds Ref:YH13275
SUFFOLK RIDING CLUB, Ipswich Ref:YH13625
THOROUGHBRED BREEDERS ASS, Newmarket Ref:YH14081
WORLINGTON RIDING CLUB, Newmarket Ref:YH15791

SURREY

ABINGER FOREST RIDING CLUB, Dorking Ref:YH00132
BHS INSURANCE HUNTER TRIALS, Camberley Ref:YH01385
BOOKHAM RIDING CLUB, East Molesey Ref:YH01629
BOOKHAM RIDING CLUB, Surbiton Ref:YH01628
BRIDGE BARN RIDING CLUB, Woking Ref:YH01871
BRITISH MORGAN HORSE SOCIETY, Godalming Ref:YH01961
BROCKHAM & DISTRICT, Tadworth Ref:YH02009
CASPIAN HORSE, Virginia Water Ref:YH02618
CHOBHAM & DISTRICT, Weybridge Ref:YH02872
E C L MARKETING, Richmond Ref:YH04399
EQUINE SVS INT, North Cheam Ref:YH04804
EWSHOT RIDING CLUB, Farnham Ref:YH04962
FARNHAM RIDERS CLUB, Farnham Ref:YH05081
FRENSHAM RIDING CLUB, Godalming Ref:YH05496
GRAHAM BROWN, Guildford Ref:YH05962
GREEN LANE STABLES, Morden Ref:YH06058
HORLEY & DISTRICT RIDING CLUB, Smallfield Ref:YH07071
HORSE RANGERS ASS, East Molesey Ref:YH07131
HURTWOOD PARK, Cranleigh Ref:YH07322
INT SPORTS MARKETING, Dorking Ref:YH07473
KINGSTON & DISTRICT, Great Bookham Ref:YH08206
LONDON UNIVERSITY POLO CLUB, Chertsey Ref:YH08791
MARK DAVIES, Cranleigh Ref:YH09151
NATIONAL ASS OF BOOKMAKERS, Surbiton Ref:YH10035
NEWLANDS CORNER RIDING CLUB, West Byfleet Ref:YH10142
PRESTIGE RACING CLUB, Epsom Ref:YH11364
PROFESSIONAL EVENT RIDERS ASS, East Horsley Ref:YH11428
RAWLEY PLANT, Godstone Ref:YH11664
REIGATE & DISTRICT, Reigate Ref:YH11745
RIDING FOR THE DISABLED ASS, Epsom Ref:YH11879
RURAL CRAFTS ASSOCIATION, Godalming Ref:YH12237
RUSSIAN HORSE SOCIETY, Epsom Ref:YH12267
SOCIETY OF EQUESTRIAN ARTISTS, Staines Ref:YH13047
STONEWAYS INSURANCE, Godalming Ref:YH13521
SUFFOLK HORSE SOCIETY, Woodbridge Ref:YH13624
UNIVERSITY OF SURREY, Guildford Ref:YH14593
VICARAGE FARM COMPETITIONS, Sunbury-on-Thames Ref:YH14705
WEAVER BROS, Redhill Ref:YH15027
WEST SURREY RIDING CLUB, Guildford Ref:YH15165
WESTERN HORSEMAN'S ASS OF GB, Ashford Ref:YH15202
WOODCOTE & DISTRICT, Worcester Park Ref:YH15677

SUSSEX (EAST)

A V S, Old Heathfield Ref:YH00065
ASA OF GB, Alfriston Ref:YH00580
BATTLE & DISTRICT RIDING CLUB, Heathfield Ref:YH01078
BROWNBREAD, Battle Ref:YH02134
BUCKINGHAM HSE, Newhaven Ref:YH02191
BUCKLAND PR, Robertsbridge Ref:YH02194
FALLABELLA SOC, Heathfield Ref:YH05041
GUILD OF MASTER CRAFTSMAN, Lewes Ref:YH06184
HEATHFIELD RIDING CLUB, Horam Ref:YH06631
KINGSWOOD AST, Robertsbridge Ref:YH08209
KWIKSPACE, Lewes Ref:YH08302
MID SUSSEX RIDING CLUB, Patcham Ref:YH09531
NATIONAL REINING HORSE ASS, Etchingham Ref:YH10042
OUSE VALLEY RIDING CLUB, Peacehaven Ref:YH10586
PONY CLUB, Robertsbridge Ref:YH11245
ROTHER VALLEY RIDING CLUB, Etchingham Ref:YH12128
SCHOOLS & UNIVERSITIES POLO, Hartfield Ref:YH12523
SOUTH PENNIE PACKHORSE, Lewes Ref:YH13104
UNIVERSITY OF SUSSEX, Brighton Ref:YH14594

SUSSEX (WEST)

ADUR VALLEY RIDING CLUB, Lancing Ref:YH00191
B M H S, Billingshurst Ref:YH00740
BHS, Hassocks Ref:YH01369
BRITISH PERCHERON HORSE, Midhurst Ref:YH01965
C R M, Horsham Ref:YH02388
COWDRAY PK POLO CLUB, Midhurst Ref:YH03523
GORING & DISTRICT RIDING CLUB, Worthing Ref:YH05933
HORSHAM & DISTRICT, Horsham Ref:YH07187
INVICTA POLOCROSSE CLUB, Ansty Ref:YH07484
JOINT COUNCIL, Chichester Ref:YH07850
KNEPP CASTLE POLO CLUB, Horsham Ref:YH08255
MAINS DISTRIBUTION SVS, Kirdford Ref:YH09039
MASTERS OF DRAGHOUNDS, Henfield Ref:YH09253
MID SUSSEX AREA BRIDLEWAYS, Hassocks Ref:YH09530
PERMIT TRAINERS ASS, Haywards Heath Ref:YH10980
POLO PONY WELFARE COMMITTEE, Petworth Ref:YH11211
R D A SOUTH DOWNS, Steyning Ref:YH11522
ROYAL NAVAL EQUESTRIAN ASS, Worthing Ref:YH12188
RSPCA, Horsham Ref:YH12204
RUDGWICK & DISTRICT, Pulborough Ref:YH12209
SOUTH OF ENGLAND AGRCLTRL SOC, Haywards Heath Ref:YH13103
SPECTRUM AGENCY, Worthing Ref:YH13189
THOROUGHBRED COMMUNICATIONS, Haywards Heath Ref:YH14085
WEST END RIDING CLUB, Burgess Hill Ref:YH15142

TYNE AND WEAR

BAY RIDING CLUB, North Shields Ref:YH01093
EQUINAME, Newcastle-upon-Tyne Ref:YH04757
NORTHERN COUNTIES, Gateshead Ref:YH10299
SPARTAN RIDING CLUB, South Shields Ref:YH13184
UNIVERSITY OF NEWCASTLE, Newcastle-upon-Tyne Ref:YH14592

WARWICKSHIRE

BDS, Warwick Ref:YH01101
BERA, Kenilworth Ref:YH01291
BERA, Rugby Ref:YH01292
BHS, Kenilworth Ref:YH01371
BHS, Solihull Ref:YH01370
BRITISH DRESSAGE, Kenilworth Ref:YH01935
BRITISH EQUESTRIAN FEDERATION, Kenilworth Ref:YH01938
BRITISH HORSE IND CONFED, Kenilworth Ref:YH01951
BRITISH HORSE TRIALS ASS, Kenilworth Ref:YH01953
BRITISH RIDING CLUBS, Kenilworth Ref:YH01970
BRITISH SHOW HACK,, Coleshill Ref:YH01971
ETTINGTON PK RIDING CLUB, Wellesbourne Ref:YH04888
FELLOWS & INSTRUCTORS, Leamington Spa Ref:YH05135
FOREST OF ARDEN RIDERS GRP, Wootton Wawen Ref:YH05345
GATE INN RIDING CLUB, Coleshill Ref:YH05671
GRAND PLAN CONSULTANCY, Southam Ref:YH05983
H M C HOPSFORD MARKETING, Coventry Ref:YH06228
HAFLINGER SOC, Warwick Ref:YH06274
HORSE & RIDER, Leamington Spa Ref:YH07095
INT PARALYMPIC EQUESTRIAN SP, Leamington Spa Ref:YH07470
INTER PARALYMPIC EQUESTRIAN, Leamington Spa Ref:YH07475
INTERNATIONAL WARWICK SCHOOL, Warwick Ref:YH07480

IRISH DRAUGHT HORSE SOCIETY, Coventry **Ref:**YH07492
J G INT EQUINE CONSULTANTS, Gaydon **Ref:**YH07584
JOINT MEASUREMENT BOARD, Kenilworth **Ref:**YH07851
M J MAC, Leamington Spa **Ref:**YH08970
N F U MUTUAL, Stratford-upon-Avon **Ref:**YH09990
N.P.S. AREA 11, Alcester **Ref:**YH10003
NAT ASS FARRIERS/BLACKSMITHS, Kenilworth **Ref:**YH10030
PONY CLUB, Kenilworth **Ref:**YH11246
RARE BREEDS SURVIVAL TRUST, Kenilworth **Ref:**YH11643
RIDING FOR THE DISABLED ASS, Kenilworth **Ref:**YH11880
ROYAL AGRICULTURAL SOCIETY, Stoneleigh **Ref:**YH12182
RUGBY RIDING CLUB, Rugby **Ref:**YH12218
SPORTS INDUSTRIES FEDERATION, Stoneleigh **Ref:**YH13234
STONELEIGH RIDING CLUB, Ryton-on-Dunsmore **Ref:**YH13518
STRATFORD SHIRE HORSE CTRE, Stratford-upon-Avon **Ref:**YH13551
UK POLOCROSSE ASSOCIATION, Silverstone **Ref:**YH14547
UK RIDERS, Leamington Spa **Ref:**YH14549
WARWICKSHIRE EQUITATION CTRE, Coventry **Ref:**YH14952

WILTSHIRE

ANSTY POLO CLUB, Salisbury **Ref:**YH00460
ARAB HORSE SOC, Marlborough **Ref:**YH00490
B M H S, Warminster **Ref:**YH00741
BAPBSH, Trowbridge **Ref:**YH00916
BERKELEY & DISTRICT, Chippenham **Ref:**YH01300
BHS, Warminster **Ref:**YH01372
BLOODSTOCK & STUD INVESTMENT, Marlborough **Ref:**YH01549
CASPIAN PONY SOC, Chippenham **Ref:**YH02619
CHRIS LEA, Salisbury **Ref:**YH02883
EVENT HORSE OWNERS ASS, Warminster **Ref:**YH04937
FOXHILL RACING PROMOTIONS, Swindon **Ref:**YH05434
HACKNEY HORSE SOC, Warminster **Ref:**YH06257
I H A, Marlborough **Ref:**YH07365
JOCKEYS EMPLOYMENT & TRAINING, Swindon **Ref:**YH07773
KENNET VALE RIDING CLUB, Chippenham **Ref:**YH08072
LAMINITIS TRUST, Chippenham **Ref:**YH08373
MOUNTED GAMES ASSOCIATION, Swindon **Ref:**YH09900
PONY CLUB, Warminster **Ref:**YH11247
ROYAL ARTILLERY, Pewsey **Ref:**YH12184
SOUTH WILTSHIRE RIDING CLUB, Warminster **Ref:**YH13124
TIDWORTH POLO CLUB, Tidworth **Ref:**YH14136
WILTSHIRE BHS BRIDLEWAYS, Salisbury **Ref:**YH15556
WINDSOR CLIVE INT, Marlborough **Ref:**YH15573
WORLD ARABIAN HORSE ORG, Swindon **Ref:**YH15783
WORLD OF EXPERIENCE, Warminster **Ref:**YH15785

WORCESTERSHIRE

AMERICAN NAT SHOW, Malvern **Ref:**YH00364
CENTAUR POLOCROSSE CLUB, Kidderminster **Ref:**YH02683
HEART OF ENGLAND TOURIST, Larkhill **Ref:**YH06618
SHROPSHIRE SOUTH RIDING CLUB, Stockton On Teme **Ref:**YH12770
STOURPORT TIGERS, Stourport-on-Severn **Ref:**YH13531
UNITED SADDLEBRED ASS, Malvern **Ref:**YH14574
WESTERN EQUESTRIAN SOCIETY, Havern **Ref:**YH15199
WORCESTER & DISTRICT, Worcester **Ref:**YH15773

YORKSHIRE (EAST)

BRIDLINGTON & DISTRICT, Bridlington **Ref:**YH01900
BRITISH HARNESS RACING CLUB, Goole **Ref:**YH01945
EAST RIDING BRIDLEWAY ASS, Driffield **Ref:**YH04484
EBOR VALE RIDING CLUB, Melbourne **Ref:**YH04531
HASTPACE DATA, Driffield **Ref:**YH06529
P M H SVS, Driffield **Ref:**YH10652
WHITE ROSE RIDING CLUB, Beverley **Ref:**YH15323
WRITERS & PHOTOGRAPHERS, Berverley **Ref:**YH15847

YORKSHIRE (NORTH)

ANIMAL INSURANCE, Thirsk **Ref:**YH00440
BHDTA, York **Ref:**YH01351
BHS, Badale **Ref:**YH01373
CLEVELAND BAY HORSE SOC, York **Ref:**YH03021
CLUB RACING, Thirsk **Ref:**YH03075
FLAT RACE JOCKEYS, Richmond **Ref:**YH05261
GALE & PHILLIPSON, Harrogate **Ref:**YH05610
GALE & PHILLIPSON, Northallerton **Ref:**YH05611
HARROGATE BRIDLEWAYS ASS, Harrogate **Ref:**YH06491
JOUSTING & ASSOCIATED SKILLS, Thirsk **Ref:**YH07948
KING FOREST ANIMAL SANCTUARY, Knaresborough **Ref:**YH08168
MALTON RACING ASS, Malton **Ref:**YH09060
MIDDLETON POINT TO POINT, Husthwaite **Ref:**YH09543
NORTH EASTERN POLOCROSSE CLUB, York **Ref:**YH10260
NORTHALLERTON RIDING CLUB, Northallerton **Ref:**YH10291
PONY CLUB, Wetherby **Ref:**YH11248
SCARBOROUGH & DISTRICT, Scarborough **Ref:**YH12486
SELBY & DISTRICT RIDING CLUB, Wilberfoss **Ref:**YH12614
STAINTONDALE PONY CLUB, Scarborough **Ref:**YH13348
VALE OF YORK PONY CLUB, Elvington **Ref:**YH14641
WETHERBY AGRICULTURAL SOCIETY, Tadcaster **Ref:**YH15243
WHITBY & DISTRICT RIDING CLUB, Whitby **Ref:**YH15295
YCHRC, York **Ref:**YH15893
YORK & AINSTY SOUTH PONY CLUB, Easingwold **Ref:**YH15914
YORK & DISTRICT RIDING CLUB, York **Ref:**YH15915

YORKSHIRE (SOUTH)

BRITISH SPOTTED PONY SOCIETY, Doncaster **Ref:**YH01978
EAST MIDLANDS DRESSAGE GRP, Doncaster **Ref:**YH04481
HALLAMSHIRE RIDING SOC, Sheffield **Ref:**YH06326
INTERNATIONAL RACING MEDIA, Doncaster **Ref:**YH07479
MOTEK PORTABLE PRODUCTS, Doncaster **Ref:**YH09873
PENISTONE & DISTRICT, Sheffield **Ref:**YH10941
TICKHILL RIDING CLUB, Doncaster **Ref:**YH14127

YORKSHIRE (WEST)

AIRE VALLEY RIDING CLUB, Bradford **Ref:**YH00221
AMATEUR JOCKEYS AST OF GB, Huddersfield **Ref:**YH00354
BETA, Wetherby **Ref:**YH01330
BHS, Pontefract **Ref:**YH01374
BRITISH EQUESTRIAN TRADE ASS, Wetherby **Ref:**YH01940
CALDERDALE SADDLE CLUB, Halifax **Ref:**YH02435
EQUESTRIAN MNGMT CONSULTANTS, Wetherby **Ref:**YH04707
HOLME VALLEY RIDING CLUB, Huddersfield **Ref:**YH06967
HORSFORTH RIDING CLUB, Rawdon **Ref:**YH07186
LOUISE LEACH, Sherburn In Elmet **Ref:**YH08843
MID YORKSHIRE RIDING CLUB, Leeds **Ref:**YH09533
NIDD VALLEY RIDING CLUB, Burley-In-Wharfedale **Ref:**YH10202
PENNINE POLOCROSSE CLUB, Wakefield **Ref:**YH10953
PENNINE RIDING CLUB, Todmorden **Ref:**YH10954
PHYLISS HARVEY, Weetwood **Ref:**YH11079
PRESS ASSOCIATION SPORT, Leeds **Ref:**YH11359
PUDSEY & DISTRICT RIDING CLUB, Bradford **Ref:**YH11448
SHIBDEN DALE RIDING CLUB, Halifax **Ref:**YH12738
SPPTT, Mankinholes **Ref:**YH13243
TOULSTON POLO CLUB, Halifax **Ref:**YH14255
UNIVERSITY OF BRADFORD, Great Horton **Ref:**YH14582
WINPENNY PHOTOGRAPHY, Otley **Ref:**YH15592
WOODNOOK ARENA, Huddersfield **Ref:**YH15726

EQUESTRIAN CENTRES

BATH & SOMERSET (NORTH EAST)

CHRISTY'S EQUESTRIAN BUREAU, Bath **Ref:**YH02892

BEDFORDSHIRE

CLGE EQUESTRIAN CTRE, Bedford **Ref:**YH03025
MOOR END STABLES, Bedford **Ref:**YH09742
STOCKWOOD PARK, Luton **Ref:**YH13498

BERKSHIRE

EAST SOLEY E C 2000, Hungerford **Ref:**YH04486
LANDS END EQUESTRIAN CTRE, Reading **Ref:**YH08386
WOODLANDS, Hungerford **Ref:**YH15705

BRISTOL

FILTON CLGE, Bristol **Ref:**YH05205

BUCKINGHAMSHIRE

ADDINGTON MANOR, Buckingham **Ref:**YH00179
BANGORS PARK FARM, Iver **Ref:**YH00883
BOW BRICKHILL TREKKING CTRE, Milton Keynes **Ref:**YH01694
BRAWLINGS FARM RIDING CTRE, Gerrards Cross **Ref:**YH01819
CHEQUERS END EQUESTRIAN CTRE, High Wycombe **Ref:**YH02812
CLASSIC EQUESTRIAN, Gerrards Cross **Ref:**YH02985
EQUESTRIAN CTRE, Amersham **Ref:**YH04696
MILTON KEYNES EVENTING, Milton Keynes **Ref:**YH09645

CAMBRIDGESHIRE

BEACONSFIELD EQUINE CTRE, Huntingdon **Ref:**YH01109
COUNTRY PURSUITS, Cambridge **Ref:**YH03421
MILL LODGE EQUESTRIAN CTRE, Wisbech **Ref:**YH09582
NORTHBROOK EQUESTRIAN CTRE, Huntingdon **Ref:**YH10294
PETERBOROUGH REGIONAL CLGE, Peterborough **Ref:**YH11018

- **PINNER, TERRY**, Huntingdon **Ref:**YH11134
- **UNIVERSITY OF CAMBRIDGE**, Cambridge **Ref:**YH14584

CHESHIRE

- **ADLINGTON EQUESTRIAN CTRE**, Macclesfield **Ref:**YH00185
- **BARROW EQUESTRIAN CTRE**, Chester **Ref:**YH01027
- **BOLD HEATH EQUESTRIAN**, Widnes **Ref:**YH01602
- **CLOVERFIELD EQUESTRIAN CTRE**, Sale **Ref:**YH03070
- **COTTON EQUESTRIAN CTRE**, Crewe **Ref:**YH03384
- **CROFT RIDING CTRE**, Warrington **Ref:**YH03617
- **DANE VALLEY EQUESTRIAN CTRE**, Congleton **Ref:**YH03865
- **HILLTOP EQUESTRIAN CTRE**, Frodsham **Ref:**YH06857
- **KELLY, SIMON**, Crewe **Ref:**YH08049
- **REASEHEATH CLGE**, Nantwich **Ref:**YH11689
- **SOUTH VIEW EQUESTRIAN CTRE**, Winsford **Ref:**YH13107

CLEVELAND

- **BUSBY HALL TREKKING CTRE**, Middlesbrough **Ref:**YH02303
- **CRIMDON PARK EQUESTRIAN CTRE**, Hartlepool **Ref:**YH03600
- **FOXHOLM STUD**, Stockton-on-Tees **Ref:**YH05437

CORNWALL

- **CLAPPER HSE RIDING CTRE**, Wadebridge **Ref:**YH02947
- **CORNISH RIDING HOLIDAYS**, Redruth **Ref:**YH03327
- **ELM PK EQUESTRIAN CTRE**, Launceston **Ref:**YH04633
- **KILLIWORGIE RIDING STABLE**, Newquay **Ref:**YH08144
- **MAER STABLES**, Bude **Ref:**YH09029
- **MULFRA TREKKING CTRE**, Penzance **Ref:**YH09931
- **SUNNYSIDE HOTEL**, Camelford **Ref:**YH13650
- **TM INT SCHOOL OF HORSEMANSHIP**, Liskeard **Ref:**YH14196
- **TRILL FARM**, Par **Ref:**YH14398

COUNTY DURHAM

- **CENTURION EQUESTRIAN CTRE**, Durham **Ref:**YH02698
- **DARLINGTON EQUESTRIAN CTRE**, Darlington **Ref:**YH03892
- **DARLINGTON EQUESTRIAN CTRE**, Haughton **Ref:**YH03893
- **EAST DURHAM & HOUGHALL**, Houghall **Ref:**YH04473
- **GO RIDING GRP**, Stanley **Ref:**YH05861
- **HIGHLING EQUESTRIAN CTRE**, Durham **Ref:**YH06798
- **IVESLEY EQUESTRIAN CTRE**, Durham **Ref:**YH07536
- **NORTHUMBRIA HORSE HOLIDAYS**, Stanley **Ref:**YH10320
- **SEAGOLD CENTURION**, Crook **Ref:**YH12587

CUMBRIA

- **GOOSEWELL TREKKING CTRE**, Keswick **Ref:**YH05920
- **GREY HORSE RIDING CTRE**, Brough **Ref:**YH06124
- **KINGWATER EQUESTRIAN CTRE**, Carlisle **Ref:**YH08214
- **LAKE DISTRICT TRAIL CTRE**, Ambleside **Ref:**YH08349
- **LAKELAND EQUESTRIAN**, Windermere **Ref:**YH08354
- **LARKRIGG RIDING SCHOOL**, Kendal **Ref:**YH08434
- **LIMEFITT PK**, Windermere **Ref:**YH08629
- **MIDDLE BAYLES LIVERY**, Alston **Ref:**YH09534
- **NEWTON RIGG**, Penrith **Ref:**YH10173
- **PARK FOOT TREKKING CTRE**, Penrith **Ref:**YH10725
- **SOCKBRIDGE PONY TREKKING CTRE**, Penrith **Ref:**YH13050

DERBYSHIRE

- **ALTON RIDING SCHOOL**, Chesterfield **Ref:**YH00344
- **BARLEYFIELDS**, Derby **Ref:**YH00952
- **C E S**, Ashbourne **Ref:**YH02370
- **CHESTERFIELD**, Chesterfield **Ref:**YH02833
- **HILLCLIFF STUD**, Belper **Ref:**YH06838
- **KNOWLE HILL EQUESTRIAN**, Derby **Ref:**YH08280
- **LEE WOOD HOTEL**, Buxton **Ref:**YH08521

DEVON

- **ARUNDELL ARMS**, Lifton **Ref:**YH00579
- **BICTON CLGE OF AGRICULTURE**, Budleigh Salterton **Ref:**YH01394
- **BRENDON MANOR RIDING STABLES**, Lynton **Ref:**YH01839
- **CHOLWELL EQUESTRIAN CTRE**, Okehampton **Ref:**YH02878
- **COOMBE PK EQUESTRIAN CTRE**, Totnes **Ref:**YH03273
- **EQUITOPIA**, Lynton **Ref:**YH04831
- **EXETER EQUESTRIAN CTRE**, Exeter **Ref:**YH04966
- **FINLAKE RIDING CTRE**, Newton Abbot **Ref:**YH05213
- **G C SEARLE & SONS**, Plymouth **Ref:**YH05573
- **HIGHER COBDEN FARM**, Exeter **Ref:**YH06778
- **HIGHER WILLYARDS FARM**, Exeter **Ref:**YH06781
- **HILLSIDE RIDING CTRE**, Princetown **Ref:**YH06853
- **MANOR FARM RIDING CTRE/LIVERY**, Okehampton **Ref:**YH09104
- **MULLACOTT EQUESTRIAN**, Ilfracombe **Ref:**YH09935
- **NEW HALL FARM**, Exeter **Ref:**YH10106
- **ROCK INN**, Newton Abbot **Ref:**YH12024
- **SILVER HORSESHOE**, Lynton **Ref:**YH12805
- **WEMBURY BAY RIDING SCHOOL**, Plymouth **Ref:**YH15103

DORSET

- **BRAMDON TREKKING CTRE**, Weymouth **Ref:**YH01789
- **FORTUNE CTRE**, Christchurch **Ref:**YH05392
- **HURN BRIDGE CTRE**, Christchurch **Ref:**YH07313
- **LANEHOUSE EQUITATION CTRE**, Weymouth **Ref:**YH08393
- **LULWORTH EQUESTRIAN CTRE**, Wareham **Ref:**YH08897
- **POUND COTTAGE RIDING CTRE**, Blandford Forum **Ref:**YH11307
- **REMPSTONE STABLES**, Wareham **Ref:**YH11751
- **TOLPUDDLE HALL**, Dorchester **Ref:**YH14213

ESSEX

- **ALEXANDER, J E**, Saffron Walden **Ref:**YH00271
- **BRETONS EQUESTRIAN CTRE**, Rainham **Ref:**YH01852
- **BUCKHATCH EQUESTRIAN CTRE**, Chelmsford **Ref:**YH02189
- **CLAY HALL**, Brentwood **Ref:**YH02994
- **COACH HSE**, Epping **Ref:**YH03102
- **COLCHESTER EQUESTRIAN CTRE**, Colchester **Ref:**YH03143
- **EPPINGDENE EQUESTRIAN CTRE**, Epping **Ref:**YH04681
- **FOLLY FOOT FARM**, Hockley **Ref:**YH05302
- **GUELDER ROSE**, Halstead **Ref:**YH06181
- **HALLINGBURY HALL**, Bishop's Stortford **Ref:**YH06331
- **HAROLDS PK RIDING CTRE**, Waltham Abbey **Ref:**YH06449
- **HOBBS CROSS EQUESTRIAN CTRE**, Epping **Ref:**YH06893
- **HOCKLEY EQUESTRIAN CTRE**, Hockley **Ref:**YH06902
- **SHOPLAND HALL EQUESTRIAN**, Rochford **Ref:**YH12758
- **WIX EQUESTRIAN CTRE**, Manningtree **Ref:**YH15636

GLOUCESTERSHIRE

- **CRISP, C (MISS)**, Westbury-on-Severn **Ref:**YH03604
- **ELM LEAZE STUD**, Badminton **Ref:**YH04631
- **MOORES FARM EQUESTRIAN CTRE**, Gloucester **Ref:**YH09771
- **SUMMERHOUSE**, Gloucester **Ref:**YH13632
- **UPCOTE CROSS COUNTRY COURSE**, Cheltenham **Ref:**YH14599

GUERNSEY

- **GUERNSEY**, St Sampsons **Ref:**YH06182

HAMPSHIRE

- **CHILLING BARN RIDING CTRE**, Southampton **Ref:**YH02856
- **CROFTON MANOR EQUESTRIAN CTRE**, Fareham **Ref:**YH03623
- **HARMSWORTH FARM**, Southampton **Ref:**YH06446
- **HOPLANDS EQUESTRIAN**, Stockbridge **Ref:**YH07058
- **INADOWN FARM STABLES**, Alton **Ref:**YH07407
- **LYNDHURST PK HOTEL**, Lyndhurst **Ref:**YH08928
- **MIRACLE TREES**, Ringwood **Ref:**YH09658
- **NRC**, Fareham **Ref:**YH10348
- **PASSFORD HSE HOTEL**, Lymington **Ref:**YH10810
- **RUSSELL EQUESTRIAN CTRE**, Southampton **Ref:**YH12252
- **SANDILANDS**, Petersfield **Ref:**YH12413
- **SOUTHERN TOURIST BOARD**, Eastleigh **Ref:**YH13144
- **SOUTHFIELD EQUESTRIAN CTRE**, Whitchurch **Ref:**YH13149
- **WELLINGTON RIDING**, Hook **Ref:**YH15075

HEREFORDSHIRE

- **COUNTY COMPETITION STUD**, Bromyard **Ref:**YH03486
- **HEREFORD RIDING CTRE**, Hereford **Ref:**YH06702
- **P G L TRAVEL**, Ross-on-Wye **Ref:**YH10640
- **SHEEPCOTE EQUESTRIAN**, Hereford **Ref:**YH12695
- **SUE ADAMS RIDING SCHOOL**, Leominster **Ref:**YH13622

HERTFORDSHIRE

- **CHIBLEY FARM STUD**, Hitchin **Ref:**YH02847
- **FIRS FARM EQUESTRIAN CTRE**, Hatfield **Ref:**YH05226
- **HERTFORDSHIRE TRAILS**, Hertford **Ref:**YH06721
- **LUFFENHALL EQUESTRIAN CTRE**, Stevenage **Ref:**YH08892
- **SOUTH MEDBURN**, Borehamwood **Ref:**YH13101
- **WILSON, R C**, Tring **Ref:**YH15545

ISLE OF MAN

- **G G H EQUITATION CTRE**, Marown **Ref:**YH05578
- **MOUNT RULE EQUESTRIAN CTRE**, Braddan **Ref:**YH09894

ISLE OF WIGHT

- **BRICKFIELDS**, Ryde **Ref:**YH01866

KENT

- **BEDGEBURY RIDING CTRE**, Goudhurst **Ref:**YH01155
- **BRAESIDE E.C**, Dover **Ref:**YH01773
- **CANTERBURY CLGE**, Canterbury **Ref:**YH02508
- **CASEY, M L**, Canterbury **Ref:**YH02615
- **CAVALRY BARN**, Ashford **Ref:**YH02663
- **COBHAM MANOR**, Maidstone **Ref:**YH03113
- **EAGLESFIELD EQUESTRIAN CTRE**, Sevenoaks **Ref:**YH04441
- **EQUINES LIVERIES**, Maidstone **Ref:**YH04809
- **FIRWOOD COURT STUD**, Herne Bay **Ref:**YH05235

FIVE OAKS EQUESTRIAN CTRE, Keston Ref:YH05254
HADLOW CLGE, Tonbridge Ref:YH06269
HEIGHTS STABLES, Westerham Ref:YH06650
HONNINGTON, Tunbridge Wells Ref:YH07019
LEYBOURNE GRANGE, West Malling Ref:YH08600
LIMES FARM EQUESTRIAN, Folkestone Ref:YH08635
MANNIX STUD, Canterbury Ref:YH09091
MAYWOOD STUD, Ashford Ref:YH09309
MOUNT MASCAL STABLES, Bexley Ref:YH09890
OLD BEXLEY EQUESTRIAN, Bexley Ref:YH10451
SOUTH EAST TOURIST BOARD, Tunbridge Wells Ref:YH13088
UPPER THRUXTED FARM, Canterbury Ref:YH14608
WHITELEAF RIDING CTRE, Sittingbourne Ref:YH15347
WILLOW FARM, Faversham Ref:YH15497
WOODLANDS, Sevenoaks Ref:YH15706
WYE COLLEGE, Ashford Ref:YH15860

LANCASHIRE

ARKENFIELD EQUESTRIAN CTRE, Chorley Ref:YH00530
ASOKA, Worsley Ref:YH00625
BARTON EQUESTRIAN CTRE, Preston Ref:YH01044
BECCONSALL, Preston Ref:YH01144
BIRCHINLEY MANOR, Rochdale Ref:YH01434
BROOMHILL, Clitheroe Ref:YH02080
CHORLEY EQUESTRIAN CTRE, Chorley Ref:YH02880
CORNFIELD FARM, Burnley Ref:YH03323
ECCLESTON, Preston Ref:YH04532
FIR TREE RIDING CTRE, Ormskirk Ref:YH05221
HERD HSE RIDING SCHOOL, Burnley Ref:YH06699
MOORVIEW, Darwen Ref:YH09782
MYERSCOUGH CLGE, Preston Ref:YH09982
OSBALDESTON RIDING CTRE, Blackburn Ref:YH10557
PANAMA SPORT HORSES, Clitheroe Ref:YH10695
RENARD RIDING CTRE, Poulton-Le-Fylde Ref:YH11753
RIBBY HALL, Preston Ref:YH11795
ROBSCOTT EQUITATION, Carnforth Ref:YH12010
ROSSENDALE & HYNDBURN EC, Accrington Ref:YH12123
WHITEGATE FARM, Bacup Ref:YH15338
WIMBOURNE EQUESTRIAN CTRE, Blackpool Ref:YH15559
WREA GREEN EQUITATION CTRE, Kirkham Ref:YH15816

LEICESTERSHIRE

DEBDALE HORSES, Leicester Ref:YH04004
HINKLEY EQUESTRIAN CTRE, Leicester Ref:YH06874
HORSE TROUGH, Loughborough Ref:YH07144
INT STUDENTS/YOUTH EXCHANGES, Leicester Ref:YH07474
MARKFIELD EQUESTRIAN, Markfield Ref:YH09161
SOMERBY EQUESTRIAN CTRE, Melton Mowbray Ref:YH13060

LINCOLNSHIRE

DE MONTFORT UNI, Grantham Ref:YH03979
FOUR WINDS, Spalding Ref:YH05413
HILL HSE, Market Rasen Ref:YH06820
LAUGHTON WOOD EQUESTRIAN CTRE, Gainsborough Ref:YH08449
LINCS RURAL ACTIVITIES, Louth Ref:YH08643
MEREHAM GRANGE, Horncastle Ref:YH09470
NORTH LINCOLNSHIRE COLLEGE, Lincoln Ref:YH10270
ORCHARD FARM EQUESTRIAN, Skegness Ref:YH10529
PARK RIDING SCHOOL, Lincoln Ref:YH10735
POPPYFIELDS, Lincoln Ref:YH11275
REDNIL EQUESTRIAN CTRE, Lincoln Ref:YH11716
SHEEPGATE EQUESTRIAN, Boston Ref:YH12696
SHEEPGATE TACK & TOGS, Boston Ref:YH12697

LINCOLNSHIRE (NORTH EAST)

R G EQUESTRIAN, Grimsby Ref:YH11536

LONDON (GREATER)

CORDWAINERS CLGE, London Ref:YH03314
DOCKLANDS EQUESTRIAN CTRE, London Ref:YH04157
HYDE PARK RIDING WEAR, London Ref:YH07345
HYDE PARK STABLES, London Ref:YH07346
LITTLEBOURNE FARM, Uxbridge Ref:YH08703
LONDON EQUESTRIAN CTRE, Finchley Ref:YH08785
LONDON EQUESTRIAN CTRE, London Ref:YH08784
ROEHAMPTON GATE, London Ref:YH12053

MANCHESTER (GREATER)

CARRINGTON RIDING, Manchester Ref:YH02589
CROFT END EQUESTRIAN CTRE, Oldham Ref:YH03613
MANCHESTER EQUESTRIAN CTRE, Manchester Ref:YH09065
MATCHMOOR RIDING CTRE, Bolton Ref:YH09257
MOSSBROOK ARENA & STUD, Astley Ref:YH09866
RYDERS FARM, Bolton Ref:YH12297

MIDLANDS (WEST)

BEARLEY CROSS STABLES, Solihull Ref:YH01121
HERON FIELD, Solihull Ref:YH06711

NORFOLK

BLACKWATER FARM, Norwich Ref:YH01501
CROFT FARM RIDING CTRE, Great Yarmouth Ref:YH03615
EASTERN CLGE EQUESTRIAN CTRE, Norwich Ref:YH04497
EASTON CLGE, Norwich Ref:YH04513
ELVEDEN EQUESTRIAN CTRE, Thetford Ref:YH04646
FOREST ARENA, Swaffham Ref:YH05332
GREENACRES RIDING SCHOOL, King's Lynn Ref:YH06079
NORFOLK CLGE, King's Lynn Ref:YH10231
RUNCTON HALL, King's Lynn Ref:YH12233
SOUTH NORFOLK EQUESTRIAN CTRE, Wymondham Ref:YH13102
WESTON PARK EQUESTRIAN CTRE, Norwich Ref:YH15224

NORTHAMPTONSHIRE

MANOR FARM RIDING SCHOOL, Wellingborough Ref:YH09106
MOULTON CLGE, Northampton Ref:YH09883
SHUCKBURGH HSE RIDING CTRE, Naseby Ref:YH12772

NORTHUMBERLAND

KIDLENDLEE TRAIL RIDING, Morpeth Ref:YH08124
REDESDALE RIDING CTRE, Otterburn Ref:YH11710
RIVERDALE HALL HOTEL, Hexham Ref:YH11921
SANDY BAY TRECKING CTRE, Ashington Ref:YH12423
WHITTON FARM HSE HOTEL, Rothbury Ref:YH15376

NOTTINGHAMSHIRE

BRACKENHURST COLLEGE, Southwell Ref:YH01741
CLGE FARM, Newark Ref:YH03026
RUFFORD PARK TRAINING CTRE, Ollerton Ref:YH12213
ST CLEMENTS LODGE, Nottingham Ref:YH13274

OXFORDSHIRE

ASTI STUD & SADDLERY, Faringdon Ref:YH00633
BURFORD SCHOOL FARM, Burford Ref:YH02239
FAIRSPEAR EQUESTRIAN CTRE, Witney Ref:YH05028
OXFORD BROOKES UNI, Oxford Ref:YH10617
PIGEON HOUSE STABLES, Witney Ref:YH11095
STANDLAKE EQUESTRIAN CTRE, Witney Ref:YH13362
THAMES VALLEY TREKKING, Henley-on-Thames Ref:YH13977
TURPINS LODGE, Banbury Ref:YH14494
UK CHASERS, Oxford Ref:YH14543
WATERSTOCK HSE TRAINING CTRE, Oxford Ref:YH14973
WEST OXFORDSHIRE COLLEGE, Witney Ref:YH15158

SHROPSHIRE

FRESHFIELDS, Market Drayton Ref:YH05499
HARPER ADAMS, Newport Ref:YH06451
HIGHGROVE SCHOOL OF RIDING, Craven Arms Ref:YH06788
HOOK FARM EQUESTRIAN CTRE, Bridgnorth Ref:YH07034
LILLESHALL EQUESTRIAN CTRE, Newport Ref:YH08620
MILL FARM RIDING CTRE, Shrewsbury Ref:YH09572
NORTH FARM RIDING EST, Ludlow Ref:YH10262
OSWESTRY EQUEST CTRE, Oswestry Ref:YH10576
TOUCHDOWN LIVERIES, Whitchurch Ref:YH14253

SOMERSET

BADGWORTH ARENA, Axbridge Ref:YH00781
BRIMSMORE EQUESTRIAN CTRE, Yeovil Ref:YH01913
BURROWHAYES FARM, Porlock Ref:YH02282
CIRCLE D RIDING CTRE, Axbridge Ref:YH02924
CONQUEST CTRE, Taunton Ref:YH03243
CURLAND EQUESTRIAN CTRE, Taunton Ref:YH03728
DIAMOND FARM RIDING CTRE, Burnham-on-Sea Ref:YH04103
EBBORLANDS, Wells Ref:YH04529
EDGCOTT HSE, Exford Ref:YH04554
FLYING START RIDING CTRE, Taunton Ref:YH05295
GREENHAM EQUESTRIAN CTRE, Wellington Ref:YH06087
MILLFIELD SCHOOL, Street Ref:YH09617
RODGROVE STUD EQUESTRIAN CTRE, Wincanton Ref:YH12048
ROYAL OAK INN, Withypool Ref:YH12189
STOCKLAND LOVELL, Bridgwater Ref:YH13493
TUFTERS, Winsford Ref:YH14447
WOOLCOTTS FARM, Dulverton Ref:YH15765
WYATT, C R & R K, Minehead Ref:YH15853

SOMERSET (NORTH)

HAND EQUESTRIAN CTRE, Clevedon Ref:YH06377
MENDIP RIDING CTRE, Churchill Ref:YH09458

STAFFORDSHIRE

ANIMAL CARE/EQUINE TRAIN ORG, Stafford Ref:YH00429

- **ASTON HILL EQUESTRIAN**, Stafford **Ref:**YH00637
- **CANNOCK CHASE TREKKING CTRE**, Stafford **Ref:**YH02504
- **FLYAWAY**, Stafford **Ref:**YH05292
- **POUND CLOSE STABLES**, Gillingham **Ref:**YH11306
- **RODBASTON**, Penkridge **Ref:**YH12040
- **RODBASTON CLGE**, Penkridge **Ref:**YH12041
- **SCHOOL OF ST MARY & ST ANNE**, Lichfield **Ref:**YH12522
- **SCROPTON**, Burton-on-Trent **Ref:**YH12569

SUFFOLK

- **BARDWELL MANOR**, Bury St Edmunds **Ref:**YH00928
- **BENTLEY RIDING CTRE**, Ipswich **Ref:**YH01286
- **BRITISH RACING SCHOOL**, Newmarket **Ref:**YH01967
- **CHURCH FARM TACK SHOP & FEEDS**, Eye **Ref:**YH02903
- **COPDOCK RIDING CTRE**, Ipswich **Ref:**YH03292
- **ENCOMPASS TRAINING SVS**, Framlingham **Ref:**YH04663
- **HADLEIGH RIDING CTRE**, Ipswich **Ref:**YH06266
- **HEYLAND, A R M A**, Bures **Ref:**YH06736
- **LINKWOOD EQUESTIAN**, Bury St Edmunds **Ref:**YH08665
- **OPEN CLGE OF EQUINE STUDIES**, Bury St Edmunds **Ref:**YH10523
- **ORWELL ARENA**, Ipswich **Ref:**YH10556
- **OTLEY CLGE**, Ipswich **Ref:**YH10577
- **STOKE BY CLARE EQUESTRIAN CTRE**, Sudbury **Ref:**YH13501
- **VALLEY FARM**, Woodbridge **Ref:**YH14651

SURREY

- **BRIDLEWAYS EQUESTRIAN CTRE**, Great Bookham **Ref:**YH01898
- **CHESSINGTON**, Chessington **Ref:**YH02830
- **CLIFF HATCH STABLES**, Woking **Ref:**YH03032
- **COULSDON CLGE**, Coulsdon **Ref:**YH03389
- **CRANLEIGH SCHOOL OF RIDING**, Cranleigh **Ref:**YH03565
- **DORKING EQUESTRIAN CTRE**, Dorking **Ref:**YH04200
- **EQUUS EQUESTRIAN CTRES**, Epsom **Ref:**YH04839
- **HACKING WITH A DIFFERENCE**, Cranleigh **Ref:**YH06255
- **MAPLE STUD EQUESTRIAN CTRE**, Cranleigh **Ref:**YH09133
- **ONLY FOALS & HORSES**, Oxted **Ref:**YH10522
- **POYNTERS**, Cobham **Ref:**YH11330
- **RIDING CTRE**, Farnham **Ref:**YH11873
- **ROYAL SCHOOL**, Haslemere **Ref:**YH12194
- **S R S**, Sunbury-on-Thames **Ref:**YH12333
- **T.T.T**, Guildford **Ref:**YH13769

SUSSEX (EAST)

- **BEAUPORT PK HOTEL**, Hastings **Ref:**YH01139
- **CROCKSTEAD PK**, Lewes **Ref:**YH03608
- **GOLDEN CROSS**, Hailsham **Ref:**YH05878
- **MISBOURNE RIDING CTRE**, Uckfield **Ref:**YH09659
- **PLUMPTON CLGE**, Lewes **Ref:**YH11183
- **WEALDEN COLLEGE**, Crowborough **Ref:**YH15018

SUSSEX (WEST)

- **BRENDON**, Brighton **Ref:**YH01835
- **BRENDON HORSE & RIDER**, Brighton **Ref:**YH01837
- **BRINSBURY COLLEGE**, Pulborough **Ref:**YH01917
- **EAST VIEW FRUIT FARM**, Haywards Heath **Ref:**YH04488
- **FERRING COUNTRY CTRE**, Worthing **Ref:**YH05171
- **HACKING IN THE COUNTRYSIDE**, Billingshurst **Ref:**YH06254
- **LAVANT HSE STABLES**, Chichester **Ref:**YH08460
- **LIGHTS**, Brighton **Ref:**YH08616
- **MOLECOMB STUD**, Chichester **Ref:**YH09712
- **NORWOOD EQUESTRIAN CTRE**, Petworth **Ref:**YH10335
- **SOUTHDOWN EQUESTRIAN CTRE**, Steyning **Ref:**YH13133
- **WILLOWBROOK RIDING CTRE**, Chichester **Ref:**YH15508
- **ZARA STUD**, Chichester **Ref:**YH15951

TYNE AND WEAR

- **GO RIDING GRP**, Ponteland **Ref:**YH05862
- **LITTLE HARLE STABLES**, Newcastle-upon-Tyne **Ref:**YH08688
- **WILLIAMS, R**, Newcastle-upon-Tyne **Ref:**YH15470

WARWICKSHIRE

- **BAXTERLEY**, Atherstone **Ref:**YH01090
- **COURT FARM RIDING CTRE**, Nuneaton **Ref:**YH03501
- **NUNEATON & NORTH WARWICKSHIRE**, Nuneaton **Ref:**YH10353
- **SPORT HORSE TRAINING CTRE**, Stratford-upon-Avon **Ref:**YH13219
- **STONELEIGH STABLES**, Kenilworth **Ref:**YH13519
- **SWALLOWFIELD EQUESTRIAN**, Solihull **Ref:**YH13686
- **WAVERLEY EQUESTRIAN CTRE**, Leamington Spa **Ref:**YH15011
- **WOOTTON GRANGE EQUESTRIAN**, Warwick **Ref:**YH15772

WILTSHIRE

- **HEYWOOD**, Westbury **Ref:**YH06737
- **HORSEMANSHIP**, Wootton Bassett **Ref:**YH07161
- **INFANTRY SADDLE CLUB**, Warminster **Ref:**YH07441
- **LACKHAM CLGE EQUESTRIAN CTRE**, Chippenham **Ref:**YH08332
- **LADYSMITHS EQUESTRIAN CTRE**, Swindon **Ref:**YH08340
- **LONGHORN**, Warminster **Ref:**YH08813
- **MALTHOUSE EQUESTRIAN CTRE**, Swindon **Ref:**YH09058
- **MILL LANE EQUESTRIAN CTRE**, Swindon **Ref:**YH09580
- **WEST LAVINGTON EQUESTRIAN**, Devizes **Ref:**YH15153
- **WIDBROOK ARABIAN STUD**, Bradford-on-Avon **Ref:**YH15388

WORCESTERSHIRE

- **BIRCHWOOD**, Bewdley **Ref:**YH01436
- **COUNTRY TREKS**, Kidderminster **Ref:**YH03433
- **DEBDALE EQUINE CTRE**, Kidderminster **Ref:**YH04003
- **FAR FOREST EQUESTRIAN CTRE**, Kidderminster **Ref:**YH05047
- **GRACELANDS**, Droitwich **Ref:**YH05958
- **HARTLEBURY EQUESTRIAN CTRE**, Kidderminster **Ref:**YH06505
- **HINDLIP EQUESTRIAN CTRE**, Hindlip **Ref:**YH06872
- **KYRE EQUESTRIAN CTRE**, Tenbury Wells **Ref:**YH08305
- **MERRYBROOK EQUESTRIAN CTRE**, Evesham **Ref:**YH09486
- **TABOR, M J & N J**, Broadway **Ref:**YH13771

YORKSHIRE (EAST)

- **BISHOP BURTON COLLEGE**, Beverley **Ref:**YH01448
- **BRAEMAR**, Hull **Ref:**YH01770
- **EAST RIDING**, Brough **Ref:**YH04483
- **NORTH HUMBERSIDE**, Hull **Ref:**YH10264

YORKSHIRE (NORTH)

- **ASKHAM BRYAN COLLEGE**, York **Ref:**YH00622
- **BILSDALE RIDING CTRE**, York **Ref:**YH01416
- **BROWSIDE PONY TREKKING CTRE**, Scarborough **Ref:**YH02148
- **CARTHORPE PONY TREKKING**, Bedale **Ref:**YH02609
- **CRAVEN CLGE**, Skipton **Ref:**YH03572
- **CROSSCOUNTRY SCHOOLING GROUND**, Scarborough **Ref:**YH03657
- **FOLLIFOOT PK**, Harrogate **Ref:**YH05300
- **FRIARS HILL STABLES**, York **Ref:**YH05501
- **HOLLINHALL RIDE & DRIVE**, Whitby **Ref:**YH06946
- **KILNSEY TREKKING CTRE**, Skipton **Ref:**YH08153
- **LITTLE PASTURE TREKKING CTRE**, Knaresborough **Ref:**YH08700
- **NABURN GRANGE RIDING CTRE**, York **Ref:**YH10008
- **ROBERTS, V J W**, Skipton **Ref:**YH11965
- **YORKSHIRE RIDING CTRE**, Harrogate **Ref:**YH15922

YORKSHIRE (SOUTH)

- **FIR TREE FARM EQUESTRIAN CTRE**, Doncaster **Ref:**YH05220
- **MOORHOUSE**, Doncaster **Ref:**YH09774
- **NORTHERN RACING COLLEGE**, Doncaster **Ref:**YH10307

YORKSHIRE (WEST)

- **MIDDLETON PK EQUESTRIAN CTRE**, Dewsbury **Ref:**YH09542
- **PARK LANE CLGE**, Leeds **Ref:**YH10729
- **TIMBERTOPS EQUESTRIAN CTRE**, Pontefract **Ref:**YH14162
- **WHITLEY EQUITATION CTRE**, Dewsbury **Ref:**YH15363

FARRIERS

BATH & SOMERSET (NORTH EAST)

- **BATH EQUESTRIAN CTRE**, Bath **Ref:**YH01070
- **BONIFACE, IAN**, Chew Magna **Ref:**YH01623
- **CURRY, COLIN J**, Bath **Ref:**YH03742
- **FORD, NIGEL STEPHEN**, Bath **Ref:**YH05325
- **PEPPARD, JOHN S J**, Bath **Ref:**YH10969
- **THATCHER, G**, Bath **Ref:**YH13979
- **YOUNG, M D**, Bath **Ref:**YH15936

BEDFORDSHIRE

- **ANDERSON, SIMON H**, Elstow **Ref:**YH00387
- **BERGER, HANS**, Haynes **Ref:**YH01296
- **BURGOYNE, ROBERT**, Kempston **Ref:**YH02252
- **COURTENAY, A L**, Toddington **Ref:**YH03503
- **CROTHERS, BILLY**, Leighton Buzzard **Ref:**YH03673
- **KNIGHT, ADAM R**, Radwell **Ref:**YH08258
- **MARTIN, KEVIN JAMES**, Leighton Buzzard **Ref:**YH09221
- **MATTHEWS, STAX D**, Luton **Ref:**YH09277
- **MCCARTIE, R**, Bedford **Ref:**YH09323
- **MOULTON, A L**, Cardington **Ref:**YH09887
- **PLATT, ANGELA D**, Flitwick **Ref:**YH11168
- **RYAN, THOMAS P**, Keysoe **Ref:**YH12287
- **SAUNDERS, BRIAN J**, Biggleswade **Ref:**YH12445
- **SAUNDERS, NEIL J**, Dunstable **Ref:**YH12451
- **TAYLOR, C**, Arlesey **Ref:**YH13898
- **TIFT, J**, Leighton Buzzard **Ref:**YH14140
- **TURNER, NIGEL D**, Stanbridge **Ref:**YH14489

BERKSHIRE

- **ADCOCK, DOMINIC R**, Windsor **Ref:**YH00178
- **ALDERTON, BARRY D**, Lambourn **Ref:**YH00259
- **BLOOMFIELD, WARWICK J**, Bracknell **Ref:**YH01554
- **BODDY, STEPHEN M**, Hungerford **Ref:**YH01594
- **BOND, DAVID**, Hungerford **Ref:**YH01617
- **BUCK, IAN**, Hungerford **Ref:**YH02186
- **CARTMELL, L A**, Lambourn **Ref:**YH02611
- **CHAPEL FORGE**, Hungerford **Ref:**YH02740
- **CHARLES, ANDREW JEREMY**, Lambourn **Ref:**YH02758
- **EQUICENTRE**, Waltham St Lawrence **Ref:**YH04737

- **FOX, F A**, Lambourn **Ref:**YH05428
- **GATESMAN, NIGEL W**, Reading **Ref:**YH05675
- **GIBBONS, PAUL M**, Newbury **Ref:**YH05741
- **HALFACRE, G W D**, Bracknell **Ref:**YH06297
- **HALLUM, DAVID J**, Newbury **Ref:**YH06335
- **HARMAN, M W**, Maidenhead **Ref:**YH06442
- **JENKINS, LLOYD P**, Windsor **Ref:**YH07734
- **KINANE, MICHAEL F**, Bracknell **Ref:**YH08164
- **KING, STUART L**, Hungerford **Ref:**YH08188
- **KNIGHT, K J**, Wokingham **Ref:**YH08262
- **LAMBOURNE, JAMES**, Newbury **Ref:**YH08370
- **MATTHEWS, DAVID J**, Maidenhead **Ref:**YH09272
- **MAY, ROBIN PETER**, Wokingham **Ref:**YH09292
- **MCCULLOCH, IAN WALKER**, Reading **Ref:**YH09340
- **PIROUET, TIMOTHY RYAN**, Newbury **Ref:**YH11150
- **REID, NOEL A**, Newbury **Ref:**YH11744
- **REILLY, VINCENT**, Newbury **Ref:**YH11747
- **SAMPSONS**, Newbury **Ref:**YH12400
- **SIDWELL, PAUL ALAN**, Maidenhead **Ref:**YH12790
- **SIMMONS, BRYNLY A**, Bracknell **Ref:**YH12827
- **SPILLER, GRAHAM**, Reading **Ref:**YH13205
- **STACEY, DONALD A**, Reading **Ref:**YH13315
- **STYLES, JAMES**, Bracknell **Ref:**YH13619
- **TOWELL, MICHAEL JAMES**, Lambourn **Ref:**YH14270
- **WHITBY, ALEXANDER J**, Windsor **Ref:**YH15296
- **WIERSMA, HAITZE**, Twyford **Ref:**YH15395
- **WILLIAMS, PAUL D**, Reading **Ref:**YH15469
- **WOODLANDS**, Hungerford **Ref:**YH15705

BRISTOL

- **BALL, H M & A H**, Bristol **Ref:**YH00851
- **C J HAWKINS & SON**, Bristol **Ref:**YH02376
- **DURBIN, J W**, Bristol **Ref:**YH04367
- **GUNTER, T J**, Bristol **Ref:**YH06193
- **HILLCREST FORGE**, Bristol **Ref:**YH06841
- **LINDSAY, I**, Bristol **Ref:**YH08653
- **SMITH, J S**, Bristol **Ref:**YH12964
- **SOMERVILLE, JASON P**, Shirehampton **Ref:**YH13067
- **STAITE, M G**, Bristol **Ref:**YH13349

BUCKINGHAMSHIRE

- **ASLETT, G**, High Wycombe **Ref:**YH00623
- **BETTISON, CARL**, Aylesbury **Ref:**YH01336
- **CHRISTIE, RUPERT W W**, Marlow **Ref:**YH02889
- **CRIGHTON, GJS & OLIVER, GA**, Marlow **Ref:**YH03598
- **CROMPTON, JOHN**, Chesham **Ref:**YH03631
- **CRYER, ANDREW N**, Marlow **Ref:**YH03693
- **EDWARDS, MARCUS L**, Windsor **Ref:**YH04584
- **EQUICTRE**, Marlow **Ref:**YH04741
- **FOSKETT, RUSSELL WILLIAM**, Chesham **Ref:**YH05394
- **HALL, ALBERT J**, Great Missenden **Ref:**YH06311
- **HEAD, SAMUEL C**, Great Brickhill **Ref:**YH06610
- **HILLSDON, ROGER C**, Marlow **Ref:**YH06851
- **HUSTON, G S**, Chesham **Ref:**YH07332
- **JENNINGS, JOHN R**, Stokenchurch **Ref:**YH07748
- **LAWTHER, J R**, Great Missenden **Ref:**YH08480
- **MYALL, AARON J**, Milton Keynes **Ref:**YH09979
- **PHILLIPS BROS**, Buckingham **Ref:**YH11047
- **PHILLIPS, TERENCE J**, Lillingstone Dayrell **Ref:**YH11066
- **RECORD, NICHOLAS J**, Amersham **Ref:**YH11690
- **ROONEY, KEVIN BARRY**, Aylesbury **Ref:**YH12077
- **ROTHERAM, G**, Aylesbury **Ref:**YH12129
- **ROTHERAM, H**, Aylesbury **Ref:**YH12130
- **SPELLER, A**, Aylesbury **Ref:**YH13194
- **SPELLER, ANDREW E**, Aylesbury **Ref:**YH13195
- **STROMSHOLM**, Milton Keynes **Ref:**YH13579
- **TERRY, JOSEPH G**, Chesham **Ref:**YH13959
- **VENN, OLIVER J**, Aylesbury **Ref:**YH14677
- **YACOMINE, P J**, Aylesbury **Ref:**YH15880

CAMBRIDGESHIRE

- **BARRATT, DAVID J**, Haslingfield **Ref:**YH01008
- **BARTLETT, ROBERT S**, Peterborough **Ref:**YH01041
- **BOND, CLIVE R**, Ely **Ref:**YH01616
- **BROOK, PHILIP J**, Ely **Ref:**YH02040
- **DRIFTEND STABLES**, Bourn **Ref:**YH04274
- **FARRIERS REGISTRATION COUNCIL**, Peterborough **Ref:**YH05091
- **FLATTERS, B**, Peterborough **Ref:**YH05264
- **FRYER, LEWIS E**, Huntingdon **Ref:**YH05529
- **GOWING, STEPHEN PETER**, March **Ref:**YH05956
- **HACKETT, KEITH J**, Huntingdon **Ref:**YH06250
- **HILL, STEPHEN J H**, Huntingdon **Ref:**YH06833
- **HONES, MARK A**, Burwell **Ref:**YH07010
- **HOWE, DAVID J**, Ely **Ref:**YH07224
- **JOHNSON, NORMAN**, Ely **Ref:**YH07830
- **LE-WECHNER, NICHOLAS J**, Ely **Ref:**YH08577
- **MASON, R J**, Peterborough **Ref:**YH09247
- **MATTHEWS, BRIAN**, Huntingdon **Ref:**YH09270
- **MOORE, C**, Cambridge **Ref:**YH09756
- **MORGAN, DAVID JOHN**, Ely **Ref:**YH09803
- **MORGAN, G W**, Peterborough **Ref:**YH09804
- **MURFITT, D G**, Ely **Ref:**YH09951
- **MURFITT, TIMOTHY J**, Soham **Ref:**YH09952
- **R C GOWING**, Ely **Ref:**YH11519
- **THOMPSON, LUKE P**, Ely **Ref:**YH14038

CHESHIRE

- **ADAMS, D C T**, Warrington **Ref:**YH00165
- **ADAMS, RICHARD A**, Warrington **Ref:**YH00172
- **ATHERTON, P V J**, Widnes **Ref:**YH00645
- **BAILEY, JOHN ANDREW**, Macclesfield **Ref:**YH00801
- **BOURNE, SIMON S**, Sandbach **Ref:**YH01685
- **BROOKE, WILLIAM N**, High Peak **Ref:**YH02044
- **BROOKS LANE SMITHY**, Middlewich **Ref:**YH02061
- **BROOKS, JONATHAN**, Altrincham **Ref:**YH02066
- **BURNS, DAVID J MAHER**, Woodford **Ref:**YH02271
- **CONSTERDINE, C J**, Macclesfield **Ref:**YH03245
- **COX, P E**, High Peak **Ref:**YH03535
- **DARLOW, G C**, Knutsford **Ref:**YH03895
- **DAVENHILL, ADAM J**, Crewe **Ref:**YH03909
- **DAWSON, KARL**, Middlewich **Ref:**YH03963
- **DUNCALF, ALAN W**, Warrington **Ref:**YH04333
- **EATON SMITHY**, Tarporley **Ref:**YH04524
- **FEARNALL STUD**, Tarporley **Ref:**YH05117
- **GORDON, PAUL T**, Northwich **Ref:**YH05926
- **GOUGH, GARRY C**, Chester **Ref:**YH05949
- **GUILFOYLE, M**, Cheadle **Ref:**YH06186
- **HARGREAVES, TERENCE D**, Northwich **Ref:**YH06429
- **HILTON, JOHN**, Tameside **Ref:**YH06865
- **HOWELL, A J**, Macclesfield **Ref:**YH07226
- **HUGHES, JOHN W**, Malpas **Ref:**YH07269
- **IAN P BRADBURY**, Macclesfield **Ref:**YH07371
- **J PRESTON & SON**, Widnes **Ref:**YH07606
- **JACKSON, PAUL**, Stockport **Ref:**YH07651
- **JOSEPH MURPHY**, Warrington **Ref:**YH07944
- **KIRKBY**, Tarporley **Ref:**YH08232
- **LINDLEY, BERNARD J**, Altrincham **Ref:**YH08648
- **MAHER-BURNS, MATTHEW J**, Macclesfield **Ref:**YH09036
- **MANIFOLD, MALCOLM T**, Hyde **Ref:**YH09079
- **MIDDLEBROOK, SIMON E**, Macclesfield **Ref:**YH09537
- **MOSS, JOHN D**, Alderley Edge **Ref:**YH09860
- **OWEN, GARETH J**, Chester **Ref:**YH10601
- **OWEN, J R**, Chester **Ref:**YH10602
- **RANDLES, JOHN M**, Congleton **Ref:**YH11631
- **ROBERTS, E N**, Chester **Ref:**YH11948
- **SALT, EDWARD M**, Tarporley **Ref:**YH12392
- **SINSTADT, M C W**, Nantwich **Ref:**YH12856
- **SMITH, ANDREW C**, Malpas **Ref:**YH12941
- **SMITH, JONATHAN C**, Malpas **Ref:**YH12971
- **SPENCER, D**, Stockport **Ref:**YH13197
- **TAYLOR, JEREMY N**, Nantwich **Ref:**YH13904
- **UNSWORTH, HARRY W**, Farndon **Ref:**YH14598
- **WELSH, JOSEPH**, Congleton **Ref:**YH15098
- **ZINON, CHRISTOPHER**, Altrincham **Ref:**YH15956

CLEVELAND

- **BROWN, KARL J**, Middlesbrough **Ref:**YH02118
- **FERNIE, A**, Norton **Ref:**YH05165
- **HAYKIN, M**, Middlesbrough **Ref:**YH06582
- **ROOKS, GORDON**, Guisborough **Ref:**YH12076
- **SMITHSON, B H**, Elwick **Ref:**YH13009
- **WATSON, EUAN MCINTOSH**, Middlesbrough **Ref:**YH14984

CORNWALL

- **BAKER, MARTYN D**, Coppathorne **Ref:**YH00824
- **BALCOMBE, KEVIN P**, Copthorne **Ref:**YH00833
- **BALL, A S**, Bodmin **Ref:**YH00849
- **BROKENSHIRE, ADRIAN KEITH**, Bodmin **Ref:**YH02022
- **BUNCE, ARTHUR LESLIE**, Helston **Ref:**YH02221
- **BUNGAY, PETER L**, Launceston **Ref:**YH02224
- **CORNWELL, RAYMOND T**, Liskeard **Ref:**YH03342
- **CRAGG, R**, Truro **Ref:**YH03543
- **FARRIER SVS**, St Ives **Ref:**YH05088
- **GRAY, GARY S**, St Just **Ref:**YH06028
- **HANN, JAMES S**, Camelford **Ref:**YH06391
- **HAYDEN, RICHARD J**, Launceston **Ref:**YH06570
- **HILLS, JOHN R**, Wadebridge **Ref:**YH06849
- **HOWIE, C J**, Saltash **Ref:**YH07232
- **JOHNSON, PAUL**, Callington **Ref:**YH07833
- **JONES, DAVID D**, Camborne **Ref:**YH07889
- **KNIGHT, P W**, Truro **Ref:**YH08263
- **LANG, JAMES H**, Mullion **Ref:**YH08396
- **LAWRIE, JOHN**, Liskeard **Ref:**YH08475
- **LONG, S P**, Truro **Ref:**YH08805
- **MALE, TREVOR**, Penzance **Ref:**YH09047
- **MARTIN, PAUL**, Par **Ref:**YH09224
- **MCNAMARA, MICHAEL F J**, Saltash **Ref:**YH09399
- **MOORE, SIMON A**, Redruth **Ref:**YH09765
- **PENCARN FORGE**, Hayle **Ref:**YH10929
- **PREECE, MARK**, Launceston **Ref:**YH11341
- **SCREATON, M**, Penzance **Ref:**YH12564
- **STEVENS, M A**, Helston **Ref:**YH13446
- **TUCKETT, GRAHAME J**, Penzance **Ref:**YH14437
- **VINCENT, JOHN**, Par **Ref:**YH14724
- **WEBBER, BRIAN**, St Austell **Ref:**YH15034
- **WILKIN, KEITH M**, Truro **Ref:**YH15416
- **WILLIAMS, J B**, Camborne **Ref:**YH15460
- **WILLS, S**, Redruth **Ref:**YH15520
- **WOODING, SIMON A**, Helston **Ref:**YH15700

COUNTY DURHAM

- **ARMSTRONG, JOHN W**, Durham **Ref:**YH00549

BELL, JOHN, Crook **Ref:**YH01225
BONE, JOSEPH, Durham **Ref:**YH01620
BRITTON, JOHN R, Durham **Ref:**YH01985
BURTON, W L, Durham **Ref:**YH02295
CASON, P, Durham **Ref:**YH02617
HESLOP, SIMON, Ebchester **Ref:**YH06722
HINDHAUGH, HENRY HALL, Old Burdon South **Ref:**YH06870
JACKSON, NEIL, Bishop Auckland **Ref:**YH07650
MOORE, W, Bishop Auckland **Ref:**YH09768
RIDLEY, GEORGE E, Stanley **Ref:**YH11887
ROSS, RUSSELL A, Consett **Ref:**YH12121
SCAIFE, ANDREW, Coatham Mundeville **Ref:**YH12480
SHAW, GARRY A, Darlington **Ref:**YH12681
TALLENTIRE & SONS, Bishop Auckland **Ref:**YH13834

CUMBRIA

ATKINSON, ROBERT W, Carlisle **Ref:**YH00652
CHARLY'S YARD SMITHY, Carlisle **Ref:**YH02770
CUTHBERT, T A K, Carlisle **Ref:**YH03760
D WATSON & SONS, Egremont **Ref:**YH03812
EBEL, KARL WALTER GUSTAV, Gretna **Ref:**YH04530
FEARHEAD, DANIEL M, Sedbergh **Ref:**YH05115
FOX, DAVID L, Millom **Ref:**YH05427
GARDNER, DEREK T, Penrith **Ref:**YH05647
GLAISTER, JAMES, Cockermouth **Ref:**YH05803
GOULDING, PHILIP, Cockermouth **Ref:**YH05951
HALE, ROGER K, Penrith **Ref:**YH06292
HANNAH, DAVID, Egremont **Ref:**YH06394
JOHNSTON, PAUL J, Workington **Ref:**YH07847
KENTDALE FARRIERS, Kendal **Ref:**YH08086
LEATHERBARROW, GORDON P, Seascale **Ref:**YH08507
MCDONALD, BRIAN, Appleby-In-Westmorland **Ref:**YH09344
MCDONALD, LIAM P, Appleby **Ref:**YH09346
MILBY, CHRISTOPHER L, Ulverston **Ref:**YH09567
MITCHELL, W J, Kendal **Ref:**YH09678
RUDD, A J, Carlisle **Ref:**YH12205
SCOTT, LESLIE, Carlisle **Ref:**YH12545
WISEMAN, ANGUS W, Kendal **Ref:**YH15609

DERBYSHIRE

AINSWORTH, DARREN R, Buxton **Ref:**YH00215
BARTLETT, WILLIAM G, South Normanton **Ref:**YH01043
BRADBURY, DOUGLAS, Chesterfield **Ref:**YH01746
BRADBURY, NEAL, Chesterfield **Ref:**YH01747
BRIDGE, MARTIN S, Tibshelf **Ref:**YH01879
BUNTING, F, Derby **Ref:**YH02227
CALEY, MARK A, Buxton **Ref:**YH02443
CHADBOURNE, C, Swadlincote **Ref:**YH02701
COCKAIN, GODFREY J, Belper **Ref:**YH03119
DOBSON, TERENCE FRANK, Ilkeston **Ref:**YH04155
DUERDEN, BRIAN ROBERT, Hope Valley **Ref:**YH04312
GIBSON, FREDERICK, Dronfield **Ref:**YH05749
GILLETT, M P, Derby **Ref:**YH05781
GRAHAM, JAMES A, Bakewell **Ref:**YH05970
GREEN, STUART E, High Peak **Ref:**YH06074
HAYBURN, J, Derby **Ref:**YH06565
HUNT, LANCE A, Belper **Ref:**YH07297
JAMES, TIMOTHY P, Melbourne **Ref:**YH07689
KING, P, Matlock **Ref:**YH08184
LANGLEY, RODNEY DONALD, Swadlincote **Ref:**YH08411
LEWIS, ROBERT I, Ashbourne **Ref:**YH08595
LONG, A D, Hatton **Ref:**YH08801
LUNNUN, NORMAN, Ashbourne **Ref:**YH08901
MARPLES, H W, Dronfield **Ref:**YH09173
MEE, JOHN S, Ashbourne **Ref:**YH09440
NORMAN LUNNUN ANIMAL HEALTH, Ashbourne **Ref:**YH10237
OLDKNOW, P L, Derby **Ref:**YH10492
POLKEY, FREDERICK C, Alvaston **Ref:**YH11203
RUSH, R G, Chesterfield **Ref:**YH12239
RUSH, ROBERT G, Chesterfield **Ref:**YH12240
RUTLAND, SEAN D, Mackworth **Ref:**YH12281
SAUNDERS, HAROLD DUNCAN, Swadlincote **Ref:**YH12448
SELBY, PAUL, Chesterfield **Ref:**YH12617
SUMMERS, J V, Barrow-on-Trent **Ref:**YH13636
WARWICK, S J, Derby **Ref:**YH14949
WARWICK, SIMON J, Breaston **Ref:**YH14950
WATKINSON, MATTHEW, Derby **Ref:**YH14981
WHITE, A, Dronfield **Ref:**YH15326
WOODWARD, CAROLINE A, Ilkeston **Ref:**YH15755
WYLES, S, Church Broughton **Ref:**YH15865

DEVON

ALFORD, H J, Cullompton **Ref:**YH00273
ASKELL, VICTOR W J, Dawlish **Ref:**YH00619
BARRASS, J, Honiton **Ref:**YH01007
BERWICK, JOHN H, Newton Abbot **Ref:**YH01322
BOYCE, P S, Okehampton **Ref:**YH01730
CANN, STEPHEN J, Otterton **Ref:**YH02500
CARNELL, R F, Newton Abbot **Ref:**YH02565
CARR, PHILIP JOHN, South Molton **Ref:**YH02571
CHILDS, ADAM, Sidmouth **Ref:**YH02852
CLARK, W L R & M E, Tiverton **Ref:**YH02969
COCKINGTON FORGE, Torquay **Ref:**YH03125
CONIBEAR, R H, Bideford **Ref:**YH03230
COSSENS, ANTHONY, Tavistock **Ref:**YH03353
CRADDOCK, STEVE A, Okehampton **Ref:**YH03539
CRIMP, B A, Beaworthy **Ref:**YH03601
DEEBLE, BEN, Yelverton **Ref:**YH04015
FARMER, L J, Newton Abbot **Ref:**YH05058
G WESTAWAY & SON, Newton Abbot **Ref:**YH05600
GALLERY, JULIAN M, Seaton **Ref:**YH05619
GLANVILLE, DAVID PETER, Winkleigh **Ref:**YH05806
GREEP, R J, Ivybridge **Ref:**YH06109
HALL, LYNN M, Seaton **Ref:**YH06316
HARRIS, IAN, Barnstaple **Ref:**YH06474
HILL, C R, Newton Abbot **Ref:**YH06827
HIRCOCK, P CHALIS, Plymouth **Ref:**YH06880
HOLLIS FARRIERS, Tiverton **Ref:**YH06949
HOLLIS HORSE/HOLLIS FARRIERS, Cullompton **Ref:**YH06950
HOPWOOD, CHRISTOPHER J, Buckfastleigh **Ref:**YH07062
INGLIS, J A, Ottery St Mary **Ref:**YH07452
JACKMAN, DAVID, Newton Abbot **Ref:**YH07640
LAKESIDE PADDOCK STUD, Ilfracombe **Ref:**YH08358
LAWRENCE, DAVID C, Torrington **Ref:**YH08471
LAWRENCE, E C, Torrington **Ref:**YH08472
LAWRENCE, R J, Umberleigh **Ref:**YH08473
LEY, CLIVE H, Ilfracombe **Ref:**YH08599
LUXTON, MARCUS N, Tiverton **Ref:**YH08912
LUXTON, STEVEN, Okehampton **Ref:**YH08913
MANN, JOHN ANTHONY, Teignmouth **Ref:**YH09082
MERCER, FRANK, Tiverton **Ref:**YH09462
MIDDLETON, LIONEL J P, South Brent **Ref:**YH09546
MORTIMORE, IAN, Yelverton **Ref:**YH09848
OLIVE, DAVID W, Honiton **Ref:**YH10496
PARKIN, KEITH JOHN, Barnstaple **Ref:**YH10764
PARTRIDGE, M A, Buckfastleigh **Ref:**YH10807
PEDRICK, R, Newton Abbot **Ref:**YH10894
PERCIVAL, MARK F B, Okehampton **Ref:**YH10972
PERSSE, BURTON S H, Cullompton **Ref:**YH10996
PIDGEON, STEVEN G, Moretonhampstead **Ref:**YH11089
RICHARDSON, ROBBIE, Newton Abbott **Ref:**YH11820
RITCHIE, CLIVE G, Crediton **Ref:**YH11915
SANSOM, B P A, Honiton **Ref:**YH12428
SECKINGTON FORGE, Winkleigh **Ref:**YH12596
SOMERS, R, Seaton **Ref:**YH13062
SPRY, RUSSELL K, Plymouth **Ref:**YH13267
STUART, G, Ottery St Mary **Ref:**YH13595
STUART, PAUL A, Feniton **Ref:**YH13597
STUARTS FARRIER SERVICE, Ottery St Mary **Ref:**YH13598
SVENSSON, MARK ANDREW, Okehampton **Ref:**YH13680
THORN MOWER FARRIER SUP, Lifton **Ref:**YH14057
TRIBE, MALCOLM, Newton Abbot **Ref:**YH14391
TUCKER, EDWARD W, Bideford **Ref:**YH14433
TULLY, GRAHAM J, Chudleigh **Ref:**YH14452
UNDERHILL, DAVID J, Newton Abbot **Ref:**YH14561
VOSPER, M, Yelverton **Ref:**YH14742
VOWDEN, T R, Newton Abbot **Ref:**YH14743
WAKELY, JAN I, Honiton **Ref:**YH14835
WARD, MICHAEL J, Holsworthy **Ref:**YH14904
WEBSTER, SHEUMAIS A, Newton Abbott **Ref:**YH15042
WEIR, M, Ivybridge **Ref:**YH15055
WESTCOTT, W M, Tiverton **Ref:**YH15188
WHITFIELD, PAUL A, Honiton **Ref:**YH15360
WILLS, R J, Exeter **Ref:**YH15519
WITHERIDGE, WILLIAM GEORGE, Barnstaple **Ref:**YH15623
WONNACOTT, DAVID J, South Brent **Ref:**YH15653
WONNACOTT, ERIC W J, Lewdown **Ref:**YH15654

DORSET

ALLEN, ROBERT T, Dorchester **Ref:**YH00301
BAILEY MOBILE, Blandford Forum **Ref:**YH00795
BARRINGTON, J M, Warmwell **Ref:**YH01023
BRIDE, D, Bournemouth **Ref:**YH01868
BROWN, ANDREW P, Poole **Ref:**YH02100
BYRNE, ROBERT, Bransgore **Ref:**YH02349
DEXTER, KIRK, Poole **Ref:**YH04099
FOX, GRAHAM P, Dorchester **Ref:**YH05429
FRANCIS, LEE M R, Ferndown **Ref:**YH05451
FREAK, N R, Sturminster Newton **Ref:**YH05475
GILL, R M, Gillingham **Ref:**YH05775
GOLDSWORTHY, C, Sherborne **Ref:**YH05894
GRAHAM C S JEANS, Blandford Forum **Ref:**YH05963
HARDING, E J, Wimborne **Ref:**YH06411
KERLEY, KEITH, Blandford Forum **Ref:**YH08097
LAIDLAW, G D W, Christchurch **Ref:**YH08345
LANGLEY, GRAHAM A, Shaftesbury **Ref:**YH08410
LATCHAM, DEAN L, Shaftesbury **Ref:**YH08444
MARCHANT, I R, Weymouth **Ref:**YH09143
MARSH, ANDREW, Corfe Mullen **Ref:**YH09188
MEADEN, ABIGAIL R L, Blandford Forum **Ref:**YH09416
MORGAN, D D P, Portland **Ref:**YH09802
OLIVER, MARK S, Bournemouth **Ref:**YH10498

PHILLIPS, LESLIE M, Dorchester Ref:YH11059
PRUST, K R, Wimborne Ref:YH11442
SLEEMAN-HISCOCK, ANTHONY IVOR, Sturminster Newton Ref:YH12894
SMITH, FREDRICK T, Dorchester Ref:YH12957
SPARKES, A J, Shaftesbury Ref:YH13175
SPARKES, PAUL J, Shaftesbury Ref:YH13176
STAPLES, LESLIE R, Blandford Ref:YH13388
SUTCLIFFE, ANTHONY W, Dorchester Ref:YH13665
THOMAS, PHILIP J, Verwood Ref:YH14027
TROWBRIDGE, B J, Shaftesbury Ref:YH14414
TUSON, PETER, Poole Ref:YH14504
VINCENT, PETER J, Sherborne Ref:YH14726
WARREN, WILLIAM J, Verwood Ref:YH14937
WATTS, NEIL D, Evershot Ref:YH15006
WHITMARSH, R A, Wareham Ref:YH15364
YATES, PETER G, Bridport Ref:YH15890

ESSEX

ACKLAND, RICHARD J, Dagenham Ref:YH00144
ADAMS, GAVIN, Ridgewell Ref:YH00166
ALLEN, G, Chelmsford Ref:YH00296
ATKINS, PAUL, Dunmow Ref:YH00649
BARNES, GEORGE EDWARD, Colchester Ref:YH00974
BELL, K J, Halstead Ref:YH01226
BIRCHER, ANDREW K, Maldon Ref:YH01432
BOWENS, BARNABY, Castle Hedingham Ref:YH01705
BRASH, DEAN, Witham Ref:YH01812
BUNDOCK, PETER M, West Thurrock Ref:YH02222
BUTLER, CARL S, Chelmsford Ref:YH02322
CLEERE, NICHOLAS S P, Wickford Ref:YH03014
CLEMENTS, IAN A, Halstead Ref:YH03018
CLOW, R A, Benfleet Ref:YH03071
COE, ALAN R, Colchester Ref:YH03132
COOPER, PAUL H, Witham Ref:YH03289
COTTER, LLOYD J, Hornchurch Ref:YH03382
CROSSLEY, RICHARD L, Billericay Ref:YH03661
CULLEN, GLYN MITCHELL, Billericay Ref:YH03703
DOBBERSON, JAMES HENRY, Tilbury Ref:YH04148
DOBBERSON, KEITH L, Bridge Ref:YH04149
DODSWORTH, KEITH D, South Benfleet Ref:YH04163
DUTTON, G, Canvey Island Ref:YH04378
ELLA, ANTHONY W, Doddinghurst Ref:YH04610
FRANKLAND, RONALD A, Waltham Abbey Ref:YH05467
GAME, DAVID C, Ingatestone Ref:YH05634
HARRIS, DEAN R, Chelmsford Ref:YH06467
HAYTER, D J, Stanford-Le-Hope Ref:YH06593
HEDGES, ANTONY A, Romford Ref:YH06643
HOLTON, IVOR J, Chelmsford Ref:YH06991
HYLTON, J H, Southminster Ref:YH07359
J TODD, Brentwood Ref:YH07622
JOHNSON, GAVIN J, Brentwood Ref:YH07824
JOSLIN, EDWARD JOHN, Halstead Ref:YH07947
KELLY, NEIL J, Southminster Ref:YH08046
LUBIN, J R B, Holland-on-Sea Ref:YH08882
MARSDEN, M A, Matching Green Ref:YH09185
MARTIN, GARY, Maldon Ref:YH09219
MAY, R S, Harwich Ref:YH09291
MCLELLAN, B M, Bishop's Stortford Ref:YH09388
MITCHELL, DAVID, Crays Hill Ref:YH09666
MOBBS, F I, Maldon Ref:YH09688
MORTLOCK, BARRIE J, Ingatestone Ref:YH09849
NEWMAN-TAYLOR, TOBIN R, Brentwood Ref:YH10153
NORTON, B J, Basildon Ref:YH10331
PARDOE, CHRISTOPHER H, Benfleet Ref:YH10713
PAY, RICHARD, Fobbing Ref:YH10845
PEARCE, ANTHONY P, Braintree Ref:YH10869
POWER, GARY, Upminster Ref:YH11326
ROBERTSON, JASON A, Romford Ref:YH11972
SARGEANT, C R, Chelmsford Ref:YH12436
SAUNDERS, E, Dunmow Ref:YH12446
SCRUTTON, I F, Manningtree Ref:YH12571
SEWELL, ERNEST CHARLES TREVOR, Fobbing Ref:YH12649
SINGH KHAKHIAN, GARY, Basildon Ref:YH12852
SINGH, PETER G, Basildon Ref:YH12854
STEVENSON, DONALD E, Ongar Ref:YH13450
TAYLOR, B W, Romford Ref:YH13896
TAYLOR, S F C, Danbury Ref:YH13910
THACKER, GRAHAM, Grays Ref:YH13972
WHITE, MARK W, Brentwood Ref:YH15334
WILLIAMS, MICHAEL, Harlow Ref:YH15466

GLOUCESTERSHIRE

BAXTER, DEREK MICHAEL, Cheltenham Ref:YH01086
BELL, MICHAEL D, Badminton Farm Ref:YH01228
BIRCH, BRIAN, Cheltenham Ref:YH01429
BROWN, A, Moreton In Marsh Ref:YH02095
BROWN, ARTHUR H, Blockley Ref:YH02101
BURT, THOMAS D, Cheltenham Ref:YH02289
CAIRNS, PETER A, Cirencester Ref:YH02420
CHALLONER, TIMOTHY V, Gloucester Ref:YH02714
COCKING, R, Moreton In Marsh Ref:YH03124
COID, STEWART, Cirencester Ref:YH03137
DEACON, NICHOLAS, Stroud Ref:YH03983
EVILL, LIONEL ALAN, Cirencester Ref:YH04959
FLETCHER, DESMOND EDWARD, Cirencester Ref:YH05275
FOLLY, CHRISTOPHER C, Dymock Ref:YH05304
GISBORNE, SIMON PATRICK, Lower Apperley Ref:YH05796
HALL, D, Gloucester Ref:YH06314
HALL, DAVID A, Quedgeley Ref:YH06315
HOPKINS, PAUL T, Cheltenham Ref:YH07054
I SINTON & SON, Cirencester Ref:YH07368
JUGGINS, PHILIP J, Cheltenham Ref:YH07960
KING, BRUCE M, Moreton In Marsh Ref:YH08175
KNIGHT, RICHARD, Cheltenham Ref:YH08265
LEATHERDALE, HOWARD M, Lechlade Ref:YH08508
LLOYD, EVAN JOHN, Stroud Ref:YH08737
LOVELL, MARTYN A, Gloucester Ref:YH08849
MARTIN, PHILLIP J, Stow-on-the-Wold Ref:YH09225
MAY, CLIVE D, Cheltenham Ref:YH09288
MCCORMICK, MICHAEL G, Cirencester Ref:YH09332
MEDCROFT, JASON R, Newent Ref:YH09433
MILLS, C D, Kings Stanley Ref:YH09632
MILLWARD, PHILIP E, Kingscote Ref:YH09640
NELSON, GARRICK S R, Longhope Ref:YH10074
NICHOLLS, N E, Dursley Ref:YH10184
NICHOLLS, WESLEY, Cheltenham Ref:YH10187
PARTRIDGE, NICHOLAS S, Cheltenham Ref:YH10808
PRICE, A C, Lydney Ref:YH11374
RACK, FRANCIS, Cirencester Ref:YH11589
RACK, W, Cirencester Ref:YH11590
RICHARDS, D C, Fairford Ref:YH11807
STAFFORD, RICHARD JOHN, Cheltenham Ref:YH13322
STRONG, ALEXANDER G, Brimpsfield Ref:YH13582
SWAN, CECIL T, Cheltenham Ref:YH13691
SWAN, CECIL T, Tewkesbury Ref:YH13690
TANNER, STEPHEN M, Horsley Ref:YH13858
THOMAS, MICHAEL JAMES, Cheltenham Ref:YH14026
WAKEFIELD, G A, Newent Ref:YH14832
WARD, JONATHAN M, Cirencester Ref:YH14901
WARD, STANLEY A, St Brivels Ref:YH14909
WELLFAIR, M, Cheltenham Ref:YH15068
WHERRETT, PETER A, Thrupp Ref:YH15278
WOOD, MERVYN, Cheltenham Ref:YH15665

GLOUCESTERSHIRE (SOUTH)

CHURCH, D E, Hanham Ref:YH02908
GILBERTSON, RICHARD D, Winterbourne Down Ref:YH05761
JEE, D G, Chipping Sodbury Ref:YH07714
SMITH, MATTHEW K, Frampton Cotterell Ref:YH12976

GUERNSEY

BEAN, PHILLIPPA J, Vale Ref:YH01118
HARGREAVES, PAUL W, Vale Ref:YH06428
LOWE, DAVID J, Castel Ref:YH08859

HAMPSHIRE

ADAMS, J, Ringwood Ref:YH00167
ADAMS, M, Lymington Ref:YH00170
ADAMS, MERVYN, Lymington Ref:YH00171
BALCOMBE, JOHN A, Aldershot Ref:YH00832
BARNES, CLIFFORD, Andover Ref:YH00973
BARTON, M A, Southampton Ref:YH01049
BEALE, C R, Lymington Ref:YH01114
BEAUMONT, J A, New Milton Ref:YH01136
BELASCO, STEPHEN R, Dibden Ref:YH01203
BIGG, STEVEN N, Southampton Ref:YH01403
BRIDGEWATER, CRAIG, Portsmouth Ref:YH01885
BROCKS, MICHAEL S, Alton Ref:YH02014
BROWN, PIERCE R, Hook Ref:YH02127
CHALMERS, ALEXANDER W, New Milton Ref:YH02715
CORDALL, I R, Fareham Ref:YH03310
CORTEN, STEPHEN, Tadley Ref:YH03346
DALY, DAVID J, Yateley Ref:YH03850
DEAN, ANDREW M, Winchester Ref:YH03990
DOYLE, DARREN L, Tadley Ref:YH04245
DRAKE, PHILIP, Lyndhurst Ref:YH04255
DUFFIN, CLIVE, Fleet Ref:YH04316
DUNNING, P L, Southampton Ref:YH04354
DUNNING, T, Southampton Ref:YH04355
ETHERIDGE, DAVID H, Bishops Waltham Ref:YH04882
F NEWMAN & SONS, Alton Ref:YH04997
FARRIER SVS, Basingstoke Ref:YH05089
FENNELL, NIGEL D, Odiham Ref:YH05147
FLETCHER, DAVID S, Fareham Ref:YH05274
GEORGES, D, Fareham Ref:YH05727
GREEN, J A H, Southampton Ref:YH06066
GRIFFITHS, DAVID W, Aldershot Ref:YH06140
HACKNEY PK, Lymington Ref:YH06258
HAMPSON, P, Bordon Ref:YH06369
HARROW, SIMON P, Emsworth Ref:YH06494
HENDERSON, PAUL F, Southampton Ref:YH06668
HOOD, C L, Swanmore Ref:YH07021
HOOF CARE, Alton Ref:YH07026
HUNT, SHOLTO A, Alton Ref:YH07298
JONES, DAVID H, Andover Ref:YH07890
JONES, ROGER M L, Lymington Ref:YH07929

KEABLE, CHRISTOPHER P, New Milton Ref:YH08014
KEELING, F J, Eastleigh Ref:YH08028
KING, R A, Havant Ref:YH08187
KIRKBY, GEORGE, Lymington Ref:YH08233
KNIGHTBRIDGE, A, Southampton Ref:YH08266
LAPIDGE, ANDREW, Southampton Ref:YH08427
LAUNDER, J W, Rowland's Castle Ref:YH08453
LINSSNER, C P, Andover Ref:YH08669
LOVEJOY, RICHARD E W, Petersfield Ref:YH08848
MALONE, B, Winchester Ref:YH09054
MANSBRIDGE, G E, Marchwood Ref:YH09121
MASKELL, TIM, Lymington Ref:YH09237
MEAKER, MARTYN A, Lymington Ref:YH09427
METCALFE, ANTHONY J, Andover Ref:YH09499
MOSS, R S, Petersfield Ref:YH09863
MOUNTIAN, ANTHONY J, Fareham Ref:YH09902
NAILOR, W C, Alton Ref:YH10012
O'ROURKE, SHAUN, Southampton Ref:YH10551
PHILLIPS, MARK J, Waltham Chase Ref:YH11060
POOLE, ANTHONY E, Liphook Ref:YH11264
POVEY, A L, Winchester Ref:YH11312
RAVENSCROFT, JAMES C, Romsey Ref:YH11658
REEVES, PAUL R, Baughurst Ref:YH11738
ROBBERTS, B A, Ringwood Ref:YH11935
ROBERTS, ALWYN, Farnborough Ref:YH11946
ROGERSON, J, Tadley Ref:YH12062
ROWE, JOSEPH ROBERT, North Baddesley Ref:YH12163
RUMSEY, WAYNE P, Southampton Ref:YH12232
SAMPSON, EDWARD, Ringwood Ref:YH12398
SAYERS, RICHARD S, Yateley Ref:YH12478
SEAGRAVE COTTAGE STABLES, Bishops Waltham Ref:YH12588
SKINNER, ROGER M, Romsey Ref:YH12877
STOCKBRIDGE, Stockbridge Ref:YH13486
STURGESS, NICHOLAS J, Curdridge Ref:YH13616
UNDERWOOD, C M, Emsworth Ref:YH14564
WEHRLE, MARCUS E, Westharting Ref:YH15049
WHYATT, D J, Ringwood Ref:YH15379
WIGGINS, R J, Basingstoke Ref:YH15399
WOODMAN, C, Hook Ref:YH15720
WOODMAN, CHRISTOPHER M, Bordon Ref:YH15721
WORLE, DEREK A, Andover Ref:YH15789
WRIGHT, ALBERT, Petersfield Ref:YH15832

HEREFORDSHIRE

BAILEY, ALAN W, Bartestree Ref:YH00797
BREAKWELL, COLIN E, Leominster Ref:YH01826
CLEATON, BRIAN E, Hereford Ref:YH03012
GREEN, M A, Hereford Ref:YH06070
JONES, M P, Pontrilas Ref:YH07915
JONES, MARK A, Dorstone Ref:YH07917
JONES, MATTHEW J, Kington Ref:YH07918
LEGGE, A M, Bromyard Ref:YH08541
LLOYD, STEPHEN DEREK, Ledbury Ref:YH08743
LOWE, ROBIN J, Weobley Marsh Ref:YH08861
PRICE, MATTHEW R, Ross-on-Wye Ref:YH11384
PRICE, ROGER J, Lugwardine Ref:YH11388
RICKELSFORD, DAVID E, Leominster Ref:YH11833
SIMPSON, JONATHAN, Leominster Ref:YH12839
STONEHEWER, GRAHAM, Leominster Ref:YH13515
SUMNER, NICHOLAS J, Fownhope Ref:YH13638
SUTTON, GRAHAM T, Hereford Ref:YH13677
UNDERWOOD, R F, Leominster Ref:YH14565
WILLIAMS, A K, Much Birch Ref:YH15445

HERTFORDSHIRE

COLE, DUNCAN L, Braughing Ref:YH03154
COLLIER, W H, Royston Ref:YH03182
COULSON, ROBERT G, New Barnet Ref:YH03390
CRIST, DAVID, Stevenage Ref:YH03605
DARBY, L W, Hemel Hempstead Ref:YH03877
DOWNHAM, TREVOR I, Bishop's Stortford Ref:YH04230
FRENCH, MARK W, Hemel Hempstead Ref:YH05493
FULLER, T W, Bishop's Stortford Ref:YH05534
HORSE & HOUNDS, Tring Ref:YH07092
HUMPHREY, MARTIN, Hemel Hempstead Ref:YH07285
JAMES, MARK ROY, Radlett Ref:YH07684
JEFFERIES, NIGEL P, Shillington Ref:YH07715
JOHNSON, TREVOR, Hertford Heath Ref:YH07840
KONIG, ANTHONY JOSEPH, Codicote Ref:YH08291
LANE, V G, Berkhamsted Ref:YH08391
LANNON, BARRY P, Welwyn Garden City Ref:YH08420
MOODY, F, Welwyn Ref:YH09737
O'SHEA, THOMAS J, Bushey Ref:YH10567
PITMAN, TERRY R, Hitchin Ref:YH11152
POPE, DAVID J, Barnet Ref:YH11266
QUINLAN, PETER G, Potters Bar Ref:YH11500
REEVE SMITH, J R M, Ware Ref:YH11735
ROBINSON, STEVEN D, Hertford Ref:YH11996
ROSS, ROBERT J, Watford Ref:YH12120
ROUSE, DAVID MICHAEL, Much Hadham Ref:YH12146
SMITH, DANIEL A, Welwyn Garden City Ref:YH12950
SMITH, J R M, Hatfield Ref:YH12963
STEVENS, BARRY G, St Albans Ref:YH13443
TAVERNER, NIGEL S, Hoddesdon Ref:YH13885
TAYLOR, P D, Royston Ref:YH13909
TERRY, GREGORY FRANCIS, Bovingdon Ref:YH13958
TOVEY, JAY D, Great Offley Ref:YH14256
WADE, A J, Flaunden Ref:YH14810
WADE, SAM, Sarratt Ref:YH14815
WALKER, RICHARD HERBERT, Malpas Ref:YH14857
WATTS, ADAM, Tring Ref:YH15004
WATTS, GARY, Northchurch Ref:YH15005
WHEELER, DEREK, Barnet Ref:YH15270

ISLE OF MAN

BARHAM, KEVIN N A, Ramsey Ref:YH00934
BOSTOCK, D R, Ramsey Ref:YH01658

ISLE OF WIGHT

BEARDSMORE, STEVEN M, Ryde Ref:YH01120
JOHNSON, NIGEL K, Ventnor Ref:YH07829
MOSS, MICHAEL R, Newport Ref:YH09861
MOUL, PETER L, Godshill Ref:YH09879
PERKIS, BARRY A, Sandown Ref:YH10979
PRITCHETT, MICHAEL J, Cowes Ref:YH11426
PURCELL, MALCOLM G, Newport Ref:YH11465
TURNER, IAN, Ryde Ref:YH14481
WEST, TIMOTHY J, Brook Ref:YH15179

JERSEY

PRYCE, DAVID J, Trinity Ref:YH11444
PRYCE, DOUGLAS F, Trinity Ref:YH11445

KENT

ANDREWS, DAVID V, Sittingbourne Ref:YH00398
ANDREWS, T, Rochester Ref:YH00404
APPS, S H, Dover Ref:YH00485
ASHTON, STUART J, Folkestone Ref:YH00615
BAKER, K D, Maidstone Ref:YH00821
BAKER, KEITH D, Maidstone Ref:YH00823
BRAY, GEOFFREY A, Ashford Ref:YH01820
BURCH, THOMAS A, Ashford Ref:YH02229
BURT, GRAEME J, Sevenoaks Ref:YH02287
BURTON, GARY S, East Farleigh Ref:YH02292
BUTCHER, K J, Deal Ref:YH02316
CASEY, DAVID L, Canterbury Ref:YH02614
CERULLO, M, Westerham Ref:YH02700
CHRISTIAN, STEPHEN, Headcorn Ref:YH02885
CLARK, CHRISTOPHER D, Goudhurst Ref:YH02962
COLLINS, STEPHEN A, Maidstone Ref:YH03190
COOK, PHILIP MICHAEL, Charing Ref:YH03257
COSTER, NOEL, Tunbridge Wells Ref:YH03356
CRAWFORD, MARTIN P, Sittingbourne Ref:YH03575
DEEPDENE STABLES, Faversham Ref:YH04021
DENNIS, EDWARD F, Maidstone Ref:YH04054
DUNMALL, PHILIP J, Maidstone Ref:YH04346
EDWARDS, M C, Ashford Ref:YH04583
FLETCHER, DOMINIC C, Groombridge Hill Ref:YH05276
FRYATT, T J, Sevenoaks Ref:YH05528
GOOD, RAYMOND D, Dartford Ref:YH05900
HEWITT, PAUL W, Erith Ref:YH06727
HOGSTON, W D, Canterbury Ref:YH06921
JACKSON, I L, Maidstone Ref:YH07647
JEFFERY, RICHARD N, Bethersden Ref:YH07720
JONES, SIMON B, Ashford Ref:YH07932
LUCK, B M, Tonbridge Ref:YH08886
MANN, TIMOTHY A, Edenbridge Ref:YH09083
MASSIE, NIGEL R, Rochester Ref:YH09249
MEADE, LOUIS, Orpington Ref:YH09412
MERCER, I J, Rochester Ref:YH09463
MINDHAM, DAVID R, Westerham Ref:YH09647
MORGAN, VINCENT E, Maidstone Ref:YH09813
NICOLA M HUNT DWCF, Sevenoaks Ref:YH10199
PATON-SMITH, JASON C, Boughton Ref:YH10823
PEACOCK, RAYMOND JAMES, Sevenoaks Ref:YH10863
PEERS, PETER S, Canterbury Ref:YH10900
PERKINS, STEPHEN, Ashford Ref:YH10978
PILKINGTON, TIMOTHY, New Romney Ref:YH11108
PITCHER, MARK S, Orpington Ref:YH11151
POLLARD, ROBERT, Deal Ref:YH11205
RAINGER, CLIVE M, Edenbridge Ref:YH11617
RICHARDSON, A M, Maidstone Ref:YH11815
RIPLEY, TYRONE T, Rochester Ref:YH11905
SANDERS, DAVID, Tonbridge Ref:YH12405
SAVAGE, P H, Sittingbourne Ref:YH12454
SKIPPON, M A, Cranbrook Ref:YH12880
SLIGHT, ERNEST G, Dartford Ref:YH12896
ST NICHOLAS FORGE, Birchington Ref:YH13283
STERN, CLIVE CHARLES, Cranbrook Ref:YH13433
STERN, EDGAR P J, Maidstone Ref:YH13434
STERN, P J, Tenterden Ref:YH13435
STERN, P M, Maidstone Ref:YH13436

SWANSCOTT, ROBERT L, Aylesford Ref:YH13694
TANTON-BROWN, JULIAN, Sittingbourne Ref:YH13861
TURNWELL, G M, Tenterden Ref:YH14493
VICKERY, MICHAEL, West Malling Ref:YH14707
WARD, BARRY P, Sheppey Ref:YH14899
WARD, K A, Tunbridge Wells Ref:YH14902
WELLSMAN, DAVID W, Sittingbourne Ref:YH15088
WEST, E C, Canterbury Ref:YH15174
WHALLEY, K R, Westerham Ref:YH15260
WHEELER, GARY M, Herne Bay Ref:YH15271
WIGGINS, CHRISTOPHER A, Maidstone Ref:YH15398
WILLARD, KEVIN J, Sevenoaks Ref:YH15428
WILLOW FARM, Maidstone Ref:YH15496
WISEMAN, PAUL, Newington Ref:YH15610

LANCASHIRE

ADDY, D L, Rochdale Ref:YH00181
ASKEW, STEVEN, Accrington Ref:YH00621
BEARDMORE FARRIER SV, Blackburn Ref:YH01119
BEECROFT, PATRICK J, Blackburn Ref:YH01184
BELL, JEFFREY, Preston Ref:YH01224
BURGIN, KRISTOPHER, Bacup Ref:YH02250
COLE, ANDREW CHARLES, Wigan Ref:YH03149
CONWAY, PAUL A, Preston Ref:YH03251
COOK, SAMUEL C, Leyland Ref:YH03258
D'ARCY, DAVID C, Blackburn Ref:YH03882
DENNISON, PAUL EDWARD, Carnforth Ref:YH04058
DURKIN, MICHAEL, Preston Ref:YH04371
GOLDER, ROBERT M, Preston Ref:YH05886
GREEN SMITHY, High Bentham Ref:YH06060
GREGORY, MAXWELL J, Preston Ref:YH06117
HANKIN, WILLIAM D & DAVID M, Preston Ref:YH06388
HOOLE, J J, Preston Ref:YH07040
HOUGHTON, R J, Blackpool Ref:YH07205
HUDSON, BRIAN, Preesall Ref:YH07255
IBEX, Preston Ref:YH07377
JOHNSON, RICHARD A, Chorley Ref:YH07837
KAY, D, Bacup Ref:YH08004
KAY, RAYMOND JAMES, Blackburn Ref:YH08005
KAYE, ANTHONY S, Barnoldswick Ref:YH08006
KAYE, HARVEY STUART, Chorley Ref:YH08008
LAMB, PETER K, Bacup Ref:YH08363
LINDLEY, B, Wigan Ref:YH08647
MATHER, ROWLAND J, Bury Ref:YH09260
NIGHTINGALE, STEPHEN A, Accrington Ref:YH10205
PICKARD, ROBERT D, Carnforth Ref:YH11080
PIMBLEY, ALEX T, Preston Ref:YH11111
RIGBY, ROBERT D E, Wigan Ref:YH11891
ROTHWELL, DAVE, Oldham Ref:YH12138
ROWLINSON, M, Blackpool Ref:YH12174
SANDERSON, BRIAN, Ormskirk Ref:YH12407
SHUTTLEWORTH, ANDREW J, Blackburn Ref:YH12776
SMITH GREEN SMITHY, Lancaster Ref:YH12936
STEAD, PAUL A, Blackpool Ref:YH13407
TAYLOR, T, Littleborough Ref:YH13912
THOMPSON, C, Rochdale Ref:YH14034
TRAVIS, P, Oldham Ref:YH14356
VALIANTS EQUESTRIAN CTRE, Preston Ref:YH14645
WATKINS, GLYNN SYLVESTER, Preston Ref:YH14978
WILSON, ANTHONY, Chorley Ref:YH15529
WOOF, PHILIP JOHN, Blackburn Ref:YH15761
WORTHINGTON, ALLAN W, Ormskirk Ref:YH15805

LEICESTERSHIRE

ALLEN, T W, Leicester Ref:YH00305
ALLINGTON, JOHN W, Melton Mowbray Ref:YH00314
ALLINGTON, JONATHAN D, Melton Mowbray Ref:YH00315
ANIMAL SCHOOL OF FARRIERY, Melton Mowbray Ref:YH00443
BEESTON, MICHAEL GUY, Coalville Ref:YH01192
BENNETT, DANIEL J, Melton Mowbray Ref:YH01270
BROWN, ANDREW N, Sileby Ref:YH02099
BROWN, LUKE R, Loughborough Ref:YH02121
DEACON, M J, Leicester Ref:YH03982
DILLON, JOHN E, Somerby Ref:YH04121
EVANS, GARY B, Melton Mowbray Ref:YH04918
GREEN, JASON L, Fleckney Ref:YH06067
GULLEY, D L, Melton Mowbray Ref:YH06189
HATTON, IAN R, Nuneaton Ref:YH06535
JOHNSON, PAUL J, Leicester Ref:YH07834
JOYCE, CHRISTOPHER G, Wigston Ref:YH07951
KEARN, RICHARD A, Shepshed Ref:YH08017
MARRIOTT, ADRIAN N, South Croxton Ref:YH09174
MASON, D W, Melton Mowbray Ref:YH09242
NORTHWOOD, GLYN, Hinckley Ref:YH10324
O'REARDON, M, Loughborough Ref:YH10540
PERRY, R L, Enderby Ref:YH10989
PHILIP DAY, Melton Mowbray Ref:YH11043
PIZER, GEOFFREY R, Melton Mowbray Ref:YH11160
PORTER, K B, Quorn Ref:YH11283
ROBERTSON, R A M, Loughborough Ref:YH11974
SELBY, TIMOTHY JOHN, Nuneaton Ref:YH12619
SMITH, GRAHAM J, Loughborough Ref:YH12959
SPECK, A W, Melton Mowbray Ref:YH13188
SWANWICK, KIM R, Melton Mowbray Ref:YH13697
TAYLOR, GEORGE S, Kibworth Ref:YH13902
VARNAM, C, Braunstone Ref:YH14662
VARNAM, PAUL A, Leicester Ref:YH14663
W SPENCE & SON, Melton Mowbray Ref:YH14798
WILLIAMS, DAMIAN D, Fleckney Ref:YH15454
WILLIAMS, J M, Oakham Ref:YH15461
WOODFORD, MICHAEL O, Hallaton Ref:YH15689
YEANDLE, ERIC, Melton Mowbray Ref:YH15896

LINCOLNSHIRE

A J PLEDGER, Stamford Ref:YH00040
ALLEN, LEE J, Grantham Ref:YH00298
BATEMAN, BRETT, Horncastle Ref:YH01065
BEECHEY, R F, Lincoln Ref:YH01171
BELL, IVON T, Grantham Ref:YH01220
BEVAN, R E M, Market Rasen Ref:YH01340
BLOOR, J O, Market Rasen Ref:YH01558
BOSWORTH, CLIVE E, Skellingthorpe Ref:YH01664
BRENNAN, MICHAEL B, Spalding Ref:YH01843
BRENNAN, SHANE P, Spalding Ref:YH01845
BUNTING, CHRISTOPHER JOHN, Spilsby Ref:YH02226
CHATTERTON, SHAUN MICHAEL, Market Rasen Ref:YH02790
D M FARRIERY, Spilsby Ref:YH03794
DALE, MAURICE & RALPH M, Louth Ref:YH03824
ELKINGTON, ANDREW JAMES, Sleaford Ref:YH04609
FAHEY, J, Lincoln Ref:YH05008
FLATTERS, MICHAEL J, Stamford Ref:YH05265
FRANKLIN, MARK A, Boston Ref:YH05469
GRAY, GLENN, Bourne Ref:YH06029
HILL ENGINEERING, Gainsborough Ref:YH06811
HILL, T, Ingham Ref:YH06834
HOUGHTON, JASPER ANTHONY, Potterhanworth Ref:YH07204
JONES, CARL (MAJOR), Grantham Ref:YH07882
JONES, P J, North Killingholme Ref:YH07921
KING, JAMES D, Grantham Ref:YH08182
LEE, GEOFFREY, Stamford Ref:YH08524
LINDER, P J, Welton Ref:YH08646
MYCAWKA, ALEXANDER H, Stamford Ref:YH09980
NICHOLLS, D E, Louth Ref:YH10182
PEARS, ROBERT A, Spilsby Ref:YH10876
PEGASUS HORSESHOES, Stamford Ref:YH10905
PLANT, MICHAEL J, Grantham Ref:YH11162
R PLANT & SON, Grantham Ref:YH11561
REDNIL EQUESTRIAN CTRE, Lincoln Ref:YH11716
SAWER, NEIL G, Boston Ref:YH12460
SMITH, NORMAN M, Market Rasen Ref:YH12981
SYKES, SCOTT S, Welton Ref:YH13724

LINCOLNSHIRE (NORTH EAST)

BARTON, J M, Grimsby Ref:YH01047
SMITH, P J, Grimsby Ref:YH12984

LINCOLNSHIRE (NORTH)

BOTTAMLEY, F D, Scunthorpe Ref:YH01665
BRAMLEY, FRANCIS N, Barton Upon Humber Ref:YH01791
CHATTERTON, M C, Brigg Ref:YH02789
CROSBY, NICHOLAS, Wootton Ref:YH03642
HOLMES, M H, Brigg Ref:YH06978

LONDON (GREATER)

CANTLE, JOHN, Chingford Ref:YH02515
COMERFORD, MICHAEL J, Muswell Hill Ref:YH03212
DIXON, M L, Kingston Upon Thames Ref:YH04143
EVANS, GORDON L, Muswell Hill Ref:YH04919
HARLEY, THOMAS H, East Ham Ref:YH06439
HYDE PK BARRACKS, London Ref:YH07348
O'NEILL, EAMONN, Hillingdon Ref:YH10516
R H A FORGE, London Ref:YH11538
RUDGE, KEITH D, Uxbridge Ref:YH12207

MANCHESTER (GREATER)

BULLEN, SIMON, Bolton Ref:YH02216
DAMPIER, J A, Bolton Ref:YH03858
GUTIERREZ-INOSTROZA, ABEL R, Bolton Ref:YH06196
JONES, R F, Stockport Ref:YH07923
JORDAN, PHILIP, Manchester Ref:YH07939
MITCHELL, HARVEY STANLEY, Stockport Ref:YH09668
SOUTHERN, JOHN, Bolton Ref:YH13147
WATSON, SIMON, Manchester Ref:YH14992
YATES, DAVID, Bolton Ref:YH15889

MERSEYSIDE

BLACKMORE, PAUL F, Prescot Ref:YH01490
CHAMBERS, KEITH R, Liverpool Ref:YH02721
CROMPTON, S W, Wirral Ref:YH03632
F BLACKMORE & SON, Liverpool Ref:YH04985
KELLY, MARTIN, Wirral Ref:YH08045
MARSHALL, BOB, Southport Ref:YH09193
MARSHALL, ROBERT C, Southport Ref:YH09203
MICHELL, K N, Wirral Ref:YH09512

- **MILOJEVIC, NEIL J**, Liverpool **Ref:**YH09644
- **PARR, IAN T**, Liverpool **Ref:**YH10785
- **SHONE, NEIL J**, St Helens **Ref:**YH12756
- **SMITH, STEVEN P L**, Thornton Hough **Ref:**YH13001
- **SUMMERS, PAUL**, Liverpool **Ref:**YH13637

MIDLANDS (WEST)

- **ABBISS, R I**, Stourbridge **Ref:**YH00098
- **ASHFORD, A & W K**, Walsall **Ref:**YH00603
- **BAGNALL, ANDREW J**, Birmingham **Ref:**YH00789
- **BEARLEY CROSS STABLES**, Solihull **Ref:**YH01121
- **CHAWNER, P D**, Birmingham **Ref:**YH02794
- **CHECKLEY, PAUL N**, Birmingham **Ref:**YH02797
- **CHESTERMAN, DANIEL J**, Wolverhampton **Ref:**YH02834
- **COX, EDWARD J**, Coventry **Ref:**YH03530
- **DYAS-HARROLD, MARK**, Stourbridge **Ref:**YH04383
- **DYAS-HARROLD, P**, Stourbridge **Ref:**YH04384
- **EDMUNDS, GARY**, Alvechurch **Ref:**YH04565
- **HICKMAN, JACKIE A**, Kingswinford **Ref:**YH06742
- **JEPHCOTT, KIM E**, Birmingham **Ref:**YH07751
- **MARSHALL, KENNETH**, Solihull **Ref:**YH09196
- **MILLWARD, GRAHAM N**, Stourbridge **Ref:**YH09639
- **NOTT, J**, Wolverhampton **Ref:**YH10338
- **ORCHARDS LIVERY STABLES**, Birmingham **Ref:**YH10537
- **PHILLIPS, RICHARD J**, Birmingham **Ref:**YH11064
- **PIMLOTT, L K**, Coventry **Ref:**YH11113
- **SMITH, N H**, Wolverhampton **Ref:**YH12980
- **SMITH, R I**, Wolverhampton **Ref:**YH12989

NORFOLK

- **ACTON, J M**, Fakenham **Ref:**YH00162
- **AIKENS, MARK L**, Norwich **Ref:**YH00210
- **ARBUTHNOT, TIMOTHY R**, Wymondham **Ref:**YH00497
- **ARMES, P J**, Norwich **Ref:**YH00537
- **BLAKE, JOHN T**, Attleborough **Ref:**YH01517
- **COUSINS, MAURICE C**, King's Lynn **Ref:**YH03513
- **FULLER, D A**, King's Lynn **Ref:**YH05532
- **GREEN, KEVIN J**, King's Lynn **Ref:**YH06068
- **GREGORY, CHARLES J N M**, King's Lynn **Ref:**YH06115
- **HARVEY, GREIG V**, Norwich **Ref:**YH06514
- **HAWES, MATTHEW D**, North Walsham **Ref:**YH06542
- **HIRD, JAMES C B**, Attleborough **Ref:**YH06881
- **HORNER, ADRIAN J**, Norwich **Ref:**YH07078
- **HORNER, JOHN D**, Aylsham **Ref:**YH07079
- **HUBBARD, D A**, Diss **Ref:**YH07250
- **HURCOMB, RICHARD I**, King's Lynn **Ref:**YH07310
- **LUSHER, RONALD MICHAEL**, King's Lynn **Ref:**YH08903
- **MARJORAM, IAN S**, Norwich **Ref:**YH09150
- **MARSHALL, STUART A**, Thetford **Ref:**YH09204
- **MARTIN, CLAIRE L**, Norwich **Ref:**YH09216
- **MILLS, ANDREW W**, Diss **Ref:**YH09631
- **MORRIS, GILES**, North Walsham **Ref:**YH09830
- **PARRY, ANDREW C**, Norwich **Ref:**YH10789
- **PELL, MARK A**, Norwich **Ref:**YH10911
- **PERUZZI, R S N**, Dereham **Ref:**YH10998
- **TURNER, GORDON GEORGE**, Downham Market **Ref:**YH14480
- **TURNER, N W**, Norwich **Ref:**YH14487
- **WELLING, JASON M**, Dereham **Ref:**YH15072

NORTHAMPTONSHIRE

- **BARRETT, JEREMY J**, Brafield On The Green **Ref:**YH01011
- **BARRONS, HENRY A**, Northampton **Ref:**YH01026
- **BAZIN, DARREN J**, Kettering **Ref:**YH01100
- **BONE, HOUSTON**, Kettering **Ref:**YH01619
- **BRADLEY, KEVIN**, Brackley **Ref:**YH01756
- **BRUDENELL, MARC**, Wellingborough **Ref:**YH02155
- **BURGESS, GRAHAM G**, Rushden **Ref:**YH02244
- **COX, JAMES W**, Wollaston **Ref:**YH03532
- **FRANKLAND, DEREK S**, Brackley **Ref:**YH05465
- **GRIGGS, KEVIN W**, Kettering **Ref:**YH06144
- **HARTGROVE, ANDREW JOHN**, Harpole **Ref:**YH06501
- **HARTGROVE, TIMOTHY G**, Kettering **Ref:**YH06502
- **HARTGROVE, TREVOR E**, Harpole **Ref:**YH06503
- **HOWITT, GORDON R**, Towcester **Ref:**YH07233
- **MIDDLETON, ADRIAN**, Kettering **Ref:**YH09545
- **PERCIVAL, ALEXANDER J**, Daventry **Ref:**YH10971
- **PHILLIPS, MICHAEL J**, Towcester **Ref:**YH11061
- **TEMPLE, BRIAN ROBERT**, Towcester **Ref:**YH13950
- **THOMPSON, GEORGE BERNARD**, Rushden **Ref:**YH14036
- **TILLEY, ASHLEY MARK E**, Northampton **Ref:**YH14151
- **WATSON, JOHN M**, Brackley **Ref:**YH14988

NORTHUMBERLAND

- **ADAMS, K**, Ashington **Ref:**YH00169
- **BATY, FRANCIS JOSEPH**, Hexham **Ref:**YH01083
- **CROSS, MICHAEL J**, Berwick-upon-Tweed **Ref:**YH03654
- **DAWSON, ROBERT**, Chappington **Ref:**YH03965
- **DUGGAN, RALPH B**, Hexham **Ref:**YH04322
- **DUNN, D**, Alnwick **Ref:**YH04350
- **GLASS, DAVID G**, Choppington **Ref:**YH05808
- **JACKSON, MATTHEW W**, Alnwick **Ref:**YH07649
- **MAYLAND, ROBERT P**, Hexham **Ref:**YH09301
- **MCDOUGALL, ERNEST**, Morpeth **Ref:**YH09348
- **PARSLOW, PHILLIP J**, Morpeth **Ref:**YH10796
- **SMITH, PETER F**, Ashington **Ref:**YH12986
- **WILLEY, DAVID**, Alnwick **Ref:**YH15433
- **WILSON, G**, Alnwick **Ref:**YH15536
- **WILSON, GORDON**, Alnwick **Ref:**YH15538
- **WILSON, GORDON**, Morpeth **Ref:**YH15537

NOTTINGHAMSHIRE

- **ARMSTRONG, BENJAMIN J**, Kirkby In Ashfield **Ref:**YH00545
- **BARNBY MOOR STABLES**, Retford **Ref:**YH00967
- **BRIGGS-PRICE, ROYSTON M**, Newark **Ref:**YH01908
- **COBB, JASON R**, Newark **Ref:**YH03111
- **CONNOLE, MARK J**, Newark **Ref:**YH03239
- **DEAKIN, SAMUEL E**, Nottingham **Ref:**YH03986
- **FORGE STABLES**, Woodborough **Ref:**YH05364
- **GILL, C G & D W**, Nottingham **Ref:**YH05771
- **GILL, D**, Nottingham **Ref:**YH05772
- **GROOBY, NICHOLAS J**, Bottesford **Ref:**YH06148
- **HALLAM, J B**, Newark **Ref:**YH06324
- **HILL, ALAN**, Newark **Ref:**YH06826
- **HUMPHREY, P O**, Nottingham **Ref:**YH07286
- **KOPEL, EDWARD R**, Cotgrave **Ref:**YH08292
- **MALLENDER BROS**, Worksop **Ref:**YH09051
- **MALTBY-SMITH, RICHARD P**, Kirkby In Ashfield **Ref:**YH09056
- **MARTIN, TERRY**, Nottingham **Ref:**YH09227
- **MURRAY, SIMON**, Westwood **Ref:**YH09969
- **NEWBERT, PAUL F**, Retford **Ref:**YH10124
- **NIXON, G**, Retford **Ref:**YH10217
- **PRICE, M A**, Nottingham **Ref:**YH11383
- **SHORT, JOHN A**, Worksop **Ref:**YH12761
- **SMITH, JOHN R**, Newark **Ref:**YH12970
- **WEBSTER, MICHAEL H**, Southwell **Ref:**YH15041
- **WELCH, ANDY**, Nottingham **Ref:**YH15058

OXFORDSHIRE

- **ANDREWS, DAVID M**, Enstone **Ref:**YH00397
- **BELCHER, IAN**, Didcot **Ref:**YH01205
- **BELCHER, MICHAEL E**, Didcot **Ref:**YH01206
- **CHERRY, R J**, Churchill **Ref:**YH02819
- **COOPER, D C**, Bampton **Ref:**YH03285
- **COX, JOHN H**, Bicester **Ref:**YH03533
- **DAVISON, ANDREW PETER**, Wantage **Ref:**YH03956
- **DEWDNEY, DEREK BARRIE**, Henley-on-Thames **Ref:**YH04096
- **GASCOIGNE, R F**, Middle Barton **Ref:**YH05667
- **GODFREY, TOM D**, Wantage **Ref:**YH05866
- **GULLEY, MICHAEL**, Chipping Norton **Ref:**YH06190
- **HALL, ALFRED**, Faringdon **Ref:**YH06313
- **HAWKINS, MARTYN R**, Didcot **Ref:**YH06550
- **HERBERT, KARN J**, Henley-on-Thames **Ref:**YH06697
- **HICKS, ANDREW G**, Enstone **Ref:**YH06745
- **HILEY, ROGER**, Bicester **Ref:**YH06808
- **HOLMES, G L**, Kidlington **Ref:**YH06976
- **JOHNSON, MARK E J**, Banbury **Ref:**YH07828
- **MARTIN, ANDREW J**, Chipping Norton **Ref:**YH09215
- **MICHAEL GULLEY FARRIER**, Banbury **Ref:**YH09510
- **MORGAN, A R**, Banbury **Ref:**YH09798
- **REED, MARTIN C**, Banbury **Ref:**YH11721
- **RICHINGS, M V**, Faringdon **Ref:**YH11826
- **SELWYN, CHRISTOPHER**, Oxford **Ref:**YH12629
- **SMITH, DAVID P**, Over Norton **Ref:**YH12952
- **SMITH, W**, Watlington **Ref:**YH13003
- **STEPHENS, ARLO R**, Banbury **Ref:**YH13423
- **STRONG, A R**, Wolvercote **Ref:**YH13581
- **TIMMS, R G**, Thame **Ref:**YH14167
- **TYSOE, JASON R**, Banbury **Ref:**YH14533
- **WATKINS, MICHAEL GEORGE**, Chipping Norton **Ref:**YH14979
- **WEBB, TREVOR MARK**, Wantage **Ref:**YH15032
- **WESTON, ALAN A**, Abingdon **Ref:**YH15226
- **WILSON, PAUL**, Kidlington **Ref:**YH15544
- **WOODWARD, MALCOLM K**, Chinnor **Ref:**YH15758
- **YOUNG, ADAM**, Henley-on-Thames **Ref:**YH15926

RUTLAND

- **FORRYAN, NICHOLAS C W**, Whissending **Ref:**YH05379

SHROPSHIRE

- **ALFORD, STEVE**, Bucknell **Ref:**YH00274
- **ASPINWALL, LAWRENCE R**, Bishops Castle **Ref:**YH00627
- **AVERY, J**, Oswestry **Ref:**YH00682
- **BAILEY, ANTHONY G**, Market Drayton **Ref:**YH00798
- **BOND, CHRISTOPHER J**, Bridgnorth **Ref:**YH01615
- **BROOME, G W**, Shrewsbury **Ref:**YH02076
- **BROWN, R**, Whitchurch **Ref:**YH02128
- **DAWES, PHILIP A P**, Shifnal **Ref:**YH03961
- **EARDLEY, LAWRENCE C**, Shifnal **Ref:**YH04449
- **HANDLEY, PETER CHARLES**, Market Drayton **Ref:**YH06379
- **MORETON WOOD FORGE**, Market Drayton **Ref:**YH09791
- **P HANDLEY & SONS**, Market Drayton **Ref:**YH10644

- PREECE, JOHN L, Shrewsbury Ref:YH11340
- PRITCHARD, GEORGE B, Oswestry Ref:YH11415
- TAYLOR, JAMES, Ellesmere Ref:YH13903
- UPPINGTON SMITHY, Shrewsbury Ref:YH14611
- WHITEHURST, A E A, Oswestry Ref:YH15346
- WILLIAMSON, TOM, Church Stretton Ref:YH15486

SOMERSET

- BARNES, A J, Somerton Ref:YH00972
- BARNES, JONATHAN R H, Glastonbury Ref:YH00975
- BISHOP, PETER J, Minehead Ref:YH01449
- BOWDEN, JONATHAN D, Highbridge Ref:YH01696
- BRETT, CHRISTOPHER P J, Frome Ref:YH01853
- CREEDY, ROBERT RAYMOND, Taunton Ref:YH03589
- CRUTCHER, STEPHEN J, Wincanton Ref:YH03692
- CURTIS, DERRICK, Taunton Ref:YH03747
- DARLINGTON, JAMES, Crewkerne Ref:YH03894
- DENNIS, ANDREW F, Bridgwater Ref:YH04052
- DENNY, J E, Dulverton Ref:YH04062
- DRAPER, MARTIN RAY, Minehead Ref:YH04260
- DYER, NICHOLAS J, Martock Ref:YH04387
- E KENT & SON, Minehead Ref:YH04413
- EDWARDS, GORDON F, Minehead Ref:YH04580
- EVERETT, ROGER H, Exford Ref:YH04950
- FORD, STEWART, Taunton Ref:YH05328
- HEATH, NICHOLAS J R, Somerton Ref:YH06624
- HOARE, NICHOLAS J, Wincanton Ref:YH06891
- JACOBS, STUART M, Minehead Ref:YH07659
- KRIS PARSONS MOBILE, Chard Ref:YH08294
- LEGG, K J, Langport Ref:YH08536
- LEGG, KEVIN J, Langport Ref:YH08537
- MALIN, MARK R W, Minehead Ref:YH09049
- MATRAVERS, DAVID P, Langport Ref:YH09266
- MATRAVERS, P J, Taunton Ref:YH09267
- MEEK, MATTHEW R, Martock Ref:YH09442
- PARSLOW, JONATHAN D, Curry Rivel Ref:YH10795
- PAULL, C W, Taunton Ref:YH10837
- PENDARVES, C, Somerton Ref:YH10931
- PERROTT, NIGEL R, Wincanton Ref:YH10986
- PHILLIPS, NIGEL, Langport Ref:YH11062
- PIKE, NIGEL S, Crewkerne Ref:YH11101
- SAUNDERS, ANDREW M, Minehead Ref:YH12444
- SHERRING, JAMES R, Bridgwater Ref:YH12730
- SHERRING, MATTHEW J, Crewkerne Ref:YH12731
- SMITH, COLIN JOHN, Yeovil Ref:YH12946
- SMITH, MICHAEL B, Wellington Ref:YH12977
- THOMPSON, RONALD, Chard Ref:YH14041
- TOOGOOD, D A P, Holford Ref:YH14231
- WAITE, COLIN, Bridgwater Ref:YH14830
- WEST ANSTEY FARM EXMOOR, Dulverton Ref:YH15124
- WHEELER, SIMON C T, Shepton Mallet Ref:YH15273
- WHEELER, T C, Bridgwater Ref:YH15274
- WHITE, BENJAMIN J, Watchet Ref:YH15327
- WOOD, RICHARD WILLIAM, Templecombe Ref:YH15668

SOMERSET (NORTH)

- BOUGOURD, WILLIAM R, Nailsea Ref:YH01671
- COLE, JUSTIN, Weston-Super-Mare Ref:YH03158
- DOWNTON, DANIEL A, Yatton Ref:YH04243
- HORNER, PAUL J, Weston-Super-Mare Ref:YH07080
- HUBBARD, DANIEL S W, Puxton Ref:YH07251
- MANNERS, ANDREW M, Clevedon Ref:YH09085
- STEER, R G, Weston-Super-Mare Ref:YH13420
- WALKER, RALPH I, Congresbury Ref:YH14855

STAFFORDSHIRE

- ABBISS, RICHARD P, Kinver Ref:YH00099
- ARMSTRONG, LESLIE, Tamworth Ref:YH00550
- ARMSTRONG, PAUL J, Tamworth Ref:YH00551
- ARNOLD, STEVEN, Uttoxeter Ref:YH00559
- ARTHERS, RICHARD A, Burton-on-Trent Ref:YH00564
- BARNBROOK, N, Stourbridge Ref:YH00966
- BASTOW, ARTHUR R, Tamworth Ref:YH01061
- BOURNE, DAVID K, Stoke-on-Trent Ref:YH01684
- CHADWICK, RUSSELL J, Leek Ref:YH02704
- DAVENPORT, P J, Stoke-on-Trent Ref:YH03910
- DAVIES, JOHN W, Stafford Ref:YH03943
- EAKINS, SAMUEL W, Stoke-on-Trent Ref:YH04443
- ELLIS, ANDREW C, Stoke-on-Trent Ref:YH04623
- FROST, T J, Stoke-on-Trent Ref:YH05522
- GRIFFITHS, COLIN A, Rugeley Ref:YH06138
- HARRISON, MARK, Eccleshall Ref:YH06485
- JONES, KARL D, Cannock Ref:YH07911
- LEESE, E, Stoke-on-Trent Ref:YH08533
- LIGHTWOOD, ROBERT IAN, Burton-on-Trent Ref:YH08618
- MARSON, KENNETH S, Newcastle-under-Lyme Ref:YH09208
- MEGAN, JASON J, Lichfield Ref:YH09445
- MELLOR, CLIVE, Stoke-on-Trent Ref:YH09455
- MOW-COP RIDING CTRE, Stoke-on-Trent Ref:YH09905
- NEWMAN, LAURENCE, Rugeley Ref:YH10148
- NICHOLLS, RUSSELL KEITH, Burton-on-Trent Ref:YH10185
- NOTT, PHILIP GEOFFREY, Rugeley Ref:YH10339
- NUNN, JONATHAN, Gnosall Ref:YH10355
- OAKES, D G, Brewood Ref:YH10376
- ONIONS, MARTIN F, Armitage Ref:YH10521
- OSMOND, T P, Stoke-on-Trent Ref:YH10570
- PEARSON, D, Leek Ref:YH10879
- RATCLIFFE, J W, Burton-on-Trent Ref:YH11650
- RATCLIFFE, P, Stoke-on-Trent Ref:YH11652
- SMITH, DAVID H, Cannock Ref:YH12951
- SMITH, I R, Wolverhampton Ref:YH12961
- STUBBS, A, Newcastle Ref:YH13602
- TOFT & STUBBS, Stoke-on-Trent Ref:YH14203
- UDALL, DAVID GEOFFREY, Little Bridgeford Ref:YH14538
- WOOD, TIMOTHY, Newcastle-under-Lyme Ref:YH15670

SUFFOLK

- ALDERTON, JAMES, Bury St Edmunds Ref:YH00260
- BARRY, DERMOT A, Bury St Edmunds Ref:YH01033
- BEADLE, MARTIN, Haverhill Ref:YH01111
- BERRY, ANDREW I, Bury St Edmunds Ref:YH01315
- BIRD, CHARLES R S, Eye Ref:YH01437
- BLAIR, KENNETH O, Newmarket Ref:YH01512
- BOYCE, DAVID J, Bury St Edmunds Ref:YH01729
- BROWN, DAVID V, Newmarket Ref:YH02107
- BUCKMAN, VINCENT J, Woodbridge Ref:YH02201
- CARD, REX T, Beccles Ref:YH02527
- CLARK, ROGER J, Ipswich Ref:YH02966
- CURTIS, MARK, Newmarket Ref:YH03750
- CURTIS, MAURICE JOHN, Ipswich Ref:YH03751
- CURTIS, NICHOLAS, Newmarket Ref:YH03752
- DELL, STEPHEN, Lowestoft Ref:YH04032
- DIXON, GEOFFREY DAVID, Bury St Edmunds Ref:YH04139
- EDWARDS, CHRISTOPHER R, Newmarket Ref:YH04578
- FINDON, EDWARD, Newmarket Ref:YH05210
- FORSYTH, GILLON S, Newmarket Ref:YH05382
- FRERE-SMITH, NICHOLAS P, Bungay Ref:YH05498
- GARRARD, STUART R, Eye Ref:YH05655
- GOLDSMITH, G R, Woodbridge Ref:YH05893
- GOODE, WILLIAM J M, Sudbury Ref:YH05901
- HARMAN, CHARLES, Newmarket Ref:YH06441
- HARRIS, ANDREW J, Newmarket Ref:YH06465
- HARVEY, PAUL B, Halesworth Ref:YH06516
- HIETT, PETER H, Newmarket Ref:YH06748
- HOLLOBONE, J C, Newmarket Ref:YH06952
- HOY, RONALD GEORGE, Ipswich Ref:YH07246
- KERSTING, MICHAEL, Lowestoft Ref:YH08104
- KNOX, THOMAS T, Woodbridge Ref:YH08289
- LAMBERT, B P, Sudbury Ref:YH08364
- MADWAR, ALLAN, Bury St Edmunds Ref:YH09026
- MOODY, GAVIN R, Newmarket Ref:YH09738
- MOORE, ANTHONY C, Ipswich Ref:YH09754
- NEWMARKET FARRIER SUPPLIES, Newmarket Ref:YH10155
- O A CURTIS & SONS, Newmarket Ref:YH10363
- OFFEN, MALCOLM J, Bury St Edmunds Ref:YH10435
- O'RIORDAN, MICHAEL J, Newmarket Ref:YH10545
- QUINLAN, NICHOLAS D, Haverhill Ref:YH11499
- READ, TERENCE J, Lowestoft Ref:YH11681
- RODD, STUART PAUL, Ipswich Ref:YH12042
- ROSE, DARREN M, Newmarket Ref:YH12097
- ROSE, MARK T, Newmarket Ref:YH12098
- RUSH, ROBERT G, Sudbury Ref:YH12241
- RUSHTON, TIMOTHY D, Haverhill Ref:YH12248
- RUST, STEVEN P, Sudbury Ref:YH12268
- RUTHERFORD, R W, Newmarket Ref:YH12274
- SMITH, DEAN C, Sudbury Ref:YH12953
- TICQUET, DAVID A, Bury St Edmunds Ref:YH14130
- TRENTER, JOHN F, Woodbridge Ref:YH14382
- TURNER, F W, Bury St Edmunds Ref:YH14479
- WARE, RONALD, Newmarket Ref:YH14914
- WOODWARD, BRIAN A, Ipswich Ref:YH15754
- WRAY, FREDERICK W, Newmarket Ref:YH15813

SURREY

- A J S FARRIERY, Redhill Ref:YH00041
- ARTHUR, JOHN C, Worcester Park Ref:YH00568
- BATES, STEPHEN P, Headley Ref:YH01068
- BEACH, WILLIAM C, Egham Ref:YH01104
- BECKERS EQUINE SVS, Egham Ref:YH01147
- BOOKHAM LODGE STUD, Cobham Ref:YH01627
- BUCKLAND, LEE P, Addlestone Ref:YH02195
- BUNTING, STANLEY G, Lingfield Ref:YH02228

BURRILL, RICHARD, Ockley **Ref:**YH02279
CHAMBERS, IAN M, Camberley **Ref:**YH02719
CHILD, RICHARD J, Guildford **Ref:**YH02851
COLLISTER, JOHN D, Woking **Ref:**YH03192
COOPER, H J, Dorking **Ref:**YH03287
CROSSLEY & GACHE, Coulsdon **Ref:**YH03658
CROSSLEY, IAN L, Coulsdon **Ref:**YH03659
CROSSLEY, NICHOLAS J, Chipstead **Ref:**YH03660
DALE, T, Guildford **Ref:**YH03825
DEVEREUX, ADRIAN J, Elstead **Ref:**YH04088
EMBLEN, JOHN G, Woking **Ref:**YH04650
FAKHOURI, ABDUL H O, Chiddingfold **Ref:**YH05037
FARRIERS EQUIPMENT, Woking **Ref:**YH05090
FISHER, TONY P, Croydon **Ref:**YH05243
GACHE, R, Lingfield **Ref:**YH05603
GALLOWAY, SIMON C, Lingfield **Ref:**YH05626
GLAZEBROOK, M S, Sutton **Ref:**YH05811
GODFREY, TIMOTHY, Farnham **Ref:**YH05865
GOLDING, MICHAEL E, Guildford **Ref:**YH05892
GOODWIN, MARTIN LEE, Chobham **Ref:**YH05911
GRAY, PHILIP M, Chertsey **Ref:**YH06031
HAMER, WAYNE, Warlingham **Ref:**YH06345
HARRISON, WILLIAM P, Leatherhead **Ref:**YH06489
HAZELTINE, J J, Dorking **Ref:**YH06603
HOLDER, MARC P, Woking **Ref:**YH06925
HOWELL, DAVID LEE, Esher **Ref:**YH07229
HURST, PAUL S, Woking **Ref:**YH07318
IBBOTSON, CHRISTOPHER J, Tadworth **Ref:**YH07373
IBBOTSON, PAUL T, Tadworth **Ref:**YH07374
IBBOTSON, PETER J, Tadworth **Ref:**YH07375
ICKE, S M, Ockley **Ref:**YH07381
IVORY, ERIC JOHN, Ewhurst **Ref:**YH07537
J A IBBOTSON & SONS, Tadworth **Ref:**YH07556
JEANS, JOHN H, Dorking **Ref:**YH07713
KAVANAGH, JOHN S, Camberley **Ref:**YH08000
KING, CHRISTOPHER G, Dorking **Ref:**YH08176
KING, PAUL D, Betchworth **Ref:**YH08186
LUDLOW-MONK, STEPHEN P, Guildford **Ref:**YH08891
MEYRICK, R M, Camberley **Ref:**YH09508
MORGAN, B A, Egham **Ref:**YH09799
PEEKE, ALBERT, Woking **Ref:**YH10897
PG SHOE, Lingfield **Ref:**YH11038
PINNEY, WILLIAM G M, Windlesham **Ref:**YH11138
PRENDERGAST, MICHAEL E, Guildford **Ref:**YH11354
QUARTERMAN, GARETH J, Tadworth **Ref:**YH11484
ROCHE, SEAN, Cranleigh **Ref:**YH12019
SAYERS, MARK, Camberley **Ref:**YH12477
SCOBELL, STEVEN CRAIG, Headley **Ref:**YH12526
SHAUN MEASURES BII, Camberley **Ref:**YH12680
SLADE, BRENT EDBROOK, Lingfield **Ref:**YH12886
SMALLPEICE, ALAN, Godalming **Ref:**YH12913
SPARROWHAWK, J A, Wallington **Ref:**YH13181
STAGG, W C, Farnham **Ref:**YH13328
STEWARTSON, WALTER E, Woking **Ref:**YH13462
TAYLOR, M, Hindhead **Ref:**YH13906
TUCKER, R, Haslemere **Ref:**YH14436
WEST, RODNEY A, Dorking **Ref:**YH15177
WOODSTOCK SOUTH STABLES, Chessington **Ref:**YH15751
WRIGHT, SIMON D, Farnham **Ref:**YH15841
YAROFF, W, Chobham **Ref:**YH15887
YORK, RAY, Cobham **Ref:**YH15918

SUSSEX (EAST)

BAKER, GRAHAM J, Lewes **Ref:**YH00818
BARNES, LEE G, Horam **Ref:**YH00976
BROWN, J H W, Hastings **Ref:**YH02114
C DEAN & SON, Lewes **Ref:**YH02366
CASSERLY, ANDREW, Uckfield **Ref:**YH02620
CORDERY, PETER W, Bexhill-on-Sea **Ref:**YH03311
DEAN, ROGER S, Newhaven **Ref:**YH03996
DUBEY, STEPHEN M, Heathfield **Ref:**YH04305
FIELDWICK, TIMOTHY, Wadhurst **Ref:**YH05198
FISHER, STEPHEN R, Nutley **Ref:**YH05242
FOREMAN, DOUGLAS G, Lewes **Ref:**YH05330
GORDON, LAWRENCE A, Telscombe Cliffs **Ref:**YH05925
GOSWELL, TREVOR M, Eastbourne **Ref:**YH05944
HARLAND, JOHN W, Lewes **Ref:**YH06434
HAYTER, JAMES W, Heathfield **Ref:**YH06594
HENRY, DAVID, Etchingham **Ref:**YH06686
HENTY, JOHN R, Eastbourne **Ref:**YH06690
HOLLIS, PAUL M, Cousley Wood **Ref:**YH06951
KNELLER, DAVID VINCENT, Newhaven **Ref:**YH08253
MARCH, ERIC, Bexhill-on-Sea **Ref:**YH09142
MARKS, SALLY K, Wadhurst **Ref:**YH09166
MARLEY, D H, Uckfield **Ref:**YH09170
MARLEY, P, Crowborough **Ref:**YH09171
MARTLEW, J W, Rye **Ref:**YH09231
NEWNHAM, JEFFREY, Bexhill-on-Sea **Ref:**YH10160
PARROTT, RICHARD M, Heathfield **Ref:**YH10788
PHILLIPS, T S R, Seaford **Ref:**YH11065
PURDIE, GARRY R, Hailsham **Ref:**YH11466
RICHARDS, GRAHAM J, Rye **Ref:**YH11809
RIDLEY, B, Uckfield **Ref:**YH11886
SKIPPON, GUY A, Heathfield **Ref:**YH12879
SOLE, DARREN B, Brighton **Ref:**YH13053
TONDO, UMBERTO R, Hastings **Ref:**YH14225
WEBSTER, J, Uckfield **Ref:**YH15038

SUSSEX (WEST)

A E LOCKWOOD & SON, Midhurst **Ref:**YH00030
ALSTON, HENRY CHARLES, Pulborough **Ref:**YH00341
BEHAN, J J, Petworth **Ref:**YH01197
BLACKSMITHS SHOP, Crawley **Ref:**YH01497
BOTTING, ROBERT W, Horsham **Ref:**YH01666
BROWNRIGG, RUSSELL P, Worthing **Ref:**YH02141
BUTTON, PETER JOHN, Patching **Ref:**YH02336
CHARD, R J, Hassocks **Ref:**YH02749
CLARK, ROBERT, Chichester **Ref:**YH02965
CLARKE, ALAN G, Worthing **Ref:**YH02971
COX, ADRIAN C S, Chichester **Ref:**YH03528
EAGER, ROSS A, Dial Post **Ref:**YH04436
FACER, JAN, Partridge Green **Ref:**YH05006
FARRIERY PRACTICE, Horsham **Ref:**YH05093
FENTON, PETER H, Arundel **Ref:**YH05153
FORGE SLINDON, Arundel **Ref:**YH05363
FROGGATT, D M, Sidlesham **Ref:**YH05512
GODDARD, D F, Worthing **Ref:**YH05863
HALL, MARK LESLIE, Horsham **Ref:**YH06318
HARRIS, SIMON P, Midhirst **Ref:**YH06482
HARROW, S, Chichester **Ref:**YH06493
HIGGS, PHILIP DOUGLAS, Horsham **Ref:**YH06751
HOGAN, M J, Worthing **Ref:**YH06918
JEFFORD, S, Arundel **Ref:**YH07722
LEWIS, DAVID G, Pulborough **Ref:**YH08590
LITTLER, MARTIN E, Worthing **Ref:**YH08708
MAYS, PHILIP, Worthing **Ref:**YH09305
MCALEAR, STUART D, Arundel **Ref:**YH09310
MONKHOUSE, PHILIP J, Midhurst **Ref:**YH09724
PACKHAM, STUART G, Worthing **Ref:**YH10664
PATTENDEN, KEVIN J, Horsham **Ref:**YH10828
PEACOCK, C J, Steyning **Ref:**YH10860
PIMM, J, Horsham **Ref:**YH11114
PIMM, JAMES V, Horsham **Ref:**YH11115
SMITH, S C, Petworth **Ref:**YH12998
STAPLES, MATTHEW, Crawley **Ref:**YH13389
STRIDE, DAVID P, West Chiltington **Ref:**YH13577
TAME, GRAEME C, Horsham **Ref:**YH13851
TFP, Horsham **Ref:**YH13971
TOLLADAY, ANDREW D, Chichester **Ref:**YH14206
UPTON, WAYNE E, Haywards Heath **Ref:**YH14617
WARNER, M V, Pulborough **Ref:**YH14926
WARNER, RONALD V, Pulborough **Ref:**YH14927
WATSON, KEITH R A, Horsham **Ref:**YH14989
WELLER, S F, Horsham **Ref:**YH15067
WELLS, G D, Wisborough Green **Ref:**YH15084
WHITE, KEVIN, Hassocks **Ref:**YH15333
WILKINSON, DONALD W, Chichester **Ref:**YH15418

TYNE AND WEAR

ALASTAIR CRAIG NURSE, Whitley Bay **Ref:**YH00242
DIAZ, FELIX, South Shields **Ref:**YH04106
GUY, JOHN, Hetton-Le-Hole **Ref:**YH06197
HARRISON, MALCOLM A, Newcastle-upon-Tyne **Ref:**YH06484
JONES, B, Newcastle-upon-Tyne **Ref:**YH07878
LECKENBY, DAVID, Newcastle-upon-Tyne **Ref:**YH08512
MCNEIL, CRAIG, Newcastle-upon-Tyne **Ref:**YH09401
MORAN, GRAEME BRYAN, North Shields **Ref:**YH09785
MOULD, DEAN S, Sunderland **Ref:**YH09880
NUNN, ERIC J, Gateshead **Ref:**YH10354
O'NEIL-MORAN, BRIAN R, North Shields **Ref:**YH10520
RAMSHAW, JOHN, Houghton Le Spring **Ref:**YH11623
STEANSON, DANIEL, Gateshead **Ref:**YH13410
STOREY, ANTHONY J, Houghton Le Spring **Ref:**YH13523

WARWICKSHIRE

ALLISON, IAN TREVOR, Coventry **Ref:**YH00318
ATLANTIC EQUINE, Rugby **Ref:**YH00653
BALCHIN, PETER W, Shipston-on-Stour **Ref:**YH00831
BEESLEY, J A, Nuneaton **Ref:**YH01188
BEESLEY, JOSEPH A, Coventry **Ref:**YH01189
BLACK, STUART B, Rugby **Ref:**YH01472
BOLTON, J, Rugby **Ref:**YH01612
BOSWELL, J, Radway **Ref:**YH01663
BRYAN, JOSEPH L, Shipston-on-Stour **Ref:**YH02165
COLE, DAVID B, Lighthorne **Ref:**YH03152
COLE, J A, Lighthorne **Ref:**YH03156
GODSON, ALAN RICHARD, Alcester **Ref:**YH05870
GOLBY, B, Coventry **Ref:**YH05875
LEWIS, DAVID CHARLES, Walton **Ref:**YH08589
MERCHANT, SIMON, Shilton **Ref:**YH09466
SMITHY, Bedworth **Ref:**YH13012
STABLES, Rugby **Ref:**YH13308
STANTON, ROBERT, Alcester **Ref:**YH13381
TONKS, IAN, Solihull **Ref:**YH14228
WALKER, R, Warwick **Ref:**YH14854

WILLIAMS, KARL, Hatton Ref:YH15462
WOODYATT, ALAN TERENCE, Warwick Ref:YH15760

WILTSHIRE

AINLEY, PETER D, Marlborough Ref:YH00213
BAKER, J, Marlborough Ref:YH00819
BAKER, PETER N, Marlborough Ref:YH00825
BUNDY, JONATHAN P, Warminster Ref:YH02223
COLLIS, W K, Salisbury Ref:YH03191
COOMBES, P F, Salisbury Ref:YH03281
DUTTON, IAN J, Swindon Ref:YH04379
FAITHFULL, JEREMY B H, Salisbury Ref:YH05035
FARRIER, Salisbury Ref:YH05087
FORD, RONALD SIMON, Chippenham Ref:YH05327
GILL, TERRY V, Swindon Ref:YH05777
GROOM, P A, Swindon Ref:YH06150
GROOM, PETER JOHN, Swindon Ref:YH06151
HAINES, T J, Leigh Ref:YH06286
HALL ROBERT, Malmesbury Ref:YH06310
HANKINSON, JOHN DEREK, Marlborough Ref:YH06389
HARDY, RUSSELL C, Salisbury Ref:YH06418
HEAD, MARTIN J, Corsham Ref:YH06609
HEWLETT & ALFORD, Salisbury Ref:YH06731
HEWLETT & ALFORD, Salisbury Ref:YH06730
HIBBERD, MICHAEL FRANCIS, Swindon Ref:YH06740
HOWES, N, Chippenham Ref:YH07231
KENNY, SHAUN J, Salisbury Ref:YH08075
LEE, THOMAS H, Warminster Ref:YH08528
LEHEUP, GEOFFREY AVENT, Chippenham Ref:YH08542
LEWIS, MARTIN J, Devizes Ref:YH08593
MAGGS, P, Chippenham Ref:YH09033
MARSHALL, ANDREW PHILIP, Marlborough Ref:YH09192
MAY, K J, Calne Ref:YH09290
MILLER, N A, Westbury Ref:YH09608
MORRISSEY, TIMOTHY P, Swindon Ref:YH09842
OLDMAN, PETER D, Pewsey Ref:YH10493
PARK, ADRIAN JOHN, Malmesbury Ref:YH10742
PATEMAN, C W, Chippenham Ref:YH10818
PERRYMAN, PHILLIP D, Devizes Ref:YH10990
PILBROW, KENNETH, Warminster Ref:YH11104
POYNTON, ANDREW PAUL, Malmesbury Ref:YH11331
RENDELL, PHILIP, Warminster Ref:YH11755
ROBERTS, M T, Chippenham Ref:YH11958
SCRUTON, CHRISTOPHER, Melksham Ref:YH12570
SMITH, JEREMY R C, Swindon Ref:YH12967
SMITH, PETER JOHN, Trowbridge Ref:YH12987
TIDMARSH, B L, Malmesbury Ref:YH14135
TURNELL, ALAN J, Marlborough Ref:YH14472
URCH, GARY, Devizes Ref:YH14619
VINE, IAN DAVID, Salisbury Ref:YH14730
WATKINS, SIMON D, Leigh Ref:YH14980
YOUNG, SIMON, Salisbury Ref:YH15940

WORCESTERSHIRE

BOND, J N, Bewdley Ref:YH01618
CAINES, GEOFFREY WILLIAM, Malvern Ref:YH02418
CHILMAN, J F, Pershore Ref:YH02857
COLLEY, J M, Bewdley Ref:YH03178
DARBY, MARTIN V, Stourport-on-Severn Ref:YH03878
EAKINS, S W, Redditch Ref:YH04442
F CASWELL & SON, Evesham Ref:YH04989
FINCH, PAUL J, Kidderminster Ref:YH05208
FRANKLIN, ROYSTON E, Malvern Ref:YH05470
HALLS, IAN S, Bromsgrove Ref:YH06334
JAMES, BRYAN GERALD, Stourport-on-Severn Ref:YH07678
JAMES, COLIN I, Stourport-on-Severn Ref:YH07679
JAMES, MARK A, Droitwich Ref:YH07683
JONES, BRIAN, Malvern Ref:YH07879
KIMBER, IAN JAMES, Malvern Ref:YH08158
LLOYD, PAUL R, Pershore Ref:YH08741
LOOKER, R D, Pershore Ref:YH08822
LYMER, KELVIN A, Grimley Ref:YH08919
MORGAN BLACKSMITHS, Malvern Ref:YH09793
MORGAN, GEOFFREY K, Malvern Ref:YH09805
MORGAN, LEE P, Fernhill Heath Ref:YH09809
OLIVER, IAN R J, Malvern Ref:YH10497
RICHMOND, DAVID GEORGE, Bewdley Ref:YH11829
SATCHELL, DOMINIC M, Malvern Ref:YH12440
SMITH, ANDREW B, Evesham Ref:YH12940
SMITH, C B, Bromsgrove Ref:YH12944
SPARREY, LIONEL, Droitwich Ref:YH13179
TYLER, DEREK P, Crowle Ref:YH14521
TYLER, S J, Redditch Ref:YH14522
WEBB, STEPHEN EDWARD, Kidderminster Ref:YH15030
WHITE, STEVEN G C, St Johns Ref:YH15335
WHITTINGTON, T J, Redditch Ref:YH15375
WILKES, MARTIN, Redditch Ref:YH15415

YORKSHIRE (EAST)

ALLERTON, S I, Driffield Ref:YH00310
BINNS, A E G, Cottingham Ref:YH01424
BINNS, ROSS BARRY, Cottingham Ref:YH01425
BINNS, T J, Beverley Ref:YH01426
BRASHILL, M, Withernsea Ref:YH01813
FRISTON, MARTIN, Driffield Ref:YH05509
GANSTEAD EQUESTRIAN CTRE, Hull Ref:YH05641
HORSLEY, ANDREW, Hull Ref:YH07191
MOORE, J, Market Weighton Ref:YH09761
MOORE, NICHOLAS J, Market Weighton Ref:YH09764
STIPETIC, ROBERT A, Driffield Ref:YH13471
THORP, SIMON P, Hornsea Ref:YH14090

YORKSHIRE (NORTH)

BAINBRIDGE, JULIAN, York Ref:YH00813
BEIGHTON, G, Leyburn Ref:YH01199
BROOKE, G M, Tadcaster Ref:YH02043
BROWNING, JARVIS, York Ref:YH02139
BUCK, RICHARD, York Ref:YH02187
COMPTON, ROBIN D, Tadcaster Ref:YH03220
DAWSON, A, Northallerton Ref:YH03962
DENTON RIDING CTRE, Scarborough Ref:YH04066
DYER, H, Northallerton Ref:YH04385
FAWCITT, ROBIN T, Moor Monkton Ref:YH05109
FOLLIFOOT PK, Harrogate Ref:YH05300
GREENLEY, ALLAN, Gowthorpe Ref:YH06096
GREENLEY, BRIAN, Malton Ref:YH06097
HALL, TIMOTHY J, Harrogate Ref:YH06319
HARDAKER, S J, Skipton Ref:YH06407
HARDCASTLE, C, Copmanthorpe Ref:YH06408
HARLAND, GARRY, Harrogate Ref:YH06433
HARLAND, PHIL, York Ref:YH06435
HEWITT, STEPHEN N, Moor Monkton Ref:YH06728
HODGSON, D C, Whitby Ref:YH06912
HOTHAM, KEVIN, Harrogate Ref:YH07200
JACKSON, SIMON D, Claxton Ref:YH07654
JEMMESON, JOHN D, Middleham Ref:YH07728
KNIGHTS, DEREK, Richmond Ref:YH08271
LEWINGTON, RICHARD W, Richmond Ref:YH08580
LONDONDERRY FARRIERS, Northallerton Ref:YH08793
LOWES, J I, Richmond Ref:YH08873
MANGER, DAVID A, Catterick Garrison Ref:YH09077
MARSHALL, KEITH WILLIAM, Skipton Ref:YH09195
MCCORMACK, JOHN, Leyburn Ref:YH09331
MILLER, F V, Leyburn Ref:YH09606
MOORE BROS, York Ref:YH09751
MORLEY, ROBERT G, Pickering Ref:YH09821
PEDLEY, JOHN D C, Harrogate Ref:YH10893
PREECE, WAYNE, Settle Ref:YH11343
READMAN, MICHAEL, Scarborough Ref:YH11683
ROBERTSON-TIERNEY, ROBERT H, Scarborough Ref:YH11976
RUSHWORTH, MARTIN D, Malton Ref:YH12249
RUSSELL, J, Richmond Ref:YH12259
S TWEDDALL & SON, Richmond Ref:YH12337
SHARPE, TIMOTHY S, Bugthorpe Ref:YH12679
SHIPLEY, ANTHONY RAYMOND, Selby Ref:YH12749
SMITH, DUNCAN R, Scarborough Ref:YH12956
STANLEY, JOHN, Northallerton Ref:YH13374
STEVENS, GUY NICHOLAS, Malton Ref:YH13444
TIERNEY, N J ROBERTSON, Scarborough Ref:YH14138
TWEDDELL, BRYAN W, Richmond Ref:YH14505
WAINWRIGHT, IAN, York Ref:YH14827
WARD, STUART J I, Thirsk Ref:YH14910

YORKSHIRE (SOUTH)

ALTON, JAMES, Sheffield Ref:YH00345
ANDERSON, JOHN C, Sheffield Ref:YH00384
ATKIN, PETER ROBERT, Sheffield Ref:YH00648
BAILEY, ERNEST L, Doncaster Ref:YH00800
DOBSON, JOHN DAVID, Rotherham Ref:YH04154
EASTMAN, CHRISTOPHER M, Sheffield Ref:YH04508
EASTWOOD, MATTHEW J, Barnsley Ref:YH04521
HALLAM, JEREMY, Doncaster Ref:YH06325
HANDSWORTH RIDING STABLES, Sheffield Ref:YH06383
HARRIS, GAVIN T, Sheffield Ref:YH06469
HAWES, ROBERT A, Sheffield Ref:YH06543
HULL, DAVID C, Doncaster Ref:YH07280
LODGE, E D, Barnsley Ref:YH08774
LOWE, EDDIE, Rotherham Ref:YH08860
LOY, JOHN S W, Barnsley Ref:YH08879
LUTON, WILLIAM A, Barnsley Ref:YH08909
MAYES, NORMAN B, Barnsley Ref:YH09294
MAYES, ROGER W, Barnsley Ref:YH09295
MILNER, WAYNE, Doncaster Ref:YH09642
MURRAY, J I, Doncaster Ref:YH09967
MURRAY, JOHN, Doncaster Ref:YH09968
PARKES, STUART J, Doncaster Ref:YH10758
SELBY, P, Rotherham Ref:YH12616
SHEPPARD, MICHAEL W, Sheffield Ref:YH12716
SMALLAGE FARM, Sheffield Ref:YH12910
SWINDIN, S J, Doncaster Ref:YH13709
THICKETT, MATTHEW C, Rotherham Ref:YH13989
VERSTER, MICHAEL J, Sheffield Ref:YH14685
WEBB, PHILIP JAMES, Mexborough Ref:YH15029
WOOD, V S, Barnsley Ref:YH15671

YORKSHIRE (WEST)

ALLEN, MELVIN, Wakefield Ref:YH00299

- **ATACK, MICHAEL J**, Wakefield **Ref:**YH00641
- **BALDWIN, DAVID C**, Leeds **Ref:**YH00840
- **BOOCOCK, MARC A**, Shipley **Ref:**YH01625
- **BOOTH, NICHOLAS H**, Bradford **Ref:**YH01636
- **BROADHEAD, G & J**, Elland **Ref:**YH01997
- **COOPER, CYRIL**, Leeds **Ref:**YH03284
- **ELLIS, LEE R**, Wakefield **Ref:**YH04626
- **EMMETT, ROBERT C**, Halifax **Ref:**YH04656
- **FIRTH, IAN J**, Ossett **Ref:**YH05234
- **GOLDTHORPE, DAVID**, Batley **Ref:**YH05895
- **HALIFAX FARRIER SUPPLIES**, Halifax **Ref:**YH06301
- **HEY, MARTIN G**, Wakefield **Ref:**YH06734
- **MACKIE, ROSS V**, East Keswick **Ref:**YH09007
- **MITCHELL, J EDWARD**, Birkenshaw **Ref:**YH09670
- **MORRIS, F**, Keighley **Ref:**YH09829
- **MYERS, PETER V**, Huddersfield **Ref:**YH09981
- **PACK, COLIN D**, Otley **Ref:**YH10662
- **PINGLE NOOK FORGE**, Huddersfield **Ref:**YH11131
- **RUSHTON, PAUL**, Ilkley **Ref:**YH12247
- **SAUNDERSON, NOEL**, Huddersfield **Ref:**YH12452
- **SMITH, J**, Bingley **Ref:**YH12962
- **TATE, RICHARD H**, Guiseley **Ref:**YH13874
- **THORNE, B**, Halifax **Ref:**YH14062
- **WARMAN, STEWART M**, Huddersfield **Ref:**YH14920
- **WHITWAM, EDWARD J**, Halifax **Ref:**YH15377
- **WOLFENDEN, SIMON**, Shipley **Ref:**YH15648
- **WOODHEAD, J**, East Bierley **Ref:**YH15694
- **WORRALL, ANDREW G**, Wakefield **Ref:**YH15794

FEED MERCHANTS

BEDFORDSHIRE

- **CHAPEL FEEDS**, Clophill **Ref:**YH02739
- **FEED BIN**, Luton **Ref:**YH05120
- **T C FEEDS**, Dunstable **Ref:**YH13732
- **W JORDANS**, Biggleswade **Ref:**YH14778

BERKSHIRE

- **BANKS SOUTHERN**, Thatcham **Ref:**YH00898
- **R HUTT & PARTNERS**, Maidenhead **Ref:**YH11546
- **TALLY HO FARM**, Windsor **Ref:**YH13840

BUCKINGHAMSHIRE

- **LANES SADDLERY & ANIMAL FEEDS**, Newport Pagnell **Ref:**YH08395
- **SPILLERS SPECIALITY FEEDS**, Milton Keynes **Ref:**YH13206
- **WIDMER FEEDS**, Princes Risborough **Ref:**YH15393

CHESHIRE

- **BOOL BY DESIGN**, Tarporley **Ref:**YH01631
- **CHELFORD FARM SUPPLIES**, Macclesfield **Ref:**YH02799
- **GREEN FARM FEEDS**, Crewe **Ref:**YH06055
- **JOHN COOK (CORN MERCHANTS)**, Macclesfield **Ref:**YH07784
- **YOUNGS**, Congleton **Ref:**YH15944

CORNWALL

- **COACHLANE FEED STORES**, Redruth **Ref:**YH03107
- **CORNWALL ANIMAL FEEDS**, Newquay **Ref:**YH03329

COUNTY DURHAM

- **FARMWAY**, Darlington **Ref:**YH05072
- **LANCHESTER COUNTRY STORE**, Lanchester **Ref:**YH08382

DERBYSHIRE

- **FRANK WRIGHT FEEDS**, Ashbourne **Ref:**YH05463
- **HILL FARM FEEDS**, Dronfield **Ref:**YH06813
- **IVANHOE FEEDS**, Swadlincote **Ref:**YH07533
- **PEAKDALE SADDLERY**, Buxton **Ref:**YH10866
- **SEALS FODDER**, Alfreton **Ref:**YH12589

DEVON

- **MOLE VALLEY FARMERS**, Holsworthy **Ref:**YH09710

DORSET

- **O Y C**, Wareham **Ref:**YH10369

ESSEX

- **BAILEYS HORSE FEEDS**, Braintree **Ref:**YH00806
- **D & F FEED SVS**, Rayleigh **Ref:**YH03770
- **DENGIE**, Maldon **Ref:**YH04045
- **ESSEX ANIMAL FEEDS**, Romford **Ref:**YH04866
- **MAYPOLE PET & GARDEN CTRE**, Witham **Ref:**YH09304
- **PULFORDS**, Great Dunmow **Ref:**YH11455
- **THOROGOODS DIRECT**, Chelmsford **Ref:**YH14079

GLOUCESTERSHIRE

- **GRIFFITHS & CLARKE**, Drybrook **Ref:**YH06135
- **HENRY COLE**, Cirencester **Ref:**YH06681
- **OXBUTTS FARM & STABLE SVS**, Cheltenham **Ref:**YH10614

HAMPSHIRE

- **DIRECT FEEDS**, Winchester **Ref:**YH04127
- **DODSON & HORRELL**, Basingstoke **Ref:**YH04161
- **FARRINGDON FEEDS**, Alton **Ref:**YH05094
- **JOHN LOADER**, Fordingbridge **Ref:**YH07799

HEREFORDSHIRE

- **BALL OF MADLEY**, Hereford **Ref:**YH00848

HERTFORDSHIRE

- **CHAMPIONSHIP FOODS**, Royston **Ref:**YH02728
- **GANWICK FODDER STORE**, Barnet **Ref:**YH05643
- **KIMBLEWICK FEEDS**, Chipperfield **Ref:**YH08160

ISLE OF WIGHT

- **DEB GROVES ANIMAL FEEDS**, Calbourne **Ref:**YH04002

JERSEY

- **LE MAISTRE BROS**, Trinity **Ref:**YH08490

KENT

- **CHILHAM FEEDS**, Canterbury **Ref:**YH02854
- **SARACEN FEEDS**, Tunbridge Wells **Ref:**YH12432

LANCASHIRE

- **OSWALDTWISTLE ANIMAL FEEDS**, Oswaldtwistle **Ref:**YH10575
- **RICHARD BATTERSBY**, Heywood **Ref:**YH11802

LEICESTERSHIRE

- **CHAMPION FEEDS EQUESTRIAN**, Market Harborough **Ref:**YH02726
- **CLAYBROOKE**, Lutterworth **Ref:**YH02996
- **COUNTRYWIDE FEEDS**, Market Harborough **Ref:**YH03447
- **FORGE FEEDS**, Ilston-on-the-Hill **Ref:**YH05362
- **SHARNFORD LODGE FEEDS/TACK**, Hinckley **Ref:**YH12676

LINCOLNSHIRE

- **FENLAND FEEDS**, Bourne **Ref:**YH05143
- **FONABY ANIMAL FEEDS**, Caistor **Ref:**YH05306
- **FOUR SEASONS FEEDS**, Grantham **Ref:**YH05411
- **LINDSEY FARM SVS**, Horncastle **Ref:**YH08655

LINCOLNSHIRE (NORTH)

- **KILLINGHOLME**, Grimsby **Ref:**YH08143

LONDON (GREATER)

- **BURY FARM FODDER STORE**, Edgware **Ref:**YH02299
- **CLGE FARM SADDLERY & FEEDS**, Finchley **Ref:**YH03027

MERSEYSIDE

- **HAMMONDS**, Huyton **Ref:**YH06362

MIDLANDS (WEST)

- **HORSESENSE**, Solihull **Ref:**YH07170

NORFOLK

- **ALLEN & PAGE**, Thetford **Ref:**YH00290
- **DARROW FARM SUPPLIES**, Diss **Ref:**YH03899
- **DEEJAY ANIMAL FEED CTRE**, Diss **Ref:**YH04016
- **G J L**, Fakenham **Ref:**YH05585
- **L A SADDLERY**, Great Yarmouth **Ref:**YH08313

NORTHAMPTONSHIRE

- **COLLINS PET FOODS**, Hardingstone **Ref:**YH03186
- **COUNTRYWISE FEEDS & NEEDS**, Kettering **Ref:**YH03484
- **DI CLARK FEEDS**, Brackley **Ref:**YH04100
- **DODSON & HORRELL**, Kettering **Ref:**YH04162

NORTHUMBERLAND

- **BEDMAX**, Belford **Ref:**YH01157
- **J S HUBBUCK**, Hexham **Ref:**YH07616

NOTTINGHAMSHIRE

- **EASY FEEDS**, Newark **Ref:**YH04522
- **EQUIFEEDS**, Retford **Ref:**YH04744
- **F MARTIN & SON**, Arnold **Ref:**YH04995
- **FORREST FEEDS**, Newark **Ref:**YH05376

OXFORDSHIRE

- **EQUI-GRASS**, Banbury **Ref:**YH04749
- **FRINGFORD FEEDS**, Bicester **Ref:**YH05507

RUTLAND

- **BADMINTON HORSE FEEDS**, Oakham **Ref:**YH00784

SHROPSHIRE

- **SHERRATT FARM SUPPLIES**, Wem **Ref:**YH12728
- **WREKIN FARMERS GARDEN CTRE**, Telford **Ref:**YH15817

SOMERSET

- **E L F FEEDS**, Minehead **Ref:**YH04414
- **MAYTREE FARM FEEDS**, Shepton Mallet **Ref:**YH09307
- **STAX SADDLERY**, Montacute **Ref:**YH13406

STAFFORDSHIRE

- **DICKSONS**, Stoke-on-Trent **Ref:**YH04119
- **DOLLIN & MORRIS**, Stafford **Ref:**YH04170

SUFFOLK

- **CHARNWOOD MILLING**, Woodbridge **Ref:**YH02773
- **CHURCH FARM TACK SHOP & FEEDS**, Eye **Ref:**YH02903
- **FEEDMARK**, Harleston **Ref:**YH05122
- **GLADWELLS**, Ipswich **Ref:**YH05802
- **K 9 PET FOODS**, Framlingham **Ref:**YH07982

SURREY

- **BALANCED FEEDS**, Malden Rushett **Ref:**YH00830
- **EGHAM ANIMAL FOOD SUPPLIES**, Egham **Ref:**YH04594
- **FROSBURY FARM FEEDS**, Guildford **Ref:**YH05518
- **J W ATTLEE**, Dorking **Ref:**YH07624

SUSSEX (EAST)

- **WINDMILL FEEDS & SADDLERY**, Heathfield **Ref:**YH15565

SUSSEX (WEST)

- **EQUITOGS**, Littlehampton **Ref:**YH04829
- **LIGHTS**, Brighton **Ref:**YH08616

TYNE AND WEAR

- **CARLTONS THE FEED MERCHANTS**, Whitley Bay **Ref:**YH02545

WARWICKSHIRE

- **A & J SADDLERY**, Southam **Ref:**YH00012
- **CREWE GARDENS**, Kenilworth **Ref:**YH03594
- **FLINT HALL FEEDS**, Newbold Pacey **Ref:**YH05285

WILTSHIRE

- **AMERICAN THOROUGHBRED**, Kilmington **Ref:**YH00365
- **CATLEY'S FARM SUPPLIES**, Devizes **Ref:**YH02652
- **JOHN TOOMER**, Swindon **Ref:**YH07815
- **OSGILIATH FEEDS**, Westbury **Ref:**YH10565

WORCESTERSHIRE

- **CORN STORES**, Redditch **Ref:**YH03321
- **EQUIMIX**, Stourport-on-Severn **Ref:**YH04756

YORKSHIRE (EAST)

- **HAIGHS**, Doncaster **Ref:**YH06282
- **SMITHS ANIMAL & PET SUPPLIES**, Cottingham **Ref:**YH13006

YORKSHIRE (NORTH)

- **DALES FEED SUPPLIES**, Thirsk **Ref:**YH03826
- **DALES PET FEED SUPPLIES**, Ripon **Ref:**YH03828
- **FOREST FEED**, Harrogate **Ref:**YH05337
- **G MAGSON FEEDS**, Pickering **Ref:**YH05588

YORKSHIRE (SOUTH)

- **BLUE CHIP**, Sheffield **Ref:**YH01565
- **COOKE, DONALD**, Rotherham **Ref:**YH03259

YORKSHIRE (WEST)

- **ACORN FEEDS**, Huddersfield **Ref:**YH00148
- **BAILEYS HORSE FEEDS**, Wakefield **Ref:**YH00808
- **BAILEYS HORSE FEEDS**, Wakefield **Ref:**YH00807
- **COUNTRY FEEDS**, Bradford **Ref:**YH03407
- **CRICKET HILL FEEDS**, Leeds **Ref:**YH03596
- **HILLAM FEEDS**, South Milford **Ref:**YH06836
- **KEITH DRAKE**, Huddersfield **Ref:**YH08033

HOLIDAYS EQUINE

CORNWALL

- **CORNISH RIDING HOLIDAYS**, Redruth **Ref:**YH03327
- **ROMANY WALKS**, Penzance **Ref:**YH12072

COUNTY DURHAM

- **ALSTON & KILLHOPE**, Bishop Auckland **Ref:**YH00339
- **NORTHUMBRIA HORSE HOLIDAYS**, Stanley **Ref:**YH10320

CUMBRIA

- **HIPSHOW FARM RIDING STABLES**, Kendal **Ref:**YH06879

DEVON

- **DARTMOOR DRIVING**, Newton Abbot **Ref:**YH03901
- **DOONE VALLEY RIDING STABLES**, Lynton **Ref:**YH04194
- **EQUITOPIA**, Lynton **Ref:**YH04831
- **NARRAMORE STUD**, Newton Abbot **Ref:**YH10023
- **SKAIGH STABLES**, Okehampton **Ref:**YH12865
- **TABRE RIDING**, Winkleigh **Ref:**YH13772
- **WEST ILKERTON FARM**, Lynton **Ref:**YH15150
- **WHITE TOR**, Tavistock **Ref:**YH15325

DORSET

- **SEACOMBE RIDING HOLIDAYS**, Swanage **Ref:**YH12581

GLOUCESTERSHIRE

- **CHURCH FARM**, Mitcheldean **Ref:**YH02895

HAMPSHIRE

- **EQUITANA HOLIDAYS**, Southampton **Ref:**YH04827
- **IN THE SADDLE**, Tadley **Ref:**YH07406
- **WELLINGTON RIDING**, Hook **Ref:**YH15075

HEREFORDSHIRE

- **ACORN ACTIVITIES**, Hereford **Ref:**YH00146
- **CAMBRIAN HORSE TRAIL NETWORK**, Hereford **Ref:**YH02467
- **P G L TRAVEL**, Ross-on-Wye **Ref:**YH10640

KENT

- **COBHAM MANOR**, Maidstone **Ref:**YH03113
- **MANNIX STUD**, Canterbury **Ref:**YH09091
- **MAYWOOD STUD**, Ashford **Ref:**YH09309

NORFOLK

- **HARRIS, J A**, Norwich **Ref:**YH06476

NORTHUMBERLAND

- **BROWN RIGG RIDING SCHOOL**, Hexham **Ref:**YH02093

OXFORDSHIRE

- **EQUITOUR/PEREGRINE HOLIDAYS**, Summertown **Ref:**YH04832

SHROPSHIRE

- **PENYCOED RIDING STABLES**, Oswestry **Ref:**YH10966

SOMERSET

- **EXMOOR WHITE HORSE INN**, Minehead **Ref:**YH04970
- **KNOWLE MANOR**, Minehead **Ref:**YH08281

SOMERSET (NORTH)

- **SHIPHAM RIDING HOLIDAYS**, Winscombe **Ref:**YH12748

WILTSHIRE

- **HAMPSLEY HOLLOW**, Calne **Ref:**YH06368
- **SAMWAYS**, Salisbury **Ref:**YH12402

YORKSHIRE (NORTH)

- **YORKSHIRE DALES**, Skipton **Ref:**YH15919
- **YORKSHIRE RIDING CTRE**, Harrogate **Ref:**YH15922

YORKSHIRE (WEST)

- **TRUEWELL HALL FARM**, Keighley **Ref:**YH14421

HORSE/RIDER ACCOM

BERKSHIRE

- **CHECKENDON**, Reading **Ref:**YH02796
- **CULLINGHOOD FARM**, Reading **Ref:**YH03705

BRISTOL

- **URCHINWOOD MANOR EQUITATION**, Bristol **Ref:**YH14620

BUCKINGHAMSHIRE

- **ADDINGTON MANOR**, Buckingham **Ref:**YH00179
- **DUNSMORE STABLES**, Wendover **Ref:**YH04358

CHESHIRE

- **ALDER ROOT RIDING CTRE**, Warrington **Ref:**YH00254
- **DINGLE BROOK FARM STABLES**, Macclesfield **Ref:**YH04125

CORNWALL

- **ROSEVIDNEY ARABIANS**, Penzance **Ref:**YH12111
- **TOR-Y-MYNYDD STUD**, Bude **Ref:**YH14248
- **TRENANCE RIDING STABLES**, Newquay **Ref:**YH14372
- **WILSON, D M**, Launceston **Ref:**YH15532

COUNTY DURHAM

- **ALSTON & KILLHOPE**, Bishop Auckland **Ref:**YH00339
- **HAMSTERLEY RIDING SCHOOL**, Bishop Auckland **Ref:**YH06372
- **IVESLEY EQUESTRIAN CTRE**, Durham **Ref:**YH07536
- **ORCHARD HSE**, Barnard Castle **Ref:**YH10534

CUMBRIA

- **ARMATHWAITE HALL**, Keswick **Ref:**YH00536
- **HORSE HIRE HOLIDAYS**, Wigton **Ref:**YH07122

DERBYSHIRE

- **HILLCLIFF STUD**, Belper **Ref:**YH06838
- **NORTHFIELD FARM**, Buxton **Ref:**YH10312
- **RINGER VILLA EQUESTRIAN CTRE**, Chesterfield **Ref:**YH11900

DEVON

- **ASHLANDS FARM**, Tavistock **Ref:**YH00606
- **COLLACOTT FARM**, Umberleigh **Ref:**YH03173
- **DARTMOOR DRIVING**, Newton Abbot **Ref:**YH03901
- **DEVENISH PITT**, Honiton **Ref:**YH04087
- **MOOR FARM**, Okehampton **Ref:**YH09743
- **NARRAMORE STUD**, Newton Abbot **Ref:**YH10023
- **WEST ILKERTON FARM**, Lynton **Ref:**YH15150
- **WHITE TOR**, Tavistock **Ref:**YH15325
- **WOODER MANOR**, Newton Abbot **Ref:**YH15685

DORSET

- **POUND COTTAGE RIDING CTRE**, Blandford Forum **Ref:**YH11307

GLOUCESTERSHIRE

- **CHURCH FARM**, Mitcheldean **Ref:**YH02895
- **COTSWOLD RIDING RAMBLES**, Cheltenham **Ref:**YH03364
- **LODGE FARM**, Tetbury **Ref:**YH08767
- **MARSDEN MANOR STUD**, Cirencester **Ref:**YH09181
- **WOODLAND**, Cheltenham **Ref:**YH15702

HAMPSHIRE

- **FOREST FARM**, Milford On Sea **Ref:**YH05335
- **HACKNEY PK**, Lymington **Ref:**YH06258
- **HOLMES, JULIA**, Petersfield **Ref:**YH06977
- **IN THE SADDLE**, Tadley **Ref:**YH07406
- **NEW PARK HOTEL**, New Forest **Ref:**YH10115
- **ROCKBOURNE**, Fordingbridge **Ref:**YH12028
- **RUSSELL, GILLIAN A**, Ringwood **Ref:**YH12258

HEREFORDSHIRE

- **CAMBRIAN HORSE TRAIL NETWORK**, Hereford **Ref:**YH02467
- **MONNINGTON**, Hereford **Ref:**YH09728

HERTFORDSHIRE

- **CONTESSA**, Ware **Ref:**YH03246
- **UPPERWOOD FARM STUD**, Hemel Hempstead **Ref:**YH14609

ISLE OF WIGHT

- **BUCKS FARM STUD**, Newport **Ref:**YH02204

KENT

- **KNOWLTON STUD**, Canterbury **Ref:**YH08286
- **WILLOW STUD**, Canterbury **Ref:**YH15503

LANCASHIRE

- **TRAILHOLME FARMHOUSE**, Morecambe **Ref:**YH14338

LEICESTERSHIRE

- **KNAPTOFT HOUSE FARM**, Lutterworth **Ref:**YH08250
- **SOMERBY EQUESTRIAN CTRE**, Melton Mowbray **Ref:**YH13060
- **SWAN LODGE**, Melton Mowbray **Ref:**YH13689

LINCOLNSHIRE

- **BUCKMINSTER LODGE**, Grantham **Ref:**YH02203
- **SPRINGFIELD FARM**, Market Rasen **Ref:**YH13253

MIDLANDS (WEST)

- **BROOKLANDS FARM**, Coventry Ref:YH02058
- **RYTON LIVESTOCK**, Coventry Ref:YH12308

NORFOLK

- **BLACKBOROUGH END**, King's Lynn Ref:YH01477
- **COURTYARD FARM**, Hunstanton Ref:YH03511

NORTHUMBERLAND

- **REIVER ANDALUSIANS**, Belford Ref:YH11750
- **STEADING**, Hexham Ref:YH13408

NOTTINGHAMSHIRE

- **CLGE FARM**, Newark Ref:YH03026

OXFORDSHIRE

- **BLEWBURY RIDING/TRAINING CTRE**, Didcot Ref:YH01539
- **DOWNLAND EQUESTRIAN**, Wantage Ref:YH04234

RUTLAND

- **OLD RECTORY**, Oakham Ref:YH10474

SHROPSHIRE

- **BRANDON-LODGE, C**, Church Stretton Ref:YH01799
- **MILL FARM RIDING CTRE**, Shrewsbury Ref:YH09572
- **PENYCOED RIDING STABLES**, Oswestry Ref:YH10966
- **TONG RIDING CTRE**, Shifnal Ref:YH14227
- **WILDING, R J**, Church Stretton Ref:YH15409

SOMERSET

- **CROWN HOTEL**, Minehead Ref:YH03681
- **DRAKES FARM**, Ilminster Ref:YH04256
- **PERITON PK RIDING STABLES**, Minehead Ref:YH10976
- **RISCOMBE FARM**, Minehead Ref:YH11908
- **STOCKLAND LOVELL**, Bridgwater Ref:YH13493

SOMERSET (NORTH)

- **BANWELL EQUESTRIAN CTRE**, Weston-Super-Mare Ref:YH00913

STAFFORDSHIRE

- **ENDON RIDING SCHOOL**, Stoke-on-Trent Ref:YH04667

SUFFOLK

- **LAURELS**, Bury St Edmunds Ref:YH08459
- **POPLAR PK**, Woodbridge Ref:YH11271

SURREY

- **ITCHELL HOME FARM**, Farnham Ref:YH07529
- **SARIAH ARABIAN STUD**, Dorking Ref:YH12439

SUSSEX (EAST)

- **SLIVERICKS**, Battle Ref:YH12899

SUSSEX (WEST)

- **EASTWOOD STUD FARM**, Petworth Ref:YH04518
- **WILLOWBROOK RIDING CTRE**, Chichester Ref:YH15508
- **ZARA STUD**, Chichester Ref:YH15951

WARWICKSHIRE

- **GREENACRES STUD**, Coventry Ref:YH06080
- **STONELEIGH STABLES**, Kenilworth Ref:YH13519

WILTSHIRE

- **LACKHAM CLGE EQUESTRIAN CTRE**, Chippenham Ref:YH08332
- **SAMWAYS**, Salisbury Ref:YH12402
- **STONAR SCHOOL**, Melksham Ref:YH13507
- **WHITE HORSE EQUESTRIAN CTRE**, Westbury Ref:YH15308

WORCESTERSHIRE

- **AVENUE RIDING CTRE**, Malvern Ref:YH00678
- **BENT, BM & SA**, Evesham Ref:YH01282
- **CARENZA, JILL**, Broadway Ref:YH02534
- **KYRE EQUESTRIAN CTRE**, Tenbury Wells Ref:YH08305
- **SAMBOURNE**, Redditch Ref:YH12396

YORKSHIRE (EAST)

- **BRAEMAR**, Hull Ref:YH01770

YORKSHIRE (NORTH)

- **FARSYDE STUD & RIDING CTRE**, Whitby Ref:YH05098
- **HOLLINHALL RIDE & DRIVE**, Whitby Ref:YH06946
- **MANOR HSE FARM**, Pickering Ref:YH09113
- **NORTHALLERTON EQUESTRIAN**, Northallerton Ref:YH10290
- **ROSET HILL FARM**, Richmond Ref:YH12108
- **SWINTON PARK**, Ripon Ref:YH13713

YORKSHIRE (SOUTH)

- **LOWER TOWNHEAD FARM**, Sheffield Ref:YH08871

YORKSHIRE (WEST)

- **LILAC FARM COURTYARD LIVERY**, Wetherby Ref:YH08619
- **WADLANDS HALL EQUESTRIAN CTRE**, Pudsey Ref:YH14817

MEDICAL SUPPORT

BATH & SOMERSET (NORTH EAST)

- **BUDD, EDWARDS & GLAS**, Langport Ref:YH02206
- **EDDY WILLIAMSON & PARTNERS**, Midsomer Norton Ref:YH04544
- **FIRS VETNRY SURGERY**, Bath Ref:YH05227
- **GOLDEN VALLEY**, Chew Magna Ref:YH05880
- **KINCAID, CLAIRE**, Bath Ref:YH08165
- **LOVE-JONES & KILLEN**, Whitchurch Ref:YH08846
- **SHEPPARD, CAWOOD & KINCAID**, Midsomer Norton Ref:YH12714
- **STATION RD VETNRY CLINIC**, Bath Ref:YH13403
- **WRENCH VETNRY GRP**, Bath Ref:YH15822
- **WRENCH VETNRY GRP**, Bath Ref:YH15821

BEDFORDSHIRE

- **ADELAIDE VETNRY CTRE**, Sandy Ref:YH00183
- **ARK HSE VETNRY SURGERY**, Leighton Buzzard Ref:YH00528
- **BURNS & WAKELY**, Bedford Ref:YH02267
- **BURNS & WAKELY**, Flitwick Ref:YH02268
- **DRAPER, GARY**, Chawston Ref:YH04257
- **GRAVENHURST**, Bedford Ref:YH06023
- **ICKNIELD VETNRY GROUP**, Dunstable Ref:YH07383
- **ICKNIELD VETNRY GROUP**, Luton Ref:YH07384
- **P W HARDING & MICHAEL NG**, Leighton Buzzard Ref:YH10659
- **PAPWORTH, H L**, Biggleswade Ref:YH10710
- **SCOTT VETNRY CLINIC**, Bedford Ref:YH12534
- **SPRINGWELL VETNRY CLINIC**, Dunstable Ref:YH13264

BERKSHIRE

- **BALDWYN, CHARLOTTE**, Bray Ref:YH00841
- **BEECHWOOD VETNRY CTRE**, Reading Ref:YH01179
- **BURGHFIELD VETNRY SURGERY**, Reading Ref:YH02248
- **COACH HSE VETNRY CLINIC**, Newbury Ref:YH03106
- **DENTON VETNRY SURGERY**, Wokingham Ref:YH04067
- **DUNN, P SCOTT**, Wokingham Ref:YH04352
- **EPSOM VETNRY REMEDIES**, Hungerford Ref:YH04684
- **EQUINE NUTRITION**, Hungerford Ref:YH04791
- **FALKLAND VETNRY CLINIC**, Newbury Ref:YH05040
- **FOREST HOUSE VETNRY GRP**, Windsor Ref:YH05339
- **GALBRAITH, KEEVILL & GLEESON**, Newbury Ref:YH05608
- **GALBRAITH, KEEVILL & GLEESON**, Thatcham Ref:YH05609
- **GURDON, MELANIE**, Newbury Ref:YH06194
- **HALL & AST**, Hungerford Ref:YH06303
- **HALL PLACE VETNRY CTRE**, Maidenhead Ref:YH06309
- **HILLSIDE STUD EQUINE SWIMMING**, Newbury Ref:YH06856
- **LAZYGRAZER**, Wokingham Ref:YH08486
- **M S F EQUINE**, Newbury Ref:YH08975
- **MARSHALL, VICTORIA**, Hungerford Ref:YH09205
- **NINE MILE VETNRY HOSPITAL**, Wokingham Ref:YH10210
- **O'GORMAN, SLATER & MAIN**, Newbury Ref:YH10438
- **O'GORMAN, SLATER & MAIN**, Thatcham Ref:YH10439
- **PARRY, JOHN LLOYD (DR)**, Cookham Ref:YH10792
- **RIDGEWAY VETNRY GROUP**, Lambourn Ref:YH11867
- **SCOTT DUNN, ANN**, Wokingham Ref:YH12531
- **SUMMERLEAZE VETNRY GROUP**, Maidenhead Ref:YH13635
- **VALLEY EQUINE**, Hungerford Ref:YH14648
- **VALLEY EQUINE HOSPITAL**, Hungerford Ref:YH14649
- **VALLEY VETNRY GROUP**, Reading Ref:YH14659
- **VETNRY CTRE**, Twyford Ref:YH14693

BRISTOL

- **ANIMAL BEDDING**, Bristol Ref:YH00427
- **FARVIS & SONS**, Bristol Ref:YH05101
- **LOVE-JONES & KILLEN**, Bedminster Ref:YH08847
- **SIMMONDS, LOUE**, Bristol Ref:YH12821

BUCKINGHAMSHIRE

- **ANIMAL THERAPY**, Aylesbury Ref:YH00444
- **CROOK, TRACY**, High Wycombe Ref:YH03636
- **EQUS HEALTH**, Aylesbury Ref:YH04835
- **FEDDERN, T A**, Milton Keynes Ref:YH05119
- **GREEN, DANA**, Olney Ref:YH06063
- **HOME OF REST FOR HORSES**, Princes Risborough Ref:YH07003
- **HULA ANIMAL RESCUE**, Milton Keynes Ref:YH07278
- **JARMAN, KAREN**, Buckingham Ref:YH07702
- **NIXON & MARSHALL**, Buckingham Ref:YH10216
- **RAGUS SUGARS**, Slough Ref:YH11608

CAMBRIDGESHIRE

- **ALDRETH VETNRY CTRE**, Ely Ref:YH00262
- **APACHE**, Huntingdon Ref:YH00473
- **ASHCROFT VETNRY SURGERY**, Hardwick Ref:YH00594
- **BELGRAVE HSE VETNRY SURGERY**, Linton Ref:YH01211
- **BOYLE, M S**, Cambridge Ref:YH01732
- **BROWN & PADDON**, Wisbech Ref:YH02090
- **BURGHLEY VETNRY CTRE**, Peterborough Ref:YH02249
- **C A J NICHOLAS**, Peterborough Ref:YH02362
- **DAVEY & DAVEY**, Whittlesford Ref:YH03912
- **GOW, ROBIN**, Great Abington Ref:YH05954
- **GRASS ROOTS**, Peterborough Ref:YH06018
- **GREEN, PETER & TONG , MATTHEW**, Huntingdon Ref:YH06071
- **INTERVET UK**, Cambridge Ref:YH07483
- **J GRIEVE & ASSOCIATES**, Cambridge Ref:YH07585
- **LYON BENNETT & AST**, Chatteries Ref:YH08937
- **LYON BENNETT & AST**, Whittlesey Ref:YH08938

- **LYON, BENNETT & AST**, March Ref:YH08939
- **MILWRIGHT, R D P**, Ely Ref:YH09646
- **PARK TONKS**, Great Abington Ref:YH10738
- **PENGELLY, PENGELLY & MIZEN**, Peterborough Ref:YH10937
- **PRESTWICH, ISOBEL**, Peterborough Ref:YH11369
- **ROBIN HUGHES-PARRY & AST**, Longstanton Ref:YH11979
- **ROBIN HUGHES-PARRY ASSOCIATES**, Cottenham Ref:YH11980
- **SMEETH SADDLERY**, Wisbech Ref:YH12925
- **TEBBUTT, NORMAN & ALASDAIR**, St Neots Ref:YH13928

CHESHIRE

- **ABBEYCROFT VETNRY CTRE**, Northwich Ref:YH00092
- **ASHBROOK EQUINE HOSP**, Knutsford Ref:YH00591
- **BARNHOUSE VETNRY SURGERY**, Chester Ref:YH00989
- **BURGESS & GRAHAM**, Northwich Ref:YH02241
- **CEDAR HEALTH**, Hazel Grove Ref:YH02673
- **CHANCE & HUNT NUTRITION**, Runcorn Ref:YH02729
- **CHRISTIAN, M K**, Kelsall Ref:YH02884
- **CLARENDON VETNRY GRP**, Altrincham Ref:YH02955
- **CLARENDON VETNRY GRP**, Sale Ref:YH02956
- **COUNTIES EQUESTRIAN SVS**, Knutsford Ref:YH03395
- **COUNTY VETNRY GRP**, Holmes Chapel Ref:YH03494
- **COUNTY VETNRY GRP**, Sandbach Ref:YH03495
- **CRANMORE VETNRY CTRE**, Childer Thornton Ref:YH03567
- **DAVIES, ZOE**, Mobberley Ref:YH03951
- **EQUIFORM NUTRITION**, Crewe Ref:YH04747
- **EVERGREEN VETNRY SURGERY**, Stockport Ref:YH04953
- **G E HUNT**, Poynton Ref:YH05576
- **GARNER, SEBASTIAN**, Knutsford Ref:YH05654
- **GATEHOUSE VETNRY HOSPITAL**, Chester Ref:YH05672
- **HALES, S J**, Malpas Ref:YH06294
- **HAMPTON VETNRY GRP**, Malpas Ref:YH06370
- **ISHERWOOD, GABRIELLE**, Macclesfield Ref:YH07516
- **LANGDALE VETNRY CTRE**, Knutsford Ref:YH08401
- **MANOR COURT VETNRY CTRE**, Chester Ref:YH09094
- **MANOR COURT VETNRY CTRE**, Tattenhall Ref:YH09093
- **MINSUPS**, Winsford Ref:YH09654
- **NANTWICH VETNRY GROUP**, Crewe Ref:YH10020
- **NANTWICH VETNRY GROUP**, Nantwich Ref:YH10019
- **POOL FARM VETNRY SURGERY**, Madeley Ref:YH11261
- **ROSE COTTAGE VETNRY CTRE**, Runcorn Ref:YH12092
- **SIMS & PARTNERS**, Congleton Ref:YH12844
- **STATION HSE VETNRY CTRE**, Altrincham Ref:YH13402
- **STORRAR PRACTICE**, Chester Ref:YH13527
- **UNIVERSITY OF LIVERPOOL**, South Wirral Ref:YH14590
- **VITACOLL EQUINE**, Warrington Ref:YH14734
- **WARD, R KEITH**, Nantwich Ref:YH14906
- **WILLOWS VETNRY GRP**, Knutsford Ref:YH15510
- **WILLOWS VETNRY GRP**, Lymm Ref:YH15511
- **WILLOWS VETNRY GRP**, Middlewich Ref:YH15512
- **WILLOWS VETNRY GRP**, Northwich Ref:YH15513
- **WILLOWS VETNRY GRP**, Warrington Ref:YH15514
- **WILLOWS VETNRY GRP**, Winsford Ref:YH15515
- **WRIGHT & MORTEN**, Congleton Ref:YH15826
- **WRIGHT & MORTEN**, Macclesfield Ref:YH15827
- **WRIGHT & MORTEN**, Wilmslow Ref:YH15828
- **WRIGHT, D G**, Chapel-En-Le-Frith Ref:YH15835
- **WRIGHT, D G**, Stockport Ref:YH15834

CLEVELAND

- **ANIMAL HEALTH CTRE**, Guisborough Ref:YH00435
- **BECK VETNRY PRACTICE**, Loftus Ref:YH01145
- **CLEVEDALE VETNRY PRACTICE**, Redcar Ref:YH03019
- **CLIFTON LODGE VETNRY GRP**, Stockton-on-Tees Ref:YH03037
- **MILLER & WHIMSTER**, Stokesley Ref:YH09600
- **VETNRY SURGERY**, Redcar Ref:YH14699
- **WILTON HSE VETNRY CTRE**, Guisborough Ref:YH15555

CORNWALL

- **ABBOTT DRAPER & FRASER**, Bodmin Ref:YH00112
- **ABBOTT DRAPER & FRASER**, Wadebridge Ref:YH00113
- **ALBERT COTTAGE**, Saltash Ref:YH00244
- **AMOS & PENNY**, Falmouth Ref:YH00370
- **ANIMAL VETNRY SVS**, Hayle Ref:YH00446
- **BOISSEAU, R**, Wadebridge Ref:YH01600
- **CALWETON VETNRY CTRE**, Callington Ref:YH02460
- **CALWETON VETNRY CTRE**, Looe Ref:YH02461
- **CALWETON VETNRY CTRE**, Saltash Ref:YH02462
- **CASTLE VETNRY GRP**, Launceston Ref:YH02638
- **CLIFTON VILLA**, Camborne Ref:YH03041
- **CLIFTON VILLA**, Truro Ref:YH03042
- **ELLIS, D**, Liskeard Ref:YH04624
- **EQUUS HEALTH**, Gunnislake Ref:YH04840
- **FRY USHER & EDWARDS**, Camborne Ref:YH05526
- **FRY USHER & EDWARDS**, Redruth Ref:YH05527
- **GREEN, CLIFTON**, Newquay Ref:YH06062
- **HARDERN YOUNG & OTTY**, Penzance Ref:YH06409
- **HEAD & HEAD**, Helston Ref:YH06606
- **HOLT, J J**, Camelford Ref:YH06988
- **KENWYN VETNRY CTRE**, Truro Ref:YH08092
- **KINGS VETNRY SURGERY**, Newquay Ref:YH08198
- **LITTLETON, C E J**, Truro Ref:YH08710
- **LOCKE & PRESTON VETNRY GRP**, Bude Ref:YH08757
- **LUXSTOWE VETNRY CTRE**, Liskeard Ref:YH08911
- **MERIDIAN RADIONICS**, Truro Ref:YH09476
- **NEWNS, J L**, Gunnislake Ref:YH10161
- **NUTE, G & P J**, Wadebridge Ref:YH10356
- **PELYN VETNRY GRP**, Lostwithiel Ref:YH10913
- **PENBODE VETNRY GRP**, Bude Ref:YH10925
- **PENMELLYN VETNRY GRP**, Padstow Ref:YH10946
- **PENMELLYN VETNRY GRP**, St Columb Ref:YH10945
- **ROSEMULLION**, Falmouth Ref:YH12106
- **ROSEMULLION VETNRY**, Helston Ref:YH12107

COUNTY DURHAM

- **CASTLE VETNRY SURGEONS**, Durham Ref:YH02639
- **CLIFTON LODGE VETNRY GRP**, Durham Ref:YH03038
- **CLIFTON LODGE VETRNRY GRP**, Durham Ref:YH03039
- **E D T**, Consett Ref:YH04401
- **SEAGOLD CENTURION**, Crook Ref:YH12587

CUMBRIA

- **ARCHWAY VETNRY PRACTICE**, Grange-Over-Sands Ref:YH00500
- **BARR & LOCKHART**, Kirkby Stephen Ref:YH00998
- **BAY VETNRY GRP**, Milnthorpe Ref:YH01094
- **BEACON VETNRY CTRE**, Wigton Ref:YH01108
- **BELLE VUE VETNRY PRACTICE**, Wigton Ref:YH01235
- **CALDEW VETNRY GRP**, Carlisle Ref:YH02437
- **CALTECH BIOTECHNOLOGY**, Carlisle Ref:YH02454
- **CARNEGIE & LINDSAY**, Brampton Ref:YH02564
- **CHURCH WALK VETNRY CTRE**, Barrow-In-Furness Ref:YH02906
- **CHURCH WALK VETNRY CTRE**, Ulverston Ref:YH02907
- **COOMARA VETNRY PRACTICE**, Carlisle Ref:YH03272
- **CRAIG ROBINSON & PARTNERS**, Carlisle Ref:YH03551
- **CROFT VETNRY GRP**, Cockermouth Ref:YH03620
- **CROFT VETNRY GRP**, Workington Ref:YH03621
- **FRAME, J & N W**, Penrith Ref:YH05440
- **GRETA BANK VETNRY CTRE**, Keswick Ref:YH06123
- **HIGHGATE VETNRY CLNC**, Kendal Ref:YH06787
- **HODGSON & HUNTER**, Cleator Moor Ref:YH06910
- **HODGSON & HUNTER**, Workington Ref:YH06911
- **J R W SEDGWICK**, Cockermouth Ref:YH07612
- **MILLCROFT VETNRY GROUP**, Cockermouth Ref:YH09595
- **MILLCROFT VETNRY GROUP**, Maryport Ref:YH09596
- **OAKHILL VETNRY GRP**, Ambleside Ref:YH10385
- **PICKLES, A C**, Penrith Ref:YH11086
- **PRESTON & BRAMLEY**, Sedbergh Ref:YH11366
- **RHAM, TRICIA**, Cockermouth Ref:YH11782
- **RICHARDSON, S P**, Ambleside Ref:YH11823
- **ROWCLIFFE HSE VETNRY**, Penrith Ref:YH12159
- **RUSHTON & BROWNE**, Broughton In Furness Ref:YH12244
- **RUSHTON & BROWNE**, Millom Ref:YH12245
- **SANSOM & DODWELL**, Windermere Ref:YH12427
- **SEDGWICK, J R W**, Egremont Ref:YH12605
- **SEDGWICK, J R W**, Keswick Ref:YH12606
- **ST BRIDGETS VETNRY CTRE**, Egremont Ref:YH13272
- **ST BRIDGETS VETNRY CTRE**, Whitehaven Ref:YH13273
- **STRAMONGATE VETNRY CTRE**, Kendal Ref:YH13546
- **TITHE BARN VETNRY CTRE**, Kirkby Lonsdale Ref:YH14188

DERBYSHIRE

- **ABBEY VETNRY GRP**, Derby Ref:YH00091
- **AMBIVET VETNRY GRP**, Heanor Ref:YH00359
- **AMBIVET VETNRY GRP**, Ripley Ref:YH00358
- **BYRON VETNRY CLINIC**, Long Eaton Ref:YH02350
- **COOPER & PARTNERS**, Repton Ref:YH03283
- **CROFT VETNRY CTRE**, Bolsover Ref:YH03619
- **FRANCIS & HERDMAN**, Bakewell Ref:YH05447

HILLCLIFF STUD, Belper **Ref:**YH06838
HOPKINSON & HURST, Alfreton **Ref:**YH07055
JAMIESON, C J, Locko Park **Ref:**YH07692
KNOX & DEVLIN, High Peak **Ref:**YH08287
MARSHALL & TILL, Derby **Ref:**YH09191
MARSHALL & TILL, Littleover **Ref:**YH09190
MCMURTY & HARDING, Ashbourne **Ref:**YH09395
NORMAN LUNNUN ANIMAL HEALTH, Ashbourne **Ref:**YH10237
OVERDALE VETNRY CTRE, Buxton **Ref:**YH10591
PETTS, KATHRINE, Matlock **Ref:**YH11034
REEVE, S C, Matlock **Ref:**YH11736
ROBINSONS, Chesterfield **Ref:**YH12003
SCARSDALE VETNRY HOSPITAL, Derby **Ref:**YH12490
SCARSDALE VETNRY HOSPITAL, Markeaton **Ref:**YH12489
SPIRE VETNRY GROUP, Chesterfield **Ref:**YH13211
WATERLOO HOUSE VETNRY SURGERY, Melbourne **Ref:**YH14969
WATERLOO HOUSE VETNRY SURGERY, Swadlincote **Ref:**YH14968

DEVON

ANIMAL BEHAVIOUR CONSULTANTS, Okehampton **Ref:**YH00428
ATKINSON & BURGESS, Bideford **Ref:**YH00650
AUSTIN, GEORGE, Ivybridge **Ref:**YH00667
BONES, Okehampton **Ref:**YH01621
BRIDGE HOUSE VETNRY, Barnstaple **Ref:**YH01873
BUSSELL, N E R, Barnstaple **Ref:**YH02315
COOMBEFIELD VETNRY HOSPITAL, Axminster **Ref:**YH03279
CULLEN, Brampton **Ref:**YH03702
D W AST, Kingsbridge **Ref:**YH03811
DAVIES, TIGER, Tiverton **Ref:**YH03948
DENIS BRINICOMBE NUTRITION, Crediton **Ref:**YH04047
DONKEY SANCTUARY, Sidmouth **Ref:**YH04184
EQWEST VETNRY CTRE, Tavistock **Ref:**YH04843
ERME VALLEY FARMERS, Ivybridge **Ref:**YH04850
FLAVIN & VERE, Crediton **Ref:**YH05266
H M THRESHER, Crediton **Ref:**YH06231
HILLCREST VETNRY CTRE, Plymouth **Ref:**YH06844
HOSGOOD, P, Exeter **Ref:**YH07195
J C EDWARDS & ASSOCIATES, Ivybridge **Ref:**YH07569
LEE & BRAIN, Honiton **Ref:**YH08516
LEWIS JONES & AST, Honiton **Ref:**YH08583
LOCKE & PRESTON VETNRY GRP, Bradworthy **Ref:**YH08758
MCDONALD, CLARE, Okehampton **Ref:**YH09345
MULLACOTT VETNRY HOSPITAL, Barnstaple **Ref:**YH09936
MULLACOTT VETNRY HOSPITAL GRP, Ilfracombe **Ref:**YH09937
MUNNINGS MITCHELL & PEPLOW, Totnes **Ref:**YH09949
NORTH PARK VETNRY GROUP, North Tawton **Ref:**YH10279
OKEFORD VETNRY CTRE, School Way **Ref:**YH10446
PENBODE VETNRY GRP, Holsworthy **Ref:**YH10927
PENBODE VETNRY GRP, Holsworthy **Ref:**YH10926
PIGGOTT & ARNOLD, Bovey Tracey **Ref:**YH11096
QUARRY HSE VETNRY CTRE, Torquay **Ref:**YH11482
RUMFORD BOND & BALDWIN, Bovey Tracey **Ref:**YH12230
SEDGECROFT STUD, Axminster **Ref:**YH12602
THRESHER, H M, Tiverton **Ref:**YH14110
TORBRIDGE VETNRY CTRE, Bideford **Ref:**YH14243
WEST RIDGE VETNRY PRAC, Tiverton **Ref:**YH15160
WOOD, JONATHAN, Crediton **Ref:**YH15664
WOODLANDS VETNRY CTRE, Ivybridge **Ref:**YH15715

DORSET

ALEXANDER TECHNIQUE TEACHER, Wimborne **Ref:**YH00267
ALEXANDER TECHNIQUE TEACHER, Wimborne **Ref:**YH00267
BREDY VETNRY CTRE, Bridport **Ref:**YH01831
CLARK, L M & GILMORE, TONY, Wareham **Ref:**YH02964
DAMORY VETNRY CLINIC, Blandford **Ref:**YH03856
DOOLEY, MICHAEL M, Broadmayne **Ref:**YH04193
DUFOSSE, TERESA, Kington **Ref:**YH04321
FIELDING, M, Weymouth **Ref:**YH05195
FORBES COPPER, Blandford **Ref:**YH05318
GETHING & BOWDITCH, Beaminster **Ref:**YH05735
HAYDON VETNRY GRP, Bridport **Ref:**YH06573
KEATES, REBEKAH, Bournemouth **Ref:**YH08020
LILLIDALE ANIMAL HEALTH, Wimborne **Ref:**YH08623
NELMES CHIROPRACTIC CLINIC, Verwood **Ref:**YH10071
OAKSFORD & BIRCH, Sherborne **Ref:**YH10405
PRIORY VETNRY GRP, Christchurch **Ref:**YH11407
SOUTHFIELD VETNRY CTRE, Dorchester **Ref:**YH13152

ESSEX

ADA COLE RESCUE STABLES, Waltham Abbey **Ref:**YH00163
CONOR FENELON, Great Dunmow **Ref:**YH03241
DUNNETT, CATHERINE (DR), Maldon **Ref:**YH04353
EQUINE HEALTH & HERBAL, Halstead **Ref:**YH04779
GUELDER ROSE, Halstead **Ref:**YH06181
HOOD, BARBARA, Saffron Walden **Ref:**YH07020
LAZARO, L, Colchester **Ref:**YH08485
PEGASUS HOLDINGS, Bishop's Stortford **Ref:**YH10904
WITHERSTONE, W A, Brentwood **Ref:**YH15625

GLOUCESTERSHIRE

ABBEY GREEN VETNRY GRP, Cheltenham **Ref:**YH00077
ABBOTSWOOD VETNRY CTRE, Yate **Ref:**YH00101
ASPINALL AULD & CLARKSON, Abbeydale **Ref:**YH00626
AUBOISE, Chaceley **Ref:**YH00658
BOURTON VALE EQUINE CLINIC, Cheltenham **Ref:**YH01690
BRAMBLES VETNRY SURGERY, Churchdown **Ref:**YH01788
BUSHY FARM EQUINE CLINIC, Berkeley **Ref:**YH02311
CLAYTON & COX, Newent **Ref:**YH03002
CODNER & CHALKLEY, Cheltenham **Ref:**YH03131
COLDICOTT, J H, Tewkesbury **Ref:**YH03147
COTSWOLD HORSE, Cirencester **Ref:**YH03363
DAVE REGAN, Moreton In Marsh **Ref:**YH03908
DAVISON, CATHERINE, Cirencester **Ref:**YH03957
ENIGMA PHYSIOTHERAPY, Moreton In Marsh **Ref:**YH04676
EQUINE SPORTS MASSAGE ASS, Cirencester **Ref:**YH04801
EQUINE SPORTS MASSAGE ASS, Dursley **Ref:**YH04802
HARVEY, SIMON F, Tewkesbury **Ref:**YH06517
JANAWAY, P H, Badminton **Ref:**YH07693
JENKINS, P, Ashleworth **Ref:**YH07735
KEARNS & REA, Tewkesbury **Ref:**YH08018
LANSDOWN VETNRY SURGEONS, Stroud **Ref:**YH08422
LESTER, MACKINNON & BENSON, Cirencester **Ref:**YH08563
NELSON VETNRY & EQUINE, Cirencester **Ref:**YH10073
OWEN, JOHN, Badminton **Ref:**YH10604
PONTING, M F, Cirencester **Ref:**YH11227
PRITCHARD, TERESA, Berkeley **Ref:**YH11424
R A C E, Churchdown **Ref:**YH11511
RIDGEWAY SCIENCE, Alvington **Ref:**YH11866
WHITEHEAD, P (DR), Prior's Norton **Ref:**YH15342
WORSLEY, R, Cirencester **Ref:**YH15801

GLOUCESTERSHIRE (SOUTH)

ANIMAL HEALTH CTRE, Filton **Ref:**YH00436
ARTIFICIAL INSEMINATION CTRE, Kingswood **Ref:**YH00575
DORAN & GRADWELL, Thornbury **Ref:**YH04195
RILEY VETNRY CLINICS, Chipping Sodbury **Ref:**YH11895
ROWE VETNRY GROUP, Patchway **Ref:**YH12160
ROWE VETNRY GROUP, Thornbury **Ref:**YH12161
ROWE VETNRY GROUP, Yate **Ref:**YH12162
WINTERBOURNE VETNRY CLINIC, Winterbourne **Ref:**YH15597

GUERNSEY

ISABELLE VETS, St Peter Port **Ref:**YH07513
NORTHSIDE VERERINARY CTRE, Vale **Ref:**YH10318
VETCARE CTRES, Alderney **Ref:**YH14689
VETCARE CTRES, Castel **Ref:**YH14690
VETCARE CTRES, St Martins **Ref:**YH14688

HAMPSHIRE

BEACH, L S, Fordingbridge **Ref:**YH01103
CEDAR VETNRY GRP, Alton **Ref:**YH02676
D L P EQUINE CONSULTANTS, Otterbourne **Ref:**YH03792
DOWNLAND VETNRY GRP, Emsworth **Ref:**YH04236
DREW, J R, Winchester **Ref:**YH04269
FOREVER LIVING PRODUCTS, Soberton **Ref:**YH05358
FORT DODGE ANIMAL HEALTH, Hedge End **Ref:**YH05386
FOSTER & SEWARD, Basingstoke **Ref:**YH05397
G N GOULD & PARTNERS, Southampton **Ref:**YH05589
JOHN ROTHERY WHOLESALE, Petersfield **Ref:**YH07809
KNOTT, J B & J E, Winchester **Ref:**YH08278
LIPHOOK EQUINE HOSPITAL, Liphook **Ref:**YH08674
MOORE, T E, Fordingbridge **Ref:**YH09767
PARSONS, G R, Liss **Ref:**YH10799
RIVERSIDE VETNRY SURGERY, Eastleigh **Ref:**YH11929
RODGERS, S E, Liss **Ref:**YH12047
SEADOWN VETNRY GROUP, Hythe **Ref:**YH12582
VETREPHARM, Fordingbridge **Ref:**YH14702
WELBAC CHIROPRACTIC CLINIC, New Milton **Ref:**YH15057
WILLIAMS, CHARLOTTE, Droxford **Ref:**YH15453

HEREFORDSHIRE

ANTHONY, F J, Bromyard **Ref:**YH00465
COUNTRYWIDE, Hereford **Ref:**YH03445
EQUINE MARKETING, Weobley **Ref:**YH04787
HUGHES, A LANCE, Hereford **Ref:**YH07258

- **JOHN HORLOCK & ASSOCIATES**, Leominster **Ref:**YH07794
- **SHEEPCOTE EQUESTRIAN**, Hereford **Ref:**YH12695

HERTFORDSHIRE

- **CALLAWAY, ELIZABETH**, Hatfield **Ref:**YH02448
- **CAMBRIDGE PET CREMATORIUM**, Royston **Ref:**YH02470
- **CHESTNUT VETNRY GRP**, Ware **Ref:**YH02837
- **CRAIB, MARGIE**, Berkhamsted **Ref:**YH03548
- **DAVIES & ROUTLEDGE**, Royston **Ref:**YH03933
- **DEAN, T S**, St Albans **Ref:**YH03997
- **FOUNDATION FOR ANIMAL HEALING**, Hitchin **Ref:**YH05407
- **HARRIS, C P**, Hertford **Ref:**YH06466
- **JONES, DAWN**, St. Albans **Ref:**YH07892
- **PARK VETNRY CTRE**, Watford **Ref:**YH10739
- **PHOENIX CLGE OF RADIONICS**, Hemel Hempstead **Ref:**YH11070
- **PRATT, JEFFERY A**, Chipperfield **Ref:**YH11339
- **SHANKS & MCEWAN PAPER BEDDING**, Hitchin **Ref:**YH12669
- **SHENTON, MAXINE**, Buntingford **Ref:**YH12708
- **STONE LANE VETNRY CLINIC**, Royston **Ref:**YH13511
- **TANT, RAY**, Wheathampstead **Ref:**YH13860
- **TODDBROOK VETNRY CTRE**, Cheshunt **Ref:**YH14199
- **TODDBROOK VETNRY CTRE**, Hoddesdon **Ref:**YH14200
- **UPPERWOOD FARM STUD**, Hemel Hempstead **Ref:**YH14609

ISLE OF MAN

- **ANGUS, S**, Ramsey **Ref:**YH00423
- **ISLE OF MAN**, Douglas **Ref:**YH07524

ISLE OF WIGHT

- **HERBERTSON, B R**, Freshwater Bay **Ref:**YH06698

JERSEY

- **MACLEOD/ALLAN/RUSHTON-TAYLOR**, St Mary **Ref:**YH09011

KENT

- **BELL EQUINE VETNRY CLINIC**, Maidstone **Ref:**YH01214
- **BIAC**, Sittingbourne **Ref:**YH01389
- **CINQUE PORTS VETNRY ASS**, Hawkhurst **Ref:**YH02922
- **CINQUE PORTS VETNRY ASS**, Tenterden **Ref:**YH02921
- **CULVERDEN VETNRY GRP**, Tunbridge Wells **Ref:**YH03709
- **EQUINE SPORT THERAPY**, Edenbridge **Ref:**YH04800
- **MAISON DIEU VETNRY CTRE**, Dover **Ref:**YH09041
- **MILBOURN EQUINE VET HOSPITAL**, Ashford **Ref:**YH09566
- **NEWNHAM COURT VETNRY GRP**, Maidstone **Ref:**YH10158
- **OXTED VETNRY CLNC**, Edenbridge **Ref:**YH10626
- **PIERSON STEWART & PARTNERS**, Cranbrook **Ref:**YH11091
- **PIERSON STEWART & PARTNERS**, Marden **Ref:**YH11092
- **PUTLANDS VETNRY SURGERY**, Tonbridge **Ref:**YH11468
- **ROGERS, ANNE**, Goudhurst **Ref:**YH12060
- **SMALLEY & BLAXLAND**, Sandwich **Ref:**YH12911
- **THEOBALD, CARON**, Greenhithe **Ref:**YH13982
- **THOMAS PETTIFER**, Romney Marsh **Ref:**YH14010
- **UPSON, ANNE & PETER**, Folkestone **Ref:**YH14613
- **VETNRY SURGERY**, Deal **Ref:**YH14700
- **WARR, TONY**, Tonbridge **Ref:**YH14929

LANCASHIRE

- **A W HELME & PARTNER**, Preston **Ref:**YH00066
- **ARGO FEEDS**, Ashton-under-Lyne **Ref:**YH00520
- **BALDRAND VETNRY PRACTICE**, Lancaster **Ref:**YH00839
- **EQUINE BEHAVIOUR**, Darwen **Ref:**YH04765
- **L S SYSTEMS**, Preston **Ref:**YH08329
- **MADDRELL, BUXTON & TAYLOR**, Leigh **Ref:**YH09021
- **NORTHERN STANDARDBREDS**, Barnoldswick **Ref:**YH10310
- **PINEWOOD VETNRY PRACTICE**, Chorley **Ref:**YH11129
- **RENARD RIDING CTRE**, Poulton-Le-Fylde **Ref:**YH11753
- **STANLEY HOUSE VETNRY SURGEONS**, Colne **Ref:**YH13370
- **TRILANCO**, Poulton-Le-Fylde **Ref:**YH14397

LEICESTERSHIRE

- **BELL, BROWN & BENTLEY**, Leicester **Ref:**YH01217
- **BEVIN BUTLER & DRUMMOND**, Market Harborough **Ref:**YH01344
- **E D SIMPSON & SON**, Leicester **Ref:**YH04400
- **ECKFORD, D A**, Oakham **Ref:**YH04534
- **EQUIHERB**, Syston **Ref:**YH04750
- **HOLISTIC RIDING**, Lutterworth **Ref:**YH06935
- **HURST SADDLERS**, Leicester **Ref:**YH07316
- **J B THORNE**, Thurmaston **Ref:**YH07566
- **MARTIN, FIONA**, Market Harborough **Ref:**YH09218
- **S L B SUPPLIES**, Coalville **Ref:**YH12329
- **WALTHAM CTRE**, Melton Mowbray **Ref:**YH14888

LINCOLNSHIRE

- **BEAUMONT, G L**, Market Rasen **Ref:**YH01135
- **BELCHFORD STUD**, Horncastle **Ref:**YH01208
- **BRANSBY HOME**, Saxilby **Ref:**YH01811
- **COOK & TIMSON**, Louth **Ref:**YH03254
- **COOL SPORT**, Brigg **Ref:**YH03269
- **F P I**, Stamford **Ref:**YH04998
- **FENWOLD VETNRY GRP**, Spilsby **Ref:**YH05157
- **IANSON, STEVE (ESQ)**, Grantham **Ref:**YH07372
- **LEVERTON**, Gainsborough **Ref:**YH08576
- **LOCHRIE, G K A**, Gainsborough **Ref:**YH08755
- **RASE VETNRY CTRE**, Market Rasen **Ref:**YH11645
- **VETNRY HOSPITAL**, Lincoln **Ref:**YH14697

LINCOLNSHIRE (NORTH EAST)

- **RASE VETNRY CTRE**, Grimsby **Ref:**YH11646

LINCOLNSHIRE (NORTH)

- **ALKBOROUGH STABLES**, Scunthorpe **Ref:**YH00282
- **EQUINE THERAPY**, Ulceby **Ref:**YH04806

LONDON (GREATER)

- **AINSWORTHS**, London **Ref:**YH00216
- **ALOE VERA EQUICARE**, Edgware **Ref:**YH00333
- **BRITISH RED CROSS**, London **Ref:**YH01969
- **BROOKE HOSPITAL FOR ANIMALS**, London **Ref:**YH02041
- **CHASE SADDLERY**, Enfield **Ref:**YH02785
- **DRUMAWHEY**, Uxbridge **Ref:**YH04285
- **HARMONY & HEALTH FORMULATIONS**, London **Ref:**YH06445
- **KIMPTON BROS**, London **Ref:**YH08162
- **LEGARD, HILARY**, London **Ref:**YH08534
- **MCCARROLL, KAY**, Hendon **Ref:**YH09319

MANCHESTER (GREATER)

- **GROVE VETNRY HOSPITAL**, Stockport **Ref:**YH06173
- **MOUNTAIN BREEZE AIR IONISERS**, Failsworth **Ref:**YH09896

MERSEYSIDE

- **JONES STRAUGHAN, & MARSDEN**, Birkenhead **Ref:**YH07874
- **TITHEBARN**, Southport **Ref:**YH14189
- **WILLIAMS, C P**, Birkenhead **Ref:**YH15452

MIDLANDS (WEST)

- **608 VETNRY GRP**, Solihull **Ref:**YH00004
- **ADAS WESTERN**, Wolverhampton **Ref:**YH00177
- **CONNAUGHT HSE VETNRY HOSPITAL**, Wolverhampton **Ref:**YH03233
- **FRANK STEPHENS & SON**, Wolverhampton **Ref:**YH05461
- **HERON FIELD**, Solihull **Ref:**YH06711
- **J G & J M JONES**, Sutton Coldfield **Ref:**YH07583
- **KEYLOCK, CARMEL**, Birmingham **Ref:**YH08115
- **KIRBY & COOK & PEGG**, Birmingham **Ref:**YH08223
- **NATURAL REMEDIES**, Walsall **Ref:**YH10054
- **OAKFIELD VETNRY GROUP**, Birmingham **Ref:**YH10382
- **PAWS & HOOFS**, Aldridge **Ref:**YH10841
- **REGENT VETNRY GROUP**, Coventry **Ref:**YH11741
- **ST GEORGE'S VETNRY CLINIC**, Wolverhampton **Ref:**YH13276
- **WILSON, WALKER & BARNBY**, Birmingham **Ref:**YH15548

NORFOLK

- **ALLEN & PAGE**, Thetford **Ref:**YH00290
- **AVIFORM**, Norwich **Ref:**YH00685
- **BARRIER ANIMAL HEALTHCARE**, Attleborough **Ref:**YH01021
- **CHAPELFIELD VETNRY**, Norwich **Ref:**YH02741
- **CURNOW, E M**, King's Lynn **Ref:**YH03732
- **FRANCIS CUPISS**, Diss **Ref:**YH05448
- **GILLHAM HOUSE VETNRY**, Fakenham **Ref:**YH05782
- **HARRIS, J A**, Norwich **Ref:**YH06476
- **LENRYS ASSOCIATES**, Attleborough **Ref:**YH08552
- **OLD GOLFHOUSE VETNRY GRP**, Thetford **Ref:**YH10459
- **RFC BED-DOWN**, Harleston **Ref:**YH11781
- **THOMSON & JOSEPH**, Norwich **Ref:**YH14046
- **WENDALS HERBS**, King's Lynn **Ref:**YH15104
- **WENSUM VALLEY VETNRY SURG**, Fakenham **Ref:**YH15109
- **WESTOVER VETNRY CTRE**, North Walsham **Ref:**YH15229
- **WOOD, J G P**, Norwich **Ref:**YH15663

NORTHAMPTONSHIRE

- **A B R FOODS**, Corby **Ref:**YH00019
- **ANIMAL HEALTH SUPPLIES**, Boughton **Ref:**YH00437
- **AVENUE VETNRY HOSP**, Kettering **Ref:**YH00680
- **BAINBRIDGE, BUTT & DALY**, Wellingborough **Ref:**YH00811
- **HAYTIP**, Towcester **Ref:**YH06595
- **HODGES, JO**, Rushden **Ref:**YH06908
- **HOLLANDS, TERESA**, Kettering **Ref:**YH06939
- **JEROME, E A**, Daventry **Ref:**YH07754
- **MAXICROP INTERNATIONAL**, Corby **Ref:**YH09284
- **NATURALLY**, Towcester **Ref:**YH10055
- **NORTHLANDS VETNRY HOSPITAL**, Kettering **Ref:**YH10315
- **SPILMAN, THOMASINA**, Yelvertoft **Ref:**YH13207
- **SPINNEY LODGE VETNRY HOSP**, Northampton **Ref:**YH13209
- **THORPE SADDLERY**, Kettering **Ref:**YH14094

NORTHUMBERLAND

- **ALN VETNRY GRP**, Alnwick **Ref:**YH00331
- **EWING & GIDLOW**, Wooler **Ref:**YH04961
- **FAIRMOOR VETNRY CTRE**, Morpeth **Ref:**YH05026

HADRIAN VETNRY GRP, Hexham Ref:YH06272
HAMPDEN & SIMONSIDE VETNRY, Alnwick Ref:YH06363
HARRIS, G W, Prudhoe Ref:YH06468
RENTON SWAN & PARTNERS, Coldstream Ref:YH11764
ROBSON & PRESCOTT, Morpeth Ref:YH12013
SIMONSIDE VETNRY CTRE, Rothbury Ref:YH12833
W E HOWDEN, Coldstream Ref:YH14761
YOUNG, PROCTOR & WAINWRIGHT, Stocksfield Ref:YH15937

NOTTINGHAMSHIRE

BARTHORPE, JANE, Newark Ref:YH01037
BRIDLE WAY & GAUNTLEYS, Newark Ref:YH01892
DAVISON VETNRY SURGEONS, Nottingham Ref:YH03955
HOLISTIC HORSECARE, Northampton Ref:YH06934
KEANE, ALLAN, Mansfield Ref:YH08015
MINSTER VETNRY CTRE, Southwell Ref:YH09653
PARK HALL STABLES, Mansfield Woodhouse Ref:YH10727

OXFORDSHIRE

ALVESCOT STUD, Carterton Ref:YH00349
AVONVALE VETNRY GRP, Banbury Ref:YH00693
BASKERVILLE, R E, Watlington Ref:YH01054
BEECHENER VETNRY SUPPLIES, Minster Lovell Ref:YH01168
CONSTANTINE, PAMELA, Witney Ref:YH03244
CORLEY, H V, Faringdon Ref:YH03318
COTSWOLD EQUINE CTRE, Burford Ref:YH03361
DALLAS KEITH, Witney Ref:YH03843
ELWELL, TERESA, Banbury Ref:YH04647
EQUI-GRASS, Banbury Ref:YH04749
FERENS, CUMMING & CORNISH, Bicester Ref:YH05158
FIELD, MICHAEL P, Barford St Michael Ref:YH05189
MARK SLINGSBY, Bicester Ref:YH09155
MCTIMONEY CHIROPRACTIC ASS, Eynsham Ref:YH09407
MCTIMONEY CHIROPRACTIC CLGE, Abingdon Ref:YH09408
MICROM, Thame Ref:YH09519
MORPHETT, S E, Milton Under Wychwood Ref:YH09823
O'DONNELL, E O, Wantage Ref:YH10432
OXFORD MCTIMONEY CHIROPRACTIC, Botley Ref:YH10619
PARKWOOD VETNRY GRP, Woodstock Ref:YH10782
QUACKERIES, Banbury Ref:YH11474
RADIONIC ASSOCIATION, Banbury Ref:YH11597
SNODGRASS EDEN & TRETHEWEY, Oxford Ref:YH13033
WALKER, GLANVILL & RICHARDS, Hook Norton Ref:YH14849

RUTLAND

GIBSONS, M W, Oakham Ref:YH05756
HOMOEOPATHY FOR HORSES, Oakham Ref:YH07009
JONES, DAVID, Oakham Ref:YH07888
SMITH, ROBIN ABEL, Rutland Ref:YH12996
TRIPLE CROWN, Oakham Ref:YH14401

SHROPSHIRE

ABBEY VETNRY CTRE, Shrewsbury Ref:YH00090
BRYNORE STUD & LIVERY STABLES, Ellesmere Ref:YH02178
CLGE HILL VETNRY GRP, Shawbury Ref:YH03028
ELEY, JANET L, Church Stretton Ref:YH04604
FYRNWY EQUINE CLINICS, Shrewsbury Ref:YH05560
HAYGATE VETNRY CTRE, Telford Ref:YH06581
NEWLANDS VETNRY GROUP, Craven Arms Ref:YH10146
ROWEN-BARBARY HORSE FEEDS, Whitchurch Ref:YH12167
STABLES FLAT, Shrewsbury Ref:YH13310
TEME VETNRY PRACTICE, Ludlow Ref:YH13945
TOUCHDOWN LIVERIES, Whitchurch Ref:YH14253
VETSEARCH EQUINE SUPPLIES UK, Bishops Castle Ref:YH14703
WINDSOR, M, Shrewsbury Ref:YH15578

SOMERSET

ARTHUR, G H (PROF), Axbridge Ref:YH00567
BAKER, COLETTE, Burnham-on-Sea Ref:YH00816
BIRT, JENNI, Wellington Ref:YH01445
BRISTOL UNIVERSITY, Langford Ref:YH01921
BROWNE WILLES WHITE & GLIDDON, Minehead Ref:YH02137
CANTI, J, Taunton Ref:YH02513
DEANE VETNRY CTRE, Taunton Ref:YH03999
DELAWARE VETNRY GRP, Castle Cary Ref:YH04029
DOWNS HSE EQUINE, Minehead Ref:YH04239
EDDY WILLIAMSON & PARTNERS, Shepton Mallet Ref:YH04545
ELLIOTT & FIELDHOUSE, Dulverton Ref:YH04617
GARSTON VETNRY GRP, Frome Ref:YH05659
GRANT & PARTNERS, Chard Ref:YH06008
GRIFFITHS, HELEN, Shepton Mallet Ref:YH06141
HILTON HERBS, Crewkerne Ref:YH06863
KENDAL, SARAH, Williton Ref:YH08059
LETHAM, SNELL & HUTCHINSON, Ilminster Ref:YH08566
MORLEY PARTNERS, Taunton Ref:YH09819
MOUNT VETNRY HOSPITAL, Wellington Ref:YH09895
RUDRAM, N, Taunton Ref:YH12210
SMITH & PARTNERS, Bridgwater Ref:YH12934
SOUTHILL VETNRY GROUP, Wincanton Ref:YH13156
STOP GAP, Wincanton Ref:YH13522
THORNEY COPSE, Wincanton Ref:YH14066
UNIVERSITY OF BRISTOL, Langford Ref:YH14583
WILLIAMS, R E, Shepton Mallet Ref:YH15471

SOMERSET (NORTH)

BEST & BEST, Portishead Ref:YH01323
CLARENDON VETNRY CTRE, Weston-Super-Mare Ref:YH02954
EQUINE DENTAL SVS, Weston-Super-Mare Ref:YH04772
FURNISS & MORTON, Weston-Super-Mare Ref:YH05551
REINBOW EQUESTRIAN PRODUCTS, Weston-Super-Mare Ref:YH11748
URCH, DAVID L, Wrington Ref:YH14618
VETNRY CTRE, Nailsea Ref:YH14695
WATKINS VETNRY SURGERY, Yatton Ref:YH14977

STAFFORDSHIRE

BLOFLOW MAGNOTHERAPY, Stoke-on-Trent Ref:YH01545
BROBERG, J O, Stafford Ref:YH02005
COUNTY VETNRY GRP, Stoke-on-Trent Ref:YH03496
DONNACHIE & TOWNLEY, Rugeley Ref:YH04186
NUTEC, Lichfield Ref:YH10357
POOL HSE VETNRY HOS, Lichfield Ref:YH11262
PREMIER NUTRITION PRODUCTS, Rugeley Ref:YH11348
ROGERS & BROCK VETNRY, Stoke-on-Trent Ref:YH12055
RUMENCO - MAIN RING, Burton-on-Trent Ref:YH12227
SPRINGWOOD VETNRY GROUP, Burton-on-Trent Ref:YH13266
THEOBALD, L & N, Stafford Ref:YH13983
VETNRY CTRE, Burton-on-Trent Ref:YH14696

SUFFOLK

ANIMAL HEALTH TRUST, Newmarket Ref:YH00438
AQUARIUS VETNRY CTRE, Brandon Ref:YH00489
BARN VETNRY PRACTICE, Ipswich Ref:YH00963
BAYER, Bury St Edmunds Ref:YH01095
BEAUFORT COTTAGE, Newmarket Ref:YH01127
DONCASTER, R A, Ipswich Ref:YH04180
EAGLE VETNRY GRP, Halesworth Ref:YH04440
EQUINE VETNRY JOURNAL, Newmarket Ref:YH04808
FROMUS VETNRY GROUP, Saxmundham Ref:YH05516
GREENWOOD, ELLIS & PARTNERS, Newmarket Ref:YH06107
HIGHCLIFF VETNRY PRACTICE, Ipswich Ref:YH06776
HOLMES, STEPHEN, Newmarket Ref:YH06979
MILL SADDLERY, Stowmarket Ref:YH09587
N S RESEARCH, Mildenhall Ref:YH09996
OAKWOOD VETNRY GRP, Harleston Ref:YH10411
PAVESCO UK, Harleston Ref:YH10838
ROSSDALE & PARTNERS, Newmarket Ref:YH12122
SMITH RYDER DAVIES & HILLIARD, Woodbridge Ref:YH12937
STOWE VETNRY GROUP, Ipswich Ref:YH13539
STOWE VETNRY GROUP, Stowmarket Ref:YH13540
SWAYNE & PARTNERS, Bury St Edmunds Ref:YH13699
SWAYNE & PARTNERS, Newmarket Ref:YH13700
SWAYNE & PARTNERS, Sudbury Ref:YH13701
TAYLOR & LEES, Sudbury Ref:YH13894
THREE RIVERS VETNRY GROUP, Beccles Ref:YH14106
UFAC, Newmarket Ref:YH14539
VIRBAC, Bury St Edmunds Ref:YH14732
WHALEY, MELISSA, Newmarket Ref:YH15257

SURREY

ADRENALINE SPORTS, Haslemere Ref:YH00188
ANIMAL ALTERNATIVES, Richmond Ref:YH00425
AVENUE VETNRY CTRE, Staple Hill Ref:YH00679
BEACON HILL SURGERY, Hindhead Ref:YH01107
BEN BATES HYDRO BATH, Camberley Ref:YH01261
COFFEY, D J, Esher Ref:YH03135
COLIN CLARK & AST, Godalming Ref:YH03171
EQUINE VETNRY CLINIC, Guildford Ref:YH04807
GAYTON VETNRY GROUP, Redhill Ref:YH05683
GIBSON, L W, Great Bookham Ref:YH05751
MEDITRINA, Caterham Ref:YH09437
MILLER, IAN, Guildford Ref:YH09607
NICOL & PARTNERS, Guildford Ref:YH10196
OXTED VETNRY CLNC, Oxted Ref:YH10627
PRIORY VETNRY SURGERY, Banstead Ref:YH11408
PRIORY VETNRY SURGERY, Redhill Ref:YH11409

- **PRIORY VETNRY SURGERY**, Reigate **Ref:**YH11411
- **PRIORY VETNRY SURGERY**, Tadworth **Ref:**YH11410
- **REIS, VICKY**, Farnham **Ref:**YH11749
- **SIMONS, M A P**, Fetcham **Ref:**YH12832
- **UNDERWOOD & CROXSON**, Guildford **Ref:**YH14562
- **UNDERWOOD & CROXSON EQUINE**, Guildford **Ref:**YH14563
- **WATERDENE VETNRY PRACTICE**, Caterham **Ref:**YH14966
- **WATERDENE VETNRY PRACTICE**, Purley **Ref:**YH14967
- **WESTCOATS VETNRY CLINIC**, Charlwood **Ref:**YH15186
- **WOODSTOCK SOUTH STABLES**, Chessington **Ref:**YH15751

SUSSEX (EAST)

- **CAMROSA EQUESTRIAN**, Wadhurst **Ref:**YH02492
- **CINQUE PORTS VETNRY ASS**, Rye **Ref:**YH02923
- **CLGE PRACT PHYTOTHERAPY**, Hailsham **Ref:**YH03029
- **CLIFFE VETNRY GRP**, Lewes **Ref:**YH03034
- **HIGHCROFT VETNRY GROUP**, Hailsham **Ref:**YH06777
- **HOWE & STARNES**, Uckfield **Ref:**YH07222
- **KIT WILSON TRUST**, Uckfield **Ref:**YH08246
- **RICKETTS, TINA**, Wadhurst **Ref:**YH11836
- **ST ANNES VETNRY GROUP**, Eastbourne **Ref:**YH13271

SUSSEX (WEST)

- **ALLPRESS, BELGRAVE & PARTNERS**, Arundel **Ref:**YH00325
- **ARTHUR LODGE VETNRY HOSP**, Horsham **Ref:**YH00566
- **BEN MAYES**, Horsham **Ref:**YH01262
- **BLAKE, JILL**, Steyning **Ref:**YH01516
- **BRENDON HORSE & RIDER**, Brighton **Ref:**YH01837
- **CINDER HILL VETNRY CLINIC**, Haywards Heath **Ref:**YH02919
- **DRAGONFLY SADDLERY**, Hassocks **Ref:**YH04252
- **HOLISTIC VET**, Chichester **Ref:**YH06936
- **HORSE HEALTH PRODUCTS**, Pulborough **Ref:**YH07121
- **KEATE, CHRIS**, Burgess Hill **Ref:**YH08019
- **MARTEN, D W**, Pulborough **Ref:**YH09210
- **ROBIN STORKEY**, Worthing **Ref:**YH11982
- **TFP**, Horsham **Ref:**YH13971
- **TOYHORSE INTERNATIONAL**, Billingshurst **Ref:**YH14306
- **TRINITY CONSULTANTS**, Bognor Regis **Ref:**YH14399
- **VACLAVEK, V (DR)**, Haywards Heath **Ref:**YH14630
- **VETNRY ACUPUNCTURE REFERRAL**, Haywards Heath **Ref:**YH14691
- **VETNRY SURGERY**, Horsham **Ref:**YH14701

TYNE AND WEAR

- **ARTHUR, M R (HON)**, Newcastle-upon-Tyne **Ref:**YH00569
- **BLYTHEMAN & PARTNERS**, Gateshead **Ref:**YH01580
- **BLYTHMAN & PARTNERS**, Gosforth **Ref:**YH01581
- **NOBLE, MARK**, Newcastle Upon Tyne **Ref:**YH10219
- **OAKLANDS VETNRY CTRE**, Yarm **Ref:**YH10393
- **STRACHAN, TYSON & HAMILTON**, Newcastle-upon-Tyne **Ref:**YH13544

WARWICKSHIRE

- **ACCIMASSU**, Studley **Ref:**YH00140
- **ACORN VETNRY CTRE**, Studley **Ref:**YH00154
- **BELL & PARTNERS**, Leamington Spa **Ref:**YH01213
- **BILTON VETNRY CTRE**, Rugby **Ref:**YH01417
- **BRAZIER, JOHN F H**, Leamington Spa **Ref:**YH01823
- **GUILD ST VETNRY CTRE**, Stratford-upon-Avon **Ref:**YH06185
- **HALINA TOMBS**, Rugby **Ref:**YH06302
- **HURLEY, BRONWEN**, Kineton **Ref:**YH07312
- **MIDLAND EQUINE THERAPY**, Kenilworth **Ref:**YH09554
- **ORTON EQUINE SWIMMING CTRE**, Atherstone **Ref:**YH10554
- **SHIPSTON MILL**, Shipston-on-Stour **Ref:**YH12751
- **THORNTON, EMMA**, Coventry **Ref:**YH14078
- **VENFIELD, CHRISTINE**, Solihull **Ref:**YH14676

WILTSHIRE

- **ARCHWAY VETNRY SURGERY**, Highworth **Ref:**YH00501
- **ARMADILLO PRODUCTS**, Salisbury **Ref:**YH00535
- **BELMONT HSE VETNRY SURGERY**, Pewsey **Ref:**YH01246
- **COATES, MARGRIT**, Redlynch **Ref:**YH03108
- **DOWNS HSE REHABILITATION CTRE**, Marlborough **Ref:**YH04240
- **ENDELL VETNRY GRP**, Salisbury **Ref:**YH04666
- **EQUINE MNGMT SOLUTIONS**, Marlborough **Ref:**YH04789
- **GEORGE VETNRY GRP**, Malmesbury **Ref:**YH05721
- **HARRIS, HILL & WARNER**, Bradford-on-Avon **Ref:**YH06471
- **HARRIS, HILL & WARNER**, Trowbridge **Ref:**YH06472
- **HARRIS, HILL & WARNER**, Warminster **Ref:**YH06473
- **HARRIS, HILL & WARNER**, Westbury **Ref:**YH06470
- **HOOPER, PENNIE**, Marlborough **Ref:**YH07044
- **LAMINITIS CLINIC**, Chippenham **Ref:**YH08372
- **PANCEUTICS**, Swindon **Ref:**YH10697
- **WESTCOURT**, Marlborough **Ref:**YH15189
- **WHITE HORSE VETNRY CLINIC**, Calne **Ref:**YH15315
- **WHITE HORSE VETNRY CLINIC**, Lyneham **Ref:**YH15316
- **WOODLANDS EQUINE VETNRY GRP**, Salisbury **Ref:**YH15708

WORCESTERSHIRE

- **ABBEY GREEN VETNRY GRP**, Broadway **Ref:**YH00078
- **DENNY, D J B**, Worcester **Ref:**YH04061
- **DUDLEY, S & M C**, Evesham **Ref:**YH04310
- **GIBBINS, JONATHON**, Malvern **Ref:**YH05738
- **MARKETING & DEVELOPMENT SVS**, Stourport-on-Severn **Ref:**YH09160
- **MCGETTIGAN & MCGETTIGAN**, Redditch **Ref:**YH09355
- **PEACE SEEDS**, Evesham **Ref:**YH10855
- **PHIPPS, A**, Pershore **Ref:**YH11068
- **STOKES, PAULA**, Redditch **Ref:**YH13505
- **TEME VETNRY PRACTICE**, Tenbury Wells **Ref:**YH13946
- **VALE VETNRY GROUP**, Stourport-on-Severn **Ref:**YH14643
- **VINE HERBAL PRODUCTS**, Broadway **Ref:**YH14729
- **WILSON, WALKER & BARNBY**, Bromsgrove **Ref:**YH15549
- **WILSON, WALKER & BARNBY**, Droitwich **Ref:**YH15550

YORKSHIRE (EAST)

- **EUROVET**, North Ferriby **Ref:**YH04909
- **GARTH HSE**, Bridlington **Ref:**YH05661
- **GARTH VETNRY GROUP**, Beeford **Ref:**YH05662
- **NORWOOD VETNRY GROUP**, Beverley **Ref:**YH10336
- **OSMONDS**, North Ferriby **Ref:**YH10571
- **PEEL VETNRY GRP**, Beverley **Ref:**YH10899
- **SEVEN SEAS VETNRY DIVISION**, Hull **Ref:**YH12640
- **STOCKCARE**, Beverley **Ref:**YH13488
- **VERMUYDEN VETNRY PRACTICE**, Goole **Ref:**YH14682

YORKSHIRE (NORTH)

- **ABBEYFIELDS VETNRY CTRE**, Tadcaster **Ref:**YH00096
- **BISHOPTON VETNRY GRP**, Ripon **Ref:**YH01452
- **BLOOM, KATRYNA**, Selby **Ref:**YH01551
- **BOOTHROYD, A**, Filey **Ref:**YH01638
- **BROADACRES NURSERIES**, Tadcaster **Ref:**YH01991
- **COLLINS, E A**, York **Ref:**YH03187
- **EASTGATE VETNRY CTRE**, Pickering **Ref:**YH04502
- **ELLIS, JANET B**, Selby **Ref:**YH04625
- **EQUINE DENTAL TECHNICAL**, York **Ref:**YH04773
- **FOREST HOUSE VETNRY SURGERY**, Knaresborough **Ref:**YH05340
- **FORSYTH & MAZONAS**, Selby **Ref:**YH05381
- **FORSYTH, MADELEINE**, Helmsley **Ref:**YH05383
- **GALTRES VETNRY SURGERY**, Alne **Ref:**YH05628
- **GRANT NORRIE & ALMOND**, Ripon **Ref:**YH06010
- **HOLMEFIELD VETNRY CTRE**, Selby **Ref:**YH06970
- **J & J L WATKINSON**, Leyburn **Ref:**YH07547
- **J C HELLENIA**, Ripon **Ref:**YH07570
- **LIFE SOURCE SUPPLEMENTS**, Ripon **Ref:**YH08610
- **LINSCOTT & BEST**, Bedale **Ref:**YH08667
- **LINSCOTT & BEST**, Ripon **Ref:**YH08668
- **MINSTER EQUINE VETNRY PRAC**, Upper Poppleton **Ref:**YH09651
- **NORTHERN EQUINE THERAPY CTRE**, Settle **Ref:**YH10303
- **PHOSYN**, York **Ref:**YH11077
- **RAE BEAN & PARTNERS**, Boroughbridge **Ref:**YH11602
- **RAINBOW EQUINE CLINIC**, Malton **Ref:**YH11615
- **STIRK & HAIZELDEN**, Ripon **Ref:**YH13472
- **SWALE VETNRY SURGERY**, Richmond **Ref:**YH13684

YORKSHIRE (SOUTH)

- **ARGO FEEDS**, Sheffield **Ref:**YH00521
- **BLUE CHIP**, Sheffield **Ref:**YH01565
- **CHANTRY VETNRY GRP**, Barnsley **Ref:**YH02735
- **CHURCHFIELD VETNRY CTRE**, Barnsley **Ref:**YH02911
- **HALLAM VETNRY CTRE**, Sheffield **Ref:**YH06323

YORKSHIRE (WEST)

- **ABBEY HSE VETNRY CLINIC**, Cleckheaton **Ref:**YH00081
- **ABBEY HSE VETNRY CLINIC**, Leeds **Ref:**YH00080
- **ABBEY HSE VETNRY CLINIC**, Leeds **Ref:**YH00082
- **AIRE VETNRY CTRE**, Leeds **Ref:**YH00222
- **AIRE VETNRY CTRE**, Leeds **Ref:**YH00223
- **BALL, VIVIENNE**, East Keswick **Ref:**YH00852
- **BAXTER, J S**, Leeds **Ref:**YH01087
- **BEECHWOOD VETNRY GRP**, Leeds **Ref:**YH01183
- **BEECHWOOD VETNRY GRP**, Leeds **Ref:**YH01182
- **BEECHWOOD VETNRY GRP**, Leeds **Ref:**YH01181
- **BEECHWOOD VETNRY GRP**, Leeds **Ref:**YH01180
- **CALDER VETNRY GRP**, Dewsbury **Ref:**YH02432
- **CALDER VETNRY GRP**, Horbury **Ref:**YH02434
- **CALDER VETNRY GRP**, Mirfield **Ref:**YH02433
- **CHANTRY VETNRY GRP**, Castleford **Ref:**YH02737
- **CHANTRY VETNRY GRP**, Wakefield **Ref:**YH02736

- **COOKSON, LORRAINE**, Leeds **Ref:**YH03267
- **CROFT HSE VETNRY CLINIC**, Batley **Ref:**YH03616
- **CROSS GREEN VETNRY CTRE**, Otley **Ref:**YH03646
- **DALES VETNRY CTRE**, Otley **Ref:**YH03830
- **DURTNELL VETNRY CTRE**, Leeds **Ref:**YH04374
- **DURTNELL VETNRY CTRE**, Leeds **Ref:**YH04375
- **EASTON & WANNOP**, Leeds **Ref:**YH04512
- **EQUINE DENTISTRY**, Wakefield **Ref:**YH04774
- **GARTH FOLD VETNRY CTRE**, Idle **Ref:**YH05660
- **GREEN, GREAVES & THOMSON**, Keighley **Ref:**YH06064
- **GREENWOOD & BROWN**, Pontefract **Ref:**YH06106
- **HALL, TONY**, Wakefield **Ref:**YH06320
- **HOLLY HSE**, Moortown **Ref:**YH06955
- **HOLMEFIELD VETNRY CTRE**, Sherburn In Elmet **Ref:**YH06971
- **HUTCHISON, DUNLOP & BAIRD**, Wetherby **Ref:**YH07337
- **KRUUSE**, Sherburn In Elmet **Ref:**YH08299
- **SPALDING, VICTORIA**, Roundhay **Ref:**YH13172
- **STEWART GREENWOOD & HODGSON**, Castleford **Ref:**YH13455
- **TACK & TURNOUT EQUESTRIAN**, Huddersfield **Ref:**YH13780
- **THORNBURY VETNRY GROUP**, Birkenshaw **Ref:**YH14059
- **THORNBURY VETNRY GRP**, Bradford **Ref:**YH14060
- **TOWER WOOD VETNRY GROUP**, Leeds **Ref:**YH14277
- **TURF VETNRY SUPPLIES**, Wetherby **Ref:**YH14468
- **TWEED HSE VETNRY SURGERY**, Leeds **Ref:**YH14506
- **WESTWOOD VETNRY SURGERY**, Boston Spa **Ref:**YH15241
- **WHITE CROSS VET HOSPITAL**, Guiseley **Ref:**YH15303

RIDING CLUBS

BATH & SOMERSET (NORTH EAST)

- **BATH RIDING CLUB**, Bath **Ref:**YH01073

BEDFORDSHIRE

- **CLGE EQUESTRIAN CTRE**, Bedford **Ref:**YH03025
- **TINSLEYS RIDING CLUB**, Oakley **Ref:**YH14176

BERKSHIRE

- **CHILTERN RIDING CLUB**, Reading **Ref:**YH02860
- **HURST RIDERS CLUB**, Hurst **Ref:**YH07315
- **MORTIMER RIDING CLUB**, Reading **Ref:**YH09846
- **THAMES VALLEY RIDING CLUB**, Maidenhead **Ref:**YH13976
- **WOKINGHAM RIDING CLUB**, Reading **Ref:**YH15645
- **WOODLANDS**, Hungerford **Ref:**YH15705

BUCKINGHAMSHIRE

- **AYLESBURY VALE RIDING CLUB**, Aylesbury **Ref:**YH00696
- **BRAWLINGS FARM RIDING CTRE**, Gerrards Cross **Ref:**YH01819
- **CHALFONT HEIGHTS RIDING CLUB**, Seer Green **Ref:**YH02709
- **EQUESTRIAN CTRE**, Amersham **Ref:**YH04696
- **GREAT MISSENDEN RIDING CLUB**, Princes Risborough **Ref:**YH06040
- **HIGH WYCOMBE RIDING CLUB**, High Wycombe **Ref:**YH06767

CAMBRIDGESHIRE

- **CAMBRIDGE & DISTRICT**, Histon **Ref:**YH02468
- **CAMBRIDGE UNIVERSITY**, Cambridge **Ref:**YH02472
- **HUNTINGDON & DISTRICT**, Huntingdon **Ref:**YH07304

CHESHIRE

- **B.R.A.T.S. RIDING CLUB**, Knutsford **Ref:**YH00756
- **BOLD HEATH EQUESTRIAN**, Widnes **Ref:**YH01602
- **BOLD RIDING CLUB**, Widnes **Ref:**YH01604
- **KRONSBEC RIDING CLUB**, Ellesmere Port **Ref:**YH08298
- **MACCLESFIELD & DISTRICT**, Macclesfield **Ref:**YH08984
- **MID CHESHIRE RIDING CLUB**, Crewe **Ref:**YH09523
- **NANTWICH RIDING CLUB**, Malpas **Ref:**YH10018
- **WERNETH LOW RIDING CLUB**, Hyde **Ref:**YH15115
- **WILMSLOW RIDING CLUB**, Altrincham **Ref:**YH15524

CLEVELAND

- **GUISBOROUGH RIDING CLUB**, Guisborough **Ref:**YH06187
- **YARM & DISTRICT RIDING CLUB**, Stockton-on-Tees **Ref:**YH15886

CORNWALL

- **CAMEL VALLEY RIDING CLUB**, Cardinham **Ref:**YH02475
- **CORNISH RIDING HOLIDAYS**, Redruth **Ref:**YH03327
- **EAST CORNWALL RIDING CLUB**, Liskeard **Ref:**YH04469
- **ENGLISH CHINA CLAYS**, St Austell **Ref:**YH04673
- **GWENNAP RIDING CLUB**, Truro **Ref:**YH06200
- **HOLSWORTHY & DISTRICT**, Bude **Ref:**YH06984
- **NEWQUAY RIDING CLUB**, Newquay **Ref:**YH10163
- **TAVY VALLEY RIDING CLUB**, Callington **Ref:**YH13887
- **THREEWATERS RIDING CLUB**, Helston **Ref:**YH14109
- **TM INT SCHOOL OF HORSEMANSHIP**, Liskeard **Ref:**YH14196
- **VERYAN RIDING CTRE**, Truro **Ref:**YH14686

COUNTY DURHAM

- **ALSTON & KILLHOPE**, Bishop Auckland **Ref:**YH00339
- **BISHOPS RIDING CLUB**, Durham **Ref:**YH01451
- **DARLINGTON & DISTRICT**, Staindrop **Ref:**YH03891
- **UNIVERSITY OF DURHAM**, Durham **Ref:**YH14585

CUMBRIA

- **JOHN PEEL RIDING CLUB**, Carlisle **Ref:**YH07806
- **LAKES RIDING CLUB**, Windermere **Ref:**YH08357

DERBYSHIRE

- **ATHERSTONE & DISTRICT**, Swadlincote **Ref:**YH00643
- **BARLEYFIELDS**, Derby **Ref:**YH00952
- **DONISTHORPE & DISTRICT**, Swadlincote **Ref:**YH04182
- **THREE SHIRES RIDING CLUB**, Buxton **Ref:**YH14108

DEVON

- **BRIDESTOWE & DISTRICT**, Yelverton **Ref:**YH01869
- **EXETER & DISTRICT**, Newton Abbot **Ref:**YH04965
- **ILFRACOMBE & DISTRICT**, Barnstaple **Ref:**YH07399
- **LAMBERTS CASTLE RIDING CLUB**, Axminster **Ref:**YH08365
- **MID DEVON RIDING CLUB**, Okehampton **Ref:**YH09524
- **NORTH DEVON RIDING CLUB**, Ilfracombe **Ref:**YH10255
- **NORTH TAWTON RIDING CLUB**, Exeter **Ref:**YH10283
- **SID & OTTER VALLEY**, Honiton **Ref:**YH12780
- **SOUTH BRENT RIDING CLUB**, Totnes **Ref:**YH13078
- **SOUTH DEVON RIDING CLUB**, Torquay **Ref:**YH13083
- **UNIVERSITY OF EXETER**, Exeter **Ref:**YH14586
- **WITHERIDGE & DISTRICT RIDING**, Tiverton **Ref:**YH15622

DORSET

- **PURBECK & DISTRICT**, Wareham **Ref:**YH11460
- **SHILLINGSTONE & DISTRICT**, Blandford **Ref:**YH12745
- **SHIPTON RIDING CLUB**, Dorchester **Ref:**YH12753
- **SOUTHERN COUNTIES RIDING CLUB**, Poole **Ref:**YH13138
- **STOUR VALLEY RIDING CLUB**, Shaftesbury **Ref:**YH13529
- **WEYMOUTH & DISTRICT**, Weymouth **Ref:**YH15253
- **WIMBORNE & DISTRICT**, Broadstone **Ref:**YH15558

ESSEX

- **BILLERICAY & DISTRICT**, Billericay **Ref:**YH01409
- **HALLINGBURY HALL**, Bishop's Stortford **Ref:**YH06331
- **HALLINGBURY RIDING CLUB**, Bishop's Stortford **Ref:**YH06332
- **INGATESTONE/BLACKMORE**, Billericay **Ref:**YH07443
- **M & B RIDING CLUB**, Dagenham **Ref:**YH08944
- **SAFFRON WALDEN & DISTRICT**, Saffron Walden **Ref:**YH12381
- **SHOPLAND HALL EQUESTRIAN**, Rochford **Ref:**YH12758
- **TENDRING HUNDRED RIDING CLUB**, Clacton-on-Sea **Ref:**YH13954
- **THURROCK RIDING CLUB**, Grays **Ref:**YH14121
- **UPMINSTER RIDING CLUB**, Aveley **Ref:**YH14603

GLOUCESTERSHIRE

- **CHELTENHAM & DISTRICT**, Cheltenham **Ref:**YH02803
- **ELM LEAZE STUD**, Badminton **Ref:**YH04631
- **EVENLODE RIDING CLUB**, Winchcombe **Ref:**YH04936
- **WEST COUNTRY POLOCROSSE CLUB**, Stroud **Ref:**YH15135

HAMPSHIRE

- **BREAKSPEAR RIDING CLUB**, Bordon **Ref:**YH01825
- **BURLEY VILLA EQUESTRIAN CTRE**, New Milton **Ref:**YH02260
- **ESSO RIDING CLUB**, Fawley **Ref:**YH04874
- **HAMBLE VALLEY RIDING CLUB**, West End **Ref:**YH06344
- **HAMPSHIRE RURAL RIDING CLUB**, Alton **Ref:**YH06366
- **IBM RIDING CLUB**, Havant **Ref:**YH07378
- **INADOWN FARM STABLES**, Alton **Ref:**YH07407
- **MEON RIDING CLUB**, Petersfield **Ref:**YH09460
- **NEW FOREST RIDING CLUB**, Hythe **Ref:**YH10104
- **NRC**, Fareham **Ref:**YH10348
- **RINGWOOD & DISTRICT**, Sway **Ref:**YH11902
- **SOLENT RIDING CLUB**, Locksheath **Ref:**YH13055
- **WELLINGTON RIDING**, Hook **Ref:**YH15075
- **WEY VALLEY RIDING CLUB**, Alton **Ref:**YH15249

HEREFORDSHIRE

- **BROMYARD & DISTRICT**, Bromyard **Ref:**YH02028

- **HEREFORD & DISTRICT**, Little Birch **Ref:**YH06700
- **VALE OF ARROW RIDING CLUB**, Woonton **Ref:**YH14637

HERTFORDSHIRE

- **CHANDLERS CROSS RIDING CLUB**, Kings Langley **Ref:**YH02731
- **CROSSROADS RIDING CLUB**, Harpenden **Ref:**YH03664
- **ESSENDON & DISTRICT**, Buntingford **Ref:**YH04864
- **HOLLY HILL RIDING CLUB**, Northaw **Ref:**YH06954
- **ICKLEFORD EQUESTRIAN**, Hitchin **Ref:**YH07382
- **LETCHWORTH BALDOCK & DISTRICT**, Baldock **Ref:**YH08565
- **NORTH MYMMS RIDING CLUB**, Hatfield **Ref:**YH10273
- **PENNIWELLS RIDING GRP**, Borehamwood **Ref:**YH10956
- **PINNERWOOD & DISTRICT**, Bushey **Ref:**YH11135
- **STEVENAGE & DISTRICT**, Stevenage **Ref:**YH13439
- **WEMBLEY RIDING CLUB**, Hemel Hempstead **Ref:**YH15102

ISLE OF WIGHT

- **ISLE OF WIGHT RIDING CLUB**, Merstone **Ref:**YH07525

JERSEY

- **JERSEY RIDING CLUB**, St Peter **Ref:**YH07756

KENT

- **BRADBOURNE RIDING CLUB**, Brenchley **Ref:**YH01744
- **CANTERBURY RIDING CLUB**, Dover **Ref:**YH02509
- **FAVERSHAM & DISTRICT**, Faversham **Ref:**YH05106
- **FAVERSHAM RIDING CLUB**, Sheerness **Ref:**YH05107
- **INVICTA RIDING CLUB**, Ashford **Ref:**YH07485
- **JOYDENS RIDING CLUB**, Bexley **Ref:**YH07953
- **MAIDSTONE & DISTRICT**, Aylesford **Ref:**YH09037
- **MANNIX STUD**, Canterbury **Ref:**YH09091
- **MOUNT MASCAL RIDING CLUB**, Sidcup **Ref:**YH09889
- **OLD BEXLEY EQUESTRIAN**, Bexley **Ref:**YH10451
- **ROYAL OAK RIDING CLUB**, Canterbury **Ref:**YH12190
- **SEVENOAKS RIDING CLUB**, Tonbridge **Ref:**YH12642
- **TUNBRIDGE WELLS RIDING CLUB**, Pembury **Ref:**YH14459

LANCASHIRE

- **ABRAM HALL RIDING CTRE**, Wigan **Ref:**YH00134
- **BACUP & DISTRICT RIDING CLUB**, Bacup **Ref:**YH00773
- **BLACKPOOL EQUESTRIAN CTRE**, Blackpool **Ref:**YH01492
- **COLNE & DISTRICT RIDING CLUB**, Colne **Ref:**YH03194
- **NORTH EAST LANCS RIDING CLUB**, Burnley **Ref:**YH10257
- **NORTH-EAST LANCASHIRE**, Burnley **Ref:**YH10297
- **OLDHAM & DISTRICT RIDING CLUB**, Oldham **Ref:**YH10490
- **OSBALDESTON RIDING CTRE**, Blackburn **Ref:**YH10557
- **RIBBLE VALLEY RIDING CLUB**, Lower Darwen **Ref:**YH11793
- **ROCHDALE & DISTRICT**, Oldham **Ref:**YH12017
- **UNIVERSITY OF LANCASTER**, Bailrigg **Ref:**YH14588
- **WESTHOUGHTON RIDING CLUB**, Wigan **Ref:**YH15217
- **WILPSHIRE RIDING CLUB**, Preston **Ref:**YH15525

LEICESTERSHIRE

- **DEBDALE HORSES**, Leicester **Ref:**YH04004
- **MELTON MOWBRAY RIDING CLUB**, Melton Mowbray **Ref:**YH09457
- **REARSBY LODGE RIDING CLUB**, Thurmaston **Ref:**YH11688
- **SUTTON BONINGTON RIDING CLUB**, Loughborough **Ref:**YH13669
- **SWAN LODGE**, Melton Mowbray **Ref:**YH13689
- **UNIVERSITY OF LEICESTER**, Leicester **Ref:**YH14589
- **WITHAM VILLA RIDING CTRE**, Leicester **Ref:**YH15620

LINCOLNSHIRE

- **LINCOLN & DISTRICT**, Lincoln **Ref:**YH08640
- **PARK RIDING SCHOOL**, Lincoln **Ref:**YH10735
- **REDNIL EQUESTRIAN CTRE**, Lincoln **Ref:**YH11716
- **SOUTH KESTEVEN & DISTRICT**, Grantham **Ref:**YH13097
- **SPALDING & DISTRICT**, Sleaford **Ref:**YH13170
- **WELTON & DISTRICT RIDING CLUB**, Gainsborough **Ref:**YH15099
- **WEST LINCOLN RIDING CLUB**, Lincoln **Ref:**YH15154

LINCOLNSHIRE (NORTH EAST)

- **NORTH LINCOLNSHIRE**, Grimsby **Ref:**YH10269
- **R G EQUESTRIAN**, Grimsby **Ref:**YH11536

LONDON (GREATER)

- **B B C RIDING CLUB**, London **Ref:**YH00716
- **BLENHEIM RIDING CLUB**, London **Ref:**YH01536
- **BOSTON MANOR RIDING CLUB**, Hanwell **Ref:**YH01660
- **BRUNEL UNIVERSITY RIDING CLUB**, Uxbridge **Ref:**YH02158
- **CHISLEHURST & DISTRICT**, Penge **Ref:**YH02869
- **CIVIL SV**, London **Ref:**YH02933
- **HARROW & DISTRICT RIDING CLUB**, Harrow **Ref:**YH06492
- **HYDE PARK HORSEMEN'S SUNDAY**, London **Ref:**YH07344
- **NORTHWOOD RIDING CLUB**, Pinner **Ref:**YH10323
- **POLYTECHNIC OF NORTH LONDON**, Holloway Road **Ref:**YH11215
- **WILLOWTREE RIDING CLUB**, Blackheath **Ref:**YH15517
- **WIMBLEDON VILLAGE STABLES**, London **Ref:**YH15557

MANCHESTER (GREATER)

- **BOLTON RIDING CLUB**, Bolton **Ref:**YH01610
- **RYDERS FARM**, Bolton **Ref:**YH12297
- **UNIVERSITY OF MANCHESTER**, Manchester **Ref:**YH14591
- **URMSTON & DISTRICT**, Manchester **Ref:**YH14621

MERSEYSIDE

- **LAFFAK RIDING CLUB**, Liverpool **Ref:**YH08341
- **WEST LANCASHIRE RIDING CLUB**, Liverpool **Ref:**YH15152

MIDLANDS (WEST)

- **ALVECHURCH RIDING CLUB**, Birmingham **Ref:**YH00348
- **EAST SHROPSHIRE RIDING CLUB**, Tettenhall Wood **Ref:**YH04485
- **MERIDEN RIDING CLUB**, Coventry **Ref:**YH09474
- **SADDLERS RIDING CLUB**, Walsall **Ref:**YH12360
- **SOLIHULL RIDING CLUB**, Solihull **Ref:**YH13058
- **SUTTON COLDFIELD & DISTRICT**, Sutton Coldfield **Ref:**YH13670
- **WALSGRAVE AMATEUR RIDING CLUB**, Coventry **Ref:**YH14874

NORFOLK

- **CROFT FARM RIDING CTRE**, Great Yarmouth **Ref:**YH03615
- **EAST ANGLIAN RIDING CLUB**, Attleborough **Ref:**YH04464
- **RUNCTON HALL**, King's Lynn **Ref:**YH12233
- **WESTON PARK EQUESTRIAN CTRE**, Norwich **Ref:**YH15224

NORTHAMPTONSHIRE

- **ALLWORK, S**, Northampton **Ref:**YH00328
- **BUCKINGHAM RIDING CLUB**, Daventry **Ref:**YH02192
- **CHERWELL VALLEY RIDING CLUB**, Daventry **Ref:**YH02822
- **MANOR FARM RIDING SCHOOL**, Wellingborough **Ref:**YH09106
- **SOUTH WARWICKSHIRE**, Daventry **Ref:**YH13114

NORTHUMBERLAND

- **BEDLINGTON BLYTH & DISTRICT**, Bedlington **Ref:**YH01156
- **CORBRIDGE & DISTRICT**, Corbridge **Ref:**YH03308
- **DRURIDGE RIDING CLUB**, Newbiggin **Ref:**YH04293

NOTTINGHAMSHIRE

- **BRACKENHURST CLGE**, Newark **Ref:**YH01740
- **CLGE FARM**, Newark **Ref:**YH03026
- **SILVER HORSESHOE RIDING CLUB**, Newark **Ref:**YH12807

OXFORDSHIRE

- **BERKSHIRE DOWNS RIDING CLUB**, Letcombe Regis **Ref:**YH01305
- **NORTH OXFORDSHIRE RIDING CLUB**, Banbury **Ref:**YH10278
- **OXFORD RIDING CLUB**, Steeple Barton **Ref:**YH10620
- **STANDLAKE EQUESTRIAN CTRE**, Witney **Ref:**YH13362

RUTLAND

- **BUCKMINSTER & DISTRICT**, Rutland **Ref:**YH02202
- **RUTLAND RIDING CLUB**, Oakham **Ref:**YH12278

SHROPSHIRE

- **DONNINGTON SADDLE CLUB**, Telford **Ref:**YH04188
- **MAELOR RIDING CLUB**, Whitchurch **Ref:**YH09027
- **SHREWSBURY & DISTRICT**, Market Drayton **Ref:**YH12768
- **WREKIN NORTH RIDING CLUB**, Telford **Ref:**YH15819

SOMERSET

- **BOWERS, HENRY**, Chard **Ref:**YH01707
- **BRENT & BERROW RIDING CLUB**, Brent Knoll **Ref:**YH01847
- **BRENT KNOLL RIDING CLUB**, Axbridge **Ref:**YH01848
- **MID SOMERSET RIDING CLUB**, Yeovil **Ref:**YH09528
- **QUANTOCK RIDING CLUB**, Bridgwater **Ref:**YH11478
- **TAUNTON & DISTRICT**, Taunton **Ref:**YH13882
- **WESSEX RIDING CLUB**, Axbridge **Ref:**YH15120

SOMERSET (NORTH)

- **BLACKDOWN RIDING CLUB**, Wrington **Ref:**YH01480

STAFFORDSHIRE

- **FOREST OF NEEDWOOD**, Burton-on-Trent **Ref:**YH05347
- **PENKRIDGE & DISTRICT**, Stafford **Ref:**YH10942
- **UNIVERSITY OF KEELE**, Keele **Ref:**YH14587

SUFFOLK

- **BARDWELL MANOR**, Bury St Edmunds **Ref:**YH00928

FINN VALLEY RIDING CLUB, Ipswich **Ref:**YH05215

FRENCH'S FARM RIDING CTRE, Ipswich **Ref:**YH05495

ST EDMUNDS RIDING CLUB, Bury St Edmunds **Ref:**YH13275

SUFFOLK RIDING CLUB, Ipswich **Ref:**YH13625

VALLEY FARM, Woodbridge **Ref:**YH14651

WORLINGTON RIDING CLUB, Newmarket **Ref:**YH15791

SURREY

ABINGER FOREST RIDING CLUB, Dorking **Ref:**YH00132

ASCOT PARK, Woking **Ref:**YH00583

BOOKHAM RIDING CLUB, East Molesey **Ref:**YH01629

BOOKHAM RIDING CLUB, Surbiton **Ref:**YH01628

BRIDGE BARN RIDING CLUB, Woking **Ref:**YH01871

BROCKHAM & DISTRICT, Tadworth **Ref:**YH02009

CHOBHAM & DISTRICT, Weybridge **Ref:**YH02872

CRANLEIGH SCHOOL OF RIDING, Cranleigh **Ref:**YH03565

EWSHOT RIDING CLUB, Farnham **Ref:**YH04962

FARNHAM RIDERS CLUB, Farnham **Ref:**YH05081

FRENSHAM RIDING CLUB, Godalming **Ref:**YH05496

HORLEY & DISTRICT RIDING CLUB, Smallfield **Ref:**YH07071

KINGSTON & DISTRICT, Great Bookham **Ref:**YH08206

NEWLANDS CORNER RIDING CLUB, West Byfleet **Ref:**YH10142

PRESTIGE RACING CLUB, Epsom **Ref:**YH11364

REIGATE & DISTRICT, Reigate **Ref:**YH11745

S R S, Sunbury-on-Thames **Ref:**YH12333

UNIVERSITY OF SURREY, Guildford **Ref:**YH14593

WEST SURREY RIDING CLUB, Guildford **Ref:**YH15165

WILDWOODS, Tadworth **Ref:**YH15413

WOODCOTE & DISTRICT, Worcester Park **Ref:**YH15677

SUSSEX (EAST)

BATTLE & DISTRICT RIDING CLUB, Heathfield **Ref:**YH01078

MID SUSSEX RIDING CLUB, Patcham **Ref:**YH09531

OUSE VALLEY RIDING CLUB, Peacehaven **Ref:**YH10586

ROTHER VALLEY RIDING CLUB, Etchingham **Ref:**YH12128

UNIVERSITY OF SUSSEX, Brighton **Ref:**YH14594

SUSSEX (WEST)

ADUR VALLEY RIDING CLUB, Lancing **Ref:**YH00191

GORING & DISTRICT RIDING CLUB, Worthing **Ref:**YH05933

HORSHAM & DISTRICT, Horsham **Ref:**YH07187

LAVANT HSE STABLES, Chichester **Ref:**YH08460

RUDGWICK & DISTRICT, Pulborough **Ref:**YH12209

WEST END RIDING CLUB, Burgess Hill **Ref:**YH15142

TYNE AND WEAR

BAY RIDING CLUB, North Shields **Ref:**YH01093

QUARRY PARK STABLES, Gateshead **Ref:**YH11483

SPARTAN RIDING CLUB, South Shields **Ref:**YH13184

UNIVERSITY OF NEWCASTLE, Newcastle-upon-Tyne **Ref:**YH14592

WARWICKSHIRE

ETTINGTON PK RIDING CLUB, Wellesbourne **Ref:**YH04888

GATE INN RIDING CLUB, Coleshill **Ref:**YH05671

RUGBY RIDING CLUB, Rugby **Ref:**YH12218

STONELEIGH RIDING CLUB, Ryton-on-Dunsmore **Ref:**YH13518

WILTSHIRE

BERKELEY & DISTRICT, Chippenham **Ref:**YH01300

KENNET VALE RIDING CLUB, Chippenham **Ref:**YH08072

SOUTH WILTSHIRE RIDING CLUB, Warminster **Ref:**YH13124

WORCESTERSHIRE

CROPTHORNE & EVESHAM VALE, Pershore **Ref:**YH03640

KYRE EQUESTRIAN CTRE, Tenbury Wells **Ref:**YH08305

SHROPSHIRE SOUTH RIDING CLUB, Stockton On Teme **Ref:**YH12770

WORCESTER & DISTRICT, Worcester **Ref:**YH15773

YORKSHIRE (EAST)

BRIDLINGTON & DISTRICT, Bridlington **Ref:**YH01900

EBOR VALE RIDING CLUB, Melbourne **Ref:**YH04531

WHITE ROSE RIDING CLUB, Beverley **Ref:**YH15323

YORKSHIRE (NORTH)

HURWORTH HUNT, Thirsk **Ref:**YH07324

NORTHALLERTON RIDING CLUB, Northallerton **Ref:**YH10291

SCARBOROUGH & DISTRICT, Scarborough **Ref:**YH12486

SELBY & DISTRICT RIDING CLUB, Wilberfoss **Ref:**YH12614

WHITBY & DISTRICT RIDING CLUB, Whitby **Ref:**YH15295

YCHRC, York **Ref:**YH15893

YORK & DISTRICT RIDING CLUB, York **Ref:**YH15915

YORKSHIRE DALES, Skipton **Ref:**YH15919

YORKSHIRE (SOUTH)

PENISTONE & DISTRICT, Sheffield **Ref:**YH10941

ROYSTON PONY CLUB, Barnsley **Ref:**YH12202

TICKHILL RIDING CLUB, Doncaster **Ref:**YH14127

YORKSHIRE (WEST)

AIRE VALLEY RIDING CLUB, Bradford **Ref:**YH00221

HOLME VALLEY RIDING CLUB, Huddersfield **Ref:**YH06967

HORSFORTH RIDING CLUB, Rawdon **Ref:**YH07186

MID YORKSHIRE RIDING CLUB, Leeds **Ref:**YH09533

NIDD VALLEY RIDING CLUB, Burley-In-Wharfedale **Ref:**YH10202

PENNINE RIDING CLUB, Todmorden **Ref:**YH10954

PUDSEY & DISTRICT RIDING CLUB, Bradford **Ref:**YH11448

SHIBDEN DALE RIDING CLUB, Halifax **Ref:**YH12738

UNIVERSITY OF BRADFORD, Great Horton **Ref:**YH14582

WHITLEY EQUITATION CTRE, Dewsbury **Ref:**YH15363

RIDING SCHOOLS

BATH & SOMERSET (NORTH EAST)

HUNSTRETE RIDING SCHOOL, Pensford **Ref:**YH07294

BEDFORDSHIRE

BACKNOE END EQUESTRIAN CTRE, Bedford **Ref:**YH00771

BROOK STABLES, Bedford **Ref:**YH02038

BROOKLYN FARM STABLES, Dunstable **Ref:**YH02060

GRANSDEN HALL, Sandy **Ref:**YH06005

LILLEY RIDING SCHOOL, Luton **Ref:**YH08621

LISCOMBE PK RIDING SCHOOL, Leighton Buzzard **Ref:**YH08678

NORTHALLETON, Biggleswade **Ref:**YH10292

ROCKLANE RIDING CTRE, Leighton Buzzard **Ref:**YH12036

STOCKWOOD PARK, Luton **Ref:**YH13498

STOCKWOOD STABLES, Luton **Ref:**YH13499

SUNSHINE RIDING SCHOOL, Luton **Ref:**YH13652

TINSLEYS RIDING SCHOOL, Bedford **Ref:**YH14177

BERKSHIRE

ASHFORD HILL RIDING SCHOOL, Thatcham **Ref:**YH00602

BANSTOCK HSE STABLES, Maidenhead **Ref:**YH00910

BAROSSA FARM RIDING STABLES, Reading **Ref:**YH00997

BEARWOOD RIDING CTRE, Wokingham **Ref:**YH01123

BOUNDARY ROAD STABLES, Maidenhead **Ref:**YH01679

BRADFIELD RIDING CTRE, Reading **Ref:**YH01748

CANE END STABLES, Reading **Ref:**YH02498

CHECKENDON, Reading **Ref:**YH02796

CLOUD STABLES, Reading **Ref:**YH03066

CROFT EQUESTRIAN CTRE, Reading **Ref:**YH03614

CULLINGHOOD FARM, Reading **Ref:**YH03705

CURRIDGE GREEN RIDING SCHOOL, Thatcham **Ref:**YH03738

GLENIFFER STABLES, Maidenhead **Ref:**YH05837

GREENGATES, Hungerford **Ref:**YH06086

HALL PLACE EQUESTRIAN CTRE, Reading **Ref:**YH06307

HEATHLANDS RIDING CTRE, Wokingham **Ref:**YH06634

SNOWBALL FARM EQUESTRIAN CTRE, Slough **Ref:**YH13037

SPANISH BIT RIDING SCHOOL, Windsor **Ref:**YH13173

WHITELOCKS FARM RIDING SCHOOL, Bracknell **Ref:**YH15350

WOODLANDS, Hungerford **Ref:**YH15705

BRISTOL

AVON RIDING CTRE, Bristol **Ref:**YH00690

CLACK MILL RIDING STABLES, Bristol **Ref:**YH02935

GORDANO VALLEY RIDING CTRE, Bristol **Ref:**YH05921

HARTLEY WOOD RIDING CTRE, Bristol **Ref:**YH06506

KINGSWESTON STABLES, Bristol **Ref:**YH08208

KINGTON RIDING STABLES, Bristol **Ref:**YH08212

LEYLAND COURT, Bristol **Ref:**YH08601

TYNINGS RIDING SCHOOL, Bristol **Ref:**YH14527

URCHINWOOD MANOR EQUITATION, Bristol **Ref:**YH14620

WAPLEY STABLES, Bristol **Ref:**YH14895

WHITE CAT STABLES, Bristol **Ref:**YH15301

BUCKINGHAMSHIRE

AESCWOOD, Beaconsfield **Ref:**YH00196

BANGORS PARK FARM, Iver **Ref:**YH00883

BRAWLINGS FARM RIDING CTRE, Gerrards Cross **Ref:**YH01819

BRYERLEY SPRINGS FARM, Milton Keynes **Ref:**YH02171

CHENIES STABLES, Chalfont St Giles **Ref:**YH02806

CHEQUERS END EQUESTRIAN CTRE, High Wycombe **Ref:**YH02812

CORHAM STABLES, Princes Risborough **Ref:**YH03315

- **CROSS KEYS FARM**, Gerrards Cross **Ref:**YH03649
- **EQUESTRIAN CTRE**, Amersham **Ref:**YH04696
- **GRAHAM-ROGERS, C**, Bourne End **Ref:**YH05973
- **GROVE EQUITATION CTRE**, High Wycombe **Ref:**YH06161
- **HARTWELL RIDING STABLES**, Aylesbury **Ref:**YH06509
- **LAKES LANE RIDING STABLES**, Newport Pagnell **Ref:**YH08356
- **LOUGHTON MANOR**, Milton Keynes **Ref:**YH08840
- **LOWER FARM STABLES**, Olney **Ref:**YH08865
- **MECA RIDING CTRE**, High Wycombe **Ref:**YH09431
- **ORCHARD END LIVERIES**, High Wycombe **Ref:**YH10528
- **RIVERSMEET STABLES**, Newport Pagnell **Ref:**YH11930
- **SHANA RIDING SCHOOL**, High Wycombe **Ref:**YH12666
- **STOWE RIDINGS**, Buckingham **Ref:**YH13538
- **TUDOR STUD FARM**, High Wycombe **Ref:**YH14444
- **WAYLANDS EQUESTRIAN CTRE**, Beaconsfield **Ref:**YH15016
- **WIDMER EQUESTRIAN CTRE**, Princes Risborough **Ref:**YH15392
- **WINKERS FARM**, Chalfont St Peter **Ref:**YH15586

CAMBRIDGESHIRE

- **COACH HSE STABLES**, Ely **Ref:**YH03104
- **CONQUEST**, Farcet Fen **Ref:**YH03242
- **CROSS LEYS FARM**, Peterborough **Ref:**YH03650
- **GRANGE FARM EQUESTRIAN CTRE**, Peterborough **Ref:**YH05988
- **GRANGE RIDING SCHOOL**, Wisbech **Ref:**YH05994
- **GUYHIRN RIDING SCHOOL**, Wisbech **Ref:**YH06198
- **HAGGIS FARM STABLES**, Cambridge **Ref:**YH06278
- **HOCKLEY GREEN RIDING STABLES**, Cambridge **Ref:**YH06903
- **LYNCH FARM EQUESTRIAN CLUB**, Peterborough **Ref:**YH08923
- **MONARCH FARM**, Huntingdon **Ref:**YH09718
- **MOORFIELD RIDING**, Peterborough **Ref:**YH09772
- **MOORFIELD TRAILER & TOWBARS**, Peterborough **Ref:**YH09773
- **MOUNT ROYAL RIDING SCHOOL**, St Neots **Ref:**YH09893
- **NEW RANGE EQUESTRIAN CTRE**, Huntingdon **Ref:**YH10119
- **NORTHBROOK EQUESTRIAN CTRE**, Huntingdon **Ref:**YH10294
- **OAKINGTON RIDING SCHOOL**, Oakington **Ref:**YH10386
- **OLD TIGER STABLES**, Ely **Ref:**YH10479
- **PARADISE RIDING CTRE**, Ely **Ref:**YH10711
- **PARKHOUSE STABLES**, Cambridge **Ref:**YH10762
- **STAUGHTON RIDING SCHOOL**, Huntingdon **Ref:**YH13404
- **SWISS COTTAGE STABLES**, Wisbech **Ref:**YH13716
- **WEST ANGLIA CLGE**, Milton **Ref:**YH15123
- **WHITE HART STABLES**, Huntingdon **Ref:**YH15305
- **WITCHAM EQUESTRIAN CTRE**, Ely **Ref:**YH15616
- **WOODHURST**, Huntingdon **Ref:**YH15697
- **YAXLEY RIDING CTRE**, Peterborough **Ref:**YH15892

CHESHIRE

- **ALDER ROOT RIDING CTRE**, Warrington **Ref:**YH00254
- **B 1ST RIDING SCHOOL**, Stockport **Ref:**YH00715
- **BARROW EQUESTRIAN CTRE**, Chester **Ref:**YH01027
- **BOLD HEATH EQUESTRIAN**, Widnes **Ref:**YH01602
- **BROOMHALL RIDING SCHOOL**, Nantwich **Ref:**YH02079
- **BURTONWOOD RIDING SCHOOL**, Warrington **Ref:**YH02296
- **CASTLE STABLES**, Malpas **Ref:**YH02635
- **CLOVERFIELD EQUESTRIAN CTRE**, Sale **Ref:**YH03070
- **COTEBROOK STUD**, Tarporley **Ref:**YH03357
- **CROFT RIDING CTRE**, Warrington **Ref:**YH03617
- **FINLOW HILL STABLES**, Macclesfield **Ref:**YH05214
- **FOXES FARM & RIDING SCHOOL**, Ellesmere Port **Ref:**YH05431
- **GLEN-JAKES RIDING SCHOOL**, Stockport **Ref:**YH05839
- **GREEN LANE RIDING SCHOOL**, Chester **Ref:**YH06057
- **HEYBROOK EQUESTRIAN CTRE**, Warrington **Ref:**YH06735
- **HOLLY TREE RIDING SCHOOL**, Knutsford **Ref:**YH06958
- **HOPE FARM RIDING SCHOOL**, Widnes **Ref:**YH07051
- **LOWTON RIDING CTRE**, Warrington **Ref:**YH08878
- **MOBBERLEY RIDING SCHOOL**, Knutsford **Ref:**YH09687
- **OAKS RIDING SCHOOL**, Sale **Ref:**YH10403
- **PEACEHAVEN RIDING CTRE**, Chester **Ref:**YH10856
- **SOUTH VIEW EQUESTRIAN CTRE**, Winsford **Ref:**YH13107
- **SOUTHFIELDS FARM**, Pen-Y-Ffordd **Ref:**YH13153
- **SUTTON MILL RIDING & SADDLERY**, Middlewich **Ref:**YH13674
- **TARDEN FARM STABLES**, Stockport **Ref:**YH13870
- **WHITEGATE**, Northwich **Ref:**YH15337
- **WILLINGTON HALL**, Tarporley **Ref:**YH15490

CLEVELAND

- **EMMERSONS**, Stokesley **Ref:**YH04655
- **ESTON EQUESTRIAN CTRE**, Middlesbrough **Ref:**YH04876
- **FORD CLOSE RIDING CTRE**, Middlesbrough **Ref:**YH05322
- **KIRKLEVINGTON RIDING SCHOOL**, Yarm **Ref:**YH08237
- **PONY WORLD**, Crimdon Dene **Ref:**YH11256
- **SALTBURN RIDING SCHOOL**, Saltburn-by-the-Sea **Ref:**YH12393
- **SOUTHBROOKE RIDING SCHOOL**, Cactote Road **Ref:**YH13130
- **STAINSBY GRANGE RIDING CTRE**, Stockton-on-Tees **Ref:**YH13346
- **STOTFOLD CREST STABLES**, Elwick **Ref:**YH13528
- **UNICORN RDA CTRE**, Middlesbrough **Ref:**YH14567
- **WOLVISTON RIDING STABLES**, Billingham **Ref:**YH15652

CORNWALL

- **BLACKACRE RIDING STABLES**, St Columb **Ref:**YH01474
- **BOSKELL RIDING CTRE**, St Austell **Ref:**YH01654
- **CHIVERTON RIDING CTRE**, Truro **Ref:**YH02871
- **CORNISH RIDING HOLIDAYS**, Redruth **Ref:**YH03327
- **CURY RIDING STABLE**, Helston **Ref:**YH03754
- **DENBY RIDING STABLES**, Bodmin **Ref:**YH04039
- **GOONBELL RIDING CTRE**, St Agnes **Ref:**YH05915
- **GOOSEFORD RIDING SCHOOL**, Saltash **Ref:**YH05916
- **GOOSEHAM BARTON STABLES**, Bude **Ref:**YH05917
- **HALLAGENNA RIDING SCHOOL**, Bodmin **Ref:**YH06321
- **LAKEFIELD EQUESTRIAN CTRE**, Camelford **Ref:**YH08351
- **LANDS END RIDING SCHOOL**, Penzance **Ref:**YH08387
- **LANJETH RIDING SCHOOL**, St Austell **Ref:**YH08418
- **MAER LANE RIDING STABLES**, Bude **Ref:**YH09028
- **NINE TOR RIDING CTRE**, Launceston **Ref:**YH10211
- **OLD MILL STABLES**, Hayle **Ref:**YH10469
- **PENHALWYN**, St Ives **Ref:**YH10939
- **POLPEVER RIDING STABLES**, Liskeard **Ref:**YH11212
- **ROMANY WALKS**, Penzance **Ref:**YH12072
- **SNOWLAND RIDING CTRE**, Par **Ref:**YH13045
- **ST LEONARDS EQUESTRIAN CTRE**, Launceston **Ref:**YH13278
- **ST MERRYN RIDING SCHOOL**, Padstow **Ref:**YH13282
- **ST VEEP RIDING STABLES**, Lostwithiel **Ref:**YH13285
- **TIMBERDOWN RIDING SCHOOL**, Callington **Ref:**YH14161
- **TM INT SCHOOL OF HORSEMANSHIP**, Liskeard **Ref:**YH14196
- **TREDOLE**, Boscastle **Ref:**YH14358
- **TREGURTHA DOWNS**, Penzance **Ref:**YH14368
- **TRENISSICK RIDING STABLES**, Newquay **Ref:**YH14375
- **TRESALLYN**, Padstow **Ref:**YH14384
- **TREVILLETT STABLES**, Tintagel **Ref:**YH14387
- **VERYAN RIDING CTRE**, Truro **Ref:**YH14686

COUNTY DURHAM

- **ALSTON & KILLHOPE**, Bishop Auckland **Ref:**YH00339
- **BEAMISH RIDING CTRE**, Stanley **Ref:**YH01117
- **BOWES MANOR EQUESTRIAN CTRE**, Chester Le Street **Ref:**YH01709
- **CENTURION EQUESTRIAN CTRE**, Durham **Ref:**YH02698
- **DARLINGTON EQUESTRIAN CTRE**, Darlington **Ref:**YH03892
- **DARLINGTON EQUESTRIAN CTRE**, Haughton **Ref:**YH03893
- **DEAF HILL**, Durham **Ref:**YH03985
- **DENNIS, JUDY**, Bishop Auckland **Ref:**YH04055
- **ETEK**, Darlington **Ref:**YH04880
- **GO RIDING GRP**, Stanley **Ref:**YH05861
- **HAMSTERLEY RIDING SCHOOL**, Bishop Auckland **Ref:**YH06372
- **HAWTHORN VILLAGE**, Seaham **Ref:**YH06557
- **HIGHLING EQUESTRIAN CTRE**, Durham **Ref:**YH06798
- **HOLE IN THE WALL**, Crook **Ref:**YH06930
- **IVESLEY EQUESTRIAN CTRE**, Durham **Ref:**YH07536
- **LOW FALLOWFIELD**, Durham **Ref:**YH08854
- **LOW FOLD RIDING CTRE**, Crook **Ref:**YH08855
- **RAYGILL**, Barnard Castle **Ref:**YH11672
- **SEAGOLD CENTURION**, Crook **Ref:**YH12587
- **SOUTH CAUSEY EQUESTRIAN CTRE**, Stanley **Ref:**YH13080
- **WEST HOPPYLAND TREKKING CTRE**, Bishop Auckland **Ref:**YH15149

CUMBRIA

- **ALLONBY RIDING SCHOOL**, Wigton **Ref:**YH00323
- **BIRKBY HALL**, Grange Over Sands **Ref:**YH01440
- **BLACKDYKE FARM RIDING CTRE**, Carlisle **Ref:**YH01481
- **BRADLEY, D**, Cleator **Ref:**YH01753
- **CALVERT TRUST ADVENTURE CTRE**, Keswick **Ref:**YH02455
- **CALVERT TRUST RIDING CTRE**, Keswick **Ref:**YH02457
- **CARGO RIDING CTRE**, Carlisle **Ref:**YH02538
- **CLAIFE/GRIZEDALE RIDING CTRE**, Ambleside **Ref:**YH02936

- **CROOK BARN STABLES**, Coniston **Ref:**YH03634
- **HOLMESCALES RIDING CTRE**, Kendal **Ref:**YH06980
- **LAKELAND EQUESTRIAN**, Windermere **Ref:**YH08354
- **LAKELAND RIDING CTRE**, Grange-Over-Sands **Ref:**YH08355
- **LARKRIGG RIDING SCHOOL**, Kendal **Ref:**YH08434
- **ROOKIN HOUSE**, Penrith **Ref:**YH12074
- **RYDAL MOUNT LIVERY STABLES**, Wigton **Ref:**YH12293
- **STONERIGG RIDING CTRE**, Carlisle **Ref:**YH13520
- **WITHERSLACK HALL**, Grange-Over-Sands **Ref:**YH15624

DERBYSHIRE

- **ALTON RIDING SCHOOL**, Chesterfield **Ref:**YH00344
- **BARLEYFIELDS**, Derby **Ref:**YH00952
- **BIRCHWOOD**, Alfreton **Ref:**YH01435
- **BREASTON EQUESTRIAN CTRE**, Derby **Ref:**YH01828
- **BRIMINGTON EQUESTRIAN CTRE**, Chesterfield **Ref:**YH01912
- **BUXTON RIDING SCHOOL**, Buxton **Ref:**YH02339
- **C E S**, Ashbourne **Ref:**YH02370
- **COWLEY RIDING SCHOOL**, Dronfield **Ref:**YH03526
- **CURBAR RIDING STABLES**, Hope Valley **Ref:**YH03727
- **ELVASTON CASTLE RIDING CTRE**, Derby **Ref:**YH04645
- **HADDON HSE**, Bakewell **Ref:**YH06261
- **HARGATE HILL**, Glossop **Ref:**YH06424
- **HOLME FARM EQUESTRIAN CTRE**, Derby **Ref:**YH06963
- **KNABBHALL EQUESTRIAN CTRE**, Matlock **Ref:**YH08249
- **KNOWLE HILL EQUESTRIAN**, Derby **Ref:**YH08280
- **LANDOWN FARM RIDING STABLES**, Derby **Ref:**YH08384
- **MOORBRIDGE RIDING STABLES**, Derby **Ref:**YH09747
- **NORTHFIELD FARM**, Buxton **Ref:**YH10312
- **QUARNHILL SCHOOL**, Kirk Ireton **Ref:**YH11481
- **RED HSE STABLES**, Matlock **Ref:**YH11698
- **RIDGEWOOD EQUESTRIAN CTRE**, Alderwasley **Ref:**YH11868
- **RINGER VILLA EQUESTRIAN CTRE**, Chesterfield **Ref:**YH11900
- **WESTWOOD FARM**, Dronfield **Ref:**YH15238
- **YEW TREE FARM STABLES**, Belper **Ref:**YH15910

DEVON

- **BABLEIGH RIDING SCHOOL**, Barnstaple **Ref:**YH00764
- **BELLE VUE VALLEY**, Exeter **Ref:**YH01234
- **BINGHAM, R J**, Lynton **Ref:**YH01422
- **BOLDTRY RIDING STABLES**, Chulmleigh **Ref:**YH01606
- **BRAKE, C J**, Cullompton **Ref:**YH01780
- **BRENDON MANOR FARM**, Lynton **Ref:**YH01838
- **BUDLEIGH SALTERTON**, Budleigh Salterton **Ref:**YH02208
- **CHESTON EQUESTRIAN CTRE**, South Brent **Ref:**YH02839
- **CHOLWELL FARM**, Tavistock **Ref:**YH02879
- **COLLACOTT FARM**, Umberleigh **Ref:**YH03173
- **CROWSNEST RIDING CTRE**, Okehampton **Ref:**YH03683
- **DEAN RIDING STABLES**, Barnstaple **Ref:**YH03989
- **DEVENISH PITT**, Honiton **Ref:**YH04087
- **DITTISCOMBE EQUESTRIAN CTRE**, Kingsbridge **Ref:**YH04136
- **EAST LAKE**, Okehampton **Ref:**YH04477
- **FITZWORTHY RIDING**, Ivybridge **Ref:**YH05251
- **GRANGE EQUESTRIAN CTRE**, Okehampton **Ref:**YH05987
- **HALDON RIDING STABLES**, Exeter **Ref:**YH06290
- **HEAZLE RIDING CTRE**, Cullompton **Ref:**YH06635
- **HIGHER WINSFORD FARM STABLES**, Bideford **Ref:**YH06782
- **HILLTOP RIDING SCHOOL**, Exeter **Ref:**YH06858
- **HONEYSUCKLE FARM**, Newton Abbot **Ref:**YH07017
- **LEAWOOD RIDING CTRE**, Okehampton **Ref:**YH08510
- **LITTLE ASH ECO-FARM & STUD**, Okehampton **Ref:**YH08683
- **LYDFORD HOUSE RIDING STABLES**, Okehampton **Ref:**YH08916
- **MULLACOTT EQUESTRIAN**, Ilfracombe **Ref:**YH09935
- **NORTH DEVON EQUESTRIAN CTRE**, Barnstaple **Ref:**YH10254
- **NORTH HAYE**, Mortonhampstead **Ref:**YH10263
- **OAKLANDS RIDING SCHOOL**, Exeter **Ref:**YH10391
- **ROSE & CROWN**, Tiverton **Ref:**YH12088
- **ROYLANDS RIDING STABLES**, Braunton **Ref:**YH12200
- **SHILSTONE ROCKS**, Newton Abbot **Ref:**YH12746
- **SOUTHDOWN FARM RIDING STABLES**, Brixham **Ref:**YH13134
- **TABRE RIDING**, Winkleigh **Ref:**YH13772
- **WEMBURY BAY RIDING SCHOOL**, Plymouth **Ref:**YH15103
- **WOOLACOMBE RIDING STABLES**, Woolacombe **Ref:**YH15763

DORSET

- **BRIDLEWAYS**, Sherborne **Ref:**YH01897
- **BRYANSTON RIDING CTRE**, Blandford Forum **Ref:**YH02168
- **CHURCH ROAD RIDING SCHOOL**, Weymouth **Ref:**YH02905
- **CLAIRE'S RIDING SCHOOL**, Wimborne **Ref:**YH02938
- **DEER PARK RIDING STABLES**, Blandford Forum **Ref:**YH04023
- **DORSET HEAVY HORSE CTRE**, Wimborne **Ref:**YH04206
- **DUDMOOR FARM**, Christchurch **Ref:**YH04311
- **EQUESTRIAN & EXAM CTRE**, Ferndown **Ref:**YH04691
- **FOREST LODGE**, Shaftesbury **Ref:**YH05342
- **GREEN COTTAGE**, Wimborne **Ref:**YH06052
- **HIGHER POUND RIDING CTRE**, Bridport **Ref:**YH06780
- **IVERS HOUSE**, Sturminster Newton **Ref:**YH07535
- **LANEHOUSE EQUITATION CTRE**, Weymouth **Ref:**YH08393
- **L'LIWETTO RIDING SCHOOL**, Sturminster Newton **Ref:**YH08731
- **LULWORTH EQUESTRIAN CTRE**, Wareham **Ref:**YH08897
- **OSMINGTON MILLS**, Weymouth **Ref:**YH10569
- **POUND COTTAGE RIDING CTRE**, Blandford Forum **Ref:**YH11307
- **REMPSTONE STABLES**, Wareham **Ref:**YH11751
- **SANDFORD PARK STABLES**, Poole **Ref:**YH12410

ESSEX

- **ALEXANDER, J E**, Saffron Walden **Ref:**YH00271
- **ASHFIELDS EQUESTRIAN CTRE**, Dunmow **Ref:**YH00599
- **ASHINGDON RIDING CTRE**, Rochford **Ref:**YH00605
- **ASHTREE EQUESTRIAN CTRE**, Chelmsford **Ref:**YH00616
- **BAMBERS GREEN RIDING CTRE**, Bishop's Stortford **Ref:**YH00876
- **BARROW FARM**, Chelmsford **Ref:**YH01028
- **BLUE SABRE RIDING SCHOOL**, Colchester **Ref:**YH01570
- **BRETONS EQUESTRIAN CTRE**, Rainham **Ref:**YH01852
- **BRIDGEFOOT FARM**, Harwich **Ref:**YH01880
- **BROOK FARM EQUESTRIAN CTRE**, Saffron Walden **Ref:**YH02034
- **BROOK FARM RIDING SCHOOL**, Ingatestone **Ref:**YH02035
- **BROOK FARM STABLES**, Colchester **Ref:**YH02036
- **BURCHES RIDING SCHOOL**, Benfleet **Ref:**YH02232
- **CHELMSFORD EQUESTRIAN CTRE**, Chelmsford **Ref:**YH02801
- **CLAY HALL**, Brentwood **Ref:**YH02994
- **COLCHESTER GARRISON**, Colchester **Ref:**YH03144
- **COLLINS, HANNAH**, Saffron Walden **Ref:**YH03188
- **DANBURY**, Chelmsford **Ref:**YH03860
- **D'ARCY RIDING STABLES**, Maldon **Ref:**YH03879
- **EASTMINSTER SCHOOL OF RIDING**, Romford **Ref:**YH04510
- **ELMWOOD EQUESTRIAN CTRE**, Burnham-on-Crouch **Ref:**YH04640
- **FOREST LODGE RIDING SCHOOL**, Epping **Ref:**YH05344
- **FOREST STABLES**, Bishop's Stortford **Ref:**YH05352
- **FOXHOUNDS RIDING SCHOOL**, Grays **Ref:**YH05438
- **GILSTON PK FARM**, Harlow **Ref:**YH05792
- **HALLINGBURY HALL**, Bishop's Stortford **Ref:**YH06331
- **HAROLDS PK RIDING CTRE**, Waltham Abbey **Ref:**YH06449
- **HAVERING PK RIDING SCHOOL**, Romford **Ref:**YH06540
- **HIGH BEECH RIDING SCHOOL**, Waltham Abbey **Ref:**YH06754
- **HILL FARM**, Chelmsford **Ref:**YH06812
- **JUHL, G**, Saffron Walden **Ref:**YH07961
- **LIMEBROOK**, Maldon **Ref:**YH08628
- **LITTLE MONTROSE**, Chelmsford **Ref:**YH08695
- **LONGWOOD EQUESTRIAN CTRE**, Basildon **Ref:**YH08820
- **MAPLE POLLARD RIDING SCHOOL**, Bishop's Stortford **Ref:**YH09132
- **MEDWAY RIDING CTRE**, Chelmsford **Ref:**YH09439
- **MILL LANE RIDING SCHOOL**, Ongar **Ref:**YH09581
- **NEWLAND HALL EQUESTRIAN CTRE**, Chelmsford **Ref:**YH10141
- **NIGHTINGALE RIDING SCHOOL**, Buckhurst Hill **Ref:**YH10204
- **PAGLESHAM SCHOOL**, Rochford **Ref:**YH10685
- **PARK FARM**, Colchester **Ref:**YH10717
- **PARK LANE RIDING SCHOOL**, Billericay **Ref:**YH10731
- **PARKLANDS FARM LIVERY**, Chelmsford **Ref:**YH10769
- **RAGWOOD RIDING CTRE**, Benfleet **Ref:**YH11609
- **RAWRETH EQUESTRIAN CTRE**, Wickford **Ref:**YH11669
- **RAYNE RIDING CTRE**, Braintree **Ref:**YH11676
- **RED STABLES FARM**, Brentwood **Ref:**YH11706
- **RUNNINGWELL STUD**, Chelmsford **Ref:**YH12236
- **SAWYERS HALL RIDING ESTAB**, Brentwood **Ref:**YH12464
- **SHAHZADA**, Dunmow **Ref:**YH12659
- **SHOPLAND HALL EQUESTRIAN**, Rochford **Ref:**YH12758
- **SOUTH VIEW RIDING SCHOOL**, Grays **Ref:**YH13109
- **ST MARGARETS RIDING SCHOOL**, Billericay **Ref:**YH13280
- **STEWARDS FARM RIDING CTRE**, Harlow **Ref:**YH13453

- **TALLY-HO RIDING SCHOOL**, Grays **Ref:**YH13844
- **TIPTREE EQUESTRIAN CTRE**, Colchester **Ref:**YH14184
- **TOWERLANDS EQUESTRIAN CTRE**, Braintree **Ref:**YH14278
- **VALLEY RIDING/LIVERY STABLES**, Ingatestone **Ref:**YH14657
- **WETHERSFIELD RIDING STABLES**, Braintree **Ref:**YH15246
- **WOODREDON RIDING SCHOOL**, Waltham Abbey **Ref:**YH15728
- **WOODREDON RIDING SCHOOL**, Waltham Abbey **Ref:**YH15729
- **WRITTLE CLGE**, Chelmsford **Ref:**YH15848

GLOUCESTERSHIRE

- **CALIFORNIA FARM RIDING SCHOOL**, Cheltenham **Ref:**YH02445
- **COLTSMOOR**, Cirencester **Ref:**YH03205
- **COTSWOLD TRAIL RIDING**, Gloucester **Ref:**YH03368
- **FOREST OF DEAN**, Lydney **Ref:**YH05346
- **HARTPURY CLGE**, Gloucester **Ref:**YH06507
- **HUNTLEY SCHOOL OF EQUITATION**, Gloucester **Ref:**YH07306
- **LITTLEDEAN RIDING CTRE**, Cinderford **Ref:**YH08707
- **LYNTRIDGE FARM RIDING STABLES**, Gloucester **Ref:**YH08935
- **MOAT FARM RIDING SCHOOL**, Cheltenham **Ref:**YH09685
- **MOORES FARM EQUESTRIAN CTRE**, Gloucester **Ref:**YH09771
- **NEWNHAM EQUESTRIAN CTRE**, Newnham **Ref:**YH10159
- **PLAYMATE CHILDRENS**, Cheltenham **Ref:**YH11172
- **SUMMERHOUSE**, Gloucester **Ref:**YH13632
- **WOODLAND**, Cheltenham **Ref:**YH15702

GUERNSEY

- **LA CARRIERE**, St Sampson **Ref:**YH08331
- **OTTERBOURNE RIDING CTRE**, Torteval **Ref:**YH10580

HAMPSHIRE

- **AMPORT RIDING SCHOOL**, Andover **Ref:**YH00372
- **APPLEMORE EQUITATION**, Southampton **Ref:**YH00480
- **ARNISS**, Fordingbridge **Ref:**YH00555
- **BROADLANDS RIDING CTRE**, Alton **Ref:**YH01999
- **BROCKS FARM**, Stockbridge **Ref:**YH02013
- **BURITON HORSE SVS**, Stockbridge **Ref:**YH02253
- **BURLEY MANOR RIDING STABLES**, Ringwood **Ref:**YH02259
- **BURLEY VILLA EQUESTRIAN CTRE**, New Milton **Ref:**YH02260
- **CLIDDESDEN RIDING SCHOOL**, Basingstoke **Ref:**YH03031
- **CLOUDBANK STABLES**, Winchester **Ref:**YH03067
- **EQUALLUS EQUESTRIAN**, Hook **Ref:**YH04685
- **FIR TREE FARM**, Fordingbridge **Ref:**YH05219
- **FOLLY FOOT FARM**, Romsey **Ref:**YH05303
- **FOREST PARK**, Brockenhurst **Ref:**YH05348
- **FOREST PINES RIDING SCHOOL**, Ringwood **Ref:**YH05349
- **FORT WIDLEY EQUESTRIAN CTRE**, Cosham **Ref:**YH05388
- **GLENEAGLES**, Southampton **Ref:**YH05832
- **HARROWAY HSE RIDING SCHOOL**, Andover **Ref:**YH06495
- **HAWLEY EQUITATION CTRE**, Camberley **Ref:**YH06553
- **HORSESHOE CTRE**, Bordon **Ref:**YH07172
- **INADOWN FARM STABLES**, Alton **Ref:**YH07407
- **KILN FARM RIDING SCHOOL**, Southampton **Ref:**YH08150
- **MERRIE STUD**, Southampton **Ref:**YH09480
- **NEW FOREST**, Dibden **Ref:**YH10096
- **NEW FOREST EQUESTRIAN CTRE**, Lymington **Ref:**YH10098
- **NEW PARK HOTEL**, New Forest **Ref:**YH10115
- **NEW PARK MANOR STABLES**, Brockenhurst **Ref:**YH10116
- **NINEHAM, T & YOUNG, J**, Brokenhurst **Ref:**YH10212
- **NRC**, Fareham **Ref:**YH10348
- **OASIS RIDING CTRE**, Southampton **Ref:**YH10413
- **OCKNELL HSE EQUESTRIAN CTRE**, Lyndhurst **Ref:**YH10427
- **PARK FARM SADDLERY**, Basingstoke **Ref:**YH10723
- **POOK LANE RIDING STABLES**, Havant **Ref:**YH11259
- **R H HANGERSLEY HEIGHT**, Ringwood **Ref:**YH11539
- **ROSHAUNA RIDING SCHOOL**, Fareham **Ref:**YH12112
- **RUSSELL EQUITATION CTRE**, Southampton **Ref:**YH12253
- **RYCROFT SCHOOL OF EQUITATION**, Hook **Ref:**YH12291
- **SILVER HORSESHOE**, Fordingbridge **Ref:**YH12806
- **STOCKBRIDGE**, Stockbridge **Ref:**YH13486
- **WELLINGTON RIDING**, Hook **Ref:**YH15075
- **YATELEY RIDING ESTABLISHMENT**, Hook **Ref:**YH15888

HEREFORDSHIRE

- **BRYNGWYN RIDING CTRE**, Kington **Ref:**YH02176
- **HEREFORD RIDING CTRE**, Hereford **Ref:**YH06702
- **LEA BAILEY RIDING SCHOOL**, Ross-on-Wye **Ref:**YH08492
- **MILL FARM RIDING SCHOOL**, Hereford **Ref:**YH09573
- **RIDDLE RIDING CTRE**, Leominster **Ref:**YH11840
- **SUE ADAMS RIDING SCHOOL**, Leominster **Ref:**YH13622
- **TIPTON HALL**, Bromyard **Ref:**YH14183
- **UPPER HENDRE CLASSICAL RIDING**, Ross-on-Wye **Ref:**YH14606

HERTFORDSHIRE

- **BARKWAY EQUESTRIAN CTRE**, Royston **Ref:**YH00948
- **BIRCH FARM**, Broxbourne **Ref:**YH01428
- **BROXBOURNEBURY RIDING SCHOOL**, Broxbourne **Ref:**YH02150
- **COLTSPRING SCHOOL OF RIDING**, Rickmansworth **Ref:**YH03206
- **CONTESSA**, Ware **Ref:**YH03246
- **COURTLANDS**, Stevenage **Ref:**YH03507
- **CROUCHFIELD**, Ware **Ref:**YH03674
- **DANECROFT RIDING**, Welwyn **Ref:**YH03866
- **ELLE-DANI FARM**, Borehamwood **Ref:**YH04612
- **GADDESDEN PLACE STABLES**, Hemel Hempstead **Ref:**YH05605
- **GREENACRES EQUESTRIAN**, Harpenden **Ref:**YH06076
- **HARPENDENBURY STABLES**, St Albans **Ref:**YH06450
- **HASTOE HILL RIDING SCHOOL**, Tring **Ref:**YH06528
- **HIGH HERTS FARM RIDING SCHOOL**, Hemel Hempstead **Ref:**YH06760
- **ICKLEFORD EQUESTRIAN**, Hitchin **Ref:**YH07382
- **MELDRETH MANOR**, Royston **Ref:**YH09451
- **MILL GREEN RIDING SCHOOL**, Hatfield **Ref:**YH09576
- **MILL RIDING CLUB**, Much Hadham **Ref:**YH09585
- **PONSBOURNE RIDING CTRE**, Hertford **Ref:**YH11224
- **ROSE HALL RIDING STABLES**, Sarratt **Ref:**YH12093
- **SOUTH MEDBURN**, Borehamwood **Ref:**YH13101
- **STAGS END**, Hemel Hempstead **Ref:**YH13342
- **TEWIN HILL SADDLERY**, Welwyn **Ref:**YH13968
- **WATFORD EQUESTRIAN CTRE**, Watford **Ref:**YH14976
- **WELWYN EQUESTRIAN**, Welwyn **Ref:**YH15101

ISLE OF MAN

- **G G H EQUITATION CTRE**, Marown **Ref:**YH05578
- **MOUNT RULE EQUESTRIAN CTRE**, Braddan **Ref:**YH09894

ISLE OF WIGHT

- **ALLENDALE, S**, Ventnor **Ref:**YH00307
- **BRICKFIELDS**, Ryde **Ref:**YH01866
- **HILL FARM RIDING SCHOOL**, Freshwater **Ref:**YH06815
- **LAKE FARM**, Ventnor **Ref:**YH08350
- **ROMANY RIDING STABLES**, Newport **Ref:**YH12070

JERSEY

- **HAIE FLEURIE**, Channel Isles **Ref:**YH06280
- **MULTINA RIDING SCHOOL**, St Ouen **Ref:**YH09944

KENT

- **APPLETREE STABLES/RIDING**, Cranbrook **Ref:**YH00481
- **BEDGEBURY RIDING CTRE**, Goudhurst **Ref:**YH01155
- **BENACRE THANET WAY**, Whitstable **Ref:**YH01263

BITCHET FARM RIDING SCHOOL, Sevenoaks **Ref:**YH01455
BLUE BARN EQUESTRIAN CTRE, Ashford **Ref:**YH01564
BRADBOURNE, Sevenoaks **Ref:**YH01743
BRAESIDE E.C, Dover **Ref:**YH01773
BURSTED MANOR RIDING CTRE, Canterbury **Ref:**YH02285
CALLUM PARK RIDING CTRE, Sittingbourne **Ref:**YH02452
CHAUCER RIDING/LIVERY STABLES, Canterbury **Ref:**YH02791
CHAVIC PK STABLES, Westerham **Ref:**YH02793
CHELSFIELD RIDING SCHOOL, Orpington **Ref:**YH02802
COBHAM MANOR, Maidstone **Ref:**YH03113
COOMBE WOOD STABLES, Folkestone **Ref:**YH03276
CORNILO RIDING, Dover **Ref:**YH03324
CRIPPENDEN STUD, Edenbridge **Ref:**YH03602
DEEPDENE STABLES, Faversham **Ref:**YH04021
DOWNE HALL STABLES, Orpington **Ref:**YH04226
EAGLESFIELD EQUESTRIAN CTRE, Sevenoaks **Ref:**YH04441
ELMWOOD FARM RIDING CTRE, Broadstairs **Ref:**YH04641
FIVE OAKS EQUESTRIAN CTRE, Keston **Ref:**YH05254
GOODNESTONE CT EQUESTRIAN, Faversham **Ref:**YH05905
GREENACRES RIDING SCHOOL, Keston **Ref:**YH06078
HAYLORS, Sheerness **Ref:**YH06584
HAYNE BARN RIDING STABLES, Hythe **Ref:**YH06587
HERONWOOD STABLES, Sevenoaks **Ref:**YH06714
HIGHSTEAD RIDING CTRE, Canterbury **Ref:**YH06800
HONNINGTON, Tunbridge Wells **Ref:**YH07019
HORSESHOES RIDING SCHOOL, Maidstone **Ref:**YH07175
KENT LIVERIES & RIDING SCHOOL, Maidstone **Ref:**YH08081
LEYBOURNE GRANGE, West Malling **Ref:**YH08600
LIMES FARM EQUESTRIAN, Folkestone **Ref:**YH08635
LOWER BELL RIDING SCHOOL, Maidstone **Ref:**YH08862
LULLINGSTONE PK, Orpington **Ref:**YH08896
LYNX PK RIDING STABLES, Cranbrook **Ref:**YH08936
MANNIX STUD, Canterbury **Ref:**YH09091
MANSTON RIDING CTRE, Ramsgate **Ref:**YH09126
MARBERDAM RIDING CTRE, Canterbury **Ref:**YH09136
MARBERDUM, Canterbury **Ref:**YH09137
MATTHEWS RIDING CTRE, Chatham **Ref:**YH09269
MINNISMOOR STABLES, Ashford **Ref:**YH09650
NELSON PARK RIDING CTRE, Birchington **Ref:**YH10072
OATHILL FARM RIDING CTRE, Canterbury **Ref:**YH10415
OLD BEXLEY EQUESTRIAN, Bexley **Ref:**YH10451
PINE RIDGE, Sevenoaks **Ref:**YH11120
POLHILL RIDING CTRE, Sevenoaks **Ref:**YH11202
RIDING FARM EQUESTRIAN CTRES, Tonbridge **Ref:**YH11875
ROOTING STREET FARM, Ashford **Ref:**YH12082
SINDOLAR, Westerham **Ref:**YH12851
SOUTHBOROUGH LANE STABLES, Bromley **Ref:**YH13128
TREWINT, Cranbrook **Ref:**YH14388
WHITELEAF RIDING CTRE, Sittingbourne **Ref:**YH15347

LANCASHIRE

ARKENFIELD EQUESTRIAN CTRE, Chorley **Ref:**YH00530
BECCONSALL, Preston **Ref:**YH01144
BEECHMOUNT EQUITATION CTRE, Thornton-Cleveleys **Ref:**YH01174
BENTGATE EQUESTRIAN CTRE, Rossendale **Ref:**YH01284
BIRTLE RIDING CTRE, Bury **Ref:**YH01447
BLACKPOOL EQUESTRIAN CTRE, Blackpool **Ref:**YH01492
BROOMHILL, Clitheroe **Ref:**YH02080
CHORLEY EQUESTRIAN CTRE, Chorley **Ref:**YH02880
CROSTONS FARM RIDING & LIVERY, Chorley **Ref:**YH03672
DALES VIEW RIDING CTRE, Barnoldswick **Ref:**YH03831
DEANDANE RIDING STABLES, Wigan **Ref:**YH03998
DICKEY STEPS RIDING CTRE, Littleborough **Ref:**YH04111
DOUGLAS FARM RIDING SCHOOL, Wigan **Ref:**YH04211
EARNSDALE FARM RIDING SCHOOL, Darwen **Ref:**YH04458
ECCLESTON, Preston **Ref:**YH04532
ELSWICK, Preston **Ref:**YH04644
EURO STYLE, Rochdale **Ref:**YH04893
FULWOOD RIDING CTRE, Preston **Ref:**YH05537
GREEN BANK, Carnforth **Ref:**YH06049
HALSALL RIDING & LIVERY CTRE, Ormskirk **Ref:**YH06336
HEDLEY RIDING SCHOOL, Bury **Ref:**YH06644
HERD HSE RIDING SCHOOL, Burnley **Ref:**YH06699
HIGHMOOR RIDING STABLES, Oldham **Ref:**YH06799
HUSTEADS RIDING SCHOOL, Oldham **Ref:**YH07330
LANDLORDS FARM, Wigan **Ref:**YH08383
LASSELL HOUSE RIDING CTRE, Wigan **Ref:**YH08441
LONGTON EQUESTRIAN CTRE, Preston **Ref:**YH08819
LORDS HOUSE FARM, Blackburn **Ref:**YH08827
MIDGELAND, Blackpool **Ref:**YH09550
OAKFIELD RIDING SCHOOL, Preston **Ref:**YH10379
OLD HALL MILL RIDING SCHOOL, Atherton **Ref:**YH10460
RENARD RIDING CTRE, Poulton-Le-Fylde **Ref:**YH11753
RIBBY HALL, Preston **Ref:**YH11795
SWORDHILL EQUESTRIAN, Blackpool **Ref:**YH13718
TOWN END FARM RIDING CTRE, Carnforth **Ref:**YH14295
VALIANTS EQUESTRIAN CTRE, Preston **Ref:**YH14645
WADDINGTON FARM, Darwen **Ref:**YH14807
WHITEGATE FARM, Bacup **Ref:**YH15338
WHITEMOOR RIDING CTRE, Colne **Ref:**YH15351
WINDMILL FARM RIDING SCHOOL, Ormskirk **Ref:**YH15563
WREA GREEN EQUITATION CTRE, Kirkham **Ref:**YH15816
WRIGHTINGTON EQUESTRIAN CTRE, Wigan **Ref:**YH15843

LEICESTERSHIRE

BROOKSBY EQUESTRIAN CTRE, Melton Mowbray **Ref:**YH02067
CLAYBROOKE STABLES, Lutterworth **Ref:**YH02997
COSSINGTON, Leicester **Ref:**YH03354
HARDWICKE LODGE STABLES, Leicester **Ref:**YH06416
IRONSTONE FARM, Holwell **Ref:**YH07507
IVANHOE EQUESTRIAN, Ashby-De-La-Zouch **Ref:**YH07532
LIMES EQUESTRIAN CTRE, Sapcote **Ref:**YH08633
LYNCHGATE FARM RIDING SCHOOL, Hinckley **Ref:**YH08925
MANOR FARM RIDING SCHOOL, Leicester **Ref:**YH09105
MARKFIELD EQUESTRIAN, Markfield **Ref:**YH09161
MEADOW SCHOOL, Loughborough **Ref:**YH09422
MEADOWS RIDING CTRE, Fleckney **Ref:**YH09426
P & G STABLES, Leicester **Ref:**YH10630
PARKVIEW RIDING SCHOOL, Leicester **Ref:**YH10777
PERRY, M A C, Lutterworth **Ref:**YH10987
SCHOOL OF NATIONAL EQUITATION, Loughborough **Ref:**YH12521
SOMERBY EQUESTRIAN CTRE, Melton Mowbray **Ref:**YH13060
SOUTH LEICESTERSHIRE, Lutterworth **Ref:**YH13099
STABLES RIDING SCHOOL, Hinckley **Ref:**YH13312
STRETTON RIDING/TRAINING CTRE, Oakham **Ref:**YH13574
THORNHILL STUD, Lutterworth **Ref:**YH14069
WITHAM VILLA RIDING CTRE, Leicester **Ref:**YH15620

LINCOLNSHIRE

BROOK HSE FARM, Louth **Ref:**YH02037
CHARNICAL RIDING CTRE, Gainsborough **Ref:**YH02772
FENBOURNE RIDING SCHOOL, Bourne **Ref:**YH05137
FOUR WINDS, Spalding **Ref:**YH05413
FUNWAY EQUESTRIAN CTRE, Skegness **Ref:**YH05540
GLEN RIVER RIDING SCHOOL, Grantham **Ref:**YH05826
HYKEHAM RIDING STABLES, North Hykeham **Ref:**YH07355
IVY LANE RIDING SCHOOL, Lincoln **Ref:**YH07540
KEY, J U, Boston **Ref:**YH08114
LAUGHTON MANOR, Sleaford **Ref:**YH08448
LAUGHTON WOOD EQUESTRIAN CTRE, Gainsborough **Ref:**YH08449
LINCS RURAL ACTIVITIES, Louth **Ref:**YH08643
LINESIDE RIDING STABLES, Boston **Ref:**YH08657
MILL VIEW FARM, Sleaford **Ref:**YH09588
ORCHARD FARM EQUESTRIAN, Skegness **Ref:**YH10529
PADDOCKS RIDING CTRE, Grantham **Ref:**YH10675
PARK RIDING SCHOOL, Lincoln **Ref:**YH10735
POPPYFIELDS, Lincoln **Ref:**YH11275
REDNIL EQUESTRIAN CTRE, Lincoln **Ref:**YH11716
S & B STABLES, Alford **Ref:**YH12309
SAXILBY RIDING SCHOOL, Lincoln **Ref:**YH12466
SHEEPGATE EQUESTRIAN, Boston **Ref:**YH12696
SHEEPGATE TACK & TOGS, Boston **Ref:**YH12697
SOUTHREY RIDING STABLES, Southrey **Ref:**YH13159
THORPE GRANGE EQUESTRIAN CTRE, Aubourn **Ref:**YH14091
UFFINGTON RIDING STABLES, Stamford **Ref:**YH14540

LINCOLNSHIRE (NORTH EAST)

R G EQUESTRIAN, Grimsby **Ref:**YH11536

LINCOLNSHIRE (NORTH)

LOPHAMS EQUESTRIAN CTRE, Barrow-upon-Humber **Ref:**YH08823
POPLARS PONY TREKKING, Scunthorpe **Ref:**YH11274
WILLOW FARM, Scunthorpe **Ref:**YH15498

LONDON (GREATER)

ABBEYFIELDS, Hayes **Ref:**YH00095
ALDBOROUGH HALL, Ilford **Ref:**YH00252

- **ALDERSBROOK RIDING SCHOOL**, London **Ref:**YH00257
- **BARNFIELD RIDING SCHOOL**, Kingston Upon Thames **Ref:**YH00985
- **BARNFIELDS**, London **Ref:**YH00986
- **BELMONT RIDING CTRE**, London **Ref:**YH01249
- **DEEN CITY FARM**, London **Ref:**YH04018
- **DOCKLANDS EQUESTRIAN CTRE**, London **Ref:**YH04157
- **DULWICH RIDING SCHOOL**, London **Ref:**YH04326
- **EALING RIDING SCHOOL**, London **Ref:**YH04444
- **FRITH MANOR EQUESTRIAN CTRE**, London **Ref:**YH05510
- **GILLIAN'S RIDING SCHOOL**, Enfield **Ref:**YH05784
- **GOULDS GREEN**, Uxbridge **Ref:**YH05952
- **HYDE PARK STABLES**, London **Ref:**YH07346
- **KENSINGTON STABLES**, London **Ref:**YH08078
- **KENTISH TOWN CITY FARM**, London **Ref:**YH08087
- **KINGS OAK EQUESTRIAN CTRE**, Enfield **Ref:**YH08196
- **KINGSTON RIDING CTRE**, Kingston Upon Thames **Ref:**YH08207
- **LEE VALLEY RIDING CTRE**, London **Ref:**YH08519
- **LITTLEBOURNE FARM**, Uxbridge **Ref:**YH08703
- **LONDON EQUESTRIAN CTRE**, Finchley **Ref:**YH08785
- **LONDON EQUESTRIAN CTRE**, London **Ref:**YH08784
- **MOTTINGHAM FARM**, London **Ref:**YH09876
- **NEWHAM RIDING SCHOOL & ASS**, Beckton **Ref:**YH10137
- **PARK LANE STABLES**, Teddington **Ref:**YH10732
- **QUEEN ELIZABETH RIDING SCHOOL**, Chingford **Ref:**YH11488
- **RIDGWAY STABLES**, London **Ref:**YH11870
- **ROSS NYE RIDING STABLES**, London **Ref:**YH12118
- **STAG LODGE STABLES**, London **Ref:**YH13326
- **SUZANNE'S RIDING SCHOOL**, Harrow **Ref:**YH13679
- **TOTTERIDGE RIDING SCHOOL**, London **Ref:**YH14251
- **TRENT PARK EQUESTRIAN CTRE**, London **Ref:**YH14378
- **WESTWAYS**, Hounslow **Ref:**YH15235
- **WILLOW TREE RIDING**, London **Ref:**YH15504
- **WIMBLEDON VILLAGE STABLES**, London **Ref:**YH15557
- **WORMWOOD SCRUBS PONY CTRE**, East Acton **Ref:**YH15793

MANCHESTER (GREATER)

- **BANK FARM**, Stockport **Ref:**YH00885
- **CARRINGTON RIDING**, Manchester **Ref:**YH02589
- **CROFT END EQUESTRIAN CTRE**, Oldham **Ref:**YH03613
- **GODLEY STUD RIDING SCHOOL**, Manchester **Ref:**YH05868
- **KENYON FARM RIDING CTRE**, Manchester **Ref:**YH08094
- **MATCHMOOR RIDING CTRE**, Bolton **Ref:**YH09257
- **MAVITA RIDING SCHOOL**, Bolton **Ref:**YH09281
- **NORTH CHESHIRE**, Manchester **Ref:**YH10246
- **OAKHILL RIDING SCHOOL**, Manchester **Ref:**YH10384
- **PONDEROSA RIDING ACADEMY**, Tyldesley **Ref:**YH11220
- **RYDERS FARM**, Bolton **Ref:**YH12297
- **STAMFORD RIDING STABLES**, Mossley **Ref:**YH13354

MERSEYSIDE

- **BARNSTON RIDING CTRE**, Wirral **Ref:**YH00991
- **BOWLERS RIDING SCHOOL**, Liverpool **Ref:**YH01716
- **CROXTETH PK RIDING CTRE**, Liverpool **Ref:**YH03685
- **GELLINGS FARM RIDING SCHOOL**, Prescot **Ref:**YH05697
- **LARTON RIDING SCHOOL**, Wirral **Ref:**YH08436
- **LONGACRES**, Liverpool **Ref:**YH08806
- **MAYPOLE FARM**, Prescot **Ref:**YH09303
- **NORTHFIELD RIDING CTRE**, St Helens **Ref:**YH10314
- **PARK LANE LIVERIES**, Wirral **Ref:**YH10730
- **ROSE COTTAGE**, Southport **Ref:**YH12090
- **TARBOCK GREEN RIDING SCHOOL**, Prescot **Ref:**YH13869
- **WEST WIRRAL RIDING SCHOOL**, Wirral **Ref:**YH15171
- **WHEATHILL RIDING CTRE**, Liverpool **Ref:**YH15268
- **WIRRAL RIDING CTRE**, Neston **Ref:**YH15603
- **WOODVILLE**, Wirral **Ref:**YH15752

MIDLANDS (WEST)

- **BOURNE VALE STABLES**, Walsall **Ref:**YH01683
- **BROOKFIELDS**, Wolverhampton **Ref:**YH02052
- **BROOKHOUSE FARM RIDING SCHOOL**, Solihull **Ref:**YH02056
- **BUBBENHALL BRIDGE**, Coventry **Ref:**YH02182
- **CASTLE HILL RIDING SCHOOL**, Coventry **Ref:**YH02627
- **FARMHOUSE STABLES**, Sutton Coldfield **Ref:**YH05064
- **FOXHILLS**, Walsall **Ref:**YH05435
- **HART, ROSEMARY**, Stourbridge **Ref:**YH06498
- **HOME LIVERY & RIDING CTRE**, Walsall **Ref:**YH07002
- **KINGSWOOD EQUESTRIAN CTRE**, Wolverhampton **Ref:**YH08210
- **MILL RIDING CTRE**, Wolverhampton **Ref:**YH09586
- **MOOR FARM STABLES**, Coventry **Ref:**YH09745
- **NORTH WORCESTERSHIRE**, Halesowen **Ref:**YH10287
- **OAKEN LAWN RIDING SCHOOL**, Wolverhampton **Ref:**YH10375
- **SANDWELL VALLEY RIDING CTRE**, West Bromwich **Ref:**YH12421
- **SEECHEM EQUESTRIAN CTRE**, Birmingham **Ref:**YH12607
- **TRUEMANS HEATH**, Solihull **Ref:**YH14420
- **VIKKIS STABLES**, Walsall **Ref:**YH14718
- **WISHAW RIDING CTRE**, Sutton Coldfield **Ref:**YH15614
- **WITHYBROOK STABLES**, Coventry **Ref:**YH15629

NORFOLK

- **BLACKBOROUGH END**, King's Lynn **Ref:**YH01477
- **BRIDGE FARM STABLES**, Mundesley **Ref:**YH01872
- **CALDECOTT HALL**, Great Yarmouth **Ref:**YH02429
- **CROFT FARM RIDING CTRE**, Great Yarmouth **Ref:**YH03615
- **EDEN MEADOWS RIDING CTRE**, Attleborough **Ref:**YH04547
- **FERN BANK RIDING SCHOOL**, Norwich **Ref:**YH05161
- **FOREST LODGE RIDING CTRE**, Holt **Ref:**YH05343
- **GREENACRES RIDING SCHOOL**, King's Lynn **Ref:**YH06079
- **HARRIS, J A**, Norwich **Ref:**YH06476
- **HOCKWOLD LODGE**, Thetford **Ref:**YH06906
- **IVY FARM EQUESTRIAN CTRE**, Swaffham **Ref:**YH07539
- **KESWICK RIDING STABLES**, Norwich **Ref:**YH08106
- **MAYWAY**, Thetford **Ref:**YH09308
- **NORFOLK SHIRE HORSE CTRE**, Cromer **Ref:**YH10232
- **NORTH NORFOLK RIDING CTRE**, Walsingham **Ref:**YH10274
- **PLAYBARN**, Poringland **Ref:**YH11169
- **RECTORY ROAD RIDING SCHOOL**, Norwich **Ref:**YH11693
- **ROSE-ACRE RIDING STABLES**, Mundesley **Ref:**YH12099
- **RUNCTON HALL**, King's Lynn **Ref:**YH12233
- **SALHOUSE EQUESTRIAN CTRE**, Norwich **Ref:**YH12387
- **STREET FARM**, King's Lynn **Ref:**YH13572
- **STRUMPSHAW RIDING CTRE**, Norwich **Ref:**YH13592
- **SWAFIELD RIDING**, North Walsham **Ref:**YH13682
- **TOP FARM EQUESTRIAN CTRE**, Norwich **Ref:**YH14236
- **WEST RUNTON RIDING STABLES**, Cromer **Ref:**YH15162
- **WESTON PARK EQUESTRIAN CTRE**, Norwich **Ref:**YH15224
- **WILLOW END EQUESTRIAN CTRE**, Diss **Ref:**YH15494
- **WILLOW FARM COTTAGE**, Norwich **Ref:**YH15499
- **WILLOW FARM RIDING SCHOOL**, Great Yarmouth **Ref:**YH15500

NORTHAMPTONSHIRE

- **A J STABLES**, Towcester **Ref:**YH00042
- **BOUGHTON MILL RIDING SCHOOL**, Northampton **Ref:**YH01669
- **BRAMPTON STABLES**, Northampton **Ref:**YH01794
- **EAST LODGE FARM RIDING EST**, Northampton **Ref:**YH04479
- **EVERGREEN RIDING STABLES**, Northampton **Ref:**YH04952
- **FOX HILL FARM EQUESTRIAN CTRE**, Northampton **Ref:**YH05422
- **GLEBE FARM EQUESTRIAN CTRE**, Wellingborough **Ref:**YH05815
- **HARRINGWORTH MANOR**, Corby **Ref:**YH06461
- **HOLDENBY RIDING SCHOOL**, Northampton **Ref:**YH06924
- **HOWARTH HOUSE RIDING SCHOOL**, Kettering **Ref:**YH07219
- **MANOR FARM RIDING SCHOOL**, Wellingborough **Ref:**YH09106

NORTHUMBERLAND

- **BENRIDGE RIDING CTRE**, Morpeth **Ref:**YH01277
- **BROWN RIGG RIDING SCHOOL**, Hexham **Ref:**YH02093
- **CALVERT TRUST KIELDER**, Hexham **Ref:**YH02456
- **FOWBERRY FARMS**, Wooler **Ref:**YH05416
- **HAGGERSTON**, Berwick-upon-Tweed **Ref:**YH06277
- **KIMMERSTON RIDING CTRE**, Wooler **Ref:**YH08161
- **PLOVER HILL RIDING SCHOOL**, Hexham **Ref:**YH11178
- **RAVENSHILL RIDING CTRE**, Hexham **Ref:**YH11660
- **THORNTON STABLES**, Berwick-upon-Tweed **Ref:**YH14075
- **WHITEHOUSE RIDING SCHOOL**, Cornhill-on-Tweed **Ref:**YH15345

NOTTINGHAMSHIRE

- **BASSINGFIELD RIDING SCHOOL**, Nottingham **Ref:**YH01057
- **BLOOMSGORSE TREKKING CTRE**, Newark **Ref:**YH01556
- **BULCOTE RIDING STABLES**, Nottingham **Ref:**YH02211
- **CARLTON FOREST**, Worksop **Ref:**YH02542
- **CLGE FARM**, Newark **Ref:**YH03026
- **CTRE - LINES**, Newark **Ref:**YH03694
- **DOVECOTE FARM**, Orston **Ref:**YH04218
- **FAIRVIEW FARM RIDING SCHOOL**, Nottingham **Ref:**YH05031

GERTRUDE RD RIDING STABLES, Nottingham **Ref:**YH05731
KIRKFIELD EQUESTRIAN CTRE, Lower Blidworth **Ref:**YH08234
LINGS LANE RIDING STABLES, Nottingham **Ref:**YH08662
LOWER PORTLAND RIDING SCHOOL, Nottingham **Ref:**YH08867
SELSTON EQUESTRIAN CTRE, Nottingham **Ref:**YH12626
SOUTH VIEW FARM EQUESTRIAN, Newark **Ref:**YH13108
ST CLEMENTS LODGE, Nottingham **Ref:**YH13274
ST LEONARD'S RIDING SCHOOL, Nottingham **Ref:**YH13279
SUTTON MANOR FARM, Retford **Ref:**YH13673
TRENT VALLEY STABLES, Southwell **Ref:**YH14381
VICTORIAN CARRIAGES, Newark **Ref:**YH14710
WELLOW PK, Newark **Ref:**YH15077

OXFORDSHIRE

ASTI STUD & SADDLERY, Faringdon **Ref:**YH00633
BLEWBURY RIDING/TRAINING CTRE, Didcot **Ref:**YH01539
CLASSICAL RIDING SCHOOL, Henley-on-Thames **Ref:**YH02990
EAST END FARM RIDING SCHOOL, Wallingford **Ref:**YH04474
FAR FURLONG RIDING SCHOOL, Chipping Norton **Ref:**YH05048
HAILEY EQUITATION CTRE, Witney **Ref:**YH06283
OAKFIELD RIDING SCHOOL, Faringdon **Ref:**YH10380
OLD MANOR HSE, Oxford **Ref:**YH10461
OXFORD RIDING SCHOOL, Oxford **Ref:**YH10621
PIGEON HOUSE STABLES, Witney **Ref:**YH11095
PIGEON HOUSE STABLES, Witney **Ref:**YH11094
SILVERDOWN, Didcot **Ref:**YH12815
STANDLAKE EQUESTRIAN CTRE, Witney **Ref:**YH13362
TURPINS LODGE, Banbury **Ref:**YH14494
TURVILLE VALLEY, Henley-on-Thames **Ref:**YH14499
VALLEY FARM EQUESTRIAN CTRE, Banbury **Ref:**YH14653
WHITE HORSE RIDING STABLES, Wantage **Ref:**YH15311

SHROPSHIRE

BERRIEWOOD FARM, Shrewsbury **Ref:**YH01313
BOW HOUSE FARM RIDING SCHOOL, Bishops Castle **Ref:**YH01695
FRESHFIELDS, Market Drayton **Ref:**YH05499
HIGHGROVE SCHOOL OF RIDING, Craven Arms **Ref:**YH06788
LILLESHALL EQUESTRIAN CTRE, Newport **Ref:**YH08620
MYNDERLEY STABLES, All Stretton **Ref:**YH09984
OAKAGE RIDING CTRE, Shrewsbury **Ref:**YH10372
OSWESTRY EQUEST CTRE, Oswestry **Ref:**YH10576
P G L YOUNG ADVENTURE CTRE, Shrewsbury **Ref:**YH10641
PRESCOTT RIDING CTRE, Shrewsbury **Ref:**YH11356
RED CASTLE RIDING CTRE, Oswestry **Ref:**YH11695
TIDDIECROSS STABLES, Wrockwardine **Ref:**YH14132
TONG RIDING CTRE, Shifnal **Ref:**YH14227
TRENCH VILLA STABLES, Ellesmere **Ref:**YH14374
WYKE OF SHIFNAL, Shifnal **Ref:**YH15863

SOMERSET

ADSBOROUGH HSE STABLES, Taunton **Ref:**YH00189
BRIMSMORE EQUESTRIAN CTRE, Yeovil **Ref:**YH01913
BURCOTT RIDING CTRE, Wells **Ref:**YH02236
BURCOTT RIDING CTRE, Wells **Ref:**YH02235
CONQUEST CTRE, Taunton **Ref:**YH03243
CROWN HOTEL, Minehead **Ref:**YH03681
CURLAND EQUESTRIAN CTRE, Taunton **Ref:**YH03728
DIAMOND FARM RIDING CTRE, Burnham-on-Sea **Ref:**YH04103
DRAKES FARM, Ilminster **Ref:**YH04256
EBBORLANDS, Wells **Ref:**YH04529
FLYING START RIDING CTRE, Taunton **Ref:**YH05295
GREGGS RIDING SCHOOL, Yeovil **Ref:**YH06113
HALF MOON RIDING STABLES, Langport **Ref:**YH06296
HORNER FARM RIDING STABLES, Minehead **Ref:**YH07077
KNOWLE MANOR, Minehead **Ref:**YH08281
LONG LANE RIDING STABLES, Wincanton **Ref:**YH08796
MILL FARM CARAVAN & CAMP SITE, Bridgwater **Ref:**YH09570
MILLHOUSE EQUESTRIAN CTRE, Taunton **Ref:**YH09620
PEVLINGS FARM, Templecombe **Ref:**YH11035
PINE LODGE RIDING HOLIDAY, Dulverton **Ref:**YH11119
PORLOCK VALE HSE/RIDING CTRE, Porlock Weir **Ref:**YH11278
RODGROVE STUD EQUESTRIAN CTRE, Wincanton **Ref:**YH12048
ROYS RIDING SCHOOL, Taunton **Ref:**YH12201
WALFORD RIDING & LIVERY EST, Taunton **Ref:**YH14843
WEBBS HILL RIDING SCHOOL, Frome **Ref:**YH15035
WEST SOMERSET RIDING CTRE, Minehead **Ref:**YH15164

SOMERSET (NORTH)

CLEVEDON RIDING, Clevedon **Ref:**YH03020
CTRE RIDING SCHOOL, Weston-Super-Mare **Ref:**YH03696
CTRE RIDING SCHOOL, Weston-Super-Mare **Ref:**YH03695
MENDIP RIDING CTRE, Churchill **Ref:**YH09458
SOUTHFIELD FARM RIDING SCHOOL, Backwell **Ref:**YH13150
SWISS VALLEY EQUESTRIAN CTRE, Clevedon **Ref:**YH13717
VOWLES RIDING STABLES, Weston-Super-Mare **Ref:**YH14744
WORLEBURY LIVERY CTRE, Weston-Super-Mare **Ref:**YH15790

STAFFORDSHIRE

ACTON HILL RIDING SCHOOL, Stafford **Ref:**YH00161
ALSAGER EQUESTRIAN CTRE, Stoke-on-Trent **Ref:**YH00335
BARLASTON RIDING CTRE, Stoke-on-Trent **Ref:**YH00949
BENTLEY HSE, Biddulph Park **Ref:**YH01285
BUTTERLAND, Stoke-on-Trent **Ref:**YH02331
CHASE SIDE, Stafford **Ref:**YH02786
DALE SCHOOL OF EQUITATION, Stafford **Ref:**YH03822
ELITE RIDING & EQUESTRIAN SVS, Cannock **Ref:**YH04607
ENDON RIDING SCHOOL, Stoke-on-Trent **Ref:**YH04667
GARTMORE RIDING SCHOOL, Burntwood **Ref:**YH05664
GUNSTONE HALL RIDING CTRE, Wolverhampton **Ref:**YH06192
INGESTRE STABLES, Stafford **Ref:**YH07445
MIDDLETON EQUESTRIAN CTRE, Tamworth **Ref:**YH09541
MODDERSHALL RIDING SCHOOL, Stone **Ref:**YH09695
MOW-COP RIDING CTRE, Stoke-on-Trent **Ref:**YH09905
POPLARS FARM RIDING SCHOOL, Stoke-on-Trent **Ref:**YH11273
PUMP HSE FARM STABLES, Stoke-on-Trent **Ref:**YH11456
RODBASTON CLGE, Penkridge **Ref:**YH12041
SCOTT, B G, Stafford **Ref:**YH12538
SCROPTON, Burton-on-Trent **Ref:**YH12569
SNOW, S J, Uttoxeter **Ref:**YH13036
STOURTON HILL STABLES, Stourbridge **Ref:**YH13532
WESTWOOD HALL FARM, Leek **Ref:**YH15239
WHITMORE RIDING SCHOOL, Newcastle **Ref:**YH15365

SUFFOLK

BARDWELL MANOR, Bury St Edmunds **Ref:**YH00928
BENTLEY RIDING CTRE, Ipswich **Ref:**YH01286
CULFORD STABLES, Bury St Edmunds **Ref:**YH03701
GROVE HSE RIDING SCHOOL, Halesworth **Ref:**YH06169
HADLEIGH RIDING CTRE, Ipswich **Ref:**YH06266
HAWKINS FARM RIDING STABLES, Stowmarket **Ref:**YH06546
HENLEY RIDING SCHOOL, Ipswich **Ref:**YH06674
HIGH BANK RIDING SCHOOL, Sudbury **Ref:**YH06753
NEWTON HALL EQUITATION CTRE, Ipswich **Ref:**YH10171
ORWELL ARENA, Ipswich **Ref:**YH10556
PAKEFIELD RIDING SCHOOL, Lowestoft **Ref:**YH10687
PARK FARM, Harleston **Ref:**YH10718
POPLAR FARM RIDING STABLES, Hundon **Ref:**YH11270
POPLAR PK, Woodbridge **Ref:**YH11271
STANTON VIEW RIDING SCHOOL, Bury St Edmunds **Ref:**YH13380
STOKE BY CLARE EQUESTRIAN CTRE, Sudbury **Ref:**YH13501
SWIFT MANOR FARM, Sudbury **Ref:**YH13706
TOLLGATE LIVERY CTRE, Felixstowe **Ref:**YH14211
TWINSTEAD RIDING SCHOOL, Sudbury **Ref:**YH14514
UGGLESHALL, Beccles **Ref:**YH14541
VALLEY FARM, Woodbridge **Ref:**YH14651
WOODLANDS, Bury St Edmunds **Ref:**YH15707

SURREY

ALL MANOR PK EQUESTRIAN CTRE, Coulsdon **Ref:**YH00285
ASCOT PARK, Woking **Ref:**YH00583
BARNES, PAT, Woking **Ref:**YH00979
BEECHWOOD, Caterham **Ref:**YH01176
BRIDLEWAYS EQUESTRIAN CTRE, Great Bookham **Ref:**YH01898
BURSTOW PK, Horley **Ref:**YH02286
CANNON, LINDA, Guildford **Ref:**YH02506
CHESSINGTON, Chessington **Ref:**YH02830
CHIPPINGS FARM, Cobham **Ref:**YH02865
CHIPPINGS FARM STABLES, Cobham **Ref:**YH02866
CLANDON PK, Guildford **Ref:**YH02943
CLOCK TOWER RIDING CTRE, Tadworth **Ref:**YH03052
CRANLEIGH SCHOOL OF RIDING, Cranleigh **Ref:**YH03565
DIAMOND CTRE, Carshalton **Ref:**YH04102
DORKING EQUESTRIAN CTRE, Dorking **Ref:**YH04200
EQUUS EQUESTRIAN CTRES, Epsom **Ref:**YH04839
FARNHAM CASTLE STABLES, Farnham **Ref:**YH05080
FARTHING DOWNS STABLES, Coulsdon **Ref:**YH05099
FENNS FARM, Woking **Ref:**YH05149

- **GARSON FARM**, Esher **Ref:**YH05658
- **GREEN LANE STABLES**, Morden **Ref:**YH06058
- **GREENWAYS FARM & STABLES**, Godalming **Ref:**YH06105
- **HATCH FARM STABLES**, Addlestone **Ref:**YH06530
- **HEADLEY GR STABLES**, Epsom **Ref:**YH06611
- **HERSHAM**, Walton-on-Thames **Ref:**YH06719
- **HIGHER PK FARM**, Woking **Ref:**YH06779
- **HUNTERSFIELD FARM RIDING CTRE**, Banstead **Ref:**YH07303
- **KILN COTTAGE**, Farnham **Ref:**YH08149
- **LANGSHOT EQUESTRIAN CTRE**, Chobham **Ref:**YH08414
- **LITTLE PADDOCKS RIDING SCHOOL**, Woking **Ref:**YH08699
- **LOWER FARM**, Cobham **Ref:**YH08864
- **OAKS PK RIDING SCHOOL**, Banstead **Ref:**YH10402
- **OLD PK STABLES**, Farnham **Ref:**YH10472
- **ONLY FOALS & HORSES**, Oxted **Ref:**YH10522
- **ORCHARD COTTAGE**, Wickham Market **Ref:**YH10527
- **POYNTERS**, Cobham **Ref:**YH11330
- **RIDING CTRE**, Farnham **Ref:**YH11873
- **ROYAL ALEXANDRA/ALBERT SCHOOL**, Reigate **Ref:**YH12183
- **S R S**, Sunbury-on-Thames **Ref:**YH12333
- **SHEYCOPSE RIDING CTRE**, Woking **Ref:**YH12737
- **SOUTH WEYLANDS EQUESTRIAN**, Walton-on-Thames **Ref:**YH13123
- **STANGRAVE HALL STABLES**, Godstone **Ref:**YH13365
- **STARSHAW STABLES**, Coulsdon **Ref:**YH13399
- **SURREY HACKING & RIDING CTRE**, Guildford **Ref:**YH13658
- **TANDRIDGE PRIORY**, Oxted **Ref:**YH13853
- **TEIZERS EQUESTRIAN CTRE**, Burstow **Ref:**YH13937
- **TRIPLE BAR RIDING CTRE**, Dorking **Ref:**YH14400
- **VALE LODGE STABLES**, Leatherhead **Ref:**YH14635
- **WAFFRONS SCHOOL OF RIDING**, Chessington **Ref:**YH14820
- **WEYBRIDGE EQUESTRIAN CTRE**, Weybridge **Ref:**YH15250
- **WILDWOODS**, Tadworth **Ref:**YH15413
- **WIX HILL RIDING STABLES**, Leatherhead **Ref:**YH15637
- **WOODRUFF EQUESTRIAN**, West Byfleet **Ref:**YH15731

SUSSEX (EAST)

- **ASHDOWN FOREST RIDING CTRE**, Uckfield **Ref:**YH00595
- **AUDIBURN RIDING STABLES**, Lewes **Ref:**YH00661
- **BEAUPORT PK RIDING SCHOOL**, St Leonards-on-Sea **Ref:**YH01140
- **BEAUPORT PK RIDING STABLES**, Battle **Ref:**YH01141
- **CANTERS END RIDING SCHOOL**, Uckfield **Ref:**YH02512
- **COGGINS MILL RIDING STABLES**, Mayfield **Ref:**YH03136
- **FLIMWELL RIDING STABLES**, Wadhurst **Ref:**YH05284
- **FOLKINGTON MANOR STABLES**, Polegate **Ref:**YH05299
- **GATEWOOD STABLES**, Polegate **Ref:**YH05676
- **HAMSEY RIDING SCHOOL**, Lewes **Ref:**YH06371
- **HIGHAM FARM**, Hastings **Ref:**YH06768
- **HORAM MANOR**, Heathfield **Ref:**YH07064
- **HYLANDS STABLES**, Hailsham **Ref:**YH07357
- **MEADOWBANK EQUESTRIAN CTRE**, Hailsham **Ref:**YH09425
- **ORCHID RIDING CTRE**, Crowborough **Ref:**YH10538
- **PEBSHAM RIDING SCHOOL**, Bexhill-on-Sea **Ref:**YH10888
- **SOUTH LODGE**, Rotherfield **Ref:**YH13100
- **TILEHURST FARM RIDING CTRE**, Hailsham **Ref:**YH14143
- **WHYDOWN PLACE EQUESTRIAN CTRE**, Bexhill-on-Sea **Ref:**YH15380
- **WINTON STREET FARM STABLES**, Polegate **Ref:**YH15600

SUSSEX (WEST)

- **ALBOURNE EQUESTRIAN CTRE**, Hassocks **Ref:**YH00248
- **ARUNDEL FARM**, Arundel **Ref:**YH00577
- **BRIDGE HSE EQUESTRIAN CTRE**, Horsham **Ref:**YH01874
- **CHESTNUTS RIDING SCHOOL**, Brighton **Ref:**YH02838
- **CLAYTON HILL STABLES**, Hassocks **Ref:**YH03003
- **DITCHLING COMMON STUD**, Burgess Hill **Ref:**YH04135
- **EATON THORNE STABLES**, Henfield **Ref:**YH04525
- **FOREST FARM**, Horsham **Ref:**YH05336
- **GRANGEFIELD**, Midhurst **Ref:**YH06000
- **HANGLETON FARM**, Worthing **Ref:**YH06386
- **HAPPY VALLEY RIDING STABLES**, Shoreham By Sea **Ref:**YH06401
- **HILLCREST FARM RIDING SCHOOL**, Horsham **Ref:**YH06840
- **LAVANT HSE STABLES**, Chichester **Ref:**YH08460
- **SANDS FARM EQUITATION CTRE**, Horsham **Ref:**YH12420
- **SOUTHDOWN EQUESTRIAN CTRE**, Steyning **Ref:**YH13133
- **TREMAINES RIDING STABLES**, Haywards Heath **Ref:**YH14370
- **WEST WOLVES RIDING CTRE**, Pulborough **Ref:**YH15172
- **WILLOWBROOK RIDING CTRE**, Chichester **Ref:**YH15508
- **WOODSIDE FARM RIDING SCHOOL**, Horsham **Ref:**YH15740
- **WOOLBEDING RIDING SCHOOL**, Midhurst **Ref:**YH15764
- **ZARA STUD**, Chichester **Ref:**YH15951

TYNE AND WEAR

- **BARTON RIDING SCHOOL**, Newcastle-upon-Tyne **Ref:**YH01045
- **DERWENTOAK RIDING CTRE**, Rowlands Gill **Ref:**YH04082
- **FINDEISEN, M S**, Newcastle-upon-Tyne **Ref:**YH05209
- **GO RIDING GRP**, Ponteland **Ref:**YH05862
- **HOLLY RIDING SCHOOL**, Newcastle-upon-Tyne **Ref:**YH06956
- **LITTLE HARLE STABLES**, Newcastle-upon-Tyne **Ref:**YH08688
- **MACKIE, HENRI**, Newcastle-upon-Tyne **Ref:**YH09005
- **MURTON RIDING SCHOOL**, Newcastle-upon-Tyne **Ref:**YH09972
- **NORTH LIZARD RIDING SCHOOL**, South Shields **Ref:**YH10271
- **PENSHAW HILL RIDING SCHOOL**, Houghton Le Spring **Ref:**YH10959
- **QUARRY PARK STABLES**, Gateshead **Ref:**YH11483
- **STEPNEY BANK STABLES**, Newcastle-upon-Tyne **Ref:**YH13429
- **WEST HERRINGTON RIDING SCHOOL**, Houghton Le Spring **Ref:**YH15148

WARWICKSHIRE

- **CALDECOTE RIDING SCHOOL**, Nuneaton **Ref:**YH02428
- **CHASE RIDING SCHOOL**, Bedworth **Ref:**YH02784
- **COTTAGE FARM RIDING STABLES**, Solihull **Ref:**YH03374
- **ETTINGTON PARK STABLES**, Stratford-upon-Avon **Ref:**YH04887
- **HOLLY RIDING SCHOOL**, Atherstone **Ref:**YH06957
- **INTERNATIONAL WARWICK SCHOOL**, Warwick **Ref:**YH07480
- **MOAT HOUSE STUD**, Henley In Arden **Ref:**YH09686
- **NASEBY HALL**, Rugby **Ref:**YH10024
- **OAKLANDS RIDING SCHOOL**, Warwick **Ref:**YH10392
- **PEBWORTH VALE SADDLERY**, Stratford-upon-Avon **Ref:**YH10890
- **PITTERN HILL**, Warwick **Ref:**YH11155
- **RADWAY RIDING SCHOOL**, Warwick **Ref:**YH11600
- **RED HSE FARM LIVERY STABLES**, Leamington Spa **Ref:**YH11696
- **STONELEIGH STABLES**, Kenilworth **Ref:**YH13519
- **SWALLOWFIELD EQUESTRIAN**, Solihull **Ref:**YH13686
- **THREE GATES EQUESTRIAN CTRE**, Moreton Morrell **Ref:**YH14103
- **UMBERSLADE EQUESTRIAN CTRE**, Solihull **Ref:**YH14558
- **WARD, ANTHONY**, Moreton Morrell **Ref:**YH14898
- **WARWICKSHIRE EQUITATION CTRE**, Coventry **Ref:**YH14952
- **WAVERLEY EQUESTRIAN CTRE**, Leamington Spa **Ref:**YH15011
- **WOODBINE RIDING STABLES**, Rugby **Ref:**YH15674
- **WOODBINE STABLES**, Rugby **Ref:**YH15675

WILTSHIRE

- **BRYMPTON RIDING SCHOOL**, Salisbury **Ref:**YH02173
- **CHIPTRICK RIDING SCHOOL**, Melksham **Ref:**YH02867
- **GROVELY**, Salisbury **Ref:**YH06175
- **HAMPSLEY HOLLOW**, Calne **Ref:**YH06368
- **HARRIS CROFT RIDING CTRE**, Swindon **Ref:**YH06462
- **HEDDINGTON WICK**, Calne **Ref:**YH06639
- **HEYWOOD**, Westbury **Ref:**YH06737
- **HILLVIEW RIDING STABLES**, Trowbridge **Ref:**YH06859
- **HULBERTS GREEN**, Chippenham **Ref:**YH07279
- **INFANTRY SADDLE CLUB**, Warminster **Ref:**YH07441
- **LACOCK RIDING CTRE**, Chippenham **Ref:**YH08333
- **MALTHOUSE EQUESTRIAN CTRE**, Swindon **Ref:**YH09058
- **MARLBOROUGH DOWNS**, Marlborough **Ref:**YH09169
- **PEWSEY VALE**, Marlborough **Ref:**YH11037
- **SOUTHVIEW FARM**, Bradford-on-Avon **Ref:**YH13160
- **SUMMERHOUSE FARM**, Malmesbury **Ref:**YH13633
- **WHITE HORSE EQUESTRIAN CTRE**, Westbury **Ref:**YH15308
- **WICKSTEAD FARM**, Swindon **Ref:**YH15387
- **WIDBROOK ARABIAN STUD**, Bradford-on-Avon **Ref:**YH15388
- **WILLIAM PUDDY WHITE HORSE**, Warminster **Ref:**YH15437

WORCESTERSHIRE

- **BEOLEY EQUESTRIAN CTRE**, Redditch **Ref:**YH01290
- **BROADCLOSE LIVERY**, Worcester **Ref:**YH01993
- **CARENZA, JILL**, Broadway **Ref:**YH02534
- **CLARKS HILL**, Evesham **Ref:**YH02980
- **HADLEY RIDING STABLES**, Droitwich **Ref:**YH06267
- **HALLOW MILLS**, Worcester **Ref:**YH06333
- **HARTLEBURY EQUESTRIAN CTRE**, Kidderminster **Ref:**YH06505
- **HEID & BRAZIER**, Stourport-on-Severn **Ref:**YH06648
- **HONEYBOURNE STABLES**, Bromsgrove **Ref:**YH07012
- **LEA CASTLE EQUESTRIAN CTRE**, Kidderminster **Ref:**YH08493
- **MANOR FARM RIDING SCHOOL**, Stourport-on-Severn **Ref:**YH09107
- **MOORLANDS**, Worcester **Ref:**YH09779
- **MOYFIELD RIDING SCHOOL**, Evesham **Ref:**YH09908

PORTMANS FARM, Upton-upon-Severn **Ref:**YH11294
RILEY HILL FARM HOLIDAYS, Cradley **Ref:**YH11894
SIX ASHES RIDING CTRE, Kidderminster **Ref:**YH12861
WALNUT STABLES, Malvern **Ref:**YH14870
WARESLEY MANOR STABLES, Kidderminster **Ref:**YH14917
WHITFORD RIDING STABLE, Bromsgrove **Ref:**YH15361

YORKSHIRE (EAST)

BLEACH YARD STABLES, Beverley **Ref:**YH01531
BURTON CONSTABLE RIDING CTRE, Hull **Ref:**YH02291
CHURCH FARM RIDING SCHOOL, Hull **Ref:**YH02899
LITTLE KELK RIDING SCHOOL, Driffield **Ref:**YH08689
MOORINGS EQUESTRIAN CTRE, Holme upon Spalding Moor **Ref:**YH09777
NORTH HUMBERSIDE, Hull **Ref:**YH10264
ROWLEY MANOR STABLES, Little Weighton **Ref:**YH12170
WOLDGATE TREKKING, Bridlington **Ref:**YH15646

YORKSHIRE (NORTH)

BARKER, A C, York **Ref:**YH00939
BELMONT LIVERY STABLE, Harrogate **Ref:**YH01247
BEWERLEY, Harrogate **Ref:**YH01347
BILSDALE RIDING CTRE, York **Ref:**YH01416
BLEACH FARM, York **Ref:**YH01530
BOGS HALL, Ripon **Ref:**YH01598
BRIGG VIEW, Filey **Ref:**YH01906
CHEQUER FARM STABLES, York **Ref:**YH02810
COTTAGE FARM STABLES, York **Ref:**YH03375
COUNTESS OF SWINTON, Ripon **Ref:**YH03394
CROSSBANK RIDING SCHOOL, Northallerton **Ref:**YH03655
DENTON RIDING CTRE, Scarborough **Ref:**YH04066
DRAUGHTON HEIGHT, Skipton **Ref:**YH04261
DUKES PLACE STABLES, Harrogate **Ref:**YH04323
EDDLETHORPE EQUESTRIAN SVS, Malton **Ref:**YH04543
ELLERBY & WEBSTER, York **Ref:**YH04613
FARSYDE STUD & RIDING CTRE, Whitby **Ref:**YH05098
FOLLIFOOT PK, Harrogate **Ref:**YH05300
FRIARS HILL STABLES, York **Ref:**YH05501
HARROGATE, Harrogate **Ref:**YH06490
HOME FARM, Malton **Ref:**YH06995
HOME FARM RIDING STABLES, Malton **Ref:**YH06999
JODHPURS, York **Ref:**YH07774
MANOR HSE FARM, Pickering **Ref:**YH09113
MILL LANE, Selby **Ref:**YH09579
MOORHOUSE RIDING CTRE, York **Ref:**YH09776
NAB BRIDGE RIDING SCHOOL, Harrogate **Ref:**YH10007
NABURN GRANGE RIDING CTRE, York **Ref:**YH10008
NORTHALLERTON EQUESTRIAN, Northallerton **Ref:**YH10290
PIMLOTT, C & N, York **Ref:**YH11112
PROSPECT FARM, Marton-cum-Grafton **Ref:**YH11435
QUEEN ETHELBURGA'S CLGE, York **Ref:**YH11489
QUEEN MARGARETS RIDING SCHOOL, York **Ref:**YH11490
RICHMOND EQUESTRIAN CTRE, Richmond **Ref:**YH11827
RIDING CTRE, Harrogate **Ref:**YH11874
ROW BROW FARM, Scarborough **Ref:**YH12151
SINNINGTON MANOR, York **Ref:**YH12855
SNAINTON RIDING CTRE, Scarborough **Ref:**YH13028
SWINTON RIDING/TREKKING CTRE, Ripon **Ref:**YH13714
WELLFIELD TREKKING CTRE, Scarborough **Ref:**YH15069
YORK RIDING SCHOOL, York **Ref:**YH15917
YORKSHIRE DALES, Skipton **Ref:**YH15919
YORKSHIRE RIDING CTRE, Harrogate **Ref:**YH15922

YORKSHIRE (SOUTH)

BARNES GREEN, Sheffield **Ref:**YH00971
BROCKHOLES FARM, Doncaster **Ref:**YH02010
GLEBE FIELD RIDING EST, Mexborough **Ref:**YH05816
GROVE HOUSE, Doncaster **Ref:**YH06168
GROVE HSE STABLES, Doncaster **Ref:**YH06170
HOWARTH LODGE RIDING CTRE, Rotherham **Ref:**YH07220
KNIGHT, G C & LINDSEY, J E, Rotherham **Ref:**YH08259
LOW ASH RIDING CTRE, Sheffield **Ref:**YH08853
MALLARD HSE, Sheffield **Ref:**YH09050
MOORHOUSE, Doncaster **Ref:**YH09775
PARKLANDS RIDING SCHOOL, Sheffield **Ref:**YH10770
PRICES, Rotherham **Ref:**YH11391
SILKSTONE EQUESTRIAN CTRE, Barnsley **Ref:**YH12800
SMELTINGS FARM RIDING CTRE, Sheffield **Ref:**YH12927
SNOWDON FARM RIDING SCHOOL, Sheffield **Ref:**YH13040

YORKSHIRE (WEST)

ACRELIFFE, Otley **Ref:**YH00159
ADEL WOOD, Leeds **Ref:**YH00182
ASTLEY RIDING CTRE, Leeds **Ref:**YH00635
BANK HSE FARM, Wakefield **Ref:**YH00891
CLIFFORD MOOR FARM, Wetherby **Ref:**YH03035
CROFTON RIDING STABLES, Wakefield **Ref:**YH03624
FIELD BOTTOM RIDING STABLES, Halifax **Ref:**YH05183
FLY LAITHE STABLES, Halifax **Ref:**YH05291
HILL CROFT FARM, Wetherby **Ref:**YH06810
HILLCROFT FARM RIDING STABLES, Wetherby **Ref:**YH06845
ILKLEY RIDING CTRE, Ilkley **Ref:**YH07400
J-SIX S C RIDING SCHOOL, Wakefield **Ref:**YH07955
LOBB STABLES RIDING SCHOOL, Todmorden **Ref:**YH08751
LONGFIELD EQUESTRIAN CTRE, Todmorden **Ref:**YH08811
LONGLEY RIDING SCHOOL, Huddersfield **Ref:**YH08815
MANOR GRANGE STUD SCHOOL, Wakefield **Ref:**YH09109
MOUNT PLEASANT STUD, Leeds **Ref:**YH09892
NETHER HALL RIDING SCHOOL, Huddersfield **Ref:**YH10082
NORLAND EQUESTRIAN CTRE, Halifax **Ref:**YH10234
NORTH IVES FARM, Horsforth **Ref:**YH10265
PARK VIEW RIDING CTRE, Huddersfield **Ref:**YH10741
PHOENIX EQUESTRIAN CTRE, Castleford **Ref:**YH11071
ROYDS HALL RIDING SCHOOL, Leeds **Ref:**YH12199
SHAY LANE STABLES, Halifax **Ref:**YH12686
STRATHMORE, Shipley **Ref:**YH13561
THROSTLE NEST RIDING SCHOOL, Bradford **Ref:**YH14113
TIMBERTOPS EQUESTRIAN CTRE, Pontefract **Ref:**YH14162
TOPS RIDING CTRE, Hebden Bridge **Ref:**YH14240
WESTWAYS RIDING SCHOOL, Leeds **Ref:**YH15236
WHITLEY EQUITATION CTRE, Dewsbury **Ref:**YH15363

RIDING WEAR RETAILERS

BEDFORDSHIRE

ARCADE SADDLERY BEDFORD, Bedford **Ref:**YH00498
BIGGLESWADE SADDLERY, Biggleswade **Ref:**YH01404
EQUISSENTIAL, Bedford **Ref:**YH04820
WADDINGTONS, Leighton Buzzard **Ref:**YH14809

BERKSHIRE

ASPREY POLO, Windsor **Ref:**YH00628
CENTELL, Reading **Ref:**YH02685
CHANGING TACK, Windsor **Ref:**YH02732
SCATS COUNTRYSTORE, Newbury **Ref:**YH12493
WOODLANDS, Hungerford **Ref:**YH15705

BRISTOL

JENNY'S TACK SHOP, Bristol **Ref:**YH07750

BUCKINGHAMSHIRE

BELLINGDON END, Chesham **Ref:**YH01238
DENNIS'S SADDLERY/RIDING WEAR, Aylesbury **Ref:**YH04059
DENNIS'S SADDLERY/RIDING WEAR, Aylesbury **Ref:**YH04060
GOHL, CHRIS, Chesham **Ref:**YH05874

CAMBRIDGESHIRE

HOOK HSE, March **Ref:**YH07035
LEO'S SADDLERY, Peterborough **Ref:**YH08555
SMEETH SADDLERY, Wisbech **Ref:**YH12925

CHESHIRE

BOLD HEATH EQUESTRIAN, Widnes **Ref:**YH01602
BOOL BY DESIGN, Tarporley **Ref:**YH01631
BOWLERS, Stockport **Ref:**YH01715
CARR & DAY & MARTIN, Wilmslow **Ref:**YH02569
CHELFORD FARM SUPPLIES, Macclesfield **Ref:**YH02799
COLBERRY SADDLERY, Ellesmere Port **Ref:**YH03142
CREWE SADDLERY, Crewe **Ref:**YH03595
DECATHLON SPORTS & LEISURE, Stockport **Ref:**YH04008
GAYNORS SADDLERY, Dukinfield **Ref:**YH05682
LANSDOWNE HORSE & RIDER, Chester **Ref:**YH08423

CLEVELAND

EQUINE EXTRAS, Stockton-on-Tees **Ref:**YH04778
HOOF'N'HOUND, Hartlepool **Ref:**YH07031
HOOF'N'HOUND, Middlesbrough **Ref:**YH07032

CORNWALL

HELSTON SADDLERY, Helston **Ref:**YH06657
HORSE & RIDER, Launceston **Ref:**YH07094
POLLY LUNN PET & AQUATICS, Truro **Ref:**YH11208
WOOFWARE, Bodmin **Ref:**YH15762

COUNTY DURHAM

FARMWAY, Darlington **Ref:**YH05072
GO RIDING GRP, Stanley **Ref:**YH05861
SEAGOLD CENTURION, Crook **Ref:**YH12587
WEST AUCKLAND COUNTRY STORE, Bishop Auckland **Ref:**YH15126

CUMBRIA

LAKELAND EQUESTRIAN, Windermere **Ref:**YH08354
LOWTHER EQUESTRIAN, Carlisle **Ref:**YH08877

DERBYSHIRE

BARLEYFIELD SADDLERY, Etwall **Ref:**YH00951
BARLEYFIELDS, Derby **Ref:**YH00952

- **COUNTRY SPORT**, Glossop **Ref:**YH03426
- **HORSE & RIDER TACK SHOP**, Nottingham **Ref:**YH07100
- **KNOWLE HILL EQUESTRIAN**, Derby **Ref:**YH08280
- **PEAKDALE SADDLERY**, Buxton **Ref:**YH10866

DEVON

- **ASHTON SADDLERY**, Exeter **Ref:**YH00613
- **CHEVAL ARMOIRE**, South Brent **Ref:**YH02840
- **ERME VALLEY FARMERS**, Ivybridge **Ref:**YH04850
- **FARMERS FRIEND**, Exeter **Ref:**YH05061
- **LEONARD COOMBE**, Newton Abbot **Ref:**YH08553
- **LUCY TURMAINE**, Beaworthy **Ref:**YH08889
- **PET & EQUINE SUPPLIES**, Okehampton **Ref:**YH11000
- **TOWN & COUNTRY SUP**, Exeter **Ref:**YH14286
- **TWYFORD FARM SUPPLIES**, Tiverton **Ref:**YH14516
- **WYCHANGER BARTON SADDLERY**, Tiverton **Ref:**YH15855

DORSET

- **COUNTRY SHOP**, Sturminster Newton **Ref:**YH03425
- **EQUUS**, Wimborne **Ref:**YH04836
- **SCATS COUNTRYSTORE**, Blandford **Ref:**YH12496
- **SCATS COUNTRYSTORE**, Dorchester **Ref:**YH12494
- **SCATS COUNTRYSTORE**, Gillingham **Ref:**YH12495
- **SIDE SADDLES**, Wimborne **Ref:**YH12787

ESSEX

- **BATTLESBRIDGE HORSE & CTRY**, Wickford **Ref:**YH01082
- **CANDLERS**, Chelmsford **Ref:**YH02496
- **CLOTHES HORSE COMPANY**, Nazeing **Ref:**YH03064
- **D & F FEED SVS**, Rayleigh **Ref:**YH03770
- **HOBBY HORSE**, Romford **Ref:**YH06897
- **INGATESTONE SADDLERY**, Ingatestone **Ref:**YH07442
- **KILN SADDLERY**, Colchester **Ref:**YH08151
- **MOORCROFT EQUESTRIAN**, Colchester **Ref:**YH09749
- **MOSS, JANETTE**, Waltham Abbey **Ref:**YH09858
- **PRIORY SADDLERY**, Colchester **Ref:**YH11403
- **SHOPLAND HALL EQUESTRIAN**, Rochford **Ref:**YH12758
- **TACK EXCHANGE**, Leigh-on-Sea **Ref:**YH13788
- **TALLY-HO RIDING SCHOOL**, Grays **Ref:**YH13844
- **THORPE TACK ROOM**, Clacton-on-Sea **Ref:**YH14095
- **UPMINSTER SADDLERY**, Upminster **Ref:**YH14604
- **YE OLDE FORGE**, Basildon **Ref:**YH15894

GLOUCESTERSHIRE

- **BILL BIRD BOOTS & SHOES**, Moreton In Marsh **Ref:**YH01407
- **HIGGS, NIGEL**, Cirencester **Ref:**YH06750
- **MORETON SADDLERY**, Moreton In Marsh **Ref:**YH09790
- **STROUD SADDLERY**, Stroud **Ref:**YH13588
- **TEWKESBURY SADDLERY**, Tewkesbury **Ref:**YH13969

HAMPSHIRE

- **CALCUTT & SONS**, Winchester **Ref:**YH02425
- **CLASSIC COLLECTION**, Alresford **Ref:**YH02983
- **COUNTRY RIDING WEAR**, Hook **Ref:**YH03424
- **HARNESS ROOM**, Lymington **Ref:**YH06447
- **HORSE CLOTHING**, Waterlooville **Ref:**YH07114
- **SCATS COUNTRYSTORE**, Alton **Ref:**YH12499
- **SCATS COUNTRYSTORE**, Andover **Ref:**YH12500
- **SCATS COUNTRYSTORE**, Basingstoke **Ref:**YH12501
- **SCATS COUNTRYSTORE**, Lymington **Ref:**YH12502
- **SCATS COUNTRYSTORE**, Romsey **Ref:**YH12497
- **SCATS COUNTRYSTORE**, Winchester **Ref:**YH12498
- **TALLY HO**, Whitchurch **Ref:**YH13839
- **WELLINGTON RIDING**, Hook **Ref:**YH15075
- **WORLD BETA EQUESTRIAN**, Waterlooville **Ref:**YH15784

HEREFORDSHIRE

- **COUNTRY YARNS & TACKROOM**, Bromyard **Ref:**YH03437
- **COUNTRYWEAR**, Hay On Wye **Ref:**YH03442
- **COUNTRYWIDE**, Hereford **Ref:**YH03445
- **HORSE & JOCKEY**, Hereford **Ref:**YH07093
- **HORSEWISE**, Hereford **Ref:**YH07178
- **SHEEPCOTE EQUESTRIAN**, Hereford **Ref:**YH12695
- **SHIRES EQUESTRIAN**, Leominster **Ref:**YH12755

HERTFORDSHIRE

- **COLEMAN CROFT**, St Albans **Ref:**YH03163
- **FIELD SPORTS**, Borehamwood **Ref:**YH05186
- **PATCHETTS**, Watford **Ref:**YH10815
- **SADDLERY**, Royston **Ref:**YH12363

ISLE OF WIGHT

- **SCATS COUNTRYSTORE**, Newport **Ref:**YH12503

JERSEY

- **LE MAISTRE BROS**, Trinity **Ref:**YH08490

KENT

- **ARIZONAS**, Tunbridge Wells **Ref:**YH00527
- **BARMINSTER TRADING**, Ashford **Ref:**YH00960
- **BIRCHALLS THE RIDING SHOP**, Maidstone **Ref:**YH01431
- **CHASKIT HSE**, Tunbridge Wells **Ref:**YH02787
- **CLASSIC EQUINE PRODUCTS**, Beckenham **Ref:**YH02987
- **CLIP CLOP SHOP**, Rochester **Ref:**YH03044
- **FROGPOOL MANOR SADDLERY**, Chislehurst **Ref:**YH05515
- **GLOVER, H F & J H**, Longfield **Ref:**YH05854
- **HOBBS PARKER**, Ashford **Ref:**YH06894
- **HORSE & COUNTRY SUPERSTORE**, Maidstone **Ref:**YH07088
- **SADDLERY & GUN ROOM**, Westerham **Ref:**YH12365
- **SCATS COUNTRYSTORE**, Canterbury **Ref:**YH12504
- **SCATS COUNTRYSTORE**, Marden **Ref:**YH12505
- **WEALDEN SADDLERY**, Tonbridge **Ref:**YH15020
- **WILLOW FARM**, Faversham **Ref:**YH15497

LANCASHIRE

- **CAUSEWAY EQUESTRIAN**, Ormskirk **Ref:**YH02662
- **DERBY HSE SADDLERY**, Wigan **Ref:**YH04071
- **EQUESTRIANA**, Blackburn **Ref:**YH04724
- **PRETTY PONIES**, Clitheroe **Ref:**YH11372
- **SNAFFLES**, Halifax **Ref:**YH13020
- **ZEBRA**, Skelmersdale **Ref:**YH15953

LEICESTERSHIRE

- **CLOTHES HORSE**, Leicester **Ref:**YH03062
- **HURST SADDLERS**, Leicester **Ref:**YH07316
- **JACK ELLIS BODY PROTECTION**, Leicester **Ref:**YH07637
- **SCHOOL OF NATIONAL EQUITATION**, Loughborough **Ref:**YH12521
- **VALE OF BELVOIR LEATHERS**, Melton Mowbray **Ref:**YH14638

LINCOLNSHIRE

- **A W RHOADES SADDLERY**, Market Rasen **Ref:**YH00068
- **BATTLE, HAYWARD & BOWER**, Lincoln **Ref:**YH01081
- **COTTAGE SADDLERY**, Boston **Ref:**YH03379
- **JONES CHARITY SADDLERY**, Grantham **Ref:**YH07873
- **SHEEPGATE EQUESTRIAN**, Boston **Ref:**YH12696
- **TACK BOX**, Lincoln **Ref:**YH13785

LINCOLNSHIRE (NORTH)

- **CROWSTONS**, Scunthorpe **Ref:**YH03684
- **KILLINGHOLME**, Grimsby **Ref:**YH08143
- **MASON, D & M**, Scunthorpe **Ref:**YH09239

LONDON (GREATER)

- **BEDFORD RIDING BREECHES**, London **Ref:**YH01152
- **BROWN, OLIVER**, London **Ref:**YH02126
- **CHASE SADDLERY**, Enfield **Ref:**YH02785
- **DECATHLON SPORTS & LEISURE**, London **Ref:**YH04009
- **DEGE & SKINNER**, London **Ref:**YH04026
- **EDWARD ROBERT SADDLERY**, Feltham **Ref:**YH04569

- **GEDDES-BODEN, LESLIE**, London **Ref:**YH05687
- **GOULDS GREEN**, Uxbridge **Ref:**YH05952
- **H HUNTSMAN & SONS**, London **Ref:**YH06225
- **HENRY POOLE**, London **Ref:**YH06685
- **HYDE PARK RIDING WEAR**, London **Ref:**YH07345
- **KENSINGTON STABLES**, London **Ref:**YH08078
- **RIDERS & SQUIRES**, London **Ref:**YH11855
- **RIDGWAY STABLES**, London **Ref:**YH11870
- **W H GIDDEN**, London **Ref:**YH14770

MANCHESTER (GREATER)

- **ALEXANDER JAMES OF PENDLEBURY**, Manchester **Ref:**YH00265
- **EQUITACK**, Bolton **Ref:**YH04823
- **HAMILTON SHOW WEAR**, Manchester **Ref:**YH06349
- **SMITHY**, Bolton **Ref:**YH13011

MERSEYSIDE

- **FORMBY SADDLERY**, Liverpool **Ref:**YH05373

MIDLANDS (WEST)

- **ARABIAN SADDLE**, Walsall **Ref:**YH00492
- **BEEBEE & BEEBEE**, Walsall **Ref:**YH01162
- **GORRINGE SPORTSWEAR**, Walsall **Ref:**YH05936
- **HARDWEAR CLOTHING**, Stourbridge **Ref:**YH06414
- **HORSESENSE**, Solihull **Ref:**YH07170
- **KIRKLAND SADDLERY**, Walsall **Ref:**YH08236
- **OVERIDER**, Coventry **Ref:**YH10593
- **WORLDWIDE EQUESTRIAN**, Walsall **Ref:**YH15788

NORFOLK

- **BRUNDALL SADDLERY**, Norwich **Ref:**YH02156
- **GORLESTON TACK ROOM**, Great Yarmouth **Ref:**YH05934
- **HORSES IN SPORT**, Diss **Ref:**YH07169
- **HORSETALK**, King's Lynn **Ref:**YH07176
- **L A SADDLERY**, Great Yarmouth **Ref:**YH08313

NORTHAMPTONSHIRE

- **BATTEN, HORACE**, Northampton **Ref:**YH01077
- **COUNTRY STYLES**, Towcester **Ref:**YH03430
- **COUNTRYWEAR BY LEWIS R LILLIE**, Kettering **Ref:**YH03443
- **COUNTY FOOTWEAR**, Kettering **Ref:**YH03487
- **EDENGATE SADDLERY**, Northampton **Ref:**YH04550
- **FAULKNERS FOOTWEAR**, Daventry **Ref:**YH05104
- **FLYING CHANGES**, Daventry **Ref:**YH05293
- **HOOKS & HOOVES**, Kettering **Ref:**YH07038
- **K & T FOOTWEAR**, Kettering **Ref:**YH07981
- **LOVESON**, Irthlingborough **Ref:**YH08851
- **WATTS & WATTS SADDLERY**, Northampton **Ref:**YH15003

NORTHUMBERLAND

- **A C BURN**, Berwick-upon-Tweed **Ref:**YH00021
- **AIR-O-WEAR**, Corbridge **Ref:**YH00225
- **FARMWAY**, Morpeth **Ref:**YH05074
- **TOTAL QUALITY EQUINE CLOTHING**, Morpeth **Ref:**YH14249
- **WILLOW WEAR**, Hexham **Ref:**YH15505

NOTTINGHAMSHIRE

- **BRIDLE WAY & GAUNTLEYS**, Newark **Ref:**YH01892
- **DECATHLON SPORTS & LEISURE**, Nottingham **Ref:**YH04010
- **HAPPY TACK**, Nottingham **Ref:**YH06400
- **HOOF ALOOF**, Nottingham **Ref:**YH07025
- **SADDLE RACK**, Nottingham **Ref:**YH12346
- **SADDLECRAFT**, Nottingham **Ref:**YH12355
- **ST CLEMENTS LODGE**, Nottingham **Ref:**YH13274

OXFORDSHIRE

- **ASTI STUD & SADDLERY**, Faringdon **Ref:**YH00633
- **HAC-TAC**, Faringdon **Ref:**YH06259
- **JODS GALORE**, Henley-on-Thames **Ref:**YH07775
- **KEN LANGFORD SADDLERY**, Abingdon **Ref:**YH08058
- **SANSOMS SADDLERY**, Witney **Ref:**YH12429
- **SCATS COUNTRYSTORE**, Faringdon **Ref:**YH12506
- **W F S COUNTRY**, Witney **Ref:**YH14766

SHROPSHIRE

- **GREENFIELDS COUNTRY PURSUITS**, Shrewsbury **Ref:**YH06084
- **HORSE & COUNTRY**, Newport **Ref:**YH07086
- **HORSE SHOP**, Bridgnorth **Ref:**YH07139
- **SHERRATT FARM SUPPLIES**, Wem **Ref:**YH12728
- **WREKIN FARMERS GARDEN CTRE**, Telford **Ref:**YH15817
- **WYNNSTAY & CLWYD FARMERS**, Oswestry **Ref:**YH15876

SOMERSET

- **BOWERS, HENRY**, Chard **Ref:**YH01707
- **MCCOY SADDLERY**, Minehead **Ref:**YH09334
- **PEGASUS**, Taunton **Ref:**YH10903
- **RIDEMOOR**, Wincanton **Ref:**YH11852
- **ROSE MILL FEEDS**, Ilminster **Ref:**YH12094
- **STAX SADDLERY**, Montacute **Ref:**YH13406
- **THORNEY COPSE**, Wincanton **Ref:**YH14066
- **W.E.S GARRETT MASTER SADDLERS**, Cheddar **Ref:**YH14803

STAFFORDSHIRE

- **DOBBINS DINER**, Tamworth **Ref:**YH04151
- **FRANCES ANN BROWN SADDLERY**, Stafford **Ref:**YH05444
- **H WOOLLEY & SON**, Uttoxeter **Ref:**YH06247
- **LARKHILL SADDLERY**, Burton-on-Trent **Ref:**YH08432

SUFFOLK

- **GIBBINS, J & C**, Woodbridge **Ref:**YH05737
- **HORSE & GARDEN**, Halesworth **Ref:**YH07089
- **HORSE BITS**, Woodbridge **Ref:**YH07105
- **HORSE REQUISITES**, Newmarket **Ref:**YH07132
- **LINKWOOD EQUESTIAN**, Bury St Edmunds **Ref:**YH08665
- **MILL SADDLERY**, Stowmarket **Ref:**YH09587
- **RIDE AWAY SADDLERY**, Ipswich **Ref:**YH11846
- **STOKE BY CLARE EQUESTRIAN CTRE**, Sudbury **Ref:**YH13501

SURREY

- **ASCOT PARK**, Woking **Ref:**YH00583
- **HASTILOW COMPETITION SADDLES**, Godalming **Ref:**YH06526
- **INJURED RIDERS FUND**, Cranleigh **Ref:**YH07458
- **SCATS COUNTRYSTORE**, Godalming **Ref:**YH12507
- **SCATS COUNTRYSTORE**, Redhill **Ref:**YH12508

SUSSEX (EAST)

- **DANDY BUSH SADDLERY**, Battle **Ref:**YH03863
- **EQUESTRIAN COUNTRY LEISURE**, Bexhill-on-Sea **Ref:**YH04695
- **HOVE TACK ROOM**, Hove **Ref:**YH07213
- **SCATS COUNTRYSTORE**, Heathfield **Ref:**YH12509
- **SOMETHING DIFFERENT**, Uckfield **Ref:**YH13068
- **STEVENS, LEONARD**, Eastbourne **Ref:**YH13445

SUSSEX (WEST)

- **BRENDON HORSE & RIDER**, Brighton **Ref:**YH01837
- **DRAGONFLY SADDLERY**, Hassocks **Ref:**YH04252
- **EQUITOGS**, Billingshurst **Ref:**YH04830
- **EQUITOGS**, Littlehampton **Ref:**YH04829
- **FELPHAM STABLES TACKROOM**, Bognor Regis **Ref:**YH05136
- **GEOFF DEAN SADDLERY**, Worthing **Ref:**YH05714
- **PENFOLD & SONS**, Haywards Heath **Ref:**YH10934
- **SCATS COUNTRYSTORE**, Billingshurst **Ref:**YH12510
- **SNOWHILL SADDLERY**, Chichester **Ref:**YH13044

TYNE AND WEAR

- **CLASSIC EQUESTRIAN**, Houghton Le Spring **Ref:**YH02986
- **GO RIDING GRP**, Ponteland **Ref:**YH05862
- **RIDERS**, North Shields **Ref:**YH11854
- **S & S SADDLERY**, Sunderland **Ref:**YH12313
- **SADDLE SHOP**, Gateshead **Ref:**YH12350
- **WEBSTER, J R**, Newcastle-upon-Tyne **Ref:**YH15040

WARWICKSHIRE

- **A & J SADDLERY**, Southam **Ref:**YH00012
- **EDWARDS' SADDLERY**, Bidford On Avon **Ref:**YH04574

- **WAVERLEY EQUESTRIAN CTRE**, Leamington Spa **Ref:**YH15011

WILTSHIRE

- **BEST BOOTS**, Chippenham **Ref:**YH01324
- **DAVID FARMER SADDLERY**, Chippenham **Ref:**YH03919
- **ELMGROVE SADDLERY**, Swindon **Ref:**YH04636
- **EQUIFOR**, Marlborough **Ref:**YH04746
- **EQUINOVA**, Salisbury **Ref:**YH04814
- **HURDCOTT LIVERY STABLES**, Salisbury **Ref:**YH07311
- **NEW EQUINE WEAR**, Malmesbury **Ref:**YH10093
- **SADDLERY**, Swindon **Ref:**YH12364
- **SCATS COUNTRYSTORE**, Devizes **Ref:**YH12512
- **SCATS COUNTRYSTORE**, Salisbury **Ref:**YH12511
- **SYDNEY INGRAM & SON**, Salisbury **Ref:**YH13722
- **WADSWICK**, Corsham **Ref:**YH14819
- **WARMINSTER SADDLERY**, Warminster **Ref:**YH14923

WORCESTERSHIRE

- **BROMSGROVE SADDLERY**, Bromsgrove **Ref:**YH02026
- **COTTAGE INDUSTRIES**, Droitwich **Ref:**YH03377
- **COUNTRYWIDE**, Worcester **Ref:**YH03446
- **EQUIMIX**, Stourport-on-Severn **Ref:**YH04756

YORKSHIRE (EAST)

- **PATRICK WILKINSON**, Beverley **Ref:**YH10825

YORKSHIRE (NORTH)

- **BEAVER HORSE SHOP**, Harrogate **Ref:**YH01143
- **BULLOCK, J A & F**, York **Ref:**YH02219
- **COUNTRY LIFE**, Northallerton **Ref:**YH03416
- **COUNTRY STILE CLOTHING**, Settle **Ref:**YH03428
- **COUNTRY STYLE CLOTHING**, Settle **Ref:**YH03429
- **GILLS SADDLERY & CANE**, Northallerton **Ref:**YH05787
- **LANGTON HORSE WEAR**, Northallerton **Ref:**YH08416
- **R & R COUNTRY**, Selby **Ref:**YH11507
- **ROBINSON**, Malton **Ref:**YH11985
- **SECOND TURNOUT**, Northallerton **Ref:**YH12598
- **YORKSHIRE RIDING SUPPLIES**, York **Ref:**YH15923

YORKSHIRE (SOUTH)

- **BITS & BOOTS**, Doncaster **Ref:**YH01456
- **HORSE & RIDER**, Doncaster **Ref:**YH07096
- **HORSE & RIDER**, Sheffield **Ref:**YH07097
- **MR ED'S**, Rotherham **Ref:**YH09915
- **THROSTLE NEST SADDLERY**, Barnsley **Ref:**YH14114
- **WILDSMITHS**, Doncaster **Ref:**YH15412

YORKSHIRE (WEST)

- **CALDENE CLOTHING**, Hebden Bridge **Ref:**YH02430
- **CLOTHES HORSE**, Boston Spa **Ref:**YH03063
- **COTTAGE INDUSTRIES**, Bradford **Ref:**YH03378
- **DAYS PET SHOP**, Bradford **Ref:**YH03971
- **DISCOUNT SADDLERY**, Huddersfield **Ref:**YH04129
- **EQUESTRIAN CLEARANCE CTRE**, Halifax **Ref:**YH04694
- **EQUITACK SADDLERY**, Wakefield **Ref:**YH04825
- **FOX SADDLERS**, Wetherby **Ref:**YH05425
- **GREAT CLOTHES**, Leeds **Ref:**YH06038
- **HERITAGE COUNTRYWEAR**, Leeds **Ref:**YH06704
- **HOOVES EQUESTRIAN**, Bradford **Ref:**YH07047
- **ILKLEY RIDING CTRE**, Ilkley **Ref:**YH07400
- **JACK LEES**, Halifax **Ref:**YH07638
- **JENKINSONS**, Dewsbury **Ref:**YH07740
- **MIDDLESTOWN SADDLERY**, Wakefield **Ref:**YH09540
- **SINCLAIR RIDING WEAR**, Leeds **Ref:**YH12849
- **TACK & TURNOUT EQUESTRIAN**, Huddersfield **Ref:**YH13780
- **WEST RIDING SUPPLIES**, Bradford **Ref:**YH15161

SADDLERY RETAILERS

BATH & SOMERSET (NORTH EAST)

- **MATTHEWS OF KEYNSHAM**, Keynsham **Ref:**YH09268

BEDFORDSHIRE

- **ARCADE SADDLERY BEDFORD**, Bedford **Ref:**YH00498
- **BIGGLESWADE SADDLERY**, Biggleswade **Ref:**YH01404
- **GRAVENHURST SADDLERY**, Bedford **Ref:**YH06024
- **K & K PET SHOPS**, Dunstable **Ref:**YH07980
- **LAGUS, S E**, Leighton Buzzard **Ref:**YH08344
- **R B EQUESTRIAN**, Leighton Buzzard **Ref:**YH11514
- **TACK HAVEN**, Dunstable **Ref:**YH13790
- **WADDINGTONS**, Leighton Buzzard **Ref:**YH14809
- **WILSTEAD SADDLERY**, Bedford **Ref:**YH15554

BERKSHIRE

- **ASPREY POLO**, Windsor **Ref:**YH00628
- **CENTELL**, Reading **Ref:**YH02685
- **CHANGING TACK**, Windsor **Ref:**YH02732
- **CROFT EQUESTRIAN CTRE**, Reading **Ref:**YH03614
- **DAVID ETON**, Windsor **Ref:**YH03918
- **DOUGLAS, EILEEN**, Sandhurst **Ref:**YH04212
- **DOUGLAS, EILEEN**, Wokingham **Ref:**YH04213
- **EQUICENTRE**, Waltham St Lawrence **Ref:**YH04737
- **FROSBURY'S**, Bracknell **Ref:**YH05519
- **LLOYD-WILLIAMS SADDLERY**, Reading **Ref:**YH08746
- **RIVERDALE**, Thatcham **Ref:**YH11920
- **SHAMLEY SADDLERY**, Maidenhead **Ref:**YH12663
- **SNOWBALL FARM EQUESTRIAN CTRE**, Slough **Ref:**YH13037
- **STABLE DOOR**, Reading **Ref:**YH13291
- **TALLY HO FARM**, Windsor **Ref:**YH13840
- **THRESHERS BARN**, Newbury **Ref:**YH14111
- **TURF & TRAVEL**, Slough **Ref:**YH14466
- **WOODLANDS**, Hungerford **Ref:**YH15705
- **WOODLANDS LEISUREWEAR**, Hungerford **Ref:**YH15709

BRISTOL

- **A T VEATER & SONS**, Bristol **Ref:**YH00062
- **C J PUDDY SADDLERY**, Bristol **Ref:**YH02378
- **EQUICRAFT SADDLERY**, Bristol **Ref:**YH04739
- **JENNY'S TACK SHOP**, Bristol **Ref:**YH07750
- **LEYLAND COURT**, Bristol **Ref:**YH08601
- **PATRICK PINKER**, Bristol **Ref:**YH10824

BUCKINGHAMSHIRE

- **ABEX HORSE & RIDER**, High Wycombe **Ref:**YH00131
- **AESCWOOD**, Beaconsfield **Ref:**YH00196
- **BEECHFIELD SADDLERY**, Grendon Underwood **Ref:**YH01172
- **BELLINGDON END**, Chesham **Ref:**YH01238
- **BRIDLEWAYS**, Burnham **Ref:**YH01896
- **C & L EQUESTRIAN**, Milton Keynes **Ref:**YH02356
- **COUNTRY EQUESTRIAN**, Milton Keynes **Ref:**YH03404
- **COX & ROBINSON**, Buckingham **Ref:**YH03527
- **CRENDON SADDLERY**, Aylesbury **Ref:**YH03591
- **D A L E**, Aylesbury **Ref:**YH03775
- **DENNIS'S SADDLERY/RIDING WEAR**, Aylesbury **Ref:**YH04059
- **DENNIS'S SADDLERY/RIDING WEAR**, Aylesbury **Ref:**YH04060
- **EQUINE DESIGN INT**, Iver **Ref:**YH04775
- **EQUITANA EQUESTIAN**, High Wycombe **Ref:**YH04826
- **G B GOMME & SON**, Princes Risborough **Ref:**YH05570
- **GEEGEES**, Milton Keynes **Ref:**YH05693
- **GOHL, CHRIS**, Chesham **Ref:**YH05874
- **LANES SADDLERY & ANIMAL FEEDS**, Newport Pagnell **Ref:**YH08395
- **SUMMERFIELDS SADDLERY**, Aylesbury **Ref:**YH13630
- **WILLOWBROOK FARM FEED & TACK**, Aylesbury **Ref:**YH15507

CAMBRIDGESHIRE

- **A FRENCH & SONS**, Cambridge **Ref:**YH00032
- **ALLTACK & ALLFEED**, Cambridge **Ref:**YH00326
- **BELTONS COUNTRY SHOP**, Peterborough **Ref:**YH01256
- **CHURCHFIELD FARM TACK SHOP**, Peterborough **Ref:**YH02910
- **E ABINGTON & SONS**, Huntingdon **Ref:**YH04396
- **GRANGE FARM EQUESTRIAN CTRE**, Peterborough **Ref:**YH05988
- **HIGHGATE FARM**, Willingham **Ref:**YH06786
- **HOOK HSE**, March **Ref:**YH07035
- **LEO'S SADDLERY**, Peterborough **Ref:**YH08555
- **LONG MELFORD**, Cambridge **Ref:**YH08798
- **LONGLAND, MICHAEL**, Huntingdon **Ref:**YH08814
- **SANDY'S SADDLERY**, Ely **Ref:**YH12426
- **SMEETH SADDLERY**, Wisbech **Ref:**YH12925
- **TACK 'N' TOGS**, Cambridge **Ref:**YH13791
- **WITCHAM EQUESTRIAN CTRE**, Ely **Ref:**YH15616

CHESHIRE

- **ALSAGER & SANDBACH SADDLERY**, Sandbach **Ref:**YH00334
- **BOOL BY DESIGN**, Tarporley **Ref:**YH01631
- **BOWLERS**, Stockport **Ref:**YH01715
- **CARR & DAY & MARTIN**, Wilmslow **Ref:**YH02569
- **CASSIDY EQUESTRIAN**, Northwich **Ref:**YH02621
- **CHELFORD FARM SUPPLIES**, Macclesfield **Ref:**YH02799
- **CHESTER SADDLERY**, Chester **Ref:**YH02832
- **COLBERRY SADDLERY**, Ellesmere Port **Ref:**YH03142
- **CREWE SADDLERY**, Crewe **Ref:**YH03595
- **DECATHLON SPORTS & LEISURE**, Stockport **Ref:**YH04008
- **DINGLE BROOK FARM STABLES**, Macclesfield **Ref:**YH04125
- **DOVE STYLE**, Chester **Ref:**YH04217
- **GAYNORS SADDLERY**, Dukinfield **Ref:**YH05682
- **KEY GREEN SADDLERY**, Congleton **Ref:**YH08113
- **LANSDOWNE HORSE & RIDER**, Chester **Ref:**YH08423
- **MACCLESFIELD SADDLERY**, Macclesfield **Ref:**YH08985
- **N W F COUNTRYWISE**, Nantwich **Ref:**YH10001
- **PEACEHAVEN RIDING CTRE**, Chester **Ref:**YH10856
- **SMITH & MORRIS**, Nantwich **Ref:**YH12932
- **STOCKFARM EQUESTRIAN SUPPLIES**, Chester **Ref:**YH13491
- **W & T GIBSON**, Frodsham **Ref:**YH14748
- **WILLIAMS, B**, Lymm **Ref:**YH15447
- **WILSONS SADDLERY**, Macclesfield **Ref:**YH15552
- **WOODVILLE FARM SADDLERY**, Sandbach **Ref:**YH15753

CLEVELAND

- **ARMSTRONG RICHARDSON**, Middlesbrough **Ref:**YH00544
- **HOOF'N'HOUND**, Hartlepool **Ref:**YH07031
- **HOOF'N'HOUND**, Middlesbrough **Ref:**YH07032

CORNWALL

- **BLISLAND HARNESS MAKERS**, Liskeard **Ref:**YH01541
- **CASTLE SADDLERY**, Liskeard **Ref:**YH02633
- **COUNTRY RIDER**, Truro **Ref:**YH03423
- **ECLIPSE**, Penzance **Ref:**YH04537
- **EQUESTRIAN STOP**, Camborne **Ref:**YH04712
- **HALLAGENNA STUD FARM**, Bodmin **Ref:**YH06322
- **HAMES SADDLERY**, Bude **Ref:**YH06346
- **HELSTON SADDLERY**, Helston **Ref:**YH06657
- **HORSE & RIDER**, Launceston **Ref:**YH07094
- **POLLY LUNN PET & AQUATICS**, Truro **Ref:**YH11208
- **S-J'S TACK ROOM**, Roche **Ref:**YH12864
- **TOKENBURY SADDLERY**, Liskeard **Ref:**YH14205

COUNTY DURHAM

- **COCKERTON SADDLERY**, Darlington **Ref:**YH03123
- **COUNTRY LEATHER SADDLERY**, Crook **Ref:**YH03414
- **FARMWAY**, Darlington **Ref:**YH05072
- **FREE & EASY SADDLE**, Barnard Castle **Ref:**YH05480
- **HORSE & RIDER SUPPLIES**, Stanley **Ref:**YH07099
- **KATANYA PETS**, Bishop Auckland **Ref:**YH07997
- **M A V SADDLERY & PET STORE**, Crook **Ref:**YH08953
- **M S RACE GEAR**, Durham **Ref:**YH08976
- **MCVICKERS, DEREK**, Consett **Ref:**YH09410
- **SADDLE SENSE**, Barnard Castle **Ref:**YH12348
- **TACK UP**, Barnard Castle **Ref:**YH13817
- **TALLY HO**, Beamish **Ref:**YH13837
- **WEST AUCKLAND COUNTRY STORE**, Bishop Auckland **Ref:**YH15126

CUMBRIA

- **BARROW SADDLERY & SUPPLIES**, Barrow-In-Furness **Ref:**YH01029
- **ESKDALE SADDLERY**, Carlisle **Ref:**YH04861
- **FOUR LEGGED FRIENDS**, Egremont **Ref:**YH05408
- **LAKELAND EQUESTRIAN**, Windermere **Ref:**YH08354
- **LANCASTER, P R**, Ulverston **Ref:**YH08381
- **LOWTHER EQUESTRIAN**, Carlisle **Ref:**YH08877
- **SCARBARROW PADDOCK SADDLERY**, Ulverston **Ref:**YH12485
- **SLACK'S**, Penrith **Ref:**YH12884
- **STEWART, L**, Carlisle **Ref:**YH13458
- **T W RELPH & SONS**, Penrith **Ref:**YH13767
- **TYNDALE FARM SERVICES**, Holmrook **Ref:**YH14525
- **W C F COUNTRY CTRES**, Wigton **Ref:**YH14757
- **W G TODD & SONS**, Kendal **Ref:**YH14767

DERBYSHIRE

- **ASHFORD FARM SUPPLIES**, Bakewell **Ref:**YH00601
- **BARLEYFIELD SADDLERY**, Etwall **Ref:**YH00951
- **BARLEYFIELDS**, Derby **Ref:**YH00952
- **BELPER SADDLERY**, Belper **Ref:**YH01252
- **BROOMBANK EQUESTRIAN**, Chesterfield **Ref:**YH02074
- **CHATSWORTH SADDLERY**, Chesterfield **Ref:**YH02788
- **COUNTRY SPORT**, Glossop **Ref:**YH03426
- **HARGATE EQUESTRIAN**, Derby **Ref:**YH06423
- **HEN MILL SADDLERY**, Clay Cross **Ref:**YH06663
- **HORSE & RIDER TACK SHOP**, Nottingham **Ref:**YH07100
- **HULLAND SADDLERY**, Ashbourne **Ref:**YH07282
- **IVANHOE FEEDS**, Swadlincote **Ref:**YH07533
- **KNOWLE HILL EQUESTRIAN**, Derby **Ref:**YH08280
- **MATLOCK SADDLERY**, Matlock **Ref:**YH09265
- **PEAKDALE SADDLERY**, Buxton **Ref:**YH10866
- **R E FARMS**, Derby **Ref:**YH11533
- **RISLEY SADDLERY**, Draycott **Ref:**YH11911
- **TACK SHACK**, Derby **Ref:**YH13805
- **TEVERSAL SADDLERY**, Alfreton **Ref:**YH13965
- **WRIGHT, L C**, Swadlincote **Ref:**YH15837

DEVON

- **ACORN SADDLERY**, South Molton **Ref:**YH00151
- **ASHTON SADDLERY**, Exeter **Ref:**YH00613
- **AVON FARMERS**, Kingsbridge **Ref:**YH00688
- **BARNSTAPLE HORSE/PET SUPP**, Barnstaple **Ref:**YH00990
- **CHAMPION SADDLERY**, Paignton **Ref:**YH02727
- **CHEVAL ARMOIRE**, South Brent **Ref:**YH02840
- **CHING SADDLERS**, Exeter **Ref:**YH02863
- **DURAL FARM ENTERPRISES**, Holsworthy **Ref:**YH04363
- **EAST DEVON SADDLERY**, Honiton **Ref:**YH04470
- **EDWIN TUCKER & SONS**, Newton Abbott **Ref:**YH04586
- **F W PERKINS**, Ottery St Mary **Ref:**YH05003
- **FARMERS FRIEND**, Exeter **Ref:**YH05061
- **LAMBERTS COUNTRY STORE**, Bideford **Ref:**YH08366
- **LEATHER WORKSHOP**, Exeter **Ref:**YH08505
- **LEONARD COOMBE**, Newton Abbot **Ref:**YH08553
- **MOLE AVON TRADING**, Axminster **Ref:**YH09707
- **MOLE AVON TRADING**, Crediton **Ref:**YH09709
- **MOLE AVON TRADING**, Okehampton **Ref:**YH09708
- **P H SADDLERS**, Winkleigh **Ref:**YH10643
- **PAYNE, MATTHEW**, Okehampton **Ref:**YH10851
- **PET & EQUINE SUPPLIES**, Okehampton **Ref:**YH11000
- **RED POST FEEDS**, Totnes **Ref:**YH11702
- **SNAFFLES SADDLERY**, Bradworthy **Ref:**YH13025
- **SOUTH DEVON EQUESTRIAN SUP**, Paignton **Ref:**YH13082
- **TAVISTOCK SADDLERY**, Tavistock **Ref:**YH13886
- **TOWN & COUNTRY SUP**, Exeter **Ref:**YH14286
- **TRAGO MILLS**, Newton Abbott **Ref:**YH14311
- **TWYFORD FARM SUPPLIES**, Tiverton **Ref:**YH14516
- **WATERMAN, M & A**, Tiverton **Ref:**YH14970
- **WEST DEVON & NORTH CORNWALL**, Holsworthy **Ref:**YH15139
- **WILLINGCOTT FARM SUPPLIES**, Woolacombe **Ref:**YH15488
- **WYCHANGER BARTON SADDLERY**, Tiverton **Ref:**YH15855

DORSET

- **BLACKMORE VALE STUD**, Gillingham **Ref:**YH01487
- **BLANDFORD SADDLERY**, Blandford Forum **Ref:**YH01524
- **BRAMBLES FARM ARABIANS**, Wimborne **Ref:**YH01787
- **COUNTRY SHOP**, Sturminster Newton **Ref:**YH03425
- **COUTISSE**, Dorchester **Ref:**YH03516
- **DORCHESTER SADDLERY**, Dorchester **Ref:**YH04198
- **DORSET COUNTY SADDLERY**, Wimborne **Ref:**YH04205
- **EQUUS**, Wimborne **Ref:**YH04836
- **HURN BRIDGE CTRE**, Christchurch **Ref:**YH07313
- **MABERS SADDLERY**, Sherborne **Ref:**YH08980
- **PURBECK PETS & EQUESTRIAN**, Wareham **Ref:**YH11462
- **SIDE SADDLES**, Wimborne **Ref:**YH12787
- **TURTONS SADDLERS & HARNESS**, Shaftesbury **Ref:**YH14496
- **WESTWAY SADDLERY**, Bridport **Ref:**YH15233

ESSEX

- **BATTLESBRIDGE HORSE & CTRY**, Wickford **Ref:**YH01082
- **BROOK FARM EQUESTRIAN CTRE**, Saffron Walden **Ref:**YH02034
- **BROOKS STABLES**, Benfleet **Ref:**YH02062
- **BROWN, N & H**, Witham **Ref:**YH02124
- **BURCHES RIDING SCHOOL**, Benfleet **Ref:**YH02232
- **CANDLERS**, Chelmsford **Ref:**YH02496
- **CLAVERING SADDLERY & LEATHER**, Saffron Walden **Ref:**YH02993
- **CLIP CLOPS SADDLERY**, Braintree **Ref:**YH03045
- **COLLINS, HANNAH**, Saffron Walden **Ref:**YH03188
- **D & F FEED SVS**, Rayleigh **Ref:**YH03770
- **D F ASSET SADDLERY**, Brentwood **Ref:**YH03783
- **D'ARCY SADDLERY**, Maldon **Ref:**YH03880
- **FAIR EARTH TRADING**, Little Oakley **Ref:**YH05011
- **FOOTPRINT SADDLERY**, Ongar **Ref:**YH05313
- **FOXHOUNDS RIDING SCHOOL**, Grays **Ref:**YH05438
- **H A C S SHOP**, Bishop's Stortford **Ref:**YH06210
- **HOBBS CROSS EQUESTRIAN CTRE**, Epping **Ref:**YH06893
- **HOBBY HORSE**, Romford **Ref:**YH06897
- **INGATESTONE SADDLERY**, Ingatestone **Ref:**YH07442
- **JOHN SKELTONS**, Benfleet **Ref:**YH07812
- **KILN SADDLERY**, Colchester **Ref:**YH08151
- **LYNFORDS**, Wickford **Ref:**YH08930
- **MARCH EQUESTRIAN**, Colchester **Ref:**YH09138
- **MARCH EQUESTRIAN**, Halstead **Ref:**YH09139
- **MOORCROFT EQUESTRIAN**, Colchester **Ref:**YH09749
- **MOSS, JANETTE**, Waltham Abbey **Ref:**YH09858
- **POND FARM**, Braintree **Ref:**YH11217
- **PRIORY SADDLERY**, Colchester **Ref:**YH11403
- **RADWINTER SADDLERY**, Saffron Walden **Ref:**YH11601
- **RAYNE RIDING CTRE**, Braintree **Ref:**YH11676
- **RUGGERY**, Romford **Ref:**YH12221
- **SHOPLAND HALL EQUESTRIAN**, Rochford **Ref:**YH12758
- **SIERRA SADDLE**, Benfleet **Ref:**YH12792
- **SOUTH VIEW SADDLERY/PET FOOD**, Grays **Ref:**YH13110
- **T S S**, Newport **Ref:**YH13764
- **TACK EXCHANGE**, Leigh-on-Sea **Ref:**YH13788
- **TALLY-HO RIDING SCHOOL**, Grays **Ref:**YH13844
- **THORPE TACK ROOM**, Clacton-on-Sea **Ref:**YH14095
- **TOWERLANDS EQUESTRIAN CTRE**, Braintree **Ref:**YH14278
- **UPMINSTER SADDLERY**, Upminster **Ref:**YH14604
- **WITHAM SADDLERY**, Witham **Ref:**YH15618
- **YE OLDE FORGE**, Basildon **Ref:**YH15894

GLOUCESTERSHIRE

- **CHELTENHAM SADDLERY**, Cheltenham **Ref:**YH02805
- **COLNE SADDLERY**, Cheltenham **Ref:**YH03197
- **COLNE SADDLERY**, Gloucester **Ref:**YH03196
- **COTSWOLD SADDLERY**, Cirencester **Ref:**YH03365
- **COURT FARM COUNTRY STORE**, Lydney **Ref:**YH03499
- **EDWARDS SADDLERY**, Moreton In Marsh **Ref:**YH04573
- **EQUESTRIAN REQUISITIES**, Stonehouse **Ref:**YH04709
- **HAWTHORN SADDLERY**, Sandhurst **Ref:**YH06556
- **HAYES J SADDLERY**, Lechlade **Ref:**YH06575
- **HIGGS, NIGEL**, Cirencester **Ref:**YH06750
- **KINGTON, JOHN**, Newent **Ref:**YH08213
- **LOCOS SADDLERY**, Tetbury **Ref:**YH08765
- **MANGAN & WEBB**, Cheltenham **Ref:**YH09076
- **MORETON SADDLERY**, Moreton In Marsh **Ref:**YH09790
- **PRESTBURY PK EQUINE SUPPLIES**, Cheltenham **Ref:**YH11360
- **ROXTON SPORTING**, Cirencester **Ref:**YH12177
- **STROUD FARM SERVICES**, Stroud **Ref:**YH13586
- **STROUD SADDLERY**, Stroud **Ref:**YH13588
- **SYDNEY FREE**, Cirencester **Ref:**YH13721
- **TEWKESBURY SADDLERY**, Tewkesbury **Ref:**YH13969

GLOUCESTERSHIRE (SOUTH)

- **BIDWELLS OF COGMILLS**, Frampton Cotterell **Ref:**YH01400
- **PORTERS**, Winterbourne **Ref:**YH11287
- **SODBURY VALE EQUESTRIAN SUP**, Stoke Gifford **Ref:**YH13051
- **STYLE PRODUCTS**, Mangotsfield **Ref:**YH13618
- **TACK ROOM**, Chipping Sodbury **Ref:**YH13799

GUERNSEY

- **GUERNSEY**, St Sampsons **Ref:**YH06182
- **LA CARRIERE**, St Sampson **Ref:**YH08331

HAMPSHIRE

- **BEGGARS ROOST SADDLERY**, Eastleigh **Ref:**YH01195
- **CALCUTT & SONS**, Winchester **Ref:**YH02425
- **CLASSIC COLLECTION**, Alresford **Ref:**YH02983
- **DAVID CATLIN**, Southampton **Ref:**YH03916
- **DECOY POND SADDLERY**, Beaulieu **Ref:**YH04013
- **DENE COUNTRY STORES**, Liphook **Ref:**YH04041
- **DIVOTS SADDLERY**, Basingstoke **Ref:**YH04137
- **FAIR OAK BARN SADDLERY**, Eastleigh **Ref:**YH05012
- **FOREST COUNTRYWEAR**, Fordingbridge **Ref:**YH05333
- **FORESTER SADDLES**, Lyndhurst **Ref:**YH05354
- **GAWTHORPE SADDLERS**, Hook **Ref:**YH05679
- **HAMPSHIRE SADDLERY**, Southampton **Ref:**YH06367
- **HANSFORDS**, Fareham **Ref:**YH06397
- **HARNESS ROOM**, Lymington **Ref:**YH06447
- **HASKER, GLENN M**, Ringwood **Ref:**YH06521
- **HIGHET JASPER SADDLER**, Farnborough **Ref:**YH06783
- **HILBURY SADDLERY**, Andover **Ref:**YH06806
- **HOPLANDS EQUESTRIAN**, Stockbridge **Ref:**YH07058
- **HORSE CLOTHING**, Waterlooville **Ref:**YH07114
- **HORSE-E-THINGS**, Fordingbridge **Ref:**YH07153
- **INCH'S SADDLERY**, Tadley **Ref:**YH07408
- **JOHN WILLIE'S SADDLE ROOM**, Ringwood **Ref:**YH07817
- **LESLEY RALPH SADDLER**, Basingstoke **Ref:**YH08557
- **LITTLE LONDON TACK SHOP**, Tadley **Ref:**YH08691
- **LYNDHURST COUNTRY CLOTHING**, Lyndhurst **Ref:**YH08927
- **M E HOWITT SADDLERS**, Alton **Ref:**YH08960
- **MALCOLM DUNNING SADDLERY**, Waterlooville **Ref:**YH09044
- **MCNEILL, IAN**, Alton **Ref:**YH09402
- **NORRIS & SONS**, Brockenhurst **Ref:**YH10244
- **OLD BASING SADDLERY**, Basingstoke **Ref:**YH10450
- **PARK FARM SADDLERY**, Basingstoke **Ref:**YH10723
- **PETERSFIELD SADDLERY**, Petersfield **Ref:**YH11022
- **RANDALL, MONICA**, Fleet **Ref:**YH11628
- **RAY'S SADDLESHOP**, Southampton **Ref:**YH11677
- **ROBJENT'S**, Stockbridge **Ref:**YH12007
- **SADDLERS WORKSHOP**, Liphook **Ref:**YH12362
- **SADDLES, SADDLES, SADDLES**, Portsmouth **Ref:**YH12371
- **SANDILANDS FARM FEEDS**, Petersfield **Ref:**YH12414
- **SCATS**, Winchester **Ref:**YH12491
- **SHAPLEY RANCH EQUINE ACCESS**, Hartley Wintney **Ref:**YH12674
- **SIMES & SON**, Aldershot **Ref:**YH12819
- **SOLENT**, Southampton **Ref:**YH13054
- **STANWELLS COUNTRY**, Brockenhurst **Ref:**YH13384
- **WELLINGTON RIDING**, Hook **Ref:**YH15075
- **WESSEX FARM & EQUI-PRODUCTS**, Ringwood **Ref:**YH15118
- **WORLD BETA EQUESTRIAN**, Waterlooville **Ref:**YH15784
- **WRIGHTS OF ROMSEY**, Romsey **Ref:**YH15846

HEREFORDSHIRE

- **BROMYARD**, Bromyard **Ref:**YH02027
- **CONCEPT SADDLERY**, Hereford **Ref:**YH03223
- **COUNTRYWIDE**, Hereford **Ref:**YH03445
- **EDWARDS BLACK SADDLERY**, Holmer **Ref:**YH04571
- **HORSE & JOCKEY**, Hereford **Ref:**YH07093
- **HORSE BEAUTIQUE**, Leominster **Ref:**YH07103
- **HORSEWISE**, Hereford **Ref:**YH07178
- **JONES, R M**, Cattle Market **Ref:**YH07925
- **JONES, R M**, Hay-on-Wye **Ref:**YH07924
- **PHIL TURNER SADDLERY**, Hoarwithy **Ref:**YH11041
- **PHILIP MORRIS & SON**, Hereford **Ref:**YH11045
- **RIDDLE SADDLERY**, Leominster **Ref:**YH11841
- **ROSS FEED**, Ross-on-Wye **Ref:**YH12114
- **SHEEPCOTE EQUESTRIAN**, Hereford **Ref:**YH12695
- **SHIRES EQUESTRIAN**, Leominster **Ref:**YH12755

HERTFORDSHIRE

- **ALAN BROWN/COUNTRY SPORTS**, Hitchin **Ref:**YH00237
- **AMBRIDGE SADDLERY**, Stevenage **Ref:**YH00361
- **CLARK'S EQUESTRIAN**, Stevenage **Ref:**YH02979
- **COLEMAN CROFT**, St Albans **Ref:**YH03163
- **FIELD SPORTS**, Borehamwood **Ref:**YH05186
- **GREINAN FARM**, Kings Langley **Ref:**YH06122
- **HILL, ALAN**, Ware **Ref:**YH06825
- **MALAN GODDARD**, Whaddon **Ref:**YH09043
- **OLD BARN SADDLERY**, Hoddesdon **Ref:**YH10448
- **PATCHETTS**, Watford **Ref:**YH10815
- **PIX FARM FEED STORE**, Hemel Hempstead **Ref:**YH11159
- **PONSBOURNE RIDING CTRE**, Hertford **Ref:**YH11224
- **RED RAE SADDLERY CTRE**, Ware **Ref:**YH11704
- **ROCHFORD & BARBER**, Hertford **Ref:**YH12022
- **SADDLERY**, Royston **Ref:**YH12363
- **SALES OF SANDON**, Buntingford **Ref:**YH12386
- **SANDON SADDLERY**, Buntingford **Ref:**YH12415
- **STABLE COLOURS**, Welwyn **Ref:**YH13289
- **TEE JAY EQUESTRIAN**, Hitchin **Ref:**YH13933
- **W PAGE & SON**, Cole Green **Ref:**YH14786
- **WATFORD EQUESTRIAN CTRE**, Watford **Ref:**YH14976
- **WIDESERVE**, Welwyn **Ref:**YH15391
- **WILKINSON, MARTIN**, St Albans **Ref:**YH15423

ISLE OF MAN

- **MANX RIDING SUPPLIES**, Onchan **Ref:**YH09128

ISLE OF WIGHT

- **BELLWOOD SADDLERY**, Cowes **Ref:**YH01243
- **EQUESTRIAN WORLD**, Cowes **Ref:**YH04721

JERSEY

- **BARETTE & GRUCHY**, St John **Ref:**YH00930
- **HAIE FLEURIE**, Channel Isles **Ref:**YH06280
- **LE MAISTRE BROS**, Trinity **Ref:**YH08490
- **SORREL SADDLERY**, St Peter **Ref:**YH13071

KENT

- **ARIZONAS**, Tunbridge Wells **Ref:**YH00527
- **BIRCHALLS THE RIDING SHOP**, Maidstone **Ref:**YH01431
- **CHASKIT HSE**, Tunbridge Wells **Ref:**YH02787
- **CLASSIC EQUINE PRODUCTS**, Beckenham **Ref:**YH02987
- **CLIP CLOP SHOP**, Rochester **Ref:**YH03044
- **DICKSON, PENNY**, Rochester **Ref:**YH04117
- **EMPORIUM**, Ashford **Ref:**YH04659
- **FARMER, M J P**, Tonbridge **Ref:**YH05059
- **FARNINGHAM SADDLERY**, Farningham **Ref:**YH05083
- **FRANDHAM KENNELS & TACK SHOP**, Dover **Ref:**YH05454
- **FROGPOOL MANOR SADDLERY**, Chislehurst **Ref:**YH05515
- **HOBBS PARKER**, Ashford **Ref:**YH06894
- **HUSBANDS SADDLERY**, West Malling **Ref:**YH07325
- **JUST THE BIT**, Maidstone **Ref:**YH07977
- **KENT WOOL GROWERS**, Ashford **Ref:**YH08083
- **LANGSTON & SON**, Tunbridge Wells **Ref:**YH08415
- **LONGFIELD & APPLEDORE**, Longfield **Ref:**YH08810
- **M HANCOCK & SON**, Ashford **Ref:**YH08966
- **MANSTON RIDING CTRE**, Ramsgate **Ref:**YH09126
- **MEREWORTH STORES & TACK SHOP**, Mereworth **Ref:**YH09472
- **MINSTER SADDLERY**, Ramsgate **Ref:**YH09652
- **OLD MILL EQUESTRIAN CTRE**, Swanley **Ref:**YH10467
- **PARK PETS**, Deal **Ref:**YH10734
- **SADDLE RACK**, Folkestone **Ref:**YH12345
- **SADDLERY & GUN ROOM**, Westerham **Ref:**YH12365
- **SANDWICH ANIMAL FEEDS**, Sandwich **Ref:**YH12422
- **SNOWBALL, BART J**, Maidstone **Ref:**YH13038
- **SPEEDGATE FARM**, Longfield **Ref:**YH13191
- **TACK-STITCH**, Tunbridge Wells **Ref:**YH13819
- **TUNBRIDGE WELLS TACK ROOM**, Tunbridge Wells **Ref:**YH14460
- **WEALDEN SADDLERY**, Tonbridge **Ref:**YH15020
- **WILLOW FARM**, Faversham **Ref:**YH15497
- **WM LILLICO & SONS**, Maidstone **Ref:**YH15641

LANCASHIRE

- **1ST CHOICE PET SUPPLIES**, Burnley Ref:YH00001
- **BEESLEYS OF BALLAM**, Lytham Ref:YH01190
- **BLACK HORSE**, Wigan Ref:YH01463
- **CANTER-ON TACK SHOP**, Darwen Ref:YH02511
- **CAUSEWAY EQUESTRIAN**, Ormskirk Ref:YH02662
- **CROSTONS FARM RIDING & LIVERY**, Chorley Ref:YH03672
- **DERBY HSE SADDLERY**, Wigan Ref:YH04071
- **EARNSDALE FARM RIDING SCHOOL**, Darwen Ref:YH04458
- **EDEN PRODUCE**, Barnoldswick Ref:YH04548
- **EQUESTRIANA**, Blackburn Ref:YH04724
- **HACKETTS SADDLERY**, Blackpool Ref:YH06253
- **HERD HSE RIDING SCHOOL**, Burnley Ref:YH06699
- **HORSE BITS SADDLERY**, Bury Ref:YH07106
- **LONGSDALE, C L**, Blackburn Ref:YH08816
- **LONGTON EQUESTRIAN CTRE**, Preston Ref:YH08819
- **MILLER SADDLERY**, Rossendale Ref:YH09602
- **OLD RUNNEL FARM**, Blackpool Ref:YH10475
- **OSWALDTWISTLE ANIMAL FEEDS**, Oswaldtwistle Ref:YH10575
- **PAUL HUTCHINSON**, Ormskirk Ref:YH10832
- **R HACKWORTH ANIMAL FEEDS**, Rochdale Ref:YH11544
- **READWOOD**, Burnley Ref:YH11684
- **ROBINSONS COUNTRY LEISURE**, Wigan Ref:YH12004
- **SNAFFLES**, Halifax Ref:YH13020
- **TAYLORS EQUESTRIAN**, Burnley Ref:YH13916
- **TROTTERS**, Burnley Ref:YH14408
- **WADDINGTON FARM**, Darwen Ref:YH14807

LEICESTERSHIRE

- **A & H GREEN HARNESSMAKERS**, Loughborough Ref:YH00010
- **APOLLO SADDLERY**, Lutterworth Ref:YH00474
- **BROWN, J W**, Melton Mowbray Ref:YH02115
- **C E COOK & SONS**, Leicester Ref:YH02369
- **CLOTHES HORSE**, Leicester Ref:YH03062
- **DADLYNGTON FIELD**, Nuneaton Ref:YH03815
- **GRIMSTON SADDLERY**, Melton Mowbray Ref:YH06145
- **HURST SADDLERS**, Leicester Ref:YH07316
- **JANES HANDMADE SADDLERY**, Melton Mowbray Ref:YH07695
- **N W F COUNTRYSTORE**, Melton Mowbray Ref:YH09997
- **PEATLING SADDLERY**, Lutterworth Ref:YH10887
- **REARSBY LODGE FEEDS**, Leicester Ref:YH11687
- **S & J SADDLERY**, Melton Mowbray Ref:YH12312
- **S MILNER & SON**, Melton Mowbray Ref:YH12330
- **SCHOOL OF NATIONAL EQUITATION**, Loughborough Ref:YH12521
- **SHARNFORD LODGE FEEDS/TACK**, Hinckley Ref:YH12676
- **STABLES**, Hinckley Ref:YH13307

LINCOLNSHIRE

- **A W RHOADES SADDLERY**, Market Rasen Ref:YH00068
- **BARNACK CTRY STORE**, Stamford Ref:YH00964
- **BETTER-TACK**, Spalding Ref:YH01334
- **BOSTON HORSE SUPPLIES**, Boston Ref:YH01659
- **COBBLETHORNS SADDLERY**, Grantham Ref:YH03112
- **COTTAGE SADDLERY**, Boston Ref:YH03379
- **HECKINGTON SUPPLIES**, Heckington Ref:YH06638
- **MANOR STABLES CRAFT WORKSHOPS**, Grantham Ref:YH09119
- **MOULTON PET STORES**, Spalding Ref:YH09884
- **POLLY PRODUCTS**, Horncastle Ref:YH11209
- **REDNIL EQUESTRIAN CTRE**, Lincoln Ref:YH11716
- **SAPPERTON STUD & SADDLERY**, Sleaford Ref:YH12431
- **SHEEPGATE TACK & TOGS**, Boston Ref:YH12697
- **SMILHAN, PETER**, Louth Ref:YH12930
- **SPORTING CHOICE**, Dunsby Ref:YH13224
- **SWALLOW SADDLERY**, Stamford Ref:YH13685
- **T M F ANIMAL FEEDS & SADDLERS**, Woodhall Spa Ref:YH13759
- **TACK BOX**, Lincoln Ref:YH13785
- **VOISE**, Allington Ref:YH14739
- **W N SHRIVE & SON**, Skegness Ref:YH14784
- **WINDRUSH SADDLERY**, Boston Ref:YH15570

LINCOLNSHIRE (NORTH EAST)

- **CLEE SADDLERY & LEATHERWORKS**, Cleethorpes Ref:YH03013
- **FOX MANIA**, Grimsby Ref:YH05424
- **THORNLEY, MARTIN**, Grimsby Ref:YH14071

LINCOLNSHIRE (NORTH)

- **CROWSTONS**, Scunthorpe Ref:YH03684
- **H SIMPSON & SON**, Scunthorpe Ref:YH06240
- **KILLINGHOLME**, Grimsby Ref:YH08143
- **MASON, D & M**, Scunthorpe Ref:YH09239

LONDON (GREATER)

- **A D L TACK & SADDLERY**, London Ref:YH00027
- **BELMONT RIDING CTRE**, London Ref:YH01249
- **BERNARD WEATHERILL**, London Ref:YH01310
- **CHASE SADDLERY**, Enfield Ref:YH02785
- **CLGE FARM SADDLERY & FEEDS**, Finchley Ref:YH03027
- **DECATHLON SPORTS & LEISURE**, London Ref:YH04009
- **EDWARD ROBERT SADDLERY**, Feltham Ref:YH04569
- **GOULDS GREEN**, Uxbridge Ref:YH05952
- **HOLLAND & HOLLAND**, Northwood Ref:YH06937
- **HORSE HOUSE**, Northwood Ref:YH07123
- **L F JOLLYES**, Enfield Ref:YH08319
- **RAWLE & SON**, London Ref:YH11663
- **RIDERS & SQUIRES**, London Ref:YH11855
- **SADDLERS SHOP**, London Ref:YH12361
- **SCHNIEDER RIDING BOOT**, London Ref:YH12515
- **W H GIDDEN**, London Ref:YH14770
- **WEST ESSEX & KERNOW SADDLERY**, Chingford Ref:YH15143

MANCHESTER (GREATER)

- **CRAINE, A**, Bolton Ref:YH03557
- **EQUITACK**, Bolton Ref:YH04823
- **GEO HOLLOWAY**, Ashton-under-Lyne Ref:YH05713
- **L FOR LEATHER**, Manchester Ref:YH08320
- **SMITHY**, Bolton Ref:YH13011
- **STERLING SPORTS SUPPLIES**, Manchester Ref:YH13432

MERSEYSIDE

- **DALE FARM SADDLERY**, Prescot Ref:YH03821
- **FORMBY SADDLERY**, Liverpool Ref:YH05373
- **MAYPOLE FARM**, Prescot Ref:YH09303
- **ROBINSONS COUNTRY LEISURE**, St Helens Ref:YH12005
- **THORNTON FARM LIVERY**, Wirral Ref:YH14073

MIDLANDS (WEST)

- **ALBRIGHTON FEEDS**, Wolverhampton Ref:YH00249
- **AMBLECOTE TACK EXCHANGE**, Stourbridge Ref:YH00360
- **ARABIAN SADDLE**, Walsall Ref:YH00492
- **ARMY & NAVY STORES**, Solihull Ref:YH00554
- **BARKER SADDLERY OF WALSALL**, Wolverhampton Ref:YH00937
- **BARRETTS OF FECKENHAM**, Wolverhampton Ref:YH01015
- **BEARLEY CROSS STABLES**, Solihull Ref:YH01121
- **BLACK COUNTRY SADDLERY**, Walsall Ref:YH01461
- **BROWNS**, Walsall Ref:YH02142
- **C V F**, Coventry Ref:YH02395
- **COBRA SADDLEMAKERS**, Walsall Ref:YH03117
- **COLT SADDLERY**, Walsall Ref:YH03201
- **COUNTY SADDLERY**, Walsall Ref:YH03491
- **DIAMOND SADDLERY**, Wolverhampton Ref:YH04104
- **FARRINGTONS SADDLE**, Walsall Ref:YH05095
- **FIELDHOUSE SADDLERY**, Walsall Ref:YH05194
- **GREENWAYS**, Birmingham Ref:YH06104
- **H W DABBS SADDLEMAKERS**, Walsall Ref:YH06245
- **HAWKINS SADDLERY**, Brierley Hill Ref:YH06547
- **HAZEL FARM**, Solihull Ref:YH06599
- **HOOPER'S SADDLERS SHOP**, Walsall Ref:YH07045
- **HORSE SHOP**, Cockshutts Lane Ref:YH07138
- **HORSESENSE**, Solihull Ref:YH07170
- **HOUND & HORSE**, Wythall Ref:YH07206
- **HUNTER SADDLERY**, Walsall Ref:YH07300
- **IRENES**, Wombourne Ref:YH07489
- **J R HORSEWEAR**, Stourbridge Ref:YH07609
- **J ROBERTS SADDLERY**, Halesowen Ref:YH07613
- **KINGS**, Walsall Ref:YH08192
- **KIRKLAND SADDLERY**, Walsall Ref:YH08236
- **MANE BRIDLES**, Walsall Ref:YH09072
- **MANOR SADDLES**, Walsall Ref:YH09118
- **OVERIDER**, Coventry Ref:YH10593
- **PADDOCK STORES**, Brierley Hill Ref:YH10671
- **PHOENIX**, Walsall Ref:YH11069
- **ROSE BANK STORES & SADDLERY**, Birmingham Ref:YH12089
- **SABRE LEATHER**, Walsall Ref:YH12339
- **SANDWELL VALLEY RIDING CTRE**, West Bromwich Ref:YH12421
- **SOUTH STAFFORDSHIRE SADDLERY**, Walsall Ref:YH13105
- **SOWERBYS OF STOURBRIDGE**, Stourbridge Ref:YH13167
- **SYMONDS SADDLERY**, Walsall Ref:YH13725
- **TOWNFIELD SADDLERS**, Coventry Ref:YH14296
- **UK SADDLES**, Walsall Ref:YH14550
- **WILLIAM POWELL & SON**, Birmingham Ref:YH15436
- **WORDSLEY SADDLERY**, Stourbridge Ref:YH15776
- **WORLDWIDE EQUESTRIAN**, Walsall Ref:YH15788

NORFOLK

- **BOJAN AT WARREN KENNELS**, Sheringham Ref:YH01601
- **BRUNDALL SADDLERY**, Norwich Ref:YH02156
- **CAISTER SADDLERY**, Caister On Sea Ref:YH02422
- **DEREHAM SADDLERY**, Dereham Ref:YH04073
- **EVERYTHING EQUESTRIAN**, Norwich Ref:YH04958
- **GEOFFREY GIBSON SADDLER**, Stibbard Ref:YH05716

- **GORLESTON TACK ROOM**, Great Yarmouth **Ref:**YH05934
- **GRANVILLE SADDLERY**, Norwich **Ref:**YH06016
- **GRANVILLE SADDLERY**, Wymondham **Ref:**YH06015
- **H & C BEART**, King's Lynn **Ref:**YH06207
- **HORSES IN SPORT**, Diss **Ref:**YH07169
- **HORSETALK**, King's Lynn **Ref:**YH07176
- **L A SADDLERY**, Great Yarmouth **Ref:**YH08313
- **MAY, JIM**, Wisbech **Ref:**YH09289
- **NORTH WALSHAM SADDLERY**, Norwich **Ref:**YH10284
- **PLAYBARN**, Poringland **Ref:**YH11169
- **SANDONS THE SADDLERY**, Dereham **Ref:**YH12416
- **TACK BARN**, Norwich **Ref:**YH13782
- **TOP TAK**, King's Lynn **Ref:**YH14238
- **TRACK & FIELD**, Dereham **Ref:**YH14307
- **WROXHAM SADDLERY**, Norwich **Ref:**YH15850

NORTHAMPTONSHIRE

- **ANDREW BOTTERILL SADDLER**, Wellingborough **Ref:**YH00389
- **EDENGATE SADDLERY**, Northampton **Ref:**YH04550
- **FLYING CHANGES**, Daventry **Ref:**YH05293
- **FOX HILL FARM EQUESTRIAN CTRE**, Northampton **Ref:**YH05422
- **GILDERS**, Kettering **Ref:**YH05762
- **GILDERS NORTHAMPTON**, Northampton **Ref:**YH05763
- **GOODTIMES LEISURE**, Kettering **Ref:**YH05909
- **GROOMERS**, Northampton **Ref:**YH06154
- **H T S EQUESTRIAN**, Wellingborough **Ref:**YH06242
- **HARLEY**, Daventry **Ref:**YH06436
- **HURSTFIELD SADDLERY**, Brackley **Ref:**YH07319
- **NORMAN & SPICER**, Daventry **Ref:**YH10235
- **O SHEPHERD & SON**, Brackley **Ref:**YH10366
- **PARKER, N**, Northampton **Ref:**YH10751
- **PET LOVE SUPPLIES**, Daventry **Ref:**YH11005
- **RIDERS INT**, Raunds **Ref:**YH11856
- **RIDING HIGH**, Towcester **Ref:**YH11882
- **SCHNIEDER RIDING BOOT**, Northampton **Ref:**YH12516
- **STUBBEN**, Corby **Ref:**YH13600
- **THORPE SADDLERY**, Kettering **Ref:**YH14094
- **TOWER FARM SADDLERS**, Northampton **Ref:**YH14273
- **UK RACING**, Daventry **Ref:**YH14548
- **WATTS & WATTS SADDLERY**, Northampton **Ref:**YH15003
- **WHITE & BISHOP**, Northampton **Ref:**YH15299

NORTHUMBERLAND

- **COOPER, SIMON**, Stocksfield **Ref:**YH03291
- **FARMWAY**, Morpeth **Ref:**YH05074
- **FORSYTH'S OF WOOLER**, Wooler **Ref:**YH05384
- **M E L**, Berwick-upon-Tweed **Ref:**YH08961
- **NORTHUMBRIAN SADDLERY**, Hexham **Ref:**YH10321
- **R L JOBSON & SON**, Alnwick **Ref:**YH11553
- **R L JOBSON & SON**, Berwick-upon-Tweed **Ref:**YH11552
- **RICKERBY**, Cornhill-on-Tweed **Ref:**YH11834
- **TACK DOCTOR**, Berwick-upon-Tweed **Ref:**YH13786
- **TYNE VALLEY SADDLERS**, Wylam **Ref:**YH14526
- **WILLOW WEAR**, Hexham **Ref:**YH15505

NOTTINGHAMSHIRE

- **ALADDIN CAVE**, Lowdham **Ref:**YH00236
- **BRIDLE WAY & GAUNTLEYS**, Newark **Ref:**YH01892
- **BROOMSIDE STUD**, Calverton **Ref:**YH02082
- **CARLTON FOREST**, Worksop **Ref:**YH02542
- **CHUKKA COVE**, Newark **Ref:**YH02893
- **DECATHLON SPORTS & LEISURE**, Nottingham **Ref:**YH04010
- **GRIFFIN, L M**, Thoroton **Ref:**YH06131
- **HOOF ALOOF**, Nottingham **Ref:**YH07025
- **NEWARK SADDLERY**, Newark **Ref:**YH10121
- **SADDLE RACK**, Nottingham **Ref:**YH12346
- **SADDLECRAFT**, Nottingham **Ref:**YH12355
- **SHELTON HSE SADDLERY**, Newark **Ref:**YH12705
- **ST CLEMENTS LODGE**, Nottingham **Ref:**YH13274
- **WELLOW PK**, Newark **Ref:**YH15077
- **WILMOTTS PET/SADDLERY STORES**, Nottingham **Ref:**YH15523

OXFORDSHIRE

- **ALICE NUTTGENS SADDLERS**, Henley-on-Thames **Ref:**YH00279
- **AMBRIDGE SADDLERY**, Watlington **Ref:**YH00362
- **ASTI STUD & SADDLERY**, Faringdon **Ref:**YH00633
- **BLAKES OF FRILFORD**, Abingdon **Ref:**YH01522
- **BLOOR, ANNE**, Banbury **Ref:**YH01557
- **CHARLBURY SADDLERY**, Chipping Norton **Ref:**YH02753
- **CHARLES HUNT & PARTNERS**, Wallingford **Ref:**YH02756
- **COOPER, S & J M**, Faringdon **Ref:**YH03290
- **DEFENCE CLOTHING & TEXTILE**, Didcot **Ref:**YH04024
- **DENCHWORTH**, Wantage **Ref:**YH04040
- **ELM OF BURFORD**, Burford **Ref:**YH04632
- **FIELD & FARM SADDLERS**, Bicester **Ref:**YH05182
- **FRIAR PK EQUESTRIAN SUP**, Henley-on-Thames **Ref:**YH05500
- **HAC-TAC**, Faringdon **Ref:**YH06259
- **JODS GALORE**, Henley-on-Thames **Ref:**YH07775
- **KEN LANGFORD SADDLERY**, Abingdon **Ref:**YH08058
- **KYLDANE FIELDSPORTS**, Charlbury **Ref:**YH08304
- **MAD HATTER**, Banbury **Ref:**YH09018
- **OUTWEAR**, Oxford **Ref:**YH10589
- **OXFORD BOOTSTORE**, Oxford **Ref:**YH10616
- **OXFORD HILL RUGS**, Witney **Ref:**YH10618
- **PETER SMITH SADDLERY**, Chipping Norton **Ref:**YH11015
- **SANSOMS SADDLERY**, Witney **Ref:**YH12429
- **STABLE GEAR**, Berrick Salome **Ref:**YH13294
- **TACK & FEED SUPPLIES**, Didcot **Ref:**YH13776
- **TEDMAN HARNESS**, Wheatley **Ref:**YH13932
- **W F S COUNTRY**, Witney **Ref:**YH14766
- **WESTFIELD SADDLERY**, Chipping Norton **Ref:**YH15213
- **WHITE HORSE COUNTRY WEAR**, Faringdon **Ref:**YH15307

RUTLAND

- **JOHNSON, SALLY**, Oakham **Ref:**YH07839
- **UPPINGHAM DRESS AGENCY**, Uppingham **Ref:**YH14610

SHROPSHIRE

- **COUNTRYWIDE STORES**, Bridgnorth **Ref:**YH03469
- **CRAZY HORSE SADDLERY**, Ludlow **Ref:**YH03582
- **EVANS, J C**, Shrewsbury **Ref:**YH04922
- **HADNELL SADDLERY**, Shrewsbury **Ref:**YH06270
- **HOORAY HENRY'S**, Much Wenlock **Ref:**YH07046
- **HORSE & COUNTRY**, Newport **Ref:**YH07086
- **HORSE SHOP**, Bridgnorth **Ref:**YH07139
- **HORSE SHOP**, Telford **Ref:**YH07140
- **HOUSEMAKERS**, Whitchurch **Ref:**YH07210
- **LLOYDS ANIMAL FEEDS**, Ludlow **Ref:**YH08745
- **N W F COUNTRYSTORE**, Market Drayton **Ref:**YH09998
- **N W F COUNTRYSTORE**, Whitchurch **Ref:**YH09999
- **NUTSHELL**, Bridgnorth **Ref:**YH10360
- **POLLY FLINDERS**, Ludlow **Ref:**YH11207
- **PRINCE & DOYLE**, Ludlow **Ref:**YH11397
- **SHERBOURNE TACK**, Ludlow **Ref:**YH12719
- **STABLES SADDLERY & FEED SHOP**, Shrewsbury **Ref:**YH13313
- **T JONES & SON**, Oswestry **Ref:**YH13755
- **WILLIAM WILLIAMS**, Bridgnorth **Ref:**YH15439
- **WYKE OF SHIFNAL**, Shifnal **Ref:**YH15863

SOMERSET

- **A W MIDGLEY & SON**, Cheddar **Ref:**YH00067
- **BADCOCK & EVERED**, Watchet **Ref:**YH00774
- **BOWERS, HENRY**, Chard **Ref:**YH01707
- **COUNTRY TRADING**, Glastonbury **Ref:**YH03432
- **HILLSIDE SADDLERS**, Yeovil **Ref:**YH06854
- **MCCOY SADDLERY**, Minehead **Ref:**YH09334
- **MOLE VALLEY FARMERS**, Frome **Ref:**YH09711
- **POPHAMS**, Highbridge **Ref:**YH11268
- **RICH & SON**, Bridgwater **Ref:**YH11798
- **RIDEMOOR**, Wincanton **Ref:**YH11852
- **ROSE MILL FEEDS**, Ilminster **Ref:**YH12094
- **SARAH ANHOLT**, Bridgwater **Ref:**YH12433
- **STABLE DOOR TRADING**, Wrantage **Ref:**YH13292
- **STAX SADDLERY**, Montacute **Ref:**YH13406
- **THORNEY COPSE**, Wincanton **Ref:**YH14066
- **UNICORN SADDLERY**, Taunton **Ref:**YH14569
- **W.E.S GARRETT MASTER SADDLERS**, Cheddar **Ref:**YH14803

SOMERSET (NORTH)

- **MURPHYS SADDLERY**, Weston-Super-Mare **Ref:**YH09961
- **VOWLES RIDING STABLES**, Weston-Super-Mare **Ref:**YH14744

STAFFORDSHIRE

- **ABNALLS FARM**, Lichfield **Ref:**YH00133
- **BOLTON GATE SADDLERY**, Stoke-on-Trent **Ref:**YH01609
- **C A DAVIES & SONS**, Uttoxeter **Ref:**YH02361
- **COPPICE EQUESTRIAN SADDLERY**, Farley **Ref:**YH03303
- **DOSTHILL SADDLERY**, Tamworth **Ref:**YH04209
- **EQUI TEC**, Dudley **Ref:**YH04729
- **FRANCES ANN BROWN SADDLERY**, Stafford **Ref:**YH05444
- **GOTHERSLEY FARM**, Stourbridge **Ref:**YH05945
- **H WOOLLEY & SON**, Uttoxeter **Ref:**YH06247
- **HORSEY THINGS**, Eccleshall **Ref:**YH07184
- **LARKHILL SADDLERY**, Burton-on-Trent **Ref:**YH08432
- **M & J SADDLERY**, Lichfield **Ref:**YH08947
- **PEGASUS SADDLERY**, Newcastle **Ref:**YH10907
- **POSH PONIES**, Stoke-on-Trent **Ref:**YH11297
- **SEABROOK FEEDS**, Sedgley **Ref:**YH12580
- **SMITH & MORRIS COUNTRY STORE**, Newcastle **Ref:**YH12933
- **WOODCROFT SADDLERS**, Stafford **Ref:**YH15681

SUFFOLK

- **BALLINGDON SADDLERY**, Sudbury **Ref:**YH00857
- **BRIDLE PATH**, Bury St Edmunds **Ref:**YH01891
- **D & D EQUESTRIAN**, Lowestoft **Ref:**YH03768
- **GIBBINS, J & C**, Woodbridge **Ref:**YH05737
- **GIBSON SADDLERS**, Newmarket **Ref:**YH05746
- **GOLDING & SON**, Newmarket **Ref:**YH05891
- **HORSE BITS**, Woodbridge **Ref:**YH07105
- **HORSE REQUISITES**, Newmarket **Ref:**YH07132
- **HORSESHOES**, Wrentham **Ref:**YH07174
- **LINKWOOD EQUESTIAN**, Bury St Edmunds **Ref:**YH08665

LONG MELFORD, Sudbury **Ref:**YH08799
MARCH EQUESTRIAN FRAMLINGHAM, Woodbridge **Ref:**YH09140
MILL SADDLERY, Stowmarket **Ref:**YH09587
R MILES SADDLER & HARNESS, Woodbridge **Ref:**YH11557
REYNOLDS, GERRY, Newmarket **Ref:**YH11778
RIDE AWAY SADDLERY, Ipswich **Ref:**YH11846
RIDE 'N' DRIVE EQUESTRIAN SUP, Beccles **Ref:**YH11848
RYLAND SADDLERS, Newmarket **Ref:**YH12305
STOKE BY CLARE EQUESTRIAN CTRE, Sudbury **Ref:**YH13501
SUFFOLK SADDLES, Ipswich **Ref:**YH13626

SURREY

ANNA'S CTRY STORE, Farnham **Ref:**YH00455
BITS & PIECES, Sunbury-on-Thames **Ref:**YH01457
BROOMELLS WORKSHOP, Dorking **Ref:**YH02077
BUTTONS SADDLERY, Woking **Ref:**YH02337
CLANDON MANOR SUPPLIES, Guildford **Ref:**YH02942
DORKING SADDLERY, Dorking **Ref:**YH04201
FARNHAM SADDLERS, Farnham **Ref:**YH05082
HASTILOW COMPETITION SADDLES, Godalming **Ref:**YH06526
HENGEST FARM SHOP, Banstead **Ref:**YH06672
INJURED RIDERS FUND, Cranleigh **Ref:**YH07458
LESTER BOWDEN, Epsom **Ref:**YH08562
LETHERS OF BROCKHAM, Betchworth **Ref:**YH08568
LETHERS OF MERSTHAM, Redhill **Ref:**YH08569
MANOR SADDLERY, Guildford **Ref:**YH09117
PETS ON PARADE, Claygate **Ref:**YH11030
RIDE & DRIVE, Horne **Ref:**YH11842
UNICORN LEATHER SADDLERY, Caterham **Ref:**YH14566
WOLDINGHAM SADDLERS, Caterham **Ref:**YH15647

SUSSEX (EAST)

ACRE & ASHDOWN FEEDS, Crowborough **Ref:**YH00156
ANDREW REILLY, Forest Row **Ref:**YH00392
BLUE RIDGE WESTERN SADDLERY, Hailsham **Ref:**YH01568
DANDY BUSH SADDLERY, Battle **Ref:**YH03863
ELMS SADDLERY & LIVERIES, Icklesham **Ref:**YH04638
FARTHING SADDLERY, Heathfield **Ref:**YH05100
H B SADDLERY, Rye **Ref:**YH06212
HORSE HOUSE, Hailsham **Ref:**YH07124
POLEGATE SADDLERY, Polegate **Ref:**YH11198
SIAN SADDLERY, Uckfield **Ref:**YH12777
SOMETHING DIFFERENT, Uckfield **Ref:**YH13068
STERLING SADDLERY, Robertsbridge **Ref:**YH13431
STEVENS, LEONARD, Eastbourne **Ref:**YH13445
TACK ROOM, Robertsbridge **Ref:**YH13802
WINDMILL FEEDS & SADDLERY, Heathfield **Ref:**YH15565
WORK SHOP, Heathfield **Ref:**YH15777

SUSSEX (WEST)

AGRIVET - KWG, Haywards Heath **Ref:**YH00204
BRENDON HORSE & RIDER, Brighton **Ref:**YH01837
BURGESS & RANDALL, Pulborough **Ref:**YH02242
COVERT, Petworth **Ref:**YH03519
DIAMOND SADDLERY, Hassocks **Ref:**YH04105
DRAGONFLY SADDLERY, Hassocks **Ref:**YH04252
E M C, Shoreham By Sea **Ref:**YH04415
EDGINGTONS, Hassocks **Ref:**YH04557
EQUITOGS, Billingshurst **Ref:**YH04830
EQUITOGS, Littlehampton **Ref:**YH04829
FELPHAM STABLES TACKROOM, Bognor Regis **Ref:**YH05136
GEOFF DEAN SADDLERY, Worthing **Ref:**YH05714
GOODROWES OF CHICHESTER, Chichester **Ref:**YH05908
HORACE FULLER, Horsham **Ref:**YH07063
HORSE BOX, Horsham **Ref:**YH07110
IFIELD PARK FEED TACK & WEAR, Crawley **Ref:**YH07389
LIGHTS, Brighton **Ref:**YH08616
M & A OUTDOOR CLOTHING, Crawley **Ref:**YH08942
MIDHURST SHOES, Midhurst **Ref:**YH09553
NORTON HIND SADDLERY, Arundel **Ref:**YH10330
OAKDENE SADDLERY, Hassocks **Ref:**YH10374
OLDWICK SADDLERY, Chichester **Ref:**YH10495
OPEN COUNTRY, Petworth **Ref:**YH10524
OUTDOORS - SCOUT SHOPS, Lancing **Ref:**YH10588
PARKERS, Horsham **Ref:**YH10753
PENFOLD & SONS, Haywards Heath **Ref:**YH10934
PENFOLDS OF CUCKFIELD, Haywards Heath **Ref:**YH10935
ROXTON, Midhurst **Ref:**YH12176
ROXTON SPORTING, Midhurst **Ref:**YH12178
SNOOTY FOX COUNTRY STORE, Petworth **Ref:**YH13035
SNOWHILL SADDLERY, Chichester **Ref:**YH13044
STOCKLEY TRADING, Littlehampton **Ref:**YH13495
T C TACK & THINGS, Burgess Hill **Ref:**YH13733
T E FRASER & SON, Midhurst **Ref:**YH13736
TACK A ROUND SADDLERY, Billingshurst **Ref:**YH13781
ZARA STUD, Chichester **Ref:**YH15951

TYNE AND WEAR

CLASSIC EQUESTRIAN, Houghton Le Spring **Ref:**YH02986
DANCESPORT & EQUESTRIAN, Gateshead **Ref:**YH03861
HORSE-WORLD, Gateshead **Ref:**YH07180
LE PREVO LEATHERS, Newcastle-upon-Tyne **Ref:**YH08491
LEATHER SHOP, Sunderland **Ref:**YH08504
MARDEN SADDLERY, Newcastle-upon-Tyne **Ref:**YH09146
PETMEALS, Boldon Colliery **Ref:**YH11028
RIDERS, North Shields **Ref:**YH11854
S & S SADDLERY, Sunderland **Ref:**YH12313
SADDLE SHOP, Gateshead **Ref:**YH12350
WEBSTER, J R, Newcastle-upon-Tyne **Ref:**YH15040

WARWICKSHIRE

A & J SADDLERY, Southam **Ref:**YH00012
ALCESTER RIDING SUPPLIES, Alcester **Ref:**YH00251
BROADHEATH SADDLERY, Warwick **Ref:**YH01998
COLEMAN, ROBIN, Kenilworth **Ref:**YH03164
COUNTRY PURSUIT, Warwick **Ref:**YH03420
EDWARDS' SADDLERY, Bidford On Avon **Ref:**YH04574
HOCKLEY HEATH RIDING SUPPLIES, Solihull **Ref:**YH06904
JODS, DOBBIES, Coventry **Ref:**YH07776
LYNMARI TACK & ACCESSORIES, Solihull **Ref:**YH08932
MONKSPATH SADDLERY, Solihull **Ref:**YH09727
NICHOLSON, CHERYL, Coventry **Ref:**YH10193
PEBWORTH VALE SADDLERY, Stratford-upon-Avon **Ref:**YH10890
PITTERN HILL, Warwick **Ref:**YH11155
RASCALS OF WARWICK, Warwick **Ref:**YH11644
RED HSE FARM LIVERY STABLES, Leamington Spa **Ref:**YH11696
RIMELL, Shipston-on-Stour **Ref:**YH11896
RUGWASH 2000, Warwick **Ref:**YH12224
SADDLERY SHOP, Stratford **Ref:**YH12367
SAXON TACK & TAILS, Rugby **Ref:**YH12471
TOWER FARM SADDLERS, Rugby **Ref:**YH14274
WAVERLEY EQUESTRIAN CTRE, Leamington Spa **Ref:**YH15011

WILTSHIRE

COUNTRY PURSUITS, Cricklade **Ref:**YH03422
DALLAS INDUSTRIES, Market Lavington **Ref:**YH03842
DAVID FARMER SADDLERY, Chippenham **Ref:**YH03919
EASTON GREY SADDLERS, Malmesbury **Ref:**YH04514
ELMGROVE SADDLERY, Swindon **Ref:**YH04636
EQUESPORT, Calne **Ref:**YH04687
EQUIFOR, Marlborough **Ref:**YH04746
EQUINOVA, Salisbury **Ref:**YH04814
FREDERICK J CHANDLER, Marlborough **Ref:**YH05478
GRANT BARNES & SON, Malmesbury **Ref:**YH06009
GREENFIELDS, Salisbury **Ref:**YH06083
HURDCOTT LIVERY STABLES, Salisbury **Ref:**YH07311
JUMPERS HORSELINE, Wootton Bassett **Ref:**YH07966
KEVINS MENSWEAR, Westbury **Ref:**YH08111
OLD DAIRY SADDLERY LTD, Swindon **Ref:**YH10454
SADDLERY, Swindon **Ref:**YH12364
SEG, Calne **Ref:**YH12611
SPORT & LEISURE, Malmesbury **Ref:**YH13217
STABLEWARE, Marlborough **Ref:**YH13314
SYDNEY INGRAM & SON, Salisbury **Ref:**YH13722
T G JEARY, Calne **Ref:**YH13741
WARMINSTER SADDLERY, Warminster **Ref:**YH14923
WHISTLEY FORGE SADDLERY, Devizes **Ref:**YH15286
WHITE HORSE SADDLERY, Salisbury **Ref:**YH15313
WYLYE VALLEY HORSE, Codford **Ref:**YH15867

WORCESTERSHIRE

BROADCLOSE LIVERY, Worcester **Ref:**YH01993
BROMSGROVE SADDLERY, Bromsgrove **Ref:**YH02026
COACH HSE SADDLERY, Hanley Castle **Ref:**YH03103
COTTAGE INDUSTRIES, Droitwich **Ref:**YH03377
COUNTRY CLASSICS, Droitwich **Ref:**YH03400
COUNTRYWIDE, Worcester **Ref:**YH03446
COUNTRYWIDE STORES, Evesham **Ref:**YH03483
DONNA LEIGH SADDLERY, Kidderminster **Ref:**YH04185
EQUIMIX, Stourport-on-Severn **Ref:**YH04756
F DURRANT & SONS, Worcester **Ref:**YH04990
GEO HEAPHY & SONS, Redditch **Ref:**YH05712
HORSEWISE CLOTHING, Worcester **Ref:**YH07179
JUST LEATHER, Worcester **Ref:**YH07975
LEA CASTLE SADDLERY, Kidderminster **Ref:**YH08494

- **LITTLE MALVERN SADDLE**, Malvern **Ref:**YH08692
- **LYNDHURST SADDLERY**, Worcester **Ref:**YH08929
- **MORGAN BLACKSMITHS**, Malvern **Ref:**YH09793
- **SAUNDERS SADDLERY**, Stourport-on-Severn **Ref:**YH12443
- **SPORTING HEIGHTS**, Kidderminster **Ref:**YH13227
- **TREEHOUSE**, Droitwich **Ref:**YH14360
- **WESCOMB SADDLERY**, Lower Strensham **Ref:**YH15116

YORKSHIRE (EAST)

- **BATA**, Beverley **Ref:**YH01062
- **DRIFFIELD DISCOUNT SADDLERY**, Driffield **Ref:**YH04273
- **ELM TREE TACK SHOP**, Halsham **Ref:**YH04635
- **HALL, ALEC W G**, Driffield **Ref:**YH06312
- **HORSE & RIDER TACK SHOP**, Hull **Ref:**YH07101
- **J J EQUESTRIAN TACK & TURNOUT**, Goole **Ref:**YH07591
- **K & B TACK SHOPS**, Bridlington **Ref:**YH07979
- **PATRICK WILKINSON**, Beverley **Ref:**YH10825
- **SMITHS ANIMAL & PET SUPPLIES**, Cottingham **Ref:**YH13006
- **STILLMEADOW TACK SHOP**, Hull **Ref:**YH13467
- **SWANLAND EQUESTRIAN CTRE**, North Ferriby **Ref:**YH13693
- **WYTON TACK SHOP**, Hull **Ref:**YH15877

YORKSHIRE (NORTH)

- **BEAVER HORSE SHOP**, Harrogate **Ref:**YH01143
- **BIT BANK**, Stokesley **Ref:**YH01454
- **BULLOCK, J A & F**, York **Ref:**YH02219
- **E K READMAN & SONS**, Scarborough **Ref:**YH04412
- **FRANCES BULLOCK'S SADDLERY**, Easingwold **Ref:**YH05446
- **GEORGE WOODALL & SONS**, Malton **Ref:**YH05722
- **GILLS SADDLERY & CANE**, Northallerton **Ref:**YH05787
- **GOLDIE, DAVID**, Skipton **Ref:**YH05887
- **GRANARY**, Whitby **Ref:**YH05980
- **HADFIELD, M A**, Malton **Ref:**YH06265
- **LANGTON HORSE WEAR**, Northallerton **Ref:**YH08416
- **R & R COUNTRY**, Selby **Ref:**YH11507
- **R C BLAND**, Harrogate **Ref:**YH11517
- **RIDE-AWAY**, York **Ref:**YH11850
- **ROBINSON**, Malton **Ref:**YH11985
- **SAM TURNER & SONS**, Northallerton **Ref:**YH12395
- **WHITE ROSE SADDLERY**, Malton **Ref:**YH15324
- **YORKSHIRE RIDING SUPPLIES**, York **Ref:**YH15923

YORKSHIRE (SOUTH)

- **ANNE WAINWRIGHT SADDLERY**, Doncaster **Ref:**YH00456
- **BITS & BOOTS**, Doncaster **Ref:**YH01456
- **DARKHORSE TINYTACK**, Barnsley **Ref:**YH03888
- **FROST, T**, Doncaster **Ref:**YH05521
- **HORSE & RIDER**, Doncaster **Ref:**YH07096
- **HORSE & RIDER**, Sheffield **Ref:**YH07097
- **HUNSHELF SADDLERY**, Sheffield **Ref:**YH07292
- **LEATHER LINES SADDLERY**, Rotherham **Ref:**YH08503
- **MILLVIEW**, Doncaster **Ref:**YH09638
- **MOORHOUSE**, Doncaster **Ref:**YH09774
- **MR ED'S**, Rotherham **Ref:**YH09915
- **PARKLANDS RIDING SCHOOL**, Sheffield **Ref:**YH10770
- **ROTHERHAM SADDLERY**, Rotherham **Ref:**YH12132
- **SMELTINGS FARM RIDING CTRE**, Sheffield **Ref:**YH12927
- **SNOWDON FARM RIDING SCHOOL**, Sheffield **Ref:**YH13040
- **THROSTLE NEST SADDLERY**, Barnsley **Ref:**YH14114
- **WILDSMITH SADDLERY**, Doncaster **Ref:**YH15410
- **WILDSMITHS**, Doncaster **Ref:**YH15412

YORKSHIRE (WEST)

- **ASTLEY RIDING CTRE**, Leeds **Ref:**YH00635
- **BARRETTS OF FECKENHAM**, Leeds **Ref:**YH01016
- **BRANDON FORGE SADDLERY**, Leeds **Ref:**YH01796
- **CLOVER HILL SADDLERY**, Halifax **Ref:**YH03069
- **COTTAGE INDUSTRIES**, Bradford **Ref:**YH03378
- **COUNTRY SUPPLIES**, Bradford **Ref:**YH03431
- **COURTYARD SADDLERY**, Collingham **Ref:**YH03512
- **DAYS PET SHOP**, Bradford **Ref:**YH03971
- **DERWENT OF LEEDS**, Holbeck **Ref:**YH04081
- **DISCOUNT SADDLERY**, Huddersfield **Ref:**YH04129
- **DRURY FARM SADDLERY**, Wakefield **Ref:**YH04294
- **EQUESTRIAN CLEARANCE CTRE**, Halifax **Ref:**YH04694
- **EQUITACK**, Wakefield **Ref:**YH04824
- **EQUITACK SADDLERY**, Wakefield **Ref:**YH04825
- **FOX SADDLERS**, Wetherby **Ref:**YH05425
- **GREAT CLOTHES**, Leeds **Ref:**YH06038
- **HILLAM FEEDS**, South Milford **Ref:**YH06836
- **HOLME VALLEY SPORTS**, Holmfirth **Ref:**YH06968
- **HOOVES EQUESTRIAN**, Bradford **Ref:**YH07047
- **HORSEBOX**, Pontefract **Ref:**YH07149
- **JACKSONS OF SILSDEN**, Keighley **Ref:**YH07657
- **KEBCOTE COUNTRYWEAR**, Hebden Bridge **Ref:**YH08021
- **KENYONS OF MORLEY**, Morley **Ref:**YH08095
- **LIVING WORLD**, Leeds **Ref:**YH08717
- **MIDDLESTOWN SADDLERY**, Wakefield **Ref:**YH09540
- **PANTOMIME HORSE**, Huddersfield **Ref:**YH10702
- **PENNINE FARM SVS**, Huddersfield **Ref:**YH10951
- **SADDLERY WORKSHOP**, Todmorden **Ref:**YH12370
- **SPENCER, ERIC**, Ilkley **Ref:**YH13198
- **STAPLETON SADDLERY**, Silsden **Ref:**YH13390
- **STIRRUPS**, Liversedge **Ref:**YH13480
- **TACK & TURNOUT EQUESTRIAN**, Huddersfield **Ref:**YH13780
- **TAILWAGGERS**, Chapel Allerton **Ref:**YH13821
- **THISTLETON FARM SADDLERY**, Knottingley **Ref:**YH14001
- **W C F COUNTRY CTRE**, Otley **Ref:**YH14756
- **WEST TACK**, Bradford **Ref:**YH15166
- **WILDERNESS VENTURES**, Featherstone **Ref:**YH15407
- **WILLIS WALKER**, Keighley **Ref:**YH15492
- **WOODS SADDLERY STORES**, Wakefield **Ref:**YH15733

STABLES/LIVERIES

BATH & SOMERSET (NORTH EAST)

- **HUNSTRETE RIDING SCHOOL**, Pensford **Ref:**YH07294
- **WELLOW TREKKING CTRE**, Bath **Ref:**YH15078

BEDFORDSHIRE

- **BACKNOE END EQUESTRIAN CTRE**, Bedford **Ref:**YH00771
- **BENNITT, CAROL**, Leighton Buzzard **Ref:**YH01276
- **BROOK STABLES**, Bedford **Ref:**YH02038
- **BROOKFIELD STABLES**, Biggleswade **Ref:**YH02050
- **BROOKLYN FARM STABLES**, Dunstable **Ref:**YH02060
- **BURMAN**, Biggleswade **Ref:**YH02262
- **CHALGRAVE MANOR**, Dunstable **Ref:**YH02710
- **CLGE EQUESTRIAN CTRE**, Bedford **Ref:**YH03025
- **DIJON STUD**, Colmworth **Ref:**YH04120
- **GRANSDEN HALL**, Sandy **Ref:**YH06005
- **GREEN END FARM**, Maulden **Ref:**YH06053
- **GROVE FARM**, Leighton Buzzard **Ref:**YH06162
- **HOME FIELD FARM**, Dunstable **Ref:**YH07001
- **LISCOMBE PK RIDING SCHOOL**, Leighton Buzzard **Ref:**YH08678
- **NEW HOUSE FARM**, Leighton Buzzard **Ref:**YH10108
- **NORTHALLETON**, Biggleswade **Ref:**YH10292
- **RAWDING, J & S M**, Leighton Buzzard **Ref:**YH11662
- **SWALLOWFIELD STABLES**, Dunstable **Ref:**YH13687
- **TINSLEYS RIDING SCHOOL**, Bedford **Ref:**YH14177
- **WOODSIDE STABLES**, Bedford **Ref:**YH15745

BERKSHIRE

- **ASTOR HOUSE AST**, Maidenhead **Ref:**YH00640
- **BANSTOCK HSE STABLES**, Maidenhead **Ref:**YH00910
- **BAROSSA FARM RIDING STABLES**, Reading **Ref:**YH00997
- **BEARWOOD RIDING CTRE**, Wokingham **Ref:**YH01123
- **BEAUMONT STABLES**, Ascot **Ref:**YH01132
- **BEAUMONT STABLES**, Maidenhead **Ref:**YH01133
- **BERKSHIRE CLGE OF AGRCLTRL**, Maidenhead **Ref:**YH01304
- **BERKSHIRE RIDING CTRE**, Windsor **Ref:**YH01306
- **BLACK, AUDREY**, Reading **Ref:**YH01470
- **CANE END STABLES**, Reading **Ref:**YH02498
- **CHECKENDON**, Reading **Ref:**YH02796
- **CLOUD STABLES**, Reading **Ref:**YH03066
- **COURTLANDS**, Wokingham **Ref:**YH03506
- **CRAGO, PAUL**, Reading **Ref:**YH03547
- **CROFT EQUESTRIAN CTRE**, Reading **Ref:**YH03614
- **CULLINGHOOD FARM**, Reading **Ref:**YH03705
- **DORNEY MEADOWS**, Maidenhead **Ref:**YH04203
- **EAST SOLEY E C 2000**, Hungerford **Ref:**YH04486
- **ERMIN ST STABLES**, Hungerford **Ref:**YH04851
- **FLETCHER, JAN**, Reading **Ref:**YH05279
- **GLENIFFER STABLES**, Maidenhead **Ref:**YH05837
- **GROVE FARM LIVERY STABLES**, Bracknell **Ref:**YH06167
- **HALL PLACE EQUESTRIAN CTRE**, Reading **Ref:**YH06307
- **HEATHLANDS RIDING CTRE**, Wokingham **Ref:**YH06634
- **ISAAC, C & D**, Newbury **Ref:**YH07511
- **J C & N C WARD**, Pangbourne **Ref:**YH07568
- **LAVENDER FARM LIVERY STABLES**, Slough **Ref:**YH08461
- **LOMAS, E A**, Maidenhead **Ref:**YH08779
- **LYFORDS MEADOW STABLES**, Ascot **Ref:**YH08917
- **MAPLE ASH LIVERY STABLES**, Newbury **Ref:**YH09130
- **MUSCHAMP STUD**, Slough **Ref:**YH09974
- **NEW FARM**, Newbury **Ref:**YH10095
- **PERRYS EQUESTRIAN SVS**, Bracknell **Ref:**YH10991
- **PINNOCKS WOOD EQUESTRIAN CTRE**, Maidenhead **Ref:**YH11139
- **PONY KIDS**, Hungerford **Ref:**YH11250

- **R HUTT & PARTNERS**, Maidenhead **Ref:**YH11546
- **ROBERTS, M & MARKS, K**, Hungerford **Ref:**YH11955
- **SNOWBALL FARM EQUESTRIAN CTRE**, Slough **Ref:**YH13037
- **SPANISH BIT RIDING SCHOOL**, Windsor **Ref:**YH13173
- **SUTTON COURT FARM**, Wokingham **Ref:**YH13671
- **TALLY HO STABLES**, Windsor **Ref:**YH13842
- **TIDMARSH STUD**, Reading **Ref:**YH14134
- **TREE TOPS PARTNERSHIP**, Bracknell **Ref:**YH14359
- **WEST END LIVERIES SUPPLIES**, Warfield **Ref:**YH15141
- **WHITELOCKS FARM RIDING SCHOOL**, Bracknell **Ref:**YH15350
- **WOKINGHAM EQUESTRIAN CTRE**, Wokingham **Ref:**YH15644
- **WOODHAVEN STUD**, Newbury **Ref:**YH15693
- **WOODLANDS**, Hungerford **Ref:**YH15705

BRISTOL

- **HAM FARM LIVERY & STUD**, Bristol **Ref:**YH06339
- **HICKS COMMON LIVERY STABLES**, Bristol **Ref:**YH06743
- **LEYLAND COURT**, Bristol **Ref:**YH08601
- **STANIORUM STABLES**, Bristol **Ref:**YH13366
- **SUNNYMEAD FARM**, Bristol **Ref:**YH13647
- **TYNINGS RIDING SCHOOL**, Bristol **Ref:**YH14527
- **URCHINWOOD MANOR EQUITATION**, Bristol **Ref:**YH14620
- **W E J KYNASTON & SONS**, Bristol **Ref:**YH14762
- **WAPLEY STABLES**, Bristol **Ref:**YH14895
- **WHITE CAT STABLES**, Bristol **Ref:**YH15301

BUCKINGHAMSHIRE

- **BANGORS PARK FARM**, Iver **Ref:**YH00883
- **BOCKMER LIVERY STABLES**, Marlow **Ref:**YH01590
- **BOCKMER LIVERY STABLES**, Marlow **Ref:**YH01591
- **BRAWLINGS FARM RIDING CTRE**, Gerrards Cross **Ref:**YH01819
- **BRYERLEY SPRINGS FARM**, Milton Keynes **Ref:**YH02171
- **CHEQUERS END EQUESTRIAN CTRE**, High Wycombe **Ref:**YH02812
- **CROSS KEYS FARM**, Gerrards Cross **Ref:**YH03649
- **D I Y LIVERY**, Great Missenden **Ref:**YH03785
- **EQUESTRIAN CTRE**, Amersham **Ref:**YH04696
- **EQUS HEALTH**, Aylesbury **Ref:**YH04835
- **FININGS FARM LIVERY YARD**, High Wycombe **Ref:**YH05212
- **FLAMSTEAD HORSE LIVERY**, Chesham **Ref:**YH05260
- **FLETCHER TOOGOOD**, Milton Keynes **Ref:**YH05272
- **GRANARY**, Milton Keynes **Ref:**YH05979
- **GROVE EQUITATION CTRE**, High Wycombe **Ref:**YH06161
- **HARTWELL RIDING STABLES**, Aylesbury **Ref:**YH06509
- **HUNTSMOOR PARK FARM**, Iver **Ref:**YH07309
- **LECKHAMPSTEAD WHARF STUD**, Buckingham **Ref:**YH08513
- **LOUGHTON MANOR**, Milton Keynes **Ref:**YH08840
- **LOWER SALDEN STABLES**, Milton Keynes **Ref:**YH08869
- **NEWBARN FARM STABLES**, Aylesbury **Ref:**YH10122
- **RADNAGE HOUSE**, High Wycombe **Ref:**YH11599
- **RIVERSMEET STABLES**, Newport Pagnell **Ref:**YH11930
- **STOWE RIDINGS**, Buckingham **Ref:**YH13538
- **WAYLANDS EQUESTRIAN CTRE**, Beaconsfield **Ref:**YH15016

CAMBRIDGESHIRE

- **BAKER, K M**, Huntingdon **Ref:**YH00822
- **BROOKFIELD LIVERY**, Cambridge **Ref:**YH02048
- **CONQUEST**, Farcet Fen **Ref:**YH03242
- **COUNTRY PURSUITS**, Cambridge **Ref:**YH03421
- **CROSS LEYS FARM**, Peterborough **Ref:**YH03650
- **DAYTON, KYM**, Wisbech **Ref:**YH03972
- **GRABELLA STUD**, Kentford **Ref:**YH05957
- **GRANGE FARM EQUESTRIAN CTRE**, Peterborough **Ref:**YH05988
- **GUYHIRN RIDING SCHOOL**, Wisbech **Ref:**YH06198
- **HAGGIS FARM STABLES**, Cambridge **Ref:**YH06278
- **HOCKLEY GREEN RIDING STABLES**, Cambridge **Ref:**YH06903
- **HOOK HSE**, March **Ref:**YH07035
- **KIDDY, S M**, Balsham **Ref:**YH08123
- **KNIGHTS END FARM**, March **Ref:**YH08268
- **NORTHBROOK EQUESTRIAN CTRE**, Huntingdon **Ref:**YH10294
- **OLD TIGER STABLES**, Ely **Ref:**YH10479
- **PARKHOUSE STABLES**, Cambridge **Ref:**YH10762
- **PINNER, TERRY**, Huntingdon **Ref:**YH11134
- **QUEENHOLME BLOODSTOCK STABLES**, Cambridge **Ref:**YH11491
- **RECTORY FARM**, Huntingdon **Ref:**YH11691
- **TOWER FARM DIY LIVERY**, Ely **Ref:**YH14272
- **WEST ANGLIA CLGE**, Milton **Ref:**YH15123
- **WITCHAM HSE FARM STUD**, Ely **Ref:**YH15617
- **WOODHURST**, Huntingdon **Ref:**YH15697

CHESHIRE

- **B 1ST RIDING SCHOOL**, Stockport **Ref:**YH00715
- **BARROW EQUESTRIAN CTRE**, Chester **Ref:**YH01027
- **CASTLE STABLES**, Malpas **Ref:**YH02635
- **CROFT RIDING CTRE**, Warrington **Ref:**YH03617
- **DINGLE BROOK FARM STABLES**, Macclesfield **Ref:**YH04125
- **FINLOW HILL STABLES**, Macclesfield **Ref:**YH05214
- **FOXES FARM & RIDING SCHOOL**, Ellesmere Port **Ref:**YH05431
- **GRANGE LIVERY STABLES**, Crewe **Ref:**YH05991
- **GREEN FARM FEEDS**, Crewe **Ref:**YH06055
- **HANKEY, R P**, Knutsford **Ref:**YH06387
- **HANNS HALL LIVERY**, Willaston **Ref:**YH06396
- **HATTON STABLES**, Warrington **Ref:**YH06533
- **HILL TOP FARM LIVERY STABLES**, Stockport **Ref:**YH06822
- **HOLLINSHEAD, DAWN**, Winsford **Ref:**YH06947
- **LAUREL FARM EQUESTRIAN CTRE**, Tarporley **Ref:**YH08457
- **M J HALE & SONS**, Willaston **Ref:**YH08968
- **MOBBERLEY RIDING SCHOOL**, Knutsford **Ref:**YH09687
- **NEW BARN FARM**, Knutsford **Ref:**YH10090
- **NEWHALL LIVERY**, Chester **Ref:**YH10136
- **OLDHAMS WOOD LIVERY**, Macclesfield **Ref:**YH10491
- **POOL BANK FARM STABLES**, Altrincham **Ref:**YH11260
- **REDGRAVE, CAROLE**, Wilmslow **Ref:**YH11711
- **SMITH & MORRIS**, Nantwich **Ref:**YH12932
- **SOUTHFIELDS FARM**, Pen-Y-Ffordd **Ref:**YH13153
- **STANNEY LANDS LIVERY**, Wilmslow **Ref:**YH13378
- **STOCKLEY FARM**, Warrington **Ref:**YH13494
- **SUTTON FIELDS FARM**, Runcorn **Ref:**YH13672
- **WHITE HALL LIVERY STABLES**, Little Budworth **Ref:**YH15304
- **WHITEGATE**, Northwich **Ref:**YH15337
- **WYNNE, M G**, Tarporley **Ref:**YH15872
- **YEW TREE FARM EQUESTRIAN CTRE**, Great Budworth **Ref:**YH15908

CLEVELAND

- **FOXHOLM STUD**, Stockton-on-Tees **Ref:**YH05437
- **LOWFIELD LIVERY STABLES**, Stockton-on-Tees **Ref:**YH08874
- **STAINSBY GRANGE RIDING CTRE**, Stockton-on-Tees **Ref:**YH13346
- **WOLVISTON RIDING STABLES**, Billingham **Ref:**YH15652

CORNWALL

- **BLACKACRE RIDING STABLES**, St Columb **Ref:**YH01474
- **BOLENOWE LIVERY STABLES**, Camborne **Ref:**YH01607
- **BOSKELL RIDING CTRE**, St Austell **Ref:**YH01654
- **BUSH LIVERY STABLES**, Saltash **Ref:**YH02306
- **CHIVERTON RIDING CTRE**, Truro **Ref:**YH02871
- **COLE, J J**, Camelford **Ref:**YH03157
- **CORNISH RIDING HOLIDAYS**, Redruth **Ref:**YH03327
- **DENBY RIDING STABLES**, Bodmin **Ref:**YH04039
- **HALLAGENNA STUD FARM**, Bodmin **Ref:**YH06322
- **HERNISS FARM LIVERY YARD**, Penryn **Ref:**YH06708
- **LANJETH RIDING SCHOOL**, St Austell **Ref:**YH08418
- **LAUREL STUD**, Truro **Ref:**YH08458
- **M J EQUESTRIAN**, Looe **Ref:**YH08967
- **NORTH CORNWALL ARENA**, Camelford **Ref:**YH10250
- **PILL FARM**, Saltash **Ref:**YH11109
- **POLPEVER RIDING STABLES**, Liskeard **Ref:**YH11212
- **ROMANY WALKS**, Penzance **Ref:**YH12072
- **S-J'S TACK ROOM**, Roche **Ref:**YH12864
- **SNOWLAND RIDING CTRE**, Par **Ref:**YH13045
- **ST LEONARDS EQUESTRIAN CTRE**, Launceston **Ref:**YH13278
- **TM INT SCHOOL OF HORSEMANSHIP**, Liskeard **Ref:**YH14196
- **TRENANCE RIDING STABLES**, Newquay **Ref:**YH14372
- **TRENAWIN STABLES**, Hayle **Ref:**YH14373
- **TRESALLYN**, Padstow **Ref:**YH14384
- **VERYAN RIDING CTRE**, Truro **Ref:**YH14686

COUNTY DURHAM

- **ALSTON & KILLHOPE**, Bishop Auckland **Ref:**YH00339
- **BEAMISH RIDING CTRE**, Stanley **Ref:**YH01117
- **BOWES MANOR EQUESTRIAN CTRE**, Chester Le Street **Ref:**YH01709
- **BROOM HALL LIVERY YARD**, Durham **Ref:**YH02072
- **CENTURION EQUESTRIAN CTRE**, Durham **Ref:**YH02698
- **COX, J**, Darlington **Ref:**YH03531
- **DARLINGTON EQUESTRIAN CTRE**, Darlington **Ref:**YH03892
- **DARLINGTON EQUESTRIAN CTRE**, Haughton **Ref:**YH03893
- **DEAF HILL**, Durham **Ref:**YH03985
- **DENE HEAD LIVERY**, Darlington **Ref:**YH04042
- **DENNIS, JUDY**, Bishop Auckland **Ref:**YH04055
- **GO RIDING GRP**, Stanley **Ref:**YH05861
- **HAMSTERLEY RIDING SCHOOL**, Bishop Auckland **Ref:**YH06372
- **HIGHLING EQUESTRIAN CTRE**, Durham **Ref:**YH06798
- **IVESLEY EQUESTRIAN CTRE**, Durham **Ref:**YH07536
- **LOW FALLOWFIELD**, Durham **Ref:**YH08854

LOW FOLD RIDING CTRE, Crook **Ref:**YH08855
LOW MEADOWS FARM LIVERY, Durham **Ref:**YH08856
NEW MOORS, Bishop Auckland **Ref:**YH10114
NEWLANDS GRANGE LIVERY YARD, Consett **Ref:**YH10143
NEWSTEAD RIDING CTRE, Darlington **Ref:**YH10166
RAYGILL, Barnard Castle **Ref:**YH11672
RICKNALL GRANGE, Newton Aycliffe **Ref:**YH11838
RICKNALL RUGS, Darlington **Ref:**YH11839
UNION HALL, Durham **Ref:**YH14570
WALKER, D A & C S, Newton Aycliffe **Ref:**YH14848

CUMBRIA

ALLONBY RIDING SCHOOL, Wigton **Ref:**YH00323
BIRKBY HALL, Grange Over Sands **Ref:**YH01440
BREED EX EQUINE STUD, Penrith **Ref:**YH01832
BUCKLEY, E H & J M, Kendal **Ref:**YH02198
CARGO RIDING CTRE, Carlisle **Ref:**YH02538
GENESIS EQUESTRIAN CTRE/STUD, Carlisle **Ref:**YH05709
GREENLANDS LIVERY STABLES, Carlisle **Ref:**YH06092
HAYESCASTLE FARM, Workington **Ref:**YH06576
KERBECK, Workington **Ref:**YH08096
KESWICK RIDING CTRE, Keswick **Ref:**YH08105
LAKELAND EQUESTRIAN, Windermere **Ref:**YH08354
LANCASTER, P R, Ulverston **Ref:**YH08381
LARKRIGG RIDING SCHOOL, Kendal **Ref:**YH08434
MIDDLE BAYLES LIVERY, Alston **Ref:**YH09534
OAKLEA LIVERY STABLES, Barrow-In-Furness **Ref:**YH10395
RYDAL MOUNT LIVERY STABLES, Wigton **Ref:**YH12293
ZALKIND, Penrith **Ref:**YH15950

DERBYSHIRE

ADLINGTON, D, Dronfield **Ref:**YH00186
ALTON RIDING SCHOOL, Chesterfield **Ref:**YH00344
AMBER HILLS EQUESTRIAN, Belper **Ref:**YH00356
BARLEYFIELDS, Derby **Ref:**YH00952
BIRCHWOOD, Alfreton **Ref:**YH01435
BRIMINGTON EQUESTRIAN CTRE, Chesterfield **Ref:**YH01912
BUXTON RIDING SCHOOL, Buxton **Ref:**YH02339
C E S, Ashbourne **Ref:**YH02370
CHESTERFIELD, Chesterfield **Ref:**YH02833
CURBAR RIDING STABLES, Hope Valley **Ref:**YH03727
DELOWEN LIVERY YARD, Derby **Ref:**YH04033
EDENSOR LIVERY STABLES, Bakewell **Ref:**YH04552
FIELD FARM, Heanor **Ref:**YH05184
HALL FARM STUD, Snarestone **Ref:**YH06306
HARGATE HILL, Glossop **Ref:**YH06424
HAWSON, C, Hope Valley **Ref:**YH06555
HILLCLIFF STUD, Belper **Ref:**YH06838
IKIN, D & D, Swadlincote **Ref:**YH07397
KNOWLE HILL EQUESTRIAN, Derby **Ref:**YH08280
LANDOWN FARM RIDING STABLES, Derby **Ref:**YH08384
MANOR FARM LIVERY, Swadlincote **Ref:**YH09100
MILL FARM DIY LIVERY STABLES, Dronfield **Ref:**YH09571
MORLEY LIVERY YARD, Ilkeston **Ref:**YH09818
NORTHFIELD FARM, Buxton **Ref:**YH10312
PARK HALL FARM EQUEST CTRE, Ilkeston **Ref:**YH10726
RED HSE STABLES, Matlock **Ref:**YH11698
RINGER VILLA EQUESTRIAN CTRE, Chesterfield **Ref:**YH11900
ROSE, C A, Ashbourne **Ref:**YH12095
SWATHWICK FARM LIVERIES, Chesterfield **Ref:**YH13698
WELLCROFT STUD, Ashbourne **Ref:**YH15065
WHITEHOUSE FARM, Alfreton **Ref:**YH15344
YEW TREE FARM STABLES, Belper **Ref:**YH15910

DEVON

BARRIBAL, Okehampton **Ref:**YH01020
BARTONS CLOSE STABLES, Teignmouth **Ref:**YH01051
BEACON COURT, Ivybridge **Ref:**YH01106
BLACKDOWN LIVERY YARD, Crediton **Ref:**YH01479
BRENDON MANOR FARM, Lynton **Ref:**YH01838
BUDLEIGH SALTERTON, Budleigh Salterton **Ref:**YH02208
CHOLWELL EQUESTRIAN CTRE, Okehampton **Ref:**YH02878
COLLAFORD FARM PARTNERSHIP, Plymouth **Ref:**YH03174
CROSSWAYS LIVERY YARD, Yelverton **Ref:**YH03665
DEAN RIDING STABLES, Barnstaple **Ref:**YH03989
DOWNE FARM, Tiverton **Ref:**YH04225
EAST LAKE, Okehampton **Ref:**YH04477
FAIRHAVEN FARM, Okehampton **Ref:**YH05021
FERNLEA, Newton Abbot **Ref:**YH05168
FORESTOKE HOLIDAYS, Newton Abbot **Ref:**YH05357
GLEBE INT ENTERPRISE, Exeter **Ref:**YH05817
GRANGE EQUESTRIAN CTRE, Okehampton **Ref:**YH05987
HALDON RIDING STABLES, Exeter **Ref:**YH06290
HALWILL ELITE LIVERY SVS, Beaworthy **Ref:**YH06338
HILLTOP RIDING SCHOOL, Exeter **Ref:**YH06858
HOLLY FARM, Exeter **Ref:**YH06953
HONEYSUCKLE FARM, Newton Abbot **Ref:**YH07017
KING, ANN, Newton Abbot **Ref:**YH08174
LEAWOOD RIDING CTRE, Okehampton **Ref:**YH08510
LITTLE ASH ECO-FARM & STUD, Okehampton **Ref:**YH08683
LOWER HALDON, Exeter **Ref:**YH08866
LYDFORD HOUSE RIDING STABLES, Okehampton **Ref:**YH08916
MANOR FARM RIDING CTRE/LIVERY, Okehampton **Ref:**YH09104
NARRAMORE STUD, Newton Abbot **Ref:**YH10023
NEAL, PAMELA, Newton Abbott **Ref:**YH10061
NEWTON FERRERS, Plymouth **Ref:**YH10170
RATCLIFF, A E, South Molton **Ref:**YH11648
ROSE & CROWN, Tiverton **Ref:**YH12088
SHILSTONE ROCKS, Newton Abbot **Ref:**YH12746
SOUTHDOWN FARM RIDING STABLES, Brixham **Ref:**YH13134
STADDON HEIGHTS FARM, Plymouth **Ref:**YH13319
STIDSTON EQUESTRIAN, South Brent **Ref:**YH13466
STRETTON-DOWNES, C, Tavistock **Ref:**YH13575
SUNNYMEADE COUNTRY HOTEL, Ilfracombe **Ref:**YH13648
UPHILL WELSH COBS, Okehampton **Ref:**YH14600
WARD, MICHAEL J, Holsworthy **Ref:**YH14904
WATTS, S E, Woolacombe **Ref:**YH15008
WEMBURY BAY RIDING SCHOOL, Plymouth **Ref:**YH15103
WHITTABOROUGH, Plympton **Ref:**YH15372
WOOD FARM STUD, Okehampton **Ref:**YH15656

DORSET

CLANDON FARM LIVERY STABLES, Dorchester **Ref:**YH02941
COLMER STUD, Bridport **Ref:**YH03193
CUCKOO HILL LIVERY CTRE, Sherborne **Ref:**YH03698
DEER PARK RIDING STABLES, Blandford Forum **Ref:**YH04023
DORSET HEAVY HORSE CTRE, Wimborne **Ref:**YH04206
DUDMOOR FARM, Christchurch **Ref:**YH04311
EQUESTRIAN & EXAM CTRE, Ferndown **Ref:**YH04691
FOREST LODGE, Shaftesbury **Ref:**YH05342
LULWORTH EQUESTRIAN CTRE, Wareham **Ref:**YH08897
POUND COTTAGE RIDING CTRE, Blandford Forum **Ref:**YH11307
PROSPECT FARM LIVERY STABLES, Dorchester **Ref:**YH11436
REMPSTONE STABLES, Wareham **Ref:**YH11751
SKINNER, ROSS, Dorchester **Ref:**YH12878
WARMWELL STUD, Dorchester **Ref:**YH14924
WESTWAY SADDLERY, Bridport **Ref:**YH15233
WINDMILL STABLES, Portland **Ref:**YH15568

ESSEX

ALEXANDER, J E, Saffron Walden **Ref:**YH00271
ARMOURY FARM LIVERY STABLES, Colchester **Ref:**YH00539
ASHFIELDS EQUESTRIAN CTRE, Dunmow **Ref:**YH00599
BIRKETT HALL LIVERY STABLE, Chelmsford **Ref:**YH01441
BLUE SABRE RIDING SCHOOL, Colchester **Ref:**YH01570
BOYLES COURT, Brentwood **Ref:**YH01733
BRAEKMAN, HELENE, Bishop's Stortford **Ref:**YH01769
BROOK FARM STABLES, Colchester **Ref:**YH02036
BROOKS STABLES, Benfleet **Ref:**YH02062
BUTTS GREEN LIVERY, Chelmsford **Ref:**YH02338
CHELMSFORD EQUESTRIAN CTRE, Chelmsford **Ref:**YH02801
COACH HSE, Epping **Ref:**YH03102
COUNTRY PADDOCKS, Brentwood **Ref:**YH03419
COURT FARM LIVERY, South Ockendon **Ref:**YH03500
D'ARCY RIDING STABLES, Maldon **Ref:**YH03879
DE BEAUVOIR, Billericay **Ref:**YH03973
EAST ANGLIAN FARM RIDES, Kelvedon **Ref:**YH04463
EASTMINSTER SCHOOL OF RIDING, Romford **Ref:**YH04510
ELM TODD, Frinton-on-Sea **Ref:**YH04634
ELMWOOD EQUESTRIAN CTRE, Burnham-on-Crouch **Ref:**YH04640
FOREST LODGE RIDING SCHOOL, Epping **Ref:**YH05344
GAME, DAVID C, Ingatestone **Ref:**YH05634
GILSTON LIVERY STABLES, Harlow **Ref:**YH05791
GLESSING, J & C, Billericay **Ref:**YH05846
H R PHILPOT & SON, Billericay **Ref:**YH06235
HALLINGBURY HALL, Bishop's Stortford **Ref:**YH06331
HARWOOD HALL LIVERY, Upminster **Ref:**YH06519
HAVERING PK RIDING SCHOOL, Romford **Ref:**YH06540
HAYCOCKS LIVERY STABLES, Colchester **Ref:**YH06567
HOBBS CROSS EQUESTRIAN CTRE, Epping **Ref:**YH06893
HOME FARM LIVERY STABLES, Colchester **Ref:**YH06997

- **KEDDIE FARM**, Rochford **Ref:**YH08022
- **LANGFORD LIVERY**, Maldon **Ref:**YH08404
- **LITTLE PADDOCK**, Colchester **Ref:**YH08698
- **LONGWOOD EQUESTRIAN CTRE**, Basildon **Ref:**YH08820
- **LYNFORDS**, Wickford **Ref:**YH08930
- **MEDWAY RIDING CTRE**, Chelmsford **Ref:**YH09439
- **MILL HILL FARM**, Chelmsford **Ref:**YH09577
- **MOOR END LIVERY YARD**, Saffron Walden **Ref:**YH09741
- **NEW LODGE SADDLERY**, Chelmsford **Ref:**YH10113
- **NEWLAND HALL EQUESTRIAN CTRE**, Chelmsford **Ref:**YH10141
- **NIGHTINGALE RIDING SCHOOL**, Buckhurst Hill **Ref:**YH10204
- **NORTON HEATH EQUESTRIAN CTRE**, Ingatestone **Ref:**YH10328
- **OAKLANDS LIVERY STABLES**, Rayleigh **Ref:**YH10390
- **PAGLESHAM SCHOOL**, Rochford **Ref:**YH10685
- **PARK LANE RIDING SCHOOL**, Billericay **Ref:**YH10731
- **PARKLANDS FARM LIVERY**, Chelmsford **Ref:**YH10769
- **PINE LODGE**, Loughton **Ref:**YH11118
- **RAWRETH EQUESTRIAN CTRE**, Wickford **Ref:**YH11669
- **RAYNE RIDING CTRE**, Braintree **Ref:**YH11676
- **RED STABLES FARM**, Brentwood **Ref:**YH11706
- **RUNNINGWELL STUD**, Chelmsford **Ref:**YH12236
- **SHOPLAND HALL EQUESTRIAN**, Rochford **Ref:**YH12758
- **STABLES**, High Ongar **Ref:**YH13306
- **STABLES**, Loughton **Ref:**YH13305
- **STAMBROOK STUD**, Halstead **Ref:**YH13352
- **STEWARDS FARM RIDING CTRE**, Harlow **Ref:**YH13453
- **SUDBURY STABLES**, Billericay **Ref:**YH13621
- **TACK ROOM**, Billericay **Ref:**YH13798
- **TALLY-HO RIDING SCHOOL**, Grays **Ref:**YH13844
- **TIPTREE EQUESTRIAN CTRE**, Colchester **Ref:**YH14184
- **TOWERLANDS EQUESTRIAN CTRE**, Braintree **Ref:**YH14278
- **TYLERS HALL**, Upminster **Ref:**YH14523
- **VALLEY RIDING/LIVERY STABLES**, Ingatestone **Ref:**YH14657
- **VALLEY STABLES**, Bishop's Stortford **Ref:**YH14658
- **WASH FARM**, Colchester **Ref:**YH14954
- **WEST BOWERS**, Maldon **Ref:**YH15129
- **WETHERSFIELD RIDING STABLES**, Braintree **Ref:**YH15246
- **WOODREDON RIDING SCHOOL**, Waltham Abbey **Ref:**YH15728

GLOUCESTERSHIRE

- **BADGEWORTH LIVERY YARD**, Cheltenham **Ref:**YH00780
- **CHURCH FARM**, Mitcheldean **Ref:**YH02895
- **COTSWOLD TRAIL RIDING**, Gloucester **Ref:**YH03368
- **CRISP, C (MISS)**, Westbury-on-Severn **Ref:**YH03604
- **ELM LEAZE STUD**, Badminton **Ref:**YH04631
- **HAWLING LODGE STABLES**, Cheltenham **Ref:**YH06554
- **HORNS FARM**, Stroud **Ref:**YH07082
- **HUNTLEY SCHOOL OF EQUITATION**, Gloucester **Ref:**YH07306
- **JAMES KEYSER**, Cirencester **Ref:**YH07670
- **KAYTE FARM EQUESTRIAN LIVERY**, Cheltenham **Ref:**YH08011
- **MIFLIN, WILLIAM**, Cirencester **Ref:**YH09563
- **PARK CORNER FARM**, Cirencester **Ref:**YH10716
- **SUMMERHOUSE**, Gloucester **Ref:**YH13632
- **WICKRIDGE**, Stroud **Ref:**YH15385
- **WILKINSON, S**, Gloucester **Ref:**YH15424
- **WOODLAND**, Cheltenham **Ref:**YH15702

GLOUCESTERSHIRE (SOUTH)

- **TACK ROOM**, Chipping Sodbury **Ref:**YH13799
- **TUDOR FARM LIVERY STABLES**, Frampton Cotterell **Ref:**YH14439

GUERNSEY

- **GUERNSEY**, St Sampsons **Ref:**YH06182
- **LA CARRIERE**, St Sampson **Ref:**YH08331

HAMPSHIRE

- **ALBANY FARM LIVERY STABLES**, Fleet **Ref:**YH00243
- **AMBERVALE**, Lymington **Ref:**YH00357
- **AMPORT RIDING SCHOOL**, Andover **Ref:**YH00372
- **ARNISS**, Fordingbridge **Ref:**YH00555
- **ASHBOURNE STABLES**, Southampton **Ref:**YH00590
- **BASTABLE M M**, Fordingbridge **Ref:**YH01058
- **BLACK KNOLL HORSE SPORTS CTRE**, Brockenhurst **Ref:**YH01467
- **BROCKS FARM**, Stockbridge **Ref:**YH02013
- **CARRON ROW STABLES**, Fareham **Ref:**YH02594
- **CLAPHAM, JENNIFER**, Hook **Ref:**YH02946
- **COCKSCOMBE FARM LIVERY**, Winchester **Ref:**YH03129
- **COTTAGE ESTATES STABLES**, Southampton **Ref:**YH03372
- **COTTAGE FARM**, Camberley **Ref:**YH03373
- **COURTHOUSE STABLES**, Petersfield **Ref:**YH03505
- **CROSS OAKS**, Romsey **Ref:**YH03651
- **DECOY POND FARM**, Brockenhurst **Ref:**YH04012
- **DIXON, J B**, Lyndhurst **Ref:**YH04140
- **EASTMOORS FARM**, Ringwood **Ref:**YH04511
- **ELEDA STABLES**, Ringwood **Ref:**YH04603
- **EQUALLUS EQUESTRIAN**, Hook **Ref:**YH04685
- **EQUINE LIVERY SVS**, Andover **Ref:**YH04785
- **FIR TREE FARM**, Fordingbridge **Ref:**YH05219
- **FLAGSTAFF STABLES**, Winchester **Ref:**YH05259
- **FLEETWATER STUD**, Lyndhurst **Ref:**YH05269
- **FOREST FARM**, Milford On Sea **Ref:**YH05335
- **FORT WIDLEY EQUESTRIAN CTRE**, Cosham **Ref:**YH05388
- **GEBBIE VALLEYS**, Lymington **Ref:**YH05686
- **GLENEAGLES**, Southampton **Ref:**YH05832
- **HARMSWORTH FARM**, Southampton **Ref:**YH06446
- **HARRIS, ANDREW**, Lymington **Ref:**YH06464
- **HEATH, F W**, Waterlooville **Ref:**YH06623
- **HIGH HURLANDS EQUESTRIAN CTRE**, Liphook **Ref:**YH06764
- **HOPLANDS EQUESTRIAN**, Stockbridge **Ref:**YH07058
- **INADOWN FARM STABLES**, Alton **Ref:**YH07407
- **KEELEY, PAULA**, Liss **Ref:**YH08027
- **KEYSTONE EQUESTRIAN**, Alton **Ref:**YH08117
- **KNIGHTSBRIDGE STABLES**, Sway **Ref:**YH08272
- **LANGFORD FARM**, Woodlands **Ref:**YH08403
- **LESTER, P**, Fareham **Ref:**YH08564
- **LYDE HOUSE LIVERIES**, Hook **Ref:**YH08915
- **MANOR FARM**, Southampton **Ref:**YH09095
- **MOYGLARE LIVERY**, Tadley **Ref:**YH09910
- **NEW PARK HOTEL**, New Forest **Ref:**YH10115
- **NEW PARK MANOR STABLES**, Brockenhurst **Ref:**YH10116
- **NINEHAM, T & YOUNG, J**, Brokenhurst **Ref:**YH10212
- **NRC**, Fareham **Ref:**YH10348
- **POOK LANE RIDING STABLES**, Havant **Ref:**YH11259
- **ROSHAUNA RIDING SCHOOL**, Fareham **Ref:**YH12112
- **RUSSELL EQUITATION CTRE**, Southampton **Ref:**YH12253
- **RUSSELL, GILLIAN A**, Ringwood **Ref:**YH12258
- **SANDILANDS**, Petersfield **Ref:**YH12413
- **SCHOOL FARM TRAINING CTRE**, Romsey **Ref:**YH12520
- **SILVER HORSESHOE**, Fordingbridge **Ref:**YH12806
- **SIMS, L**, Andover **Ref:**YH12846
- **SOUTH SWAY FARM**, Lymington **Ref:**YH13106
- **SOUTHFIELD EQUESTRIAN CTRE**, Whitchurch **Ref:**YH13149
- **SPARSHOLT COLLEGE**, Winchester **Ref:**YH13183
- **STOCKBRIDGE**, Stockbridge **Ref:**YH13486
- **T J STUD & LIVERY STABLE**, Southampton **Ref:**YH13754
- **VALESMOOR FARM**, New Milton **Ref:**YH14644
- **WALSH, P**, Newbury **Ref:**YH14879
- **WELLINGTON RIDING**, Hook **Ref:**YH15075
- **WICKHAM STABLES**, Fareham **Ref:**YH15383

HEREFORDSHIRE

- **COUNTY COMPETITION STUD**, Bromyard **Ref:**YH03486
- **DOYLE, MARK**, Leominster **Ref:**YH04249
- **LEA BAILEY RIDING SCHOOL**, Ross-on-Wye **Ref:**YH08492
- **MONNINGTON**, Hereford **Ref:**YH09728
- **NEWCOMB, SALLY**, Hereford **Ref:**YH10130
- **PEARSON, S R**, Bromyard **Ref:**YH10882
- **SEABORN, J**, Ledbury **Ref:**YH12579

HERTFORDSHIRE

- **ARKLEY LIVERY STABLES**, Barnet **Ref:**YH00532
- **BARKWAY EQUESTRIAN CTRE**, Royston **Ref:**YH00948
- **BIRCH FARM**, Broxbourne **Ref:**YH01428
- **BOSWELL STABLES**, Hertford **Ref:**YH01662
- **BROOK END**, Royston **Ref:**YH02032
- **CALDECOTE FARM LIVERY**, Watford **Ref:**YH02427
- **CATLIPS FARM LIVERY STABLES**, Rickmansworth **Ref:**YH02653
- **CHESFIELD EQUESTRIAN CTRE**, Hitchin **Ref:**YH02823
- **COLTSFOOT FARM LIVERY**, Knebworth **Ref:**YH03204
- **COUNTY LIVERY**, Hertford **Ref:**YH03489
- **CROUCHFIELD**, Ware **Ref:**YH03674
- **FOURFIELDS FARM**, Hertford **Ref:**YH05414
- **GREENACRES EQUESTRIAN**, Harpenden **Ref:**YH06076
- **GROVE LIVERY STABLES**, Harpenden **Ref:**YH06171
- **HARTS FARM**, Watford **Ref:**YH06508
- **HIGH HERTS FARM RIDING SCHOOL**, Hemel Hempstead **Ref:**YH06760
- **HOSKINS FARM LIVERY STABLES**, Sawbridgeworth **Ref:**YH07197
- **ICKLEFORD EQUESTRIAN**, Hitchin **Ref:**YH07382
- **IVORY, K T**, Radlett **Ref:**YH07538
- **LEASEY BRIDGE LIVERY STABLES**, St Albans **Ref:**YH08502
- **LOVELY VIEW STABLES**, Royston **Ref:**YH08850
- **MELDRETH MANOR**, Royston **Ref:**YH09451
- **MILL RIDING CLUB**, Much Hadham **Ref:**YH09585
- **MYMMS HALL LIVERY STABLES**, Potters Bar **Ref:**YH09983
- **OAKLANDS CLGE**, St Albans **Ref:**YH10389
- **OLD FORGE**, St Albans **Ref:**YH10457
- **PATCHETTS**, Watford **Ref:**YH10815
- **PEDEN, D W**, Waltham Cross **Ref:**YH10892
- **PONSBOURNE RIDING CTRE**, Hertford **Ref:**YH11224
- **POYNDERS END FARM**, Hitchin **Ref:**YH11329
- **ROSE HALL RIDING STABLES**, Sarratt **Ref:**YH12093

- **RYDAL MOUNT**, Potters Bar **Ref:**YH12292
- **SANDRIDGEBURY**, St Albans **Ref:**YH12419
- **SOUTH MEDBURN**, Borehamwood **Ref:**YH13101
- **STAGS END**, Hemel Hempstead **Ref:**YH13342
- **TRAINING & LIVERY CTRE**, Welwyn **Ref:**YH14342
- **UPPERWOOD FARM STUD**, Hemel Hempstead **Ref:**YH14609
- **VALLEY FARM**, Rickmansworth **Ref:**YH14650
- **WELWYN EQUESTRIAN**, Welwyn **Ref:**YH15101
- **WOODGREEN FARM**, Waltham Cross **Ref:**YH15692

ISLE OF MAN

- **G G H EQUITATION CTRE**, Marown **Ref:**YH05578
- **ITTON COURT STUD**, The Braaid **Ref:**YH07531
- **MANX RIDING SUPPLIES**, Onchan **Ref:**YH09128

ISLE OF WIGHT

- **COOK'S CASTLE FARM**, Ventnor **Ref:**YH03265
- **COTTON, W J**, Ventnor **Ref:**YH03386
- **FAIRFIELDS FARM**, Ryde **Ref:**YH05020
- **GREAT PAN FARM STABLES**, Newport **Ref:**YH06041
- **JONES, E A & C**, Newport **Ref:**YH07895
- **LAKE FARM**, Ventnor **Ref:**YH08350

JERSEY

- **HAIE FLEURIE**, Channel Isles **Ref:**YH06280
- **SORREL SADDLERY**, St Peter **Ref:**YH13071

KENT

- **BADGERS COURT LIVERY**, Sevenoaks **Ref:**YH00779
- **BALI HAI FARM**, Kemsing **Ref:**YH00846
- **BEDGEBURY RIDING CTRE**, Goudhurst **Ref:**YH01155
- **BEKESBOURNE STABLES**, Canterbury **Ref:**YH01200
- **BIRCHES LIVERY STABLES**, Whitstable **Ref:**YH01433
- **BLACKDALE FARM LIVERIES**, Dartford **Ref:**YH01478
- **BLUE BARN EQUESTRIAN CTRE**, Ashford **Ref:**YH01564
- **BRAESIDE E.C**, Dover **Ref:**YH01773
- **BRENLEY FARM LIVERY**, Faversham **Ref:**YH01841
- **BROMLEY COMMON LIVERIES**, Bromley **Ref:**YH02023
- **BURCHWOOD STABLES**, Cobham **Ref:**YH02233
- **CASTLEWOOD LIVERY**, Sittingbourne **Ref:**YH02647
- **CHAFFORD FARM**, Tunbridge Wells **Ref:**YH02708
- **CHAUCER RIDING/LIVERY STABLES**, Canterbury **Ref:**YH02791
- **CHAVIC PK STABLES**, Westerham **Ref:**YH02793
- **CHELSFIELD RIDING SCHOOL**, Orpington **Ref:**YH02802
- **COBHAM MANOR**, Maidstone **Ref:**YH03113
- **COOMBE WOOD STABLES**, Folkestone **Ref:**YH03276
- **DOWNE COURT RIDING CTRE**, Orpington **Ref:**YH04224
- **DUCKHURST FARM**, Staplehurst **Ref:**YH04307
- **EAGLESFIELD EQUESTRIAN CTRE**, Sevenoaks **Ref:**YH04441
- **ELMWOOD FARM RIDING CTRE**, Broadstairs **Ref:**YH04641
- **ELWORTHY, S**, Broadstairs **Ref:**YH04648
- **EQUINE SPORT THERAPY**, Edenbridge **Ref:**YH04800
- **EQUINES LIVERIES**, Maidstone **Ref:**YH04809
- **FAIRBOURNE STABLES**, Maidstone **Ref:**YH05015
- **FIVE OAKS EQUESTRIAN CTRE**, Keston **Ref:**YH05254
- **FOREST VIEW**, Sidcup **Ref:**YH05353
- **FRANDHAM KENNELS & TACK SHOP**, Dover **Ref:**YH05454
- **FRIDAY FIELD STABLES**, Sittingbourne **Ref:**YH05502
- **GABRIELS FARM**, Edenbridge **Ref:**YH05602
- **GLENWOOD RIDING**, Canterbury **Ref:**YH05845
- **GOODNESTONE CT EQUESTRIAN**, Faversham **Ref:**YH05905
- **GREENACRES RIDING SCHOOL**, Keston **Ref:**YH06078
- **GREENHILLS FARM**, Dover **Ref:**YH06090
- **HAYLORS**, Sheerness **Ref:**YH06584
- **HEIGHTS STABLES**, Westerham **Ref:**YH06650
- **HEMESLEY LIVERY STABLES**, Longfield **Ref:**YH06660
- **HEMPSTEAD STUD**, Cranbrook **Ref:**YH06662
- **HERONWOOD STABLES**, Sevenoaks **Ref:**YH06714
- **HIGH ELMS LIVERY**, Canterbury **Ref:**YH06757
- **HIGHSTEAD RIDING CTRE**, Canterbury **Ref:**YH06800
- **HODSTOLL STREET LIVERIES**, Sevenoaks **Ref:**YH06916
- **HOGBROOK RIDING SCHOOL**, Dover **Ref:**YH06919
- **HOME FARM STABLES**, Chislehurst **Ref:**YH07000
- **HONNINGTON**, Tunbridge Wells **Ref:**YH07019
- **HOP GARDEN STABLES**, Maidstone **Ref:**YH07048
- **HOWES, E A**, Tenterden **Ref:**YH07230
- **INGLEDEN PARK RIDING CTRE**, Tenterden **Ref:**YH07447
- **JENNER, B A**, West Malling **Ref:**YH07744
- **KENT LIVERIES**, Maidstone **Ref:**YH08080
- **KENT LIVERIES & RIDING SCHOOL**, Maidstone **Ref:**YH08081
- **LASLETT, E E**, Sandwich **Ref:**YH08438
- **LEYBOURNE GRANGE**, West Malling **Ref:**YH08600
- **LIMES FARM EQUESTRIAN**, Folkestone **Ref:**YH08635
- **LITTLE FORSHAM FARM STABLES**, Cranbrook **Ref:**YH08687
- **LYNX PK RIDING STABLES**, Cranbrook **Ref:**YH08936
- **MACE FARM**, Sevenoaks **Ref:**YH08993
- **MANNIX STUD**, Canterbury **Ref:**YH09091
- **MANOR LIVERY**, Westerham **Ref:**YH09114
- **MANSTON RIDING CTRE**, Ramsgate **Ref:**YH09126
- **MARBERDUM**, Canterbury **Ref:**YH09137
- **MINNISMOOR STABLES**, Ashford **Ref:**YH09650
- **OATHILL FARM RIDING CTRE**, Canterbury **Ref:**YH10415
- **OLD BEXLEY EQUESTRIAN**, Bexley **Ref:**YH10451
- **OLD STABLES**, Sevenoaks **Ref:**YH10477
- **PEATE, JEFFREY**, Tunbridge Wells **Ref:**YH10885
- **QUADRANGLE**, Sevenoaks **Ref:**YH11475
- **ROOTING STREET FARM**, Ashford **Ref:**YH12082
- **SANDHILL FARM STABLES**, Tunbridge Wells **Ref:**YH12411
- **SOUTHBOROUGH LANE STABLES**, Bromley **Ref:**YH13128
- **SPEEDGATE FARM**, Longfield **Ref:**YH13191
- **STIDOLPH'S LIVERY**, Sevenoaks **Ref:**YH13465
- **TILI FARM LIVERIES**, Tatsfield **Ref:**YH14146
- **TREWINT**, Cranbrook **Ref:**YH14388
- **WARRIGAL FARM LIVERY STABLES**, Dartford **Ref:**YH14941
- **WHITELEAF RIDING CTRE**, Sittingbourne **Ref:**YH15347
- **WILLOW FARM**, Faversham **Ref:**YH15497
- **WILLOW FARM**, Swanley **Ref:**YH15495
- **WILLOW STUD**, Canterbury **Ref:**YH15503
- **WOODLANDS**, Sevenoaks **Ref:**YH15706

LANCASHIRE

- **ABRAM HALL RIDING CTRE**, Wigan **Ref:**YH00134
- **ARKENFIELD EQUESTRIAN CTRE**, Chorley **Ref:**YH00530
- **BECCONSALL**, Preston **Ref:**YH01144
- **BEECHMOUNT EQUITATION CTRE**, Thornton-Cleveleys **Ref:**YH01174
- **BICKERSTAFFE HALL STABLE YARD**, Ormskirk **Ref:**YH01392
- **BLACKPOOL EQUESTRIAN CTRE**, Blackpool **Ref:**YH01492
- **BOUNDARY FARM CARRIAGES**, Wigan **Ref:**YH01677
- **BROOKFIELD GREEN FARM**, Ormskirk **Ref:**YH02047
- **BROOMHILL**, Clitheroe **Ref:**YH02080
- **CALICO LIVERY STABLES**, Wigan **Ref:**YH02444
- **CHARITY FARM LIVERY STABLES**, Wigan **Ref:**YH02751
- **CHORLEY EQUESTRIAN CTRE**, Chorley **Ref:**YH02880
- **CHURCH FARM LIVERY STABLES**, Ormskirk **Ref:**YH02897
- **CORNFIELD FARM**, Burnley **Ref:**YH03323
- **CROSTONS FARM RIDING & LIVERY**, Chorley **Ref:**YH03672
- **DALES VIEW RIDING CTRE**, Barnoldswick **Ref:**YH03831
- **DRAKE HSE DIY STABLES**, Clitheroe **Ref:**YH04254
- **EARNSDALE FARM RIDING SCHOOL**, Darwen **Ref:**YH04458
- **ELSWICK**, Preston **Ref:**YH04644
- **FLIGHT VIEW**, Poulton-Le-Fylde **Ref:**YH05283
- **FULWOOD RIDING CTRE**, Preston **Ref:**YH05537
- **GREEN BANK**, Carnforth **Ref:**YH06049
- **HALSALL RIDING & LIVERY CTRE**, Ormskirk **Ref:**YH06336
- **HERD HSE RIDING SCHOOL**, Burnley **Ref:**YH06699
- **HOLMESWOOD STUD**, Preston **Ref:**YH06983
- **HUSTEADS RIDING SCHOOL**, Oldham **Ref:**YH07330
- **LAUND VIEW STABLES**, Burnley **Ref:**YH08451
- **MARSHALL, M C**, Heywood **Ref:**YH09199
- **MARSHALL, MICHELLE**, Heywood **Ref:**YH09200
- **MAXY HOUSE FARM LIVERY**, Preston **Ref:**YH09286
- **MEWS COTTAGE STABLES**, Ormskirk **Ref:**YH09506
- **NETHERWOOD FARM**, Burnley **Ref:**YH10083
- **OSBALDESTON RIDING CTRE**, Blackburn **Ref:**YH10557
- **PANAMA SPORT HORSES**, Clitheroe **Ref:**YH10695
- **RENARD RIDING CTRE**, Poulton-Le-Fylde **Ref:**YH11753
- **ROBERTSON, S A S**, Carnforth **Ref:**YH11975
- **ROBSCOTT EQUITATION**, Carnforth **Ref:**YH12010
- **ROSSENDALE & HYNDBURN EC**, Accrington **Ref:**YH12123
- **SILVER BIRCH STABLES**, Heywood **Ref:**YH12803
- **SOUGH FARM**, Darwen **Ref:**YH13073
- **TONG END LIVERY STABLES**, Rochdale **Ref:**YH14226
- **TOWN END FARM RIDING CTRE**, Carnforth **Ref:**YH14295
- **VALIANTS EQUESTRIAN CTRE**, Preston **Ref:**YH14645
- **WADDINGTON FARM**, Darwen **Ref:**YH14807
- **WHITEGATE FARM**, Bacup **Ref:**YH15338
- **WHITEMOOR RIDING CTRE**, Colne **Ref:**YH15351

LEICESTERSHIRE

- **BLABY MILL STABLES**, Leicester **Ref:**YH01459
- **BROOKSBY EQUESTRIAN CTRE**, Melton Mowbray **Ref:**YH02067

- **CANAAN FARM**, Loughborough **Ref:**YH02493
- **CLAYBROOKE STABLES**, Lutterworth **Ref:**YH02997
- **COSSINGTON**, Leicester **Ref:**YH03354
- **DEBDALE HORSES**, Leicester **Ref:**YH04004
- **GLENDALE EQUESTRIAN FEEDS**, Leicester **Ref:**YH05830
- **HARDWICKE LODGE STABLES**, Leicester **Ref:**YH06416
- **HEATHER HALL**, Heather **Ref:**YH06626
- **HILL, N & J A**, Lutterworth **Ref:**YH06832
- **HOME FARM LIVERY**, Coalville **Ref:**YH06996
- **HORSE TROUGH**, Loughborough **Ref:**YH07144
- **LIMES EQUESTRIAN CTRE**, Sapcote **Ref:**YH08633
- **LYNCHGATE FARM RIDING SCHOOL**, Hinckley **Ref:**YH08925
- **MANOR HOUSE STUD**, Queniborough **Ref:**YH09111
- **MARKFIELD EQUESTRIAN**, Markfield **Ref:**YH09161
- **MEADOW SCHOOL**, Loughborough **Ref:**YH09422
- **P & G STABLES**, Leicester **Ref:**YH10630
- **PADDOCKS**, Rothley **Ref:**YH10673
- **PINE TREE LIVERY**, Leicester **Ref:**YH11122
- **RICH, BARBARA**, Melton Mowbray **Ref:**YH11800
- **SCHOOL OF NATIONAL EQUITATION**, Loughborough **Ref:**YH12521
- **SHIELDS, J GILLIES**, Castle Donington **Ref:**YH12741
- **SOMERBY EQUESTRIAN CTRE**, Melton Mowbray **Ref:**YH13060
- **SPRING, JEREMY**, Cosby **Ref:**YH13248
- **SWAN LODGE**, Melton Mowbray **Ref:**YH13689
- **WILSON, LENNOX**, Rutland **Ref:**YH15540
- **WITHAM VILLA RIDING CTRE**, Leicester **Ref:**YH15620

LINCOLNSHIRE

- **AISBY HSE RACING STABLES**, Grantham **Ref:**YH00226
- **AUSTER LODGE LIVERY YARD**, Bourne **Ref:**YH00666
- **BELCHFORD STUD**, Horncastle **Ref:**YH01208
- **BEST/THOROUGHBRED RACING GB**, Louth **Ref:**YH01327
- **BRING YOUR HORSE ON HOLIDAY**, Louth **Ref:**YH01915
- **BROOK HSE FARM**, Louth **Ref:**YH02037
- **CHARNICAL RIDING CTRE**, Gainsborough **Ref:**YH02772
- **EAGLE HALL EST**, Lincoln **Ref:**YH04437
- **FOUR WINDS**, Spalding **Ref:**YH05413
- **FUNWAY EQUESTRIAN CTRE**, Skegness **Ref:**YH05540
- **GLEN RIVER RIDING SCHOOL**, Grantham **Ref:**YH05826
- **GORSE FARM LIVERY STABLES**, Sleaford **Ref:**YH05940
- **IVY LANE RIDING SCHOOL**, Lincoln **Ref:**YH07540
- **KEY, J U**, Boston **Ref:**YH08114
- **KIRBY HSE COTTAGE**, Grantham **Ref:**YH08224
- **LAUGHTON WOOD EQUESTRIAN CTRE**, Gainsborough **Ref:**YH08449
- **LINESIDE RIDING STABLES**, Boston **Ref:**YH08657
- **OAKWOOD RIDING SERVICES**, Spalding **Ref:**YH10410
- **ORCHARD FARM EQUESTRIAN**, Skegness **Ref:**YH10529
- **POPPYFIELDS**, Lincoln **Ref:**YH11275
- **REDNIL EQUESTRIAN CTRE**, Lincoln **Ref:**YH11716
- **S & B STABLES**, Alford **Ref:**YH12309
- **SAXILBY RIDING SCHOOL**, Lincoln **Ref:**YH12466

LINCOLNSHIRE (NORTH EAST)

- **R G EQUESTRIAN**, Grimsby **Ref:**YH11536

LINCOLNSHIRE (NORTH)

- **E A JAQUES**, Scunthorpe **Ref:**YH04395
- **WILLOW FARM**, Scunthorpe **Ref:**YH15498

LONDON (GREATER)

- **ALDER, R**, Uxbridge **Ref:**YH00256
- **ALDERSBROOK RIDING SCHOOL**, London **Ref:**YH00257
- **BARNFIELDS**, London **Ref:**YH00986
- **BELMONT RIDING CTRE**, London **Ref:**YH01249
- **BRAYSIDE FARM DIY LIVERY**, Enfield **Ref:**YH01822
- **DOCKLANDS EQUESTRIAN CTRE**, London **Ref:**YH04157
- **DRUMAWHEY**, Uxbridge **Ref:**YH04285
- **FRITH MANOR EQUESTRIAN CTRE**, London **Ref:**YH05510
- **GILLIAN'S RIDING SCHOOL**, Enfield **Ref:**YH05784
- **GOULDS GREEN**, Uxbridge **Ref:**YH05952
- **GROVE FARM**, Stanmore **Ref:**YH06164
- **KINGS OAK EQUESTRIAN CTRE**, Enfield **Ref:**YH08196
- **KINGSTON RIDING CTRE**, Kingston Upon Thames **Ref:**YH08207
- **LEE VALLEY RIDING CTRE**, London **Ref:**YH08519
- **LITTLEBOURNE FARM**, Uxbridge **Ref:**YH08703
- **LONDON EQUESTRIAN CTRE**, Finchley **Ref:**YH08785
- **LONDON EQUESTRIAN CTRE**, London **Ref:**YH08784
- **LOWDHAM LODGE**, Uxbridge **Ref:**YH08858
- **LOWER PRIORY FARM**, Stanmore **Ref:**YH08868
- **LYNCH COTTAGE FARM**, Totteridge Common **Ref:**YH08922
- **OLD FARM STABLES**, Hampton **Ref:**YH10456
- **PINNERWOOD ARABIAN STUD**, Hatch End **Ref:**YH11136
- **QUEEN ELIZABETH RIDING SCHOOL**, Chingford **Ref:**YH11488
- **RIDGWAY STABLES**, London **Ref:**YH11870
- **ROEHAMPTON GATE**, London **Ref:**YH12053
- **STAG LODGE STABLES**, London **Ref:**YH13326
- **SUZANNE'S RIDING SCHOOL**, Harrow **Ref:**YH13679
- **TRENT PARK EQUESTRIAN CTRE**, London **Ref:**YH14378
- **WHITE HSE STABLES**, Enfield **Ref:**YH15319
- **WIMBLEDON VILLAGE STABLES**, London **Ref:**YH15557

MANCHESTER (GREATER)

- **CARRINGTON RIDING**, Manchester **Ref:**YH02589
- **CROFT END EQUESTRIAN CTRE**, Oldham **Ref:**YH03613
- **GODLEY STUD RIDING SCHOOL**, Manchester **Ref:**YH05868
- **HARPER FOLD STABLES**, Manchester **Ref:**YH06452
- **HOUGH FARM**, Manchester **Ref:**YH07201
- **KENYON FARM RIDING CTRE**, Manchester **Ref:**YH08094
- **LOMAX, M & J**, Bolton **Ref:**YH08781
- **MIDDLEWOOD LIVERY STABLES**, Stockport **Ref:**YH09548
- **MOSSBROOK ARENA & STUD**, Astley **Ref:**YH09866
- **NEW HILL FARM**, Manchester **Ref:**YH10107
- **OAKHILL RIDING SCHOOL**, Manchester **Ref:**YH10384
- **RYDERS FARM**, Bolton **Ref:**YH12297
- **SHORESIDE STABLES**, Manchester **Ref:**YH12759

MERSEYSIDE

- **BACKWOOD LIVERY SERVICES**, Neston **Ref:**YH00772
- **BANK FARM**, Wirral **Ref:**YH00886
- **BEACHLEY STABLES**, Liverpool **Ref:**YH01105
- **BOWLERS RIDING SCHOOL**, Liverpool **Ref:**YH01716
- **DEE FARM LIVERY STABLES**, Wirral **Ref:**YH04014
- **HORNBY, W M**, Southport **Ref:**YH07075
- **LARTON LIVERY**, Wirral **Ref:**YH08435
- **MAYPOLE FARM**, Prescot **Ref:**YH09303
- **PARK LANE LIVERIES**, Wirral **Ref:**YH10730
- **PATTEN, D**, Prescot **Ref:**YH10827
- **RABY HOUSE STABLES**, Neston **Ref:**YH11571
- **ROSE COTTAGE**, Southport **Ref:**YH12090
- **TARBOCK GREEN RIDING SCHOOL**, Prescot **Ref:**YH13869
- **THORNTON FARM LIVERY**, Wirral **Ref:**YH14073
- **THURSTASTON HALL FARM**, Wirral **Ref:**YH14123
- **WARREN FARM STABLES**, Liverpool **Ref:**YH14930
- **WHEATHILL RIDING CTRE**, Liverpool **Ref:**YH15268

MIDLANDS (WEST)

- **BARN COTTAGE LIVERY STABLES**, Solihull **Ref:**YH00961
- **BEARLEY CROSS STABLES**, Solihull **Ref:**YH01121
- **BIRCH, MICHAEL E**, Wolverhampton **Ref:**YH01430
- **BOURNE VALE STABLES**, Walsall **Ref:**YH01683
- **BROOKFIELDS**, Wolverhampton **Ref:**YH02052
- **BUBBENHALL BRIDGE**, Coventry **Ref:**YH02182
- **CASTLE HILL RIDING SCHOOL**, Coventry **Ref:**YH02627
- **CHARLEY, B**, Coventry **Ref:**YH02763
- **CROOK COTTAGE STABLES**, Walsall **Ref:**YH03635
- **FARMHOUSE STABLES**, Sutton Coldfield **Ref:**YH05064
- **FOUR OAKS LIVERY**, Sutton Coldfield **Ref:**YH05409
- **FOXHILLS**, Walsall **Ref:**YH05435
- **GORSE FARM ARENA**, Aldridge **Ref:**YH05939
- **HART, ROSEMARY**, Stourbridge **Ref:**YH06498
- **HAZEL FARM**, Solihull **Ref:**YH06599
- **HILTON PARK STABLES**, Wolverhampton **Ref:**YH06864
- **HOME LIVERY & RIDING CTRE**, Walsall **Ref:**YH07002
- **LEE MARSDEN EQUESTRIAN**, Sutton Coldfield **Ref:**YH08517
- **MOOR FARM STABLES**, Coventry **Ref:**YH09745
- **NORTH WORCESTERSHIRE**, Halesowen **Ref:**YH10287
- **SANDWELL VALLEY RIDING CTRE**, West Bromwich **Ref:**YH12421
- **SEECHEM EQUESTRIAN CTRE**, Birmingham **Ref:**YH12607
- **W S WALTON & SONS**, Dudley **Ref:**YH14796
- **WISHAW RIDING CTRE**, Sutton Coldfield **Ref:**YH15614
- **WITHYBROOK STABLES**, Coventry **Ref:**YH15629

NORFOLK

- **BINTREE MANOR LIVERIES**, Dereham **Ref:**YH01427
- **BLACKBOROUGH END**, King's Lynn **Ref:**YH01477
- **BLOOM, M J**, Wymondham **Ref:**YH01552
- **BRIDGE FARM STABLES**, Mundesley **Ref:**YH01872
- **CALDECOTT HALL**, Great Yarmouth **Ref:**YH02429
- **CHURCH FARM LIVERY STABLES**, Great Yarmouth **Ref:**YH02898
- **COUSINS, S D J**, King's Lynn **Ref:**YH03514
- **CROFT FARM RIDING CTRE**, Great Yarmouth **Ref:**YH03615
- **CROSSWAYS LIVERY YARD**, Great Yarmouth **Ref:**YH03666
- **D I Y STABLING**, Norwich **Ref:**YH03786

- **DISS LIVERY CTRE**, Diss **Ref:**YH04132
- **EDEN MEADOWS RIDING CTRE**, Attleborough **Ref:**YH04547
- **F J LUCAS STABLES**, King's Lynn **Ref:**YH04994
- **FERRY FARM LIVERY YARD**, Norwich **Ref:**YH05172
- **FOREST LODGE RIDING CTRE**, Holt **Ref:**YH05343
- **FRITTON LAKE**, Great Yarmouth **Ref:**YH05511
- **GRANGE FARM LIVERY**, Norwich **Ref:**YH05990
- **HARDINGHAM FARMS**, Norwich **Ref:**YH06413
- **HARRIS, J A**, Norwich **Ref:**YH06476
- **HIGHFIELD EQUESTRIAN CTRE**, Great Yarmouth **Ref:**YH06784
- **HILLCREST LIVERY CTRE**, Great Yarmouth **Ref:**YH06842
- **HOCKWOLD LODGE**, Thetford **Ref:**YH06906
- **KESWICK RIDING STABLES**, Norwich **Ref:**YH08106
- **MEADOW FARM EQUESTRIAN CTRE**, Norwich **Ref:**YH09418
- **MILL FARM STABLES**, Great Witchingham **Ref:**YH09574
- **RECTORY ROAD RIDING SCHOOL**, Norwich **Ref:**YH11693
- **ROSE-ACRE RIDING STABLES**, Mundesley **Ref:**YH12099
- **RUNCTON HALL**, King's Lynn **Ref:**YH12233
- **STREET FARM**, King's Lynn **Ref:**YH13572
- **STRUMPSHAW HALL**, Norwich **Ref:**YH13591
- **STRUMPSHAW RIDING CTRE**, Norwich **Ref:**YH13592
- **SUSSEX FARM STABLES**, King's Lynn **Ref:**YH13661
- **SWAFIELD RIDING**, North Walsham **Ref:**YH13682
- **THOMPSON BRANCASTER FARMS**, King's Lynn **Ref:**YH14030
- **TOP FARM EQUESTRIAN CTRE**, Norwich **Ref:**YH14236
- **WESTON PARK EQUESTRIAN CTRE**, Norwich **Ref:**YH15224
- **WILLOW FARM RIDING SCHOOL**, Great Yarmouth **Ref:**YH15500

NORTHAMPTONSHIRE

- **A J STABLES**, Towcester **Ref:**YH00042
- **ALLWORK, S**, Northampton **Ref:**YH00328
- **ASHTON STABLES**, Northampton **Ref:**YH00614
- **BLETSOE BROWN**, Northampton **Ref:**YH01538
- **BRAMPTON STABLES**, Northampton **Ref:**YH01794
- **BROOK FARM**, Wellingborough **Ref:**YH02033
- **EAST LODGE FARM RIDING EST**, Northampton **Ref:**YH04479
- **GLEBE FARM EQUESTRIAN CTRE**, Wellingborough **Ref:**YH05815
- **GRANGE STABLES**, Kettering **Ref:**YH05998
- **GREENACRES LIVERY CTRE**, Towcester **Ref:**YH06077
- **HARRINGWORTH MANOR**, Corby **Ref:**YH06461
- **MANDI'S LIVERIES**, Northampton **Ref:**YH09071
- **RATHBONE, K**, Ravensthorpe **Ref:**YH11654
- **THREE SHIRES LIVERY CTRE**, Wellingborough **Ref:**YH14107
- **TOP FARM**, Wellingborough **Ref:**YH14235
- **YELVERTOFT EQUESTRIAN CTRE**, Yelvertoft **Ref:**YH15900

NORTHUMBERLAND

- **BENRIDGE RIDING CTRE**, Morpeth **Ref:**YH01277
- **CHARLTON, R B**, Hexham **Ref:**YH02766
- **DALGISH, S**, Hexham **Ref:**YH03840
- **FOWBERRY FARMS**, Wooler **Ref:**YH05416
- **HAGGERSTON**, Berwick-upon-Tweed **Ref:**YH06277
- **HARGREAVE EQUINE SVS**, Chathill **Ref:**YH06425
- **THORNLEY GATE LIVERIES**, Hexham **Ref:**YH14070
- **WINDY EDGE STABLES**, Alnwick **Ref:**YH15580
- **WOOPERTON**, Alnwick **Ref:**YH15770

NOTTINGHAMSHIRE

- **ARKENFIELD STABLES**, Nottingham **Ref:**YH00531
- **BAKER, RICHARD**, Nottingham **Ref:**YH00826
- **BARNFIELDS**, Keyworth **Ref:**YH00987
- **BROOMSIDE STUD**, Calverton **Ref:**YH02082
- **CARLTON FOREST**, Worksop **Ref:**YH02542
- **CARR, S J**, Worksop **Ref:**YH02574
- **CAULDWELL LIVERY STABLES**, Sutton-In-Ashfield **Ref:**YH02658
- **CHERRY TREE RIDING CTRE**, New Brinsley **Ref:**YH02817
- **CLGE FARM**, Newark **Ref:**YH03026
- **CTRE - LINES**, Newark **Ref:**YH03694
- **DANETHORPE LIVERY SVS**, Newark **Ref:**YH03868
- **DAVEY, R**, Nottingham **Ref:**YH03913
- **FIRBECK**, Worksop **Ref:**YH05222
- **HODSOCK STABLES**, Worksop **Ref:**YH06915
- **HOLME FARM LIVERY**, Newark **Ref:**YH06964
- **KIRKFIELD EQUESTRIAN CTRE**, Lower Blidworth **Ref:**YH08234
- **LANEHAM LIVERY STABLE**, Retford **Ref:**YH08392
- **MANOR FARM LIVERY YARD**, Gotham **Ref:**YH09102
- **NEWTON CROFT COUNTRY**, Nottingham **Ref:**YH10169
- **PLEASLEY PARK LIVERY**, Mansfield **Ref:**YH11174
- **RICHARDSON STABLES**, Nottingham **Ref:**YH11814
- **SADDLE RACK**, Nottingham **Ref:**YH12346
- **ST CLEMENTS LODGE**, Nottingham **Ref:**YH13274
- **SUTTON MANOR FARM**, Retford **Ref:**YH13673
- **TRENT VALLEY STABLES**, Southwell **Ref:**YH14381
- **VICTORIAN CARRIAGES**, Newark **Ref:**YH14710
- **WELLOW PK**, Newark **Ref:**YH15077
- **WOODSIDE FARM STABLES**, Mansfield **Ref:**YH15741
- **WOODSIDE LIVERY STABLES**, Nottingham **Ref:**YH15743

OXFORDSHIRE

- **ARLINGTON POLO**, Kidlington **Ref:**YH00533
- **ASTI STUD & SADDLERY**, Faringdon **Ref:**YH00633
- **BLACKHEATH LIVERY STABLES**, Burford **Ref:**YH01484
- **EAST END FARM RIDING SCHOOL**, Wallingford **Ref:**YH04474
- **FRIEZE FARM LIVERIES**, Henley-on-Thames **Ref:**YH05505
- **GODINGTON STUD**, Bicester **Ref:**YH05867
- **GRAMPS HILL RIDING CTRE**, Wantage **Ref:**YH05978
- **HOME FARM LIVERY YARD**, Kidlington **Ref:**YH06998
- **J M EDMUNDS KENNS FARM**, Carterton **Ref:**YH07596
- **JEFFERY, C A**, Witney **Ref:**YH07717
- **LOWER FARM**, Wallingford **Ref:**YH08863
- **MALTHOUSE TRAINING CTRE**, Abingdon **Ref:**YH09059
- **MANOR FARM**, Oxford **Ref:**YH09096
- **NEW HOUSE LIVERY**, Abingdon **Ref:**YH10109
- **OLD MANOR HSE**, Oxford **Ref:**YH10461
- **PIGEON HOUSE STABLES**, Witney **Ref:**YH11095
- **PONYTEL**, Banbury **Ref:**YH11258
- **SILVERDOWN**, Didcot **Ref:**YH12815
- **STANDLAKE EQUESTRIAN CTRE**, Witney **Ref:**YH13362
- **TURPINS LODGE**, Banbury **Ref:**YH14494
- **VALLEY FARM EQUESTRIAN CTRE**, Banbury **Ref:**YH14653
- **WESTFIELD SADDLERY**, Chipping Norton **Ref:**YH15213
- **WHITE HORSE STABLES**, Faringdon **Ref:**YH15314
- **YEW TREE STABLES**, Witney **Ref:**YH15911

RUTLAND

- **BARROW STABLES**, Oakham **Ref:**YH01030
- **MANTON LODGE STABLES**, Rutland **Ref:**YH09127
- **PURBRICK, LIZZIE**, Oakham **Ref:**YH11463

SHROPSHIRE

- **BERRIEWOOD FARM**, Shrewsbury **Ref:**YH01313
- **BOW HOUSE FARM RIDING SCHOOL**, Bishops Castle **Ref:**YH01695
- **BRYNORE STUD & LIVERY STABLES**, Ellesmere **Ref:**YH02178
- **CHARTERS, SUE**, Ludlow **Ref:**YH02776
- **CRANN, P F**, Bridgnorth **Ref:**YH03568
- **G & K CRADDOCK & SONS**, Whitchurch **Ref:**YH05563
- **HANCOCK, J & V**, Telford **Ref:**YH06375
- **HIGHGROVE SCHOOL OF RIDING**, Craven Arms **Ref:**YH06788
- **LILLESHALL EQUESTRIAN CTRE**, Newport **Ref:**YH08620
- **MIDDLE FARM**, Newport **Ref:**YH09535
- **MILL FARM RIDING CTRE**, Shrewsbury **Ref:**YH09572
- **OSWESTRY EQUEST CTRE**, Oswestry **Ref:**YH10576
- **PRESCOTT RIDING CTRE**, Shrewsbury **Ref:**YH11356
- **ROWAN, J**, Church Stretton **Ref:**YH12156
- **TOUCHDOWN LIVERIES**, Whitchurch **Ref:**YH14253
- **TRENCH VILLA STABLES**, Ellesmere **Ref:**YH14374
- **W BRYAN HORSE SERVICES**, Shrewsbury **Ref:**YH14753
- **WOOD FARM STUD**, Wellington **Ref:**YH15657
- **WYKE OF SHIFNAL**, Shifnal **Ref:**YH15863

SOMERSET

- **ADSBOROUGH HSE STABLES**, Taunton **Ref:**YH00189
- **ALSTONE COURT RIDING ESTB**, Highbridge **Ref:**YH00342
- **BADGWORTH ARENA**, Axbridge **Ref:**YH00781
- **BRIMSMORE EQUESTRIAN CTRE**, Yeovil **Ref:**YH01913
- **BROAD ACRES STABLES**, Somerton **Ref:**YH01988
- **BURCOTT RIDING CTRE**, Wells **Ref:**YH02235
- **BURCOTT RIDING CTRE**, Wells **Ref:**YH02236
- **CALLOW, W J**, Taunton **Ref:**YH02451
- **COURT FARM STABLES**, Exford **Ref:**YH03502
- **CROWN HOTEL**, Minehead **Ref:**YH03681
- **CUTTHORNE**, Minehead **Ref:**YH03762
- **DRAKES FARM**, Ilminster **Ref:**YH04256
- **DRAYDON FARM**, Dulverton **Ref:**YH04262
- **DUNKERY**, Minehead **Ref:**YH04343
- **EBBORLANDS**, Wells **Ref:**YH04529
- **HALF MOON RIDING STABLES**, Langport **Ref:**YH06296
- **HINDON FARM**, Minehead **Ref:**YH06873
- **LONG LANE RIDING STABLES**, Wincanton **Ref:**YH08796
- **LYNG COURT LIVERY**, Taunton **Ref:**YH08931
- **MILLHOUSE EQUESTRIAN CTRE**, Taunton **Ref:**YH09620
- **MINEHEAD HARRIERS & FOXHOUNDS**, Templecombe **Ref:**YH09649
- **PEVLINGS FARM**, Templecombe **Ref:**YH11035
- **PORLOCK VALE HSE/RIDING CTRE**, Porlock Weir **Ref:**YH11278
- **RISCOMBE FARM**, Minehead **Ref:**YH11908

- **RODGROVE STUD EQUESTRIAN CTRE**, Wincanton **Ref:**YH12048
- **SCOTTS RIDING STABLES**, Bridgwater **Ref:**YH12562
- **SHRUB FARM LIVERY YARD**, Brent Knoll **Ref:**YH12771
- **SPARKFORD SAWMILLS**, Yeovil **Ref:**YH13177
- **WINDMILL HILL EQUESTRIAN CTRE**, Ilminster **Ref:**YH15566

SOMERSET (NORTH)

- **CLEVEDON RIDING**, Clevedon **Ref:**YH03020
- **SMART, JAYNE**, Banwell **Ref:**YH12922
- **SOUTHFIELD FARM RIDING SCHOOL**, Backwell **Ref:**YH13150
- **VOWLES RIDING STABLES**, Weston-Super-Mare **Ref:**YH14744

STAFFORDSHIRE

- **ABNALLS FARM**, Lichfield **Ref:**YH00133
- **ALDERSHAWE LIVERY YARD**, Lichfield **Ref:**YH00258
- **ALSAGER EQUESTRIAN CTRE**, Stoke-on-Trent **Ref:**YH00335
- **ASHMORE BROOK DAIRY FARM**, Lichfield **Ref:**YH00609
- **BARLASTON RIDING CTRE**, Stoke-on-Trent **Ref:**YH00949
- **BENTLEY HSE**, Biddulph Park **Ref:**YH01285
- **CHEADLE EQUESTRIAN CTRE**, Stoke-on-Trent **Ref:**YH02795
- **COPPICE EQUESTRIAN SADDLERY**, Farley **Ref:**YH03303
- **DAISY LANE LIVERY YARD**, Burton-on-Trent **Ref:**YH03816
- **DAVISON, RICHARD**, Uttoxeter **Ref:**YH03959
- **ELITE RIDING & EQUESTRIAN SVS**, Cannock **Ref:**YH04607
- **ENDON RIDING SCHOOL**, Stoke-on-Trent **Ref:**YH04667
- **GOTHERSLEY FARM**, Stourbridge **Ref:**YH05945
- **GRANGE FARM LIVERIES**, Stoke-on-Trent **Ref:**YH05989
- **GUNSTONE HALL RIDING CTRE**, Wolverhampton **Ref:**YH06192
- **HEART OF ENGLAND EQUESTRIAN**, Stone **Ref:**YH06617
- **HOLLYWALL FARM & STABLES**, Stoke-on-Trent **Ref:**YH06959
- **INGESTRE STABLES**, Stafford **Ref:**YH07445
- **LADYMOOR GATE**, Stoke-on-Trent **Ref:**YH08339
- **MAPLES LIVERY CTRE**, Lichfield **Ref:**YH09134
- **OFFLEY BROOK LIVERY STABLES**, Eccleshall **Ref:**YH10436
- **RODBASTON CLGE**, Penkridge **Ref:**YH12041
- **SANT, C J**, Newcastle **Ref:**YH12430
- **SCOTT, B G**, Stafford **Ref:**YH12538
- **SCROPTON**, Burton-on-Trent **Ref:**YH12569
- **SIMMONS, W H & K A**, Stafford **Ref:**YH12829
- **SMITH & MORRIS COUNTRY STORE**, Newcastle **Ref:**YH12933
- **WOODHOUSE STABLES**, Burton-on-Trent **Ref:**YH15695

SUFFOLK

- **BARDWELL MANOR**, Bury St Edmunds **Ref:**YH00928
- **BRANDON RIDING ACADEMY**, Brandon **Ref:**YH01797
- **CHILLESFORD STABLES**, Woodbridge **Ref:**YH02855
- **CHIMNEY MILL GALLERIES**, Bury St Edmunds **Ref:**YH02862
- **COUNTRY FARM LIVERY YARD**, Sudbury **Ref:**YH03405
- **CULFORD STABLES**, Bury St Edmunds **Ref:**YH03701
- **EARLSWAY FARM**, Halesworth **Ref:**YH04454
- **EDMUNDSON, P W J**, Woodbridge **Ref:**YH04567
- **GILLAM HALL STABLES**, Bury St Edmunds **Ref:**YH05778
- **GLEVERING HALL FARM**, Woodbridge **Ref:**YH05847
- **GROVE FARM DRIVING & LIVERY**, Mildenhall **Ref:**YH06166
- **HAAG, R**, Stowmarket **Ref:**YH06248
- **HARDWICK STABLES**, Bury St Edmunds **Ref:**YH06415
- **HERITAGE COAST STUD**, Woodbridge **Ref:**YH06703
- **HIGH HSE**, Stowmarket **Ref:**YH06762
- **HONEYHILL FARM RIDING STABLES**, Bury St Edmunds **Ref:**YH07014
- **LAVENHAM HALL LIVERIES**, Lavenham **Ref:**YH08462
- **LINKWOOD EQUESTIAN**, Bury St Edmunds **Ref:**YH08665
- **NEWTON HALL EQUITATION CTRE**, Ipswich **Ref:**YH10171
- **ORWELL ARENA**, Ipswich **Ref:**YH10556
- **PARK FARM**, Harleston **Ref:**YH10718
- **PARK FARM STABLES**, Newmarket **Ref:**YH10724
- **POPLAR PK**, Woodbridge **Ref:**YH11271
- **POTTERS TYE**, Sudbury **Ref:**YH11301
- **STOKE BY CLARE EQUESTRIAN CTRE**, Sudbury **Ref:**YH13501
- **TOLLGATE LIVERY CTRE**, Felixstowe **Ref:**YH14211
- **UGGLESHALL**, Beccles **Ref:**YH14541
- **VALLEY FARM**, Woodbridge **Ref:**YH14651
- **WOODLANDS**, Bury St Edmunds **Ref:**YH15707
- **WOOLMER COTTAGE STABLES**, Newmarket **Ref:**YH15768

SURREY

- **ALL MANOR PK EQUESTRIAN CTRE**, Coulsdon **Ref:**YH00285
- **ASCOT PARK**, Woking **Ref:**YH00583
- **BARKER, J**, Chessington **Ref:**YH00943
- **BARNES, PAT**, Woking **Ref:**YH00979
- **BEECHWOOD**, Caterham **Ref:**YH01176
- **BERKELEY EQUESTRIAN SVS**, Kingswood **Ref:**YH01301
- **BRIDLEWAYS EQUESTRIAN CTRE**, Great Bookham **Ref:**YH01898
- **BRILLS FARM**, Oxted **Ref:**YH01911
- **BUSHY PLAT LIVERY STABLES**, Dorking **Ref:**YH02313
- **CHALK PIT FARM STABLES**, Leatherhead **Ref:**YH02711
- **CHIPPINGS FARM**, Cobham **Ref:**YH02865
- **CHIPPINGS FARM STABLES**, Cobham **Ref:**YH02866
- **CLANDON MANOR SUPPLIES**, Guildford **Ref:**YH02942
- **CLANDON PK**, Guildford **Ref:**YH02943
- **CLOCK TOWER RIDING CTRE**, Tadworth **Ref:**YH03052
- **COPPER HORSE STABLES**, Egham **Ref:**YH03300
- **COURTLANDS LIVERY STABLES**, Banstead **Ref:**YH03508
- **CRANLEIGH SCHOOL OF RIDING**, Cranleigh **Ref:**YH03565
- **DELL PK FARM**, Egham **Ref:**YH04031
- **DUNSFOLD RYSE STABLES**, Chiddingfold **Ref:**YH04357
- **EBBISHAM FARM**, Tadworth **Ref:**YH04528
- **FAIRHOLME FARM LIVERY STABLE**, Banstead **Ref:**YH05023
- **FARTHING DOWNS STABLES**, Coulsdon **Ref:**YH05099
- **FENNS FARM**, Woking **Ref:**YH05149
- **FOUR SEASONS**, Epsom **Ref:**YH05410
- **GARSON FARM**, Esher **Ref:**YH05658
- **GRAVETTS LANE STABLES**, Guildford **Ref:**YH06025
- **GREEN LANE FARM**, Guildford **Ref:**YH06056
- **GREENFIELD FARM STABLES**, Leatherhead **Ref:**YH06082
- **GREENWAYS FARM & STABLES**, Godalming **Ref:**YH06105
- **HALLEGA STABLES**, Epsom **Ref:**YH06328
- **HAMMOND LIVERY STABLES**, Chessington **Ref:**YH06359
- **HATCH FARM STABLES**, Addlestone **Ref:**YH06530
- **HEADLEY GR STABLES**, Epsom **Ref:**YH06611
- **HEATHFIELDS FARM LIVERY**, Woking **Ref:**YH06632
- **HEDGE FARM LIVERIES**, Godalming **Ref:**YH06640
- **HIGHLANDS FARM STABLES**, Leatherhead **Ref:**YH06796
- **HIGHLEA STUD & LIVERY STABLES**, Tadworth **Ref:**YH06797
- **HOOKE FARM LIVERY STABLES**, Leatherhead **Ref:**YH07037
- **HUNTERSFIELD FARM RIDING CTRE**, Banstead **Ref:**YH07303
- **HURSTFIELDS EQUESTRIAN CTRE**, Tadworth **Ref:**YH07321
- **JOYSONS HILL**, Whyteleafe **Ref:**YH07954
- **KENILWORTH EQUESTRIAN CTRE**, Leatherhead **Ref:**YH08063
- **LANGSHOT EQUESTRIAN CTRE**, Chobham **Ref:**YH08414
- **LARKENSHAW FARM**, Woking **Ref:**YH08429
- **LEMANS BARN FARM**, Cranleigh **Ref:**YH08550
- **LITTLE BROOK EQUESTRIAN**, Lingfield **Ref:**YH08685
- **LOCKNER FARM**, Guildford **Ref:**YH08760
- **LODGE LIVERIES**, Cobham **Ref:**YH08771
- **LONGSHAW STABLES**, Coulsdon **Ref:**YH08817
- **LOWER FARM**, Cobham **Ref:**YH08864
- **MANOR FARM LIVERY STABLES**, Richmond **Ref:**YH09101
- **MANOR PK LIVERY STABLES**, Chertsey **Ref:**YH09116
- **NEW LODGE FARM LIVERY STABLES**, Carshalton **Ref:**YH10111
- **OLD FARM**, Ripley **Ref:**YH10455
- **OLD FORGE**, Reigate **Ref:**YH10458
- **OLD PK STABLES**, Farnham **Ref:**YH10472
- **OLDENCRAIG EQUESTRIAN CTRE**, Lingfield **Ref:**YH10484
- **OVERHILL LIVERY STABLES**, Farnham **Ref:**YH10592
- **PACHESHAM EQUESTRIAN CTRE**, Leatherhead **Ref:**YH10661
- **PARK STABLES**, Dorking **Ref:**YH10737
- **PETERSHAM FARM**, Richmond **Ref:**YH11023
- **POYNTERS**, Cobham **Ref:**YH11330
- **RIDGEWOOD RIDING CTRE**, Reigate **Ref:**YH11869
- **RUNNINGWELL STABLES**, Oxted **Ref:**YH12235
- **S R S**, Sunbury-on-Thames **Ref:**YH12333
- **SMALL, M E**, Croydon **Ref:**YH12908
- **STANGRAVE HALL STABLES**, Godstone **Ref:**YH13365
- **STARSHAW STABLES**, Coulsdon **Ref:**YH13399
- **TANGYE, JOHN**, Guildford **Ref:**YH13855
- **TEIZERS EQUESTRIAN CTRE**, Burstow **Ref:**YH13937
- **TILFORD HOUSE FARM**, Farnham **Ref:**YH14144
- **TRIPLE BAR RIDING CTRE**, Dorking **Ref:**YH14400
- **TRUXFORD RIDING CTRE**, Godalming **Ref:**YH14423
- **UPPER RIDGEWAY FARM**, Godalming **Ref:**YH14607
- **VALE LODGE STABLES**, Leatherhead **Ref:**YH14635
- **VICTORIA FARM**, Woking **Ref:**YH14708
- **WAFFRONS SCHOOL OF RIDING**, Chessington **Ref:**YH14820
- **WEST WEYLANDS FARM**, Walton-on-Thames **Ref:**YH15169
- **WHITEWOOD HSE FARM**, Horley **Ref:**YH15359
- **WINDACRES FARM**, Horley **Ref:**YH15561
- **WISHANGER EQUESTRIAN CTRE**, Farnham **Ref:**YH15612
- **WISHANGER LIVERIES**, Farnham **Ref:**YH15613

WOODCOTE FARM, West Horsley **Ref:**YH15678
WOODRUFF EQUESTRIAN, West Byfleet **Ref:**YH15731
WOODSIDE STABLES, Godalming **Ref:**YH15746
WOODSTOCK SOUTH STABLES, Chessington **Ref:**YH15751
WOOLFORDS FARM LIVERY STABLES, Godalming **Ref:**YH15767

SUSSEX (EAST)

ASHDOWN FOREST RIDING CTRE, Uckfield **Ref:**YH00595
BARNES FARM RETIREMENT, Robertsbridge **Ref:**YH00970
CANTERS END RIDING SCHOOL, Uckfield **Ref:**YH02512
CHURCH FARM & STUD, Lewes **Ref:**YH02896
ELMS SADDLERY & LIVERIES, Icklesham **Ref:**YH04638
GLENGORSE STABLES, Battle **Ref:**YH05836
GOLDEN CROSS, Hailsham **Ref:**YH05878
GROVEBRIDGE LIVERY YARD, Heathfield **Ref:**YH06174
HIGHAM FARM, Hastings **Ref:**YH06768
HOLE FARM, Uckfield **Ref:**YH06928
JOHN BIRON EQUESTRIAN, Heathfield **Ref:**YH07781
ROBIN POST STABLES, Hailsham **Ref:**YH11981
ROCK LANE, Bexhill-on-Sea **Ref:**YH12025
SLYES FARM, Hailsham **Ref:**YH12904
SOUTH LODGE, Rotherfield **Ref:**YH13100
ST IVES LIVERY, Hartfield **Ref:**YH13277
WINTON STREET FARM STABLES, Polegate **Ref:**YH15600

SUSSEX (WEST)

ALBOURNE EQUESTRIAN CTRE, Hassocks **Ref:**YH00248
ASHWATER LIVERIES, Horsham **Ref:**YH00617
BADGER WOOD FARM STABLES, Fulking **Ref:**YH00777
BADGER WOOD TRAINING/LIVERY, Henfield **Ref:**YH00778
BELMOREDEAN, West Grinstead **Ref:**YH01251
BOXGROVE COMPETITION STABLES, Chichester **Ref:**YH01726
BRIDGE HSE EQUESTRIAN CTRE, Horsham **Ref:**YH01874
BROADFIELD STABLES, Steyning **Ref:**YH01995
C & C EQUINE SVS, Billingshurst **Ref:**YH02353
CARPENTER, E J, Arundel **Ref:**YH02568
CHEPHURST FARM LIVERIES, Horsham **Ref:**YH02807
CLAYTON HILL STABLES, Hassocks **Ref:**YH03003
COBB, I, Pulborough **Ref:**YH03110
DITCHLING COMMON STUD, Burgess Hill **Ref:**YH04135
EATON THORNE STABLES, Henfield **Ref:**YH04525
FOREST FARM, Horsham **Ref:**YH05336
GOSPELS FARM, Hassocks **Ref:**YH05943
HAM HSE STABLES, Haywards Heath **Ref:**YH06340
HANGLETON FARM, Worthing **Ref:**YH06386
HAPPY VALLEY RIDING STABLES, Shoreham By Sea **Ref:**YH06401
HIGHLANDER EQUINE CTRE, Lancing **Ref:**YH06794
KENT, A, Midhurst **Ref:**YH08084
LASSETTER, JOHN F, Chichester **Ref:**YH08442
LAVANT HSE STABLES, Chichester **Ref:**YH08460
LAVANT HSE STABLES, Chichester **Ref:**YH08460
LORDINGTON LIVERY, Chichester **Ref:**YH08826
MANNINGS LIVERIES, Henfield **Ref:**YH09089
MOLECOMB STUD, Chichester **Ref:**YH09712
NICOL, C, Horsham **Ref:**YH10198
NORTHBROOK FARM, Worthing **Ref:**YH10295
NORWOOD EQUESTRIAN CTRE, Petworth **Ref:**YH10335
PATCHING LIVERY YARD, Worthing **Ref:**YH10816
REDMIRE STABLES & BUILDINGS, Storrington **Ref:**YH11715
RIVERSIDE EQUESTRIAN CTRE, Lancing **Ref:**YH11924
ROGERS FARM, Worthing **Ref:**YH12058
SELSEY RIDING CTRE, Selsey **Ref:**YH12625
SIRETT, R T, Worthing **Ref:**YH12859
SYMONDSBURY STUD, Haywards Heath **Ref:**YH13726
TOWNS, I, Chichester **Ref:**YH14298
TREMAINES RIDING STABLES, Haywards Heath **Ref:**YH14370
WILLOWBROOK RIDING CTRE, Chichester **Ref:**YH15508
ZARA STUD, Chichester **Ref:**YH15951

TYNE AND WEAR

DUNSTON WEST FARM, Newcastle-upon-Tyne **Ref:**YH04360
E G WATSON & PARTNERS, Whitley Bay **Ref:**YH04406
GIRSONFIELD STUD, Otterburn **Ref:**YH05795
GO RIDING GRP, Ponteland **Ref:**YH05862
HYLTON LIVERY, East Boldon **Ref:**YH07358
LITTLE HARLE STABLES, Newcastle-upon-Tyne **Ref:**YH08688
MACKIE, HENRI, Newcastle-upon-Tyne **Ref:**YH09005
NORTH LIZARD RIDING SCHOOL, South Shields **Ref:**YH10271
PAULINE ROBSON LIVERY, Newcastle-upon-Tyne **Ref:**YH10836
QUARRY PARK STABLES, Gateshead **Ref:**YH11483
WILLIAMS, R, Newcastle-upon-Tyne **Ref:**YH15470

WARWICKSHIRE

ACCIMASSU, Studley **Ref:**YH00140
BEECHWOOD LIVERY/TRAINING, Berkswell **Ref:**YH01178
CALDECOTE RIDING SCHOOL, Nuneaton **Ref:**YH02428
CARRY ON RIDING STABLES, Warwick **Ref:**YH02602
COCKRAM, R A, Radway **Ref:**YH03127
ETTINGTON PARK STABLES, Stratford-upon-Avon **Ref:**YH04887
FINWOOD BARN, Warwick **Ref:**YH05218
GREENACRES STUD, Coventry **Ref:**YH06080
HOLE FARM LIVERY STABLES, Solihull **Ref:**YH06929
HOLLY RIDING SCHOOL, Atherstone **Ref:**YH06957
HOPSFORD HALL LIVERY YARD, Coventry **Ref:**YH07060
INTERNATIONAL WARWICK SCHOOL, Warwick **Ref:**YH07480
KINGSWOOD FARM HOUSE, Kenilworth **Ref:**YH08211
LITTLE MANOR FARM, Warwick **Ref:**YH08693
LODGE FARM LIVERIES, Hatton **Ref:**YH08769
NEWLEY, K & L, Coventry **Ref:**YH10147
PEBWORTH VALE SADDLERY, Stratford-upon-Avon **Ref:**YH10890
RED HSE FARM LIVERY STABLES, Leamington Spa **Ref:**YH11696
SNOWFORD HILL FARM, Rugby **Ref:**YH13043
SWALLOWFIELD EQUESTRIAN, Solihull **Ref:**YH13686
VERO, FELICITY, Nuneaton **Ref:**YH14683
WARD, ANTHONY, Moreton Morrell **Ref:**YH14898
WARWICKSHIRE CLGE HORSE UNIT, Warwick **Ref:**YH14951
WOODBINE STABLES, Rugby **Ref:**YH15675
WOOTTON COURT FARM, Warwick **Ref:**YH15771

WILTSHIRE

CHARLBURY FARM, Swindon **Ref:**YH02752
COPPERFIELD STABLES, Salisbury **Ref:**YH03302
FARROW, C, Salisbury **Ref:**YH05096
FORD FARM STABLES, Chippenham **Ref:**YH05323
FREEWARREN FARM, Marlborough **Ref:**YH05486
GREENACRES, Salisbury **Ref:**YH06075
GROVELY, Salisbury **Ref:**YH06175
HADDON STUD, Marlborough **Ref:**YH06263
HARRIS CROFT RIDING CTRE, Swindon **Ref:**YH06462
HEYWOOD, Westbury **Ref:**YH06737
HILLVIEW RIDING STABLES, Trowbridge **Ref:**YH06859
HOLY OAK HILL, Swindon **Ref:**YH06992
HORSEMANSHIP, Wootton Bassett **Ref:**YH07161
HUDDS FARM, Bradford-on-Avon **Ref:**YH07254
HURDCOTT LIVERY STABLES, Salisbury **Ref:**YH07311
INFANTRY SADDLE CLUB, Warminster **Ref:**YH07441
LADYSMITHS EQUESTRIAN CTRE, Swindon **Ref:**YH08340
LANES FARM D I Y STABLES, Swindon **Ref:**YH08394
MALTHOUSE EQUESTRIAN CTRE, Swindon **Ref:**YH09058
MARDEN GRANGE LIVERY STABLES, Devizes **Ref:**YH09145
MIDWAY MANOR, Bradford-on-Avon **Ref:**YH09562
ORMEROD, GILES, Salisbury **Ref:**YH10548
PEWSEY VALE, Marlborough **Ref:**YH11037
SAMWAYS, Salisbury **Ref:**YH12402
SOUTH FARM LIVERY YARD, Swindon **Ref:**YH13092
STONAR SCHOOL, Melksham **Ref:**YH13507
TATE, S E, Salisbury **Ref:**YH13876
TIDBALL, F G, Swindon **Ref:**YH14131
TOLLARD PARK EQUESTRIAN CTRE, Salisbury **Ref:**YH14207
TYAN CONNEMARA STUD, Salisbury **Ref:**YH14518
WHITE HORSE EQUESTRIAN CTRE, Westbury **Ref:**YH15308
WICKSTEAD FARM, Swindon **Ref:**YH15387
WIDBROOK ARABIAN STUD, Bradford-on-Avon **Ref:**YH15388

WORCESTERSHIRE

ABBOTTS MORTON LIVERY YARD, Worcester **Ref:**YH00115
ALLMAN, R P & G E J, Evesham **Ref:**YH00321
BENT, BM & SA, Evesham **Ref:**YH01282
CLARKS HILL, Evesham **Ref:**YH02980
COLLEY, ANNE, Bewdley **Ref:**YH03177
CROWFIELDS EQUESTRIAN SVS, Bromsgrove **Ref:**YH03678
DITCHAM, JANET, Kidderminster **Ref:**YH04134
EILBERG, FERDI, Redditch **Ref:**YH04598
EQUINE RESOURCES, Malvern **Ref:**YH04796
FAR FOREST EQUESTRIAN CTRE, Kidderminster **Ref:**YH05047
GRACELANDS, Droitwich **Ref:**YH05958
HACKETT, L, Broadway **Ref:**YH06251
HADLEY RIDING STABLES, Droitwich **Ref:**YH06267
HARTLEBURY EQUESTRIAN CTRE, Kidderminster **Ref:**YH06505
HIGH CRUNDALLS STABLES, Bewdley **Ref:**YH06756
HILLOCKS FARM, Kidderminster **Ref:**YH06847
HOLLIES FARM, Kidderminster **Ref:**YH06941
HONEYBOURNE STABLES, Bromsgrove **Ref:**YH07012

KNOLL & OAKTREE FARMS, Worcester **Ref:**YH08276
KYRE EQUESTRIAN CTRE, Tenbury Wells **Ref:**YH08305
MOORLANDS, Worcester **Ref:**YH09779
PERSHORE & HINDLIP CLGE, Hindlip **Ref:**YH10993
SAMBOURNE, Redditch **Ref:**YH12396
SEVERN VALLEY LIVERY CTRE, Stourport-on-Severn **Ref:**YH12645
SOLCUM STUD & STABLES, Kidderminster **Ref:**YH13052
STABLE, Redditch **Ref:**YH13287
WARRINGTON, S, Little Witley **Ref:**YH14943
WHITFORD RIDING STABLE, Bromsgrove **Ref:**YH15361
WITS END STABLES, Worcester **Ref:**YH15634

YORKSHIRE (EAST)

AIKE GRANGE STUD, Driffield **Ref:**YH00207
BLEACH YARD STABLES, Beverley **Ref:**YH01531
BRAEMAR, Hull **Ref:**YH01770
CHURCH FARMS, Beverley **Ref:**YH02904
EAST RIDING, Brough **Ref:**YH04483
HIGH BELTHORPE LIVERY, Bishop Wilton **Ref:**YH06755
HIGH FARM STABLES, Beverley **Ref:**YH06758
METHAM GRANGE STABLES, Brough **Ref:**YH09502
NORTH HUMBERSIDE, Hull **Ref:**YH10264
RISTON WHINS LIVERY YARD, Beverley **Ref:**YH11913
ROWLEY MANOR STABLES, Little Weighton **Ref:**YH12170
RYEHILL, Hull **Ref:**YH12301
SKERNE LEYS FARM, Driffield **Ref:**YH12869
SWANLAND EQUESTRIAN CTRE, North Ferriby **Ref:**YH13693
WOLDGATE TREKKING, Bridlington **Ref:**YH15646

YORKSHIRE (NORTH)

AVISON, PENNY, York **Ref:**YH00686
B & B LIVERY, Northallerton **Ref:**YH00709
BARKER, A C, York **Ref:**YH00939
BELMONT LIVERY STABLE, Harrogate **Ref:**YH01247
BEWERLEY, Harrogate **Ref:**YH01347
BILSDALE RIDING CTRE, York **Ref:**YH01416
BOGS HALL, Ripon **Ref:**YH01598
BRIGG VIEW, Filey **Ref:**YH01906
CHEQUER FARM STABLES, York **Ref:**YH02810
COTTAGE FARM STABLES, York **Ref:**YH03375
DRIVER, J G & A S, Haxby **Ref:**YH04277
FOLLIFOOT PK, Harrogate **Ref:**YH05300
FRIARS HILL STABLES, York **Ref:**YH05501
GROSMONT HSE, Whitby **Ref:**YH06157
HARROGATE, Harrogate **Ref:**YH06490
HUTTON HALL FARM, Ripon **Ref:**YH07339
LIME TREE FARM, Ripon **Ref:**YH08627
M K M RACING, Leyburn **Ref:**YH08972
MANOR FARM, Pickering **Ref:**YH09097
MILL LANE, Selby **Ref:**YH09579
NABURN GRANGE RIDING CTRE, York **Ref:**YH10008
NORTHERN EQUINE THERAPY CTRE, Settle **Ref:**YH10303
PIMLOTT, C & N, York **Ref:**YH11112
QUEEN ETHELBURGA'S CLGE, York **Ref:**YH11489
RICHMOND EQUESTRIAN CTRE, Richmond **Ref:**YH11827
RIDING CTRE, Harrogate **Ref:**YH11874
ROSE COTTAGE FARM, York **Ref:**YH12091
RUSSELL, G T, Malton **Ref:**YH12257
SAXBY, ALAN K, Northallerton **Ref:**YH12465
SEDBURYS FARM, Richmond **Ref:**YH12600
SNAINTON RIDING CTRE, Scarborough **Ref:**YH13028
SPALDING, C M, Richmond **Ref:**YH13171
STOCKWELL STUD LIVERY STABLES, Tadcaster **Ref:**YH13497
TEAL COTTAGE STUD, Welburn **Ref:**YH13922
WHALTON STUD, Harrogate **Ref:**YH15262
WILSON, C, Pickering **Ref:**YH15531
YORK RIDING SCHOOL, York **Ref:**YH15917
YORKSHIRE RIDING CTRE, Harrogate **Ref:**YH15922

YORKSHIRE (SOUTH)

BARBER, A, Sheffield **Ref:**YH00920
BELLE VUE STABLES, Doncaster **Ref:**YH01233
BRANDSTONE FARM LIVERIES, Doncaster **Ref:**YH01810
CLOUGH FIELDS STABLES, Sheffield **Ref:**YH03068
FINNINGLEY LIVERY CTRE, Doncaster **Ref:**YH05217
GLEBE FIELD RIDING EST, Mexborough **Ref:**YH05816
GROVE HSE STABLES, Doncaster **Ref:**YH06170
HOWARTH LODGE RIDING CTRE, Rotherham **Ref:**YH07220
MALLARD HSE, Sheffield **Ref:**YH09050
MASSARELLA, Sheffield **Ref:**YH09248
MOORHOUSE, Doncaster **Ref:**YH09774
OAK LODGE LIVERIES, Sheffield **Ref:**YH10370
PARKLANDS RIDING SCHOOL, Sheffield **Ref:**YH10770
PRICES, Rotherham **Ref:**YH11391
SANDALL BEAT STABLES, Doncaster **Ref:**YH12403
SIDDALL, J K & J, Sheffield **Ref:**YH12782
SMELTINGS FARM RIDING CTRE, Sheffield **Ref:**YH12927
SNOWDON FARM RIDING SCHOOL, Sheffield **Ref:**YH13040
SYKEHOUSE ARENA, Doncaster **Ref:**YH13723
WINTERINGHAM FARM LIVERY CTRE, Doncaster **Ref:**YH15598

YORKSHIRE (WEST)

ASH ROYD LIVERY STABLES, Huddersfield **Ref:**YH00588
ASTLEY RIDING CTRE, Leeds **Ref:**YH00635
BANK HSE FARM, Wakefield **Ref:**YH00891
BARTON, R & J, Wilsden **Ref:**YH01050
BLACUP TRAINING GRP, Halifax **Ref:**YH01504
BROCKADALE ARABIANS, Pontefract **Ref:**YH02006
BROOKFIELDS LIVERY STABLES, Bradford **Ref:**YH02053
BUCKSTONES LIVERY YARD, Sutton In Craven **Ref:**YH02205
BURNETT, P A, Leeds **Ref:**YH02265
CHAPPELOW, A, Mirfield **Ref:**YH02748
CHERRY TREE LIVERY STABLES, Wetherby **Ref:**YH02816
CLIFFORD MOOR FARM, Wetherby **Ref:**YH03035
CROFTON RIDING STABLES, Wakefield **Ref:**YH03624
EASTVIEW STABLES, Leeds **Ref:**YH04516
EQUINE ENTERPRISES, South Milford **Ref:**YH04777
FACTORY FARM, Huddersfield **Ref:**YH05007
FARFIELD LIVERY, Ilkley **Ref:**YH05052
GARFORTH LIVERY YARD, Leeds **Ref:**YH05651
HALLAS LANE LIVERY STABLES, Bradford **Ref:**YH06327
HAREWOOD LIVERY STABLES, Leeds **Ref:**YH06421
HEIGHTS HSE, Todmorden **Ref:**YH06649
HILLCROFT FARM RIDING STABLES, Wetherby **Ref:**YH06845
HOBSON, J H, Bingley **Ref:**YH06900
HONLEY LIVERY STABLES, Huddersfield **Ref:**YH07018
HOPTON, Mirfield **Ref:**YH07061
HUGHES, HELEN, Leeds **Ref:**YH07267
ILKLEY RIDING CTRE, Ilkley **Ref:**YH07400
LANTWOOD STABLES, Leeds **Ref:**YH08424
LATHAM FARM, Cleckheaton **Ref:**YH08445
LILAC FARM COURTYARD LIVERY, Wetherby **Ref:**YH08619
MANOR GRANGE STUD SCHOOL, Wakefield **Ref:**YH09109
MOORSIDE EQUESTRIAN, Shipley **Ref:**YH09780
MOUNT PLEASANT STUD, Leeds **Ref:**YH09892
OWLET FARM LIVERY STABLES, Leeds **Ref:**YH10613
PARKSWOOD ANGLO-ARAB STUD, Weeton **Ref:**YH10775
RICHMOND, PETER, Wetherby **Ref:**YH11830
RIGTON CARR FARM, Bardsey **Ref:**YH11893
ROYDS HALL RIDING SCHOOL, Leeds **Ref:**YH12199
SHAY LANE STABLES, Halifax **Ref:**YH12686
SPRINGFIELD LIVERY, Keighley **Ref:**YH13254
SYCAMORE HOUSE FARM, Leeds **Ref:**YH13719
THISTLETON FARM SADDLERY, Knottingley **Ref:**YH14001
THREE ACRES LIVERY STABLES, Leeds **Ref:**YH14101
WIKEFIELD FARM LIVERIES, Leeds **Ref:**YH15402
WILLOW ROYD STABLES, Halifax **Ref:**YH15502
WOODLAND STABLES, Huddersfield **Ref:**YH15703

STUD FARMS

CHESHIRE

COTEBROOK STUD, Tarporley **Ref:**YH03357

ESSEX

MOORAH STUD, Maldon **Ref:**YH09746

HAMPSHIRE

T J STUD & LIVERY STABLE, Southampton **Ref:**YH13754

HERTFORDSHIRE

CHIBLEY FARM STUD, Hitchin **Ref:**YH02847
OAKLEIGH FARM, Welwyn **Ref:**YH10396
UPPERWOOD FARM STUD, Hemel Hempstead **Ref:**YH14609

KENT

FIRWOOD COURT STUD, Herne Bay **Ref:**YH05235

LANCASHIRE

FLIGHT VIEW, Poulton-Le-Fylde **Ref:**YH05283
SOUGH FARM, Darwen **Ref:**YH13073

NORTHAMPTONSHIRE

NOBOTTLE STUD, Nobottle **Ref:**YH10224

NORTHUMBERLAND

CHESTERS STUD, Hexham **Ref:**YH02835
GOLDENMOOR, Alnwick **Ref:**YH05885

STAFFORDSHIRE

HARNOR STUD, Leek **Ref:**YH06448

SUFFOLK

CHEVELEY PK, Newmarket **Ref:**YH02842
CROCKFORDS STUD, Newmarket **Ref:**YH03607
LANGHAM HALL, Bury St Edmunds **Ref:**YH08406

SURREY

CHASE FARM STUD, Ashtead **Ref:**YH02781
HAZELWOOD STUD, Warlingham **Ref:**YH06604

SUSSEX (WEST)

BRENDON, Brighton **Ref:**YH01835
BRENDON HORSE & RIDER, Brighton **Ref:**YH01837
WORTH ARABIAN STUD, Crawley **Ref:**YH15803

TYNE AND WEAR

- **GIRSONFIELD STUD**, Otterburn Ref:YH05795

WARWICKSHIRE

- **CLAVERDON**, Warwick Ref:YH02992

SUPPLIES

BATH & SOMERSET (NORTH EAST)

- **CLUTTON HILL AGRICULTURAL SVS**, Clutton Ref:YH03077
- **HEXT BROTHERS**, Bath Ref:YH06733
- **LANSDOWN ACTION RUGS**, Bath Ref:YH08421
- **TAPSONS**, Midsomer Norton Ref:YH13867

BEDFORDSHIRE

- **ARCADE SADDLERY BEDFORD**, Bedford Ref:YH00498
- **BANKS OF SANDY**, Sandy Ref:YH00897
- **BANKS, M C**, Sandy Ref:YH00901
- **BEECHCROFT ANIMAL FEEDS**, Steppingley Ref:YH01167
- **BIGGLESWADE SADDLERY**, Biggleswade Ref:YH01404
- **BOWLEY & COLEMAN TRUCKS**, Bedford Ref:YH01717
- **BROWNS PET SHOP**, Luton Ref:YH02146
- **EQUINE AFFAIRS**, Bedford Ref:YH04760
- **FEED BIN**, Luton Ref:YH05120
- **GRAVENHURST SADDLERY**, Bedford Ref:YH06024
- **HANDMADE SHOES UK**, Leighton Buzzard Ref:YH06381
- **K-VEST UK**, Sandy Ref:YH08301
- **MCCULLAM**, Little Staughton Ref:YH09339
- **MORPHEUS**, Luton Ref:YH09824
- **PARTNERS PET SUPERMARKET**, Bedford Ref:YH10803
- **SHERPA FEEDS**, Dunstable Ref:YH12727
- **W JORDANS**, Biggleswade Ref:YH14778

BERKSHIRE

- **ATLAS SHOWJUMPS**, Reading Ref:YH00654
- **BANKS SOUTHERN**, Thatcham Ref:YH00898
- **BERKSHIRE ROSETTES**, Reading Ref:YH01307
- **BEXMINSTER**, Reading Ref:YH01349
- **CARSON, ROBERT**, Hungerford Ref:YH02604
- **COOKHAM EQUESTRIAN**, Upper Basildon Ref:YH03264
- **COUNTRYWIDE STORES**, Reading Ref:YH03448
- **DALGETY AGRCLTRL**, Reading Ref:YH03833
- **EPSOM VETNRY REMEDIES**, Hungerford Ref:YH04684
- **EQUESTRIA.NET**, Windsor Ref:YH04689
- **GOLDENEYE**, Newbury Ref:YH05882
- **LASSALE WATCHES**, Maidenhead Ref:YH08440
- **LEISURE VISION**, Newbury Ref:YH08548
- **MAYS-SMITH, ELIZA (LADY)**, Newbury Ref:YH09306
- **PERCY STONE**, Pangbourne Ref:YH10974
- **PETFOOD EXPRESS**, Maidenhead Ref:YH11026
- **PONYMANIA MAIL ORDER**, Newbury Ref:YH11257
- **RACING & FOOTBALL OUTLOOK**, Newbury Ref:YH11582
- **RACING REVIEW**, Newbury Ref:YH11586
- **RIDERS REPAIRS**, Reading Ref:YH11859
- **SCATS COUNTRYSTORE**, Newbury Ref:YH12493
- **SNAFFLES SADDLERY**, Reading Ref:YH13023
- **UNICORN SADDLERY**, Reading Ref:YH14568
- **VALLEY EQUINE**, Hungerford Ref:YH14648
- **WALKER, ALAN YUILL**, Kintbury Ref:YH14846
- **WITNEY SHOW SERVICES**, Hungerford Ref:YH15631
- **WM LILLICO & SON**, Hungerford Ref:YH15640
- **WOODCRAY FEEDS**, Wokingham Ref:YH15680
- **WOODLANDS**, Hungerford Ref:YH15705

BRISTOL

- **ANIMAL BEDDING**, Bristol Ref:YH00427
- **EQUINE LAUNDRY**, Bristol Ref:YH04783
- **ON THE HOOF**, Victoria Park Ref:YH10510

BUCKINGHAMSHIRE

- **BELLINGDON END**, Chesham Ref:YH01238
- **BRITISH BREEDER**, Buckingham Ref:YH01931
- **CLASSIC DRESSAGE COLLECTION**, Chesham Ref:YH02984
- **COUNTRYWIDE STORES**, Tingewick Ref:YH03450
- **DIAMOND CONSULTING SVS**, Aylesbury Ref:YH04101
- **EQUS HEALTH**, Aylesbury Ref:YH04835
- **GIBSON, SUSAN**, Wooburn Green Ref:YH05753
- **HERBERT, IVOR**, High Wycombe Ref:YH06695
- **JAYCLARE SADDLERY**, Milton Keynes Ref:YH07712
- **JOLLYES**, Milton Keynes Ref:YH07852
- **JOSEPH, J**, Amersham Ref:YH07945
- **LIDSTONE FARMS**, Slough Ref:YH08607
- **NATURAL HORSE FOOD**, Princes Risborough Ref:YH10052
- **OAKWOOD EQUESTRIAN**, Buckingham Ref:YH10408
- **PATCHES**, High Wycombe Ref:YH10814
- **R & S PRICE**, Milton Keynes Ref:YH11508
- **TUBBY-BOXES INTERNAL STABLING**, Milton Keynes Ref:YH14429
- **WHITAKERS EQUESTRIAN**, Aylesbury Ref:YH15293
- **WOODROW, A**, High Wycombe Ref:YH15730

CAMBRIDGESHIRE

- **BAILY'S HUNTING DIRECTORY**, Cambridge Ref:YH00809
- **BANKS CARGILL AGRICULTURE**, Huntingdon Ref:YH00896
- **BENWELL, LIZ**, Wisbech Ref:YH01289
- **CLARK & BUTCHER**, Ely Ref:YH02960
- **COOGAN, A B**, Ely Ref:YH03252
- **DURRANT, R C**, Cambridge Ref:YH04372
- **EQUI-VIDEO & EQUISETTE**, Peterborough Ref:YH04834
- **GILL FOX COUNTRY CLOTHES**, Huntingdon Ref:YH05769
- **GOW, ROBIN**, Great Abington Ref:YH05954
- **GRABELLA STUD**, Kentford Ref:YH05957
- **H E PRINGLE**, Bourn Ref:YH06220
- **HANDSOME HORSES**, Cambridge Ref:YH06382
- **HOOK HSE**, March Ref:YH07035
- **INGENUS**, Peterborough Ref:YH07444
- **INT COUNTRY CLOTHING RETAILER**, Peterborough Ref:YH07466
- **JANSWEAR**, Huntingdon Ref:YH07699
- **LONG MELFORD**, Cambridge Ref:YH08798
- **NEWSUM, GILLIAN**, Swavesey Ref:YH10167
- **PEARSON, MICHAEL**, Harston Ref:YH10881
- **PEGASUS**, Peterborough Ref:YH10901
- **ROBB & SON**, St Ives Ref:YH11932
- **SAWSTON FARM FEEDS**, Pampisford Ref:YH12462
- **SIMPSONS MANU**, Ely Ref:YH12843
- **SMEETH SADDLERY**, Wisbech Ref:YH12925
- **STUDLAND SERVICES**, Oundle Ref:YH13611
- **SUNDOWN STRAW**, Huntingdon Ref:YH13643
- **THODY, M & P**, Huntingdon Ref:YH14002
- **WASTE WARRIOR PRODUCTS**, March Ref:YH14960
- **WHITWORTH BROS**, Peterborough Ref:YH15378
- **WINNERS OF PETERBOROUGH**, Peterborough Ref:YH15589
- **YOUR HORSE MAGAZINE**, Peterborough Ref:YH15947

CHESHIRE

- **ABBEY SADDLERY & CRAFTS**, Knutsford Ref:YH00085
- **ASHTON HALL EQUESTRIAN CTRE**, Sale Ref:YH00612
- **BARLOW, JOHN (SIR)**, Nantwich Ref:YH00958
- **BERNARD CORBETT**, Malpas Ref:YH01309
- **BODEN & DAVIES**, Stockport Ref:YH01595
- **BOOL BY DESIGN**, Tarporley Ref:YH01631
- **BOWLERS**, Stockport Ref:YH01715
- **BUTLER, F L**, Pen-Y-Ffordd Ref:YH02325
- **CARDEN, J**, Macclesfield Ref:YH02528
- **CLYDESDALE TIMBER PRODUCTS**, High Peak Ref:YH03082
- **COLBERRY SADDLERY**, Ellesmere Port Ref:YH03142
- **COURTLEA NUMNAHS**, Ellesmere Port Ref:YH03509
- **CREWE SADDLERY**, Crewe Ref:YH03595
- **DANE VALLEY**, Macclesfield Ref:YH03864
- **EQUINE INNOVATIONS**, Hyde Ref:YH04781
- **EQUINE PRODUCTS**, Nantwich Ref:YH04794
- **ESTATE SUPPLIES & SVS**, Altrincham Ref:YH04875
- **EVEQUE LEISURE EQUIPMENT**, Northwich Ref:YH04948
- **GAYNORS SADDLERY**, Dukinfield Ref:YH05682
- **GRAHAMS**, Sale Ref:YH05974
- **GREEN FARM FEEDS**, Crewe Ref:YH06055
- **HEPWORTH MINERAL & CHEMICALS**, Sandbach Ref:YH06693
- **HOOFPRINT**, Knutsford Ref:YH07033
- **JOHN COOK (CORN MERCHANTS)**, Macclesfield Ref:YH07784
- **K Y P LEATHER**, Mobberley Ref:YH07993
- **KINSEY, T R**, Ashton Ref:YH08219
- **LANSDOWNE HORSE & RIDER**, Chester Ref:YH08423
- **LE GUP**, Mobberley Ref:YH08489
- **LIFELIGHTS**, Mobberley Ref:YH08611
- **MILLENNIUM ANIMAL BEDDING**, Warrington Ref:YH09598
- **NUTRI-MECH UK**, Malpas Ref:YH10359
- **PET FOOD & HORSE SUPPLIES**, Macclesfield Ref:YH11003
- **PET FOOD DISCOUNT CTRE**, Hyde Ref:YH11004
- **PETER HUNTER**, Tarporley Ref:YH11010
- **POINTER**, Lymm Ref:YH11193
- **RUGZ**, Northwich Ref:YH12225
- **SHAW, MARGARET**, Warrington Ref:YH12683
- **SHENTON, C W**, Wilmslow Ref:YH12707
- **STIRRUPS**, Crewe Ref:YH13478
- **STOCKFARM EQUESTRIAN SUPPLIES**, Chester Ref:YH13491
- **SUGAR BROOK FARM FEEDS**, Altrincham Ref:YH13627
- **TOPSPEC**, Nantwich Ref:YH14241
- **VELCLEAN BRUSH**, Crewe Ref:YH14674

CLEVELAND

- **ARMSTRONG RICHARDSON**, Middlesbrough Ref:YH00544
- **BAXTERS OF YARM**, Yarm Ref:YH01091
- **CAINE, E M**, Chop Gate Ref:YH02417
- **DE BOIZ**, Middlesbrough Ref:YH03974
- **EQUINE EXTRAS**, Stockton-on-Tees Ref:YH04778
- **FARMWAY**, Stokesley Ref:YH05070
- **FEED-EM**, Guisborough Ref:YH05121
- **FRANK, S**, Ingleby Barwick Ref:YH05464
- **HADRIAN EQUINE**, Stockton-on-Tees Ref:YH06271
- **HOOF'N'HOUND**, Hartlepool Ref:YH07031
- **HOOF'N'HOUND**, Middlesbrough Ref:YH07032
- **HORNER-HARKER, S**, Stockton-on-Tees Ref:YH07081
- **PARK, I**, Eaglescliffe Ref:YH10743
- **SAWNEY, J**, Middlesbrough Ref:YH12461
- **WADE, J**, Stockton-on-Tees Ref:YH14812

WOLVISTON ANIMAL FEEDS, Billingham Ref:YH15651

CORNWALL

BLOOMFIELD, D E F, Launceston Ref:YH01553
CORNISH CALCIFIED SEAWEED, Truro Ref:YH03325
CORNWALL FARMERS, Callington Ref:YH03330
CORNWALL FARMERS, Camborne Ref:YH03331
CORNWALL FARMERS, Camelford Ref:YH03332
CORNWALL FARMERS, Helston Ref:YH03333
CORNWALL FARMERS, Liskeard Ref:YH03334
CORNWALL FARMERS, Penzance Ref:YH03335
CORNWALL FARMERS, St Austell Ref:YH03336
CORNWALL FARMERS, Truro Ref:YH03337
CORNWALL FARMERS, Wadebridge Ref:YH03338
CORNWALL PAPER, Redruth Ref:YH03341
COUNTRY STABLING, Hayle Ref:YH03427
D MAY & SONS, St Austell Ref:YH03796
DALGETY AGRCLTRL, Launceston Ref:YH03835
DENNIS, W W, Bude Ref:YH04056
DOWNFIELD FARM SHOP, Gunnislake Ref:YH04229
DU PLESSIS, J M, Saltash Ref:YH04304
EQUESTRIAN STOP, Camborne Ref:YH04712
F W MASTERS & SON, Bodmin Ref:YH05002
FENNSMITH, TONY, Kilkhampton Ref:YH05150
FORGE COTTAGE SADDLERY, Camborne Ref:YH05361
HAMMER 'N' HOE, Falmouth Ref:YH06358
HELSTON SADDLERY, Helston Ref:YH06657
HORSE STUFF & RIDERWEAR, Truro Ref:YH07141
LE GRICE, T C, Penzance Ref:YH08488
NANTURRIAN STUD FARM, Falmouth Ref:YH10017
NICHOLLS & SONS, Helston Ref:YH10181
POLLY LUNN PET & AQUATICS, Truro Ref:YH11208
RICKARD, T R, St Austell Ref:YH11832
SMITH, M M, Launceston Ref:YH12975
TEAGLE MACHINERY, Truro Ref:YH13921
W RICHARDS & SON, Bodmin Ref:YH14793
WALTER BAILEY, St Austell Ref:YH14882
WILSON HORSEWEAR, Redruth Ref:YH15528
WOOFWARE, Bodmin Ref:YH15762

COUNTY DURHAM

EAST DURHAM, Durham Ref:YH04472
EGGLESTON WOODCHIPS, Lanchester Ref:YH04593
ELLIOTT, E A, Rushyford Ref:YH04620
FARMWAY, Darlington Ref:YH05071
FARMWAY, Darlington Ref:YH05072
FORSTER, D M, Heighington Ref:YH05380
FORT, J R, Brandon Ref:YH05389
GO RIDING GRP, Stanley Ref:YH05861
GRAHAM, HUGH, Consett Ref:YH05968
H GARNHAM & SON, Sacriston Ref:YH06224
HELLENS, J A, Chester Le Street Ref:YH06653
LANCHESTER COUNTRY STORE, Lanchester Ref:YH08382
MADDOX, Elton Ref:YH09020
MASON, N B, Crook Ref:YH09246
MCCUNE, D, Bishopton Ref:YH09342
NEEDHAM, P, Barnard Castle Ref:YH10069
RICHARDSONS DESIGNS, Burnhope Ref:YH11824
ROBINSON, S J, Coatham Mundeville Ref:YH11995
SHAFTO'S FARM SHOP, Stanley Ref:YH12658
TALLENTIRE, M L, Bishop Auckland Ref:YH13835
W M MCIVOR & SON, Ferry Hill Ref:YH14780
WAGGOTT, N, Spennymoor Ref:YH14825

CUMBRIA

AXECROFT, Maryport Ref:YH00694
BENSON, LAUREL, Maryport Ref:YH01279
BREED EX EQUINE STUD, Penrith Ref:YH01832
BROCKBANK, J E, Wigton Ref:YH02007
BURNS PET FOODS, Workington Ref:YH02269
BUTTERWORTH, B, Appleby-In-Westmorland Ref:YH02334
CARRS AGRICULTURE, Carlisle Ref:YH02596
CARRS AGRICULTURE, Penrith Ref:YH02597
CHADWICK, S G, Aspatria Ref:YH02705
COCKBURN, R G, Carlisle Ref:YH03122
COUNTRY COLLECTION, Brampton Ref:YH03401
D A HARRISON & SONS, Carlisle Ref:YH03774
FOSTER, LOUIS, Maryport Ref:YH05401
FURNESS & S CUMBERLAND SUPPLY, Ulverston Ref:YH05545
GET SMART, Barrow-In-Furness Ref:YH05732
GRASSGARTH HORSE FEEDS, Kendal Ref:YH06019
GRAYLING BOOKS, Penrith Ref:YH06034
HARRISON, PAM, Carlisle Ref:YH06486
HAYNES, J C, Kendal Ref:YH06589
INMAN, JENNY, Kendal Ref:YH07459
J & E PETFOODS, Whitehaven Ref:YH07545
J JORDAN & SONS, Windermere Ref:YH07593
J W WILKINSON, Kendal Ref:YH07628
JESTIN, F, Wigton Ref:YH07762
KINGFISHER, Ulverston Ref:YH08191
LIVESTOCK SUPPLIES INTL, Milnthorpe Ref:YH08715
LOWTHER EQUESTRIAN, Carlisle Ref:YH08877
MACDONALD, D W, Cockermouth Ref:YH08988
MAUREEN'S SADDLERY, Carlisle Ref:YH09280
MCCARTEN, ELAINE, Cleator Ref:YH09321
MILLARD, SUE, Tebay Ref:YH09592
O'HARA, JOHNNIE, Carlisle Ref:YH10442
OLD STABLES, Penrith Ref:YH10476
STOREY, F S, Carlisle Ref:YH13524
SWINDLEHURST, D G, Carlisle Ref:YH13710

DERBYSHIRE

ALTON RIDING SCHOOL, Chesterfield Ref:YH00344
ARMSON, RICHARD, Melbourne Ref:YH00541
BARLEYFIELD SADDLERY, Etwall Ref:YH00951
BARLEYFIELDS, Derby Ref:YH00952
BARLOW, R, Denby Village Ref:YH00959
BRINDLE AND WHITE, New Mills Ref:YH01914
C W G, Buxton Ref:YH02396
COUNTRY SPORT, Glossop Ref:YH03426
DENTEX (NORTH WEST), Glossop Ref:YH04065
HOOFBEATS & PAWPRINTS, Chesterfield Ref:YH07030
HOUSE OF ST WILFIDS, Barrow-on-Trent Ref:YH07209
HULLAND EQUESTRIAN, Matlock Ref:YH07281
J B PET SUPPLIES, Belper Ref:YH07565
J R FEEDS, Ilkeston Ref:YH07608
L W & H B GIBSON & SON, Chesterfield Ref:YH08330
NORMAN LUNNUN ANIMAL HEALTH, Ashbourne Ref:YH10237
O V WEBSTER & SON, Ticknall Ref:YH10367
PEAKDALE SADDLERY, Buxton Ref:YH10866
PRESTIGE PRESENTATIONS, Chesterfield Ref:YH11363
R E FARMS, Ashbourne Ref:YH11534
RICCHI, REGALI, Chesterfield Ref:YH11796
ROBINSONS, Chesterfield Ref:YH12003
ROBINSONS, Derby Ref:YH12002
RUTH LEE RIDING SERVICES, Derby Ref:YH12272
S & E JOHNSON, Matlock Ref:YH12310
SEALS FODDER, Alfreton Ref:YH12589
SHALLY, LAURA, Allestree Ref:YH12662
TAYLORS OF SOUTH WINGFIELD, South Wingfield Ref:YH13917
THOMAS IRVING, Chesterfield Ref:YH14007
THOMPSON, MARGOT, Snarestone Ref:YH14039
TOWN & COUNTRY SUPPLIES, Ashbourne Ref:YH14287
WESTHILLS EQUINE SUPPLIES, Matlock Ref:YH15216
WM EYRE & SONS, Hope Valley Ref:YH15639

DEVON

AGRITRADERS, Exeter Ref:YH00203
ANIMAL EDIBLES, Exeter Ref:YH00431
ANTHONY WALLIS FARM/EQUINE, Umberleigh Ref:YH00464
ASH ROSETTES, Ivybridge Ref:YH00587
ASHTON SADDLERY, Exeter Ref:YH00613
BOCM PAULS, Exeter Ref:YH01592
BRACKENBURY, R, Totnes Ref:YH01737
BYSTOCK PAPER BEDDING, Exmouth Ref:YH02351
CARTER, J, Dawlish Ref:YH02607
CLIPPER SHARP, Cullompton Ref:YH03046
COLLACOMBE FARM, Tavistock Ref:YH03172
COMFY PET & PEOPLE PRODUCTS, Exeter Ref:YH03213
CORNWALL FARMERS, Hatherleigh Ref:YH03339
CORNWALL FARMERS, Holsworthy Ref:YH03340
CREDITON MILLING, Crediton Ref:YH03586
DARK HORSE, Okehampton Ref:YH03887
DARTMOOR ROSETTES, Exeter Ref:YH03905
DEVON & CORNWALL FARMS, Tavistock Ref:YH04092
E J SNELL & SONS, Barnstaple Ref:YH04409
EQUINE ADVISORY SV, Newton Abbot Ref:YH04759
ERME VALLEY FARMERS, Ivybridge Ref:YH04850
FELL, R S, Plymouth Ref:YH05133
FREQUENCY PRECISION, Okehampton Ref:YH05497
FROSTS ROSETTES, Paignton Ref:YH05523
G C HAYBALL, Axminster Ref:YH05571
GRANNY'S TACK ROOM, Torquay Ref:YH06004
H & K SIMS, Buckfastleigh Ref:YH06208
HAPS PET & ANIMAL FEEDS, Exeter Ref:YH06402
HOLD YOUR HORSES, Exeter Ref:YH06922
HOWARD-CHAPPELL, A S E, Totnes Ref:YH07218
LEONARD COOMBE, Newton Abbot Ref:YH08553
LIBBY'S, Plymouth Ref:YH08602
LIMPET ANTI-SLIP SADDLE PADS, Ottery St Mary Ref:YH08638
LUSCOMBE ARENA CONSTRUCTION, Newton Abbot Ref:YH08902
MAIN RING ROSETTES, Torquay Ref:YH09038
MARK WESTAWAY & SON, Paignton Ref:YH09157
MAXIMILLIAN STUD, North Tawton Ref:YH09285
MITCHELL, DAVID, Cullompton Ref:YH09665

- **MOLE VALLEY FARMERS**, Holsworthy Ref:YH09710
- **MULLACOTT EQUESTRIAN**, Ilfracombe Ref:YH09935
- **OGLE, M B**, Buckfastleigh Ref:YH10437
- **OWL LEATHERCRAFT**, Newton Abbot Ref:YH10612
- **PIKE, S L**, Sidmouth Ref:YH11102
- **PINCOMBE, R W**, South Molton Ref:YH11116
- **RACING ANCILLARY SERVICES**, Honiton Ref:YH11583
- **REED, W J**, Umberleigh Ref:YH11723
- **REX AGRICULTURE**, Barnstaple Ref:YH11772
- **ROE, G L**, Yelverton Ref:YH12051
- **RUGGIT**, South Brent Ref:YH12222
- **SARGENT & SONS**, Sidmouth Ref:YH12437
- **SIDE SADDLE LADY**, Exeter Ref:YH12786
- **SLADES COUNTRYWISE**, Honiton Ref:YH12887
- **SOUCH, A**, Bideford Ref:YH13072
- **SOUTH WEST HORSE**, Tiverton Ref:YH13115
- **STOCKSHOP WOLSELEY**, Exeter Ref:YH13496
- **TACK & COUNTRY**, Plymouth Ref:YH13775
- **TAMAR LAKE PRODUCTS**, Holsworthy Ref:YH13847
- **TOM WILLCOCKS**, Plymouth Ref:YH14216
- **TOWN & COUNTRY SUP**, Exeter Ref:YH14286
- **TURNER, D C**, Plymouth Ref:YH14477
- **TURTON, S F**, Plymouth Ref:YH14495
- **TWYFORD FARM SUPPLIES**, Tiverton Ref:YH14516
- **VAUTERHILL STUD**, Umberleigh Ref:YH14669
- **WARREN'S TACK**, Okehampton Ref:YH14940
- **WEST COUNTRY VIDEOS**, Plymouth Ref:YH15138
- **WILLIAMS, NICK**, South Molton Ref:YH15468
- **WONNACOTT, L J**, Lifton Ref:YH15655
- **WRATTEN, SARAH**, Cheriton Bishop Ref:YH15812
- **WYCHANGER BARTON SADDLERY**, Tiverton Ref:YH15855

DORSET

- **BARTLETT**, Bridport Ref:YH01039
- **BLAKEMORE VALE SADDLERY**, Gillingham Ref:YH01520
- **CARTER, S M**, Shaftesbury Ref:YH02608
- **D B I INSURANCE**, Bournemouth Ref:YH03778
- **DENEWEAR**, Dorchester Ref:YH04044
- **ELLIOTT, BRIAN**, Weymouth Ref:YH04618
- **EQUUS**, Wimborne Ref:YH04836
- **HARDY, R C C**, Gillingham Ref:YH06417
- **HUNTER CHASERS**, Wimborne Ref:YH07299
- **HURN BRIDGE CTRE**, Christchurch Ref:YH07313
- **JULIP HORSES**, Dorchester Ref:YH07964
- **JUMP FOR JOY SHOWJUMPS**, Beaminster Ref:YH07965
- **MARABOUT ANIMAL FEEDS**, Dorchester Ref:YH09135
- **MITCHELL, C W**, Dorchester Ref:YH09664
- **O Y C**, Wareham Ref:YH10369
- **POINT TO POINT & HUNTER CHASE**, Dorchester Ref:YH11192
- **SCATS COUNTRYSTORE**, Blandford Ref:YH12496
- **SCATS COUNTRYSTORE**, Dorchester Ref:YH12494
- **SCATS COUNTRYSTORE**, Gillingham Ref:YH12495
- **SELBY, TERRY**, Wimborne Ref:YH12618
- **STICKLAND, G W**, Sturminster Newton Ref:YH13463
- **THREE LEGGED CROSS SADDLERY**, Three Legged Cross Ref:YH14105
- **WATERMAN, S**, Dorchester Ref:YH14971
- **WESTCOTT WEATHERVANES**, Poole Ref:YH15187
- **WESTERN HORSE SUPPLIES**, West Moors Ref:YH15201
- **WESTERN HORSE SUPPLIES**, Wimborne Ref:YH15200
- **WHITE, CHRISTINA**, Weymouth Ref:YH15328
- **WILKINSON, J V**, Blandford Forum Ref:YH15421

ESSEX

- **BAILEYS HORSE FEEDS**, Braintree Ref:YH00806
- **BAKER, JENNY**, Colchester Ref:YH00820
- **BARLING TACK SHOP**, Rochford Ref:YH00955
- **BELMONT STABLING**, Loughton Ref:YH01250
- **BILLERICAY FARM SVS**, Billericay Ref:YH01411
- **BREYER MODEL HORSES**, Great Dunmow Ref:YH01857
- **BRITISH DRESSAGE**, Bishop's Stortford Ref:YH01934
- **C W G**, Ongar Ref:YH02397
- **CARRIAGEHOUSE INSURANCE**, Colchester Ref:YH02582
- **CLOTHES HORSE COMPANY**, Nazeing Ref:YH03064
- **COUNTRY & DISTANCE RIDER**, Saffron Walden Ref:YH03397
- **D & H ANIMAL HUSBANDRY**, Epping Ref:YH03773
- **DESIGNER BROWBANDS**, Benfleet Ref:YH04084
- **E T A**, West Thurrock Ref:YH04427
- **EQUINE HEALTH & HERBAL**, Halstead Ref:YH04779
- **ESSEX ANIMAL FEEDS**, Romford Ref:YH04866
- **ESSEX RIDER**, Basildon Ref:YH04872
- **GALLOPS**, Colchester Ref:YH05624
- **HALLINGBURY HALL**, Bishop's Stortford Ref:YH06331
- **HEMCORE**, Bishop's Stortford Ref:YH06659
- **JESSOP, A E M**, Chelmsford Ref:YH07760
- **KENNEDY, B J**, Maldon Ref:YH08067
- **LEWIS, ANTHONY**, Chigwell Ref:YH08586
- **LONGWOOD FEED CTRE**, Upminster Ref:YH08821
- **MANOR FARM FEEDS**, Upminster Ref:YH09098
- **MONCUR, J & M**, Nazeing Ref:YH09721
- **MOORCROFT EQUESTRIAN**, Colchester Ref:YH09749
- **O F A H SADDLERY**, Billericay Ref:YH10364
- **OSMAN, BRIAN**, Colchester Ref:YH10568
- **POOLE FARM HORSE/ANIMAL FEED**, Great Yeldham Ref:YH11263
- **PULFORDS**, Great Dunmow Ref:YH11455
- **RIDE OUT**, Dunmow Ref:YH11849
- **RYDER'S ROSETTES**, South Woodham Ferrers Ref:YH12299
- **SADLERS FARM FEEDS**, Bowers Gifford Ref:YH12375
- **SHOPLAND HALL EQUESTRIAN**, Rochford Ref:YH12758
- **SIERRA SADDLE**, Benfleet Ref:YH12792
- **SIMMONS, J C**, Abridge Ref:YH12828
- **SOUTH EAST SHAVINGS**, Upminster Ref:YH13087
- **SOUTH ESSEX FEED CTRE**, Basildon Ref:YH13090
- **STANTONS METSA PRIMA**, Tilbury Ref:YH13382
- **STOKES, R & S**, Rayleigh Ref:YH13506
- **TACK EXCHANGE**, Leigh-on-Sea Ref:YH13788
- **TROTTERS INDEPENDENT SADDLERY**, Horndon-on-The Hill Ref:YH14411
- **TUKE, DIANA R**, Saffron Walden Ref:YH14449
- **VIDEO CLASSIFIED**, Rayleigh Ref:YH14713
- **WHITE, F E**, Chelmsford Ref:YH15330
- **YEATS, J**, Waltham Abbey Ref:YH15897

GLOUCESTERSHIRE

- **A A SHERWOOD**, Cirencester Ref:YH00017
- **ABBOTT**, Cirencester Ref:YH00102
- **ANDREWS, SUE**, Stroud Ref:YH00403
- **B G W SPECTRAFLECT**, Cheltenham Ref:YH00722
- **BARCLAY, A**, Moreton In Marsh Ref:YH00924
- **BENNETT, C J**, Dymock Ref:YH01269
- **COTSWOLD GRASS SEEDS**, Moreton In Marsh Ref:YH03362
- **COUNTRY & EQUESTRIAN**, Gloucester Ref:YH03398
- **COUNTRY MATTERS**, Cirencester Ref:YH03417
- **COUNTRYWIDE STORES**, Bourton-on-The Water Ref:YH03451
- **COUNTRYWIDE STORES**, Cirencester Ref:YH03452
- **COUNTRYWIDE STORES**, Gloucester Ref:YH03454
- **COUNTRYWIDE STORES**, Gloucester Ref:YH03453
- **COUNTRYWIDE STORES**, Tewkesbury Ref:YH03455
- **EQUIFIELD SVS**, Stonehouse Ref:YH04745
- **EQUINE RESPONSE**, Badminton Ref:YH04797
- **EVANS, H J**, Chipping Campden Ref:YH04920
- **GIBSON, P L**, Cheltenham Ref:YH05752
- **GILL WALKER SADDLERY**, Dursley Ref:YH05770
- **GILL, S A**, Moreton In Marsh Ref:YH05776
- **GLOUCESTER MIXED FEEDS**, Witcombe Ref:YH05851
- **HAVEN HOMES**, Dursley Ref:YH06538
- **HAWTHORN SADDLERY**, Sandhurst Ref:YH06556
- **HENRIQUES, M R Q**, Cirencester Ref:YH06678
- **HENRY COLE**, Cirencester Ref:YH06681
- **HORIZONT**, Gloucester Ref:YH07068
- **HUGHES, R L**, Cheltenham Ref:YH07272
- **J S EQUINE**, Gloucester Ref:YH07614
- **J T EQUI-SPORT**, Stroud Ref:YH07621
- **JAMES KEYSER**, Cirencester Ref:YH07670
- **KIDD, JANE**, Aldsworth Ref:YH08122
- **LAIT, MAURICE H**, Cheltenham Ref:YH08348
- **LANGRISH, BOB**, Stroud Ref:YH08412
- **LISTER SHEARING EQUIPMENT**, Dursley Ref:YH08680
- **M C WESTERN**, Gloucester Ref:YH08957
- **MORETON SADDLERY**, Moreton In Marsh Ref:YH09790
- **NOCK, S**, Cheltenham Ref:YH10226
- **P S B ANIMAL HEALTH**, Tetbury Ref:YH10657
- **PERRETT, A C J**, Cheltenham Ref:YH10983
- **RATCLIFFE, L J**, Cranham Ref:YH11651
- **REVINGTON, H & SPARKES, S**, Stroud Ref:YH11770
- **RICHARDSON, S L**, Cheltenham Ref:YH11822
- **RIDEOUT, NIGEL**, Moreton In Marsh Ref:YH11853
- **ROLFE, JOHN**, Berkeley Ref:YH12066
- **RUG-RITE**, Cirencester Ref:YH12223
- **SAVORY, KEITH**, Cirencester Ref:YH12458
- **SELECT FEEDS & SEED**, Westbury-on-Severn Ref:YH12620
- **SIMPLY BY DESIGN**, Gloucester Ref:YH12834
- **SMITH, RICHARD J**, Badminton Ref:YH12994
- **SOUTH AMERICAN TRADE SERVICES**, Cirencester Ref:YH13075
- **SOUTHWICK FARM**, Tewkesbury Ref:YH13163
- **STROUD SADDLERY**, Stroud Ref:YH13588
- **T H WHITE**, Tetbury Ref:YH13745
- **TETBURY**, Chaceley Ref:YH13962
- **TEWKESBURY SADDLERY**, Tewkesbury Ref:YH13969
- **THICK, N K**, Dymock Ref:YH13988
- **TIM BLAKE SADDLERY**, Gloucester Ref:YH14159
- **TRAPP, J W**, Forthampton Ref:YH14355
- **WICKFIELD STUD**, Cheltenham Ref:YH15382

- **WILESMITH, M S**, Dymock **Ref:**YH15414
- **WOODSIDE EQUESTRIAN**, Cheltenham **Ref:**YH15739

GLOUCESTERSHIRE (SOUTH)

- **A NICHOLS**, Chipping Sodbury **Ref:**YH00054
- **COUNTRYWIDE STORES**, Thornbury **Ref:**YH03456
- **CROMWELLS OF OLVESTON**, Olveston **Ref:**YH03633
- **HUTCHINSON, LYNNE**, Thornbury **Ref:**YH07336
- **JOLLYES**, Longwell Green **Ref:**YH07860
- **WEYLODE**, Old Sodbury **Ref:**YH15252

HAMPSHIRE

- **ABBOTT**, Alton **Ref:**YH00103
- **ANDREW GOOD VIDEO PRODUCERS**, Sholing **Ref:**YH00390
- **ANGELA MASKELL**, Lymington **Ref:**YH00408
- **BRITISH SHOW JUMP STORES**, Aldershot **Ref:**YH01972
- **CALCUTT & SONS**, Winchester **Ref:**YH02425
- **CORBETT, R A C**, Cheriton **Ref:**YH03307
- **COUNTRYWIDE**, Liphook **Ref:**YH03444
- **DAVIS, J S & P A**, Petersfield **Ref:**YH03952
- **DODSON & HORRELL**, Basingstoke **Ref:**YH04161
- **EASI-LOADER**, Brockenhurst **Ref:**YH04460
- **EQUESTRIAN EVENT INSURANCE**, Ringwood **Ref:**YH04701
- **EQUESTRIAN SVS FENCING**, Southampton **Ref:**YH04716
- **EQUI FILE**, Lymington **Ref:**YH04727
- **FLEETWATER STUD**, Lyndhurst **Ref:**YH05269
- **FORGE TRADING**, Winchester **Ref:**YH05365
- **FRAMPTON ZIEGLER AGRICULTURE**, Ringwood **Ref:**YH05443
- **GOLD CUP FEEDS**, Romsey **Ref:**YH05876
- **HAMILTON-FAIRLEY, A J**, Basingstoke **Ref:**YH06354
- **HOPLANDS EQUESTRIAN**, Stockbridge **Ref:**YH07058
- **HORSE VOGUE**, Basingstoke **Ref:**YH07145
- **JAMES MEADE**, Andover **Ref:**YH07673
- **JOHN LOADER**, Fordingbridge **Ref:**YH07799
- **JOLLYES**, Portsmouth **Ref:**YH07861
- **KATIE WHETREN**, Totton **Ref:**YH07998
- **KILIJARO**, Basingstoke **Ref:**YH08137
- **LEATHER WORKSHOP**, Ringwood **Ref:**YH08506
- **LISA HUNT EQUESTRIAN**, Copythorne **Ref:**YH08677
- **LOCKYERS ANIMAL PROVISIONS**, New Milton **Ref:**YH08764
- **LONG ACRE FEEDS**, Botley **Ref:**YH08795
- **M J HAYWARD & SONS**, Fordingbridge **Ref:**YH08969
- **MOYGLARE LIVERY**, Tadley **Ref:**YH09910
- **ORVIS CO INC**, Andover **Ref:**YH10555
- **P BOX - WORKING SADDLER**, Ringwood **Ref:**YH10634
- **QUALITY IRRIGATION**, Aldershot **Ref:**YH11476
- **RAWLINGS, M A**, Alton **Ref:**YH11665
- **ROWLEY, CHARLES**, Eastleigh **Ref:**YH12171
- **SCATS COUNTRYSTORE**, Alton **Ref:**YH12499
- **SCATS COUNTRYSTORE**, Andover **Ref:**YH12500
- **SCATS COUNTRYSTORE**, Basingstoke **Ref:**YH12501
- **SCATS COUNTRYSTORE**, Lymington **Ref:**YH12502
- **SCATS COUNTRYSTORE**, Romsey **Ref:**YH12497
- **SCATS COUNTRYSTORE**, Winchester **Ref:**YH12498
- **SHEDFIELD EQUESTRIAN NURSERY**, Southampton **Ref:**YH12693
- **SHERGOLD**, Southampton **Ref:**YH12722
- **THOROUGHBRED INFORMATION SVS**, Alresford **Ref:**YH14087
- **TROTTERS**, Havant **Ref:**YH14407
- **W J PARDEY & SON**, Fordingbridge **Ref:**YH14777
- **WESSEX MACHINERY**, Bordon **Ref:**YH15119
- **WESTBOURNE ANIMAL FEEDS**, Westbourne **Ref:**YH15183
- **WITNEY RUG COMPANY**, Winchester **Ref:**YH15630
- **WOODINGTON FEEDS**, Romsey **Ref:**YH15701

HEREFORDSHIRE

- **ABBOTT**, Hereford **Ref:**YH00104
- **ABBOTT**, Kington **Ref:**YH00105
- **AMTEX**, Leominster **Ref:**YH00374
- **BEVAN, E G**, Ullingswick **Ref:**YH01337
- **BREESE, J C**, Ledbury **Ref:**YH01833
- **BROWN, I R**, Leominster **Ref:**YH02110
- **CAM EQUESTRIAN JOINERY/EQUIP**, Hereford **Ref:**YH02463
- **COUNTRY YARNS & TACKROOM**, Bromyard **Ref:**YH03437
- **COUNTRYWIDE**, Hereford **Ref:**YH03445
- **COUNTRYWIDE STORES**, Bromyard **Ref:**YH03458
- **COUNTRYWIDE STORES**, Ledbury **Ref:**YH03457
- **COUNTRYWIDE STORES**, Leominster **Ref:**YH03459
- **DAVIES, P S**, Bromyard **Ref:**YH03945
- **EUROPEAN EQUESTRIAN**, Hereford **Ref:**YH04908
- **EVANS, J T**, Bromyard **Ref:**YH04924
- **FARMWELL**, Hereford **Ref:**YH05079
- **FRANCIS WILLEY**, Bromyard **Ref:**YH05449
- **FRANK H DALE**, Leominster **Ref:**YH05456
- **FRASER, J M**, Westhide **Ref:**YH05474
- **HAY & BRECON FARMERS**, Hay-on-Wye **Ref:**YH06558
- **HORSE & JOCKEY**, Hereford **Ref:**YH07093
- **ISAACS STORES**, Ledbury **Ref:**YH07512
- **JOHNSON, S M**, Madley **Ref:**YH07838
- **LOCKS GARAGE FEEDS**, Allensmore **Ref:**YH08761
- **MORTON, T**, Leominster **Ref:**YH09853
- **PHILLIPS STRUCTURES**, Hereford **Ref:**YH11050
- **PHILLIPS, C E**, Clifford **Ref:**YH11052
- **PIONEER ANIMAL FEEDS**, Ledbury **Ref:**YH11141
- **POWELL, G J**, Abbeydore **Ref:**YH11317
- **PRICE, C G**, Hay-on-Wye **Ref:**YH11375
- **PRICE, W**, Leominster **Ref:**YH11390
- **R T ANIMAL FEEDS**, Hereford **Ref:**YH11564
- **SHEEPCOTE EQUESTRIAN**, Hereford **Ref:**YH12695
- **SHIRES EQUESTRIAN**, Leominster **Ref:**YH12755
- **SMITH, G R**, Ross-on-Wye **Ref:**YH12958
- **SNAFFLES EQUESTRIAN**, Ross On Wye **Ref:**YH13021
- **SOCK**, Hereford **Ref:**YH13049
- **TIDY-TACK**, Ross-on-Wye **Ref:**YH14137
- **TURNERS**, Kington **Ref:**YH14492
- **WESTHIDE TRUST**, Hereford **Ref:**YH15215

HERTFORDSHIRE

- **ANIMAL FAYRE**, Cheshunt **Ref:**YH00432
- **ARNOLD HITCHCOCK**, Buntingford **Ref:**YH00557
- **BLACKMORE, A G**, Little Berkhamsted **Ref:**YH01489
- **BOSSY'S BIBS**, Tring **Ref:**YH01657
- **BOXMOOR SHOWJUMPS**, Hemel Hempstead **Ref:**YH01727
- **C U & PHOSCO**, Ware **Ref:**YH02394
- **CHALLENGER DISTRIBUTION**, Royston **Ref:**YH02712
- **COLEMAN CROFT**, St Albans **Ref:**YH03163
- **COLESDALE FARM SVS**, Potters Bar **Ref:**YH03168
- **EQUETECH**, Bushey **Ref:**YH04726
- **EQUITECHNICAL**, Harpenden **Ref:**YH04828
- **G J W TITMUSS**, Wheathampstead **Ref:**YH05586
- **HAZEL END FARM SHOP**, Bishop's Stortford **Ref:**YH06598
- **HERTFORD HORSE CLOTHING**, Hertford **Ref:**YH06720
- **HODGE, H B**, Ware **Ref:**YH06907
- **IVORY, K T**, Radlett **Ref:**YH07538
- **JOHNSON, M A**, Buntingford **Ref:**YH07827
- **MANOR HOUSE FARM STUD**, Tring **Ref:**YH09110
- **MARTIN PICKERING**, Potters Bar **Ref:**YH09213
- **N S R COMMUNICATIONS**, Rickmansworth **Ref:**YH09995
- **P S A EQUESTRIAN SVS**, Shenley **Ref:**YH10656
- **PARTNERS PET SUPERMARKET**, Barnet **Ref:**YH10804
- **PARTNERS PET SUPERMARKET**, St Albans **Ref:**YH10805
- **PATCHETTS**, Watford **Ref:**YH10815
- **PREMIERE ROSETTE COMPANY**, Harpenden **Ref:**YH11352
- **SADDLERY**, Royston **Ref:**YH12363
- **SPORBORG, C H**, Ware **Ref:**YH13215
- **STRANGEWAYS FEEDS**, Borehamwood **Ref:**YH13549
- **STREATHER HAYWARD FARMS**, Baldock **Ref:**YH13570
- **SUMMER FRESH**, Colney Heath **Ref:**YH13629
- **W MOSS & SONS**, Stevenage **Ref:**YH14783
- **WHITE HORSES**, Welwyn **Ref:**YH15317

ISLE OF MAN

- **MANAGRAKEM, N W F**, Douglas **Ref:**YH09063

ISLE OF WIGHT

- **ARENA FARM & PET SUPPLIES**, Wootton **Ref:**YH00513
- **JOLLYES**, Newport **Ref:**YH07862
- **P & G FARM SUPPLIES**, Newport **Ref:**YH10629
- **SCATS**, Newport **Ref:**YH12492
- **SCATS COUNTRYSTORE**, Newport **Ref:**YH12503
- **TRUMOR FEEDS**, Newport **Ref:**YH14422
- **WINDMILL FARM SUPPLIES**, Ryde **Ref:**YH15564

JERSEY

- **DAVID DUMOSCH**, St John **Ref:**YH03917
- **LE MAISTRE BROS**, Trinity **Ref:**YH08490

KENT

- **ARIZONAS**, Tunbridge Wells **Ref:**YH00527
- **BARN TACK & TACKLE SHOP**, Edenbridge **Ref:**YH00962
- **BARRADALE FARM**, Headcorn **Ref:**YH01005
- **BAVERSTOCK CTRY SALES**, Westerham Hill **Ref:**YH01084
- **BOWEN, S A**, Canterbury **Ref:**YH01703
- **BROADFEED**, Tunbridge Wells **Ref:**YH01994
- **CHILHAM FEEDS**, Canterbury **Ref:**YH02854
- **CRAWFORD, PAT**, Nettlestead **Ref:**YH03576
- **DEAN, RICHARD**, Maidstone **Ref:**YH03995
- **E WILLIAMS FARMERS**, Dartford **Ref:**YH04432
- **EQUESTRIAN ASPECTS**, Hartley **Ref:**YH04692
- **EQUINN**, Westerham **Ref:**YH04811
- **FRENCH, S**, Gravesend **Ref:**YH05494
- **FROGPOOL MANOR SADDLERY**, Chislehurst **Ref:**YH05515
- **GILLET COOK**, Faversham **Ref:**YH05780
- **GLOVER, H F & J H**, Longfield **Ref:**YH05854
- **GRAIN HARVESTERS**, Canterbury **Ref:**YH05976
- **HILLS, T**, Ashford **Ref:**YH06850
- **HOMEWOOD, J S**, Ashford **Ref:**YH07007
- **HORSE & COUNTRY SUPERSTORE**, Maidstone **Ref:**YH07088
- **HORSE BOOKS**, Maidstone **Ref:**YH07108
- **HORSEFLEX UK**, Wrotham **Ref:**YH07156
- **K G L C FEEDS**, Sundridge **Ref:**YH07987
- **LEDGER, R**, Sittingbourne **Ref:**YH08515

- **MANE TO TAIL SUPPLIES**, Canterbury **Ref:**YH09074
- **MANSFIELD, T J**, Ashford **Ref:**YH09124
- **OAKLEY'S HORSE & ANIMAL FEED**, Bromley Common **Ref:**YH10400
- **PANVERT, J F**, Tonbridge **Ref:**YH10705
- **PAYNE, NIKKI**, Egerton **Ref:**YH10852
- **REESTACK**, Tonbridge **Ref:**YH11734
- **ROSE, C J**, Rochester **Ref:**YH12096
- **SADDLERY & GUN ROOM**, Westerham **Ref:**YH12365
- **SCATS COUNTRYSTORE**, Canterbury **Ref:**YH12504
- **SCATS COUNTRYSTORE**, Marden **Ref:**YH12505
- **SEVERS, MALCOLM**, Sevenoaks **Ref:**YH12647
- **SMARDEN EQUESTRIAN SERVICES**, Ashford **Ref:**YH12916
- **SOUTHERN COUNTIES ROSETTES**, Tonbridge **Ref:**YH13139
- **STABLEITE**, Sittingbourne **Ref:**YH13303
- **SUPPLE, K R**, Wrotham **Ref:**YH13657
- **SUTCLIFFE ELECTRONICS**, Ashford **Ref:**YH13664
- **THANET SHOW JUMPS**, Ashford **Ref:**YH13978
- **THOMPSON, A**, Dartford **Ref:**YH14031
- **TILLBROOK FEEDS**, Meopham **Ref:**YH14149
- **TRADEWINDS**, Sittingbourne **Ref:**YH14309
- **WARR, S**, Tonbridge **Ref:**YH14928
- **WEALDEN SADDLERY**, Tonbridge **Ref:**YH15020
- **WEBB, T M**, Tonbridge **Ref:**YH15031
- **WILLOW FARM**, Faversham **Ref:**YH15497

LANCASHIRE

- **ANTHEL EQUINE SUPPLIES**, Blackpool **Ref:**YH00461
- **AQUAPLAST**, Skelmersdale **Ref:**YH00488
- **ARKENFIELD EQUESTRIAN CTRE**, Chorley **Ref:**YH00530
- **ASHTON AGRICULTURE**, Clitheroe **Ref:**YH00610
- **B B EQUESTRIAN**, Preston **Ref:**YH00717
- **BADMINTON HORSE FEEDS**, Blackburn **Ref:**YH00783
- **BERRY'S HORSEFEEDS**, Blackburn **Ref:**YH01320
- **BLACKPOOL WORKSPACE**, Blackpool **Ref:**YH01493
- **CARRS BILLINGTON**, Clitheroe **Ref:**YH02598
- **CARRS BILLINGTON**, Preston **Ref:**YH02599
- **COUNTRY LAUNDRY SVS**, Preston **Ref:**YH03413
- **COUNTRY VOGUE**, Preston **Ref:**YH03435
- **CROSTON CORN MILLS**, Preston **Ref:**YH03671
- **DERBY HSE SADDLERY**, Wigan **Ref:**YH04071
- **EATON, J M**, Wennington **Ref:**YH04526
- **EQUESTRIAN**, Bury **Ref:**YH04690
- **EQUESTRIANA**, Blackburn **Ref:**YH04724
- **EQUIMAC**, Preston **Ref:**YH04753
- **ESPRO EQUESTRIAN & SPORTSWEAR**, Wigan **Ref:**YH04862
- **HARGREAVES BANNISTER**, Colne **Ref:**YH06426
- **HASLEM, ROBERT**, Preston **Ref:**YH06524
- **HERD HSE RIDING SCHOOL**, Burnley **Ref:**YH06699
- **JOHN HATTON AGRICULTURAL**, Wyresdale Road **Ref:**YH07792
- **KENYON BROTHERS**, Ormskirk **Ref:**YH08093
- **LAXTON, TREVOR**, Clitheroe **Ref:**YH08482
- **LIDUN PET FOODS**, Lytham **Ref:**YH08608
- **LITTLE OAKS SHOWJUMPS**, Preston **Ref:**YH08697
- **M & M OILS**, Heywood **Ref:**YH08948
- **MORDAX STUDS**, Burnley **Ref:**YH09787
- **PAUL HUTCHINSON**, Ormskirk **Ref:**YH10832
- **PRETTY PONIES**, Clitheroe **Ref:**YH11372
- **PYE, W & J**, Lancaster **Ref:**YH11470
- **QUAY EQUESTRIAN**, Lancaster **Ref:**YH11485
- **RICHARD BATTERSBY**, Heywood **Ref:**YH11802
- **RISING BRIDGE CORN**, Accrington **Ref:**YH11909
- **ROSETTES DIRECT**, Accrington **Ref:**YH12110
- **S G ANIMAL FEEDS**, Blackburn **Ref:**YH12325
- **SELLERS, F H & D D**, Bury **Ref:**YH12623
- **SNAFFLES**, Halifax **Ref:**YH13020
- **SOUTH WEST LANCASHIRE FARMERS**, Skelmersdale **Ref:**YH13116
- **STANAH HORSE FEEDS**, Thornton-Cleveleys **Ref:**YH13358
- **T ASCROFT & SON**, Preston **Ref:**YH13730
- **TOWN & COUNTRY**, Chorley **Ref:**YH14283
- **UNIVERSAL ROOFING SYSTEMS**, Low Bentham **Ref:**YH14576
- **WHALLEY CORN MILLS**, Blackburn **Ref:**YH15258
- **WILSONS TIMBER SHAVINGS**, Burnley **Ref:**YH15553
- **ZEBRA**, Skelmersdale **Ref:**YH15953

LEICESTERSHIRE

- **ARENA SHOW JUMPS**, Oakham **Ref:**YH00515
- **ASHFIELD SUBS MANAGEMENT**, Market Harborough **Ref:**YH00598
- **BARBER, F**, Rothley **Ref:**YH00921
- **BUTTERCUP FEEDS**, Melton Mowbray **Ref:**YH02329
- **C W G**, Melton Mowbray **Ref:**YH02398
- **CHAMPION FEEDS EQUESTRIAN**, Market Harborough **Ref:**YH02726
- **CHARNWOOD PET SUPPLIES**, Rothley **Ref:**YH02774
- **CHEVRON EQUINE UK**, Leicester **Ref:**YH02845
- **CLOTHES HORSE**, Leicester **Ref:**YH03062
- **EUROMEC**, Market Harborough **Ref:**YH04902
- **FLEXTOL**, Astley **Ref:**YH05282
- **FOOT FETISH**, Melton Mowbray **Ref:**YH05310
- **FOSSE DRYBED**, Whetstone **Ref:**YH05396
- **GREENHILL MILLING**, Coalville **Ref:**YH06088
- **HERRICK, H**, Thurlaston **Ref:**YH06716
- **HOWS RACESAFE**, Market Harborough **Ref:**YH07244
- **HURST SADDLERS**, Leicester **Ref:**YH07316
- **JACQUES, RODNEY**, Sharnford **Ref:**YH07660
- **JOLLYES**, Coalville **Ref:**YH07863
- **L A EQUESTRIAN**, Leicester **Ref:**YH08310
- **L A EQUESTRIAN**, Leicester **Ref:**YH08309
- **MILLINGTON, CHARLES**, Arnesby **Ref:**YH09624
- **NAPIER, MILES**, Market Harborough **Ref:**YH10021
- **PALMERS**, Hinckley **Ref:**YH10692
- **RI-DRY**, Lutterworth **Ref:**YH11888
- **S L B SUPPLIES**, Coalville **Ref:**YH12329
- **SAGITTARIUS BLOODSTOCK AGENCY**, Melton Mowbray **Ref:**YH12382
- **SCHOOL OF NATIONAL EQUITATION**, Loughborough **Ref:**YH12521
- **SID WILSON**, Leicester **Ref:**YH12781
- **SKINNER, C MCINNES**, Melton Mowbray **Ref:**YH12874
- **SMITH, ROY J**, Loughborough **Ref:**YH12997
- **STABLECARE**, Lutterworth **Ref:**YH13300
- **SWEDISH COTTAGE ANIMAL FEEDS**, Earl Shilton **Ref:**YH13702
- **T L C EQUESTRIAN**, Market Harborough **Ref:**YH13757
- **TACK SHACK**, Loughborough **Ref:**YH13808
- **WATCHORN, KELLY**, Melton Mowbray **Ref:**YH14962
- **WORMALL, JILL**, Ibstock **Ref:**YH15792

LINCOLNSHIRE

- **A W RHOADES SADDLERY**, Market Rasen **Ref:**YH00068
- **ACORN RUGS**, Market Rasen **Ref:**YH00150
- **ADVANTA**, Sleaford **Ref:**YH00193
- **BAINES, P**, Louth **Ref:**YH00814
- **BARK PRODUCTS**, Lincoln **Ref:**YH00935
- **BARROWBY FEEDS**, Barrowby **Ref:**YH01031
- **BATTLE, HAYWARD & BOWER**, Lincoln **Ref:**YH01081
- **BEALBY, S M V**, Grantham **Ref:**YH01112
- **BELVOIR HORSE PRODUCTS**, Grantham **Ref:**YH01259
- **BIRDBROOK ROSETTES**, Saxilby **Ref:**YH01438
- **BOWLBY, P T S**, Grantham **Ref:**YH01712
- **BUCKLEY, J R**, Lincoln **Ref:**YH02199
- **C W G**, Market Rasen **Ref:**YH02400
- **C W G**, Stamford **Ref:**YH02399
- **F B FOREMAN & SONS**, Mablethorpe **Ref:**YH04982
- **G HOWSAM & SON**, Boston **Ref:**YH05582
- **HYKEHAM ANIMAL FEEDS**, Lincoln **Ref:**YH07354
- **LINDSEY FARM SVS**, Horncastle **Ref:**YH08655
- **MERCHANT, D**, Carlton Le Moorland **Ref:**YH09465
- **PIG & WHISTLE ROCKING HORSES**, North Somercotes **Ref:**YH11093
- **POLLY PRODUCTS**, Horncastle **Ref:**YH11209
- **SNOWFLAKE WOODSHAVING**, Boston **Ref:**YH13042
- **STRAGGLETHORPE ROCKER**, Brant Broughton **Ref:**YH13545
- **TACK BOX**, Lincoln **Ref:**YH13785
- **TYLER ANIMAL SYSTEMS**, Grantham **Ref:**YH14520
- **WINERGY**, Grantham **Ref:**YH15582
- **WOODPECKER PRODUCTS**, Gainsborough **Ref:**YH15727

LINCOLNSHIRE (NORTH EAST)

- **COUPLAND, J**, Grimsby **Ref:**YH03498
- **SMITH, DIANA**, Grimsby **Ref:**YH12954

LINCOLNSHIRE (NORTH)

- **AVERY, S B**, Barrow Haven **Ref:**YH00683
- **CROWSTONS**, Scunthorpe **Ref:**YH03684
- **MASON, D & M**, Scunthorpe **Ref:**YH09239
- **NAME PLATES**, Ulceby **Ref:**YH10014
- **NATIONWIDE EQUESTRIAN**, Scunthorpe **Ref:**YH10047
- **TORIC TROPHIES**, Immingham **Ref:**YH14244

LONDON (GREATER)

- **BADMINTON SPORTING DIARY**, London **Ref:**YH00788
- **BELL, JAKI**, London **Ref:**YH01223
- **CHASE SADDLERY**, Enfield **Ref:**YH02785
- **CONTINENTAL IND SUPPLIES**, London **Ref:**YH03248
- **COUNTRY ILLUSTRATED MAGAZINE**, London **Ref:**YH03410
- **EQUESTRIAN RECORD BOOKS**, London **Ref:**YH04708
- **EVENTERS DIRECT**, Eltham **Ref:**YH04939
- **FARMVIEW SYSTEMS**, Friern Park **Ref:**YH05069
- **FIELD**, London **Ref:**YH05181
- **GARVEY, ARNOLD**, London **Ref:**YH05665
- **HORSE & HOUND**, London **Ref:**YH07090
- **LAWSON, CHARLOTTE**, London **Ref:**YH08477
- **LOCK, JAMES**, London **Ref:**YH08756
- **LONDON COMMUNICATIONS**, Regents Park **Ref:**YH08783
- **MCGRATH, CHRIS**, Merton Park **Ref:**YH09362
- **OSTERLEY BOOKSHOP**, Osterley **Ref:**YH10573
- **PACEMAKER & THOROUGHBRED**, Teddington **Ref:**YH10660
- **PATEY**, London **Ref:**YH10820
- **PETERS FRASER & DUNLOPS**, London **Ref:**YH11021
- **PHILLIPS BROS**, Camberwell **Ref:**YH11048
- **RACING POST**, Canary Wharf **Ref:**YH11585
- **REDESDALE RESEARCH COMPANY**, London **Ref:**YH11709
- **REEL THING**, London **Ref:**YH11726
- **ROYAL MEWS**, London **Ref:**YH12187
- **SEAMAN, JULIAN**, London **Ref:**YH12591

- **SPORTING LIFE**, London **Ref:**YH13228
- **SPORTING LIFE WEEKENDER**, Canary Wharf **Ref:**YH13229
- **SPORTING TWENTY-PAGER**, London **Ref:**YH13232
- **SPORTSPAGES**, London **Ref:**YH13237
- **THOROUGHBRED BUSINESS GUIDE**, London **Ref:**YH14082
- **TRANS ATLANTIC FILMS**, London **Ref:**YH14347
- **UNIVERSITY DIAGNOSTICS**, Teddington **Ref:**YH14580
- **USA PRO JOCKEYS APPAREL**, Uxbridge **Ref:**YH14622
- **WESTMACOTT, SAM**, Yeading **Ref:**YH15220
- **WILLIAMS, MICHAEL**, Harrow-on-the-Hill **Ref:**YH15467

MANCHESTER (GREATER)

- **BROWZERS**, Manchester **Ref:**YH02149
- **EQUITACK**, Bolton **Ref:**YH04823
- **J & D WOODS**, Bolton **Ref:**YH07544
- **JOLLYES**, Manchester **Ref:**YH07864
- **MILLERS TRADING POST**, Oldham **Ref:**YH09615
- **SPORTSPAGES**, Manchester **Ref:**YH13238
- **STABLEMATES**, Bolton **Ref:**YH13304

MERSEYSIDE

- **ANIMAL WORLD**, Southport **Ref:**YH00448
- **JAMES E. JAMES**, Liverpool **Ref:**YH07665

MIDLANDS (WEST)

- **ALLENS SPORTINGMAN'S BOOKSHOP**, Solihull **Ref:**YH00308
- **ARABIAN SADDLE**, Walsall **Ref:**YH00492
- **ARDEN WOOD SHAVINGS**, Solihull **Ref:**YH00502
- **AULTON & BUTLER**, Walsall **Ref:**YH00664
- **B WHEELWRIGHT & SON**, Birmingham **Ref:**YH00751
- **BRITISH EQUINE COLLECTORS**, Coventry **Ref:**YH01942
- **CENTRAL EQUESTRIAN WHOLESALE**, Walsall **Ref:**YH02688
- **CLEAN, B**, Coventry **Ref:**YH03008
- **CROFT BRIDLES**, Walsall **Ref:**YH03612
- **DIAMOND SADDLERY**, Wolverhampton **Ref:**YH04104
- **EARLSWOOD SVS**, Coventry **Ref:**YH04457
- **EQUESTRIAN BRIDLE**, Walsall **Ref:**YH04693
- **EQUINE INNOVATIONS**, Wolverhampton **Ref:**YH04782
- **EQUINE SWIMMING POOLS**, Coventry **Ref:**YH04805
- **F C ROBERTS & SON**, Kingswinford **Ref:**YH04988
- **FAZ**, Coventry **Ref:**YH05112
- **FINE ENGLISH BRIDLES**, Walsall **Ref:**YH05211
- **FISHER FOUNDRIES**, Birmingham **Ref:**YH05236
- **GARDEN IMAGES**, Solihull **Ref:**YH05644
- **GLOBE ORGANIC SVS**, Solihull **Ref:**YH05848
- **GREENSFORGE**, Kingswinford **Ref:**YH06100
- **HORSESHOE & FARRIER SUPPLIES**, Sutton Coldfield **Ref:**YH07171
- **HUNGRY HORSE**, Sutton Coldfield **Ref:**YH07289
- **J & A MAIL ORDER**, Walsall **Ref:**YH07542
- **JAMES COTTERELL & SONS**, Walsall **Ref:**YH07664
- **JOHNSON BROTHERS**, Walsall **Ref:**YH07822
- **LARIOT EQUESTRIAN SUPPLIES**, Walsall **Ref:**YH08428
- **LAUNDRY MACHINE**, Birmingham **Ref:**YH08454
- **MCARDLE FABRICATIONS**, Coventry **Ref:**YH09312
- **MONARCH EQUESTRIAN**, Willenhall **Ref:**YH09717
- **MULBERRY BUSH**, Coventry **Ref:**YH09930
- **MULTI-SHRED**, Lanesfiels **Ref:**YH09945
- **OVERIDER**, Coventry **Ref:**YH10593
- **P J COYNE**, Walsall **Ref:**YH10647
- **PONY SADDLE**, Walsall **Ref:**YH11254
- **PREMIER GIRTHS MANUFACTURING**, Walsall **Ref:**YH11346
- **PROLITE**, Walsall **Ref:**YH11432
- **QUEST WHOLESALERS**, Walsall **Ref:**YH11495
- **RANCH HSE WESTERN WARE INT**, Dudley **Ref:**YH11626
- **ROXANA HORSE & PET SUPPLIES**, Birmingham **Ref:**YH12175
- **SADDLE & BRIDLE**, Walsall **Ref:**YH12340
- **SARGENT, C B**, Walsall **Ref:**YH12438
- **SCHOOL FARM PETS & SUPPLIES**, Walsall **Ref:**YH12519
- **STEEDSMAN**, Walsall **Ref:**YH13413
- **STURMAN, JOHN**, Warley **Ref:**YH13617
- **THOROWGOOD**, Walsall **Ref:**YH14089
- **VALE BROTHERS**, Walsall **Ref:**YH14632

NORFOLK

- **ANIMAL CRACKERS**, Norwich **Ref:**YH00430
- **BARRIER ANIMAL HEALTHCARE**, Attleborough **Ref:**YH01021
- **BEXWELL TRACTORS**, Downham Market **Ref:**YH01350
- **C W G**, East Dereham **Ref:**YH02401
- **CHAFF-CUTTERS ANIMAL SUPPLIES**, Norwich **Ref:**YH02707
- **CREST-A-BED**, Attleborough **Ref:**YH03593
- **DARROW FARM SUPPLIES**, Diss **Ref:**YH03899
- **DEEJAY ANIMAL FEED CTRE**, Diss **Ref:**YH04016
- **DIXONS DUSTLESS**, Diss **Ref:**YH04145
- **EQUINE CLOTHING**, Downham Market **Ref:**YH04770
- **FERNDALE FARM SUPPLIES**, Diss **Ref:**YH05162
- **FIESTA ROSETTES & TROPHIES**, Norwich **Ref:**YH05199
- **H BANHAM**, Fakenham **Ref:**YH06213
- **HORSES IN SPORT**, Diss **Ref:**YH07169
- **HORSETALK**, King's Lynn **Ref:**YH07176
- **JOLLYES**, East Dereham **Ref:**YH07865
- **KEN'S CORN STORES**, Norwich **Ref:**YH08076
- **KONGSKILDE UK**, Holt **Ref:**YH08290
- **L K F ANIMAL BEDDING**, Banham **Ref:**YH08324
- **L S SADDLERY**, King's Lynn **Ref:**YH08328
- **MARRS**, Thetford **Ref:**YH09179
- **MOULHAM & HORN**, King's Lynn **Ref:**YH09882
- **NEVILLE BLAKEY FEEDSTUFFS**, Pulham St Mary **Ref:**YH10086
- **NICHOLSON FARM MACHINERY**, Downham Market **Ref:**YH10189
- **RACING TIMES**, North Walsham **Ref:**YH11587
- **RFC BED-DOWN**, Harleston **Ref:**YH11781
- **SAVAGE, E A**, Thetford **Ref:**YH12453
- **SHEPCO**, Great Yarmouth **Ref:**YH12710
- **WORDINGHAM, L**, Fakenham **Ref:**YH15775
- **WYMONDHAM PET & GARDEN**, Wymondham **Ref:**YH15869

NORTHAMPTONSHIRE

- **BATTEN, HORACE**, Northampton **Ref:**YH01077
- **BUCKLEY BITS**, Northampton **Ref:**YH02197
- **C W G**, Towcester **Ref:**YH02402
- **CHIRON EQUESTRIAN BOOKS**, Wellingborough **Ref:**YH02868
- **CONNELL, ANNE (LADY)**, Brackley **Ref:**YH03236
- **COUNTRYWISE FEEDS & NEEDS**, Kettering **Ref:**YH03484
- **CROFT & CO**, Brackley **Ref:**YH03610
- **D A WATTS**, Wellingborough **Ref:**YH03777
- **DAVIES BENAKI**, Roade **Ref:**YH03934
- **DODSON & HORRELL**, Kettering **Ref:**YH04162
- **EDENGATE SADDLERY**, Northampton **Ref:**YH04550
- **EQUIMAT**, Kettering **Ref:**YH04755
- **GREGORY ENTERPRISES**, Northampton **Ref:**YH06114
- **H O E**, Daventry **Ref:**YH06232
- **HEMMINGS, A W**, Duston **Ref:**YH06661
- **JOLLYES**, Kettering **Ref:**YH07866
- **LATIMER & CRICK**, Northampton **Ref:**YH08447
- **LIGHTFOOT INT**, Daventry **Ref:**YH08613
- **LOGGIN, C W**, Brackley **Ref:**YH08775
- **LOVESON**, Irthlingborough **Ref:**YH08851
- **MACARTHUR, JENNY**, Towcester **Ref:**YH08981
- **MARROWELL FARM SVS**, West Haddon **Ref:**YH09178
- **NATURALLY**, Towcester **Ref:**YH10055
- **PIDGEON, G**, Brackley **Ref:**YH11088
- **RACING CALENDAR**, Wellingborough **Ref:**YH11584
- **RUFFLES ROSETTES**, Northampton **Ref:**YH12212
- **STALLION BOOK**, Wellingborough **Ref:**YH13350
- **TURWESTON HILL FARM SUP**, Brackley **Ref:**YH14500
- **WATTS & WATTS SADDLERY**, Northampton **Ref:**YH15003
- **WRATHALL, J G G**, Northampton **Ref:**YH15811

NORTHUMBERLAND

- **A C BURN**, Berwick-upon-Tweed **Ref:**YH00021
- **ALDER, D S**, Belford **Ref:**YH00255
- **ARABLE FARM SUPPLIES**, Alnwick **Ref:**YH00493
- **AYNSLEY, J W F**, Morpeth **Ref:**YH00697
- **BEDMAX**, Belford **Ref:**YH01157
- **DRAPER, JUDITH**, Berwick-upon-Tweed **Ref:**YH04258
- **EQUIDIRECT**, Alnwick **Ref:**YH04742
- **FAL TEXTILE INDUSTRIES**, Blyth **Ref:**YH05038
- **FARMWAY**, Hexham **Ref:**YH05075
- **FARMWAY**, Morpeth **Ref:**YH05074
- **FARMWAY**, Wooler **Ref:**YH05073
- **GIBSON, T M**, Hexham **Ref:**YH05754
- **GLEDSON, J L**, Hexham **Ref:**YH05823
- **GREEN**, Morpeth **Ref:**YH06048
- **HAYMAX**, Belford **Ref:**YH06586
- **LAMB, K M**, Seahouses **Ref:**YH08362
- **LANE FARM SHOP**, Bedlington **Ref:**YH08389
- **LOGIC ATV EQUIPMENT**, Hexham **Ref:**YH08777
- **MARSHALL, L A**, Morpeth **Ref:**YH09197
- **NORTH NORTHUMBERLAND**, Denwick **Ref:**YH10275
- **RENWICK**, Morpeth **Ref:**YH11767
- **RIDERS JOURNAL**, Coldstream **Ref:**YH11857
- **ROBSON & COWAN**, Morpeth **Ref:**YH12011
- **ROBSON, E H**, Morpeth **Ref:**YH12014
- **ROBSON, T L A**, Alnwick **Ref:**YH12016
- **SCOTT, D W**, Hexham **Ref:**YH12541
- **SINCLAIR FEEDS**, Berwick-upon-Tweed **Ref:**YH12848
- **SPOTTISWOOD, P**, Hexham **Ref:**YH13242
- **WALTON, J B**, Morpeth **Ref:**YH14892
- **WHITE, G F**, Alnwick **Ref:**YH15331
- **WILLOW WEAR**, Hexham **Ref:**YH15505

NOTTINGHAMSHIRE

- **AERBORN EQUESTRIAN**, Nottingham **Ref:**YH00195
- **ARENASPRAY**, Hoveringham **Ref:**YH00518
- **B J W EQUINE SVS**, Thurgarton **Ref:**YH00734
- **BETHELL, W A**, Arnold **Ref:**YH01333
- **BRIDLE WAY & GAUNTLEYS**, Newark **Ref:**YH01892
- **BROOMSIDE STUD**, Calverton **Ref:**YH02082
- **C E COBB & SONS**, Newark **Ref:**YH02368
- **C W G**, Newark **Ref:**YH02403
- **C W G**, Worksop **Ref:**YH02404
- **CAREYS**, Southwell **Ref:**YH02537
- **CAUNTON GRASS DRIERS**, Newark **Ref:**YH02660

- **CHUKKA COVE**, Newark **Ref:**YH02893
- **COTON, F**, Epperstone **Ref:**YH03359
- **DIRTY DOBBINS**, Mansfield Woodhouse **Ref:**YH04128
- **F MARTIN & SON**, Arnold **Ref:**YH04995
- **HARDY, W**, Lambley **Ref:**YH06419
- **HAYES FARM FEEDS**, Newstead Village **Ref:**YH06574
- **HAYFIELD SADDLERY REPAIRS**, Worksop **Ref:**YH06580
- **HOOF ALOOF**, Nottingham **Ref:**YH07025
- **JACKSON, ROGER**, Nottingham **Ref:**YH07653
- **K-FEEDS**, Retford **Ref:**YH08118
- **LANGFORD SADDLERY**, Nottingham **Ref:**YH08405
- **LEE, C F**, Hoveringham **Ref:**YH08523
- **MALLENDER BROS**, Worksop **Ref:**YH09051
- **MERRIVALE TRADING**, Nottingham **Ref:**YH09483
- **MITEL MARKETING**, Papplewick **Ref:**YH09682
- **NEWBOULT & THORP**, Retford **Ref:**YH10125
- **OLD MILL ANIMAL FEEDS**, Mansfield Woodhouse **Ref:**YH10466
- **PAPER BEDDING SUPPLIES**, Newark **Ref:**YH10707
- **POGSON, CHARLES**, Newark **Ref:**YH11189
- **RAKE 'N' LIFT**, Edwalton **Ref:**YH11618
- **SADDLE RACK**, Nottingham **Ref:**YH12346
- **SADDLECRAFT**, Nottingham **Ref:**YH12355
- **SCAN FIRE + SECURITY SERVICES**, Colwick **Ref:**YH12483
- **SHOW WINNER PRODUCTS**, Newark **Ref:**YH12765
- **ST CLEMENTS LODGE**, Nottingham **Ref:**YH13274
- **W H OTTLEY**, Retford **Ref:**YH14772
- **WALTER HARRISON & SONS**, Radcliffe-on-Trent **Ref:**YH14883
- **WELLS AGRICULTURAL**, Edwalton **Ref:**YH15079
- **WILLIAM BAILEY AGRICULTURAL**, Newark **Ref:**YH15434

OXFORDSHIRE

- **ABBOTT**, Chipping Norton **Ref:**YH00108
- **ADAS**, Kidlington **Ref:**YH00176
- **ALDEN EQUIFEEDS**, Didcot **Ref:**YH00253
- **ASTI STUD & SADDLERY**, Faringdon **Ref:**YH00633
- **BODICOTE FLYOVER FARM SHOP**, Banbury **Ref:**YH01596
- **CASWELL, LESLEY**, Chinnor **Ref:**YH02648
- **COUNTRYWIDE STORES**, Chipping Norton **Ref:**YH03463
- **COUNTRYWIDE STORES**, Oxford **Ref:**YH03464
- **COURTHILL STABLES**, Wantage **Ref:**YH03504
- **CROFT & CO**, Banbury **Ref:**YH03611
- **DOBBINS CLOBBER**, Thame **Ref:**YH04150
- **EQUI-GRASS**, Banbury **Ref:**YH04749
- **EUROCLIP 2000**, Banbury **Ref:**YH04895
- **FRAMPTON HSE STABLES**, East Hendred **Ref:**YH05442
- **GRANGE SALES**, Banbury **Ref:**YH05997
- **GREATHEAD, T R**, Chipping Norton **Ref:**YH06046
- **HARPER, R C**, Banbury **Ref:**YH06455
- **JENNINGS FARM PRODUCE**, Garsington **Ref:**YH07746
- **JODS GALORE**, Henley-on-Thames **Ref:**YH07775
- **JOHN ROWING SADDLERY**, Banbury **Ref:**YH07810
- **KIRBY, J**, Wantage **Ref:**YH08228
- **LAUNTON SADDLERY**, Bicester **Ref:**YH08456
- **MANE LINE**, Oxford **Ref:**YH09073
- **MATHEW, ROBIN**, Burford **Ref:**YH09262
- **MICROM**, Thame **Ref:**YH09519
- **OATHILL FARM SUPPLIES**, Banbury **Ref:**YH10416
- **ODELL, S M**, Chipping Norton **Ref:**YH10431
- **O'NEILL, J G**, Bicester **Ref:**YH10517
- **PEARCE, H & C**, Thame **Ref:**YH10871
- **SCATS COUNTRYSTORE**, Faringdon **Ref:**YH12506
- **SCHUMACHER, GEORGE**, Faringdon **Ref:**YH12524
- **SEENEY'S ANIMAL & PET FOODS**, Water Eaton **Ref:**YH12610
- **SHOW JUMPERS**, Banbury **Ref:**YH12764
- **SMITH, ALAN**, Clanfield **Ref:**YH12939
- **SOLOCOMB**, Abingdon **Ref:**YH13059
- **TACK SHOP**, Carterton **Ref:**YH13813
- **TETCHWICK FEED SUPPLIES**, Kidlington **Ref:**YH13963
- **W F S COUNTRY**, Witney **Ref:**YH14766
- **WALEY-COHEN, ROBERT B**, Banbury **Ref:**YH14840
- **WEATHERBEETA**, Banbury **Ref:**YH15023
- **WHARTON ELECTRONICS**, Thame **Ref:**YH15263
- **WHITE HORSE ANIMAL FEEDS**, Wantage **Ref:**YH15306
- **WORKHORSE SERVICES**, Hornton **Ref:**YH15779

RUTLAND

- **CLAYTON, MICHAEL**, Oakham **Ref:**YH03005
- **EQUI-DRENCH**, Knossington **Ref:**YH04743
- **LANDS' END**, Oakham **Ref:**YH08385
- **MANOR FARM FEEDS**, Rutland **Ref:**YH09099
- **STABLE EXPRESS**, Oakham **Ref:**YH13293
- **STAMFORD ANIMAL & PET SUP**, Oakham **Ref:**YH13353
- **W'UNDERWEAR**, Oakham **Ref:**YH15852
- **YOUNG, J R A**, Oakham **Ref:**YH15932

SHROPSHIRE

- **4 SEASONS MARQUEE & FURNITURE**, Whitchurch **Ref:**YH00003
- **A & A PEATE**, Oswestry **Ref:**YH00005
- **BARKER HICKMAN**, Shifnal **Ref:**YH00936
- **BERKELEY**, Telford **Ref:**YH01299
- **BICKERTON, P E**, Market Drayton **Ref:**YH01393
- **BLACK, C J**, Oswestry **Ref:**YH01471
- **BOUNDARY GATE SADDLERY**, Bridgnorth **Ref:**YH01678
- **BRI - TAC**, Church Stretton **Ref:**YH01858
- **BRYNORE STUD & LIVERY STABLES**, Ellesmere **Ref:**YH02178
- **CAMBER, N B**, Shrewsbury **Ref:**YH02465
- **CARADOC CLOTHING**, Bridgnorth **Ref:**YH02525
- **COMPASS EQUESTRIAN PRODUCTS**, Oswestry **Ref:**YH03216
- **COUNTRYWIDE STORES**, Bishops Castle **Ref:**YH03468
- **COUNTRYWIDE STORES**, Craven Arms **Ref:**YH03470
- **DALTON, J N**, Shifnal **Ref:**YH03847
- **DAVID BAKER FARM SUPPLIES**, Oswestry **Ref:**YH03915
- **DENMAR SUPPLIES**, Shrewsbury **Ref:**YH04048
- **EDDIE PALIN DISTRIBUTION**, Market Drayton **Ref:**YH04541
- **GITTINS, H W**, Market Drayton **Ref:**YH05799
- **GREENFIELDS COUNTRY PURSUITS**, Shrewsbury **Ref:**YH06084
- **GRIFFITHS & SIMPSON**, Market Drayton **Ref:**YH06136
- **GRIFFITHS & SIMPSON**, Newport **Ref:**YH06137
- **HEAD TO HOOF**, Market Drayton **Ref:**YH06608
- **J B HORSE SUPPLIES**, Market Drayton **Ref:**YH07564
- **LLOYDS ANIMAL FEEDS**, Oswestry **Ref:**YH08744
- **NAG TAGS**, Telford **Ref:**YH10009
- **NATIONAL FOALING BANK**, Newport **Ref:**YH10037
- **NEEDHAM, J L**, Ludlow **Ref:**YH10068
- **RUG OSTLER**, Oswestry **Ref:**YH12216
- **SLATER, M**, Market Drayton **Ref:**YH12891
- **STAN CHEADLE CLIPPER SVS**, Ludlow **Ref:**YH13356
- **TOUCHDOWN LIVERIES**, Whitchurch **Ref:**YH14253
- **WREKIN FARMERS GARDEN CTRE**, Telford **Ref:**YH15817
- **WYKE OF SHIFNAL**, Shifnal **Ref:**YH15863
- **WYNNSTAY & CLWYD FARMERS**, Oswestry **Ref:**YH15876

SOMERSET

- **ABBAS MARQUEE HIRE**, Wincanton **Ref:**YH00073
- **ALSTONE COURT RIDING ESTB**, Highbridge **Ref:**YH00342
- **ANGELA BROMWICH**, Cheddar **Ref:**YH00407
- **ANIMAL FEED SHOP**, Bridgwater **Ref:**YH00433
- **BADMINTON HORSE FEEDS**, Bridgwater **Ref:**YH00785
- **BLACKTHORN SHAVINGS**, Highbridge **Ref:**YH01499
- **CHURCHES, M R**, Glastonbury **Ref:**YH02909
- **COLE, H T**, Taunton **Ref:**YH03155
- **COUNTRYWIDE STORES**, Bridgwater **Ref:**YH03472
- **COUNTRYWIDE STORES**, Marksbury **Ref:**YH03471
- **DAWE, N J**, Bridgwater **Ref:**YH03960
- **DAY, H**, Taunton **Ref:**YH03967
- **DELBRIDGE, G L**, Minehead **Ref:**YH04030
- **DUNN, ALLAN**, Minehead **Ref:**YH04349
- **DUNN, NIGEL**, Taunton **Ref:**YH04351
- **EXMOOR WHOLESALE**, Dulverton **Ref:**YH04971
- **FARMPET SUPPLIES**, Taunton **Ref:**YH05068
- **GANE, A R**, Somerton **Ref:**YH05640
- **GREAT WESTERN TACK**, Chantry **Ref:**YH06043
- **GREENWAY, V G**, Taunton **Ref:**YH06103
- **GRIFFIN NUU MED**, Bridgwater **Ref:**YH06130
- **HEMBROW, S J R**, Taunton **Ref:**YH06658
- **HILTON HERBS**, Crewkerne **Ref:**YH06863
- **IMPACT SIGNS**, Wellington **Ref:**YH07402
- **JACKSON, TONY**, Chard **Ref:**YH07656
- **JAMES, W D**, Taunton **Ref:**YH07690
- **JEREMY FRANKS TACK REPAIRS**, Templecombe **Ref:**YH07752
- **JUST REWARDS**, Bridgwater **Ref:**YH07976
- **K C EQUESTRIAN**, Wellington **Ref:**YH07984
- **KRAIBURG**, Bridgwater **Ref:**YH08293
- **LAMBSKIN MARKETING**, Somerton **Ref:**YH08371
- **MANELINE, B G I**, Bridgwater **Ref:**YH09075
- **MCCOY SADDLERY**, Minehead **Ref:**YH09334
- **MCKENZIE-COLES, W G**, Taunton **Ref:**YH09384
- **MEDLAND SANDERS & TWOSE**, Yeovil **Ref:**YH09438
- **MINTY, D J**, Dulverton **Ref:**YH09657
- **MOORE & SONS**, Frome **Ref:**YH09750
- **NYTACK EQUESTRIAN**, Wells **Ref:**YH10362
- **PAYNE, J R**, Dulverton **Ref:**YH10848
- **PETER STUNT COUNTRY PURSUITS**, Taunton **Ref:**YH11016
- **POLDEN LEA STABLES**, Bridgwater **Ref:**YH11197
- **R E D ROSETTES**, Bridgwater **Ref:**YH11531
- **RIDEMOOR**, Wincanton **Ref:**YH11852
- **ROSE MILL FEEDS**, Ilminster **Ref:**YH12094
- **S S EQUESTRIAN VIDEO**, Yeovil **Ref:**YH12335
- **SCOTT, E**, Taunton **Ref:**YH12542
- **SCOTT, E B**, Axbridge **Ref:**YH12543
- **SCRIVEN, B**, Taunton **Ref:**YH12566
- **SCRIVENS, J**, Taunton **Ref:**YH12567
- **SMALL, L G**, Somerton **Ref:**YH12907
- **SNELL, C F & J E**, Crewkerne **Ref:**YH13029
- **SOUTHALL, J**, Wincanton **Ref:**YH13126
- **STAX SADDLERY**, Montacute **Ref:**YH13406
- **STEPHENS, V A**, Taunton **Ref:**YH13424
- **TAKEL, FRANCES**, Dulverton **Ref:**YH13827

TAPLIN, E J, Minehead **Ref:**YH13865
THORNEY COPSE, Wincanton **Ref:**YH14066
THOROUGHBRED CLOTHING, Simonsbath **Ref:**YH14083
TRISCOMBE STABLES, Taunton **Ref:**YH14404
TUCKER, F G, Wedmore **Ref:**YH14434
W.E.S GARRETT MASTER SADDLERS, Cheddar **Ref:**YH14803
WELLINGTON PET GARDEN, Wellington **Ref:**YH15074
WEST COUNTRY FEEDS, Taunton **Ref:**YH15134
WRANTAGE MILLS, Taunton **Ref:**YH15810

SOMERSET (NORTH)

ABBOTT, Banwell **Ref:**YH00109
ALBERT E JAMES & SON, Barrow Gurney **Ref:**YH00245
NAILSEA PET CTRE, Nailsea **Ref:**YH10013
SANDFORD ANIMAL FEEDS, Sandford **Ref:**YH12409
SPRINGFIELD, Claverham **Ref:**YH13252

STAFFORDSHIRE

A & F WILLIAMSON & SONS, Stoke-on-Trent **Ref:**YH00007
A K FEEDS, Shenstone **Ref:**YH00044
ABBOTSWOOD SHOW JUMPS, Rugeley **Ref:**YH00100
BOCM PAULS, Newcastle-under-Lyme **Ref:**YH01593
BRADLEY, PAUL, Stoke-on-Trent **Ref:**YH01759
BROOKES, REGINALD, Lichfield **Ref:**YH02046
C W G, Burton-on-Trent **Ref:**YH02405
CAMBIDGE, B R, Brewood **Ref:**YH02466
CLASSIC RACING BOOKS, Stoke-on-Trent **Ref:**YH02988
CRESSWELL, J K S, Stoke-on-Trent **Ref:**YH03592
DOBBINS DINER, Tamworth **Ref:**YH04151
EQUINE CLEANING SVS, Burton-on-Trent **Ref:**YH04769
FLYAWAY, Stafford **Ref:**YH05292
FRANCES ANN BROWN SADDLERY, Stafford **Ref:**YH05444
G & M PET SUPPLIES, Burntwood **Ref:**YH05567
GOLDEN FLEECE, Lichfield **Ref:**YH05879
HAYNET, Lichfield **Ref:**YH06591
HIGH ASH CTRY STORE, Rugeley **Ref:**YH06752
HILLCREST STABLES, Levedale **Ref:**YH06843
INTERNET HORSE, Stoke-on-Trent **Ref:**YH07481
KINGDOM PRODUCTS, Stafford **Ref:**YH08190
L E SLANEY & SON, Uttoxeter **Ref:**YH08318
LARKHILL SADDLERY, Burton-on-Trent **Ref:**YH08432
MEARS, E & S, Stafford **Ref:**YH09429
MOSS, T, Cheadle **Ref:**YH09864
O WARNER, KEITH, Brewood **Ref:**YH10368
OWEN, F M, Rugeley **Ref:**YH10600
ROOS FEEDS, Rugeley **Ref:**YH12080
RUMSEY, A J, Stourbridge **Ref:**YH12231
STAFFORDSHIRE HORSE WORLD, Stoke-on-Trent **Ref:**YH13324

SUFFOLK

BARNARD BROTHERS, Ipswich **Ref:**YH00965
BRAYBAY COUNTRY KNITWEAR, Bury St Edmunds **Ref:**YH01821
BRITISH RACING HERITAGE, Newmarket **Ref:**YH01966
BURTON, V & S, Lowestoft **Ref:**YH02294
C E ALDRIDGE, Bury St Edmunds **Ref:**YH02367
C W G, Bury St Edmunds **Ref:**YH02406
CANTILLON, DON, Newmarket **Ref:**YH02514
CAULFIELD, ANDREW M, Bury St Edmunds **Ref:**YH02659
CHEVAL D'OR, Lowestoft **Ref:**YH02841
CHURCH FARM TACK SHOP & FEEDS, Eye **Ref:**YH02903
COUNTRYSIDE, Ipswich **Ref:**YH03439
CROSSWAYS SV CTRE, Bungay **Ref:**YH03667
D M P MACHINERY, Bury St Edmunds **Ref:**YH03795
DALGETY AGRCLTRL, Bury St Edmunds **Ref:**YH03837
DALGETY AGRCLTRL, Newmarket **Ref:**YH03838
E Q, Harleston **Ref:**YH04422
E V J POSTAL BOOKSHOP, Newmarket **Ref:**YH04430
EQUIBRIEF, Stowmarket **Ref:**YH04735
EQUINE VETNRY JOURNAL, Newmarket **Ref:**YH04808
FARM & COUNTRY, Harleston **Ref:**YH05055
FEEDSAFE, Ipswich **Ref:**YH05125
FRANK HARVEY INT, Stowmarket **Ref:**YH05458
GALLOPON, Ipswich **Ref:**YH05623
GARROD'S SADDLERY, Harleston **Ref:**YH05657
GENESIS GREEN STUD, Newmarket **Ref:**YH05710
GEOFFREY SALE, Newmarket **Ref:**YH05717
GERNI SALES & SERVICE, Bury St Edmunds **Ref:**YH05730
GIBSON SADDLERS, Newmarket **Ref:**YH05746
GLADWELLS, Ipswich **Ref:**YH05802
HOBBLES GREEN ANIMAL FEEDS, Newmarket **Ref:**YH06892
HORSE & GARDEN, Halesworth **Ref:**YH07089
HORSE IT, Woodbridge **Ref:**YH07126
HORSE REQUISITES, Newmarket **Ref:**YH07132
HORSESHOES, Wrentham **Ref:**YH07174
HYDRO AGRI, Bury St Edmunds **Ref:**YH07352
INTERNATIONAL RACING BUREAU, Newmarket **Ref:**YH07478
JAKOBSON, TONY, Bury St Edmunds **Ref:**YH07662
LASAR EUROPE, Bury St Edmunds **Ref:**YH08437
LINKWOOD EQUESTIAN, Bury St Edmunds **Ref:**YH08665
LONG MELFORD, Sudbury **Ref:**YH08799
MACKENZIE, IAIN, Newmarket **Ref:**YH09002
MILL SADDLERY, Stowmarket **Ref:**YH09587
MORT, LIZ, Hadleigh **Ref:**YH09845
ORWELL ARENA, Ipswich **Ref:**YH10556
PADDOCK MAINTENANCE COMPANY, Ipswich **Ref:**YH10669
PARKER BROTHERS, Bury St Edmunds **Ref:**YH10744
R T'S SADDLERY, Newmarket **Ref:**YH11567
R W TAYLOR ANIMAL FEEDS, Haverhill **Ref:**YH11568
RACKHAM, E R & R T, Woodbridge **Ref:**YH11592
RIDE AWAY SADDLERY, Ipswich **Ref:**YH11846
SEEDEE PET FOODS, Sudbury **Ref:**YH12608
STABLECARE, Newmarket **Ref:**YH13301
STOKE BY CLARE EQUESTRIAN CTRE, Sudbury **Ref:**YH13501
STOREY, MARTIN J, Ipswich **Ref:**YH13525
STOWE ANIMAL HEALTH, Stowmarket **Ref:**YH13537
SUFFOLK ANIMAL FEED, Bury St Edmunds **Ref:**YH13623
SUFFOLK SADDLES, Ipswich **Ref:**YH13626
T A T SERVICES, Newmarket **Ref:**YH13729
TERRA-VAC, Haverhill **Ref:**YH13955
THURLOW NUNN STANDEN, Newmarket **Ref:**YH14120
TINDALLS BOOKSHOP, Newmarket **Ref:**YH14171
WAY, R E & G B, Newmarket **Ref:**YH15014
WESTBRINK FARMS, Newmarket **Ref:**YH15184
WHYTE, J W, Beccles **Ref:**YH15381

SURREY

A & H FEEDS, Ashtead **Ref:**YH00008
A & H FEEDS, Leatherhead **Ref:**YH00009
A C F ANIMAL BEDDING, Haslemere **Ref:**YH00024
ADDLESTONE HARDWARE, Addlestone **Ref:**YH00180
ALBURY ANIMAL FEEDS, Guildford **Ref:**YH00250
ASCOT PARK, Woking **Ref:**YH00583
AUSTIN, KATE, Haslemere **Ref:**YH00668
BACKHURST OF NORMANDY, Guildford **Ref:**YH00770
BUTTONS SADDLERY, Woking **Ref:**YH02337
COLLINS, M J, Horley **Ref:**YH03189
COUNTRYWIDE STORES, Redhill **Ref:**YH03473
CURZON, G E, Staines **Ref:**YH03755
ELLIOT RIGHT WAY BOOKS, Tadworth **Ref:**YH04615
FIELDGUARD, Cranleigh **Ref:**YH05193
FORT WHEELBARROWS, Woking **Ref:**YH05387
GILL & PUNTER RACING SUPPLIES, Dorking **Ref:**YH05768
GREIG, D R, Cranleigh **Ref:**YH06120
H F S SUPPLIES, Horley **Ref:**YH06222
HAINES ROSETTE, Addlestone **Ref:**YH06285
HAMLYN-WRIGHT HORSE RUGS, Cobham **Ref:**YH06356
HASTILOW COMPETITION SADDLES, Godalming **Ref:**YH06526
HEATHFIELD PK STABLES, Reigate **Ref:**YH06630
HORSE BITZ, Ashford **Ref:**YH07107
J W ATTLEE, Dorking **Ref:**YH07624
JASPERS, Lingfield **Ref:**YH07710
KNIGHT & BUTLER, Lingfield **Ref:**YH08256
LINGFIELD TACK, Lingfield **Ref:**YH08660
MURPHY, GENEVIEVE, Warlingham **Ref:**YH09956
MY BEAUTIFUL HORSES, Haslemere **Ref:**YH09978
ONE STOP TACK SHOP, East Molesey **Ref:**YH10513
OUTBACK TRADING, South Croydon **Ref:**YH10587
PADD FARM SHOP, Egham **Ref:**YH10665
PREMIER SHOW JUMPS, Horley **Ref:**YH11350
PRICE, N, Lingfield **Ref:**YH11385
ROBERT STEVENS, Dorking **Ref:**YH11943
ROKER'S TACK SHOP, Guildford **Ref:**YH12064
RUGGED, Woking **Ref:**YH12220
RUSTICS, Lingfield **Ref:**YH12269
SCATS COUNTRYSTORE, Godalming **Ref:**YH12507
SCATS COUNTRYSTORE, Redhill **Ref:**YH12508
SECRETT FARM SHOP, Godalming **Ref:**YH12599
STAR COMFORT RUBBER MATTING, Guildford **Ref:**YH13392
STRATUS DEVELOPMENTS, Mitcham **Ref:**YH13566
SUPERPET THE HORSE SHOP, Banstead **Ref:**YH13656
SUPERPET THE HORSE SHOP, Epsom **Ref:**YH13654
SUPERPET THE HORSE SHOP, Tadworth **Ref:**YH13655
THEW, ARNOTT, Wallington **Ref:**YH13987
TILITA ROSETTES, Warlingham **Ref:**YH14147
TRIPLE CROWN FENCE, Guildford **Ref:**YH14403
WATES, A T A, Dorking **Ref:**YH14975
WISEWEAR, Dorking **Ref:**YH15611

SUSSEX (EAST)

ANGLO EUROPEAN STUDBOOK, Crowborough **Ref:**YH00419
BATTLE EQUINE HEALTH, Battle **Ref:**YH01079
BOOK STORE, Ukfield **Ref:**YH01626

DICKSON & CHURCH, Forest Row Ref:YH04115
EURO-MECH, Brighton Ref:YH04903
FARAMUS, ANTOINETTE, Crowborough Ref:YH05050
FURNASIA, Burwash Ref:YH05544
JOLLYES, Hailsham Ref:YH07867
LUSTED FEEDS, Hankham Ref:YH08907
MILLS, A M, Heathfield Ref:YH09629
NET INFO WORKS, Hove Ref:YH10080
PARKWAY, Northiam Ref:YH10779
PEASRIDGE, S S, Rye Ref:YH10884
PENTATALE, Heathfield Ref:YH10960
SCATS COUNTRYSTORE, Heathfield Ref:YH12509
SMITH, M J, Heathfield Ref:YH12974
SOMETHING DIFFERENT, Uckfield Ref:YH13068
STEVENS, LEONARD, Eastbourne Ref:YH13445
WARMAN, JANICE, Crowborough Ref:YH14919
WRENN'S ANIMAL FEEDS, Robertsbridge Ref:YH15824
YOUNG, V P, Hastings Ref:YH15941

SUSSEX (WEST)

ABBOTT, Crawley Ref:YH00110
ABBOTT, Haywards Heath Ref:YH00111
ALL TIME EQUESTRIAN, Crawley Ref:YH00286
BARTHOLOMEWS, Chichester Ref:YH01036
BERRY, N, East Grinstead Ref:YH01317
BRENDON HORSE & RIDER, Brighton Ref:YH01837
CRAWLEY DOWN SADDLERY, Crawley Ref:YH03578
DAM, Shoreham By Sea Ref:YH03853
DIXON, F H, Haywards Heath Ref:YH04138
DRAGONFLY SADDLERY, Hassocks Ref:YH04252
E M C, Shoreham By Sea Ref:YH04415
EQUINE AMERICA, Broadbridge Heath Ref:YH04761
EQUITOGS, Billingshurst Ref:YH04830
EQUITOGS, Littlehampton Ref:YH04829
FONSECA, M & A, Pulborough Ref:YH05307
FUTURE DISTRIBUTION UK, Crawley Ref:YH05555
GEOFF DEAN SADDLERY, Worthing Ref:YH05714
GIVONS, J, Haywards Heath Ref:YH05801
GRANARY HORSE FEEDS, Chichester Ref:YH05981
H M SCARTERFIELD & SONS, Chichester Ref:YH06230
HIGHBROOK FENCING, Ardingly Ref:YH06772
HORSHAM PET CTRE, Horsham Ref:YH07188
J B ARENAS, Brighton Ref:YH07559
KIDBY INTERNATIONAL, Singleton Ref:YH08119
LIGHTS, Brighton Ref:YH08616
LOWER SPARR FARM, Billingshurst Ref:YH08870
LUKIN, P D, Arundel Ref:YH08895
MARTIN BIRD PRODUCTIONS, Horsham Ref:YH09211
MEDATA EQUESTRIAN, Arundel Ref:YH09432
MIDHURST GRANARIES, Midhurst Ref:YH09552
ONE STOP, Billingshurst Ref:YH10512
ORCHARD FARM FEEDS, East Grinstead Ref:YH10530
PENFOLD & SONS, Haywards Heath Ref:YH10934
POWELLS OF COOLHAM, Horsham Ref:YH11323
PROLITE, Pulborough Ref:YH11433
SCATS COUNTRYSTORE, Billingshurst Ref:YH12510
SNOWHILL SADDLERY, Chichester Ref:YH13044
TAYLOR, A J, Streat Hassocks Ref:YH13895
TEAM GROUP, Petworth Ref:YH13925
TEDFOULD FARM MNGMT SVS, Billingshurst Ref:YH13931
TFP, Horsham Ref:YH13971
TOWER SOUND & COMMUNICATIONS, Horsham Ref:YH14276
TRACK RIGHT, Hassocks Ref:YH14308
WATT TO WEAR, Horsham Ref:YH14998
WESTBROOK AGRICULTURAL SUP, Rudgwick Ref:YH15185

TYNE AND WEAR

ARTHUR, V R, Newcastle-upon-Tyne Ref:YH00571
B M ENGLISH & SON, Houghton Le Spring Ref:YH00738
BLOND, A J LE, Houghton Le Spring Ref:YH01546
E SWINBURN & SON, Newcastle-upon-Tyne Ref:YH04426
EQUINE PRODUCTS, Newcastle-upon-Tyne Ref:YH04795
ESSENTIALLY EQUINE, Houghton Le Spring Ref:YH04865
GO RIDING GRP, Ponteland Ref:YH05862
H C S, North Shields Ref:YH06215
HAMILTON, A, Newcastle-upon-Tyne Ref:YH06351
JOLLYES, Newcastle-upon-Tyne Ref:YH07868
PROTAC, East Boldon Ref:YH11438
RIDE IN STYLE, Sunderland Ref:YH11847
RIDERS, North Shields Ref:YH11854
S & S SADDLERY, Sunderland Ref:YH12313

WARWICKSHIRE

ATHAG LTD, Atherstone Ref:YH00642
B & G SERVICES, Studley Ref:YH00712
BAKER, D J, Rugby Ref:YH00817
BDS, Warwick Ref:YH01101
BLYTH MILL, Birmingham Ref:YH01577
BUTLER, D A, Rugby Ref:YH02323
CALDECOTE RIDING SCHOOL, Nuneaton Ref:YH02428
COUNTRYWIDE STORES, Nuneaton Ref:YH03474
COUNTRYWIDE STORES, Rugby Ref:YH03475
COUNTRYWIDE STORES, Stratford-upon-Avon Ref:YH03476
DARLOWS, Butlers Marston Ref:YH03896
EDWARDS' SADDLERY, Bidford On Avon Ref:YH04574
ENGLAND, E M V, Rugby Ref:YH04671
FYNA-LITE, Alcester Ref:YH05558
GRAPES VILLA FARM SUPPLIES, Coventry Ref:YH06017
HUTSBY, G, Wellesbourne Ref:YH07338
JOLLYES, Stratford-upon-Avon Ref:YH07869
LYNMARI TACK & ACCESSORIES, Solihull Ref:YH08932
MUMFORD, H S & G R, Nuneaton Ref:YH09947
NET-WEAR, Nuneaton Ref:YH10084
PEACHEY, H E, Stratford-upon-Avon Ref:YH10857
RACECOURSE & COVERTSIDE, Hampton Magna Ref:YH11573
SHERIDAN, FELIX, Rowington Ref:YH12723
SPORTSMARK, Warwick Ref:YH13236
TEAM CHASER, Leamington Spa Ref:YH13924
TROTTERS EQUESTRIAN SUPPLIES, Kenilworth Ref:YH14410
WAVERLEY EQUESTRIAN CTRE, Leamington Spa Ref:YH15011
WINDRIDGE STORES, Coventry Ref:YH15569

WILTSHIRE

BEST BOOTS, Chippenham Ref:YH01324
BLOODSTOCK PUBLICATIONS, Marlborough Ref:YH01550
CONDRY, HUGH & SUE, Salisbury Ref:YH03225
COUNTRYWIDE STORES, Chippenham Ref:YH03477
COUNTRYWIDE STORES, Melksham Ref:YH03478
COUNTRYWIDE STORES, Swindon Ref:YH03479
E P C, Warminster Ref:YH04419
EASTON GREY SADDLERS, Malmesbury Ref:YH04514
ELMGROVE SADDLERY, Swindon Ref:YH04636
EQUESTRIAN MATTING, Chippenham Ref:YH04706
EQUESTRIAN SVS, Chippenham Ref:YH04715
EQUI LIFE, Chippenham Ref:YH04728
EQUIBALE, Chippenham Ref:YH04732
EQUIFOR, Marlborough Ref:YH04746
EQUINOVA, Warminster Ref:YH04813
EQUI-SURE, Corsham Ref:YH04822
GALE, BARBARA, Malmesbury Ref:YH05612
GILMORE, JIM, Malmesbury Ref:YH05789
GRO-WELL FEEDS, Melksham Ref:YH06176
IRRIGATION SYSTEMS & SERVICES, Salisbury Ref:YH07508
J & K ANIMAL FEEDS, Warminster Ref:YH07549
JOHN TOOMER, Swindon Ref:YH07815
JOLLYES, Chippenham Ref:YH07870
KENLIN TRADING, Swindon Ref:YH08064
KEYSLEY HORSE RUGS, Salisbury Ref:YH08116
L J'S EQUESTRIAN, Swindon Ref:YH08323
M C A TACK, Westbury Ref:YH08955
M M T SERVICES, Marlborough Ref:YH08973
MULLIS, ROBERT, Swindon Ref:YH09943
NEW EQUINE WEAR, Malmesbury Ref:YH10093
OSGILIATH FEEDS, Westbury Ref:YH10565
PEMBROKE FARM FEEDS, Salisbury Ref:YH10917
S & J DISTRIBUTORS, Swindon Ref:YH12311
SCATS COUNTRYSTORE, Devizes Ref:YH12512
SCATS COUNTRYSTORE, Salisbury Ref:YH12511
T H WHITE, Marlborough Ref:YH13746

WORCESTERSHIRE

A & M MARKETING, Evesham Ref:YH00014
BEALE FEEDS, Bromsgrove Ref:YH01113
BROMSGROVE SADDLERY, Bromsgrove Ref:YH02026
COACH HSE SADDLERY, Hanley Castle Ref:YH03103
CORN STORES, Redditch Ref:YH03321
COUNTRYWIDE, Worcester Ref:YH03446
COUNTRYWIDE STORES, Bromsgrove Ref:YH03482
COUNTRYWIDE STORES, Kidderminster Ref:YH03480
COUNTRYWIDE STORES, Upton-upon-Severn Ref:YH03481
DOWSON, H B, Pershore Ref:YH04244
EQUIMIX, Stourport-on-Severn Ref:YH04756
EQUINE & CANINE SUPPLIES, Worcester Ref:YH04758
ERIC FIRKINS FARM SUPPLIES, Stourport-on-Severn Ref:YH04844
EVANS, MARTIN, Kidderminster Ref:YH04928
FOREST HARNESS, Bewdley Ref:YH05338
HOLLINGSWORTH, A F, Redditch Ref:YH06944
HUGHES, A L, Malvern Ref:YH07257
JOHN BARNETT, Worcester Ref:YH07779
JOHN SCOTT SPORTING BOOKS, Abberley Ref:YH07811
JUMPS FOR JOY, Worcester Ref:YH07969
M F HOWARD & SONS, Droitwich Ref:YH08962
PASTURES CLEAN, Broadway Ref:YH10813
PILKINGTON, J, Malvern Ref:YH11106
PIONEER ANIMAL FEEDS, Upton-upon-Severn Ref:YH11142

- **ROBINS, ADRIAN J**, Kidderminster **Ref:**YH11984
- **RUG LAUDRY**, Worcester **Ref:**YH12215
- **SADIK, A M**, Kidderminster **Ref:**YH12373
- **STRONG, PETER**, Wolverley **Ref:**YH13584
- **TANWOOD STUD**, Kidderminster **Ref:**YH13862
- **W H SUTTON & SONS**, Kidderminster **Ref:**YH14775
- **WESTON, M H**, Hindlip **Ref:**YH15227
- **WILSONS PET & ANIMAL CTRE**, Bromsgrove **Ref:**YH15551

YORKSHIRE (EAST)

- **A & E WOODWARD**, Hull **Ref:**YH00006
- **ASS BLOOD STOCK CONS**, Bridlington **Ref:**YH00629
- **BRANDSBY AGRIC TRADING ASS**, Driffield **Ref:**YH01800
- **CURTIS, J W P**, Driffield **Ref:**YH03749
- **DALGETY AGRCLTRL**, Driffield **Ref:**YH03839
- **FARMWAY**, Driffield **Ref:**YH05076
- **HAIGHS**, Doncaster **Ref:**YH06282
- **MARSHALLS**, Holme upon Spalding Moor **Ref:**YH09207
- **MERCHANT PET & ANIMAL FEED**, Driffield **Ref:**YH09464
- **N P R DATATAG DIVISION**, Hull **Ref:**YH09993
- **NORTH RIDING ROSETTES**, Bridlington **Ref:**YH10280
- **NORTHERN STRAW**, Goole **Ref:**YH10311
- **PATRICK WILKINSON**, Beverley **Ref:**YH10825
- **SEXTON, JOHN**, Beverley **Ref:**YH12650
- **SIGNFORD**, Beverley **Ref:**YH12794
- **SMITHY**, Driffield **Ref:**YH13013
- **TEMPLE, B M**, Driffield **Ref:**YH13949
- **TIMSBURY INTERNATIONAL**, Driffield **Ref:**YH14168
- **TOMKINSON, A**, Pocklington **Ref:**YH14222

YORKSHIRE (NORTH)

- **ALL 4 PETS**, Malton **Ref:**YH00283
- **BIT BANK**, Stokesley **Ref:**YH01454
- **BRANDSBY AGRIC TRADING ASS**, Kirkbymoorside **Ref:**YH01801
- **BRANDSBY AGRIC TRADING ASSOC**, Easingwold **Ref:**YH01803
- **BRANDSBY AGRIC TRADING ASSOC**, Helmsley **Ref:**YH01805
- **BRANDSBY AGRIC TRADING ASSOC**, Scarborough **Ref:**YH01807
- **BRANDSBY AGRIC TRADING ASSOC**, Whitby **Ref:**YH01806
- **BRANDSBY AGRIC TRADING ASSOC**, Whitby **Ref:**YH01804
- **BRANDSBY AGRIC TRADING ASSOC**, York **Ref:**YH01808
- **BULLOCK, J A & F**, York **Ref:**YH02219
- **CLARKE, W H**, Thirsk **Ref:**YH02976
- **CURRIE, D P & J A**, Settle **Ref:**YH03739
- **DALES PET FEED SUPPLIES**, Ripon **Ref:**YH03828
- **DEBOIZ**, Thirsk **Ref:**YH04005
- **DON WEAR TEXTILES**, Green Hammerton **Ref:**YH04173
- **EQUINE AMERICA**, Richmond **Ref:**YH04762
- **F GREEN & SON**, Gargrave **Ref:**YH04992
- **FARMWAY**, Leyburn **Ref:**YH05078
- **FARMWAY**, Thirsk **Ref:**YH05077
- **FOSS FEEDS**, Acaster Malbis **Ref:**YH05395
- **FRIMBLE OF RIPON**, Ripon **Ref:**YH05506
- **GILLS SADDLERY & CANE**, Northallerton **Ref:**YH05787
- **H WADDINGTON**, Skipton **Ref:**YH06246
- **HARKER, G A**, Northallerton **Ref:**YH06431
- **HORSEFEEDSUK**, Harrogate **Ref:**YH07154
- **HUGILL, J D**, Northallerton **Ref:**YH07275
- **JAMESON, W E**, Ripon **Ref:**YH07691
- **JOHNSON, ELIZABETH**, Bedale **Ref:**YH07823
- **JUST AS GOOD**, Thirsk **Ref:**YH07972
- **KARL BUTLER BUSINESS**, Malton **Ref:**YH07996
- **KIRBY, F**, Northallerton **Ref:**YH08227
- **KNIGHT EQUESTRIAN SUPPLIES**, Harrogate **Ref:**YH08257
- **LOAFERS**, Lower Dunsforth **Ref:**YH08750
- **NICHOLSON EQUESTRIAN SVS**, Harrogate **Ref:**YH10188
- **ORDE-POWLETT, H**, Leyburn **Ref:**YH10539
- **ORMSTON, J M**, Richmond **Ref:**YH10550
- **PICKERING, JOHN T**, Helmsley **Ref:**YH11084
- **R & R COUNTRY**, Selby **Ref:**YH11507
- **RIDING STOCK**, York **Ref:**YH11884
- **ROCKING HORSE SHOP**, Pocklington **Ref:**YH12034
- **ROOS FEEDS NORTH**, Malton **Ref:**YH12081
- **RUSSELL, P A**, Claxton **Ref:**YH12262
- **SCULPTURE TO WEAR**, Leyburn **Ref:**YH12574
- **SKELTON, J**, Skipton **Ref:**YH12866
- **SMITH, WILLIAM J**, Richmond **Ref:**YH13004
- **SWIERS, J E**, Helperby **Ref:**YH13705
- **TAYLOR, F**, Richmond **Ref:**YH13901
- **TUER, E W**, Northallerton **Ref:**YH14446
- **TURNER, S J**, Ripon **Ref:**YH14490
- **W M THOMPSON**, Murton **Ref:**YH14781
- **WALMSLEY, J W**, Tadcaster **Ref:**YH14868
- **WALTON, KATE**, Leyburn **Ref:**YH14893
- **WARD, S A**, Northallerton **Ref:**YH14908
- **WATT FENCES**, Catterick Garrison **Ref:**YH14997
- **WESTERMAN, BARRY**, Riccall **Ref:**YH15196
- **WESTWICK EQUESTRIAN SERVICES**, Thirsk **Ref:**YH15237
- **WOOD, R S**, Nawton **Ref:**YH15667
- **WOODS SHOW JUMPS**, Malton **Ref:**YH15734

YORKSHIRE (SOUTH)

- **AXIENT**, Rotherham **Ref:**YH00695
- **BOWMAN, CAROL**, Doncaster **Ref:**YH01720
- **BROWN, D H**, Maltby **Ref:**YH02105
- **CONISBROUGH PETS**, Doncaster **Ref:**YH03231
- **COOKE, DONALD**, Rotherham **Ref:**YH03259
- **DOOK, C M A**, Doncaster **Ref:**YH04191
- **EASTWOOD, D**, Barnsley **Ref:**YH04519
- **FLINTWYK ENGINEERING**, Doncaster **Ref:**YH05287
- **FRIENDSHIP ESTATES**, Doncaster **Ref:**YH05503
- **HORSE & RIDER**, Sheffield **Ref:**YH07097
- **HORSE PARAPHENALIA**, Sheffield **Ref:**YH07127
- **HUMBLE ORIGINS INT**, Sheffield **Ref:**YH07284
- **INT RACECOURSE MNGMT**, Doncaster **Ref:**YH07471
- **JOLLYES**, Doncaster **Ref:**YH07871
- **MURPHY HIRE**, Sheffield **Ref:**YH09955
- **R & P FEEDERS**, Sheffield **Ref:**YH11506
- **ROCKING HORSE CLOTHING**, Rotherham **Ref:**YH12033
- **SHOWJUMP INT**, Barnsley **Ref:**YH12766
- **STABLE-DRY & EQUIBALE**, Doncaster **Ref:**YH13302
- **THROSTLE NEST SADDLERY**, Barnsley **Ref:**YH14114
- **TWIBELL, J**, Sheffield **Ref:**YH14511
- **WILSON FEEDS**, Doncaster **Ref:**YH15527

YORKSHIRE (WEST)

- **ACORN FEEDS**, Huddersfield **Ref:**YH00148
- **B WORTLEY & SON**, Huddersfield **Ref:**YH00752
- **BADMINTON HORSE FEEDS**, Sherburn In Elmet **Ref:**YH00786
- **BARDSEY MILLS**, Otley **Ref:**YH00927
- **BINNS BOOKS**, Knottingley **Ref:**YH01423
- **BLACK HORSE ACCESSORIES**, Leeds **Ref:**YH01464
- **BLUE BARN**, Otley **Ref:**YH01563
- **BROWN, T**, Wakefield **Ref:**YH02132
- **CALDENE CLOTHING**, Hebden Bridge **Ref:**YH02430
- **CARMAN EQUESTRIAN SUPPLIES**, Bradford **Ref:**YH02546
- **CLASSY PONIES**, Dewsbury **Ref:**YH02991
- **COUNTRY COVERS**, Leeds **Ref:**YH03402
- **CRICKET HILL FEEDS**, Leeds **Ref:**YH03596
- **DAMART**, Bingley **Ref:**YH03854
- **DAYS PET SHOP**, Bradford **Ref:**YH03971
- **ELIZABETH GREENWOOD**, Halifax **Ref:**YH04608
- **EQUINE EASY CLEAR**, Dewsbury **Ref:**YH04776
- **EQUITACK SADDLERY**, Wakefield **Ref:**YH04825
- **F & STROKER & SONS**, Leeds **Ref:**YH04981
- **F W TINGLE & SONS**, Wakefield **Ref:**YH05004
- **FARMERS IMPLEMENT SUPPLY**, Wakefield **Ref:**YH05063
- **FREELANCE FEATURES**, Otley **Ref:**YH05483
- **GRATTAN**, Ingleby Road **Ref:**YH06022
- **GREETLAND & DISTRICT TRAD SOC**, Halifax **Ref:**YH06112
- **H THORNBER**, Halifax **Ref:**YH06244
- **HOOVES EQUESTRIAN**, Bradford **Ref:**YH07047
- **HUTCHINSON, A**, Wakefield **Ref:**YH07335
- **J R COUNTRY & PET SUPPLIES**, Wetherby **Ref:**YH07607
- **JAMES BURNHILL & SON**, Cleckheaton **Ref:**YH07663
- **JENKINSONS**, Dewsbury **Ref:**YH07740
- **JUST JODS**, Wakefield **Ref:**YH07974
- **KAYES ANIMAL FEEDS**, Wyke **Ref:**YH08010
- **KEITH DRAKE**, Huddersfield **Ref:**YH08033
- **KIPPAX**, Leeds **Ref:**YH08222
- **MEARCLOUGH FARM FEEDS**, Halifax **Ref:**YH09428
- **MIDDLESTOWN SADDLERY**, Wakefield **Ref:**YH09540
- **OSCARS PET & EQUINE SUPPLIES**, Wetherby **Ref:**YH10564
- **PETE'S TACK**, Bingley **Ref:**YH11025
- **PLOWRIGHT, G S**, Wakefield **Ref:**YH11180
- **PONY PIT-STOP**, Bradford **Ref:**YH11251
- **PUDSEY AGRICULTURAL SVS**, Pudsey **Ref:**YH11449
- **QUALTEX**, Hebden Bridge **Ref:**YH11477
- **RATCATCHER**, Guiseley **Ref:**YH11647
- **RIDGEWAY LEATHER**, Addingham **Ref:**YH11864
- **SCARLETT RIBBONS**, Halifax **Ref:**YH12488
- **SILVER FOX EQUESTRIAN**, Liversedge **Ref:**YH12804
- **SIMCOCK, R**, Halifax **Ref:**YH12818
- **STEPHENSONS ANIMAL FEEDS**, Todmorden **Ref:**YH13427
- **STYLO MATCHMAKERS INT**, Bradford **Ref:**YH13620
- **TACK & TURNOUT EQUESTRIAN**, Huddersfield **Ref:**YH13780
- **TIMEFORM ORGANISATION**, Halifax **Ref:**YH14164
- **VAUX BROS**, Pontefract **Ref:**YH14670
- **WEST RIDING SUPPLIES**, Bradford **Ref:**YH15161

TRACKS/COURSES

BATH & SOMERSET (NORTH EAST)

- **H S JACKSON & SON**, Bath **Ref:**YH06237
- **HUNSTRETE RIDING SCHOOL**, Pensford **Ref:**YH07294

BEDFORDSHIRE

- **CLGE EQUESTRIAN CTRE**, Bedford **Ref:**YH03025

BERKSHIRE

- **ALAN HADLEY**, Reading **Ref:**YH00239
- **ASCOT RACECOURSE**, Ascot **Ref:**YH00584
- **HALL PLACE EQUESTRIAN CTRE**, Reading **Ref:**YH06307
- **MARTIN COLLINS ENTERPRISES**, Hungerford **Ref:**YH09212
- **NEW FARM**, Newbury **Ref:**YH10095

NEWBURY RACECOURSE, Newbury Ref:YH10126
WINDSOR RACING, Windsor Ref:YH15577
WOODLANDS, Hungerford Ref:YH15705

BUCKINGHAMSHIRE

ARDENLEA ENTERPRISES, Princes Risborough Ref:YH00503
EQUESTRIAN CTRE, Amersham Ref:YH04696

CAMBRIDGESHIRE

HUNTINGDON STEEPLECHASE, Huntingdon Ref:YH07305

CHESHIRE

CHESTER RACE, Chester Ref:YH02831
H S JACKSON & SON, Tattenhall Ref:YH06238
RINGWOOD ARENAS, Tarporley Ref:YH11903

CLEVELAND

REDCAR RACECOURSE, Redcar Ref:YH11707
SEDGEFIELD STEEPLECHASES, Stockton-on-Tees Ref:YH12603

CORNWALL

MOORE, K & A E, Launceston Ref:YH09762
ST LEONARDS EQUESTRIAN CTRE, Launceston Ref:YH13278

COUNTY DURHAM

BEAMISH RIDING CTRE, Stanley Ref:YH01117
LOW FOLD RIDING CTRE, Crook Ref:YH08855
LOW MEADOWS FARM LIVERY, Durham Ref:YH08856
NEW MOORS, Bishop Auckland Ref:YH10114
RAYGILL, Barnard Castle Ref:YH11672
WITTON CASTLE RACEWAY, Bishop Auckland Ref:YH15635

CUMBRIA

BREED EX EQUINE STUD, Penrith Ref:YH01832
CARLISLE RACECOURSE, Carlisle Ref:YH02540
CARTMEL RACECOURSE, Grange-Over-Sands Ref:YH02610
HAYESCASTLE FARM, Workington Ref:YH06576
KESWICK RIDING CTRE, Keswick Ref:YH08105
MIDDLE BAYLES LIVERY, Alston Ref:YH09534

DERBYSHIRE

BARLEYFIELDS, Derby Ref:YH00952
BRITTON, CHARLES, Buxton Ref:YH01984
PRESTIGE SPORTS SERVICES, Buxton Ref:YH11365

DEVON

COLLACOTT FARM, Umberleigh Ref:YH03173
DURALOCK, Plymouth Ref:YH04365
EXETER STEEPLECHASE, Exeter Ref:YH04967
GRANGE EQUESTRIAN CTRE, Okehampton Ref:YH05987
HONEYSUCKLE FARM, Newton Abbot Ref:YH07017
NEWTON ABBOT RACECOURSE, Newton Abbot Ref:YH10168

DORSET

EQUESTRIAN & EXAM CTRE, Ferndown Ref:YH04691
SKINNER, ROSS, Dorchester Ref:YH12878

ESSEX

CLAY HALL, Brentwood Ref:YH02994
FURNESS FARM CROSS COUNTRY, Ingatestone Ref:YH05546
HOBBS CROSS EQUESTRIAN CTRE, Epping Ref:YH06893
SUDBURY STABLES, Billericay Ref:YH13621
WILLOWS SHOW JUMPING CLUB, Loughton Ref:YH15509

GLOUCESTERSHIRE

CHELTENHAM RACECOURSE, Cheltenham Ref:YH02804
DENNY, L, Moreton-in-Marsh Ref:YH04063
DORMIT RIDING SURFACES, Cirencester Ref:YH04202
FENCING IN THE MIDLANDS, Moreton In Marsh Ref:YH05139
MELCOURT INDUSTRIES, Tetbury Ref:YH09450
SUMMERHOUSE, Gloucester Ref:YH13632
UPCOTE CROSS COUNTRY COURSE, Cheltenham Ref:YH14599
W F EQUESTRIAN SURFACES, Cheltenham Ref:YH14765
WOODLAND, Cheltenham Ref:YH15702

GLOUCESTERSHIRE (SOUTH)

BATH RACECOURSE, Yate Ref:YH01071
TACK ROOM, Chipping Sodbury Ref:YH13799

HAMPSHIRE

BROCKWOOD PARK HORSE TRIALS, Alresford Ref:YH02016
DECOY POND FARM, Brockenhurst Ref:YH04012
DRI-EX GALLOPS, Fordingbridge Ref:YH04272
EAST STREET STABLES, Lymington Ref:YH04487
EQUITRED, Southampton Ref:YH04833
FIRGO FARM CROSS CTRY COURSE, Whitchurch Ref:YH05225
HARRIS, ANDREW, Lymington Ref:YH06464
HOPLANDS EQUESTRIAN, Stockbridge Ref:YH07058
SOUTHFIELD EQUESTRIAN CTRE, Whitchurch Ref:YH13149

HEREFORDSHIRE

HEREFORD RACECOURSE, Eaton Bishop Ref:YH06701

HERTFORDSHIRE

GREAT WESTWOOD, Chipperfield Ref:YH06044

KENT

BALI HAI FARM, Kemsing Ref:YH00846
FOREST VIEW, Sidcup Ref:YH05353
H S JACKSON & SON, Ashford Ref:YH06239

LANCASHIRE

ELSWICK, Preston Ref:YH04644
OSBALDESTON RIDING CTRE, Blackburn Ref:YH10557
THROUGHBRED SURFACES, Preston Ref:YH14115

LEICESTERSHIRE

BROOKSBY EQUESTRIAN CTRE, Melton Mowbray Ref:YH02067
GLENDALE EQUESTRIAN FEEDS, Leicester Ref:YH05830
LAZYLAWN, Oakham Ref:YH08487
LEICESTER RACECOURSE, Oadby Ref:YH08544
LONGDON STUD MATTING, Huncote Ref:YH08809
MEADOWS RIDING CTRE, Fleckney Ref:YH09426
QUORN, Melton Mowbray Ref:YH11503
VISCORIDE, Lutterworth Ref:YH14733

LINCOLNSHIRE

ARENA UK, Grantham Ref:YH00517
GREAT PONTON UK CHASERS, Grantham Ref:YH06042
HOOD, J S F, Grange-De-Lings Ref:YH07024
MARKET RASEN RACECOURSE, Market Rasen Ref:YH09159

LONDON (GREATER)

BELMONT RIDING CTRE, London Ref:YH01249

MERSEYSIDE

AINTREE RACECOURSE, Aintree Ref:YH00217
HAYDOCK PK RACECOURSE, Newton-Le-Willows Ref:YH06571
HIGHCLARE WOODCHIPS SUPPLIES, Bootle Ref:YH06774

MIDLANDS (WEST)

FOXHILLS, Walsall Ref:YH05435
MANCHESTER PLASTICS, Wolverhampton Ref:YH09067
WOLVERHAMPTON RACECOURSE, Wolverhampton Ref:YH15650

NORFOLK

ANGLIA WOODCHIP, Norwich Ref:YH00416
FAKENHAM RACECOURSE, Fakenham Ref:YH05036
GREAT YARMOUTH RACECOURSE, Great Yarmouth Ref:YH06045
WESTON PARK EQUESTRIAN CTRE, Norwich Ref:YH15224
WRENINGHAM TROTTING RACEWAY, Norwich Ref:YH15823

NORTHAMPTONSHIRE

AMEGA SCIENCES, Daventry Ref:YH00363
BRYLINE RIDING SURFACES, Roade Ref:YH02172
RUSHTON HALL FARM, Kettering Ref:YH12246
TOWCESTER RACECOURSE, Towcester Ref:YH14268
WASHBROOK FARM, Daventry Ref:YH14955

NORTHUMBERLAND

CHARLTON, R B, Hexham Ref:YH02766
HARGREAVE EQUINE SVS, Chathill Ref:YH06425
HEXHAM STEEPLECHASE, Hexham Ref:YH06732
KELSO RACES, Wooler Ref:YH08051
WOOPERTON, Alnwick Ref:YH15770

NOTTINGHAMSHIRE

CLGE FARM, Newark Ref:YH03026
NEWTON CROFT COUNTRY, Nottingham Ref:YH10169
NOTTINGHAM RACECOURSE, Nottingham Ref:YH10344
SOUTHWELL RACE COURSE, Newark Ref:YH13161
WELLOW PK, Newark Ref:YH15077

OXFORDSHIRE

AUTOTRAK PORTABLE ROADWAYS, Bicester Ref:YH00674
DURALOCK, Chipping Norton Ref:YH04366
NEW HOUSE LIVERY, Abingdon Ref:YH10109
RYCOTE FARMS, Oxford Ref:YH12290
THAMES VALLEY FENCING, Chiselhampton Ref:YH13975

RUTLAND

MANTON LODGE STABLES, Rutland Ref:YH09127

SHROPSHIRE

LUDLOW RACECOURSE, Ludlow Ref:YH08890
RANSFORDS, Bishops Castle Ref:YH11636
SOMMERFIELD FLEXABOARD, Telford Ref:YH13069
WALFORD COLLEGE, Shrewsbury Ref:YH14842
WYKE OF SHIFNAL, Shifnal Ref:YH15863

SOMERSET

STOCKLAND LOVELL, Bridgwater Ref:YH13493
TAUNTON RACECOURSE, Taunton Ref:YH13883
WINCANTON RACES, Wincanton Ref:YH15560
WINDMILL HILL EQUESTRIAN CTRE, Ilminster Ref:YH15566

WITHAM VALE CONTRACTORS, Yeovil **Ref:**YH15619

SOMERSET (NORTH)

MENDIP RIDING CTRE, Churchill **Ref:**YH09458

MENDIP WOODSHAVINGS, Blagdon **Ref:**YH09459

STAFFORDSHIRE

ALSAGER EQUESTRIAN CTRE, Stoke-on-Trent **Ref:**YH00335

OFFLEY BROOK LIVERY STABLES, Eccleshall **Ref:**YH10436

UTTOXETER RACECOURSE, Uttoxeter **Ref:**YH14626

SUFFOLK

NEWMARKET RACECOURSES TRUST, Newmarket **Ref:**YH10157

NORCROFT EQUESTRIAN DVLP, Bury St Edmunds **Ref:**YH10230

POPLAR PK, Woodbridge **Ref:**YH11271

UGGLESHALL, Beccles **Ref:**YH14541

SURREY

ALWYN HOLDEN, Newdigate **Ref:**YH00352

ARDENLEA ENTERPRISES, Epsom **Ref:**YH00504

BARNES, PAT, Woking **Ref:**YH00979

CHASE FARM, Hindhead **Ref:**YH02780

CHOBHAM CHASERS CROSS COUNTRY, Woking **Ref:**YH02873

DUNSFOLD RYSE STABLES, Chiddingfold **Ref:**YH04357

EPSOM DOWNS RACECOURSE, Epsom **Ref:**YH04682

FOLKESTONE RACECOURSE, Lingfield **Ref:**YH05298

HURSTFIELDS EQUESTRIAN CTRE, Tadworth **Ref:**YH07321

KEMPTON PK RACECOURSES, Sunbury-on-Thames **Ref:**YH08056

LINGFIELD PARK RACECOURSE, Lingfield **Ref:**YH08659

MERRIST WOOD CLGE, Guildford **Ref:**YH09482

SANDOWN PARK RACECOURSE, Esher **Ref:**YH12417

TANGYE, JOHN, Guildford **Ref:**YH13855

TRIPLE CROWN FENCE, Guildford **Ref:**YH14403

WINDACRES FARM, Horley **Ref:**YH15561

SUSSEX (EAST)

BRIGHTON RACECOURSE, Brighton **Ref:**YH01909

PARKWAY, Heathfield **Ref:**YH10780

PLUMPTON RACECOURSE, Plumpton **Ref:**YH11184

SUSSEX (WEST)

FONTWELL PK RACECOURSE, Arundel **Ref:**YH05309

GOODWOOD RACECOURSE, Chichester **Ref:**YH05914

TYNE AND WEAR

NEWCASTLE RACES, Newcastle-upon-Tyne **Ref:**YH10128

WARWICKSHIRE

ACCIMASSU, Studley **Ref:**YH00140

INTERNATIONAL WARWICK SCHOOL, Warwick **Ref:**YH07480

RED HSE FARM LIVERY STABLES, Leamington Spa **Ref:**YH11696

STONELEIGH STABLES, Kenilworth **Ref:**YH13519

STRATFORD-ON-AVON RACECOURSE, Stratford-upon-Avon **Ref:**YH13553

WARWICK RACECOURSE COMPANY, Warwick **Ref:**YH14946

WILTSHIRE

BUSH, N, Chippenham **Ref:**YH02308

HEYWOOD, Westbury **Ref:**YH06737

MIDWAY MANOR, Bradford-on-Avon **Ref:**YH09562

SALISBURY RACECOURSE, Salisbury **Ref:**YH12388

STONAR SCHOOL, Melksham **Ref:**YH13507

WEST WILTS, Trowbridge **Ref:**YH15170

WORCESTERSHIRE

HILLOCKS FARM, Kidderminster **Ref:**YH06847

KYRE EQUESTRIAN CTRE, Tenbury Wells **Ref:**YH08305

PERSHORE & HINDLIP CLGE, Hindlip **Ref:**YH10993

TABOR, M J & N J, Broadway **Ref:**YH13771

WORCESTER RACECOURSE, Worcester **Ref:**YH15774

YORKSHIRE (EAST)

BEVERLEY RACE, Beverley **Ref:**YH01343

REWCASTLE, K, North Cave **Ref:**YH11771

YORKSHIRE (NORTH)

CATTERICK RACECOURSE, Richmond **Ref:**YH02655

EDDLETHORPE EQUESTRIAN SVS, Malton **Ref:**YH04543

ESCRICK PK RIDEWAYS, York **Ref:**YH04859

RAINBOW ARENA'S, Harrogate **Ref:**YH11613

RIPON RACE, Ripon **Ref:**YH11907

RUSSELL, G T, Malton **Ref:**YH12257

STOCKWELL STUD LIVERY STABLES, Tadcaster **Ref:**YH13497

SWINTON PARK, Ripon **Ref:**YH13713

THIRSK RACECOURSE, Thirsk **Ref:**YH13999

YORK RACE COMMITTEE, York **Ref:**YH15916

YORKSHIRE (SOUTH)

DONCASTER RACECOURSE, Doncaster **Ref:**YH04179

SNOWDON FARM RIDING SCHOOL, Sheffield **Ref:**YH13040

YORKSHIRE (WEST)

FACTORY FARM, Huddersfield **Ref:**YH05007

LILAC FARM COURTYARD LIVERY, Wetherby **Ref:**YH08619

PARNHAM LANDSCAPES, Leeds **Ref:**YH10784

PONTEFRACT PK RACE, Pontefract **Ref:**YH11225

WETHERBY STEEPLECHASE, Wetherby **Ref:**YH15244

WIKEFIELD FARM LIVERIES, Leeds **Ref:**YH15402

TRAINERS

BATH & SOMERSET (NORTH EAST)

CONKWELL GRANGE STUD, Bath **Ref:**YH03232

HORLER, M A, Bath **Ref:**YH07070

HUNSTRETE RIDING SCHOOL, Pensford **Ref:**YH07294

BEDFORDSHIRE

CAROE, C J E, Thurleigh **Ref:**YH02567

GRANSDEN HALL, Sandy **Ref:**YH06005

ROWAN LODGE, Shefford **Ref:**YH12154

TURNER, NICK, Biggleswade **Ref:**YH14488

BERKSHIRE

ARBUTHNOT, D W P, Hungerford **Ref:**YH00496

B W HILLS SOUTHBANK, Hungerford **Ref:**YH00750

BALDING, IAN, Newbury **Ref:**YH00836

BEAUMONT STABLES, Maidenhead **Ref:**YH01133

BECKETT, R, Hungerford **Ref:**YH01148

BLANSHARD, M T W, Hungerford **Ref:**YH01526

BURGOYNE, PAUL, Hungerford **Ref:**YH02251

CASTLE PIECE RACING STABLES, Hungerford **Ref:**YH02630

CHANCE, NOEL, Hungerford **Ref:**YH02730

CHANNON, M, Newbury **Ref:**YH02734

CHARLIE MANN RACING, Hungerford **Ref:**YH02764

COOMBE PK RACING STABLES, Reading **Ref:**YH03274

COURTLANDS, Wokingham **Ref:**YH03506

CRAGO, KAREN, Reading **Ref:**YH03546

DE HAAN, B, Hungerford **Ref:**YH03978

DELAMERE COTTAGE STABLES, Hungerford **Ref:**YH04028

DOYLE, JACQUELINE, Hungerford **Ref:**YH04247

EAST SOLEY E C 2000, Hungerford **Ref:**YH04486

EASTBURY COTTAGE STABLES, Hungerford **Ref:**YH04489

EQUICENTRE, Waltham St Lawrence **Ref:**YH04737

FETHERSTON-GODLEY, M J, Newbury **Ref:**YH05173

FOUR SEASONS RACING, Hungerford **Ref:**YH05412

GASELEE, N, Hungerford **Ref:**YH05669

HAMILTON RACING, Hungerford **Ref:**YH06348

HEADS FARM STABLES, Newbury **Ref:**YH06613

HENDERSON, N J, Hungerford **Ref:**YH06667

HILL HSE STABLES, Hungerford **Ref:**YH06821

HILLS, J W, Hungerford **Ref:**YH06848

HILLSIDE STUD, Hungerford **Ref:**YH06855

JAMES, E, Hungerford **Ref:**YH07681

JONES, M A, Hungerford **Ref:**YH07914

JONES, MERRITA, Hungerford **Ref:**YH07919

K S CUNDELL & PARTNERS, Newbury **Ref:**YH07991

KEEPERS STABLES, Newbury **Ref:**YH08031

KINGS FARM STABLES, Hungerford **Ref:**YH08193

KINGWOOD HOUSE STABLES, Hungerford **Ref:**YH08215

LAMBOURN RACEHORSE TRANSPORT, Hungerford **Ref:**YH08367

LIMES FARM STABLES, Hungerford **Ref:**YH08636

LINKSLADE STABLES, Hungerford **Ref:**YH08664

LIPLANDS STABLES, Newbury **Ref:**YH08676

MANNING, PAT, Reading **Ref:**YH09088

MARK PITMAN RACING, Hungerford **Ref:**YH09154

MARKS, D, Hungerford **Ref:**YH09164

MARKS, KELLY, Hungerford **Ref:**YH09165

MEEHAN, BRIAN, Hungerford **Ref:**YH09441

MORRISON, H, Newbury **Ref:**YH09837

MUIR, WILLIAM R, Hungerford **Ref:**YH09921

NEARDOWN STABLES, Hungerford **Ref:**YH10062

NEWLANDS STABLES, Hungerford **Ref:**YH10145

NORMAN BERRY RACING, Hungerford **Ref:**YH10236

OSBOURNE, J, Hungerford **Ref:**YH10562

PARK HSE STABLES, Newbury **Ref:**YH10728

PARSONAGE FARM RACING STABLES, Hungerford **Ref:**YH10797

PEACHEY, KA, Maidenhead **Ref:**YH10858

PERISI, J S, Windsor **Ref:**YH10975

PORTER, JOHN, Hungerford **Ref:**YH11282

RACE HORSE TRAINER, Hungerford **Ref:**YH11572

RIBBLESDALE PARK, Ascot **Ref:**YH11794

SAXON GATE STABLES, Hungerford **Ref:**YH12468

SAXON HSE STABLES, Hungerford **Ref:**YH12469

SHERWOOD STABLES, Hungerford **Ref:**YH12732

SHERWOOD, O M C, Hungerford **Ref:**YH12733

SHERWOOD, S E H, Hungerford **Ref:**YH12734

SMART, BRYAN, Hungerford **Ref:**YH12921

SOUTH BANK STABLES, Hungerford **Ref:**YH13077

STILLWELL, R L M, Wokingham **Ref:**YH13468

STRONGE, R M, Newbury **Ref:**YH13585

- TIDMARSH STUD, Reading Ref:YH14134
- UPSHIRE FARM STABLES, Lambourn Ref:YH14612
- WEST HAMILTON STABLES, Newbury Ref:YH15147
- WHITCOOMBE HOUSE STABLES, Hungerford Ref:YH15298
- WILLONYX RACING, Reading Ref:YH15493
- WOODLANDS, Hungerford Ref:YH15705

BUCKINGHAMSHIRE

- BARKER, K J, Burnham Ref:YH00944
- BUSH, KAREN, Great Missenden Ref:YH02307
- CATHERINE WRIGHT, Aylesbury Ref:YH02649
- CHEQUERS END EQUESTRIAN CTRE, High Wycombe Ref:YH02812
- CRAWFORD-BROWN, FIONA, Ludgershall Ref:YH03577
- CRIPPIN, I C, Chesham Ref:YH03603
- CULLINAN, J, Aylesbury Ref:YH03704
- DORTON GRANGE STABLES, Aylesbury Ref:YH04208
- GEORGE, K M, Princes Risborough Ref:YH05724
- HARVEY, JUDY, Milton Keynes Ref:YH06515
- ROBBINS, M A, Amersham Ref:YH11936
- ROBESON, P, Newport Pagnell Ref:YH11977
- WATSON, GILLIAN, Great Missenden Ref:YH14986
- WHITAKERS, Princes Risborough Ref:YH15292

CAMBRIDGESHIRE

- FOX END STABLES, Rampton Ref:YH05419
- HOOK HSE, March Ref:YH07035
- KNIGHTS END FARM, March Ref:YH08268
- PINNER, TERRY, Huntingdon Ref:YH11134
- ROSACH STUD, Wisbech Ref:YH12087
- SLY, P M, Peterborough Ref:YH12903
- WITCHAM HSE FARM STUD, Ely Ref:YH15617

CHESHIRE

- BAYLISS, RACHEL, Congleton Ref:YH01097
- BEVIS, RICHARD, Malpas Ref:YH01345
- BILLINGTON, GEOFF, Nantwich Ref:YH01414
- BOLD HEATH EQUESTRIAN, Widnes Ref:YH01602
- CALDWELL, T H, Warrington Ref:YH02439
- CARRUTHERS, RICHARD, Frodsham Ref:YH02601
- COTTON EQUESTRIAN CTRE, Crewe Ref:YH03384
- EQUESTRIAN SKILLS, Crewe Ref:YH04711
- FOLLY FARM STABLES, Tarporley Ref:YH05301
- GREENWAY FARM, Congleton Ref:YH06102
- MATHER, F E, Stockport Ref:YH09259
- MCCAIN, D, Cholmondeley Ref:YH09316
- MULLINEAUX, M, Tarporley Ref:YH09939
- PORTLANDS STUD, Congleton Ref:YH11293
- RACEWOOD, Tarporley Ref:YH11581
- ROBERTS, STUART, Crewe Ref:YH11962
- ROBINSON, P, Stalybridge Ref:YH11992
- SANDY BROW RACING STABLES, Tarporley Ref:YH12424
- SENIOR, A, Macclesfield Ref:YH12634
- WILLIAMSON, LISA, Chester Ref:YH15485
- WYNNE, M G, Tarporley Ref:YH15872

CLEVELAND

- BARR, R E, Stokesley Ref:YH01001
- CANDLER, B, Thornaby Ref:YH02495
- CLOSE, J, Stockton-on-Tees Ref:YH03060
- FOXHOLM STUD, Stockton-on-Tees Ref:YH05437
- GRANT, CHRIS, Stockton-on-Tees Ref:YH06011
- JONES, ALAN, Redcar Ref:YH07877
- REVELEY, C, Saltburn-by-the-Sea Ref:YH11769

CORNWALL

- ASTLEY, D, Penzance Ref:YH00636
- PARKINS, WENDY, Bodmin Ref:YH10766
- PLUESS, KERENSA, Bude Ref:YH11181
- ST LEONARDS EQUESTRIAN CTRE, Launceston Ref:YH13278
- VERYAN RIDING CTRE, Truro Ref:YH14686
- WILLIAMS ENDURANCE, Uskard Ref:YH15442

COUNTY DURHAM

- BROUGH, L E, Durham Ref:YH02087
- CRAGGS, R, Durham Ref:YH03544
- DIXON, KAREN, Barnard Castle Ref:YH04142
- DODS, M, Darlington Ref:YH04160
- E D T, Consett Ref:YH04401
- ELLISON RACEHORSE TRAINER, Durham Ref:YH04629
- JOHNSON, J H, Crook Ref:YH07826
- MOISER, PHILLIP, Stanley Ref:YH09705
- NEW MOORS, Bishop Auckland Ref:YH10114
- SMITH, D, Bishop Auckland Ref:YH12947
- STOREY, W L, Consett Ref:YH13526
- TEASDALE, D, Bishop Auckland Ref:YH13926
- WALKER, L, Barnard Castle Ref:YH14853
- WATSON, F, Durham Ref:YH14985

CUMBRIA

- BAINBRIDGE, J S, Kirkby Stephen Ref:YH00812
- BARNES, M A, Carlisle Ref:YH00978
- BARNES, M A, Penrith Ref:YH00977
- BIRKBECK, H W, Kirkby Stephen Ref:YH01439
- BIRKBY HALL, Grange Over Sands Ref:YH01440
- BOUSFIELD, D, Penrith Ref:YH01693
- BREED EX EQUINE STUD, Penrith Ref:YH01832
- BROWN, I H, Kirkby Stephen Ref:YH02109
- BUCKLEY, E H & J M, Kendal Ref:YH02198
- CUMBRIA SCHOOL OF SADDLERY, Penrith Ref:YH03715
- CUTHBERT, T A K, Carlisle Ref:YH03760
- FISHER, R F, Ulverston Ref:YH05241
- GOULDING, J, Cockermouth Ref:YH05950
- HULLOCK, A, Appleby Ref:YH07283
- KENDALL, R, Kirkby Stephen Ref:YH08060
- KIRK, C, Penrith Ref:YH08231
- LAKELAND EQUESTRIAN, Windermere Ref:YH08354
- MOFFATT, D, Grange-Over-Sands Ref:YH09700
- MURTAGH, F P, Carlisle Ref:YH09971
- OAKDEN, JAMES, Windermere Ref:YH10373
- O'NEILL, J J, Penrith Ref:YH10518
- RICHARDS, N G, Penrith Ref:YH11811
- SAYER, H D, Penrith Ref:YH12474
- SOWERBY, G, Appleby Ref:YH13165
- SOWERBY, W T, Appleby Ref:YH13166
- TODHUNTER, MARTIN, Ulverston Ref:YH14202
- ZALKIND, Penrith Ref:YH15950

DERBYSHIRE

- BARLEYFIELDS, Derby Ref:YH00952
- CALKE ABBEY RACING STABLES, Swadlincote Ref:YH02446
- CHESTERFIELD, Chesterfield Ref:YH02833
- CLINTON, P L, Ashbourne Ref:YH03043
- COWLEY RIDING SCHOOL, Dronfield Ref:YH03526
- DODD, C, Matlock Ref:YH04158
- ELVASTON CASTLE RIDING CTRE, Derby Ref:YH04645
- HILLCLIFF STUD, Belper Ref:YH06838
- HOLME FARM EQUESTRIAN CTRE, Derby Ref:YH06963
- JONES, EMMA-JANE, Chesterfield Ref:YH07897
- MACKIE, W J W, Church Broughton Ref:YH09008
- PELL, DAVID, Ilkeston Ref:YH10910
- POLLARD, V, Ashbourne Ref:YH11206
- RED HSE STABLES, Matlock Ref:YH11698

DEVON

- BARRIBAL, Okehampton Ref:YH01020
- BARWELL, C R, Tiverton Ref:YH01052
- BLEEKMAN, E & C, Cullompton Ref:YH01533
- BRAGG, MIRANDA, Buckfastleigh Ref:YH01775
- BRAKE, C J, Cullompton Ref:YH01780
- COLE, DEBORAH, South Molton Ref:YH03153
- COLE, S N, Tiverton Ref:YH03160
- COTTRELL, L G, Cullompton Ref:YH03387
- DUTFIELD, P N, Seaton Ref:YH04376
- EQUITOPIA, Lynton Ref:YH04831
- FROST, R G, Buckfastleigh Ref:YH05520
- GLEBE INT ENTERPRISE, Exeter Ref:YH05817
- HALWILL ELITE LIVERY SVS, Beaworthy Ref:YH06338
- HILL, TONY, South Molton Ref:YH06835
- HOWE, H S, Tiverton Ref:YH07225
- KILEY-WORTHINGTON, M (DR), Okehampton Ref:YH08133
- MILLMAN, B R, Cullompton Ref:YH09625
- MOFFETT, HEATHER, Totnes Ref:YH09701
- NEWCOMBE, A G, Barnstaple Ref:YH10132
- NEWTON FERRERS, Plymouth Ref:YH10170
- PIPE, K, Cullompton Ref:YH11144
- REEDER, PENNY, Okehampton Ref:YH11724
- STEART HOUSE RACING STABLES, Tiverton Ref:YH13411
- TALAWATER QUARTER HORSES, Yelverton Ref:YH13830
- TUGGYS, Branscombe Ref:YH14448
- WARD, MICHAEL J, Holsworthy Ref:YH14904
- WEST DOWN RACING STABLES, South Molton Ref:YH15140
- WILLIAMS, S D, South Molton Ref:YH15478
- WOOD FARM STUD, Okehampton Ref:YH15656

DORSET

- ALNER, R H, Blandford Ref:YH00332
- BUCKLER, R H, Bridport Ref:YH02196
- EQUESTRIAN & EXAM CTRE, Ferndown Ref:YH04691
- KAYE, GILES, Wimborne Ref:YH08007
- MITCHELL, N R, Dorchester Ref:YH09675
- O Y C, Wareham Ref:YH10369
- POUND COTTAGE RIDING CTRE, Blandford Forum Ref:YH11307
- PROSPECT FARM LIVERY STABLES, Dorchester Ref:YH11436
- THOMSON, N B, Shaftesbury Ref:YH14053
- TIZZARD, C, Sherborne Ref:YH14194
- TURNER, W G M, Sherborne Ref:YH14491
- WEEDON, M J, Weymouth Ref:YH15046

ESSEX

- ALLINSON, JONATHAN, Colchester Ref:YH00316
- CLASSICAL DRESSAGE, Upminster Ref:YH02989
- CLAY HALL, Brentwood Ref:YH02994
- COACH HSE, Epping Ref:YH03102
- COTTON, SARAH, Chelmsford Ref:YH03385
- DANBURY, Chelmsford Ref:YH03860
- HALLINGBURY HALL, Bishop's Stortford Ref:YH06331
- HUTCHESON, TOM, Boxall Ref:YH07333
- LEWIS, ANNETTE, Chigwell Ref:YH08585
- MERRETT, D T, Colchester Ref:YH09479
- ROYSTONS TRAINING YARD, Colchester Ref:YH12203
- RUNNINGWELL STUD, Chelmsford Ref:YH12236
- TALLY-HO RIDING SCHOOL, Grays Ref:YH13844
- TAYLOR, D J W, Southend Ref:YH13899
- WETHERSFIELD RIDING STABLES, Braintree Ref:YH15246

GLOUCESTERSHIRE

- **BABBAGE, N M**, Cheltenham **Ref:**YH00761
- **BRAZINGTON, R G**, Redmarley **Ref:**YH01824
- **BROWN, ALISTAIR**, Cheltenham **Ref:**YH02098
- **DENNY, L**, Moreton-in-Marsh **Ref:**YH04063
- **EVANS, ANNE-MARIE & RICHARD**, Moreton In Marsh **Ref:**YH04916
- **FERNEYHOUGH, R J & OLIVER, A M**, Stonehouse **Ref:**YH05163
- **FOX HILL RACING**, Cheltenham **Ref:**YH05423
- **GEORGE, SARAH**, Dursley **Ref:**YH05725
- **GRASSICK, L P**, Cheltenham **Ref:**YH06020
- **GROVE FARM**, Moreton In Marsh **Ref:**YH06163
- **HICKS, C M**, Cheltenham **Ref:**YH06746
- **HYND, MIKE**, Hucclecote **Ref:**YH07360
- **J A, WILSON**, Cheltenham **Ref:**YH07557
- **JUPP, BARBARA**, Cirencester **Ref:**YH07970
- **KANLET**, Cheltenham **Ref:**YH07995
- **MAYCOCK, ADAM**, Cheltenham **Ref:**YH09293
- **MIFLIN, WILLIAM**, Cirencester **Ref:**YH09563
- **OLIVER, R N**, Newent **Ref:**YH10499
- **O'NEILL, OWEN**, Cheltenham **Ref:**YH10519
- **PHILLIPS, J G**, Cirencester **Ref:**YH11057
- **PHILLIPS, R**, Cheltenham **Ref:**YH11063
- **PRITCHARD, P L J (DR)**, Berkeley **Ref:**YH11420
- **ROE, G**, Stroud **Ref:**YH12050
- **SCUDIMORE, PETER**, Cheltenham **Ref:**YH12573
- **SIMON, (CPT), TOMLINSON C**, Tetbury **Ref:**YH12831
- **SMITH, J S**, Tirley **Ref:**YH12965
- **SMITH, R J**, Cheltenham **Ref:**YH12991
- **SMITH, R J**, Naunton **Ref:**YH12992
- **SPRING BANK STABLES**, Stroud **Ref:**YH13244
- **TAFFS, PHILIPPA**, Cheltenham **Ref:**YH13820
- **TALLAND SCHOOL OF EQUITATION**, Cirencester **Ref:**YH13833
- **TAYLOR, SARAH**, Cheltenham **Ref:**YH13911
- **TOWNSEND, K**, Moreton In Marsh **Ref:**YH14299
- **TUCK, J C**, Didmarton **Ref:**YH14431
- **TUCKER, ANGELA**, Tetbury **Ref:**YH14432
- **TUDOR RACING STABLES**, Newnham **Ref:**YH14442
- **TWISTON-DAVIES, N A**, Cheltenham **Ref:**YH14515
- **WATSON, T R**, Winchcombe **Ref:**YH14993
- **WINTLE, D J**, Cheltenham **Ref:**YH15599

HAMPSHIRE

- **AMBERVALE**, Lymington **Ref:**YH00357
- **BALDINGS**, Andover **Ref:**YH00838
- **BOWER, L J**, Alresford **Ref:**YH01706
- **BRIDGER, J J**, Liphook **Ref:**YH01882
- **CATHERSTON**, Stockbridge **Ref:**YH02650
- **CLEVERLY, TANYA**, Church Crookham **Ref:**YH03024
- **CORBETT, MARK**, Tadley **Ref:**YH03306
- **COTTAGE STABLES**, Andover **Ref:**YH03380
- **CROFTON MANOR EQUESTRIAN CTRE**, Fareham **Ref:**YH03623
- **CUNNINGHAM-BROWN, K**, Stockbridge **Ref:**YH03726
- **ELEDA STABLES**, Ringwood **Ref:**YH04603
- **FIR TREE FARM**, Fordingbridge **Ref:**YH05219
- **FOREST FARM**, Milford On Sea **Ref:**YH05335
- **FROXFIELD TRAINING CTRE**, Alton **Ref:**YH05524
- **GLENEAGLES**, Southampton **Ref:**YH05832
- **GREEN, LUCINDA**, Andover **Ref:**YH06069
- **HARROWAY HSE RIDING SCHOOL**, Andover **Ref:**YH06495
- **HILL FARM STABLES**, Stockbridge **Ref:**YH06816
- **HOLMES, J W**, Alresford **Ref:**YH06974
- **HOPLANDS EQUESTRIAN**, Stockbridge **Ref:**YH07058
- **HORSEPOWER**, Alton **Ref:**YH07163
- **IEDEMA, BARRY**, Romsey **Ref:**YH07388
- **INHURST FARM STABLES**, Basingstoke **Ref:**YH07456
- **KEELEY, PAULA**, Liss **Ref:**YH08027
- **LONDON, MOIRA**, Lymington **Ref:**YH08792
- **MADGWICK, M J**, Denmead **Ref:**YH09023
- **MAYHEW, BOB**, Petersfield **Ref:**YH09298
- **MORSTEAD STABLES**, Winchester **Ref:**YH09844
- **MOYGLARE LIVERY**, Tadley **Ref:**YH09910
- **RAWLINS FARM**, Tadley **Ref:**YH11667
- **RITCHENS, P C**, Stockbridge **Ref:**YH11914
- **SEAVILL, C A S**, Petersfield **Ref:**YH12595
- **SOUTHFIELD EQUESTRIAN CTRE**, Whitchurch **Ref:**YH13149
- **TUNWORTH DOWN STABLES**, Basingstoke **Ref:**YH14463
- **TURNER, DAVID**, Ringwood **Ref:**YH14478
- **WELLINGTON RIDING**, Hook **Ref:**YH15075
- **WHITSBURY MANOR**, Fordingbridge **Ref:**YH15370

HEREFORDSHIRE

- **ARAMSTONE STABLES**, Hereford **Ref:**YH00494
- **ARROW TRAINING**, Leominster **Ref:**YH00562
- **ARROW VAULTING GRP**, Leominster **Ref:**YH00563
- **BRYAN, W & K**, Hereford **Ref:**YH02167
- **CARO, D J**, Ledbury **Ref:**YH02566
- **COUNTY COMPETITION STUD**, Bromyard **Ref:**YH03486
- **CULSHAW, D**, Bromyard **Ref:**YH03708
- **DOYLE, MARK**, Leominster **Ref:**YH04249
- **DUMBELL, LUCY**, Ross On Wye **Ref:**YH04327
- **EACOCK, KAREN**, Leominster **Ref:**YH04435
- **HASKETT, ISOBEL**, Ross-on-Wye **Ref:**YH06522
- **HOOLEY, C & A**, Hereford **Ref:**YH07041
- **HOPE END RACING**, Ledbury **Ref:**YH07050
- **JORDAN, FRANK T J**, Leominster **Ref:**YH07938
- **MONNINGTON**, Hereford **Ref:**YH09728
- **NEWCOMB, SALLY**, Hereford **Ref:**YH10130
- **PRICE, C J**, Leominster **Ref:**YH11376
- **PRICE, RICHARD**, Hereford **Ref:**YH11387
- **SHEEPCOTE EQUESTRIAN**, Hereford **Ref:**YH12695
- **SHEPPARD, M I**, Ledbury **Ref:**YH12715
- **STILWELL, ELAINE**, Dilwyn **Ref:**YH13469
- **STONE HSE STABLE**, Hereford **Ref:**YH13510
- **SUE ADAMS RIDING SCHOOL**, Leominster **Ref:**YH13622

HERTFORDSHIRE

- **BARTON, JOHN**, Royston **Ref:**YH01048
- **COPELAND, JIM**, New Barnet **Ref:**YH03294
- **COPELAND, STUART**, New Barnet **Ref:**YH03295
- **DRESSAGE TRAINING CTRE**, Radlett **Ref:**YH04268
- **FOX FIELD FARM RACING STABLES**, Royston **Ref:**YH05421
- **HARRIS, P W**, Berkhamsted **Ref:**YH06479
- **HARRIS, P W**, Tring **Ref:**YH06478
- **HARVEY, A**, Bishop's Stortford **Ref:**YH06513
- **IVORY, K T**, Radlett **Ref:**YH07538
- **JACKSON, CHRIS**, New Barnet **Ref:**YH07645
- **JENKINS, J**, Royston **Ref:**YH07733
- **LAYTON, T**, Ware **Ref:**YH08484
- **MEES, RON**, Hatfield **Ref:**YH09443
- **PEVSNER, DANIEL**, Hitchin **Ref:**YH11036
- **STANLEY, ANDREA**, Baldock **Ref:**YH13373
- **TRAINING & LIVERY CTRE**, Welwyn **Ref:**YH14342

ISLE OF MAN

- **G G H EQUITATION CTRE**, Marown **Ref:**YH05578

ISLE OF WIGHT

- **GREAT PAN FARM STABLES**, Newport **Ref:**YH06041

JERSEY

- **ARTHUR, STEPHEN**, St Mary **Ref:**YH00570
- **BROCQ, JOAN LE**, St Peter **Ref:**YH02017
- **GREEN BANK RACING STABLES**, St Peter **Ref:**YH06050
- **MALEARD, A**, St Owen **Ref:**YH09048
- **VIBERT, ALYSON**, St Ouen **Ref:**YH14704

KENT

- **BALL, CHRISTINE**, Orpington **Ref:**YH00850
- **BEST, J R**, Maidstone **Ref:**YH01326
- **BRADBOURNE**, Sevenoaks **Ref:**YH01743
- **BRAESIDE E.C**, Dover **Ref:**YH01773
- **CANTERBURY CARRIAGES**, Dover **Ref:**YH02507
- **CHAFFORD FARM**, Tunbridge Wells **Ref:**YH02708
- **CHAVIC PK STABLES**, Westerham **Ref:**YH02793
- **CHERRETT, TOM B**, Sittingbourne **Ref:**YH02813
- **CLARK, RON & JULIE**, Tunbridge Wells **Ref:**YH02967
- **CLAYTON, PENNIE**, Dartford **Ref:**YH03006
- **DANIEL O'BRIEN RACING**, Tonbridge **Ref:**YH03870
- **ELLISON COURT**, Ashford **Ref:**YH04628
- **EQUINE SPORT THERAPY**, Edenbridge **Ref:**YH04800
- **EQUINES LIVERIES**, Maidstone **Ref:**YH04809
- **FOREST VIEW**, Sidcup **Ref:**YH05353
- **FRIDAY FIELD STABLES**, Sittingbourne **Ref:**YH05502
- **HOWES, E A**, Tenterden **Ref:**YH07230
- **KING, D J**, Canterbury **Ref:**YH08177
- **MCMORRIS, KATE**, Tonbridge **Ref:**YH09393
- **NEW BARN STUD**, Eynsford **Ref:**YH10091
- **PANNETT**, Sevenoaks **Ref:**YH10699
- **PHILLIPS, A K**, Ashford **Ref:**YH11051
- **REYNOLDS, SIMON**, Sittingbourne **Ref:**YH11780
- **SANDHILL FARM STABLES**, Tunbridge Wells **Ref:**YH12411
- **SOUTHFIELD STABLES**, Maidstone **Ref:**YH13151
- **TREWINT**, Cranbrook **Ref:**YH14388
- **TURNER, JACKY**, Sidcup **Ref:**YH14484
- **TURNER, MIKE**, Sidcup **Ref:**YH14486
- **WHITMORE, S**, Edenbridge **Ref:**YH15367
- **WIGGINS, CELIA**, Faversham **Ref:**YH15397

LANCASHIRE

- **ABRAM HALL RIDING CTRE**, Wigan **Ref:**YH00134
- **ALDRED, J D**, Preston **Ref:**YH00261
- **ALSTON, ERIC**, Preston **Ref:**YH00340
- **ARKENFIELD EQUESTRIAN CTRE**, Chorley **Ref:**YH00530
- **ASOKA**, Worsley **Ref:**YH00625
- **ATHERTON, JENNY**, Bickerstaffe **Ref:**YH00644
- **BOUNDARY FARM CARRIAGES**, Wigan **Ref:**YH01677
- **BROOKFIELDS STABLES**, Westhead **Ref:**YH02054
- **DOUGLAS FARM RIDING SCHOOL**, Wigan **Ref:**YH04211
- **HARRIS, R M**, Adlington **Ref:**YH06481
- **KILROE, R J**, Preston **Ref:**YH08154
- **LUCAS, R & M**, Chorley **Ref:**YH08884
- **MARSHALL, MICHELLE**, Heywood **Ref:**YH09200
- **MCBANE, SUSAN**, Longridge **Ref:**YH09313
- **MOSS SIDE RACING STABLES**, Lancaster **Ref:**YH09856
- **PANAMA SPORT HORSES**, Clitheroe **Ref:**YH10695
- **REES, GERALDINE**, Preston **Ref:**YH11730
- **ROBSCOTT EQUITATION**, Carnforth **Ref:**YH12010
- **VALLEY PADDOCKS RACING**, Clitheroe **Ref:**YH14656
- **WAKEFIELD, HILARY**, Lancaster **Ref:**YH14833

- WHITEGATE FARM, Bacup Ref:YH15338
- WILSON, J H, Preston Ref:YH15539

LEICESTERSHIRE

- ACKERMANN, D H W, Oakham Ref:YH00143
- ALLEN, DONNA, Leicester Ref:YH00295
- CREATON, N A, Coalville Ref:YH03583
- CZERPAK, J D, Market Harborough Ref:YH03767
- EASTWELL HALL STABLES, Melton Mowbray Ref:YH04517
- FELGATE, P S, Melton Mowbray Ref:YH05128
- HALL FARM STABLES, Melton Mowbray Ref:YH06305
- HOLT, J R, Peckleton Ref:YH06989
- KERRY, JOHN, Melton Mowbray Ref:YH08102
- LOMAX, CHRISTIE, Market Harborough Ref:YH08780
- MACAULEY, N J, Melton Mowbray Ref:YH08983
- MACLEAN, TINA, Scraptoft Ref:YH09010
- MORGAN, K A, Melton Mowbray Ref:YH09808
- PARSONAGE, GARY, Melton Mowbray Ref:YH10798
- PICKERING, J A, Hinckley Ref:YH11083
- SMITH, D MURRAY, Market Harborough Ref:YH12949
- SPRING, JEREMY, Cosby Ref:YH13248
- TILL, J A, Glenfield Ref:YH14148
- WALKER, RICHARD, Melton Mowbray Ref:YH14856
- WALLACE, JANE, Market Harborough Ref:YH14864
- WHARTON TRAINING STABLES, Melton Mowbray Ref:YH15264
- WHARTON, J R H, Melton Mowbray Ref:YH15265
- WILSON, MELANIE, Seagrave Ref:YH15542
- WITHAM VILLA RIDING CTRE, Leicester Ref:YH15620

LINCOLNSHIRE

- BELTON, C, Louth Ref:YH01255
- CLAPHAM, DIANA, Grantham Ref:YH02945
- EQUINE MNGMT & TRAINING, Stamford Ref:YH04788
- EVENTERS INT, Grantham Ref:YH04940
- GOLLINGS, S, Louth Ref:YH05898
- HENSON, LUCY, Lincoln Ref:YH06689
- JAMES GIVEN RACING, Gainsborough Ref:YH07668
- L DUNNING SHOW JUMPING, Lincoln Ref:YH08317
- LAMYMAN, S, Louth Ref:YH08378
- LANNI, JOHN, Grantham Ref:YH08419
- LIMES FARM, Grantham Ref:YH08634
- LIMESTONE STUD, Gainsborough Ref:YH08637
- MONTEITH, HELEN, Grantham Ref:YH09731
- MONTEITH, PETER, Grantham Ref:YH09732
- MOUNT HOUSE STABLES, Gainsborough Ref:YH09888
- NORTHERN BLOODSTOCK, Louth Ref:YH10298
- OAKWOOD RIDING SERVICES, Spalding Ref:YH10410
- POPPYFIELDS, Lincoln Ref:YH11275
- SMITH, C, Wellingore Ref:YH12943
- SPICER, R C, Spalding Ref:YH13202
- SPRINGFIELD FARM, Market Rasen Ref:YH13253
- WALTON, HELEN L, Grantham Ref:YH14891
- WARD, V C, Grantham Ref:YH14911
- WOODLANDS STABLES, Market Rasen Ref:YH15711

LINCOLNSHIRE (NORTH EAST)

- R G EQUESTRIAN, Grimsby Ref:YH11536
- STRAWSON, VIRGINIA, Grimsby Ref:YH13569

LONDON (GREATER)

- BELMONT RACING STABLES, Mill Hill Ref:YH01248
- BELMONT RIDING CTRE, London Ref:YH01249
- BUNN, CLAUDIA, Pershore Ref:YH02225
- CARRINGTON, WALTER, London Ref:YH02590
- DOCKLANDS CARRIAGE DRIVING, East Ham Ref:YH04156
- HORSE HOUSE, Northwood Ref:YH07123
- ISSEA - GB, London Ref:YH07527
- NATURAL PARTNERSHIP, London Ref:YH10053
- WOOD HALL STUD, Shenley Ref:YH15658

MANCHESTER (GREATER)

- HADFIELD, G, Manchester Ref:YH06264

MERSEYSIDE

- WAY, LAURA, Liverpool Ref:YH15013

MIDLANDS (WEST)

- BEARLEY CROSS STABLES, Solihull Ref:YH01121
- DOMINION RACING STABLES, Alvechurch Ref:YH04172
- FOXHILLS, Walsall Ref:YH05435
- POOLE, JOHN, Alvechurch Ref:YH11265
- ROBINS NEST STABLES, Wolverhampton Ref:YH11983
- WOLVERHAMPTON RACECOURSE, Wolverhampton Ref:YH15650

NORFOLK

- CROFT FARM RIDING CTRE, Great Yarmouth Ref:YH03615
- GREENACRES RIDING SCHOOL, King's Lynn Ref:YH06079
- HEATHER ARABIAN RACING STUD, Norwich Ref:YH06625
- HIGH HSE EVENTING CTRE, King's Lynn Ref:YH06763
- JOHN PARKER, Diss Ref:YH07804
- LEWIS, J E, Norwich Ref:YH08592
- MCCONNOCHIE, J, Norwich Ref:YH09329
- MCMULLEN, R P, King's Lynn Ref:YH09394
- NORTH FARM RACING STABLES, Norwich Ref:YH10261
- PAWLEY, ZARA, Kings Lynn Ref:YH10840
- PRODDROMOW, GEORGE, East Harling Ref:YH11427
- RUNCTON HALL, King's Lynn Ref:YH12233
- THOMPSON, EMILY, King's Lynn Ref:YH14035
- YARHAM, A, Great Yarmouth Ref:YH15885

NORTHAMPTONSHIRE

- ASHTON STABLES, Northampton Ref:YH00614
- BAILEY, K C, Daventry Ref:YH00802
- BRAMPTON STABLES, Northampton Ref:YH01794
- CROSS COUNTRY HORSE TRANSPORT, Northampton Ref:YH03643
- JONES, J D, Kettering Ref:YH07907
- KENWARD, ALLISON, Towcester Ref:YH08090
- MOBLEY, HELEN, Brackley Ref:YH09694
- ROUNDGREY, Towcester Ref:YH12141
- SHUCKBURGH HSE RIDING CTRE, Naseby Ref:YH12772
- SMYTH-OSBOURNE, J, Towcester Ref:YH13016
- STOCKDALE, TIM, Roade Ref:YH13490
- SULBY HALL, Northampton Ref:YH13628
- TAYLOR, NIGEL & ANN, Daventry Ref:YH13907
- UPSON, J R, Towcester Ref:YH14614
- WESLEY, SOPHIE, Towcester Ref:YH15117
- WHITMORE, SUE, Wellingborough Ref:YH15368

NORTHUMBERLAND

- CHARLTON, J I A, Stocksfield Ref:YH02767
- DODDS, J P, Alnwick Ref:YH04159
- FLEMING, BARBARA SLANE, Alnwick Ref:YH05270
- HALDANE, J S, Mindrum Ref:YH06289
- HARGREAVE EQUINE SVS, Chathill Ref:YH06425
- JOICEY, (LADY), Cornhill-on-Tweed Ref:YH07849
- LEADBETTER, S J, Berwick-upon-Tweed Ref:YH08498
- PALLINSBURN STABLES, Cornhill-on-Tweed Ref:YH10690
- PITTENDRIGH, P I, Wylam Ref:YH11154
- THOMPSON, V, Alnwick Ref:YH14045
- WOOPERTON, Alnwick Ref:YH15770

NOTTINGHAMSHIRE

- ARKENFIELD STABLES, Nottingham Ref:YH00531
- AVERHAM PK, Newark Ref:YH00681
- BOWRING, S R, Mansfield Ref:YH01724
- BRADWELL, JANE, Cotgrave Ref:YH01766
- BRENNAN, OWEN, Worksop Ref:YH01844
- CLGE FARM, Newark Ref:YH03026
- COUTTS, JANET, Nottingham Ref:YH03517
- CTRE - LINES, Newark Ref:YH03694
- FIRBECK, Worksop Ref:YH05222
- HOLISTIC HORSECARE, Northampton Ref:YH06934
- KIRKFIELD STABLES, Lower Blidworth Ref:YH08235
- LANEHAM LIVERY STABLE, Retford Ref:YH08392
- MARVIN, R F, Newark Ref:YH09233
- PELL, NATALIE, Ruddington Ref:YH10912
- PINEWOOD STABLES, Worksop Ref:YH11127
- POLGLASE, MARK, Southwell Ref:YH11200
- PYRAH, MALCOLM, Nottingham Ref:YH11471
- ROBINSON, LISA, Nottingham Ref:YH11991
- ROWLAND, M E, Lower Blidworth Ref:YH12168
- SAVILLE, LOUISE, Newark Ref:YH12456
- TRAINING BARN 7, Newark Ref:YH14343
- VICTORIAN CARRIAGES, Newark Ref:YH14710
- WELLOW PK, Newark Ref:YH15077
- WOODWARD, GARRY, Worksop Ref:YH15757

OXFORDSHIRE

- ANTWICK STUD, Wantage Ref:YH00466
- ARLINGTON POLO, Kidlington Ref:YH00533
- ASKER HORSESPORTS, Henley-on-Thames Ref:YH00620
- BOSLEY, M R, Wantage Ref:YH01655
- BOWLBY EQUINE, Wantage Ref:YH01711
- BRADSTOCK, MARK, Wantage Ref:YH01764
- CANDY, H, Wantage Ref:YH02497
- CASE, BENJAMIN, Banbury Ref:YH02613
- CHURN STABLES, Didcot Ref:YH02916
- COACH HSE STABLES, Wantage Ref:YH03105
- COMPTON BEAUCHAMP ESTS, Didcot Ref:YH03218
- DREWE, C J, Didcot Ref:YH04270
- EAST MANTON STABLES, Wantage Ref:YH04480
- EDGECOTE HSE STABLES, Banbury Ref:YH04555
- FAIRSPEAR EQUESTRIAN CTRE, Witney Ref:YH05028
- FAURIE, E, Chipping Norton Ref:YH05105
- FLETCHER, GRAHAM, Farringdon Ref:YH05277
- FRENCH DAVIS, D, Wantage Ref:YH05488
- GANDOLFO, D R, Wantage Ref:YH05639
- GODINGTON STUD, Bicester Ref:YH05867
- HALL PLACE STABLES, Wantage Ref:YH06308
- HIATT, P W, Banbury Ref:YH06739
- IRVING, HEATHER, Banbury Ref:YH07510
- JARVIS, A P, Didcot Ref:YH07705
- JOHN WEBBER & PARTNERS, Banbury Ref:YH07816
- JOHNSON-HOUGHTON, R F, Didcot Ref:YH07842
- KETTLE, CAROLINE, Blewbury Ref:YH08108

KNIGHT, HENRIETTA, Wantage **Ref:**YH08261
LAW, GRAHAM, Chipping Norton **Ref:**YH08469
LUCKETT, GEOFF, Banbury **Ref:**YH08887
MANOR FARM RACING STABLES, Wantage **Ref:**YH09103
MARK USHER RACING, Wantage **Ref:**YH09156
MCCOURT RACING, Wantage **Ref:**YH09333
MORLOCK, C, Wantage **Ref:**YH09822
OLD MANOR STABLES, Wantage **Ref:**YH10463
P F I COLE, Wantage **Ref:**YH10638
STEPHANIE MEADOWS, Chipping Norton **Ref:**YH13422
TATLOW, D J, Chipping Norton **Ref:**YH13878
TEDMAN HARNESS, Wheatley **Ref:**YH13932
THINK EQUUS, Kidlington **Ref:**YH13995
THORNER, GRAHAM, Wantage **Ref:**YH14063
TURVILLE VALLEY, Henley-on-Thames **Ref:**YH14499
WHITESHOOT STABLES, Blewbury **Ref:**YH15357
WILKINSON, M J, Banbury **Ref:**YH15422

RUTLAND

BARROW STABLES, Oakham **Ref:**YH01030
COMPETITION HORSES, Oakham **Ref:**YH03217
LAMPARD, DI, Oakham **Ref:**YH08375
MANTON LODGE STABLES, Rutland **Ref:**YH09127
PURBRICK, LIZZIE, Oakham **Ref:**YH11463
SEDERHOLM, LARS, Oakham **Ref:**YH12601

SHROPSHIRE

BARRATT, L J, Oswestry **Ref:**YH01009
BRISBOURNE, MARK, Shrewsbury **Ref:**YH01918
BROAD ACRE, Bridgnorth **Ref:**YH01987
BROOKSHAW, S A, Shrewsbury **Ref:**YH02068
CHARTERS, SUE, Ludlow **Ref:**YH02776
DALTON, HEATHER, Shifnal **Ref:**YH03846
DOWNTON HALL STABLES, Ludlow **Ref:**YH04242
JENKS, WILLIAM P, Bridgnorth **Ref:**YH07742
MARTIN, S, Shrewsbury **Ref:**YH09226
OSWESTRY EQUEST CTRE, Oswestry **Ref:**YH10576
OUGHTON, A, Bucknell **Ref:**YH10583
PREECE, W G, Telford **Ref:**YH11342
W BRYAN HORSE SERVICES, Shrewsbury **Ref:**YH14753
WALL, T R, Church Stretton **Ref:**YH14861

SOMERSET

BARFORD PK RACING STABLES, Bridgwater **Ref:**YH00932
BLUE MOUNTAIN FARM, Wells **Ref:**YH01567
BOSSINGTON DRESSAGE STABLES, Minehead **Ref:**YH01656
COOK, ANGELA, Wiveliscombe **Ref:**YH03255
EQUISENSE, Bruton **Ref:**YH04818
FARRELL, P, Chard **Ref:**YH05086
FOALE, D, Street **Ref:**YH05296
GADD, CELIA, Brent Knoll **Ref:**YH05604
GLEBE STABLES, Minehead **Ref:**YH05819
HAM, G A, Axbridge **Ref:**YH06342
HAWKE, N, Woolminstone **Ref:**YH06544
HODGES, R J, Somerton **Ref:**YH06909
HOLEMOOR HOUSE STABLES, Chard **Ref:**YH06931
KNIGHT, GEORGE, Taunton **Ref:**YH08260
P F & B NICHOLLS RACING, Shepton Mallet **Ref:**YH10637
PIPE, M C, Wellington **Ref:**YH11145
POPHAM, C L, Taunton **Ref:**YH11267
PRIMMORE FARM HORSES, Bridgwater **Ref:**YH11396
RODFORD, P, Martock **Ref:**YH12045
RYALL, B J M, Yeovil **Ref:**YH12283
SANDHILL RACING STABLES, Minehead **Ref:**YH12412
SMALL, ROSALIND, South Petherton **Ref:**YH12909
STICKLEBALL HILL FARM, Glastonbury **Ref:**YH13464
SUTTON OAKS, Bridgwater **Ref:**YH13675
WINDMILL HILL EQUESTRIAN CTRE, Ilminster **Ref:**YH15566

SOMERSET (NORTH)

BLIXEN-FINECKE, H (BARON), Winscombe **Ref:**YH01542
GUBB, TONY, Nailsea **Ref:**YH06179
RACECOURSE FARM, Portbury **Ref:**YH11575
SMART, JAYNE, Banwell **Ref:**YH12922

STAFFORDSHIRE

ANFIELD HSE RACING STABLES, Uttoxeter **Ref:**YH00406
BALLANTYNE, CLAIRE, Stafford **Ref:**YH00853
BARNETT, G W, Stoke-on-Trent **Ref:**YH00983
BAXTER, S E, Lichfield **Ref:**YH01088
BROWN, CAROLINE, Burton-on-Trent **Ref:**YH02104
CLAY, W, Stoke-on-Trent **Ref:**YH02995
DALTON, P T, Burton-on-Trent **Ref:**YH03848
DAVISON, RICHARD, Uttoxeter **Ref:**YH03959
DUNSTON HEATH, Stafford **Ref:**YH04359
FORBES, A L, Uttoxeter **Ref:**YH05319
GLAZZARD, G, Stafford **Ref:**YH05813
HAZEL SLADE STABLES, Hednesford **Ref:**YH06600
HOLLINSHEAD, R, Rugeley **Ref:**YH06948
INGESTRE STABLES, Stafford **Ref:**YH07445
LEAVY, B D, Stoke-on-Trent **Ref:**YH08509
LEES, T D, Pelsall **Ref:**YH08532
MORGAN, B C, Burton-on-Trent **Ref:**YH09800
OFFLEY BROOK LIVERY STABLES, Eccleshall **Ref:**YH10436
PLANT, JANET, Woodseaves **Ref:**YH11161
ROUNDMEADOWS RACING STABLES, Stoke-on-Trent **Ref:**YH12144
SCROPTON, Burton-on-Trent **Ref:**YH12569
STREETER, A, Leek **Ref:**YH13573
WOODSIDE RACING STABLES, Tamworth **Ref:**YH15744

SUFFOLK

AKBARY, H, Newmarket **Ref:**YH00230
ALLEN, C N, Newmarket **Ref:**YH00293
BANKS, J E, Newmarket **Ref:**YH00900
BELL, M L, Newmarket **Ref:**YH01227
BEVERLEY HSE STABLES, Newmarket **Ref:**YH01341
BOB JONES, Newmarket **Ref:**YH01587
BOWEN, JOHN, Mendlesham **Ref:**YH01701
BRAVERY, G C, Newmarket **Ref:**YH01818
BRITTAIN, C E, Newmarket **Ref:**YH01981
BROWN, M A, Newmarket **Ref:**YH02122
CALDER PARK STABLES, Newmarket **Ref:**YH02431
CALLAGHAN, N A, Newmarket **Ref:**YH02447
CANTILLON, DON, Newmarket **Ref:**YH02514
CARRIAGEWAY STABLES, Newmarket **Ref:**YH02584
CECIL, H R A, Newmarket **Ref:**YH02671
CECIL, JULIE, Newmarket **Ref:**YH02672
CLAREHAVEN STABLES, Newmarket **Ref:**YH02950
COLLINGRIDGE, H J, Newmarket **Ref:**YH03184
COSGROVE, D J S, Newmarket **Ref:**YH03351
COWELL, ROBERT, Newmarket **Ref:**YH03524
CRAWLEY, E & R, Newmarket **Ref:**YH03579
CUMANI, L, Newmarket **Ref:**YH03710
CUMANI, L M, Newmarket **Ref:**YH03711
CURLEY, B J, Newmarket **Ref:**YH03730
CURLEY, B J, Newmarket **Ref:**YH03729
D'ARCY, PAUL, Newmarket **Ref:**YH03883
DUFFIELD, GILLIAN, Newmarket **Ref:**YH04315
DWYER, C A, Newmarket **Ref:**YH04381
EASAWAY, Newmarket **Ref:**YH04459
EUSTACE, J M P, Newmarket **Ref:**YH04911
EVE LODGE STABLES, Newmarket **Ref:**YH04934
FANSHAWE, J R, Newmarket **Ref:**YH05045
GAINSBOROUGH STABLES, Newmarket **Ref:**YH05606
GILBERT, J, Bury St Edmunds **Ref:**YH05759
GILLIGAN, P L, Newmarket **Ref:**YH05785
GODOLPHIN MNGMT, Newmarket **Ref:**YH05869
GRAHAM LODGE STABLES, Newmarket **Ref:**YH05965
GRAHAM, N, Newmarket **Ref:**YH05972
GREEN RIDGE STABLES, Newmarket **Ref:**YH06059
GROVE FARM DRIVING & LIVERY, Mildenhall **Ref:**YH06166
GUEST, R, Newmarket **Ref:**YH06183
HAAG, R, Stowmarket **Ref:**YH06248
HACKNESS VILLA STABLES, Newmarket **Ref:**YH06256
HAGGAS, W, Newmarket **Ref:**YH06276
HAINE, D, Newmarket **Ref:**YH06284
HAMILTON STABLES, Newmarket **Ref:**YH06350
HANBURY, B, Newmarket **Ref:**YH06374
HERRINGSWELL BLOODSTOCK CTRE, Bury St Edmunds **Ref:**YH06717
HINTLESHAM RACING, Ipswich **Ref:**YH06876
HOEG-MUDD, CLEA, Woodbridge **Ref:**YH06917
HOLDEN, MAUREEN, Bungay **Ref:**YH06923
HOWLING, PAUL, Newmarket **Ref:**YH07243
HUBBARD, G A, Woodbridge **Ref:**YH07252
INDUNA STABLES, Newmarket **Ref:**YH07439
J ALLEN, Newmarket **Ref:**YH07558
J N PEARCE RACING TRAINERS, Newmarket **Ref:**YH07603
JAMES NICHOL, Newmarket **Ref:**YH07674
JARVIS, M A, Newmarket **Ref:**YH07706
JARVIS, W, Newmarket **Ref:**YH07708
JEREMY NOSEDA, Newmarket **Ref:**YH07753
JOHN SNOWDON HARNESS MAKER, Woodbridge **Ref:**YH07813
JONES, R W, Newmarket **Ref:**YH07927
JULIA FIELDEN RACING, Newmarket **Ref:**YH07962
KELLEWAY, GAY, Newmarket **Ref:**YH08042
LINDEN LODGE STABLES, Newmarket **Ref:**YH08645
LITTMODEN, N P, Newmarket **Ref:**YH08711
LONGSTONES, Newmarket **Ref:**YH08818
MCHALE, DENISE, Newmarket **Ref:**YH09370
MCMATH, B J, Newmarket **Ref:**YH09392
MOSS, JOHN, Woodbridge **Ref:**YH09859
MUSSON, W J, Newmarket **Ref:**YH09976
NICHOL, J, Newmarket **Ref:**YH10180
O'GORMAN, W, Newmarket **Ref:**YH10440
OLD TWELVE STABLES, Newmarket **Ref:**YH10480
O'NEILL, E, Newmarket **Ref:**YH10515
ORWELL ARENA, Ipswich **Ref:**YH10556
PAYNE, J W, Newmarket **Ref:**YH10849
PHILIP MCENTEE RACING, Newmarket **Ref:**YH11044
PRESCOTT, MARK (SIR), Newmarket **Ref:**YH11358
RED HSE STABLES, Newmarket **Ref:**YH11699
RINGER, D S, Newmarket **Ref:**YH11901
RYAN, M J, Newmarket **Ref:**YH12285
SAFFRON HOUSE STABLES, Newmarket **Ref:**YH12380
SEAN WOODS RACING, Newmarket **Ref:**YH12592
SHADOWFAX STABLE, Newmarket **Ref:**YH12655
SHIPPY'S JOCKEY AGENCY, Newmarket **Ref:**YH12750
STANLEY HOUSE STABLES, Newmarket **Ref:**YH13369
STOCKBRIDGE HOUSE STABLES, Newmarket **Ref:**YH13487

STOKE BY CLARE EQUESTRIAN CTRE, Sudbury **Ref:**YH13501
STOUTE, MICHAEL (SIR), Newmarket **Ref:**YH13534
STUBBS, LINDA, Newmarket **Ref:**YH13603
TOLLER, J A R, Newmarket **Ref:**YH14210
TOMPKINS, M H, Newmarket **Ref:**YH14223
UGGLESHALL, Beccles **Ref:**YH14541
VALLEY FARM, Woodbridge **Ref:**YH14651
WADHAM, Newmarket **Ref:**YH14816
WALROND, SALLIE, Bury St Edmunds **Ref:**YH14871
WIGHAM, M, Newmarket **Ref:**YH15400
WILLIAMS, S C, Newmarket **Ref:**YH15477
WOODLANDS, Bury St Edmunds **Ref:**YH15707
WRAGG, G, Newmarket **Ref:**YH15808

SURREY

AKEHURST, JOHN, Epsom **Ref:**YH00232
ASCOT PARK, Woking **Ref:**YH00583
BOLTON, M J, Oxted **Ref:**YH01613
BOULTON, ANDREA, Whyteleafe **Ref:**YH01675
CASEY, W T, Dorking **Ref:**YH02616
CEDAR POINT STABLES, Epsom **Ref:**YH02674
CHARTWELL STABLES, Epsom **Ref:**YH02777
CLEAR HEIGHT STABLES, Epsom **Ref:**YH03009
CRANLEIGH SCHOOL OF RIDING, Cranleigh **Ref:**YH03565
CROFTS, ANDY, Albury **Ref:**YH03625
CROWDER, CHARLOTTE, Warlingham **Ref:**YH03676
DOW, S, Epsom **Ref:**YH04220
DUNMORE-FRANCIS, VALERIE, Old Coulsdon **Ref:**YH04348
DURDANS STABLES, Epsom **Ref:**YH04368
FORGEHILL STUD, South Godstone **Ref:**YH05367
GAY KALLIWAY RACING, Lingfield **Ref:**YH05680
HAYNES, MICHAEL J, Epsom **Ref:**YH06590
HILDEN, D, Croydon **Ref:**YH06807
HORSES GALORE, Dunsfold **Ref:**YH07168
INGRAM, ROGER, Epsom **Ref:**YH07455
JONES, T M, Guildford **Ref:**YH07934
LEWIS, G, Epsom **Ref:**YH08591
LONG, J E, Caterham **Ref:**YH08803
LORETTA LODGE RACING STABLE, Epsom **Ref:**YH08831
MCCARTHY, TIM, Godstone **Ref:**YH09322
MCGREGOR RACING, Epsom **Ref:**YH09366
MITCHELL, P, Epsom **Ref:**YH09676
MORRIS, NICKY, Stanwell **Ref:**YH09834
PEARCE, B A, Lingfield **Ref:**YH10870
POWELL, BRYNLEY, Farnham **Ref:**YH11315
POWELL, T E, Reigate **Ref:**YH11322
ROBERTS, D A, Redhill **Ref:**YH11947
ROBINSON, DEIRDRE, Lingfield **Ref:**YH11986
SANDERS, BROOKE, Epsom **Ref:**YH12404
SOUTH HATCH STABLES, Epsom **Ref:**YH13095
T.T.T, Guildford **Ref:**YH13769
THUNDRY COMPETITION HORSES, Godalming **Ref:**YH14117
TOWNSLEY, P LAXTON, Godalming **Ref:**YH14300
UPLANDS STUD, Godalming **Ref:**YH14601
VICTORIA FARM, Woking **Ref:**YH14708
WENDOVER STABLES, Epsom **Ref:**YH15106
WINKWORTH, P, Chiddingfold **Ref:**YH15587
WOODSTOCK SOUTH STABLES, Chessington **Ref:**YH15751

SUSSEX (EAST)

BROWN BREAD HORSE RESCUE CTRE, Battle **Ref:**YH02092
BUTLER, P, Lewes **Ref:**YH02326
CARR, R R, Robertsbridge **Ref:**YH02572
ENRIGHT, G P, Lewes **Ref:**YH04680
FFITCH-HEYES, J, Lewes **Ref:**YH05175
FLOWER, M, Jevington **Ref:**YH05289
GREEN, CAROL & STOKES, MARIE, Hastings **Ref:**YH06061
GRISSELL, D M, Robertsbridge **Ref:**YH06146
INGLESIDE RACING STABLES, Brighton **Ref:**YH07451
LITTLE MEADOWS, Hailsham **Ref:**YH08694
MCGOVERN, T P, Lewes **Ref:**YH09359
MERRYWEATHERS, Hailsham **Ref:**YH09490
NEWTON-SMITH, A M, Polegate **Ref:**YH10175
PIPER, JUDI, Hailsham **Ref:**YH11146
POULTON, J C, Lewes **Ref:**YH11304
POULTON, J R, Lewes **Ref:**YH11305
ROBERTS, M J, Hailsham **Ref:**YH11957
SMART, JOHN, Uckfield **Ref:**YH12923
WEBSTER, J, Uckfield **Ref:**YH15038
WINDMILL LODGE STABLES, Lewes **Ref:**YH15567

SUSSEX (WEST)

ARNOLD, T J, Pulborough **Ref:**YH00560
B M F, Petworth **Ref:**YH00739
B M M LEATHERS, Petworth **Ref:**YH00743
BADGER WOOD TRAINING/LIVERY, Henfield **Ref:**YH00778
BRENDON, Brighton **Ref:**YH01835
BRENDON HORSE & RIDER, Brighton **Ref:**YH01837
CASTLE STABLES, Arundel **Ref:**YH02636
COOMBELANDS RACING STABLES, Pulborough **Ref:**YH03280
CYZER, C, Horsham **Ref:**YH03766
DACE, L A, Pulborough **Ref:**YH03814
EASTMERE STABLES, Chichester **Ref:**YH04509
EDWARDS, S, Pulborough **Ref:**YH04585
GIFFORD, J T, Worthing **Ref:**YH05757
H E I, Pulborough **Ref:**YH06218
HARTLAND CARRIAGE SUPPLIES, Rudgwick **Ref:**YH06504
HORGAN, C A, Pulborough **Ref:**YH07066
LADY HERRIES STABLES, Littlehampton **Ref:**YH08336
LASSETTER, JOHN F, Chichester **Ref:**YH08442
LAVANT HSE STABLES, Chichester **Ref:**YH08460
MANNINGS LIVERIES, Henfield **Ref:**YH09089
MINTA WINN CARRIAGE DRIVING, Billingshurst **Ref:**YH09655
MOLECOMB STUD, Chichester **Ref:**YH09712
MORRISON, LIZ, Billingshurst **Ref:**YH09838
RICHARDS, L, Chichester **Ref:**YH11810
ROWE, R, Pulborough **Ref:**YH12165
SHOVELSTRODE RACING, East Grinstead **Ref:**YH12763
SMITH, DINA, Pulborough **Ref:**YH12955
WADE, J & A, Midhurst **Ref:**YH14813
WADE, JONNY, Midhurst **Ref:**YH14814
WEEDON, C, Pulborough **Ref:**YH15045
WELLS, L, Billingshurst **Ref:**YH15086
WINDRUSH STABLES, Findon **Ref:**YH15571
WOODMAN, S, Chichester **Ref:**YH15722
WOODMANS STABLES, Ashington **Ref:**YH15723
ZARA STUD, Chichester **Ref:**YH15951

TYNE AND WEAR

BARTON RIDING SCHOOL, Newcastle-upon-Tyne **Ref:**YH01045
BYERLEY STUD, Newcastle-upon-Tyne **Ref:**YH02346
CUNNINGHAM, W S, Yarm **Ref:**YH03725
JOHNSON, R W, Newcastle-upon-Tyne **Ref:**YH07836
LITTLE HARLE STABLES, Newcastle-upon-Tyne **Ref:**YH08688
MACKIE, HENRI, Newcastle-upon-Tyne **Ref:**YH09005
MAW, J D, Sunderland **Ref:**YH09282
MCKEOWN, W J, Newcastle-upon-Tyne **Ref:**YH09385
REED, W G, Newcastle-upon-Tyne **Ref:**YH11722
SCOTT, ANDY, Newcastle-upon-Tyne **Ref:**YH12537

WARWICKSHIRE

ACCIMASSU, Studley **Ref:**YH00140
ALLEN, J S, Alcester **Ref:**YH00297
ALSCOT PARK STABLES, Stratford-upon-Avon **Ref:**YH00336
BANKFIELD RACING STABLES, Stratford-upon-Avon **Ref:**YH00894
BARRACLOUGH, M F, Warwick **Ref:**YH01004
BERA, Kenilworth **Ref:**YH01291
BRADLEY, A S, Coventry **Ref:**YH01752
BRIDGWATER, MARY, Lapworth **Ref:**YH01888
CLAYDON HORSE EXERCISERS, Southam **Ref:**YH02999
COTON EQUITANA, Rugby **Ref:**YH03358
DICKEN, ROBIN, Stratford-upon-Avon **Ref:**YH04110
HADLEY, STEPHEN, Kineton **Ref:**YH06268
IRELAND, KEITH, Nuneaton **Ref:**YH07488
KING, A, Stratford-upon-Avon **Ref:**YH08172
MILLHOUSE RACING, Alcester **Ref:**YH09621
MOAT HOUSE STUD, Henley In Arden **Ref:**YH09686
PRITCHARD, P A, Shipston-on-Stour **Ref:**YH11419
RANKIN, JULIA, Alcester **Ref:**YH11635
RUMER FARM STUD & STABLES, Welford-on-Avon **Ref:**YH12229
STARKEY, JANE, Leamington Spa **Ref:**YH13395
TED EDGAR, Warwick **Ref:**YH13930
WOOTTON GRANGE EQUESTRIAN, Warwick **Ref:**YH15772

WILTSHIRE

ALAN KING RACING, Swindon **Ref:**YH00240
BENSON, SUE, Devizes **Ref:**YH01280
BEST-TURNER, W DE, Marlborough **Ref:**YH01328
BONITA RACING STABLES, Marlborough **Ref:**YH01624
BURGESS, PAT, Salisbury **Ref:**YH02246
CHAMBERLAIN, A J, Swindon **Ref:**YH02717
CHARLTON, ROGER J, Marlborough **Ref:**YH02768
COPPERFIELD STABLES, Salisbury **Ref:**YH03302
DE GILES, J A T, Swindon **Ref:**YH03976
EARLE, S A, Marlborough **Ref:**YH04452
FORD FARM STABLES, Chippenham **Ref:**YH05323
GOSDEN, J H M, Marlborough **Ref:**YH05941
HADDON STUD, Marlborough **Ref:**YH06263
HANNON, R, Marlborough **Ref:**YH06395
HAYNES, H E, Swindon **Ref:**YH06588
HIGHLANDS FARM RACING STABLES, Marlborough **Ref:**YH06795
HOLDERNESS-RODDAM, JANE, Chippenham **Ref:**YH06926
HORSEMANSHIP, Wootton Bassett **Ref:**YH07161
IDOVER HOUSE STABLES, Swindon **Ref:**YH07387
INGLESHAM POLO CTRE, Swindon **Ref:**YH07450
J A B OLD, Swindon **Ref:**YH07553
KING, J S & PM, Swindon **Ref:**YH08181
LANE, CHARLIE, Warminster **Ref:**YH08390
LYON, POLLY, Malmesbury **Ref:**YH08940
MALTHOUSE EQUESTRIAN CTRE, Swindon **Ref:**YH09058
MANNERS, JOHN, Swindon **Ref:**YH09086
MEADE, MARTYN, Malmesbury **Ref:**YH09413
MEADE, RICHARD, Chippenham **Ref:**YH09415
NAYLOR, J R J (DR), Salisbury **Ref:**YH10059
NICHOLSON, ANDREW, Devizes **Ref:**YH10190
ORMEROD, GILES, Salisbury **Ref:**YH10548

PEACOCK, R E, Malmesbury **Ref:**YH10862
SALAMAN, M, Marlborough **Ref:**YH12385
SCIMGEOUR, ANNABEL, Marlborough **Ref:**YH12525
STONAR SCHOOL, Melksham **Ref:**YH13507
WANLESS, MARY, Box **Ref:**YH14894
WEST KINGTON STUD, Chippenham **Ref:**YH15151
WILSFORD STABLES, Salisbury **Ref:**YH15526
WYLYE STUD, Salisbury **Ref:**YH15866
YOUNG, JUDY, Calne **Ref:**YH15935

WORCESTERSHIRE

AUTY, I, Hallow **Ref:**YH00676
CARROLL, A W, Flavell **Ref:**YH02592
COLLEY, ANNE, Bewdley **Ref:**YH03177
DORAN, B N, Broadway **Ref:**YH04196
EILBERG, FERDI, Redditch **Ref:**YH04598
EQUINE RESOURCES, Malvern **Ref:**YH04796
EVANS, SALLYANN & LISA, Bromsgrove **Ref:**YH04932
FAR FOREST EQUESTRIAN CTRE, Kidderminster **Ref:**YH05047
HEID & BRAZIER, Stourport-on-Severn **Ref:**YH06648
HINDLIP EQUESTRIAN CTRE, Hindlip **Ref:**YH06872
INGRAM, PAUL, Kidderminster **Ref:**YH07454
JACKSON, C F C, Malvern **Ref:**YH07644
JAMES, A P, Tenbury Wells **Ref:**YH07677
JUCKES, R T, Worcester **Ref:**YH07956
KINNERSLEY RACING STABLES, Severn Stoke **Ref:**YH08218
KYRE EQUESTRIAN CTRE, Tenbury Wells **Ref:**YH08305
LAST EMPIRE STABLES, Suckley **Ref:**YH08443
LEA CASTLE EQUESTRIAN CTRE, Kidderminster **Ref:**YH08493
LYMER, WENDY, Grimley **Ref:**YH08920
MANOR FARM RIDING SCHOOL, Stourport-on-Severn **Ref:**YH09107
MILL END RACING, Pershore **Ref:**YH09569
PEASEBROOK, Broadway **Ref:**YH10883
PERSHORE & HINDLIP CLGE, Hindlip **Ref:**YH10993
SMITH, N A, Worcester **Ref:**YH12979
SOLCUM STUD & STABLES, Kidderminster **Ref:**YH13052
TATE, MARTIN, Kidderminster **Ref:**YH13873
TURBLES, Malvern **Ref:**YH14465
WARRINGTON, S, Little Witley **Ref:**YH14943
WELLMAN, M, Upton-upon-Severn **Ref:**YH15076
WORSLEY RACING STABLES, Worcester **Ref:**YH15800
YARDLEY, G H, Malvern **Ref:**YH15883
YARDLEY, GEORGE HENRY, Malvern **Ref:**YH15884

YORKSHIRE (EAST)

BLEACH YARD STABLES, Beverley **Ref:**YH01531
CHURCH FARMS, Beverley **Ref:**YH02904
CURTIS, CARL, Goole **Ref:**YH03745
HEATH RACING STABLES, Beverley **Ref:**YH06622
NASH, J, Driffield **Ref:**YH10026
SOWERSBY, M E, Goodmanham **Ref:**YH13168

YORKSHIRE (NORTH)

ALEXANDER, HAMISH, York **Ref:**YH00270
ANDY COOK RACING, Leyburn **Ref:**YH00405
ASHGILL STABLES, Leyburn **Ref:**YH00604
BARKER TRAINING, Richmond **Ref:**YH00938
BARKER, DAVID, Richmond **Ref:**YH00941
BARNHOUSE RACING STABLES, Richmond **Ref:**YH00988
BARRON, T D, Thirsk **Ref:**YH01025
BARROWBY RIDING CTRE, Harrogate **Ref:**YH01032
BARTLE, G M, Tadcaster **Ref:**YH01038
BEAUMONT, P, York **Ref:**YH01137
BELLWOOD COTTAGE STABLES, Malton **Ref:**YH01242
BETHEL, J D W, Leyburn **Ref:**YH01332
BOOTH, C B B, York **Ref:**YH01634
BRECONGILL STABLES, Leyburn **Ref:**YH01830
BRIGG VIEW, Filey **Ref:**YH01906
BRITTAIN, M, York **Ref:**YH01982
BROWN, M IAN, Richmond **Ref:**YH02123
BYCROFT, N, York **Ref:**YH02345
CAMACHO RACING, Malton **Ref:**YH02464
CARR, J M, Malton **Ref:**YH02570
CASTLE STABLES, Richmond **Ref:**YH02637
CHAPMAN, D W, York **Ref:**YH02744
COLDBECK, J D & N, Whitby **Ref:**YH03145
COMMON FARM STABLES, York **Ref:**YH03215
DUFFIELD, ANN, Leyburn **Ref:**YH04314
EASTERBY, M H, Malton **Ref:**YH04493
EASTERBY, M W, York **Ref:**YH04494
ETHERINGTON, T J, Malton **Ref:**YH04883
EYRE, J L, Thirsk **Ref:**YH04976
FAHEY, R, Malton **Ref:**YH05009
FAIRHURST, C W, Leyburn **Ref:**YH05024
FELL VIEW STABLES, Leyburn **Ref:**YH05132
FITZGERALD, J G, Malton **Ref:**YH05247
FLETCHER, KAREN, Thirsk **Ref:**YH05280
GILYHEAD, G M, Knaresborough **Ref:**YH05793
HASLAM, P C, Leyburn **Ref:**YH06523
HETHERTON, JAMES, Malton **Ref:**YH06725
HOLGATE, T, Skipton **Ref:**YH06932
HOLMES, G, Pickering **Ref:**YH06975
INCISA, DON ENRICO, Leyburn **Ref:**YH07409
JOUSTING & ASSOCIATED SKILLS, Thirsk **Ref:**YH07948
KELLY, G P, Sheriff Hutton **Ref:**YH08044
KETTLEWELL, S E, Leyburn **Ref:**YH08109
LOCKWOOD, A, Malton **Ref:**YH08762
MARK JOHNSTON RACING, Leyburn **Ref:**YH09153
MATCHMAKER HORSE & PONY, York **Ref:**YH09256
MICKY HAMMOND RACING, Leyburn **Ref:**YH09517
MOORE, GEORGE, Leyburn **Ref:**YH09759
MULHOLLAND, T, Thirsk **Ref:**YH09933
MURRAY, B W, Malton **Ref:**YH09963
MUSLEY BANK STABLES, Malton **Ref:**YH09975
NABURN GRANGE RIDING CTRE, York **Ref:**YH10008
NAUGHTON, A M, Richmond **Ref:**YH10056
NEWSTEAD COTTAGE STABLES, Malton **Ref:**YH10165
NICHOLSON, MYLES, Harrogate **Ref:**YH10194
PARKES, J E, Upper Helmsley **Ref:**YH10757
PARRINGTON, M C, Skipton **Ref:**YH10786
ROTHWELL, B, Malton **Ref:**YH12137
ROW BROW FARM, Scarborough **Ref:**YH12151
RYAN, KEVIN, Thirsk **Ref:**YH12284
SAXBY, ALAN K, Northallerton **Ref:**YH12465
SIDDALL, L C, Tadcaster **Ref:**YH12783
SLEE, C, Coverham **Ref:**YH12893
SNAINTON RIDING CTRE, Scarborough **Ref:**YH13028
SPALDING, C M, Richmond **Ref:**YH13171
SPIGOT LODGE, Leyburn **Ref:**YH13203
SPRING COTTAGE STABLES, Melton **Ref:**YH13245
TATE, ROBIN, Thirsk **Ref:**YH13875
TATE, TOM, Tadcaster **Ref:**YH13877
THORNDALE FARM STABLES, Richmond **Ref:**YH14061
TINKLER, NIGEL, Malton **Ref:**YH14173
TINNING, BILL, Thornton-Le-Clay **Ref:**YH14174
TUPGILL PARK STABLES, Leyburn **Ref:**YH14464
TURNELL, ANDY, Thirsk **Ref:**YH14473
TURNER, J R, Helperby **Ref:**YH14482
WAINWRIGHT, J S, Malton **Ref:**YH14829
WEATHERILL, P S, Harrogate **Ref:**YH15026
WILSON, N, Kirby Underdale **Ref:**YH15543
WOODHOUSE, R D E, York **Ref:**YH15696
WYNBURY STABLES, Leyburn **Ref:**YH15870
YORKSHIRE RIDING CTRE, Harrogate **Ref:**YH15922

YORKSHIRE (SOUTH)

BALDING, JOHN, Doncaster **Ref:**YH00837
NORTON, J, Barnsley **Ref:**YH10332
THOMPSON, R, Doncaster **Ref:**YH14040

YORKSHIRE (WEST)

BLACUP TRAINING GRP, Halifax **Ref:**YH01504
CHADWICK, SUE, Huddersfield **Ref:**YH02706
DAWSON, P G, Halton **Ref:**YH03964
MANOR GRANGE STUD SCHOOL, Wakefield **Ref:**YH09109
METCALFE, STUART, Ilkley **Ref:**YH09501
MIDGLEY, A D, Hobberley Lane **Ref:**YH09551
NICHOL, D W, Bradford **Ref:**YH10179
ROBERTS, V C, Pontefract **Ref:**YH11964
SMITH, S J, Bingley **Ref:**YH13000
SYCAMORE HOUSE FARM, Leeds **Ref:**YH13719
WHITAKER, R M, Leeds **Ref:**YH15291
WRB RACING, Leeds **Ref:**YH15814

TRANSPORT/HORSE BOXES

BATH & SOMERSET (NORTH EAST)

AVON TRAILER TOWBAR CTRE, Bath **Ref:**YH00691
CHAVES HORSE TRANSPORT, Bath **Ref:**YH02792
HITCH N LIFT TRAILERS, Bath **Ref:**YH06886
RAWLINGS, P S, Bath **Ref:**YH11666

BEDFORDSHIRE

ASHCRAFT EQUESTRIAN, Haynes **Ref:**YH00592
C R DAY'S MOTORS, Dunstable **Ref:**YH02387
COOPER, JOHN, Shefford **Ref:**YH03288
EASIRAMP SYSTEMS, Leighton Buzzard **Ref:**YH04461
F & R CAWLEY, Dunstable **Ref:**YH04980
GROOMS LIVESTOCK TRANSPORT, Leighton Buzzard **Ref:**YH06156
GROOMS LIVESTOCK TRANSPORT, Leighton Buzzard **Ref:**YH06155
MILLER, T F, Bedford **Ref:**YH09613
SOUTHERN HAY COACH BUILDERS, Bedford **Ref:**YH13140
TRAIL-A-BRAKE SYSTEMS, Leighton Buzzard **Ref:**YH14314
TRAILER RESOURCES, Leighton Buzzard **Ref:**YH14327
VENTURE COACHWORKS, Dunstable **Ref:**YH14678
VULCAN TOWING CTRE, Luton **Ref:**YH14745

BERKSHIRE

A TO B, Wokingham **Ref:**YH00063
ACORN TRAILER HIRE, Reading **Ref:**YH00152
ALLTRUCK TRAILER RENTAL, Thatcham **Ref:**YH00327
A-ZEP TRANSPORT, Reading **Ref:**YH00706
B M VEALE & SON, Reading **Ref:**YH00744
BARRY, JOHN F J, Newbury **Ref:**YH01034
BRACKNELL HORSE TRANSPORT, Wokingham **Ref:**YH01742
C N HORSE BOX INT, Reading **Ref:**YH02382
C R BLACK & SONS, Reading **Ref:**YH02386
CROSSWAYS TRANSPORT, Crowthorne **Ref:**YH03668
EQUINE CHAUFFEUR SVS, Reading **Ref:**YH04768
ERMIN ST STABLES, Hungerford **Ref:**YH04851
FRANCIS, M E D, Hungerford **Ref:**YH05452

- **HAYDEN WEBB CARRIAGES**, Reading **Ref:**YH06568
- **HINCHLIFFE, M J**, Hungerford **Ref:**YH06867
- **HORSE BOX & TRAILER OWNERS**, Newbury **Ref:**YH07111
- **INDESPENSION**, Reading **Ref:**YH07411
- **KRONE COMMERCIAL TRAILERS**, Hungerford **Ref:**YH08296
- **PARKES INT TRANSPORT**, Newbury **Ref:**YH10755
- **RHINO TRAILER HIRE**, Reading **Ref:**YH11787
- **T L TRAILER SERVICES**, Sandhurst **Ref:**YH13758
- **T N T INT AVIATION SVS**, Windsor **Ref:**YH13761
- **VINCENT TRAILERS**, Thatcham **Ref:**YH14723
- **WOODLANDS**, Hungerford **Ref:**YH15705

BRISTOL

- **DOWNEND TRAILOR SVS**, Bristol **Ref:**YH04227
- **G HARRAWAY & SONS**, Bristol **Ref:**YH05581
- **GENERAL TRAILERS**, Bristol **Ref:**YH05704
- **PAGE, R G**, Bristol **Ref:**YH10682
- **PEARCE, A W**, Bristol **Ref:**YH10868
- **SHORT, JAMES H**, Bristol **Ref:**YH12760
- **SMALL, K W**, Bristol **Ref:**YH12906
- **U PULL TRAILERS**, Bristol **Ref:**YH14537
- **WESTERN TRAILERS**, Bristol **Ref:**YH15208

BUCKINGHAMSHIRE

- **BATES, AL**, Aylesbury **Ref:**YH01066
- **BROSHUIS TRAILERS**, Princes Risborough **Ref:**YH02084
- **C S HORSEBOXES**, High Wycombe **Ref:**YH02390
- **CARTWHEEL TRAILERS**, Gerrards Cross **Ref:**YH02612
- **CENTRAL TRAILER RENTCO**, Aylesbury **Ref:**YH02691
- **CITY TRUCK RENTALS**, Milton Keynes **Ref:**YH02932
- **FLATMOBILE**, Great Missenden **Ref:**YH05263
- **FORREST HORSE TRANSPORT**, Milton Keynes **Ref:**YH05377
- **HILL HIRE**, Milton Keynes **Ref:**YH06817
- **HOPCROFT TRANSPORT**, Aylesbury **Ref:**YH07049
- **NEWMAN, R & J**, High Wycombe **Ref:**YH10151
- **PEN & PADDOCK**, Long Crendon **Ref:**YH10921
- **S E BURNELL**, Aylesbury **Ref:**YH12323
- **TAYLOR, DAVID**, High Wycombe **Ref:**YH13900

CAMBRIDGESHIRE

- **BARNWELL TRAILERS**, Peterborough **Ref:**YH00992
- **CAMBRIDGE TRAILERS**, Cambridge **Ref:**YH02471
- **CENTURION INT HORSE TRANSPORT**, Reach **Ref:**YH02699
- **COLLIER, W E**, Ely **Ref:**YH03181
- **COUNTRY VEHICLES**, Ely **Ref:**YH03434
- **CUSTOM TRAILERS**, Ely **Ref:**YH03758
- **DYER, J**, Ely **Ref:**YH04386
- **ENGLISH BROTHERS**, Wisbech **Ref:**YH04672
- **F S TRAILERS & TOWBARS CTRE**, St Ives **Ref:**YH05000
- **FARM-INSTALL**, St Neots **Ref:**YH05065
- **FENLAND TRAILER PARTS**, Peterborough **Ref:**YH05144
- **GENERAL TRAILERS**, Peterborough **Ref:**YH05705
- **HATCHAM**, Ely **Ref:**YH06531
- **IRELAND, D**, Wisbech **Ref:**YH07487
- **N B SANDERS**, Peterborough **Ref:**YH09987
- **RATCLIFFE, J M**, Ely **Ref:**YH11649
- **SHAMROCK HORSEBOXES**, Ely **Ref:**YH12664
- **T I P**, Peterborough **Ref:**YH13747
- **TALLY-HO TRAILERS**, Huntingdon **Ref:**YH13845
- **THOROUGHBRED COACHBUILDERS**, Ely **Ref:**YH14084
- **WESTON, V J**, Peterborough **Ref:**YH15228
- **WILKINSON BROS**, Cambridge **Ref:**YH15417

CHESHIRE

- **A C TRAILERS**, Crewe **Ref:**YH00026
- **A L G TRAILER HIRE**, Northwich **Ref:**YH00047
- **CONGLETON TRAILER HIRE**, Congleton **Ref:**YH03228
- **CONGLETON TRAILERS**, Congleton **Ref:**YH03229
- **CURTAINSIDER**, Sandbach **Ref:**YH03744
- **DINGLE BROOK FARM STABLES**, Macclesfield **Ref:**YH04125
- **E P TOWING**, Chester **Ref:**YH04421
- **EAST CHESHIRE TRAILERS**, Macclesfield **Ref:**YH04467
- **FIELD, LINDSEY**, Warrington **Ref:**YH05188
- **FOXLEA HORSE BOXES**, Warrington **Ref:**YH05439
- **FRANCIS, W D**, Malpas **Ref:**YH05453
- **G COOKE COACHBUILDERS**, Crewe **Ref:**YH05574
- **GOODMAN HORSE BOX SVS**, Ellesmere Port **Ref:**YH05904
- **HENRY CARRIAGE CARTS**, Crewe **Ref:**YH06680
- **HORSEBOX BITS**, Warrington **Ref:**YH07150
- **INDESPENSION**, Altrincham **Ref:**YH07412
- **KIDD, D**, Macclesfield **Ref:**YH08121
- **LANSDOWNE HORSE & RIDER**, Chester **Ref:**YH08423
- **M6 TRAILER RENTAL**, Warrington **Ref:**YH08978
- **MOTTRAM ST ANDREW**, Macclesfield **Ref:**YH09878
- **NORBROOK TRAILERS**, Warrington **Ref:**YH10227
- **OMEGA TRAILERS**, Warrington **Ref:**YH10509
- **PETERLEA TOWING & TRAILER**, Stockport **Ref:**YH11019
- **QUINLAN, F W**, Hyde **Ref:**YH11498
- **REDGRAVE, CAROLE**, Wilmslow **Ref:**YH11711
- **T I P C T R TRAILER RENTAL**, Sale **Ref:**YH13749
- **TOWBARS NORTH WEST**, Warrington **Ref:**YH14265
- **WARRINGTON TRAILER CTRE**, Warrington **Ref:**YH14942
- **WOODFORD TRAILERS**, Stockport **Ref:**YH15688

CLEVELAND

- **C T C MARINE & LEISURE GROUP**, Middlesbrough **Ref:**YH02392
- **CLEVELAND TRAILER CTRE**, Middlesbrough **Ref:**YH03022
- **JOHN MOORHOUSE**, Stockton-on-Tees **Ref:**YH07802
- **JOPLING SELF TOW HIRE**, Middlesbrough **Ref:**YH07937
- **TL TRAILER SERVICES**, Billingham **Ref:**YH14195
- **W H HORSEBOXES**, Nunthorpe **Ref:**YH14771
- **WHITEHALL TRAILERS**, Stockton-on-Tees **Ref:**YH15340

CORNWALL

- **BODMIN TRAILER CTRE**, Bodmin **Ref:**YH01597
- **CITADEL TRAILERS**, Liskeard **Ref:**YH02928
- **DAVEY'S LIVESTOCK TRANSPORT**, Launceston **Ref:**YH03914
- **EQUESTRIAN STOP**, Camborne **Ref:**YH04712
- **FISHER, ANN**, Bodmin **Ref:**YH05237
- **GOODFELLOWS**, Wadebridge **Ref:**YH05903
- **GORDON MARTIN & SON**, Bodmin **Ref:**YH05924
- **HARLEY HORSEBOXES**, Truro **Ref:**YH06437
- **HOSKING, J A**, Penzance **Ref:**YH07196
- **JONES, P T**, St Austell **Ref:**YH07922
- **LIZARD TRAILER SVS**, Helston **Ref:**YH08718
- **M & S HAULIERS**, Saltash **Ref:**YH08950
- **MASON, G K**, Launceston **Ref:**YH09244
- **MORLEY BONNER**, Redruth **Ref:**YH09817
- **P & L LUCK HORSE TRANSPORT**, Liskeard **Ref:**YH10631
- **P R J ENGINEERING**, Launceston **Ref:**YH10655
- **ROWE, ROB**, Bodmin **Ref:**YH12166
- **TAMAR VALLEY TRANSPORT**, Callington **Ref:**YH13849
- **TRAILER LAND**, Liskeard **Ref:**YH14323
- **TYRONE SNELL TRAILERS**, Penryn **Ref:**YH14531
- **VANSTONE, B**, Bude **Ref:**YH14660

COUNTY DURHAM

- **ACRUM LODGE STUD**, Bishop Auckland **Ref:**YH00160
- **BOWES MANOR EQUESTRIAN CTRE**, Chester Le Street **Ref:**YH01709
- **BROOM HALL LIVERY YARD**, Durham **Ref:**YH02072
- **CENTRAL TRAILER RENTCO**, Darlington **Ref:**YH02692
- **CUMMINGS, R C**, Chester Le Street **Ref:**YH03721
- **GIGANT UK**, Shildon **Ref:**YH05758
- **GRICE, W A**, Darlington **Ref:**YH06127
- **HEDLEYS ALARMS/TOWING CTRE**, Durham **Ref:**YH06646
- **KEWAL TRAILER PRODUCTS**, Darlington **Ref:**YH08112
- **MONKHOUSE, TONY**, Bishop Auckland **Ref:**YH09725
- **MOOREHOUSE HORSEBOXES**, Whinney Hill **Ref:**YH09770
- **P MONKHOUSE HAULAGE**, Bishop Auckland **Ref:**YH10653
- **PR PROFESSIONAL SERVICES**, Consett **Ref:**YH11336
- **STANLEY TOWBAR CTRE**, Chester Le Street **Ref:**YH13372
- **TINSLEY TRAILERS**, Darlington **Ref:**YH14175
- **W S HODGSON**, Barnard Castle **Ref:**YH14794
- **WIDDAS, A**, Bishop Auckland **Ref:**YH15389
- **WIDDAS, TONY**, Cockfield **Ref:**YH15390

CUMBRIA

- **C T C**, Carlisle **Ref:**YH02391
- **CUMBRIA WELDING & TRAILERS**, Kendal **Ref:**YH03717
- **KENNEDY, R R & K**, Brampton **Ref:**YH08069
- **NEWTON HORSEFEEDS & TRAILER**, Penrith **Ref:**YH10172
- **STOBART, D T**, Brampton **Ref:**YH13483
- **THWAITES, R G**, Penrith **Ref:**YH14124
- **WALLING, R H**, Kendal **Ref:**YH14866

DERBYSHIRE

- **ABBEY TRAILERS**, Derby **Ref:**YH00086
- **BAKEWELL TRAILERS**, Hope Valley **Ref:**YH00827
- **BARLEYFIELDS**, Derby **Ref:**YH00952
- **C E S**, Ashbourne **Ref:**YH02370
- **CHESTERFIELD**, Chesterfield **Ref:**YH02833
- **EUROFLEET RENTAL**, Swadlincote **Ref:**YH04899
- **GENERAL TRAILER ENGINEERING**, Swadlincote **Ref:**YH05703
- **GLENTEL TRAILERS**, Derby **Ref:**YH05844
- **HEDGEHOG EQUESTRIAN**, Ashbourne **Ref:**YH06641
- **HIGH PEAK TRAILERS**, High Peak **Ref:**YH06765
- **HOPKINSON, S R**, Chesterfield **Ref:**YH07057
- **INDESPENSION**, Derby **Ref:**YH07416
- **J A HOPKINSON & SON**, Chesterfield **Ref:**YH07555
- **KEMP, J T**, High Peak **Ref:**YH08054
- **KING OF THE ROAD TRAILERS**, Chesterfield **Ref:**YH08169
- **MARCH, BILL**, Chesterfield **Ref:**YH09141
- **TRAILER MEN**, Chesterfield **Ref:**YH14324
- **WITHINGTON HILL STABLES**, High Peak **Ref:**YH15626

DEVON

- **ADMIRAL TRAILERS**, Tiverton **Ref:**YH00187
- **BAMPTON CATTLE TRANSPORT**, Tiverton **Ref:**YH00878
- **BENNEY TRAILERS**, Ivybridge **Ref:**YH01274
- **BRAMBER TRAILERS**, Cullompton **Ref:**YH01786
- **C & M TRAILERS**, South Brent **Ref:**YH02357
- **CHAMBERS, S C**, Totnes **Ref:**YH02722
- **CLAIRE HOWARTH**, Exeter **Ref:**YH02937
- **DENYER, I D & C R M**, Tiverton **Ref:**YH04069
- **G & C HORSE TRANSPORT**, Totnes **Ref:**YH05562
- **HUISH ENGINEERING**, Exeter **Ref:**YH07277
- **J H COMMERCIALS**, Barnstaple **Ref:**YH07586
- **J WATTS & SONS**, Barnstaple **Ref:**YH07631
- **J WATTS & SONS**, Braunton **Ref:**YH07632
- **KING, P**, Tedburn St Mary **Ref:**YH08185
- **LES LEY HORSE TRANSPORT**, Brixham **Ref:**YH08556
- **LYNTON CROSS TRAILER CTRE**, Ilfracombe **Ref:**YH08933
- **NEPTUNE TRAILERS**, Torquay **Ref:**YH10078
- **NOVA ENGINEERING**, Newton Abbot **Ref:**YH10346
- **NOVA TRAILERS**, Exeter **Ref:**YH10347
- **OASIS TRAILER CTRE**, Braunton **Ref:**YH10414
- **PENGELLY, DAVID**, Cullompton **Ref:**YH10936
- **REEVES, MARK**, St Mary **Ref:**YH11737
- **ROBDALE CAR TRAILERS**, Barnstaple **Ref:**YH11937
- **SLUGGETT, S J**, Holsworthy **Ref:**YH12902
- **TAMAR TRAILER CTRE**, Plymouth **Ref:**YH13848
- **TORBAY TRAILER & TOWBARS**, Paignton **Ref:**YH14242
- **TRAILAMANSYSTEMS**, Tiverton **Ref:**YH14315
- **TRAIL-A-WAY**, Exeter **Ref:**YH14316
- **WALKE, L**, South Brent **Ref:**YH14844
- **WESTERN TOWING**, Newton Abbot **Ref:**YH15206
- **WESTERN TOWING ATTACHMENTS**, Exeter **Ref:**YH15207
- **WHITE HORSE MOTORS**, Exeter **Ref:**YH15309
- **WILLIAMS, W R**, Exeter **Ref:**YH15481
- **WINDUSS HORSEBOXES**, Crediton **Ref:**YH15579
- **YEOFORD TRAILERS**, Crediton **Ref:**YH15903

DORSET

- **BOURNEMOUTH TRAILER CTRE**, Wimborne **Ref:**YH01688
- **BRIDPORT TRAILERS**, Bridport **Ref:**YH01902
- **C K TRAILERS**, Poole **Ref:**YH02379
- **EAGLE TRAILERS**, Poole **Ref:**YH04439
- **FIVE SQUARE MOTORS**, Shaftesbury **Ref:**YH05256
- **FOOT, P B**, Sturminster Newton **Ref:**YH05311
- **HIRE A TRAILER**, Bournemouth **Ref:**YH06882
- **JOHN REID & SONS**, Christchurch **Ref:**YH07808
- **LINE 1**, Wimborne **Ref:**YH08656
- **MITCHELL, J**, Sturminster Newton **Ref:**YH09669
- **PARKSTONE TRAILER HIRE**, Poole **Ref:**YH10774
- **PETS TO VETS**, Bournemouth **Ref:**YH11031
- **PRIDDLE, KEITH**, Bournemouth **Ref:**YH11393
- **SHAFTESBURY TRAILER**, Shaftesbury **Ref:**YH12657
- **STANDFIELD, M J**, Dorchester **Ref:**YH13360
- **STOWER VALLEY HORSEBOXES**, Sturminster Newton **Ref:**YH13541
- **TOLLER TRAILERS**, Dorchester **Ref:**YH14209
- **TOWBAR**, Bournemouth **Ref:**YH14262
- **WAREHAM, TONY**, Blandford Forum **Ref:**YH14915
- **WESSEX TRAILERS**, Dorchester **Ref:**YH15122

ESSEX

- **ANGLIA TOWING EQUIPMENT**, Colchester **Ref:**YH00414
- **ARIAN TRAILERS**, Chelmsford **Ref:**YH00525
- **BRIDGEWATER SHIPPING**, Harwich **Ref:**YH01884
- **C & K EQUINE SVS**, Chelmsford **Ref:**YH02355
- **CHELMER TRAILERS**, Chelmsford **Ref:**YH02800
- **COACH HSE**, Epping **Ref:**YH03102
- **COCKS, L R**, Dagenham **Ref:**YH03128
- **COLNE CARGO TRANSPORT SVS**, Colchester **Ref:**YH03195
- **EMSLIE HORSE BOXES**, Harlow **Ref:**YH04661
- **EQUESTRIAN TRANSPORT SVS**, Maldon **Ref:**YH04718
- **ESSEX TRAILER SALES**, Grays **Ref:**YH04873
- **FRUEHAUF, CRANE**, Barking **Ref:**YH05525
- **GRIFFIN ENGINEERING**, Dunmow **Ref:**YH06129
- **I P D COACHBUILDERS**, Ongar **Ref:**YH07367
- **JAMES, SIMON**, Romford **Ref:**YH07687
- **LTT IMMINGHAM**, South Ockendon **Ref:**YH08881
- **M P TRAILERS**, Burnham-on-Crouch **Ref:**YH08974
- **MALDON TRAILER SVS**, Rainham **Ref:**YH09046
- **MOBILE TRANSPORT MAINTENANCE**, Dagenham **Ref:**YH09693
- **MONTRACON**, Barking **Ref:**YH09734
- **ORSETT HORSEBOX REPAIRERS**, Wickford **Ref:**YH10553
- **SMITH, B J**, Clacton-on-Sea **Ref:**YH12942
- **THORPE HORSE BOXES**, Clacton-on-Sea **Ref:**YH14092
- **TOWRITE**, Upminster **Ref:**YH14301
- **TRAILER YARD**, Chigwell **Ref:**YH14331
- **UPSON, T B**, Colchester **Ref:**YH14615
- **W MARTIN & SON**, Braintree **Ref:**YH14782
- **WORLDWIDE ANIMAL TRAVEL**, Brentwood **Ref:**YH15787

GLOUCESTERSHIRE

- **BAYLISS, M G**, Cheltenham **Ref:**YH01096
- **BISLEY TRANSPORT SVS**, Stroud **Ref:**YH01453
- **BRASTOCK, R W**, Badminton **Ref:**YH01816
- **CAMERON HORSE TRANSPORT**, Stroud **Ref:**YH02477
- **CIRENCESTER GARAGE**, Cirencester **Ref:**YH02926
- **COTSWOLD TRAILERS**, Cheltenham **Ref:**YH03370
- **COTSWOLD TRAILERS**, Gloucester **Ref:**YH03369
- **D R W TRAILERS**, Longhope **Ref:**YH03806
- **FOOTE TRANSPORT**, Stonehouse **Ref:**YH05312
- **GAMBLE, KEN**, Cheltenham **Ref:**YH05631
- **GLOUCESTER FABRICATIONS**, Gloucester **Ref:**YH05850
- **GREEN BROS**, Tewkesbury **Ref:**YH06051
- **GROVE FARM**, Moreton In Marsh **Ref:**YH06163
- **KING, E & M J**, Stroud **Ref:**YH08179
- **LEVACE HORSEBOXES**, Gloucester **Ref:**YH08571
- **MARSCOM**, Cheltenham **Ref:**YH09180
- **MUMFORD SPECIALIST VEHICLES**, Stroud **Ref:**YH09946
- **P J N**, Tewkesbury **Ref:**YH10648
- **RUSHMERE FARM CARRIAGES**, Coleford **Ref:**YH12243
- **SOUTHWICK FARM**, Tewkesbury **Ref:**YH13163
- **WATSONIAN SQUIRE**, Moreton In Marsh **Ref:**YH14995

GUERNSEY

- **GUERNSEY**, St Sampsons **Ref:**YH06182

HAMPSHIRE

- **ALLIED TRAILER RENTAL**, Alton **Ref:**YH00312
- **BLENDWORTH TRAILER CTRE**, Rowland's Castle **Ref:**YH01534
- **BOURNEMOUTH HORSE TRANSPORT**, Ringwood **Ref:**YH01687
- **CENTRAL TRAILER RENTCO**, Southampton **Ref:**YH02693
- **CINDERELLA CARRIAGES**, Romsey **Ref:**YH02920
- **DIBDIN, D A**, Fordingbridge **Ref:**YH04107
- **EDWARDS, C J**, Romsey **Ref:**YH04577
- **EQUICRUISER**, Alton **Ref:**YH04740
- **FRECOL AUTO SVS**, Fleet **Ref:**YH05476
- **GRAY, D**, Basingstoke **Ref:**YH06027
- **H E MILLINGTON & SONS**, Havant **Ref:**YH06219
- **HAMPSHIRE CARRIAGE**, Bordon **Ref:**YH06364
- **HANDLING AIDS**, Ringwood **Ref:**YH06380
- **HARMANS HAULAGE CONTRACTORS**, Bordon **Ref:**YH06444
- **HAYLING TRAILER**, Hayling Island **Ref:**YH06583
- **HINDHEAD TRAILER CTRE**, Liss **Ref:**YH06871
- **INDESPENSION**, Southampton **Ref:**YH07420
- **NEW FOREST AUTOS**, Southampton **Ref:**YH10097
- **NEW FOREST HORSE BOXES**, Lymington **Ref:**YH10099
- **O M C HORSEBOX REPAIRS**, Bordon **Ref:**YH10365
- **OWEN MILLS HAULAGE**, Southampton **Ref:**YH10598
- **PEDEN BLOODSTOCK**, Hook **Ref:**YH10891
- **PET CARRIER SVS**, Havant **Ref:**YH11002
- **PETS TO VETS**, Southsea **Ref:**YH11032
- **PRESTIGE**, Ringwood **Ref:**YH11362
- **R M TRAILERS**, Alresford **Ref:**YH11556
- **RAFFERTY NEWMAN**, Petersfield **Ref:**YH11603
- **RAYMARK TRAILERS**, Southampton **Ref:**YH11674
- **RICKETTS, A G**, Camberley **Ref:**YH11835
- **ROLLS LIVESTOCK HAULAGE**, Andover **Ref:**YH12068
- **S G TRAILER REPAIRS**, Southampton **Ref:**YH12327
- **SHOOTER TOWBARS & TRAILERS**, Andover **Ref:**YH12757
- **SOUTHERN TRAILERS**, Alton **Ref:**YH13146
- **SPEEDFIT**, Basingstoke **Ref:**YH13190
- **STUBBINGTON TRAILERS**, Fareham **Ref:**YH13601
- **T A HULME & SONS**, Southampton **Ref:**YH13728
- **TEST VALLEY GARAGE**, Stockbridge **Ref:**YH13961
- **TOP FLIGHT HORSE BOXES**, Southampton **Ref:**YH14237
- **TOW BAR & TRAILER EQUIPMENT**, Farnborough **Ref:**YH14259
- **TOWING LOGISTICS**, Southampton **Ref:**YH14280
- **TRAILER CARE**, Eastleigh **Ref:**YH14317
- **WARWICK BROS**, Alresford **Ref:**YH14944
- **WEYHILL HORSE TRANSPORT**, Andover **Ref:**YH15251

HEREFORDSHIRE

- **KINGSLAND STABLING**, Leominster **Ref:**YH08203
- **P R B HORSE BOXES**, Leominster **Ref:**YH10654
- **SHIE NEWTON TRAILERS**, Ledbury **Ref:**YH12739
- **WEST MIDLAND HORSE BOX CTRE**, Ledbury **Ref:**YH15156

HERTFORDSHIRE

- **ARROW TRAILERS**, Hatfield **Ref:**YH00561
- **BLAIN'S TRAILERS & TYRES**, Hemel Hempstead **Ref:**YH01508
- **C M TRAILERS**, Bovingdon **Ref:**YH02381

- **COUNTRYSIDE COACHWORKS**, Royston **Ref:**YH03441
- **G T TOWING**, Potters Bar **Ref:**YH05597
- **OAKLEY COACHBUILDERS**, Ware **Ref:**YH10398
- **ROCHIN TRAILERS**, Tring **Ref:**YH12023
- **ROWE, L J**, Bovingdon **Ref:**YH12164
- **SOUTHERN MOBILE**, Bushey **Ref:**YH13141
- **UPPERWOOD FARM STUD**, Hemel Hempstead **Ref:**YH14609

KENT

- **AUTO REPAIRS MECHANICAL**, Bexley **Ref:**YH00670
- **BEESLEY LIVESTOCK HAULAGE**, Cranbrook **Ref:**YH01187
- **BRISLEY BOXES**, Ashford **Ref:**YH01919
- **BRITANNIA TOWING CTRE**, Canterbury **Ref:**YH01922
- **BROMLEY TOWBARS & TRAILERS**, Bromley **Ref:**YH02024
- **CASTLE HILL TRAILERS**, Tonbridge **Ref:**YH02628
- **COOPER, DAVID**, Erith **Ref:**YH03286
- **DENNETT & PARKER**, Sandwich **Ref:**YH04051
- **ENGLISH INT HORSE TRANSPORT**, Dartford **Ref:**YH04675
- **EQUINES LIVERIES**, Maidstone **Ref:**YH04809
- **FARNINGHAM SADDLERY**, Farningham **Ref:**YH05083
- **FOREST VIEW**, Sidcup **Ref:**YH05353
- **G & K SVS**, Ashford **Ref:**YH05564
- **G & L TRAILERS**, Ashford **Ref:**YH05566
- **HERNE BAY**, Herne Bay **Ref:**YH06707
- **HERON CONVERSIONS**, Tunbridge Wells **Ref:**YH06710
- **HORSEFERRY TRANSPORT**, Swanley **Ref:**YH07155
- **JOHN PARKER INTERNATIONAL**, Hythe **Ref:**YH07805
- **L A S TRAILERS**, Canterbury **Ref:**YH08312
- **LONGFIELD & APPLEDORE**, Longfield **Ref:**YH08810
- **MERRIWORTH TRAILERS**, Erith **Ref:**YH09484
- **MOBILE TOWBARS**, Rochester **Ref:**YH09692
- **PAGE, JOHN**, Ashford **Ref:**YH10681
- **PASSMORES PORTABLE BUILDINGS**, Rochester **Ref:**YH10812
- **PRICE, P E**, Canterbury **Ref:**YH11386
- **RICHMONDS HORSE TRANSPORT**, Cobham **Ref:**YH11831
- **RUMENS, A E**, Cranbrook **Ref:**YH12228
- **SPORT LEISURE & TRAILERS**, Orpington **Ref:**YH13220
- **STARLINE HORSE BOXES**, Edenbridge **Ref:**YH13397
- **TILLS HORSE TRANSPORT**, Maidstone **Ref:**YH14153
- **TOW & TRAIL**, Sevenoaks **Ref:**YH14257
- **TRIDENT TRAILERS**, Canterbury **Ref:**YH14393
- **TRIDENT TRAILERS**, Maidstone **Ref:**YH14396
- **TRIDENT TRAILERS**, Sittingbourne **Ref:**YH14395
- **TRIDENT TRAILERS**, Tunbridge Wells **Ref:**YH14394
- **VAS**, Dartford **Ref:**YH14664
- **VERRALL, VERNON**, Cranbrook **Ref:**YH14684
- **WAGGONWORKS TRAILERS**, Canterbury **Ref:**YH14824

LANCASHIRE

- **ARDERN HORSEBOXES**, Wigan **Ref:**YH00506
- **BELL TRAILERS**, Nelson **Ref:**YH01216
- **BLUE ROSE**, Preston **Ref:**YH01569
- **CARAVAN CORNER**, Blackpool **Ref:**YH02526
- **CONWAY PRODUCTS**, Wigan **Ref:**YH03250
- **CRAFTSMEN HORSE BOXES**, Wigan **Ref:**YH03542
- **CRANE, LES**, Ormskirk **Ref:**YH03562
- **CUMMINGS, G B & R**, Preston **Ref:**YH03720
- **DELTA ENGINEERING**, Preston **Ref:**YH04037
- **DENNISON TRAILERS**, Lancaster **Ref:**YH04057
- **E S G SVS**, Bury **Ref:**YH04424
- **HARGREAVES, G**, Burnley **Ref:**YH06427
- **HORSEBOX UPHOLSTERY**, Westhoughton **Ref:**YH07151
- **INDESPENSION**, Blackburn **Ref:**YH07421
- **INTERTRADE ENGINEERING**, Oldham **Ref:**YH07482
- **J WAREING & SON**, Preston **Ref:**YH07630
- **MAUDSLEY COMMERCIAL BODIES**, Darwen **Ref:**YH09278
- **MAUDSLEY HORSEBOXES**, Darwen **Ref:**YH09279
- **MERCURY TRAILERS**, Burnley **Ref:**YH09467
- **MILLER TRAILERS**, Blackpool **Ref:**YH09604
- **MILLER TRAILERS**, Burnley **Ref:**YH09603
- **MUNRO COMMERCIALS**, Burscough **Ref:**YH09950
- **MURRAY, DAVID**, Oldham **Ref:**YH09965
- **NOBLET, G V**, Chorley **Ref:**YH10222
- **NOTEHOME**, Salford **Ref:**YH10337
- **NUTTALL, JOHN**, Preston **Ref:**YH10361
- **PENNINE LEISURE PRODUCTS**, Accrington **Ref:**YH10952
- **PRESCOTT, J & W**, Preston **Ref:**YH11357
- **R J & I WELLS**, Preston **Ref:**YH11547
- **TAYLORED HIRE**, Skelmersdale **Ref:**YH13915
- **THOMPSON, ALAN**, Carnforth **Ref:**YH14032
- **TRAILERCARE**, Preston **Ref:**YH14332
- **TRUCK-TEK**, Preston **Ref:**YH14419
- **VIKING TRAILERS**, Bacup **Ref:**YH14717
- **WESTWOOD HORSE BOXES**, Heywood **Ref:**YH15240

LEICESTERSHIRE

- **ALISTAIRE CLARKE TRANSPORT**, Scraptoft **Ref:**YH00281
- **BRITISH HORSE**, Leicester **Ref:**YH01948
- **CHAMBERS, J W**, Loughborough **Ref:**YH02720
- **E H HUTTON**, Melton Mowbray **Ref:**YH04407
- **G T TRAILERS**, Lutterworth **Ref:**YH05598
- **HARLOW BROTHERS**, Loughborough **Ref:**YH06440
- **HEALEY ENGINEERING**, Oakham **Ref:**YH06614
- **HERRICK HORSEBOXES**, Kirkby Mallory **Ref:**YH06715
- **KING TRAILERS**, Market Harborough **Ref:**YH08170
- **LANGROP TRAILERS CTRE**, Leicester **Ref:**YH08413
- **PEGASUS TRAILERS**, Hinckley **Ref:**YH10908
- **ROCKINGHAM LANDROVERS**, Market Harborough **Ref:**YH12035
- **TOWRITE FABRICATIONS**, Market Harborough **Ref:**YH14302
- **W E STURGESS & SONS**, Leicester **Ref:**YH14764

LINCOLNSHIRE

- **ARTIC TRAILERS**, Market Rasen **Ref:**YH00574
- **BAILEY TRAILERS**, Sleaford **Ref:**YH00796
- **BEEVER, C R**, Grantham **Ref:**YH01193
- **BIRTILL ENGINEERING**, Grantham **Ref:**YH01446
- **BLADES LIVESTOCK TRANSPORT**, Lincoln **Ref:**YH01505
- **CHAPMAN, COLIN**, Spilsby **Ref:**YH02743
- **COSGROVE & SON**, Market Rasen **Ref:**YH03350
- **DAVIES, H L L**, Grantham **Ref:**YH03941
- **EMPIRE STABLES**, Lincoln **Ref:**YH04658
- **GISSING, M**, Market Rasen **Ref:**YH05797
- **GRAYLEASE RENTALS**, Spalding **Ref:**YH06032
- **HIGGINS, G B**, Lincoln **Ref:**YH06749
- **HOLMES JOINERY**, Market Rasen **Ref:**YH06972
- **K LITTLEWORTH & SON**, Horncastle **Ref:**YH07988
- **LINTRAN**, Lincoln **Ref:**YH08670
- **MCARA**, Market Rasen **Ref:**YH09311
- **PORTLAND TOWING CTRE**, Lincoln **Ref:**YH11292
- **REDNIL EQUESTRIAN CTRE**, Lincoln **Ref:**YH11716
- **RICHARD GRICE TRAILERS**, Market Rasen **Ref:**YH11803
- **SCOTT TRAILERS**, Lincoln **Ref:**YH12533
- **SPORTY TRAILERS**, Gainsborough **Ref:**YH13239
- **WOODLANDS STABLES**, Market Rasen **Ref:**YH15711

LINCOLNSHIRE (NORTH EAST)

- **A P M COMMERCIALS**, Immingham **Ref:**YH00056
- **CLAYDEN ENGINEERING**, Grimsby **Ref:**YH02998
- **CRANE FRUEHAUF**, Immingham **Ref:**YH03560
- **GRAYLEASE RENTALS**, Grimsby **Ref:**YH06033
- **UK TRAILER PARTS**, Grimsby **Ref:**YH14551

LINCOLNSHIRE (NORTH)

- **INDESPENSION**, Scunthorpe **Ref:**YH07422
- **KRONE COMMERCIAL TRAILERS**, Ulceby **Ref:**YH08297
- **LOCKWOOD, C A**, Scunthorpe **Ref:**YH08763
- **TITAN TRAILERS**, Scunthorpe **Ref:**YH14187
- **WEIGHT MASTER TRAILERS**, Scunthorpe **Ref:**YH15050

LONDON (GREATER)

- **ANIMAL TRANSPORTATION**, London **Ref:**YH00445
- **FLETTNER VENTILATOR**, London **Ref:**YH05281
- **INDESPENSION**, London **Ref:**YH07423
- **L H H ANIMAL FEEDS**, Enfield **Ref:**YH08321
- **NEATE BRAKE CONTROLS**, Feltham **Ref:**YH10063
- **TOWING, D C**, Harrow **Ref:**YH14282
- **TRAILER SERVICES**, London **Ref:**YH14328
- **YARBOROUGH, RACHEL**, Edgware **Ref:**YH15882

MANCHESTER (GREATER)

- **ANIMAL AIRLINES**, Manchester **Ref:**YH00424
- **B K HILL TRAILERS**, Stockport **Ref:**YH00735
- **BATESON TRAILERS**, Stockport **Ref:**YH01069
- **FISHWICKS HORSEBOXES**, Bolton **Ref:**YH05244
- **HILL HIRE**, Manchester **Ref:**YH06819
- **INDESPENSION**, Bolton **Ref:**YH07425
- **INDESPENSION**, Bolton **Ref:**YH07424
- **INDESPENSION**, Bolton **Ref:**YH07426
- **LYNTON TRAILERS**, Manchester **Ref:**YH08934
- **MANCHESTER TOWBAR/TRAILER**, Manchester **Ref:**YH09068
- **RYDER TOWING EQUIPMENT**, Manchester **Ref:**YH12294
- **RYDERS FARM**, Bolton **Ref:**YH12297
- **SKYMASTER AIRCARGO**, Manchester **Ref:**YH12882
- **T I P TRAILER RENTAL**, Manchester **Ref:**YH13751
- **TOW BAR SERVICES**, Bolton **Ref:**YH14260
- **TRANSRENT**, Manchester **Ref:**YH14352
- **WILD TRAILER SERVICES**, Manchester **Ref:**YH15405

MERSEYSIDE

- **BANCROFT GRACEY**, Birkenhead **Ref:**YH00881
- **BATHER, D L**, Neston **Ref:**YH01074
- **ERIC HIGNETT ENGINEERING**, Neston **Ref:**YH04846
- **FORMBY TRAILERS**, Liverpool **Ref:**YH05374
- **G P TRAILERS & TOWBARS**, Southport **Ref:**YH05590
- **PETCARE ANIMAL SITTING SVS**, Liverpool **Ref:**YH11008

- **PORT SUNLIGHT TRAILER**, Wirral Ref:YH11279
- **RYDERS INTERNATIONAL**, Liverpool Ref:YH12298
- **TOWBARS & TRAILERS**, Southport Ref:YH14264
- **TRAILER EXPRESS**, Birkenhead Ref:YH14321
- **WIRRALL TRAILERS**, Birkenhead Ref:YH15604

MIDLANDS (WEST)

- **A H P TRAILERS**, Wolverhampton Ref:YH00035
- **A T E GROUP**, Wolverhampton Ref:YH00059
- **B J COMPONENTS**, Birmingham Ref:YH00732
- **B L R S**, Birmingham Ref:YH00736
- **CRUMP, D G**, Stourbridge Ref:YH03690
- **DEREK POINTON**, Coventry Ref:YH04074
- **EJECTORS UK**, Smethwick Ref:YH04600
- **EUROEJECTORS**, Bilston Ref:YH04896
- **FOXHILLS**, Walsall Ref:YH05435
- **INDESPENSION**, Halesowen Ref:YH07427
- **JONES, WATSON**, Bilston Ref:YH07936
- **LOVE, GORDON**, Birmingham Ref:YH08845
- **M & G TRAILERS**, Stourbridge Ref:YH08946
- **MAYPOLE**, Birmingham Ref:YH09302
- **MIDLAND TRAILER REPAIRS**, Birmingham Ref:YH09556
- **MIDLANDS EQUITRANS**, Walsall Ref:YH09558
- **OLDBURY COMPONENTS**, Wednesbury Ref:YH10482
- **S B S**, Wolverhampton Ref:YH12316
- **SHELDON TRAILER HIRE & SALES**, Solihull Ref:YH12702
- **STS AUTOELECTRICS**, Birmingham Ref:YH13593
- **T & A TRAILERS**, Walsall Ref:YH13727
- **TIP TRAILER RENTAL**, Wolverhampton Ref:YH14178
- **TOWCRAFT**, Rowley Regis Ref:YH14269
- **TOWING SHOP**, Walsall Ref:YH14281
- **TRAILER ENGINEERING**, Cradley Heath Ref:YH14320
- **WHITES**, Sutton Coldfield Ref:YH15355

NORFOLK

- **ANGLIA TRAILER MAILER**, Great Yarmouth Ref:YH00415
- **CRANE FRUEHAUF**, Dereham Ref:YH03561
- **DEREHAM CONVERSIONS**, Dereham Ref:YH04072
- **EQUILUXE ENGINEERING**, King's Lynn Ref:YH04752
- **F W HUME & SONS**, Diss Ref:YH05001
- **FENLAND TRAILERS**, Thetford Ref:YH05145
- **FITZROY TRAILERS**, Great Yarmouth Ref:YH05249
- **GENERAL TRAILERS**, Dereham Ref:YH05707
- **GOTTS, A R**, Norwich Ref:YH05946
- **HALL FARM FORAGE**, Happisburgh Ref:YH06304
- **HORSE BOXES WELDING**, Attleborough Ref:YH07113
- **INDESPENSION**, Norwich Ref:YH07428
- **KEITH GOOCH TRAILERS**, Norwich Ref:YH08035
- **LODDON**, Norwich Ref:YH08766
- **MID-NORFOLK CANOPIES/TRAILERS**, Dereham Ref:YH09561
- **NORWICH TRAILER CTRE**, Norwich Ref:YH10334
- **PAGE TRAILERS**, Great Yarmouth Ref:YH10678
- **PAYNE BROS**, Fakenham Ref:YH10846
- **REYNOLDS MOTORS**, Cromer Ref:YH11775
- **ROPER SERVICES**, Norwich Ref:YH12083
- **TIRUS EQUESTRIAN PRODUCTS**, Norwich Ref:YH14185
- **TOW-WIN EQUIPMENT**, Norwich Ref:YH14304
- **TRUCKS 'N' TRAILERS**, Norwich Ref:YH14418
- **TRUCKS 'N' TRAILERS**, Norwich Ref:YH14417
- **WOOLNOUGH, B & S**, Dereham Ref:YH15769
- **WRIGHT TRAILER**, Norwich Ref:YH15830
- **WRIGHT, W G**, Norwich Ref:YH15842

NORTHAMPTONSHIRE

- **AAPS**, Wellingborough Ref:YH00070
- **BRIAN JAMES TRAILERS**, Daventry Ref:YH01861
- **BURWELL HILL GARAGES**, Brackley Ref:YH02298
- **DRYDEN TRAILERS**, Northampton Ref:YH04299
- **EQUIBRAND**, Charwelton Ref:YH04734
- **F H BURGESS**, Northampton Ref:YH04993
- **H S E**, Corby Ref:YH06236
- **INDESPENSION**, Northampton Ref:YH07429
- **KETTERING TRAILER CTRE**, Kettering Ref:YH08107
- **LOGGIN, MERRICK**, Brackley Ref:YH08776
- **MANOR FARM RIDING SCHOOL**, Wellingborough Ref:YH09106
- **MEU**, Kettering Ref:YH09505
- **MOBILE PROMOTIONS COMPANY**, Titchmarsh Ref:YH09689
- **SCOTTS OF THRAPSTON**, Kettering Ref:YH12561
- **TOWABILITY TRAILERS**, Wellingborough Ref:YH14261
- **TRAILOAD TRAILERS**, Corby Ref:YH14339
- **WESTAWAY MOTORS**, Maidwell Ref:YH15182

NORTHUMBERLAND

- **BROWN TRAILERS**, Cramlington Ref:YH02094
- **CLASSIC CARRIAGES**, Mindrum Ref:YH02982
- **DALE TRAILERS**, Alnwick Ref:YH03823
- **HUNTERS**, Stocksfield Ref:YH07301
- **KENT BROS**, Morpeth Ref:YH08079

NOTTINGHAMSHIRE

- **APPLEYARD TRAILERS**, Nottingham Ref:YH00484
- **BENNINGTON CARRIAGES**, Newark Ref:YH01275
- **BINGHAM TRAILERS**, Nottingham Ref:YH01421
- **BROOKS, J V**, Nottingham Ref:YH02065
- **DEAKIN, STEWART E**, Sutton-In-Ashfield Ref:YH03987
- **DUNNS TRAILERS**, Nottingham Ref:YH04356
- **INDESPENSION**, Nottingham Ref:YH07430
- **L H WOODHOUSE**, Ruddington Ref:YH08322
- **LANGAR ENGINEERING**, Nottingham Ref:YH08398
- **LILLEY, M J**, Nottingham Ref:YH08622
- **NOTTINGHAM HORSE TRANSPORT**, Nottingham Ref:YH10340
- **NOTTINGHAM TRAILER SPARES**, Nottingham Ref:YH10345
- **RANCH TRUCKS & TRAILERS**, Nottingham Ref:YH11627
- **S E B INTERNATIONAL**, Nottingham Ref:YH12322
- **T WILSON & SON**, Mansfield Ref:YH13768
- **TOW BAR & TRAILER CTRE**, Worksop Ref:YH14258
- **WHITTAKER HORSE BOXES**, Retford Ref:YH15373

OXFORDSHIRE

- **BANBURY TRAILERS**, Banbury Ref:YH00880
- **BICESTER TRAILERS**, Bicester Ref:YH01391
- **CENTAUR TRANSPORT**, Bicester Ref:YH02684
- **CROSS COUNTRY VEHICLES**, Witney Ref:YH03644
- **D J SLATTER HORSE TRANSPORT**, Chipping Norton Ref:YH03788
- **E P BARRUS**, Bicester Ref:YH04418
- **F N PILE & SON**, Banbury Ref:YH04996
- **HINCHLIFFE, M**, Faringdon Ref:YH06866
- **HOPPER**, Banbury Ref:YH07059
- **J S FRASER PROPERTIES**, Witney Ref:YH07615
- **J WALLINGTON & SONS**, Bicester Ref:YH07629
- **KUBOTA**, Thame Ref:YH08300
- **OLYMPIC COACHBUILDERS**, Abingdon Ref:YH10505
- **P FROUD & SON**, Wantage Ref:YH10639
- **PREMIER TRAILERS**, Henley-on-Thames Ref:YH11351
- **VENTURENEED**, Wallingford Ref:YH14680

SHROPSHIRE

- **BACHE, R E**, Bridgnorth Ref:YH00765
- **BORDER TRAILER WORKS**, Oswestry Ref:YH01646
- **BULKRITE TRUCK BODIES**, Shrewsbury Ref:YH02212
- **CHALLONER, JOHN**, Bucknell Ref:YH02713
- **D S PINCHES & SONS**, Shrewsbury Ref:YH03808
- **E T C SAW MILLS**, Ellesmere Ref:YH04428
- **EVANS & BROOKS**, Ludlow Ref:YH04912
- **G H BRADSHAW & SONS**, Whitchurch Ref:YH05579
- **H F PUGH & SONS**, Craven Arms Ref:YH06221
- **JERVIS, JOHN**, Ludlow Ref:YH07758
- **K P COMMERCIALS**, Shrewsbury Ref:YH07990
- **NORTH SHROPSHIRE TRAILER CTRE**, Market Drayton Ref:YH10282
- **REYNOLDS, M H**, Craven Arms Ref:YH11779
- **TEME TRAILERS**, Craven Arms Ref:YH13944
- **TRAILERS & COMPONENTS**, Craven Arms Ref:YH14336
- **TRUCK & TRAILER EQUIPMENT**, Craven Arms Ref:YH14416
- **WHITE, K B**, Ludlow Ref:YH15332
- **YEOWARD, R**, Ludlow Ref:YH15907

SOMERSET

- **BAILEY, RALPH**, Bridgwater Ref:YH00805
- **BRIDGWATER TRAILER CTRE**, Bridgwater Ref:YH01887
- **BUFFALO TRAILER SYSTEMS**, Yeovil Ref:YH02210
- **CRUICKSHANK TRAILERS**, Crewkerne Ref:YH03688
- **D & G HORSE TRANSPORTATION**, Cheddar Ref:YH03772
- **EQUESTRIAN ENGINEERING**, Templecombe Ref:YH04700
- **HILLYERS HORSE BOXES**, Street Ref:YH06862
- **J A E TRAILERS**, Ilminster Ref:YH07554
- **LAMPERT TRAILERS**, Somerton Ref:YH08376
- **PASSMORE, M J**, Minehead Ref:YH10811
- **RICHARDS, PETER**, Shepton Mallet Ref:YH11812
- **SELWAY, K D**, Frome Ref:YH12627
- **SPARKFORD SAWMILLS**, Yeovil Ref:YH13177
- **STEVE'S TRAILERS**, Minehead Ref:YH13452
- **SUTTON OAKS**, Bridgwater Ref:YH13675
- **TOWER FARM TRAILERS**, Bruton Ref:YH14275
- **VINCENTS OF YEOVIL**, Yeovil Ref:YH14727
- **WALTER, ALAN**, Taunton Ref:YH14884
- **YEOVIL TRAILERS**, Yeovil Ref:YH15906

SOMERSET (NORTH)

- **BOULTERS OF BANWELL**, Banwell Ref:YH01673
- **SMART HORSEBOXES**, Banwell Ref:YH12918
- **SMART HORSEBOXES**, Weston-Super-Mare Ref:YH12917
- **SOUTH WEST TRAILERS**, Weston-Super-Mare Ref:YH13119
- **SPRINGFIELD**, Claverham Ref:YH13252

STAFFORDSHIRE

- **AZTEC TRAILER**, Tamworth Ref:YH00708
- **BAILEY, M F**, Stone Ref:YH00803
- **BESWICK, H F**, Leek Ref:YH01329

- **D R G TRAILERS**, Cannock **Ref:**YH03804
- **DAVID LEWIS INT**, Burton-on-Trent **Ref:**YH03922
- **DEELEYS**, Burton-on-Trent **Ref:**YH04017
- **DOWNES, T W**, Stoke-on-Trent **Ref:**YH04228
- **ELLMORE HORSE TRANSPORT**, Lichfield **Ref:**YH04630
- **HANFORD TRAILER SPARES**, Stoke-on-Trent **Ref:**YH06385
- **HATFIELD'S HORSE TRANSPORT**, Stafford **Ref:**YH06532
- **HAYWOOD DESIGN**, Stafford **Ref:**YH06596
- **INDESPENSION**, Stoke-on-Trent **Ref:**YH07431
- **LEEK TRAILERS**, Leek **Ref:**YH08531
- **LUKE TRAILERS**, Leek **Ref:**YH08893
- **PYE, E**, Leek **Ref:**YH11469
- **SNIPE TRAILERS**, Cannock **Ref:**YH13031
- **STAFFORDSHIRE TRAILERS**, Lichfield **Ref:**YH13325
- **STURGE TRAILERS**, Newcastle **Ref:**YH13613
- **TRAILERCARE**, Stoke-on-Trent **Ref:**YH14333
- **W BARKER & SONS**, Rugeley **Ref:**YH14752
- **WHALLEY'S LIVESTOCK**, Tamworth **Ref:**YH15261
- **WOFFORD INT HORSE TRANSPORT**, Lichfield **Ref:**YH15643

SUFFOLK

- **ALSION THOM TRANSPORT**, Newmarket **Ref:**YH00337
- **ANGLIA HORSE TRANSPORT**, Ipswich **Ref:**YH00413
- **ANGLIAN TRAILER CTRE**, Bury St Edmunds **Ref:**YH00417
- **BILL FELLOWES TRAILERS**, Newmarket **Ref:**YH01408
- **BLOSS, B**, Ipswich **Ref:**YH01560
- **COLLEASE TRAILER RENTALS**, Felixstowe **Ref:**YH03175
- **COUNTY COACHBUILDERS**, Hadleigh **Ref:**YH03485
- **D BLOWERS**, Halesworth **Ref:**YH03781
- **D BLOWERS**, Halesworth **Ref:**YH03782
- **D BLOWERS**, Halesworth **Ref:**YH03780
- **EDWARDS TRAILERS**, Bury St Edmunds **Ref:**YH04575
- **EQUISAVE HORSE AMBULANCES**, Newmarket **Ref:**YH04816
- **GOUDY, RAY**, Stowmarket **Ref:**YH05948
- **HARRIS OF WHEPSTEAD**, Bury St Edmunds **Ref:**YH06463
- **HI TECH MAINTENANCE**, Felixstowe **Ref:**YH06738
- **HTL**, Bury St Edmunds **Ref:**YH07249
- **HUGHES RACEHORSE TRANSPORT**, Newmarket **Ref:**YH07256
- **HUNTON LEGG**, Ipswich **Ref:**YH07307
- **INDESPENSION**, Ipswich **Ref:**YH07432
- **INT RACEHORSE TRANSPORT**, Newmarket **Ref:**YH07472
- **J.SAVILL INT HORSE TRANSPORT**, Newmarket **Ref:**YH07635
- **M C INT HORSE TRANSPORT**, Newmarket **Ref:**YH08956
- **MELLON & BODEN**, Bury St Edmunds **Ref:**YH09454
- **MERIDIAN TRAILERS**, Beccles **Ref:**YH09477
- **ORWELL ARENA**, Ipswich **Ref:**YH10556
- **OWEN FARMING TRANSPORT**, Bury St Edmunds **Ref:**YH10597
- **PARKES INT TRANSPORT**, Newmarket **Ref:**YH10756
- **R T NELSON & SON**, Beccles **Ref:**YH11565
- **RAPIDO HORSE SERVICES**, Newmarket **Ref:**YH11640
- **S D H COACHWORKS**, Bury St Edmunds **Ref:**YH12321
- **T I P EUROPE**, Felixstowe **Ref:**YH13750
- **THOM, ALISON**, Newmarket **Ref:**YH14003
- **TIP-CTR EUROPE**, Felixstowe **Ref:**YH14180
- **TREASURE SEEKERS**, Newmarket **Ref:**YH14357
- **UNIVERSAL TRAILERS**, Ipswich **Ref:**YH14578
- **W & G SERVICES**, Felixstowe **Ref:**YH14747
- **WELTON NORTHSEN**, Felixstowe **Ref:**YH15100

SURREY

- **ASCOT HORSE BOXES INT**, Redhill **Ref:**YH00582
- **ASCOT PARK**, Woking **Ref:**YH00583
- **ASCOT TIMBER BUILDINGS**, Haslemere **Ref:**YH00585
- **B & R INT HORSE TRANSPORT**, Farnham **Ref:**YH00714
- **B H C COACH BUILDERS**, Staines **Ref:**YH00724
- **BARNCRAFT**, Lingfield **Ref:**YH00968
- **CROYDON HORSE & CATTLE**, Warlingham **Ref:**YH03686
- **HARMANS**, Haslemere **Ref:**YH06443
- **I T A**, Walton-on-Thames **Ref:**YH07369
- **INDESPENSION**, Redhill **Ref:**YH07433
- **J CROOK & SONS**, Ashford **Ref:**YH07577
- **NATIONWIDE PROP/PET SITTERS**, Worcester Park **Ref:**YH10048
- **NORMANDY HORSE TRAILERS**, Guildford **Ref:**YH10241
- **PET CABS**, Croydon **Ref:**YH11001
- **ROVERTOW**, Warlingham **Ref:**YH12150
- **S R S**, Sunbury-on-Thames **Ref:**YH12333
- **STANWELL TRAILERS**, Staines **Ref:**YH13383
- **TOW-SAFE TRAILER HIRE & SALES**, Chertsey **Ref:**YH14303
- **TRAILER CTRE**, Croydon **Ref:**YH14318
- **TRAILER CTRE**, Guildford **Ref:**YH14319
- **TRAIL-O-WAY**, Walton-on-Thames **Ref:**YH14340
- **TRANS-PET**, Morden **Ref:**YH14348
- **TURNER, A**, Woking **Ref:**YH14474
- **WESTLANDS**, Horley **Ref:**YH15218
- **WOODSTOCK SOUTH STABLES**, Chessington **Ref:**YH15751

SUSSEX (EAST)

- **B & B TRAILERS**, Uckfield **Ref:**YH00710
- **B C M TRAILER HIRE**, Hailsham **Ref:**YH00719
- **BATTLE TRAILERS**, Battle **Ref:**YH01080
- **BLYTHE HAULAGE**, Wadhurst **Ref:**YH01579
- **G A COMMERCIALS**, Pevensey **Ref:**YH05569
- **GREENSLADE HORSE TRAILERS**, Robertsbridge **Ref:**YH06101
- **GUMTREE ENTERPRISES**, Plumpton **Ref:**YH06191
- **HERONDEN INT HORSE TRANSPORT**, Rye **Ref:**YH06713
- **HOAD, R P C**, Lewes **Ref:**YH06890
- **HOBDEN, W J**, Heathfield **Ref:**YH06898
- **HYLAND LIVESTOCK CARRYING**, Robertsbridge **Ref:**YH07356
- **LEVADE SYSTEMS**, Hartfield **Ref:**YH08572
- **MARCO TRAILERS**, Newhaven **Ref:**YH09144
- **SILVERDALE TRANSPORT**, Robertsbridge **Ref:**YH12814
- **TICEHURST, G J**, Mayfield **Ref:**YH14125
- **TRAILER HIRE**, Hastings **Ref:**YH14322

SUSSEX (WEST)

- **A C DAWSON & SONS**, Horsham **Ref:**YH00023
- **C A BOWERS & SONS**, Crawley **Ref:**YH02360
- **DAVID WILSON'S TRAILERS**, Horsted Keynes **Ref:**YH03925
- **DOVETAIL TRAILER**, Chichester **Ref:**YH04219
- **DUNCAN ENGLAND ENTERPRISES**, Horsham **Ref:**YH04334
- **H T GREEN & SON**, Billingshurst **Ref:**YH06241
- **HEDGERS HORSE TRANSPORT**, Chichester **Ref:**YH06642
- **INSTONE AIR SERVICES**, Pulborough **Ref:**YH07463
- **L M COMMERCIALS**, Chichester **Ref:**YH08325
- **PEPER HAROW HORSE TRAILERS**, Horsham **Ref:**YH10968
- **SLINFOLD TRAILERS**, Horsham **Ref:**YH12898
- **SUSSEX TOWING BRACKETS**, Worthing **Ref:**YH13663
- **UNIVERSAL TRAILERS**, Billingshurst **Ref:**YH14579
- **WOODRUFF, RAY**, Horsham **Ref:**YH15732
- **WORTHING TRAILERS & TOWBARS**, Worthing **Ref:**YH15804

TYNE AND WEAR

- **A & J TRAILER MADE**, Newcastle-upon-Tyne **Ref:**YH00013
- **CENTRAL TRAILER RENTCO**, Gateshead **Ref:**YH02695
- **HOUGHTON TRAILERS**, Houghton Le Spring **Ref:**YH07203
- **IFOR WILLIAMS TRAILERS**, Blaydon-on-Tyne **Ref:**YH07393
- **INDESPENSION**, Newcastle-upon-Tyne **Ref:**YH07434
- **JOSEPH BAILEY & SONS**, Houghton Le Spring **Ref:**YH07942
- **QUARRY PARK STABLES**, Gateshead **Ref:**YH11483
- **R L PROUDLOCK & SONS**, Newcastle-upon-Tyne **Ref:**YH11554
- **SUNDERLAND TRAILER & TOWING**, Sunderland **Ref:**YH13642
- **TRAILERCO**, Houghton Le Spring **Ref:**YH14334

WARWICKSHIRE

- **A M S**, Nuneaton **Ref:**YH00051
- **BLT TRAILERS**, Warwick **Ref:**YH01561
- **HENLEY TIMBER**, Solihull **Ref:**YH06675
- **HIRONS, G T**, Warwick **Ref:**YH06884
- **OLDFIELD, JOHN**, Leamington Spa **Ref:**YH10487
- **PEAK TRAILERS**, Alcester **Ref:**YH10865
- **PITTHAM & BODILY**, Southam **Ref:**YH11156
- **RHINO BODIES**, Warwick **Ref:**YH11786
- **RUGBY TRAILER CTRE**, Rugby **Ref:**YH12219
- **T I P C T R**, Nuneaton **Ref:**YH13748
- **T SPIERS & SONS**, Warwick **Ref:**YH13765
- **WALKER, IAN**, Warwick **Ref:**YH14850
- **WARWICK BUILDINGS**, Rugby **Ref:**YH14945
- **WARWICKSHIRE TRAILERS**, Solihull **Ref:**YH14953
- **WHITEHALL, G**, Rugby **Ref:**YH15341

WILTSHIRE

- **A J STOKES & SONS**, Warminster **Ref:**YH00043
- **AMESBURY TRAILER HIRE**, Salisbury **Ref:**YH00366
- **AUTO TRAILER SERVICES**, Chippenham **Ref:**YH00671
- **BRYANTS TRANSPORT**, Calne **Ref:**YH02169
- **BUTLER TRAILERS**, Calne **Ref:**YH02321
- **CHIPPENHAM TRAILER HIRE**, Chippenham **Ref:**YH02864
- **COPPERFIELD STABLES**, Salisbury **Ref:**YH03302
- **CORBRIDGE FABRICATIONS**, Marlborough **Ref:**YH03309
- **DEVIZES TRAILER CTRE**, Devizes **Ref:**YH04091
- **FIELDFARE TRAILERS**, Salisbury **Ref:**YH05192
- **FOXHAVEN STABLES**, Westbury **Ref:**YH05432
- **GEORGE SMITH HORSEBOXES**, Salisbury **Ref:**YH05719
- **JON WILLIAM STABLES**, Chippenham **Ref:**YH07872
- **MALMESBURY TRAILERS**, Malmesbury **Ref:**YH09053
- **SWINDON VOLVO TRAILER HIRE**, Swindon **Ref:**YH13711
- **TATE, J**, Salisbury **Ref:**YH13872
- **W A ANNETTS & SON**, Salisbury **Ref:**YH14749
- **WARDALL BLOODSTOCK SHIPPING**, Salisbury **Ref:**YH14912

WORCESTERSHIRE

- **ANCHOR TRAILERS**, Kidderminster **Ref:**YH00377
- **AUTOTOW**, Redditch **Ref:**YH00673
- **BARROD HORSE BOXES**, Stourport-on-Severn **Ref:**YH01024
- **CASTLE HORSEBOXES**, Kidderminster **Ref:**YH02629
- **CENTRIFORCE**, Worcester **Ref:**YH02697
- **COTTRILL EQSTN VEHICLE SVS**, Worcester **Ref:**YH03388
- **COUNTASH TRAILERS**, Kidderminster **Ref:**YH03392
- **E S EVERITT**, Redditch **Ref:**YH04423
- **FRONT RUNNER RACE**, Malvern **Ref:**YH05517
- **HAZLEWOOD TRAILERS**, Evesham **Ref:**YH06605
- **LONGBRIDGE ENGINEERING**, Bromsgrove **Ref:**YH08807
- **LOWES GARAGE SVS**, Worcester **Ref:**YH08872
- **OAKLAND HORSEBOXES**, Little Witley **Ref:**YH10388
- **P D LEVI & SON**, Droitwich **Ref:**YH10635
- **PERSHORE TRANSPORT**, Evesham **Ref:**YH10994
- **RAXTER MOTOR ENGINEERING**, Bromsgrove **Ref:**YH11671
- **SPENCER, G**, Malvern **Ref:**YH13199
- **TARRINGTON TRAILERS**, Bromsgrove **Ref:**YH13871
- **TOMICK TRAILERS**, Droitwich **Ref:**YH14220
- **VALE AUTOBUILD**, Pershore **Ref:**YH14631
- **WALKERS OF WORCESTERSHIRE**, Kidderminster **Ref:**YH14859
- **WICKHAM TRAILER HIRE**, Evesham **Ref:**YH15384

YORKSHIRE (EAST)

- **C T R**, Hull **Ref:**YH02393
- **EASTERBY TRAILERS**, Driffield **Ref:**YH04491
- **GUTHRIE RIGBY**, Holme upon Spalding Moor **Ref:**YH06195
- **HAIRSINE TRAILER REPAIRS**, Hull **Ref:**YH06288
- **JACKSON, ADRIAN**, Hull **Ref:**YH07642
- **JENNISON, A P**, Driffield **Ref:**YH07749
- **TRAILER PRODUCTION**, Goole **Ref:**YH14325

YORKSHIRE (NORTH)

- **B GREGSON & SON**, Harrogate **Ref:**YH00723
- **BECKHOUSE CARRIAGES**, Pickering **Ref:**YH01149
- **BROWN, A D**, Malton **Ref:**YH02096
- **C & C HORSE TRANSPORT**, Thirsk **Ref:**YH02354
- **CARL BROWN HORSE TRANSPORT**, York **Ref:**YH02539
- **CAWOOD, WILLIAM**, Malton **Ref:**YH02668
- **COUNTY GARAGE**, York **Ref:**YH03488
- **DALES HORSE BOXES**, Skipton **Ref:**YH03827
- **DURALOC**, Thirsk **Ref:**YH04364
- **E DODSWORTH & SON**, York **Ref:**YH04402
- **E WARD & SON**, York **Ref:**YH04431
- **EUROLEASE**, Thirsk **Ref:**YH04901
- **FLETCHER TRAILERS**, Richmond **Ref:**YH05273
- **FRED WADDINGTON & SON**, Richmond **Ref:**YH05477
- **FRIARS HILL STABLES**, York **Ref:**YH05501
- **G & A HORSE TRANSPORT**, Harrogate **Ref:**YH05561
- **GOODRICKS EQUESTRIAN**, Osbaldwick **Ref:**YH05907
- **GRAHAM EDWARDS TRAILERS**, York **Ref:**YH05964
- **HI-LINE HORSEBOXES**, Cawood **Ref:**YH06809
- **HORSE BOX SERVICES**, Selby **Ref:**YH07112
- **I J A ENGINEERING**, Thirsk **Ref:**YH07366
- **J M BELL & SON**, Thirsk **Ref:**YH07595
- **J S W & SON COACHBUILDERS**, Northallerton **Ref:**YH07619
- **M A FABRICATION**, Pickering **Ref:**YH08952
- **R A BUSBY & SON**, Richmond **Ref:**YH11510
- **RICHARDSON RICE**, York **Ref:**YH11813
- **S A S TRAILERS**, Thirsk **Ref:**YH12315
- **SCALING TRAILERS**, York **Ref:**YH12481
- **SCE**, Richmond **Ref:**YH12513
- **TOCKWITH TRAILER HIRE**, York **Ref:**YH14197
- **UTILITY INTERNATIONAL**, Northallerton **Ref:**YH14624

YORKSHIRE (SOUTH)

- **AUTAUX-SEYMOUR**, Doncaster **Ref:**YH00669
- **BAKEWELL TRAILERS**, Sheffield **Ref:**YH00828
- **BDS**, Sheffield **Ref:**YH01102
- **CADDY TRAILORS**, Sheffield **Ref:**YH02410
- **EUROFLEET RENTAL**, Sheffield **Ref:**YH04900
- **GB TRUCK & TRAILER RENTAL**, Rotherham **Ref:**YH05685
- **JOHN HUDSON**, Doncaster **Ref:**YH07795
- **MOBILE TOWBAR SERVICES**, Sheffield **Ref:**YH09691
- **MONTRACON**, Doncaster **Ref:**YH09735
- **NEEDHAM, J**, Doncaster **Ref:**YH10067
- **ROWLING, W W**, Doncaster **Ref:**YH12173
- **S W TRAILER HIRE**, Barnsley **Ref:**YH12338
- **SPRINGVALE CARRIAGES**, Sheffield **Ref:**YH13262
- **STAG TRAILERS**, Sheffield **Ref:**YH13327
- **T P TRAILERS**, Doncaster **Ref:**YH13762
- **TRAILER SUPPLIES**, Doncaster **Ref:**YH14330
- **WHEATON TRUCK & TRAILER SALES**, Barnsley **Ref:**YH15269

YORKSHIRE (WEST)

- **A RUDD & SON**, Leeds **Ref:**YH00057
- **ARMITAGES TRAILERS**, Knottingley **Ref:**YH00538
- **B T H HIRE & SALES**, Leeds **Ref:**YH00749
- **BARNES & WINDER**, Leeds **Ref:**YH00969
- **BARS R US**, Castleford **Ref:**YH01035
- **BRADLEY DOUBLELOCK**, Bingley **Ref:**YH01749
- **BRIGG, W NORRIS**, Bradford **Ref:**YH01907
- **BROWNBRIDGE, JOSEPH**, Pontefract **Ref:**YH02136
- **C W S HORSEBOX WINDOWS**, Leeds **Ref:**YH02408
- **CENTRAL TRAILER RENTCO**, Leeds **Ref:**YH02696
- **EDWARDS MOBILE TOW BARS**, Brighouse **Ref:**YH04572
- **EUR-O-WAY TRAILER HIRE**, Keighley **Ref:**YH04910
- **EVERALL HORSE BOXES**, Otley **Ref:**YH04949
- **GARFORTH LIVERY YARD**, Leeds **Ref:**YH05651
- **GENERAL TRAILERS**, Ossett **Ref:**YH05708
- **HIGHWOOD**, Ossett **Ref:**YH06803
- **HIGHWOOD HORSEBOXES**, Wakefield **Ref:**YH06804
- **HILLAM TRAILERS**, Cleckheaton **Ref:**YH06837
- **HODGSONS MINIBUS HIRE**, Keighley **Ref:**YH06914
- **INDESPENSION**, Leeds **Ref:**YH07435
- **J C RIDDIOUGH**, Bingley **Ref:**YH07574
- **J C RIDDIOUGH TRAILER SALES**, Bradford **Ref:**YH07575
- **JENKINSONS HUDDERSFIELD**, Huddersfield **Ref:**YH07741
- **KINSLEY GREEN FARM**, Pontefract **Ref:**YH08221
- **KLIPONOFF TRAILER HIRE/SALES**, Halifax **Ref:**YH08248
- **LATHAM FARM**, Cleckheaton **Ref:**YH08445
- **M & B TRAILER SALES**, Dewsbury **Ref:**YH08945
- **MALT KILN TRAILERS**, Sowerby Bridge **Ref:**YH09055
- **MILLEECA HORSEBOXES**, Leeds **Ref:**YH09597
- **MTS MOBILE TRAILER SERVICES**, Castleford **Ref:**YH09919
- **PARKER MERCHANTING**, Rothwell **Ref:**YH10746
- **RUSKIN HORSE DRAWN CARRIAGES**, Leeds **Ref:**YH12250
- **S C S TRAILER SERVICES**, Bradford **Ref:**YH12318
- **SWILLINGTON TRAILER CTRE**, Leeds **Ref:**YH13707
- **T C TRAILER**, Keighley **Ref:**YH13734
- **TAYLORS TRAILERS**, Huddersfield **Ref:**YH13919
- **TIP TRAILER RENTAL**, Knottingley **Ref:**YH14179
- **TOWBARS SERVICES**, Wakefield **Ref:**YH14266
- **TRI TRAILER RENTALS**, Dewsbury **Ref:**YH14390
- **VEHICLE WINDOW CTRE**, Castleford **Ref:**YH14673
- **WATSON TRAILERS**, Batley **Ref:**YH14982
- **WATSON, R J**, Dewsbury **Ref:**YH14990
- **YORKSHIRE EQUESTRIAN FLOORING**, Leeds **Ref:**YH15920

ARENAS

COUNTY CORK

- **CASTLEWHITE**, Cork **Ref:**YH02646

COUNTY OFFALY

- **ANNAGHARVEY FARM**, Tullamore **Ref:**YH00450

BLACKSMITHS

COUNTY CORK

- **CASTLEWHITE**, Cork **Ref:**YH02646

BLOOD STOCK AGENCIES

COUNTY DUBLIN

- **EDDIE BRENNAN**, Dublin **Ref:**YH04540

COUNTY KILDARE

- **OAKLODGE STUD**, Naas **Ref:**YH10401

COUNTY OFFALY

- **ETTER SPORTS HORSES**, Bellmont **Ref:**YH04886

BREEDERS

COUNTY CARLOW

- **CARTER, EDWARD**, Busherstown **Ref:**YH02606

COUNTY CORK

- **CASTLEWHITE**, Cork **Ref:**YH02646

COUNTY KILDARE

- **ABBERVILLE & MEADOW CT STUD**, The Curragh **Ref:**YH00074
- **AIRLIE STUD**, Maynooth **Ref:**YH00224
- **BARODA STUD**, Newbridge **Ref:**YH00993
- **BARRETTSTOWN FARM**, Newbridge **Ref:**YH01018
- **BROADFIELD STUD**, Naas **Ref:**YH01996
- **BROGUESTOWN STUD**, Kill **Ref:**YH02020
- **BROWNSTOWN STUD**, The Curragh **Ref:**YH02147
- **CASTLEMARTIN STUD**, Kildare **Ref:**YH02644
- **CORDUFF STUD**, Kildare **Ref:**YH03313
- **COTTAGE STUD**, Kilcock **Ref:**YH03381
- **DAMASTOWN STUD**, Kilcock **Ref:**YH03855
- **DERRINSTOWN STUD**, Maynooth **Ref:**YH04078
- **DERRYVARROGE STUD**, Naas **Ref:**YH04080
- **EYREFIELD LODGE STUD**, The Curragh **Ref:**YH04978
- **FORENAUGHTS STUD**, Naas **Ref:**YH05331
- **GILLTOWN STUD**, Kilcullen **Ref:**YH05788
- **GRANGEMORE STUD**, The Curragh **Ref:**YH06002
- **HEBERTSTOWN STUD FARM**, Newbridge **Ref:**YH06636
- **JIGGINSTOWN HOUSE STABLES**, Naas **Ref:**YH07766
- **KILDANGAN STUD**, Kildare **Ref:**YH08130
- **KILDARAGH STUD**, Kildangan **Ref:**YH08131
- **LOUGHBROWN STUD**, The Curragh **Ref:**YH08839
- **LOUGHTOWN STUD**, Naas **Ref:**YH08841
- **MORRISTOWN LATTIN STUD**, Naas **Ref:**YH09843
- **MOYGLARE STUD**, Maynooth **Ref:**YH09911
- **NEW IRISH SANT PANCRAZIO**, Newbridge **Ref:**YH10110
- **NEWBERRY STUD FARM**, Kildare **Ref:**YH10123
- **NEWTON STUD**, Naas **Ref:**YH10174
- **OAKLAWN STUD**, Kildare **Ref:**YH10394
- **OAKLODGE STUD**, Naas **Ref:**YH10401
- **OLD MEADOW STUD**, Naas **Ref:**YH10464
- **OWENSTOWN STUD**, Maynooth **Ref:**YH10610
- **PIER HSE STUD**, The Curragh **Ref:**YH11090
- **RATHASKER STUD**, Naas **Ref:**YH11653
- **SUNNYHILL STUD**, Kildare **Ref:**YH13646
- **YEOMANSTOWN STUD**, Naas **Ref:**YH15905

COUNTY KILKENNY

- **BANOGUE STUD**, Callan **Ref:**YH00907

COUNTY MAYO

- **ASHFORD EQUESTRIAN CTRE**, Mayo **Ref:**YH00600

COUNTY MEATH

- **SHEKLETON, ALAN**, Carrickmacross **Ref:**YH12700

COUNTY OFFALY

- **ETTER SPORTS HORSES**, Bellmont **Ref:**YH04886

CLUBS/ASSOCIATIONS

COUNTY CORK

- **EVENTING IRELAND**, Douglas **Ref:**YH04941
- **IRISH HORSE SOCIETY**, Cobh **Ref:**YH07495
- **IRISH PIEBALD & SKEWBALD ASS**, Fermoy **Ref:**YH07498
- **LADY JOCKEY ASSOCIATION**, Cork **Ref:**YH08337

COUNTY DUBLIN

- **EQUESTRIAN FEDERATION**, Castleknock **Ref:**YH04703
- **IHA**, Dublin **Ref:**YH07395
- **LEOPARDSTOWN CLUB**, Dublin **Ref:**YH08554

COUNTY GALWAY

- **EVENTING IRELAND**, Ballinasloe **Ref:**YH04943
- **GALWAY RACE COMMITTEE**, Ballybrit **Ref:**YH05629

COUNTY KILDARE

- **EVENTING IRELAND**, Kilcock **Ref:**YH04945
- **EVENTING IRELAND**, Kill **Ref:**YH04944
- **KILDARE HORSE DEVELOPMENT**, The Curragh **Ref:**YH08132
- **NAAS RACECOURSE**, Naas **Ref:**YH10006
- **WEATHERBYS IRELAND**, Naas **Ref:**YH15025

COUNTY MAYO

- **IRISH DRAUGHT HORSE SOCIETY**, Mayo **Ref:**YH07491

COUNTY OFFALY

- **WESTERN RIDING ASS OF IRELAND**, Shannon **Ref:**YH15205

COUNTY WEXFORD

- **EVENTING IRELAND**, Gorey **Ref:**YH04946

EQUESTRIAN CENTRES

COUNTY CLARE

- **BANNER EQUESTRIAN**, Ennis **Ref:**YH00906
- **WILLIE DALY RIDING SCHOOL**, Ennistymon **Ref:**YH15487

COUNTY CORK

- **BANTRY HORSE RIDING**, Bantry **Ref:**YH00912
- **CASTLEWHITE**, Cork **Ref:**YH02646

COUNTY DUBLIN

- **CALLIAGHSTOWN EQUESTRIAN**, Rathcoole **Ref:**YH02449

COUNTY GALWAY

- **CLEGGAN TREKKING CTRE**, Connemara **Ref:**YH03015
- **FARM EQUESTRIAN CTRE**, Loughrea **Ref:**YH05056

COUNTY KERRY

- **BLACKVALLEY EQUESTRIAN**, Derrycarna **Ref:**YH01500
- **EAGLE LODGE EQUESTRIAN CTRE**, Tralee **Ref:**YH04438

COUNTY KILDARE

- **ABBEYFIELD EQUESTRIAN FARM**, Clane **Ref:**YH00093
- **ACORN EQUESTRIAN CTRE**, Maynooth **Ref:**YH00147
- **BOROHARD EQUESTRIAN CTRE**, Naas **Ref:**YH01652
- **COILOG EVENTING**, Naas **Ref:**YH03139
- **COPPERALLEY EQUESTRIAN CTRE**, Maynooth **Ref:**YH03301
- **KILKEA LODGE FARM**, Castledermot **Ref:**YH08138
- **KILL EQUESTRIAN CTRE**, Kill **Ref:**YH08140
- **NAAS RACECOURSE**, Naas **Ref:**YH10006
- **OSBERTOWN RIDING CTRE**, Naas **Ref:**YH10558
- **PUNCHESTOWN NATIONAL CTRE**, Naas **Ref:**YH11458

COUNTY LIMERICK

- **ADARE EQUESTRIAN CTRE**, Adare **Ref:**YH00175

COUNTY MAYO

- **ASHFORD EQUESTRIAN CTRE**, Mayo **Ref:**YH00600
- **CLAREMORRIS**, Claremorris **Ref:**YH02952

COUNTY MEATH

- **BACHELORS LODGE**, Navan **Ref:**YH00766
- **BROADMEADOW**, Ashbourne **Ref:**YH02001

COUNTY OFFALY

- **BIRR EQUESTRIAN CTRE**, Birr **Ref:**YH01443

COUNTY SLIGO

- **BALLINA EQUESTRIAN CTRE**, Ballina **Ref:**YH00855

COUNTY TIPPERARY

- **BALLINTOHER EQUESTRIAN CTRE**, Nenagh **Ref:**YH00862
- **CAHIR EQUESTRIAN CTRE**, Cahir **Ref:**YH02416
- **CLONMEL EQUESTRIAN CTRE**, Clonmel **Ref:**YH03057

COUNTY WEXFORD

- **CARNE RIDING STABLES**, Wexford **Ref:**YH02563

COUNTY WICKLOW

- **BEL-AIR HOTEL & EQUESTRIAN**, Ashford **Ref:**YH01202

FARRIERS

COUNTY CORK

- **CASTLEWHITE**, Cork **Ref:**YH02646

COUNTY TIPPERARY

- **O'CONNELL, PATRICK**, Bansha **Ref:**YH10429
- **O'CONNELL, PATRICK**, Bansha **Ref:**YH10430

FEED MERCHANTS

COUNTY GALWAY

- **EQUI-GRASS**, Athenry **Ref:**YH04748

HOLIDAYS

COUNTY CLARE

- **WILLIE DALY RIDING SCHOOL**, Ennistymon **Ref:**YH15487

COUNTY LAOIS

- **KILVAHAN**, Portlaoise **Ref:**YH08155

COUNTY OFFALY

- **ANNAGHARVEY FARM**, Tullamore **Ref:**YH00450

COUNTY TIPPERARY

- **DAVERN EQUESTRIAN CTRE**, Clonmel **Ref:**YH03911

HORSE/RIDER ACCOM

COUNTY CAVAN

- **REDHILLS EQUESTRIAN**, Redhills **Ref:**YH11713

COUNTY CLARE

- **CLARE EQUESTRIAN CTRE**, Ennis **Ref:**YH02949

COUNTY GALWAY

- **FEENEY'S EQUESTRIAN CTRE**, Galway **Ref:**YH05127

COUNTY MEATH

- **BROADMEADOW**, Ashbourne **Ref:**YH02001

COUNTY TIPPERARY

- **CAHIR EQUESTRIAN CTRE**, Cahir **Ref:**YH02416

COUNTY WICKLOW

- **BEL-AIR HOTEL & EQUESTRIAN**, Ashford **Ref:**YH01202
- **CLARA GUESTHOUSE**, Rathdrum **Ref:**YH02948

MEDICAL SUPPORT

COUNTY CLARE

- **MURPHY CLIPPING SV**, O'Briansbridge **Ref:**YH09953

COUNTY DUBLIN

- **COLEMANS OF SANDYFORD**, Dublin **Ref:**YH03166

COUNTY GALWAY

- **EQUI-GRASS**, Athenry **Ref:**YH04748

COUNTY KILDARE

- **GRANGEMORE STUD**, The Curragh **Ref:**YH06002

RIDING CLUBS

COUNTY CORK

- **CASTLEWHITE**, Cork **Ref:**YH02646
- **GREYBROOK RIDING SCHOOL**, Cork **Ref:**YH06125

COUNTY WICKLOW

- **BEL-AIR HOTEL & EQUESTRIAN**, Ashford **Ref:**YH01202

RIDING SCHOOLS

COUNTY CARLOW

- **CARRIGBEG RIDING SCHOOL**, Bagenalstown **Ref:**YH02588

COUNTY CAVAN

- **REDHILLS EQUESTRIAN**, Redhills **Ref:**YH11713

COUNTY CLARE

- **BANNER EQUESTRIAN**, Ennis **Ref:**YH00906
- **CLARE EQUESTRIAN CTRE**, Ennis **Ref:**YH02949
- **CLONLARA EQUESTRIAN CTRE**, Clonlara **Ref:**YH03056

COUNTY CORK

- **BALLYBURDEN RIDING**, Ballincollig **Ref:**YH00865
- **BANTRY HORSE RIDING**, Bantry **Ref:**YH00912
- **BLARNEY RIDING CTRE**, Blarney **Ref:**YH01528
- **CASTLEWHITE**, Cork **Ref:**YH02646
- **DUNMANWAY RIDING SCHOOL**, Dunmanway **Ref:**YH04347
- **GREYBROOK RIDING SCHOOL**, Cork **Ref:**YH06125

COUNTY DUBLIN

- **BROOKE LODGE**, Sandyford **Ref:**YH02042
- **CALLIAGHSTOWN EQUESTRIAN**, Rathcoole **Ref:**YH02449
- **CARRICKMINES EQUESTRIAN CTRE**, Dublin **Ref:**YH02587
- **PADDOCKS RIDING CTRE**, Sandyford **Ref:**YH10674
- **RATHFARNHAN EQUESTRIAN CTRE**, Dublin **Ref:**YH11655
- **THORNTON PARK**, Dublin **Ref:**YH14074

COUNTY GALWAY

- **AILLECROSS EQUESTRIAN CTRE**, Loughrea **Ref:**YH00211
- **FEENEY'S EQUESTRIAN CTRE**, Galway **Ref:**YH05127
- **ROCKMOUNT RIDING CTRE**, Claregalway **Ref:**YH12037

COUNTY KERRY

- **ABBEYGLEN**, Milltown **Ref:**YH00097
- **CURRAGH COTTAGE LEISURE**, Tralee **Ref:**YH03735

COUNTY MEATH

- **BACHELORS LODGE**, Navan **Ref:**YH00766
- **BLACKHALL EQUESTRIAN CTRE**, Little Kilcloone **Ref:**YH01483

COUNTY OFFALY

- **BIRR EQUESTRIAN CTRE**, Birr **Ref:**YH01443

COUNTY SLIGO

- **BALLINA EQUESTRIAN CTRE**, Ballina **Ref:**YH00855

COUNTY TIPPERARY

- **BALLINTOHER EQUESTRIAN CTRE**, Nenagh **Ref:**YH00862
- **CLONMEL EQUESTRIAN CTRE**, Clonmel **Ref:**YH03057
- **DAVERN EQUESTRIAN CTRE**, Clonmel **Ref:**YH03911

COUNTY WATERFORD

- **CONNORS, MICK**, Woodstown **Ref:**YH03240

COUNTY WESTMEATH

- **ABBEY ACRE**, Westmeath **Ref:**YH00075
- **AUBURN**, Athlone **Ref:**YH00659

COUNTY WICKLOW

- **BRENNANSTOWN RIDING SCHOOL**, Bray **Ref:**YH01846
- **BROOMFIELD RIDING CTRE**, Tinahely **Ref:**YH02078
- **COOLADOYLE RIDING SCHOOL**, Newtownmountkennedy **Ref:**YH03270

RIDING WEAR RETAILERS

COUNTY CORK

- **BUCAS**, Cork **Ref:**YH02184

COUNTY DUBLIN

- **COLEMANS OF SANDYFORD**, Dublin **Ref:**YH03166
- **EQUESTRIAN DIRECT SALES**, Dublin **Ref:**YH04699

COUNTY KERRY

- **BRIDLES & BITS**, Tralee **Ref:**YH01893

COUNTY KILKENNY

- **EUROFARM**, Kilkenny **Ref:**YH04898

COUNTY LIMERICK

- **COUNTRY DRESSER**, Adare **Ref:**YH03403

COUNTY LOUTH

- **HORSEWARE**, Dundalk **Ref:**YH07177

COUNTY MEATH

- **CLARKE'S SPORTSDEN**, Navan **Ref:**YH02978

COUNTY WESTMEATH

- **TALLY HO**, Athlone **Ref:**YH13838

COUNTY WICKLOW

- **EQUESTRIAN LEATHERS**, Bray **Ref:**YH04704

SADDLERY RETAILERS

COUNTY CORK

- **CLONAKILTY SADDLERY**, Clonakilty **Ref:**YH03054
- **CORK SADDLERY**, Cork **Ref:**YH03317

COUNTY DUBLIN

- **EQUESTRIAN DIRECT SALES**, Dublin **Ref:**YH04699
- **MURT O'BRIEN SADDLERS**, Rathcoole **Ref:**YH09970

COUNTY KERRY

- **BRIDLES & BITS**, Tralee **Ref:**YH01893

COUNTY KILDARE

- **CLANCY DECLAN SADDLERY**, Newbridge **Ref:**YH02940

COUNTY KILKENNY

- **EUROFARM**, Kilkenny **Ref:**YH04898

COUNTY LIMERICK

- **COUNTRY DRESSER**, Adare **Ref:**YH03403

COUNTY MAYO

- **ABRAM, DAVID**, Bohola **Ref:**YH00135

COUNTY MEATH

- **CLARKE'S SPORTSDEN**, Navan **Ref:**YH02978

COUNTY MONAGHAN

- **FRANK WARD**, Carrickmacross **Ref:**YH05462

COUNTY WATERFORD

- **BLACKWATER SADDLERY**, Tallow **Ref:**YH01502

COUNTY WESTMEATH

- **WEBBWEAR**, Multyfarnham **Ref:**YH15036

COUNTY WICKLOW

- **BALLINTESKIN TACK**, Wicklow **Ref:**YH00861
- **EQUESTRIAN LEATHERS**, Bray **Ref:**YH04704

STABLES/LIVERIES

COUNTY CARLOW

- **CARTER, EDWARD**, Busherstown **Ref:**YH02606

COUNTY CAVAN

- **REDHILLS EQUESTRIAN**, Redhills **Ref:**YH11713

COUNTY CLARE

- **BANNER EQUESTRIAN**, Ennis **Ref:**YH00906
- **CLARE EQUESTRIAN CTRE**, Ennis **Ref:**YH02949

COUNTY CORK

- **CASTLEWHITE**, Cork **Ref:**YH02646
- **KILBYRNE STABLES**, Doneraile **Ref:**YH08127

COUNTY DONEGAL

- **LENAMORE STABLES**, Donegal **Ref:**YH08551

COUNTY DUBLIN

- **ASHTON EQUESTRIAN CTRE**, Dublin **Ref:**YH00611
- **CARRICKMINES EQUESTRIAN CTRE**, Dublin **Ref:**YH02587
- **RATHFARNHAN EQUESTRIAN CTRE**, Dublin **Ref:**YH11655

COUNTY GALWAY

- **AILLECROSS EQUESTRIAN CTRE**, Loughrea **Ref:**YH00211

COUNTY KERRY

- **ABBEYGLEN**, Milltown **Ref:**YH00097

COUNTY KILDARE

- **BOROHARD EQUESTRIAN CTRE**, Naas **Ref:**YH01652
- **COILOG EVENTING**, Naas **Ref:**YH03139
- **GRANGEMORE STUD**, The Curragh **Ref:**YH06002
- **HEBERTSTOWN STUD FARM**, Newbridge **Ref:**YH06636
- **LEGGA LIVERY & SALES**, Naas **Ref:**YH08538
- **YEOMANSTOWN STUD**, Naas **Ref:**YH15905

COUNTY MAYO

- **CLAREMORRIS**, Claremorris **Ref:**YH02952

COUNTY MEATH

- **BACHELORS LODGE**, Navan **Ref:**YH00766

BLACKHALL EQUESTRIAN CTRE, Little Kilcloone Ref:YH01483

COUNTY SLIGO
BALLINA EQUESTRIAN CTRE, Ballina Ref:YH00855

COUNTY TIPPERARY
CAHIR EQUESTRIAN CTRE, Cahir Ref:YH02416
CLONMEL EQUESTRIAN CTRE, Clonmel Ref:YH03057

COUNTY WESTMEATH
WEBBWEAR, Multyfarnham Ref:YH15036

COUNTY WICKLOW
BRENNANSTOWN RIDING SCHOOL, Bray Ref:YH01846

STUD FARMS

COUNTY KILDARE
FORENAUGHTS STUD, Naas Ref:YH05331
OAKLODGE STUD, Naas Ref:YH10401

SUPPLIES

COUNTY CARLOW
BOLGER, J S, Coolcullen Ref:YH01608
HORSE POWER TRANSPORT, Milford Ref:YH07129
MULLINS PATK, Doninga Goresbridge Ref:YH09940
MULLINS, W P, Bagenalstown Ref:YH09942

COUNTY CAVAN
FAIRTOWN RACING, Cavan Ref:YH05029

COUNTY CLARE
CASTLEFERGUS RIDING STABLES, Quin Ref:YH02642
COSTELLO TOM, Newmarket-on-Fergus Ref:YH03355
MCGRATH'S SADDLERY, Ennis Ref:YH09364
STUBBEN, Ennistymon Ref:YH13599
WEST CLARE SADDLERY, Ennistymon Ref:YH15132

COUNTY CORK
BALLYKENLEY RIDING SCHOOL, Cork Ref:YH00868
BANTRY BRIDLE, Bantry Ref:YH00911
BEE WOODCRAFT, Ardmore Ref:YH01160
BUCAS, Cork Ref:YH02184
CLONAKILTY SADDLERY, Clonakilty Ref:YH03054
CORK RACECOURSE MALLOW, Mallow Ref:YH03316
CROWLEY, JOHN, Midleton Ref:YH03679
GREYBROOK RIDING SCHOOL, Cork Ref:YH06125
HITCHMOUGH RIDING SCHOOL, Monkstown Ref:YH06888
HORGAN, TIMOTHY, Bandon Ref:YH07067
J W GREEN, Cork Ref:YH07625
LEE SADDLERY, Bandon Ref:YH08518
MALLOW RACE CO, Mallow Ref:YH09052
MANLEY, JOHN, Blackpool Ref:YH09081
O'BRIEN'S, Bandon Ref:YH10424
O'RIORDAN RIDING CTRE, Whitechurch Ref:YH10544
SKEVANISH EQUESTRIAN, Cork Ref:YH12871
SOUTHERN TRAILER SYSTEMS, Cork Ref:YH13145
TACK ROOM, Cork Ref:YH13796

COUNTY DUBLIN
ASS OF IRISH RACECOURSES, Dublin Ref:YH00630
COLEMANS OF SANDYFORD, Dublin Ref:YH03166
DREAPER JIM, Dublin Ref:YH04263
EDDIE BRENNAN, Dublin Ref:YH04540
EQUESTRIAN DIRECT SALES, Dublin Ref:YH04699
EURO MECH, Dublin Ref:YH04892
GREER S & SON, Dublin Ref:YH06110
IRISH THOROUGHBRED MARKETING, Dublin Ref:YH07502
MICHO, MICHAEL, Dublin Ref:YH09515
MURT O'BRIEN SADDLERS, Rathcoole Ref:YH09970
NAGWARE, Dublin Ref:YH10010
PHOENIX PK RACECOURSE, Dublin Ref:YH11075
T CONNOLLY & SONS, Dublin Ref:YH13735
TONY GOODWIN & SONS, Dublin Ref:YH14229
TOTE ACCOUNT, Dublin Ref:YH14250

COUNTY GALWAY
DEVANEYS, Galway Ref:YH04086
EQUI-GRASS, Athenry Ref:YH04748
JENNINGS, E, Tuam Ref:YH07747
LYNCH, GERRY, Craughwell Ref:YH08924
O'BRIEN, VAL, Athenry Ref:YH10423
RACEDAY EVENTS, Ballybrit Ref:YH11576

COUNTY KERRY
BRIDLES & BITS, Tralee Ref:YH01893
HORAN T & SONS, Kerry Ref:YH07065
IRISH EQUIMARKET, Tralee Ref:YH07494
KERRY FARM SUPPLIES, Tralee Ref:YH08101

COUNTY KILDARE
BERNEY BROS, Kilcullen Ref:YH01312
BROWNE, LIAM, Curragh Ref:YH02138
BURKE PATRICK, Kildare Ref:YH02255
CANTY, JOSEPH M, Kildare Ref:YH02517
CANTY, PHILIP, Kildare Ref:YH02518
COOGAN, JAMES, Kildare Ref:YH03253
CUSACK, OLIVER, Bishopland Ref:YH03757
DOOLEY ANDREW FARRIER SV, Kilcullen Ref:YH04192
EQUESTRIAN WORLD, Maynooth Ref:YH04720
FRENCH FURZE STABLES, Curragh Ref:YH05489
GILLESPIE, D.F., Curragh Ref:YH05779
HARLEY, JEREMY, Rathbride Ref:YH06438
HOLMESTEAD SADDLERY, Kill Ref:YH06982
INT BLOODSTOCK FINANCE, Naas Ref:YH07465
IRISH EQUESTRIAN PRODUCTS, Kildare Ref:YH07493
IRISH NATIONAL STUD, Kildare Ref:YH07497
M J O'BRIEN SADDLERY, Newbridge Ref:YH08971
MADDEN, NIALL, Naas Ref:YH09019
MCCARTON, GERALD, Kilcullen Ref:YH09325
MCGRATH, NEIL S, Curragh Ref:YH09363
MOORE, ARTHUR, Naas Ref:YH09755
MULHERN, J E, Rathbride Ref:YH09932
MURPHY, SAM, Monasterevin Ref:YH09960
O'BRIEN, CHARLES, Curragh Ref:YH10419
O'BRIEN, MICHAEL, Naas Ref:YH10422
O'DONOVAN, RICHARD, Kildare Ref:YH10433
OSBORNE PK, Naas Ref:YH10559
O'TOOLE, M L, Maddenstown Ref:YH10579
PRENDERGAST, P J, Kildare Ref:YH11355
REGAN, T A, Curragh Ref:YH11739
REGISTRY OFFICE TURF CLUB, Curragh Ref:YH11742
RIDGE MANOR STABLES, Milltown Ref:YH11863
ROPER, W M, Clifden Ref:YH12086
STACK, GERARD, Kildare Ref:YH13317
UNIVERSAL TRAILERS, Newbridge Ref:YH14577
WESTWOOD, IFOR WILLIAMS, Naas Ref:YH15242

COUNTY KILKENNY
ABBEY RACING, Kilkenny Ref:YH00084
BERGIN, TOM, Johnstown Ref:YH01298
EUROFARM, Kilkenny Ref:YH04898
JERPOINT LIVERY, Thomastown Ref:YH07755
O'SHEA, JOHN, Callan Ref:YH10566
PORTER'S SADDLERY, Dungarvan Ref:YH11288
STANLEY HUNTER, Freshford Ref:YH13371
TOWN & COUNTY SPORTS SHOP, Kilkenny Ref:YH14294

COUNTY LAOIS
AIR PURIFICATION SYSTEMS, Portlaoise Ref:YH00218
GERALD, ROBINSON, Portlaoise Ref:YH05729

COUNTY LEITRIM
O'CALLAGHAN, JAS, Mohill Ref:YH10425
SOXLINE, Leitrim Ref:YH13169

COUNTY LIMERICK
BURKE BLOODSTOCK TRANSPORT, Limerick Ref:YH02254
COUNTRY DRESSER, Adare Ref:YH03403
FENNELL, JOHN, Rathkeale Ref:YH05146
GAMMELL EQUESTRIAN, Rathluirc Ref:YH05637
HOURIGAN, M L, Patrickswell Ref:YH07207
KELLEHER, NEAL, Kilmallock Ref:YH08041
MCNAMARA, ERIC, Rathkeale Ref:YH09398
MORRISSEY, JIM, Charleville Ref:YH09841
O'CONNELL, JAMES, Limerick Ref:YH10428
PREMIER MOLASSES, Foynes Ref:YH11347
PURCELL JAMES, Limerick Ref:YH11464
TOM WALLACE SADDLERS, Limerick Ref:YH14215

COUNTY LONGFORD
A M CARR & SONS, Longford Ref:YH00049

COUNTY LOUTH
COX, JOHN R, Dundalk Ref:YH03534
DUNDALK RACE, Dundalk Ref:YH04339
HORSEWARE, Dundalk Ref:YH07177

COUNTY MAYO
BALLINROBE RACECOURSE, Ballinrobe Ref:YH00858
DEVANEY, JOSEPH, Enniscrone Ref:YH04085
JOHN, JOYCE, Claremorris Ref:YH07819

COUNTY MEATH
CLARKE'S SPORTSDEN, Navan Ref:YH02978
COYLE, JAMES, Navan Ref:YH03537
CUNNINGHAM, M I, Navan Ref:YH03724
GRANGE SADDLERY, Kells Ref:YH05995
J, MORGAN, Ballivor Ref:YH07634
KAUNTZE MICHAEL, Ashbourne Ref:YH07999
KAVANAGH, MARY & PETER, Boharmeen Ref:YH08001
LARKIN, JOHN, Trim Ref:YH08433
MEADE, NOEL, Kilpatrick Ref:YH09414
NAVAN RACE, Navan Ref:YH10057

COUNTY MONAGHAN
MONAGHAN SADDLERY WORKSHOP, Monaghan Ref:YH09715

COUNTY OFFALY
MCNAMARA'S, Birr Ref:YH09400
WALSH EMMETT FARM SUPPLIES, Tullamore Ref:YH14876

COUNTY ROSCOMMON
CASTLECOOTE STORES, Roscommon Ref:YH02641
MANNION, W, Glenamaddy Ref:YH09090
MURPHY EQUESTRIAN, Strokestown Ref:YH09954

COUNTY SLIGO
HORSEBED STABLE SUPPLIES, Collooney Ref:YH07148
MCDONAGH, ANDREW, Boyle Ref:YH09343

COUNTY TIPPERARY

- **BALLINROBE TRANSPORT**, Templemore **Ref:**YH00859
- **BRENNAN RICHARD FENCING SV**, Thurles **Ref:**YH01842
- **BYRNE, MICHAEL J**, Cahir **Ref:**YH02348
- **CARROLL, MICHAEL J**, Cloughjordan **Ref:**YH02593
- **CROKE, MICHAEL**, Fethard **Ref:**YH03628
- **DANL, KINANE**, Thurles **Ref:**YH03874
- **EGAN, CHRISTINE**, Ethard **Ref:**YH04589
- **EQUISTOCK**, Fethard **Ref:**YH04821
- **JAS, DOYLE**, Holycross **Ref:**YH07709
- **JOHN, RYAN**, Thurles **Ref:**YH07820
- **MALACHY, RYAN**, Tipperary **Ref:**YH09042
- **MURPHY, J G**, Fethard **Ref:**YH09957
- **NEVIN, RICHARD**, Fethard **Ref:**YH10089
- **O'MARA, THOMOND**, Bansha **Ref:**YH10507
- **SLIEVENAMON SADDLERY**, Clonmel **Ref:**YH12895
- **STACK, TOMMY**, Golden **Ref:**YH13318
- **THURLES RACE**, Thurles **Ref:**YH14118
- **TIPPERARY RACE COURSE**, Tipperary **Ref:**YH14181
- **TIPPERARY TACK**, Fethard **Ref:**YH14182
- **TOORACURRAGH HARNESS SHOP**, Ballymacarbry **Ref:**YH14233
- **WALSH, DAVID**, Tipperary Town **Ref:**YH14877
- **WINNING FARE TACK**, Killenaule **Ref:**YH15591

COUNTY WATERFORD

- **CURLEY, ERIC**, Tallow **Ref:**YH03731
- **DE BROMHEAD, HARRY**, Knockeen **Ref:**YH03975
- **KILCANNON HOUSE TACK SHOP**, Cappagh **Ref:**YH08128
- **MURRAY, BERNARD**, Tramore **Ref:**YH09964
- **O'BRIEN, JIMMY**, Ballyduff **Ref:**YH10421
- **PADDOCK RIDING**, Waterford **Ref:**YH10670
- **QUEALLY, JOHN**, Dungarvan **Ref:**YH11487
- **TACK ROOM**, Waterford **Ref:**YH13797

COUNTY WESTMEATH

- **ASHES EQUESTRIAN CTRE**, Mullingar **Ref:**YH00596
- **COUNIHAN RACHEL**, Ballinagore **Ref:**YH03391
- **HYDE PARK STUD**, Killucan **Ref:**YH07347
- **JOYCE M A**, Mullingar **Ref:**YH07950
- **MICHAEL, KIERNAN**, Mullingar **Ref:**YH09511
- **WEBB WEAR**, Mullingar **Ref:**YH15028
- **WEBBWEAR**, Multyfarnham **Ref:**YH15036

COUNTY WEXFORD

- **BAILEY ERNIE**, New Ross **Ref:**YH00793
- **BORLEIGH MANOR STUD**, Gorey **Ref:**YH01651
- **DOYLE, P.J.**, Gorey **Ref:**YH04250
- **GIBBON WM A.**, Foulksmills **Ref:**YH05739
- **LUKE, DOYLE**, New Ross **Ref:**YH08894
- **MURPHY, LARRY**, Wexford **Ref:**YH09958
- **O'TOOLE, ANN F**, Wicklow **Ref:**YH10578
- **SOUTH EAST EQUESTRIAN**, Wexford **Ref:**YH13086
- **SPORTS**, Bettyville **Ref:**YH13233
- **WEXFORD COUNTRY STORE**, Wexford **Ref:**YH15247

COUNTY WICKLOW

- **AIGLE INTERNATIONAL**, Wicklow **Ref:**YH00206
- **BOWENS VICTOR**, Colbinstown **Ref:**YH01704
- **DRAGONHOLD STABLES**, Newcastle **Ref:**YH04253
- **MACKEY EQUESTRIAN WHOLESALE**, Donard **Ref:**YH09003
- **ROB, EVANS**, Greystones **Ref:**YH11931

TRACKS/COURSES

COUNTY KERRY

- **KILLARNEY RACE**, Killarney **Ref:**YH08141
- **LISTOWEL RACE CO RACECOURSE**, Listowel **Ref:**YH08682

COUNTY KILDARE

- **CURRAGH RACE COURSE OFFICE**, Curragh **Ref:**YH03737
- **NAAS RACECOURSE**, Naas **Ref:**YH10006

COUNTY LIMERICK

- **LIMERICK RACE**, Limerick **Ref:**YH08631

COUNTY MEATH

- **FAIRYHOUSE RACE COURSE**, Meath **Ref:**YH05034

COUNTY SLIGO

- **COUNTY SLIGO RACES**, Sligo **Ref:**YH03492

TRAINERS

COUNTY CARLOW

- **FENNISCOURT STABLES**, Bagenalstown **Ref:**YH05148
- **HUGHES, PATRICK**, Bagenalstown **Ref:**YH07271

COUNTY CORK

- **CASTLEWHITE**, Cork **Ref:**YH02646
- **PINEGROVE STABLES**, Cork **Ref:**YH11125

COUNTY KILDARE

- **BERRY, FRANK**, Kilcullen **Ref:**YH01316
- **BRASSIL, MARTIN**, Kildare **Ref:**YH01815
- **BURNS, JAMES G**, The Curragh **Ref:**YH02273
- **CUSACK, GERALD A**, Naas **Ref:**YH03756
- **ENNIS, FRANCIS**, The Curragh **Ref:**YH04677
- **ENNIS, FRANK**, Curragh **Ref:**YH04678
- **GORMAN, JIM**, The Curragh **Ref:**YH05935
- **GRASSICK, MICHAEL**, The Curragh **Ref:**YH06021
- **GROOME, JIMMY**, Kildare **Ref:**YH06152
- **HALFORD, MICHAEL**, Curragh **Ref:**YH06299
- **HANLEY, DAVID**, The Curragh **Ref:**YH06390
- **HAYDEN, JOHN**, Kilcullen **Ref:**YH06569
- **HUGHES, DESMOND T**, Kildare **Ref:**YH07264
- **HUGHES, DESSIE**, Kildare **Ref:**YH07265
- **KENNEDY, VIVIAN**, The Curragh **Ref:**YH08071
- **MCCREERY, P D**, Clane **Ref:**YH09336
- **MCCREERY, PETER**, Clane **Ref:**YH09337
- **MOORE, ARTHUR**, Naas **Ref:**YH09755
- **MULLHERN, JOHN**, The Curragh **Ref:**YH09938
- **NAAS RACECOURSE**, Naas **Ref:**YH10006
- **OAKES, IRENE**, Stroud **Ref:**YH10377
- **OSBORNE, ROBERT**, Naas **Ref:**YH10560
- **OXX, JOHN**, Kildare **Ref:**YH10628
- **PRENDERGAST, KEVIN**, Kildare **Ref:**YH11353
- **ROCHE, CHRISTY**, Kildare **Ref:**YH12018
- **ROPER, MARK**, The Curragh **Ref:**YH12085
- **SCOTT, HOMER**, Castledermot **Ref:**YH12544
- **TAAFFE, TOM**, Straffan **Ref:**YH13770
- **WALSH, TED**, Kill **Ref:**YH14880
- **WELD, D K**, Curragh **Ref:**YH15061

COUNTY KILKENNY

- **MULLINS, A**, Kilkenny **Ref:**YH09941

COUNTY MAYO

- **ASHFORD EQUESTRIAN CTRE**, Mayo **Ref:**YH00600

COUNTY TIPPERARY

- **HORSEY HABIT**, Tipperary **Ref:**YH07181
- **MORRIS, MICHAEL**, Fethard **Ref:**YH09833
- **O'GRADY, EDWARD J**, Thurles **Ref:**YH10441

COUNTY WATERFORD

- **DEBROMHEAD, HARRY**, Knockeen **Ref:**YH04006

COUNTY WICKLOW

- **EVANS, ALFRED D**, Delgany **Ref:**YH04915

TRANSPORT/HORSE BOXES

COUNTY CARLOW

- **AGRI SERVICES**, Bagenalstown **Ref:**YH00201

COUNTY CORK

- **MCSWEENEY TRAILERS**, Bandon **Ref:**YH09406

COUNTY DUBLIN

- **EDDIE BRENNAN**, Dublin **Ref:**YH04540
- **INDESPENSION**, Tallaght **Ref:**YH07414

COUNTY KILDARE

- **RONAN GRASSICK BLOODSTOCK TNSPRT**, Naas **Ref:**YH12073

COUNTY LAOIS

- **HENRY FINGLETON**, Portlaoise **Ref:**YH06683

COUNTY LIMERICK

- **INDESPENSION**, Limerick **Ref:**YH07415

COUNTY MEATH

- **COUNTY TRAILERS**, Enfield **Ref:**YH03493

COUNTY ROSCOMMON

- **BRADLEY DOUBLELOCK LTD**, Athlone **Ref:**YH01750

NORTHERN IRELAND

ARENAS

COUNTY LONDONDERRY

- **ARDMORE STABLES**, Londonderry **Ref:**YH00511
- **EGLINTON EQUESTRIAN CLUB**, Eglinton **Ref:**YH04595
- **FAUGHANVALE STABLES**, Londonderry **Ref:**YH05102

COUNTY TYRONE

- **ECCLESVILLE CTRE**, Omagh **Ref:**YH04533

BLACKSMITHS

COUNTY ARMAGH

- **LIME PARK EQUESTRIAN**, Craigavon **Ref:**YH08626

BLOOD STOCK AGENCIES

COUNTY ANTRIM

- **BUSER, M**, Lisburn **Ref:**YH02305

COUNTY DOWN

- **MOSSVALE BLOODSTOCK SALES**, Newry **Ref:**YH09870

COUNTY TYRONE

- **EAMONN RICE BLOOD STOCK**, Dungannon **Ref:**YH04447

BREEDERS

COUNTY ANTRIM

- **ANDREWS, JOHN**, Toomebridge **Ref:**YH00400
- **BELL, D**, Ballyclare **Ref:**YH01218
- **BELL, T**, Larne **Ref:**YH01230
- **CRAIGS STUD**, Ballyclare **Ref:**YH03555
- **DUNLOP, H F**, Ballymena **Ref:**YH04344
- **GILBERT, K F**, Ballyclare **Ref:**YH05760
- **GLASS, JOHN**, Ballycastle **Ref:**YH05810
- **HUSTON, D N**, Belfast **Ref:**YH07331
- **LUSK EQUESTRIAN**, Lisburn **Ref:**YH08905
- **MACKEAN, P**, Antrim **Ref:**YH08998
- **STEVENSON, J M**, Belfast **Ref:**YH13451
- **TULLYROE STUD**, Crumlin **Ref:**YH14457

COUNTY ARMAGH

- **ALFRED BULLER BLOODSTOCK**, Craigavon **Ref:**YH00275
- **BALLINTEGGART STUD**, Portadown **Ref:**YH00860
- **BULLER, A W**, Craigavon **Ref:**YH02218
- **N I S P G**, Mowhan **Ref:**YH09991

COUNTY DOWN

- **ALLEN, SUZANNE**, Bainbridge **Ref:**YH00303
- **MAGHERADARTIN SHETLAND STUD**, Hillsborough **Ref:**YH09034
- **MCCABE, JIM**, Downpatrick **Ref:**YH09315
- **MCCONVEY, J**, Downpatrick **Ref:**YH09330
- **MCIVOR, A**, Dromore **Ref:**YH09378
- **MILLHOLLOW STUD**, Downpatrick **Ref:**YH09619
- **NORTHERN IRELAND HORSE BOARD**, Newtownards **Ref:**YH10305
- **PORTER, NOEL**, Guildford **Ref:**YH11285

COUNTY LONDONDERRY

- **MCCOLLUM, JEANNIE**, Coleraine **Ref:**YH09328
- **SPARKLING STUDS**, Londonderry **Ref:**YH13178

COUNTY TYRONE

- **KEE, W R**, Strabane **Ref:**YH08025
- **WATTERS, R J**, Omagh **Ref:**YH15001

CLUBS/ASSOCIATIONS

COUNTY ANTRIM

- **BALLYCORR RIDING CLUB**, Ballyclare **Ref:**YH00867
- **BEECHES RIDING CLUB**, Newtownabbey **Ref:**YH01170
- **BHS DEVELOPMENT (N IRE)**, Belfast **Ref:**YH01377
- **BHS RIDING CLUBS**, Belfast **Ref:**YH01386
- **DERRY & ANTRIM**, Antrim **Ref:**YH04079
- **EAST ANTRIM HOUNDS**, Ballyclare **Ref:**YH04466
- **G & L MNGMT CONSULTANTS**, Ballymoney **Ref:**YH05565
- **GLEN'S RIDING CLUB**, Ballymena **Ref:**YH05842
- **HALF BRED HORSE BREEDERS SOC**, Belfast **Ref:**YH06295
- **KILLYLESS RIDING CLUB**, Ballymena **Ref:**YH08146
- **LAGAN VALLEY RIDING CLUB**, Belfast **Ref:**YH08343
- **MID ANTRIM PONY CLUB**, Ballymena **Ref:**YH09521
- **MID ULSTER SHOWJUMPERS**, Ballymena **Ref:**YH09532
- **NATIONAL PONY SOCIETY**, Larne **Ref:**YH10040
- **NATIONAL PONY SOCIETY**, Lisburn **Ref:**YH10039
- **NORTH DOWN HARRIERS PONY CLUB**, Belfast **Ref:**YH10256
- **NORTHERN IRELAND DRIVING CLUB**, Lisburn **Ref:**YH10304
- **NORTHERN IRELAND SHOWS ASS**, Belfast **Ref:**YH10306
- **PONY CLUB**, Carrickfergus **Ref:**YH11233
- **REDHALL RIDING CLUB**, Carrickfergus **Ref:**YH11712
- **ROYAL ULSTER AGRICULTURAL SOC**, Belfast **Ref:**YH12196
- **ULSTER PONY SOCIETY**, Lisburn **Ref:**YH14556
- **UNIVERSITY OF ULSTER**, Newtownabbey **Ref:**YH14596
- **USPCA**, Lisburn **Ref:**YH14623
- **WEST BELFAST**, Belfast **Ref:**YH15127

COUNTY ARMAGH

- **BALLYKNOCK RIDING CLUB**, Lurgan **Ref:**YH00869
- **IVEAGH BRANCH**, Portadown **Ref:**YH07534
- **N I S P G**, Mowhan **Ref:**YH09991
- **NICDA**, Trandragee **Ref:**YH10177

COUNTY DOWN

- **ARDS RIDING CLUB**, Bangor **Ref:**YH00512
- **B H S-N I CHAIRMAN**, Hillsborough **Ref:**YH00728
- **BALLYNAHINCH & DISTRICT**, Hillsborough **Ref:**YH00872
- **CAPALL RIDING CLUB**, Comber **Ref:**YH02519
- **CIVIL SV (NORTHERN IRELAND)**, Moneyrea **Ref:**YH02934
- **DOWN ROYAL CORPORATION**, Downpatrick **Ref:**YH04222
- **DRESSAGE IRELAND**, Carryduff **Ref:**YH04267
- **EAST DOWN FOXHOUNDS**, Saintfield **Ref:**YH04471
- **EVENTING IRELAND**, Killyleagh **Ref:**YH04942
- **GRANSHA EQUESTRIAN**, Bangor **Ref:**YH06006
- **ILDRA**, Dromore **Ref:**YH07398
- **IRISH DRAUGHT HORSE SOCIETY**, Dromore **Ref:**YH07490
- **IRISH PONY SOCIETY**, Ballynahinch **Ref:**YH07499
- **IRISH THOROUGHBRED**, Crossgar **Ref:**YH07501
- **NEWCASTLE & DISTRICT**, Castlewellan **Ref:**YH10127
- **NIWHA**, Donaghadee **Ref:**YH10214
- **RIDING FOR THE DISABLED ASS**, Dromara **Ref:**YH11876
- **SIDE-SADDLE ASS**, Comber **Ref:**YH12789
- **SJAI**, Saintfield **Ref:**YH12863
- **WARRENPOINT RIDING CLUB**, Warrenpoint **Ref:**YH14938

COUNTY FERMANAGH

- **ERNE LAKELAND RIDING CLUB**, Enniskillen **Ref:**YH04852
- **FERMANAGH HARRIERS**, Enniskillen **Ref:**YH05160
- **IRISH SPORT HORSE DEVELOPMENT**, Enniskillen **Ref:**YH07500
- **MEDICAL EQUESTRIAN ASS**, Enniskillen **Ref:**YH09435

COUNTY LONDONDERRY

- **BANN VALLEY RIDING CLUB**, Coleraine **Ref:**YH00905
- **NORTH COAST RIDING CLUB**, Aghadowey **Ref:**YH10248
- **ROUTE HUNT BRANCH**, Coleraine **Ref:**YH12148
- **UNIVERSITY OF ULSTER**, Coleraine **Ref:**YH14597

COUNTY TYRONE

- **SEEIN RIDING CLUB**, Sion Mills **Ref:**YH12609
- **TULLYLAGAN**, Cookstown **Ref:**YH14453
- **TULLYLAGAN PONY CLUB**, Cookstown **Ref:**YH14454

EQUESTRIAN CENTRES

COUNTY ANTRIM

- **BURN EQUESTRIAN CLUB**, Belfast **Ref:**YH02263
- **CONNEL HILL RIDING CTRE**, Antrim **Ref:**YH03235
- **CULLYBURN EQUESTRIAN CTRE**, Newtownabbey **Ref:**YH03707
- **LOUGH NEAGH EQUESTRIAN CTRE**, Lisburn **Ref:**YH08836
- **LOUGHAVEEMA TREKKING CTRE**, Ballycastle **Ref:**YH08837

COUNTY ARMAGH

- **LIME PARK EQUESTRIAN**, Craigavon **Ref:**YH08626

COUNTY DOWN

- **ARDMINNAN EQUESTRIAN CTRE**, Newtownards **Ref:**YH00510
- **GRANSHA EQUESTRIAN CTRE**, Bangor **Ref:**YH06007
- **KING BROS**, Castlewellan **Ref:**YH08167
- **MOSSVALE EQUESTRIAN CTRE**, Dromore **Ref:**YH09871
- **MOUNT PLEASANT**, Castlewellan **Ref:**YH09891
- **MOURNE TRAIL RIDING CTRE**, Newcastle **Ref:**YH09904

COUNTY FERMANAGH

- **DRUMHONEY STABLES**, Enniskillen **Ref:**YH04291
- **ENNISKILLEN CLGE**, Enniskillen **Ref:**YH04679

COUNTY LONDONDERRY

- **COOL RIDING STABLES**, Londonderry **Ref:**YH03268
- **DRUMSAMNEY EQUESTRIAN CTRE**, Magherafelt **Ref:**YH04292
- **EGLINTON EQUESTRIAN CLUB**, Eglinton **Ref:**YH04595
- **FORT CTRE**, Maghera **Ref:**YH05385
- **MARSH KYFE RIDING SCHOOL**, Magherafelt **Ref:**YH09186

COUNTY TYRONE

- **EDERGOLE RIDING CTRE**, Cookstown **Ref:**YH04553

FARRIERS

COUNTY ANTRIM

- **BEECHVALE FARRIER SUPPLIES**, Lisburn **Ref:**YH01175

COUNTY ARMAGH

- **LIME PARK EQUESTRIAN**, Craigavon **Ref:**YH08626

COUNTY DOWN

- **PAYNE, SAMUEL M**, Dundonald **Ref:**YH10853

COUNTY TYRONE

- **CUMMINS, M J**, Omagh **Ref:**YH03722
- **LAVERTY, M**, Dungannon **Ref:**YH08465

FEED MERCHANTS

COUNTY ANTRIM

- **DOAGH FARM FEEDS**, Doagh **Ref:**YH04147
- **EQUESTRIAN FARM FEEDS**, Lisburn **Ref:**YH04702

COUNTY DOWN

- **FEEDWELL ANIMAL FOOD**, Castlewellan **Ref:**YH05126

COUNTY LONDONDERRY

- **CORNDALE ANIMAL FEEDS**, Limavady **Ref:**YH03322

HOLIDAYS

COUNTY DOWN

- **MOUNT PLEASANT**, Castlewellan **Ref:**YH09891

HORSE/RIDER ACCOM

- **MOUNT PLEASANT**, Castlewellan **Ref:**YH09891

COUNTY LONDONDERRY

- **MADDYBENNY RIDING CTRE**, Coleraine **Ref:**YH09022

MEDICAL SUPPORT

COUNTY ANTRIM

- **GLENBURN VETNRY CLNC**, Crumlin **Ref:**YH05829
- **GRANGE EQUESTRIAN**, Newtownabbey **Ref:**YH05986
- **JARDEN, J**, Crumlin **Ref:**YH07701

COUNTY ARMAGH

- **HOWARD ALLEN SEEDS**, Craigavon **Ref:**YH07215

COUNTY DOWN

- **KELLY, SHARON**, Saintfield **Ref:**YH08048

COUNTY FERMANAGH

- **MEDICAL EQUESTRIAN ASS**, Enniskillen **Ref:**YH09435

COUNTY LONDONDERRY

- **CLARKE, CROCKETT & JAMISON**, Magherafelt **Ref:**YH02973
- **E G CAMPBELL**, Drumahoe **Ref:**YH04405
- **RAMSEY, J**, Coleraine **Ref:**YH11621

COUNTY TYRONE

- **PARKVIEW VETNRY GRP**, Strabane **Ref:**YH10778
- **POTTIE, A D**, Fintona **Ref:**YH11302

RIDING CLUBS

COUNTY ANTRIM

- **BALLYCORR RIDING CLUB**, Ballyclare **Ref:**YH00867
- **BURN EQUESTRIAN CLUB**, Belfast **Ref:**YH02263
- **GLEN'S RIDING CLUB**, Ballymena **Ref:**YH05842
- **KILLYLESS RIDING CLUB**, Ballymena **Ref:**YH08146
- **LAGAN VALLEY RIDING CLUB**, Belfast **Ref:**YH08343
- **REDHALL RIDING CLUB**, Carrickfergus **Ref:**YH11712

COUNTY ARMAGH

- **BALLYKNOCK RIDING CLUB**, Lurgan **Ref:**YH00869
- **LIMEPARK RIDING CLUB**, Moira **Ref:**YH08630

COUNTY DOWN

- **ARDS RIDING CLUB**, Bangor **Ref:**YH00512
- **BALLYNAHINCH & DISTRICT**, Hillsborough **Ref:**YH00872
- **CAPALL RIDING CLUB**, Comber **Ref:**YH02519
- **CIVIL SV (NORTHERN IRELAND)**, Moneyrea **Ref:**YH02934
- **CRAIGANTLET RIDING CLUB**, Newtownards **Ref:**YH03552
- **GRANSHA EQUESTRIAN**, Bangor **Ref:**YH06006
- **KILKEEL & DISTRICT**, Newry **Ref:**YH08139
- **LECALE RIDING CLUB**, Downpatrick **Ref:**YH08511
- **LESSANS RIDING CLUB**, Ballygowan **Ref:**YH08560
- **NEWCASTLE & DISTRICT**, Castlewellan **Ref:**YH10127
- **WARRENPOINT RIDING CLUB**, Warrenpoint **Ref:**YH14938

COUNTY FERMANAGH

- **ERNE LAKELAND RIDING CLUB**, Enniskillen **Ref:**YH04852

COUNTY LONDONDERRY

- **BANN VALLEY RIDING CLUB**, Coleraine **Ref:**YH00905
- **EGLINTON EQUESTRIAN CLUB**, Eglinton **Ref:**YH04595
- **FAUGHANVALE STABLES**, Londonderry **Ref:**YH05102

COUNTY TYRONE

- **SEEIN RIDING CLUB**, Sion Mills **Ref:**YH12609

RIDING SCHOOLS

COUNTY ANTRIM

- **BEECHES EQUESTRIAN CTRE**, Ballyclare **Ref:**YH01169
- **BIRR HSE RIDING CTRE**, Belfast **Ref:**YH01444
- **BROOKLANDS EQUITARE**, Lisburn **Ref:**YH02057
- **BURN EQUESTRIAN CLUB**, Belfast **Ref:**YH02263
- **CASTLEHILL EQUESTRIAN CTRE**, Ballymena **Ref:**YH02643
- **DRUMAHEGLIS RIDING SCHOOL**, Ballymoney **Ref:**YH04283
- **GALGORM MANOR EQUESTRIAN CTRE**, Ballymena **Ref:**YH05614
- **GALGORM PARKS RIDING SCHOOL**, Ballymena **Ref:**YH05615
- **KILLOAN RIDING CTRE**, Ballymena **Ref:**YH08145
- **LAGAN VALLEY EQUESTRIAN CTRE**, Belfast **Ref:**YH08342
- **RAINBOW EQUESTRIAN CTRE**, Larne **Ref:**YH11614
- **STIRLING, J**, Ballyclare **Ref:**YH13473

COUNTY ARMAGH

- **LIME PARK EQUESTRIAN**, Craigavon **Ref:**YH08626
- **RICHHILL EQUESTRIAN CTRE**, Richhill **Ref:**YH11825

COUNTY DOWN

- **BALLYKNOCK RIDING SCHOOL**, Hillsborough **Ref:**YH00870
- **BALLYNAHINCH RIDING CTRE**, Ballynahinch **Ref:**YH00873
- **BRENTFORD RIDING SCHOOL**, Comber **Ref:**YH01849
- **DRUMGOOLAND HOUSE**, Downpatrick **Ref:**YH04290
- **LESSANS RIDING STABLES**, Ballynahinch **Ref:**YH08561
- **MILLBRIDGE RIDING CTRE**, Newtownards **Ref:**YH09594
- **MONTALTO FARM & FORESTRY**, Ballynahinch **Ref:**YH09730
- **NEWCASTLE RIDING CTRE**, Castlewellan **Ref:**YH10129
- **PENINSULA EQUESTRIAN ACADEMY**, Newtownards **Ref:**YH10940
- **ROCKFIELD EQUESTRIAN CTRE**, Newtownards **Ref:**YH12029
- **TULLYMURRY EQUESTRIAN CTRE**, Downpatrick **Ref:**YH14455

COUNTY FERMANAGH

- **LAKEVIEW HORSE RIDING CTRE**, Enniskillen **Ref:**YH08359
- **NECARNE CASTLE**, Enniskillen **Ref:**YH10066

COUNTY LONDONDERRY

- **ARDMORE STABLES**, Londonderry **Ref:**YH00511
- **FAUGHANVALE STABLES**, Londonderry **Ref:**YH05102
- **HILL FARM RIDING CTRE**, Coleraine **Ref:**YH06814
- **ISLAND EQUESTRIAN CTRE**, Coleraine **Ref:**YH07520
- **MADDYBENNY RIDING CTRE**, Coleraine **Ref:**YH09022
- **MARSH KYFE RIDING SCHOOL**, Magherafelt **Ref:**YH09186
- **TIMBERTOPS RIDING CTRE**, Coleraine **Ref:**YH14163

COUNTY TYRONE

- **EDERGOLE RIDING CTRE**, Cookstown **Ref:**YH04553
- **MOY RIDING SCHOOL**, Dungannon **Ref:**YH09907
- **TULLYWHISKER RIDING SCHOOL**, Strabane **Ref:**YH14458

RIDING WEAR RETAILERS

COUNTY ANTRIM

- **BRACKEN EQUESTRIAN**, Belfast **Ref:**YH01736
- **COUNTRY CLASSICS**, Lisburn **Ref:**YH03399
- **OLD MILL**, Carrickfergus **Ref:**YH10465

COUNTY ARMAGH

- **ANNAGHMORE SADDLERY**, Craigavon **Ref:**YH00451
- **PREMIER SADDLERY**, Armagh **Ref:**YH11349

COUNTY DOWN

- **HOLMESTEAD SADDLERY**, Downpatrick **Ref:**YH06981

COUNTY LONDONDERRY

- **BLAKES EQUESTRIAN**, Coleraine **Ref:**YH01521
- **HAVEN SADDLERY**, Magherafelt **Ref:**YH06539

SADDLERY RETAILERS

COUNTY ANTRIM

- **BRACKEN EQUESTRIAN**, Belfast **Ref:**YH01736
- **OLD MILL**, Carrickfergus **Ref:**YH10465
- **ROSS LODGE SADDLERY**, Ballymena **Ref:**YH12117
- **ROWAN RIDING WEAR**, Lisburn **Ref:**YH12155

COUNTY ARMAGH

- **ANNAGHMORE SADDLERY**, Craigavon **Ref:**YH00451
- **PREMIER SADDLERY**, Armagh **Ref:**YH11349
- **STINSON, J D**, Armagh **Ref:**YH13470

COUNTY DOWN

- **ANNAHILT SADDLERY**, Hillsborough **Ref:**YH00452
- **CARROWDORE SADDLERY**, Newtownards **Ref:**YH02595
- **GENERAL STORE**, Ballynahinch **Ref:**YH05702
- **HOLMESTEAD SADDLERY**, Downpatrick **Ref:**YH06981
- **KIDD SADDLERY**, Banbridge **Ref:**YH08120
- **M & B EQUESTRIAN**, Killinchy **Ref:**YH08943
- **MCCULLY BROS**, Newtownards **Ref:**YH09341
- **SMYTHS**, Newry **Ref:**YH13017

COUNTY LONDONDERRY

- **BLAKES EQUESTRIAN**, Coleraine **Ref:**YH01521
- **DEENY'S**, Claudy **Ref:**YH04019
- **HAVEN SADDLERY**, Magherafelt **Ref:**YH06539

COUNTY TYRONE

- **MCILVEEN, W M**, Omagh **Ref:**YH09371
- **OMAGH**, Omagh **Ref:**YH10506

STABLES/LIVERIES

COUNTY ANTRIM

- **ASHFIELD EQUESTRIAN**, Larne **Ref:**YH00597
- **BEECHES EQUESTRIAN CTRE**, Ballyclare **Ref:**YH01169
- **BIRR HSE RIDING CTRE**, Belfast **Ref:**YH01444
- **BURN EQUESTRIAN CLUB**, Belfast **Ref:**YH02263
- **CASTLEHILL EQUESTRIAN CTRE**, Ballymena **Ref:**YH02643
- **DRUMAHEGLIS RIDING SCHOOL**, Ballymoney **Ref:**YH04283
- **GALGORM MANOR EQUESTRIAN CTRE**, Ballymena **Ref:**YH05614
- **LAGAN VALLEY EQUESTRIAN CTRE**, Belfast **Ref:**YH08342
- **LUSK EQUESTRIAN**, Lisburn **Ref:**YH08905
- **TULLYNEWBANK STABLES**, Glenavy **Ref:**YH14456

COUNTY ARMAGH

- **BALLINTEGGART STUD**, Portadown **Ref:**YH00860
- **LIME PARK EQUESTRIAN**, Craigavon **Ref:**YH08626
- **LOUGHVIEW STABLES**, Lurgan **Ref:**YH08842
- **RICHHILL EQUESTRIAN CTRE**, Richhill **Ref:**YH11825

COUNTY DOWN

- **BALLYKNOCK RIDING SCHOOL**, Hillsborough **Ref:**YH00870
- **BALLYNAHINCH RIDING CTRE**, Ballynahinch **Ref:**YH00873
- **LESSANS RIDING STABLES**, Ballynahinch **Ref:**YH08561
- **MILLBRIDGE RIDING CTRE**, Newtownards **Ref:**YH09594
- **NEWCASTLE RIDING CTRE**, Castlewellan **Ref:**YH10129
- **PENINSULA EQUESTRIAN ACADEMY**, Newtownards **Ref:**YH10940
- **WOOD LODGE STABLES**, Castlewellan **Ref:**YH15659

COUNTY LONDONDERRY

- **ARDMORE STABLES**, Londonderry **Ref:**YH00511
- **DRUMSAMNEY EQUESTRIAN CTRE**, Magherafelt **Ref:**YH04292

FAUGHANVALE STABLES, Londonderry Ref:YH05102
HILL FARM RIDING CTRE, Coleraine Ref:YH06814
ISLAND EQUESTRIAN CTRE, Coleraine Ref:YH07520

COUNTY TYRONE

MOY RIDING SCHOOL, Dungannon Ref:YH09907

STUD FARMS

COUNTY ARMAGH

ALFRED BULLER BLOODSTOCK, Craigavon Ref:YH00275
BALLINTEGGART STUD, Portadown Ref:YH00860

SUPPLIES

COUNTY ANTRIM

ANDREWS MILLING, Belfast Ref:YH00396
BADMINTON HORSE FEEDS, Lisburn Ref:YH00782
BLAIR, R & K, Ballyclare Ref:YH01513
CHRISTIE & JEFFERS, Ballymoney Ref:YH02887
CHRISTIES ANIMAL GROOMING, Ballymoney Ref:YH02891
D P MULHOLLAND & SONS, Crumlin Ref:YH03803
E.CO IRELAND, Ballymena Ref:YH04434
GRANGE EQUESTRIAN, Newtownabbey Ref:YH05986
JOHN THOMPSON & SONS, Belfast Ref:YH07814
JOLLYES, Ballymena Ref:YH07853
JOLLYES, Glengormley Ref:YH07854
JOLLYES, Lisburn Ref:YH07855
LINDSAY RUGS, Newtownabbey Ref:YH08652
MILLAR FEEDS, Ballymena Ref:YH09591
OLD MILL WHIPS, Carrickfergus Ref:YH10471
T K S, Ballymena Ref:YH13756
WALKER, JIMMY, Belfast Ref:YH14852

COUNTY ARMAGH

FANE VALLEY, Armagh Ref:YH05043
HONEYHILL ROSETTES, Portadown Ref:YH07015

COUNTY DOWN

BALL BROTHERS, Dromara Ref:YH00847
BOOKLINE, Downpatrick Ref:YH01630
D B S FARM SUPPLIES, Dromara Ref:YH03779
DRUM-A-HOY, Saintfield Ref:YH04284
FANE VALLEY, Banbridge Ref:YH05044
HOLMESTEAD SADDLERY, Downpatrick Ref:YH06981
JAMES GLOVER & SONS, Crossgar Ref:YH07669
JOLLYES, Bangor Ref:YH07856
JOLLYES, Newry Ref:YH07857
MOURNE ROSETTES, Hillsborough Ref:YH09903
O'HARES, Castlewellan Ref:YH10444
OLD MANOR MILL, Newtownards Ref:YH10462
P LAVELLE & SONS, Newry Ref:YH10651
R W TOASE, Newry Ref:YH11569
SHIELDS, THOMAS, Newry Ref:YH12742
SOUTH ARMAGH FARMING, Newry Ref:YH13076
SOUTHDOWN FEEDS, Rathfriland Ref:YH13135
WATSONS FARM FEEDS, Downpatrick Ref:YH14996
WEIR, Ballynahinch Ref:YH15051

COUNTY FERMANAGH

JOLLYES, Eniskillen Ref:YH07858

COUNTY LONDONDERRY

ARCHIBALD, Coleraine Ref:YH00499
BLAKES EQUESTRIAN, Coleraine Ref:YH01521
HAVEN SADDLERY, Magherafelt Ref:YH06539
MOYOLA CANVAS, Maghera Ref:YH09912
QUIGLEY, H D, Dungiven Ref:YH11497
STEWART ROBINSON, Limavady Ref:YH13456

COUNTY TYRONE

BLUEGRASS HORSE FEEDS, Dungannon Ref:YH01573
CLEMENTS, D, Augher Ref:YH03016
DONNELLY & SON, Fintona Ref:YH04187
HACKETTS, Omagh Ref:YH06252
LECKPATRICK AGRCLTRL SVS, Strabane Ref:YH08514
MCLERNON, P, Dungannon Ref:YH09391

TRACKS/COURSES

COUNTY ANTRIM

DOWN ROYAL RACECOURSE, Lisburn Ref:YH04223

COUNTY ARMAGH

RICHHILL EQUESTRIAN CTRE, Richhill Ref:YH11825

COUNTY DOWN

DOWNPATRICK RACECOURSE, Downpatrick Ref:YH04237

COUNTY LONDONDERRY

MARSH KYFE RIDING SCHOOL, Magherafelt Ref:YH09186

COUNTY TYRONE

MOY RIDING SCHOOL, Dungannon Ref:YH09907

TRAINERS

COUNTY ANTRIM

ROCK SEMEN CTRE, Ballymena Ref:YH12026
ROSS, J B, Newtownabbey Ref:YH12119

COUNTY DOWN

BLACKWOOD, LADY PERDITA, Newtownards Ref:YH01503
GILL, J, Ballynahinch Ref:YH05773
SMILEY, ERIC, Ballynahinch Ref:YH12929
WOOD LODGE STABLES, Castlewellan Ref:YH15659

COUNTY LONDONDERRY

FAUGHANVALE STABLES, Londonderry Ref:YH05102
FORT CTRE, Maghera Ref:YH05385

COUNTY TYRONE

WOODS, L, Strabane Ref:YH15738

TRANSPORT/HORSE BOXES

COUNTY ANTRIM

ASHCROFT TRAILER HIRE, Newtownabbey Ref:YH00593
BROWN, C N, Lisburn Ref:YH02103
BROWNS COACHWORKS, Lisburn Ref:YH02143
C B R, Newtownabbey Ref:YH02364
DUFFIN, W, Ballymena Ref:YH04318
DUNCRUE TRAILERS, Newtownabbey Ref:YH04337
G R M TRAILERS, Ballymena Ref:YH05592
GENERAL TRAILERS, Newtownabbey Ref:YH05706
GRAHAM, LINDSAY, Ballyclare Ref:YH05971
HANNA TRAILERS, Belfast Ref:YH06393
HIRECO NI, Belfast Ref:YH06883
HORNER COMPONENTS, Lisburn Ref:YH07076
INDESPENSION, Newtownabbey Ref:YH07413
LAVERTY LIVESTOCK, Ballymena Ref:YH08464
LUSK TRANSPORT, Lisburn Ref:YH08906
MCCAULEY TRAILERS, Antrim Ref:YH09327
MCGRATH TRAILERS, Belfast Ref:YH09360
METAL MART, Belfast Ref:YH09497
MONTRACON, Newtownabbey Ref:YH09733
NEVILLE GRAHAM, Ballyclare Ref:YH10087
NICHOLSON, BRIAN, Crumlin Ref:YH10192
NICHOLSON, BRIAN, Lisburn Ref:YH10191
S D C TRAILERS, Antrim Ref:YH12319

COUNTY ARMAGH

FULLERTON CAR & TRAILER, Craigavon Ref:YH05535
HAMMOND, DAVID, Craigavon Ref:YH06360
MONARCH ENGINEERING, Armagh Ref:YH09716
NEILL, IVOR, Craigavon Ref:YH10070
W T WAITE & SONS, Craigavon Ref:YH14800

COUNTY DOWN

FAWCETT, GEORGE, Ballynahinch Ref:YH05108
GEDDIS TRANSPORT, Helens Bay Ref:YH05689
MCILWAINE TRAILERS, Hillsborough Ref:YH09372
MET ART, Newry Ref:YH09493

COUNTY LONDONDERRY

A J C LAMONT, Coleraine Ref:YH00038
ANDMAR TRAILER CTRE, Londonderry Ref:YH00388
MCGURK, M, Magherafelt Ref:YH09369
PURBECK HORSE BOXES, Londonderry Ref:YH11461

COUNTY TYRONE

CROOKS TRAILERS, Cookstown Ref:YH03639
CROOKS TRAILERS, Cookstown Ref:YH03638
EAMONN RICE BLOOD STOCK, Dungannon Ref:YH04447
NUGENT TRAILERS, Dungannon Ref:YH10352
PARKS, DAVID, Dungannon Ref:YH10772

ARENAS

ABERDEENSHIRE

- **RIDINGHILL STUD**, Fraserburgh **Ref:**YH11885

AYRSHIRE (EAST)

- **DEAN CASTLE RIDING CTRE**, Kilmarnock **Ref:**YH03988
- **ROWALLAN ACTIVITY CTRE**, Kilmarnock **Ref:**YH12152

AYRSHIRE (NORTH)

- **CAIRNHOUSE RIDING CTRE**, Isle Of Arran **Ref:**YH02419

EDINBURGH (CITY OF)

- **TOWER FARM**, Edinburgh **Ref:**YH14271

GLASGOW (CITY OF)

- **BUSBY EQUITATION CTRE**, Busby **Ref:**YH02302

ISLE OF SKYE

- **SKYE RIDING CTRE**, Portree **Ref:**YH12881

PERTH AND KINROSS

- **EASTERTON ARENAS**, Auchterarder **Ref:**YH04499
- **GLEN EAGLES EQUESTRIAN**, Auchterarder **Ref:**YH05825
- **GLENMARKIE**, Blairgowrie **Ref:**YH05840

BLACKSMITHS

ABERDEEN (CITY OF)

- **ANDERSON, IAN**, Aberdeen **Ref:**YH00383
- **BTC**, Aberdeen **Ref:**YH02181
- **MOIR, DAVID**, Aberdeen **Ref:**YH09702

ABERDEENSHIRE

- **ANDERSON, D**, Banchory **Ref:**YH00381
- **BELMONT BLACKSMITH**, Banchory **Ref:**YH01244
- **E STRACHAN**, Inverurie **Ref:**YH04425
- **JOHN FINDLATER & SON**, Westhill **Ref:**YH07788
- **KELMAN ENGINEERING**, Turriff **Ref:**YH08050
- **MORRISON, S J**, Turriff **Ref:**YH09839
- **MORRISON, WILLIAM G**, Huntly **Ref:**YH09840
- **SMIDDY, FYVIE**, Turriff **Ref:**YH12928
- **SMITH, A G**, Keith **Ref:**YH12938
- **STRACHAN, ARTHUR E**, Banchory **Ref:**YH13543
- **STUART, L G**, Peterhead **Ref:**YH13596
- **TAWSE, JAMES E**, Stonehaven **Ref:**YH13890

ANGUS

- **ALGATE FABRACATES**, Arbroath **Ref:**YH00277
- **ANGUS MCMURTRIE**, Dundee **Ref:**YH00422
- **BLACKLITE**, Dundee **Ref:**YH01486
- **CAMERON, D N & R**, Arbroath **Ref:**YH02478
- **CAMERON, D N & R**, Arbroath **Ref:**YH02479
- **D P FENWICK**, Dundee **Ref:**YH03802
- **E N ROBERTSON & SON**, Forfar **Ref:**YH04417
- **GARLOWBANK SMITHY**, Kirriemuir **Ref:**YH05653
- **GRANT, G B**, Dundee **Ref:**YH06012
- **J & J FABRICATION**, Dundee **Ref:**YH07546
- **J & J STEWART**, Arbroath **Ref:**YH07548
- **KENNEDY & CHEETHAM**, Forfar **Ref:**YH08066
- **MARK FABRICATION**, Dundee **Ref:**YH09152
- **MARKS FABRICATIONS**, Dundee **Ref:**YH09162

ARGYLL AND BUTE

- **BUTE BLACKSMITHS**, Rothesay **Ref:**YH02318
- **CLYDEBANK WELDING**, Clydebank **Ref:**YH03080
- **CURRIE, G H**, Dunoon **Ref:**YH03740
- **WELDMECH SERVICES**, Taynuilt **Ref:**YH15064
- **WEST COAST WELDING**, Lochgilphead **Ref:**YH15133

AYRSHIRE (EAST)

- **ANVIL ENGINEERING**, Kilmarnock **Ref:**YH00467

AYRSHIRE (NORTH)

- **CALVIN**, Irvine **Ref:**YH02459
- **FORGE**, Largs **Ref:**YH05359

AYRSHIRE (SOUTH)

- **D MCCULLOCH & SON**, Maybole **Ref:**YH03797
- **GILMOUR, JOHN**, Prestwick **Ref:**YH05790
- **MORRELL ANTHONY & SONS**, Girvan **Ref:**YH09825

DUMFRIES AND GALLOWAY

- **CURRIE, ROBERT J**, Moffat **Ref:**YH03741
- **DONALDSON, J & W**, Moffat **Ref:**YH04176
- **DOUGLAS, JOHN L**, Newton Stewart **Ref:**YH04214
- **J HARKNESS & SONS**, Dumfries **Ref:**YH07588
- **J MCKIRDLE & SONS**, Dumfries **Ref:**YH07600
- **JOHN GIBSON & SONS**, Dumfries **Ref:**YH07791
- **JOHN MCKNIGHT & SON**, Stranraer **Ref:**YH07801
- **MUTEHILL SMITHY**, Kirkcudbright **Ref:**YH09977
- **PIPERS FORGE**, Castle Douglas **Ref:**YH11148
- **SEGGIE, A**, Dumfries **Ref:**YH12612
- **STEELE, J A**, Dumfries **Ref:**YH13419

EDINBURGH (CITY OF)

- **ABEL ENGINEERING**, Edinburgh **Ref:**YH00117
- **ALEXANDER**, Edinburgh **Ref:**YH00264
- **BANKS BLACKSMITHS**, Edinburgh **Ref:**YH00895
- **CAMERON, JOHN**, Edinburgh **Ref:**YH02481
- **COCKBURN ENGINEERING**, Edinburgh **Ref:**YH03120
- **CRAMOND BRIG**, Edinburgh **Ref:**YH03558
- **EDINBURGH FABRICATIONS**, Edinburgh **Ref:**YH04562
- **GLASGOW & WEIR**, Edinburgh **Ref:**YH05807
- **GRANGE METALWORK**, Edinburgh **Ref:**YH05992
- **HORSBURGH, THOMAS**, Edinburgh **Ref:**YH07084
- **JAMES MACKINTOSH & SON**, Edinburgh **Ref:**YH07672
- **JJG BLACKSMITHS**, Edinburgh **Ref:**YH07769
- **JOHNSON, P**, Newbridge **Ref:**YH07831
- **MCDOUGALL, A**, Edinburgh **Ref:**YH09347
- **MCLENNAN, ALEXANDER**, Edinburgh **Ref:**YH09389
- **NEWHAVEN BLACKSMITHS**, Edinburgh **Ref:**YH10138
- **R THOMPSON**, Edinburgh **Ref:**YH11566
- **SPENCER, WALTER**, Edinburgh **Ref:**YH13201
- **STEEL FABRICATIONS**, Currie **Ref:**YH13414
- **SUTHERLAND, G**, Edinburgh **Ref:**YH13667

FALKIRK

- **FORTHSIDE FABRICATION**, Bonnybridge **Ref:**YH05391
- **JOHN JENKINS & SON**, Falkirk **Ref:**YH07796

FIFE

- **ALLEN, SANDY**, Kirkcaldy **Ref:**YH00302
- **B M K FABRICATION**, Glenrothes **Ref:**YH00742
- **DON, J S**, Newport-on-Tay **Ref:**YH04174
- **EDNIE, JAS P**, Leven **Ref:**YH04568
- **FENTON FABRICATION**, Cupar **Ref:**YH05152
- **H C STAR METALS**, Burntisland **Ref:**YH06216
- **HENDERSON FABRICATION**, St Andrews **Ref:**YH06665
- **IRVINE ENGINEERING**, St Andrews **Ref:**YH07509
- **LAWSON, SCOTT**, Tayport **Ref:**YH08479
- **MCLEOD & HUNTER**, Dunfermline **Ref:**YH09390
- **MILLER, R**, Cupar **Ref:**YH09610
- **RENTOUL, ROBIN**, Kirkcaldy **Ref:**YH11765

GLASGOW (CITY OF)

- **ALEX MCDERMID & SON**, Glasgow **Ref:**YH00263
- **AMRAK ENGINEERING**, Glasgow **Ref:**YH00373
- **ANCHOR TO NEEDLE FABRICATIONS**, Glasgow **Ref:**YH00376
- **BLAIR, J K**, Glasgow **Ref:**YH01510
- **BLAIR, J K**, Glasgow **Ref:**YH01511
- **BROWN, J**, Glasgow **Ref:**YH02113
- **CRAIG & BUCHANAN**, Glasgow **Ref:**YH03549
- **CRAIG BUILDERS ENGINEERS**, Glasgow **Ref:**YH03550
- **CROWN WELDING**, Glasgow **Ref:**YH03682
- **CRUICKSHANKS, T & D**, Glasgow **Ref:**YH03689
- **D M E FABRICATIONS 1984**, Glasgow **Ref:**YH03793
- **D R PATERSON GRP**, Glasgow **Ref:**YH03805
- **D TOBIAS**, Glasgow **Ref:**YH03810
- **DERMAX**, Glasgow **Ref:**YH04076
- **DERMAX IND SVS**, Glasgow **Ref:**YH04077
- **GALLACHER, A**, Glasgow **Ref:**YH05616
- **LAMOND, A**, Glasgow **Ref:**YH08374
- **LYLE, W**, Glasgow **Ref:**YH08918
- **M H M BLACKSMITHS**, Glasgow **Ref:**YH08964
- **MACPHERSON T J & SON**, Glasgow **Ref:**YH09015
- **MCEWAN BROS**, Glasgow **Ref:**YH09350
- **OMEGA BLACKSMITHS**, Glasgow **Ref:**YH10508
- **PARKHEAD WELDING**, Glasgow **Ref:**YH10761
- **RENFREW, W G**, Glasgow **Ref:**YH11758
- **SCROLL FACTORY**, Glasgow **Ref:**YH12568
- **SILLARS, A L**, Glasgow **Ref:**YH12801
- **STAR BLACKSMITH**, Glasgow **Ref:**YH13391
- **WELDING, A M**, Glasgow **Ref:**YH15062

HIGHLANDS

- **FRASER, J D**, Inverness **Ref:**YH05472
- **L A SMITH**, Dingwall **Ref:**YH08315
- **MACKENZIE, G A**, Dornoch **Ref:**YH09001
- **MARSHALL, W**, Nairn **Ref:**YH09206
- **MCBEAN, W F**, Nairn **Ref:**YH09314
- **RENOUF, PAUL**, Lairg **Ref:**YH11761
- **TOMATIN SMITHY**, Inverness **Ref:**YH14218

INVERCLYDE

- **BOAG DESIGN BLACKSMITHS**, Greenock **Ref:**YH01582

LANARKSHIRE (NORTH)

- **ANVIL PRODUCTS**, Wishaw **Ref:**YH00469
- **BELHAVEN ENGINEERING**, Wishaw **Ref:**YH01212
- **KIRK RD SMIDDY**, Shotts **Ref:**YH08230
- **MCLEAN, H S**, Airdrie **Ref:**YH09387
- **MORGAN BLACKSMITH**, Airdrie **Ref:**YH09792
- **MUIRHEAD BLACKSMITHS**, Glasgow **Ref:**YH09925
- **R & D BLACKSMITHS**, Motherwell **Ref:**YH11504
- **R MILLER BLACKSMITH**, Wishaw **Ref:**YH11558

LANARKSHIRE (SOUTH)

- **CAMPBELL, FINDLAY**, Hamilton **Ref:**YH02484
- **HUTTON, C D**, Glasgow **Ref:**YH07340
- **INDUSTRI ART**, Glasgow **Ref:**YH07440
- **JACKTON SMIDDY**, Glasgow **Ref:**YH07658
- **LEGGATE, J**, Lanark **Ref:**YH08539

LOTHIAN (EAST)

- **ANDERSON, ALEC A**, East Linton **Ref:**YH00380
- **D A W ENGINEERING**, North Berwick **Ref:**YH03776
- **HARROWER, HENRY**, Haddington **Ref:**YH06496
- **HOGG, W**, Tranent **Ref:**YH06920

LOTHIAN (MID)

- **A M FABRICATIONS**, Bonnyrigg **Ref:**YH00050
- **ABEL ENGINEERING**, Dalkeith **Ref:**YH00118
- **G FITZSIMMONS & SON**, Rosewell **Ref:**YH05577
- **GILHOOLEY ENGINEERING**, Loanhead **Ref:**YH05766
- **INNES, J**, Musselburgh **Ref:**YH07460
- **KAY ENGINEERING**, Bonnyrigg **Ref:**YH08002
- **LOTHIAN FABRICATIONS**, Rosewell **Ref:**YH08832
- **PAXTON & CLARK**, Bonnyrigg **Ref:**YH10843
- **TURNER, ANDREW**, Penicuik **Ref:**YH14475
- **WHITEHILL FORGE & WORKS**, Rosewell **Ref:**YH15343

LOTHIAN (WEST)

- **BROWN, A T**, Kirknewton **Ref:**YH02097
- **EDINBURGH FABRICATION**, Broxburn **Ref:**YH04561
- **G & M RODGER**, Bathgate **Ref:**YH05568
- **HARRIS, J**, West Calder **Ref:**YH06475
- **METAL COMPONENT FABRICATORS**, Bathgate **Ref:**YH09496
- **QUEENSFERRY METALS**, South Queensferry **Ref:**YH11492
- **WYMAN-GORDON**, Livingston **Ref:**YH15868
- **YOUNG, D M**, Broxburn **Ref:**YH15928

MORAY

- **TERRIS, J & D G**, Grantown-on-Spey **Ref:**YH13956

ORKNEY ISLES

- **TAIT, T A**, Orkney **Ref:**YH13825
- **W REDLAND & SON**, Stromness **Ref:**YH14792

PERTH AND KINROSS

- **BELL, STEVEN A**, Perth **Ref:**YH01229
- **CUMMING, J W**, Aberfeldy **Ref:**YH03719
- **DONALDSON, ROBERT**, Kinross **Ref:**YH04177
- **J MITCHELL**, Perth **Ref:**YH07601
- **J, MILLER**, Blairgowrie **Ref:**YH07633
- **KING, A & L**, Auchterarder **Ref:**YH08173
- **MEDDICKS, J**, Perth **Ref:**YH09434
- **MUIRHEAD BLACKSMITH**, Perth **Ref:**YH09924
- **NEW FORGE**, Perth **Ref:**YH10105
- **PATTERSON, W**, Crieff **Ref:**YH10829
- **SMITH, R H**, Perth **Ref:**YH12988
- **THOM, ALLAN**, Blairgowrie **Ref:**YH14004
- **THOMSON, D W**, Perth **Ref:**YH14051

RENFREWSHIRE

- **ADFAB FABRICATIONS**, Port Glasgow **Ref:**YH00184
- **BLACKSTOCK, L**, Bridge Of Weir **Ref:**YH01498
- **D L FABRICATIONS**, Paisley **Ref:**YH03790
- **IRONART FABRICATIONS**, Lochwinnoch **Ref:**YH07505
- **J & W WROUGHT IRONWORK**, Paisley **Ref:**YH07552
- **MCPHERSON A BLACKSMITHS**, Johnstone **Ref:**YH09404
- **THOMSON W. A**, Paisley **Ref:**YH14048

SCOTTISH BORDERS

- **JEFFREY, A T**, West Linton **Ref:**YH07724
- **KEDDIE T & R**, Selkirk **Ref:**YH08023
- **NOBLE, R**, Eyemouth **Ref:**YH10220
- **TELFER, JOHN**, Hawick **Ref:**YH13939
- **WEIR, W S**, Peebles **Ref:**YH15056
- **WELDING, P C**, Peebles **Ref:**YH15063

SHETLAND ISLANDS

- **BRUCE WILCOCK**, Shetland **Ref:**YH02154

STIRLING

- **B, MCPHEE**, Stirling **Ref:**YH00753
- **HENDRY, JAMES**, Stirling **Ref:**YH06669
- **HOWDEN**, Denny **Ref:**YH07221
- **MARSHALL, JOHN**, Stirling **Ref:**YH09194

BLOOD STOCK AGENCIES

ABERDEENSHIRE

- **CRAGINETHERTY**, Turriff **Ref:**YH03545
- **HJEMDAL**, Turriff **Ref:**YH06889

AYRSHIRE (SOUTH)

- **CREE LODGE**, Ayr **Ref:**YH03587
- **I C S BLOODSTOCK**, Mauchline **Ref:**YH07364
- **JAMES M BARCLAY & SON**, Maybole **Ref:**YH07671
- **SEMEX**, Prestwick **Ref:**YH12631

EDINBURGH (CITY OF)

- **SEROLOGICALS**, Edinburgh **Ref:**YH12636

SCOTTISH BORDERS

- **DONCASTER BLOODSTOCK SALES**, Hawick **Ref:**YH04178
- **SCOTTISH BLOODSTOCK AGENCY**, Jedburgh **Ref:**YH12550

BREEDERS

ABERDEEN (CITY OF)

- **ABERDEEN RARE BREEDS PK**, Aberdeen **Ref:**YH00124
- **BOWLEY, HAZEL**, Aberdeen **Ref:**YH01718
- **BRITISH BAVARIAN WARMBLOOD**, Aberdeen **Ref:**YH01927
- **CHRISTIE, NORMAN**, Aberdeen **Ref:**YH02888
- **CLOTHIE SHETLAND PONY STUD**, Dyce **Ref:**YH03065
- **GREENFERNS STUD**, Portlethen **Ref:**YH06081
- **RYOVAN ARABIAN STUD**, Dyce **Ref:**YH12307
- **WHITEMYRES STUD LIVERY YARD**, Aberdeen **Ref:**YH15353

ABERDEENSHIRE

- **ASGARD STUD**, Inverurie **Ref:**YH00586
- **BEE, M**, Inverurie **Ref:**YH01161
- **BEKON HAFLINGER STUD**, Methlick **Ref:**YH01201
- **BIRKLAND STUD**, Banchory **Ref:**YH01442
- **BROGAR PONY STUD**, Methlick **Ref:**YH02019
- **CRAGINETHERTY**, Turriff **Ref:**YH03545
- **DENMILL HIGHLAND PONY STUD**, Alford **Ref:**YH04049
- **DONALD, GEORGE**, Huntly **Ref:**YH04175
- **GAMMIE, J W**, Laurencekirk **Ref:**YH05638
- **GLEN TANAR EQUESTRIAN CTRE**, Aboyne **Ref:**YH05827
- **HAYBRAKE SHETLAND PONY STUD**, Inverurie **Ref:**YH06564
- **HJEMDAL**, Turriff **Ref:**YH06889
- **MAINS OF BADENSCOTH**, Inverurie **Ref:**YH09040
- **MANAR STUD & RIDING CTRE**, Alford **Ref:**YH09064
- **MCINTOSH, WILLIAM G**, Macduff **Ref:**YH09377
- **MILL OF URAS EQUESTRIAN**, Stonehaven **Ref:**YH09583
- **PITMEDDEN STUD**, Inverurie **Ref:**YH11153
- **RAVENSHEAR, J**, Huntly **Ref:**YH11659
- **RIDINGHILL STUD**, Fraserburgh **Ref:**YH11885
- **RUSSELL, S**, Peterhead **Ref:**YH12263
- **SCOTHORSE**, Maryculter **Ref:**YH12530
- **SKINNER, GEORGE M**, Inverurie **Ref:**YH12875
- **STEVENS**, Banchory **Ref:**YH13440
- **STONEHAVEN ICELANDICS**, Stonehaven **Ref:**YH13513
- **TOMINTOUL RIDING CTRE**, Ballindalloch **Ref:**YH14221
- **WESTPARK SHETLAND PONY STUD**, Turriff **Ref:**YH15230

ANGUS

- **BALHALL RIDING STABLES**, Brechin **Ref:**YH00845
- **BROWN, RAYMOND**, Forfar **Ref:**YH02131
- **COMPTON, J C**, Forfar **Ref:**YH03219
- **DALBRACK HIGHLAND PONY STUD**, Brechin **Ref:**YH03819
- **GOW, D J H**, Forfar **Ref:**YH05953
- **GREENHILL, A**, Forfar **Ref:**YH06089
- **MACDONALD, A R**, Kirriemuir **Ref:**YH08987
- **WHITEGATE STUD**, Forfar **Ref:**YH15339

ARGYLL AND BUTE

- **APPALOOSA HOLIDAYS**, Lochgilphead **Ref:**YH00475
- **BOASE, N & L**, Lochgilphead **Ref:**YH01585
- **ERRAY**, Isle Of Mull **Ref:**YH04853
- **MAPLE LEAF QUARTER HORSES**, Rosneath **Ref:**YH09131
- **ROCKHILL FARM**, Dalmally **Ref:**YH12031
- **ROCKHILL HANOVERIAN STUD**, Dalmally **Ref:**YH12032

AYRSHIRE (EAST)

- **CLUNY HACKNEY STUD**, Galston **Ref:**YH03076
- **MCINNES, WILLIAM**, Kilmarnock **Ref:**YH09375
- **MERRYLEES, G**, Kilmarnock **Ref:**YH09488
- **MITCHELL, TOM**, Kilmarnock **Ref:**YH09677
- **MUIRDYKE STUD FARM**, Cumnock **Ref:**YH09922

AYRSHIRE (NORTH)

- **CRAIGWEIL ARABIAN STUD**, Irvine **Ref:**YH03556
- **SMITH, JAMES HARRY**, Kilwinning **Ref:**YH12966

AYRSHIRE (SOUTH)

- **CREE LODGE**, Ayr **Ref:**YH03587
- **I C S**, Mauchline **Ref:**YH07363
- **JAMES M BARCLAY & SON**, Maybole **Ref:**YH07671
- **O'NEIL, HUGH**, Ayr **Ref:**YH10514
- **THOM, J G**, Ayr **Ref:**YH14005
- **YOUNG, JAMES W**, Ayr **Ref:**YH15934

CLACKMANNANSHIRE

- **LUCEY, P E**, Alloa **Ref:**YH08885
- **SIBBALD, ROBERT**, Dollar **Ref:**YH12779
- **TRANSY SHETLAND PONY STUD**, Dollar **Ref:**YH14354

DUMFRIES AND GALLOWAY

- **AGNEW, R & A**, Stranraer **Ref:**YH00199
- **EASTLANDS**, Langholm **Ref:**YH04507
- **GALLOWAY, TOM**, Newton Stewart **Ref:**YH05627
- **LOVE, ANDREW**, Stranraer **Ref:**YH08844
- **MACMILLAN, WILLIAM G**, Lockerbie **Ref:**YH09013
- **MCGEOGH, J & I**, Stranraer **Ref:**YH09354
- **MEIKLE WELSH COBS**, Castle Douglas **Ref:**YH09447
- **MRS HUNT**, Terregles **Ref:**YH09917
- **SHAW, WALTER H**, Stranraer **Ref:**YH12684
- **SMITH, JOHN (JNR)**, Newton Stewart **Ref:**YH12969
- **THOMSON, J L**, Thornhill **Ref:**YH14052

EDINBURGH (CITY OF)

- **CLYDESDALE HORSE SOC**, Edinburgh **Ref:**YH03081
- **DAVDOR STUD**, Currie **Ref:**YH03907
- **LAWRIE, D**, Balerno **Ref:**YH08474
- **ROBERTSON, E C**, Dalkeith **Ref:**YH11968

FALKIRK

- **COWAN STABLES**, Falkirk **Ref:**YH03520
- **TAYLOR, JOHN S**, Slamannan **Ref:**YH13905

FIFE

- **ALEXANDER, N W**, Glenrothes **Ref:**YH00272
- **ALLAN, W K A**, Freuchie **Ref:**YH00289
- **BRADY, RON**, Saline **Ref:**YH01768
- **BRAITHWAITE, C G**, Cupar **Ref:**YH01779
- **BROWN, R & F**, Cupar **Ref:**YH02129
- **LOW-MITCHELL, D I**, Leven **Ref:**YH08876
- **MOORE, W**, Kelty **Ref:**YH09769
- **PUDDLEDUB STUD**, Kirkcaldy **Ref:**YH11447
- **WAXWING STUD**, Saline **Ref:**YH15012

GLASGOW (CITY OF)

- **BARR, ANGELINE**, Glasgow **Ref:**YH01000
- **BUSBY EQUITATION CTRE**, Busby **Ref:**YH02302
- **CHRISTIE**, Glasgow **Ref:**YH02886
- **LEAHY, P N**, Glasgow **Ref:**YH08500

HIGHLANDS

- **CROILA STABLES**, Newtonmore **Ref:**YH03627
- **DARMADY, JOHN**, Lybster **Ref:**YH03897
- **GETHIN, M**, Inverness **Ref:**YH05734
- **JOHNSTONE**, Muir Of Ord **Ref:**YH07848
- **MACDONALD, PETER**, Sleat **Ref:**YH08989
- **MCKAY, J & S**, Portree **Ref:**YH09379
- **MILLER, W & M**, Nairn **Ref:**YH09614
- **MURRAY, ALEXANDER C**, Wick **Ref:**YH09962
- **ORMISTON, EWAN C**, Kingussie **Ref:**YH10549
- **SCORRAIG EXMOOR PONIES**, Garve **Ref:**YH12528
- **WALFORD**, Broadford **Ref:**YH14841
- **WATT, R**, Sutherland **Ref:**YH15000

ISLE OF SKYE

- **SKYE RIDING CTRE**, Portree **Ref:**YH12881

LANARKSHIRE (NORTH)

- **LAIRD, ALEXANDER**, Shotts **Ref:**YH08347

LANARKSHIRE (SOUTH)

- **BABES, G**, Glasgow **Ref:**YH00763
- **DARHO STUD & EQUESTRIAN SVS**, Auchengray **Ref:**YH03886
- **GEMMELL, WILLIAM**, Lesmahagow **Ref:**YH05699
- **HILLSIDE CLYSDALE STUD**, Lesmahagow **Ref:**YH06852
- **MOUNTAIN TOP MORGANS**, Forth **Ref:**YH09897
- **STEEL, A & E**, Strathaven **Ref:**YH13416
- **STEWART, J**, Kirkmuirhill **Ref:**YH13457
- **STEWART, W**, Lanark **Ref:**YH13460
- **SUMMERHILL STUD**, Lanark **Ref:**YH13631
- **WEIR, D**, Sandilands **Ref:**YH15052

LOTHIAN (EAST)

- **DUNCRAHILL STUD**, Tranent **Ref:**YH04336
- **MACGREGOR, E & I**, Dunbar **Ref:**YH08997
- **SIMPSON**, North Berwick **Ref:**YH12836
- **THORBURN, ELSPETH**, North Berwick **Ref:**YH14055

LOTHIAN (MID)

- **NOBLE, ANNETTE**, Penicuik **Ref:**YH10218
- **PENTLAND HILLS ICELANDICS**, Penicuik **Ref:**YH10961
- **PERPOP STUD**, Roslin **Ref:**YH10981

LOTHIAN (WEST)

- **MACFARLANE, THOMAS W**, West Calder **Ref:**YH08996
- **NIMMO, M C**, Broxburn **Ref:**YH10207

MORAY

- **BENNETT, JAMES G**, Buckie **Ref:**YH01271
- **SHENVAL FARM**, Ballindalloch **Ref:**YH12709
- **YOUNG, IAN**, Fochabers **Ref:**YH15930

PERTH AND KINROSS

- **ALEXANDER, G & B**, Blairgowrie **Ref:**YH00269
- **ANNANDALE SHETLAND PONY STUD**, Alyth **Ref:**YH00454
- **ARMOURY STABLES**, Pitlochry **Ref:**YH00540
- **BAIRD, GEORGE M**, Blairgowrie **Ref:**YH00815
- **BLAIR CASTLE TREKKING CTRE**, Pitlochry **Ref:**YH01509
- **BLAIRHILL STUD**, Kinross **Ref:**YH01515
- **BREWSTER, T & C**, Perth **Ref:**YH01856
- **CAMPMUIR QUARTER HORSES**, Coupar Angus **Ref:**YH02491
- **DICKSON, F**, Perth **Ref:**YH04116
- **EASTERTON ARENAS**, Auchterarder **Ref:**YH04499
- **FAIRWAYS CLYDESDALE CTRE**, Glencarse **Ref:**YH05033
- **FENTON**, Dunning **Ref:**YH05151
- **MCGILLIVRAY, D & M**, Comrie **Ref:**YH09357
- **MUIRTON STUD**, Crieff **Ref:**YH09928
- **RIMMER, M**, Dunblane **Ref:**YH11898
- **TILLYRIE RACING**, Kinross **Ref:**YH14155

RENFREWSHIRE

- **THOS MITCHELL & SON**, Uplawmoor **Ref:**YH14098

SCOTTISH BORDERS

- **BROKEN SPOKE**, West Linton **Ref:**YH02021
- **DOUGLAS, W J**, Jedburgh **Ref:**YH04215
- **DUN, J M**, Heriot **Ref:**YH04330
- **FLOORS STUD**, Kelso **Ref:**YH05288
- **HAMILTON, H B**, Innerleithen **Ref:**YH06353
- **KELLOE PK STUD**, Duns **Ref:**YH08043
- **LOCH, SYLVIA (LADY)**, Kelso **Ref:**YH08754
- **MACTAGGART, A B**, Hawick **Ref:**YH09017
- **OLIVER, RHONA**, Hawick **Ref:**YH10500
- **OVER WHITLAW STABLES**, Selkirk **Ref:**YH10590
- **ROWCHESTER ARABIANS**, Duns **Ref:**YH12158
- **SCOTT, C**, Hawick **Ref:**YH12539
- **SLIGHT, K**, Lauder **Ref:**YH12897
- **WEST TARF ICELANDIC HORSES**, West Linton **Ref:**YH15167
- **YOUNG, J W**, Kelso **Ref:**YH15933

SHETLAND ISLANDS

- **BROOTHOM PONIES**, Shetland **Ref:**YH02083

STIRLING

- **CARRICK, CHARLES W**, Kippen **Ref:**YH02585
- **LOMONDSIDE STUD**, Glasgow **Ref:**YH08782
- **MCGREGOR, HUGH SCOTT**, Stirling **Ref:**YH09367
- **MYOTHILL HSE EQUESTRIAN CTRE**, Denny **Ref:**YH09985
- **ROBERT BREWSTER & SON**, Causewayhead **Ref:**YH11939

CLUBS/ASSOCIATIONS

ABERDEEN (CITY OF)

- **ABERDEEN DISTRICT COUNCIL**, Aberdeen **Ref:**YH00123
- **BRITISH BAVARIAN WARMBLOOD**, Aberdeen **Ref:**YH01927
- **UNIVERSITY OF ABERDEEN**, Aberdeen **Ref:**YH14581

ABERDEENSHIRE

- **BHS**, Ellon **Ref:**YH01352
- **BRITISH HORSE LOGGERS**, Inverurie **Ref:**YH01952
- **BUCHAN RIDING CLUB**, Fraserburgh **Ref:**YH02185
- **FJORD HORSE REGISTRY**, Inverurie **Ref:**YH05257
- **GORDON DRESSAGE GROUP**, Banchory **Ref:**YH05923
- **KINCARDINE COUNTY RIDING CLUB**, Stonehaven **Ref:**YH08166
- **STRATH ISLA RIDING CLUB**, Huntly **Ref:**YH13554

ARGYLL AND BUTE

- **ARGYLL RIDING CLUB**, Argyll **Ref:**YH00522
- **BUTE PONY & RIDING CLUB**, Ettrick Bay **Ref:**YH02319
- **GARELOCH RIDING CLUB**, Helensburgh **Ref:**YH05650

AYRSHIRE (EAST)

- **BSPS AREA SCOTTISH BRANCH**, Kilmaurs **Ref:**YH02180
- **ERISKAY PONY SOC**, Fenwick **Ref:**YH04849
- **KILMAURS FARMERS SOC**, Kilmaurs **Ref:**YH08148

AYRSHIRE (NORTH)

- **RENFREWSHIRE RIDING CLUB**, Kilbirnie **Ref:**YH11759

AYRSHIRE (SOUTH)

- **AILSA RIDING CLUB**, Girvan **Ref:**YH00212
- **AYR RIDING CLUB**, Monkton **Ref:**YH00699
- **AYR RIDING CLUB DRESSAGE**, Maybole **Ref:**YH00700

DUMFRIES AND GALLOWAY

- **BHS**, Castle Douglas **Ref:**YH01354
- **PONY CLUB**, Kirkcudbright **Ref:**YH11235
- **SCOTTISH EQUESTRIAN ASS**, Thornhill **Ref:**YH12554
- **SOUTH WEST SCOTLAND**, Lockerbie **Ref:**YH13118
- **STRANRAER & DISTRICT**, Stanraer **Ref:**YH13550

EDINBURGH (CITY OF)

- **CLYDESDALE HORSE SOC**, Edinburgh **Ref:**YH03081
- **DUNDEE & PERTH POLO CLUB**, Edinburgh **Ref:**YH04340
- **DUNEDIN TRAINING GRP**, Edinburgh **Ref:**YH04341
- **SCOTTISH DRESSAGE GROUP**, Balerno **Ref:**YH12551
- **W C SERVICES**, Edinburgh **Ref:**YH14758

FALKIRK

- **GLENBRAE RIDING CLUB**, Westquarter **Ref:**YH05828
- **ICELANDIC HORSE SOCIETY**, Falkirk **Ref:**YH07379
- **T S RIDING CLUB**, Polmont **Ref:**YH13763

FIFE

- **BHS**, Leslie **Ref:**YH01355
- **FIFE AGRICULTURAL ASS**, St Andrews **Ref:**YH05200
- **FIFE RIDING CLUB**, Kirkcaldy **Ref:**YH05202
- **FORTH VIEW RIDING CLUB**, Dunfermline **Ref:**YH05390
- **SPORTS MARKETING SURVEYS**, Byfleet **Ref:**YH13235
- **STRATHMORE & DISTRICT**, Newport On Tay **Ref:**YH13562
- **WALLACE RIDING CLUB**, Cairneyhill **Ref:**YH14863

GLASGOW (CITY OF)

- **BARRHEAD RIDING CLUB**, Glasgow **Ref:**YH01019
- **SEIS**, Glasgow **Ref:**YH12613
- **STRATHKELVIN RIDING CLUB**, Glasgow **Ref:**YH13560

HIGHLANDS

- **B H S SCOTLAND-HIGHLAND**, Spittal **Ref:**YH00726
- **B H S-SCOTLAND-HIGHLAND**, Drumnadrochit **Ref:**YH00729
- **BADENOCH RIDING CLUB**, Nethybridge **Ref:**YH00776
- **CAITHNESS RIDING CLUB**, Halkirk **Ref:**YH02423
- **CALEDONIAN RIDING CLUB**, Culbokie **Ref:**YH02442
- **STRATHPEFFER HIGHLAND**, Stratheffer **Ref:**YH13564

LANARKSHIRE (NORTH)

- **MONKLANDS & DISTRICT**, Airdrie **Ref:**YH09726
- **NORTH LANARKSHIRE RIDING CLUB**, Cumbernauld **Ref:**YH10267

LANARKSHIRE (SOUTH)

- **BHS**, Lemahagowh **Ref:**YH01358
- **BRITISH SHOW JUMPING ASS**, Strathaven **Ref:**YH01973
- **POLNOON CASTLE RIDERS ASS**, East Kilbride **Ref:**YH11210

LOTHIAN (EAST)

- **HORSE DRIVING TRIALS**, North Berwick **Ref:**YH07120
- **ICELANDIC HORSE SOCIETY OF GB**, North Berwick **Ref:**YH07380
- **NORTH LAMMERMUIR RIDING CLUB**, Tranent **Ref:**YH10266

LOTHIAN (MID)

- **BEHAVIOUR & WELFARE**, Roslin **Ref:**YH01198
- **BHS**, Roslin **Ref:**YH01361
- **EDINBURGH & DISTRICT**, Loanhead **Ref:**YH04558
- **EQUINE BEHAVIOUR FORUM**, Penicuik **Ref:**YH04766
- **WORKING TOGETHER FOR EQUINES**, Roslin **Ref:**YH15781

LOTHIAN (WEST)

- **ALMOND RIDING CLUB**, West Calder **Ref:**YH00329
- **BHS**, Bathgate **Ref:**YH01362
- **BRITISH SHOW PONY SOCIETY**, Bathgate **Ref:**YH01974
- **EDINBURGH POLO CLUB**, Kirknewton **Ref:**YH04563
- **SIMPLY ROSETTES**, Fauldhouse **Ref:**YH12835
- **WEST LOTHIAN BRIDLEWAYS ASS**, Linlithgow **Ref:**YH15155

MORAY

- **ABCIS**, Ballindalloch **Ref:**YH00116
- **PONY CLUB**, Forres **Ref:**YH11241
- **STRATHISLA RIDING CLUB**, Keith **Ref:**YH13559

ORKNEY ISLES

- **ORKNEY RIDING CLUB**, Kirkwall **Ref:**YH10546

PERTH AND KINROSS

- **BHS**, Crieff **Ref:**YH01366
- **BHS (SCOTLAND)**, Crieff **Ref:**YH01375
- **GENERAL ACCIDENT**, Perth **Ref:**YH05701
- **GREENLOANING EQUINE CARE**, Dunblane **Ref:**YH06098
- **HIGHLAND PONY SOC**, Perth **Ref:**YH06792
- **SCS**, Perth **Ref:**YH12572
- **SHETLAND PONY STUD BOOK SOC**, Perth **Ref:**YH12736
- **STRATHEARN RIDING CLUB**, Pitlochry **Ref:**YH13556
- **TAYBANK RIDING CLUB**, Collace **Ref:**YH13891
- **TREKKING AND RIDING SOCIETY**, Killin **Ref:**YH14369
- **TRSS**, Aberfeldy **Ref:**YH14415

RENFREWSHIRE

- **KILMACOLM RIDING CLUB**, Kilbarchan **Ref:**YH08147

SCOTTISH BORDERS

- **BHS**, Kelso **Ref:**YH01367
- **ETTRICK FOREST RIDERS ASS**, Jedburgh **Ref:**YH04889
- **N.P.S. SCOTTISH SHOW KINROSS**, Gordon **Ref:**YH10005
- **PEEBLES & DISTRICT**, Peebles **Ref:**YH10895
- **PPSA AREA SECRETARY**, Galashiels **Ref:**YH11335
- **SCOTTISH ENDURANCE RIDING**, Borders **Ref:**YH12552
- **SCOTTISH TEXTILE ASSOCIATION**, Galashiels **Ref:**YH12559
- **SOUTH LAMMERMUIR RIDING CLUB**, Duns **Ref:**YH13098

STIRLING

- **BHS**, Stirling **Ref:**YH01368
- **STRATHENDRICK RIDING CLUB**, Kippen **Ref:**YH13557

EQUESTRIAN CENTRES

ABERDEEN (CITY OF)

- **ABERDEEN CLGE**, Aberdeen **Ref:**YH00122
- **EQUESTRIAN CTRE AT LOANHEAD**, Aberdeen **Ref:**YH04698
- **HOME FARM**, Aberdeen **Ref:**YH06994

ABERDEENSHIRE

- **CORRYLAIR FARM TREKKING CTRE**, Huntly **Ref:**YH03344
- **EDEN EQUESTRIAN CTRE**, Turriff **Ref:**YH04546
- **MANAR STUD & RIDING CTRE**, Alford **Ref:**YH09064
- **RIDINGHILL STUD**, Fraserburgh **Ref:**YH11885
- **STONEHAVEN TREKKING CTRE**, Stonehaven **Ref:**YH13514

ANGUS

- **MUIRHEAD**, Muirhead **Ref:**YH09923

ARGYLL AND BUTE

- **BALLIVICAR FARM**, Isle Of Islay **Ref:**YH00863
- **COILESSAN**, Arrochar **Ref:**YH03138
- **COLGRAIN EQUESTRIAN CTRE**, Helensburgh **Ref:**YH03170
- **CORROW TREKKING CTRE**, Cairndow **Ref:**YH03343
- **EQUI VENTURE**, Barcaldine **Ref:**YH04730
- **MULL OF KINTYRE**, Campbeltown **Ref:**YH09934
- **ROCKSIDE FARM TREKKING CTRE**, Isle Of Islay **Ref:**YH12038
- **TAYINLOAN TREKKING CTRE**, Tarbert **Ref:**YH13892
- **VELVET PATH TREKKING CTRE**, Dunoon **Ref:**YH14675

AYRSHIRE (EAST)

- **MUIRMILL INTERNATIONAL E C**, Kilmarnock **Ref:**YH09927
- **ROWALLAN ACTIVITY CTRE**, Kilmarnock **Ref:**YH12152

AYRSHIRE (NORTH)

- **CAIRNHOUSE RIDING CTRE**, Isle Of Arran **Ref:**YH02419
- **CLOYBURN TREKKING CTRE**, Brodick **Ref:**YH03073

AYRSHIRE (SOUTH)

- **AYRSHIRE EQUITATION CTRE**, Ayr **Ref:**YH00704
- **HORSE SENSE**, Girvan **Ref:**YH07137

CLACKMANNANSHIRE

- **DEVON EQUESTRIAN**, Alloa **Ref:**YH04094
- **GLENDEVON YOUTH HOSTEL**, Dollar **Ref:**YH05831
- **ROYAL SCHOOL**, Dollar **Ref:**YH12192

DUMFRIES AND GALLOWAY

- **CHARIOTS OF FIRE DRIVING CTRE**, Lockerbie **Ref:**YH02750
- **DALMAKERRAN EQUESTRIAN CTRE**, Thornhill **Ref:**YH03844

EDINBURGH (CITY OF)

- **TOWER FARM**, Edinburgh **Ref:**YH14271

FIFE

- **DABBS**, Cupar **Ref:**YH03813
- **DUNVEGAN EQUESTRIAN CTRE**, Cupar **Ref:**YH04362

GLASGOW (CITY OF)

- **BUSBY EQUITATION CTRE**, Busby **Ref:**YH02302
- **LINN PARK EQUESTRIAN CTRE**, Glasgow **Ref:**YH08666

HIGHLANDS

- **BEVERLEY HYMERS SADDLERY**, Halkirk **Ref:**YH01342
- **GRAMPIAN HIGHLAND RIDING**, Carrbridge **Ref:**YH05977
- **HEBRIDEAN TREKKING HOLIDAYS**, Small Isles **Ref:**YH06637
- **HIGHLAND RIDING CTRE**, Inverness **Ref:**YH06793
- **LATHERON RIDING CTRE**, Caithness **Ref:**YH08446
- **LOGIE FARM**, Nairn **Ref:**YH08778
- **NORTH COAST ADVENTURE HOLS**, Sutherland **Ref:**YH10247
- **THURSO COLLEGE**, Thurso **Ref:**YH14122

ISLE OF SKYE

- **SKYE RIDING CTRE**, Portree **Ref:**YH12881

LANARKSHIRE (NORTH)

- **DRUMBEG EQUINE CTRE**, Glasgow **Ref:**YH04286

LANARKSHIRE (SOUTH)

- **CLYDE VALLEY TREKKING CTRE**, Carluke **Ref:**YH03079
- **HILLHEAD**, Carluke **Ref:**YH06846
- **JUMPS**, Carluke **Ref:**YH07967

LOTHIAN (MID)

- **BRAIDWOOD HSE EQUESTRIAN CTRE**, Silverburn **Ref:**YH01776
- **EDINBURGH EQUESTRIAN CTRE**, Dalkeith **Ref:**YH04560
- **PENTLAND HILLS ICELANDICS**, Penicuik **Ref:**YH10961
- **ROYAL SCHOOL**, Roslin **Ref:**YH12193
- **SCOTTISH FARRIER**, Roslin **Ref:**YH12557

LOTHIAN (WEST)

- **FIELDINGS EQUESTRIAN CTRE**, Bathgate **Ref:**YH05196
- **OATRIDGE**, Broxburn **Ref:**YH10417

MORAY

- **SHENVAL FARM**, Ballindalloch **Ref:**YH12709
- **STRATHSPEY HIGHLAND PONY CTRE**, Grantown-on-Spey **Ref:**YH13565

PERTH AND KINROSS

- **CLAISH FARM PONY TREKKING**, Callander **Ref:**YH02939
- **FAIRWAYS CLYDESDALE CTRE**, Glencarse **Ref:**YH05033
- **GLEN EAGLES EQUESTRIAN**, Auchterarder **Ref:**YH05825
- **GLEN EAGLES EQUESTRIAN**, Auchterarder **Ref:**YH05825
- **GLENISLA HOTEL**, Alyth **Ref:**YH05838
- **GLENMARKIE**, Blairgowrie **Ref:**YH05840

RENFREWSHIRE

- **MEADOW PK**, Johnstone **Ref:**YH09421

SCOTTISH BORDERS

- **COWDENKNOWES EQUI CTRE**, Earlston **Ref:**YH03522
- **MANOR TREKKING CTRE**, Peebles **Ref:**YH09120
- **WESTERTOUN**, Gordon **Ref:**YH15212

STIRLING

- **MYOTHILL HSE EQUESTRIAN CTRE**, Denny **Ref:**YH09985

FARRIERS

ABERDEEN (CITY OF)

- **NICOL, A**, Aberdeen **Ref:**YH10197

ABERDEENSHIRE

- **AIKEN, RONALD G**, Peterhead **Ref:**YH00208
- **CHAPMAN, DUNCAN**, Aboyne **Ref:**YH02745
- **CHAPMAN, WILLIAM**, Tarland **Ref:**YH02747
- **DAVIDSON, ALISTAIR**, Aboyne **Ref:**YH03928
- **PLAYLE, J**, Fraserburgh **Ref:**YH11170
- **PLAYLE, KENNETH R**, Keith **Ref:**YH11171
- **PORTER, LESLIE**, New Pitsligo **Ref:**YH11284
- **TANNER, R**, Turriff **Ref:**YH13857

ANGUS
- **BALFOUR, JAMES S**, Kirriemuir **Ref:**YH00843
- **BALFOUR, K P & P F**, Dundee **Ref:**YH00844
- **CAMPBELL, SCOTT J**, Forfar **Ref:**YH02487
- **JARRETT, EDWIN**, Arbroath **Ref:**YH07703
- **MACPHERSON, JOHN**, Montrose **Ref:**YH09016
- **WILLIAMSON, GORDON FERRIER**, Forfar **Ref:**YH15484

ARGYLL AND BUTE
- **MORGAN, JAMES REGINALD**, Isle Of Mull **Ref:**YH09807
- **ROBB, C A**, Inveraray **Ref:**YH11933
- **WITHAM, JIM**, Dunoon **Ref:**YH15621

AYRSHIRE (EAST)
- **FERRIE, J & A**, Newmilns **Ref:**YH05169
- **MCCRAE, JOHN & HODGE, C**, Cumnock **Ref:**YH09335
- **ROBINSON, PAUL**, Galston **Ref:**YH11993

AYRSHIRE (NORTH)
- **DAVIDSON, SCOTT G**, Dalry **Ref:**YH03930
- **MARSHALL, ROBERT**, Beith **Ref:**YH09202
- **SMITH, JAMES HARRY**, Kilwinning **Ref:**YH12966

AYRSHIRE (SOUTH)
- **MORIARTY, KEVIN J D**, Mossblown **Ref:**YH09816
- **REID, JOHN R**, Coylton **Ref:**YH11743

CLACKMANNANSHIRE
- **MCKEAND, B W**, Tillicoultry **Ref:**YH09381

DUMFRIES AND GALLOWAY
- **AITCHISON, G W**, Lockerbie **Ref:**YH00228
- **ALLAN, JAMES W**, Kirkconnel **Ref:**YH00288
- **COCHRANE, STUART M**, Dalbeattie **Ref:**YH03118
- **FERRIE, J C**, Newton Stewart **Ref:**YH05170
- **KENNEDY, ROBERT M**, Georgetown **Ref:**YH08070
- **MARTIN, EDWARD**, Thornhill **Ref:**YH09217
- **MARTIN, MURRAY**, Lockerbie **Ref:**YH09223
- **SLONE, JOHN**, Barrow-In-Furness **Ref:**YH12900
- **THOMSON, A J**, Lockerbie **Ref:**YH14049
- **TRESIDDER, ROGER M**, Annan **Ref:**YH14385
- **TWEEDIE, THOMAS**, Newton Stewart **Ref:**YH14507
- **YOUNG, GORDON**, Dumfries **Ref:**YH15929

EDINBURGH (CITY OF)
- **MACNAUGHTON, DONALD**, Edinburgh **Ref:**YH09014
- **ROBB, RUARAIDH C**, Dalkeith **Ref:**YH11934

FIFE
- **CHESHIRE, RONALD**, Glenrothes **Ref:**YH02828
- **CRAWFORD, DOUGLAS A**, Ladybank **Ref:**YH03574
- **FRANKS, MICHAEL R**, East Wemyss **Ref:**YH05471
- **GRIEVE, GEORGE WISHART**, Glenrothes **Ref:**YH06128
- **HOOD, G**, Cupar **Ref:**YH07022
- **KER-RAMSAY, ROBERT N**, Kirkcaldy **Ref:**YH08098
- **STRONACH, JOHN**, Dunfermline **Ref:**YH13580
- **WILSON, DAVID**, Ballmullo **Ref:**YH15533
- **WILSON, DAVID G**, Ceres **Ref:**YH15534

GLASGOW (CITY OF)
- **JARVIE, JAMES**, Glasgow **Ref:**YH07704
- **ORR, CHRISTOPHER J**, Milton Of Campsie **Ref:**YH10552
- **WADE, IAN**, Barrhead **Ref:**YH14811

HIGHLANDS
- **BARRATT, T**, Nairn **Ref:**YH01010
- **HALLIDAY, J**, Nairn **Ref:**YH06330
- **HEDLEY, K H**, Lairg **Ref:**YH06645
- **LESLIE, A C**, Newtonmore **Ref:**YH08559
- **MACDONALD, S**, Inverness **Ref:**YH08990
- **MCGUIRE, STEWART**, Tain **Ref:**YH09368
- **PAPE, R ROBIN**, Beauly **Ref:**YH10706

LANARKSHIRE (NORTH)
- **GREIG, COLIN A R**, Airdrie **Ref:**YH06119
- **HENDERSON, FRANCIS**, Airdrie **Ref:**YH06666
- **WATSON, W**, Wishaw **Ref:**YH14994

LANARKSHIRE (SOUTH)
- **AIRD, JOHN W**, Lesmahagow **Ref:**YH00220
- **ARMSTRONG, STEWART A**, Lanark **Ref:**YH00553
- **BEVRIDGE**, Carluke **Ref:**YH01346
- **BORLAND, DAVID J**, East Kilbride **Ref:**YH01649
- **BURNS, DAVID H**, Biggar **Ref:**YH02270
- **NIMMO, J ALASTAIR**, Biggar **Ref:**YH10206
- **PATERSON, ALEXANDER MILLER**, Braehead Forth **Ref:**YH10819
- **RENSON, MICHAEL D**, Lanark **Ref:**YH11762
- **TELFER, THOMAS**, Carnwath **Ref:**YH13940
- **W, WATSON**, Carluke **Ref:**YH14802
- **WEIR, J**, East Kilbride **Ref:**YH15053

LOTHIAN (EAST)
- **DUFF, A**, Tranent **Ref:**YH04313
- **RITCHIE, IAIN BURNS**, Haddington **Ref:**YH11916
- **RUSSELL, MARK ROBSON**, Haddington **Ref:**YH12261

LOTHIAN (MID)
- **TELFER, J**, Roslin **Ref:**YH13938

LOTHIAN (WEST)
- **DENHOLM, LESLIE**, Whitburn **Ref:**YH04046
- **HARRELL, CHRISTOPHER J**, East Clader **Ref:**YH06457

MORAY
- **DUFFY, THOMAS**, Arberlour **Ref:**YH04320
- **LINDRIDGE, KEITH P**, Keith **Ref:**YH08651
- **ROBERTS, GORDON**, Forres **Ref:**YH11952
- **SIMPSON, ANDREW W**, Elgin **Ref:**YH12837

ORKNEY ISLES
- **TAIT, THOMAS A**, Stromness **Ref:**YH13826

PERTH AND KINROSS
- **ARMSTRONG, J A**, Glencarse **Ref:**YH00548
- **BROWN, DAVID R**, Inchture **Ref:**YH02106
- **CHALMERS, ALISTAIR N**, Blairgowrie **Ref:**YH02716
- **DOIG, W G**, Balbeggie **Ref:**YH04165
- **ERSKINE, DOUGLAS J**, Gairney Bank **Ref:**YH04857
- **MCFADZEAN, ROBERT L**, Dunning **Ref:**YH09352
- **WEST, GEORGE**, Auchterarder **Ref:**YH15175

RENFREWSHIRE
- **BROWN, JAMES C**, Lochwinnoch **Ref:**YH02116
- **KILGOUR, Y**, Lochwinnoch **Ref:**YH08136

SCOTTISH BORDERS
- **ALLISON, W P**, Hawick **Ref:**YH00320
- **COCKBURN, CHARLES KERR**, Earlston **Ref:**YH03121
- **CROW, ANDREW M**, Jedburgh **Ref:**YH03675
- **HOOK, ELLIOT W G**, Hawick **Ref:**YH07036
- **JEFFREY THOMAS & SON**, Galashiels **Ref:**YH07723
- **JOHN NISBET**, Eyemouth **Ref:**YH07803
- **JOHNSTON, G J**, Kelso **Ref:**YH07845
- **PEEBLES HYDRO STABLES**, Peebles **Ref:**YH10896
- **SCOT, J & A**, Selkirk **Ref:**YH12529
- **SMITHY, LINDEAN**, Galashiels **Ref:**YH13015
- **THREADGALL, FRANCIS JOHN**, Lauder **Ref:**YH14100
- **WHALEY, J H**, Duns **Ref:**YH15256
- **YOUNG, D A**, Selkirk **Ref:**YH15927

SHETLAND ISLANDS
- **BRUCE WILCOCK**, Shetland **Ref:**YH02154

STIRLING
- **ADAMSON, J**, Stirling **Ref:**YH00174
- **FRASER, J L**, Drymen **Ref:**YH05473
- **MITCHELL, K A**, Stirling **Ref:**YH09674
- **MOIR, JOHN ANDERSON**, Bridge Of Allan **Ref:**YH09704

FEED MERCHANTS

ABERDEENSHIRE
- **FEEDMIX**, Turriff **Ref:**YH05123
- **NORVITE**, Insch **Ref:**YH10333

ANGUS
- **FEEDMIX**, Kirriemuir **Ref:**YH05124

ARGYLL AND BUTE
- **TACKLE & TACK**, Oban **Ref:**YH13818

CLACKMANNANSHIRE
- **E & S FEEDS**, Tillicoultry **Ref:**YH04394

FALKIRK
- **COUNTRY FEEDS LARBERT**, Larbert **Ref:**YH03408
- **D H F ANIMAL FEEDS**, Airth **Ref:**YH03784

LANARKSHIRE (SOUTH)
- **COUNTRY FEEDS**, Blantyre **Ref:**YH03406

ORKNEY ISLES
- **HAMISH MACLEAN FARM PRODUCTS**, Kirkwall **Ref:**YH06355

HOLIDAYS

DUMFRIES AND GALLOWAY
- **CHARIOTS OF FIRE DRIVING CTRE**, Lockerbie **Ref:**YH02750
- **ETTRICK STABLES**, Thornhill **Ref:**YH04890

HIGHLANDS
- **LOGIE FARM**, Nairn **Ref:**YH08778

HORSE/RIDER ACCOM

ABERDEEN (CITY OF)
- **HAYFIELD RIDING**, Aberdeen **Ref:**YH06578

ABERDEENSHIRE
- **ABERQUEST**, Turriff **Ref:**YH00128
- **STRATHORN FARM**, Inverurie **Ref:**YH13563

ARGYLL AND BUTE
- **CASTLE RIDING CTRE**, Lochgilphead **Ref:**YH02631
- **LETTERSHUNA RIDING CTRE**, Appin **Ref:**YH08570

AYRSHIRE (EAST)
- **ROWALLAN ACTIVITY CTRE**, Kilmarnock **Ref:**YH12152

AYRSHIRE (SOUTH)
- **AYRSHIRE EQUITATION CTRE**, Ayr **Ref:**YH00704

DUMFRIES AND GALLOWAY
- **CHARIOTS OF FIRE DRIVING CTRE**, Lockerbie **Ref:**YH02750
- **DALMAKERRAN EQUESTRIAN CTRE**, Thornhill **Ref:**YH03844

FIFE
- **SHIELDBANK**, Dunfermline **Ref:**YH12740

HIGHLANDS
- **LOCH NESS RIDING**, Inverness **Ref:**YH08752

LANARKSHIRE (NORTH)
- **WOODSIDE VILLA**, Airdrie **Ref:**YH15748

LOTHIAN (EAST)
- **CLARK, SHEILA**, Haddington **Ref:**YH02968

LOTHIAN (MID)
- **COUSLAND PK FARM**, Dalkeith **Ref:**YH03515

LOTHIAN (WEST)
- **CRAIGHEAD**, Fauldhouse **Ref:**YH03553

PERTH AND KINROSS
- **EASTERTON FARM**, Auchterarder **Ref:**YH04500
- **GLEN EAGLES EQUESTRIAN**, Auchterarder **Ref:**YH05825

RENFREWSHIRE
- **MID GAVIN FARM**, Johnstone **Ref:**YH09527

SCOTTISH BORDERS
- **BAILEY MILL**, Newcastleton **Ref:**YH00794
- **FERNIEHIRST MILL RIDING CTRE**, Jedburgh **Ref:**YH05167
- **WHISGILLS RIDING CTRE**, Newcastleton **Ref:**YH15285

MEDICAL SUPPORT

ABERDEEN (CITY OF)
- **TOWN & COUNTRY VETNRY**, Aberdeen **Ref:**YH14289
- **TOWN & COUNTRY VETNRY GROUP**, Kingswells **Ref:**YH14291
- **TOWN & COUNTRY VETNRY GRP**, Aberdeen **Ref:**YH14292

ABERDEENSHIRE
- **BELLEVUE VETNRY GRP**, Banff **Ref:**YH01237
- **DONVIEW VETNRY CTRE**, Inverurie **Ref:**YH04190
- **NORTH EASTERN FARMERS**, Inverurie **Ref:**YH10258
- **POLESBURN VETNRY CTRE**, Ellon **Ref:**YH11199
- **ROBSON & PARTNERS**, Laurencekirk **Ref:**YH12012
- **RUSSELL & WOOD**, Insch **Ref:**YH12251
- **STRATHBOGIE VETNRY CTRE**, Huntly **Ref:**YH13555
- **TOWN & COUNTRY VETNRY**, Westhill **Ref:**YH14290
- **TOWN & COUNTRY VETNRY GRP**, Banchory **Ref:**YH14293
- **WOODSIDE VETNRY GRP**, Torphins **Ref:**YH15747

ANGUS
- **KNEEN, J E**, Arbroath **Ref:**YH08252
- **MACFARLANE GOVAN, A L**, Arbroath **Ref:**YH08994
- **MACFARLANE GOVAN, A L**, Montrose **Ref:**YH08995
- **THRUMS VETNRY GROUP**, Kirriemuir **Ref:**YH14116

ARGYLL AND BUTE
- **LISTER, M**, Lochgilphead **Ref:**YH08681
- **TACKLE & TACK**, Oban **Ref:**YH13818

AYRSHIRE (EAST)
- **CROSSRIGGS VETNRY CLINIC**, Cumnock **Ref:**YH03663
- **JAMES GIBB**, Galston **Ref:**YH07667
- **MACKENZIE BRYSON & MARSHALL**, Kilmarnock **Ref:**YH08999

AYRSHIRE (NORTH)
- **WARWICK, JOHN T**, Kilwinning **Ref:**YH14948

AYRSHIRE (SOUTH)
- **ALEXANDER, D C S**, Mauchline **Ref:**YH00268
- **BARR & MACMILLAN**, Mauchline **Ref:**YH00999
- **DALBLAIR VETNRY SURGERY**, Ayr **Ref:**YH03818
- **OTTERSWICK**, Mauchine **Ref:**YH10581

DUMFRIES AND GALLOWAY
- **BARD VETNRY GRP**, Dumfries **Ref:**YH00926
- **DUNLOPS**, Troqueer **Ref:**YH04345
- **FIRTH VETNRY CTRE**, Annan **Ref:**YH05232
- **JESSIMAN, D C**, Kirkcudbright **Ref:**YH07759
- **MILLER & COCHRANE**, Stranraer **Ref:**YH09599

EDINBURGH (CITY OF)
- **MACKIE & BRECHIN**, Kirkliston **Ref:**YH09004
- **SCOTT, ALEX**, Kinkliston **Ref:**YH12536
- **THISTLE VETNRY CTRE**, Edinburgh **Ref:**YH14000

FALKIRK
- **VETNRY CLINIC**, Falkirk **Ref:**YH14692

FIFE
- **BROOKWICK WARD**, Glenrothes **Ref:**YH02070
- **SCOTTISH ANIMAL PHYSIOTHERAPY**, Strathmiglo **Ref:**YH12549

GLASGOW (CITY OF)
- **ROSS & BICKERTON**, Glasgow **Ref:**YH12113

HIGHLANDS
- **CONANVET**, Dingwall **Ref:**YH03222
- **EASTGATE VETNRY PRACTICE**, Inverness **Ref:**YH04503
- **G C MACINTYRE & PARTNERS**, Dingwall **Ref:**YH05572
- **MCCARROLL, KAY**, Evanton **Ref:**YH09318
- **MCGREGOR & PARTNERS**, Wick **Ref:**YH09365
- **VETNRY CTRE**, Invergordon **Ref:**YH14694
- **WALL, A E**, Sutherland **Ref:**YH14860

INVERCLYDE
- **ABBEY VET GRP**, Greenock **Ref:**YH00087

LANARKSHIRE (SOUTH)
- **ACORN VETNRY CTRE**, Lanark **Ref:**YH00153
- **ARMAC VETNRY GRP**, Biggar **Ref:**YH00534
- **BEGG & PARTNERS**, Strathaven **Ref:**YH01194
- **CLIVE VALLEY VETNRY PRACTICE**, Lanark **Ref:**YH03050
- **TOP CROP ORGANICS**, Law **Ref:**YH14234
- **VITAL MAX**, Forth **Ref:**YH14735

LOTHIAN (EAST)
- **DUNBAR EQUINE**, Dunbar **Ref:**YH04331
- **GORDON, R**, Musselburgh **Ref:**YH05927

LOTHIAN (MID)
- **CUDDEFORD, DEREK (DR)**, Roslin **Ref:**YH03700
- **EASTER BUSH VETNRY CTRE**, Roslin **Ref:**YH04490
- **MARSDEN, DEBBIE (DR)**, Dalkeith **Ref:**YH09183

MORAY
- **MORAY COAST VET GROUP**, Forres **Ref:**YH09786
- **SHANKS & MCLEAN**, Aberlour **Ref:**YH12670

PERTH AND KINROSS
- **ASHWORTH VETNRY GRP**, Crieff **Ref:**YH00618
- **CAMERON & GREIG**, Milnathort **Ref:**YH02476
- **DAVIDSONS VETNRY SUPPLIES**, Blairgowrie **Ref:**YH03931
- **FAIR CITY VETNRY GRP**, Perth **Ref:**YH05010
- **GREENLOANING EQUINE CARE**, Dunblane **Ref:**YH06098
- **HARBIT & RYDER**, Aberfeldy **Ref:**YH06403
- **NATURAL APPROACH**, Bankfoot **Ref:**YH10051

RENFREWSHIRE
- **ABBEY VET GRP**, Paisley **Ref:**YH00088

SCOTTISH BORDERS
- **BORTHWICK, A J**, Selkirk **Ref:**YH01653
- **GIBSON & GIBSON**, Galashiels **Ref:**YH05743
- **MERLIN VETS**, Kelso **Ref:**YH09478
- **ROGERSON & PARTNERS**, Galashiels **Ref:**YH12061

STIRLING
- **BROADLEYS VETNRY HOSPITAL**, Stirling **Ref:**YH02000

(continued)
- **GLENSIDE ORGANICS**, Throsk **Ref:**YH05843

RIDING CLUBS

ABERDEENSHIRE
- **BUCHAN RIDING CLUB**, Fraserburgh **Ref:**YH02185
- **KINCARDINE COUNTY RIDING CLUB**, Stonehaven **Ref:**YH08166
- **STRATH ISLA RIDING CLUB**, Huntly **Ref:**YH13554

ARGYLL AND BUTE
- **ARGYLL RIDING CLUB**, Argyll **Ref:**YH00522
- **BUTE PONY & RIDING CLUB**, Ettrick Bay **Ref:**YH02319
- **GARELOCH RIDING CLUB**, Helensburgh **Ref:**YH05650

AYRSHIRE (EAST)
- **ROWALLAN ACTIVITY CTRE**, Kilmarnock **Ref:**YH12152

AYRSHIRE (NORTH)
- **RENFREWSHIRE RIDING CLUB**, Kilbirnie **Ref:**YH11759

AYRSHIRE (SOUTH)
- **AILSA RIDING CLUB**, Girvan **Ref:**YH00212
- **AYR RIDING CLUB**, Monkton **Ref:**YH00699

DUMFRIES AND GALLOWAY
- **SOUTH WEST SCOTLAND**, Lockerbie **Ref:**YH13118
- **STRANRAER & DISTRICT**, Stanraer **Ref:**YH13550

DUNBARTONSHIRE (WEST)
- **LEVEN VALLEY RIDING CLUB**, Dunbarton **Ref:**YH08573

FALKIRK
- **GLENBRAE RIDING CLUB**, Westquarter **Ref:**YH05828
- **T S RIDING CLUB**, Polmont **Ref:**YH13763

FIFE
- **FIFE RIDING CLUB**, Kirkcaldy **Ref:**YH05202
- **FORTH VIEW RIDING CLUB**, Dunfermline **Ref:**YH05390
- **SHIELDBANK**, Dunfermline **Ref:**YH12740
- **STRATHMORE & DISTRICT**, Newport On Tay **Ref:**YH13562
- **WALLACE RIDING CLUB**, Cairneyhill **Ref:**YH14863

GLASGOW (CITY OF)
- **BARRHEAD RIDING CLUB**, Glasgow **Ref:**YH01019
- **STRATHKELVIN RIDING CLUB**, Glasgow **Ref:**YH13560

HIGHLANDS
- **BADENOCH RIDING CLUB**, Nethybridge **Ref:**YH00776
- **CAITHNESS RIDING CLUB**, Halkirk **Ref:**YH02423
- **CALEDONIAN RIDING CLUB**, Culbokie **Ref:**YH02442

ISLE OF SKYE
- **SKYE RIDING CTRE**, Portree **Ref:**YH12881

LANARKSHIRE (NORTH)
- **NORTH LANARKSHIRE RIDING CLUB**, Cumbernauld **Ref:**YH10267

LOTHIAN (EAST)
- **NORTH LAMMERMUIR RIDING CLUB**, Tranent **Ref:**YH10266

LOTHIAN (MID)
- **EDINBURGH & DISTRICT**, Loanhead **Ref:**YH04558
- **EDINBURGH EQUESTRIAN CTRE**, Dalkeith **Ref:**YH04560
- **PENTLAND HILLS ICELANDICS**, Penicuik **Ref:**YH10961

LOTHIAN (WEST)
- **ALMOND RIDING CLUB**, West Calder **Ref:**YH00329

MORAY

- **STRATHISLA RIDING CLUB**, Keith **Ref:**YH13559

ORKNEY ISLES

- **ORKNEY RIDING CLUB**, Kirkwall **Ref:**YH10546

PERTH AND KINROSS

- **EQUI-CARE**, Perth **Ref:**YH04736
- **GLEN EAGLES EQUESTRIAN**, Auchterarder **Ref:**YH05825
- **STRATHEARN RIDING CLUB**, Pitlochry **Ref:**YH13556
- **TAYBANK RIDING CLUB**, Collace **Ref:**YH13891

RENFREWSHIRE

- **KILMACOLM RIDING CLUB**, Kilbarchan **Ref:**YH08147

SCOTTISH BORDERS

- **PEEBLES & DISTRICT**, Peebles **Ref:**YH10895
- **SCOTTISH ENDURANCE RIDING**, Borders **Ref:**YH12552
- **SOUTH LAMMERMUIR RIDING CLUB**, Duns **Ref:**YH13098

STIRLING

- **STRATHENDRICK RIDING CLUB**, Kippen **Ref:**YH13557

RIDING SCHOOLS

ABERDEEN (CITY OF)

- **BURNSIDE STABLES**, Aberdeen **Ref:**YH02274
- **GROVE RIDING CTRE**, Aberdeen **Ref:**YH06172
- **HAYFIELD RIDING**, Aberdeen **Ref:**YH06578
- **HAYFIELD SADDLERY**, Aberdeen **Ref:**YH06579
- **REDWING RIDING SCHOOL**, Aberdeen **Ref:**YH11717
- **SESSNIE EQUESTRIAN**, Aberdeen **Ref:**YH12637

ABERDEENSHIRE

- **ANNANDALE EQUESTRIAN CTRE**, Peterhead **Ref:**YH00453
- **BRIDESWELL RIDING CTRE**, Alford **Ref:**YH01870
- **EDEN EQUESTRIAN CTRE**, Turriff **Ref:**YH04546
- **ERROISTON EQUESTRIAN CTRE**, Peterhead **Ref:**YH04854
- **GLEN TANAR EQUESTRIAN CTRE**, Aboyne **Ref:**YH05827
- **HIGHLAND HORSE BACK**, Huntly **Ref:**YH06790
- **LADYMIRE EQUESTRIAN CTRE**, Ellon **Ref:**YH08338
- **SKINNER, GEORGE M**, Inverurie **Ref:**YH12875
- **TERTOWIE CTRE**, Kinellar **Ref:**YH13960
- **TROTTS EQUESTRIAN CTRE**, Stonehaven **Ref:**YH14413
- **WESTERTON RIDING CTRE**, Huntly **Ref:**YH15211

ANGUS

- **BALHALL RIDING STABLES**, Brechin **Ref:**YH00845
- **DENMILL STABLES**, Kirriemuir **Ref:**YH04050
- **KIRRIEMUIR HORSE SUPPLIES**, Kirriemuir **Ref:**YH08240
- **MUIRHEAD STABLES**, Dundee **Ref:**YH09926
- **PATHHEAD STABLES**, Kirriemuir **Ref:**YH10821
- **ROWAN LEA RIDING SCHOOL**, Carnoustie **Ref:**YH12153
- **SHANDON SCHOOL OF EQUITATION**, Dundee **Ref:**YH12668

ARGYLL AND BUTE

- **APPALOOSA HOLIDAYS**, Lochgilphead **Ref:**YH00475
- **ARGYLL TRAIL RIDING**, Lochgilphead **Ref:**YH00523
- **CASTLE RIDING CTRE**, Lochgilphead **Ref:**YH02631
- **COLGRAIN EQUESTRIAN CTRE**, Helensburgh **Ref:**YH03170
- **KINGARTH TREKKING CTRE**, Isle Of Bute **Ref:**YH08189
- **LETTERSHUNA RIDING CTRE**, Appin **Ref:**YH08570
- **MELFORT RIDING CTRE**, Oban **Ref:**YH09452
- **ROTHESAY RIDING CTRE**, Rothesay **Ref:**YH12134
- **TIGNABRUAICH**, Tighnabruaich **Ref:**YH14142

AYRSHIRE (EAST)

- **BARGOWER RIDING SCHOOL**, Kilmarnock **Ref:**YH00933
- **DALLARS RIDING SCHOOL**, Kilmarnock **Ref:**YH03841
- **DEAN CASTLE RIDING CTRE**, Kilmarnock **Ref:**YH03988
- **MOSSBACK RIDING SCHOOL**, Cumnock **Ref:**YH09865
- **MUIRMILL INTERNATIONAL E C**, Kilmarnock **Ref:**YH09927
- **ROWALLAN ACTIVITY CTRE**, Kilmarnock **Ref:**YH12152

AYRSHIRE (NORTH)

- **BROOM FARM RIDING SCHOOL**, Stevenston **Ref:**YH02071
- **CAIRNHOUSE RIDING CTRE**, Isle Of Arran **Ref:**YH02419
- **CLOYBURN TREKKING CTRE**, Brodick **Ref:**YH03073
- **FERGUSHILL RIDING STABLES**, Kilwinning **Ref:**YH05159
- **KELBURN COUNTRY CTRE**, Fairlie **Ref:**YH08039
- **MILLPORT RIDING SCHOOL**, Millport **Ref:**YH09627
- **TANDLEVIEW STABLES**, Beith **Ref:**YH13852

AYRSHIRE (SOUTH)

- **AYRSHIRE EQUITATION CTRE**, Ayr **Ref:**YH00704
- **CRAIGIE BYRE RIDING SCHOOL**, Prestwick **Ref:**YH03554
- **ROSEMOUNT RIDING SVS**, Prestwick **Ref:**YH12105
- **SHANTER RIDING CTRE**, Girvan **Ref:**YH12672

DUMFRIES AND GALLOWAY

- **BAREND RIDING CTRE**, Dalbeattie **Ref:**YH00929
- **CHARIOTS OF FIRE DRIVING CTRE**, Lockerbie **Ref:**YH02750
- **DEEP WATER EQUITATION CTRE**, Dumfries **Ref:**YH04020
- **ETTRICK STABLES**, Thornhill **Ref:**YH04890
- **LONE PINE RIDING CTRE**, Moffat **Ref:**YH08794
- **ROSEBANK HORSE & PONY CTRE**, Dumfries **Ref:**YH12100

DUNBARTONSHIRE (WEST)

- **DUNCRYNE**, Alexandria **Ref:**YH04338

EDINBURGH (CITY OF)

- **DRUM RIDING**, Edinburgh **Ref:**YH04282
- **TOWER FARM**, Edinburgh **Ref:**YH14271

FALKIRK

- **CAMPBELL, CARNET**, Slamannan **Ref:**YH02483
- **MILNHOLM**, Falkirk **Ref:**YH09643

FIFE

- **ANGLE PARK**, Cupar **Ref:**YH00409
- **BARBARAFIELD RIDING SCHOOL**, Cupar **Ref:**YH00919
- **DABBS**, Cupar **Ref:**YH03813
- **GLENROTHES RIDING CTRE**, Glenrothes **Ref:**YH05841
- **KILCONQUHAR RIDING STABLES**, Leven **Ref:**YH08129
- **KINSHALDY RIDING STABLES**, St Andrews **Ref:**YH08220
- **RIDING STABLES**, Lochgelly **Ref:**YH11883

GLASGOW (CITY OF)

- **BUSBY EQUITATION CTRE**, Busby **Ref:**YH02302
- **DUMBRECK RIDING SCHOOL**, Glasgow **Ref:**YH04328
- **EASTERTON STABLES**, Glasgow **Ref:**YH04501
- **GREYFRIARS RIDING SCHOOL**, Glasgow **Ref:**YH06126
- **HAZELDEN SADDLERY**, Glasgow **Ref:**YH06602
- **KENMURE RIDING SCHOOL**, Glasgow **Ref:**YH08065
- **ROUNDKNOWE FARM**, Glasgow **Ref:**YH12143
- **SAUCHENHALL RIDING SCHOOL**, Kirkintilloch **Ref:**YH12442
- **WOODEND**, Glasgow **Ref:**YH15684

HIGHLANDS

- **ACHALONE ACTIVITIES**, Halkirk **Ref:**YH00141
- **ALVIE STABLES**, Kingussie **Ref:**YH00350
- **ANDERSON, P A**, Fortrose **Ref:**YH00386
- **BLACK ISLE RIDING CTRE**, Inverness **Ref:**YH01466
- **CARRBRIDGE PONY TREKKING CTRE**, Carrbridge **Ref:**YH02577
- **HEATHERFIELD RIDING CTRE**, Nairn **Ref:**YH06627
- **HIGHLAND RIDING CTRE**, Inverness **Ref:**YH06793
- **LOGIE FARM**, Nairn **Ref:**YH08778
- **LYTH STABLES**, Wick **Ref:**YH08941
- **NORTHWILDS RIDING CTRE**, Tain **Ref:**YH10322
- **PORTREE RIDING/TREKKING CTRE**, Portree **Ref:**YH11296
- **SEAFORTH RIDING CTRE**, Dingwall **Ref:**YH12585
- **TORLUNDY RIDING CTRE**, Fort William **Ref:**YH14245

INVERCLYDE

- **ARDGOWAN**, Greenock **Ref:**YH00507

ISLE OF SKYE

- **SKYE RIDING CTRE**, Portree **Ref:**YH12881

LANARKSHIRE (NORTH)

- **TANNOCK STABLES**, Cumbernauld **Ref:**YH13859

LANARKSHIRE (SOUTH)

- **EAST KILBRIDE RIDING SCHOOL**, Glasgow **Ref:**YH04476
- **HILLHEAD**, Carluke **Ref:**YH06846
- **JUMPS**, Carluke **Ref:**YH07967
- **LETHAME HOUSE EQUESTRIAN CTRE**, Strathaven **Ref:**YH08567
- **MID DRUMLOCH**, Hamilton **Ref:**YH09526
- **SCOTTISH EQUESTRIAN COMPLEX**, Lanark **Ref:**YH12555

LOTHIAN (EAST)

- **APPIN EQUESTRIAN CTRE**, Haddington **Ref:**YH00478
- **HARELAW EQUESTRIAN CTRE**, Longniddry **Ref:**YH06420
- **WHITELOCH FARM STABLES**, Tranent **Ref:**YH15349

LOTHIAN (MID)

- **EASTER BUSH VETNRY CTRE**, Roslin **Ref:**YH04490
- **EDINBURGH & LASSWADE**, Lasswade **Ref:**YH04559

LOTHIAN (WEST)

- **CHAMPFLEURIE STABLES**, Bathgate **Ref:**YH02725
- **GRANGE RIDING CTRE**, West Calder **Ref:**YH05993
- **HOLMES RIDING STABLES**, Bathgate **Ref:**YH06973
- **HOUSTON FARM RIDING SCHOOL**, Broxburn **Ref:**YH07212

MORAY

- **ABERLOUR RIDING/TREKKING CTRE**, Aberlour **Ref:**YH00127
- **CRANNA, P**, Aberlour **Ref:**YH03569
- **SEAFIELD RIDING CTRE**, Forres **Ref:**YH12583

PERTH AND KINROSS

- **ALICHMORE RIDING/LIVERY CTRE**, Crieff **Ref:**YH00280
- **BALNAKILLY RIDING CTRE**, Kirkmichael **Ref:**YH00874
- **CALEDONIAN EQUESTRIAN CTRE**, Perth **Ref:**YH02440
- **CRIEFF HYDRO HOTEL STABLES**, Crieff **Ref:**YH03597
- **EQUI-CARE**, Perth **Ref:**YH04736
- **GLEN EAGLES EQUESTRIAN**, Auchterarder **Ref:**YH05825
- **GLENFARG RIDING SCHOOL**, Perth **Ref:**YH05834
- **GLENMARKIE**, Blairgowrie **Ref:**YH05840
- **LOCH TAY HIGHLAND**, Killin **Ref:**YH08753
- **TEEN RANCH SCOTLAND**, Inchture **Ref:**YH13935

RENFREWSHIRE

- **FORDBANK EQUE CTRE**, Johnstone **Ref:**YH05329
- **GLEDDOCH RIDING SCHOOL**, Port Glasgow **Ref:**YH05822
- **MEADOW PK**, Johnstone **Ref:**YH09421

SCOTTISH BORDERS

- **BAILEY MILL**, Newcastleton **Ref:**YH00794
- **BOWHILL STABLES**, Selkirk **Ref:**YH01710
- **DRYDEN RIDING CTRE**, Selkirk **Ref:**YH04298
- **FERNIEHIRST MILL RIDING CTRE**, Jedburgh **Ref:**YH05167
- **HAZELDEAN RIDING CTRE**, Hawick **Ref:**YH06601
- **NENTHORN STABLES**, Kelso **Ref:**YH10077
- **PEEBLES HYDRO STABLES**, Peebles **Ref:**YH10896
- **WESTERTOUN**, Gordon **Ref:**YH15212
- **WHISGILLS RIDING CTRE**, Newcastleton **Ref:**YH15285

SHETLAND ISLANDS

- **BROOTHOM PONIES**, Shetland **Ref:**YH02083

STIRLING

- **DRUMBRAE FARM AND RIDING CTRE**, Stirling **Ref:**YH04287
- **EASTERHILL**, Gartmore **Ref:**YH04495
- **LOMONDSIDE STUD**, Glasgow **Ref:**YH08782
- **MYOTHILL HSE EQUESTRIAN CTRE**, Denny **Ref:**YH09985

RIDING WEAR RETAILERS

ABERDEEN (CITY OF)

- **COUNTRY WAYS**, Aberdeen **Ref:**YH03436

ABERDEENSHIRE

- **MILLER PLANT**, Inverurie **Ref:**YH09601

ANGUS

- **KIRRIEMUIR HORSE SUPPLIES**, Kirriemuir **Ref:**YH08240
- **PATHHEAD STABLES**, Kirriemuir **Ref:**YH10821

ARGYLL AND BUTE

- **TACKLE & TACK**, Oban **Ref:**YH13818
- **WHAT EVERY HORSE WANTS**, Helensburgh **Ref:**YH15266

AYRSHIRE (SOUTH)

- **CROCKET EQUESTRIAN**, Ayr **Ref:**YH03606

DUMFRIES AND GALLOWAY

- **GEE GEE'S**, Dumfries **Ref:**YH05690

EDINBURGH (CITY OF)

- **DRUM MOORE FARM SHOP**, Edinburgh **Ref:**YH04281
- **STIRLINGSHIRE SADDLERY**, Edinburgh **Ref:**YH13474

GLASGOW (CITY OF)

- **BUSBY EQUITATION CTRE**, Busby **Ref:**YH02302
- **EVERYTHING EQUESTRIAN**, Busby **Ref:**YH04957
- **JET SET**, Glasgow **Ref:**YH07763
- **WARD SADDLERY**, Glasgow **Ref:**YH14897

HIGHLANDS

- **BEVERLEY HYMERS SADDLERY**, Halkirk **Ref:**YH01342
- **RADDERY EQUINE**, Fortrose **Ref:**YH11593
- **SEAFORTH SADDLERS**, Inverness **Ref:**YH12586

LOTHIAN (EAST)

- **J S MAIN & SONS**, Haddington **Ref:**YH07617
- **WILLIAM MAIN SADDLER**, Dunbar **Ref:**YH15435

LOTHIAN (MID)

- **R H MILLER**, Dalkeith **Ref:**YH11541

LOTHIAN (WEST)

- **GRANGE SADDLERY**, West Calder **Ref:**YH05996

MORAY

- **GREENFIELDS SADDLERY**, Elgin **Ref:**YH06085
- **HOOFBEAT**, Forres **Ref:**YH07028

PERTH AND KINROSS

- **EQUI-CARE**, Perth **Ref:**YH04736
- **GLEN EAGLES EQUESTRIAN**, Auchterarder **Ref:**YH05825
- **MCCASH'S**, Perth **Ref:**YH09326

SCOTTISH BORDERS

- **A C BURN**, Jedburgh **Ref:**YH00022

SADDLERY RETAILERS

ABERDEEN (CITY OF)

- **COUNTRY WAYS**, Aberdeen **Ref:**YH03436
- **HAYFIELD SADDLERY**, Aberdeen **Ref:**YH06579
- **SESSNIE EQUESTRIAN**, Aberdeen **Ref:**YH12637

ABERDEENSHIRE

- **ANNANDALE EQUESTRIAN CTRE**, Peterhead **Ref:**YH00453
- **AUCHENHAMPER SUFFOLK**, Banff **Ref:**YH00660
- **GILKHORN FARM SADDLERY**, Peterhead **Ref:**YH05767
- **HARBRO FARM SALES**, Turriff **Ref:**YH06404
- **HORSE & RIDER OUTFITTERS**, Stonehaven **Ref:**YH07098
- **MICHIE, ERIC**, Huntly **Ref:**YH09514
- **MILL OF URAS EQUESTRIAN**, Stonehaven **Ref:**YH09583
- **TACK SHOP**, Banchory **Ref:**YH13810

ANGUS

- **CHODASIEWICZ, S**, Dundee **Ref:**YH02875
- **CONCHIE, DAVID**, Carnoustie **Ref:**YH03224

ARGYLL AND BUTE

- **ISLAY FARMERS**, Isle Of Islay **Ref:**YH07523
- **TACKLE & TACK**, Oban **Ref:**YH13818
- **WHAT EVERY HORSE WANTS**, Helensburgh **Ref:**YH15266

AYRSHIRE (SOUTH)

- **CROCKET EQUESTRIAN**, Ayr **Ref:**YH03606
- **JET SET SADDLERY**, Prestwick **Ref:**YH07764
- **SCOTTISH SIDE SADDLES**, Dunlop **Ref:**YH12558

DUMFRIES AND GALLOWAY

- **DEEP WATER EQUITATION CTRE**, Dumfries **Ref:**YH04020
- **GEE GEE'S**, Dumfries **Ref:**YH05690
- **PATTIES OF DUMFRIES**, Dumfries **Ref:**YH10830
- **W C F COUNTRY CTRE**, Castle Douglas **Ref:**YH14754
- **WM MURRAY FARMCARE**, Dumfries **Ref:**YH15642

EDINBURGH (CITY OF)

- **DRUM FEEDS**, Edinburgh **Ref:**YH04280
- **DRUM MOORE FARM SHOP**, Edinburgh **Ref:**YH04281
- **JOHN DICKSON & SON**, Edinburgh **Ref:**YH07786
- **MANACRAFT LEATHER**, Edinburgh **Ref:**YH09062
- **STEWART CHRISTIE**, Edinburgh **Ref:**YH13454
- **STIRLINGSHIRE SADDLERY**, Edinburgh **Ref:**YH13474

FALKIRK

- **CENTRAL SADDLERY**, Falkirk **Ref:**YH02690

FIFE

- **EUROPA**, Lochgelly **Ref:**YH04904

GLASGOW (CITY OF)

- **BUSBY EQUITATION CTRE**, Busby **Ref:**YH02302
- **EVERYTHING EQUESTRIAN**, Busby **Ref:**YH04957
- **GREAVES SPORTS**, Glasgow **Ref:**YH06047
- **HAZELDEN SADDLERY**, Glasgow **Ref:**YH06602
- **JET SET**, Glasgow **Ref:**YH07763
- **WARD SADDLERY**, Glasgow **Ref:**YH14897

HIGHLANDS

- **BEVERLEY HYMERS SADDLERY**, Halkirk **Ref:**YH01342
- **BITS 'N' BOBS**, Caithness **Ref:**YH01458
- **DERELOCHY SADDLER**, Nairn **Ref:**YH04075
- **RADDERY EQUINE**, Fortrose **Ref:**YH11593
- **ROSS-SHIRE HORSE TALK**, Tain **Ref:**YH12125
- **SEAFORTH SADDLERS**, Inverness **Ref:**YH12586

LANARKSHIRE (SOUTH)

- **MILLBRAE SADDLERY**, Glasgow **Ref:**YH09593
- **STONEHOUSE SADDLERY/PET CTRE**, Stonehouse **Ref:**YH13517
- **THOMSON CRAFT SADDLERY**, Carluke **Ref:**YH14047
- **WELLGATE SADDLERY**, Lanark **Ref:**YH15070

LOTHIAN (EAST)

- **J S MAIN & SONS**, Haddington **Ref:**YH07617
- **WILLIAM MAIN SADDLER**, Dunbar **Ref:**YH15435

LOTHIAN (MID)

- **GEORGES SADDLERY**, Newbridge **Ref:**YH05726
- **R H MILLER**, Dalkeith **Ref:**YH11541

LOTHIAN (WEST)

- **GRANGE SADDLERY**, West Calder **Ref:**YH05996
- **TACK RACK**, Bathgate **Ref:**YH13792
- **TIGGA'S SADDLERY**, Wester Calder **Ref:**YH14141

MORAY

- **GAMMACK, C A**, Aberlour **Ref:**YH05636
- **GREENFIELDS SADDLERY**, Elgin **Ref:**YH06085
- **HOOFBEAT**, Forres **Ref:**YH07028
- **OBERON SADDLERY**, Buckie **Ref:**YH10418
- **PALS**, Cullen **Ref:**YH10694

ORKNEY ISLES

- **SUNNYBRAE FEEDS**, Kirkwall **Ref:**YH13645

PERTH AND KINROSS

- **EQUI-CARE**, Perth **Ref:**YH04736
- **GLEN EAGLES EQUESTRIAN**, Auchterarder **Ref:**YH05825
- **HOUSE OF BRUAR**, Blair Atholl **Ref:**YH07208

RENFREWSHIRE
- **MCROSTIE'S**, Howwood **Ref:**YH09405

SCOTTISH BORDERS
- **D THOMSON & SON**, Jedburgh **Ref:**YH03809
- **LEE VALLEY SADDLERY**, Earlston **Ref:**YH08520
- **MCNAB SADDLERS**, Kelso **Ref:**YH09397
- **MCNAB SADDLERS**, Selkirk **Ref:**YH09396
- **R H MILLER AGRICULTURAL**, Hawick **Ref:**YH11543
- **SPORT OF KINGS**, Hawick **Ref:**YH13221
- **WESTERKIRK SADDLERY**, Newcastleton **Ref:**YH15193

STIRLING
- **CAERDACH**, Drymen **Ref:**YH02414
- **EASTERHILL**, Gartmore **Ref:**YH04495
- **MYOTHILL HSE EQUESTRIAN CTRE**, Denny **Ref:**YH09985
- **W C F COUNTRY CTRE**, Kildean **Ref:**YH14755

STABLES/LIVERIES

ABERDEEN (CITY OF)
- **ALTRIES STABLES**, Aberdeen **Ref:**YH00346
- **BRIDGE OF DON EQUESTRIAN CTRE**, Dyce **Ref:**YH01876
- **BURNSIDE STABLES**, Aberdeen **Ref:**YH02274
- **GROVE RIDING CTRE**, Aberdeen **Ref:**YH06172
- **HAYFIELD SADDLERY**, Aberdeen **Ref:**YH06579
- **REDWING RIDING SCHOOL**, Aberdeen **Ref:**YH11717
- **SESSNIE EQUESTRIAN**, Aberdeen **Ref:**YH12637
- **SUNNYSIDE**, Aberdeen **Ref:**YH13649
- **WHITEMYRES STUD**, Aberdeen **Ref:**YH15352
- **WHITEMYRES STUD LIVERY YARD**, Aberdeen **Ref:**YH15353

ABERDEENSHIRE
- **ANNANDALE EQUESTRIAN CTRE**, Peterhead **Ref:**YH00453
- **ARDMIDDLE LIVERY STABLES**, Turriff **Ref:**YH00509
- **BRAESIDE EQUESTRIAN CTRE**, Inverurie **Ref:**YH01774
- **EDEN EQUESTRIAN CTRE**, Turriff **Ref:**YH04546
- **GLEN TANAR EQUESTRIAN CTRE**, Aboyne **Ref:**YH05827
- **LADYMIRE EQUESTRIAN CTRE**, Ellon **Ref:**YH08338
- **MERGIE LIVERY STABLES**, Stonehaven **Ref:**YH09473
- **MILL OF URAS EQUESTRIAN**, Stonehaven **Ref:**YH09583
- **SKINNER, GEORGE M**, Inverurie **Ref:**YH12875
- **SPRINGFIELD STABLES**, Huntly **Ref:**YH13258

ANGUS
- **BALRUDDERY STABLES**, Dundee **Ref:**YH00875
- **KIRRIEMUIR HORSE SUPPLIES**, Kirriemuir **Ref:**YH08240
- **MIDDLER, C**, Dundee **Ref:**YH09539
- **MUIRHEAD STABLES**, Dundee **Ref:**YH09926
- **PATHHEAD STABLES**, Kirriemuir **Ref:**YH10821
- **ROBERTSON, G**, Dundee **Ref:**YH11969
- **ROWAN LEA RIDING SCHOOL**, Carnoustie **Ref:**YH12153

ARGYLL AND BUTE
- **ARGYLL TRAIL RIDING**, Lochgilphead **Ref:**YH00523
- **BLACKS LIVERY STABLES**, Helensburgh **Ref:**YH01494
- **COLGRAIN EQUESTRIAN CTRE**, Helensburgh **Ref:**YH03170
- **LETTERSHUNA RIDING CTRE**, Appin **Ref:**YH08570
- **LITTLE RAHANE**, Helensburgh **Ref:**YH08701

AYRSHIRE (EAST)
- **BARGOWER RIDING SCHOOL**, Kilmarnock **Ref:**YH00933
- **BLAIRFIELD FARM STUD**, Kilmarnock **Ref:**YH01514
- **DEAN CASTLE RIDING CTRE**, Kilmarnock **Ref:**YH03988
- **HARPERLAND LIVERY**, Kilmarnock **Ref:**YH06456
- **MOSSBACK RIDING SCHOOL**, Cumnock **Ref:**YH09865
- **MUIRDYKE STUD FARM**, Cumnock **Ref:**YH09922
- **MUIRMILL INTERNATIONAL E C**, Kilmarnock **Ref:**YH09927
- **ROWALLAN ACTIVITY CTRE**, Kilmarnock **Ref:**YH12152

AYRSHIRE (NORTH)
- **BROOM FARM RIDING SCHOOL**, Stevenston **Ref:**YH02071
- **CAIRNHOUSE RIDING CTRE**, Isle Of Arran **Ref:**YH02419
- **KELBURN COUNTRY CTRE**, Fairlie **Ref:**YH08039
- **MILLSTONFORD**, West Kilbride **Ref:**YH09637
- **TANDLEVIEW STABLES**, Beith **Ref:**YH13852

AYRSHIRE (SOUTH)
- **DRUMCOYLE LIVERY YARD**, Ayr **Ref:**YH04289
- **ROSEMOUNT RIDING SVS**, Prestwick **Ref:**YH12105
- **SHANTER RIDING CTRE**, Girvan **Ref:**YH12672

CLACKMANNANSHIRE
- **SIMMONS, AVRIL**, Dollar **Ref:**YH12826

DUMFRIES AND GALLOWAY
- **BAREND RIDING CTRE**, Dalbeattie **Ref:**YH00929
- **CHARIOTS OF FIRE DRIVING CTRE**, Lockerbie **Ref:**YH02750
- **DALESIDE EQUESTRIAN CTRE**, Annan **Ref:**YH03832
- **ETTRICK STABLES**, Thornhill **Ref:**YH04890

EDINBURGH (CITY OF)
- **MORTON MAINS LIVERY**, Edinburgh **Ref:**YH09850
- **ROBERTSON, E C**, Dalkeith **Ref:**YH11968
- **TOWER FARM**, Edinburgh **Ref:**YH14271

FALKIRK
- **CAMPBELL, CARNET**, Slamannan **Ref:**YH02483
- **HAYFIELD LIVERY**, Bonnybridge **Ref:**YH06577
- **WOODEND**, Falkirk **Ref:**YH15683

FIFE
- **ANGLE PARK**, Cupar **Ref:**YH00409
- **DABBS**, Cupar **Ref:**YH03813
- **DRUMCARROW**, St Andrews **Ref:**YH04288
- **GLENROTHES RIDING CTRE**, Glenrothes **Ref:**YH05841
- **KINNEAR, TERRY**, Dunfermline **Ref:**YH08217
- **PUDDLEDUB STUD**, Kirkcaldy **Ref:**YH11447
- **REMUS EQUESTRIAN**, Lochgelly **Ref:**YH11752
- **WEST PITCORTHI STABLES**, Anstruther **Ref:**YH15159

GLASGOW (CITY OF)
- **BUSBY EQUITATION CTRE**, Busby **Ref:**YH02302
- **DUMBRECK RIDING SCHOOL**, Glasgow **Ref:**YH04328
- **EASTERTON STABLES**, Glasgow **Ref:**YH04501
- **HAZELDEN SADDLERY**, Glasgow **Ref:**YH06602
- **KENMURE RIDING SCHOOL**, Glasgow **Ref:**YH08065
- **WOODEND**, Glasgow **Ref:**YH15684

HIGHLANDS
- **ACHALONE ACTIVITIES**, Halkirk **Ref:**YH00141
- **FOXHOLE LIVERY STABLE**, Beauly **Ref:**YH05436
- **HIGHLAND RIDING CTRE**, Inverness **Ref:**YH06793
- **LOGIE FARM**, Nairn **Ref:**YH08778

ISLE OF SKYE
- **SKYE RIDING CTRE**, Portree **Ref:**YH12881

LANARKSHIRE (NORTH)
- **DRUMBEG EQUINE CTRE**, Glasgow **Ref:**YH04286
- **TANNOCK STABLES**, Cumbernauld **Ref:**YH13859

LANARKSHIRE (SOUTH)
- **HIGHBURN STABLES**, Lanark **Ref:**YH06773
- **HILLHEAD**, Carluke **Ref:**YH06846
- **JUMPS**, Carluke **Ref:**YH07967
- **LETHAME HOUSE EQUESTRIAN CTRE**, Strathaven **Ref:**YH08567
- **MID DRUMLOCH**, Hamilton **Ref:**YH09526
- **NEWHOUSE FARM**, Glasgow **Ref:**YH10140
- **SCOTTISH EQUESTRIAN COMPLEX**, Lanark **Ref:**YH12555
- **WATT, C**, Glasgow **Ref:**YH14999

LOTHIAN (EAST)
- **ORCHARD FIELD LIVERY STABLES**, Tranent **Ref:**YH10533
- **TRANENT RIDING CTRE**, Tranent **Ref:**YH14346
- **WEST FENTON LIVERY**, North Berwick **Ref:**YH15145

LOTHIAN (MID)
- **COUSLAND PK FARM**, Dalkeith **Ref:**YH03515
- **EDINBURGH & LASSWADE**, Lasswade **Ref:**YH04559
- **EDINBURGH EQUESTRIAN CTRE**, Dalkeith **Ref:**YH04560
- **PENTLAND HILLS ICELANDICS**, Penicuik **Ref:**YH10961

LOTHIAN (WEST)
- **CHAMPFLEURIE STABLES**, Bathgate **Ref:**YH02725
- **FERNIEHAUGH LIVERY STABLES**, Penicuik **Ref:**YH05166
- **FORBES & SON**, Linlithgow **Ref:**YH05317
- **HOLMES RIDING STABLES**, Bathgate **Ref:**YH06973
- **HOUSTON FARM RIDING SCHOOL**, Broxburn **Ref:**YH07212
- **WESTMUIR RIDING CTRE**, Broxburn **Ref:**YH15221

MORAY
- **CRANNA, P**, Aberlour **Ref:**YH03569
- **SHENVAL FARM**, Ballindalloch **Ref:**YH12709

PERTH AND KINROSS
- **ALICHMORE RIDING/LIVERY CTRE**, Crieff **Ref:**YH00280
- **CALEDONIAN EQUESTRIAN CTRE**, Perth **Ref:**YH02440
- **CRIEFF HYDRO HOTEL STABLES**, Crieff **Ref:**YH03597
- **EASTERTON ARENAS**, Auchterarder **Ref:**YH04499
- **EQUI-CARE**, Perth **Ref:**YH04736
- **GLEN EAGLES EQUESTRIAN**, Auchterarder **Ref:**YH05825
- **GLENMARKIE**, Blairgowrie **Ref:**YH05840
- **LOCH TAY HIGHLAND**, Killin **Ref:**YH08753
- **RAMSBOTTOM, J**, Dunblane **Ref:**YH11620
- **TULLOCHVILLE LIVERY YARD**, Aberfeldy **Ref:**YH14451

RENFREWSHIRE
- **FORDBANK EQUE CTRE**, Johnstone **Ref:**YH05329
- **GLEDDOCH RIDING SCHOOL**, Port Glasgow **Ref:**YH05822
- **MEADOW PK**, Johnstone **Ref:**YH09421

SCOTTISH BORDERS
- **BAILEY MILL**, Newcastleton **Ref:**YH00794
- **BOWHILL STABLES**, Selkirk **Ref:**YH01710
- **FURNESS, J**, Lauder **Ref:**YH05548
- **NENTHORN STABLES**, Kelso **Ref:**YH10077
- **OVER WHITLAW STABLES**, Selkirk **Ref:**YH10590
- **STARK, IAN**, Selkirk **Ref:**YH13394
- **WESTERTOUN**, Gordon **Ref:**YH15212
- **WHISGILLS RIDING CTRE**, Newcastleton **Ref:**YH15285

STIRLING
- **EASTERHILL**, Gartmore **Ref:**YH04495
- **LOMONDSIDE STUD**, Glasgow **Ref:**YH08782
- **MYOTHILL HSE EQUESTRIAN CTRE**, Denny **Ref:**YH09985

STUD FARMS

ARGYLL AND BUTE
- **ROCKHILL HANOVERIAN STUD**, Dalmally **Ref:**YH12032

AYRSHIRE (EAST)
- **BLAIRFIELD FARM STUD**, Kilmarnock **Ref:**YH01514

FIFE
- **PUDDLEDUB STUD**, Kirkcaldy **Ref:**YH11447

SUPPLIES

ABERDEEN (CITY OF)
- **HAPPY HORSE**, Aberdeen **Ref:**YH06399

ABERDEENSHIRE
- **COUNTRY JUMPKINS BAKER-MAC**, Alford **Ref:**YH03411
- **FEEDMIX**, Turriff **Ref:**YH05123
- **HARBRO FARM SALES**, Inverurie **Ref:**YH06405
- **HIGHLAND PONY GAZETTE**, Alford **Ref:**YH06791
- **LOVETT, I**, Stonehaven **Ref:**YH08852
- **MILL OF URAS EQUESTRIAN**, Stonehaven **Ref:**YH09583
- **MILLER PLANT**, Inverurie **Ref:**YH09601
- **NORTH EASTERN FARMERS**, Inverurie **Ref:**YH10258
- **SARAH'S ROSETTES**, Ellon **Ref:**YH12434
- **TOWNS & CARNIE**, Inverurie **Ref:**YH14297
- **TROJAN EQUESTRIAN**, Fraserburgh **Ref:**YH14405

ANGUS
- **BLACKLITE**, Dundee **Ref:**YH01486
- **FEEDMIX**, Kirriemuir **Ref:**YH05124
- **KIRRIEMUIR HORSE SUPPLIES**, Kirriemuir **Ref:**YH08240
- **MACDONALD, A R**, Kirriemuir **Ref:**YH08987
- **NORTH EASTERN FARMERS**, Forfar **Ref:**YH10259
- **PATHHEAD STABLES**, Kirriemuir **Ref:**YH10821
- **SCOTTISH EQUESTRIAN**, Forfar **Ref:**YH12553

ARGYLL AND BUTE
- **ARGYLL WEATHERWISE**, Oban **Ref:**YH00524
- **GREENLEES**, Southend **Ref:**YH06095
- **QUEST HORSE CLOTHING**, Innellan **Ref:**YH11494
- **TACKLE & TACK**, Oban **Ref:**YH13818
- **WHAT EVERY HORSE WANTS**, Helensburgh **Ref:**YH15266

AYRSHIRE (EAST)
- **ROBERTSON, DAVID**, Kilmarnock **Ref:**YH11967
- **SOMERVILLE, J & M**, Kilmarnock **Ref:**YH13066
- **WALKER & TEMPLETON**, Kilmarnock **Ref:**YH14845

AYRSHIRE (NORTH)
- **EQUICO**, Kilwinning **Ref:**YH04738
- **GOLDIE, T**, Kilwinning **Ref:**YH05890

AYRSHIRE (SOUTH)
- **OTTERSWICK**, Mauchine **Ref:**YH10581
- **VICTORIA ROSETTES**, Girvan **Ref:**YH14709

CLACKMANNANSHIRE
- **MACKIE, JAMES A**, Alloa **Ref:**YH09006

DUMFRIES AND GALLOWAY
- **ESKDALE HARNESS**, Lockerbie **Ref:**YH04860
- **GEE GEE'S**, Dumfries **Ref:**YH05690
- **MCKENZIE AGRICULTURAL**, Ruthwell **Ref:**YH09383
- **MCNEILL, P A**, Newton Stewart **Ref:**YH09403
- **NELSON, W M**, Torthorwald **Ref:**YH10076
- **PAISLEY, R**, Langholm **Ref:**YH10686
- **RIDE & GROOM**, Gretna **Ref:**YH11844
- **ROBERT THORNE**, Annan **Ref:**YH11944
- **ROBINSON, JOSEPH**, Annan **Ref:**YH11989

EDINBURGH (CITY OF)
- **STIRLINGSHIRE SADDLERY**, Edinburgh **Ref:**YH13474

FIFE
- **A T HOGG**, Cupar **Ref:**YH00061
- **ANDREWS, J**, Cupar **Ref:**YH00399
- **ARMSTRONG, I & E**, Falkland **Ref:**YH00547
- **BILLINGE, J N R**, Cupar **Ref:**YH01412
- **KEITH GARRY FENCING**, Freuchie **Ref:**YH08034
- **RODGER, J & T**, Cupar **Ref:**YH12046
- **WEIR, J C (HON)**, Cupar **Ref:**YH15054

GLASGOW (CITY OF)
- **BUSBY EQUITATION CTRE**, Busby **Ref:**YH02302
- **HORSE & HOUND FEED SUPPLIES**, Milngavie **Ref:**YH07091
- **SCOTTISH FARMER**, Glasgow **Ref:**YH12556
- **WM ALEXANDER & SON**, Glasgow **Ref:**YH15638

HIGHLANDS
- **CLYNE ENGINEERING**, Glenurquhart **Ref:**YH03101
- **FOXHOLE LIVERY STABLE**, Beauly **Ref:**YH05436
- **H P T SADDLERY**, Newtonmore **Ref:**YH06233
- **HIGHLAND EQUESTRIAN SVS**, Inverness **Ref:**YH06789
- **N D S ANIMAL FEEDS**, Nairn **Ref:**YH09988
- **NORTHFIELD HORSE SUPPLIES**, Invergordon **Ref:**YH10313
- **RADDERY EQUINE**, Fortrose **Ref:**YH11593
- **SEAFORTH SADDLERS**, Inverness **Ref:**YH12586

INVERCLYDE
- **RUSSELL, A**, Kilmacolm **Ref:**YH12255

LANARKSHIRE (NORTH)
- **BARTLETT, R A**, Airdrie **Ref:**YH01040
- **CLIPPETY CLOP**, Cumbernauld **Ref:**YH03048
- **RED ROSETTE PET PRODUCTS**, Airdrie **Ref:**YH11705

LANARKSHIRE (SOUTH)
- **SCOT-TACK**, Larkhall **Ref:**YH12548
- **YOUNG, W G**, Carluke **Ref:**YH15942

LOTHIAN (EAST)
- **J S MAIN & SONS**, Haddington **Ref:**YH07617
- **WILLIAM MAIN SADDLER**, Dunbar **Ref:**YH15435

LOTHIAN (MID)
- **EQUINE NEWS**, Penicuik **Ref:**YH04790
- **R H MILLER**, Dalkeith **Ref:**YH11541
- **ROBINSON'S RUG WASH**, Carrington **Ref:**YH12006

LOTHIAN (WEST)
- **BERTRAM, IAN**, Broxburn **Ref:**YH01321
- **CLEAR ROUND ORIGINALS**, Bathgate **Ref:**YH03010
- **DAVID THOMSON**, Livingston **Ref:**YH03924
- **WESTER WOODSIDE FARM FEEDS**, Linlithgow **Ref:**YH15191

MORAY
- **A & I SUPPLIES**, Elgin **Ref:**YH00011
- **GREENFIELDS SADDLERY**, Elgin **Ref:**YH06085
- **THERAPY SYSTEMS**, Aberlour **Ref:**YH13985

PERTH AND KINROSS
- **2 XCEL**, Perth **Ref:**YH00002
- **BREMNER, BLACK**, Aberfeldy **Ref:**YH01834
- **EQUI-CARE**, Perth **Ref:**YH04736
- **MCCASH'S**, Perth **Ref:**YH09326
- **TAINSH, W**, Cromrie **Ref:**YH13822
- **W A THOMSON PLANT HIRE**, Aberfeldy **Ref:**YH14750

RENFREWSHIRE
- **RIVERBANK POULTRY**, Bridge Of Weir **Ref:**YH11918
- **T F R C**, Lochwinnoch **Ref:**YH13738

SCOTTISH BORDERS
- **A C BURN**, Jedburgh **Ref:**YH00022
- **A J B SPENCE & SON**, Eyemouth **Ref:**YH00037
- **AMOS, W**, Hawick **Ref:**YH00371
- **BEWLEY, J R**, Jedburgh **Ref:**YH01348
- **BORDER SHOWJUMPING EQUIPMENT**, Duns **Ref:**YH01645
- **COLTHERD, W S**, Selkirk **Ref:**YH03202
- **G R S NIXON**, Selkirk **Ref:**YH05593
- **GRAHAM, H O**, Jedburgh **Ref:**YH05967
- **J HOGARTH**, Kelso **Ref:**YH07589
- **R H MILLER**, Peebles **Ref:**YH11542
- **SHIELS, R**, Tedburgh **Ref:**YH12743
- **TEVIOT HORSEWEAR DIRECT**, Hawick **Ref:**YH13966
- **TEVIOT TOWN & COUNTRY**, Hawick **Ref:**YH13967
- **THOMSON, A M**, Duns **Ref:**YH14050
- **THOMSON, R W**, Hawick **Ref:**YH14054
- **WELLS, A H MACTAGGART**, Hawick **Ref:**YH15081
- **WELLS, F & H**, Galashiels **Ref:**YH15083
- **WIGHT, A J**, Cockburnspath **Ref:**YH15401

STIRLING
- **CARRUTHERS ROSETTE**, Balfron Station **Ref:**YH02600

TRACKS/COURSES

ABERDEENSHIRE
- **LADYMIRE EQUESTRIAN CTRE**, Ellon **Ref:**YH08338
- **TACK SHOP**, Banchory **Ref:**YH13810

ARGYLL AND BUTE
- **ARGYLL TRAIL RIDING**, Lochgilphead **Ref:**YH00523

AYRSHIRE (EAST)
- **DEAN CASTLE RIDING CTRE**, Kilmarnock **Ref:**YH03988
- **ROWALLAN ACTIVITY CTRE**, Kilmarnock **Ref:**YH12152

AYRSHIRE (SOUTH)
- **AYR RACECOURSE**, Ayr **Ref:**YH00698

FIFE
- **BRAESIDE**, Cupar **Ref:**YH01772
- **SALTIRE STABLES**, Cupar **Ref:**YH12394

LANARKSHIRE (SOUTH)
- **HAMILTON PK RACE COURSE**, Hamilton **Ref:**YH06347

PERTH AND KINROSS
- **EASTERTON ARENAS**, Auchterarder **Ref:**YH04499
- **ERROL RACEWAY**, Perth **Ref:**YH04856
- **GLEN EAGLES EQUESTRIAN**, Auchterarder **Ref:**YH05825
- **PERTH HUNT**, Perth **Ref:**YH10997

SCOTTISH BORDERS
- **BOWHILL STABLES**, Selkirk **Ref:**YH01710

TRAINERS

ABERDEEN (CITY OF)
- **HAYFIELD SADDLERY**, Aberdeen **Ref:**YH06579
- **SUNNYSIDE**, Aberdeen **Ref:**YH13649

ABERDEENSHIRE
- **EDEN EQUESTRIAN CTRE**, Turriff **Ref:**YH04546
- **HOBGOBLINS**, Aboyne **Ref:**YH06899
- **MANAR STUD & RIDING CTRE**, Alford **Ref:**YH09064
- **SKINNER, GEORGE M**, Inverurie **Ref:**YH12875

ANGUS
- **LIDDLE, H T**, Forfar **Ref:**YH08606

ARGYLL AND BUTE
- **APPALOOSA HOLIDAYS**, Lochgilphead **Ref:**YH00475
- **ARGYLL TRAIL RIDING**, Lochgilphead **Ref:**YH00523
- **STUART, FIONA**, Alexandria **Ref:**YH13594

AYRSHIRE (EAST)
- **GOLDIE, ROBERT H**, Kilmarnock **Ref:**YH05889

AYRSHIRE (SOUTH)
- **CREE LODGE**, Ayr **Ref:**YH03587
- **CREE LODGE RACING STABLES**, Ayr **Ref:**YH03588
- **MCGAWN, D**, Ayr **Ref:**YH09353

DUMFRIES AND GALLOWAY
- **CHARIOTS OF FIRE DRIVING CTRE**, Lockerbie **Ref:**YH02750
- **LUNGO, L**, Dumfries **Ref:**YH08900
- **MEIKLE WELSH COBS**, Castle Douglas **Ref:**YH09447
- **PARKER, C**, Lockerbie **Ref:**YH10747

FIFE
- **BARCLAY, J**, Leslie **Ref:**YH00925
- **BLYTH, J**, Kirkcaldy **Ref:**YH01578
- **BRADBURNE, S**, Cupar **Ref:**YH01745
- **DABBS**, Cupar **Ref:**YH03813
- **DRYSDALE, A**, Boreland **Ref:**YH04300
- **EDENSIDE**, St Andrews **Ref:**YH04551
- **LOW-MITCHELL, D I**, Leven **Ref:**YH08876
- **PEARSON, D**, Thorton **Ref:**YH10878
- **ROSEBANK STABLES**, Cowdenbeath **Ref:**YH12101
- **WOOD, T C**, Lochgelly **Ref:**YH15669

GLASGOW (CITY OF)
- **FORREST, W**, Glasgow **Ref:**YH05378
- **GOLDIE, J S**, Uplawmoor **Ref:**YH05888

HIGHLANDS
- **HIGHLAND RIDING CTRE**, Inverness **Ref:**YH06793
- **LOCH NESS RIDING**, Inverness **Ref:**YH08752

ISLE OF SKYE
- **SKYE RIDING CTRE**, Portree **Ref:**YH12881

LANARKSHIRE (NORTH)
- **KENNEDY, R**, Wishaw **Ref:**YH08068
- **LAIRD, ALEXANDER**, Shotts **Ref:**YH08347
- **NIMMO, R W F**, Newarthill **Ref:**YH10208
- **O'BRIEN, H H**, Stepps **Ref:**YH10420
- **RIVERSIDE RACING STABLES**, Wishaw **Ref:**YH11925

LANARKSHIRE (SOUTH)
- **BELSTANE RACING**, Carluke **Ref:**YH01253

LOTHIAN (EAST)
- **TILTON HOUSE STABLES**, Dunbar **Ref:**YH14158

MORAY
- **MUIRYHALL STABLES**, Elgin **Ref:**YH09929

PERTH AND KINROSS
- **CARSTAIRS, H**, Auchterarder **Ref:**YH02605
- **DRYSDALE, G**, Kinross **Ref:**YH04301
- **EASTERTON ARENAS**, Auchterarder **Ref:**YH04499
- **EQUI-CARE**, Perth **Ref:**YH04736
- **GIAMANDREA, J**, Auchterarder **Ref:**YH05736
- **GLEN EAGLES EQUESTRIAN**, Auchterarder **Ref:**YH05825
- **GLENMARKIE**, Blairgowrie **Ref:**YH05840
- **HAY, A M**, Milnathort **Ref:**YH06563
- **LOCH TAY HIGHLAND**, Killin **Ref:**YH08753
- **MCILWRAITH, A M**, Auchterarder **Ref:**YH09373
- **NORMILE, LUCY**, Glenfarg **Ref:**YH10242
- **RUSSELL, LUCINDA V**, Kinross **Ref:**YH12260
- **TILLYRIE RACING**, Kinross **Ref:**YH14155

SCOTTISH BORDERS
- **AYTON CASTLE**, Eyemouth **Ref:**YH00705
- **BROKEN SPOKE**, West Linton **Ref:**YH02021
- **KEMP, W T**, Duns **Ref:**YH08055
- **LEGGATE, JENNY**, Greenlaw **Ref:**YH08540
- **LOCH, SYLVIA (LADY)**, Kelso **Ref:**YH08754
- **MACTAGGART, A B**, Hawick **Ref:**YH09017
- **OLIVER, RHONA**, Hawick **Ref:**YH10500
- **OVER WHITLAW STABLES**, Selkirk **Ref:**YH10590
- **STARK, IAN**, Selkirk **Ref:**YH13394
- **TELFORD, R**, Eyemouth **Ref:**YH13943
- **WESTERTOUN**, Gordon **Ref:**YH15212
- **WHILLANS, A C**, Hawick **Ref:**YH15280
- **WHILLANS, D**, Hawick **Ref:**YH15281

STIRLING
- **MYOTHILL HSE EQUESTRIAN CTRE**, Denny **Ref:**YH09985

TRANSPORT/HORSE BOXES

ABERDEEN (CITY OF)
- **MOIR, H & F**, Aberdeen **Ref:**YH09703

ABERDEENSHIRE
- **ABERDEEN TRAILERS**, Turriff **Ref:**YH00125
- **BEEDIE BROS**, Fraserburgh **Ref:**YH01185
- **EDEN EQUESTRIAN CTRE**, Turriff **Ref:**YH04546
- **EMSLIE, COLIN**, Inverurie **Ref:**YH04662
- **GRAY & ADAMS**, Fraserburgh **Ref:**YH06026
- **GREIG, JOHN**, Peterhead **Ref:**YH06121
- **WESTERTON BOXES**, Old Meldrum **Ref:**YH15210

ANGUS
- **MCINTOSH, DUNCAN R**, Brechin **Ref:**YH09376
- **MONIFIETH TRAILERS**, Dundee **Ref:**YH09722

ARGYLL AND BUTE
- **TRAIL WEST**, Oban **Ref:**YH14313

AYRSHIRE (EAST)
- **FENWICK MOBILE EXHIBITIONS**, Kilmarnock **Ref:**YH05154

AYRSHIRE (NORTH)
- **VOLVO BUS**, Irvine **Ref:**YH14740

AYRSHIRE (SOUTH)
- **AYR TRAILER CTRE**, Ayr **Ref:**YH00701
- **AYRSHIRE EQUITATION CTRE**, Ayr **Ref:**YH00704
- **JENKINSON, T H**, Ayr **Ref:**YH07738
- **MARINE MECHANICAL**, Troon **Ref:**YH09149

DUMFRIES AND GALLOWAY
- **A KERR HAULAGE**, Kirkcudbright **Ref:**YH00045
- **B R I INT**, Annan **Ref:**YH00746
- **JENKINSON, T H**, Castle Douglas **Ref:**YH07739
- **R DAVIDSON & SONS**, Dumfries **Ref:**YH11528

EDINBURGH (CITY OF)
- **INDESPENSION**, Edinburgh **Ref:**YH07417

FALKIRK
- **ARTIC TRAILER SERVICES**, Falkirk **Ref:**YH00572
- **J C M**, Falkirk **Ref:**YH07572

FIFE
- **DABBS**, Cupar **Ref:**YH03813
- **GO 4 IT**, Cupar **Ref:**YH05859
- **TRAILER REFURB**, Dunfermline **Ref:**YH14326
- **WALKER, W**, St Andrews **Ref:**YH14858

GLASGOW (CITY OF)
- **ANDREW GRAY**, Glasgow **Ref:**YH00391
- **DISCOUNT TOWBAR SUPPLIES**, Glasgow **Ref:**YH04130
- **INDESPENSION**, Glasgow **Ref:**YH07419
- **SCOTT HALLEYS**, Milngavie **Ref:**YH12532

HIGHLANDS
- **A J GRANT & SONS**, Inverness **Ref:**YH00039
- **IFOR WILLIAMS TRAILERS**, Caithness **Ref:**YH07392
- **ROBERTSON, NEIL**, Spean Bridge **Ref:**YH11973
- **TRANSPORTAPET**, Beauly **Ref:**YH14351
- **W D MACRAE**, Inverness **Ref:**YH14760

LANARKSHIRE (NORTH)
- **HILL HIRE**, Bellshill **Ref:**YH06818

LANARKSHIRE (SOUTH)
- **SAMRO TRAILER UK**, Glasgow **Ref:**YH12401

LOTHIAN (EAST)
- **EQUIBOX**, Haddington **Ref:**YH04733
- **H & S EUROPEAN TRANSPORT**, Longniddry **Ref:**YH06209
- **LOTHIAN TRAILER CTRE**, Tranent **Ref:**YH08833

LOTHIAN (MID)
- **BOWLEA TRAILERS**, Penicuik **Ref:**YH01713
- **MIDLOTHIAN'S TOWBAR CTRE**, Bonnyrigg **Ref:**YH09560
- **PETER BECK TRAILERS**, Lasswade **Ref:**YH11009
- **S D C TRAILERS**, Dalkeith **Ref:**YH12320

LOTHIAN (WEST)
- **CENTRAL TRAILER RENTCO**, Bathgate **Ref:**YH02694

ORKNEY ISLES
- **DRURY TRANSPORT**, Orkney **Ref:**YH04296

PERTH AND KINROSS
- **AUTOW CTRE**, Perth **Ref:**YH00675
- **GLEN EAGLES EQUESTRIAN**, Auchterarder **Ref:**YH05825
- **HORSE TRANSPORT**, Milnathort **Ref:**YH07142
- **KAY TRAILERS**, Kinross **Ref:**YH08003
- **MITCHELL, JAMES K**, Crieff **Ref:**YH09671
- **STRUAN MOTORS**, Perth **Ref:**YH13590
- **WHITESIDE TRAILERS**, Perth **Ref:**YH15358

RENFREWSHIRE
- **TURNBULL TRAILERS**, Paisley **Ref:**YH14470

SCOTTISH BORDERS
- **CARRIAGES**, Innerleithen **Ref:**YH02583
- **ERIC GILLIE**, Kelso **Ref:**YH04845

STIRLING
- **ARTIC TRAILER SERVICES**, Stirling **Ref:**YH00573
- **PETER MCKENZIE & SON**, Stirling **Ref:**YH11012
- **PETER MCKENZIE & SON**, Stirling **Ref:**YH11011

ARENAS

CEREDIGION

- **RHEIDOL RIDING CTRE**, Aberystwyth **Ref:**YH11784

GLAMORGAN (VALE OF)

- **CIMLA TREKKING**, Neath **Ref:**YH02918

ISLE OF ANGLESEY

- **TAL Y FOEL RIDING CTRE**, Anglesey **Ref:**YH13829

PEMBROKESHIRE

- **OASIS PARK EQUESTRIAN CTRE**, Narberth **Ref:**YH10412

POWYS

- **BROMPTON HALL**, Montgomery **Ref:**YH02025
- **CANTREF**, Brecon **Ref:**YH02516
- **GOLDEN CASTLE**, Crickhowell **Ref:**YH05877

SWANSEA

- **TANKEY LAKE LIVERY**, Swansea **Ref:**YH13856

BLACKSMITHS

CAERPHILLY

- **MILL FORGE**, Hengoed **Ref:**YH09575

CARMARTHENSHIRE

- **B.E.M.**, Newcastle Emlyn **Ref:**YH00754
- **HOWLETT, ANDREW**, Llanybydder **Ref:**YH07241
- **INCUS DESIGNS**, Carmarthen **Ref:**YH07410
- **J R THOMAS & SON**, Llanelli **Ref:**YH07611
- **JONES, D A G**, Carmarthen **Ref:**YH07885
- **PAGE, ALEC**, Lampeter **Ref:**YH10679

CEREDIGION

- **BURRELL, RAYMOND**, Aberystwyth **Ref:**YH02277
- **W E LEWIS & SON**, Aberystwyth **Ref:**YH14763

CONWY

- **WILLIAMS, B**, Colwyn Bay **Ref:**YH15448

DENBIGHSHIRE

- **ABSOLAM EVANS & SON**, Llangollen **Ref:**YH00138

GLAMORGAN (VALE OF)

- **CITY FORGE**, Cardiff **Ref:**YH02931
- **HARRY, RICHARD J**, Cardiff **Ref:**YH06497
- **MORGAN, R W J**, Barry **Ref:**YH09812
- **WHELAN, J G**, Cardiff **Ref:**YH15277

ISLE OF ANGLESEY

- **W R WILLIAMS & SON**, Holyhead **Ref:**YH14791

MONMOUTHSHIRE

- **MORGAN, R**, Usk **Ref:**YH09811

PEMBROKESHIRE

- **E B OWEN & SON**, Narberth **Ref:**YH04398
- **R D DAVIES & SON**, Tenby **Ref:**YH11527
- **THOMAS, J E**, Newport **Ref:**YH14023

POWYS

- **CANTREF**, Brecon **Ref:**YH02516
- **IAN DENNIS PARTNERSHIP**, Brecon **Ref:**YH07370
- **PRICE, D A**, Builth Wells **Ref:**YH11377

BLOOD STOCK AGENCIES

RHONDDA CYNON TAFF

- **RICHARDS, GRAHAM**, Cilfynydd **Ref:**YH11808

BREEDERS

BLAENAU GWENT

- **BRAKE, DAVID & JANET**, Ebbw Vale **Ref:**YH01781
- **DAVIES, R & J**, Ebbw Vale **Ref:**YH03947
- **HARPER, D & R**, Ebbw Vale **Ref:**YH06454
- **WALTERS, J K & M S**, Tredegar **Ref:**YH14887

BRIDGEND

- **COOKE, J & S**, Bridgend **Ref:**YH03261
- **WESTRA DONKEY STUD**, Bridgend **Ref:**YH15231

CAERPHILLY

- **BROWN, C**, Blackwood **Ref:**YH02102
- **DOWDING, BRIAN H**, Blackwood **Ref:**YH04221
- **GARRETT, DAI**, Bargoed **Ref:**YH05656
- **JENKINS, W J P**, Blackwood **Ref:**YH07737
- **JENNA LIVESTOCK**, Rudry **Ref:**YH07743
- **JONES, J P**, Hengoed **Ref:**YH07908
- **ROBERTS, M D**, Blackwood **Ref:**YH11956

CARMARTHENSHIRE

- **AUSDAN STUD**, Lampeter **Ref:**YH00665
- **BLAENWAUN STUD**, Llanwrda **Ref:**YH01507
- **BOWEN, E & M**, Ammanford **Ref:**YH01700
- **BRENTON**, Carmarthen **Ref:**YH01850
- **BYCHAN STUD**, Llandeilo **Ref:**YH02344
- **CARMARTHENSHIRE**, Cardigan **Ref:**YH02559
- **CEFN GLAN STUD**, Carmarthen **Ref:**YH02677
- **CHARLTON, S**, Newcastle Emlyn **Ref:**YH02769
- **CLARKE, P**, Llansadwrn **Ref:**YH02975
- **D L DAVIES & SON**, Llandysul **Ref:**YH03789
- **DAVIES, D**, Carmarthen **Ref:**YH03936
- **DAVIES, W B**, Carmarthen **Ref:**YH03949
- **DOBBS, P J**, Llangadog **Ref:**YH04152
- **EISENFARN STUD**, Llanelli **Ref:**YH04599
- **EVERITT, S & H**, Llangadog **Ref:**YH04954
- **GIRDLER, K & C**, Carmarthen **Ref:**YH05794
- **HOOPER, K E**, Llanelli **Ref:**YH07043
- **JEHAN, F W**, Llandeilo **Ref:**YH07727
- **JENKINS, A & E**, Ammanford **Ref:**YH07730
- **JONES, C**, Llandysul **Ref:**YH07880
- **KINGSETTLE STUD**, Llandsyssul **Ref:**YH08202
- **LEWIS, MEGAN**, Llanwrda **Ref:**YH08594
- **LEWIS, W D**, Clynderwen **Ref:**YH08597
- **LLETY**, Carmarthen **Ref:**YH08729
- **M H W S J FRATERNITY**, Llanwrda **Ref:**YH08965
- **MILLER, R & DAVIES, M**, Ferryside **Ref:**YH09611
- **MORGAN EQUINE STUD**, Llandeilo **Ref:**YH09795
- **PEARCE, J & A**, Carmarthen **Ref:**YH10872
- **PENCADER STUD**, Pencader **Ref:**YH10928
- **READING, R H**, Carmarthen **Ref:**YH11682
- **RHYDHIR STUD**, Carmarthen **Ref:**YH11792
- **RIPMAN, BARBARA**, Carmarthen **Ref:**YH11906
- **RIVERSDALE**, Carmarthen **Ref:**YH11923
- **RUTHERFORD, E**, Llandeilo **Ref:**YH12273
- **SCHMITT, H & U**, Llandysul **Ref:**YH12514
- **SHERMANDELL MORGANS**, Llandeilo **Ref:**YH12725
- **SIANWOOD STUD**, Llandovery **Ref:**YH12778
- **SMALL-LAND PONY STUD**, Carmarthen **Ref:**YH12912
- **STALLIONS AT TACKEXCHANGE**, Llanelli **Ref:**YH13351
- **STEVENS, R**, Llandysul **Ref:**YH13447
- **TACK EXCHANGE**, Llanelli **Ref:**YH13787
- **TANYFOEL MORGANS**, Llandysul **Ref:**YH13863
- **THOMAS, D G B**, Carmarthen **Ref:**YH14017
- **THOMAS, D J**, Kidwelly **Ref:**YH14018
- **TOWY VALLEY PONY STUD**, Llandovery **Ref:**YH14305

CEREDIGION

- **D & D JONES & SON**, Tregaron **Ref:**YH03769
- **DAVIES, ERIC**, Lampeter **Ref:**YH03940
- **DOWNLAND PONY STUD**, Llangoedmor **Ref:**YH04235
- **EVANS, J H**, Lampeter **Ref:**YH04923
- **EVANS, T E**, Aberaeron **Ref:**YH04933
- **FFOSLAS STUD**, Lampeter **Ref:**YH05179
- **G JONES BROS**, Llanon **Ref:**YH05587
- **GRANGEWAY STUD**, Lampeter **Ref:**YH06003
- **HOYLES, C**, Lampeter **Ref:**YH07247
- **J M JONES**, Llanon **Ref:**YH07597
- **JAMES, T H**, Aberystwyth **Ref:**YH07688
- **JONES, D & R**, Llanon **Ref:**YH07884
- **JONES, G M**, Tregaron **Ref:**YH07901
- **KINNARD, D W & A M**, Tregaron **Ref:**YH08216
- **LLOYD, I J R**, Pennant **Ref:**YH08739
- **LLOYD, S**, Lampeter **Ref:**YH08742
- **MORRIS, D**, Aberystwyth **Ref:**YH09828
- **MORRIS, H & H A**, Tregaron **Ref:**YH09831
- **NANTGWINAU WELSH COBS**, Lampeter **Ref:**YH10016
- **NEBO STUD**, Llanon **Ref:**YH10065
- **PARC - STUD**, Lampeter **Ref:**YH10712
- **ROBERTS, R**, Lampeter **Ref:**YH11959
- **WILLIAMS, F**, Aberystwyth **Ref:**YH15456
- **WILLS, G J**, Aberystwyth **Ref:**YH15518

CONWY

- **ABERCONWY STUD**, Colwyn Bay **Ref:**YH00120
- **BENFIELD, M**, Colwyn Bay **Ref:**YH01265
- **JONES, G W**, Abergele **Ref:**YH07902
- **LLWYNGARTH WELSH COBS**, Colwyn Bay **Ref:**YH08748
- **MORRIS, J, C & S**, Colwyn Bay **Ref:**YH09832
- **OLDFIELD, D T**, Bryn Hyfryd Park **Ref:**YH10486
- **PRITCHARD, S**, Denbigh **Ref:**YH11423

DENBIGHSHIRE

- **BALE-WILLIAMS, A M**, Chirk **Ref:**YH00842
- **JOHNSON, J**, Llangollen **Ref:**YH07825
- **LEE, P**, Rhyl **Ref:**YH08525
- **LLANNERCH EQUESTRIAN CTRE**, St Asaph **Ref:**YH08726
- **MORWYN STUD**, Ruthin **Ref:**YH09854

FLINTSHIRE

- **DRINKWATER, J**, Garden City **Ref:**YH04275
- **LEVERETT, C J & S**, Holywell **Ref:**YH08575
- **LIGHTFOOT, R**, Mold **Ref:**YH08614
- **MANNOG**, Holywell **Ref:**YH09092
- **VLACQ STUD**, Mold **Ref:**YH14738

GLAMORGAN (VALE OF)

- **ALGER, A**, Cardiff **Ref:**YH00278
- **ARGAE HSE STABLES**, Dinas Powys **Ref:**YH00519
- **DAVIES & ANDERSON, J & C**, Cardiff **Ref:**YH03932
- **EDDINS, J M & S M**, Cardiff **Ref:**YH04542
- **GOGGIN, F M**, Merthyr Tydfil **Ref:**YH05873
- **HOMFRAY, S**, Crowbridge **Ref:**YH07008
- **KIRBY, E M**, Cardiff **Ref:**YH08226
- **LEADBITTER, P M & F**, Cardiff **Ref:**YH08499
- **MEREDITH, D P**, Merthyr Tydfil **Ref:**YH09469
- **PALMER, D W**, St Nicholas **Ref:**YH10691
- **PICKERSTON STUD**, Barry **Ref:**YH11085
- **RUSSELL LUSITANO STUD**, St Nicholas **Ref:**YH12254
- **SEVERN QUARTER HORSES**, Cowbridge **Ref:**YH12644
- **THOMAS, J T**, Llantwit Major **Ref:**YH14024
- **WILLIAMS, B**, Cardiff **Ref:**YH15449

GWYNEDD

- **ABERSOCH MARCHROS STUD**, Abersoch **Ref:**YH00129
- **DWYFOR RIDING CTRE**, Criccieth **Ref:**YH04382
- **GRIFFITH, W H**, Caernarfon **Ref:**YH06134
- **JONES, J**, Caernarfon **Ref:**YH07906
- **JONES, W T**, Tywyn **Ref:**YH07935
- **MEREDITH, D & S**, Dolgellau **Ref:**YH09468
- **NASH, A**, Bala **Ref:**YH10025
- **PEN-LLEYN RIDING CTRE**, Pwllheli **Ref:**YH10943

PENRHYN STUD FARM, Caernarfon **Ref:**YH10958
STRICK, J, Pwllheli **Ref:**YH13576

ISLE OF ANGLESEY

AUGUST APPALOOSAS, Holyhead **Ref:**YH00663
BRACKENDENE STUD, Anglesey **Ref:**YH01738
COOKE, G A, Menai Bridge **Ref:**YH03260
E EDWARDS & SON, Llangefni **Ref:**YH04403
E, THOMAS & WILLIAMS, R, Holyhead **Ref:**YH04433
EVANS, J T, Llangefni **Ref:**YH04925
HENDY EQUESTRIAN, Holyhead **Ref:**YH06670
JONES, K M, Holyhead **Ref:**YH07909
LLOYD, E, Holyhead **Ref:**YH08736
OWENS, R, Gaerwen **Ref:**YH10608
PARRY, G & M, Holyhead **Ref:**YH10791
ROBERTS, E W, Ty Croes **Ref:**YH11950
STANFORD EVENTING HORSES, Holyhead **Ref:**YH13363
TAL Y FOEL RIDING CTRE, Anglesey **Ref:**YH13829
THOMAS, V & M, Holyhead **Ref:**YH14029

MONMOUTHSHIRE

BATT, J A, Abergavenny **Ref:**YH01076
BELCHER, RACHAEL, Chepstow **Ref:**YH01207
EARLSWOOD RIDING CTRE, Chepstow **Ref:**YH04455
EARLSWOOD STUD, Chepstow **Ref:**YH04456
GLEBEDALE, Abergavenny **Ref:**YH05821
GROUCOTT, W & MORRIS, T A, Crumlin **Ref:**YH06159
LAN GARTH STUD, Llanvihangel-Ystern-Llewern **Ref:**YH08379
LANGARTH, Monmouth **Ref:**YH08399
PEMBRIDGE PERFORMANCE HORSES, Monmouth **Ref:**YH10916
POULTER, D M, Monmouth **Ref:**YH11303
POWELL, JOHN C, Abergavenny **Ref:**YH11319
REES, G, Tredegar **Ref:**YH11729
ROBINSON, R & V, Usk **Ref:**YH11994
ROTHERDALE STUD, Abergavenny **Ref:**YH12131
TAWMARSH STUD, Abergavenny **Ref:**YH13889
THOMAS, D, Blackwood **Ref:**YH14015
TICEHURST, LESLEY J, Abergavenny **Ref:**YH14126
TOKENBOW STUD, Usk **Ref:**YH14204
WOODLANDER STUD, Raglan **Ref:**YH15704

NEATH PORT TALBOT

DYKES, J H & D J, North Cornelly **Ref:**YH04392

NEWPORT

PRICE, M & G, Wentloog **Ref:**YH11382
WILLIAMS, A J, Llandevaud **Ref:**YH15444
WILLIAMS, L J, Magor **Ref:**YH15463
WILLIAMS, M, Bassaleg **Ref:**YH15464

PEMBROKESHIRE

ALLEN, T E, Clynderwen **Ref:**YH00304
CAMPBELL, W M, Pembroke **Ref:**YH02488
DOLRHANOG RIDING CTRE, Newport **Ref:**YH04171
EAST NOLTON RIDING STABLES, Haverfordwest **Ref:**YH04482
FILMSTONE FARM, Narberth **Ref:**YH05204
HASGUARD SHETLAND PONY STUD, Haverfordwest **Ref:**YH06520
PHILLIPS, F S L, Saundersfoot **Ref:**YH11056
REED, J M, Haverfordwest **Ref:**YH11720
TALLY HO FARM, Pembroke **Ref:**YH13841
THOMAS, B, Clynderwen **Ref:**YH14013
TREFOEL STUD, Crymych **Ref:**YH14363
WATSON, R W D & P, Narberth **Ref:**YH14991

POWYS

ANDREW, R M, Welshpool **Ref:**YH00395
APPALOOSAS, NOCONA, Knighton **Ref:**YH00476
BASSETT, A, Cardiff **Ref:**YH01056
BERNARD, JENNIFER, Montgomery **Ref:**YH01311
BRANDSBY DARTMOORS, Welshpool **Ref:**YH01809
CHILTERN CONNEMARA, Presteigne **Ref:**YH02858
COED Y WERN, Brecon **Ref:**YH03134
CURRY, JOAN, Builth Wells **Ref:**YH03743
DELROSA QUARTER HORSES, Presteigne **Ref:**YH04034
EQUINE SEARCH, Llanfyllin **Ref:**YH04798
GETHIN, D, Newtown **Ref:**YH05733
JANTON STUD, Llangammarch Wells **Ref:**YH07700
JONES, A & M, Newton **Ref:**YH07875
JONES, D T, Machynlleth **Ref:**YH07887
JONES, H G, Llanbrynmair **Ref:**YH07904
KILLINEY, Llandrindod Wells **Ref:**YH08142
MARL STUD MARL CRIS STUD, Brecon **Ref:**YH09167
NORRIS, PAULINE, Newtown **Ref:**YH10245
PRICE, G, Brecon **Ref:**YH11378
PUGH, P, Newtown **Ref:**YH11452
REED, ANGELA, Brecon **Ref:**YH11719
REES, K M & W P, Brecon **Ref:**YH11731
SHEPPARD, P J, Brecon **Ref:**YH12717
THOMAS, D, Talgarth **Ref:**YH14016
VAUGHAN, P, Llanidloes **Ref:**YH14666
WILLAIMS, G & R, Llandinam **Ref:**YH15426

RHONDDA CYNON TAFF

DAVIES, E W (DR), Pontyclun **Ref:**YH03939
MANCHIP, R & M, Llanharry **Ref:**YH09070
POUNDER, W C & GREEN, B A, Pontypridd **Ref:**YH11311
PRICHARD, D, J & T, Llantrisant **Ref:**YH11392
WOODLEY, G, Aberdare **Ref:**YH15719

SWANSEA

PHILLIPS, D J, Swansea **Ref:**YH11054

TORFAEN

COBLEY, CHRIS & MARRIE, Pontypool **Ref:**YH03116
COWARD, J R, Pontypool **Ref:**YH03521
PHILLIPS, C M, Blaenavon **Ref:**YH11053
ROSEDALE STUD, Cwmbran **Ref:**YH12102

WREXHAM

BROAD, E P, Wrexham **Ref:**YH01990
EMRAL STUD, Worthenbury **Ref:**YH04660

CLUBS/ASSOCIATIONS

BLAENAU GWENT

COLOURED HORSE & PONY SOC, Tredegar **Ref:**YH03199

BRIDGEND

KENFIG HILL & DISTRICT, Ewenny **Ref:**YH08062
PORTHCAWL HORSE & PONY GRP, Porthcawl **Ref:**YH11289
PORTHCAWL HORSE SHOW SOC, North Cornelly **Ref:**YH11290
SKER RIDING CLUB, North Cornelly **Ref:**YH12868

CAERPHILLY

BEDWELLTY, Blackwood **Ref:**YH01158
BHS WALES, Caerphilly **Ref:**YH01387
GELLIGAER POINT TO POINT, Blackwood **Ref:**YH05696

CARMARTHENSHIRE

AMMAN VALLEY PONY CLUB, Ammanford **Ref:**YH00368
BRITISH PALOMINO SOCIETY, Llandysul **Ref:**YH01964
CARMARTHENSHIRE, Cardigan **Ref:**YH02559
FENWICK, W J GODDARD, Lampeter **Ref:**YH05156
FJORD HORSE SOC, Lampeter **Ref:**YH05258
INT MINIATURE HORSE/PONY SOC, Llanwrda **Ref:**YH07469
LIPIZZANER NATIONAL STUDBOOK, Lampeter **Ref:**YH08675
LLUEST HORSE & PONY TRUST, Llangadog **Ref:**YH08747
M H W S J FRATERNITY, Llanwrda **Ref:**YH08965
PONY CLUB, Ammanford **Ref:**YH11230

CEREDIGION

BHS WALES, Aberystwyth **Ref:**YH01388
DYFFRYN CLETTWR RIDING CLUB, Aberaeron **Ref:**YH04389
DYFFRYN PAITH RIDING GRP, Lampeter **Ref:**YH04390
IGER, Aberystwyth **Ref:**YH07394
TIVYSIDE RIDING CLUB, Cardigan **Ref:**YH14193
TREGARON PONY TREKKING ASS, Tregaron **Ref:**YH14364
VALE OF AERON RIDING CLUB, Lampeter **Ref:**YH14636
WELSH PONY AND COB SOCIETY, Aberystwyth **Ref:**YH15095

CONWY

BHS, Abergele **Ref:**YH01353

DENBIGHSHIRE

CLWYD WELSH PONY & COB ASS, Ruthin **Ref:**YH03078
WEXHAM & DISTRICT BRIDLEWAYS, Ruthin **Ref:**YH15248

GWYNEDD

BHS, Bodedern **Ref:**YH01356
CAERNARFONSHIRE RIDING CLUB, Caernarfon **Ref:**YH02415

ISLE OF ANGLESEY

INT EQUINE LOGISTICS, Llanfairpwllgwyn **Ref:**YH07468

MONMOUTHSHIRE

SOC FOR THE WELFARE OF HORSES, Monmouth **Ref:**YH13046
VALE OF USK RIDING CLUB, Abergavenny **Ref:**YH14640
WYE VALLEY RIDING CLUB, Chepstow **Ref:**YH15861

NEATH PORT TALBOT

AFON RIDING CLUB, Neath Port Talbot **Ref:**YH00198

PEMBROKESHIRE

PPSA AREA SECRETARY, Haverfordwest **Ref:**YH11334

POWYS

B H S WALES DEVELOP OFFICER, Sennybridge **Ref:**YH00727
B H S-WALES-POWYS REGION, Llangurig **Ref:**YH00730
BHS CHAIRMAN, Llandrindod Wells **Ref:**YH01376
BRITISH ANDALUSIAN SOCIETY, Montgomery **Ref:**YH01923
DOLFOR RIDING CLUB, Welshpool **Ref:**YH04167
LLANELWEDD RIDING CLUB, Brecon **Ref:**YH08722
PONY CLUB, Llangorse **Ref:**YH11243
VYRNWY VALLEY RIDING CLUB, Llanymynech **Ref:**YH14746
WELSH RIDING & TREKKING ASS, Brecon **Ref:**YH15096

RHONDDA CYNON TAFF

RHONDDA RIDING CLUB, Rhondda **Ref:**YH11790

SWANSEA

GOWER RIDING CLUB, Swansea **Ref:**YH05955
UNIVERSITY OF SWANSEA RIDING CLUB, Swansea **Ref:**YH14595

TORFAEN

- **BLAENAVON STIRRUP CLUB**, Blaenavon **Ref:**YH01506

WREXHAM

- **EAST CLWYD RIDING CLUB**, Coedpoeth **Ref:**YH04468

EQUESTRIAN CENTRES

BRIDGEND

- **E K M EQUESTRIAN**, Bridgend **Ref:**YH04411

CARMARTHENSHIRE

- **CARMARTHENSHIRE CLGE**, Carmarthen **Ref:**YH02561
- **CARMARTHENSHIRE CLGE**, Llanelli **Ref:**YH02560
- **COWIN EQUESTRIAN CTRE**, Burry Port **Ref:**YH03525
- **CWM EQUESTRIAN CTRE**, Ceredigion **Ref:**YH03763
- **CWMTYDU RIDING STABLES**, New Quay **Ref:**YH03764
- **DREFACH EQUESTRIAN CTRE**, Llanelli **Ref:**YH04264
- **FFYNNOCYLL**, Whitland **Ref:**YH05180
- **FIVE SAINTS**, Llanwrda **Ref:**YH05255
- **GWERSYLL YR URDD/URDD CAMP**, Llandysul **Ref:**YH06203
- **HOME PARK RIDING CTRE**, Llandovery **Ref:**YH07004
- **MARROS RIDING CTRE**, Carmarthen **Ref:**YH09177
- **PEMBREY PARK EQUEST CTRE**, Llanelli **Ref:**YH10915
- **REES, S R**, Llandysul **Ref:**YH11733
- **SIR JOHN HILL FARM**, Laugharne **Ref:**YH12858
- **THOMAS SHOW TEAM**, Carmarthen **Ref:**YH14011

CEREDIGION

- **GILFACH HOLIDAY VILLAGE**, Aberaeron **Ref:**YH05765
- **MAESGLAS MOUNTAIN RIDERS**, Tregaron **Ref:**YH09030
- **PANT RHYN TREKKING CTRE**, New Quay **Ref:**YH10701
- **PONTERWYD TREKING CTRE**, Aberystwyth **Ref:**YH11226
- **RHEIDOL RIDING CTRE**, Aberystwyth **Ref:**YH11784
- **WELSH INS OF RURAL STUDIES**, Aberystwyth **Ref:**YH15092

DENBIGHSHIRE

- **GLYN VALLEY HOTEL**, Llangollen **Ref:**YH05857
- **LLANNERCH EQUESTRIAN CTRE**, St Asaph **Ref:**YH08726

GLAMORGAN (VALE OF)

- **CIMLA TREKKING**, Neath **Ref:**YH02918

GWYNEDD

- **ABERSOCH RIDING/TREKKING CTRE**, Pwllheli **Ref:**YH00130
- **BWLCHGWYN FARM**, Arthog **Ref:**YH02341
- **DAVIES, D A & H A**, Caernarfon **Ref:**YH03937
- **DOLBADARN TREKKING**, Llanberis **Ref:**YH04166
- **MEIFOD-ISAF**, Dyffryn Ardudwy **Ref:**YH09446
- **RHIWIAU RIDING CTRE**, Llanfairfechan **Ref:**YH11788
- **SNOWDONIA RIDING STABLES**, Caernarfon **Ref:**YH13041

ISLE OF ANGLESEY

- **ANGLESEY EQUESTRIAN CTRE**, Holyhead **Ref:**YH00410
- **CELT 'N' GAEL CTRE**, Holyhead **Ref:**YH02679
- **GORS WEN RIDING STABLES**, Holyhead **Ref:**YH05938
- **TAL Y FOEL RIDING CTRE**, Anglesey **Ref:**YH13829
- **TYN-MORFA RIDING CTRE**, Rhosneigr **Ref:**YH14529

MONMOUTHSHIRE

- **GRANGE TREKKING**, Abergavenny **Ref:**YH05999
- **PEGASUS PONY TREKKING CTRE**, Abergavenny **Ref:**YH10906
- **PONY TREKKING CTRE**, Abergavenny **Ref:**YH11255

PEMBROKESHIRE

- **CASTELLAN RIDING ACADEMY**, Boncath **Ref:**YH02623
- **DOLRHANOG RIDING CTRE**, Newport **Ref:**YH04171
- **DUNES RIDING**, Narberth **Ref:**YH04342
- **ISLAND FARM RIDING STABLES**, Saundersfoot **Ref:**YH07521
- **OASIS PARK EQUESTRIAN CTRE**, Narberth **Ref:**YH10412
- **PEMBROKESHIRE CLGE**, Haverfordwest **Ref:**YH10918
- **PLUMSTONE TREKKING CTRE**, Haverfordwest **Ref:**YH11185
- **RAVEL FARM**, Crymych **Ref:**YH11656

POWYS

- **BROMPTON HALL**, Montgomery **Ref:**YH02025
- **CADARN TRAIL RIDING FARM**, Brecon **Ref:**YH02409
- **CANTREF**, Brecon **Ref:**YH02516
- **ELLESMERE**, Brecon **Ref:**YH04614
- **GOLDEN CASTLE**, Crickhowell **Ref:**YH05877
- **HILL VALLEY RIDING CTRE**, Crickhowell **Ref:**YH06823
- **LLANGENNY PONY TREKKING CTRE**, Crickhowell **Ref:**YH08724
- **LLANGORSE RIDING**, Brecon **Ref:**YH08725
- **LLETTY MAWR TREKKING**, Welshpool **Ref:**YH08728
- **NEWCOURT FARM**, Glasbury **Ref:**YH10135
- **RANGE RIDES**, Llandrindod Wells **Ref:**YH11634
- **RHAYADER PONY TREKKING ASS**, Rhayader **Ref:**YH11783
- **STABLES HOTEL**, Crickhowell **Ref:**YH13311
- **STAR INN TREKKING CTRE**, Llanbrynmair **Ref:**YH13393
- **TREGOYD MOUNTAIN RIDERS**, Brecon **Ref:**YH14367

RHONDDA CYNON TAFF

- **TALYGARN**, Pontyclun **Ref:**YH13846

SWANSEA

- **DAN-YR-OGOF**, Swansea **Ref:**YH03875
- **PEN-Y-FEDW RIDING CTRE**, Swansea **Ref:**YH10967
- **PITTON CROSS TREKKING CTRE**, Swansea **Ref:**YH11157
- **SOUTH WALES CARRIAGE DRIVING**, Swansea **Ref:**YH13111

WREXHAM

- **BROUGHTON HALL**, Wrexham **Ref:**YH02088
- **YALE COLLEGE**, Wrexham **Ref:**YH15881

FARRIERS

BLAENAU GWENT

- **EDWARDS, JOHN**, Abertillery **Ref:**YH04582

BRIDGEND

- **DAVID, GLYN O**, Maesteg **Ref:**YH03926
- **DAVID, O J**, Maesteg **Ref:**YH03927
- **GALLIERS, MARK E**, Bridgend **Ref:**YH05621
- **SHILLAM, H G**, Bridgend **Ref:**YH12744

CAERPHILLY

- **GRIFFITHS, DAVID**, Rudry **Ref:**YH06139
- **GRIFFITHS, KEVIN**, Hengoed **Ref:**YH06142
- **PARTIS, COLIN**, Bargoed **Ref:**YH10802

CARMARTHENSHIRE

- **BAILEY, DESMOND EARL**, Llanybydder **Ref:**YH00799
- **BURNETT, LEE**, Ammanford **Ref:**YH02264
- **D L MORGAN & SON**, Llanwrda **Ref:**YH03791
- **DAVIES, MARK**, Kidwelly **Ref:**YH03944
- **GRANT, LEWIS**, Carmarthen **Ref:**YH06013
- **GRIFFIN, T R**, Ammanford **Ref:**YH06133
- **HOLTOM, GILES E**, Llandeilo **Ref:**YH06990
- **JACKSON, BRIAN FRANK**, Llandysul **Ref:**YH07643
- **KAYE, HILARY LOIS**, Llandovery **Ref:**YH08009
- **LEWIS, A S**, Carmarthen **Ref:**YH08584
- **LLOYD, KEVIN**, Llandovery **Ref:**YH08740
- **RAIL, P A**, Llandysul **Ref:**YH11611
- **THOMAS, A**, Llanelli **Ref:**YH14012
- **THOMAS, D J M**, Llanybydder **Ref:**YH14019
- **WAGG, R G**, Llandysul **Ref:**YH14822
- **WAGG, RAYMOND GEORGE**, Llandysul **Ref:**YH14823
- **WILLIAMS, ROBERT C**, Burry Port **Ref:**YH15475
- **WILLIAMS, ROBIN**, Carmarthen **Ref:**YH15476
- **WOODWARD, R S**, Llanelli **Ref:**YH15759
- **YOUNGMAN, NICHOLAS EDWARD**, Llanelli **Ref:**YH15943

CEREDIGION

- **BENSON, T F J**, Llanon **Ref:**YH01281
- **BOOTH, THOMAS M**, Llanon **Ref:**YH01637
- **DAVIS, V C M**, Aberystwyth **Ref:**YH03954
- **GLOVER, STEVEN P**, Cardigan **Ref:**YH05856
- **WILLIAMS, RICHARD H**, Lampeter **Ref:**YH15473

CONWY

- **JONES, DYFED W**, Denbigh **Ref:**YH07894
- **YOUNGSON, FRASER W**, Coed Lyn **Ref:**YH15945

DENBIGHSHIRE

- **EAMES, J S**, Rhyl **Ref:**YH04446
- **HUGHES, G**, St Asaph **Ref:**YH07266
- **JONES, I G**, Ruthin **Ref:**YH07905
- **MARSDEN, A J**, St Asaph **Ref:**YH09182
- **PUGHE, J S**, Llangollen **Ref:**YH11454
- **WAKEFIELD, JASON T**, Chirk **Ref:**YH14834

FLINTSHIRE

- **ANDERSON, JOHN F**, Mold **Ref:**YH00385
- **CHILTON, S L**, Mold **Ref:**YH02861
- **HUGHES, IAN G**, Mold **Ref:**YH07268
- **JONES, DAVID THOMAS**, Mold **Ref:**YH07891
- **JONES, KENNETH**, Mold **Ref:**YH07912
- **ROBERTS, E P**, Mold **Ref:**YH11949
- **ROGERS, A**, Mold **Ref:**YH12059
- **SMITH, PAUL G**, Mold **Ref:**YH12985

GLAMORGAN (VALE OF)

- **A GRIFFITHS & SON**, Treharris **Ref:**YH00033
- **CROFTS, JOHN D**, Cardiff **Ref:**YH03626
- **JONES, MARC T**, Merthyr Tydfil **Ref:**YH07916
- **PAGE, CLIVE**, Cilfrew **Ref:**YH10680
- **PAYNE, MARK A**, Cardiff **Ref:**YH10850
- **POMFRET, J B**, Cardiff **Ref:**YH11216
- **PRITCHARD, RUSSELL J**, Cowbridge **Ref:**YH11422
- **ROONEY, STEPHEN P**, Cardiff **Ref:**YH12078
- **ROONEY, T P**, Cardiff **Ref:**YH12079
- **SEARL, RICHARD MICHAEL**, Cardiff **Ref:**YH12593
- **WHITNEY, A**, Neath **Ref:**YH15369

GWYNEDD

- **EVANS, IFOR WYN**, Pwllheli **Ref:**YH04921
- **JAMES, PAUL ELLIS**, Bangor **Ref:**YH07686
- **MILLS, ALAN JOHN**, Pwllheli **Ref:**YH09630
- **PRITCHARD, H G**, Caernarfon **Ref:**YH11416
- **ROBERTS, EDWIN**, Caernarfon **Ref:**YH11951

ISLE OF ANGLESEY

- **FITZPATRICK, JAMES B**, Beaumaris **Ref:**YH05248
- **LEE, WILLIAM P**, Ty Croes **Ref:**YH08529

MONMOUTHSHIRE

- **BROWN, NIGEL R**, Abergavenny **Ref:**YH02125

- **BRUNGER, ANTHONY R**, Abergavenny **Ref:**YH02159
- **FARRIERY CTRE**, Usk **Ref:**YH05092
- **KEDWARD, TIMOTHY J**, Monmouth **Ref:**YH08024
- **LALLEY, A F**, Chepstow **Ref:**YH08361
- **PACKER, C S**, Chepstow **Ref:**YH10663
- **PARSONS, ROYSTON J**, Abergavenny **Ref:**YH10801
- **STOCKHAM, G J**, Abergavenny **Ref:**YH13492
- **WILLIAMS, RICHARD JOHN**, Chepstow **Ref:**YH15474

NEATH PORT TALBOT

- **DAVISON, HOWARD**, Pontardawe **Ref:**YH03958
- **REES, D W**, Neath **Ref:**YH11728
- **SAUNDERS, MICHAEL**, Pontrhydyfen **Ref:**YH12450

NEWPORT

- **DEACON, JOSEPH LYNDON**, Llanvaches **Ref:**YH03981
- **JONES, H B**, Lower Machen **Ref:**YH07903
- **RUDDICK, MARK A**, Sudbrook **Ref:**YH12206

PEMBROKESHIRE

- **BYRNE, J T**, Kilgetty **Ref:**YH02347
- **CUMINE, DENIS HAROLD**, Haverfordwest **Ref:**YH03718
- **GAMBLE, SEAN**, Milford Haven **Ref:**YH05632
- **GLOVER, STEVEN**, Haverfordwest **Ref:**YH05855
- **SELBY, J**, Crymych **Ref:**YH12615
- **THOMPSON, ARTHUR RICHARD**, Narberth **Ref:**YH14033

POWYS

- **BLURTON, JAMES P**, Welshpool **Ref:**YH01576
- **BOUNDY, C J**, Montgomery **Ref:**YH01680
- **BRYAN, FRANCIS HAROLD**, Brecon **Ref:**YH02164
- **EATON, STEPHEN G**, Caersws **Ref:**YH04527
- **EVANS, DAVID T C**, Brecon **Ref:**YH04917
- **FULLER, C A**, Brecon **Ref:**YH05531
- **HANDEL, PETER**, Welshpool **Ref:**YH06378
- **JAMES, NICHOLAS J**, Caereinion **Ref:**YH07685
- **JONES, EDWARD GLYN**, Machynlleth **Ref:**YH07896
- **LEE, RICHARD A**, Presteigne **Ref:**YH08527
- **WOODALL, PAUL**, Welshpool **Ref:**YH15672

RHONDDA CYNON TAFF

- **GRUNEWALD, P**, Pontyclun **Ref:**YH06177
- **HUGHES, BRIAN**, Porth **Ref:**YH07261
- **HUGHES, KEVIN G**, Porthcawl **Ref:**YH07270
- **HUGHES, S A**, Porth **Ref:**YH07273
- **LEWIS, THOMAS HUGH**, Aberdare **Ref:**YH08596
- **PARRY-JONES, A W**, Pontypridd **Ref:**YH10794

SWANSEA

- **BOWEN, ADRIAN R G**, Swansea **Ref:**YH01698

TORFAEN

- **MORGAN, CLIVE J**, Pontypool **Ref:**YH09801
- **MORGAN, LEE W**, Pontypool **Ref:**YH09810
- **RICHARDS, CHRISTOPHER D**, Abersychan **Ref:**YH11806

WREXHAM

- **HAMMOND, WILLIAM E**, Bwlchgwyn **Ref:**YH06361
- **SPOOR, DAVID RUSSELL**, Wrexham **Ref:**YH13214
- **WILLIAMS, G H**, Holt **Ref:**YH15457

FEED MERCHANTS

CARMARTHENSHIRE

- **BERRY ANIMAL FEEDS**, Kidwelly **Ref:**YH01314

GWYNEDD

- **DOLGELLAU FARMERS**, Dolgellau **Ref:**YH04168

MONMOUTHSHIRE

- **ROSS FEED**, Monmouth **Ref:**YH12115

PEMBROKESHIRE

- **CASTLEMORRIS FEEDS**, Haverfordwest **Ref:**YH02645

RHONDDA CYNON TAFF

- **DRYSGOED FARM FEEDS**, Pontypridd **Ref:**YH04302

HOLIDAYS

GWYNEDD

- **RHIWIAU RIDING CTRE**, Llanfairfechan **Ref:**YH11788

MONMOUTHSHIRE

- **BLACK MOUNTAIN HOLIDAYS**, Abergavenny **Ref:**YH01468

NEATH PORT TALBOT

- **L & A HOLIDAY & RIDING CTRE**, Port Talbot **Ref:**YH08306

POWYS

- **CANTREF**, Brecon **Ref:**YH02516
- **GLAN YR AFON HOLIDAYS**, Welshpool **Ref:**YH05804
- **TREGOYD MOUNTAIN RIDERS**, Brecon **Ref:**YH14367

WREXHAM

- **EQUESTRIAN CTRE**, Wrexham **Ref:**YH04697

HORSE/RIDER ACCOM

CARMARTHENSHIRE

- **FLYING M RANCH**, Carmarthen **Ref:**YH05294
- **RIVERSDALE**, Carmarthen **Ref:**YH11923
- **WELSH LONG DISTANCE**, Carmarthen **Ref:**YH15093

CEREDIGION

- **NANTGWINAU WELSH COBS**, Lampeter **Ref:**YH10016

DENBIGHSHIRE

- **MORWYN STUD**, Ruthin **Ref:**YH09854
- **PENGWERN MILL DRIVING STABLES**, Llangollen **Ref:**YH10938

GWYNEDD

- **ABERSOCH MARCHROS STUD**, Abersoch **Ref:**YH00129
- **TY COCH FARM & TREKKING CTRE**, Betws-Y-Coed **Ref:**YH14517

ISLE OF ANGLESEY

- **CROMLECH MANOR FARM**, Tyn-Y-Gongl **Ref:**YH03630

PEMBROKESHIRE

- **PEMBROKESHIRE RIDING CTRE**, Pembroke **Ref:**YH10920

POWYS

- **GLAN YR AFON HOLIDAYS**, Welshpool **Ref:**YH05804

WREXHAM

- **EQUESTRIAN CTRE**, Wrexham **Ref:**YH04697

MEDICAL SUPPORT

CARMARTHENSHIRE

- **ALLEN & PARTNERS**, Whitland **Ref:**YH00291
- **GIBSON & JONES**, Llanelli **Ref:**YH05744
- **STRONG, M G**, Newcastle Emlyn **Ref:**YH13583
- **THOMAS & PERCY**, Llandeilo **Ref:**YH14006
- **TYSUL VETNRY GROUP**, Llandysul **Ref:**YH14534

DENBIGHSHIRE

- **LLANNERCH EQUESTRIAN CTRE**, St Asaph **Ref:**YH08726

FLINTSHIRE

- **STRACHAN & WIGNALL**, Mold **Ref:**YH13542

GLAMORGAN (VALE OF)

- **PARK VETNRY GRP**, Cardiff **Ref:**YH10740

GWYNEDD

- **HILL, E BARBOUR**, Bangor **Ref:**YH06829
- **JENKINS, G M**, Tywyn **Ref:**YH07731
- **PINDER, P J**, Llanfairfechan **Ref:**YH11117
- **TUDOR & LAWSON**, Dolgellau **Ref:**YH14438

ISLE OF ANGLESEY

- **BIMEDA**, Llangefni **Ref:**YH01418
- **FINCH, A C & J J**, Llangefni **Ref:**YH05207
- **MILFEDDYGON BODRWNSIWN**, Rhosneigr **Ref:**YH09568

MONMOUTHSHIRE

- **ABBEY VETNRY CTRE**, Abergavenny **Ref:**YH00089
- **CROSSCOUNTRY EQUINE CLINIC**, Chepstow **Ref:**YH03656
- **DRYBRIDGE VETNRY CLINIC**, Monmouth **Ref:**YH04297
- **MCEWEN, J C**, Chepstow **Ref:**YH09351
- **NATURAL ANIMAL FEEDS**, Raglan **Ref:**YH10050
- **SPORTABAC**, Abergavenny **Ref:**YH13222
- **VETNRY HOSPITAL**, Usk **Ref:**YH14698

PEMBROKESHIRE

- **GWAUN VETNRY GRP**, Pembroke **Ref:**YH06199
- **PETERS & PARTNERS**, Haverfordwest **Ref:**YH11020
- **WILLIAMS & LINGE**, Narberth **Ref:**YH15441

POWYS

- **ABBEY EQUINE CTRE**, Crickhowell **Ref:**YH00076
- **ADVANCED EQUINE DENTISTRY**, Llanidloes **Ref:**YH00192
- **BOUNDY, TERRY**, Montgomery **Ref:**YH01681
- **FYRNWY EQUINE CLINICS**, Llanymynech **Ref:**YH05559
- **JENKINS, G M**, Maghynlleth **Ref:**YH07732
- **THOMAS JONES**, Newtown **Ref:**YH14008

RHONDDA CYNON TAFF

- **FFOREST UCHAF**, Pontypridd **Ref:**YH05178
- **HUGHES, AMANDA**, Porth **Ref:**YH07259

SWANSEA

- **GIBSON & JONES**, Swansea **Ref:**YH05745

WREXHAM

- **COUNTIES EQUESTRIAN SVS**, Wrexham **Ref:**YH03396
- **GREETHAM, RACHEL**, Bwlchgwyn **Ref:**YH06111

RIDING CLUBS

BRIDGEND

- **KENFIG HILL & DISTRICT**, Ewenny **Ref:**YH08062
- **SKER RIDING CLUB**, North Cornelly **Ref:**YH12868

CEREDIGION

- **DYFFRYN CLETTWR RIDING CLUB**, Aberaeron **Ref:**YH04389
- **TIVYSIDE RIDING CLUB**, Cardigan **Ref:**YH14193
- **VALE OF AERON RIDING CLUB**, Lampeter **Ref:**YH14636

DENBIGHSHIRE

- **CLWYD WELSH PONY & COB ASS**, Ruthin **Ref:**YH03078

GWYNEDD

- **CAERNARFONSHIRE RIDING CLUB**, Caernarfon **Ref:**YH02415
- **RHIWIAU RIDING CTRE**, Llanfairfechan **Ref:**YH11788

MONMOUTHSHIRE
- **VALE OF USK RIDING CLUB**, Abergavenny **Ref:**YH14640
- **WYE VALLEY RIDING CLUB**, Chepstow **Ref:**YH15861

PEMBROKESHIRE
- **DUNES RIDING**, Narberth **Ref:**YH04342

POWYS
- **CANTREF**, Brecon **Ref:**YH02516
- **DOLFOR RIDING CLUB**, Welshpool **Ref:**YH04167
- **LLANELWEDD RIDING CLUB**, Brecon **Ref:**YH08722
- **VYRNWY VALLEY RIDING CLUB**, Llanymynech **Ref:**YH14746

RHONDDA CYNON TAFF
- **RHONDDA RIDING CLUB**, Rhondda **Ref:**YH11790

SWANSEA
- **GOWER RIDING CLUB**, Swansea **Ref:**YH05955
- **UNIVERSITY OF SWANSEA RIDING CLUB**, Swansea **Ref:**YH14595

WREXHAM
- **EAST CLWYD RIDING CLUB**, Coedpoeth **Ref:**YH04468

RIDING SCHOOLS

BRIDGEND
- **E K M EQUESTRIAN**, Bridgend **Ref:**YH04411
- **SOUTH WALES EQUESTRIAN CTRE**, Bridgend **Ref:**YH13112

CAERPHILLY
- **BEAU COURT**, Newport **Ref:**YH01126
- **GROESWEN RIDING STABLES**, Caerphilly **Ref:**YH06147
- **ROCKWOOD RIDING CTRE**, Caerphilly **Ref:**YH12039
- **RUDRY RIDING STABLES**, Caerphilly **Ref:**YH12211

CARMARTHENSHIRE
- **BLUE WELL RIDING CTRE**, Pencader **Ref:**YH01571
- **CAE IAGO RIDING CTRE**, Llanwrda **Ref:**YH02413
- **CLYN-DU RIDING CTRE**, Burry Port **Ref:**YH03100
- **COWIN EQUESTRIAN CTRE**, Burry Port **Ref:**YH03525
- **CWM EQUESTRIAN CTRE**, Ceredigion **Ref:**YH03763
- **GLYNHIR LODGE STABLES**, Ammanford **Ref:**YH05858
- **STARLIGHT RIDING CTRE**, Newcastle Emlyn **Ref:**YH13396
- **TREFACH RIDING CTRE**, Clynderwen **Ref:**YH14362
- **WELSH EQUITATION CTRE**, Carmarthen **Ref:**YH15091

CEREDIGION
- **DYFED RIDING CTRE**, Cardigan **Ref:**YH04388
- **MOELFRYN RIDING CTRE**, Aberystwyth **Ref:**YH09699
- **RHEIDOL RIDING CTRE**, Aberystwyth **Ref:**YH11784
- **WINDY GAIL STABLES**, Blaenannerch **Ref:**YH15581

CONWY
- **ABERCONWY EQUESTRIAN CTRE**, Llandudno Junction **Ref:**YH00119
- **PINEWOOD STABLES**, Llechwedd **Ref:**YH11126
- **TYNLLWYN RIDING SCHOOL**, Colwyn Bay **Ref:**YH14528

DENBIGHSHIRE
- **DOLGOED RIDING SCHOOL**, St Asaph **Ref:**YH04169
- **LLANNERCH EQUESTRIAN CTRE**, St Asaph **Ref:**YH08726
- **RUTHIN RIDING**, Ruthin **Ref:**YH12276

FLINTSHIRE
- **ALYN BANK**, Mold **Ref:**YH00353
- **BRIDLEWOOD EQUESTRIAN CTRE**, Holywell **Ref:**YH01899
- **LYNDEN FARM**, Holywell **Ref:**YH08926
- **PANT GLAS MAWR**, Holywell **Ref:**YH10700

GLAMORGAN (VALE OF)
- **CARDIFF CITY RIDING SCHOOL**, Cardiff **Ref:**YH02530
- **CARDIFF RIDING SCHOOL**, Cardiff **Ref:**YH02531
- **CIMLA TREKKING**, Neath **Ref:**YH02918
- **DIMLANDS FARM RIDING SCHOOL**, Llantwit Major **Ref:**YH04122
- **DOWNS SIDE RIDING CTRE**, Penarth **Ref:**YH04241
- **LIEGE MANOR**, Cardiff **Ref:**YH08609
- **PEN-MAEN LIVERY YARD**, Cowbridge **Ref:**YH10944

GWYNEDD
- **ABERGWYNANT FARM**, Dolgellau **Ref:**YH00126
- **COLEG MEIRION-DWYFOR**, Caernarfon **Ref:**YH03162
- **DWYFOR RIDING CTRE**, Criccieth **Ref:**YH04382
- **PEN ISAR FARM**, Bala **Ref:**YH10922
- **PEN-LLEYN RIDING CTRE**, Pwllheli **Ref:**YH10943
- **PLAS-Y-CELYN**, Caernarfon **Ref:**YH11165
- **RHIWIAU RIDING CTRE**, Llanfairfechan **Ref:**YH11788
- **RHOSYN GWYN EQUESTRIAN CTRE**, Caernarfon **Ref:**YH11791
- **SNOWDONIA RIDING STABLES**, Caernarfon **Ref:**YH13041

ISLE OF ANGLESEY
- **ANGLESEY EQUESTRIAN CTRE**, Holyhead **Ref:**YH00410
- **GORS WEN FARM**, Holyhead **Ref:**YH05937
- **HEWITTS RIDING STABLES**, Benllech Bay **Ref:**YH06729
- **LLANDDONA**, Beaumaris **Ref:**YH08720
- **TAL Y FOEL RIDING CTRE**, Anglesey **Ref:**YH13829

MONMOUTHSHIRE
- **EARLSWOOD RIDING CTRE**, Chepstow **Ref:**YH04455
- **GRANGE TREKKING**, Abergavenny **Ref:**YH05999
- **GWENT TERTIARY**, Usk **Ref:**YH06202
- **PONDEROSA EQUESTRIAN CTRE**, Pontypool **Ref:**YH11219
- **SEVERNVALE EQUESTRIAN CTRE**, Chepstow **Ref:**YH12646

NEATH PORT TALBOT
- **PANT-Y-SAIS**, Neath Port Talbot **Ref:**YH10703

NEWPORT
- **SPRINGFIELD RIDING STABLES**, Wentloog **Ref:**YH13256

PEMBROKESHIRE
- **BOWLINGS RIDING SCHOOL**, Haverfordwest **Ref:**YH01719
- **CROSSWELL**, Crymych **Ref:**YH03669
- **DOLRHANOG RIDING CTRE**, Newport **Ref:**YH04171
- **DUNES RIDING**, Narberth **Ref:**YH04342
- **HEATHERTON RIDING STABLES**, Saundersfoot **Ref:**YH06628
- **LLANWNDA STABLES**, Goodwick **Ref:**YH08727
- **MAESGWYNNE RIDING STABLES**, Fishguard **Ref:**YH09031
- **NORCHARD FARM RIDING SCHOOL**, Tenby **Ref:**YH10228
- **OASIS PARK EQUESTRIAN CTRE**, Narberth **Ref:**YH10412
- **PEMBROKESHIRE RIDING CTRE**, Pembroke **Ref:**YH10920
- **SEALYHAM ACTIVITY CTRE**, Haverfordwest **Ref:**YH12590

POWYS
- **BROMPTON HALL**, Montgomery **Ref:**YH02025
- **CANTREF**, Brecon **Ref:**YH02516
- **GOLDEN CASTLE**, Crickhowell **Ref:**YH05877
- **HEART OF WALES RIDING SCHOOL**, Llandrindod Wells **Ref:**YH06619
- **LLETTY MAWR TREKKING**, Welshpool **Ref:**YH08728
- **MILL PONY TREKKING CTRE**, Newtown **Ref:**YH09584
- **OVERLAND PONY TREK**, Llandrindod Wells **Ref:**YH10594
- **RIVERSIDE RIDING CTRE**, Crickhowell **Ref:**YH11927
- **TRANS-WALES TRAILS**, Brecon **Ref:**YH14353
- **TREGOYD MOUNTAIN RIDERS**, Brecon **Ref:**YH14367
- **UNDERHILL RIDING STABLES**, Llandrindod Wells **Ref:**YH14560

RHONDDA CYNON TAFF
- **GREENMEADOW RIDING CTRE**, Aberdare **Ref:**YH06099
- **TALYGARN**, Pontyclun **Ref:**YH13846

SWANSEA
- **COPLEY**, Swansea **Ref:**YH03297
- **EDWARDS, J T**, Swansea **Ref:**YH04581
- **FORGEMILL**, Swansea **Ref:**YH05368
- **GREEN FARM**, Swansea **Ref:**YH06054
- **PENTRE RIDING STABLES**, Swansea **Ref:**YH10962
- **WOODLANDS RIDING SCHOOL**, Swansea **Ref:**YH15710

WREXHAM
- **CHAPEL FARM**, Wrexham **Ref:**YH02738
- **EQUESTRIAN CTRE**, Wrexham **Ref:**YH04697

RIDING WEAR RETAILERS

BLAENAU GWENT
- **DAVIES RIDING BOOTS**, Ebbw Vale **Ref:**YH03935

CARMARTHENSHIRE
- **MORGAN EQUINE**, Llandeilo **Ref:**YH09794
- **STALLIONS AT TACKEXCHANGE**, Llanelli **Ref:**YH13351
- **TACK EXCHANGE**, Llanelli **Ref:**YH13787

CEREDIGION
- **ROGERS & TAYLOR**, Aberystwyth **Ref:**YH12056
- **VALIENT SADDLERY**, Cardigan **Ref:**YH14646

DENBIGHSHIRE
- **WYNNSTAY & CLWYD FARMERS**, St Asaph **Ref:**YH15874

FLINTSHIRE
- **T F S**, Buckley **Ref:**YH13739

GLAMORGAN (VALE OF)
- **AYRES, JOHN**, Cardiff **Ref:**YH00702
- **CARDIFF SPORTSGEAR**, Cardiff **Ref:**YH02532

GWYNEDD
- **BRONALLT**, Caernarfon **Ref:**YH02029

ISLE OF ANGLESEY
- **BATT, F J**, Pentraeth **Ref:**YH01075

MONMOUTHSHIRE
- **CHEPSTOW SADDLERY**, Chepstow **Ref:**YH02809

PEMBROKESHIRE
- **BOULSTON**, Haverfordwest **Ref:**YH01672
- **COUNTRY LIFE**, Haverfordwest **Ref:**YH03415

POWYS
- **BROMPTON HALL**, Montgomery **Ref:**YH02025

- **CHOICE SADDLERY**, Knighton **Ref:**YH02876
- **WYNNSTAY & CLWYD FARMERS**, Llansanffraid **Ref:**YH15875

RHONDDA CYNON TAFF
- **BOOTS & SADDLES**, Tonypandy **Ref:**YH01640

SWANSEA
- **D MORGAN & SONS**, Swansea **Ref:**YH03799
- **HORSE CTRE**, Swansea **Ref:**YH07116

WREXHAM
- **ACRE HSE EQUESTRIAN**, Wrexham **Ref:**YH00158
- **BLINKERS EQUESTRIAN**, Wrexham **Ref:**YH01540

SADDLERY RETAILERS

BRIDGEND
- **THOMAS, HUW R**, Bridgend **Ref:**YH14022
- **WILLIAMS & EVANS**, Bridgend **Ref:**YH15440

CAERPHILLY
- **HYPERION SADDLERY**, Bargoed **Ref:**YH07361
- **MACAULAYS TACK SHOP**, Blackwood **Ref:**YH08982

CARMARTHENSHIRE
- **H PITTAM SADDLERY**, Llandysul **Ref:**YH06234
- **HORSE CTRE**, Llandysul **Ref:**YH07115
- **PLAS EQUESTRIAN**, Carmarthen **Ref:**YH11164
- **STALLIONS AT TACKEXCHANGE**, Llanelli **Ref:**YH13351
- **TACK EXCHANGE**, Llanelli **Ref:**YH13787

CEREDIGION
- **HELLMAN, GLENN**, Ystrad Meurig **Ref:**YH06655
- **ROGERS & TAYLOR**, Aberystwyth **Ref:**YH12056
- **VALIENT SADDLERY**, Cardigan **Ref:**YH14646

CONWY
- **COLWYN TACK CTRE**, Colwyn Bay **Ref:**YH03208
- **PEN-Y-BINC FARM**, Colwyn Bay **Ref:**YH10964

DENBIGHSHIRE
- **GARTH-ROBERTS, GORDON**, Denbigh **Ref:**YH05663

FLINTSHIRE
- **BRIDLEWOOD EQUESTRIAN CTRE**, Holywell **Ref:**YH01899
- **MOLD VALLEY SADDLERY**, Mold **Ref:**YH09706

GLAMORGAN (VALE OF)
- **AYRES, JOHN**, Cardiff **Ref:**YH00702
- **CARDIFF SPORTSGEAR**, Cardiff **Ref:**YH02532
- **HORSEGUARDS**, Cardiff **Ref:**YH07157
- **J M P SADDLERY**, Cardiff **Ref:**YH07598
- **JOHN REES**, Barry **Ref:**YH07807
- **S J B SADDLERY**, Neath **Ref:**YH12328
- **SNAFFLES SADDLERY**, Cowbridge **Ref:**YH13026

GWYNEDD
- **BRONALLT**, Caernarfon **Ref:**YH02029
- **EIFIONYDD FARMERS**, Pwllheli **Ref:**YH04596
- **HERON BARN SADDLERY**, Arthog **Ref:**YH06709
- **TACK & STITCH SADDLERY**, Pwllheli **Ref:**YH13777

ISLE OF ANGLESEY
- **A C G S EQUESTRIAN**, Bodorgan **Ref:**YH00025
- **BATT, F J**, Pentraeth **Ref:**YH01075
- **MOELFRE LEATHER WORKSHOP**, Moelfre **Ref:**YH09698
- **TYN-MORFA RIDING CTRE**, Rhosneigr **Ref:**YH14529

MONMOUTHSHIRE
- **CHEPSTOW SADDLERY**, Chepstow **Ref:**YH02809
- **JONES, R M**, Abergavenny **Ref:**YH07926
- **VILLAGE STORES**, Monmouth **Ref:**YH14721

NEATH PORT TALBOT
- **R DAYCOCK & SON**, Talbach **Ref:**YH11529
- **ZOAR HORSE & COUNTRY CTRE**, Neath Port Talbot **Ref:**YH15957

NEWPORT
- **CALDICOT SADDLERY**, Portskewett **Ref:**YH02438
- **GWENT SADDLERY**, Newport **Ref:**YH06201
- **N J CRIDDLE**, Newport **Ref:**YH09992
- **NEWCOMBES HORSE & DOG SHOP**, Newport **Ref:**YH10134

PEMBROKESHIRE
- **BOULSTON**, Haverfordwest **Ref:**YH01672
- **CASTLEMORRIS FEEDS**, Haverfordwest **Ref:**YH02645
- **HIDE TO HARNESS**, Narberth **Ref:**YH06747
- **PEGASUS**, Haverfordwest **Ref:**YH10902
- **PEMBROKESHIRE EQUESTRIAN**, Haverfordwest **Ref:**YH10919
- **PEMBROKESHIRE RIDING CTRE**, Pembroke **Ref:**YH10920

POWYS
- **ALAN PRICE**, Crickhowell **Ref:**YH00241
- **BROMPTON HALL**, Montgomery **Ref:**YH02025
- **CHOICE SADDLERY**, Knighton **Ref:**YH02876
- **CRADOC TACK**, Brecon **Ref:**YH03541
- **HORSEMAN'S STOP**, Abercrave **Ref:**YH07160
- **LLANFYLLIN SADDLERY**, Llanfyllin **Ref:**YH08723
- **LLWYNON**, Brecon **Ref:**YH08749
- **NICHOLLS, W**, Crickhowell **Ref:**YH10186

RHONDDA CYNON TAFF
- **BOOTS & SADDLES**, Tonypandy **Ref:**YH01640

SWANSEA
- **CROSS STORES**, Swansea **Ref:**YH03653
- **HORSE CTRE**, Swansea **Ref:**YH07116

WREXHAM
- **ACRE HSE EQUESTRIAN**, Wrexham **Ref:**YH00158
- **BLINKERS EQUESTRIAN**, Wrexham **Ref:**YH01540
- **N W F COUNTRYSTORE**, Wrexham **Ref:**YH10000
- **TOWN & COUNTRY SUPPLIES**, Bangor-on-Dee **Ref:**YH14288

STABLES/LIVERIES

BRIDGEND
- **E K M EQUESTRIAN**, Bridgend **Ref:**YH04411
- **FFORDD GYRAITH LIVERY STABLES**, Cefn Cribwr **Ref:**YH05177
- **SOUTH WALES EQUESTRIAN CTRE**, Bridgend **Ref:**YH13112

CAERPHILLY
- **BEAU COURT**, Newport **Ref:**YH01126
- **GRAIG FAWR LIVERY YARD**, Caerphilly **Ref:**YH05975
- **GROESWEN RIDING STABLES**, Caerphilly **Ref:**YH06147
- **ROCKWOOD RIDING CTRE**, Caerphilly **Ref:**YH12039

CARMARTHENSHIRE
- **DINESWR RIDING CTRE**, Ammanford **Ref:**YH04124
- **PEMBREY EQUESTRIAN**, Burry Port **Ref:**YH10914
- **PENCADER STUD**, Pencader **Ref:**YH10928
- **STALLIONS AT TACKEXCHANGE**, Llanelli **Ref:**YH13351
- **TREFACH RIDING CTRE**, Clynderwen **Ref:**YH14362
- **WELSH EQUITATION CTRE**, Carmarthen **Ref:**YH15091

CEREDIGION
- **MOELFRYN RIDING CTRE**, Aberystwyth **Ref:**YH09699
- **RHEIDOL RIDING CTRE**, Aberystwyth **Ref:**YH11784
- **WINDY GAIL STABLES**, Blaenannerch **Ref:**YH15581

CONWY
- **ABERCONWY EQUESTRIAN CTRE**, Llandudno Junction **Ref:**YH00119
- **FOULKES, JUSTIN & CHRISTINE**, Colwyn Bay **Ref:**YH05406

DENBIGHSHIRE
- **CARRINGTON-SYKES**, Denbigh **Ref:**YH02591
- **CLAREMONT EQUESTRIAN CTRE**, Ruthin **Ref:**YH02951
- **LLANNERCH EQUESTRIAN CTRE**, St Asaph **Ref:**YH08726

FLINTSHIRE
- **CLAYTON, J**, Mold **Ref:**YH03004
- **LYNDEN FARM**, Holywell **Ref:**YH08926

GLAMORGAN (VALE OF)
- **ARGAE HSE STABLES**, Dinas Powys **Ref:**YH00519
- **CARDIFF RIDING SCHOOL**, Cardiff **Ref:**YH02531
- **CIMLA TREKKING**, Neath **Ref:**YH02918
- **PEN-MAEN LIVERY YARD**, Cowbridge **Ref:**YH10944
- **PICKERSTON STUD**, Barry **Ref:**YH11085

GWYNEDD
- **ABERSOCH MARCHROS STUD**, Abersoch **Ref:**YH00129
- **DWYFOR RIDING CTRE**, Criccieth **Ref:**YH04382
- **MEREDITH, D & S**, Dolgellau **Ref:**YH09468
- **PEN ISAR FARM**, Bala **Ref:**YH10922
- **RHOSYN GWYN EQUESTRIAN CTRE**, Caernarfon **Ref:**YH11791
- **SNOWDONIA RIDING STABLES**, Caernarfon **Ref:**YH13041

ISLE OF ANGLESEY
- **ANGLESEY EQUESTRIAN CTRE**, Holyhead **Ref:**YH00410
- **BRACKENDENE STUD**, Anglesey **Ref:**YH01738
- **TAL Y FOEL RIDING CTRE**, Anglesey **Ref:**YH13829
- **TYN-MORFA RIDING CTRE**, Rhosneigr **Ref:**YH14529

MONMOUTHSHIRE
- **BEAUMONT, REBECCA**, Abergavenny **Ref:**YH01138
- **EARLSWOOD RIDING CTRE**, Chepstow **Ref:**YH04455
- **GROVE FARM**, Abergavenny **Ref:**YH06165
- **HORNWALK EQUESTRIAN**, Monmouth **Ref:**YH07083
- **PONDEROSA EQUESTRIAN CTRE**, Pontypool **Ref:**YH11219
- **SEVERNVALE EQUESTRIAN CTRE**, Chepstow **Ref:**YH12646

NEATH PORT TALBOT
- **WAUN FAWR FARM**, Pontardawe **Ref:**YH15009

PEMBROKESHIRE
- **FILMSTONE FARM**, Narberth **Ref:**YH05204
- **HEATHERTON RIDING STABLES**, Saundersfoot **Ref:**YH06628
- **LLANWNDA STABLES**, Goodwick **Ref:**YH08727
- **MOOR FARM RIDING STABLES**, Haverfordwest **Ref:**YH09744

- **PEMBROKESHIRE RIDING CTRE**, Pembroke **Ref:**YH10920
- **TALLY HO FARM**, Pembroke **Ref:**YH13841

POWYS

- **BROMPTON HALL**, Montgomery **Ref:**YH02025
- **CILWYCH FARM**, Bwlch **Ref:**YH02917
- **CWRT ISAF FARM**, Crickhowell **Ref:**YH03765
- **FOREST INN**, New Radnor **Ref:**YH05341
- **GLAN YR AFON HOLIDAYS**, Welshpool **Ref:**YH05804
- **GOLDEN CASTLE**, Crickhowell **Ref:**YH05877
- **LION ROYAL HOTEL**, Rhayader **Ref:**YH08671
- **LLETTY MAWR TREKKING**, Welshpool **Ref:**YH08728
- **MARL STUD MARL CRIS STUD**, Brecon **Ref:**YH09167
- **RIVERSIDE RIDING CTRE**, Crickhowell **Ref:**YH11927
- **TRANS-WALES TRAILS**, Brecon **Ref:**YH14353

RHONDDA CYNON TAFF

- **YNYSCRUG STUD**, Tonyrefail **Ref:**YH15912

SWANSEA

- **COPLEY**, Swansea **Ref:**YH03297
- **FORGEMILL**, Swansea **Ref:**YH05368
- **GREEN FARM**, Swansea **Ref:**YH06054
- **PENTRE RIDING STABLES**, Swansea **Ref:**YH10962
- **PRIORY STABLES**, Swansea **Ref:**YH11405
- **SOUTH WALES CARRIAGE DRIVING**, Swansea **Ref:**YH13111
- **TANKEY LAKE LIVERY**, Swansea **Ref:**YH13856
- **WAUN FAWR FARM**, Swansea **Ref:**YH15010

WREXHAM

- **BILLINGTON, G**, Wrexham **Ref:**YH01413
- **CHAPEL FARM**, Wrexham **Ref:**YH02738
- **ROBERTS, SHELAGH**, Penycae **Ref:**YH11961

STUD FARMS

CEREDIGION

- **MAESMYNACH STUD**, Lampeter **Ref:**YH09032
- **MOELFRYN RIDING CTRE**, Aberystwyth **Ref:**YH09699

MONMOUTHSHIRE

- **LANGARTH**, Monmouth **Ref:**YH08399

SUPPLIES

BLAENAU GWENT

- **HARRIMAN, JOHN**, Tredegar **Ref:**YH06460
- **PRICE, J K**, Ebbw Vale **Ref:**YH11381
- **WARD, R & S**, Newport **Ref:**YH14905

BRIDGEND

- **COUNTRYWIDE STORES**, Bridgend **Ref:**YH03449
- **HARVESTERS FARM SUPPLIES**, Bridgend **Ref:**YH06511
- **LLOYD, D M**, Brynmenyn **Ref:**YH08735
- **THOMAS, D**, Aberkenfig **Ref:**YH14014
- **WALTERS PET & GARDEN STORES**, Bridgend **Ref:**YH14885
- **WINNERS ANIMAL PET SHOP**, Pyle **Ref:**YH15588

CAERPHILLY

- **EXPRESS PET SUPPLIES**, Hengoed **Ref:**YH04973

CARMARTHENSHIRE

- **CARMARTHEN & PUMSAINT FARMERS**, Carmarthen **Ref:**YH02549
- **CARMARTHEN & PUMSAINT FARMERS**, Carmarthen **Ref:**YH02554
- **CARMARTHEN & PUMSAINT FARMERS**, Carmarthen **Ref:**YH02550
- **CARMARTHEN & PUMSAINT FARMERS**, Kidwelly **Ref:**YH02551
- **CARMARTHEN & PUMSAINT FARMERS**, Llandeilo **Ref:**YH02547
- **CARMARTHEN & PUMSAINT FARMERS**, Llandeilo **Ref:**YH02555
- **CARMARTHEN & PUMSAINT FARMERS**, Llandovery **Ref:**YH02548
- **CARMARTHEN & PUMSAINT FARMERS**, Llangadog **Ref:**YH02553
- **CARMARTHEN & PUMSAINT FARMERS**, Llanybydder **Ref:**YH02552
- **CARMARTHEN & PUMSAINT FARMERS**, St Clears **Ref:**YH02556
- **CARMARTHEN & PUMSAINT FARMERS**, Whitland **Ref:**YH02557
- **CLYNDERWEN & CARDIGAN**, Whitland **Ref:**YH03083
- **CLYNDERWEN & CARDIGANSHIRE**, Newcastle Emlyn **Ref:**YH03087
- **DALGETY AGRCLTRL**, Carmarthen **Ref:**YH03834
- **DOUCH, SELWYN**, Carmarthen **Ref:**YH04210
- **EQUINE SHOP**, Carmarthen **Ref:**YH04799
- **EVANS, M V**, Carmarthen **Ref:**YH04927
- **GRIFFITHS, S G**, Carmarthen **Ref:**YH06143
- **HICKLING, L M**, Carmarthen **Ref:**YH06741
- **J BIBBY AGRICULTURE**, Carmarthen **Ref:**YH07567
- **MORGAN EQUINE**, Llandeilo **Ref:**YH09794
- **PEARCE, K R**, Laugharne **Ref:**YH10873
- **PENCADER STUD**, Pencader **Ref:**YH10928
- **PLAS EQUESTRIAN**, Carmarthen **Ref:**YH11164
- **PLAS-Y-MAES**, Llanelli **Ref:**YH11166
- **POLY PROP**, Llandysul **Ref:**YH11213
- **SHUFFLEBOTTOM**, Cross Hands **Ref:**YH12773
- **SIDEBOTTOM, J**, Llandysul **Ref:**YH12788
- **STALLIONS AT TACKEXCHANGE**, Llanelli **Ref:**YH13351
- **TACK EXCHANGE**, Llanelli **Ref:**YH13787
- **TEAL, V J**, St Clears **Ref:**YH13923
- **THERMATEX**, Cardigan **Ref:**YH13986

CEREDIGION

- **CAPTAIN RUGWASH**, Cardigan **Ref:**YH02524
- **CARMARTHEN & PUMSAINT FARMERS**, Pontardulais **Ref:**YH02558
- **CLYNDERWEN & CARDIGAN**, Lampeter **Ref:**YH03084
- **CLYNDERWEN & CARDIGANSHIRE**, Aberystwyth **Ref:**YH03088
- **CLYNDERWEN & CARDIGANSHIRE**, Cardigan **Ref:**YH03089
- **CLYNDERWEN & CARDIGANSHIRE**, Tregaron **Ref:**YH03090
- **JONES, G E**, Lampeter **Ref:**YH07900
- **ROGERS & TAYLOR**, Aberystwyth **Ref:**YH12056
- **TY-LLYN TACK**, Aberystwyth **Ref:**YH14524
- **W D LEWIS & SON**, Lampeter **Ref:**YH14759
- **WERN EQUESTRIAN SERVICES**, New Quay **Ref:**YH15112

CONWY

- **GWYN LEWIS FARM SUPPLIES**, Abergele **Ref:**YH06205
- **OWEN, E HOLLISTER**, Denbigh **Ref:**YH10599

DENBIGHSHIRE

- **ACRE HSE EQUESTRIAN**, Acrefair **Ref:**YH00157
- **CORWEN & DISTRICT FARMERS**, Corwen **Ref:**YH03347
- **ERIC WILLIAMS LEATHER-CRAFT**, Corwen **Ref:**YH04847
- **MASTERS DISPLAYS**, Ruthin **Ref:**YH09250
- **WYNNSTAY & CLWYD FARMERS**, St Asaph **Ref:**YH15874

FLINTSHIRE

- **G REES AGRICULTURAL MERCHANTS**, Mold **Ref:**YH05596
- **HORSES**, Wrexham **Ref:**YH07167
- **JOLLYES**, Flint **Ref:**YH07859
- **LLONG MILL**, Mold **Ref:**YH08732
- **MOLD VALLEY SADDLERY**, Mold **Ref:**YH09706
- **T F S**, Buckley **Ref:**YH13739

GLAMORGAN (VALE OF)

- **AYRES, JOHN**, Cardiff **Ref:**YH00702
- **CLARK OF DOWLAIS**, Merthyr **Ref:**YH02961
- **CLYNDERWEN & CARDIGANSHIRE**, Lladon **Ref:**YH03091
- **DAVIES, D J**, Resolven **Ref:**YH03938
- **HORSE RUG WASH**, Cardiff **Ref:**YH07136
- **TUDOR, J W**, Pencoed **Ref:**YH14445
- **VALLEY FEEDS**, Merthyr Tydfil **Ref:**YH14655

GWYNEDD

- **BRONALLT**, Caernarfon **Ref:**YH02029
- **CLYNDERWEN & CARDIGAN**, Llanbedr **Ref:**YH03085
- **CLYNDERWEN & CARDIGANSHIRE**, Bala **Ref:**YH03092
- **CLYNDERWEN & CARDIGANSHIRE**, Bala **Ref:**YH03093
- **D & F HORSE SUPPLIES**, Caernarfon **Ref:**YH03771
- **EVANS, RHYS**, Bangor **Ref:**YH04931
- **W H EVANS**, Garndolbenmaen **Ref:**YH14769

ISLE OF ANGLESEY

- **BATT, F J**, Pentraeth **Ref:**YH01075
- **CLYNDERWEN & CARDIGANSHIRE**, Gaerwen **Ref:**YH03094
- **DUFFY, J A & P**, Llanfair **Ref:**YH04319
- **SHEAR EASE**, Amlwch **Ref:**YH12688

MONMOUTHSHIRE

- **ABBOTT**, Monmouth **Ref:**YH00106
- **BROWN, R L**, Abergavenny **Ref:**YH02130
- **CAREY, D N**, Raglan **Ref:**YH02535
- **CHEPSTOW SADDLERY**, Chepstow **Ref:**YH02809
- **CLIPPERS**, Chepstow **Ref:**YH03047
- **COUNTRYWIDE STORES**, Abergavenny **Ref:**YH03460
- **COUNTRYWIDE STORES**, Chepstow **Ref:**YH03461
- **COUNTRYWIDE STORES**, Raglan **Ref:**YH03462
- **HAWKINS, J E**, Usk **Ref:**YH06548
- **LIVERMORE, R E A**, Usk **Ref:**YH08713
- **NATURAL ANIMAL FEEDS**, Raglan **Ref:**YH10050
- **ROSS FEED**, Monmouth **Ref:**YH12115
- **WELSH RIDING COAT**, Abergavenny **Ref:**YH15097

NEWPORT

- **HAWKINS, JOANNE**, Rogerstone **Ref:**YH06549
- **K B M F AUDIO**, Llanvaches **Ref:**YH07983
- **PRICE, J J E**, Llandevaud **Ref:**YH11380
- **PRICE, T J**, Chepstow **Ref:**YH11389
- **SHEEDY, W R**, Newport **Ref:**YH12694

PEMBROKESHIRE

- **ARMSTRONG MOWERS**, Haverfordwest **Ref:**YH00543
- **BOULSTON**, Haverfordwest **Ref:**YH01672
- **CLYNDERWEN & CARDIGAN**, Johnston **Ref:**YH03086
- **CLYNDERWEN & CARDIGANSHIRE**, Clynderwen **Ref:**YH03095
- **CLYNDERWEN & CARDIGANSHIRE**, Crymych **Ref:**YH03097
- **CLYNDERWEN & CARDIGANSHIRE**, Narberth **Ref:**YH03096
- **CLYNDERWEN & CARDIGANSHIRE**, Tenby **Ref:**YH03098
- **EVANS, M**, Pembroke **Ref:**YH04926
- **PEGASUS**, Haverfordwest **Ref:**YH10902
- **SMART R'S**, Narberth **Ref:**YH12920

POWYS

- **ANDERSON, I F F**, Welshpool **Ref:**YH00382
- **BLOOR, RAY**, Montgomery **Ref:**YH01559
- **BROMPTON HALL**, Montgomery **Ref:**YH02025
- **BROYD, A E**, Crickhowell **Ref:**YH02152

- **CLYNDERWEN & CARDIGANSHIRE**, Machynlleth **Ref:**YH03099
- **CONTROL TECHNIQUES**, Newtown **Ref:**YH03249
- **COUNTRYWIDE STORES**, Llandrindod Wells **Ref:**YH03465
- **COUNTRYWIDE STORES**, Presteigne **Ref:**YH03466
- **COUNTRYWIDE STORES**, Welshpool **Ref:**YH03467
- **CROWE, C D**, Montgomery **Ref:**YH03677
- **DALGETY AGRCLTRL**, Knighton **Ref:**YH03836
- **ECKLEY, B J**, Brecon **Ref:**YH04535
- **GITTENS, W R**, Welshpool **Ref:**YH05798
- **HAY & BRECON FARMERS**, Brecon **Ref:**YH06560
- **HAY & BRECON FARMERS**, Brecon **Ref:**YH06559
- **HAY & BRECON FARMERS**, Builth Wells **Ref:**YH06561
- **HAY & BRECON FARMERS**, Llandrindod Wells **Ref:**YH06562
- **NORRIS, PAULINE**, Newtown **Ref:**YH10245
- **PARRY, K G**, Welshpool **Ref:**YH10793
- **PENBAULLT ROSETTES**, Llangammarch Wells **Ref:**YH10924
- **PRICE, A**, Presteigne **Ref:**YH11373
- **PRICE, G M**, Brecon **Ref:**YH11379
- **R A OWEN & SONS**, Llandinam **Ref:**YH11513
- **SMITHS INDUSTRIES WATCH**, Ystradgynlais **Ref:**YH13008
- **STAVELEY PEDIGREE LIMOUSINS**, Llandrindod Wells **Ref:**YH13405
- **WEST BULTHY EQUESTRIAN**, Welshpool **Ref:**YH15130
- **WYNNSTAY & CLWYD FARMERS**, Llansanffraid **Ref:**YH15875

RHONDDA CYNON TAFF

- **WINNERS OF WALES**, Pontyclun **Ref:**YH15590

SWANSEA

- **D MORGAN & SON**, Swansea **Ref:**YH03798
- **D MORGAN & SONS**, Swansea **Ref:**YH03799
- **KILVEY TACK**, Swansea **Ref:**YH08156
- **MABBETT, JOHN**, Swansea **Ref:**YH08979
- **MR POTTER'S TROTTERS**, Swansea **Ref:**YH09916
- **WEST WALES FOODS**, Swansea **Ref:**YH15168

TORFAEN

- **CUNNINGHAM & REED**, Cwmbran **Ref:**YH03723
- **PAPERSHRED**, Cwmbran **Ref:**YH10708
- **PETSTOP**, Cwmbran **Ref:**YH11033

WREXHAM

- **ACRE HSE EQUESTRIAN**, Wrexham **Ref:**YH00158
- **BLINKERS EQUESTRIAN**, Wrexham **Ref:**YH01540
- **CHARLES OWEN**, Wrexham **Ref:**YH02757
- **LLOYD, F**, Bangor-on-Dee **Ref:**YH08738

TRACKS/COURSES

CARMARTHENSHIRE

- **AMMAN VALLEY RACEWAY**, Ammanford **Ref:**YH00369

CEREDIGION

- **WALES & THE WEST HARNESS**, Aberystwyth **Ref:**YH14838

CONWY

- **T I R PRINCE RACEWAY**, Abergele **Ref:**YH13752

DENBIGHSHIRE

- **LLANNERCH EQUESTRIAN CTRE**, St Asaph **Ref:**YH08726

FLINTSHIRE

- **BABELL CROSS CTRY**, Holywell **Ref:**YH00762

GLAMORGAN (VALE OF)

- **ARGAE HSE STABLES**, Dinas Powys **Ref:**YH00519
- **CIMLA TREKKING**, Neath **Ref:**YH02918
- **PENCOED CLGE**, Pencoed **Ref:**YH10930

GWYNEDD

- **PRITCHARD, E**, Blaenau Ffestiniog **Ref:**YH11412
- **RHOSYN GWYN EQUESTRIAN CTRE**, Caernarfon **Ref:**YH11791

ISLE OF ANGLESEY

- **BRACKENDENE STUD**, Anglesey **Ref:**YH01738
- **GORS WEN FARM**, Holyhead **Ref:**YH05937

MONMOUTHSHIRE

- **CHEPSTOW RACECOURSE**, Chepstow **Ref:**YH02808
- **SEVERNVALE EQUESTRIAN CTRE**, Chepstow **Ref:**YH12646

PEMBROKESHIRE

- **EAST NOLTON RIDING STABLES**, Haverfordwest **Ref:**YH04482

POWYS

- **CANTREF**, Brecon **Ref:**YH02516
- **UNDERHILL RIDING STABLES**, Llandrindod Wells **Ref:**YH14560

WREXHAM

- **BANGOR-ON-DEE RACES**, Bangor-on-Dee **Ref:**YH00882

TRAINERS

BLAENAU GWENT

- **BURCHELL, DAVID**, Ebbw Vale **Ref:**YH02230

BRIDGEND

- **E K M EQUESTRIAN**, Bridgend **Ref:**YH04411

CAERPHILLY

- **B J LLEWELLYN**, Bargoed **Ref:**YH00733

CARMARTHENSHIRE

- **ELLIOTT, D**, Llandysul **Ref:**YH04619
- **EQUISECRETS**, Lampeter **Ref:**YH04817
- **HOWELL, CASTELL**, Llandysul **Ref:**YH07227
- **JAMES, D W**, Ammanford **Ref:**YH07680
- **JONES, A W**, Ammanford **Ref:**YH07876
- **PENCADER STUD**, Pencader **Ref:**YH10928
- **RIPMAN, BARBARA**, Carmarthen **Ref:**YH11906
- **THOMAS, H T**, Ammanford **Ref:**YH14021

CEREDIGION

- **BHS WALES**, Aberystwyth **Ref:**YH01388
- **RHEIDOL RIDING CTRE**, Aberystwyth **Ref:**YH11784

DENBIGHSHIRE

- **LEE, C**, Rhuddlan **Ref:**YH08522
- **LEE, P**, Rhyl **Ref:**YH08525

FLINTSHIRE

- **OWENS, R M L**, Mold **Ref:**YH10609

GLAMORGAN (VALE OF)

- **CHASE FARM**, Llantwit Major **Ref:**YH02779
- **CIMLA TREKKING**, Neath **Ref:**YH02918
- **LIEGE MANOR**, Cardiff **Ref:**YH08609
- **PALLING, BRYN**, Cowbridge **Ref:**YH10689
- **PEN-MAEN LIVERY YARD**, Cowbridge **Ref:**YH10944
- **SEVERN QUARTER HORSES**, Cowbridge **Ref:**YH12644
- **TY-WYTH-NEWYDD STABLES**, Cowbridge **Ref:**YH14535

GWYNEDD

- **PEN-LLEYN RIDING CTRE**, Pwllheli **Ref:**YH10943

ISLE OF ANGLESEY

- **PRITCHARD, K V**, Holyhead **Ref:**YH11417
- **STANFORD EVENTING HORSES**, Holyhead **Ref:**YH13363

MONMOUTHSHIRE

- **BEAUMONT, REBECCA**, Abergavenny **Ref:**YH01138
- **BRADLEY, J M**, Chepstow **Ref:**YH01754
- **DAVIES, J D J**, Abergavenny **Ref:**YH03942
- **JOHNSEY, CLAIRE**, Chepstow **Ref:**YH07821
- **RICH, P**, Usk **Ref:**YH11801
- **WINTER, ERIC**, Chepstow **Ref:**YH15593
- **WOODLANDER STUD**, Raglan **Ref:**YH15704

NEWPORT

- **CEFN LLOGELL RACING STABLES**, Coed Kernew **Ref:**YH02678
- **PAYNE STEEPLECHASE FENCES**, Highcross **Ref:**YH10847

PEMBROKESHIRE

- **BOWEN, PETER**, Haverfordwest **Ref:**YH01702
- **FILMSTONE FARM**, Narberth **Ref:**YH05204
- **LAVIS, H W**, Haverfordwest **Ref:**YH08467
- **OASIS PARK EQUESTRIAN CTRE**, Narberth **Ref:**YH10412

POWYS

- **BROMPTON HALL**, Montgomery **Ref:**YH02025
- **CARREG DRESSAGE**, Machynlleth **Ref:**YH02578
- **EVANS, P D**, Welshpool **Ref:**YH04929
- **GOLDEN CASTLE**, Crickhowell **Ref:**YH05877
- **LEE, RICHARD**, Presteigne **Ref:**YH08526
- **LEE, RICHARD A**, Presteigne **Ref:**YH08527
- **LLETTY MAWR TREKKING**, Welshpool **Ref:**YH08728
- **PHILLIPS, E R**, Presteigne **Ref:**YH11055

RHONDDA CYNON TAFF

- **JONES, DEREK H**, Pontypridd **Ref:**YH07893

SWANSEA

- **MOYSE, ROWENA**, Swansea **Ref:**YH09914
- **SOUTH WALES CARRIAGE DRIVING**, Swansea **Ref:**YH13111

WREXHAM

- **BLINKERS EQUESTRIAN**, Wrexham **Ref:**YH01540

TRANSPORT/HORSE BOXES

BRIDGEND

- **AVONRIDE**, Maesteg **Ref:**YH00692
- **ETS TRAILERS & TOWBARS**, Bridgend **Ref:**YH04885

CAERPHILLY

- **BRIAN DAVIES MOTORS**, Caerphilly **Ref:**YH01860

CARMARTHENSHIRE

- **BANK FARM TRAILERS**, Carmarthen **Ref:**YH00887
- **C L H TRAILERS**, Carmarthen **Ref:**YH02380
- **CROSS HANDS TRAILER CTRE**, Llanelli **Ref:**YH03647
- **D I Y TRAILERS**, Llandysul **Ref:**YH03787
- **HAFOD TRAILERS**, Llandysul **Ref:**YH06275
- **LLANELLI TRAILER CTRE**, Llanelli **Ref:**YH08721

CEREDIGION

- **L CLARK**, Llanrhystud **Ref:**YH08316
- **MORGAN, H R**, Bow Street **Ref:**YH09806
- **RHEIDOL RIDING CTRE**, Aberystwyth **Ref:**YH11784
- **T EBENEZER & SON**, Tregaron **Ref:**YH13737

CONWY

- **TRAILERMATE PRODUCTS**, Llandudno **Ref:**YH14335

DENBIGHSHIRE

- **IFOR WILLIAMS**, Corwen **Ref:**YH07391

FLINTSHIRE

- **DAWSONSRENTALS**, Mold **Ref:**YH03966
- **DIXON-BATE**, Deeside **Ref:**YH04144
- **MIDDLEWOOD**, Mold **Ref:**YH09547

- **TRAILERWAY**, Flint **Ref:**YH14337
- **WILCOX COACH WORKS**, Mold **Ref:**YH15404

GLAMORGAN (VALE OF)

- **CARDIFF TRAILER CTRE**, Cardiff **Ref:**YH02533
- **CELTIC TRAILERS**, Neath **Ref:**YH02680
- **HAULRITE TRAILERS**, Penarth **Ref:**YH06536
- **INDESPENSION**, Cardiff **Ref:**YH07418

GWYNEDD

- **WILLIAMS, HUMPHREY**, Pwllheli **Ref:**YH15459

ISLE OF ANGLESEY

- **TRAILER SERVICES BANGOR**, Menai Bridge **Ref:**YH14329
- **TYN-MORFA RIDING CTRE**, Rhosneigr **Ref:**YH14529

NEATH PORT TALBOT

- **TOWBAR CTRE**, Neath **Ref:**YH14263

NEWPORT

- **BANK FARM TRAILERS**, Newport **Ref:**YH00888
- **GEMS CLEARWAY**, Newport **Ref:**YH05700

PEMBROKESHIRE

- **BANK FARM TRAILERS**, Narberth **Ref:**YH00889
- **BEE LINE TOWBAR/TRAILER CTRE**, Milford Haven **Ref:**YH01159
- **BRYAN, B D**, Narberth **Ref:**YH02163
- **KILGETTY TRAILER HIRE**, Kilgetty **Ref:**YH08135

POWYS

- **BROMPTON HALL**, Montgomery **Ref:**YH02025
- **GAMIC TRAILERS**, Newtown **Ref:**YH05635
- **GOLDEN CASTLE**, Crickhowell **Ref:**YH05877

SWANSEA

- **BANK FARM TRAILERS**, Swansea **Ref:**YH00890

WREXHAM

- **BELGRAVE COACH BUILDERS**, Wrexham **Ref:**YH01210
- **CLARKE'S EQUINE COACHWORKS**, Wrexham **Ref:**YH02977

SECTION 3A

Lesson Prices

This section helps you to locate a business by Country, by County within the Lesson Price range.

Lesson Prices are grouped into ranges of half hourly rates. However, in some cases, the 60 minute rate will be displayed. If a business offers lessons at £15.00 for 1 hour for example, they will be displayed in the under £10.00 for 30 minutes section. The type of lesson offered is also listed.

E.g. **England, Under £25,**
Derbyshire:
Moorfield Riding Stables
£15.00 for 30 Minutes
(one-to-one)

Once you have located a business using this section you can then refer to the company's detailed profile in Section 1.

UNDER £10

BEDFORDSHIRE

ALTERNATIVE RIDING SCHOOL
YH00343
£12.00 for 60 minutes (one-to-one)

STOCKWOOD PARK
YH13498
£18.00 for 60 minutes (one-to-one)

SUNSHINE RIDING SCHOOL
YH13652
£9.00 for 30 minutes (one-to-one)

CHESHIRE

CROFT RIDING CTRE
YH03617
£10.00 for 60 minutes (child)
£12.00 for 60 minutes (adult)

CORNWALL

HELSTON SADDLERY
YH06657
£6.00 for 30 minutes (one-to-one)

COUNTY DURHAM

ALSTON & KILLHOPE
YH00339
£8.00 for 60 minutes (child)
£9.00 for 60 minutes (adult)

BOWES MANOR EQUESTRIAN CTRE
YH01709
£15.00 for 60 minutes (one-to-one)

DARLINGTON EQUESTRIAN CTRE
YH03892
£7.50 for 30 minutes (one-to-one)

DARLINGTON EQUESTRIAN CTRE
YH03893
£7.50 for 30 minutes (adult)

DENNIS, JUDY
YH04055
£5.00 for 30 minutes (child)
£9.00 for 60 minutes (adult)

HAMSTERLEY RIDING SCHOOL
YH06372
£9.00 for 60 minutes (one-to-one)

HIGHLING EQUESTRIAN CTRE
YH06798
£7.00 for 30 minutes (one-to-one)

CUMBRIA

ALLONBY RIDING SCHOOL
YH00323
£8.50 for 30 minutes (one-to-one)

DEVON

DONKEY SANCTUARY
YH04184
Free for 60 minutes (child)
Free for 60 minutes (one-to-one)
Free for 60 minutes (adult)
Free for 30 minutes (adult)
Free for 30 minutes (one-to-one)
Free for 30 minutes (child)

HALDON RIDING STABLES
YH06290
£8.00 for 30 minutes (one-to-one)

MULLACOTT EQUESTRIAN
YH09935
£7.00 for 30 minutes (one-to-one)

DORSET

REMPSTONE STABLES
YH11751
£8.50 for 30 minutes (one-to-one)

ESSEX

ASHINGDON RIDING CTRE
YH00605
£7.00 for 30 minutes (one-to-one)

BROOK FARM STABLES
YH02036
£8.50 for 30 minutes (child)

TALLY-HO RIDING SCHOOL
YH13844
£7.50 for 30 minutes (one-to-one)

HEREFORDSHIRE

TIPTON HALL
YH14183
£8.00 for 60 minutes (child)
£16.00 for 60 minutes (adult)

ISLE OF WIGHT

ROMANY RIDING STABLES
YH12070
£5.00 for 30 minutes (one-to-one)

LANCASHIRE

BLACKPOOL EQUESTRIAN CTRE
YH01492
£8.50 for 30 minutes (one-to-one)

RENARD RIDING CTRE
YH11753
£8.50 for 30 minutes (one-to-one)

WAKEFIELD, HILARY
YH14833
£15.00 for 60 minutes (one-to-one)

LINCOLNSHIRE

S & B STABLES
YH12309
£12.00 for 60 minutes (one-to-one)

LONDON (GREATER)

ABBEYFIELDS
YH00095
£17.00 for 60 minutes (child)

QUEEN ELIZABETH RIDING SCHOOL
YH11488
£12.00 for 60 minutes (child)
£16.00 for 60 minutes (adult)

MANCHESTER (GREATER)

MATCHMOOR RIDING CTRE
YH09257
£9.50 for 30 minutes (one-to-one)

MIDLANDS (WEST)

MOOR FARM STABLES
YH09745
£9.00 for 30 minutes (adult)
£9.00 for 30 minutes (child)

WITHYBROOK STABLES
YH15629
£17.00 for 60 minutes (child)

NOTTINGHAMSHIRE

SUTTON MANOR FARM
YH13673
£6.00 for 30 minutes (one-to-one)

OXFORDSHIRE

EAST END FARM RIDING SCHOOL
YH04474
£7.00 for 30 minutes (one-to-one)

SOMERSET

ALSTONE COURT RIDING ESTB
YH00342
£6.00 for 30 minutes (child)
£6.50 for 30 minutes (adult)
£12.50 for 60 minutes (child)
£13.50 for 60 minutes (adult)

BURCOTT RIDING CTRE
YH02236
£9.00 for 30 minutes (child)

ROYS RIDING SCHOOL
YH12201
£5.00 for 60 minutes (child)
£10.00 for 60 minutes (adult)

SOMERSET (NORTH)

CTRE RIDING SCHOOL
YH03696
£10.00 for 60 minutes (child)
£15.00 for 60 minutes (adult)

STAFFORDSHIRE

BARLASTON RIDING CTRE
YH00949
£8.00 for 30 minutes (adult)

SURREY

BEECHWOOD
YH01176
£8.00 for 30 minutes (one-to-one)

WILTSHIRE

WHITE HORSE EQUESTRIAN CTRE
YH15308
£19.00 for 60 minutes (one-to-one)

WORCESTERSHIRE

HALLOW MILLS
YH06333
£8.00 for 30 minutes (child)

YORKSHIRE (NORTH)

FRIARS HILL STABLES
YH05501
£7.50 for 30 minutes (one-to-one)

HOME FARM
YH06995
£9.00 for 30 minutes (one-to-one)

MILL LANE
YH09579
£7.00 for 30 minutes (child)

YORKSHIRE (SOUTH)

PRICES
YH11391
£9.00 for 30 minutes (one-to-one)

YORKSHIRE (WEST)

ASTLEY RIDING CTRE
YH00635
£8.50 for 30 minutes (one-to-one)

CROFTON RIDING STABLES
YH03624
£5.50 for 30 minutes (one-to-one)

WESTWAYS RIDING SCHOOL
YH15236
£13.00 for 60 minutes (child)
£13.50 for 60 minutes (adult)

UNDER £25

BEDFORDSHIRE

BROOK STABLES
YH02038
£14.00 for 30 minutes (child)
£16.00 for 30 minutes (adult)

BRSC
YH02153
£10.00 for 30 minutes (one-to-one)

STOCKWOOD PARK
YH13498
£10.00 for 30 minutes (one-to-one)

BERKSHIRE

EAST SOLEY E C 2000
YH04486
£20.00 for 30 minutes (one-to-one)

PEACHEY, KA
YH10858
£15.00 for 30 minutes (one-to-one)

SHELTON FARM
YH12704
£11.00 for 30 minutes (one-to-one)

BUCKINGHAMSHIRE

BRAWLINGS FARM RIDING CTRE
YH01819
£22.00 for 30 minutes (one-to-one)

CATHERINE WRIGHT
YH02649
£15.00 for 30 minutes (one-to-one)

EQUESTRIAN CTRE
YH04696
£21.00 for 30 minutes (one-to-one)

CAMBRIDGESHIRE

NORTHBROOK EQUESTRIAN CTRE
YH10294
£15.00 for 30 minutes (one-to-one)

OLD TIGER STABLES
YH10479
£15.00 for 30 minutes (one-to-one)

CHESHIRE

BARROW EQUESTRIAN CTRE
YH01027
£10.00 for 30 minutes (one-to-one)

CROFT RIDING CTRE
YH03617
£12.00 for 30 minutes (one-to-one)

CLEVELAND

KIRKLEVINGTON RIDING SCHOOL
YH08237
£16.00 for 30 minutes (one-to-one)
£20.00 for 60 minutes (one-to-one)
£20.00 for 60 minutes (adult)

WOLVISTON RIDING STABLES
YH15652
£10.00 for 30 minutes (one-to-one)

CORNWALL

LAUREL STUD
YH08458
£10.00 for 30 minutes (one-to-one)

TM INT SCHOOL OF HORSEMANSHIP
YH14196
£15.00 for 30 minutes (one-to-one)

VERYAN RIDING CTRE
YH14686
£11.00 for 30 minutes (one-to-one)

COUNTY DURHAM

BOWES MANOR EQUESTRIAN CTRE
YH01709
£10.00 for 30 minutes (one-to-one)

BROOM HALL LIVERY YARD
YH02072
£10.00 for 30 minutes (one-to-one)

CENTURION EQUESTRIAN CTRE
YH02698
£13.50 for 30 minutes (adult)
£13.50 for 30 minutes (child)

SEAGOLD CENTURION
YH12587
£13.50 for 30 minutes (one-to-one)

CUMBRIA

LARKRIGG RIDING SCHOOL
YH08434
£15.00 for 30 minutes (one-to-one)

DERBYSHIRE

ALTON RIDING SCHOOL
YH00344
£11.00 for 30 minutes (one-to-one)

BARLEYFIELDS
YH00952
£14.00 for 30 minutes (one-to-one)

C E S
YH02370
£15.00 for 30 minutes (one-to-one)

CHESTERFIELD
YH02833
£20.00 for 30 minutes (one-to-one)

HADDON HSE
YH06261
£15.00 for 30 minutes (one-to-one)

HILLCLIFF STUD
YH06838
£10.00 for 30 minutes (one-to-one)

MOORBRIDGE RIDING STABLES
YH09747
£15.00 for 30 minutes (one-to-one)

DEVON

WEST ILKERTON FARM
YH15150
£12.50 for 30 minutes (one-to-one)

DORSET

ALEXANDER TECHNIQUE TEACHER
YH00267
£20.00 for 30 minutes (one-to-one)

LULWORTH EQUESTRIAN CTRE
YH08897
£13.50 for 30 minutes (one-to-one)

WARMWELL STUD
YH14924
£15.00 for 30 minutes (one-to-one)

ESSEX

BLUE SABRE RIDING SCHOOL
YH01570
£12.00 for 30 minutes (one-to-one)

BROOK FARM STABLES
YH02036
£10.00 for 30 minutes (adult)

CLAY HALL
YH02994
£15.00 for 30 minutes (one-to-one)

COACH HSE
YH03102
£15.00 for 30 minutes (one-to-one)

COLCHESTER GARRISON
YH03144
£13.00 for 30 minutes (one-to-one)

ELMWOOD EQUESTRIAN CTRE
YH04640
£15.00 for 30 minutes (one-to-one)

HALLINGBURY HALL
YH06331
£16.00 for 30 minutes (one-to-one)

LIMEBROOK
YH08628
£12.00 for 30 minutes (one-to-one)

RAGWOOD RIDING CTRE
YH11609
£17.00 for 30 minutes (one-to-one)

SHAHZADA
YH12659
£14.00 for 30 minutes (one-to-one)

SHOPLAND HALL EQUESTRIAN
YH12758
£15.00 for 30 minutes (one-to-one)

TIPTREE EQUESTRIAN CTRE
YH14184
£14.50 for 30 minutes (adult)

VALLEY RIDING/LIVERY STABLES
YH14657
£10.00 for 30 minutes (one-to-one)

WETHERSFIELD RIDING STABLES
YH15246
£15.00 for 30 minutes (one-to-one)

HAMPSHIRE

BURLEY VILLA EQUESTRIAN CTRE
YH02260
£18.00 for 30 minutes (one-to-one)

EQUALLUS EQUESTRIAN
YH04685
£17.00 for 30 minutes (child)
£19.00 for 30 minutes (adult)

FOREST FARM
YH05335
£10.00 for 30 minutes (one-to-one)

INADOWN FARM STABLES
YH07407
£18.00 for 30 minutes (one-to-one)

KILN FARM RIDING SCHOOL
YH08150
£15.00 for 30 minutes (adult)
£15.00 for 30 minutes (child)

MERRIE STUD
YH09480
£18.00 for 30 minutes (one-to-one)

MOYGLARE LIVERY
YH09910
£15.00 for 30 minutes (one-to-one)

NRC
YH10348
£12.50 for 30 minutes (one-to-one)

WELLINGTON RIDING
YH15075
£14.25 for 30 minutes (one-to-one)

HEREFORDSHIRE

COUNTY COMPETITION STUD
YH03486
£10.00 for 30 minutes (one-to-one)

SHEEPCOTE EQUESTRIAN
YH12695
£20.00 for 30 minutes (one-to-one)

SUE ADAMS RIDING SCHOOL
YH13622
£15.00 for 30 minutes (one-to-one)

HERTFORDSHIRE

CROUCHFIELD
YH03674
£10.00 for 30 minutes (one-to-one)

ICKLEFORD EQUESTRIAN
YH07382
£15.00 for 30 minutes (child)
£17.00 for 30 minutes (adult)

ROSE HALL RIDING STABLES
YH12093
£15.00 for 30 minutes (child)

£16.00 for 30 minutes (adult)

SOUTH MEDBURN
YH13101
£20.00 for 30 minutes (one-to-one)

ISLE OF WIGHT

BRICKFIELDS
YH01866
£16.00 for 30 minutes (one-to-one)

LAKE FARM
YH08350
£10.00 for 30 minutes (child)
£12.00 for 30 minutes (adult)

KENT

BRAESIDE E.C
YH01773
£16.00 for 30 minutes (one-to-one)

CLAYTON, PENNIE
YH03006
£18.00 for 30 minutes (one-to-one)

COBHAM MANOR
YH03113
£18.50 for 30 minutes (adult)
£36.00 for 60 minutes (adult)

FRIDAY FIELD STABLES
YH05502
£15.00 for 30 minutes (one-to-one)

HONNINGTON
YH07019
£17.50 for 30 minutes (child)
£20.00 for 30 minutes (one-to-one)

LEYBOURNE GRANGE
YH08600
£10.00 for 30 minutes (one-to-one)

MANNIX STUD
YH09091
£15.00 for 30 minutes (one-to-one)

OLD BEXLEY EQUESTRIAN
YH10451
£12.00 for 30 minutes (one-to-one)

PINE RIDGE
YH11120
£16.00 for 30 minutes (one-to-one)

WHITELEAF RIDING CTRE
YH15347
£15.00 for 30 minutes (one-to-one)

LANCASHIRE

1ST CHOICE PET SUPPLIES
YH00001
£10.00 for 30 minutes (adult)

ARKENFIELD EQUESTRIAN CTRE
YH00530
£18.00 for 30 minutes (one-to-one)

BARTON EQUESTRIAN CTRE
YH01044
£15.00 for 30 minutes (one-to-one)

BECCONSALL
YH01144
£18.00 for 30 minutes (one-to-one)

CHORLEY EQUESTRIAN CTRE
YH02880
£14.00 for 30 minutes (one-to-one)

DALES VIEW RIDING CTRE
YH03831
£13.00 for 30 minutes (one-to-one)

DEANDANE RIDING STABLES
YH03998
£13.00 for 30 minutes (one-to-one)

GREEN BANK
YH06049
£14.00 for 30 minutes (one-to-one)

HERD HSE RIDING SCHOOL
YH06699
£12.00 for 30 minutes (adult)
£12.00 for 30 minutes (one-to-one)

HUSTEADS RIDING SCHOOL
YH07330
£15.00 for 30 minutes (one-to-one)

MOORVIEW
YH09782
£11.00 for 30 minutes (child)
£12.00 for 30 minutes (adult)

RIBBY HALL
YH11795
£15.00 for 30 minutes (one-to-one)
£22.00 for 60 minutes (one-to-one)

WHITEGATE FARM
YH15338
£12.00 for 30 minutes (one-to-one)

LEICESTERSHIRE

COSSINGTON
YH03354
£13.00 for 30 minutes (one-to-one)

P & G STABLES
YH10630
£12.00 for 30 minutes (one-to-one)

SCHOOL OF NATIONAL EQUITATION
YH12521
£14.25 for 30 minutes (one-to-one)

SOMERBY EQUESTRIAN CTRE
YH13060
£16.20 for 30 minutes (one-to-one)

SWAN LODGE
YH13689
£10.00 for 30 minutes (one-to-one)

WITHAM VILLA RIDING CTRE
YH15620
£18.00 for 30 minutes (one-to-one)

LINCOLNSHIRE

PADDOCKS RIDING CTRE
YH10675
£15.00 for 30 minutes (one-to-one)

POPPYFIELDS
YH11275
£15.00 for 30 minutes (one-to-one)

SHEEPGATE EQUESTRIAN
YH12696
£15.00 for 30 minutes (one-to-one)

LINCOLNSHIRE (NORTH EAST)

R G EQUESTRIAN
YH11536
£10.00 for 30 minutes (one-to-one)

LONDON (GREATER)

ABBEYFIELDS
YH00095
£11.00 for 30 minutes (child)
£14.00 for 30 minutes (adult)
£20.00 for 60 minutes (adult)

ALDERSBROOK RIDING SCHOOL
YH00257
£14.00 for 30 minutes (one-to-one)

BARNFIELDS
YH00986
£16.00 for 30 minutes (one-to-one)

CIVIL SV
YH02933
£23.00 for 30 minutes (one-to-one)

DRUMAWHEY
YH04285
£15.00 for 30 minutes (one-to-one)

GOULDS GREEN
YH05952
£17.50 for 30 minutes (one-to-one)

HYDE PARK STABLES
YH07346
£35.00 for 60 minutes (one-to-one)

ISSEA - GB
YH07527
£18.00 for 30 minutes (one-to-one)

LEE VALLEY RIDING CTRE
YH08519
£23.00 for 30 minutes (one-to-one)

LITTLEBOURNE FARM
YH08703
£20.00 for 60 minutes (child)
£25.00 for 60 minutes (adult)

LONDON EQUESTRIAN CTRE
YH08784
£19.00 for 30 minutes (one-to-one)

LONDON EQUESTRIAN CTRE
YH08785
£19.00 for 30 minutes (one-to-one)

MOTTINGHAM FARM
YH09876
£13.00 for 30 minutes (one-to-one)

NATURAL PARTNERSHIP
YH10053
£20.00 for 30 minutes (one-to-one)

RIDGWAY STABLES
YH11870
£17.00 for 30 minutes (one-to-one)
£34.00 for 60 minutes (one-to-one)

SUZANNE'S RIDING SCHOOL
YH13679
£17.00 for 30 minutes (one-to-one)

WILLOW TREE RIDING
YH15504
£14.50 for 30 minutes (one-to-one)

MANCHESTER (GREATER)

CARRINGTON RIDING
YH02589
£13.00 for 30 minutes (one-to-one)

EQUITACK
YH04823
£10.00 for 30 minutes (one-to-one)

GODLEY STUD RIDING SCHOOL
YH05868
£11.00 for 30 minutes (one-to-one)

OAKHILL RIDING SCHOOL
YH10384
£15.00 for 30 minutes (one-to-one)

RYDERS FARM
YH12297
£18.00 for 30 minutes (one-to-one)

STAMFORD RIDING STABLES
YH13354
£10.50 for 30 minutes (one-to-one)

MERSEYSIDE

BOWLERS RIDING SCHOOL
YH01716
£12.50 for 30 minutes (child)
£14.50 for 30 minutes (adult)
£14.50 for 30 minutes (one-to-one)

CROXTETH PK RIDING CTRE
YH03685
£13.50 for 30 minutes (one-to-one)

LONGACRES
YH08806
£14.50 for 30 minutes (one-to-one)

PARK LANE LIVERIES
YH10730
£12.00 for 30 minutes (child)
£13.00 for 30 minutes (adult)
£13.00 for 30 minutes (one-to-one)

TARBOCK GREEN RIDING SCHOOL
YH13869
£12.50 for 30 minutes (adult)
£25.00 for 60 minutes (one-to-one)

MIDLANDS (WEST)

BEARLEY CROSS STABLES
YH01121
£12.00 for 30 minutes (one-to-one)

BUBBENHALL BRIDGE
YH02182
£13.00 for 30 minutes (one-to-one)

FOXHILLS
YH05435
£14.00 for 30 minutes (adult)

TRUEMANS HEATH
YH14420
£13.00 for 30 minutes (one-to-one)

WITHYBROOK STABLES
YH15629
£20.00 for 60 minutes (adult)

NORFOLK

CROFT FARM RIDING CTRE
YH03615
£13.00 for 30 minutes (one-to-one)

GREENACRES RIDING SCHOOL
YH06079
£15.00 for 30 minutes (one-to-one)

MAYWAY
YH09308
£20.00 for 60 minutes (one-to-one)

RUNCTON HALL
YH12233
£11.50 for 30 minutes (one-to-one)

WESTON PARK EQUESTRIAN CTRE
YH15224
£17.50 for 30 minutes (one-to-one)

NORTHAMPTONSHIRE

BOUGHTON MILL RIDING SCHOOL
YH01669
£10.00 for 30 minutes (one-to-one)

HARRINGWORTH MANOR
YH06461
£12.00 for 30 minutes (one-to-one)

MANOR FARM RIDING SCHOOL
YH09106
£16.50 for 30 minutes (one-to-one)

NORTHUMBERLAND

REDESDALE RIDING CTRE
YH11710
£13.00 for 30 minutes (one-to-one)

SINDERHOPE PONY TREKKING CTRE
YH12850
£10.00 for 30 minutes (one-to-one)

WOOPERTON
YH15770
£15.00 for 30 minutes (one-to-one)

NOTTINGHAMSHIRE

CLGE FARM
YH03026
£12.50 for 30 minutes (one-to-one)

CTRE - LINES
YH03694
£18.00 for 30 minutes (one-to-one)

LANEHAM LIVERY STABLE
YH08392
£15.00 for 30 minutes (one-to-one)

OXFORDSHIRE

GODINGTON STUD
YH05867
£20.00 for 30 minutes (one-to-one)

PIGEON HOUSE STABLES
YH11095
£15.00 for 30 minutes (one-to-one)

STANDLAKE EQUESTRIAN CTRE
YH13362
£15.00 for 30 minutes (one-to-one)

TURPINS LODGE
YH14494
£22.00 for 30 minutes (one-to-one)

RUTLAND

BARROW STABLES
YH01030
£12.50 for 30 minutes (one-to-one)

SCURRY DRIVING ASSOCIATION
YH12578
£20.00 for 30 minutes (one-to-one)

SHROPSHIRE

FRESHFIELDS
YH05499
£14.00 for 30 minutes (one-to-one)

HIGHGROVE SCHOOL OF RIDING
YH06788
£10.00 for 30 minutes (one-to-one)

OSWESTRY EQUEST CTRE
YH10576
£12.00 for 30 minutes (one-to-one)

SOMERSET

ADSBOROUGH HSE STABLES
YH00189
£12.00 for 30 minutes (one-to-one)

BRIMSMORE EQUESTRIAN CTRE
YH01913
£11.00 for 30 minutes (child)
£12.00 for 30 minutes (adult)

BURCOTT RIDING CTRE
YH02236
£12.00 for 30 minutes (adult)

EBBORLANDS
YH04529
£10.00 for 30 minutes (one-to-one)

KNOWLE MANOR
YH08281
£10.00 for 30 minutes (one-to-one)

PEVLINGS FARM
YH11035
£11.50 for 30 minutes (one-to-one)

SOMERSET (NORTH)

CLEVEDON RIDING
YH03020
£15.00 for 30 minutes (child)
£18.00 for 30 minutes (adult)

MENDIP RIDING CTRE
YH09458
£10.50 for 30 minutes (one-to-one)

STAFFORDSHIRE

DOBBINS DINER
YH04151
£15.00 for 30 minutes (one-to-one)

RODBASTON CLGE
YH12041
£20.00 for 30 minutes (one-to-one)

SCROPTON
YH12569
£15.00 for 30 minutes (one-to-one)

SUFFOLK

BENTLEY RIDING CTRE
YH01286
£13.00 for 30 minutes (one-to-one)
£25.00 for 60 minutes (one-to-one)

CULFORD STABLES
YH03701
£11.00 for 30 minutes (one-to-one)

ORWELL ARENA
YH10556
£10.00 for 30 minutes (one-to-one)

POPLAR PK
YH11271
£20.00 for 30 minutes (one-to-one)

STOKE BY CLARE EQUESTRIAN CTRE
YH13501
£15.00 for 30 minutes (one-to-one)

VALLEY FARM
YH14651
£16.00 for 30 minutes (one-to-one)

SURREY

BRIDLEWAYS EQUESTRIAN CTRE
YH01898
£20.00 for 30 minutes (one-to-one)

BURSTOW PK
YH02286
£16.00 for 30 minutes (one-to-one)

CRANLEIGH SCHOOL OF RIDING
YH03565
£13.50 for 30 minutes (one-to-one)

DORKING EQUESTRIAN CTRE
YH04200
£23.00 for 30 minutes (one-to-one)

EBBISHAM FARM
YH04528
£18.00 for 30 minutes (one-to-one)

GREEN LANE STABLES
YH06058
£23.50 for 30 minutes (one-to-one)

RIDING CTRE
YH11873
£15.00 for 30 minutes (one-to-one)

S R S
YH12333
£20.00 for 30 minutes (one-to-one)

TANDRIDGE PRIORY
YH13853
£11.00 for 30 minutes (one-to-one)

SUSSEX (EAST)

HAMSEY RIDING SCHOOL
YH06371
£13.00 for 30 minutes (one-to-one)

SOUTH LODGE
YH13100
£12.00 for 30 minutes (child)

SUSSEX (WEST)

LAVANT HSE STABLES
YH08460
£20.00 for 30 minutes (one-to-one)

WILLOWBROOK RIDING CTRE
YH15508
£11.50 for 30 minutes (one-to-one)

ZARA STUD
YH15951
£15.00 for 30 minutes (one-to-one)

TYNE AND WEAR

LITTLE HARLE STABLES
YH08688
£15.00 for 30 minutes (one-to-one)

QUARRY PARK STABLES
YH11483
£15.00 for 30 minutes (one-to-one)

WARWICKSHIRE

CALDECOTE RIDING SCHOOL
YH02428
£11.50 for 30 minutes (one-to-one)

WAVERLEY EQUESTRIAN CTRE
YH15011
£16.00 for 30 minutes (one-to-one)

WOOTTON GRANGE EQUESTRIAN
YH15772
£15.00 for 30 minutes (one-to-one)

WILTSHIRE

HORSEMANSHIP
YH07161
£15.00 for 30 minutes (one-to-one)

INFANTRY SADDLE CLUB
YH07441
£15.00 for 30 minutes (one-to-one)

MALTHOUSE EQUESTRIAN CTRE
YH09058
£15.00 for 30 minutes (one-to-one)

MARLBOROUGH DOWNS
YH09169
£30.00 for 60 minutes (adult)

WHITE HORSE EQUESTRIAN CTRE
YH15308
£15.00 for 30 minutes (one-to-one)

WIDBROOK ARABIAN STUD
YH15388
£15.00 for 30 minutes (one-to-one)

WORCESTERSHIRE

CARENZA, JILL
YH02534
£10.00 for 30 minutes (child)
£30.00 for 60 minutes (adult)

HALLOW MILLS
YH06333
£10.00 for 30 minutes (adult)

HEID & BRAZIER
YH06648
£12.50 for 30 minutes (one-to-one)

KYRE EQUESTRIAN CTRE
YH08305
£15.00 for 30 minutes (one-to-one)

MOYFIELD RIDING SCHOOL
YH09908
£12.00 for 30 minutes (one-to-one)

WALNUT STABLES
YH14870
£12.00 for 30 minutes (one-to-one)

YORKSHIRE (NORTH)

BLEACH FARM
YH01530
£21.00 for 60 minutes (one-to-one)

BOGS HALL
YH01598
£10.00 for 30 minutes (one-to-one)

BRIGG VIEW
YH01906
£15.00 for 30 minutes (one-to-one)

JODHPURS
YH07774
£14.00 for 30 minutes (child)
£16.00 for 30 minutes (adult)

MILL LANE
YH09579
£10.00 for 30 minutes (one-to-one)

MOORHOUSE RIDING CTRE
YH09776
£12.00 for 30 minutes (one-to-one)

NABURN GRANGE RIDING CTRE
YH10008
£15.00 for 30 minutes (child)
£20.00 for 30 minutes (adult)

RIDING CTRE
YH11874
£23.00 for 30 minutes (one-to-one)

YORKSHIRE DALES
YH15919
£15.00 for 30 minutes (one-to-one)

YORKSHIRE (SOUTH)

BARNES GREEN
YH00971
£12.00 for 30 minutes (one-to-one)
£20.00 for 60 minutes (one-to-one)

GROVE HOUSE
YH06168
£10.00 for 30 minutes (child)
£11.00 for 30 minutes (adult)

MALLARD HSE
YH09050
£11.00 for 30 minutes (child)
£12.00 for 30 minutes (adult)

YORKSHIRE (WEST)

ADEL WOOD
YH00182
£14.00 for 30 minutes (adult)
£24.00 for 60 minutes (adult)

BANK HSE FARM
YH00891
£15.00 for 30 minutes (one-to-one)

BLACUP TRAINING GRP
YH01504
£12.00 for 30 minutes (one-to-one)

NORLAND EQUESTRIAN CTRE
YH10234
£13.00 for 30 minutes (one-to-one)

TIMBERTOPS EQUESTRIAN CTRE
YH14162
£30.00 for 60 minutes (one-to-one)

WHITLEY EQUITATION CTRE
YH15363
£10.00 for 30 minutes (child)
£12.00 for 30 minutes (adult)

UNDER £50

CUMBRIA

LAKELAND EQUESTRIAN
YH08354
£28.00 for 30 minutes (one-to-one)

DEVON

WHITE TOR
YH15325
£25.00 for 30 minutes (one-to-one)

HAMPSHIRE

HOPLANDS EQUESTRIAN
YH07058
£25.00 for 30 minutes (one-to-one)

RYCROFT SCHOOL OF EQUITATION
YH12291
£30.00 for 30 minutes (adult)

HERTFORDSHIRE

COURTLANDS
YH03507
£25.00 for 30 minutes (one-to-one)

LANCASHIRE

PANAMA SPORT HORSES
YH10695
£25.00 for 30 minutes (one-to-one)

LINCOLNSHIRE

UFFINGTON RIDING STABLES
YH14540
£25.00 for 30 minutes (one-to-one)

LONDON (GREATER)

KENSINGTON STABLES
YH08078
£55.00 for 60 minutes (one-to-one)

SUFFOLK

BARDWELL MANOR
YH00928
£25.00 for 30 minutes (one-to-one)

SURREY

CHESSINGTON
YH02830
£25.00 for 30 minutes (one-to-one)

ORCHARD COTTAGE
YH10527
£31.00 for 30 minutes (one-to-one)

WOODSTOCK SOUTH STABLES
YH15751
£25.00 for 30 minutes (one-to-one)

WILTSHIRE

HAMPSLEY HOLLOW
YH06368
£25.00 for 30 minutes (one-to-one)

UNDER £75

SURREY

ASCOT PARK
YH00583
£50.00 for 30 minutes (one-to-one)

IRELAND

UNDER £10

COUNTY CLARE

BANNER EQUESTRIAN
YH00906
£7.00 for 30 minutes (child)

COUNTY DUBLIN

BROOKE LODGE
YH02042
£11.00 for 60 minutes (child)
£12.00 for 60 minutes (adult)

COUNTY MEATH

BLACKHALL EQUESTRIAN CTRE
YH01483
£9.50 for 30 minutes (child)

COUNTY TIPPERARY

CAHIR EQUESTRIAN CTRE
YH02416
£15.24 for 60 minutes (child)
£19.05 for 60 minutes (adult)

UNDER £25

COUNTY CAVAN

REDHILLS EQUESTRIAN
YH11713
£10.50 for 30 minutes (one-to-one)

COUNTY CLARE

BANNER EQUESTRIAN
YH00906
£10.00 for 30 minutes (adult)

COUNTY DUBLIN

CALLIAGHSTOWN EQUESTRIAN
YH02449
£10.00 for 30 minutes (child)
£15.00 for 30 minutes (adult)

RATHFARNHAN EQUESTRIAN CTRE
YH11655
£25.00 for 60 minutes (one-to-one)

COUNTY KERRY

ABBEYGLEN
YH00097
£15.00 for 30 minutes (one-to-one)

COUNTY LIMERICK

ADARE EQUESTRIAN CTRE
YH00175
£12.00 for 30 minutes (one-to-one)

COUNTY MEATH

BLACKHALL EQUESTRIAN CTRE
YH01483
£11.50 for 30 minutes (adult)

COUNTY TIPPERARY

CLONMEL EQUESTRIAN CTRE
YH03057
£15.00 for 30 minutes (child)
£20.00 for 30 minutes (adult)

UNDER £50

COUNTY WICKLOW

BEL-AIR HOTEL & EQUESTRIAN
YH01202
£35.00 for 30 minutes (one-to-one)

NORTHERN IRELAND

UNDER £10

COUNTY ANTRIM

GALGORM PARKS RIDING SCHOOL
YH05615
£7.00 for 60 minutes (one-to-one)

COUNTY ARMAGH

LIME PARK EQUESTRIAN
YH08626
£16.00 for 60 minutes (child)

COUNTY DOWN

GRANSHA EQUESTRIAN CTRE
YH06007
£10.00 for 60 minutes (child)
£10.00 for 60 minutes (adult)

LESSANS RIDING STABLES
YH08561
£9.00 for 60 minutes (child)
£10.00 for 60 minutes (adult)

COUNTY LONDONDERRY

ARDMORE STABLES
YH00511
£7.00 for 60 minutes (child)
£8.00 for 60 minutes (adult)

FAUGHANVALE STABLES
YH05102
£8.00 for 60 minutes (child)
£9.00 for 60 minutes (adult)

HILL FARM RIDING CTRE
YH06814
£12.00 for 60 minutes (one-to-one)

ISLAND EQUESTRIAN CTRE
YH07520
£10.00 for 60 minutes (child)

MARSH KYFE RIDING SCHOOL
YH09186
£10.00 for 60 minutes (one-to-one)

COUNTY TYRONE

EDERGOLE RIDING CTRE
YH04553
£10.00 for 60 minutes (one-to-one)

MOY RIDING SCHOOL
YH09907
£15.00 for 60 minutes (adult)
£15.00 for 60 minutes (child)

TULLYWHISKER RIDING SCHOOL
YH14458
£7.00 for 30 minutes (adult)
£7.00 for 30 minutes (child)
£7.00 for 30 minutes (one-to-one)

UNDER £25

COUNTY ANTRIM

BURN EQUESTRIAN CLUB
YH02263
£14.50 for 30 minutes (one-to-one)

COUNTY ARMAGH

LIME PARK EQUESTRIAN
YH08626
£20.00 for 60 minutes (adult)

COUNTY DOWN

LESSANS RIDING STABLES
YH08561
£20.00 for 60 minutes (one-to-one)

MILLBRIDGE RIDING CTRE
YH09594
£30.00 for 60 minutes (adult)

COUNTY TYRONE

MOY RIDING SCHOOL
YH09907
£10.00 for 30 minutes (child)
£10.00 for 30 minutes (adult)

UNDER £10

ANGUS

KIRRIEMUIR HORSE SUPPLIES
YH08240
£8.50 for 30 minutes (one-to-one)

PATHHEAD STABLES
YH10821
£8.50 for 30 minutes (one-to-one)

AYRSHIRE (NORTH)

CAIRNHOUSE RIDING CTRE
YH02419
£7.50 for 30 minutes (one-to-one)

TANDLEVIEW STABLES
YH13852
£16.00 for 60 minutes (one-to-one)

EDINBURGH (CITY OF)

TOWER FARM
YH14271
£17.50 for 60 minutes (one-to-one)

FIFE

ANGLE PARK
YH00409
£8.00 for 30 minutes (one-to-one)

LOTHIAN (WEST)

HOLMES RIDING STABLES
YH06973
£9.00 for 30 minutes (one-to-one)

SCOTTISH BORDERS

BAILEY MILL
YH00794
£9.00 for 30 minutes (one-to-one)

FERNIEHIRST MILL RIDING CTRE
YH05167
£7.50 for 30 minutes (one-to-one)

UNDER £25

ABERDEENSHIRE

EDEN EQUESTRIAN CTRE
YH04546
£10.00 for 30 minutes (one-to-one)

ARGYLL AND BUTE

APPALOOSA HOLIDAYS
YH00475
£17.00 for 30 minutes (one-to-one)

COLGRAIN EQUESTRIAN CTRE
YH03170
£12.00 for 30 minutes (one-to-one)

AYRSHIRE (EAST)

BARGOWER RIDING SCHOOL
YH00933
£15.00 for 30 minutes (one-to-one)

DEAN CASTLE RIDING CTRE
YH03988
£15.00 for 30 minutes (one-to-one)

ROWALLAN ACTIVITY CTRE
YH12152
£15.00 for 30 minutes (one-to-one)

AYRSHIRE (NORTH)

BROOM FARM RIDING SCHOOL
YH02071
£10.00 for 30 minutes (one-to-one)

AYRSHIRE (SOUTH)

ROSEMOUNT RIDING SVS
YH12105
£11.75 for 30 minutes (one-to-one)

SHANTER RIDING CTRE
YH12672
£10.00 for 30 minutes (one-to-one)

CLACKMANNANSHIRE

DEVON EQUESTRIAN
YH04094
£12.00 for 30 minutes (one-to-one)
£22.00 for 60 minutes (one-to-one)

FIFE

BRAESIDE
YH01772
£25.00 for 60 minutes (one-to-one)

RIDING STABLES
YH11883
£15.00 for 30 minutes (one-to-one)

GLASGOW (CITY OF)

BUSBY EQUITATION CTRE
YH02302
£16.00 for 30 minutes (one-to-one)

EASTERTON STABLES
YH04501
£12.00 for 30 minutes (one-to-one)

WOODEND
YH15684
£12.00 for 30 minutes (one-to-one)

HIGHLANDS

HIGHLAND RIDING CTRE
YH06793
£17.50 for 30 minutes (one-to-one)

LOCH NESS RIDING
YH08752
£15.00 for 30 minutes (one-to-one)

LOGIE FARM
YH08778
£22.00 for 30 minutes (one-to-one)

INVERCLYDE

ARDGOWAN
YH00507
£12.00 for 30 minutes (one-to-one)

ISLE OF SKYE

SKYE RIDING CTRE
YH12881
£15.00 for 30 minutes (one-to-one)

LANARKSHIRE (SOUTH)

HILLHEAD
YH06846
£10.00 for 30 minutes (one-to-one)

JUMPS
YH07967
£15.00 for 30 minutes (one-to-one)

MID DRUMLOCH
YH09526
£12.00 for 30 minutes (one-to-one)

LOTHIAN (EAST)

APPIN EQUESTRIAN CTRE
YH00478
£18.50 for 30 minutes (one-to-one)

HARELAW EQUESTRIAN CTRE
YH06420
£10.00 for 30 minutes (one-to-one)

LOTHIAN (MID)

EASTER BUSH VETNRY CTRE
YH04490
£15.00 for 30 minutes (one-to-one)

EDINBURGH & LASSWADE
YH04559
£16.00 for 30 minutes (one-to-one)

LOTHIAN (WEST)

GRANGE RIDING CTRE
YH05993
£17.00 for 30 minutes (one-to-one)

HOUSTON FARM RIDING SCHOOL
YH07212
£14.50 for 30 minutes (one-to-one)

MORAY

SHENVAL FARM
YH12709
£10.00 for 30 minutes (one-to-one)

PERTH AND KINROSS

EQUI-CARE
YH04736
£16.00 for 30 minutes (one-to-one)

GLENMARKIE
YH05840
£13.00 for 30 minutes (one-to-one)
£23.00 for 60 minutes (one-to-one)

RENFREWSHIRE

MEADOW PK
YH09421
£13.00 for 30 minutes (one-to-one)

SCOTTISH BORDERS

WESTERTOUN
YH15212
£10.00 for 30 minutes (one-to-one)

UNDER £10

CARMARTHENSHIRE

CWMTYDU RIDING STABLES
YH03764
£10.00 for 60 minutes (adult)
£10.00 for 60 minutes (child)

STARLIGHT RIDING CTRE
YH13396
£10.00 for 60 minutes (child)
£10.00 for 60 minutes (adult)

CEREDIGION

DYFED RIDING CTRE
YH04388
£17.00 for 60 minutes (one-to-one)

ISLE OF ANGLESEY

LLANDDONA
YH08720
£8.00 for 30 minutes (one-to-one)
£12.00 for 60 minutes (one-to-one)

NEWPORT

SPRINGFIELD RIDING STABLES
YH13256
£9.00 for 60 minutes (child)

PEMBROKESHIRE

CROSSWELL
YH03669
£4.00 for 30 minutes (one-to-one)

DOLRHANOG RIDING CTRE
YH04171
£7.00 for 30 minutes (one-to-one)

LLANWNDA STABLES
YH08727
£6.00 for 30 minutes (one-to-one)

OASIS PARK EQUESTRIAN CTRE
YH10412
£6.00 for 30 minutes (one-to-one)
£12.00 for 60 minutes (one-to-one)

POWYS

LLANGORSE RIDING
YH08725
£9.00 for 30 minutes (one-to-one)

UNDERHILL RIDING STABLES
YH14560
£9.00 for 60 minutes (adult)
£9.00 for 60 minutes (child)

SWANSEA

GREEN FARM
YH06054
£8.00 for 30 minutes (one-to-one)

UNDER £25

BRIDGEND

E K M EQUESTRIAN
YH04411
£13.00 for 30 minutes (one-to-one)

CAERPHILLY

ROCKWOOD RIDING CTRE
YH12039
£11.50 for 30 minutes (one-to-one)

CARMARTHENSHIRE

PENCADER STUD
YH10928
£20.00 for 30 minutes (one-to-one)

CEREDIGION

MOELFRYN RIDING CTRE
YH09699
£10.00 for 30 minutes (one-to-one)

RHEIDOL RIDING CTRE
YH11784
£10.00 for 30 minutes (one-to-one)

DENBIGHSHIRE

LLANNERCH EQUESTRIAN CTRE
YH08726
£14.00 for 30 minutes (one-to-one)

GLAMORGAN (VALE OF)

LIEGE MANOR
YH08609
£18.00 for 30 minutes (child)

GWYNEDD

RHIWIAU RIDING CTRE
YH11788
£12.00 for 30 minutes (one-to-one)

SNOWDONIA RIDING STABLES
YH13041
£10.00 for 30 minutes (one-to-one)

ISLE OF ANGLESEY

TAL Y FOEL RIDING CTRE
YH13829
£12.50 for 30 minutes (one-to-one)

TYN-MORFA RIDING CTRE
YH14529
£10.00 for 30 minutes (one-to-one)

PEMBROKESHIRE

DUNES RIDING
YH04342
£10.00 for 30 minutes (one-to-one)

POWYS

BROMPTON HALL
YH02025
£15.00 for 30 minutes (one-to-one)

CANTREF
YH02516
£10.00 for 30 minutes (one-to-one)

RIVERSIDE RIDING CTRE
YH11927
£12.00 for 30 minutes (one-to-one)

RHONDDA CYNON TAFF

TALYGARN
YH13846
£12.00 for 30 minutes (one-to-one)

SWANSEA

COPLEY
YH03297
£13.50 for 30 minutes (one-to-one)

FORGEMILL
YH05368
£16.50 for 30 minutes (one-to-one)

PENTRE RIDING STABLES
YH10962
£10.00 for 30 minutes (one-to-one)

WREXHAM

CHAPEL FARM
YH02738
£12.00 for 30 minutes (one-to-one)

EQUESTRIAN CTRE
YH04697
£16.00 for 30 minutes (one-to-one)

UNDER £50

GLAMORGAN (VALE OF)

LIEGE MANOR
YH08609
£25.00 for 30 minutes (one-to-one)

SECTION 3B

Livery Prices by Weekly Rate

This section helps you to locate a business by Country, by County within the Livery Price range.

Livery Prices are grouped by weekly rates. The type of livery is also listed, stating whether it is full, part or DIY.

e.g. **England, Under £25, Norfolk: Fritton Lake £10.00 for DIY**

Once you have located a business using this section you can then refer to the company's detailed profile in Section 1.

ENGLAND

UNDER £25

CHESHIRE

GRANGE LIVERY STABLES
YH05991
£21.50 for DIY

CORNWALL

SNOWLAND RIDING CTRE
YH13045
£10.00 for DIY

COUNTY DURHAM

DARLINGTON EQUESTRIAN CTRE
YH03893
£15.00 for DIY

LOW MEADOWS FARM LIVERY
YH08856
£16.00 for DIY

NEWSTEAD RIDING CTRE
YH10166
£20.00 for DIY

CUMBRIA

GREENLANDS LIVERY STABLES
YH06092
£20.00 for DIY

RYDAL MOUNT LIVERY STABLES
YH12293
£12.00 for DIY

ESSEX

BIRKETT HALL LIVERY STABLE
YH01441
£20.00 for DIY

COUNTRY PADDOCKS
YH03419
£22.75 for DIY

KEDDIE FARM
YH08022
£12.00 for DIY

MOOR END LIVERY YARD
YH09741
£22.50 for DIY

GLOUCESTERSHIRE (SOUTH)

TUDOR FARM LIVERY STABLES
YH14439
£15.00 for DIY

HAMPSHIRE

COCKSCOMBE FARM LIVERY
YH03129
£20.00 for DIY

NEW PARK HOTEL
YH10115
£20.00 for DIY

KENT

STIDOLPH'S LIVERY
YH13465
£20.00 for DIY

LANCASHIRE

CALICO LIVERY STABLES
YH02444
£13.50 for DIY

CHARITY FARM LIVERY STABLES
YH02751
£16.00 for DIY

MAXY HOUSE FARM LIVERY
YH09286
£22.50 for DIY

LINCOLNSHIRE

EAGLE HALL EST
YH04437
£20.00 for DIY

MANCHESTER (GREATER)

GODLEY STUD RIDING SCHOOL
YH05868
£13.00 for DIY

KENYON FARM RIDING CTRE
YH08094
£17.50 for DIY

MIDDLEWOOD LIVERY STABLES
YH09548
£20.00 for DIY

SHORESIDE STABLES
YH12759
£11.00 for DIY

MERSEYSIDE

DEE FARM LIVERY STABLES
YH04014
£18.00 for DIY

THORNTON FARM LIVERY
YH14073
£20.00 for DIY

MIDLANDS (WEST)

MOOR FARM STABLES
YH09745
£20.00 for DIY

NORFOLK

CROSSWAYS LIVERY YARD
YH03666
£21.00 for DIY

DISS LIVERY CTRE
YH04132
£14.00 for DIY

FRITTON LAKE
YH05511
£10.00 for DIY

HILLCREST LIVERY CTRE
YH06842
£19.00 for DIY

NORTHAMPTONSHIRE

MANDI'S LIVERIES
YH09071
£14.00 for DIY

NOTTINGHAMSHIRE

LANEHAM LIVERY STABLE
YH08392
£15.00 for DIY

STAFFORDSHIRE

BARLASTON RIDING CTRE
YH00949
£20.00 for DIY

WARWICKSHIRE

RED HSE FARM LIVERY STABLES
YH11696
£20.00 for DIY

WILTSHIRE

HURDCOTT LIVERY STABLES
YH07311
£21.00 for DIY

SOUTH FARM LIVERY YARD
YH13092
£21.00 for DIY

YORKSHIRE (EAST)

BRAEMAR
YH01770
£15.00 for DIY

YORKSHIRE (NORTH)

STOCKWELL STUD LIVERY STABLES
YH13497
£24.00 for DIY

YORKSHIRE (WEST)

MOORSIDE EQUESTRIAN
YH09780
£21.00 for DIY

NEW HALL LIVERY YARD
YH02205
£20.00 for DIY

OWLET FARM LIVERY STABLES
YH10613
£17.00 for DIY

THREE ACRES LIVERY STABLES
YH14101
£16.00 for DIY

WOODLAND STABLES
YH15703
£13.00 for DIY

UNDER £50

BRISTOL

HICKS COMMON LIVERY STABLES
YH06743
£27.50 for DIY

CHESHIRE

HANNS HALL LIVERY
YH06396
£25.00 for DIY

CORNWALL

SNOWLAND RIDING CTRE
YH13045
£30.00 for Full

COUNTY DURHAM

DENE HEAD LIVERY
YH04042
£26.00 for DIY

CUMBRIA

LAKELAND EQUESTRIAN
YH08354
£45.00 for DIY

MIDDLE BAYLES LIVERY
YH09534
£45.00 for Part

HERTFORDSHIRE

ARKLEY LIVERY STABLES
YH00532
£25.00 for DIY

GROVE LIVERY STABLES
YH06171
£36.00 for DIY

KENT

HIGH ELMS LIVERY
YH06757
£40.00 for DIY

LINCOLNSHIRE

BUCKMINSTER LODGE
YH02203
£40.00 for Full

POPPYFIELDS
YH11275

£35.00 for Full

MERSEYSIDE

TARBOCK GREEN RIDING SCHOOL
YH13869
£30.00 for Full

NORFOLK

FERRY FARM LIVERY YARD
YH05172
£45.00 for Part

NORTHAMPTONSHIRE

MANDI'S LIVERIES
YH09071
£45.00 for Part

SOMERSET

BRIMSMORE EQUESTRIAN CTRE
YH01913
£25.00 for DIY

SOMERSET (NORTH)

CLEVEDON RIDING
YH03020
£25.00 for DIY

STAFFORDSHIRE

MAPLES LIVERY YARD
YH09134
£45.00 for DIY

SUFFOLK

COUNTRY FARM LIVERY YARD
YH03405
£32.50 for DIY

SURREY

BRILLS FARM
YH01911
£25.00 for DIY

WOODRUFF EQUESTRIAN
YH15731
£25.00 for DIY

SUSSEX (WEST)

PATCHING LIVERY YARD
YH10816
£25.00 for DIY

WORCESTERSHIRE

BENT, BM & SA
YH01282
£40.00 for DIY

YORKSHIRE (NORTH)

MILL LANE
YH09579
£45.00 for Full

YORKSHIRE (WEST)

BROOKFIELDS LIVERY STABLES
YH02053
£38.00 for Part

GARFORTH LIVERY YARD
YH05651
£25.00 for DIY

HALLAS LANE LIVERY STABLES
YH06327
£25.00 for DIY
£45.00 for Part

THREE ACRES LIVERY STABLES
YH14101
£40.00 for Full

UNDER £75

CHESHIRE

DINGLE BROOK FARM STABLES
YH04125
£60.00 for Part

COUNTY DURHAM

DENE HEAD LIVERY
YH04042
£55.00 for Full

CUMBRIA

GREENLANDS LIVERY STABLES
YH06092
£70.00 for Full

LAKELAND EQUESTRIAN
YH08354
£65.00 for Full

MIDDLE BAYLES LIVERY
YH09534
£60.00 for Full

ESSEX

MOOR END LIVERY YARD
YH09741
£65.00 for Part

NIGHTINGALE RIDING SCHOOL
YH10204
£55.00 for Part
£70.00 for Full

VALLEY RIDING/LIVERY STABLES
YH14657
£60.00 for Full

HAMPSHIRE

NEW PARK HOTEL
YH10115
£55.00 for Part

KENT

BIRCHES LIVERY STABLES
YH01433
£55.00 for Full

HIGH ELMS LIVERY
YH06757
£58.00 for Part
£72.00 for Full

LINCOLNSHIRE

EAGLE HALL EST
YH04437
£52.00 for Part

MERSEYSIDE

RABY HOUSE STABLES
YH11571
£55.00 for Part

MIDLANDS (WEST)

BUBBENHALL BRIDGE
YH02182
£57.50 for Part

WITHYBROOK STABLES
YH15629
£70.00 for Full

NORFOLK

FERRY FARM LIVERY YARD
YH05172
£60.00 for Full

NORTHAMPTONSHIRE

EAST LODGE FARM RIDING EST
YH04479
£60.00 for Part

MANDI'S LIVERIES
YH09071
£70.00 for Full

NOTTINGHAMSHIRE

LANEHAM LIVERY STABLE
YH08392
£70.00 for Full

STAFFORDSHIRE

MAPLES LIVERY YARD
YH09134
£55.00 for Part
£65.00 for Full

SUFFOLK

BARDWELL MANOR
YH00928
£63.00 for Full

COUNTRY FARM LIVERY YARD
YH03405
£50.00 for Part

SURREY

OVERHILL LIVERY STABLES
YH10592
£67.00 for Full

WOOLFORDS FARM LIVERY STABLES
YH15767
£58.00 for DIY

WILTSHIRE

HURDCOTT LIVERY STABLES
YH07311
£60.00 for Part

MARDEN GRANGE LIVERY STABLES
YH09145
£55.00 for Part
£70.00 for Full

WORCESTERSHIRE

ABBOTTS MORTON LIVERY YARD
YH00115
£55.00 for Part

SEVERN VALLEY LIVERY CTRE
YH12645
£55.00 for Full

YORKSHIRE (EAST)

BRAEMAR
YH01770
£53.00 for Full

YORKSHIRE (NORTH)

COTTAGE FARM STABLES
YH03375
£50.00 for Full

YORKSHIRE (WEST)

BROOKFIELDS LIVERY STABLES
YH02053
£58.00 for Full

GARFORTH LIVERY YARD
YH05651
£50.00 for Part

MOORSIDE EQUESTRIAN
YH09780
£66.00 for Full

NEW HALL LIVERY YARD
YH02205
£55.00 for Part

£75 AND ABOVE

CHESHIRE

DINGLE BROOK FARM STABLES
YH04125
£80.00 for Full

GRANGE LIVERY STABLES
YH05991
£80.00 for Full

DORSET

CUCKOO HILL LIVERY CTRE
YH03698
£95.00 for Full

ESSEX

GILSTON LIVERY STABLES
YH05791
£75.00 for Part
£95.00 for Full

LITTLE PADDOCK
YH08698
£80.00 for Full

MOOR END LIVERY YARD
YH09741
£85.00 for Full

HAMPSHIRE

NEW PARK HOTEL
YH10115
£80.00 for Full

HERTFORDSHIRE

ARKLEY LIVERY STABLES
YH00532
£80.00 for Full
£120.00 for Part

LEASEY BRIDGE LIVERY STABLES
YH08502
£90.00 for Part
£120.00 for Full

KENT

COBHAM MANOR
YH03113
£100.00 for Full

LANCASHIRE

CALICO LIVERY STABLES
YH02444
£95.00 for Full

LONDON (GREATER)

LEE VALLEY RIDING CTRE
YH08519
£82.00 for Part

MANCHESTER (GREATER)

MOSSBROOK ARENA & STUD
YH09866
£80.00 for Full

MERSEYSIDE

RABY HOUSE STABLES
YH11571
£80.00 for Full

THORNTON FARM LIVERY
YH14073
£85.00 for Full

NORTHAMPTONSHIRE

ASHTON STABLES
YH00614
£75.00 for Part
£110.00 for Full

EAST LODGE FARM RIDING EST
YH04479
£85.00 for Full

OXFORDSHIRE

ASTI STUD & SADDLERY
YH00633
£92.75 for Part
£112.00 for Full

SOMERSET

BADGWORTH ARENA
YH00781
£85.00 for Full

SURREY

ASCOT PARK
YH00583
£125.00 for Full

MANOR PK LIVERY STABLES
YH09116
£90.00 for Part
£95.00 for Full

WOOLFORDS FARM LIVERY STABLES
YH15767
£95.00 for Part

SUSSEX (WEST)

PATCHING LIVERY YARD
YH10816
£80.00 for Full

TYNE AND WEAR

LITTLE HARLE STABLES
YH08688
£80.00 for Full

WILTSHIRE

HURDCOTT LIVERY STABLES
YH07311
£90.00 for Full

WORCESTERSHIRE

BENT, BM & SA
YH01282
£80.00 for Part
£100.00 for Full

YORKSHIRE (EAST)

RISTON WHINS LIVERY YARD
YH11913
£100.00 for Full

YORKSHIRE (WEST)

GARFORTH LIVERY YARD
YH05651
£75.00 for Full

IRELAND

UNDER £75

COUNTY KILDARE

LEGGA LIVERY & SALES
YH08538
£63.55 for Full

NORTHERN IRELAND

UNDER £25

COUNTY DOWN

GRANSHA EQUESTRIAN CTRE
YH06007
£22.50 for DIY

LESSANS RIDING STABLES
YH08561
£20.00 for DIY

UNDER £50

COUNTY ANTRIM

LAGAN VALLEY EQUESTRIAN CTRE
YH08342
£48.00 for Full

COUNTY ARMAGH

BALLINTEGGART STUD
YH00860
£25.00 for DIY

LOUGHVIEW STABLES
YH08842
£35.00 for Part

COUNTY DOWN

LESSANS RIDING STABLES
YH08561
£25.00 for Part

COUNTY LONDONDERRY

HILL FARM RIDING CTRE
YH06814
£35.00 for Full

UNDER £75

COUNTY ARMAGH

LOUGHVIEW STABLES
YH08842
£50.00 for Full

COUNTY DOWN

GRANSHA EQUESTRIAN CTRE
YH06007
£65.00 for Full

LESSANS RIDING STABLES
YH08561
£50.00 for Full

MOUNT PLEASANT
YH09891
£60.00 for Full

WOOD LODGE STABLES
YH15659
£50.00 for Full

COUNTY LONDONDERRY

FAUGHANVALE STABLES
YH05102
£55.00 for Full

SPARKLING STUDS
YH13178
£50.00 for Full

SCOTLAND

UNDER £25

AYRSHIRE (EAST)

HARPERLAND LIVERY
YH06456
£15.00 for DIY

AYRSHIRE (SOUTH)

SHANTER RIDING CTRE
YH12672
£20.00 for DIY

HIGHLANDS

FOXHOLE LIVERY STABLE
YH05436
£14.00 for DIY

LANARKSHIRE (SOUTH)

MID DRUMLOCH
YH09526
£23.00 for DIY

LOTHIAN (EAST)

WEST FENTON LIVERY
YH15145
£20.00 for Part

UNDER £50

AYRSHIRE (SOUTH)

DRUMCOYLE LIVERY YARD
YH04289
£25.00 for DIY

ROSEMOUNT RIDING SVS
YH12105
£25.00 for DIY
£34.00 for Part

UNDER £75

AYRSHIRE (EAST)

BARGOWER RIDING SCHOOL
YH00933
£55.00 for Full

AYRSHIRE (SOUTH)

DRUMCOYLE LIVERY YARD
YH04289
£50.00 for Part

ROSEMOUNT RIDING SVS
YH12105
£58.00 for Full

LANARKSHIRE (SOUTH)

JUMPS
YH07967
£60.00 for Full

LOTHIAN (MID)

EDINBURGH EQUESTRIAN CTRE
YH04560
£70.00 for Full

LOTHIAN (WEST)

FERNIEHAUGH LIVERY STABLES
YH05166
£55.00 for Full

£75 AND ABOVE

LOTHIAN (MID)

COUSLAND PK FARM
YH03515
£77.00 for Full

PERTH AND KINROSS

GLEN EAGLES EQUESTRIAN
YH05825
£127.00 for Full

WALES

UNDER £25

CEREDIGION

MOELFRYN RIDING CTRE
YH09699
£10.00 for DIY

PEMBROKESHIRE

MOOR FARM RIDING STABLES
YH09744
£15.00 for DIY

SWANSEA

GREEN FARM
YH06054
£20.00 for Part

WAUN FAWR FARM
YH15010
£15.00 for DIY

UNDER £50

DENBIGHSHIRE

CLAREMONT EQUESTRIAN CTRE
YH02951
£33.00 for DIY

GLAMORGAN (VALE OF)

PEN-MAEN LIVERY YARD
YH10944
£25.00 for DIY

SWANSEA

PENTRE RIDING STABLES
YH10962
£35.00 for Full

SECTION 4A

Business Profile

This section allows you to search alphabetically for services related to equine breeding and wellbeing. Companies are listed by Country, by County.

The Business Profile can be used in two different ways. You can search by the particular service you require.

e.g. **Animal Behaviourist : Ambervale Farm**

Or, you can look at the profile of one particular company in order to see what service/s they offer.

e.g. **Equitack : Clipper Maintenance**

Once you have located a business using this section you can then refer to the company's detailed profile in Section 1.

Business Profile
Breeding and Wellbeing

by Country by County

	Ambulance Services	Animal Behaviourist	Artificial Insemination	Bloodstock Advice	Bloodstock Agency	Breaking In Horses	Breeding Advice	Chiropractics	Clipper Maintenance	Complementary Medicine	Dentistry Skills	Dust Control	Emergency Services	Farrier Services	Groom	Groom Services	Herbalists	Holistic Medicine	Homeopathy	Horse Ambulance	Horse Psychiatry	Horse Sitter	Horse Walker	Laser & Ultrasound	Nutritionists	Osteopathy	Physiotherapy	Respiratory Disease control	Shoe Fitting Skills	Solarium	Stud Services	Swimming Pool Centre	Trotting Services	Vaccination	Veterinary Labs	Veterinary Practice	Veterinary Skills
ENGLAND																																					
BATH & SOMERSET (NORTH EAST)																																					
BATH EQUESTRIAN CTRE, Bath (YH01070)														●																							
BONIFACE, IAN, Chew Magna (YH01623)														●																							
BUDD, EDWARDS & GLAS, Langport (YH02206)																																				●	
CURRY, COLIN J, Bath (YH03742)														●																							
EDDY WILLIAMSON & PARTNERS, Midsomer Norton (YH04544)																																				●	
FIRS VETNRY SURGERY, Bath (YH05227)																																				●	
FORD, NIGEL STEPHEN, Bath (YH05325)														●																							
GOLDEN VALLEY, Chew Magna (YH05880)																																				●	
KINCAID, CLAIRE, Bath (YH08165)																											●										
LOVE-JONES & KILLEN, Whitchurch (YH08846)																																				●	
PEPPARD, JOHN S J, Bath (YH10969)														●																							
SHEPPARD, CAWOOD & KINCAID, Midsomer Norton (YH12714)																																				●	
STATION RD VETNRY CLINIC, Bath (YH13403)																																				●	
THATCHER, G, Bath (YH13979)														●																							
WRENCH VETNRY GRP, Bath (YH15822)																																				●	
WRENCH VETNRY GRP, Bath (YH15821)																																				●	
YOUNG, M D, Bath (YH15936)														●																							
BEDFORDSHIRE																																					
ADELAIDE VETNRY CTRE, Sandy (YH00183)																																				●	
ANDERSON, SIMON H, Elstow (YH00387)														●																							
ARCADE SADDLERY BEDFORD, Bedford (YH00498)									●																												
ARK HSE VETNRY SURGERY, Leighton Buzzard (YH00528)																																				●	
BERGER, HANS, Haynes (YH01296)														●																							
BURGOYNE, ROBERT, Kempston (YH02252)														●																							
BURNS & WAKELY, Flitwick (YH02268)																																				●	
BURNS & WAKELY, Bedford (YH02267)																																				●	
COURTENAY, A L, Toddington (YH03503)														●																							
CROTHERS, BILLY, Leighton Buzzard (YH03673)														●																							
DRAPER, GARY, Chawston (YH04257)											●																										

Business Profile
Breeding and Wellbeing

by Country by County	Ambulance Services	Animal Behaviourist	Artificial Insemination	Bloodstock Advice	Bloodstock Agency	Breaking In Horses	Breeding Advice	Chiropractics	Clipper Maintenance	Complementary Medicine	Dentistry Skills	Dust Control	Emergency Services	Farrier Services	Groom	Groom Services	Herbalists	Holistic Medicine	Homeopathy	Horse Ambulance	Horse Psychiatry	Horse Sitter	Horse Walker	Laser & Ultrasound	Nutritionists	Osteopathy	Physiotherapy	Respiratory Disease control	Shoe Fitting Skills	Solarium	Stud Services	Swimming Pool Centre	Trotting Services	Vaccination	Veterinary Labs	Veterinary Practice	Veterinary Skills
GRAVENHURST, Bedford (YH06023)																									●												
HOME FIELD FARM, Dunstable (YH07001)														●		●							●														
ICKNIELD VETNRY GROUP, Luton (YH07384)																																				●	
ICKNIELD VETNRY GROUP, Dunstable (YH07383)																																				●	
KNIGHT, ADAM R, Radwell (YH08258)														●																							
MARTIN, KEVIN JAMES, Leighton Buzzard (YH09221)														●																							
MATTHEWS, STAX D, Luton (YH09277)														●																							
MCCARTIE, R, Bedford (YH09323)														●																							
METCALFE, DAVID, Dunstable (YH09500)					●																																
MOULTON, A L, Cardington (YH09887)														●																							
P W HARDING & MICHAEL NG, Leighton Buzzard (YH10659)																																				●	
PAPWORTH, H L, Biggleswade (YH10710)																																				●	
PLATT, ANGELA D, Flitwick (YH11168)														●																							
RYAN, THOMAS P, Keysoe (YH12287)														●																							
SALSA STUD, Chawston (YH12391)				●			●																								●						
SAUNDERS, BRIAN J, Biggleswade (YH12445)														●																							
SAUNDERS, NEIL J, Dunstable (YH12451)														●																							
SCOTT VETNRY CLINIC, Bedford (YH12534)																																				●	
SPRINGWELL VETNRY CLINIC, Dunstable (YH13264)																																				●	
SWALLOWFIELD STABLES, Dunstable (YH13687)														●		●																					
TAYLOR, C, Arlesey (YH13898)														●																							
TURNER, NIGEL D, Stanbridge (YH14489)														●																							
BERKSHIRE																																					
ADCOCK, DOMINIC R, Windsor (YH00178)														●																							
ALDERTON, BARRY D, Lambourn (YH00259)														●																							
BALDWYN, CHARLOTTE, Bray (YH00841)								●		●																●	●										
BEECHWOOD VETNRY CTRE, Reading (YH01179)																																				●	
BERESFORD BLOODSTOCK SERVICES, Binfield (YH01293)					●																																
BLOODHORSE INT, Hungerford (YH01547)				●	●																																
BLOOMFIELD, WARWICK J, Bracknell (YH01554)														●																							
BODDY, STEPHEN M, Hungerford (YH01594)														●																							
BOND, DAVID, Hungerford (YH01617)														●																							

Business Profile
Breeding and Wellbeing

by Country by County

	Ambulance Services	Animal Behaviourist	Artificial Insemination	Bloodstock Advice	Bloodstock Agency	Breaking In Horses	Breeding Advice	Chiropractics	Clipper Maintenance	Complementary Medicine	Dentistry Skills	Dust Control	Emergency Services	Farrier Services	Groom	Groom Services	Herbalists	Holistic Medicine	Homeopathy	Horse Ambulance	Horse Psychiatry	Horse Sitter	Horse Walker	Laser & Ultrasound	Nutritionists	Osteopathy	Physiotherapy	Respiratory Disease control	Shoe Fitting Skills	Solarium	Stud Services	Swimming Pool Centre	Trotting Services	Vaccination	Veterinary Labs	Veterinary Practice	Veterinary Skills
BRITISH BLOODSTOCK AGENCY, Hungerford (YH01928)					●																																
BUCK, IAN, Hungerford (YH02186)														●																							
BURGHFIELD VETNRY SURGERY, Reading (YH02248)																																				●	
CARTMELL, L A, Lambourn (YH02611)														●																							
CHAPEL FORGE, Hungerford (YH02740)														●															●								
CHARLES EGERTON BLOODSTOCK, Newbury (YH02755)					●																																
CHARLES, ANDREW JEREMY, Lambourn (YH02758)														●																							
CHECKENDON, Reading (YH02796)																																●					
COACH HSE VETNRY CLINIC, Newbury (YH03106)																																				●	
DENTON VETNRY SURGERY, Wokingham (YH04067)																																				●	
DUNN, P SCOTT, Wokingham (YH04352)																																				●	
EQUICENTRE, Waltham St Lawrence (YH04737)											●			●		●																					
EQUINE NUTRITION, Hungerford (YH04791)																									●												
FALKLAND VETNRY CLINIC, Newbury (YH05040)																																				●	
FOREST HOUSE VETNRY GRP, Windsor (YH05339)																																				●	
FOX, F A, Lambourn (YH05428)														●																							
GALBRAITH, KEEVILL & GLEESON, Thatcham (YH05609)																																				●	
GALBRAITH, KEEVILL & GLEESON, Newbury (YH05608)																																				●	
GATESMAN, NIGEL W, Reading (YH05675)														●																							
GIBBONS, PAUL M, Newbury (YH05741)														●																							
GORDIAN TROELLER BLOODSTOCK, Upper Bucklebury (YH05922)					●																																
GURDON, MELANIE, Newbury (YH06194)																											●										
HALFACRE, G W D, Bracknell (YH06297)														●																							
HALL & AST, Hungerford (YH06303)					●																															●	●
HALL PLACE VETNRY CTRE, Maidenhead (YH06309)																																				●	
HALLUM, DAVID J, Newbury (YH06335)														●																							
HARMAN, M W, Maidenhead (YH06442)														●																							
HIGHCLERE THOROUGHBRED RACING, Newbury (YH06775)					●																																
HILLSIDE STUD, Hungerford (YH06855)					●																																
HORSE BOX & TRAILER OWNERS, Newbury (YH07111)													●																								
JENKINS, LLOYD P, Windsor (YH07734)														●																							
KINANE, MICHAEL F, Bracknell (YH08164)														●																							

Business Profile
Breeding and Wellbeing

by Country by County	Ambulance Services	Animal Behaviourist	Artificial Insemination	Bloodstock Advice	Bloodstock Agency	Breaking In Horses	Breeding Advice	Chiropractics	Clipper Maintenance	Complementary Medicine	Dentistry Skills	Dust Control	Emergency Services	Farrier Services	Groom	Groom Services	Herbalists	Holistic Medicine	Homeopathy	Horse Ambulance	Horse Psychiatry	Horse Sitter	Horse Walker	Laser & Ultrasound	Nutritionists	Osteopathy	Physiotherapy	Respiratory Disease control	Shoe Fitting Skills	Solarium	Stud Services	Swimming Pool Centre	Trotting Services	Vaccination	Veterinary Labs	Veterinary Practice	Veterinary Skills
KING, STUART L, Hungerford (YH08188)														●																							
KNIGHT, K J, Wokingham (YH08262)														●																							
LAMBOURNE, JAMES, Newbury (YH08370)														●																							
LILLINGSTON BLOODSTOCK, Reading (YH08624)					●																																
M S F EQUINE, Newbury (YH08975)											●																										
MARKS, KELLY, Hungerford (YH09165)		●																			●																
MARSHALL, VICTORIA, Hungerford (YH09205)																											●										
MATTHEWS, DAVID J, Maidenhead (YH09272)														●																							
MAY, ROBIN PETER, Wokingham (YH09292)														●																							
MCCULLOCH, IAN WALKER, Reading (YH09340)														●																							
MUSCHAMP STUD, Slough (YH09974)			●																																		
NELSON, PETER, Reading (YH10075)					●																																
NINE MILE VETNRY HOSPITAL, Wokingham (YH10210)																																				●	
O'GORMAN, SLATER & MAIN, Thatcham (YH10439)																																				●	
O'GORMAN, SLATER & MAIN, Newbury (YH10438)																																			●	●	
PARK HSE STABLES, Newbury (YH10728)														●																							
PIROUET, TIMOTHY RYAN, Newbury (YH11150)														●																							
PORTER, JOHN, Hungerford (YH11282)						●																															
REID, NOEL A, Newbury (YH11744)														●																							
REILLY, VINCENT, Newbury (YH11747)														●																							
RIDGEWAY VETNRY GROUP, Lambourn (YH11867)																																				●	
ROBERTS, M & MARKS, K, Hungerford (YH11955)		●																																			
SAMPSONS, Newbury (YH12400)														●																							
SCOTT DUNN, ANN, Wokingham (YH12531)																											●										
SIDWELL, PAUL ALAN, Maidenhead (YH12790)														●																							
SIMMONS, BRYNLY A, Bracknell (YH12827)														●																							
SPILLER, GRAHAM, Reading (YH13205)														●																							
STACEY, DONALD A, Reading (YH13315)														●																							
STYLES, JAMES, Bracknell (YH13619)														●																							
SUMMERLEAZE VETNRY GROUP, Maidenhead (YH13635)																																				●	
TOWELL, MICHAEL JAMES, Lambourn (YH14270)														●																							
VALLEY EQUINE HOSPITAL, Hungerford (YH14649)																																				●	

Business Profile
Breeding and Wellbeing

by Country by County

	Ambulance Services	Animal Behaviourist	Artificial Insemination	Bloodstock Advice	Bloodstock Agency	Breaking In Horses	Breeding Advice	Chiropractics	Clipper Maintenance	Complementary Medicine	Dentistry Skills	Dust Control	Emergency Services	Farrier Services	Groom	Groom Services	Herbalists	Holistic Medicine	Homeopathy	Horse Ambulance	Horse Psychiatry	Horse Sitter	Horse Walker	Laser & Ultrasound	Nutritionists	Osteopathy	Physiotherapy	Respiratory Disease control	Shoe Fitting Skills	Solarium	Stud Services	Swimming Pool Centre	Trotting Services	Vaccination	Veterinary Labs	Veterinary Practice	Veterinary Skills
VALLEY VETNRY GROUP, Reading (YH14659)																																				●	
VETNRY CTRE, Twyford (YH14693)																																				●	
W H PONSONBY, Newbury (YH14774)					●																																
WHITBY, ALEXANDER J, Windsor (YH15296)														●																							
WIERSMA, HAITZE, Twyford (YH15395)														●																							
WILLIAMS, PAUL D, Reading (YH15469)														●																							
BRISTOL																																					
BALL, H M & A H, Bristol (YH00851)														●																							
C J HAWKINS & SON, Bristol (YH02376)														●																							
GARWAY HAFLINGERS, Bristol (YH05666)							●																								●						
GUNTER, T J, Bristol (YH06193)														●																							
HILLCREST FORGE, Bristol (YH06841)														●																							
LINDSAY, I, Bristol (YH08653)														●																							
LOVE-JONES & KILLEN, Bedminster (YH08847)																																				●	
SIMMONDS, LOUE, Bristol (YH12821)																											●										
SMITH, J S, Bristol (YH12964)														●																							
SOMERVILLE, JASON P, Shirehampton (YH13067)														●																							
STAITE, M G, Bristol (YH13349)														●																							
BUCKINGHAMSHIRE																																					
ANIMAL THERAPY, Aylesbury (YH00444)																											●										
ASLETT, G, High Wycombe (YH00623)														●																							
BELLINGDON END, Chesham (YH01238)									●																												
BETTISON, CARL, Aylesbury (YH01336)														●																							
CHEQUERS END EQUESTRIAN CTRE, High Wycombe (YH02812)						●																															
CHRISTIE, RUPERT W W, Marlow (YH02889)														●																							
CRAWFORD-BROWN, FIONA, Ludgershall (YH03577)										●																											
CRIGHTON, GJS & OLIVER, GA, Marlow (YH03598)														●																							
CROMPTON, JOHN, Chesham (YH03631)														●																							
CROOK, TRACY, High Wycombe (YH03636)								●																		●	●										
CRYER, ANDREW N, Marlow (YH03693)														●																							
EDWARDS, MARCUS L, Windsor (YH04584)														●																							
EQUICTRE, Marlow (YH04741)														●																							

Business Profile
Breeding and Wellbeing

by Country by County	Ambulance Services	Animal Behaviourist	Artificial Insemination	Bloodstock Advice	Bloodstock Agency	Breaking In Horses	Breeding Advice	Chiropractics	Clipper Maintenance	Complementary Medicine	Dentistry Skills	Dust Control	Emergency Services	Farrier Services	Groom	Groom Services	Herbalists	Holistic Medicine	Homeopathy	Horse Ambulance	Horse Psychiatry	Horse Sitter	Horse Walker	Laser & Ultrasound	Nutritionists	Osteopathy	Physiotherapy	Respiratory Disease control	Shoe Fitting Skills	Solarium	Stud Services	Swimming Pool Centre	Trotting Services	Vaccination	Veterinary Labs	Veterinary Practice	Veterinary Skills
EQUS HEALTH, Aylesbury (YH04835)										●									●																		
FEDDERN, T A, Milton Keynes (YH05119)			●																																	●	
FOSKETT, RUSSELL WILLIAM, Chesham (YH05394)														●																							
GREEN, DANA, Olney (YH06063)								●		●																●	●										
HALL, ALBERT J, Great Missenden (YH06311)														●																							
HEAD, SAMUEL C, Great Brickhill (YH06610)														●																							
HILLSDON, ROGER C, Marlow (YH06851)														●																							
HUSTON, G S, Chesham (YH07332)														●																							
JARMAN, KAREN, Buckingham (YH07702)								●																		●	●										
JENNINGS, JOHN R, Stokenchurch (YH07748)														●																							
LAWTHER, J R, Great Missenden (YH08480)														●																							
MYALL, AARON J, Milton Keynes (YH09979)														●																							
NIXON & MARSHALL, Buckingham (YH10216)																																				●	
PHILLIPS, TERENCE J, Lillingstone Dayrell (YH11066)														●																							
RECORD, NICHOLAS J, Amersham (YH11690)														●																							
ROONEY, KEVIN BARRY, Aylesbury (YH12077)														●																							
ROTHERAM, G, Aylesbury (YH12129)														●																							
ROTHERAM, H, Aylesbury (YH12130)														●																							
SPELLER, ANDREW E, Aylesbury (YH13195)														●																							
SPILLERS SPECIALITY FEEDS, Milton Keynes (YH13206)																									●												
TERRY, JOSEPH G, Chesham (YH13959)														●																							
VENN, OLIVER J, Aylesbury (YH14677)														●																							
WILL EDMEADES BLOODSTOCK, Great Horwood (YH15425)					●																																
YACOMINE, P J, Aylesbury (YH15880)														●																							
CAMBRIDGESHIRE																																					
ALDRETH VETNRY CTRE, Ely (YH00262)																																				●	
ANGLIA BLOODSTOCK, Ely (YH00412)					●																																
APACHE, Huntingdon (YH00473)		●						●		●								●	●		●			●	●	●	●										
ASHCROFT VETNRY SURGERY, Hardwick (YH00594)																																				●	
BARRATT, DAVID J, Haslingfield (YH01008)														●																							
BARTLETT, ROBERT S, Peterborough (YH01041)														●																							
BELGRAVE HSE VETNRY SURGERY, Linton (YH01211)																																				●	

Business Profile
Breeding and Wellbeing

by Country by County	Ambulance Services	Animal Behaviourist	Artificial Insemination	Bloodstock Advice	Bloodstock Agency	Breaking In Horses	Breeding Advice	Chiropractics	Clipper Maintenance	Complementary Medicine	Dentistry Skills	Dust Control	Emergency Services	Farrier Services	Groom	Groom Services	Herbalists	Holistic Medicine	Homeopathy	Horse Ambulance	Horse Psychiatry	Horse Sitter	Horse Walker	Laser & Ultrasound	Nutritionists	Osteopathy	Physiotherapy	Respiratory Disease control	Shoe Fitting Skills	Solarium	Stud Services	Swimming Pool Centre	Trotting Services	Vaccination	Veterinary Labs	Veterinary Practice	Veterinary Skills
BOND, CLIVE R, Ely (YH01616)														●																							
BOYLE, M S, Cambridge (YH01732)																																				●	
BROOK, PHILIP J, Ely (YH02040)														●																							
BROWN & PADDON, Wisbech (YH02090)																																				●	
BURGHLEY VETNRY CTRE, Peterborough (YH02249)																																				●	
C A J NICHOLAS, Peterborough (YH02362)																																				●	
DAVEY & DAVEY, Whittlesford (YH03912)																																				●	
DRIFTEND STABLES, Bourn (YH04274)														●																							
FLATTERS, B, Peterborough (YH05264)														●																							
FLUOROCARBON BLOODSTOCK, Ely (YH05290)					●																																
FRYER, LEWIS E, Huntingdon (YH05529)														●																							
GOWING, STEPHEN PETER, March (YH05956)														●																							
GREEN, PETER & TONG , MATTHEW, Huntingdon (YH06071)																																				●	
HACKETT, KEITH J, Huntingdon (YH06250)														●																							
HILL, STEPHEN J H, Huntingdon (YH06833)														●																							
HONES, MARK A, Burwell (YH07010)														●																							
HOOK HSE, March (YH07035)		●				●									●	●					●	●									●						
HOWE, DAVID J, Ely (YH07224)														●																							
J GRIEVE & ASSOCIATES, Cambridge (YH07585)																																				●	
JOHNSON, NORMAN, Ely (YH07830)														●																							
LE-WECHNER, NICHOLAS J, Ely (YH08577)														●																							
LYON BENNETT & AST, Chatteries (YH08937)																																				●	
LYON BENNETT & AST, Whittlesey (YH08938)																																				●	
LYON, BENNETT & AST, March (YH08939)																																				●	
MASON, R J, Peterborough (YH09247)														●																							
MATTHEWS, BRIAN, Huntingdon (YH09270)														●																							
MILWRIGHT, R D P, Ely (YH09646)																																				●	
MORGAN, DAVID JOHN, Ely (YH09803)														●																							
MORGAN, G W, Peterborough (YH09804)														●																							
MURFITT, D G, Ely (YH09951)														●																							
MURFITT, TIMOTHY J, Soham (YH09952)														●																							
NORTHBROOK EQUESTRIAN CTRE, Huntingdon (YH10294)															●	●																					

www.hccyourhorse.com

Business Profile
Breeding and Wellbeing

by Country by County

	Ambulance Services	Animal Behaviourist	Artificial Insemination	Bloodstock Advice	Bloodstock Agency	Breaking In Horses	Breeding Advice	Chiropractics	Clipper Maintenance	Complementary Medicine	Dentistry Skills	Dust Control	Emergency Services	Farrier Services	Groom	Groom Services	Herbalists	Holistic Medicine	Homeopathy	Horse Ambulance	Horse Psychiatry	Horse Sitter	Horse Walker	Laser & Ultrasound	Nutritionists	Osteopathy	Physiotherapy	Respiratory Disease control	Shoe Fitting Skills	Solarium	Stud Services	Swimming Pool Centre	Trotting Services	Vaccination	Veterinary Labs	Veterinary Practice	Veterinary Skills
PENGELLY, PENGELLY & MIZEN, Peterborough (YH10937)																																				●	
PINNER, TERRY, Huntingdon (YH11134)		●																																			
PRESTWICH, ISOBEL, Peterborough (YH11369)								●																		●	●										
R C GOWING, Ely (YH11519)														●																							
ROBIN HUGHES-PARRY & AST, Longstanton (YH11979)																																				●	
ROBIN HUGHES-PARRY ASSOCIATES, Cottenham (YH11980)																																				●	
SADLER, LINDA, Ely (YH12374)					●																																
SIMPSONS MANU, Ely (YH12843)									●																												
SMEETH SADDLERY, Wisbech (YH12925)																			●																		
TEBBUTT, N F & A C F, Huntingdon (YH13927)										●																										●	
TEBBUTT, NORMAN & ALASDAIR, St Neots (YH13928)																																				●	
THOMPSON, LUKE P, Ely (YH14038)														●																							
WITCHAM HSE FARM STUD, Ely (YH15617)			●				●																														
CHESHIRE																																					
ABBEYCROFT VETNRY CTRE, Northwich (YH00092)																																				●	
ADAMS, D C T, Warrington (YH00165)														●																							
ADAMS, RICHARD A, Warrington (YH00172)														●																							
ASHBROOK EQUINE HOSP, Knutsford (YH00591)																																				●	
ATHERTON, P V J, Widnes (YH00645)														●																							
BAILEY, JOHN ANDREW, Macclesfield (YH00801)														●																							
BARNHOUSE VETNRY SURGERY, Chester (YH00989)																																				●	
BOURNE, SIMON S, Sandbach (YH01685)														●																							
BROOKE, WILLIAM N, High Peak (YH02044)														●																							
BROOKS LANE SMITHY, Middlewich (YH02061)														●																							
BROOKS, JONATHAN, Altrincham (YH02066)														●																							
BURGESS & GRAHAM, Northwich (YH02241)																																				●	
BURNS, DAVID J MAHER, Woodford (YH02271)														●																							
CHRISTIAN, M K, Kelsall (YH02884)																																				●	
CLARENDON VETNRY GRP, Altrincham (YH02955)																																				●	
CLARENDON VETNRY GRP, Sale (YH02956)																																				●	
CONSTERDINE, C J, Macclesfield (YH03245)														●																							
COUNTIES EQUESTRIAN SVS, Knutsford (YH03395)																				●																	

Business Profile
Breeding and Wellbeing

by Country by County

	Ambulance Services	Animal Behaviourist	Artificial Insemination	Bloodstock Advice	Bloodstock Agency	Breaking In Horses	Breeding Advice	Chiropractics	Clipper Maintenance	Complementary Medicine	Dentistry Skills	Dust Control	Emergency Services	Farrier Services	Groom	Groom Services	Herbalists	Holistic Medicine	Homeopathy	Horse Ambulance	Horse Psychiatry	Horse Sitter	Horse Walker	Laser & Ultrasound	Nutritionists	Osteopathy	Physiotherapy	Respiratory Disease control	Shoe Fitting Skills	Solarium	Stud Services	Swimming Pool Centre	Trotting Services	Vaccination	Veterinary Labs	Veterinary Practice	Veterinary Skills
COUNTY VETNRY GRP, Holmes Chapel (YH03494)																																				●	
COUNTY VETNRY GRP, Sandbach (YH03495)																																				●	
COX, P E, High Peak (YH03535)														●																							
CRANMORE VETNRY CTRE, Childer Thornton (YH03567)																																				●	
CROFT RIDING CTRE, Warrington (YH03617)						●																															
DARLOW, G C, Knutsford (YH03895)														●																							
DAVENHILL, ADAM J, Crewe (YH03909)														●																							
DAVIES, ZOE, Mobberley (YH03951)																									●												
DAWSON, KARL, Middlewich (YH03963)														●																							
DUNCALF, ALAN W, Warrington (YH04333)														●																							
EATON SMITHY, Tarporley (YH04524)														●																							
EQUIFORM NUTRITION, Crewe (YH04747)																									●												
EVERGREEN VETNRY SURGERY, Stockport (YH04953)																																				●	
FEARNALL, Tarporley (YH05116)							●																														
FEARNALL STUD, Tarporley (YH05117)														●																							
G E HUNT, Poynton (YH05576)																																				●	
GATEHOUSE VETNRY HOSPITAL, Chester (YH05672)																																				●	
GAYNORS SADDLERY, Dukinfield (YH05682)									●	●									●																		
GORDON, PAUL T, Northwich (YH05926)														●																							
GOUGH, GARRY C, Chester (YH05949)														●																							
GUILFOYLE, M, Cheadle (YH06186)														●																							
HALES, S J, Malpas (YH06294)																																				●	
HAMPTON VETNRY GRP, Malpas (YH06370)																																				●	
HARGREAVES, TERENCE D, Northwich (YH06429)														●																							
HILTON, JOHN, Tameside (YH06865)														●																							
HOWELL, A J, Macclesfield (YH07226)														●																							
HUGHES, JOHN W, Malpas (YH07269)														●																							
IAN P BRADBURY, Macclesfield (YH07371)														●																							
ISHERWOOD, GABRIELLE, Macclesfield (YH07516)																											●										
J PRESTON & SON, Widnes (YH07606)														●																							
JACKSON, PAUL, Stockport (YH07651)														●																							
JOSEPH MURPHY, Warrington (YH07944)														●																							

Business Profile
Breeding and Wellbeing

by Country by County	Ambulance Services	Animal Behaviourist	Artificial Insemination	Bloodstock Advice	Bloodstock Agency	Breaking In Horses	Breeding Advice	Chiropractics	Clipper Maintenance	Complementary Medicine	Dentistry Skills	Dust Control	Emergency Services	Farrier Services	Groom	Groom Services	Herbalists	Holistic Medicine	Homeopathy	Horse Ambulance	Horse Psychiatry	Horse Sitter	Horse Walker	Laser & Ultrasound	Nutritionists	Osteopathy	Physiotherapy	Respiratory Disease control	Shoe Fitting Skills	Solarium	Stud Services	Swimming Pool Centre	Trotting Services	Vaccination	Veterinary Labs	Veterinary Practice	Veterinary Skills
KIRKBY, Tarporley (YH08232)														●															●								
LANGDALE VETNRY CTRE, Knutsford (YH08401)																																				●	
LANSDOWNE HORSE & RIDER, Chester (YH08423)									●	●									●						●			●									
LINDLEY, BERNARD J, Altrincham (YH08648)														●																							
MAHER-BURNS, MATTHEW J, Macclesfield (YH09036)														●																							
MANIFOLD, MALCOLM T, Hyde (YH09079)														●																							
MANOR COURT VETNRY CTRE, Chester (YH09094)																																				●	
MANOR COURT VETNRY CTRE, Tattenhall (YH09093)																																				●	
MIDDLEBROOK, SIMON E, Macclesfield (YH09537)														●																							
MOSS, JOHN D, Alderley Edge (YH09860)														●																							
NANTWICH VETNRY GROUP, Nantwich (YH10019)																																				●	
NANTWICH VETNRY GROUP, Crewe (YH10020)																																				●	
NORCLIFFE SHIRES, Macclesfield (YH10229)				●																																	
OWEN, GARETH J, Chester (YH10601)														●																							
OWEN, J R, Chester (YH10602)														●																							
PICKMERE, Knutsford (YH11087)							●																								●						
POOL FARM VETNRY SURGERY, Madeley (YH11261)																																				●	
RANDLES, JOHN M, Congleton (YH11631)														●																							
ROBERTS, E N, Chester (YH11948)														●																							
ROSE COTTAGE VETNRY CTRE, Runcorn (YH12092)																																				●	
SALT, EDWARD M, Tarporley (YH12392)														●																							
SIMS & PARTNERS, Congleton (YH12844)																																				●	
SINSTADT, M C W, Nantwich (YH12856)														●																							
SMITH, ANDREW C, Malpas (YH12941)														●																							
SMITH, JONATHAN C, Malpas (YH12971)														●																							
SPENCER, D, Stockport (YH13197)														●																							
SPRINGWATER STUD, Nantwich (YH13263)																									●						●						
STATION HSE VETNRY CTRE, Altrincham (YH13402)																																				●	
STORRAR PRACTICE, Chester (YH13527)																																				●	
TAYLOR, JEREMY N, Nantwich (YH13904)														●																							
TOPSPEC, Nantwich (YH14241)																									●												
UNIVERSITY OF LIVERPOOL, South Wirral (YH14590)																																				●	

Business Profile
Breeding and Wellbeing

by Country by County

Name	Ambulance Services	Animal Behaviourist	Artificial Insemination	Bloodstock Advice	Bloodstock Agency	Breaking In Horses	Breeding Advice	Chiropractics	Clipper Maintenance	Complementary Medicine	Dentistry Skills	Dust Control	Emergency Services	Farrier Services	Groom	Groom Services	Herbalists	Holistic Medicine	Homeopathy	Horse Ambulance	Horse Psychiatry	Horse Sitter	Horse Walker	Laser & Ultrasound	Nutritionists	Osteopathy	Physiotherapy	Respiratory Disease control	Shoe Fitting Skills	Solarium	Stud Services	Swimming Pool Centre	Trotting Services	Vaccination	Veterinary Labs	Veterinary Practice	Veterinary Skills
UNSWORTH, HARRY W, Farndon (YH14598)														●																							
WARD, R KEITH, Nantwich (YH14906)																																				●	
WELSH, JOSEPH, Congleton (YH15098)														●																							
WILLOWS VETNRY GRP, Winsford (YH15515)																																				●	
WILLOWS VETNRY GRP, Warrington (YH15514)																																				●	
WILLOWS VETNRY GRP, Northwich (YH15513)																																				●	
WILLOWS VETNRY GRP, Middlewich (YH15512)																																				●	
WILLOWS VETNRY GRP, Lymm (YH15511)																																				●	
WILLOWS VETNRY GRP, Knutsford (YH15510)																																				●	
WRIGHT & MORTEN, Congleton (YH15826)																																				●	
WRIGHT & MORTEN, Wilmslow (YH15828)																																				●	
WRIGHT & MORTEN, Macclesfield (YH15827)																																				●	
WRIGHT, D G, Stockport (YH15834)																																				●	
WRIGHT, D G, Chapel-En-Le-Frith (YH15835)																																				●	
WYNNE, M G, Tarporley (YH15872)						●																															
ZINON, CHRISTOPHER, Altrincham (YH15956)														●																							
CLEVELAND																																					
ANIMAL HEALTH CTRE, Guisborough (YH00435)																																				●	
BECK VETNRY PRACTICE, Loftus (YH01145)																																				●	
BROWN, KARL J, Middlesbrough (YH02118)														●																							
CLEVEDALE VETNRY PRACTICE, Redcar (YH03019)																																				●	
CLIFTON LODGE VETNRY GRP, Stockton-on-Tees (YH03037)																																				●	
FERNIE, A, Norton (YH05165)														●																							
FOXHOLM STUD, Stockton-on-Tees (YH05437)																															●						
HAYKIN, M, Middlesbrough (YH06582)														●																							
HOOF'N'HOUND, Hartlepool (YH07031)																			●																		
MILLER & WHIMSTER, Stokesley (YH09600)																																				●	
ROOKS, GORDON, Guisborough (YH12076)														●																							
SMITHSON, B H, Elwick (YH13009)														●																							
VETNRY SURGERY, Redcar (YH14699)																																				●	
WATSON, EUAN MCINTOSH, Middlesbrough (YH14984)														●																							
WILTON HSE VETNRY CTRE, Guisborough (YH15555)																																				●	

Business Profile
Breeding and Wellbeing

by Country by County

	Ambulance Services	Animal Behaviourist	Artificial Insemination	Bloodstock Advice	Bloodstock Agency	Breaking In Horses	Breeding Advice	Chiropractics	Clipper Maintenance	Complementary Medicine	Dentistry Skills	Dust Control	Emergency Services	Farrier Services	Groom	Groom Services	Herbalists	Holistic Medicine	Homeopathy	Horse Ambulance	Horse Psychiatry	Horse Sitter	Horse Walker	Laser & Ultrasound	Nutritionists	Osteopathy	Physiotherapy	Respiratory Disease control	Shoe Fitting Skills	Solarium	Stud Services	Swimming Pool Centre	Trotting Services	Vaccination	Veterinary Labs	Veterinary Practice	Veterinary Skills
CORNWALL																																					
ABBOTT DRAPER & FRASER, Bodmin (YH00112)																																				●	
ABBOTT DRAPER & FRASER, Wadebridge (YH00113)																																				●	
ALBERT COTTAGE, Saltash (YH00244)																																				●	
AMOS & PENNY, Falmouth (YH00370)																																				●	
ANIMAL VETNRY SVS, Hayle (YH00446)																																				●	
BAKER, MARTYN D, Coppathorne (YH00824)														●																							
BALCOMBE, KEVIN P, Copthorne (YH00833)														●																							
BARRACLOUGH, A & S, Launceston (YH01003)										●																											
BOISSEAU, R, Wadebridge (YH01600)								●																		●	●										
BROKENSHIRE, ADRIAN KEITH, Bodmin (YH02022)														●																							
BUNCE, ARTHUR LESLIE, Helston (YH02221)														●																							
BUNGAY, PETER L, Launceston (YH02224)														●																							
CALWETON VETNRY CTRE, Callington (YH02460)																																				●	
CALWETON VETNRY CTRE, Looe (YH02461)																																				●	
CALWETON VETNRY CTRE, Saltash (YH02462)																																				●	
CASTLE VETNRY GRP, Launceston (YH02638)																																				●	
CLIFTON VILLA, Camborne (YH03041)																																				●	
CLIFTON VILLA, Truro (YH03042)																																				●	
CORNWELL, RAYMOND T, Liskeard (YH03342)														●																							
CRAGG, R, Truro (YH03543)														●																							
ELLIS, D, Liskeard (YH04624)																																				●	
FARRIER SVS, St Ives (YH05088)														●															●								
FRY USHER & EDWARDS, Camborne (YH05526)																																				●	
FRY USHER & EDWARDS, Redruth (YH05527)																																				●	
GRAY, GARY S, St Just (YH06028)														●																							
GREEN, CLIFTON, Newquay (YH06062)																																				●	
GWINEAR & DISTRICT FARMERS, Camborne (YH06204)										●																											
HANN, JAMES S, Camelford (YH06391)														●																							
HARDERN YOUNG & OTTY, Penzance (YH06409)																																				●	
HAYDEN, RICHARD J, Launceston (YH06570)														●																							
HEAD & HEAD, Helston (YH06606)																																				●	

Business Profile
Breeding and Wellbeing

by Country by County	Ambulance Services	Animal Behaviourist	Artificial Insemination	Bloodstock Advice	Bloodstock Agency	Breaking In Horses	Breeding Advice	Chiropractics	Clipper Maintenance	Complementary Medicine	Dentistry Skills	Dust Control	Emergency Services	Farrier Services	Groom	Groom Services	Herbalists	Holistic Medicine	Homeopathy	Horse Ambulance	Horse Psychiatry	Horse Sitter	Horse Walker	Laser & Ultrasound	Nutritionists	Osteopathy	Physiotherapy	Respiratory Disease control	Shoe Fitting Skills	Solarium	Stud Services	Swimming Pool Centre	Trotting Services	Vaccination	Veterinary Labs	Veterinary Practice	Veterinary Skills
HELSTON SADDLERY, Helston (YH06657)									●																												
HILLS, JOHN R, Wadebridge (YH06849)														●																							
HOLT, J J, Camelford (YH06988)																																				●	
JOHNSON, PAUL, Callington (YH07833)														●																							
JONES, DAVID D, Camborne (YH07889)														●																							
KENWYN VETNRY CTRE, Truro (YH08092)																																				●	
KINGS VETNRY SURGERY, Newquay (YH08198)																																				●	
KNIGHT, P W, Truro (YH08263)														●																							
LANG, JAMES H, Mullion (YH08396)														●																							
LAUREL STUD, Truro (YH08458)							●																														
LAWRIE, JOHN, Liskeard (YH08475)														●																							
LITTLETON, C E J, Truro (YH08710)																																				●	
LOCKE & PRESTON VETNRY GRP, Bude (YH08757)																																				●	
LONG, S P, Truro (YH08805)														●																							
LUXSTOWE VETNRY CTRE, Liskeard (YH08911)																																				●	
MAER STABLES, Bude (YH09029)										●																											
MALE, TREVOR, Penzance (YH09047)														●																							
MARTIN, PAUL, Par (YH09224)														●																							
MCNAMARA, MICHAEL F J, Saltash (YH09399)														●																							
MERIDIAN RADIONICS, Truro (YH09476)										●																											
MOORE, SIMON A, Redruth (YH09765)														●																							
NEWNS, J L, Gunnislake (YH10161)										●																										●	
NUTE, G & P J, Wadebridge (YH10356)																																				●	
PELYN VETNRY GRP, Lostwithiel (YH10913)																																				●	
PENBODE VETNRY GRP, Bude (YH10925)																																				●	
PENCARN FORGE, Hayle (YH10929)														●																							
PENMELLYN VETNRY GRP, St Columb (YH10945)																																				●	
PENMELLYN VETNRY GRP, Padstow (YH10946)																																				●	
PREECE, MARK, Launceston (YH11341)														●																							
ROSEMULLION, Falmouth (YH12106)																																				●	
ROSEMULLION VETNRY, Helston (YH12107)																																				●	
ROSEVIDNEY ARABIANS, Penzance (YH12111)							●																														

Business Profile
Breeding and Wellbeing

by Country by County	Ambulance Services	Animal Behaviourist	Artificial Insemination	Bloodstock Advice	Bloodstock Agency	Breaking In Horses	Breeding Advice	Chiropractics	Clipper Maintenance	Complementary Medicine	Dentistry Skills	Dust Control	Emergency Services	Farrier Services	Groom	Groom Services	Herbalists	Holistic Medicine	Homeopathy	Horse Ambulance	Horse Psychiatry	Horse Sitter	Horse Walker	Laser & Ultrasound	Nutritionists	Osteopathy	Physiotherapy	Respiratory Disease control	Shoe Fitting Skills	Solarium	Stud Services	Swimming Pool Centre	Trotting Services	Vaccination	Veterinary Labs	Veterinary Practice	Veterinary Skills
SCREATON, M, Penzance (YH12564)														●																							
STEVENS, Helston (YH13441)					●																																
STEVENS, M A, Helston (YH13446)														●																							
TM INT SCHOOL OF HORSEMANSHIP, Liskeard (YH14196)		●																																			
TUCKETT, GRAHAME J, Penzance (YH14437)														●																							
VINCENT, JOHN, Par (YH14724)														●																							
WEBBER, BRIAN, St Austell (YH15034)														●																							
WILKIN, KEITH M, Truro (YH15416)														●																							
WILLIAMS, J B, Camborne (YH15460)														●																							
WILLS, S, Redruth (YH15520)														●																							
WOODING, SIMON A, Helston (YH15700)														●																							
COUNTY DURHAM																																					
ACRUM LODGE STUD, Bishop Auckland (YH00160)				●			●																								●						
ALSTON & KILLHOPE, Bishop Auckland (YH00339)																						●															
ARMSTRONG, JOHN W, Durham (YH00549)														●																							
BELL, JOHN, Crook (YH01225)														●																							
BONE, JOSEPH, Durham (YH01620)														●																							
BOWES MANOR EQUESTRIAN CTRE, Chester Le Street (YH01709)						●																															
BRITTON, JOHN R, Durham (YH01985)														●																							
BURTON, W L, Durham (YH02295)														●																							
CASON, P, Durham (YH02617)														●																							
CASTLE VETNRY SURGEONS, Durham (YH02639)																																				●	
CLIFTON LODGE VETNRY GRP, Durham (YH03038)																																				●	
CLIFTON LODGE VETRNRY GRP, Durham (YH03039)																																				●	
E D T, Consett (YH04401)											●																										
FARMWAY, Darlington (YH05072)																									●												
GO RIDING GRP, Stanley (YH05861)																●							●														
HESLOP, SIMON, Ebchester (YH06722)														●																							
HIGHWELL STUD, Darlington (YH06802)			●				●																								●						
HINDHAUGH, HENRY HALL, Old Burdon South (YH06870)														●																							
JACKSON, NEIL, Bishop Auckland (YH07650)														●																							
MOORE, W, Bishop Auckland (YH09768)														●																							

Business Profile
Breeding and Wellbeing

by Country by County

	Ambulance Services	Animal Behaviourist	Artificial Insemination	Bloodstock Advice	Bloodstock Agency	Breaking In Horses	Breeding Advice	Chiropractics	Clipper Maintenance	Complementary Medicine	Dentistry Skills	Dust Control	Emergency Services	Farrier Services	Groom	Groom Services	Herbalists	Holistic Medicine	Homeopathy	Horse Ambulance	Horse Psychiatry	Horse Sitter	Horse Walker	Laser & Ultrasound	Nutritionists	Osteopathy	Physiotherapy	Respiratory Disease control	Shoe Fitting Skills	Solarium	Stud Services	Swimming Pool Centre	Trotting Services	Vaccination	Veterinary Labs	Veterinary Practice	Veterinary Skills
RIDLEY, GEORGE E, Stanley (YH11887)														●																							
ROSS, RUSSELL A, Consett (YH12121)														●																							
SCAIFE, ANDREW, Coatham Mundeville (YH12480)														●																							
SHAW, GARRY A, Darlington (YH12681)														●																							
TALLENTIRE & SONS, Bishop Auckland (YH13834)														●																							
CUMBRIA																																					
ARCHWAY VETNRY PRACTICE, Grange-Over-Sands (YH00500)																																				●	
ATKINSON, ROBERT W, Carlisle (YH00652)														●																							
BARR & LOCKHART, Kirkby Stephen (YH00998)																																				●	
BAY VETNRY GRP, Milnthorpe (YH01094)																																				●	
BEACON VETNRY CTRE, Wigton (YH01108)																																				●	
BELLE VUE VETNRY PRACTICE, Wigton (YH01235)																																				●	
BLACK, WENDY, Windermere (YH01473)							●																														
CALDEW VETNRY GRP, Carlisle (YH02437)																																				●	
CARNEGIE & LINDSAY, Brampton (YH02564)																																				●	
CHARLY'S YARD SMITHY, Carlisle (YH02770)														●																							
CHURCH WALK VETNRY CTRE, Ulverston (YH02907)																																				●	
CHURCH WALK VETNRY CTRE, Barrow-In-Furness (YH02906)																																				●	
COOMARA VETNRY PRACTICE, Carlisle (YH03272)																																				●	
CRAIG ROBINSON & PARTNERS, Carlisle (YH03551)																																				●	
CROFT VETNRY GRP, Cockermouth (YH03620)																																				●	
CROFT VETNRY GRP, Workington (YH03621)																																				●	
CUTHBERT, T A K, Carlisle (YH03760)														●																							
D WATSON & SONS, Egremont (YH03812)														●																							
EBEL, KARL WALTER GUSTAV, Gretna (YH04530)														●																							
FEARHEAD, DANIEL M, Sedbergh (YH05115)														●																							
FOX, DAVID L, Millom (YH05427)														●																							
FRAME, J & N W, Penrith (YH05440)																																				●	
GARDNER, DEREK T, Penrith (YH05647)														●																							
GET SMART, Barrow-In-Furness (YH05732)									●																												
GLAISTER, JAMES, Cockermouth (YH05803)														●																							
GOULDING, PHILIP, Cockermouth (YH05951)														●																							

Business Profile
Breeding and Wellbeing

by Country by County

	Ambulance Services	Animal Behaviourist	Artificial Insemination	Bloodstock Advice	Bloodstock Agency	Breaking In Horses	Breeding Advice	Chiropractics	Clipper Maintenance	Complementary Medicine	Dentistry Skills	Dust Control	Emergency Services	Farrier Services	Groom	Groom Services	Herbalists	Holistic Medicine	Homeopathy	Horse Ambulance	Horse Psychiatry	Horse Sitter	Horse Walker	Laser & Ultrasound	Nutritionists	Osteopathy	Physiotherapy	Respiratory Disease control	Shoe Fitting Skills	Solarium	Stud Services	Swimming Pool Centre	Trotting Services	Vaccination	Veterinary Labs	Veterinary Practice	Veterinary Skills
GRETA BANK VETNRY CTRE, Keswick (YH06123)																																				●	
HALE, ROGER K, Penrith (YH06292)														●																							
HANNAH, DAVID, Egremont (YH06394)														●																							
HIGHGATE VETNRY CLNC, Kendal (YH06787)																																				●	
HODGSON & HUNTER, Cleator Moor (YH06910)																																				●	
HODGSON & HUNTER, Workington (YH06911)																																				●	
J R W SEDGWICK, Cockermouth (YH07612)																																				●	
JOHNSTON, PAUL J, Workington (YH07847)														●																							
KENTDALE FARRIERS, Kendal (YH08086)														●																							
KERBECK, Workington (YH08096)							●																								●						
LAKELAND EQUESTRIAN, Windermere (YH08354)																							●														
LEATHERBARROW, GORDON P, Seascale (YH08507)														●																							
MCDONALD, BRIAN, Appleby-In-Westmorland (YH09344)														●																							
MCDONALD, LIAM P, Appleby (YH09346)														●																							
MIDDLE BAYLES LIVERY, Alston (YH09534)																●						●															
MILBY, CHRISTOPHER L, Ulverston (YH09567)														●																							
MILLCROFT VETNRY GROUP, Maryport (YH09596)																																				●	
MILLCROFT VETNRY GROUP, Cockermouth (YH09595)																																				●	
MITCHELL, W J, Kendal (YH09678)														●																							
OAKHILL VETNRY GRP, Ambleside (YH10385)																																				●	
PICKLES, A C, Penrith (YH11086)																																				●	
PRESTON & BRAMLEY, Sedbergh (YH11366)																																				●	
RHAM, TRICIA, Cockermouth (YH11782)								●																		●	●										
RICHARDSON, S P, Ambleside (YH11823)																																				●	
ROWCLIFFE HSE VETNRY, Penrith (YH12159)																																				●	
RUDD, A J, Carlisle (YH12205)														●																							
RUSHTON & BROWNE, Broughton In Furness (YH12244)																																				●	
RUSHTON & BROWNE, Millom (YH12245)																																				●	
SANSOM & DODWELL, Windermere (YH12427)																																				●	
SCOTT, LESLIE, Carlisle (YH12545)														●																							
SEDGWICK, J R W, Keswick (YH12606)																																				●	
SEDGWICK, J R W, Egremont (YH12605)																																				●	

Business Profile
Breeding and Wellbeing

by Country by County

	Ambulance Services	Animal Behaviourist	Artificial Insemination	Bloodstock Advice	Bloodstock Agency	Breaking In Horses	Breeding Advice	Chiropractics	Clipper Maintenance	Complementary Medicine	Dentistry Skills	Dust Control	Emergency Services	Farrier Services	Groom	Groom Services	Herbalists	Holistic Medicine	Homeopathy	Horse Ambulance	Horse Psychiatry	Horse Sitter	Horse Walker	Laser & Ultrasound	Nutritionists	Osteopathy	Physiotherapy	Respiratory Disease control	Shoe Fitting Skills	Solarium	Stud Services	Swimming Pool Centre	Trotting Services	Vaccination	Veterinary Labs	Veterinary Practice	Veterinary Skills
ST BRIDGETS VETNRY CTRE, Whitehaven (YH13273)																																				●	
ST BRIDGETS VETNRY CTRE, Egremont (YH13272)																																				●	
STAINMORE STUD, Kirkby Stephen (YH13345)							●																														
STRAMONGATE VETNRY CTRE, Kendal (YH13546)																																				●	
TITHE BARN VETNRY CTRE, Kirkby Lonsdale (YH14188)																																				●	
WISEMAN, ANGUS W, Kendal (YH15609)														●																							
DERBYSHIRE																																					
ABBEY VETNRY GRP, Derby (YH00091)																																				●	
AINSWORTH, DARREN R, Buxton (YH00215)														●																							
ALTON RIDING SCHOOL, Chesterfield (YH00344)							●																								●						
AMBIVET VETNRY GRP, Heanor (YH00359)																																				●	
AMBIVET VETNRY GRP, Ripley (YH00358)																																				●	
BARTLETT, WILLIAM G, South Normanton (YH01043)														●																							
BRADBURY, DOUGLAS, Chesterfield (YH01746)														●																							
BRADBURY, NEAL, Chesterfield (YH01747)														●																							
BRIDGE, MARTIN S, Tibshelf (YH01879)														●																							
BUNTING, F, Derby (YH02227)														●																							
BYRON VETNRY CLINIC, Long Eaton (YH02350)																																				●	
C E S, Ashbourne (YH02370)		●		●	●		●		●		●		●	●	●	●				●		●	●	●													●
CALEY, MARK A, Buxton (YH02443)														●																							
CHADBOURNE, C, Swadlincote (YH02701)														●																							
COCKAIN, GODFREY J, Belper (YH03119)														●																							
COOPER & PARTNERS, Repton (YH03283)																																				●	
CROFT VETNRY CTRE, Bolsover (YH03619)																																				●	
DOBSON, TERENCE FRANK, Ilkeston (YH04155)														●																							
DUERDEN, BRIAN ROBERT, Hope Valley (YH04312)														●																							
FRANCIS & HERDMAN, Bakewell (YH05447)																																				●	
GIBSON, FREDERICK, Dronfield (YH05749)														●																							
GILLETT, M P, Derby (YH05781)														●																							
GRAHAM, JAMES A, Bakewell (YH05970)														●																							
GREEN, STUART E, High Peak (YH06074)														●																							
HAYBURN, J, Derby (YH06565)														●																							

Business Profile
Breeding and Wellbeing

by Country by County	Ambulance Services	Animal Behaviourist	Artificial Insemination	Bloodstock Advice	Bloodstock Agency	Breaking In Horses	Breeding Advice	Chiropractics	Clipper Maintenance	Complementary Medicine	Dentistry Skills	Dust Control	Emergency Services	Farrier Services	Groom	Groom Services	Herbalists	Holistic Medicine	Homeopathy	Horse Ambulance	Horse Psychiatry	Horse Sitter	Horse Walker	Laser & Ultrasound	Nutritionists	Osteopathy	Physiotherapy	Respiratory Disease control	Shoe Fitting Skills	Solarium	Stud Services	Swimming Pool Centre	Trotting Services	Vaccination	Veterinary Labs	Veterinary Practice	Veterinary Skills
HILLCLIFF STUD, Belper (YH06838)		●																			●																
HOPKINSON & HURST, Alfreton (YH07055)																																				●	
HUNT, LANCE A, Belper (YH07297)														●																							
IVANHOE FEEDS, Swadlincote (YH07533)										●																											
JAMES, TIMOTHY P, Melbourne (YH07689)														●																							
JAMIESON, C J, Locko Park (YH07692)																																				●	
KING, P, Matlock (YH08184)														●																							
KNOX & DEVLIN, High Peak (YH08287)																																				●	
LANGLEY, RODNEY DONALD, Swadlincote (YH08411)														●																							
LEWIS, ROBERT I, Ashbourne (YH08595)														●																							
LONG, A D, Hatton (YH08801)														●																							
LUNNUN, NORMAN, Ashbourne (YH08901)														●																							
MARPLES, H W, Dronfield (YH09173)														●																							
MARSHALL & TILL, Derby (YH09191)																																				●	
MARSHALL & TILL, Littleover (YH09190)																																				●	
MCMURTY & HARDING, Ashbourne (YH09395)																																				●	
MEE, JOHN S, Ashbourne (YH09440)														●																							
NORMAN LUNNUN ANIMAL HEALTH, Ashbourne (YH10237)														●																							
OLDKNOW, P L, Derby (YH10492)														●																							
OVERDALE VETNRY CTRE, Buxton (YH10591)																																				●	
PEAKDALE SADDLERY, Buxton (YH10866)									●	●									●																		
PETTS, KATHRINE, Matlock (YH11034)								●																		●	●										
POLKEY, FREDERICK C, Alvaston (YH11203)														●																							
REEVE, S C, Matlock (YH11736)																																				●	
RINGER VILLA EQUESTRIAN CTRE, Chesterfield (YH11900)						●																															
RUSH, ROBERT G, Chesterfield (YH12240)														●																							
RUTLAND, SEAN D, Mackworth (YH12281)														●																							
SAUNDERS, HAROLD DUNCAN, Swadlincote (YH12448)														●																							
SCARSDALE VETNRY HOSPITAL, Markeaton (YH12489)																																				●	
SCARSDALE VETNRY HOSPITAL, Derby (YH12490)																																				●	
SELBY, PAUL, Chesterfield (YH12617)														●																							
SPIRE VETNRY GROUP, Chesterfield (YH13211)																																				●	

Business Profile
Breeding and Wellbeing

by Country by County	Ambulance Services	Animal Behaviourist	Artificial Insemination	Bloodstock Advice	Bloodstock Agency	Breaking In Horses	Breeding Advice	Chiropractics	Clipper Maintenance	Complementary Medicine	Dentistry Skills	Dust Control	Emergency Services	Farrier Services	Groom	Groom Services	Herbalists	Holistic Medicine	Homeopathy	Horse Ambulance	Horse Psychiatry	Horse Sitter	Horse Walker	Laser & Ultrasound	Nutritionists	Osteopathy	Physiotherapy	Respiratory Disease control	Shoe Fitting Skills	Solarium	Stud Services	Swimming Pool Centre	Trotting Services	Vaccination	Veterinary Labs	Veterinary Practice	Veterinary Skills
SUMMERS, J V, Barrow-on-Trent (YH13636)														●																							
WARWICK, SIMON J, Breaston (YH14950)														●																							
WATERLOO HOUSE VETNRY SURGERY, Swadlincote (YH14968)																																				●	
WATERLOO HOUSE VETNRY SURGERY, Melbourne (YH14969)																																				●	
WATKINSON, MATTHEW, Derby (YH14981)														●																							
WHITE, A, Dronfield (YH15326)														●																							
WOODWARD, CAROLINE A, Ilkeston (YH15755)														●																							
WYLES, S, Church Broughton (YH15865)														●																							
DEVON																																					
ALFORD, H J, Cullompton (YH00273)														●																							
ANIMAL BEHAVIOUR CONSULTANTS, Okehampton (YH00428)		●																							●						●						
ASKELL, VICTOR W J, Dawlish (YH00619)														●																							
ATKINSON & BURGESS, Bideford (YH00650)																																				●	
AUSTIN, GEORGE, Ivybridge (YH00667)																																				●	
BARONS, D H, Kingsbridge (YH00995)					●																																
BARRASS, J, Honiton (YH01007)														●																							
BARWELL, C R, Tiverton (YH01052)					●																																
BERWICK, JOHN H, Newton Abbot (YH01322)														●																							
BOYCE, P S, Okehampton (YH01730)														●																							
BRIDGE HOUSE VETNRY, Barnstaple (YH01873)																																				●	
BUSSELL, N E R, Barnstaple (YH02315)																																				●	
C J HORSE TRANSPORT, Tavistock (YH02377)			●																																		
CANN, STEPHEN J, Otterton (YH02500)														●																							
CARNELL, R F, Newton Abbot (YH02565)														●																							
CARR, PHILIP JOHN, South Molton (YH02571)														●																							
CHILDS, ADAM, Sidmouth (YH02852)														●																							
CLARK, W L R & M E, Tiverton (YH02969)														●																							
CLIPPER SHARP, Cullompton (YH03046)									●																												
CONIBEAR, R H, Bideford (YH03230)														●																							
COOMBEFIELD VETNRY HOSPITAL, Axminster (YH03279)																																				●	
COSSENS, ANTHONY, Tavistock (YH03353)														●																							
CRADDOCK, STEVE A, Okehampton (YH03539)														●																							

www.hccyourhorse.com

Business Profile
Breeding and Wellbeing

by Country by County

	Ambulance Services	Animal Behaviourist	Artificial Insemination	Bloodstock Advice	Bloodstock Agency	Breaking In Horses	Breeding Advice	Chiropractics	Clipper Maintenance	Complementary Medicine	Dentistry Skills	Dust Control	Emergency Services	Farrier Services	Groom	Groom Services	Herbalists	Holistic Medicine	Homeopathy	Horse Ambulance	Horse Psychiatry	Horse Sitter	Horse Walker	Laser & Ultrasound	Nutritionists	Osteopathy	Physiotherapy	Respiratory Disease control	Shoe Fitting Skills	Solarium	Stud Services	Swimming Pool Centre	Trotting Services	Vaccination	Veterinary Labs	Veterinary Practice	Veterinary Skills
CRIMP, B A, Beaworthy (YH03601)														●																							
CULLEN, Brampton (YH03702)																																				●	
DEEBLE, BEN, Yelverton (YH04015)														●																							
EQUITOPIA, Lynton (YH04831)		●																																			
EQWEST VETNRY CTRE, Tavistock (YH04843)								●			●															●	●									●	
ERME VALLEY FARMERS, Ivybridge (YH04850)									●							●																					
FARMER, L J, Newton Abbot (YH05058)														●																							
FEU, DIANA DU, Axminster (YH05174)								●																		●	●										
FIRSEDGE, Beaworthy (YH05228)							●																														
FLAVIN & VERE, Crediton (YH05266)										●																										●	
G WESTAWAY & SON, Newton Abbot (YH05600)														●																							
GALLERY, JULIAN M, Seaton (YH05619)														●																							
GLANVILLE, DAVID PETER, Winkleigh (YH05806)														●																							
GREEP, R J, Ivybridge (YH06109)														●																							
H M THRESHER, Crediton (YH06231)																																				●	
HALL, LYNN M, Seaton (YH06316)														●																							
HARRIS, IAN, Barnstaple (YH06474)														●																							
HILL, C R, Newton Abbot (YH06827)														●																							
HILLCREST VETNRY CTRE, Plymouth (YH06844)																																				●	
HIRCOCK, P CHALIS, Plymouth (YH06880)														●																							
HOLLIS FARRIERS, Tiverton (YH06949)														●																							
HOLLIS HORSE/HOLLIS FARRIERS, Cullompton (YH06950)														●																							
HOLMEDOWN, Beaworthy (YH06969)							●																														
HOPWOOD, CHRISTOPHER J, Buckfastleigh (YH07062)														●																							
HOSGOOD, P, Exeter (YH07195)											●																										
INGLIS, J A, Ottery St Mary (YH07452)														●																							
J C EDWARDS & ASSOCIATES, Ivybridge (YH07569)																																				●	
JACKMAN, DAVID, Newton Abbot (YH07640)														●																							
LAKESIDE PADDOCK STUD, Ilfracombe (YH08358)														●																							
LAWRENCE, DAVID C, Torrington (YH08471)														●																							
LAWRENCE, R J, Umberleigh (YH08473)														●																							
LEE & BRAIN, Honiton (YH08516)																																				●	

Business Profile
Breeding and Wellbeing

by Country by County

by Country by County	Ambulance Services	Animal Behaviourist	Artificial Insemination	Bloodstock Advice	Bloodstock Agency	Breaking In Horses	Breeding Advice	Chiropractics	Clipper Maintenance	Complementary Medicine	Dentistry Skills	Dust Control	Emergency Services	Farrier Services	Groom	Groom Services	Herbalists	Holistic Medicine	Homeopathy	Horse Ambulance	Horse Psychiatry	Horse Sitter	Horse Walker	Laser & Ultrasound	Nutritionists	Osteopathy	Physiotherapy	Respiratory Disease control	Shoe Fitting Skills	Solarium	Stud Services	Swimming Pool Centre	Trotting Services	Vaccination	Veterinary Labs	Veterinary Practice	Veterinary Skills
LEONARD COOMBE, Newton Abbot (YH08553)									●																												
LEWIS JONES & AST, Honiton (YH08583)																																				●	
LEY, CLIVE H, Ilfracombe (YH08599)														●																							
LOCKE & PRESTON VETNRY GRP, Bradworthy (YH08758)																																				●	
LUXTON, MARCUS N, Tiverton (YH08912)														●																							
LUXTON, STEVEN, Okehampton (YH08913)														●																							
MANN, JOHN ANTHONY, Teignmouth (YH09082)														●																							
MAXIMILLIAN STUD, North Tawton (YH09285)			●																																		
MCDONALD, CLARE, Okehampton (YH09345)								●																		●	●										
MERCER, FRANK, Tiverton (YH09462)														●																							
MIDDLETON, LIONEL J P, South Brent (YH09546)														●																							
MORTIMORE, IAN, Yelverton (YH09848)														●																							
MULLACOTT EQUESTRIAN, Ilfracombe (YH09935)															●							●									●						
MULLACOTT VETNRY HOSPITAL, Barnstaple (YH09936)																																				●	
MULLACOTT VETNRY HOSPITAL GRP, Ilfracombe (YH09937)										●	●																									●	
MUNNINGS MITCHELL & PEPLOW, Totnes (YH09949)																																				●	
NORTH PARK VETNRY GROUP, North Tawton (YH10279)																																				●	
OKEFORD VETNRY CTRE, School Way (YH10446)																																				●	
OLIVE, DAVID W, Honiton (YH10496)														●																							
PARKIN, KEITH JOHN, Barnstaple (YH10764)														●																							
PARTRIDGE, M A, Buckfastleigh (YH10807)														●																							
PEDRICK, R, Newton Abbot (YH10894)														●																							
PENBODE VETNRY GRP, Holsworthy (YH10927)																																				●	
PENBODE VETNRY GRP, Holsworthy (YH10926)																																				●	
PERCIVAL, MARK F B, Okehampton (YH10972)														●																							
PERSSE, BURTON S H, Cullompton (YH10996)														●																							
PIDGEON, STEVEN G, Moretonhampstead (YH11089)														●																							
PIGGOTT & ARNOLD, Bovey Tracey (YH11096)																																				●	
QUARRY HSE VETNRY CTRE, Torquay (YH11482)																																				●	
RICHARDSON, ROBBIE, Newton Abbott (YH11820)														●																							
RITCHIE, CLIVE G, Crediton (YH11915)														●																							
RUMFORD BOND & BALDWIN, Bovey Tracey (YH12230)																																				●	

Business Profile
Breeding and Wellbeing

by Country by County

	Ambulance Services	Animal Behaviourist	Artificial Insemination	Bloodstock Advice	Bloodstock Agency	Breaking In Horses	Breeding Advice	Chiropractics	Clipper Maintenance	Complementary Medicine	Dentistry Skills	Dust Control	Emergency Services	Farrier Services	Groom	Groom Services	Herbalists	Holistic Medicine	Homeopathy	Horse Ambulance	Horse Psychiatry	Horse Sitter	Horse Walker	Laser & Ultrasound	Nutritionists	Osteopathy	Physiotherapy	Respiratory Disease control	Shoe Fitting Skills	Solarium	Stud Services	Swimming Pool Centre	Trotting Services	Vaccination	Veterinary Labs	Veterinary Practice	Veterinary Skills
SANSOM, B P A, Honiton (YH12428)														●																							
SECKINGTON FORGE, Winkleigh (YH12596)														●																							
SEDGECROFT STUD, Axminster (YH12602)																											●				●						
SOMERS, R, Seaton (YH13062)														●																							
SOUTH DEVON EQUESTRIAN SUP, Paignton (YH13082)										●																											
SPRY, RUSSELL K, Plymouth (YH13267)														●																							
STIDSTON EQUESTRIAN, South Brent (YH13466)						●																															
STOCKSHOP WOLSELEY, Exeter (YH13496)									●																												
STUART, G, Ottery St Mary (YH13595)														●																							
STUART, PAUL A, Feniton (YH13597)														●																							
SVENSSON, MARK ANDREW, Okehampton (YH13680)														●																							
TALAWATER QUARTER HORSES, Yelverton (YH13830)							●																								●						
THRESHER, H M, Tiverton (YH14110)																																				●	
TORBRIDGE VETNRY CTRE, Bideford (YH14243)																																				●	
TRIBE, MALCOLM, Newton Abbot (YH14391)														●																							
TUCKER, EDWARD W, Bideford (YH14433)														●																							
TULLY, GRAHAM J, Chudleigh (YH14452)														●																							
UNDERHILL, DAVID J, Newton Abbot (YH14561)														●																							
VOSPER, M, Yelverton (YH14742)														●																							
VOWDEN, T R, Newton Abbot (YH14743)														●																							
WAKELY, JAN I, Honiton (YH14835)														●																							
WARD, MICHAEL J, Holsworthy (YH14904)														●																							
WEBSTER, SHEUMAIS A, Newton Abbott (YH15042)														●																							
WEIR, M, Ivybridge (YH15055)														●																							
WEST RIDGE VETNRY PRAC, Tiverton (YH15160)																																				●	
WESTCOTT, W M, Tiverton (YH15188)														●																							
WHITFIELD, PAUL A, Honiton (YH15360)														●																							
WILLS, R J, Exeter (YH15519)														●																							
WITHERIDGE, WILLIAM GEORGE, Barnstaple (YH15623)														●																							
WONNACOTT, DAVID J, South Brent (YH15653)														●																							
WONNACOTT, ERIC W J, Lewdown (YH15654)														●																							
WOOD, JONATHAN, Crediton (YH15664)																																				●	

Business Profile
Breeding and Wellbeing

by Country by County

	Ambulance Services	Animal Behaviourist	Artificial Insemination	Bloodstock Advice	Bloodstock Agency	Breaking In Horses	Breeding Advice	Chiropractics	Clipper Maintenance	Complementary Medicine	Dentistry Skills	Dust Control	Emergency Services	Farrier Services	Groom	Groom Services	Herbalists	Holistic Medicine	Homeopathy	Horse Ambulance	Horse Psychiatry	Horse Sitter	Horse Walker	Laser & Ultrasound	Nutritionists	Osteopathy	Physiotherapy	Respiratory Disease control	Shoe Fitting Skills	Solarium	Stud Services	Swimming Pool Centre	Trotting Services	Vaccination	Veterinary Labs	Veterinary Practice	Veterinary Skills
WOODLANDS VETNRY CTRE, Ivybridge (YH15715)																																				●	
DORSET																																					
ALEXANDER TECHNIQUE TEACHER, Wimborne (YH00267)										●																											
ALLEN, ROBERT T, Dorchester (YH00301)														●																							
BAILEY MOBILE, Blandford Forum (YH00795)														●																							
BARRINGTON, J M, Warmwell (YH01023)														●																							
BRAMBLES FARM ARABIANS, Wimborne (YH01787)																															●						
BREDY VETNRY CTRE, Bridport (YH01831)																																				●	
BRIDE, D, Bournemouth (YH01868)														●																							
BROWN, ANDREW P, Poole (YH02100)														●																							
BYRNE, ROBERT, Bransgore (YH02349)														●																							
CENTRAL PREFIX REGISTER, Shaftesbury (YH02689)							●																								●						
CLARK, L M & GILMORE, TONY, Wareham (YH02964)								●		●																●	●										
COLMER STUD, Bridport (YH03193)																															●						
DAMORY VETNRY CLINIC, Blandford (YH03856)																																				●	
DEXTER, KIRK, Poole (YH04099)														●																							
DUFOSSE, TERESA, Kington (YH04321)																											●										
ESS, Dorchester (YH04863)													●																								
FIELDING, M, Weymouth (YH05195)																																				●	
FORBES COPPER, Blandford (YH05318)										●																											
FOX, GRAHAM P, Dorchester (YH05429)														●																							
FRANCIS, LEE M R, Ferndown (YH05451)														●																							
FREAK, N R, Sturminster Newton (YH05475)														●																							
GETHING & BOWDITCH, Beaminster (YH05735)																																				●	
GILL, R M, Gillingham (YH05775)														●																							
GOLDSWORTHY, C, Sherborne (YH05894)														●																							
GRAHAM C S JEANS, Blandford Forum (YH05963)														●																							
HARDING, E J, Wimborne (YH06411)														●																							
HAYDON VETNRY GRP, Bridport (YH06573)																																				●	
HURN BRIDGE CTRE, Christchurch (YH07313)										●																											
KEATES, REBEKAH, Bournemouth (YH08020)																											●										
KERLEY, KEITH, Blandford Forum (YH08097)														●																							

Business Profile
Breeding and Wellbeing

by Country by County	Ambulance Services	Animal Behaviourist	Artificial Insemination	Bloodstock Advice	Bloodstock Agency	Breaking In Horses	Breeding Advice	Chiropractics	Clipper Maintenance	Complementary Medicine	Dentistry Skills	Dust Control	Emergency Services	Farrier Services	Groom	Groom Services	Herbalists	Holistic Medicine	Homeopathy	Horse Ambulance	Horse Psychiatry	Horse Sitter	Horse Walker	Laser & Ultrasound	Nutritionists	Osteopathy	Physiotherapy	Respiratory Disease control	Shoe Fitting Skills	Solarium	Stud Services	Swimming Pool Centre	Trotting Services	Vaccination	Veterinary Labs	Veterinary Practice	Veterinary Skills
LAIDLAW, G D W, Christchurch (YH08345)														●																							
LANGLEY, GRAHAM A, Shaftesbury (YH08410)														●																							
LATCHAM, DEAN L, Shaftesbury (YH08444)														●																							
LONDON THOROUGHBRED SVS, Wimborne (YH08790)					●																																
MARCHANT, I R, Weymouth (YH09143)														●																							
MARSH, ANDREW, Corfe Mullen (YH09188)														●																							
MEADEN, ABIGAIL R L, Blandford Forum (YH09416)														●																							
MORGAN, D D P, Portland (YH09802)														●																							
NELMES CHIROPRACTIC CLINIC, Verwood (YH10071)								●																		●	●										
O Y C, Wareham (YH10369)		●		●			●														●																
OAKSFORD & BIRCH, Sherborne (YH10405)																																				●	
OLIVER, MARK S, Bournemouth (YH10498)														●																							
PHILLIPS, LESLIE M, Dorchester (YH11059)														●																							
PRIORY VETNRY GRP, Christchurch (YH11407)																																				●	
PRUST, K R, Wimborne (YH11442)														●																							
RAFIQUE, M, Sturminster Newton (YH11605)					●																																
SLEEMAN-HISCOCK, ANTHONY IVOR, Sturminster Newton (YH12894)														●																							
SMITH, FREDRICK T, Dorchester (YH12957)														●																							
SOUTHFIELD VETNRY CTRE, Dorchester (YH13152)																																				●	
SPARKES, A J, Shaftesbury (YH13175)														●																							
SPARKES, PAUL J, Shaftesbury (YH13176)														●																							
STABLE MINDS, Ferndown (YH13297)																															●						
STAPLES, LESLIE R, Blandford (YH13388)														●																							
STARROCK STUD, Shaftesbury (YH13398)							●																								●						
SUTCLIFFE, ANTHONY W, Dorchester (YH13665)														●																							
THOMAS, PHILIP J, Verwood (YH14027)														●																							
TROWBRIDGE, B J, Shaftesbury (YH14414)														●																							
TUSON, PETER, Poole (YH14504)														●																							
VINCENT, PETER J, Sherborne (YH14726)														●																							
WARMWELL STUD, Dorchester (YH14924)							●		●					●		●						●															
WARREN, WILLIAM J, Verwood (YH14937)														●																							
WATTS, NEIL D, Evershot (YH15006)														●																							

Business Profile
Breeding and Wellbeing

by Country by County

	Ambulance Services	Animal Behaviourist	Artificial Insemination	Bloodstock Advice	Bloodstock Agency	Breaking In Horses	Breeding Advice	Chiropractics	Clipper Maintenance	Complementary Medicine	Dentistry Skills	Dust Control	Emergency Services	Farrier Services	Groom	Groom Services	Herbalists	Holistic Medicine	Homeopathy	Horse Ambulance	Horse Psychiatry	Horse Sitter	Horse Walker	Laser & Ultrasound	Nutritionists	Osteopathy	Physiotherapy	Respiratory Disease control	Shoe Fitting Skills	Solarium	Stud Services	Swimming Pool Centre	Trotting Services	Vaccination	Veterinary Labs	Veterinary Practice	Veterinary Skills
WHITMARSH, R A, Wareham (YH15364)														●																							
YATES, PETER G, Bridport (YH15890)														●																							
ESSEX																																					
ACKLAND, RICHARD J, Dagenham (YH00144)														●																							
ADAMS, GAVIN, Ridgewell (YH00166)														●																							
ALLEN, G, Chelmsford (YH00296)														●																							
ATKINS, PAUL, Dunmow (YH00649)														●																							
BAILEYS HORSE FEEDS, Braintree (YH00806)																									●												
BARNES, GEORGE EDWARD, Colchester (YH00974)														●																							
BELL, K J, Halstead (YH01226)														●																							
BIRCHER, ANDREW K, Maldon (YH01432)														●																							
BOWENS, BARNABY, Castle Hedingham (YH01705)														●																							
BRASH, DEAN, Witham (YH01812)														●																							
BROOK FARM STABLES, Colchester (YH02036)																						●	●														
BUNDOCK, PETER M, West Thurrock (YH02222)														●																							
BUTLER, CARL S, Chelmsford (YH02322)														●																							
CLEERE, NICHOLAS S P, Wickford (YH03014)														●																							
CLEMENTS, IAN A, Halstead (YH03018)														●																							
CLOW, R A, Benfleet (YH03071)														●																							
COE, ALAN R, Colchester (YH03132)														●																							
CONOR FENELON, Great Dunmow (YH03241)			●																																●	●	
COOPER, PAUL H, Witham (YH03289)														●																							
COTTER, LLOYD J, Hornchurch (YH03382)														●																							
CROSSLEY, RICHARD L, Billericay (YH03661)														●																							
CULLEN, GLYN MITCHELL, Billericay (YH03703)														●																							
DANBURY, Chelmsford (YH03860)						●																															
DENGIE, Maldon (YH04045)																									●												
DOBBERSON, JAMES HENRY, Tilbury (YH04148)														●																							
DOBBERSON, KEITH L, Bridge (YH04149)														●																							
DODSWORTH, KEITH D, South Benfleet (YH04163)														●																							
DUNNETT, CATHERINE (DR), Maldon (YH04353)																									●												
DUTTON, G, Canvey Island (YH04378)														●																							

Business Profile
Breeding and Wellbeing

by Country by County	Ambulance Services	Animal Behaviourist	Artificial Insemination	Bloodstock Advice	Bloodstock Agency	Breaking In Horses	Breeding Advice	Chiropractics	Clipper Maintenance	Complementary Medicine	Dentistry Skills	Dust Control	Emergency Services	Farrier Services	Groom	Groom Services	Herbalists	Holistic Medicine	Homeopathy	Horse Ambulance	Horse Psychiatry	Horse Sitter	Horse Walker	Laser & Ultrasound	Nutritionists	Osteopathy	Physiotherapy	Respiratory Disease control	Shoe Fitting Skills	Solarium	Stud Services	Swimming Pool Centre	Trotting Services	Vaccination	Veterinary Labs	Veterinary Practice	Veterinary Skills
ELLA, ANTHONY W, Doddinghurst (YH04610)														●																							
ELM TODD, Frinton-on-Sea (YH04634)																●																					
EQUINE HEALTH & HERBAL, Halstead (YH04779)										●																											
FRANKLAND, RONALD A, Waltham Abbey (YH05467)														●																							
GAME, DAVID C, Ingatestone (YH05634)														●																							
GILSTON LIVERY STABLES, Harlow (YH05791)																●																					
HARRIS, DEAN R, Chelmsford (YH06467)														●																							
HAYTER, D J, Stanford-Le-Hope (YH06593)														●																							
HEDGES, ANTONY A, Romford (YH06643)														●																							
HOLTON, IVOR J, Chelmsford (YH06991)														●																							
HOOD, BARBARA, Saffron Walden (YH07020)								●																		●	●										
HYLTON, J H, Southminster (YH07359)														●															●								
IMPEY, LINDA, Chelmsford (YH07404)							●																														
J TODD, Brentwood (YH07622)														●																							
JOHNSON, GAVIN J, Brentwood (YH07824)														●																							
JOSLIN, EDWARD JOHN, Halstead (YH07947)														●																							
KELLY, NEIL J, Southminster (YH08046)														●																							
KILN SADDLERY, Colchester (YH08151)									●																												
LANGFORD LIVERY, Maldon (YH08404)																●																					
LAZARO, L, Colchester (YH08485)											●																										
LITTLE PADDOCK, Colchester (YH08698)														●		●																					●
LONGWOOD EQUESTRIAN CTRE, Basildon (YH08820)								●																		●	●										
LUBIN, J R B, Holland-on-Sea (YH08882)														●																							
MARSDEN, M A, Matching Green (YH09185)														●																							
MARTIN, GARY, Maldon (YH09219)														●																							
MAY, R S, Harwich (YH09291)														●																							
MCLELLAN, B M, Bishop's Stortford (YH09388)														●																							
MITCHELL, DAVID, Crays Hill (YH09666)														●																							
MOBBS, F I, Maldon (YH09688)														●															●								
MOORAH STUD, Maldon (YH09746)														●																	●						
MORTLOCK, BARRIE J, Ingatestone (YH09849)														●																							
MOSS, JANETTE, Waltham Abbey (YH09858)									●																												

Business Profile
Breeding and Wellbeing

by Country by County

	Ambulance Services	Animal Behaviourist	Artificial Insemination	Bloodstock Advice	Bloodstock Agency	Breaking In Horses	Breeding Advice	Chiropractics	Clipper Maintenance	Complementary Medicine	Dentistry Skills	Dust Control	Emergency Services	Farrier Services	Groom	Groom Services	Herbalists	Holistic Medicine	Homeopathy	Horse Ambulance	Horse Psychiatry	Horse Sitter	Horse Walker	Laser & Ultrasound	Nutritionists	Osteopathy	Physiotherapy	Respiratory Disease control	Shoe Fitting Skills	Solarium	Stud Services	Swimming Pool Centre	Trotting Services	Vaccination	Veterinary Labs	Veterinary Practice	Veterinary Skills
NEWMAN-TAYLOR, TOBIN R, Brentwood (YH10153)														●																							
NIGHTINGALE RIDING SCHOOL, Buckhurst Hill (YH10204)																●																					
NORTON, B J, Basildon (YH10331)														●																							
PARDOE, CHRISTOPHER H, Benfleet (YH10713)														●																							
PAY, RICHARD, Fobbing (YH10845)														●																							
PEARCE, ANTHONY P, Braintree (YH10869)														●																							
PINE LODGE, Loughton (YH11118)																●																					
POWER, GARY, Upminster (YH11326)														●																							
PRIORY SADDLERY, Colchester (YH11403)									●																												
ROBERTSON, JASON A, Romford (YH11972)														●																							
SARGEANT, C R, Chelmsford (YH12436)														●																							
SAUNDERS, E, Dunmow (YH12446)														●																							
SCRUTTON, I F, Manningtree (YH12571)														●																							
SEVEN SAINTS RARE BREEDS, Colchester (YH12639)		●																																			
SEWELL, ERNEST CHARLES TREVOR, Fobbing (YH12649)														●																							
SHAHZADA, Dunmow (YH12659)				●			●																														
SINGH KHAKHIAN, GARY, Basildon (YH12852)											●			●																							
SINGH, PETER G, Basildon (YH12854)														●																							
STEVENSON, DONALD E, Ongar (YH13450)														●																							
TACK EXCHANGE, Leigh-on-Sea (YH13788)									●																												
TAYLOR, B W, Romford (YH13896)														●																							
TAYLOR, D J W, Southend (YH13899)																																				●	
TAYLOR, S F C, Danbury (YH13910)														●																							
THACKER, GRAHAM, Grays (YH13972)														●																							
TIPTREE EQUESTRIAN CTRE, Colchester (YH14184)																●																					
VALLEY RIDING/LIVERY STABLES, Ingatestone (YH14657)														●		●													●								●
WASH FARM, Colchester (YH14954)																							●														
WETHERSFIELD RIDING STABLES, Braintree (YH15246)		●														●					●																
WHITE, MARK W, Brentwood (YH15334)														●																							
WILLIAMS, MICHAEL, Harlow (YH15466)														●																							
WITHERSTONE, W A, Brentwood (YH15625)											●																										
WIX EQUESTRIAN CTRE, Manningtree (YH15636)																	●																				

Business Profile
Breeding and Wellbeing

by Country by County

	Ambulance Services	Animal Behaviourist	Artificial Insemination	Bloodstock Advice	Bloodstock Agency	Breaking In Horses	Breeding Advice	Chiropractics	Clipper Maintenance	Complementary Medicine	Dentistry Skills	Dust Control	Emergency Services	Farrier Services	Groom	Groom Services	Herbalists	Holistic Medicine	Homeopathy	Horse Ambulance	Horse Psychiatry	Horse Sitter	Horse Walker	Laser & Ultrasound	Nutritionists	Osteopathy	Physiotherapy	Respiratory Disease control	Shoe Fitting Skills	Solarium	Stud Services	Swimming Pool Centre	Trotting Services	Vaccination	Veterinary Labs	Veterinary Practice	Veterinary Skills
GLOUCESTERSHIRE																																					
ABBEY GREEN VETNRY GRP, Cheltenham (YH00077)																																				●	
ABBOTSWOOD VETNRY CTRE, Yate (YH00101)																																				●	
ASPINALL AULD & CLARKSON, Abbeydale (YH00626)																																				●	
AUBOISE, Chaceley (YH00658)												●																									
BAXTER, DEREK MICHAEL, Cheltenham (YH01086)														●																							
BELL, MICHAEL D, Badminton Farm (YH01228)														●																							
BIRCH, BRIAN, Cheltenham (YH01429)														●																							
BOURTON VALE EQUINE CLINIC, Cheltenham (YH01690)																																				●	
BRAMBLES VETNRY SURGERY, Churchdown (YH01788)																																				●	
BROWN, A, Moreton In Marsh (YH02095)														●																							
BROWN, ARTHUR H, Blockley (YH02101)														●																							
BURT, THOMAS D, Cheltenham (YH02289)														●																							
BUSHY FARM EQUINE CLINIC, Berkeley (YH02311)																																				●	
CAIRNS, PETER A, Cirencester (YH02420)														●																							
CHALLONER, TIMOTHY V, Gloucester (YH02714)														●																							
CHURCH FARM, Mitcheldean (YH02895)																●																					
CLAYTON & COX, Newent (YH03002)																																				●	
COCKING, R, Moreton In Marsh (YH03124)														●																							
CODNER & CHALKLEY, Cheltenham (YH03131)																																				●	
COID, STEWART, Cirencester (YH03137)														●																							
COLDICOTT, J H, Tewkesbury (YH03147)																																				●	
DAVE REGAN, Moreton In Marsh (YH03908)											●																										
DAVISON, CATHERINE, Cirencester (YH03957)								●		●																●	●										
DEACON, NICHOLAS, Stroud (YH03983)														●																							
ELM LEAZE STUD, Badminton (YH04631)																							●														
ENIGMA PHYSIOTHERAPY, Moreton In Marsh (YH04676)								●																		●	●										
EQUINE SPORTS MASSAGE ASS, Dursley (YH04802)										●								●									●										
EVANS, ANNE-MARIE & RICHARD, Moreton In Marsh (YH04916)											●																										
EVILL, LIONEL ALAN, Cirencester (YH04959)														●																							
FLETCHER, DESMOND EDWARD, Cirencester (YH05275)														●																							
FOLLY, CHRISTOPHER C, Dymock (YH05304)														●																							

Business Profile

Breeding and Wellbeing

by Country by County

	Ambulance Services	Animal Behaviourist	Artificial Insemination	Bloodstock Advice	Bloodstock Agency	Breaking In Horses	Breeding Advice	Chiropractics	Clipper Maintenance	Complementary Medicine	Dentistry Skills	Dust Control	Emergency Services	Farrier Services	Groom	Groom Services	Herbalists	Holistic Medicine	Homeopathy	Horse Ambulance	Horse Psychiatry	Horse Sitter	Horse Walker	Laser & Ultrasound	Nutritionists	Osteopathy	Physiotherapy	Respiratory Disease control	Shoe Fitting Skills	Solarium	Stud Services	Swimming Pool Centre	Trotting Services	Vaccination	Veterinary Labs	Veterinary Practice	Veterinary Skills
GISBORNE, SIMON PATRICK, Lower Apperley (YH05796)														●																							
HALL, DAVID A, Quedgeley (YH06315)														●																							
HARVEY, SIMON F, Tewkesbury (YH06517)																																				●	
HENRY COLE, Cirencester (YH06681)												●																									
HOPKINS, PAUL T, Cheltenham (YH07054)														●																							
HOWSON, GEOFFREY, Cheltenham (YH07245)				●	●																																
I SINTON & SON, Cirencester (YH07368)														●																							
J C PRICE, Stonehouse (YH07573)									●																												
JANAWAY, P H, Badminton (YH07693)																																				●	
JENKINS, P, Ashleworth (YH07735)											●																										
JUGGINS, PHILIP J, Cheltenham (YH07960)														●																							
KEARNS & REA, Tewkesbury (YH08018)																																				●	
KING, BRUCE M, Moreton In Marsh (YH08175)														●																							
KNIGHT, RICHARD, Cheltenham (YH08265)														●																							
LANSDOWN VETNRY SURGEONS, Stroud (YH08422)																																				●	
LEATHERDALE, HOWARD M, Lechlade (YH08508)														●																							
LESTER, MACKINNON & BENSON, Cirencester (YH08563)																																				●	
LLOYD, EVAN JOHN, Stroud (YH08737)														●																							
LOVELL, MARTYN A, Gloucester (YH08849)														●																							
MARTIN, PHILLIP J, Stow-on-the-Wold (YH09225)														●																							
MAY, CLIVE D, Cheltenham (YH09288)														●																							
MCCORMICK, MICHAEL G, Cirencester (YH09332)														●																							
MEDCROFT, JASON R, Newent (YH09433)														●																							
MILLS, C D, Kings Stanley (YH09632)														●																							
MILLWARD, PHILIP E, Kingscote (YH09640)														●																							
NELSON, GARRICK S R, Longhope (YH10074)														●																							
NICHOLLS, N E, Dursley (YH10184)														●																							
NICHOLLS, WESLEY, Cheltenham (YH10187)														●																							
OLYMPIC BLOODSTOCK, Moreton In Marsh (YH10503)					●																																
OWEN, JOHN, Badminton (YH10604)																																				●	
PARK CORNER FARM, Cirencester (YH10716)																●																					
PARTRIDGE, NICHOLAS S, Cheltenham (YH10808)														●																							

Business Profile
Breeding and Wellbeing

by Country by County	Ambulance Services	Animal Behaviourist	Artificial Insemination	Bloodstock Advice	Bloodstock Agency	Breaking In Horses	Breeding Advice	Chiropractics	Clipper Maintenance	Complementary Medicine	Dentistry Skills	Dust Control	Emergency Services	Farrier Services	Groom	Groom Services	Herbalists	Holistic Medicine	Homeopathy	Horse Ambulance	Horse Psychiatry	Horse Sitter	Horse Walker	Laser & Ultrasound	Nutritionists	Osteopathy	Physiotherapy	Respiratory Disease control	Shoe Fitting Skills	Solarium	Stud Services	Swimming Pool Centre	Trotting Services	Vaccination	Veterinary Labs	Veterinary Practice	Veterinary Skills
PONTING, M F, Cirencester (YH11227)																																				●	
PRICE, A C, Lydney (YH11374)														●																							
PRITCHARD, TERESA, Berkeley (YH11424)								●																		●	●										
RACK, FRANCIS, Cirencester (YH11589)														●																							
RACK, W, Cirencester (YH11590)														●																							
RICHARDS, D C, Fairford (YH11807)														●																							
STAFFORD, RICHARD JOHN, Cheltenham (YH13322)														●																							
STRONG, ALEXANDER G, Brimpsfield (YH13582)														●																							
STROUD SADDLERY, Stroud (YH13588)									●																												
SWAN, CECIL T, Tewkesbury (YH13690)														●																							
TANNER, STEPHEN M, Horsley (YH13858)														●																							
TEWKESBURY SADDLERY, Tewkesbury (YH13969)									●																												
THOMAS, MICHAEL JAMES, Cheltenham (YH14026)														●																							
TOWNSEND, K, Moreton In Marsh (YH14299)								●																		●	●										
TWEENHILLS FARM & STUD, Gloucester (YH14508)					●																																
WAKEFIELD, G A, Newent (YH14832)														●																							
WARD, JONATHAN M, Cirencester (YH14901)														●																							
WARD, STANLEY A, St Brivels (YH14909)														●																							
WELLFAIR, M, Cheltenham (YH15068)														●																							
WHERRETT, PETER A, Thrupp (YH15278)														●																							
WILLESLEY EQUINE CLINIC, Tetbury (YH15430)			●																																	●	
WOOD, MERVYN, Cheltenham (YH15665)														●																							
WORSLEY, R, Cirencester (YH15801)										●																											
GLOUCESTERSHIRE (SOUTH)																																					
ANIMAL HEALTH CTRE, Filton (YH00436)																																				●	
ARTIFICIAL INSEMINATION CTRE, Kingswood (YH00575)			●																																		
CHURCH, D E, Hanham (YH02908)														●																							
DORAN & GRADWELL, Thornbury (YH04195)																																				●	
GILBERTSON, RICHARD D, Winterbourne Down (YH05761)														●																							
JEE, D G, Chipping Sodbury (YH07714)														●																							
RILEY VETNRY CLINICS, Chipping Sodbury (YH11895)																																				●	
ROWE VETNRY GROUP, Patchway (YH12160)																																				●	

Business Profile
Breeding and Wellbeing

by Country by County

	Ambulance Services	Animal Behaviourist	Artificial Insemination	Bloodstock Advice	Bloodstock Agency	Breaking In Horses	Breeding Advice	Chiropractics	Clipper Maintenance	Complementary Medicine	Dentistry Skills	Dust Control	Emergency Services	Farrier Services	Groom	Groom Services	Herbalists	Holistic Medicine	Homeopathy	Horse Ambulance	Horse Psychiatry	Horse Sitter	Horse Walker	Laser & Ultrasound	Nutritionists	Osteopathy	Physiotherapy	Respiratory Disease control	Shoe Fitting Skills	Solarium	Stud Services	Swimming Pool Centre	Trotting Services	Vaccination	Veterinary Labs	Veterinary Practice	Veterinary Skills
ROWE VETNRY GROUP, Yate (YH12162)																																				●	
ROWE VETNRY GROUP, Thornbury (YH12161)																																				●	
SMITH, MATTHEW K, Frampton Cotterell (YH12976)														●																							
WINTERBOURNE VETNRY CLINIC, Winterbourne (YH15597)																																				●	
GUERNSEY																																					
BEAN, PHILLIPPA J, Vale (YH01118)														●																							
HARGREAVES, PAUL W, Vale (YH06428)														●																							
ISABELLE VETS, St Peter Port (YH07513)																																				●	
LOWE, DAVID J, Castel (YH08859)														●																							
NORTHSIDE VERERINARY CTRE, Vale (YH10318)																																				●	
VETCARE CTRES, Castel (YH14690)																																				●	
VETCARE CTRES, Alderney (YH14689)																																				●	
VETCARE CTRES, St Martins (YH14688)																																				●	
HAMPSHIRE																																					
ADAMS, J, Ringwood (YH00167)														●																							
ADAMS, MERVYN, Lymington (YH00171)														●																							
AMBERVALE, Lymington (YH00357)		●																																			
BALCOMBE, JOHN A, Aldershot (YH00832)														●																							
BARNES, CLIFFORD, Andover (YH00973)														●																							
BARTON, M A, Southampton (YH01049)														●																							
BEACH, L S, Fordingbridge (YH01103)																																				●	
BEALE, C R, Lymington (YH01114)											●			●																							
BEAUMONT, J A, New Milton (YH01136)														●																							
BELASCO, STEPHEN R, Dibden (YH01203)														●																							
BIGG, STEVEN N, Southampton (YH01403)														●																							
BRIDGEWATER, CRAIG, Portsmouth (YH01885)														●																							
BROCKS FARM, Stockbridge (YH02013)																●																					
BROCKS, MICHAEL S, Alton (YH02014)														●																							
BROWN, PIERCE R, Hook (YH02127)														●																							
CALCUTT & SONS, Winchester (YH02425)									●																												
CATHERSTON, Stockbridge (YH02650)																							●														
CEDAR VETNRY GRP, Alton (YH02676)																																				●	

Business Profile
Breeding and Wellbeing

by Country by County	Ambulance Services	Animal Behaviourist	Artificial Insemination	Bloodstock Advice	Bloodstock Agency	Breaking In Horses	Breeding Advice	Chiropractics	Clipper Maintenance	Complementary Medicine	Dentistry Skills	Dust Control	Emergency Services	Farrier Services	Groom	Groom Services	Herbalists	Holistic Medicine	Homeopathy	Horse Ambulance	Horse Psychiatry	Horse Sitter	Horse Walker	Laser & Ultrasound	Nutritionists	Osteopathy	Physiotherapy	Respiratory Disease control	Shoe Fitting Skills	Solarium	Stud Services	Swimming Pool Centre	Trotting Services	Vaccination	Veterinary Labs	Veterinary Practice	Veterinary Skills
CHALMERS, ALEXANDER W, New Milton (YH02715)														●																							
CORDALL, I R, Fareham (YH03310)														●																							
CORTEN, STEPHEN, Tadley (YH03346)														●																							
D L P EQUINE CONSULTANTS, Otterbourne (YH03792)																									●												
DALY, DAVID J, Yateley (YH03850)														●																							
DEAN, ANDREW M, Winchester (YH03990)														●																							
DOWNLAND VETNRY GRP, Emsworth (YH04236)																																				●	
DOYLE, DARREN L, Tadley (YH04245)														●																							
DRAKE, PHILIP, Lyndhurst (YH04255)														●																							
DREW, J R, Winchester (YH04269)																																				●	
DUFFIN, CLIVE, Fleet (YH04316)														●																							
DUNNING, P L, Southampton (YH04354)														●																							
DUNNING, T, Southampton (YH04355)														●																							
EQUALLUS EQUESTRIAN, Hook (YH04685)																●																					
ETHERIDGE, DAVID H, Bishops Waltham (YH04882)														●																							
F NEWMAN & SONS, Alton (YH04997)														●																							
FARRIER SVS, Basingstoke (YH05089)														●																							
FENNELL, NIGEL D, Odiham (YH05147)														●																							
FLETCHER, DAVID S, Fareham (YH05274)														●																							
FOREST COUNTRYWEAR, Fordingbridge (YH05333)										●		●													●												
FOREVER LIVING PRODUCTS, Soberton (YH05358)										●																											
FOSTER & SEWARD, Basingstoke (YH05397)																																				●	
G N GOULD & PARTNERS, Southampton (YH05589)																																				●	
GEORGES, D, Fareham (YH05727)														●																							
GREEN, J A H, Southampton (YH06066)														●																							
GRIFFITHS, DAVID W, Aldershot (YH06140)														●																							
HACKNEY PK, Lymington (YH06258)														●															●								
HAMPSON, P, Bordon (YH06369)														●																							
HARMSWORTH FARM, Southampton (YH06446)																●																					
HARRIS, ANDREW, Lymington (YH06464)					●																																
HARROW, SIMON P, Emsworth (YH06494)														●																							
HENDERSON, PAUL F, Southampton (YH06668)														●																							

Business Profile
Breeding and Wellbeing

by Country by County

	Ambulance Services	Animal Behaviourist	Artificial Insemination	Bloodstock Advice	Bloodstock Agency	Breaking In Horses	Breeding Advice	Chiropractics	Clipper Maintenance	Complementary Medicine	Dentistry Skills	Dust Control	Emergency Services	Farrier Services	Groom	Groom Services	Herbalists	Holistic Medicine	Homeopathy	Horse Ambulance	Horse Psychiatry	Horse Sitter	Horse Walker	Laser & Ultrasound	Nutritionists	Osteopathy	Physiotherapy	Respiratory Disease control	Shoe Fitting Skills	Solarium	Stud Services	Swimming Pool Centre	Trotting Services	Vaccination	Veterinary Labs	Veterinary Practice	Veterinary Skills
HOOD, C L, Swanmore (YH07021)														●																							
HUNT, SHOLTO A, Alton (YH07298)														●																							
JONES, DAVID H, Andover (YH07890)														●																							
JONES, ROGER M L, Lymington (YH07929)														●																							
KEABLE, CHRISTOPHER P, New Milton (YH08014)														●																							
KEELEY, PAULA, Liss (YH08027)										●																											
KEELING, F J, Eastleigh (YH08028)														●																							
KING, R A, Havant (YH08187)														●																							
KIRKBY, GEORGE, Lymington (YH08233)														●																							
KNIGHTBRIDGE, A, Southampton (YH08266)														●																							
KNOTT, J B & J E, Winchester (YH08278)																																				●	
LAPIDGE, ANDREW, Southampton (YH08427)														●																							
LAUNDER, J W, Rowland's Castle (YH08453)														●																							
LINSSNER, C P, Andover (YH08669)														●																							
LIPHOOK EQUINE HOSPITAL, Liphook (YH08674)											●																									●	
LOVEJOY, RICHARD E W, Petersfield (YH08848)														●																							
MALONE, B, Winchester (YH09054)														●																							
MANSBRIDGE, G E, Marchwood (YH09121)														●																							
MASKELL, TIM, Lymington (YH09237)														●																							
MAYHEW, BOB, Petersfield (YH09298)							●																								●						
MEAKER, MARTYN A, Lymington (YH09427)														●																							
METCALFE, ANTHONY J, Andover (YH09499)														●																							
MOORE, T E, Fordingbridge (YH09767)																																				●	
MOSS, R S, Petersfield (YH09863)														●																							
MOUNTIAN, ANTHONY J, Fareham (YH09902)														●																							
NAILOR, W C, Alton (YH10012)														●																							
O'ROURKE, SHAUN, Southampton (YH10551)														●																							
PARSONS, G R, Liss (YH10799)										●																											
PERRYS PLACE, Brokenhurst (YH10992)														●		●																					
PHILLIPS, MARK J, Waltham Chase (YH11060)														●																							
POOLE, ANTHONY E, Liphook (YH11264)														●																							
POVEY, A L, Winchester (YH11312)														●																							

Business Profile
Breeding and Wellbeing

by Country by County

	Ambulance Services	Animal Behaviourist	Artificial Insemination	Bloodstock Advice	Bloodstock Agency	Breaking In Horses	Breeding Advice	Chiropractics	Clipper Maintenance	Complementary Medicine	Dentistry Skills	Dust Control	Emergency Services	Farrier Services	Groom	Groom Services	Herbalists	Holistic Medicine	Homeopathy	Horse Ambulance	Horse Psychiatry	Horse Sitter	Horse Walker	Laser & Ultrasound	Nutritionists	Osteopathy	Physiotherapy	Respiratory Disease control	Shoe Fitting Skills	Solarium	Stud Services	Swimming Pool Centre	Trotting Services	Vaccination	Veterinary Labs	Veterinary Practice	Veterinary Skills
RAVENSCROFT, JAMES C, Romsey (YH11658)														●																							
REDENHAM PK STUD, Andover (YH11708)				●	●		●																														
REEVES, PAUL R, Baughurst (YH11738)														●																							
RIVERSIDE VETNRY SURGERY, Eastleigh (YH11929)																																				●	
ROBBERTS, B A, Ringwood (YH11935)														●																							
ROBERTS, ALWYN, Farnborough (YH11946)														●																							
RODGERS, S E, Liss (YH12047)																																				●	
ROWE, JOSEPH ROBERT, North Baddesley (YH12163)														●																							
RUMSEY, WAYNE P, Southampton (YH12232)														●																							
SAMPSON, EDWARD, Ringwood (YH12398)														●																							
SANDILANDS, Petersfield (YH12413)							●																														
SAYERS, RICHARD S, Yateley (YH12478)														●																							
SEADOWN VETNRY GROUP, Hythe (YH12582)																																				●	
SEAGRAVE COTTAGE STABLES, Bishops Waltham (YH12588)														●																							
SKINNER, ROGER M, Romsey (YH12877)														●																							
SOUTHWEST BLOODSTOCK, Alton (YH13162)					●																																
STOCKBRIDGE, Stockbridge (YH13486)														●																							
STURGESS, NICHOLAS J, Curdridge (YH13616)														●																							
TRICKLEDOWN STUD, Stockbridge (YH14392)					●																																
UK AST OF HOLISTIC NUTRITION, Hook (YH14542)										●															●												
UNDERWOOD, C M, Emsworth (YH14564)														●																							
WEHRLE, MARCUS E, Westharting (YH15049)														●																							
WELBAC CHIROPRACTIC CLINIC, New Milton (YH15057)								●																		●	●										
WELLINGTON RIDING, Hook (YH15075)														●		●							●														
WHYATT, D J, Ringwood (YH15379)														●																							
WIGGINS, R J, Basingstoke (YH15399)														●																							
WILLIAMS, CHARLOTTE, Droxford (YH15453)																											●										
WOODMAN, CHRISTOPHER M, Bordon (YH15721)														●																							
WORLE, DEREK A, Andover (YH15789)														●																							
WRIGHT, ALBERT, Petersfield (YH15832)														●																							
HEREFORDSHIRE																																					
ANTHONY, F J, Bromyard (YH00465)																																				●	

Business Profile
Breeding and Wellbeing

by Country by County

	Ambulance Services	Animal Behaviourist	Artificial Insemination	Bloodstock Advice	Bloodstock Agency	Breaking In Horses	Breeding Advice	Chiropractics	Clipper Maintenance	Complementary Medicine	Dentistry Skills	Dust Control	Emergency Services	Farrier Services	Groom	Groom Services	Herbalists	Holistic Medicine	Homeopathy	Horse Ambulance	Horse Psychiatry	Horse Sitter	Horse Walker	Laser & Ultrasound	Nutritionists	Osteopathy	Physiotherapy	Respiratory Disease control	Shoe Fitting Skills	Solarium	Stud Services	Swimming Pool Centre	Trotting Services	Vaccination	Veterinary Labs	Veterinary Practice	Veterinary Skills
BAILEY, ALAN W, Bartestree (YH00797)														●																							
BREAKWELL, COLIN E, Leominster (YH01826)														●																							
BRIGHTWELLS BLOODSTOCK, Hereford (YH01910)					●																																
BROMYARD, Bromyard (YH02027)										●																											
COUNTRYWIDE, Hereford (YH03445)									●																												
COUNTRYWIDE STORES, Ledbury (YH03457)												●																									
COUNTY COMPETITION STUD, Bromyard (YH03486)															●																●						
DAVID SMYLY, Dorstone (YH03923)					●																																
DOYLE, MARK, Leominster (YH04249)														●																							
ECKLEY, R J, Kington (YH04536)					●																																
EQUINE MARKETING, Weobley (YH04787)										●																											
GREEN, M A, Hereford (YH06070)														●																							
HOOLEY, C & A, Hereford (YH07041)						●																															
HUGHES, A LANCE, Hereford (YH07258)																																				●	
JOHN HORLOCK & ASSOCIATES, Leominster (YH07794)																																				●	
JONES, M P, Pontrilas (YH07915)														●																							
JONES, MARK A, Dorstone (YH07917)														●																							
JONES, MATTHEW J, Kington (YH07918)														●																							
LEGGE, A M, Bromyard (YH08541)														●																							
LLOYD, STEPHEN DEREK, Ledbury (YH08743)														●																							
LOWE, ROBIN J, Weobley Marsh (YH08861)														●																							
MONNINGTON, Hereford (YH09728)			●	●		●	●																								●						
PRICE, MATTHEW R, Ross-on-Wye (YH11384)														●																							
PRICE, ROGER J, Lugwardine (YH11388)														●																							
RICKELSFORD, DAVID E, Leominster (YH11833)														●																							
SHEEPCOTE EQUESTRIAN, Hereford (YH12695)							●																							●							
SIMPSON, JONATHAN, Leominster (YH12839)														●																							
STONEHEWER, GRAHAM, Leominster (YH13515)														●																							
SUE ADAMS RIDING SCHOOL, Leominster (YH13622)		●																			●						●										
SUMNER, NICHOLAS J, Fownhope (YH13638)														●																							
SUTTON, GRAHAM T, Hereford (YH13677)														●																							
UNDERWOOD, R F, Leominster (YH14565)														●																							

Business Profile
Breeding and Wellbeing

by Country by County	Ambulance Services	Animal Behaviourist	Artificial Insemination	Bloodstock Advice	Bloodstock Agency	Breaking In Horses	Breeding Advice	Chiropractics	Clipper Maintenance	Complementary Medicine	Dentistry Skills	Dust Control	Emergency Services	Farrier Services	Groom	Groom Services	Herbalists	Holistic Medicine	Homeopathy	Horse Ambulance	Horse Psychiatry	Horse Sitter	Horse Walker	Laser & Ultrasound	Nutritionists	Osteopathy	Physiotherapy	Respiratory Disease control	Shoe Fitting Skills	Solarium	Stud Services	Swimming Pool Centre	Trotting Services	Vaccination	Veterinary Labs	Veterinary Practice	Veterinary Skills
WILLIAMS, A K, Much Birch (YH15445)														●																							
HERTFORDSHIRE																																					
BRITISH LIVESTOCK, Buntingford (YH01959)					●																																
CALLAWAY, ELIZABETH, Hatfield (YH02448)								●		●																●	●										
CHESTNUT VETNRY GRP, Ware (YH02837)																																				●	
COLE, DUNCAN L, Braughing (YH03154)														●																							
COLLIER, W H, Royston (YH03182)														●																							
COULSON, ROBERT G, New Barnet (YH03390)														●																							
CRAIB, MARGIE, Berkhamsted (YH03548)								●																		●	●										
CRIST, DAVID, Stevenage (YH03605)														●																							
CROUCHFIELD, Ware (YH03674)							●							●		●																					
DARBY, L W, Hemel Hempstead (YH03877)														●																							
DAVIES & ROUTLEDGE, Royston (YH03933)																																				●	
DEAN, T S, St Albans (YH03997)																																				●	
DOWNHAM, TREVOR I, Bishop's Stortford (YH04230)														●																							
FOUNDATION FOR ANIMAL HEALING, Hitchin (YH05407)										●																											
FRENCH, MARK W, Hemel Hempstead (YH05493)														●																							
FULLER, T W, Bishop's Stortford (YH05534)														●																							
HARRIS, C P, Hertford (YH06466)																																				●	
HARTFORD BLOODSTOCK, Welwyn Garden City (YH06500)					●																																
HORSE & HOUNDS, Tring (YH07092)														●																							
HUMPHREY, MARTIN, Hemel Hempstead (YH07285)														●																							
JAMES, MARK ROY, Radlett (YH07684)														●																							
JEFFERIES, NIGEL P, Shillington (YH07715)														●																							
JOHNSON, TREVOR, Hertford Heath (YH07840)														●																							
JONES, DAWN, St. Albans (YH07892)																											●										
KONIG, ANTHONY JOSEPH, Codicote (YH08291)														●																							
LANE, V G, Berkhamsted (YH08391)														●																							
LANNON, BARRY P, Welwyn Garden City (YH08420)														●																							
MOODY, F, Welwyn (YH09737)														●																							
O'SHEA, THOMAS J, Bushey (YH10567)														●																							
PARK VETNRY CTRE, Watford (YH10739)																																				●	

Business Profile
Breeding and Wellbeing

by Country by County

	Ambulance Services	Animal Behaviourist	Artificial Insemination	Bloodstock Advice	Bloodstock Agency	Breaking In Horses	Breeding Advice	Chiropractics	Clipper Maintenance	Complementary Medicine	Dentistry Skills	Dust Control	Emergency Services	Farrier Services	Groom	Groom Services	Herbalists	Holistic Medicine	Homeopathy	Horse Ambulance	Horse Psychiatry	Horse Sitter	Horse Walker	Laser & Ultrasound	Nutritionists	Osteopathy	Physiotherapy	Respiratory Disease control	Shoe Fitting Skills	Solarium	Stud Services	Swimming Pool Centre	Trotting Services	Vaccination	Veterinary Labs	Veterinary Practice	Veterinary Skills
PATCHETTS, Watford (YH10815)														●	●	●							●														
PEVSNER, DANIEL, Hitchin (YH11036)								●																		●	●										
PHOENIX CLGE OF RADIONICS, Hemel Hempstead (YH11070)								●		●															●	●	●										
PITMAN, TERRY R, Hitchin (YH11152)														●																							
POPE, DAVID J, Barnet (YH11266)														●																							
PRATT, JEFFERY A, Chipperfield (YH11339)										●																											
QUINLAN, PETER G, Potters Bar (YH11500)														●																							
ROBINSON, STEVEN D, Hertford (YH11996)														●																							
ROSS, ROBERT J, Watford (YH12120)														●																							
ROUSE, DAVID MICHAEL, Much Hadham (YH12146)														●																							
RYDAL MOUNT, Potters Bar (YH12292)														●		●																					
SADDLERY, Royston (YH12363)									●																												
SHANKS & MCEWAN PAPER BEDDING, Hitchin (YH12669)												●																									
SHENTON, MAXINE, Buntingford (YH12708)								●																		●	●										
SMITH, DANIEL A, Welwyn Garden City (YH12950)														●																							
SMITH, J R M, Hatfield (YH12963)														●																							
SOUTH MEDBURN, Borehamwood (YH13101)														●		●																					
STEVENS, BARRY G, St Albans (YH13443)														●																							
STONE LANE VETNRY CLINIC, Royston (YH13511)																																				●	
TANT, RAY, Wheathampstead (YH13860)								●																		●	●										
TAVERNER, NIGEL S, Hoddesdon (YH13885)														●																							
TAYLOR, P D, Royston (YH13909)														●																							
TERRY, GREGORY FRANCIS, Bovingdon (YH13958)														●																							
TODDBROOK VETNRY CTRE, Hoddesdon (YH14200)																																				●	
TODDBROOK VETNRY CTRE, Cheshunt (YH14199)																																				●	
TOVEY, JAY D, Great Offley (YH14256)														●																							
UPPERWOOD FARM STUD, Hemel Hempstead (YH14609)			●	●			●																●								●						
WADE, A J, Flaunden (YH14810)														●																							
WADE, SAM, Sarratt (YH14815)														●																							
WALKER, RICHARD HERBERT, Malpas (YH14857)														●																							
WATTS, ADAM, Tring (YH15004)														●																							
WATTS, GARY, Northchurch (YH15005)														●																							

Business Profile
Breeding and Wellbeing

by Country by County

	Ambulance Services	Animal Behaviourist	Artificial Insemination	Bloodstock Advice	Bloodstock Agency	Breaking In Horses	Breeding Advice	Chiropractics	Clipper Maintenance	Complementary Medicine	Dentistry Skills	Dust Control	Emergency Services	Farrier Services	Groom	Groom Services	Herbalists	Holistic Medicine	Homeopathy	Horse Ambulance	Horse Psychiatry	Horse Sitter	Horse Walker	Laser & Ultrasound	Nutritionists	Osteopathy	Physiotherapy	Respiratory Disease control	Shoe Fitting Skills	Solarium	Stud Services	Swimming Pool Centre	Trotting Services	Vaccination	Veterinary Labs	Veterinary Practice	Veterinary Skills
WHEELER, DEREK, Barnet (YH15270)														●																							
WIDESERVE, Welwyn (YH15391)										●																											
ISLE OF MAN																																					
ANGUS, S, Ramsey (YH00423)																																				●	
BARHAM, KEVIN N A, Ramsey (YH00934)														●																							
BOSTOCK, D R, Ramsey (YH01658)														●																							
ISLE OF WIGHT																																					
BEARDSMORE, STEVEN M, Ryde (YH01120)														●																							
GREAT PAN FARM STABLES, Newport (YH06041)						●																															
HERBERTSON, B R, Freshwater Bay (YH06698)								●																		●	●										
JOHNSON, NIGEL K, Ventnor (YH07829)														●																							
MOSS, MICHAEL R, Newport (YH09861)														●																							
MOUL, PETER L, Godshill (YH09879)														●																							
PERKIS, BARRY A, Sandown (YH10979)														●																							
PRITCHETT, MICHAEL J, Cowes (YH11426)														●																							
PURCELL, MALCOLM G, Newport (YH11465)														●																							
TURNER, IAN, Ryde (YH14481)														●																							
WEST, TIMOTHY J, Brook (YH15179)														●																							
JERSEY																																					
MACLEOD/ALLAN/RUSHTON-TAYLOR, St Mary (YH09011)																																				●	
PRYCE, DAVID J, Trinity (YH11444)														●																							
PRYCE, DOUGLAS F, Trinity (YH11445)														●																							
KENT																																					
ANDREWS, DAVID V, Sittingbourne (YH00398)														●																							
ANDREWS, T, Rochester (YH00404)														●																							
APPS, S H, Dover (YH00485)														●																							
ASHTON, STUART J, Folkestone (YH00615)														●																							
BAKER, KEITH D, Maidstone (YH00823)														●																							
BELL EQUINE VETNRY CLINIC, Maidstone (YH01214)																																				●	
BIAC, Sittingbourne (YH01389)																									●												
BRAY, GEOFFREY A, Ashford (YH01820)														●																							
BURCH, THOMAS A, Ashford (YH02229)														●																							

Business Profile
Breeding and Wellbeing

by Country by County

	Ambulance Services	Animal Behaviourist	Artificial Insemination	Bloodstock Advice	Bloodstock Agency	Breaking In Horses	Breeding Advice	Chiropractics	Clipper Maintenance	Complementary Medicine	Dentistry Skills	Dust Control	Emergency Services	Farrier Services	Groom	Groom Services	Herbalists	Holistic Medicine	Homeopathy	Horse Ambulance	Horse Psychiatry	Horse Sitter	Horse Walker	Laser & Ultrasound	Nutritionists	Osteopathy	Physiotherapy	Respiratory Disease control	Shoe Fitting Skills	Solarium	Stud Services	Swimming Pool Centre	Trotting Services	Vaccination	Veterinary Labs	Veterinary Practice	Veterinary Skills
BURT, GRAEME J, Sevenoaks (YH02287)														●																							
BURTON, GARY S, East Farleigh (YH02292)														●																							
BUTCHER, K J, Deal (YH02316)														●																							
CASEY, DAVID L, Canterbury (YH02614)														●																							
CERULLO, M, Westerham (YH02700)														●																							
CHRISTIAN, STEPHEN, Headcorn (YH02885)														●																							
CINQUE PORTS VETNRY ASS, Tenterden (YH02921)																																				●	
CINQUE PORTS VETNRY ASS, Hawkhurst (YH02922)																																				●	
CLARK, CHRISTOPHER D, Goudhurst (YH02962)														●																							
COLLINS, STEPHEN A, Maidstone (YH03190)														●																							
COOK, PHILIP MICHAEL, Charing (YH03257)														●																							
COSTER, NOEL, Tunbridge Wells (YH03356)														●																							
CRAWFORD, MARTIN P, Sittingbourne (YH03575)														●																							
CULVERDEN VETNRY GRP, Tunbridge Wells (YH03709)																																				●	
DEEPDENE STABLES, Faversham (YH04021)														●																							
DENNIS, EDWARD F, Maidstone (YH04054)														●																							
DUNMALL, PHILIP J, Maidstone (YH04346)														●																							
EDWARDS, M C, Ashford (YH04583)														●																							
ELMHURST BLOODSTOCK, Tonbridge (YH04637)					●																																
EQUINE SPORT THERAPY, Edenbridge (YH04800)								●		●								●	●								●										
EQUINES LIVERIES, Maidstone (YH04809)							●																								●						
EQUINN, Westerham (YH04811)										●																											
FLETCHER, DOMINIC C, Groombridge Hill (YH05276)														●																							
FOREST VIEW, Sidcup (YH05353)																						●															
FRIDAY FIELD STABLES, Sittingbourne (YH05502)		●																																			
FRYATT, T J, Sevenoaks (YH05528)														●																							
GOOD, RAYMOND D, Dartford (YH05900)														●																							
HAYSELDEN, Cranbrook (YH06592)							●																														
HEWITT, PAUL W, Erith (YH06727)														●																							
HOGSTON, W D, Canterbury (YH06921)														●																							
JEFFERY, RICHARD N, Bethersden (YH07720)														●																							
JONES, SIMON B, Ashford (YH07932)														●																							

Business Profile
Breeding and Wellbeing

by Country by County	Ambulance Services	Animal Behaviourist	Artificial Insemination	Bloodstock Advice	Bloodstock Agency	Breaking In Horses	Breeding Advice	Chiropractics	Clipper Maintenance	Complementary Medicine	Dentistry Skills	Dust Control	Emergency Services	Farrier Services	Groom	Groom Services	Herbalists	Holistic Medicine	Homeopathy	Horse Ambulance	Horse Psychiatry	Horse Sitter	Horse Walker	Laser & Ultrasound	Nutritionists	Osteopathy	Physiotherapy	Respiratory Disease control	Shoe Fitting Skills	Solarium	Stud Services	Swimming Pool Centre	Trotting Services	Vaccination	Veterinary Labs	Veterinary Practice	Veterinary Skills
LUCK, B M, Tonbridge (YH08886)														●																							
MAISON DIEU VETNRY CTRE, Dover (YH09041)																																				●	
MANN, TIMOTHY A, Edenbridge (YH09083)														●																							
MASSIE, NIGEL R, Rochester (YH09249)														●																							
MEADE, LOUIS, Orpington (YH09412)														●																							
MERCER, I J, Rochester (YH09463)														●																							
MILBOURN EQUINE VET HOSPITAL, Ashford (YH09566)																																				●	
MINDHAM, DAVID R, Westerham (YH09647)														●																							
MORGAN, VINCENT E, Maidstone (YH09813)														●																							
NEWNHAM COURT VETNRY GRP, Maidstone (YH10158)																																				●	
NICOLA M HUNT DWCF, Sevenoaks (YH10199)														●																							
OXTED VETNRY CLNC, Edenbridge (YH10626)																																				●	
PATON-SMITH, JASON C, Boughton (YH10823)														●																							
PEACOCK, RAYMOND JAMES, Sevenoaks (YH10863)														●																							
PEERS, PETER S, Canterbury (YH10900)														●																							
PERKINS, STEPHEN, Ashford (YH10978)														●																							
PIERSON STEWART & PARTNERS, Cranbrook (YH11091)																																				●	
PIERSON STEWART & PARTNERS,, Marden (YH11092)																																				●	
PILKINGTON, TIMOTHY, New Romney (YH11108)														●																							
PITCHER, MARK S, Orpington (YH11151)														●																							
POLLARD, ROBERT, Deal (YH11205)														●																							
PUTLANDS VETNRY SURGERY, Tonbridge (YH11468)																																				●	
RAINGER, CLIVE M, Edenbridge (YH11617)														●																							
RICHARDSON, A M, Maidstone (YH11815)														●																							
RIPLEY, TYRONE T, Rochester (YH11905)														●																							
ROGERS, ANNE, Goudhurst (YH12060)										●																											
SADDLE RACK, Folkestone (YH12345)									●																												
SADDLERY & GUN ROOM, Westerham (YH12365)									●																				●								
SANDERS, DAVID, Tonbridge (YH12405)														●																							
SARACEN FEEDS, Tunbridge Wells (YH12432)																									●												
SAVAGE, P H, Sittingbourne (YH12454)														●																							
SKIPPON, M A, Cranbrook (YH12880)														●																							

Business Profile
Breeding and Wellbeing

by Country by County	Ambulance Services	Animal Behaviourist	Artificial Insemination	Bloodstock Advice	Bloodstock Agency	Breaking In Horses	Breeding Advice	Chiropractics	Clipper Maintenance	Complementary Medicine	Dentistry Skills	Dust Control	Emergency Services	Farrier Services	Groom	Groom Services	Herbalists	Holistic Medicine	Homeopathy	Horse Ambulance	Horse Psychiatry	Horse Sitter	Horse Walker	Laser & Ultrasound	Nutritionists	Osteopathy	Physiotherapy	Respiratory Disease control	Shoe Fitting Skills	Solarium	Stud Services	Swimming Pool Centre	Trotting Services	Vaccination	Veterinary Labs	Veterinary Practice	Veterinary Skills
SLIGHT, ERNEST G, Dartford (YH12896)														●																							
SMALLEY & BLAXLAND, Sandwich (YH12911)																																				●	
ST NICHOLAS FORGE, Birchington (YH13283)														●																							
STERN, CLIVE CHARLES, Cranbrook (YH13433)														●																							
STERN, EDGAR P J, Maidstone (YH13434)														●																							
STERN, P J, Tenterden (YH13435)														●																							
STERN, P M, Maidstone (YH13436)														●																							
SWANSCOTT, ROBERT L, Aylesford (YH13694)														●																							
TANTON-BROWN, JULIAN, Sittingbourne (YH13861)														●																							
THEOBALD, CARON, Greenhithe (YH13982)																											●										
TURNWELL, G M, Tenterden (YH14493)														●																							
UPSON, ANNE & PETER, Folkestone (YH14613)								●																		●	●										
VETNRY SURGERY, Deal (YH14700)																																				●	
VICKERY, MICHAEL, West Malling (YH14707)														●																							
WARD, BARRY P, Sheppey (YH14899)														●																							
WARD, K A, Tunbridge Wells (YH14902)														●																							
WARR, TONY, Tonbridge (YH14929)																																				●	●
WEALDEN SADDLERY, Tonbridge (YH15020)									●																												
WELLSMAN, DAVID W, Sittingbourne (YH15088)														●																							
WEST, E C, Canterbury (YH15174)														●																							
WHALLEY, K R, Westerham (YH15260)														●																							
WHEELER, GARY M, Herne Bay (YH15271)														●																							
WIGGINS, CHRISTOPHER A, Maidstone (YH15398)														●																							
WILLARD, KEVIN J, Sevenoaks (YH15428)														●																							
WILLOW FARM, Maidstone (YH15496)														●																							
WILLOW FARM, Faversham (YH15497)									●																												
WISEMAN, PAUL, Newington (YH15610)														●																							
WOODLANDS, Sevenoaks (YH15706)																●																					
LANCASHIRE																																					
A W HELME & PARTNER, Preston (YH00066)																																				●	
ADDY, D L, Rochdale (YH00181)														●																							
ALDRED, J D, Preston (YH00261)							●																														

Business Profile
Breeding and Wellbeing

by Country by County

	Ambulance Services	Animal Behaviourist	Artificial Insemination	Bloodstock Advice	Bloodstock Agency	Breaking In Horses	Breeding Advice	Chiropractics	Clipper Maintenance	Complementary Medicine	Dentistry Skills	Dust Control	Emergency Services	Farrier Services	Groom	Groom Services	Herbalists	Holistic Medicine	Homeopathy	Horse Ambulance	Horse Psychiatry	Horse Sitter	Horse Walker	Laser & Ultrasound	Nutritionists	Osteopathy	Physiotherapy	Respiratory Disease control	Shoe Fitting Skills	Solarium	Stud Services	Swimming Pool Centre	Trotting Services	Vaccination	Veterinary Labs	Veterinary Practice	Veterinary Skills
ARKENFIELD EQUESTRIAN CTRE, Chorley (YH00530)															●																						
ASKEW, STEVEN, Accrington (YH00621)														●																							
ASOKA, Worsley (YH00625)		●					●			●								●	●		●										●						
BALDRAND VETNRY PRACTICE, Lancaster (YH00839)																																				●	
BEARDMORE FARRIER SV, Blackburn (YH01119)														●																							
BEECROFT, PATRICK J, Blackburn (YH01184)														●																							
BELL, JEFFREY, Preston (YH01224)														●																							
BROOKFIELD GREEN FARM, Ormskirk (YH02047)														●																							
BROOKFIELDS, Ormskirk (YH02051)				●	●		●																														
BURGIN, KRISTOPHER, Bacup (YH02250)														●																							
COLE, ANDREW CHARLES, Wigan (YH03149)														●																							
CONWAY, PAUL A, Preston (YH03251)														●																							
COOK, SAMUEL C, Leyland (YH03258)														●																							
D'ARCY, DAVID C, Blackburn (YH03882)														●																							
DENNISON, PAUL EDWARD, Carnforth (YH04058)														●																							
DURKIN, MICHAEL, Preston (YH04371)														●																							
EQUINE BEHAVIOUR, Darwen (YH04765)		●								●																●	●										
GOLDER, ROBERT M, Preston (YH05886)														●																							
GREEN BANK, Carnforth (YH06049)																●																					
GREEN SMITHY, High Bentham (YH06060)														●																							
GREGORY, MAXWELL J, Preston (YH06117)														●																							
HANKIN, WILLIAM D & DAVID M, Preston (YH06388)														●																							
HARKER, MICHAEL, Bury (YH06432)					●																																
HOOLE, J J, Preston (YH07040)														●																							
HOUGHTON, R J, Blackpool (YH07205)														●																							
HUDSON, BRIAN, Preesall (YH07255)														●																							
IBEX, Preston (YH07377)														●															●								
JOHNSON, RICHARD A, Chorley (YH07837)														●																							
KAY, D, Bacup (YH08004)														●																							
KAY, RAYMOND JAMES, Blackburn (YH08005)														●																							
KAYE, ANTHONY S, Barnoldswick (YH08006)														●																							
KAYE, HARVEY STUART, Chorley (YH08008)														●																							

Business Profile
Breeding and Wellbeing

by Country by County	Ambulance Services	Animal Behaviourist	Artificial Insemination	Bloodstock Advice	Bloodstock Agency	Breaking In Horses	Breeding Advice	Chiropractics	Clipper Maintenance	Complementary Medicine	Dentistry Skills	Dust Control	Emergency Services	Farrier Services	Groom	Groom Services	Herbalists	Holistic Medicine	Homeopathy	Horse Ambulance	Horse Psychiatry	Horse Sitter	Horse Walker	Laser & Ultrasound	Nutritionists	Osteopathy	Physiotherapy	Respiratory Disease control	Shoe Fitting Skills	Solarium	Stud Services	Swimming Pool Centre	Trotting Services	Vaccination	Veterinary Labs	Veterinary Practice	Veterinary Skills
L S SYSTEMS, Preston (YH08329)												●																									
LAMB, PETER K, Bacup (YH08363)														●																							
LINDLEY, B, Wigan (YH08647)														●																							
MADDRELL, BUXTON & TAYLOR, Leigh (YH09021)																																				●	
MATHER, ROWLAND J, Bury (YH09260)														●																							
MCBANE, SUSAN, Longridge (YH09313)								●		●																●	●										
MOSS SIDE RACING STABLES, Lancaster (YH09856)																							●														
NAYLORS SADDLERY STORES, Rochdale (YH10060)								●																		●	●										
NIGHTINGALE, STEPHEN A, Accrington (YH10205)														●																							
OAKLEIGH STUD FARM, Preston (YH10397)					●																																
OXENDALE, Blackburn (YH10615)							●																														
PANAMA SPORT HORSES, Clitheroe (YH10695)				●												●							●														
PICKARD, ROBERT D, Carnforth (YH11080)														●																							
PIMBLEY, ALEX T, Preston (YH11111)														●																							
PINEWOOD VETNRY PRACTICE, Chorley (YH11129)																																				●	
RIGBY, ROBERT D E, Wigan (YH11891)														●																							
ROSSENDALE & HYNDBURN EC, Accrington (YH12123)																							●														
ROTHWELL, DAVE, Oldham (YH12138)														●																							
ROWLINSON, M, Blackpool (YH12174)														●																							
SANDERSON, BRIAN, Ormskirk (YH12407)														●																							
SHUTTLEWORTH, ANDREW J, Blackburn (YH12776)														●																							
SMITH GREEN SMITHY, Lancaster (YH12936)														●																							
STANLEY HOUSE VETNRY SURGEONS, Colne (YH13370)																																				●	
STEAD, PAUL A, Blackpool (YH13407)														●																							
TAYLOR, T, Littleborough (YH13912)														●																							
THOMPSON, C, Rochdale (YH14034)														●																							
TRAVIS, P, Oldham (YH14356)														●																							
VALIANTS EQUESTRIAN CTRE, Preston (YH14645)														●																							
WATKINS, GLYNN SYLVESTER, Preston (YH14978)														●																							
WILSON, ANTHONY, Chorley (YH15529)														●																							
WOOF, PHILIP JOHN, Blackburn (YH15761)														●																							
WORTHINGTON, ALLAN W, Ormskirk (YH15805)														●																							

Business Profile
Breeding and Wellbeing

by Country by County

	Ambulance Services	Animal Behaviourist	Artificial Insemination	Bloodstock Advice	Bloodstock Agency	Breaking In Horses	Breeding Advice	Chiropractics	Clipper Maintenance	Complementary Medicine	Dentistry Skills	Dust Control	Emergency Services	Farrier Services	Groom	Groom Services	Herbalists	Holistic Medicine	Homeopathy	Horse Ambulance	Horse Psychiatry	Horse Sitter	Horse Walker	Laser & Ultrasound	Nutritionists	Osteopathy	Physiotherapy	Respiratory Disease control	Shoe Fitting Skills	Solarium	Stud Services	Swimming Pool Centre	Trotting Services	Vaccination	Veterinary Labs	Veterinary Practice	Veterinary Skills
LEICESTERSHIRE																																					
ALLEN, T W, Leicester (YH00305)														●																							
ALLINGTON, JOHN W, Melton Mowbray (YH00314)														●																							
ALLINGTON, JONATHAN D, Melton Mowbray (YH00315)														●																							
ANIMAL SCHOOL OF FARRIERY, Melton Mowbray (YH00443)														●																							
BEESTON, MICHAEL GUY, Coalville (YH01192)														●																							
BELL, BROWN & BENTLEY, Leicester (YH01217)																																				●	
BENNETT, DANIEL J, Melton Mowbray (YH01270)														●																							
BEVIN BUTLER & DRUMMOND, Market Harborough (YH01344)																																				●	
BROWN, ANDREW N, Sileby (YH02099)														●																							
BROWN, LUKE R, Loughborough (YH02121)														●																							
CANAAN FARM, Loughborough (YH02493)																●																					
CLOTHES HORSE, Leicester (YH03062)									●	●					●																						
COSSINGTON, Leicester (YH03354)																●																					
CRANSWICK, Melton Mowbray (YH03570)				●			●																														
DEACON, M J, Leicester (YH03982)														●																							
DILLON, JOHN E, Somerby (YH04121)														●																							
E D SIMPSON & SON, Leicester (YH04400)										●																											
ECKFORD, D A, Oakham (YH04534)																																				●	
EQUIHERB, Syston (YH04750)										●																											
EVANS, GARY B, Melton Mowbray (YH04918)														●																							
GREEN, JASON L, Fleckney (YH06067)														●																							
GULLEY, D L, Melton Mowbray (YH06189)														●																							
HATTON, IAN R, Nuneaton (YH06535)														●																							
HOLISTIC RIDING, Lutterworth (YH06935)																		●																			
HURST SADDLERS, Leicester (YH07316)									●																												
J B THORNE, Thurmaston (YH07566)												●																									
JOHNSON, PAUL J, Leicester (YH07834)														●																							
JOYCE, CHRISTOPHER G, Wigston (YH07951)														●																							
KEARN, RICHARD A, Shepshed (YH08017)														●																							
LOMAX, CHRISTIE, Market Harborough (YH08780)						●																															
MARRIOTT, ADRIAN N, South Croxton (YH09174)														●																							

Business Profile
Breeding and Wellbeing

by Country by County

	Ambulance Services	Animal Behaviourist	Artificial Insemination	Bloodstock Advice	Bloodstock Agency	Breaking In Horses	Breeding Advice	Chiropractics	Clipper Maintenance	Complementary Medicine	Dentistry Skills	Dust Control	Emergency Services	Farrier Services	Groom	Groom Services	Herbalists	Holistic Medicine	Homeopathy	Horse Ambulance	Horse Psychiatry	Horse Sitter	Horse Walker	Laser & Ultrasound	Nutritionists	Osteopathy	Physiotherapy	Respiratory Disease control	Shoe Fitting Skills	Solarium	Stud Services	Swimming Pool Centre	Trotting Services	Vaccination	Veterinary Labs	Veterinary Practice	Veterinary Skills
MARTIN, FIONA, Market Harborough (YH09218)																										●											
MASON, D W, Melton Mowbray (YH09242)														●																							
NORTHWOOD, GLYN, Hinckley (YH10324)														●																							
O'REARDON, M, Loughborough (YH10540)														●																							
PERRY, R L, Enderby (YH10989)														●																							
PHILIP DAY, Melton Mowbray (YH11043)														●																							
PIZER, GEOFFREY R, Melton Mowbray (YH11160)														●																							
PORTER, K B, Quorn (YH11283)														●																							
ROBERTSON, R A M, Loughborough (YH11974)														●																							
ROTHERWOOD STUD, Ashby-De-La-Zouch (YH12133)			●																												●						
S L B SUPPLIES, Coalville (YH12329)										●																											
SAGITTARIUS BLOODSTOCK AGENCY, Melton Mowbray (YH12382)					●																																
SCHOOL OF NATIONAL EQUITATION, Loughborough (YH12521)																●							●														
SELBY, TIMOTHY JOHN, Nuneaton (YH12619)														●																							
SMITH, GRAHAM J, Loughborough (YH12959)														●																							
SPECK, A W, Melton Mowbray (YH13188)														●																							
SWANWICK, KIM R, Melton Mowbray (YH13697)														●																							
TAYLOR, GEORGE S, Kibworth (YH13902)														●																							
TOULSON, V, Melton Mowbray (YH14254)							●																														
VARNAM, C, Braunstone (YH14662)														●																							
VARNAM, PAUL A, Leicester (YH14663)														●																							
W SPENCE & SON, Melton Mowbray (YH14798)														●																							
WALTHAM CTRE, Melton Mowbray (YH14888)																									●												
WILLIAMS, DAMIAN D, Fleckney (YH15454)														●																							
WILLIAMS, J M, Oakham (YH15461)														●																							
WOODFORD, MICHAEL O, Hallaton (YH15689)														●																							
YEANDLE, ERIC, Melton Mowbray (YH15896)														●																							
LINCOLNSHIRE																																					
A J PLEDGER, Stamford (YH00040)														●																							
ALLEN, LEE J, Grantham (YH00298)														●																							
BATEMAN, BRETT, Horncastle (YH01065)														●																							
BEAUMONT, G L, Market Rasen (YH01135)																																				●	

Business Profile
Breeding and Wellbeing

by Country by County

	Ambulance Services	Animal Behaviourist	Artificial Insemination	Bloodstock Advice	Bloodstock Agency	Breaking In Horses	Breeding Advice	Chiropractics	Clipper Maintenance	Complementary Medicine	Dentistry Skills	Dust Control	Emergency Services	Farrier Services	Groom	Groom Services	Herbalists	Holistic Medicine	Homeopathy	Horse Ambulance	Horse Psychiatry	Horse Sitter	Horse Walker	Laser & Ultrasound	Nutritionists	Osteopathy	Physiotherapy	Respiratory Disease control	Shoe Fitting Skills	Solarium	Stud Services	Swimming Pool Centre	Trotting Services	Vaccination	Veterinary Labs	Veterinary Practice	Veterinary Skills
BEECHEY, R F, Lincoln (YH01171)														●																							
BELCHFORD STUD, Horncastle (YH01208)											●																										
BELL, IVON T, Grantham (YH01220)														●																							
BEST/THOROUGHBRED RACING GB, Louth (YH01327)				●	●		●																								●						
BEVAN, R E M, Market Rasen (YH01340)														●																							
BLOOR, J O, Market Rasen (YH01558)														●																							
BOSWORTH, CLIVE E, Skellingthorpe (YH01664)														●																							
BRENNAN, MICHAEL B, Spalding (YH01843)														●																							
BRENNAN, SHANE P, Spalding (YH01845)														●																							
BUNTING, CHRISTOPHER JOHN, Spilsby (YH02226)														●																							
CHATTERTON, SHAUN MICHAEL, Market Rasen (YH02790)														●																							
COOK & TIMSON, Louth (YH03254)																																				●	
COOL SPORT, Brigg (YH03269)								●		●																●	●										●
COSGROVE & SON, Market Rasen (YH03350)							●																														
DALE, MAURICE & RALPH M, Louth (YH03824)														●																							
ELKINGTON, ANDREW JAMES, Sleaford (YH04609)														●																							
EQUINE MNGMT & TRAINING, Stamford (YH04788)						●																															
F P I, Stamford (YH04998)										●							●		●																		
FENWOLD VETNRY GRP, Spilsby (YH05157)																																				●	
FLATTERS, MICHAEL J, Stamford (YH05265)														●																							
FRANKLIN, MARK A, Boston (YH05469)														●																							
GOLLINGS, JAYNE, Louth (YH05897)					●																																
GRAY, GLENN, Bourne (YH06029)														●																							
HENSON, LUCY, Lincoln (YH06689)						●																															
HILL ENGINEERING, Gainsborough (YH06811)														●																							
HILL, T, Ingham (YH06834)														●																							
HOUGHTON, JASPER ANTHONY, Potterhanworth (YH07204)														●																							
IANSON, STEVE (ESQ), Grantham (YH07372)											●																										
J & M L HENFREY & SON, Spalding (YH07551)						●																															
JONES, CARL (MAJOR), Grantham (YH07882)														●																							
JONES, P J, North Killingholme (YH07921)														●																							
KING, JAMES D, Grantham (YH08182)														●																							

Business Profile
Breeding and Wellbeing

by Country by County

	Ambulance Services	Animal Behaviourist	Artificial Insemination	Bloodstock Advice	Bloodstock Agency	Breaking In Horses	Breeding Advice	Chiropractics	Clipper Maintenance	Complementary Medicine	Dentistry Skills	Dust Control	Emergency Services	Farrier Services	Groom	Groom Services	Herbalists	Holistic Medicine	Homeopathy	Horse Ambulance	Horse Psychiatry	Horse Sitter	Horse Walker	Laser & Ultrasound	Nutritionists	Osteopathy	Physiotherapy	Respiratory Disease control	Shoe Fitting Skills	Solarium	Stud Services	Swimming Pool Centre	Trotting Services	Vaccination	Veterinary Labs	Veterinary Practice	Veterinary Skills
LEE, GEOFFREY, Stamford (YH08524)														●																							
LINDER, P J, Welton (YH08646)														●																							
LOCHRIE, G K A, Gainsborough (YH08755)																																				●	
MOORE, A J & R A, Boston (YH09753)							●																														
MYCAWKA, ALEXANDER H, Stamford (YH09980)														●																							
NICHOLLS, D E, Louth (YH10182)														●																							
OAKWOOD RIDING SERVICES, Spalding (YH10410)										●																											
PEARS, ROBERT A, Spilsby (YH10876)														●																							
PEGASUS HORSESHOES, Stamford (YH10905)														●																							
PLANT, MICHAEL J, Grantham (YH11162)														●																							
POPPYFIELDS, Lincoln (YH11275)												●																									
R PLANT & SON, Grantham (YH11561)														●																							
RASE VETNRY CTRE, Market Rasen (YH11645)								●			●															●	●									●	
REDNIL EQUESTRIAN CTRE, Lincoln (YH11716)														●																							
SAWER, NEIL G, Boston (YH12460)														●																							
SMITH, NORMAN M, Market Rasen (YH12981)														●																							
SYKES, SCOTT S, Welton (YH13724)														●																							
TACK BOX, Lincoln (YH13785)									●																												
TEMPLE TRINE STUD, Boston (YH13948)						●																									●						
VETNRY HOSPITAL, Lincoln (YH14697)																																				●	
W N SHRIVE & SON, Skegness (YH14784)										●																											
LINCOLNSHIRE (NORTH EAST)																																					
BARTON, J M, Grimsby (YH01047)														●																							
R G EQUESTRIAN, Grimsby (YH11536)															●	●							●														
RASE VETNRY CTRE, Grimsby (YH11646)											●																									●	
SMITH, P J, Grimsby (YH12984)														●																							
LINCOLNSHIRE (NORTH)																																					
ALKBOROUGH STABLES, Scunthorpe (YH00282)								●																		●	●										
BOTTAMLEY, F D, Scunthorpe (YH01665)														●																							
BRAMLEY, FRANCIS N, Barton Upon Humber (YH01791)														●																							
CHATTERTON, M C, Brigg (YH02789)														●																							
CROSBY, NICHOLAS, Wootton (YH03642)														●																							

Business Profile
Breeding and Wellbeing

by Country by County

	Ambulance Services	Animal Behaviourist	Artificial Insemination	Bloodstock Advice	Bloodstock Agency	Breaking In Horses	Breeding Advice	Chiropractics	Clipper Maintenance	Complementary Medicine	Dentistry Skills	Dust Control	Emergency Services	Farrier Services	Groom	Groom Services	Herbalists	Holistic Medicine	Homeopathy	Horse Ambulance	Horse Psychiatry	Horse Sitter	Horse Walker	Laser & Ultrasound	Nutritionists	Osteopathy	Physiotherapy	Respiratory Disease control	Shoe Fitting Skills	Solarium	Stud Services	Swimming Pool Centre	Trotting Services	Vaccination	Veterinary Labs	Veterinary Practice	Veterinary Skills
EQUINE THERAPY, Ulceby (YH04806)										●								●						●		●											
HOLMES, M H, Brigg (YH06978)														●																							
LONDON (GREATER)																																					
A D L TACK & SADDLERY, London (YH00027)									●	●																											
AINSWORTHS, London (YH00216)										●																											
ALOE VERA EQUICARE, Edgware (YH00333)										●																											
CANTLE, JOHN, Chingford (YH02515)														●																							
CENTAUR BLOODSTOCK, Kingston Upon Thames (YH02682)					●																																
COMERFORD, MICHAEL J, Muswell Hill (YH03212)														●																							
COPSEM STUD, Chessington (YH03304)							●																														
DIXON, M L, Kingston Upon Thames (YH04143)														●																							
DRUMAWHEY, Uxbridge (YH04285)										●															●												
EVANS, GORDON L, Muswell Hill (YH04919)														●																							
GORDON-WATSON BLOODSTOCK, London (YH05929)					●																																
GORDON-WATSON, CHARLES, London (YH05930)				●	●																																
HARLEY, THOMAS H, East Ham (YH06439)														●																							
HARMONY & HEALTH FORMULATIONS, London (YH06445)										●		●																									
HYDE PK BARRACKS, London (YH07348)														●															●								
LEGARD, HILARY, London (YH08534)							●			●								●																			
MCCARROLL, KAY, Hendon (YH09319)								●																		●	●										
O'NEILL, EAMONN, Hillingdon (YH10516)														●																							
PERSIAN BLOODSTOCK, Feltham (YH10995)					●																																
R B I BLOODSTOCK, South Kensington (YH11515)					●																																
R H A FORGE, London (YH11538)														●															●								
RIDGWAY STABLES, London (YH11870)															●																						
RUDGE, KEITH D, Uxbridge (YH12207)														●																							
MANCHESTER (GREATER)																																					
BULLEN, SIMON, Bolton (YH02216)														●																							
DAMPIER, J A, Bolton (YH03858)														●																							
EQUITACK, Bolton (YH04823)		●							●					●			●		●												●						
GROVE VETNRY HOSPITAL, Stockport (YH06173)																																				●	
GUTIERREZ-INOSTROZA, ABEL R, Bolton (YH06196)														●																							

Business Profile
Breeding and Wellbeing

by Country by County

	Ambulance Services	Animal Behaviourist	Artificial Insemination	Bloodstock Advice	Bloodstock Agency	Breaking In Horses	Breeding Advice	Chiropractics	Clipper Maintenance	Complementary Medicine	Dentistry Skills	Dust Control	Emergency Services	Farrier Services	Groom	Groom Services	Herbalists	Holistic Medicine	Homeopathy	Horse Ambulance	Horse Psychiatry	Horse Sitter	Horse Walker	Laser & Ultrasound	Nutritionists	Osteopathy	Physiotherapy	Respiratory Disease control	Shoe Fitting Skills	Solarium	Stud Services	Swimming Pool Centre	Trotting Services	Vaccination	Veterinary Labs	Veterinary Practice	Veterinary Skills
JONES, R F, Stockport (YH07923)														●																							
JORDAN, PHILIP, Manchester (YH07939)														●																							
MITCHELL, HARVEY STANLEY, Stockport (YH09668)														●																							
RYDERS FARM, Bolton (YH12297)											●	●		●																							●
SOUTHERN, JOHN, Bolton (YH13147)														●																							
WATSON, SIMON, Manchester (YH14992)														●																							
YATES, DAVID, Bolton (YH15889)														●																							
MERSEYSIDE																																					
BLACKMORE, PAUL F, Prescot (YH01490)														●																							
CHAMBERS, KEITH R, Liverpool (YH02721)														●																							
CROMPTON, S W, Wirral (YH03632)														●																							
F BLACKMORE & SON, Liverpool (YH04985)														●																							
JONES STRAUGHAN, & MARSDEN, Birkenhead (YH07874)																																				●	
KELLY, MARTIN, Wirral (YH08045)														●																							
MARSHALL, ROBERT C, Southport (YH09203)														●																							
MICHELL, K N, Wirral (YH09512)														●																							
MILOJEVIC, NEIL J, Liverpool (YH09644)														●																							
PARR, IAN T, Liverpool (YH10785)														●																							
SHONE, NEIL J, St Helens (YH12756)														●																							
SMITH, STEVEN P L, Thornton Hough (YH13001)														●																							
SUMMERS, PAUL, Liverpool (YH13637)														●																							
WILLIAMS, C P, Birkenhead (YH15452)																																				●	
MIDLANDS (WEST)																																					
608 VETNRY GRP, Solihull (YH00004)																																				●	
ABBISS, R I, Stourbridge (YH00098)														●																							
ADAS WESTERN, Wolverhampton (YH00177)																									●												
ASHFORD, A & W K, Walsall (YH00603)														●															●								
BAGNALL, ANDREW J, Birmingham (YH00789)														●																							
BEARLEY CROSS STABLES, Solihull (YH01121)						●				●				●	●							●	●														●
BRITISH ARABIAN BLOODSTOCK, Birmingham (YH01926)					●																																
C V F, Coventry (YH02395)									●																												
CHAWNER, P D, Birmingham (YH02794)														●																							

www.hccyourhorse.com

Business Profile
Breeding and Wellbeing

by Country by County	Ambulance Services	Animal Behaviourist	Artificial Insemination	Bloodstock Advice	Bloodstock Agency	Breaking In Horses	Breeding Advice	Chiropractics	Clipper Maintenance	Complementary Medicine	Dentistry Skills	Dust Control	Emergency Services	Farrier Services	Groom	Groom Services	Herbalists	Holistic Medicine	Homeopathy	Horse Ambulance	Horse Psychiatry	Horse Sitter	Horse Walker	Laser & Ultrasound	Nutritionists	Osteopathy	Physiotherapy	Respiratory Disease control	Shoe Fitting Skills	Solarium	Stud Services	Swimming Pool Centre	Trotting Services	Vaccination	Veterinary Labs	Veterinary Practice	Veterinary Skills
CHECKLEY, PAUL N, Birmingham (YH02797)														●																							
CHESTERMAN, DANIEL J, Wolverhampton (YH02834)														●																							
CONNAUGHT HSE VETNRY HOSPITAL, Wolverhampton (YH03233)																																				●	
COX, EDWARD J, Coventry (YH03530)														●																							
DYAS-HARROLD, MARK, Stourbridge (YH04383)														●																							
DYAS-HARROLD, P, Stourbridge (YH04384)														●																							
EDMUNDS, GARY, Alvechurch (YH04565)														●																							
HICKMAN, JACKIE A, Kingswinford (YH06742)														●																							
J G & J M JONES, Sutton Coldfield (YH07583)																																				●	
JEPHCOTT, KIM E, Birmingham (YH07751)														●																							
KEYLOCK, CARMEL, Birmingham (YH08115)																											●										
KIRBY & COOK & PEGG, Birmingham (YH08223)																																				●	
MARSHALL, KENNETH, Solihull (YH09196)														●																							
MILLWARD, GRAHAM N, Stourbridge (YH09639)														●																							
MOOR FARM STABLES, Coventry (YH09745)														●		●																					
NATURAL REMEDIES, Walsall (YH10054)										●																											
NEWCOMBE & EAST, Brownhills (YH10131)																																				●	
OAKFIELD VETNRY GROUP, Birmingham (YH10382)																																				●	
ORCHARDS LIVERY STABLES, Birmingham (YH10537)														●																							
PAWS & HOOFS, Aldridge (YH10841)										●																											
PHILLIPS, RICHARD J, Birmingham (YH11064)														●																							
PIMLOTT, L K, Coventry (YH11113)														●																							
REGENT VETNRY GROUP, Coventry (YH11741)																																				●	
SMITH, R I, Wolverhampton (YH12989)														●																							
ST GEORGE'S VETNRY CLINIC, Wolverhampton (YH13276)																																				●	
WILSON, WALKER & BARNBY, Birmingham (YH15548)																																				●	
NORFOLK																																					
ACTON, J M, Fakenham (YH00162)														●																							
AIKENS, MARK L, Norwich (YH0021C)														●																							
ALLEN & PAGE, Thetford (YH00290)																									●												
ARBUTHNOT, TIMOTHY R, Wymondham (YH00497)														●																							
ARMES, P J, Norwich (YH00537)														●																							

Business Profile
Breeding and Wellbeing

by Country by County

	Ambulance Services	Animal Behaviourist	Artificial Insemination	Bloodstock Advice	Bloodstock Agency	Breaking In Horses	Breeding Advice	Chiropractics	Clipper Maintenance	Complementary Medicine	Dentistry Skills	Dust Control	Emergency Services	Farrier Services	Groom	Groom Services	Herbalists	Holistic Medicine	Homeopathy	Horse Ambulance	Horse Psychiatry	Horse Sitter	Horse Walker	Laser & Ultrasound	Nutritionists	Osteopathy	Physiotherapy	Respiratory Disease control	Shoe Fitting Skills	Solarium	Stud Services	Swimming Pool Centre	Trotting Services	Vaccination	Veterinary Labs	Veterinary Practice	Veterinary Skills
BARRIER ANIMAL HEALTHCARE, Attleborough (YH01021)									●																												
BERGH APTON STUD, Norwich (YH01297)					●																																
BLAKE, JOHN T, Attleborough (YH01517)														●																							
CHAPELFIELD VETNRY, Norwich (YH02741)																																				●	
COUSINS, MAURICE C, King's Lynn (YH03513)														●																							
CURNOW, E M, King's Lynn (YH03732)																																				●	
FREEMAN, KEITH, Norwich (YH05485)					●																																
GILLHAM HOUSE VETNRY, Fakenham (YH05782)																																				●	
GREEN, KEVIN J, King's Lynn (YH06068)														●																							
GREGORY, CHARLES J N M, King's Lynn (YH06115)														●																							
HARVEY, GREIG V, Norwich (YH06514)														●																							
HAWES, MATTHEW D, North Walsham (YH06542)														●																							
HIRD, JAMES C B, Attleborough (YH06881)														●																							
HORNER, ADRIAN J, Norwich (YH07078)														●																							
HORNER, JOHN D, Aylsham (YH07079)														●																							
HUBBARD, D A, Diss (YH07250)														●																							
HURCOMB, RICHARD I, King's Lynn (YH07310)														●																							
LUSHER, RONALD MICHAEL, King's Lynn (YH08903)														●																							
MANNING, L, Norwich (YH09087)										●																											
MARJORAM, IAN S, Norwich (YH09150)														●																							
MARSHALL, STUART A, Thetford (YH09204)														●																							
MARTIN, CLAIRE L, Norwich (YH09216)														●																							
MAYWAY, Thetford (YH09308)							●																														
MILLS, ANDREW W, Diss (YH09631)														●																							
MORRIS, GILES, North Walsham (YH09830)														●																							
OLD GOLFHOUSE VETNRY GRP, Thetford (YH10459)																																				●	
PARRY, ANDREW C, Norwich (YH10789)														●																							
PELL, MARK A, Norwich (YH10911)														●																							
PERUZZI, R S N, Dereham (YH10998)														●																							
RFC BED-DOWN, Harleston (YH11781)												●																●									
SANDONS THE SADDLERY, Dereham (YH12416)									●																												
SAVAGE, E A, Thetford (YH12453)									●																												

www.hccyourhorse.com

Business Profile
Breeding and Wellbeing

by Country by County

	Ambulance Services	Animal Behaviourist	Artificial Insemination	Bloodstock Advice	Bloodstock Agency	Breaking In Horses	Breeding Advice	Chiropractics	Clipper Maintenance	Complementary Medicine	Dentistry Skills	Dust Control	Emergency Services	Farrier Services	Groom	Groom Services	Herbalists	Holistic Medicine	Homeopathy	Horse Ambulance	Horse Psychiatry	Horse Sitter	Horse Walker	Laser & Ultrasound	Nutritionists	Osteopathy	Physiotherapy	Respiratory Disease control	Shoe Fitting Skills	Solarium	Stud Services	Swimming Pool Centre	Trotting Services	Vaccination	Veterinary Labs	Veterinary Practice	Veterinary Skills
TIRUS EQUESTRIAN PRODUCTS, Norwich (YH14185)												●																									
TURNER, GORDON GEORGE, Downham Market (YH14480)														●																							
TURNER, N W, Norwich (YH14487)														●																							
WELLING, JASON M, Dereham (YH15072)														●																							
WENDALS HERBS, King's Lynn (YH15104)										●																											
WENSUM VALLEY VETNRY SURG, Fakenham (YH15109)																																				●	
WESTOVER VETNRY CTRE, North Walsham (YH15229)																																				●	
WOOD, J G P, Norwich (YH15663)																																				●	
WROXHAM SADDLERY, Norwich (YH15850)										●																											
NORTHAMPTONSHIRE																																					
ANIMAL HEALTH SUPPLIES, Boughton (YH00437)			●							●								●	●					●													
AVENUE VETNRY HOSP, Kettering (YH00680)																																				●	
BAILEY, K C, Daventry (YH00802)																							●														
BAINBRIDGE, BUTT & DALY, Wellingborough (YH00811)																																				●	
BARRETT, JEREMY J, Brafield On The Green (YH01011)														●																							
BARRONS, HENRY A, Northampton (YH01026)														●																							
BAZIN, DARREN J, Kettering (YH01100)														●																							
BONE, HOUSTON, Kettering (YH01619)														●																							
BRADLEY, KEVIN, Brackley (YH01756)														●																							
BROOK FARM, Wellingborough (YH02033)																●							●														
BRUDENELL, MARC, Wellingborough (YH02155)														●																							
BURGESS, GRAHAM G, Rushden (YH02244)														●																							
COX, JAMES W, Wollaston (YH03532)														●																							
EDENGATE SADDLERY, Northampton (YH04550)									●																												
EQUINE SVS, Wellingborough (YH04803)					●																																
FRANKLAND, DEREK S, Brackley (YH05465)														●																							
GRIGGS, KEVIN W, Kettering (YH06144)														●																							
HARTGROVE, ANDREW JOHN, Harpole (YH06501)														●																							
HARTGROVE, TIMOTHY G, Kettering (YH06502)														●																							
HARTGROVE, TREVOR E, Harpole (YH06503)														●																							
HAYTIP, Towcester (YH06595)												●																									
HODGES, JO, Rushden (YH06908)								●		●															●	●											

Business Profile
Breeding and Wellbeing

by Country by County

	Ambulance Services	Animal Behaviourist	Artificial Insemination	Bloodstock Advice	Bloodstock Agency	Breaking In Horses	Breeding Advice	Chiropractics	Clipper Maintenance	Complementary Medicine	Dentistry Skills	Dust Control	Emergency Services	Farrier Services	Groom	Groom Services	Herbalists	Holistic Medicine	Homeopathy	Horse Ambulance	Horse Psychiatry	Horse Sitter	Horse Walker	Laser & Ultrasound	Nutritionists	Osteopathy	Physiotherapy	Respiratory Disease control	Shoe Fitting Skills	Solarium	Stud Services	Swimming Pool Centre	Trotting Services	Vaccination	Veterinary Labs	Veterinary Practice	Veterinary Skills
HOLLANDS, TERESA, Kettering (YH06939)																									●												
HOWITT, GORDON R, Towcester (YH07233)														●																							
JEROME, E A, Daventry (YH07754)																																				●	
MIDDLETON, ADRIAN, Kettering (YH09545)														●																							
NATURALLY, Towcester (YH10055)										●									●																		
NOBOTTLE STUD, Nobottle (YH10224)														●																	●						
NORTHLANDS VETNRY HOSPITAL, Kettering (YH10315)																																				●	
PERCIVAL, ALEXANDER J, Daventry (YH10971)														●																							
PHILLIPS, MICHAEL J, Towcester (YH11061)														●																							
SPILMAN, THOMASINA, Yelvertoft (YH13207)								●		●																●	●										
SPINNEY LODGE VETNRY HOSP, Northampton (YH13209)																																				●	
TEMPLE, BRIAN ROBERT, Towcester (YH13950)														●																							
THOMPSON, GEORGE BERNARD, Rushden (YH14036)														●																							
THREE SHIRES LIVERY CTRE, Wellingborough (YH14107)														●																							
TILLEY, ASHLEY MARK E, Northampton (YH14151)														●																							
WATSON, JOHN M, Brackley (YH14988)														●																							
WATTS & WATTS SADDLERY, Northampton (YH15003)															●																						
NORTHUMBERLAND																																					
A C BURN, Berwick-upon-Tweed (YH00021)									●										●																		
ADAMS, K, Ashington (YH00169)														●																							
ALN VETNRY GRP, Alnwick (YH00331)																																				●	
BATY, FRANCIS JOSEPH, Hexham (YH01083)														●																							
CHESTERS STUD, Hexham (YH02835)																															●						
CROSS, MICHAEL J, Berwick-upon-Tweed (YH03654)														●																							
DAWSON, ROBERT, Chappington (YH03965)														●																							
DUGGAN, RALPH B, Hexham (YH04322)														●																							
DUNN, D, Alnwick (YH04350)														●																							
EQUILINK, Alnwick (YH04751)							●									●																					
EWING & GIDLOW, Wooler (YH04961)																																				●	
FAIRMOOR VETNRY CTRE, Morpeth (YH05026)																																				●	
FARMWAY, Morpeth (YH05074)									●																●												
GLASS, DAVID G, Choppington (YH05808)														●																							

Business Profile
Breeding and Wellbeing

by Country by County	Ambulance Services	Animal Behaviourist	Artificial Insemination	Bloodstock Advice	Bloodstock Agency	Breaking In Horses	Breeding Advice	Chiropractics	Clipper Maintenance	Complementary Medicine	Dentistry Skills	Dust Control	Emergency Services	Farrier Services	Groom	Groom Services	Herbalists	Holistic Medicine	Homeopathy	Horse Ambulance	Horse Psychiatry	Horse Sitter	Horse Walker	Laser & Ultrasound	Nutritionists	Osteopathy	Physiotherapy	Respiratory Disease control	Shoe Fitting Skills	Solarium	Stud Services	Swimming Pool Centre	Trotting Services	Vaccination	Veterinary Labs	Veterinary Practice	Veterinary Skills
GOLDENMOOR, Alnwick (YH05885)				●			●																								●						
HADRIAN VETNRY GRP, Hexham (YH06272)																																				●	
HAMPDEN & SIMONSIDE VETNRY, Alnwick (YH06363)																																				●	
HARRIS, G W, Prudhoe (YH06468)																																				●	
JACKSON, MATTHEW W, Alnwick (YH07649)														●																							
MAYLAND, ROBERT P, Hexham (YH09301)														●																							
MCDOUGALL, ERNEST, Morpeth (YH09348)														●																							
NORTHERN EQUINE SERVICES, Morpeth (YH10302)					●																																
PARSLOW, PHILLIP J, Morpeth (YH10796)														●																							
RENTON SWAN & PARTNERS, Coldstream (YH11764)																																				●	
ROBSON & PRESCOTT, Morpeth (YH12013)																																				●	
SIMONSIDE VETNRY CTRE, Rothbury (YH12833)																																				●	
SMITH, PETER F, Ashington (YH12986)														●																							
WILLEY, DAVID, Alnwick (YH15433)														●																							
WILSON, G, Alnwick (YH15536)														●																							
YOUNG, PROCTOR & WAINWRIGHT, Stocksfield (YH15937)																																				●	
NOTTINGHAMSHIRE																																					
ARENASPRAY, Hoveringham (YH00518)												●																									
ARMSTRONG, BENJAMIN J, Kirkby In Ashfield (YH00545)														●																							
BARNBY MOOR STABLES, Retford (YH00967)														●																							
BARTHORPE, JANE, Newark (YH01037)											●																										
BRIDLE WAY & GAUNTLEYS, Newark (YH01892)		●						●	●																		●										
BRIGGS-PRICE, ROYSTON M, Newark (YH01908)														●																							
CHUKKA COVE, Newark (YH02893)									●																												
COBB, JASON R, Newark (YH03111)														●																							
CONNOLE, MARK J, Newark (YH03239)														●																							
CTRE - LINES, Newark (YH03694)		●																			●																
DAVISON VETNRY SURGEONS, Nottingham (YH03955)																																				●	
DEAKIN, SAMUEL E, Nottingham (YH03986)														●																							
FORGE STABLES, Woodborough (YH05364)														●																							
GEE, M P, Worksop (YH05691)											●																										
GILL, C G & D W, Nottingham (YH05771)														●																							

Business Profile
Breeding and Wellbeing

by Country by County	Ambulance Services	Animal Behaviourist	Artificial Insemination	Bloodstock Advice	Bloodstock Agency	Breaking In Horses	Breeding Advice	Chiropractics	Clipper Maintenance	Complementary Medicine	Dentistry Skills	Dust Control	Emergency Services	Farrier Services	Groom	Groom Services	Herbalists	Holistic Medicine	Homeopathy	Horse Ambulance	Horse Psychiatry	Horse Sitter	Horse Walker	Laser & Ultrasound	Nutritionists	Osteopathy	Physiotherapy	Respiratory Disease control	Shoe Fitting Skills	Solarium	Stud Services	Swimming Pool Centre	Trotting Services	Vaccination	Veterinary Labs	Veterinary Practice	Veterinary Skills
GROOBY, NICHOLAS J, Bottesford (YH06148)														●																							
HALLAM, J B, Newark (YH06324)														●																							
HILL, ALAN, Newark (YH06826)														●																							
HOLISTIC HORSECARE, Northampton (YH06934)		●								●								●			●																
HUMPHREY, P O, Nottingham (YH07286)														●																							
KEANE, ALLAN, Mansfield (YH08015)											●																										
KOPEL, EDWARD R, Cotgrave (YH08292)														●																							
MALLENDER BROS, Worksop (YH09051)														●																							
MALTBY-SMITH, RICHARD P, Kirkby In Ashfield (YH09056)														●																							
MARTIN, TERRY, Nottingham (YH09227)														●																							
MINSTER VETNRY CTRE, Southwell (YH09653)																																				●	
MURRAY, SIMON, Westwood (YH09969)														●																							
NEWBERT, PAUL F, Retford (YH10124)														●																							
NIXON, G, Retford (YH10217)														●																							
PARK HALL STABLES, Mansfield Woodhouse (YH10727)																																				●	
PRICE, M A, Nottingham (YH11383)														●																							
SADDLECRAFT, Nottingham (YH12355)									●	●																											
SHELTON HSE SADDLERY, Newark (YH12705)										●																											
SHORT, JOHN A, Worksop (YH12761)														●																							
SMITH, JOHN R, Newark (YH12970)														●																							
WEBSTER, MICHAEL H, Southwell (YH15041)														●																							
WELCH, ANDY, Nottingham (YH15058)														●																							
OXFORDSHIRE																																					
ADAS, Kidlington (YH00176)																									●												
ALVESCOT STUD, Carterton (YH00349)			●							●								●	●												●						
ANDREWS, DAVID M, Enstone (YH00397)														●																							
ASKER HORSESPORTS, Henley-on-Thames (YH00620)																									●												
ASTI STUD & SADDLERY, Faringdon (YH00633)									●	●																											
AVONVALE VETNRY GRP, Banbury (YH00693)																																				●	
BAHVS, Faringdon (YH00792)										●															●											●	
BASKERVILLE, R E, Watlington (YH01054)																																				●	
BEECHENER VETNRY SUPPLIES, Minster Lovell (YH01168)										●																											

Business Profile
Breeding and Wellbeing

by Country by County	Ambulance Services	Animal Behaviourist	Artificial Insemination	Bloodstock Advice	Bloodstock Agency	Breaking In Horses	Breeding Advice	Chiropractics	Clipper Maintenance	Complementary Medicine	Dentistry Skills	Dust Control	Emergency Services	Farrier Services	Groom	Groom Services	Herbalists	Holistic Medicine	Homeopathy	Horse Ambulance	Horse Psychiatry	Horse Sitter	Horse Walker	Laser & Ultrasound	Nutritionists	Osteopathy	Physiotherapy	Respiratory Disease control	Shoe Fitting Skills	Solarium	Stud Services	Swimming Pool Centre	Trotting Services	Vaccination	Veterinary Labs	Veterinary Practice	Veterinary Skills
BELCHER, IAN, Didcot (YH01205)														●																							
BELCHER, MICHAEL E, Didcot (YH01206)														●																							
BRAIN INTERNATIONAL, Woodstock (YH01778)					●																																
CHERRY, R J, Churchill (YH02819)														●																							
CONSTANTINE, PAMELA, Witney (YH03244)																											●										
COOPER, D C, Bampton (YH03285)														●																							
CORLEY, H V, Faringdon (YH03318)								●																		●	●										
COTSWOLD EQUINE CTRE, Burford (YH03361)								●																		●	●										
COX, JOHN H, Bicester (YH03533)														●																							
DAVISON, ANDREW PETER, Wantage (YH03956)														●																							
DEWDNEY, DEREK BARRIE, Henley-on-Thames (YH04096)														●																							
ELWELL, TERESA, Banbury (YH04647)								●																													
EUROCLIP 2000, Banbury (YH04895)									●																												
FERENS, CUMMING & CORNISH, Bicester (YH05158)																																				●	
FIELD, MICHAEL P, Barford St Michael (YH05189)											●																										
GASCOIGNE, R F, Middle Barton (YH05667)														●																							
GODFREY, TOM D, Wantage (YH05866)														●																							
GODINGTON STUD, Bicester (YH05867)				●			●	●																							●						
GULLEY, MICHAEL, Chipping Norton (YH06190)														●																							
HALL, ALFRED, Faringdon (YH06313)														●																							
HAWKINS, MARTYN R, Didcot (YH06550)														●																							
HERBERT, KARN J, Henley-on-Thames (YH06697)														●																							
HICKS, ANDREW G, Enstone (YH06745)														●																							
HILEY, ROGER, Bicester (YH06808)														●																							
HOLMES, G L, Kidlington (YH06976)														●																							
HPA, Faringdon (YH07248)														●																							
JOHNSON, MARK E J, Banbury (YH07828)														●																							
MARK SLINGSBY, Bicester (YH09155)											●																										
MARTIN, ANDREW J, Chipping Norton (YH09215)														●																							
MCTIMONEY CHIROPRACTIC ASS, Eynsham (YH09407)								●		●																●	●										
MCTIMONEY CHIROPRACTIC CLGE, Abingdon (YH09408)								●		●																●	●										
MICROM, Thame (YH09519)			●																																		

Business Profile
Breeding and Wellbeing

by Country by County

	Ambulance Services	Animal Behaviourist	Artificial Insemination	Bloodstock Advice	Bloodstock Agency	Breaking In Horses	Breeding Advice	Chiropractics	Clipper Maintenance	Complementary Medicine	Dentistry Skills	Dust Control	Emergency Services	Farrier Services	Groom	Groom Services	Herbalists	Holistic Medicine	Homeopathy	Horse Ambulance	Horse Psychiatry	Horse Sitter	Horse Walker	Laser & Ultrasound	Nutritionists	Osteopathy	Physiotherapy	Respiratory Disease control	Shoe Fitting Skills	Solarium	Stud Services	Swimming Pool Centre	Trotting Services	Vaccination	Veterinary Labs	Veterinary Practice	Veterinary Skills
MORGAN, A R, Banbury (YH09798)													●																							
MORPHETT, S E, Milton Under Wychwood (YH09823)							●																	●	●										
O'DONNELL, E O, Wantage (YH10432)							●																	●	●										
OXFORD MCTIMONEY CHIROPRACTIC, Botley (YH10619)							●																	●	●										
PARKWOOD VETNRY GRP, Woodstock (YH10782)																																			●	
RADIONIC ASSOCIATION, Banbury (YH11597)									●																											
REED, MARTIN C, Banbury (YH11721)													●																							
RICHARD PITMAN BLOODSTOCK, Wantage (YH11805)				●																																
RICHINGS, M V, Faringdon (YH11826)													●																							
SANSOMS SADDLERY, Witney (YH12429)								●	●				●																						
SELWYN, CHRISTOPHER, Oxford (YH12629)													●																							
SMITH, DAVID P, Over Norton (YH12952)													●																							
SMITH, W, Watlington (YH13003)													●																							
SNODGRASS EDEN & TRETHEWEY, Oxford (YH13033)																																			●	
STEPHENS, ARLO R, Banbury (YH13423)													●																							
STRONG, A R, Wolvercote (YH13581)													●																							
THINK EQUUS, Kidlington (YH13995)		●							●										●																
TIMMS, R G, Thame (YH14167)													●																							
TYSOE, JASON R, Banbury (YH14533)													●																							
WALKER, GLANVILL & RICHARDS, Hook Norton (YH14849)																																			●	
WATKINS, MICHAEL GEORGE, Chipping Norton (YH14979)													●																							
WEBB, TREVOR MARK, Wantage (YH15032)													●																							
WESTON, ALAN A, Abingdon (YH15226)													●																							
WILSON, PAUL, Kidlington (YH15544)													●																							
WOODWARD, MALCOLM K, Chinnor (YH15758)													●																							
YOUNG, ADAM, Henley-on-Thames (YH15926)													●																							
RUTLAND																																					
FORRYAN, NICHOLAS C W, Whissending (YH05379)													●																							
GIBSONS, M W, Oakham (YH05756)																																			●	
HOMOEOPATHY FOR HORSES, Oakham (YH07009)									●																											
JONES, DAVID, Oakham (YH07888)							●		●														●	●										
SMITH, ROBIN ABEL, Rutland (YH12996)										●																										

Business Profile
Breeding and Wellbeing

by Country by County

Name	Ambulance Services	Animal Behaviourist	Artificial Insemination	Bloodstock Advice	Bloodstock Agency	Breaking In Horses	Breeding Advice	Chiropractics	Clipper Maintenance	Complementary Medicine	Dentistry Skills	Dust Control	Emergency Services	Farrier Services	Groom	Groom Services	Herbalists	Holistic Medicine	Homeopathy	Horse Ambulance	Horse Psychiatry	Horse Sitter	Horse Walker	Laser & Ultrasound	Nutritionists	Osteopathy	Physiotherapy	Respiratory Disease control	Shoe Fitting Skills	Solarium	Stud Services	Swimming Pool Centre	Trotting Services	Vaccination	Veterinary Labs	Veterinary Practice	Veterinary Skills
TRIPLE CROWN, Oakham (YH14401)										●																											
SHROPSHIRE																																					
ABBEY VETNRY CTRE, Shrewsbury (YH00090)																																				●	
ALFORD, STEVE, Bucknell (YH00274)														●																							
ASPINWALL, LAWRENCE R, Bishops Castle (YH00627)														●																							
AVERY, J, Oswestry (YH00682)														●																							
BAILEY, ANTHONY G, Market Drayton (YH00798)														●																							
BOND, CHRISTOPHER J, Bridgnorth (YH01615)														●																							
BROOME, G W, Shrewsbury (YH02076)														●																							
BRYNORE STUD & LIVERY STABLES, Ellesmere (YH02178)		●								●																											
CHARLES BRITTON CONSTRUCTION, Ellesmere (YH02754)																							●														
CLGE HILL VETNRY GRP, Shawbury (YH03028)																																				●	
DAWES, PHILIP A P, Shifnal (YH03961)														●																							
EARDLEY, LAWRENCE C, Shifnal (YH04449)														●																							
ELEY, JANET L, Church Stretton (YH04604)																																				●	
FYRNWY EQUINE CLINICS, Shrewsbury (YH05560)																																				●	
HAMAR, ROSITA J, Bishops Castle (YH06343)							●																								●						
HANDLEY, PETER CHARLES, Market Drayton (YH06379)														●																							
HAYGATE VETNRY CTRE, Telford (YH06581)																																				●	
HIGHGROVE SCHOOL OF RIDING, Craven Arms (YH06788)																●																					
MARTIN, MICHAEL, Shrewsbury (YH09222)							●																														
MISTHAVEN, Tern Hill (YH09661)				●			●																														
NEWLANDS VETNRY GROUP, Craven Arms (YH10146)																																				●	
NOCK DEIGHTON AGRICULTURAL, Bridgnorth (YH10225)					●																																
NORTH FARM RIDING EST, Ludlow (YH10262)																				●																	
OSWESTRY EQUEST CTRE, Oswestry (YH10576)																						●															
P HANDLEY & SONS, Market Drayton (YH10644)														●																							
PREECE, JOHN L, Shrewsbury (YH11340)														●																							
PRITCHARD, GEORGE B, Oswestry (YH11415)														●																							
ROWEN-BARBARY HORSE FEEDS, Whitchurch (YH12167)																									●												
STABLES FLAT, Shrewsbury (YH13310)											●																										
STAN CHEADLE CLIPPER SVS, Ludlow (YH13356)									●																												

Business Profile
Breeding and Wellbeing

by Country by County

	Ambulance Services	Animal Behaviourist	Artificial Insemination	Bloodstock Advice	Bloodstock Agency	Breaking In Horses	Breeding Advice	Chiropractics	Clipper Maintenance	Complementary Medicine	Dentistry Skills	Dust Control	Emergency Services	Farrier Services	Groom	Groom Services	Herbalists	Holistic Medicine	Homeopathy	Horse Ambulance	Horse Psychiatry	Horse Sitter	Horse Walker	Laser & Ultrasound	Nutritionists	Osteopathy	Physiotherapy	Respiratory Disease control	Shoe Fitting Skills	Solarium	Stud Services	Swimming Pool Centre	Trotting Services	Vaccination	Veterinary Labs	Veterinary Practice	Veterinary Skills
TEME VETNRY PRACTICE, Ludlow (YH13945)																																				●	
TOUCHDOWN LIVERIES, Whitchurch (YH14253)										●		●						●										●									
TREMLOWS HALL STUD, Whitchurch (YH14371)			●				●																								●						
VETSEARCH EQUINE SUPPLIES UK, Bishops Castle (YH14703)										●															●												
W BRYAN HORSE SERVICES, Shrewsbury (YH14753)		●																																			
WHITEHURST, A E A, Oswestry (YH15346)														●																							
WILDING, R J, Church Stretton (YH15409)							●																														
WINDSOR, M, Shrewsbury (YH15578)								●		●																●	●										
WYKE OF SHIFNAL, Shifnal (YH15863)												●																									
SOMERSET																																					
ARTHUR, G H (PROF), Axbridge (YH00567)																																				●	
BAKER, COLETTE, Burnham-on-Sea (YH00816)																											●										
BARNES, A J, Somerton (YH00972)														●																							
BARNES, JONATHAN R H, Glastonbury (YH00975)														●																							
BIRT, JENNI, Wellington (YH01445)																											●										
BISHOP, PETER J, Minehead (YH01449)														●																							
BOWDEN, JONATHAN D, Highbridge (YH01696)														●																							
BRETT, CHRISTOPHER P J, Frome (YH01853)														●																							
BRISTOL UNIVERSITY, Langford (YH01921)																																				●	
BROWNE WILLES WHITE & GLIDDON, Minehead (YH02137)																																				●	
BURCOTT RIDING CTRE, Wells (YH02236)																							●														
CANTI, J, Taunton (YH02513)																		●																			
COOK, ANGELA, Wiveliscombe (YH03255)										●																											
CREEDY, ROBERT RAYMOND, Taunton (YH03589)														●																							
CRUTCHER, STEPHEN J, Wincanton (YH03692)														●																							
CURTIS, DERRICK, Taunton (YH03747)														●																							
DARLINGTON, JAMES, Crewkerne (YH03894)														●																							
DEANE VETNRY CTRE, Taunton (YH03999)																																				●	
DELAWARE VETNRY GRP, Castle Cary (YH04029)																																				●	
DELBRIDGE, G L, Minehead (YH04030)									●																												
DENNIS, ANDREW F, Bridgwater (YH04052)														●																							
DENNY, J E, Dulverton (YH04062)														●																							

Business Profile
Breeding and Wellbeing

by Country by County	Ambulance Services	Animal Behaviourist	Artificial Insemination	Bloodstock Advice	Bloodstock Agency	Breaking In Horses	Breeding Advice	Chiropractics	Clipper Maintenance	Complementary Medicine	Dentistry Skills	Dust Control	Emergency Services	Farrier Services	Groom	Groom Services	Herbalists	Holistic Medicine	Homeopathy	Horse Ambulance	Horse Psychiatry	Horse Sitter	Horse Walker	Laser & Ultrasound	Nutritionists	Osteopathy	Physiotherapy	Respiratory Disease control	Shoe Fitting Skills	Solarium	Stud Services	Swimming Pool Centre	Trotting Services	Vaccination	Veterinary Labs	Veterinary Practice	Veterinary Skills
DOWNS HSE EQUINE, Minehead (YH04239)								●																		●	●										
DRAPER, MARTIN RAY, Minehead (YH04260)														●																							
DUNKERY, Minehead (YH04343)							●																														
DYER, NICHOLAS J, Martock (YH04387)														●																							
E KENT & SON, Minehead (YH04413)														●																							
EDDY WILLIAMSON & PARTNERS, Shepton Mallet (YH04545)																																				●	
EDWARDS, GORDON F, Minehead (YH04580)														●																							
ELLIOTT & FIELDHOUSE, Dulverton (YH04617)																																				●	
EVERETT, ROGER H, Exford (YH04950)														●																							
FORD, STEWART, Taunton (YH05328)														●																							
GARSTON VETNRY GRP, Frome (YH05659)																																				●	
GRANT & PARTNERS, Chard (YH06008)																																				●	
GRIFFITHS, HELEN, Shepton Mallet (YH06141)																											●										
HEATH, NICHOLAS J R, Somerton (YH06624)														●																							
HILTON HERBS, Crewkerne (YH06863)										●							●		●																		
HOARE, NICHOLAS J, Wincanton (YH06891)														●																							
JACOBS, STUART M, Minehead (YH07659)														●																							
KENDAL, SARAH, Williton (YH08059)								●																		●	●										
KRIS PARSONS MOBILE, Chard (YH08294)														●																							
LEGG, KEVIN J, Langport (YH08537)														●																							
LETHAM, SNELL & HUTCHINSON, Ilminster (YH08566)																																				●	
MALIN, MARK R W, Minehead (YH09049)														●																							
MATRAVERS, DAVID P, Langport (YH09266)														●																							
MATRAVERS, P J, Taunton (YH09267)														●																							
MEEK, MATTHEW R, Martock (YH09442)														●																							
MORLEY PARTNERS, Taunton (YH09819)																																				●	
MOUNT VETNRY HOSPITAL, Wellington (YH09895)																																				●	
PARSLOW, JONATHAN D, Curry Rivel (YH10795)														●																							
PAULL, C W, Taunton (YH10837)														●																							
PENDARVES, C, Somerton (YH10931)														●																							
PERROTT, NIGEL R, Wincanton (YH10986)														●																							
PHILLIPS, NIGEL, Langport (YH11062)														●																							

Business Profile
Breeding and Wellbeing

by Country by County

by Country by County	Ambulance Services	Animal Behaviourist	Artificial Insemination	Bloodstock Advice	Bloodstock Agency	Breaking In Horses	Breeding Advice	Chiropractics	Clipper Maintenance	Complementary Medicine	Dentistry Skills	Dust Control	Emergency Services	Farrier Services	Groom	Groom Services	Herbalists	Holistic Medicine	Homeopathy	Horse Ambulance	Horse Psychiatry	Horse Sitter	Horse Walker	Laser & Ultrasound	Nutritionists	Osteopathy	Physiotherapy	Respiratory Disease control	Shoe Fitting Skills	Solarium	Stud Services	Swimming Pool Centre	Trotting Services	Vaccination	Veterinary Labs	Veterinary Practice	Veterinary Skills
PIKE, NIGEL S, Crewkerne (YH11101)														●																							
RADIONIC & RADIESTHESIC, Wincanton (YH11596)										●																											
RIDEMOOR, Wincanton (YH11852)									●										●																●		
ROSE MILL FEEDS, Ilminster (YH12094)										●									●																		
RUDRAM, N, Taunton (YH12210)																																				●	
SAUNDERS, ANDREW M, Minehead (YH12444)														●																							
SHERRING, JAMES R, Bridgwater (YH12730)														●																							
SHERRING, MATTHEW J, Crewkerne (YH12731)														●																							
SMITH & PARTNERS, Bridgwater (YH12934)																																				●	
SMITH, COLIN JOHN, Yeovil (YH12946)														●																							
SMITH, MICHAEL B, Wellington (YH12977)														●																							
SOUTHILL VETNRY GROUP, Wincanton (YH13156)																																				●	
STAX SADDLERY, Montacute (YH13406)									●	●									●																		
STICKLEBALL HILL FARM, Glastonbury (YH13464)						●																															
STOP GAP, Wincanton (YH13522)																									●												
TAWBITTS EXMOORS, Minehead (YH13888)						●	●																														
THOMPSON, RONALD, Chard (YH14041)														●																							
THORNEY COPSE, Wincanton (YH14066)										●									●																		
TOOGOOD, D A P, Holford (YH14231)														●																							
UNIVERSITY OF BRISTOL, Langford (YH14583)																																				●	
W.E.S GARRETT MASTER SADDLERS, Cheddar (YH14803)									●	●																											
WAITE, COLIN, Bridgwater (YH14830)														●																							
WEST ANSTEY FARM EXMOOR, Dulverton (YH15124)														●																							
WHEELER, SIMON C T, Shepton Mallet (YH15273)														●																							
WHEELER, T C, Bridgwater (YH15274)														●																							
WHITE, BENJAMIN J, Watchet (YH15327)														●																							
WILLIAMS, R E, Shepton Mallet (YH15471)																																				●	
WOOD, RICHARD WILLIAM, Templecombe (YH15668)														●																							
SOMERSET (NORTH)																																					
BEST & BEST, Portishead (YH01323)																																				●	
BOUGOURD, WILLIAM R, Nailsea (YH01671)														●																							
CLARENDON VETNRY CTRE, Weston-Super-Mare (YH02954)																																				●	

Business Profile
Breeding and Wellbeing

by Country by County	Ambulance Services	Animal Behaviourist	Artificial Insemination	Bloodstock Advice	Bloodstock Agency	Breaking In Horses	Breeding Advice	Chiropractics	Clipper Maintenance	Complementary Medicine	Dentistry Skills	Dust Control	Emergency Services	Farrier Services	Groom	Groom Services	Herbalists	Holistic Medicine	Homeopathy	Horse Ambulance	Horse Psychiatry	Horse Sitter	Horse Walker	Laser & Ultrasound	Nutritionists	Osteopathy	Physiotherapy	Respiratory Disease control	Shoe Fitting Skills	Solarium	Stud Services	Swimming Pool Centre	Trotting Services	Vaccination	Veterinary Labs	Veterinary Practice	Veterinary Skills
COLE, JUSTIN, Weston-Super-Mare (YH03158)														●																							
DOWNTON, DANIEL A, Yatton (YH04243)														●																							
EQUINE DENTAL SVS, Weston-Super-Mare (YH04772)											●																										
FURNISS & MORTON, Weston-Super-Mare (YH05551)																																				●	
HORNER, PAUL J, Weston-Super-Mare (YH07080)														●																							
HUBBARD, DANIEL S W, Puxton (YH07251)														●																							
MANNERS, ANDREW M, Clevedon (YH09085)														●																							
STEER, R G, Weston-Super-Mare (YH13420)														●																							
URCH, DAVID L, Wrington (YH14618)																																				●	
VETNRY CTRE, Nailsea (YH14695)																																				●	
WALKER, RALPH I, Congresbury (YH14855)														●																							
WATKINS VETNRY SURGERY, Yatton (YH14977)																																				●	
STAFFORDSHIRE																																					
ABBISS, RICHARD P, Kinver (YH00099)														●																							
ARMSTRONG, LESLIE, Tamworth (YH00550)														●																							
ARMSTRONG, PAUL J, Tamworth (YH00551)														●																							
ARNOLD, STEVEN, Uttoxeter (YH00559)														●																							
ARTHERS, RICHARD A, Burton-on-Trent (YH00564)														●																							
BARNBROOK, N, Stourbridge (YH00966)														●																							
BASTOW, ARTHUR R, Tamworth (YH01061)														●																							
BLOFLOW MAGNOTHERAPY, Stoke-on-Trent (YH01545)										●																											
BOURNE, DAVID K, Stoke-on-Trent (YH01684)														●																							
BROBERG, J O, Stafford (YH02005)																																				●	
CHADWICK, RUSSELL J, Leek (YH02704)														●																							
COUNTY VETNRY GRP, Stoke-on-Trent (YH03496)																																				●	
DAVENPORT, P J, Stoke-on-Trent (YH03910)														●																							
DAVIES, JOHN W, Stafford (YH03943)														●																							
DOBBINS DINER, Tamworth (YH04151)							●																														
DONNACHIE & TOWNLEY, Rugeley (YH04186)																																				●	
EAKINS, SAMUEL W, Stoke-on-Trent (YH04443)														●																							
ELLIS, ANDREW C, Stoke-on-Trent (YH04623)														●																							
FRANCES ANN BROWN SADDLERY, Stafford (YH05444)								●	●																												

Business Profile
Breeding and Wellbeing

by Country by County

	Ambulance Services	Animal Behaviourist	Artificial Insemination	Bloodstock Advice	Bloodstock Agency	Breaking In Horses	Breeding Advice	Chiropractics	Clipper Maintenance	Complementary Medicine	Dentistry Skills	Dust Control	Emergency Services	Farrier Services	Groom	Groom Services	Herbalists	Holistic Medicine	Homeopathy	Horse Ambulance	Horse Psychiatry	Horse Sitter	Horse Walker	Laser & Ultrasound	Nutritionists	Osteopathy	Physiotherapy	Respiratory Disease control	Shoe Fitting Skills	Solarium	Stud Services	Swimming Pool Centre	Trotting Services	Vaccination	Veterinary Labs	Veterinary Practice	Veterinary Skills
FROST, T J, Stoke-on-Trent (YH05522)														●																							
GRIFFITHS, COLIN A, Rugeley (YH06138)														●																							
HARRISON, MARK, Eccleshall (YH06485)														●																							
JONES, KARL D, Cannock (YH07911)														●																							
LEESE, E, Stoke-on-Trent (YH08533)														●																							
LIGHTWOOD, ROBERT IAN, Burton-on-Trent (YH08618)														●																							
MARSON, KENNETH S, Newcastle-under-Lyme (YH09208)														●																							
MEGAN, JASON J, Lichfield (YH09445)														●																							
MELLOR, CLIVE, Stoke-on-Trent (YH09455)														●																							
MOW-COP RIDING CTRE, Stoke-on-Trent (YH09905)														●																							
NEWMAN, LAURENCE, Rugeley (YH10148)														●																							
NICHOLLS, RUSSELL KEITH, Burton-on-Trent (YH10185)														●																							
NOTT, PHILIP GEOFFREY, Rugeley (YH10339)														●																							
NUNN, JONATHAN, Gnosall (YH10355)														●																							
NUTEC, Lichfield (YH10357)										●															●												
OAKES, D G, Brewood (YH10376)														●																							
ONIONS, MARTIN F, Armitage (YH10521)														●																							
OSMOND, T P, Stoke-on-Trent (YH10570)														●																							
PEARSON, D, Leek (YH10879)														●																							
POOL HSE VETNRY HOS, Lichfield (YH11262)																																				●	
RATCLIFFE, J W, Burton-on-Trent (YH11650)														●																							
RATCLIFFE, P, Stoke-on-Trent (YH11652)														●																							
ROGERS & BROCK VETNRY, Stoke-on-Trent (YH12055)																																				●	
RUMENCO - MAIN RING, Burton-on-Trent (YH12227)																									●												
SCROPTON, Burton-on-Trent (YH12569)																														●							
SMITH, DAVID H, Cannock (YH12951)														●																							
SMITH, I R, Wolverhampton (YH12961)														●																							
SPRINGWOOD VETNRY GROUP, Burton-on-Trent (YH13266)																																				●	
STUBBS, A, Newcastle (YH13602)														●																							
THEOBALD, L & N, Stafford (YH13983)																																				●	
TOFT & STUBBS, Stoke-on-Trent (YH14203)														●																							
UDALL, DAVID GEOFFREY, Little Bridgeford (YH14538)														●																							

Business Profile
Breeding and Wellbeing

by Country by County

	Ambulance Services	Animal Behaviourist	Artificial Insemination	Bloodstock Advice	Bloodstock Agency	Breaking In Horses	Breeding Advice	Chiropractics	Clipper Maintenance	Complementary Medicine	Dentistry Skills	Dust Control	Emergency Services	Farrier Services	Groom	Groom Services	Herbalists	Holistic Medicine	Homeopathy	Horse Ambulance	Horse Psychiatry	Horse Sitter	Horse Walker	Laser & Ultrasound	Nutritionists	Osteopathy	Physiotherapy	Respiratory Disease control	Shoe Fitting Skills	Solarium	Stud Services	Swimming Pool Centre	Trotting Services	Vaccination	Veterinary Labs	Veterinary Practice	Veterinary Skills
VETNRY CTRE, Burton-on-Trent (YH14696)																																				●	
WOOD, TIMOTHY, Newcastle-under-Lyme (YH15670)														●																							
YSWAIN WELSH COBS, Cannock (YH15949)			●				●																								●						
SUFFOLK																																					
A H B INSURANCE, Newmarket (YH00034)				●																																	
ALDERTON, JAMES, Bury St Edmunds (YH00260)														●																							
ANDREW SIME, Newmarket (YH00393)					●																																
ANIMAL HEALTH TRUST, Newmarket (YH00438)																																				●	
AQUARIUS VETNRY CTRE, Brandon (YH00489)																																				●	
ARABIAN BLOODSTOCK AGENCY, Raydon (YH00491)					●																																
BARN VETNRY PRACTICE, Ipswich (YH00963)																																				●	
BARNES, RAYMOND, Newmarket (YH00980)					●																																
BARRY, DERMOT A, Bury St Edmunds (YH01033)														●																							
BEADLE, MARTIN, Haverhill (YH01111)														●																							
BEAUFORT COTTAGE, Newmarket (YH01127)																																				●	
BERRY, ANDREW I, Bury St Edmunds (YH01315)														●																							
BIRD, CHARLES R S, Eye (YH01437)														●																							
BLAIR, KENNETH O, Newmarket (YH01512)														●																							
BOYCE, DAVID J, Bury St Edmunds (YH01729)														●																							
BRITISH BLOODSTOCK AGENCY, Newmarket (YH01929)				●	●		●									●																					
BROWN, DAVID V, Newmarket (YH02107)														●																							
BUCKMAN, VINCENT J, Woodbridge (YH02201)														●																							
BULWER-LONG, T, Newmarket (YH02220)					●																																
CARD, REX T, Beccles (YH02527)														●																							
CHERRY-DOWNS BLOODSTOCK, Newmarket (YH02820)					●																																
CHEVELEY PK, Newmarket (YH02842)							●																								●						
CLARK, ROGER J, Ipswich (YH02966)														●																							
CROCKFORDS STUD, Newmarket (YH03607)																															●						
CURRAGH BLOODSTOCK AGENCY, Newmarket (YH03734)					●																																
CURTIS, MARK, Newmarket (YH03750)														●																							
CURTIS, MAURICE JOHN, Ipswich (YH03751)														●																							
CURTIS, NICHOLAS, Newmarket (YH03752)														●																							

Business Profile

Breeding and Wellbeing

by Country by County

	Ambulance Services	Animal Behaviourist	Artificial Insemination	Bloodstock Advice	Bloodstock Agency	Breaking In Horses	Breeding Advice	Chiropractics	Clipper Maintenance	Complementary Medicine	Dentistry Skills	Dust Control	Emergency Services	Farrier Services	Groom	Groom Services	Herbalists	Holistic Medicine	Homeopathy	Horse Ambulance	Horse Psychiatry	Horse Sitter	Horse Walker	Laser & Ultrasound	Nutritionists	Osteopathy	Physiotherapy	Respiratory Disease control	Shoe Fitting Skills	Solarium	Stud Services	Swimming Pool Centre	Trotting Services	Vaccination	Veterinary Labs	Veterinary Practice	Veterinary Skills
DELL, STEPHEN, Lowestoft (YH04032)														●																							
DELTA BLOOD STOCK MNGMT, Newmarket (YH04035)					●																																
DIXON, GEOFFREY DAVID, Bury St Edmunds (YH04139)														●																							
DONCASTER, R A, Ipswich (YH04180)																																				●	
EAGLE VETNRY GRP, Halesworth (YH04440)																																				●	
ECLIPSE MNGMT, Newmarket (YH04538)					●																																
EDWARDS, CHRISTOPHER R, Newmarket (YH04578)														●																							
EQUINE BEHAVIOUR FORUM, Newmarket (YH04767)		●																																			
EQUISAVE HORSE AMBULANCES, Newmarket (YH04816)																				●																	
FAIRFIELD BLOODSTOCK, Woodbridge (YH05017)					●					●																											
FBA, Newmarket (YH05113)					●																																
FEEDMARK, Harleston (YH05122)																									●												
FINDON, EDWARD, Newmarket (YH05210)														●																							
FORSYTH, GILLON S, Newmarket (YH05382)														●																							
FOSTER BLOODSTOCK, Bury St Edmunds (YH05399)							●																														
FRERE-SMITH, NICHOLAS P, Bungay (YH05498)														●																							
FROMUS VETNRY GROUP, Saxmundham (YH05516)																																				●	
GARRARD, STUART R, Eye (YH05655)														●																							
GOLDSMITH, G R, Woodbridge (YH05893)														●																							
GOODE, WILLIAM J M, Sudbury (YH05901)														●																							
GREENWOOD, ELLIS & PARTNERS, Newmarket (YH06107)																																				●	
HARMAN, CHARLES, Newmarket (YH06441)														●																							
HARRIS, ANDREW J, Newmarket (YH06465)														●																							
HARVEY, PAUL B, Halesworth (YH06516)														●																							
HERITAGE COAST STUD, Woodbridge (YH06703)				●	●		●																								●						
HERRINGSWELL BLOODSTOCK CTRE, Bury St Edmunds (YH06717)						●																															
HIETT, PETER H, Newmarket (YH06748)														●																							
HIGH HSE, Stowmarket (YH06762)								●						●		●																					
HIGHCLIFF VETNRY PRACTICE, Ipswich (YH06776)																																				●	
HILL, GEORGE, Newmarket (YH06830)					●																																
HOLLOBONE, J C, Newmarket (YH06952)														●																							
HOLMES, STEPHEN, Newmarket (YH06979)											●																										

Business Profile
Breeding and Wellbeing

by Country by County

	Ambulance Services	Animal Behaviourist	Artificial Insemination	Bloodstock Advice	Bloodstock Agency	Breaking In Horses	Breeding Advice	Chiropractics	Clipper Maintenance	Complementary Medicine	Dentistry Skills	Dust Control	Emergency Services	Farrier Services	Groom	Groom Services	Herbalists	Holistic Medicine	Homeopathy	Horse Ambulance	Horse Psychiatry	Horse Sitter	Horse Walker	Laser & Ultrasound	Nutritionists	Osteopathy	Physiotherapy	Respiratory Disease control	Shoe Fitting Skills	Solarium	Stud Services	Swimming Pool Centre	Trotting Services	Vaccination	Veterinary Labs	Veterinary Practice	Veterinary Skills
HOY, RONALD GEORGE, Ipswich (YH07246)														●																							
HUGO LASCELLES BLOODSTOCK, Bury St Edmunds (YH07276)					●																																
JILL LAMB BLOODSTOCK, Newmarket (YH07767)					●																																
JOHN FERGUSON BLOODSTOCK, Newmarket (YH07787)					●																																
KERSTING, MICHAEL, Lowestoft (YH08104)														●																							
KNOX, THOMAS T, Woodbridge (YH08289)														●																							
LAMBERT, B P, Sudbury (YH08364)														●																							
MADWAR, ALLAN, Bury St Edmunds (YH09026)														●																							
MEAD GOODBODY, Newmarket (YH09411)					●																																
MILL SADDLERY, Stowmarket (YH09587)									●																												
MOODY, GAVIN R, Newmarket (YH09738)														●																							
MOORE, ANTHONY C, Ipswich (YH09754)														●																							
N S RESEARCH, Mildenhall (YH09996)																									●												
O A CURTIS & SONS, Newmarket (YH10363)														●																							
OAKWOOD VETNRY GRP, Harleston (YH10411)																																				●	
OFFEN, MALCOLM J, Bury St Edmunds (YH10435)														●																							
O'RIORDAN, MICHAEL J, Newmarket (YH10545)														●																							
ORWELL ARENA, Ipswich (YH10556)																●																					
POPLAR PK, Woodbridge (YH11271)														●		●																					
QUINLAN, NICHOLAS D, Haverhill (YH11499)														●																							
READ, TERENCE J, Lowestoft (YH11681)														●																							
RICHARD O'GORMAN BLOODSTOCK, Newmarket (YH11804)					●																																
RODD, STUART PAUL, Ipswich (YH12042)														●																							
ROSE, DARREN M, Newmarket (YH12097)														●																							
ROSE, MARK T, Newmarket (YH12098)														●																							
ROSSDALE & PARTNERS, Newmarket (YH12122)			●																																	●	
RUSH, ROBERT G, Sudbury (YH12241)														●																							
RUSHTON, TIMOTHY D, Haverhill (YH12248)														●																							
RUST, STEVEN P, Sudbury (YH12268)														●																							
RUTHERFORD, R W, Newmarket (YH12274)														●																							
SEYMOUR BLOODSTOCK, Newmarket (YH12651)					●																																
SHADOWFAX STABLE, Newmarket (YH12655)					●																																

Business Profile
Breeding and Wellbeing

by Country by County

	Ambulance Services	Animal Behaviourist	Artificial Insemination	Bloodstock Advice	Bloodstock Agency	Breaking In Horses	Breeding Advice	Chiropractics	Clipper Maintenance	Complementary Medicine	Dentistry Skills	Dust Control	Emergency Services	Farrier Services	Groom	Groom Services	Herbalists	Holistic Medicine	Homeopathy	Horse Ambulance	Horse Psychiatry	Horse Sitter	Horse Walker	Laser & Ultrasound	Nutritionists	Osteopathy	Physiotherapy	Respiratory Disease control	Shoe Fitting Skills	Solarium	Stud Services	Swimming Pool Centre	Trotting Services	Vaccination	Veterinary Labs	Veterinary Practice	Veterinary Skills
SIDE HILL STUD, Newmarket (YH12784)					●																																
SMITH RYDER DAVIES & HILLIARD, Woodbridge (YH12937)																																				●	
SMITH, DEAN C, Sudbury (YH12953)														●																							
STOKE BY CLARE EQUESTRIAN CTRE, Sudbury (YH13501)		●													●	●					●		●														
STOWE VETNRY GROUP, Stowmarket (YH13540)																																				●	
STOWE VETNRY GROUP, Ipswich (YH13539)																																				●	
SWAYNE & PARTNERS, Sudbury (YH13701)																																				●	
SWAYNE & PARTNERS, Bury St Edmunds (YH13699)																																				●	
SWAYNE & PARTNERS, Newmarket (YH13700)																																				●	
TAYLOR & LEES, Sudbury (YH13894)																																				●	
THREE RIVERS VETNRY GROUP, Beccles (YH14106)																																				●	
TICQUET, DAVID A, Bury St Edmunds (YH14130)														●																							
TIM VIGORS BLOODSTOCK, Newmarket (YH14160)					●																																
TRENTER, JOHN F, Woodbridge (YH14382)														●																							
TURNER, F W, Bury St Edmunds (YH14479)														●																							
UFAC, Newmarket (YH14539)																									●												
VALLEY FARM, Woodbridge (YH14651)																															●						
VIVIAN PRATT, Felixstowe (YH14737)				●	●																																
WARE, RONALD, Newmarket (YH14914)														●																							
WHALEY, MELISSA, Newmarket (YH15257)																											●										
WOODS, A J, Bury St Edmunds (YH15735)					●																																
WOODWARD, BRIAN A, Ipswich (YH15754)														●																							
WRAGG, PETER, Newmarket (YH15809)					●																																
WRAY, FREDERICK W, Newmarket (YH15813)														●																							
SURREY																																					
A J S FARRIERY, Redhill (YH00041)														●																							
ADDLESTONE HARDWARE, Addlestone (YH00180)									●																												
ADRENALINE SPORTS, Haslemere (YH00188)										●																											
ALLAN BLOODLINES, West Byfleet (YH00287)					●																																
ANIMAL ALTERNATIVES, Richmond (YH00425)										●																											
ARTHUR, JOHN C, Worcester Park (YH00568)														●																							
ASCOT PARK, Woking (YH00583)				●											●	●																					

Business Profile
Breeding and Wellbeing

by Country by County

	Ambulance Services	Animal Behaviourist	Artificial Insemination	Bloodstock Advice	Bloodstock Agency	Breaking In Horses	Breeding Advice	Chiropractics	Clipper Maintenance	Complementary Medicine	Dentistry Skills	Dust Control	Emergency Services	Farrier Services	Groom	Groom Services	Herbalists	Holistic Medicine	Homeopathy	Horse Ambulance	Horse Psychiatry	Horse Sitter	Horse Walker	Laser & Ultrasound	Nutritionists	Osteopathy	Physiotherapy	Respiratory Disease control	Shoe Fitting Skills	Solarium	Stud Services	Swimming Pool Centre	Trotting Services	Vaccination	Veterinary Labs	Veterinary Practice	Veterinary Skills
AVENUE VETNRY CTRE, Staple Hill (YH00679)																																				●	
BALANCED FEEDS, Malden Rushett (YH00830)																									●												
BATES, STEPHEN P, Headley (YH01068)														●																							
BEACH, WILLIAM C, Egham (YH01104)														●																							
BEACON HILL SURGERY, Hindhead (YH01107)																																				●	
BECKERS EQUINE SVS, Egham (YH01147)														●																							
BEECHWOOD BLOODSTOCK, Weybridge (YH01177)					●																																
BEN BATES HYDRO BATH, Camberley (YH01261)										●																											
BOOKHAM LODGE STUD, Cobham (YH01627)														●																							
BOYD & PARTNERS, Staines (YH01731)																																				●	
BUCKLAND, LEE P, Addlestone (YH02195)														●																							
BUNTING, STANLEY G, Lingfield (YH02228)														●																							
BURRILL, RICHARD, Ockley (YH02279)														●																							
CHAMBERS, IAN M, Camberley (YH02719)														●																							
CHILD, RICHARD J, Guildford (YH02851)														●																							
CLAYGATE SPORTS HORSES, Esher (YH03000)					●																																
COFFEY, D J, Esher (YH03135)																																				●	
COLIN CLARK & AST, Godalming (YH03171)																																				●	
COLLISTER, JOHN D, Woking (YH03192)														●																							
COOPER, H J, Dorking (YH03287)														●																							
CRANLEIGH SCHOOL OF RIDING, Cranleigh (YH03565)																●																					
CROSSLEY, IAN L, Coulsdon (YH03659)														●																							
CROSSLEY, NICHOLAS J, Chipstead (YH03660)														●																							
DALE, T, Guildford (YH03825)														●																							
DEVEREUX, ADRIAN J, Elstead (YH04088)														●																							
EBBISHAM FARM, Tadworth (YH04528)															●								●														
EMBLEN, JOHN G, Woking (YH04650)														●																							
EQUINE VETNRY CLINIC, Guildford (YH04807)										●																										●	
FAKHOURI, ABDUL H O, Chiddingfold (YH05037)														●																							
FISHER, TONY P, Croydon (YH05243)														●																							
GACHE, R, Lingfield (YH05603)														●																							
GALLOWAY, SIMON C, Lingfield (YH05626)														●																							

Business Profile

Breeding and Wellbeing

by Country by County	Ambulance Services	Animal Behaviourist	Artificial Insemination	Bloodstock Advice	Bloodstock Agency	Breaking In Horses	Breeding Advice	Chiropractics	Clipper Maintenance	Complementary Medicine	Dentistry Skills	Dust Control	Emergency Services	Farrier Services	Groom	Groom Services	Herbalists	Holistic Medicine	Homeopathy	Horse Ambulance	Horse Psychiatry	Horse Sitter	Horse Walker	Laser & Ultrasound	Nutritionists	Osteopathy	Physiotherapy	Respiratory Disease control	Shoe Fitting Skills	Solarium	Stud Services	Swimming Pool Centre	Trotting Services	Vaccination	Veterinary Labs	Veterinary Practice	Veterinary Skills
GAYTON VETNRY GROUP, Redhill (YH05683)																																				●	
GIBSON, L W, Great Bookham (YH05751)																																				●	
GLAZEBROOK, M S, Sutton (YH05811)														●																							
GLENFIELDS STUD, Chiddingfold (YH05835)																															●						
GODFREY, TIMOTHY, Farnham (YH05865)														●																							
GOLDING, MICHAEL E, Guildford (YH05892)														●																							
GOODWIN, MARTIN LEE, Chobham (YH05911)														●																							
GRAY, PHILIP M, Chertsey (YH06031)														●																							
HAMER, WAYNE, Warlingham (YH06345)														●																							
HARRISON, WILLIAM P, Leatherhead (YH06489)														●																							
HASTILOW COMPETITION SADDLES, Godalming (YH06526)									●	●																											
HAZELTINE, J J, Dorking (YH06603)														●																							
HOLDER, MARC P, Woking (YH06925)														●																							
HOWELL, DAVID LEE, Esher (YH07229)														●																							
HURST, PAUL S, Woking (YH07318)														●																							
IBBOTSON, CHRISTOPHER J, Tadworth (YH07373)														●																							
IBBOTSON, PAUL T, Tadworth (YH07374)														●																							
IBBOTSON, PETER J, Tadworth (YH07375)														●																							
ICKE, S M, Ockley (YH07381)														●																							
IVORY, ERIC JOHN, Ewhurst (YH07537)								●						●												●	●										
JEANS, JOHN H, Dorking (YH07713)														●																							
KAVANAGH, JOHN S, Camberley (YH08000)														●																							
KEAR, BILL, Dorking (YH08016)																							●														
KING, CHRISTOPHER G, Dorking (YH08176)														●																							
KING, PAUL D, Betchworth (YH08186)														●																							
LOCKNER FARM, Guildford (YH08760)				●																																	
LORETTA LODGE RACING STABLE, Epsom (YH08831)					●																																
LUDLOW-MONK, STEPHEN P, Guildford (YH08891)														●																							
MCCALL, DAVID, Woking (YH09317)					●																																
MEDITRINA, Caterham (YH09437)										●																											
MEYRICK, R M, Camberley (YH09508)														●																							
MILLER, IAN, Guildford (YH09607)								●																		●	●										

Business Profile
Breeding and Wellbeing

by Country by County	Ambulance Services	Animal Behaviourist	Artificial Insemination	Bloodstock Advice	Bloodstock Agency	Breaking In Horses	Breeding Advice	Chiropractics	Clipper Maintenance	Complementary Medicine	Dentistry Skills	Dust Control	Emergency Services	Farrier Services	Groom	Groom Services	Herbalists	Holistic Medicine	Homeopathy	Horse Ambulance	Horse Psychiatry	Horse Sitter	Horse Walker	Laser & Ultrasound	Nutritionists	Osteopathy	Physiotherapy	Respiratory Disease control	Shoe Fitting Skills	Solarium	Stud Services	Swimming Pool Centre	Trotting Services	Vaccination	Veterinary Labs	Veterinary Practice	Veterinary Skills
MORGAN, B A, Egham (YH09799)														●																							
NICOL & PARTNERS, Guildford (YH10196)																																				●	
OXTED VETNRY CLNC, Oxted (YH10627)																																				●	
PEEKE, ALBERT, Woking (YH10897)														●																							
PINNEY, WILLIAM G M, Windlesham (YH11138)														●																							
PRENDERGAST, MICHAEL E, Guildford (YH11354)														●																							
PRIORY VETNRY SURGERY, Banstead (YH11408)																																				●	
PRIORY VETNRY SURGERY, Redhill (YH11409)																																				●	
PRIORY VETNRY SURGERY, Tadworth (YH11410)																																				●	
PRIORY VETNRY SURGERY, Reigate (YH11411)																																				●	
QUARTERMAN, GARETH J, Tadworth (YH11484)														●																							
REIS, VICKY, Farnham (YH11749)																											●										
RIDING CTRE, Farnham (YH11873)															●																						
ROCHE, SEAN, Cranleigh (YH12019)														●																							
S R S, Sunbury-on-Thames (YH12333)																		●																			
SAYERS, MARK, Camberley (YH12477)														●																							
SCOBELL, STEVEN CRAIG, Headley (YH12526)														●																							
SHAUN MEASURES BII, Camberley (YH12680)														●																							
SIMONS, M A P, Fetcham (YH12832)																																				●	
SLADE, BRENT EDBROOK, Lingfield (YH12886)														●																							
SMALLPEICE, ALAN, Godalming (YH12913)														●																							
SPARROWHAWK, J A, Wallington (YH13181)														●																							
STAGG, W C, Farnham (YH13328)														●																							
STEWARTSON, WALTER E, Woking (YH13462)														●																							
SUPERPET THE HORSE SHOP, Tadworth (YH13655)									●																												
SUPERPET THE HORSE SHOP, Epsom (YH13654)									●																												
SUPERPET THE HORSE SHOP, Banstead (YH13656)									●																												
TAYLOR, M, Hindhead (YH13906)														●																							
TUCKER, R, Haslemere (YH14436)														●																							
UNDERWOOD & CROXSON, Guildford (YH14562)																																				●	
UNDERWOOD & CROXSON EQUINE, Guildford (YH14563)																																				●	
VICTORIA FARM, Woking (YH14708)																														●							

Business Profile
Breeding and Wellbeing

by Country by County

	Ambulance Services	Animal Behaviourist	Artificial Insemination	Bloodstock Advice	Bloodstock Agency	Breaking In Horses	Breeding Advice	Chiropractics	Clipper Maintenance	Complementary Medicine	Dentistry Skills	Dust Control	Emergency Services	Farrier Services	Groom	Groom Services	Herbalists	Holistic Medicine	Homeopathy	Horse Ambulance	Horse Psychiatry	Horse Sitter	Horse Walker	Laser & Ultrasound	Nutritionists	Osteopathy	Physiotherapy	Respiratory Disease control	Shoe Fitting Skills	Solarium	Stud Services	Swimming Pool Centre	Trotting Services	Vaccination	Veterinary Labs	Veterinary Practice	Veterinary Skills
WATERDENE VETNRY PRACTICE, Caterham (YH14966)																																				●	
WATERDENE VETNRY PRACTICE, Purley (YH14967)																																				●	
WEST, RODNEY A, Dorking (YH15177)														●																							
WESTCOATS VETNRY CLINIC, Charlwood (YH15186)			●							●	●																									●	
WOODSTOCK SOUTH STABLES, Chessington (YH15751)										●								●																			
WRIGHT, SIMON D, Farnham (YH15841)														●																							
YAROFF, W, Chobham (YH15887)														●																							
YORK, RAY, Cobham (YH15918)														●																							
SUSSEX (EAST)																																					
BAKER, GRAHAM J, Lewes (YH00818)														●																							
BARNES, LEE G, Horam (YH00976)														●																							
BROWN, J H W, Hastings (YH02114)														●																							
C DEAN & SON, Lewes (YH02366)				●										●																							
CAMROSA EQUESTRIAN, Wadhurst (YH02492)										●																											
CASSERLY, ANDREW, Uckfield (YH02620)														●																							
CINQUE PORTS VETNRY ASS, Rye (YH02923)																																				●	
CLIFFE VETNRY GRP, Lewes (YH03034)																																				●	
CORDERY, PETER W, Bexhill-on-Sea (YH03311)														●																							
CROCKSTEAD PK, Lewes (YH03608)																																				●	●
DEAN, ROGER S, Newhaven (YH03996)														●																							
DUBEY, STEPHEN M, Heathfield (YH04305)														●																							
FIELDWICK, TIMOTHY, Wadhurst (YH05198)														●																							
FISHER, STEPHEN R, Nutley (YH05242)														●																							
FOREMAN, DOUGLAS G, Lewes (YH05330)														●																							
GORDON, LAWRENCE A, Telscombe Cliffs (YH05925)														●																							
GOSWELL, TREVOR M, Eastbourne (YH05944)														●																							
HARLAND, JOHN W, Lewes (YH06434)														●																							
HAYTER, JAMES W, Heathfield (YH06594)														●																							
HENRY, DAVID, Etchingham (YH06686)														●																							
HENTY, JOHN R, Eastbourne (YH06690)														●																							
HIGHCROFT VETNRY GROUP, Hailsham (YH06777)																																				●	
HOLLIS, PAUL M, Cousley Wood (YH06951)														●																							

Business Profile
Breeding and Wellbeing

by Country by County

	Ambulance Services	Animal Behaviourist	Artificial Insemination	Bloodstock Advice	Bloodstock Agency	Breaking In Horses	Breeding Advice	Chiropractics	Clipper Maintenance	Complementary Medicine	Dentistry Skills	Dust Control	Emergency Services	Farrier Services	Groom	Groom Services	Herbalists	Holistic Medicine	Homeopathy	Horse Ambulance	Horse Psychiatry	Horse Sitter	Horse Walker	Laser & Ultrasound	Nutritionists	Osteopathy	Physiotherapy	Respiratory Disease control	Shoe Fitting Skills	Solarium	Stud Services	Swimming Pool Centre	Trotting Services	Vaccination	Veterinary Labs	Veterinary Practice	Veterinary Skills
HOWE & STARNES, Uckfield (YH07222)																																				●	
KNELLER, DAVID VINCENT, Newhaven (YH08253)														●																							
LITTLE MEADOWS, Hailsham (YH08694)							●																														
MARCH, ERIC, Bexhill-on-Sea (YH09142)														●																							
MARKS, SALLY K, Wadhurst (YH09166)														●																							
MARLEY, D H, Uckfield (YH09170)														●																							
MARLEY, P, Crowborough (YH09171)														●																							
MARTLEW, J W, Rye (YH09231)														●																							
MOORCROFT CTRE, Battle (YH09748)		●																			●																
NEWNHAM, JEFFREY, Bexhill-on-Sea (YH10160)														●																							
PARROTT, RICHARD M, Heathfield (YH10788)														●																							
PEASRIDGE, S S, Rye (YH10884)									●																												
PHILLIPS, T S R, Seaford (YH11065)														●																							
PURDIE, GARRY R, Hailsham (YH11466)														●																							
RICHARDS, GRAHAM J, Rye (YH11809)														●																							
RICKETTS, TINA, Wadhurst (YH11836)								●		●																●	●										
RIDLEY, B, Uckfield (YH11886)														●																							
SKIPPON, GUY A, Heathfield (YH12879)														●																							
SOLE, DARREN B, Brighton (YH13053)														●																							
ST ANNES VETNRY GROUP, Eastbourne (YH13271)																																				●	
STEVENS, LEONARD, Eastbourne (YH13445)									●																												
TONDO, UMBERTO R, Hastings (YH14225)														●																							
WEBSTER, J, Uckfield (YH15038)														●																							
SUSSEX (WEST)																																					
A E LOCKWOOD & SON, Midhurst (YH00030)														●																							
ALBOURNE EQUESTRIAN CTRE, Hassocks (YH00248)										●								●																			
ALL ENGLAND JUMPING COURSE, Haywards Heath (YH00284)											●																										
ALLPRESS, BELGRAVE & PARTNERS, Arundel (YH00325)																																				●	
ALSTON, HENRY CHARLES, Pulborough (YH00341)														●																							
ARTHUR LODGE VETNRY HOSP, Horsham (YH00566)																																				●	
BEHAN, J J, Petworth (YH01197)														●																							
BEN MAYES, Horsham (YH01262)																																				●	

Business Profile
Breeding and Wellbeing

by Country by County

	Ambulance Services	Animal Behaviourist	Artificial Insemination	Bloodstock Advice	Bloodstock Agency	Breaking In Horses	Breeding Advice	Chiropractics	Clipper Maintenance	Complementary Medicine	Dentistry Skills	Dust Control	Emergency Services	Farrier Services	Groom	Groom Services	Herbalists	Holistic Medicine	Homeopathy	Horse Ambulance	Horse Psychiatry	Horse Sitter	Horse Walker	Laser & Ultrasound	Nutritionists	Osteopathy	Physiotherapy	Respiratory Disease control	Shoe Fitting Skills	Solarium	Stud Services	Swimming Pool Centre	Trotting Services	Vaccination	Veterinary Labs	Veterinary Practice	Veterinary Skills
BLACKSMITHS SHOP, Crawley (YH01497)														●																							
BLAKE, JILL, Steyning (YH01516)																		●																			
BOTTING, ROBERT W, Horsham (YH01666)														●																							
BRENDON, Brighton (YH01835)			●	●		●	●																								●						
BROWNRIGG, RUSSELL P, Worthing (YH02141)														●																							
BUTTON, PETER JOHN, Patching (YH02336)														●																							
CHARD, R J, Hassocks (YH02749)														●																							
CINDER HILL VETNRY CLINIC, Haywards Heath (YH02919)																																				●	
CLARK, ROBERT, Chichester (YH02965)														●																							
CLARKE, ALAN G, Worthing (YH02971)														●																							
COX, ADRIAN C S, Chichester (YH03528)														●																							
DRAGONFLY SADDLERY, Hassocks (YH04252)									●																												
EAGER, ROSS A, Dial Post (YH04436)														●																							
FACER, JAN, Partridge Green (YH05006)														●																							
FARRIERY PRACTICE, Horsham (YH05093)														●																							
FENTON, PETER H, Arundel (YH05153)														●																							
FROGGATT, D M, Sidlesham (YH05512)														●																							
GODDARD, D F, Worthing (YH05863)														●																							
HALL, MARK LESLIE, Horsham (YH06318)														●																							
HARRIS, SIMON P, Midhirst (YH06482)														●																							
HIGGS, PHILIP DOUGLAS, Horsham (YH06751)														●																							
HOGAN, M J, Worthing (YH06918)														●																							
HOLISTIC VET, Chichester (YH06936)																		●	●						●											●	●
HORACE FULLER, Horsham (YH07063)									●																												
JEFFORD, S, Arundel (YH07722)														●																							
KEATE, CHRIS, Burgess Hill (YH08019)											●																										
LAKIN BLOODSTOCK, Wisborough Green (YH08360)					●																																
LEWIS, DAVID G, Pulborough (YH08590)														●																							
LIGHTS, Brighton (YH08616)																									●												
LITTLER, MARTIN E, Worthing (YH08708)														●																							
LONDON STUD, Pulborough (YH08789)																															●						
MARTEN, D W, Pulborough (YH09210)																																				●	

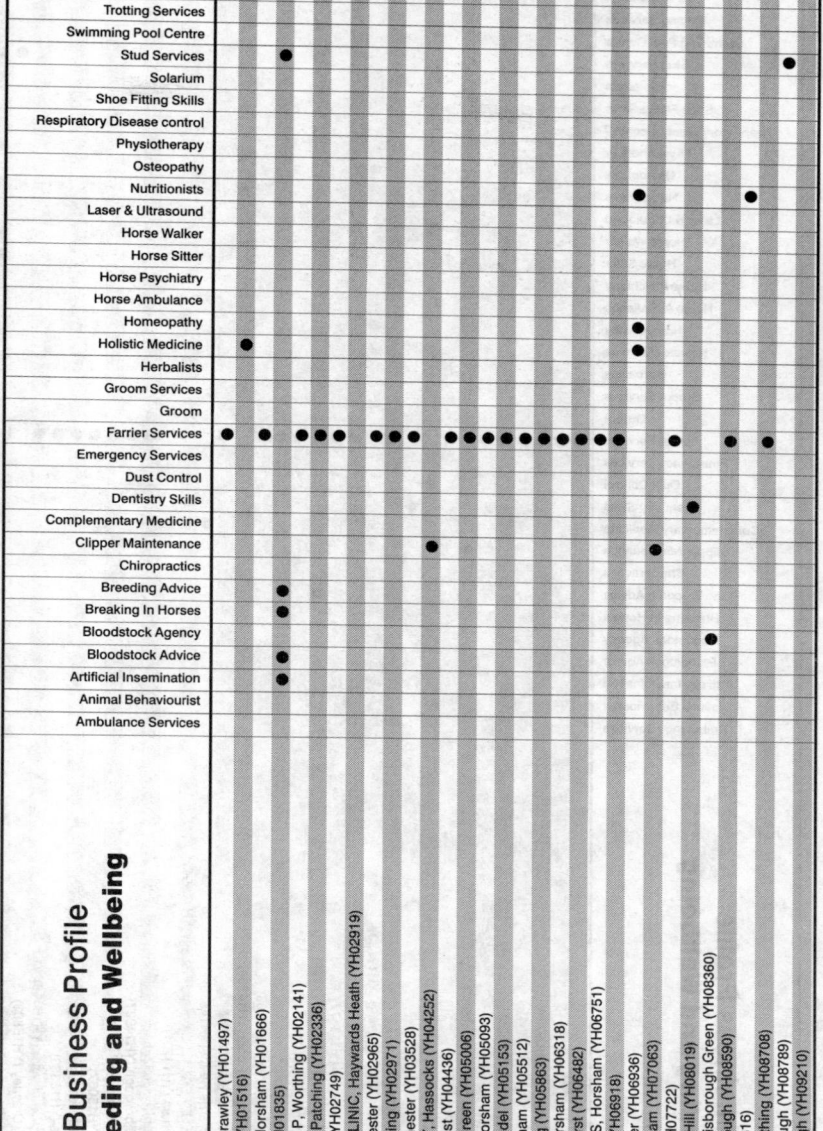

Business Profile
Breeding and Wellbeing

by Country by County	Ambulance Services	Animal Behaviourist	Artificial Insemination	Bloodstock Advice	Bloodstock Agency	Breaking In Horses	Breeding Advice	Chiropractics	Clipper Maintenance	Complementary Medicine	Dentistry Skills	Dust Control	Emergency Services	Farrier Services	Groom	Groom Services	Herbalists	Holistic Medicine	Homeopathy	Horse Ambulance	Horse Psychiatry	Horse Sitter	Horse Walker	Laser & Ultrasound	Nutritionists	Osteopathy	Physiotherapy	Respiratory Disease control	Shoe Fitting Skills	Solarium	Stud Services	Swimming Pool Centre	Trotting Services	Vaccination	Veterinary Labs	Veterinary Practice	Veterinary Skills
MAYS, PHILIP, Worthing (YH09305)														●																							
MCALEAR, STUART D, Arundel (YH09310)														●																							
MONKHOUSE, PHILIP J, Midhurst (YH09724)														●																							
PACKHAM, STUART G, Worthing (YH10664)														●																							
PATTENDEN, KEVIN J, Horsham (YH10828)														●																							
PEACOCK, C J, Steyning (YH10860)														●																							
PENFOLD & SONS, Haywards Heath (YH10934)									●																												
PIMM, JAMES V, Horsham (YH11115)														●																							
RENTOKIL INTITAL, East Grinstead (YH11763)												●																									
ROBIN STORKEY, Worthing (YH11982)											●																										
SMITH, S C, Petworth (YH12998)														●																							
SOUTHDOWN EQUESTRIAN CTRE, Steyning (YH13133)																		●	●							●											
STAPLES, MATTHEW, Crawley (YH13389)														●																							
STRIDE, DAVID P, West Chiltington (YH13577)														●																							
SYMONDSBURY STUD, Haywards Heath (YH13726)							●																								●						
TAME, GRAEME C, Horsham (YH13851)														●																							
TFP, Horsham (YH13971)														●															●								
TOLLADAY, ANDREW D, Chichester (YH14206)														●																							
TRINITY CONSULTANTS, Bognor Regis (YH14399)																									●												
UPTON, WAYNE E, Haywards Heath (YH14617)														●																							
VACLAVEK, V (DR), Haywards Heath (YH14630)										●																											
VETNRY ACUPUNCTURE REFERRAL, Haywards Heath (YH14691)										●																											
VETNRY SURGERY, Horsham (YH14701)																																				●	
WARNER, M V, Pulborough (YH14926)														●																							
WARNER, RONALD V, Pulborough (YH14927)														●																							
WATSON, KEITH R A, Horsham (YH14989)														●																							
WELLER, S F, Horsham (YH15067)														●																							
WELLS, G D, Wisborough Green (YH15084)														●																							
WHITE, KEVIN, Hassocks (YH15333)														●																							
WILKINSON, DONALD W, Chichester (YH15418)														●																							
WORTH ARABIAN STUD, Crawley (YH15803)																															●						
ZARA STUD, Chichester (YH15951)							●															●	●				●			●	●						

Business Profile
Breeding and Wellbeing

by Country by County

	Ambulance Services	Animal Behaviourist	Artificial Insemination	Bloodstock Advice	Bloodstock Agency	Breaking In Horses	Breeding Advice	Chiropractics	Clipper Maintenance	Complementary Medicine	Dentistry Skills	Dust Control	Emergency Services	Farrier Services	Groom	Groom Services	Herbalists	Holistic Medicine	Homeopathy	Horse Ambulance	Horse Psychiatry	Horse Sitter	Horse Walker	Laser & Ultrasound	Nutritionists	Osteopathy	Physiotherapy	Respiratory Disease control	Shoe Fitting Skills	Solarium	Stud Services	Swimming Pool Centre	Trotting Services	Vaccination	Veterinary Labs	Veterinary Practice	Veterinary Skills
TYNE AND WEAR																																					
ALASTAIR CRAIG NURSE, Whitley Bay (YH00242)														●																							
ARTHUR, M R (HON), Newcastle-upon-Tyne (YH00569)								●																		●	●										
BLYTHEMAN & PARTNERS, Gateshead (YH01580)																																				●	
BLYTHMAN & PARTNERS, Gosforth (YH01581)																																				●	
DIAZ, FELIX, South Shields (YH04106)														●																							
EQUINE PRODUCTS, Newcastle-upon-Tyne (YH04795)																									●												
GIRSONFIELD STUD, Otterburn (YH05795)							●																								●						
GO RIDING GRP, Ponteland (YH05862)																●							●														
GUY, JOHN, Hetton-Le-Hole (YH06197)														●																							
H C S, North Shields (YH06215)									●																												
HARRISON, MALCOLM A, Newcastle-upon-Tyne (YH06484)														●																							
JONES, B, Newcastle-upon-Tyne (YH07878)														●																							
LECKENBY, DAVID, Newcastle-upon-Tyne (YH08512)														●																							
LITTLE HARLE STABLES, Newcastle-upon-Tyne (YH08688)		●																																			
MCNEIL, CRAIG, Newcastle-upon-Tyne (YH09401)														●																							
MORAN, GRAEME BRYAN, North Shields (YH09785)														●																							
MOULD, DEAN S, Sunderland (YH09880)														●																							
NOBLE, MARK, Newcastle Upon Tyne (YH10219)																											●										
NUNN, ERIC J, Gateshead (YH10354)														●																							
OAKLANDS VETNRY CTRE, Yarm (YH10393)																																				●	
O'NEIL-MORAN, BRIAN R, North Shields (YH10520)														●																							
RAMSHAW, JOHN, Houghton Le Spring (YH11623)														●																							
STEANSON, DANIEL, Gateshead (YH13410)														●																							
STOREY, ANTHONY J, Houghton Le Spring (YH13523)														●																							
STRACHAN, TYSON & HAMILTON, Newcastle-upon-Tyne (YH13544)																																				●	
WARWICKSHIRE																																					
A & J SADDLERY, Southam (YH00012)									●																												
ACCIMASSU, Studley (YH00140)			●	●			●			●							●	●			●										●						
ACORN VETNRY CTRE, Studley (YH00154)																																				●	
ALLISON, IAN TREVOR, Coventry (YH00318)														●																							
BALCHIN, PETER W, Shipston-on-Stour (YH00831)														●																							

Business Profile
Breeding and Wellbeing

by Country by County	Ambulance Services	Animal Behaviourist	Artificial Insemination	Bloodstock Advice	Bloodstock Agency	Breaking In Horses	Breeding Advice	Chiropractics	Clipper Maintenance	Complementary Medicine	Dentistry Skills	Dust Control	Emergency Services	Farrier Services	Groom	Groom Services	Herbalists	Holistic Medicine	Homeopathy	Horse Ambulance	Horse Psychiatry	Horse Sitter	Horse Walker	Laser & Ultrasound	Nutritionists	Osteopathy	Physiotherapy	Respiratory Disease control	Shoe Fitting Skills	Solarium	Stud Services	Swimming Pool Centre	Trotting Services	Vaccination	Veterinary Labs	Veterinary Practice	Veterinary Skills
BEESLEY, JOSEPH A, Coventry (YH01189)														●																							
BELL & PARTNERS, Leamington Spa (YH01213)			●																																	●	
BILTON VETNRY CTRE, Rugby (YH01417)																																				●	
BLACK, STUART B, Rugby (YH01472)														●																							
BOSWELL, J, Radway (YH01663)														●																							
BRAZIER, JOHN F H, Leamington Spa (YH01823)																																				●	
BRYAN, JOSEPH L, Shipston-on-Stour (YH02165)														●																							
COCKRAM, R A, Radway (YH03127)			●																																		
COLE, DAVID B, Lighthorne (YH03152)														●																							
COLE, J A, Lighthorne (YH03156)														●																							
GODSON, ALAN RICHARD, Alcester (YH05870)														●																							
GOLBY, B, Coventry (YH05875)														●																							
GUILD ST VETNRY CTRE, Stratford-upon-Avon (YH06185)																																				●	
HALINA TOMBS, Rugby (YH06302)																											●										
HURLEY, BRONWEN, Kineton (YH07312)								●																		●	●										
LEWIS, DAVID CHARLES, Walton (YH08589)														●																							
MERCHANT, SIMON, Shilton (YH09466)														●																							
SHIPSTON MILL, Shipston-on-Stour (YH12751)										●																											
STABLES, Rugby (YH13308)														●																							
STANTON, ROBERT, Alcester (YH13381)														●																							
THORNTON, EMMA, Coventry (YH14078)																											●										
TONKS, IAN, Solihull (YH14228)														●																							
VENFIELD, CHRISTINE, Solihull (YH14676)								●																		●	●										
WALKER, R, Warwick (YH14854)														●																							
WILLIAMS, KARL, Hatton (YH15462)														●																							
WOODYATT, ALAN TERENCE, Warwick (YH15760)														●																							
WILTSHIRE																																					
AINLEY, PETER D, Marlborough (YH00213)														●																							
AMERICAN THOROUGHBRED, Kilmington (YH00365)																									●												
ARCHWAY VETNRY SURGERY, Highworth (YH00501)																																				●	
ARMADILLO PRODUCTS, Salisbury (YH00535)										●																											
BAKER, J, Marlborough (YH00819)														●																							

Business Profile
Breeding and Wellbeing

by Country by County

	Ambulance Services	Animal Behaviourist	Artificial Insemination	Bloodstock Advice	Bloodstock Agency	Breaking In Horses	Breeding Advice	Chiropractics	Clipper Maintenance	Complementary Medicine	Dentistry Skills	Dust Control	Emergency Services	Farrier Services	Groom	Groom Services	Herbalists	Holistic Medicine	Homeopathy	Horse Ambulance	Horse Psychiatry	Horse Sitter	Horse Walker	Laser & Ultrasound	Nutritionists	Osteopathy	Physiotherapy	Respiratory Disease control	Shoe Fitting Skills	Solarium	Stud Services	Swimming Pool Centre	Trotting Services	Vaccination	Veterinary Labs	Veterinary Practice	Veterinary Skills
BAKER, PETER N, Marlborough (YH00825)														●																							
BELMONT HSE VETNRY SURGERY, Pewsey (YH01246)																																				●	
BRITISH RACING SERVICES, Malmesbury (YH01968)					●																																
BUNDY, JONATHAN P, Warminster (YH02223)														●																							
COATES, MARGRIT, Redlynch (YH03108)										●																											
COLLIS, W K, Salisbury (YH03191)														●																							
COOMBES, P F, Salisbury (YH03281)														●																							
DOWNS HSE REHABILITATION CTRE, Marlborough (YH04240)								●																		●	●										
DUTTON, IAN J, Swindon (YH04379)														●																							
ENDELL VETNRY GRP, Salisbury (YH04666)																																				●	
EQUINE MNGMT SOLUTIONS, Marlborough (YH04789)		●																																			
FAITHFULL, JEREMY B H, Salisbury (YH05035)														●																							
FARRIER, Salisbury (YH05087)														●																							
FONTHILL STUD, Salisbury (YH05308)						●																															
FORD, RONALD SIMON, Chippenham (YH05327)														●																							
GENUS EQUINE, Chippenham (YH05711)			●	●			●																								●						●
GEORGE VETNRY GRP, Malmesbury (YH05721)																																				●	
GILL, TERRY V, Swindon (YH05777)														●																							
GROOM, P A, Swindon (YH06150)														●																							
GROOM, PETER JOHN, Swindon (YH06151)														●																							
GROVELY, Salisbury (YH06175)														●		●																					
HAINES, T J, Leigh (YH06286)														●																							
HALL ROBERT, Malmesbury (YH06310)														●																							
HANKINSON, JOHN DEREK, Marlborough (YH06389)														●																							
HARDY, RUSSELL C, Salisbury (YH06418)														●																							
HARRIS, HILL & WARNER, Warminster (YH06473)																																				●	
HARRIS, HILL & WARNER, Westbury (YH06470)																																				●	
HARRIS, HILL & WARNER, Bradford-on-Avon (YH06471)																																				●	
HARRIS, HILL & WARNER, Trowbridge (YH06472)																																				●	
HEAD, MARTIN J, Corsham (YH06609)														●																							
HEDDINGTON WICK, Calne (YH06639)						●																															
HEWLETT & ALFORD, Salisbury (YH06731)														●																							

Business Profile
Breeding and Wellbeing

by Country by County	Ambulance Services	Animal Behaviourist	Artificial Insemination	Bloodstock Advice	Bloodstock Agency	Breaking In Horses	Breeding Advice	Chiropractics	Clipper Maintenance	Complementary Medicine	Dentistry Skills	Dust Control	Emergency Services	Farrier Services	Groom	Groom Services	Herbalists	Holistic Medicine	Homeopathy	Horse Ambulance	Horse Psychiatry	Horse Sitter	Horse Walker	Laser & Ultrasound	Nutritionists	Osteopathy	Physiotherapy	Respiratory Disease control	Shoe Fitting Skills	Solarium	Stud Services	Swimming Pool Centre	Trotting Services	Vaccination	Veterinary Labs	Veterinary Practice	Veterinary Skills
HEWLETT & ALFORD, Salisbury (YH06730)														●																							
HEYWOOD, Westbury (YH06737)																							●														
HIBBERD, MICHAEL FRANCIS, Swindon (YH06740)														●																							
HOOPER, PENNIE, Marlborough (YH07044)								●		●																●	●										
HOWES, N, Chippenham (YH07231)														●																							
HUDDS FARM, Bradford-on-Avon (YH07254)														●		●																					
HURDCOTT LIVERY STABLES, Salisbury (YH07311)										●																											
I H A, Marlborough (YH07365)		●																																			
KENNY, SHAUN J, Salisbury (YH08075)														●																							
LAMINITIS CLINIC, Chippenham (YH08372)																																				●	
LEE, THOMAS H, Warminster (YH08528)														●																							
LEHEUP, GEOFFREY AVENT, Chippenham (YH08542)														●																							
LEWIS, MARTIN J, Devizes (YH08593)														●																							
MAGGS, P, Chippenham (YH09033)														●																							
MALMESBURY TRAILERS, Malmesbury (YH09053)													●							●																	
MALTHOUSE EQUESTRIAN CTRE, Swindon (YH09058)		●																																			
MARSHALL, ANDREW PHILIP, Marlborough (YH09192)														●																							
MAY, K J, Calne (YH09290)														●																							
MILLER, N A, Westbury (YH09608)														●																							
MORRISSEY, TIMOTHY P, Swindon (YH09842)														●																							
NICHOLSON, ANDREW, Devizes (YH10190)					●																																
OLDMAN, PETER D, Pewsey (YH10493)														●																							
PARK, ADRIAN JOHN, Malmesbury (YH10742)														●																							
PATEMAN, C W, Chippenham (YH10818)														●																							
PERRYMAN, PHILLIP D, Devizes (YH10990)														●																							
PILBROW, KENNETH, Warminster (YH11104)														●																							
POYNTON, ANDREW PAUL, Malmesbury (YH11331)														●																							
RAILTON, JAMIE, Chippenham (YH11612)					●																																
RENDELL, PHILIP, Warminster (YH11755)														●																							
ROBERTS, M T, Chippenham (YH11958)														●																							
SAMWAYS, Salisbury (YH12402)																															●						
SCRUTON, CHRISTOPHER, Melksham (YH12570)														●																							

Business Profile
Breeding and Wellbeing

by Country by County

	Ambulance Services	Animal Behaviourist	Artificial Insemination	Bloodstock Advice	Bloodstock Agency	Breaking In Horses	Breeding Advice	Chiropractics	Clipper Maintenance	Complementary Medicine	Dentistry Skills	Dust Control	Emergency Services	Farrier Services	Groom	Groom Services	Herbalists	Holistic Medicine	Homeopathy	Horse Ambulance	Horse Psychiatry	Horse Sitter	Horse Walker	Laser & Ultrasound	Nutritionists	Osteopathy	Physiotherapy	Respiratory Disease control	Shoe Fitting Skills	Solarium	Stud Services	Swimming Pool Centre	Trotting Services	Vaccination	Veterinary Labs	Veterinary Practice	Veterinary Skills
SMITH, JEREMY R C, Swindon (YH12967)														●																							
SMITH, PETER JOHN, Trowbridge (YH12987)														●																							
TIDMARSH, B L, Malmesbury (YH14135)														●																							
TURNELL, ALAN J, Marlborough (YH14472)														●																							
TYAN CONNEMARA STUD, Salisbury (YH14518)							●																								●						
URCH, GARY, Devizes (YH14619)														●																							
VINE, IAN DAVID, Salisbury (YH14730)														●																							
WATKINS, SIMON D, Leigh (YH14980)														●																							
WEST KINGTON STUD, Chippenham (YH15151)			●	●			●																								●						
WEST WILTS, Trowbridge (YH15170)																							●														
WESTCOURT, Marlborough (YH15189)		●				●																															
WHITE HORSE VETNRY CLINIC, Lyneham (YH15316)										●																										●	
WHITE HORSE VETNRY CLINIC, Calne (YH15315)										●																										●	
WOODLANDS EQUINE VETNRY GRP, Salisbury (YH15708)																																				●	
WYLYE STUD, Salisbury (YH15866)						●																															
YOUNG, SIMON, Salisbury (YH15940)														●																							
WORCESTERSHIRE																																					
ABBEY GREEN VETNRY GRP, Broadway (YH00078)																																				●	
BIRCHWOOD, Bewdley (YH01436)														●																							
BOND, J N, Bewdley (YH01618)														●																							
BROMSGROVE SADDLERY, Bromsgrove (YH02026)																●																					
CAINES, GEOFFREY WILLIAM, Malvern (YH02418)														●																							
CARENZA, JILL, Broadway (YH02534)						●																															
CHILMAN, J F, Pershore (YH02857)														●																							
COLLEY, J M, Bewdley (YH03178)														●																							
CROWFIELDS EQUESTRIAN SVS, Bromsgrove (YH03678)											●																										
DARBY, MARTIN V, Stourport-on-Severn (YH03878)														●																							
DENNY, D J B, Worcester (YH04061)																																				●	
DUDLEY, S & M C, Evesham (YH04310)								●																		●	●										
EQUIMIX, Stourport-on-Severn (YH04756)									●	●					●																						
F CASWELL & SON, Evesham (YH04989)														●																							
FINCH, PAUL J, Kidderminster (YH05208)														●																							

Business Profile
Breeding and Wellbeing

by Country by County

	Ambulance Services	Animal Behaviourist	Artificial Insemination	Bloodstock Advice	Bloodstock Agency	Breaking In Horses	Breeding Advice	Chiropractics	Clipper Maintenance	Complementary Medicine	Dentistry Skills	Dust Control	Emergency Services	Farrier Services	Groom	Groom Services	Herbalists	Holistic Medicine	Homeopathy	Horse Ambulance	Horse Psychiatry	Horse Sitter	Horse Walker	Laser & Ultrasound	Nutritionists	Osteopathy	Physiotherapy	Respiratory Disease control	Shoe Fitting Skills	Solarium	Stud Services	Swimming Pool Centre	Trotting Services	Vaccination	Veterinary Labs	Veterinary Practice	Veterinary Skills
FRANKLIN, ROYSTON E, Malvern (YH05470)														●																							
GIBBINS, JONATHON, Malvern (YH05738)								●																		●	●										
HALLS, IAN S, Bromsgrove (YH06334)														●																							
HARTLEBURY EQUESTRIAN CTRE, Kidderminster (YH06505)						●																															
HEID & BRAZIER, Stourport-on-Severn (YH06648)		●																			●																
HENRY FIELDS STUD, Pershore (YH06682)			●	●	●		●																														
JAMES, BRYAN GERALD, Stourport-on-Severn (YH07678)														●																							
JAMES, COLIN I, Stourport-on-Severn (YH07679)														●																							
JAMES, MARK A, Droitwich (YH07683)														●																							
JONES, BRIAN, Malvern (YH07879)														●																							
KIMBER, IAN JAMES, Malvern (YH08158)														●																							
LLOYD, PAUL R, Pershore (YH08741)														●																							
LOOKER, R D, Pershore (YH08822)														●																							
LYMER, KELVIN A, Grimley (YH08919)														●																							
MARKETING & DEVELOPMENT SVS, Stourport-on-Severn (YH09160)										●																											
MCGETTIGAN & MCGETTIGAN, Redditch (YH09355)																																				●	
MOORLANDS, Worcester (YH09779)														●		●																					
MORGAN BLACKSMITHS, Malvern (YH09793)														●																							
MORGAN, GEOFFREY K, Malvern (YH09805)														●																							
MORGAN, LEE P, Fernhill Heath (YH09809)														●																							
NORTH COTSWOLD STUD, Broadway (YH10251)					●																																
OLIVER, IAN R J, Malvern (YH10497)														●																							
PASTURES CLEAN, Broadway (YH10813)												●																									
PHIPPS, A, Pershore (YH11068)										●																											
RICHMOND, DAVID GEORGE, Bewdley (YH11829)														●																							
SATCHELL, DOMINIC M, Malvern (YH12440)														●																							
SEVERN VALLEY LIVERY CTRE, Stourport-on-Severn (YH12645)															●	●																					
SMITH, ANDREW B, Evesham (YH12940)														●																							
SMITH, C B, Bromsgrove (YH12944)														●																							
SMITH-MAXWELL, A L, Upton-upon-Severn (YH13005)							●																					●			●						
SPARREY, LIONEL, Droitwich (YH13179)														●																							
STOKES, PAULA, Redditch (YH13505)								●																		●	●										

Business Profile
Breeding and Wellbeing

by Country by County

Name	Ambulance Services	Animal Behaviourist	Artificial Insemination	Bloodstock Advice	Bloodstock Agency	Breaking In Horses	Breeding Advice	Chiropractics	Clipper Maintenance	Complementary Medicine	Dentistry Skills	Dust Control	Emergency Services	Farrier Services	Groom	Groom Services	Herbalists	Holistic Medicine	Homeopathy	Horse Ambulance	Horse Psychiatry	Horse Sitter	Horse Walker	Laser & Ultrasound	Nutritionists	Osteopathy	Physiotherapy	Respiratory Disease control	Shoe Fitting Skills	Solarium	Stud Services	Swimming Pool Centre	Trotting Services	Vaccination	Veterinary Labs	Veterinary Practice	Veterinary Skills
TEME VETNRY PRACTICE, Tenbury Wells (YH13946)																																				●	
TYLER, DEREK P, Crowle (YH14521)														●																							
TYLER, S J, Redditch (YH14522)														●																							
VALE VETNRY GROUP, Stourport-on-Severn (YH14643)																																				●	
VINE HERBAL PRODUCTS, Broadway (YH14729)										●																											
WARRINGTON, S, Little Witley (YH14943)															●	●																					
WEBB, STEPHEN EDWARD, Kidderminster (YH15030)														●																							
WHITE, STEVEN G C, St Johns (YH15335)														●																							
WHITTINGTON, T J, Redditch (YH15375)														●																							
WILKES, MARTIN, Redditch (YH15415)														●																							
WILSON, WALKER & BARNBY, Bromsgrove (YH15549)																																				●	
WILSON, WALKER & BARNBY, Droitwich (YH15550)																																				●	
WITS END STABLES, Worcester (YH15634)														●									●														
YORKSHIRE (EAST)																																					
A & E WOODWARD, Hull (YH00006)									●																												
AIKE GRANGE STUD, Driffield (YH00207)						●																															
ALLERTON, S I, Driffield (YH00310)														●																							
ASS BLOOD STOCK CONS, Bridlington (YH00629)					●																																
BINNS, A E G, Cottingham (YH01424)														●																							
BINNS, ROSS BARRY, Cottingham (YH01425)														●																							
BINNS, T J, Beverley (YH01426)														●																							
BRASHILL, M, Withernsea (YH01813)														●																							
DEARING, R, Driffield (YH04001)						●																															
EUROVET, North Ferriby (YH04909)												●													●												
FRISTON, MARTIN, Driffield (YH05509)														●																							
GANSTEAD EQUESTRIAN CTRE, Hull (YH05641)														●																							
GARTH HSE, Bridlington (YH05661)																																				●	
GARTH VETNRY GROUP, Beeford (YH05662)																																				●	
HORSLEY, ANDREW, Hull (YH07191)														●																							
MELBOURNE HALL STUD, Melbourne (YH09449)							●																														
MOORE, J, Market Weighton (YH09761)														●																							
MOORE, NICHOLAS J, Market Weighton (YH09764)														●																							

Business Profile
Breeding and Wellbeing

by Country by County

	Ambulance Services	Animal Behaviourist	Artificial Insemination	Bloodstock Advice	Bloodstock Agency	Breaking In Horses	Breeding Advice	Chiropractics	Clipper Maintenance	Complementary Medicine	Dentistry Skills	Dust Control	Emergency Services	Farrier Services	Groom	Groom Services	Herbalists	Holistic Medicine	Homeopathy	Horse Ambulance	Horse Psychiatry	Horse Sitter	Horse Walker	Laser & Ultrasound	Nutritionists	Osteopathy	Physiotherapy	Respiratory Disease control	Shoe Fitting Skills	Solarium	Stud Services	Swimming Pool Centre	Trotting Services	Vaccination	Veterinary Labs	Veterinary Practice	Veterinary Skills
NORWOOD VETNRY GROUP, Beverley (YH10336)																																				●	
PEEL VETNRY GRP, Beverley (YH10899)																																				●	
RISTON WHINS LIVERY YARD, Beverley (YH11913)						●									●																						
RYEHILL, Hull (YH12301)														●																							
STIPETIC, ROBERT A, Driffield (YH13471)														●																							
THORP, SIMON P, Hornsea (YH14090)														●																							
VERMUYDEN VETNRY PRACTICE, Goole (YH14682)																																				●	
YORKSHIRE (NORTH)																																					
ABBEYFIELDS VETNRY CTRE, Tadcaster (YH00096)																																				●	
ANDY COOK RACING, Leyburn (YH00405)																							●							●		●					
BAINBRIDGE, JULIAN, York (YH00813)														●																							
BARRACA BLOODSTOCK, Thirsk (YH01002)					●																																
BEAVER HORSE SHOP, Harrogate (YH01143)									●																												
BEIGHTON, G, Leyburn (YH01199)														●																							
BEWERLEY, Harrogate (YH01347)														●		●																					
BISHOPTON VETNRY GRP, Ripon (YH01452)																																				●	
BLOOM, KATRYNA, Selby (YH01551)								●																		●	●										
BOGS HALL, Ripon (YH01598)														●																							
BOOTHROYD, A, Filey (YH01638)																																				●	
BRIGG VIEW, Filey (YH01906)						●																															
BROADACRES NURSERIES, Tadcaster (YH01991)																		●																			
BROOKE, G M, Tadcaster (YH02043)														●																							
BROWNING, JARVIS, York (YH02139)														●																							
BUCK, RICHARD, York (YH02187)														●																							
COLLINS, E A, York (YH03187)																																				●	
COMPTON, ROBIN D, Tadcaster (YH03220)														●																							
DAWSON, A, Northallerton (YH03962)														●																							
DELAHOOKE, JAMES STUART, Richmond (YH04027)					●																																
DENTON RIDING CTRE, Scarborough (YH04066)														●																							
DYER, H, Northallerton (YH04385)														●																							
EASTGATE VETNRY CTRE, Pickering (YH04502)																																				●	
ELLIS, JANET B, Selby (YH04625)								●																		●	●										

Business Profile

Breeding and Wellbeing

by Country by County

	Ambulance Services	Animal Behaviourist	Artificial Insemination	Bloodstock Advice	Bloodstock Agency	Breaking In Horses	Breeding Advice	Chiropractics	Clipper Maintenance	Complementary Medicine	Dentistry Skills	Dust Control	Emergency Services	Farrier Services	Groom	Groom Services	Herbalists	Holistic Medicine	Homeopathy	Horse Ambulance	Horse Psychiatry	Horse Sitter	Horse Walker	Laser & Ultrasound	Nutritionists	Osteopathy	Physiotherapy	Respiratory Disease control	Shoe Fitting Skills	Solarium	Stud Services	Swimming Pool Centre	Trotting Services	Vaccination	Veterinary Labs	Veterinary Practice	Veterinary Skills
FAWCITT, ROBIN T, Moor Monkton (YH05109)														●																							
FOLLIFOOT PK, Harrogate (YH05300)														●																							
FOREST HOUSE VETNRY SURGERY, Knaresborough (YH05340)																																				●	
FORSYTH & MAZONAS, Selby (YH05381)																																				●	
FORSYTH, MADELEINE, Helmsley (YH05383)																																				●	
FRIARS HILL STABLES, York (YH05501)																●							●														
GALTRES VETNRY SURGERY, Alne (YH05628)																																				●	
GRANT NORRIE & ALMOND, Ripon (YH06010)																																				●	
GREENLEY, ALLAN, Gowthorpe (YH06096)														●																							
GREENLEY, BRIAN, Malton (YH06097)														●																							
HALL, TIMOTHY J, Harrogate (YH06319)														●																							
HARDAKER, S J, Skipton (YH06407)														●																							
HARDCASTLE, C, Copmanthorpe (YH06408)														●																							
HARLAND, GARRY, Harrogate (YH06433)														●																							
HARLAND, PHIL, York (YH06435)														●																							
HEWITT, STEPHEN N, Moor Monkton (YH06728)														●																							
HODGSON, D C, Whitby (YH06912)														●																							
HOLMEFIELD VETNRY CTRE, Selby (YH06970)																																				●	
HOTHAM, KEVIN, Harrogate (YH07200)														●																							
J & J L WATKINSON, Leyburn (YH07547)																																				●	
J C HELLENIA, Ripon (YH07570)										●																											
JACKSON, SIMON D, Claxton (YH07654)														●																							
JEMMESON, JOHN D, Middleham (YH07728)														●																							
KNIGHTS, DEREK, Richmond (YH08271)														●																							
LEWINGTON, RICHARD W, Richmond (YH08580)														●																							
LINSCOTT & BEST, Ripon (YH08668)																																				●	
LINSCOTT & BEST, Bedale (YH08667)																																				●	
LOWES, J I, Richmond (YH08873)														●																							
MANGER, DAVID A, Catterick Garrison (YH09077)														●																							
MARSHALL, KEITH WILLIAM, Skipton (YH09195)														●																							
MCCORMACK, JOHN, Leyburn (YH09331)														●																							
MIDDLEHAM SWIMMING POOL, Leyburn (YH09538)																																●					

Business Profile
Breeding and Wellbeing

by Country by County

	Ambulance Services	Animal Behaviourist	Artificial Insemination	Bloodstock Advice	Bloodstock Agency	Breaking In Horses	Breeding Advice	Chiropractics	Clipper Maintenance	Complementary Medicine	Dentistry Skills	Dust Control	Emergency Services	Farrier Services	Groom	Groom Services	Herbalists	Holistic Medicine	Homeopathy	Horse Ambulance	Horse Psychiatry	Horse Sitter	Horse Walker	Laser & Ultrasound	Nutritionists	Osteopathy	Physiotherapy	Respiratory Disease control	Shoe Fitting Skills	Solarium	Stud Services	Swimming Pool Centre	Trotting Services	Vaccination	Veterinary Labs	Veterinary Practice	Veterinary Skills
MILL LANE, Selby (YH09579)														●																							
MILLER, F V, Leyburn (YH09606)														●																							
MINSTER EQUINE VETNRY PRAC, Upper Poppleton (YH09651)																																				●	
MORLEY, ROBERT G, Pickering (YH09821)														●																							
NABURN GRANGE RIDING CTRE, York (YH10008)																							●														
NORTHERN EQUINE THERAPY CTRE, Settle (YH10303)								●		●																●	●										
PEDLEY, JOHN D C, Harrogate (YH10893)														●																							
PREECE, WAYNE, Settle (YH11343)														●																							
R & R COUNTRY, Selby (YH11507)									●																●												
RAE BEAN & PARTNERS, Boroughbridge (YH11602)																																				●	
RAINBOW EQUINE CLINIC, Malton (YH11615)																																				●	
READMAN, MICHAEL, Scarborough (YH11683)														●																							
ROBERTSON-TIERNEY, ROBERT H, Scarborough (YH11976)														●																							
ROBINSON, Malton (YH11985)									●																												
ROSE COTTAGE FARM, York (YH12091)														●		●																					
RUSHWORTH, MARTIN D, Malton (YH12249)														●																							
RUSSELL, J, Richmond (YH12259)														●																							
SHARPE, TIMOTHY S, Bugthorpe (YH12679)														●																							
SHIPLEY, ANTHONY RAYMOND, Selby (YH12749)														●																							
SINNINGTON MANOR, York (YH12855)																															●						
SMITH, DUNCAN R, Scarborough (YH12956)														●																							
SPALDING, C M, Richmond (YH13171)					●																																
STANLEY, JOHN, Northallerton (YH13374)														●																							
STEVENS, GUY NICHOLAS, Malton (YH13444)														●																							
STIRK & HAIZELDEN, Ripon (YH13472)																																				●	
STUD FARM, York (YH13606)			●				●																								●						
SWALE VETNRY SURGERY, Richmond (YH13684)																																				●	
SWINBANK, ALAN, Richmond (YH13708)					●																																
TEAL COTTAGE STUD, Welburn (YH13922)							●																														
TIERNEY, N J ROBERTSON, Scarborough (YH14138)														●																							
TWEDDELL, BRYAN W, Richmond (YH14505)														●																							
WAINWRIGHT, IAN, York (YH14827)														●																							

Business Profile
Breeding and Wellbeing

by Country by County

	Ambulance Services	Animal Behaviourist	Artificial Insemination	Bloodstock Advice	Bloodstock Agency	Breaking In Horses	Breeding Advice	Chiropractics	Clipper Maintenance	Complementary Medicine	Dentistry Skills	Dust Control	Emergency Services	Farrier Services	Groom	Groom Services	Herbalists	Holistic Medicine	Homeopathy	Horse Ambulance	Horse Psychiatry	Horse Sitter	Horse Walker	Laser & Ultrasound	Nutritionists	Osteopathy	Physiotherapy	Respiratory Disease control	Shoe Fitting Skills	Solarium	Stud Services	Swimming Pool Centre	Trotting Services	Vaccination	Veterinary Labs	Veterinary Practice	Veterinary Skills
WARD, STUART J I, Thirsk (YH14910)														●																							
YORKSHIRE DALES, Skipton (YH15919)							●																														
YORKSHIRE (SOUTH)																																					
ALTON, JAMES, Sheffield (YH00345)														●																							
ANDERSON, JOHN C, Sheffield (YH00384)														●																							
ARGO FEEDS, Sheffield (YH00521)																									●												
ATKIN, PETER ROBERT, Sheffield (YH00648)														●																							
BAILEY, ERNEST L, Doncaster (YH00800)														●																							
CHANTRY VETNRY GRP, Barnsley (YH02735)																																				●	
CHURCHFIELD VETNRY CTRE, Barnsley (YH02911)																																				●	
DARKHORSE TINYTACK, Barnsley (YH03888)							●																								●						
DOBSON, JOHN DAVID, Rotherham (YH04154)														●																							
EASTMAN, CHRISTOPHER M, Sheffield (YH04508)														●																							
EASTWOOD, MATTHEW J, Barnsley (YH04521)														●																							
FINNINGLEY LIVERY CTRE, Doncaster (YH05217)														●		●																					
HALLAM VETNRY CTRE, Sheffield (YH06323)																																				●	
HALLAM, JEREMY, Doncaster (YH06325)														●																							
HANDSWORTH RIDING STABLES, Sheffield (YH06383)														●																							
HARRIS, GAVIN T, Sheffield (YH06469)														●																							
HAWES, ROBERT A, Sheffield (YH06543)														●																							
HULL, DAVID C, Doncaster (YH07280)														●																							
LODGE, E D, Barnsley (YH08774)														●																							
LOWE, EDDIE, Rotherham (YH08860)														●																							
LOY, JOHN S W, Barnsley (YH08879)														●																							
LUTON, WILLIAM A, Barnsley (YH08909)														●																							
MALLARD HSE, Sheffield (YH09050)														●		●																					
MAYES, NORMAN B, Barnsley (YH09294)														●																							
MAYES, ROGER W, Barnsley (YH09295)														●																							
MILNER, WAYNE, Doncaster (YH09642)														●																							
MOORHOUSE, Doncaster (YH09774)						●								●	●																						
MURRAY, J I, Doncaster (YH09967)														●																							
MURRAY, JOHN, Doncaster (YH09968)														●																							

Business Profile
Breeding and Wellbeing

by Country by County

	Ambulance Services	Animal Behaviourist	Artificial Insemination	Bloodstock Advice	Bloodstock Agency	Breaking In Horses	Breeding Advice	Chiropractics	Clipper Maintenance	Complementary Medicine	Dentistry Skills	Dust Control	Emergency Services	Farrier Services	Groom	Groom Services	Herbalists	Holistic Medicine	Homeopathy	Horse Ambulance	Horse Psychiatry	Horse Sitter	Horse Walker	Laser & Ultrasound	Nutritionists	Osteopathy	Physiotherapy	Respiratory Disease control	Shoe Fitting Skills	Solarium	Stud Services	Swimming Pool Centre	Trotting Services	Vaccination	Veterinary Labs	Veterinary Practice	Veterinary Skills
PARKES, STUART J, Doncaster (YH10758)														●																							
PININA STUD, Doncaster (YH11133)																															●						
PRICES, Rotherham (YH11391)								●						●		●																					
SANDALL BEAT STABLES, Doncaster (YH12403)														●		●																					
SHEPPARD, MICHAEL W, Sheffield (YH12716)														●																							
SMALLAGE FARM, Sheffield (YH12910)														●																							
STABLE-DRY & EQUIBALE, Doncaster (YH13302)																												●									
SWINDIN, S J, Doncaster (YH13709)														●																							
THICKETT, MATTHEW C, Rotherham (YH13989)														●																							
VERSTER, MICHAEL J, Sheffield (YH14685)														●																							
WEBB, PHILIP JAMES, Mexborough (YH15029)														●																							
WOOD, V S, Barnsley (YH15671)														●																							
YORKSHIRE (WEST)																																					
ABBEY HSE VETNRY CLINIC, Cleckheaton (YH00081)																																				●	
ABBEY HSE VETNRY CLINIC, Leeds (YH00080)																																				●	
ABBEY HSE VETNRY CLINIC, Leeds (YH00082)																																				●	
AIRE VETNRY CTRE, Leeds (YH00222)																																				●	
AIRE VETNRY CTRE, Leeds (YH00223)																																				●	
ALLEN, MELVIN, Wakefield (YH00299)														●																							
ASTLEY RIDING CTRE, Leeds (YH00635)																															●						
ATACK, MICHAEL J, Wakefield (YH00641)														●																							
BALDWIN, DAVID C, Leeds (YH00840)														●																							
BALL, VIVIENNE, East Keswick (YH00852)								●																		●	●										
BARDSEY MILLS, Otley (YH00927)																									●			●									
BAXTER, J S, Leeds (YH01087)																																				●	
BEECHWOOD VETNRY GRP, Leeds (YH01181)																																				●	
BEECHWOOD VETNRY GRP, Leeds (YH01180)																																				●	
BEECHWOOD VETNRY GRP, Leeds (YH01183)																																				●	
BEECHWOOD VETNRY GRP, Leeds (YH01182)																																				●	
BLACUP TRAINING GRP, Halifax (YH01504)															●	●															●						
BOOCOCK, MARC A, Shipley (YH01625)														●																							
BOOTH, NICHOLAS H, Bradford (YH01636)														●																							

Business Profile
Breeding and Wellbeing

by Country by County

by Country by County	Ambulance Services	Animal Behaviourist	Artificial Insemination	Bloodstock Advice	Bloodstock Agency	Breaking In Horses	Breeding Advice	Chiropractics	Clipper Maintenance	Complementary Medicine	Dentistry Skills	Dust Control	Emergency Services	Farrier Services	Groom	Groom Services	Herbalists	Holistic Medicine	Homeopathy	Horse Ambulance	Horse Psychiatry	Horse Sitter	Horse Walker	Laser & Ultrasound	Nutritionists	Osteopathy	Physiotherapy	Respiratory Disease control	Shoe Fitting Skills	Solarium	Stud Services	Swimming Pool Centre	Trotting Services	Vaccination	Veterinary Labs	Veterinary Practice	Veterinary Skills
BROADHEAD, G & J, Elland (YH01997)														●																							
CALDER VETNRY GRP, Dewsbury (YH02432)																																				●	
CALDER VETNRY GRP, Mirfield (YH02433)																																				●	
CALDER VETNRY GRP, Horbury (YH02434)																																				●	
CHANTRY VETNRY GRP, Castleford (YH02737)																																				●	
CHANTRY VETNRY GRP, Wakefield (YH02736)																																				●	
CHAPPELOW, A, Mirfield (YH02748)														●		●																					
COOKSON, LORRAINE, Leeds (YH03267)								●		●																●	●										
COOPER, CYRIL, Leeds (YH03284)														●																							
CROFT HSE VETNRY CLINIC, Batley (YH03616)																																				●	
CROFTON RIDING STABLES, Wakefield (YH03624)														●		●																					
CROSS GREEN VETNRY CTRE, Otley (YH03646)																																				●	
DALES VETNRY CTRE, Otley (YH03830)																																				●	
DISCOUNT SADDLERY, Huddersfield (YH04129)										●									●																		
DURTNELL VETNRY CTRE, Leeds (YH04374)																																				●	
DURTNELL VETNRY CTRE, Leeds (YH04375)																																				●	
EASTON & WANNOP, Leeds (YH04512)																																				●	
EASTVIEW STABLES, Leeds (YH04516)						●								●																							
ELLIS, LEE R, Wakefield (YH04626)														●																							
EMMETT, ROBERT C, Halifax (YH04656)														●																							
EQUINE DENTISTRY, Wakefield (YH04774)											●																									●	●
EQUINE ENTERPRISES, South Milford (YH04777)														●		●																					
FIRTH, IAN J, Ossett (YH05234)														●															●								
GARTH FOLD VETNRY CTRE, Idle (YH05660)																																				●	
GOLDTHORPE, DAVID, Batley (YH05895)														●																							
GREEN, GREAVES & THOMSON, Keighley (YH06064)																																				●	
GREENWOOD & BROWN, Pontefract (YH06106)																																				●	
HALL, TONY, Wakefield (YH06320)																									●												
HEY, MARTIN G, Wakefield (YH06734)														●																							
HIGHWOOD STUD, Wakefield (YH06805)																															●						
HOLLY HSE, Moortown (YH06955)																																				●	
HOLMEFIELD VETNRY CTRE, Sherburn In Elmet (YH06971)																																				●	

Business Profile
Breeding and Wellbeing

by Country by County	Ambulance Services	Animal Behaviourist	Artificial Insemination	Bloodstock Advice	Bloodstock Agency	Breaking In Horses	Breeding Advice	Chiropractics	Clipper Maintenance	Complementary Medicine	Dentistry Skills	Dust Control	Emergency Services	Farrier Services	Groom	Groom Services	Herbalists	Holistic Medicine	Homeopathy	Horse Ambulance	Horse Psychiatry	Horse Sitter	Horse Walker	Laser & Ultrasound	Nutritionists	Osteopathy	Physiotherapy	Respiratory Disease control	Shoe Fitting Skills	Solarium	Stud Services	Swimming Pool Centre	Trotting Services	Vaccination	Veterinary Labs	Veterinary Practice	Veterinary Skills
HUTCHISON, DUNLOP & BAIRD, Wetherby (YH07337)																																			●	
KADAN STUD, Bradford (YH07994)							●																														
MACKIE, ROSS V, East Keswick (YH09007)														●																							
MITCHELL, J EDWARD, Birkenshaw (YH09670)														●																							
MORRIS, F, Keighley (YH09829)														●																							
MYERS, PETER V, Huddersfield (YH09981)														●																							
PACK, COLIN D, Otley (YH10662)														●																							
PINGLE NOOK FORGE, Huddersfield (YH11131)														●																							
RICHMOND, PETER, Wetherby (YH11830)					●																																
RUSHTON, PAUL, Ilkley (YH12247)														●																							
SAUNDERSON, NOEL, Huddersfield (YH12452)														●																							
SMITH, J, Bingley (YH12962)														●																							
SPALDING, VICTORIA, Roundhay (YH13172)								●																		●	●										
STEWART GREENWOOD & HODGSON, Castleford (YH13455)																																			●	
TACK & TURNOUT EQUESTRIAN, Huddersfield (YH13780)										●							●								●												
TATE, RICHARD H, Guiseley (YH13874)														●																							
THORNBURY VETNRY GROUP, Birkenshaw (YH14059)																																			●	
THORNBURY VETNRY GRP, Bradford (YH14060)																																			●	
THORNE, B, Halifax (YH14062)														●																							
TOWER WOOD VETNRY GROUP, Leeds (YH14277)										●																									●	
TWEED HSE VETNRY SURGERY, Leeds (YH14506)																																			●	
WARMAN, STEWART M, Huddersfield (YH14920)														●																							
WESTWOOD VETNRY SURGERY, Boston Spa (YH15241)																																			●	
WHITE CROSS VET HOSPITAL, Guiseley (YH15303)																																			●	
WHITWAM, EDWARD J, Halifax (YH15377)														●																							
WOLFENDEN, SIMON, Shipley (YH15648)														●																							
WOODHEAD, J, East Bierley (YH15694)														●																							
WORRALL, ANDREW G, Wakefield (YH15794)														●																							

Business Profile
Breeding and Wellbeing

by Country by County	Ambulance Services	Animal Behaviourist	Artificial Insemination	Bloodstock Advice	Bloodstock Agency	Breaking In Horses	Breeding Advice	Chiropractics	Clipper Maintenance	Complementary Medicine	Dentistry Skills	Dust Control	Emergency Services	Farrier Services	Groom	Groom Services	Herbalists	Holistic Medicine	Homeopathy	Horse Ambulance	Horse Psychiatry	Horse Sitter	Horse Walker	Laser & Ultrasound	Nutritionists	Osteopathy	Physiotherapy	Respiratory Disease control	Shoe Fitting Skills	Solarium	Stud Services	Swimming Pool Centre	Trotting Services	Vaccination	Veterinary Labs	Veterinary Practice	Veterinary Skills
IRELAND																																					
COUNTY CARLOW																																					
CARTER, EDWARD, Busherstown (YH02606)						●																															
COUNTY CLARE																																					
MURPHY CLIPPING SV, O'Briansbridge (YH09953)									●																												
COUNTY KILDARE																																					
ABBEYFIELD EQUESTRIAN FARM, Clane (YH00093)																							●														
AIRLIE STUD, Maynooth (YH00224)							●																														
BARODA STUD, Newbridge (YH00993)							●																														
BARRETTSTOWN FARM, Newbridge (YH01018)							●																●														
BROADFIELD STUD, Naas (YH01996)							●																														
BROGUESTOWN STUD, Kill (YH02020)							●																														
BROWNSTOWN STUD, The Curragh (YH02147)							●																														
CASTLEMARTIN STUD, Kildare (YH02644)							●																														
CORDUFF STUD, Kildare (YH03313)							●																														
CURRAGH EQUINE, Suncroft (YH03736)																							●														
FORENAUGHTS STUD, Naas (YH05331)																															●						
GRANGEMORE STUD, The Curragh (YH06002)						●																															
GRASSICK, MICHAEL, The Curragh (YH06021)																							●														
HUGHES, DESSIE, Kildare (YH07265)																							●														
IRISH EQUESTRIAN PRODUCTS, Kildare (YH07493)															●																						
KILDARE HORSE DEVELOPMENT, The Curragh (YH08132)				●																																	
LEGGA LIVERY & SALES, Naas (YH08538)						●																															
MOORE, ARTHUR, Naas (YH09755)																							●														
NEWTON STUD, Naas (YH10174)																							●														
OAKES, IRENE, Stroud (YH10377)																							●														
OAKLODGE STUD, Naas (YH10401)				●																																	
OXX, JOHN, Kildare (YH10628)																							●														
PIER HSE STUD, The Curragh (YH11090)							●																														
YEOMANSTOWN STUD, Naas (YH15905)																							●														

Business Profile
Breeding and Wellbeing

by Country by County

	Ambulance Services	Animal Behaviourist	Artificial Insemination	Bloodstock Advice	Bloodstock Agency	Breaking In Horses	Breeding Advice	Chiropractics	Clipper Maintenance	Complementary Medicine	Dentistry Skills	Dust Control	Emergency Services	Farrier Services	Groom	Groom Services	Herbalists	Holistic Medicine	Homeopathy	Horse Ambulance	Horse Psychiatry	Horse Sitter	Horse Walker	Laser & Ultrasound	Nutritionists	Osteopathy	Physiotherapy	Respiratory Disease control	Shoe Fitting Skills	Solarium	Stud Services	Swimming Pool Centre	Trotting Services	Vaccination	Veterinary Labs	Veterinary Practice	Veterinary Skills
COUNTY KILKENNY																																					
BANOGUE STUD, Callan (YH00907)							●																								●						
COUNTY MAYO																																					
ASHFORD EQUESTRIAN CTRE, Mayo (YH00600)							●																														
COUNTY MEATH																																					
BLACKHALL EQUESTRIAN CTRE, Little Kilcloone (YH01483)																							●														
COUNTY OFFALY																																					
ETTER SPORTS HORSES, Bellmont (YH04886)			●	●	●		●																								●						
COUNTY SLIGO																																					
BALLINA EQUESTRIAN CTRE, Ballina (YH00855)																														●							
COUNTY WESTMEATH																																					
WEBBWEAR, Multyfarnham (YH15036)															●	●						●															

Business Profile
Breeding and Wellbeing

by Country by County

	Ambulance Services	Animal Behaviourist	Artificial Insemination	Bloodstock Advice	Bloodstock Agency	Breaking In Horses	Breeding Advice	Chiropractics	Clipper Maintenance	Complementary Medicine	Dentistry Skills	Dust Control	Emergency Services	Farrier Services	Groom	Groom Services	Herbalists	Holistic Medicine	Homeopathy	Horse Ambulance	Horse Psychiatry	Horse Sitter	Horse Walker	Laser & Ultrasound	Nutritionists	Osteopathy	Physiotherapy	Respiratory Disease control	Shoe Fitting Skills	Solarium	Stud Services	Swimming Pool Centre	Trotting Services	Vaccination	Veterinary Labs	Veterinary Practice	Veterinary Skills
NORTHERN IRELAND																																					
COUNTY ANTRIM																																					
GLENBURN VETNRY CLNC, Crumlin (YH05829)																																				●	
JARDEN, J, Crumlin (YH07701)								●																		●	●										
TULLYROE STUD, Crumlin (YH14457)							●																														
COUNTY ARMAGH																																					
BALLINTEGGART STUD, Portadown (YH00860)			●																																		
HOWARD ALLEN SEEDS, Craigavon (YH07215)										●																											
COUNTY DOWN																																					
HOLMESTEAD SADDLERY, Downpatrick (YH06981)										●																											
KELLY, SHARON, Saintfield (YH08048)																											●										
MAGHERADARTIN SHETLAND STUD, Hillsborough (YH09034)																															●						
NORTHERN IRELAND HORSE BOARD, Newtownards (YH10305)							●																														
PAYNE, SAMUEL M, Dundonald (YH10853)														●																							
WOOD LODGE STABLES, Castlewellan (YH15659)						●																															
COUNTY LONDONDERRY																																					
CLARKE, CROCKETT & JAMISON, Magherafelt (YH02973)																																				●	
E G CAMPBELL, Drumahoe (YH04405)																																				●	
HAVEN SADDLERY, Magherafelt (YH06539)										●							●																				
MADDYBENNY RIDING CTRE, Coleraine (YH09022)						●																															
RAMSEY, J, Coleraine (YH11621)																																				●	
SPARKLING STUDS, Londonderry (YH13178)																															●						
COUNTY TYRONE																																					
EAMONN RICE BLOOD STOCK, Dungannon (YH04447)				●	●																																
PARKVIEW VETNRY GRP, Strabane (YH10778)																																				●	
POTTIE, A D, Fintona (YH11302)																																				●	

Business Profile
Breeding and Wellbeing

by Country by County

	Ambulance Services	Animal Behaviourist	Artificial Insemination	Bloodstock Advice	Bloodstock Agency	Breaking In Horses	Breeding Advice	Chiropractics	Clipper Maintenance	Complementary Medicine	Dentistry Skills	Dust Control	Emergency Services	Farrier Services	Groom	Groom Services	Herbalists	Holistic Medicine	Homeopathy	Horse Ambulance	Horse Psychiatry	Horse Sitter	Horse Walker	Laser & Ultrasound	Nutritionists	Osteopathy	Physiotherapy	Respiratory Disease control	Shoe Fitting Skills	Solarium	Stud Services	Swimming Pool Centre	Trotting Services	Vaccination	Veterinary Labs	Veterinary Practice	Veterinary Skills
SCOTLAND																																					
ABERDEEN (CITY OF)																																					
NICOL, A, Aberdeen (YH10197)														●																							
SUNNYSIDE, Aberdeen (YH13649)						●																															
TOWN & COUNTRY VETNRY, Aberdeen (YH14289)										●																										●	
TOWN & COUNTRY VETNRY GROUP, Kingswells (YH14291)										●																										●	
TOWN & COUNTRY VETNRY GRP, Aberdeen (YH14292)										●																										●	
ABERDEENSHIRE																																					
AIKEN, RONALD G, Peterhead (YH00208)														●																							
BELLEVUE VETNRY GRP, Banff (YH01237)																																				●	
CHAPMAN, DUNCAN, Aboyne (YH02745)														●																							
CHAPMAN, WILLIAM, Tarland (YH02747)														●																							
CRAGINETHERTY, Turriff (YH03545)				●	●		●																								●						
DAVIDSON, ALISTAIR, Aboyne (YH03928)														●																							
DONVIEW VETNRY CTRE, Inverurie (YH04190)																																				●	
HARBRO FARM SALES, Turriff (YH06404)																									●												
HJEMDAL, Turriff (YH06889)				●	●		●																														
MILL OF URAS EQUESTRIAN, Stonehaven (YH09583)											●				●	●																					●
PLAYLE, J, Fraserburgh (YH11170)														●																							
PLAYLE, KENNETH R, Keith (YH11171)														●																							
POLESBURN VETNRY CTRE, Ellon (YH11199)																																				●	
PORTER, LESLIE, New Pitsligo (YH11284)														●																							
RIDINGHILL STUD, Fraserburgh (YH11885)							●																														
ROBSON & PARTNERS, Laurencekirk (YH12012)																																				●	
RUSSELL & WOOD, Insch (YH12251)																																				●	
STRATHBOGIE VETNRY CTRE, Huntly (YH13555)																																				●	
TANNER, R, Turriff (YH13857)														●																							
TOWN & COUNTRY VETNRY, Westhill (YH14290)										●																										●	
TOWN & COUNTRY VETNRY GRP, Banchory (YH14293)										●																										●	
WOODSIDE VETNRY GRP, Torphins (YH15747)																																				●	

Business Profile
Breeding and Wellbeing

by Country by County

	Ambulance Services	Animal Behaviourist	Artificial Insemination	Bloodstock Advice	Bloodstock Agency	Breaking In Horses	Breeding Advice	Chiropractics	Clipper Maintenance	Complementary Medicine	Dentistry Skills	Dust Control	Emergency Services	Farrier Services	Groom	Groom Services	Herbalists	Holistic Medicine	Homeopathy	Horse Ambulance	Horse Psychiatry	Horse Sitter	Horse Walker	Laser & Ultrasound	Nutritionists	Osteopathy	Physiotherapy	Respiratory Disease control	Shoe Fitting Skills	Solarium	Stud Services	Swimming Pool Centre	Trotting Services	Vaccination	Veterinary Labs	Veterinary Practice	Veterinary Skills
ANGUS																																					
BALFOUR, JAMES S, Kirriemuir (YH00843)														●																							
BALFOUR, K P & P F, Dundee (YH00844)														●																							
CAMPBELL, SCOTT J, Forfar (YH02487)														●																							
JARRETT, EDWIN, Arbroath (YH07703)														●																							
KNEEN, J E, Arbroath (YH08252)																																				●	
MACFARLANE GOVAN, A L, Montrose (YH08995)																																				●	
MACFARLANE GOVAN, A L, Arbroath (YH08994)																																				●	
MACPHERSON, JOHN, Montrose (YH09016)														●																							
THRUMS VETNRY GROUP, Kirriemuir (YH14116)																																				●	
WHITEGATE STUD, Forfar (YH15339)																															●						
WILLIAMSON, GORDON FERRIER, Forfar (YH15484)														●																							
ARGYLL AND BUTE																																					
COLGRAIN EQUESTRIAN CTRE, Helensburgh (YH03170)						●																															
LISTER, M, Lochgilphead (YH08681)																																				●	
MORGAN, JAMES REGINALD, Isle Of Mull (YH09807)														●																							
ROBB, C A, Inveraray (YH11933)														●																							
TACKLE & TACK, Oban (YH13818)									●	●															●												
WITHAM, JIM, Dunoon (YH15621)														●																							
AYRSHIRE (EAST)																																					
CROSSRIGGS VETNRY CLINIC, Cumnock (YH03663)																																				●	
FERRIE, J & A, Newmilns (YH05169)														●																							
MACKENZIE BRYSON & MARSHALL, Kilmarnock (YH08999)																																				●	
MCCRAE, JOHN & HODGE, C, Cumnock (YH09335)														●																							
ROBINSON, PAUL, Galston (YH11993)														●																							
AYRSHIRE (NORTH)																																					
DAVIDSON, SCOTT G, Dalry (YH03930)														●																							
MARSHALL, ROBERT, Beith (YH09202)														●																							
SMITH, JAMES HARRY, Kilwinning (YH12966)														●																							
WARWICK, JOHN T, Kilwinning (YH14948)																											●										
AYRSHIRE (SOUTH)																																					
ALEXANDER, D C S, Mauchline (YH00268)																																				●	

Business Profile
Breeding and Wellbeing

by Country by County	Ambulance Services	Animal Behaviourist	Artificial Insemination	Bloodstock Advice	Bloodstock Agency	Breaking In Horses	Breeding Advice	Chiropractics	Clipper Maintenance	Complementary Medicine	Dentistry Skills	Dust Control	Emergency Services	Farrier Services	Groom	Groom Services	Herbalists	Holistic Medicine	Homeopathy	Horse Ambulance	Horse Psychiatry	Horse Sitter	Horse Walker	Laser & Ultrasound	Nutritionists	Osteopathy	Physiotherapy	Respiratory Disease control	Shoe Fitting Skills	Solarium	Stud Services	Swimming Pool Centre	Trotting Services	Vaccination	Veterinary Labs	Veterinary Practice	Veterinary Skills
BARR & MACMILLAN, Mauchline (YH00999)																																				●	
CREE LODGE, Ayr (YH03587)					●																																
CREE LODGE RACING STABLES, Ayr (YH03588)						●																															
DALBLAIR VETNRY SURGERY, Ayr (YH03818)																																				●	
I C S, Mauchline (YH07363)			●																																		
I C S BLOODSTOCK, Mauchline (YH07364)					●																																
JAMES M BARCLAY & SON, Maybole (YH07671)				●	●		●																														
MORIARTY, KEVIN J D, Mossblown (YH09816)														●																							
OTTERSWICK, Mauchine (YH10581)			●																																		
REID, JOHN R, Coylton (YH11743)														●																							
THOM, J G, Ayr (YH14005)																															●						
CLACKMANNANSHIRE																																					
MACKIE, JAMES A, Alloa (YH09006)										●		●													●												
MCKEAND, B W, Tillicoultry (YH09381)														●																							
DUMFRIES AND GALLOWAY																																					
AITCHISON, G W, Lockerbie (YH00228)														●																							
ALLAN, JAMES W, Kirkconnel (YH00288)														●																							
BARD VETNRY GRP, Dumfries (YH00926)																																				●	
CHARIOTS OF FIRE DRIVING CTRE, Lockerbie (YH02750)						●																															
COCHRANE, STUART M, Dalbeattie (YH03118)														●																							
FERRIE, J C, Newton Stewart (YH05170)														●																							
FIRTH VETNRY CTRE, Annan (YH05232)																																				●	
GEE GEE'S, Dumfries (YH05690)									●										●										●								
JESSIMAN, D C, Kirkcudbright (YH07759)																																				●	
KENNEDY, ROBERT M, Georgetown (YH08070)														●																							
MARTIN, EDWARD, Thornhill (YH09217)														●																							
MARTIN, MURRAY, Lockerbie (YH09223)														●																							
MILLER & COCHRANE, Stranraer (YH09599)																																				●	
ROBERT THORNE, Annan (YH11944)									●																												
SLONE, JOHN, Barrow-In-Furness (YH12900)														●																							
THOMSON, A J, Lockerbie (YH14049)														●																							
TRESIDDER, ROGER M, Annan (YH14385)														●																							

Business Profile
Breeding and Wellbeing

by Country by County

Name	Ambulance Services	Animal Behaviourist	Artificial Insemination	Bloodstock Advice	Bloodstock Agency	Breaking In Horses	Breeding Advice	Chiropractics	Clipper Maintenance	Complementary Medicine	Dentistry Skills	Dust Control	Emergency Services	Farrier Services	Groom	Groom Services	Herbalists	Holistic Medicine	Homeopathy	Horse Ambulance	Horse Psychiatry	Horse Sitter	Horse Walker	Laser & Ultrasound	Nutritionists	Osteopathy	Physiotherapy	Respiratory Disease control	Shoe Fitting Skills	Solarium	Stud Services	Swimming Pool Centre	Trotting Services	Vaccination	Veterinary Labs	Veterinary Practice	Veterinary Skills
TWEEDIE, THOMAS, Newton Stewart (YH14507)														●																							
YOUNG, GORDON, Dumfries (YH15929)														●																							
EDINBURGH (CITY OF)																																					
DRUM FEEDS, Edinburgh (YH04280)										●																											
MACKIE & BRECHIN, Kirkliston (YH09004)																																				●	
MACNAUGHTON, DONALD, Edinburgh (YH09014)														●																							
ROBB, RUARAIDH C, Dalkeith (YH11934)														●																							
SCOTT, ALEX, Kinkliston (YH12536)											●																										
STIRLINGSHIRE SADDLERY, Edinburgh (YH13474)										●																											
THISTLE VETNRY CTRE, Edinburgh (YH14000)																																				●	
FALKIRK																																					
VETNRY CLINIC, Falkirk (YH14692)																																				●	
FIFE																																					
BROOKWICK WARD, Glenrothes (YH02070)									●																												
CHESHIRE, RONALD, Glenrothes (YH02828)														●																							
CRAWFORD, DOUGLAS A, Ladybank (YH03574)														●																							
DRUMCARROW, St Andrews (YH04288)																●																					
FRANKS, MICHAEL R, East Wemyss (YH05471)														●																							
GRIEVE, GEORGE WISHART, Glenrothes (YH06128)														●																							
KER-RAMSAY, ROBERT N, Kirkcaldy (YH08098)														●																							
LOW-MITCHELL, D I, Leven (YH08876)			●																																		
PUDDLEDUB STUD, Kirkcaldy (YH11447)							●																								●						
SCOTTISH ANIMAL PHYSIOTHERAPY, Strathmiglo (YH12549)																											●										
STRONACH, JOHN, Dunfermline (YH13580)														●																							
WAXWING STUD, Saline (YH15012)			●																																		
WILSON, DAVID, Ballmullo (YH15533)														●																							
WILSON, DAVID G, Ceres (YH15534)														●																							
GLASGOW (CITY OF)																																					
EASTERTON STABLES, Glasgow (YH04501)														●		●																					
JARVIE, JAMES, Glasgow (YH07704)														●																							
ORR, CHRISTOPHER J, Milton Of Campsie (YH10552)														●																							
ROSS & BICKERTON, Glasgow (YH12113)																																				●	

Business Profile
Breeding and Wellbeing

by Country by County	Ambulance Services	Animal Behaviourist	Artificial Insemination	Bloodstock Advice	Bloodstock Agency	Breaking In Horses	Breeding Advice	Chiropractics	Clipper Maintenance	Complementary Medicine	Dentistry Skills	Dust Control	Emergency Services	Farrier Services	Groom	Groom Services	Herbalists	Holistic Medicine	Homeopathy	Horse Ambulance	Horse Psychiatry	Horse Sitter	Horse Walker	Laser & Ultrasound	Nutritionists	Osteopathy	Physiotherapy	Respiratory Disease control	Shoe Fitting Skills	Solarium	Stud Services	Swimming Pool Centre	Trotting Services	Vaccination	Veterinary Labs	Veterinary Practice	Veterinary Skills
WADE, IAN, Barrhead (YH14811)														●																							
HIGHLANDS																																					
BARRATT, T, Nairn (YH01010)														●																							
CONANVET, Dingwall (YH03222)																																				●	
EASTGATE VETNRY PRACTICE, Inverness (YH04503)																																				●	
G C MACINTYRE & PARTNERS, Dingwall (YH05572)																																				●	
HEDLEY, K H, Lairg (YH06645)														●																							
LESLIE, A C, Newtonmore (YH08559)														●																							
MACDONALD, S, Inverness (YH08990)														●																							
MCCARROLL, KAY, Evanton (YH09318)								●																		●	●										
MCGREGOR & PARTNERS, Wick (YH09365)																																				●	
PAPE, R ROBIN, Beauly (YH10706)														●																							
SCORRAIG EXMOOR PONIES, Garve (YH12528)																															●						
SEAFORTH SADDLERS, Inverness (YH12586)																			●																		
VETNRY CTRE, Invergordon (YH14694)																																				●	
WALL, A E, Sutherland (YH14860)																																				●	
INVERCLYDE																																					
ABBEY VET GRP, Greenock (YH00087)																																				●	
LANARKSHIRE (NORTH)																																					
GREIG, COLIN A R, Airdrie (YH06119)														●																							
HENDERSON, FRANCIS, Airdrie (YH06666)														●																							
LAIRD, ALEXANDER, Shotts (YH08347)						●																															
WATSON, W, Wishaw (YH14994)														●																							
LANARKSHIRE (SOUTH)																																					
ACORN VETNRY CTRE, Lanark (YH00153)																																				●	
AIRD, JOHN W, Lesmahagow (YH00220)														●																							
ARMAC VETNRY GRP, Biggar (YH00534)																																				●	
ARMSTRONG, STEWART A, Lanark (YH00553)														●																							
BEGG & PARTNERS, Strathaven (YH01194)																																				●	
BEVRIDGE, Carluke (YH01346)														●																							
BORLAND, DAVID J, East Kilbride (YH01649)														●																							
BURNS, DAVID H, Biggar (YH02270)														●																							

Business Profile
Breeding and Wellbeing

by Country by County

	Ambulance Services	Animal Behaviourist	Artificial Insemination	Bloodstock Advice	Bloodstock Agency	Breaking In Horses	Breeding Advice	Chiropractics	Clipper Maintenance	Complementary Medicine	Dentistry Skills	Dust Control	Emergency Services	Farrier Services	Groom	Groom Services	Herbalists	Holistic Medicine	Homeopathy	Horse Ambulance	Horse Psychiatry	Horse Sitter	Horse Walker	Laser & Ultrasound	Nutritionists	Osteopathy	Physiotherapy	Respiratory Disease control	Shoe Fitting Skills	Solarium	Stud Services	Swimming Pool Centre	Trotting Services	Vaccination	Veterinary Labs	Veterinary Practice	Veterinary Skills
CLIVE VALLEY VETNRY PRACTICE, Lanark (YH03050)																																				●	
HILLSIDE CLYSDALE STUD, Lesmahagow (YH06852)				●			●																								●						
NIMMO, J ALASTAIR, Biggar (YH10206)														●																							
PATERSON, ALEXANDER MILLER, Braehead Forth (YH10819)														●																							
RENSON, MICHAEL D, Lanark (YH11762)														●																							
TELFER, THOMAS, Carnwath (YH13940)														●																							
VITAL MAX, Forth (YH14735)										●																											
WEIR, J, East Kilbride (YH15053)														●																							
LOTHIAN (EAST)																																					
DUFF, A, Tranent (YH04313)														●																							
DUNBAR EQUINE, Dunbar (YH04331)								●		●																●	●										
DUNCRAHILL STUD, Tranent (YH04336)			●																																		
GORDON, R, Musselburgh (YH05927)																																				●	
J S MAIN & SONS, Haddington (YH07617)									●																												
RITCHIE, IAIN BURNS, Haddington (YH11916)														●																							
RUSSELL, MARK ROBSON, Haddington (YH12261)														●																							
LOTHIAN (MID)																																					
CUDDEFORD, DEREK (DR), Roslin (YH03700)																									●												
EQUINE BEHAVIOUR FORUM, Penicuik (YH04766)		●																																			
MARSDEN, DEBBIE (DR), Dalkeith (YH09183)		●																			●																
TELFER, J, Roslin (YH13938)														●																							
LOTHIAN (WEST)																																					
DENHOLM, LESLIE, Whitburn (YH04046)														●																							
HARRELL, CHRISTOPHER J, East Clader (YH06457)														●																							
MORAY																																					
ABCIS, Ballindalloch (YH00116)				●			●																														
DUFFY, THOMAS, Arberlour (YH04320)														●																							
GREENFIELDS SADDLERY, Elgin (YH06085)									●																												
LINDRIDGE, KEITH P, Keith (YH08651)														●																							
MORAY COAST VET GROUP, Forres (YH09786)																																				●	
ROBERTS, GORDON, Forres (YH11952)														●																							
SHANKS & MCLEAN, Aberlour (YH12670)																																				●	

www.hccyourhorse.com

Business Profile
Breeding and Wellbeing

by Country by County

	Ambulance Services	Animal Behaviourist	Artificial Insemination	Bloodstock Advice	Bloodstock Agency	Breaking In Horses	Breeding Advice	Chiropractics	Clipper Maintenance	Complementary Medicine	Dentistry Skills	Dust Control	Emergency Services	Farrier Services	Groom	Groom Services	Herbalists	Holistic Medicine	Homeopathy	Horse Ambulance	Horse Psychiatry	Horse Sitter	Horse Walker	Laser & Ultrasound	Nutritionists	Osteopathy	Physiotherapy	Respiratory Disease control	Shoe Fitting Skills	Solarium	Stud Services	Swimming Pool Centre	Trotting Services	Vaccination	Veterinary Labs	Veterinary Practice	Veterinary Skills
SHENVAL FARM, Ballindalloch (YH12709)							●																								●						
SIMPSON, ANDREW W, Elgin (YH12837)														●																							
THERAPY SYSTEMS, Aberlour (YH13985)										●																											
ORKNEY ISLES																																					
MCCARROLL, KAY, Kirkwall (YH09320)								●																													
TAIT, THOMAS A, Stromness (YH13826)														●																							
PERTH AND KINROSS																																					
ARMSTRONG, J A, Glencarse (YH00548)														●																							
ASHWORTH VETNRY GRP, Crieff (YH00618)																																				●	
BROWN, DAVID R, Inchture (YH02106)														●																							
CAMERON & GREIG, Milnathort (YH02476)																																				●	
CHALMERS, ALISTAIR N, Blairgowrie (YH02716)														●																							
DAVIDSONS VETNRY SUPPLIES, Blairgowrie (YH03931)										●																											
DOIG, W G, Balbeggie (YH04165)														●																							
EQUI-CARE, Perth (YH04736)															●	●																					●
ERSKINE, DOUGLAS J, Gairney Bank (YH04857)														●																							
FAIR CITY VETNRY GRP, Perth (YH05010)																																				●	
GLEN EAGLES EQUESTRIAN, Auchterarder (YH05825)		●								●					●		●	●	●		●						●			●							●
GLENMARKIE, Blairgowrie (YH05840)															●	●														●	●						
HARBIT & RYDER, Aberfeldy (YH06403)																																				●	
MCFADZEAN, ROBERT L, Dunning (YH09352)														●																							
NATURAL APPROACH, Bankfoot (YH10051)										●																											
NORMILE, LUCY, Glenfarg (YH10242)																							●														
SHETLAND PONY STUD BOOK SOC, Perth (YH12736)							●																														
TILLYRIE RACING, Kinross (YH14155)				●																																	
WEST, GEORGE, Auchterarder (YH15175)														●																							
RENFREWSHIRE																																					
ABBEY VET GRP, Paisley (YH00088)																																				●	
BROWN, JAMES C, Lochwinnoch (YH02116)														●																							
KILGOUR, Y, Lochwinnoch (YH08136)														●																							
SCOTTISH BORDERS																																					
A C BURN, Jedburgh (YH00022)									●										●																		

Business Profile
Breeding and Wellbeing

by Country by County

	Ambulance Services	Animal Behaviourist	Artificial Insemination	Bloodstock Advice	Bloodstock Agency	Breaking In Horses	Breeding Advice	Chiropractics	Clipper Maintenance	Complementary Medicine	Dentistry Skills	Dust Control	Emergency Services	Farrier Services	Groom	Groom Services	Herbalists	Holistic Medicine	Homeopathy	Horse Ambulance	Horse Psychiatry	Horse Sitter	Horse Walker	Laser & Ultrasound	Nutritionists	Osteopathy	Physiotherapy	Respiratory Disease control	Shoe Fitting Skills	Solarium	Stud Services	Swimming Pool Centre	Trotting Services	Vaccination	Veterinary Labs	Veterinary Practice	Veterinary Skills
ALLISON, W P, Hawick (YH00320)														●																							
COCKBURN, CHARLES KERR, Earlston (YH03121)														●																							
CROW, ANDREW M, Jedburgh (YH03675)														●																							
DONCASTER BLOODSTOCK SALES, Hawick (YH04178)					●																																
GIBSON & GIBSON, Galashiels (YH05743)																																				●	
HOOK, ELLIOT W G, Hawick (YH07036)														●																							
JOHN NISBET, Eyemouth (YH07803)														●																							
JOHNSTON, G J, Kelso (YH07845)														●																							
MCNAB SADDLERS, Selkirk (YH09396)																●		●	●																		
MCNAB SADDLERS, Kelso (YH09397)																●																					
MERLIN VETS, Kelso (YH09478)																																				●	
OVER WHITLAW STABLES, Selkirk (YH10590)																															●						
PEEBLES HYDRO STABLES, Peebles (YH10896)														●																							
ROGERSON & PARTNERS, Galashiels (YH12061)																																				●	
SCOT, J & A, Selkirk (YH12529)														●																							
SCOTTISH BLOODSTOCK AGENCY, Jedburgh (YH12550)					●																																
SMITHY, LINDEAN, Galashiels (YH13015)														●																							
TELFORD, R, Eyemouth (YH13943)						●																															
THREADGALL, FRANCIS JOHN, Lauder (YH14100)														●																							
WESTERTOUN, Gordon (YH15212)																						●															
WHALEY, J H, Duns (YH15256)														●																							
YOUNG, D A, Selkirk (YH15927)														●																							
SHETLAND ISLANDS																																					
BRUCE WILCOCK, Shetland (YH02154)														●															●								
STIRLING																																					
ADAMSON, J, Stirling (YH00174)														●																							
BROADLEYS VETNRY HOSPITAL, Stirling (YH02000)																																				●	
FRASER, J L, Drymen (YH05473)														●																							
MITCHELL, K A, Stirling (YH09674)														●																							
MOIR, JOHN ANDERSON, Bridge Of Allan (YH09704)														●																							

Business Profile
Breeding and Wellbeing

by Country by County

	Ambulance Services	Animal Behaviourist	Artificial Insemination	Bloodstock Advice	Bloodstock Agency	Breaking In Horses	Breeding Advice	Chiropractics	Clipper Maintenance	Complementary Medicine	Dentistry Skills	Dust Control	Emergency Services	Farrier Services	Groom	Groom Services	Herbalists	Holistic Medicine	Homeopathy	Horse Ambulance	Horse Psychiatry	Horse Sitter	Horse Walker	Laser & Ultrasound	Nutritionists	Osteopathy	Physiotherapy	Respiratory Disease control	Shoe Fitting Skills	Solarium	Stud Services	Swimming Pool Centre	Trotting Services	Vaccination	Veterinary Labs	Veterinary Practice	Veterinary Skills
WALES																																					
BLAENAU GWENT																																					
EDWARDS, JOHN, Abertillery (YH04582)														●																							
BRIDGEND																																					
DAVID, GLYN O, Maesteg (YH03926)														●																							
DAVID, O J, Maesteg (YH03927)														●																							
E K M EQUESTRIAN, Bridgend (YH04411)							●																								●						
GALLIERS, MARK E, Bridgend (YH05621)														●																							
CAERPHILLY																																					
GRIFFITHS, DAVID, Rudry (YH06139)														●																							
GRIFFITHS, KEVIN, Hengoed (YH06142)														●																							
PARTIS, COLIN, Bargoed (YH10802)														●																							
CARMARTHENSHIRE																																					
ALLEN & PARTNERS, Whitland (YH00291)																																				●	
BAILEY, DESMOND EARL, Llanybydder (YH00799)														●																							
BURNETT, LEE, Ammanford (YH02264)														●																							
D L MORGAN & SON, Llanwrda (YH03791)														●																							
DAVIES, MARK, Kidwelly (YH03944)														●																							
EQUISECRETS, Lampeter (YH04817)		●																																			
GIBSON & JONES, Llanelli (YH05744)																																				●	
GRANT, LEWIS, Carmarthen (YH06013)														●																							
GRIFFIN, T R, Ammanford (YH06133)														●																							
HOLTOM, GILES E, Llandeilo (YH06990)														●																							
HORSE CTRE, Llandysul (YH07115)									●																												
JACKSON, BRIAN FRANK, Llandysul (YH07643)														●																							
KAYE, HILARY LOIS, Llandovery (YH08009)														●																							
LEWIS, A S, Carmarthen (YH08584)														●																							
LLOYD, KEVIN, Llandovery (YH08740)														●																							
MORGAN EQUINE STUD, Llandeilo (YH09795)																															●						
PENCADER STUD, Pencader (YH10928)			●				●																								●						
RAIL, P A, Llandysul (YH11611)														●																							

Business Profile
Breeding and Wellbeing

by Country by County

	Ambulance Services	Animal Behaviourist	Artificial Insemination	Bloodstock Advice	Bloodstock Agency	Breaking In Horses	Breeding Advice	Chiropractics	Clipper Maintenance	Complementary Medicine	Dentistry Skills	Dust Control	Emergency Services	Farrier Services	Groom	Groom Services	Herbalists	Holistic Medicine	Homeopathy	Horse Ambulance	Horse Psychiatry	Horse Sitter	Horse Walker	Laser & Ultrasound	Nutritionists	Osteopathy	Physiotherapy	Respiratory Disease control	Shoe Fitting Skills	Solarium	Stud Services	Swimming Pool Centre	Trotting Services	Vaccination	Veterinary Labs	Veterinary Practice	Veterinary Skills
RIVERSDALE, Carmarthen (YH11923)							●																														
RUTHERFORD, E, Llandeilo (YH12273)							●																														
SHERMANDELL MORGANS, Llandeilo (YH12725)				●																																	
STALLIONS AT TACKEXCHANGE, Llanelli (YH13351)				●			●																								●						
STRONG, M G, Newcastle Emlyn (YH13583)																																				●	
TACK EXCHANGE, Llanelli (YH13787)																															●						
THOMAS & PERCY, Llandeilo (YH14006)																																				●	
THOMAS, A, Llanelli (YH14012)														●																							
THOMAS, D J M, Llanybydder (YH14019)														●																							
TYSUL VETNRY GROUP, Llandysul (YH14534)																																				●	
WAGG, RAYMOND GEORGE, Llandysul (YH14823)														●																							
WILLIAMS, ROBERT C, Burry Port (YH15475)														●																							
WILLIAMS, ROBIN, Carmarthen (YH15476)														●																							
WOODWARD, R S, Llanelli (YH15759)														●																							
YOUNGMAN, NICHOLAS EDWARD, Llanelli (YH15943)														●																							
CEREDIGION																																					
BENSON, T F J, Llanon (YH01281)														●																							
BHS WALES, Aberystwyth (YH01388)													●							●																	
BOOTH, THOMAS M, Llanon (YH01637)														●																							
DAVIS, V C M, Aberystwyth (YH03954)														●																							
GLOVER, STEVEN P, Cardigan (YH05856)														●																							
IGER, Aberystwyth (YH07394)																									●												
MOELFRYN RIDING CTRE, Aberystwyth (YH09699)							●																														
WILLIAMS, RICHARD H, Lampeter (YH15473)														●																							
CONWY																																					
JONES, DYFED W, Denbigh (YH07894)														●																							
YOUNGSON, FRASER W, Coed Lyn (YH15945)														●																							
DENBIGHSHIRE																																					
EAMES, J S, Rhyl (YH04446)														●																							
HUGHES, G, St Asaph (YH07266)														●																							
JONES, I G, Ruthin (YH07905)														●																							
LLANNERCH EQUESTRIAN CTRE, St Asaph (YH08726)																							●							●		●	●				

Business Profile
Breeding and Wellbeing

by Country by County

	Ambulance Services	Animal Behaviourist	Artificial Insemination	Bloodstock Advice	Bloodstock Agency	Breaking In Horses	Breeding Advice	Chiropractics	Clipper Maintenance	Complementary Medicine	Dentistry Skills	Dust Control	Emergency Services	Farrier Services	Groom	Groom Services	Herbalists	Holistic Medicine	Homeopathy	Horse Ambulance	Horse Psychiatry	Horse Sitter	Horse Walker	Laser & Ultrasound	Nutritionists	Osteopathy	Physiotherapy	Respiratory Disease control	Shoe Fitting Skills	Solarium	Stud Services	Swimming Pool Centre	Trotting Services	Vaccination	Veterinary Labs	Veterinary Practice	Veterinary Skills
MORWYN STUD, Ruthin (YH09854)							●																														
PUGHE, J S, Llangollen (YH11454)														●																							
WAKEFIELD, JASON T, Chirk (YH14834)														●																							
FLINTSHIRE																																					
ANDERSON, JOHN F, Mold (YH00385)														●																							
HUGHES, IAN G, Mold (YH07268)														●																							
JONES, DAVID THOMAS, Mold (YH07891)														●																							
JONES, KENNETH, Mold (YH07912)														●																							
MANNOG, Holywell (YH09092)																															●						
ROBERTS, E P, Mold (YH11949)														●																							
ROGERS, A, Mold (YH12059)														●																							
SMITH, PAUL G, Mold (YH12985)														●																							
STRACHAN & WIGNALL, Mold (YH13542)																																				●	
GLAMORGAN (VALE OF)																																					
A GRIFFITHS & SON, Treharris (YH00033)														●																							
CIMLA TREKKING, Neath (YH02918)														●	●																						
CROFTS, JOHN D, Cardiff (YH03626)														●																							
JONES, MARC T, Merthyr Tydfil (YH07916)														●																							
LIEGE MANOR, Cardiff (YH08609)															●																						
PAGE, CLIVE, Cilfrew (YH10680)														●																							
PAYNE, MARK A, Cardiff (YH10850)														●																							
POMFRET, J B, Cardiff (YH11216)														●																							
PRITCHARD, RUSSELL J, Cowbridge (YH11422)														●																							
ROONEY, STEPHEN P, Cardiff (YH12078)														●																							
ROONEY, T P, Cardiff (YH12079)														●																							
SEARL, RICHARD MICHAEL, Cardiff (YH12593)														●																							
WHITNEY, A, Neath (YH15369)														●																							
GWYNEDD																																					
EVANS, IFOR WYN, Pwllheli (YH04921)														●																							
HILL, E BARBOUR, Bangor (YH06829)											●																									●	
JAMES, PAUL ELLIS, Bangor (YH07686)														●																							
JENKINS, G M, Tywyn (YH07731)																																				●	

Business Profile
Breeding and Wellbeing

by Country by County

	Ambulance Services	Animal Behaviourist	Artificial Insemination	Bloodstock Advice	Bloodstock Agency	Breaking In Horses	Breeding Advice	Chiropractics	Clipper Maintenance	Complementary Medicine	Dentistry Skills	Dust Control	Emergency Services	Farrier Services	Groom	Groom Services	Herbalists	Holistic Medicine	Homeopathy	Horse Ambulance	Horse Psychiatry	Horse Sitter	Horse Walker	Laser & Ultrasound	Nutritionists	Osteopathy	Physiotherapy	Respiratory Disease control	Shoe Fitting Skills	Solarium	Stud Services	Swimming Pool Centre	Trotting Services	Vaccination	Veterinary Labs	Veterinary Practice	Veterinary Skills
MILLS, ALAN JOHN, Pwllheli (YH09630)														●																							
PINDER, P J, Llanfairfechan (YH11117)																																				●	
PRITCHARD, H G, Caernarfon (YH11416)														●																							
ROBERTS, EDWIN, Caernarfon (YH11951)														●																							
TUDOR & LAWSON, Dolgellau (YH14438)																																				●	
ISLE OF ANGLESEY																																					
AUGUST APPALOOSAS, Holyhead (YH00663)							●																														
FINCH, A C & J J, Llangefni (YH05207)																																				●	
FITZPATRICK, JAMES B, Beaumaris (YH05248)														●																							
HENDY EQUESTRIAN, Holyhead (YH06670)											●																										
LEE, WILLIAM P, Ty Croes (YH08529)														●																							
MILFEDDYGON BODRWNSIWN, Rhosneigr (YH09568)																																				●	
SHEAR EASE, Amlwch (YH12688)									●																												
MONMOUTHSHIRE																																					
ABBEY VETNRY CTRE, Abergavenny (YH00089)																																				●	
BEAUMONT, REBECCA, Abergavenny (YH01138)						●																															
BROWN, NIGEL R, Abergavenny (YH02125)														●																							
BRUNGER, ANTHONY R, Abergavenny (YH02159)														●																							
CLIPPERS, Chepstow (YH03047)									●																												
CROSSCOUNTRY EQUINE CLINIC, Chepstow (YH03656)																																				●	
DRYBRIDGE VETNRY CLINIC, Monmouth (YH04297)																																				●	
FARRIERY CTRE, Usk (YH05092)														●																							
GLEBEDALE, Abergavenny (YH05821)				●			●																														
KEDWARD, TIMOTHY J, Monmouth (YH08024)														●																							
LALLEY, A F, Chepstow (YH08361)														●																							
LANGARTH, Monmouth (YH08399)							●																								●						
MCEWEN, J C, Chepstow (YH09351)																																				●	
NATURAL ANIMAL FEEDS, Raglan (YH10050)										●															●												
PACKER, C S, Chepstow (YH10663)														●																							
PARSONS, ROYSTON J, Abergavenny (YH10801)														●																							
STOCKHAM, G J, Abergavenny (YH13492)														●																							
VETNRY HOSPITAL, Usk (YH14698)																																				●	

Business Profile
Breeding and Wellbeing

by Country by County	Ambulance Services	Animal Behaviourist	Artificial Insemination	Bloodstock Advice	Bloodstock Agency	Breaking In Horses	Breeding Advice	Chiropractics	Clipper Maintenance	Complementary Medicine	Dentistry Skills	Dust Control	Emergency Services	Farrier Services	Groom	Groom Services	Herbalists	Holistic Medicine	Homeopathy	Horse Ambulance	Horse Psychiatry	Horse Sitter	Horse Walker	Laser & Ultrasound	Nutritionists	Osteopathy	Physiotherapy	Respiratory Disease control	Shoe Fitting Skills	Solarium	Stud Services	Swimming Pool Centre	Trotting Services	Vaccination	Veterinary Labs	Veterinary Practice	Veterinary Skills
WILLIAMS, RICHARD JOHN, Chepstow (YH15474)														●																							
WOODLANDER STUD, Raglan (YH15704)						●																															
NEATH PORT TALBOT																																					
DAVISON, HOWARD, Pontardawe (YH03958)														●																							
REES, D W, Neath (YH11728)														●																							
SAUNDERS, MICHAEL, Pontrhydyfen (YH12450)														●																							
NEWPORT																																					
DEACON, JOSEPH LYNDON, Llanvaches (YH03981)														●																							
JONES, H B, Lower Machen (YH07903)														●																							
RUDDICK, MARK A, Sudbrook (YH12206)														●																							
PEMBROKESHIRE																																					
BYRNE, J T, Kilgetty (YH02347)														●																							
CUMINE, DENIS HAROLD, Haverfordwest (YH03718)														●																							
FILMSTONE FARM, Narberth (YH05204)		●				●															●																
GAMBLE, SEAN, Milford Haven (YH05632)														●																							
GWAUN VETNRY GRP, Pembroke (YH06199)																																				●	
PEMBROKESHIRE EQUESTRIAN, Haverfordwest (YH10919)																													●								
PETERS & PARTNERS, Haverfordwest (YH11020)																																				●	
SELBY, J, Crymych (YH12615)														●																							
THOMPSON, ARTHUR RICHARD, Narberth (YH14033)														●																							
WILLIAMS & LINGE, Narberth (YH15441)																																				●	
POWYS																																					
ABBEY EQUINE CTRE, Crickhowell (YH00076)																																				●	
ADVANCED EQUINE DENTISTRY, Llanidloes (YH00192)											●																										
BLURTON, JAMES P, Welshpool (YH01576)														●																							
BOUNDY, C J, Montgomery (YH01680)														●																							
BOUNDY, TERRY, Montgomery (YH01681)																																				●	
BRYAN, FRANCIS HAROLD, Brecon (YH02164)														●																							
CHOICE SADDLERY, Knighton (YH02876)									●																												
COED Y WERN, Brecon (YH03134)																																				●	
CONTROL TECHNIQUES, Newtown (YH03249)																							●														
EATON, STEPHEN G, Caersws (YH04527)														●																							

Business Profile
Breeding and Wellbeing

by Country by County	Ambulance Services	Animal Behaviourist	Artificial Insemination	Bloodstock Advice	Bloodstock Agency	Breaking In Horses	Breeding Advice	Chiropractics	Clipper Maintenance	Complementary Medicine	Dentistry Skills	Dust Control	Emergency Services	Farrier Services	Groom	Groom Services	Herbalists	Holistic Medicine	Homeopathy	Horse Ambulance	Horse Psychiatry	Horse Sitter	Horse Walker	Laser & Ultrasound	Nutritionists	Osteopathy	Physiotherapy	Respiratory Disease control	Shoe Fitting Skills	Solarium	Stud Services	Swimming Pool Centre	Trotting Services	Vaccination	Veterinary Labs	Veterinary Practice	Veterinary Skills
EVANS, DAVID T C, Brecon (YH04917)														●																							
FOREST INN, New Radnor (YH05341)										●																											
FULLER, C A, Brecon (YH05531)														●																							
FYRNWY EQUINE CLINICS, Llanymynech (YH05559)																																				●	
GOLDEN CASTLE, Crickhowell (YH05877)																																		●			
HANDEL, PETER, Welshpool (YH06378)														●																							
JAMES, NICHOLAS J, Caereinion (YH07685)														●																							
JENKINS, G M, Maghynlleth (YH07732)																																				●	
JONES, EDWARD GLYN, Machynlleth (YH07896)														●																							
JONES, H G, Llanbrynmair (YH07904)																															●						
LEE, RICHARD A, Presteigne (YH08527)														●																							
NORRIS, PAULINE, Newtown (YH10245)				●			●																														
THOMAS JONES, Newtown (YH14008)																																				●	
WOODALL, PAUL, Welshpool (YH15672)														●																							
RHONDDA CYNON TAFF																																					
GRUNEWALD, P, Pontyclun (YH06177)														●																							
HUGHES, AMANDA, Porth (YH07259)											●																										
HUGHES, BRIAN, Porth (YH07261)														●															●								
HUGHES, KEVIN G, Porthcawl (YH07270)														●																							
HUGHES, S A, Porth (YH07273)														●																							
LEWIS, THOMAS HUGH, Aberdare (YH08596)														●																							
PARRY-JONES, A W, Pontypridd (YH10794)														●																							
RICHARDS, GRAHAM, Cilfynydd (YH11808)					●																																
YNYSCRUG STUD, Tonyrefail (YH15912)											●																										
SWANSEA																																					
BOWEN, ADRIAN R G, Swansea (YH01698)														●																							
COPLEY, Swansea (YH03297)						●																															
GIBSON & JONES, Swansea (YH05745)																																				●	
PRIORY STABLES, Swansea (YH11405)															●	●																					
SOUTH WALES CARRIAGE DRIVING, Swansea (YH13111)		●																																			
TORFAEN																																					
MORGAN, CLIVE J, Pontypool (YH09801)														●																							

www.hccyourhorse.com

Business Profile
Breeding and Wellbeing

by Country by County	Ambulance Services	Animal Behaviourist	Artificial Insemination	Bloodstock Advice	Bloodstock Agency	Breaking In Horses	Breeding Advice	Chiropractics	Clipper Maintenance	Complementary Medicine	Dentistry Skills	Dust Control	Emergency Services	Farrier Services	Groom	Groom Services	Herbalists	Holistic Medicine	Homeopathy	Horse Ambulance	Horse Psychiatry	Horse Sitter	Horse Walker	Laser & Ultrasound	Nutritionists	Osteopathy	Physiotherapy	Respiratory Disease control	Shoe Fitting Skills	Solarium	Stud Services	Swimming Pool Centre	Trotting Services	Vaccination	Veterinary Labs	Veterinary Practice	Veterinary Skills
MORGAN, LEE W, Pontypool (YH09810)														●																							
RICHARDS, CHRISTOPHER D, Abersychan (YH11806)														●																							
WREXHAM																																					
CHAPEL FARM, Wrexham (YH02738)						●								●		●																					
COUNTIES EQUESTRIAN SVS, Wrexham (YH03396)																				●																	
GREETHAM, RACHEL, Bwlchgwyn (YH06111)								●																		●	●										
HAMMOND, WILLIAM E, Bwlchgwyn (YH06361)														●																							
SPOOR, DAVID RUSSELL, Wrexham (YH13214)														●																							
WILLIAMS, G H, Holt (YH15457)														●																							

SECTION 4B

Business Profile

This section allows you to search for services related to training, courses, arenas, buildings and pasture. Companies are listed by Country, by County.

The Business Profile can be used in two different ways. You can search by the particular service you require.

e.g. **Training (Dressage) : Arrow Training**

Or, you can look at the profile of one particular company in order to see what service/s they offer.

e.g. **Robert Stevens**
Equestrian Contractor : Building Repairs

Once you have located a business using this section you can then refer to the company's detailed profile in Section 1.

Business Profile

Training (shaded area) **Course, Arena, Buildings and Pasture**

by Country by County

Name	Coaches	Harness Trainer	Dressage Training	Polo Trainer	Side-saddle specialist	Side-saddle trainer	Trainers	Training (1 to 1)	Training (Children)	Training (Disabled)	Training (Dressage)	Training (Flat)	Training (Freelance)	Training (Group)	Training (Horse Breaking)	Training (Jockey)	Training (Jumps)	Training (Personnel)	Training (Point-to-Point)	Training (Riding)	Training (SteepleChase)	Training (To become a Trainer)	Training for Examination	Work with Children 10-16	Work with Children under 10	Work with Senior Citizens	Work with Students	Work with the Disabled
ENGLAND																												
BATH & SOMERSET (NORTH EAST)																												
CONKWELL GRANGE STUD, Bath (YH03232)							●																					
H E F MORRIS, Bath (YH06217)																												
H S JACKSON & SON, Bath (YH06237)																												
HORLER, M A, Bath (YH07070)							●																					
HUNSTRETE RIDING SCHOOL, Pensford (YH07294)							●																					
SOMERLAP FOREST PRODUCTS, Compton Martin (YH13061)																												
BEDFORDSHIRE																												
ALTERNATIVE RIDING SCHOOL, Luton (YH00343)									●	●														●	●			
ARCADE SADDLERY BEDFORD, Bedford (YH00498)																								●	●	●	●	●
BENNITT, CAROL, Leighton Buzzard (YH01276)													●															
BROOK STABLES, Bedford (YH02038)								●	●					●			●			●				●	●	●	●	
BRSC, Bedford (YH02153)								●					●															
CAROE, C J E, Thurleigh (YH02567)							●																					
CLGE EQUESTRIAN CTRE, Bedford (YH03025)			●								●						●											
GRANSDEN HALL, Sandy (YH06005)			●				●				●																	
NORTHALLETON, Biggleswade (YH10292)													●											●	●	●	●	●
ROWAN LODGE, Shefford (YH12154)			●								●																	
SALSA STUD, Chawston (YH12391)																												
STOCKWOOD PARK, Luton (YH13498)								●	●					●			●			●			●	●		●	●	
SUNSHINE RIDING SCHOOL, Luton (YH13652)								●	●					●										●	●			
TURNER, NICK, Biggleswade (YH14488)							●																					
BERKSHIRE																												
B W HILLS SOUTHBANK, Hungerford (YH00750)							●																					
BALDING, IAN, Newbury (YH00836)							●																					
BEAUMONT STABLES, Maidenhead (YH01133)			●				●				●																	
BECKETT, R, Hungerford (YH01148)							●																					
BERKSHIRE CLGE OF AGRCLTRL, Maidenhead (YH01304)																							●					
BLANSHARD, M T W, Hungerford (YH01526)							●																					
BRIDGES, C & M, Reading (YH01883)																												

Name	Architectural Advice	Architectural Planning	Arenas (large) for hire	Arenas (small) for hire	Arenas Indoor (Build)	Arenas Outdoor (Build)	Building Maintenance	Building Repairs	Cross Country Course (Build)	Cross Country Course (Design)	Fencing (Build)	Gates (Build)	Outbuildings (Build)	Pasture Supply	Pasture Support	Property Services	Racing Tracks (Build)	Show Jumps (Design)	Stables (Build)	Stables (Design)	Swimming Pools (Build)	Swimming Pools (Design)
ENGLAND																						
BATH & SOMERSET (NORTH EAST)																						
CONKWELL GRANGE STUD, Bath (YH03232)																						
H E F MORRIS, Bath (YH06217)																●						
H S JACKSON & SON, Bath (YH06237)											●											
HORLER, M A, Bath (YH07070)																						
HUNSTRETE RIDING SCHOOL, Pensford (YH07294)																						
SOMERLAP FOREST PRODUCTS, Compton Martin (YH13061)											●											
BEDFORDSHIRE																						
ALTERNATIVE RIDING SCHOOL, Luton (YH00343)																						
ARCADE SADDLERY BEDFORD, Bedford (YH00498)																						
BENNITT, CAROL, Leighton Buzzard (YH01276)																						
BROOK STABLES, Bedford (YH02038)																						
BRSC, Bedford (YH02153)																						
CAROE, C J E, Thurleigh (YH02567)																						
CLGE EQUESTRIAN CTRE, Bedford (YH03025)			●	●																		
GRANSDEN HALL, Sandy (YH06005)																						
NORTHALLETON, Biggleswade (YH10292)			●																			
ROWAN LODGE, Shefford (YH12154)																						
SALSA STUD, Chawston (YH12391)														●								
STOCKWOOD PARK, Luton (YH13498)																						
SUNSHINE RIDING SCHOOL, Luton (YH13652)																						
TURNER, NICK, Biggleswade (YH14488)																						
BERKSHIRE																						
B W HILLS SOUTHBANK, Hungerford (YH00750)																						
BALDING, IAN, Newbury (YH00836)																						
BEAUMONT STABLES, Maidenhead (YH01133)																						
BECKETT, R, Hungerford (YH01148)																						
BERKSHIRE CLGE OF AGRCLTRL, Maidenhead (YH01304)																						
BLANSHARD, M T W, Hungerford (YH01526)																						
BRIDGES, C & M, Reading (YH01883)															●							

Business Profile
Training (shaded area)
Course, Arena, Buildings and Pasture

by Country by County

	Coaches	Harness Trainer	Dressage Training	Polo Trainer	Side-saddle specialist	Side-saddle trainer	Trainers	Training (1 to 1)	Training (Children)	Training (Disabled)	Training (Dressage)	Training (Flat)	Training (Freelance)	Training (Group)	Training (Horse Breaking)	Training (Jockey)	Training (Jumps)	Training (Personnel)	Training (Point-to-Point)	Training (Riding)	Training (SteepleChase)	Training (To become a Trainer)	Training for Examination	Work with Children 10-16	Work with Children under 10	Work with Senior Citizens	Work with Students	Work with the Disabled	Architectural Advice	Architectural Planning	Arenas (large) for hire	Arenas (small) for hire	Arenas Indoor (Build)	Arenas Outdoor (Build)	Building Maintenance	Building Repairs	Cross Country Course (Build)	Cross Country Course (Design)	Fencing (Build)	Gates (Build)	Outbuildings (Build)	Pasture Supply	Pasture Support	Property Services	Racing Tracks (Build)	Show Jumps (Design)	Stables (Build)	Stables (Design)	Swimming Pools (Build)	Swimming Pools (Design)
BURGOYNE, PAUL, Hungerford (YH02251)							●																																											
C R BLACK & SONS, Reading (YH02386)																																							●											
CASTLE PIECE RACING STABLES, Hungerford (YH02630)							●																																											
CHANCE, NOEL, Hungerford (YH02730)							●																																											
CHANNON, M, Newbury (YH02734)							●																																											
CHECKENDON, Reading (YH02796)								●	●		●			●			●		●	●		●	●																											
COOMBE PK RACING STABLES, Reading (YH03274)							●																																											
COURTLANDS, Wokingham (YH03506)			●																																															
CRAGO, KAREN, Reading (YH03546)			●				●				●																																							
CRAGO, PAUL, Reading (YH03547)																	●																																	
CULLINGHOOD FARM, Reading (YH03705)																								●	●	●	●																							
DE HAAN, B, Hungerford (YH03978)							●																																											
DELAMERE COTTAGE STABLES, Hungerford (YH04028)							●																																											
DOYLE, JACQUELINE, Hungerford (YH04247)							●																																											
EAST SOLEY E C 2000, Hungerford (YH04486)			●				●		●		●																				●	●																		
EASTBURY COTTAGE STABLES, Hungerford (YH04489)							●																																											
EQUICENTRE, Waltham St Lawrence (YH04737)				●																																														
GASELEE, N, Hungerford (YH05669)							●																																											
HEADS FARM STABLES, Newbury (YH06613)							●																																											
HENDERSON, N J, Hungerford (YH06667)							●																																											
HILL HSE STABLES, Hungerford (YH06821)							●																																											
HILLSIDE STUD, Hungerford (YH06855)							●																																											
J C & N C WARD, Pangbourne (YH07568)																																							●											
JAMES, E, Hungerford (YH07681)												●					●				●																													
JONES, M A, Hungerford (YH07914)							●																																											
K S CUNDELL & PARTNERS, Newbury (YH07991)							●																																											
KEEPERS STABLES, Newbury (YH08031)							●																																											
KINGS FARM STABLES, Hungerford (YH08193)							●																																											
KINGWOOD HOUSE STABLES, Hungerford (YH08215)							●																																											
LAMBOURN RACEHORSE TRANSPORT, Hungerford (YH08367)							●																																											
LAZYGRAZER, Wokingham (YH08486)																																											●							
LINKSLADE STABLES, Hungerford (YH08664)							●																																											

Business Profile

Training (shaded area) Course, Arena, Buildings and Pasture

by Country by County

	Coaches	Harness Trainer	Dressage Training	Polo Trainer	Side-saddle specialist	Side-saddle trainer	Trainers	Training (1 to 1)	Training (Children)	Training (Disabled)	Training (Dressage)	Training (Flat)	Training (Freelance)	Training (Group)	Training (Horse Breaking)	Training (Jockey)	Training (Jumps)	Training (Personnel)	Training (Point-to-Point)	Training (Riding)	Training (SteepleChase)	Training (To become a Trainer)	Training for Examination	Work with Children 10-16	Work with Children under 10	Work with Senior Citizens	Work with Students	Work with the Disabled
LIPLANDS STABLES, Newbury (YH08676)							●																					
MAGNA CARTA POLO, Ascot (YH09035)				●																								
MANNING, PAT, Reading (YH09088)			●				●				●		●															
MARK PITMAN RACING, Hungerford (YH09154)							●																					
MARKS, D, Hungerford (YH09164)							●																					
MARKS, KELLY, Hungerford (YH09165)															●													
MORRISON, H, Newbury (YH09837)							●																					
NEARDOWN STABLES, Hungerford (YH10062)							●																					
NEWLANDS STABLES, Hungerford (YH10145)							●																					
OSBOURNE, J, Hungerford (YH10562)							●																					
PARK HSE STABLES, Newbury (YH10728)							●																					
PARSONAGE FARM RACING STABLES, Hungerford (YH10797)							●																					
PEACHEY, KA, Maidenhead (YH10858)		●																										
PERISI, J S, Windsor (YH10975)		●																										
PORTER, JOHN, Hungerford (YH11282)							●																					
SAXON GATE STABLES, Hungerford (YH12468)							●																					
SAXON HSE STABLES, Hungerford (YH12469)							●																					
SHELTON FARM, Reading (YH12704)	●							●		●													●	●		●	●	●
SHERWOOD STABLES, Hungerford (YH12732)							●																					
SHERWOOD, O M C, Hungerford (YH12733)							●																					
SHERWOOD, S E H, Hungerford (YH12734)							●																					
SOUTH BANK STABLES, Hungerford (YH13077)							●																					
STRONGE, R M, Newbury (YH13585)							●																					
TIDMARSH STUD, Reading (YH14134)			●								●																	
UPSHIRE FARM STABLES, Lambourn (YH14612)							●																					
WEST HAMILTON STABLES, Newbury (YH15147)							●																					
WHITCOOMBE HOUSE STABLES, Hungerford (YH15298)							●																					
WOKINGHAM EQUESTRIAN CTRE, Wokingham (YH15644)			●																									
BRISTOL																												
FILTON CLGE, Bristol (YH05205)																							●					
URCHINWOOD MANOR EQUITATION, Bristol (YH14620)									●															●	●		●	
BUCKINGHAMSHIRE																												

	Architectural Advice	Architectural Planning	Arenas (large) for hire	Arenas (small) for hire	Arenas Indoor (Build)	Arenas Outdoor (Build)	Building Maintenance	Building Repairs	Cross Country Course (Build)	Cross Country Course (Design)	Fencing (Build)	Gates (Build)	Outbuildings (Build)	Pasture Supply	Pasture Support	Property Services	Racing Tracks (Build)	Show Jumps (Design)	Stables (Build)	Stables (Design)	Swimming Pools (Build)	Swimming Pools (Design)
LIPLANDS STABLES, Newbury (YH08676)																						
MAGNA CARTA POLO, Ascot (YH09035)																						
MANNING, PAT, Reading (YH09088)																						
MARK PITMAN RACING, Hungerford (YH09154)																						
MARKS, D, Hungerford (YH09164)																						
MARKS, KELLY, Hungerford (YH09165)																						
MORRISON, H, Newbury (YH09837)																						
NEARDOWN STABLES, Hungerford (YH10062)																						
NEWLANDS STABLES, Hungerford (YH10145)																						
OSBOURNE, J, Hungerford (YH10562)																						
PARK HSE STABLES, Newbury (YH10728)																						
PARSONAGE FARM RACING STABLES, Hungerford (YH10797)																						
PEACHEY, KA, Maidenhead (YH10858)																						
PERISI, J S, Windsor (YH10975)																						
PORTER, JOHN, Hungerford (YH11282)																						
SAXON GATE STABLES, Hungerford (YH12468)																						
SAXON HSE STABLES, Hungerford (YH12469)																						
SHELTON FARM, Reading (YH12704)																						
SHERWOOD STABLES, Hungerford (YH12732)																						
SHERWOOD, O M C, Hungerford (YH12733)																						
SHERWOOD, S E H, Hungerford (YH12734)																						
SOUTH BANK STABLES, Hungerford (YH13077)																						
STRONGE, R M, Newbury (YH13585)																						
TIDMARSH STUD, Reading (YH14134)																						
UPSHIRE FARM STABLES, Lambourn (YH14612)																						
WEST HAMILTON STABLES, Newbury (YH15147)																						
WHITCOOMBE HOUSE STABLES, Hungerford (YH15298)																						
WOKINGHAM EQUESTRIAN CTRE, Wokingham (YH15644)																						
BRISTOL																						
FILTON CLGE, Bristol (YH05205)																						
URCHINWOOD MANOR EQUITATION, Bristol (YH14620)																						
BUCKINGHAMSHIRE																						

Business Profile
Training (shaded area) **Course, Arena, Buildings and Pasture**

by Country by County

Business	Coaches	Harness Trainer	Dressage Training	Polo Trainer	Side-saddle specialist	Side-saddle trainer	Trainers	Training (1 to 1)	Training (Children)	Training (Disabled)	Training (Dressage)	Training (Flat)	Training (Freelance)	Training (Group)	Training (Horse Breaking)	Training (Jockey)	Training (Jumps)	Training (Personnel)	Training (Point-to-Point)	Training (Riding)	Training (SteepleChase)	Training (To become a Trainer)	Training for Examination	Work with Children 10-16	Work with Children under 10	Work with Senior Citizens	Work with Students	Work with the Disabled	Architectural Advice	Architectural Planning	Arenas (large) for hire	Arenas (small) for hire	Arenas Indoor (Build)	Arenas Outdoor (Build)	Building Maintenance	Building Repairs	Cross Country Course (Build)	Cross Country Course (Design)	Fencing (Build)	Gates (Build)	Outbuildings (Build)	Pasture Supply	Pasture Support	Property Services	Racing Tracks (Build)	Show Jumps (Design)	Stables (Build)	Stables (Design)	Swimming Pools (Build)	Swimming Pools (Design)
ADDINGTON MANOR, Buckingham (YH00179)																															●	●																		
ARDENLEA ENTERPRISES, Princes Risborough (YH00503)																																					●							●						
BALANCE, Aylesbury (YH00829)													●																																					
BARKER, K J, Burnham (YH00944)							●																																											
BRAWLINGS FARM RIDING CTRE, Gerrards Cross (YH01819)																								●	●	●	●	●																						
BRYERLEY SPRINGS FARM, Milton Keynes (YH02171)													●		●																																			
BUSH, KAREN, Great Missenden (YH02307)			●				●				●		●																																					
CATHERINE WRIGHT, Aylesbury (YH02649)								●					●	●						●																														
CRAWFORD-BROWN, FIONA, Ludgershall (YH03577)							●						●																																					
CULLINAN, J, Aylesbury (YH03704)							●																																											
DEVILS HORSEMEN, Milton Keynes (YH04090)	●																														●																			
DORTON GRANGE STABLES, Aylesbury (YH04208)							●																																											
EQUESTRIAN CTRE, Amersham (YH04696)								●	●	●		●		●	●		●			●				●	●	●		●			●		●	●																
EQUS HEALTH, Aylesbury (YH04835)																																●																		
GEORGE, K M, Princes Risborough (YH05724)							●																																											
GRAHAM-ROGERS, C, Bourne End (YH05973)																				●																														
HARVEY, JUDY, Milton Keynes (YH06515)			●				●				●		●																																					
MILTON KEYNES EVENTING, Milton Keynes (YH09645)							●																																											
PEN & PADDOCK, Long Crendon (YH10921)																																							●			●	●							
ROBBINS, M A, Amersham (YH11936)							●																																											
ROBESON, P, Newport Pagnell (YH11977)							●																																											
S R OSBORN & SON, Newport Pagnell (YH12332)																																							●											
SIMMONS, Marlow (YH12822)																																												●						
SOUTH BUCKS ESTATES, Beaconsfield (YH13079)																																							●											
WATSON, GILLIAN, Great Missenden (YH14986)							●																																											
WAYLANDS EQUESTRIAN CTRE, Beaconsfield (YH15016)																	●																																	
WEST WYCOMBE PARK POLO CLUB, West Wycombe (YH15173)							●																								●																			
WHITAKERS, Princes Risborough (YH15292)																	●																																	
CAMBRIDGESHIRE																																																		
ARENA STRUCTURES, St Ives (YH00516)																																	●	●																
ENGLISH BROTHERS, Wisbech (YH04672)																																							●											
FENCING CONTRACTOR, Peterborough (YH05138)																																					●		●											

Business Profile

Training (shaded area)
Course, Arena, Buildings and Pasture

by Country by County

Business	Coaches	Harness Trainer	Dressage Training	Polo Trainer	Side-saddle specialist	Side-saddle trainer	Trainers	Training (1 to 1)	Training (Children)	Training (Disabled)	Training (Dressage)	Training (Flat)	Training (Freelance)	Training (Group)	Training (Horse Breaking)	Training (Jockey)	Training (Jumps)	Training (Personnel)	Training (Point-to-Point)	Training (Riding)	Training (SteepleChase)	Training (To become a Trainer)	Training for Examination	Work with Children 10-16	Work with Children under 10	Work with Senior Citizens	Work with Students	Work with the Disabled	Architectural Advice	Architectural Planning	Arenas (large) for hire	Arenas (small) for hire	Arenas Indoor (Build)	Arenas Outdoor (Build)	Building Maintenance	Building Repairs	Cross Country Course (Build)	Cross Country Course (Design)	Fencing (Build)	Gates (Build)	Outbuildings (Build)	Pasture Supply	Pasture Support	Property Services	Racing Tracks (Build)	Show Jumps (Design)	Stables (Build)	Stables (Design)	Swimming Pools (Build)	Swimming Pools (Design)
FOX END STABLES, Rampton (YH05419)							●																																											
HOOK HSE, March (YH07035)															●									●		●																								
KEITH WARTH & ASSOCIATES, Babraham (YH08037)																																												●						
KNIGHTS END FARM, March (YH08268)			●								●	●																			●	●																		
NORTHBROOK EQUESTRIAN CTRE, Huntingdon (YH10294)			●					●	●	●	●	●		●	●		●			●		●	●	●	●	●	●					●	●																	
OLD TIGER STABLES, Ely (YH10479)								●	●	●	●			●	●		●			●			●	●	●	●	●	●																						
PEGASUS, Peterborough (YH10901)																																							●							●				
PINNER, TERRY, Huntingdon (YH11134)															●																																			
SLY, P M, Peterborough (YH12903)							●																																											
SMEETH SADDLERY, Wisbech (YH12925)																								●	●	●	●	●																						
STUDLAND SERVICES, Oundle (YH13611)																																										●								
WEST ANGLIA CLGE, Milton (YH15123)																							●				●																							
WITCHAM HSE FARM STUD, Ely (YH15617)			●				●				●				●																	●																		
CHESHIRE																																																		
ALDER ROOT RIDING CTRE, Warrington (YH00254)								●	●	●	●			●			●						●																											
BARROW EQUESTRIAN CTRE, Chester (YH01027)																				●												●																		
BAYLISS, RACHEL, Congleton (YH01097)							●																																											
BEVIS, RICHARD, Malpas (YH01345)							●																																											
BILLINGTON, GEOFF, Nantwich (YH01414)																	●																																	
CALDWELL, T H, Warrington (YH02439)							●																																											
CARRUTHERS, RICHARD, Frodsham (YH02601)			●				●	●	●		●		●				●			●		●	●	●			●											●												
CLYDESDALE TIMBER PRODUCTS, High Peak (YH03082)																																															●	●		
COTTON EQUESTRIAN CTRE, Crewe (YH03384)			●				●				●																																							
CROFT RIDING CTRE, Warrington (YH03617)																								●	●																									
DECATHLON SPORTS & LEISURE, Stockport (YH04008)																								●	●																									
DUTTON, Holmes Chapel (YH04377)		●																																																
FOLLY FARM STABLES, Tarporley (YH05301)							●																																											
GAYNORS SADDLERY, Dukinfield (YH05682)																								●	●	●	●	●																						
GO ENTERTAINMENTS, Congleton (YH05860)																															●	●																		
GREENWAY FARM, Congleton (YH06102)			●				●																																											
H S JACKSON & SON, Tattenhall (YH06238)																																							●											
HOLLINSHEAD, DAWN, Winsford (YH06947)													●																																					

www.hccyourhorse.com

Business Profile
Training (shaded area) **Course, Arena, Buildings and Pasture**

by Country by County	Coaches	Harness Trainer	Dressage Training	Polo Trainer	Side-saddle specialist	Side-saddle trainer	Trainers	Training (1 to 1)	Training (Children)	Training (Disabled)	Training (Dressage)	Training (Flat)	Training (Freelance)	Training (Group)	Training (Horse Breaking)	Training (Jockey)	Training (Jumps)	Training (Personnel)	Training (Point-to-Point)	Training (Riding)	Training (SteepleChase)	Training (To become a Trainer)	Training for Examination	Work with Children 10-16	Work with Children under 10	Work with Senior Citizens	Work with Students	Work with the Disabled	Architectural Advice	Architectural Planning	Arenas (large) for hire	Arenas (small) for hire	Arenas Indoor (Build)	Arenas Outdoor (Build)	Building Maintenance	Building Repairs	Cross Country Course (Build)	Cross Country Course (Design)	Fencing (Build)	Gates (Build)	Outbuildings (Build)	Pasture Supply	Pasture Support	Property Services	Racing Tracks (Build)	Show Jumps (Design)	Stables (Build)	Stables (Design)	Swimming Pools (Build)	Swimming Pools (Design)
LANSDOWNE HORSE & RIDER, Chester (YH08423)																								●	●																									
MATHER, F E, Stockport (YH09259)		●																																																
MCCAIN, D, Cholmondeley (YH09316)							●																																											
MULLINEAUX, M, Tarporley (YH09939)							●																																											
NUTRI-MECH UK, Malpas (YH10359)																																										●								
PETER HUNTER, Tarporley (YH11010)																																									●									
RINGWOOD FENCING, Chester (YH11904)																																							●											
ROBERTS, STUART, Crewe (YH11962)							●																																											
ROBINSON, P, Stalybridge (YH11992)		●																																																
SANDY BROW RACING STABLES, Tarporley (YH12424)							●																																											
SENIOR, A, Macclesfield (YH12634)							●																																											
SOUTH VIEW EQUESTRIAN CTRE, Winsford (YH13107)																															●																			
STANNEY LANDS LIVERY, Wilmslow (YH13378)															●																																			
WILLIAMSON, LISA, Chester (YH15485)							●																																											
WYNNE, M G, Tarporley (YH15872)							●										●																																	
CLEVELAND																																																		
BARR, R E, Stokesley (YH01001)							●																																											
CANDLER, B, Thornaby (YH02495)							●										●																				●													
CLOSE, J, Stockton-on-Tees (YH03060)		●																																																
FARMWAY, Stokesley (YH05070)																																									●									
FOXHOLM STUD, Stockton-on-Tees (YH05437)			●					●	●		●		●	●	●																																			
GRANT, CHRIS, Stockton-on-Tees (YH06011)							●																																											
HOOF'N'HOUND, Hartlepool (YH07031)																								●	●																									
JONES, ALAN, Redcar (YH07877)													●																																					
REVELEY, C, Saltburn-by-the-Sea (YH11769)							●																																											
STAINSBY GRANGE RIDING CTRE, Stockton-on-Tees (YH13346)																	●																				●													
UNICORN RDA CTRE, Middlesbrough (YH14567)										●																																								
WOLVISTON RIDING STABLES, Billingham (YH15652)								●	●		●		●	●			●			●			●	●	●	●	●																							
CORNWALL																																																		
ABRS, Penzance (YH00137)																							●																											
ASTLEY, D, Penzance (YH00636)			●				●				●		●				●																																	
CORNISH CALCIFIED SEAWEED, Truro (YH03325)																																									●									

Business Profile

Training (shaded area) Course, Arena, Buildings and Pasture

by Country by County

Business	Coaches	Harness Trainer	Dressage Training	Polo Trainer	Side-saddle specialist	Side-saddle trainer	Trainers	Training (1 to 1)	Training (Children)	Training (Disabled)	Training (Dressage)	Training (Flat)	Training (Freelance)	Training (Group)	Training (Horse Breaking)	Training (Jockey)	Training (Jumps)	Training (Personnel)	Training (Point-to-Point)	Training (Riding)	Training (SteepleChase)	Training (To become a Trainer)	Training for Examination	Work with Children 10-16	Work with Children under 10	Work with Senior Citizens	Work with Students	Work with the Disabled
CORNISH RIDING HOLIDAYS, Redruth (YH03327)									●		●			●	●		●			●								
GWINEAR & DISTRICT FARMERS, Camborne (YH06204)																												
HELSTON SADDLERY, Helston (YH06657)									●				●											●	●			
LAUREL STUD, Truro (YH08458)							●	●					●							●								
MOORE, K & A E, Launceston (YH09762)																												
ROMANY WALKS, Penzance (YH12072)								●	●		●			●			●	●		●		●	●					
ROSEVIDNEY ARABIANS, Penzance (YH12111)	●																											
SNOWLAND RIDING CTRE, Par (YH13045)								●	●	●	●	●		●			●						●	●	●			
ST LEONARDS EQUESTRIAN CTRE, Launceston (YH13278)							●						●				●											
STAGS, Truro (YH13330)																												
STAGS, Launceston (YH13329)																												
TALL TREES, Camelford (YH13831)											●	●																
TEAGLE MACHINERY, Truro (YH13921)																												
TM INT SCHOOL OF HORSEMANSHIP, Liskeard (YH14196)			●					●	●	●	●				●			●		●			●	●	●	●	●	●
VERYAN RIDING CTRE, Truro (YH14686)								●	●	●	●	●		●	●			●		●			●	●	●	●	●	●
WILLIAMS ENDURANCE, Uskard (YH15442)							●																					
COUNTY DURHAM																												
ALSTON & KILLHOPE, Bishop Auckland (YH00339)								●							●					●				●	●	●		●
BOWES MANOR EQUESTRIAN CTRE, Chester Le Street (YH01709)																												
BROOM HALL LIVERY YARD, Durham (YH02072)							●	●	●	●	●	●	●	●	●		●	●		●			●	●	●	●	●	●
BROUGH, L E, Durham (YH02087)		●																										
CENTURION EQUESTRIAN CTRE, Durham (YH02698)								●	●	●				●			●							●	●			●
CRAGGS, R, Durham (YH03544)							●																					
DARLINGTON EQUESTRIAN CTRE, Darlington (YH03892)																								●	●			
DENE HEAD LIVERY, Darlington (YH04042)																												
DIXON, KAREN, Barnard Castle (YH04142)							●																					
DODS, M, Darlington (YH04160)							●																					
E D T, Consett (YH04401)							●																					
EAST DURHAM & HOUGHALL, Houghall (YH04473)																							●					
FARMWAY, Darlington (YH05072)																												
GO RIDING GRP, Stanley (YH05861)			●					●	●	●	●			●								●	●					
HAMSTERLEY RIDING SCHOOL, Bishop Auckland (YH06372)								●	●					●					●									

Business	Architectural Advice	Architectural Planning	Arenas (large) for hire	Arenas (small) for hire	Arenas Indoor (Build)	Arenas Outdoor (Build)	Building Maintenance	Building Repairs	Cross Country Course (Build)	Cross Country Course (Design)	Fencing (Build)	Gates (Build)	Outbuildings (Build)	Pasture Supply	Pasture Support	Property Services	Racing Tracks (Build)	Show Jumps (Design)	Stables (Build)	Stables (Design)	Swimming Pools (Build)	Swimming Pools (Design)
CORNISH RIDING HOLIDAYS, Redruth (YH03327)																						
GWINEAR & DISTRICT FARMERS, Camborne (YH06204)											●			●								
HELSTON SADDLERY, Helston (YH06657)																						
LAUREL STUD, Truro (YH08458)																						
MOORE, K & A E, Launceston (YH09762)											●											
ROMANY WALKS, Penzance (YH12072)																						
ROSEVIDNEY ARABIANS, Penzance (YH12111)																						
SNOWLAND RIDING CTRE, Par (YH13045)																						
ST LEONARDS EQUESTRIAN CTRE, Launceston (YH13278)																						
STAGS, Truro (YH13330)																●						
STAGS, Launceston (YH13329)																●						
TALL TREES, Camelford (YH13831)			●																			
TEAGLE MACHINERY, Truro (YH13921)															●							
TM INT SCHOOL OF HORSEMANSHIP, Liskeard (YH14196)																						
VERYAN RIDING CTRE, Truro (YH14686)				●																		
WILLIAMS ENDURANCE, Uskard (YH15442)																						
COUNTY DURHAM																						
ALSTON & KILLHOPE, Bishop Auckland (YH00339)							●	●				●										
BOWES MANOR EQUESTRIAN CTRE, Chester Le Street (YH01709)			●	●																		
BROOM HALL LIVERY YARD, Durham (YH02072)			●																			
BROUGH, L E, Durham (YH02087)																						
CENTURION EQUESTRIAN CTRE, Durham (YH02698)																						
CRAGGS, R, Durham (YH03544)																						
DARLINGTON EQUESTRIAN CTRE, Darlington (YH03892)																						
DENE HEAD LIVERY, Darlington (YH04042)				●														●	●	●		
DIXON, KAREN, Barnard Castle (YH04142)																						
DODS, M, Darlington (YH04160)																						
E D T, Consett (YH04401)																						
EAST DURHAM & HOUGHALL, Houghall (YH04473)																						
FARMWAY, Darlington (YH05072)											●	●										
GO RIDING GRP, Stanley (YH05861)																						
HAMSTERLEY RIDING SCHOOL, Bishop Auckland (YH06372)																						

www.hccyourhorse.com

Business Profile

Training (shaded area)

Course, Arena, Buildings and Pasture

by Country by County

	Coaches	Harness Trainer	Dressage Training	Polo Trainer	Side-saddle specialist	Side-saddle trainer	Trainers	Training (1 to 1)	Training (Children)	Training (Disabled)	Training (Dressage)	Training (Flat)	Training (Freelance)	Training (Group)	Training (Horse Breaking)	Training (Jockey)	Training (Jumps)	Training (Personnel)	Training (Point-to-Point)	Training (Riding)	Training (SteepleChase)	Training (To become a Trainer)	Training for Examination	Work with Children 10-16	Work with Children under 10	Work with Senior Citizens	Work with Students	Work with the Disabled
HIGHLING EQUESTRIAN CTRE, Durham (YH06798)								●	●			●		●	●		●			●				●	●			
HIGHWELL STUD, Darlington (YH06802)			●				●				●				●					●			●					
JOHNSON, J H, Crook (YH07826)							●																					
KING, D W, Crook (YH08178)																												
LIVEWIRE GATES & FENCING, Barnard Castle (YH08716)																												
NEW MOORS, Bishop Auckland (YH10114)			●				●				●																	
PADDOCK LINES, Barnard Castle (YH10667)																												
SEAGOLD CENTURION, Crook (YH12587)								●	●	●				●						●				●	●		●	●
SMITH, D, Bishop Auckland (YH12947)							●																					
STOREY, W L, Consett (YH13526)							●																					
TEASDALE, D, Bishop Auckland (YH13926)		●																										
WALKER, L, Barnard Castle (YH14853)		●																										
WATSON, F, Durham (YH14985)							●																					
CUMBRIA																												
ALLONBY RIDING SCHOOL, Wigton (YH00323)								●	●								●			●		●		●	●			
BAINBRIDGE, J S, Kirkby Stephen (YH00812)		●																										
BARNES, M A, Carlisle (YH00978)							●																					
BIRKBECK, H W, Kirkby Stephen (YH01439)		●																										
BIRKBY HALL, Grange Over Sands (YH01440)			●				●				●		●															
BLACKDYKE FARM RIDING CTRE, Carlisle (YH01481)																												
BLAYLOCK, J A, Brampton (YH01529)		●																										
BOUSFIELD, C J & J, Appleby-In-Westmorland (YH01692)		●																										
BOUSFIELD, D, Penrith (YH01693)		●																										
BREED EX EQUINE STUD, Penrith (YH01832)		●					●										●											
BROWN, I H, Kirkby Stephen (YH02109)		●																										
CARGO RIDING CTRE, Carlisle (YH02538)								●	●		●			●			●						●					
CUMBRIA SCHOOL OF SADDLERY, Penrith (YH03715)																		●					●				●	
CUTHBERT, T A K, Carlisle (YH03760)							●																					
FISHER, R F, Ulverston (YH05241)							●																					
GET SMART, Barrow-In-Furness (YH05732)																												
GOODRICK, H, Ulverston (YH05906)																												
GOULDING, J, Cockermouth (YH05950)							●																					

	Architectural Advice	Architectural Planning	Arenas (large) for hire	Arenas (small) for hire	Arenas Indoor (Build)	Arenas Outdoor (Build)	Building Maintenance	Building Repairs	Cross Country Course (Build)	Cross Country Course (Design)	Fencing (Build)	Gates (Build)	Outbuildings (Build)	Pasture Supply	Pasture Support	Property Services	Racing Tracks (Build)	Show Jumps (Design)	Stables (Build)	Stables (Design)	Swimming Pools (Build)	Swimming Pools (Design)
HIGHLING EQUESTRIAN CTRE, Durham (YH06798)																						
HIGHWELL STUD, Darlington (YH06802)																						
JOHNSON, J H, Crook (YH07826)																						
KING, D W, Crook (YH08178)									●													
LIVEWIRE GATES & FENCING, Barnard Castle (YH08716)											●											
NEW MOORS, Bishop Auckland (YH10114)																						
PADDOCK LINES, Barnard Castle (YH10667)											●											
SEAGOLD CENTURION, Crook (YH12587)			●																			
SMITH, D, Bishop Auckland (YH12947)																						
STOREY, W L, Consett (YH13526)																						
TEASDALE, D, Bishop Auckland (YH13926)																						
WALKER, L, Barnard Castle (YH14853)																						
WATSON, F, Durham (YH14985)																						
CUMBRIA																						
ALLONBY RIDING SCHOOL, Wigton (YH00323)			●																			
BAINBRIDGE, J S, Kirkby Stephen (YH00812)																						
BARNES, M A, Carlisle (YH00978)																						
BIRKBECK, H W, Kirkby Stephen (YH01439)																						
BIRKBY HALL, Grange Over Sands (YH01440)																						
BLACKDYKE FARM RIDING CTRE, Carlisle (YH01481)									●													
BLAYLOCK, J A, Brampton (YH01529)																						
BOUSFIELD, C J & J, Appleby-In-Westmorland (YH01692)																						
BOUSFIELD, D, Penrith (YH01693)																						
BREED EX EQUINE STUD, Penrith (YH01832)																						
BROWN, I H, Kirkby Stephen (YH02109)																						
CARGO RIDING CTRE, Carlisle (YH02538)																						
CUMBRIA SCHOOL OF SADDLERY, Penrith (YH03715)																						
CUTHBERT, T A K, Carlisle (YH03760)																						
FISHER, R F, Ulverston (YH05241)																						
GET SMART, Barrow-In-Furness (YH05732)	●	●																				
GOODRICK, H, Ulverston (YH05906)									●													
GOULDING, J, Cockermouth (YH05950)																						

Business Profile

Training (shaded area) Course, Arena, Buildings and Pasture

by Country by County

	Coaches	Harness Trainer	Dressage Training	Polo Trainer	Side-saddle specialist	Side-saddle trainer	Trainers	Training (1 to 1)	Training (Children)	Training (Disabled)	Training (Dressage)	Training (Flat)	Training (Freelance)	Training (Group)	Training (Horse Breaking)	Training (Jockey)	Training (Jumps)	Training (Personnel)	Training (Point-to-Point)	Training (Riding)	Training (SteepleChase)	Training (To become a Trainer)	Training for Examination	Work with Children 10-16	Work with Children under 10	Work with Senior Citizens	Work with Students	Work with the Disabled	Architectural Advice	Architectural Planning	Arenas (large) for hire	Arenas (small) for hire	Arenas Indoor (Build)	Arenas Outdoor (Build)	Building Maintenance	Building Repairs	Cross Country Course (Build)	Cross Country Course (Design)	Fencing (Build)	Gates (Build)	Outbuildings (Build)	Pasture Supply	Pasture Support	Property Services	Racing Tracks (Build)	Show Jumps (Design)	Stables (Build)	Stables (Design)	Swimming Pools (Build)	Swimming Pools (Design)
HULLOCK, A, Appleby (YH07283)		●																																																
KESWICK RIDING CTRE, Keswick (YH08105)													●																																					
KIRK, C, Penrith (YH08231)		●																																																
LAKELAND EQUESTRIAN, Windermere (YH08354)								●	●		●		●	●	●		●	●		●		●	●	●	●		●																							
LARKRIGG RIDING SCHOOL, Kendal (YH08434)			●																●		●		●	●	●		●				●																			
LEWNEY, E, Ulverston (YH08598)		●																																																
LOWTHER EQUESTRIAN, Carlisle (YH08877)																								●	●	●	●																							
MIDDLE BAYLES LIVERY, Alston (YH09534)																																●		●																
MOFFATT, D, Grange-Over-Sands (YH09700)							●																																											
MURTAGH, F P, Carlisle (YH09971)							●																																											
OAKDEN, JAMES, Windermere (YH10373)							●																																											
O'NEILL, J J, Penrith (YH10518)							●																																											
RICHARDS, N G, Penrith (YH11811)							●																																											
SAYER, H D, Penrith (YH12474)							●																																											
SLACK, EVELYN, Appleby (YH12883)		●																																																
SOCKBRIDGE PONY TREKKING CTRE, Penrith (YH13050)																								●	●	●	●																							
SOWERBY, G, Appleby (YH13165)		●																																																
SOWERBY, W T, Appleby (YH13166)		●																																																
T W RELPH & SONS, Penrith (YH13767)																																										●								
TODHUNTER, MARTIN, Ulverston (YH14202)							●																																											
ZALKIND, Penrith (YH15950)			●				●				●						●																																	
DERBYSHIRE																																																		
ALTON RIDING SCHOOL, Chesterfield (YH00344)			●			●		●	●	●	●			●	●		●			●			●	●	●	●	●	●																						
BARLEYFIELDS, Derby (YH00952)			●					●	●	●	●	●		●	●		●			●				●	●	●	●	●			●	●																		
BRAILSFORD STABLES, Ashbourne (YH01777)	●																																																	
C E S, Ashbourne (YH02370)			●								●		●					●	●					●	●	●	●	●				●						●												
C W G, Buxton (YH02396)																																										●								
CALKE ABBEY RACING STABLES, Swadlincote (YH02446)							●																																											
CHESTERFIELD, Chesterfield (YH02833)			●				●	●	●		●		●	●			●	●		●				●	●	●	●				●	●																		
CLINTON, P L, Ashbourne (YH03043)							●																																											
COWLEY RIDING SCHOOL, Dronfield (YH03526)			●				●				●																																							
DODD, C, Matlock (YH04158)		●																																																

Business Profile

Training (shaded area)

Course, Arena, Buildings and Pasture

by Country by County

	Coaches	Harness Trainer	Dressage Training	Polo Trainer	Side-saddle specialist	Side-saddle trainer	Trainers	Training (1 to 1)	Training (Children)	Training (Disabled)	Training (Dressage)	Training (Flat)	Training (Freelance)	Training (Group)	Training (Horse Breaking)	Training (Jockey)	Training (Jumps)	Training (Personnel)	Training (Point-to-Point)	Training (Riding)	Training (SteepleChase)	Training (To become a Trainer)	Training for Examination	Work with Children 10-16	Work with Children under 10	Work with Senior Citizens	Work with Students	Work with the Disabled	Architectural Advice	Architectural Planning	Arenas (large) for hire	Arenas (small) for hire	Arenas Indoor (Build)	Arenas Outdoor (Build)	Building Maintenance	Building Repairs	Cross Country Course (Build)	Cross Country Course (Design)	Fencing (Build)	Gates (Build)	Outbuildings (Build)	Pasture Supply	Pasture Support	Property Services	Racing Tracks (Build)	Show Jumps (Design)	Stables (Build)	Stables (Design)	Swimming Pools (Build)	Swimming Pools (Design)
ELVASTON CASTLE RIDING CTRE, Derby (YH04645)			●				●				●																																							
HILLCLIFF STUD, Belper (YH06838)			●					●			●						●							●		●	●					●																		
HOLME FARM EQUESTRIAN CTRE, Derby (YH06963)							●																																											
IVANHOE FEEDS, Swadlincote (YH07533)																																										●								
JONES, EMMA-JANE, Chesterfield (YH07897)							●																																											
KNOWLE HILL EQUESTRIAN, Derby (YH08280)								●	●					●	●								●									●																		
MACKIE, W J W, Church Broughton (YH09008)							●																																											
MOORBRIDGE RIDING STABLES, Derby (YH09747)									●																																									
NORTHFIELD FARM, Buxton (YH10312)		●																																																
PEAKDALE SADDLERY, Buxton (YH10866)																								●	●	●	●	●																						
POLLARD, V, Ashbourne (YH11206)			●				●				●		●																																					
RED HSE STABLES, Matlock (YH11698)							●																																											
RINGER VILLA EQUESTRIAN CTRE, Chesterfield (YH11900)							●		●	●																		●																						
ROBINSONS, Derby (YH12002)																																									●									
S & E JOHNSON, Matlock (YH12310)																																										●								
DEVON																																																		
BARRIBAL, Okehampton (YH01020)							●																																											
BARWELL, C R, Tiverton (YH01052)							●																																											
BINGHAM, R J, Lynton (YH01422)																												●																						
BLEEKMAN, E & C, Cullompton (YH01533)							●																																											
BRAGG, MIRANDA, Buckfastleigh (YH01775)							●																																											
BRAKE, C J, Cullompton (YH01780)							●																																											
CLIPPER SHARP, Cullompton (YH03046)																																							●											
COLE, DEBORAH, South Molton (YH03153)							●																																											
COLE, S N, Tiverton (YH03160)							●																																											
COLLACOTT FARM, Umberleigh (YH03173)								●				●		●			●																																	
COTTRELL, L G, Cullompton (YH03387)							●																																											
DONKEY SANCTUARY, Sidmouth (YH04184)										●																		●																						
DURALOCK, Plymouth (YH04365)																																							●											
DUTFIELD, P N, Seaton (YH04376)							●																																											
EDWIN TUCKER & SONS, Newton Abbott (YH04586)																																										●								
EQUITOPIA, Lynton (YH04831)			●				●	●			●		●	●	●					●																														

Business Profile

Training (shaded area) **Course, Arena, Buildings and Pasture**

by Country by County

	Coaches	Harness Trainer	Dressage Training	Polo Trainer	Side-saddle specialist	Side-saddle trainer	Trainers	Training (1 to 1)	Training (Children)	Training (Disabled)	Training (Dressage)	Training (Flat)	Training (Freelance)	Training (Group)	Training (Horse Breaking)	Training (Jockey)	Training (Jumps)	Training (Personnel)	Training (Point-to-Point)	Training (Riding)	Training (SteepleChase)	Training (To become a Trainer)	Training for Examination	Work with Children 10-16	Work with Children under 10	Work with Senior Citizens	Work with Students	Work with the Disabled	Architectural Advice	Architectural Planning	Arenas (large) for hire	Arenas (small) for hire	Arenas Indoor (Build)	Arenas Outdoor (Build)	Building Maintenance	Building Repairs	Cross Country Course (Build)	Cross Country Course (Design)	Fencing (Build)	Gates (Build)	Outbuildings (Build)	Pasture Supply	Pasture Support	Property Services	Racing Tracks (Build)	Show Jumps (Design)	Stables (Build)	Stables (Design)	Swimming Pools (Build)	Swimming Pools (Design)
FROST, R G, Buckfastleigh (YH05520)							●																																												
GLEBE INT ENTERPRISE, Exeter (YH05817)											●																																						
GRAHAM, FERGUS, Newton Abbott (YH05966)													●																																				
HALDON RIDING STABLES, Exeter (YH06290)																								●	●	●	●	●																						
HALWILL ELITE LIVERY SVS, Beaworthy (YH06338)			●				●				●																																						
HILL, TONY, South Molton (YH06835)													●																																				
HOLLY FARM, Exeter (YH06953)																															●	●																		
HOWE, H S, Tiverton (YH07225)							●																																												
J R SERPELL & SON, Plymouth (YH07610)																																										●								
KILEY-WORTHINGTON, M (DR), Okehampton (YH08133)			●				●				●																																						
KING, ANN, Newton Abbot (YH08174)															●																																		
LEONARD COOMBE, Newton Abbot (YH08553)																								●	●			●																						
LUSCOMBE ARENA CONSTRUCTION, Newton Abbot (YH08902)																																	●	●																
MILLMAN, B R, Cullompton (YH09625)							●																																												
MOFFETT, HEATHER, Totnes (YH09701)			●				●				●																																						
MOLE AVON TRADING, Crediton (YH09709)																																										●								
MULLACOTT EQUESTRIAN, Ilfracombe (YH09935)								●	●	●				●	●		●			●				●	●	●	●	●				●																		
NEWCOMBE, A G, Barnstaple (YH10132)							●																																												
NEWTON FERRERS, Plymouth (YH10170)			●				●				●						●																																
REEDER, PENNY, Okehampton (YH11724)													●																																				
RENE, P, Tiverton (YH11757)													●																																				
SHERRATT, GUY, South Molton (YH12729)																																																		
STAGS, Barnstaple (YH13333)																																												●						
STAGS, Exeter (YH13331)																																												●						
STAGS, Tiverton (YH13332)																																												●						
STAGS, Totnes (YH13335)																																												●						
STAGS, Plymouth (YH13338)																																												●						
STAGS, Kingsbridge (YH13337)																																												●						
STAGS, Honiton (YH13336)																																												●						
STAGS, South Molton (YH13334)																																												●						
STEART HOUSE RACING STABLES, Tiverton (YH13411)							●																																												
TALAWATER QUARTER HORSES, Yelverton (YH13830)									●															●																										

www.hccyourhorse.com

Business Profile

Training (shaded area) Course, Arena, Buildings and Pasture

by Country by County

	Coaches	Harness Trainer	Dressage Training	Polo Trainer	Side-saddle specialist	Side-saddle trainer	Trainers	Training (1 to 1)	Training (Children)	Training (Disabled)	Training (Dressage)	Training (Flat)	Training (Freelance)	Training (Group)	Training (Horse Breaking)	Training (Jockey)	Training (Jumps)	Training (Personnel)	Training (Point-to-Point)	Training (Riding)	Training (SteepleChase)	Training (To become a Trainer)	Training for Examination	Work with Children 10-16	Work with Children under 10	Work with Senior Citizens	Work with Students	Work with the Disabled	Architectural Advice	Architectural Planning	Arenas (large) for hire	Arenas (small) for hire	Arenas Indoor (Build)	Arenas Outdoor (Build)	Building Maintenance	Building Repairs	Cross Country Course (Build)	Cross Country Course (Design)	Fencing (Build)	Gates (Build)	Outbuildings (Build)	Pasture Supply	Pasture Support	Property Services	Racing Tracks (Build)	Show Jumps (Design)	Stables (Build)	Stables (Design)	Swimming Pools (Build)	Swimming Pools (Design)
TUGGYS, Branscombe (YH14448)			●				●				●																																							
WARD, MICHAEL J, Holsworthy (YH14904)							●																																											
WEST DEVON & NORTH CORNWALL, Holsworthy (YH15139)																																										●								
WEST DOWN RACING STABLES, South Molton (YH15140)							●																																											
WEST ILKERTON FARM, Lynton (YH15150)																								●	●	●	●	●																						
WILLIAMS, S D, South Molton (YH15478)							●																																											
WOOD FARM STUD, Okehampton (YH15656)							●																														●		●											
WYCHANGER BARTON SADDLERY, Tiverton (YH15855)					●																																													
DORSET																																																		
ALEXANDER TECHNIQUE TEACHER, Wimborne (YH00267)																								●	●	●	●	●																						
ALNER, R H, Blandford (YH00332)							●																																											
BUCKLER, R H, Bridport (YH02196)							●																																											
EQUESTRIAN & EXAM CTRE, Ferndown (YH04691)							●																								●																			
HURN BRIDGE CTRE, Christchurch (YH07313)																															●																			
KAYE, GILES, Wimborne (YH08007)							●																																											
LANEHOUSE EQUITATION CTRE, Weymouth (YH08393)								●	●	●	●									●				●	●		●	●																						
LULWORTH EQUESTRIAN CTRE, Wareham (YH08897)								●	●					●						●				●	●						●																			
MITCHELL, N R, Dorchester (YH09675)							●																																											
OAKFIELD ICELANDIC HORSES, Verwood (YH10378)													●																																					
POUND COTTAGE RIDING CTRE, Blandford Forum (YH11307)								●	●	●	●			●				●		●			●									●																		
PROSPECT FARM LIVERY STABLES, Dorchester (YH11436)			●				●				●		●																																					
REMPSTONE STABLES, Wareham (YH11751)																								●	●																									
SIDE SADDLES, Wimborne (YH12787)					●																																													
THOMSON, N B, Shaftesbury (YH14053)							●																																											
TIZZARD, C, Sherborne (YH14194)							●																																											
TURNER, W G M, Sherborne (YH14491)							●																																											
WARMWELL STUD, Dorchester (YH14924)								●					●		●				●	●			●								●											●								
WEEDON, M J, Weymouth (YH15046)							●																																											
ESSEX																																																		
ALLINSON, JONATHAN, Colchester (YH00316)			●				●										●																																	
ASHINGDON RIDING CTRE, Rochford (YH00605)								●	●					●										●	●																									
BARLING TACK SHOP, Rochford (YH00955)								●						●																																				

Business Profile

Training (shaded area) Course, Arena, Buildings and Pasture

by Country by County

	Coaches	Harness Trainer	Dressage Training	Polo Trainer	Side-saddle specialist	Side-saddle trainer	Trainers	Training (1 to 1)	Training (Children)	Training (Disabled)	Training (Dressage)	Training (Flat)	Training (Freelance)	Training (Group)	Training (Horse Breaking)	Training (Jockey)	Training (Jumps)	Training (Personnel)	Training (Point-to-Point)	Training (Riding)	Training (SteepleChase)	Training (To become a Trainer)	Training for Examination	Work with Children 10-16	Work with Children under 10	Work with Senior Citizens	Work with Students	Work with the Disabled	Architectural Advice	Architectural Planning	Arenas (large) for hire	Arenas (small) for hire	Arenas Indoor (Build)	Arenas Outdoor (Build)	Building Maintenance	Building Repairs	Cross Country Course (Build)	Cross Country Course (Design)	Fencing (Build)	Gates (Build)	Outbuildings (Build)	Pasture Supply	Pasture Support	Property Services	Racing Tracks (Build)	Show Jumps (Design)	Stables (Build)	Stables (Design)	Swimming Pools (Build)	Swimming Pools (Design)
BLUE SABRE RIDING SCHOOL, Colchester (YH01570)																								●	●																									
BROOK FARM STABLES, Colchester (YH02036)							●		●	●										●								●																						
C W G, Ongar (YH02397)																																										●								
CLAY HALL, Brentwood (YH02994)			●					●	●		●		●	●			●			●			●	●	●	●	●																							
COACH HSE, Epping (YH03102)		●	●						●		●		●		●					●			●									●																		
COLCHESTER GARRISON, Colchester (YH03144)								●	●	●	●			●			●			●				●	●	●	●	●																						
COTTON, SARAH, Chelmsford (YH03385)							●						●																																					
DANBURY, Chelmsford (YH03860)							●								●																																			
D'ARCY RIDING STABLES, Maldon (YH03879)								●	●	●				●			●			●																														
ELMWOOD EQUESTRIAN CTRE, Burnham-on-Crouch (YH04640)								●	●					●			●			●				●	●	●	●																							
ESSEX FENCING, Wickford (YH04870)																																							●											
H R PHILPOT & SON, Billericay (YH06235)																																										●	●							
HALLINGBURY HALL, Bishop's Stortford (YH06331)																								●	●		●																							
J ODDY & SONS, Chelmsford (YH07604)																																							●											
JUHL, G, Saffron Walden (YH07961)									●																																									
LEWIS, ANNETTE, Chigwell (YH08585)																	●																																	
LIMEBROOK, Maldon (YH08628)								●	●		●			●			●			●				●	●	●	●																							
MERRETT, D T, Colchester (YH09479)			●				●				●						●																																	
NIGHTINGALE RIDING SCHOOL, Buckhurst Hill (YH10204)								●	●	●										●				●	●	●	●																							
PARK FARM, Colchester (YH10717)								●	●		●			●			●			●		●	●	●	●	●	●																							
PARK LANE RIDING SCHOOL, Billericay (YH10731)																															●																			
RAGWOOD RIDING CTRE, Benfleet (YH11609)								●	●		●			●			●			●			●	●	●	●	●																							
RAYNE RIDING CTRE, Braintree (YH11676)								●	●	●	●			●			●			●		●	●	●	●	●	●	●																						
RUNNINGWELL STUD, Chelmsford (YH12236)			●				●				●						●																																	
SEVEN SAINTS RARE BREEDS, Colchester (YH12639)																															●																			
SHAHZADA, Dunmow (YH12659)							●	●	●	●				●			●			●				●	●	●	●	●																						
SHOPLAND HALL EQUESTRIAN, Rochford (YH12758)									●	●	●	●		●			●			●			●	●	●	●	●	●				●																		
STABLES, Loughton (YH13305)			●								●																																							
TALLY-HO RIDING SCHOOL, Grays (YH13844)			●					●	●		●	●	●	●			●			●				●	●						●	●																		
TAYLOR, D J W, Southend (YH13899)							●																																											
TIPTREE EQUESTRIAN CTRE, Colchester (YH14184)								●	●					●			●			●				●	●	●	●																							
UPMINSTER SADDLERY, Upminster (YH14604)																												●																						

www.hccyourhorse.com

Business Profile

Training (shaded area) Course, Arena, Buildings and Pasture

by Country by County

by Country by County	Coaches	Harness Trainer	Dressage Training	Polo Trainer	Side-saddle specialist	Side-saddle trainer	Trainers	Training (1 to 1)	Training (Children)	Training (Disabled)	Training (Dressage)	Training (Flat)	Training (Freelance)	Training (Group)	Training (Horse Breaking)	Training (Jockey)	Training (Jumps)	Training (Personnel)	Training (Point-to-Point)	Training (Riding)	Training (SteepleChase)	Training (To become a Trainer)	Training for Examination	Work with Children 10-16	Work with Children under 10	Work with Senior Citizens	Work with Students	Work with the Disabled
VALLEY RIDING/LIVERY STABLES, Ingatestone (YH14657)								●	●		●	●		●			●			●		●	●	●	●	●	●	
WETHERSFIELD RIDING STABLES, Braintree (YH15246)			●					●	●		●	●	●		●					●								
WILLOWS SHOW JUMPING CLUB, Loughton (YH15509)													●				●											
GLOUCESTERSHIRE																												
BABBAGE, N M, Cheltenham (YH00761)							●																					
BEAUFORT POLO CLUB, Tetbury (YH01128)				●			●																	●			●	
BRAMLEY & WELLESLEY, Gloucester (YH01790)																												
BRAZINGTON, R G, Redmarley (YH01824)							●																					
BROWN, ALISTAIR, Cheltenham (YH02098)			●				●				●																	
COTSWOLD GRASS SEEDS, Moreton In Marsh (YH03362)																												
DENNY, L, Moreton-in-Marsh (YH04063)							●																					
DONEY, JON, Tewkesbury (YH04181)																												
ELM LEAZE STUD, Badminton (YH04631)																												
EVANS, ANNE-MARIE & RICHARD, Moreton In Marsh (YH04916)							●																					
FENCING IN THE MIDLANDS, Moreton In Marsh (YH05139)																												
FERNEYHOUGH, R J & OLIVER, A M, Stonehouse (YH05163)																	●											
GRASSICK, L P, Cheltenham (YH06020)							●																					
GROVE FARM, Moreton In Marsh (YH06163)							●																					
HARTPURY CLGE, Gloucester (YH06507)																												
HENRY COLE, Cirencester (YH06681)																												
HICKS, C M, Cheltenham (YH06746)							●																					
J A, WILSON, Cheltenham (YH07557)							●																					
J C PRICE, Stonehouse (YH07573)																												
JUPP, BARBARA, Cirencester (YH07970)			●				●				●		●															
MARSDEN MANOR STUD, Cirencester (YH09181)																												
MIFLIN, WILLIAM, Cirencester (YH09563)							●						●															
PARK CORNER FARM, Cirencester (YH10716)																												
PHILLIPS, R, Cheltenham (YH11063)							●																					
PLAYMATE CHILDRENS, Cheltenham (YH11172)																												
PRITCHARD, P L J (DR), Berkeley (YH11420)							●																					
ROCKHAMPTON EQUESTRIAN CTRE, Berkeley (YH12030)																	●											
ROE, G, Stroud (YH12050)							●																					

by Country by County	Architectural Advice	Architectural Planning	Arenas (large) for hire	Arenas (small) for hire	Arenas Indoor (Build)	Arenas Outdoor (Build)	Building Maintenance	Building Repairs	Cross Country Course (Build)	Cross Country Course (Design)	Fencing (Build)	Gates (Build)	Outbuildings (Build)	Pasture Supply	Pasture Support	Property Services	Racing Tracks (Build)	Show Jumps (Design)	Stables (Build)	Stables (Design)	Swimming Pools (Build)	Swimming Pools (Design)
VALLEY RIDING/LIVERY STABLES, Ingatestone (YH14657)																						
WETHERSFIELD RIDING STABLES, Braintree (YH15246)				●																		
WILLOWS SHOW JUMPING CLUB, Loughton (YH15509)			●																			
GLOUCESTERSHIRE																						
BABBAGE, N M, Cheltenham (YH00761)																						
BEAUFORT POLO CLUB, Tetbury (YH01128)																						
BRAMLEY & WELLESLEY, Gloucester (YH01790)											●					●						
BRAZINGTON, R G, Redmarley (YH01824)																						
BROWN, ALISTAIR, Cheltenham (YH02098)																						
COTSWOLD GRASS SEEDS, Moreton In Marsh (YH03362)														●								
DENNY, L, Moreton-in-Marsh (YH04063)																						
DONEY, JON, Tewkesbury (YH04181)																		●				
ELM LEAZE STUD, Badminton (YH04631)				●																		
EVANS, ANNE-MARIE & RICHARD, Moreton In Marsh (YH04916)																						
FENCING IN THE MIDLANDS, Moreton In Marsh (YH05139)									●		●											
FERNEYHOUGH, R J & OLIVER, A M, Stonehouse (YH05163)																						
GRASSICK, L P, Cheltenham (YH06020)																						
GROVE FARM, Moreton In Marsh (YH06163)																						
HARTPURY CLGE, Gloucester (YH06507)			●																			
HENRY COLE, Cirencester (YH06681)														●								
HICKS, C M, Cheltenham (YH06746)																						
J A, WILSON, Cheltenham (YH07557)																						
J C PRICE, Stonehouse (YH07573)											●											
JUPP, BARBARA, Cirencester (YH07970)																						
MARSDEN MANOR STUD, Cirencester (YH09181)			●																			
MIFLIN, WILLIAM, Cirencester (YH09563)																						
PARK CORNER FARM, Cirencester (YH10716)														●								
PHILLIPS, R, Cheltenham (YH11063)																						
PLAYMATE CHILDRENS, Cheltenham (YH11172)											●											
PRITCHARD, P L J (DR), Berkeley (YH11420)																						
ROCKHAMPTON EQUESTRIAN CTRE, Berkeley (YH12030)																						
ROE, G, Stroud (YH12050)																						

Business Profile

Training (shaded area) Course, Arena, Buildings and Pasture

by Country by County

	Coaches	Harness Trainer	Dressage Training	Polo Trainer	Side-saddle specialist	Side-saddle trainer	Trainers	Training (1 to 1)	Training (Children)	Training (Disabled)	Training (Dressage)	Training (Flat)	Training (Freelance)	Training (Group)	Training (Horse Breaking)	Training (Jockey)	Training (Jumps)	Training (Personnel)	Training (Point-to-Point)	Training (Riding)	Training (SteepleChase)	Training (To become a Trainer)	Training for Examination	Work with Children 10-16	Work with Children under 10	Work with Senior Citizens	Work with Students	Work with the Disabled	Architectural Advice	Architectural Planning	Arenas (large) for hire	Arenas (small) for hire	Arenas Indoor (Build)	Arenas Outdoor (Build)	Building Maintenance	Building Repairs	Cross Country Course (Build)	Cross Country Course (Design)	Fencing (Build)	Gates (Build)	Outbuildings (Build)	Pasture Supply	Pasture Support	Property Services	Racing Tracks (Build)	Show Jumps (Design)	Stables (Build)	Stables (Design)	Swimming Pools (Build)	Swimming Pools (Design)
ROYAL AGRICULTURAL CLGE, Cirencester (YH12180)																							●																											
SIMON, (CPT), TOMLINSON C, Tetbury (YH12831)							●																																											
SMITH, J S, Tirley (YH12965)							●																																											
SMITH, R J, Naunton (YH12992)							●																																											
SPRING BANK STABLES, Stroud (YH13244)							●																																											
STROUD SADDLERY, Stroud (YH13588)					●																			●	●	●	●	●																						
SUMMERHOUSE, Gloucester (YH13632)																						●	●				●																							
TALLAND SCHOOL OF EQUITATION, Cirencester (YH13833)			●				●				●		●																																					
TAYLER & FLETCHER, Stow-on-the-Wold (YH13893)																																												●						
TAYLOR, SARAH, Cheltenham (YH13911)							●																																											
TUCK, J C, Didmarton (YH14431)							●																																											
TUCKER, ANGELA, Tetbury (YH14432)			●				●				●																																							
TWISTON-DAVIES, N A, Cheltenham (YH14515)							●																																											
WATSON, T R, Winchcombe (YH14993)							●																																											
WINTLE, D J, Cheltenham (YH15599)							●																																											
WOODLAND, Cheltenham (YH15702)								●	●	●	●			●			●			●				●	●	●	●	●																						
WYATT, N J S, Moreton In Marsh (YH15854)																																					●													
HAMPSHIRE																																																		
AMBERVALE, Lymington (YH00357)							●		●																																									
ARNISS, Fordingbridge (YH00555)								●	●	●	●			●			●							●	●			●																						
ASHBOURNE STABLES, Southampton (YH00590)																	●																																	
B & M FENCING, Hook (YH00713)																																							●											
BALDINGS, Andover (YH00838)							●																																											
BENNETT, ROD, Andover (YH01273)																																					●													
BLACK KNOLL HORSE SPORTS CTRE, Brockenhurst (YH01467)																															●																			
BOWER, L J, Alresford (YH01706)							●																																											
BRIDGER, J J, Liphook (YH01882)												●									●																													
BROCKS FARM, Stockbridge (YH02013)								●	●	●	●			●			●			●		●																												
BURITON HORSE SVS, Stockbridge (YH02253)					●	●					●				●		●		●	●		●																												
BURLEY VILLA EQUESTRIAN CTRE, New Milton (YH02260)								●	●					●						●				●	●	●																								
CLEVERLY, TANYA, Church Crookham (YH03024)							●																																											
CORBETT, MARK, Tadley (YH03306)							●																																											

www.hccyourhorse.com

Business Profile
Training (shaded area) Course, Arena, Buildings and Pasture

by Country by County

	Coaches	Harness Trainer	Dressage Training	Polo Trainer	Side-saddle specialist	Side-saddle trainer	Trainers	Training (1 to 1)	Training (Children)	Training (Disabled)	Training (Dressage)	Training (Flat)	Training (Freelance)	Training (Group)	Training (Horse Breaking)	Training (Jockey)	Training (Jumps)	Training (Personnel)	Training (Point-to-Point)	Training (Riding)	Training (SteepleChase)	Training (To become a Trainer)	Training for Examination	Work with Children 10-16	Work with Children under 10	Work with Senior Citizens	Work with Students	Work with the Disabled	Architectural Advice	Architectural Planning	Arenas (large) for hire	Arenas (small) for hire	Arenas Indoor (Build)	Arenas Outdoor (Build)	Building Maintenance	Building Repairs	Cross Country Course (Build)	Cross Country Course (Design)	Fencing (Build)	Gates (Build)	Outbuildings (Build)	Pasture Supply	Pasture Support	Property Services	Racing Tracks (Build)	Show Jumps (Design)	Stables (Build)	Stables (Design)	Swimming Pools (Build)	Swimming Pools (Design)
COTTAGE ESTATES STABLES, Southampton (YH03372)																																															●	●		
COTTAGE STABLES, Andover (YH03380)							●																																											
CROFTON MANOR EQUESTRIAN CTRE, Fareham (YH03623)			●				●				●																																							
CUNNINGHAM-BROWN, K, Stockbridge (YH03726)							●																																											
DOYLE, KEITH, Eversley (YH04248)																	●																																	
ELEDA STABLES, Ringwood (YH04603)			●				●				●																																							
ELLIS, Alton (YH04621)																																												●						
EQUALLUS EQUESTRIAN, Hook (YH04685)							●	●	●	●	●			●						●			●	●	●	●	●	●																						
EQUESTRIAN SVS FENCING, Southampton (YH04716)																																		●					●											
FIR TREE FARM, Fordingbridge (YH05219)			●				●				●						●																																	
FLEETWATER STUD, Lyndhurst (YH05269)																																											●							
FOREST FARM, Milford On Sea (YH05335)		●						●						●						●			●								●																			
FOREST PARK, Brockenhurst (YH05348)								●						●									●	●			●																							
FROXFIELD TRAINING CTRE, Alton (YH05524)									●								●			●																														
HARMSWORTH FARM, Southampton (YH06446)								●																																										
HARROWAY HSE RIDING SCHOOL, Andover (YH06495)							●																																											
HILL FARM STABLES, Stockbridge (YH06816)							●																																											
HOPLANDS EQUESTRIAN, Stockbridge (YH07058)			●				●	●			●						●														●																			
HORSEPOWER, Alton (YH07163)							●																																											
IEDEMA, BARRY, Romsey (YH07388)			●				●				●		●																																					
INADOWN FARM STABLES, Alton (YH07407)								●	●	●	●	●					●	●		●			●	●	●		●	●																						
INHURST FARM STABLES, Basingstoke (YH07456)							●																																											
J B CORRIE & CO, Petersfield (YH07561)																																							●											
J ELLIS & SONS, Bordon (YH07580)																																										●								
KEELEY, PAULA, Liss (YH08027)			●				●				●																																							
KILN FARM RIDING SCHOOL, Southampton (YH08150)								●	●					●			●																																	
LONDON, MOIRA, Lymington (YH08792)													●																																					
MADGWICK, M J, Denmead (YH09023)							●																																											
MCNEILL, IAN, Alton (YH09402)																																							●											
MERRIE STUD, Southampton (YH09480)																								●	●																									
MORSTEAD STABLES, Winchester (YH09844)							●																																											
MOYGLARE LIVERY, Tadley (YH09910)			●					●			●		●	●						●																														

Business Profile

Training (shaded area) Course, Arena, Buildings and Pasture

by Country by County

by Country by County	Coaches	Harness Trainer	Dressage Training	Polo Trainer	Side-saddle specialist	Side-saddle trainer	Trainers	Training (1 to 1)	Training (Children)	Training (Disabled)	Training (Dressage)	Training (Flat)	Training (Freelance)	Training (Group)	Training (Horse Breaking)	Training (Jockey)	Training (Jumps)	Training (Personnel)	Training (Point-to-Point)	Training (Riding)	Training (SteepleChase)	Training (To become a Trainer)	Training for Examination	Work with Children 10-16	Work with Children under 10	Work with Senior Citizens	Work with Students	Work with the Disabled	Architectural Advice	Architectural Planning	Arenas (large) for hire	Arenas (small) for hire	Arenas Indoor (Build)	Arenas Outdoor (Build)	Building Maintenance	Building Repairs	Cross Country Course (Build)	Cross Country Course (Design)	Fencing (Build)	Gates (Build)	Outbuildings (Build)	Pasture Supply	Pasture Support	Property Services	Racing Tracks (Build)	Show Jumps (Design)	Stables (Build)	Stables (Design)	Swimming Pools (Build)	Swimming Pools (Design)
NRC, Fareham (YH10348)																								●	●	●	●	●																						
RAFFERTY NEWMAN, Petersfield (YH11603)																																											●							
RAWLINS FARM, Tadley (YH11667)								●																																										
REDENHAM PK STUD, Andover (YH11708)															●																																			
RENOUARD, STEPHEN G, Romsey (YH11760)																																					●													
RYCROFT SCHOOL OF EQUITATION, Hook (YH12291)							●	●	●			●		●			●	●		●		●	●	●	●	●	●																							
SADDLES, SADDLES, SADDLES, Portsmouth (YH12371)																								●	●	●	●	●																						
SEAVILL, C A S, Petersfield (YH12595)							●																																											
SIMMONS, Basingstoke (YH12823)																																												●						
SOUTHFIELD EQUESTRIAN CTRE, Whitchurch (YH13149)															●																																			
TUNWORTH DOWN STABLES, Basingstoke (YH14463)							●																																											
TURNER, DAVID, Ringwood (YH14478)													●																																					
WALSH & CO, Brockenhurst (YH14875)																																												●						
WELLINGTON RIDING, Hook (YH15075)			●					●	●	●	●	●		●	●		●	●		●		●	●	●	●	●	●	●																						
WESSEX MACHINERY, Bordon (YH15119)																																											●							
WHITSBURY MANOR, Fordingbridge (YH15370)							●																																											
HEREFORDSHIRE																																																		
AMTEX, Leominster (YH00374)																																											●							
ARAMSTONE STABLES, Hereford (YH00494)							●																																											
ARROW TRAINING, Leominster (YH00562)			●				●				●		●				●																																	
BORDER ESTATES, Leominster (YH01643)																																												●						
CAM EQUESTRIAN JOINERY/EQUIP, Hereford (YH02463)																																							●											
CARO, D J, Ledbury (YH02566)							●																																											
COUNTRYWIDE, Hereford (YH03445)																													●	●												●	●							
COUNTRYWIDE STORES, Ledbury (YH03457)																																										●	●							
COUNTY COMPETITION STUD, Bromyard (YH03486)			●				●	●	●		●		●		●		●	●		●			●	●			●																							
CULSHAW, D, Bromyard (YH03708)			●				●				●																																							
DOYLE, MARK, Leominster (YH04249)															●				●																															
EACOCK, KAREN, Leominster (YH04435)			●				●				●																																							
HOPE END RACING, Ledbury (YH07050)							●																																											
JONES, R M, Hay-on-Wye (YH07924)																																										●								
JORDAN, FRANK T J, Leominster (YH07938)							●																																											

Business Profile
Training (shaded area) Course, Arena, Buildings and Pasture

by Country by County	Coaches	Harness Trainer	Dressage Training	Polo Trainer	Side-saddle specialist	Side-saddle trainer	Trainers	Training (1 to 1)	Training (Children)	Training (Disabled)	Training (Dressage)	Training (Flat)	Training (Freelance)	Training (Group)	Training (Horse Breaking)	Training (Jockey)	Training (Jumps)	Training (Personnel)	Training (Point-to-Point)	Training (Riding)	Training (SteepleChase)	Training (To become a Trainer)	Training for Examination	Work with Children 10-16	Work with Children under 10	Work with Senior Citizens	Work with Students	Work with the Disabled	Architectural Advice	Architectural Planning	Arenas (large) for hire	Arenas (small) for hire	Arenas Indoor (Build)	Arenas Outdoor (Build)	Building Maintenance	Building Repairs	Cross Country Course (Build)	Cross Country Course (Design)	Fencing (Build)	Gates (Build)	Outbuildings (Build)	Pasture Supply	Pasture Support	Property Services	Racing Tracks (Build)	Show Jumps (Design)	Stables (Build)	Stables (Design)	Swimming Pools (Build)	Swimming Pools (Design)
MONNINGTON, Hereford (YH09728)															●					●		●					●																								
NEWCOMB, SALLY, Hereford (YH10130)			●				●	●			●		●							●			●																												
P G L TRAVEL, Ross-on-Wye (YH10640)																								●	●																										
PRICE, C J, Leominster (YH11376)							●																																												
PRICE, RICHARD, Hereford (YH11387)							●																																												
SHEEPCOTE EQUESTRIAN, Hereford (YH12695)			●																								●																								
SHEPPARD, M I, Ledbury (YH12715)							●																																												
SIMPSON, JONATHAN, Leominster (YH12839)							●																																												
STILWELL, ELAINE, Dilwyn (YH13469)		●																																																	
STONE HSE STABLE, Hereford (YH13510)							●																																												
SUE ADAMS RIDING SCHOOL, Leominster (YH13622)	●		●					●	●	●	●			●	●					●		●	●	●	●	●	●	●				●																			
TIPTON HALL, Bromyard (YH14183)								●	●	●				●			●							●	●	●	●	●																							
WALL, Y L, Bromyard (YH14862)													●																																						
HERTFORDSHIRE																																																			
BEESONS, Hertford (YH01191)																													●	●														●							
CONTESSA, Ware (YH03246)			●					●			●			●									●																												
COURTLANDS, Stevenage (YH03507)								●	●					●						●			●	●	●	●	●																								
CROUCHFIELD, Ware (YH03674)								●	●	●	●			●			●							●	●	●	●	●			●																●				
DRESSAGE TRAINING CTRE, Radlett (YH04268)							●				●																																								
GREENACRES EQUESTRIAN, Harpenden (YH06076)																	●																																		
HARRIS, P W, Berkhamsted (YH06479)							●																																												
ICKLEFORD EQUESTRIAN, Hitchin (YH07382)			●					●	●		●			●			●			●			●	●	●	●	●																								
IVORY, K T, Radlett (YH07538)							●																																												
JENKINS, J, Royston (YH07733)							●																																												
LAYTON, T, Ware (YH08484)			●				●				●		●																																						
MEES, RON, Hatfield (YH09443)							●																																												
ONE JUMP AHEAD, Hertford (YH10511)																																							●												
PATCHETTS, Watford (YH10815)																															●	●																			
PENNIWELLS RIDING GRP, Borehamwood (YH10956)										●																																									
PEVSNER, DANIEL, Hitchin (YH11036)			●				●				●																																								
POYNDERS END FARM, Hitchin (YH11329)													●																																						
ROSE HALL RIDING STABLES, Sarratt (YH12093)								●	●					●			●		●	●			●	●	●																										

Business Profile

Training (shaded area) Course, Arena, Buildings and Pasture

by Country by County

	Coaches	Harness Trainer	Dressage Training	Polo Trainer	Side-saddle specialist	Side-saddle trainer	Trainers	Training (1 to 1)	Training (Children)	Training (Disabled)	Training (Dressage)	Training (Flat)	Training (Freelance)	Training (Group)	Training (Horse Breaking)	Training (Jockey)	Training (Jumps)	Training (Personnel)	Training (Point-to-Point)	Training (Riding)	Training (SteepleChase)	Training (To become a Trainer)	Training for Examination	Work with Children 10-16	Work with Children under 10	Work with Senior Citizens	Work with Students	Work with the Disabled
SOUTH MEDBURN, Borehamwood (YH13101)								●	●		●			●			●					●	●	●	●	●	●	
STANLEY, ANDREA, Baldock (YH13373)			●				●				●																	
TRAINING & LIVERY CTRE, Welwyn (YH14342)							●																					
UPPERWOOD FARM STUD, Hemel Hempstead (YH14609)																												
WELWYN EQUESTRIAN, Welwyn (YH15101)									●					●										●	●			
ISLE OF MAN																												
G G H EQUITATION CTRE, Marown (YH05578)			●				●				●																	
ISLE OF WIGHT																												
BRICKFIELDS, Ryde (YH01866)								●	●					●										●	●			
GREAT PAN FARM STABLES, Newport (YH06041)															●													
LAKE FARM, Ventnor (YH08350)								●				●		●						●								
ROMANY RIDING STABLES, Newport (YH12070)								●	●		●			●			●			●			●	●	●	●	●	
JERSEY																												
ARTHUR, STEPHEN, St Mary (YH00570)							●																					
BARETTE & GRUCHY, St John (YH00930)																												
BROCQ, JOAN LE, St Peter (YH02017)							●																					
GREEN BANK RACING STABLES, St Peter (YH06050)							●																					
MALEARD, A, St Owen (YH09048)							●																					
VIBERT, ALYSON, St Ouen (YH14704)							●																					
KENT																												
BALL, CHRISTINE, Orpington (YH00850)			●				●				●		●															
BEDGEBURY RIDING CTRE, Goudhurst (YH01155)																						●	●					
BEST, J R, Maidstone (YH01326)							●																					
BIAC, Sittingbourne (YH01389)																												
BLUE BARN EQUESTRIAN CTRE, Ashford (YH01564)																	●											
BRADBOURNE, Sevenoaks (YH01743)							●																					
BRAESIDE E.C, Dover (YH01773)			●				●	●	●		●	●	●	●	●		●					●	●				●	
BRITISH GATES & TIMBER, Ashford (YH01943)																												
BROMLEY COMMON LIVERIES, Bromley (YH02023)																	●											
CANTERBURY CARRIAGES, Dover (YH02507)							●																					
CHART STABLES, Ashford (YH02775)																												
CHASE FENCING SUPPLIES, Tonbridge (YH02782)																												

	Architectural Advice	Architectural Planning	Arenas (large) for hire	Arenas (small) for hire	Arenas Indoor (Build)	Arenas Outdoor (Build)	Building Maintenance	Building Repairs	Cross Country Course (Build)	Cross Country Course (Design)	Fencing (Build)	Gates (Build)	Outbuildings (Build)	Pasture Supply	Pasture Support	Property Services	Racing Tracks (Build)	Show Jumps (Design)	Stables (Build)	Stables (Design)	Swimming Pools (Build)	Swimming Pools (Design)
SOUTH MEDBURN, Borehamwood (YH13101)																						
STANLEY, ANDREA, Baldock (YH13373)																						
TRAINING & LIVERY CTRE, Welwyn (YH14342)																						
UPPERWOOD FARM STUD, Hemel Hempstead (YH14609)	●	●																				
WELWYN EQUESTRIAN, Welwyn (YH15101)																						
ISLE OF MAN																						
G G H EQUITATION CTRE, Marown (YH05578)																						
ISLE OF WIGHT																						
BRICKFIELDS, Ryde (YH01866)																						
GREAT PAN FARM STABLES, Newport (YH06041)																						
LAKE FARM, Ventnor (YH08350)																						
ROMANY RIDING STABLES, Newport (YH12070)																						
JERSEY																						
ARTHUR, STEPHEN, St Mary (YH00570)																						
BARETTE & GRUCHY, St John (YH00930)											●			●								
BROCQ, JOAN LE, St Peter (YH02017)																						
GREEN BANK RACING STABLES, St Peter (YH06050)																						
MALEARD, A, St Owen (YH09048)																						
VIBERT, ALYSON, St Ouen (YH14704)																						
KENT																						
BALL, CHRISTINE, Orpington (YH00850)																						
BEDGEBURY RIDING CTRE, Goudhurst (YH01155)																						
BEST, J R, Maidstone (YH01326)																						
BIAC, Sittingbourne (YH01389)														●								
BLUE BARN EQUESTRIAN CTRE, Ashford (YH01564)																						
BRADBOURNE, Sevenoaks (YH01743)																						
BRAESIDE E.C, Dover (YH01773)																						
BRITISH GATES & TIMBER, Ashford (YH01943)											●											
BROMLEY COMMON LIVERIES, Bromley (YH02023)									●													
CANTERBURY CARRIAGES, Dover (YH02507)																						
CHART STABLES, Ashford (YH02775)																			●	●		
CHASE FENCING SUPPLIES, Tonbridge (YH02782)											●											

Business Profile

Training (shaded area) Course, Arena, Buildings and Pasture

by Country by County

by Country by County	Coaches	Harness Trainer	Dressage Training	Polo Trainer	Side-saddle specialist	Side-saddle trainer	Trainers	Training (1 to 1)	Training (Children)	Training (Disabled)	Training (Dressage)	Training (Flat)	Training (Freelance)	Training (Group)	Training (Horse Breaking)	Training (Jockey)	Training (Jumps)	Training (Personnel)	Training (Point-to-Point)	Training (Riding)	Training (SteepleChase)	Training (To become a Trainer)	Training for Examination	Work with Children 10-16	Work with Children under 10	Work with Senior Citizens	Work with Students	Work with the Disabled	Architectural Advice	Architectural Planning	Arenas (large) for hire	Arenas (small) for hire	Arenas Indoor (Build)	Arenas Outdoor (Build)	Building Maintenance	Building Repairs	Cross Country Course (Build)	Cross Country Course (Design)	Fencing (Build)	Gates (Build)	Outbuildings (Build)	Pasture Supply	Pasture Support	Property Services	Racing Tracks (Build)	Show Jumps (Design)	Stables (Build)	Stables (Design)	Swimming Pools (Build)	Swimming Pools (Design)
CHAVIC PK STABLES, Westerham (YH02793)							●																																											
CLARK, RON & JULIE, Tunbridge Wells (YH02967)													●																																					
CLAYTON, PENNIE, Dartford (YH03006)			●				●	●			●		●	●								●																												
COBHAM MANOR, Maidstone (YH03113)								●	●	●	●	●		●			●						●	●	●	●		●																						
DANIEL O'BRIEN RACING, Tonbridge (YH03870)							●																																											
DUCKHURST FARM, Staplehurst (YH04307)																																					●													
ELECTRIC FENCING DIRECT, Tonbridge (YH04602)																																							●											
EQUINE SPORT THERAPY, Edenbridge (YH04800)			●										●																																					
EQUINES LIVERIES, Maidstone (YH04809)	●																																																	
EQUUS, Maidstone (YH04837)																																												●						
FOREST VIEW, Sidcup (YH05353)																															●																			
FRIDAY FIELD STABLES, Sittingbourne (YH05502)								●					●	●	●																																			
FROGPOOL MANOR SADDLERY, Chislehurst (YH05515)																								●	●																									
H S JACKSON & SON, Ashford (YH06239)																																							●											
HEIGHTS STABLES, Westerham (YH06650)																	●							●							●																			
HOBBS PARKER, Ashford (YH06894)																																												●						
HONNINGTON, Tunbridge Wells (YH07019)								●	●		●			●								●	●	●	●																									
KING, D J, Canterbury (YH08177)							●																																											
LEYBOURNE GRANGE, West Malling (YH08600)								●	●	●	●	●		●			●			●				●	●	●	●	●																						
LIMES FARM EQUESTRIAN, Folkestone (YH08635)			●					●	●		●	●		●			●						●				●																							
M HANCOCK & SON, Ashford (YH08966)																																										●								
MANNIX STUD, Canterbury (YH09091)								●	●	●		●	●	●				●		●		●	●	●	●																									
MARBERDUM, Canterbury (YH09137)									●															●	●																									
MAYWOOD STUD, Ashford (YH09309)											●		●																																					
MOUNT MASCAL STABLES, Bexley (YH09890)								●	●	●	●			●						●			●	●	●	●	●	●																						
NEW BARN STUD, Eynsford (YH10091)		●																																																
OLD BEXLEY EQUESTRIAN, Bexley (YH10451)			●						●		●												●	●	●						●	●																		
PHILLIPS, A K, Ashford (YH11051)		●																																																
PINE RIDGE, Sevenoaks (YH11120)								●	●					●										●	●																									
QUADRANGLE, Sevenoaks (YH11475)																																●																		
RIDING FARM EQUESTRIAN CTRES, Tonbridge (YH11875)																	●																																	
SANDHILL FARM STABLES, Tunbridge Wells (YH12411)			●				●				●																																							

Business Profile

Training (shaded area) **Course, Arena, Buildings and Pasture**

by Country by County

	Coaches	Harness Trainer	Dressage Training	Polo Trainer	Side-saddle specialist	Side-saddle trainer	Trainers	Training (1 to 1)	Training (Children)	Training (Disabled)	Training (Dressage)	Training (Flat)	Training (Freelance)	Training (Group)	Training (Horse Breaking)	Training (Jockey)	Training (Jumps)	Training (Personnel)	Training (Point-to-Point)	Training (Riding)	Training (SteepleChase)	Training (To become a Trainer)	Training for Examination	Work with Children 10-16	Work with Children under 10	Work with Senior Citizens	Work with Students	Work with the Disabled	Architectural Advice	Architectural Planning	Arenas (large) for hire	Arenas (small) for hire	Arenas Indoor (Build)	Arenas Outdoor (Build)	Building Maintenance	Building Repairs	Cross Country Course (Build)	Cross Country Course (Design)	Fencing (Build)	Gates (Build)	Outbuildings (Build)	Pasture Supply	Pasture Support	Property Services	Racing Tracks (Build)	Show Jumps (Design)	Stables (Build)	Stables (Design)	Swimming Pools (Build)	Swimming Pools (Design)
SOUTHFIELD STABLES, Maidstone (YH13151)							●																																											
THANET SHOW JUMPS, Ashford (YH13978)																																														●				
TREWINT, Cranbrook (YH14388)								●	●	●	●			●	●					●			●	●	●	●	●	●																						
WHITELEAF RIDING CTRE, Sittingbourne (YH15347)								●	●	●		●	●	●	●		●			●		●	●																											
WHITMORE, S, Edenbridge (YH15367)			●				●				●																																							
WIGGINS, CELIA, Faversham (YH15397)			●				●				●																																							
WILLOW FARM, Faversham (YH15497)																															●	●																		
WM LILLICO & SONS, Maidstone (YH15641)																																										●								
WOODLANDS, Sevenoaks (YH15706)			●																																															
LANCASHIRE																																																		
A T F, Preston (YH00060)																																					●		●											
ABRAM HALL RIDING CTRE, Wigan (YH00134)								●			●	●	●	●	●		●			●											●																			
ALDRED, J D, Preston (YH00261)							●																																											
ALMOND, M, Chorley (YH00330)																																					●													
ALSTON, ERIC, Preston (YH00340)							●																																											
ARKENFIELD EQUESTRIAN CTRE, Chorley (YH00530)			●					●	●	●	●			●		●		●		●			●	●	●	●	●	●			●	●							●			●								
ASOKA, Worsley (YH00625)			●				●	●						●	●					●		●																												
ATHERTON, JENNY, Bickerstaffe (YH00644)			●				●				●		●																																					
BARTON EQUESTRIAN CTRE, Preston (YH01044)								●							●		●			●												●																		
BECCONSALL, Preston (YH01144)			●					●	●		●			●			●						●	●	●	●	●																							
BLACKPOOL EQUESTRIAN CTRE, Blackpool (YH01492)																		●		●																														
BOUNDARY FARM CARRIAGES, Wigan (YH01677)		●					●																																											
BROOKFIELDS STABLES, Westhead (YH02054)							●																																											
BROOMHILL, Clitheroe (YH02080)								●	●		●			●			●			●																														
CHORLEY EQUESTRIAN CTRE, Chorley (YH02880)							●	●	●					●			●			●			●	●	●																									
DALES VIEW RIDING CTRE, Barnoldswick (YH03831)																								●	●																									
DEANDANE RIDING STABLES, Wigan (YH03998)								●			●			●			●							●	●																									
DOUGLAS FARM RIDING SCHOOL, Wigan (YH04211)							●																																											
ECCLESTON, Preston (YH04532)									●																																									
EQUINE BEHAVIOUR, Darwen (YH04765)			●				●				●		●																																					
GREEN BANK, Carnforth (YH06049)								●	●					●			●					●	●	●	●	●	●																							
HARKER, MICHAEL, Bury (YH06432)																	●																																	

www.hccyourhorse.com

Business Profile

Training (shaded area)
Course, Arena, Buildings and Pasture

by Country by County	Coaches	Harness Trainer	Dressage Training	Polo Trainer	Side-saddle specialist	Side-saddle trainer	Trainers	Training (1 to 1)	Training (Children)	Training (Disabled)	Training (Dressage)	Training (Flat)	Training (Freelance)	Training (Group)	Training (Horse Breaking)	Training (Jockey)	Training (Jumps)	Training (Personnel)	Training (Point-to-Point)	Training (Riding)	Training (SteepleChase)	Training (To become a Trainer)	Training for Examination	Work with Children 10-16	Work with Children under 10	Work with Senior Citizens	Work with Students	Work with the Disabled	Architectural Advice	Architectural Planning	Arenas (large) for hire	Arenas (small) for hire	Arenas Indoor (Build)	Arenas Outdoor (Build)	Building Maintenance	Building Repairs	Cross Country Course (Build)	Cross Country Course (Design)	Fencing (Build)	Gates (Build)	Outbuildings (Build)	Pasture Supply	Pasture Support	Property Services	Racing Tracks (Build)	Show Jumps (Design)	Stables (Build)	Stables (Design)	Swimming Pools (Build)	Swimming Pools (Design)
HARRIS, R M, Adlington (YH06481)													●																																					
HERD HSE RIDING SCHOOL, Burnley (YH06699)									●											●				●	●	●		●																						
HORSE BITS SADDLERY, Bury (YH07106)																								●	●		●																							
HUSTEADS RIDING SCHOOL, Oldham (YH07330)								●	●	●	●	●	●	●	●		●			●				●	●	●		●			●																			
KILROE, R J, Preston (YH08154)											●																																							
LORDS HOUSE FARM, Blackburn (YH08827)																												●																						
MARRIOTT, K, Blackpool (YH09175)													●				●																																	
MARSHALL, MICHELLE, Heywood (YH09200)			●				●				●		●																																					
MCBANE, SUSAN, Longridge (YH09313)			●				●				●		●																																					
MOORVIEW, Darwen (YH09782)								●	●					●						●				●	●	●	●					●																		
NETHERWOOD FARM, Burnley (YH10083)																				●																														
PANAMA SPORT HORSES, Clitheroe (YH10695)							●	●							●		●			●	●																													
REES, GERALDINE, Preston (YH11730)							●																																											
RENARD RIDING CTRE, Poulton-Le-Fylde (YH11753)								●	●			●		●						●				●	●	●	●																							
RIBBY HALL, Preston (YH11795)								●	●		●			●			●			●				●	●	●	●	●																						
RICHARD BATTERSBY, Heywood (YH11802)																																										●								
ROBSCOTT EQUITATION, Carnforth (YH12010)															●				●	●		●	●				●					●																		
ROSSENDALE & HYNDBURN EC, Accrington (YH12123)																															●																			
ROUTLEDGE, K, Burnley (YH12149)																																					●													
SNAFFLES, Halifax (YH13020)																									●																									
SOUTH WEST LANCASHIRE FARMERS, Skelmersdale (YH13116)																																										●								
VALIANTS EQUESTRIAN CTRE, Preston (YH14645)																															●																			
WHITEGATE FARM, Bacup (YH15338)								●	●			●		●			●			●			●	●	●						●																			
LEICESTERSHIRE																																																		
ACKERMANN, D H W, Oakham (YH00143)							●										●																																	
BRITISH HORSE, Leicester (YH01948)																																												●						
BROOKSBY EQUESTRIAN CTRE, Melton Mowbray (YH02067)																															●																			
C W G, Melton Mowbray (YH02398)																																										●								
COSSINGTON, Leicester (YH03354)								●	●	●	●			●			●			●			●	●	●	●	●	●																						
COUNTRYWIDE FEEDS, Market Harborough (YH03447)																																										●								
CREATON, N A, Coalville (YH03583)			●				●				●		●				●																																	
CZERPAK, J D, Market Harborough (YH03767)							●																																											

Business Profile
Training (shaded area) **Course, Arena, Buildings and Pasture**

by Country by County	Coaches	Harness Trainer	Dressage Training	Polo Trainer	Side-saddle specialist	Side-saddle trainer	Trainers	Training (1 to 1)	Training (Children)	Training (Disabled)	Training (Dressage)	Training (Flat)	Training (Freelance)	Training (Group)	Training (Horse Breaking)	Training (Jockey)	Training (Jumps)	Training (Personnel)	Training (Point-to-Point)	Training (Riding)	Training (SteepleChase)	Training (To become a Trainer)	Training for Examination	Work with Children 10-16	Work with Children under 10	Work with Senior Citizens	Work with Students	Work with the Disabled	Architectural Advice	Architectural Planning	Arenas (large) for hire	Arenas (small) for hire	Arenas Indoor (Build)	Arenas Outdoor (Build)	Building Maintenance	Building Repairs	Cross Country Course (Build)	Cross Country Course (Design)	Fencing (Build)	Gates (Build)	Outbuildings (Build)	Pasture Supply	Pasture Support	Property Services	Racing Tracks (Build)	Show Jumps (Design)	Stables (Build)	Stables (Design)	Swimming Pools (Build)	Swimming Pools (Design)
DEBDALE HORSES, Leicester (YH04004)			●				●	●	●		●			●	●					●																														
E D SIMPSON & SON, Leicester (YH04400)																																										●								
EASTWELL HALL STABLES, Melton Mowbray (YH04517)							●																																											
EUROMEC, Market Harborough (YH04902)																																											●							
FELGATE, P S, Melton Mowbray (YH05128)							●																																											
HALL FARM STABLES, Melton Mowbray (YH06305)							●																																											
HARDWICKE LODGE STABLES, Leicester (YH06416)									●																																									
HOLISTIC RIDING, Lutterworth (YH06935)								●																																										
HOLT, J R, Peckleton (YH06989)																			●																															
IVANHOE EQUESTRIAN, Ashby-De-La-Zouch (YH07532)									●											●																														
J D GOODACRE & SON, Melton Mowbray (YH07578)																																							●											
LOMAX, CHRISTIE, Market Harborough (YH08780)							●								●																																			
LYNCHGATE FARM RIDING SCHOOL, Hinckley (YH08925)								●	●					●										●	●																									
MACAULEY, N J, Melton Mowbray (YH08983)							●																																											
MORGAN, K A, Melton Mowbray (YH09808)																●																																		
P & G STABLES, Leicester (YH10630)								●	●					●			●			●				●		●	●	●																						
PALMERS, Hinckley (YH10692)																																										●								
PARSONAGE, GARY, Melton Mowbray (YH10798)							●						●																																					
PERRY, M A C, Lutterworth (YH10987)									●	●														●	●			●																						
PICKERING, J A, Hinckley (YH11083)							●																																											
SCHOOL OF NATIONAL EQUITATION, Loughborough (YH12521)			●		●				●		●									●	●			●	●	●	●	●																						
SMITH, D MURRAY, Market Harborough (YH12949)							●																																											
SOMERBY EQUESTRIAN CTRE, Melton Mowbray (YH13060)																								●	●	●	●	●																						
SPRING, JEREMY, Cosby (YH13248)			●				●				●		●																																					
SWAN LODGE, Melton Mowbray (YH13689)								●	●		●			●			●			●			●	●	●	●	●																							
TILL, J A, Glenfield (YH14148)		●																																																
VISCORIDE, Lutterworth (YH14733)																															●			●																
WALKER, RICHARD, Melton Mowbray (YH14856)							●																																											
WALLACE, JANE, Market Harborough (YH14864)							●																																											
WHARTON, J R H, Melton Mowbray (YH15265)							●																																											
WITHAM VILLA RIDING CTRE, Leicester (YH15620)	●		●					●	●	●	●	●	●	●			●			●		●	●	●	●	●	●	●			●	●																		
LINCOLNSHIRE																																																		

Business Profile
Training (shaded area)
Course, Arena, Buildings and Pasture

by Country by County

Name	Coaches	Harness Trainer	Dressage Training	Polo Trainer	Side-saddle specialist	Side-saddle trainer	Trainers	Training (1 to 1)	Training (Children)	Training (Disabled)	Training (Dressage)	Training (Flat)	Training (Freelance)	Training (Group)	Training (Horse Breaking)	Training (Jockey)	Training (Jumps)	Training (Personnel)	Training (Point-to-Point)	Training (Riding)	Training (SteepleChase)	Training (To become a Trainer)	Training for Examination	Work with Children 10-16	Work with Children under 10	Work with Senior Citizens	Work with Students	Work with the Disabled	Architectural Advice	Architectural Planning	Arenas (large) for hire	Arenas (small) for hire	Arenas Indoor (Build)	Arenas Outdoor (Build)	Building Maintenance	Building Repairs	Cross Country Course (Build)	Cross Country Course (Design)	Fencing (Build)	Gates (Build)	Outbuildings (Build)	Pasture Supply	Pasture Support	Property Services	Racing Tracks (Build)	Show Jumps (Design)	Stables (Build)	Stables (Design)	Swimming Pools (Build)	Swimming Pools (Design)
A W RHOADES SADDLERY, Market Rasen (YH00068)																								●			●	●																						
ADVANTA, Sleaford (YH00193)																																										●								
ARENA UK, Grantham (YH00517)																	●														●																			
AZTEC FENCING, Spalding (YH00707)																																							●											
BELTON, C, Louth (YH01255)							●						●																																					
BROOK HSE FARM, Louth (YH02037)									●	●																																								
BUCKMINSTER LODGE, Grantham (YH02203)																								●	●																									
C W G, Stamford (YH02399)																																										●								
C W G, Market Rasen (YH02400)																																										●								
CALDERS & GRANDIDGE, Boston (YH02436)																																							●											
CHARNICAL RIDING CTRE, Gainsborough (YH02772)									●								●																																	
CLAPHAM, DIANA, Grantham (YH02945)							●																																											
EMPIRE STABLES, Lincoln (YH04658)																																							●											
EVENTERS INT, Grantham (YH04940)							●													●																														
GLEN RIVER RIDING SCHOOL, Grantham (YH05826)								●	●					●									●																											
GOLLINGS, S, Louth (YH05898)							●																																											
GREAT PONTON UK CHASERS, Grantham (YH06042)			●																													●																		
HENSON, LUCY, Lincoln (YH06689)							●																																											
HILL HSE, Market Rasen (YH06820)								●	●	●	●			●			●						●								●	●																		
HOLMES JOINERY, Market Rasen (YH06972)																																							●											
JAMES GIVEN RACING, Gainsborough (YH07668)							●					●									●																													
KEY, J U, Boston (YH08114)								●	●	●				●																																				
LAMYMAN, S, Louth (YH08378)							●																																											
LANNI, JOHN, Grantham (YH08419)																	●																				●													
LAUGHTON WOOD EQUESTRIAN CTRE, Gainsborough (YH08449)								●	●	●				●			●																																	
LIMES FARM, Grantham (YH08634)																																							●											
LIMESTONE STUD, Gainsborough (YH08637)							●																																											
MILL VIEW FARM, Sleaford (YH09588)								●	●	●	●						●																																	
MONTEITH, HELEN, Grantham (YH09731)							●																																											
MONTEITH, PETER, Grantham (YH09732)							●																																											
MOUNT HOUSE STABLES, Gainsborough (YH09888)							●																																											
OAKWOOD RIDING SERVICES, Spalding (YH10410)			●				●				●		●																																					

Business Profile

Training (shaded area)

Course, Arena, Buildings and Pasture

by Country by County	Coaches	Harness Trainer	Dressage Training	Polo Trainer	Side-saddle specialist	Side-saddle trainer	Trainers	Training (1 to 1)	Training (Children)	Training (Disabled)	Training (Dressage)	Training (Flat)	Training (Freelance)	Training (Group)	Training (Horse Breaking)	Training (Jockey)	Training (Jumps)	Training (Personnel)	Training (Point-to-Point)	Training (Riding)	Training (SteepleChase)	Training (To become a Trainer)	Training for Examination	Work with Children 10-16	Work with Children under 10	Work with Senior Citizens	Work with Students	Work with the Disabled	Architectural Advice	Architectural Planning	Arenas (large) for hire	Arenas (small) for hire	Arenas Indoor (Build)	Arenas Outdoor (Build)	Building Maintenance	Building Repairs	Cross Country Course (Build)	Cross Country Course (Design)	Fencing (Build)	Gates (Build)	Outbuildings (Build)	Pasture Supply	Pasture Support	Property Services	Racing Tracks (Build)	Show Jumps (Design)	Stables (Build)	Stables (Design)	Swimming Pools (Build)	Swimming Pools (Design)
ORCHARD FARM EQUESTRIAN, Skegness (YH10529)								●	●					●			●															●																			
PADDOCKS RIDING CTRE, Grantham (YH10675)								●		●	●			●						●								●																							
PARK RIDING SCHOOL, Lincoln (YH10735)									●	●										●			●																												
POPPYFIELDS, Lincoln (YH11275)			●				●	●	●		●		●	●			●			●		●	●	●	●	●					●																				
REDNIL EQUESTRIAN CTRE, Lincoln (YH11716)								●	●	●	●			●			●			●				●	●	●		●				●																			
S & B STABLES, Alford (YH12309)								●	●	●	●			●			●						●																												
SHEEPGATE EQUESTRIAN, Boston (YH12696)								●	●		●			●			●						●																												
SHEEPGATE TACK & TOGS, Boston (YH12697)											●												●								●																				
SMITH, C, Wellingore (YH12943)							●																																												
SPICER, R C, Spalding (YH13202)							●																																												
THORPE, MERVYN, Stamford (YH14096)																																							●												
TYLER ANIMAL SYSTEMS, Grantham (YH14520)																																							●												
UFFINGTON RIDING STABLES, Stamford (YH14540)								●	●					●	●									●	●																										
W N SHRIVE & SON, Skegness (YH14784)																																									●									
WALTON, HELEN L, Grantham (YH14891)							●																																												
WARD, V C, Grantham (YH14911)							●																																												
LINCOLNSHIRE (NORTH EAST)																																																			
R G EQUESTRIAN, Grimsby (YH11536)															●		●	●		●			●	●	●	●	●	●				●																			
STRAWSON, VIRGINIA, Grimsby (YH13569)							●																																												
LINCOLNSHIRE (NORTH)																																																			
FORBEK FARM, Scunthorpe (YH05316)																							●																												
LONDON (GREATER)																																																			
ALDBOROUGH HALL, Ilford (YH00252)								●	●		●			●			●			●		●	●	●	●	●	●	●																							
ALDERSBROOK RIDING SCHOOL, London (YH00257)									●	●																																								
BARNFIELDS, London (YH00986)								●	●	●				●						●		●	●																												
BELMONT RACING STABLES, Mill Hill (YH01248)							●																																												
BELMONT RIDING CTRE, London (YH01249)							●																																												
BUNN, CLAUDIA, Pershore (YH02225)							●																																												
CARRINGTON, WALTER, London (YH02590)													●																																						
CIVIL SV, London (YH02933)								●		●				●																																					
DECATHLON SPORTS & LEISURE, London (YH04009)																								●	●																										
DOCKLANDS CARRIAGE DRIVING, East Ham (YH04156)							●																																												

Business Profile

Training (shaded area)

Course, Arena, Buildings and Pasture

by Country by County

by Country by County	Coaches	Harness Trainer	Dressage Training	Polo Trainer	Side-saddle specialist	Side-saddle trainer	Trainers	Training (1 to 1)	Training (Children)	Training (Disabled)	Training (Dressage)	Training (Flat)	Training (Freelance)	Training (Group)	Training (Horse Breaking)	Training (Jockey)	Training (Jumps)	Training (Personnel)	Training (Point-to-Point)	Training (Riding)	Training (SteepleChase)	Training (To become a Trainer)	Training for Examination	Work with Children 10-16	Work with Children under 10	Work with Senior Citizens	Work with Students	Work with the Disabled
DOCKLANDS EQUESTRIAN CTRE, London (YH04157)																												●
DUFFIN, JULIA, Ealing (YH04317)					●																							
GOULDS GREEN, Uxbridge (YH05952)								●	●	●				●			●											
HORSE HOUSE, Northwood (YH07123)							●																					
HOWKINS & HARRISON, London (YH07234)																												
HYDE PARK RIDING WEAR, London (YH07345)			●					●	●		●			●														
HYDE PARK STABLES, London (YH07346)								●	●					●														
ISSEA - GB, London (YH07527)								●	●					●														
KENSINGTON STABLES, London (YH08078)								●			●			●														
KINGS OAK EQUESTRIAN CTRE, Enfield (YH08196)																	●											
L H H ANIMAL FEEDS, Enfield (YH08321)																												
LEE VALLEY RIDING CTRE, London (YH08519)								●	●	●	●			●			●			●			●					●
LITTLEBOURNE FARM, Uxbridge (YH08703)								●	●	●	●			●			●											
LONDON EQUESTRIAN CTRE, London (YH08784)								●	●	●	●			●			●											
LONDON EQUESTRIAN CTRE, Finchley (YH08785)								●	●		●			●			●						●	●	●			
MOTTINGHAM FARM, London (YH09876)								●	●					●														
NATURAL PARTNERSHIP, London (YH10053)							●	●					●	●	●													
QUEEN ELIZABETH RIDING SCHOOL, Chingford (YH11488)									●											●								
RIDGWAY STABLES, London (YH11870)																									●			
STAGS, London (YH13339)																												
SUZANNE'S RIDING SCHOOL, Harrow (YH13679)								●	●	●	●			●									●					
WILLOW TREE RIDING, London (YH15504)								●	●	●				●														●
WIMBLEDON VILLAGE STABLES, London (YH15557)											●																	
WOOD HALL STUD, Shenley (YH15658)							●																					
MANCHESTER (GREATER)																												
CARRINGTON RIDING, Manchester (YH02589)								●	●					●										●	●			
CROFT END EQUESTRIAN CTRE, Oldham (YH03613)											●						●											
EQUITACK, Bolton (YH04823)								●						●	●		●							●	●	●	●	●
GODLEY STUD RIDING SCHOOL, Manchester (YH05868)								●	●		●			●			●						●	●	●			
HADFIELD, G, Manchester (YH06264)		●																										
KENYON FARM RIDING CTRE, Manchester (YH08094)								●	●		●			●			●							●	●			
MATCHMOOR RIDING CTRE, Bolton (YH09257)								●	●	●	●	●	●	●	●		●			●		●	●	●	●			●

by Country by County	Architectural Advice	Architectural Planning	Arenas (large) for hire	Arenas (small) for hire	Arenas Indoor (Build)	Arenas Outdoor (Build)	Building Maintenance	Building Repairs	Cross Country Course (Build)	Cross Country Course (Design)	Fencing (Build)	Gates (Build)	Outbuildings (Build)	Pasture Supply	Pasture Support	Property Services	Racing Tracks (Build)	Show Jumps (Design)	Stables (Build)	Stables (Design)	Swimming Pools (Build)	Swimming Pools (Design)
DOCKLANDS EQUESTRIAN CTRE, London (YH04157)																						
DUFFIN, JULIA, Ealing (YH04317)																						
GOULDS GREEN, Uxbridge (YH05952)																						
HORSE HOUSE, Northwood (YH07123)																						
HOWKINS & HARRISON, London (YH07234)																●						
HYDE PARK RIDING WEAR, London (YH07345)																						
HYDE PARK STABLES, London (YH07346)																						
ISSEA - GB, London (YH07527)																						
KENSINGTON STABLES, London (YH08078)																						
KINGS OAK EQUESTRIAN CTRE, Enfield (YH08196)																						
L H H ANIMAL FEEDS, Enfield (YH08321)											●			●	●							
LEE VALLEY RIDING CTRE, London (YH08519)																						
LITTLEBOURNE FARM, Uxbridge (YH08703)																						
LONDON EQUESTRIAN CTRE, London (YH08784)																						
LONDON EQUESTRIAN CTRE, Finchley (YH08785)																						
MOTTINGHAM FARM, London (YH09876)																						
NATURAL PARTNERSHIP, London (YH10053)																						
QUEEN ELIZABETH RIDING SCHOOL, Chingford (YH11488)																						
RIDGWAY STABLES, London (YH11870)																						
STAGS, London (YH13339)																●						
SUZANNE'S RIDING SCHOOL, Harrow (YH13679)																						
WILLOW TREE RIDING, London (YH15504)																						
WIMBLEDON VILLAGE STABLES, London (YH15557)																						
WOOD HALL STUD, Shenley (YH15658)																						
MANCHESTER (GREATER)																						
CARRINGTON RIDING, Manchester (YH02589)				●																		
CROFT END EQUESTRIAN CTRE, Oldham (YH03613)																						
EQUITACK, Bolton (YH04823)																						
GODLEY STUD RIDING SCHOOL, Manchester (YH05868)																						
HADFIELD, G, Manchester (YH06264)																						
KENYON FARM RIDING CTRE, Manchester (YH08094)																						
MATCHMOOR RIDING CTRE, Bolton (YH09257)																						

Business Profile

Training (shaded area) **Course, Arena, Buildings and Pasture**

by Country by County

Company	Coaches	Harness Trainer	Dressage Training	Polo Trainer	Side-saddle specialist	Side-saddle trainer	Trainers	Training (1 to 1)	Training (Children)	Training (Disabled)	Training (Dressage)	Training (Flat)	Training (Freelance)	Training (Group)	Training (Horse Breaking)	Training (Jockey)	Training (Jumps)	Training (Personnel)	Training (Point-to-Point)	Training (Riding)	Training (SteepleChase)	Training (To become a Trainer)	Training for Examination	Work with Children 10-16	Work with Children under 10	Work with Senior Citizens	Work with Students	Work with the Disabled	Architectural Advice	Architectural Planning	Arenas (large) for hire	Arenas (small) for hire	Arenas Indoor (Build)	Arenas Outdoor (Build)	Building Maintenance	Building Repairs	Cross Country Course (Build)	Cross Country Course (Design)	Fencing (Build)	Gates (Build)	Outbuildings (Build)	Pasture Supply	Pasture Support	Property Services	Racing Tracks (Build)	Show Jumps (Design)	Stables (Build)	Stables (Design)	Swimming Pools (Build)	Swimming Pools (Design)
MOSSBROOK ARENA & STUD, Astley (YH09866)																															●																			
OAKHILL RIDING SCHOOL, Manchester (YH10384)								●	●		●			●			●							●	●																									
RYDERS FARM, Bolton (YH12297)			●					●	●	●	●			●			●			●				●	●	●	●	●			●											●								
SHORESIDE STABLES, Manchester (YH12759)															●																																			
STAMFORD RIDING STABLES, Mossley (YH13354)								●	●					●						●		●	●		●																									
MERSEYSIDE																																																		
BARNSTON RIDING CTRE, Wirral (YH00991)								●	●					●									●																											
BOWLERS RIDING SCHOOL, Liverpool (YH01716)								●	●	●	●			●			●						●	●	●	●		●																						
CROXTETH PK RIDING CTRE, Liverpool (YH03685)								●	●		●			●			●							●	●																									
LONGACRES, Liverpool (YH08806)																								●	●	●	●	●																						
PARK LANE LIVERIES, Wirral (YH10730)								●	●	●	●						●							●	●																									
TARBOCK GREEN RIDING SCHOOL, Prescot (YH13869)								●	●	●	●	●		●			●						●	●	●																									
MIDLANDS (WEST)																																																		
ALBRIGHTON FEEDS, Wolverhampton (YH00249)																																										●								
BEARLEY CROSS STABLES, Solihull (YH01121)									●				●		●		●			●												●																		
BUBBENHALL BRIDGE, Coventry (YH02182)								●	●	●				●									●	●	●																									
CASTLE HILL RIDING SCHOOL, Coventry (YH02627)						●		●	●		●	●		●	●		●						●																											
DOMINION RACING STABLES, Alvechurch (YH04172)							●																																											
DRIVALL, Halesowen (YH04276)																																							●											
FOXHILLS, Walsall (YH05435)			●				●	●	●		●			●	●		●			●				●	●							●																		
GALLAGHER POWER FENCE, Coventry (YH05617)																																							●											
GORSE FARM ARENA, Aldridge (YH05939)																	●																																	
HOWKINS & HARRISON, Coventry (YH07235)																																												●						
KINGSWOOD EQUESTRIAN CTRE, Wolverhampton (YH08210)									●	●	●	●					●																																	
MOOR FARM STABLES, Coventry (YH09745)								●	●		●	●		●			●						●	●	●	●	●																							
OVERIDER, Coventry (YH10593)																								●	●		●																							
POOLE, JOHN, Alvechurch (YH11265)							●										●																																	
SEECHEM EQUESTRIAN CTRE, Birmingham (YH12607)																	●																																	
TOM HOOPER FENCING, Birmingham (YH14214)																																							●											
TRUEMANS HEATH, Solihull (YH14420)								●	●	●	●	●		●	●		●	●		●			●	●	●	●	●	●																						
WITHYBROOK STABLES, Coventry (YH15629)								●	●	●	●	●		●			●						●																											
WOLVERHAMPTON RACECOURSE, Wolverhampton (YH15650)							●																																											

www.hccyourhorse.com

Business Profile
Training (shaded area)
Course, Arena, Buildings and Pasture

by Country by County

	Coaches	Harness Trainer	Dressage Training	Polo Trainer	Side-saddle specialist	Side-saddle trainer	Trainers	Training (1 to 1)	Training (Children)	Training (Disabled)	Training (Dressage)	Training (Flat)	Training (Freelance)	Training (Group)	Training (Horse Breaking)	Training (Jockey)	Training (Jumps)	Training (Personnel)	Training (Point-to-Point)	Training (Riding)	Training (SteepleChase)	Training (To become a Trainer)	Training for Examination	Work with Children 10-16	Work with Children under 10	Work with Senior Citizens	Work with Students	Work with the Disabled	Architectural Advice	Architectural Planning	Arenas (large) for hire	Arenas (small) for hire	Arenas Indoor (Build)	Arenas Outdoor (Build)	Building Maintenance	Building Repairs	Cross Country Course (Build)	Cross Country Course (Design)	Fencing (Build)	Gates (Build)	Outbuildings (Build)	Pasture Supply	Pasture Support	Property Services	Racing Tracks (Build)	Show Jumps (Design)	Stables (Build)	Stables (Design)	Swimming Pools (Build)	Swimming Pools (Design)
NORFOLK																																																		
BARRIER ANIMAL HEALTHCARE, Attleborough (YH01021)																																											●							
BEXWELL TRACTORS, Downham Market (YH01350)																																											●							
BLACKBOROUGH END, King's Lynn (YH01477)																															●																			
C W G, East Dereham (YH02401)																																										●								
CROFT FARM RIDING CTRE, Great Yarmouth (YH03615)								●	●	●	●	●		●	●					●		●	●					●																						
F J LUCAS STABLES, King's Lynn (YH04994)																																															●	●		
GREENACRES RIDING SCHOOL, King's Lynn (YH06079)							●	●			●		●	●			●			●				●	●																									
H & C BEART, King's Lynn (YH06207)																																										●								
HEATHER ARABIAN RACING STUD, Norwich (YH06625)							●																																											
HIGH HSE EVENTING CTRE, King's Lynn (YH06763)							●																																											
HORSETALK, King's Lynn (YH07176)																								●	●	●	●	●																						
J C SCHAAY TIMBER BUILDINGS, Diss (YH07576)																																							●					●						
JOHN PARKER, Diss (YH07804)							●																																											
KONGSKILDE UK, Holt (YH08290)																																											●							
LEWIS, J E, Norwich (YH08592)													●																																					
LODDON, Norwich (YH08766)																																							●											
MAYWAY, Thetford (YH09308)									●															●	●																									
NICHOLSON FARM MACHINERY, Downham Market (YH10189)																																											●							
NORTH FARM RACING STABLES, Norwich (YH10261)							●																																											
PAWLEY, ZARA, Kings Lynn (YH10840)			●				●				●		●				●																																	
PRODDROMOW, GEORGE, East Harling (YH11427)							●																																											
RUNCTON HALL, King's Lynn (YH12233)			●					●	●	●	●			●	●			●		●			●	●	●	●	●	●			●	●					●													
THOMPSON, EMILY, King's Lynn (YH14035)							●																																											
WESTON PARK EQUESTRIAN CTRE, Norwich (YH15224)																								●	●		●				●																			
YARHAM, A, Great Yarmouth (YH15885)		●																																																
NORTHAMPTONSHIRE																																																		
ASHTON STABLES, Northampton (YH00614)											●									●																														
BAILEY, K C, Daventry (YH00802)							●																																											
BOUGHTON MILL RIDING SCHOOL, Northampton (YH01669)								●	●		●	●		●			●							●	●																									
BRAMPTON STABLES, Northampton (YH01794)			●				●				●																																							
BROOK FARM, Wellingborough (YH02033)								●	●		●			●																		●																		

Business Profile

Training (shaded area) Course, Arena, Buildings and Pasture

by Country by County

	Coaches	Harness Trainer	Dressage Training	Polo Trainer	Side-saddle specialist	Side-saddle trainer	Trainers	Training (1 to 1)	Training (Children)	Training (Disabled)	Training (Dressage)	Training (Flat)	Training (Freelance)	Training (Group)	Training (Horse Breaking)	Training (Jockey)	Training (Jumps)	Training (Personnel)	Training (Point-to-Point)	Training (Riding)	Training (SteepleChase)	Training (To become a Trainer)	Training for Examination	Work with Children 10-16	Work with Children under 10	Work with Senior Citizens	Work with Students	Work with the Disabled	Architectural Advice	Architectural Planning	Arenas (large) for hire	Arenas (small) for hire	Arenas Indoor (Build)	Arenas Outdoor (Build)	Building Maintenance	Building Repairs	Cross Country Course (Build)	Cross Country Course (Design)	Fencing (Build)	Gates (Build)	Outbuildings (Build)	Pasture Supply	Pasture Support	Property Services	Racing Tracks (Build)	Show Jumps (Design)	Stables (Build)	Stables (Design)	Swimming Pools (Build)	Swimming Pools (Design)
BRYLINE RIDING SURFACES, Roade (YH02172)																																							●											
C W G, Towcester (YH02402)																																										●								
CROSS COUNTRY HORSE TRANSPORT, Northampton (YH03643)							●																																											
EAST LODGE FARM RIDING EST, Northampton (YH04479)									●	●	●	●		●	●		●							●	●																									
EDENGATE SADDLERY, Northampton (YH04550)																								●	●		●																							
HARRINGWORTH MANOR, Corby (YH06461)								●	●	●		●		●			●							●	●	●	●	●																						
HARVEST SVS, West Farndon (YH06510)																																															●	●		
HENRY H BLETSOE & SON, Kettering (YH06684)																																												●						
HOWKINS & HARRISON, Northampton (YH07236)																																												●						
MANOR FARM RIDING SCHOOL, Wellingborough (YH09106)																								●	●	●	●	●																						
MOBLEY, HELEN, Brackley (YH09694)							●																																											
MOULTON CLGE, Northampton (YH09883)																							●				●																							
NORMAN & SPICER, Daventry (YH10235)																																										●								
SHUCKBURGH HSE RIDING CTRE, Naseby (YH12772)			●				●				●						●																																	
SMYTH-OSBOURNE, J, Towcester (YH13016)							●																																											
STOCKDALE, TIM, Roade (YH13490)																	●																																	
STUBBEN, Corby (YH13600)											●													●																										
TAYLOR, NIGEL & ANN, Daventry (YH13907)							●																																											
THREE SHIRES LIVERY CTRE, Wellingborough (YH14107)																																●		●																
UPSON, J R, Towcester (YH14614)							●																																											
WATTS & WATTS SADDLERY, Northampton (YH15003)					●																																													
WHITMORE, SUE, Wellingborough (YH15368)													●																																					
NORTHUMBERLAND																																																		
CHARLTON, J I A, Stocksfield (YH02767)							●																																											
DODDS, J P, Alnwick (YH04159)							●																																											
EQUILINK, Alnwick (YH04751)																																												●						
FARMWAY, Morpeth (YH05074)																																							●	●										
FLEMING, BARBARA SLANE, Alnwick (YH05270)			●				●				●		●																																					
HALDANE, J S, Mindrum (YH06289)							●																																											
JOICEY, (LADY), Cornhill-on-Tweed (YH07849)			●				●				●																																							
LOGIC ATV EQUIPMENT, Hexham (YH08777)																																											●							
PALLINSBURN STABLES, Cornhill-on-Tweed (YH10690)							●																																											

Business Profile

Training (shaded area) Course, Arena, Buildings and Pasture

by Country by County

	Coaches	Harness Trainer	Dressage Training	Polo Trainer	Side-saddle specialist	Side-saddle trainer	Trainers	Training (1 to 1)	Training (Children)	Training (Disabled)	Training (Dressage)	Training (Flat)	Training (Freelance)	Training (Group)	Training (Horse Breaking)	Training (Jockey)	Training (Jumps)	Training (Personnel)	Training (Point-to-Point)	Training (Riding)	Training (SteepleChase)	Training (To become a Trainer)	Training for Examination	Work with Children 10-16	Work with Children under 10	Work with Senior Citizens	Work with Students	Work with the Disabled	Architectural Advice	Architectural Planning	Arenas (large) for hire	Arenas (small) for hire	Arenas Indoor (Build)	Arenas Outdoor (Build)	Building Maintenance	Building Repairs	Cross Country Course (Build)	Cross Country Course (Design)	Fencing (Build)	Gates (Build)	Outbuildings (Build)	Pasture Supply	Pasture Support	Property Services	Racing Tracks (Build)	Show Jumps (Design)	Stables (Build)	Stables (Design)	Swimming Pools (Build)	Swimming Pools (Design)
REDESDALE RIDING CTRE, Otterburn (YH11710)			●					●	●		●						●			●			●	●	●	●	●	●																						
SINDERHOPE PONY TREKKING CTRE, Hexham (YH12850)								●	●					●						●				●	●																									
THOMPSON, V, Alnwick (YH14045)							●																																											
WOOPERTON, Alnwick (YH15770)			●				●	●			●		●	●	●		●			●			●				●					●	●				●	●												
NOTTINGHAMSHIRE																																																		
ANDREW, M, Worksop (YH00394)																																					●													
AVERHAM PK, Newark (YH00681)							●																																											
BOWRING, S R, Mansfield (YH01724)							●																																											
BRENNAN, OWEN, Worksop (YH01844)							●																																											
BRIDLE WAY & GAUNTLEYS, Newark (YH01892)																																			●							●								
C W G, Worksop (YH02404)																																										●								
CLGE FARM, Newark (YH03026)			●					●	●	●	●	●	●	●			●			●			●	●	●		●	●																						
CTRE - LINES, Newark (YH03694)			●				●	●			●		●	●	●					●																														
DECATHLON SPORTS & LEISURE, Nottingham (YH04010)																								●	●																									
F MARTIN & SON, Arnold (YH04995)																																							●											
FIRBECK, Worksop (YH05222)			●				●				●		●				●																																	
HODSOCK STABLES, Worksop (YH06915)													●																																					
HOLISTIC HORSECARE, Northampton (YH06934)							●	●	●				●	●	●			●		●		●	●	●	●	●	●	●																						
KIRKFIELD STABLES, Lower Blidworth (YH08235)																	●																																	
LANEHAM LIVERY STABLE, Retford (YH08392)								●		●	●		●	●						●																														
LINGS LANE RIDING STABLES, Nottingham (YH08662)								●	●	●										●																														
MALLENDER BROS, Worksop (YH09051)																																								●										
MANSFIELD SAND, Mansfield (YH09123)																																	●	●											●					
MARVIN, R F, Newark (YH09233)							●																																											
PEARSON, A, Worksop (YH10877)																																					●													
PINEWOOD STABLES, Worksop (YH11127)							●																																											
POLGLASE, MARK, Southwell (YH11200)							●																																											
PYRAH, MALCOLM, Nottingham (YH11471)													●				●																																	
ROWLAND, M E, Lower Blidworth (YH12168)							●																																											
ST CLEMENTS LODGE, Nottingham (YH13274)								●	●		●	●		●						●				●	●	●	●																							
SUTTON MANOR FARM, Retford (YH13673)											●									●				●																										
TRAINING BARN 7, Newark (YH14343)							●																																											

Business Profile
Training (shaded area)
Course, Arena, Buildings and Pasture

by Country by County

by Country by County	Coaches	Harness Trainer	Dressage Training	Polo Trainer	Side-saddle specialist	Side-saddle trainer	Trainers	Training (1 to 1)	Training (Children)	Training (Disabled)	Training (Dressage)	Training (Flat)	Training (Freelance)	Training (Group)	Training (Horse Breaking)	Training (Jockey)	Training (Jumps)	Training (Personnel)	Training (Point-to-Point)	Training (Riding)	Training (SteepleChase)	Training (To become a Trainer)	Training for Examination	Work with Children 10-16	Work with Children under 10	Work with Senior Citizens	Work with Students	Work with the Disabled	Architectural Advice	Architectural Planning	Arenas (large) for hire	Arenas (small) for hire	Arenas Indoor (Build)	Arenas Outdoor (Build)	Building Maintenance	Building Repairs	Cross Country Course (Build)	Cross Country Course (Design)	Fencing (Build)	Gates (Build)	Outbuildings (Build)	Pasture Supply	Pasture Support	Property Services	Racing Tracks (Build)	Show Jumps (Design)	Stables (Build)	Stables (Design)	Swimming Pools (Build)	Swimming Pools (Design)
VICTORIAN CARRIAGES, Newark (YH14710)							●																																											
WELLOW PK, Newark (YH15077)							●																																											
WOODWARD, GARRY, Worksop (YH15757)							●																																											
OXFORDSHIRE																																																		
ADAS, Kidlington (YH00176)																																										●		●						
ANTWICK STUD, Wantage (YH00466)							●																																											
ARLINGTON POLO, Kidlington (YH00533)							●																																											
ASTI STUD & SADDLERY, Faringdon (YH00633)			●					●	●		●	●	●	●										●	●																									
BLACKHEATH LIVERY STABLES, Burford (YH01484)													●																																					
BLEWBURY RIDING/TRAINING CTRE, Didcot (YH01539)								●	●	●	●			●																																				
BOSLEY, M R, Wantage (YH01655)							●																																											
BOWLBY EQUINE, Wantage (YH01711)							●																																											
CANDY, H, Wantage (YH02497)							●																																											
CHURN STABLES, Didcot (YH02916)							●																																											
CLAYSON-HASELWOOD, Banbury (YH03001)																																												●						
COACH HSE STABLES, Wantage (YH03105)							●																																											
DOBBINS CLOBBER, Thame (YH04150)																																										●								
DREWE, C J, Didcot (YH04270)							●																																											
DURALOCK, Chipping Norton (YH04366)																																							●											
E P BARRUS, Bicester (YH04418)																																											●							
EAST END FARM RIDING SCHOOL, Wallingford (YH04474)									●				●											●	●							●																		
EAST MANTON STABLES, Wantage (YH04480)							●																																											
EDGECOTE HSE STABLES, Banbury (YH04555)							●																																											
ETHERINGTON-SMITH, MICHAEL, Banbury (YH04884)																																					●													
FAIRSPEAR EQUESTRIAN CTRE, Witney (YH05028)							●																																											
FAURIE, E, Chipping Norton (YH05105)			●				●				●																																							
FRENCH DAVIS, D, Wantage (YH05488)							●																																											
GANDOLFO, D R, Wantage (YH05639)							●																																											
GODINGTON STUD, Bicester (YH05867)			●								●				●					●			●				●																							
H J WEBB & SON, Faringdon (YH06227)																																							●					●						
HALL PLACE STABLES, Wantage (YH06308)							●																																											
HIATT, P W, Banbury (YH06739)							●																																											

www.hccyourhorse.com

Business Profile

Training (shaded area) Course, Arena, Buildings and Pasture

by Country by County

Name	Coaches	Harness Trainer	Dressage Training	Polo Trainer	Side-saddle specialist	Side-saddle trainer	Trainers	Training (1 to 1)	Training (Children)	Training (Disabled)	Training (Dressage)	Training (Flat)	Training (Freelance)	Training (Group)	Training (Horse Breaking)	Training (Jockey)	Training (Jumps)	Training (Personnel)	Training (Point-to-Point)	Training (Riding)	Training (SteepleChase)	Training (To become a Trainer)	Training for Examination	Work with Children 10-16	Work with Children under 10	Work with Senior Citizens	Work with Students	Work with the Disabled
IRVING, HEATHER, Banbury (YH07510)							●																					
JARVIS, A P, Didcot (YH07705)							●																					
JODS GALORE, Henley-on-Thames (YH07775)																								●	●			
JOHN WEBBER & PARTNERS, Banbury (YH07816)							●																					
JOHNSON-HOUGHTON, R F, Didcot (YH07842)							●																					
KNIGHT, HENRIETTA, Wantage (YH08261)							●						●															
LUCKETT, GEOFF, Banbury (YH08887)																	●											
MANOR FARM RACING STABLES, Wantage (YH09103)							●																					
MORLOCK, C, Wantage (YH09822)							●																					
NEW HOUSE LIVERY, Abingdon (YH10109)																												
OLD MANOR STABLES, Wantage (YH10463)							●																					
P F I COLE, Wantage (YH10638)							●																					
PIGEON HOUSE STABLES, Witney (YH11095)								●	●			●		●			●	●		●			●	●			●	
SIMMONS, Henley-on-Thames (YH12824)																												
STANDLAKE EQUESTRIAN CTRE, Witney (YH13362)			●		●	●			●		●			●						●			●	●	●	●	●	●
STEPHANIE MEADOWS, Chipping Norton (YH13422)							●																					
TEDMAN HARNESS, Wheatley (YH13932)							●																					
THAMES VALLEY, Oxford (YH13973)																												
THAMES VALLEY FENCING, Chiselhampton (YH13975)																												
THINK EQUUS, Kidlington (YH13995)			●					●	●		●	●	●	●	●		●	●		●		●						
TURPINS LODGE, Banbury (YH14494)																								●	●		●	
TURVILLE VALLEY, Henley-on-Thames (YH14499)			●				●				●																	
WHITESHOOT STABLES, Blewbury (YH15357)							●																					
WILKINSON, M J, Banbury (YH15422)							●																					
RUTLAND																												
BADMINTON HORSE FEEDS, Oakham (YH00784)																												
BARROW STABLES, Oakham (YH01030)							●																					
COMPETITION HORSES, Oakham (YH03217)			●				●										●											
LAMPARD, DI, Oakham (YH08375)																	●											
MANTON LODGE STABLES, Rutland (YH09127)			●				●				●		●															
PURBRICK, LIZZIE, Oakham (YH11463)							●																					
SEDERHOLM, LARS, Oakham (YH12601)							●										●											

Name	Architectural Advice	Architectural Planning	Arenas (large) for hire	Arenas (small) for hire	Arenas Indoor (Build)	Arenas Outdoor (Build)	Building Maintenance	Building Repairs	Cross Country Course (Build)	Cross Country Course (Design)	Fencing (Build)	Gates (Build)	Outbuildings (Build)	Pasture Supply	Pasture Support	Property Services	Racing Tracks (Build)	Show Jumps (Design)	Stables (Build)	Stables (Design)	Swimming Pools (Build)	Swimming Pools (Design)
IRVING, HEATHER, Banbury (YH07510)																						
JARVIS, A P, Didcot (YH07705)																						
JODS GALORE, Henley-on-Thames (YH07775)																						
JOHN WEBBER & PARTNERS, Banbury (YH07816)																						
JOHNSON-HOUGHTON, R F, Didcot (YH07842)																						
KNIGHT, HENRIETTA, Wantage (YH08261)																						
LUCKETT, GEOFF, Banbury (YH08887)																						
MANOR FARM RACING STABLES, Wantage (YH09103)																						
MORLOCK, C, Wantage (YH09822)																						
NEW HOUSE LIVERY, Abingdon (YH10109)				●																		
OLD MANOR STABLES, Wantage (YH10463)																						
P F I COLE, Wantage (YH10638)																						
PIGEON HOUSE STABLES, Witney (YH11095)																						
SIMMONS, Henley-on-Thames (YH12824)																●						
STANDLAKE EQUESTRIAN CTRE, Witney (YH13362)			●		●																	
STEPHANIE MEADOWS, Chipping Norton (YH13422)																						
TEDMAN HARNESS, Wheatley (YH13932)																						
THAMES VALLEY, Oxford (YH13973)					●	●					●											
THAMES VALLEY FENCING, Chiselhampton (YH13975)			●								●											
THINK EQUUS, Kidlington (YH13995)																						
TURPINS LODGE, Banbury (YH14494)																						
TURVILLE VALLEY, Henley-on-Thames (YH14499)																						
WHITESHOOT STABLES, Blewbury (YH15357)																						
WILKINSON, M J, Banbury (YH15422)																						
RUTLAND																						
BADMINTON HORSE FEEDS, Oakham (YH00784)														●								
BARROW STABLES, Oakham (YH01030)																						
COMPETITION HORSES, Oakham (YH03217)																						
LAMPARD, DI, Oakham (YH08375)																						
MANTON LODGE STABLES, Rutland (YH09127)																						
PURBRICK, LIZZIE, Oakham (YH11463)																						
SEDERHOLM, LARS, Oakham (YH12601)																						

Business Profile

Training (shaded area) Course, Arena, Buildings and Pasture

by Country by County

	Coaches	Harness Trainer	Dressage Training	Polo Trainer	Side-saddle specialist	Side-saddle trainer	Trainers	Training (1 to 1)	Training (Children)	Training (Disabled)	Training (Dressage)	Training (Flat)	Training (Freelance)	Training (Group)	Training (Horse Breaking)	Training (Jockey)	Training (Jumps)	Training (Personnel)	Training (Point-to-Point)	Training (Riding)	Training (SteepleChase)	Training (To become a Trainer)	Training for Examination	Work with Children 10-16	Work with Children under 10	Work with Senior Citizens	Work with Students	Work with the Disabled
SHROPSHIRE																												
BARRATT, L J, Oswestry (YH01009)							●																					
BRISBOURNE, MARK, Shrewsbury (YH01918)							●																					
BROAD ACRE, Bridgnorth (YH01987)							●																					
BROOKSHAW, S A, Shrewsbury (YH02068)							●																					
BROWNS OF WEM, Shrewsbury (YH02145)																												
BRYNORE STUD & LIVERY STABLES, Ellesmere (YH02178)													●		●									●	●	●	●	●
BURWARTON EST TIMBER, Bridgnorth (YH02297)																												
C J BLACKSMITHS, Shrewsbury (YH02375)																										●	●	●
CHARLES BRITTON CONSTRUCTION, Ellesmere (YH02754)																												
CHARTERS, SUE, Ludlow (YH02776)			●				●		●		●		●				●			●		●	●					
CRANN, P F, Bridgnorth (YH03568)																	●											
DALTON, HEATHER, Shifnal (YH03846)							●																					
DOWNTON HALL STABLES, Ludlow (YH04242)							●																					
FRESHFIELDS, Market Drayton (YH05499)																								●	●			
HAMAR, ROSITA J, Bishops Castle (YH06343)																												
HIGHGROVE SCHOOL OF RIDING, Craven Arms (YH06788)			●				●																	●	●		●	
JENKS, WILLIAM P, Bridgnorth (YH07742)							●																					
MARTIN, MICHAEL, Shrewsbury (YH09222)			●																									
MARTIN, S, Shrewsbury (YH09226)			●				●				●		●															
N W F COUNTRYSTORE, Market Drayton (YH09998)																												
NORTH FARM RIDING EST, Ludlow (YH10262)																								●	●	●	●	●
OSWESTRY EQUEST CTRE, Oswestry (YH10576)			●					●	●	●		●		●	●		●	●		●		●	●	●	●	●	●	●
PREECE, W G, Telford (YH11342)							●																					
PURKIS, IAN B, Ellesmere (YH11467)																												
RANSFORDS, Bishops Castle (YH11636)																												
TONG RIDING CTRE, Shifnal (YH14227)							●		●		●												●					
TOUCHDOWN LIVERIES, Whitchurch (YH14253)															●													
W BRYAN HORSE SERVICES, Shrewsbury (YH14753)															●		●		●									
WALL, T R, Church Stretton (YH14861)							●																					
WILDING, R J, Church Stretton (YH15409)																			●									
WYKE OF SHIFNAL, Shifnal (YH15863)																												

	Architectural Advice	Architectural Planning	Arenas (large) for hire	Arenas (small) for hire	Arenas Indoor (Build)	Arenas Outdoor (Build)	Building Maintenance	Building Repairs	Cross Country Course (Build)	Cross Country Course (Design)	Fencing (Build)	Gates (Build)	Outbuildings (Build)	Pasture Supply	Pasture Support	Property Services	Racing Tracks (Build)	Show Jumps (Design)	Stables (Build)	Stables (Design)	Swimming Pools (Build)	Swimming Pools (Design)
SHROPSHIRE																						
BARRATT, L J, Oswestry (YH01009)																						
BRISBOURNE, MARK, Shrewsbury (YH01918)																						
BROAD ACRE, Bridgnorth (YH01987)																						
BROOKSHAW, S A, Shrewsbury (YH02068)																						
BROWNS OF WEM, Shrewsbury (YH02145)																●						
BRYNORE STUD & LIVERY STABLES, Ellesmere (YH02178)																						
BURWARTON EST TIMBER, Bridgnorth (YH02297)											●											
C J BLACKSMITHS, Shrewsbury (YH02375)																						
CHARLES BRITTON CONSTRUCTION, Ellesmere (YH02754)					●	●						●	●				●		●	●		
CHARTERS, SUE, Ludlow (YH02776)																						
CRANN, P F, Bridgnorth (YH03568)																						
DALTON, HEATHER, Shifnal (YH03846)																						
DOWNTON HALL STABLES, Ludlow (YH04242)																						
FRESHFIELDS, Market Drayton (YH05499)																						
HAMAR, ROSITA J, Bishops Castle (YH06343)				●																		
HIGHGROVE SCHOOL OF RIDING, Craven Arms (YH06788)			●																			
JENKS, WILLIAM P, Bridgnorth (YH07742)																						
MARTIN, MICHAEL, Shrewsbury (YH09222)																●						
MARTIN, S, Shrewsbury (YH09226)																						
N W F COUNTRYSTORE, Market Drayton (YH09998)														●								
NORTH FARM RIDING EST, Ludlow (YH10262)																						
OSWESTRY EQUEST CTRE, Oswestry (YH10576)				●																		
PREECE, W G, Telford (YH11342)																						
PURKIS, IAN B, Ellesmere (YH11467)											●											
RANSFORDS, Bishops Castle (YH11636)											●											
TONG RIDING CTRE, Shifnal (YH14227)																						
TOUCHDOWN LIVERIES, Whitchurch (YH14253)			●	●																		
W BRYAN HORSE SERVICES, Shrewsbury (YH14753)																						
WALL, T R, Church Stretton (YH14861)																						
WILDING, R J, Church Stretton (YH15409)																						
WYKE OF SHIFNAL, Shifnal (YH15863)														●								

Business Profile

Training (shaded area) Course, Arena, Buildings and Pasture

by Country by County

SOMERSET	Coaches	Harness Trainer	Dressage Training	Polo Trainer	Side-saddle specialist	Side-saddle trainer	Trainers	Training (1 to 1)	Training (Children)	Training (Disabled)	Training (Dressage)	Training (Flat)	Training (Freelance)	Training (Group)	Training (Horse Breaking)	Training (Jockey)	Training (Jumps)	Training (Personnel)	Training (Point-to-Point)	Training (Riding)	Training (SteepleChase)	Training (To become a Trainer)	Training for Examination
ADSBOROUGH HSE STABLES, Taunton (YH00189)																							
BADCOCK & EVERED, Watchet (YH00774)																							
BADGWORTH ARENA, Axbridge (YH00781)																							
BARFORD PK RACING STABLES, Bridgwater (YH00932)							●																
BLUE MOUNTAIN FARM, Wells (YH01567)							●																
BOSSINGTON DRESSAGE STABLES, Minehead (YH01656)			●				●				●												
BRIMSMORE EQUESTRIAN CTRE, Yeovil (YH01913)								●	●	●	●	●		●			●						●
BURCOTT RIDING CTRE, Wells (YH02236)								●	●		●	●		●	●		●						
CONQUEST CTRE, Taunton (YH03243)								●															
COOK, ANGELA, Wiveliscombe (YH03255)							●																
DRAKES FARM, Ilminster (YH04256)									●														●
EBBORLANDS, Wells (YH04529)								●	●	●	●			●			●			●		●	●
FARRELL, P, Chard (YH05086)							●																
FOALE, D, Street (YH05296)							●																
GADD, CELIA, Brent Knoll (YH05604)			●				●				●												
GLEBE STABLES, Minehead (YH05819)							●																
HAM, G A, Axbridge (YH06342)							●																
HAWKE, N, Woolminstone (YH06544)							●																
HODGES, R J, Somerton (YH06909)							●																
HOLEMOOR HOUSE STABLES, Chard (YH06931)							●																
KNIGHT, GEORGE, Taunton (YH08260)							●																
P F & B NICHOLLS RACING, Shepton Mallet (YH10637)							●																
PEVLINGS FARM, Templecombe (YH11035)																							
PIPE, M C, Wellington (YH11145)							●																
POPHAM, C L, Taunton (YH11267)							●																
PRIMMORE FARM HORSES, Bridgwater (YH11396)			●				●		●		●		●				●					●	
RODFORD, P, Martock (YH12045)							●																
ROYS RIDING SCHOOL, Taunton (YH12201)								●	●			●		●			●						
RYALL, B J M, Yeovil (YH12283)							●																
SANDHILL RACING STABLES, Minehead (YH12412)							●																
SMALL, ROSALIND, South Petherton (YH12909)							●						●										

SOMERSET	Work with Children 10-16	Work with Children under 10	Work with Senior Citizens	Work with Students	Work with the Disabled	Architectural Advice	Architectural Planning	Arenas (large) for hire	Arenas (small) for hire	Arenas Indoor (Build)	Arenas Outdoor (Build)	Building Maintenance	Building Repairs	Cross Country Course (Build)	Cross Country Course (Design)	Fencing (Build)	Gates (Build)	Outbuildings (Build)	Pasture Supply	Pasture Support	Property Services	Racing Tracks (Build)	Show Jumps (Design)	Stables (Build)	Stables (Design)	Swimming Pools (Build)	Swimming Pools (Design)
ADSBOROUGH HSE STABLES, Taunton (YH00189)	●	●	●	●																							
BADCOCK & EVERED, Watchet (YH00774)																			●								
BADGWORTH ARENA, Axbridge (YH00781)								●	●																		
BARFORD PK RACING STABLES, Bridgwater (YH00932)																											
BLUE MOUNTAIN FARM, Wells (YH01567)																											
BOSSINGTON DRESSAGE STABLES, Minehead (YH01656)																											
BRIMSMORE EQUESTRIAN CTRE, Yeovil (YH01913)	●	●																									
BURCOTT RIDING CTRE, Wells (YH02236)	●	●																									
CONQUEST CTRE, Taunton (YH03243)					●																						
COOK, ANGELA, Wiveliscombe (YH03255)																											
DRAKES FARM, Ilminster (YH04256)																											
EBBORLANDS, Wells (YH04529)	●	●	●	●	●			●																			
FARRELL, P, Chard (YH05086)																											
FOALE, D, Street (YH05296)																											
GADD, CELIA, Brent Knoll (YH05604)																											
GLEBE STABLES, Minehead (YH05819)																											
HAM, G A, Axbridge (YH06342)																											
HAWKE, N, Woolminstone (YH06544)																											
HODGES, R J, Somerton (YH06909)																											
HOLEMOOR HOUSE STABLES, Chard (YH06931)																											
KNIGHT, GEORGE, Taunton (YH08260)																											
P F & B NICHOLLS RACING, Shepton Mallet (YH10637)																											
PEVLINGS FARM, Templecombe (YH11035)	●	●																									
PIPE, M C, Wellington (YH11145)																											
POPHAM, C L, Taunton (YH11267)																											
PRIMMORE FARM HORSES, Bridgwater (YH11396)																											
RODFORD, P, Martock (YH12045)																											
ROYS RIDING SCHOOL, Taunton (YH12201)	●	●																									
RYALL, B J M, Yeovil (YH12283)																											
SANDHILL RACING STABLES, Minehead (YH12412)																											
SMALL, ROSALIND, South Petherton (YH12909)																											

Business Profile

Training (shaded area) Course, Arena, Buildings and Pasture

by Country by County	Coaches	Harness Trainer	Dressage Training	Polo Trainer	Side-saddle specialist	Side-saddle trainer	Trainers	Training (1 to 1)	Training (Children)	Training (Disabled)	Training (Dressage)	Training (Flat)	Training (Freelance)	Training (Group)	Training (Horse Breaking)	Training (Jockey)	Training (Jumps)	Training (Personnel)	Training (Point-to-Point)	Training (Riding)	Training (SteepleChase)	Training (To become a Trainer)	Training for Examination	Work with Children 10-16	Work with Children under 10	Work with Senior Citizens	Work with Students	Work with the Disabled	Architectural Advice	Architectural Planning	Arenas (large) for hire	Arenas (small) for hire	Arenas Indoor (Build)	Arenas Outdoor (Build)	Building Maintenance	Building Repairs	Cross Country Course (Build)	Cross Country Course (Design)	Fencing (Build)	Gates (Build)	Outbuildings (Build)	Pasture Supply	Pasture Support	Property Services	Racing Tracks (Build)	Show Jumps (Design)	Stables (Build)	Stables (Design)	Swimming Pools (Build)	Swimming Pools (Design)
SPARKFORD SAWMILLS, Yeovil (YH13177)																																							●												
STAGS, Dulverton (YH13340)																																												●							
STAGS, Wellington (YH13341)																																												●							
SUTTON OAKS, Bridgwater (YH13675)							●					●					●																																		
THORNEY COPSE, Wincanton (YH14066)																								●	●		●																								
W.E.S GARRETT MASTER SADDLERS, Cheddar (YH14803)					●																																														
WINDMILL HILL EQUESTRIAN CTRE, Ilminster (YH15566)							●						●																		●																				
WYATT, C R & R K, Minehead (YH15853)																										●																									
SOMERSET (NORTH)																																																			
ALBERT E JAMES & SON, Barrow Gurney (YH00245)																																										●									
BANWELL EQUESTRIAN CTRE, Weston-Super-Mare (YH00913)																				●																															
BLIXEN-FINECKE, H (BARON), Winscombe (YH01542)													●																																						
CLEVEDON RIDING, Clevedon (YH03020)								●	●	●	●			●			●							●	●																										
CTRE RIDING SCHOOL, Weston-Super-Mare (YH03696)								●	●	●				●										●	●																										
HAND EQUESTRIAN CTRE, Clevedon (YH06377)																															●	●																			
MENDIP RIDING CTRE, Churchill (YH09458)								●	●	●	●	●		●			●			●				●							●	●																			
RACECOURSE FARM, Portbury (YH11575)							●																																												
SMART, JAYNE, Banwell (YH12922)							●																																												
STAFFORDSHIRE																																																			
A K FEEDS, Shenstone (YH00044)																																										●									
BALLANTYNE, CLAIRE, Stafford (YH00853)			●				●				●		●																																						
BARLASTON RIDING CTRE, Stoke-on-Trent (YH00949)								●	●	●	●	●		●	●		●																																		
BARNETT, G W, Stoke-on-Trent (YH00983)							●																																												
BAXTER, S E, Lichfield (YH01088)							●																																												
BENTLEY HSE, Biddulph Park (YH01285)																															●																				
BOB ELLIS EQUESTRIAN SVS, Brewood (YH01586)																																					●														
BROWN, CAROLINE, Burton-on-Trent (YH02104)													●																																						
C W G, Burton-on-Trent (YH02405)																																										●									
CLAY, W, Stoke-on-Trent (YH02995)							●																																												
DALTON, P T, Burton-on-Trent (YH03848)							●																																												
DAVISON, RICHARD, Uttoxeter (YH03959)			●				●				●																																								
DOBBINS DINER, Tamworth (YH04151)			●					●	●	●	●	●	●		●		●	●		●		●	●	●	●		●																								

Business Profile

Training (shaded area) **Course, Arena, Buildings and Pasture**

by Country by County

Name	Coaches	Harness Trainer	Dressage Training	Polo Trainer	Side-saddle specialist	Side-saddle trainer	Trainers	Training (1 to 1)	Training (Children)	Training (Disabled)	Training (Dressage)	Training (Flat)	Training (Freelance)	Training (Group)	Training (Horse Breaking)	Training (Jockey)	Training (Jumps)	Training (Personnel)	Training (Point-to-Point)	Training (Riding)	Training (SteepleChase)	Training (To become a Trainer)	Training for Examination	Work with Children 10-16	Work with Children under 10	Work with Senior Citizens	Work with Students	Work with the Disabled	Architectural Advice	Architectural Planning	Arenas (large) for hire	Arenas (small) for hire	Arenas Indoor (Build)	Arenas Outdoor (Build)	Building Maintenance	Building Repairs	Cross Country Course (Build)	Cross Country Course (Design)	Fencing (Build)	Gates (Build)	Outbuildings (Build)	Pasture Supply	Pasture Support	Property Services	Racing Tracks (Build)	Show Jumps (Design)	Stables (Build)	Stables (Design)	Swimming Pools (Build)	Swimming Pools (Design)
FORBES, A L, Uttoxeter (YH05319)							●																																											
FRANCES ANN BROWN SADDLERY, Stafford (YH05444)																								●	●	●	●	●																						
HAZEL SLADE STABLES, Hednesford (YH06600)							●																																											
HOLLINSHEAD, R, Rugeley (YH06948)							●																																											
HORSEY THINGS, Eccleshall (YH07184)																																										●								
INGESTRE STABLES, Stafford (YH07445)			●				●				●																																							
LEAVY, B D, Stoke-on-Trent (YH08509)							●																																											
LEES, T D, Pelsall (YH08532)		●																																																
OFFLEY BROOK LIVERY STABLES, Eccleshall (YH10436)			●				●				●		●				●																																	
PLANT, JANET, Woodseaves (YH11161)			●				●				●		●																								●													
RODBASTON, Penkridge (YH12040)																							●				●																							
RODBASTON CLGE, Penkridge (YH12041)								●	●					●						●			●																											
ROUNDMEADOWS RACING STABLES, Stoke-on-Trent (YH12144)							●																																											
SCROPTON, Burton-on-Trent (YH12569)		●	●				●	●	●	●	●		●	●	●		●			●			●	●		●	●	●																						
STREETER, A, Leek (YH13573)							●																																											
WOFFORD INT HORSE TRANSPORT, Lichfield (YH15643)													●																																					
WOODSIDE RACING STABLES, Tamworth (YH15744)							●																																											
SUFFOLK																																																		
AKBARY, H, Newmarket (YH00230)							●																																											
ALLEN, C N, Newmarket (YH00293)							●																																											
BARDWELL MANOR, Bury St Edmunds (YH00928)								●			●			●								●	●	●	●		●																							
BELL, M L, Newmarket (YH01227)							●																																											
BENTLEY RIDING CTRE, Ipswich (YH01286)								●	●		●			●			●			●				●	●	●	●																							
BEVERLEY HSE STABLES, Newmarket (YH01341)							●																																											
BOB JONES, Newmarket (YH01587)												●																																						
BOWEN, JOHN, Mendlesham (YH01701)			●				●				●																																							
BRAVERY, G C, Newmarket (YH01818)							●																																											
BRITTAIN, C E, Newmarket (YH01981)							●																																											
BROWN, M A, Newmarket (YH02122)			●				●				●																																							
C W G, Bury St Edmunds (YH02406)																																										●								
CALDER PARK STABLES, Newmarket (YH02431)							●																																											
CALLAGHAN, N A, Newmarket (YH02447)							●																																											

Business Profile

Training (shaded area) **Course, Arena, Buildings and Pasture**

by Country by County

	Coaches	Harness Trainer	Dressage Training	Polo Trainer	Side-saddle specialist	Side-saddle trainer	Trainers	Training (1 to 1)	Training (Children)	Training (Disabled)	Training (Dressage)	Training (Flat)	Training (Freelance)	Training (Group)	Training (Horse Breaking)	Training (Jockey)	Training (Jumps)	Training (Personnel)	Training (Point-to-Point)	Training (Riding)	Training (SteepleChase)	Training (To become a Trainer)	Training for Examination	Work with Children 10-16	Work with Children under 10	Work with Senior Citizens	Work with Students	Work with the Disabled	Architectural Advice	Architectural Planning	Arenas (large) for hire	Arenas (small) for hire	Arenas Indoor (Build)	Arenas Outdoor (Build)	Building Maintenance	Building Repairs	Cross Country Course (Build)	Cross Country Course (Design)	Fencing (Build)	Gates (Build)	Outbuildings (Build)	Pasture Supply	Pasture Support	Property Services	Racing Tracks (Build)	Show Jumps (Design)	Stables (Build)	Stables (Design)	Swimming Pools (Build)	Swimming Pools (Design)
CANTILLON, DON, Newmarket (YH02514)							●																																											
CARRIAGEWAY STABLES, Newmarket (YH02584)							●																																											
CECIL, H R A, Newmarket (YH02671)							●																																											
CHASE FENCING SUPPLIES, Brandon (YH02783)																																							●											
CHURCH FARM TACK SHOP & FEEDS, Eye (YH02903)																																●																		
CLAREHAVEN STABLES, Newmarket (YH02950)							●																																											
COLLINGRIDGE, H J, Newmarket (YH03184)							●																																											
COSGROVE, D J S, Newmarket (YH03351)							●																																											
COUNTRYSIDE, Ipswich (YH03439)																																						●								●				
COWELL, ROBERT, Newmarket (YH03524)							●																																											
CULFORD STABLES, Bury St Edmunds (YH03701)								●	●					●						●			●																											
CUMANI, L M, Newmarket (YH03711)							●																																											
CURLEY, B J, Newmarket (YH03730)							●																																											
CURLEY, B J, Newmarket (YH03729)							●																																											
D M P MACHINERY, Bury St Edmunds (YH03795)																																											●							
D'ARCY, PAUL, Newmarket (YH03883)							●																																											
DUFFIELD, GILLIAN, Newmarket (YH04315)							●																																											
DWYER, C A, Newmarket (YH04381)							●																																											
EUSTACE, J M P, Newmarket (YH04911)							●																																											
EVE LODGE STABLES, Newmarket (YH04934)							●																																											
FANSHAWE, J R, Newmarket (YH05045)							●																																											
FEEDSAFE, Ipswich (YH05125)																																										●								
GALLOPON, Ipswich (YH05623)																																		●																
GILBERT, J, Bury St Edmunds (YH05759)							●																																											
GILLIGAN, P L, Newmarket (YH05785)							●																																											
GODOLPHIN MNGMT, Newmarket (YH05869)							●																																											
GRAHAM LODGE STABLES, Newmarket (YH05965)							●																																											
GRAHAM, N, Newmarket (YH05972)							●																																											
GREEN RIDGE STABLES, Newmarket (YH06059)							●																																											
GROVE FARM DRIVING & LIVERY, Mildenhall (YH06166)							●																																											
GUEST, R, Newmarket (YH06183)							●																																											
HACKNESS VILLA STABLES, Newmarket (YH06256)							●																																											

www.hccyourhorse.com

Business Profile

Training (shaded area) Course, Arena, Buildings and Pasture

by Country by County

	Coaches	Harness Trainer	Dressage Training	Polo Trainer	Side-saddle specialist	Side-saddle trainer	Trainers	Training (1 to 1)	Training (Children)	Training (Disabled)	Training (Dressage)	Training (Flat)	Training (Freelance)	Training (Group)	Training (Horse Breaking)	Training (Jockey)	Training (Jumps)	Training (Personnel)	Training (Point-to-Point)	Training (Riding)	Training (SteepleChase)	Training (To become a Trainer)	Training for Examination	Work with Children 10-16	Work with Children under 10	Work with Senior Citizens	Work with Students	Work with the Disabled	Architectural Advice	Architectural Planning	Arenas (large) for hire	Arenas (small) for hire	Arenas Indoor (Build)	Arenas Outdoor (Build)	Building Maintenance	Building Repairs	Cross Country Course (Build)	Cross Country Course (Design)	Fencing (Build)	Gates (Build)	Outbuildings (Build)	Pasture Supply	Pasture Support	Property Services	Racing Tracks (Build)	Show Jumps (Design)	Stables (Build)	Stables (Design)	Swimming Pools (Build)	Swimming Pools (Design)
HAGGAS, W, Newmarket (YH06276)							●																																											
HAINE, D, Newmarket (YH06284)							●																																											
HAMILTON STABLES, Newmarket (YH06350)							●																																											
HANBURY, B, Newmarket (YH06374)							●																																											
HOEG-MUDD, CLEA, Woodbridge (YH06917)			●				●				●						●																																	
HOLDEN, MAUREEN, Bungay (YH06923)																	●																																	
HORSE REQUISITES, Newmarket (YH07132)																																										●	●							
HOWLING, PAUL, Newmarket (YH07243)							●																																											
HTL, Bury St Edmunds (YH07249)							●																																											
HUBBARD, G A, Woodbridge (YH07252)							●																																											
HYDRO AGRI, Bury St Edmunds (YH07352)																																										●								
INDUNA STABLES, Newmarket (YH07439)							●																																											
J ALLEN, Newmarket (YH07558)							●																																											
J N PEARCE RACING TRAINERS, Newmarket (YH07603)							●																																											
JAMES NICHOL, Newmarket (YH07674)							●																																											
JARVIS, M A, Newmarket (YH07706)							●																																											
JARVIS, W, Newmarket (YH07708)							●																																											
JEREMY NOSEDA, Newmarket (YH07753)							●																																											
JOHN SNOWDON HARNESS MAKER, Woodbridge (YH07813)							●																																											
JONES, R W, Newmarket (YH07927)							●																																											
JULIA FIELDEN RACING, Newmarket (YH07962)							●																																											
KELLEWAY, GAY, Newmarket (YH08042)							●																																											
L S K, Bury St Edmunds (YH08327)																																												●						
L S K, Stowmarket (YH08326)																																												●						
LEGEND SVS, Bury St Edmunds (YH08535)																																					●													
LINDEN LODGE STABLES, Newmarket (YH08645)							●																																											
LITTMODEN, N P, Newmarket (YH08711)							●																																											
MCHALE, DENISE, Newmarket (YH09370)							●																																											
MCMATH, B J, Newmarket (YH09392)							●																																											
MOUNTFOLD, Bures (YH09901)																																							●				●							
MUSSON, W J, Newmarket (YH09976)							●																																											
NORCROFT EQUESTRIAN DVLP, Bury St Edmunds (YH10230)																																							●					●						

Business Profile
Training (shaded area) **Course, Arena, Buildings and Pasture**

by Country by County

Name	Coaches	Harness Trainer	Dressage Training	Polo Trainer	Side-saddle specialist	Side-saddle trainer	Trainers	Training (1 to 1)	Training (Children)	Training (Disabled)	Training (Dressage)	Training (Flat)	Training (Freelance)	Training (Group)	Training (Horse Breaking)	Training (Jockey)	Training (Jumps)	Training (Personnel)	Training (Point-to-Point)	Training (Riding)	Training (SteepleChase)	Training (To become a Trainer)	Training for Examination	Work with Children 10-16	Work with Children under 10	Work with Senior Citizens	Work with Students	Work with the Disabled	Architectural Advice	Architectural Planning	Arenas (large) for hire	Arenas (small) for hire	Arenas Indoor (Build)	Arenas Outdoor (Build)	Building Maintenance	Building Repairs	Cross Country Course (Build)	Cross Country Course (Design)	Fencing (Build)	Gates (Build)	Outbuildings (Build)	Pasture Supply	Pasture Support	Property Services	Racing Tracks (Build)	Show Jumps (Design)	Stables (Build)	Stables (Design)	Swimming Pools (Build)	Swimming Pools (Design)
O'GORMAN, W, Newmarket (YH10440)							●																																											
OLD TWELVE STABLES, Newmarket (YH10480)							●																																											
O'NEILL, E, Newmarket (YH10515)							●																																											
OPEN CLGE OF EQUINE STUDIES, Bury St Edmunds (YH10523)																							●																											
ORWELL ARENA, Ipswich (YH10556)			●					●			●		●		●		●			●				●	●			●			●																			
PADDOCK MAINTENANCE COMPANY, Ipswich (YH10669)																																										●	●							
PAKEFIELD RIDING SCHOOL, Lowestoft (YH10687)								●	●	●	●	●	●	●			●			●			●	●	●	●	●	●																						
PAYNE, J W, Newmarket (YH10849)							●																																											
PHILIP MCENTEE RACING, Newmarket (YH11044)							●																																											
POPLAR PK, Woodbridge (YH11271)								●	●		●			●			●			●				●	●	●	●	●																						
PRESCOTT, MARK (SIR), Newmarket (YH11358)							●																																											
RED HSE STABLES, Newmarket (YH11699)							●																																											
RYAN, M J, Newmarket (YH12285)							●																																											
SAFFRON HOUSE STABLES, Newmarket (YH12380)							●																																											
SEAN WOODS RACING, Newmarket (YH12592)							●																																											
SHADOWFAX STABLE, Newmarket (YH12655)							●																																											
STANLEY HOUSE STABLES, Newmarket (YH13369)							●																																											
STOCKBRIDGE HOUSE STABLES, Newmarket (YH13487)							●																																											
STOKE BY CLARE EQUESTRIAN CTRE, Sudbury (YH13501)			●					●	●	●	●			●	●								●	●	●		●	●			●																			
STOUTE, MICHAEL (SIR), Newmarket (YH13534)							●																																											
STUBBS, LINDA, Newmarket (YH13603)							●																																											
TERRA-VAC, Haverhill (YH13955)																																											●							
TOLLER, J A R, Newmarket (YH14210)							●																																											
TOMPKINS, M H, Newmarket (YH14223)							●																																											
UGGLESHALL, Beccles (YH14541)							●																																											
VALLEY FARM, Woodbridge (YH14651)						●			●	●	●									●			●	●	●	●	●	●				●																		
WADHAM, Newmarket (YH14816)							●																																											
WALROND, SALLIE, Bury St Edmunds (YH14871)							●						●																																					
WIGHAM, M, Newmarket (YH15400)							●																																											
WILLIAMS, S C, Newmarket (YH15477)							●																																											
WOODLANDS, Bury St Edmunds (YH15707)							●	●	●		●						●			●				●	●	●	●										●													
WRAGG, G, Newmarket (YH15808)							●																																											

www.hccyourhorse.com

Business Profile

Training (shaded area)
Course, Arena, Buildings and Pasture

by Country by County

	Coaches	Harness Trainer	Dressage Training	Polo Trainer	Side-saddle specialist	Side-saddle trainer	Trainers	Training (1 to 1)	Training (Children)	Training (Disabled)	Training (Dressage)	Training (Flat)	Training (Freelance)	Training (Group)	Training (Horse Breaking)	Training (Jockey)	Training (Jumps)	Training (Personnel)	Training (Point-to-Point)	Training (Riding)	Training (SteepleChase)	Training (To become a Trainer)	Training for Examination	Work with Children 10-16	Work with Children under 10	Work with Senior Citizens	Work with Students	Work with the Disabled	Architectural Advice	Architectural Planning	Arenas (large) for hire	Arenas (small) for hire	Arenas Indoor (Build)	Arenas Outdoor (Build)	Building Maintenance	Building Repairs	Cross Country Course (Build)	Cross Country Course (Design)	Fencing (Build)	Gates (Build)	Outbuildings (Build)	Pasture Supply	Pasture Support	Property Services	Racing Tracks (Build)	Show Jumps (Design)	Stables (Build)	Stables (Design)	Swimming Pools (Build)	Swimming Pools (Design)
SURREY																																																		
ADDLESTONE HARDWARE, Addlestone (YH00180)																																											●							
AGRIQUESTRIAN CONSULTANTS, Epsom (YH00202)																													●	●			●	●			●	●			●						●	●	●	●
ARDENLEA ENTERPRISES, Epsom (YH00504)																																					●							●						
ASCOT PARK, Woking (YH00583)	●			●			●	●					●	●	●					●											●																			
BEECHWOOD, Caterham (YH01176)									●					●						●				●	●		●	●																						
BOLTON, M J, Oxted (YH01613)							●																																											
BOULTON, ANDREA, Whyteleafe (YH01675)							●																																											
BRIDLEWAYS EQUESTRIAN CTRE, Great Bookham (YH01898)						●		●	●		●	●		●			●			●		●	●	●	●	●	●																							
BURSTOW PK, Horley (YH02286)			●					●	●		●			●						●				●	●																									
CASEY, W T, Dorking (YH02616)							●																																											
CEDAR POINT STABLES, Epsom (YH02674)							●																																											
CHARTWELL STABLES, Epsom (YH02777)							●																																											
CHESSINGTON, Chessington (YH02830)								●	●	●	●			●			●			●				●	●	●	●	●																						
CLEAR HEIGHT STABLES, Epsom (YH03009)							●																																											
CRANLEIGH SCHOOL OF RIDING, Cranleigh (YH03565)							●	●	●		●		●	●	●		●			●		●		●	●		●																							
CROWN AXXESS, Guildford (YH03680)																																							●											
DORKING EQUESTRIAN CTRE, Dorking (YH04200)			●		●	●		●	●		●			●			●			●				●	●	●	●																							
DUNMORE-FRANCIS, VALERIE, Old Coulsdon (YH04348)			●				●				●																																							
DURDANS STABLES, Epsom (YH04368)							●																																											
EBBISHAM FARM, Tadworth (YH04528)			●					●			●	●			●		●			●			●				●				●	●																		
FORGEHILL STUD, South Godstone (YH05367)							●																																											
GREEN LANE STABLES, Morden (YH06058)			●					●	●		●			●			●			●				●	●		●																							
HATCH FARM STABLES, Addlestone (YH06530)									●											●				●	●																									
HILDEN, D, Croydon (YH06807)		●																																																
JONES, T M, Guildford (YH07934)							●																																											
KEAR, BILL, Dorking (YH08016)																																	●	●	●	●			●		●						●			
LINGFIELD PARK RACECOURSE, Lingfield (YH08659)							●																																											
LOCKNER FARM, Guildford (YH08760)								●					●	●				●	●	●																														
LONG, J E, Caterham (YH08803)							●																																											
LORETTA LODGE RACING STABLE, Epsom (YH08831)							●																																											
MCCARTHY, TIM, Godstone (YH09322)							●																																											

Business Profile

Training (shaded area) **Course, Arena, Buildings and Pasture**

by Country by County	Coaches	Harness Trainer	Dressage Training	Polo Trainer	Side-saddle specialist	Side-saddle trainer	Trainers	Training (1 to 1)	Training (Children)	Training (Disabled)	Training (Dressage)	Training (Flat)	Training (Freelance)	Training (Group)	Training (Horse Breaking)	Training (Jockey)	Training (Jumps)	Training (Personnel)	Training (Point-to-Point)	Training (Riding)	Training (SteepleChase)	Training (To become a Trainer)	Training for Examination	Work with Children 10-16	Work with Children under 10	Work with Senior Citizens	Work with Students	Work with the Disabled	Architectural Advice	Architectural Planning	Arenas (large) for hire	Arenas (small) for hire	Arenas Indoor (Build)	Arenas Outdoor (Build)	Building Maintenance	Building Repairs	Cross Country Course (Build)	Cross Country Course (Design)	Fencing (Build)	Gates (Build)	Outbuildings (Build)	Pasture Supply	Pasture Support	Property Services	Racing Tracks (Build)	Show Jumps (Design)	Stables (Build)	Stables (Design)	Swimming Pools (Build)	Swimming Pools (Design)
MITCHELL, P, Epsom (YH09676)							●																																												
OAKS PK RIDING SCHOOL, Banstead (YH10402)								●	●				●						●				●	●																									
ORCHARD COTTAGE, Wickham Market (YH10527)																								●	●		●																							
PEARCE, B A, Lingfield (YH10870)							●																																												
PELHAMS, Godalming (YH10909)																																												●						
POWELL, BRYNLEY, Farnham (YH11315)							●																																												
POWELL, T E, Reigate (YH11322)							●																																												
POYNTERS, Cobham (YH11330)							●		●					●			●			●				●	●																									
RIDING CTRE, Farnham (YH11873)			●					●	●	●			●						●				●	●																									
ROBERT LEECH, Oxted (YH11940)																																												●						
ROBERT LEECH, Purley (YH11941)																																												●						
ROBERT LEECH, Croydon (YH11942)																																												●						
ROBERT STEVENS, Dorking (YH11943)																																			●	●														
ROBINSON, DEIRDRE, Lingfield (YH11986)			●				●				●																																								
S R S, Sunbury-on-Thames (YH12333)								●	●	●	●	●	●	●	●		●	●		●		●		●	●	●	●	●			●																					
SANDERS, BROOKE, Epsom (YH12404)							●																																												
SIMMONS, Godalming (YH12825)																																												●						
SOUTH HATCH STABLES, Epsom (YH13095)							●																																												
STARSHAW STABLES, Coulsdon (YH13399)								●	●				●			●			●				●	●																									
SUPERPET THE HORSE SHOP, Banstead (YH13656)		●																																																
T.T.T, Guildford (YH13769)			●								●										●																													
TANDRIDGE PRIORY, Oxted (YH13853)								●	●				●						●																															
TILHILL ECONOMIC FORESTRY, Farnham (YH14145)																																							●										
TOWNSLEY, P LAXTON, Godalming (YH14300)							●																																												
TRIPLE CROWN FENCE, Guildford (YH14403)																																							●							●				
UPLANDS STUD, Godalming (YH14601)			●				●				●																																								
VICTORIA FARM, Woking (YH14708)			●					●	●		●		●	●	●		●	●		●		●	●																											
WENDOVER STABLES, Epsom (YH15106)							●																																												
WILDWOODS, Tadworth (YH15413)								●	●		●			●			●	●		●			●	●	●	●	●																									
WINKWORTH, P, Chiddingfold (YH15587)							●																																												
WOODSTOCK SOUTH STABLES, Chessington (YH15751)			●								●		●																																						
SUSSEX (EAST)																																																		

Business Profile
Training (shaded area) Course, Arena, Buildings and Pasture
by Country by County

	Coaches	Harness Trainer	Dressage Training	Polo Trainer	Side-saddle specialist	Side-saddle trainer	Trainers	Training (1 to 1)	Training (Children)	Training (Disabled)	Training (Dressage)	Training (Flat)	Training (Freelance)	Training (Group)	Training (Horse Breaking)	Training (Jockey)	Training (Jumps)	Training (Personnel)	Training (Point-to-Point)	Training (Riding)	Training (SteepleChase)	Training (To become a Trainer)	Training for Examination	Work with Children 10-16	Work with Children under 10	Work with Senior Citizens	Work with Students	Work with the Disabled	Architectural Advice	Architectural Planning	Arenas (large) for hire	Arenas (small) for hire	Arenas Indoor (Build)	Arenas Outdoor (Build)	Building Maintenance	Building Repairs	Cross Country Course (Build)	Cross Country Course (Design)	Fencing (Build)	Gates (Build)	Outbuildings (Build)	Pasture Supply	Pasture Support	Property Services	Racing Tracks (Build)	Show Jumps (Design)	Stables (Build)	Stables (Design)	Swimming Pools (Build)	Swimming Pools (Design)
BROWN BREAD HORSE RESCUE CTRE, Battle (YH02092)									●	●																																								
BUTLER, P, Lewes (YH02326)							●																																											
CALEDONIAN FENCING, Lewes (YH02441)																																							●											
CROCKSTEAD PK, Lewes (YH03608)																															●	●																		
DELTA CONSTRUCTION, Uckfield (YH04036)																																															●	●		
DEWHURST STABLING, Wadhurst (YH04097)																																															●	●		
DOWNS FENCING, Lewes (YH04238)																																							●											
FARMIX, Wadhurst (YH05066)																																										●								
FLOWER, M, Jevington (YH05289)							●																																											
G A COMMERCIALS, Pevensey (YH05569)							●																																											
GOLDEN CROSS, Hailsham (YH05878)			●														●														●																			
GREEN, CAROL & STOKES, MARIE, Hastings (YH06061)			●				●				●						●																																	
GRISSELL, D M, Robertsbridge (YH06146)							●																																											
HAMSEY RIDING SCHOOL, Lewes (YH06371)								●	●					●			●			●				●	●	●	●																							
HOLE FARM, Uckfield (YH06928)								●			●						●			●																														
INGLESIDE RACING STABLES, Brighton (YH07451)							●																																											
LITTLE MEADOWS, Hailsham (YH08694)							●	●					●		●																																			
MCGOVERN, T P, Lewes (YH09359)							●																																											
MISBOURNE RIDING CTRE, Uckfield (YH09659)																										●	●																							
MITCHELL, K & K, Uckfield (YH09673)																																							●											
MOORCROFT CTRE, Battle (YH09748)							●																																											
NEWTON-SMITH, A M, Polegate (YH10175)							●																																											
PARKWAY, Heathfield (YH10780)																																										●								
PARKWAY, Northiam (YH10779)																																													●					
PIPER, JUDI, Hailsham (YH11146)							●										●																																	
POULTON, J C, Lewes (YH11304)							●																																											
POULTON, J R, Lewes (YH11305)							●																																											
ROBERTS, M J, Hailsham (YH11957)							●																																											
RUSSELL, S C, Heathfield (YH12265)																																							●											
SMART, JOHN, Uckfield (YH12923)							●						●				●																																	
SOMETHING DIFFERENT, Uckfield (YH13068)																								●	●																									
SOUTH LODGE, Rotherfield (YH13100)								●	●											●				●	●																									

Business Profile

Training (shaded area) Course, Arena, Buildings and Pasture

by Country by County

	Coaches	Harness Trainer	Dressage Training	Polo Trainer	Side-saddle specialist	Side-saddle trainer	Trainers	Training (1 to 1)	Training (Children)	Training (Disabled)	Training (Dressage)	Training (Flat)	Training (Freelance)	Training (Group)
STEVENS, LEONARD, Eastbourne (YH13445)					●									
WEBSTER, J, Uckfield (YH15038)							●							
WINDMILL LODGE STABLES, Lewes (YH15567)							●							
SUSSEX (WEST)														
ALBOURNE EQUESTRIAN CTRE, Hassocks (YH00248)								●	●	●	●			●
ARNOLD, T J, Pulborough (YH00560)							●							
B M F, Petworth (YH00739)							●							
B M M LEATHERS, Petworth (YH00743)			●				●				●		●	
BRENDON, Brighton (YH01835)							●							
BRENDON HORSE & RIDER, Brighton (YH01837)							●							
BROADFIELD STABLES, Steyning (YH01995)														
CASTLE STABLES, Arundel (YH02636)							●							
CHURCHILL, Wisborough Green (YH02912)														
COOMBELANDS RACING STABLES, Pulborough (YH03280)							●							
CYZER, C, Horsham (YH03766)							●							
DACE, L A, Pulborough (YH03814)							●							
DRAGONFLY SADDLERY, Hassocks (YH04252)														
EASTMERE STABLES, Chichester (YH04509)							●							
EDWARDS, S, Pulborough (YH04585)							●							
FERRING COUNTRY CTRE, Worthing (YH05171)										●				
GEORGE PERKS BROS, Crawley (YH05718)														
GIFFORD, J T, Worthing (YH05757)							●							
H J BURT & SON, Steyning (YH06226)														
HANGLETON FARM, Worthing (YH06386)														
HARTLAND CARRIAGE SUPPLIES, Rudgwick (YH06504)		●					●							
HENRY ADAMS, Storrington (YH06679)														
HIGHBROOK FENCING, Ardingly (YH06772)														
HORACE FULLER, Horsham (YH07063)														
HORGAN, C A, Pulborough (YH07066)							●							
LADY HERRIES STABLES, Littlehampton (YH08336)							●							
LASSETTER, JOHN F, Chichester (YH08442)			●				●				●		●	
LAVANT HSE STABLES, Chichester (YH08460)			●					●	●		●			●

	Training (Horse Breaking)	Training (Jockey)	Training (Jumps)	Training (Personnel)	Training (Point-to-Point)	Training (Riding)	Training (SteepleChase)	Training (To become a Trainer)	Training for Examination	Work with Children 10-16	Work with Children under 10	Work with Senior Citizens	Work with Students	Work with the Disabled
STEVENS, LEONARD, Eastbourne (YH13445)														
WEBSTER, J, Uckfield (YH15038)														
WINDMILL LODGE STABLES, Lewes (YH15567)														
SUSSEX (WEST)														
ALBOURNE EQUESTRIAN CTRE, Hassocks (YH00248)									●	●	●	●	●	●
ARNOLD, T J, Pulborough (YH00560)														
B M F, Petworth (YH00739)														
B M M LEATHERS, Petworth (YH00743)														
BRENDON, Brighton (YH01835)	●													
BRENDON HORSE & RIDER, Brighton (YH01837)														
BROADFIELD STABLES, Steyning (YH01995)														
CASTLE STABLES, Arundel (YH02636)														
CHURCHILL, Wisborough Green (YH02912)														
COOMBELANDS RACING STABLES, Pulborough (YH03280)														
CYZER, C, Horsham (YH03766)														
DACE, L A, Pulborough (YH03814)														
DRAGONFLY SADDLERY, Hassocks (YH04252)											●			
EASTMERE STABLES, Chichester (YH04509)														
EDWARDS, S, Pulborough (YH04585)														
FERRING COUNTRY CTRE, Worthing (YH05171)														●
GEORGE PERKS BROS, Crawley (YH05718)														
GIFFORD, J T, Worthing (YH05757)														
H J BURT & SON, Steyning (YH06226)														
HANGLETON FARM, Worthing (YH06386)			●											
HARTLAND CARRIAGE SUPPLIES, Rudgwick (YH06504)														
HENRY ADAMS, Storrington (YH06679)														
HIGHBROOK FENCING, Ardingly (YH06772)														
HORACE FULLER, Horsham (YH07063)														
HORGAN, C A, Pulborough (YH07066)														
LADY HERRIES STABLES, Littlehampton (YH08336)														
LASSETTER, JOHN F, Chichester (YH08442)														
LAVANT HSE STABLES, Chichester (YH08460)			●			●		●	●	●	●		●	

	Architectural Advice	Architectural Planning	Arenas (large) for hire	Arenas (small) for hire	Arenas Indoor (Build)	Arenas Outdoor (Build)	Building Maintenance	Building Repairs	Cross Country Course (Build)	Cross Country Course (Design)	Fencing (Build)	Gates (Build)	Outbuildings (Build)	Pasture Supply	Pasture Support	Property Services	Racing Tracks (Build)	Show Jumps (Design)	Stables (Build)	Stables (Design)	Swimming Pools (Build)	Swimming Pools (Design)
STEVENS, LEONARD, Eastbourne (YH13445)																						
WEBSTER, J, Uckfield (YH15038)																						
WINDMILL LODGE STABLES, Lewes (YH15567)																						
SUSSEX (WEST)																						
ALBOURNE EQUESTRIAN CTRE, Hassocks (YH00248)																						
ARNOLD, T J, Pulborough (YH00560)																						
B M F, Petworth (YH00739)																						
B M M LEATHERS, Petworth (YH00743)																						
BRENDON, Brighton (YH01835)																						
BRENDON HORSE & RIDER, Brighton (YH01837)			●	●											●							
BROADFIELD STABLES, Steyning (YH01995)																			●			
CASTLE STABLES, Arundel (YH02636)																						
CHURCHILL, Wisborough Green (YH02912)																●						
COOMBELANDS RACING STABLES, Pulborough (YH03280)																						
CYZER, C, Horsham (YH03766)																						
DACE, L A, Pulborough (YH03814)																						
DRAGONFLY SADDLERY, Hassocks (YH04252)																						
EASTMERE STABLES, Chichester (YH04509)																						
EDWARDS, S, Pulborough (YH04585)																						
FERRING COUNTRY CTRE, Worthing (YH05171)																						
GEORGE PERKS BROS, Crawley (YH05718)											●											
GIFFORD, J T, Worthing (YH05757)																						
H J BURT & SON, Steyning (YH06226)																●						
HANGLETON FARM, Worthing (YH06386)																						
HARTLAND CARRIAGE SUPPLIES, Rudgwick (YH06504)																						
HENRY ADAMS, Storrington (YH06679)																●						
HIGHBROOK FENCING, Ardingly (YH06772)											●											
HORACE FULLER, Horsham (YH07063)											●											
HORGAN, C A, Pulborough (YH07066)																						
LADY HERRIES STABLES, Littlehampton (YH08336)																						
LASSETTER, JOHN F, Chichester (YH08442)																						
LAVANT HSE STABLES, Chichester (YH08460)																						

www.hccyourhorse.com

Business Profile

Training (shaded area)

Course, Arena, Buildings and Pasture

by Country by County

by Country by County	Coaches	Harness Trainer	Dressage Training	Polo Trainer	Side-saddle specialist	Side-saddle trainer	Trainers	Training (1 to 1)	Training (Children)	Training (Disabled)	Training (Dressage)	Training (Flat)	Training (Freelance)	Training (Group)	Training (Horse Breaking)	Training (Jockey)	Training (Jumps)	Training (Personnel)	Training (Point-to-Point)	Training (Riding)	Training (SteepleChase)	Training (To become a Trainer)	Training for Examination	Work with Children 10-16	Work with Children under 10	Work with Senior Citizens	Work with Students	Work with the Disabled
LIGHTS, Brighton (YH08616)																												
MANNINGS LIVERIES, Henfield (YH09089)			●				●				●																	
MINTA WINN CARRIAGE DRIVING, Billingshurst (YH09655)							●																					
MOLECOMB STUD, Chichester (YH09712)			●				●		●	●	●																	
MORRISON, LIZ, Billingshurst (YH09838)			●				●				●		●															
NICOL, C, Horsham (YH10198)																	●											
REDMIRE STABLES & BUILDINGS, Storrington (YH11715)																												
RICHARDS, L, Chichester (YH11810)							●																					
ROWE, R, Pulborough (YH12165)							●																					
SELSEY RIDING CTRE, Selsey (YH12625)													●															
SHOVELSTRODE RACING, East Grinstead (YH12763)							●																					
SMITH, DINA, Pulborough (YH12955)							●																					
SOUTHDOWN EQUESTRIAN CTRE, Steyning (YH13133)								●	●	●				●			●			●				●	●	●	●	●
SYMONDSBURY STUD, Haywards Heath (YH13726)																												
WADE, J & A, Midhurst (YH14813)							●																					
WADE, JONNY, Midhurst (YH14814)							●																					
WEEDON, C, Pulborough (YH15045)							●																					
WELLS, L, Billingshurst (YH15086)							●																					
WEST WOLVES RIDING CTRE, Pulborough (YH15172)								●	●	●				●			●							●	●			●
WILLOWBROOK RIDING CTRE, Chichester (YH15508)								●	●					●						●				●	●	●	●	
WINDRUSH STABLES, Findon (YH15571)							●																					
WOODMAN, S, Chichester (YH15722)							●																					
WOODMANS STABLES, Ashington (YH15723)							●																					
WYNN, JOHN, Haywards Heath (YH15871)																												
ZARA STUD, Chichester (YH15951)			●				●				●				●					●								
TYNE AND WEAR																												
BARTON RIDING SCHOOL, Newcastle-upon-Tyne (YH01045)			●				●				●																	
BYERLEY STUD, Newcastle-upon-Tyne (YH02346)							●																					
CUNNINGHAM, W S, Yarm (YH03725)							●																					
GO RIDING GRP, Ponteland (YH05862)			●					●	●	●	●			●								●	●					
JOHNSON, R W, Newcastle-upon-Tyne (YH07836)							●																					
JOSEPH BAILEY & SONS, Houghton Le Spring (YH07942)																												

by Country by County	Architectural Advice	Architectural Planning	Arenas (large) for hire	Arenas (small) for hire	Arenas Indoor (Build)	Arenas Outdoor (Build)	Building Maintenance	Building Repairs	Cross Country Course (Build)	Cross Country Course (Design)	Fencing (Build)	Gates (Build)	Outbuildings (Build)	Pasture Supply	Pasture Support	Property Services	Racing Tracks (Build)	Show Jumps (Design)	Stables (Build)	Stables (Design)	Swimming Pools (Build)	Swimming Pools (Design)
LIGHTS, Brighton (YH08616)															●							
MANNINGS LIVERIES, Henfield (YH09089)																						
MINTA WINN CARRIAGE DRIVING, Billingshurst (YH09655)																						
MOLECOMB STUD, Chichester (YH09712)																						
MORRISON, LIZ, Billingshurst (YH09838)																						
NICOL, C, Horsham (YH10198)																						
REDMIRE STABLES & BUILDINGS, Storrington (YH11715)																			●	●		
RICHARDS, L, Chichester (YH11810)																						
ROWE, R, Pulborough (YH12165)																						
SELSEY RIDING CTRE, Selsey (YH12625)																						
SHOVELSTRODE RACING, East Grinstead (YH12763)																						
SMITH, DINA, Pulborough (YH12955)																						
SOUTHDOWN EQUESTRIAN CTRE, Steyning (YH13133)																						
SYMONDSBURY STUD, Haywards Heath (YH13726)			●																			
WADE, J & A, Midhurst (YH14813)																						
WADE, JONNY, Midhurst (YH14814)																						
WEEDON, C, Pulborough (YH15045)																						
WELLS, L, Billingshurst (YH15086)																						
WEST WOLVES RIDING CTRE, Pulborough (YH15172)																						
WILLOWBROOK RIDING CTRE, Chichester (YH15508)				●																		
WINDRUSH STABLES, Findon (YH15571)																						
WOODMAN, S, Chichester (YH15722)																						
WOODMANS STABLES, Ashington (YH15723)																						
WYNN, JOHN, Haywards Heath (YH15871)											●											
ZARA STUD, Chichester (YH15951)			●																			
TYNE AND WEAR																						
BARTON RIDING SCHOOL, Newcastle-upon-Tyne (YH01045)																						
BYERLEY STUD, Newcastle-upon-Tyne (YH02346)																						
CUNNINGHAM, W S, Yarm (YH03725)																						
GO RIDING GRP, Ponteland (YH05862)																						
JOHNSON, R W, Newcastle-upon-Tyne (YH07836)																						
JOSEPH BAILEY & SONS, Houghton Le Spring (YH07942)											●											

Business Profile
Training (shaded area) **Course, Arena, Buildings and Pasture**

by Country by County

Name	Coaches	Harness Trainer	Dressage Training	Polo Trainer	Side-saddle specialist	Side-saddle trainer	Trainers	Training (1 to 1)	Training (Children)	Training (Disabled)	Training (Dressage)	Training (Flat)	Training (Freelance)	Training (Group)	Training (Horse Breaking)	Training (Jockey)	Training (Jumps)	Training (Personnel)	Training (Point-to-Point)	Training (Riding)	Training (SteepleChase)	Training (To become a Trainer)	Training for Examination	Work with Children 10-16	Work with Children under 10	Work with Senior Citizens	Work with Students	Work with the Disabled
LITTLE HARLE STABLES, Newcastle-upon-Tyne (YH08688)			●					●		●	●		●							●		●	●				●	
MACKIE, HENRI, Newcastle-upon-Tyne (YH09005)			●				●				●		●															
MAW, J D, Sunderland (YH09282)		●																										
MCKEOWN, W J, Newcastle-upon-Tyne (YH09385)							●																					
QUARRY PARK STABLES, Gateshead (YH11483)								●	●					●			●			●				●	●			
REED, W G, Newcastle-upon-Tyne (YH11722)							●																					
RIDERS, North Shields (YH11854)																								●	●			
S & S SADDLERY, Sunderland (YH12313)																								●	●	●	●	●
SCOTT, ANDY, Newcastle-upon-Tyne (YH12537)							●																					
TURNBULL, T M, Newcastle-upon-Tyne (YH14471)		●																										
WARWICKSHIRE																												
A & J SADDLERY, Southam (YH00012)																								●	●	●	●	●
ACCIMASSU, Studley (YH00140)			●						●						●													
ALLEN, J S, Alcester (YH00297)							●																					
ALSCOT PARK STABLES, Stratford-upon-Avon (YH00336)							●																					
BERA, Kenilworth (YH01291)							●																					
BHS, Kenilworth (YH01371)			●																			●	●				●	
BLYTH MILL, Birmingham (YH01577)																												
BRADLEY, A S, Coventry (YH01752)																	●											
BRIDGWATER, MARY, Lapworth (YH01888)							●																					
CALDECOTE RIDING SCHOOL, Nuneaton (YH02428)																							●	●	●	●	●	●
COTON EQUITANA, Rugby (YH03358)							●																					
HADLEY, STEPHEN, Kineton (YH06268)							●						●				●											
HOWKINS & HARRISON, Henley-In-Arden (YH07239)																												
HOWKINS & HARRISON, Atherstone (YH07238)																												
KING, A, Stratford-upon-Avon (YH08172)							●																					
MOAT HOUSE STUD, Henley In Arden (YH09686)							●																					
PRITCHARD, P A, Shipston-on-Stour (YH11419)							●																					
RANKIN, JULIA, Alcester (YH11635)													●															
STARKEY, JANE, Leamington Spa (YH13395)							●																					
STONELEIGH STABLES, Kenilworth (YH13519)							●	●	●					●									●					
SWALLOWFIELD EQUESTRIAN, Solihull (YH13686)											●																	

Name	Architectural Advice	Architectural Planning	Arenas (large) for hire	Arenas (small) for hire	Arenas Indoor (Build)	Arenas Outdoor (Build)	Building Maintenance	Building Repairs	Cross Country Course (Build)	Cross Country Course (Design)	Fencing (Build)	Gates (Build)	Outbuildings (Build)	Pasture Supply	Pasture Support	Property Services	Racing Tracks (Build)	Show Jumps (Design)	Stables (Build)	Stables (Design)	Swimming Pools (Build)	Swimming Pools (Design)
LITTLE HARLE STABLES, Newcastle-upon-Tyne (YH08688)				●																		
MACKIE, HENRI, Newcastle-upon-Tyne (YH09005)																						
MAW, J D, Sunderland (YH09282)																						
MCKEOWN, W J, Newcastle-upon-Tyne (YH09385)																						
QUARRY PARK STABLES, Gateshead (YH11483)																						
REED, W G, Newcastle-upon-Tyne (YH11722)																						
RIDERS, North Shields (YH11854)																						
S & S SADDLERY, Sunderland (YH12313)																						
SCOTT, ANDY, Newcastle-upon-Tyne (YH12537)																						
TURNBULL, T M, Newcastle-upon-Tyne (YH14471)																						
WARWICKSHIRE																						
A & J SADDLERY, Southam (YH00012)																						
ACCIMASSU, Studley (YH00140)	●	●			●	●							●						●	●	●	●
ALLEN, J S, Alcester (YH00297)																						
ALSCOT PARK STABLES, Stratford-upon-Avon (YH00336)																						
BERA, Kenilworth (YH01291)																						
BHS, Kenilworth (YH01371)																						
BLYTH MILL, Birmingham (YH01577)														●								
BRADLEY, A S, Coventry (YH01752)																						
BRIDGWATER, MARY, Lapworth (YH01888)																						
CALDECOTE RIDING SCHOOL, Nuneaton (YH02428)				●																		
COTON EQUITANA, Rugby (YH03358)																						
HADLEY, STEPHEN, Kineton (YH06268)																						
HOWKINS & HARRISON, Henley-In-Arden (YH07239)																●						
HOWKINS & HARRISON, Atherstone (YH07238)																●						
KING, A, Stratford-upon-Avon (YH08172)																						
MOAT HOUSE STUD, Henley In Arden (YH09686)																						
PRITCHARD, P A, Shipston-on-Stour (YH11419)																						
RANKIN, JULIA, Alcester (YH11635)																						
STARKEY, JANE, Leamington Spa (YH13395)																						
STONELEIGH STABLES, Kenilworth (YH13519)																						
SWALLOWFIELD EQUESTRIAN, Solihull (YH13686)																						

Business Profile
Training (shaded area)
Course, Arena, Buildings and Pasture

by Country by County

	Coaches	Harness Trainer	Dressage Training	Polo Trainer	Side-saddle specialist	Side-saddle trainer	Trainers	Training (1 to 1)	Training (Children)	Training (Disabled)	Training (Dressage)	Training (Flat)	Training (Freelance)	Training (Group)	Training (Horse Breaking)	Training (Jockey)	Training (Jumps)	Training (Personnel)	Training (Point-to-Point)	Training (Riding)	Training (SteepleChase)	Training (To become a Trainer)	Training for Examination	Work with Children 10-16	Work with Children under 10	Work with Senior Citizens	Work with Students	Work with the Disabled	Architectural Advice	Architectural Planning	Arenas (large) for hire	Arenas (small) for hire	Arenas Indoor (Build)	Arenas Outdoor (Build)	Building Maintenance	Building Repairs	Cross Country Course (Build)	Cross Country Course (Design)	Fencing (Build)	Gates (Build)	Outbuildings (Build)	Pasture Supply	Pasture Support	Property Services	Racing Tracks (Build)	Show Jumps (Design)	Stables (Build)	Stables (Design)	Swimming Pools (Build)	Swimming Pools (Design)
TED EDGAR, Warwick (YH13930)																	●																																	
UK CHASERS & RIDERS, Leamington Spa (YH14545)																															●	●					●	●												
WAVERLEY EQUESTRIAN CTRE, Leamington Spa (YH15011)				●					●	●														●			●	●			●						●	●												
WOOTTON GRANGE EQUESTRIAN, Warwick (YH15772)								●				●	●	●	●		●							●		●	●																							
WILTSHIRE																																																		
ALAN KING RACING, Swindon (YH00240)							●																																											
BARRIERS INT, Malmesbury (YH01022)																																					●		●											
BENSON, SUE, Devizes (YH01280)							●																																											
BEST-TURNER, W DE, Marlborough (YH01328)							●																																											
BONITA RACING STABLES, Marlborough (YH01624)							●																																											
BURGESS, PAT, Salisbury (YH02246)							●						●																																					
CHAMBERLAIN, A J, Swindon (YH02717)							●																																											
CHARLTON, ROGER J, Marlborough (YH02768)							●																																											
DE GILES, J A T, Swindon (YH03976)							●																																											
EARLE, S A, Marlborough (YH04452)							●																																											
EASTON GREY SADDLERS, Malmesbury (YH04514)								●					●	●																																				
EQUIFOR, Marlborough (YH04746)	●																																																	
EQUINE MNGMT SOLUTIONS, Marlborough (YH04789)													●																																					
FONTHILL STUD, Salisbury (YH05308)							●																																											
GOSDEN, J H M, Marlborough (YH05941)							●																																											
GREENACRES, Salisbury (YH06075)			●					●																																										
GROVELY, Salisbury (YH06175)								●	●			●		●			●			●				●	●	●	●																							
HADDON STUD, Marlborough (YH06263)			●				●				●		●																																					
HAMPSLEY HOLLOW, Calne (YH06368)								●	●	●	●			●			●			●				●	●	●	●	●																						
HANNON, R, Marlborough (YH06395)							●																																											
HAYNES, H E, Swindon (YH06588)							●																																											
HEDDINGTON WICK, Calne (YH06639)								●	●	●				●			●							●	●																									
HIGHLANDS FARM RACING STABLES, Marlborough (YH06795)							●																																											
HOLDERNESS-RODDAM, JANE, Chippenham (YH06926)			●				●				●		●				●																																	
HORSEMANSHIP, Wootton Bassett (YH07161)							●	●						●				●		●												●																		
HULBERTS GREEN, Chippenham (YH07279)																												●																						
HURDCOTT LIVERY STABLES, Salisbury (YH07311)																															●																			

Business Profile

Training (shaded area) **Course, Arena, Buildings and Pasture**

by Country by County

	Coaches	Harness Trainer	Dressage Training	Polo Trainer	Side-saddle specialist	Side-saddle trainer	Trainers	Training (1 to 1)	Training (Children)	Training (Disabled)	Training (Dressage)	Training (Flat)	Training (Freelance)	Training (Group)	Training (Horse Breaking)	Training (Jockey)	Training (Jumps)	Training (Personnel)	Training (Point-to-Point)	Training (Riding)	Training (SteepleChase)	Training (To become a Trainer)	Training for Examination	Work with Children 10-16	Work with Children under 10	Work with Senior Citizens	Work with Students	Work with the Disabled	Architectural Advice	Architectural Planning	Arenas (large) for hire	Arenas (small) for hire	Arenas Indoor (Build)	Arenas Outdoor (Build)	Building Maintenance	Building Repairs	Cross Country Course (Build)	Cross Country Course (Design)	Fencing (Build)	Gates (Build)	Outbuildings (Build)	Pasture Supply	Pasture Support	Property Services	Racing Tracks (Build)	Show Jumps (Design)	Stables (Build)	Stables (Design)	Swimming Pools (Build)	Swimming Pools (Design)
INFANTRY SADDLE CLUB, Warminster (YH07441)			●						●	●	●						●			●				●	●			●			●	●																		
INGLESHAM POLO CTRE, Swindon (YH07450)							●																																											
IRRIGATION SYSTEMS & SERVICES, Salisbury (YH07508)																																											●							
J A B OLD, Swindon (YH07553)							●																																											
KING, J S & PM, Swindon (YH08181)												●									●																													
LACKHAM CLGE EQUESTRIAN CTRE, Chippenham (YH08332)																						●	●				●																							
LANE, CHARLIE, Warminster (YH08390)							●						●																																					
LYON, POLLY, Malmesbury (YH08940)							●																																											
MALTHOUSE EQUESTRIAN CTRE, Swindon (YH09058)			●				●	●	●		●			●			●	●		●			●	●	●	●	●					●																		
MANNERS, JOHN, Swindon (YH09086)							●																																											
MARLBOROUGH DOWNS, Marlborough (YH09169)								●	●		●			●			●			●				●	●	●	●																							
MEADE, RICHARD, Chippenham (YH09415)							●																																											
NAYLOR, J R J (DR), Salisbury (YH10059)							●																																											
NICHOLSON, ANDREW, Devizes (YH10190)							●																																											
ORMEROD, GILES, Salisbury (YH10548)							●																																											
PEACOCK, R E, Malmesbury (YH10862)							●																																											
PEWSEY VALE, Marlborough (YH11037)								●	●					●			●			●			●																											
RURAL SCENE, Marlborough (YH12238)																																												●						
SALAMAN, M, Marlborough (YH12385)							●																																											
SCIMGEOUR, ANNABEL, Marlborough (YH12525)			●				●				●		●																																					
SOUTHVIEW FARM, Bradford-on-Avon (YH13160)									●					●						●				●	●	●	●																							
STONAR SCHOOL, Melksham (YH13507)			●				●				●		●				●														●																			
TOLLARD PARK EQUESTRIAN CTRE, Salisbury (YH14207)													●																																					
WANLESS, MARY, Box (YH14894)			●				●				●		●																																					
WEST KINGTON STUD, Chippenham (YH15151)																											●																							
WHITE HORSE EQUESTRIAN CTRE, Westbury (YH15308)								●	●	●				●										●	●	●	●	●																						
WIDBROOK ARABIAN STUD, Bradford-on-Avon (YH15388)								●	●		●	●		●			●			●																														
WILLIS BROS, Malmesbury (YH15491)																																							●											
WILSFORD STABLES, Salisbury (YH15526)							●																																											
WYLYE STUD, Salisbury (YH15866)							●																																											
WORCESTERSHIRE																																																		
AUTY, I, Hallow (YH00676)			●				●				●		●																																					

Business Profile
Training (shaded area) **Course, Arena, Buildings and Pasture**

by Country by County

by Country by County	Coaches	Harness Trainer	Dressage Training	Polo Trainer	Side-saddle specialist	Side-saddle trainer	Trainers	Training (1 to 1)	Training (Children)	Training (Disabled)	Training (Dressage)	Training (Flat)	Training (Freelance)	Training (Group)	Training (Horse Breaking)	Training (Jockey)	Training (Jumps)	Training (Personnel)	Training (Point-to-Point)	Training (Riding)	Training (SteepleChase)	Training (To become a Trainer)	Training for Examination	Work with Children 10-16	Work with Children under 10	Work with Senior Citizens	Work with Students	Work with the Disabled	Architectural Advice	Architectural Planning	Arenas (large) for hire	Arenas (small) for hire	Arenas Indoor (Build)	Arenas Outdoor (Build)	Building Maintenance	Building Repairs	Cross Country Course (Build)	Cross Country Course (Design)	Fencing (Build)	Gates (Build)	Outbuildings (Build)	Pasture Supply	Pasture Support	Property Services	Racing Tracks (Build)	Show Jumps (Design)	Stables (Build)	Stables (Design)	Swimming Pools (Build)	Swimming Pools (Design)
BIRCHWOOD, Bewdley (YH01436)								●																																										
CARENZA, JILL, Broadway (YH02534)								●	●					●										●	●	●	●																							
CARROLL, A W, Flavell (YH02592)							●																																											
CLARKS HILL, Evesham (YH02980)								●	●					●										●	●																									
COLLEY, ANNE, Bewdley (YH03177)							●						●																																					
CROWFIELDS EQUESTRIAN SVS, Bromsgrove (YH03678)													●																																					
DORAN, B N, Broadway (YH04196)							●																																											
EILBERG, FERDI, Redditch (YH04598)			●				●				●		●																																					
EQUINE RESOURCES, Malvern (YH04796)							●																																											
EVANS, SALLYANN & LISA, Bromsgrove (YH04932)			●				●				●																																							
FAR FOREST EQUESTRIAN CTRE, Kidderminster (YH05047)			●				●				●																																							
GRACELANDS, Droitwich (YH05958)																																●																		
HALLOW MILLS, Worcester (YH06333)								●	●		●			●			●			●			●	●	●	●	●																							
HARTLEBURY EQUESTRIAN CTRE, Kidderminster (YH06505)								●	●	●	●			●			●			●			●	●	●		●	●																						
HEID & BRAZIER, Stourport-on-Severn (YH06648)							●	●					●	●	●					●			●																											
HENRY FIELDS STUD, Pershore (YH06682)																			●																															
HINDLIP EQUESTRIAN CTRE, Hindlip (YH06872)			●				●				●		●				●																																	
INGRAM, PAUL, Kidderminster (YH07454)			●				●				●		●																																					
JACKSON, C F C, Malvern (YH07644)							●																																											
JAMES, A P, Tenbury Wells (YH07677)							●																																											
JUCKES, R T, Worcester (YH07956)							●																																											
JUMPS FOR JOY, Worcester (YH07969)																																														●				
KINNERSLEY RACING STABLES, Severn Stoke (YH08218)							●																																											
KYRE EQUESTRIAN CTRE, Tenbury Wells (YH08305)								●			●		●	●			●			●				●							●											●								
LAST EMPIRE STABLES, Suckley (YH08443)							●																																											
LEA CASTLE EQUESTRIAN CTRE, Kidderminster (YH08493)							●																																											
LYMER, WENDY, Grimley (YH08920)													●																																					
M & M TIMBER, Kidderminster (YH08949)																													●										●					●						
MILL END RACING, Pershore (YH09569)							●																																											
MOORLANDS, Worcester (YH09779)									●	●	●			●			●			●				●	●	●	●	●																						
MOYFIELD RIDING SCHOOL, Evesham (YH09908)						●		●	●	●	●			●						●				●	●	●	●																							
PEASEBROOK, Broadway (YH10883)							●																																											

Business Profile

Training (shaded area) Course, Arena, Buildings and Pasture

by Country by County

	Coaches	Harness Trainer	Dressage Training	Polo Trainer	Side-saddle specialist	Side-saddle trainer	Trainers	Training (1 to 1)	Training (Children)	Training (Disabled)	Training (Dressage)	Training (Flat)	Training (Freelance)	Training (Group)	Training (Horse Breaking)	Training (Jockey)	Training (Jumps)	Training (Personnel)	Training (Point-to-Point)	Training (Riding)	Training (SteepleChase)	Training (To become a Trainer)	Training for Examination	Work with Children 10-16	Work with Children under 10	Work with Senior Citizens	Work with Students	Work with the Disabled	Architectural Advice	Architectural Planning	Arenas (large) for hire	Arenas (small) for hire	Arenas Indoor (Build)	Arenas Outdoor (Build)	Building Maintenance	Building Repairs	Cross Country Course (Build)	Cross Country Course (Design)	Fencing (Build)	Gates (Build)	Outbuildings (Build)	Pasture Supply	Pasture Support	Property Services	Racing Tracks (Build)	Show Jumps (Design)	Stables (Build)	Stables (Design)	Swimming Pools (Build)	Swimming Pools (Design)
PERSHORE & HINDLIP CLGE, Hindlip (YH10993)			●				●				●						●														●																			
SMITH, N A, Worcester (YH12979)							●																																											
SOLCUM STUD & STABLES, Kidderminster (YH13052)			●				●				●																																							
TATE, MARTIN, Kidderminster (YH13873)							●																																											
WALKERS OF WORCESTERSHIRE, Kidderminster (YH14859)																																							●											
WALNUT STABLES, Malvern (YH14870)			●					●	●		●			●			●			●				●	●	●	●																							
WARRINGTON, S, Little Witley (YH14943)			●				●	●	●		●		●	●			●			●			●	●	●	●	●				●																			
WELLMAN, M, Upton-upon-Severn (YH15076)			●				●				●		●																																					
YARDLEY, GEORGE HENRY, Malvern (YH15884)							●																																											
YORKSHIRE (EAST)																																																		
AIKE GRANGE STUD, Driffield (YH00207)			●								●													●	●		●	●			●																			
BISHOP BURTON COLLEGE, Beverley (YH01448)																							●																											
BLEACH YARD STABLES, Beverley (YH01531)			●				●				●																																							
BURTON CONSTABLE RIDING CTRE, Hull (YH02291)								●			●			●			●							●	●	●	●	●																						
CURTIS, CARL, Goole (YH03745)																	●																				●													
EAST RIDING, Brough (YH04483)																	●																																	
GEE, MICHAEL, Holme upon Spalding Moor (YH05692)																																					●													
HEATH RACING STABLES, Beverley (YH06622)							●																																											
NASH, J, Driffield (YH10026)							●																																											
NORTH HUMBERSIDE, Hull (YH10264)			●					●	●		●	●	●	●						●		●	●																											
RISTON WHINS LIVERY YARD, Beverley (YH11913)																			●																															
SOWERSBY, M E, Goodmanham (YH13168)							●																																											
YORKSHIRE (NORTH)																																																		
ALEXANDER, HAMISH, York (YH00270)							●																																											
ASHGILL STABLES, Leyburn (YH00604)							●																																											
BARKER, DAVID, Richmond (YH00941)							●																																											
BARNHOUSE RACING STABLES, Richmond (YH00988)							●																																											
BARRON, T D, Thirsk (YH01025)							●																																											
BARROWBY RIDING CTRE, Harrogate (YH01032)													●																																					
BARTLE, G M, Tadcaster (YH01038)													●																																					
BEAUMONT, P, York (YH01137)							●																																											
BELLWOOD COTTAGE STABLES, Malton (YH01242)							●																																											

Business Profile
Training (shaded area) Course, Arena, Buildings and Pasture

by Country by County

	Coaches	Harness Trainer	Dressage Training	Polo Trainer	Side-saddle specialist	Side-saddle trainer	Trainers	Training (1 to 1)	Training (Children)	Training (Disabled)	Training (Dressage)	Training (Flat)	Training (Freelance)	Training (Group)	Training (Horse Breaking)	Training (Jockey)	Training (Jumps)	Training (Personnel)	Training (Point-to-Point)	Training (Riding)	Training (SteepleChase)	Training (To become a Trainer)	Training for Examination	Work with Children 10-16	Work with Children under 10	Work with Senior Citizens	Work with Students	Work with the Disabled	Architectural Advice	Architectural Planning	Arenas (large) for hire	Arenas (small) for hire	Arenas Indoor (Build)	Arenas Outdoor (Build)	Building Maintenance	Building Repairs	Cross Country Course (Build)	Cross Country Course (Design)	Fencing (Build)	Gates (Build)	Outbuildings (Build)	Pasture Supply	Pasture Support	Property Services	Racing Tracks (Build)	Show Jumps (Design)	Stables (Build)	Stables (Design)	Swimming Pools (Build)	Swimming Pools (Design)
BEWERLEY, Harrogate (YH01347)								●	●	●	●			●			●			●			●	●	●	●	●	●																						
BLEACH FARM, York (YH01530)								●	●		●			●			●			●				●	●	●	●																							
BOGS HALL, Ripon (YH01598)								●	●	●				●										●	●	●	●	●																						
BOOTH, C B B, York (YH01634)							●																																											
BOULTON & COOPER, Malton (YH01674)																																												●						
BRANDSBY AGRIC TRADING ASS, Malton (YH01802)																																							●			●								
BRECONGILL STABLES, Leyburn (YH01830)							●																																											
BRIGG VIEW, Filey (YH01906)			●					●	●		●			●			●			●			●	●	●	●	●																							
BRITTAIN, M, York (YH01982)							●																																											
BROADACRES NURSERIES, Tadcaster (YH01991)																								●	●	●	●	●																						
BROWN, M IAN, Richmond (YH02123)			●				●				●																																							
CAMACHO RACING, Malton (YH02464)							●																																											
CASTLE STABLES, Richmond (YH02637)							●																																											
CHAPMAN, D W, York (YH02744)							●																																											
COMMON FARM STABLES, York (YH03215)							●																																											
COTTAGE FARM STABLES, York (YH03375)																								●	●																									
CRAVEN CLGE, Skipton (YH03572)																							●																											
DUFFIELD, ANN, Leyburn (YH04314)							●																																											
EASTERBY, M H, Malton (YH04493)							●																																											
EASTERBY, M W, York (YH04494)							●																																											
ETHERINGTON, T J, Malton (YH04883)							●																																											
EYRE, J L, Thirsk (YH04976)							●																																											
FAHEY, R, Malton (YH05009)							●																																											
FAIRHURST, C W, Leyburn (YH05024)							●																																											
FELL VIEW STABLES, Leyburn (YH05132)							●																																											
FITZGERALD, J G, Malton (YH05247)							●																																											
FLETCHER, KAREN, Thirsk (YH05280)																	●																																	
FOLLIFOOT PK, Harrogate (YH05300)									●	●														●	●			●																						
FRIARS HILL STABLES, York (YH05501)						●		●	●	●			●	●	●		●		●	●			●	●	●	●	●	●				●																		
GILYHEAD, G M, Knaresborough (YH05793)		●																																																
HASLAM, P C, Leyburn (YH06523)							●																																											
HETHERTON, JAMES, Malton (YH06725)							●																																											

Business Profile

Training (shaded area)
Course, Arena, Buildings and Pasture

by Country by County

Name	Coaches	Harness Trainer	Dressage Training	Polo Trainer	Side-saddle specialist	Side-saddle trainer	Trainers	Training (1 to 1)	Training (Children)	Training (Disabled)	Training (Dressage)	Training (Flat)	Training (Freelance)	Training (Group)	Training (Horse Breaking)	Training (Jockey)	Training (Jumps)	Training (Personnel)	Training (Point-to-Point)	Training (Riding)	Training (SteepleChase)	Training (To become a Trainer)	Training for Examination	Work with Children 10-16	Work with Children under 10	Work with Senior Citizens	Work with Students	Work with the Disabled	Architectural Advice	Architectural Planning	Arenas (large) for hire	Arenas (small) for hire	Arenas Indoor (Build)	Arenas Outdoor (Build)	Building Maintenance	Building Repairs	Cross Country Course (Build)	Cross Country Course (Design)	Fencing (Build)	Gates (Build)	Outbuildings (Build)	Pasture Supply	Pasture Support	Property Services	Racing Tracks (Build)	Show Jumps (Design)	Stables (Build)	Stables (Design)	Swimming Pools (Build)	Swimming Pools (Design)
HOLGATE, T, Skipton (YH06932)		●																																																
HOLMES, G, Pickering (YH06975)							●																																											
HOME FARM, Malton (YH06995)								●	●		●			●			●			●			●	●	●	●	●																							
INCISA, DON ENRICO, Leyburn (YH07409)							●																																											
JODHPURS, York (YH07774)								●	●		●			●			●			●				●	●	●	●																							
JOUSTING & ASSOCIATED SKILLS, Thirsk (YH07948)							●	●			●							●		●		●	●	●			●	●																						
KELLY, G P, Sheriff Hutton (YH08044)							●																																											
KETTLEWELL, S E, Leyburn (YH08109)							●																																											
LANGTON HORSE WEAR, Northallerton (YH08416)																								●	●																									
LOCKWOOD, A, Malton (YH08762)							●																																											
MANOR HSE FARM, Pickering (YH09113)							●	●												●																														
MARK JOHNSTON RACING, Leyburn (YH09153)							●																																											
MILL LANE, Selby (YH09579)								●	●					●			●	●		●			●	●	●	●	●	●				●																		
MOORE, GEORGE, Leyburn (YH09759)							●																																											
MOORHOUSE RIDING CTRE, York (YH09776)								●	●	●	●			●			●			●			●	●	●	●	●	●																						
MULHOLLAND, T, Thirsk (YH09933)							●																																											
MURRAY, B W, Malton (YH09963)							●																																											
MUSLEY BANK STABLES, Malton (YH09975)							●																																											
NABURN GRANGE RIDING CTRE, York (YH10008)								●	●		●	●	●	●	●		●			●		●	●	●	●	●	●	●																						
NAUGHTON, A M, Richmond (YH10056)							●																																											
NEWSTEAD COTTAGE STABLES, Malton (YH10165)							●																																											
NICHOLSON, MYLES, Harrogate (YH10194)			●				●				●		●				●																																	
NORTHALLERTON EQUESTRIAN, Northallerton (YH10290)								●		●				●												●	●	●																						
PARKES, J E, Upper Helmsley (YH10757)							●																																											
PARRINGTON, M C, Skipton (YH10786)		●																																																
R & R COUNTRY, Selby (YH11507)																																																●		
RIDING CTRE, Harrogate (YH11874)			●					●	●	●	●			●			●		●				●	●	●	●	●	●																						
ROBINSON, W R, Scarborough (YH12001)																	●																				●													
ROSE COTTAGE FARM, York (YH12091)																																●																		
ROTHWELL, B, Malton (YH12137)							●																																											
ROW BROW FARM, Scarborough (YH12151)			●				●				●																																							
RYAN, KEVIN, Thirsk (YH12284)							●																																											

Business Profile
Training (shaded area) **Course, Arena, Buildings and Pasture**

by Country by County

by Country by County	Coaches	Harness Trainer	Dressage Training	Polo Trainer	Side-saddle specialist	Side-saddle trainer	Trainers	Training (1 to 1)	Training (Children)	Training (Disabled)	Training (Dressage)	Training (Flat)	Training (Freelance)	Training (Group)	Training (Horse Breaking)	Training (Jockey)	Training (Jumps)	Training (Personnel)	Training (Point-to-Point)	Training (Riding)	Training (SteepleChase)	Training (To become a Trainer)	Training for Examination	Work with Children 10-16	Work with Children under 10	Work with Senior Citizens	Work with Students	Work with the Disabled	Architectural Advice	Architectural Planning	Arenas (large) for hire	Arenas (small) for hire	Arenas Indoor (Build)	Arenas Outdoor (Build)	Building Maintenance	Building Repairs	Cross Country Course (Build)	Cross Country Course (Design)	Fencing (Build)	Gates (Build)	Outbuildings (Build)	Pasture Supply	Pasture Support	Property Services	Racing Tracks (Build)	Show Jumps (Design)	Stables (Build)	Stables (Design)	Swimming Pools (Build)	Swimming Pools (Design)
SIDDALL, L C, Tadcaster (YH12783)							●																																											
SINNINGTON MANOR, York (YH12855)			●					●					●	●	●																																			
SLEE, C, Coverham (YH12893)		●																																																
SNAINTON RIDING CTRE, Scarborough (YH13028)			●				●				●																																							
SPALDING, C M, Richmond (YH13171)							●																																											
SPIGOT LODGE, Leyburn (YH13203)							●																																											
SPRING COTTAGE STABLES, Melton (YH13245)							●																																											
TATE, ROBIN, Thirsk (YH13875)							●																																											
TATE, TOM, Tadcaster (YH13877)							●																																											
TEAL COTTAGE STUD, Welburn (YH13922)																			●																															
THORNDALE FARM STABLES, Richmond (YH14061)							●																																											
TINKLER, NIGEL, Malton (YH14173)							●																																											
TINNING, BILL, Thornton-Le-Clay (YH14174)							●																																											
TURNELL, ANDY, Thirsk (YH14473)							●																																											
TURNER, J R, Helperby (YH14482)							●																																											
WAINWRIGHT, J S, Malton (YH14829)							●																																											
WATT FENCES, Catterick Garrison (YH14997)																																					●	●	●							●				
WEATHERILL, P S, Harrogate (YH15026)		●																																																
WILSON, N, Kirby Underdale (YH15543)							●																																											
WOODHOUSE, R D E, York (YH15696)							●																																											
WYNBURY STABLES, Leyburn (YH15870)							●																																											
YORKSHIRE DALES, Skipton (YH15919)								●	●		●	●	●	●									●	●	●	●	●	●																						
YORKSHIRE RIDING CTRE, Harrogate (YH15922)			●				●	●			●			●						●		●	●	●		●	●																							
YORKSHIRE (SOUTH)																																																		
BALDING, JOHN, Doncaster (YH00837)							●																																											
BARNES GREEN, Sheffield (YH00971)								●	●					●			●			●			●	●	●	●	●																							
BROCKHOLES FARM, Doncaster (YH02010)								●	●	●	●			●			●			●			●	●	●	●	●	●																						
DARKHORSE TINYTACK, Barnsley (YH03888)																								●	●			●																						
EQUESTRUCT, Sheffield (YH04725)																																												●						
GROVE HOUSE, Doncaster (YH06168)								●	●	●				●									●	●	●	●	●	●																						
MALLARD HSE, Sheffield (YH09050)								●	●		●			●			●						●	●	●	●	●																							
MOORHOUSE, Doncaster (YH09775)								●	●	●	●			●			●			●			●	●	●	●	●	●																						

Business Profile

Training (shaded area) **Course, Arena, Buildings and Pasture**

by Country by County

	Coaches	Harness Trainer	Dressage Training	Polo Trainer	Side-saddle specialist	Side-saddle trainer	Trainers	Training (1 to 1)	Training (Children)	Training (Disabled)	Training (Dressage)	Training (Flat)	Training (Freelance)	Training (Group)	Training (Horse Breaking)	Training (Jockey)	Training (Jumps)	Training (Personnel)	Training (Point-to-Point)	Training (Riding)	Training (SteepleChase)	Training (To become a Trainer)	Training for Examination	Work with Children 10-16	Work with Children under 10	Work with Senior Citizens	Work with Students	Work with the Disabled	Architectural Advice	Architectural Planning	Arenas (large) for hire	Arenas (small) for hire	Arenas Indoor (Build)	Arenas Outdoor (Build)	Building Maintenance	Building Repairs	Cross Country Course (Build)	Cross Country Course (Design)	Fencing (Build)	Gates (Build)	Outbuildings (Build)	Pasture Supply	Pasture Support	Property Services	Racing Tracks (Build)	Show Jumps (Design)	Stables (Build)	Stables (Design)	Swimming Pools (Build)	Swimming Pools (Design)
NORTHERN RACING COLLEGE, Doncaster (YH10307)																●		●		●		●					●																							
NORTON, J, Barnsley (YH10332)							●																																											
PARKLANDS RIDING SCHOOL, Sheffield (YH10770)								●	●					●						●																														
PRICES, Rotherham (YH11391)								●	●	●		●		●			●			●			●	●	●	●	●	●																						
ROYSTON PONY CLUB, Barnsley (YH12202)									●	●							●			●				●	●		●	●																						
SHOWJUMP INT, Barnsley (YH12766)																																					●	●								●				
SILKSTONE EQUESTRIAN CTRE, Barnsley (YH12800)								●	●	●		●		●			●			●				●	●	●	●	●																						
SYKEHOUSE ARENA, Doncaster (YH13723)											●						●																																	
THOMPSON, R, Doncaster (YH14040)							●						●																																					
YORKSHIRE (WEST)																																																		
ACRELIFFE, Otley (YH00159)					●	●		●	●	●				●						●			●		●																									
ASTLEY RIDING CTRE, Leeds (YH00635)									●						●		●			●				●	●		●				●																			
BANK HSE FARM, Wakefield (YH00891)								●	●	●				●						●				●	●	●	●	●																						
BARTON, R & J, Wilsden (YH01050)																	●																																	
BETA, Wetherby (YH01330)																		●																																
BLACUP TRAINING GRP, Halifax (YH01504)			●				●	●			●		●	●	●		●	●		●		●	●				●				●	●																		
BRADMAN, N, Pontefract (YH01761)																	●																				●													
BROWNS FENCING, Liversedge (YH02144)																																							●											
CHADWICK, SUE, Huddersfield (YH02706)							●																																											
CLIFFORD MOOR FARM, Wetherby (YH03035)								●	●					●						●																														
CROFTON RIDING STABLES, Wakefield (YH03624)								●	●					●			●			●				●	●																									
DAWSON, P G, Halton (YH03964)		●																																																
DISCOUNT SADDLERY, Huddersfield (YH04129)					●																																													
EASTVIEW STABLES, Leeds (YH04516)								●					●	●													●					●		●																
EASTWOOD, M, Huddersfield (YH04520)		●																																																
EQUITACK SADDLERY, Wakefield (YH04825)																												●																						
EVENT SVS, Halifax (YH04938)																																							●											
FARMERS IMPLEMENT SUPPLY, Wakefield (YH05063)																																											●							
GOODWIN, P, Wakefield (YH05912)																																					●													
HOPTON, Mirfield (YH07061)															●		●	●													●						●				●	●	●			●	●			
ILKLEY RIDING CTRE, Ilkley (YH07400)								●	●					●						●				●	●																									
JAMES BURNHILL & SON, Cleckheaton (YH07663)																																										●								

Business Profile
Training (shaded area)
Course, Arena, Buildings and Pasture

by Country by County

	Coaches	Harness Trainer	Dressage Training	Polo Trainer	Side-saddle specialist	Side-saddle trainer	Trainers	Training (1 to 1)	Training (Children)	Training (Disabled)	Training (Dressage)	Training (Flat)	Training (Freelance)	Training (Group)	Training (Horse Breaking)	Training (Jockey)	Training (Jumps)	Training (Personnel)	Training (Point-to-Point)	Training (Riding)	Training (SteepleChase)	Training (To become a Trainer)	Training for Examination	Work with Children 10-16	Work with Children under 10	Work with Senior Citizens	Work with Students	Work with the Disabled
LATHAM FARM, Cleckheaton (YH08445)																												
MANOR GRANGE STUD SCHOOL, Wakefield (YH09109)			●				●				●																	
METCALFE, STUART, Ilkley (YH09501)			●				●				●																	
MIDGLEY, A D, Hobberley Lane (YH09551)													●															
NICHOL, D W, Bradford (YH10179)		●																										
NORLAND EQUESTRIAN CTRE, Halifax (YH10234)							●	●	●	●	●	●	●	●						●					●			
PARNHAM LANDSCAPES, Leeds (YH10784)																												
ROBERTS, V C, Pontefract (YH11964)																	●											
SMITH, S J, Bingley (YH13000)							●																					
SYCAMORE HOUSE FARM, Leeds (YH13719)													●															
THROSTLE NEST RIDING SCHOOL, Bradford (YH14113)							●	●	●	●				●								●	●					
TIMBERTOPS EQUESTRIAN CTRE, Pontefract (YH14162)								●	●		●			●			●					●						
TRUEWELL HALL FARM, Keighley (YH14421)								●	●					●						●								
WESTWAYS RIDING SCHOOL, Leeds (YH15236)								●	●					●											●			
WHITAKER, R M, Leeds (YH15291)							●																					
WHITLEY EQUITATION CTRE, Dewsbury (YH15363)								●	●	●				●			●			●		●	●					
WRB RACING, Leeds (YH15814)												●					●											

	Architectural Advice	Architectural Planning	Arenas (large) for hire	Arenas (small) for hire	Arenas Indoor (Build)	Arenas Outdoor (Build)	Building Maintenance	Building Repairs	Cross Country Course (Build)	Cross Country Course (Design)	Fencing (Build)	Gates (Build)	Outbuildings (Build)	Pasture Supply	Pasture Support	Property Services	Racing Tracks (Build)	Show Jumps (Design)	Stables (Build)	Stables (Design)	Swimming Pools (Build)	Swimming Pools (Design)
LATHAM FARM, Cleckheaton (YH08445)												●										
MANOR GRANGE STUD SCHOOL, Wakefield (YH09109)																						
METCALFE, STUART, Ilkley (YH09501)																						
MIDGLEY, A D, Hobberley Lane (YH09551)																						
NICHOL, D W, Bradford (YH10179)																						
NORLAND EQUESTRIAN CTRE, Halifax (YH10234)																						
PARNHAM LANDSCAPES, Leeds (YH10784)											●											
ROBERTS, V C, Pontefract (YH11964)																						
SMITH, S J, Bingley (YH13000)																						
SYCAMORE HOUSE FARM, Leeds (YH13719)																						
THROSTLE NEST RIDING SCHOOL, Bradford (YH14113)																						
TIMBERTOPS EQUESTRIAN CTRE, Pontefract (YH14162)																						
TRUEWELL HALL FARM, Keighley (YH14421)																						
WESTWAYS RIDING SCHOOL, Leeds (YH15236)																						
WHITAKER, R M, Leeds (YH15291)																						
WHITLEY EQUITATION CTRE, Dewsbury (YH15363)																						
WRB RACING, Leeds (YH15814)																						

Business Profile
Training (shaded area)
Course, Arena, Buildings and Pasture

by Country by County

	Coaches	Harness Trainer	Dressage Training	Polo Trainer	Side-saddle specialist	Side-saddle trainer	Trainers	Training (1 to 1)	Training (Children)	Training (Disabled)	Training (Dressage)	Training (Flat)	Training (Freelance)	Training (Group)	Training (Horse Breaking)	Training (Jockey)	Training (Jumps)	Training (Personnel)	Training (Point-to-Point)	Training (Riding)	Training (SteepleChase)	Training (To become a Trainer)	Training for Examination	Work with Children 10-16	Work with Children under 10	Work with Senior Citizens	Work with Students	Work with the Disabled	Architectural Advice	Architectural Planning	Arenas (large) for hire	Arenas (small) for hire	Arenas Indoor (Build)	Arenas Outdoor (Build)	Building Maintenance	Building Repairs	Cross Country Course (Build)	Cross Country Course (Design)	Fencing (Build)	Gates (Build)	Outbuildings (Build)	Pasture Supply	Pasture Support	Property Services	Racing Tracks (Build)	Show Jumps (Design)	Stables (Build)	Stables (Design)	Swimming Pools (Build)	Swimming Pools (Design)
IRELAND																																																		
COUNTY CARLOW																																																		
CARRIGBEG RIDING SCHOOL, Bagenalstown (YH02588)									●					●			●			●				●	●	●	●																							
FENNISCOURT STABLES, Bagenalstown (YH05148)							●																																											
COUNTY CAVAN																																																		
CAVAN EQUESTRIAN CTRE, Cavan (YH02664)									●								●														●																			
REDHILLS EQUESTRIAN, Redhills (YH11713)								●	●	●	●			●			●			●		●	●																											
COUNTY CLARE																																																		
BANNER EQUESTRIAN, Ennis (YH00906)								●	●		●			●			●			●				●	●	●	●																							
COUNTY CORK																																																		
BANTRY HORSE RIDING, Bantry (YH00912)									●	●				●						●				●	●	●	●	●																						
BEE WOODCRAFT, Ardmore (YH01160)																																							●								●	●		
BLARNEY RIDING CTRE, Blarney (YH01528)								●	●		●			●						●																														
CASTLEWHITE, Cork (YH02646)									●	●										●			●	●	●		●	●																						
CHURCHTOWN RIDING SCHOOL, Mallow (YH02915)									●																																									
CLONAKILTY EQUESTRIAN CTRE, Clonakilty (YH03053)								●	●		●			●			●			●																														
PINEGROVE STABLES, Cork (YH11125)												●							●		●																													
COUNTY DUBLIN																																																		
CALLIAGHSTOWN EQUESTRIAN, Rathcoole (YH02449)									●		●			●			●			●				●	●	●	●																							
CARRICKMINES EQUESTRIAN CTRE, Dublin (YH02587)								●	●		●			●			●			●																														
RATHFARNHAN EQUESTRIAN CTRE, Dublin (YH11655)								●	●	●	●			●						●				●	●	●	●	●																						
THORNTON PARK, Dublin (YH14074)									●					●						●		●	●	●	●	●	●																							
COUNTY GALWAY																																																		
ROCKMOUNT RIDING CTRE, Claregalway (YH12037)									●					●						●																														
COUNTY KERRY																																																		
ABBEYGLEN, Milltown (YH00097)								●	●	●				●						●				●	●	●	●	●																						
CURRAGH COTTAGE LEISURE, Tralee (YH03735)									●					●						●																														
COUNTY KILDARE																																																		
BERRY, FRANK, Kilcullen (YH01316)							●																																											
BRASSIL, MARTIN, Kildare (YH01815)							●																																											
BURNS, JAMES G, The Curragh (YH02273)							●																																											

Business Profile
Training (shaded area) Course, Arena, Buildings and Pasture

by Country by County

Name	Coaches	Harness Trainer	Dressage Training	Polo Trainer	Side-saddle specialist	Side-saddle trainer	Trainers	Training (1 to 1)	Training (Children)	Training (Disabled)	Training (Dressage)	Training (Flat)	Training (Freelance)	Training (Group)	Training (Horse Breaking)	Training (Jockey)	Training (Jumps)	Training (Personnel)	Training (Point-to-Point)	Training (Riding)	Training (SteepleChase)	Training (To become a Trainer)	Training for Examination	Work with Children 10-16	Work with Children under 10	Work with Senior Citizens	Work with Students	Work with the Disabled	Architectural Advice	Architectural Planning	Arenas (large) for hire	Arenas (small) for hire	Arenas Indoor (Build)	Arenas Outdoor (Build)	Building Maintenance	Building Repairs	Cross Country Course (Build)	Cross Country Course (Design)	Fencing (Build)	Gates (Build)	Outbuildings (Build)	Pasture Supply	Pasture Support	Property Services	Racing Tracks (Build)	Show Jumps (Design)	Stables (Build)	Stables (Design)	Swimming Pools (Build)	Swimming Pools (Design)
CUSACK, GERALD A, Naas (YH03756)							●																																											
ENNIS, FRANCIS, The Curragh (YH04677)							●																																											
ENNIS, FRANK, Curragh (YH04678)							●																																											
GORMAN, JIM, The Curragh (YH05935)							●																																											
GRASSICK, MICHAEL, The Curragh (YH06021)							●																																											
GROOME, JIMMY, Kildare (YH06152)							●																																											
HALFORD, MICHAEL, Curragh (YH06299)							●																																											
HANLEY, DAVID, The Curragh (YH06390)							●																																											
HAYDEN, JOHN, Kilcullen (YH06569)							●																																											
HUGHES, DESMOND T, Kildare (YH07264)							●																																											
HUGHES, DESSIE, Kildare (YH07265)							●																																											
KENNEDY, VIVIAN, The Curragh (YH08071)							●																																											
MOORE, ARTHUR, Naas (YH09755)							●																																											
MULLHERN, JOHN, The Curragh (YH09938)							●																																											
NAAS RACECOURSE, Naas (YH10006)																																													●					
OAKES, IRENE, Stroud (YH10377)							●																																											
OSBORNE, ROBERT, Naas (YH10560)							●																																											
OXX, JOHN, Kildare (YH10628)							●																																											
PRENDERGAST, KEVIN, Kildare (YH11353)							●																																											
ROCHE, CHRISTY, Kildare (YH12018)							●									●																																		
ROPER, MARK, The Curragh (YH12085)							●																																											
SCOTT, HOMER, Castledermot (YH12544)							●																																											
TAAFFE, TOM, Straffan (YH13770)							●																																											
WALSH, TED, Kill (YH14880)							●																																											
WELD, D K, Curragh (YH15061)							●																																											
YEOMANSTOWN STUD, Naas (YH15905)							●																																											
COUNTY KILKENNY																																																		
MULLINS, A, Kilkenny (YH09941)							●																																											
COUNTY LIMERICK																																																		
ADARE EQUESTRIAN CTRE, Adare (YH00175)								●	●					●						●		●	●	●	●	●	●																							
COUNTY MEATH																																																		
BACHELORS LODGE, Navan (YH00766)								●	●					●						●				●	●	●	●																							

Business Profile
Training (shaded area)
Course, Arena, Buildings and Pasture

by Country by County

	Coaches	Harness Trainer	Dressage Training	Polo Trainer	Side-saddle specialist	Side-saddle trainer	Trainers	Training (1 to 1)	Training (Children)	Training (Disabled)	Training (Dressage)	Training (Flat)	Training (Freelance)	Training (Group)	Training (Horse Breaking)	Training (Jockey)	Training (Jumps)	Training (Personnel)	Training (Point-to-Point)	Training (Riding)	Training (SteepleChase)	Training (To become a Trainer)	Training for Examination	Work with Children 10-16	Work with Children under 10	Work with Senior Citizens	Work with Students	Work with the Disabled	Architectural Advice	Architectural Planning	Arenas (large) for hire	Arenas (small) for hire	Arenas Indoor (Build)	Arenas Outdoor (Build)	Building Maintenance	Building Repairs	Cross Country Course (Build)	Cross Country Course (Design)	Fencing (Build)	Gates (Build)	Outbuildings (Build)	Pasture Supply	Pasture Support	Property Services	Racing Tracks (Build)	Show Jumps (Design)	Stables (Build)	Stables (Design)	Swimming Pools (Build)	Swimming Pools (Design)
BLACKHALL EQUESTRIAN CTRE, Little Kilcloone (YH01483)								●	●	●				●						●				●	●	●	●	●																						
COUNTY OFFALY																																																		
ANNAGHARVEY FARM, Tullamore (YH00450)									●								●			●																														
BIRR EQUESTRIAN CTRE, Birr (YH01443)									●					●						●																														
COUNTY SLIGO																																																		
BALLINA EQUESTRIAN CTRE, Ballina (YH00855)								●	●					●			●			●																														
COUNTY TIPPERARY																																																		
BALLINTOHER EQUESTRIAN CTRE, Nenagh (YH00862)									●					●						●																														
CLONMEL EQUESTRIAN CTRE, Clonmel (YH03057)								●	●	●				●						●				●	●	●	●	●																						
DAVERN EQUESTRIAN CTRE, Clonmel (YH03911)									●					●						●																														
MORRIS, MICHAEL, Fethard (YH09833)							●																																											
O'GRADY, EDWARD J, Thurles (YH10441)							●																																											
COUNTY WATERFORD																																																		
CONNORS, MICK, Woodstown (YH03240)									●					●						●				●	●	●	●	●																						
DEBROMHEAD, HARRY, Knockeen (YH04006)							●																																											
COUNTY WESTMEATH																																																		
WEBBWEAR, Multyfarnham (YH15036)															●																																			
COUNTY WICKLOW																																																		
BEL-AIR HOTEL & EQUESTRIAN, Ashford (YH01202)																				●																														
BRENNANSTOWN RIDING SCHOOL, Bray (YH01846)																							●																											
BROOMFIELD RIDING CTRE, Tinahely (YH02078)																	●			●				●	●	●	●																							
COOLADOYLE RIDING SCHOOL, Newtownmountkennedy (YH03270)									●					●						●			●	●	●		●																							
NORTHERN IRELAND																																																		
COUNTY ANTRIM																																																		
BURN EQUESTRIAN CLUB, Belfast (YH02263)								●	●					●										●	●																									
GALGORM PARKS RIDING SCHOOL, Ballymena (YH05615)											●			●			●							●	●																									
STIRLING, J, Ballyclare (YH13473)							●																																											
COUNTY ARMAGH																																																		
HOWARD ALLEN SEEDS, Craigavon (YH07215)																																										●								
LIME PARK EQUESTRIAN, Craigavon (YH08626)								●	●	●	●	●		●			●						●	●	●			●																						
LOUGHVIEW STABLES, Lurgan (YH08842)															●																																			

www.hccyourhorse.com

Business Profile

Training (shaded area) Course, Arena, Buildings and Pasture

by Country by County

Name	Coaches	Harness Trainer	Dressage Training	Polo Trainer	Side-saddle specialist	Side-saddle trainer	Trainers	Training (1 to 1)	Training (Children)	Training (Disabled)	Training (Dressage)	Training (Flat)	Training (Freelance)	Training (Group)	Training (Horse Breaking)	Training (Jockey)	Training (Jumps)	Training (Personnel)	Training (Point-to-Point)	Training (Riding)	Training (SteepleChase)	Training (To become a Trainer)	Training for Examination	Work with Children 10-16	Work with Children under 10	Work with Senior Citizens	Work with Students	Work with the Disabled	Architectural Advice	Architectural Planning	Arenas (large) for hire	Arenas (small) for hire	Arenas Indoor (Build)	Arenas Outdoor (Build)	Building Maintenance	Building Repairs	Cross Country Course (Build)	Cross Country Course (Design)	Fencing (Build)	Gates (Build)	Outbuildings (Build)	Pasture Supply	Pasture Support	Property Services	Racing Tracks (Build)	Show Jumps (Design)	Stables (Build)	Stables (Design)	Swimming Pools (Build)	Swimming Pools (Design)
COUNTY DOWN																																																		
FAWCETT, GEORGE, Ballynahinch (YH05108)	●																																						●								●			
HOLMESTEAD SADDLERY, Downpatrick (YH06981)																								●	●	●	●	●																						
LESSANS RIDING STABLES, Ballynahinch (YH08561)																								●	●	●	●	●																						
MOUNT PLEASANT, Castlewellan (YH09891)								●	●	●				●																																				
NEWCASTLE RIDING CTRE, Castlewellan (YH10129)																								●	●																									
R W TOASE, Newry (YH11569)																																										●								
SMILEY, ERIC, Ballynahinch (YH12929)							●																																											
WOOD LODGE STABLES, Castlewellan (YH15659)							●																																											
COUNTY FERMANAGH																																																		
DRUMHONEY STABLES, Enniskillen (YH04291)																								●				●																						
NECARNE CASTLE, Enniskillen (YH10066)																							●																											
COUNTY LONDONDERRY																																																		
ARCHIBALD, Coleraine (YH00499)																																										●								
ARDMORE STABLES, Londonderry (YH00511)									●		●						●																																	
EGLINTON EQUESTRIAN CLUB, Eglinton (YH04595)																															●	●																		
FAUGHANVALE STABLES, Londonderry (YH05102)								●	●	●				●					●			●	●																											
FORT CTRE, Maghera (YH05385)									●	●																		●																						
HILL FARM RIDING CTRE, Coleraine (YH06814)								●	●	●				●									●																											
ISLAND EQUESTRIAN CTRE, Coleraine (YH07520)																								●	●																									
MADDYBENNY RIDING CTRE, Coleraine (YH09022)								●	●					●			●			●		●	●																											
MARSH KYFE RIDING SCHOOL, Magherafelt (YH09186)								●	●		●	●		●			●																																	
MCCOLLUM, JEANNIE, Coleraine (YH09328)													●																																					
COUNTY TYRONE																																																		
ECCLESVILLE CTRE, Omagh (YH04533)																															●	●																		
EDERGOLE RIDING CTRE, Cookstown (YH04553)								●	●		●	●		●		●	●						●																											
MOY RIDING SCHOOL, Dungannon (YH09907)																								●	●																									
TULLYWHISKER RIDING SCHOOL, Strabane (YH14458)								●	●	●				●			●																																	

Business Profile

Training (shaded area) Course, Arena, Buildings and Pasture

by Country by County

	Coaches	Harness Trainer	Dressage Training	Polo Trainer	Side-saddle specialist	Side-saddle trainer	Trainers	Training (1 to 1)	Training (Children)	Training (Disabled)	Training (Dressage)	Training (Flat)	Training (Freelance)	Training (Group)	Training (Horse Breaking)	Training (Jockey)	Training (Jumps)	Training (Personnel)	Training (Point-to-Point)	Training (Riding)	Training (SteepleChase)	Training (To become a Trainer)	Training for Examination	Work with Children 10-16	Work with Children under 10	Work with Senior Citizens	Work with Students	Work with the Disabled	Architectural Advice	Architectural Planning	Arenas (large) for hire	Arenas (small) for hire	Arenas Indoor (Build)	Arenas Outdoor (Build)	Building Maintenance	Building Repairs	Cross Country Course (Build)	Cross Country Course (Design)	Fencing (Build)	Gates (Build)	Outbuildings (Build)	Pasture Supply	Pasture Support	Property Services	Racing Tracks (Build)	Show Jumps (Design)	Stables (Build)	Stables (Design)	Swimming Pools (Build)	Swimming Pools (Design)
SCOTLAND																																																		
ABERDEEN (CITY OF)																																																		
HAYFIELD RIDING, Aberdeen (YH06578)								●	●		●			●			●			●		●	●																											
HAYFIELD SADDLERY, Aberdeen (YH06579)							●						●																																					
SUNNYSIDE, Aberdeen (YH13649)							●																																											
ABERDEENSHIRE																																																		
EDEN EQUESTRIAN CTRE, Turriff (YH04546)								●	●	●				●	●					●				●	●			●																						
LOVETT, I, Stonehaven (YH08852)																													●								●							●						
MANAR STUD & RIDING CTRE, Alford (YH09064)			●				●				●																																							
MILL OF URAS EQUESTRIAN, Stonehaven (YH09583)									●									●		●				●	●	●					●	●	●	●								●								
RIDINGHILL STUD, Fraserburgh (YH11885)											●				●		●			●											●																			
SKINNER, GEORGE M, Inverurie (YH12875)							●																																											
ANGUS																																																		
BLACKLITE, Dundee (YH01486)																																			●	●				●	●					●	●	●		
KIRRIEMUIR HORSE SUPPLIES, Kirriemuir (YH08240)			●						●	●		●			●					●			●	●	●	●		●			●	●																		
LIDDLE, H T, Forfar (YH08606)		●																																																
PATHHEAD STABLES, Kirriemuir (YH10821)			●						●	●		●			●					●			●	●	●	●		●			●	●																		
ARGYLL AND BUTE																																																		
APPALOOSA HOLIDAYS, Lochgilphead (YH00475)																												●				●																		
ARGYLL TRAIL RIDING, Lochgilphead (YH00523)			●				●				●		●				●																																	
CASTLE RIDING CTRE, Lochgilphead (YH02631)								●	●					●			●			●																														
COLGRAIN EQUESTRIAN CTRE, Helensburgh (YH03170)							●	●	●	●	●		●	●	●							●	●	●	●		●					●																		
CORROW TREKKING CTRE, Cairndow (YH03343)																								●																										
STUART, FIONA, Alexandria (YH13594)							●																																											
TACKLE & TACK, Oban (YH13818)																								●	●	●		●														●	●							
AYRSHIRE (EAST)																																																		
BARGOWER RIDING SCHOOL, Kilmarnock (YH00933)									●	●														●	●																									
DEAN CASTLE RIDING CTRE, Kilmarnock (YH03988)									●											●			●	●	●	●	●				●																			
GOLDIE, ROBERT H, Kilmarnock (YH05889)							●																																											
MUIRMILL INTERNATIONAL E C, Kilmarnock (YH09927)								●	●	●				●										●	●			●			●																			
ROWALLAN ACTIVITY CTRE, Kilmarnock (YH12152)	●		●					●	●		●	●	●	●			●			●		●	●	●	●						●	●					●	●												

www.hccyourhorse.com

Business Profile

Training (shaded area)

Course, Arena, Buildings and Pasture

by Country by County

	Coaches	Harness Trainer	Dressage Training	Polo Trainer	Side-saddle specialist	Side-saddle trainer	Trainers	Training (1 to 1)	Training (Children)	Training (Disabled)	Training (Dressage)	Training (Flat)	Training (Freelance)	Training (Group)	Training (Horse Breaking)	Training (Jockey)	Training (Jumps)	Training (Personnel)	Training (Point-to-Point)	Training (Riding)	Training (SteepleChase)	Training (To become a Trainer)	Training for Examination	Work with Children 10-16	Work with Children under 10	Work with Senior Citizens	Work with Students	Work with the Disabled	Architectural Advice	Architectural Planning	Arenas (large) for hire	Arenas (small) for hire	Arenas Indoor (Build)	Arenas Outdoor (Build)	Building Maintenance	Building Repairs	Cross Country Course (Build)	Cross Country Course (Design)	Fencing (Build)	Gates (Build)	Outbuildings (Build)	Pasture Supply	Pasture Support	Property Services	Racing Tracks (Build)	Show Jumps (Design)	Stables (Build)	Stables (Design)	Swimming Pools (Build)	Swimming Pools (Design)
WALKER & TEMPLETON, Kilmarnock (YH14845)																																										●								
AYRSHIRE (NORTH)																																																		
BROOM FARM RIDING SCHOOL, Stevenston (YH02071)								●	●					●										●	●																									
FERGUSHILL RIDING STABLES, Kilwinning (YH05159)								●	●	●	●			●			●							●	●																									
TANDLEVIEW STABLES, Beith (YH13852)								●	●	●														●	●																									
AYRSHIRE (SOUTH)																																																		
AYRSHIRE EQUITATION CTRE, Ayr (YH00704)								●			●	●		●			●						●																											
CREE LODGE, Ayr (YH03587)							●																																											
HORSE SENSE, Girvan (YH07137)														●																																				
MCGAWN, D, Ayr (YH09353)							●																																											
ROSEMOUNT RIDING SVS, Prestwick (YH12105)								●	●	●	●	●		●	●									●	●			●																						
SHANTER RIDING CTRE, Girvan (YH12672)								●	●	●	●	●		●	●		●							●	●																									
CLACKMANNANSHIRE																																																		
DEVON EQUESTRIAN, Alloa (YH04094)																															●	●																		
SIMMONS, AVRIL, Dollar (YH12826)													●																																					
DUMFRIES AND GALLOWAY																																																		
DOUGLAS, JOHN L, Newton Stewart (YH04214)																																										●								
FORBES, JANE (LADY), Castle Douglas (YH05320)																																					●													
GEE GEE'S, Dumfries (YH05690)																								●	●		●																							
LUNGO, L, Dumfries (YH08900)							●																																											
MEIKLE WELSH COBS, Castle Douglas (YH09447)							●																																											
PARKER, C, Lockerbie (YH10747)							●																																											
W C F COUNTRY CTRE, Castle Douglas (YH14754)																																										●								
WM MURRAY FARMCARE, Dumfries (YH15642)																																										●								
EDINBURGH (CITY OF)																																																		
DRUM RIDING, Edinburgh (YH04282)										●																		●																						
LAWRIE, D, Balerno (YH08474)		●																																																
STIRLINGSHIRE SADDLERY, Edinburgh (YH13474)																								●	●	●	●	●																						
TOWER FARM, Edinburgh (YH14271)								●	●	●	●			●			●							●	●	●	●	●			●	●	●	●																
FALKIRK																																																		
COUNTRY FEEDS LARBERT, Larbert (YH03408)																																										●								
COWAN STABLES, Falkirk (YH03520)		●																																																

Business Profile

Training (shaded area) **Course, Arena, Buildings and Pasture**

by Country by County	Coaches	Harness Trainer	Dressage Training	Polo Trainer	Side-saddle specialist	Side-saddle trainer	Trainers	Training (1 to 1)	Training (Children)	Training (Disabled)	Training (Dressage)	Training (Flat)	Training (Freelance)	Training (Group)	Training (Horse Breaking)	Training (Jockey)	Training (Jumps)	Training (Personnel)	Training (Point-to-Point)	Training (Riding)	Training (SteepleChase)	Training (To become a Trainer)	Training for Examination	Work with Children 10-16	Work with Children under 10	Work with Senior Citizens	Work with Students	Work with the Disabled	Architectural Advice	Architectural Planning	Arenas (large) for hire	Arenas (small) for hire	Arenas Indoor (Build)	Arenas Outdoor (Build)	Building Maintenance	Building Repairs	Cross Country Course (Build)	Cross Country Course (Design)	Fencing (Build)	Gates (Build)	Outbuildings (Build)	Pasture Supply	Pasture Support	Property Services	Racing Tracks (Build)	Show Jumps (Design)	Stables (Build)	Stables (Design)	Swimming Pools (Build)	Swimming Pools (Design)
MILNHOLM, Falkirk (YH09643)								●	●					●			●							●	●	●	●																							
FIFE																																																		
ANGLE PARK, Cupar (YH00409)			●					●	●	●	●	●	●	●			●	●		●			●	●	●	●	●	●																						
BARCLAY, J, Leslie (YH00925)							●																																											
BLYTH, J, Kirkcaldy (YH01578)		●																																																
BRADBURNE, S, Cupar (YH01745)							●																																											
DABBS, Cupar (YH03813)			●				●																																											
DRYSDALE, A, Boreland (YH04300)		●																																																
EDENSIDE, St Andrews (YH04551)							●								●																																			
KEITH GARRY FENCING, Freuchie (YH08034)																																							●											
MOORE, W, Kelty (YH09769)		●																																																
PEARSON, D, Thorton (YH10878)		●																																																
RIDING STABLES, Lochgelly (YH11883)								●	●	●	●			●			●			●			●	●	●	●	●	●																						
ROSEBANK STABLES, Cowdenbeath (YH12101)		●																																																
SALTIRE STABLES, Cupar (YH12394)																																							●											
WOOD, T C, Lochgelly (YH15669)		●																																																
GLASGOW (CITY OF)																																																		
BUSBY EQUITATION CTRE, Busby (YH02302)								●	●	●	●	●	●	●									●																											
EASTERTON STABLES, Glasgow (YH04501)								●	●	●	●	●	●	●			●			●			●	●	●	●	●	●																						
EVERYTHING EQUESTRIAN, Busby (YH04957)								●	●	●	●	●	●	●									●																											
FORREST, W, Glasgow (YH05378)		●																																																
GOLDIE, J S, Uplawmoor (YH05888)							●																																											
KENMURE RIDING SCHOOL, Glasgow (YH08065)																	●																																	
ROUNDKNOWE FARM, Glasgow (YH12143)																				●																														
WILSON, T, Glasgow (YH15546)																																					●													
WOODEND, Glasgow (YH15684)							●	●	●	●	●			●			●			●		●	●	●	●	●	●	●																						
HIGHLANDS																																																		
BEVERLEY HYMERS SADDLERY, Halkirk (YH01342)																								●	●		●	●									●	●									●	●		
HIGHLAND EQUESTRIAN SVS, Inverness (YH06789)																																							●											
HIGHLAND RIDING CTRE, Inverness (YH06793)	●		●				●	●	●	●	●			●	●		●			●				●	●	●		●																						
LOCH NESS RIDING, Inverness (YH08752)	●																																																	
LOGIE FARM, Nairn (YH08778)									●		●			●	●			●		●			●	●	●		●																							

Business Profile
Training (shaded area) Course, Arena, Buildings and Pasture

by Country by County	Coaches	Harness Trainer	Dressage Training	Polo Trainer	Side-saddle specialist	Side-saddle trainer	Trainers	Training (1 to 1)	Training (Children)	Training (Disabled)	Training (Dressage)	Training (Flat)	Training (Freelance)	Training (Group)	Training (Horse Breaking)	Training (Jockey)	Training (Jumps)	Training (Personnel)	Training (Point-to-Point)	Training (Riding)	Training (SteepleChase)	Training (To become a Trainer)	Training for Examination	Work with Children 10-16	Work with Children under 10	Work with Senior Citizens	Work with Students	Work with the Disabled	Architectural Advice	Architectural Planning	Arenas (large) for hire	Arenas (small) for hire	Arenas Indoor (Build)	Arenas Outdoor (Build)	Building Maintenance	Building Repairs	Cross Country Course (Build)	Cross Country Course (Design)	Fencing (Build)	Gates (Build)	Outbuildings (Build)	Pasture Supply	Pasture Support	Property Services	Racing Tracks (Build)	Show Jumps (Design)	Stables (Build)	Stables (Design)	Swimming Pools (Build)	Swimming Pools (Design)
RADDERY EQUINE, Fortrose (YH11593)																												●																						
INVERCLYDE																																																		
ARDGOWAN, Greenock (YH00507)								●	●					●										●	●	●	●																							
ISLE OF SKYE																																																		
SKYE RIDING CTRE, Portree (YH12881)										●				●				●		●			●	●	●	●	●	●																						
LANARKSHIRE (NORTH)																																																		
KENNEDY, R, Wishaw (YH08068)		●																																																
NIMMO, R W F, Newarthill (YH10208)		●																																																
O'BRIEN, H H, Stepps (YH10420)		●																																																
RIVERSIDE RACING STABLES, Wishaw (YH11925)							●																																											
LANARKSHIRE (SOUTH)																																																		
BELSTANE RACING, Carluke (YH01253)							●																																											
BLACKIE, G, Carluke (YH01485)																																					●													
DARHO STUD & EQUESTRIAN SVS, Auchengray (YH03886)																																												●						
FOSTER, R, Strathaven (YH05402)																																					●													
FOX, J & M, Stonehouse (YH05430)																																					●													
GALLOWAY & MACLEOD, Larkhall (YH05625)																																										●								
HILLHEAD, Carluke (YH06846)								●	●					●			●							●	●	●	●																							
JUMPS, Carluke (YH07967)								●			●			●			●				●																													
MID DRUMLOCH, Hamilton (YH09526)								●	●	●				●			●			●				●	●	●	●	●																						
RENDALL, K, Carluke (YH11754)																																					●													
ROBERTSON, A, Strathaven (YH11966)																																					●													
TOP CROP ORGANICS, Law (YH14234)																																										●								
LOTHIAN (EAST)																																																		
APPIN EQUESTRIAN CTRE, Haddington (YH00478)								●	●		●			●																																				
HARELAW EQUESTRIAN CTRE, Longniddry (YH06420)								●	●	●				●			●																																	
TILTON HOUSE STABLES, Dunbar (YH14158)							●																																											
LOTHIAN (MID)																																																		
BOWLEA TRAILERS, Penicuik (YH01713)																																			●					●				●				●		
EASTER BUSH VETNRY CTRE, Roslin (YH04490)								●			●			●			●						●																											
EDINBURGH & LASSWADE, Lasswade (YH04559)								●	●	●	●			●			●																																	
LOTHIAN (WEST)																																																		

Business Profile

Training (shaded area)
Course, Arena, Buildings and Pasture

by Country by County

	Coaches	Harness Trainer	Dressage Training	Polo Trainer	Side-saddle specialist	Side-saddle trainer	Trainers	Training (1 to 1)	Training (Children)	Training (Disabled)	Training (Dressage)	Training (Flat)	Training (Freelance)	Training (Group)	Training (Horse Breaking)	Training (Jockey)	Training (Jumps)	Training (Personnel)	Training (Point-to-Point)	Training (Riding)	Training (SteepleChase)	Training (To become a Trainer)	Training for Examination	Work with Children 10-16	Work with Children under 10	Work with Senior Citizens	Work with Students	Work with the Disabled
GRANGE RIDING CTRE, West Calder (YH05993)			●					●	●		●			●			●						●					
HOLMES RIDING STABLES, Bathgate (YH06973)								●	●	●				●			●							●	●	●		●
HOUSTON FARM RIDING SCHOOL, Broxburn (YH07212)								●	●	●	●			●														
OATRIDGE, Broxburn (YH10417)																							●					
WELLS, E, Linlithgow (YH15082)																												
MORAY																												
GREENFIELDS SADDLERY, Elgin (YH06085)																								●	●	●	●	●
MUIRYHALL STABLES, Elgin (YH09929)			●				●				●		●															
SHENVAL FARM, Ballindalloch (YH12709)															●													
PERTH AND KINROSS																												
CALEDONIAN EQUESTRIAN CTRE, Perth (YH02440)																												
CARSTAIRS, H, Auchterarder (YH02605)			●				●				●		●															
CLAISH FARM PONY TREKKING, Callander (YH02939)	●								●																			
DRYSDALE, G, Kinross (YH04301)		●																										
EASTERTON ARENAS, Auchterarder (YH04499)			●				●				●																	
EQUI-CARE, Perth (YH04736)			●				●	●	●		●	●	●	●	●	●	●	●		●		●	●	●	●	●	●	●
GIAMANDREA, J, Auchterarder (YH05736)		●																										
GLEN EAGLES EQUESTRIAN, Auchterarder (YH05825)			●		●	●	●	●	●	●	●		●	●	●		●	●		●		●	●	●	●	●	●	●
GLENFARG RIDING SCHOOL, Perth (YH05834)									●	●										●				●	●			●
GLENMARKIE, Blairgowrie (YH05840)							●	●	●			●	●	●	●		●	●		●				●	●	●	●	
HAY, A M, Milnathort (YH06563)													●															
J B CORRIE, Blairgowrie (YH07560)																												
LOCH TAY HIGHLAND, Killin (YH08753)			●				●				●																	
MCILWRAITH, A M, Auchterarder (YH09373)													●															
NORMILE, LUCY, Glenfarg (YH10242)							●					●			●	●	●		●		●							
RUSSELL, LUCINDA V, Kinross (YH12260)							●																					
TILLYRIE RACING, Kinross (YH14155)							●					●				●	●		●		●	●						
TORNADO WIRE, Crieff (YH14246)																												
RENFREWSHIRE																												
CANNEY, R, Greenock (YH02501)																												
DREGHORN, R, Lochwinnoch (YH04265)																												
FORDBANK EQUE CTRE, Johnstone (YH05329)										●																		

	Architectural Advice	Architectural Planning	Arenas (large) for hire	Arenas (small) for hire	Arenas Indoor (Build)	Arenas Outdoor (Build)	Building Maintenance	Building Repairs	Cross Country Course (Build)	Cross Country Course (Design)	Fencing (Build)	Gates (Build)	Outbuildings (Build)	Pasture Supply	Pasture Support	Property Services	Racing Tracks (Build)	Show Jumps (Design)	Stables (Build)	Stables (Design)	Swimming Pools (Build)	Swimming Pools (Design)
GRANGE RIDING CTRE, West Calder (YH05993)																						
HOLMES RIDING STABLES, Bathgate (YH06973)																						
HOUSTON FARM RIDING SCHOOL, Broxburn (YH07212)																						
OATRIDGE, Broxburn (YH10417)																						
WELLS, E, Linlithgow (YH15082)									●													
MORAY																						
GREENFIELDS SADDLERY, Elgin (YH06085)																						
MUIRYHALL STABLES, Elgin (YH09929)																						
SHENVAL FARM, Ballindalloch (YH12709)																						
PERTH AND KINROSS																						
CALEDONIAN EQUESTRIAN CTRE, Perth (YH02440)									●													
CARSTAIRS, H, Auchterarder (YH02605)																						
CLAISH FARM PONY TREKKING, Callander (YH02939)																						
DRYSDALE, G, Kinross (YH04301)																						
EASTERTON ARENAS, Auchterarder (YH04499)																						
EQUI-CARE, Perth (YH04736)				●					●	●	●	●						●				
GIAMANDREA, J, Auchterarder (YH05736)																						
GLEN EAGLES EQUESTRIAN, Auchterarder (YH05825)			●	●	●									●								
GLENFARG RIDING SCHOOL, Perth (YH05834)																						
GLENMARKIE, Blairgowrie (YH05840)				●										●								
HAY, A M, Milnathort (YH06563)																						
J B CORRIE, Blairgowrie (YH07560)											●											
LOCH TAY HIGHLAND, Killin (YH08753)																						
MCILWRAITH, A M, Auchterarder (YH09373)																						
NORMILE, LUCY, Glenfarg (YH10242)																						
RUSSELL, LUCINDA V, Kinross (YH12260)																						
TILLYRIE RACING, Kinross (YH14155)																						
TORNADO WIRE, Crieff (YH14246)											●											
RENFREWSHIRE																						
CANNEY, R, Greenock (YH02501)									●													
DREGHORN, R, Lochwinnoch (YH04265)									●													
FORDBANK EQUE CTRE, Johnstone (YH05329)																						

www.hccyourhorse.com

Business Profile

Training (shaded area) **Course, Arena, Buildings and Pasture**

by Country by County

	Coaches	Harness Trainer	Dressage Training	Polo Trainer	Side-saddle specialist	Side-saddle trainer	Trainers	Training (1 to 1)	Training (Children)	Training (Disabled)	Training (Dressage)	Training (Flat)	Training (Freelance)	Training (Group)	Training (Horse Breaking)	Training (Jockey)	Training (Jumps)	Training (Personnel)	Training (Point-to-Point)	Training (Riding)	Training (SteepleChase)	Training (To become a Trainer)	Training for Examination	Work with Children 10-16	Work with Children under 10	Work with Senior Citizens	Work with Students	Work with the Disabled	Architectural Advice	Architectural Planning	Arenas (large) for hire	Arenas (small) for hire	Arenas Indoor (Build)	Arenas Outdoor (Build)	Building Maintenance	Building Repairs	Cross Country Course (Build)	Cross Country Course (Design)	Fencing (Build)	Gates (Build)	Outbuildings (Build)	Pasture Supply	Pasture Support	Property Services	Racing Tracks (Build)	Show Jumps (Design)	Stables (Build)	Stables (Design)	Swimming Pools (Build)	Swimming Pools (Design)
MEADOW PK, Johnstone (YH09421)									●					●						●				●	●																									
MORE, W A, Dean Park (YH09788)																																					●													
SCOTTISH BORDERS																																																		
AYTON CASTLE, Eyemouth (YH00705)							●																																											
BAILEY MILL, Newcastleton (YH00794)									●											●			●	●	●										●	●					●						●			
BOWHILL STABLES, Selkirk (YH01710)																																						●												
BROKEN SPOKE, West Linton (YH02021)							●																																											
KEMP, W T, Duns (YH08055)							●																																											
LEGGATE, JENNY, Greenlaw (YH08540)			●				●				●		●																																					
LOCH, SYLVIA (LADY), Kelso (YH08754)			●				●				●																																							
MACTAGGART, A B, Hawick (YH09017)							●																																											
MCNAB SADDLERS, Kelso (YH09397)																																					●													
MCNAB SADDLERS, Selkirk (YH09396)																																					●													
OLIVER, RHONA, Hawick (YH10500)							●																																											
OVER WHITLAW STABLES, Selkirk (YH10590)																			●																															
STARK, IAN, Selkirk (YH13394)							●																																											
TELFORD, R, Eyemouth (YH13943)							●																																											
WESTERTOUN, Gordon (YH15212)			●					●	●		●		●	●	●		●	●		●		●	●	●	●		●				●																			
WHILLANS, A C, Hawick (YH15280)							●																																											
WHILLANS, D, Hawick (YH15281)							●																																											
STIRLING																																																		
GLENSIDE ORGANICS, Throsk (YH05843)																																										●								
HENDRY, JAMES, Stirling (YH06669)																																								●						●				
MYOTHILL HSE EQUESTRIAN CTRE, Denny (YH09985)			●				●				●		●				●																																	

Business Profile

Training (shaded area)

Course, Arena, Buildings and Pasture

by Country by County

	Coaches	Harness Trainer	Dressage Training	Polo Trainer	Side-saddle specialist	Side-saddle trainer	Trainers	Training (1 to 1)	Training (Children)	Training (Disabled)	Training (Dressage)	Training (Flat)	Training (Freelance)	Training (Group)	Training (Horse Breaking)	Training (Jockey)	Training (Jumps)	Training (Personnel)	Training (Point-to-Point)	Training (Riding)	Training (SteepleChase)	Training (To become a Trainer)	Training for Examination	Work with Children 10-16	Work with Children under 10	Work with Senior Citizens	Work with Students	Work with the Disabled	Architectural Advice	Architectural Planning	Arenas (large) for hire	Arenas (small) for hire	Arenas Indoor (Build)	Arenas Outdoor (Build)	Building Maintenance	Building Repairs	Cross Country Course (Build)	Cross Country Course (Design)	Fencing (Build)	Gates (Build)	Outbuildings (Build)	Pasture Supply	Pasture Support	Property Services	Racing Tracks (Build)	Show Jumps (Design)	Stables (Build)	Stables (Design)	Swimming Pools (Build)	Swimming Pools (Design)
WALES																																																		
BRIDGEND																																																		
E K M EQUESTRIAN, Bridgend (YH04411)			●					●	●	●	●		●	●	●					●		●	●	●		●	●	●				●														●				
CAERPHILLY																																																		
B J LLEWELLYN, Bargoed (YH00733)							●					●					●																																	
BEAU COURT, Newport (YH01126)							●	●	●					●																																				
ROCKWOOD RIDING CTRE, Caerphilly (YH12039)								●	●			●		●						●				●	●																									
CARMARTHENSHIRE																																																		
BROWN, JOHN, Llanwrda (YH02117)																																							●											
CARMARTHEN & PUMSAINT FARMERS, Llandeilo (YH02547)																																										●								
ELLIOTT, D, Llandysul (YH04619)							●																																											
EQUISECRETS, Lampeter (YH04817)											●				●																																			
HOWELL, CASTELL, Llandysul (YH07227)			●				●				●																																							
JAMES, D W, Ammanford (YH07680)		●																																																
JONES, A W, Ammanford (YH07876)		●																																																
PENCADER STUD, Pencader (YH10928)								●					●	●	●					●																														
PLAS EQUESTRIAN, Carmarthen (YH11164)					●																																													
RIPMAN, BARBARA, Carmarthen (YH11906)			●				●				●		●																																					
STALLIONS AT TACKEXCHANGE, Llanelli (YH13351)													●							●																														
THOMAS SHOW TEAM, Carmarthen (YH14011)																								●	●																									
THOMAS, H T, Ammanford (YH14021)		●																																																
CEREDIGION																																																		
BHS WALES, Aberystwyth (YH01388)																							●	●	●		●	●															●							
EVANS, J H, Lampeter (YH04923)		●																																																
IGER, Aberystwyth (YH07394)																																										●								
MOELFRYN RIDING CTRE, Aberystwyth (YH09699)									●															●	●	●		●																						
RHEIDOL RIDING CTRE, Aberystwyth (YH11784)			●					●	●	●	●	●	●	●	●		●			●		●	●	●	●	●	●	●				●																		
CONWY																																																		
T I R PRINCE RACEWAY, Abergele (YH13752)		●																																																
TYNLLWYN RIDING SCHOOL, Colwyn Bay (YH14528)																								●	●	●	●	●																						
DENBIGHSHIRE																																																		

www.hccyourhorse.com

Business Profile

Training (shaded area) **Course, Arena, Buildings and Pasture**

by Country by County	Coaches	Harness Trainer	Dressage Training	Polo Trainer	Side-saddle specialist	Side-saddle trainer	Trainers	Training (1 to 1)	Training (Children)	Training (Disabled)	Training (Dressage)	Training (Flat)	Training (Freelance)	Training (Group)	Training (Horse Breaking)	Training (Jockey)	Training (Jumps)	Training (Personnel)	Training (Point-to-Point)	Training (Riding)	Training (SteepleChase)	Training (To become a Trainer)	Training for Examination	Work with Children 10-16	Work with Children under 10	Work with Senior Citizens	Work with Students	Work with the Disabled	Architectural Advice	Architectural Planning	Arenas (large) for hire	Arenas (small) for hire	Arenas Indoor (Build)	Arenas Outdoor (Build)	Building Maintenance	Building Repairs	Cross Country Course (Build)	Cross Country Course (Design)	Fencing (Build)	Gates (Build)	Outbuildings (Build)	Pasture Supply	Pasture Support	Property Services	Racing Tracks (Build)	Show Jumps (Design)	Stables (Build)	Stables (Design)	Swimming Pools (Build)	Swimming Pools (Design)
A P E S ROCKING HORSES, Denbigh (YH00055)																									●																									
LEE, C, Rhuddlan (YH08522)		●																																																
LEE, P, Rhyl (YH08525)		●																																																
LLANNERCH EQUESTRIAN CTRE, St Asaph (YH08726)								●	●	●				●			●			●			●	●	●	●	●	●				●																		
MORWYN STUD, Ruthin (YH09854)																																			●	●														
FLINTSHIRE																																																		
ALYN BANK, Mold (YH00353)								●						●																																				
OWENS, R M L, Mold (YH10609)		●																																																
T F S, Buckley (YH13739)																																								●										
WELSH COLLEGE OF HORTICULTURE, Mold (YH15090)																							●																											
GLAMORGAN (VALE OF)																																																		
ARGAE HSE STABLES, Dinas Powys (YH00519)																															●																			
CIMLA TREKKING, Neath (YH02918)								●	●	●	●						●			●		●	●																											
JOHN REES, Barry (YH07807)																																										●								
LIEGE MANOR, Cardiff (YH08609)							●	●	●	●				●			●			●		●	●	●	●	●	●	●																						
PALLING, BRYN, Cowbridge (YH10689)							●					●		●		●					●																													
PEN-MAEN LIVERY YARD, Cowbridge (YH10944)							●																																											
SEVERN QUARTER HORSES, Cowbridge (YH12644)							●																																											
TY-WYTH-NEWYDD STABLES, Cowbridge (YH14535)							●																																											
GWYNEDD																																																		
BRONALLT, Caernarfon (YH02029)																																●																		
DWYFOR RIDING CTRE, Criccieth (YH04382)													●																																					
PEN-LLEYN RIDING CTRE, Pwllheli (YH10943)			●				●				●																																							
RHIWIAU RIDING CTRE, Llanfairfechan (YH11788)								●	●	●										●			●	●	●		●	●																						
SNOWDONIA RIDING STABLES, Caernarfon (YH13041)																							●	●	●		●																							
ISLE OF ANGLESEY																																																		
ANGLESEY EQUESTRIAN CTRE, Holyhead (YH00410)								●	●	●	●			●			●			●																														
LLANDDONA, Beaumaris (YH08720)								●	●					●										●	●	●	●																							
STANFORD EVENTING HORSES, Holyhead (YH13363)							●						●																																					
TAL Y FOEL RIDING CTRE, Anglesey (YH13829)																								●	●	●	●	●																						
TYN-MORFA RIDING CTRE, Rhosneigr (YH14529)															●					●																														
MONMOUTHSHIRE																																																		

Business Profile

Training (shaded area) **Course, Arena, Buildings and Pasture**

by Country by County

	Coaches	Harness Trainer	Dressage Training	Polo Trainer	Side-saddle specialist	Side-saddle trainer	Trainers	Training (1 to 1)	Training (Children)	Training (Disabled)	Training (Dressage)	Training (Flat)	Training (Freelance)	Training (Group)	Training (Horse Breaking)	Training (Jockey)	Training (Jumps)	Training (Personnel)	Training (Point-to-Point)	Training (Riding)	Training (SteepleChase)	Training (To become a Trainer)	Training for Examination	Work with Children 10-16	Work with Children under 10	Work with Senior Citizens	Work with Students	Work with the Disabled	Architectural Advice	Architectural Planning	Arenas (large) for hire	Arenas (small) for hire	Arenas Indoor (Build)	Arenas Outdoor (Build)	Building Maintenance	Building Repairs	Cross Country Course (Build)	Cross Country Course (Design)	Fencing (Build)	Gates (Build)	Outbuildings (Build)	Pasture Supply	Pasture Support	Property Services	Racing Tracks (Build)	Show Jumps (Design)	Stables (Build)	Stables (Design)	Swimming Pools (Build)	Swimming Pools (Design)
BEAUMONT, REBECCA, Abergavenny (YH01138)							●																																											
BRADLEY, J M, Chepstow (YH01754)							●																																											
CHEPSTOW SADDLERY, Chepstow (YH02809)																								●	●	●	●	●																						
DAVIES, J D J, Abergavenny (YH03942)							●																																											
JOHNSEY, CLAIRE, Chepstow (YH07821)							●																																											
MONTAGUE HARRIS, Abergavenny (YH09729)																																												●						
RICH, P, Usk (YH11801)							●																																											
WINTER, ERIC, Chepstow (YH15593)							●										●																																	
NEATH PORT TALBOT																																																		
ZOAR HORSE & COUNTRY CTRE, Neath Port Talbot (YH15957)																																										●								
NEWPORT																																																		
CEFN LLOGELL RACING STABLES, Coed Kernew (YH02678)							●																																											
SPRINGFIELD RIDING STABLES, Wentloog (YH13256)																								●	●		●																							
PEMBROKESHIRE																																																		
ARMSTRONG MOWERS, Haverfordwest (YH00543)																																											●							
BOWEN, PETER, Haverfordwest (YH01702)							●																																											
CROSSWELL, Crymych (YH03669)								●	●					●	●		●	●	●	●				●	●	●																								
DOLRHANOG RIDING CTRE, Newport (YH04171)							●	●	●		●		●	●	●	●	●			●	●		●	●	●	●	●	●																						
DUNES RIDING, Narberth (YH04342)								●	●	●				●						●			●	●	●	●	●	●																						
FILMSTONE FARM, Narberth (YH05204)			●					●			●		●		●		●			●			●																											
LAVIS, H W, Haverfordwest (YH08467)							●																																											
LLANWNDA STABLES, Goodwick (YH08727)																								●	●	●	●							●																
OASIS PARK EQUESTRIAN CTRE, Narberth (YH10412)								●	●	●				●	●					●				●	●	●	●	●				●																		
POWYS																																																		
BROMPTON HALL, Montgomery (YH02025)								●	●	●	●	●		●	●		●	●	●	●	●		●	●	●	●	●	●			●																			
CANTREF, Brecon (YH02516)								●	●	●				●						●				●			●				●																			
CARREG DRESSAGE, Machynlleth (YH02578)			●																																															
EVANS, P D, Welshpool (YH04929)							●																																											
GOLDEN CASTLE, Crickhowell (YH05877)								●	●	●			●	●			●	●		●			●								●	●																		
LEE, RICHARD A, Presteigne (YH08527)							●																																											
LLANGORSE RIDING, Brecon (YH08725)																								●																										
NORRIS, PAULINE, Newtown (YH10245)																											●																							

Business Profile

Training (shaded area)

Course, Arena, Buildings and Pasture

by Country by County

	Coaches	Harness Trainer	Dressage Training	Polo Trainer	Side-saddle specialist	Side-saddle trainer	Trainers	Training (1 to 1)	Training (Children)	Training (Disabled)	Training (Dressage)	Training (Flat)	Training (Freelance)	Training (Group)	Training (Horse Breaking)	Training (Jockey)	Training (Jumps)	Training (Personnel)	Training (Point-to-Point)	Training (Riding)	Training (SteepleChase)	Training (To become a Trainer)	Training for Examination	Work with Children 10-16	Work with Children under 10	Work with Senior Citizens	Work with Students	Work with the Disabled	Architectural Advice	Architectural Planning	Arenas (large) for hire	Arenas (small) for hire	Arenas Indoor (Build)	Arenas Outdoor (Build)	Building Maintenance	Building Repairs	Cross Country Course (Build)	Cross Country Course (Design)	Fencing (Build)	Gates (Build)	Outbuildings (Build)	Pasture Supply	Pasture Support	Property Services	Racing Tracks (Build)	Show Jumps (Design)	Stables (Build)	Stables (Design)	Swimming Pools (Build)	Swimming Pools (Design)
PHILLIPS, E R, Presteigne (YH11055)		●																																																
RIVERSIDE RIDING CTRE, Crickhowell (YH11927)																								●	●		●	●																						
UNDERHILL RIDING STABLES, Llandrindod Wells (YH14560)																							●	●	●																									
RHONDDA CYNON TAFF																																																		
JONES, DEREK H, Pontypridd (YH07893)							●																																											
TALYGARN, Pontyclun (YH13846)								●	●		●	●		●			●						●	●	●	●	●	●																						
SWANSEA																																																		
COPLEY, Swansea (YH03297)						●		●	●		●			●			●			●			●																											
FORGEMILL, Swansea (YH05368)													●											●	●	●	●	●																						
GREEN FARM, Swansea (YH06054)								●	●	●				●										●	●			●																						
PENTRE RIDING STABLES, Swansea (YH10962)								●	●	●				●						●				●	●	●	●	●																						
SOUTH WALES CARRIAGE DRIVING, Swansea (YH13111)		●	●					●			●		●		●					●			●	●		●	●																							
TANKEY LAKE LIVERY, Swansea (YH13856)																															●	●										●								
WREXHAM																																																		
BLINKERS EQUESTRIAN, Wrexham (YH01540)													●											●	●	●	●	●																						
CHAPEL FARM, Wrexham (YH02738)								●	●	●				●									●	●	●	●	●	●																						
EQUESTRIAN CTRE, Wrexham (YH04697)								●	●		●			●			●			●			●	●	●	●	●																							

SECTION 4C

Business Profile

This section allows you to search for businesses that offer general equine Services.
Companies are listed by Country, by County.

The Business Profile can be used in two different ways. You can search by the particular service you require.

e.g. Engraving :
Stroud Saddlery

Or, you can look at the profile of one particular company in order to see what service/s they offer.

e.g. H J Burt & Son : Valuer

Once you have located a business using this section you can then refer to the company's detailed profile in Section 1.

Business Profile
General Equine

by Country by County

	Artist	Blacksmith	Business Consultancy	Commentating for Events	Competition Horses	Competition Riders	Cross Country Course	Dressage Riders	Driving Centre	Driving Competitors	Driving Services	Engraving	Equine Holidays	Event Management	Event Riders	Forge	Harness Race Course	Harness Racing Horses	Harness Racing Skills	Harness Retailer	Horse Sale Agency	Horsebox Hire	International Arena	Jockey	Jockey Supply	Photographer	Point-to-Point Course	Polo Pitch	Portraits	Racecourse Flat	Racecourse Steeplechase	Racing Investment	Repairs Rugs	Repairs Saddles	Riding Club	Rug Cleaning	Saddler	School (Indoor)	School (Outdoor)	Sculptor	Shipping Agent	Show Jump Course	Show Jumping arena	Stabling Centre	Tack Shop	Taxidermy	Trail Riding Centre	Transport	Transport Overseas	Trekking Centre	Valuer	Website design	Wheelwright
ENGLAND																																																					
BATH & SOMERSET (NORTH EAST)																																																					
CHAVES HORSE TRANSPORT, Bath (YH02792)																																																●					
DE SOUSA, NICOLA, Bath (YH03980)															●																																						
HORLER, M A, Bath (YH07070)											●																																										●
HUNSTRETE RIDING SCHOOL, Pensford (YH07294)							●														●																							●									
MATTHEWS OF KEYNSHAM, Keynsham (YH09268)																																					●																
MICKLEBURGH, ROBERT, Bath (YH09516)															●																																						
WELLOW TREKKING CTRE, Bath (YH15078)													●								●																							●									
BEDFORDSHIRE																																																					
ARCADE SADDLERY BEDFORD, Bedford (YH00498)																																	●	●		●	●																
BACKNOE END EQUESTRIAN CTRE, Bedford (YH00771)																																												●									
BENNITT, CAROL, Leighton Buzzard (YH01276)																																												●									
BIGGLESWADE SADDLERY, Biggleswade (YH01404)																																	●	●		●	●								●								
BROOK STABLES, Bedford (YH02038)							●																															●		●													
BROOKLYN FARM STABLES, Dunstable (YH02060)																																												●									
BURMAN, Biggleswade (YH02262)																																												●									
CLGE EQUESTRIAN CTRE, Bedford (YH03025)							●		●					●														●										●		●		●	●	●									
DICK, C, Dunstable (YH04109)									●	●																																											
DIJON STUD, Colmworth (YH04120)																																												●									
EQUISSENTIAL, Bedford (YH04820)																																		●																			
GRANSDEN HALL, Sandy (YH06005)																																												●									
GRAVENHURST SADDLERY, Bedford (YH06024)																																	●	●		●	●																
GREEN END FARM, Maulden (YH06053)																																												●									
K & K PET SHOPS, Dunstable (YH07980)																																					●																
LAGUS, S E, Leighton Buzzard (YH08344)																																		●																			
NORTHALLETON, Biggleswade (YH10292)													●																									●		●				●									
PARRIS, STEPHEN M, Bedford (YH10787)																											●																										
R B EQUESTRIAN, Leighton Buzzard (YH11514)																																	●	●		●	●																
RAWDING, J & S M, Leighton Buzzard (YH11662)																																												●									
ROWAN LODGE, Shefford (YH12154)																																						●															

Business Profile
General Equine

by Country by County

Business	Artist	Blacksmith	Business Consultancy	Commentating for Events	Competition Horses	Competition Riders	Cross Country Course	Dressage Riders	Driving Centre	Driving Competitors	Driving Services	Engraving	Equine Holidays	Event Management	Event Riders	Forge	Harness Race Course	Harness Racing Horses
SALSA STUD, Chawston (YH12391)					●													
STOCKWOOD PARK, Luton (YH13498)																		
STOCKWOOD STABLES, Luton (YH13499)									●									
SUNSHINE RIDING SCHOOL, Luton (YH13652)																		
TACK HAVEN, Dunstable (YH13790)																		
TINSLEYS RIDING SCHOOL, Bedford (YH14177)																		
TURNER, NICK, Biggleswade (YH14488)															●			
VULCAN TOWING CTRE, Luton (YH14745)																		
WADDINGTONS, Leighton Buzzard (YH14809)																		
WILSTEAD SADDLERY, Bedford (YH15554)																		
BERKSHIRE																		
BANSTOCK HSE STABLES, Maidenhead (YH00910)																		
BARRY, JOHN F J, Newbury (YH01034)																		
BEARWOOD RIDING CTRE, Wokingham (YH01123)																		
BEAUMONT STABLES, Maidenhead (YH01133)																		
BERKSHIRE CLGE OF AGRCLTRL, Maidenhead (YH01304)																		
BERKSHIRE RIDING CTRE, Windsor (YH01306)																		
BLACK, AUDREY, Reading (YH01470)																		
BURLEY LODGE STUD, Reading (YH02258)																		
CANE END STABLES, Reading (YH02498)																		
CENTELL, Reading (YH02685)																		
CHANGING TACK, Windsor (YH02732)																		
CHECKENDON, Reading (YH02796)					●	●	●						●					
CLOUD STABLES, Reading (YH03066)																		
COUNTRYWIDE STORES, Reading (YH03448)																		
COURTLANDS, Wokingham (YH03506)																		
CRAGO, PAUL, Reading (YH03547)																		
CROFT EQUESTRIAN CTRE, Reading (YH03614)																		
CULLINGHOOD FARM, Reading (YH03705)													●					
DAISYCHAIN PHOTOGRAPHIC, Newbury (YH03817)																		
DAVID ETON, Windsor (YH03918)																		
DOUGLAS, EILEEN, Wokingham (YH04213)																		

Business	Harness Racing Skills	Harness Retailer	Horse Sale Agency	Horsebox Hire	International Arena	Jockey	Jockey Supply	Photographer	Point-to-Point Course	Polo Pitch	Portraits	Racecourse Flat	Racecourse Steeplechase	Racing Investment	Repairs Rugs	Repairs Saddles	Riding Club	Rug Cleaning
SALSA STUD, Chawston (YH12391)																		
STOCKWOOD PARK, Luton (YH13498)																		
STOCKWOOD STABLES, Luton (YH13499)																		
SUNSHINE RIDING SCHOOL, Luton (YH13652)																		
TACK HAVEN, Dunstable (YH13790)															●	●		●
TINSLEYS RIDING SCHOOL, Bedford (YH14177)																		
TURNER, NICK, Biggleswade (YH14488)																		
VULCAN TOWING CTRE, Luton (YH14745)				●														
WADDINGTONS, Leighton Buzzard (YH14809)																		
WILSTEAD SADDLERY, Bedford (YH15554)															●	●		●
BERKSHIRE																		
BANSTOCK HSE STABLES, Maidenhead (YH00910)																		
BARRY, JOHN F J, Newbury (YH01034)																		
BEARWOOD RIDING CTRE, Wokingham (YH01123)																		
BEAUMONT STABLES, Maidenhead (YH01133)																		
BERKSHIRE CLGE OF AGRCLTRL, Maidenhead (YH01304)																		
BERKSHIRE RIDING CTRE, Windsor (YH01306)																		
BLACK, AUDREY, Reading (YH01470)																		
BURLEY LODGE STUD, Reading (YH02258)			●															
CANE END STABLES, Reading (YH02498)																		
CENTELL, Reading (YH02685)		●																
CHANGING TACK, Windsor (YH02732)															●			●
CHECKENDON, Reading (YH02796)																		
CLOUD STABLES, Reading (YH03066)																		
COUNTRYWIDE STORES, Reading (YH03448)																		
COURTLANDS, Wokingham (YH03506)					●													
CRAGO, PAUL, Reading (YH03547)			●															
CROFT EQUESTRIAN CTRE, Reading (YH03614)																		
CULLINGHOOD FARM, Reading (YH03705)																		
DAISYCHAIN PHOTOGRAPHIC, Newbury (YH03817)									●									
DAVID ETON, Windsor (YH03918)															●	●		
DOUGLAS, EILEEN, Wokingham (YH04213)															●	●		●

Business	Saddler	School (Indoor)	School (Outdoor)	Sculptor	Shipping Agent	Show Jump Course	Show Jumping arena	Stabling Centre	Tack Shop	Taxidermy	Trail Riding Centre	Transport	Transport Overseas	Trekking Centre	Valuer	Website design	Wheelwright
SALSA STUD, Chawston (YH12391)																	
STOCKWOOD PARK, Luton (YH13498)				●													
STOCKWOOD STABLES, Luton (YH13499)																	
SUNSHINE RIDING SCHOOL, Luton (YH13652)				●													
TACK HAVEN, Dunstable (YH13790)	●																
TINSLEYS RIDING SCHOOL, Bedford (YH14177)								●									
TURNER, NICK, Biggleswade (YH14488)																	
VULCAN TOWING CTRE, Luton (YH14745)																	
WADDINGTONS, Leighton Buzzard (YH14809)	●																
WILSTEAD SADDLERY, Bedford (YH15554)	●																
BERKSHIRE																	
BANSTOCK HSE STABLES, Maidenhead (YH00910)								●									
BARRY, JOHN F J, Newbury (YH01034)												●					
BEARWOOD RIDING CTRE, Wokingham (YH01123)								●									
BEAUMONT STABLES, Maidenhead (YH01133)								●									
BERKSHIRE CLGE OF AGRCLTRL, Maidenhead (YH01304)								●									
BERKSHIRE RIDING CTRE, Windsor (YH01306)								●									
BLACK, AUDREY, Reading (YH01470)								●									
BURLEY LODGE STUD, Reading (YH02258)																	
CANE END STABLES, Reading (YH02498)								●									
CENTELL, Reading (YH02685)	●								●								
CHANGING TACK, Windsor (YH02732)																	
CHECKENDON, Reading (YH02796)		●		●		●											
CLOUD STABLES, Reading (YH03066)								●									
COUNTRYWIDE STORES, Reading (YH03448)	●																
COURTLANDS, Wokingham (YH03506)				●													
CRAGO, PAUL, Reading (YH03547)								●									
CROFT EQUESTRIAN CTRE, Reading (YH03614)	●							●									
CULLINGHOOD FARM, Reading (YH03705)																	
DAISYCHAIN PHOTOGRAPHIC, Newbury (YH03817)																	
DAVID ETON, Windsor (YH03918)	●																
DOUGLAS, EILEEN, Wokingham (YH04213)	●																

Business Profile
General Equine

by Country by County

	Artist	Blacksmith	Business Consultancy	Commentating for Events	Competition Horses	Competition Riders	Cross Country Course	Dressage Riders	Driving Centre	Driving Competitors	Driving Services	Engraving	Equine Holidays	Event Management	Event Riders	Forge	Harness Race Course	Harness Racing Horses	Harness Racing Skills	Harness Retailer	Horse Sale Agency	Horsebox Hire	International Arena	Jockey	Jockey Supply	Photographer	Point-to-Point Course	Polo Pitch	Portraits	Racecourse Flat	Racecourse Steeplechase	Racing Investment	Repairs Rugs	Repairs Saddles	Riding Club	Rug Cleaning	Saddler	School (Indoor)	School (Outdoor)	Sculptor	Shipping Agent	Show Jump Course	Show Jumping arena	Stabling Centre	Tack Shop	Taxidermy	Trail Riding Centre	Transport	Transport Overseas	Trekking Centre	Valuer	Website design	Wheelwright
EAST SOLEY E C 2000, Hungerford (YH04486)																																						●		●		●		●									
EQUICENTRE, Waltham St Lawrence (YH04737)															●																																						
EQUINE CHAUFFEUR SVS, Reading (YH04768)																																																●					
ERMIN ST STABLES, Hungerford (YH04851)																																												●				●					
FANTASTIC FEATURES, Sandhurst (YH05046)																											●																										
FISHER, J T, Reading (YH05240)																					●																																
FROSBURY'S, Bracknell (YH05519)																																					●																
HALL PLACE EQUESTRIAN CTRE, Reading (YH06307)							●																																					●									
HARRIES, STELLA, Bracknell (YH06458)																					●																																
HEATHLANDS RIDING CTRE, Wokingham (YH06634)																																												●									
HINCHLIFFE, M J, Hungerford (YH06867)																																																●					
HOUSEMAN, S, Reading (YH07211)																				●																																	
INDESPENSION, Reading (YH07411)																						●																															
ISAAC, C & D, Newbury (YH07511)																																												●									
J C & N C WARD, Pangbourne (YH07568)																																												●									
LAMBOURN RACEHORSE TRANSPORT, Hungerford (YH08367)																																																●					
LYFORDS MEADOW STABLES, Ascot (YH08917)																																												●									
MARKS, KELLY, Hungerford (YH09165)																																							●														
MARNER, FIONA, Hungerford (YH09172)																											●																										
MUSCHAMP STUD, Slough (YH09974)																																												●									
NEW FARM, Newbury (YH10095)							●																																					●									
PARKES INT TRANSPORT, Newbury (YH10755)																																									●												
PEACHEY, KA, Maidenhead (YH10858)											●									●																												●					
PERRYS EQUESTRIAN SVS, Bracknell (YH10991)																																												●									
PINNOCKS WOOD EQUESTRIAN CTRE, Maidenhead (YH11139)																																												●									
PLEASURE PRINTS AREA C, Newbury (YH11176)																											●																										
RACEHORSE TRANSPORTERS ASS, Reading (YH11579)																																									●							●					
RIDERS REPAIRS, Reading (YH11859)																																	●	●																			
RIVERDALE, Thatcham (YH11920)																				●													●	●		●	●																
ROBERTS, M & MARKS, K, Hungerford (YH11955)																																												●									
SCATS COUNTRYSTORE, Newbury (YH12493)																																	●			●																	
SHAMLEY SADDLERY, Maidenhead (YH12663)																																	●	●		●	●								●								

Business Profile
General Equine

by Country by County

	Artist	Blacksmith	Business Consultancy	Commentating for Events	Competition Horses	Competition Riders	Cross Country Course	Dressage Riders	Driving Centre	Driving Competitors	Driving Services	Engraving	Equine Holidays	Event Management	Event Riders	Forge	Harness Race Course	Harness Racing Horses	Harness Racing Skills	Harness Retailer	Horse Sale Agency	Horsebox Hire	International Arena	Jockey	Jockey Supply	Photographer	Point-to-Point Course	Polo Pitch	Portraits	Racecourse Flat	Racecourse Steeplechase	Racing Investment	Repairs Rugs	Repairs Saddles	Riding Club	Rug Cleaning	Saddler	School (Indoor)	School (Outdoor)	Sculptor	Shipping Agent	Show Jump Course	Show Jumping arena	Stabling Centre	Tack Shop	Taxidermy	Trail Riding Centre	Transport	Transport Overseas	Trekking Centre	Valuer	Website design	Wheelwright
SHELTON FARM, Reading (YH12704)									●	●	●																																										
SNOWBALL FARM EQUESTRIAN CTRE, Slough (YH13037)													●																								●							●									
SPANISH BIT RIDING SCHOOL, Windsor (YH13173)																																												●									
STABLE DOOR, Reading (YH13291)																																	●	●		●	●																
T N T INT AVIATION SVS, Windsor (YH13761)																																									●							●					
TALLY HO FARM, Windsor (YH13840)																																					●																
THIMBLEBY & SHORTLAND, Reading (YH13991)																					●																																
THRESHERS BARN, Newbury (YH14111)																																					●																
TIDMARSH STUD, Reading (YH14134)					●																																																
TURF & TRAVEL, Slough (YH14466)																				●																●	●																
WEST END LIVERIES SUPPLIES, Warfield (YH15141)																																												●									
WHITELOCKS FARM RIDING SCHOOL, Bracknell (YH15350)																																												●									
WOKINGHAM EQUESTRIAN CTRE, Wokingham (YH15644)							●								●																												●										
WOODHAVEN STUD, Newbury (YH15693)																																												●									
WOODLANDS, Hungerford (YH15705)																								●									●	●		●																	
WOODLANDS LEISUREWEAR, Hungerford (YH15709)																																					●																
BRISTOL																																																					
A T VEATER & SONS, Bristol (YH00062)																																	●	●			●																
CLIFTON CARRIAGES, Bristol (YH03036)											●																																										
EQUICRAFT SADDLERY, Bristol (YH04739)																																				●	●																
JENNY'S TACK SHOP, Bristol (YH07750)																																	●	●			●																
KINGSDOWN PICTURES, Stapleton (YH08201)																											●																										
KINGTON RIDING STABLES, Bristol (YH08212)													●																																								
LEYLAND COURT, Bristol (YH08601)																																					●							●									
PATRICK PINKER, Bristol (YH10824)																																					●																
TYNINGS RIDING SCHOOL, Bristol (YH14527)																																												●									
URCHINWOOD MANOR EQUITATION, Bristol (YH14620)							●																							●								●		●					●								
WHITE CAT STABLES, Bristol (YH15301)													●																															●									
BUCKINGHAMSHIRE																																																					
ABEX HORSE & RIDER, High Wycombe (YH00131)																						●															●											●					
ADDINGTON MANOR, Buckingham (YH00179)																							●																														
AESCWOOD, Beaconsfield (YH00196)																																					●																

Business Profile
General Equine

by Country by County	Artist	Blacksmith	Business Consultancy	Commentating for Events	Competition Horses	Competition Riders	Cross Country Course	Dressage Riders	Driving Centre	Driving Competitors	Driving Services	Engraving	Equine Holidays	Event Management	Event Riders	Forge	Harness Race Course	Harness Racing Horses	Harness Racing Skills	Harness Retailer	Horse Sale Agency	Horsebox Hire	International Arena	Jockey	Jockey Supply	Photographer	Point-to-Point Course	Polo Pitch	Portraits	Racecourse Flat	Racecourse Steeplechase	Racing Investment	Repairs Rugs	Repairs Saddles	Riding Club	Rug Cleaning	Saddler	School (Indoor)	School (Outdoor)	Sculptor	Shipping Agent	Show Jump Course	Show Jumping arena	Stabling Centre	Tack Shop	Taxidermy	Trail Riding Centre	Transport	Transport Overseas	Trekking Centre	Valuer	Website design	Wheelwright
BATES, AL, Aylesbury (YH01066)																																																●					
BEECHFIELD SADDLERY, Grendon Underwood (YH01172)																																					●																
BELLINGDON END, Chesham (YH01238)																				●													●	●		●	●																
BOCKMER LIVERY STABLES, Marlow (YH01590)																																												●									
BOW BRICKHILL TREKKING CTRE, Milton Keynes (YH01694)																																																		●			
BRAWLINGS FARM RIDING CTRE, Gerrards Cross (YH01819)																																						●		●		●											
BRIDLEWAYS, Burnham (YH01896)																																					●																
BRYERLEY SPRINGS FARM, Milton Keynes (YH02171)																																								●		●											
C & L EQUESTRIAN, Milton Keynes (YH02356)																																					●																
COUNTRY EQUESTRIAN, Milton Keynes (YH03404)																																	●	●		●	●																
COUNTRYWIDE STORES, Tingewick (YH03450)																																					●																
COX & ROBINSON, Buckingham (YH03527)																																					●																
CRAWFORD-BROWN, FIONA, Ludgershall (YH03577)											●																																										
CRENDON SADDLERY, Aylesbury (YH03591)																																					●																
DENNIS'S SADDLERY/RIDING WEAR, Aylesbury (YH04059)																																					●																
DENNIS'S SADDLERY/RIDING WEAR, Aylesbury (YH04060)																																					●																
DEVILS HORSEMEN, Milton Keynes (YH04090)											●																																										
DUNSMORE STABLES, Wendover (YH04358)																																												●									
EQUESTRIAN CTRE, Amersham (YH04696)																																						●		●				●									
EQUINE DESIGN INT, Iver (YH04775)																																					●																
EQUITANA EQUESTIAN, High Wycombe (YH04826)																																					●																
EQUS HEALTH, Aylesbury (YH04835)																																	●			●																	
FLETCHER TOOGOOD, Milton Keynes (YH05272)																																												●									
FORREST HORSE TRANSPORT, Milton Keynes (YH05377)																																																●					
G B GOMME & SON, Princes Risborough (YH05570)																																					●																
GEEGEES, Milton Keynes (YH05693)																																					●																
GIBSON, SUSAN, Wooburn Green (YH05753)																																	●	●																			
GOHL, CHRIS, Chesham (YH05874)																																	●	●																			
GROVE EQUITATION CTRE, High Wycombe (YH06161)													●																															●									
HARTWELL RIDING STABLES, Aylesbury (YH06509)																																												●									
HARVEY, JUDY, Milton Keynes (YH06515)								●																																													
HOOF PRINTS, Haddenham (YH07027)																											●																										

Business Profile
General Equine

by Country by County

	Artist	Blacksmith	Business Consultancy	Commentating for Events	Competition Horses	Competition Riders	Cross Country Course	Dressage Riders	Driving Centre	Driving Competitors	Driving Services	Engraving	Equine Holidays	Event Management	Event Riders	Forge	Harness Race Course	Harness Racing Horses	Harness Racing Skills	Harness Retailer	Horse Sale Agency	Horsebox Hire	International Arena	Jockey	Jockey Supply	Photographer	Point-to-Point Course	Polo Pitch	Portraits	Racecourse Flat	Racecourse Steeplechase	Racing Investment	Repairs Rugs	Repairs Saddles	Riding Club	Rug Cleaning	Saddler	School (Indoor)	School (Outdoor)	Sculptor	Shipping Agent	Show Jump Course	Show Jumping arena	Stabling Centre	Tack Shop	Taxidermy	Trail Riding Centre	Transport	Transport Overseas	Trekking Centre	Valuer	Website design	Wheelwright
HUNTSMOOR PARK FARM, Iver (YH07309)																																												●									
JOHN BRITTER PHOTOGRAPHY, Buckingham (YH07782)																											●																										
LECKHAMPSTEAD WHARF STUD, Buckingham (YH08513)																																												●									
LOUGHTON MANOR, Milton Keynes (YH08840)													●																															●									
M V R PHOTOGRAPHIC, Chesham (YH08977)																											●																										
MILLER, EMMA DOUGLAS, Great Missenden (YH09605)															●																																						
MILTON KEYNES EVENTING, Milton Keynes (YH09645)					●	●	●																								●							●		●		●	●										
NEWBARN FARM STABLES, Aylesbury (YH10122)																					●																							●									
NEWMAN, R & J, High Wycombe (YH10151)																																																●					
PATCHES, High Wycombe (YH10814)																																	●	●		●																	
RADNAGE HOUSE, High Wycombe (YH11599)							●																															●															
RIVERSMEET STABLES, Newport Pagnell (YH11930)																																												●									
ROBBINS, M A, Amersham (YH11936)										●	●																																										
S E BURNELL, Aylesbury (YH12323)																																									●												
SHANA RIDING SCHOOL, High Wycombe (YH12666)													●																																			●					
SIMMONS, Marlow (YH12822)			●																																																●		
STOWE RIDINGS, Buckingham (YH13538)															●																													●									
SUMMERFIELDS SADDLERY, Aylesbury (YH13630)																																					●																
WAYLANDS EQUESTRIAN CTRE, Beaconsfield (YH15016)																					●																							●									
WIDMER FEEDS, Princes Risborough (YH15393)																																					●																
WILLOWBROOK FARM FEED & TACK, Aylesbury (YH15507)																																	●	●			●																
CAMBRIDGESHIRE																																																					
A FRENCH & SONS, Cambridge (YH00032)																																					●																
ALLTACK & ALLFEED, Cambridge (YH00326)																				●													●	●		●	●																
BARRETT, R, Chatteris (YH01013)										●																																											
BELTONS COUNTRY SHOP, Peterborough (YH01256)																																					●																
BROOKFIELD SHIRES, Huntingdon (YH02049)																				●																																	
CENTURION INT HORSE TRANSPORT, Reach (YH02699)																																																●					
CHURCHFIELD FARM TACK SHOP, Peterborough (YH02910)																																					●																
CONQUEST, Farcet Fen (YH03242)																																												●									
COUNTRY PURSUITS, Cambridge (YH03421)							●																																			●		●									
COUNTRY VEHICLES, Ely (YH03434)																																																●					

Business Profile
General Equine

by Country by County

Category	CROSS LEYS FARM, Peterborough (YH03650)	DAYTON, KYM, Wisbech (YH03972)	E ABINGTON & SONS, Huntingdon (YH04396)	EQUESTRIAN SVS THORNEY, Peterborough (YH04717)	GRABELLA STUD, Kentford (YH05957)	GRANGE FARM EQUESTRIAN CTRE, Peterborough (YH05988)	GUYHIRN RIDING SCHOOL, Wisbech (YH06198)	HAGGIS FARM STABLES, Cambridge (YH06278)	HIGHGATE FARM, Willingham (YH06786)	HOOK HSE, March (YH07035)	INGENUS, Peterborough (YH07444)	JANICE GORDON, Peterborough (YH07697)	KIDDY, S M, Balsham (YH08123)	KNIGHTS END FARM, March (YH08268)	LEJEUNE, Ely (YH08549)	LONG MELFORD, Cambridge (YH08798)	LONGLAND, MICHAEL, Huntingdon (YH08814)	MOORE, STEVE, Wisbech (YH09766)	MORTON, LAURIE, Ely (YH09852)	NEW RANGE EQUESTRIAN CTRE, Huntingdon (YH10119)	NORTHBROOK EQUESTRIAN CTRE, Huntingdon (YH10294)	OAKINGTON RIDING SCHOOL, Oakington (YH10386)	OLD TIGER STABLES, Ely (YH10479)	PARKHOUSE STABLES, Cambridge (YH10762)	PINNER, TERRY, Huntingdon (YH11134)	QUEENHOLME BLOODSTOCK STABLES, Cambridge (YH11491)	RATCLIFFE, J M, Ely (YH11649)	RECTORY FARM, Huntingdon (YH11691)	ROBB & SON, St Ives (YH11932)	SANDY'S SADDLERY, Ely (YH12426)	SHIRE HORSE SOC, Peterborough (YH12754)	SMEETH SADDLERY, Wisbech (YH12925)
Wheelwright																																
Website design																																
Valuer																																
Trekking Centre																																
Transport Overseas																																
Transport																											●					
Trail Riding Centre																																
Taxidermy																																
Tack Shop										●						●																
Stabling Centre	●	●			●	●	●	●		●			●								●			●	●	●		●				
Show Jumping arena																																
Show Jump Course																																
Shipping Agent																																
Sculptor														●							●		●									
School (Outdoor)															●																	
School (Indoor)														●							●											
Saddler			●			●			●								●													●		●
Rug Cleaning											●			●																		●
Riding Club																																
Repairs Saddles																																●
Repairs Rugs																●													●			●
Racing Investment																																
Racecourse Steeplechase																																
Racecourse Flat																																
Portraits												●																				
Polo Pitch																																
Point-to-Point Course				●														●	●													
Photographer																																
Jockey Supply																																
Jockey																																
International Arena														●																		
Horsebox Hire																																
Horse Sale Agency																															●	
Harness Retailer																													●	●		
Harness Racing Skills																																
Harness Racing Horses																																
Harness Race Course																																
Forge																																
Event Riders																										●						
Event Management																																
Equine Holidays										●										●	●	●										
Engraving																																
Driving Services																																
Driving Competitors																																
Driving Centre																																
Dressage Riders														●							●											
Cross Country Course																																
Competition Riders														●																		
Competition Horses														●																		
Commentating for Events																																
Business Consultancy																																
Blacksmith																																
Artist												●			●																	

www.hccyourhorse.com

Business Profile
General Equine

by Country by County	Artist	Blacksmith	Business Consultancy	Commentating for Events	Competition Horses	Competition Riders	Cross Country Course	Dressage Riders	Driving Centre	Driving Competitors	Driving Services	Engraving	Equine Holidays	Event Management	Event Riders	Forge	Harness Race Course	Harness Racing Horses	Harness Racing Skills	Harness Retailer	Horse Sale Agency	Horsebox Hire	International Arena	Jockey	Jockey Supply	Photographer	Point-to-Point Course	Polo Pitch	Portraits	Racecourse Flat	Racecourse Steeplechase	Racing Investment	Repairs Rugs	Repairs Saddles	Riding Club	Rug Cleaning	Saddler	School (Indoor)	School (Outdoor)	Sculptor	Shipping Agent	Show Jump Course	Show Jumping arena	Stabling Centre	Tack Shop	Taxidermy	Trail Riding Centre	Transport	Transport Overseas	Trekking Centre	Valuer	Website design	Wheelwright
SWISS COTTAGE STABLES, Wisbech (YH13716)													●																																								
TACK 'N' TOGS, Cambridge (YH13791)																																				●	●																
WEST ANGLIA CLGE, Milton (YH15123)																																												●									
WITCHAM EQUESTRIAN CTRE, Ely (YH15616)																																					●																
WITCHAM HSE FARM STUD, Ely (YH15617)								●													●																			●													
WOODHURST, Huntingdon (YH15697)													●																															●									
CHESHIRE																																																					
ALLMAN, RAY & MARK, Crewe (YH00322)																					●																																
B 1ST RIDING SCHOOL, Stockport (YH00715)																																												●									
BARROW EQUESTRIAN CTRE, Chester (YH01027)																																						●						●									
BELLCROWN, Malpas (YH01231)																				●																																	
BOOL BY DESIGN, Tarporley (YH01631)																																	●	●		●	●								●								
BOWLERS, Stockport (YH01715)																						●											●	●		●	●											●					
BROOMHALL RIDING SCHOOL, Nantwich (YH02079)													●																																								
CARRUTHERS, RICHARD, Frodsham (YH02601)					●	●		●							●																																						
CASSIDY EQUESTRIAN, Northwich (YH02621)																																					●																
CASTLE STABLES, Malpas (YH02635)																																												●									
CHELFORD FARM SUPPLIES, Macclesfield (YH02799)																																	●			●																	
CHESTER SADDLERY, Chester (YH02832)																																	●	●			●																
COLBERRY SADDLERY, Ellesmere Port (YH03142)																																	●	●		●	●								●								
COTTON EQUESTRIAN CTRE, Crewe (YH03384)								●																																													
CREWE SADDLERY, Crewe (YH03595)																																	●	●		●	●								●								
CROFT RIDING CTRE, Warrington (YH03617)							●																															●		●		●		●	●								
DECATHLON SPORTS & LEISURE, Stockport (YH04008)																																													●								
DINGLE BROOK FARM STABLES, Macclesfield (YH04125)						●																																										●					
DOVE STYLE, Chester (YH04217)																																					●																
EQUIPORT, Northwich (YH04815)																																										●	●										
FIELD, LINDSEY, Warrington (YH05188)																																																●					
FOXES FARM & RIDING SCHOOL, Ellesmere Port (YH05431)																																												●									
FRANCIS, W D, Malpas (YH05453)																																									●							●					
GAYNORS SADDLERY, Dukinfield (YH05682)																																	●	●		●	●								●								
GREEN FARM FEEDS, Crewe (YH06055)																																				●																	

Business Profile
General Equine

by Country by County

	Artist	Blacksmith	Business Consultancy	Commentating for Events	Competition Horses	Competition Riders	Cross Country Course	Dressage Riders	Driving Centre	Driving Competitors	Driving Services	Engraving	Equine Holidays	Event Management	Event Riders	Forge	Harness Race Course	Harness Racing Horses	Harness Racing Skills	Harness Retailer	Horse Sale Agency	Horsebox Hire	International Arena	Jockey	Jockey Supply	Photographer	Point-to-Point Course	Polo Pitch	Portraits	Racecourse Flat	Racecourse Steeplechase	Racing Investment	Repairs Rugs	Repairs Saddles	Riding Club	Rug Cleaning	Saddler	School (Indoor)	School (Outdoor)	Sculptor	Shipping Agent	Show Jump Course	Show Jumping arena	Stabling Centre	Tack Shop	Taxidermy	Trail Riding Centre	Transport	Transport Overseas	Trekking Centre	Valuer	Website design	Wheelwright
HANNS HALL LIVERY, Willaston (YH06396)																																												●									
HOLLINSHEAD, DAWN, Winsford (YH06947)															●																													●									
HUGHES, CLINT, Chester (YH07263)																											●																										
INDESPENSION, Altrincham (YH07412)																						●																															
K Y P LEATHER, Mobberley (YH07993)																																	●	●																			
KEY GREEN SADDLERY, Congleton (YH08113)																																	●	●			●																
LANSDOWNE HORSE & RIDER, Chester (YH08423)																									●								●	●		●	●								●								
LEIGH, J, Warrington (YH08547)																					●																																
LEVER, J S, Warrington (YH08574)																					●																																
M J HALE & SONS, Willaston (YH08968)																																												●									
MACCLESFIELD SADDLERY, Macclesfield (YH08985)																																	●	●			●																
MARSDEN, JOHN, Macclesfield (YH09184)															●																																						
MOBBERLEY RIDING SCHOOL, Knutsford (YH09687)																																												●									
MOSS, PHILIP, Congleton (YH09862)																																									●												
N W F COUNTRYWISE, Nantwich (YH10001)																																					●																
PEACEHAVEN RIDING CTRE, Chester (YH10856)																																					●																
PENN HOUSE PUBLISHING, Knutsford (YH10947)				●																																																	
POOL BANK FARM STABLES, Altrincham (YH11260)																																												●									
REDGRAVE, CAROLE, Wilmslow (YH11711)																		●															●	●			●											●					
ROBERTS, STUART, Crewe (YH11962)									●		●																																										
RUGZ, Northwich (YH12225)																																	●	●		●																	
SANDERSONS T C M, Winsford (YH12408)																																																					●
SMITH & MORRIS, Nantwich (YH12932)																																					●							●									
SOUTH VIEW EQUESTRIAN CTRE, Winsford (YH13107)																					●																																
SOUTHFIELDS FARM, Pen-Y-Ffordd (YH13153)																																												●									
STOCKFARM EQUESTRIAN SUPPLIES, Chester (YH13491)																																					●																
STOCKLEY FARM, Warrington (YH13494)					●																																	●		●													
TOWN & COUNTRY PRODUCTIONS, Malpas (YH14285)																											●																										
VIETOR, BERND, Macclesfield (YH14714)															●																																						
W & T GIBSON, Frodsham (YH14748)																																					●																
WHITE HALL LIVERY STABLES, Little Budworth (YH15304)																																												●									
WILLIAMS, B, Lymm (YH15447)																																					●																

Business Profile
General Equine

by Country by County

	Artist	Blacksmith	Business Consultancy	Commentating for Events	Competition Horses	Competition Riders	Cross Country Course	Dressage Riders	Driving Centre	Driving Competitors	Driving Services	Engraving	Equine Holidays	Event Management	Event Riders	Forge	Harness Race Course	Harness Racing Horses	Harness Racing Skills	Harness Retailer	Horse Sale Agency	Horsebox Hire	International Arena	Jockey	Jockey Supply	Photographer	Point-to-Point Course	Polo Pitch	Portraits	Racecourse Flat	Racecourse Steeplechase	Racing Investment	Repairs Rugs	Repairs Saddles	Riding Club	Rug Cleaning	Saddler	School (Indoor)	School (Outdoor)	Sculptor	Shipping Agent	Show Jump Course	Show Jumping arena	Stabling Centre	Tack Shop	Taxidermy	Trail Riding Centre	Transport	Transport Overseas	Trekking Centre	Valuer	Website design	Wheelwright
WILSONS SADDLERY, Macclesfield (YH15552)																																					●																
WOODVILLE FARM SADDLERY, Sandbach (YH15753)																																					●																
WYNNE, M G, Tarporley (YH15872)																																												●									
YEW TREE FARM EQUESTRIAN CTRE, Great Budworth (YH15908)																																													●								
CLEVELAND																																																					
ARMSTRONG RICHARDSON, Middlesbrough (YH00544)												●																									●																
ESTON EQUESTRIAN CTRE, Middlesbrough (YH04876)													●																																								
FOXHOLM STUD, Stockton-on-Tees (YH05437)					●		●	●																																●		●		●									
HOOF'N'HOUND, Hartlepool (YH07031)																																	●			●									●								
JOHN MOORHOUSE, Stockton-on-Tees (YH07802)																																																●					
LOWFIELD LIVERY STABLES, Stockton-on-Tees (YH08874)																																												●									
ROBINSON, KIRSTI, Stokesley (YH11990)															●																																						
STAINSBY GRANGE RIDING CTRE, Stockton-on-Tees (YH13346)													●																															●									
W H HORSEBOXES, Nunthorpe (YH14771)																																																●					
WHITEHALL TRAILERS, Stockton-on-Tees (YH15340)																																																●					
CORNWALL																																																					
BLACKACRE RIDING STABLES, St Columb (YH01474)																																												●									
BLISLAND HARNESS MAKERS, Liskeard (YH01541)																																	●	●			●																
BOLENOWE LIVERY STABLES, Camborne (YH01607)																																												●									
BOSKELL RIDING CTRE, St Austell (YH01654)																																												●									
BUSH LIVERY STABLES, Saltash (YH02306)																																												●									
CHIVERTON RIDING CTRE, Truro (YH02871)																																												●									
CLAPPER HSE RIDING CTRE, Wadebridge (YH02947)													●																																								
COLE, J J, Camelford (YH03157)																																												●									
CORNISH RIDING HOLIDAYS, Redruth (YH03327)													●																									●		●		●								●			
COUNTRY RIDER, Truro (YH03423)																																					●																
ECLIPSE, Penzance (YH04537)																																					●																
EQUESTRIAN STOP, Camborne (YH04712)																																					●																
FARRIER SVS, St Ives (YH05088)		●														●																																					
FORGE COTTAGE SADDLERY, Camborne (YH05361)																																	●	●																			
GOODFELLOWS, Wadebridge (YH05903)																																																					●
GOOSEHAM BARTON STABLES, Bude (YH05917)													●																																								

Business Profile
General Equine

by Country by County

Business	Artist	Blacksmith	Business Consultancy	Commentating for Events	Competition Horses	Competition Riders	Cross Country Course	Dressage Riders	Driving Centre	Driving Competitors	Driving Services	Engraving	Equine Holidays	Event Management	Event Riders	Forge	Harness Race Course	Harness Racing Horses	Harness Racing Skills	Harness Retailer	Horse Sale Agency	Horsebox Hire	International Arena	Jockey	Jockey Supply	Photographer
GOTTS, H J, Redruth (YH05947)																										
HALLAGENNA STUD FARM, Bodmin (YH06322)													●													
HELSTON SADDLERY, Helston (YH06657)																										
HERNISS FARM LIVERY YARD, Penryn (YH06708)																										
KILLIWORGIE RIDING STABLE, Newquay (YH08144)													●													
M J EQUESTRIAN, Looe (YH08967)																										
MAER STABLES, Bude (YH09029)													●													
MAY ROSE FARM, Camelford (YH09287)																					●					
MITCHELL, HAMISH, Bodmin (YH09667)																										
NANTURRIAN STUD FARM, Falmouth (YH10017)																					●					
NINE TOR RIDING CTRE, Launceston (YH10211)													●													
NORTH CORNWALL ARENA, Camelford (YH10250)																										
OLD MILL STABLES, Hayle (YH10469)													●													
P & L LUCK HORSE TRANSPORT, Liskeard (YH10631)																										
PENHALWYN, St Ives (YH10939)													●													
PERRAN SANDS, Perranporth (YH10982)																										
POLPEVER RIDING STABLES, Liskeard (YH11212)																										
RIDE & DRIVE SUPPLIES, Helston (YH11843)											●									●						
ROMANY WALKS, Penzance (YH12072)							●						●													
ROSEVIDNEY ARABIANS, Penzance (YH12111)	●												●													
S-J'S TACK ROOM, Roche (YH12864)																										
SNOWLAND RIDING CTRE, Par (YH13045)							●																			
ST LEONARDS EQUESTRIAN CTRE, Launceston (YH13278)													●													
SUNNYSIDE HOTEL, Camelford (YH13650)													●													
TALL TREES, Camelford (YH13831)																										
TM INT SCHOOL OF HORSEMANSHIP, Liskeard (YH14196)													●													
TRENANCE RIDING STABLES, Newquay (YH14372)																										
TRENAWIN STABLES, Hayle (YH14373)																										
TRENISSICK RIDING STABLES, Newquay (YH14375)													●													
TRESALLYN, Padstow (YH14384)													●													
VERYAN RIDING CTRE, Truro (YH14686)																										
WIEGERSMA, HENDRIK J, Penzance (YH15394)																					●					

Business	Point-to-Point Course	Polo Pitch	Portraits	Racecourse Flat	Racecourse Steeplechase	Racing Investment	Repairs Rugs	Repairs Saddles	Riding Club	Rug Cleaning	Saddler	School (Indoor)	School (Outdoor)	Sculptor	Shipping Agent	Show Jump Course	Show Jumping arena	Stabling Centre	Tack Shop	Taxidermy	Trail Riding Centre	Transport	Transport Overseas	Trekking Centre	Valuer	Website design	Wheelwright
GOTTS, H J, Redruth (YH05947)																											●
HALLAGENNA STUD FARM, Bodmin (YH06322)											●							●									
HELSTON SADDLERY, Helston (YH06657)							●	●			●			●					●								
HERNISS FARM LIVERY YARD, Penryn (YH06708)																		●									
KILLIWORGIE RIDING STABLE, Newquay (YH08144)																											
M J EQUESTRIAN, Looe (YH08967)																		●									
MAER STABLES, Bude (YH09029)																											
MAY ROSE FARM, Camelford (YH09287)																											
MITCHELL, HAMISH, Bodmin (YH09667)	●																										
NANTURRIAN STUD FARM, Falmouth (YH10017)																											
NINE TOR RIDING CTRE, Launceston (YH10211)																											
NORTH CORNWALL ARENA, Camelford (YH10250)																		●									
OLD MILL STABLES, Hayle (YH10469)																											
P & L LUCK HORSE TRANSPORT, Liskeard (YH10631)															●							●					
PENHALWYN, St Ives (YH10939)																											
PERRAN SANDS, Perranporth (YH10982)																								●			
POLPEVER RIDING STABLES, Liskeard (YH11212)																		●									
RIDE & DRIVE SUPPLIES, Helston (YH11843)																											●
ROMANY WALKS, Penzance (YH12072)														●		●											
ROSEVIDNEY ARABIANS, Penzance (YH12111)			●																								
S-J'S TACK ROOM, Roche (YH12864)											●							●									
SNOWLAND RIDING CTRE, Par (YH13045)												●		●				●									
ST LEONARDS EQUESTRIAN CTRE, Launceston (YH13278)																		●									
SUNNYSIDE HOTEL, Camelford (YH13650)																											
TALL TREES, Camelford (YH13831)												●		●		●	●										
TM INT SCHOOL OF HORSEMANSHIP, Liskeard (YH14196)																											
TRENANCE RIDING STABLES, Newquay (YH14372)																								●			
TRENAWIN STABLES, Hayle (YH14373)																		●									
TRENISSICK RIDING STABLES, Newquay (YH14375)																											
TRESALLYN, Padstow (YH14384)														●										●			
VERYAN RIDING CTRE, Truro (YH14686)									●			●		●				●									
WIEGERSMA, HENDRIK J, Penzance (YH15394)																											

Business Profile
General Equine

by Country by County

	Artist	Blacksmith	Business Consultancy	Commentating for Events	Competition Horses	Competition Riders	Cross Country Course	Dressage Riders	Driving Centre	Driving Competitors	Driving Services	Engraving	Equine Holidays	Event Management	Event Riders	Forge	Harness Race Course	Harness Racing Horses	Harness Racing Skills	Harness Retailer	Horse Sale Agency	Horsebox Hire	International Arena	Jockey	Jockey Supply	Photographer	Point-to-Point Course	Polo Pitch	Portraits	Racecourse Flat	Racecourse Steeplechase	Racing Investment	Repairs Rugs	Repairs Saddles	Riding Club	Rug Cleaning	Saddler	School (Indoor)	School (Outdoor)	Sculptor	Shipping Agent	Show Jump Course	Show Jumping arena	Stabling Centre	Tack Shop	Taxidermy	Trail Riding Centre	Transport	Transport Overseas	Trekking Centre	Valuer	Website design	Wheelwright
COUNTY DURHAM																																																					
ACRUM LODGE STUD, Bishop Auckland (YH00160)																																																●					
ALSTON & KILLHOPE, Bishop Auckland (YH00339)													●																						●					●							●			●			
BEAMISH RIDING CTRE, Stanley (YH01117)													●																															●									
BOWES MANOR EQUESTRIAN CTRE, Chester Le Street (YH01709)						●																●																	●		●				●				●				
BROOM HALL LIVERY YARD, Durham (YH02072)					●			●							●							●																				●	●	●									
C R SADDLERY, Bishop Auckland (YH02389)																				●																																	
CENTURION EQUESTRIAN CTRE, Durham (YH02698)							●																															●		●													
COUNTRY LEATHER SADDLERY, Crook (YH03414)																																					●																
DARLINGTON EQUESTRIAN CTRE, Darlington (YH03892)																																						●		●				●									
DEAF HILL, Durham (YH03985)																																												●									
DENE HEAD LIVERY, Darlington (YH04042)		●																																		●								●									
DENNIS, JUDY, Bishop Auckland (YH04055)													●																															●									
DIXON, KAREN, Barnard Castle (YH04142)															●																																						
FARMWAY, Darlington (YH05072)																																	●	●		●	●								●								
FREE & EASY SADDLE, Barnard Castle (YH05480)																																					●																
GO RIDING GRP, Stanley (YH05861)														●							●														●			●		●		●		●	●								
GRAHAM, HUGH, Consett (YH05968)																																	●	●																			
HAMSTERLEY RIDING SCHOOL, Bishop Auckland (YH06372)																																			●					●													
HIGHWELL STUD, Darlington (YH06802)					●								●																									●		●				●							●		
HORSE & RIDER SUPPLIES, Stanley (YH07099)																																					●																
IVESLEY EQUESTRIAN CTRE, Durham (YH07536)							●						●																															●									
KATANYA PETS, Bishop Auckland (YH07997)																																					●																
LOW FOLD RIDING CTRE, Crook (YH08855)							●																																					●									
M A V SADDLERY & PET STORE, Crook (YH08953)																																					●																
M S RACE GEAR, Durham (YH08976)																																	●	●			●																
MCVICKERS, DEREK, Consett (YH09410)																																					●																
NEW MOORS, Bishop Auckland (YH10114)							●																																					●									
NORTHUMBRIA HORSE HOLIDAYS, Stanley (YH10320)													●																																								
ORCHARD HSE, Barnard Castle (YH10534)																																												●									
RAYGILL, Barnard Castle (YH11672)							●						●																															●									
RICKNALL GRANGE, Newton Aycliffe (YH11838)																																						●															

Business Profile
General Equine

by Country by County	Artist	Blacksmith	Business Consultancy	Commentating for Events	Competition Horses	Competition Riders	Cross Country Course	Dressage Riders	Driving Centre	Driving Competitors	Driving Services	Engraving	Equine Holidays	Event Management	Event Riders	Forge	Harness Race Course	Harness Racing Horses	Harness Racing Skills	Harness Retailer	Horse Sale Agency	Horsebox Hire	International Arena	Jockey	Jockey Supply	Photographer	Point-to-Point Course	Polo Pitch	Portraits	Racecourse Flat	Racecourse Steeplechase	Racing Investment	Repairs Rugs	Repairs Saddles	Riding Club	Rug Cleaning	Saddler	School (Indoor)	School (Outdoor)	Sculptor	Shipping Agent	Show Jump Course	Show Jumping arena	Stabling Centre	Tack Shop	Taxidermy	Trail Riding Centre	Transport	Transport Overseas	Trekking Centre	Valuer	Website design	Wheelwright
RICKNALL RUGS, Darlington (YH11839)																																	●			●																	
ROBSON, JAMES, Wolsingham (YH12015)										●																																											
SADDLE SENSE, Barnard Castle (YH12348)																																	●	●		●	●																
SEAGOLD CENTURION, Crook (YH12587)							●																															●		●		●	●	●									
TACK UP, Barnard Castle (YH13817)																																					●																
TALLY HO, Beamish (YH13837)																																					●																
WALKER, D A & C S, Newton Aycliffe (YH14848)																																	●																				
WEST HOPPYLAND TREKKING CTRE, Bishop Auckland (YH15149)														●																																							
WIDDAS, TONY, Cockfield (YH15390)																																																●					
WITTON CASTLE RACEWAY, Bishop Auckland (YH15635)																	●																																				
CUMBRIA																																																					
ALLONBY RIDING SCHOOL, Wigton (YH00323)																																	●	●			●			●				●						●			
ARMATHWAITE HALL, Keswick (YH00536)													●																																								
BARROW SADDLERY & SUPPLIES, Barrow-In-Furness (YH01029)																																						●															
BENSON, LAUREL, Maryport (YH01279)																																	●	●																			
BIRKBY HALL, Grange Over Sands (YH01440)									●		●		●																															●									
BOWMAN, GEORGE, Penrith (YH01721)										●																																											
BREED EX EQUINE STUD, Penrith (YH01832)											●										●																							●				●					
CALVERT TRUST ADVENTURE CTRE, Keswick (YH02455)													●																																								
CARGO RIDING CTRE, Carlisle (YH02538)							●																																	●		●											
CLAIFE/GRIZEDALE RIDING CTRE, Ambleside (YH02936)													●																																								
CROOK BARN STABLES, Coniston (YH03634)																																																		●			
CUMBRIA SCHOOL OF SADDLERY, Penrith (YH03715)													●																				●	●			●																
CUMBRIA TOURIST BOARD, Windermere (YH03716)													●																																								
EDEN VALLEY TROTTING ASS, Kirkby Stephen (YH04549)																	●																																				
ESKDALE SADDLERY, Carlisle (YH04861)																																					●																
EXPO LIFE, Carlisle (YH04972)																											●																										
FOUR LEGGED FRIENDS, Egremont (YH05408)																																					●																
GOOSEWELL TREKKING CTRE, Keswick (YH05920)													●																																					●			
GREENLANDS LIVERY STABLES, Carlisle (YH06092)																																												●									
GREY HORSE RIDING CTRE, Brough (YH06124)													●																																								
HAYESCASTLE FARM, Workington (YH06576)																																												●									

Business Profile
General Equine

by Country by County

by Country by County	Artist	Blacksmith	Business Consultancy	Commentating for Events	Competition Horses	Competition Riders	Cross Country Course	Dressage Riders	Driving Centre	Driving Competitors	Driving Services	Engraving	Equine Holidays	Event Management	Event Riders	Forge	Harness Race Course	Harness Racing Horses	Harness Racing Skills	Harness Retailer	Horse Sale Agency	Horsebox Hire	International Arena	Jockey	Jockey Supply	Photographer	Point-to-Point Course	Polo Pitch	Portraits	Racecourse Flat	Racecourse Steeplechase	Racing Investment	Repairs Rugs	Repairs Saddles	Riding Club	Rug Cleaning	Saddler	School (Indoor)	School (Outdoor)	Sculptor	Shipping Agent	Show Jump Course	Show Jumping arena	Stabling Centre	Tack Shop	Taxidermy	Trail Riding Centre	Transport	Transport Overseas	Trekking Centre	Valuer	Website design	Wheelwright
HIPSHOW FARM RIDING STABLES, Kendal (YH06879)																																															●						
HORSE HIRE HOLIDAYS, Wigton (YH07122)													●																																		●			●			
INMAN, JENNY, Kendal (YH07459)																																	●	●																			
KERBECK, Workington (YH08096)													●																											●													
KESWICK RIDING CTRE, Keswick (YH08105)							●																																					●									
LAKE DISTRICT TRAIL CTRE, Ambleside (YH08349)													●																																								
LAKELAND EQUESTRIAN, Windermere (YH08354)					●	●							●		●																									●				●			●			●			
LANCASTER, P R, Ulverston (YH08381)																						●															●							●				●					
LARKRIGG RIDING SCHOOL, Kendal (YH08434)					●	●		●																																●				●						●			
LEACH, S J, Ulverston (YH08496)																				●													●	●																			
LIMEFITT PK, Windermere (YH08629)													●																																					●			
LIVESTOCK SUPPLIES INTL, Milnthorpe (YH08715)																					●																																
MCCARTEN, ELAINE, Cleator (YH09321)																																	●	●																			
MIDDLE BAYLES LIVERY, Alston (YH09534)													●																											●							●						
OAKDEN, JAMES, Windermere (YH10373)															●																																						
PARK FOOT TREKKING CTRE, Penrith (YH10725)													●																																								
PARKFOOT TREKKING CTRE, Ullswater (YH10759)																																																		●			
ROOKIN HOUSE, Penrith (YH12074)													●																											●										●			
SCARBARROW PADDOCK SADDLERY, Ulverston (YH12485)																																					●																
SLACK'S, Penrith (YH12884)																																	●	●			●																
SOCKBRIDGE PONY TREKKING CTRE, Penrith (YH13050)																																																		●			
STEWART, L, Carlisle (YH13458)																																	●	●			●																
T W RELPH & SONS, Penrith (YH13767)																																					●																
TYNDALE FARM SERVICES, Holmrook (YH14525)																																					●																
W C F COUNTRY CTRES, Wigton (YH14757)																																					●																
W G TODD & SONS, Kendal (YH14767)																																					●																
ZALKIND, Penrith (YH15950)																																				●								●									
DERBYSHIRE																																																					
ALTON RIDING SCHOOL, Chesterfield (YH00344)					●								●																				●					●		●		●	●								●		
AMBER HILLS EQUESTRIAN, Belper (YH00356)																																												●									
ASHFORD FARM SUPPLIES, Bakewell (YH00601)																																					●																
BAGSHAWS AGRICULTURAL, Ashbourne (YH00791)																																																			●		

Business Profile
General Equine

by Country by County

	Artist	Blacksmith	Business Consultancy	Commentating for Events	Competition Horses	Competition Riders	Cross Country Course	Dressage Riders	Driving Centre	Driving Competitors	Driving Services	Engraving	Equine Holidays	Event Management	Event Riders	Forge	Harness Race Course	Harness Racing Horses	Harness Racing Skills	Harness Retailer	Horse Sale Agency	Horsebox Hire
BARLEYFIELD SADDLERY, Etwall (YH00951)																						
BARLEYFIELDS, Derby (YH00952)							●						●									
BIRCHWOOD, Alfreton (YH01435)																						
BRAILSFORD STABLES, Ashbourne (YH01777)											●											
BRIMINGTON EQUESTRIAN CTRE, Chesterfield (YH01912)													●									
BROOMBANK EQUESTRIAN, Chesterfield (YH02074)																						
BUXTON RIDING SCHOOL, Buxton (YH02339)																						
C E S, Ashbourne (YH02370)	●	●			●	●		●		●	●		●								●	●
CHESTERFIELD, Chesterfield (YH02833)					●	●		●														●
COUNTRY SPORT, Glossop (YH03426)																						
CURBAR RIDING STABLES, Hope Valley (YH03727)							●															
EDENSOR LIVERY STABLES, Bakewell (YH04552)																						
ELVASTON CASTLE RIDING CTRE, Derby (YH04645)													●									
FIELD FARM, Heanor (YH05184)																						
FRANCIS, K, Dronfield (YH05450)																					●	
HADDON HSE, Bakewell (YH06261)							●						●								●	
HARGATE EQUESTRIAN, Derby (YH06423)																						
HARGATE HILL, Glossop (YH06424)																						
HEN MILL SADDLERY, Clay Cross (YH06663)																						
HIGH PEAK TRAILERS, High Peak (YH06765)																						
HILLCLIFF STUD, Belper (YH06838)	●				●	●							●		●							
HOLME FARM EQUESTRIAN CTRE, Derby (YH06963)									●		●											
HULLAND SADDLERY, Ashbourne (YH07282)																				●		
IKIN, D & D, Swadlincote (YH07397)																						
INDESPENSION, Derby (YH07416)																						●
IVANHOE FEEDS, Swadlincote (YH07533)																						
JONES, EMMA-JANE, Chesterfield (YH07897)															●							
KNABBHALL EQUESTRIAN CTRE, Matlock (YH08249)													●									
KNOWLE HILL EQUESTRIAN, Derby (YH08280)							●						●									
LEE WOOD HOTEL, Buxton (YH08521)													●									
MANOR FARM LIVERY, Swadlincote (YH09100)																						
MATLOCK SADDLERY, Matlock (YH09265)																						

	International Arena	Jockey	Jockey Supply	Photographer	Point-to-Point Course	Polo Pitch	Portraits	Racecourse Flat	Racecourse Steeplechase	Racing Investment	Repairs Rugs	Repairs Saddles	Riding Club	Rug Cleaning	Saddler	School (Indoor)	School (Outdoor)	Sculptor	Shipping Agent	Show Jump Course	Show Jumping arena	Stabling Centre	Tack Shop	Taxidermy	Trail Riding Centre	Transport	Transport Overseas	Trekking Centre	Valuer	Website design	Wheelwright
BARLEYFIELD SADDLERY, Etwall (YH00951)											●	●		●									●								
BARLEYFIELDS, Derby (YH00952)													●		●	●		●		●	●	●	●			●					
BIRCHWOOD, Alfreton (YH01435)																						●									
BRAILSFORD STABLES, Ashbourne (YH01777)																															
BRIMINGTON EQUESTRIAN CTRE, Chesterfield (YH01912)																						●									
BROOMBANK EQUESTRIAN, Chesterfield (YH02074)															●																
BUXTON RIDING SCHOOL, Buxton (YH02339)																						●									
C E S, Ashbourne (YH02370)																		●				●				●				●	
CHESTERFIELD, Chesterfield (YH02833)																		●				●									
COUNTRY SPORT, Glossop (YH03426)																							●								
CURBAR RIDING STABLES, Hope Valley (YH03727)																				●											
EDENSOR LIVERY STABLES, Bakewell (YH04552)																						●									
ELVASTON CASTLE RIDING CTRE, Derby (YH04645)																															
FIELD FARM, Heanor (YH05184)																						●									
FRANCIS, K, Dronfield (YH05450)																															
HADDON HSE, Bakewell (YH06261)																		●		●								●			
HARGATE EQUESTRIAN, Derby (YH06423)															●																
HARGATE HILL, Glossop (YH06424)																						●									
HEN MILL SADDLERY, Clay Cross (YH06663)															●																
HIGH PEAK TRAILERS, High Peak (YH06765)																										●					
HILLCLIFF STUD, Belper (YH06838)																●		●				●									
HOLME FARM EQUESTRIAN CTRE, Derby (YH06963)																															
HULLAND SADDLERY, Ashbourne (YH07282)											●	●			●																
IKIN, D & D, Swadlincote (YH07397)																						●									
INDESPENSION, Derby (YH07416)																															
IVANHOE FEEDS, Swadlincote (YH07533)															●																
JONES, EMMA-JANE, Chesterfield (YH07897)																															
KNABBHALL EQUESTRIAN CTRE, Matlock (YH08249)																															
KNOWLE HILL EQUESTRIAN, Derby (YH08280)																●						●						●			
LEE WOOD HOTEL, Buxton (YH08521)																															
MANOR FARM LIVERY, Swadlincote (YH09100)																						●									
MATLOCK SADDLERY, Matlock (YH09265)											●	●		●	●																

www.hccyourhorse.com

Business Profile
General Equine

by Country by County	Artist	Blacksmith	Business Consultancy	Commentating for Events	Competition Horses	Competition Riders	Cross Country Course	Dressage Riders	Driving Centre	Driving Competitors	Driving Services	Engraving	Equine Holidays	Event Management	Event Riders	Forge	Harness Race Course	Harness Racing Horses	Harness Racing Skills	Harness Retailer	Horse Sale Agency	Horsebox Hire	International Arena	Jockey	Jockey Supply	Photographer	Point-to-Point Course	Polo Pitch	Portraits	Racecourse Flat	Racecourse Steeplechase	Racing Investment	Repairs Rugs	Repairs Saddles	Riding Club	Rug Cleaning	Saddler	School (Indoor)	School (Outdoor)	Sculptor	Shipping Agent	Show Jump Course	Show Jumping arena	Stabling Centre	Tack Shop	Taxidermy	Trail Riding Centre	Transport	Transport Overseas	Trekking Centre	Valuer	Website design	Wheelwright
MOORBRIDGE RIDING STABLES, Derby (YH09747)																																								●													
NORTHFIELD FARM, Buxton (YH10312)													●																																					●			
PARK HALL FARM EQUEST CTRE, Ilkeston (YH10726)																																												●									
PEAKDALE SADDLERY, Buxton (YH10866)																																	●	●		●	●								●								
QUARNHILL SCHOOL, Kirk Ireton (YH11481)													●																																								
R E FARMS, Derby (YH11533)																				●													●	●			●																
RED HSE STABLES, Matlock (YH11698)									●		●																																	●									
RINGER VILLA EQUESTRIAN CTRE, Chesterfield (YH11900)																																								●													
RISLEY SADDLERY, Draycott (YH11911)																																					●																
ROGUES GALLERY, Mackworth (YH12063)																											●																										
SWATHWICK FARM LIVERIES, Chesterfield (YH13698)																																												●									
TACK SHACK, Derby (YH13805)																																					●																
TEVERSAL SADDLERY, Alfreton (YH13965)																																					●																
WELLCROFT STUD, Ashbourne (YH15065)																																												●									
WRIGHT, L C, Swadlincote (YH15837)																				●													●	●			●																
YEW TREE FARM STABLES, Belper (YH15910)																					●																							●									
DEVON																																																					
ACORN SADDLERY, South Molton (YH00151)																																	●	●			●																
ARUNDELL ARMS, Lifton (YH00579)													●																																								
ASHLANDS FARM, Tavistock (YH00606)													●																																								
AVON FARMERS, Kingsbridge (YH00688)																																					●																
BARNSTAPLE HORSE/PET SUPP, Barnstaple (YH00990)																																	●	●			●																
BARRIBAL, Okehampton (YH01020)									●		●		●																																								
BARTONS CLOSE STABLES, Teignmouth (YH01051)																																												●									
BARWELL, C R, Tiverton (YH01052)																																																●					
BINGHAM, R J, Lynton (YH01422)													●																																								
BOLDTRY RIDING STABLES, Chulmleigh (YH01606)													●																																								
BRAKE, C J, Cullompton (YH01780)																					●																																
BRENDON MANOR RIDING STABLES, Lynton (YH01839)													●																																								
BUDLEIGH SALTERTON, Budleigh Salterton (YH02208)																																												●									
C J HORSE TRANSPORT, Tavistock (YH02377)				●																																												●					
CHESTON EQUESTRIAN CTRE, South Brent (YH02839)													●																																								

Business Profile
General Equine

by Country by County

by Country by County	Artist	Blacksmith	Business Consultancy	Commentating for Events	Competition Horses	Competition Riders	Cross Country Course	Dressage Riders	Driving Centre	Driving Competitors	Driving Services	Engraving	Equine Holidays	Event Management	Event Riders	Forge	Harness Race Course	Harness Racing Horses	Harness Racing Skills	Harness Retailer	Horse Sale Agency	Horsebox Hire	International Arena	Jockey	Jockey Supply	Photographer	Point-to-Point Course
CHING SADDLERS, Exeter (YH02863)																											
CHOLWELL EQUESTRIAN CTRE, Okehampton (YH02878)																											
CLAIRE HOWARTH, Exeter (YH02937)																											
CLIPPER SHARP, Cullompton (YH03046)																											
COLLACOTT FARM, Umberleigh (YH03173)							●																				
COLLAFORD FARM PARTNERSHIP, Plymouth (YH03174)																											
COOMBE STUDIO, Bovey Tracey (YH03275)																											
CRAWSHAW, ALWYN, Dawlish (YH03580)	●																										
DARTMOOR DRIVING, Newton Abbot (YH03901)									●		●		●														
DEVENISH PITT, Honiton (YH04087)													●														
DOONE VALLEY RIDING STABLES, Lynton (YH04194)													●														
DOWNE FARM, Tiverton (YH04225)																											
DURAL FARM ENTERPRISES, Holsworthy (YH04363)																											
DURALOCK, Plymouth (YH04365)																						●					
EAST DEVON SADDLERY, Honiton (YH04470)																											
EAST LAKE, Okehampton (YH04477)													●														
EDWIN TUCKER & SONS, Newton Abbott (YH04586)																											
EQUITOPIA, Lynton (YH04831)	●												●														
ERME VALLEY FARMERS, Ivybridge (YH04850)																											
F W PERKINS, Ottery St Mary (YH05003)																											
FARLAP EQUESTRIAN PHOTOGRAPHY, Lewdown (YH05053)																											●
FARMERS FRIEND, Exeter (YH05061)																											
FENIX CARRIAGE DRIVING CTRE, Tiverton (YH05141)									●																		
FERNLEA, Newton Abbot (YH05168)																											
FITZWORTHY RIDING, Ivybridge (YH05251)													●														
G C SEARLE & SONS, Plymouth (YH05573)																											
GLEBE INT ENTERPRISE, Exeter (YH05817)					●			●																			
GRAHAM, FERGUS, Newton Abbott (YH05966)																					●						
GRANGE EQUESTRIAN CTRE, Okehampton (YH05987)							●						●														
HALDON RIDING STABLES, Exeter (YH06290)																											
HALWILL ELITE LIVERY SVS, Beaworthy (YH06338)																											
HEAZLE RIDING CTRE, Cullompton (YH06635)																					●						

by Country by County	Polo Pitch	Portraits	Racecourse Flat	Racecourse Steeplechase	Racing Investment	Repairs Rugs	Repairs Saddles	Riding Club	Rug Cleaning	Saddler	School (Indoor)	School (Outdoor)	Sculptor	Shipping Agent	Show Jump Course	Show Jumping arena	Stabling Centre	Tack Shop	Taxidermy	Trail Riding Centre	Transport	Transport Overseas	Trekking Centre	Valuer	Website design	Wheelwright
CHING SADDLERS, Exeter (YH02863)						●	●			●																
CHOLWELL EQUESTRIAN CTRE, Okehampton (YH02878)																●										
CLAIRE HOWARTH, Exeter (YH02937)																					●					
CLIPPER SHARP, Cullompton (YH03046)										●																
COLLACOTT FARM, Umberleigh (YH03173)													●													
COLLAFORD FARM PARTNERSHIP, Plymouth (YH03174)																	●									
COOMBE STUDIO, Bovey Tracey (YH03275)		●																								
CRAWSHAW, ALWYN, Dawlish (YH03580)																										
DARTMOOR DRIVING, Newton Abbot (YH03901)																										
DEVENISH PITT, Honiton (YH04087)										●	●		●													
DOONE VALLEY RIDING STABLES, Lynton (YH04194)																										
DOWNE FARM, Tiverton (YH04225)																	●									
DURAL FARM ENTERPRISES, Holsworthy (YH04363)										●																
DURALOCK, Plymouth (YH04365)																					●					
EAST DEVON SADDLERY, Honiton (YH04470)										●																
EAST LAKE, Okehampton (YH04477)																	●									
EDWIN TUCKER & SONS, Newton Abbott (YH04586)						●	●		●	●																
EQUITOPIA, Lynton (YH04831)																				●			●			
ERME VALLEY FARMERS, Ivybridge (YH04850)						●			●									●								
F W PERKINS, Ottery St Mary (YH05003)										●																
FARLAP EQUESTRIAN PHOTOGRAPHY, Lewdown (YH05053)																										
FARMERS FRIEND, Exeter (YH05061)																		●								
FENIX CARRIAGE DRIVING CTRE, Tiverton (YH05141)																										
FERNLEA, Newton Abbot (YH05168)																	●									
FITZWORTHY RIDING, Ivybridge (YH05251)																										
G C SEARLE & SONS, Plymouth (YH05573)																							●			
GLEBE INT ENTERPRISE, Exeter (YH05817)																										
GRAHAM, FERGUS, Newton Abbott (YH05966)																										
GRANGE EQUESTRIAN CTRE, Okehampton (YH05987)																										
HALDON RIDING STABLES, Exeter (YH06290)													●										●			
HALWILL ELITE LIVERY SVS, Beaworthy (YH06338)																	●									
HEAZLE RIDING CTRE, Cullompton (YH06635)																										

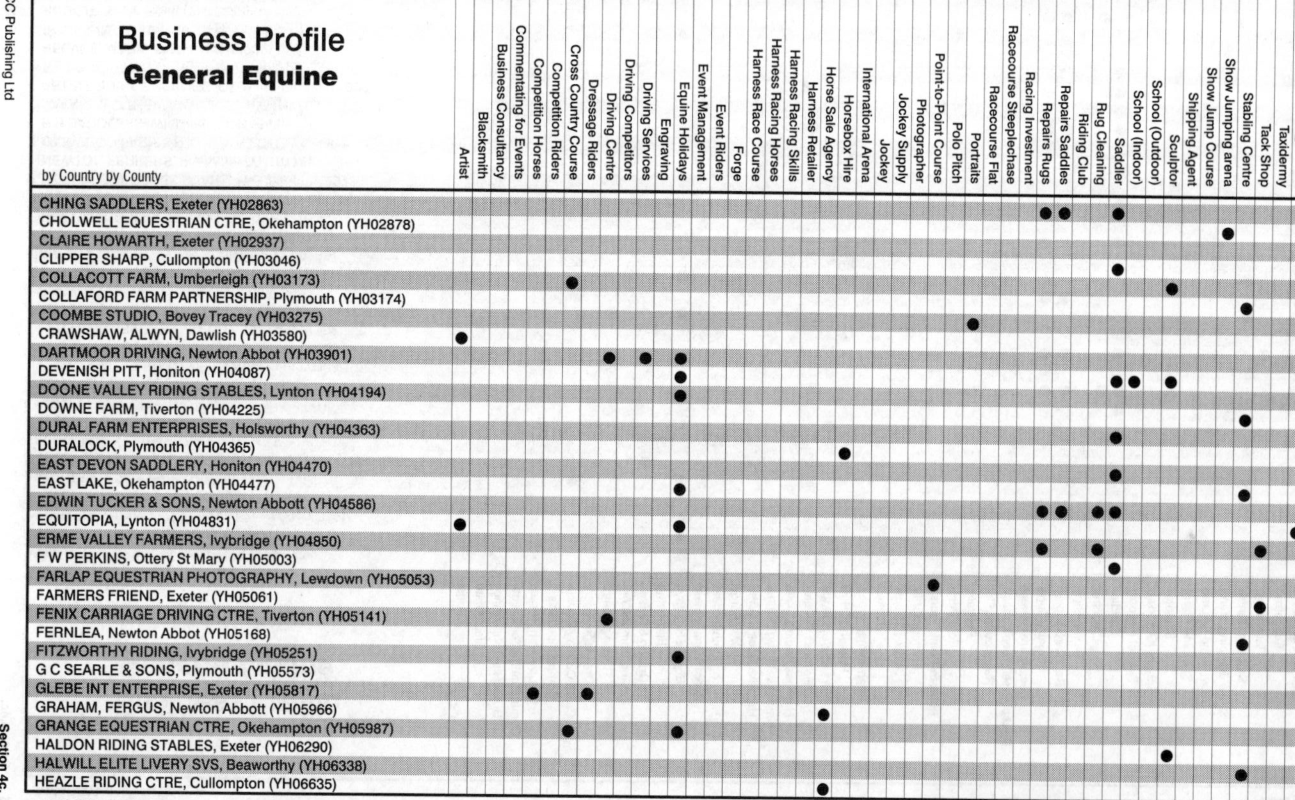

Business Profile
General Equine

by Country by County	Artist	Blacksmith	Business Consultancy	Commentating for Events	Competition Horses	Competition Riders	Cross Country Course	Dressage Riders	Driving Centre	Driving Competitors	Driving Services	Engraving	Equine Holidays	Event Management	Event Riders	Forge	Harness Race Course	Harness Racing Horses	Harness Racing Skills	Harness Retailer	Horse Sale Agency	Horsebox Hire	International Arena	Jockey	Jockey Supply	Photographer	Point-to-Point Course	Polo Pitch	Portraits	Racecourse Flat	Racecourse Steeplechase	Racing Investment	Repairs Rugs	Repairs Saddles	Riding Club	Rug Cleaning	Saddler	School (Indoor)	School (Outdoor)	Sculptor	Shipping Agent	Show Jump Course	Show Jumping arena	Stabling Centre	Tack Shop	Taxidermy	Trail Riding Centre	Transport	Transport Overseas	Trekking Centre	Valuer	Website design	Wheelwright
HIGHER COBDEN FARM, Exeter (YH06778)													●																																								
HIGHER WILLYARDS FARM, Exeter (YH06781)													●																																								
HILLSIDE RIDING CTRE, Princetown (YH06853)													●																																								
HILLTOP RIDING SCHOOL, Exeter (YH06858)																																												●									
HONEYSUCKLE FARM, Newton Abbot (YH07017)							●						●																															●									
KILEY-WORTHINGTON, M (DR), Okehampton (YH08133)											●																																										
KING, MARY ELIZABETH, Sidmouth (YH08183)															●																																						
LAKESIDE PADDOCK STUD, Ilfracombe (YH08358)																					●																																
LAMBERTS COUNTRY STORE, Bideford (YH08366)																																					●																
LEATHER WORKSHOP, Exeter (YH08505)																				●													●	●		●	●																
LEAWOOD RIDING CTRE, Okehampton (YH08510)																																												●									
LEONARD COOMBE, Newton Abbot (YH08553)																																	●	●			●								●								
LES LEY HORSE TRANSPORT, Brixham (YH08556)																																																●					
LITTLE ASH ECO-FARM & STUD, Okehampton (YH08683)									●				●																															●									
LUCY TURMAINE, Beaworthy (YH08889)																																	●	●																			
LYDFORD HOUSE RIDING STABLES, Okehampton (YH08916)													●																															●									
MAXIMILLIAN STUD, North Tawton (YH09285)																					●																																
MOLE AVON TRADING, Axminster (YH09707)																																					●																
MOLE AVON TRADING, Crediton (YH09709)																																					●																
MOLE AVON TRADING, Okehampton (YH09708)																																					●																
MULLACOTT EQUESTRIAN, Ilfracombe (YH09935)							●						●																											●							●			●			
NEWTON FERRERS, Plymouth (YH10170)																																												●									
OAKWOOD FARM STUD/RIDING CTRE, Newton Abbot (YH10409)														●																																							
P H SADDLERS, Winkleigh (YH10643)																				●													●	●			●																
PAYNE, MATTHEW, Okehampton (YH10851)																				●																	●																
PET & EQUINE SUPPLIES, Okehampton (YH11000)																																					●																
RED POST FEEDS, Totnes (YH11702)																																					●																
REEVES, MARK, St Mary (YH11737)																																																●					
ROCK INN, Newton Abbot (YH12024)													●																																								
RUGGIT, South Brent (YH12222)																																	●	●		●																	
SAWDYE & HARRIS, Ashburton (YH12459)																																																			●		
SILVER HORSESHOE, Lynton (YH12805)													●																																								

Business Profile
General Equine

by Country by County

Business	Artist	Blacksmith	Business Consultancy	Commentating for Events	Competition Horses	Competition Riders	Cross Country Course	Dressage Riders	Driving Centre	Driving Competitors	Driving Services	Engraving	Equine Holidays	Event Management	Event Riders	Forge	Harness Race Course	Harness Racing Horses	Harness Racing Skills	Harness Retailer	Horse Sale Agency	Horsebox Hire	International Arena	Jockey	Jockey Supply	Photographer	Point-to-Point Course	Polo Pitch	Portraits	Racecourse Flat	Racecourse Steeplechase	Racing Investment	Repairs Rugs	Repairs Saddles	Riding Club	Rug Cleaning	Saddler	School (Indoor)	School (Outdoor)	Sculptor	Shipping Agent	Show Jump Course	Show Jumping arena	Stabling Centre	Tack Shop	Taxidermy	Trail Riding Centre	Transport	Transport Overseas	Trekking Centre	Valuer	Website design	Wheelwright
SKAIGH STABLES, Okehampton (YH12865)													●																																								
SNAFFLES SADDLERY, Bradworthy (YH13025)																				●													●	●			●																
SOUTH DEVON EQUESTRIAN SUP, Paignton (YH13082)																				●													●	●		●	●																
SOUTHDOWN FARM RIDING STABLES, Brixham (YH13134)													●																															●									
STADDON HEIGHTS FARM, Plymouth (YH13319)																																												●									
STANLEY-RICKETTS, JOY, Honiton (YH13376)	●																												●																								
STRETTON-DOWNES, C, Tavistock (YH13575)																																												●									
SUNNYMEADE COUNTRY HOTEL, Ilfracombe (YH13648)													●																																								
TABRE RIDING, Winkleigh (YH13772)													●																																								
TALAWATER QUARTER HORSES, Yelverton (YH13830)					●																																																
TAMAR TRAILER CTRE, Plymouth (YH13848)																						●																										●					
TAVISTOCK SADDLERY, Tavistock (YH13886)																																	●	●			●																
TOWN & COUNTRY SUP, Exeter (YH14286)																						●											●	●		●	●											●					
TRAGO MILLS, Newton Abbott (YH14311)																																					●																
TWYFORD FARM SUPPLIES, Tiverton (YH14516)																																					●																
WARD, MICHAEL J, Holsworthy (YH14904)											●																						●	●										●									
WATERMAN, M & A, Tiverton (YH14970)																																					●																
WEMBURY BAY RIDING SCHOOL, Plymouth (YH15103)																																								●			●							●			
WEST DEVON & NORTH CORNWALL, Holsworthy (YH15139)																																					●																
WEST ILKERTON FARM, Lynton (YH15150)	●										●		●																																								
WHITE HORSE MOTORS, Exeter (YH15309)																																																●					
WHITE TOR, Tavistock (YH15325)													●																																		●						
WHITTABOROUGH, Plympton (YH15372)																																												●									
WILLINGCOTT FARM SUPPLIES, Woolacombe (YH15488)																																					●																
WOOD FARM STUD, Okehampton (YH15656)																																												●									
WYCHANGER BARTON SADDLERY, Tiverton (YH15855)																																	●	●		●	●			●					●								
DORSET																																																					
BLACKMORE VALE STUD, Gillingham (YH01487)																				●													●	●			●																
BLANDFORD SADDLERY, Blandford Forum (YH01524)																																	●	●			●																
CLAIRE'S RIDING SCHOOL, Wimborne (YH02938)													●																																								
COUTISSE, Dorchester (YH03516)																																	●	●			●																
DEER PARK RIDING STABLES, Blandford Forum (YH04023)													●																																								

www.hccyourhorse.com

www.hccyourhorse.com

Business Profile
General Equine

by Country by County	Artist	Blacksmith	Business Consultancy	Commentating for Events	Competition Horses	Competition Riders	Cross Country Course	Dressage Riders	Driving Centre	Driving Competitors	Driving Services	Engraving	Equine Holidays	Event Management	Event Riders	Forge	Harness Race Course	Harness Racing Horses	Harness Racing Skills	Harness Retailer	Horse Sale Agency	Horsebox Hire	International Arena	Jockey	Jockey Supply	Photographer	Point-to-Point Course	Polo Pitch	Portraits	Racecourse Flat	Racecourse Steeplechase	Racing Investment	Repairs Rugs	Repairs Saddles	Riding Club	Rug Cleaning	Saddler	School (Indoor)	School (Outdoor)	Sculptor	Shipping Agent	Show Jump Course	Show Jumping arena	Stabling Centre	Tack Shop	Taxidermy	Trail Riding Centre	Transport	Transport Overseas	Trekking Centre	Valuer	Website design	Wheelwright
DORCHESTER SADDLERY, Dorchester (YH04198)																																					●																
DORSET HEAVY HORSE CTRE, Wimborne (YH04206)																																												●									
DUDMOOR FARM, Christchurch (YH04311)													●																															●									
EQUESTRIAN & EXAM CTRE, Ferndown (YH04691)							●				●										●																	●						●	●								
EQUUS, Wimborne (YH04836)																																	●	●		●	●								●								
FLEET, K L, Sherborne (YH05267)																				●																																	
FOREST LODGE, Shaftesbury (YH05342)													●																															●									
HARRIET GLEN DESIGN, Dorchester (YH06459)																																							●														
HURN BRIDGE CTRE, Christchurch (YH07313)							●																										●	●		●									●								
LULWORTH EQUESTRIAN CTRE, Wareham (YH08897)							●						●																											●			●	●						●			
POUND COTTAGE RIDING CTRE, Blandford Forum (YH11307)													●																									●		●													
PROSPECT FARM LIVERY STABLES, Dorchester (YH11436)																																												●									
PURBECK PETS & EQUESTRIAN, Wareham (YH11462)																																	●	●			●																
REMPSTONE STABLES, Wareham (YH11751)													●																											●				●						●			
SCATS COUNTRYSTORE, Blandford (YH12496)																																	●			●																	
SCATS COUNTRYSTORE, Dorchester (YH12494)																																	●			●																	
SCATS COUNTRYSTORE, Gillingham (YH12495)																																	●			●																	
SEACOMBE RIDING HOLIDAYS, Swanage (YH12581)													●																																								
SIDE SADDLES, Wimborne (YH12787)																																													●								
SIER, JOHN, Christchurch (YH12791)				●																																																	
SIMMONDS & SAMPSON, Wimborne (YH12820)																																																			●		
SKINNER, ROSS, Dorchester (YH12878)							●																																					●									
SOUTHERN COUNTIES AUCTIONEERS, Shaftesbury (YH13136)																																																			●		
SPEER, EMMA, Wareham (YH13192)															●																																						
STABLE MINDS, Ferndown (YH13297)					●																																																
TOLLER TRAILERS, Dorchester (YH14209)																						●																										●					
TOLPUDDLE HALL, Dorchester (YH14213)													●																																								
TURTONS SADDLERS & HARNESS, Shaftesbury (YH14496)																				●													●	●			●																
WARMWELL STUD, Dorchester (YH14924)					●		●																	●	●															●													
WESTWAY SADDLERY, Bridport (YH15233)																																					●							●									
WHITE, CHRISTINA, Weymouth (YH15328)																										●																											

ESSEX

Business Profile
General Equine

by Country by County

Business	Artist	Blacksmith	Business Consultancy	Commentating for Events	Competition Horses	Competition Riders	Cross Country Course	Dressage Riders	Driving Centre	Driving Competitors	Driving Services	Engraving	Equine Holidays	Event Management	Event Riders	Forge	Harness Race Course	Harness Racing Horses	Harness Racing Skills	Harness Retailer	Horse Sale Agency	Horsebox Hire	International Arena	Jockey	Jockey Supply	Photographer	Point-to-Point Course	Polo Pitch	Portraits	Racecourse Flat	Racecourse Steeplechase	Racing Investment	Repairs Rugs	Repairs Saddles	Riding Club	Rug Cleaning	Saddler	School (Indoor)	School (Outdoor)	Sculptor	Shipping Agent	Show Jump Course	Show Jumping arena	Stabling Centre	Tack Shop	Taxidermy	Trail Riding Centre	Transport	Transport Overseas	Trekking Centre	Valuer	Website design	Wheelwright
ACCESS TRAVEL, Hornchurch (YH00139)													●																												●												
ASHFIELDS EQUESTRIAN CTRE, Dunmow (YH00599)																					●																							●									
BARLING TACK SHOP, Rochford (YH00955)																																													●								
BATTLESBRIDGE HORSE & CTRY, Wickford (YH01082)																																	●												●								
BENTLEY STABLES, Brentwood (YH01287)																					●																																
BRAEKMAN, HELENE, Bishop's Stortford (YH01769)																																												●									
BRIDGEWATER SHIPPING, Harwich (YH01884)																																									●												
BROOK FARM EQUESTRIAN CTRE, Saffron Walden (YH02034)																																					●																
BROOK FARM RIDING SCHOOL, Ingatestone (YH02035)													●																																								
BROOKS STABLES, Benfleet (YH02062)																																				●	●							●									
BROWN, N & H, Witham (YH02124)																				●																	●																
BURCHES RIDING SCHOOL, Benfleet (YH02232)																																					●																
CANDLERS, Chelmsford (YH02496)																																	●	●			●								●								
CHELMSFORD EQUESTRIAN CTRE, Chelmsford (YH02801)																																												●									
CLAY HALL, Brentwood (YH02994)									●	●	●				●																									●													
CLIP CLOPS SADDLERY, Braintree (YH03045)																																				●	●																
COACH HSE, Epping (YH03102)					●	●		●																														●		●				●									
COLCHESTER GARRISON, Colchester (YH03144)																																						●		●			●										
COTTON, SARAH, Chelmsford (YH03385)															●																																						
D F ASSET SADDLERY, Brentwood (YH03783)																				●																	●																
DANBURY, Chelmsford (YH03860)									●																																												
D'ARCY RIDING STABLES, Maldon (YH03879)											●																													●		●											
D'ARCY SADDLERY, Maldon (YH03880)																																	●	●		●	●								●								
DE BEAUVOIR, Billericay (YH03973)													●																															●									
EAST ANGLIAN FARM RIDES, Kelvedon (YH04463)																																												●									
EASTMINSTER SCHOOL OF RIDING, Romford (YH04510)																																												●									
ELMWOOD EQUESTRIAN CTRE, Burnham-on-Crouch (YH04640)								●																																	●		●										
FAIR EARTH TRADING, Little Oakley (YH05011)																																	●	●			●																
FOOTPRINT SADDLERY, Ongar (YH05313)																																					●																
FOREST LODGE RIDING SCHOOL, Epping (YH05344)																																												●									
FOXHOUNDS RIDING SCHOOL, Grays (YH05438)																																					●																
FURNESS FARM CROSS COUNTRY, Ingatestone (YH05546)							●																																														

Business Profile
General Equine

by Country by County

Business	Artist	Blacksmith	Business Consultancy	Commentating for Events	Competition Horses	Competition Riders	Cross Country Course	Dressage Riders	Driving Centre	Driving Competitors	Driving Services	Engraving	Equine Holidays	Event Management	Event Riders	Forge	Harness Race Course	Harness Racing Horses	Harness Racing Skills	Harness Retailer	Horse Sale Agency	Horsebox Hire	International Arena	Jockey	Jockey Supply	Photographer	Point-to-Point Course	Polo Pitch	Portraits	Racecourse Flat	Racecourse Steeplechase	Racing Investment	Repairs Rugs	Repairs Saddles	Riding Club	Rug Cleaning	Saddler	School (Indoor)	School (Outdoor)	Sculptor	Shipping Agent	Show Jump Course	Show Jumping arena	Stabling Centre	Tack Shop	Taxidermy	Trail Riding Centre	Transport	Transport Overseas	Trekking Centre	Valuer	Website design	Wheelwright
GAME, DAVID C, Ingatestone (YH05634)																																											●									
H A C S SHOP, Bishop's Stortford (YH06210)																																				●																
HAVERING PK RIDING SCHOOL, Romford (YH06540)																																											●									
HAYCOCKS LIVERY STABLES, Colchester (YH06567)																																											●									
HOBBS CROSS EQUESTRIAN CTRE, Epping (YH06893)							●																										●	●			●							●									
HOBBY HORSE, Romford (YH06897)																																		●			●								●								
HUNNABLE, CHRIS & SAM, Halstead (YH07291)															●																																						
INGATESTONE SADDLERY, Ingatestone (YH07442)																																	●	●		●	●								●								
JARVIS, P, Bishop's Stortford (YH07707)																											●																										
JOHN SKELTONS, Benfleet (YH07812)																																					●								●								
KEDDIE FARM, Rochford (YH08022)																																												●									
KILN SADDLERY, Colchester (YH08151)																																	●	●		●	●								●								
LANGFORD LIVERY, Maldon (YH08404)																																								●													
LIMEBROOK, Maldon (YH08628)																																						●		●		●											
LITTLE PADDOCK, Colchester (YH08698)																																								●													
LONGWOOD EQUESTRIAN CTRE, Basildon (YH08820)																																												●									
LYNFORDS, Wickford (YH08930)																																					●							●									
M P TRAILERS, Burnham-on-Crouch (YH08974)																						●																															
MARCH EQUESTRIAN, Halstead (YH09139)																																					●																
MARCH EQUESTRIAN, Colchester (YH09138)																																					●																
MEDWAY RIDING CTRE, Chelmsford (YH09439)																																												●									
MOOR END LIVERY YARD, Saffron Walden (YH09741)																																												●									
MOORCROFT EQUESTRIAN, Colchester (YH09749)																																													●								
MOSS, JANETTE, Waltham Abbey (YH09858)																																	●	●		●	●								●								
MOSTYN GALLERIES, Ilford (YH09872)																													●																								
NEW LODGE SADDLERY, Chelmsford (YH10113)																																												●									
NEWLAND HALL EQUESTRIAN CTRE, Chelmsford (YH10141)																																												●									
NORTON HEATH EQUESTRIAN CTRE, Ingatestone (YH10328)																																												●									
O F A H SADDLERY, Billericay (YH10364)																																	●	●																			
OAKLANDS LIVERY STABLES, Rayleigh (YH10390)																																												●									
PAGLESHAM SCHOOL, Rochford (YH10685)																																												●									
PARK FARM, Colchester (YH10717)																																						●		●		●	●										

Business Profile

General Equine

by Country by County

Business	Artist	Blacksmith	Business Consultancy	Commentating for Events	Competition Horses	Competition Riders	Cross Country Course	Dressage Riders	Driving Centre	Driving Competitors	Driving Services	Engraving	Equine Holidays	Event Management	Event Riders	Forge	Harness Race Course	Harness Racing Horses
PARK LANE RIDING SCHOOL, Billericay (YH10731)																		
PARKLANDS FARM LIVERY, Chelmsford (YH10769)																		
PINE LODGE, Loughton (YH11118)																		
POND FARM, Braintree (YH11217)																		
PRIORY SADDLERY, Colchester (YH11403)																		
RADWINTER SADDLERY, Saffron Walden (YH11601)																		
RAGWOOD RIDING CTRE, Benfleet (YH11609)																		
RAWRETH EQUESTRIAN CTRE, Wickford (YH11669)																		
RAYNE RIDING CTRE, Braintree (YH11676)																		
RED STABLES FARM, Brentwood (YH11706)																		
RUGGERY, Romford (YH12221)																		
RUNNINGWELL STUD, Chelmsford (YH12236)																		
SCOTT, R J, Billericay (YH12546)																		
SHOPLAND HALL EQUESTRIAN, Rochford (YH12758)					●		●								●			
SIERRA SADDLE, Benfleet (YH12792)	●																	
SOUTH VIEW SADDLERY/PET FOOD, Grays (YH13110)																		
STABLES, High Ongar (YH13306)																		
STAMBROOK STUD, Halstead (YH13352)																		
STEWARDS FARM RIDING CTRE, Harlow (YH13453)																		
SUDBURY STABLES, Billericay (YH13621)							●											
T S S, Newport (YH13764)																		
TACK EXCHANGE, Leigh-on-Sea (YH13788)																		
TACK ROOM, Billericay (YH13798)																		
TALLY-HO RIDING SCHOOL, Grays (YH13844)								●										
TAYLOR, D J W, Southend (YH13899)										●	●							
THORPE TACK ROOM, Clacton-on-Sea (YH14095)																		
TIPTREE EQUESTRIAN CTRE, Colchester (YH14184)																		
TOWERLANDS EQUESTRIAN CTRE, Braintree (YH14278)																		
TUKE, DIANA R, Saffron Walden (YH14449)																		
UPMINSTER SADDLERY, Upminster (YH14604)																		
VALLEY RIDING/LIVERY STABLES, Ingatestone (YH14657)																		
WASH FARM, Colchester (YH14954)																		

Business	Harness Racing Skills	Harness Retailer	Horse Sale Agency	Horsebox Hire	International Arena	Jockey	Jockey Supply	Photographer	Point-to-Point Course	Polo Pitch	Portraits	Racecourse Flat	Racecourse Steeplechase	Racing Investment	Repairs Rugs	Repairs Saddles	Riding Club	Rug Cleaning
PARK LANE RIDING SCHOOL, Billericay (YH10731)																		
PARKLANDS FARM LIVERY, Chelmsford (YH10769)																		
PINE LODGE, Loughton (YH11118)																		
POND FARM, Braintree (YH11217)																		
PRIORY SADDLERY, Colchester (YH11403)															●	●		
RADWINTER SADDLERY, Saffron Walden (YH11601)																		
RAGWOOD RIDING CTRE, Benfleet (YH11609)																		
RAWRETH EQUESTRIAN CTRE, Wickford (YH11669)																		
RAYNE RIDING CTRE, Braintree (YH11676)																		
RED STABLES FARM, Brentwood (YH11706)																		
RUGGERY, Romford (YH12221)															●			●
RUNNINGWELL STUD, Chelmsford (YH12236)																		
SCOTT, R J, Billericay (YH12546)			●															
SHOPLAND HALL EQUESTRIAN, Rochford (YH12758)																		
SIERRA SADDLE, Benfleet (YH12792)																●		
SOUTH VIEW SADDLERY/PET FOOD, Grays (YH13110)																		
STABLES, High Ongar (YH13306)																		
STAMBROOK STUD, Halstead (YH13352)																		
STEWARDS FARM RIDING CTRE, Harlow (YH13453)																		
SUDBURY STABLES, Billericay (YH13621)																		
T S S, Newport (YH13764)																		
TACK EXCHANGE, Leigh-on-Sea (YH13788)															●			●
TACK ROOM, Billericay (YH13798)																		
TALLY-HO RIDING SCHOOL, Grays (YH13844)				●														
TAYLOR, D J W, Southend (YH13899)																		
THORPE TACK ROOM, Clacton-on-Sea (YH14095)															●	●		
TIPTREE EQUESTRIAN CTRE, Colchester (YH14184)																		
TOWERLANDS EQUESTRIAN CTRE, Braintree (YH14278)																		
TUKE, DIANA R, Saffron Walden (YH14449)									●									
UPMINSTER SADDLERY, Upminster (YH14604)																		
VALLEY RIDING/LIVERY STABLES, Ingatestone (YH14657)																		
WASH FARM, Colchester (YH14954)																		

Business	Saddler	School (Indoor)	School (Outdoor)	Sculptor	Shipping Agent	Show Jump Course	Show Jumping arena	Stabling Centre	Tack Shop	Taxidermy	Trail Riding Centre	Transport	Transport Overseas	Trekking Centre	Valuer	Website design	Wheelwright
PARK LANE RIDING SCHOOL, Billericay (YH10731)								●									
PARKLANDS FARM LIVERY, Chelmsford (YH10769)								●									
PINE LODGE, Loughton (YH11118)		●		●													
POND FARM, Braintree (YH11217)	●																
PRIORY SADDLERY, Colchester (YH11403)	●								●								
RADWINTER SADDLERY, Saffron Walden (YH11601)	●																
RAGWOOD RIDING CTRE, Benfleet (YH11609)		●		●		●											
RAWRETH EQUESTRIAN CTRE, Wickford (YH11669)								●									
RAYNE RIDING CTRE, Braintree (YH11676)	●	●		●			●		●								
RED STABLES FARM, Brentwood (YH11706)								●									
RUGGERY, Romford (YH12221)																	
RUNNINGWELL STUD, Chelmsford (YH12236)								●									
SCOTT, R J, Billericay (YH12546)																	
SHOPLAND HALL EQUESTRIAN, Rochford (YH12758)	●	●		●		●		●									
SIERRA SADDLE, Benfleet (YH12792)	●		●														
SOUTH VIEW SADDLERY/PET FOOD, Grays (YH13110)	●																
STABLES, High Ongar (YH13306)								●									
STAMBROOK STUD, Halstead (YH13352)								●									
STEWARDS FARM RIDING CTRE, Harlow (YH13453)								●									
SUDBURY STABLES, Billericay (YH13621)								●									
T S S, Newport (YH13764)	●																
TACK EXCHANGE, Leigh-on-Sea (YH13788)	●								●								
TACK ROOM, Billericay (YH13798)								●									
TALLY-HO RIDING SCHOOL, Grays (YH13844)		●		●													
TAYLOR, D J W, Southend (YH13899)																	
THORPE TACK ROOM, Clacton-on-Sea (YH14095)									●								
TIPTREE EQUESTRIAN CTRE, Colchester (YH14184)		●		●		●											
TOWERLANDS EQUESTRIAN CTRE, Braintree (YH14278)	●																
TUKE, DIANA R, Saffron Walden (YH14449)																	
UPMINSTER SADDLERY, Upminster (YH14604)	●								●								
VALLEY RIDING/LIVERY STABLES, Ingatestone (YH14657)				●		●											
WASH FARM, Colchester (YH14954)		●		●													

Business Profile
General Equine

by Country by County

	Artist	Blacksmith	Business Consultancy	Commentating for Events	Competition Horses	Competition Riders	Cross Country Course	Dressage Riders	Driving Centre	Driving Competitors	Driving Services	Engraving	Equine Holidays	Event Management	Event Riders	Forge	Harness Race Course	Harness Racing Horses	Harness Racing Skills	Harness Retailer	Horse Sale Agency	Horsebox Hire	International Arena	Jockey	Jockey Supply	Photographer	Point-to-Point Course	Polo Pitch	Portraits	Racecourse Flat	Racecourse Steeplechase	Racing Investment	Repairs Rugs	Repairs Saddles	Riding Club	Rug Cleaning	Saddler	School (Indoor)	School (Outdoor)	Sculptor	Shipping Agent	Show Jump Course	Show Jumping arena	Stabling Centre	Tack Shop	Taxidermy	Trail Riding Centre	Transport	Transport Overseas	Trekking Centre	Valuer	Website design	Wheelwright
WEST BOWERS, Maldon (YH15129)																																												●									
WHIRLEDGE & NOTT, Great Dunmow (YH15284)																																																			●		
WILLOWS SHOW JUMPING CLUB, Loughton (YH15509)							●																																														
WITHAM SADDLERY, Witham (YH15618)																																	●			●	●								●								
WIX EQUESTRIAN CTRE, Manningtree (YH15636)							●																															●				●											
WOODREDON RIDING SCHOOL, Waltham Abbey (YH15728)																																												●									
YE OLDE FORGE, Basildon (YH15894)																																		●		●	●								●								
GLOUCESTERSHIRE																																																					
BADGEWORTH LIVERY YARD, Cheltenham (YH00780)																																												●									
BEAUFORT POLO CLUB, Tetbury (YH01128)														●														●										●		●													
BROWN, ALISTAIR, Cheltenham (YH02098)								●																																													
BURTON, NICK, Hartpury (YH02293)															●																																						
CHELTENHAM SADDLERY, Cheltenham (YH02805)																				●																	●																
CHURCH FARM, Mitcheldean (YH02895)							●						●																											●		●											
COLNE SADDLERY, Gloucester (YH03196)																																		●			●																
COTSWOLD SADDLERY, Cirencester (YH03365)																																	●	●		●	●																
COTSWOLD TRAIL RIDING, Gloucester (YH03368)																																															●			●			
COUNTRYWIDE STORES, Gloucester (YH03454)																																					●																
COURT FARM COUNTRY STORE, Lydney (YH03499)																																					●																
DALY, PAT, Berkley (YH03852)																					●																																
DENNY, L, Moreton-in-Marsh (YH04063)							●														●																																
DUTTON, PHILLIP, Tetbury (YH04380)															●																																						
EDWARDS SADDLERY, Moreton In Marsh (YH04573)																																					●																
ELM LEAZE STUD, Badminton (YH04631)					●																														●			●		●													
EQUESTRIAN REQUISITIES, Stonehouse (YH04709)																																					●																
EVANS, ANNE-MARIE & RICHARD, Moreton In Marsh (YH04916)															●																																						
FOREST OF DEAN, Lydney (YH05346)													●																																								
GAMBLE, KEN, Cheltenham (YH05631)																																																●					
GROVE FARM, Moreton In Marsh (YH06163)																								●																								●					
HAYES J SADDLERY, Lechlade (YH06575)																																	●	●			●																
HENRY COLE, Cirencester (YH06681)																																				●																	
HIGGS, NIGEL, Cirencester (YH06750)																				●																																	

Business Profile
General Equine

by Country by County	Artist	Blacksmith	Business Consultancy	Commentating for Events	Competition Horses	Competition Riders	Cross Country Course	Dressage Riders	Driving Centre	Driving Competitors	Driving Services	Engraving	Equine Holidays	Event Management	Event Riders	Forge	Harness Race Course	Harness Racing Horses	Harness Racing Skills	Harness Retailer	Horse Sale Agency	Horsebox Hire	International Arena	Jockey	Jockey Supply	Photographer	Point-to-Point Course	Polo Pitch	Portraits	Racecourse Flat	Racecourse Steeplechase	Racing Investment	Repairs Rugs	Repairs Saddles	Riding Club	Rug Cleaning	Saddler	School (Indoor)	School (Outdoor)	Sculptor	Shipping Agent	Show Jump Course	Show Jumping arena	Stabling Centre	Tack Shop	Taxidermy	Trail Riding Centre	Transport	Transport Overseas	Trekking Centre	Valuer	Website design	Wheelwright
HUNTLEY SCHOOL OF EQUITATION, Gloucester (YH07306)																																												●									
HURWITZ, STANLEY, Cirencester (YH07323)																											●																										
LANGRISH, BOB, Stroud (YH08412)																											●																										
LAW, LESLIE & HARRIET, Highnam (YH08470)															●																																						
LITTLEDEAN RIDING CTRE, Cinderford (YH08707)													●																																								
LODGE FARM, Tetbury (YH08767)													●																																								
MANGAN & WEBB, Cheltenham (YH09076)																																		●			●								●								
MARSDEN MANOR STUD, Cirencester (YH09181)																																						●															
MIFLIN, WILLIAM, Cirencester (YH09563)															●																													●									
MORETON SADDLERY, Moreton In Marsh (YH09790)																																	●	●		●	●																
NASHEND STUD, Stroud (YH10028)													●																																								
PARK CORNER FARM, Cirencester (YH10716)													●																															●									
PARKIN, BERNARD, Cheltenham (YH10763)																											●																										
POND, STEPHEN, Staunton (YH11218)																				●																																	
PRESTBURY PK EQUINE SUPPLIES, Cheltenham (YH11360)																																					●																
RATCLIFFE, L J, Cranham (YH11651)																																	●	●																			
REVINGTON, H & SPARKES, S, Stroud (YH11770)																											●																										
ROXTON SPORTING, Cirencester (YH12177)																																					●																
RUSHMERE FARM CARRIAGES, Coleford (YH12243)											●																																										
SAVORY, KEITH, Cirencester (YH12458)																																	●	●																			
SPARROW, KEVIN, Cirencester (YH13180)																											●																										
STROUD FARM SERVICES, Stroud (YH13586)																																					●																
STROUD SADDLERY, Stroud (YH13588)												●									●												●	●		●	●								●								
SUMMERHOUSE, Gloucester (YH13632)							●																																					●									
SYDNEY FREE, Cirencester (YH13721)																																	●	●			●																
TAIT, BLYTH, Cheltenham (YH13823)															●																																						
TALLAND SCHOOL OF EQUITATION, Cirencester (YH13833)								●					●		●																																						
TAYLER & FLETCHER, Stow-on-the-Wold (YH13893)																													●																						●		
TAYLOR, SARAH, Cheltenham (YH13911)															●																																						
TEWKESBURY SADDLERY, Tewkesbury (YH13969)																																		●			●								●								
TIM BLAKE SADDLERY, Gloucester (YH14159)																																	●	●																			
TUCKER, ANGELA, Tetbury (YH14432)															●																																						

www.hccyourhorse.com

Business Profile
General Equine

by Country by County	Artist	Blacksmith	Business Consultancy	Commentating for Events	Competition Horses	Competition Riders	Cross Country Course	Dressage Riders	Driving Centre	Driving Competitors	Driving Services	Engraving	Equine Holidays	Event Management	Event Riders	Forge	Harness Race Course	Harness Racing Horses	Harness Racing Skills	Harness Retailer	Horse Sale Agency	Horsebox Hire	International Arena	Jockey	Jockey Supply	Photographer	Point-to-Point Course	Polo Pitch	Portraits	Racecourse Flat	Racecourse Steeplechase	Racing Investment	Repairs Rugs	Repairs Saddles	Riding Club	Rug Cleaning	Saddler	School (Indoor)	School (Outdoor)	Sculptor	Shipping Agent	Show Jump Course	Show Jumping arena	Stabling Centre	Tack Shop	Taxidermy	Trail Riding Centre	Transport	Transport Overseas	Trekking Centre	Valuer	Website design	Wheelwright
TUCKER, MICHAEL, Tetbury (YH14435)				●																																																	
UPCOTE CROSS COUNTRY COURSE, Cheltenham (YH14599)							●																																														
WOODLAND, Cheltenham (YH15702)							●						●																											●		●								●			
GLOUCESTERSHIRE (SOUTH)																																																					
BIDWELLS OF COGMILLS, Frampton Cotterell (YH01400)																																					●																
PORTERS, Winterbourne (YH11287)																																					●																
SODBURY VALE EQUESTRIAN SUP, Stoke Gifford (YH13051)																																					●																
STYLE PRODUCTS, Mangotsfield (YH13618)																																					●																
TACK ROOM, Chipping Sodbury (YH13799)							●																														●							●									
TUDOR FARM LIVERY STABLES, Frampton Cotterell (YH14439)																																												●									
GUERNSEY																																																					
GUERNSEY, St Sampsons (YH06182)																						●															●				●			●				●					
LA CARRIERE, St Sampson (YH08331)																																					●							●									
HAMPSHIRE																																																					
ALLIGATOR SADDLERY, Romsey (YH00313)												●																								●																	
AMBERVALE, Lymington (YH00357)						●					●		●																																								
AMPORT RIDING SCHOOL, Andover (YH00372)																																												●									
ANGELA MASKELL, Lymington (YH00408)																																	●	●																			
ANNETTE YARROW, Fordingbridge (YH00457)	●																																																				
ARNISS, Fordingbridge (YH00555)																																								●				●									
ASHBOURNE STABLES, Southampton (YH00590)																																												●									
BLACK KNOLL HORSE SPORTS CTRE, Brockenhurst (YH01467)									●				●																															●									
BLUNDELL, REX G, Southampton (YH01574)				●																																																	
BROADLANDS RIDING CTRE, Alton (YH01999)													●																																								
BROCKWOOD PARK HORSE TRIALS, Alresford (YH02016)							●																																														
BULLEN, SARAH, Winchester (YH02215)															●																																						
BURITON HORSE SVS, Stockbridge (YH02253)																																						●		●													
BURLEY VILLA EQUESTRIAN CTRE, New Milton (YH02260)																																															●						
CALCUTT & SONS, Winchester (YH02425)																																	●	●		●	●								●								
CAMPBELL, NICHOLAS, Ringwood (YH02486)															●																																						
CATHERSTON, Stockbridge (YH02650)					●	●																																●		●													
CHARLES, P, Alton (YH02760)																				●																																	

Business Profile
General Equine

by Country by County

Business	Artist	Blacksmith	Business Consultancy	Commentating for Events	Competition Horses	Competition Riders	Cross Country Course	Dressage Riders	Driving Centre	Driving Competitors	Driving Services	Engraving	Equine Holidays	Event Management	Event Riders	Forge	Harness Race Course	Harness Racing Horses
CLAPHAM, JENNIFER, Hook (YH02946)																		
CLASSIC CARRIAGE, Lymington (YH02981)													●					
CLEVERLY, TANYA, Church Crookham (YH03024)															●			
COCKSCOMBE FARM LIVERY, Winchester (YH03129)																		
CORBETT, MARK, Tadley (YH03306)															●			
COUNTRY RIDING WEAR, Hook (YH03424)																		
COURTHOUSE STABLES, Petersfield (YH03505)																		
CROFTON MANOR EQUESTRIAN CTRE, Fareham (YH03623)							●											
DAVID CATLIN, Southampton (YH03916)																		
DECOY POND FARM, Brockenhurst (YH04012)							●											
DECOY POND SADDLERY, Beaulieu (YH04013)																		
DENE COUNTRY STORES, Liphook (YH04041)																		
DIVOTS SADDLERY, Basingstoke (YH04137)																		
DOYLE, KEITH, Eversley (YH04248)																		
EAST STREET STABLES, Lymington (YH04487)													●					
ELEDA STABLES, Ringwood (YH04603)																		
EQUITANA HOLIDAYS, Southampton (YH04827)													●					
EXBURY, Southampton (YH04963)																		
FAIR OAK BARN SADDLERY, Eastleigh (YH05012)																		
FIR TREE FARM, Fordingbridge (YH05219)													●					
FLEETWATER STUD, Lyndhurst (YH05269)																		
FOREST COUNTRYWEAR, Fordingbridge (YH05333)																		
FOREST FARM, Milford On Sea (YH05335)					●	●			●	●	●		●	●				
FORT WIDLEY EQUESTRIAN CTRE, Cosham (YH05388)													●					
G J GARNER & SON, Romsey (YH05584)																		
GAWTHORPE SADDLERS, Hook (YH05679)																		
GEBBIE VALLEYS, Lymington (YH05686)																		
GLENEAGLES, Southampton (YH05832)							●						●					
GREEN, LUCINDA, Andover (YH06069)															●			
HACKNEY PK, Lymington (YH06258)													●					
HAMPSHIRE SADDLERY, Southampton (YH06367)																		
HANSFORDS, Fareham (YH06397)																		

Business	Harness Racing Skills	Harness Retailer	Horse Sale Agency	Horsebox Hire	International Arena	Jockey	Jockey Supply	Photographer	Point-to-Point Course	Polo Pitch	Portraits	Racecourse Flat	Racecourse Steeplechase	Racing Investment	Repairs Rugs	Repairs Saddles	Riding Club	Rug Cleaning
CLAPHAM, JENNIFER, Hook (YH02946)																		
CLASSIC CARRIAGE, Lymington (YH02981)																		
CLEVERLY, TANYA, Church Crookham (YH03024)																		
COCKSCOMBE FARM LIVERY, Winchester (YH03129)																		
CORBETT, MARK, Tadley (YH03306)																		
COUNTRY RIDING WEAR, Hook (YH03424)																●		
COURTHOUSE STABLES, Petersfield (YH03505)																		
CROFTON MANOR EQUESTRIAN CTRE, Fareham (YH03623)			●															
DAVID CATLIN, Southampton (YH03916)																		
DECOY POND FARM, Brockenhurst (YH04012)																		
DECOY POND SADDLERY, Beaulieu (YH04013)																		
DENE COUNTRY STORES, Liphook (YH04041)																		●
DIVOTS SADDLERY, Basingstoke (YH04137)																		
DOYLE, KEITH, Eversley (YH04248)			●															
EAST STREET STABLES, Lymington (YH04487)																		
ELEDA STABLES, Ringwood (YH04603)																		
EQUITANA HOLIDAYS, Southampton (YH04827)																		
EXBURY, Southampton (YH04963)																		
FAIR OAK BARN SADDLERY, Eastleigh (YH05012)																		
FIR TREE FARM, Fordingbridge (YH05219)																		
FLEETWATER STUD, Lyndhurst (YH05269)																		
FOREST COUNTRYWEAR, Fordingbridge (YH05333)		●													●	●		●
FOREST FARM, Milford On Sea (YH05335)																		
FORT WIDLEY EQUESTRIAN CTRE, Cosham (YH05388)																		
G J GARNER & SON, Romsey (YH05584)																		
GAWTHORPE SADDLERS, Hook (YH05679)															●	●		
GEBBIE VALLEYS, Lymington (YH05686)			●															
GLENEAGLES, Southampton (YH05832)																		
GREEN, LUCINDA, Andover (YH06069)																		
HACKNEY PK, Lymington (YH06258)																		
HAMPSHIRE SADDLERY, Southampton (YH06367)																		
HANSFORDS, Fareham (YH06397)																		

Business	Saddler	School (Indoor)	School (Outdoor)	Sculptor	Shipping Agent	Show Jump Course	Show Jumping arena	Stabling Centre	Tack Shop	Taxidermy	Trail Riding Centre	Transport	Transport Overseas	Trekking Centre	Valuer	Website design	Wheelwright
CLAPHAM, JENNIFER, Hook (YH02946)								●									
CLASSIC CARRIAGE, Lymington (YH02981)								●									
CLEVERLY, TANYA, Church Crookham (YH03024)																	
COCKSCOMBE FARM LIVERY, Winchester (YH03129)								●									
CORBETT, MARK, Tadley (YH03306)																	
COUNTRY RIDING WEAR, Hook (YH03424)	●																
COURTHOUSE STABLES, Petersfield (YH03505)								●									
CROFTON MANOR EQUESTRIAN CTRE, Fareham (YH03623)																	
DAVID CATLIN, Southampton (YH03916)	●																
DECOY POND FARM, Brockenhurst (YH04012)								●									
DECOY POND SADDLERY, Beaulieu (YH04013)	●																
DENE COUNTRY STORES, Liphook (YH04041)	●																
DIVOTS SADDLERY, Basingstoke (YH04137)	●																
DOYLE, KEITH, Eversley (YH04248)																	
EAST STREET STABLES, Lymington (YH04487)																	
ELEDA STABLES, Ringwood (YH04603)								●									
EQUITANA HOLIDAYS, Southampton (YH04827)																	
EXBURY, Southampton (YH04963)																	●
FAIR OAK BARN SADDLERY, Eastleigh (YH05012)	●																
FIR TREE FARM, Fordingbridge (YH05219)								●									
FLEETWATER STUD, Lyndhurst (YH05269)								●									
FOREST COUNTRYWEAR, Fordingbridge (YH05333)	●																
FOREST FARM, Milford On Sea (YH05335)				●				●									
FORT WIDLEY EQUESTRIAN CTRE, Cosham (YH05388)								●									
G J GARNER & SON, Romsey (YH05584)																	●
GAWTHORPE SADDLERS, Hook (YH05679)	●																
GEBBIE VALLEYS, Lymington (YH05686)								●									
GLENEAGLES, Southampton (YH05832)								●									
GREEN, LUCINDA, Andover (YH06069)																	
HACKNEY PK, Lymington (YH06258)																	
HAMPSHIRE SADDLERY, Southampton (YH06367)	●																
HANSFORDS, Fareham (YH06397)	●																

Business Profile
General Equine

by Country by County	Artist	Blacksmith	Business Consultancy	Commentating for Events	Competition Horses	Competition Riders	Cross Country Course	Dressage Riders	Driving Centre	Driving Competitors	Driving Services	Engraving	Equine Holidays	Event Management	Event Riders	Forge	Harness Race Course	Harness Racing Horses	Harness Racing Skills	Harness Retailer	Horse Sale Agency	Horsebox Hire	International Arena	Jockey	Jockey Supply	Photographer	Point-to-Point Course	Polo Pitch	Portraits	Racecourse Flat	Racecourse Steeplechase	Racing Investment	Repairs Rugs	Repairs Saddles	Riding Club	Rug Cleaning	Saddler	School (Indoor)	School (Outdoor)	Sculptor	Shipping Agent	Show Jump Course	Show Jumping arena	Stabling Centre	Tack Shop	Taxidermy	Trail Riding Centre	Transport	Transport Overseas	Trekking Centre	Valuer	Website design	Wheelwright
HARRIS, ANDREW, Lymington (YH06464)							●								●																													●									
HARROWAY HSE RIDING SCHOOL, Andover (YH06495)													●																																								
HASKER, GLENN M, Ringwood (YH06521)																																	●	●			●																
HIGH HURLANDS EQUESTRIAN CTRE, Liphook (YH06764)																																												●									
HILBURY SADDLERY, Andover (YH06806)																																	●	●			●																
HOPLANDS EQUESTRIAN, Stockbridge (YH07058)					●	●		●							●								●														●	●				●	●										
HORSE-E-THINGS, Fordingbridge (YH07153)																																					●																
HORSEPOWER, Alton (YH07163)									●		●																																										
IEDEMA, BARRY, Romsey (YH07388)								●																																													
IN THE SADDLE, Tadley (YH07406)													●																																								
INADOWN FARM STABLES, Alton (YH07407)																																												●									
INCH'S SADDLERY, Tadley (YH07408)																																					●																
INDESPENSION, Southampton (YH07420)																						●																															
J & M ASSOCIATES, Andover (YH07550)				●																																																	
JOHN WILLIE'S SADDLE ROOM, Ringwood (YH07817)																				●																	●																
KATIE WHETREN, Totton (YH07998)																																	●	●																			
KEELEY, PAULA, Liss (YH08027)																																												●									
KEYSTONE EQUESTRIAN, Alton (YH08117)					●																																																
KILN FARM RIDING SCHOOL, Southampton (YH08150)																																								●		●											
KNIGHTSBRIDGE STABLES, Sway (YH08272)															●																																						
LANGFORD FARM, Woodlands (YH08403)																																												●									
LEATHER WORKSHOP, Ringwood (YH08506)																																	●	●																			
LESLEY RALPH SADDLER, Basingstoke (YH08557)																				●													●	●			●																
LESTER, P, Fareham (YH08564)																																												●									
LITTLE LONDON TACK SHOP, Tadley (YH08691)																																					●																
LYNDHURST COUNTRY CLOTHING, Lyndhurst (YH08927)																																					●																
LYNDHURST PK HOTEL, Lyndhurst (YH08928)													●																																								
M E HOWITT SADDLERS, Alton (YH08960)																																					●																
MALCOLM DUNNING SADDLERY, Waterlooville (YH09044)																						●															●											●					
MANOR FARM, Southampton (YH09095)																																												●									
MCNEILL, IAN, Alton (YH09402)																																					●																
MERRIE STUD, Southampton (YH09480)																																								●													

Business Profile
General Equine

by Country by County	Artist	Blacksmith	Business Consultancy	Commentating for Events	Competition Horses	Competition Riders	Cross Country Course	Dressage Riders	Driving Centre	Driving Competitors	Driving Services	Engraving	Equine Holidays	Event Management	Event Riders	Forge	Harness Race Course	Harness Racing Horses	Harness Racing Skills	Harness Retailer	Horse Sale Agency	Horsebox Hire	International Arena	Jockey	Jockey Supply	Photographer
MIRACLE TREES, Ringwood (YH09658)													●													
MOYGLARE LIVERY, Tadley (YH09910)																										
NEW FOREST, Dibden (YH10096)													●													
NEW FOREST EQUESTRIAN CTRE, Lymington (YH10098)													●													
NEW PARK HOTEL, New Forest (YH10115)							●																			
NEW PARK MANOR STABLES, Brockenhurst (YH10116)													●													
NINEHAM, T & YOUNG, J, Brokenhurst (YH10212)																										
NORRIS & SONS, Brockenhurst (YH10244)																										
NRC, Fareham (YH10348)							●																●			
OASIS RIDING CTRE, Southampton (YH10413)													●													
OLD BASING SADDLERY, Basingstoke (YH10450)																										
P BOX - WORKING SADDLER, Ringwood (YH10634)																										
PARK FARM SADDLERY, Basingstoke (YH10723)																										
PASSFORD HSE HOTEL, Lymington (YH10810)													●													
PEDEN BLOODSTOCK, Hook (YH10891)																										
PETERSFIELD SADDLERY, Petersfield (YH11022)																										
POOK LANE RIDING STABLES, Havant (YH11259)																										
PREETHA BALSE, Fareham (YH11344)								●							●											
RANDALL, MONICA, Fleet (YH11628)																										
RAWLINS FARM, Tadley (YH11667)																										
RAY'S SADDLESHOP, Southampton (YH11677)																										
REDENHAM PK STUD, Andover (YH11708)													●													
RIDGWAY, SHARON, Andover (YH11872)															●											
ROBJENT'S, Stockbridge (YH12007)																										
ROBLEY, RACHEL, Romsey (YH12008)															●											
ROCKBOURNE, Fordingbridge (YH12028)													●													
ROSHAUNA RIDING SCHOOL, Fareham (YH12112)																										
RUSSELL EQUITATION CTRE, Southampton (YH12253)													●													
RYCROFT SCHOOL OF EQUITATION, Hook (YH12291)									●																	
SADDLERS WORKSHOP, Liphook (YH12362)																				●						
SADDLES, SADDLES, SADDLES, Portsmouth (YH12371)															●											
SANDILANDS FARM FEEDS, Petersfield (YH12414)																										

by Country by County	Point-to-Point Course	Polo Pitch	Portraits	Racecourse Flat	Racecourse Steeplechase	Racing Investment	Repairs Rugs	Repairs Saddles	Riding Club	Rug Cleaning	Saddler	School (Indoor)	School (Outdoor)	Sculptor	Shipping Agent	Show Jump Course	Show Jumping arena	Stabling Centre	Tack Shop	Taxidermy	Trail Riding Centre	Transport	Transport Overseas	Trekking Centre	Valuer	Website design	Wheelwright
MIRACLE TREES, Ringwood (YH09658)																											
MOYGLARE LIVERY, Tadley (YH09910)												●															
NEW FOREST, Dibden (YH10096)																											
NEW FOREST EQUESTRIAN CTRE, Lymington (YH10098)																											
NEW PARK HOTEL, New Forest (YH10115)														●		●											
NEW PARK MANOR STABLES, Brockenhurst (YH10116)																		●									
NINEHAM, T & YOUNG, J, Brokenhurst (YH10212)																		●									
NORRIS & SONS, Brockenhurst (YH10244)											●																
NRC, Fareham (YH10348)									●			●		●		●	●	●									
OASIS RIDING CTRE, Southampton (YH10413)																											
OLD BASING SADDLERY, Basingstoke (YH10450)											●																
P BOX - WORKING SADDLER, Ringwood (YH10634)							●	●			●																
PARK FARM SADDLERY, Basingstoke (YH10723)											●																
PASSFORD HSE HOTEL, Lymington (YH10810)																											
PEDEN BLOODSTOCK, Hook (YH10891)															●							●					
PETERSFIELD SADDLERY, Petersfield (YH11022)							●	●			●																
POOK LANE RIDING STABLES, Havant (YH11259)																		●									
PREETHA BALSE, Fareham (YH11344)																											
RANDALL, MONICA, Fleet (YH11628)							●	●			●																
RAWLINS FARM, Tadley (YH11667)												●		●													
RAY'S SADDLESHOP, Southampton (YH11677)								●			●																
REDENHAM PK STUD, Andover (YH11708)																		●									
RIDGWAY, SHARON, Andover (YH11872)																											
ROBJENT'S, Stockbridge (YH12007)											●																
ROBLEY, RACHEL, Romsey (YH12008)																											
ROCKBOURNE, Fordingbridge (YH12028)																											
ROSHAUNA RIDING SCHOOL, Fareham (YH12112)																		●									
RUSSELL EQUITATION CTRE, Southampton (YH12253)																		●									
RYCROFT SCHOOL OF EQUITATION, Hook (YH12291)												●		●													
SADDLERS WORKSHOP, Liphook (YH12362)							●	●			●																
SADDLES, SADDLES, SADDLES, Portsmouth (YH12371)											●								●								
SANDILANDS FARM FEEDS, Petersfield (YH12414)											●																

www.hccyourhorse.com

Business Profile
General Equine

by Country by County

by Country by County	Artist	Blacksmith	Business Consultancy	Commentating for Events	Competition Horses	Competition Riders	Cross Country Course	Dressage Riders	Driving Centre	Driving Competitors	Driving Services	Engraving	Equine Holidays	Event Management	Event Riders	Forge	Harness Race Course	Harness Racing Horses	Harness Racing Skills	Harness Retailer	Horse Sale Agency	Horsebox Hire	International Arena	Jockey	Jockey Supply	Photographer	Point-to-Point Course
SCATS, Winchester (YH12491)																											
SCATS COUNTRYSTORE, Alton (YH12499)																											
SCATS COUNTRYSTORE, Lymington (YH12502)																											
SCATS COUNTRYSTORE, Winchester (YH12498)																											
SCATS COUNTRYSTORE, Andover (YH12500)																											
SCATS COUNTRYSTORE, Romsey (YH12497)																											
SCATS COUNTRYSTORE, Basingstoke (YH12501)																											
SCHOOL FARM TRAINING CTRE, Romsey (YH12520)																											
SHAPLEY RANCH EQUINE ACCESS, Hartley Wintney (YH12674)																											
SILVER HORSESHOE, Fordingbridge (YH12806)													●														
SIMES & SON, Aldershot (YH12819)																											
SIMMONS, Basingstoke (YH12823)			●																								
SIMS, L, Andover (YH12846)																											
SOLENT, Southampton (YH13054)																											
SOUTHERN TOURIST BOARD, Eastleigh (YH13144)													●														
SOUTHFIELD EQUESTRIAN CTRE, Whitchurch (YH13149)					●		●																				
SPARSHOLT COLLEGE, Winchester (YH13183)																											
STANWELLS COUNTRY, Brockenhurst (YH13384)																											
STOCKBRIDGE, Stockbridge (YH13486)																											
TACK ROOM, Southampton (YH13800)																											
TRICKLEDOWN STUD, Stockbridge (YH14392)																					●						
TURNER, J S E, Whitchurch (YH14483)				●																							
VALESMOOR FARM, New Milton (YH14644)																											
WALSH, P, Newbury (YH14879)																											
WELCH, FRED, Hook (YH15060)																					●						
WELLINGTON RIDING, Hook (YH15075)					●	●	●	●					●	●	●								●				
WESSEX FARM & EQUI-PRODUCTS, Ringwood (YH15118)																											
WEYHILL HORSE TRANSPORT, Andover (YH15251)																						●					
WICKHAM STABLES, Fareham (YH15383)																											
WRIGHTS OF ROMSEY, Romsey (YH15846)																											
HEREFORDSHIRE																											
ACORN ACTIVITIES, Hereford (YH00146)													●														

by Country by County	Polo Pitch	Portraits	Racecourse Flat	Racecourse Steeplechase	Racing Investment	Repairs Rugs	Repairs Saddles	Riding Club	Rug Cleaning	Saddler	School (Indoor)	School (Outdoor)	Sculptor	Shipping Agent	Show Jump Course	Show Jumping arena	Stabling Centre	Tack Shop	Taxidermy	Trail Riding Centre	Transport	Transport Overseas	Trekking Centre	Valuer	Website design	Wheelwright
SCATS, Winchester (YH12491)										●																
SCATS COUNTRYSTORE, Alton (YH12499)						●			●																	
SCATS COUNTRYSTORE, Lymington (YH12502)						●			●																	
SCATS COUNTRYSTORE, Winchester (YH12498)						●			●									●								
SCATS COUNTRYSTORE, Andover (YH12500)						●			●																	
SCATS COUNTRYSTORE, Romsey (YH12497)						●			●																	
SCATS COUNTRYSTORE, Basingstoke (YH12501)						●			●																	
SCHOOL FARM TRAINING CTRE, Romsey (YH12520)																	●									
SHAPLEY RANCH EQUINE ACCESS, Hartley Wintney (YH12674)										●																
SILVER HORSESHOE, Fordingbridge (YH12806)																	●									
SIMES & SON, Aldershot (YH12819)						●	●			●																
SIMMONS, Basingstoke (YH12823)																								●		
SIMS, L, Andover (YH12846)																	●									
SOLENT, Southampton (YH13054)						●	●			●																
SOUTHERN TOURIST BOARD, Eastleigh (YH13144)																										
SOUTHFIELD EQUESTRIAN CTRE, Whitchurch (YH13149)													●		●	●	●									
SPARSHOLT COLLEGE, Winchester (YH13183)																	●									
STANWELLS COUNTRY, Brockenhurst (YH13384)									●	●																
STOCKBRIDGE, Stockbridge (YH13486)																	●									
TACK ROOM, Southampton (YH13800)						●	●																			
TRICKLEDOWN STUD, Stockbridge (YH14392)																										
TURNER, J S E, Whitchurch (YH14483)																										
VALESMOOR FARM, New Milton (YH14644)																	●									
WALSH, P, Newbury (YH14879)																	●									
WELCH, FRED, Hook (YH15060)																										
WELLINGTON RIDING, Hook (YH15075)								●			●		●		●	●	●	●								
WESSEX FARM & EQUI-PRODUCTS, Ringwood (YH15118)										●																
WEYHILL HORSE TRANSPORT, Andover (YH15251)														●							●					
WICKHAM STABLES, Fareham (YH15383)																	●									
WRIGHTS OF ROMSEY, Romsey (YH15846)						●	●			●																
HEREFORDSHIRE																										
ACORN ACTIVITIES, Hereford (YH00146)																							●			

Business Profile
General Equine

by Country by County

	Artist	Blacksmith	Business Consultancy	Commentating for Events	Competition Horses	Competition Riders	Cross Country Course	Dressage Riders	Driving Centre	Driving Competitors	Driving Services	Engraving	Equine Holidays	Event Management	Event Riders	Forge	Harness Race Course	Harness Racing Horses	Harness Racing Skills	Harness Retailer	Horse Sale Agency	Horsebox Hire	International Arena	Jockey	Jockey Supply	Photographer	Point-to-Point Course	Polo Pitch	Portraits	Racecourse Flat	Racecourse Steeplechase	Racing Investment	Repairs Rugs	Repairs Saddles	Riding Club	Rug Cleaning	Saddler	School (Indoor)	School (Outdoor)	Sculptor	Shipping Agent	Show Jump Course	Show Jumping arena	Stabling Centre	Tack Shop	Taxidermy	Trail Riding Centre	Transport	Transport Overseas	Trekking Centre	Valuer	Website design	Wheelwright
ANIMAL ARTISTRY, Bromyard (YH00426)	●																																																				
BRIGHTWELLS BLOODSTOCK, Hereford (YH01910)																					●																														●		
BROMYARD, Bromyard (YH02027)																				●													●	●			●																
BRYNGWYN RIDING CTRE, Kington (YH02176)													●																																								
CAMBRIAN HORSE TRAIL NETWORK, Hereford (YH02467)													●																																								
CONCEPT SADDLERY, Hereford (YH03223)																																	●	●		●	●																
COUNTRYWEAR, Hay On Wye (YH03442)																																					●																
COUNTRYWIDE, Hereford (YH03445)																																	●			●									●								
COUNTRYWIDE STORES, Bromyard (YH03458)																																					●																
COUNTRYWIDE STORES, Ledbury (YH03457)																																					●																
COUNTY COMPETITION STUD, Bromyard (YH03486)					●	●		●																																●				●									
EDWARDS BLACK SADDLERY, Holmer (YH04571)																																					●																
FARMWELL, Hereford (YH05079)																																					●																
HORSE BEAUTIQUE, Leominster (YH07103)																																					●																
HORSEWISE, Hereford (YH07178)																																					●																
ISAACS STORES, Ledbury (YH07512)																																					●																
JONES, R M, Cattle Market (YH07925)																																					●																
JONES, R M, Hay-on-Wye (YH07924)																																					●																
LEA BAILEY RIDING SCHOOL, Ross-on-Wye (YH08492)																																												●									
MONNINGTON, Hereford (YH09728)	●																																						●														
NEWCOMB, SALLY, Hereford (YH10130)					●	●		●																														●		●													
P G L TRAVEL, Ross-on-Wye (YH10640)													●																																					●			
PEARSON, S R, Bromyard (YH10882)																																												●									
PHIL TURNER SADDLERY, Hoarwithy (YH11041)																																					●																
PHILIP MORRIS & SON, Hereford (YH11045)																																					●																
RIDDLE RIDING CTRE, Leominster (YH11840)													●																																								
RIDDLE SADDLERY, Leominster (YH11841)																																					●																
SEABORN, J, Ledbury (YH12579)																																												●									
SHEEPCOTE EQUESTRIAN, Hereford (YH12695)								●																														●		●													
SIMPSON, JONATHAN, Leominster (YH12839)		●																																																			
SUE ADAMS RIDING SCHOOL, Leominster (YH13622)					●	●		●							●																				●			●		●		●											
TIPTON HALL, Bromyard (YH14183)																																						●															

Business Profile
General Equine

by Country by County

	Artist	Blacksmith	Business Consultancy	Commentating for Events	Competition Horses	Competition Riders	Cross Country Course	Dressage Riders	Driving Centre	Driving Competitors	Driving Services	Engraving	Equine Holidays	Event Management	Event Riders	Forge	Harness Race Course	Harness Racing Horses	Harness Racing Skills	Harness Retailer	Horse Sale Agency	Horsebox Hire	International Arena	Jockey	Jockey Supply	Photographer	Point-to-Point Course	Polo Pitch	Portraits	Racecourse Flat	Racecourse Steeplechase	Racing Investment	Repairs Rugs	Repairs Saddles	Riding Club	Rug Cleaning	Saddler	School (Indoor)	School (Outdoor)	Sculptor	Shipping Agent	Show Jump Course	Show Jumping arena	Stabling Centre	Tack Shop	Taxidermy	Trail Riding Centre	Transport	Transport Overseas	Trekking Centre	Valuer	Website design	Wheelwright
WALL, Y L, Bromyard (YH14862)								●																																													
HERTFORDSHIRE																																																					
ADVERTISING ANSWERS, Bishop's Stortford (YH00194)			●																																																		
ALAN BROWN/COUNTRY SPORTS, Hitchin (YH00237)																																					●																
AMBRIDGE SADDLERY, Stevenage (YH00361)																				●													●	●			●																
BARKWAY EQUESTRIAN CTRE, Royston (YH00948)																																												●									
BEESONS, Hertford (YH01191)																																																			●		
BIRCH FARM, Broxbourne (YH01428)																																												●									
BOSWELL STABLES, Hertford (YH01662)																																												●									
CHESFIELD EQUESTRIAN CTRE, Hitchin (YH02823)																																												●									
CLARK'S EQUESTRIAN, Stevenage (YH02979)																						●											●	●			●											●					
COLEMAN CROFT, St Albans (YH03163)																																	●	●			●								●								
CONTESSA, Ware (YH03246)								●					●																									●		●													
COUNTY LIVERY, Hertford (YH03489)																																												●									
CROUCHFIELD, Ware (YH03674)																																										●	●										
G T TOWING, Potters Bar (YH05597)																						●																										●					
GREAT WESTWOOD, Chipperfield (YH06044)							●																																														
GREENACRES EQUESTRIAN, Harpenden (YH06076)																					●																							●									
GREINAN FARM, Kings Langley (YH06122)																																					●																
HERTFORDSHIRE TRAILS, Hertford (YH06721)													●																																								
HIGH HERTS FARM RIDING SCHOOL, Hemel Hempstead (YH06760)																																														●							
HILL, ALAN, Ware (YH06825)																																					●																
HOSKINS FARM LIVERY STABLES, Sawbridgeworth (YH07197)																																												●									
IVORY, K T, Radlett (YH07538)																																												●									
LUFFENHALL EQUESTRIAN CTRE, Stevenage (YH08892)																																												●									
MALAN GODDARD, Whaddon (YH09043)																																	●	●			●																
MELDRETH MANOR, Royston (YH09451)																																												●									
MILL RIDING CLUB, Much Hadham (YH09585)																																												●									
OAKLANDS CLGE, St Albans (YH10389)																																												●									
OLD BARN SADDLERY, Hoddesdon (YH10448)																																					●																
OLD FORGE, St Albans (YH10457)																																												●									

Business Profile
General Equine

by Country by County	Artist	Blacksmith	Business Consultancy	Commentating for Events	Competition Horses	Competition Riders	Cross Country Course	Dressage Riders	Driving Centre	Driving Competitors	Driving Services	Engraving	Equine Holidays	Event Management	Event Riders	Forge	Harness Race Course	Harness Racing Horses	Harness Racing Skills	Harness Retailer	Horse Sale Agency	Horsebox Hire	International Arena	Jockey	Jockey Supply	Photographer	Point-to-Point Course	Polo Pitch	Portraits	Racecourse Flat	Racecourse Steeplechase	Racing Investment	Repairs Rugs	Repairs Saddles	Riding Club	Rug Cleaning	Saddler	School (Indoor)	School (Outdoor)	Sculptor	Shipping Agent	Show Jump Course	Show Jumping arena	Stabling Centre	Tack Shop	Taxidermy	Trail Riding Centre	Transport	Transport Overseas	Trekking Centre	Valuer	Website design	Wheelwright
PATCHETTS, Watford (YH10815)							●																															●		●			●		●								
PIX FARM FEED STORE, Hemel Hempstead (YH11159)																																					●																
PONSBOURNE RIDING CTRE, Hertford (YH11224)																																					●							●									
POYNDERS END FARM, Hitchin (YH11329)																																												●									
RED RAE SADDLERY CTRE, Ware (YH11704)																				●																	●																
ROCHFORD & BARBER, Hertford (YH12022)																																					●																
ROSE HALL RIDING STABLES, Sarratt (YH12093)							●																																	●										●			
ROWE, L J, Bovingdon (YH12164)																																																●					
SADDLERY, Royston (YH12363)																																	●	●		●	●								●								
SALES OF SANDON, Buntingford (YH12386)																																					●																
SANDON SADDLERY, Buntingford (YH12415)																				●													●	●			●																
SOUTHERN MOBILE, Bushey (YH13141)																						●																										●					
STABLE COLOURS, Welwyn (YH13289)																																					●																
STAGS END, Hemel Hempstead (YH13342)																																												●									
STANLEY, ANDREA, Baldock (YH13373)								●							●																																						
TEE JAY EQUESTRIAN, Hitchin (YH13933)																																	●	●			●																
THELWALL, P A, Royston (YH13981)				●																																																	
UPPERWOOD FARM STUD, Hemel Hempstead (YH14609)			●		●								●																											●													
W PAGE & SON, Cole Green (YH14786)																																					●																
WATFORD EQUESTRIAN CTRE, Watford (YH14976)																																					●																
WELWYN EQUESTRIAN, Welwyn (YH15101)																																						●		●		●	●										
WIDESERVE, Welwyn (YH15391)																																					●																
WILKINSON, MARTIN, St Albans (YH15423)																				●																	●																
YOUTH HOSTELS ASSOCIATION, St Albans (YH15948)													●																																								
ISLE OF MAN																																																					
G G H EQUITATION CTRE, Marown (YH05578)																																												●									
ITTON COURT STUD, The Braaid (YH07531)																					●																							●									
MANX RIDING SUPPLIES, Onchan (YH09128)																																					●							●									
ISLE OF WIGHT																																																					
BRICKFIELDS, Ryde (YH01866)																																					●	●		●													
EQUESTRIAN WORLD, Cowes (YH04721)																																					●																
JONES, E A & C, Newport (YH07895)													●																																								

Business Profile
General Equine

by Country by County	Artist	Blacksmith	Business Consultancy	Commentating for Events	Competition Horses	Competition Riders	Cross Country Course	Dressage Riders	Driving Centre	Driving Competitors	Driving Services	Engraving	Equine Holidays	Event Management	Event Riders	Forge	Harness Race Course	Harness Racing Horses	Harness Racing Skills	Harness Retailer	Horse Sale Agency	Horsebox Hire	International Arena	Jockey	Jockey Supply	Photographer	Point-to-Point Course	Polo Pitch	Portraits	Racecourse Flat	Racecourse Steeplechase	Racing Investment	Repairs Rugs	Repairs Saddles	Riding Club	Rug Cleaning	Saddler	School (Indoor)	School (Outdoor)	Sculptor	Shipping Agent	Show Jump Course	Show Jumping arena	Stabling Centre	Tack Shop	Taxidermy	Trail Riding Centre	Transport	Transport Overseas	Trekking Centre	Valuer	Website design	Wheelwright
LAKE FARM, Ventnor (YH08350)																																						●		●													
SCATS COUNTRYSTORE, Newport (YH12503)																																	●			●																	
JERSEY																																																					
BARETTE & GRUCHY, St John (YH00930)																																	●	●			●																
HAIE FLEURIE, Channel Isles (YH06280)																																					●							●									
LE MAISTRE BROS, Trinity (YH08490)																																					●																
SORREL SADDLERY, St Peter (YH13071)																																					●							●									
KENT																																																					
BALI HAI FARM, Kemsing (YH00846)							●																																					●									
BARMINSTER TRADING, Ashford (YH00960)																																	●			●																	
BEDGEBURY RIDING CTRE, Goudhurst (YH01155)							●																															●		●													
BIGWOOD, FIONA, Westerham (YH01406)								●																																													
BIRCHALLS THE RIDING SHOP, Maidstone (YH01431)																																				●	●																
BLACK FORGE ART, Tenterden (YH01462)		●																																																			
BLUE BARN EQUESTRIAN CTRE, Ashford (YH01564)													●																															●									
BRADBOURNE, Sevenoaks (YH01743)									●		●																																										
BRAESIDE E.C, Dover (YH01773)					●	●		●																																●		●		●									
BROMLEY COMMON LIVERIES, Bromley (YH02023)																																												●									
BURCHWOOD STABLES, Cobham (YH02233)																																												●									
BURGE, MARK, Sevenoaks (YH02240)				●																																																	
CANTERBURY CARRIAGES, Dover (YH02507)									●		●																																										
CARRIAGE CONNECTIONS, Marden (YH02580)											●																																										
CAVALRY BARN, Ashford (YH02663)													●																																								
CHAUCER RIDING/LIVERY STABLES, Canterbury (YH02791)																																												●									
CHAVIC PK STABLES, Westerham (YH02793)										●	●																																	●									
CHELSFIELD RIDING SCHOOL, Orpington (YH02802)																																												●									
CLAYTON, PENNIE, Dartford (YH03006)								●																																													
COBHAM MANOR, Maidstone (YH03113)													●																									●		●			●	●	●								
COOMBE WOOD STABLES, Folkestone (YH03276)																																												●									
CROFORD COACH BUILDERS, Ashford (YH03609)																																																					●
DICKSON, PENNY, Rochester (YH04117)																				●													●	●			●																
DOWNE COURT RIDING CTRE, Orpington (YH04224)																																												●									

Business Profile
General Equine

by Country by County	Artist	Blacksmith	Business Consultancy	Commentating for Events	Competition Horses	Competition Riders	Cross Country Course	Dressage Riders	Driving Centre	Driving Competitors	Driving Services	Engraving	Equine Holidays	Event Management	Event Riders	Forge	Harness Race Course	Harness Racing Horses	Harness Racing Skills	Harness Retailer	Horse Sale Agency	Horsebox Hire	International Arena	Jockey	Jockey Supply	Photographer	Point-to-Point Course	Polo Pitch	Portraits	Racecourse Flat	Racecourse Steeplechase	Racing Investment	Repairs Rugs	Repairs Saddles	Riding Club	Rug Cleaning	Saddler	School (Indoor)	School (Outdoor)	Sculptor	Shipping Agent	Show Jump Course	Show Jumping arena	Stabling Centre	Tack Shop	Taxidermy	Trail Riding Centre	Transport	Transport Overseas	Trekking Centre	Valuer	Website design	Wheelwright
DUCKHURST FARM, Staplehurst (YH04307)													●								●																							●									
EAGLESFIELD EQUESTRIAN CTRE, Sevenoaks (YH04441)													●																															●									
ELMWOOD FARM RIDING CTRE, Broadstairs (YH04641)																																												●									
ELWORTHY, S, Broadstairs (YH04648)																																												●									
EMPORIUM, Ashford (YH04659)																																					●																
ENGLISH INT HORSE TRANSPORT, Dartford (YH04675)																																																●					
EQUINE PICTURES, Ashford (YH04792)																											●																										
EQUINE SPORT THERAPY, Edenbridge (YH04800)					●										●																																						
EQUINES LIVERIES, Maidstone (YH04809)					●																																																
FAIRBOURNE CARRIAGES, Maidstone (YH05014)																																																					●
FARMER, M J P, Tonbridge (YH05059)																				●																	●																
FARNINGHAM SADDLERY, Farningham (YH05083)																						●											●	●		●												●					
FIVE OAK GREEN STUD, Tonbridge (YH05253)																					●																																
FIVE OAKS EQUESTRIAN CTRE, Keston (YH05254)																																												●									
FOREST VIEW, Sidcup (YH05353)							●																																	●		●		●									
FRANDHAM KENNELS & TACK SHOP, Dover (YH05454)																																					●							●									
FRIDAY FIELD STABLES, Sittingbourne (YH05502)																																								●													
FROGPOOL MANOR SADDLERY, Chislehurst (YH05515)												●																					●	●		●	●			●					●								
GLENWOOD RIDING, Canterbury (YH05845)																																												●									
GOODNESTONE CT EQUESTRIAN, Faversham (YH05905)																																												●									
GREENACRES RIDING SCHOOL, Keston (YH06078)																																												●									
GREENHILLS FARM, Dover (YH06090)																																												●									
HAYLORS, Sheerness (YH06584)																																												●									
HEIGHTS STABLES, Westerham (YH06650)																																								●		●	●										
HIGHSTEAD RIDING CTRE, Canterbury (YH06800)																																												●									
HOBBS PARKER, Ashford (YH06894)																																																			●		
HOGBROOK RIDING SCHOOL, Dover (YH06919)																																												●									
HORSEFERRY TRANSPORT, Swanley (YH07155)																																																●					
HORSESHOES RIDING SCHOOL, Maidstone (YH07175)													●																																								
HUSBANDS SADDLERY, West Malling (YH07325)																																	●	●			●																
INGLEDEN PARK RIDING CTRE, Tenterden (YH07447)																																												●									
JOHN PARKER INTERNATIONAL, Hythe (YH07805)																																									●							●			●		

Business Profile
General Equine

by Country by County	Artist	Blacksmith	Business Consultancy	Commentating for Events	Competition Horses	Competition Riders	Cross Country Course	Dressage Riders	Driving Centre	Driving Competitors	Driving Services	Engraving	Equine Holidays	Event Management	Event Riders	Forge	Harness Race Course	Harness Racing Horses	Harness Racing Skills	Harness Retailer	Horse Sale Agency	Horsebox Hire	International Arena	Jockey	Jockey Supply	Photographer	Point-to-Point Course	Polo Pitch	Portraits	Racecourse Flat	Racecourse Steeplechase	Racing Investment	Repairs Rugs	Repairs Saddles	Riding Club	Rug Cleaning	Saddler	School (Indoor)	School (Outdoor)	Sculptor	Shipping Agent	Show Jump Course	Show Jumping arena	Stabling Centre	Tack Shop	Taxidermy	Trail Riding Centre	Transport	Transport Overseas	Trekking Centre	Valuer	Website design	Wheelwright
JONES, D J, Staplehurst (YH07886)																					●																																
JUST DANDY, Rochester (YH07973)											●																																										
JUST THE BIT, Maidstone (YH07977)																																					●																
KENT LIVERIES & RIDING SCHOOL, Maidstone (YH08081)																																												●									
KENT WOOL GROWERS, Ashford (YH08083)																																					●																
LANGSTON & SON, Tunbridge Wells (YH08415)																																					●																
LEYBOURNE GRANGE, West Malling (YH08600)																																						●		●		●		●									
LIMES FARM EQUESTRIAN, Folkestone (YH08635)							●	●																														●		●		●											
LITTLE FORSHAM FARM STABLES, Cranbrook (YH08687)																																												●									
LITTLE LONDON HORSES, Canterbury (YH08690)																					●																																
LONGFIELD & APPLEDORE, Longfield (YH08810)																																					●																
LYNX PK RIDING STABLES, Cranbrook (YH08936)													●																															●									
M HANCOCK & SON, Ashford (YH08966)																																					●																
MACE FARM, Sevenoaks (YH08993)																																												●									
MANE TO TAIL SUPPLIES, Canterbury (YH09074)																																	●	●		●	●																
MANNIX STUD, Canterbury (YH09091)													●																						●			●		●													
MANOR LIVERY, Westerham (YH09114)																																												●									
MANSTON RIDING CTRE, Ramsgate (YH09126)																																					●							●									
MAYWOOD STUD, Ashford (YH09309)											●		●																																								
MEREWORTH STORES & TACK SHOP, Mereworth (YH09472)																																					●																
MINNISMOOR STABLES, Ashford (YH09650)													●																															●									
MINSTER SADDLERY, Ramsgate (YH09652)																																					●																
MOUNT MASCAL STABLES, Bexley (YH09890)							●																												●			●		●		●	●	●									
OATHILL FARM RIDING CTRE, Canterbury (YH10415)																																												●									
OLD BEXLEY EQUESTRIAN, Bexley (YH10451)																																			●								●	●									
OLD MILL EQUESTRIAN CTRE, Swanley (YH10467)																																					●																
OLD STABLES, Sevenoaks (YH10477)																																												●									
PAGE, JOHN, Ashford (YH10681)																						●																										●					
PARK PETS, Deal (YH10734)																																					●																
PINE RIDGE, Sevenoaks (YH11120)																																								●													
QUADRANGLE, Sevenoaks (YH11475)																																								●													
REESTACK, Tonbridge (YH11734)																																	●	●																			

Business Profile
General Equine

by Country by County	Artist	Blacksmith	Business Consultancy	Commentating for Events	Competition Horses	Competition Riders	Cross Country Course	Dressage Riders	Driving Centre	Driving Competitors	Driving Services	Engraving	Equine Holidays	Event Management	Event Riders	Forge	Harness Race Course	Harness Racing Horses	Harness Racing Skills	Harness Retailer	Horse Sale Agency	Horsebox Hire	International Arena	Jockey	Jockey Supply	Photographer	Point-to-Point Course	Polo Pitch	Portraits	Racecourse Flat	Racecourse Steeplechase	Racing Investment	Repairs Rugs	Repairs Saddles	Riding Club	Rug Cleaning	Saddler	School (Indoor)	School (Outdoor)	Sculptor	Shipping Agent	Show Jump Course	Show Jumping arena	Stabling Centre	Tack Shop	Taxidermy	Trail Riding Centre	Transport	Transport Overseas	Trekking Centre	Valuer	Website design	Wheelwright
RICHMONDS HORSE TRANSPORT, Cobham (YH11831)																																																●	●				
RIDING FARM EQUESTRIAN CTRES, Tonbridge (YH11875)																					●																																
ROOTING STREET FARM, Ashford (YH12082)																																												●									
RULER, JOHN, Bromley (YH12226)																											●																										
SADDLE RACK, Folkestone (YH12345)																																					●																
SADDLERY & GUN ROOM, Westerham (YH12365)																																	●	●		●	●																
SANDHILL FARM STABLES, Tunbridge Wells (YH12411)																																												●									
SANDWICH ANIMAL FEEDS, Sandwich (YH12422)																																					●																
SCATS COUNTRYSTORE, Marden (YH12505)																																	●			●																	
SCATS COUNTRYSTORE, Canterbury (YH12504)																																	●			●																	
SNOWBALL, BART J, Maidstone (YH13038)																																	●	●			●																
SOUTH EAST TOURIST BOARD, Tunbridge Wells (YH13088)													●																																								
SOUTHBOROUGH LANE STABLES, Bromley (YH13128)																																												●									
SPEEDGATE FARM, Longfield (YH13191)																																					●							●									
STANDEN CONNEMARAS, Cranbrook (YH13359)					●																																																
TACK-STITCH, Tunbridge Wells (YH13819)																				●													●	●		●	●																
TILI FARM LIVERIES, Tatsfield (YH14146)																																												●									
TILLS HORSE TRANSPORT, Maidstone (YH14153)																																																●					
TRIDENT TRAILERS, Canterbury (YH14393)																						●																															
TRIDENT TRAILERS, Tunbridge Wells (YH14394)																						●																															
TUNBRIDGE WELLS TACK ROOM, Tunbridge Wells (YH14460)																																	●	●		●	●																
UPPER THRUXTED FARM, Canterbury (YH14608)													●																																								
WARRIGAL FARM LIVERY STABLES, Dartford (YH14941)																																												●									
WEALDEN SADDLERY, Tonbridge (YH15020)																																	●	●		●	●								●								
WHITELEAF RIDING CTRE, Sittingbourne (YH15347)							●																															●		●		●		●									
WILLOW FARM, Faversham (YH15497)																																	●	●		●	●	●		●					●								
WM LILLICO & SONS, Maidstone (YH15641)																																					●																
WRIGHT, RAY, West Wickham (YH15840)																											●																										
LANCASHIRE																																																					
1ST CHOICE PET SUPPLIES, Burnley (YH00001)																																					●																
ABBEY PHOTO, Preston (YH00083)																											●																										
ABRAM HALL RIDING CTRE, Wigan (YH00134)				●	●																														●					●				●									

Business Profile
General Equine

by Country by County	Artist	Blacksmith	Business Consultancy	Commentating for Events	Competition Horses	Competition Riders	Cross Country Course	Dressage Riders	Driving Centre	Driving Competitors	Driving Services	Engraving	Equine Holidays	Event Management	Event Riders	Forge	Harness Race Course	Harness Racing Horses	Harness Racing Skills	Harness Retailer	Horse Sale Agency	Horsebox Hire	International Arena	Jockey	Jockey Supply	Photographer	Point-to-Point Course	Polo Pitch	Portraits	Racecourse Flat	Racecourse Steeplechase	Racing Investment	Repairs Rugs	Repairs Saddles	Riding Club	Rug Cleaning	Saddler	School (Indoor)	School (Outdoor)	Sculptor	Shipping Agent	Show Jump Course	Show Jumping arena	Stabling Centre	Tack Shop	Taxidermy	Trail Riding Centre	Transport	Transport Overseas	Trekking Centre	Valuer	Website design	Wheelwright
ARKENFIELD EQUESTRIAN CTRE, Chorley (YH00530)					●	●	●	●							●																			●		●		●		●				●									
ASOKA, Worsley (YH00625)				●				●																																													
BARTON EQUESTRIAN CTRE, Preston (YH01044)																																						●		●		●	●										
BECCONSALL, Preston (YH01144)																																						●		●			●										
BEECHMOUNT EQUITATION CTRE, Thornton-Cleveleys (YH01174)																																													●								
BEESLEYS OF BALLAM, Lytham (YH01190)																																					●																
BICKERSTAFFE HALL STABLE YARD, Ormskirk (YH01392)																																												●									
BLACK HORSE, Wigan (YH01463)																																					●																
BLACKPOOL EQUESTRIAN CTRE, Blackpool (YH01492)																																								●													
BLACKPOOL WORKSPACE, Blackpool (YH01493)																																	●			●																	
BOUNDARY FARM CARRIAGES, Wigan (YH01677)									●		●		●																																								
BRAKEWELL, JEANETTE, Chorley (YH01785)															●																																						
BROOMHILL, Clitheroe (YH02080)							●																															●		●					●								
CALICO LIVERY STABLES, Wigan (YH02444)																																												●									
CANTER-ON TACK SHOP, Darwen (YH02511)																																	●	●		●	●																
CARRS BILLINGTON, Preston (YH02599)																																					●																
CARRS BILLINGTON, Clitheroe (YH02598)																																					●																
CHARITY FARM LIVERY STABLES, Wigan (YH02751)																																												●									
CHORLEY EQUESTRIAN CTRE, Chorley (YH02880)							●																															●		●		●											
COUNTRY LAUNDRY SVS, Preston (YH03413)																																				●																	
CROSTONS FARM RIDING & LIVERY, Chorley (YH03672)																																					●							●									
CUCKSON CARRIAGE WHEELS, Skelmersdale (YH03699)											●																																										●
DEANDANE RIDING STABLES, Wigan (YH03998)							●																															●		●													
DERBY HSE SADDLERY, Wigan (YH04071)					●	●		●																									●	●			●																
DOUGLAS FARM RIDING SCHOOL, Wigan (YH04211)											●		●																																								
EARNSDALE FARM RIDING SCHOOL, Darwen (YH04458)																																					●							●									
ECCLESTON, Preston (YH04532)							●																																			●	●										
EDEN PRODUCE, Barnoldswick (YH04548)																																					●																
ELSWICK, Preston (YH04644)							●														●																							●									
EQUESTRIANA, Blackburn (YH04724)																																	●			●									●								
EQUINE ART, Preston (YH04764)	●																																																				
FOTO SPORT, Ormskirk (YH05404)																											●																										

Business Profile
General Equine

by Country by County

Name	Artist	Blacksmith	Business Consultancy	Commentating for Events	Competition Horses	Competition Riders	Cross Country Course	Dressage Riders	Driving Centre	Driving Competitors	Driving Services	Engraving	Equine Holidays	Event Management	Event Riders	Forge	Harness Race Course	Harness Racing Horses	Harness Racing Skills	Harness Retailer	Horse Sale Agency	Horsebox Hire	International Arena	Jockey	Jockey Supply	Photographer	Point-to-Point Course
FULWOOD RIDING CTRE, Preston (YH05537)																											
GREEN BANK, Carnforth (YH06049)																											
HALSALL RIDING & LIVERY CTRE, Ormskirk (YH06336)																											
HARKER, MICHAEL, Bury (YH06432)																					●						
HASLEM, ROBERT, Preston (YH06524)																											
HERD HSE RIDING SCHOOL, Burnley (YH06699)													●														
HOLMESWOOD STUD, Preston (YH06983)																											
HORSE BITS SADDLERY, Bury (YH07106)																											
JACKSON, JOANNA, Clitheroe (YH07648)								●																			
JERUSALEM FARM, Colne (YH07757)																											
JOSEPH HOWARD & SON, Preston (YH07943)																					●						
KAYE, HARVEY STUART, Chorley (YH08008)																					●						
LANDLORDS FARM, Wigan (YH08383)													●														
LONGTON EQUESTRIAN CTRE, Preston (YH08819)																											
MARSHALL, MICHELLE, Heywood (YH09200)																											
MEWS COTTAGE STABLES, Ormskirk (YH09506)																											
MILLER SADDLERY, Rossendale (YH09602)																				●							
MOORVIEW, Darwen (YH09782)																											
MOSS SIDE RACING STABLES, Lancaster (YH09856)																											
NETHERWOOD FARM, Burnley (YH10083)																											
OAKLEIGH STUD FARM, Preston (YH10397)																					●						
OLD RUNNEL FARM, Blackpool (YH10475)																											
OSWALDTWISTLE ANIMAL FEEDS, Oswaldtwistle (YH10575)																											
PANAMA SPORT HORSES, Clitheroe (YH10695)																											
PAUL HUTCHINSON, Ormskirk (YH10832)																											
POLLARD, G S, Chorley (YH11204)																											
R HACKWORTH ANIMAL FEEDS, Rochdale (YH11544)																											
READWOOD, Burnley (YH11684)																											
RENARD RIDING CTRE, Poulton-Le-Fylde (YH11753)													●														
RIBBY HALL, Preston (YH11795)																											
ROBERTSON, S A S, Carnforth (YH11975)																											
ROBINSONS COUNTRY LEISURE, Wigan (YH12004)																											

Name	Polo Pitch	Portraits	Racecourse Flat	Racecourse Steeplechase	Racing Investment	Repairs Rugs	Repairs Saddles	Riding Club	Rug Cleaning	Saddler	School (Indoor)	School (Outdoor)	Sculptor	Shipping Agent	Show Jump Course	Show Jumping arena	Stabling Centre	Tack Shop	Taxidermy	Trail Riding Centre	Transport	Transport Overseas	Trekking Centre	Valuer	Website design	Wheelwright
FULWOOD RIDING CTRE, Preston (YH05537)																	●									
GREEN BANK, Carnforth (YH06049)											●		●		●	●										
HALSALL RIDING & LIVERY CTRE, Ormskirk (YH06336)																	●									
HARKER, MICHAEL, Bury (YH06432)																										
HASLEM, ROBERT, Preston (YH06524)																										●
HERD HSE RIDING SCHOOL, Burnley (YH06699)											●				●			●								
HOLMESWOOD STUD, Preston (YH06983)																	●									
HORSE BITS SADDLERY, Bury (YH07106)										●																
JACKSON, JOANNA, Clitheroe (YH07648)																										
JERUSALEM FARM, Colne (YH07757)									●																	
JOSEPH HOWARD & SON, Preston (YH07943)																										
KAYE, HARVEY STUART, Chorley (YH08008)																										
LANDLORDS FARM, Wigan (YH08383)																										
LONGTON EQUESTRIAN CTRE, Preston (YH08819)						●	●			●																
MARSHALL, MICHELLE, Heywood (YH09200)																	●									
MEWS COTTAGE STABLES, Ormskirk (YH09506)																	●									
MILLER SADDLERY, Rossendale (YH09602)						●	●		●	●																
MOORVIEW, Darwen (YH09782)											●		●		●											
MOSS SIDE RACING STABLES, Lancaster (YH09856)											●															
NETHERWOOD FARM, Burnley (YH10083)											●		●		●		●									
OAKLEIGH STUD FARM, Preston (YH10397)																										
OLD RUNNEL FARM, Blackpool (YH10475)										●																
OSWALDTWISTLE ANIMAL FEEDS, Oswaldtwistle (YH10575)										●																
PANAMA SPORT HORSES, Clitheroe (YH10695)											●		●		●	●										
PAUL HUTCHINSON, Ormskirk (YH10832)						●	●																			
POLLARD, G S, Chorley (YH11204)						●	●																			
R HACKWORTH ANIMAL FEEDS, Rochdale (YH11544)										●																
READWOOD, Burnley (YH11684)										●																
RENARD RIDING CTRE, Poulton-Le-Fylde (YH11753)											●						●									
RIBBY HALL, Preston (YH11795)											●		●		●	●										
ROBERTSON, S A S, Carnforth (YH11975)																	●				●					
ROBINSONS COUNTRY LEISURE, Wigan (YH12004)										●																

Business Profile
General Equine

by Country by County	Artist	Blacksmith	Business Consultancy	Commentating for Events	Competition Horses	Competition Riders	Cross Country Course	Dressage Riders	Driving Centre	Driving Competitors	Driving Services	Engraving	Equine Holidays	Event Management	Event Riders	Forge	Harness Race Course	Harness Racing Horses	Harness Racing Skills	Harness Retailer	Horse Sale Agency	Horsebox Hire	International Arena	Jockey	Jockey Supply	Photographer	Point-to-Point Course	Polo Pitch	Portraits	Racecourse Flat	Racecourse Steeplechase	Racing Investment	Repairs Rugs	Repairs Saddles	Riding Club	Rug Cleaning	Saddler	School (Indoor)	School (Outdoor)	Sculptor	Shipping Agent	Show Jump Course	Show Jumping arena	Stabling Centre	Tack Shop	Taxidermy	Trail Riding Centre	Transport	Transport Overseas	Trekking Centre	Valuer	Website design	Wheelwright
ROBSCOTT EQUITATION, Carnforth (YH12010)																																												●									
ROSSENDALE & HYNDBURN EC, Accrington (YH12123)							●																																				●										
SILVER BIRCH STABLES, Heywood (YH12803)																																												●									
SNAFFLES, Halifax (YH13020)																																													●								
STUD & STABLE PHOTOGRAPHY, Unsworth (YH13605)																											●																										
TAYLORS EQUESTRIAN, Burnley (YH13916)																																				●	●																
TOWN END FARM RIDING CTRE, Carnforth (YH14295)																																												●									
TROTTERS, Burnley (YH14408)																																	●	●			●																
VALIANTS EQUESTRIAN CTRE, Preston (YH14645)																					●																							●									
WADDINGTON FARM, Darwen (YH14807)																																					●							●									
WHITAKER, A S, Clitheroe (YH15287)																																																					●
WHITEGATE FARM, Bacup (YH15338)																																								●													
WHITEMOOR RIDING CTRE, Colne (YH15351)																																												●									
LEICESTERSHIRE																																																					
A & H GREEN HARNESSMAKERS, Loughborough (YH00010)																				●													●	●			●																
ALISTAIRE CLARKE TRANSPORT, Scraptoft (YH00281)																																																●					
BARRETT, MARGARET, Market Bosworth (YH01012)	●																																																				
BLABY MILL STABLES, Leicester (YH01459)																																												●									
BRITISH HORSE, Leicester (YH01948)																						●																										●					
BROOKSBY EQUESTRIAN CTRE, Melton Mowbray (YH02067)							●						●																																								
BROWN, J W, Melton Mowbray (YH02115)																																					●																
C E COOK & SONS, Leicester (YH02369)																																					●																
CLAYBROOKE STABLES, Lutterworth (YH02997)																																						●															
CLOTHES HORSE, Leicester (YH03062)																																	●	●		●	●								●								
COSSINGTON, Leicester (YH03354)																																						●		●		●											
DADLYNGTON FIELD, Nuneaton (YH03815)																																					●																
DEBDALE HORSES, Leicester (YH04004)					●	●							●																						●					●													
DTA, Leicester (YH04303)																																	●	●		●									●								
DYKE, J D, Market Harborough (YH04391)				●																																																	
GLENDALE EQUESTRIAN FEEDS, Leicester (YH05830)							●																																					●									
HARDWICKE LODGE STABLES, Leicester (YH06416)																																								●													
HEATHER HALL, Heather (YH06626)																																												●									

Business Profile
General Equine

by Country by County	Artist	Blacksmith	Business Consultancy	Commentating for Events	Competition Horses	Competition Riders	Cross Country Course	Dressage Riders	Driving Centre	Driving Competitors	Driving Services	Engraving	Equine Holidays	Event Management	Event Riders	Forge	Harness Race Course	Harness Racing Horses	Harness Racing Skills	Harness Retailer	Horse Sale Agency	Horsebox Hire	International Arena	Jockey	Jockey Supply	Photographer	Point-to-Point Course	Polo Pitch	Portraits	Racecourse Flat	Racecourse Steeplechase	Racing Investment	Repairs Rugs	Repairs Saddles	Riding Club	Rug Cleaning	Saddler	School (Indoor)	School (Outdoor)	Sculptor	Shipping Agent	Show Jump Course	Show Jumping arena	Stabling Centre	Tack Shop	Taxidermy	Trail Riding Centre	Transport	Transport Overseas	Trekking Centre	Valuer	Website design	Wheelwright
HERRICK, H, Thurlaston (YH06716)																																	●	●		●																	
HILL, N & J A, Lutterworth (YH06832)																																												●									
HOME FARM LIVERY, Coalville (YH06996)																																												●									
HORSE TROUGH, Loughborough (YH07144)																																													●								
HURST SADDLERS, Leicester (YH07316)												●																					●	●		●	●								●								
INT STUDENTS/YOUTH EXCHANGES, Leicester (YH07474)													●																																								
IVANHOE EQUESTRIAN, Ashby-De-La-Zouch (YH07532)																																						●		●													
JANES HANDMADE SADDLERY, Melton Mowbray (YH07695)																				●																	●																
KNAPTOFT HOUSE FARM, Lutterworth (YH08250)																																												●									
LEICESTER RACECOURSE, Oadby (YH08544)																														●	●																						
LIMES EQUESTRIAN CTRE, Sapcote (YH08633)													●																															●									
LOMAX, CHRISTIE, Market Harborough (YH08780)															●																																						
MANOR HOUSE STUD, Queniborough (YH09111)																																												●									
MARKFIELD EQUESTRIAN, Markfield (YH09161)																																												●									
MEADOW SCHOOL, Loughborough (YH09422)																																												●									
MEADOWS RIDING CTRE, Fleckney (YH09426)							●																																														
MORGAN, K A, Melton Mowbray (YH09808)																								●																													
N W F COUNTRYSTORE, Melton Mowbray (YH09997)																																					●																
P & G STABLES, Leicester (YH10630)																																								●		●											
PADDOCKS, Rothley (YH10673)																																												●									
PARSONAGE, GARY, Melton Mowbray (YH10798)															●																																						
QUENBY HALL STUD & STABLES, Hungarton (YH11493)																					●																																
REARSBY LODGE FEEDS, Leicester (YH11687)																																					●																
RICH, BARBARA, Melton Mowbray (YH11800)																					●																							●									
ROBERTSON, J P, Oakham (YH11970)																					●																																
S & J SADDLERY, Melton Mowbray (YH12312)																																					●																
S L B SUPPLIES, Coalville (YH12329)													●																																								
S MILNER & SON, Melton Mowbray (YH12330)																																	●	●		●	●																
SAGITTARIUS BLOODSTOCK AGENCY, Melton Mowbray (YH12382)																						●																															
SCHOOL OF NATIONAL EQUITATION, Loughborough (YH12521)																																						●		●		●			●								
SHARNFORD LODGE FEEDS/TACK, Hinckley (YH12676)																																	●	●		●	●																
SHEFFIELD, JOHN-PAUL, Lutterworth (YH12699)															●																																						

www.hccyourhorse.com

Business Profile
General Equine

by Country by County	Artist	Blacksmith	Business Consultancy	Commentating for Events	Competition Horses	Competition Riders	Cross Country Course	Dressage Riders	Driving Centre	Driving Competitors	Driving Services	Engraving	Equine Holidays	Event Management	Event Riders	Forge	Harness Race Course	Harness Racing Horses	Harness Racing Skills	Harness Retailer	Horse Sale Agency	Horsebox Hire	International Arena	Jockey	Jockey Supply	Photographer	Point-to-Point Course	Polo Pitch	Portraits	Racecourse Flat	Racecourse Steeplechase	Racing Investment	Repairs Rugs	Repairs Saddles	Riding Club	Rug Cleaning	Saddler	School (Indoor)	School (Outdoor)	Sculptor	Shipping Agent	Show Jump Course	Show Jumping arena	Stabling Centre	Tack Shop	Taxidermy	Trail Riding Centre	Transport	Transport Overseas	Trekking Centre	Valuer	Website design	Wheelwright
SHIELDS, J GILLIES, Castle Donington (YH12741)																																												●									
SOUTH LEICESTERSHIRE, Lutterworth (YH13099)													●																																								
SPRING, JEREMY, Cosby (YH13248)													●		●																													●									
STABLECARE, Lutterworth (YH13300)																																				●																	
STABLES, Hinckley (YH13307)																																					●																
STRETTON RIDING/TRAINING CTRE, Oakham (YH13574)													●									●																										●					
SWAN LODGE, Melton Mowbray (YH13689)							●																																				●	●									
VERE PHILLIPPS, Loughborough (YH14681)																					●																																
WALKER, RICHARD, Melton Mowbray (YH14856)															●																																						
WATCHORN, KELLY, Melton Mowbray (YH14962)																																	●	●																			
WITHAM VILLA RIDING CTRE, Leicester (YH15620)					●	●		●					●																						●			●		●				●									
LINCOLNSHIRE																																																					
A W RHOADES SADDLERY, Market Rasen (YH00068)																																	●	●			●								●								
ACORN RUGS, Market Rasen (YH00150)																																	●	●																			
ARENA UK, Grantham (YH00517)																					●																																
AUSTER LODGE LIVERY YARD, Bourne (YH00666)																																												●									
BARNACK CTRY STORE, Stamford (YH00964)																																					●																
BEEVER, C R, Grantham (YH01193)																																																●					
BEST/THOROUGHBRED RACING GB, Louth (YH01327)																					●											●																					
BETTER-TACK, Spalding (YH01334)																																					●																
BOSTON HORSE SUPPLIES, Boston (YH01659)																																					●																
BRIAN CHAPMAN SPORTING ARTIST, Spilsby (YH01859)	●																																																				
BRING YOUR HORSE ON HOLIDAY, Louth (YH01915)													●																																								
BROOK HSE FARM, Louth (YH02037)																																												●									
CHARNICAL RIDING CTRE, Gainsborough (YH02772)																																												●									
CLAPHAM, DIANA, Grantham (YH02945)															●																																						
COBBLETHORNS SADDLERY, Grantham (YH03112)																				●																																	
COSGROVE & SON, Market Rasen (YH03350)						●																																										●					
CUTTERIDGE, SARAH, Spalding (YH03761)															●																																						
FAIRMOUNT STUDIOS, Boston (YH05027)	●																																																				
FUNWAY EQUESTRIAN CTRE, Skegness (YH05540)													●																															●									
GREAT PONTON UK CHASERS, Grantham (YH06042)							●																																					●									

Business Profile
General Equine

by Country by County	Artist	Blacksmith	Business Consultancy	Commentating for Events	Competition Horses	Competition Riders	Cross Country Course	Dressage Riders	Driving Centre	Driving Competitors	Driving Services	Engraving	Equine Holidays	Event Management	Event Riders	Forge	Harness Race Course	Harness Racing Horses	Harness Racing Skills	Harness Retailer	Horse Sale Agency	Horsebox Hire	International Arena	Jockey	Jockey Supply	Photographer	Point-to-Point Course	Polo Pitch	Portraits	Racecourse Flat	Racecourse Steeplechase	Racing Investment	Repairs Rugs	Repairs Saddles	Riding Club	Rug Cleaning	Saddler	School (Indoor)	School (Outdoor)	Sculptor	Shipping Agent	Show Jump Course	Show Jumping arena	Stabling Centre	Tack Shop	Taxidermy	Trail Riding Centre	Transport	Transport Overseas	Trekking Centre	Valuer	Website design	Wheelwright
HECKINGTON SUPPLIES, Heckington (YH06638)																																					●																
HENEAGE, ROBERT, Lincoln (YH06671)				●																																																	
HENSON, LUCY, Lincoln (YH06689)															●																																						
HERBERT, JOHN FITZ, Grantham (YH06696)				●																																																	
HILL HSE, Market Rasen (YH06820)				●	●	●	●																															●		●		●	●	●									
HOOD, J S F, Grange-De-Lings (YH07024)							●																																														
IVY LANE RIDING SCHOOL, Lincoln (YH07540)																																												●									
JANET JENKINSON CARTOONS, Brant Broughton (YH07696)	●																																																				
JOHNSON, TRICIA, Sleaford (YH07841)																					●																																
KEY, J U, Boston (YH08114)																																						●		●		●											
LANNI, JOHN, Grantham (YH08419)																					●																																
LAUGHTON WOOD EQUESTRIAN CTRE, Gainsborough (YH08449)																																													●								
LIMES FARM, Grantham (YH08634)																																														●							
LINDALL HARNESS & SADDLERY, Woodhall Spa (YH08644)																				●													●	●																			
LINDSEY FARM SVS, Horncastle (YH08655)																																					●																
LINESIDE RIDING STABLES, Boston (YH08657)																																												●									
MANOR STABLES CRAFT WORKSHOPS, Grantham (YH09119)																				●													●	●			●																
MONTEITH, HELEN, Grantham (YH09731)															●																																						
MOORE, C L (MAJ), Market Rasen (YH09757)				●																																																	
OAKWOOD RIDING SERVICES, Spalding (YH10410)																																												●									
ORCHARD FARM EQUESTRIAN, Skegness (YH10529)																																						●		●				●									
PARK RIDING SCHOOL, Lincoln (YH10735)							●						●																											●		●	●										
PETER ORR PHOTOGRAPHY, Spilsby (YH11013)																											●																										
POPPYFIELDS, Lincoln (YH11275)					●										●								●																	●		●											
REDNIL EQUESTRIAN CTRE, Lincoln (YH11716)											●											●																●		●					●			●					
ROGER HEATON, Grantham (YH12054)	●																												●																								
S & B STABLES, Alford (YH12309)																																												●									
SAPPERTON STUD & SADDLERY, Sleaford (YH12431)																																					●																
SAXILBY RIDING SCHOOL, Lincoln (YH12466)																																												●									
SHEEPGATE EQUESTRIAN, Boston (YH12696)																																						●		●			●										
SHEEPGATE TACK & TOGS, Boston (YH12697)																																						●		●													
SMILHAN, PETER, Louth (YH12930)																				●																	●																

Business Profile
General Equine

by Country by County

	Artist	Blacksmith	Business Consultancy	Commentating for Events	Competition Horses	Competition Riders	Cross Country Course	Dressage Riders	Driving Centre	Driving Competitors	Driving Services	Engraving	Equine Holidays	Event Management	Event Riders	Forge	Harness Race Course	Harness Racing Horses	Harness Racing Skills	Harness Retailer	Horse Sale Agency	Horsebox Hire	International Arena	Jockey	Jockey Supply	Photographer	Point-to-Point Course	Polo Pitch	Portraits	Racecourse Flat	Racecourse Steeplechase	Racing Investment	Repairs Rugs	Repairs Saddles	Riding Club	Rug Cleaning	Saddler	School (Indoor)	School (Outdoor)	Sculptor	Shipping Agent	Show Jump Course	Show Jumping arena	Stabling Centre	Tack Shop	Taxidermy	Trail Riding Centre	Transport	Transport Overseas	Trekking Centre	Valuer	Website design	Wheelwright
SPORTING CHOICE, Dunsby (YH13224)																																					●																
SPRINGFIELD FARM, Market Rasen (YH13253)																																												●									
SWALLOW SADDLERY, Stamford (YH13685)																																					●																
T M F ANIMAL FEEDS & SADDLERS, Woodhall Spa (YH13759)																																					●																
TACK BOX, Lincoln (YH13785)																																	●	●		●	●								●								
THORPE, MERVYN, Stamford (YH14096)		●																																																			
TYLER ANIMAL SYSTEMS, Grantham (YH14520)																																														●							
UFFINGTON RIDING STABLES, Stamford (YH14540)							●																																	●		●											
VOISE, Allington (YH14739)												●																					●	●			●																
W N SHRIVE & SON, Skegness (YH14784)																																					●																
LINCOLNSHIRE (NORTH EAST)																																																					
CLEE SADDLERY & LEATHERWORKS, Cleethorpes (YH03013)																																	●	●			●																
FOX MANIA, Grimsby (YH05424)																																					●																
R G EQUESTRIAN, Grimsby (YH11536)					●	●	●																												●					●		●	●	●									
THORNLEY, MARTIN, Grimsby (YH14071)																																					●																
WALKER, J B & V D, Grimsby (YH14851)																					●																																
LINCOLNSHIRE (NORTH)																																																					
CROWSTONS, Scunthorpe (YH03684)																																				●																	
H SIMPSON & SON, Scunthorpe (YH06240)																																					●																
INDESPENSION, Scunthorpe (YH07422)																						●																															
KILLINGHOLME, Grimsby (YH08143)																																					●																
MASON, D & M, Scunthorpe (YH09239)																																													●								
NAME PLATES, Ulceby (YH10014)												●																																									
LONDON (GREATER)																																																					
A D L TACK & SADDLERY, London (YH00027)												●																					●	●		●	●								●								
ALDBOROUGH HALL, Ilford (YH00252)							●																															●		●		●	●										
ALDERSBROOK RIDING SCHOOL, London (YH00257)																																								●													
BARNFIELDS, London (YH00986)																																								●													
BELMONT RIDING CTRE, London (YH01249)							●																														●							●									
BERNARD WEATHERILL, London (YH01310)																																					●																
BUNN, CLAUDIA, Pershore (YH02225)										●	●																																										
BUTTERWORTH, NINETTA, London (YH02335)	●																																																				

Business Profile
General Equine

by Country by County

Name	Artist	Blacksmith	Business Consultancy	Commentating for Events	Competition Horses	Competition Riders	Cross Country Course	Dressage Riders	Driving Centre	Driving Competitors	Driving Services	Engraving	Equine Holidays	Event Management	Event Riders	Forge	Harness Race Course	Harness Racing Horses	Harness Racing Skills	Harness Retailer	Horse Sale Agency	Horsebox Hire	International Arena	Jockey	Jockey Supply	Photographer
CHASE SADDLERY, Enfield (YH02785)																										
CIVIL SV, London (YH02933)																										
CLGE FARM SADDLERY & FEEDS, Finchley (YH03027)																										
DECATHLON SPORTS & LEISURE, London (YH04009)																										
DOCKLANDS CARRIAGE DRIVING, East Ham (YH04156)											●															
DRUMAWHEY, Uxbridge (YH04285)																										
DUFFIN, JULIA, Ealing (YH04317)																										
EDWARD ROBERT SADDLERY, Feltham (YH04569)																				●						
EQUESTRIAN TRAVELLERS CLUB, London (YH04719)													●													
FRITH MANOR EQUESTRIAN CTRE, London (YH05510)																										
FURTH, ELIZABETH, London (YH05553)																										
GILLIAN'S RIDING SCHOOL, Enfield (YH05784)																										
GLOBEPOST TRAVEL, London (YH05849)													●													
GOULDS GREEN, Uxbridge (YH05952)																										
GREEN, RICHARD, London (YH06072)	●																									
GROVE FARM, Stanmore (YH06164)																										
HOLLAND & HOLLAND, Northwood (YH06937)												●														
HORSE HOUSE, Northwood (YH07123)																										
HYDE PARK HORSEMEN'S SUNDAY, London (YH07344)																										
HYDE PARK RIDING WEAR, London (YH07345)																										
HYDE PARK STABLES, London (YH07346)																										
ISSEA - GB, London (YH07527)				●																						
KEITH PROWSE HOSPITALITY, Wembley (YH08036)													●													
KENSINGTON STABLES, London (YH08078)																										
KINGS OAK EQUESTRIAN CTRE, Enfield (YH08196)																					●					
KINGSTON RIDING CTRE, Kingston Upon Thames (YH08207)																										
KRISLAN TRAVEL, London (YH08295)													●													
L F JOLLYES, Enfield (YH08319)																										
L H H ANIMAL FEEDS, Enfield (YH08321)																						●				
LEE VALLEY RIDING CTRE, London (YH08519)							●						●													
LEGARD, HILARY, London (YH08534)					●																					
LITTLEBOURNE FARM, Uxbridge (YH08703)																										

Name	Point-to-Point Course	Polo Pitch	Portraits	Racecourse Flat	Racecourse Steeplechase	Racing Investment	Repairs Rugs	Repairs Saddles	Riding Club	Rug Cleaning	Saddler	School (Indoor)	School (Outdoor)	Sculptor	Shipping Agent	Show Jump Course	Show Jumping arena	Stabling Centre	Tack Shop	Taxidermy	Trail Riding Centre	Transport	Transport Overseas	Trekking Centre	Valuer	Website design	Wheelwright
CHASE SADDLERY, Enfield (YH02785)										●																	
CIVIL SV, London (YH02933)									●																		
CLGE FARM SADDLERY & FEEDS, Finchley (YH03027)											●																
DECATHLON SPORTS & LEISURE, London (YH04009)																			●								
DOCKLANDS CARRIAGE DRIVING, East Ham (YH04156)																											
DRUMAWHEY, Uxbridge (YH04285)												●		●													
DUFFIN, JULIA, Ealing (YH04317)											●																
EDWARD ROBERT SADDLERY, Feltham (YH04569)																											
EQUESTRIAN TRAVELLERS CLUB, London (YH04719)																											
FRITH MANOR EQUESTRIAN CTRE, London (YH05510)											●							●									
FURTH, ELIZABETH, London (YH05553)	●																										
GILLIAN'S RIDING SCHOOL, Enfield (YH05784)																		●									
GLOBEPOST TRAVEL, London (YH05849)																											
GOULDS GREEN, Uxbridge (YH05952)																		●	●								
GREEN, RICHARD, London (YH06072)																											
GROVE FARM, Stanmore (YH06164)																		●									
HOLLAND & HOLLAND, Northwood (YH06937)											●																
HORSE HOUSE, Northwood (YH07123)							●	●		●	●																
HYDE PARK HORSEMEN'S SUNDAY, London (YH07344)									●																		
HYDE PARK RIDING WEAR, London (YH07345)														●							●						
HYDE PARK STABLES, London (YH07346)																			●								
ISSEA - GB, London (YH07527)																											
KEITH PROWSE HOSPITALITY, Wembley (YH08036)																											
KENSINGTON STABLES, London (YH08078)																			●								
KINGS OAK EQUESTRIAN CTRE, Enfield (YH08196)																		●									
KINGSTON RIDING CTRE, Kingston Upon Thames (YH08207)																		●									
KRISLAN TRAVEL, London (YH08295)																											
L F JOLLYES, Enfield (YH08319)											●																
L H H ANIMAL FEEDS, Enfield (YH08321)																						●					
LEE VALLEY RIDING CTRE, London (YH08519)												●		●				●	●								
LEGARD, HILARY, London (YH08534)																											
LITTLEBOURNE FARM, Uxbridge (YH08703)												●		●		●	●										

Business Profile
General Equine

by Country by County	Artist	Blacksmith	Business Consultancy	Commentating for Events	Competition Horses	Competition Riders	Cross Country Course	Dressage Riders	Driving Centre	Driving Competitors	Driving Services	Engraving	Equine Holidays	Event Management	Event Riders	Forge	Harness Race Course	Harness Racing Horses	Harness Racing Skills	Harness Retailer	Horse Sale Agency	Horsebox Hire	International Arena	Jockey	Jockey Supply	Photographer	Point-to-Point Course
LONDON EQUESTRIAN CTRE, Finchley (YH08785)																											
LONDON EQUESTRIAN CTRE, London (YH08784)																											
LOWDHAM LODGE, Uxbridge (YH08858)																											
LOWER PRIORY FARM, Stanmore (YH08868)																											
LYNCH COTTAGE FARM, Totteridge Common (YH08922)																											
MARIE STERNER, Brook Green (YH09148)																											●
PHOTO SOURCE, London (YH11078)																											●
PINNERWOOD ARABIAN STUD, Hatch End (YH11136)																											
RAWLE & SON, London (YH11663)																											
RIDGWAY STABLES, London (YH11870)					●																						
ROEHAMPTON GATE, London (YH12053)																											
ROSS NYE RIDING STABLES, London (YH12118)													●														
ROUCH WILMOT, London (YH12140)																											●
SADDLERS SHOP, London (YH12361)																											
SCHNIEDER RIDING BOOT, London (YH12515)																											
SELWYN, GEORGE, London (YH12630)																											●
SMYTHSON, London (YH13018)												●															
SOUTHERN SHOWS GROUP, London (YH13142)				●																							●
SPORT & GENERAL PRESS AGENCY, London (YH13216)																											●
SPORTING PICTURES, Holborn (YH13231)																											●
STAG LODGE STABLES, London (YH13326)																											
STURDY, CONAN, London (YH13612)																											
SUZANNE'S RIDING SCHOOL, Harrow (YH13679)							●																				
TRENT PARK EQUESTRIAN CTRE, London (YH14378)																											
WEST ESSEX & KERNOW SADDLERY, Chingford (YH15143)																											
WILLOW TREE RIDING, London (YH15504)																											
WIMBLEDON VILLAGE STABLES, London (YH15557)						●																					
MANCHESTER (GREATER)																											
CARRINGTON RIDING, Manchester (YH02589)																											
CROFT END EQUESTRIAN CTRE, Oldham (YH03613)																											
EQUITACK, Bolton (YH04823)						●														●	●	●					
GEO HOLLOWAY, Ashton-under-Lyne (YH05713)																											

by Country by County	Polo Pitch	Portraits	Racecourse Flat	Racecourse Steeplechase	Racing Investment	Repairs Rugs	Repairs Saddles	Riding Club	Rug Cleaning	Saddler	School (Indoor)	School (Outdoor)	Sculptor	Shipping Agent	Show Jump Course	Show Jumping arena	Stabling Centre	Tack Shop	Taxidermy	Trail Riding Centre	Transport	Transport Overseas	Trekking Centre	Valuer	Website design	Wheelwright
LONDON EQUESTRIAN CTRE, Finchley (YH08785)											●		●			●	●									
LONDON EQUESTRIAN CTRE, London (YH08784)											●		●			●	●									
LOWDHAM LODGE, Uxbridge (YH08858)																	●									
LOWER PRIORY FARM, Stanmore (YH08868)																	●									
LYNCH COTTAGE FARM, Totteridge Common (YH08922)																	●									
MARIE STERNER, Brook Green (YH09148)																										
PHOTO SOURCE, London (YH11078)																										
PINNERWOOD ARABIAN STUD, Hatch End (YH11136)								●									●									
RAWLE & SON, London (YH11663)						●	●			●																
RIDGWAY STABLES, London (YH11870)																		●								
ROEHAMPTON GATE, London (YH12053)													●													
ROSS NYE RIDING STABLES, London (YH12118)																										
ROUCH WILMOT, London (YH12140)																										
SADDLERS SHOP, London (YH12361)										●																
SCHNIEDER RIDING BOOT, London (YH12515)										●																
SELWYN, GEORGE, London (YH12630)																										
SMYTHSON, London (YH13018)																										
SOUTHERN SHOWS GROUP, London (YH13142)																										
SPORT & GENERAL PRESS AGENCY, London (YH13216)																										
SPORTING PICTURES, Holborn (YH13231)																										
STAG LODGE STABLES, London (YH13326)																	●									
STURDY, CONAN, London (YH13612)												●														
SUZANNE'S RIDING SCHOOL, Harrow (YH13679)											●		●				●									
TRENT PARK EQUESTRIAN CTRE, London (YH14378)																	●									
WEST ESSEX & KERNOW SADDLERY, Chingford (YH15143)						●	●			●																
WILLOW TREE RIDING, London (YH15504)											●															
WIMBLEDON VILLAGE STABLES, London (YH15557)																	●									
MANCHESTER (GREATER)																										
CARRINGTON RIDING, Manchester (YH02589)											●		●													
CROFT END EQUESTRIAN CTRE, Oldham (YH03613)											●		●		●											
EQUITACK, Bolton (YH04823)						●	●		●									●			●					
GEO HOLLOWAY, Ashton-under-Lyne (YH05713)						●	●			●																

Business Profile
General Equine

by Country by County	Artist	Blacksmith	Business Consultancy	Commentating for Events	Competition Horses	Competition Riders	Cross Country Course	Dressage Riders	Driving Centre	Driving Competitors	Driving Services	Engraving	Equine Holidays	Event Management	Event Riders	Forge	Harness Race Course	Harness Racing Horses	Harness Racing Skills	Harness Retailer	Horse Sale Agency	Horsebox Hire	International Arena	Jockey	Jockey Supply	Photographer	Point-to-Point Course	Polo Pitch	Portraits	Racecourse Flat	Racecourse Steeplechase	Racing Investment	Repairs Rugs	Repairs Saddles	Riding Club	Rug Cleaning	Saddler	School (Indoor)	School (Outdoor)	Sculptor	Shipping Agent	Show Jump Course	Show Jumping arena	Stabling Centre	Tack Shop	Taxidermy	Trail Riding Centre	Transport	Transport Overseas	Trekking Centre	Valuer	Website design	Wheelwright
GIBPRINT, Manchester (YH05742)																										●																											
GODLEY STUD RIDING SCHOOL, Manchester (YH05868)																																						●		●										●			
HARPER FOLD STABLES, Manchester (YH06452)																																								●													
INDESPENSION, Bolton (YH07425)																						●																															
INDESPENSION, Bolton (YH07426)																						●																															
INDESPENSION, Bolton (YH07424)																						●																										●					
KENYON FARM RIDING CTRE, Manchester (YH08094)																																						●		●													
L FOR LEATHER, Manchester (YH08320)																				●													●	●		●	●																
MATCHMOOR RIDING CTRE, Bolton (YH09257)																																								●										●			
OAKHILL RIDING SCHOOL, Manchester (YH10384)																																												●									
RYDERS FARM, Bolton (YH12297)													●									●													●	●		●		●		●											
SHORESIDE STABLES, Manchester (YH12759)																																													●								
SMITHY, Bolton (YH13011)																																	●			●									●								
STABLEMATES, Bolton (YH13304)																																	●	●											●								
STAMFORD RIDING STABLES, Mossley (YH13354)																																								●													
STERLING SPORTS SUPPLIES, Manchester (YH13432)																																					●																
SWEET, PETER & MARILYN, Bolton (YH13703)																											●																										
MERSEYSIDE																																																					
BANK FARM, Wirral (YH00886)																																												●									
BARNSTON RIDING CTRE, Wirral (YH00991)																																				●		●		●					●								
BOWLERS RIDING SCHOOL, Liverpool (YH01716)																																						●		●													
CROXTETH PK RIDING CTRE, Liverpool (YH03685)							●																																	●					●								
DALE FARM SADDLERY, Prescot (YH03821)																																					●																
DEE FARM LIVERY STABLES, Wirral (YH04014)																																												●									
MAYPOLE FARM, Prescot (YH09303)																					●																●							●									
NORTHFIELD RIDING CTRE, St Helens (YH10314)													●																																								
PARK LANE LIVERIES, Wirral (YH10730)																																						●															
RABY HOUSE STABLES, Neston (YH11571)																																												●									
ROBINSONS COUNTRY LEISURE, St Helens (YH12005)																																					●																
ROSE COTTAGE, Southport (YH12090)																																												●									
TARBOCK GREEN RIDING SCHOOL, Prescot (YH13869)																																								●													
THORNTON FARM LIVERY, Wirral (YH14073)																																					●							●									

www.hccyourhorse.com

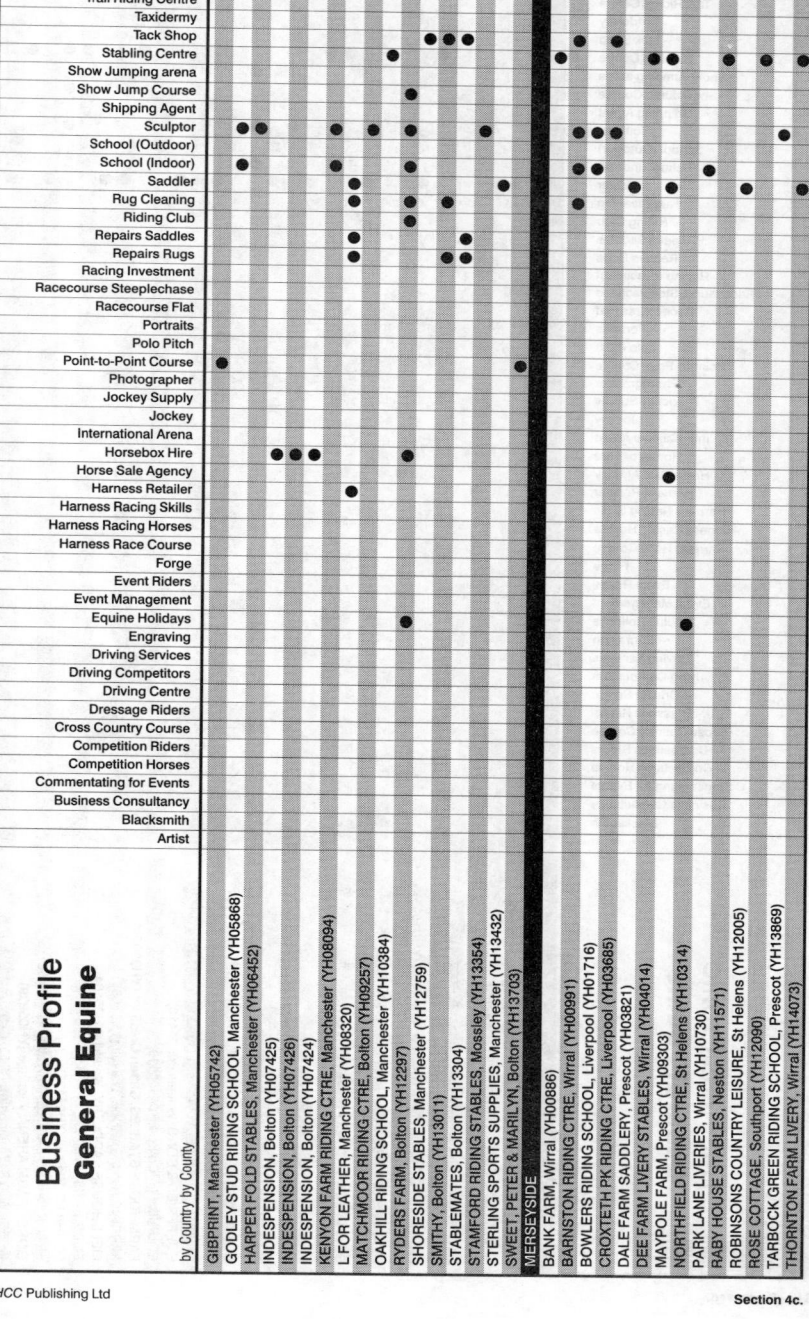

Business Profile
General Equine

by Country by County	Artist	Blacksmith	Business Consultancy	Commentating for Events	Competition Horses	Competition Riders	Cross Country Course	Dressage Riders	Driving Centre	Driving Competitors	Driving Services	Engraving	Equine Holidays	Event Management	Event Riders	Forge	Harness Race Course	Harness Racing Horses	Harness Racing Skills	Harness Retailer	Horse Sale Agency	Horsebox Hire	International Arena	Jockey	Jockey Supply	Photographer	Point-to-Point Course	Polo Pitch	Portraits	Racecourse Flat	Racecourse Steeplechase	Racing Investment	Repairs Rugs	Repairs Saddles	Riding Club	Rug Cleaning	Saddler	School (Indoor)	School (Outdoor)	Sculptor	Shipping Agent	Show Jump Course	Show Jumping arena	Stabling Centre	Tack Shop	Taxidermy	Trail Riding Centre	Transport	Transport Overseas	Trekking Centre	Valuer	Website design	Wheelwright
WHEATHILL RIDING CTRE, Liverpool (YH15268)																																											●									
MIDLANDS (WEST)																																																					
ALBRIGHTON FEEDS, Wolverhampton (YH00249)																																					●																
AMBLECOTE TACK EXCHANGE, Stourbridge (YH00360)																																					●																
ARMY & NAVY STORES, Solihull (YH00554)																																					●																
B & D HORSE DRAWN, Birmingham (YH00711)																				●																																	
B WHEELWRIGHT & SON, Birmingham (YH00751)																																																					●
BARN COTTAGE LIVERY STABLES, Solihull (YH00961)																																											●									
BARRETTS OF FECKENHAM, Wolverhampton (YH01015)																																					●																
BEAMAN, J, Brierley Hill (YH01116)																					●																																
BEARLEY CROSS STABLES, Solihull (YH01121)		●																			●	●											●															●					
BLACK COUNTRY SADDLERY, Walsall (YH01461)																																					●																
BOURNE VALE STABLES, Walsall (YH01683)													●								●																							●									
BROOKFIELDS, Wolverhampton (YH02052)													●																															●									
BROWNS, Walsall (YH02142)																				●																	●																
BUBBENHALL BRIDGE, Coventry (YH02182)							●																																	●								●					
C V F, Coventry (YH02395)																																					●																
CASTLE HILL RIDING SCHOOL, Coventry (YH02627)							●																															●		●			●										
CLEAN, B, Coventry (YH03008)																																	●	●		●																	
COUNTY SADDLERY, Walsall (YH03491)																																					●																
DIAMOND SADDLERY, Wolverhampton (YH04104)																																					●																
E JEFFRIES & SONS, Walsall (YH04410)																																					●																
EQUINIMITY, Coventry (YH04810)																											●																										
FARMHOUSE STABLES, Sutton Coldfield (YH05064)																																												●									
FARRINGTONS SADDLE, Walsall (YH05095)																																					●																
FIELDHOUSE SADDLERY, Walsall (YH05194)																																					●																
FOUR OAKS LIVERY, Sutton Coldfield (YH05409)																																												●									
FOXHILLS, Walsall (YH05435)					●		●																																	●		●		●				●					
FRANK BAINES SADDLERY, Walsall (YH05455)																																					●																
GORSE FARM ARENA, Aldridge (YH05939)																																												●									
GREENWAYS, Birmingham (YH06104)																																					●																
H W DABBS SADDLEMAKERS, Walsall (YH06245)																																					●																

Business Profile
General Equine

by Country by County

	Artist	Blacksmith	Business Consultancy	Commentating for Events	Competition Horses	Competition Riders	Cross Country Course	Dressage Riders	Driving Centre	Driving Competitors	Driving Services	Engraving	Equine Holidays	Event Management	Event Riders	Forge	Harness Race Course	Harness Racing Horses	Harness Racing Skills	Harness Retailer	Horse Sale Agency	Horsebox Hire	International Arena	Jockey	Jockey Supply	Photographer	Point-to-Point Course	Polo Pitch	Portraits	Racecourse Flat	Racecourse Steeplechase	Racing Investment	Repairs Rugs	Repairs Saddles	Riding Club	Rug Cleaning	Saddler	School (Indoor)	School (Outdoor)	Sculptor	Shipping Agent	Show Jump Course	Show Jumping arena	Stabling Centre	Tack Shop	Taxidermy	Trail Riding Centre	Transport	Transport Overseas	Trekking Centre	Valuer	Website design	Wheelwright
HARDWEAR CLOTHING, Stourbridge (YH06414)																																					●																
HAZEL FARM, Solihull (YH06599)																																	●	●		●	●							●									
HOOPER'S SADDLERS SHOP, Walsall (YH07045)																																					●																
HORSE SHOP, Cockshutts Lane (YH07138)																																					●																
HORSESENSE, Solihull (YH07170)																																					●																
HOUND & HORSE, Wythall (YH07206)																																					●																
INDESPENSION, Halesowen (YH07427)																						●																															
IRENES, Wombourne (YH07489)																																					●																
J R HORSEWEAR, Stourbridge (YH07609)																																					●																
J ROBERTS SADDLERY, Halesowen (YH07613)																																					●																
JAMES COTTERELL & SONS, Walsall (YH07664)																																					●																
KINGS, Walsall (YH08192)																																					●																
KINGSWOOD EQUESTRIAN CTRE, Wolverhampton (YH08210)							●																															●		●			●										
LAUNDRY MACHINE, Birmingham (YH08454)																																				●																	
MOOR FARM STABLES, Coventry (YH09745)							●																																	●													
NORTH WORCESTERSHIRE, Halesowen (YH10287)																																												●									
ORCHARDS LIVERY STABLES, Birmingham (YH10537)																					●																																
OVERIDER, Coventry (YH10593)													●																																								
P J COYNE, Walsall (YH10647)																																	●	●																			
PADDOCK STORES, Brierley Hill (YH10671)																																					●																
PENORCHARDS FARM, Halesowen (YH10957)																					●																																
PHOENIX, Walsall (YH11069)																																					●																
POOLE, JOHN, Alvechurch (YH11265)																					●																																
ROSE BANK STORES & SADDLERY, Birmingham (YH12089)																																					●																
SADDLE & BRIDLE, Walsall (YH12340)																																	●	●																			
SANDWELL VALLEY RIDING CTRE, West Bromwich (YH12421)													●																								●							●									
SEECHEM EQUESTRIAN CTRE, Birmingham (YH12607)																					●																							●									
SOWERBYS OF STOURBRIDGE, Stourbridge (YH13167)																																					●																
SUNRAY STUD, Walsall (YH13651)																																				●																	
SYMONDS SADDLERY, Walsall (YH13725)																																					●																
THOROWGOOD, Walsall (YH14089)																																					●																
TOWNFIELD SADDLERS, Coventry (YH14296)																																					●																

Business Profile
General Equine

by Country by County	Artist	Blacksmith	Business Consultancy	Commentating for Events	Competition Horses	Competition Riders	Cross Country Course	Dressage Riders	Driving Centre	Driving Competitors	Driving Services	Engraving	Equine Holidays	Event Management	Event Riders	Forge	Harness Race Course	Harness Racing Horses	Harness Racing Skills	Harness Retailer	Horse Sale Agency	Horsebox Hire	International Arena	Jockey	Jockey Supply	Photographer	Point-to-Point Course	Polo Pitch	Portraits	Racecourse Flat	Racecourse Steeplechase	Racing Investment	Repairs Rugs	Repairs Saddles	Riding Club	Rug Cleaning	Saddler	School (Indoor)	School (Outdoor)	Sculptor	Shipping Agent	Show Jump Course	Show Jumping arena	Stabling Centre	Tack Shop	Taxidermy	Trail Riding Centre	Transport	Transport Overseas	Trekking Centre	Valuer	Website design	Wheelwright
WILLIAM POWELL & SON, Birmingham (YH15436)																																					●																
WISHAW RIDING CTRE, Sutton Coldfield (YH15614)																																												●									
WITHYBROOK STABLES, Coventry (YH15629)																																						●		●			●										
WOLVERHAMPTON RACECOURSE, Wolverhampton (YH15650)																	●																																				
WORDSLEY SADDLERY, Stourbridge (YH15776)																																					●																
NORFOLK																																																					
BEST CLEANING SV, Diss (YH01325)																																	●	●		●																	
BINTREE MANOR LIVERIES, Dereham (YH01427)																																												●									
BLACKBOROUGH END, King's Lynn (YH01477)																																												●									
BLOOM, M J, Wymondham (YH01552)																																												●									
BOJAN AT WARREN KENNELS, Sheringham (YH01601)																																					●																
BOON, TERRY, Norwich (YH01632)															●																																						
BRIDGE FARM STABLES, Mundesley (YH01872)													●																															●									
BRITTON, VANESSA, Thetford (YH01986)																											●																										
CAISTER SADDLERY, Caister On Sea (YH02422)																																	●	●			●																
CALDECOTT HALL, Great Yarmouth (YH02429)																																												●									
CHURCH FARM LIVERY STABLES, Great Yarmouth (YH02898)																																												●									
COUSINS, S D J, King's Lynn (YH03514)																																												●									
CROFT FARM RIDING CTRE, Great Yarmouth (YH03615)																																			●			●		●													
CROSSWAYS LIVERY YARD, Great Yarmouth (YH03666)																																											●										
DARROW FARM SUPPLIES, Diss (YH03899)																																					●																
DEREHAM SADDLERY, Dereham (YH04073)																																	●	●			●																
EASTON CLGE, Norwich (YH04513)							●																															●		●													
EDEN MEADOWS RIDING CTRE, Attleborough (YH04547)																																												●									
EVERYTHING EQUESTRIAN, Norwich (YH04958)																																					●																
FOREST LODGE RIDING CTRE, Holt (YH05343)																																												●									
G J L, Fakenham (YH05585)																																	●			●																	
GEOFFREY GIBSON SADDLER, Stibbard (YH05716)																																					●																
GRANE STUD, Norwich (YH05985)					●																																																
GRANGE FARM LIVERY, Norwich (YH05990)																																												●									
GRANVILLE SADDLERY, Norwich (YH06016)																																				●	●																
GRANVILLE SADDLERY, Wymondham (YH06015)																																				●	●																

Business Profile

General Equine

by Country by County	Artist	Blacksmith	Business Consultancy	Commentating for Events	Competition Horses	Competition Riders	Cross Country Course	Dressage Riders	Driving Centre	Driving Competitors	Driving Services	Engraving	Equine Holidays	Event Management	Event Riders	Forge	Harness Race Course	Harness Racing Horses	Harness Racing Skills	Harness Retailer	Horse Sale Agency	Horsebox Hire	International Arena	Jockey	Jockey Supply	Photographer	Point-to-Point Course	Polo Pitch	Portraits	Racecourse Flat	Racecourse Steeplechase	Racing Investment	Repairs Rugs	Repairs Saddles	Riding Club	Rug Cleaning	Saddler	School (Indoor)	School (Outdoor)	Sculptor	Shipping Agent	Show Jump Course	Show Jumping arena	Stabling Centre	Tack Shop	Taxidermy	Trail Riding Centre	Transport	Transport Overseas	Trekking Centre	Valuer	Website design	Wheelwright
GREENACRES RIDING SCHOOL, King's Lynn (YH06079)							●																																	●		●											
H & C BEART, King's Lynn (YH06207)																																	●	●			●																
HALL FARM FORAGE, Happisburgh (YH06304)																						●																										●					
HARDINGHAM FARMS, Norwich (YH06413)																																												●									
HIGHFIELD EQUESTRIAN CTRE, Great Yarmouth (YH06784)																																								●				●									
HILLCREST LIVERY CTRE, Great Yarmouth (YH06842)																																												●									
HOCKWOLD LODGE, Thetford (YH06906)													●																															●									
HORSES IN SPORT, Diss (YH07169)																				●																	●								●								
HORSETALK, King's Lynn (YH07176)																																	●	●		●	●								●								
INDESPENSION, Norwich (YH07428)																						●																															
JOHN PARKER, Diss (YH07804)									●		●																																										
L S SADDLERY, King's Lynn (YH08328)																																	●	●																			
LESLIE LANE, Mundesley (YH08558)																											●																										
MAY, JIM, Wisbech (YH09289)																																					●																
MILL FARM STABLES, Great Witchingham (YH09574)																																												●									
NORTH NORFOLK RIDING CTRE, Walsingham (YH10274)													●																																								
OLD BUCKENHAM STUD, Attleborough (YH10453)																					●																																
P H PHOTOGRAPHY, Kings Lynn (YH10642)																											●																										
PLAYBARN, Poringland (YH11169)																																					●																
RECTORY ROAD RIDING SCHOOL, Norwich (YH11693)													●																															●									
REYNOLDS, ANTHONY, Diss (YH11776)																											●																										
ROSE-ACRE RIDING STABLES, Mundesley (YH12099)													●																															●									
RUNCTON HALL, King's Lynn (YH12233)					●	●	●						●																						●			●				●	●	●									
RYDER, JUSTINE, King's Lynn (YH12295)														●																																							
SANDONS THE SADDLERY, Dereham (YH12416)																																					●																
SAVAGE, E A, Thetford (YH12453)																																	●	●		●																	
SHEPCO, Great Yarmouth (YH12710)																																	●	●																			
STREET FARM, King's Lynn (YH13572)																																												●									
STRUMPSHAW RIDING CTRE, Norwich (YH13592)																																												●									
SUSSEX FARM STABLES, King's Lynn (YH13661)																																												●									
SWAFIELD RIDING, North Walsham (YH13682)													●																															●									
TACK BARN, Norwich (YH13782)																																	●	●			●																

Business Profile
General Equine

by Country by County	Artist	Blacksmith	Business Consultancy	Commentating for Events	Competition Horses	Competition Riders	Cross Country Course	Dressage Riders	Driving Centre	Driving Competitors	Driving Services	Engraving	Equine Holidays	Event Management	Event Riders	Forge	Harness Race Course	Harness Racing Horses	Harness Racing Skills	Harness Retailer	Horse Sale Agency	Horsebox Hire	International Arena	Jockey	Jockey Supply	Photographer	Point-to-Point Course	Polo Pitch	Portraits	Racecourse Flat	Racecourse Steeplechase	Racing Investment	Repairs Rugs	Repairs Saddles	Riding Club	Rug Cleaning	Saddler	School (Indoor)	School (Outdoor)	Sculptor	Shipping Agent	Show Jump Course	Show Jumping arena	Stabling Centre	Tack Shop	Taxidermy	Trail Riding Centre	Transport	Transport Overseas	Trekking Centre	Valuer	Website design	Wheelwright
THOMPSON, EMILY, King's Lynn (YH14035)															●																																						
TOP FARM EQUESTRIAN CTRE, Norwich (YH14236)													●																															●									
TOP TAK, King's Lynn (YH14238)																																					●																
TRACK & FIELD, Dereham (YH14307)																																	●	●			●																
WEST RUNTON RIDING STABLES, Cromer (YH15162)													●																																								
WESTON PARK EQUESTRIAN CTRE, Norwich (YH15224)							●						●																						●			●		●				●									
WILLOW FARM COTTAGE, Norwich (YH15499)													●																																								
WILLOW FARM RIDING SCHOOL, Great Yarmouth (YH15500)																																												●									
WRENINGHAM TROTTING RACEWAY, Norwich (YH15823)																	●																																				
WROXHAM SADDLERY, Norwich (YH15850)																																	●	●			●																
NORTHAMPTONSHIRE																																																					
ANDREW BOTTERILL SADDLER, Wellingborough (YH00389)																				●													●	●		●	●																
ASHTON STABLES, Northampton (YH00614)					●	●																																						●									
BLETSOE BROWN, Northampton (YH01538)																																												●				●					
BRAMPTON STABLES, Northampton (YH01794)																																												●									
BROOK FARM, Wellingborough (YH02033)																																												●									
COUNTRYWISE FEEDS & NEEDS, Kettering (YH03484)																																					●																
CROSS COUNTRY HORSE TRANSPORT, Northampton (YH03643)												●											●																										●				
D A WATTS, Wellingborough (YH03777)																																																					●
EAST LODGE FARM RIDING EST, Northampton (YH04479)							●						●																									●		●													
EDENGATE SADDLERY, Northampton (YH04550)																				●													●	●		●									●								
FAULKNERS FOOTWEAR, Daventry (YH05104)																																					●																
FLYING CHANGES, Daventry (YH05293)																					●																●																
FOX HILL FARM EQUESTRIAN CTRE, Northampton (YH05422)																																					●																
GILDERS, Kettering (YH05762)																																					●																
GILDERS NORTHAMPTON, Northampton (YH05763)																																					●																
GOODTIMES LEISURE, Kettering (YH05909)																																					●																
GREENACRES LIVERY CTRE, Towcester (YH06077)																																												●									
GROOMERS, Northampton (YH06154)																																					●																
H T S EQUESTRIAN, Wellingborough (YH06242)																																					●																
HARLEY, Daventry (YH06436)																																					●																
HARRINGWORTH MANOR, Corby (YH06461)							●																																	●			●										

Business Profile
General Equine

by Country by County	Artist	Blacksmith	Business Consultancy	Commentating for Events	Competition Horses	Competition Riders	Cross Country Course	Dressage Riders	Driving Centre	Driving Competitors	Driving Services	Engraving	Equine Holidays	Event Management	Event Riders	Forge	Harness Race Course	Harness Racing Horses	Harness Racing Skills	Harness Retailer	Horse Sale Agency	Horsebox Hire	International Arena	Jockey	Jockey Supply	Photographer	Point-to-Point Course	Polo Pitch	Portraits	Racecourse Flat	Racecourse Steeplechase	Racing Investment	Repairs Rugs	Repairs Saddles	Riding Club	Rug Cleaning	Saddler	School (Indoor)	School (Outdoor)	Sculptor	Shipping Agent	Show Jump Course	Show Jumping arena	Stabling Centre	Tack Shop	Taxidermy	Trail Riding Centre	Transport	Transport Overseas	Trekking Centre	Valuer	Website design	Wheelwright
HENRY H BLETSOE & SON, Kettering (YH06684)																																																			●		
HOLDENBY RIDING SCHOOL, Northampton (YH06924)													●																																								
HOOKS & HOOVES, Kettering (YH07038)																																													●								
HORSE INDEX, Silverstone (YH07125)																					●																																
HURSTFIELD SADDLERY, Brackley (YH07319)																																					●																
INDESPENSION, Northampton (YH07429)																						●																															
MANDI'S LIVERIES, Northampton (YH09071)							●																																	●				●									
MANOR FARM RIDING SCHOOL, Wellingborough (YH09106)																					●	●													●					●													
MEU, Kettering (YH09505)																						●																										●					
MOBILE PROMOTIONS COMPANY, Titchmarsh (YH09689)																						●																										●					
MOULTON CLGE, Northampton (YH09883)							●																															●		●													
NORMAN & SPICER, Daventry (YH10235)																																					●																
PARKER, N, Northampton (YH10751)																																	●	●		●	●																
PET LOVE SUPPLIES, Daventry (YH11005)																																					●																
RATHBONE, K, Ravensthorpe (YH11654)																																												●									
RIDERS INT, Raunds (YH11856)																																					●																
RIDING HIGH, Towcester (YH11882)																																					●																
RUSHTON HALL FARM, Kettering (YH12246)							●																																														
SCHNIEDER RIDING BOOT, Northampton (YH12516)																																					●																
SULBY HALL, Northampton (YH13628)						●																																															
TAYLOR, NIGEL & ANN, Daventry (YH13907)															●																																						
THREE SHIRES LIVERY CTRE, Wellingborough (YH14107)																						●																						●									
TOWER FARM SADDLERS, Northampton (YH14273)																																					●																
UK RACING, Daventry (YH14548)																																					●																
WASHBROOK FARM, Daventry (YH14955)							●																																														
WATTS & WATTS SADDLERY, Northampton (YH15003)																																	●	●		●	●		●						●								
WHITE & BISHOP, Northampton (YH15299)																																					●																
YELVERTOFT EQUESTRIAN CTRE, Yelvertoft (YH15900)																																												●									
NORTHUMBERLAND																																																					
A C BURN, Berwick-upon-Tweed (YH00021)																																	●			●																	
BENRIDGE RIDING CTRE, Morpeth (YH01277)																																												●									
BROWN RIGG RIDING SCHOOL, Hexham (YH02093)													●																																								

Business Profile
General Equine

by Country by County

Business	Artist	Blacksmith	Business Consultancy	Commentating for Events	Competition Horses	Competition Riders	Cross Country Course	Dressage Riders	Driving Centre	Driving Competitors	Driving Services	Engraving	Equine Holidays	Event Management	Event Riders	Forge	Harness Race Course	Harness Racing Horses
BROWN TRAILERS, Cramlington (YH02094)																		
BROWN, GEOFF, Stamfordham (YH02108)										●								
CHARLTON, R B, Hexham (YH02766)							●											
COOPER, SIMON, Stocksfield (YH03291)																		
EQUILINK, Alnwick (YH04751)					●													
FARMWAY, Morpeth (YH05074)																		
FORSYTH'S OF WOOLER, Wooler (YH05384)																		
FOWBERRY FARMS, Wooler (YH05416)																		
JOICEY, (LADY), Cornhill-on-Tweed (YH07849)								●										
KIDLENDLEE TRAIL RIDING, Morpeth (YH08124)													●					
KIMMERSTON RIDING CTRE, Wooler (YH08161)													●					
M E L, Berwick-upon-Tweed (YH08961)																		
NICHOL, CHARLOTTE, Hexham (YH10178)															●			
NICK MORRIS PHOTOGRAPHY, Alnwick (YH10195)																		
NORTHUMBRIAN SADDLERY, Hexham (YH10321)																		
PLOVER HILL RIDING SCHOOL, Hexham (YH11178)													●					
R L JOBSON & SON, Alnwick (YH11553)																		
R L JOBSON & SON, Berwick-upon-Tweed (YH11552)																		
RAVENSHILL RIDING CTRE, Hexham (YH11660)													●					
REDESDALE RIDING CTRE, Otterburn (YH11710)											●		●					
RICKERBY, Cornhill-on-Tweed (YH11834)																		
RIVERDALE HALL HOTEL, Hexham (YH11921)													●					
SINDERHOPE PONY TREKKING CTRE, Hexham (YH12850)																		
STEVE NEWMAN PHOTOGRAPHY, Belford (YH13438)																		
TACK DOCTOR, Berwick-upon-Tweed (YH13786)																		
THORNLEY GATE LIVERIES, Hexham (YH14070)																		
TYNE VALLEY SADDLERS, Wylam (YH14526)																		
WHITTON FARM HSE HOTEL, Rothbury (YH15376)													●					
WILLOW WEAR, Hexham (YH15505)																		
WOOPERTON, Alnwick (YH15770)					●	●	●											
NOTTINGHAMSHIRE																		
ALADDIN CAVE, Lowdham (YH00236)																		

Business	Harness Racing Skills	Harness Retailer	Horse Sale Agency	Horsebox Hire	International Arena	Jockey	Jockey Supply	Photographer	Point-to-Point Course	Polo Pitch	Portraits	Racecourse Flat	Racecourse Steeplechase	Racing Investment	Repairs Rugs	Repairs Saddles	Riding Club	Rug Cleaning
BROWN TRAILERS, Cramlington (YH02094)				●														
BROWN, GEOFF, Stamfordham (YH02108)																		
CHARLTON, R B, Hexham (YH02766)																		
COOPER, SIMON, Stocksfield (YH03291)		●													●	●		
EQUILINK, Alnwick (YH04751)			●															
FARMWAY, Morpeth (YH05074)															●	●		●
FORSYTH'S OF WOOLER, Wooler (YH05384)																		
FOWBERRY FARMS, Wooler (YH05416)																		
JOICEY, (LADY), Cornhill-on-Tweed (YH07849)																		
KIDLENDLEE TRAIL RIDING, Morpeth (YH08124)																		
KIMMERSTON RIDING CTRE, Wooler (YH08161)																		
M E L, Berwick-upon-Tweed (YH08961)															●	●		
NICHOL, CHARLOTTE, Hexham (YH10178)																		
NICK MORRIS PHOTOGRAPHY, Alnwick (YH10195)									●									
NORTHUMBRIAN SADDLERY, Hexham (YH10321)															●	●		
PLOVER HILL RIDING SCHOOL, Hexham (YH11178)																		
R L JOBSON & SON, Alnwick (YH11553)		●																
R L JOBSON & SON, Berwick-upon-Tweed (YH11552)																		
RAVENSHILL RIDING CTRE, Hexham (YH11660)																		
REDESDALE RIDING CTRE, Otterburn (YH11710)																		
RICKERBY, Cornhill-on-Tweed (YH11834)																		
RIVERDALE HALL HOTEL, Hexham (YH11921)																		
SINDERHOPE PONY TREKKING CTRE, Hexham (YH12850)																		
STEVE NEWMAN PHOTOGRAPHY, Belford (YH13438)									●									
TACK DOCTOR, Berwick-upon-Tweed (YH13786)															●	●		
THORNLEY GATE LIVERIES, Hexham (YH14070)																		
TYNE VALLEY SADDLERS, Wylam (YH14526)															●	●		●
WHITTON FARM HSE HOTEL, Rothbury (YH15376)																		
WILLOW WEAR, Hexham (YH15505)															●			●
WOOPERTON, Alnwick (YH15770)																		
NOTTINGHAMSHIRE																		
ALADDIN CAVE, Lowdham (YH00236)																		

Business	Saddler	School (Indoor)	School (Outdoor)	Sculptor	Shipping Agent	Show Jump Course	Show Jumping arena	Stabling Centre	Tack Shop	Taxidermy	Trail Riding Centre	Transport	Transport Overseas	Trekking Centre	Valuer	Website design	Wheelwright
BROWN TRAILERS, Cramlington (YH02094)												●					
BROWN, GEOFF, Stamfordham (YH02108)																	
CHARLTON, R B, Hexham (YH02766)								●									
COOPER, SIMON, Stocksfield (YH03291)	●																
EQUILINK, Alnwick (YH04751)																	
FARMWAY, Morpeth (YH05074)	●								●								
FORSYTH'S OF WOOLER, Wooler (YH05384)	●																
FOWBERRY FARMS, Wooler (YH05416)								●									
JOICEY, (LADY), Cornhill-on-Tweed (YH07849)																	
KIDLENDLEE TRAIL RIDING, Morpeth (YH08124)																	
KIMMERSTON RIDING CTRE, Wooler (YH08161)																	
M E L, Berwick-upon-Tweed (YH08961)	●																
NICHOL, CHARLOTTE, Hexham (YH10178)																	
NICK MORRIS PHOTOGRAPHY, Alnwick (YH10195)																	
NORTHUMBRIAN SADDLERY, Hexham (YH10321)	●																
PLOVER HILL RIDING SCHOOL, Hexham (YH11178)																	
R L JOBSON & SON, Alnwick (YH11553)	●																
R L JOBSON & SON, Berwick-upon-Tweed (YH11552)	●																
RAVENSHILL RIDING CTRE, Hexham (YH11660)																	
REDESDALE RIDING CTRE, Otterburn (YH11710)																	
RICKERBY, Cornhill-on-Tweed (YH11834)	●																
RIVERDALE HALL HOTEL, Hexham (YH11921)																	
SINDERHOPE PONY TREKKING CTRE, Hexham (YH12850)				●										●			
STEVE NEWMAN PHOTOGRAPHY, Belford (YH13438)																	
TACK DOCTOR, Berwick-upon-Tweed (YH13786)	●																
THORNLEY GATE LIVERIES, Hexham (YH14070)								●									
TYNE VALLEY SADDLERS, Wylam (YH14526)	●																
WHITTON FARM HSE HOTEL, Rothbury (YH15376)																	
WILLOW WEAR, Hexham (YH15505)																	
WOOPERTON, Alnwick (YH15770)		●				●		●									
NOTTINGHAMSHIRE																	
ALADDIN CAVE, Lowdham (YH00236)	●																

Business Profile
General Equine

by Country by County

	Artist	Blacksmith	Business Consultancy	Commentating for Events	Competition Horses	Competition Riders	Cross Country Course	Dressage Riders	Driving Centre	Driving Competitors	Driving Services	Engraving	Equine Holidays	Event Management	Event Riders	Forge	Harness Race Course	Harness Racing Horses	Harness Racing Skills	Harness Retailer	Horse Sale Agency	Horsebox Hire	International Arena	Jockey	Jockey Supply	Photographer
B J W EQUINE SVS, Thurgarton (YH00734)																										
BARNFIELDS, Keyworth (YH00987)																										
BLOOMSGORSE TREKKING CTRE, Newark (YH01556)													●													
BRIDLE WAY & GAUNTLEYS, Newark (YH01892)																										
BROOMSIDE STUD, Calverton (YH02082)																										
CARLTON FOREST, Worksop (YH02542)																										
CHERRY ANN WILE PHOTOGRAPHY, Hucknall (YH02814)																										
CHERRY TREE RIDING CTRE, New Brinsley (YH02817)																										
CHUKKA COVE, Newark (YH02893)																										
CLGE FARM, Newark (YH03026)							●						●		●											
CTRE - LINES, Newark (YH03694)					●	●		●																		
DECATHLON SPORTS & LEISURE, Nottingham (YH04010)																										
DIRTY DOBBINS, Mansfield Woodhouse (YH04128)																										
DOVECOTE FARM, Orston (YH04218)																										
F MARTIN & SON, Arnold (YH04995)																				●						
FIRBECK, Worksop (YH05222)																					●					
GASCOINES, Southwell (YH05668)																										
GRIFFIN, L M, Thoroton (YH06131)																				●						
HAYFIELD SADDLERY REPAIRS, Worksop (YH06580)																										
HODSOCK STABLES, Worksop (YH06915)																										
HOLISTIC HORSECARE, Northampton (YH06934)													●													
HOLME FARM LIVERY, Newark (YH06964)																										
HOOF ALOOF, Nottingham (YH07025)																										
INDESPENSION, Nottingham (YH07430)																						●				
KIRKFIELD EQUESTRIAN CTRE, Lower Blidworth (YH08234)																										
KIRKFIELD STABLES, Lower Blidworth (YH08235)																					●					
LANEHAM LIVERY STABLE, Retford (YH08392)																										
LINGS LANE RIDING STABLES, Nottingham (YH08662)																										
MALLENDER BROS, Worksop (YH09051)		●			●											●										
MANOR FARM LIVERY YARD, Gotham (YH09102)																										
NEWCOMBE, P & A, Worksop (YH10133)																										
NEWTON CROFT COUNTRY, Nottingham (YH10169)							●																			

	Point-to-Point Course	Polo Pitch	Portraits	Racecourse Flat	Racecourse Steeplechase	Racing Investment	Repairs Rugs	Repairs Saddles	Riding Club	Rug Cleaning	Saddler	School (Indoor)	School (Outdoor)	Sculptor	Shipping Agent	Show Jump Course	Show Jumping arena	Stabling Centre	Tack Shop	Taxidermy	Trail Riding Centre	Transport	Transport Overseas	Trekking Centre	Valuer	Website design	Wheelwright
B J W EQUINE SVS, Thurgarton (YH00734)							●	●		●																	
BARNFIELDS, Keyworth (YH00987)																		●									
BLOOMSGORSE TREKKING CTRE, Newark (YH01556)																											
BRIDLE WAY & GAUNTLEYS, Newark (YH01892)										●																	
BROOMSIDE STUD, Calverton (YH02082)							●	●			●							●									
CARLTON FOREST, Worksop (YH02542)											●							●									
CHERRY ANN WILE PHOTOGRAPHY, Hucknall (YH02814)	●																										
CHERRY TREE RIDING CTRE, New Brinsley (YH02817)																		●									
CHUKKA COVE, Newark (YH02893)							●	●		●	●																
CLGE FARM, Newark (YH03026)									●					●													
CTRE - LINES, Newark (YH03694)														●													
DECATHLON SPORTS & LEISURE, Nottingham (YH04010)																			●								
DIRTY DOBBINS, Mansfield Woodhouse (YH04128)										●																	
DOVECOTE FARM, Orston (YH04218)														●		●											
F MARTIN & SON, Arnold (YH04995)																			●								
FIRBECK, Worksop (YH05222)																		●									
GASCOINES, Southwell (YH05668)																									●		
GRIFFIN, L M, Thoroton (YH06131)							●	●			●																
HAYFIELD SADDLERY REPAIRS, Worksop (YH06580)							●	●																			
HODSOCK STABLES, Worksop (YH06915)																		●									
HOLISTIC HORSECARE, Northampton (YH06934)																											
HOLME FARM LIVERY, Newark (YH06964)																		●									
HOOF ALOOF, Nottingham (YH07025)											●								●								
INDESPENSION, Nottingham (YH07430)																											
KIRKFIELD EQUESTRIAN CTRE, Lower Blidworth (YH08234)																		●									
KIRKFIELD STABLES, Lower Blidworth (YH08235)																											
LANEHAM LIVERY STABLE, Retford (YH08392)																		●									
LINGS LANE RIDING STABLES, Nottingham (YH08662)														●													
MALLENDER BROS, Worksop (YH09051)																											●
MANOR FARM LIVERY YARD, Gotham (YH09102)																		●									
NEWCOMBE, P & A, Worksop (YH10133)							●	●																			
NEWTON CROFT COUNTRY, Nottingham (YH10169)																		●									

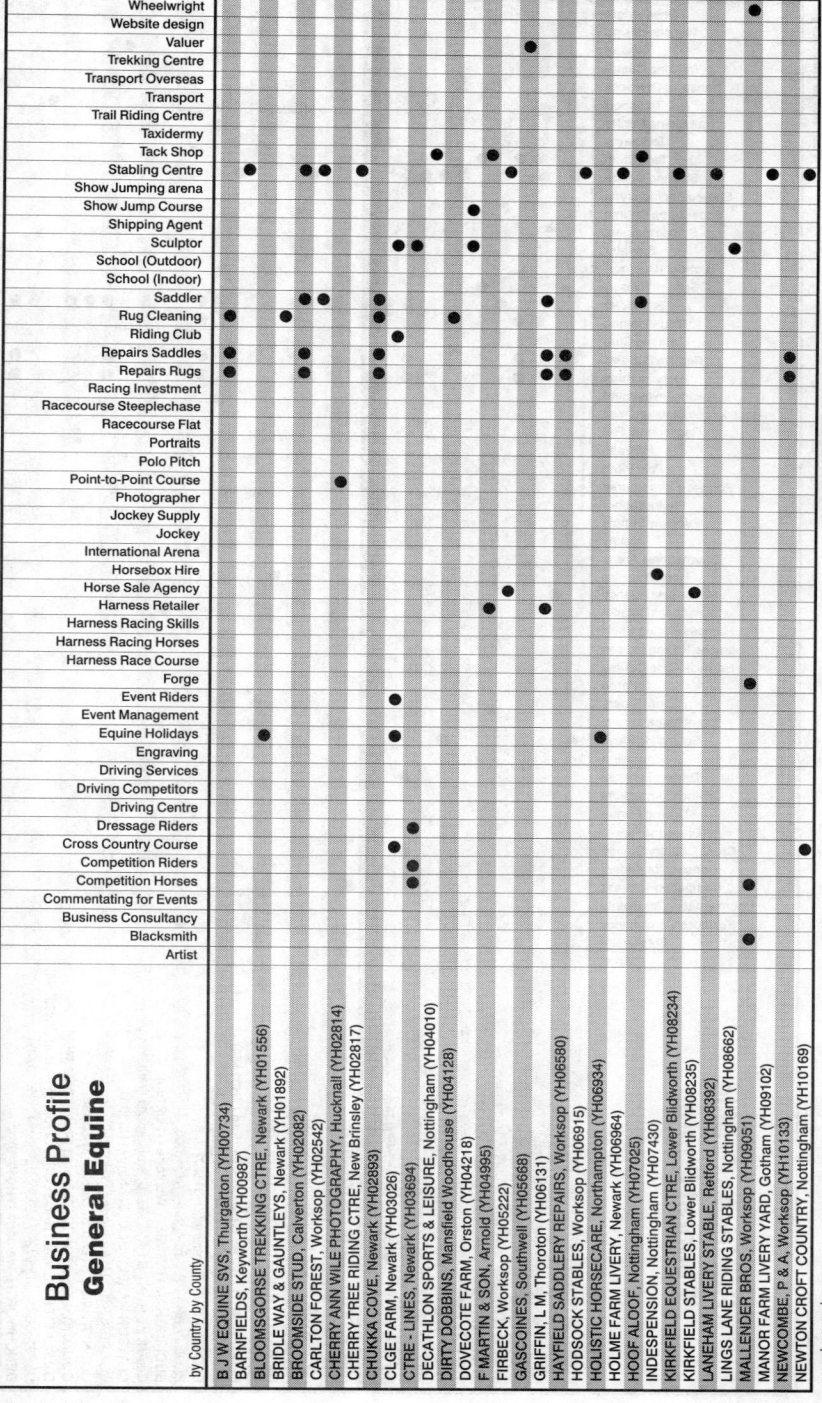

Business Profile
General Equine

by Country by County	Artist	Blacksmith	Business Consultancy	Commentating for Events	Competition Horses	Competition Riders	Cross Country Course	Dressage Riders	Driving Centre	Driving Competitors	Driving Services	Engraving	Equine Holidays	Event Management	Event Riders	Forge	Harness Race Course	Harness Racing Horses	Harness Racing Skills	Harness Retailer	Horse Sale Agency	Horsebox Hire	International Arena	Jockey	Jockey Supply	Photographer	Point-to-Point Course	Polo Pitch	Portraits	Racecourse Flat	Racecourse Steeplechase	Racing Investment	Repairs Rugs	Repairs Saddles	Riding Club	Rug Cleaning	Saddler	School (Indoor)	School (Outdoor)	Sculptor	Shipping Agent	Show Jump Course	Show Jumping arena	Stabling Centre	Tack Shop	Taxidermy	Trail Riding Centre	Transport	Transport Overseas	Trekking Centre	Valuer	Website design	Wheelwright
PLEASLEY PARK LIVERY, Mansfield (YH11174)													●																															●									
PYRAH, MALCOLM, Nottingham (YH11471)																					●																																
SADDLE RACK, Nottingham (YH12346)																																	●			●								●	●								
SADDLECRAFT, Nottingham (YH12355)																																	●	●		●									●								
SHELTON HSE SADDLERY, Newark (YH12705)																																					●																
ST CLEMENTS LODGE, Nottingham (YH13274)																																						●							●								
SUTTON MANOR FARM, Retford (YH13673)																																												●									
TRENT VALLEY STABLES, Southwell (YH14381)													●																															●									
VICTORIAN CARRIAGES, Newark (YH14710)									●		●																																	●									
WELLOW PK, Newark (YH15077)							●				●																						●	●			●							●									
WILMOTTS PET/SADDLERY STORES, Nottingham (YH15523)																																					●																
OXFORDSHIRE																																																					
ALVESCOT STUD, Carterton (YH00349)					●																																																
AMBRIDGE SADDLERY, Watlington (YH00362)																				●													●	●			●																
ARLINGTON POLO, Kidlington (YH00533)																																												●									
ASTI STUD & SADDLERY, Faringdon (YH00633)													●																				●	●		●	●			●		●			●								
BANBURY TRAILERS, Banbury (YH00880)																						●																															
BERGENDORFF, FREDERICK, Banbury (YH01295)															●																																						
BLACKHEATH LIVERY STABLES, Burford (YH01484)																																												●									
BLAKES OF FRILFORD, Abingdon (YH01522)																																					●																
BLOOR, ANNE, Banbury (YH01557)																																	●	●		●	●																
BLUE ZEBRA PR, Ardington (YH01572)			●																																																		
BUCKINGHAM HARNESS, Wantage (YH02190)																				●																																	
CHARLES HUNT & PARTNERS, Wallingford (YH02756)																																					●																
CLAYSON-HASELWOOD, Banbury (YH03001)																																																			●		
COOPER, S & J M, Faringdon (YH03290)																																	●	●			●																
COUNTRYWIDE STORES, Oxford (YH03464)																																					●																
COUNTRYWIDE STORES, Chipping Norton (YH03463)																																					●																
D J SLATTER HORSE TRANSPORT, Chipping Norton (YH03788)																																																●					
DEFENCE CLOTHING & TEXTILE, Didcot (YH04024)																																					●																
DENCHWORTH, Wantage (YH04040)																																	●	●			●																
EAST END FARM RIDING SCHOOL, Wallingford (YH04474)																																								●													

Business Profile
General Equine

by Country by County	Artist	Blacksmith	Business Consultancy	Commentating for Events	Competition Horses	Competition Riders	Cross Country Course	Dressage Riders	Driving Centre	Driving Competitors	Driving Services	Engraving	Equine Holidays	Event Management	Event Riders	Forge	Harness Race Course	Harness Racing Horses	Harness Racing Skills	Harness Retailer	Horse Sale Agency	Horsebox Hire	International Arena	Jockey	Jockey Supply	Photographer	Point-to-Point Course	Polo Pitch	Portraits	Racecourse Flat	Racecourse Steeplechase	Racing Investment	Repairs Rugs	Repairs Saddles	Riding Club	Rug Cleaning	Saddler	School (Indoor)	School (Outdoor)	Sculptor	Shipping Agent	Show Jump Course	Show Jumping arena	Stabling Centre	Tack Shop	Taxidermy	Trail Riding Centre	Transport	Transport Overseas	Trekking Centre	Valuer	Website design	Wheelwright
ELLIOT, GINNY, Middle Barton (YH04616)															●																																						
ELM OF BURFORD, Burford (YH04632)																																					●																	
EQUITOUR/PEREGRINE HOLIDAYS, Summertown (YH04832)													●																																									
ETHERINGTON-SMITH, MICHAEL, Banbury (YH04884)				●																																																		
FAURIE, E, Chipping Norton (YH05105)								●																																														
FIELD & FARM SADDLERS, Bicester (YH05182)																																	●	●		●	●																	
FRIAR PK EQUESTRIAN SUP, Henley-on-Thames (YH05500)																																					●																	
GITTINS, STEPHEN, Chipping Norton (YH05800)																					●																																	
GODINGTON STUD, Bicester (YH05867)					●			●							●																																						
HALL PLACE STABLES, Wantage (YH06308)																					●																																	
HIATT, P W, Banbury (YH06739)																																																●					
HINCHLIFFE, M, Faringdon (YH06866)																																																●	●				
HORSE DRAWN WEDDING CARRIAGES, Oxford (YH07119)											●																																										●
JODS GALORE, Henley-on-Thames (YH07775)																																	●	●			●								●								
JOHN ROWING SADDLERY, Banbury (YH07810)																																	●	●																			
KELLARD, SARAH, Over Norton (YH08040)															●																																						
KEN LANGFORD SADDLERY, Abingdon (YH08058)																																					●																	
KYLDANE FIELDSPORTS, Charlbury (YH08304)																																					●																	
LAW, GRAHAM, Chipping Norton (YH08469)															●																																						
MAD HATTER, Banbury (YH09018)																																					●																	
MALTHOUSE TRAINING CTRE, Abingdon (YH09059)																																												●									
MANOR FARM, Oxford (YH09096)																																												●									
MISTRAL, Cassington (YH09662)			●																																																			
N A S T A, Bicester (YH09986)															●																																						
NEW HOUSE LIVERY, Abingdon (YH10109)							●																																	●				●								●	
OUTWEAR, Oxford (YH10589)																																					●																	
OXFORD BOOTSTORE, Oxford (YH10616)																																					●																	
OXFORD HILL RUGS, Witney (YH10618)																																					●																	
PETER SMITH SADDLERY, Chipping Norton (YH11015)																																	●	●			●																	
PIGEON HOUSE STABLES, Witney (YH11095)																																								●							●			●			
PONYTEL, Banbury (YH11258)																																												●									
RYAN, MATT, Wantage (YH12286)															●																																						

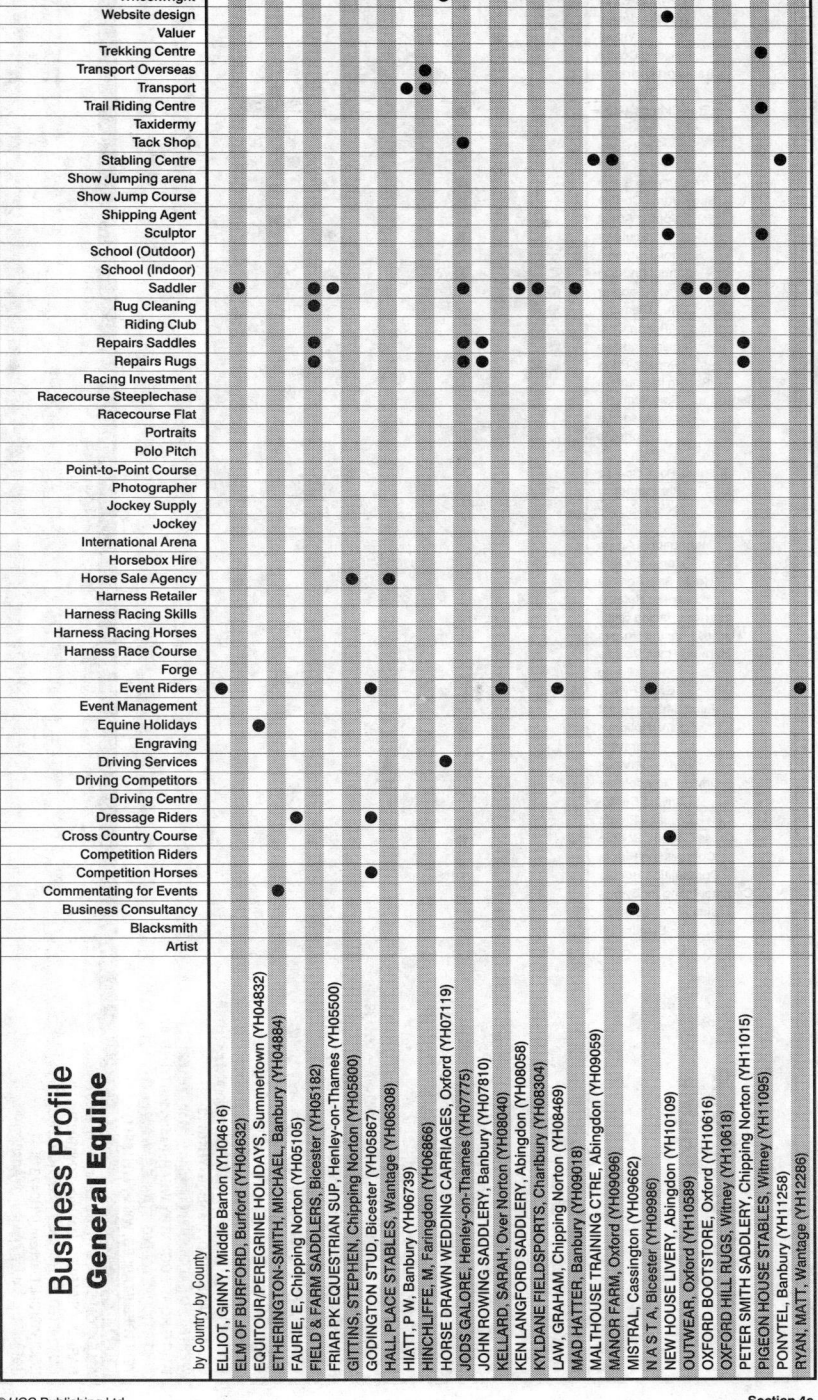

Business Profile

General Equine

by Country by County	Artist	Blacksmith	Business Consultancy	Commentating for Events	Competition Horses	Competition Riders	Cross Country Course	Dressage Riders	Driving Centre	Driving Competitors	Driving Services	Engraving	Equine Holidays	Event Management	Event Riders	Forge	Harness Race Course	Harness Racing Horses	Harness Racing Skills	Harness Retailer	Horse Sale Agency	Horsebox Hire	International Arena	Jockey	Jockey Supply	Photographer
RYCOTE FARMS, Oxford (YH12290)							●																			
SANSOMS SADDLERY, Witney (YH12429)																										
SCATS COUNTRYSTORE, Faringdon (YH12506)																										
SILVERDOWN, Didcot (YH12815)																										
SIMMONS, Henley-on-Thames (YH12824)			●																							
STABLE GEAR, Berrick Salome (YH13294)																										
STANDLAKE EQUESTRIAN CTRE, Witney (YH13362)							●						●													
STEPHANIE MEADOWS, Chipping Norton (YH13422)															●											
TACK & FEED SUPPLIES, Didcot (YH13776)																										
TACK SHOP, Carterton (YH13813)																										
TEDMAN HARNESS, Wheatley (YH13932)										●	●									●						
THAMES VALLEY TREKKING, Henley-on-Thames (YH13977)													●													
TUDOR PHOTOGRAPHY, Banbury (YH14441)																										
TURPINS LODGE, Banbury (YH14494)																										
UK CHASERS, Oxford (YH14544)							●																			
VALLEY FARM EQUESTRIAN CTRE, Banbury (YH14653)																										
VENTURENEED, Wallingford (YH14680)																										
W F S COUNTRY, Witney (YH14766)																										
WARDINGTON STUD FARM, Banbury (YH14913)																					●					
WATERSTOCK HSE TRAINING CTRE, Waterstock (YH14974)															●											
WERN FRANK STUD, Wantage (YH15113)															●											
WESTFIELD SADDLERY, Chipping Norton (YH15213)																										
WHITE HORSE COUNTRY WEAR, Faringdon (YH15307)																										
WHITE HORSE RIDING STABLES, Wantage (YH15311)													●													
YEW TREE STABLES, Witney (YH15911)																										
RUTLAND																										
ALLEXTON EQUESTRIAN, Oakham (YH00311)																					●					
BARROW STABLES, Oakham (YH01030)																										
COMPETITION HORSES, Oakham (YH03217)															●											
EQUI VISION, Oakham (YH04731)				●																						
JOHNSON, SALLY, Oakham (YH07839)																										
MANTON LODGE STABLES, Rutland (YH09127)							●																			

by Country by County	Point-to-Point Course	Polo Pitch	Portraits	Racecourse Flat	Racecourse Steeplechase	Racing Investment	Repairs Rugs	Repairs Saddles	Riding Club	Rug Cleaning	Saddler	School (Indoor)	School (Outdoor)	Sculptor	Shipping Agent	Show Jump Course	Show Jumping arena	Stabling Centre	Tack Shop	Taxidermy	Trail Riding Centre	Transport	Transport Overseas	Trekking Centre	Valuer	Website design	Wheelwright
RYCOTE FARMS, Oxford (YH12290)																											
SANSOMS SADDLERY, Witney (YH12429)							●	●		●	●								●								
SCATS COUNTRYSTORE, Faringdon (YH12506)							●			●																	
SILVERDOWN, Didcot (YH12815)																		●									
SIMMONS, Henley-on-Thames (YH12824)																									●		
STABLE GEAR, Berrick Salome (YH13294)											●																
STANDLAKE EQUESTRIAN CTRE, Witney (YH13362)												●		●			●	●			●						
STEPHANIE MEADOWS, Chipping Norton (YH13422)																											
TACK & FEED SUPPLIES, Didcot (YH13776)											●																
TACK SHOP, Carterton (YH13813)																			●								
TEDMAN HARNESS, Wheatley (YH13932)											●																
THAMES VALLEY TREKKING, Henley-on-Thames (YH13977)																											
TUDOR PHOTOGRAPHY, Banbury (YH14441)	●																										
TURPINS LODGE, Banbury (YH14494)												●		●		●	●	●									
UK CHASERS, Oxford (YH14544)																											
VALLEY FARM EQUESTRIAN CTRE, Banbury (YH14653)																		●									
VENTURENEED, Wallingford (YH14680)															●							●					
W F S COUNTRY, Witney (YH14766)											●																
WARDINGTON STUD FARM, Banbury (YH14913)																											
WATERSTOCK HSE TRAINING CTRE, Waterstock (YH14974)																											
WERN FRANK STUD, Wantage (YH15113)																											
WESTFIELD SADDLERY, Chipping Norton (YH15213)											●							●									
WHITE HORSE COUNTRY WEAR, Faringdon (YH15307)											●																
WHITE HORSE RIDING STABLES, Wantage (YH15311)																											
YEW TREE STABLES, Witney (YH15911)																		●									
RUTLAND																											
ALLEXTON EQUESTRIAN, Oakham (YH00311)																											
BARROW STABLES, Oakham (YH01030)																		●									
COMPETITION HORSES, Oakham (YH03217)																											
EQUI VISION, Oakham (YH04731)																											
JOHNSON, SALLY, Oakham (YH07839)							●	●		●	●																
MANTON LODGE STABLES, Rutland (YH09127)																		●									

Business Profile
General Equine

by Country by County

by Country by County	PURBRICK, LIZZIE, Oakham (YH11463)	SCURRY DRIVING ASSOCIATION, Oakham (YH12578)	UPPINGHAM DRESS AGENCY, Uppingham (YH14610)	SHROPSHIRE	BERRIEWOOD FARM, Shrewsbury (YH01313)	BOUNDARY GATE SADDLERY, Bridgnorth (YH01678)	BOW HOUSE FARM RIDING SCHOOL, Bishops Castle (YH01695)	BRANDON-LODGE, C, Church Stretton (YH01799)	BRI - TAC, Church Stretton (YH01858)	C J BLACKSMITHS, Shrewsbury (YH02375)	CAUGHLEY PORCELAIN, Shewsbury (YH02657)	CHARTERS, SUE, Ludlow (YH02776)	COUNTRYWIDE STORES, Bridgnorth (YH03469)	CRANN, P F, Bridgnorth (YH03568)	CRAZY HORSE SADDLERY, Ludlow (YH03582)	EQUEST, Market Drayton (YH04688)	EVANS, J C, Shrewsbury (YH04922)	HAMAR, ROSITA J, Bishops Castle (YH06343)	HANCOCK, J & V, Telford (YH06375)	HIGHGROVE SCHOOL OF RIDING, Craven Arms (YH06788)	HOORAY HENRY'S, Much Wenlock (YH07046)	HORN, CAMILLA, Bucknell (YH07072)	HORSE SHOP, Telford (YH07140)	HORSE SHOP, Bridgnorth (YH07139)	HOUSEMAKERS, Whitchurch (YH07210)	LILLESHALL EQUESTRIAN CTRE, Newport (YH08620)	LLOYDS ANIMAL FEEDS, Ludlow (YH08745)	MIDDLE FARM, Newport (YH09535)	MILL FARM RIDING CTRE, Shrewsbury (YH09572)	MYNDERLEY STABLES, All Stretton (YH09984)	N W F COUNTRYSTORE, Whitchurch (YH09999)	N W F COUNTRYSTORE, Market Drayton (YH09998)
Wheelwright																																
Website design																																
Valuer																																
Trekking Centre																																
Transport Overseas																																
Transport																	●															
Trail Riding Centre																																
Taxidermy																																
Tack Shop							●																						●			
Stabling Centre	●				●									●					●	●						●		●				
Show Jumping arena																																
Show Jump Course																				●												
Shipping Agent																																
Sculptor																				●												
School (Outdoor)											●																					
School (Indoor)																																
Saddler			●										●		●		●				●		●	●	●		●		●		●	●
Rug Cleaning																							●									
Riding Club																																
Repairs Saddles						●			●						●		●															
Repairs Rugs						●			●						●		●															
Racing Investment																																
Racecourse Steeplechase																																
Racecourse Flat																																
Portraits																																
Polo Pitch																																
Point-to-Point Course																						●										
Photographer																																
Jockey Supply																																
Jockey																																
International Arena																																
Horsebox Hire																	●															
Horse Sale Agency														●		●		●	●													
Harness Retailer																																
Harness Racing Skills																																
Harness Racing Horses																																
Harness Race Course																																
Forge										●																						
Event Riders	●											●																				
Event Management																																
Equine Holidays					●															●									●	●		
Engraving																																
Driving Services		●																														
Driving Competitors																																
Driving Centre																																
Dressage Riders																																
Cross Country Course																				●												
Competition Riders																																
Competition Horses								●										●														
Commentating for Events																																
Business Consultancy																																
Blacksmith										●																						
Artist											●																					

www.hccyourhorse.com

Business Profile
General Equine

by Country by County	Artist	Blacksmith	Business Consultancy	Commentating for Events	Competition Horses	Competition Riders	Cross Country Course	Dressage Riders	Driving Centre	Driving Competitors	Driving Services	Engraving	Equine Holidays	Event Management	Event Riders	Forge	Harness Race Course	Harness Racing Horses	Harness Racing Skills	Harness Retailer	Horse Sale Agency	Horsebox Hire	International Arena	Jockey	Jockey Supply	Photographer	Point-to-Point Course	Polo Pitch	Portraits	Racecourse Flat	Racecourse Steeplechase	Racing Investment	Repairs Rugs	Repairs Saddles	Riding Club	Rug Cleaning	Saddler	School (Indoor)	School (Outdoor)	Sculptor	Shipping Agent	Show Jump Course	Show Jumping arena	Stabling Centre	Tack Shop	Taxidermy	Trail Riding Centre	Transport	Transport Overseas	Trekking Centre	Valuer	Website design	Wheelwright
NATIONAL FOALING BANK, Newport (YH10037)				●																																																	
NOCK DEIGHTON AGRICULTURAL, Bridgnorth (YH10225)																																																			●		
NUTSHELL, Bridgnorth (YH10360)																																					●																
OAKAGE RIDING CTRE, Shrewsbury (YH10372)													●																																								
OSWESTRY EQUEST CTRE, Oswestry (YH10576)					●	●							●		●																							●		●		●		●									
P G L YOUNG ADVENTURE CTRE, Shrewsbury (YH10641)													●																																								
PENYCOED RIDING STABLES, Oswestry (YH10966)													●																																								
POLLY FLINDERS, Ludlow (YH11207)																																					●																
PRESCOTT RIDING CTRE, Shrewsbury (YH11356)													●																															●									
PRINCE & DOYLE, Ludlow (YH11397)																																					●																
SHERBOURNE TACK, Ludlow (YH12719)																																					●																
SLATER, M, Market Drayton (YH12891)													●																																								
STABLES SADDLERY & FEED SHOP, Shrewsbury (YH13313)																																					●																
T JONES & SON, Oswestry (YH13755)																																					●																
TERRY DAVIS, Craven Arms (YH13957)																				●																																	
TONG RIDING CTRE, Shifnal (YH14227)													●																									●		●		●											
TOUCHDOWN LIVERIES, Whitchurch (YH14253)																																				●		●		●				●									
TRENCH VILLA STABLES, Ellesmere (YH14374)																																												●									
W BRYAN HORSE SERVICES, Shrewsbury (YH14753)					●																																																
WACKLEY LODGE FARM, Shrewsbury (YH14804)																					●																																
WALFORD COLLEGE, Shrewsbury (YH14842)							●																																														
WILLIAM WILLIAMS, Bridgnorth (YH15439)																																					●																
WOOD FARM STUD, Wellington (YH15657)																																												●									
WYKE OF SHIFNAL, Shifnal (YH15863)																																	●	●			●							●									
SOMERSET																																																					
A W MIDGLEY & SON, Cheddar (YH00067)																																					●																
ADSBOROUGH HSE STABLES, Taunton (YH00189)																																								●				●									
ALSTONE COURT RIDING ESTB, Highbridge (YH00342)																																													●								
ANDREWS, R T, Dulverton (YH00402)																					●																																
ANGELA BROMWICH, Cheddar (YH00407)																																	●	●			●																
ARMSTRONG, BRIAN, Wincanton (YH00546)																											●																										
ASH, RICHARD W J, Somerton (YH00589)		●																																																			

Business Profile
General Equine

by Country by County

Business	Artist	Blacksmith	Business Consultancy	Commentating for Events	Competition Horses	Competition Riders	Cross Country Course	Dressage Riders	Driving Centre	Driving Competitors	Driving Services	Engraving	Equine Holidays	Event Management	Event Riders	Forge	Harness Race Course	Harness Racing Horses	Harness Racing Skills	Harness Retailer	Horse Sale Agency	Horsebox Hire	International Arena	Jockey	Jockey Supply	Photographer	Point-to-Point Course	Polo Pitch	Portraits	Racecourse Flat	Racecourse Steeplechase	Racing Investment	Repairs Rugs	Repairs Saddles	Riding Club	Rug Cleaning	Saddler	School (Indoor)	School (Outdoor)	Sculptor	Shipping Agent	Show Jump Course	Show Jumping arena	Stabling Centre	Tack Shop	Taxidermy	Trail Riding Centre	Transport	Transport Overseas	Trekking Centre	Valuer	Website design	Wheelwright
BADCOCK & EVERED, Watchet (YH00774)																																	●	●		●	●																
BOWERS, HENRY, Chard (YH01707)																																													●								
BRAKE, V, Ilminster (YH01784)																					●																																
BRENDON HILL, Watchet (YH01836)					●																																																
BRIMSMORE EQUESTRIAN CTRE, Yeovil (YH01913)							●																															●		●													
BURCOTT RIDING CTRE, Wells (YH02236)							●																																	●													
BURCOTT RIDING CTRE, Wells (YH02235)																																												●									
BURROWHAYES FARM, Porlock (YH02282)													●																																								
COUNTRY TRADING, Glastonbury (YH03432)																																					●																
COURT FARM STABLES, Exford (YH03502)													●																															●									
CROWN HOTEL, Minehead (YH03681)													●																															●									
DRAKES FARM, Ilminster (YH04256)							●						●																									●		●		●											
DRAYDON FARM, Dulverton (YH04262)																																												●									
DUNKERY, Minehead (YH04343)													●																															●									
EBBORLANDS, Wells (YH04529)													●																																								
EDGCOTT HSE, Exford (YH04554)													●																																								
EXMOOR WHITE HORSE INN, Minehead (YH04970)													●																																								
HINDON FARM, Minehead (YH06873)													●																																								
HORNER FARM RIDING STABLES, Minehead (YH07077)													●																																								
HORSESHOE FARM, Bruton (YH07173)																				●																																	
JEREMY FRANKS TACK REPAIRS, Templecombe (YH07752)																																	●	●																			
JOHN MCDONALD, Dulverton (YH07800)																				●																																	
KIT HOUGHTON PHOTOGRAPHY, Bridgwater (YH08244)																											●																										
KNOWLE MANOR, Minehead (YH08281)							●						●																																					●			
LONG LANE RIDING STABLES, Wincanton (YH08796)																																												●									
MAYTREE FARM FEEDS, Shepton Mallet (YH09307)																						●											●	●		●	●											●					
MCCOY SADDLERY, Minehead (YH09334)																																	●	●			●								●								
MILL FARM CARAVAN & CAMP SITE, Bridgwater (YH09570)													●																																								
MILLHOUSE EQUESTRIAN CTRE, Taunton (YH09620)																																												●									
MINEHEAD HARRIERS & FOXHOUNDS, Templecombe (YH09649)																																													●								
MOLE VALLEY FARMERS, Frome (YH09711)																																					●																
NEWMAN, SOPHIE, Crewkerne (YH10152)															●																																						

Business Profile
General Equine

by Country by County

by Country by County	Artist	Blacksmith	Business Consultancy	Commentating for Events	Competition Horses	Competition Riders	Cross Country Course	Dressage Riders	Driving Centre	Driving Competitors	Driving Services	Engraving	Equine Holidays	Event Management	Event Riders	Forge	Harness Race Course	Harness Racing Horses
PARKER, KATIE, Frome (YH10750)															●			
PINE LODGE RIDING HOLIDAY, Dulverton (YH11119)													●					
POPHAMS, Highbridge (YH11268)																		
PORLOCK VALE HSE/RIDING CTRE, Porlock Weir (YH11278)													●					
RICH & SON, Bridgwater (YH11798)																		
RIDEMOOR, Wincanton (YH11852)																		
RISCOMBE FARM, Minehead (YH11908)																		
RODGROVE STUD EQUESTRIAN CTRE, Wincanton (YH12048)													●					
ROSE MILL FEEDS, Ilminster (YH12094)																		
ROYAL OAK INN, Withypool (YH12189)													●					
ROYS RIDING SCHOOL, Taunton (YH12201)																		
SARAH ANHOLT, Bridgwater (YH12433)																		
SCOTTS RIDING STABLES, Bridgwater (YH12562)													●					
SHRUB FARM LIVERY YARD, Brent Knoll (YH12771)																		
STABLE DOOR TRADING, Wrantage (YH13292)																		
STAX SADDLERY, Montacute (YH13406)																		
STOCKLAND LOVELL, Bridgwater (YH13493)							●											
SUTTON OAKS, Bridgwater (YH13675)					●													
TAKEL, FRANCES, Dulverton (YH13827)																		
THORNEY COPSE, Wincanton (YH14066)																		
TUFTERS, Winsford (YH14447)													●					
UNICORN SADDLERY, Taunton (YH14569)																		
W.E.S GARRETT MASTER SADDLERS, Cheddar (YH14803)																		
WEST ANSTEY FARM EXMOOR, Dulverton (YH15124)													●					
WINDMILL HILL EQUESTRIAN CTRE, Ilminster (YH15566)							●								●			
WOOLCOTTS FARM, Dulverton (YH15765)													●					
SOMERSET (NORTH)																		
CARNABY, IAN, Nailsea (YH02562)				●														
CLEVEDON RIDING, Clevedon (YH03020)							●											
CTRE RIDING SCHOOL, Weston-Super-Mare (YH03696)																		
HAND EQUESTRIAN CTRE, Clevedon (YH06377)																		
MENDIP RIDING CTRE, Churchill (YH09458)							●						●					

by Country by County	Harness Racing Skills	Harness Retailer	Horse Sale Agency	Horsebox Hire	International Arena	Jockey	Jockey Supply	Photographer	Point-to-Point Course	Polo Pitch	Portraits	Racecourse Flat	Racecourse Steeplechase	Racing Investment	Repairs Rugs	Repairs Saddles	Riding Club	Rug Cleaning
PARKER, KATIE, Frome (YH10750)																		
PINE LODGE RIDING HOLIDAY, Dulverton (YH11119)																		
POPHAMS, Highbridge (YH11268)																		
PORLOCK VALE HSE/RIDING CTRE, Porlock Weir (YH11278)																		
RICH & SON, Bridgwater (YH11798)		●																
RIDEMOOR, Wincanton (YH11852)							●								●	●		●
RISCOMBE FARM, Minehead (YH11908)																		
RODGROVE STUD EQUESTRIAN CTRE, Wincanton (YH12048)																		
ROSE MILL FEEDS, Ilminster (YH12094)															●	●		●
ROYAL OAK INN, Withypool (YH12189)																		
ROYS RIDING SCHOOL, Taunton (YH12201)																		
SARAH ANHOLT, Bridgwater (YH12433)															●	●		
SCOTTS RIDING STABLES, Bridgwater (YH12562)																		
SHRUB FARM LIVERY YARD, Brent Knoll (YH12771)																		
STABLE DOOR TRADING, Wrantage (YH13292)																		
STAX SADDLERY, Montacute (YH13406)															●	●		●
STOCKLAND LOVELL, Bridgwater (YH13493)																		
SUTTON OAKS, Bridgwater (YH13675)				●														
TAKEL, FRANCES, Dulverton (YH13827)															●	●		
THORNEY COPSE, Wincanton (YH14066)															●	●		●
TUFTERS, Winsford (YH14447)																		
UNICORN SADDLERY, Taunton (YH14569)															●	●		
W.E.S GARRETT MASTER SADDLERS, Cheddar (YH14803)		●					●								●	●		●
WEST ANSTEY FARM EXMOOR, Dulverton (YH15124)																		
WINDMILL HILL EQUESTRIAN CTRE, Ilminster (YH15566)																		
WOOLCOTTS FARM, Dulverton (YH15765)																		
SOMERSET (NORTH)																		
CARNABY, IAN, Nailsea (YH02562)																		
CLEVEDON RIDING, Clevedon (YH03020)																		
CTRE RIDING SCHOOL, Weston-Super-Mare (YH03696)																		
HAND EQUESTRIAN CTRE, Clevedon (YH06377)																		
MENDIP RIDING CTRE, Churchill (YH09458)																		

by Country by County	Saddler	School (Indoor)	School (Outdoor)	Sculptor	Shipping Agent	Show Jump Course	Show Jumping arena	Stabling Centre	Tack Shop	Taxidermy	Trail Riding Centre	Transport	Transport Overseas	Trekking Centre	Valuer	Website design	Wheelwright
PARKER, KATIE, Frome (YH10750)																	
PINE LODGE RIDING HOLIDAY, Dulverton (YH11119)																	
POPHAMS, Highbridge (YH11268)	●																
PORLOCK VALE HSE/RIDING CTRE, Porlock Weir (YH11278)																	
RICH & SON, Bridgwater (YH11798)	●																
RIDEMOOR, Wincanton (YH11852)	●								●								
RISCOMBE FARM, Minehead (YH11908)								●									
RODGROVE STUD EQUESTRIAN CTRE, Wincanton (YH12048)								●									
ROSE MILL FEEDS, Ilminster (YH12094)									●								
ROYAL OAK INN, Withypool (YH12189)																	
ROYS RIDING SCHOOL, Taunton (YH12201)				●													
SARAH ANHOLT, Bridgwater (YH12433)	●																
SCOTTS RIDING STABLES, Bridgwater (YH12562)								●									
SHRUB FARM LIVERY YARD, Brent Knoll (YH12771)								●									
STABLE DOOR TRADING, Wrantage (YH13292)	●																
STAX SADDLERY, Montacute (YH13406)									●								
STOCKLAND LOVELL, Bridgwater (YH13493)				●			●										
SUTTON OAKS, Bridgwater (YH13675)												●					
TAKEL, FRANCES, Dulverton (YH13827)																	
THORNEY COPSE, Wincanton (YH14066)	●								●								
TUFTERS, Winsford (YH14447)																	
UNICORN SADDLERY, Taunton (YH14569)	●																
W.E.S GARRETT MASTER SADDLERS, Cheddar (YH14803)	●								●								
WEST ANSTEY FARM EXMOOR, Dulverton (YH15124)																	
WINDMILL HILL EQUESTRIAN CTRE, Ilminster (YH15566)								●									
WOOLCOTTS FARM, Dulverton (YH15765)																	
SOMERSET (NORTH)																	
CARNABY, IAN, Nailsea (YH02562)																	
CLEVEDON RIDING, Clevedon (YH03020)				●													
CTRE RIDING SCHOOL, Weston-Super-Mare (YH03696)				●													
HAND EQUESTRIAN CTRE, Clevedon (YH06377)		●		●			●	●									
MENDIP RIDING CTRE, Churchill (YH09458)				●		●	●							●			

Business Profile
General Equine

by Country by County	Artist	Blacksmith	Business Consultancy	Commentating for Events	Competition Horses	Competition Riders	Cross Country Course	Dressage Riders	Driving Centre	Driving Competitors	Driving Services	Engraving	Equine Holidays	Event Management	Event Riders	Forge	Harness Race Course	Harness Racing Horses	Harness Racing Skills	Harness Retailer	Horse Sale Agency	Horsebox Hire	International Arena	Jockey	Jockey Supply	Photographer	Point-to-Point Course	Polo Pitch	Portraits	Racecourse Flat	Racecourse Steeplechase	Racing Investment	Repairs Rugs	Repairs Saddles	Riding Club	Rug Cleaning	Saddler	School (Indoor)	School (Outdoor)	Sculptor	Shipping Agent	Show Jump Course	Show Jumping arena	Stabling Centre	Tack Shop	Taxidermy	Trail Riding Centre	Transport	Transport Overseas	Trekking Centre	Valuer	Website design	Wheelwright
MURPHYS SADDLERY, Weston-Super-Mare (YH09961)																																					●																
SHIPHAM RIDING HOLIDAYS, Winscombe (YH12748)													●																																								
SMART, JAYNE, Banwell (YH12922)															●																													●									
SOUTHFIELD FARM RIDING SCHOOL, Backwell (YH13150)																																												●									
VOWLES RIDING STABLES, Weston-Super-Mare (YH14744)																																					●							●									
WORLEBURY LIVERY CTRE, Weston-Super-Mare (YH15790)													●																																								
STAFFORDSHIRE																																																					
ABNALLS FARM, Lichfield (YH00133)																																					●							●									
ALSAGER EQUESTRIAN CTRE, Stoke-on-Trent (YH00335)							●																																					●									
ANSLOW, JENNIFER R, Wolverhampton (YH00459)																											●																										
ASHMORE BROOK DAIRY FARM, Lichfield (YH00609)																																												●									
BALLANTYNE, TONI, Eccleshall (YH00854)																											●																										
BARLASTON RIDING CTRE, Stoke-on-Trent (YH00949)							●																															●					●										
BENTLEY HSE, Biddulph Park (YH01285)																																												●									
BOLTON GATE SADDLERY, Stoke-on-Trent (YH01609)																																					●																
BOWDLER, T, Stafford (YH01697)																					●																																
BROOKES, JOSEPHINE, Stafford (YH02045)																					●																																
BROWN, CAROLINE, Burton-on-Trent (YH02104)															●																																						
C A DAVIES & SONS, Uttoxeter (YH02361)																																					●																
CANNOCK CHASE TREKKING CTRE, Stafford (YH02504)																																																		●			
CHEADLE EQUESTRIAN CTRE, Stoke-on-Trent (YH02795)																																												●									
COPPICE EQUESTRIAN SADDLERY, Farley (YH03303)																																					●							●									
COX, ROBERT, Stafford (YH03536)	●																																																				
DAISY LANE LIVERY YARD, Burton-on-Trent (YH03816)																																												●									
DAVID LEWIS INT, Burton-on-Trent (YH03922)																																									●							●					
DAVISON, RICHARD, Uttoxeter (YH03959)								●																																				●									
DOBBINS DINER, Tamworth (YH04151)					●			●							●																														●								
DOSTHILL SADDLERY, Tamworth (YH04209)																																	●	●		●	●																
ELLMORE HORSE TRANSPORT, Lichfield (YH04630)																																																●					
ENDON RIDING SCHOOL, Stoke-on-Trent (YH04667)													●								●																							●									
EQUI TEC, Dudley (YH04729)																																					●																
EQUINE CLEANING SVS, Burton-on-Trent (YH04769)																																				●																	

Business Profile
General Equine

by Country by County	Artist	Blacksmith	Business Consultancy	Commentating for Events	Competition Horses	Competition Riders	Cross Country Course	Dressage Riders	Driving Centre	Driving Competitors	Driving Services	Engraving	Equine Holidays	Event Management	Event Riders	Forge	Harness Race Course	Harness Racing Horses	Harness Racing Skills	Harness Retailer	Horse Sale Agency	Horsebox Hire	International Arena	Jockey	Jockey Supply	Photographer	Point-to-Point Course	Polo Pitch	Portraits	Racecourse Flat	Racecourse Steeplechase	Racing Investment	Repairs Rugs	Repairs Saddles	Riding Club	Rug Cleaning	Saddler	School (Indoor)	School (Outdoor)	Sculptor	Shipping Agent	Show Jump Course	Show Jumping arena	Stabling Centre	Tack Shop	Taxidermy	Trail Riding Centre	Transport	Transport Overseas	Trekking Centre	Valuer	Website design	Wheelwright
FRANCES ANN BROWN SADDLERY, Stafford (YH05444)																																				●	●								●								
GOTHERSLEY FARM, Stourbridge (YH05945)																																					●							●									
GUNSTONE HALL RIDING CTRE, Wolverhampton (YH06192)																																												●									
H WOOLLEY & SON, Uttoxeter (YH06247)																				●													●	●																			
HEART OF ENGLAND EQUESTRIAN, Stone (YH06617)																																												●									
HORSEY THINGS, Eccleshall (YH07184)																																				●	●																
INDESPENSION, Stoke-on-Trent (YH07431)																						●																															
INGESTRE STABLES, Stafford (YH07445)																																												●									
INTERNATIONAL PERFORMANCE, Brewde (YH07477)																					●																																
JONES, COLIN, Burntwood (YH07883)																											●																										
JONES, SUZANNE, Cannock (YH07933)																											●																										
LADYMOOR GATE, Stoke-on-Trent (YH08339)																																												●									
LARKHILL SADDLERY, Burton-on-Trent (YH08432)																				●													●	●		●	●								●								
MOW-COP RIDING CTRE, Stoke-on-Trent (YH09905)													●																																								
OFFLEY BROOK LIVERY STABLES, Eccleshall (YH10436)							●																																					●									
PEGASUS SADDLERY, Newcastle (YH10907)																																					●																
POSH PONIES, Stoke-on-Trent (YH11297)																																	●	●		●	●																
POUND CLOSE STABLES, Gillingham (YH11306)													●																																								
RODBASTON CLGE, Penkridge (YH12041)																																											●										
SCROPTON, Burton-on-Trent (YH12569)					●	●		●	●	●	●		●																						●			●		●			●	●									
SEABROOK FEEDS, Sedgley (YH12580)																					●																●																
SMITH & MORRIS COUNTRY STORE, Newcastle (YH12933)																																				●	●							●									
WOFFORD INT HORSE TRANSPORT, Lichfield (YH15643)																																									●							●					
SUFFOLK																																																					
ANGLIA HORSE TRANSPORT, Ipswich (YH00413)																																																●					
BALLINGDON SADDLERY, Sudbury (YH00857)																																		●																			
BENTLEY RIDING CTRE, Ipswich (YH01286)																																						●															
BOB JONES, Newmarket (YH01587)																																																●					
BRANDON RIDING ACADEMY, Brandon (YH01797)																																												●									
BRIDLE PATH, Bury St Edmunds (YH01891)																																					●																
BRITISH BLOODSTOCK AGENCY, Newmarket (YH01929)																																																●	●				
CARRIAGE OCCASIONS, Red Lodge (YH02581)											●																																										

Business Profile
General Equine

by Country by County

Company	Artist	Blacksmith	Business Consultancy	Commentating for Events	Competition Horses	Competition Riders	Cross Country Course	Dressage Riders	Driving Centre	Driving Competitors	Driving Services	Engraving	Equine Holidays	Event Management	Event Riders	Forge	Harness Race Course	Harness Racing Horses	Harness Racing Skills	Harness Retailer	Horse Sale Agency	Horsebox Hire	International Arena	Jockey	Jockey Supply	Photographer	Point-to-Point Course	Polo Pitch	Portraits	Racecourse Flat	Racecourse Steeplechase	Racing Investment	Repairs Rugs	Repairs Saddles	Riding Club	Rug Cleaning	Saddler	School (Indoor)	School (Outdoor)	Sculptor	Shipping Agent	Show Jump Course	Show Jumping arena	Stabling Centre	Tack Shop	Taxidermy	Trail Riding Centre	Transport	Transport Overseas	Trekking Centre	Valuer	Website design	Wheelwright
CHIMNEY MILL GALLERIES, Bury St Edmunds (YH02862)																																												●									
COLORLABS INT, Newmarket (YH03198)																											●																										
CURRAGH BLOODSTOCK AGENCY, Newmarket (YH03734)																																									●												
D & D EQUESTRIAN, Lowestoft (YH03768)																																					●																
DALY, G M, Newmarket (YH03851)																				●																																	
EARLSWAY FARM, Halesworth (YH04454)																																												●									
FBA, Newmarket (YH05113)																																									●												
FRANK HARVEY INT, Stowmarket (YH05458)																																	●	●																			
GIBSON SADDLERS, Newmarket (YH05746)																																	●	●		●																	
GOLDING & SON, Newmarket (YH05891)																																					●																
GROVE FARM DRIVING & LIVERY, Mildenhall (YH06166)									●		●																																	●									
HERITAGE COAST STUD, Woodbridge (YH06703)					●										●																																					●	
HERRINGSWELL BLOODSTOCK CTRE, Bury St Edmunds (YH06717)						●																																								●							
HOEG-MUDD, CLEA, Woodbridge (YH06917)															●																																						
HOOFBEATS, Newmarket (YH07029)													●																																								
HORSE & GARDEN, Halesworth (YH07089)																																	●	●			●																
HORSE REQUISITES, Newmarket (YH07132)												●																									●																
HORSESHOES, Wrentham (YH07174)																																					●																
HTL, Bury St Edmunds (YH07249)																																																●	●				
HUGHES RACEHORSE TRANSPORT, Newmarket (YH07256)																																																●					
INDESPENSION, Ipswich (YH07432)																						●																															
INT RACEHORSE TRANSPORT, Newmarket (YH07472)																																									●							●					
J.SAVILL INT HORSE TRANSPORT, Newmarket (YH07635)																																									●								●				
JOHN SNOWDON HARNESS MAKER, Woodbridge (YH07813)										●	●									●																																	
L S K, Bury St Edmunds (YH08327)																																																			●		
L S K, Stowmarket (YH08326)																																																			●		
LAURELS, Bury St Edmunds (YH08459)													●																																								
LAVENHAM HALL LIVERIES, Lavenham (YH08462)																																												●									
LONG MELFORD, Sudbury (YH08799)																																	●	●			●								●								
M C INT HORSE TRANSPORT, Newmarket (YH08956)																																																●	●				
MARCH EQUESTRIAN FRAMLINGHAM, Woodbridge (YH09140)																																					●																

Business Profile
General Equine

by Country by County

Business	Artist	Blacksmith	Business Consultancy	Commentating for Events	Competition Horses	Competition Riders	Cross Country Course	Dressage Riders	Driving Centre	Driving Competitors	Driving Services	Engraving	Equine Holidays	Event Management	Event Riders	Forge
MIKE DANIELL, Woodbridge (YH09564)											●		●			
MILL SADDLERY, Stowmarket (YH09587)																
NATIONAL STUD, Newmarket (YH10045)													●			
NEWMARKET PHOTONEWS AGENCY, Bury St Edmunds (YH10156)																
NEWTON HALL EQUITATION CTRE, Ipswich (YH10171)													●			
ORWELL ARENA, Ipswich (YH10556)					●			●								
PAKEFIELD RIDING SCHOOL, Lowestoft (YH10687)																
PARK FARM, Harleston (YH10718)																
PARK FARM STABLES, Newmarket (YH10724)																
POPLAR PK, Woodbridge (YH11271)							●						●			
POTTERS TYE, Sudbury (YH11301)																
R MILES SADDLER & HARNESS, Woodbridge (YH11557)																
R T'S SADDLERY, Newmarket (YH11567)																
RAPIDO HORSE SERVICES, Newmarket (YH11640)																
REYNOLDS, GERRY, Newmarket (YH11778)												●				
RIDE AWAY SADDLERY, Ipswich (YH11846)																
RIDE 'N' DRIVE EQUESTRIAN SUP, Beccles (YH11848)																
RYLAND SADDLERS, Newmarket (YH12305)																
SAMPSON, LESLEY, Newmarket (YH12399)																
SHADOWFAX STABLE, Newmarket (YH12655)																
STABLECARE, Newmarket (YH13301)																
STOKE BY CLARE EQUESTRIAN CTRE, Sudbury (YH13501)					●	●		●					●		●	
STOWE ANIMAL HEALTH, Stowmarket (YH13537)																
SUFFOLK SADDLES, Ipswich (YH13626)																
SWIFT MANOR FARM, Sudbury (YH13706)																
TOLLGATE LIVERY CTRE, Felixstowe (YH14211)																
TWINSTEAD RIDING SCHOOL, Sudbury (YH14514)													●			
UGGLESHALL, Beccles (YH14541)							●				●		●			
VALLEY FARM, Woodbridge (YH14651)									●							
WALROND, SALLIE, Bury St Edmunds (YH14871)									●		●					
WILLIAMS, C M, Newmarket (YH15451)																
WOODLANDS, Bury St Edmunds (YH15707)																

Business	Harness Race Course	Harness Racing Horses	Harness Racing Skills	Harness Retailer	Horse Sale Agency	Horsebox Hire	International Arena	Jockey	Jockey Supply	Photographer	Point-to-Point Course	Polo Pitch	Portraits	Racecourse Flat	Racecourse Steeplechase	Racing Investment	Repairs Rugs	Repairs Saddles	Riding Club
MIKE DANIELL, Woodbridge (YH09564)																			
MILL SADDLERY, Stowmarket (YH09587)																	●	●	
NATIONAL STUD, Newmarket (YH10045)																			
NEWMARKET PHOTONEWS AGENCY, Bury St Edmunds (YH10156)												●							
NEWTON HALL EQUITATION CTRE, Ipswich (YH10171)																			
ORWELL ARENA, Ipswich (YH10556)																			
PAKEFIELD RIDING SCHOOL, Lowestoft (YH10687)																			
PARK FARM, Harleston (YH10718)																			
PARK FARM STABLES, Newmarket (YH10724)																			
POPLAR PK, Woodbridge (YH11271)																			
POTTERS TYE, Sudbury (YH11301)																			
R MILES SADDLER & HARNESS, Woodbridge (YH11557)				●													●	●	
R T'S SADDLERY, Newmarket (YH11567)																	●	●	
RAPIDO HORSE SERVICES, Newmarket (YH11640)																			
REYNOLDS, GERRY, Newmarket (YH11778)																	●	●	
RIDE AWAY SADDLERY, Ipswich (YH11846)																			
RIDE 'N' DRIVE EQUESTRIAN SUP, Beccles (YH11848)																	●	●	
RYLAND SADDLERS, Newmarket (YH12305)																		●	
SAMPSON, LESLEY, Newmarket (YH12399)											●								
SHADOWFAX STABLE, Newmarket (YH12655)					●														
STABLECARE, Newmarket (YH13301)																			
STOKE BY CLARE EQUESTRIAN CTRE, Sudbury (YH13501)					●														
STOWE ANIMAL HEALTH, Stowmarket (YH13537)																			
SUFFOLK SADDLES, Ipswich (YH13626)																		●	
SWIFT MANOR FARM, Sudbury (YH13706)					●														
TOLLGATE LIVERY CTRE, Felixstowe (YH14211)																			
TWINSTEAD RIDING SCHOOL, Sudbury (YH14514)																			
UGGLESHALL, Beccles (YH14541)																			
VALLEY FARM, Woodbridge (YH14651)																			
WALROND, SALLIE, Bury St Edmunds (YH14871)																			
WILLIAMS, C M, Newmarket (YH15451)											●								
WOODLANDS, Bury St Edmunds (YH15707)																			

Business	Rug Cleaning	Saddler	School (Indoor)	School (Outdoor)	Sculptor	Shipping Agent	Show Jump Course	Show Jumping arena	Stabling Centre	Tack Shop	Taxidermy	Trail Riding Centre	Transport	Transport Overseas	Trekking Centre	Valuer	Website design	Wheelwright
MIKE DANIELL, Woodbridge (YH09564)																		
MILL SADDLERY, Stowmarket (YH09587)	●	●																
NATIONAL STUD, Newmarket (YH10045)																		
NEWMARKET PHOTONEWS AGENCY, Bury St Edmunds (YH10156)																		
NEWTON HALL EQUITATION CTRE, Ipswich (YH10171)									●									
ORWELL ARENA, Ipswich (YH10556)			●		●			●	●				●					
PAKEFIELD RIDING SCHOOL, Lowestoft (YH10687)			●		●		●											
PARK FARM, Harleston (YH10718)									●									
PARK FARM STABLES, Newmarket (YH10724)									●									
POPLAR PK, Woodbridge (YH11271)									●									
POTTERS TYE, Sudbury (YH11301)									●									
R MILES SADDLER & HARNESS, Woodbridge (YH11557)		●																
R T'S SADDLERY, Newmarket (YH11567)																		
RAPIDO HORSE SERVICES, Newmarket (YH11640)						●							●					
REYNOLDS, GERRY, Newmarket (YH11778)	●																	
RIDE AWAY SADDLERY, Ipswich (YH11846)										●								
RIDE 'N' DRIVE EQUESTRIAN SUP, Beccles (YH11848)		●																
RYLAND SADDLERS, Newmarket (YH12305)																		
SAMPSON, LESLEY, Newmarket (YH12399)																		
SHADOWFAX STABLE, Newmarket (YH12655)													●					
STABLECARE, Newmarket (YH13301)	●																	
STOKE BY CLARE EQUESTRIAN CTRE, Sudbury (YH13501)			●		●				●	●								
STOWE ANIMAL HEALTH, Stowmarket (YH13537)		●																
SUFFOLK SADDLES, Ipswich (YH13626)		●																
SWIFT MANOR FARM, Sudbury (YH13706)																		
TOLLGATE LIVERY CTRE, Felixstowe (YH14211)									●									
TWINSTEAD RIDING SCHOOL, Sudbury (YH14514)																		
UGGLESHALL, Beccles (YH14541)									●									
VALLEY FARM, Woodbridge (YH14651)			●														●	
WALROND, SALLIE, Bury St Edmunds (YH14871)																		
WILLIAMS, C M, Newmarket (YH15451)																		
WOODLANDS, Bury St Edmunds (YH15707)									●									

Business Profile
General Equine

by Country by County

	Artist	Blacksmith	Business Consultancy	Commentating for Events	Competition Horses	Competition Riders	Cross Country Course	Dressage Riders	Driving Centre	Driving Competitors	Driving Services	Engraving	Equine Holidays	Event Management	Event Riders	Forge
WOOLMER COTTAGE STABLES, Newmarket (YH15768)																
SURREY																
ANNA'S CTRY STORE, Farnham (YH00455)																
ASCOT PARK, Woking (YH00583)			●	●	●	●							●	●		
B & R INT HORSE TRANSPORT, Farnham (YH00714)																
BARKER, J, Chessington (YH00943)																
BARNES, PAT, Woking (YH00979)							●									
BEECHWOOD, Caterham (YH01176)																
BERKELEY EQUESTRIAN SVS, Kingswood (YH01301)																
BITS & PIECES, Sunbury-on-Thames (YH01457)																
BRIDLEWAYS EQUESTRIAN CTRE, Great Bookham (YH01898)																
BROOMELLS WORKSHOP, Dorking (YH02077)																
BURSTOW PK, Horley (YH02286)																
BUTTONS SADDLERY, Woking (YH02337)																
CHALK PIT FARM STABLES, Leatherhead (YH02711)																
CHAMBERS, G W, Guildford (YH02718)																
CHASE FARM, Hindhead (YH02780)																
CHESSINGTON, Chessington (YH02830)																
CHIPPINGS FARM STABLES, Cobham (YH02866)																
CHOBHAM CHASERS CROSS COUNTRY, Woking (YH02873)							●									
CLANDON MANOR SUPPLIES, Guildford (YH02942)																
CLAYGATE SPORTS HORSES, Esher (YH03000)					●											
CLOCK TOWER RIDING CTRE, Tadworth (YH03052)																
CLUB PRO-AM, Richmond (YH03074)																
COE, NICOLA, Dorking (YH03133)															●	
COUNTRYWIDE STORES, Redhill (YH03473)																
COURTLANDS LIVERY STABLES, Banstead (YH03508)																
CRANHAM, GERRY, Coulsdon (YH03564)																
CRANLEIGH SCHOOL OF RIDING, Cranleigh (YH03565)						●									●	
CROFTS, ANDY, Albury (YH03625)															●	
DORKING EQUESTRIAN CTRE, Dorking (YH04200)																
DUNSFOLD RYSE STABLES, Chiddingfold (YH04357)							●									

	Harness Race Course	Harness Racing Horses	Harness Racing Skills	Harness Retailer	Horse Sale Agency	Horsebox Hire	International Arena	Jockey	Jockey Supply	Photographer	Point-to-Point Course	Polo Pitch	Portraits	Racecourse Flat	Racecourse Steeplechase	Racing Investment	Repairs Rugs	Repairs Saddles
WOOLMER COTTAGE STABLES, Newmarket (YH15768)																		
SURREY																		
ANNA'S CTRY STORE, Farnham (YH00455)																		
ASCOT PARK, Woking (YH00583)				●		●						●						
B & R INT HORSE TRANSPORT, Farnham (YH00714)																		
BARKER, J, Chessington (YH00943)																		
BARNES, PAT, Woking (YH00979)																		
BEECHWOOD, Caterham (YH01176)							●											
BERKELEY EQUESTRIAN SVS, Kingswood (YH01301)																		
BITS & PIECES, Sunbury-on-Thames (YH01457)																		
BRIDLEWAYS EQUESTRIAN CTRE, Great Bookham (YH01898)																		
BROOMELLS WORKSHOP, Dorking (YH02077)																	●	●
BURSTOW PK, Horley (YH02286)																		
BUTTONS SADDLERY, Woking (YH02337)																	●	●
CHALK PIT FARM STABLES, Leatherhead (YH02711)																		
CHAMBERS, G W, Guildford (YH02718)																		
CHASE FARM, Hindhead (YH02780)																		
CHESSINGTON, Chessington (YH02830)																		
CHIPPINGS FARM STABLES, Cobham (YH02866)																		
CHOBHAM CHASERS CROSS COUNTRY, Woking (YH02873)																		
CLANDON MANOR SUPPLIES, Guildford (YH02942)																		
CLAYGATE SPORTS HORSES, Esher (YH03000)																		
CLOCK TOWER RIDING CTRE, Tadworth (YH03052)																		
CLUB PRO-AM, Richmond (YH03074)																		
COE, NICOLA, Dorking (YH03133)																		
COUNTRYWIDE STORES, Redhill (YH03473)																		
COURTLANDS LIVERY STABLES, Banstead (YH03508)																		
CRANHAM, GERRY, Coulsdon (YH03564)											●							
CRANLEIGH SCHOOL OF RIDING, Cranleigh (YH03565)																		
CROFTS, ANDY, Albury (YH03625)																		
DORKING EQUESTRIAN CTRE, Dorking (YH04200)																		
DUNSFOLD RYSE STABLES, Chiddingfold (YH04357)																		

	Riding Club	Rug Cleaning	Saddler	School (Indoor)	School (Outdoor)	Sculptor	Shipping Agent	Show Jump Course	Show Jumping arena	Stabling Centre	Tack Shop	Taxidermy	Trail Riding Centre	Transport	Transport Overseas	Trekking Centre	Valuer	Website design	Wheelwright
WOOLMER COTTAGE STABLES, Newmarket (YH15768)										●									
SURREY																			
ANNA'S CTRY STORE, Farnham (YH00455)			●																
ASCOT PARK, Woking (YH00583)	●					●								●					
B & R INT HORSE TRANSPORT, Farnham (YH00714)														●					
BARKER, J, Chessington (YH00943)										●									
BARNES, PAT, Woking (YH00979)										●									
BEECHWOOD, Caterham (YH01176)						●			●										
BERKELEY EQUESTRIAN SVS, Kingswood (YH01301)										●									
BITS & PIECES, Sunbury-on-Thames (YH01457)			●																
BRIDLEWAYS EQUESTRIAN CTRE, Great Bookham (YH01898)						●													
BROOMELLS WORKSHOP, Dorking (YH02077)			●																
BURSTOW PK, Horley (YH02286)						●													
BUTTONS SADDLERY, Woking (YH02337)		●	●																
CHALK PIT FARM STABLES, Leatherhead (YH02711)										●									
CHAMBERS, G W, Guildford (YH02718)														●					
CHASE FARM, Hindhead (YH02780)								●	●										
CHESSINGTON, Chessington (YH02830)						●													
CHIPPINGS FARM STABLES, Cobham (YH02866)										●									
CHOBHAM CHASERS CROSS COUNTRY, Woking (YH02873)																			
CLANDON MANOR SUPPLIES, Guildford (YH02942)			●							●									
CLAYGATE SPORTS HORSES, Esher (YH03000)																			
CLOCK TOWER RIDING CTRE, Tadworth (YH03052)										●									
CLUB PRO-AM, Richmond (YH03074)			●																
COE, NICOLA, Dorking (YH03133)																			
COUNTRYWIDE STORES, Redhill (YH03473)			●																
COURTLANDS LIVERY STABLES, Banstead (YH03508)										●									
CRANHAM, GERRY, Coulsdon (YH03564)																			
CRANLEIGH SCHOOL OF RIDING, Cranleigh (YH03565)						●				●									
CROFTS, ANDY, Albury (YH03625)																			
DORKING EQUESTRIAN CTRE, Dorking (YH04200)				●		●													
DUNSFOLD RYSE STABLES, Chiddingfold (YH04357)										●									

Business Profile
General Equine

by Country by County	Artist	Blacksmith	Business Consultancy	Commentating for Events	Competition Horses	Competition Riders	Cross Country Course	Dressage Riders	Driving Centre	Driving Competitors	Driving Services	Engraving	Equine Holidays	Event Management	Event Riders	Forge	Harness Race Course	Harness Racing Horses	Harness Racing Skills	Harness Retailer	Horse Sale Agency	Horsebox Hire	International Arena	Jockey	Jockey Supply	Photographer	Point-to-Point Course	Polo Pitch	Portraits	Racecourse Flat	Racecourse Steeplechase	Racing Investment	Repairs Rugs	Repairs Saddles	Riding Club	Rug Cleaning	Saddler	School (Indoor)	School (Outdoor)	Sculptor	Shipping Agent	Show Jump Course	Show Jumping arena	Stabling Centre	Tack Shop	Taxidermy	Trail Riding Centre	Transport	Transport Overseas	Trekking Centre	Valuer	Website design	Wheelwright
EBBISHAM FARM, Tadworth (YH04528)					●										●																		●			●								●									
EQUARIUS, New Malden (YH04686)																					●																																
EQUUS EQUESTRIAN CTRES, Epsom (YH04839)													●																																								
FARNHAM SADDLERS, Farnham (YH05082)																																					●																
FARTHING DOWNS STABLES, Coulsdon (YH05099)																																												●									
FROSBURY FARM FEEDS, Guildford (YH05518)																																					●																
FUNNELL, PIPPA, Dorking (YH05539)															●																																						
GREEN LANE FARM, Guildford (YH06056)																																												●									
GREEN LANE STABLES, Morden (YH06058)																																								●													
GREENFIELD FARM STABLES, Leatherhead (YH06082)																																												●									
GREENWAYS FARM & STABLES, Godalming (YH06105)																																												●									
GUIVER, DAVID, Wallington (YH06188)																											●																										
HAMLYN-WRIGHT HORSE RUGS, Cobham (YH06356)																																	●	●		●	●																
HASTILOW COMPETITION SADDLES, Godalming (YH06526)																																	●	●		●	●								●								
HEADLEY GR STABLES, Epsom (YH06611)																																												●									
HENGEST FARM SHOP, Banstead (YH06672)																																					●																
HERMANN, ANNA, Effingham (YH06706)															●																																						
HIGHLANDS FARM STABLES, Leatherhead (YH06796)																																												●									
HIGHLEA STUD & LIVERY STABLES, Tadworth (YH06797)																																												●									
HORSES GALORE, Dunsfold (YH07168)																					●																																
HUNTERSFIELD FARM RIDING CTRE, Banstead (YH07303)																																												●									
HURSTFIELDS EQUESTRIAN CTRE, Tadworth (YH07321)							●																																					●									
HURTWOOD PARK, Cranleigh (YH07322)																												●																									
INDESPENSION, Redhill (YH07433)																						●																															
INJURED RIDERS FUND, Cranleigh (YH07458)																																					●																
ITCHELL HOME FARM, Farnham (YH07529)																																												●									
JUDE, Richmond (YH07959)	●																																																				
JULIETTE WETTERN SADDLER, Cobham (YH07963)																				●													●	●																			
KENILWORTH EQUESTRIAN CTRE, Leatherhead (YH08063)													●																															●									
LANGSHOT EQUESTRIAN CTRE, Chobham (YH08414)																																												●									
LARKENSHAW FARM, Woking (YH08429)																																												●									
LESTER BOWDEN, Epsom (YH08562)																																					●																

Business Profile
General Equine

by Country by County

by Country by County	Artist	Blacksmith	Business Consultancy	Commentating for Events	Competition Horses	Competition Riders	Cross Country Course	Dressage Riders	Driving Centre	Driving Competitors	Driving Services	Engraving	Equine Holidays	Event Management	Event Riders	Forge	Harness Race Course	Harness Racing Horses	Harness Racing Skills	Harness Retailer	Horse Sale Agency	Horsebox Hire	International Arena	Jockey	Jockey Supply	Photographer	Point-to-Point Course	Polo Pitch	Portraits	Racecourse Flat	Racecourse Steeplechase	Racing Investment	Repairs Rugs	Repairs Saddles	Riding Club	Rug Cleaning	Saddler	School (Indoor)	School (Outdoor)	Sculptor	Shipping Agent	Show Jump Course	Show Jumping arena	Stabling Centre	Tack Shop	Taxidermy	Trail Riding Centre	Transport	Transport Overseas	Trekking Centre	Valuer	Website design	Wheelwright
LETHERS OF BROCKHAM, Betchworth (YH08568)																																	●	●			●																
LETHERS OF MERSTHAM, Redhill (YH08569)																																	●	●			●																
LINGFIELD TACK, Lingfield (YH08660)																																													●								
LITTLE BROOK EQUESTRIAN, Lingfield (YH08685)																																												●									
LOWER FARM, Cobham (YH08864)																																												●									
MANOR SADDLERY, Guildford (YH09117)																																	●	●			●																
MASON, CLAIRE, Farnham (YH09238)															●																																						
MATTHEWS, M P, Dorking (YH09275)										●																																											
MERRIST WOOD CLGE, Guildford (YH09482)							●																																														
MITCHELL, P, Epsom (YH09676)																																																●					
OAKS PK RIDING SCHOOL, Banstead (YH10402)																																								●													
OLD FARM, Ripley (YH10455)																																												●									
OLD FORGE, Reigate (YH10458)																																												●									
OLD PK STABLES, Farnham (YH10472)													●																															●									
OLDENCRAIG EQUESTRIAN CTRE, Lingfield (YH10484)																																												●									
ONE STOP TACK SHOP, East Molesey (YH10513)																																													●								
ORCHARD COTTAGE, Wickham Market (YH10527)							●																															●		●													
PACHESHAM EQUESTRIAN CTRE, Leatherhead (YH10661)																																												●									
PARK STABLES, Dorking (YH10737)																																												●									
PELHAMS, Godalming (YH10909)																																																			●		
PETS ON PARADE, Claygate (YH11030)																																					●																
PLEASURE PRINTS, Walton-on-Thames (YH11175)																											●																										
POWELL, BRYNLEY, Farnham (YH11315)															●																																						
POWER, DURGA, Dorking (YH11325)																					●																																
POYNTERS, Cobham (YH11330)					●																																			●				●									
PRICE, N, Lingfield (YH11385)																																	●	●																			
RAPER-ZULLIG, Oxted (YH11639)																											●																										
RIDE & DRIVE, Horne (YH11842)																				●																																	
RIDGEWOOD RIDING CTRE, Reigate (YH11869)																																				●								●									
RIDING CTRE, Farnham (YH11873)					●	●		●							●																									●													
ROKER'S TACK SHOP, Guildford (YH12064)																																	●	●																			
RUNNINGWELL STABLES, Oxted (YH12235)																																												●									

Business Profile
General Equine

by Country by County	Artist	Blacksmith	Business Consultancy	Commentating for Events	Competition Horses	Competition Riders	Cross Country Course	Dressage Riders	Driving Centre	Driving Competitors	Driving Services	Engraving	Equine Holidays	Event Management	Event Riders	Forge	Harness Race Course	Harness Racing Horses	Harness Racing Skills	Harness Retailer	Horse Sale Agency	Horsebox Hire	International Arena	Jockey	Jockey Supply	Photographer	Point-to-Point Course	Polo Pitch	Portraits	Racecourse Flat	Racecourse Steeplechase	Racing Investment	Repairs Rugs	Repairs Saddles	Riding Club	Rug Cleaning	Saddler	School (Indoor)	School (Outdoor)	Sculptor	Shipping Agent	Show Jump Course	Show Jumping arena	Stabling Centre	Tack Shop	Taxidermy	Trail Riding Centre	Transport	Transport Overseas	Trekking Centre	Valuer	Website design	Wheelwright
RUSSIAN HORSE SOCIETY, Epsom (YH12267)																						●																																
S R S, Sunbury-on-Thames (YH12333)							●															●																		●		●		●									
SARIAH ARABIAN STUD, Dorking (YH12439)													●																																								
SCATS COUNTRYSTORE, Redhill (YH12508)																																	●			●																	
SCATS COUNTRYSTORE, Godalming (YH12507)																																	●			●																	
SIMMONS, Godalming (YH12825)			●																																																●		
SMALL, M E, Croydon (YH12908)																																												●									
STANGRAVE HALL STABLES, Godstone (YH13365)																																												●									
STARSHAW STABLES, Coulsdon (YH13399)																																								●				●									
STEVENS, ROBERT, Hazlemere (YH13448)															●																																						
SUPERPET THE HORSE SHOP, Tadworth (YH13655)																				●													●			●																	
SUPERPET THE HORSE SHOP, Banstead (YH13656)																																	●			●																	
SUPERPET THE HORSE SHOP, Epsom (YH13654)																				●													●			●																	
T.T.T, Guildford (YH13769)								●																																													
TANDRIDGE PRIORY, Oxted (YH13853)																																								●													
TANGYE, JOHN, Guildford (YH13855)							●																																				●									
TEIZERS EQUESTRIAN CTRE, Burstow (YH13937)																																												●									
TRIPLE BAR RIDING CTRE, Dorking (YH14400)													●																														●									
TRUXFORD RIDING CTRE, Godalming (YH14423)																																												●									
UNICORN LEATHER SADDLERY, Caterham (YH14566)																																	●	●		●	●																
UPLANDS STUD, Godalming (YH14601)								●																																													
UPPER RIDGEWAY FARM, Godalming (YH14607)																																												●									
VALE LODGE STABLES, Leatherhead (YH14635)																																												●									
VICTORIA FARM, Woking (YH14708)					●	●		●						●	●																										●			●	●									
WAFFRONS SCHOOL OF RIDING, Chessington (YH14820)																																												●									
WHIPPS, TONY, Effingham (YH15283)															●																																						
WHITEWOOD HSE FARM, Horley (YH15359)																																												●									
WILDWOODS, Tadworth (YH15413)					●	●	●						●																												●		●	●										
WINDACRES FARM, Horley (YH15561)							●																																				●									
WISE, Alfold (YH15607)																						●																																
WISHANGER EQUESTRIAN CTRE, Farnham (YH15612)																																												●									
WOLDINGHAM SADDLERS, Caterham (YH15617)																				●													●	●			●																

Business Profile
General Equine

by Country by County	Artist	Blacksmith	Business Consultancy	Commentating for Events	Competition Horses	Competition Riders	Cross Country Course	Dressage Riders	Driving Centre	Driving Competitors	Driving Services	Engraving	Equine Holidays	Event Management	Event Riders	Forge	Harness Race Course	Harness Racing Horses	Harness Racing Skills	Harness Retailer	Horse Sale Agency	Horsebox Hire	International Arena	Jockey	Jockey Supply	Photographer	Point-to-Point Course	Polo Pitch	Portraits	Racecourse Flat	Racecourse Steeplechase	Racing Investment	Repairs Rugs	Repairs Saddles	Riding Club	Rug Cleaning	Saddler	School (Indoor)	School (Outdoor)	Sculptor	Shipping Agent	Show Jump Course	Show Jumping arena	Stabling Centre	Tack Shop	Taxidermy	Trail Riding Centre	Transport	Transport Overseas	Trekking Centre	Valuer	Website design	Wheelwright
WOODCOTE FARM, West Horsley (YH15678)																																												●									
WOODSTOCK SOUTH STABLES, Chessington (YH15751)					●	●		●																																●				●									
SUSSEX (EAST)																																																					
ACRE & ASHDOWN FEEDS, Crowborough (YH00156)																																	●	●		●	●																
ANDREW REILLY, Forest Row (YH00392)																																					●																
ASHDOWN FOREST RIDING CTRE, Uckfield (YH00595)																																												●									
BARNES FARM RETIREMENT, Robertsbridge (YH00970)																																												●									
BEAUPORT PK HOTEL, Hastings (YH01139)													●																																								
BLUE RIDGE WESTERN SADDLERY, Hailsham (YH01568)																																					●																
BUCKLAND PR, Robertsbridge (YH02194)			●																								●																										
C DEAN & SON, Lewes (YH02366)		●														●																																					
CANTERS END RIDING SCHOOL, Uckfield (YH02512)																																												●									
CAREY, R G, Battle (YH02536)											●																																										●
CHURCH FARM & STUD, Lewes (YH02896)																																												●									
CROCKSTEAD PK, Lewes (YH03608)							●																															●							●								
DANDY BUSH SADDLERY, Battle (YH03863)																																		●			●								●								
ELMS SADDLERY & LIVERIES, Icklesham (YH04638)																																					●							●									
FARRANT, TAMARA, Robertsbridge (YH05085)																											●																										
FARTHING SADDLERY, Heathfield (YH05100)																																					●																
GOLDEN CROSS, Hailsham (YH05878)					●	●									●																							●		●		●	●	●									
GRISSELL, D M, Robertsbridge (YH06146)																																																●					
H B SADDLERY, Rye (YH06212)																																					●																
HAMSEY RIDING SCHOOL, Lewes (YH06371)																																						●		●													
HERONDEN INT HORSE TRANSPORT, Rye (YH06713)																																																●					
HIGHAM FARM, Hastings (YH06768)																																												●									
HOLE FARM, Uckfield (YH06928)																																						●						●									
HORAM MANOR, Heathfield (YH07064)													●																																								
HORSE HOUSE, Hailsham (YH07124)																																					●																
JOHN BIRON EQUESTRIAN, Heathfield (YH07781)																																												●									
LITTLE MEADOWS, Hailsham (YH08694)					●	●																																															
MEL FORDHAM, Uckfield (YH09448)																											●																										
MEPHAM, KIRSTY, Uckfield (YH09461)								●																																													

www.hccyourhorse.com

Business Profile
General Equine

by Country by County	Artist	Blacksmith	Business Consultancy	Commentating for Events	Competition Horses	Competition Riders	Cross Country Course	Dressage Riders	Driving Centre	Driving Competitors	Driving Services	Engraving	Equine Holidays	Event Management	Event Riders	Forge	Harness Race Course	Harness Racing Horses	Harness Racing Skills	Harness Retailer	Horse Sale Agency	Horsebox Hire	International Arena	Jockey	Jockey Supply	Photographer	Point-to-Point Course	Polo Pitch	Portraits	Racecourse Flat	Racecourse Steeplechase	Racing Investment	Repairs Rugs	Repairs Saddles	Riding Club	Rug Cleaning	Saddler	School (Indoor)	School (Outdoor)	Sculptor	Shipping Agent	Show Jump Course	Show Jumping arena	Stabling Centre	Tack Shop	Taxidermy	Trail Riding Centre	Transport	Transport Overseas	Trekking Centre	Valuer	Website design	Wheelwright
MOORCROFT CTRE, Battle (YH09748)								●																																													
POLEGATE SADDLERY, Polegate (YH11198)																																	●	●			●																
ROCK LANE, Bexhill-on-Sea (YH12025)																																												●									
SCATS COUNTRYSTORE, Heathfield (YH12509)																																	●			●																	
SIAN SADDLERY, Uckfield (YH12777)																																	●	●		●	●																
SILVERDALE TRANSPORT, Robertsbridge (YH12814)																																									●							●					
SLYES FARM, Hailsham (YH12904)																																												●									
SOMETHING DIFFERENT, Uckfield (YH13068)																																	●	●		●	●								●								
SOUTH EASTERN EQUESTRIAN SVS, Wadhurst (YH13089)				●																																																	
SOUTH LODGE, Rotherfield (YH13100)																																								●													
ST IVES LIVERY, Hartfield (YH13277)																																												●									
STERLING SADDLERY, Robertsbridge (YH13431)																																					●																
STEVENS, LEONARD, Eastbourne (YH13445)																				●																	●																
TACK ROOM, Robertsbridge (YH13802)																																	●	●			●																
VINE, W E, Hailsham (YH14731)									●																																												
WINTON STREET FARM STABLES, Polegate (YH15600)																																												●									
WORK SHOP, Heathfield (YH15777)																																					●																
SUSSEX (WEST)																																																					
AGRIVET - KWG, Haywards Heath (YH00204)																																					●																
ALBOURNE EQUESTRIAN CTRE, Hassocks (YH00248)																																						●		●		●	●										
ALL TIME EQUESTRIAN, Crawley (YH00286)																																	●	●		●	●																
BADGER WOOD FARM STABLES, Fulking (YH00777)																																												●									
BELMOREDEAN, West Grinstead (YH01251)																																												●									
BOXGROVE COMPETITION STABLES, Chichester (YH01726)					●																																																
BRENDON, Brighton (YH01835)					●	●																																															
BRENDON HORSE & RIDER, Brighton (YH01837)		●																															●				●								●								
BRIDGE HSE EQUESTRIAN CTRE, Horsham (YH01874)																																												●									
BURGESS & RANDALL, Pulborough (YH02242)																																					●																
C & C EQUINE SVS, Billingshurst (YH02353)																																						●															
C R M, Horsham (YH02388)																																				●																	
COBB, I, Pulborough (YH03110)																																												●									
COVERT, Petworth (YH03519)																																					●																

Business Profile
General Equine

by Country by County

by Country by County	Artist	Blacksmith	Business Consultancy	Commentating for Events	Competition Horses	Competition Riders	Cross Country Course	Dressage Riders	Driving Centre	Driving Competitors	Driving Services	Engraving	Equine Holidays	Event Management	Event Riders	Forge	Harness Race Course	Harness Racing Horses	Harness Racing Skills	Harness Retailer	Horse Sale Agency	Horsebox Hire	International Arena	Jockey	Jockey Supply	Photographer	Point-to-Point Course	Polo Pitch	Portraits	Racecourse Flat	Racecourse Steeplechase	Racing Investment	Repairs Rugs	Repairs Saddles	Riding Club	Rug Cleaning	Saddler	School (Indoor)	School (Outdoor)	Sculptor	Shipping Agent	Show Jump Course	Show Jumping arena	Stabling Centre	Tack Shop	Taxidermy	Trail Riding Centre	Transport	Transport Overseas	Trekking Centre	Valuer	Website design	Wheelwright
CRAWLEY DOWN SADDLERY, Crawley (YH03578)																																	●	●		●																	
DEAN, GEOFF, Worthing (YH03991)																	●	●		●														●			●																
DIAMOND SADDLERY, Hassocks (YH04105)																				●																	●																
DRAGONFLY SADDLERY, Hassocks (YH04252)												●																					●	●		●	●								●								
E M C, Shoreham By Sea (YH04415)																				●																																	
EAST VIEW FRUIT FARM, Haywards Heath (YH04488)																																																		●			
EASTWOOD STUD FARM, Petworth (YH04518)																																												●									
EATON THORNE STABLES, Henfield (YH04525)																																												●									
EDGINGTONS, Hassocks (YH04557)																																					●																
EQUITOGS, Billingshurst (YH04830)																																	●	●		●	●																
EQUITOGS, Littlehampton (YH04829)																																	●	●		●	●																
GEOFF DEAN SADDLERY, Worthing (YH05714)											●	●								●													●	●		●	●																
GIFFORD, J T, Worthing (YH05757)															●																																						
GILLIAN HARRIS, Chichester (YH05783)	●																																																				
GOODROWES OF CHICHESTER, Chichester (YH05908)																																					●																
H J BURT & SON, Steyning (YH06226)																																																			●		
HAM HSE STABLES, Haywards Heath (YH06340)																																												●									
HANGLETON FARM, Worthing (YH06386)																																												●									
HARTLAND CARRIAGE SUPPLIES, Rudgwick (YH06504)									●	●	●									●																																	
HEDGERS HORSE TRANSPORT, Chichester (YH06642)																																																●	●				
HIGHLANDER EQUINE CTRE, Lancing (YH06794)																																												●									
HOOPER, FRANCES, Billingshurst (YH07042)															●																																						
HORACE FULLER, Horsham (YH07063)																																					●																
HORSE BOX, Horsham (YH07110)																																					●																
HORSE RACING ABROAD, Haywards Heath (YH07130)													●																																								
IFIELD PARK FEED TACK & WEAR, Crawley (YH07389)																																					●																
INSTONE AIR SERVICES, Pulborough (YH07463)																																																●					
LASSETTER, JOHN F, Chichester (YH08442)				●				●																																				●									
LAVANT HSE STABLES, Chichester (YH08460)																																			●					●		●		●									
LEWIS, CLARE, Horstead Keynes (YH08587)															●																																						
LIGHTS, Brighton (YH08616)																																					●																
M & A OUTDOOR CLOTHING, Crawley (YH08942)																																					●																

Business Profile
General Equine

by Country by County

	Artist	Blacksmith	Business Consultancy	Commentating for Events	Competition Horses	Competition Riders	Cross Country Course	Dressage Riders	Driving Centre	Driving Competitors	Driving Services	Engraving	Equine Holidays	Event Management	Event Riders	Forge	Harness Race Course	Harness Racing Horses	Harness Racing Skills	Harness Retailer	Horse Sale Agency	Horsebox Hire	International Arena	Jockey	Jockey Supply	Photographer	Point-to-Point Course	Polo Pitch	Portraits	Racecourse Flat	Racecourse Steeplechase	Racing Investment	Repairs Rugs	Repairs Saddles	Riding Club	Rug Cleaning	Saddler	School (Indoor)	School (Outdoor)	Sculptor	Shipping Agent	Show Jump Course	Show Jumping arena	Stabling Centre	Tack Shop	Taxidermy	Trail Riding Centre	Transport	Transport Overseas	Trekking Centre	Valuer	Website design	Wheelwright
MANNINGS LIVERIES, Henfield (YH09089)																																												●									
MIDHURST SHOES, Midhurst (YH09553)																																					●																
MINTA WINN CARRIAGE DRIVING, Billingshurst (YH09655)									●	●	●																																										
MOLECOMB STUD, Chichester (YH09712)					●	●		●																														●		●													
NEWMAN, PHIL, Pulborough (YH10149)				●																																																	
NICOL, C, Horsham (YH10198)																					●																							●									
NORTHBROOK FARM, Worthing (YH10295)																																												●									
NORTON HIND SADDLERY, Arundel (YH10330)																																		●																			
OAKDENE SADDLERY, Hassocks (YH10374)																																					●																
OLDWICK SADDLERY, Chichester (YH10495)																																					●																
ONE STOP, Billingshurst (YH10512)																																	●			●																	
OPEN COUNTRY, Petworth (YH10524)																																					●																
OUTDOORS - SCOUT SHOPS, Lancing (YH10588)																																					●																
PARKERS, Horsham (YH10753)																																					●																
PENFOLD & SONS, Haywards Heath (YH10934)																																	●	●		●	●																
PENFOLDS OF CUCKFIELD, Haywards Heath (YH10935)																																					●																
PEPER HAROW HORSE TRAILERS, Horsham (YH10968)																																																●				●	
RAHMATALLAH, S, Billingshurst (YH11610)													●																																								
RAPKYNS, Horsham (YH11641)																					●																																
ROUSE, SARAH, Midhurst (YH12147)				●																																																	
ROXTON, Midhurst (YH12176)																																	●	●			●																
ROXTON SPORTING, Midhurst (YH12178)																																					●																
SCATS COUNTRYSTORE, Billingshurst (YH12510)																																	●			●																	
SELSEY RIDING CTRE, Selsey (YH12625)																																												●									
SHARON TONG, Steyning (YH12677)	●																												●																								
SIRETT, R T, Worthing (YH12859)																																												●									
SNOOTY FOX COUNTRY STORE, Petworth (YH13035)																																					●																
SNOWHILL SADDLERY, Chichester (YH13044)																				●																																	
STOCKLEY TRADING, Littlehampton (YH13495)																																					●																
SYMONDSBURY STUD, Haywards Heath (YH13726)																																								●				●									
T C TACK & THINGS, Burgess Hill (YH13733)																																					●																
T E FRASER & SON, Midhurst (YH13736)																																					●																

Business Profile
General Equine

by Country by County	Artist	Blacksmith	Business Consultancy	Commentating for Events	Competition Horses	Competition Riders	Cross Country Course	Dressage Riders	Driving Centre	Driving Competitors	Driving Services	Engraving	Equine Holidays	Event Management	Event Riders	Forge	Harness Race Course	Harness Racing Horses	Harness Racing Skills	Harness Retailer	Horse Sale Agency	Horsebox Hire	International Arena	Jockey	Jockey Supply	Photographer	Point-to-Point Course	Polo Pitch	Portraits	Racecourse Flat	Racecourse Steeplechase	Racing Investment	Repairs Rugs	Repairs Saddles	Riding Club	Rug Cleaning	Saddler	School (Indoor)	School (Outdoor)	Sculptor	Shipping Agent	Show Jump Course	Show Jumping arena	Stabling Centre	Tack Shop	Taxidermy	Trail Riding Centre	Transport	Transport Overseas	Trekking Centre	Valuer	Website design	Wheelwright
TACK A ROUND SADDLERY, Billingshurst (YH13781)																																	●	●			●																
TOWNS, I, Chichester (YH14298)																																												●									
UNIVERSAL TRAILERS, Billingshurst (YH14579)																						●																										●					
WEST WOLVES RIDING CTRE, Pulborough (YH15172)							●																															●		●		●											
WILLOWBROOK RIDING CTRE, Chichester (YH15508)													●								●																			●				●						●			
ZARA STUD, Chichester (YH15951)					●								●																									●						●	●								
TYNE AND WEAR																																																					
BAIN, FIONA M, Gosforth (YH00810)																											●																										
CUNNINGHAM, W S, Yarm (YH03725)																																																●					
DANCESPORT & EQUESTRIAN, Gateshead (YH03861)																																					●																
GIRSONFIELD STUD, Otterburn (YH05795)																																												●									
GO RIDING GRP, Ponteland (YH05862)														●							●														●			●		●		●		●	●								
HORSE-WORLD, Gateshead (YH07180)																																					●																
INDESPENSION, Newcastle-upon-Tyne (YH07434)																						●																															
JOSEPH BAILEY & SONS, Houghton Le Spring (YH07942)																																																					●
LE PREVO LEATHERS, Newcastle-upon-Tyne (YH08491)																																					●																
LEATHER SHOP, Sunderland (YH08504)																																					●																
LITTLE HARLE STABLES, Newcastle-upon-Tyne (YH08688)					●	●		●							●																									●				●									
MACKIE, HENRI, Newcastle-upon-Tyne (YH09005)																																												●									
MARDEN SADDLERY, Newcastle-upon-Tyne (YH09146)																																					●																
NORTH LIZARD RIDING SCHOOL, South Shields (YH10271)																																												●									
PETMEALS, Boldon Colliery (YH11028)																																					●																
QUARRY PARK STABLES, Gateshead (YH11483)	●																																		●					●								●		●			
REAL TIME IMAGING, Sunderland (YH11685)																											●																										
RIDERS, North Shields (YH11854)																																				●									●								
S & S SADDLERY, Sunderland (YH12313)																				●																									●								
SADDLE SHOP, Gateshead (YH12350)																																	●	●		●	●																
TURF PICTURES, Houghton Le Spring (YH14467)																											●																										
WEBSTER, J R, Newcastle-upon-Tyne (YH15040)																																					●																
WARWICKSHIRE																																																					
A & J SADDLERY, Southam (YH00012)																																	●	●		●	●								●								
ACCIMASSU, Studley (YH00140)					●						●			●																																							

Business Profile
General Equine

by Country by County	Artist	Blacksmith	Business Consultancy	Commentating for Events	Competition Horses	Competition Riders	Cross Country Course	Dressage Riders	Driving Centre	Driving Competitors	Driving Services	Engraving	Equine Holidays	Event Management	Event Riders	Forge	Harness Race Course	Harness Racing Horses	Harness Racing Skills	Harness Retailer	Horse Sale Agency	Horsebox Hire	International Arena	Jockey	Jockey Supply	Photographer	Point-to-Point Course	Polo Pitch	Portraits	Racecourse Flat	Racecourse Steeplechase	Racing Investment	Repairs Rugs	Repairs Saddles	Riding Club	Rug Cleaning	Saddler	School (Indoor)	School (Outdoor)	Sculptor	Shipping Agent	Show Jump Course	Show Jumping arena	Stabling Centre	Tack Shop	Taxidermy	Trail Riding Centre	Transport	Transport Overseas	Trekking Centre	Valuer	Website design	Wheelwright
ALCESTER RIDING SUPPLIES, Alcester (YH00251)																																					●																
BEECHWOOD LIVERY/TRAINING, Berkswell (YH01178)																																												●									
BROADHEATH SADDLERY, Warwick (YH01998)																																					●																
BROADWELL CROSS COUNTRY, Rugby (YH02004)							●																																														
CALDECOTE RIDING SCHOOL, Nuneaton (YH02428)																																								●					●								
CARRY ON RIDING STABLES, Warwick (YH02602)																																												●									
COCKRAM, R A, Radway (YH03127)																																												●									
COLEMAN, ROBIN, Kenilworth (YH03164)																				●													●	●			●																
COTON EQUITANA, Rugby (YH03358)											●																																										
COTTAGE FARM RIDING STABLES, Solihull (YH03374)													●																																								
COUNTRY PURSUIT, Warwick (YH03420)																																	●	●			●																
COUNTRYWIDE STORES, Rugby (YH03475)																																					●																
COUNTRYWIDE STORES, Nuneaton (YH03474)																																					●																
COUNTRYWIDE STORES, Stratford-upon-Avon (YH03476)																																					●																
DARLOWS, Butlers Marston (YH03896)	●																																						●														
EDWARDS' SADDLERY, Bidford On Avon (YH04574)																																	●	●		●	●								●								
GRAPES VILLA FARM SUPPLIES, Coventry (YH06017)																																					●																
GREENACRES STUD, Coventry (YH06080)																																												●									
H M C HOPSFORD MARKETING, Coventry (YH06228)																											●																										
HADLEY, STEPHEN, Kineton (YH06268)				●																	●																																
HOCKLEY HEATH RIDING SUPPLIES, Solihull (YH06904)																																					●																
HOLLY RIDING SCHOOL, Atherstone (YH06957)																																												●									
HOPSFORD HALL LIVERY YARD, Coventry (YH07060)																																												●									
INT PARALYMPIC EQUESTRIAN SP, Leamington Spa (YH07470)								●		●																																											
INTERNATIONAL WARWICK SCHOOL, Warwick (YH07480)							●						●																															●									
JODS, DOBBIES, Coventry (YH07776)																																					●																
JOHN WRIGHT PHOTOGRAPHY, Warwick (YH07818)																											●																										
KINGSWOOD FARM HOUSE, Kenilworth (YH08211)																																												●									
LODGE FARM LIVERIES, Hatton (YH08769)																																												●									
MOAT HOUSE STUD, Henley In Arden (YH09686)																					●																																
MONKSPATH SADDLERY, Solihull (YH09727)																																					●																
NICHOLSON, CHERYL, Coventry (YH10193)																				●													●	●			●																

Business Profile
General Equine

by Country by County	Artist	Blacksmith	Business Consultancy	Commentating for Events	Competition Horses	Competition Riders	Cross Country Course	Dressage Riders	Driving Centre	Driving Competitors	Driving Services	Engraving	Equine Holidays	Event Management	Event Riders	Forge	Harness Race Course	Harness Racing Horses	Harness Racing Skills	Harness Retailer	Horse Sale Agency	Horsebox Hire	International Arena	Jockey	Jockey Supply	Photographer	Point-to-Point Course	Polo Pitch	Portraits	Racecourse Flat	Racecourse Steeplechase	Racing Investment	Repairs Rugs	Repairs Saddles	Riding Club	Rug Cleaning	Saddler	School (Indoor)	School (Outdoor)	Sculptor	Shipping Agent	Show Jump Course	Show Jumping arena	Stabling Centre	Tack Shop	Taxidermy	Trail Riding Centre	Transport	Transport Overseas	Trekking Centre	Valuer	Website design	Wheelwright
OUSBEY'S HARNESS ROOM, Atherstone (YH10585)																				●																																	
PEBWORTH VALE SADDLERY, Stratford-upon-Avon (YH10890)																																					●							●									
PERRY, MICHELLE, Tanworth-In-Arden (YH10988)	●																																																				
PITTERN HILL, Warwick (YH11155)																																					●																
RASCALS OF WARWICK, Warwick (YH11644)																																					●																
RED HSE FARM LIVERY STABLES, Leamington Spa (YH11696)							●																														●							●									
RIMELL, Shipston-on-Stour (YH11896)																																					●																
RISSIK, DAVID, Stratford-upon-Avon (YH11912)															●																																						
RUGWASH 2000, Warwick (YH12224)																																					●																
SADDLERY SHOP, Stratford (YH12367)																																					●																
SAXON TACK & TAILS, Rugby (YH12471)																																					●																
SNOWFORD HILL FARM, Rugby (YH13043)																																												●									
STONELEIGH STABLES, Kenilworth (YH13519)							●																					●										●		●													
THOMPSON, STEFANIE, Rugby (YH14043)															●																																						
TOWER FARM SADDLERS, Rugby (YH14274)																																	●	●			●																
UK CHASERS & RIDERS, Leamington Spa (YH14545)							●																																														
UMBERSLADE EQUESTRIAN CTRE, Solihull (YH14558)																					●	●																										●					
VERO, FELICITY, Nuneaton (YH14683)				●																																								●									
WARD, ANTHONY, Moreton Morrell (YH14898)													●																															●									
WARWICKSHIRE CLGE HORSE UNIT, Warwick (YH14951)																																												●									
WAVERLEY EQUESTRIAN CTRE, Leamington Spa (YH15011)				●									●															●										●		●			●		●								
WOODBINE STABLES, Rugby (YH15675)																						●																						●				●					
WOOTTON COURT FARM, Warwick (YH15771)																																												●									
WOOTTON GRANGE EQUESTRIAN, Warwick (YH15772)																																											●										
WILTSHIRE																																																					
B M H S, Warminster (YH00741)																																												●									
BRASS TACKS, Chippenham (YH01814)												●																																									
BRYMPTON RIDING SCHOOL, Salisbury (YH02173)													●																																								
BUSH, N, Chippenham (YH02308)							●																																														
CARDEN, SUSAN M M, Chippenham (YH02529)																											●																										
CHIPPENHAM TRAILER HIRE, Chippenham (YH02864)																						●																										●					
COPPERFIELD STABLES, Salisbury (YH03302)																																																●					

Business Profile
General Equine

by Country by County

	Artist	Blacksmith	Business Consultancy	Commentating for Events	Competition Horses	Competition Riders	Cross Country Course	Dressage Riders	Driving Centre	Driving Competitors	Driving Services	Engraving	Equine Holidays	Event Management	Event Riders	Forge	Harness Race Course	Harness Racing Horses	Harness Racing Skills	Harness Retailer	Horse Sale Agency	Horsebox Hire	International Arena	Jockey	Jockey Supply	Photographer	Point-to-Point Course	Polo Pitch	Portraits	Racecourse Flat	Racecourse Steeplechase	Racing Investment	Repairs Rugs	Repairs Saddles	Riding Club	Rug Cleaning	Saddler	School (Indoor)	School (Outdoor)	Sculptor	Shipping Agent	Show Jump Course	Show Jumping arena	Stabling Centre	Tack Shop	Taxidermy	Trail Riding Centre	Transport	Transport Overseas	Trekking Centre	Valuer	Website design	Wheelwright
COUNTRY PURSUITS, Cricklade (YH03422)																																					●																
DALLAS INDUSTRIES, Market Lavington (YH03842)																																					●																
DAVID FARMER SADDLERY, Chippenham (YH03919)																				●													●	●			●																
EASTON GREY SADDLERS, Malmesbury (YH04514)																				●													●	●		●	●																
ELMGROVE SADDLERY, Swindon (YH04636)																																	●	●		●	●								●								
EQUESPORT, Calne (YH04687)																																					●																
EQUIFOR, Marlborough (YH04746)										●	●									●														●		●																●	
FARROW, C, Salisbury (YH05096)													●																															●									
FOXHILL RACING PROMOTIONS, Swindon (YH05434)													●																																								
FREDERICK J CHANDLER, Marlborough (YH05478)																																					●																
FREDERICKS, CLAYTON, Salisbury (YH05479)															●																																						
GENUS EQUINE, Chippenham (YH05711)					●																																																
GEORGE SMITH HORSEBOXES, Salisbury (YH05719)																						●																										●					
GRANT BARNES & SON, Malmesbury (YH06009)																																	●	●			●								●								
GREENACRES, Salisbury (YH06075)																																								●													
GREENFIELDS, Salisbury (YH06083)																																					●																
GROVELY, Salisbury (YH06175)																																								●		●											
HADDON STUD, Marlborough (YH06263)																																												●									
HAMPSLEY HOLLOW, Calne (YH06368)													●																									●		●		●											
HARRIS CROFT RIDING CTRE, Swindon (YH06462)																																												●									
HEDDINGTON WICK, Calne (YH06639)																																								●													
HEYWOOD, Westbury (YH06737)							●																															●		●			●										
HOLDERNESS-RODDAM, JANE, Chippenham (YH06926)															●																																						
HUDDS FARM, Bradford-on-Avon (YH07254)																																												●									
HURDCOTT LIVERY STABLES, Salisbury (YH07311)													●																				●			●									●								
INFANTRY SADDLE CLUB, Warminster (YH07441)							●																															●		●		●											
JONES, ERIC, Mere (YH07898)																											●																										
JUMPERS HORSELINE, Wootton Bassett (YH07966)																																					●																
KEVINS MENSWEAR, Westbury (YH08111)																																					●																
KEYSLEY HORSE RUGS, Salisbury (YH08116)																																				●																	
LACKHAM CLGE EQUESTRIAN CTRE, Chippenham (YH08332)																																						●		●													
LANE, CHARLIE, Warminster (YH08390)				●																																																	

Business Profile
General Equine

by Country by County

	LONGHORN, Warminster (YH08813)	LOWBRIDGE STABLES, Calne (YH08857)	LYON, POLLY, Malmesbury (YH08940)	MACDONALD-HALL, ANNI, Salisbury (YH08992)	MALMESBURY TRAILERS, Malmesbury (YH09053)	MALTHOUSE EQUESTRIAN CTRE, Swindon (YH09058)	MARLBOROUGH DOWNS, Marlborough (YH09169)	MEADE, RICHARD, Chippenham (YH09415)	MIDWAY MANOR, Bradford-on-Avon (YH09562)	NICHOLSON, ANDREW, Devizes (YH10190)	OAKSEY, (LORD), Malmesbury (YH10404)	OLD DAIRY SADDLERY LTD, Swindon (YH10454)	ORMEROD, GILES, Salisbury (YH10548)	PATS VIGORS PHOTOGRAPHY, Melksham (YH10826)	PEWSEY VALE, Marlborough (YH11037)	POWELL, RODNEY, Swindon (YH11321)
Wheelwright																
Website design																
Valuer																
Trekking Centre	●															
Transport Overseas																
Transport					●											
Trail Riding Centre																
Taxidermy																
Tack Shop																
Stabling Centre						●			●				●			
Show Jumping arena																
Show Jump Course							●								●	
Shipping Agent																
Sculptor						●									●	
School (Outdoor)																
School (Indoor)						●	●								●	
Saddler												●				
Rug Cleaning												●				
Riding Club						●										
Repairs Saddles												●				
Repairs Rugs												●				
Racing Investment																
Racecourse Steeplechase																
Racecourse Flat																
Portraits																
Polo Pitch																
Point-to-Point Course						●								●		
Photographer																
Jockey Supply																
Jockey																
International Arena																
Horsebox Hire					●											
Horse Sale Agency		●								●						
Harness Retailer																
Harness Racing Skills																
Harness Racing Horses																
Harness Race Course																
Forge																
Event Riders			●							●						●
Event Management																
Equine Holidays																
Engraving																
Driving Services																
Driving Competitors																
Driving Centre																
Dressage Riders				●		●										
Cross Country Course							●		●							
Competition Riders						●										
Competition Horses						●										
Commentating for Events								●			●					
Business Consultancy																
Blacksmith																
Artist																

	ROE, M A, Swindon (YH12052)	ROSEGARTH STUD, Devizes (YH12103)	SADDLERY, Swindon (YH12364)	SAMWAYS, Salisbury (YH12402)	SCATS COUNTRYSTORE, Salisbury (YH12511)	SCATS COUNTRYSTORE, Devizes (YH12512)	SCIMGEOUR, ANNABEL, Marlborough (YH12525)	SEG, Calne (YH12611)	SOUTH FARM LIVERY YARD, Swindon (YH13092)	SOUTHVIEW FARM, Bradford-on-Avon (YH13160)	SPORT & LEISURE, Malmesbury (YH13217)	STABLEWARE, Marlborough (YH13314)	STONAR SCHOOL, Melksham (YH13507)	SYDNEY INGRAM & SON, Salisbury (YH13722)	T G JEARY, Calne (YH13741)	TOLLARD PARK EQUESTRIAN CTRE, Salisbury (YH14207)
Wheelwright																
Website design																
Valuer																
Trekking Centre																
Transport Overseas																
Transport																
Trail Riding Centre				●												
Taxidermy																
Tack Shop			●													
Stabling Centre									●							●
Show Jumping arena																
Show Jump Course																
Shipping Agent																
Sculptor										●						
School (Outdoor)																
School (Indoor)																
Saddler			●	●				●			●	●		●	●	
Rug Cleaning					●	●										
Riding Club																
Repairs Saddles			●	●										●		
Repairs Rugs			●	●	●	●								●		
Racing Investment																
Racecourse Steeplechase																
Racecourse Flat																
Portraits																
Polo Pitch																
Point-to-Point Course																
Photographer																
Jockey Supply																
Jockey																
International Arena																
Horsebox Hire																
Horse Sale Agency	●															
Harness Retailer																
Harness Racing Skills																
Harness Racing Horses																
Harness Race Course																
Forge																
Event Riders		●														
Event Management																
Equine Holidays				●												
Engraving																
Driving Services																
Driving Competitors																
Driving Centre																
Dressage Riders							●									
Cross Country Course													●			
Competition Riders																
Competition Horses																
Commentating for Events																
Business Consultancy																
Blacksmith																
Artist																

www.hccyourhorse.com

Business Profile
General Equine

by Country by County

	Artist	Blacksmith	Business Consultancy	Commentating for Events	Competition Horses	Competition Riders	Cross Country Course	Dressage Riders	Driving Centre	Driving Competitors	Driving Services	Engraving	Equine Holidays	Event Management	Event Riders	Forge	Harness Race Course	Harness Racing Horses	Harness Racing Skills	Harness Retailer	Horse Sale Agency	Horsebox Hire	International Arena	Jockey	Jockey Supply	Photographer	Point-to-Point Course	Polo Pitch	Portraits	Racecourse Flat	Racecourse Steeplechase	Racing Investment	Repairs Rugs	Repairs Saddles	Riding Club	Rug Cleaning	Saddler	School (Indoor)	School (Outdoor)	Sculptor	Shipping Agent	Show Jump Course	Show Jumping arena	Stabling Centre	Tack Shop	Taxidermy	Trail Riding Centre	Transport	Transport Overseas	Trekking Centre	Valuer	Website design	Wheelwright
WADSWICK, Corsham (YH14819)																																	●	●			●																
WARDALL BLOODSTOCK SHIPPING, Salisbury (YH14912)																																									●							●					
WARMINSTER SADDLERY, Warminster (YH14923)																																		●			●								●								
WEST KINGTON STUD, Chippenham (YH15151)					●	●	●								●																									●		●		●									
WEST WILTS, Trowbridge (YH15170)							●																															●		●													
WHISTLEY FORGE SADDLERY, Devizes (YH15286)																																					●																
WHITE HORSE EQUESTRIAN CTRE, Westbury (YH15308)													●																									●												●			
WHITE HORSE SADDLERY, Salisbury (YH15313)																																	●	●		●	●																
WICKSTEAD FARM, Swindon (YH15387)																																												●									
WIDBROOK ARABIAN STUD, Bradford-on-Avon (YH15388)																																						●		●													
WILLIAM PUDDY WHITE HORSE, Warminster (YH15437)													●																																								
WILMOT, GUY, Marlborough (YH15521)																											●																										
WYLYE VALLEY HORSE, Codford (YH15867)																																					●																
YEO, JANCIS, Chippenham (YH15902)															●																																						
WORCESTERSHIRE																																																					
ALLMAN, R P & G E J, Evesham (YH00321)																																												●									
BENT, BM & SA, Evesham (YH01282)																						●																															
BIRCHWOOD, Bewdley (YH01436)																																								●													
BROADCLOSE LIVERY, Worcester (YH01993)																																					●																
BROMSGROVE SADDLERY, Bromsgrove (YH02026)					●	●		●												●													●	●											●								
CARENZA, JILL, Broadway (YH02534)																																								●													
COLLEY, ANNE, Bewdley (YH03177)																																												●									
COUNTRY CLASSICS, Droitwich (YH03400)																																					●																
COUNTRYWIDE, Worcester (YH03446)																																					●																
COUNTRYWIDE STORES, Upton-upon-Severn (YH03481)																																					●																
COUNTRYWIDE STORES, Bromsgrove (YH03482)																																					●																
COUNTRYWIDE STORES, Evesham (YH03483)																																					●																
COUNTRYWIDE STORES, Kidderminster (YH03480)																																					●																
CROWFIELDS EQUESTRIAN SVS, Bromsgrove (YH03678)																																												●									
DITCHAM, JANET, Kidderminster (YH04134)													●																																								
DONNA LEIGH SADDLERY, Kidderminster (YH04185)																																					●																
EILBERG, FERDI, Redditch (YH04598)								●																																				●									

Business Profile
General Equine

by Country by County	Artist	Blacksmith	Business Consultancy	Commentating for Events	Competition Horses	Competition Riders	Cross Country Course	Dressage Riders	Driving Centre	Driving Competitors	Driving Services	Engraving	Equine Holidays	Event Management	Event Riders	Forge	Harness Race Course	Harness Racing Horses	Harness Racing Skills	Harness Retailer	Horse Sale Agency	Horsebox Hire	International Arena	Jockey	Jockey Supply	Photographer	Point-to-Point Course	Polo Pitch	Portraits	Racecourse Flat	Racecourse Steeplechase	Racing Investment	Repairs Rugs	Repairs Saddles	Riding Club	Rug Cleaning	Saddler	School (Indoor)	School (Outdoor)	Sculptor	Shipping Agent	Show Jump Course	Show Jumping arena	Stabling Centre	Tack Shop	Taxidermy	Trail Riding Centre	Transport	Transport Overseas	Trekking Centre	Valuer	Website design	Wheelwright
EQUIMIX, Stourport-on-Severn (YH04756)																																	●	●		●	●								●								
EQUINE RESOURCES, Malvern (YH04796)																																												●									
EVANS, SALLYANN & LISA, Bromsgrove (YH04932)								●							●																																						
F DURRANT & SONS, Worcester (YH04990)																																					●																
FAR FOREST EQUESTRIAN CTRE, Kidderminster (YH05047)																																												●									
FOREST HARNESS, Bewdley (YH05338)																				●																																	
GEO HEAPHY & SONS, Redditch (YH05712)																																					●																
GRACELANDS, Droitwich (YH05958)																																						●		●			●										
HACKETT, L, Broadway (YH06251)																																												●									
HANN, PRISCILLA, Kidderminster (YH06392)																																							●														
HARTLEBURY EQUESTRIAN CTRE, Kidderminster (YH06505)															●																							●		●		●		●						●			
HEID & BRAZIER, Stourport-on-Severn (YH06648)					●	●																																		●													
HIGH CRUNDALLS STABLES, Bewdley (YH06756)																																												●									
HIGHWAY GALLERY, Upton-upon-Severn (YH06801)	●																																																				
HILLOCKS FARM, Kidderminster (YH06847)							●																																					●									
HONEYBOURNE STABLES, Bromsgrove (YH07012)																																												●									
HORSEWISE CLOTHING, Worcester (YH07179)																																					●																
JUST LEATHER, Worcester (YH07975)																																					●																
KYRE EQUESTRIAN CTRE, Tenbury Wells (YH08305)							●						●		●																							●		●				●									
LEA CASTLE EQUESTRIAN CTRE, Kidderminster (YH08493)									●		●		●									●																										●					
LEA CASTLE SADDLERY, Kidderminster (YH08494)																																					●																
LITTLE MALVERN SADDLE, Malvern (YH08692)																				●																	●																
LYNDHURST SADDLERY, Worcester (YH08929)																																					●																
MOORLANDS, Worcester (YH09779)																																						●															
MORGAN BLACKSMITHS, Malvern (YH09793)																																					●																
MOYFIELD RIDING SCHOOL, Evesham (YH09908)							●																															●		●		●											
OAKLAND HORSEBOXES, Little Witley (YH10388)																						●																										●					
PERSHORE & HINDLIP CLGE, Hindlip (YH10993)							●																																					●									
RANDLE, TIM, Kidderminster (YH11630)															●																																						
RILEY HILL FARM HOLIDAYS, Cradley (YH11894)													●																																								
ROBINS, ADRIAN J, Kidderminster (YH11984)																																	●	●																			
RUG LAUDRY, Worcester (YH12215)																																				●																	

www.hccyourhorse.com

Business Profile
General Equine

by Country by County

by Country by County	Artist	Blacksmith	Business Consultancy	Commentating for Events	Competition Horses	Competition Riders	Cross Country Course	Dressage Riders	Driving Centre	Driving Competitors	Driving Services	Engraving	Equine Holidays	Event Management	Event Riders	Forge	Harness Race Course	Harness Racing Horses
RYAN-BELL, CAROLYNE, Evesham (YH12288)															●			
SAUNDERS SADDLERY, Stourport-on-Severn (YH12443)																		
SMITH-MAXWELL, A L, Upton-upon-Severn (YH13005)					●								●					
SOLCUM STUD & STABLES, Kidderminster (YH13052)																		
SPORTING HEIGHTS, Kidderminster (YH13227)																		
TABOR, M J & N J, Broadway (YH13771)							●											
TREEHOUSE, Droitwich (YH14360)																		
TURVEY, F C, Kidderminster (YH14497)																		
W H SUTTON & SONS, Kidderminster (YH14775)																		
WALNUT STABLES, Malvern (YH14870)																		
WARRINGTON, S, Little Witley (YH14943)					●	●		●					●		●			
WATSON, ERICA, Broadway (YH14983)															●			
WESCOMB SADDLERY, Lower Strensham (YH15116)																		
WHITFORD RIDING STABLE, Bromsgrove (YH15361)																		
WITS END STABLES, Worcester (YH15634)																		
YORKSHIRE (EAST)																		
ASS BLOOD STOCK CONS, Bridlington (YH00629)																		
BANKS, R T, Beverley (YH00903)																		
BATA, Beverley (YH01062)																		
BELL, J F & C R (ESQ), Howden (YH01222)																		
BLEACH YARD STABLES, Beverley (YH01531)																		
BRAEMAR, Hull (YH01770)							●											
BURTON CONSTABLE RIDING CTRE, Hull (YH02291)					●													
CHURCH FARMS, Beverley (YH02904)					●													
DALGETY AGRCLTRL, Driffield (YH03839)																		
EAST RIDING, Brough (YH04483)					●	●												
ELM TREE TACK SHOP, Halsham (YH04635)																		
FARMWAY, Driffield (YH05076)																		
GEE, MICHAEL, Holme upon Spalding Moor (YH05692)															●			
HALL, ALEC W G, Driffield (YH06312)																		
HIGH BELTHORPE LIVERY, Bishop Wilton (YH06755)																		
HORSE & RIDER TACK SHOP, Hull (YH07101)																		

by Country by County	Harness Racing Skills	Harness Retailer	Horse Sale Agency	Horsebox Hire	International Arena	Jockey	Jockey Supply	Photographer	Point-to-Point Course	Polo Pitch	Portraits	Racecourse Flat	Racecourse Steeplechase	Racing Investment	Repairs Rugs	Repairs Saddles	Riding Club	Rug Cleaning
RYAN-BELL, CAROLYNE, Evesham (YH12288)																		
SAUNDERS SADDLERY, Stourport-on-Severn (YH12443)																		
SMITH-MAXWELL, A L, Upton-upon-Severn (YH13005)									●					●				
SOLCUM STUD & STABLES, Kidderminster (YH13052)			●															
SPORTING HEIGHTS, Kidderminster (YH13227)																		
TABOR, M J & N J, Broadway (YH13771)																		
TREEHOUSE, Droitwich (YH14360)																		
TURVEY, F C, Kidderminster (YH14497)			●															
W H SUTTON & SONS, Kidderminster (YH14775)																		
WALNUT STABLES, Malvern (YH14870)																		
WARRINGTON, S, Little Witley (YH14943)																		
WATSON, ERICA, Broadway (YH14983)																		
WESCOMB SADDLERY, Lower Strensham (YH15116)																		
WHITFORD RIDING STABLE, Bromsgrove (YH15361)																		
WITS END STABLES, Worcester (YH15634)																		
YORKSHIRE (EAST)																		
ASS BLOOD STOCK CONS, Bridlington (YH00629)																		
BANKS, R T, Beverley (YH00903)			●															
BATA, Beverley (YH01062)																		
BELL, J F & C R (ESQ), Howden (YH01222)			●															
BLEACH YARD STABLES, Beverley (YH01531)																		
BRAEMAR, Hull (YH01770)																		
BURTON CONSTABLE RIDING CTRE, Hull (YH02291)																	●	
CHURCH FARMS, Beverley (YH02904)																		
DALGETY AGRCLTRL, Driffield (YH03839)																		
EAST RIDING, Brough (YH04483)																		
ELM TREE TACK SHOP, Halsham (YH04635)																		
FARMWAY, Driffield (YH05076)																		
GEE, MICHAEL, Holme upon Spalding Moor (YH05692)																		
HALL, ALEC W G, Driffield (YH06312)																		
HIGH BELTHORPE LIVERY, Bishop Wilton (YH06755)																		
HORSE & RIDER TACK SHOP, Hull (YH07101)																		

by Country by County	Saddler	School (Indoor)	School (Outdoor)	Sculptor	Shipping Agent	Show Jump Course	Show Jumping arena	Stabling Centre	Tack Shop	Taxidermy	Trail Riding Centre	Transport	Transport Overseas	Trekking Centre	Valuer	Website design	Wheelwright
RYAN-BELL, CAROLYNE, Evesham (YH12288)																	
SAUNDERS SADDLERY, Stourport-on-Severn (YH12443)	●											●					
SMITH-MAXWELL, A L, Upton-upon-Severn (YH13005)																	
SOLCUM STUD & STABLES, Kidderminster (YH13052)								●									
SPORTING HEIGHTS, Kidderminster (YH13227)	●																
TABOR, M J & N J, Broadway (YH13771)																	
TREEHOUSE, Droitwich (YH14360)	●																
TURVEY, F C, Kidderminster (YH14497)																	
W H SUTTON & SONS, Kidderminster (YH14775)																	●
WALNUT STABLES, Malvern (YH14870)				●													
WARRINGTON, S, Little Witley (YH14943)				●				●									
WATSON, ERICA, Broadway (YH14983)																	
WESCOMB SADDLERY, Lower Strensham (YH15116)	●																
WHITFORD RIDING STABLE, Bromsgrove (YH15361)								●									
WITS END STABLES, Worcester (YH15634)				●													
YORKSHIRE (EAST)																	
ASS BLOOD STOCK CONS, Bridlington (YH00629)					●												
BANKS, R T, Beverley (YH00903)																	
BATA, Beverley (YH01062)	●																
BELL, J F & C R (ESQ), Howden (YH01222)																	
BLEACH YARD STABLES, Beverley (YH01531)								●									
BRAEMAR, Hull (YH01770)				●		●											
BURTON CONSTABLE RIDING CTRE, Hull (YH02291)							●										
CHURCH FARMS, Beverley (YH02904)																	
DALGETY AGRCLTRL, Driffield (YH03839)	●																
EAST RIDING, Brough (YH04483)																	
ELM TREE TACK SHOP, Halsham (YH04635)	●																
FARMWAY, Driffield (YH05076)	●																
GEE, MICHAEL, Holme upon Spalding Moor (YH05692)																	
HALL, ALEC W G, Driffield (YH06312)	●																
HIGH BELTHORPE LIVERY, Bishop Wilton (YH06755)								●									
HORSE & RIDER TACK SHOP, Hull (YH07101)	●																

Business Profile
General Equine

by Country by County

	Artist	Blacksmith	Business Consultancy	Commentating for Events	Competition Horses	Competition Riders	Cross Country Course	Dressage Riders	Driving Centre	Driving Competitors	Driving Services	Engraving	Equine Holidays	Event Management	Event Riders	Forge	Harness Race Course	Harness Racing Horses	Harness Racing Skills	Harness Retailer	Horse Sale Agency	Horsebox Hire	International Arena	Jockey	Jockey Supply	Photographer	Point-to-Point Course	Polo Pitch	Portraits	Racecourse Flat	Racecourse Steeplechase	Racing Investment	Repairs Rugs	Repairs Saddles	Riding Club	Rug Cleaning	Saddler	School (Indoor)	School (Outdoor)	Sculptor	Shipping Agent	Show Jump Course	Show Jumping arena	Stabling Centre	Tack Shop	Taxidermy	Trail Riding Centre	Transport	Transport Overseas	Trekking Centre	Valuer	Website design	Wheelwright
J J EQUESTRIAN TACK & TURNOUT, Goole (YH07591)																																					●																
K & B TACK SHOPS, Bridlington (YH07979)																																	●	●			●																
NORTH HUMBERSIDE, Hull (YH10264)													●																									●															
PATRICK WILKINSON, Beverley (YH10825)																																	●	●		●	●								●								
R J A ROBSON & SON, Bridlington (YH11548)		●																																																			
RISTON WHINS LIVERY YARD, Beverley (YH11913)																																																●					
ROWLEY MANOR STABLES, Little Weighton (YH12170)																																												●									
RYEHILL, Hull (YH12301)																																												●									
SKERNE LEYS FARM, Driffield (YH12869)																																												●									
SMITHS ANIMAL & PET SUPPLIES, Cottingham (YH13006)																																					●																
SMITHY, Driffield (YH13013)		●																																																			
STILLMEADOW TACK SHOP, Hull (YH13467)																																					●																
SWANLAND EQUESTRIAN CTRE, North Ferriby (YH13693)																																					●							●									
WYTON TACK SHOP, Hull (YH15877)																																					●																
YORKSHIRE (NORTH)																																																					
AVISON, PENNY, York (YH00686)																																												●									
B & B LIVERY, Northallerton (YH00709)																																												●									
B GREGSON & SON, Harrogate (YH00723)																						●																										●					
BARKER, A C, York (YH00939)																																												●									
BEAVER HORSE SHOP, Harrogate (YH01143)																																	●	●		●	●													●			
BELL, HELEN, Thirsk (YH01219)															●																																						
BELMONT LIVERY STABLE, Harrogate (YH01247)																																												●									
BEWERLEY, Harrogate (YH01347)																																						●		●		●								●			
BHDTA, York (YH01351)											●																																										
BIELBYS OF SCARBOROUGH, Scarborough (YH01401)												●																																									
BLEACH FARM, York (YH01530)																																								●		●											
BOGS HALL, Ripon (YH01598)																																						●		●													
BRIGG VIEW, Filey (YH01906)															●																							●		●													
BROWSIDE PONY TREKKING CTRE, Scarborough (YH02148)													●																																								
C & C HORSE TRANSPORT, Thirsk (YH02354)																																																●					
CARL BROWN HORSE TRANSPORT, York (YH02539)																																																●					
COUNTESS OF SWINTON, Ripon (YH03394)													●																																								

Business Profile
General Equine

by Country by County

by Country by County	Artist	Blacksmith	Business Consultancy	Commentating for Events	Competition Horses	Competition Riders	Cross Country Course	Dressage Riders	Driving Centre	Driving Competitors	Driving Services	Engraving	Equine Holidays	Event Management	Event Riders	Forge	Harness Race Course	Harness Racing Horses
DRIVER, J G & A S, Haxby (YH04277)																		
E K READMAN & SONS, Scarborough (YH04412)																		
ESCRICK PK RIDEWAYS, York (YH04859)							●											
FARSYDE STUD & RIDING CTRE, Whitby (YH05098)													●					
FLETCHER, KAREN, Thirsk (YH05280)																		
FOLLIFOOT PK, Harrogate (YH05300)					●								●			●		
FRANCES BULLOCK'S SADDLERY, Easingwold (YH05446)																		
FRIARS HILL STABLES, York (YH05501)					●								●					
FURNESS, ROBIN, Northallerton (YH05550)	●																	
G & A HORSE TRANSPORT, Harrogate (YH05561)																		
GEORGE WOODALL & SONS, Malton (YH05722)																		
GILLS SADDLERY & CANE, Northallerton (YH05787)																		
GOLDIE, DAVID, Skipton (YH05887)																		
GRANARY, Whitby (YH05980)																		
HARROGATE, Harrogate (YH06490)													●					
HOLLINHALL RIDE & DRIVE, Whitby (YH06946)							●		●		●							
HOME FARM, Malton (YH06995)																		
HORSE RIDING HOLIDAYS, Hovingham (YH07135)													●					
HORSEFEEDSUK, Harrogate (YH07154)																		
HUTTON HALL FARM, Ripon (YH07339)																		
JODHPURS, York (YH07774)							●											
JOUSTING & ASSOCIATED SKILLS, Thirsk (YH07948)														●				
KILNSEY TREKKING CTRE, Skipton (YH08153)													●					
LANGTON HORSE WEAR, Northallerton (YH08416)																		
LODGE, DIANA ROSEMARY, Skipton (YH08773)	●																	
M K M RACING, Leyburn (YH08972)																		
MATCHMAKER HORSE & PONY, York (YH09256)							●											
MILL LANE, Selby (YH09579)							●											
MOORE, CHRISTINE M, Tadcaster (YH09758)				●														
MOORHOUSE RIDING CTRE, York (YH09776)							●											
NABURN GRANGE RIDING CTRE, York (YH10008)					●	●	●						●		●			
NICHOLSON, MYLES, Harrogate (YH10194)															●			

by Country by County	Harness Racing Skills	Harness Retailer	Horse Sale Agency	Horsebox Hire	International Arena	Jockey	Jockey Supply	Photographer	Point-to-Point Course	Polo Pitch	Portraits	Racecourse Flat	Racecourse Steeplechase	Racing Investment	Repairs Rugs	Repairs Saddles	Riding Club	Rug Cleaning
DRIVER, J G & A S, Haxby (YH04277)																		
E K READMAN & SONS, Scarborough (YH04412)																		
ESCRICK PK RIDEWAYS, York (YH04859)																		
FARSYDE STUD & RIDING CTRE, Whitby (YH05098)																		
FLETCHER, KAREN, Thirsk (YH05280)			●															
FOLLIFOOT PK, Harrogate (YH05300)																		
FRANCES BULLOCK'S SADDLERY, Easingwold (YH05446)															●	●		●
FRIARS HILL STABLES, York (YH05501)				●														
FURNESS, ROBIN, Northallerton (YH05550)																		
G & A HORSE TRANSPORT, Harrogate (YH05561)																		
GEORGE WOODALL & SONS, Malton (YH05722)																		
GILLS SADDLERY & CANE, Northallerton (YH05787)															●	●		●
GOLDIE, DAVID, Skipton (YH05887)																		
GRANARY, Whitby (YH05980)																		
HARROGATE, Harrogate (YH06490)																		
HOLLINHALL RIDE & DRIVE, Whitby (YH06946)																		
HOME FARM, Malton (YH06995)																		
HORSE RIDING HOLIDAYS, Hovingham (YH07135)																		
HORSEFEEDSUK, Harrogate (YH07154)																		
HUTTON HALL FARM, Ripon (YH07339)																		
JODHPURS, York (YH07774)																		
JOUSTING & ASSOCIATED SKILLS, Thirsk (YH07948)																		
KILNSEY TREKKING CTRE, Skipton (YH08153)																		
LANGTON HORSE WEAR, Northallerton (YH08416)		●													●	●		●
LODGE, DIANA ROSEMARY, Skipton (YH08773)																		
M K M RACING, Leyburn (YH08972)																		
MATCHMAKER HORSE & PONY, York (YH09256)			●															
MILL LANE, Selby (YH09579)																		
MOORE, CHRISTINE M, Tadcaster (YH09758)																		
MOORHOUSE RIDING CTRE, York (YH09776)																		
NABURN GRANGE RIDING CTRE, York (YH10008)																		
NICHOLSON, MYLES, Harrogate (YH10194)																		

by Country by County	Saddler	School (Indoor)	School (Outdoor)	Sculptor	Shipping Agent	Show Jump Course	Show Jumping arena	Stabling Centre	Tack Shop	Taxidermy	Trail Riding Centre	Transport	Transport Overseas	Trekking Centre	Valuer	Website design	Wheelwright
DRIVER, J G & A S, Haxby (YH04277)								●									
E K READMAN & SONS, Scarborough (YH04412)	●																
ESCRICK PK RIDEWAYS, York (YH04859)																	
FARSYDE STUD & RIDING CTRE, Whitby (YH05098)				●													
FLETCHER, KAREN, Thirsk (YH05280)																	
FOLLIFOOT PK, Harrogate (YH05300)		●		●		●		●									
FRANCES BULLOCK'S SADDLERY, Easingwold (YH05446)	●																
FRIARS HILL STABLES, York (YH05501)		●				●		●				●		●			
FURNESS, ROBIN, Northallerton (YH05550)																	
G & A HORSE TRANSPORT, Harrogate (YH05561)												●					
GEORGE WOODALL & SONS, Malton (YH05722)	●																
GILLS SADDLERY & CANE, Northallerton (YH05787)	●																
GOLDIE, DAVID, Skipton (YH05887)	●																
GRANARY, Whitby (YH05980)	●																
HARROGATE, Harrogate (YH06490)								●									
HOLLINHALL RIDE & DRIVE, Whitby (YH06946)				●													
HOME FARM, Malton (YH06995)				●													
HORSE RIDING HOLIDAYS, Hovingham (YH07135)																	
HORSEFEEDSUK, Harrogate (YH07154)																●	
HUTTON HALL FARM, Ripon (YH07339)								●									
JODHPURS, York (YH07774)		●		●													
JOUSTING & ASSOCIATED SKILLS, Thirsk (YH07948)		●		●													
KILNSEY TREKKING CTRE, Skipton (YH08153)																	
LANGTON HORSE WEAR, Northallerton (YH08416)									●								
LODGE, DIANA ROSEMARY, Skipton (YH08773)																	
M K M RACING, Leyburn (YH08972)								●									
MATCHMAKER HORSE & PONY, York (YH09256)								●									
MILL LANE, Selby (YH09579)		●		●		●											
MOORE, CHRISTINE M, Tadcaster (YH09758)																	
MOORHOUSE RIDING CTRE, York (YH09776)		●		●		●											
NABURN GRANGE RIDING CTRE, York (YH10008)		●		●		●											
NICHOLSON, MYLES, Harrogate (YH10194)																	

Business Profile
General Equine

by Country by County	NORMAN, JILL, Whixley (YH10238)	NORTH OF ENGLAND SADDLE, Bedale (YH10277)	NORTHALLERTON EQUESTRIAN, Northallerton (YH10290)	NORTHERN EQUINE THERAPY CTRE, Settle (YH10303)	PIMLOTT, C & N, York (YH11112)	R & R COUNTRY, Selby (YH11507)	R C BLAND, Harrogate (YH11517)	RICHMOND EQUESTRIAN CTRE, Richmond (YH11827)	RIDE-AWAY, York (YH11850)	RIDING CTRE, Harrogate (YH11874)	ROBERTS, V J W, Skipton (YH11965)	ROBINSON, Malton (YH11985)	ROSE COTTAGE FARM, York (YH12091)	ROY PARKER PHOTOGRAPHY, Scarborough (YH12179)	RUSSELL, ALEC, Huttons Ambo (YH12256)	RUSSELL, G T, Malton (YH12257)	SALLY ARNUP, York (YH12389)	SAM TURNER & SONS, Northallerton (YH12395)	SCULPTURE TO WEAR, Leyburn (YH12575)	SIMPSON, PETER D, Malton (YH12841)	SINNINGTON MANOR, York (YH12855)	SNAINTON RIDING CTRE, Scarborough (YH13028)	SPALDING, C M, Richmond (YH13171)	STEPHENSON & SON, York (YH13425)	STOCKWELL STUD LIVERY STABLES, Tadcaster (YH13497)	SWINTON PARK, Ripon (YH13713)	SWINTON RIDING/TREKKING CTRE, Ripon (YH13714)	TEAL COTTAGE STUD, Welburn (YH13922)	WELLFIELD TREKKING CTRE, Scarborough (YH15069)	WESTERMAN, BARRY, Riccall (YH15196)	WHALTON STUD, Harrogate (YH15262)	WHITE ROSE SADDLERY, Malton (YH15324)
Wheelwright																																
Website design																																
Valuer																								●								
Trekking Centre																																
Transport Overseas																																
Transport																																
Trail Riding Centre																										●						
Taxidermy																																
Tack Shop												●																				
Stabling Centre			●	●	●			●								●						●	●		●			●			●	
Show Jumping arena																																
Show Jump Course													●																			
Shipping Agent																																
Sculptor			●							●			●																			
School (Outdoor)																	●		●													
School (Indoor)			●							●			●																			
Saddler						●	●					●						●														●
Rug Cleaning						●						●																				●
Riding Club																																
Repairs Saddles		●				●						●																		●		●
Repairs Rugs		●				●						●																		●		●
Racing Investment																																
Racecourse Steeplechase																																
Racecourse Flat																																
Portraits																	●															
Polo Pitch																																
Point-to-Point Course														●	●					●												
Photographer																																
Jockey Supply									●																							
Jockey																																
International Arena																																
Horsebox Hire																																
Horse Sale Agency																																
Harness Retailer																																
Harness Racing Skills																																
Harness Racing Horses																																
Harness Race Course																																
Forge																																
Event Riders																																
Event Management																																
Equine Holidays			●					●			●										●	●				●	●		●			
Engraving																																
Driving Services																																
Driving Competitors																																
Driving Centre																																
Dressage Riders																																
Cross Country Course			●							●						●									●	●						
Competition Riders			●																													
Competition Horses			●																													
Commentating for Events	●																															
Business Consultancy																																
Blacksmith																																
Artist																	●															

Business Profile
General Equine

by Country by County	Artist	Blacksmith	Business Consultancy	Commentating for Events	Competition Horses	Competition Riders	Cross Country Course	Dressage Riders	Driving Centre	Driving Competitors	Driving Services	Engraving	Equine Holidays	Event Management	Event Riders	Forge	Harness Race Course	Harness Racing Horses	Harness Racing Skills	Harness Retailer	Horse Sale Agency	Horsebox Hire	International Arena	Jockey	Jockey Supply	Photographer	Point-to-Point Course	Polo Pitch	Portraits	Racecourse Flat	Racecourse Steeplechase	Racing Investment	Repairs Rugs	Repairs Saddles	Riding Club	Rug Cleaning	Saddler	School (Indoor)	School (Outdoor)	Sculptor	Shipping Agent	Show Jump Course	Show Jumping arena	Stabling Centre	Tack Shop	Taxidermy	Trail Riding Centre	Transport	Transport Overseas	Trekking Centre	Valuer	Website design	Wheelwright
YORK RIDING SCHOOL, York (YH15917)													●								●																							●									
YORKSHIRE DALES, Skipton (YH15919)													●																																		●			●			
YORKSHIRE RIDING CTRE, Harrogate (YH15922)					●	●	●	●					●		●																							●		●		●	●										
YORKSHIRE RIDING SUPPLIES, York (YH15923)																																					●								●								
YORKSHIRE (SOUTH)																																																					
ANNE WAINWRIGHT SADDLERY, Doncaster (YH00456)																																					●																
BARNES GREEN, Sheffield (YH00971)																																								●													
BROCKHOLES FARM, Doncaster (YH02010)							●																															●		●		●			●								
CLOUGH FIELDS STABLES, Sheffield (YH03068)																																												●									
COPLEY, JOSEPHINE, Doncaster (YH03299)	●																																																				
DARKHORSE TINYTACK, Barnsley (YH03888)					●						●									●	●																●								●								
EASTWOOD, D, Barnsley (YH04519)																																	●	●		●																	
FROST, T, Doncaster (YH05521)																																					●																
GLEBE FIELD RIDING EST, Mexborough (YH05816)																																												●									
GROVE HOUSE, Doncaster (YH06168)							●																																			●			●								
HALES, ALFRED (SNR), Sheffield (YH06293)											●																																										
HORSE & RIDER, Sheffield (YH07097)																																					●								●								
HORSE & RIDER, Doncaster (YH07096)																																	●			●	●								●								
HOWARTH LODGE RIDING CTRE, Rotherham (YH07220)																																												●									
HUNSHELF SADDLERY, Sheffield (YH07292)																																					●																
LEATHER LINES SADDLERY, Rotherham (YH08503)																																	●	●			●																
MALLARD HSE, Sheffield (YH09050)																																								●		●											
MASSARELLA, Sheffield (YH09248)																																												●									
MILLVIEW, Doncaster (YH09638)																																	●	●		●	●																
MOORHOUSE, Doncaster (YH09774)																																					●	●							●								
MOORHOUSE, Doncaster (YH09775)																																						●					●										
MR ED'S, Rotherham (YH09915)																																	●	●		●	●								●								
NORTHERN RACING COLLEGE, Doncaster (YH10307)																																						●		●			●										
PARKLANDS RIDING SCHOOL, Sheffield (YH10770)																																					●							●									
PRICES, Rotherham (YH11391)																																								●		●											
ROTHERHAM SADDLERY, Rotherham (YH12132)																																					●																
ROYSTON PONY CLUB, Barnsley (YH12202)																																			●							●	●										

Business Profile

General Equine

by Country by County	Artist	Blacksmith	Business Consultancy	Commentating for Events	Competition Horses	Competition Riders	Cross Country Course	Dressage Riders	Driving Centre	Driving Competitors	Driving Services	Engraving	Equine Holidays	Event Management	Event Riders	Forge	Harness Race Course	Harness Racing Horses	Harness Racing Skills	Harness Retailer	Horse Sale Agency	Horsebox Hire	International Arena	Jockey	Jockey Supply	Photographer	Point-to-Point Course	Polo Pitch	Portraits	Racecourse Flat	Racecourse Steeplechase	Racing Investment	Repairs Rugs	Repairs Saddles	Riding Club	Rug Cleaning	Saddler	School (Indoor)	School (Outdoor)	Sculptor	Shipping Agent	Show Jump Course	Show Jumping arena	Stabling Centre	Tack Shop	Taxidermy	Trail Riding Centre	Transport	Transport Overseas	Trekking Centre	Valuer	Website design	Wheelwright
SANDALL BEAT STABLES, Doncaster (YH12403)																																								●													
SILKSTONE EQUESTRIAN CTRE, Barnsley (YH12800)																																						●		●													
SMELTINGS FARM RIDING CTRE, Sheffield (YH12927)																																					●							●									
SNOWDON FARM RIDING SCHOOL, Sheffield (YH13040)							●																														●							●									
SPRINGVALE CARRIAGES, Sheffield (YH13262)									●		●																																										
SYKEHOUSE ARENA, Doncaster (YH13723)					●																																							●									
THROSTLE NEST SADDLERY, Barnsley (YH14114)																																●	●			●																
WILDSMITH SADDLERY, Doncaster (YH15410)																																					●																
WILDSMITHS, Doncaster (YH15412)																																●	●		●	●																
YORKSHIRE (WEST)																																																					
ACRELIFFE, Otley (YH00159)							●																														●		●			●										
ANTHONY WAKEHAM CONSULTING, Wetherby (YH00463)			●																																																	
ASTLEY RIDING CTRE, Leeds (YH00635)					●	●	●																																	●		●			●								
BANK HSE FARM, Wakefield (YH00891)																																								●													
BARNES & WINDER, Leeds (YH00969)																						●																										●					
BARRETTS OF FECKENHAM, Leeds (YH01016)																																					●																
BARTON, R & J, Wilsden (YH01050)																																												●									
BETA, Wetherby (YH01330)			●																																																	
BLACUP TRAINING GRP, Halifax (YH01504)					●	●	●	●							●																									●		●		●									
BRADMAN, N, Pontefract (YH01761)				●																																																	
BRANDON FORGE SADDLERY, Leeds (YH01796)																																●	●		●									●								
BUCKSTONES LIVERY YARD, Sutton In Craven (YH02205)																																												●									
CANNING, SUSAN, Leeds (YH02502)	●																																																				
CHADWICK, SUE, Huddersfield (YH02706)															●																																						
CHAMELEON PHOTOGRAPHY, Huddersfield (YH02724)																											●																										
CHERRY TREE LIVERY STABLES, Wetherby (YH02816)																																												●									
CLIFFORD MOOR FARM, Wetherby (YH03035)																																								●													
CLOTHES HORSE, Boston Spa (YH03063)																																					●																
CLOVER HILL SADDLERY, Halifax (YH03069)																																●	●			●																
COUNTRY FEEDS, Bradford (YH03407)																																					●																
COUNTRY SUPPLIES, Bradford (YH03431)																																					●																
COURTYARD SADDLERY, Collingham (YH03512)																																					●																

www.hccyourhorse.com

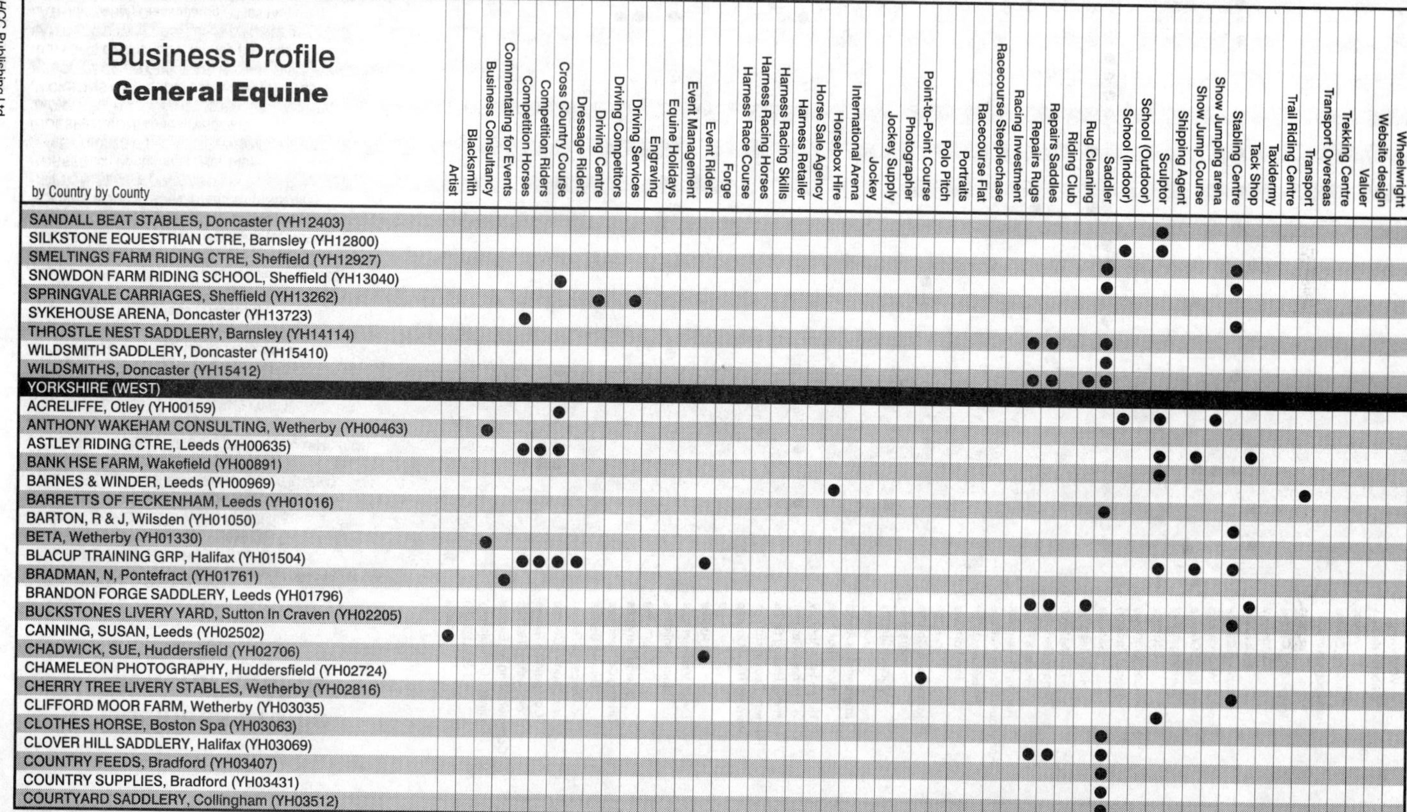

Business Profile
General Equine

by Country by County	Artist	Blacksmith	Business Consultancy	Commentating for Events	Competition Horses	Competition Riders	Cross Country Course	Dressage Riders	Driving Centre	Driving Competitors	Driving Services	Engraving	Equine Holidays	Event Management	Event Riders	Forge	Harness Race Course	Harness Racing Horses	Harness Racing Skills	Harness Retailer	Horse Sale Agency	Horsebox Hire	International Arena	Jockey	Jockey Supply	Photographer	Point-to-Point Course	Polo Pitch	Portraits	Racecourse Flat	Racecourse Steeplechase	Racing Investment	Repairs Rugs	Repairs Saddles	Riding Club	Rug Cleaning	Saddler	School (Indoor)	School (Outdoor)	Sculptor	Shipping Agent	Show Jump Course	Show Jumping arena	Stabling Centre	Tack Shop	Taxidermy	Trail Riding Centre	Transport	Transport Overseas	Trekking Centre	Valuer	Website design	Wheelwright
CROFTON RIDING STABLES, Wakefield (YH03624)																																						●		●		●											
DALE COCHRANE, Keighley (YH03820)	●																																																				
DAYS PET SHOP, Bradford (YH03971)																																					●								●								
DERWENT OF LEEDS, Holbeck (YH04081)																																					●																
DISCOUNT SADDLERY, Huddersfield (YH04129)																				●					●												●																
DRURY FARM SADDLERY, Wakefield (YH04294)																																					●																
EASTVIEW STABLES, Leeds (YH04516)					●	●	●																																	●		●	●	●									
EQUESTRIAN CLEARANCE CTRE, Halifax (YH04694)																				●																																	
EQUITACK, Wakefield (YH04824)																																					●																
EQUITACK SADDLERY, Wakefield (YH04825)																																					●								●								
F W TINGLE & SONS, Wakefield (YH05004)																																																					●
FACTORY FARM, Huddersfield (YH05007)							●																																					●									
FLY LAITHE STABLES, Halifax (YH05291)													●																																								
FOX SADDLERS, Wetherby (YH05425)																																													●								
GREAT CLOTHES, Leeds (YH06038)																																					●																
HALLAS LANE LIVERY STABLES, Bradford (YH06327)																																						●				●		●									
HELEN J BRAY STUDIO, Huddersfield (YH06652)																											●																										
HILLAM FEEDS, South Milford (YH06836)																																					●								●								
HOLME VALLEY SPORTS, Holmfirth (YH06968)																																					●																
HONLEY LIVERY STABLES, Huddersfield (YH07018)																																												●									
HOOVES EQUESTRIAN, Bradford (YH07047)																																	●			●																	
HOPTON, Mirfield (YH07061)		●					●															●																						●									
HORSEBOX, Pontefract (YH07149)																																					●																
ILKLEY RIDING CTRE, Ilkley (YH07400)						●																														●								●						●			
INDESPENSION, Leeds (YH07435)																						●																															
JACK LEES, Halifax (YH07638)																																					●																
JACKSONS OF SILSDEN, Keighley (YH07657)																																					●																
KEBCOTE COUNTRYWEAR, Hebden Bridge (YH08021)																																					●																
KENYONS OF MORLEY, Morley (YH08095)																																					●																
LANTWOOD STABLES, Leeds (YH08424)																																												●									
LATHAM FARM, Cleckheaton (YH08445)										●	●		●							●																								●									
LILAC FARM COURTYARD LIVERY, Wetherby (YH08619)							●																																					●									

Business Profile
General Equine

by Country by County

by Country by County	Artist	Blacksmith	Business Consultancy	Commentating for Events	Competition Horses	Competition Riders	Cross Country Course	Dressage Riders	Driving Centre	Driving Competitors	Driving Services	Engraving	Equine Holidays	Event Management	Event Riders	Forge	Harness Race Course	Harness Racing Horses	Harness Racing Skills	Harness Retailer	Horse Sale Agency	Horsebox Hire	International Arena	Jockey	Jockey Supply	Photographer	Point-to-Point Course	Polo Pitch	Portraits	Racecourse Flat	Racecourse Steeplechase	Racing Investment
LIVING WORLD, Leeds (YH08717)																																
LONGFIELD EQUESTRIAN CTRE, Todmorden (YH08811)													●																			
MANOR GRANGE STUD SCHOOL, Wakefield (YH09109)																																
MIDDLESTOWN SADDLERY, Wakefield (YH09540)																																
MOORSIDE EQUESTRIAN, Shipley (YH09780)																																
MOUNT PLEASANT STUD, Leeds (YH09892)																																
NORLAND EQUESTRIAN CTRE, Halifax (YH10234)																																
OWLET FARM LIVERY STABLES, Leeds (YH10613)																																
PANTOMIME HORSE, Huddersfield (YH10702)																																
PARKSWOOD ANGLO-ARAB STUD, Weeton (YH10775)																																
PENNINE FARM SVS, Huddersfield (YH10951)																																
PETER PITTS, Headingley (YH11014)				●																												
PETE'S TACK, Bingley (YH11025)																																
RICHMOND, PETER, Wetherby (YH11830)																					●											
RIGTON CARR FARM, Bardsey (YH11893)																																
ROBERTS, JOHN, Pontefract (YH11953)																					●											
ROYDS HALL RIDING SCHOOL, Leeds (YH12199)																																
RUSKIN HORSE DRAWN CARRIAGES, Leeds (YH12250)																																
SADDLERY WORKSHOP, Todmorden (YH12370)																																
SHAY LANE STABLES, Halifax (YH12686)																																
SMITH, HARVEY, Bingley (YH12960)																					●											
SPENCER, ERIC, Ilkley (YH13198)																																
SPRINGFIELD LIVERY, Keighley (YH13254)																																
STAPLETON SADDLERY, Silsden (YH13390)																																
STIRRUPS, Liversedge (YH13480)																																
TACK & TURNOUT EQUESTRIAN, Huddersfield (YH13780)																																
TAILWAGGERS, Chapel Allerton (YH13821)																																
THISTLETON FARM SADDLERY, Knottingley (YH14001)																																
TIMBERTOPS EQUESTRIAN CTRE, Pontefract (YH14162)																																
TRUEWELL HALL FARM, Keighley (YH14421)													●																			
W C F COUNTRY CTRE, Otley (YH14756)																																
WEST TACK, Bradford (YH15166)																																

by Country by County	Repairs Rugs	Repairs Saddles	Riding Club	Rug Cleaning	Saddler	School (Indoor)	School (Outdoor)	Sculptor	Shipping Agent	Show Jump Course	Show Jumping arena	Stabling Centre	Tack Shop	Taxidermy	Trail Riding Centre	Transport	Transport Overseas	Trekking Centre	Valuer	Website design	Wheelwright
LIVING WORLD, Leeds (YH08717)					●																
LONGFIELD EQUESTRIAN CTRE, Todmorden (YH08811)																					
MANOR GRANGE STUD SCHOOL, Wakefield (YH09109)												●									
MIDDLESTOWN SADDLERY, Wakefield (YH09540)	●	●		●									●								
MOORSIDE EQUESTRIAN, Shipley (YH09780)												●									
MOUNT PLEASANT STUD, Leeds (YH09892)												●									
NORLAND EQUESTRIAN CTRE, Halifax (YH10234)								●										●			
OWLET FARM LIVERY STABLES, Leeds (YH10613)												●									
PANTOMIME HORSE, Huddersfield (YH10702)					●																
PARKSWOOD ANGLO-ARAB STUD, Weeton (YH10775)												●									
PENNINE FARM SVS, Huddersfield (YH10951)					●																
PETER PITTS, Headingley (YH11014)																					
PETE'S TACK, Bingley (YH11025)	●	●																			
RICHMOND, PETER, Wetherby (YH11830)												●									
RIGTON CARR FARM, Bardsey (YH11893)												●									
ROBERTS, JOHN, Pontefract (YH11953)																					
ROYDS HALL RIDING SCHOOL, Leeds (YH12199)												●									
RUSKIN HORSE DRAWN CARRIAGES, Leeds (YH12250)																					●
SADDLERY WORKSHOP, Todmorden (YH12370)	●	●		●	●																
SHAY LANE STABLES, Halifax (YH12686)												●									
SMITH, HARVEY, Bingley (YH12960)																					
SPENCER, ERIC, Ilkley (YH13198)					●																
SPRINGFIELD LIVERY, Keighley (YH13254)												●									
STAPLETON SADDLERY, Silsden (YH13390)					●																
STIRRUPS, Liversedge (YH13480)					●																
TACK & TURNOUT EQUESTRIAN, Huddersfield (YH13780)	●			●									●								
TAILWAGGERS, Chapel Allerton (YH13821)					●																
THISTLETON FARM SADDLERY, Knottingley (YH14001)					●							●									
TIMBERTOPS EQUESTRIAN CTRE, Pontefract (YH14162)						●				●								●			
TRUEWELL HALL FARM, Keighley (YH14421)																					
W C F COUNTRY CTRE, Otley (YH14756)					●																
WEST TACK, Bradford (YH15166)					●																

Business Profile
General Equine

by Country by County

by Country by County	Artist	Blacksmith	Business Consultancy	Commentating for Events	Competition Horses	Competition Riders	Cross Country Course	Dressage Riders	Driving Centre	Driving Competitors	Driving Services	Engraving	Equine Holidays	Event Management	Event Riders	Forge	Harness Race Course	Harness Racing Horses
WESTWAYS RIDING SCHOOL, Leeds (YH15236)																		
WHITLEY EQUITATION CTRE, Dewsbury (YH15363)					●	●	●											
WIKEFIELD FARM LIVERIES, Leeds (YH15402)							●											
WILDERNESS VENTURES, Featherstone (YH15407)																		
WILLIS WALKER, Keighley (YH15492)												●						
WINPENNY PHOTOGRAPHY, Otley (YH15592)																		
WOODS SADDLERY STORES, Wakefield (YH15733)																		
YORKSHIRE EQUESTRIAN FLOORING, Leeds (YH15920)																		

by Country by County	Harness Racing Skills	Harness Retailer	Horse Sale Agency	Horsebox Hire	International Arena	Jockey	Jockey Supply	Photographer	Point-to-Point Course	Polo Pitch	Portraits	Racecourse Flat	Racecourse Steeplechase	Racing Investment	Repairs Rugs	Repairs Saddles	Riding Club	Rug Cleaning
WESTWAYS RIDING SCHOOL, Leeds (YH15236)																		
WHITLEY EQUITATION CTRE, Dewsbury (YH15363)																		
WIKEFIELD FARM LIVERIES, Leeds (YH15402)																		
WILDERNESS VENTURES, Featherstone (YH15407)																		
WILLIS WALKER, Keighley (YH15492)																		
WINPENNY PHOTOGRAPHY, Otley (YH15592)									●									
WOODS SADDLERY STORES, Wakefield (YH15733)																		
YORKSHIRE EQUESTRIAN FLOORING, Leeds (YH15920)				●														

by Country by County	Saddler	School (Indoor)	School (Outdoor)	Sculptor	Shipping Agent	Show Jump Course	Show Jumping arena	Stabling Centre	Tack Shop	Taxidermy	Trail Riding Centre	Transport	Transport Overseas	Trekking Centre	Valuer	Website design	Wheelwright
WESTWAYS RIDING SCHOOL, Leeds (YH15236)				●													
WHITLEY EQUITATION CTRE, Dewsbury (YH15363)				●		●								●			
WIKEFIELD FARM LIVERIES, Leeds (YH15402)								●									
WILDERNESS VENTURES, Featherstone (YH15407)	●																
WILLIS WALKER, Keighley (YH15492)	●																
WINPENNY PHOTOGRAPHY, Otley (YH15592)																	
WOODS SADDLERY STORES, Wakefield (YH15733)	●																
YORKSHIRE EQUESTRIAN FLOORING, Leeds (YH15920)												●					

Business Profile
General Equine

by Country by County

Business	Artist	Blacksmith	Business Consultancy	Commentating for Events	Competition Horses	Competition Riders	Cross Country Course	Dressage Riders	Driving Centre	Driving Competitors	Driving Services	Engraving	Equine Holidays	Event Management	Event Riders	Forge	Harness Race Course	Harness Racing Horses	Harness Racing Skills	Harness Retailer	Horse Sale Agency	Horsebox Hire	International Arena	Jockey	Jockey Supply	Photographer	Point-to-Point Course	Polo Pitch	Portraits	Racecourse Flat	Racecourse Steeplechase	Racing Investment	Repairs Rugs	Repairs Saddles	Riding Club	Rug Cleaning	Saddler	School (Indoor)	School (Outdoor)	Sculptor	Shipping Agent	Show Jump Course	Show Jumping arena	Stabling Centre	Tack Shop	Taxidermy	Trail Riding Centre	Transport	Transport Overseas	Trekking Centre	Valuer	Website design	Wheelwright
IRELAND																																																					
COUNTY CARLOW																																																					
AGRI SERVICES, Bagenalstown (YH00201)																						●																										●	●				
CARRIGBEG RIDING SCHOOL, Bagenalstown (YH02588)							●																															●		●													
CARTER, EDWARD, Busherstown (YH02606)																																												●									
COUNTY CAVAN																																																					
CAVAN EQUESTRIAN CTRE, Cavan (YH02664)							●														●																	●		●										●			
REDHILLS EQUESTRIAN, Redhills (YH11713)																																						●		●		●											
COUNTY CLARE																																																					
BANNER EQUESTRIAN, Ennis (YH00906)																																						●		●													
BURREN RIDING CTRE, Ballyvaughan (YH02278)													●																																		●			●			
CLARE EQUESTRIAN CTRE, Ennis (YH02949)							●																															●		●										●			
CLONLARA EQUESTRIAN CTRE, Clonlara (YH03056)							●																															●		●										●			
WILLIE DALY RIDING SCHOOL, Ennistymon (YH15487)													●																																		●			●			
COUNTY CORK																																																					
BANTRY HORSE RIDING, Bantry (YH00912)							●																															●		●													
BLARNEY RIDING CTRE, Blarney (YH01528)																																								●													
CASTLEWHITE, Cork (YH02646)																																			●			●		●		●					●			●			
CLONAKILTY EQUESTRIAN CTRE, Clonakilty (YH03053)																					●																	●		●				●						●			
CORK SADDLERY, Cork (YH03317)																																					●																
COUNTY DUBLIN																																																					
BROOKE LODGE, Sandyford (YH02042)							●																															●												●			
CALLIAGHSTOWN EQUESTRIAN, Rathcoole (YH02449)							●						●																									●		●													
CALLIAGHSTOWN RIDING CTRE, Rathcoole (YH02450)													●																																								
CARRICKMINES EQUESTRIAN CTRE, Dublin (YH02587)							●																															●		●										●			
EQUESTRIAN DIRECT SALES, Dublin (YH04699)																																													●								
INDESPENSION, Tallaght (YH07414)																						●																															
PORTRAITS, Dublin (YH11295)	●																																																				
RATHFARNHAN EQUESTRIAN CTRE, Dublin (YH11655)																																						●		●				●									
THORNTON PARK, Dublin (YH14074)																																						●		●					●								

Business Profile
General Equine

by Country by County

	Artist	Blacksmith	Business Consultancy	Commentating for Events	Competition Horses	Competition Riders	Cross Country Course	Dressage Riders	Driving Centre	Driving Competitors	Driving Services	Engraving	Equine Holidays	Event Management	Event Riders	Forge	Harness Race Course	Harness Racing Horses	Harness Racing Skills	Harness Retailer	Horse Sale Agency	Horsebox Hire	International Arena	Jockey	Jockey Supply	Photographer	Point-to-Point Course	Polo Pitch	Portraits	Racecourse Flat	Racecourse Steeplechase	Racing Investment	Repairs Rugs	Repairs Saddles	Riding Club	Rug Cleaning	Saddler	School (Indoor)	School (Outdoor)	Sculptor	Shipping Agent	Show Jump Course	Show Jumping arena	Stabling Centre	Tack Shop	Taxidermy	Trail Riding Centre	Transport	Transport Overseas	Trekking Centre	Valuer	Website design	Wheelwright
COUNTY GALWAY																																																					
CLEGGAN TREKKING CTRE, Connemara (YH03015)													●																																					●			
CONNEMARA PONY BREEDERS, Clifden (YH03237)														●																																							
FEENEY'S EQUESTRIAN CTRE, Galway (YH05127)													●																																					●			
ROCKMOUNT RIDING CTRE, Claregalway (YH12037)							●																															●		●										●			
COUNTY KERRY																																																					
ABBEYGLEN, Milltown (YH00097)																																						●		●													
BLACKVALLEY EQUESTRIAN, Derrycarna (YH01500)													●																																								
BRIDLES & BITS, Tralee (YH01893)																																													●								
BURKE'S HORSE TREKKING CTRE, Glenbiegh (YH02256)																																																		●			
CURRAGH COTTAGE LEISURE, Tralee (YH03735)																																																		●			
COUNTY KILDARE																																																					
ABBEYFIELD EQUESTRIAN FARM, Clane (YH00093)							●																																														
ACORN EQUESTRIAN CTRE, Maynooth (YH00147)							●																																														
BOROHARD EQUESTRIAN CTRE, Naas (YH01652)					●	●																																						●									
COILOG EVENTING, Naas (YH03139)							●																															●		●													
HUGHES, DESSIE, Kildare (YH07265)																																						●															
IRISH EQUESTRIAN PRODUCTS, Kildare (YH07493)																									●											●																	
LANGAN, ANNIE, Curragh (YH08397)	●																																																				
LEGGA LIVERY & SALES, Naas (YH08538)																					●																							●									
NAAS RACECOURSE, Naas (YH10006)					●	●																	●							●	●																						
NIALL'S STABLE SVS, Curragh (YH10176)																																				●																	
PUNCHESTOWN NATIONAL CTRE, Naas (YH11458)							●																																														
COUNTY KILKENNY																																																					
EUROFARM, Kilkenny (YH04898)																																													●								
COUNTY LIMERICK																																																					
ADARE EQUESTRIAN CTRE, Adare (YH00175)																																								●													
COUNTRY DRESSER, Adare (YH03403)																																													●								
INDESPENSION, Limerick (YH07415)																						●																															
COUNTY MAYO																																																						
ABRAM, DAVID, Bohola (YH00135)																				●																																	
BARLEYHILL PONY TREKKING, Bohola (YH00953)																																																		●			

Business Profile
General Equine

by Country by County	Artist	Blacksmith	Business Consultancy	Commentating for Events	Competition Horses	Competition Riders	Cross Country Course	Dressage Riders	Driving Centre	Driving Competitors	Driving Services	Engraving	Equine Holidays	Event Management	Event Riders	Forge	Harness Race Course	Harness Racing Horses	Harness Racing Skills	Harness Retailer	Horse Sale Agency	Horsebox Hire	International Arena	Jockey	Jockey Supply	Photographer	Point-to-Point Course	Polo Pitch	Portraits	Racecourse Flat	Racecourse Steeplechase	Racing Investment	Repairs Rugs	Repairs Saddles	Riding Club	Rug Cleaning	Saddler	School (Indoor)	School (Outdoor)	Sculptor	Shipping Agent	Show Jump Course	Show Jumping arena	Stabling Centre	Tack Shop	Taxidermy	Trail Riding Centre	Transport	Transport Overseas	Trekking Centre	Valuer	Website design	Wheelwright
CLAREMORRIS, Claremorris (YH02952)														●																							●	●		●		●		●	●								
COUNTY MEATH																																																					
BACHELORS LODGE, Navan (YH00766)							●						●																																								
BLACKHALL EQUESTRIAN CTRE, Little Kilcloone (YH01483)																																								●													
BROADMEADOW, Ashbourne (YH02001)																																						●		●				●									
CLARKE'S SPORTSDEN, Navan (YH02978)																																													●								
COUNTY MONAGHAN																																																					
FRANK WARD, Carrickmacross (YH05462)																																					●																
COUNTY OFFALY																																																					
ANNAGHARVEY FARM, Tullamore (YH00450)							●																															●		●		●								●			
BIRR EQUESTRIAN CTRE, Birr (YH01443)																																						●		●													
ETTER SPORTS HORSES, Bellmont (YH04886)					●																																																
COUNTY SLIGO																																																					
BALLINA EQUESTRIAN CTRE, Ballina (YH00855)																																										●								●			
COUNTY TIPPERARY																																																					
BALLINTOHER EQUESTRIAN CTRE, Nenagh (YH00862)																																						●		●										●			
CAHIR EQUESTRIAN CTRE, Cahir (YH02416)																																						●												●			
DAVERN EQUESTRIAN CTRE, Clonmel (YH03911)													●																																								
COUNTY WATERFORD																																																					
BLACKWATER SADDLERY, Tallow (YH01502)																																	●	●			●																
CONNORS, MICK, Woodstown (YH03240)																																						●															
COUNTY WESTMEATH																																																					
WEBBWEAR, Multyfarnham (YH15036)																																	●	●		●																	
COUNTY WEXFORD																																																					
CARNE RIDING STABLES, Wexford (YH02563)																																																		●			
COUNTY WICKLOW																																																					
BEL-AIR HOTEL & EQUESTRIAN, Ashford (YH01202)													●																						●																		
BROOMFIELD RIDING CTRE, Tinahely (YH02078)																																						●				●											
CLARA GUESTHOUSE, Rathdrum (YH02948)													●																																					●			
COOLADOYLE RIDING SCHOOL, Newtownmountkennedy (YH03270)																																										●											

Business Profile
General Equine

by Country by County

by Country by County	Artist	Blacksmith	Business Consultancy	Commentating for Events	Competition Horses	Competition Riders	Cross Country Course	Dressage Riders	Driving Centre	Driving Competitors	Driving Services	Engraving	Equine Holidays	Event Management	Event Riders	Forge	Harness Race Course	Harness Racing Horses	Harness Racing Skills	Harness Retailer	Horse Sale Agency	Horsebox Hire	International Arena	Jockey	Jockey Supply	Photographer	Point-to-Point Course	Polo Pitch	Portraits	Racecourse Flat	Racecourse Steeplechase	Racing Investment	Repairs Rugs	Repairs Saddles	Riding Club	Rug Cleaning	Saddler	School (Indoor)	School (Outdoor)	Sculptor	Shipping Agent	Show Jump Course	Show Jumping arena	Stabling Centre	Tack Shop	Taxidermy	Trail Riding Centre	Transport	Transport Overseas	Trekking Centre	Valuer	Website design	Wheelwright
NORTHERN IRELAND																																																					
COUNTY ANTRIM																																																					
ASHFIELD EQUESTRIAN, Larne (YH00597)																																																	●			
BEECHES EQUESTRIAN CTRE, Ballyclare (YH01169)																																																	●			
BIRR HSE RIDING CTRE, Belfast (YH01444)													●																															●									
BRACKEN EQUESTRIAN, Belfast (YH01736)																																				●	●								●								
CULLYBURN EQUESTRIAN CTRE, Newtownabbey (YH03707)																																																	●			
DRUMAHEGLIS RIDING SCHOOL, Ballymoney (YH04283)																																												●									
GALGORM MANOR EQUESTRIAN CTRE, Ballymena (YH05614)																																																	●			
GALGORM PARKS RIDING SCHOOL, Ballymena (YH05615)																																						●		●													
GRANGE EQUESTRIAN, Newtownabbey (YH05986)																																	●			●																	
INDESPENSION, Newtownabbey (YH07413)																						●																															
KIRKPATRICK, JOE, Belfast (YH08238)																											●																										
LAGAN VALLEY EQUESTRIAN CTRE, Belfast (YH08342)																																												●									
LINDSAY RUGS, Newtownabbey (YH08652)																																				●																	
LOUGHAVEEMA TREKKING CTRE, Ballycastle (YH08837)													●																																								
LUSK EQUESTRIAN, Lisburn (YH08905)							●																															●		●													
NICHOLSON, BRIAN, Lisburn (YH10191)																																																●					
OLD MILL, Carrickfergus (YH10465)																																													●								
ROSS LODGE SADDLERY, Ballymena (YH12117)																																					●																
ROWAN RIDING WEAR, Lisburn (YH12155)																																				●	●																
TULLYNEWBANK STABLES, Glenavy (YH14456)																																												●									
TULLYROE STUD, Crumlin (YH14457)					●																																																
COUNTY ARMAGH																																																					
ANNAGHMORE SADDLERY, Craigavon (YH00451)																																				●	●								●								
BALLINTEGGART STUD, Portadown (YH00860)																																												●									
LIME PARK EQUESTRIAN, Craigavon (YH08626)							●																															●		●			●	●	●								
PREMIER SADDLERY, Armagh (YH11349)																																				●									●								
RICHHILL EQUESTRIAN CTRE, Richhill (YH11825)							●						●																															●									
COUNTY DOWN																																																					
ANNAHILT SADDLERY, Hillsborough (YH00452)																				●													●	●			●																

Business Profile
General Equine

by Country by County

Business	Artist	Blacksmith	Business Consultancy	Commentating for Events	Competition Horses	Competition Riders	Cross Country Course	Dressage Riders	Driving Centre	Driving Competitors	Driving Services	Engraving	Equine Holidays	Event Management	Event Riders	Forge	Harness Race Course	Harness Racing Horses	Harness Racing Skills	Harness Retailer	Horse Sale Agency	Horsebox Hire	International Arena	Jockey	Jockey Supply	Photographer	Point-to-Point Course	Polo Pitch	Portraits	Racecourse Flat	Racecourse Steeplechase	Racing Investment	Repairs Rugs	Repairs Saddles	Riding Club	Rug Cleaning	Saddler	School (Indoor)	School (Outdoor)	Sculptor	Shipping Agent	Show Jump Course	Show Jumping arena	Stabling Centre	Tack Shop	Taxidermy	Trail Riding Centre	Transport	Transport Overseas	Trekking Centre	Valuer	Website design	Wheelwright
BALLYKNOCK RIDING SCHOOL, Hillsborough (YH00870)													●																															●									
BALLYNAHINCH RIDING CTRE, Ballynahinch (YH00873)													●																															●									
DRUMGOOLAND HOUSE, Downpatrick (YH04290)													●																																								
GEDDIS TRANSPORT, Helens Bay (YH05689)																																																●					
GENERAL STORE, Ballynahinch (YH05702)																																					●																
GRANSHA EQUESTRIAN CTRE, Bangor (YH06007)																																						●		●			●	●									
HOLMESTEAD SADDLERY, Downpatrick (YH06981)																																	●	●			●								●								
KIDD SADDLERY, Banbridge (YH08120)																																					●																
LESSANS RIDING STABLES, Ballynahinch (YH08561)							●																															●		●				●						●			
M & B EQUESTRIAN, Killinchy (YH08943)																				●																	●																
MILLBRIDGE RIDING CTRE, Newtownards (YH09594)													●																															●									
MOUNT PLEASANT, Castlewellan (YH09891)													●																															●						●			
MOURNE TRAIL RIDING CTRE, Newcastle (YH09904)																																															●						
NEWCASTLE RIDING CTRE, Castlewellan (YH10129)													●																															●									
PENINSULA EQUESTRIAN ACADEMY, Newtownards (YH10940)													●																															●									
SMILEY, ERIC, Ballynahinch (YH12929)															●																																						
SMYTHS, Newry (YH13017)																																					●																
TULLYMURRY EQUESTRIAN CTRE, Downpatrick (YH14455)													●																																								
WOOD LODGE STABLES, Castlewellan (YH15659)																																												●									
COUNTY FERMANAGH																																																					
DRUMHONEY STABLES, Enniskillen (YH04291)																																																		●			
COUNTY LONDONDERRY																																																					
ARDMORE STABLES, Londonderry (YH00511)																																						●		●													
BLAKES EQUESTRIAN, Coleraine (YH01521)																				●													●	●			●								●								
DEENY'S, Claudy (YH04019)																																					●																
DRUMSAMNEY EQUESTRIAN CTRE, Magherafelt (YH04292)							●																																														
EGLINTON EQUESTRIAN CLUB, Eglinton (YH04595)																					●																						●										
FAUGHANVALE STABLES, Londonderry (YH05102)																																			●			●		●		●	●	●	●		●			●			
HAVEN SADDLERY, Magherafelt (YH06539)																				●													●	●		●									●								
HILL FARM RIDING CTRE, Coleraine (YH06814)																																			●					●										●			
ISLAND EQUESTRIAN CTRE, Coleraine (YH07520)																																						●						●									
MADDYBENNY RIDING CTRE, Coleraine (YH09022)							●						●																									●					●										

Business Profile
General Equine

by Country by County	Artist	Blacksmith	Business Consultancy	Commentating for Events	Competition Horses	Competition Riders	Cross Country Course	Dressage Riders	Driving Centre	Driving Competitors	Driving Services	Engraving	Equine Holidays	Event Management	Event Riders	Forge	Harness Race Course	Harness Racing Horses	Harness Racing Skills	Harness Retailer	Horse Sale Agency	Horsebox Hire	International Arena	Jockey	Jockey Supply	Photographer	Point-to-Point Course	Polo Pitch	Portraits	Racecourse Flat	Racecourse Steeplechase	Racing Investment	Repairs Rugs	Repairs Saddles	Riding Club	Rug Cleaning	Saddler	School (Indoor)	School (Outdoor)	Sculptor	Shipping Agent	Show Jump Course	Show Jumping arena	Stabling Centre	Tack Shop	Taxidermy	Trail Riding Centre	Transport	Transport Overseas	Trekking Centre	Valuer	Website design	Wheelwright
MARSH KYFE RIDING SCHOOL, Magherafelt (YH09186)							●																																	●										●			
SPARKLING STUDS, Londonderry (YH13178)																																												●									
COUNTY TYRONE																																																					
EAMONN RICE BLOOD STOCK, Dungannon (YH04447)																																																●					
MCILVEEN, W M, Omagh (YH09371)																				●																	●																
MOY RIDING SCHOOL, Dungannon (YH09907)							●						●																															●									
OMAGH, Omagh (YH10506)																																					●																
SCOTLAND																																																					
ABERDEEN (CITY OF)																																																					
ALTRIES STABLES, Aberdeen (YH00346)																																												●									
BRIDGE OF DON EQUESTRIAN CTRE, Dyce (YH01876)																																												●									
COUNTRY WAYS, Aberdeen (YH03436)																				●																	●																
GROVE RIDING CTRE, Aberdeen (YH06172)																																												●									
HAYFIELD RIDING, Aberdeen (YH06578)							●																					●										●		●			●										
HAYFIELD SADDLERY, Aberdeen (YH06579)													●								●																●				●							●					
HOME FARM, Aberdeen (YH06994)													●																																								
REDWING RIDING SCHOOL, Aberdeen (YH11717)																																												●									
SESSNIE EQUESTRIAN, Aberdeen (YH12637)																																					●							●									
SUNNYSIDE, Aberdeen (YH13649)									●		●																											●					●	●									
WHITEMYRES STUD, Aberdeen (YH15352)																																												●									
ABERDEENSHIRE																																																					
ABERDEEN & NORTHERN MARTS, Inverurie (YH00121)																					●																																
ANNANDALE EQUESTRIAN CTRE, Peterhead (YH00453)																																					●							●									
ARDMIDDLE LIVERY STABLES, Turriff (YH00509)																																												●									
AUCHENHAMPER SUFFOLK, Banff (YH00660)																																					●																
BRAESIDE EQUESTRIAN CTRE, Inverurie (YH01774)																																												●									
BRIDESWELL RIDING CTRE, Alford (YH01870)									●				●																																								
EDEN EQUESTRIAN CTRE, Turriff (YH04546)													●									●																●		●													
GAMMIE, J W, Laurencekirk (YH05638)																					●																																
GILKHORN FARM SADDLERY, Peterhead (YH05767)																				●													●	●			●																
GLEN TANAR EQUESTRIAN CTRE, Aboyne (YH05827)													●																																								

Business Profile
General Equine

by Country by County	Artist	Blacksmith	Business Consultancy	Commentating for Events	Competition Horses	Competition Riders	Cross Country Course	Dressage Riders	Driving Centre	Driving Competitors	Driving Services	Engraving	Equine Holidays	Event Management	Event Riders	Forge	Harness Race Course	Harness Racing Horses	Harness Racing Skills	Harness Retailer	Horse Sale Agency	Horsebox Hire	International Arena	Jockey	Jockey Supply	Photographer	Point-to-Point Course	Polo Pitch	Portraits	Racecourse Flat	Racecourse Steeplechase	Racing Investment	Repairs Rugs	Repairs Saddles	Riding Club	Rug Cleaning	Saddler	School (Indoor)	School (Outdoor)	Sculptor	Shipping Agent	Show Jump Course	Show Jumping arena	Stabling Centre	Tack Shop	Taxidermy	Trail Riding Centre	Transport	Transport Overseas	Trekking Centre	Valuer	Website design	Wheelwright
HARBRO FARM SALES, Turriff (YH06404)																																					●																
HIGHLAND HORSE BACK, Huntly (YH06790)													●																																								
HOBGOBLINS, Aboyne (YH06899)																																	●	●																			
HORSE & RIDER OUTFITTERS, Stonehaven (YH07098)																																					●																
LADYMIRE EQUESTRIAN CTRE, Ellon (YH08338)							●																																					●									
MAINS OF BADENSCOTH, Inverurie (YH09040)																					●																																
MICHIE, ERIC, Huntly (YH09514)																				●																	●																
MILL OF URAS EQUESTRIAN, Stonehaven (YH09583)																																	●			●		●		●		●	●		●								
RIDINGHILL STUD, Fraserburgh (YH11885)																																						●		●													
SCOTHORSE, Maryculter (YH12530)																					●																																
SKINNER, GEORGE M, Inverurie (YH12875)									●		●																																	●									
SPRINGFIELD STABLES, Huntly (YH13258)																																												●									
STONEHAVEN TREKKING CTRE, Stonehaven (YH13514)													●																																								
TACK SHOP, Banchory (YH13810)							●																														●																
TOMINTOUL RIDING CTRE, Ballindalloch (YH14221)													●																																								
ANGUS																																																					
BLACKLITE, Dundee (YH01486)		●																																																			
CHODASIEWICZ, S, Dundee (YH02875)																				●													●	●																			
CONCHIE, DAVID, Carnoustie (YH03224)																																					●								●								
KIRRIEMUIR HORSE SUPPLIES, Kirriemuir (YH08240)													●									●											●			●				●		●		●	●					●			
MUIRHEAD, Muirhead (YH09923)													●																																								
PATHHEAD STABLES, Kirriemuir (YH10821)													●									●											●			●				●		●		●	●					●			
ROWAN LEA RIDING SCHOOL, Carnoustie (YH12153)																																												●									
ARGYLL AND BUTE																																																					
APPALOOSA HOLIDAYS, Lochgilphead (YH00475)																																								●										●			
ARGYLL TRAIL RIDING, Lochgilphead (YH00523)							●						●																															●									
BALLIVICAR FARM, Isle Of Islay (YH00863)													●																																								
BLACKS LIVERY STABLES, Helensburgh (YH01494)																																												●									
CASTLE RIDING CTRE, Lochgilphead (YH02631)							●						●																																		●			●			
COILESSAN, Arrochar (YH03138)													●																																								
COLGRAIN EQUESTRIAN CTRE, Helensburgh (YH03170)							●																															●		●		●	●										
CORROW TREKKING CTRE, Cairndow (YH03343)													●																																								

Business Profile
General Equine

by Country by County	Artist	Blacksmith	Business Consultancy	Commentating for Events	Competition Horses	Competition Riders	Cross Country Course	Dressage Riders	Driving Centre	Driving Competitors	Driving Services	Engraving	Equine Holidays	Event Management	Event Riders	Forge	Harness Race Course	Harness Racing Horses	Harness Racing Skills	Harness Retailer	Horse Sale Agency	Horsebox Hire	International Arena	Jockey	Jockey Supply	Photographer	Point-to-Point Course	Polo Pitch	Portraits	Racecourse Flat	Racecourse Steeplechase	Racing Investment	Repairs Rugs	Repairs Saddles	Riding Club	Rug Cleaning	Saddler	School (Indoor)	School (Outdoor)	Sculptor	Shipping Agent	Show Jump Course	Show Jumping arena	Stabling Centre	Tack Shop	Taxidermy	Trail Riding Centre	Transport	Transport Overseas	Trekking Centre	Valuer	Website design	Wheelwright
EQUI VENTURE, Barcaldine (YH04730)													●																																								
ISLAY FARMERS, Isle Of Islay (YH07523)																																					●																
KINGARTH TREKKING CTRE, Isle Of Bute (YH08189)																																																		●			
LETTERSHUNA RIDING CTRE, Appin (YH08570)													●																															●									
LITTLE RAHANE, Helensburgh (YH08701)																																															●						
MELFORT RIDING CTRE, Oban (YH09452)													●																																								
MULL OF KINTYRE, Campbeltown (YH09934)													●																																								
ROCKSIDE FARM TREKKING CTRE, Isle Of Islay (YH12038)													●																																								
ROTHESAY RIDING CTRE, Rothesay (YH12134)													●																																								
STUART, FIONA, Alexandria (YH13594)															●																																						
TACKLE & TACK, Oban (YH13818)																																	●			●									●								
TAYINLOAN TREKKING CTRE, Tarbert (YH13892)													●																																								
TIGNABRUAICH, Tighnabruaich (YH14142)													●																																								
VELVET PATH TREKKING CTRE, Dunoon (YH14675)													●																																								
WHAT EVERY HORSE WANTS, Helensburgh (YH15266)																																	●	●		●									●								
AYRSHIRE (EAST)																																																					
BARGOWER RIDING SCHOOL, Kilmarnock (YH00933)							●																															●		●													
BLAIRFIELD FARM STUD, Kilmarnock (YH01514)							●																																														
DEAN CASTLE RIDING CTRE, Kilmarnock (YH03988)							●						●																											●		●		●	●			●		●			
FENWICK MOBILE EXHIBITIONS, Kilmarnock (YH05154)																						●																															
HARPERLAND LIVERY, Kilmarnock (YH06456)																																												●									
MUIRDYKE STUD FARM, Cumnock (YH09922)													●																															●									
MUIRMILL INTERNATIONAL E C, Kilmarnock (YH09927)					●	●																																●		●		●	●		●								
ROWALLAN ACTIVITY CTRE, Kilmarnock (YH12152)				●	●	●							●	●									●															●		●		●	●	●	●					●			
AYRSHIRE (NORTH)																																																					
BROOM FARM RIDING SCHOOL, Stevenston (YH02071)																																						●															
CAIRNHOUSE RIDING CTRE, Isle Of Arran (YH02419)													●																											●										●			
CLOYBURN TREKKING CTRE, Brodick (YH03073)													●																																					●			
FERGUSHILL RIDING STABLES, Kilwinning (YH05159)					●	●	●																															●		●													
KELBURN COUNTRY CTRE, Fairlie (YH08039)													●																															●									
MILLSTONFORD, West Kilbride (YH09637)																																												●									
TANDLEVIEW STABLES, Beith (YH13852)																																								●													

Business Profile
General Equine

by Country by County

Business	Artist	Blacksmith	Business Consultancy	Commentating for Events	Competition Horses	Competition Riders	Cross Country Course	Dressage Riders	Driving Centre	Driving Competitors	Driving Services	Engraving	Equine Holidays	Event Management	Event Riders	Forge	Harness Race Course	Harness Racing Horses	Harness Racing Skills	Harness Retailer	Horse Sale Agency	Horsebox Hire	International Arena	Jockey	Jockey Supply	Photographer	Point-to-Point Course	Polo Pitch	Portraits	Racecourse Flat	Racecourse Steeplechase	Racing Investment	Repairs Rugs	Repairs Saddles	Riding Club	Rug Cleaning	Saddler	School (Indoor)	School (Outdoor)	Sculptor	Shipping Agent	Show Jump Course	Show Jumping arena	Stabling Centre	Tack Shop	Taxidermy	Trail Riding Centre	Transport	Transport Overseas	Trekking Centre	Valuer	Website design	Wheelwright
AYRSHIRE (SOUTH)																																																					
AYRSHIRE EQUITATION CTRE, Ayr (YH00704)							●						●																									●		●		●			●								
CROCKET EQUESTRIAN, Ayr (YH03606)																																													●								
DRUMCOYLE LIVERY YARD, Ayr (YH04289)																																												●									
I C S BLOODSTOCK, Mauchline (YH07364)																					●																																
JET SET SADDLERY, Prestwick (YH07764)																																					●																
ROSEMOUNT RIDING SVS, Prestwick (YH12105)																																						●		●		●											
SCOTTISH SIDE SADDLES, Dunlop (YH12558)																																	●	●			●																
SHANTER RIDING CTRE, Girvan (YH12672)																																								●													
CLACKMANNANSHIRE																																																					
DEVON EQUESTRIAN, Alloa (YH04094)																																						●		●													
GLENDEVON YOUTH HOSTEL, Dollar (YH05831)													●																																								
LUCEY, P E, Alloa (YH08885)										●																																											
ROYAL SCHOOL, Dollar (YH12192)													●																																								
SIMMONS, AVRIL, Dollar (YH12826)																																												●									
DUMFRIES AND GALLOWAY																																																					
B R I INT, Annan (YH00746)																																																●					
BAREND RIDING CTRE, Dalbeattie (YH00929)													●																															●									
DALESIDE EQUESTRIAN CTRE, Annan (YH03832)																																												●									
DEEP WATER EQUITATION CTRE, Dumfries (YH04020)																																					●																
DOUGLAS, JOHN L, Newton Stewart (YH04214)		●																																																			
ESKDALE HARNESS, Lockerbie (YH04860)																				●													●	●																			
ETTRICK STABLES, Thornhill (YH04890)													●																																								
FORBES, JOHN (SIR), Castle Douglas (YH05321)																											●																										
GEE GEE'S, Dumfries (YH05690)																				●	●	●											●	●		●	●								●								
MCGEOGH, J & I, Stranraer (YH09354)																					●																																
MRS HUNT, Terregles (YH09917)																					●																																
PATTIES OF DUMFRIES, Dumfries (YH10830)																																					●																
ROBERT THORNE, Annan (YH11944)																																												●									
W C F COUNTRY CTRE, Castle Douglas (YH14754)																																					●																
WM MURRAY FARMCARE, Dumfries (YH15642)																																				●	●																
YOUNG, GORDON, Dumfries (YH15929)																						●																										●					

Business Profile
General Equine

by Country by County

	Artist	Blacksmith	Business Consultancy	Commentating for Events	Competition Horses	Competition Riders	Cross Country Course	Dressage Riders	Driving Centre	Driving Competitors	Driving Services	Engraving	Equine Holidays	Event Management	Event Riders	Forge	Harness Race Course	Harness Racing Horses	Harness Racing Skills	Harness Retailer	Horse Sale Agency	Horsebox Hire	International Arena	Jockey	Jockey Supply	Photographer	Point-to-Point Course	Polo Pitch	Portraits	Racecourse Flat	Racecourse Steeplechase	Racing Investment	Repairs Rugs	Repairs Saddles	Riding Club	Rug Cleaning	Saddler	School (Indoor)	School (Outdoor)	Sculptor	Shipping Agent	Show Jump Course	Show Jumping arena	Stabling Centre	Tack Shop	Taxidermy	Trail Riding Centre	Transport	Transport Overseas	Trekking Centre	Valuer	Website design	Wheelwright
DUNBARTONSHIRE (WEST)																																																					
DUNCRYNE, Alexandria (YH04338)																																																	●			
EDINBURGH (CITY OF)																																																				
DAVDOR STUD, Currie (YH03907)																										●																										
DRUM FEEDS, Edinburgh (YH04280)																			●													●	●		●	●																
INDESPENSION, Edinburgh (YH07417)																					●																															
JOHN DICKSON & SON, Edinburgh (YH07786)																																				●																
MANACRAFT LEATHER, Edinburgh (YH09062)																																●	●			●																
ROBERTSON, E C, Dalkeith (YH11968)																																											●									
STEWART CHRISTIE, Edinburgh (YH13454)																																				●																
STIRLINGSHIRE SADDLERY, Edinburgh (YH13474)																																●	●		●	●								●								
TOWER FARM, Edinburgh (YH14271)						●																															●		●		●		●	●					●			
FALKIRK																																																				
CAMPBELL, CARNET, Slamannan (YH02483)												●																															●									
COWAN STABLES, Falkirk (YH03520)																																															●					
MILNHOLM, Falkirk (YH09643)																																																	●			
FIFE																																																				
ANGLE PARK, Cupar (YH00409)					●	●					●		●																										●				●									
BRADY, RON, Saline (YH01768)																				●																																
BRAESIDE, Cupar (YH01772)						●																																														
DABBS, Cupar (YH03813)																																					●		●								●					
DRYSDALE, A, Boreland (YH04300)																				●																																
EDENSIDE, St Andrews (YH04551)																																					●		●		●											
GLENROTHES RIDING CTRE, Glenrothes (YH05841)												●																															●									
KINNEAR, TERRY, Dunfermline (YH08217)																				●																							●									
LOW-MITCHELL, D I, Leven (YH08876)																																					●		●													
PUDDLEDUB STUD, Kirkcaldy (YH11447)				●																																																
RIDING STABLES, Lochgelly (YH11883)																																					●				●			●								
TIVENDALE, D A, Cupar (YH14190)																										●																										
WEST PITCORTHI STABLES, Anstruther (YH15159)												●																															●									
GLASGOW (CITY OF)																																																				
BUSBY EQUITATION CTRE, Busby (YH02302)																																●	●		●	●	●				●		●	●								

Business Profile
General Equine

by Country by County	Artist	Blacksmith	Business Consultancy	Commentating for Events	Competition Horses	Competition Riders	Cross Country Course	Dressage Riders	Driving Centre	Driving Competitors	Driving Services	Engraving	Equine Holidays	Event Management	Event Riders	Forge	Harness Race Course	Harness Racing Horses	Harness Racing Skills	Harness Retailer	Horse Sale Agency	Horsebox Hire	International Arena	Jockey	Jockey Supply	Photographer	Point-to-Point Course	Polo Pitch	Portraits	Racecourse Flat	Racecourse Steeplechase	Racing Investment	Repairs Rugs	Repairs Saddles	Riding Club	Rug Cleaning	Saddler	School (Indoor)	School (Outdoor)	Sculptor	Shipping Agent	Show Jump Course	Show Jumping arena	Stabling Centre	Tack Shop	Taxidermy	Trail Riding Centre	Transport	Transport Overseas	Trekking Centre	Valuer	Website design	Wheelwright
DUMBRECK RIDING SCHOOL, Glasgow (YH04328)																																												●									
EVERYTHING EQUESTRIAN, Busby (YH04957)																																						●				●		●	●								
GREAVES SPORTS, Glasgow (YH06047)																																					●																
HAZELDEN SADDLERY, Glasgow (YH06602)																																												●									
INDESPENSION, Glasgow (YH07419)																						●																															
KENMURE RIDING SCHOOL, Glasgow (YH08065)																																												●									
HIGHLANDS																																																					
ACHALONE ACTIVITIES, Halkirk (YH00141)													●																															●									
BEVERLEY HYMERS SADDLERY, Halkirk (YH01342)																																					●	●		●					●								
BITS 'N' BOBS, Caithness (YH01458)																																					●																
BLACK ISLE RIDING CTRE, Inverness (YH01466)																																								●										●			
CARRBRIDGE PONY TREKKING CTRE, Carrbridge (YH02577)																																																		●			
CROILA STABLES, Newtonmore (YH03627)										●			●									●																										●					
DERELOCHY SADDLER, Nairn (YH04075)																																					●																
FOXHOLE LIVERY STABLE, Beauly (YH05436)	●																												●																								
GRAMPIAN HIGHLAND RIDING, Carrbridge (YH05977)													●																																								
H P T SADDLERY, Newtonmore (YH06233)																																	●	●																			
HEBRIDEAN TREKKING HOLIDAYS, Small Isles (YH06637)													●																																					●			
HIGHLAND RIDING CTRE, Inverness (YH06793)								●					●																									●		●		●	●	●						●			
LOCH NESS RIDING, Inverness (YH08752)													●																									●		●		●		●									
LOGIE FARM, Nairn (YH08778)							●						●																											●				●						●			
NORTH COAST ADVENTURE HOLS, Sutherland (YH10247)													●																																								
ORMISTON, EWAN C, Kingussie (YH10549)										●																																											
PORTREE RIDING/TREKKING CTRE, Portree (YH11296)													●																																								
ROSS-SHIRE HORSE TALK, Tain (YH12125)																																					●																
SEAFORTH SADDLERS, Inverness (YH12586)																																	●	●		●	●								●								
TORLUNDY RIDING CTRE, Fort William (YH14245)													●																																								
INVERCLYDE																																																					
ARDGOWAN, Greenock (YH00507)																																								●		●			●								
ISLE OF SKYE																																																					
SKYE RIDING CTRE, Portree (YH12881)													●																							●				●							●	●		●			

Business Profile
General Equine

by Country by County

by Country by County	Artist	Blacksmith	Business Consultancy	Commentating for Events	Competition Horses	Competition Riders	Cross Country Course	Dressage Riders	Driving Centre	Driving Competitors	Driving Services	Engraving	Equine Holidays	Event Management	Event Riders	Forge	Harness Race Course	Harness Racing Horses	Harness Racing Skills	Harness Retailer	Horse Sale Agency	Horsebox Hire	International Arena	Jockey	Jockey Supply	Photographer	Point-to-Point Course	Polo Pitch	Portraits	Racecourse Flat	Racecourse Steeplechase	Racing Investment	Repairs Rugs	Repairs Saddles	Riding Club	Rug Cleaning	Saddler	School (Indoor)	School (Outdoor)	Sculptor	Shipping Agent	Show Jump Course	Show Jumping arena	Stabling Centre	Tack Shop	Taxidermy	Trail Riding Centre	Transport	Transport Overseas	Trekking Centre	Valuer	Website design	Wheelwright
LANARKSHIRE (NORTH)																																																					
CLIPPETY CLOP, Cumbernauld (YH03048)																																					●																
KIRK RD SMIDDY, Shotts (YH08230)		●																																																			
LAIRD, ALEXANDER, Shotts (YH08347)																																						●															
TANNOCK STABLES, Cumbernauld (YH13859)																																												●									
LANARKSHIRE (SOUTH)																																																					
HILLHEAD, Carluke (YH06846)																																						●					●										
HILLSIDE CLYSDALE STUD, Lesmahagow (YH06852)				●									●														●																										
JUMPS, Carluke (YH07967)							●																															●					●										
LETHAME HOUSE EQUESTRIAN CTRE, Strathaven (YH08567)																																												●									
MID DRUMLOCH, Hamilton (YH09526)																																						●		●			●	●									
MILLBRAE SADDLERY, Glasgow (YH09593)																																	●	●			●																
SCOTTISH EQUESTRIAN COMPLEX, Lanark (YH12555)													●																															●									
STONEHOUSE SADDLERY/PET CTRE, Stonehouse (YH13517)																																					●																
THOMSON CRAFT SADDLERY, Carluke (YH14047)												●																									●																
WELLGATE SADDLERY, Lanark (YH15070)																																					●																
LOTHIAN (EAST)																																																					
APPIN EQUESTRIAN CTRE, Haddington (YH00478)																																						●															
GROSSICK, JOHN, Longniddry (YH06158)																											●																										
H & S EUROPEAN TRANSPORT, Longniddry (YH06209)																																																●					
HARELAW EQUESTRIAN CTRE, Longniddry (YH06420)																																						●		●													
J S MAIN & SONS, Haddington (YH07617)																																	●	●		●	●								●								
ORCHARD FIELD LIVERY STABLES, Tranent (YH10533)																																												●									
WEST FENTON LIVERY, North Berwick (YH15145)																																								●				●									
WHITELOCH FARM STABLES, Tranent (YH15349)													●																																								
LOTHIAN (MID)																																																					
BOWLEA TRAILERS, Penicuik (YH01713)																																																●					
COUSLAND PK FARM, Dalkeith (YH03515)																																												●									
EASTER BUSH VETNRY CTRE, Roslin (YH04490)																																						●															
EDINBURGH & LASSWADE, Lasswade (YH04559)																																						●		●													
EDINBURGH EQUESTRIAN CTRE, Dalkeith (YH04560)							●																																	●			●										
EQUINE BEHAVIOUR FORUM, Penicuik (YH04766)																																					●																

Business Profile
General Equine

by Country by County	Artist	Blacksmith	Business Consultancy	Commentating for Events	Competition Horses	Competition Riders	Cross Country Course	Dressage Riders	Driving Centre	Driving Competitors	Driving Services	Engraving	Equine Holidays	Event Management	Event Riders	Forge	Harness Race Course	Harness Racing Horses	Harness Racing Skills	Harness Retailer	Horse Sale Agency	Horsebox Hire	International Arena	Jockey	Jockey Supply	Photographer	Point-to-Point Course	Polo Pitch	Portraits	Racecourse Flat	Racecourse Steeplechase	Racing Investment	Repairs Rugs	Repairs Saddles	Riding Club	Rug Cleaning	Saddler	School (Indoor)	School (Outdoor)	Sculptor	Shipping Agent	Show Jump Course	Show Jumping arena	Stabling Centre	Tack Shop	Taxidermy	Trail Riding Centre	Transport	Transport Overseas	Trekking Centre	Valuer	Website design	Wheelwright
GEORGES SADDLERY, Newbridge (YH05726)																																					●																
ROBINSON'S RUG WASH, Carrington (YH12006)																																				●																	
LOTHIAN (WEST)																																																					
CRAIGHEAD, Fauldhouse (YH03553)									●		●																																										
FERNIEHAUGH LIVERY STABLES, Penicuik (YH05166)							●																																	●				●									
GRANGE RIDING CTRE, West Calder (YH05993)								●																																													
GRANGE SADDLERY, West Calder (YH05996)																																													●								
HOLMES RIDING STABLES, Bathgate (YH06973)							●																															●		●			●	●									
PATCHWORK, West Calder (YH10817)																																	●																				
TACK RACK, Bathgate (YH13792)																																					●																
TIGGA'S SADDLERY, Wester Calder (YH14141)																																				●	●																
WESTMUIR RIDING CTRE, Broxburn (YH15221)																																												●									
MORAY																																																					
ABERLOUR RIDING/TREKKING CTRE, Aberlour (YH00127)													●																																								
CRANNA, P, Aberlour (YH03569)													●																															●									
GAMMACK, C A, Aberlour (YH05636)																																	●				●																
GREENFIELDS SADDLERY, Elgin (YH06085)																				●									●				●	●			●								●								
OBERON SADDLERY, Buckie (YH10418)																																	●	●			●																
PALS, Cullen (YH10694)																																					●																
SHENVAL FARM, Ballindalloch (YH12709)													●																															●			●						
STRATHSPEY HIGHLAND PONY CTRE, Grantown-on-Spey (YH13565)																																																				●	
ORKNEY ISLES																																																					
SUNNYBRAE FEEDS, Kirkwall (YH13645)																																					●																
PERTH AND KINROSS																																																					
2 XCEL, Perth (YH00002)																																	●			●																	
BALNAKILLY RIDING CTRE, Kirkmichael (YH00874)													●																																								
BLAIR CASTLE TREKKING CTRE, Pitlochry (YH01509)													●																																								
BREWSTER, T & C, Perth (YH01856)										●																																											
CALEDONIAN EQUESTRIAN CTRE, Perth (YH02440)													●																															●									
CRIEFF HYDRO HOTEL STABLES, Crieff (YH03597)																																												●									
EASTERTON ARENAS, Auchterarder (YH04499)																																												●									

www.hccyourhorse.com

Business Profile
General Equine

by Country by County	Artist	Blacksmith	Business Consultancy	Commentating for Events	Competition Horses	Competition Riders	Cross Country Course	Dressage Riders	Driving Centre	Driving Competitors	Driving Services	Engraving	Equine Holidays	Event Management	Event Riders	Forge	Harness Race Course	Harness Racing Horses	Harness Racing Skills	Harness Retailer	Horse Sale Agency	Horsebox Hire	International Arena	Jockey	Jockey Supply	Photographer
EQUI-CARE, Perth (YH04736)					●								●								●					
ERROL RACEWAY, Perth (YH04856)																	●									
GLEN EAGLES EQUESTRIAN, Auchterarder (YH05825)							●	●	●	●	●		●	●	●								●			
GLENFARG RIDING SCHOOL, Perth (YH05834)																										
GLENISLA HOTEL, Alyth (YH05838)													●													
GLENMARKIE, Blairgowrie (YH05840)					●								●													
HORSE TRANSPORT, Milnathort (YH07142)																						●				
HOUSE OF BRUAR, Blair Atholl (YH07208)																										
J J S PHOTOGRAPHY, Perth (YH07592)																										
LOCH TAY HIGHLAND, Killin (YH08753)													●													
MCCASH'S, Perth (YH09326)																										
PERTH HUNT, Perth (YH10997)																	●									
TULLOCHVILLE LIVERY YARD, Aberfeldy (YH14451)																										
RENFREWSHIRE																										
GLEDDOCH RIDING SCHOOL, Port Glasgow (YH05822)																										
MCROSTIE'S, Howwood (YH09405)																				●						
MEADOW PK, Johnstone (YH09421)																										
SCOTTISH BORDERS																										
A C BURN, Jedburgh (YH00022)																										
BAILEY MILL, Newcastleton (YH00794)													●													
BOWHILL STABLES, Selkirk (YH01710)							●																			
BROKEN SPOKE, West Linton (YH02021)									●		●															
D THOMSON & SON, Jedburgh (YH03809)																										
DONCASTER BLOODSTOCK SALES, Hawick (YH04178)																					●					
DRYDEN RIDING CTRE, Selkirk (YH04298)																										
ERIC GILLIE, Kelso (YH04845)																										
FERNIEHIRST MILL RIDING CTRE, Jedburgh (YH05167)																										
FURNESS, J, Lauder (YH05548)																										
HAZELDEAN RIDING CTRE, Hawick (YH06601)													●													
MCNAB SADDLERS, Selkirk (YH09396)																				●						
MCNAB SADDLERS, Kelso (YH09397)																				●						
NENTHORN STABLES, Kelso (YH10077)													●													

by Country by County	Point-to-Point Course	Polo Pitch	Portraits	Racecourse Flat	Racecourse Steeplechase	Racing Investment	Repairs Rugs	Repairs Saddles	Riding Club	Rug Cleaning	Saddler	School (Indoor)	School (Outdoor)	Sculptor	Shipping Agent	Show Jump Course	Show Jumping arena	Stabling Centre	Tack Shop	Taxidermy	Trail Riding Centre	Transport	Transport Overseas	Trekking Centre	Valuer	Website design	Wheelwright
EQUI-CARE, Perth (YH04736)									●		●			●				●	●					●			
ERROL RACEWAY, Perth (YH04856)																											
GLEN EAGLES EQUESTRIAN, Auchterarder (YH05825)									●	●		●		●		●	●	●	●		●			●			
GLENFARG RIDING SCHOOL, Perth (YH05834)												●		●													
GLENISLA HOTEL, Alyth (YH05838)																											
GLENMARKIE, Blairgowrie (YH05840)									●					●				●						●			
HORSE TRANSPORT, Milnathort (YH07142)															●							●					
HOUSE OF BRUAR, Blair Atholl (YH07208)											●																
J J S PHOTOGRAPHY, Perth (YH07592)	●																										
LOCH TAY HIGHLAND, Killin (YH08753)																		●									
MCCASH'S, Perth (YH09326)							●			●									●								
PERTH HUNT, Perth (YH10997)																											
TULLOCHVILLE LIVERY YARD, Aberfeldy (YH14451)																		●									
RENFREWSHIRE																											
GLEDDOCH RIDING SCHOOL, Port Glasgow (YH05822)																		●									
MCROSTIE'S, Howwood (YH09405)							●	●			●																
MEADOW PK, Johnstone (YH09421)												●		●													
SCOTTISH BORDERS																											
A C BURN, Jedburgh (YH00022)							●			●																	
BAILEY MILL, Newcastleton (YH00794)														●										●			
BOWHILL STABLES, Selkirk (YH01710)																											
BROKEN SPOKE, West Linton (YH02021)							●	●																			
D THOMSON & SON, Jedburgh (YH03809)											●																
DONCASTER BLOODSTOCK SALES, Hawick (YH04178)																									●		
DRYDEN RIDING CTRE, Selkirk (YH04298)																								●			
ERIC GILLIE, Kelso (YH04845)																						●					
FERNIEHIRST MILL RIDING CTRE, Jedburgh (YH05167)																					●						
FURNESS, J, Lauder (YH05548)																		●									
HAZELDEAN RIDING CTRE, Hawick (YH06601)																											
MCNAB SADDLERS, Selkirk (YH09396)							●	●		●	●								●								
MCNAB SADDLERS, Kelso (YH09397)							●	●		●	●								●								
NENTHORN STABLES, Kelso (YH10077)																		●									

Business Profile
General Equine

by Country by County	Artist	Blacksmith	Business Consultancy	Commentating for Events	Competition Horses	Competition Riders	Cross Country Course	Dressage Riders	Driving Centre	Driving Competitors	Driving Services	Engraving	Equine Holidays	Event Management	Event Riders	Forge	Harness Race Course	Harness Racing Horses	Harness Racing Skills	Harness Retailer	Horse Sale Agency	Horsebox Hire	International Arena	Jockey	Jockey Supply	Photographer	Point-to-Point Course	Polo Pitch	Portraits	Racecourse Flat	Racecourse Steeplechase	Racing Investment	Repairs Rugs	Repairs Saddles	Riding Club	Rug Cleaning	Saddler	School (Indoor)	School (Outdoor)	Sculptor	Shipping Agent	Show Jump Course	Show Jumping arena	Stabling Centre	Tack Shop	Taxidermy	Trail Riding Centre	Transport	Transport Overseas	Trekking Centre	Valuer	Website design	Wheelwright
OVER WHITLAW STABLES, Selkirk (YH10590)																								●																													
PEEBLES HYDRO STABLES, Peebles (YH10896)													●																																								
R H MILLER AGRICULTURAL, Hawick (YH11543)																																					●																
SPORT OF KINGS, Hawick (YH13221)																																					●																
STARK, IAN, Selkirk (YH13394)															●																													●									
WEST TARF ICELANDIC HORSES, West Linton (YH15167)																																																			●		
WESTERKIRK SADDLERY, Newcastleton (YH15193)																																	●	●			●																
WESTERTOUN, Gordon (YH15212)					●	●	●						●		●																							●		●		●	●	●									
WHISGILLS RIDING CTRE, Newcastleton (YH15285)													●																																								
SHETLAND ISLANDS																																																					
BROOTHOM PONIES, Shetland (YH02083)													●																																								
BRUCE WILCOCK, Shetland (YH02154)		●																																																			
STIRLING																																																					
CAERDACH, Drymen (YH02414)																																	●	●			●																
EASTERHILL, Gartmore (YH04495)													●																								●							●									
HENDRY, JAMES, Stirling (YH06669)		●																																					●														
LOMONDSIDE STUD, Glasgow (YH08782)																																												●									
MYOTHILL HSE EQUESTRIAN CTRE, Denny (YH09985)									●																								●	●			●							●									
W C F COUNTRY CTRE, Kildean (YH14755)																																					●																

www.hccyourhorse.com

Business Profile
General Equine

by Country by County

	Artist	Blacksmith	Business Consultancy	Commentating for Events	Competition Horses	Competition Riders	Cross Country Course	Dressage Riders	Driving Centre	Driving Competitors	Driving Services	Engraving	Equine Holidays	Event Management	Event Riders	Forge	Harness Race Course	Harness Racing Horses	Harness Racing Skills	Harness Retailer	Horse Sale Agency	Horsebox Hire	International Arena	Jockey	Jockey Supply	Photographer	Point-to-Point Course	Polo Pitch	Portraits	Racecourse Flat	Racecourse Steeplechase	Racing Investment	Repairs Rugs	Repairs Saddles	Riding Club	Rug Cleaning	Saddler	School (Indoor)	School (Outdoor)	Sculptor	Shipping Agent	Show Jump Course	Show Jumping arena	Stabling Centre	Tack Shop	Taxidermy	Trail Riding Centre	Transport	Transport Overseas	Trekking Centre	Valuer	Website design	Wheelwright
WALES																																																					
BLAENAU GWENT																																																					
KIERNAN, LYDIA, Brecon (YH08125)	●																																																				
BRIDGEND																																																					
E K M EQUESTRIAN, Bridgend (YH04411)								●																			●													●												●	
FFORDD GYRAITH LIVERY STABLES, Cefn Cribwr (YH05177)																																												●									
SOUTH WALES EQUESTRIAN CTRE, Bridgend (YH13112)													●																															●									
THOMAS, HUW R, Bridgend (YH14022)																																					●																
WILLIAMS & EVANS, Bridgend (YH15440)																																					●																
CAERPHILLY																																																					
HYPERION SADDLERY, Bargoed (YH07361)																																	●	●			●																
JENNA LIVESTOCK, Rudry (YH07743)																					●																																
MACAULAYS TACK SHOP, Blackwood (YH08982)																																					●																
ROCKWOOD RIDING CTRE, Caerphilly (YH12039)																																						●												●			
WILLIAMS, TED, Blackwood (YH15479)				●																																																	
CARMARTHENSHIRE																																																					
ALAN ELLISON, Llandeilo (YH00238)	●																																																				
AMMAN VALLEY RACEWAY, Ammanford (YH00369)																	●																																				
BERRY ANIMAL FEEDS, Kidwelly (YH01314)																																					●																
BLUE WELL RIDING CTRE, Pencader (YH01571)													●																																								
CAE IAGO RIDING CTRE, Llanwrda (YH02413)													●																																								
CLYN-DU RIDING CTRE, Burry Port (YH03100)																																			●																		
CWMTYDU RIDING STABLES, New Quay (YH03764)																																																		●			
DAVIES, MARK, Kidwelly (YH03944)																●																																					
DINESWR RIDING CTRE, Ammanford (YH04124)													●																															●									
DOBBS, P J, Llangadog (YH04152)																					●																																
DUNBAR, DEBBIE, Newcastle Emlyn (YH04332)	●																																						●														
FENWICK, W J GODDARD, Lampeter (YH05156)				●																																																	
FFYNNOCYLL, Whitland (YH05180)													●																																								
FIVE SAINTS, Llanwrda (YH05255)													●																																					●			
GLYNHIR LODGE STABLES, Ammanford (YH05858)													●																																								

Business Profile
General Equine

by Country by County	Artist	Blacksmith	Business Consultancy	Commentating for Events	Competition Horses	Competition Riders	Cross Country Course	Dressage Riders	Driving Centre	Driving Competitors	Driving Services	Engraving	Equine Holidays	Event Management	Event Riders	Forge	Harness Race Course	Harness Racing Horses	Harness Racing Skills	Harness Retailer	Horse Sale Agency	Horsebox Hire	International Arena	Jockey	Jockey Supply	Photographer	Point-to-Point Course	Polo Pitch	Portraits	Racecourse Flat	Racecourse Steeplechase	Racing Investment	Repairs Rugs	Repairs Saddles	Riding Club	Rug Cleaning	Saddler	School (Indoor)	School (Outdoor)	Sculptor	Shipping Agent	Show Jump Course	Show Jumping arena	Stabling Centre	Tack Shop	Taxidermy	Trail Riding Centre	Transport	Transport Overseas	Trekking Centre	Valuer	Website design	Wheelwright
GWERSYLL YR URDD/URDD CAMP, Llandysul (YH06203)													●																																								
H PITTAM SADDLERY, Llandysul (YH06234)																																	●	●			●																
HICKLING, L M, Carmarthen (YH06741)																																	●	●																			
HOME PARK RIDING CTRE, Llandovery (YH07004)													●																																								
HORSE CTRE, Llandysul (YH07115)																																	●	●			●																
HOWELL, CASTELL, Llandysul (YH07227)													●																																								
PEMBREY PARK EQUEST CTRE, Llanelli (YH10915)													●																																								
PENCADER STUD, Pencader (YH10928)					●																																																
PLAS EQUESTRIAN, Carmarthen (YH11164)					●						●									●														●			●								●								
PLAS-Y-MAES, Llanelli (YH11166)																																	●	●																			
PLEASURE PRINTS AREA D, Llanwrda (YH11177)																											●																										
RIPMAN, BARBARA, Carmarthen (YH11906)																					●																																
RIVERSDALE, Carmarthen (YH11923)																																												●									
SIR JOHN HILL FARM, Laugharne (YH12858)													●																																								
STALLIONS AT TACKEXCHANGE, Llanelli (YH13351)					●								●							●	●												●	●		●	●							●	●								
STARLIGHT RIDING CTRE, Newcastle Emlyn (YH13396)																																								●													
TACK EXCHANGE, Llanelli (YH13787)					●															●	●												●	●		●	●								●								
THERMATEX, Cardigan (YH13986)																																	●	●		●																	
THOMAS SHOW TEAM, Carmarthen (YH14011)					●			●																																													
TREFACH RIDING CTRE, Clynderwen (YH14362)													●																															●									
WELSH EQUITATION CTRE, Carmarthen (YH15091)													●																															●									
WILLETTS, J, Llandysul (YH15432)																																																					●
CEREDIGION																																																					
CAPTAIN RUGWASH, Cardigan (YH02524)																																	●	●		●																	
DAVIS, V C M, Aberystwyth (YH03954)		●																																																			
DYFED RIDING CTRE, Cardigan (YH04388)																																						●															
GILFACH HOLIDAY VILLAGE, Aberaeron (YH05765)													●																																								
HELLMAN, GLENN, Ystrad Meurig (YH06655)																																	●	●			●																
L CLARK, Llanrhystud (YH08316)																																																●					
MAESGLAS MOUNTAIN RIDERS, Tregaron (YH09030)													●																																								
MOELFRYN RIDING CTRE, Aberystwyth (YH09699)																																						●						●									
PANT RHYN TREKKING CTRE, New Quay (YH10701)													●																																								

Business Profile
General Equine

by Country by County

	Artist	Blacksmith	Business Consultancy	Commentating for Events	Competition Horses	Competition Riders	Cross Country Course	Dressage Riders	Driving Centre	Driving Competitors	Driving Services	Engraving	Equine Holidays	Event Management	Event Riders	Forge	Harness Race Course	Harness Racing Horses	Harness Racing Skills	Harness Retailer	Horse Sale Agency	Horsebox Hire	International Arena	Jockey	Jockey Supply	Photographer	Point-to-Point Course	Polo Pitch	Portraits	Racecourse Flat	Racecourse Steeplechase	Racing Investment	Repairs Rugs	Repairs Saddles	Riding Club	Rug Cleaning	Saddler	School (Indoor)	School (Outdoor)	Sculptor	Shipping Agent	Show Jump Course	Show Jumping arena	Stabling Centre	Tack Shop	Taxidermy	Trail Riding Centre	Transport	Transport Overseas	Trekking Centre	Valuer	Website design	Wheelwright
RHEIDOL RIDING CTRE, Aberystwyth (YH11784)							●	●																														●		●		●	●	●				●		●			
ROGERS & TAYLOR, Aberystwyth (YH12056)																																	●				●																
TREGARON PONY TREKKING ASS, Tregaron (YH14364)													●																																								
VALIENT SADDLERY, Cardigan (YH14646)																																					●																
WALES & THE WEST HARNESS, Aberystwyth (YH14838)																	●																																				
WERN EQUESTRIAN SERVICES, New Quay (YH15112)													●																																								
WINDY GAIL STABLES, Blaenannerch (YH15581)													●																															●									
CONWY																																																					
ABERCONWY EQUESTRIAN CTRE, Llandudno Junction (YH00119)										●																																			●								
COLWYN TACK CTRE, Colwyn Bay (YH03208)																																	●	●			●																
FOULKES, JUSTIN & CHRISTINE, Colwyn Bay (YH05406)																																												●									
OLDFIELD, D T, Bryn Hyfryd Park (YH10486)																					●																																
PEN-Y-BINC FARM, Colwyn Bay (YH10964)																																				●	●																
PINEWOOD STABLES, Llechwedd (YH11126)													●																																								
T I R PRINCE RACEWAY, Abergele (YH13752)																	●																																				
TYNLLWYN RIDING SCHOOL, Colwyn Bay (YH14528)																																						●		●													
DENBIGHSHIRE																																																					
A P E S ROCKING HORSES, Denbigh (YH00055)																																							●														
CLWYD WELSH PONY & COB ASS, Ruthin (YH03078)																																			●																		
ERIC WILLIAMS LEATHER-CRAFT, Corwen (YH04847)																																	●	●																			
GARTH-ROBERTS, GORDON, Denbigh (YH05663)																																					●																
GLYN VALLEY HOTEL, Llangollen (YH05857)													●																																								
LLANNERCH EQUESTRIAN CTRE, St Asaph (YH08726)					●		●						●					●	●																			●		●				●						●			
MORWYN STUD, Ruthin (YH09854)																					●																																
OWEN, TUFFY, St Asaph (YH10606)															●																																						
PUGHE, J S, Llangollen (YH11454)													●																																								
RUTHIN FARMERS AUCTION, Ruthin (YH12275)																																																			●		
FLINTSHIRE																																																					
ALYN BANK, Mold (YH00353)																																								●													
BABELL CROSS CTRY, Holywell (YH00762)							●																																														
BRIDLEWOOD EQUESTRIAN CTRE, Holywell (YH01899)																																					●																
LIGHTFOOT, R, Mold (YH08614)																					●																																

Business Profile
General Equine

by Country by County	Artist	Blacksmith	Business Consultancy	Commentating for Events	Competition Horses	Competition Riders	Cross Country Course	Dressage Riders	Driving Centre	Driving Competitors	Driving Services	Engraving	Equine Holidays	Event Management	Event Riders	Forge	Harness Race Course	Harness Racing Horses	Harness Racing Skills	Harness Retailer	Horse Sale Agency	Horsebox Hire	International Arena	Jockey	Jockey Supply	Photographer	Point-to-Point Course	Polo Pitch	Portraits	Racecourse Flat	Racecourse Steeplechase	Racing Investment	Repairs Rugs	Repairs Saddles	Riding Club	Rug Cleaning	Saddler	School (Indoor)	School (Outdoor)	Sculptor	Shipping Agent	Show Jump Course	Show Jumping arena	Stabling Centre	Tack Shop	Taxidermy	Trail Riding Centre	Transport	Transport Overseas	Trekking Centre	Valuer	Website design	Wheelwright
LYNDEN FARM, Holywell (YH08926)													●																															●									
MANNOG, Holywell (YH09092)					●																																																
GLAMORGAN (VALE OF)																																																					
ARGAE HSE STABLES, Dinas Powys (YH00519)							●																																					●									
AYRES, JOHN, Cardiff (YH00702)																																				●																
CARDIFF RIDING SCHOOL, Cardiff (YH02531)							●																														●															
CARDIFF SPORTSGEAR, Cardiff (YH02532)																																			●									●								
CIMLA TREKKING, Neath (YH02918)											●		●																																								
HORSE RUG WASH, Cardiff (YH07136)																																	●			●																	
HORSEGUARDS, Cardiff (YH07157)																																				●																
INDESPENSION, Cardiff (YH07418)																						●																															
J M P SADDLERY, Cardiff (YH07598)																																				●																
JOHN REES, Barry (YH07807)																																				●																
PENCOED CLGE, Pencoed (YH10930)							●																																														
PEN-MAEN LIVERY YARD, Cowbridge (YH10944)													●																															●									
PICKERSTON STUD, Barry (YH11085)																																												●									
S J B SADDLERY, Neath (YH12328)																																				●																
SNAFFLES SADDLERY, Cowbridge (YH13026)																																				●																
GWYNEDD																																																					
ABERGWYNANT FARM, Dolgellau (YH00126)													●																																								
ABERSOCH MARCHROS STUD, Abersoch (YH00129)													●																									●								●									
ABERSOCH RIDING/TREKKING CTRE, Pwllheli (YH00130)													●																																								
BRONALLT, Caernarfon (YH02029)																																					●							●								
BWLCHGWYN FARM, Arthog (YH02341)																																																	●			
CHAS MEDFORTH, Caernarfon (YH02778)																																																		●		
DOLBADARN TREKKING, Llanberis (YH04166)													●																																								
DOLGELLAU FARMERS, Dolgellau (YH04168)																																				●																
DWYFOR RIDING CTRE, Criccieth (YH04382)													●																															●									
EIFIONYDD FARMERS, Pwllheli (YH04596)																																				●																
HERON BARN SADDLERY, Arthog (YH06709)																				●													●	●			●																
MEIFOD-ISAF, Dyffryn Ardudwy (YH09446)													●																																								
PEN ISAR FARM, Bala (YH10922)													●																															●									

Business Profile
General Equine

by Country by County

by Country by County	Artist	Blacksmith	Business Consultancy	Commentating for Events	Competition Horses	Competition Riders	Cross Country Course	Dressage Riders	Driving Centre	Driving Competitors	Driving Services	Engraving	Equine Holidays	Event Management	Event Riders	Forge	Harness Race Course	Harness Racing Horses	Harness Racing Skills	Harness Retailer	Horse Sale Agency	Horsebox Hire	International Arena	Jockey	Jockey Supply	Photographer
PEN-LLEYN RIDING CTRE, Pwllheli (YH10943)													●													
PLAS-Y-CELYN, Caernarfon (YH11165)													●													
RHIWIAU RIDING CTRE, Llanfairfechan (YH11788)							●																			
RHOSYN GWYN EQUESTRIAN CTRE, Caernarfon (YH11791)							●																			
SNOWDONIA RIDING STABLES, Caernarfon (YH13041)																										
TACK & STITCH SADDLERY, Pwllheli (YH13777)																						●				
TY COCH FARM & TREKKING CTRE, Betws-Y-Coed (YH14517)																										
ISLE OF ANGLESEY																										
A C G S EQUESTRIAN, Bodorgan (YH00025)																										
ANGLESEY EQUESTRIAN CTRE, Holyhead (YH00410)							●																			
BRACKENDENE STUD, Anglesey (YH01738)							●																			
CROMLECH MANOR FARM, Tyn-Y-Gongl (YH03630)													●													
GORS WEN FARM, Holyhead (YH05937)													●													
LLANDDONA, Beaumaris (YH08720)													●													
MOELFRE LEATHER WORKSHOP, Moelfre (YH09698)																										
TYN-MORFA RIDING CTRE, Rhosneigr (YH14529)					●																					
MONMOUTHSHIRE																										
BEAUMONT, REBECCA, Abergavenny (YH01138)															●											
BEVAN, LYNNE, Abergavenny (YH01339)															●											
BLACK MOUNTAIN HOLIDAYS, Abergavenny (YH01468)													●													
CHEPSTOW SADDLERY, Chepstow (YH02809)																										
COUNTRYWIDE STORES, Abergavenny (YH03460)																										
COUNTRYWIDE STORES, Raglan (YH03462)																										
EARLSWOOD RIDING CTRE, Chepstow (YH04455)																										
GRANGE TREKKING, Abergavenny (YH05999)													●													
HORNWALK EQUESTRIAN, Monmouth (YH07083)																										
JONES, R M, Abergavenny (YH07926)																										
LANGARTH, Monmouth (YH08399)					●																					
MONTAGUE HARRIS, Abergavenny (YH09729)																										
PEGASUS PONY TREKKING CTRE, Abergavenny (YH10906)													●													
PONDEROSA EQUESTRIAN CTRE, Pontypool (YH11219)																										
SEVERNVALE EQUESTRIAN CTRE, Chepstow (YH12646)							●																			

by Country by County	Point-to-Point Course	Polo Pitch	Portraits	Racecourse Flat	Racecourse Steeplechase	Racing Investment	Repairs Rugs	Repairs Saddles	Riding Club	Rug Cleaning	Saddler	School (Indoor)	School (Outdoor)	Sculptor	Shipping Agent	Show Jump Course	Show Jumping arena	Stabling Centre	Tack Shop	Taxidermy	Trail Riding Centre	Transport	Transport Overseas	Trekking Centre	Valuer	Website design	Wheelwright
PEN-LLEYN RIDING CTRE, Pwllheli (YH10943)																											
PLAS-Y-CELYN, Caernarfon (YH11165)																											
RHIWIAU RIDING CTRE, Llanfairfechan (YH11788)														●		●											
RHOSYN GWYN EQUESTRIAN CTRE, Caernarfon (YH11791)																		●									
SNOWDONIA RIDING STABLES, Caernarfon (YH13041)														●										●			
TACK & STITCH SADDLERY, Pwllheli (YH13777)											●											●					
TY COCH FARM & TREKKING CTRE, Betws-Y-Coed (YH14517)																								●			
ISLE OF ANGLESEY																											
A C G S EQUESTRIAN, Bodorgan (YH00025)											●																
ANGLESEY EQUESTRIAN CTRE, Holyhead (YH00410)												●		●		●	●	●						●			
BRACKENDENE STUD, Anglesey (YH01738)																											
CROMLECH MANOR FARM, Tyn-Y-Gongl (YH03630)																		●									
GORS WEN FARM, Holyhead (YH05937)																											
LLANDDONA, Beaumaris (YH08720)														●													
MOELFRE LEATHER WORKSHOP, Moelfre (YH09698)							●	●			●																
TYN-MORFA RIDING CTRE, Rhosneigr (YH14529)												●				●		●				●		●			
MONMOUTHSHIRE																											
BEAUMONT, REBECCA, Abergavenny (YH01138)																											
BEVAN, LYNNE, Abergavenny (YH01339)																											
BLACK MOUNTAIN HOLIDAYS, Abergavenny (YH01468)																											
CHEPSTOW SADDLERY, Chepstow (YH02809)							●	●		●	●																
COUNTRYWIDE STORES, Abergavenny (YH03460)											●																
COUNTRYWIDE STORES, Raglan (YH03462)											●																
EARLSWOOD RIDING CTRE, Chepstow (YH04455)																		●									
GRANGE TREKKING, Abergavenny (YH05999)																								●			
HORNWALK EQUESTRIAN, Monmouth (YH07083)												●						●									
JONES, R M, Abergavenny (YH07926)											●																
LANGARTH, Monmouth (YH08399)																											
MONTAGUE HARRIS, Abergavenny (YH09729)																									●		
PEGASUS PONY TREKKING CTRE, Abergavenny (YH10906)																											
PONDEROSA EQUESTRIAN CTRE, Pontypool (YH11219)																		●									
SEVERNVALE EQUESTRIAN CTRE, Chepstow (YH12646)																		●									

Business Profile
General Equine

by Country by County	Artist	Blacksmith	Business Consultancy	Commentating for Events	Competition Horses	Competition Riders	Cross Country Course	Dressage Riders	Driving Centre	Driving Competitors	Driving Services	Engraving	Equine Holidays	Event Management	Event Riders	Forge	Harness Race Course	Harness Racing Horses	Harness Racing Skills	Harness Retailer	Horse Sale Agency	Horsebox Hire	International Arena	Jockey	Jockey Supply	Photographer	Point-to-Point Course	Polo Pitch	Portraits	Racecourse Flat	Racecourse Steeplechase	Racing Investment	Repairs Rugs	Repairs Saddles	Riding Club	Rug Cleaning	Saddler	School (Indoor)	School (Outdoor)	Sculptor	Shipping Agent	Show Jump Course	Show Jumping arena	Stabling Centre	Tack Shop	Taxidermy	Trail Riding Centre	Transport	Transport Overseas	Trekking Centre	Valuer	Website design	Wheelwright
VILLAGE STORES, Monmouth (YH14721)																																	●	●			●																
WINTER, ERIC, Chepstow (YH15593)															●																																						
NEATH PORT TALBOT																																																					
L & A HOLIDAY & RIDING CTRE, Port Talbot (YH08306)													●																																								
PANT-Y-SAIS, Neath Port Talbot (YH10703)													●																																								
R DAYCOCK & SON, Talbach (YH11529)																																					●																
WAUN FAWR FARM, Pontardawe (YH15009)																																												●									
ZOAR HORSE & COUNTRY CTRE, Neath Port Talbot (YH15957)																																					●																
NEWPORT																																																					
CALDICOT SADDLERY, Portskewett (YH02438)																																	●	●			●																
GWENT SADDLERY, Newport (YH06201)																																					●																
N J CRIDDLE, Newport (YH09992)																																					●																
NEWCOMBES HORSE & DOG SHOP, Newport (YH10134)																																					●																
PRICE, M & G, Wentloog (YH11382)																					●																																
SPRINGFIELD RIDING STABLES, Wentloog (YH13256)																																						●															
WILLIAMS, M, Bassaleg (YH15464)																					●																																
PEMBROKESHIRE																																																					
BOULSTON, Haverfordwest (YH01672)																																					●																
BOWLINGS RIDING SCHOOL, Haverfordwest (YH01719)													●																																								
CASTELLAN RIDING ACADEMY, Boncath (YH02623)													●																																								
CASTLEMORRIS FEEDS, Haverfordwest (YH02645)																																					●																
CROSSWELL, Crymych (YH03669)																																								●							●			●			
DOLRHANOG RIDING CTRE, Newport (YH04171)							●																																	●		●					●			●			
DUNES RIDING, Narberth (YH04342)													●																						●					●							●			●			
EAST NOLTON RIDING STABLES, Haverfordwest (YH04482)													●																																					●			
FILMSTONE FARM, Narberth (YH05204)					●	●		●							●																									●				●									
HIDE TO HARNESS, Narberth (YH06747)																				●													●	●																			
ISLAND FARM RIDING STABLES, Saundersfoot (YH07521)													●																																								
LLANWNDA STABLES, Goodwick (YH08727)																																								●										●			
MAESGWYNNE RIDING STABLES, Fishguard (YH09031)													●																																								
MOOR FARM RIDING STABLES, Haverfordwest (YH09744)							●																															●		●				●									
OASIS PARK EQUESTRIAN CTRE, Narberth (YH10412)													●							●																		●															

Business Profile
General Equine

by Country by County

	Artist	Blacksmith	Business Consultancy	Commentating for Events	Competition Horses	Competition Riders	Cross Country Course	Dressage Riders	Driving Centre	Driving Competitors	Driving Services	Engraving	Equine Holidays	Event Management	Event Riders	Forge	Harness Race Course	Harness Racing Horses	Harness Racing Skills	Harness Retailer	Horse Sale Agency	Horsebox Hire	International Arena	Jockey	Jockey Supply	Photographer	Point-to-Point Course	Polo Pitch	Portraits	Racecourse Flat	Racecourse Steeplechase	Racing Investment	Repairs Rugs	Repairs Saddles	Riding Club	Rug Cleaning	Saddler	School (Indoor)	School (Outdoor)	Sculptor	Shipping Agent	Show Jump Course	Show Jumping arena	Stabling Centre	Tack Shop	Taxidermy	Trail Riding Centre	Transport	Transport Overseas	Trekking Centre	Valuer	Website design	Wheelwright
PEGASUS, Haverfordwest (YH10902)																																		●			●																
PEMBROKESHIRE EQUESTRIAN, Haverfordwest (YH10919)																													●																								
PEMBROKESHIRE RIDING CTRE, Pembroke (YH10920)													●									●															●							●				●					
RAVEL FARM, Crymych (YH11656)													●																																								
SEALYHAM ACTIVITY CTRE, Haverfordwest (YH12590)													●																																								
TALLY HO FARM, Pembroke (YH13841)																																												●									
POWYS																																																					
ALAN PRICE, Crickhowell (YH00241)																																	●	●			●																
BROMPTON HALL, Montgomery (YH02025)					●		●														●	●											●	●		●	●	●		●		●	●	●	●			●	●				
CADARN TRAIL RIDING FARM, Brecon (YH02409)													●																																					●			
CANTREF, Brecon (YH02516)													●																											●							●			●		●	
CARREG DRESSAGE, Machynlleth (YH02578)								●																																													
CHOICE SADDLERY, Knighton (YH02876)																																	●	●			●								●								
COUNTRYWIDE STORES, Welshpool (YH03467)																																					●																
COUNTRYWIDE STORES, Presteigne (YH03466)																																					●																
COUNTRYWIDE STORES, Llandrindod Wells (YH03465)																																					●																
CRADOC TACK, Brecon (YH03541)																				●																																	
CWRT ISAF FARM, Crickhowell (YH03765)																																												●				●					
ELLESMERE, Brecon (YH04614)													●																																					●			
EQUINE SEARCH, Llanfyllin (YH04798)																					●																																
FOREST INN, New Radnor (YH05341)																				●																																	
GLAN YR AFON HOLIDAYS, Welshpool (YH05804)	●												●																●															●									
GOLDEN CASTLE, Crickhowell (YH05877)					●	●							●		●																							●		●				●			●	●					
HEART OF WALES RIDING SCHOOL, Llandrindod Wells (YH06619)														●																																							
HILL VALLEY RIDING CTRE, Crickhowell (YH06823)													●																																								
HORSEMAN'S STOP, Abercrave (YH07160)																																					●																
JIM MEADS - PHOTOGRAPHER, Caersws (YH07768)																											●																										
LION ROYAL HOTEL, Rhayader (YH08671)													●																																					●			
LLANFYLLIN SADDLERY, Llanfyllin (YH08723)																																					●																
LLANGENNY PONY TREKKING CTRE, Crickhowell (YH08724)													●																																					●			
LLANGORSE RIDING, Brecon (YH08725)													●																																					●			
LLETTY MAWR TREKKING, Welshpool (YH08728)																																																		●			

Business Profile
General Equine

by Country by County

	Artist	Blacksmith	Business Consultancy	Commentating for Events	Competition Horses	Competition Riders	Cross Country Course	Dressage Riders	Driving Centre	Driving Competitors	Driving Services	Engraving	Equine Holidays	Event Management	Event Riders	Forge	Harness Race Course	Harness Racing Horses	Harness Racing Skills	Harness Retailer	Horse Sale Agency	Horsebox Hire	International Arena	Jockey	Jockey Supply	Photographer	Point-to-Point Course	Polo Pitch	Portraits	Racecourse Flat	Racecourse Steeplechase	Racing Investment	Repairs Rugs	Repairs Saddles	Riding Club	Rug Cleaning	Saddler	School (Indoor)	School (Outdoor)	Sculptor	Shipping Agent	Show Jump Course	Show Jumping arena	Stabling Centre	Tack Shop	Taxidermy	Trail Riding Centre	Transport	Transport Overseas	Trekking Centre	Valuer	Website design	Wheelwright
LLWYNON, Brecon (YH08749)																				●													●	●		●	●			●					●								
MARL STUD MARL CRIS STUD, Brecon (YH09167)																																												●									
MATTHEWS, SALLY, Builth Wells (YH09276)																																							●														
MILL PONY TREKKING CTRE, Newtown (YH09584)													●																																								
NEWCOURT FARM, Glasbury (YH10135)													●																																								
NICHOLLS, W, Crickhowell (YH10186)																																					●																
OVERLAND PONY TREK, Llandrindod Wells (YH10594)													●																																					●			
RANGE RIDES, Llandrindod Wells (YH11634)													●																																								
RHAYADER PONY TREKKING ASS, Rhayader (YH11783)													●																																								
SHEPPARD, P J, Brecon (YH12717)													●																																								
STABLES HOTEL, Crickhowell (YH13311)													●																																								
STAR INN TREKKING CTRE, Llanbrynmair (YH13393)													●																																								
TRANS-WALES TRAILS, Brecon (YH14353)													●																															●									
TREGOYD MOUNTAIN RIDERS, Brecon (YH14367)																																															●			●			
UNDERHILL RIDING STABLES, Llandrindod Wells (YH14560)							●																																	●													
WERN RIDING CTRE, Crickhowell (YH15114)													●																																								
RHONDDA CYNON TAFF																																																					
BOOTS & SADDLES, Tonypandy (YH01640)																																													●								
GREENMEADOW RIDING CTRE, Aberdare (YH06099)													●																																								
TALYGARN, Pontyclun (YH13846)							●																															●		●			●										
YNYSCRUG STUD, Tonyrefail (YH15912)																																												●									
SWANSEA																																																					
COPLEY, Swansea (YH03297)													●																															●									
CROSS STORES, Swansea (YH03653)																																					●																
D MORGAN & SON, Swansea (YH03798)																																													●								
D MORGAN & SONS, Swansea (YH03799)																																					●																
DAN-YR-OGOF, Swansea (YH03875)																																																		●			
EDWARDS, J T, Swansea (YH04581)													●																																								
FORGEMILL, Swansea (YH05368)													●																															●			●			●			
GREEN FARM, Swansea (YH06054)																																								●													
PENTRE RIDING STABLES, Swansea (YH10962)													●																																					●			
PRIORY STABLES, Swansea (YH11405)																																								●				●									

www.hccyourhorse.com

Business Profile
General Equine

by Country by County	Artist	Blacksmith	Business Consultancy	Commentating for Events	Competition Horses	Competition Riders	Cross Country Course	Dressage Riders	Driving Centre	Driving Competitors	Driving Services	Engraving	Equine Holidays	Event Management	Event Riders	Forge	Harness Race Course	Harness Racing Horses	Harness Racing Skills	Harness Retailer	Horse Sale Agency	Horsebox Hire	International Arena	Jockey	Jockey Supply	Photographer	Point-to-Point Course	Polo Pitch	Portraits	Racecourse Flat	Racecourse Steeplechase	Racing Investment	Repairs Rugs	Repairs Saddles	Riding Club	Rug Cleaning	Saddler	School (Indoor)	School (Outdoor)	Sculptor	Shipping Agent	Show Jump Course	Show Jumping arena	Stabling Centre	Tack Shop	Taxidermy	Trail Riding Centre	Transport	Transport Overseas	Trekking Centre	Valuer	Website design	Wheelwright
PUNNETT, L, Swansea (YH11459)				●																																																	
SOUTH WALES CARRIAGE DRIVING, Swansea (YH13111)								●	●	●	●																																	●									
TANKEY LAKE LIVERY, Swansea (YH13856)													●									●																		●				●									
WOODLANDS RIDING SCHOOL, Swansea (YH15710)													●																																								
WREXHAM																																																					
ACRE HSE EQUESTRIAN, Wrexham (YH00158)																											●																		●								
BLINKERS EQUESTRIAN, Wrexham (YH01540)																																				●									●								
CHAPEL FARM, Wrexham (YH02738)																																								●			●										
COUNTIES EQUESTRIAN SVS, Wrexham (YH03396)																																																●					
EQUESTRIAN CTRE, Wrexham (YH04697)							●																															●		●		●											
N W F COUNTRYSTORE, Wrexham (YH10000)																																					●																
TOWN & COUNTRY SUPPLIES, Bangor-on-Dee (YH14288)																																					●																

SECTION 5

Owners and Breeders

This section allows you to search for companies that own and/or breed a particular breed of horse. Companies are listed by Country, by County.

Breeds are sorted alphabetically:

Section 5A - A to Er
Section 5B - Ev to N
Section 5C - P to Y

The Owners and Breeders grid can be used in two different ways. You can search by a particular breed of horse you are looking for.

e.g. **Dartmoor : Brook Stables**

Or, you can look at the profile of a particular company in order to see what horses they own and/or breed.

e.g. **Scottsway Stud : Connemara**

There is a key to identify whether the business owns, breeds or owns and breeds.

Once you have located a business using this section you can then refer to the company's detailed profile in Section 1.

Owners & Breeders of Horses and Ponies

Breeds A-E

by Country by County Key: ○=own ●=breed ◉=both

	Albino	All Crosses	American Saddlebred	American Bashkir Curly	American Quarter Horse	Andalusian	Appaloosa	Arab Anglo	Arab Horse	Arab Caspian	Arab Polish	Ardennes	Belgian Warm Blooded	British Riding Pony	Camargue	Caspian	Caspian Mini	Cleveland Bay	Clydesdale	Cobs	Cold Blooded	Coloured Horse	Competition Horse	Competition Pony	Connemara	Cremello	Cross	Dales	Danish Warmblood	Dartmoor	Deer Pony	Donkey	Dressage	Driving Horses	Driving Pony	Dutch Warm Blood	Endurance	Endurance Pony	Eriskay Pony
ENGLAND																																							
BATH & SOMERSET (NORTH EAST)																																							
CONKWELL GRANGE STUD - Bath (YH03232)									●																														
BEDFORDSHIRE																																							
BIGGLESWADE SADDLERY - Biggleswade (YH01404)									○													○																	
BROOK STABLES - Bedford (YH02038)								○																						○									
COURTENAY, A L - Toddington (YH03503)																						●																	
DIJON STUD - Colmworth (YH04120)									●																														
EVERKERRY - Leighton Buzzard (YH04955)																														●									
HOLLINGDON GRANGE - Leighton Buzzard (YH06943)																						●																	
RAWDING, J & S M - Leighton Buzzard (YH11662)																							●																
SALSA STUD - Chawston (YH12391)																							◉										◉						
SMITH, N - Flitwick (YH12978)																						●																	
STAPLEFORD MILL FARM STUD - Leighton Buzzard (YH13387)																						●	●																
YEGUADA IBERICA - Knotting (YH15898)						●																																	
BERKSHIRE																																							
BROXDOWN STUD - Maidenhead (YH02151)																														●									
CLEVELANDS STUD - Windsor (YH03023)																		●																					
COURTLANDS - Wokingham (YH03506)																																	○						
EAST SOLEY E C 2000 - Hungerford (YH04486)																							○										○						
HARRIES, STELLA - Bracknell (YH06458)																							●																
HEADLEY STUD - Thatcham (YH06612)																																	●						
PARKVIEW ANDALUSIANS - Wokingham (YH10776)						●																																	
BUCKINGHAMSHIRE																																							
APPLEACRE DARTMOORS - Wendover (YH00479)																														●									
BARKER, K J - Burnham (YH00944)								●	●																														
BRAWLINGS FARM RIDING CTRE - Gerrards Cross (YH01819)																							○																
CATHERINE WRIGHT - Aylesbury (YH02649)					◉																																		
D A L E - Aylesbury (YH03775)					○																																		
DEEPMILL STUD - Great Missenden (YH04022)																														●									
DEVILS HORSEMEN - Milton Keynes (YH04090)						◉																																	

Owners & Breeders of Horses and Ponies

Breeds A-E

by Country by County Key: ○=own ●=breed ◉=both

	Albino	All Crosses	American Saddlebred	American Bashkir Curly	American Quarter Horse	Andalusian	Appaloosa	Arab Anglo	Arab Horse	Arab Caspian	Arab Polish	Ardennes	Belgian Warm Blooded	British Riding Pony	Camargue	Caspian	Caspian Mini	Cleveland Bay	Clydesdale	Cobs	Cold Blooded	Coloured Horse	Competition Horse	Competition Pony	Connemara	Cremello	Cross	Dales	Danish Warmblood	Dartmoor	Deer Pony	Donkey	Dressage	Driving Horses	Driving Pony	Dutch Warm Blood	Endurance	Endurance Pony	Eriskay Pony
GRAFTON DONKEY STUD - Lillingstone Lovell (YH05960)																																●							
LECKHAMPSTEAD WHARF STUD - Buckingham (YH08513)																						●	●																
MEARS, IVAN - Great Brickhill (YH09430)																						●																	
RADNAGE HOUSE - High Wycombe (YH11599)																					○																		
RAGLAN HOUSE ANDALUSIAN STUD - Aston Clinton (YH11606)						●																																	
SINGH, ANITA - Chesham (YH12853)						●																																	
TALLENTS STUD - Buckingham (YH13836)																							●		●														
WYCHWOOD STUD - Mursley (YH15857)						●																																	
CAMBRIDGESHIRE																																							
APPALOOSAS, RODEGA - Histon (YH00477)							◉																																
BRITISH SKEWBALD/PIEBALD ASS - Ely (YH01975)																						●																	
FENGATE DARTMOORS - Warboys (YH05140)																														●									
HIGHBARN DARTMOORS - Trumpington (YH06771)																														●									
HOOK HSE - March (YH07035)								○																															
KNIGHTS END FARM - March (YH08268)																																	○						
NORTHBROOK EQUESTRIAN CTRE - Huntingdon (YH10294)						○															○	○											○						
SCOTTSWAY STUD - Castle Camps (YH12563)																									●														
THOMPSON, S - Ely (YH14042)																									●														
WEST ANGLIA CLGE - Milton (YH15123)					●																																		
WITCHAM HSE FARM STUD - Ely (YH15617)																							○										○						
WULFSTAN - Welney (YH15851)																						◉																	
CHESHIRE																																							
BENNETT, R - Heatley (YH01272)																						●																	
CARRUTHERS, RICHARD - Frodsham (YH02601)																							○										○						
COLBERRY SADDLERY - Ellesmere Port (YH03142)																																○							
EARDLEY, ANGELA - Hough (YH04448)																						●																	

Owners & Breeders of Horses and Ponies
Breeds A-E

by Country by County   Key: ○=own ●=breed ◉=both

by Country by County	Albino	All Crosses	American Saddlebred	American Bashkir Curly	American Quarter Horse	Andalusian	Appaloosa	Arab Anglo	Arab Horse	Arab Caspian	Arab Polish	Ardennes	Belgian Warm Blooded	British Riding Pony	Camargue	Caspian	Caspian Mini	Cleveland Bay	Clydesdale	Cobs	Cold Blooded	Coloured Horse	Competition Horse	Competition Pony	Connemara	Cremello	Cross	Dales	Danish Warmblood	Dartmoor	Deer Pony	Donkey	Dressage	Driving Horses	Driving Pony	Dutch Warm Blood	Endurance	Endurance Pony	Eriskay Pony
IRELAND																																							
COUNTY CLARE																																							
BURREN RIDING CTRE - Ballyvaughan (YH02278)																									○														
COUNTY CORK																																							
CASTLEWHITE - Cork (YH02646)																				◉		◉			◉														
COUNTY DUBLIN																																							
CALLIAGHSTOWN EQUESTRIAN - Rathcoole (YH02449)																									◉														
COUNTY KERRY																																							
CURRAGH COTTAGE LEISURE - Tralee (YH03735)																									○														
COUNTY MAYO																																							
ASHFORD EQUESTRIAN CTRE - Mayo (YH00600)																									●														
COUNTY OFFALY																																							
ETTER SPORTS HORSES - Bellmont (YH04886)								◉															◉										◉						
COUNTY WATERFORD																																							
BLACKWATER SADDLERY - Tallow (YH01502)																						○			◉														

Owners & Breeders of Horses and Ponies

Breeds A-E

by Country by County

Key: ○=own ●=breed ◉=both

	Albino	All Crosses	American Saddlebred	American Bashkir Curly	American Quarter Horse	Andalusian	Appaloosa	Arab Anglo	Arab Horse	Arab Caspian	Arab Polish	Ardennes	Belgian Warm Blooded	British Riding Pony	Camargue	Caspian	Caspian Mini	Cleveland Bay	Clydesdale	Cobs	Cold Blooded	Coloured Horse	Competition Horse	Competition Pony	Connemara	Cremello	Cross	Dales	Danish Warmblood	Dartmoor	Deer Pony	Donkey	Dressage	Driving Horses	Driving Pony	Dutch Warm Blood	Endurance	Endurance Pony	Eriskay Pony
NORTHERN IRELAND																																						
COUNTY ANTRIM																																						
ANDREWS, JOHN - Toomebridge (YH00400)																			●																			
GLASS, JOHN - Ballycastle (YH05810)																			●																			
LUSK EQUESTRIAN - Lisburn (YH08905)																							●															
COUNTY ARMAGH																																						
ALFRED BULLER BLOODSTOCK - Craigavon (YH00275)																							●															
COUNTY DOWN																																						
ALLEN, SUZANNE - Bainbridge (YH00303)																																						●
HOLMESTEAD SADDLERY - Downpatrick (YH06981)																									◉													
MCCABE, JIM - Downpatrick (YH09315)																			●																			
MCIVOR, A - Dromore (YH09378)																						●																
PORTER, NOEL - Guildford (YH11285)																			●																			
COUNTY LONDONDERRY																																						
FORT CTRE - Maghera (YH05385)	○				○																○			○													
MCCOLLUM, JEANNIE - Coleraine (YH09328)																							●															
COUNTY TYRONE																																						
TULLYWHISKER RIDING SCHOOL - Strabane (YH14458)															○																							
SCOTLAND																																						
ABERDEEN (CITY OF)																																						
ABERDEEN DISTRICT COUNCIL - Aberdeen (YH00123)																			●																			●
BOWLEY, HAZEL - Aberdeen (YH01718)																			●																			
CHRISTIE, NORMAN - Aberdeen (YH02888)																			●																			
GREENFERNS STUD - Portlethen (YH06081)																														●									
ABERDEENSHIRE																																						
BEE, M - Inverurie (YH01161)																						●																
BROGAR PONY STUD - Methlick (YH02019)																						●																
DONALD, GEORGE - Huntly (YH04175)							●																															
EDEN EQUESTRIAN CTRE - Turriff (YH04546)																							○															
MCINTOSH, WILLIAM G - Macduff (YH09377)							●																															
RIDINGHILL STUD - Fraserburgh (YH11885)																											◉											

Owners & Breeders of Horses and Ponies
Breeds A-E

by Country by County   Key: ○=own ●=breed ◉=both

	Albino	All Crosses	American Saddlebred	American Bashkir Curly	American Quarter Horse	Andalusian	Appaloosa	Arab Anglo	Arab Horse	Arab Caspian	Arab Polish	Ardennes	Belgian Warm Blooded	British Riding Pony	Camargue	Caspian	Caspian Mini	Cleveland Bay	Clydesdale	Cobs	Cold Blooded	Coloured Horse	Competition Horse	Competition Pony	Connemara	Cremello	Cross	Dales	Danish Warmblood	Dartmoor	Deer Pony	Donkey	Dressage	Driving Horses	Driving Pony	Dutch Warm Blood	Endurance	Endurance Pony	Eriskay Pony
RUSSELL, S - Peterhead (YH12263)																																●							
SKINNER, GEORGE M - Inverurie (YH12875)																			●																				
STEVENS - Banchory (YH13440)																							●																
TOMINTOUL RIDING CTRE - Ballindalloch (YH14221)																																							●
ANGUS																																							
BROWN, RAYMOND - Forfar (YH02131)																			●																				
GREENHILL, A - Forfar (YH06089)																			●																				
KIRRIEMUIR HORSE SUPPLIES - Kirriemuir (YH08240)																				○		○																	
MACDONALD, A R - Kirriemuir (YH08987)																							●																
PATHHEAD STABLES - Kirriemuir (YH10821)																				○		○																	
WHITEGATE STUD - Forfar (YH15339)																						◉	●																
ARGYLL AND BUTE																																							
APPALOOSA HOLIDAYS - Lochgilphead (YH00475)							◉																																
BOASE, N & L - Lochgilphead (YH01585)							●																																
COLGRAIN EQUESTRIAN CTRE - Helensburgh (YH03170)																							○										○						○
WHAT EVERY HORSE WANTS - Helensburgh (YH15266)					○																																		
AYRSHIRE (EAST)																																							
MCINNES, WILLIAM - Kilmarnock (YH09375)																			●																				
MITCHELL, TOM - Kilmarnock (YH09677)																			●																				
ROWALLAN ACTIVITY CTRE - Kilmarnock (YH12152)																						○	○																
AYRSHIRE (NORTH)																																							
CAIRNHOUSE RIDING CTRE - Isle Of Arran (YH02419)																			○														○						
CRAIGWEIL ARABIAN STUD - Irvine (YH03556)									●																														
FERGUSHILL RIDING STABLES - Kilwinning (YH05159)																						○																	
AYRSHIRE (SOUTH)																																							
I C S - Mauchline (YH07363)																							●		●														
I C S BLOODSTOCK - Mauchline (YH07364)																							●																
JAMES M BARCLAY & SON - Maybole (YH07671)																			●																				
O'NEIL, HUGH - Ayr (YH10514)																			●																				
ROSEMOUNT RIDING SVS - Prestwick (YH12105)																							○																
YOUNG, JAMES W - Ayr (YH15934)																			◉																				

Owners & Breeders of Horses and Ponies

Breeds A-E

by Country by County

Key: ○=own ●=breed ◉=both

by Country by County	Albino	All Crosses	American Saddlebred	American Bashkir Curly	American Quarter Horse	Andalusian	Appaloosa	Arab Anglo	Arab Horse	Arab Caspian	Arab Polish	Ardennes	Belgian Warm Blooded	British Riding Pony	Camargue	Caspian	Caspian Mini	Cleveland Bay	Clydesdale	Cobs	Cold Blooded	Coloured Horse	Competition Horse	Competition Pony	Connemara	Cremello	Cross	Dales	Danish Warmblood	Dartmoor	Deer Pony	Donkey	Dressage	Driving Horses	Driving Pony	Dutch Warm Blood	Endurance	Endurance Pony	Eriskay Pony
CLACKMANNANSHIRE																																							
SIBBALD, ROBERT - Dollar (YH12779)																			●																				
TRANSY SHETLAND PONY STUD - Dollar (YH14354)																									●														
DUMFRIES AND GALLOWAY																																							
AGNEW, R & A - Stranraer (YH00199)																			●																				
EASTLANDS - Langholm (YH04507)																									●														
GALLOWAY, TOM - Newton Stewart (YH05627)																			●																				
LOVE, ANDREW - Stranraer (YH08844)																			●																				
SHAW, WALTER H - Stranraer (YH12684)																			●																				
SMITH, JOHN (JNR) - Newton Stewart (YH12969)																			●																				
THOMSON, J L - Thornhill (YH14052)																			●																				
EDINBURGH (CITY OF)																																							
CLYDESDALE HORSE SOC - Edinburgh (YH03081)																			●																				
FALKIRK																																							
TAYLOR, JOHN S - Slamannan (YH13905)																			●																				
FIFE																																							
ANGLE PARK - Cupar (YH00409)							○	○											○			○	○							○			○						
BROWN, R & F - Cupar (YH02129)																			●																				
LOW-MITCHELL, D I - Leven (YH08876)																																				●			
WALES																																							
BLAENAU GWENT																																							
COLOURED HORSE & PONY SOC - Tredegar (YH03199)																						●																	
BRIDGEND																																							
E K M EQUESTRIAN - Bridgend (YH04411)																																	○						
WESTRA DONKEY STUD - Bridgend (YH15231)																																●							
CAERPHILLY																																							
ROCKWOOD RIDING CTRE - Caerphilly (YH12039)	○																					○																	
CARMARTHENSHIRE																																							
BLAENWAUN STUD - Llanwrda (YH01507)																									●														
BYCHAN STUD - Llandeilo (YH02344)									●																														
JEHAN, F W - Llandeilo (YH07727)																		●																					

Owners & Breeders of Horses and Ponies
Breeds A-E

by Country by County Key: ○=own ●=breed ◉=both

	Albino	All Crosses	American Saddlebred	American Bashkir Curly	American Quarter Horse	Andalusian	Appaloosa	Arab Anglo	Arab Horse	Arab Caspian	Arab Polish	Ardennes	Belgian Warm Blooded	British Riding Pony	Camargue	Caspian	Caspian Mini	Cleveland Bay	Clydesdale	Cobs	Cold Blooded	Coloured Horse	Competition Horse	Competition Pony	Connemara	Cremello	Cross	Dales	Danish Warmblood	Dartmoor	Deer Pony	Donkey	Dressage	Driving Horses	Driving Pony	Dutch Warm Blood	Endurance	Endurance Pony	Eriskay Pony
KINGSETTLE STUD - Llandsyssul (YH08202)									●																														
LEWIS, MEGAN - Llanwrda (YH08594)									●																														
PENCADER STUD - Pencader (YH10928)																							◉																
PLAS EQUESTRIAN - Carmarthen (YH11164)									○													○																	
RHYDHIR STUD - Carmarthen (YH11792)																						●																	
RIVERSDALE - Carmarthen (YH11923)																									●		●												
RUTHERFORD, E - Llandeilo (YH12273)																																	●			●			●
STALLIONS AT TACKEXCHANGE - Llanelli (YH13351)																						◉	◉																
TACK EXCHANGE - Llanelli (YH13787)																						◉																	
CEREDIGION																																							
GRANGEWAY STUD - Lampeter (YH06003)								●																															
MOELFRYN RIDING CTRE - Aberystwyth (YH09699)																		◉																					
RHEIDOL RIDING CTRE - Aberystwyth (YH11784)																																	○						
WILLS, G J - Aberystwyth (YH15518)																		●																					
CONWY																																							
BENFIELD, M - Colwyn Bay (YH01265)																									●														
DENBIGHSHIRE																																							
LLANNERCH EQUESTRIAN CTRE - St Asaph (YH08726)																							○																
FLINTSHIRE																																							
DRINKWATER, J - Garden City (YH04275)																						●																	
MANNOG - Holywell (YH09092)							◉																																
VLACQ STUD - Mold (YH14738)								●	●														●																
GLAMORGAN (VALE OF)																																							
ALGER, A - Cardiff (YH00278)																						●																	
ARGAE HSE STABLES - Dinas Powys (YH00519)																							●																
PALMER, D W - St Nicholas (YH10691)																		●																					
GWYNEDD																																							
BRONALLT - Caernarfon (YH02029)								◉	◉																														
JONES, J - Caernarfon (YH07906)																		●																					
PENRYHN STUD FARM - Caernarfon (YH10958)																		●																					
STRICK, J - Pwllheli (YH13576)																									●														

Owners & Breeders of Horses and Ponies
Breeds A-E

by Country by County

Key: ○=own ●=breed ◉=both

	Albino	All Crosses	American Saddlebred	American Bashkir Curly	American Quarter Horse	Andalusian	Appaloosa	Arab Anglo	Arab Horse	Arab Caspian	Arab Polish	Ardennes	Belgian Warm Blooded	British Riding Pony	Camargue	Caspian	Caspian Mini	Cleveland Bay	Clydesdale	Cobs	Cold Blooded	Coloured Horse	Competition Horse	Competition Pony	Connemara	Cremello	Cross	Dales	Danish Warmblood	Dartmoor	Deer Pony	Donkey	Dressage	Driving Horses	Driving Pony	Dutch Warm Blood	Endurance	Endurance Pony	Eriskay Pony
ISLE OF ANGLESEY																																							
AUGUST APPALOOSAS - Holyhead (YH00663)							●																																
BRACKENDENE STUD - Anglesey (YH01738)								●	●													●	●																
HENDY EQUESTRIAN - Holyhead (YH06670)																							●																
STANFORD EVENTING HORSES - Holyhead (YH13363)																							●																
TYN-MORFA RIDING CTRE - Rhosneigr (YH14529)																							◉																
MONMOUTHSHIRE																																							
BELCHER, RACHAEL - Chepstow (YH01207)							●																																
EARLSWOOD RIDING CTRE - Chepstow (YH04455)																		●																					
EARLSWOOD STUD - Chepstow (YH04456)																		●																					
GRANGE TREKKING - Abergavenny (YH05999)	○							○	○													◉	◉					○											
POWELL, JOHN C - Abergavenny (YH11319)							●																																
TAWMARSH STUD - Abergavenny (YH13889)								●	●														●																
TICEHURST, LESLEY J - Abergavenny (YH14126)							●																																
TOKENBOW STUD - Usk (YH14204)																						●																	
WOODLANDER STUD - Raglan (YH15704)																									●														
PEMBROKESHIRE																																							
ALLEN, T E - Clynderwen (YH00304)									●																														
CAMPBELL, W M - Pembroke (YH02488)																						●																	
CROSSWELL - Crymych (YH03669)																						○	○																
DOLRHANOG RIDING CTRE - Newport (YH04171)																					◉		◉																

Owners & Breeders of Horses and Ponies

Breeds E-N

by Country by County

Key: ○=own ●=breed ◉=both

	Eventing	Exmoor	Falabella	Fell Pony	Friesian	Gelderland	General Riding Horses	Hackney	Haflinger	Hanoverian	Harness Racing Horse	Highland Pony	Hispano Arab	Holstein	Hunter	Iberian Sports	Icelandic Horse	Irish Cob	Irish Cross	Irish Draught Cross	Irish Draught	Irish Sports Horses	Jumping Pony	KWPN	Light/Riding Horse	Lipizzaner	Lundy Pony	Lusitano	Miniature	Moorlands	Morab	Morgan	Mountain	Mule	National Hunt Racehorses	Native Breeds	New Forest	Norfolk Cob	Norwegian Fjord
ENGLAND																																							
BATH & SOMERSET (NORTH EAST)																																							
KNOWLES, E - Bath (YH08284)				●																																			
LPPS - Paulton (YH08880)																											◉												
BEDFORDSHIRE																																							
BARKER, E - Harrold (YH00942)		●																																					
BIGGLESWADE SADDLERY - Biggleswade (YH01404)																		○																			○		
LIMERICK STUD - Gamlingay (YH08632)									●																														
RAWDING, J & S M - Leighton Buzzard (YH11662)															●										●														
SALSA STUD - Chawston (YH12391)	◉									◉					◉																								
STAGSDEN HAFLINGERS - Stagsden (YH13343)									●																														
STAPLEFORD MILL FARM STUD - Leighton Buzzard (YH13387)															●										●														
SUNSHINE RIDING SCHOOL - Luton (YH13652)																									○														
YEGUADA IBERICA - Knotting (YH15898)																												●											
BERKSHIRE																																							
EAST SOLEY E C 2000 - Hungerford (YH04486)												○																											
HUNGERFORD PARK EST - Hungerford (YH07287)												●																											
MUSCHAMP STUD - Slough (YH09974)										●																													
PRIORY STUD - White Waltham (YH11406)																																					●		
SHELTON FARM - Reading (YH12704)					○																																		
BRISTOL																																							
CLIFTON CARRIAGES - Bristol (YH03036)								○																															
GARWAY HAFLINGERS - Bristol (YH05666)									◉																														
BUCKINGHAMSHIRE																																							
COLQUHOUN, ELIZABETH - Buckingham (YH03200)																																						●	
DEVILS HORSEMEN - Milton Keynes (YH04090)																										◉		◉						○					
GLANFIELD, J - Iver (YH05805)		●																																					
GRAY, P J - Iver (YH06030)								●																															
SEDGEHILL SHETLAND PONY STUD - Chesham (YH12604)																									●														
TALLENTS STUD - Buckingham (YH13836)																									●														
WYCHWOOD STUD - Mursley (YH15857)																												●											

Owners & Breeders of Horses and Ponies
Breeds E-N

by Country by County Key: ○=own ●=breed ◉=both

	Eventing	Exmoor	Falabella	Fell Pony	Friesian	Gelderland	General Riding Horses	Hackney	Haflinger	Hanoverian	Harness Racing Horse	Highland Pony	Hispano Arab	Holstein	Hunter	Iberian Sports	Icelandic Horse	Irish Cob	Irish Cross	Irish Draught Cross	Irish Draught	Irish Sports Horses	Jumping Pony	KWPN	Light/Riding Horse	Lipizzaner	Lundy Pony	Lusitano	Miniature	Moorlands	Morab	Morgan	Mountain	Mule	National Hunt Racehorses	Native Breeds	New Forest	Norfolk Cob	Norwegian Fjord
CAMBRIDGESHIRE																																							
HOOK HSE - March (YH07035)		◉																																					
KNIGHTS END FARM - March (YH08268)										○																													
NORTHBROOK EQUESTRIAN CTRE - Huntingdon (YH10294)																									○			○									○		
PENNIES STUD - Wisbech (YH10950)																													●										
PROSPECT STUD - Grantchester (YH11437)																									●														
WARD, M & W - Ely (YH14903)																									●														
WELLS PARK FARM - Whittlesford (YH15080)																																●							
WHITE, F B - Teversham (YH15329)															●					●					●														
WITCHAM HSE FARM STUD - Ely (YH15617)										◉															◉														
CHESHIRE																																							
CARRUTHERS, RICHARD - Frodsham (YH02601)	○																																						
CREWE SADDLERY - Crewe (YH03595)																													○										
DOVE STYLE - Chester (YH04217)															●					●																			
DUTTON - Holmes Chapel (YH04377)											●																												
MORRIS, S & HUNTON, J - Audlem (YH09835)																									●														
PICKMERE - Knutsford (YH11087)																									●														
REDGRAVE, CAROLE - Wilmslow (YH11711)											◉																												
SOUTHERN, R - Chester (YH13148)																									●														
WORTHINGTON, D - Macclesfield (YH15806)															●																								
CLEVELAND																																							
FOXHOLM STUD - Stockton-on-Tees (YH05437)						◉				◉															◉														
HARFORTH, J F - Middlesbrough (YH06422)															●																								
LAWSON, P A - Guisborough (YH08478)				●																																			
WOLVISTON RIDING STABLES - Billingham (YH15652)	○	○																		○					○												○		
CORNWALL																																							
CHADWICK, R - Truro (YH02703)				●																																			
HAWKLANDS STUD - Jacobstow (YH06551)																				●																			
LANTYAN STUD - Lostwithiel (YH08425)																									●														

Owners & Breeders of Horses and Ponies

Breeds E-N

by Country by County

Key: ○=own ●=breed ◉=both

	Eventing	Exmoor	Falabella	Fell Pony	Friesian	Gelderland	General Riding Horses	Hackney	Haflinger	Hanoverian	Harness Racing Horse	Highland Pony	Hispano Arab	Holstein	Hunter	Iberian Sports	Icelandic Horse	Irish Cob	Irish Cross	Irish Draught Cross	Irish Draught	Irish Sports Horses	Jumping Pony	KWPN	Light/Riding Horse	Lipizzaner	Lundy Pony	Lusitano	Miniature	Moorlands	Morab	Morgan	Mountain	Mule	National Hunt Racehorses	Native Breeds	New Forest	Norfolk Cob	Norwegian Fjord
IRELAND																																							
COUNTY CLARE																																							
BURREN RIDING CTRE - Ballyvaughan (YH02278)															○					○																			
COUNTY CORK																																							
CASTLEWHITE - Cork (YH02646)															◉					◉																			
COUNTY DUBLIN																																							
CALLIAGHSTOWN EQUESTRIAN - Rathcoole (YH02449)															◉																								
COUNTY KILDARE																																							
LEGGA LIVERY & SALES - Naas (YH08538)																						●																	
COUNTY MAYO																																							
ASHFORD EQUESTRIAN CTRE - Mayo (YH00600)																				●		●																	
COUNTY OFFALY																																							
ETTER SPORTS HORSES - Bellmont (YH04886)	◉														◉							◉																	
COUNTY WATERFORD																																							
BLACKWATER SADDLERY - Tallow (YH01502)															◉					●																			
NORTHERN IRELAND																																							
COUNTY ANTRIM																																							
CRAIGS STUD - Ballyclare (YH03555)																																●							
TULLYROE STUD - Crumlin (YH14457)	◉																			◉																			
COUNTY ARMAGH																																							
ALFRED BULLER BLOODSTOCK - Craigavon (YH00275)																																			●				
BALLINTEGGART STUD - Portadown (YH00860)																				●		●																	
COUNTY DOWN																																							
FAWCETT, GEORGE - Ballynahinch (YH05108)					◉																																		
COUNTY LONDONDERRY																																							
FORT CTRE - Maghera (YH05385)															○					○					○														
COUNTY TYRONE																																							
TULLYWHISKER RIDING SCHOOL - Strabane (YH14458)																				○																			

Owners & Breeders of Horses and Ponies

Breeds E-N

by Country by County

Key: ○=own ●=breed ◉=both

	Eventing	Exmoor	Falabella	Fell Pony	Friesian	Gelderland	General Riding Horses	Hackney	Haflinger	Hanoverian	Harness Racing Horse	Highland Pony	Hispano Arab	Holstein	Hunter	Iberian Sports	Icelandic Horse	Irish Cob	Irish Cross	Irish Draught Cross	Irish Draught	Irish Sports Horses	Jumping Pony	KWPN	Light/Riding Horse	Lipizzaner	Lundy Pony	Lusitano	Miniature	Moorlands	Morab	Morgan	Mountain	Mule	National Hunt Racehorses	Native Breeds	New Forest	Norfolk Cob	Norwegian Fjord
SCOTLAND																																							
ABERDEEN (CITY OF)																																							
ABERDEEN DISTRICT COUNCIL - Aberdeen (YH00123)		●																																					
ABERDEEN RARE BREEDS PK - Aberdeen (YH00124)		●																																					
ABERDEENSHIRE																																							
ASGARD STUD - Inverurie (YH00586)																																							●
BEKON HAFLINGER STUD - Methlick (YH01201)									●																														
CRAGINETHERTY - Turriff (YH03545)												◉																											
DENMILL HIGHLAND PONY STUD - Alford (YH04049)												●																											
EDEN EQUESTRIAN CTRE - Turriff (YH04546)				○								○																											
GAMMIE, J W - Laurencekirk (YH05638)											●																												
GLEN TANAR EQUESTRIAN CTRE - Aboyne (YH05827)																																							●
HJEMDAL - Turriff (YH06889)																																							◉
MILL OF URAS EQUESTRIAN - Stonehaven (YH09583)										○																													
PITMEDDEN STUD - Inverurie (YH11153)															●																								
RAVENSHEAR, J - Huntly (YH11659)				●																																			
STEVENS - Banchory (YH13440)															●																								
STONEHAVEN ICELANDICS - Stonehaven (YH13513)																	●																						
TOMINTOUL RIDING CTRE - Ballindalloch (YH14221)												●																											
ANGUS																																							
COMPTON, J C - Forfar (YH03219)												●																											
DALBRACK HIGHLAND PONY STUD - Brechin (YH03819)												●																											
GOW, D J H - Forfar (YH05953)												●																											
KIRRIEMUIR HORSE SUPPLIES - Kirriemuir (YH08240)												○													○														
MACDONALD, A R - Kirriemuir (YH08987)															●										●														
PATHHEAD STABLES - Kirriemuir (YH10821)												○													○														
ARGYLL AND BUTE																																							
ROCKHILL HANOVERIAN STUD - Dalmally (YH12032)										●																													
WHAT EVERY HORSE WANTS - Helensburgh (YH15266)																				○																			
AYRSHIRE (EAST)																																							
BLAIRFIELD FARM STUD - Kilmarnock (YH01514)																				●																			

Owners & Breeders of Horses and Ponies

Breeds E-N

by Country by County   Key: ○=own ●=breed ◉=both

	Eventing	Exmoor	Falabella	Fell Pony	Friesian	Gelderland	General Riding Horses	Hackney	Haflinger	Hanoverian	Harness Racing Horse	Highland Pony	Hispano Arab	Holstein	Hunter	Iberian Sports	Icelandic Horse	Irish Cob	Irish Cross	Irish Draught Cross	Irish Draught	Irish Sports Horses	Jumping Pony	KWPN	Light/Riding Horse	Lipizzaner	Lundy Pony	Lusitano	Miniature	Moorlands	Morab	Morgan	Mountain	Mule	National Hunt Racehorses	Native Breeds	New Forest	Norfolk Cob	Norwegian Fjord
CLUNY HACKNEY STUD - Galston (YH03076)								●																															
MUIRDYKE STUD FARM - Cumnock (YH09922)				●											●																								
AYRSHIRE (NORTH)																																							
CAIRNHOUSE RIDING CTRE - Isle Of Arran (YH02419)		○													○					○					○														
AYRSHIRE (SOUTH)																																							
I C S - Mauchline (YH07363)										●					●					●					●														
ROSEMOUNT RIDING SVS - Prestwick (YH12105)																			○																				
CLACKMANNANSHIRE																																							
LUCEY, P E - Alloa (YH08885)															●																								
DUMFRIES AND GALLOWAY																																							
DALMAKERRAN EQUESTRIAN CTRE - Thornhill (YH03844)				●																																			
EDINBURGH (CITY OF)																																							
LAWRIE, D - Balerno (YH08474)											●																												
ROBERTSON, E C - Dalkeith (YH11968)															●																								
FALKIRK																																							
COWAN STABLES - Falkirk (YH03520)											●																												
MILNHOLM - Falkirk (YH09643)																							○																
FIFE																																							
ALLAN, W K A - Freuchie (YH00289)												●																											
ANGLE PARK - Cupar (YH00409)																									○				○										
LOW-MITCHELL, D I - Leven (YH08876)	●																																						
MOORE, W - Kelty (YH09769)											●																												
PUDDLEDUB STUD - Kirkcaldy (YH11447)	●																								◉														
HIGHLANDS																																							
CROILA STABLES - Newtonmore (YH03627)												●																											
DARMADY, JOHN - Lybster (YH03897)																	●																						
HIGHLAND RIDING CTRE - Inverness (YH06793)		○										○			○					○																			○
LOGIE FARM - Nairn (YH08778)												○								○					○														
ORMISTON, EWAN C - Kingussie (YH10549)												●																											
SCORRAIG EXMOOR PONIES - Garve (YH12528)		◉		○																																			
ISLE OF SKYE																																							

www.hccyourhorse.com

Owners & Breeders of Horses and Ponies

Breeds E-N

by Country by County

Key: ○=own ●=breed ◉=both

	Eventing	Exmoor	Falabella	Fell Pony	Friesian	Gelderland	General Riding Horses	Hackney	Haflinger	Hanoverian	Harness Racing Horse	Highland Pony	Hispano Arab	Holstein	Hunter	Iberian Sports	Icelandic Horse	Irish Cob	Irish Cross	Irish Draught Cross	Irish Draught	Irish Sports Horses	Jumping Pony	KWPN	Light/Riding Horse	Lipizzaner	Lundy Pony	Lusitano	Miniature	Moorlands	Morab	Morgan	Mountain	Mule	National Hunt Racehorses	Native Breeds	New Forest	Norfolk Cob	Norwegian Fjord
SKYE RIDING CTRE - Portree (YH12881)												◉																											
LANARKSHIRE (NORTH)																																							
LAIRD, ALEXANDER - Shotts (YH08347)	●																																						
LANARKSHIRE (SOUTH)																																							
MOUNTAIN TOP MORGANS - Forth (YH09897)																																●							
WALES																																							
BRIDGEND																																							
E K M EQUESTRIAN - Bridgend (YH04411)										◉																													
CAERPHILLY																																							
BEAU COURT - Newport (YH01126)										●					●																								
ROCKWOOD RIDING CTRE - Caerphilly (YH12039)																		○		○																			
CARMARTHENSHIRE																																							
AUSDAN STUD - Lampeter (YH00665)					●																					●													●
LEWIS, W D - Clynderwen (YH08597)															●										●														
M H W S J FRATERNITY - Llanwrda (YH08965)																													●										
MORGAN EQUINE - Llandeilo (YH09794)										●																													
PENCADER STUD - Pencader (YH10928)															◉																								
PLAS EQUESTRIAN - Carmarthen (YH11164)																													○								○		
SHERMANDELL MORGANS - Llandeilo (YH12725)																																◉							
STALLIONS AT TACKEXCHANGE - Llanelli (YH13351)															◉					◉																			
STEVENS, R - Llandysul (YH13447)																				●																			
TACK EXCHANGE - Llanelli (YH13787)															◉										◉														
TANYFOEL MORGANS - Llandysul (YH13863)																																●							
THOMAS SHOW TEAM - Carmarthen (YH14011)															○																								
THOMAS, D G B - Carmarthen (YH14017)																									●														
CEREDIGION																																							
EVANS, J H - Lampeter (YH04923)											●																												
MOELFRYN RIDING CTRE - Aberystwyth (YH09699)															◉										◉														
RHEIDOL RIDING CTRE - Aberystwyth (YH11784)	○									○										○					○														
DENBIGHSHIRE																																							

Owners & Breeders of Horses and Ponies

Breeds E-N

by Country by County   Key: ○=own ●=breed ◉=both

	Eventing	Exmoor	Falabella	Fell Pony	Friesian	Gelderland	General Riding Horses	Hackney	Haflinger	Hanoverian	Harness Racing Horse	Highland Pony	Hispano Arab	Holstein	Hunter	Iberian Sports	Icelandic Horse	Irish Cob	Irish Cross	Irish Draught Cross	Irish Draught	Irish Sports Horses	Jumping Pony	KWPN	Light/Riding Horse	Lipizzaner	Lundy Pony	Lusitano	Miniature	Moorlands	Morab	Morgan	Mountain	Mule	National Hunt Racehorses	Native Breeds	New Forest	Norfolk Cob	Norwegian Fjord
LLANNERCH EQUESTRIAN CTRE - St Asaph (YH08726)										○	○				○																								
FLINTSHIRE																																							
MANNOG - Holywell (YH09092)																									●														
VLACQ STUD - Mold (YH14738)																									●														
GLAMORGAN (VALE OF)																																							
PICKERSTON STUD - Barry (YH11085)																									●														
RUSSELL LUSITANO STUD - St Nicholas (YH12254)																												●											
GWYNEDD																																							
PEN-LLEYN RIDING CTRE - Pwllheli (YH10943)																												●											
PENRYHN STUD FARM - Caernarfon (YH10958)															●																								
ISLE OF ANGLESEY																																							
BRACKENDENE STUD - Anglesey (YH01738)															●										●														
HENDY EQUESTRIAN - Holyhead (YH06670)																				●																			
MONMOUTHSHIRE																																							
CHEPSTOW SADDLERY - Chepstow (YH02809)																				○																			
GRANGE TREKKING - Abergavenny (YH05999)				○																																			
LANGARTH - Monmouth (YH08399)																									●														
POULTER, D M - Monmouth (YH11303)		●																																					
NEATH PORT TALBOT																																							
DYKES, J H & D J - North Cornelly (YH04392)																																	●						
PEMBROKESHIRE																																							
CROSSWELL - Crymych (YH03669)	○														◉																								
DOLRHANOG RIDING CTRE - Newport (YH04171)	◉														◉										◉														
DUNES RIDING - Narberth (YH04342)										○															○												○		
EAST NOLTON RIDING STABLES - Haverfordwest (YH04482)															●																								
OASIS PARK EQUESTRIAN CTRE - Narberth (YH10412)										○																													
PHILLIPS, F S L - Saundersfoot (YH11056)																									●														
REED, J M - Haverfordwest (YH11720)																																	●						
POWYS																																							
BASSETT, A - Cardiff (YH01056)															●										●														
CANTREF - Brecon (YH02516)	○			○								○			○					○					○												○	○	

www.hccyourhorse.com

Owners & Breeders of Horses and Ponies
Breeds E-N

by Country by County Key: ○=own ●=breed ◉=both

	Eventing	Exmoor	Falabella	Fell Pony	Friesian	Gelderland	General Riding Horses	Hackney	Haflinger	Hanoverian	Harness Racing Horse	Highland Pony	Hispano Arab
COED Y WERN - Brecon (YH03134)		◉											
GETHIN, D - Newtown (YH05733)													
GLAN YR AFON HOLIDAYS - Welshpool (YH05804)													
GOLDEN CASTLE - Crickhowell (YH05877)	○												
LLETTY MAWR TREKKING - Welshpool (YH08728)						○							
NORRIS, PAULINE - Newtown (YH10245)				◉									
SHEPPARD, P J - Brecon (YH12717)													
WILLAIMS, G & R - Llandinam (YH15426)													

	Holstein	Hunter	Iberian Sports	Icelandic Horse	Irish Cob	Irish Cross	Irish Draught Cross	Irish Draught	Irish Sports Horses	Jumping Pony	KWPN	Light/Riding Horse	Lipizzaner
COED Y WERN - Brecon (YH03134)													
GETHIN, D - Newtown (YH05733)		●										●	
GLAN YR AFON HOLIDAYS - Welshpool (YH05804)												○	
GOLDEN CASTLE - Crickhowell (YH05877)		○											
LLETTY MAWR TREKKING - Welshpool (YH08728)											○		
NORRIS, PAULINE - Newtown (YH10245)													
SHEPPARD, P J - Brecon (YH12717)		●											
WILLAIMS, G & R - Llandinam (YH15426)													

	Lundy Pony	Lusitano	Miniature	Moorlands	Morab	Morgan	Mountain	Mule	National Hunt Racehorses	Native Breeds	New Forest	Norfolk Cob	Norwegian Fjord
COED Y WERN - Brecon (YH03134)													
GETHIN, D - Newtown (YH05733)													
GLAN YR AFON HOLIDAYS - Welshpool (YH05804)													
GOLDEN CASTLE - Crickhowell (YH05877)													
LLETTY MAWR TREKKING - Welshpool (YH08728)													
NORRIS, PAULINE - Newtown (YH10245)													
SHEPPARD, P J - Brecon (YH12717)													
WILLAIMS, G & R - Llandinam (YH15426)							●						

Owners & Breeders of Horses and Ponies

Breeds P-Y

by Country by County

Key: ○=own ●=breed ◉=both

	Palomino	Part Breds	PB Welsh	Percheron	Piebald	Pinto	Point To Pointers	Polo Pony	Pony Hunter	Quarter Horse	Riding Pony	Selle Francais	Shetland	Shire	Show Cobs	Show Hacks	Show Hunters	Show Jumpers	Show Jumping Pony	Show Pony	Skewbald	Sports Horse	Spotted Pony	Suffolk	Tersk	Thoroughbred	Thoroughbred Flat	Thoroughbred Hanoverian	Thoroughbred Steeplechase	Trakehener	Veteran	Warm Blooded	Warmblood	Welsh Cob	Welsh Part Bred	Welsh Pony	Western Horse	Working Hunter	Working Pony	Young Stock
ENGLAND																																								
BATH & SOMERSET (NORTH EAST)																																								
CONKWELL GRANGE STUD - Bath (YH03232)																													●											
HORLER, M A - Bath (YH07070)														●																										
BEDFORDSHIRE																																								
ALTERNATIVE RIDING SCHOOL - Luton (YH00343)													○																							○				
BIGGLESWADE SADDLERY - Biggleswade (YH01404)																																○								
BLOOMSBURY STUD - Woburn (YH01555)																											●		●											
BROOK STABLES - Bedford (YH02038)													○																					○						
GIBBONS, P & S - Bedford (YH05740)																																		●		●				
HOLME GROVE FARM - Biggleswade (YH06965)																														●										
HOLME PK STUD - Biggleswade (YH06966)																														●										
HOWE, B M - Cranfield (YH07223)	●																																	●		●				
RAWDING, J & S M - Leighton Buzzard (YH11662)																											●		●				●							
RISINGHOE CASTLE STUD - Goldington (YH11910)											●																													
SALSA STUD - Chawston (YH12391)	◉																													◉		◉	●			○				
STAPLEFORD MILL FARM STUD - Leighton Buzzard (YH13387)																																	●							
SUNSHINE RIDING SCHOOL - Luton (YH13652)											○																							○		○				
BERKSHIRE																																								
BERRYMAN-HORNE, A - Slough (YH01319)																																		●		●				
BLOODHORSE INT - Hungerford (YH01547)																											●		●											
BOARD-JONES, S - Windsor (YH01584)											●																							●		●				
BOOTH, A - Reading (YH01633)																																		●		●				
CHIEVELEY MANOR STUD - Newbury (YH02850)																											●													
CLIVEDEN STUD - Maidenhead (YH03051)																											●													
EQUICENTRE - Waltham St Lawrence (YH04737)								○																																
EWAR STUD FARM - Wokingham (YH04960)																											●													
GAINSBOROUGH STUD MNGMT - Newbury (YH05607)																											●													
HARRIES, STELLA - Bracknell (YH06458)											●																													
HEADLEY STUD - Thatcham (YH06612)																			●																					
HEATHERWOLD STUD - Newbury (YH06629)														●													●													

Owners & Breeders of Horses and Ponies
Breeds P-Y

by Country by County Key: ○=own ●=breed ◉=both

	Palomino	Part Breds	PB Welsh	Percheron	Piebald	Pinto	Point To Pointers	Polo Pony	Pony Hunter	Quarter Horse	Riding Pony	Selle Francais	Shetland	Shire	Show Cobs	Show Hacks	Show Hunters	Show Jumpers	Show Jumping Pony	Show Pony	Skewbald	Sports Horse	Spotted Pony	Suffolk	Tersk	Thoroughbred	Thoroughbred Flat	Thoroughbred Hanoverian	Thoroughbred Steeplechase	Trakehener	Veteran	Warm Blooded	Warmblood	Welsh Cob	Welsh Part Bred	Welsh Pony	Western Horse	Working Hunter	Working Pony	Young Stock
HILLSIDE STUD - Hungerford (YH06855)											●																●		●											
ISAAC, C & D - Newbury (YH07511)																																		●		●				
JUDDMONTE FARMS - Wargrave On Thames (YH07957)																											●													
KINGWOOD HOUSE STABLES - Hungerford (YH08215)																											●													
MUSCHAMP STUD - Slough (YH09974)																														●			●							
PEACHEY, KA - Maidenhead (YH10858)														○																										
SHELTON FARM - Reading (YH12704)																																		○		○				
SPRINGBOURNE & BLANCHE WELSH - Newbury (YH13250)																																		●		●				
WATERSHIP DOWN STUD - Newbury (YH14972)																											●													
WHEELERSLAND STUD - Thatcham (YH15276)																											●													
WOODHAVEN STUD - Newbury (YH15693)																											●		●											
BRISTOL																																								
URCHINWOOD MANOR EQUITATION - Bristol (YH14620)																																	●							
BUCKINGHAMSHIRE																																								
CATHERINE WRIGHT - Aylesbury (YH02649)										◉																											◉			
CLARKE, CELIA - Buckingham (YH02972)																						●										●								
CLARKE, D - Marlow (YH02974)																																		●		●				
COLQUHOUN, ELIZABETH - Buckingham (YH03200)								●																																
D A L E - Aylesbury (YH03775)						○				○																											○			
FAIR WINTER - Milton Keynes (YH05013)																											●													
HEDSOR STUD - Bourne End (YH06647)																											●													
MCKIE, V - Twyford (YH09386)																													●											
PANAYIOTOU, E - Gerrards Cross (YH10696)																																		●		●				
R HUNT - Penn (YH11545)																																		●		●				
RADNAGE HOUSE - High Wycombe (YH11599)											○																													

Owners & Breeders of Horses and Ponies
Breeds P-Y

by Country by County

Key: ○=own ●=breed ◉=both

	Palomino	Part Breds	PB Welsh	Percheron	Piebald	Pinto	Point To Pointers	Polo Pony	Pony Hunter	Quarter Horse	Riding Pony	Selle Francais	Shetland	Shire	Show Cobs	Show Hacks	Show Hunters	Show Jumpers	Show Jumping Pony	Show Pony	Skewbald	Sports Horse	Spotted Pony	Suffolk	Tersk	Thoroughbred	Thoroughbred Flat	Thoroughbred Hanoverian	Thoroughbred Steeplechase	Trakehener	Veteran	Warm Blooded	Warmblood	Welsh Cob	Welsh Part Bred	Welsh Pony	Western Horse	Working Hunter	Working Pony	Young Stock
IRELAND																																								
COUNTY CORK																																								
CASTLEWHITE - Cork (YH02646)											◉											◉																		
COUNTY KILDARE																																								
LEGGA LIVERY & SALES - Naas (YH08538)		●																																						
COUNTY KILKENNY																																								
BANOGUE STUD - Callan (YH00907)			●																																	●				
COUNTY OFFALY																																								
ETTER SPORTS HORSES - Bellmont (YH04886)											◉	◉																				◉								◉
COUNTY WATERFORD																																								
BLACKWATER SADDLERY - Tallow (YH01502)											●																													
NORTHERN IRELAND																																								
COUNTY ANTRIM																																								
BELL, D - Ballyclare (YH01218)													●																											
BELL, T - Larne (YH01230)													●																											
CRAIGS STUD - Ballyclare (YH03555)																													●											
GILBERT, K F - Ballyclare (YH05760)													●																											
HUSTON, D N - Belfast (YH07331)													●																											
STEVENSON, J M - Belfast (YH13451)													●																											
COUNTY ARMAGH																																								
N I S P G - Mowhan (YH09991)													●																											
COUNTY DOWN																																								
MAGHERADARTIN SHETLAND STUD - Hillsborough (YH09034)													◉																											
COUNTY LONDONDERRY																																								
FORT CTRE - Maghera (YH05385)											○																													
SPARKLING STUDS - Londonderry (YH13178)																			●																					
COUNTY TYRONE																																								
KEE, W R - Strabane (YH08025)													●																											
TULLYWHISKER RIDING SCHOOL - Strabane (YH14458)																																				○				

Owners & Breeders of Horses and Ponies
Breeds P-Y

by Country by County

Key: ○=own ●=breed ◉=both

	Palomino	Part Breds	PB Welsh	Percheron	Piebald	Pinto	Point To Pointers	Polo Pony	Pony Hunter	Quarter Horse	Riding Pony	Selle Francais	Shetland	Shire	Show Cobs	Show Hacks	Show Hunters	Show Jumpers	Show Jumping Pony	Show Pony	Skewbald	Sports Horse	Spotted Pony	Suffolk	Tersk	Thoroughbred	Thoroughbred Flat	Thoroughbred Hanoverian	Thoroughbred Steeplechase	Trakehener	Veteran	Warm Blooded	Warmblood	Welsh Cob	Welsh Part Bred	Welsh Pony	Western Horse	Working Hunter	Working Pony	Young Stock
SCOTLAND																																								
ABERDEEN (CITY OF)																																								
CLOTHIE SHETLAND PONY STUD - Dyce (YH03065)													●																											
RYOVAN ARABIAN STUD - Dyce (YH12307)																																		●		●				
ABERDEENSHIRE																																								
BROGAR PONY STUD - Methlick (YH02019)													●																											
EDEN EQUESTRIAN CTRE - Turriff (YH04546)	○										○		○																			○				○				
HAYBRAKE SHETLAND PONY STUD - Inverurie (YH06564)													●																											
MANAR STUD & RIDING CTRE - Alford (YH09064)										●																														
MILL OF URAS EQUESTRIAN - Stonehaven (YH09583)											○																					●		○						
PITMEDDEN STUD - Inverurie (YH11153)													●																											
RIDINGHILL STUD - Fraserburgh (YH11885)																										◉			◉			◉								
WESTPARK SHETLAND PONY STUD - Turriff (YH15230)													●																											
ANGUS																																								
BALHALL RIDING STABLES - Brechin (YH00845)										●																														
KIRRIEMUIR HORSE SUPPLIES - Kirriemuir (YH08240)											○		○																					○		○				
PATHHEAD STABLES - Kirriemuir (YH10821)											○		○																					○		○				
ARGYLL AND BUTE																																								
COLGRAIN EQUESTRIAN CTRE - Helensburgh (YH03170)											○																									○				
ERRAY - Isle Of Mull (YH04853)													◉																											
MAPLE LEAF QUARTER HORSES - Rosneath (YH09131)										●																														
ROCKHILL HANOVERIAN STUD - Dalmally (YH12032)													●																											
WHAT EVERY HORSE WANTS - Helensburgh (YH15266)																																○								
AYRSHIRE (NORTH)																																								
CAIRNHOUSE RIDING CTRE - Isle Of Arran (YH02419)											○																							○		○				
FERGUSHILL RIDING STABLES - Kilwinning (YH05159)																																				○				
SMITH, JAMES HARRY - Kilwinning (YH12966)											●																													
AYRSHIRE (SOUTH)																																								
CREE LODGE - Ayr (YH03587)																											●		●											
I C S - Mauchline (YH07363)											●	●															●		●	●			●	●		●				
CLACKMANNANSHIRE																																								

Owners & Breeders of Horses and Ponies
Breeds P-Y

by Country by County

Key: ○=own ●=breed ◉=both

	Palomino	Part Breds	PB Welsh	Percheron	Piebald	Pinto	Point To Pointers	Polo Pony	Pony Hunter	Quarter Horse	Riding Pony	Selle Francais	Shetland	Shire	Show Cobs	Show Hacks	Show Hunters	Show Jumpers	Show Jumping Pony	Show Pony	Skewbald	Sports Horse	Spotted Pony	Suffolk	Tersk	Thoroughbred	Thoroughbred Flat	Thoroughbred Hanoverian	Thoroughbred Steeplechase	Trakehener	Veteran	Warm Blooded	Warmblood	Welsh Cob	Welsh Part Bred	Welsh Pony	Western Horse	Working Hunter	Working Pony	Young Stock
TRANSY SHETLAND PONY STUD - Dollar (YH14354)													●																											
DUMFRIES AND GALLOWAY																																								
EASTLANDS - Langholm (YH04507)													●																●											
MACMILLAN, WILLIAM G - Lockerbie (YH09013)																													●											
MEIKLE WELSH COBS - Castle Douglas (YH09447)																						●												◉						
MRS HUNT - Terregles (YH09917)											●																													
EDINBURGH (CITY OF)																																								
DAVDOR STUD - Currie (YH03907)																																		●		●				
ROBERTSON, E C - Dalkeith (YH11968)																																	●							
FIFE																																								
ALEXANDER, N W - Glenrothes (YH00272)																											●													
ANGLE PARK - Cupar (YH00409)											○		○																○					○		○				
BRAITHWAITE, C G - Cupar (YH01779)											●																		●											
LOW-MITCHELL, D I - Leven (YH08876)																													●											
PUDDLEDUB STUD - Kirkcaldy (YH11447)																											●		●											
WAXWING STUD - Saline (YH15012)											●																							●		●				
HIGHLANDS																																								
BEVERLEY HYMERS SADDLERY - Halkirk (YH01342)													◉																											
FOXHOLE LIVERY STABLE - Beauly (YH05436)																																○								
GETHIN, M - Inverness (YH05734)											●																							●		●				
HIGHLAND RIDING CTRE - Inverness (YH06793)											○		○																					○		○				
LATHERON RIDING CTRE - Caithness (YH08446)											●																													
LOCH NESS RIDING - Inverness (YH08752)																									○															
LOGIE FARM - Nairn (YH08778)	○										○		○																					○		○				
RADDERY EQUINE - Fortrose (YH11593)																																				◉				
ISLE OF SKYE																																								
SKYE RIDING CTRE - Portree (YH12881)											○		○																											
LANARKSHIRE (NORTH)																																								
LAIRD, ALEXANDER - Shotts (YH08347)																		●				●																		
LANARKSHIRE (SOUTH)																																								
SUMMERHILL STUD - Lanark (YH13631)																											●						●							

Owners & Breeders of Horses and Ponies

Breeds P-Y

by Country by County

Key: ○=own ●=breed ◉=both

	Palomino	Part Breds	PB Welsh	Percheron	Piebald	Pinto	Point To Pointers	Polo Pony	Pony Hunter	Quarter Horse	Riding Pony	Selle Francais	Shetland	Shire	Show Cobs	Show Hacks	Show Hunters	Show Jumpers	Show Jumping Pony	Show Pony	Skewbald	Sports Horse	Spotted Pony	Suffolk	Tersk	Thoroughbred	Thoroughbred Flat	Thoroughbred Hanoverian	Thoroughbred Steeplechase	Trakehener	Veteran	Warm Blooded	Warmblood	Welsh Cob	Welsh Part Bred	Welsh Pony	Western Horse	Working Hunter	Working Pony	Young Stock
LOTHIAN (EAST)																																								
DUNCRAHILL STUD - Tranent (YH04336)										●																														
LOTHIAN (MID)																																								
PERPOP STUD - Roslin (YH10981)											●																●		●					●		●				
LOTHIAN (WEST)																																								
NIMMO, M C - Broxburn (YH10207)																																		●		●				

Owners & Breeders of Horses and Ponies

Breeds P-Y

by Country by County

Key: ○=own ●=breed ◉=both

	Palomino	Part Breds	PB Welsh	Percheron	Piebald	Pinto	Point To Pointers	Polo Pony	Pony Hunter	Quarter Horse	Riding Pony	Selle Francais	Shetland	Shire	Show Cobs	Show Hacks	Show Hunters	Show Jumpers	Show Jumping Pony	Show Pony	Skewbald	Sports Horse	Spotted Pony	Suffolk	Tersk	Thoroughbred	Thoroughbred Flat	Thoroughbred Hanoverian	Thoroughbred Steeplechase	Trakehener	Veteran	Warm Blooded	Warmblood	Welsh Cob	Welsh Part Bred	Welsh Pony	Western Horse	Working Hunter	Working Pony	Young Stock
WALES																																								
BLAENAU GWENT																																								
BRAKE, DAVID & JANET - Ebbw Vale (YH01781)																																		●		●				
DAVIES, R & J - Ebbw Vale (YH03947)																																		●		●				
HARPER, D & R - Ebbw Vale (YH06454)																																		●		●				
WALTERS, J K & M S - Tredegar (YH14887)																																		●		●				
BRIDGEND																																								
COOKE, J & S - Bridgend (YH03261)																																		●		●				
CAERPHILLY																																								
BROWN, C - Blackwood (YH02102)																																		●		●				
GARRETT, DAI - Bargoed (YH05656)																																		●		●				
JENKINS, W J P - Blackwood (YH07737)																																		●		●				
JONES, J P - Hengoed (YH07908)																																				●				
ROBERTS, M D - Blackwood (YH11956)																																		●		●				
ROCKWOOD RIDING CTRE - Caerphilly (YH12039)																																		○	○	○				
CARMARTHENSHIRE																																								
ALAN ELLISON - Llandeilo (YH00238)																																		○						
AUSDAN STUD - Lampeter (YH00665)																							●																	
BOWEN, E & M - Ammanford (YH01700)																																		●		●				
CARMARTHENSHIRE - Cardigan (YH02559)																																		●		●				
CHARLTON, S - Newcastle Emlyn (YH02769)																																		●		●				
CLARKE, P - Llansadwrn (YH02975)																																		●		●				
D L DAVIES & SON - Llandysul (YH03789)																																		●		●				
DAVIES, D - Carmarthen (YH03936)																																		●		●				
DAVIES, W B - Carmarthen (YH03949)																																		●		●				
EVERITT, S & H - Llangadog (YH04954)																																		●		●				
GIRDLER, K & C - Carmarthen (YH05794)																																		●		●				
HOOPER, K E - Llanelli (YH07043)																																		●		●				
JENKINS, A & E - Ammanford (YH07730)																																		●		●				
JONES, C - Llandysul (YH07880)																																		●		●				
KINGSETTLE STUD - Llandsyssul (YH08202)	●																																							

Owners & Breeders of Horses and Ponies
Breeds P-Y

by Country by County   Key: ○=own ●=breed ◉=both

Name	Palomino	Part Breds	PB Welsh	Percheron	Piebald	Pinto	Point To Pointers	Polo Pony	Pony Hunter	Quarter Horse	Riding Pony	Selle Francais	Shetland	Shire	Show Cobs	Show Hacks	Show Hunters	Show Jumpers	Show Jumping Pony	Show Pony	Skewbald	Sports Horse	Spotted Pony	Suffolk	Tersk	Thoroughbred	Thoroughbred Flat	Thoroughbred Hanoverian	Thoroughbred Steeplechase	Trakehener	Veteran	Warm Blooded	Warmblood	Welsh Cob	Welsh Part Bred	Welsh Pony	Western Horse	Working Hunter	Working Pony	Young Stock
LEWIS, MEGAN - Llanwrda (YH08594)																																		●		●				
LLETY - Carmarthen (YH08729)																											●		●											
PEARCE, J & A - Carmarthen (YH10872)																																		●		●				
PENCADER STUD - Pencader (YH10928)																											●		●			◉								
PLAS EQUESTRIAN - Carmarthen (YH11164)		○	○								○												○													○				
READING, R H - Carmarthen (YH11682)																																		●		●				
RIPMAN, BARBARA - Carmarthen (YH11906)																																	●							
RIVERSDALE - Carmarthen (YH11923)																										●														
RUTHERFORD, E - Llandeilo (YH12273)																		●														●								
SCHMITT, H & U - Llandysul (YH12514)																																		●		●				
SIANWOOD STUD - Llandovery (YH12778)																																		●		●				
SMALL-LAND PONY STUD - Carmarthen (YH12912)											●																							●		●				
STALLIONS AT TACKEXCHANGE - Llanelli (YH13351)																																◉								
STEVENS, R - Llandysul (YH13447)																																		●		●				
TACK EXCHANGE - Llanelli (YH13787)																						◉										◉								
THOMAS SHOW TEAM - Carmarthen (YH14011)											○																		○							○				
THOMAS, D J - Kidwelly (YH14018)																																		●		●				
TOWY VALLEY PONY STUD - Llandovery (YH14305)											●																													
CEREDIGION																																								
D & D JONES & SON - Tregaron (YH03769)																																		●		●				
DOWNLAND PONY STUD - Llangoedmor (YH04235)																																		●		●				
EVANS, T E - Aberaeron (YH04933)																																		●		●				
FFOSLAS STUD - Lampeter (YH05179)																																		●		●				
G JONES BROS - Llanon (YH05587)																																		●		●				
GRANGEWAY STUD - Lampeter (YH06003)																																		●		●				

SECTION 6

Products Supplied

This section allows you to search for products supplied. Companies are listed by Country, by County.

Products are sorted alphabetically:

Section 6A - A to Gl
Section 6B - Gr to Ri
Section 6C - Ri to W

The Products Supplied grid can be used in two different ways. You can search by the particular product you require in order to see which company/companies supply it.

e.g. Bedding : Frosbury's

Or, you can look at the profile of one particular company in order to see what product/s they supply.

e.g. Chapel Feeds : Feeds

Once you have located a business using this section you can then refer to the company's detailed profile in Section 1.

Products Supplied
A - G

by Country by County

	Air Conditioning	Air Purifiers	Aloe Vera	Back Supports	Bedding	Bits	Body Protectors	Books	Boot Holders	Boot Jacks	Boot Scrapers	Boots	Boxes	Breeding Equipment	Breeding Supplies	Bridles	Bridlework	Carriages	Carts	CD's	Cleaning Equipment	Cleaning Supplies	Clippers	Closed Circuit TV	Clothes (Bespoke)	Clothes (Standard)	Coolers	Corn	Cross Country Jumps	Cushion Web	Damp Hay	Disposable A.V Liners	Disposable Equitainer	Driving Collars	Driving Harness	Dust Free Shavings	Electric Fencing	Exercise Equipment	Farm Equipment	Feed	Feed Racks	Feed Supplements	Fencing	Fertilisers	Fire Baskets	Flooring Supply (Arenas)	Fly Repellent	Gallops	Gates	Girths	Gloves	Mail Order Facilities
ENGLAND																																																				
BATH & SOMERSET (NORTH EAST)																																																				
CLUTTON HILL AGRICULTURAL SVS, Clutton (YH03077)																												●												●												
HEXT BROTHERS, Bath (YH06733)																												●												●												
MATTHEWS OF KEYNSHAM, Keynsham (YH09268)																												●												●												
SOMERLAP FOREST PRODUCTS, Compton Martin (YH13061)																																								●												
TAPSONS, Midsomer Norton (YH13867)																												●												●												
BEDFORDSHIRE																																																				
ARCADE SADDLERY BEDFORD, Bedford (YH00498)								●				●											●			●																●										
BANKS OF SANDY, Sandy (YH00897)																												●												●												
BEECHCROFT ANIMAL FEEDS, Steppingley (YH01167)																												●												●												
BIGGLESWADE SADDLERY, Biggleswade (YH01404)								●				●					●						●			●																●										
BROWNS PET SHOP, Luton (YH02146)																												●												●												
CHAPEL FEEDS, Clophill (YH02739)																												●												●												
EQUISSENTIAL, Bedford (YH04820)												●														●																										
FEED BIN, Luton (YH05120)																																								●		●										
GRAVENHURST, Bedford (YH06023)																												●												●												
GRAVENHURST SADDLERY, Bedford (YH06024)												●														●														●		●										
K & K PET SHOPS, Dunstable (YH07980)																												●												●												
LAGUS, S E, Leighton Buzzard (YH08344)																●																																				
MCCULLAM, Little Staughton (YH09339)																												●												●												
PARTNERS PET SUPERMARKET, Bedford (YH10803)																												●												●												
R B EQUESTRIAN, Leighton Buzzard (YH11514)																												●												●												
SALSA STUD, Chawston (YH12391)													●										●																	●		●							●			
SHERPA FEEDS, Dunstable (YH12727)																												●												●												
STOCKWOOD STABLES, Luton (YH13499)																		●																																		
SUNSHINE RIDING SCHOOL, Luton (YH13652)												●																																								
T C FEEDS, Dunstable (YH13732)																												●												●												
VULCAN TOWING CTRE, Luton (YH14745)													●																																							
W JORDANS, Biggleswade (YH14778)																																								●												
WADDINGTONS, Leighton Buzzard (YH14809)												●														●																										

A - G

by Country by County	Air Conditioning	Air Purifiers	Aloe Vera	Back Supports	Bedding	Bits	Body Protectors	Books	Boot Holders	Boot Jacks	Boot Scrapers	Boots	Boxes	Breeding Equipment	Breeding Supplies	Bridles	Bridlework	Carriages	Carts	CD's	Cleaning Equipment	Cleaning Supplies	Clippers	Closed Circuit TV	Clothes (Bespoke)	Clothes (Standard)	Coolers	Corn	Cross Country Jumps	Cushion Web	Damp Hay	Disposable A.V Liners	Disposable Equitainer	Driving Collars	Driving Harness	Dust Free Shavings	Electric Fencing	Exercise Equipment	Farm Equipment	Feed	Feed Racks	Feed Supplements	Fencing	Fertilisers	Fire Baskets	Flooring Supply (Arenas)	Fly Repellent	Gallops	Gates	Girths	Gloves	Mail Order Facilities
BERKSHIRE																																																				
ASPREY POLO, Windsor (YH00628)																										●																										
BANKS SOUTHERN, Thatcham (YH00898)																												●												●												
BRIDGES, C & M, Reading (YH01883)																		●																																		
CENTELL, Reading (YH02685)																										●		●												●												
CHANGING TACK, Windsor (YH02732)						●						●				●										●																										
COUNTRYWIDE STORES, Reading (YH03448)																												●												●												
DALGETY AGRCLTRL, Reading (YH03833)																												●												●												
EAST SOLEY E C 2000, Hungerford (YH04486)																								●																												
FROSBURY'S, Bracknell (YH05519)					●																							●												●												
J C & N C WARD, Pangbourne (YH07568)					●																																			●												
LAZYGRAZER, Wokingham (YH08486)																																								●												
MILLS, J C, Newbury (YH09634)																																								●												
PEACHEY, KA, Maidenhead (YH10858)																			●																																	
PERCY STONE, Pangbourne (YH10974)																												●												●												
RIVERDALE, Thatcham (YH11920)																																			●																	
SCATS COUNTRYSTORE, Newbury (YH12493)												●											●					●												●		●										
SHAMLEY SADDLERY, Maidenhead (YH12663)																																			●																	
SHELTON FARM, Reading (YH12704)																		●																																		
STABLE DOOR, Reading (YH13291)																																								●												
TALLY HO FARM, Windsor (YH13840)																												●												●												
THIMBLEBY & SHORTLAND, Reading (YH13991)																		●																					●													
THRESHERS BARN, Newbury (YH14111)																												●												●												
VALLEY EQUINE, Hungerford (YH14648)																																										●										●
WM LILLICO & SON, Hungerford (YH15640)																												●												●												
WOODCRAY FEEDS, Wokingham (YH15680)																												●												●												
WOODLANDS, Hungerford (YH15705)					●							●																										●														
BRISTOL																																																				
A T VEATER & SONS, Bristol (YH00062)																												●												●												
ANIMAL BEDDING, Bristol (YH00427)					●																																															
EQUICRAFT SADDLERY, Bristol (YH04739)																												●												●												
JENNY'S TACK SHOP, Bristol (YH07750)																												●												●												

Products Supplied

A - G

by Country by County

Company	Air Conditioning	Air Purifiers	Aloe Vera	Back Supports	Bedding	Bits	Body Protectors	Books	Boot Holders	Boot Jacks	Boot Scrapers	Boots	Boxes	Breeding Equipment	Breeding Supplies	Bridles	Bridlework	Carriages	Carts	CD's	Cleaning Equipment	Cleaning Supplies	Clippers	Closed Circuit TV	Clothes (Bespoke)	Clothes (Standard)	Coolers	Corn	Cross Country Jumps	Cushion Web	Damp Hay	Disposable A.V Liners	Disposable Equitainer	Driving Collars	Driving Harness	Dust Free Shavings	Electric Fencing	Exercise Equipment	Farm Equipment	Feed	Feed Racks	Feed Supplements	Fencing	Fertilisers	Fire Baskets	Flooring Supply (Arenas)	Fly Repellent	Gallops	Gates	Girths	Gloves	Mail Order Facilities
BUCKINGHAMSHIRE																																																				
BEECHFIELD SADDLERY, Grendon Underwood (YH01172)																												●												●												
BELLINGDON END, Chesham (YH01238)					●			●				●											●			●		●											●	●		●	●									
BRIDLEWAYS, Burnham (YH01896)																												●												●												
C & L EQUESTRIAN, Milton Keynes (YH02356)																												●												●												
COUNTRYWIDE STORES, Tingewick (YH03450)																												●												●												
COX & ROBINSON, Buckingham (YH03527)																												●												●												
CRAWFORD-BROWN, FIONA, Ludgershall (YH03577)																		●																																		
D A L E, Aylesbury (YH03775)																																																				●
DENNIS'S SADDLERY/RIDING WEAR, Aylesbury (YH04059)												●														●																									●	
DENNIS'S SADDLERY/RIDING WEAR, Aylesbury (YH04060)																										●																									●	
DEVILS HORSEMEN, Milton Keynes (YH04090)																		●	●																●																	
EQUESTRIAN CTRE, Amersham (YH04696)								●																●		●																										
EQUS HEALTH, Aylesbury (YH04835)																																										●										
FLETCHER TOOGOOD, Milton Keynes (YH05272)																												●												●												
G B GOMME & SON, Princes Risborough (YH05570)																												●												●												
JOLLYES, Milton Keynes (YH07852)																												●												●												
LIDSTONE FARMS, Slough (YH08607)																												●												●												
MECA RIDING CTRE, High Wycombe (YH09431)																												●												●												
NATURAL HORSE FOOD, Princes Risborough (YH10052)																												●												●												
PENN TACK & FEED CTRE, High Wycombe (YH10948)																												●												●												
R & S PRICE, Milton Keynes (YH11508)																												●												●												
RAGUS SUGARS, Slough (YH11608)																																										●										
SPILLERS SPECIALITY FEEDS, Milton Keynes (YH13206)																																								●		●										
WIDMER FEEDS, Princes Risborough (YH15393)																												●												●												
WILLOWBROOK FARM FEED & TACK, Aylesbury (YH15507)																												●												●												
CAMBRIDGESHIRE																																																				
A FRENCH & SONS, Cambridge (YH00032)																												●												●												
ALLTACK & ALLFEED, Cambridge (YH00326)																												●												●												
APACHE, Huntingdon (YH00473)								●																																												
BAILY'S HUNTING DIRECTORY, Cambridge (YH00809)								●																																												
BANKS CARGILL AGRICULTURE, Huntingdon (YH00896)					●																																			●		●		●								

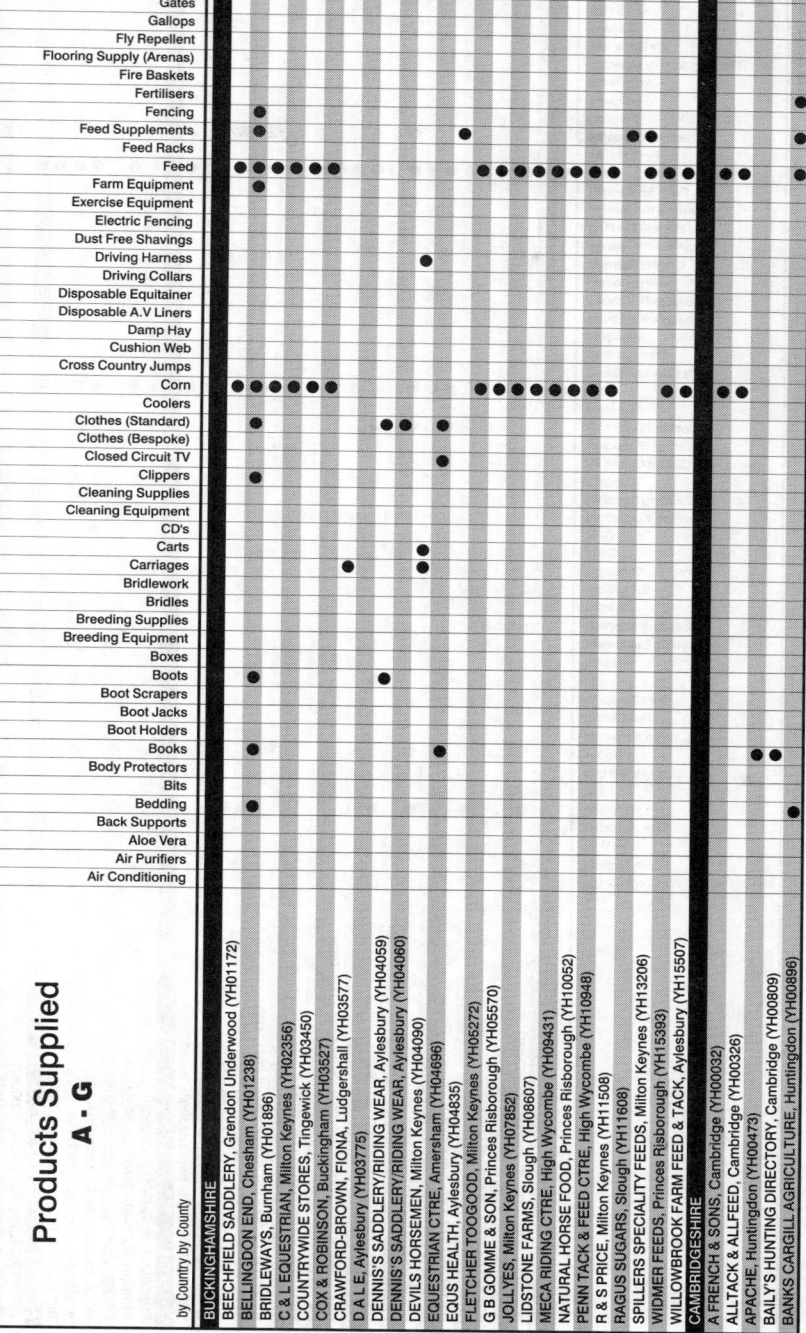

Products Supplied
A - G

by Country by County	Air Conditioning	Air Purifiers	Aloe Vera	Back Supports	Bedding	Bits	Body Protectors	Books	Boot Holders	Boot Jacks	Boot Scrapers	Boots	Boxes	Breeding Equipment	Breeding Supplies	Bridles	Bridlework	Carriages	Carts	CD's	Cleaning Equipment	Cleaning Supplies	Clippers	Closed Circuit TV	Clothes (Bespoke)	Clothes (Standard)	Coolers	Corn	Cross Country Jumps	Cushion Web	Damp Hay	Disposable A.V Liners	Disposable Equitainer	Driving Collars	Driving Harness	Dust Free Shavings	Electric Fencing	Exercise Equipment	Farm Equipment	Feed	Feed Racks	Feed Supplements	Fencing	Fertilisers	Fire Baskets	Flooring Supply (Arenas)	Fly Repellent	Gallops	Gates	Girths	Gloves	Mail Order Facilities
BELTONS COUNTRY SHOP, Peterborough (YH01256)																												●												●												
CLARK & BUTCHER, Ely (YH02960)																												●												●												
COUNTRY PURSUITS, Cambridge (YH03421)					●																																			●												
COUNTRY VEHICLES, Ely (YH03434)													●																																							
GRABELLA STUD, Kentford (YH05957)														●	●																																					
GRASS ROOTS, Peterborough (YH06018)					●																																			●												
H E PRINGLE, Bourn (YH06220)																												●												●												
HIGHGATE FARM, Willingham (YH06786)																												●												●												
HOOK HSE, March (YH07035)					●			●																		●		●												●		●										
INTERVET UK, Cambridge (YH07483)																																										●										
LONG MELFORD, Cambridge (YH08798)					●							●											●			●														●		●										
LONGLAND, MICHAEL, Huntingdon (YH08814)																												●												●												
NORTHBROOK EQUESTRIAN CTRE, Huntingdon (YH10294)													●																																							
PARK TONKS, Great Abington (YH10738)																																										●										
PEGASUS, Peterborough (YH10901)																													●																							
R C GOWING, Ely (YH11519)																																							●													
SAWSTON FARM FEEDS, Pampisford (YH12462)																												●												●												
SMEETH SADDLERY, Wisbech (YH12925)					●																																					●										
SUNDOWN STRAW, Huntingdon (YH13643)					●																																															
THODY, M & P, Huntingdon (YH14002)																												●												●												
WHITWORTH BROS, Peterborough (YH15378)																												●												●												
CHESHIRE																																																				
BELLCROWN, Malpas (YH01231)																		●																																		
BERNARD CORBETT, Malpas (YH01309)																												●												●												
BODEN & DAVIES, Stockport (YH01595)					●																																															
BOOL BY DESIGN, Tarporley (YH01631)					●							●								●					●	●		●												●		●										●
BOWLERS, Stockport (YH01715)								●				●														●		●												●		●										
BUTLER, F L, Pen-Y-Ffordd (YH02325)																												●												●												
CASSIDY EQUESTRIAN, Northwich (YH02621)																												●												●												
CEDAR HEALTH, Hazel Grove (YH02673)																																										●										
CHANCE & HUNT NUTRITION, Runcorn (YH02729)																																										●										
CHELFORD FARM SUPPLIES, Macclesfield (YH02799)					●			●				●											●			●		●												●		●										

Products Supplied
A - G

by Country by County

	Air Conditioning	Air Purifiers	Aloe Vera	Back Supports	Bedding	Bits	Body Protectors	Books	Boot Holders	Boot Jacks	Boot Scrapers	Boots	Boxes	Breeding Equipment	Breeding Supplies	Bridles	Bridlework	Carriages	Carts	CD's	Cleaning Equipment	Cleaning Supplies	Clippers	Closed Circuit TV	Clothes (Bespoke)	Clothes (Standard)
COLBERRY SADDLERY, Ellesmere Port (YH03142)								●																		●
CREWE SADDLERY, Crewe (YH03595)								●																		
DANE VALLEY, Macclesfield (YH03864)					●																					
DECATHLON SPORTS & LEISURE, Stockport (YH04008)												●											●			●
DOVE STYLE, Chester (YH04217)																		●								
EQUIFORM NUTRITION, Crewe (YH04747)																										
ESTATE SUPPLIES & SVS, Altrincham (YH04875)																										
GAYNORS SADDLERY, Dukinfield (YH05682)																					●		●		●	●
GO ENTERTAINMENTS, Congleton (YH05860)																		●								
GREEN FARM FEEDS, Crewe (YH06055)					●																					
HORSE DRAWN CARRIAGES, Macclesfield (YH07117)																		●								
JOHN COOK (CORN MERCHANTS), Macclesfield (YH07784)																										
KEY GREEN SADDLERY, Congleton (YH08113)																										
KIRKBY, Tarporley (YH08232)																										
LANSDOWNE HORSE & RIDER, Chester (YH08423)					●			●				●		●							●		●		●	●
M J HALE & SONS, Willaston (YH08968)																										
MILLENNIUM ANIMAL BEDDING, Warrington (YH09598)					●																					
MINSUPS, Winsford (YH09654)																										
N W F COUNTRYWISE, Nantwich (YH10001)																										
PET FOOD & HORSE SUPPLIES, Macclesfield (YH11003)																										
PET FOOD DISCOUNT CTRE, Hyde (YH11004)																										
RINGWOOD FENCING, Chester (YH11904)																										
SHENTON, C W, Wilmslow (YH12707)																										
SMITH & MORRIS, Nantwich (YH12932)																										
STOCKFARM EQUESTRIAN SUPPLIES, Chester (YH13491)														●	●											
SUGAR BROOK FARM FEEDS, Altrincham (YH13627)																										
TOPSPEC, Nantwich (YH14241)																										
VITACOLL EQUINE, Warrington (YH14734)																										
W & T GIBSON, Frodsham (YH14748)																										
WILLIAMS, B, Lymm (YH15447)																										
WILSONS SADDLERY, Macclesfield (YH15552)																										
WOODVILLE FARM SADDLERY, Sandbach (YH15753)																										

	Coolers	Corn	Cross Country Jumps	Cushion Web	Damp Hay	Disposable A.V Liners	Disposable Equitainer	Driving Collars	Driving Harness	Dust Free Shavings	Electric Fencing	Exercise Equipment	Farm Equipment	Feed	Feed Racks	Feed Supplements	Fencing	Fertilisers	Fire Baskets	Flooring Supply (Arenas)	Fly Repellent	Gallops	Gates	Girths	Gloves	Mail Order Facilities
COLBERRY SADDLERY, Ellesmere Port (YH03142)																										●
CREWE SADDLERY, Crewe (YH03595)																										
DANE VALLEY, Macclesfield (YH03864)																										
DECATHLON SPORTS & LEISURE, Stockport (YH04008)																	●									
DOVE STYLE, Chester (YH04217)																										
EQUIFORM NUTRITION, Crewe (YH04747)														●		●										
ESTATE SUPPLIES & SVS, Altrincham (YH04875)		●												●												
GAYNORS SADDLERY, Dukinfield (YH05682)									●					●		●										
GO ENTERTAINMENTS, Congleton (YH05860)																										
GREEN FARM FEEDS, Crewe (YH06055)		●												●		●		●								
HORSE DRAWN CARRIAGES, Macclesfield (YH07117)																										
JOHN COOK (CORN MERCHANTS), Macclesfield (YH07784)		●												●												
KEY GREEN SADDLERY, Congleton (YH08113)		●												●												
KIRKBY, Tarporley (YH08232)														●												
LANSDOWNE HORSE & RIDER, Chester (YH08423)		●										●	●	●		●	●	●								●
M J HALE & SONS, Willaston (YH08968)		●												●												
MILLENNIUM ANIMAL BEDDING, Warrington (YH09598)																										
MINSUPS, Winsford (YH09654)														●		●										
N W F COUNTRYWISE, Nantwich (YH10001)		●												●												
PET FOOD & HORSE SUPPLIES, Macclesfield (YH11003)		●												●												
PET FOOD DISCOUNT CTRE, Hyde (YH11004)		●												●												
RINGWOOD FENCING, Chester (YH11904)		●												●												
SHENTON, C W, Wilmslow (YH12707)		●												●												
SMITH & MORRIS, Nantwich (YH12932)		●												●												
STOCKFARM EQUESTRIAN SUPPLIES, Chester (YH13491)		●												●												
SUGAR BROOK FARM FEEDS, Altrincham (YH13627)		●												●												
TOPSPEC, Nantwich (YH14241)														●		●										●
VITACOLL EQUINE, Warrington (YH14734)																●										
W & T GIBSON, Frodsham (YH14748)		●												●		●										
WILLIAMS, B, Lymm (YH15447)		●												●												
WILSONS SADDLERY, Macclesfield (YH15552)		●												●												
WOODVILLE FARM SADDLERY, Sandbach (YH15753)		●												●												

Products Supplied
A - G

by Country by County

Company	Air Conditioning	Air Purifiers	Aloe Vera	Back Supports	Bedding	Bits	Body Protectors	Books	Boot Holders	Boot Jacks	Boot Scrapers	Boots	Boxes	Breeding Equipment	Breeding Supplies	Bridles	Bridlework	Carriages	Carts	CD's	Cleaning Equipment	Cleaning Supplies	Clippers	Closed Circuit TV	Clothes (Bespoke)	Clothes (Standard)	Coolers	Corn	Cross Country Jumps	Cushion Web	Damp Hay	Disposable A.V Liners	Disposable Equitainer	Driving Collars	Driving Harness	Dust Free Shavings	Electric Fencing	Exercise Equipment	Farm Equipment	Feed	Feed Racks	Feed Supplements	Fencing	Fertilisers	Fire Baskets	Flooring Supply (Arenas)	Fly Repellent	Gallops	Gates	Girths	Gloves	Mail Order Facilities
YOUNGS, Congleton (YH15944)																												●												●		●										
CLEVELAND																																																				
ARMSTRONG RICHARDSON, Middlesbrough (YH00544)												●														●		●									●			●		●										●
EQUINE EXTRAS, Stockton-on-Tees (YH04778)								●				●														●														●		●										
FARMWAY, Stokesley (YH05070)																												●												●												
FEED-EM, Guisborough (YH05121)																												●												●												
HADRIAN EQUINE, Stockton-on-Tees (YH06271)																																																				●
HOOF'N'HOUND, Hartlepool (YH07031)					●			●				●											●			●														●		●										
HOOF'N'HOUND, Middlesbrough (YH07032)																										●																										
WOLVISTON ANIMAL FEEDS, Billingham (YH15651)																												●												●												
CORNWALL																																																				
BLISLAND HARNESS MAKERS, Liskeard (YH01541)																																			●																	
BUSH LIVERY STABLES, Saltash (YH02306)					●																																			●												
COACHLANE FEED STORES, Redruth (YH03107)																												●												●												
CORNWALL ANIMAL FEEDS, Newquay (YH03329)																												●												●												
CORNWALL FARMERS, Liskeard (YH03334)					●							●														●		●												●		●										
CORNWALL FARMERS, Callington (YH03330)					●							●																●												●		●										
CORNWALL FARMERS, Wadebridge (YH03338)					●							●											●			●		●												●		●										
CORNWALL FARMERS, Penzance (YH03335)					●							●																●												●		●										
CORNWALL FARMERS, Truro (YH03337)					●							●														●		●												●		●										
CORNWALL FARMERS, St Austell (YH03336)																												●												●												
CORNWALL FARMERS, Helston (YH03333)																												●												●												
CORNWALL FARMERS, Camelford (YH03332)																												●												●												
CORNWALL FARMERS, Camborne (YH03331)																												●												●												
CORNWALL PAPER, Redruth (YH03341)					●																																															
D MAY & SONS, St Austell (YH03796)																												●												●												
DALGETY AGRCLTRL, Launceston (YH03835)																												●												●												
DOWNFIELD FARM SHOP, Gunnislake (YH04229)																												●												●												
ECLIPSE, Penzance (YH04537)																												●												●												
EQUESTRIAN STOP, Camborne (YH04712)						●																																														●
EQUUS HEALTH, Gunnislake (YH04840)																																										●										
F W MASTERS & SON, Bodmin (YH05002)																												●												●												

Products Supplied

A - G

by Country by County

	Air Conditioning	Air Purifiers	Aloe Vera	Back Supports	Bedding	Bits	Body Protectors	Books	Boot Holders	Boot Jacks	Boot Scrapers	Boots	Boxes
FENNSMITH, TONY, Kilkhampton (YH05150)													
GOTTS, H J, Redruth (YH05947)													
GWINEAR & DISTRICT FARMERS, Camborne (YH06204)													
HALLAGENNA STUD FARM, Bodmin (YH06322)													
HAMMER 'N' HOE, Falmouth (YH06358)													
HELSTON SADDLERY, Helston (YH06657)								●					
HORSE & RIDER, Launceston (YH07094)												●	
LE GRICE, T C, Penzance (YH08488)													
NANTURRIAN STUD FARM, Falmouth (YH10017)													
NICHOLLS & SONS, Helston (YH10181)													
POLLY LUNN PET & AQUATICS, Truro (YH11208)												●	
RICKARD, T R, St Austell (YH11832)													
RIDE & DRIVE SUPPLIES, Helston (YH11843)													
ROSEVIDNEY ARABIANS, Penzance (YH12111)					●								
ST LEONARDS EQUESTRIAN CTRE, Launceston (YH13278)													
W RICHARDS & SON, Bodmin (YH14793)													
WALTER BAILEY, St Austell (YH14882)													
WOOFWARE, Bodmin (YH15762)													
COUNTY DURHAM													
ALSTON & KILLHOPE, Bishop Auckland (YH00339)													
BOWES MANOR EQUESTRIAN CTRE, Chester Le Street (YH01709)					●								
BROOM HALL LIVERY YARD, Durham (YH02072)													
C R SADDLERY, Bishop Auckland (YH02389)													
DENE HEAD LIVERY, Darlington (YH04042)									●	●	●		●
EGGLESTON WOODCHIPS, Lanchester (YH04593)					●								
FARMWAY, Darlington (YH05071)													
FARMWAY, Darlington (YH05072)					●			●				●	
H GARNHAM & SON, Sacriston (YH06224)													
LANCHESTER COUNTRY STORE, Lanchester (YH08382)													
M A V SADDLERY & PET STORE, Crook (YH08953)													
MADDOX, Elton (YH09020)													
SADDLE SENSE, Barnard Castle (YH12348)													

	Breeding Equipment	Breeding Supplies	Bridles	Bridlework	Carriages	Carts	CD's	Cleaning Equipment	Cleaning Supplies	Clippers	Closed Circuit TV	Clothes (Bespoke)	Clothes (Standard)
FENNSMITH, TONY, Kilkhampton (YH05150)													
GOTTS, H J, Redruth (YH05947)													
GWINEAR & DISTRICT FARMERS, Camborne (YH06204)													
HALLAGENNA STUD FARM, Bodmin (YH06322)													
HAMMER 'N' HOE, Falmouth (YH06358)													
HELSTON SADDLERY, Helston (YH06657)										●			
HORSE & RIDER, Launceston (YH07094)													●
LE GRICE, T C, Penzance (YH08488)	●	●											
NANTURRIAN STUD FARM, Falmouth (YH10017)	●	●											
NICHOLLS & SONS, Helston (YH10181)													
POLLY LUNN PET & AQUATICS, Truro (YH11208)										●			●
RICKARD, T R, St Austell (YH11832)													
RIDE & DRIVE SUPPLIES, Helston (YH11843)					●	●							
ROSEVIDNEY ARABIANS, Penzance (YH12111)													
ST LEONARDS EQUESTRIAN CTRE, Launceston (YH13278)													
W RICHARDS & SON, Bodmin (YH14793)													
WALTER BAILEY, St Austell (YH14882)													
WOOFWARE, Bodmin (YH15762)													●
COUNTY DURHAM													
ALSTON & KILLHOPE, Bishop Auckland (YH00339)													
BOWES MANOR EQUESTRIAN CTRE, Chester Le Street (YH01709)													
BROOM HALL LIVERY YARD, Durham (YH02072)											●		
C R SADDLERY, Bishop Auckland (YH02389)					●								
DENE HEAD LIVERY, Darlington (YH04042)													
EGGLESTON WOODCHIPS, Lanchester (YH04593)													
FARMWAY, Darlington (YH05071)													
FARMWAY, Darlington (YH05072)										●		●	●
H GARNHAM & SON, Sacriston (YH06224)													
LANCHESTER COUNTRY STORE, Lanchester (YH08382)													●
M A V SADDLERY & PET STORE, Crook (YH08953)													
MADDOX, Elton (YH09020)													
SADDLE SENSE, Barnard Castle (YH12348)			●										

	Coolers	Corn	Cross Country Jumps	Cushion Web	Damp Hay	Disposable A.V Liners	Disposable Equitainer	Driving Collars	Driving Harness	Dust Free Shavings	Electric Fencing	Exercise Equipment	Farm Equipment
FENNSMITH, TONY, Kilkhampton (YH05150)		●											
GOTTS, H J, Redruth (YH05947)													●
GWINEAR & DISTRICT FARMERS, Camborne (YH06204)		●											
HALLAGENNA STUD FARM, Bodmin (YH06322)		●											
HAMMER 'N' HOE, Falmouth (YH06358)		●											
HELSTON SADDLERY, Helston (YH06657)													
HORSE & RIDER, Launceston (YH07094)													
LE GRICE, T C, Penzance (YH08488)													
NANTURRIAN STUD FARM, Falmouth (YH10017)													
NICHOLLS & SONS, Helston (YH10181)		●											
POLLY LUNN PET & AQUATICS, Truro (YH11208)		●											
RICKARD, T R, St Austell (YH11832)		●											
RIDE & DRIVE SUPPLIES, Helston (YH11843)								●	●				
ROSEVIDNEY ARABIANS, Penzance (YH12111)													
ST LEONARDS EQUESTRIAN CTRE, Launceston (YH13278)		●											
W RICHARDS & SON, Bodmin (YH14793)		●											
WALTER BAILEY, St Austell (YH14882)		●											
WOOFWARE, Bodmin (YH15762)													
COUNTY DURHAM													
ALSTON & KILLHOPE, Bishop Auckland (YH00339)													
BOWES MANOR EQUESTRIAN CTRE, Chester Le Street (YH01709)													
BROOM HALL LIVERY YARD, Durham (YH02072)													
C R SADDLERY, Bishop Auckland (YH02389)												●	
DENE HEAD LIVERY, Darlington (YH04042)													
EGGLESTON WOODCHIPS, Lanchester (YH04593)													
FARMWAY, Darlington (YH05071)		●											
FARMWAY, Darlington (YH05072)												●	●
H GARNHAM & SON, Sacriston (YH06224)		●											
LANCHESTER COUNTRY STORE, Lanchester (YH08382)		●											
M A V SADDLERY & PET STORE, Crook (YH08953)		●											
MADDOX, Elton (YH09020)		●											
SADDLE SENSE, Barnard Castle (YH12348)													

	Feed	Feed Racks	Feed Supplements	Fencing	Fertilisers	Fire Baskets	Flooring Supply (Arenas)	Fly Repellent	Gallops	Gates	Girths	Gloves	Mail Order Facilities
FENNSMITH, TONY, Kilkhampton (YH05150)	●												
GOTTS, H J, Redruth (YH05947)													
GWINEAR & DISTRICT FARMERS, Camborne (YH06204)	●												
HALLAGENNA STUD FARM, Bodmin (YH06322)	●												
HAMMER 'N' HOE, Falmouth (YH06358)	●												
HELSTON SADDLERY, Helston (YH06657)													
HORSE & RIDER, Launceston (YH07094)													
LE GRICE, T C, Penzance (YH08488)													
NANTURRIAN STUD FARM, Falmouth (YH10017)													
NICHOLLS & SONS, Helston (YH10181)	●												
POLLY LUNN PET & AQUATICS, Truro (YH11208)	●		●										
RICKARD, T R, St Austell (YH11832)	●												
RIDE & DRIVE SUPPLIES, Helston (YH11843)													
ROSEVIDNEY ARABIANS, Penzance (YH12111)													●
ST LEONARDS EQUESTRIAN CTRE, Launceston (YH13278)	●												
W RICHARDS & SON, Bodmin (YH14793)	●												
WALTER BAILEY, St Austell (YH14882)	●												
WOOFWARE, Bodmin (YH15762)													
COUNTY DURHAM													
ALSTON & KILLHOPE, Bishop Auckland (YH00339)										●			
BOWES MANOR EQUESTRIAN CTRE, Chester Le Street (YH01709)													
BROOM HALL LIVERY YARD, Durham (YH02072)													
C R SADDLERY, Bishop Auckland (YH02389)													
DENE HEAD LIVERY, Darlington (YH04042)													
EGGLESTON WOODCHIPS, Lanchester (YH04593)	●												
FARMWAY, Darlington (YH05071)	●												
FARMWAY, Darlington (YH05072)	●		●	●	●					●			
H GARNHAM & SON, Sacriston (YH06224)	●												
LANCHESTER COUNTRY STORE, Lanchester (YH08382)	●		●										
M A V SADDLERY & PET STORE, Crook (YH08953)	●												
MADDOX, Elton (YH09020)	●												
SADDLE SENSE, Barnard Castle (YH12348)													

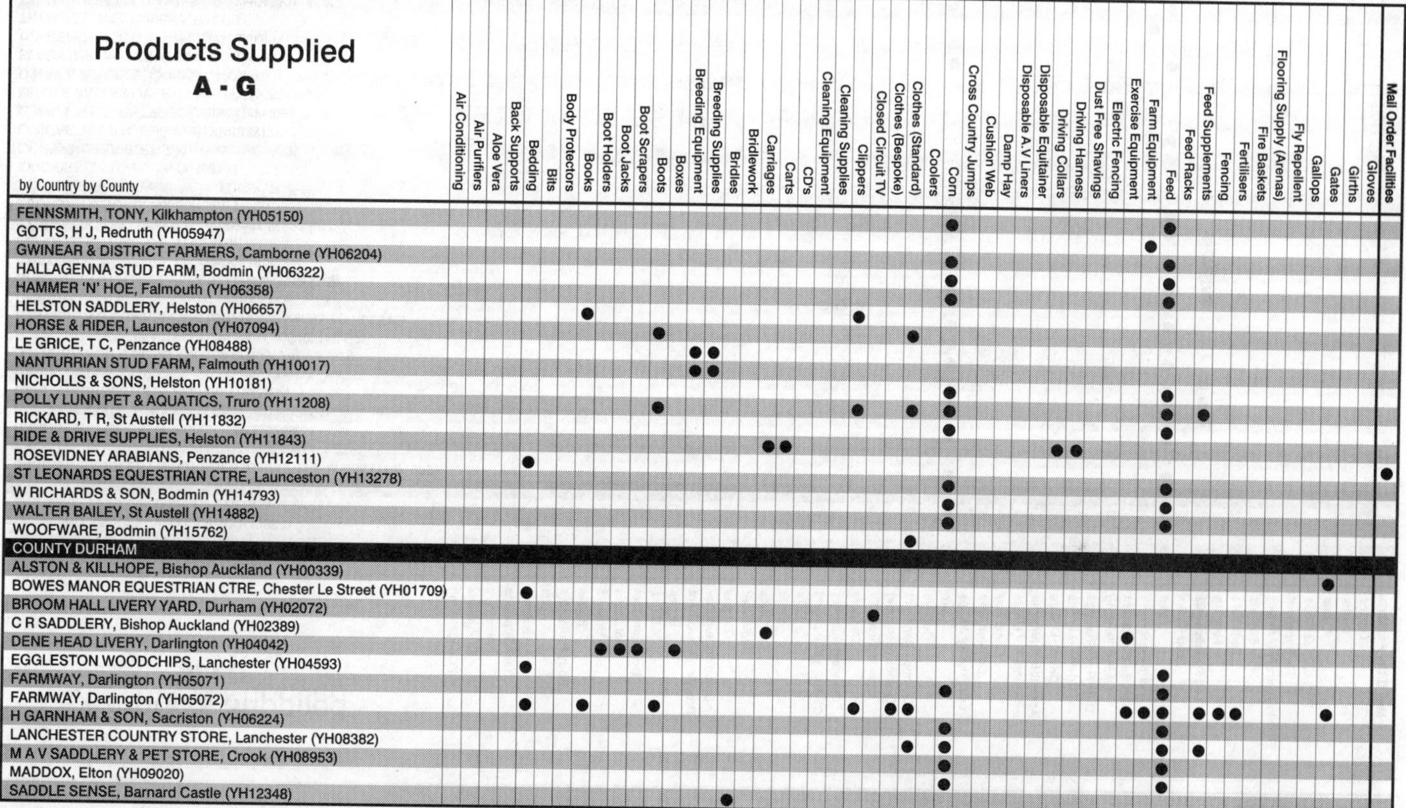

Products Supplied
A - G

by Country by County

Company	Air Conditioning	Air Purifiers	Aloe Vera	Back Supports	Bedding	Bits	Body Protectors	Books	Boot Holders	Boot Jacks	Boot Scrapers	Boots	Boxes	Breeding Equipment	Breeding Supplies	Bridles	Bridlework	Carriages	Carts	CD's	Cleaning Equipment	Cleaning Supplies	Clippers	Closed Circuit TV	Clothes (Bespoke)	Clothes (Standard)
SEAGOLD CENTURION, Crook (YH12587)																										●
TALLENTIRE, M L, Bishop Auckland (YH13835)																										
THINFORD SADDLERY, Durham (YH13994)					●																					
W M MCIVOR & SON, Ferry Hill (YH14780)																										
CUMBRIA																										
BARROW SADDLERY & SUPPLIES, Barrow-In-Furness (YH01029)																										
BREED EX EQUINE STUD, Penrith (YH01832)														●	●											
BURNS PET FOODS, Workington (YH02269)																										
CALTECH BIOTECHNOLOGY, Carlisle (YH02454)																										
CARRS AGRICULTURE, Penrith (YH02597)																										
CARRS AGRICULTURE, Carlisle (YH02596)																										
D A HARRISON & SONS, Carlisle (YH03774)																										
FOUR LEGGED FRIENDS, Egremont (YH05408)																										
FURNESS & S CUMBERLAND SUPPLY, Ulverston (YH05545)																										
GET SMART, Barrow-In-Furness (YH05732)																					●	●	●			
GRASSGARTH HORSE FEEDS, Kendal (YH06019)																										
GRAYLING BOOKS, Penrith (YH06034)								●																		
INMAN, JENNY, Kendal (YH07459)																●										
J & E PETFOODS, Whitehaven (YH07545)																										
J JORDAN & SONS, Windermere (YH07593)																										
J W WILKINSON, Kendal (YH07628)																										
KINGFISHER, Ulverston (YH08191)					●																					
LAKELAND EQUESTRIAN, Windermere (YH08354)								●				●														
LANCASTER, P R, Ulverston (YH08381)																										
LOWTHER EQUESTRIAN, Carlisle (YH08877)																										
MIDDLE BAYLES LIVERY, Alston (YH09534)																								●		
O'HARA, JOHNNIE, Carlisle (YH10442)																●										
SLACK'S, Penrith (YH12884)																										
T W RELPH & SONS, Penrith (YH13767)																										
THWAITES, R G, Penrith (YH14124)																										
TYNDALE FARM SERVICES, Holmrook (YH14525)																										
W C F COUNTRY CTRES, Wigton (YH14757)																										

Company	Coolers	Corn	Cross Country Jumps	Cushion Web	Damp Hay	Disposable A.V Liners	Disposable Equitainer	Driving Collars	Driving Harness	Dust Free Shavings	Electric Fencing	Exercise Equipment	Farm Equipment	Feed	Feed Racks	Feed Supplements	Fencing	Fertilisers	Fire Baskets	Flooring Supply (Arenas)	Fly Repellent	Gallops	Gates	Girths	Gloves	Mail Order Facilities
SEAGOLD CENTURION, Crook (YH12587)																										
TALLENTIRE, M L, Bishop Auckland (YH13835)		●												●												
THINFORD SADDLERY, Durham (YH13994)																										
W M MCIVOR & SON, Ferry Hill (YH14780)		●												●												
CUMBRIA																										
BARROW SADDLERY & SUPPLIES, Barrow-In-Furness (YH01029)		●												●												
BREED EX EQUINE STUD, Penrith (YH01832)																										
BURNS PET FOODS, Workington (YH02269)		●												●												
CALTECH BIOTECHNOLOGY, Carlisle (YH02454)														●		●										
CARRS AGRICULTURE, Penrith (YH02597)		●												●		●										
CARRS AGRICULTURE, Carlisle (YH02596)		●												●		●										
D A HARRISON & SONS, Carlisle (YH03774)		●												●												
FOUR LEGGED FRIENDS, Egremont (YH05408)		●												●												
FURNESS & S CUMBERLAND SUPPLY, Ulverston (YH05545)		●												●												
GET SMART, Barrow-In-Furness (YH05732)																										
GRASSGARTH HORSE FEEDS, Kendal (YH06019)		●												●												
GRAYLING BOOKS, Penrith (YH06034)																										
INMAN, JENNY, Kendal (YH07459)																										
J & E PETFOODS, Whitehaven (YH07545)		●												●												
J JORDAN & SONS, Windermere (YH07593)		●												●												
J W WILKINSON, Kendal (YH07628)	●																									
KINGFISHER, Ulverston (YH08191)																										
LAKELAND EQUESTRIAN, Windermere (YH08354)																										
LANCASTER, P R, Ulverston (YH08381)														●												
LOWTHER EQUESTRIAN, Carlisle (YH08877)									●																	
MIDDLE BAYLES LIVERY, Alston (YH09534)																										
O'HARA, JOHNNIE, Carlisle (YH10442)																								●		●
SLACK'S, Penrith (YH12884)		●												●												
T W RELPH & SONS, Penrith (YH13767)		●												●												
THWAITES, R G, Penrith (YH14124)													●													
TYNDALE FARM SERVICES, Holmrook (YH14525)		●												●												
W C F COUNTRY CTRES, Wigton (YH14757)		●												●												

Products Supplied
A - G
by Country by County

Company	Air Conditioning	Air Purifiers	Aloe Vera	Back Supports	Bedding	Bits	Body Protectors	Books	Boot Holders	Boot Jacks	Boot Scrapers	Boots	Boxes	Breeding Equipment	Breeding Supplies	Bridles	Bridlework	Carriages	Carts	CD's	Cleaning Equipment	Cleaning Supplies	Clippers	Closed Circuit TV	Clothes (Bespoke)	Clothes (Standard)
W G TODD & SONS, Kendal (YH14767)																										
DERBYSHIRE																										
ALTON RIDING SCHOOL, Chesterfield (YH00344)																								●		
ASHFORD FARM SUPPLIES, Bakewell (YH00601)																										
BARLEYFIELD SADDLERY, Etwall (YH00951)					●							●													●	●
BARLEYFIELDS, Derby (YH00952)																										●
BRAILSFORD STABLES, Ashbourne (YH01777)																		●								
C E S, Ashbourne (YH02370)					●							●	●					●			●		●		●	●
C W G, Buxton (YH02396)					●							●														●
COUNTRY SPORT, Glossop (YH03426)																										●
DENTEX (NORTH WEST), Glossop (YH04065)																										
ECTON CARRIAGES, Buxton (YH04539)																		●								
FRANK WRIGHT FEEDS, Ashbourne (YH05463)																										
FURNESS, P M & J J, Matlock (YH05549)								●																		
HARGATE EQUESTRIAN, Derby (YH06423)																										
HILL FARM FEEDS, Dronfield (YH06813)																										
HORSE & RIDER TACK SHOP, Nottingham (YH07100)												●														●
HULLAND SADDLERY, Ashbourne (YH07282)																										
IVANHOE FEEDS, Swadlincote (YH07533)												●											●			●
J B PET SUPPLIES, Belper (YH07565)																										
J R FEEDS, Ilkeston (YH07608)																										
MATLOCK SADDLERY, Matlock (YH09265)																										
NORMAN LUNNUN ANIMAL HEALTH, Ashbourne (YH10237)																										
O V WEBSTER & SON, Ticknall (YH10367)														●	●											
PEAKDALE SADDLERY, Buxton (YH10866)																					●		●		●	●
R E FARMS, Ashbourne (YH11534)																										
R E FARMS, Derby (YH11533)																										
S & E JOHNSON, Matlock (YH12310)																										
SEALS FODDER, Alfreton (YH12589)																										
TACK SHACK, Derby (YH13805)																										
TAYLORS OF SOUTH WINGFIELD, South Wingfield (YH13917)																										
TEVERSAL SADDLERY, Alfreton (YH13965)																										

Company	Coolers	Corn	Cross Country Jumps	Cushion Web	Damp Hay	Disposable A.V Liners	Disposable Equitainer	Driving Collars	Driving Harness	Dust Free Shavings	Electric Fencing	Exercise Equipment	Farm Equipment	Feed	Feed Racks	Feed Supplements	Fencing	Fertilisers	Fire Baskets	Flooring Supply (Arenas)	Fly Repellent	Gallops	Gates	Girths	Gloves	Mail Order Facilities
W G TODD & SONS, Kendal (YH14767)		●												●												
DERBYSHIRE																										
ALTON RIDING SCHOOL, Chesterfield (YH00344)																										
ASHFORD FARM SUPPLIES, Bakewell (YH00601)		●												●												
BARLEYFIELD SADDLERY, Etwall (YH00951)														●		●										
BARLEYFIELDS, Derby (YH00952)														●												
BRAILSFORD STABLES, Ashbourne (YH01777)																										
C E S, Ashbourne (YH02370)		●										●		●												
C W G, Buxton (YH02396)														●		●										
COUNTRY SPORT, Glossop (YH03426)																										●
DENTEX (NORTH WEST), Glossop (YH04065)																				●						
ECTON CARRIAGES, Buxton (YH04539)																										
FRANK WRIGHT FEEDS, Ashbourne (YH05463)																●										
FURNESS, P M & J J, Matlock (YH05549)																										
HARGATE EQUESTRIAN, Derby (YH06423)		●												●												
HILL FARM FEEDS, Dronfield (YH06813)		●												●												
HORSE & RIDER TACK SHOP, Nottingham (YH07100)																										
HULLAND SADDLERY, Ashbourne (YH07282)		●												●												
IVANHOE FEEDS, Swadlincote (YH07533)		●												●												
J B PET SUPPLIES, Belper (YH07565)		●												●												
J R FEEDS, Ilkeston (YH07608)		●												●												
MATLOCK SADDLERY, Matlock (YH09265)		●												●												
NORMAN LUNNUN ANIMAL HEALTH, Ashbourne (YH10237)																●										
O V WEBSTER & SON, Ticknall (YH10367)																										
PEAKDALE SADDLERY, Buxton (YH10866)		●							●					●		●										
R E FARMS, Ashbourne (YH11534)		●												●												
R E FARMS, Derby (YH11533)		●												●												
S & E JOHNSON, Matlock (YH12310)		●												●												
SEALS FODDER, Alfreton (YH12589)		●												●		●										
TACK SHACK, Derby (YH13805)		●												●												
TAYLORS OF SOUTH WINGFIELD, South Wingfield (YH13917)		●												●												
TEVERSAL SADDLERY, Alfreton (YH13965)		●												●												

Products Supplied

A - G

by Country by County	Air Conditioning	Air Purifiers	Aloe Vera	Back Supports	Bedding	Bits	Body Protectors	Books	Boot Holders	Boot Jacks	Boot Scrapers	Boots	Boxes	Breeding Equipment	Breeding Supplies	Bridles	Bridlework	Carriages	Carts	CD's	Cleaning Equipment	Cleaning Supplies	Clippers	Closed Circuit TV	Clothes (Bespoke)	Clothes (Standard)	Coolers	Corn	Cross Country Jumps	Cushion Web	Damp Hay	Disposable A.V Liners	Disposable Equitainer	Driving Collars	Driving Harness	Dust Free Shavings	Electric Fencing	Exercise Equipment	Farm Equipment	Feed	Feed Racks	Feed Supplements	Fencing	Fertilisers	Fire Baskets	Flooring Supply (Arenas)	Fly Repellent	Gallops	Gates	Girths	Gloves	Mail Order Facilities
THOMAS IRVING, Chesterfield (YH14007)																											●											●												
TOWN & COUNTRY SUPPLIES, Ashbourne (YH14287)																											●											●												
WESTHILLS EQUINE SUPPLIES, Matlock (YH15216)																											●											●												
WM EYRE & SONS, Hope Valley (YH15639)																											●											●												
DEVON																																																				
AGRITRADERS, Exeter (YH00203)																											●											●												
ANIMAL EDIBLES, Exeter (YH00431)																											●											●												
AVON FARMERS, Kingsbridge (YH00688)																											●											●												
BARNSTAPLE HORSE/PET SUPP, Barnstaple (YH00990)																											●											●												
BOCM PAULS, Exeter (YH01592)																											●											●												
BONES, Okehampton (YH01621)																																									●										
BYSTOCK PAPER BEDDING, Exmouth (YH02351)					●																																															
CARTER, J, Dawlish (YH02607)														●	●																																					
CLIPPER SHARP, Cullompton (YH03046)																							●																													
COLLACOMBE FARM, Tavistock (YH03172)																											●											●												
CORNWALL FARMERS, Hatherleigh (YH03339)																											●											●												
CORNWALL FARMERS, Holsworthy (YH03340)																											●											●												
CREDITON MILLING, Crediton (YH03586)																											●											●												
D W AST, Kingsbridge (YH03811)																																									●										
DAVIES, TIGER, Tiverton (YH03948)																																									●										
DENIS BRINICOMBE NUTRITION, Crediton (YH04047)																																									●										
DEVON & CORNWALL FARMS, Tavistock (YH04092)					●	●						●				●										●		●												●		●									●	
E J SNELL & SONS, Barnstaple (YH04409)																											●											●												
EDWIN TUCKER & SONS, Newton Abbott (YH04586)																											●											●												
ERME VALLEY FARMERS, Ivybridge (YH04850)								●				●									●		●			●		●											●	●		●	●						●			
F W PERKINS, Ottery St Mary (YH05003)																											●											●												
FARMERS FRIEND, Exeter (YH05061)																									●												●														
G C HAYBALL, Axminster (YH05571)																											●											●												
H & K SIMS, Buckfastleigh (YH06208)					●																																															
HAPS PET & ANIMAL FEEDS, Exeter (YH06402)																											●											●												
HOLLY FARM, Exeter (YH06953)					●																																															
J R SERPELL & SON, Plymouth (YH07610)																											●											●												

Products Supplied

A - G

by Country by County	Air Conditioning	Air Purifiers	Aloe Vera	Back Supports	Bedding	Bits	Body Protectors	Books	Boot Holders	Boot Jacks	Boot Scrapers	Boots	Boxes	Breeding Equipment	Breeding Supplies	Bridles	Bridlework	Carriages	Carts	CD's	Cleaning Equipment	Cleaning Supplies	Clippers	Closed Circuit TV	Clothes (Bespoke)	Clothes (Standard)	Coolers	Corn	Cross Country Jumps	Cushion Web	Damp Hay	Disposable A.V Liners	Disposable Equitainer	Driving Collars	Driving Harness	Dust Free Shavings	Electric Fencing	Exercise Equipment	Farm Equipment	Feed	Feed Racks	Feed Supplements	Fencing	Fertilisers	Fire Baskets	Flooring Supply (Arenas)	Fly Repellent	Gallops	Gates	Girths	Gloves	Mail Order Facilities
LAMBERTS COUNTRY STORE, Bideford (YH08366)																												●												●												
LEONARD COOMBE, Newton Abbot (YH08553)												●									●		●			●																										
LIMPET ANTI-SLIP SADDLE PADS, Ottery St Mary (YH08638)																																																				●
LITTLE ASH ECO-FARM & STUD, Okehampton (YH08683)																																							●													
MARK WESTAWAY & SON, Paignton (YH09157)																																								●		●										
MAXIMILLIAN STUD, North Tawton (YH09285)														●	●																																					
MOLE AVON TRADING, Okehampton (YH09708)																												●												●												
MOLE AVON TRADING, Axminster (YH09707)																												●												●												
MOLE AVON TRADING, Crediton (YH09709)																												●												●												
MOLE VALLEY FARMERS, Holsworthy (YH09710)																																								●												
MULLACOTT EQUESTRIAN, Ilfracombe (YH09935)					●																							●												●		●										
PET & EQUINE SUPPLIES, Okehampton (YH11000)												●											●			●																										
RED POST FEEDS, Totnes (YH11702)																												●												●												
REX AGRICULTURE, Barnstaple (YH11772)																												●												●												
SARGENT & SONS, Sidmouth (YH12437)																												●												●												
SIDE SADDLE LADY, Exeter (YH12786)								●																		●																										●
SLADES COUNTRYWISE, Honiton (YH12887)																												●												●												
SOUTH DEVON EQUESTRIAN SUP, Paignton (YH13082)																												●												●												
STOCKSHOP WOLSELEY, Exeter (YH13496)																							●														●		●				●									
TOM WILLCOCKS, Plymouth (YH14216)																												●												●												
TOWN & COUNTRY SUP, Exeter (YH14286)												●														●		●												●		●										
TRAGO MILLS, Newton Abbott (YH14311)																												●												●												
TWYFORD FARM SUPPLIES, Tiverton (YH14516)												●																●												●												
VAUTERHILL STUD, Umberleigh (YH14669)														●	●																																					
WARD, MICHAEL J, Holsworthy (YH14904)																		●																																		
WATERMAN, M & A, Tiverton (YH14970)																												●												●												
WEST DEVON & NORTH CORNWALL, Holsworthy (YH15139)																												●												●												
WEST ILKERTON FARM, Lynton (YH15150)								●											●															●	●				●													
WILLINGCOTT FARM SUPPLIES, Woolacombe (YH15488)																												●												●												
WYCHANGER BARTON SADDLERY, Tiverton (YH15855)						●		●				●				●										●														●		●										●
DORSET																																																				
BARTLETT, Bridport (YH01039)																												●												●												

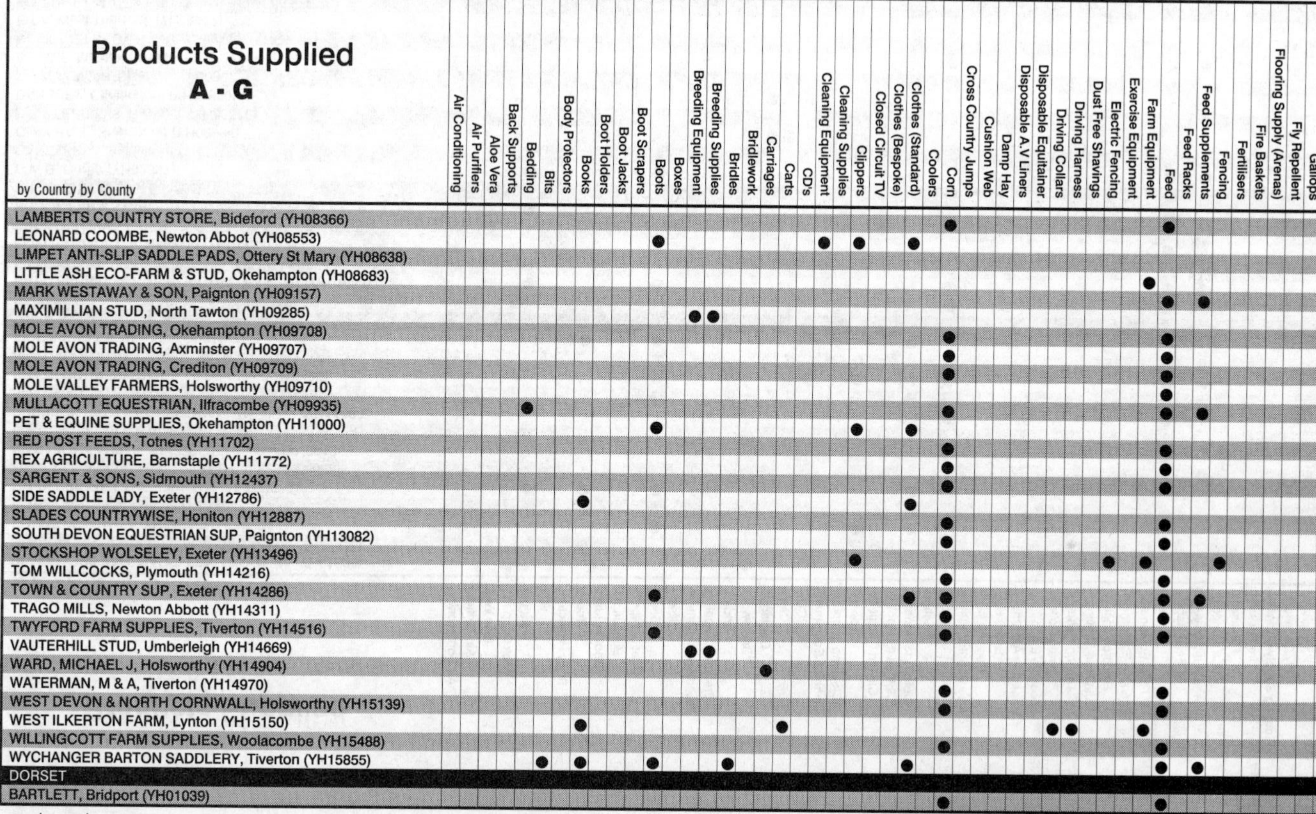

www.hccyourhorse.com

Products Supplied
A - G

by Country by County

by Country by County	Air Conditioning	Air Purifiers	Aloe Vera	Back Supports	Bedding	Bits	Body Protectors	Books	Boot Holders	Boot Jacks	Boot Scrapers	Boots	Boxes	Breeding Equipment	Breeding Supplies	Bridles	Bridlework
BLAKEMORE VALE SADDLERY, Gillingham (YH01520)																	●
BLANDFORD SADDLERY, Blandford Forum (YH01524)								●									
EQUUS, Wimborne (YH04836)												●					
HORSE BITS, Wimborne (YH07104)												●					
HURN BRIDGE CTRE, Christchurch (YH07313)					●			●				●					
LILLIDALE ANIMAL HEALTH, Wimborne (YH08623)																	
MARABOUT ANIMAL FEEDS, Dorchester (YH09135)																	
O Y C, Wareham (YH10369)					●												
PURBECK PETS & EQUESTRIAN, Wareham (YH11462)																	
SCATS COUNTRYSTORE, Blandford (YH12496)												●					
SCATS COUNTRYSTORE, Gillingham (YH12495)												●					
SCATS COUNTRYSTORE, Dorchester (YH12494)												●					
SIDE SADDLES, Wimborne (YH12787)								●				●					
ESSEX																	
BAILEYS HORSE FEEDS, Braintree (YH00806)																	
BATTLESBRIDGE HORSE & CTRY, Wickford (YH01082)					●							●					
BILLERICAY FARM SVS, Billericay (YH01411)					●												
BOYLES COURT, Brentwood (YH01733)																	
BREYER MODEL HORSES, Great Dunmow (YH01857)																	
BROOK FARM STABLES, Colchester (YH02036)					●												
BROOKS STABLES, Benfleet (YH02062)																	
C W G, Ongar (YH02397)					●							●					
CANDLERS, Chelmsford (YH02496)												●					
CLAY HALL, Brentwood (YH02994)																	
D & F FEED SVS, Rayleigh (YH03770)																	
DANBURY, Chelmsford (YH03860)																	
DE BEAUVOIR, Billericay (YH03973)																	
DENGIE, Maldon (YH04045)																	
DESIGNER BROWBANDS, Benfleet (YH04084)																	
E T A, West Thurrock (YH04427)																	
EQUINE HEALTH & HERBAL, Halstead (YH04779)																	
ESSEX ANIMAL FEEDS, Romford (YH04866)					●												

by Country by County	Carriages	Carts	CD's	Cleaning Equipment	Cleaning Supplies	Clippers	Closed Circuit TV	Clothes (Bespoke)	Clothes (Standard)	Coolers	Corn	Cross Country Jumps	Cushion Web	Damp Hay	Disposable A.V Liners	Disposable Equitainer	Driving Collars
BLAKEMORE VALE SADDLERY, Gillingham (YH01520)																	
BLANDFORD SADDLERY, Blandford Forum (YH01524)																	
EQUUS, Wimborne (YH04836)						●			●								
HORSE BITS, Wimborne (YH07104)									●								
HURN BRIDGE CTRE, Christchurch (YH07313)									●								
LILLIDALE ANIMAL HEALTH, Wimborne (YH08623)																	
MARABOUT ANIMAL FEEDS, Dorchester (YH09135)											●						
O Y C, Wareham (YH10369)																	
PURBECK PETS & EQUESTRIAN, Wareham (YH11462)											●						
SCATS COUNTRYSTORE, Blandford (YH12496)						●			●		●						
SCATS COUNTRYSTORE, Gillingham (YH12495)						●			●		●						
SCATS COUNTRYSTORE, Dorchester (YH12494)						●			●		●						
SIDE SADDLES, Wimborne (YH12787)									●								
ESSEX																	
BAILEYS HORSE FEEDS, Braintree (YH00806)											●						
BATTLESBRIDGE HORSE & CTRY, Wickford (YH01082)											●						
BILLERICAY FARM SVS, Billericay (YH01411)																	
BOYLES COURT, Brentwood (YH01733)																	
BREYER MODEL HORSES, Great Dunmow (YH01857)																	
BROOK FARM STABLES, Colchester (YH02036)																	
BROOKS STABLES, Benfleet (YH02062)											●						
C W G, Ongar (YH02397)									●								
CANDLERS, Chelmsford (YH02496)						●			●								
CLAY HALL, Brentwood (YH02994)	●	●															
D & F FEED SVS, Rayleigh (YH03770)									●		●						
DANBURY, Chelmsford (YH03860)	●																
DE BEAUVOIR, Billericay (YH03973)											●						
DENGIE, Maldon (YH04045)											●						
DESIGNER BROWBANDS, Benfleet (YH04084)					●				●								
E T A, West Thurrock (YH04427)																	
EQUINE HEALTH & HERBAL, Halstead (YH04779)																	
ESSEX ANIMAL FEEDS, Romford (YH04866)											●						

by Country by County	Driving Harness	Dust Free Shavings	Electric Fencing	Exercise Equipment	Farm Equipment	Feed	Feed Racks	Feed Supplements	Fencing	Fertilisers	Fire Baskets	Flooring Supply (Arenas)	Fly Repellent	Gallops	Gates	Girths	Gloves	Mail Order Facilities
BLAKEMORE VALE SADDLERY, Gillingham (YH01520)																		
BLANDFORD SADDLERY, Blandford Forum (YH01524)																		
EQUUS, Wimborne (YH04836)																		
HORSE BITS, Wimborne (YH07104)						●												
HURN BRIDGE CTRE, Christchurch (YH07313)																		
LILLIDALE ANIMAL HEALTH, Wimborne (YH08623)								●										
MARABOUT ANIMAL FEEDS, Dorchester (YH09135)						●												
O Y C, Wareham (YH10369)						●												
PURBECK PETS & EQUESTRIAN, Wareham (YH11462)						●												
SCATS COUNTRYSTORE, Blandford (YH12496)						●		●										
SCATS COUNTRYSTORE, Gillingham (YH12495)						●		●										
SCATS COUNTRYSTORE, Dorchester (YH12494)						●		●										
SIDE SADDLES, Wimborne (YH12787)																		●
ESSEX																		
BAILEYS HORSE FEEDS, Braintree (YH00806)						●		●										
BATTLESBRIDGE HORSE & CTRY, Wickford (YH01082)						●		●										
BILLERICAY FARM SVS, Billericay (YH01411)																		
BOYLES COURT, Brentwood (YH01733)						●												
BREYER MODEL HORSES, Great Dunmow (YH01857)																		●
BROOK FARM STABLES, Colchester (YH02036)						●												
BROOKS STABLES, Benfleet (YH02062)						●												
C W G, Ongar (YH02397)						●		●										
CANDLERS, Chelmsford (YH02496)																		
CLAY HALL, Brentwood (YH02994)																		
D & F FEED SVS, Rayleigh (YH03770)						●		●	●	●								
DANBURY, Chelmsford (YH03860)																		
DE BEAUVOIR, Billericay (YH03973)						●												
DENGIE, Maldon (YH04045)						●		●										
DESIGNER BROWBANDS, Benfleet (YH04084)																	●	●
E T A, West Thurrock (YH04427)												●						
EQUINE HEALTH & HERBAL, Halstead (YH04779)						●		●										●
ESSEX ANIMAL FEEDS, Romford (YH04866)						●												

Products Supplied
A - G

by Country by County

Company	Air Conditioning	Air Purifiers	Aloe Vera	Back Supports	Bedding	Bits	Body Protectors	Books	Boot Holders	Boot Jacks	Boot Scrapers	Boots	Boxes	Breeding Equipment	Breeding Supplies	Bridles	Bridlework	Carriages	Carts	CD's	Cleaning Equipment	Cleaning Supplies	Clippers	Closed Circuit TV	Clothes (Bespoke)	Clothes (Standard)	Coolers	Corn	Cross Country Jumps	Cushion Web	Damp Hay	Disposable A.V Liners	Disposable Equitainer	Driving Collars	Driving Harness	Dust Free Shavings	Electric Fencing	Exercise Equipment	Farm Equipment	Feed	Feed Racks	Feed Supplements	Fencing	Fertilisers	Fire Baskets	Flooring Supply (Arenas)	Fly Repellent	Gallops	Gates	Girths	Gloves	Mail Order Facilities
ESSEX FENCING, Wickford (YH04870)																																											●									
H A C S SHOP, Bishop's Stortford (YH06210)																												●												●												
H R PHILPOT & SON, Billericay (YH06235)																												●												●												
HEMCORE, Bishop's Stortford (YH06659)					●																																															
HOBBY HORSE, Romford (YH06897)												●											●		●	●																										
INGATESTONE SADDLERY, Ingatestone (YH07442)												●											●		●	●																										
KILN SADDLERY, Colchester (YH08151)					●							●											●			●														●												
LEWIS, ANTHONY, Chigwell (YH08586)																												●												●												
LINGWOOD SHIRE PROMOTIONS, Brentwood (YH08663)																		●																																		
LONGWOOD FEED CTRE, Upminster (YH08821)																												●												●												
MANOR FARM FEEDS, Upminster (YH09098)																												●												●												
MARCH EQUESTRIAN, Halstead (YH09139)					●																							●												●												
MARCH EQUESTRIAN, Colchester (YH09138)					●																							●												●		●										
MAYPOLE PET & GARDEN CTRE, Witham (YH09304)																												●												●												
MONCUR, J & M, Nazeing (YH09721)																												●												●												
MOORCROFT EQUESTRIAN, Colchester (YH09749)																							●			●																	●						●			●
MOSS, JANETTE, Waltham Abbey (YH09858)												●											●		●	●														●												
NIGHTINGALE RIDING SCHOOL, Buckhurst Hill (YH10204)					●																																			●												
PEGASUS HOLDINGS, Bishop's Stortford (YH10904)																																										●										
PINE LODGE, Loughton (YH11118)					●																																			●												
POOLE FARM HORSE/ANIMAL FEED, Great Yeldham (YH11263)																												●												●												
PRIORY SADDLERY, Colchester (YH11403)					●			●															●			●														●												
PULFORDS, Great Dunmow (YH11455)					●																							●												●		●										
RADWINTER SADDLERY, Saffron Walden (YH11601)																												●												●												
RUGGERY, Romford (YH12221)																									●																											
SADLERS FARM FEEDS, Bowers Gifford (YH12375)																												●												●												
SHOPLAND HALL EQUESTRIAN, Rochford (YH12758)												●														●														●		●										
SIERRA SADDLE, Benfleet (YH12792)																																																				●
SOUTH ESSEX FEED CTRE, Basildon (YH13090)																												●												●												
SOUTH VIEW SADDLERY/PET FOOD, Grays (YH13110)																												●												●												
STANTONS METSA PRIMA, Tilbury (YH13382)					●																																															
STOKES, R & S, Rayleigh (YH13506)					●																							●												●												

Products Supplied
A - G

by Country by County	Air Conditioning	Air Purifiers	Aloe Vera	Back Supports	Bedding	Bits	Body Protectors	Books	Boot Holders	Boot Jacks	Boot Scrapers	Boots	Boxes	Breeding Equipment	Breeding Supplies	Bridles	Bridlework	Carriages	Carts	CD's	Cleaning Equipment	Cleaning Supplies	Clippers	Closed Circuit TV	Clothes (Bespoke)	Clothes (Standard)	Coolers	Corn	Cross Country Jumps	Cushion Web	Damp Hay	Disposable A.V Liners	Disposable Equitainer	Driving Collars	Driving Harness	Dust Free Shavings	Electric Fencing	Exercise Equipment	Farm Equipment	Feed	Feed Racks	Feed Supplements	Fencing	Fertilisers	Fire Baskets	Flooring Supply (Arenas)	Fly Repellent	Gallops	Gates	Girths	Gloves	Mail Order Facilities
T S S, Newport (YH13764)																												●												●												
TACK EXCHANGE, Leigh-on-Sea (YH13788)												●											●			●																										
TALLY-HO RIDING SCHOOL, Grays (YH13844)					●							●									●																			●		●										
THOROGOODS DIRECT, Chelmsford (YH14079)																																								●												
THORPE TACK ROOM, Clacton-on-Sea (YH14095)												●											●			●																										
TOWERLANDS EQUESTRIAN CTRE, Braintree (YH14278)					●																							●												●												
TUKE, DIANA R, Saffron Walden (YH14449)								●																																												
UPMINSTER SADDLERY, Upminster (YH14604)								●				●											●		●	●																										
WIX EQUESTRIAN CTRE, Manningtree (YH15636)																																								●		●										
YE OLDE FORGE, Basildon (YH15894)																●																																				
YEATS, J, Waltham Abbey (YH15897)																												●												●												
GLOUCESTERSHIRE																																																				
A A SHERWOOD, Cirencester (YH00017)																												●												●												
ABBOTT, Cirencester (YH00102)					●																																			●												
AUBOISE, Chaceley (YH00658)					●																																			●												
BILL BIRD BOOTS & SHOES, Moreton In Marsh (YH01407)												●																																								
CHELTENHAM SADDLERY, Cheltenham (YH02805)																												●												●												
COLNE SADDLERY, Gloucester (YH03196)																												●												●												
COTSWOLD HORSE, Cirencester (YH03363)																																										●										
COUNTRY & EQUESTRIAN, Gloucester (YH03398)								●																																												
COUNTRY MATTERS, Cirencester (YH03417)																												●												●												
COUNTRYWIDE STORES, Bourton-on-The Water (YH03451)																												●												●												
COUNTRYWIDE STORES, Gloucester (YH03453)																												●												●												
COUNTRYWIDE STORES, Tewkesbury (YH03455)																												●												●												
COUNTRYWIDE STORES, Cirencester (YH03452)																												●												●												
COUNTRYWIDE STORES, Gloucester (YH03454)																												●												●												
COURT FARM COUNTRY STORE, Lydney (YH03499)																												●												●												
DONEY, JON, Tewkesbury (YH04181)																													●																							
EQUESTRIAN REQUISITIES, Stonehouse (YH04709)																												●												●												
GLOUCESTER MIXED FEEDS, Witcombe (YH05851)																												●												●												
GRIFFITHS & CLARKE, Drybrook (YH06135)																												●												●												
HAVEN HOMES, Dursley (YH06538)																												●												●												

Products Supplied
A - G

by Country by County	Air Conditioning	Air Purifiers	Aloe Vera	Back Supports	Bedding	Bits	Body Protectors	Books	Boot Holders	Boot Jacks	Boot Scrapers	Boots	Boxes	Breeding Equipment	Breeding Supplies	Bridles	Bridlework	Carriages	Carts	CD's	Cleaning Equipment	Cleaning Supplies	Clippers	Closed Circuit TV	Clothes (Bespoke)	Clothes (Standard)	Coolers	Corn	Cross Country Jumps	Cushion Web	Damp Hay	Disposable A.V Liners	Disposable Equitainer	Driving Collars	Driving Harness	Dust Free Shavings	Electric Fencing	Exercise Equipment	Farm Equipment	Feed	Feed Racks	Feed Supplements	Fencing	Fertilisers	Fire Baskets	Flooring Supply (Arenas)	Fly Repellent	Gallops	Gates	Girths	Gloves	Mail Order Facilities
HENRY COLE, Cirencester (YH06681)					●																							●												●		●										
HORIZONT, Gloucester (YH07068)																																											●									
LISTER SHEARING EQUIPMENT, Dursley (YH08680)																							●																													
MANGAN & WEBB, Cheltenham (YH09076)												●														●																										
MORETON SADDLERY, Moreton In Marsh (YH09790)																										●																										
NELSON VETNRY & EQUINE, Cirencester (YH10073)																																										●										
OXBUTTS FARM & STABLE SVS, Cheltenham (YH10614)																												●												●												
P S B ANIMAL HEALTH, Tetbury (YH10657)																												●												●												
PRESTBURY PK EQUINE SUPPLIES, Cheltenham (YH11360)																												●												●												
RIDGEWAY SCIENCE, Alvington (YH11866)																																										●										
SELECT FEEDS & SEED, Westbury-on-Severn (YH12620)																												●												●												
SOUTH AMERICAN TRADE SERVICES, Cirencester (YH13075)												●													●																											
STROUD FARM SERVICES, Stroud (YH13586)																												●												●												
STROUD SADDLERY, Stroud (YH13588)								●				●											●			●																●										●
T H WHITE, Tetbury (YH13745)																												●												●												
TETBURY, Chaceley (YH13962)																												●												●												
TEWKESBURY SADDLERY, Tewkesbury (YH13969)								●				●											●		●	●																										●
GLOUCESTERSHIRE (SOUTH)																																																				
A NICHOLS, Chipping Sodbury (YH00054)																												●												●												
ARTIFICIAL INSEMINATION CTRE, Kingswood (YH00575)														●	●																																					
BIDWELLS OF COGMILLS, Frampton Cotterell (YH01400)																												●												●												
COUNTRYWIDE STORES, Thornbury (YH03456)																												●												●												
CROMWELLS OF OLVESTON, Olveston (YH03633)																												●												●												
JOLLYES, Longwell Green (YH07860)																												●												●												
PORTERS, Winterbourne (YH11287)								●																				●												●												
WEYLODE, Old Sodbury (YH15252)																												●												●												
HAMPSHIRE																																																				
ABBOTT, Alton (YH00103)																												●												●												
AMBERVALE, Lymington (YH00357)																		●	●																																	
B & M FENCING, Hook (YH00713)																																											●									
CALCUTT & SONS, Winchester (YH02425)																							●																	●	●												●
COUNTRY RIDING WEAR, Hook (YH03424)								●				●				●									●	●																										

www.hccyourhorse.com

Products Supplied
A - G

by Country by County

by Country by County	Air Conditioning	Air Purifiers	Aloe Vera	Back Supports	Bedding	Bits	Body Protectors	Books	Boot Holders	Boot Jacks	Boot Scrapers	Boots	Boxes	Breeding Equipment	Breeding Supplies	Bridles	Bridlework	Carriages	Carts	CD's	Cleaning Equipment	Cleaning Supplies	Clippers
DAVIS, J S & P A, Petersfield (YH03952)																							
DENE COUNTRY STORES, Liphook (YH04041)																							
DIRECT FEEDS, Winchester (YH04127)																							
DODSON & HORRELL, Basingstoke (YH04161)					●																		
EQUESTRIAN SVS FENCING, Southampton (YH04716)																							
EXBURY, Southampton (YH04963)																		●					
FAIR OAK BARN SADDLERY, Eastleigh (YH05012)																							
FLEETWATER STUD, Lyndhurst (YH05269)														●	●								
FOREST COUNTRYWEAR, Fordingbridge (YH05333)								●															
FOREST FARM, Milford On Sea (YH05335)																		●	●				
FORESTER SADDLES, Lyndhurst (YH05354)																							
FRAMPTON ZIEGLER AGRICULTURE, Ringwood (YH05443)																							
GAWTHORPE SADDLERS, Hook (YH05679)																							
GEBBIE VALLEYS, Lymington (YH05686)																		●					
GOLD CUP FEEDS, Romsey (YH05876)																							
HASKER, GLENN M, Ringwood (YH06521)												●											
HOPLANDS EQUESTRIAN, Stockbridge (YH07058)					●							●											
HORSEPOWER, Alton (YH07163)																		●					
J ELLIS & SONS, Bordon (YH07580)																							
JOHN LOADER, Fordingbridge (YH07799)																							
JOHN ROTHERY WHOLESALE, Petersfield (YH07809)																							
JOLLYES, Portsmouth (YH07861)																							
LESLEY RALPH SADDLER, Basingstoke (YH08557)																							
LOCKYERS ANIMAL PROVISIONS, New Milton (YH08764)																							
LONG ACRE FEEDS, Botley (YH08795)																							
M J HAYWARD & SONS, Fordingbridge (YH08969)																							
MCNEILL, IAN, Alton (YH09402)																							
NORRIS & SONS, Brockenhurst (YH10244)																							
PARK FARM SADDLERY, Basingstoke (YH10723)																							
ROWLEY, CHARLES, Eastleigh (YH12171)																							
RYCROFT SCHOOL OF EQUITATION, Hook (YH12291)												●											
SANDILANDS FARM FEEDS, Petersfield (YH12414)																							

by Country by County	Closed Circuit TV	Clothes (Bespoke)	Clothes (Standard)	Coolers	Corn	Cross Country Jumps	Cushion Web	Damp Hay	Disposable A.V Liners	Disposable Equitainer	Driving Collars	Driving Harness	Dust Free Shavings	Electric Fencing	Exercise Equipment	Farm Equipment	Feed	Feed Racks	Feed Supplements	Fencing	Fertilisers	Fire Baskets	Flooring Supply (Arenas)	Fly Repellent	Gallops	Gates	Girths	Gloves	Mail Order Facilities
DAVIS, J S & P A, Petersfield (YH03952)					●												●												
DENE COUNTRY STORES, Liphook (YH04041)					●												●												
DIRECT FEEDS, Winchester (YH04127)					●												●		●										
DODSON & HORRELL, Basingstoke (YH04161)					●												●												
EQUESTRIAN SVS FENCING, Southampton (YH04716)																				●									
EXBURY, Southampton (YH04963)																													
FAIR OAK BARN SADDLERY, Eastleigh (YH05012)					●												●												
FLEETWATER STUD, Lyndhurst (YH05269)					●												●												
FOREST COUNTRYWEAR, Fordingbridge (YH05333)																													
FOREST FARM, Milford On Sea (YH05335)												●																	
FORESTER SADDLES, Lyndhurst (YH05354)																													●
FRAMPTON ZIEGLER AGRICULTURE, Ringwood (YH05443)					●												●												
GAWTHORPE SADDLERS, Hook (YH05679)					●												●												
GEBBIE VALLEYS, Lymington (YH05686)																													
GOLD CUP FEEDS, Romsey (YH05876)					●												●												
HASKER, GLENN M, Ringwood (YH06521)			●																										
HOPLANDS EQUESTRIAN, Stockbridge (YH07058)																	●		●										●
HORSEPOWER, Alton (YH07163)																													
J ELLIS & SONS, Bordon (YH07580)					●												●												
JOHN LOADER, Fordingbridge (YH07799)					●												●		●										
JOHN ROTHERY WHOLESALE, Petersfield (YH07809)																			●										
JOLLYES, Portsmouth (YH07861)					●												●												
LESLEY RALPH SADDLER, Basingstoke (YH08557)												●																	
LOCKYERS ANIMAL PROVISIONS, New Milton (YH08764)					●												●												
LONG ACRE FEEDS, Botley (YH08795)					●												●												
M J HAYWARD & SONS, Fordingbridge (YH08969)					●												●												
MCNEILL, IAN, Alton (YH09402)					●												●												
NORRIS & SONS, Brockenhurst (YH10244)					●												●												
PARK FARM SADDLERY, Basingstoke (YH10723)					●												●												
ROWLEY, CHARLES, Eastleigh (YH12171)					●												●												
RYCROFT SCHOOL OF EQUITATION, Hook (YH12291)			●																										
SANDILANDS FARM FEEDS, Petersfield (YH12414)					●												●												

Products Supplied
A - G

by Country by County	Air Conditioning	Air Purifiers	Aloe Vera	Back Supports	Bedding	Bits	Body Protectors	Books	Boot Holders	Boot Jacks	Boot Scrapers	Boots	Boxes	Breeding Equipment	Breeding Supplies	Bridles	Bridlework	Carriages	Carts	CD's	Cleaning Equipment	Cleaning Supplies	Clippers	Closed Circuit TV	Clothes (Bespoke)	Clothes (Standard)	Coolers	Corn	Cross Country Jumps	Cushion Web	Damp Hay	Disposable A.V Liners	Disposable Equitainer	Driving Collars	Driving Harness	Dust Free Shavings	Electric Fencing	Exercise Equipment	Farm Equipment	Feed	Feed Racks	Feed Supplements	Fencing	Fertilisers	Fire Baskets	Flooring Supply (Arenas)	Fly Repellent	Gallops	Gates	Girths	Gloves	Mail Order Facilities
SCATS, Winchester (YH12491)																												●												●												
SCATS COUNTRYSTORE, Romsey (YH12497)												●											●			●		●												●		●										
SCATS COUNTRYSTORE, Winchester (YH12498)												●														●		●												●												
SCATS COUNTRYSTORE, Alton (YH12499)												●											●			●		●												●		●										
SCATS COUNTRYSTORE, Andover (YH12500)												●														●		●												●		●										
SCATS COUNTRYSTORE, Basingstoke (YH12501)												●											●			●		●												●		●										
SCATS COUNTRYSTORE, Lymington (YH12502)												●											●			●		●												●		●										
SHAPLEY RANCH EQUINE ACCESS, Hartley Wintney (YH12674)																												●												●												
SHERGOLD, Southampton (YH12722)																												●												●												
THOROUGHBRED INFORMATION SVS, Alresford (YH14087)														●	●																																					
TROTTERS, Havant (YH14407)					●																							●												●		●										
VETREPHARM, Fordingbridge (YH14702)																																										●										
W J PARDEY & SON, Fordingbridge (YH14777)																												●												●												
WELLINGTON RIDING, Hook (YH15075)								●				●									●				●	●												●														
WESTBOURNE ANIMAL FEEDS, Westbourne (YH15183)																												●												●												
WOODINGTON FEEDS, Romsey (YH15701)																												●												●												
WRIGHTS OF ROMSEY, Romsey (YH15846)																												●												●												
HEREFORDSHIRE																																																				
ABBOTT, Hereford (YH00104)																												●												●												
BALL OF MADLEY, Hereford (YH00848)																												●												●												
BROMYARD, Bromyard (YH02027)																												●												●												
COUNTRYWIDE, Hereford (YH03445)												●									●		●		●	●		●											●	●		●	●	●					●			
COUNTRYWIDE STORES, Leominster (YH03459)																												●												●												
COUNTRYWIDE STORES, Ledbury (YH03457)																												●												●												
COUNTRYWIDE STORES, Bromyard (YH03458)																												●												●												
EQUINE MARKETING, Weobley (YH04787)																																								●		●										
FRANCIS WILLEY, Bromyard (YH05449)																												●												●												
HAY & BRECON FARMERS, Hay-on-Wye (YH06558)																												●												●												
HORSE & JOCKEY, Hereford (YH07093)												●														●														●												
HORSE BEAUTIQUE, Leominster (YH07103)																												●												●												
HORSEWISE, Hereford (YH07178)								●				●														●																										
JONES, R M, Hay-on-Wye (YH07924)																												●												●												

Products Supplied
A - G

by Country by County

	Air Conditioning	Air Purifiers	Aloe Vera	Back Supports	Bedding	Bits	Body Protectors	Books	Boot Holders	Boot Jacks	Boot Scrapers	Boots	Boxes	Breeding Equipment	Breeding Supplies	Bridles	Bridlework	Carriages	Carts	CD's	Cleaning Equipment	Cleaning Supplies	Clippers	Closed Circuit TV	Clothes (Bespoke)	Clothes (Standard)	Coolers	Corn	Cross Country Jumps	Cushion Web	Damp Hay	Disposable A.V Liners	Disposable Equitainer	Driving Collars	Driving Harness	Dust Free Shavings	Electric Fencing	Exercise Equipment	Farm Equipment	Feed	Feed Racks	Feed Supplements	Fencing	Fertilisers	Fire Baskets	Flooring Supply (Arenas)	Fly Repellent	Gallops	Gates	Girths	Gloves	Mail Order Facilities
JONES, R M, Cattle Market (YH07925)																												●												●												
LOCKS GARAGE FEEDS, Allensmore (YH08761)																												●												●												
PIONEER ANIMAL FEEDS, Ledbury (YH11141)																												●												●												
R T ANIMAL FEEDS, Hereford (YH11564)																												●												●												
ROSS FEED, Ross-on-Wye (YH12114)																												●												●												
SHIRES EQUESTRIAN, Leominster (YH12755)						●																				●																										
TURNERS, Kington (YH14492)					●																							●												●				●								
HERTFORDSHIRE																																																				
ANIMAL FAYRE, Cheshunt (YH00432)																												●												●												
ARNOLD HITCHCOCK, Buntingford (YH00557)																												●												●												
CHALLENGER DISTRIBUTION, Royston (YH02712)																																										●										
CHAMPIONSHIP FOODS, Royston (YH02728)																																										●										
CLARK'S EQUESTRIAN, Stevenage (YH02979)																												●												●												
COLEMAN CROFT, St Albans (YH03163)								●				●									●		●			●														●		●										●
COLESDALE FARM SVS, Potters Bar (YH03168)																												●												●												
FIELD SPORTS, Borehamwood (YH05186)																										●																										
FOX FEEDS, Buntingford (YH05420)																												●												●												
G J W TITMUSS, Wheathampstead (YH05586)																												●												●												
GANWICK FODDER STORE, Barnet (YH05643)																												●												●												
GREINAN FARM, Kings Langley (YH06122)																												●												●												
HAZEL END FARM SHOP, Bishop's Stortford (YH06598)																												●												●												
HILL, ALAN, Ware (YH06825)																												●												●												
IVORY, K T, Radlett (YH07538)														●	●																																					
KIMBLEWICK FEEDS, Chipperfield (YH08160)																												●												●												
MANOR HOUSE FARM STUD, Tring (YH09110)														●	●																																					
OLD BARN SADDLERY, Hoddesdon (YH10448)																												●												●												
P S A EQUESTRIAN SVS, Shenley (YH10656)																												●												●												
PARTNERS PET SUPERMARKET, St Albans (YH10805)																												●												●												
PARTNERS PET SUPERMARKET, Barnet (YH10804)																												●												●												
PATCHETTS, Watford (YH10815)												●														●														●		●										
PIX FARM FEED STORE, Hemel Hempstead (YH11159)																												●												●												
POUND FARM FEEDS, Datchworth (YH11308)																												●												●												

Products Supplied
A - G

by Country by County

Name	Air Conditioning	Air Purifiers	Aloe Vera	Back Supports	Bedding	Bits	Body Protectors	Books	Boot Holders	Boot Jacks	Boot Scrapers	Boots	Boxes	Breeding Equipment	Breeding Supplies	Bridles	Bridlework	Carriages	Carts	CD's	Cleaning Equipment	Cleaning Supplies	Clippers	Closed Circuit TV	Clothes (Bespoke)	Clothes (Standard)	Coolers	Corn	Cross Country Jumps	Cushion Web	Damp Hay	Disposable A.V Liners	Disposable Equitainer	Driving Collars	Driving Harness	Dust Free Shavings	Electric Fencing	Exercise Equipment	Farm Equipment	Feed	Feed Racks	Feed Supplements	Fencing	Fertilisers	Fire Baskets	Flooring Supply (Arenas)	Fly Repellent	Gallops	Gates	Girths	Gloves	Mail Order Facilities
ROCHFORD & BARBER, Hertford (YH12022)																												●												●												
SADDLERY, Royston (YH12363)												●											●																●	●		●										
SALES OF SANDON, Buntingford (YH12386)																												●												●												
SANDON SADDLERY, Buntingford (YH12415)								●																																												
STABLE COLOURS, Welwyn (YH13289)																												●												●												
STRANGEWAYS FEEDS, Borehamwood (YH13549)																												●												●												
STREATHER HAYWARD FARMS, Baldock (YH13570)																												●												●												
SUMMER FRESH, Colney Heath (YH13629)																												●												●												
UPPERWOOD FARM STUD, Hemel Hempstead (YH14609)																																										●										
W MOSS & SONS, Stevenage (YH14783)																												●												●												
W PAGE & SON, Cole Green (YH14786)																												●												●												
WIDESERVE, Welwyn (YH15391)																								●																												
ISLE OF MAN																																																				
MANAGRAKEM, N W F, Douglas (YH09063)																												●												●												
MANX RIDING SUPPLIES, Onchan (YH09128)																												●												●												
ISLE OF WIGHT																																																			
ARENA FARM & PET SUPPLIES, Wootton (YH00513)																												●												●												
BRICKFIELDS, Ryde (YH01866)																		●																																		
DEB GROVES ANIMAL FEEDS, Calbourne (YH04002)																												●												●		●										
JOLLYES, Newport (YH07862)																												●												●												
JONES, E A & C, Newport (YH07895)																																								●												
P & G FARM SUPPLIES, Newport (YH10629)																												●												●												
SCATS, Newport (YH12492)																												●												●												
SCATS COUNTRYSTORE, Newport (YH12503)												●											●			●		●												●		●										
TRUMOR FEEDS, Newport (YH14422)																												●												●												
WINDMILL FARM SUPPLIES, Ryde (YH15564)																												●												●												
JERSEY																																																			
BARETTE & GRUCHY, St John (YH00930)																												●												●												
DAVID DUMOSCH, St John (YH03917)																												●												●												
HAIE FLEURIE, Channel Isles (YH06280)																												●												●												
LE MAISTRE BROS, Trinity (YH08490)												●											●			●		●												●		●										
KENT																																																			

Products Supplied
A - G

by Country by County

by Country by County	Air Conditioning	Air Purifiers	Aloe Vera	Back Supports	Bedding	Bits	Body Protectors	Books	Boot Holders	Boot Jacks	Boot Scrapers	Boots	Boxes	Breeding Equipment	Breeding Supplies	Bridles	Bridlework	Carriages	Carts	CD's	Cleaning Equipment	Cleaning Supplies	Clippers	Closed Circuit TV	Clothes (Bespoke)	Clothes (Standard)
ARIZONAS, Tunbridge Wells (YH00527)								●				●														●
BA GREEN CROP DRIERS, Hythe (YH00758)																										
BARMINSTER TRADING, Ashford (YH00960)												●													●	●
BARRADALE FARM, Headcorn (YH01005)																										
BAVERSTOCK CTRY SALES, Westerham Hill (YH01084)																										
BIRCHALLS THE RIDING SHOP, Maidstone (YH01431)								●				●											●			●
BROADFEED, Tunbridge Wells (YH01994)																										
CANTERBURY CARRIAGES, Dover (YH02507)																		●								
CHELSFIELD RIDING SCHOOL, Orpington (YH02802)																										
CHILHAM FEEDS, Canterbury (YH02854)																										
COBHAM MANOR, Maidstone (YH03113)												●														●
E WILLIAMS FARMERS, Dartford (YH04432)																										
ELECTRIC FENCING DIRECT, Tonbridge (YH04602)																										
EMPORIUM, Ashford (YH04659)																										
FAIRBOURNE CARRIAGES, Maidstone (YH05014)																		●								
FORAGES, J T, Cranbrook (YH05315)					●																					
FOREST VIEW, Sidcup (YH05353)													●													
FROGPOOL MANOR SADDLERY, Chislehurst (YH05515)					●			●				●											●		●	●
GILLET COOK, Faversham (YH05780)																										
GLOVER, H F & J H, Longfield (YH05854)																										
GOODNESTONE CT EQUESTRIAN, Faversham (YH05905)																										
GRAIN HARVESTERS, Canterbury (YH05976)																										
HOBBS PARKER, Ashford (YH06894)												●							●						●	●
HORSE & COUNTRY SUPERSTORE, Maidstone (YH07088)												●														●
HORSE BOOKS, Maidstone (YH07108)								●																		
JUST DANDY, Rochester (YH07973)																		●								
JUST THE BIT, Maidstone (YH07977)																										
K G L C FEEDS, Sundridge (YH07987)																										
KENT WOOL GROWERS, Ashford (YH08083)																										
LUCK, B M, Tonbridge (YH08886)																										
M HANCOCK & SON, Ashford (YH08966)																										
MANSTON RIDING CTRE, Ramsgate (YH09126)																										

by Country by County	Coolers	Corn	Cross Country Jumps	Cushion Web	Damp Hay	Disposable A.V Liners	Disposable Equitainer	Driving Collars	Driving Harness	Dust Free Shavings	Electric Fencing	Exercise Equipment	Farm Equipment	Feed	Feed Racks	Feed Supplements	Fencing	Fertilisers	Fire Baskets	Flooring Supply (Arenas)	Fly Repellent	Gallops	Gates	Girths	Gloves	Mail Order Facilities
ARIZONAS, Tunbridge Wells (YH00527)																										●
BA GREEN CROP DRIERS, Hythe (YH00758)														●												
BARMINSTER TRADING, Ashford (YH00960)																										
BARRADALE FARM, Headcorn (YH01005)		●												●												
BAVERSTOCK CTRY SALES, Westerham Hill (YH01084)		●												●												
BIRCHALLS THE RIDING SHOP, Maidstone (YH01431)														●												
BROADFEED, Tunbridge Wells (YH01994)		●												●												
CANTERBURY CARRIAGES, Dover (YH02507)																										
CHELSFIELD RIDING SCHOOL, Orpington (YH02802)		●												●												
CHILHAM FEEDS, Canterbury (YH02854)		●												●												
COBHAM MANOR, Maidstone (YH03113)																										
E WILLIAMS FARMERS, Dartford (YH04432)		●												●												
ELECTRIC FENCING DIRECT, Tonbridge (YH04602)											●						●									
EMPORIUM, Ashford (YH04659)		●												●												
FAIRBOURNE CARRIAGES, Maidstone (YH05014)																										
FORAGES, J T, Cranbrook (YH05315)														●												
FOREST VIEW, Sidcup (YH05353)																										
FROGPOOL MANOR SADDLERY, Chislehurst (YH05515)		●												●		●	●									●
GILLET COOK, Faversham (YH05780)		●												●												
GLOVER, H F & J H, Longfield (YH05854)		●												●												
GOODNESTONE CT EQUESTRIAN, Faversham (YH05905)		●												●												
GRAIN HARVESTERS, Canterbury (YH05976)		●												●												
HOBBS PARKER, Ashford (YH06894)																										
HORSE & COUNTRY SUPERSTORE, Maidstone (YH07088)														●												
HORSE BOOKS, Maidstone (YH07108)																										
JUST DANDY, Rochester (YH07973)																										
JUST THE BIT, Maidstone (YH07977)		●												●												
K G L C FEEDS, Sundridge (YH07987)		●												●												
KENT WOOL GROWERS, Ashford (YH08083)		●												●												
LUCK, B M, Tonbridge (YH08886)													●													
M HANCOCK & SON, Ashford (YH08966)		●												●												
MANSTON RIDING CTRE, Ramsgate (YH09126)		●												●												

Products Supplied
A - G

by Country by County	Air Conditioning	Air Purifiers	Aloe Vera	Back Supports	Bedding	Bits	Body Protectors	Books	Boot Holders	Boot Jacks	Boot Scrapers	Boots	Boxes	Breeding Equipment	Breeding Supplies	Bridles	Bridlework	Carriages	Carts	CD's	Cleaning Equipment	Cleaning Supplies	Clippers	Closed Circuit TV	Clothes (Bespoke)	Clothes (Standard)	Coolers	Corn	Cross Country Jumps	Cushion Web	Damp Hay	Disposable A.V Liners	Disposable Equitainer	Driving Collars	Driving Harness	Dust Free Shavings	Electric Fencing	Exercise Equipment	Farm Equipment	Feed	Feed Racks	Feed Supplements	Fencing	Fertilisers	Fire Baskets	Flooring Supply (Arenas)	Fly Repellent	Gallops	Gates	Girths	Gloves	Mail Order Facilities
MAYWOOD STUD, Ashford (YH09309)								●																																												
MINSTER SADDLERY, Ramsgate (YH09652)																												●												●												
MOUNT MASCAL STABLES, Bexley (YH09890)																																								●												
OAKLEY'S HORSE & ANIMAL FEED, Bromley Common (YH10400)																												●												●												
OLD MILL EQUESTRIAN CTRE, Swanley (YH10467)																												●												●												
PARK PETS, Deal (YH10734)																												●												●												
ROSE, C J, Rochester (YH12096)																												●												●												
S RANSLEY & SONS, Ashford (YH12334)																												●												●												
SADDLE RACK, Folkestone (YH12345)																												●												●												
SADDLERY & GUN ROOM, Westerham (YH12365)								●				●											●			●																●										
SANDWICH ANIMAL FEEDS, Sandwich (YH12422)																												●												●												
SARACEN FEEDS, Tunbridge Wells (YH12432)																												●												●		●										
SCATS COUNTRYSTORE, Marden (YH12505)												●											●			●		●												●		●										
SCATS COUNTRYSTORE, Canterbury (YH12504)												●											●			●		●												●		●										
SNOWBALL, BART J, Maidstone (YH13038)																												●												●												
SPEEDGATE FARM, Longfield (YH13191)																												●												●												
STABLEITE, Sittingbourne (YH13303)					●																																															
THANET SHOW JUMPS, Ashford (YH13978)																																						●														
THOMAS PETTIFER, Romney Marsh (YH14010)																																										●										
THOMPSON, A, Dartford (YH14031)																												●												●												
TILLBROOK FEEDS, Meopham (YH14149)																												●												●												
TUNBRIDGE WELLS TACK ROOM, Tunbridge Wells (YH14460)																												●												●												
WEALDEN SADDLERY, Tonbridge (YH15020)												●											●		●	●																										●
WEBB, T M, Tonbridge (YH15031)																												●												●												
WESTGATE GROUP, Romney Marsh (YH15214)																																										●										
WILLOW FARM, Faversham (YH15497)					●			●				●											●			●														●		●	●									●
WM LILLICO & SONS, Maidstone (YH15641)																												●												●												
LANCASHIRE																																																				
1ST CHOICE PET SUPPLIES, Burnley (YH00001)																												●												●												
ARGO FEEDS, Ashton-under-Lyne (YH00520)																												●												●		●										
ARKENFIELD EQUESTRIAN CTRE, Chorley (YH00530)					●																			●																												
ASHTON AGRICULTURE, Clitheroe (YH00610)																												●												●												

Products Supplied
A - G

by Country by County

Company	Air Conditioning	Air Purifiers	Aloe Vera	Back Supports	Bedding	Bits	Body Protectors	Books	Boot Holders	Boot Jacks	Boot Scrapers	Boots	Boxes	Breeding Equipment	Breeding Supplies	Bridles	Bridlework	Carriages	Carts	CD's	Cleaning Equipment	Cleaning Supplies	Clippers	Closed Circuit TV	Clothes (Bespoke)	Clothes (Standard)
BADMINTON HORSE FEEDS, Blackburn (YH00783)																										
BEESLEYS OF BALLAM, Lytham (YH01190)																										
BERRY'S HORSEFEEDS, Blackburn (YH01320)																										
BLACK HORSE, Wigan (YH01463)																										
BOUNDARY FARM CARRIAGES, Wigan (YH01677)																		●								
BROOMHILL, Clitheroe (YH02080)												●														●
CARRS BILLINGTON, Clitheroe (YH02598)																										
CARRS BILLINGTON, Preston (YH02599)																										
CROSTON CORN MILLS, Preston (YH03671)																										
DERBY HSE SADDLERY, Wigan (YH04071)					●																				●	●
EDEN PRODUCE, Barnoldswick (YH04548)																										
EQUESTRIAN SURFACES, Burnley (YH04714)																										
EQUESTRIANA, Blackburn (YH04724)																	●						●			●
ESPRO EQUESTRIAN & SPORTSWEAR, Wigan (YH04862)																										●
HARGREAVES BANNISTER, Colne (YH06426)																										
HORSE BITS SADDLERY, Bury (YH07106)								●																		●
HUSTEADS RIDING SCHOOL, Oldham (YH07330)					●																					
JERUSALEM FARM, Colne (YH07757)												●											●			●
KENYON BROTHERS, Ormskirk (YH08093)																										
LIDUN PET FOODS, Lytham (YH08608)																										
NORTHERN STANDARDBREDS, Barnoldswick (YH10310)																										
OLD RUNNEL FARM, Blackpool (YH10475)																										
OSWALDTWISTLE ANIMAL FEEDS, Oswaldtwistle (YH10575)																										
PRETTY PONIES, Clitheroe (YH11372)												●													●	
PYE, W & J, Lancaster (YH11470)																										
QUAY EQUESTRIAN, Lancaster (YH11485)																										
R & E BAMFORD, Leyland (YH11505)																										
R HACKWORTH ANIMAL FEEDS, Rochdale (YH11544)																										
READWOOD, Burnley (YH11684)					●																					
RICHARD BATTERSBY, Heywood (YH11802)																										
RISING BRIDGE CORN, Accrington (YH11909)																										
ROBINSONS COUNTRY LEISURE, Wigan (YH12004)																										

Company	Coolers	Corn	Cross Country Jumps	Cushion Web	Damp Hay	Disposable A.V Liners	Disposable Equitainer	Driving Collars	Driving Harness	Dust Free Shavings	Electric Fencing	Exercise Equipment	Farm Equipment	Feed	Feed Racks	Feed Supplements	Fencing	Fertilisers	Fire Baskets	Flooring Supply (Arenas)	Fly Repellent	Gallops	Gates	Girths	Gloves	Mail Order Facilities
BADMINTON HORSE FEEDS, Blackburn (YH00783)		●												●												
BEESLEYS OF BALLAM, Lytham (YH01190)		●												●												
BERRY'S HORSEFEEDS, Blackburn (YH01320)		●												●												
BLACK HORSE, Wigan (YH01463)		●												●												
BOUNDARY FARM CARRIAGES, Wigan (YH01677)																										
BROOMHILL, Clitheroe (YH02080)																										
CARRS BILLINGTON, Clitheroe (YH02598)		●												●												
CARRS BILLINGTON, Preston (YH02599)		●												●												
CROSTON CORN MILLS, Preston (YH03671)		●												●												
DERBY HSE SADDLERY, Wigan (YH04071)														●		●										●
EDEN PRODUCE, Barnoldswick (YH04548)		●												●												
EQUESTRIAN SURFACES, Burnley (YH04714)																				●						
EQUESTRIANA, Blackburn (YH04724)																										
ESPRO EQUESTRIAN & SPORTSWEAR, Wigan (YH04862)																										
HARGREAVES BANNISTER, Colne (YH06426)		●												●												
HORSE BITS SADDLERY, Bury (YH07106)																●										
HUSTEADS RIDING SCHOOL, Oldham (YH07330)																										
JERUSALEM FARM, Colne (YH07757)																										
KENYON BROTHERS, Ormskirk (YH08093)		●												●												
LIDUN PET FOODS, Lytham (YH08608)		●												●												
NORTHERN STANDARDBREDS, Barnoldswick (YH10310)																●										
OLD RUNNEL FARM, Blackpool (YH10475)		●												●												
OSWALDTWISTLE ANIMAL FEEDS, Oswaldtwistle (YH10575)		●												●												
PRETTY PONIES, Clitheroe (YH11372)																										
PYE, W & J, Lancaster (YH11470)		●												●												
QUAY EQUESTRIAN, Lancaster (YH11485)																●								●		
R & E BAMFORD, Leyland (YH11505)		●												●												
R HACKWORTH ANIMAL FEEDS, Rochdale (YH11544)		●												●												
READWOOD, Burnley (YH11684)		●												●												
RICHARD BATTERSBY, Heywood (YH11802)		●												●		●										
RISING BRIDGE CORN, Accrington (YH11909)		●												●												
ROBINSONS COUNTRY LEISURE, Wigan (YH12004)		●												●												

Products Supplied
A - G

by Country by County

Company	Air Conditioning	Air Purifiers	Aloe Vera	Back Supports	Bedding	Bits	Body Protectors	Books	Boot Holders	Boot Jacks	Boot Scrapers	Boots	Boxes	Breeding Equipment	Breeding Supplies	Bridles	Bridlework	Carriages	Carts	CD's	Cleaning Equipment	Cleaning Supplies	Clippers	Closed Circuit TV	Clothes (Bespoke)	Clothes (Standard)	Coolers	Corn	Cross Country Jumps	Cushion Web	Damp Hay	Disposable A.V Liners	Disposable Equitainer	Driving Collars	Driving Harness	Dust Free Shavings	Electric Fencing	Exercise Equipment	Farm Equipment	Feed	Feed Racks	Feed Supplements	Fencing	Fertilisers	Fire Baskets	Flooring Supply (Arenas)	Fly Repellent	Gallops	Gates	Girths	Gloves	Mail Order Facilities
S G ANIMAL FEEDS, Blackburn (YH12325)																												●												●												
SELLERS, F H & D D, Bury (YH12623)																												●												●												
SNAFFLES, Halifax (YH13020)								●				●													●	●																●										
SOUTH WEST LANCASHIRE FARMERS, Skelmersdale (YH13116)																												●												●												
SPARE MOMENTS, Lancaster (YH13174)																												●												●												
STANAH HORSE FEEDS, Thornton-Cleveleys (YH13358)																												●												●												
T ASCROFT & SON, Preston (YH13730)																												●												●												
TOWN & COUNTRY, Chorley (YH14283)																												●												●												
TRILANCO, Poulton-Le-Fylde (YH14397)																																										●										
TROTTERS, Burnley (YH14408)																												●												●												
WHALLEY CORN MILLS, Blackburn (YH15258)																												●												●												
WILSONS TIMBER SHAVINGS, Burnley (YH15553)					●																																															
ZEBRA, Skelmersdale (YH15953)																									●																											
LEICESTERSHIRE																																																				
BARBER, F, Rothley (YH00921)																												●												●												
BUTTERCUP FEEDS, Melton Mowbray (YH02329)																												●												●												
C E COOK & SONS, Leicester (YH02369)																												●												●												
C W G, Melton Mowbray (YH02398)					●							●														●														●		●										
CHAMPION FEEDS EQUESTRIAN, Market Harborough (YH02726)																												●												●												
CLAYBROOKE, Lutterworth (YH02996)																												●												●		●										
CLOTHES HORSE, Leicester (YH03062)								●				●											●			●														●		●										
COUNTRYMAN'S GALLERY, Market Harborough (YH03438)								●																																												
COUNTRYWIDE FEEDS, Market Harborough (YH03447)																												●												●												
DADLYNGTON FIELD, Nuneaton (YH03815)																												●												●												
DTA, Leicester (YH04303)												●											●		●	●																										
E D SIMPSON & SON, Leicester (YH04400)																								●				●												●												
FORGE FEEDS, Ilston-on-the-Hill (YH05362)																												●												●												
FOSSE DRYBED, Whetstone (YH05396)					●																																															
FRISBY FLYERS HORSEBALL CLUB, Seagrave (YH05508)								●																																												
GREENHILL MILLING, Coalville (YH06088)																												●												●												
HOWS RACESAFE, Market Harborough (YH07244)							●																																													
HURST SADDLERS, Leicester (YH07316)								●				●											●		●	●												●		●		●										●

Products Supplied
A - G

by Country by County

	Air Conditioning	Air Purifiers	Aloe Vera	Back Supports	Bedding	Bits	Body Protectors	Books	Boot Holders	Boot Jacks	Boot Scrapers	Boots	Boxes	Breeding Equipment	Breeding Supplies	Bridles	Bridlework	Carriages	Carts	CD's	Cleaning Equipment	Cleaning Supplies	Clippers	Closed Circuit TV	Clothes (Bespoke)	Clothes (Standard)	Coolers	Corn	Cross Country Jumps	Cushion Web	Damp Hay	Disposable A.V Liners	Disposable Equitainer	Driving Collars	Driving Harness	Dust Free Shavings	Electric Fencing	Exercise Equipment	Farm Equipment	Feed	Feed Racks	Feed Supplements	Fencing	Fertilisers	Fire Baskets	Flooring Supply (Arenas)	Fly Repellent	Gallops	Gates	Girths	Gloves	Mail Order Facilities
JACK ELLIS BODY PROTECTION, Leicester (YH07637)							●																																													
JACQUES, RODNEY, Sharnford (YH07660)																												●												●												
JOLLYES, Coalville (YH07863)																												●												●												
N W F COUNTRYSTORE, Melton Mowbray (YH09997)																												●												●												
PALMERS, Hinckley (YH10692)																																												●								
REARSBY LODGE FEEDS, Leicester (YH11687)																												●												●												
S L B SUPPLIES, Coalville (YH12329)					●																							●												●		●										
SAGITTARIUS BLOODSTOCK AGENCY, Melton Mowbray (YH12382)														●	●																																					
SCHOOL OF NATIONAL EQUITATION, Loughborough (YH12521)												●													●	●														●		●										
SHARNFORD LODGE FEEDS/TACK, Hinckley (YH12676)																												●												●												
STABLES, Hinckley (YH13307)																												●												●												
SWEDISH COTTAGE ANIMAL FEEDS, Earl Shilton (YH13702)																												●												●												
VALE OF BELVOIR LEATHERS, Melton Mowbray (YH14638)																									●																											
LINCOLNSHIRE																																																				
A W RHOADES SADDLERY, Market Rasen (YH00068)																										●														●		●										
AZTEC FENCING, Spalding (YH00707)																																											●									
BAINES, P, Louth (YH00814)																												●												●												
BARNACK CTRY STORE, Stamford (YH00964)																												●												●												
BARROWBY FEEDS, Barrowby (YH01031)																												●												●												
BATTLE, HAYWARD & BOWER, Lincoln (YH01081)					●							●														●														●		●										
BELVOIR HORSE FEEDS, Boothby Graffoe Heath (YH01258)					●																																			●												
BELVOIR HORSE PRODUCTS, Grantham (YH01259)					●																																															
BETTER-TACK, Spalding (YH01334)					●																							●												●												
BOSTON HORSE SUPPLIES, Boston (YH01659)																												●												●												
C W G, Stamford (YH02399)					●							●														●														●		●										
C W G, Market Rasen (YH02400)					●							●														●														●		●										
COOL SPORT, Brigg (YH03269)																										●																										
COTTAGE SADDLERY, Boston (YH03379)												●														●																										
F B FOREMAN & SONS, Mablethorpe (YH04982)																												●												●												
F P I, Stamford (YH04998)																																										●										●
FENLAND FEEDS, Bourne (YH05143)																												●												●												
FONABY ANIMAL FEEDS, Caistor (YH05306)																												●												●												

Products Supplied
A - G

by Country by County

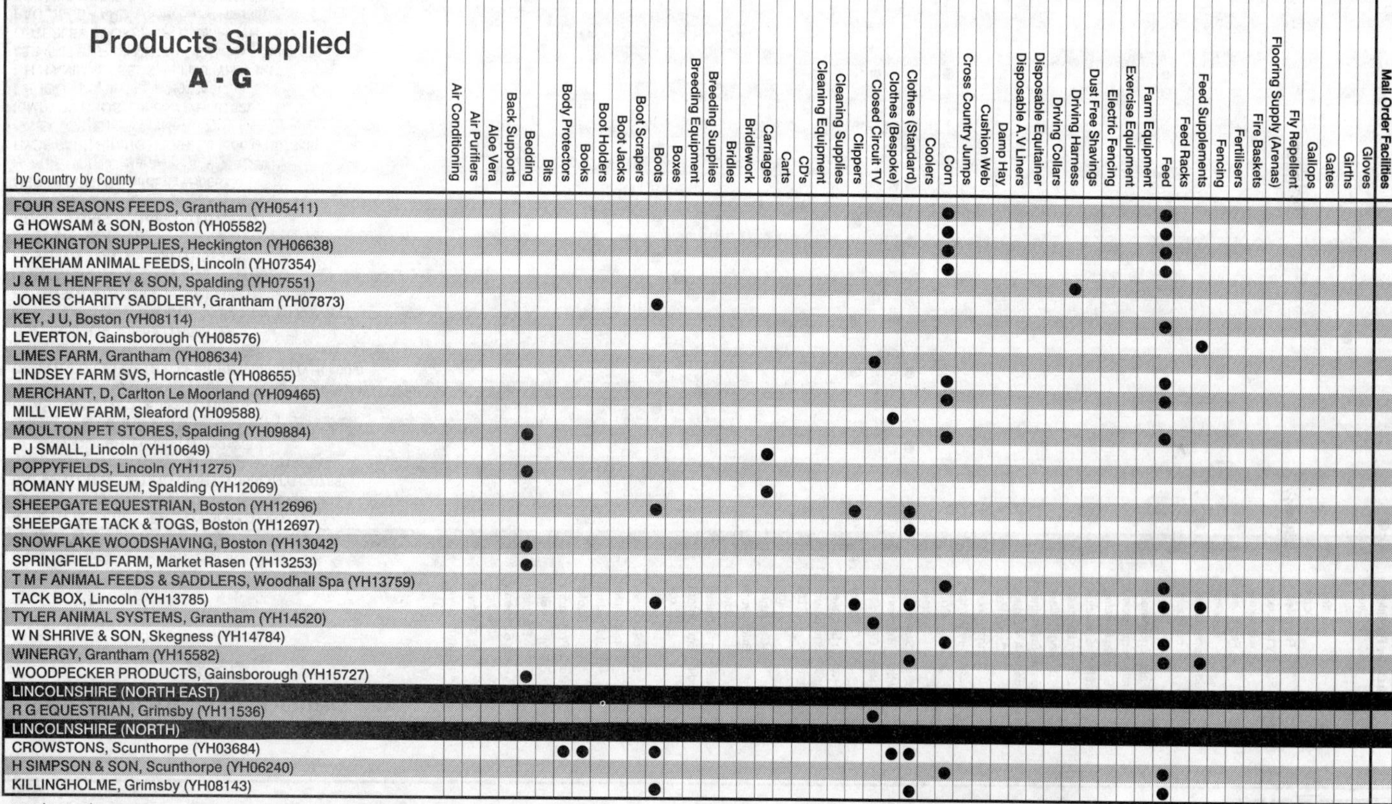

Name	Air Conditioning	Air Purifiers	Aloe Vera	Back Supports	Bedding	Bits	Body Protectors	Books	Boot Holders	Boot Jacks	Boot Scrapers	Boots	Boxes	Breeding Equipment	Breeding Supplies	Bridles	Bridlework	Carriages	Carts	CD's	Cleaning Equipment	Cleaning Supplies	Clippers	Closed Circuit TV	Clothes (Bespoke)	Clothes (Standard)	Coolers	Corn	Cross Country Jumps	Cushion Web	Damp Hay	Disposable A.V Liners	Disposable Equitainer	Driving Collars	Driving Harness	Dust Free Shavings	Electric Fencing	Exercise Equipment	Farm Equipment	Feed	Feed Racks	Feed Supplements	Fencing	Fertilisers	Fire Baskets	Flooring Supply (Arenas)	Fly Repellent	Gallops	Gates	Girths	Gloves	Mail Order Facilities
FOUR SEASONS FEEDS, Grantham (YH05411)																												●												●												
G HOWSAM & SON, Boston (YH05582)																												●												●												
HECKINGTON SUPPLIES, Heckington (YH06638)																												●												●												
HYKEHAM ANIMAL FEEDS, Lincoln (YH07354)																												●												●												
J & M L HENFREY & SON, Spalding (YH07551)																																			●																	
JONES CHARITY SADDLERY, Grantham (YH07873)												●																																								
KEY, J U, Boston (YH08114)																																								●												
LEVERTON, Gainsborough (YH08576)																																										●										
LIMES FARM, Grantham (YH08634)																								●																												
LINDSEY FARM SVS, Horncastle (YH08655)																												●												●												
MERCHANT, D, Carlton Le Moorland (YH09465)																												●												●												
MILL VIEW FARM, Sleaford (YH09588)																									●																											
MOULTON PET STORES, Spalding (YH09884)					●																							●												●												
P J SMALL, Lincoln (YH10649)																		●																																		
POPPYFIELDS, Lincoln (YH11275)					●																																															
ROMANY MUSEUM, Spalding (YH12069)																		●																																		
SHEEPGATE EQUESTRIAN, Boston (YH12696)												●											●			●																										
SHEEPGATE TACK & TOGS, Boston (YH12697)																										●																										
SNOWFLAKE WOODSHAVING, Boston (YH13042)					●																																															
SPRINGFIELD FARM, Market Rasen (YH13253)					●																																															
T M F ANIMAL FEEDS & SADDLERS, Woodhall Spa (YH13759)																												●												●												
TACK BOX, Lincoln (YH13785)												●											●			●														●		●										
TYLER ANIMAL SYSTEMS, Grantham (YH14520)																								●																												
W N SHRIVE & SON, Skegness (YH14784)																												●												●												
WINERGY, Grantham (YH15582)																										●														●		●										
WOODPECKER PRODUCTS, Gainsborough (YH15727)					●																																															
LINCOLNSHIRE (NORTH EAST)																																																				
R G EQUESTRIAN, Grimsby (YH11536)																								●																												
LINCOLNSHIRE (NORTH)																																																			
CROWSTONS, Scunthorpe (YH03684)							●	●				●													●	●																										
H SIMPSON & SON, Scunthorpe (YH06240)																												●												●												
KILLINGHOLME, Grimsby (YH08143)												●														●														●												

Products Supplied
A - G

by Country by County	Air Conditioning	Air Purifiers	Aloe Vera	Back Supports	Bedding	Bits	Body Protectors	Books	Boot Holders	Boot Jacks	Boot Scrapers	Boots	Boxes	Breeding Equipment	Breeding Supplies	Bridles	Bridlework	Carriages	Carts	CD's	Cleaning Equipment	Cleaning Supplies	Clippers	Closed Circuit TV	Clothes (Bespoke)	Clothes (Standard)	Coolers	Corn	Cross Country Jumps	Cushion Web	Damp Hay	Disposable A.V Liners	Disposable Equitainer	Driving Collars	Driving Harness	Dust Free Shavings	Electric Fencing	Exercise Equipment	Farm Equipment	Feed	Feed Racks	Feed Supplements	Fencing	Fertilisers	Fire Baskets	Flooring Supply (Arenas)	Fly Repellent	Gallops	Gates	Girths	Gloves	Mail Order Facilities
MASON, D & M, Scunthorpe (YH09239)																							●																													
LONDON (GREATER)																																																					
A D L TACK & SADDLERY, London (YH00027)								●															●			●																●										●
AINSWORTHS, London (YH00216)								●																																												
BADMINTON SPORTING DIARY, London (YH00788)								●																																												
BELMONT RIDING CTRE, London (YH01249)																												●												●												
BROWN, OLIVER, London (YH02126)																										●																										
BURY FARM FODDER STORE, Edgware (YH02299)																												●												●												
CHASE SADDLERY, Enfield (YH02785)												●											●																													
CLGE FARM SADDLERY & FEEDS, Finchley (YH03027)																												●												●												
DECATHLON SPORTS & LEISURE, London (YH04009)												●											●			●																	●									
DEGE & SKINNER, London (YH04026)																									●																											
DUFFIN, JULIA, Ealing (YH04317)																																																		●		
EDWARD ROBERT SADDLERY, Feltham (YH04569)								●															●		●																											
FARMVIEW SYSTEMS, Friern Park (YH05069)														●	●									●																												
FLETTNER VENTILATOR, London (YH05281)													●																																							
FOSTER & SON, London (YH05398)												●																																								
GEDDES-BODEN, LESLIE, London (YH05687)																										●																										●
GOULDS GREEN, Uxbridge (YH05952)					●							●											●																													
HARMONY & HEALTH FORMULATIONS, London (YH06445)																																										●										
HENRY POOLE, London (YH06685)																									●																											
HORSE HOUSE, Northwood (YH07123)																												●												●												
HYDE PARK RIDING WEAR, London (YH07345)												●														●																										
ISSEA - GB, London (YH07527)								●																																												
KIMPTON BROS, London (YH08162)																																										●										
L F JOLLYES, Enfield (YH08319)																												●												●												
L H H ANIMAL FEEDS, Enfield (YH08321)					●																			●				●												●												
LEE VALLEY RIDING CTRE, London (YH08519)																		●																																		
OSTERLEY BOOKSHOP, Osterley (YH10573)								●																																												
PAGET, EDWARD, Hampton (YH10684)												●																																								
PHILLIPS BROS, Camberwell (YH11048)					●																																															
RACETECH, Raynes Park (YH11580)																								●																												

Products Supplied
A - G

by Country by County	Air Conditioning	Air Purifiers	Aloe Vera	Back Supports	Bedding	Bits	Body Protectors	Books	Boot Holders	Boot Jacks	Boot Scrapers	Boots	Boxes	Breeding Equipment	Breeding Supplies	Bridles	Bridlework	Carriages	Carts	CD's	Cleaning Equipment	Cleaning Supplies	Clippers	Closed Circuit TV	Clothes (Bespoke)	Clothes (Standard)	Coolers	Corn	Cross Country Jumps	Cushion Web	Damp Hay	Disposable A.V Liners	Disposable Equitainer	Driving Collars	Driving Harness	Dust Free Shavings	Electric Fencing	Exercise Equipment	Farm Equipment	Feed	Feed Racks	Feed Supplements	Fencing	Fertilisers	Fire Baskets	Flooring Supply (Arenas)	Fly Repellent	Gallops	Gates	Girths	Gloves	Mail Order Facilities
REEL THING, London (YH11726)								●																																												
RIDERS & SQUIRES, London (YH11855)												●											●																													
RIDGWAY STABLES, London (YH11870)																										●																										
SCHNIEDER RIDING BOOT, London (YH12515)												●																																								
SPORTSPAGES, London (YH13237)								●																																												
UNIVERSITY DIAGNOSTICS, Teddington (YH14580)														●	●																																					
WIMBLEDON VILLAGE STABLES, London (YH15557)																								●																												
MANCHESTER (GREATER)																																																				
ALEXANDER JAMES OF PENDLEBURY, Manchester (YH00265)												●													●																											
BROWZERS, Manchester (YH02149)								●																																												●
EQUITACK, Bolton (YH04823)															●								●												●							●										●
JOLLYES, Manchester (YH07864)																												●												●												
MOUNTAIN BREEZE AIR IONISERS, Failsworth (YH09896)																																										●										
RYDERS FARM, Bolton (YH12297)																					●		●			●													●	●												
SHORESIDE STABLES, Manchester (YH12759)												●														●														●												
SMITHY, Bolton (YH13011)																										●														●		●										
SPORTSPAGES, Manchester (YH13238)								●																																												
STABLEMATES, Bolton (YH13304)																																								●		●										
MERSEYSIDE																																																				
ANIMAL WORLD, Southport (YH00448)																												●												●												
BARNSTON RIDING CTRE, Wirral (YH00991)												●														●																										
CROXTETH PK RIDING CTRE, Liverpool (YH03685)												●														●																										
FORMBY SADDLERY, Liverpool (YH05373)												●											●																	●												
HAMMONDS, Huyton (YH06362)																												●												●		●										
LARTON LIVERY, Wirral (YH08435)																												●												●												
ROBINSONS COUNTRY LEISURE, St Helens (YH12005)																												●												●												
TITHEBARN, Southport (YH14189)																																										●										
MIDLANDS (WEST)																																																				
ALBION SADDLEMAKERS, Walsall (YH00247)				●																																																
ALBRIGHTON FEEDS, Wolverhampton (YH00249)																												●												●												
ARDEN WOOD SHAVINGS, Solihull (YH00502)					●																																															
BEARLEY CROSS STABLES, Solihull (YH01121)					●																		●																				●									

www.hccyourhorse.com

Products Supplied
A - G

by Country by County

Company	Air Conditioning	Air Purifiers	Aloe Vera	Back Supports	Bedding	Bits	Body Protectors	Books	Boot Holders	Boot Jacks	Boot Scrapers	Boots	Boxes	Breeding Equipment	Breeding Supplies	Bridles	Bridlework	Carriages	Carts	CD's	Cleaning Equipment	Cleaning Supplies	Clippers	Closed Circuit TV	Clothes (Bespoke)	Clothes (Standard)	Coolers	Corn	Cross Country Jumps	Cushion Web	Damp Hay	Disposable A.V Liners	Disposable Equitainer	Driving Collars	Driving Harness	Dust Free Shavings	Electric Fencing	Exercise Equipment	Farm Equipment	Feed	Feed Racks	Feed Supplements	Fencing	Fertilisers	Fire Baskets	Flooring Supply (Arenas)	Fly Repellent	Gallops	Gates	Girths	Gloves	Mail Order Facilities
BOURNE VALE STABLES, Walsall (YH01683)																												●												●												
BROWNS, Walsall (YH02142)																●																																				
C V F, Coventry (YH02395)																												●												●												
DRIVALL, Halesowen (YH04276)																																					●						●									
E JEFFRIES & SONS, Walsall (YH04410)																	●																																			
EQUESTRIAN BRIDLE, Walsall (YH04693)																●																																				
F C ROBERTS & SON, Kingswinford (YH04988)																												●												●												
FINE ENGLISH BRIDLES, Walsall (YH05211)																	●																																			
FRANK STEPHENS & SON, Wolverhampton (YH05461)					●																							●												●		●										
GORRINGE SPORTSWEAR, Walsall (YH05936)																										●																										
GREENSFORGE, Kingswinford (YH06100)																												●												●												
HAZEL FARM, Solihull (YH06599)																												●												●												
HORSESENSE, Solihull (YH07170)												●														●		●												●		●										
HOUND & HORSE, Wythall (YH07206)																												●												●												
HUNGRY HORSE, Sutton Coldfield (YH07289)																												●												●												
JAMES COTTERELL & SONS, Walsall (YH07664)						●																																														
JOHNSON BROTHERS, Walsall (YH07822)																												●												●												
MULTI-SHRED, Lanesfiels (YH09945)					●																																															
OLD PORTWAY FARM, Rowley Regis (YH10473)																												●												●												
OVERIDER, Coventry (YH10593)							●					●													●	●																										●
PADDOCK STORES, Brierley Hill (YH10671)																												●												●												
PROLITE, Walsall (YH11432)				●																																																
ROSE BANK STORES & SADDLERY, Birmingham (YH12089)																												●												●												
SABRE LEATHER, Walsall (YH12339)																●																																		●		
SCHOOL FARM PETS & SUPPLIES, Walsall (YH12519)																												●												●												
STURMAN, JOHN, Warley (YH13617)																												●												●												
NORFOLK																																																				
ABBOTT, Norwich (YH00107)																												●												●												
ALLEN & PAGE, Thetford (YH00290)																																								●												
ANGLIA WOODCHIP, Norwich (YH00416)					●																																															
ANIMAL CRACKERS, Norwich (YH00430)																												●												●												
AVIFORM, Norwich (YH00685)																																										●										

Products Supplied
A - G

by Country by County

Products Supplied	BARRIER ANIMAL HEALTHCARE, Attleborough (YH01021)	BLACKBOROUGH END, King's Lynn (YH01477)	BOJAN AT WARREN KENNELS, Sheringham (YH01601)	C W G, East Dereham (YH02401)	CHAFF-CUTTERS ANIMAL SUPPLIES, Norwich (YH02707)	DARROW FARM SUPPLIES, Diss (YH03899)	DEEJAY ANIMAL FEED CTRE, Diss (YH04016)	DEREHAM SADDLERY, Dereham (YH04073)	DIXONS DUSTLESS, Diss (YH04145)	EQUINE CLOTHING, Downham Market (YH04770)	EVERYTHING EQUESTRIAN, Norwich (YH04958)	FRANCIS CUPISS, Diss (YH05448)	G J L, Fakenham (YH05585)	GRANVILLE SADDLERY, Wymondham (YH06015)	GRANVILLE SADDLERY, Norwich (YH06016)	H & C BEART, King's Lynn (YH06207)	H BANHAM, Fakenham (YH06213)	HALL FARM FORAGE, Happisburgh (YH06304)	HORSES IN SPORT, Diss (YH07169)	HORSETALK, King's Lynn (YH07176)	JOLLYES, East Dereham (YH07865)	KEN'S CORN STORES, Norwich (YH08076)	L K F ANIMAL BEDDING, Banham (YH08324)	LENRYS ASSOCIATES, Attleborough (YH08552)	MOULHAM & HORN, King's Lynn (YH09882)	NEVILLE BLAKEY FEEDSTUFFS, Pulham St Mary (YH10086)	RFC BED-DOWN, Harleston (YH11781)	RUNCTON HALL, King's Lynn (YH12233)	THOMSON & JOSEPH, Norwich (YH14046)	TOP TAK, King's Lynn (YH14238)	WENDALS HERBS, King's Lynn (YH15104)	WROXHAM SADDLERY, Norwich (YH15850)
Mail Order Facilities										●									●													
Gloves																																
Girths																																
Gates																																
Gallops																																
Fly Repellent	●																															
Flooring Supply (Arenas)																																
Fire Baskets																																
Fertilisers													●																			
Fencing																																
Feed Supplements	●			●								●	●							●				●					●		●	
Feed Racks																																
Feed			●	●	●	●	●	●			●		●	●	●	●	●	●			●	●			●	●				●		●
Farm Equipment																																
Exercise Equipment																																
Electric Fencing																																
Dust Free Shavings																																
Driving Harness																																
Driving Collars																																
Disposable Equitainer																																
Disposable A.V Liners																																
Damp Hay																																
Cushion Web																																
Cross Country Jumps																																
Corn			●		●	●	●	●					●	●	●	●	●	●			●	●			●	●				●		●
Coolers																																
Clothes (Standard)				●															●	●												
Clothes (Bespoke)																			●													
Closed Circuit TV																																
Clippers																												●				
Cleaning Supplies																																
Cleaning Equipment	●																															
CD's																																
Carts																																
Carriages																																
Bridlework																																
Bridles																				●												
Breeding Supplies																																
Breeding Equipment																																
Boxes																																
Boots		●		●															●	●												
Boot Scrapers																																
Boot Jacks																																
Boot Holders																																
Books																																
Body Protectors																				●												
Bits																				●												
Bedding				●					●				●			●		●					●				●					
Back Supports																																
Aloe Vera																																
Air Purifiers																																
Air Conditioning																																

www.hccyourhorse.com

Products Supplied
A - G

by Country by County

Company	Air Conditioning	Air Purifiers	Aloe Vera	Back Supports	Bedding	Bits	Body Protectors	Books	Boot Holders	Boot Jacks	Boot Scrapers	Boots	Boxes	Breeding Equipment	Breeding Supplies	Bridles	Bridlework	Carriages	Carts	CD's	Cleaning Equipment	Cleaning Supplies	Clippers	Closed Circuit TV	Clothes (Bespoke)	Clothes (Standard)
WYMONDHAM PET & GARDEN, Wymondham (YH15869)																										
NORTHAMPTONSHIRE																										
A B R FOODS, Corby (YH00019)																										
BATTEN, HORACE, Northampton (YH01077)												●														
BLETSOE BROWN, Northampton (YH01538)																										
BROOK FARM, Wellingborough (YH02033)					●																					
BUCKLEY BITS, Northampton (YH02197)						●																				
C W G, Towcester (YH02402)					●							●														●
CHIRON EQUESTRIAN BOOKS, Wellingborough (YH02868)								●																		
COLLINS PET FOODS, Hardingstone (YH03186)																										
COUNTRY STYLES, Towcester (YH03430)												●														●
COUNTRYWISE FEEDS & NEEDS, Kettering (YH03484)																										
COUNTY FOOTWEAR, Kettering (YH03487)												●														
CROFT & CO, Brackley (YH03610)																										
CROSS COUNTRY HORSE TRANSPORT, Northampton (YH03643)																		●								
DI CLARK FEEDS, Brackley (YH04100)																										
DODSON & HORRELL, Kettering (YH04162)																										
EDENGATE SADDLERY, Northampton (YH04550)								●												●	●		●			●
EQUIMAT, Kettering (YH04755)					●																					
FAULKNERS FOOTWEAR, Daventry (YH05104)												●														
GROOMERS, Northampton (YH06154)																										
H O E, Daventry (YH06232)																										
HARLEY, Daventry (YH06436)																										
HOOKS & HOOVES, Kettering (YH07038)												●														●
JOLLYES, Kettering (YH07866)																										
K & T FOOTWEAR, Kettering (YH07981)												●														●
LATIMER & CRICK, Northampton (YH08447)																										
LOVESON, Irthlingborough (YH08851)																										●
MARROWELL FARM SVS, West Haddon (YH09178)																										
MAXICROP INTERNATIONAL, Corby (YH09284)																										
NORMAN & SPICER, Daventry (YH10235)																										
O SHEPHERD & SON, Brackley (YH10366)																●										

Company	Coolers	Corn	Cross Country Jumps	Cushion Web	Damp Hay	Disposable A.V Liners	Disposable Equitainer	Driving Collars	Driving Harness	Dust Free Shavings	Electric Fencing	Exercise Equipment	Farm Equipment	Feed	Feed Racks	Feed Supplements	Fencing	Fertilisers	Fire Baskets	Flooring Supply (Arenas)	Fly Repellent	Gallops	Gates	Girths	Gloves	Mail Order Facilities
WYMONDHAM PET & GARDEN, Wymondham (YH15869)		●												●												
NORTHAMPTONSHIRE																										
A B R FOODS, Corby (YH00019)																●										
BATTEN, HORACE, Northampton (YH01077)																										●
BLETSOE BROWN, Northampton (YH01538)		●												●												
BROOK FARM, Wellingborough (YH02033)																										
BUCKLEY BITS, Northampton (YH02197)																										
C W G, Towcester (YH02402)														●		●										
CHIRON EQUESTRIAN BOOKS, Wellingborough (YH02868)																										
COLLINS PET FOODS, Hardingstone (YH03186)		●												●												
COUNTRY STYLES, Towcester (YH03430)																										
COUNTRYWISE FEEDS & NEEDS, Kettering (YH03484)		●												●												
COUNTY FOOTWEAR, Kettering (YH03487)																										
CROFT & CO, Brackley (YH03610)		●												●												
CROSS COUNTRY HORSE TRANSPORT, Northampton (YH03643)																										
DI CLARK FEEDS, Brackley (YH04100)		●												●		●										
DODSON & HORRELL, Kettering (YH04162)		●												●		●										
EDENGATE SADDLERY, Northampton (YH04550)									●																	
EQUIMAT, Kettering (YH04755)																										
FAULKNERS FOOTWEAR, Daventry (YH05104)																										
GROOMERS, Northampton (YH06154)		●												●												
H O E, Daventry (YH06232)		●												●		●										
HARLEY, Daventry (YH06436)																										●
HOOKS & HOOVES, Kettering (YH07038)														●												
JOLLYES, Kettering (YH07866)		●												●												
K & T FOOTWEAR, Kettering (YH07981)																										●
LATIMER & CRICK, Northampton (YH08447)		●												●												
LOVESON, Irthlingborough (YH08851)																									●	
MARROWELL FARM SVS, West Haddon (YH09178)		●												●												
MAXICROP INTERNATIONAL, Corby (YH09284)																●										
NORMAN & SPICER, Daventry (YH10235)		●												●												
O SHEPHERD & SON, Brackley (YH10366)																										

Products Supplied
A - G

by Country by County

by Country by County	Air Conditioning	Air Purifiers	Aloe Vera	Back Supports	Bedding	Bits	Body Protectors	Books	Boot Holders	Boot Jacks	Boot Scrapers	Boots	Boxes	Breeding Equipment	Breeding Supplies	Bridles	Bridlework	Carriages	Carts	CD's	Cleaning Equipment	Cleaning Supplies	Clippers	Closed Circuit TV	Clothes (Bespoke)	Clothes (Standard)
PARKER, N, Northampton (YH10751)																										
PET LOVE SUPPLIES, Daventry (YH11005)																										
R E TRICKERS, Northampton (YH11535)												●														
RIDERS INT, Raunds (YH11856)																										
SCHNIEDER RIDING BOOT, Northampton (YH12516)												●														
STUBBEN, Corby (YH13600)																●										
THORPE SADDLERY, Kettering (YH14094)				●																						
THREE SHIRES LIVERY CTRE, Wellingborough (YH14107)					●								●													
TURWESTON HILL FARM SUP, Brackley (YH14500)																										
WATTS & WATTS SADDLERY, Northampton (YH15003)					●			●				●											●			●
WOODFLAKES OF DAVENTRY, Daventry (YH15686)					●																					
YOUR CARRIAGE AWAITS, Northampton (YH15946)																		●								
NORTHUMBERLAND																										
A C BURN, Berwick-upon-Tweed (YH00021)					●							●											●			●
ARABLE FARM SUPPLIES, Alnwick (YH00493)																										
BEDMAX, Belford (YH01157)					●																					
CHESTERS STUD, Hexham (YH02835)																										
EQUILINK, Alnwick (YH04751)			●																							
FARMWAY, Wooler (YH05073)																										
FARMWAY, Morpeth (YH05074)					●			●				●											●		●	●
FARMWAY, Hexham (YH05075)																										
FORSYTH'S OF WOOLER, Wooler (YH05384)																										
GREEN, Morpeth (YH06048)																										
HAYMAX, Belford (YH06586)																										
J S HUBBUCK, Hexham (YH07616)																										
LANE FARM SHOP, Bedlington (YH08389)																										
NORTH NORTHUMBERLAND, Denwick (YH10275)														●	●											
NORTHUMBRIAN SADDLERY, Hexham (YH10321)																										
R L JOBSON & SON, Berwick-upon-Tweed (YH11552)																										
R L JOBSON & SON, Alnwick (YH11553)																										
REDESDALE RIDING CTRE, Otterburn (YH11710)					●																					
RICKERBY, Cornhill-on-Tweed (YH11834)																										

by Country by County	Coolers	Corn	Cross Country Jumps	Cushion Web	Damp Hay	Disposable A.V Liners	Disposable Equitainer	Driving Collars	Driving Harness	Dust Free Shavings	Electric Fencing	Exercise Equipment	Farm Equipment	Feed	Feed Racks	Feed Supplements	Fencing	Fertilisers	Fire Baskets	Flooring Supply (Arenas)	Fly Repellent	Gallops	Gates	Girths	Gloves	Mail Order Facilities
PARKER, N, Northampton (YH10751)									●																	
PET LOVE SUPPLIES, Daventry (YH11005)		●												●												
R E TRICKERS, Northampton (YH11535)																										
RIDERS INT, Raunds (YH11856)		●												●												
SCHNIEDER RIDING BOOT, Northampton (YH12516)																										
STUBBEN, Corby (YH13600)																										
THORPE SADDLERY, Kettering (YH14094)																										
THREE SHIRES LIVERY CTRE, Wellingborough (YH14107)																										
TURWESTON HILL FARM SUP, Brackley (YH14500)		●												●												
WATTS & WATTS SADDLERY, Northampton (YH15003)								●	●					●		●										
WOODFLAKES OF DAVENTRY, Daventry (YH15686)														●												
YOUR CARRIAGE AWAITS, Northampton (YH15946)																										
NORTHUMBERLAND																										
A C BURN, Berwick-upon-Tweed (YH00021)		●												●		●							●			
ARABLE FARM SUPPLIES, Alnwick (YH00493)		●												●												
BEDMAX, Belford (YH01157)														●												
CHESTERS STUD, Hexham (YH02835)														●												
EQUILINK, Alnwick (YH04751)																										●
FARMWAY, Wooler (YH05073)		●												●												
FARMWAY, Morpeth (YH05074)													●	●		●	●	●					●			
FARMWAY, Hexham (YH05075)		●												●												
FORSYTH'S OF WOOLER, Wooler (YH05384)		●												●												
GREEN, Morpeth (YH06048)		●												●												
HAYMAX, Belford (YH06586)		●												●												
J S HUBBUCK, Hexham (YH07616)		●												●		●										
LANE FARM SHOP, Bedlington (YH08389)		●												●												
NORTH NORTHUMBERLAND, Denwick (YH10275)																										
NORTHUMBRIAN SADDLERY, Hexham (YH10321)		●												●												
R L JOBSON & SON, Berwick-upon-Tweed (YH11552)		●												●												
R L JOBSON & SON, Alnwick (YH11553)		●												●												
REDESDALE RIDING CTRE, Otterburn (YH11710)																										
RICKERBY, Cornhill-on-Tweed (YH11834)		●												●												

Products Supplied
A - G

by Country by County	Air Conditioning	Air Purifiers	Aloe Vera	Back Supports	Bedding	Bits	Body Protectors	Books	Boot Holders	Boot Jacks	Boot Scrapers	Boots	Boxes	Breeding Equipment	Breeding Supplies	Bridles	Bridlework	Carriages	Carts	CD's	Cleaning Equipment	Cleaning Supplies	Clippers	Closed Circuit TV	Clothes (Bespoke)	Clothes (Standard)	Coolers	Corn	Cross Country Jumps	Cushion Web	Damp Hay	Disposable A.V Liners	Disposable Equitainer	Driving Collars	Driving Harness	Dust Free Shavings	Electric Fencing	Exercise Equipment	Farm Equipment	Feed	Feed Racks	Feed Supplements	Fencing	Fertilisers	Fire Baskets	Flooring Supply (Arenas)	Fly Repellent	Gallops	Gates	Girths	Gloves	Mail Order Facilities
ROBSON & COWAN, Morpeth (YH12011)																												●												●												
SINCLAIR FEEDS, Berwick-upon-Tweed (YH12848)																												●												●												
W E HOWDEN, Coldstream (YH14761)																																										●										
WILLOW WEAR, Hexham (YH15505)								●				●								●			●			●																●										
NOTTINGHAMSHIRE																																																				
AERBORN EQUESTRIAN, Nottingham (YH00195)												●														●	●			●																						
ALADDIN CAVE, Lowdham (YH00236)																												●												●												
BRIDLE WAY & GAUNTLEYS, Newark (YH01892)					●			●				●									●		●			●														●		●							●			●
BROOMSIDE STUD, Calverton (YH02082)														●	●																																					
C E COBB & SONS, Newark (YH02368)																												●												●												
C W G, Worksop (YH02404)					●							●														●														●		●										
C W G, Newark (YH02403)					●							●														●														●		●										
CARLTON FOREST, Worksop (YH02542)																												●												●												
CAUNTON GRASS DRIERS, Newark (YH02660)					●																							●												●												
CHUKKA COVE, Newark (YH02893)																												●												●												
DECATHLON SPORTS & LEISURE, Nottingham (YH04010)												●											●			●																	●									
EASY FEEDS, Newark (YH04522)																												●												●												
EQUIFEEDS, Retford (YH04744)																												●												●												
F MARTIN & SON, Arnold (YH04995)					●																		●					●									●			●		●	●									
FORREST FEEDS, Newark (YH05376)																												●												●												
HAYES FARM FEEDS, Newstead Village (YH06574)																												●												●												
HOLISTIC HORSECARE, Northampton (YH06934)																																																				●
HOOF ALOOF, Nottingham (YH07025)																										●																										
K-FEEDS, Retford (YH08118)																												●												●												
MALLENDER BROS, Worksop (YH09051)					●																																												●			
OLD MILL ANIMAL FEEDS, Mansfield Woodhouse (YH10466)																												●												●												
OSBOURNES, Retford (YH10563)					●																																			●												
OSS-I-CHAFF, Newark (YH10572)					●																																			●												
SADDLE RACK, Nottingham (YH12346)					●			●				●											●			●														●		●										
SADDLECRAFT, Nottingham (YH12355)						●		●				●									●		●		●	●								●	●			●				●										●
SHELTON HSE SADDLERY, Newark (YH12705)																												●												●												
ST CLEMENTS LODGE, Nottingham (YH13274)																																								●		●	●									

Products Supplied
A - G

by Country by County	Air Conditioning	Air Purifiers	Aloe Vera	Back Supports	Bedding	Bits	Body Protectors	Books	Boot Holders	Boot Jacks	Boot Scrapers	Boots	Boxes	Breeding Equipment	Breeding Supplies	Bridles	Bridlework	Carriages	Carts	CD's	Cleaning Equipment	Cleaning Supplies	Clippers	Closed Circuit TV	Clothes (Bespoke)	Clothes (Standard)	Coolers	Corn	Cross Country Jumps	Cushion Web	Damp Hay	Disposable A.V Liners	Disposable Equitainer	Driving Collars	Driving Harness	Dust Free Shavings	Electric Fencing	Exercise Equipment	Farm Equipment	Feed	Feed Racks	Feed Supplements	Fencing	Fertilisers	Fire Baskets	Flooring Supply (Arenas)	Fly Repellent	Gallops	Gates	Girths	Gloves	Mail Order Facilities
VICTORIAN CARRIAGES, Newark (YH14710)																		●																																		
W H OTTLEY, Retford (YH14772)																												●												●												
WALTER HARRISON & SONS, Radcliffe-on-Trent (YH14883)																												●												●												
WELLOW PK, Newark (YH15077)																												●												●												
WELLS AGRICULTURAL, Edwalton (YH15079)																												●												●												
WILLIAM BAILEY AGRICULTURAL, Newark (YH15434)																												●												●												
WILMOTTS PET/SADDLERY STORES, Nottingham (YH15523)																												●												●												
OXFORDSHIRE																																																				
ABBOTT, Chipping Norton (YH00108)																												●												●												
ALDEN EQUIFEEDS, Didcot (YH00253)																												●												●												
ASTI STUD & SADDLERY, Faringdon (YH00633)								●				●											●			●												●		●		●										●
BLAKES OF FRILFORD, Abingdon (YH01522)																												●												●												
BODICOTE FLYOVER FARM SHOP, Banbury (YH01596)																												●												●												
CHARLES HUNT & PARTNERS, Wallingford (YH02756)																												●												●												
COUNTRYWIDE STORES, Oxford (YH03464)																												●												●												
COUNTRYWIDE STORES, Chipping Norton (YH03463)																												●												●												
CROFT & CO, Banbury (YH03611)																												●												●												
DALLAS KEITH, Witney (YH03843)																																										●										
DOBBINS CLOBBER, Thame (YH04150)																																								●												
EQUI-GRASS, Banbury (YH04749)																																								●												
FIELD & FARM SADDLERS, Bicester (YH05182)																												●												●												
FRIAR PK EQUESTRIAN SUP, Henley-on-Thames (YH05500)																												●												●												
FRINGFORD FEEDS, Bicester (YH05507)																												●												●												
GARDNER, C D, Banbury (YH05646)					●																							●												●												
HAC-TAC, Faringdon (YH06259)																										●																										
HORSE DRAWN WEDDING CARRIAGES, Oxford (YH07119)																		●																																		
JENNINGS FARM PRODUCE, Garsington (YH07746)																												●												●												
JODS GALORE, Henley-on-Thames (YH07775)								●																	●	●																										●
KEN LANGFORD SADDLERY, Abingdon (YH08058)																										●																										
MICROM, Thame (YH09519)								●							●																	●	●																			
OATHILL FARM SUPPLIES, Banbury (YH10416)																												●												●												
PEARCE, H & C, Thame (YH10871)																												●												●												

www.hccyourhorse.com

Products Supplied

A - G

by Country by County

Company	Air Conditioning	Air Purifiers	Aloe Vera	Back Supports	Bedding	Bits	Body Protectors	Books	Boot Holders	Boot Jacks	Boot Scrapers	Boots	Boxes	Breeding Equipment	Breeding Supplies	Bridles	Bridlework	Carriages	Carts	CD's	Cleaning Equipment	Cleaning Supplies	Clippers	Closed Circuit TV	Clothes (Bespoke)	Clothes (Standard)	Coolers	Corn	Cross Country Jumps	Cushion Web	Damp Hay	Disposable A.V Liners	Disposable Equitainer	Driving Collars	Driving Harness	Dust Free Shavings	Electric Fencing	Exercise Equipment	Farm Equipment	Feed	Feed Racks	Feed Supplements	Fencing	Fertilisers	Fire Baskets	Flooring Supply (Arenas)	Fly Repellent	Gallops	Gates	Girths	Gloves	Mail Order Facilities
R S ASSEMBLIES, Bicester (YH11562)																												●												●												
SANSOMS SADDLERY, Witney (YH12429)								●				●								●	●		●		●	●												●				●										●
SCATS COUNTRYSTORE, Faringdon (YH12506)												●											●			●		●												●		●										
SEENEY'S ANIMAL & PET FOODS, Water Eaton (YH12610)																												●												●												
STANDLAKE EQUESTRIAN CTRE, Witney (YH13362)								●																																												
TACK & FEED SUPPLIES, Didcot (YH13776)																												●												●												
TETCHWICK FEED SUPPLIES, Kidlington (YH13963)																												●												●												
TOMPKINS, R J, Banbury (YH14224)					●																																			●												
W F S COUNTRY, Witney (YH14766)												●														●		●												●		●										
WEATHERBEETA, Banbury (YH15023)																									●																											
WHITE HORSE ANIMAL FEEDS, Wantage (YH15306)																												●												●												
RUTLAND																																																				
BADMINTON HORSE FEEDS, Oakham (YH00784)																																								●		●										
MANOR FARM FEEDS, Rutland (YH09099)																												●												●												
STABLE EXPRESS, Oakham (YH13293)																												●												●												
STAMFORD ANIMAL & PET SUP, Oakham (YH13353)																												●												●												
TRIPLE CROWN, Oakham (YH14401)																												●												●		●										
W'UNDERWEAR, Oakham (YH15852)																																																				●
SHROPSHIRE																																																				
A & A PEATE, Oswestry (YH00005)																												●												●												
BARKER HICKMAN, Shifnal (YH00936)																												●												●												
BURWARTON EST TIMBER, Bridgnorth (YH02297)					●																																															
C J BLACKSMITHS, Shrewsbury (YH02375)											●							●																											●							●
CAMBER, N B, Shrewsbury (YH02465)																												●												●												
CHARLES BRITTON CONSTRUCTION, Ellesmere (YH02754)																																														●		●	●			
COUNTRYWIDE STORES, Craven Arms (YH03470)																												●												●												
COUNTRYWIDE STORES, Bridgnorth (YH03469)																												●												●												
COUNTRYWIDE STORES, Bishops Castle (YH03468)																												●												●												
DAVID BAKER FARM SUPPLIES, Oswestry (YH03915)																												●												●												
EDDIE PALIN DISTRIBUTION, Market Drayton (YH04541)												●																									●					●	●									
GRIFFITHS & SIMPSON, Market Drayton (YH06136)																												●												●												
GRIFFITHS & SIMPSON, Newport (YH06137)																												●												●												

Products Supplied

A - G

by Country by County	Air Conditioning	Air Purifiers	Aloe Vera	Back Supports	Bedding	Bits	Body Protectors	Books	Boot Holders	Boot Jacks	Boot Scrapers	Boots	Boxes	Breeding Equipment	Breeding Supplies	Bridles	Bridlework	Carriages	Carts	CD's	Cleaning Equipment	Cleaning Supplies	Clippers	Closed Circuit TV	Clothes (Bespoke)	Clothes (Standard)	Coolers	Corn	Cross Country Jumps	Cushion Web	Damp Hay	Disposable A.V Liners	Disposable Equitainer	Driving Collars	Driving Harness	Dust Free Shavings	Electric Fencing	Exercise Equipment	Farm Equipment	Feed	Feed Racks	Feed Supplements	Fencing	Fertilisers	Fire Baskets	Flooring Supply (Arenas)	Fly Repellent	Gallops	Gates	Girths	Gloves	Mail Order Facilities
HEAD TO HOOF, Market Drayton (YH06608)																																																				●
HOORAY HENRY'S, Much Wenlock (YH07046)																												●												●												
HORSE SHOP, Bridgnorth (YH07139)												●														●		●												●												
LLOYDS ANIMAL FEEDS, Ludlow (YH08745)																												●												●												
LLOYDS ANIMAL FEEDS, Oswestry (YH08744)																												●												●												
MORRIS HOLDINGS, Oswestry (YH09827)																					●																															
N W F COUNTRYSTORE, Whitchurch (YH09999)																												●												●												
N W F COUNTRYSTORE, Market Drayton (YH09998)																												●												●												
NATIONAL FOALING BANK, Newport (YH10037)														●	●													●												●												
PRINCE & DOYLE, Ludlow (YH11397)																												●												●												
ROWEN-BARBARY HORSE FEEDS, Whitchurch (YH12167)																												●												●		●										
SHERBOURNE TACK, Ludlow (YH12719)																												●												●												
SHERRATT FARM SUPPLIES, Wem (YH12728)																												●												●												
STABLES SADDLERY & FEED SHOP, Shrewsbury (YH13313)																												●												●												
STAN CHEADLE CLIPPER SVS, Ludlow (YH13356)																							●																													
TOUCHDOWN LIVERIES, Whitchurch (YH14253)					●																										●					●				●		●										
TREMLOWS HALL STUD, Whitchurch (YH14371)														●																																						
WELLINGTON CARRIAGE, Telford (YH15073)																		●																																		
WREKIN FARMERS GARDEN CTRE, Telford (YH15817)																										●		●												●		●										
WYKE OF SHIFNAL, Shifnal (YH15863)														●	●													●												●												
WYNNSTAY & CLWYD FARMERS, Oswestry (YH15876)												●																												●												
SOMERSET																																																				
ANIMAL FEED SHOP, Bridgwater (YH00433)																												●												●												
BADCOCK & EVERED, Watchet (YH00774)																												●												●												
BADMINTON HORSE FEEDS, Bridgwater (YH00785)																												●												●												
BOWERS, HENRY, Chard (YH01707)												●											●			●																●										
COUNTRY TRADING, Glastonbury (YH03432)																												●												●												
COUNTRYWIDE STORES, Marksbury (YH03471)																												●												●												
COUNTRYWIDE STORES, Bridgwater (YH03472)																												●												●												
DUNN, NIGEL, Taunton (YH04351)					●																																															
E L F FEEDS, Minehead (YH04414)																												●												●												
EXMOOR WHOLESALE, Dulverton (YH04971)					●																							●									●			●		●	●									

Products Supplied
A - G

by Country by County

by Country by County	Air Conditioning	Air Purifiers	Aloe Vera	Back Supports	Bedding	Bits	Body Protectors	Books	Boot Holders	Boot Jacks	Boot Scrapers	Boots	Boxes	Breeding Equipment	Breeding Supplies	Bridles	Bridlework	Carriages	Carts	CD's	Cleaning Equipment	Cleaning Supplies	Clippers	Closed Circuit TV	Clothes (Bespoke)	Clothes (Standard)
FARMPET SUPPLIES, Taunton (YH05068)																										
GANE, A R, Somerton (YH05640)																										
HILTON HERBS, Crewkerne (YH06863)												●														
MAYTREE FARM FEEDS, Shepton Mallet (YH09307)																										
MCCOY SADDLERY, Minehead (YH09334)												●											●			●
MEDLAND SANDERS & TWOSE, Yeovil (YH09438)																										
MOLE VALLEY FARMERS, Frome (YH09711)																										
MOORE & SONS, Frome (YH09750)																										
POPHAMS, Highbridge (YH11268)																										
RICH & SON, Bridgwater (YH11798)																										
RIDEMOOR, Wincanton (YH11852)					●			●				●			●								●		●	●
ROSE MILL FEEDS, Ilminster (YH12094)					●			●																		●
SNELL, C F & J E, Crewkerne (YH13029)																										
STAX SADDLERY, Montacute (YH13406)					●																					●
THORNEY COPSE, Wincanton (YH14066)					●			●				●											●			●
UNICORN SADDLERY, Taunton (YH14569)																										
W.E.S GARRETT MASTER SADDLERS, Cheddar (YH14803)					●			●				●									●		●		●	●
WELLINGTON PET GARDEN, Wellington (YH15074)																										
WEST COUNTRY FEEDS, Taunton (YH15134)																										
WRANTAGE MILLS, Taunton (YH15810)																										
SOMERSET (NORTH)																										
ALBERT E JAMES & SON, Barrow Gurney (YH00245)																										
MURPHYS SADDLERY, Weston-Super-Mare (YH09961)																										
NAILSEA PET CTRE, Nailsea (YH10013)																										
REINBOW EQUESTRIAN PRODUCTS, Weston-Super-Mare (YH11748)																										
SANDFORD ANIMAL FEEDS, Sandford (YH12409)																										
SPRINGFIELD, Claverham (YH13252)																								●		
STROUTS, J M (DR), Nailsea (YH13589)																		●								
STAFFORDSHIRE																										
A & F WILLIAMSON & SONS, Stoke-on-Trent (YH00007)																										
A K FEEDS, Shenstone (YH00044)																										
BOCM PAULS, Newcastle-under-Lyme (YH01593)																										

by Country by County	Coolers	Corn	Cross Country Jumps	Cushion Web	Damp Hay	Disposable A.V Liners	Disposable Equitainer	Driving Collars	Driving Harness	Dust Free Shavings	Electric Fencing	Exercise Equipment	Farm Equipment	Feed	Feed Racks	Feed Supplements	Fencing	Fertilisers	Fire Baskets	Flooring Supply (Arenas)	Fly Repellent	Gallops	Gates	Girths	Gloves	Mail Order Facilities
FARMPET SUPPLIES, Taunton (YH05068)		●												●												
GANE, A R, Somerton (YH05640)		●												●												
HILTON HERBS, Crewkerne (YH06863)																●										
MAYTREE FARM FEEDS, Shepton Mallet (YH09307)		●												●												
MCCOY SADDLERY, Minehead (YH09334)																										●
MEDLAND SANDERS & TWOSE, Yeovil (YH09438)		●												●												
MOLE VALLEY FARMERS, Frome (YH09711)		●												●												
MOORE & SONS, Frome (YH09750)		●												●												
POPHAMS, Highbridge (YH11268)		●												●												
RICH & SON, Bridgwater (YH11798)									●																	
RIDEMOOR, Wincanton (YH11852)													●	●		●	●									●
ROSE MILL FEEDS, Ilminster (YH12094)		●												●		●	●									
SNELL, C F & J E, Crewkerne (YH13029)		●												●												
STAX SADDLERY, Montacute (YH13406)														●		●										
THORNEY COPSE, Wincanton (YH14066)		●										●		●		●	●									●
UNICORN SADDLERY, Taunton (YH14569)		●												●												
W.E.S GARRETT MASTER SADDLERS, Cheddar (YH14803)		●							●			●		●		●										
WELLINGTON PET GARDEN, Wellington (YH15074)		●												●												
WEST COUNTRY FEEDS, Taunton (YH15134)		●												●												
WRANTAGE MILLS, Taunton (YH15810)		●												●												
SOMERSET (NORTH)																										
ALBERT E JAMES & SON, Barrow Gurney (YH00245)		●												●												
MURPHYS SADDLERY, Weston-Super-Mare (YH09961)		●												●												
NAILSEA PET CTRE, Nailsea (YH10013)		●												●												
REINBOW EQUESTRIAN PRODUCTS, Weston-Super-Mare (YH11748)																	●									
SANDFORD ANIMAL FEEDS, Sandford (YH12409)		●												●												
SPRINGFIELD, Claverham (YH13252)																										
STROUTS, J M (DR), Nailsea (YH13589)																										
STAFFORDSHIRE																										
A & F WILLIAMSON & SONS, Stoke-on-Trent (YH00007)		●												●												
A K FEEDS, Shenstone (YH00044)		●												●												
BOCM PAULS, Newcastle-under-Lyme (YH01593)		●												●												

Products Supplied

A - G

by Country by County

Company	Air Conditioning	Air Purifiers	Aloe Vera	Back Supports	Bedding	Bits	Body Protectors	Books	Boot Holders	Boot Jacks	Boot Scrapers	Boots	Boxes	Breeding Equipment	Breeding Supplies	Bridles	Bridlework	Carriages	Carts	CD's	Cleaning Equipment	Cleaning Supplies	Clippers	Closed Circuit TV
BOLTON GATE SADDLERY, Stoke-on-Trent (YH01609)																								
BRITISH HORSE FEEDS, Stafford (YH01949)																								
C A DAVIES & SONS, Uttoxeter (YH02361)																								
C W G, Burton-on-Trent (YH02405)					●							●												
CLASSIC RACING BOOKS, Stoke-on-Trent (YH02988)								●																
COPPICE EQUESTRIAN SADDLERY, Farley (YH03303)																								
DAISY LANE LIVERY YARD, Burton-on-Trent (YH03816)																								
DAMPHAY PRODUCTS, Eccleshall (YH03857)																								
DICKSONS, Stoke-on-Trent (YH04119)																								
DOBBINS DINER, Tamworth (YH04151)					●			●				●									●			
DOLLIN & MORRIS, Stafford (YH04170)																								
DOSTHILL SADDLERY, Tamworth (YH04209)																								
FRANCES ANN BROWN SADDLERY, Stafford (YH05444)								●				●									●		●	
G & M PET SUPPLIES, Burntwood (YH05567)																								
GOTHERSLEY FARM, Stourbridge (YH05945)																								
HIGH ASH CTRY STORE, Rugeley (YH06752)																								
HORSEY THINGS, Eccleshall (YH07184)																								
HOSSNOSH FEEDS, Uttoxeter (YH07198)																								
KINGDOM PRODUCTS, Stafford (YH08190)																								
LARKHILL SADDLERY, Burton-on-Trent (YH08432)												●												
LUSITANO BREED SOC, Leek (YH08904)														●	●									
M & J SADDLERY, Lichfield (YH08947)																								
MEARS, E & S, Stafford (YH09429)																								
MOSS, T, Cheadle (YH09864)																								
NUTEC, Lichfield (YH10357)																								
POSH PONIES, Stoke-on-Trent (YH11297)																								
PREMIER NUTRITION PRODUCTS, Rugeley (YH11348)																								
ROOS FEEDS, Rugeley (YH12080)					●																			
RUMENCO - MAIN RING, Burton-on-Trent (YH12227)																								
SCROPTON, Burton-on-Trent (YH12569)																		●	●					
SEABROOK FEEDS, Sedgley (YH12580)																								
SMITH & MORRIS COUNTRY STORE, Newcastle (YH12933)								●																

Company	Clothes (Bespoke)	Clothes (Standard)	Coolers	Corn	Cross Country Jumps	Cushion Web	Damp Hay	Disposable A.V Liners	Disposable Equitainer	Driving Collars	Driving Harness	Dust Free Shavings	Electric Fencing	Exercise Equipment	Farm Equipment	Feed	Feed Racks	Feed Supplements	Fencing	Fertilisers	Fire Baskets	Flooring Supply (Arenas)	Fly Repellent	Gallops	Gates	Girths	Gloves	Mail Order Facilities
BOLTON GATE SADDLERY, Stoke-on-Trent (YH01609)				●												●												
BRITISH HORSE FEEDS, Stafford (YH01949)				●												●												
C A DAVIES & SONS, Uttoxeter (YH02361)				●												●												
C W G, Burton-on-Trent (YH02405)		●														●		●										
CLASSIC RACING BOOKS, Stoke-on-Trent (YH02988)																												
COPPICE EQUESTRIAN SADDLERY, Farley (YH03303)				●												●												
DAISY LANE LIVERY YARD, Burton-on-Trent (YH03816)				●												●												
DAMPHAY PRODUCTS, Eccleshall (YH03857)				●												●												
DICKSONS, Stoke-on-Trent (YH04119)				●												●		●										
DOBBINS DINER, Tamworth (YH04151)		●		●										●		●		●										
DOLLIN & MORRIS, Stafford (YH04170)				●												●		●										
DOSTHILL SADDLERY, Tamworth (YH04209)				●												●												
FRANCES ANN BROWN SADDLERY, Stafford (YH05444)																		●										
G & M PET SUPPLIES, Burntwood (YH05567)				●												●												
GOTHERSLEY FARM, Stourbridge (YH05945)				●												●												
HIGH ASH CTRY STORE, Rugeley (YH06752)				●												●												
HORSEY THINGS, Eccleshall (YH07184)				●												●												
HOSSNOSH FEEDS, Uttoxeter (YH07198)				●												●												
KINGDOM PRODUCTS, Stafford (YH08190)																●		●										
LARKHILL SADDLERY, Burton-on-Trent (YH08432)		●		●							●					●		●	●									
LUSITANO BREED SOC, Leek (YH08904)																												
M & J SADDLERY, Lichfield (YH08947)																		●										
MEARS, E & S, Stafford (YH09429)				●												●												
MOSS, T, Cheadle (YH09864)				●												●												
NUTEC, Lichfield (YH10357)																		●										
POSH PONIES, Stoke-on-Trent (YH11297)				●												●												
PREMIER NUTRITION PRODUCTS, Rugeley (YH11348)																		●										
ROOS FEEDS, Rugeley (YH12080)				●												●												
RUMENCO - MAIN RING, Burton-on-Trent (YH12227)																●		●										
SCROPTON, Burton-on-Trent (YH12569)											●																	
SEABROOK FEEDS, Sedgley (YH12580)				●												●												
SMITH & MORRIS COUNTRY STORE, Newcastle (YH12933)				●												●												

www.hccyourhorse.com

Products Supplied
A - G

by Country by County

	Air Conditioning	Air Purifiers	Aloe Vera	Back Supports	Bedding	Bits	Body Protectors	Books	Boot Holders	Boot Jacks	Boot Scrapers	Boots	Boxes	Breeding Equipment	Breeding Supplies	Bridles	Bridlework	Carriages	Carts	CD's	Cleaning Equipment	Cleaning Supplies	Clippers	Closed Circuit TV	Clothes (Bespoke)	Clothes (Standard)
SUFFOLK																										
BARNARD BROTHERS, Ipswich (YH00965)																										
BAYER, Bury St Edmunds (YH01095)																										
BLACKSMITHS SHOP, Woodbridge (YH01496)																										
BRIDLE PATH, Bury St Edmunds (YH01891)																										
BURTON, V & S, Lowestoft (YH02294)																										
BURYFEEDS, Bury St Edmunds (YH02300)																										
C E ALDRIDGE, Bury St Edmunds (YH02367)																										
C W G, Bury St Edmunds (YH02406)					●							●														●
CARRIAGE OCCASIONS, Red Lodge (YH02581)																		●								
CHARNWOOD MILLING, Woodbridge (YH02773)																										
CHURCH FARM TACK SHOP & FEEDS, Eye (YH02903)					●							●					●									●
CROSSWAYS SV CTRE, Bungay (YH03667)					●							●														
D & D EQUESTRIAN, Lowestoft (YH03768)																										
DALGETY AGRCLTRL, Bury St Edmunds (YH03837)																										
DALGETY AGRCLTRL, Newmarket (YH03838)																										
E V J POSTAL BOOKSHOP, Newmarket (YH04430)								●																		
FARM & COUNTRY, Harleston (YH05055)																										
FEEDMARK, Harleston (YH05122)																										
FEEDSAFE, Ipswich (YH05125)																										
FOSTER BLOODSTOCK, Bury St Edmunds (YH05399)														●												
GENESIS GREEN STUD, Newmarket (YH05710)														●	●											
GIBSON SADDLERS, Newmarket (YH05746)												●				●									●	●
GLADWELLS, Ipswich (YH05802)					●																					
GROVE FARM DRIVING & LIVERY, Mildenhall (YH06166)																		●								
HOBBLES GREEN ANIMAL FEEDS, Newmarket (YH06892)																										
HORSE & GARDEN, Halesworth (YH07089)					●			●																		●
HORSE REQUISITES, Newmarket (YH07132)												●		●	●									●		●
HORSESHOES, Wrentham (YH07174)					●																					
K 9 PET FOODS, Framlingham (YH07982)																										
LASAR EUROPE, Bury St Edmunds (YH08437)																										
LAVENHAM LEISURE, Sudbury (YH08463)																										●

	Coolers	Corn	Cross Country Jumps	Cushion Web	Damp Hay	Disposable A.V Liners	Disposable Equitainer	Driving Collars	Driving Harness	Dust Free Shavings	Electric Fencing	Exercise Equipment	Farm Equipment	Feed	Feed Racks	Feed Supplements	Fencing	Fertilisers	Fire Baskets	Flooring Supply (Arenas)	Fly Repellent	Gallops	Gates	Girths	Gloves	Mail Order Facilities
SUFFOLK																										
BARNARD BROTHERS, Ipswich (YH00965)		●												●												
BAYER, Bury St Edmunds (YH01095)																●										
BLACKSMITHS SHOP, Woodbridge (YH01496)													●													
BRIDLE PATH, Bury St Edmunds (YH01891)		●												●												
BURTON, V & S, Lowestoft (YH02294)		●												●												
BURYFEEDS, Bury St Edmunds (YH02300)		●												●												
C E ALDRIDGE, Bury St Edmunds (YH02367)		●												●												
C W G, Bury St Edmunds (YH02406)														●		●										
CARRIAGE OCCASIONS, Red Lodge (YH02581)																										
CHARNWOOD MILLING, Woodbridge (YH02773)		●												●		●										
CHURCH FARM TACK SHOP & FEEDS, Eye (YH02903)														●		●										
CROSSWAYS SV CTRE, Bungay (YH03667)																●										
D & D EQUESTRIAN, Lowestoft (YH03768)		●												●												
DALGETY AGRCLTRL, Bury St Edmunds (YH03837)		●												●												
DALGETY AGRCLTRL, Newmarket (YH03838)		●												●												
E V J POSTAL BOOKSHOP, Newmarket (YH04430)																										
FARM & COUNTRY, Harleston (YH05055)		●												●												
FEEDMARK, Harleston (YH05122)		●												●		●										
FEEDSAFE, Ipswich (YH05125)		●												●												
FOSTER BLOODSTOCK, Bury St Edmunds (YH05399)																										
GENESIS GREEN STUD, Newmarket (YH05710)																										
GIBSON SADDLERS, Newmarket (YH05746)																								●		
GLADWELLS, Ipswich (YH05802)		●												●		●										
GROVE FARM DRIVING & LIVERY, Mildenhall (YH06166)																										
HOBBLES GREEN ANIMAL FEEDS, Newmarket (YH06892)		●												●												
HORSE & GARDEN, Halesworth (YH07089)		●												●		●										
HORSE REQUISITES, Newmarket (YH07132)		●												●												
HORSESHOES, Wrentham (YH07174)		●												●		●										●
K 9 PET FOODS, Framlingham (YH07982)		●												●												
LASAR EUROPE, Bury St Edmunds (YH08437)																				●						
LAVENHAM LEISURE, Sudbury (YH08463)																										●

Products Supplied
A - G

by Country by County	Air Conditioning	Air Purifiers	Aloe Vera	Back Supports	Bedding	Bits	Body Protectors	Books	Boot Holders	Boot Jacks	Boot Scrapers	Boots	Boxes	Breeding Equipment	Breeding Supplies	Bridles	Bridlework	Carriages	Carts	CD's	Cleaning Equipment	Cleaning Supplies	Clippers	Closed Circuit TV	Clothes (Bespoke)	Clothes (Standard)	Coolers	Corn	Cross Country Jumps	Cushion Web	Damp Hay	Disposable A.V Liners	Disposable Equitainer	Driving Collars	Driving Harness	Dust Free Shavings	Electric Fencing	Exercise Equipment	Farm Equipment	Feed	Feed Racks	Feed Supplements	Fencing	Fertilisers	Fire Baskets	Flooring Supply (Arenas)	Fly Repellent	Gallops	Gates	Girths	Gloves	Mail Order Facilities
LONG MELFORD, Sudbury (YH08799)					●							●											●			●		●												●		●										
MARCH EQUESTRIAN FRAMLINGHAM, Woodbridge (YH09140)					●																							●												●												
MILL SADDLERY, Stowmarket (YH09587)					●			●				●									●		●			●														●		●										●
MOUNTFOLD, Bures (YH09901)																								●																												
OAKLEY, N W, Bury St Edmunds (YH10399)																																							●													
ORWELL ARENA, Ipswich (YH10556)					●																																			●												
PARKER BROTHERS, Bury St Edmunds (YH10744)																												●												●												
PAVESCO UK, Harleston (YH10838)																																										●										
R W TAYLOR ANIMAL FEEDS, Haverhill (YH11568)																												●												●												
RACKHAM, E R & R T, Woodbridge (YH11592)																												●												●												
RIDE AWAY SADDLERY, Ipswich (YH11846)																							●																			●										
RIDE 'N' DRIVE EQUESTRIAN SUP, Beccles (YH11848)																												●												●												
RYLAND SADDLERS, Newmarket (YH12305)																●																																				
SEEDEE PET FOODS, Sudbury (YH12608)																												●												●												
STOKE BY CLARE EQUESTRIAN CTRE, Sudbury (YH13501)					●																																			●		●										
STOREY, MARTIN J, Ipswich (YH13525)																					●																															
STOW FEEDS, Stowmarket (YH13536)																												●												●												
SUFFOLK ANIMAL FEED, Bury St Edmunds (YH13623)																												●												●												
SUFFOLK SADDLES, Ipswich (YH13626)												●													●																											
TERRA-VAC, Haverhill (YH13955)																					●																															
TINDALLS BOOKSHOP, Newmarket (YH14171)								●																																												
UFAC, Newmarket (YH14539)																												●												●												
WAY, R E & G B, Newmarket (YH15014)								●																																												
WESTBRINK FARMS, Newmarket (YH15184)					●																																			●												
SURREY																																																				
A & H FEEDS, Ashtead (YH00008)																												●												●												
A & H FEEDS, Leatherhead (YH00009)																												●												●												
A C F ANIMAL BEDDING, Haslemere (YH00024)					●																																															
ALBURY ANIMAL FEEDS, Guildford (YH00250)																												●												●												
ANIMAL ALTERNATIVES, Richmond (YH00425)																																																●					
ANNA'S CTRY STORE, Farnham (YH00455)																												●												●												
ASCOT PARK, Woking (YH00583)								●				●													●																											●

Products Supplied
A - G

by Country by County	Air Conditioning	Air Purifiers	Aloe Vera	Back Supports	Bedding	Bits	Body Protectors	Books	Boot Holders	Boot Jacks	Boot Scrapers	Boots	Boxes	Breeding Equipment	Breeding Supplies	Bridles	Bridlework	Carriages	Carts	CD's	Cleaning Equipment	Cleaning Supplies	Clippers	Closed Circuit TV	Clothes (Bespoke)	Clothes (Standard)	Coolers	Corn	Cross Country Jumps	Cushion Web	Damp Hay	Disposable A.V Liners	Disposable Equitainer	Driving Collars	Driving Harness	Dust Free Shavings	Electric Fencing	Exercise Equipment	Farm Equipment	Feed	Feed Racks	Feed Supplements	Fencing	Fertilisers	Fire Baskets	Flooring Supply (Arenas)	Fly Repellent	Gallops	Gates	Girths	Gloves	Mail Order Facilities
BACKHURST OF NORMANDY, Guildford (YH00770)																												●												●												
BALANCED FEEDS, Malden Rushett (YH00830)																												●												●		●										
BITS & PIECES, Sunbury-on-Thames (YH01457)																												●												●												
BOYD & PARTNERS, Staines (YH01731)																																							●													
BROOMELLS WORKSHOP, Dorking (YH02077)																										●																										
BUTTONS SADDLERY, Woking (YH02337)								●				●													●	●																										
CLANDON MANOR SUPPLIES, Guildford (YH02942)																												●												●												
COUNTRYWIDE STORES, Redhill (YH03473)																												●												●												
CROWN AXXESS, Guildford (YH03680)																																											●									
CURZON, G E, Staines (YH03755)																												●												●												
EGHAM ANIMAL FOOD SUPPLIES, Egham (YH04594)																												●												●												
ELLIOT RIGHT WAY BOOKS, Tadworth (YH04615)								●																																												
FIELDGUARD, Cranleigh (YH05193)					●																●																●						●									●
FROSBURY FARM FEEDS, Guildford (YH05518)					●																							●												●												
HASTILOW COMPETITION SADDLES, Godalming (YH06526)					●																		●			●		●												●		●										●
HENGEST FARM SHOP, Banstead (YH06672)																												●												●												
J W ATTLEE, Dorking (YH07624)																												●												●		●										
JASPERS, Lingfield (YH07710)																												●												●												
KEAR, BILL, Dorking (YH08016)																																														●						
LETHERS OF BROCKHAM, Betchworth (YH08568)												●														●																●										
LETHERS OF MERSTHAM, Redhill (YH08569)												●														●																●										
LINGFIELD TACK, Lingfield (YH08660)												●														●																●										
MANOR SADDLERY, Guildford (YH09117)												●																																								
ONE STOP TACK SHOP, East Molesey (YH10513)												●																																								
ORCHARD POYLE, Egham (YH10535)																		●																																		
PADD FARM SHOP, Egham (YH10665)																												●												●												
PETS ON PARADE, Claygate (YH11030)																												●												●												
RIDE & DRIVE, Horne (YH11842)						●											●																		●																	
RIDGEWOOD RIDING CTRE, Reigate (YH11869)																												●												●												
ROKER'S TACK SHOP, Guildford (YH12064)					●			●				●														●														●		●										
S R S, Sunbury-on-Thames (YH12333)			●																																																	
SCATS COUNTRYSTORE, Redhill (YH12508)												●											●			●		●												●		●										

Products Supplied
A - G

by Country by County	Air Conditioning	Air Purifiers	Aloe Vera	Back Supports	Bedding	Bits	Body Protectors	Books	Boot Holders	Boot Jacks	Boot Scrapers	Boots	Boxes	Breeding Equipment	Breeding Supplies	Bridles	Bridlework	Carriages	Carts	CD's	Cleaning Equipment	Cleaning Supplies	Clippers	Closed Circuit TV	Clothes (Bespoke)	Clothes (Standard)	Coolers	Corn	Cross Country Jumps	Cushion Web	Damp Hay	Disposable A.V Liners	Disposable Equitainer	Driving Collars	Driving Harness	Dust Free Shavings	Electric Fencing	Exercise Equipment	Farm Equipment	Feed	Feed Racks	Feed Supplements	Fencing	Fertilisers	Fire Baskets	Flooring Supply (Arenas)	Fly Repellent	Gallops	Gates	Girths	Gloves	Mail Order Facilities
SCATS COUNTRYSTORE, Godalming (YH12507)												●											●			●		●												●		●										
SECRETT FARM SHOP, Godalming (YH12599)																												●												●												
SUPERPET THE HORSE SHOP, Epsom (YH13654)					●			●																		●												●		●		●										●
SUPERPET THE HORSE SHOP, Banstead (YH13656)					●			●																		●												●		●		●										
SUPERPET THE HORSE SHOP, Tadworth (YH13655)					●			●																		●												●		●		●										
T.T.T, Guildford (YH13769)					●																																															
TANGYE, JOHN, Guildford (YH13855)																												●												●												
THEW, ARNOTT, Wallington (YH13987)																												●												●												
TRIPLE CROWN FENCE, Guildford (YH14403)																																											●									
WOLDINGHAM SADDLERS, Caterham (YH15647)																																			●																	
YORK, RAY, Cobham (YH15918)																																								●												
SUSSEX (EAST)																																																				
ACRE & ASHDOWN FEEDS, Crowborough (YH00156)																												●												●												
BOOK STORE, Ukfield (YH01626)								●																																												
CROCKSTEAD PK, Lewes (YH03608)																										●																										
DANDY BUSH SADDLERY, Battle (YH03863)																																										●										
DICKSON & CHURCH, Forest Row (YH04115)																												●												●												
FARMIX, Wadhurst (YH05066)					●																							●												●												
HORSE HOUSE, Hailsham (YH07124)																												●												●												
JOLLYES, Hailsham (YH07867)																												●												●												
LUSTED FEEDS, Hankham (YH08907)																												●												●												
PEASRIDGE, S S, Rye (YH10884)																								●																												
POLEGATE SADDLERY, Polegate (YH11198)																												●												●												
SCATS COUNTRYSTORE, Heathfield (YH12509)												●											●			●		●												●		●										
SOMETHING DIFFERENT, Uckfield (YH13068)												●														●																										
STEVENS, LEONARD, Eastbourne (YH13445)					●							●	●										●			●		●										●		●		●										
TACK ROOM, Robertsbridge (YH13802)																												●												●												
VINE, W E, Hailsham (YH14731)																		●																																		
WRENN'S ANIMAL FEEDS, Robertsbridge (YH15824)																												●												●												
SUSSEX (WEST)																																																				
A V BAKER & SONS, Chichester (YH00064)					●																																			●												
AGRIVET - KWG, Haywards Heath (YH00204)																												●												●												

www.hccyourhorse.com

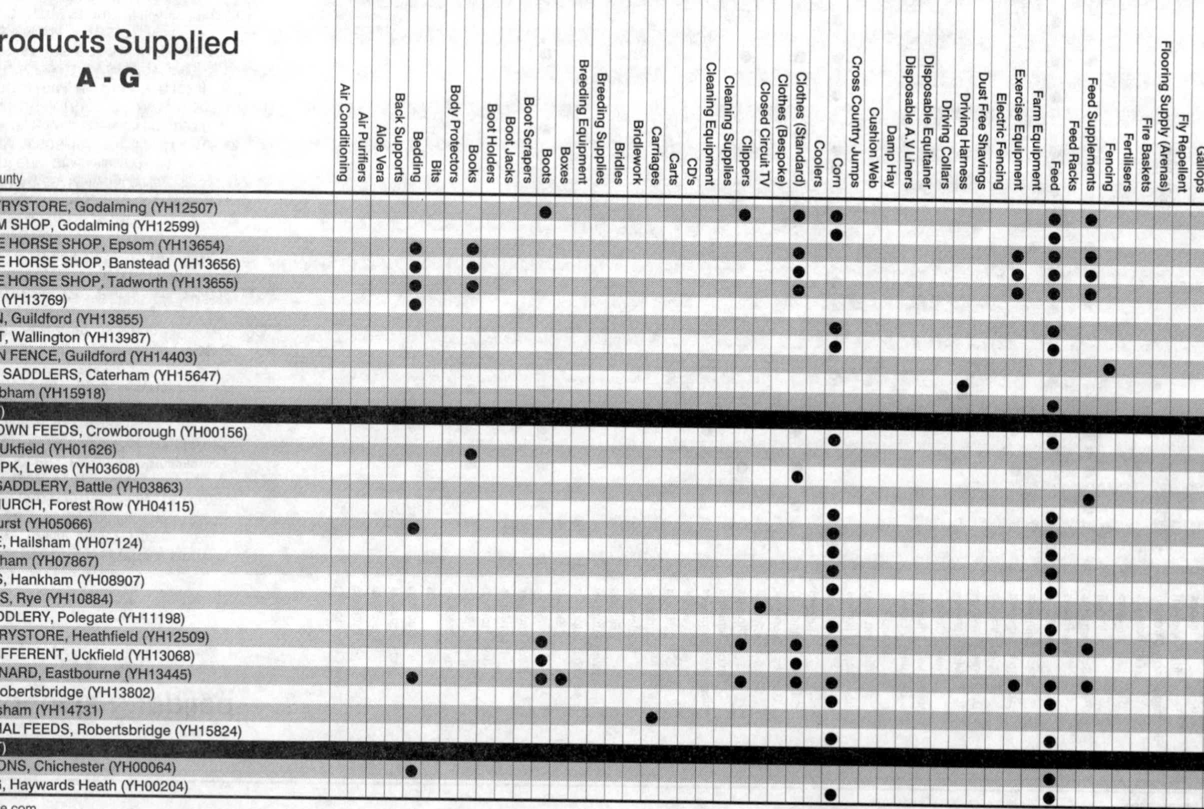

Products Supplied
A - G

by Country by County	Air Conditioning	Air Purifiers	Aloe Vera	Back Supports	Bedding	Bits	Body Protectors	Books	Boot Holders	Boot Jacks	Boot Scrapers	Boots	Boxes	Breeding Equipment	Breeding Supplies	Bridles	Bridlework	Carriages	Carts	CD's	Cleaning Equipment	Cleaning Supplies	Clippers	Closed Circuit TV	Clothes (Bespoke)	Clothes (Standard)	Coolers	Corn	Cross Country Jumps	Cushion Web	Damp Hay	Disposable A.V Liners	Disposable Equitainer	Driving Collars	Driving Harness	Dust Free Shavings	Electric Fencing	Exercise Equipment	Farm Equipment	Feed	Feed Racks	Feed Supplements	Fencing	Fertilisers	Fire Baskets	Flooring Supply (Arenas)	Fly Repellent	Gallops	Gates	Girths	Gloves	Mail Order Facilities
ALL TIME EQUESTRIAN, Crawley (YH00286)												●														●																●										
BARTHOLOMEWS, Chichester (YH01036)																												●												●												
BRENDON HORSE & RIDER, Brighton (YH01837)					●			●				●		●							●		●			●		●										●	●	●		●	●									
CRAWLEY DOWN SADDLERY, Crawley (YH03578)												●														●																●										
DEAN, GEOFF, Worthing (YH03991)																																			●																	
DRAGONFLY SADDLERY, Hassocks (YH04252)								●				●											●			●												●				●										●
EQUINE AMERICA, Broadbridge Heath (YH04761)																																										●										
EQUITOGS, Billingshurst (YH04830)					●							●									●					●														●		●										
EQUITOGS, Littlehampton (YH04829)					●							●									●					●														●		●										
GEOFF DEAN SADDLERY, Worthing (YH05714)								●				●																						●	●																	
GRANARY HORSE FEEDS, Chichester (YH05981)																												●												●												
H M SCARTERFIELD & SONS, Chichester (YH06230)																												●												●												
HARTLAND CARRIAGE SUPPLIES, Rudgwick (YH06504)																		●																																		
HORACE FULLER, Horsham (YH07063)																					●																															
HORSE HEALTH PRODUCTS, Pulborough (YH07121)																																								●		●										
HORSHAM PET CTRE, Horsham (YH07188)																												●												●												
IFIELD PARK FEED TACK & WEAR, Crawley (YH07389)																												●												●												
LIGHTS, Brighton (YH08616)					●																																		●	●		●										
LONDON STUD, Pulborough (YH08789)															●																																					
M & A OUTDOOR CLOTHING, Crawley (YH08942)												●														●																										
MIDHURST GRANARIES, Midhurst (YH09552)																												●												●												
OLDWICK SADDLERY, Chichester (YH10495)																												●												●												
ORCHARD FARM FEEDS, East Grinstead (YH10530)																												●												●												
PENFOLD & SONS, Haywards Heath (YH10934)												●														●																										
PEPER HAROW HORSE TRAILERS, Horsham (YH10968)													●																																							
POWELLS OF COOLHAM, Horsham (YH11323)																												●												●												
RENTOKIL INTITAL, East Grinstead (YH11763)		●																						●																												
SCATS COUNTRYSTORE, Billingshurst (YH12510)												●											●			●		●												●		●										
SHARON TONG, Steyning (YH12677)																																																				●
SNOOTY FOX COUNTRY STORE, Petworth (YH13035)																												●												●												
SNOWHILL SADDLERY, Chichester (YH13044)												●														●									●																	
TACK A ROUND SADDLERY, Billingshurst (YH13781)												●														●																										

Products Supplied
A - G

by Country by County

	Air Conditioning	Air Purifiers	Aloe Vera	Back Supports	Bedding	Bits	Body Protectors	Books	Boot Holders	Boot Jacks	Boot Scrapers	Boots	Boxes	Breeding Equipment	Breeding Supplies	Bridles	Bridlework	Carriages	Carts	CD's	Cleaning Equipment	Cleaning Supplies	Clippers	Closed Circuit TV	Clothes (Bespoke)	Clothes (Standard)	Coolers	Corn	Cross Country Jumps	Cushion Web	Damp Hay	Disposable A.V Liners	Disposable Equitainer	Driving Collars	Driving Harness	Dust Free Shavings	Electric Fencing	Exercise Equipment	Farm Equipment	Feed	Feed Racks	Feed Supplements	Fencing	Fertilisers	Fire Baskets	Flooring Supply (Arenas)	Fly Repellent	Gallops	Gates	Girths	Gloves	Mail Order Facilities
TFP, Horsham (YH13971)																				●																				●												
TRACK RIGHT, Hassocks (YH14308)																					●					●																										●
WESTBROOK AGRICULTURAL SUP, Rudgwick (YH15185)																												●												●												
TYNE AND WEAR																																																				
B M ENGLISH & SON, Houghton Le Spring (YH00738)																												●												●												
CARLTONS THE FEED MERCHANTS, Whitley Bay (YH02545)																												●												●												
E SWINBURN & SON, Newcastle-upon-Tyne (YH04426)																												●												●												
EQUINE PRODUCTS, Newcastle-upon-Tyne (YH04795)																																								●		●										
H C S, North Shields (YH06215)																							●														●						●									●
JOLLYES, Newcastle-upon-Tyne (YH07868)																												●												●												
JOSEPH BAILEY & SONS, Houghton Le Spring (YH07942)																																							●													
NORTH LIZARD RIDING SCHOOL, South Shields (YH10271)																												●												●												
PETMEALS, Boldon Colliery (YH11028)																												●												●												
QUARRY PARK STABLES, Gateshead (YH11483)																			●																																	
RIDE IN STYLE, Sunderland (YH11847)																										●																										
RIDERS, North Shields (YH11854)												●														●														●		●										
S & S SADDLERY, Sunderland (YH12313)																																			●																	
SADDLE SHOP, Gateshead (YH12350)												●														●														●		●										
WEBSTER, J R, Newcastle-upon-Tyne (YH15040)												●														●																										
WARWICKSHIRE																																																				
A & J SADDLERY, Southam (YH00012)					●			●				●											●		●	●														●		●										
ACCIMASSU, Studley (YH00140)															●																																					
BHS, Kenilworth (YH01371)								●												●																																●
BLYTH MILL, Birmingham (YH01577)																												●												●												
COUNTRY PURSUIT, Warwick (YH03420)								●																																												
COUNTRYWIDE STORES, Rugby (YH03475)																												●												●												
COUNTRYWIDE STORES, Stratford-upon-Avon (YH03476)																												●												●												
COUNTRYWIDE STORES, Nuneaton (YH03474)																												●												●												
CREWE GARDENS, Kenilworth (YH03594)																												●												●		●										
FLINT HALL FEEDS, Newbold Pacey (YH05285)																												●												●												
GRAPES VILLA FARM SUPPLIES, Coventry (YH06017)																												●												●												
HOCKLEY HEATH RIDING SUPPLIES, Solihull (YH06904)																												●												●												

www.hccyourhorse.com

by Country by County

Company	Air Conditioning	Air Purifiers	Aloe Vera	Back Supports	Bedding	Bits	Body Protectors	Books	Boot Holders	Boot Jacks	Boot Scrapers	Boots	Boxes	Breeding Equipment	Breeding Supplies	Bridles	Bridlework	Carriages	Carts	CD's	Cleaning Equipment	Cleaning Supplies	Clippers	Closed Circuit TV	Clothes (Bespoke)	Clothes (Standard)	Coolers	Corn	Cross Country Jumps	Cushion Web	Damp Hay	Disposable A.V Liners	Disposable Equitainer	Driving Collars	Driving Harness	Dust Free Shavings	Electric Fencing	Exercise Equipment	Farm Equipment	Feed	Feed Racks	Feed Supplements	Fencing	Fertilisers	Fire Baskets	Flooring Supply (Arenas)	Fly Repellent	Gallops	Gates	Girths	Gloves	Mail Order Facilities
JOLLYES, Stratford-upon-Avon (YH07869)																												●												●												
MONKSPATH SADDLERY, Solihull (YH09727)																												●												●												
MUMFORD, H S & G R, Nuneaton (YH09947)																												●												●												
OUSBEY CARRIAGES, Statford-on-Avon (YH10584)																		●																																		
RACECOURSE & COVERTSIDE, Hampton Magna (YH11573)								●																																												
SHIPSTON MILL, Shipston-on-Stour (YH12751)																												●												●												
TOWER FARM SADDLERS, Rugby (YH14274)																												●												●												
WARWICKSHIRE TRAILERS, Solihull (YH14953)																																																				●
WAVERLEY EQUESTRIAN CTRE, Leamington Spa (YH15011)																										●														●		●										
WESTERN RIDING, Rugby (YH15204)								●																																												
WINDRIDGE STORES, Coventry (YH15569)																												●												●												
WILTSHIRE																																																				
AMERICAN THOROUGHBRED, Kilmington (YH00365)																												●												●		●										
BEST BOOTS, Chippenham (YH01324)												●																																								●
BLOODSTOCK PUBLICATIONS, Marlborough (YH01550)								●						●	●																																					
CATLEY'S FARM SUPPLIES, Devizes (YH02652)																																								●												
COUNTRYWIDE STORES, Melksham (YH03478)																												●												●												
COUNTRYWIDE STORES, Chippenham (YH03477)																												●												●												
COUNTRYWIDE STORES, Swindon (YH03479)																												●												●												
E P C, Warminster (YH04419)																																										●										
EASTON GREY SADDLERS, Malmesbury (YH04514)																									●									●	●																	
ELMGROVE SADDLERY, Swindon (YH04636)												●											●			●														●												
EQUI LIFE, Chippenham (YH04728)								●																																		●										
EQUIFOR, Marlborough (YH04746)																		●	●															●	●							●										
FARROW, C, Salisbury (YH05096)																		●																																		
GENUS EQUINE, Chippenham (YH05711)														●	●					●																																
GEORGE SMITH HORSEBOXES, Salisbury (YH05719)	●	●											●											●																												
GRANT BARNES & SON, Malmesbury (YH06009)																						●																														
GRO-WELL FEEDS, Melksham (YH06176)																																								●												
HURDCOTT LIVERY STABLES, Salisbury (YH07311)																																										●										
J & K ANIMAL FEEDS, Warminster (YH07549)																												●												●												
JOHN TOOMER, Swindon (YH07815)																												●												●		●										

Products Supplied
A - G

by Country by County

Company	Air Conditioning	Air Purifiers	Aloe Vera	Back Supports	Bedding	Bits	Body Protectors	Books	Boot Holders	Boot Jacks	Boot Scrapers	Boots	Boxes	Breeding Equipment	Breeding Supplies	Bridles	Bridlework	Carriages	Carts	CD's	Cleaning Equipment	Cleaning Supplies	Clippers	Closed Circuit TV	Clothes (Bespoke)	Clothes (Standard)	Coolers	Corn	Cross Country Jumps	Cushion Web	Damp Hay	Disposable A.V Liners	Disposable Equitainer	Driving Collars	Driving Harness	Dust Free Shavings	Electric Fencing	Exercise Equipment	Farm Equipment	Feed	Feed Racks	Feed Supplements	Fencing	Fertilisers	Fire Baskets	Flooring Supply (Arenas)	Fly Repellent	Gallops	Gates	Girths	Gloves	Mail Order Facilities
JOLLYES, Chippenham (YH07870)																												●												●												
M M T SERVICES, Marlborough (YH08973)																												●												●												
NEW EQUINE WEAR, Malmesbury (YH10093)												●																																								
OLD DAIRY SADDLERY LTD, Swindon (YH10454)																												●												●												
OSGILIATH FEEDS, Westbury (YH10565)																												●												●												
PANCEUTICS, Swindon (YH10697)																																										●										
PEMBROKE FARM FEEDS, Salisbury (YH10917)																												●												●												
SADDLERY, Swindon (YH12364)												●														●																										
SCATS COUNTRYSTORE, Salisbury (YH12511)												●											●			●		●												●		●										
SCATS COUNTRYSTORE, Devizes (YH12512)												●											●			●		●												●		●										
STABLEWARE, Marlborough (YH13314)																												●												●												
SYDNEY INGRAM & SON, Salisbury (YH13722)												●														●																										
T G JEARY, Calne (YH13741)																												●												●												
T H WHITE, Marlborough (YH13746)																												●												●												
WADSWICK, Corsham (YH14819)												●														●														●		●										
WEST KINGTON STUD, Chippenham (YH15151)														●	●																																					
WORCESTERSHIRE																																																				
A & M MARKETING, Evesham (YH00014)								●																																												
BEALE FEEDS, Bromsgrove (YH01113)																												●												●												
BENT, BM & SA, Evesham (YH01282)																																										●										
BROMSGROVE SADDLERY, Bromsgrove (YH02026)								●															●															●				●										
CORN STORES, Redditch (YH03321)																												●												●												
COUNTRYWIDE, Worcester (YH03446)												●														●		●												●		●										
COUNTRYWIDE STORES, Evesham (YH03483)																												●												●												
COUNTRYWIDE STORES, Upton-upon-Severn (YH03481)																												●												●												
COUNTRYWIDE STORES, Bromsgrove (YH03482)																												●												●												
COUNTRYWIDE STORES, Kidderminster (YH03480)																												●												●												
DONNA LEIGH SADDLERY, Kidderminster (YH04185)																												●												●												
EQUIMIX, Stourport-on-Severn (YH04756)					●			●				●								●	●		●			●												●		●		●										●
EQUINE & CANINE SUPPLIES, Worcester (YH04758)																												●												●												
ERIC FIRKINS FARM SUPPLIES, Stourport-on-Severn (YH04844)																												●												●												
HUGHES, A L, Malvern (YH07257)																												●												●												

www.hccyourhorse.com

Products Supplied
A - G

by Country by County	Air Conditioning	Air Purifiers	Aloe Vera	Back Supports	Bedding	Bits	Body Protectors	Books	Boot Holders	Boot Jacks	Boot Scrapers	Boots	Boxes	Breeding Equipment	Breeding Supplies	Bridles	Bridlework	Carriages	Carts	CD's	Cleaning Equipment	Cleaning Supplies	Clippers	Closed Circuit TV	Clothes (Bespoke)	Clothes (Standard)	Coolers	Corn	Cross Country Jumps	Cushion Web	Damp Hay	Disposable A.V Liners	Disposable Equitainer	Driving Collars	Driving Harness	Dust Free Shavings	Electric Fencing	Exercise Equipment	Farm Equipment	Feed	Feed Racks	Feed Supplements	Fencing	Fertilisers	Fire Baskets	Flooring Supply (Arenas)	Fly Repellent	Gallops	Gates	Girths	Gloves	Mail Order Facilities
JOHN BARNETT, Worcester (YH07779)																												●												●												
JOHN SCOTT SPORTING BOOKS, Abberley (YH07811)								●																																												
LEA CASTLE EQUESTRIAN CTRE, Kidderminster (YH08493)																		●																																		
LEA CASTLE SADDLERY, Kidderminster (YH08494)																												●												●												
MARKETING & DEVELOPMENT SVS, Stourport-on-Severn (YH09160)																													●												●											
MORGAN BLACKSMITHS, Malvern (YH09793)																												●												●												
PASTURES CLEAN, Broadway (YH10813)																					●																															
PEACE SEEDS, Evesham (YH10855)																																										●										
PHIPPS, A, Pershore (YH11068)																																																				●
PIONEER ANIMAL FEEDS, Upton-upon-Severn (YH11142)																												●												●												
VINE HERBAL PRODUCTS, Broadway (YH14729)																																										●										
WILSONS PET & ANIMAL CTRE, Bromsgrove (YH15551)																												●												●												
WITS END STABLES, Worcester (YH15634)																																								●												
YORKSHIRE (EAST)																																																				
ASS BLOOD STOCK CONS, Bridlington (YH00629)														●	●																																					
BATA, Beverley (YH01062)																												●												●												
BRANDSBY AGRIC TRADING ASS, Driffield (YH01800)																												●												●												
DALGETY AGRCLTRL, Driffield (YH03839)																												●												●												
EUROVET, North Ferriby (YH04909)																																								●		●										
FARMWAY, Driffield (YH05076)																												●												●												
HAIGHS, Doncaster (YH06282)					●																																			●												
HASTPACE DATA, Driffield (YH06529)																								●																												
K & B TACK SHOPS, Bridlington (YH07979)																												●												●												
MARSHALLS, Holme upon Spalding Moor (YH09207)					●																																															
MERCHANT PET & ANIMAL FEED, Driffield (YH09464)																												●												●												
OSMONDS, North Ferriby (YH10571)																																										●										
PATRICK WILKINSON, Beverley (YH10825)												●											●		●	●												●				●										●
SEVEN SEAS VETNRY DIVISION, Hull (YH12640)																																										●										
SIGNFORD, Beverley (YH12794)					●																																															
SMITHS ANIMAL & PET SUPPLIES, Cottingham (YH13006)																												●												●												
SMITHY, Driffield (YH13013)						●																																														
STILLMEADOW TACK SHOP, Hull (YH13467)																												●												●												

Products Supplied
A - G

by Country by County

Business	Air Conditioning	Air Purifiers	Aloe Vera	Back Supports	Bedding	Bits	Body Protectors	Books	Boot Holders	Boot Jacks	Boot Scrapers	Boots	Boxes	Breeding Equipment	Breeding Supplies	Bridles	Bridlework	Carriages	Carts	CD's	Cleaning Equipment	Cleaning Supplies	Clippers	Closed Circuit TV	Clothes (Bespoke)	Clothes (Standard)	Coolers	Corn	Cross Country Jumps	Cushion Web	Damp Hay	Disposable A.V Liners	Disposable Equitainer	Driving Collars	Driving Harness	Dust Free Shavings	Electric Fencing	Exercise Equipment	Farm Equipment	Feed	Feed Racks	Feed Supplements	Fencing	Fertilisers	Fire Baskets	Flooring Supply (Arenas)	Fly Repellent	Gallops	Gates	Girths	Gloves	Mail Order Facilities
STOCKCARE, Beverley (YH13488)																																										●										
WYTON TACK SHOP, Hull (YH15877)																												●												●												
YORKSHIRE (NORTH)																																																				
ALL 4 PETS, Malton (YH00283)																												●												●												
B & B LIVERY, Northallerton (YH00709)					●																																			●												
BEAVER HORSE SHOP, Harrogate (YH01143)												●											●			●														●		●										
BIELBYS OF SCARBOROUGH, Scarborough (YH01401)																												●												●												
BIT BANK, Stokesley (YH01454)						●											●																																	●		●
BRANDSBY AGRIC TRADING ASS, Malton (YH01802)																												●												●												
BRANDSBY AGRIC TRADING ASS, Kirkbymoorside (YH01801)																												●												●												
BRANDSBY AGRIC TRADING ASSOC, Whitby (YH01806)																												●												●												
BRANDSBY AGRIC TRADING ASSOC, Scarborough (YH01807)																												●												●												
BRANDSBY AGRIC TRADING ASSOC, Whitby (YH01804)																												●												●												
BRANDSBY AGRIC TRADING ASSOC, York (YH01808)																												●												●												
BRANDSBY AGRIC TRADING ASSOC, Easingwold (YH01803)																												●												●												
BRANDSBY AGRIC TRADING ASSOC, Helmsley (YH01805)																												●												●												
BULLOCK, J A & F, York (YH02219)					●																																			●		●										
BURGESS ENDEAVOUR, Pickering (YH02243)																																								●												
DALES FEED SUPPLIES, Thirsk (YH03826)																												●												●												
DALES PET FEED SUPPLIES, Ripon (YH03828)																												●												●												
DENNIS, CHRISTOPHER J, Knaresborough (YH04053)								●																																												
E K READMAN & SONS, Scarborough (YH04412)																												●												●												
EDDLETHORPE EQUESTRIAN SVS, Malton (YH04543)																																								●												
F GREEN & SON, Gargrave (YH04992)																												●												●												
FARMWAY, Leyburn (YH05078)																												●												●												
FARMWAY, Thirsk (YH05077)																												●												●												
FOREST FEED, Harrogate (YH05337)																												●												●												
FOSS FEEDS, Acaster Malbis (YH05395)																												●												●												
FRANCES BULLOCK'S SADDLERY, Easingwold (YH05446)																												●												●												
G MAGSON FEEDS, Pickering (YH05588)																												●												●												
GILLS SADDLERY & CANE, Northallerton (YH05787)					●							●													●	●														●		●										
GRANARY, Whitby (YH05980)																												●												●												

Products Supplied

A - G

by Country by County

Company	Air Conditioning	Air Purifiers	Aloe Vera	Back Supports	Bedding	Bits	Body Protectors	Books	Boot Holders	Boot Jacks	Boot Scrapers	Boots	Boxes	Breeding Equipment	Breeding Supplies	Bridles	Bridlework	Carriages	Carts	CD's	Cleaning Equipment	Cleaning Supplies	Clippers	Closed Circuit TV	Clothes (Bespoke)	Clothes (Standard)	Coolers	Corn	Cross Country Jumps	Cushion Web	Damp Hay	Disposable A.V Liners	Disposable Equitainer	Driving Collars	Driving Harness	Dust Free Shavings	Electric Fencing	Exercise Equipment	Farm Equipment	Feed	Feed Racks	Feed Supplements	Fencing	Fertilisers	Fire Baskets	Flooring Supply (Arenas)	Fly Repellent	Gallops	Gates	Girths	Gloves	Mail Order Facilities
H WADDINGTON, Skipton (YH06246)																												●												●												
HOLMAN, A E & A B, Selby (YH06961)					●																																															
JAMESON, W E, Ripon (YH07691)																												●												●												
LANGTON HORSE WEAR, Northallerton (YH08416)																										●																●										
LIFE SOURCE SUPPLEMENTS, Ripon (YH08610)																																										●										
MILL LANE, Selby (YH09579)																																								●		●										
PHOSYN, York (YH11077)																																										●										
PICKERING, JOHN T, Helmsley (YH11084)								●																																												
R & R COUNTRY, Selby (YH11507)					●																●		●			●		●												●		●				●						●
R C BLAND, Harrogate (YH11517)																												●												●												
RIDE-AWAY, York (YH11850)								●															●																	●		●										●
ROBINSON, Malton (YH11985)												●											●			●														●		●										●
ROOS FEEDS NORTH, Malton (YH12081)																												●												●												
SECOND TURNOUT, Northallerton (YH12598)												●														●																										
VITALIN EQUINE FEEDS, Ripon (YH14736)																												●												●												
W M THOMPSON, Murton (YH14781)																												●												●												
WHITE ROSE SADDLERY, Malton (YH15324)												●														●																										
YORKSHIRE RIDING SUPPLIES, York (YH15923)								●				●														●																										
YORKSHIRE (SOUTH)																																																				
ANNE WAINWRIGHT SADDLERY, Doncaster (YH00456)																												●												●												
ARGO FEEDS, Sheffield (YH00521)																												●												●		●										
AXIENT, Rotherham (YH00695)														●	●																																					
BLUE CHIP, Sheffield (YH01565)																																								●		●										●
CONISBROUGH PETS, Doncaster (YH03231)																												●												●		●										
COOKE, DONALD, Rotherham (YH03259)																												●												●												
DARKHORSE TINYTACK, Barnsley (YH03888)														●	●				●				●											●	●			●					●									●
EASTWOOD, D, Barnsley (YH04519)																												●												●												
FLINTWYK ENGINEERING, Doncaster (YH05287)																								●																												
FRIENDSHIP ESTATES, Doncaster (YH05503)					●																																			●		●										
HALES, ALFRED (SNR), Sheffield (YH06293)																		●																																		
HORSE & RIDER, Doncaster (YH07096)												●														●																●										
HORSE & RIDER, Sheffield (YH07097)								●				●											●			●														●		●										●

Products Supplied
A - G

by Country by County	Air Conditioning	Air Purifiers	Aloe Vera	Back Supports	Bedding	Bits	Body Protectors	Books	Boot Holders	Boot Jacks	Boot Scrapers	Boots	Boxes	Breeding Equipment	Breeding Supplies	Bridles	Bridlework	Carriages	Carts	CD's	Cleaning Equipment	Cleaning Supplies	Clippers	Closed Circuit TV	Clothes (Bespoke)	Clothes (Standard)	Coolers	Corn	Cross Country Jumps	Cushion Web	Damp Hay	Disposable A.V Liners	Disposable Equitainer	Driving Collars	Driving Harness	Dust Free Shavings	Electric Fencing	Exercise Equipment	Farm Equipment	Feed	Feed Racks	Feed Supplements	Fencing	Fertilisers	Fire Baskets	Flooring Supply (Arenas)	Fly Repellent	Gallops	Gates	Girths	Gloves	Mail Order Facilities
JOLLYES, Doncaster (YH07871)																												●												●												
MILLVIEW, Doncaster (YH09638)												●														●																										
MR ED'S, Rotherham (YH09915)												●											●			●																										
PARKLANDS RIDING SCHOOL, Sheffield (YH10770)																												●												●												
SPRINGVALE CARRIAGES, Sheffield (YH13262)																		●																																		
STABLE-DRY & EQUIBALE, Doncaster (YH13302)					●																							●																								
THROSTLE NEST SADDLERY, Barnsley (YH14114)												●													●	●																										
WILDSMITHS, Doncaster (YH15412)												●													●	●														●		●										
WILSON FEEDS, Doncaster (YH15527)																												●												●												
YORKSHIRE (WEST)																																																				
ACORN FEEDS, Huddersfield (YH00148)																												●												●		●										
ASTLEY RIDING CTRE, Leeds (YH00635)																																								●												
B T H HIRE & SALES, Leeds (YH00749)																																																				●
B WORTLEY & SON, Huddersfield (YH00752)																												●												●												
BADMINTON HORSE FEEDS, Sherburn In Elmet (YH00786)																												●												●												
BAILEYS HORSE FEEDS, Wakefield (YH00807)																																								●		●										
BAILEYS HORSE FEEDS, Wakefield (YH00808)																																								●		●										
BARDSEY MILLS, Otley (YH00927)					●																							●											●	●		●										
BETA, Wetherby (YH01330)								●																																												
BINNS BOOKS, Knottingley (YH01423)								●																																												
BLUE BARN, Otley (YH01563)																												●												●												
BRANDON FORGE SADDLERY, Leeds (YH01796)								●				●									●		●			●												●				●										
BROWNS FENCING, Liversedge (YH02144)																																											●									
CALDENE CLOTHING, Hebden Bridge (YH02430)																									●	●																										
COUNTRY FEEDS, Bradford (YH03407)																												●												●												
CRICKET HILL FEEDS, Leeds (YH03596)																												●												●												
DAYS PET SHOP, Bradford (YH03971)												●														●														●		●										
DISCOUNT SADDLERY, Huddersfield (YH04129)					●	●	●	●				●									●		●		●	●								●	●			●	●			●	●									●
EASTVIEW STABLES, Leeds (YH04516)													●																																							
EQUESTRIAN CLEARANCE CTRE, Halifax (YH04694)																																																				●
EQUITACK SADDLERY, Wakefield (YH04825)																							●												●							●	●									●
FOX SADDLERS, Wetherby (YH05425)								●				●													●	●																●										●

by Country by County

	Air Conditioning	Air Purifiers	Aloe Vera	Back Supports	Bedding	Bits	Body Protectors	Books	Boot Holders	Boot Jacks	Boot Scrapers	Boots	Boxes	Breeding Equipment	Breeding Supplies	Bridles	Bridlework	Carriages	Carts	CD's	Cleaning Equipment	Cleaning Supplies	Clippers	Closed Circuit TV	Clothes (Bespoke)	Clothes (Standard)	Coolers	Corn	Cross Country Jumps	Cushion Web	Damp Hay	Disposable A.V Liners	Disposable Equitainer	Driving Collars	Driving Harness	Dust Free Shavings	Electric Fencing	Exercise Equipment	Farm Equipment	Feed	Feed Racks	Feed Supplements	Fencing	Fertilisers	Fire Baskets	Flooring Supply (Arenas)	Fly Repellent	Gallops	Gates	Girths	Gloves	Mail Order Facilities
GREETLAND & DISTRICT TRAD SOC, Halifax (YH06112)																												●												●												
H THORNBER, Halifax (YH06244)																												●												●												
HILLAM FEEDS, South Milford (YH06836)					●							●											●					●												●		●										
HILLAM TRAILERS, Cleckheaton (YH06837)													●																										●													
HOOVES EQUESTRIAN, Bradford (YH07047)						●											●				●				●	●	●																									●
HOPTON, Mirfield (YH07061)					●																			●															●													
HUTCHINSON, A, Wakefield (YH07335)																												●												●												
ILKLEY RIDING CTRE, Ilkley (YH07400)																										●																										
J R COUNTRY & PET SUPPLIES, Wetherby (YH07607)																												●												●												
JAMES BURNHILL & SON, Cleckheaton (YH07663)																												●												●												
JENKINSONS, Dewsbury (YH07740)																					●																					●										
KAYES ANIMAL FEEDS, Wyke (YH08010)																												●												●												
KEITH DRAKE, Huddersfield (YH08033)																												●												●												
KENYONS OF MORLEY, Morley (YH08095)																												●												●												
KIPPAX, Leeds (YH08222)					●							●																●												●		●										
KRUUSE, Sherburn In Elmet (YH08299)																																										●										
LATHAM FARM, Cleckheaton (YH08445)																		●	●															●	●														●			
LIVING WORLD, Leeds (YH08717)																												●												●												
MEARCLOUGH FARM FEEDS, Halifax (YH09428)																												●												●												
MIDDLESTOWN SADDLERY, Wakefield (YH09540)								●				●											●			●									●		●	●				●										
OSCARS PET & EQUINE SUPPLIES, Wetherby (YH10564)																												●												●												
PENNINE FARM SVS, Huddersfield (YH10951)																																										●										
PUDSEY AGRICULTURAL SVS, Pudsey (YH11449)																												●												●												
QUALTEX, Hebden Bridge (YH11477)																											●																									
RIGTON CARR FARM, Bardsey (YH11893)																																								●												
SINCLAIR RIDING WEAR, Leeds (YH12849)																										●																										
STAPLETON SADDLERY, Silsden (YH13390)																												●												●												
STEPHENSONS ANIMAL FEEDS, Todmorden (YH13427)																												●												●												
STYLO MATCHMAKERS INT, Bradford (YH13620)																																																		●		
TACK & TURNOUT EQUESTRIAN, Huddersfield (YH13780)																									●	●		●											●	●		●	●									●
TAILWAGGERS, Chapel Allerton (YH13821)																												●												●												
TURF VETNRY SUPPLIES, Wetherby (YH14468)																																										●										

Products Supplied
A - G

by Country by County

	Air Conditioning	Air Purifiers	Aloe Vera	Back Supports	Bedding	Bits	Body Protectors	Books	Boot Holders	Boot Jacks	Boot Scrapers	Boots	Boxes	Breeding Equipment	Breeding Supplies	Bridles	Bridlework	Carriages	Carts	CD's	Cleaning Equipment	Cleaning Supplies	Clippers	Closed Circuit TV	Clothes (Bespoke)	Clothes (Standard)	Coolers	Corn	Cross Country Jumps	Cushion Web	Damp Hay	Disposable A.V Liners	Disposable Equitainer	Driving Collars	Driving Harness	Dust Free Shavings	Electric Fencing	Exercise Equipment	Farm Equipment	Feed	Feed Racks	Feed Supplements	Fencing	Fertilisers	Fire Baskets	Flooring Supply (Arenas)	Fly Repellent	Gallops	Gates	Girths	Gloves	Mail Order Facilities
VAUX BROS, Pontefract (YH14670)																												●												●												
YORKSHIRE EQUESTRIAN FLOORING, Leeds (YH15920)					●																																															
IRELAND																																																				
COUNTY CARLOW																																																				
BEHAN D & E, Carlow (YH01196)																																														●						
COUNTY CLARE																																																				
MURPHY CLIPPING SV, O'Briansbridge (YH09953)																							●																													
COUNTY CORK																																																				
BEE WOODCRAFT, Ardmore (YH01160)																																											●									
BUCAS, Cork (YH02184)																											●																							●		
COUNTY DUBLIN																																																				
COLEMANS OF SANDYFORD, Dublin (YH03166)						●	●					●				●										●																								●		●
EQUESTRIAN DIRECT SALES, Dublin (YH04699)								●				●											●			●																										
COUNTY KERRY																																																				
BRIDLES & BITS, Tralee (YH01893)						●						●				●										●																●										
COUNTY KILDARE																																																				
IRISH EQUESTRIAN PRODUCTS, Kildare (YH07493)												●											●			●												●														●
COUNTY KILKENNY																																																				
EUROFARM, Kilkenny (YH04898)												●				●										●																									●	
COUNTY LIMERICK																																																				
COUNTRY DRESSER, Adare (YH03403)												●														●																										
COUNTY LOUTH																																																				
HORSEWARE, Dundalk (YH07177)																										●																										
COUNTY MAYO																																																				
ABRAM, DAVID, Bohola (YH00135)																●																																				
COUNTY MEATH																																																				
CLARKE'S SPORTSDEN, Navan (YH02978)												●														●																										
COUNTY ROSCOMMON																																																				
MURPHY EQUESTRIAN, Strokestown (YH09954)																								●																												●
COUNTY WESTMEATH																																																				
TALLY HO, Athlone (YH13838)												●														●																										

www.hccyourhorse.com

Products Supplied
A - G

by Country by County	Air Conditioning	Air Purifiers	Aloe Vera	Back Supports	Bedding	Bits	Body Protectors	Books	Boot Holders	Boot Jacks	Boot Scrapers	Boots	Boxes	Breeding Equipment	Breeding Supplies	Bridles	Bridlework	Carriages	Carts	CD's	Cleaning Equipment	Cleaning Supplies	Clippers	Closed Circuit TV	Clothes (Bespoke)	Clothes (Standard)	Coolers	Corn	Cross Country Jumps	Cushion Web	Damp Hay	Disposable A.V Liners	Disposable Equitainer	Driving Collars	Driving Harness	Dust Free Shavings	Electric Fencing	Exercise Equipment	Farm Equipment	Feed	Feed Racks	Feed Supplements	Fencing	Fertilisers	Fire Baskets	Flooring Supply (Arenas)	Fly Repellent	Gallops	Gates	Girths	Gloves	Mail Order Facilities
WEBBWEAR, Multyfarnham (YH15036)																					●																															
COUNTY WICKLOW																																																				
EQUESTRIAN LEATHERS, Bray (YH04704)				●			●					●										●																														
NORTHERN IRELAND																																																				
COUNTY ANTRIM																																																				
ANDREWS MILLING, Belfast (YH00396)																												●												●												
BADMINTON HORSE FEEDS, Lisburn (YH00782)																												●												●												
BLAIR, R & K, Ballyclare (YH01513)																												●												●												
BRACKEN EQUESTRIAN, Belfast (YH01736)												●														●																										
BROWN, C N, Lisburn (YH02103)																		●																																		
CHRISTIE & JEFFERS, Ballymoney (YH02887)																												●												●												
COUNTRY CLASSICS, Lisburn (YH03399)												●														●																										
D P MULHOLLAND & SONS, Crumlin (YH03803)																												●												●												
DOAGH FARM FEEDS, Doagh (YH04147)																												●												●		●										
EQUESTRIAN FARM FEEDS, Lisburn (YH04702)																												●												●												
GRANGE EQUESTRIAN, Newtownabbey (YH05986)					●																		●														●			●		●										
JOHN THOMPSON & SONS, Belfast (YH07814)																												●												●												
JOLLYES, Lisburn (YH07855)																												●												●												
JOLLYES, Ballymena (YH07853)																												●												●												
JOLLYES, Glengormley (YH07854)																												●												●												
MILLAR FEEDS, Ballymena (YH09591)																												●												●												
OLD MILL, Carrickfergus (YH10465)												●														●																										
ROSS LODGE SADDLERY, Ballymena (YH12117)																												●												●												
ROWAN RIDING WEAR, Lisburn (YH12155)																												●												●												
T K S, Ballymena (YH13756)																												●												●												
COUNTY ARMAGH																																																				
ANNAGHMORE SADDLERY, Craigavon (YH00451)												●											●																	●												
FANE VALLEY, Armagh (YH05043)																												●												●												
HOWARD ALLEN SEEDS, Craigavon (YH07215)					●																							●												●												
LIME PARK EQUESTRIAN, Craigavon (YH08626)																																								●												
PREMIER SADDLERY, Armagh (YH11349)												●											●			●																										

Products Supplied

A - G

by Country by County

by Country by County	Air Conditioning	Air Purifiers	Aloe Vera	Back Supports	Bedding	Bits	Body Protectors	Books	Boot Holders	Boot Jacks	Boot Scrapers	Boots	Boxes	Breeding Equipment	Breeding Supplies	Bridles	Bridlework
STINSON, J D, Armagh (YH13470)												●					
COUNTY DOWN																	
ANNAHILT SADDLERY, Hillsborough (YH00452)																	
BALL BROTHERS, Dromara (YH00847)																	
BOOKLINE, Downpatrick (YH01630)								●									
D B S FARM SUPPLIES, Dromara (YH03779)																	
DRUM-A-HOY, Saintfield (YH04284)																	
FANE VALLEY, Banbridge (YH05044)																	
FAWCETT, GEORGE, Ballynahinch (YH05108)					●								●				
FEEDWELL ANIMAL FOOD, Castlewellan (YH05126)																	
GENERAL STORE, Ballynahinch (YH05702)																	
HOLMESTEAD SADDLERY, Downpatrick (YH06981)						●		●				●	●				
JAMES GLOVER & SONS, Crossgar (YH07669)																	
JOLLYES, Bangor (YH07856)																	
JOLLYES, Newry (YH07857)																	
KIDD SADDLERY, Banbridge (YH08120)																	
M & B EQUESTRIAN, Killinchy (YH08943)																	
O'HARES, Castlewellan (YH10444)																	
OLD MANOR MILL, Newtownards (YH10462)																	
P LAVELLE & SONS, Newry (YH10651)																	
R W TOASE, Newry (YH11569)																	
SHIELDS, THOMAS, Newry (YH12742)																	
SOUTH ARMAGH FARMING, Newry (YH13076)																	
SOUTHDOWN FEEDS, Rathfriland (YH13135)																	
WATSONS FARM FEEDS, Downpatrick (YH14996)																	
WEIR, Ballynahinch (YH15051)					●												
COUNTY FERMANAGH																	
JOLLYES, Eniskillen (YH07858)																	
COUNTY LONDONDERRY																	
ARCHIBALD, Coleraine (YH00499)																	
ARDMORE STABLES, Londonderry (YH00511)																	
BLAKES EQUESTRIAN, Coleraine (YH01521)																	

by Country by County	Carriages	Carts	CD's	Cleaning Equipment	Cleaning Supplies	Clippers	Closed Circuit TV	Clothes (Bespoke)	Clothes (Standard)	Coolers	Corn	Cross Country Jumps	Cushion Web	Damp Hay	Disposable A.V Liners	Disposable Equitainer	Driving Collars
STINSON, J D, Armagh (YH13470)									●								
COUNTY DOWN																	
ANNAHILT SADDLERY, Hillsborough (YH00452)											●						
BALL BROTHERS, Dromara (YH00847)											●						
BOOKLINE, Downpatrick (YH01630)																	
D B S FARM SUPPLIES, Dromara (YH03779)											●						
DRUM-A-HOY, Saintfield (YH04284)											●						
FANE VALLEY, Banbridge (YH05044)											●						
FAWCETT, GEORGE, Ballynahinch (YH05108)	●	●															
FEEDWELL ANIMAL FOOD, Castlewellan (YH05126)											●						
GENERAL STORE, Ballynahinch (YH05702)											●						
HOLMESTEAD SADDLERY, Downpatrick (YH06981)						●			●								
JAMES GLOVER & SONS, Crossgar (YH07669)											●						
JOLLYES, Bangor (YH07856)											●						
JOLLYES, Newry (YH07857)											●						
KIDD SADDLERY, Banbridge (YH08120)											●						
M & B EQUESTRIAN, Killinchy (YH08943)											●						
O'HARES, Castlewellan (YH10444)											●						
OLD MANOR MILL, Newtownards (YH10462)											●						
P LAVELLE & SONS, Newry (YH10651)											●						
R W TOASE, Newry (YH11569)											●						
SHIELDS, THOMAS, Newry (YH12742)											●						
SOUTH ARMAGH FARMING, Newry (YH13076)											●						
SOUTHDOWN FEEDS, Rathfriland (YH13135)											●						
WATSONS FARM FEEDS, Downpatrick (YH14996)											●						
WEIR, Ballynahinch (YH15051)											●						
COUNTY FERMANAGH																	
JOLLYES, Eniskillen (YH07858)											●						
COUNTY LONDONDERRY																	
ARCHIBALD, Coleraine (YH00499)											●						
ARDMORE STABLES, Londonderry (YH00511)																	
BLAKES EQUESTRIAN, Coleraine (YH01521)								●									●

by Country by County	Driving Harness	Dust Free Shavings	Electric Fencing	Exercise Equipment	Farm Equipment	Feed	Feed Racks	Feed Supplements	Fencing	Fertilisers	Fire Baskets	Flooring Supply (Arenas)	Fly Repellent	Gallops	Gates	Girths	Gloves	Mail Order Facilities
STINSON, J D, Armagh (YH13470)																		
COUNTY DOWN																		
ANNAHILT SADDLERY, Hillsborough (YH00452)						●												
BALL BROTHERS, Dromara (YH00847)						●												
BOOKLINE, Downpatrick (YH01630)																		
D B S FARM SUPPLIES, Dromara (YH03779)						●												
DRUM-A-HOY, Saintfield (YH04284)						●												
FANE VALLEY, Banbridge (YH05044)						●												
FAWCETT, GEORGE, Ballynahinch (YH05108)									●									
FEEDWELL ANIMAL FOOD, Castlewellan (YH05126)						●												
GENERAL STORE, Ballynahinch (YH05702)						●												
HOLMESTEAD SADDLERY, Downpatrick (YH06981)								●										
JAMES GLOVER & SONS, Crossgar (YH07669)						●												
JOLLYES, Bangor (YH07856)						●												
JOLLYES, Newry (YH07857)						●												
KIDD SADDLERY, Banbridge (YH08120)						●												
M & B EQUESTRIAN, Killinchy (YH08943)						●												
O'HARES, Castlewellan (YH10444)						●												
OLD MANOR MILL, Newtownards (YH10462)						●												
P LAVELLE & SONS, Newry (YH10651)						●												
R W TOASE, Newry (YH11569)						●												
SHIELDS, THOMAS, Newry (YH12742)						●												
SOUTH ARMAGH FARMING, Newry (YH13076)						●												
SOUTHDOWN FEEDS, Rathfriland (YH13135)						●												
WATSONS FARM FEEDS, Downpatrick (YH14996)						●												
WEIR, Ballynahinch (YH15051)						●		●										
COUNTY FERMANAGH																		
JOLLYES, Eniskillen (YH07858)						●												
COUNTY LONDONDERRY																		
ARCHIBALD, Coleraine (YH00499)						●												
ARDMORE STABLES, Londonderry (YH00511)						●												
BLAKES EQUESTRIAN, Coleraine (YH01521)	●																	

www.hccyourhorse.com

Products Supplied
A - G

by Country by County	Air Conditioning	Air Purifiers	Aloe Vera	Back Supports	Bedding	Bits	Body Protectors	Books	Boot Holders	Boot Jacks	Boot Scrapers	Boots	Boxes	Breeding Equipment	Breeding Supplies	Bridles	Bridlework	Carriages	Carts	CD's	Cleaning Equipment	Cleaning Supplies	Clippers	Closed Circuit TV	Clothes (Bespoke)	Clothes (Standard)	Coolers	Corn	Cross Country Jumps	Cushion Web	Damp Hay	Disposable A.V Liners	Disposable Equitainer	Driving Collars	Driving Harness	Dust Free Shavings	Electric Fencing	Exercise Equipment	Farm Equipment	Feed	Feed Racks	Feed Supplements	Fencing	Fertilisers	Fire Baskets	Flooring Supply (Arenas)	Fly Repellent	Gallops	Gates	Girths	Gloves	Mail Order Facilities
CORNDALE ANIMAL FEEDS, Limavady (YH03322)																												●												●												
DEENY'S, Claudy (YH04019)																												●												●												
DRUMSAMNEY EQUESTRIAN CTRE, Magherafelt (YH04292)																		●																																		
HAVEN SADDLERY, Magherafelt (YH06539)												●													●	●														●		●										●
MARSH KYFE RIDING SCHOOL, Magherafelt (YH09186)																		●	●																																	
QUIGLEY, H D, Dungiven (YH11497)																												●												●												
STEWART ROBINSON, Limavady (YH13456)																												●												●												
COUNTY TYRONE																																																				
BLUEGRASS HORSE FEEDS, Dungannon (YH01573)																												●												●												
CLEMENTS, D, Augher (YH03016)																												●												●												
DONNELLY & SON, Fintona (YH04187)																												●												●												
HACKETTS, Omagh (YH06252)																												●												●												
LECKPATRICK AGRCLTRL SVS, Strabane (YH08514)																												●												●												
MCLERNON, P, Dungannon (YH09391)																												●												●												
OMAGH, Omagh (YH10506)																												●												●												
SCOTLAND																																																				
ABERDEEN (CITY OF)																																																				
COUNTRY WAYS, Aberdeen (YH03436)												●														●																										
HAPPY HORSE, Aberdeen (YH06399)																												●												●												
HAYFIELD RIDING, Aberdeen (YH06578)																									●	●																										
SESSNIE EQUESTRIAN, Aberdeen (YH12637)																												●												●												
ABERDEENSHIRE																																																				
AUCHENHAMPER SUFFOLK, Banff (YH00660)																												●												●												
FEEDMIX, Turriff (YH05123)																												●												●		●										
GILKHORN FARM SADDLERY, Peterhead (YH05767)																												●												●												
HARBRO FARM SALES, Inverurie (YH06405)																												●												●												
HARBRO FARM SALES, Turriff (YH06404)																												●												●												
MILL OF URAS EQUESTRIAN, Stonehaven (YH09583)					●							●											●																	●		●										
MILLER PLANT, Inverurie (YH09601)												●											●			●		●												●												
NORTH EASTERN FARMERS, Inverurie (YH10258)																												●												●		●										
NORVITE, Insch (YH10333)																												●											●	●		●										
SKINNER, GEORGE M, Inverurie (YH12875)																		●																																		

Products Supplied
A - G

by Country by County

Company	Air Conditioning	Air Purifiers	Aloe Vera	Back Supports	Bedding	Bits	Body Protectors	Books	Boot Holders	Boot Jacks	Boot Scrapers	Boots	Boxes	Breeding Equipment	Breeding Supplies	Bridles	Bridlework	Carriages	Carts	CD's	Cleaning Equipment	Cleaning Supplies	Clippers	Closed Circuit TV	Clothes (Bespoke)	Clothes (Standard)	Coolers	Corn	Cross Country Jumps	Cushion Web	Damp Hay	Disposable A.V Liners	Disposable Equitainer	Driving Collars	Driving Harness	Dust Free Shavings	Electric Fencing	Exercise Equipment	Farm Equipment	Feed	Feed Racks	Feed Supplements	Fencing	Fertilisers	Fire Baskets	Flooring Supply (Arenas)	Fly Repellent	Gallops	Gates	Girths	Gloves	Mail Order Facilities
TACK SHOP, Banchory (YH13810)																											●											●												
TOWNS & CARNIE, Inverurie (YH14297)																											●											●												
ANGUS																																																				
BLACKLITE, Dundee (YH01486)																																																●			
FEEDMIX, Kirriemuir (YH05124)																											●											●		●										
KIRRIEMUIR HORSE SUPPLIES, Kirriemuir (YH08240)					●			●				●											●			●														●		●	●									
MACDONALD, A R, Kirriemuir (YH08987)														●	●																																					
NORTH EASTERN FARMERS, Forfar (YH10259)																											●											●												
PATHHEAD STABLES, Kirriemuir (YH10821)					●			●				●											●			●														●		●	●									
ARGYLL AND BUTE																																																				
BALLIVICAR FARM, Isle Of Islay (YH00863)					●																																															
ISLAY FARMERS, Isle Of Islay (YH07523)																											●											●												
TACKLE & TACK, Oban (YH13818)					●			●				●			●						●		●			●		●						●	●			●	●	●		●										●
WHAT EVERY HORSE WANTS, Helensburgh (YH15266)								●																		●																										●
AYRSHIRE (EAST)																																																				
FERRIE, J & A, Newmilns (YH05169)																										●																										
JAMES GIBB, Galston (YH07667)																											●											●		●										
ROWALLAN ACTIVITY CTRE, Kilmarnock (YH12152)					●																																	●														
SOMERVILLE, J & M, Kilmarnock (YH13066)																											●											●												
WALKER & TEMPLETON, Kilmarnock (YH14845)																											●											●												
AYRSHIRE (SOUTH)																																																				
AYRSHIRE EQUITATION CTRE, Ayr (YH00704)												●														●																										
CROCKET EQUESTRIAN, Ayr (YH03606)												●																																								
OTTERSWICK, Mauchine (YH10581)								●						●	●																																					●
CLACKMANNANSHIRE																																																				
E & S FEEDS, Tillicoultry (YH04394)																											●											●												
MACKIE, JAMES A, Alloa (YH09006)																					●																															
DUMFRIES AND GALLOWAY																																																				
DOUGLAS, JOHN L, Newton Stewart (YH04214)																																							●										●			
DUNLOPS, Troqueer (YH04345)																																										●										
GEE GEE'S, Dumfries (YH05690)					●			●				●								●					●	●														●		●	●									●
MCKENZIE AGRICULTURAL, Ruthwell (YH09383)																											●											●												

Products Supplied
A - G

by Country by County

	Air Conditioning	Air Purifiers	Aloe Vera	Back Supports	Bedding	Bits	Body Protectors	Books	Boot Holders	Boot Jacks	Boot Scrapers	Boots	Boxes	Breeding Equipment	Breeding Supplies	Bridles	Bridlework	Carriages	Carts	CD's	Cleaning Equipment	Cleaning Supplies	Clippers	Closed Circuit TV	Clothes (Bespoke)	Clothes (Standard)
ROBERT THORNE, Annan (YH11944)					●																					
W C F COUNTRY CTRE, Castle Douglas (YH14754)																										
WM MURRAY FARMCARE, Dumfries (YH15642)																										
EDINBURGH (CITY OF)																										
DRUM FEEDS, Edinburgh (YH04280)																										
DRUM MOORE FARM SHOP, Edinburgh (YH04281)																										
STIRLINGSHIRE SADDLERY, Edinburgh (YH13474)								●				●											●			●
FALKIRK																										
COUNTRY FEEDS LARBERT, Larbert (YH03408)					●																					
D H F ANIMAL FEEDS, Airth (YH03784)																										
FIFE																										
ARMSTRONG, I & E, Falkland (YH00547)																										
EUROPA, Lochgelly (YH04904)																										
REMUS EQUESTRIAN, Lochgelly (YH11752)													●													
RODGER, J & T, Cupar (YH12046)																										
SALTIRE STABLES, Cupar (YH12394)																								●		
GLASGOW (CITY OF)																										
BUSBY EQUITATION CTRE, Busby (YH02302)								●												●			●			●
EVERYTHING EQUESTRIAN, Busby (YH04957)								●												●						●
HORSE & HOUND FEED SUPPLIES, Milngavie (YH07091)																										
JET SET, Glasgow (YH07763)																										●
WM ALEXANDER & SON, Glasgow (YH15638)																										
HIGHLANDS																										
BITS 'N' BOBS, Caithness (YH01458)																										
CROILA STABLES, Newtonmore (YH03627)																		●								
FOXHOLE LIVERY STABLE, Beauly (YH05436)					●																					
N D S ANIMAL FEEDS, Nairn (YH09988)																										
NORTHFIELD HORSE SUPPLIES, Invergordon (YH10313)																										
ORMISTON, EWAN C, Kingussie (YH10549)																		●								
RADDERY EQUINE, Fortrose (YH11593)								●									●								●	
SEAFORTH SADDLERS, Inverness (YH12586)								●				●											●			●
LANARKSHIRE (NORTH)																										

	Coolers	Corn	Cross Country Jumps	Cushion Web	Damp Hay	Disposable A.V Liners	Disposable Equitainer	Driving Collars	Driving Harness	Dust Free Shavings	Electric Fencing	Exercise Equipment	Farm Equipment	Feed	Feed Racks	Feed Supplements	Fencing	Fertilisers	Fire Baskets	Flooring Supply (Arenas)	Fly Repellent	Gallops	Gates	Girths	Gloves	Mail Order Facilities
ROBERT THORNE, Annan (YH11944)		●												●		●		●								
W C F COUNTRY CTRE, Castle Douglas (YH14754)		●												●												
WM MURRAY FARMCARE, Dumfries (YH15642)		●												●												
EDINBURGH (CITY OF)																										
DRUM FEEDS, Edinburgh (YH04280)		●												●												
DRUM MOORE FARM SHOP, Edinburgh (YH04281)														●												
STIRLINGSHIRE SADDLERY, Edinburgh (YH13474)												●														
FALKIRK																										
COUNTRY FEEDS LARBERT, Larbert (YH03408)		●												●		●										
D H F ANIMAL FEEDS, Airth (YH03784)		●												●												
FIFE																										
ARMSTRONG, I & E, Falkland (YH00547)		●												●												
EUROPA, Lochgelly (YH04904)																										●
REMUS EQUESTRIAN, Lochgelly (YH11752)																										
RODGER, J & T, Cupar (YH12046)		●												●												
SALTIRE STABLES, Cupar (YH12394)																										
GLASGOW (CITY OF)																										
BUSBY EQUITATION CTRE, Busby (YH02302)																										
EVERYTHING EQUESTRIAN, Busby (YH04957)																										
HORSE & HOUND FEED SUPPLIES, Milngavie (YH07091)		●												●												
JET SET, Glasgow (YH07763)																										
WM ALEXANDER & SON, Glasgow (YH15638)		●												●												
HIGHLANDS																										
BITS 'N' BOBS, Caithness (YH01458)		●												●												
CROILA STABLES, Newtonmore (YH03627)													●													
FOXHOLE LIVERY STABLE, Beauly (YH05436)																										
N D S ANIMAL FEEDS, Nairn (YH09988)		●												●												
NORTHFIELD HORSE SUPPLIES, Invergordon (YH10313)		●												●												
ORMISTON, EWAN C, Kingussie (YH10549)													●													
RADDERY EQUINE, Fortrose (YH11593)												●														●
SEAFORTH SADDLERS, Inverness (YH12586)												●				●										
LANARKSHIRE (NORTH)																										

Products Supplied
A - G

by Country by County

Company	Air Conditioning	Air Purifiers	Aloe Vera	Back Supports	Bedding	Bits	Body Protectors	Books	Boot Holders	Boot Jacks	Boot Scrapers	Boots	Boxes	Breeding Equipment	Breeding Supplies	Bridles	Bridlework	Carriages	Carts	CD's	Cleaning Equipment	Cleaning Supplies	Clippers	Closed Circuit TV	Clothes (Bespoke)	Clothes (Standard)
CLIPPETY CLOP, Cumbernauld (YH03048)																										
KIRK RD SMIDDY, Shotts (YH08230)																										
RED ROSETTE PET PRODUCTS, Airdrie (YH11705)																										
LANARKSHIRE (SOUTH)																										
COUNTRY FEEDS, Blantyre (YH03406)																										
GALLOWAY & MACLEOD, Larkhall (YH05625)																										
STONEHOUSE SADDLERY/PET CTRE, Stonehouse (YH13517)																										
TOP CROP ORGANICS, Law (YH14234)																										
VITAL MAX, Forth (YH14735)																										
LOTHIAN (EAST)																										
J S MAIN & SONS, Haddington (YH07617)								●				●									●		●			●
LOTHIAN (MID)																										
BOWLEA TRAILERS, Penicuik (YH01713)																										
R H MILLER, Dalkeith (YH11541)					●							●														●
LOTHIAN (WEST)																										
BERTRAM, IAN, Broxburn (YH01321)																										
CRAIGHEAD, Fauldhouse (YH03553)																		●								
DAVID THOMSON, Livingston (YH03924)																										
GRANGE SADDLERY, West Calder (YH05996)												●														●
WESTER WOODSIDE FARM FEEDS, Linlithgow (YH15191)																										
MORAY																										
A & I SUPPLIES, Elgin (YH00011)																										
GREENFIELDS SADDLERY, Elgin (YH06085)					●			●				●									●		●		●	●
PALS, Cullen (YH10694)																										
ORKNEY ISLES																										
HAMISH MACLEAN FARM PRODUCTS, Kirkwall (YH06355)																										
SUNNYBRAE FEEDS, Kirkwall (YH13645)																										
PERTH AND KINROSS																										
BREMNER, BLACK, Aberfeldy (YH01834)																										
DAVIDSONS VETNRY SUPPLIES, Blairgowrie (YH03931)																										
EQUI-CARE, Perth (YH04736)																										●
GLEN EAGLES EQUESTRIAN, Auchterarder (YH05825)																		●								

Company	Coolers	Corn	Cross Country Jumps	Cushion Web	Damp Hay	Disposable A.V Liners	Disposable Equitainer	Driving Collars	Driving Harness	Dust Free Shavings	Electric Fencing	Exercise Equipment	Farm Equipment	Feed	Feed Racks	Feed Supplements	Fencing	Fertilisers	Fire Baskets	Flooring Supply (Arenas)	Fly Repellent	Gallops	Gates	Girths	Gloves	Mail Order Facilities
CLIPPETY CLOP, Cumbernauld (YH03048)		●												●												
KIRK RD SMIDDY, Shotts (YH08230)															●											
RED ROSETTE PET PRODUCTS, Airdrie (YH11705)		●												●												
LANARKSHIRE (SOUTH)																										
COUNTRY FEEDS, Blantyre (YH03406)		●												●												
GALLOWAY & MACLEOD, Larkhall (YH05625)		●												●												
STONEHOUSE SADDLERY/PET CTRE, Stonehouse (YH13517)		●												●												
TOP CROP ORGANICS, Law (YH14234)																●										
VITAL MAX, Forth (YH14735)																●										
LOTHIAN (EAST)																										
J S MAIN & SONS, Haddington (YH07617)													●			●	●									●
LOTHIAN (MID)																										
BOWLEA TRAILERS, Penicuik (YH01713)																	●						●			
R H MILLER, Dalkeith (YH11541)														●		●										
LOTHIAN (WEST)																										
BERTRAM, IAN, Broxburn (YH01321)		●												●												
CRAIGHEAD, Fauldhouse (YH03553)																										
DAVID THOMSON, Livingston (YH03924)		●												●												
GRANGE SADDLERY, West Calder (YH05996)																										
WESTER WOODSIDE FARM FEEDS, Linlithgow (YH15191)		●												●												
MORAY																										
A & I SUPPLIES, Elgin (YH00011)		●												●												
GREENFIELDS SADDLERY, Elgin (YH06085)									●					●		●										●
PALS, Cullen (YH10694)		●												●												
ORKNEY ISLES																										
HAMISH MACLEAN FARM PRODUCTS, Kirkwall (YH06355)		●												●												
SUNNYBRAE FEEDS, Kirkwall (YH13645)		●												●												
PERTH AND KINROSS																										
BREMNER, BLACK, Aberfeldy (YH01834)		●												●												
DAVIDSONS VETNRY SUPPLIES, Blairgowrie (YH03931)		●												●												
EQUI-CARE, Perth (YH04736)			●																							
GLEN EAGLES EQUESTRIAN, Auchterarder (YH05825)									●																	

Products Supplied
A - G

by Country by County	Air Conditioning	Air Purifiers	Aloe Vera	Back Supports	Bedding	Bits	Body Protectors	Books	Boot Holders	Boot Jacks	Boot Scrapers	Boots	Boxes	Breeding Equipment	Breeding Supplies	Bridles	Bridlework	Carriages	Carts	CD's	Cleaning Equipment	Cleaning Supplies	Clippers	Closed Circuit TV	Clothes (Bespoke)	Clothes (Standard)	Coolers	Corn	Cross Country Jumps	Cushion Web	Damp Hay	Disposable A.V Liners	Disposable Equitainer	Driving Collars	Driving Harness	Dust Free Shavings	Electric Fencing	Exercise Equipment	Farm Equipment	Feed	Feed Racks	Feed Supplements	Fencing	Fertilisers	Fire Baskets	Flooring Supply (Arenas)	Fly Repellent	Gallops	Gates	Girths	Gloves	Mail Order Facilities
MCCASH'S, Perth (YH09326)												●														●		●												●		●		●								
NATURAL APPROACH, Bankfoot (YH10051)								●																																												
NORMILE, LUCY, Glenfarg (YH10242)					●																																															
SHETLAND PONY STUD BOOK SOC, Perth (YH12736)								●																																												●
TAINSH, W, Cromrie (YH13822)																												●												●												
RENFREWSHIRE																																																				
RIVERBANK POULTRY, Bridge Of Weir (YH11918)																												●												●												
T F R C, Lochwinnoch (YH13738)																												●												●												
SCOTTISH BORDERS																																																				
A C BURN, Jedburgh (YH00022)					●							●											●			●		●												●		●							●			
A J B SPENCE & SON, Eyemouth (YH00037)																												●												●												
BROKEN SPOKE, West Linton (YH02021)																		●																																		
J HOGARTH, Kelso (YH07589)																												●												●												
MCNAB SADDLERS, Selkirk (YH09396)												●					●				●		●		●	●		●							●					●		●										●
MCNAB SADDLERS, Kelso (YH09397)												●					●				●		●		●	●		●							●					●		●										●
R H MILLER, Peebles (YH11542)					●																					●														●		●										
R H MILLER AGRICULTURAL, Hawick (YH11543)																												●												●												
TEVIOT TOWN & COUNTRY, Hawick (YH13967)																												●												●												
WELLS, F & H, Galashiels (YH15083)																												●												●												
STIRLING																																																				
EASTERHILL, Gartmore (YH04495)																												●												●												
GLENSIDE ORGANICS, Throsk (YH05843)																																										●										
HENDRY, JAMES, Stirling (YH06669)																																																	●			
W C F COUNTRY CTRE, Kildean (YH14755)																												●												●												

Products Supplied
A - G
by Country by County

	Air Conditioning	Air Purifiers	Aloe Vera	Back Supports	Bedding	Bits	Body Protectors	Books	Boot Holders	Boot Jacks	Boot Scrapers	Boots	Boxes	Breeding Equipment	Breeding Supplies	Bridles	Bridlework	Carriages	Carts	CD's	Cleaning Equipment	Cleaning Supplies	Clippers	Closed Circuit TV	Clothes (Bespoke)	Clothes (Standard)	Coolers	Corn	Cross Country Jumps	Cushion Web	Damp Hay	Disposable A.V Liners	Disposable Equitainer	Driving Collars	Driving Harness	Dust Free Shavings	Electric Fencing	Exercise Equipment	Farm Equipment	Feed	Feed Racks	Feed Supplements	Fencing	Fertilisers	Fire Baskets	Flooring Supply (Arenas)	Fly Repellent	Gallops	Gates	Girths	Gloves	Mail Order Facilities
WALES																																																				
BLAENAU GWENT																																																				
DAVIES RIDING BOOTS, Ebbw Vale (YH03935)												●																																								●
WARD, R & S, Newport (YH14905)																												●												●												
BRIDGEND																																																				
COUNTRYWIDE STORES, Bridgend (YH03449)																												●												●												
E K M EQUESTRIAN, Bridgend (YH04411)																							●																													
HARVESTERS FARM SUPPLIES, Bridgend (YH06511)																												●												●												
WALTERS PET & GARDEN STORES, Bridgend (YH14885)																												●												●												
WINNERS ANIMAL PET SHOP, Pyle (YH15588)																												●												●												
CAERPHILLY																																																				
EXPRESS PET SUPPLIES, Hengoed (YH04973)																												●												●												
CARMARTHENSHIRE																																																				
AUSDAN STUD, Lampeter (YH00665)																		●																																		
BERRY ANIMAL FEEDS, Kidwelly (YH01314)																												●												●												
CARMARTHEN & PUMSAINT FARMERS, Kidwelly (YH02551)																												●												●												
CARMARTHEN & PUMSAINT FARMERS, Whitland (YH02557)																												●												●												
CARMARTHEN & PUMSAINT FARMERS, St Clears (YH02556)																												●												●												
CARMARTHEN & PUMSAINT FARMERS, Llandeilo (YH02555)																												●												●												
CARMARTHEN & PUMSAINT FARMERS, Carmarthen (YH02554)																												●												●												
CARMARTHEN & PUMSAINT FARMERS, Llanybydder (YH02552)																												●												●												
CARMARTHEN & PUMSAINT FARMERS, Carmarthen (YH02550)																												●												●												
CARMARTHEN & PUMSAINT FARMERS, Llandeilo (YH02547)					●																							●												●												
CARMARTHEN & PUMSAINT FARMERS, Carmarthen (YH02549)																												●												●												
CARMARTHEN & PUMSAINT FARMERS, Llandovery (YH02548)																												●												●												
CARMARTHEN & PUMSAINT FARMERS, Llangadog (YH02553)																												●												●												
CLYNDERWEN & CARDIGAN, Whitland (YH03083)																												●												●												
CLYNDERWEN & CARDIGANSHIRE, Newcastle Emlyn (YH03087)																												●												●												
DALGETY AGRCLTRL, Carmarthen (YH03834)																												●												●												
EVANS, M V, Carmarthen (YH04927)					●																																			●												
HORSE CTRE, Llandysul (YH07115)																												●												●												

Products Supplied
A - G

by Country by County

by Country by County	Air Conditioning	Air Purifiers	Aloe Vera	Back Supports	Bedding	Bits	Body Protectors	Books	Boot Holders	Boot Jacks	Boot Scrapers	Boots	Boxes	Breeding Equipment	Breeding Supplies	Bridles	Bridlework	Carriages	Carts	CD's	Cleaning Equipment	Cleaning Supplies	Clippers	Closed Circuit TV	Clothes (Bespoke)	Clothes (Standard)
J BIBBY AGRICULTURE, Carmarthen (YH07567)																										
MORGAN EQUINE, Llandeilo (YH09794)																										●
PENCADER STUD, Pencader (YH10928)																										
PLAS EQUESTRIAN, Carmarthen (YH11164)														●	●											
STALLIONS AT TACKEXCHANGE, Llanelli (YH13351)																							●			●
TACK EXCHANGE, Llanelli (YH13787)												●											●			●
CEREDIGION																										
BHS WALES, Aberystwyth (YH01388)								●																		
CARMARTHEN & PUMSAINT FARMERS, Pontardulais (YH02558)																										
CLYNDERWEN & CARDIGAN, Lampeter (YH03084)																										
CLYNDERWEN & CARDIGANSHIRE, Aberystwyth (YH03088)																										
CLYNDERWEN & CARDIGANSHIRE, Cardigan (YH03089)																										
CLYNDERWEN & CARDIGANSHIRE, Tregaron (YH03090)																										
ROGERS & TAYLOR, Aberystwyth (YH12056)												●														●
VALIENT SADDLERY, Cardigan (YH14646)												●											●			●
W D LEWIS & SON, Lampeter (YH14759)																										
CONWY																										
COLWYN TACK CTRE, Colwyn Bay (YH03208)																										
GWYN LEWIS FARM SUPPLIES, Abergele (YH06205)																										
PEN-Y-BINC FARM, Colwyn Bay (YH10964)																										
DENBIGHSHIRE																										
CORWEN & DISTRICT FARMERS, Corwen (YH03347)																										
GARTH-ROBERTS, GORDON, Denbigh (YH05663)																										
WYNNSTAY & CLWYD FARMERS, St Asaph (YH15874)												●														●
FLINTSHIRE																										
G REES AGRICULTURAL MERCHANTS, Mold (YH05596)																										
JOLLYES, Flint (YH07859)																										
LLONG MILL, Mold (YH08732)																										
T F S, Buckley (YH13739)					●							●														●
GLAMORGAN (VALE OF)																										
AYRES, JOHN, Cardiff (YH00702)												●														●
CARDIFF SPORTSGEAR, Cardiff (YH02532)												●														●

by Country by County	Coolers	Corn	Cross Country Jumps	Cushion Web	Damp Hay	Disposable A.V Liners	Disposable Equitainer	Driving Collars	Driving Harness	Dust Free Shavings	Electric Fencing	Exercise Equipment	Farm Equipment	Feed	Feed Racks	Feed Supplements	Fencing	Fertilisers	Fire Baskets	Flooring Supply (Arenas)	Fly Repellent	Gallops	Gates	Girths	Gloves	Mail Order Facilities
J BIBBY AGRICULTURE, Carmarthen (YH07567)		●												●												
MORGAN EQUINE, Llandeilo (YH09794)																										●
PENCADER STUD, Pencader (YH10928)														●												
PLAS EQUESTRIAN, Carmarthen (YH11164)								●	●			●														●
STALLIONS AT TACKEXCHANGE, Llanelli (YH13351)																										●
TACK EXCHANGE, Llanelli (YH13787)								●	●																	●
CEREDIGION																										
BHS WALES, Aberystwyth (YH01388)																										
CARMARTHEN & PUMSAINT FARMERS, Pontardulais (YH02558)		●												●												
CLYNDERWEN & CARDIGAN, Lampeter (YH03084)		●												●		●										
CLYNDERWEN & CARDIGANSHIRE, Aberystwyth (YH03088)		●												●		●										
CLYNDERWEN & CARDIGANSHIRE, Cardigan (YH03089)		●												●												
CLYNDERWEN & CARDIGANSHIRE, Tregaron (YH03090)		●												●												
ROGERS & TAYLOR, Aberystwyth (YH12056)		●												●		●										
VALIENT SADDLERY, Cardigan (YH14646)																										
W D LEWIS & SON, Lampeter (YH14759)		●												●												
CONWY																										
COLWYN TACK CTRE, Colwyn Bay (YH03208)		●												●												
GWYN LEWIS FARM SUPPLIES, Abergele (YH06205)		●												●												
PEN-Y-BINC FARM, Colwyn Bay (YH10964)		●												●												
DENBIGHSHIRE																										
CORWEN & DISTRICT FARMERS, Corwen (YH03347)		●												●												
GARTH-ROBERTS, GORDON, Denbigh (YH05663)		●												●												
WYNNSTAY & CLWYD FARMERS, St Asaph (YH15874)														●												
FLINTSHIRE																										
G REES AGRICULTURAL MERCHANTS, Mold (YH05596)		●												●												
JOLLYES, Flint (YH07859)		●												●												
LLONG MILL, Mold (YH08732)		●												●												
T F S, Buckley (YH13739)		●							●					●		●	●	●								
GLAMORGAN (VALE OF)																										
AYRES, JOHN, Cardiff (YH00702)		●												●												
CARDIFF SPORTSGEAR, Cardiff (YH02532)																										

Products Supplied
A - G

by Country by County

Company	Air Conditioning	Air Purifiers	Aloe Vera	Back Supports	Bedding	Bits	Body Protectors	Books	Boot Holders	Boot Jacks	Boot Scrapers	Boots	Boxes	Breeding Equipment	Breeding Supplies	Bridles	Bridlework	Carriages	Carts	CD's	Cleaning Equipment	Cleaning Supplies	Clippers	Closed Circuit TV	Clothes (Bespoke)	Clothes (Standard)	Coolers	Corn	Cross Country Jumps	Cushion Web	Damp Hay	Disposable A.V Liners	Disposable Equitainer	Driving Collars	Driving Harness	Dust Free Shavings	Electric Fencing	Exercise Equipment	Farm Equipment	Feed	Feed Racks	Feed Supplements	Fencing	Fertilisers	Fire Baskets	Flooring Supply (Arenas)	Fly Repellent	Gallops	Gates	Girths	Gloves	Mail Order Facilities
CIMLA TREKKING, Neath (YH02918)					●																		●												●					●		●										
CLARK OF DOWLAIS, Merthyr (YH02961)																												●												●												
CLYNDERWEN & CARDIGANSHIRE, Lladon (YH03091)																												●												●												
JOHN REES, Barry (YH07807)																												●												●												
VALLEY FEEDS, Merthyr Tydfil (YH14655)																												●												●												
GWYNEDD																																																				
BRONALLT, Caernarfon (YH02029)					●			●				●														●									●					●		●										
CLYNDERWEN & CARDIGAN, Llanbedr (YH03085)																												●												●												
CLYNDERWEN & CARDIGANSHIRE, Bala (YH03093)																												●												●												
CLYNDERWEN & CARDIGANSHIRE, Bala (YH03092)																												●												●												
DOLGELLAU FARMERS, Dolgellau (YH04168)																												●												●												
EIFIONYDD FARMERS, Pwllheli (YH04596)																												●												●		●										
EVANS, RHYS, Bangor (YH04931)																												●												●												
HERON BARN SADDLERY, Arthog (YH06709)																												●												●												
TACK & STITCH SADDLERY, Pwllheli (YH13777)																												●												●												
W H EVANS, Garndolbenmaen (YH14769)																												●												●												
ISLE OF ANGLESEY																																																				
A C G S EQUESTRIAN, Bodorgan (YH00025)																												●												●												
BIMEDA, Llangefni (YH01418)																																										●										
CLYNDERWEN & CARDIGANSHIRE, Gaerwen (YH03094)																												●												●												
DUFFY, J A & P, Llanfair (YH04319)																												●												●												
SHEAR EASE, Amlwch (YH12688)																							●																													●
MONMOUTHSHIRE																																																				
ABBOTT, Monmouth (YH00106)																												●												●												
CHEPSTOW SADDLERY, Chepstow (YH02809)								●				●											●			●														●		●										
COUNTRYWIDE STORES, Raglan (YH03462)																												●												●												
COUNTRYWIDE STORES, Chepstow (YH03461)																												●												●												
COUNTRYWIDE STORES, Abergavenny (YH03460)																												●												●												
JONES, R M, Abergavenny (YH07926)																												●												●												
NATURAL ANIMAL FEEDS, Raglan (YH10050)																																								●		●										
ROSS FEED, Monmouth (YH12115)																												●												●												
SPORTABAC, Abergavenny (YH13222)				●			●																																													

www.hccyourhorse.com

Products Supplied
A - G

by Country by County	Air Conditioning	Air Purifiers	Aloe Vera	Back Supports	Bedding	Bits	Body Protectors	Books	Boot Holders	Boot Jacks	Boot Scrapers	Boots	Boxes	Breeding Equipment	Breeding Supplies	Bridles	Bridlework	Carriages	Carts	CD's	Cleaning Equipment	Cleaning Supplies	Clippers	Closed Circuit TV	Clothes (Bespoke)	Clothes (Standard)	Coolers	Corn	Cross Country Jumps	Cushion Web	Damp Hay	Disposable A.V Liners	Disposable Equitainer	Driving Collars	Driving Harness	Dust Free Shavings	Electric Fencing	Exercise Equipment	Farm Equipment	Feed	Feed Racks	Feed Supplements	Fencing	Fertilisers	Fire Baskets	Flooring Supply (Arenas)	Fly Repellent	Gallops	Gates	Girths	Gloves	Mail Order Facilities
VILLAGE STORES, Monmouth (YH14721)																											●											●													
NEATH PORT TALBOT																																																				
R DAYCOCK & SON, Talbach (YH11529)																											●											●													
ZOAR HORSE & COUNTRY CTRE, Neath Port Talbot (YH15957)																											●											●													
NEWPORT																																																				
GWENT SADDLERY, Newport (YH06201)																											●											●													
N J CRIDDLE, Newport (YH09992)																											●											●													
NEWCOMBES HORSE & DOG SHOP, Newport (YH10134)																											●											●													
PEMBROKESHIRE																																																			
BOULSTON, Haverfordwest (YH01672)					●							●														●		●												●		●										
CASTLEMORRIS FEEDS, Haverfordwest (YH02645)																											●											●													
CLYNDERWEN & CARDIGAN, Johnston (YH03086)																											●											●													
CLYNDERWEN & CARDIGANSHIRE, Clynderwen (YH03095)																											●											●													
CLYNDERWEN & CARDIGANSHIRE, Narberth (YH03096)																											●											●													
CLYNDERWEN & CARDIGANSHIRE, Crymych (YH03097)																											●											●													
CLYNDERWEN & CARDIGANSHIRE, Tenby (YH03098)																											●											●													
PEGASUS, Haverfordwest (YH10902)																									●		●											●													●
PEMBROKESHIRE EQUESTRIAN, Haverfordwest (YH10919)								●				●								●	●				●	●																										●
POWYS																																																				
BROMPTON HALL, Montgomery (YH02025)					●			●				●											●		●	●														●		●										●
CANTREF, Brecon (YH02516)					●								●																											●												
CHILTERN CONNEMARA, Presteigne (YH02858)								●																																												●
CHOICE SADDLERY, Knighton (YH02876)												●				●					●		●			●																										
CLYNDERWEN & CARDIGANSHIRE, Machynlleth (YH03099)																											●											●													
COUNTRYWIDE STORES, Llandrindod Wells (YH03465)																											●											●													
COUNTRYWIDE STORES, Presteigne (YH03466)																											●											●													
COUNTRYWIDE STORES, Welshpool (YH03467)																											●											●													
CRADOC TACK, Brecon (YH03541)															●																																					
CROWE, C D, Montgomery (YH03677)																											●											●													
CWRT ISAF FARM, Crickhowell (YH03765)																																							●													
DALGETY AGRCLTRL, Knighton (YH03836)																											●											●													
HAY & BRECON FARMERS, Brecon (YH06560)																											●											●													

Products Supplied
A - G

by Country by County	Air Conditioning	Air Purifiers	Aloe Vera	Back Supports	Bedding	Bits	Body Protectors	Books	Boot Holders	Boot Jacks	Boot Scrapers	Boots	Boxes	Breeding Equipment	Breeding Supplies	Bridles	Bridlework	Carriages	Carts	CD's	Cleaning Equipment	Cleaning Supplies	Clippers	Closed Circuit TV	Clothes (Bespoke)	Clothes (Standard)	Coolers	Corn	Cross Country Jumps	Cushion Web	Damp Hay	Disposable A.V Liners	Disposable Equitainer	Driving Collars	Driving Harness	Dust Free Shavings	Electric Fencing	Exercise Equipment	Farm Equipment	Feed	Feed Racks	Feed Supplements	Fencing	Fertilisers	Fire Baskets	Flooring Supply (Arenas)	Fly Repellent	Gallops	Gates	Girths	Gloves	Mail Order Facilities
HAY & BRECON FARMERS, Builth Wells (YH06561)																												●												●												
HAY & BRECON FARMERS, Llandrindod Wells (YH06562)																												●												●												
HAY & BRECON FARMERS, Brecon (YH06559)																												●												●												
NICHOLLS, W, Crickhowell (YH10186)																												●												●												
R A OWEN & SONS, Llandinam (YH11513)																												●												●												
WYNNSTAY & CLWYD FARMERS, Llansanffraid (YH15875)												●														●														●												
RHONDDA CYNON TAFF																																																				
BOOTS & SADDLES, Tonypandy (YH01640)												●											●			●									●																	
DRYSGOED FARM FEEDS, Pontypridd (YH04302)																												●												●		●										
SWANSEA																																																				
CROSS STORES, Swansea (YH03653)																												●												●												
D MORGAN & SON, Swansea (YH03798)					●							●									●					●														●		●	●									
D MORGAN & SONS, Swansea (YH03799)																												●												●												
HORSE CTRE, Swansea (YH07116)												●														●		●												●												
SOUTH WALES CARRIAGE DRIVING, Swansea (YH13111)																		●	●																●																	
WEST WALES FOODS, Swansea (YH15168)																												●												●												
TORFAEN																																																				
CUNNINGHAM & REED, Cwmbran (YH03723)																												●												●												
PAPERSHRED, Cwmbran (YH10708)					●																																															
PETSTOP, Cwmbran (YH11033)																												●												●												
WREXHAM																																																				
ACRE HSE EQUESTRIAN, Wrexham (YH00158)												●											●			●																										●
BLINKERS EQUESTRIAN, Wrexham (YH01540)								●				●								●																																●
CHARLES OWEN, Wrexham (YH02757)							●																																												●	
N W F COUNTRYSTORE, Wrexham (YH10000)																												●												●												

Products Supplied
G - R

by Country by County

	Grain	Grooming Products	Half Chaps	Halters	Harness	Harness Racing Equipment	Hats	Hay	Hay Baskets	Hay Cratchers	Haylage	Head Collars	Heaters	Herbal Remedies	Herbs	Horse Boots	Horse Feeds	Horse Rugs	Horsebox Accessories	Horsebox Equipment	Horseboxes	Immune Support (Respiratory)	Immune Support (S. P. V.Synd.)	Insoles	Insurance	Ironmongery
ENGLAND																										
BATH & SOMERSET (NORTH EAST)																										
CANADA HAY, Bath (YH02494)								●																		
SOMERLAP FOREST PRODUCTS, Compton Martin (YH13061)								●																		
BEDFORDSHIRE																										
ARCADE SADDLERY BEDFORD, Bedford (YH00498)							●																			
BIGGLESWADE SADDLERY, Biggleswade (YH01404)							●																			
C R DAY'S MOTORS, Dunstable (YH02387)																				●						
EQUISSENTIAL, Bedford (YH04820)							●																			
GRAVENHURST, Bedford (YH06023)								●																		
GRAVENHURST SADDLERY, Bedford (YH06024)							●																			
MORPHEUS, Luton (YH09824)																										
SUNSHINE RIDING SCHOOL, Luton (YH13652)							●																			
T C FEEDS, Dunstable (YH13732)								●																		
VULCAN TOWING CTRE, Luton (YH14745)																				●						
WADDINGTONS, Leighton Buzzard (YH14809)							●																			
BERKSHIRE																										
BEXMINSTER, Reading (YH01349)								●																		
BLOODHORSE INT, Hungerford (YH01547)																									●	
CHANGING TACK, Windsor (YH02732)																		●								
EQUICENTRE, Waltham St Lawrence (YH04737)								●																		
FROSBURY'S, Bracknell (YH05519)								●																		
GORDIAN TROELLER BLOODSTOCK, Upper Bucklebury (YH05922)																									●	
HORSE BOX & TRAILER OWNERS, Newbury (YH07111)																				●					●	
INDESPENSION, Reading (YH07411)																					●					
J C & N C WARD, Pangbourne (YH07568)								●																		
KBIS, Newbury (YH08013)																									●	
LASSALE WATCHES, Maidenhead (YH08440)																										
LAZYGRAZER, Wokingham (YH08486)								●																		
MILLS, J C, Newbury (YH09634)								●																		
R HUTT & PARTNERS, Maidenhead (YH11546)								●																		

	Jewel Combs	Jodhpurs	Jump Cups	Kings	Leather Stirrups	Mini Muck Spreaders	Model Horses	Modified Panels	Numnahs	Outbuildings	Pad Clip	Paper Bedding	Partitions	Pasture Toppers	Performance Rugs	Photo Finish Equipment	Photography Equipment	Pledgers	Polo Equipment	Poly Jumps	Protective Clothing	Reins	Remedies	Ribbons	Riding Hats	Mail Order Facilities
ENGLAND																										
BATH & SOMERSET (NORTH EAST)																										
CANADA HAY, Bath (YH02494)																										
SOMERLAP FOREST PRODUCTS, Compton Martin (YH13061)																										
BEDFORDSHIRE																										
ARCADE SADDLERY BEDFORD, Bedford (YH00498)																										
BIGGLESWADE SADDLERY, Biggleswade (YH01404)																										
C R DAY'S MOTORS, Dunstable (YH02387)																										
EQUISSENTIAL, Bedford (YH04820)																										
GRAVENHURST, Bedford (YH06023)																										
GRAVENHURST SADDLERY, Bedford (YH06024)																										
MORPHEUS, Luton (YH09824)									●																	
SUNSHINE RIDING SCHOOL, Luton (YH13652)																										
T C FEEDS, Dunstable (YH13732)																										
VULCAN TOWING CTRE, Luton (YH14745)																										
WADDINGTONS, Leighton Buzzard (YH14809)																										
BERKSHIRE																										
BEXMINSTER, Reading (YH01349)																										
BLOODHORSE INT, Hungerford (YH01547)																										
CHANGING TACK, Windsor (YH02732)		●																								
EQUICENTRE, Waltham St Lawrence (YH04737)																		●	●							
FROSBURY'S, Bracknell (YH05519)																										
GORDIAN TROELLER BLOODSTOCK, Upper Bucklebury (YH05922)																										
HORSE BOX & TRAILER OWNERS, Newbury (YH07111)																										
INDESPENSION, Reading (YH07411)																										
J C & N C WARD, Pangbourne (YH07568)																										
KBIS, Newbury (YH08013)																										
LASSALE WATCHES, Maidenhead (YH08440)																●										
LAZYGRAZER, Wokingham (YH08486)																										
MILLS, J C, Newbury (YH09634)																										
R HUTT & PARTNERS, Maidenhead (YH11546)																										

Products Supplied
G - R

by Country by County	Grain	Grooming Products	Half Chaps	Halters	Harness	Harness Racing Equipment	Hats	Hay	Hay Baskets	Hay Cratchers	Haylage	Head Collars	Heaters	Herbal Remedies	Herbs	Horse Boots	Horse Feeds	Horse Rugs	Horsebox Accessories	Horsebox Equipment	Horseboxes	Immune Support (Respiratory)	Immune Support (S. P. V.Synd.)	Insoles	Insurance	Ironmongery	Jewel Combs	Jodhpurs	Jump Cups	Kings	Leather Stirrups	Mini Muck Spreaders	Model Horses	Modified Panels	Numnahs	Outbuildings	Pad Clip	Paper Bedding	Partitions	Pasture Toppers	Performance Rugs	Photo Finish Equipment	Photography Equipment	Pledgers	Polo Equipment	Poly Jumps	Protective Clothing	Reins	Remedies	Ribbons	Riding Hats	Mail Order Facilities
SCATS COUNTRYSTORE, Newbury (YH12493)							●																																													
SHAMLEY SADDLERY, Maidenhead (YH12663)																																													●							
STABLE DOOR, Reading (YH13291)								●																																												
TALLY HO FARM, Windsor (YH13840)																																													●							
VALLEY EQUINE, Hungerford (YH14648)																																																				●
VINCENT TRAILERS, Thatcham (YH14723)																				●																																
WOODLANDS, Hungerford (YH15705)							●																																													
BRISTOL																																																				
ANIMAL BEDDING, Bristol (YH00427)																																						●														
BUCKINGHAMSHIRE																																																				
ARDENLEA ENTERPRISES, Princes Risborough (YH00503)													●																										●													
BANKERS EQUINE DIRECT, High Wycombe (YH00893)																									●																											
BELLINGDON END, Chesham (YH01238)							●	●						●																																						
D A L E, Aylesbury (YH03775)																																	●																			●
DENNIS'S SADDLERY/RIDING WEAR, Aylesbury (YH04060)																												●																								
DENNIS'S SADDLERY/RIDING WEAR, Aylesbury (YH04059)																												●																								
EQUESTRIAN CTRE, Amersham (YH04696)							●																																													
EQUS HEALTH, Aylesbury (YH04835)														●	●																																		●			
SPILLERS SPECIALITY FEEDS, Milton Keynes (YH13206)																	●																																			
WEST WYCOMBE PARK POLO CLUB, West Wycombe (YH15173)																																													●							
CAMBRIDGESHIRE																																																				
APACHE, Huntingdon (YH00473)														●																																						
BANKS CARGILL AGRICULTURE, Huntingdon (YH00896)	●																																																			
C FRANKS & SONS, Ely (YH02371)								●																																												
CLARK & BUTCHER, Ely (YH02960)								●																																												
COUNTRY VEHICLES, Ely (YH03434)																				●	●																															
DURRANT, R C, Cambridge (YH04372)								●																																												
ENGLISH BROTHERS, Wisbech (YH04672)																																							●													
GRASS ROOTS, Peterborough (YH06018)								●																																												
HOOK HSE, March (YH07035)							●																																													
LONG MELFORD, Cambridge (YH08798)							●																												●																	
NORTHBROOK EQUESTRIAN CTRE, Huntingdon (YH10294)							●	●																																												

Products Supplied
G - R

by Country by County	Grain	Grooming Products	Half Chaps	Halters	Harness	Harness Racing Equipment	Hats	Hay	Hay Baskets	Hay Cratchers	Haylage	Head Collars	Heaters	Herbal Remedies	Herbs	Horse Boots	Horse Feeds	Horse Rugs	Horsebox Accessories	Horsebox Equipment	Horseboxes	Immune Support (Respiratory)	Immune Support (S. P. V.Synd.)	Insoles	Insurance	Ironmongery	Jewel Combs	Jodhpurs	Jump Cups	Kings	Leather Stirrups	Mini Muck Spreaders	Model Horses	Modified Panels	Numnahs	Outbuildings	Pad Clip	Paper Bedding	Partitions	Pasture Toppers	Performance Rugs	Photo Finish Equipment	Photography Equipment	Pledgers	Polo Equipment	Poly Jumps	Protective Clothing	Reins	Remedies	Ribbons	Riding Hats	Mail Order Facilities
PEARSON, MICHAEL, Harston (YH10881)																																	●																			
ROBB & SON, St Ives (YH11932)				●																																												●				
CHESHIRE																																																				
BOOL BY DESIGN, Tarporley (YH01631)							●							●																																						●
BOWLERS, Stockport (YH01715)								●																																												
CHELFORD FARM SUPPLIES, Macclesfield (YH02799)	●						●																																													
COLBERRY SADDLERY, Ellesmere Port (YH03142)							●																																													●
DECATHLON SPORTS & LEISURE, Stockport (YH04008)							●																																													
EQUIFORM NUTRITION, Crewe (YH04747)								●																																												
EQUINE INNOVATIONS, Hyde (YH04781)																		●																																		
GAYNORS SADDLERY, Dukinfield (YH05682)							●							●																																						
GREEN FARM FEEDS, Crewe (YH06055)	●							●																																												
HORSEBOX BITS, Warrington (YH07150)																				●																																
INDESPENSION, Altrincham (YH07412)																					●																															
LANSDOWNE HORSE & RIDER, Chester (YH08423)	●					●	●	●						●							●																								●							●
LAWSHIELD UK, Warrington (YH08476)																									●																											
MINSUPS, Winsford (YH09654)								●																																												
RACEWOOD, Tarporley (YH11581)																																													●							
SPENCER LAVERY AST, Hale (YH13196)																									●																											
TOPSPEC, Nantwich (YH14241)																																																				●
W & T GIBSON, Frodsham (YH14748)								●																																												
YOUNGS, Congleton (YH15944)								●																																												
CLEVELAND																																																				
ARMSTRONG RICHARDSON, Middlesbrough (YH00544)	●						●																																													●
EQUINE EXTRAS, Stockton-on-Tees (YH04778)							●																																													
HADRIAN EQUINE, Stockton-on-Tees (YH06271)																		●																																		●
HOOF'N'HOUND, Middlesbrough (YH07032)							●																																													
HOOF'N'HOUND, Hartlepool (YH07031)	●						●	●						●																																						
JOHN MOORHOUSE, Stockton-on-Tees (YH07802)																			●	●	●																															
W H HORSEBOXES, Nunthorpe (YH14771)																			●	●	●																															
CORNWALL																																																				
ANDREWS, JULIE, Launceston (YH00401)																									●																											

www.hccyourhorse.com

Products Supplied
G - R

by Country by County	Grain	Grooming Products	Half Chaps	Halters	Harness	Harness Racing Equipment	Hats	Hay	Hay Baskets	Hay Cratchers	Haylage	Head Collars	Heaters	Herbal Remedies	Herbs	Horse Boots	Horse Feeds	Horse Rugs	Horsebox Accessories	Horsebox Equipment	Horseboxes	Immune Support (Respiratory)	Immune Support (S. P. V.Synd.)	Insoles	Insurance	Ironmongery	Jewel Combs	Jodhpurs	Jump Cups	Kings	Leather Stirrups	Mini Muck Spreaders	Model Horses	Modified Panels	Numnahs	Outbuildings	Pad Clip	Paper Bedding	Partitions	Pasture Toppers	Performance Rugs	Photo Finish Equipment	Photography Equipment	Pledgers	Polo Equipment	Poly Jumps	Protective Clothing	Reins	Remedies	Ribbons	Riding Hats	Mail Order Facilities
BLISLAND HARNESS MAKERS, Liskeard (YH01541)					●							●																																								
BUSH LIVERY STABLES, Saltash (YH02306)								●																																												
CORNWALL FARMERS, Liskeard (YH03334)	●						●																																													
CORNWALL FARMERS, Callington (YH03330)	●						●																																													
CORNWALL FARMERS, Penzance (YH03335)	●						●																																													
CORNWALL FARMERS, Truro (YH03337)	●						●																																													
CORNWALL FARMERS, Wadebridge (YH03338)	●						●																																													
DOIDGE, T R, Launceston (YH04164)								●																																												
EQUESTRIAN STOP, Camborne (YH04712)																																																				●
HELSTON SADDLERY, Helston (YH06657)																					●																															
HORSE & RIDER, Launceston (YH07094)							●																																													
P R J ENGINEERING, Launceston (YH10655)																				●																																
POLLY LUNN PET & AQUATICS, Truro (YH11208)							●																																													
RIDE & DRIVE SUPPLIES, Helston (YH11843)														●																																						
ROSEVIDNEY ARABIANS, Penzance (YH12111)								●																																												●
ST LEONARDS EQUESTRIAN CTRE, Launceston (YH13278)													●																																							
WOOFWARE, Bodmin (YH15762)																●																																				
COUNTY DURHAM																																																				
DENE HEAD LIVERY, Darlington (YH04042)																																							●													
EGGLESTON WOODCHIPS, Lanchester (YH04593)								●																																												
FARMWAY, Darlington (YH05072)	●						●																																													
GO RIDING GRP, Stanley (YH05861)								●																																												
W S HODGSON, Barnard Castle (YH14794)																																							●													
CUMBRIA																																																				
ALLONBY RIDING SCHOOL, Wigton (YH00323)								●																																												
CALTECH BIOTECHNOLOGY, Carlisle (YH02454)								●																																												
GET SMART, Barrow-In-Furness (YH05732)		●																																																		
INMAN, JENNY, Kendal (YH07459)																		●																																		
J W WILKINSON, Kendal (YH07628)																		●																																		
KINGFISHER, Ulverston (YH08191)																																						●														
LAKELAND EQUESTRIAN, Windermere (YH08354)							●																																													
LANCASTER, P R, Ulverston (YH08381)								●																																												

Products Supplied
G - R

by Country by County

by Country by County	Grain	Grooming Products	Half Chaps	Halters	Harness	Harness Racing Equipment	Hats	Hay	Hay Baskets	Hay Cratchers	Haylage	Head Collars	Heaters	Herbal Remedies	Herbs	Horse Boots	Horse Feeds	Horse Rugs	Horsebox Accessories	Horsebox Equipment	Horseboxes	Immune Support (Respiratory)	Immune Support (S. P. V.Synd.)	Insoles	Insurance	Ironmongery	Jewel Combs	Jodhpurs	Jump Cups	Kings	Leather Stirrups	Mini Muck Spreaders	Model Horses	Modified Panels	Numnahs	Outbuildings	Pad Clip	Paper Bedding	Partitions	Pasture Toppers	Performance Rugs	Photo Finish Equipment	Photography Equipment	Pledgers	Polo Equipment	Poly Jumps	Protective Clothing	Reins	Remedies	Ribbons	Riding Hats	Mail Order Facilities
O'HARA, JOHNNIE, Carlisle (YH10442)					●																																											●				●
DERBYSHIRE																																																				
BARLEYFIELD SADDLERY, Etwall (YH00951)														●																																						
C E S, Ashbourne (YH02370)							●													●	●				●																											
C W G, Buxton (YH02396)							●																																													
COUNTRY SPORT, Glossop (YH03426)							●																																													●
HORSE & RIDER TACK SHOP, Nottingham (YH07100)							●																																													
INDESPENSION, Derby (YH07416)																					●																															
IVANHOE FEEDS, Swadlincote (YH07533)							●																																													
PEAKDALE SADDLERY, Buxton (YH10866)	●						●							●																																						
DEVON																																																				
BARWELL, C R, Tiverton (YH01052)																									●																											
DEVON & CORNWALL FARMS, Tavistock (YH04092)	●	●			●		●										●	●										●										●										●		●	●	
EASTLAKE INSURANCE, Plymouth (YH04506)																									●																											
ERME VALLEY FARMERS, Ivybridge (YH04850)							●																																													
FARMERS FRIEND, Exeter (YH05061)							●																																													
HOLLY FARM, Exeter (YH06953)														●																																						
HUISH ENGINEERING, Exeter (YH07277)																				●																																
J R SERPELL & SON, Plymouth (YH07610)								●																																												
LEONARD COOMBE, Newton Abbot (YH08553)							●																																													
LIMPET ANTI-SLIP SADDLE PADS, Ottery St Mary (YH08638)																																			●																	●
MULLACOTT EQUESTRIAN, Ilfracombe (YH09935)	●							●																																												
OTTERY INSURANCE SVS, Ottery St Mary (YH10582)																									●																											
PET & EQUINE SUPPLIES, Okehampton (YH11000)							●																																													
SIDE SADDLE LADY, Exeter (YH12786)																																																				●
TOWN & COUNTRY SUP, Exeter (YH14286)							●	●												●																																
TWYFORD FARM SUPPLIES, Tiverton (YH14516)							●		●																																											
WHITE HORSE MOTORS, Exeter (YH15309)																				●																																
WINDUSS HORSEBOXES, Crediton (YH15579)																				●																																
WISCOMBE HAYLAGE, Colyton (YH15606)											●																																									
WYCHANGER BARTON SADDLERY, Tiverton (YH15855)							●																																													●
DORSET																																																				

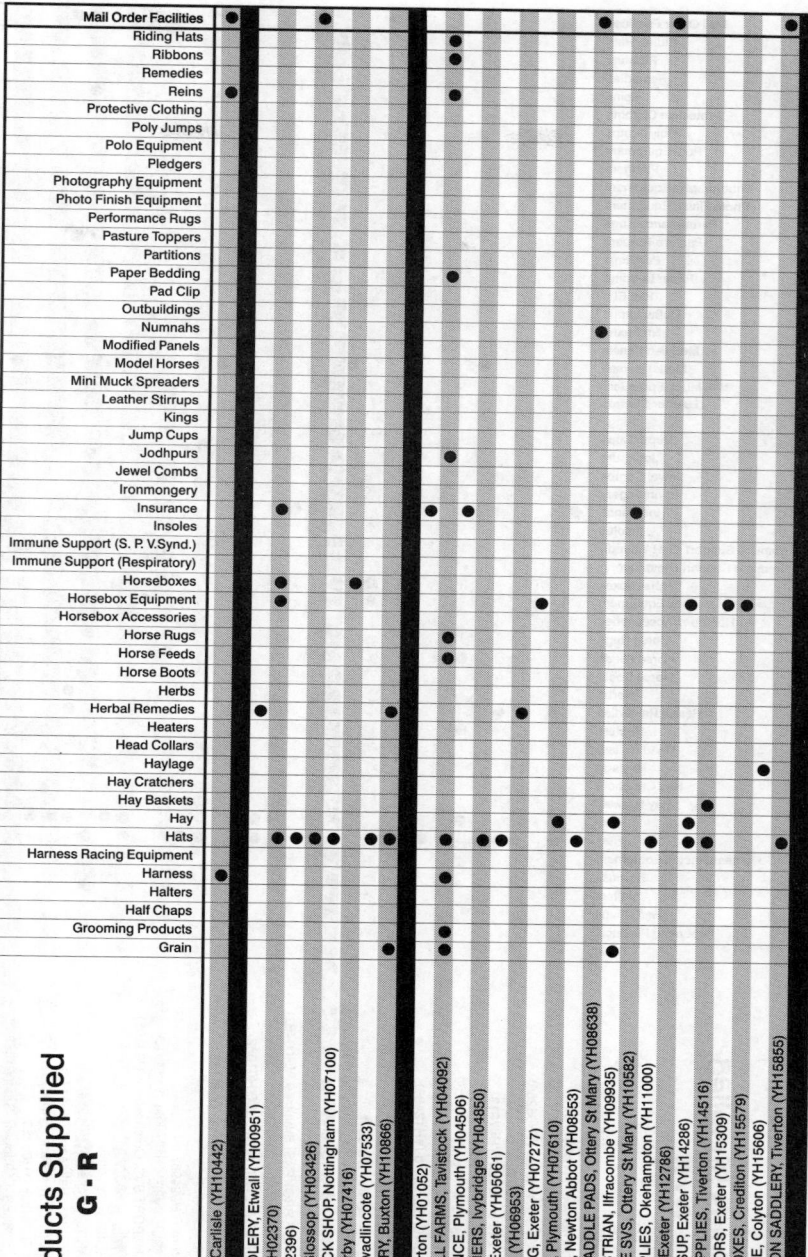

Products Supplied
G - R

by Country by County	Grain	Grooming Products	Half Chaps	Halters	Harness	Harness Racing Equipment	Hats	Hay	Hay Baskets	Hay Cratchers	Haylage	Head Collars	Heaters	Herbal Remedies	Herbs	Horse Boots	Horse Feeds	Horse Rugs	Horsebox Accessories	Horsebox Equipment	Horseboxes	Immune Support (Respiratory)	Immune Support (S. P. V.Synd.)	Insoles	Insurance	Ironmongery	Jewel Combs	Jodhpurs	Jump Cups	Kings	Leather Stirrups	Mini Muck Spreaders	Model Horses	Modified Panels	Numnahs	Outbuildings	Pad Clip	Paper Bedding	Partitions	Pasture Toppers	Performance Rugs	Photo Finish Equipment	Photography Equipment	Pledgers	Polo Equipment	Poly Jumps	Protective Clothing	Reins	Remedies	Ribbons	Riding Hats	Mail Order Facilities
D B I INSURANCE, Bournemouth (YH03778)																									●																											
EQUUS, Wimborne (YH04836)							●							●																																						
FIVE SQUARE MOTORS, Shaftesbury (YH05256)																				●																																
HORSE BITS, Wimborne (YH07104)							●																																													
HURN BRIDGE CTRE, Christchurch (YH07313)							●							●																																						
JULIP HORSES, Dorchester (YH07964)																																	●																			
O Y C, Wareham (YH10369)								●					●				●																																			
SCATS COUNTRYSTORE, Dorchester (YH12494)							●																																													
SCATS COUNTRYSTORE, Blandford (YH12496)							●																																													
SCATS COUNTRYSTORE, Gillingham (YH12495)							●																																													
SIDE SADDLES, Wimborne (YH12787)							●																																													●
TOLLER TRAILERS, Dorchester (YH14209)																				●	●																															
TURTONS SADDLERS & HARNESS, Shaftesbury (YH14496)																																	●																			
ESSEX																																																				
ALLISON & PARTNERS, Witham (YH00317)																									●																											
APPLEWELL INSURANCE BROKERS, Braintree (YH00482)																									●																											
BAILEYS HORSE FEEDS, Braintree (YH00806)								●																																												
BATTLESBRIDGE HORSE & CTRY, Wickford (YH01082)							●	●																																												
BOYLES COURT, Brentwood (YH01733)								●																																												
BREYER MODEL HORSES, Great Dunmow (YH01857)																																	●																			●
C W G, Ongar (YH02397)							●																																													
CANDLERS, Chelmsford (YH02496)							●																																													
CARRIAGEHOUSE INSURANCE, Colchester (YH02582)																									●																											
COLNE CARGO TRANSPORT SVS, Colchester (YH03195)																				●																																
D & F FEED SVS, Rayleigh (YH03770)	●						●	●																																												
DENGIE, Maldon (YH04045)								●																																												
DESIGNER BROWBANDS, Benfleet (YH04084)		●		●			●											●										●							●													●		●		●
EQUINE HEALTH & HERBAL, Halstead (YH04779)								●						●	●																																					●
ESSEX HAY & STRAW, Clacton-on-Sea (YH04871)								●																																												
H R PHILPOT & SON, Billericay (YH06235)								●																																												
HADDON ROCKING HORSES, Clacton-on-Sea (YH06262)																																	●																			
HOBBY HORSE, Romford (YH06897)							●																																													

Products Supplied
G - R

by Country by County

	Grain	Grooming Products	Half Chaps	Halters	Harness	Harness Racing Equipment	Hats	Hay	Hay Baskets	Hay Cratchers	Haylage	Head Collars	Heaters	Herbal Remedies	Herbs	Horse Boots	Horse Feeds	Horse Rugs	Horsebox Accessories	Horsebox Equipment	Horseboxes	Immune Support (Respiratory)	Immune Support (S. P. V.Synd.)	Insoles	Insurance	Ironmongery	Jewel Combs	Jodhpurs	Jump Cups	Kings	Leather Stirrups	Mini Muck Spreaders	Model Horses	Modified Panels	Numnahs	Outbuildings	Pad Clip	Paper Bedding	Partitions	Pasture Toppers	Performance Rugs	Photo Finish Equipment	Photography Equipment	Pledgers	Polo Equipment	Poly Jumps	Protective Clothing	Reins	Remedies	Ribbons	Riding Hats	Mail Order Facilities
INGATESTONE SADDLERY, Ingatestone (YH07442)							●																																													
KILN SADDLERY, Colchester (YH08151)							●																																													
M P TRAILERS, Burnham-on-Crouch (YH08974)																					●																															
MOORCROFT EQUESTRIAN, Colchester (YH09749)		●																●																	●																	●
MOSS, JANETTE, Waltham Abbey (YH09858)							●																																													
PRIORY SADDLERY, Colchester (YH11403)							●																																													
SHOPLAND HALL EQUESTRIAN, Rochford (YH12758)							●							●																																						
SIERRA SADDLE, Benfleet (YH12792)																																																				●
SOUTH ESSEX INSURANCE, South Ockendon (YH13091)																									●																											
TACK EXCHANGE, Leigh-on-Sea (YH13788)							●																																													
TALLY-HO RIDING SCHOOL, Grays (YH13844)							●	●												●																																
THORPE TACK ROOM, Clacton-on-Sea (YH14095)							●																																													
TOWRITE, Upminster (YH14301)																				●																																
UPMINSTER SADDLERY, Upminster (YH14604)							●																																													
GLOUCESTERSHIRE																																																				
ABBOTT, Cirencester (YH00102)								●																																												
BEAUFORT POLO CLUB, Tetbury (YH01128)																																													●							
CIRENCESTER GARAGE, Cirencester (YH02926)																				●																																
COTSWOLD TRAILERS, Cheltenham (YH03370)																				●																																
GLOUCESTER FABRICATIONS, Gloucester (YH05850)																				●	●																															
HAYES J SADDLERY, Lechlade (YH06575)																																													●							
HENRY COLE, Cirencester (YH06681)														●	●																							●														
LOCOS SADDLERY, Tetbury (YH08765)																																													●							
MANGAN & WEBB, Cheltenham (YH09076)							●																																													
PARK CORNER FARM, Cirencester (YH10716)								●																																												
RIVERMEAD INSURANCE, Lechlade (YH11922)																									●																											
ROLFE, JOHN, Berkeley (YH12066)																																	●																			
ROXTON SPORTING, Cirencester (YH12177)																																													●							
SOUTH AMERICAN TRADE SERVICES, Cirencester (YH13075)							●																																						●							
SOUTHWICK FARM, Tewkesbury (YH13163)								●																																												
STROUD SADDLERY, Stroud (YH13588)							●							●																																						●
TEWKESBURY SADDLERY, Tewkesbury (YH13969)							●																																													●

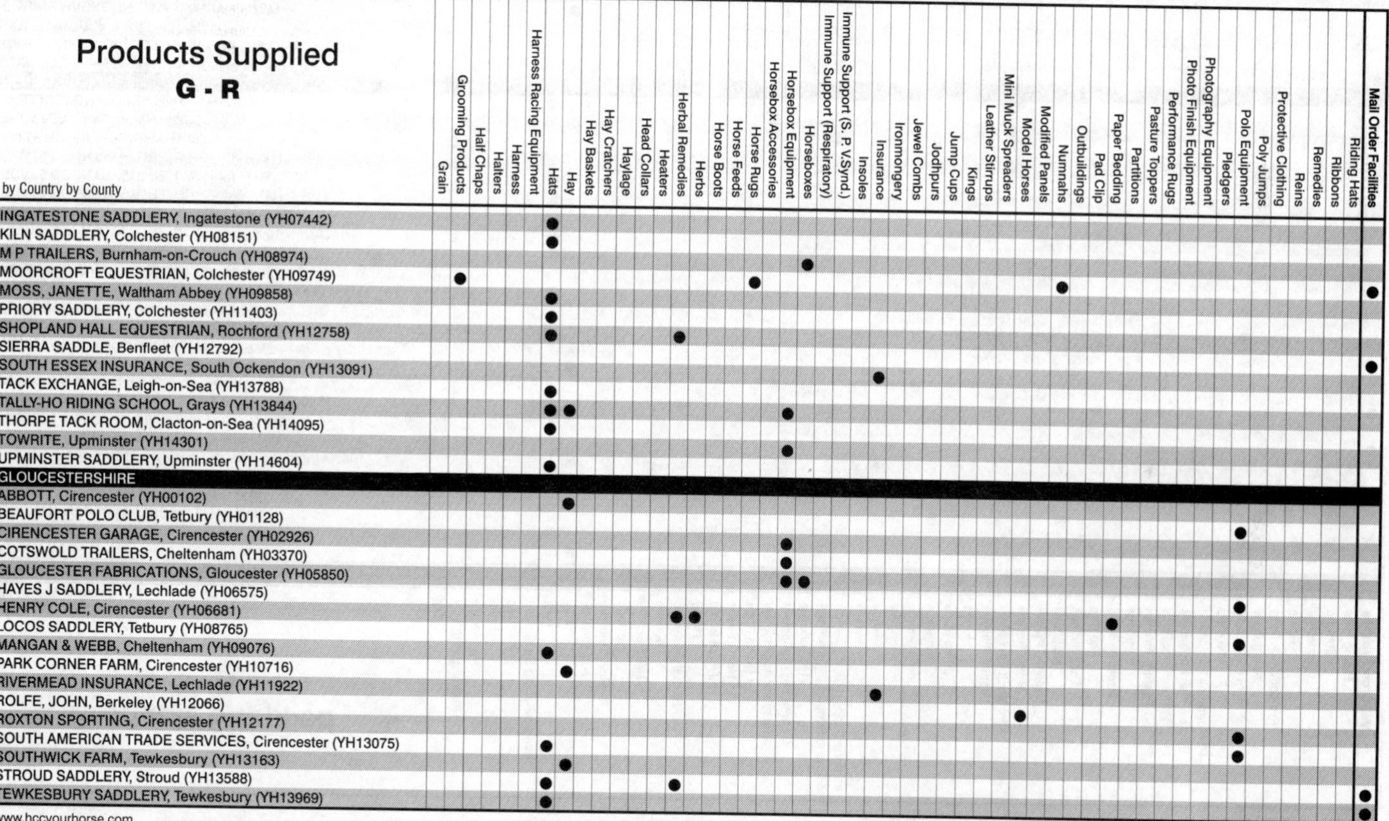

Products Supplied
G - R

by Country by County	Grain	Grooming Products	Half Chaps	Halters	Harness	Harness Racing Equipment	Hats	Hay	Hay Baskets	Hay Cratchers	Haylage	Head Collars	Heaters	Herbal Remedies	Herbs	Horse Boots	Horse Feeds	Horse Rugs	Horsebox Accessories	Horsebox Equipment	Horseboxes	Immune Support (Respiratory)	Immune Support (S. P. V.Synd.)	Insoles	Insurance	Ironmongery	Jewel Combs	Jodhpurs	Jump Cups	Kings	Leather Stirrups	Mini Muck Spreaders	Model Horses	Modified Panels	Numnahs	Outbuildings	Pad Clip	Paper Bedding	Partitions	Pasture Toppers	Performance Rugs	Photo Finish Equipment	Photography Equipment	Pledgers	Polo Equipment	Poly Jumps	Protective Clothing	Reins	Remedies	Ribbons	Riding Hats	Mail Order Facilities
HAMPSHIRE																																																				
ABBOTT, Alton (YH00103)								●																																					●							●
CALCUTT & SONS, Winchester (YH02425)							●																																												●	
COUNTRY RIDING WEAR, Hook (YH03424)																												●							●																	
DAVID CATLIN, Southampton (YH03916)																														●																						
DIRECT FEEDS, Winchester (YH04127)	●							●																																												
EQUESTRIAN EVENT INSURANCE, Ringwood (YH04701)																									●																											
FORESTER SADDLES, Lyndhurst (YH05354)																																																				●
HASKER, GLENN M, Ringwood (YH06521)							●																														●															●
HOPLANDS EQUESTRIAN, Stockbridge (YH07058)														●																																						
INDESPENSION, Southampton (YH07420)																					●																															
J ELLIS & SONS, Bordon (YH07580)								●																																												
JOHN LOADER, Fordingbridge (YH07799)								●																																												
LEATHER WORKSHOP, Ringwood (YH08506)																																													●							
MCNEILL, IAN, Alton (YH09402)																																							●													
RYCROFT SCHOOL OF EQUITATION, Hook (YH12291)							●																																													
SADDLES, SADDLES, SADDLES, Portsmouth (YH12371)																																		●																		
SCATS COUNTRYSTORE, Romsey (YH12497)							●																																													
SCATS COUNTRYSTORE, Alton (YH12499)							●																																													
SCATS COUNTRYSTORE, Andover (YH12500)							●																																													
SCATS COUNTRYSTORE, Basingstoke (YH12501)							●																																													
SCATS COUNTRYSTORE, Lymington (YH12502)							●																																													
SCATS COUNTRYSTORE, Winchester (YH12498)							●																																													
TALLY HO, Whitchurch (YH13839)			●																									●																								
TROTTERS, Havant (YH14407)								●																																												
WELLINGTON RIDING, Hook (YH15075)							●																																													
HEREFORDSHIRE																																																				
ABBOTT, Hereford (YH00104)								●																																												
CAM EQUESTRIAN JOINERY/EQUIP, Hereford (YH02463)																																							●													
COUNTRYWIDE, Hereford (YH03445)	●						●							●																																						
EQUINE MARKETING, Weobley (YH04787)								●																																												
HORSE & JOCKEY, Hereford (YH07093)							●																																													

Products Supplied
G - R

by Country by County	Grain	Grooming Products	Half Chaps	Halters	Harness	Harness Racing Equipment	Hats	Hay	Hay Baskets	Hay Cratchers	Haylage	Head Collars	Heaters	Herbal Remedies	Herbs	Horse Boots	Horse Feeds	Horse Rugs	Horsebox Accessories	Horsebox Equipment	Horseboxes	Immune Support (Respiratory)	Immune Support (S. P. V.Synd.)	Insoles	Insurance	Ironmongery	Jewel Combs	Jodhpurs	Jump Cups	Kings	Leather Stirrups	Mini Muck Spreaders	Model Horses	Modified Panels	Numnahs	Outbuildings	Pad Clip	Paper Bedding	Partitions	Pasture Toppers	Performance Rugs	Photo Finish Equipment	Photography Equipment	Pledgers	Polo Equipment	Poly Jumps	Protective Clothing	Reins	Remedies	Ribbons	Riding Hats	Mail Order Facilities
HORSEWISE, Hereford (YH07178)							●																																													
SHIRES EQUESTRIAN, Leominster (YH12755)												●				●		●										●																								
TURNERS, Kington (YH14492)	●																																																		●	
HERTFORDSHIRE																																																				
CHOLESBURY, Tring (YH02877)								●																																												
COLEMAN CROFT, St Albans (YH03163)							●	●																																												
FIELDFARE, Waltham Cross (YH05191)								●																																												●
FOX FEEDS, Buntingford (YH05420)								●																																												
G T TOWING, Potters Bar (YH05597)																					●																															
MARSH PRIVATE CLIENT SVS, Hitchin (YH09187)																									●																											
PATCHETTS, Watford (YH10815)							●								●																																					
POUND FARM FEEDS, Datchworth (YH11308)								●																																												
SADDLERY, Royston (YH12363)							●																																													
SHEARWATER INSURANCE SVS, Waltham Cross (YH12692)																									●																											
UPPERWOOD FARM STUD, Hemel Hempstead (YH14609)								●																																												
WHITE HORSES, Welwyn (YH15317)																																	●																			
ISLE OF WIGHT																																																				
JONES, E A & C, Newport (YH07895)								●																																												
SCATS COUNTRYSTORE, Newport (YH12503)							●																																													
JERSEY																																																				
LE MAISTRE BROS, Trinity (YH08490)							●																																													
KENT																																																				
ARIZONAS, Tunbridge Wells (YH00527)							●																																													
BA GREEN CROP DRIERS, Hythe (YH00758)								●																																												●
BARMINSTER TRADING, Ashford (YH00960)							●																																													
BIRCHALLS THE RIDING SHOP, Maidstone (YH01431)							●							●																																						
BRITISH EQUESTRIAN BROKERS, Tonbridge (YH01937)																									●																											
CHASKIT HSE, Tunbridge Wells (YH02787)																		●																																		
COBHAM MANOR, Maidstone (YH03113)							●	●																																												
DICKSON, PENNY, Rochester (YH04117)					●																																															
ELMHURST BLOODSTOCK, Tonbridge (YH04637)																									●																											
EQUINE SPORT THERAPY, Edenbridge (YH04800)														●																																						

by Country by County

	Grain	Grooming Products	Half Chaps	Halters	Harness	Harness Racing Equipment	Hats	Hay	Hay Baskets	Hay Cratchers	Haylage	Head Collars	Heaters	Herbal Remedies	Herbs	Horse Boots	Horse Feeds	Horse Rugs	Horsebox Accessories	Horsebox Equipment	Horseboxes	Immune Support (Respiratory)	Immune Support (S. P. V.Synd.)	Insoles	Insurance	Ironmongery	Jewel Combs	Jodhpurs	Jump Cups	Kings	Leather Stirrups	Mini Muck Spreaders	Model Horses	Modified Panels	Numnahs	Outbuildings	Pad Clip	Paper Bedding	Partitions	Pasture Toppers	Performance Rugs	Photo Finish Equipment	Photography Equipment	Pledgers	Polo Equipment	Poly Jumps	Protective Clothing	Reins	Remedies	Ribbons	Riding Hats	Mail Order Facilities
EQUUS INSURANCE, Orpington (YH04842)																									●																											
FARNINGHAM SADDLERY, Farningham (YH05083)																									●																				●							
FORAGES, J T, Cranbrook (YH05315)								●																																												
FOREST VIEW, Sidcup (YH05353)																					●																															
FROGPOOL MANOR SADDLERY, Chislehurst (YH05515)	●						●	●						●																																						●
HOBBS PARKER, Ashford (YH06894)							●																																													
HORSE & COUNTRY SUPERSTORE, Maidstone (YH07088)							●																																													
LONGFIELD & APPLEDORE, Longfield (YH08810)																					●																															
MOUNT MASCAL STABLES, Bexley (YH09890)								●																																												
S RANSLEY & SONS, Ashford (YH12334)								●																																												
SADDLERY & GUN ROOM, Westerham (YH12365)							●																																													
SARACEN FEEDS, Tunbridge Wells (YH12432)	●							●																																												
SCATS COUNTRYSTORE, Marden (YH12505)							●																																													
SCATS COUNTRYSTORE, Canterbury (YH12504)							●																																													
STEVENSON BROS, Ashford (YH13449)																																	●																			
TRIDENT TRAILERS, Canterbury (YH14393)																				●	●																															
TRIDENT TRAILERS, Tunbridge Wells (YH14394)																				●	●																															
WEALDEN SADDLERY, Tonbridge (YH15020)							●																																													●
WILLOW FARM, Faversham (YH15497)							●	●						●																			●																			●
WM LILLICO & SONS, Maidstone (YH15641)								●																																												
LANCASHIRE																																																				
ABRAM HALL RIDING CTRE, Wigan (YH00134)								●																																												
ASOKA, Worsley (YH00625)														●																																						
BLACKPOOL WORKSPACE, Blackpool (YH01493)																		●																																		
BROOKFIELD GREEN FARM, Ormskirk (YH02047)								●																																												
BROOMHILL, Clitheroe (YH02080)							●																																													
CARRS BILLINGTON, Preston (YH02599)		●															●																																			
CARRS BILLINGTON, Clitheroe (YH02598)		●															●																																			
DERBY HSE SADDLERY, Wigan (YH04071)																																																				●
EQUESTRIANA, Blackburn (YH04724)							●																																													
HORSE BITS SADDLERY, Bury (YH07106)							●																																													
HORSEBOX UPHOLSTERY, Westhoughton (YH07151)																				●																																

Products Supplied
G - R

by Country by County

	Grain	Grooming Products	Half Chaps	Halters	Harness	Harness Racing Equipment	Hats	Hay	Hay Baskets	Hay Cratchers	Haylage	Head Collars	Heaters	Herbal Remedies	Herbs	Horse Boots	Horse Feeds	Horse Rugs	Horsebox Accessories	Horsebox Equipment	Horseboxes	Immune Support (Respiratory)	Immune Support (S. P. V.Synd.)	Insoles	Insurance	Ironmongery	Jewel Combs	Jodhpurs	Jump Cups	Kings	Leather Stirrups	Mini Muck Spreaders	Model Horses	Modified Panels	Numnahs	Outbuildings	Pad Clip	Paper Bedding	Partitions	Pasture Toppers	Performance Rugs	Photo Finish Equipment	Photography Equipment	Pledgers	Polo Equipment	Poly Jumps	Protective Clothing	Reins	Remedies	Ribbons	Riding Hats	Mail Order Facilities
HUSTEADS RIDING SCHOOL, Oldham (YH07330)								●																																												
JERUSALEM FARM, Colne (YH07757)							●																																													
M E FRENCH, Preston (YH08959)																									●																											
MAUDSLEY HORSEBOXES, Darwen (YH09279)																				●																																
MILLER TRAILERS, Burnley (YH09603)																					●																															
MILLIN INSURANCE SVS, Parbold (YH09623)																									●																											
PRETTY PONIES, Clitheroe (YH11372)							●																																													
QUAY EQUESTRIAN, Lancaster (YH11485)												●				●		●			●																															
R & E BAMFORD, Leyland (YH11505)								●						●																																						
RICHARD BATTERSBY, Heywood (YH11802)								●																																												
SNAFFLES, Halifax (YH13020)							●																					●																								
WHITEGATE FARM, Bacup (YH15338)								●																																												
WORLD OF HORSES I T L, Layland (YH15786)																									●																											
LEICESTERSHIRE																																																				
BRITISH HORSE, Leicester (YH01948)																				●	●				●																											
C W G, Melton Mowbray (YH02398)							●																																													
CLOTHES HORSE, Leicester (YH03062)							●	●						●																																						
DTA, Leicester (YH04303)							●																												●																	
E H HUTTON, Melton Mowbray (YH04407)																				●																																
EASTLAKE & BEACHELL, Leicester (YH04505)																									●																											
GLENDALE EQUESTRIAN FEEDS, Leicester (YH05830)																																	●																			
HARLOW BROTHERS, Loughborough (YH06440)																																							●													
HURST SADDLERS, Leicester (YH07316)							●							●																																						●
PEGASUS TRAILERS, Hinckley (YH10908)																				●																																
S L B SUPPLIES, Coalville (YH12329)	●													●																																						
SAGITTARIUS BLOODSTOCK AGENCY, Melton Mowbray (YH12382)																									●																											
SCHOOL OF NATIONAL EQUITATION, Loughborough (YH12521)							●																																													
SHARNFORD LODGE FEEDS/TACK, Hinckley (YH12676)								●																																												
TOWRITE FABRICATIONS, Market Harborough (YH14302)																					●																															
LINCOLNSHIRE																																																				
BATTLE, HAYWARD & BOWER, Lincoln (YH01081)							●																																													
BEEVER, C R, Grantham (YH01193)																				●																																

www.hccyourhorse.com

Products Supplied
G - R

by Country by County

by Country by County	Grain	Grooming Products	Half Chaps	Halters	Harness	Harness Racing Equipment	Hats	Hay	Hay Baskets	Hay Cratchers	Haylage	Head Collars	Heaters	Herbal Remedies	Herbs	Horse Boots	Horse Feeds	Horse Rugs	Horsebox Accessories	Horsebox Equipment	Horseboxes	Immune Support (Respiratory)	Immune Support (S. P. V.Synd.)	Insoles	Insurance	Ironmongery
BELVOIR HORSE FEEDS, Boothby Graffoe Heath (YH01258)								●																		
C W G, Stamford (YH02399)							●																			
C W G, Market Rasen (YH02400)							●																			
COOL SPORT, Brigg (YH03269)							●																			
COSGROVE & SON, Market Rasen (YH03350)								●																		
COTTAGE SADDLERY, Boston (YH03379)							●																			
EAGLE HALL EST, Lincoln (YH04437)								●																		
F P I, Stamford (YH04998)														●	●											
GREAT PONTON UK CHASERS, Grantham (YH06042)								●																		
LIMES FARM, Grantham (YH08634)													●													
MCARA, Market Rasen (YH09311)																				●						
PIG & WHISTLE ROCKING HORSES, North Somercotes (YH11093)																										
POPPYFIELDS, Lincoln (YH11275)								●			●															
REDNIL EQUESTRIAN CTRE, Lincoln (YH11716)								●																		
SHEEPGATE EQUESTRIAN, Boston (YH12696)							●																			
STRAGGLETHORPE ROCKER, Brant Broughton (YH13545)																										
TACK BOX, Lincoln (YH13785)		●					●																			
TYLER ANIMAL SYSTEMS, Grantham (YH14520)													●													
WINERGY, Grantham (YH15582)							●																			
LINCOLNSHIRE (NORTH)																										
CROWSTONS, Scunthorpe (YH03684)							●							●				●								
INDESPENSION, Scunthorpe (YH07422)																				●	●					
KILLINGHOLME, Grimsby (YH08143)							●	●																		
MASON, D & M, Scunthorpe (YH09239)							●																			
LONDON (GREATER)																										
A D L TACK & SADDLERY, London (YH00027)							●							●												
BLOODLINES, London (YH01548)																									●	
BURY FARM FODDER STORE, Edgware (YH02299)								●																		
BYAS MOSLEY, London (YH02343)																									●	
CHASE SADDLERY, Enfield (YH02785)							●																			
DECATHLON SPORTS & LEISURE, London (YH04009)							●																			
DUFFIN, JULIA, Ealing (YH04317)																										

by Country by County	Jewel Combs	Jodhpurs	Jump Cups	Kings	Leather Stirrups	Mini Muck Spreaders	Model Horses	Modified Panels	Numnahs	Outbuildings	Pad Clip	Paper Bedding	Partitions	Pasture Toppers	Performance Rugs	Photo Finish Equipment	Photography Equipment	Pledgers	Polo Equipment	Poly Jumps	Protective Clothing	Reins	Remedies	Ribbons	Riding Hats	Mail Order Facilities
BELVOIR HORSE FEEDS, Boothby Graffoe Heath (YH01258)																										
C W G, Stamford (YH02399)																										
C W G, Market Rasen (YH02400)																										
COOL SPORT, Brigg (YH03269)																			●							
COSGROVE & SON, Market Rasen (YH03350)																										
COTTAGE SADDLERY, Boston (YH03379)																										
EAGLE HALL EST, Lincoln (YH04437)																										
F P I, Stamford (YH04998)																										●
GREAT PONTON UK CHASERS, Grantham (YH06042)																										
LIMES FARM, Grantham (YH08634)																										
MCARA, Market Rasen (YH09311)																										
PIG & WHISTLE ROCKING HORSES, North Somercotes (YH11093)							●																			
POPPYFIELDS, Lincoln (YH11275)																										
REDNIL EQUESTRIAN CTRE, Lincoln (YH11716)																										
SHEEPGATE EQUESTRIAN, Boston (YH12696)																										
STRAGGLETHORPE ROCKER, Brant Broughton (YH13545)							●																			
TACK BOX, Lincoln (YH13785)																										
TYLER ANIMAL SYSTEMS, Grantham (YH14520)																										
WINERGY, Grantham (YH15582)																										
LINCOLNSHIRE (NORTH)																										
CROWSTONS, Scunthorpe (YH03684)																										
INDESPENSION, Scunthorpe (YH07422)																										
KILLINGHOLME, Grimsby (YH08143)																										
MASON, D & M, Scunthorpe (YH09239)																										
LONDON (GREATER)																										
A D L TACK & SADDLERY, London (YH00027)																										●
BLOODLINES, London (YH01548)																										
BURY FARM FODDER STORE, Edgware (YH02299)																										
BYAS MOSLEY, London (YH02343)																										
CHASE SADDLERY, Enfield (YH02785)																										
DECATHLON SPORTS & LEISURE, London (YH04009)																										
DUFFIN, JULIA, Ealing (YH04317)					●																					

Products Supplied
G - R

by Country by County	Grain	Grooming Products	Half Chaps	Halters	Harness	Harness Racing Equipment	Hats	Hay	Hay Baskets	Hay Cratchers	Haylage	Head Collars	Heaters	Herbal Remedies	Herbs	Horse Boots	Horse Feeds	Horse Rugs	Horsebox Accessories	Horsebox Equipment	Horseboxes	Immune Support (S. P. V.Synd.)	Immune Support (Respiratory)	Insoles	Insurance	Ironmongery	Jewel Combs	Jodhpurs	Jump Cups	Kings	Leather Stirrups	Mini Muck Spreaders	Model Horses	Modified Panels	Numnahs	Outbuildings	Pad Clip	Paper Bedding	Partitions	Pasture Toppers	Performance Rugs	Photo Finish Equipment	Photography Equipment	Pledgers	Polo Equipment	Poly Jumps	Protective Clothing	Reins	Remedies	Ribbons	Riding Hats	Mail Order Facilities
EDWARD ROBERT SADDLERY, Feltham (YH04569)					●																																															
GEDDES-BODEN, LESLIE, London (YH05687)																																																				●
GOULDS GREEN, Uxbridge (YH05952)							●	●																																												
HUGHES-GIBB, London (YH07274)																									●																											
HYDE PARK RIDING WEAR, London (YH07345)							●																																						●							
HYDE PARK STABLES, London (YH07346)																																													●							
KENSINGTON STABLES, London (YH08078)																																													●							
L H H ANIMAL FEEDS, Enfield (YH08321)								●																																												
LOCK, JAMES, London (YH08756)																																																			●	
PATEY, London (YH10820)							●																																												●	
PET PLAN, Brentford (YH11006)																									●																											
RACETECH, Raynes Park (YH11580)																																										●										
RIDERS & SQUIRES, London (YH11855)							●																																													
SCHNIEDER RIDING BOOT, London (YH12515)																																													●							
SHEARWATER CORPORATE SVS, Colindale (YH12691)																									●																											
STURDY, CONAN, London (YH13612)																					●																															
SUN ALLIANCE, London (YH13639)																									●																											
WINDSOR INSURANCE BROKERS, London (YH15575)																									●																											
YARBOROUGH, RACHEL, Edgware (YH15882)																				●																																
MANCHESTER (GREATER)																																																				
B R ROUND, Stockport (YH00747)																									●																											
BROWZERS, Manchester (YH02149)																																																				●
EQUITACK, Bolton (YH04823)							●							●											●								●																			●
INDESPENSION, Bolton (YH07425)																					●																															
INDESPENSION, Bolton (YH07426)																					●																															
J & D WOODS, Bolton (YH07544)																																	●																			
RYDERS FARM, Bolton (YH12297)								●																																												
SHORESIDE STABLES, Manchester (YH12759)								●																																												
MERSEYSIDE																																																				
BARNSTON RIDING CTRE, Wirral (YH00991)							●																																													
FORMBY SADDLERY, Liverpool (YH05373)							●																																													
MIDLANDS (WEST)																																																				

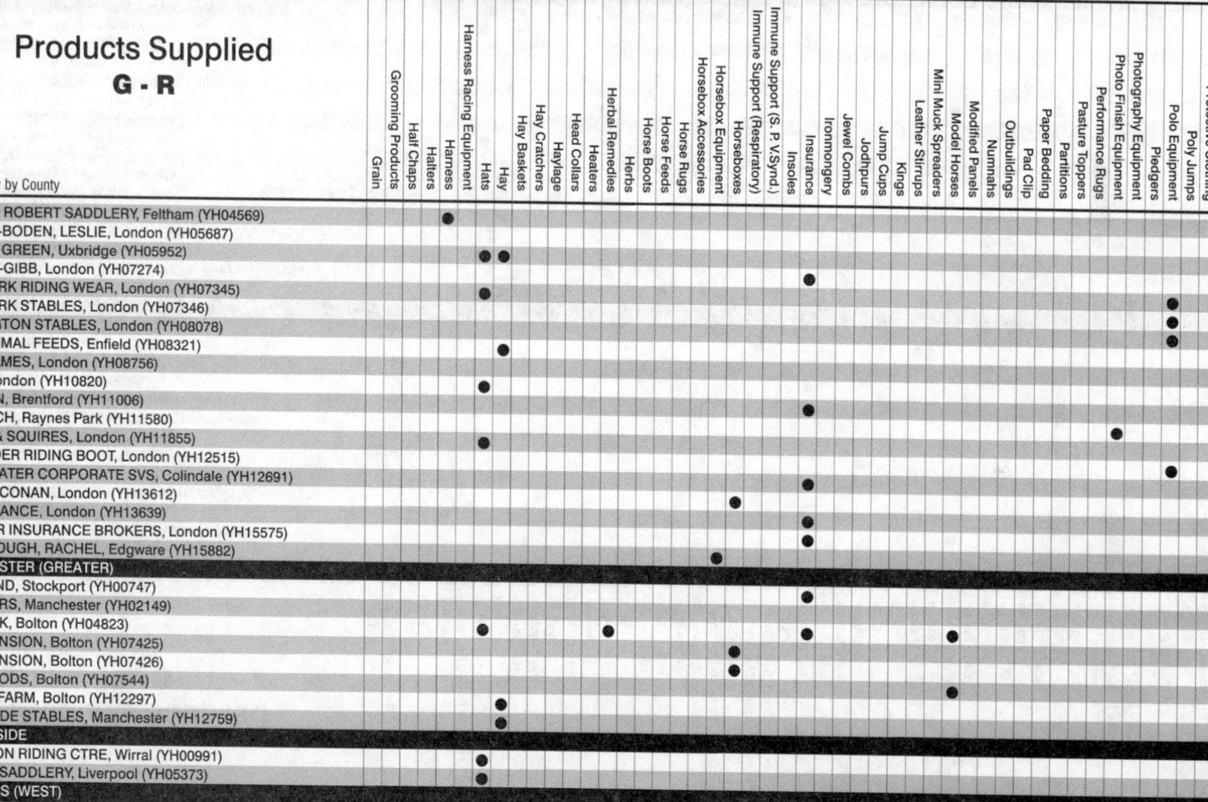

Products Supplied G - R

by Country by County

by Country by County	Grain	Grooming Products	Half Chaps	Halters	Harness	Harness Racing Equipment	Hats	Hay	Hay Baskets	Hay Cratchers	Haylage	Head Collars	Heaters	Herbal Remedies	Herbs	Horse Boots	Horse Feeds	Horse Rugs	Horsebox Accessories	Horsebox Equipment	Horseboxes	Immune Support (Respiratory)	Immune Support (S. P. V.Synd.)	Insoles	Insurance	Ironmongery	Jewel Combs	Jodhpurs	Jump Cups	Kings	Leather Stirrups	Mini Muck Spreaders	Model Horses	Modified Panels	Numnahs	Outbuildings	Pad Clip	Paper Bedding	Partitions	Pasture Toppers	Performance Rugs	Photo Finish Equipment	Photography Equipment	Pledgers	Polo Equipment	Poly Jumps	Protective Clothing	Reins	Remedies	Ribbons	Riding Hats	Mail Order Facilities
ALBION SADDLEMAKERS, Walsall (YH00247)																																			●																	
ANTHONY D EVANS, Coventry (YH00462)																									●																											
BRITISH EQUINE COLLECTORS, Coventry (YH01942)																																	●																			
BROWNS, Walsall (YH02142)					●																																															
DIAMOND SADDLERY, Wolverhampton (YH04104)																		●																																		
FRANK STEPHENS & SON, Wolverhampton (YH05461)								●																																												
GORRINGE SPORTSWEAR, Walsall (YH05936)																												●																								
HORSESENSE, Solihull (YH07170)							●																																													
INDESPENSION, Halesowen (YH07427)																					●																															
MONARCH EQUESTRIAN, Willenhall (YH09717)													●																										●													
OVERIDER, Coventry (YH10593)							●																		●																											●
PROLITE, Walsall (YH11432)																●																			●												●					
SABRE LEATHER, Walsall (YH12339)																															●																					
VALE BROTHERS, Walsall (YH14632)		●																																																		
NORFOLK																																																				
ALLEN & PAGE, Thetford (YH00290)								●									●																																			
BARRIER ANIMAL HEALTHCARE, Attleborough (YH01021)														●																																						
C W G, East Dereham (YH02401)							●																																													
EQUINE CLOTHING, Downham Market (YH04770)																●																			●						●											●
EVERYTHING EQUESTRIAN, Norwich (YH04958)								●																																												
G J L, Fakenham (YH05585)								●			●																																									
H & C BEART, King's Lynn (YH06207)								●												●																																
HORSES IN SPORT, Diss (YH07169)			●																									●																								●
HORSETALK, King's Lynn (YH07176)		●					●											●																																		
INDESPENSION, Norwich (YH07428)																					●																															
J C SCHAAY TIMBER BUILDINGS, Diss (YH07576)																																	●						●													
LENRYS ASSOCIATES, Attleborough (YH08552)		●																																																		
LODDON, Norwich (YH08766)																																							●													
REYNOLDS MOTORS, Cromer (YH11775)																				●																																
RUNCTON HALL, King's Lynn (YH12233)							●																																													
TIRUS EQUESTRIAN PRODUCTS, Norwich (YH14185)																				●																																
NORTHAMPTONSHIRE																																																				

Products Supplied
G - R

by Country by County	Grain	Grooming Products	Half Chaps	Halters	Harness	Harness Racing Equipment	Hats	Hay	Hay Baskets	Hay Cratchers	Haylage	Head Collars	Heaters	Herbal Remedies	Herbs	Horse Boots	Horse Feeds	Horse Rugs	Horsebox Accessories	Horsebox Equipment	Horseboxes	Immune Support (Respiratory)	Immune Support (S. P. V.Synd.)	Insoles	Insurance	Ironmongery	Jewel Combs	Jodhpurs	Jump Cups	Kings	Leather Stirrups	Mini Muck Spreaders	Model Horses	Modified Panels	Numnahs	Outbuildings	Pad Clip	Paper Bedding	Partitions	Pasture Toppers	Performance Rugs	Photo Finish Equipment	Photography Equipment	Pledgers	Polo Equipment	Poly Jumps	Protective Clothing	Reins	Remedies	Ribbons	Riding Hats	Mail Order Facilities
BATTEN, HORACE, Northampton (YH01077)																																																				●
BUCKLEY BITS, Northampton (YH02197)		●																																																		
BURWELL HILL GARAGES, Brackley (YH02298)																				●																																
C W G, Towcester (YH02402)							●																																													
COUNTRY STYLES, Towcester (YH03430)							●																																													
EDENGATE SADDLERY, Northampton (YH04550)														●																																						
EQUIBRAND, Charwelton (YH04734)																				●																																
EQUIMAT, Kettering (YH04755)																				●																																
HARLEY, Daventry (YH06436)																																																				●
INDESPENSION, Northampton (YH07429)																					●																															
K & T FOOTWEAR, Kettering (YH07981)																																																				●
LIGHTFOOT INT, Daventry (YH08613)																				●																																
LOVESON, Irthlingborough (YH08851)			●															●										●																								
MANOR FARM RIDING SCHOOL, Wellingborough (YH09106)																					●																															
NATURALLY, Towcester (YH10055)														●																																						
NORMAN & SPICER, Daventry (YH10235)																																													●							
R P LOVATT INSURANCE, Brackley (YH11559)																									●																											
STUBBEN, Corby (YH13600)												●																			●										●				●							
THORPE SADDLERY, Kettering (YH14094)																●								●																												
THREE SHIRES LIVERY CTRE, Wellingborough (YH14107)								●																																												
WATTS & WATTS SADDLERY, Northampton (YH15003)														●																																						
WEATHERBYS, Wellingborough (YH15024)																									●																											
WOODFLAKES OF DAVENTRY, Daventry (YH15686)								●																																												
NORTHUMBERLAND																																																				
A C BURN, Berwick-upon-Tweed (YH00021)	●													●																																						
AIR-O-WEAR, Corbridge (YH00225)																																															●					
BEDMAX, Belford (YH01157)								●																																												
BROWN TRAILERS, Cramlington (YH02094)																				●																																
CHESTERS STUD, Hexham (YH02835)								●																																												
DICKINSON, T M, Morpeth (YH04114)								●																																												
EQUILINK, Alnwick (YH04751)																									●																											●
FAL TEXTILE INDUSTRIES, Blyth (YH05038)																		●																																		

www.hccyourhorse.com

Products Supplied
G - R

by Country by County

	Grain	Grooming Products	Half Chaps	Halters	Harness	Harness Racing Equipment	Hats	Hay	Hay Baskets	Hay Cratchers	Haylage	Head Collars	Heaters	Herbal Remedies	Herbs	Horse Boots	Horse Feeds	Horse Rugs	Horsebox Accessories	Horsebox Equipment	Horseboxes	Immune Support (Respiratory)	Immune Support (S. P. V.Synd.)	Insoles	Insurance	Ironmongery	Jewel Combs	Jodhpurs	Jump Cups	Kings	Leather Stirrups	Mini Muck Spreaders	Model Horses	Modified Panels	Numnahs	Outbuildings	Pad Clip	Paper Bedding	Partitions	Pasture Toppers	Performance Rugs	Photo Finish Equipment	Photography Equipment	Pledgers	Polo Equipment	Poly Jumps	Protective Clothing	Reins	Remedies	Ribbons	Riding Hats	Mail Order Facilities
FARMWAY, Morpeth (YH05074)							●							●																																						
HAYMAX, Belford (YH06586)								●																																												
J S HUBBUCK, Hexham (YH07616)								●																																												
WILLOW WEAR, Hexham (YH15505)							●																																													
NOTTINGHAMSHIRE																																																				
AERBORN EQUESTRIAN, Nottingham (YH00195)																		●																	●																	
BRIDLE WAY & GAUNTLEYS, Newark (YH01892)							●	●						●																																						●
C W G, Worksop (YH02404)							●																																													
C W G, Newark (YH02403)							●																																													
CAUNTON GRASS DRIERS, Newark (YH02660)								●																																												
DECATHLON SPORTS & LEISURE, Nottingham (YH04010)							●																																													
EASY FEEDS, Newark (YH04522)								●																																												
EUROBALE, Nottingham (YH04894)								●																																												
F MARTIN & SON, Arnold (YH04995)	●	●						●																																							●					
HOLISTIC HORSECARE, Northampton (YH06934)																																																				●
HOOF ALOOF, Nottingham (YH07025)							●																																													
INDESPENSION, Nottingham (YH07430)																					●																															
MALLENDER BROS, Worksop (YH09051)								●			●																																									
MITEL MARKETING, Papplewick (YH09682)																				●																																
OSBOURNES, Retford (YH10563)								●																																												
OSS-I-CHAFF, Newark (YH10572)								●																																												
PAPER BEDDING SUPPLIES, Newark (YH10707)																																						●														
SADDLE RACK, Nottingham (YH12346)							●							●																																						
SADDLECRAFT, Nottingham (YH12355)		●	●				●																					●																			●					●
ST CLEMENTS LODGE, Nottingham (YH13274)							●	●																																												
OXFORDSHIRE																																																				
ABBOTT, Chipping Norton (YH00108)								●																																												
ASTI STUD & SADDLERY, Faringdon (YH00633)							●											●															●																			●
BANBURY TRAILERS, Banbury (YH00880)																				●	●																															
DOBBINS CLOBBER, Thame (YH04150)								●										●																	●																	
ELITE FORAGE, Wallingford (YH04605)								●																																												
EQUI-GRASS, Banbury (YH04749)								●																																												

Products Supplied
G - R

by Country by County

	Grain	Grooming Products	Half Chaps	Halters	Harness	Harness Racing Equipment	Hats	Hay	Hay Baskets	Hay Cratchers	Haylage	Head Collars	Heaters	Herbal Remedies	Herbs	Horse Boots	Horse Feeds	Horse Rugs	Horsebox Accessories	Horsebox Equipment	Horseboxes	Immune Support (Respiratory)	Immune Support (S. P. V.Synd.)	Insoles	Insurance	Ironmongery	Jewel Combs	Jodhpurs	Jump Cups	Kings	Leather Stirrups	Mini Muck Spreaders	Model Horses	Modified Panels	Numnahs	Outbuildings	Pad Clip	Paper Bedding	Partitions	Pasture Toppers	Performance Rugs	Photo Finish Equipment	Photography Equipment	Pledgers	Polo Equipment	Poly Jumps	Protective Clothing	Reins	Remedies	Ribbons	Riding Hats	Mail Order Facilities
F S JUDGE & SONS, Faringdon (YH04999)								●																																												
FARMKEY, Banbury (YH05067)																				●																																
GARDNER, C D, Banbury (YH05646)								●																																												
JODS GALORE, Henley-on-Thames (YH07775)							●																																													●
MATHEWS COMFORT, Henley-on-Thames (YH09263)																									●																											
NEW HOUSE LIVERY, Abingdon (YH10109)								●																																												
OXFORD HILL RUGS, Witney (YH10618)																		●																																		
R S ASSEMBLIES, Bicester (YH11562)								●																																												
SANSOMS SADDLERY, Witney (YH12429)							●																																													●
SCATS COUNTRYSTORE, Faringdon (YH12506)							●																																													
TOMPKINS, R J, Banbury (YH14224)								●																																												
W F S COUNTRY, Witney (YH14766)							●																																													
WEATHERBEETA, Banbury (YH15023)																●																																				
RUTLAND																																																				
BADMINTON HORSE FEEDS, Oakham (YH00784)								●									●																																			
TRIPLE CROWN, Oakham (YH14401)								●																																												
W'UNDERWEAR, Oakham (YH15852)																																																				●
SHROPSHIRE																																																			
BULLDOG SECURITY, Much Wenlock (YH02214)																				●																																
C J BLACKSMITHS, Shrewsbury (YH02375)									●	●																			●																							●
CHARLES BRITTON CONSTRUCTION, Ellesmere (YH02754)																																				●			●													
DAVIES, R, Shrewsbury (YH03946)								●																																												
EDDIE PALIN DISTRIBUTION, Market Drayton (YH04541)		●																																																		
EVANS, J C, Shrewsbury (YH04922)																				●																																
HEAD TO HOOF, Market Drayton (YH06608)																		●																																		●
HIGHGROVE SCHOOL OF RIDING, Craven Arms (YH06788)							●																																													
HORSE SHOP, Bridgnorth (YH07139)							●																																													
N W F COUNTRYSTORE, Market Drayton (YH09998)																				●																																
TERRY DAVIS, Craven Arms (YH13957)					●																																															
TOUCHDOWN LIVERIES, Whitchurch (YH14253)															●																																					
WYKE OF SHIFNAL, Shifnal (YH15863)													●																																							
WYNNSTAY & CLWYD FARMERS, Oswestry (YH15876)							●																																													

Products Supplied
G - R

by Country by County	Grain	Grooming Products	Half Chaps	Halters	Harness	Harness Racing Equipment	Hats	Hay	Hay Baskets	Hay Cratchers	Haylage	Head Collars	Heaters	Herbal Remedies	Herbs	Horse Boots	Horse Feeds	Horse Rugs	Horsebox Accessories	Horsebox Equipment	Horseboxes	Immune Support (Respiratory)	Immune Support (S. P. V.Synd.)	Insoles	Insurance	Ironmongery	Jewel Combs	Jodhpurs	Jump Cups	Kings	Leather Stirrups	Mini Muck Spreaders	Model Horses	Modified Panels	Numnahs	Outbuildings	Pad Clip	Paper Bedding	Partitions	Pasture Toppers	Performance Rugs	Photo Finish Equipment	Photography Equipment	Pledgers	Polo Equipment	Poly Jumps	Protective Clothing	Reins	Remedies	Ribbons	Riding Hats	Mail Order Facilities
SOMERSET																																																				
BOWERS, HENRY, Chard (YH01707)							●																																													
COUNTRYWIDE STORES, Bridgwater (YH03472)								●																																												
EQUESTRIAN ENGINEERING, Templecombe (YH04700)																				●																																
HILLYERS HORSE BOXES, Street (YH06862)																				●	●																		●													
HILTON HERBS, Crewkerne (YH06863)														●	●																																					
MANELINE, B G I, Bridgwater (YH09075)																											●																									
MCCOY SADDLERY, Minehead (YH09334)							●							●																																						●
RIDEMOOR, Wincanton (YH11852)							●							●																			●												●							●
ROSE MILL FEEDS, Ilminster (YH12094)	●						●	●						●	●																																					
SPARKFORD SAWMILLS, Yeovil (YH13177)																																							●													
STAX SADDLERY, Montacute (YH13406)							●							●																																						
THORNEY COPSE, Wincanton (YH14066)	●						●	●						●						●																																●
W.E.S GARRETT MASTER SADDLERS, Cheddar (YH14803)	●					●	●							●																															●							
SOMERSET (NORTH)																																																				
SMART HORSEBOXES, Banwell (YH12918)																				●																																
SPRINGFIELD, Claverham (YH13252)																				●																																
STAFFORDSHIRE																																																				
BRITISH HORSE FEEDS, Stafford (YH01949)								●																																												
DAMPHAY PRODUCTS, Eccleshall (YH03857)								●																																												
DOBBINS DINER, Tamworth (YH04151)	●						●							●																																						
DOLLIN & MORRIS, Stafford (YH04170)	●							●																																												
FRANCES ANN BROWN SADDLERY, Stafford (YH05444)							●							●																																						
HOSSNOSH FEEDS, Uttoxeter (YH07198)								●																																												
INDESPENSION, Stoke-on-Trent (YH07431)																					●																															
KINGDOM PRODUCTS, Stafford (YH08190)								●																																												
LARKHILL SADDLERY, Burton-on-Trent (YH08432)					●		●																																													
ROOS FEEDS, Rugeley (YH12080)								●																																												
RUMENCO - MAIN RING, Burton-on-Trent (YH12227)								●																																												
STAFFORDSHIRE TRAILERS, Lichfield (YH13325)																				●																																
SUFFOLK																																																				
A H B INSURANCE, Newmarket (YH00034)																									●																											

Products Supplied
G - R

by Country by County	Grain	Grooming Products	Half Chaps	Halters	Harness	Harness Racing Equipment	Hats	Hay	Hay Baskets	Hay Cratchers	Haylage	Head Collars	Heaters	Herbal Remedies	Herbs	Horse Boots	Horse Feeds	Horse Rugs	Horsebox Accessories	Horsebox Equipment	Horseboxes	Immune Support (Respiratory)	Immune Support (S. P. V.Synd.)	Insoles	Insurance	Ironmongery	Jewel Combs	Jodhpurs	Jump Cups	Kings	Leather Stirrups	Mini Muck Spreaders	Model Horses	Modified Panels	Numnahs	Outbuildings	Pad Clip	Paper Bedding	Partitions	Pasture Toppers	Performance Rugs	Photo Finish Equipment	Photography Equipment	Pledgers	Polo Equipment	Poly Jumps	Protective Clothing	Reins	Remedies	Ribbons	Riding Hats	Mail Order Facilities
B G I BLOODSTOCK/INSURANCE, Newmarket (YH00721)																									●																											
BRADSTOCK HAMILTON & PARTNERS, Newmarket (YH01763)																									●																											
BURYFEEDS, Bury St Edmunds (YH02300)								●																																												
C W G, Bury St Edmunds (YH02406)							●																																													
CHARNWOOD MILLING, Woodbridge (YH02773)								●																																												
CHURCH FARM TACK SHOP & FEEDS, Eye (YH02903)							●											●																																		
CROSSWAYS SV CTRE, Bungay (YH03667)							●	●										●																																		
CURRAGH BLOODSTOCK AGENCY, Newmarket (YH03734)																									●																											
GIBSON SADDLERS, Newmarket (YH05746)							●																												●													●				
GLADWELLS, Ipswich (YH05802)								●							●																																					
HERITAGE COAST STUD, Woodbridge (YH06703)								●																																												
HORSE REQUISITES, Newmarket (YH07132)							●						●																																●							
HORSESHOES, Wrentham (YH07174)															●																																					●
INDESPENSION, Ipswich (YH07432)																					●																															
J B FENWICK & SON, Newmarket (YH07563)								●																																												
K 9 PET FOODS, Framlingham (YH07982)								●																																												
LAVENHAM LEISURE, Sudbury (YH08463)																		●																																		●
LONG MELFORD, Sudbury (YH08799)							●																												●																	
MILL SADDLERY, Stowmarket (YH09587)							●																																													●
MOUNTFOLD, Bures (YH09901)													●																																							
NORCROFT EQUESTRIAN DVLP, Bury St Edmunds (YH10230)																																							●													
ORWELL ARENA, Ipswich (YH10556)								●																																												
RIDE AWAY SADDLERY, Ipswich (YH11846)							●																																													
STOKE BY CLARE EQUESTRIAN CTRE, Sudbury (YH13501)							●	●																																												
STOREY, MARTIN J, Ipswich (YH13525)													●																																							
STOW FEEDS, Stowmarket (YH13536)								●																																												
SUFFOLK SADDLES, Ipswich (YH13626)							●																																													
UFAC, Newmarket (YH14539)								●																																												
VALLEY FARM, Woodbridge (YH14651)								●																																												
WESTBRINK FARMS, Newmarket (YH15184)								●									●																																			
SURREY																																																				
AGRIQUESTRIAN CONSULTANTS, Epsom (YH00202)																																				●			●													

www.hccyourhorse.com

Products Supplied
G - R

by Country by County

	Grain	Grooming Products	Half Chaps	Halters	Harness	Harness Racing Equipment	Hats	Hay	Hay Baskets	Hay Cratchers	Haylage	Head Collars	Heaters	Herbal Remedies	Herbs	Horse Boots	Horse Feeds	Horse Rugs	Horsebox Accessories	Horsebox Equipment	Horseboxes	Immune Support (Respiratory)	Immune Support (S. P. V.Synd.)	Insoles	Insurance	Ironmongery	Jewel Combs	Jodhpurs	Jump Cups	Kings	Leather Stirrups	Mini Muck Spreaders	Model Horses	Modified Panels	Numnahs	Outbuildings	Pad Clip	Paper Bedding	Partitions	Pasture Toppers	Performance Rugs	Photo Finish Equipment	Photography Equipment	Pledgers	Polo Equipment	Poly Jumps	Protective Clothing	Reins	Remedies	Ribbons	Riding Hats	Mail Order Facilities
ANIMAL ALTERNATIVES, Richmond (YH00425)																						●	●																													
ARDENLEA ENTERPRISES, Epsom (YH00504)													●																										●													
ASCOT PARK, Woking (YH00583)																					●																								●							●
BALANCED FEEDS, Malden Rushett (YH00830)								●																																												
BUTTONS SADDLERY, Woking (YH02337)							●																																													
CHRIS HAY, Dorking (YH02881)								●																																												
CHRIS HAY, Dorking (YH02882)								●																																												
CLUB PRO-AM, Richmond (YH03074)																																													●							
FIELDGUARD, Cranleigh (YH05193)																																																				●
FROSBURY FARM FEEDS, Guildford (YH05518)								●																																												
GRAHAM BROWN, Guildford (YH05962)																									●																											
HASTILOW COMPETITION SADDLES, Godalming (YH06526)	●						●	●						●				●																											●							●
INDESPENSION, Redhill (YH07433)																					●																															
LETHERS OF BROCKHAM, Betchworth (YH08568)							●																																													
LETHERS OF MERSTHAM, Redhill (YH08569)							●																																													
LINGFIELD TACK, Lingfield (YH08660)							●							●	●																																					
ONE STOP TACK SHOP, East Molesey (YH10513)							●																																													
RIDE & DRIVE, Horne (YH11842)					●																																															
ROKER'S TACK SHOP, Guildford (YH12064)							●	●																																												
SCATS COUNTRYSTORE, Redhill (YH12508)							●																																													
SCATS COUNTRYSTORE, Godalming (YH12507)							●																																													
STONEWAYS INSURANCE, Godalming (YH13521)																									●																											
SUPERPET THE HORSE SHOP, Epsom (YH13654)																																																				●
YORK, RAY, Cobham (YH15918)								●																																												
SUSSEX (EAST)																																																				
ANDREW REILLY, Forest Row (YH00392)																														●																						
BROWN BREAD HORSE RESCUE CTRE, Battle (YH02092)																									●																											
BUCKINGHAM HSE, Newhaven (YH02191)																									●																											
FARMIX, Wadhurst (YH05066)								●																																												
G A COMMERCIALS, Pevensey (YH05569)																				●																																
GREENSLADE HORSE TRAILERS, Robertsbridge (YH06101)																				●																																
GUMTREE ENTERPRISES, Plumpton (YH06191)																				●																																

Products Supplied
G - R

by Country by County	Grain	Grooming Products	Half Chaps	Halters	Harness	Harness Racing Equipment	Hats	Hay	Hay Baskets	Hay Cratchers	Haylage	Head Collars	Heaters	Herbal Remedies	Herbs	Horse Boots	Horse Feeds	Horse Rugs	Horsebox Accessories	Horsebox Equipment	Horseboxes	Immune Support (Respiratory)	Immune Support (S. P. V.Synd.)	Insoles	Insurance	Ironmongery	Jewel Combs	Jodhpurs	Jump Cups	Kings	Leather Stirrups	Mini Muck Spreaders	Model Horses	Modified Panels	Numnahs	Outbuildings	Pad Clip	Paper Bedding	Partitions	Pasture Toppers	Performance Rugs	Photo Finish Equipment	Photography Equipment	Pledgers	Polo Equipment	Poly Jumps	Protective Clothing	Reins	Remedies	Ribbons	Riding Hats	Mail Order Facilities
LEVADE SYSTEMS, Hartfield (YH08572)																																							●													
SCATS COUNTRYSTORE, Heathfield (YH12509)							●																																													
SOUTH LODGE, Rotherfield (YH13100)																																	●																			
STEVENS, LEONARD, Eastbourne (YH13445)	●						●							●																																						
SUSSEX (WEST)																																																				
A V BAKER & SONS, Chichester (YH00064)																	●																																			
ALL TIME EQUESTRIAN, Crawley (YH00286)							●																																													
BRENDON HORSE & RIDER, Brighton (YH01837)							●	●						●																																						
COUNTY ROSETTES, Hassocks (YH03490)																																																		●		
CRAWLEY DOWN SADDLERY, Crawley (YH03578)							●																																													
DEAN, GEOFF, Worthing (YH03991)						●																																														
DIAMOND SADDLERY, Hassocks (YH04105)					●																																															
DRAGONFLY SADDLERY, Hassocks (YH04252)							●							●																																						●
EQUINE AMERICA, Broadbridge Heath (YH04761)		●																																																		
EQUITOGS, Billingshurst (YH04830)							●	●																																												
EQUITOGS, Littlehampton (YH04829)							●	●																																												
GEOFF DEAN SADDLERY, Worthing (YH05714)					●		●																																													
HORSE HEALTH PRODUCTS, Pulborough (YH07121)								●																																												
LIGHTS, Brighton (YH08616)								●						●																																						
PENFOLD & SONS, Haywards Heath (YH10934)							●																																													
ROXTON, Midhurst (YH12176)																																													●							
ROXTON SPORTING, Midhurst (YH12178)																																													●							
SCATS COUNTRYSTORE, Billingshurst (YH12510)							●																																													
SHARON TONG, Steyning (YH12677)																																																				●
SNOWHILL SADDLERY, Chichester (YH13044)							●																																													
SYMONDSBURY STUD, Haywards Heath (YH13726)								●																																												
TACK A ROUND SADDLERY, Billingshurst (YH13781)							●																																													
TRACK RIGHT, Hassocks (YH14308)							●																																													●
WATT TO WEAR, Horsham (YH14998)																																													●							
TYNE AND WEAR																																																				
EQUINE PRODUCTS, Newcastle-upon-Tyne (YH04795)								●																																												
GO RIDING GRP, Ponteland (YH05862)								●																																												

Products Supplied
G - R

by Country by County	Grain	Grooming Products	Half Chaps	Halters	Harness	Harness Racing Equipment	Hats	Hay	Hay Baskets	Hay Cratchers	Haylage	Head Collars	Heaters	Herbal Remedies	Herbs	Horse Boots	Horse Feeds	Horse Rugs	Horsebox Accessories	Horsebox Equipment	Horseboxes	Immune Support (Respiratory)	Immune Support (S. P. V.Synd.)	Insoles	Insurance	Ironmongery	Jewel Combs	Jodhpurs	Jump Cups	Kings	Leather Stirrups	Mini Muck Spreaders	Model Horses	Modified Panels	Numnahs	Outbuildings	Pad Clip	Paper Bedding	Partitions	Pasture Toppers	Performance Rugs	Photo Finish Equipment	Photography Equipment	Pledgers	Polo Equipment	Poly Jumps	Protective Clothing	Reins	Remedies	Ribbons	Riding Hats	Mail Order Facilities
H C S, North Shields (YH06215)																																																				●
INDESPENSION, Newcastle-upon-Tyne (YH07434)																					●																															
JOSEPH BAILEY & SONS, Houghton Le Spring (YH07942)																																							●													
RIDERS, North Shields (YH11854)							●							●																																						
S & S SADDLERY, Sunderland (YH12313)							●																																													
SADDLE SHOP, Gateshead (YH12350)							●																																													
WEBSTER, J R, Newcastle-upon-Tyne (YH15040)							●																																													
WARWICKSHIRE																																																				
A & J SADDLERY, Southam (YH00012)							●	●						●																																						
ACCIMASSU, Studley (YH00140)														●																						●																
ATHAG LTD, Atherstone (YH00642)																																							●													
BHS, Kenilworth (YH01371)																									●																											●
CALDECOTE RIDING SCHOOL, Nuneaton (YH02428)							●																																													
COLEMAN, ROBIN, Kenilworth (YH03164)																																	●												●							
HORSE & RIDER, Leamington Spa (YH07095)																									●																											
M J MAC, Leamington Spa (YH08970)																									●																											
N F U MUTUAL, Stratford-upon-Avon (YH09990)																									●																											
OUSBEY CARRIAGES, Statford-on-Avon (YH10584)																																	●																			
SPORTSMARK, Warwick (YH13236)																																													●							
WARWICK BUILDINGS, Rugby (YH14945)																																							●													
WARWICKSHIRE TRAILERS, Solihull (YH14953)																																																				●
WAVERLEY EQUESTRIAN CTRE, Leamington Spa (YH15011)							●	●																																					●							
WILTSHIRE																																																				
AMERICAN THOROUGHBRED, Kilmington (YH00365)								●																																												
ARMADILLO PRODUCTS, Salisbury (YH00535)																●																																				
BEST BOOTS, Chippenham (YH01324)																																																				●
BLOODSTOCK & STUD INVESTMENT, Marlborough (YH01549)																									●																											
CHRIS LEA, Salisbury (YH02883)																									●																											
DAVID FARMER SADDLERY, Chippenham (YH03919)					●																							●																								
ELMGROVE SADDLERY, Swindon (YH04636)							●																																													
GEORGE SMITH HORSEBOXES, Salisbury (YH05719)													●							●	●																		●													
GRANT BARNES & SON, Malmesbury (YH06009)		●																																																		

Products Supplied
G - R

by Country by County

	Grain	Grooming Products	Half Chaps	Halters	Harness	Harness Racing Equipment	Hats	Hay	Hay Baskets	Hay Cratchers	Haylage	Head Collars	Heaters	Herbal Remedies	Herbs	Horse Boots	Horse Feeds	Horse Rugs	Horsebox Accessories	Horsebox Equipment	Horseboxes	Immune Support (Respiratory)	Immune Support (S. P. V.Synd.)	Insoles	Insurance	Ironmongery
HURDCOTT LIVERY STABLES, Salisbury (YH07311)							●							●												
MALTHOUSE EQUESTRIAN CTRE, Swindon (YH09058)																										
NEW EQUINE WEAR, Malmesbury (YH10093)		●																								
SADDLERY, Swindon (YH12364)							●																			
SAMWAYS, Salisbury (YH12402)								●																		
SCATS COUNTRYSTORE, Salisbury (YH12511)							●																			
SCATS COUNTRYSTORE, Devizes (YH12512)							●																			
SEG, Calne (YH12611)																										
SYDNEY INGRAM & SON, Salisbury (YH13722)							●																			
TIDWORTH POLO CLUB, Tidworth (YH14136)																										
WADSWICK, Corsham (YH14819)							●																			
WORCESTERSHIRE																										
BENT, BM & SA, Evesham (YH01282)								●													●					
CASTLE HORSEBOXES, Kidderminster (YH02629)																				●	●					
CENTRIFORCE, Worcester (YH02697)																				●						
COTTRILL EQSTN VEHICLE SVS, Worcester (YH03388)																					●					
COUNTRYWIDE, Worcester (YH03446)							●																			
EQUIMIX, Stourport-on-Severn (YH04756)	●						●																			
EQUINE RESOURCES, Malvern (YH04796)																									●	
KYRE EQUESTRIAN CTRE, Tenbury Wells (YH08305)	●							●																		
OAKLAND HORSEBOXES, Little Witley (YH10388)																				●						
PHIPPS, A, Pershore (YH11068)																										
ROPER, J H, Suckley (YH12084)																									●	
SMITH-MAXWELL, A L, Upton-upon-Severn (YH13005)								●																		
WITS END STABLES, Worcester (YH15634)								●																		
YORKSHIRE (EAST)																										
ASS BLOOD STOCK CONS, Bridlington (YH00629)																									●	
EUROVET, North Ferriby (YH04909)								●																		
HAIGHS, Doncaster (YH06282)								●																		
HOOD, J R, Driffield (YH07023)								●																		
NORTHERN STRAW, Goole (YH10311)								●																		
PATRICK WILKINSON, Beverley (YH10825)							●																			

	Jewel Combs	Jodhpurs	Jump Cups	Kings	Leather Stirrups	Mini Muck Spreaders	Model Horses	Modified Panels	Numnahs	Outbuildings	Pad Clip	Paper Bedding	Partitions	Pasture Toppers	Performance Rugs	Photo Finish Equipment	Photography Equipment	Pledgers	Polo Equipment	Poly Jumps	Protective Clothing	Reins	Remedies	Ribbons	Riding Hats	Mail Order Facilities
HURDCOTT LIVERY STABLES, Salisbury (YH07311)																										
MALTHOUSE EQUESTRIAN CTRE, Swindon (YH09058)																	●									
NEW EQUINE WEAR, Malmesbury (YH10093)																										
SADDLERY, Swindon (YH12364)																										
SAMWAYS, Salisbury (YH12402)																										
SCATS COUNTRYSTORE, Salisbury (YH12511)																										
SCATS COUNTRYSTORE, Devizes (YH12512)																										
SEG, Calne (YH12611)																			●							
SYDNEY INGRAM & SON, Salisbury (YH13722)																										
TIDWORTH POLO CLUB, Tidworth (YH14136)																			●							
WADSWICK, Corsham (YH14819)																										
WORCESTERSHIRE																										
BENT, BM & SA, Evesham (YH01282)																										
CASTLE HORSEBOXES, Kidderminster (YH02629)																										
CENTRIFORCE, Worcester (YH02697)													●													
COTTRILL EQSTN VEHICLE SVS, Worcester (YH03388)																										
COUNTRYWIDE, Worcester (YH03446)																										
EQUIMIX, Stourport-on-Severn (YH04756)																			●							●
EQUINE RESOURCES, Malvern (YH04796)																										
KYRE EQUESTRIAN CTRE, Tenbury Wells (YH08305)																										
OAKLAND HORSEBOXES, Little Witley (YH10388)																										
PHIPPS, A, Pershore (YH11068)																										●
ROPER, J H, Suckley (YH12084)																										
SMITH-MAXWELL, A L, Upton-upon-Severn (YH13005)																										
WITS END STABLES, Worcester (YH15634)																										
YORKSHIRE (EAST)																										
ASS BLOOD STOCK CONS, Bridlington (YH00629)																										
EUROVET, North Ferriby (YH04909)																										
HAIGHS, Doncaster (YH06282)																										
HOOD, J R, Driffield (YH07023)																										
NORTHERN STRAW, Goole (YH10311)																										
PATRICK WILKINSON, Beverley (YH10825)																										●

Products Supplied
G - R

by Country by County

Company	Grain	Grooming Products	Half Chaps	Halters	Harness	Harness Racing Equipment	Hats	Hay	Hay Baskets	Hay Cratchers	Haylage	Head Collars	Heaters	Herbal Remedies	Herbs	Horse Boots	Horse Feeds	Horse Rugs	Horsebox Accessories	Horsebox Equipment	Horseboxes	Immune Support (Respiratory)	Immune Support (S. P. V.Synd.)	Insoles	Insurance	Ironmongery	Jewel Combs	Jodhpurs	Jump Cups	Kings	Leather Stirrups	Mini Muck Spreaders	Model Horses	Modified Panels	Numnahs	Outbuildings	Pad Clip	Paper Bedding	Partitions	Pasture Toppers	Performance Rugs	Photo Finish Equipment	Photography Equipment	Pledgers	Polo Equipment	Poly Jumps	Protective Clothing	Reins	Remedies	Ribbons	Riding Hats	Mail Order Facilities
YORKSHIRE (NORTH)																																																				
ANIMAL INSURANCE, Thirsk (YH00440)																									●																											
B & B LIVERY, Northallerton (YH00709)								●																																												
BEAVER HORSE SHOP, Harrogate (YH01143)							●																																													
BIT BANK, Stokesley (YH01454)																																																				●
BURGESS ENDEAVOUR, Pickering (YH02243)								●																																												
BUSHELL, ANN, Richmond (YH02309)																																	●																			
E & L INSURANCE, Ouseburn (YH04393)																									●																											
EDDLETHORPE EQUESTRIAN SVS, Malton (YH04543)								●																																												
F BAYRAM & SONS, York (YH04984)								●																																												
FRANCES BULLOCK'S SADDLERY, Easingwold (YH05446)								●																																												
GALE & PHILLIPSON, Northallerton (YH05611)																									●																											
GALE & PHILLIPSON, Harrogate (YH05610)																									●																											
GILLS SADDLERY & CANE, Northallerton (YH05787)							●																																													
HI-LINE HORSEBOXES, Cawood (YH06809)																				●																			●													
HOLMAN, A E & A B, Selby (YH06961)								●																																												
HORSEFEEDSUK, Harrogate (YH07154)																	●																																			
J S W & SON COACHBUILDERS, Northallerton (YH07619)																				●																			●													
LANGTON HORSE WEAR, Northallerton (YH08416)							●																																													
PRATT, IAN, Sutton-on-Forest (YH11338)																									●																											
R & R COUNTRY, Selby (YH11507)								●																																												●
RIDE-AWAY, York (YH11850)							●							●				●																																	●	●
ROBINSON, Malton (YH11985)							●																																													●
ROCKING HORSE SHOP, Pocklington (YH12034)																																	●																			
SECOND TURNOUT, Northallerton (YH12598)							●																																													
TEAL COTTAGE STUD, Welburn (YH13922)																					●																															
VITALIN EQUINE FEEDS, Ripon (YH14736)								●																																												
WHITE ROSE SADDLERY, Malton (YH15324)							●																																													
YORKSHIRE (SOUTH)																																																				
ARGO FEEDS, Sheffield (YH00521)								●																																												
BLUE CHIP, Sheffield (YH01565)														●	●																																					●
DARKHORSE TINYTACK, Barnsley (YH03888)																																																				●

Products Supplied
G - R

by Country by County

	Grain	Grooming Products	Half Chaps	Halters	Harness	Harness Racing Equipment	Hats	Hay	Hay Baskets	Hay Cratchers	Haylage	Head Collars	Heaters	Herbal Remedies	Herbs	Horse Boots	Horse Feeds	Horse Rugs	Horsebox Accessories	Horsebox Equipment	Horseboxes	Immune Support (Respiratory)	Immune Support (S. P. V.Synd.)	Insoles	Insurance	Ironmongery	Jewel Combs	Jodhpurs	Jump Cups	Kings	Leather Stirrups	Mini Muck Spreaders	Model Horses	Modified Panels	Numnahs	Outbuildings	Pad Clip	Paper Bedding	Partitions	Pasture Toppers	Performance Rugs	Photo Finish Equipment	Photography Equipment	Pledgers	Polo Equipment	Poly Jumps	Protective Clothing	Reins	Remedies	Ribbons	Riding Hats	Mail Order Facilities
FRIENDSHIP ESTATES, Doncaster (YH05503)								●																																												
HORSE & RIDER, Sheffield (YH07097)							●																																													●
HORSE & RIDER, Doncaster (YH07096)							●																																													
MILLVIEW, Doncaster (YH09638)							●																																													
MR ED'S, Rotherham (YH09915)							●																																													
STABLE-DRY & EQUIBALE, Doncaster (YH13302)								●			●																																									
THROSTLE NEST SADDLERY, Barnsley (YH14114)							●																																													
WILDSMITHS, Doncaster (YH15412)							●																																													
YORKSHIRE (WEST)																																																				
B T H HIRE & SALES, Leeds (YH00749)																																																				●
BAILEYS HORSE FEEDS, Wakefield (YH00808)																	●																																			
BAILEYS HORSE FEEDS, Wakefield (YH00807)																	●																																			
BARDSEY MILLS, Otley (YH00927)	●													●																																						
BRADLEY DOUBLELOCK, Bingley (YH01749)																				●																																
BRANDON FORGE SADDLERY, Leeds (YH01796)							●							●																			●																			
CALDENE CLOTHING, Hebden Bridge (YH02430)							●																																													
DAYS PET SHOP, Bradford (YH03971)							●																																							●						
DISCOUNT SADDLERY, Huddersfield (YH04129)		●					●							●				●																														●				●
EASTVIEW STABLES, Leeds (YH04516)								●																																												
EQUESTRIAN CLEARANCE CTRE, Halifax (YH04694)																																																				●
EQUITACK SADDLERY, Wakefield (YH04825)							●							●																																						●
F & STROKER & SONS, Leeds (YH04981)								●																																												
FOX SADDLERS, Wetherby (YH05425)																																																				●
HIGHWOOD, Ossett (YH06803)																				●																																
HIGHWOOD HORSEBOXES, Wakefield (YH06804)																				●																																
HILLAM FEEDS, South Milford (YH06836)							●	●																																												
HILLAM TRAILERS, Cleckheaton (YH06837)																																							●													
HOOVES EQUESTRIAN, Bradford (YH07047)		●																●										●																								●
HOPTON, Mirfield (YH07061)								●												●																																
INDESPENSION, Leeds (YH07435)																					●																															
JENKINSONS, Dewsbury (YH07740)		●					●																																													
KIPPAX, Leeds (YH08222)							●											●																																		

www.hccyourhorse.com

Products Supplied
G - R

by Country by County	Grain	Grooming Products	Half Chaps	Halters	Harness	Harness Racing Equipment	Hats	Hay	Hay Baskets	Hay Cratchers	Haylage	Head Collars	Heaters	Herbal Remedies	Herbs	Horse Boots	Horse Feeds	Horse Rugs	Horsebox Accessories	Horsebox Equipment	Horseboxes	Immune Support (Respiratory)	Immune Support (S. P. V.Synd.)	Insoles	Insurance	Ironmongery	Jewel Combs	Jodhpurs	Jump Cups	Kings	Leather Stirrups	Mini Muck Spreaders	Model Horses	Modified Panels	Numnahs	Outbuildings	Pad Clip	Paper Bedding	Partitions	Pasture Toppers	Performance Rugs	Photo Finish Equipment	Photography Equipment	Pledgers	Polo Equipment	Poly Jumps	Protective Clothing	Reins	Remedies	Ribbons	Riding Hats	Mail Order Facilities
MIDDLESTOWN SADDLERY, Wakefield (YH09540)							●							●																			●																		●	
PARKER MERCHANTING, Rothwell (YH10746)																				●																																
PUDSEY AGRICULTURAL SVS, Pudsey (YH11449)								●																																												
QUALTEX, Hebden Bridge (YH11477)																●		●																																		
RIGTON CARR FARM, Bardsey (YH11893)								●																																												
SIMCOCK, R, Halifax (YH12818)								●																																												
STYLO MATCHMAKERS INT, Bradford (YH13620)												●						●																	●																	
TACK & TURNOUT EQUESTRIAN, Huddersfield (YH13780)														●																																						●
VEHICLE WINDOW CTRE, Castleford (YH14673)																			●	●																																
YORKSHIRE EQUESTRIAN FLOORING, Leeds (YH15920)																				●																																
IRELAND																																																				
COUNTY CORK																																																				
BUCAS, Cork (YH02184)				●												●		●																																		
COUNTY DUBLIN																																																				
COLEMANS OF SANDYFORD, Dublin (YH03166)			●	●			●					●																●							●												●	●			●	●
EQUESTRIAN DIRECT SALES, Dublin (YH04699)							●																																													
INDESPENSION, Tallaght (YH07414)																					●																															
COUNTY KERRY																																																			
BRIDLES & BITS, Tralee (YH01893)							●																												●																	
COUNTY KILDARE																																																			
INT BLOODSTOCK FINANCE, Naas (YH07465)																									●																											
IRISH EQUESTRIAN PRODUCTS, Kildare (YH07493)						●	●																																													●
COUNTY KILKENNY																																																			
EUROFARM, Kilkenny (YH04898)		●	●	●			●					●						●										●																			●					
COUNTY LIMERICK																																																			
COUNTRY DRESSER, Adare (YH03403)							●											●																																		
INDESPENSION, Limerick (YH07415)																					●																															
COUNTY LOUTH																																																			
HORSEWARE, Dundalk (YH07177)																		●																																		
COUNTY MAYO																																																			
ABRAM, DAVID, Bohola (YH00135)					●																																															
COUNTY MEATH																																																			

Products Supplied

G - R

by Country by County

	Grain	Grooming Products	Half Chaps	Halters	Harness	Harness Racing Equipment	Hats	Hay	Hay Baskets	Hay Cratchers	Haylage	Head Collars	Heaters	Herbal Remedies	Herbs	Horse Boots	Horse Feeds	Horse Rugs	Horsebox Accessories	Horsebox Equipment	Horseboxes	Immune Support (Respiratory)	Immune Support (S. P. V.Synd.)	Insoles	Insurance	Ironmongery	Jewel Combs	Jodhpurs	Jump Cups	Kings	Leather Stirrups	Mini Muck Spreaders	Model Horses	Modified Panels	Numnahs	Outbuildings	Pad Clip	Paper Bedding	Partitions	Pasture Toppers	Performance Rugs	Photo Finish Equipment	Photography Equipment	Pledgers	Polo Equipment	Poly Jumps	Protective Clothing	Reins	Remedies	Ribbons	Riding Hats	Mail Order Facilities
CLARKE'S SPORTSDEN, Navan (YH02978)							●																																													
COUNTY MONAGHAN																																																				
FRANK WARD, Carrickmacross (YH05462)			●																																												●					
COUNTY ROSCOMMON																																																				
MURPHY EQUESTRIAN, Strokestown (YH09954)																																																				●
COUNTY WESTMEATH																																																				
TALLY HO, Athlone (YH13838)			●																									●																								
COUNTY WICKLOW																																																				
EQUESTRIAN LEATHERS, Bray (YH04704)			●				●					●				●																			●																	
NORTHERN IRELAND																																																				
COUNTY ANTRIM																																																				
AON MCMILLEN, Belfast (YH00472)																									●																											
BRACKEN EQUESTRIAN, Belfast (YH01736)							●																																													
COUNTRY CLASSICS, Lisburn (YH03399)							●																																													
DOAGH FARM FEEDS, Doagh (YH04147)	●																																																			
GRANGE EQUESTRIAN, Newtownabbey (YH05986)														●																																			●			
INDESPENSION, Newtownabbey (YH07413)																					●																															
OLD MILL, Carrickfergus (YH10465)							●																																													
ROWAN RIDING WEAR, Lisburn (YH12155)													●																																							
COUNTY ARMAGH																																																				
ANNAGHMORE SADDLERY, Craigavon (YH00451)							●																																													
LIME PARK EQUESTRIAN, Craigavon (YH08626)								●																																												
PREMIER SADDLERY, Armagh (YH11349)							●																																													
STINSON, J D, Armagh (YH13470)							●																																													
COUNTY DOWN																																																				
HOLMESTEAD SADDLERY, Downpatrick (YH06981)							●							●																															●							
WEIR, Ballynahinch (YH15051)	●													●																																						
COUNTY LONDONDERRY																																																				
HAVEN SADDLERY, Magherafelt (YH06539)														●																																						●

Products Supplied
G - R

by Country by County

Supplier	Grain	Grooming Products	Half Chaps	Halters	Harness	Harness Racing Equipment	Hats	Hay	Hay Baskets	Hay Cratchers	Haylage	Head Collars	Heaters	Herbal Remedies	Herbs	Horse Boots	Horse Feeds	Horse Rugs	Horsebox Accessories	Horsebox Equipment	Horseboxes	Immune Support (Respiratory)	Immune Support (S. P. V.Synd.)	Insoles	Insurance	Ironmongery	Jewel Combs	Jodhpurs	Jump Cups	Kings	Leather Stirrups	Mini Muck Spreaders	Model Horses	Modified Panels	Numnahs	Outbuildings	Pad Clip	Paper Bedding	Partitions	Pasture Toppers	Performance Rugs	Photo Finish Equipment	Photography Equipment	Pledgers	Polo Equipment	Poly Jumps	Protective Clothing	Reins	Remedies	Ribbons	Riding Hats	Mail Order Facilities
SCOTLAND																																																				
ABERDEEN (CITY OF)																																																				
COUNTRY WAYS, Aberdeen (YH03436)							●																																													
HAYFIELD SADDLERY, Aberdeen (YH06579)																									●																											
ABERDEENSHIRE																																																				
CRAGINETHERTY, Turriff (YH03545)								●																																												
FEEDMIX, Turriff (YH05123)								●																																												
MILL OF URAS EQUESTRIAN, Stonehaven (YH09583)							●	●																																												
MILLER PLANT, Inverurie (YH09601)							●							●																																						
SARAH'S ROSETTES, Ellon (YH12434)																																																		●		
TROJAN EQUESTRIAN, Fraserburgh (YH14405)			●															●																																		
ANGUS																																																				
BLACKLITE, Dundee (YH01486)																				●																●																
FEEDMIX, Kirriemuir (YH05124)								●																																												
KIRRIEMUIR HORSE SUPPLIES, Kirriemuir (YH08240)							●	●						●																																						
PATHHEAD STABLES, Kirriemuir (YH10821)							●	●						●																																						
ARGYLL AND BUTE																																																				
TACKLE & TACK, Oban (YH13818)	●						●	●						●																			●																			●
WHAT EVERY HORSE WANTS, Helensburgh (YH15266)							●																																													●
AYRSHIRE (EAST)																																																				
FERRIE, J & A, Newmilns (YH05169)																		●																																		
JAMES GIBB, Galston (YH07667)								●																																												
AYRSHIRE (SOUTH)																																																				
AYR TRAILER CTRE, Ayr (YH00701)																					●																															
AYRSHIRE EQUITATION CTRE, Ayr (YH00704)							●																																													
CROCKET EQUESTRIAN, Ayr (YH03606)							●																																													
OTTERSWICK, Mauchine (YH10581)																																																				●
DUMFRIES AND GALLOWAY																																																				
DOUGLAS, JOHN L, Newton Stewart (YH04214)																				●												●								●												
GEE GEE'S, Dumfries (YH05690)							●							●																			●																			●
ROBERT THORNE, Annan (YH11944)														●	●																																					

Products Supplied
G - R

by Country by County

	Grain	Grooming Products	Half Chaps	Halters	Harness	Harness Racing Equipment	Hats	Hay	Hay Baskets	Hay Cratchers	Haylage	Head Collars	Heaters	Herbal Remedies	Herbs	Horse Boots	Horse Feeds	Horse Rugs	Horsebox Accessories	Horsebox Equipment	Horseboxes	Immune Support (Respiratory)	Immune Support (S. P. V.Synd.)	Insoles	Insurance	Ironmongery	Jewel Combs	Jodhpurs	Jump Cups	Kings	Leather Stirrups	Mini Muck Spreaders	Model Horses	Modified Panels	Numnahs	Outbuildings	Pad Clip	Paper Bedding	Partitions	Pasture Toppers	Performance Rugs	Photo Finish Equipment	Photography Equipment	Pledgers	Polo Equipment	Poly Jumps	Protective Clothing	Reins	Remedies	Ribbons	Riding Hats	Mail Order Facilities
EDINBURGH (CITY OF)																																																				
DRUM FEEDS, Edinburgh (YH04280)								●																																					●							
INDESPENSION, Edinburgh (YH07417)																					●																															
STIRLINGSHIRE SADDLERY, Edinburgh (YH13474)							●							●																																						
FALKIRK																																																				
J C M, Falkirk (YH07572)																				●																																
FIFE																																																				
EUROPA, Lochgelly (YH04904)																																																				●
SALTIRE STABLES, Cupar (YH12394)																																							●													
GLASGOW (CITY OF)																																																				
INDESPENSION, Glasgow (YH07419)																					●																															
SEIS, Glasgow (YH12613)																									●																											
HIGHLANDS																																																				
RADDERY EQUINE, Fortrose (YH11593)							●																																						●							●
SEAFORTH SADDLERS, Inverness (YH12586)							●							●																																						
ISLE OF SKYE																																																				
SKYE RIDING CTRE, Portree (YH12881)							●																																													
LANARKSHIRE (NORTH)																																																				
KIRK RD SMIDDY, Shotts (YH08230)																										●																										
LANARKSHIRE (SOUTH)																																																				
GALLOWAY & MACLEOD, Larkhall (YH05625)								●																																												
LOTHIAN (EAST)																																																				
J S MAIN & SONS, Haddington (YH07617)							●																																													●
LOTHIAN (MID)																																																				
BOWLEA TRAILERS, Penicuik (YH01713)																																				●																
GEORGES SADDLERY, Newbridge (YH05726)																																	●												●							
R H MILLER, Dalkeith (YH11541)																		●																																●		
LOTHIAN (WEST)																																																				
CLEAR ROUND ORIGINALS, Bathgate (YH03010)																																	●																			
TIGGA'S SADDLERY, Wester Calder (YH14141)																																													●							
MORAY																																																				
GREENFIELDS SADDLERY, Elgin (YH06085)						●	●	●						●																			●												●							●

Products Supplied
G - R

by Country by County	Grain	Grooming Products	Half Chaps	Halters	Harness	Harness Racing Equipment	Hats	Hay	Hay Baskets	Hay Cratchers	Haylage	.Head Collars	Heaters	Herbal Remedies	Herbs	Horse Boots	Horse Feeds	Horse Rugs	Horsebox Accessories	Horsebox Equipment	Horseboxes	Immune Support (Respiratory)	Immune Support (S. P. V.Synd.)	Insoles	Insurance	Ironmongery	Jewel Combs	Jodhpurs	Jump Cups	Kings	Leather Stirrups	Mini Muck Spreaders	Model Horses	Modified Panels	Numnahs	Outbuildings	Pad Clip	Paper Bedding	Partitions	Pasture Toppers	Performance Rugs	Photo Finish Equipment	Photography Equipment	Pledgers	Polo Equipment	Poly Jumps	Protective Clothing	Reins	Remedies	Ribbons	Riding Hats	Mail Order Facilities
THERAPY SYSTEMS, Aberlour (YH13985)													●																																							
PERTH AND KINROSS																																																				
EQUI-CARE, Perth (YH04736)							●																																													
GENERAL ACCIDENT, Perth (YH05701)																									●																											
GLEN EAGLES EQUESTRIAN, Auchterarder (YH05825)														●																																						
MCCASH'S, Perth (YH09326)	●						●	●							●													●																								
SHETLAND PONY STUD BOOK SOC, Perth (YH12736)																																																				●
SCOTTISH BORDERS																																																			
A C BURN, Jedburgh (YH00022)	●													●																																						
MCNAB SADDLERS, Kelso (YH09397)							●							●						●																																●
MCNAB SADDLERS, Selkirk (YH09396)							●							●						●																																●
R H MILLER, Peebles (YH11542)							●	●																																												

Products Supplied

G - R

by Country by County

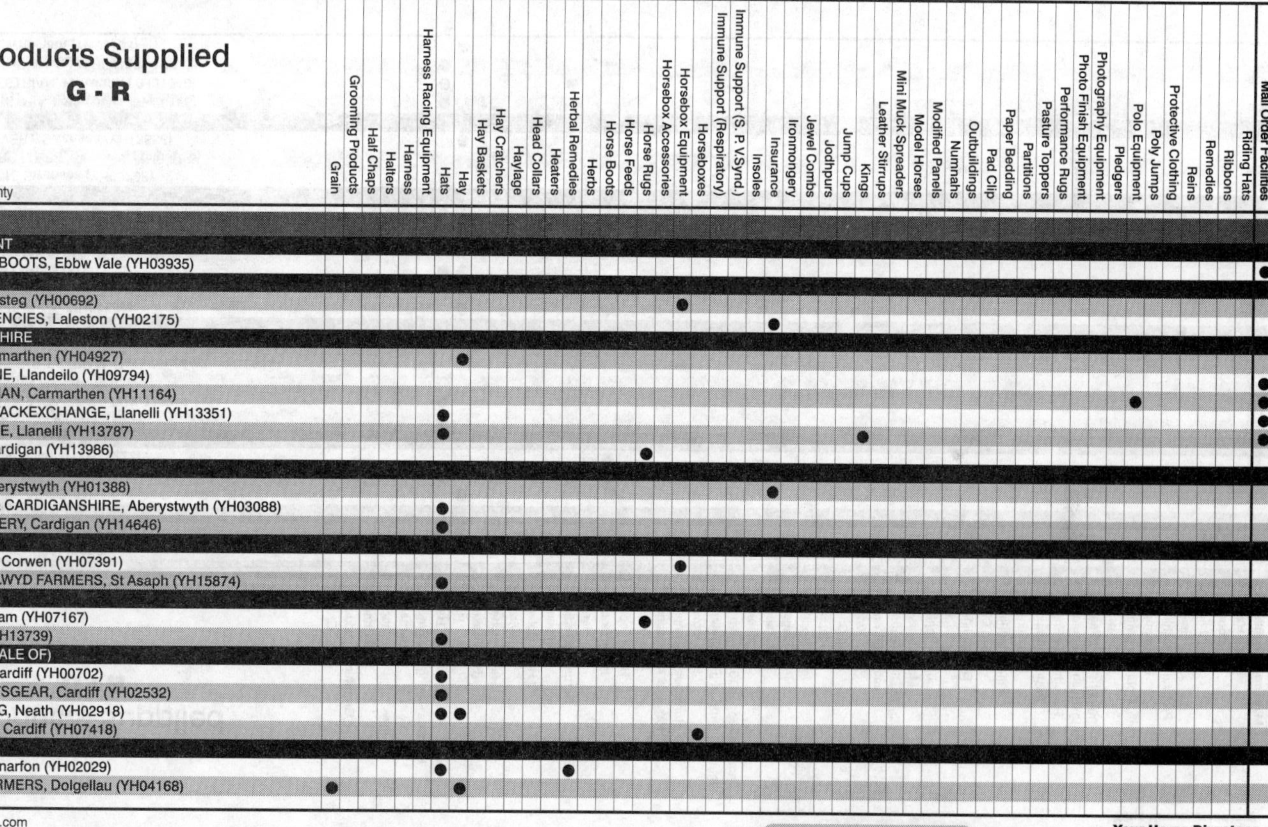

	Grain	Grooming Products	Half Chaps	Halters	Harness	Harness Racing Equipment	Hats	Hay	Hay Baskets	Hay Cratchers	Haylage	Head Collars	Heaters	Herbal Remedies	Herbs	Horse Boots	Horse Feeds	Horse Rugs	Horsebox Accessories	Horsebox Equipment	Horseboxes	Immune Support (Respiratory)	Immune Support (S. P. V.Synd.)	Insoles	Insurance	Ironmongery	Jewel Combs	Jodhpurs	Jump Cups	Kings	Leather Stirrups	Mini Muck Spreaders	Model Horses	Modified Panels	Numnahs	Outbuildings	Pad Clip	Paper Bedding	Partitions	Pasture Toppers	Performance Rugs	Photo Finish Equipment	Photography Equipment	Pledgers	Polo Equipment	Poly Jumps	Protective Clothing	Reins	Remedies	Ribbons	Riding Hats	**Mail Order Facilities**
WALES																																																				
BLAENAU GWENT																																																				
DAVIES RIDING BOOTS, Ebbw Vale (YH03935)																																																				●
BRIDGEND																																																				
AVONRIDE, Maesteg (YH00692)																				●																																
BRYNAVON AGENCIES, Laleston (YH02175)																									●																											
CARMARTHENSHIRE																																																				
EVANS, M V, Carmarthen (YH04927)								●																																												
MORGAN EQUINE, Llandeilo (YH09794)																																																				●
PLAS EQUESTRIAN, Carmarthen (YH11164)																																													●							●
STALLIONS AT TACKEXCHANGE, Llanelli (YH13351)							●																																													●
TACK EXCHANGE, Llanelli (YH13787)							●																							●																						●
THERMATEX, Cardigan (YH13986)																		●																																		
CEREDIGION																																																				
BHS WALES, Aberystwyth (YH01388)																									●																											
CLYNDERWEN & CARDIGANSHIRE, Aberystwyth (YH03088)							●																																													
VALIENT SADDLERY, Cardigan (YH14646)							●																																													
DENBIGHSHIRE																																																				
IFOR WILLIAMS, Corwen (YH07391)																				●																																
WYNNSTAY & CLWYD FARMERS, St Asaph (YH15874)							●																																													
FLINTSHIRE																																																				
HORSES, Wrexham (YH07167)																		●																																		
T F S, Buckley (YH13739)							●																																													
GLAMORGAN (VALE OF)																																																				
AYRES, JOHN, Cardiff (YH00702)							●																																													
CARDIFF SPORTSGEAR, Cardiff (YH02532)							●																																													
CIMLA TREKKING, Neath (YH02918)							●	●																																												
INDESPENSION, Cardiff (YH07418)																					●																															
GWYNEDD																																																				
BRONALLT, Caernarfon (YH02029)							●							●																																						
DOLGELLAU FARMERS, Dolgellau (YH04168)	●							●																																												

www.hccyourhorse.com

Products Supplied
G - R

by Country by County	Grain	Grooming Products	Half Chaps	Halters	Harness	Harness Racing Equipment	Hats	Hay	Hay Baskets	Hay Cratchers	Haylage	Head Collars	Heaters	Herbal Remedies	Herbs	Horse Boots	Horse Feeds	Horse Rugs	Horsebox Accessories	Horsebox Equipment	Horseboxes	Immune Support (Respiratory)	Immune Support (S. P. V.Synd.)	Insoles	Insurance	Ironmongery	Jewel Combs	Jodhpurs	Jump Cups	Kings	Leather Stirrups	Mini Muck Spreaders	Model Horses	Modified Panels	Numnahs	Outbuildings	Pad Clip	Paper Bedding	Partitions	Pasture Toppers	Performance Rugs	Photo Finish Equipment	Photography Equipment	Pledgers	Polo Equipment	Poly Jumps	Protective Clothing	Reins	Remedies	Ribbons	Riding Hats	Mail Order Facilities
ISLE OF ANGLESEY																																																				
SHEAR EASE, Amlwch (YH12688)																																																				●
TYN-MORFA RIDING CTRE, Rhosneigr (YH14529)								●																																												
MONMOUTHSHIRE																																																				
ABBOTT, Monmouth (YH00106)								●																																												
CHEPSTOW SADDLERY, Chepstow (YH02809)							●							●																																						
SPORTABAC, Abergavenny (YH13222)																●																																				
PEMBROKESHIRE																																																				
BOULSTON, Haverfordwest (YH01672)							●																																													
LLANWNDA STABLES, Goodwick (YH08727)							●																																													
PEGASUS, Haverfordwest (YH10902)																																																				●
PEMBROKESHIRE EQUESTRIAN, Haverfordwest (YH10919)																				●																																●
QUITS EQUESTRIAN, Haverfordwest (YH11501)																									●																											
POWYS																																																				
BLOOR, RAY, Montgomery (YH01559)								●																																												
BROMPTON HALL, Montgomery (YH02025)							●	●																																												●
CANTREF, Brecon (YH02516)							●	●																																												
CHILTERN CONNEMARA, Presteigne (YH02858)																																																				●
CWRT ISAF FARM, Crickhowell (YH03765)								●																																												
WYNNSTAY & CLWYD FARMERS, Llansanffraid (YH15875)							●																																													
SWANSEA																																																				
D MORGAN & SON, Swansea (YH03798)							●																																													
MR POTTER'S TROTTERS, Swansea (YH09916)																																	●																			
TANKEY LAKE LIVERY, Swansea (YH13856)								●																																												
WREXHAM																																																				
ACRE HSE EQUESTRIAN, Wrexham (YH00158)							●																																													●
BLINKERS EQUESTRIAN, Wrexham (YH01540)							●							●																																						●
CHARLES OWEN, Wrexham (YH02757)							●																																													
FAULKNER, R M, Wrexham (YH05103)								●																																												

Products Supplied
R - W

by Country by County

Company	Riding Wear	Rocking Horse	Rosettes	Rubber Matting	Rubs & Creams	Saddle Pads	Saddles	Sash	Sea Clay	Second Hand Equipment	Security Products	Seed	Shavings	Show Jumps	Show Saddles	Show Stationery	Shredded Paper	Skin Feed Supplements	Snowflake Shavings	Solarium Equipment	Sperm Counter	Stable Bandages	Stable Equipment	Stable Fittings	Stage Warmer	Stainless Steel Bits	Stalls	Stirrups	Straw	Supplements	Sweatshirts	Tack	Tactile Webbing	Timing Equipment	Towbars	Trad Wooden Show Jump Equip	Trailer Accessories	Trailers	Training Aids	Traps	Travel Bandages	Treadmills (Build)	Treadmills (Supply)	Trophies	Videos	Vitamins	Weathervanes	Western Tack	Whips	Witter	Worming Products	Mail Order Facilities
ENGLAND																																																				
BEDFORDSHIRE																																																				
ARCADE SADDLERY BEDFORD, Bedford (YH00498)			●				●																									●																				
BIGGLESWADE SADDLERY, Biggleswade (YH01404)							●																									●																				
BRSC, Bedford (YH02153)							●																																													
C R DAY'S MOTORS, Dunstable (YH02387)																																					●															
EASIRAMP SYSTEMS, Leighton Buzzard (YH04461)																																						●														
GRAVENHURST SADDLERY, Bedford (YH06024)							●																																													
LAGUS, S E, Leighton Buzzard (YH08344)							●																																													
MORPHEUS, Luton (YH09824)						●																																														
SALSA STUD, Chawston (YH12391)																											●		●																							
TRAIL-A-BRAKE SYSTEMS, Leighton Buzzard (YH14314)																																						●														
VULCAN TOWING CTRE, Luton (YH14745)																																			●		●	●												●		
WADDINGTONS, Leighton Buzzard (YH14809)							●																																													
BERKSHIRE																																																				
ATLAS SHOWJUMPS, Reading (YH00654)														●																																						
BERKSHIRE ROSETTES, Reading (YH01307)			●																																																	
BEXMINSTER, Reading (YH01349)																													●																							
CENTELL, Reading (YH02685)							●																									●																				
CHANGING TACK, Windsor (YH02732)	●						●																																													
GOLDENEYE, Newbury (YH05882)																																													●							
HORSE BOX & TRAILER OWNERS, Newbury (YH07111)																																					●															
J C & N C WARD, Pangbourne (YH07568)													●																●																							
LASSALE WATCHES, Maidenhead (YH08440)																																		●																		
LEISURE VISION, Newbury (YH08548)																																													●							
LLOYD-WILLIAMS SADDLERY, Reading (YH08746)							●																																													
R HUTT & PARTNERS, Maidenhead (YH11546)																													●																							
SCATS COUNTRYSTORE, Newbury (YH12493)																																●																			●	
SHAMLEY SADDLERY, Maidenhead (YH12663)							●																																													
VALLEY EQUINE, Hungerford (YH14648)																																																				●
VINCENT TRAILERS, Thatcham (YH14723)																																					●															

www.hccyourhorse.com

Products Supplied
R - W

by Country by County	Riding Wear	Rocking Horse	Rosettes	Rubber Matting	Rubs & Creams	Saddle Pads	Saddles	Sash	Sea Clay	Second Hand Equipment	Security Products	Seed	Shavings	Show Jumps	Show Saddles	Show Stationery	Shredded Paper	Skin Feed Supplements	Snowflake Shavings	Solarium Equipment	Sperm Counter	Stable Bandages	Stable Equipment	Stable Fittings	Stage Warmer	Stainless Steel Bits	Stalls	Stirrups	Straw	Supplements	Sweatshirts	Tack	Tactile Webbing	Timing Equipment	Towbars	Trad Wooden Show Jump Equip	Trailer Accessories	Trailers	Training Aids	Traps	Travel Bandages	Treadmills (Build)	Treadmills (Supply)	Trophies	Videos	Vitamins	Weathervanes	Western Tack	Whips	Witter	Worming Products	Mail Order Facilities
WOODLANDS, Hungerford (YH15705)							●						●				●															●																				
BRISTOL																																																				
ANIMAL BEDDING, Bristol (YH00427)																	●																																			
JENNY'S TACK SHOP, Bristol (YH07750)																																●																				
BUCKINGHAMSHIRE																																																				
ARDENLEA ENTERPRISES, Princes Risborough (YH00503)														●													●																●									
BALANCE, Aylesbury (YH00829)							●																																●													
BELLINGDON END, Chesham (YH01238)							●						●				●												●			●																				
D A L E, Aylesbury (YH03775)							●																									●																●				●
DENNIS'S SADDLERY/RIDING WEAR, Aylesbury (YH04060)	●						●																																													
DENNIS'S SADDLERY/RIDING WEAR, Aylesbury (YH04059)	●						●																																													
EQUINE DESIGN INT, Iver (YH04775)																																							●													
HERBERT, IVOR, High Wycombe (YH06695)																																													●							
SOUTH BUCKS ESTATES, Beaconsfield (YH13079)														●																																						
WHITAKERS EQUESTRIAN, Aylesbury (YH15293)														●																																						
CAMBRIDGESHIRE																																																				
ALLTACK & ALLFEED, Cambridge (YH00326)														●																																						
BANKS CARGILL AGRICULTURE, Huntingdon (YH00896)												●	●																																							
C FRANKS & SONS, Ely (YH02371)																													●																							
CAMBRIDGE TRAILERS, Cambridge (YH02471)																																					●	●														
CHURCHFIELD FARM TACK SHOP, Peterborough (YH02910)														●																																						
DURRANT, R C, Cambridge (YH04372)																													●																							
ENGLISH BROTHERS, Wisbech (YH04672)																											●																									
EQUI-VIDEO & EQUISETTE, Peterborough (YH04834)																																													●							
HOOK HSE, March (YH07035)							●			●																																										
LEJEUNE, Ely (YH08549)																																												●								
LONG MELFORD, Cambridge (YH08798)							●						●																			●																				
NORTHBROOK EQUESTRIAN CTRE, Huntingdon (YH10294)																																						●	●													
PEARSON, MICHAEL, Harston (YH10881)		●																																																		
PEGASUS, Peterborough (YH10901)														●																																						
ROBB & SON, St Ives (YH11932)																																●																				
SMEETH SADDLERY, Wisbech (YH12925)							●						●																			●																				

Products Supplied
R - W

by Country by County

Company	Riding Wear	Rocking Horse	Rosettes	Rubber Matting	Rubs & Creams	Saddle Pads	Saddles	Sash	Sea Clay	Second Hand Equipment	Security Products	Seed	Shavings
SUNDOWN STRAW, Huntingdon (YH13643)													●
CHESHIRE													
BOOL BY DESIGN, Tarporley (YH01631)							●						●
BOWLERS, Stockport (YH01715)							●						
CHELFORD FARM SUPPLIES, Macclesfield (YH02799)												●	●
COLBERRY SADDLERY, Ellesmere Port (YH03142)							●						
CREWE SADDLERY, Crewe (YH03595)							●						●
DECATHLON SPORTS & LEISURE, Stockport (YH04008)							●						
DINGLE BROOK FARM STABLES, Macclesfield (YH04125)							●						
GAYNORS SADDLERY, Dukinfield (YH05682)							●						
GREEN FARM FEEDS, Crewe (YH06055)												●	●
GREENWAY FARM, Congleton (YH06102)													
HORSEBOX BITS, Warrington (YH07150)													
LANSDOWNE HORSE & RIDER, Chester (YH08423)							●					●	●
MACCLESFIELD SADDLERY, Macclesfield (YH08985)													
RACEWOOD, Tarporley (YH11581)		●											
REDGRAVE, CAROLE, Wilmslow (YH11711)							●						
TOPSPEC, Nantwich (YH14241)													
CLEVELAND													
ARMSTRONG RICHARDSON, Middlesbrough (YH00544)							●						
EQUINE EXTRAS, Stockton-on-Tees (YH04778)													
HADRIAN EQUINE, Stockton-on-Tees (YH06271)													
HOOF'N'HOUND, Hartlepool (YH07031)							●						●
HOOF'N'HOUND, Middlesbrough (YH07032)							●						
JOHN MOORHOUSE, Stockton-on-Tees (YH07802)										●			
W H HORSEBOXES, Nunthorpe (YH14771)													
CORNWALL													
BLISLAND HARNESS MAKERS, Liskeard (YH01541)		●											
BODMIN TRAILER CTRE, Bodmin (YH01597)													
CORNWALL FARMERS, Penzance (YH03335)													●
CORNWALL FARMERS, Truro (YH03337)													●
CORNWALL FARMERS, Callington (YH03330)													●

Company	Show Jumps	Show Saddles	Show Stationery	Shredded Paper	Skin Feed Supplements	Snowflake Shavings	Solarium Equipment	Sperm Counter	Stable Bandages	Stable Equipment	Stable Fittings	Stage Warmer	Stainless Steel Bits
SUNDOWN STRAW, Huntingdon (YH13643)													
CHESHIRE													
BOOL BY DESIGN, Tarporley (YH01631)													
BOWLERS, Stockport (YH01715)													
CHELFORD FARM SUPPLIES, Macclesfield (YH02799)													
COLBERRY SADDLERY, Ellesmere Port (YH03142)													
CREWE SADDLERY, Crewe (YH03595)													
DECATHLON SPORTS & LEISURE, Stockport (YH04008)													
DINGLE BROOK FARM STABLES, Macclesfield (YH04125)		●											
GAYNORS SADDLERY, Dukinfield (YH05682)		●											
GREEN FARM FEEDS, Crewe (YH06055)						●							
GREENWAY FARM, Congleton (YH06102)													
HORSEBOX BITS, Warrington (YH07150)													
LANSDOWNE HORSE & RIDER, Chester (YH08423)													
MACCLESFIELD SADDLERY, Macclesfield (YH08985)	●												
RACEWOOD, Tarporley (YH11581)													
REDGRAVE, CAROLE, Wilmslow (YH11711)													
TOPSPEC, Nantwich (YH14241)													
CLEVELAND													
ARMSTRONG RICHARDSON, Middlesbrough (YH00544)													
EQUINE EXTRAS, Stockton-on-Tees (YH04778)													
HADRIAN EQUINE, Stockton-on-Tees (YH06271)													
HOOF'N'HOUND, Hartlepool (YH07031)													
HOOF'N'HOUND, Middlesbrough (YH07032)													
JOHN MOORHOUSE, Stockton-on-Tees (YH07802)													
W H HORSEBOXES, Nunthorpe (YH14771)													
CORNWALL													
BLISLAND HARNESS MAKERS, Liskeard (YH01541)													
BODMIN TRAILER CTRE, Bodmin (YH01597)													
CORNWALL FARMERS, Penzance (YH03335)													
CORNWALL FARMERS, Truro (YH03337)													
CORNWALL FARMERS, Callington (YH03330)													

Company	Stalls	Stirrups	Straw	Supplements	Sweatshirts	Tack	Tactile Webbing	Timing Equipment	Towbars	Trad Wooden Show Jump Equip	Trailer Accessories	Trailers	Training Aids
SUNDOWN STRAW, Huntingdon (YH13643)			●										
CHESHIRE													
BOOL BY DESIGN, Tarporley (YH01631)						●							
BOWLERS, Stockport (YH01715)						●							
CHELFORD FARM SUPPLIES, Macclesfield (YH02799)													
COLBERRY SADDLERY, Ellesmere Port (YH03142)						●							
CREWE SADDLERY, Crewe (YH03595)						●							
DECATHLON SPORTS & LEISURE, Stockport (YH04008)						●							
DINGLE BROOK FARM STABLES, Macclesfield (YH04125)													
GAYNORS SADDLERY, Dukinfield (YH05682)						●							
GREEN FARM FEEDS, Crewe (YH06055)			●										
GREENWAY FARM, Congleton (YH06102)						●							
HORSEBOX BITS, Warrington (YH07150)											●		
LANSDOWNE HORSE & RIDER, Chester (YH08423)			●			●						●	●
MACCLESFIELD SADDLERY, Macclesfield (YH08985)								●					
RACEWOOD, Tarporley (YH11581)													●
REDGRAVE, CAROLE, Wilmslow (YH11711)													
TOPSPEC, Nantwich (YH14241)													
CLEVELAND													
ARMSTRONG RICHARDSON, Middlesbrough (YH00544)						●							
EQUINE EXTRAS, Stockton-on-Tees (YH04778)													
HADRIAN EQUINE, Stockton-on-Tees (YH06271)													
HOOF'N'HOUND, Hartlepool (YH07031)			●										
HOOF'N'HOUND, Middlesbrough (YH07032)						●							
JOHN MOORHOUSE, Stockton-on-Tees (YH07802)												●	
W H HORSEBOXES, Nunthorpe (YH14771)											●	●	
CORNWALL													
BLISLAND HARNESS MAKERS, Liskeard (YH01541)						●							
BODMIN TRAILER CTRE, Bodmin (YH01597)												●	
CORNWALL FARMERS, Penzance (YH03335)						●							
CORNWALL FARMERS, Truro (YH03337)						●							
CORNWALL FARMERS, Callington (YH03330)													

Company	Traps	Travel Bandages	Treadmills (Build)	Treadmills (Supply)	Trophies	Videos	Vitamins	Weathervanes	Western Tack	Whips	Witter	Worming Products	Mail Order Facilities
SUNDOWN STRAW, Huntingdon (YH13643)													
CHESHIRE													
BOOL BY DESIGN, Tarporley (YH01631)													●
BOWLERS, Stockport (YH01715)						●							
CHELFORD FARM SUPPLIES, Macclesfield (YH02799)												●	
COLBERRY SADDLERY, Ellesmere Port (YH03142)													●
CREWE SADDLERY, Crewe (YH03595)													
DECATHLON SPORTS & LEISURE, Stockport (YH04008)					●								
DINGLE BROOK FARM STABLES, Macclesfield (YH04125)													
GAYNORS SADDLERY, Dukinfield (YH05682)												●	
GREEN FARM FEEDS, Crewe (YH06055)													
GREENWAY FARM, Congleton (YH06102)													
HORSEBOX BITS, Warrington (YH07150)													
LANSDOWNE HORSE & RIDER, Chester (YH08423)													●
MACCLESFIELD SADDLERY, Macclesfield (YH08985)													
RACEWOOD, Tarporley (YH11581)													
REDGRAVE, CAROLE, Wilmslow (YH11711)													
TOPSPEC, Nantwich (YH14241)													●
CLEVELAND													
ARMSTRONG RICHARDSON, Middlesbrough (YH00544)					●								●
EQUINE EXTRAS, Stockton-on-Tees (YH04778)						●							
HADRIAN EQUINE, Stockton-on-Tees (YH06271)												●	●
HOOF'N'HOUND, Hartlepool (YH07031)													
HOOF'N'HOUND, Middlesbrough (YH07032)													
JOHN MOORHOUSE, Stockton-on-Tees (YH07802)													
W H HORSEBOXES, Nunthorpe (YH14771)													
CORNWALL													
BLISLAND HARNESS MAKERS, Liskeard (YH01541)													
BODMIN TRAILER CTRE, Bodmin (YH01597)													
CORNWALL FARMERS, Penzance (YH03335)													
CORNWALL FARMERS, Truro (YH03337)													
CORNWALL FARMERS, Callington (YH03330)													

www.hccyourhorse.com

Products Supplied
R - W

by Country by County	Riding Wear	Rocking Horse	Rosettes	Rubber Matting	Rubs & Creams	Saddle Pads	Saddles	Sash	Sea Clay	Second Hand Equipment	Security Products	Seed	Shavings	Show Jumps	Show Saddles	Show Stationery	Shredded Paper	Skin Feed Supplements	Snowflake Shavings	Solarium Equipment	Sperm Counter	Stable Bandages	Stable Equipment	Stable Fittings	Stage Warmer	Stainless Steel Bits	Stalls	Stirrups	Straw	Supplements	Sweatshirts	Tack	Tactile Webbing	Timing Equipment	Towbars	Trad Wooden Show Jump Equip	Trailer Accessories	Trailers	Training Aids	Traps	Travel Bandages	Treadmills (Build)	Treadmills (Supply)	Trophies	Videos	Vitamins	Weathervanes	Western Tack	Whips	Witter	Worming Products	Mail Order Facilities
CORNWALL FARMERS, Liskeard (YH03334)													●																			●																				
CORNWALL FARMERS, Wadebridge (YH03338)																																●																				
DOIDGE, T R, Launceston (YH04164)																													●																							
EQUESTRIAN STOP, Camborne (YH04712)							●																															●														●
HELSTON SADDLERY, Helston (YH06657)							●																																													
HORSE & RIDER, Launceston (YH07094)							●																									●																				
LAUREL STUD, Truro (YH08458)							●																																									●				
P R J ENGINEERING, Launceston (YH10655)																																					●															
POLLY LUNN PET & AQUATICS, Truro (YH11208)							●																									●																				
RIDE & DRIVE SUPPLIES, Helston (YH11843)							●																									●								●												
ROMANY WALKS, Penzance (YH12072)																																							●													
ROSEVIDNEY ARABIANS, Penzance (YH12111)																													●																							●
ST LEONARDS EQUESTRIAN CTRE, Launceston (YH13278)														●																																						
TM INT SCHOOL OF HORSEMANSHIP, Liskeard (YH14196)																																						●														
WILLIAMS ENDURANCE, Uskard (YH15442)																																													●							
COUNTY DURHAM																																																				
ALSTON & KILLHOPE, Bishop Auckland (YH00339)													●																																							
DENE HEAD LIVERY, Darlington (YH04042)														●																																						
FARMWAY, Darlington (YH05072)							●					●	●																			●																				
G PRUDHOE, Faverdale (YH05591)			●																																									●								
GO RIDING GRP, Stanley (YH05861)													●																																							
KATANYA PETS, Bishop Auckland (YH07997)																																●																				
LANCHESTER COUNTRY STORE, Lanchester (YH08382)																																																			●	
RICHARDSONS DESIGNS, Burnhope (YH11824)			●																																									●								
SADDLE SENSE, Barnard Castle (YH12348)							●																									●																				
W S HODGSON, Barnard Castle (YH14794)																											●																									
CUMBRIA																																																				
ALLONBY RIDING SCHOOL, Wigton (YH00323)													●																																							
CUMBRIA SCHOOL OF SADDLERY, Penrith (YH03715)							●																									●																				
ESKDALE SADDLERY, Carlisle (YH04861)							●																																													
GET SMART, Barrow-In-Furness (YH05732)					●																																															
LAKELAND EQUESTRIAN, Windermere (YH08354)							●																									●													●							

Products Supplied
R - W

by Country by County	Riding Wear	Rocking Horse	Rosettes	Rubber Matting	Rubs & Creams	Saddle Pads	Saddles	Sash	Sea Clay	Second Hand Equipment	Security Products	Seed	Shavings	Show Jumps	Show Saddles	Show Stationery	Shredded Paper	Skin Feed Supplements	Snowflake Shavings	Solarium Equipment	Sperm Counter	Stable Bandages	Stable Equipment	Stable Fittings	Stage Warmer	Stainless Steel Bits	Stalls	Stirrups	Straw	Supplements	Sweatshirts	Tack	Tactile Webbing	Timing Equipment	Towbars	Trad Wooden Show Jump Equip	Trailer Accessories	Trailers	Training Aids	Traps	Travel Bandages	Treadmills (Build)	Treadmills (Supply)	Trophies	Videos	Vitamins	Weathervanes	Western Tack	Whips	Witter	Worming Products	Mail Order Facilities
LOWTHER EQUESTRIAN, Carlisle (YH08877)							●																									●																				
O'HARA, JOHNNIE, Carlisle (YH10442)																																●																				●
DERBYSHIRE																																																				
BARLEYFIELD SADDLERY, Etwall (YH00951)							●						●																			●																				
BARLEYFIELDS, Derby (YH00952)							●						●																			●																				
BARLOW, R, Denby Village (YH00959)														●																																						
C E S, Ashbourne (YH02370)							●																									●					●	●														
C W G, Buxton (YH02396)																																																			●	
COUNTRY SPORT, Glossop (YH03426)							●																									●																				●
HIGH PEAK TRAILERS, High Peak (YH06765)																																					●	●														
HORSE & RIDER TACK SHOP, Nottingham (YH07100)																																●																				
HULLAND SADDLERY, Ashbourne (YH07282)														●																															●							
IVANHOE FEEDS, Swadlincote (YH07533)																																●																				
KNOWLE HILL EQUESTRIAN, Derby (YH08280)																											●					●																				
NORMAN LUNNUN ANIMAL HEALTH, Ashbourne (YH10237)																																																			●	
PEAKDALE SADDLERY, Buxton (YH10866)							●						●																			●																			●	
PRESTIGE PRESENTATIONS, Chesterfield (YH11363)			●																																									●								
RISLEY SADDLERY, Draycott (YH11911)																																													●							
DEVON																																																				
ASH ROSETTES, Ivybridge (YH00587)			●																																																	
DARTMOOR ROSETTES, Exeter (YH03905)			●																																									●								
DEVON & CORNWALL FARMS, Tavistock (YH04092)	●																																																●		●	
EAST DEVON SADDLERY, Honiton (YH04470)							●																																													
ERME VALLEY FARMERS, Ivybridge (YH04850)							●						●																			●																				
FARMERS FRIEND, Exeter (YH05061)							●																									●																				
FROSTS ROSETTES, Paignton (YH05523)			●																																																	
HUISH ENGINEERING, Exeter (YH07277)																																					●	●														
LEONARD COOMBE, Newton Abbot (YH08553)							●																									●																				
LIMPET ANTI-SLIP SADDLE PADS, Ottery St Mary (YH08638)						●																										●																				●
MAIN RING ROSETTES, Torquay (YH09038)			●																																																	
MULLACOTT EQUESTRIAN, Ilfracombe (YH09935)													●																●																							
PAYNE, MATTHEW, Okehampton (YH10851)							●																																													

Products Supplied
R - W

by Country by County

	Riding Wear	Rocking Horse	Rosettes	Rubber Matting	Rubs & Creams	Saddle Pads	Saddles	Sash	Sea Clay	Second Hand Equipment	Security Products	Seed	Shavings	Show Jumps	Show Saddles	Show Stationery	Shredded Paper	Skin Feed Supplements	Snowflake Shavings	Solarium Equipment	Sperm Counter	Stable Bandages	Stable Equipment	Stable Fittings	Stage Warmer	Stainless Steel Bits	Stalls	Stirrups	Straw	Supplements	Sweatshirts	Tack	Tactile Webbing	Timing Equipment	Towbars	Trad Wooden Show Jump Equip	Trailer Accessories	Trailers	Training Aids	Traps	Travel Bandages	Treadmills (Build)	Treadmills (Supply)	Trophies	Videos	Vitamins	Weathervanes	Western Tack	Whips	Witter	Worming Products	Mail Order Facilities
PET & EQUINE SUPPLIES, Okehampton (YH11000)																																●																				
SIDE SADDLE LADY, Exeter (YH12786)																															●																					●
STOCKSHOP WOLSELEY, Exeter (YH13496)																																●																				
TOWN & COUNTRY SUP, Exeter (YH14286)																																					●															
TWYFORD FARM SUPPLIES, Tiverton (YH14516)							●																									●																				
WEST COUNTRY VIDEOS, Plymouth (YH15138)																																													●							
WHITE HORSE MOTORS, Exeter (YH15309)																																						●														
WINDUSS HORSEBOXES, Crediton (YH15579)																																					●															
WOOD FARM STUD, Okehampton (YH15656)														●																																						
WYCHANGER BARTON SADDLERY, Tiverton (YH15855)							●							●																		●							●													●
DORSET																																																				
BLAKEMORE VALE SADDLERY, Gillingham (YH01520)																																●																				
BRAMBLES FARM ARABIANS, Wimborne (YH01787)			●																																																	
DORCHESTER SADDLERY, Dorchester (YH04198)							●																																													
DORSET COUNTY SADDLERY, Wimborne (YH04205)							●																																													
DORSET HEAVY HORSE CTRE, Wimborne (YH04206)			●																																																	
EQUESTRIAN & EXAM CTRE, Ferndown (YH04691)																																●																				
EQUUS, Wimborne (YH04836)							●																									●							●													
FIVE SQUARE MOTORS, Shaftesbury (YH05256)																																					●															
HORSE BITS, Wimborne (YH07104)							●																									●																			●	
HURN BRIDGE CTRE, Christchurch (YH07313)													●																			●							●												●	
JULIP HORSES, Dorchester (YH07964)		●																																																		
JUMP FOR JOY SHOWJUMPS, Beaminster (YH07965)														●																																						
O Y C, Wareham (YH10369)													●																																							
PEEKS THE EVENT MAKERS, Christchurch (YH10898)			●																																																	
POUND COTTAGE RIDING CTRE, Blandford Forum (YH11307)																																							●													
SCATS COUNTRYSTORE, Blandford (YH12496)																																●																			●	
SCATS COUNTRYSTORE, Dorchester (YH12494)																																●																			●	
SCATS COUNTRYSTORE, Gillingham (YH12495)																																●																			●	
SIDE SADDLES, Wimborne (YH12787)							●			●																																			●							●
TOLLER TRAILERS, Dorchester (YH14209)																																					●	●														
TURTONS SADDLERS & HARNESS, Shaftesbury (YH14496)		●																																																		

Products Supplied
R - W

by Country by County

	Riding Wear	Rocking Horse	Rosettes	Rubber Matting	Rubs & Creams	Saddle Pads	Saddles	Sash	Sea Clay	Second Hand Equipment	Security Products	Seed	Shavings	Show Jumps	Show Saddles	Show Stationery	Shredded Paper
WEST COUNTRY ROSETTES, Gillingham (YH15136)			●														
ESSEX																	
ANGLIA TOWING EQUIPMENT, Colchester (YH00414)											●						
BARLING TACK SHOP, Rochford (YH00955)																	
BATTLESBRIDGE HORSE & CTRY, Wickford (YH01082)												●					
BOYLES COURT, Brentwood (YH01733)																	
BREYER MODEL HORSES, Great Dunmow (YH01857)		●															
BRIANA ELECTRONICS, Southminster (YH01862)																	
BROOK FARM STABLES, Colchester (YH02036)																	
C W G, Ongar (YH02397)																	
CANDLERS, Chelmsford (YH02496)							●										
CARRIAGEHOUSE INSURANCE, Colchester (YH02582)																	
COLNE CARGO TRANSPORT SVS, Colchester (YH03195)																	
D & F FEED SVS, Rayleigh (YH03770)												●					
D'ARCY SADDLERY, Maldon (YH03880)																	
DESIGNER BROWBANDS, Benfleet (YH04084)	●		●		●												
EQUINE HEALTH & HERBAL, Halstead (YH04779)																	
ESSEX HAY & STRAW, Clacton-on-Sea (YH04871)																	
FAIR EARTH TRADING, Little Oakley (YH05011)														●			
FOOTPRINT SADDLERY, Ongar (YH05313)							●										
HADDON ROCKING HORSES, Clacton-on-Sea (YH06262)		●															
HOBBY HORSE, Romford (YH06897)							●										
INGATESTONE SADDLERY, Ingatestone (YH07442)							●										
JOHN SKELTONS, Benfleet (YH07812)							●										
KILN SADDLERY, Colchester (YH08151)							●										
MAYPOLE PET & GARDEN CTRE, Witham (YH09304)																	
MOORCROFT EQUESTRIAN, Colchester (YH09749)						●											
MOSS, JANETTE, Waltham Abbey (YH09858)							●										
POWERLINE PRODUCTIONS, Romford (YH11328)																	
PRIORY SADDLERY, Colchester (YH11403)							●										
RAYNE RIDING CTRE, Braintree (YH11676)																	
RUGGERY, Romford (YH12221)							●										

	Skin Feed Supplements	Snowflake Shavings	Solarium Equipment	Sperm Counter	Stable Bandages	Stable Equipment	Stable Fittings	Stage Warmer	Stainless Steel Bits	Stalls	Stirrups	Straw	Supplements	Sweatshirts	Tack	Tactile Webbing	Timing Equipment
WEST COUNTRY ROSETTES, Gillingham (YH15136)																	
ESSEX																	
ANGLIA TOWING EQUIPMENT, Colchester (YH00414)																	
BARLING TACK SHOP, Rochford (YH00955)															●		
BATTLESBRIDGE HORSE & CTRY, Wickford (YH01082)												●			●		
BOYLES COURT, Brentwood (YH01733)												●					
BREYER MODEL HORSES, Great Dunmow (YH01857)																	
BRIANA ELECTRONICS, Southminster (YH01862)																	
BROOK FARM STABLES, Colchester (YH02036)										●							
C W G, Ongar (YH02397)																	
CANDLERS, Chelmsford (YH02496)															●		
CARRIAGEHOUSE INSURANCE, Colchester (YH02582)																	
COLNE CARGO TRANSPORT SVS, Colchester (YH03195)																	
D & F FEED SVS, Rayleigh (YH03770)												●			●		
D'ARCY SADDLERY, Maldon (YH03880)															●		
DESIGNER BROWBANDS, Benfleet (YH04084)																	
EQUINE HEALTH & HERBAL, Halstead (YH04779)																	
ESSEX HAY & STRAW, Clacton-on-Sea (YH04871)												●					
FAIR EARTH TRADING, Little Oakley (YH05011)																	
FOOTPRINT SADDLERY, Ongar (YH05313)																	
HADDON ROCKING HORSES, Clacton-on-Sea (YH06262)																	
HOBBY HORSE, Romford (YH06897)															●		
INGATESTONE SADDLERY, Ingatestone (YH07442)															●		
JOHN SKELTONS, Benfleet (YH07812)															●		
KILN SADDLERY, Colchester (YH08151)															●		
MAYPOLE PET & GARDEN CTRE, Witham (YH09304)															●		
MOORCROFT EQUESTRIAN, Colchester (YH09749)															●		
MOSS, JANETTE, Waltham Abbey (YH09858)															●		
POWERLINE PRODUCTIONS, Romford (YH11328)																	
PRIORY SADDLERY, Colchester (YH11403)															●		
RAYNE RIDING CTRE, Braintree (YH11676)															●		
RUGGERY, Romford (YH12221)															●		

	Towbars	Trad Wooden Show Jump Equip	Trailer Accessories	Trailers	Training Aids	Traps	Travel Bandages	Treadmills (Build)	Treadmills (Supply)	Trophies	Videos	Vitamins	Weathervanes	Western Tack	Whips	Witter	Worming Products	Mail Order Facilities
WEST COUNTRY ROSETTES, Gillingham (YH15136)																		
ESSEX																		
ANGLIA TOWING EQUIPMENT, Colchester (YH00414)	●		●	●														
BARLING TACK SHOP, Rochford (YH00955)																		
BATTLESBRIDGE HORSE & CTRY, Wickford (YH01082)																		
BOYLES COURT, Brentwood (YH01733)																		
BREYER MODEL HORSES, Great Dunmow (YH01857)																		●
BRIANA ELECTRONICS, Southminster (YH01862)											●							
BROOK FARM STABLES, Colchester (YH02036)																		
C W G, Ongar (YH02397)																	●	
CANDLERS, Chelmsford (YH02496)																		
CARRIAGEHOUSE INSURANCE, Colchester (YH02582)			●															
COLNE CARGO TRANSPORT SVS, Colchester (YH03195)			●															
D & F FEED SVS, Rayleigh (YH03770)																		
D'ARCY SADDLERY, Maldon (YH03880)																		
DESIGNER BROWBANDS, Benfleet (YH04084)																		●
EQUINE HEALTH & HERBAL, Halstead (YH04779)												●						●
ESSEX HAY & STRAW, Clacton-on-Sea (YH04871)																		
FAIR EARTH TRADING, Little Oakley (YH05011)																		
FOOTPRINT SADDLERY, Ongar (YH05313)																		
HADDON ROCKING HORSES, Clacton-on-Sea (YH06262)																		
HOBBY HORSE, Romford (YH06897)																		
INGATESTONE SADDLERY, Ingatestone (YH07442)																		
JOHN SKELTONS, Benfleet (YH07812)														●				
KILN SADDLERY, Colchester (YH08151)																		
MAYPOLE PET & GARDEN CTRE, Witham (YH09304)																		
MOORCROFT EQUESTRIAN, Colchester (YH09749)							●											●
MOSS, JANETTE, Waltham Abbey (YH09858)																		
POWERLINE PRODUCTIONS, Romford (YH11328)											●							
PRIORY SADDLERY, Colchester (YH11403)																		
RAYNE RIDING CTRE, Braintree (YH11676)																		
RUGGERY, Romford (YH12221)																		

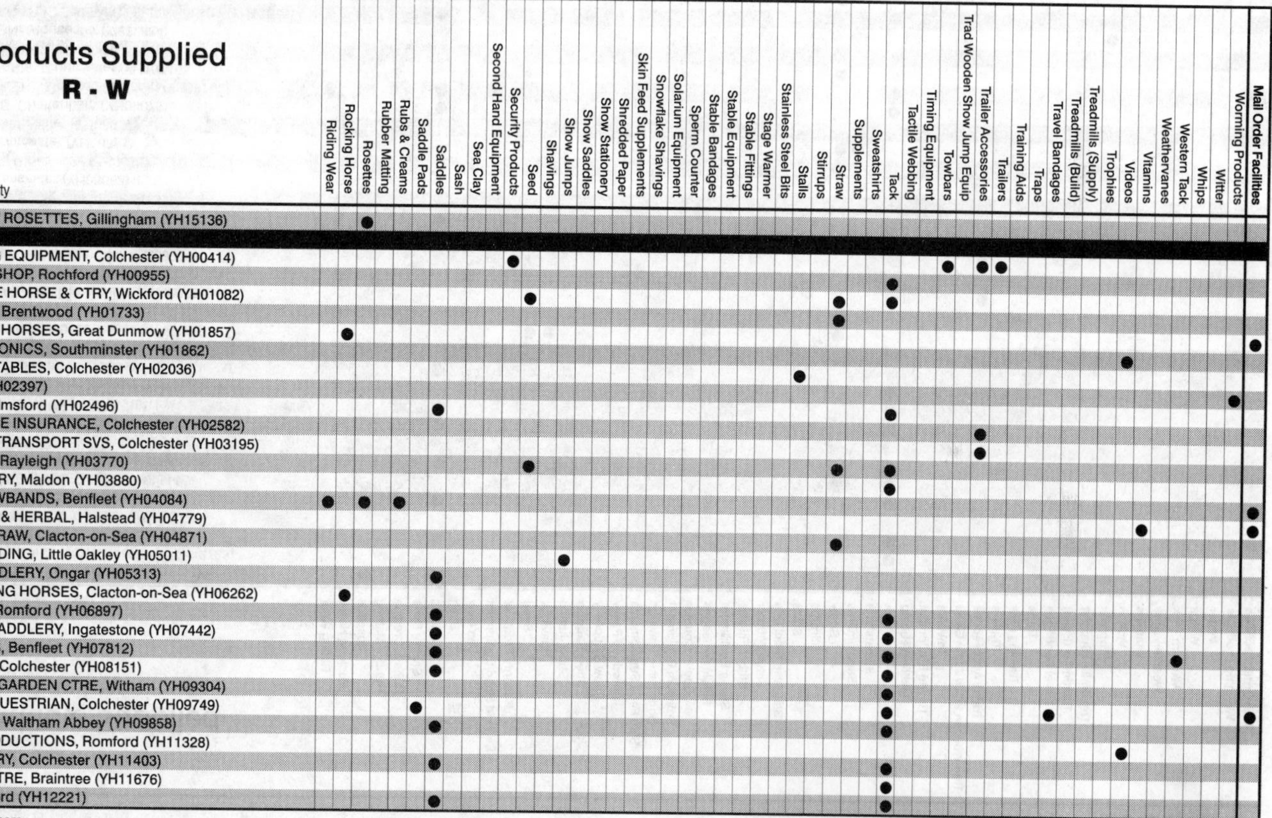

Products Supplied
R - W

by Country by County	Riding Wear	Rocking Horse	Rosettes	Rubber Matting	Rubs & Creams	Saddle Pads	Saddles	Sash	Sea Clay	Second Hand Equipment	Security Products	Seed	Shavings	Show Jumps	Show Saddles	Show Stationery	Shredded Paper	Skin Feed Supplements	Snowflake Shavings	Solarium Equipment	Sperm Counter	Stable Bandages	Stable Equipment	Stable Fittings	Stage Warmer	Stainless Steel Bits
RYDER'S ROSETTES, South Woodham Ferrers (YH12299)			●																							
SHOPLAND HALL EQUESTRIAN, Rochford (YH12758)																										
SIERRA SADDLE, Benfleet (YH12792)							●																			
SOUTH EAST SHAVINGS, Upminster (YH13087)													●													
TACK EXCHANGE, Leigh-on-Sea (YH13788)							●																			
TALLY-HO RIDING SCHOOL, Grays (YH13844)													●													
THORPE TACK ROOM, Clacton-on-Sea (YH14095)							●																			
TOWRITE, Upminster (YH14301)																										
UPMINSTER SADDLERY, Upminster (YH14604)							●																			
WITHAM SADDLERY, Witham (YH15618)							●																			
WIX EQUESTRIAN CTRE, Manningtree (YH15636)																										
YE OLDE FORGE, Basildon (YH15894)							●																			
GLOUCESTERSHIRE																										
ABBOTT, Cirencester (YH00102)												●	●													
B G W SPECTRAFLECT, Cheltenham (YH00722)																										
CIRENCESTER GARAGE, Cirencester (YH02926)																										
COTSWOLD SADDLERY, Cirencester (YH03365)																										
COTSWOLD TRAILERS, Cheltenham (YH03370)																										
DONEY, JON, Tewkesbury (YH04181)														●												
EDWARDS SADDLERY, Moreton In Marsh (YH04573)							●																			
EQUINE RESPONSE, Badminton (YH04797)																										
GOLDENEYE, Cirencester (YH05883)																										
HARTPURY CLGE, Gloucester (YH06507)																										
HENRY COLE, Cirencester (YH06681)													●													
M C WESTERN, Gloucester (YH08957)														●												
MANGAN & WEBB, Cheltenham (YH09076)							●																			
MORETON SADDLERY, Moreton in Marsh (YH09790)	●						●																			
PARK CORNER FARM, Cirencester (YH10716)																										
ROLFE, JOHN, Berkeley (YH12066)		●																								
SIMPLY BY DESIGN, Gloucester (YH12834)																										
SOUTH AMERICAN TRADE SERVICES, Cirencester (YH13075)							●																			
SOUTHWICK FARM, Tewkesbury (YH13163)																										

by Country by County	Stalls	Stirrups	Straw	Supplements	Sweatshirts	Tack	Tactile Webbing	Timing Equipment	Towbars	Trad Wooden Show Jump Equip	Trailer Accessories	Trailers	Training Aids	Traps	Travel Bandages	Treadmills (Build)	Treadmills (Supply)	Trophies	Videos	Vitamins	Weathervanes	Western Tack	Whips	Witter	Worming Products	Mail Order Facilities
RYDER'S ROSETTES, South Woodham Ferrers (YH12299)																		●								
SHOPLAND HALL EQUESTRIAN, Rochford (YH12758)						●																				
SIERRA SADDLE, Benfleet (YH12792)						●																				●
SOUTH EAST SHAVINGS, Upminster (YH13087)																										
TACK EXCHANGE, Leigh-on-Sea (YH13788)						●																				
TALLY-HO RIDING SCHOOL, Grays (YH13844)			●			●																				
THORPE TACK ROOM, Clacton-on-Sea (YH14095)						●																				
TOWRITE, Upminster (YH14301)									●																	
UPMINSTER SADDLERY, Upminster (YH14604)						●																				
WITHAM SADDLERY, Witham (YH15618)						●																				
WIX EQUESTRIAN CTRE, Manningtree (YH15636)						●																				
YE OLDE FORGE, Basildon (YH15894)																										
GLOUCESTERSHIRE																										
ABBOTT, Cirencester (YH00102)			●																							
B G W SPECTRAFLECT, Cheltenham (YH00722)													●													
CIRENCESTER GARAGE, Cirencester (YH02926)											●															
COTSWOLD SADDLERY, Cirencester (YH03365)																			●							
COTSWOLD TRAILERS, Cheltenham (YH03370)											●															
DONEY, JON, Tewkesbury (YH04181)																										
EDWARDS SADDLERY, Moreton In Marsh (YH04573)																										
EQUINE RESPONSE, Badminton (YH04797)																			●							
GOLDENEYE, Cirencester (YH05883)																			●							
HARTPURY CLGE, Gloucester (YH06507)																	●									
HENRY COLE, Cirencester (YH06681)			●	●																						
M C WESTERN, Gloucester (YH08957)																										
MANGAN & WEBB, Cheltenham (YH09076)						●																				
MORETON SADDLERY, Moreton in Marsh (YH09790)						●																				
PARK CORNER FARM, Cirencester (YH10716)			●																							
ROLFE, JOHN, Berkeley (YH12066)																										
SIMPLY BY DESIGN, Gloucester (YH12834)																		●								
SOUTH AMERICAN TRADE SERVICES, Cirencester (YH13075)						●																				
SOUTHWICK FARM, Tewkesbury (YH13163)			●																							

Products Supplied
R - W

by Country by County

	Riding Wear	Rocking Horse	Rosettes	Rubber Matting	Rubs & Creams	Saddle Pads	Saddles	Sash	Sea Clay	Second Hand Equipment	Security Products	Seed	Shavings	Show Jumps	Show Saddles	Show Stationery	Shredded Paper	Skin Feed Supplements	Snowflake Shavings	Solarium Equipment	Sperm Counter	Stable Bandages	Stable Equipment	Stable Fittings	Stage Warmer	Stainless Steel Bits	Stalls	Stirrups	Straw	Supplements	Sweatshirts	Tack	Tactile Webbing	Timing Equipment	Towbars	Trad Wooden Show Jump Equip	Trailer Accessories	Trailers	Training Aids	Traps	Travel Bandages	Treadmills (Build)	Treadmills (Supply)	Trophies	Videos	Vitamins	Weathervanes	Western Tack	Whips	Witter	Worming Products	Mail Order Facilities
STROUD SADDLERY, Stroud (YH13588)							●																									●						●							●							●
TEWKESBURY SADDLERY, Tewkesbury (YH13969)							●																									●																				●
HAMPSHIRE																																																				
ALLIGATOR SADDLERY, Romsey (YH00313)			●																																									●								
AMBERVALE, Lymington (YH00357)		●																																																		
ANDREW GOOD VIDEO PRODUCERS, Sholing (YH00390)																																													●							
BRITISH SHOW JUMP STORES, Aldershot (YH01972)														●																																						
CALCUTT & SONS, Winchester (YH02425)							●																									●																				●
COUNTRY RIDING WEAR, Hook (YH03424)	●						●																									●																				
DAVID CATLIN, Southampton (YH03916)							●																									●																				
FOREST COUNTRYWEAR, Fordingbridge (YH05333)																																							●													
FOREST FARM, Milford On Sea (YH05335)																																								●												
FORESTER SADDLES, Lyndhurst (YH05354)							●																																													●
FORT DODGE ANIMAL HEALTH, Hedge End (YH05386)																																																			●	
HOPLANDS EQUESTRIAN, Stockbridge (YH07058)									●																																											●
JOHN WILLIE'S SADDLE ROOM, Ringwood (YH07817)							●																																													
LANGFORD FARM, Woodlands (YH08403)														●																																						
LESLEY RALPH SADDLER, Basingstoke (YH08557)																																●																				
MCNEILL, IAN, Alton (YH09402)																											●																									
MOYGLARE LIVERY, Tadley (YH09910)																																						●														
PARKER, GILL, Andover (YH10749)																																												●								
RAY'S SADDLESHOP, Southampton (YH11677)							●																																													
SADDLES, SADDLES, SADDLES, Portsmouth (YH12371)							●																									●																				
SCATS COUNTRYSTORE, Romsey (YH12497)																																●																		●		
SCATS COUNTRYSTORE, Winchester (YH12498)																																●																		●		
SCATS COUNTRYSTORE, Andover (YH12500)																																●																		●		
SCATS COUNTRYSTORE, Basingstoke (YH12501)																																●																		●		
SCATS COUNTRYSTORE, Alton (YH12499)																																●																		●		
SCATS COUNTRYSTORE, Lymington (YH12502)																																●																		●		
SOLENT, Southampton (YH13054)							●																									●																				
TALLY HO, Whitchurch (YH13839)	●																																																			
TROTTERS, Havant (YH14407)																													●																							

www.hccyourhorse.com

Products Supplied
R - W

by Country by County

	Riding Wear	Rocking Horse	Rosettes	Rubber Matting	Rubs & Creams	Saddle Pads	Saddles	Sash	Sea Clay	Second Hand Equipment	Security Products	Seed	Shavings	Show Jumps	Show Saddles	Show Stationery	Shredded Paper	Skin Feed Supplements	Snowflake Shavings	Solarium Equipment	Sperm Counter	Stable Bandages	Stable Equipment	Stable Fittings	Stage Warmer	Stainless Steel Bits	Stalls	Stirrups	Straw	Supplements	Sweatshirts	Tack	Tactile Webbing	Timing Equipment	Towbars	Trad Wooden Show Jump Equip	Trailer Accessories	Trailers	Training Aids	Traps	Travel Bandages	Treadmills (Build)	Treadmills (Supply)	Trophies	Videos	Vitamins	Weathervanes	Western Tack	Whips	Witter	Worming Products	Mail Order Facilities
WELLINGTON RIDING, Hook (YH15075)																																							●						●							
HEREFORDSHIRE																																																				
CAM EQUESTRIAN JOINERY/EQUIP, Hereford (YH02463)														●													●												●						●							
COUNTRYWIDE, Hereford (YH03445)												●	●																			●							●													
HORSE & JOCKEY, Hereford (YH07093)							●																									●																				
ROSS FEED, Ross-on-Wye (YH12114)																																●																				
SHIRES EQUESTRIAN, Leominster (YH12755)	●						●																●																													
TURNERS, Kington (YH14492)												●	●																																							
HERTFORDSHIRE																																																				
BARKWAY EQUESTRIAN CTRE, Royston (YH00948)			●																																																	
BOXMOOR SHOWJUMPS, Hemel Hempstead (YH01727)														●																																						
C M TRAILERS, Bovingdon (YH02381)																																					●	●														
CHOLESBURY, Tring (YH02877)																													●																							
COLEMAN CROFT, St Albans (YH03163)			●				●																						●			●																				●
CONTESSA, Ware (YH03246)																																													●							
FIELD SPORTS, Borehamwood (YH05186)							●																																													
FIELDFARE, Waltham Cross (YH05191)																													●																							
G T TOWING, Potters Bar (YH05597)																																						●														
N S R COMMUNICATIONS, Rickmansworth (YH09995)																																		●																		
ONE JUMP AHEAD, Hertford (YH10511)														●																																						
PATCHETTS, Watford (YH10815)																																●																				
PHOENIX CLGE OF RADIONICS, Hemel Hempstead (YH11070)																																													●							
PREMIERE ROSETTE COMPANY, Harpenden (YH11352)			●																																									●								
SADDLERY, Royston (YH12363)							●						●																			●																				
SANDON SADDLERY, Buntingford (YH12415)			●																																																	
SOUTHERN MOBILE, Bushey (YH13141)																																						●														
UPPERWOOD FARM STUD, Hemel Hempstead (YH14609)																													●																							
WHITE HORSES, Welwyn (YH15317)		●																																																		
ISLE OF WIGHT																																																				
BRICKFIELDS, Ryde (YH01866)							●																																													
SCATS COUNTRYSTORE, Newport (YH12503)																																●																			●	
JERSEY																																																				

Products Supplied
R - W

by Country by County	Riding Wear	Rocking Horse	Rosettes	Rubber Matting	Rubs & Creams	Saddle Pads	Saddles	Sash	Sea Clay	Second Hand Equipment	Security Products	Seed	Shavings	Show Jumps	Show Saddles	Show Stationery	Shredded Paper	Skin Feed Supplements	Snowflake Shavings	Solarium Equipment	Sperm Counter	Stable Bandages	Stable Equipment	Stable Fittings	Stage Warmer	Stainless Steel Bits	Stalls	Stirrups	Straw	Supplements	Sweatshirts	Tack	Tactile Webbing	Timing Equipment	Towbars	Trad Wooden Show Jump Equip	Trailer Accessories	Trailers	Training Aids	Traps	Travel Bandages	Treadmills (Build)	Treadmills (Supply)	Trophies	Videos	Vitamins	Weathervanes	Western Tack	Whips	Witter	Worming Products	Mail Order Facilities
LE MAISTRE BROS, Trinity (YH08490)							●																									●																				●	
KENT																																																					
ARIZONAS, Tunbridge Wells (YH00527)							●																									●																●				●
BARMINSTER TRADING, Ashford (YH00960)							●																									●																				
BIRCHALLS THE RIDING SHOP, Maidstone (YH01431)							●																									●													●							
BROMLEY TOWBARS & TRAILERS, Bromley (YH02024)																																			●																	
CHASKIT HSE, Tunbridge Wells (YH02787)	●																																																			
DICKSON, PENNY, Rochester (YH04117)							●																																													
FORAGES, J T, Cranbrook (YH05315)																													●																							
FROGPOOL MANOR SADDLERY, Chislehurst (YH05515)							●						●				●												●			●							●						●							●
G & K SVS, Ashford (YH05564)				●																																		●														
HOBBS PARKER, Ashford (YH06894)							●																									●						●														
HORSE & COUNTRY SUPERSTORE, Maidstone (YH07088)																																●																				
MAYWOOD STUD, Ashford (YH09309)																																													●							
MOUNT MASCAL STABLES, Bexley (YH09890)													●																●																							
SADDLERY & GUN ROOM, Westerham (YH12365)							●																									●													●							
SCATS COUNTRYSTORE, Canterbury (YH12504)																																●																			●	
SCATS COUNTRYSTORE, Marden (YH12505)																																●																			●	
SOUTHERN COUNTIES ROSETTES, Tonbridge (YH13139)			●																																																	
STEVENSON BROS, Ashford (YH13449)		●																																																		
THANET SHOW JUMPS, Ashford (YH13978)														●																																						
TRIDENT TRAILERS, Tunbridge Wells (YH14394)																																						●														
TRIDENT TRAILERS, Canterbury (YH14393)																																						●														
TUNBRIDGE WELLS TACK ROOM, Tunbridge Wells (YH14460)																																													●							
WEALDEN SADDLERY, Tonbridge (YH15020)							●																									●																				●
WILLOW FARM, Faversham (YH15497)							●						●																●			●							●						●							●
LANCASHIRE																																																				
ABRAM HALL RIDING CTRE, Wigan (YH00134)													●																																							
ARKENFIELD EQUESTRIAN CTRE, Chorley (YH00530)													●																●																							
ASOKA, Worsley (YH00625)																																							●													
BROOKFIELD GREEN FARM, Ormskirk (YH02047)																													●																							
BROOMHILL, Clitheroe (YH02080)																																●																				

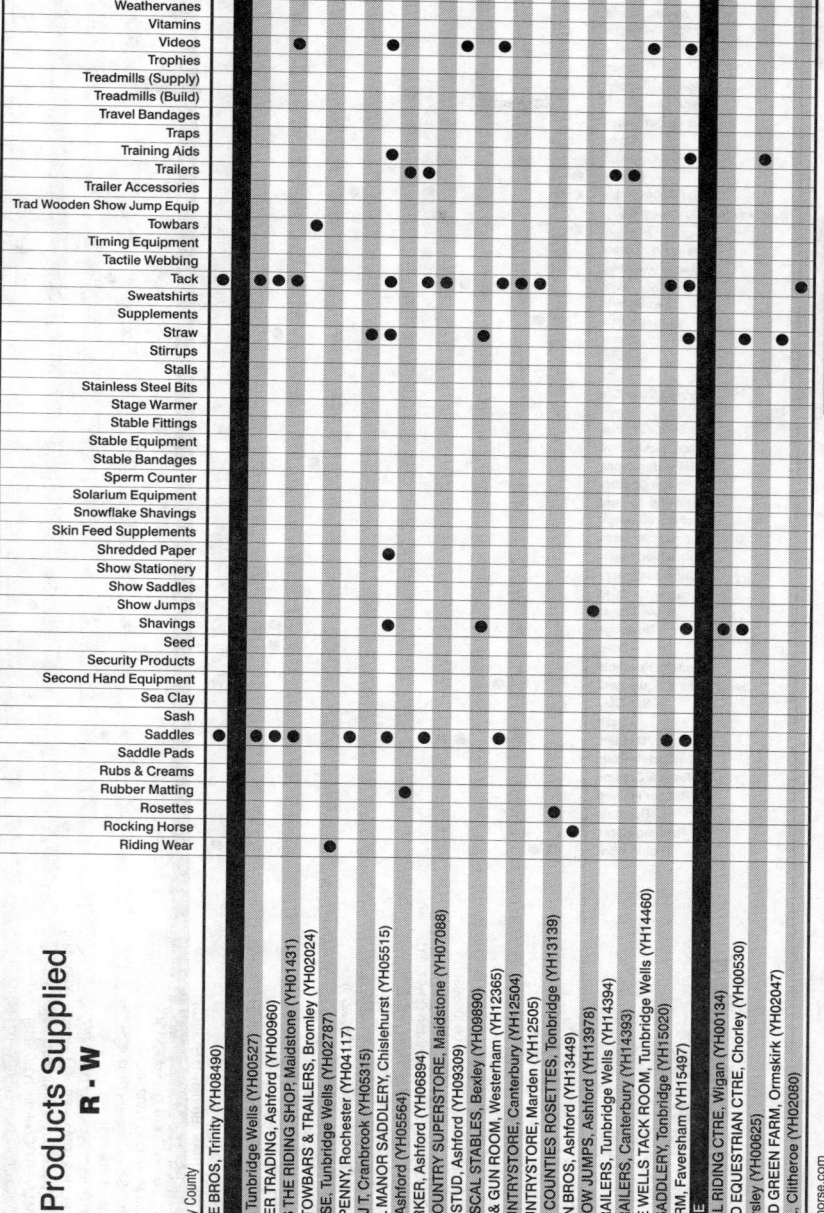

Products Supplied
R - W

by Country by County

	Riding Wear	Rocking Horse	Rosettes	Rubber Matting	Rubs & Creams	Saddle Pads	Saddles	Sash	Sea Clay	Second Hand Equipment	Security Products	Seed	Shavings	Show Jumps	Show Saddles	Show Stationery	Shredded Paper	Skin Feed Supplements	Snowflake Shavings	Solarium Equipment	Sperm Counter	Stable Bandages	Stable Equipment	Stable Fittings	Stage Warmer	Stainless Steel Bits	Stalls	Stirrups	Straw	Supplements	Sweatshirts	Tack	Tactile Webbing	Timing Equipment	Towbars	Trad Wooden Show Jump Equip	Trailer Accessories	Trailers	Training Aids	Traps	Travel Bandages	Treadmills (Build)	Treadmills (Supply)	Trophies	Videos	Vitamins	Weathervanes	Western Tack	Whips	Witter	Worming Products	Mail Order Facilities
CARAVAN CORNER, Blackpool (YH02526)																																			●		●	●														
CARRS BILLINGTON, Clitheroe (YH02598)	●																													●																						
CARRS BILLINGTON, Preston (YH02599)	●																													●																						
DERBY HSE SADDLERY, Wigan (YH04071)							●						●																										●													●
EQUESTRIANA, Blackburn (YH04724)							●			●																						●																				
ESPRO EQUESTRIAN & SPORTSWEAR, Wigan (YH04862)	●																																																			
HERD HSE RIDING SCHOOL, Burnley (YH06699)							●																									●																				
HORSE BITS SADDLERY, Bury (YH07106)							●																									●																				
HORSEBOX UPHOLSTERY, Westhoughton (YH07151)																																					●															
HUSTEADS RIDING SCHOOL, Oldham (YH07330)																													●		●																					
JERUSALEM FARM, Colne (YH07757)							●																									●																				
LITTLE OAKS SHOWJUMPS, Preston (YH08697)														●																																						
MAUDSLEY HORSEBOXES, Darwen (YH09279)																																					●															
MILLER TRAILERS, Burnley (YH09603)																																						●														
QUAY EQUESTRIAN, Lancaster (YH11485)																						●																													●	
R & E BAMFORD, Leyland (YH11505)																														●																						
RICHARD BATTERSBY, Heywood (YH11802)												●	●																●																							
ROBINSONS COUNTRY LEISURE, Wigan (YH12004)														●																																						
ROSETTES DIRECT, Accrington (YH12110)			●																																																	
SNAFFLES, Halifax (YH13020)	●						●			●																						●																				
TAYLORS EQUESTRIAN, Burnley (YH13916)														●																																						
LEICESTERSHIRE																																																				
BROWN, J W, Melton Mowbray (YH02115)							●																																													
C W G, Melton Mowbray (YH02398)																																																			●	
CLOTHES HORSE, Leicester (YH03062)							●						●																●			●													●							
DTA, Leicester (YH04303)							●			●																						●																				
E H HUTTON, Melton Mowbray (YH04407)																																					●															
GLENDALE EQUESTRIAN FEEDS, Leicester (YH05830)		●																																																		
HARLOW BROTHERS, Loughborough (YH06440)																											●																									
HOME FARM LIVERY, Coalville (YH06996)														●																																						
HORSE TROUGH, Loughborough (YH07144)																																●																				
HURST SADDLERS, Leicester (YH07316)							●										●															●																			●	●

Products Supplied
R - W

by Country by County

Company	Riding Wear	Rocking Horse	Rosettes	Rubber Matting	Rubs & Creams	Saddle Pads	Saddles	Sash	Sea Clay	Second Hand Equipment	Security Products	Seed	Shavings	Show Jumps	Show Saddles	Show Stationery	Shredded Paper	Skin Feed Supplements	Snowflake Shavings	Solarium Equipment	Sperm Counter	Stable Bandages	Stable Equipment	Stable Fittings	Stage Warmer	Stainless Steel Bits	Stalls	Stirrups	Straw	Supplements	Sweatshirts	Tack	Tactile Webbing	Timing Equipment	Towbars	Trad Wooden Show Jump Equip	Trailer Accessories	Trailers	Training Aids	Traps	Travel Bandages	Treadmills (Build)	Treadmills (Supply)	Trophies	Videos	Vitamins	Weathervanes	Western Tack	Whips	Witter	Worming Products	Mail Order Facilities
L A EQUESTRIAN, Leicester (YH08309)																						●																														
PEGASUS TRAILERS, Hinckley (YH10908)																																					●	●														
S & J SADDLERY, Melton Mowbray (YH12312)														●																																						
S L B SUPPLIES, Coalville (YH12329)													●				●												●																							
SCHOOL OF NATIONAL EQUITATION, Loughborough (YH12521)													●																			●																				
SHARNFORD LODGE FEEDS/TACK, Hinckley (YH12676)																																●																				
TOWRITE FABRICATIONS, Market Harborough (YH14302)																							●															●														
VISCORIDE, Lutterworth (YH14733)																																●																				
LINCOLNSHIRE																																																				
A W RHOADES SADDLERY, Market Rasen (YH00068)							●																									●																				
BATTLE, HAYWARD & BOWER, Lincoln (YH01081)																																●																				
BIRDBROOK ROSETTES, Saxilby (YH01438)			●																																																	
BOB PAULEY PA HIRE, Stamford (YH01589)																																		●																		
C W G, Market Rasen (YH02400)																																																			●	
C W G, Stamford (YH02399)																																																			●	
COSGROVE & SON, Market Rasen (YH03350)																													●																							
EAGLE HALL EST, Lincoln (YH04437)																													●																							
EMPIRE STABLES, Lincoln (YH04658)																																											●									
F P I, Stamford (YH04998)					●																																															●
HILL HSE, Market Rasen (YH06820)																																								●												
HOLMES JOINERY, Market Rasen (YH06972)														●																																						
KEY, J U, Boston (YH08114)																																●																				
LIMES FARM, Grantham (YH08634)																																							●				●									
LINDSEY FARM SVS, Horncastle (YH08655)																																●																				
MCARA, Market Rasen (YH09311)																																					●															
PIG & WHISTLE ROCKING HORSES, North Somercotes (YH11093)		●																																																		
POLLY PRODUCTS, Horncastle (YH11209)						●	●																																		●											
POPPYFIELDS, Lincoln (YH11275)													●																																							
REDNIL EQUESTRIAN CTRE, Lincoln (YH11716)																													●																							
RICHARD GRICE TRAILERS, Market Rasen (YH11803)																																					●	●														
SCOTT TRAILERS, Lincoln (YH12533)																																						●														
SHARP, ELIZABETH, Grantham (YH12678)																																												●								

Products Supplied
R - W

by Country by County	Riding Wear	Rocking Horse	Rosettes	Rubber Matting	Rubs & Creams	Saddle Pads	Saddles	Sash	Sea Clay	Second Hand Equipment	Security Products	Seed	Shavings	Show Jumps	Show Saddles	Show Stationery	Shredded Paper	Skin Feed Supplements	Snowflake Shavings	Solarium Equipment	Sperm Counter	Stable Bandages	Stable Equipment	Stable Fittings	Stage Warmer	Stainless Steel Bits	Stalls	Stirrups	Straw	Supplements	Sweatshirts	Tack	Tactile Webbing	Timing Equipment	Towbars	Trad Wooden Show Jump Equip	Trailer Accessories	Trailers	Training Aids	Traps	Travel Bandages	Treadmills (Build)	Treadmills (Supply)	Trophies	Videos	Vitamins	Weathervanes	Western Tack	Whips	Witter	Worming Products	Mail Order Facilities
STRAGGLETHORPE ROCKER, Brant Broughton (YH13545)		●																																																		
SWALLOW SADDLERY, Stamford (YH13685)							●																																													
TACK BOX, Lincoln (YH13785)							●																									●																			●	
THORPE, MERVYN, Stamford (YH14096)														●																																						
TYLER ANIMAL SYSTEMS, Grantham (YH14520)																																							●				●									
WINERGY, Grantham (YH15582)																															●																					
LINCOLNSHIRE (NORTH)																																																				
CROWSTONS, Scunthorpe (YH03684)					●									●																●		●							●						●							
KILLINGHOLME, Grimsby (YH08143)							●						●																●			●																				
MASON, D & M, Scunthorpe (YH09239)							●																									●																				
TORIC TROPHIES, Immingham (YH14244)																																												●								
LONDON (GREATER)																																																				
A D L TACK & SADDLERY, London (YH00027)							●																									●													●							●
CHASE SADDLERY, Enfield (YH02785)							●																																												●	
DECATHLON SPORTS & LEISURE, London (YH04009)							●																									●												●								
DUFFIN, JULIA, Ealing (YH04317)							●																					●				●																				
EDWARD ROBERT SADDLERY, Feltham (YH04569)							●																																													
GEDDES-BODEN, LESLIE, London (YH05687)																																																				●
GOULDS GREEN, Uxbridge (YH05952)							●						●																●			●																				
L H H ANIMAL FEEDS, Enfield (YH08321)														●																															●							
R B I PROMOTIONS, South Kensington (YH11516)																																													●							
RACETECH, Raynes Park (YH11580)																											●							●											●							
RAWLE & SON, London (YH11663)																																													●							
REDESDALE RESEARCH COMPANY, London (YH11709)																																		●																		
RIDERS & SQUIRES, London (YH11855)							●																																													
SEAMAN, JULIAN, London (YH12591)																																													●							
TRANS ATLANTIC FILMS, London (YH14347)																																													●							
YARBOROUGH, RACHEL, Edgware (YH15882)																																					●															
MANCHESTER (GREATER)																																																				
BATESON TRAILERS, Stockport (YH01069)																																					●	●														
BROWZERS, Manchester (YH02149)																																																				●
CRAINE, A, Bolton (YH03557)							●																																													

Products Supplied
R - W

by Country by County

	Riding Wear	Rocking Horse	Rosettes	Rubber Matting	Rubs & Creams	Saddle Pads	Saddles	Sash	Sea Clay	Second Hand Equipment	Security Products	Seed	Shavings	Show Jumps	Show Saddles	Show Stationery	Shredded Paper	Skin Feed Supplements	Snowflake Shavings	Solarium Equipment	Sperm Counter	Stable Bandages	Stable Equipment	Stable Fittings	Stage Warmer	Stainless Steel Bits	Stalls	Stirrups	Straw	Supplements	Sweatshirts	Tack	Tactile Webbing	Timing Equipment	Towbars	Trad Wooden Show Jump Equip	Trailer Accessories	Trailers	Training Aids	Traps	Travel Bandages	Treadmills (Build)	Treadmills (Supply)	Trophies	Videos	Vitamins	Weathervanes	Western Tack	Whips	Witter	Worming Products	Mail Order Facilities
EQUITACK, Bolton (YH04823)			●				●																									●													●							●
INDESPENSION, Bolton (YH07424)																																						●														
J & D WOODS, Bolton (YH07544)		●																																																		
PETS & PONIES, Ashton-under-Lyne (YH11029)	●																																																			
RYDERS FARM, Bolton (YH12297)													●				●												●			●																				
SHORESIDE STABLES, Manchester (YH12759)							●																																													
SMITHY, Bolton (YH13011)																																●																				
STABLEMATES, Bolton (YH13304)							●																									●																				
MERSEYSIDE																																																				
BARNSTON RIDING CTRE, Wirral (YH00991)							●																																													
FORMBY SADDLERY, Liverpool (YH05373)							●																																												●	
MIDLANDS (WEST)																																																				
ALBION SADDLEMAKERS, Walsall (YH00247)							●																																													
BEARLEY CROSS STABLES, Solihull (YH01121)													●																			●																				
BLACK COUNTRY SADDLERY, Walsall (YH01461)							●																																													
BRITISH EQUINE COLLECTORS, Coventry (YH01942)		●																																																		
BROWNS, Walsall (YH02142)							●																									●																				
COLT SADDLERY, Walsall (YH03201)							●																																													
COUNTY SADDLERY, Walsall (YH03491)							●																																													
COVENTRY SILVERCRAFT, Coventry (YH03518)																																												●								
DIAMOND SADDLERY, Wolverhampton (YH04104)					●		●																																													
E JEFFRIES & SONS, Walsall (YH04410)							●																																													
FRANK BAINES SADDLERY, Walsall (YH05455)							●																																													
GORSE FARM ARENA, Aldridge (YH05939)														●																																						
H W DABBS SADDLEMAKERS, Walsall (YH06245)							●																																													
HOOPER'S SADDLERS SHOP, Walsall (YH07045)							●																																													
JAMES COTTERELL & SONS, Walsall (YH07664)																												●				●																				
MONARCH EQUESTRIAN, Willenhall (YH09717)														●													●																●									
OVERIDER, Coventry (YH10593)	●																															●																				●
PHOENIX, Walsall (YH11069)							●																																													
PROLITE, Walsall (YH11432)						●																●																														
THOROWGOOD, Walsall (YH14089)						●	●																																													

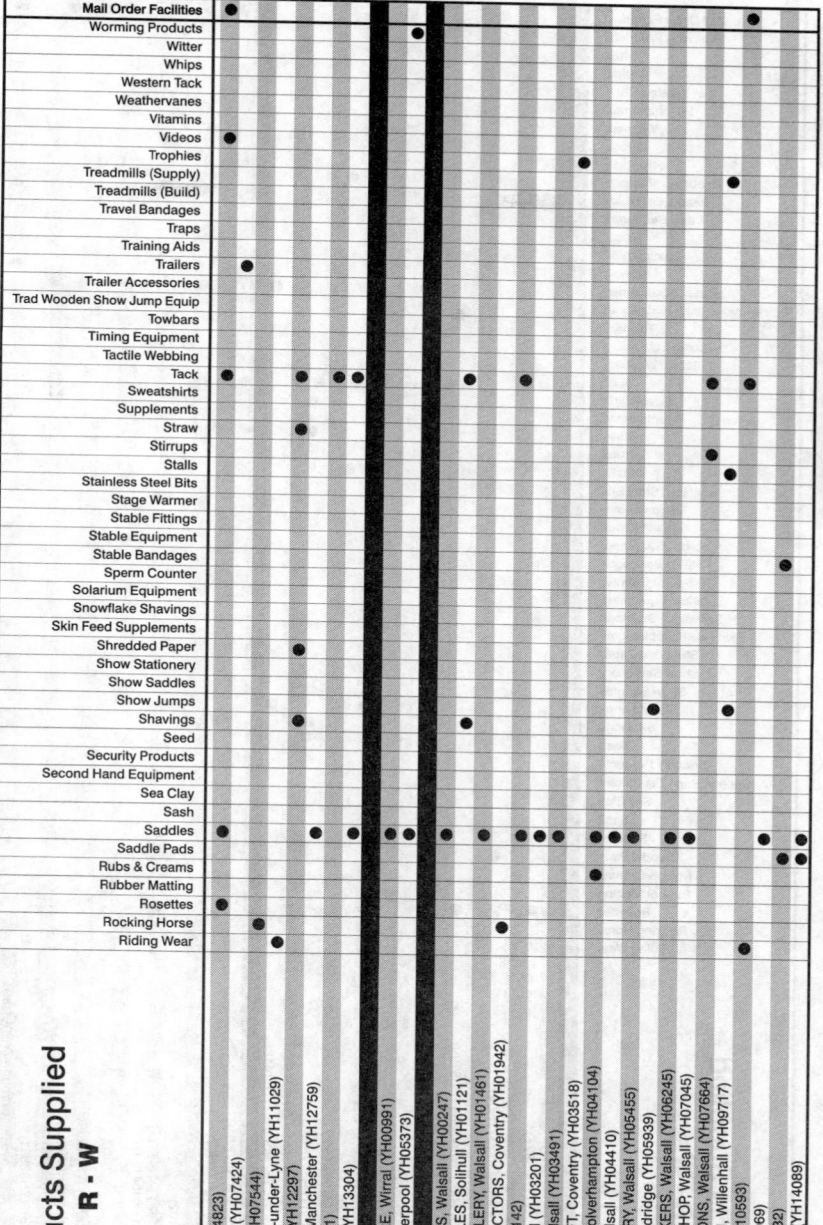

Products Supplied
R - W

by Country by County

	Riding Wear	Rocking Horse	Rosettes	Rubber Matting	Rubs & Creams	Saddle Pads	Saddles	Sash	Sea Clay	Second Hand Equipment	Security Products	Seed	Shavings	Show Jumps	Show Saddles	Show Stationery	Shredded Paper	Skin Feed Supplements	Snowflake Shavings	Solarium Equipment	Sperm Counter	Stable Bandages	Stable Equipment	Stable Fittings	Stage Warmer	Stainless Steel Bits
NORFOLK																										
C W G, East Dereham (YH02401)																										
DARBY ROSETTES, Norwich (YH03876)			●																							
EQUILUXE ENGINEERING, King's Lynn (YH04752)																										
EQUINE CLOTHING, Downham Market (YH04770)						●																				
EVERYTHING EQUESTRIAN, Norwich (YH04958)														●												
FIESTA ROSETTES & TROPHIES, Norwich (YH05199)			●																							
G J L, Fakenham (YH05585)													●				●									
H & C BEART, King's Lynn (YH06207)																										
HORSES IN SPORT, Diss (YH07169)																										
HORSETALK, King's Lynn (YH07176)							●																●			
J C SCHAAY TIMBER BUILDINGS, Diss (YH07576)		●												●												
LODDON, Norwich (YH08766)																										
REYNOLDS MOTORS, Cromer (YH11775)																										
RFC BED-DOWN, Harleston (YH11781)													●													
SHOWTIME ROSETTES, Thorpe Abbotts (YH12767)			●																							
TIRUS EQUESTRIAN PRODUCTS, Norwich (YH14185)														●												
NORTHAMPTONSHIRE																										
BATTEN, HORACE, Northampton (YH01077)																										
BROOK FARM, Wellingborough (YH02033)													●													
BURWELL HILL GARAGES, Brackley (YH02298)																										
C W G, Towcester (YH02402)																										
EDENGATE SADDLERY, Northampton (YH04550)			●				●			●																
EQUIBRAND, Charwelton (YH04734)																										
EQUIMAT, Kettering (YH04755)																										
HARLEY, Daventry (YH06436)																										
HOOKS & HOOVES, Kettering (YH07038)																										
K & T FOOTWEAR, Kettering (YH07981)																										
LIGHTFOOT INT, Daventry (YH08613)																										
LOVESON, Irthlingborough (YH08851)	●																									
MANOR FARM RIDING SCHOOL, Wellingborough (YH09106)																										
MOBILE PROMOTIONS COMPANY, Titchmarsh (YH09689)																										

	Stalls	Stirrups	Straw	Supplements	Sweatshirts	Tack	Tactile Webbing	Timing Equipment	Towbars	Trad Wooden Show Jump Equip	Trailer Accessories	Trailers	Training Aids	Traps	Travel Bandages	Treadmills (Build)	Treadmills (Supply)	Trophies	Videos	Vitamins	Weathervanes	Western Tack	Whips	Witter	Worming Products	Mail Order Facilities
NORFOLK																										
C W G, East Dereham (YH02401)																									●	
DARBY ROSETTES, Norwich (YH03876)																										
EQUILUXE ENGINEERING, King's Lynn (YH04752)												●														
EQUINE CLOTHING, Downham Market (YH04770)															●											●
EVERYTHING EQUESTRIAN, Norwich (YH04958)																										
FIESTA ROSETTES & TROPHIES, Norwich (YH05199)																										
G J L, Fakenham (YH05585)			●																							
H & C BEART, King's Lynn (YH06207)											●															
HORSES IN SPORT, Diss (YH07169)						●																				●
HORSETALK, King's Lynn (YH07176)						●																				
J C SCHAAY TIMBER BUILDINGS, Diss (YH07576)	●																									
LODDON, Norwich (YH08766)	●																●									
REYNOLDS MOTORS, Cromer (YH11775)											●	●														
RFC BED-DOWN, Harleston (YH11781)			●																							
SHOWTIME ROSETTES, Thorpe Abbotts (YH12767)																										
TIRUS EQUESTRIAN PRODUCTS, Norwich (YH14185)											●															
NORTHAMPTONSHIRE																										
BATTEN, HORACE, Northampton (YH01077)																										●
BROOK FARM, Wellingborough (YH02033)			●																							
BURWELL HILL GARAGES, Brackley (YH02298)											●															
C W G, Towcester (YH02402)																									●	
EDENGATE SADDLERY, Northampton (YH04550)						●							●						●							
EQUIBRAND, Charwelton (YH04734)											●															
EQUIMAT, Kettering (YH04755)											●															
HARLEY, Daventry (YH06436)																										●
HOOKS & HOOVES, Kettering (YH07038)						●																				
K & T FOOTWEAR, Kettering (YH07981)																										●
LIGHTFOOT INT, Daventry (YH08613)											●															
LOVESON, Irthlingborough (YH08851)																										
MANOR FARM RIDING SCHOOL, Wellingborough (YH09106)												●														
MOBILE PROMOTIONS COMPANY, Titchmarsh (YH09689)												●														

Products Supplied
R - W
by Country by County

	Riding Wear	Rocking Horse	Rosettes	Rubber Matting	Rubs & Creams	Saddle Pads	Saddles	Sash	Sea Clay	Second Hand Equipment	Security Products	Seed	Shavings	Show Jumps	Show Saddles	Show Stationery	Shredded Paper	Skin Feed Supplements	Snowflake Shavings	Solarium Equipment	Sperm Counter	Stable Bandages	Stable Equipment	Stable Fittings	Stage Warmer	Stainless Steel Bits	Stalls	Stirrups	Straw	Supplements	Sweatshirts	Tack	Tactile Webbing	Timing Equipment	Towbars	Trad Wooden Show Jump Equip	Trailer Accessories	Trailers	Training Aids	Traps	Travel Bandages	Treadmills (Build)	Treadmills (Supply)	Trophies	Videos	Vitamins	Weathervanes	Western Tack	Whips	Witter	Worming Products	Mail Order Facilities
O SHEPHERD & SON, Brackley (YH10366)							●																																													
PARKER, N, Northampton (YH10751)																																●																				
RUFFLES ROSETTES, Northampton (YH12212)			●																																																	
STUBBEN, Corby (YH13600)							●																			●		●				●							●													
THORPE SADDLERY, Kettering (YH14094)																																●																				
THREE SHIRES LIVERY CTRE, Wellingborough (YH14107)																													●																							
WATTS & WATTS SADDLERY, Northampton (YH15003)							●						●																			●							●						●							
WOODFLAKES OF DAVENTRY, Daventry (YH15686)			●																																																	
NORTHUMBERLAND																																																				
A C BURN, Berwick-upon-Tweed (YH00021)												●	●				●													●																					●	
BROWN TRAILERS, Cramlington (YH02094)																																					●	●														
DICKINSON, T M, Morpeth (YH04114)																													●																							
EQUILINK, Alnwick (YH04751)																																●						●														●
FARMWAY, Morpeth (YH05074)							●					●	●																			●																				
J S HUBBUCK, Hexham (YH07616)																																																			●	
WILLOW WEAR, Hexham (YH15505)							●																									●							●						●							
NOTTINGHAMSHIRE																																																				
AERBORN EQUESTRIAN, Nottingham (YH00195)																						●											●								●											
BRIDLE WAY & GAUNTLEYS, Newark (YH01892)							●						●	●			●												●			●					●		●						●							●
C W G, Worksop (YH02404)																																																			●	
C W G, Newark (YH02403)																																																			●	
CAREYS, Southwell (YH02537)			●																																																	
DECATHLON SPORTS & LEISURE, Nottingham (YH04010)							●																									●												●								
EUROBALE, Nottingham (YH04894)																													●																							
F MARTIN & SON, Arnold (YH04995)	●				●									●																																					●	
HOLISTIC HORSECARE, Northampton (YH06934)																																													●							●
HOOF ALOOF, Nottingham (YH07025)							●																									●																				
MALLENDER BROS, Worksop (YH09051)														●															●																							
MARTIN'S SHOWJUMPS, Trowell (YH09228)														●																																						
MERRIVALE TRADING, Nottingham (YH09483)																																											●									
MITEL MARKETING, Papplewick (YH09682)																																					●															
NEWBOULT & THORP, Retford (YH10125)																											●																									

www.hccyourhorse.com

Products Supplied
R - W

by Country by County	Riding Wear	Rocking Horse	Rosettes	Rubber Matting	Rubs & Creams	Saddle Pads	Saddles	Sash	Sea Clay	Second Hand Equipment	Security Products	Seed	Shavings	Show Jumps	Show Saddles	Show Stationery	Shredded Paper	Skin Feed Supplements	Snowflake Shavings	Solarium Equipment	Sperm Counter	Stable Bandages	Stable Equipment	Stable Fittings	Stage Warmer	Stainless Steel Bits	Stalls	Stirrups	Straw	Supplements	Sweatshirts	Tack	Tactile Webbing	Timing Equipment	Towbars	Trad Wooden Show Jump Equip	Trailer Accessories	Trailers	Training Aids	Traps	Travel Bandages	Treadmills (Build)	Treadmills (Supply)	Trophies	Videos	Vitamins	Weathervanes	Western Tack	Whips	Witter	Worming Products	Mail Order Facilities
NOTTINGHAM TRAILER SPARES, Nottingham (YH10345)																																					●	●														
PAPER BEDDING SUPPLIES, Newark (YH10707)																	●																																			
SADDLE RACK, Nottingham (YH12346)							●						●																			●																				
SADDLECRAFT, Nottingham (YH12355)	●						●																●									●							●						●							●
ST CLEMENTS LODGE, Nottingham (YH13274)							●						●																●			●																				
WELLOW PK, Newark (YH15077)														●																																						
OXFORDSHIRE																																																				
ASKER HORSESPORTS, Henley-on-Thames (YH00620)														●																									●													
ASTI STUD & SADDLERY, Faringdon (YH00633)							●						●																																●							●
BANBURY TRAILERS, Banbury (YH00880)																																					●	●														
BLOOR, ANNE, Banbury (YH01557)		●																																																		
CASTLE ROSETTES, Wallingford (YH02632)			●																																																	
DOBBINS CLOBBER, Thame (YH04150)	●					●	●																																													
ELITE FORAGE, Wallingford (YH04605)																													●																							
F S JUDGE & SONS, Faringdon (YH04999)																													●																							
FARMKEY, Banbury (YH05067)																																					●															
HAC-TAC, Faringdon (YH06259)	●																																																			
JODS GALORE, Henley-on-Thames (YH07775)							●																									●							●						●							●
KEN LANGFORD SADDLERY, Abingdon (YH08058)							●																																													
KUBOTA, Thame (YH08300)																																						●														
MICROM, Thame (YH09519)																					●				●																											
SANSOMS SADDLERY, Witney (YH12429)							●																									●							●						●							●
SCATS COUNTRYSTORE, Faringdon (YH12506)																																●																			●	
W F S COUNTRY, Witney (YH14766)							●																									●																				
WEATHERBEETA, Banbury (YH15023)	●						●																																													
WHARTON ELECTRONICS, Thame (YH15263)																																		●																		
RUTLAND																																																				
W'UNDERWEAR, Oakham (YH15852)																																																				●
SHROPSHIRE																																																				
A & M SADDLERY, Ellesmere (YH00015)	●						●																																													
BULLDOG SECURITY, Much Wenlock (YH02214)											●																										●															
C J BLACKSMITHS, Shrewsbury (YH02375)																																															●					●

Products Supplied
R - W

by Country by County

	Riding Wear	Rocking Horse	Rosettes	Rubber Matting	Rubs & Creams	Saddle Pads	Saddles	Sash	Sea Clay	Second Hand Equipment	Security Products	Seed	Shavings	Show Jumps	Show Saddles	Show Stationery	Shredded Paper	Skin Feed Supplements	Snowflake Shavings	Solarium Equipment	Sperm Counter	Stable Bandages	Stable Equipment	Stable Fittings	Stage Warmer	Stainless Steel Bits	Stalls	Stirrups	Straw	Supplements	Sweatshirts	Tack	Tactile Webbing	Timing Equipment	Towbars	Trad Wooden Show Jump Equip	Trailer Accessories	Trailers	Training Aids	Traps	Travel Bandages	Treadmills (Build)	Treadmills (Supply)	Trophies	Videos	Vitamins	Weathervanes	Western Tack	Whips	Witter	Worming Products	Mail Order Facilities
CHARLES BRITTON CONSTRUCTION, Ellesmere (YH02754)														●													●																									
DAVIES, R, Shrewsbury (YH03946)																													●																							
EVANS, J C, Shrewsbury (YH04922)																																					●	●														
HEAD TO HOOF, Market Drayton (YH06608)																																																				●
HORSE SHOP, Telford (YH07140)							●																																													
HORSE SHOP, Bridgnorth (YH07139)							●																									●																				
N W F COUNTRYSTORE, Market Drayton (YH09998)																																					●															
NATIONAL FOALING BANK, Newport (YH10037)																																													●							
TOUCHDOWN LIVERIES, Whitchurch (YH14253)													●																																							
W BRYAN HORSE SERVICES, Shrewsbury (YH14753)																																						●														
WREKIN FARMERS GARDEN CTRE, Telford (YH15817)																																																			●	
WYKE OF SHIFNAL, Shifnal (YH15863)														●																																						
WYNNSTAY & CLWYD FARMERS, Oswestry (YH15876)																																														●					●	
SOMERSET																																																				
BOWERS, HENRY, Chard (YH01707)							●																									●																				
EBBORLANDS, Wells (YH04529)																																							●													
EQUESTRIAN ENGINEERING, Templecombe (YH04700)																																					●															
EXMOOR WHOLESALE, Dulverton (YH04971)																																														●					●	
HILTON HERBS, Crewkerne (YH06863)					●																																								●							
JUST REWARDS, Bridgwater (YH07976)			●																																																	
MAYTREE FARM FEEDS, Shepton Mallet (YH09307)														●																																						
MCCOY SADDLERY, Minehead (YH09334)							●																									●																				●
R E D ROSETTES, Bridgwater (YH11531)			●																																																	
RICH & SON, Bridgwater (YH11798)							●																																													
RIDEMOOR, Wincanton (YH11852)							●						●				●												●			●							●						●							●
RODGROVE STUD EQUESTRIAN CTRE, Wincanton (YH12048)																																							●				●									
ROSE MILL FEEDS, Ilminster (YH12094)							●					●	●				●												●	●		●																				
S S EQUESTRIAN VIDEO, Yeovil (YH12335)																																													●							
SPARKFORD SAWMILLS, Yeovil (YH13177)																											●																									
STAX SADDLERY, Montacute (YH13406)							●						●																			●																				
THORNEY COPSE, Wincanton (YH14066)							●						●																●			●					●		●						●							●
W.E.S GARRETT MASTER SADDLERS, Cheddar (YH14803)							●						●																			●							●													

www.hccyourhorse.com

www.hccyourhorse.com

Products Supplied
R - W

by Country by County

	Riding Wear	Rocking Horse	Rosettes	Rubber Matting	Rubs & Creams	Saddle Pads	Saddles	Sash	Sea Clay	Second Hand Equipment	Security Products	Seed	Shavings	Show Jumps	Show Saddles	Show Stationery	Shredded Paper	Skin Feed Supplements	Snowflake Shavings	Solarium Equipment	Sperm Counter	Stable Bandages	Stable Equipment	Stable Fittings	Stage Warmer	Stainless Steel Bits
WITHAM VALE CONTRACTORS, Yeovil (YH15619)														●												
SOMERSET (NORTH)																										
SMART HORSEBOXES, Banwell (YH12918)																										
SPRINGFIELD, Claverham (YH13252)																										
STAFFORDSHIRE																										
ABBOTSWOOD SHOW JUMPS, Rugeley (YH00100)														●												
B I S, Stoke-on-Trent (YH00731)			●																							
C W G, Burton-on-Trent (YH02405)																										
COUNTY WHIPS, Burton-on-Trent (YH03497)																										
DOBBINS DINER, Tamworth (YH04151)												●	●				●									
FRANCES ANN BROWN SADDLERY, Stafford (YH05444)							●																			
LARKHILL SADDLERY, Burton-on-Trent (YH08432)							●						●													
SCROPTON, Burton-on-Trent (YH12569)																										
STAFFORDSHIRE TRAILERS, Lichfield (YH13325)																										
SUFFOLK																										
BALLINGDON SADDLERY, Sudbury (YH00857)							●																			
C W G, Bury St Edmunds (YH02406)																										
CHURCH FARM TACK SHOP & FEEDS, Eye (YH02903)													●													
COUNTRYSIDE, Ipswich (YH03439)														●												
CROSSWAYS SV CTRE, Bungay (YH03667)													●													
EQUISAVE HORSE AMBULANCES, Newmarket (YH04816)																										
GIBSON SADDLERS, Newmarket (YH05746)							●																●			
GLADWELLS, Ipswich (YH05802)													●													
HERITAGE COAST STUD, Woodbridge (YH06703)																										
HORSE & GARDEN, Halesworth (YH07089)																										
HORSE REQUISITES, Newmarket (YH07132)							●																			
HORSESHOES, Wrentham (YH07174)													●													
J B FENWICK & SON, Newmarket (YH07563)																										
LAVENHAM LEISURE, Sudbury (YH08463)																										
LEGEND SVS, Bury St Edmunds (YH08535)														●												
LONG MELFORD, Sudbury (YH08799)							●						●													
MILL SADDLERY, Stowmarket (YH09587)							●						●													

	Stalls	Stirrups	Straw	Supplements	Sweatshirts	Tack	Tactile Webbing	Timing Equipment	Towbars	Trad Wooden Show Jump Equip	Trailer Accessories	Trailers	Training Aids	Traps	Travel Bandages	Treadmills (Build)	Treadmills (Supply)	Trophies	Videos	Vitamins	Weathervanes	Western Tack	Whips	Witter	Worming Products	Mail Order Facilities
WITHAM VALE CONTRACTORS, Yeovil (YH15619)																										
SOMERSET (NORTH)																										
SMART HORSEBOXES, Banwell (YH12918)											●															
SPRINGFIELD, Claverham (YH13252)											●	●					●									
STAFFORDSHIRE																										
ABBOTSWOOD SHOW JUMPS, Rugeley (YH00100)																										
B I S, Stoke-on-Trent (YH00731)																										
C W G, Burton-on-Trent (YH02405)																									●	
COUNTY WHIPS, Burton-on-Trent (YH03497)																							●			
DOBBINS DINER, Tamworth (YH04151)																										
FRANCES ANN BROWN SADDLERY, Stafford (YH05444)						●																				
LARKHILL SADDLERY, Burton-on-Trent (YH08432)						●																				
SCROPTON, Burton-on-Trent (YH12569)														●												
STAFFORDSHIRE TRAILERS, Lichfield (YH13325)											●															
SUFFOLK																										
BALLINGDON SADDLERY, Sudbury (YH00857)																										
C W G, Bury St Edmunds (YH02406)																									●	
CHURCH FARM TACK SHOP & FEEDS, Eye (YH02903)						●																	●			
COUNTRYSIDE, Ipswich (YH03439)																										
CROSSWAYS SV CTRE, Bungay (YH03667)			●			●																				
EQUISAVE HORSE AMBULANCES, Newmarket (YH04816)												●														
GIBSON SADDLERS, Newmarket (YH05746)						●																				
GLADWELLS, Ipswich (YH05802)			●																	●						
HERITAGE COAST STUD, Woodbridge (YH06703)			●																							
HORSE & GARDEN, Halesworth (YH07089)																									●	
HORSE REQUISITES, Newmarket (YH07132)	●					●											●									
HORSESHOES, Wrentham (YH07174)																									●	●
J B FENWICK & SON, Newmarket (YH07563)			●																							
LAVENHAM LEISURE, Sudbury (YH08463)																										●
LEGEND SVS, Bury St Edmunds (YH08535)																										
LONG MELFORD, Sudbury (YH08799)						●																				
MILL SADDLERY, Stowmarket (YH09587)						●									●											●

Products Supplied
R - W

by Country by County	Riding Wear	Rocking Horse	Rosettes	Rubber Matting	Rubs & Creams	Saddle Pads	Saddles	Sash	Sea Clay	Second Hand Equipment	Security Products	Seed	Shavings	Show Jumps	Show Saddles	Show Stationery	Shredded Paper	Skin Feed Supplements	Snowflake Shavings	Solarium Equipment	Sperm Counter	Stable Bandages	Stable Equipment	Stable Fittings	Stage Warmer	Stainless Steel Bits	Stalls	Stirrups	Straw	Supplements	Sweatshirts	Tack	Tactile Webbing	Timing Equipment	Towbars	Trad Wooden Show Jump Equip	Trailer Accessories	Trailers	Training Aids	Traps	Travel Bandages	Treadmills (Build)	Treadmills (Supply)	Trophies	Videos	Vitamins	Weathervanes	Western Tack	Whips	Witter	Worming Products	Mail Order Facilities
NORCROFT EQUESTRIAN DVLP, Bury St Edmunds (YH10230)																											●																●									
REYNOLDS, GERRY, Newmarket (YH11778)							●																																													
RIDE AWAY SADDLERY, Ipswich (YH11846)							●																									●																				
RYLAND SADDLERS, Newmarket (YH12305)							●																●									●																				
STOKE BY CLARE EQUESTRIAN CTRE, Sudbury (YH13501)													●																																							
SUFFOLK SADDLES, Ipswich (YH13626)							●																									●																				
VALLEY FARM, Woodbridge (YH14651)																													●																							
VIRBAC, Bury St Edmunds (YH14732)																																																			●	
WESTBRINK FARMS, Newmarket (YH15184)													●						●										●																							
SURREY																																																				
A C F ANIMAL BEDDING, Haslemere (YH00024)																	●												●																							
ANIMAL ALTERNATIVES, Richmond (YH00425)																		●																																		
ARDENLEA ENTERPRISES, Epsom (YH00504)														●													●																●									
ASCOT PARK, Woking (YH00583)							●						●																			●													●							●
BALANCED FEEDS, Malden Rushett (YH00830)																														●																						
BROOMELLS WORKSHOP, Dorking (YH02077)							●																									●																				
BUTTONS SADDLERY, Woking (YH02337)							●																									●																				
CHRIS HAY, Dorking (YH02881)																													●																							
CHRIS HAY, Dorking (YH02882)																													●																							
FARNHAM SADDLERS, Farnham (YH05082)							●																																													
FIELDGUARD, Cranleigh (YH05193)																							●																													●
GREEN LANE STABLES, Morden (YH06058)							●																									●																				
HAINES ROSETTE, Addlestone (YH06285)			●																																																	
HASTILOW COMPETITION SADDLES, Godalming (YH06526)							●						●	●															●			●							●													●
KEAR, BILL, Dorking (YH08016)																											●																									
LETHERS OF BROCKHAM, Betchworth (YH08568)							●																									●																				
LETHERS OF MERSTHAM, Redhill (YH08569)							●																									●																				
LINGFIELD TACK, Lingfield (YH08660)																																●																				
MANOR SADDLERY, Guildford (YH09117)							●																									●																				
ONE STOP TACK SHOP, East Molesey (YH10513)																																●																				
PREMIER SHOW JUMPS, Horley (YH11350)														●																																						
RIDE & DRIVE, Horne (YH11842)																																●																				

www.hccyourhorse.com

Products Supplied
R - W

by Country by County

	Riding Wear	Rocking Horse	Rosettes	Rubber Matting	Rubs & Creams	Saddle Pads	Saddles	Sash	Sea Clay	Second Hand Equipment	Security Products	Seed	Shavings	Show Jumps	Show Saddles	Show Stationery	Shredded Paper	Skin Feed Supplements	Snowflake Shavings	Solarium Equipment	Sperm Counter	Stable Bandages	Stable Equipment	Stable Fittings	Stage Warmer	Stainless Steel Bits
ROKER'S TACK SHOP, Guildford (YH12064)													●													
RUSTICS, Lingfield (YH12269)														●												
S R S, Sunbury-on-Thames (YH12333)					●																					
SCATS COUNTRYSTORE, Redhill (YH12508)																										
SCATS COUNTRYSTORE, Godalming (YH12507)																										
SUPERPET THE HORSE SHOP, Tadworth (YH13655)							●						●										●			
SUPERPET THE HORSE SHOP, Banstead (YH13656)							●						●										●			
SUPERPET THE HORSE SHOP, Epsom (YH13654)							●						●										●			
TILITA ROSETTES, Warlingham (YH14147)			●																							
TRIPLE CROWN FENCE, Guildford (YH14403)														●												
WOLDINGHAM SADDLERS, Caterham (YH15647)							●																			
SUSSEX (EAST)																										
ANDREW REILLY, Forest Row (YH00392)							●																			
CROCKSTEAD PK, Lewes (YH03608)							●																			
DANDY BUSH SADDLERY, Battle (YH03863)							●																			
EURO-MECH, Brighton (YH04903)																										
FARMIX, Wadhurst (YH05066)																										
G A COMMERCIALS, Pevensey (YH05569)																										
GREENSLADE HORSE TRAILERS, Robertsbridge (YH06101)																										
GUMTREE ENTERPRISES, Plumpton (YH06191)																										
LEVADE SYSTEMS, Hartfield (YH08572)																										
SCATS COUNTRYSTORE, Heathfield (YH12509)																										
SOMETHING DIFFERENT, Uckfield (YH13068)							●																			
SOUTH LODGE, Rotherfield (YH13100)																										
STEVENS, LEONARD, Eastbourne (YH13445)							●						●													
SUSSEX (WEST)																										
ALL TIME EQUESTRIAN, Crawley (YH00286)																										
BRENDON HORSE & RIDER, Brighton (YH01837)							●						●	●												
COUNTY ROSETTES, Hassocks (YH03490)			●																							
CRAWLEY DOWN SADDLERY, Crawley (YH03578)							●																			
DAVID WILSON'S TRAILERS, Horsted Keynes (YH03925)																										
DEAN, GEOFF, Worthing (YH03991)							●																			

	Stalls	Stirrups	Straw	Supplements	Sweatshirts	Tack	Tactile Webbing	Timing Equipment	Towbars	Trad Wooden Show Jump Equip	Trailer Accessories	Trailers	Training Aids	Traps	Travel Bandages	Treadmills (Build)	Treadmills (Supply)	Trophies	Videos	Vitamins	Weathervanes	Western Tack	Whips	Witter	Worming Products	Mail Order Facilities
ROKER'S TACK SHOP, Guildford (YH12064)						●													●							
RUSTICS, Lingfield (YH12269)																										
S R S, Sunbury-on-Thames (YH12333)																										
SCATS COUNTRYSTORE, Redhill (YH12508)						●																			●	
SCATS COUNTRYSTORE, Godalming (YH12507)						●																			●	
SUPERPET THE HORSE SHOP, Tadworth (YH13655)						●																				
SUPERPET THE HORSE SHOP, Banstead (YH13656)						●																				
SUPERPET THE HORSE SHOP, Epsom (YH13654)						●																				●
TILITA ROSETTES, Warlingham (YH14147)																										
TRIPLE CROWN FENCE, Guildford (YH14403)																										
WOLDINGHAM SADDLERS, Caterham (YH15647)						●																			●	
SUSSEX (EAST)																										
ANDREW REILLY, Forest Row (YH00392)																										
CROCKSTEAD PK, Lewes (YH03608)																										
DANDY BUSH SADDLERY, Battle (YH03863)																										
EURO-MECH, Brighton (YH04903)																	●									
FARMIX, Wadhurst (YH05066)			●																							
G A COMMERCIALS, Pevensey (YH05569)											●	●														
GREENSLADE HORSE TRAILERS, Robertsbridge (YH06101)											●	●														
GUMTREE ENTERPRISES, Plumpton (YH06191)											●															
LEVADE SYSTEMS, Hartfield (YH08572)	●																									
SCATS COUNTRYSTORE, Heathfield (YH12509)						●																			●	
SOMETHING DIFFERENT, Uckfield (YH13068)																										
SOUTH LODGE, Rotherfield (YH13100)																		●								
STEVENS, LEONARD, Eastbourne (YH13445)																										
SUSSEX (WEST)																										
ALL TIME EQUESTRIAN, Crawley (YH00286)						●																				
BRENDON HORSE & RIDER, Brighton (YH01837)				●		●													●						●	
COUNTY ROSETTES, Hassocks (YH03490)																										
CRAWLEY DOWN SADDLERY, Crawley (YH03578)						●																				
DAVID WILSON'S TRAILERS, Horsted Keynes (YH03925)												●														
DEAN, GEOFF, Worthing (YH03991)																										

Products Supplied
R - W

by Country by County

Company	Riding Wear	Rocking Horse	Rosettes	Rubber Matting	Rubs & Creams	Saddle Pads	Saddles	Sash	Sea Clay	Second Hand Equipment	Security Products	Seed	Shavings	Show Jumps	Show Saddles	Show Stationery	Shredded Paper	Skin Feed Supplements	Snowflake Shavings	Solarium Equipment	Sperm Counter	Stable Bandages	Stable Equipment	Stable Fittings	Stage Warmer	Stainless Steel Bits	Stalls	Stirrups	Straw	Supplements	Sweatshirts	Tack	Tactile Webbing	Timing Equipment	Towbars	Trad Wooden Show Jump Equip	Trailer Accessories	Trailers	Training Aids	Traps	Travel Bandages	Treadmills (Build)	Treadmills (Supply)	Trophies	Videos	Vitamins	Weathervanes	Western Tack	Whips	Witter	Worming Products	Mail Order Facilities
DIAMOND SADDLERY, Hassocks (YH04105)							●																																													
DRAGONFLY SADDLERY, Hassocks (YH04252)			●				●																									●							●						●							●
E M C, Shoreham By Sea (YH04415)																																●																				
EQUINE AMERICA, Broadbridge Heath (YH04761)					●																																															
EQUITOGS, Littlehampton (YH04829)							●						●																●			●																				
EQUITOGS, Billingshurst (YH04830)							●						●																●			●																				
FFOOKS FLAGS, Pulborough (YH05176)														●																																						
GEOFF DEAN SADDLERY, Worthing (YH05714)							●																									●																				
H E I, Pulborough (YH06218)																																							●													
LIGHTS, Brighton (YH08616)												●	●																			●																				
LOWER SPARR FARM, Billingshurst (YH08870)				●																																						●	●									
MARTIN BIRD PRODUCTIONS, Horsham (YH09211)																																													●							
NORTON HIND SADDLERY, Arundel (YH10330)							●																									●																				
PARKERS, Horsham (YH10753)							●																																													
PENFOLD & SONS, Haywards Heath (YH10934)							●																									●																				
PEPER HAROW HORSE TRAILERS, Horsham (YH10968)																																					●	●														
ROUSE, SARAH, Midhurst (YH12147)																																													●							
SCATS COUNTRYSTORE, Billingshurst (YH12510)																																●																			●	
SHARON TONG, Steyning (YH12677)																																																				●
SNOWHILL SADDLERY, Chichester (YH13044)							●																									●																				
TACK A ROUND SADDLERY, Billingshurst (YH13781)							●																									●																				
TFP, Horsham (YH13971)													●																																●							
TRACK RIGHT, Hassocks (YH14308)																																●							●													●
WILLOWBROOK RIDING CTRE, Chichester (YH15508)																																						●														
ZARA STUD, Chichester (YH15951)							●																									●																				
TYNE AND WEAR																																																				
GO RIDING GRP, Ponteland (YH05862)													●																																							
H C S, North Shields (YH06215)					●																																															●
JOSEPH BAILEY & SONS, Houghton Le Spring (YH07942)																										●												●														
QUARRY PARK STABLES, Gateshead (YH11483)																																							●													
RIDE IN STYLE, Sunderland (YH11847)																																●																				
RIDERS, North Shields (YH11854)							●																									●																				

Products Supplied
R - W

by Country by County	Riding Wear	Rocking Horse	Rosettes	Rubber Matting	Rubs & Creams	Saddle Pads	Saddles	Sash	Sea Clay	Second Hand Equipment	Security Products	Seed	Shavings	Show Jumps	Show Saddles	Show Stationery	Shredded Paper	Skin Feed Supplements	Snowflake Shavings	Solarium Equipment	Sperm Counter	Stable Bandages	Stable Equipment	Stable Fittings	Stage Warmer	Stainless Steel Bits	Stalls	Stirrups	Straw	Supplements	Sweatshirts	Tack	Tactile Webbing	Timing Equipment	Towbars	Trad Wooden Show Jump Equip	Trailer Accessories	Trailers	Training Aids	Traps	Travel Bandages	Treadmills (Build)	Treadmills (Supply)	Trophies	Videos	Vitamins	Weathervanes	Western Tack	Whips	Witter	Worming Products	Mail Order Facilities
S & S SADDLERY, Sunderland (YH12313)																																●																				
SADDLE SHOP, Gateshead (YH12350)							●																									●																				
WEBSTER, J R, Newcastle-upon-Tyne (YH15040)							●																																													
WARWICKSHIRE																																																				
A & J SADDLERY, Southam (YH00012)							●						●																			●																			●	
ACCIMASSU, Studley (YH00140)																											●																									
ATHAG LTD, Atherstone (YH00642)																											●																									
BHS, Kenilworth (YH01371)																																													●							●
CLAYDON HORSE EXERCISERS, Southam (YH02999)																																											●									
COLEMAN, ROBIN, Kenilworth (YH03164)		●																																																		
DARLOWS, Butlers Marston (YH03896)			●																																									●								
GRAPES VILLA FARM SUPPLIES, Coventry (YH06017)																																																			●	
OUSBEY CARRIAGES, Statford-on-Avon (YH10584)		●																																																		
SHIPSTON MILL, Shipston-on-Stour (YH12751)																																													●							
SPORTSMARK, Warwick (YH13236)														●																																						
WARWICK BUILDINGS, Rugby (YH14945)																											●																									
WARWICKSHIRE TRAILERS, Solihull (YH14953)																																					●	●														●
WAVERLEY EQUESTRIAN CTRE, Leamington Spa (YH15011)													●																			●																				
WESTERN RIDING, Rugby (YH15204)																																													●							
WILTSHIRE																																																				
ARMADILLO PRODUCTS, Salisbury (YH00535)						●																																														
BEST BOOTS, Chippenham (YH01324)																																																				●
CARDEN, SUSAN M M, Chippenham (YH02529)																																													●							
DAVID FARMER SADDLERY, Chippenham (YH03919)	●																																																			
EASTON GREY SADDLERS, Malmesbury (YH04514)							●																									●																				
ELMGROVE SADDLERY, Swindon (YH04636)							●																									●																				
EQUI-SURE, Corsham (YH04822)				●																																																
GEORGE SMITH HORSEBOXES, Salisbury (YH05719)																																					●	●														
GRANT BARNES & SON, Malmesbury (YH06009)							●																									●																				
HURDCOTT LIVERY STABLES, Salisbury (YH07311)							●																									●																				
I H A, Marlborough (YH07365)																																							●													
JOHN TOOMER, Swindon (YH07815)																																																			●	

Products Supplied
R - W

by Country by County

	Riding Wear	Rocking Horse	Rosettes	Rubber Matting	Rubs & Creams	Saddle Pads	Saddles	Sash	Sea Clay	Second Hand Equipment	Security Products	Seed	Shavings	Show Jumps	Show Saddles	Show Stationery	Shredded Paper	Skin Feed Supplements	Snowflake Shavings	Solarium Equipment	Sperm Counter	Stable Bandages	Stable Equipment	Stable Fittings	Stage Warmer	Stainless Steel Bits	Stalls	Stirrups	Straw	Supplements	Sweatshirts	Tack	Tactile Webbing	Timing Equipment	Towbars	Trad Wooden Show Jump Equip	Trailer Accessories	Trailers	Training Aids	Traps	Travel Bandages	Treadmills (Build)	Treadmills (Supply)	Trophies	Videos	Vitamins	Weathervanes	Western Tack	Whips	Witter	Worming Products	Mail Order Facilities
MALMESBURY TRAILERS, Malmesbury (YH09053)																																					●														
MULLIS, ROBERT, Swindon (YH09943)		●																																																		
NEW EQUINE WEAR, Malmesbury (YH10093)						●																																		●											
SADDLERY, Swindon (YH12364)							●																								●																				
SCATS COUNTRYSTORE, Salisbury (YH12511)																																●																			●	
SCATS COUNTRYSTORE, Devizes (YH12512)																																●																			●	
SYDNEY INGRAM & SON, Salisbury (YH13722)							●																								●			●																	
WADSWICK, Corsham (YH14819)							●																								●																			●	
WARMINSTER SADDLERY, Warminster (YH14923)							●																								●																				
WILLIS BROS, Malmesbury (YH15491)														●																																						
WORCESTERSHIRE																																																				
BENT, BM & SA, Evesham (YH01282)																													●																							
BROMSGROVE SADDLERY, Bromsgrove (YH02026)							●																																													
CENTRIFORCE, Worcester (YH02697)																											●										●															
COUNTRYWIDE, Worcester (YH03446)							●						●																			●																			●	
EQUIMIX, Stourport-on-Severn (YH04756)							●						●																			●													●							●
JUMPS FOR JOY, Worcester (YH07969)														●																																						
M & M TIMBER, Kidderminster (YH08949)														●																																						
OAKLAND HORSEBOXES, Little Witley (YH10388)																																					●															
PHIPPS, A, Pershore (YH11068)																																																				●
SMITH-MAXWELL, A L, Upton-upon-Severn (YH13005)																													●																							
WITS END STABLES, Worcester (YH15634)													●																																							
YORKSHIRE (EAST)																																																				
DRIFFIELD DISCOUNT SADDLERY, Driffield (YH04273)							●																																													
HAIGHS, Doncaster (YH06282)																													●																							
HASTPACE DATA, Driffield (YH06529)																																		●																		
HOOD, J R, Driffield (YH07023)																													●																							
NORTH RIDING ROSETTES, Bridlington (YH10280)			●																																																	
NORTHERN STRAW, Goole (YH10311)																													●																							
PATRICK WILKINSON, Beverley (YH10825)							●																								●																				●
SMITHY, Driffield (YH13013)																												●											●													
YORKSHIRE (NORTH)																																																				

www.hccyourhorse.com

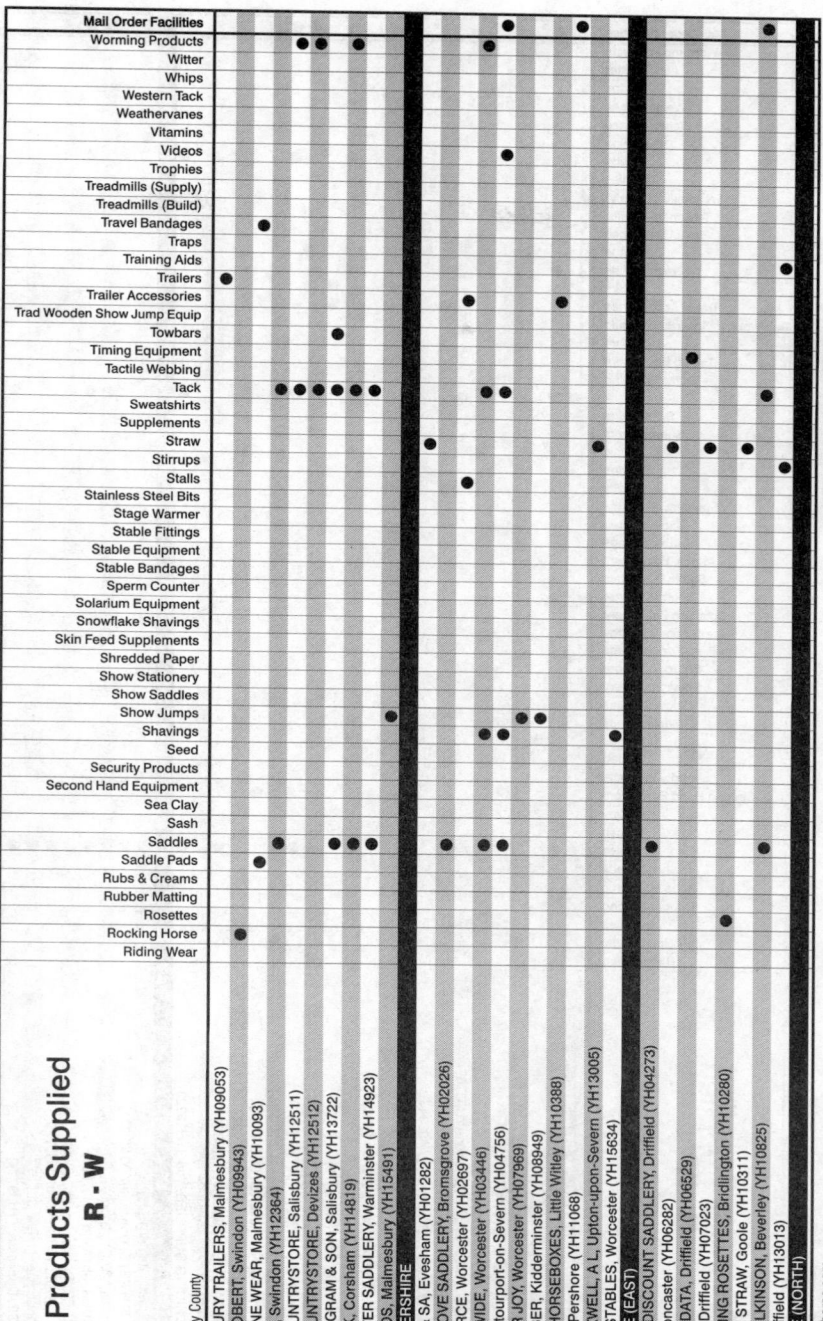

Products Supplied
R - W

by Country by County	Riding Wear	Rocking Horse	Rosettes	Rubber Matting	Rubs & Creams	Saddle Pads	Saddles	Sash	Sea Clay	Second Hand Equipment	Security Products	Seed	Shavings	Show Jumps	Show Saddles	Show Stationery	Shredded Paper	Skin Feed Supplements	Snowflake Shavings	Solarium Equipment	Sperm Counter	Stable Bandages	Stable Equipment	Stable Fittings	Stage Warmer	Stainless Steel Bits	Stalls	Stirrups	Straw	Supplements	Sweatshirts	Tack	Tactile Webbing	Timing Equipment	Towbars	Trad Wooden Show Jump Equip	Trailer Accessories	Trailers	Training Aids	Traps	Travel Bandages	Treadmills (Build)	Treadmills (Supply)	Trophies	Videos	Vitamins	Weathervanes	Western Tack	Whips	Witter	Worming Products	Mail Order Facilities
BEAVER HORSE SHOP, Harrogate (YH01143)							●																									●																				
BIT BANK, Stokesley (YH01454)							●																									●							●													●
BULLOCK, J A & F, York (YH02219)													●																																							
BUSHELL, ANN, Richmond (YH02309)		●																																										●								
E WARD & SON, York (YH04431)																																						●														
F BAYRAM & SONS, York (YH04984)																													●																							
GILLS SADDLERY & CANE, Northallerton (YH05787)							●																									●																				
HI-LINE HORSEBOXES, Cawood (YH06809)																											●										●															
HOLLINHALL RIDE & DRIVE, Whitby (YH06946)																																								●												
HOLMAN, A E & A B, Selby (YH06961)																													●																							
J S W & SON COACHBUILDERS, Northallerton (YH07619)																											●										●	●														
LANGTON HORSE WEAR, Northallerton (YH08416)																																●																				
R & R COUNTRY, Selby (YH11507)							●						●	●															●			●							●						●							●
RICHARDSON RICE, York (YH11813)																																					●	●														
RIDE-AWAY, York (YH11850)	●						●						●										●							●		●													●							●
ROBINSON, Malton (YH11985)							●																									●													●							●
ROCKING HORSE SHOP, Pocklington (YH12034)		●																																																		
SECOND TURNOUT, Northallerton (YH12598)										●																																										
WATT FENCES, Catterick Garrison (YH14997)														●																																						
WHITE ROSE SADDLERY, Malton (YH15324)							●																																													
WOODS SHOW JUMPS, Malton (YH15734)														●																																						
YORKSHIRE RIDING SUPPLIES, York (YH15923)							●																									●													●							
YORKSHIRE (SOUTH)																																																				
BLUE CHIP, Sheffield (YH01565)																																														●						●
CONISBROUGH PETS, Doncaster (YH03231)							●																																													
DARKHORSE TINYTACK, Barnsley (YH03888)							●																									●								●												●
HORSE & RIDER, Sheffield (YH07097)							●																									●													●						●	●
HORSE & RIDER, Doncaster (YH07096)							●																									●																				
HUNSHELF SADDLERY, Sheffield (YH07292)							●																																													
MILLVIEW, Doncaster (YH09638)							●																																													
MOORHOUSE, Doncaster (YH09774)							●																									●																				
MR ED'S, Rotherham (YH09915)							●																																													

Products Supplied

R - W

by Country by County

by Country by County	Riding Wear	Rocking Horse	Rosettes	Rubber Matting	Rubs & Creams	Saddle Pads	Saddles	Sash	Sea Clay	Second Hand Equipment	Security Products	Seed	Shavings
ROSETTE COMPANY, Barnsley (YH12109)			●										
SHOWJUMP INT, Barnsley (YH12766)													
STABLE-DRY & EQUIBALE, Doncaster (YH13302)													●
THROSTLE NEST SADDLERY, Barnsley (YH14114)													
WILDSMITHS, Doncaster (YH15412)							●						
YORKSHIRE (WEST)													
ACORN FEEDS, Huddersfield (YH00148)													
B T H HIRE & SALES, Leeds (YH00749)													
BARDSEY MILLS, Otley (YH00927)													●
BLACUP TRAINING GRP, Halifax (YH01504)													
BRADLEY DOUBLELOCK, Bingley (YH01749)													
BRANDON FORGE SADDLERY, Leeds (YH01796)													
COURTYARD SADDLERY, Collingham (YH03512)							●						
DALE COCHRANE, Keighley (YH03820)			●										
DAYS PET SHOP, Bradford (YH03971)							●						
DISCOUNT SADDLERY, Huddersfield (YH04129)			●				●					●	
EQUESTRIAN CLEARANCE CTRE, Halifax (YH04694)							●						
EQUITACK SADDLERY, Wakefield (YH04825)							●						
F & STROKER & SONS, Leeds (YH04981)													
FOX SADDLERS, Wetherby (YH05425)							●						
HALLAS LANE LIVERY STABLES, Bradford (YH06327)													
HIGHWOOD, Ossett (YH06803)													
HILLAM FEEDS, South Milford (YH06836)													
HILLAM TRAILERS, Cleckheaton (YH06837)													
HOOVES EQUESTRIAN, Bradford (YH07047)							●						
JENKINSONS, Dewsbury (YH07740)							●						
KIPPAX, Leeds (YH08222)													
LATHAM FARM, Cleckheaton (YH08445)													
MIDDLESTOWN SADDLERY, Wakefield (YH09540)	●						●			●			
MOORSIDE EQUESTRIAN, Shipley (YH09780)													
MTS MOBILE TRAILER SERVICES, Castleford (YH09919)													
PARKER MERCHANTING, Rothwell (YH10746)													

by Country by County	Show Jumps	Show Saddles	Show Stationery	Shredded Paper	Skin Feed Supplements	Snowflake Shavings	Solarium Equipment	Sperm Counter	Stable Bandages	Stable Equipment	Stable Fittings	Stage Warmer	Stainless Steel Bits
ROSETTE COMPANY, Barnsley (YH12109)													
SHOWJUMP INT, Barnsley (YH12766)	●												
STABLE-DRY & EQUIBALE, Doncaster (YH13302)													
THROSTLE NEST SADDLERY, Barnsley (YH14114)													
WILDSMITHS, Doncaster (YH15412)													
YORKSHIRE (WEST)													
ACORN FEEDS, Huddersfield (YH00148)													
B T H HIRE & SALES, Leeds (YH00749)													
BARDSEY MILLS, Otley (YH00927)													
BLACUP TRAINING GRP, Halifax (YH01504)													
BRADLEY DOUBLELOCK, Bingley (YH01749)													
BRANDON FORGE SADDLERY, Leeds (YH01796)													
COURTYARD SADDLERY, Collingham (YH03512)													
DALE COCHRANE, Keighley (YH03820)													
DAYS PET SHOP, Bradford (YH03971)	●												
DISCOUNT SADDLERY, Huddersfield (YH04129)	●										●		
EQUESTRIAN CLEARANCE CTRE, Halifax (YH04694)													
EQUITACK SADDLERY, Wakefield (YH04825)													
F & STROKER & SONS, Leeds (YH04981)													
FOX SADDLERS, Wetherby (YH05425)													
HALLAS LANE LIVERY STABLES, Bradford (YH06327)													
HIGHWOOD, Ossett (YH06803)													
HILLAM FEEDS, South Milford (YH06836)													
HILLAM TRAILERS, Cleckheaton (YH06837)													
HOOVES EQUESTRIAN, Bradford (YH07047)													
JENKINSONS, Dewsbury (YH07740)													
KIPPAX, Leeds (YH08222)													
LATHAM FARM, Cleckheaton (YH08445)													
MIDDLESTOWN SADDLERY, Wakefield (YH09540)											●		
MOORSIDE EQUESTRIAN, Shipley (YH09780)													
MTS MOBILE TRAILER SERVICES, Castleford (YH09919)													
PARKER MERCHANTING, Rothwell (YH10746)													

by Country by County	Stalls	Stirrups	Straw	Supplements	Sweatshirts	Tack	Tactile Webbing	Timing Equipment	Towbars	Trad Wooden Show Jump Equip	Trailer Accessories	Trailers	Training Aids
ROSETTE COMPANY, Barnsley (YH12109)													
SHOWJUMP INT, Barnsley (YH12766)								●		●			
STABLE-DRY & EQUIBALE, Doncaster (YH13302)													
THROSTLE NEST SADDLERY, Barnsley (YH14114)						●							
WILDSMITHS, Doncaster (YH15412)						●							
YORKSHIRE (WEST)													
ACORN FEEDS, Huddersfield (YH00148)						●							
B T H HIRE & SALES, Leeds (YH00749)											●	●	
BARDSEY MILLS, Otley (YH00927)													
BLACUP TRAINING GRP, Halifax (YH01504)													●
BRADLEY DOUBLELOCK, Bingley (YH01749)											●		
BRANDON FORGE SADDLERY, Leeds (YH01796)						●							●
COURTYARD SADDLERY, Collingham (YH03512)													
DALE COCHRANE, Keighley (YH03820)													
DAYS PET SHOP, Bradford (YH03971)						●							
DISCOUNT SADDLERY, Huddersfield (YH04129)		●											●
EQUESTRIAN CLEARANCE CTRE, Halifax (YH04694)						●							
EQUITACK SADDLERY, Wakefield (YH04825)						●							
F & STROKER & SONS, Leeds (YH04981)			●										
FOX SADDLERS, Wetherby (YH05425)													
HALLAS LANE LIVERY STABLES, Bradford (YH06327)	●												
HIGHWOOD, Ossett (YH06803)											●		
HILLAM FEEDS, South Milford (YH06836)						●							
HILLAM TRAILERS, Cleckheaton (YH06837)											●	●	
HOOVES EQUESTRIAN, Bradford (YH07047)													
JENKINSONS, Dewsbury (YH07740)						●							
KIPPAX, Leeds (YH08222)						●							
LATHAM FARM, Cleckheaton (YH08445)	●										●	●	
MIDDLESTOWN SADDLERY, Wakefield (YH09540)						●							
MOORSIDE EQUESTRIAN, Shipley (YH09780)	●												
MTS MOBILE TRAILER SERVICES, Castleford (YH09919)									●				
PARKER MERCHANTING, Rothwell (YH10746)											●		

by Country by County	Traps	Travel Bandages	Treadmills (Build)	Treadmills (Supply)	Trophies	Videos	Vitamins	Weathervanes	Western Tack	Whips	Witter	Worming Products	Mail Order Facilities
ROSETTE COMPANY, Barnsley (YH12109)													
SHOWJUMP INT, Barnsley (YH12766)													
STABLE-DRY & EQUIBALE, Doncaster (YH13302)													
THROSTLE NEST SADDLERY, Barnsley (YH14114)													
WILDSMITHS, Doncaster (YH15412)													
YORKSHIRE (WEST)													
ACORN FEEDS, Huddersfield (YH00148)													
B T H HIRE & SALES, Leeds (YH00749)													●
BARDSEY MILLS, Otley (YH00927)												●	
BLACUP TRAINING GRP, Halifax (YH01504)													
BRADLEY DOUBLELOCK, Bingley (YH01749)													
BRANDON FORGE SADDLERY, Leeds (YH01796)													
COURTYARD SADDLERY, Collingham (YH03512)													
DALE COCHRANE, Keighley (YH03820)													
DAYS PET SHOP, Bradford (YH03971)												●	
DISCOUNT SADDLERY, Huddersfield (YH04129)					●	●							●
EQUESTRIAN CLEARANCE CTRE, Halifax (YH04694)													●
EQUITACK SADDLERY, Wakefield (YH04825)													●
F & STROKER & SONS, Leeds (YH04981)													
FOX SADDLERS, Wetherby (YH05425)						●							●
HALLAS LANE LIVERY STABLES, Bradford (YH06327)													
HIGHWOOD, Ossett (YH06803)													
HILLAM FEEDS, South Milford (YH06836)													
HILLAM TRAILERS, Cleckheaton (YH06837)													
HOOVES EQUESTRIAN, Bradford (YH07047)									●				●
JENKINSONS, Dewsbury (YH07740)													
KIPPAX, Leeds (YH08222)													
LATHAM FARM, Cleckheaton (YH08445)													
MIDDLESTOWN SADDLERY, Wakefield (YH09540)													
MOORSIDE EQUESTRIAN, Shipley (YH09780)													
MTS MOBILE TRAILER SERVICES, Castleford (YH09919)													
PARKER MERCHANTING, Rothwell (YH10746)													

Products Supplied
R - W

by Country by County

	Riding Wear	Rocking Horse	Rosettes	Rubber Matting	Rubs & Creams	Saddle Pads	Saddles	Sash	Sea Clay	Second Hand Equipment	Security Products	Seed	Shavings	Show Jumps	Show Saddles	Show Stationery	Shredded Paper	Skin Feed Supplements	Snowflake Shavings	Solarium Equipment	Sperm Counter	Stable Bandages	Stable Equipment	Stable Fittings	Stage Warmer	Stainless Steel Bits	Stalls	Stirrups	Straw	Supplements	Sweatshirts	Tack	Tactile Webbing	Timing Equipment	Towbars	Trad Wooden Show Jump Equip	Trailer Accessories	Trailers	Training Aids	Traps	Travel Bandages	Treadmills (Build)	Treadmills (Supply)	Trophies	Videos	Vitamins	Weathervanes	Western Tack	Whips	Witter	Worming Products	Mail Order Facilities
PENNINE FARM SVS, Huddersfield (YH10951)																																														●					●	
QUALTEX, Hebden Bridge (YH11477)						●																																														
RUSKIN HORSE DRAWN CARRIAGES, Leeds (YH12250)																																						●														
SIMCOCK, R, Halifax (YH12818)																													●																							
SINCLAIR RIDING WEAR, Leeds (YH12849)	●																																																			
T C TRAILER, Keighley (YH13734)																																					●	●														
TACK & TURNOUT EQUESTRIAN, Huddersfield (YH13780)							●																						●			●																				●
WESTWAYS RIDING SCHOOL, Leeds (YH15236)																																							●													
WILLIS WALKER, Keighley (YH15492)																																												●								
WINPENNY PHOTOGRAPHY, Otley (YH15592)																																													●							
YORKSHIRE EQUESTRIAN FLOORING, Leeds (YH15920)																																					●	●					●									
IRELAND																																																				
COUNTY CORK																																																				
BUCAS, Cork (YH02184)	●																																																			
COUNTY DUBLIN																																																				
COLEMANS OF SANDYFORD, Dublin (YH03166)	●																											●				●																				●
EQUESTRIAN DIRECT SALES, Dublin (YH04699)							●																									●																				
COUNTY KERRY																																																				
BRIDLES & BITS, Tralee (YH01893)							●			●																						●																				
COUNTY KILDARE																																																				
IRISH EQUESTRIAN PRODUCTS, Kildare (YH07493)							●																									●							●													●
COUNTY KILKENNY																																																				
EUROFARM, Kilkenny (YH04898)						●																										●																				
COUNTY LIMERICK																																																				
COUNTRY DRESSER, Adare (YH03403)							●																									●																				
COUNTY LOUTH																																																				
HORSEWARE, Dundalk (YH07177)	●																																																			
COUNTY MAYO																																																				
ABRAM, DAVID, Bohola (YH00135)							●																									●																				
CLAREMORRIS, Claremorris (YH02952)							●							●																		●																				
COUNTY MEATH																																																				

Products Supplied
R - W

by Country by County	Riding Wear	Rocking Horse	Rosettes	Rubber Matting	Rubs & Creams	Saddle Pads	Saddles	Sash	Sea Clay	Second Hand Equipment	Security Products	Seed	Shavings	Show Jumps	Show Saddles	Show Stationery	Shredded Paper	Skin Feed Supplements	Snowflake Shavings	Solarium Equipment	Sperm Counter	Stable Bandages	Stable Equipment	Stable Fittings	Stage Warmer	Stainless Steel Bits	Stalls	Stirrups	Straw	Supplements	Sweatshirts	Tack	Tactile Webbing	Timing Equipment	Towbars	Trad Wooden Show Jump Equip	Trailer Accessories	Trailers	Training Aids	Traps	Travel Bandages	Treadmills (Build)	Treadmills (Supply)	Trophies	Videos	Vitamins	Weathervanes	Western Tack	Whips	Witter	Worming Products	Mail Order Facilities
CLARKE'S SPORTSDEN, Navan (YH02978)																																●																				
COUNTY TRAILERS, Enfield (YH03493)																																						●														
COUNTY ROSCOMMON																																																				
MURPHY EQUESTRIAN, Strokestown (YH09954)																																													●							●
COUNTY WESTMEATH																																																				
TALLY HO, Athlone (YH13838)	●																																																			
WEBBWEAR, Multyfarnham (YH15036)							●																																													
COUNTY WICKLOW																																																				
BALLINTESKIN TACK, Wicklow (YH00861)																																●																				
EQUESTRIAN LEATHERS, Bray (YH04704)						●																																														
NORTHERN IRELAND																																																				
COUNTY ANTRIM																																																				
BRACKEN EQUESTRIAN, Belfast (YH01736)							●																									●																			●	
BROWNS COACHWORKS, Lisburn (YH02143)																																						●														
GRANGE EQUESTRIAN, Newtownabbey (YH05986)				●									●										●																													
OLD MILL, Carrickfergus (YH10465)							●																																													
COUNTY ARMAGH																																																				
ANNAGHMORE SADDLERY, Craigavon (YH00451)							●																									●																				
HONEYHILL ROSETTES, Portadown (YH07015)			●																																																●	
LIME PARK EQUESTRIAN, Craigavon (YH08626)							●																						●			●																				
PREMIER SADDLERY, Armagh (YH11349)							●																									●																				
STINSON, J D, Armagh (YH13470)							●																																													
COUNTY DOWN																																																				
FAWCETT, GEORGE, Ballynahinch (YH05108)													●																											●												
HOLMESTEAD SADDLERY, Downpatrick (YH06981)							●							●																		●		●					●						●							
MOURNE ROSETTES, Hillsborough (YH09903)			●																																																	
SMYTHS, Newry (YH13017)							●																									●												●								
WEIR, Ballynahinch (YH15051)													●																																							
COUNTY LONDONDERRY																																																				
BLAKES EQUESTRIAN, Coleraine (YH01521)							●																																													
FAUGHANVALE STABLES, Londonderry (YH05102)																										●						●																				
HAVEN SADDLERY, Magherafelt (YH06539)																																●																				

www.hccyourhorse.com

Products Supplied
R - W

by Country by County

	Riding Wear	Rocking Horse	Rosettes	Rubber Matting	Rubs & Creams	Saddle Pads	Saddles	Sash	Sea Clay	Second Hand Equipment	Security Products	Seed	Shavings	Show Jumps	Show Saddles	Show Stationery	Shredded Paper	Skin Feed Supplements	Snowflake Shavings	Solarium Equipment	Sperm Counter	Stable Bandages	Stable Equipment	Stable Fittings	Stage Warmer	Stainless Steel Bits	Stalls	Stirrups	Straw	Supplements	Sweatshirts	Tack	Tactile Webbing	Timing Equipment	Towbars	Trad Wooden Show Jump Equip	Trailer Accessories	Trailers	Training Aids	Traps	Travel Bandages	Treadmills (Build)	Treadmills (Supply)	Trophies	Videos	Vitamins	Weathervanes	Western Tack	Whips	Witter	Worming Products	Mail Order Facilities
SCOTLAND																																																				
ABERDEENSHIRE																																																				
COUNTRY JUMPKINS BAKER-MAC, Alford (YH03411)														●																																						
CRAGINETHERTY, Turriff (YH03545)																													●																							
FEEDMIX, Turriff (YH05123)																													●																							
GILKHORN FARM SADDLERY, Peterhead (YH05767)														●																																						
MILL OF URAS EQUESTRIAN, Stonehaven (YH09583)													●																			●																				
NORTH EASTERN FARMERS, Inverurie (YH10258)																																																			●	
SARAH'S ROSETTES, Ellon (YH12434)			●					●								●																												●								
ANGUS																																																				
BLACKLITE, Dundee (YH01486)														●																																						
CONCHIE, DAVID, Carnoustie (YH03224)							●																																													
KIRRIEMUIR HORSE SUPPLIES, Kirriemuir (YH08240)							●						●				●												●			●																				
PATHHEAD STABLES, Kirriemuir (YH10821)							●						●				●												●			●																				
ARGYLL AND BUTE																																																				
CASTLE RIDING CTRE, Lochgilphead (YH02631)																																						●														
TACKLE & TACK, Oban (YH13818)			●				●					●	●	●			●															●							●					●								●
WHAT EVERY HORSE WANTS, Helensburgh (YH15266)							●																									●																				●
AYRSHIRE (EAST)																																																				
FENWICK MOBILE EXHIBITIONS, Kilmarnock (YH05154)																																					●	●														
AYRSHIRE (SOUTH)																																																				
AYR TRAILER CTRE, Ayr (YH00701)																																					●	●														
AYRSHIRE EQUITATION CTRE, Ayr (YH00704)							●																																													
CROCKET EQUESTRIAN, Ayr (YH03606)							●																																													
OTTERSWICK, Mauchine (YH10581)																																													●							●
VICTORIA ROSETTES, Girvan (YH14709)			●																																																	
DUMFRIES AND GALLOWAY																																																				
DOUGLAS, JOHN L, Newton Stewart (YH04214)																																						●														
GEE GEE'S, Dumfries (YH05690)		●	●				●						●				●															●												●	●							●
ROBERT THORNE, Annan (YH11944)													●				●												●																							
EDINBURGH (CITY OF)																																																				

Products Supplied
R - W

by Country by County	Riding Wear	Rocking Horse	Rosettes	Rubber Matting	Rubs & Creams	Saddle Pads	Saddles	Sash	Sea Clay	Second Hand Equipment	Security Products	Seed	Shavings	Show Jumps	Show Saddles	Show Stationery	Shredded Paper	Skin Feed Supplements	Snowflake Shavings	Solarium Equipment	Sperm Counter	Stable Bandages	Stable Equipment	Stable Fittings	Stage Warmer	Stainless Steel Bits	Stalls	Stirrups	Straw	Supplements	Sweatshirts	Tack	Tactile Webbing	Timing Equipment	Towbars	Trad Wooden Show Jump Equip	Trailer Accessories	Trailers	Training Aids	Traps	Travel Bandages	Treadmills (Build)	Treadmills (Supply)	Trophies	Videos	Vitamins	Weathervanes	Western Tack	Whips	Witter	Worming Products	Mail Order Facilities
STIRLINGSHIRE SADDLERY, Edinburgh (YH13474)							●																									●													●							
FALKIRK																																																				
COUNTRY FEEDS LARBERT, Larbert (YH03408)													●																																							
J C M, Falkirk (YH07572)																																					●	●														
FIFE																																																				
EUROPA, Lochgelly (YH04904)							●																									●																				●
KEITH GARRY FENCING, Freuchie (YH08034)														●																																						
RIDING STABLES, Lochgelly (YH11883)																																●																				
SALTIRE STABLES, Cupar (YH12394)														●													●																									
GLASGOW (CITY OF)																																																				
BUSBY EQUITATION CTRE, Busby (YH02302)							●																									●																				
EVERYTHING EQUESTRIAN, Busby (YH04957)																																●													●							
HAZELDEN SADDLERY, Glasgow (YH06602)			●																																																	
JET SET, Glasgow (YH07763)							●																																													
HIGHLANDS																																																				
DERELOCHY SADDLER, Nairn (YH04075)							●																																													
IFOR WILLIAMS TRAILERS, Caithness (YH07392)																																						●														
RADDERY EQUINE, Fortrose (YH11593)	●																											●				●		●					●													●
SEAFORTH SADDLERS, Inverness (YH12586)							●																									●							●						●							
INVERCLYDE																																																				
ARDGOWAN, Greenock (YH00507)																																●																				
LANARKSHIRE (SOUTH)																																																			
HILLSIDE CLYSDALE STUD, Lesmahagow (YH06852)																																													●							
THOMSON CRAFT SADDLERY, Carluke (YH14047)																																												●								
LOTHIAN (EAST)																																																				
J S MAIN & SONS, Haddington (YH07617)							●																									●																				●
LOTHIAN TRAILER CTRE, Tranent (YH08833)																																						●														
LOTHIAN (MID)																																																			
BOWLEA TRAILERS, Penicuik (YH01713)																																					●	●														
GEORGES SADDLERY, Newbridge (YH05726)		●																																																		
R H MILLER, Dalkeith (YH11541)	●						●																									●																			●	
LOTHIAN (WEST)																																																			

Products Supplied
R - W

by Country by County

	Riding Wear	Rocking Horse	Rosettes	Rubber Matting	Rubs & Creams	Saddle Pads	Saddles	Sash	Sea Clay	Second Hand Equipment	Security Products	Seed	Shavings	Show Jumps	Show Saddles	Show Stationery	Shredded Paper	Skin Feed Supplements	Snowflake Shavings	Solarium Equipment	Sperm Counter	Stable Bandages	Stable Equipment	Stable Fittings	Stage Warmer	Stainless Steel Bits	Stalls	Stirrups	Straw	Supplements	Sweatshirts	Tack	Tactile Webbing	Timing Equipment	Towbars	Trad Wooden Show Jump Equip	Trailer Accessories	Trailers	Training Aids	Traps	Travel Bandages	Treadmills (Build)	Treadmills (Supply)	Trophies	Videos	Vitamins	Weathervanes	Western Tack	Whips	Witter	Worming Products	Mail Order Facilities
CLEAR ROUND ORIGINALS, Bathgate (YH03010)		●												●																																						
GRANGE SADDLERY, West Calder (YH05996)																																●																			●	
SIMPLY ROSETTES, Fauldhouse (YH12835)			●																																																	
MORAY																																																				
GREENFIELDS SADDLERY, Elgin (YH06085)							●						●	●																		●													●							●
PERTH AND KINROSS																																																				
AUTOW CTRE, Perth (YH00675)																																			●		●	●														
EASTERTON ARENAS, Auchterarder (YH04499)																																											●									
EQUI-CARE, Perth (YH04736)			●											●																		●												●								
GLEN EAGLES EQUESTRIAN, Auchterarder (YH05825)							●													●												●							●						●							
MCCASH'S, Perth (YH09326)													●				●													●		●													●						●	
SHETLAND PONY STUD BOOK SOC, Perth (YH12736)																																													●							●
SCOTTISH BORDERS																																																				
A C BURN, Jedburgh (YH00022)												●	●				●													●																					●	
BORDER SHOWJUMPING EQUIPMENT, Duns (YH01645)														●																																						
MCNAB SADDLERS, Selkirk (YH09396)							●																									●																				●
MCNAB SADDLERS, Kelso (YH09397)							●																									●																				●
R H MILLER, Peebles (YH11542)													●																●																						●	
STIRLING																																																				
CARRUTHERS ROSETTE, Balfron Station (YH02600)			●																																																	
HENDRY, JAMES, Stirling (YH06669)														●																																						
WALES																																																				
BLAENAU GWENT																																																				
DAVIES RIDING BOOTS, Ebbw Vale (YH03935)																																																				●
BRIDGEND																																																				
AVONRIDE, Maesteg (YH00692)																																					●	●														
E K M EQUESTRIAN, Bridgend (YH04411)														●																																						
CARMARTHENSHIRE																																																				
EVANS, M V, Carmarthen (YH04927)																													●																							
HORSE CTRE, Llandysul (YH07115)																																													●							
MORGAN EQUINE, Llandeilo (YH09794)																																																				●
PLAS EQUESTRIAN, Carmarthen (YH11164)																																●							●													●

Products Supplied
R - W

by Country by County	Riding Wear	Rocking Horse	Rosettes	Rubber Matting	Rubs & Creams	Saddle Pads	Saddles	Sash	Sea Clay	Second Hand Equipment	Security Products	Seed	Shavings
POLY PROP, Llandysul (YH11213)													
STALLIONS AT TACKEXCHANGE, Llanelli (YH13351)							●						
TACK EXCHANGE, Llanelli (YH13787)							●			●			
CEREDIGION													
RHEIDOL RIDING CTRE, Aberystwyth (YH11784)													
VALIENT SADDLERY, Cardigan (YH14646)							●						
CONWY													
JONES, G W, Abergele (YH07902)			●										
DENBIGHSHIRE													
A P E S ROCKING HORSES, Denbigh (YH00055)		●											
IFOR WILLIAMS, Corwen (YH07391)													
MORWYN STUD, Ruthin (YH09854)													
WYNNSTAY & CLWYD FARMERS, St Asaph (YH15874)													
FLINTSHIRE													
T F S, Buckley (YH13739)												●	●
GLAMORGAN (VALE OF)													
AYRES, JOHN, Cardiff (YH00702)							●						
CARDIFF SPORTSGEAR, Cardiff (YH02532)							●						
CIMLA TREKKING, Neath (YH02918)			●										
DOWNS SIDE RIDING CTRE, Penarth (YH04241)													
LIEGE MANOR, Cardiff (YH08609)													
GWYNEDD													
BRONALLT, Caernarfon (YH02029)							●						●
ISLE OF ANGLESEY													
SHEAR EASE, Amlwch (YH12688)													
TYN-MORFA RIDING CTRE, Rhosneigr (YH14529)													
MONMOUTHSHIRE													
CHEPSTOW SADDLERY, Chepstow (YH02809)							●						●
ROSS FEED, Monmouth (YH12115)													
NEWPORT													
PAYNE STEEPLECHASE FENCES, Highcross (YH10847)													
PEMBROKESHIRE													

by Country by County	Show Jumps	Show Saddles	Show Stationery	Shredded Paper	Skin Feed Supplements	Snowflake Shavings	Solarium Equipment	Sperm Counter	Stable Bandages	Stable Equipment	Stable Fittings	Stage Warmer	Stainless Steel Bits
POLY PROP, Llandysul (YH11213)	●												
STALLIONS AT TACKEXCHANGE, Llanelli (YH13351)													
TACK EXCHANGE, Llanelli (YH13787)													
CEREDIGION													
RHEIDOL RIDING CTRE, Aberystwyth (YH11784)													
VALIENT SADDLERY, Cardigan (YH14646)													
CONWY													
JONES, G W, Abergele (YH07902)													
DENBIGHSHIRE													
A P E S ROCKING HORSES, Denbigh (YH00055)													
IFOR WILLIAMS, Corwen (YH07391)													
MORWYN STUD, Ruthin (YH09854)	●												
WYNNSTAY & CLWYD FARMERS, St Asaph (YH15874)													
FLINTSHIRE													
T F S, Buckley (YH13739)													
GLAMORGAN (VALE OF)													
AYRES, JOHN, Cardiff (YH00702)													
CARDIFF SPORTSGEAR, Cardiff (YH02532)													
CIMLA TREKKING, Neath (YH02918)													
DOWNS SIDE RIDING CTRE, Penarth (YH04241)													
LIEGE MANOR, Cardiff (YH08609)													
GWYNEDD													
BRONALLT, Caernarfon (YH02029)													
ISLE OF ANGLESEY													
SHEAR EASE, Amlwch (YH12688)													
TYN-MORFA RIDING CTRE, Rhosneigr (YH14529)													
MONMOUTHSHIRE													
CHEPSTOW SADDLERY, Chepstow (YH02809)													
ROSS FEED, Monmouth (YH12115)													
NEWPORT													
PAYNE STEEPLECHASE FENCES, Highcross (YH10847)	●												
PEMBROKESHIRE													

by Country by County	Stalls	Stirrups	Straw	Supplements	Sweatshirts	Tack	Tactile Webbing	Timing Equipment	Towbars	Trad Wooden Show Jump Equip	Trailer Accessories	Trailers	Training Aids
POLY PROP, Llandysul (YH11213)													
STALLIONS AT TACKEXCHANGE, Llanelli (YH13351)													
TACK EXCHANGE, Llanelli (YH13787)						●							
CEREDIGION													
RHEIDOL RIDING CTRE, Aberystwyth (YH11784)													●
VALIENT SADDLERY, Cardigan (YH14646)													
CONWY													
JONES, G W, Abergele (YH07902)													
DENBIGHSHIRE													
A P E S ROCKING HORSES, Denbigh (YH00055)													
IFOR WILLIAMS, Corwen (YH07391)											●	●	
MORWYN STUD, Ruthin (YH09854)													
WYNNSTAY & CLWYD FARMERS, St Asaph (YH15874)													
FLINTSHIRE													
T F S, Buckley (YH13739)			●			●							
GLAMORGAN (VALE OF)													
AYRES, JOHN, Cardiff (YH00702)						●							
CARDIFF SPORTSGEAR, Cardiff (YH02532)						●							
CIMLA TREKKING, Neath (YH02918)													
DOWNS SIDE RIDING CTRE, Penarth (YH04241)						●							
LIEGE MANOR, Cardiff (YH08609)													●
GWYNEDD													
BRONALLT, Caernarfon (YH02029)						●						●	●
ISLE OF ANGLESEY													
SHEAR EASE, Amlwch (YH12688)													
TYN-MORFA RIDING CTRE, Rhosneigr (YH14529)								●					
MONMOUTHSHIRE													
CHEPSTOW SADDLERY, Chepstow (YH02809)						●							
ROSS FEED, Monmouth (YH12115)						●							
NEWPORT													
PAYNE STEEPLECHASE FENCES, Highcross (YH10847)													●
PEMBROKESHIRE													

by Country by County	Traps	Travel Bandages	Treadmills (Build)	Treadmills (Supply)	Trophies	Videos	Vitamins	Weathervanes	Western Tack	Whips	Witter	Worming Products	Mail Order Facilities
POLY PROP, Llandysul (YH11213)													
STALLIONS AT TACKEXCHANGE, Llanelli (YH13351)													●
TACK EXCHANGE, Llanelli (YH13787)													●
CEREDIGION													
RHEIDOL RIDING CTRE, Aberystwyth (YH11784)													
VALIENT SADDLERY, Cardigan (YH14646)													
CONWY													
JONES, G W, Abergele (YH07902)													
DENBIGHSHIRE													
A P E S ROCKING HORSES, Denbigh (YH00055)													
IFOR WILLIAMS, Corwen (YH07391)													
MORWYN STUD, Ruthin (YH09854)													
WYNNSTAY & CLWYD FARMERS, St Asaph (YH15874)							●					●	
FLINTSHIRE													
T F S, Buckley (YH13739)													
GLAMORGAN (VALE OF)													
AYRES, JOHN, Cardiff (YH00702)													
CARDIFF SPORTSGEAR, Cardiff (YH02532)													
CIMLA TREKKING, Neath (YH02918)													
DOWNS SIDE RIDING CTRE, Penarth (YH04241)													
LIEGE MANOR, Cardiff (YH08609)													
GWYNEDD													
BRONALLT, Caernarfon (YH02029)													
ISLE OF ANGLESEY													
SHEAR EASE, Amlwch (YH12688)													●
TYN-MORFA RIDING CTRE, Rhosneigr (YH14529)													
MONMOUTHSHIRE													
CHEPSTOW SADDLERY, Chepstow (YH02809)													
ROSS FEED, Monmouth (YH12115)													
NEWPORT													
PAYNE STEEPLECHASE FENCES, Highcross (YH10847)													
PEMBROKESHIRE													

Products Supplied
R - W

by Country by County	Riding Wear	Rocking Horse	Rosettes	Rubber Matting	Rubs & Creams	Saddle Pads	Saddles	Sash	Sea Clay	Second Hand Equipment	Security Products	Seed	Shavings	Show Jumps	Show Saddles	Show Stationery	Shredded Paper	Skin Feed Supplements	Snowflake Shavings	Solarium Equipment	Sperm Counter	Stable Bandages	Stable Equipment	Stable Fittings	Stage Warmer	Stainless Steel Bits	Stalls	Stirrups	Straw	Supplements	Sweatshirts	Tack	Tactile Webbing	Timing Equipment	Towbars	Trad Wooden Show Jump Equip	Trailer Accessories	Trailers	Training Aids	Traps	Travel Bandages	Treadmills (Build)	Treadmills (Supply)	Trophies	Videos	Vitamins	Weathervanes	Western Tack	Whips	Witter	Worming Products	Mail Order Facilities
BOULSTON, Haverfordwest (YH01672)							●																															●														
PEGASUS, Haverfordwest (YH10902)							●																																													●
PEMBROKESHIRE EQUESTRIAN, Haverfordwest (YH10919)							●																									●																				●
POWYS																																																				
BLOOR, RAY, Montgomery (YH01559)																													●																							
BROMPTON HALL, Montgomery (YH02025)							●						●																●			●																				●
CHILTERN CONNEMARA, Presteigne (YH02858)																																																				
CHOICE SADDLERY, Knighton (YH02876)							●																									●																				
CRADOC TACK, Brecon (YH03541)							●																																													
LLANFYLLIN SADDLERY, Llanfyllin (YH08723)							●																																													
LLWYNON, Brecon (YH08749)							●																									●																				
PENBAULLT ROSETTES, Llangammarch Wells (YH10924)			●																																																	
SMITHS INDUSTRIES WATCH, Ystradgynlais (YH13008)																																		●																		
WYNNSTAY & CLWYD FARMERS, Llansanffraid (YH15875)																																														●					●	
RHONDDA CYNON TAFF																																																				
BOOTS & SADDLES, Tonypandy (YH01640)							●																									●																				
WINNERS OF WALES, Pontyclun (YH15590)			●																																																	
SWANSEA																																																				
D MORGAN & SON, Swansea (YH03798)													●																			●																				
HORSE CTRE, Swansea (YH07116)							●																									●																				
MR POTTER'S TROTTERS, Swansea (YH09916)		●																																																		
SOUTH WALES CARRIAGE DRIVING, Swansea (YH13111)																																								●												
WREXHAM																																																				
ACRE HSE EQUESTRIAN, Wrexham (YH00158)							●																									●																				●
BLINKERS EQUESTRIAN, Wrexham (YH01540)							●																									●																				●
FAULKNER, R M, Wrexham (YH05103)																													●																							

SECTION 7

Brands Supplied.

Companies are listed by Country, by County.

Products are sorted alphabetically:

Section 7A - A to D
Section 7B - E to Jo
Section 7C - Ju to P
Section 7D - Q to Z

The Brands Supplied grid can be used in two different ways. You can search by a particular brand in order to see which company/companies supply it.

E.g. Champion : Jods Galore

Or, you can look at the profile of one particular company in order to see what brand/s they supply.

e.g. Saddle Rack (The) : Loveson

Once you have located a business using this section you can then refer to the company's detailed profile in Section 1.

Brands Supplied

A - D

by Country by County

	Aerborn	Aigle	Air-o-Wear	Albion	Allen & Page	Apaloosa	Arait	Arenas	Ash Horseshoes	Aubiose	Badminton	Bahill	Baileys	Barbour	Bardsey Mill	Barrier H	Basic	Bates	Bedmax	Bio-Barley	Bioflow	Blue Chip	Bucas	Butlet	Cair	Caldene	Casco Helmets	Cavallo	CDS Products	Champion	Charles Owen	Charnwood Mill Products	Chatham	Cliff Barnsby	Codlivine	Corta Flex	Cottage Craft	Colt Combi	Commissions	Contour Saddles	Dark Horse	Dengie	Deflect	Dever	Dodson & Horrell	Dollin & Morris	Driza Bone	Dublin
ENGLAND																																																
BEDFORDSHIRE																																																
BIGGLESWADE SADDLERY, Biggleswade (YH01404)	●																																															
BERKSHIRE																																																
SCATS COUNTRYSTORE, Newbury (YH12493)														●																												●			●			
SHAMLEY SADDLERY, Maidenhead (YH12663)																																					●											
WOODLANDS, Hungerford (YH15705)																														●																		
BUCKINGHAMSHIRE																																																
DENNIS'S SADDLERY/RIDING WEAR, Aylesbury (YH04059)			●																																													
DENNIS'S SADDLERY/RIDING WEAR, Aylesbury (YH04060)			●																																													
CAMBRIDGESHIRE																																																
LONG MELFORD, Cambridge (YH08798)																																																●
SMEETH SADDLERY, Wisbech (YH12925)																														●																		
CHESHIRE																																																
BOOL BY DESIGN, Tarporley (YH01631)						●																														●												
GAYNORS SADDLERY, Dukinfield (YH05682)																														●							●											
GREEN FARM FEEDS, Crewe (YH06055)											●		●																																●			
LANSDOWNE HORSE & RIDER, Chester (YH08423)																		●													●																	
COUNTY DURHAM																																																
FARMWAY, Darlington (YH05072)																																					●								●			
LANCHESTER COUNTRY STORE, Lanchester (YH08382)													●	●																												●			●			
DERBYSHIRE																																																
BARLEYFIELD SADDLERY, Etwall (YH00951)																																					●								●			
BARLEYFIELDS, Derby (YH00952)																															●					●									●			
C E S, Ashbourne (YH02370)														●																	●																	
COUNTRY SPORT, Glossop (YH03426)																															●									●								
SEALS FODDER, Alfreton (YH12589)													●																													●			●			
DEVON																																																
FARMERS FRIEND, Exeter (YH05061)														●												●				●							●											
HOLLY FARM, Exeter (YH06953)											●																																					
MULLACOTT EQUESTRIAN, Ilfracombe (YH09935)								●																																								

Brands Supplied
A - D

by Country by County	Aerborn	Aigle	Air-o-Wear	Albion	Allen & Page	Apaloosa	Arait	Arenas	Ash Horseshoes	Aubiose	Badminton	Bahill	Baileys	Barbour	Bardsey Mill	Barrier H	Basic	Bates	Bedmax	Bio-Barley	Bioflow	Blue Chip	Bucas	Butlet	Cair	Caldene	Casco Helmets	Cavallo	CDS Products	Champion	Charles Owen	Charnwood Mill Products	Chatham	Cliff Barnsby	Codlivine	Corta Flex	Cottage Craft	Colt Combi	Commissions	Contour Saddles	Dark Horse	Dengie	Deflect	Dever	Dodson & Horrell	Dollin & Morris	Driza Bone	Dublin
TOWN & COUNTRY SUP, Exeter (YH14286)																																										●			●			
DORSET																																																
EQUUS, Wimborne (YH04836)																														●							●											
HURN BRIDGE CTRE, Christchurch (YH07313)																																					●											
SCATS COUNTRYSTORE, Gillingham (YH12495)														●																												●			●			
SCATS COUNTRYSTORE, Blandford (YH12496)														●																												●			●			
SCATS COUNTRYSTORE, Dorchester (YH12494)														●																												●			●			
ESSEX																																																
BAILEYS HORSE FEEDS, Braintree (YH00806)													●																																			
D & F FEED SVS, Rayleigh (YH03770)													●																													●			●			
DENGIE, Maldon (YH04045)																																										●						
TALLY-HO RIDING SCHOOL, Grays (YH13844)																														●																		
GLOUCESTERSHIRE																																																
HENRY COLE, Cirencester (YH06681)											●		●																													●						
MORETON SADDLERY, Moreton In Marsh (YH09790)																												●																				
STROUD SADDLERY, Stroud (YH13588)				●																						●				●																		
TEWKESBURY SADDLERY, Tewkesbury (YH13969)		●												●												●				●																		
HAMPSHIRE																																																
COUNTRY RIDING WEAR, Hook (YH03424)		●					●							●												●								●													●	
DAVID CATLIN, Southampton (YH03916)				●																																												
HOPLANDS EQUESTRIAN, Stockbridge (YH07058)																				●																●												
SCATS COUNTRYSTORE, Lymington (YH12502)														●																												●			●			
SCATS COUNTRYSTORE, Basingstoke (YH12501)														●																												●			●			
SCATS COUNTRYSTORE, Andover (YH12500)														●																												●			●			
SCATS COUNTRYSTORE, Winchester (YH12498)														●																												●			●			
SCATS COUNTRYSTORE, Romsey (YH12497)														●																												●			●			
SCATS COUNTRYSTORE, Alton (YH12499)														●																												●			●			
HEREFORDSHIRE																																																
COUNTRYWIDE, Hereford (YH03445)													●			●																										●			●			
TURNERS, Kington (YH14492)																																										●						
HERTFORDSHIRE																																																
PATCHETTS, Watford (YH10815)			●																							●					●						●											

Brands Supplied
A - D

by Country by County	Aerborn	Aigle	Air-o-Wear	Albion	Allen & Page	Apaloosa	Arait	Arenas	Ash Horseshoes	Aubiose	Badminton	Bahill	Baileys	Barbour	Bardsey Mill	Barrier H	Basic	Bates	Bedmax	Bio-Barley	Bioflow	Blue Chip	Bucas	Butlet	Cair	Caldene	Casco Helmets	Cavallo	CDS Products	Champion	Charles Owen	Charnwood Mill Products	Chatham	Cliff Barnsby	Codlivine	Corta Flex	Cottage Craft	Colt Combi	Commissions	Contour Saddles	Dark Horse	Dengie	Deflect	Dever	Dodson & Horrell	Dollin & Morris	Driza Bone	Dublin
ISLE OF WIGHT																																																
SCATS COUNTRYSTORE, Newport (YH12503)														●																												●			●			
KENT																																																
FROGPOOL MANOR SADDLERY, Chislehurst (YH05515)				●										●																																		
SADDLERY & GUN ROOM, Westerham (YH12365)																																		●														
SCATS COUNTRYSTORE, Marden (YH12505)														●																												●			●			
SCATS COUNTRYSTORE, Canterbury (YH12504)														●																												●			●			
LANCASHIRE																																																
EQUESTRIANA, Blackburn (YH04724)																															●																	
HORSE BITS SADDLERY, Bury (YH07106)														●												●																						
RICHARD BATTERSBY, Heywood (YH11802)					●								●																													●			●			
LEICESTERSHIRE																																																
CLAYBROOKE, Lutterworth (YH02996)													●																													●			●			
CLOTHES HORSE, Leicester (YH03062)			●																											●																		
DTA, Leicester (YH04303)																														●																		
LINCOLNSHIRE																																																
BATTLE, HAYWARD & BOWER, Lincoln (YH01081)																																			●													
RICHARD GRICE TRAILERS, Market Rasen (YH11803)												●						●																														
SHEEPGATE TACK & TOGS, Boston (YH12697)																																					●											
LINCOLNSHIRE (NORTH)																																																
CROWSTONS, Scunthorpe (YH03684)																																				●												●
MASON, D & M, Scunthorpe (YH09239)																																					●											
LONDON (GREATER)																																																
HYDE PARK RIDING WEAR, London (YH07345)																												●		●																		
RIDGWAY STABLES, London (YH11870)																														●																		
MERSEYSIDE																																																
HAMMONDS, Huyton (YH06362)											●		●																																●			
MIDLANDS (WEST)																																																
ALBION SADDLEMAKERS, Walsall (YH00247)				●																																												
NORFOLK																																																
ALLEN & PAGE, Thetford (YH00290)					●																																											
BARRIER ANIMAL HEALTHCARE, Attleborough (YH01021)																●																																

www.hccyourhorse.com

Brands Supplied
A - D

by Country by County	Aerborn	Aigle	Air-o-Wear	Albion	Allen & Page	Apaloosa	Arait	Arenas	Ash Horseshoes	Aubiose	Badminton	Bahill	Baileys	Barbour	Bardsey Mill	Barrier H	Basic	Bates	Bedmax	Bio-Barley	Bioflow	Blue Chip	Bucas	Butlet	Cair	Caldene	Casco Helmets	Cavallo	CDS Products	Champion	Charles Owen	Charnwood Mill Products	Chatham	Cliff Barnsby	Codlivine	Corta Flex	Cottage Craft	Colt Combi	Commissions	Contour Saddles	Dark Horse	Dengie	Deflect	Dever	Dodson & Horrell	Dollin & Morris	Driza Bone	Dublin
DARROW FARM SUPPLIES, Diss (YH03899)					●																																											
G J L, Fakenham (YH05585)					●						●		●																													●			●			
HORSETALK, King's Lynn (YH07176)		●																								●									●													●
NORTHAMPTONSHIRE																																																
DODSON & HORRELL, Kettering (YH04162)																																													●			
NORTHUMBERLAND																																																
A C BURN, Berwick-upon-Tweed (YH00021)																																										●			●			
AIR-O-WEAR, Corbridge (YH00225)			●																																													
WILLOW WEAR, Hexham (YH15505)																																																●
NOTTINGHAMSHIRE																																																
SADDLE RACK, Nottingham (YH12346)																														●																		
SADDLECRAFT, Nottingham (YH12355)																																						●										
ST CLEMENTS LODGE, Nottingham (YH13274)																																																●
OXFORDSHIRE																																																
JODS GALORE, Henley-on-Thames (YH07775)																														●																		●
SANSOMS SADDLERY, Witney (YH12429)			●																											●																		●
SCATS COUNTRYSTORE, Faringdon (YH12506)														●																												●			●			
WEATHERBEETA, Banbury (YH15023)																		●																														●
RUTLAND																																																
BADMINTON HORSE FEEDS, Oakham (YH00784)											●																																					
SHROPSHIRE																																																
BRYNORE STUD & LIVERY STABLES, Ellesmere (YH02178)																					●																											
C J BLACKSMITHS, Shrewsbury (YH02375)																																							●									
CHARLES BRITTON CONSTRUCTION, Ellesmere (YH02754)								●																																								
HORSE SHOP, Telford (YH07140)				●																					●									●														
TOUCHDOWN LIVERIES, Whitchurch (YH14253)													●																																			
SOMERSET																																																
RIDEMOOR, Wincanton (YH11852)																										●																						●
ROSE MILL FEEDS, Ilminster (YH12094)													●																													●			●			
THORNEY COPSE, Wincanton (YH14066)																																	●			●												
W.E.S GARRETT MASTER SADDLERS, Cheddar (YH14803)																										●																						
SUFFOLK																																																

Brands Supplied
A - D

by Country by County	Aerborn	Aigle	Air-o-Wear	Albion	Allen & Page	Apaloosa	Arait	Arenas	Ash Horseshoes	Aubiose	Badminton	Bahill	Baileys	Barbour	Bardsey Mill	Barrier H	Basic	Bates	Bedmax	Bio-Barley	Bioflow	Blue Chip	Bucas	Butlet	Cair	Caldene	Casco Helmets	Cavallo	CDS Products	Champion	Charles Owen	Charnwood Mill Products	Chatham	Cliff Barnsby	Codlivine	Corta Flex	Cottage Craft	Colt Combi	Commissions	Contour Saddles	Dark Horse	Dengie	Deflect	Dever	Dodson & Horrell	Dollin & Morris	Driza Bone	Dublin
GLADWELLS, Ipswich (YH05802)											●		●																													●			●			
HORSESHOES, Wrentham (YH07174)													●																													●						
LINKWOOD EQUESTIAN, Bury St Edmunds (YH08665)																															●																	
LONG MELFORD, Sudbury (YH08799)																																																●
MILL SADDLERY, Stowmarket (YH09587)																		●								●																						
RIDE AWAY SADDLERY, Ipswich (YH11846)																														●																		
WESTBRINK FARMS, Newmarket (YH15184)										●			●																													●						
SURREY																																																
ANIMAL ALTERNATIVES, Richmond (YH00425)																																											●					
FIELDGUARD, Cranleigh (YH05193)		●																																														
HASTILOW COMPETITION SADDLES, Godalming (YH06526)																																													●			
LINGFIELD TACK, Lingfield (YH08660)																										●					●																	
SCATS COUNTRYSTORE, Redhill (YH12508)														●																												●			●			
SCATS COUNTRYSTORE, Godalming (YH12507)														●																												●			●			
SUPERPET THE HORSE SHOP, Epsom (YH13654)																										●										●												
SUSSEX (EAST)																																																
ANDREW REILLY, Forest Row (YH00392)				●																					●																							
SCATS COUNTRYSTORE, Heathfield (YH12509)														●																												●			●			
SUSSEX (WEST)																																																
DRAGONFLY SADDLERY, Hassocks (YH04252)														●																				●														
GEOFF DEAN SADDLERY, Worthing (YH05714)																																		●														
LIGHTS, Brighton (YH08616)					●																	●																				●			●			
SCATS COUNTRYSTORE, Billingshurst (YH12510)														●																												●			●			
WARWICKSHIRE																																																
A & J SADDLERY, Southam (YH00012)														●												●																			●			
WOOTTON GRANGE EQUESTRIAN, Warwick (YH15772)																								●																								
WILTSHIRE																																																
HURDCOTT LIVERY STABLES, Salisbury (YH07311)																●																																
SCATS COUNTRYSTORE, Devizes (YH12512)														●																												●			●			
SCATS COUNTRYSTORE, Salisbury (YH12511)														●																												●			●			
WORCESTERSHIRE																																																
COUNTRYWIDE, Worcester (YH03446)													●	●																												●			●			●

Brands Supplied
A - D

by Country by County

by Country by County	Aerborn	Aigle	Air-o-Wear	Albion	Allen & Page	Apaloosa	Arait	Arenas	Ash Horseshoes	Aubiose	Badminton	Bahill	Baileys	Barbour	Bardsey Mill	Barrier H	Basic	Bates	Bedmax	Bio-Barley	Bioflow	Blue Chip	Bucas	Butlet
EQUIMIX, Stourport-on-Severn (YH04756)																								
YORKSHIRE (EAST)																								
PATRICK WILKINSON, Beverley (YH10825)				●																				
YORKSHIRE (NORTH)																								
HORSEFEEDSUK, Harrogate (YH07154)					●								●		●				●			●		
LANGTON HORSE WEAR, Northallerton (YH08416)			●																					
RIDE-AWAY, York (YH11850)																								
YORKSHIRE (SOUTH)																								
BLUE CHIP, Sheffield (YH01565)																						●		
DARKHORSE TINYTACK, Barnsley (YH03888)																								
YORKSHIRE (WEST)																								
ACORN FEEDS, Huddersfield (YH00148)													●											
BAILEYS HORSE FEEDS, Wakefield (YH00807)													●											
BAILEYS HORSE FEEDS, Wakefield (YH00808)													●											
BARDSEY MILLS, Otley (YH00927)													●		●							●		
CALDENE CLOTHING, Hebden Bridge (YH02430)																								
EQUITACK SADDLERY, Wakefield (YH04825)		●																						
MIDDLESTOWN SADDLERY, Wakefield (YH09540)																								
STYLO MATCHMAKERS INT, Bradford (YH13620)																								
IRELAND																								
COUNTY CORK																								
BUCAS, Cork (YH02184)																							●	
COUNTY DUBLIN																								
COLEMANS OF SANDYFORD, Dublin (YH03166)	●																						●	
COUNTY KERRY																								
BRIDLES & BITS, Tralee (YH01893)		●																						
COUNTY KILDARE																								
IRISH EQUESTRIAN PRODUCTS, Kildare (YH07493)									●								●							
COUNTY KILKENNY																								
EUROFARM, Kilkenny (YH04898)	●	●																						
COUNTY MEATH																								
CLARKE'S SPORTSDEN, Navan (YH02978)		●												●										

by Country by County	Cair	Caldene	Casco Helmets	Cavallo	CDS Products	Champion	Charles Owen	Charnwood Mill Products	Chatham	Cliff Barnsby	Codlivine	Corta Flex	Cottage Craft	Colt Combi	Commissions	Contour Saddles	Dark Horse	Dengie	Deflect	Dever	Dodson & Horrell	Dollin & Morris	Driza Bone	Dublin
EQUIMIX, Stourport-on-Severn (YH04756)							●														●			
YORKSHIRE (EAST)																								
PATRICK WILKINSON, Beverley (YH10825)																								
YORKSHIRE (NORTH)																								
HORSEFEEDSUK, Harrogate (YH07154)					●			●										●			●	●		
LANGTON HORSE WEAR, Northallerton (YH08416)						●							●							●				
RIDE-AWAY, York (YH11850)		●					●						●											
YORKSHIRE (SOUTH)																								
BLUE CHIP, Sheffield (YH01565)																								
DARKHORSE TINYTACK, Barnsley (YH03888)																	●							
YORKSHIRE (WEST)																								
ACORN FEEDS, Huddersfield (YH00148)																								
BAILEYS HORSE FEEDS, Wakefield (YH00807)																								
BAILEYS HORSE FEEDS, Wakefield (YH00808)																								
BARDSEY MILLS, Otley (YH00927)																		●			●			
CALDENE CLOTHING, Hebden Bridge (YH02430)		●																						
EQUITACK SADDLERY, Wakefield (YH04825)													●											
MIDDLESTOWN SADDLERY, Wakefield (YH09540)							●																	●
STYLO MATCHMAKERS INT, Bradford (YH13620)													●											
IRELAND																								
COUNTY CORK																								
BUCAS, Cork (YH02184)																								
COUNTY DUBLIN																								
COLEMANS OF SANDYFORD, Dublin (YH03166)							●						●											●
COUNTY KERRY																								
BRIDLES & BITS, Tralee (YH01893)		●				●							●											
COUNTY KILDARE																								
IRISH EQUESTRIAN PRODUCTS, Kildare (YH07493)																								
COUNTY KILKENNY																								
EUROFARM, Kilkenny (YH04898)																								
COUNTY MEATH																								
CLARKE'S SPORTSDEN, Navan (YH02978)																								

Brands Supplied
A - D

by Country by County	NORTHERN IRELAND	COUNTY ANTRIM	DOAGH FARM FEEDS, Doagh (YH04147)	COUNTY DOWN	HOLMESTEAD SADDLERY, Downpatrick (YH06981)	SCOTLAND	ARGYLL AND BUTE	TACKLE & TACK, Oban (YH13818)	WHAT EVERY HORSE WANTS, Helensburgh (YH15266)	AYRSHIRE (EAST)	FERRIE, J & A, Newmilns (YH05169)	DUMFRIES AND GALLOWAY	GEE GEE'S, Dumfries (YH05690)	ROBERT THORNE, Annan (YH11944)	FALKIRK	COUNTRY FEEDS LARBERT, Larbert (YH03408)	GLASGOW (CITY OF)	BUSBY EQUITATION CTRE, Busby (YH02302)	EVERYTHING EQUESTRIAN, Busby (YH04957)	LOTHIAN (MID)	R H MILLER, Dalkeith (YH11541)	PERTH AND KINROSS	MCCASH'S, Perth (YH09326)	SCOTTISH BORDERS	A C BURN, Jedburgh (YH00022)
Dublin																			●		●				
Driza Bone																									
Dollin & Morris																									
Dodson & Horrell														●		●					●		●		●
Dever																					●				
Deflect																									
Dengie			●																		●		●		●
Dark Horse																									
Contour Saddles																									
Commissions																									
Colt Combi																									
Cottage Craft								●	●		●		●												
Corta Flex																									
Codlivine																							●		
Cliff Barnsby																					●				
Chatham																									
Charnwood Mill Products																									
Charles Owen								●	●		●		●												
Champion																									
CDS Products																									
Cavallo																		●	●		●				
Casco Helmets																									
Caldene													●								●				
Cair																									
Butlet																									
Bucas																									
Blue Chip														●											
Bioflow																									
Bio-Barley																									
Bedmax																●									
Bates																									
Basic																									
Barrier H																									
Bardsey Mill																									
Barbour					●																				
Baileys														●							●		●		
Bahill																									
Badminton																					●				
Aubiose																									
Ash Horseshoes																									
Arenas																									
Arait																									
Apaloosa																									
Allen & Page																									
Albion																									
Air-o-Wear													●												
Aigle																					●				
Aerborn																									

Brands Supplied

A - D

by Country by County

	Aerborn	Aigle	Air-o-Wear	Albion	Allen & Page	Apaloosa	Arait	Arenas	Ash Horseshoes	Aubiose	Badminton	Bahill	Baileys	Barbour	Bardsey Mill	Barrier H	Basic	Bates	Bedmax	Bio-Barley	Bioflow	Blue Chip	Bucas	Butlet	Cair	Caldene	Casco Helmets	Cavallo	CDS Products	Champion	Charles Owen	Charnwood Mill Products	Chatham	Cliff Barnsby	Codlivine	Corta Flex	Cottage Craft	Colt Combi	Commissions	Contour Saddles	Dark Horse	Dengie	Deflect	Dever	Dodson & Horrell	Dollin & Morris	Driza Bone	Dublin
WALES																																																
CARMARTHENSHIRE																																																
PENCADER STUD, Pencader (YH10928)																																													●			
FLINTSHIRE																																																
T F S, Buckley (YH13739)													●																													●			●			●
GWYNEDD																																																
BRONALLT, Caernarfon (YH02029)																											●										●											
PEMBROKESHIRE																																																
BOULSTON, Haverfordwest (YH01672)																																										●			●			
PEMBROKESHIRE EQUESTRIAN, Haverfordwest (YH10919)																																		●			●										●	●
POWYS																																																
LLWYNON, Brecon (YH08749)		●		●																						●		●						●			●											●

Brands Supplied
E - J

by Country by County

	ECC Carriages	Ecoflow	Equetech	Equibale	Equiform	Equilibra	Equilife	Equimax	Equine America	Equinox	Equipoise PREbiotic
ENGLAND											
BERKSHIRE											
SHAMLEY SADDLERY, Maidenhead (YH12663)											
WOODLANDS, Hungerford (YH15705)											
BUCKINGHAMSHIRE											
DENNIS'S SADDLERY/RIDING WEAR, Aylesbury (YH04060)											
DENNIS'S SADDLERY/RIDING WEAR, Aylesbury (YH04059)											
CHESHIRE											
BOOL BY DESIGN, Tarporley (YH01631)											
CREWE SADDLERY, Crewe (YH03595)											
GAYNORS SADDLERY, Dukinfield (YH05682)											
LANSDOWNE HORSE & RIDER, Chester (YH08423)			●								
CLEVELAND											
ARMSTRONG RICHARDSON, Middlesbrough (YH00544)									●		
COUNTY DURHAM											
FARMWAY, Darlington (YH05072)											
LANCHESTER COUNTRY STORE, Lanchester (YH08382)											
CUMBRIA											
LOWTHER EQUESTRIAN, Carlisle (YH08877)											
DERBYSHIRE											
BARLEYFIELD SADDLERY, Etwall (YH00951)											
BARLEYFIELDS, Derby (YH00952)											
PEAKDALE SADDLERY, Buxton (YH10866)											
DEVON											
FARMERS FRIEND, Exeter (YH05061)											
DORSET											
EQUUS, Wimborne (YH04836)											
HURN BRIDGE CTRE, Christchurch (YH07313)											
TOLLER TRAILERS, Dorchester (YH14209)											
ESSEX											
D & F FEED SVS, Rayleigh (YH03770)						●					

	Eraquell	Euro Hunter	Eurostar	Exselle	Fal	Field Master	Fieldhouse	Flair	Forester	FPI
ENGLAND										
BERKSHIRE										
SHAMLEY SADDLERY, Maidenhead (YH12663)							●			
WOODLANDS, Hungerford (YH15705)										
BUCKINGHAMSHIRE										
DENNIS'S SADDLERY/RIDING WEAR, Aylesbury (YH04060)										
DENNIS'S SADDLERY/RIDING WEAR, Aylesbury (YH04059)										
CHESHIRE										
BOOL BY DESIGN, Tarporley (YH01631)					●					
CREWE SADDLERY, Crewe (YH03595)										
GAYNORS SADDLERY, Dukinfield (YH05682)							●			
LANSDOWNE HORSE & RIDER, Chester (YH08423)										
CLEVELAND										
ARMSTRONG RICHARDSON, Middlesbrough (YH00544)										
COUNTY DURHAM										
FARMWAY, Darlington (YH05072)					●					
LANCHESTER COUNTRY STORE, Lanchester (YH08382)										
CUMBRIA										
LOWTHER EQUESTRIAN, Carlisle (YH08877)										
DERBYSHIRE										
BARLEYFIELD SADDLERY, Etwall (YH00951)										
BARLEYFIELDS, Derby (YH00952)							●			
PEAKDALE SADDLERY, Buxton (YH10866)							●			
DEVON										
FARMERS FRIEND, Exeter (YH05061)										
DORSET										
EQUUS, Wimborne (YH04836)							●			
HURN BRIDGE CTRE, Christchurch (YH07313)										
TOLLER TRAILERS, Dorchester (YH14209)										
ESSEX										
D & F FEED SVS, Rayleigh (YH03770)										

	Frank Baines	Gatehouse	Georg Schumacher	Gibbins	Gorringe	Griffin NU-Med	Hac Tac	Hamilton Thorne	Harkaway	Harry Dabbs	Harry Hall
ENGLAND											
BERKSHIRE											
SHAMLEY SADDLERY, Maidenhead (YH12663)											
WOODLANDS, Hungerford (YH15705)											●
BUCKINGHAMSHIRE											
DENNIS'S SADDLERY/RIDING WEAR, Aylesbury (YH04060)						●					
DENNIS'S SADDLERY/RIDING WEAR, Aylesbury (YH04059)						●					
CHESHIRE											
BOOL BY DESIGN, Tarporley (YH01631)			●								
CREWE SADDLERY, Crewe (YH03595)											●
GAYNORS SADDLERY, Dukinfield (YH05682)											
LANSDOWNE HORSE & RIDER, Chester (YH08423)	●										
CLEVELAND											
ARMSTRONG RICHARDSON, Middlesbrough (YH00544)											●
COUNTY DURHAM											
FARMWAY, Darlington (YH05072)						●					●
LANCHESTER COUNTRY STORE, Lanchester (YH08382)											
CUMBRIA											
LOWTHER EQUESTRIAN, Carlisle (YH08877)										●	
DERBYSHIRE											
BARLEYFIELD SADDLERY, Etwall (YH00951)											●
BARLEYFIELDS, Derby (YH00952)											●
PEAKDALE SADDLERY, Buxton (YH10866)											●
DEVON											
FARMERS FRIEND, Exeter (YH05061)											●
DORSET											
EQUUS, Wimborne (YH04836)							●				
HURN BRIDGE CTRE, Christchurch (YH07313)											●
TOLLER TRAILERS, Dorchester (YH14209)											
ESSEX											
D & F FEED SVS, Rayleigh (YH03770)											

	Hastilow Saddles	Haymax	Herbilix	Honeychop Horse Feed	Horse Ware	Horsefair	Horslyx	Ideal	Hunter	Ifor Williams	IV Horse	Jaguar	Jeffries	John Whittaker
ENGLAND														
BERKSHIRE														
SHAMLEY SADDLERY, Maidenhead (YH12663)														
WOODLANDS, Hungerford (YH15705)														
BUCKINGHAMSHIRE														
DENNIS'S SADDLERY/RIDING WEAR, Aylesbury (YH04060)														
DENNIS'S SADDLERY/RIDING WEAR, Aylesbury (YH04059)														
CHESHIRE														
BOOL BY DESIGN, Tarporley (YH01631)														
CREWE SADDLERY, Crewe (YH03595)														
GAYNORS SADDLERY, Dukinfield (YH05682)												●		
LANSDOWNE HORSE & RIDER, Chester (YH08423)														
CLEVELAND														
ARMSTRONG RICHARDSON, Middlesbrough (YH00544)														
COUNTY DURHAM														
FARMWAY, Darlington (YH05072)														
LANCHESTER COUNTRY STORE, Lanchester (YH08382)								●						
CUMBRIA														
LOWTHER EQUESTRIAN, Carlisle (YH08877)											●			
DERBYSHIRE														
BARLEYFIELD SADDLERY, Etwall (YH00951)														
BARLEYFIELDS, Derby (YH00952)														
PEAKDALE SADDLERY, Buxton (YH10866)												●		
DEVON														
FARMERS FRIEND, Exeter (YH05061)														
DORSET														
EQUUS, Wimborne (YH04836)					●									
HURN BRIDGE CTRE, Christchurch (YH07313)												●		
TOLLER TRAILERS, Dorchester (YH14209)									●					
ESSEX														
D & F FEED SVS, Rayleigh (YH03770)				●										

Brands Supplied
E - J

by Country by County	ECC Carriages	Ecoflow	Equetech	Equibale	Equiform	Equilibra	Equilife	Equimax	Equine America	Equinox	Equipoise PREbiotic	Eraquell	Euro Hunter	Eurostar	Exselle	Fal	Field Master	Fieldhouse	Flair	Forester	FPI	Frank Baines	Gatehouse	Georg Schumacher	Gibbins	Gorringe	Griffin NU-Med	Hac Tac	Hamilton Thorne	Harkaway	Harry Dabbs	Harry Hall	Hastilow Saddles	Haymax	Herbilix	Honeychop Horse Feed	Horse Ware	Horsefair	Horslyx	Ideal	Hunter	Ifor Williams	IV Horse	Jaguar	Jeffries	John Whittaker
THORPE TACK ROOM, Clacton-on-Sea (YH14095)																																●														
UPMINSTER SADDLERY, Upminster (YH14604)																																●												●		
GLOUCESTERSHIRE																																														
MORETON SADDLERY, Moreton In Marsh (YH09790)									●																												●							●		
STROUD SADDLERY, Stroud (YH13588)																																												●		
TEWKESBURY SADDLERY, Tewkesbury (YH13969)																		●																										●		
HAMPSHIRE																																														
COUNTRY RIDING WEAR, Hook (YH03424)														●	●	●																														
DAVID CATLIN, Southampton (YH03916)															●			●																					●					●		
DIRECT FEEDS, Winchester (YH04127)																																							●							
FORESTER SADDLES, Lyndhurst (YH05354)																				●																										
HOPLANDS EQUESTRIAN, Stockbridge (YH07058)									●																																					
SADDLES, SADDLES, SADDLES, Portsmouth (YH12371)																				●																			●							
HEREFORDSHIRE																																														
COUNTRYWIDE, Hereford (YH03445)																																					●									
HERTFORDSHIRE																																														
PATCHETTS, Watford (YH10815)																●																●					●									
UPPERWOOD FARM STUD, Hemel Hempstead (YH14609)					●																																									
KENT																																														
FROGPOOL MANOR SADDLERY, Chislehurst (YH05515)																																					●									
LANCASHIRE																																														
EQUESTRIANA, Blackburn (YH04724)									●	●																																				
HORSE BITS SADDLERY, Bury (YH07106)																																												●		
LEICESTERSHIRE																																														
CLOTHES HORSE, Leicester (YH03062)																●												●				●												●		
LINCOLNSHIRE																																														
POPPYFIELDS, Lincoln (YH11275)				●																																										
RICHARD GRICE TRAILERS, Market Rasen (YH11803)																																									●					
SHEEPGATE TACK & TOGS, Boston (YH12697)									●							●										●																				
TACK BOX, Lincoln (YH13785)																			●																											
LINCOLNSHIRE (NORTH)																																														
CROWSTONS, Scunthorpe (YH03684)									●																		●																			

Brands Supplied
E - J

by Country by County	ECC Carriages	Ecoflow	Equetech	Equibale	Equiform	Equilibra	Equilife	Equimax	Equine America	Equinox	Equipoise PREbiotic	Eraquell	Euro Hunter	Eurostar	Exselle	Fal	Field Master	Fieldhouse	Flair	Forester	FPI	Frank Baines	Gatehouse	Georg Schumacher	Gibbins	Gorringe	Griffin NU-Med	Hac Tac	Hamilton Thorne	Harkaway	Harry Dabbs	Harry Hall	Hastilow Saddles	Haymax	Herbilix	Honeychop Horse Feed	Horse Ware	Horsefair	Horslyx	Ideal	Hunter	Ifor Williams	IV Horse	Jaguar	Jeffries	John Whittaker
MASON, D & M, Scunthorpe (YH09239)																															●												●		
LONDON (GREATER)																																														
HYDE PARK RIDING WEAR, London (YH07345)																															●														
RIDGWAY STABLES, London (YH11870)																					●		●									●														
MANCHESTER (GREATER)																																														
EQUITACK, Bolton (YH04823)																															●										●				
MIDLANDS (WEST)																																														
FRANK BAINES SADDLERY, Walsall (YH05455)																						●																								
H W DABBS SADDLEMAKERS, Walsall (YH06245)																															●															
NORFOLK																																														
DARROW FARM SUPPLIES, Diss (YH03899)							●																																							
HORSES IN SPORT, Diss (YH07169)														●																															●	
NORTHAMPTONSHIRE																																														
EDENGATE SADDLERY, Northampton (YH04550)																		●																												
THORPE SADDLERY, Kettering (YH14094)									●																																					
WATTS & WATTS SADDLERY, Northampton (YH15003)																															●														
NORTHUMBERLAND																																														
FAL TEXTILE INDUSTRIES, Blyth (YH05038)																●																														
WILLOW WEAR, Hexham (YH15505)																									●							●					●									
NOTTINGHAMSHIRE																																														
NOTTINGHAM TRAILER SPARES, Nottingham (YH10345)																																									●					
SADDLE RACK, Nottingham (YH12346)																										●																				
ST CLEMENTS LODGE, Nottingham (YH13274)									●																							●														
OXFORDSHIRE																																														
ASTI STUD & SADDLERY, Faringdon (YH00633)																																					●									
DOBBINS CLOBBER, Thame (YH04150)							●																																							
HAC-TAC, Faringdon (YH06259)																												●																		
JODS GALORE, Henley-on-Thames (YH07775)																		●																										●		
MICROM, Thame (YH09519)																													●																	
SANSOMS SADDLERY, Witney (YH12429)									●																		●					●												●		
SHROPSHIRE																																														
BRYNORE STUD & LIVERY STABLES, Ellesmere (YH02178)		●																																												

www.hccyourhorse.com

Brands Supplied
E - J

by Country by County	ECC Carriages	Ecoflow	Equetech	Equibale	Equiform	Equilibra	Equilife	Equimax	Equine America	Equinox	Equipoise PREbiotic	Eraquell	Euro Hunter	Eurostar	Exselle	Fal	Field Master	Fieldhouse	Flair	Forester	FPI	Frank Baines	Gatehouse	Georg Schumacher	Gibbins	Gorringe	Griffin NU-Med	Hac Tac	Hamilton Thorne	Harkaway	Harry Dabbs	Harry Hall	Hastilow Saddles	Haymax	Herbilix	Honeychop Horse Feed	Horse Ware	Horsefair	Horslyx	Ideal	Hunter	Ifor Williams	IV Horse	Jaguar	Jeffries	John Whittaker
HORSE SHOP, Telford (YH07140)																		●	●																				●							
SOMERSET																																														
RIDEMOOR, Wincanton (YH11852)														●																							●							●		
THORNEY COPSE, Wincanton (YH14066)																												●				●														
W.E.S GARRETT MASTER SADDLERS, Cheddar (YH14803)																																●														
STAFFORDSHIRE																																														
DICKSONS, Stoke-on-Trent (YH04119)																																							●							
SUFFOLK																																														
CHURCH FARM TACK SHOP & FEEDS, Eye (YH02903)																											●																			
GIBSON SADDLERS, Newmarket (YH05746)									●																												●									
LINKWOOD EQUESTIAN, Bury St Edmunds (YH08665)																																												●		
MILL SADDLERY, Stowmarket (YH09587)									●							●																							●							
RIDE AWAY SADDLERY, Ipswich (YH11846)																																●														
VIRBAC, Bury St Edmunds (YH14732)								●				●																																		
SURREY																																														
ANIMAL ALTERNATIVES, Richmond (YH00425)											●																																			
BROOMELLS WORKSHOP, Dorking (YH02077)									●																																					
HASTILOW COMPETITION SADDLES, Godalming (YH06526)																																	●				●									
LINGFIELD TACK, Lingfield (YH08660)									●							●																●														
SUSSEX (EAST)																																														
ANDREW REILLY, Forest Row (YH00392)																			●			●																								
SUSSEX (WEST)																																														
BRENDON HORSE & RIDER, Brighton (YH01837)									●																																			●	●	
DRAGONFLY SADDLERY, Hassocks (YH04252)																		●																			●									
EQUINE AMERICA, Broadbridge Heath (YH04761)									●																																					
GEOFF DEAN SADDLERY, Worthing (YH05714)																																								●				●		
WARWICKSHIRE																																														
A & J SADDLERY, Southam (YH00012)																																●														
WILTSHIRE																																														
EQUIFOR, Marlborough (YH04746)	●																																													
GRO-WELL FEEDS, Melksham (YH06176)						●																																								
HURDCOTT LIVERY STABLES, Salisbury (YH07311)									●							●																														

Brands Supplied
E - J

by Country by County	ECC Carriages	Ecoflow	Equetech	Equibale	Equiform	Equilibra	Equilife	Equimax	Equine America	Equinox	Equipoise PREbiotic	Eraquell	Euro Hunter	Eurostar	Exselle	Fal	Field Master	Fieldhouse	Flair	Forester	FPI	Frank Baines	Gatehouse	Georg Schumacher	Gibbins	Gorringe	Griffin NU-Med	Hac Tac	Hamilton Thorne	Harkaway	Harry Dabbs	Harry Hall	Hastilow Saddles	Haymax	Herbilix	Honeychop Horse Feed	Horse Ware	Horsefair	Horslyx	Ideal	Hunter	Ifor Williams	IV Horse	Jaguar	Jeffries	John Whittaker
WARMINSTER SADDLERY, Warminster (YH14923)																																●														
WORCESTERSHIRE																																														
BROMSGROVE SADDLERY, Bromsgrove (YH02026)																											●	●																	●	
EQUIMIX, Stourport-on-Severn (YH04756)																											●																			
YORKSHIRE (EAST)																																														
PATRICK WILKINSON, Beverley (YH10825)																																												●		
YORKSHIRE (NORTH)																																														
HORSEFEEDSUK, Harrogate (YH07154)						●																												●	●	●		●	●							
LANGTON HORSE WEAR, Northallerton (YH08416)																●																														
RIDE-AWAY, York (YH11850)																												●				●														
YORKSHIRE (WEST)																																														
BRANDON FORGE SADDLERY, Leeds (YH01796)														●		●																●												●		
CALDENE CLOTHING, Hebden Bridge (YH02430)																	●													●																
DAYS PET SHOP, Bradford (YH03971)							●																									●														
EQUITACK SADDLERY, Wakefield (YH04825)																																●														
STYLO MATCHMAKERS INT, Bradford (YH13620)																																●														
IRELAND																																														
COUNTY KERRY																																														
BRIDLES & BITS, Tralee (YH01893)																																●														
COUNTY KILDARE																																														
IRISH EQUESTRIAN PRODUCTS, Kildare (YH07493)													●																																	
COUNTY LOUTH																																														
HORSEWARE, Dundalk (YH07177)																																					●									
NORTHERN IRELAND																																														
COUNTY DOWN																																														
HOLMESTEAD SADDLERY, Downpatrick (YH06981)																												●																		
SCOTLAND																																														
ARGYLL AND BUTE																																														
TACKLE & TACK, Oban (YH13818)																																●														
WHAT EVERY HORSE WANTS, Helensburgh (YH15266)																		●																			●					●				
AYRSHIRE (EAST)																																														

Brands Supplied
E - J

by Country by County	ECC Carriages	Ecoflow	Equetech	Equibale	Equiform	Equilibra	Equilife	Equimax	Equine America	Equinox	Equipoise PREbiotic	Eraquell	Euro Hunter	Eurostar	Exselle	Fal	Field Master	Fieldhouse	Flair	Forester	FPI	Frank Baines	Gatehouse	Georg Schumacher	Gibbins	Gorringe	Griffin NU-Med	Hac Tac	Hamilton Thorne	Harkaway	Harry Dabbs	Harry Hall	Hastilow Saddles	Haymax	Herbilix	Honeychop Horse Feed	Horse Ware	Horsefair	Horslyx	Ideal	Hunter	Ifor Williams	IV Horse	Jaguar	Jeffries	John Whittaker
FERRIE, J & A, Newmilns (YH05169)																										●						●										●				
DUMFRIES AND GALLOWAY																																														
GEE GEE'S, Dumfries (YH05690)																										●	●																			
FALKIRK																																														
COUNTRY FEEDS LARBERT, Larbert (YH03408)																																		●												
GLASGOW (CITY OF)																																														
BUSBY EQUITATION CTRE, Busby (YH02302)																																●													●	
EVERYTHING EQUESTRIAN, Busby (YH04957)																																●													●	
LANARKSHIRE (NORTH)																																														
CLIPPETY CLOP, Cumbernauld (YH03048)																																							●							
LOTHIAN (MID)																																														
R H MILLER, Dalkeith (YH11541)			●													●		●								●		●				●												●		
MORAY																																														
GREENFIELDS SADDLERY, Elgin (YH06085)																●			●																											
PERTH AND KINROSS																																														
MCCASH'S, Perth (YH09326)																																●														
WALES																																														
CARMARTHENSHIRE																																														
TACK EXCHANGE, Llanelli (YH13787)																		●																												
GLAMORGAN (VALE OF)																																														
CARDIFF SPORTSGEAR, Cardiff (YH02532)																																●														
GWYNEDD																																														
BRONALLT, Caernarfon (YH02029)																																●												●		
PEMBROKESHIRE																																														
PEMBROKESHIRE EQUESTRIAN, Haverfordwest (YH10919)																																					●									
POWYS																																														
LLWYNON, Brecon (YH08749)									●							●											●										●		●					●		

Brands Supplied
J - P

by Country by County	Julip	Just Togs	Kawasaki	Kingshead	Kyra-K	Landrover	Le Chameau	Lemetex	Lenrys Associates	Limpet	Lincoln	Liscop	Liveryman	Loveson	Lucinda Green	Lyn Ryes Products	Magnetic Rugs	Mane Master	Mark Todd	Marksway HorseHage	Masta	Mears	Michael Whittaker	Mollichaff	Morris & Nolan	Mountain Horse	Mountain World	Mustad	Mustang	Musto	Mycoplex Cordyceps	Mycoplex Coriolus	Myler	Myur	N.A.F	Nags Rags	Nanny Blue	New Equine Wear	Ornella Prosperi	Pegasus	Pessoa	Phoenix	Pikeur	Poly Pads	Probalance	Professional Choice	Puffa
ENGLAND																																															
BERKSHIRE																																															
SCATS COUNTRYSTORE, Newbury (YH12493)															●															●																	●
SHAMLEY SADDLERY, Maidenhead (YH12663)																																									●						
WOODLANDS, Hungerford (YH15705)																																							●								●
CAMBRIDGESHIRE																																															
PEGASUS, Peterborough (YH10901)																																								●							
SMEETH SADDLERY, Wisbech (YH12925)																					●																							●			
CHESHIRE																																															
BOOL BY DESIGN, Tarporley (YH01631)															●																												●				
GAYNORS SADDLERY, Dukinfield (YH05682)														●																																	
LANSDOWNE HORSE & RIDER, Chester (YH08423)		●																																	●												
CLEVELAND																																															
ARMSTRONG RICHARDSON, Middlesbrough (YH00544)																														●					●												●
COUNTY DURHAM																																															
FARMWAY, Darlington (YH05072)																																			●												
LANCHESTER COUNTRY STORE, Lanchester (YH08382)																																															●
CUMBRIA																																															
J W WILKINSON, Kendal (YH07628)				●																																											
DERBYSHIRE																																															
BARLEYFIELD SADDLERY, Etwall (YH00951)														●							●																										
C E S, Ashbourne (YH02370)		●																			●																										
PEAKDALE SADDLERY, Buxton (YH10866)		●																																	●												●
DEVON																																															
FARMERS FRIEND, Exeter (YH05061)																																															●
LIMPET ANTI-SLIP SADDLE PADS, Ottery St Mary (YH08638)										●																																					
MARK WESTAWAY & SON, Paignton (YH09157)																				●				●																							
DORSET																																															
EQUUS, Wimborne (YH04836)																																			●												
SCATS COUNTRYSTORE, Dorchester (YH12494)															●															●																	●
SCATS COUNTRYSTORE, Gillingham (YH12495)															●															●																	●

Brands Supplied
J - P

by Country by County	Julip	Just Togs	Kawasaki	Kingshead	Kyra-K	Landrover	Le Chameau	Lemetex	Lenrys Associates	Limpet	Lincoln	Liscop	Liveryman	Loveson	Lucinda Green	Lyn Ryes Products	Magnetic Rugs	Mane Master	Mark Todd	Marksway HorseHage	Masta	Mears	Michael Whittaker	Mollichaff	Morris & Nolan	Mountain Horse	Mountain World	Mustad	Mustang	Musto	Mycoplex Cordyceps	Mycoplex Coriolus	Myler	Myur	N.A.F	Nags Rags	Nanny Blue	New Equine Wear	Ornella Prosperi	Pegasus	Pessoa	Phoenix	Pikeur	Poly Pads	Probalance	Professional Choice	Puffa
SCATS COUNTRYSTORE, Blandford (YH12496)															●															●																	●
ESSEX																																															
D & F FEED SVS, Rayleigh (YH03770)																				●				●																							
MOSS, JANETTE, Waltham Abbey (YH09858)					●																					●																					●
THORPE TACK ROOM, Clacton-on-Sea (YH14095)																																															●
UPMINSTER SADDLERY, Upminster (YH14604)		●																																													●
GLOUCESTERSHIRE																																															
HENRY COLE, Cirencester (YH06681)																																			●												
MORETON SADDLERY, Moreton In Marsh (YH09790)					●			●																						●													●				●
HAMPSHIRE																																															
COUNTRY RIDING WEAR, Hook (YH03424)					●		●																							●													●				●
DAVID CATLIN, Southampton (YH03916)																																									●						
SCATS COUNTRYSTORE, Romsey (YH12497)															●															●																	●
SCATS COUNTRYSTORE, Lymington (YH12502)															●															●																	●
SCATS COUNTRYSTORE, Basingstoke (YH12501)															●															●																	●
SCATS COUNTRYSTORE, Andover (YH12500)															●															●																	●
SCATS COUNTRYSTORE, Alton (YH12499)															●															●																	●
SCATS COUNTRYSTORE, Winchester (YH12498)															●															●																	●
HEREFORDSHIRE																																															
COUNTRYWIDE, Hereford (YH03445)																																			●												
TURNERS, Kington (YH14492)											●																																				
HERTFORDSHIRE																																															
PATCHETTS, Watford (YH10815)					●																									●					●								●				
ISLE OF WIGHT																																															
SCATS COUNTRYSTORE, Newport (YH12503)															●															●																	●
KENT																																															
ARIZONAS, Tunbridge Wells (YH00527)																																														●	
FROGPOOL MANOR SADDLERY, Chislehurst (YH05515)																														●																	
SCATS COUNTRYSTORE, Marden (YH12505)															●															●																	●
SCATS COUNTRYSTORE, Canterbury (YH12504)															●															●																	●
LANCASHIRE																																															
EQUESTRIANA, Blackburn (YH04724)																																										●					

Brands Supplied
J - P

by Country by County

by Country by County	Julip	Just Togs	Kawasaki	Kingshead	Kyra-K	Landrover	Le Chameau	Lemetex	Lenrys Associates	Limpet	Lincoln	Liscop	Liveryman	Loveson	Lucinda Green	Lyn Ryes Products	Magnetic Rugs	Mane Master	Mark Todd	Marksway HorseHage	Masta	Mears	Michael Whittaker	Mollichaff	Morris & Nolan	Mountain Horse	Mountain World	Mustad	Mustang	Musto	Mycoplex Cordyceps	Mycoplex Coriolus	Myler	Myur	N.A.F	Nags Rags	Nanny Blue	New Equine Wear	Ornella Prosperi	Pegasus	Pessoa	Phoenix	Pikeur	Poly Pads	Probalance	Professional Choice	Puffa
HORSE BITS SADDLERY, Bury (YH07106)																														●																	●
ZEBRA, Skelmersdale (YH15953)															●																																
LEICESTERSHIRE																																															
CLAYBROOKE, Lutterworth (YH02996)																																			●												
CLOTHES HORSE, Leicester (YH03062)																										●									●												●
DTA, Leicester (YH04303)					●																																					●					
LINCOLNSHIRE																																															
BATTLE, HAYWARD & BOWER, Lincoln (YH01081)											●																																				
SHEEPGATE TACK & TOGS, Boston (YH12697)																						●								●																	
WINERGY, Grantham (YH15582)																																												●			
LINCOLNSHIRE (NORTH)																																															
CROWSTONS, Scunthorpe (YH03684)																						●														●											
MASON, D & M, Scunthorpe (YH09239)																					●									●																	●
LONDON (GREATER)																																															
HYDE PARK RIDING WEAR, London (YH07345)					●																					●																					
RIDGWAY STABLES, London (YH11870)	●																																														
MANCHESTER (GREATER)																																															
EQUITACK, Bolton (YH04823)														●																																	
MIDLANDS (WEST)																																															
DIAMOND SADDLERY, Wolverhampton (YH04104)				●																																											
NORFOLK																																															
G J L, Fakenham (YH05585)																				●																											
HORSES IN SPORT, Diss (YH07169)																			●																			●									
HORSETALK, King's Lynn (YH07176)											●														●																						
NORTHAMPTONSHIRE																																															
EDENGATE SADDLERY, Northampton (YH04550)		●																																													
LOVESON, Irthlingborough (YH08851)														●																																	
THORPE SADDLERY, Kettering (YH14094)																	●																														
NORTHUMBERLAND																																															
WILLOW WEAR, Hexham (YH15505)																					●																										●
NOTTINGHAMSHIRE																																															
BRIDLE WAY & GAUNTLEYS, Newark (YH01892)														●					●																												●

Brands Supplied
J - P

by Country by County

	Julip	Just Togs	Kawasaki	Kingshead	Kyra-K	Landrover	Le Chameau	Lemetex	Lenrys Associates	Limpet	Lincoln	Liscop	Liveryman	Loveson	Lucinda Green	Lyn Ryes Products	Magnetic Rugs	Mane Master	Mark Todd	Marksway HorseHage	Masta	Mears	Michael Whittaker	Mollichaff	Morris & Nolan	Mountain Horse	Mountain World	Mustad	Mustang	Musto	Mycoplex Cordyceps	Mycoplex Coriolus	Myler	Myur	N.A.F	Nags Rags	Nanny Blue	New Equine Wear	Ornella Prosperi	Pegasus	Pessoa	Phoenix	Pikeur	Poly Pads	Probalance	Professional Choice	Puffa
SADDLE RACK, Nottingham (YH12346)														●																														●			●
ST CLEMENTS LODGE, Nottingham (YH13274)																					●																										●
OXFORDSHIRE																																															
ASTI STUD & SADDLERY, Faringdon (YH00633)																																		●													
JODS GALORE, Henley-on-Thames (YH07775)																														●																	●
SANSOMS SADDLERY, Witney (YH12429)																														●														●			
SCATS COUNTRYSTORE, Faringdon (YH12506)															●															●																	●
SHROPSHIRE																																															
TOUCHDOWN LIVERIES, Whitchurch (YH14253)																				●																											
SOMERSET																																															
MANELINE, B G I, Bridgwater (YH09075)																		●																													
RIDEMOOR, Wincanton (YH11852)																														●			●														●
ROSE MILL FEEDS, Ilminster (YH12094)																				●																											
THORNEY COPSE, Wincanton (YH14066)		●																	●		●					●																					
W.E.S GARRETT MASTER SADDLERS, Cheddar (YH14803)						●								●							●																										
SUFFOLK																																															
GIBSON SADDLERS, Newmarket (YH05746)					●																					●												●									
GLADWELLS, Ipswich (YH05802)																				●																											
HORSESHOES, Wrentham (YH07174)																				●																											
LINKWOOD EQUESTIAN, Bury St Edmunds (YH08665)									●														●																								
RIDE AWAY SADDLERY, Ipswich (YH11846)														●																																	
WESTBRINK FARMS, Newmarket (YH15184)																				●																											
SURREY																																															
ANIMAL ALTERNATIVES, Richmond (YH00425)																															●	●															
HASTILOW COMPETITION SADDLES, Godalming (YH06526)		●																																							●		●				
LINGFIELD TACK, Lingfield (YH08660)					●																●																						●				●
SCATS COUNTRYSTORE, Godalming (YH12507)															●															●																	●
SCATS COUNTRYSTORE, Redhill (YH12508)															●															●																	●
SUPERPET THE HORSE SHOP, Epsom (YH13654)																			●							●				●																	
SUSSEX (EAST)																																															
SCATS COUNTRYSTORE, Heathfield (YH12509)															●															●																	●
SUSSEX (WEST)																																															

Brands Supplied
J - P

by Country by County	Julip	Just Togs	Kawasaki	Kingshead	Kyra-K	Landrover	Le Chameau	Lemetex	Lenrys Associates	Limpet	Lincoln	Liscop	Liveryman	Loveson	Lucinda Green	Lyn Ryes Products	Magnetic Rugs	Mane Master	Mark Todd	Marksway HorseHage	Masta	Mears	Michael Whittaker	Mollichaff	Morris & Nolan	Mountain Horse	Mountain World	Mustad	Mustang	Musto	Mycoplex Cordyceps	Mycoplex Coriolus	Myler	Myur	N.A.F	Nags Rags	Nanny Blue	New Equine Wear	Ornella Prosperi	Pegasus	Pessoa	Phoenix	Pikeur	Poly Pads	Probalance	Professional Choice	Puffa
BRENDON HORSE & RIDER, Brighton (YH01837)																														●																	
DRAGONFLY SADDLERY, Hassocks (YH04252)		●																																													
GEOFF DEAN SADDLERY, Worthing (YH05714)		●																																													●
LIGHTS, Brighton (YH08616)																				●																											
PEPER HAROW HORSE TRAILERS, Horsham (YH10968)																																								●							
SCATS COUNTRYSTORE, Billingshurst (YH12510)															●															●																	●
TYNE AND WEAR																																															
H C S, North Shields (YH06215)													●																																		
WARWICKSHIRE																																															
A & J SADDLERY, Southam (YH00012)																				●															●												
WAVERLEY EQUESTRIAN CTRE, Leamington Spa (YH15011)																						●																									
WILTSHIRE																																															
ARMADILLO PRODUCTS, Salisbury (YH00535)																	●																														
BEST BOOTS, Chippenham (YH01324)							●																																								
HURDCOTT LIVERY STABLES, Salisbury (YH07311)				●															●																●									●			
NEW EQUINE WEAR, Malmesbury (YH10093)																																						●									
SCATS COUNTRYSTORE, Salisbury (YH12511)															●															●																	●
SCATS COUNTRYSTORE, Devizes (YH12512)															●															●																	●
WORCESTERSHIRE																																															
COUNTRYWIDE, Worcester (YH03446)																														●																	●
EQUIMIX, Stourport-on-Severn (YH04756)																														●																	●
YORKSHIRE (EAST)																																															
PATRICK WILKINSON, Beverley (YH10825)																														●					●												●
YORKSHIRE (NORTH)																																															
HORSEFEEDSUK, Harrogate (YH07154)									●															●																					●		
RIDE-AWAY, York (YH11850)														●																●																	●
YORKSHIRE (WEST)																																															
BARDSEY MILLS, Otley (YH00927)																				●															●												
BRANDON FORGE SADDLERY, Leeds (YH01796)																			●		●	●				●																					
DAYS PET SHOP, Bradford (YH03971)																																															●
EQUITACK SADDLERY, Wakefield (YH04825)													●																																		
MIDDLESTOWN SADDLERY, Wakefield (YH09540)														●																					●												

www.hccyourhorse.com

Brands Supplied
J - P

by Country by County	Julip	Just Togs	Kawasaki	Kingshead	Kyra-K	Landrover	Le Chameau	Lemetex	Lenrys Associates	Limpet	Lincoln	Liscop	Liveryman	Loveson	Lucinda Green	Lyn Ryes Products	Magnetic Rugs	Mane Master	Mark Todd	Marksway HorseHage	Masta	Mears	Michael Whittaker	Mollichaff	Morris & Nolan	Mountain Horse	Mountain World	Mustad	Mustang	Musto	Mycoplex Cordyceps	Mycoplex Coriolus	Myler	Myur	N.A.F	Nags Rags	Nanny Blue	New Equine Wear	Ornella Prosperi	Pegasus	Pessoa	Phoenix	Pikeur	Poly Pads	Probalance	Professional Choice	Puffa
STYLO MATCHMAKERS INT, Bradford (YH13620)																					●																										
IRELAND																																															
COUNTY KERRY																																															
BRIDLES & BITS, Tralee (YH01893)																										●																					
COUNTY KILDARE																																															
IRISH EQUESTRIAN PRODUCTS, Kildare (YH07493)												●															●	●	●																		
COUNTY KILKENNY																																															
EUROFARM, Kilkenny (YH04898)														●																																	
NORTHERN IRELAND																																															
COUNTY ANTRIM																																															
GRANGE EQUESTRIAN, Newtownabbey (YH05986)			●																																												
COUNTY DOWN																																															
HOLMESTEAD SADDLERY, Downpatrick (YH06981)																										●				●			●										●				
SCOTLAND																																															
ABERDEENSHIRE																																															
MILL OF URAS EQUESTRIAN, Stonehaven (YH09583)																																			●												
ARGYLL AND BUTE																																															
WHAT EVERY HORSE WANTS, Helensburgh (YH15266)																					●																										
AYRSHIRE (EAST)																																															
FERRIE, J & A, Newmilns (YH05169)																					●																										
DUMFRIES AND GALLOWAY																																															
GEE GEE'S, Dumfries (YH05690)																					●					●																●					
GLASGOW (CITY OF)																																															
BUSBY EQUITATION CTRE, Busby (YH02302)					●																					●																					●
EVERYTHING EQUESTRIAN, Busby (YH04957)					●																					●																					●
LOTHIAN (MID)																																															
R H MILLER, Dalkeith (YH11541)		●			●										●				●							●																	●				●
PERTH AND KINROSS																																															
MCCASH'S, Perth (YH09326)																				●										●					●												●

Brands Supplied
J - P

by Country by County	Julip	Just Togs	Kawasaki	Kingshead	Kyra-K	Landrover	Le Chameau	Lemetex	Lenrys Associates	Limpet	Lincoln	Liscop	Liveryman	Loveson	Lucinda Green	Lyn Ryes Products	Magnetic Rugs	Mane Master	Mark Todd	Marksway HorseHage	Masta	Mears	Michael Whittaker	Mollichaff	Morris & Nolan	Mountain Horse	Mountain World	Mustad	Mustang	Musto	Mycoplex Cordyceps	Mycoplex Coriolus	Myler	Myur	N.A.F	Nags Rags	Nanny Blue	New Equine Wear	Ornella Prosperi	Pegasus	Pessoa	Phoenix	Pikeur	Poly Pads	Probalance	Professional Choice	Puffa
WALES																																															
CARMARTHENSHIRE																																															
TACK EXCHANGE, Llanelli (YH13787)		●																																													
FLINTSHIRE																																															
T F S, Buckley (YH13739)																																			●												
MONMOUTHSHIRE																																															
NATURAL ANIMAL FEEDS, Raglan (YH10050)																																			●												
PEMBROKESHIRE																																															
BOULSTON, Haverfordwest (YH01672)																																															●
PEMBROKESHIRE EQUESTRIAN, Haverfordwest (YH10919)																										●											●										
POWYS																																															
LLWYNON, Brecon (YH08749)																										●																	●				

Brands Supplied
Q - Z

by Country by County	Quorn Sportswear	Rambo	Rectiligne	Regent	Renegade	Richardson Rice	Rockies	Rodney Powall	Ryder	Sabre	Saddle Master	Saddlecraft	San Giorgio	Saracen Horse Feeds	Sarm Hippique	Sergio Graso	Shayler	Shepherds	Shires	Silver Royal	Skin Rite	Small Tractors	Spillers	Stubben	Stylo	Tally Ho	Tedman	Thermatex	Thorowgood	Tiny Tack	Toggi	Top Score	Topspec	Tredstep	Triple Crown	Weatherbeeta	Webster	Wendals	Wessex	Westgates	Winergy	Wintec	Woof	World Beater	Zilco
ENGLAND																																													
BEDFORDSHIRE																																													
BIGGLESWADE SADDLERY, Biggleswade (YH01404)																													●													●			
BERKSHIRE																																													
SCATS COUNTRYSTORE, Newbury (YH12493)																							●								●														
SHAMLEY SADDLERY, Maidenhead (YH12663)																	●		●																							●			
WOODLANDS, Hungerford (YH15705)																															●														
BUCKINGHAMSHIRE																																													
DENNIS'S SADDLERY/RIDING WEAR, Aylesbury (YH04059)																																		●											
DENNIS'S SADDLERY/RIDING WEAR, Aylesbury (YH04060)																																		●											
SPILLERS SPECIALITY FEEDS, Milton Keynes (YH13206)																							●																						
CAMBRIDGESHIRE																																													
ROBB & SON, St Ives (YH11932)																																		●											
SMEETH SADDLERY, Wisbech (YH12925)																			●												●					●									
CHESHIRE																																													
BOOL BY DESIGN, Tarporley (YH01631)																								●							●														
CREWE SADDLERY, Crewe (YH03595)		●																																											
GAYNORS SADDLERY, Dukinfield (YH05682)																																								●					
GREEN FARM FEEDS, Crewe (YH06055)																							●										●					●							
LANSDOWNE HORSE & RIDER, Chester (YH08423)																																				●									
TOPSPEC, Nantwich (YH14241)																																	●												
COUNTY DURHAM																																													
FARMWAY, Darlington (YH05072)																															●					●									
LANCHESTER COUNTRY STORE, Lanchester (YH08382)																							●																						
CUMBRIA																																													
LOWTHER EQUESTRIAN, Carlisle (YH08877)									●																																				
DERBYSHIRE																																													
BARLEYFIELD SADDLERY, Etwall (YH00951)											●																																		
BARLEYFIELDS, Derby (YH00952)				●															●																					●					
C E S, Ashbourne (YH02370)																								●	●																				
COUNTRY SPORT, Glossop (YH03426)								●																					●							●						●			

www.hccyourhorse.com

Brands Supplied
Q - Z

by Country by County	Quorn Sportswear	Rambo	Rectiligne	Regent	Renegade	Richardson Rice	Rockies	Rodney Powell	Ryder	Sabre	Saddle Master	Saddlecraft	San Giorgio	Saracen Horse Feeds	Sarm Hippique	Sergio Graso	Shayler	Shepherds	Shires	Silver Royal	Skin Rite	Small Tractors	Spillers	Stubben	Stylo	Tally Ho	Tedman	Thermatex	Thorowgood	Tiny Tack	Toggi	Top Score	Topspec	Tredstep	Triple Crown	Weatherbeeta	Webster	Wendals	Wessex	Westgates	Winergy	Wintec	Woof	World Beater	Zilco
PEAKDALE SADDLERY, Buxton (YH10866)																									●																				
SEALS FODDER, Alfreton (YH12589)																							●										●												
DEVON																																													
FARMERS FRIEND, Exeter (YH05061)		●																											●																
TOWN & COUNTRY SUP, Exeter (YH14286)																							●																						
DORSET																																													
EQUUS, Wimborne (YH04836)				●																											●														
HURN BRIDGE CTRE, Christchurch (YH07313)																			●						●											●								●	
SCATS COUNTRYSTORE, Gillingham (YH12495)																							●								●														
SCATS COUNTRYSTORE, Dorchester (YH12494)																							●								●														
SCATS COUNTRYSTORE, Blandford (YH12496)																							●								●														
ESSEX																																													
D & F FEED SVS, Rayleigh (YH03770)							●							●									●												●						●				
MOSS, JANETTE, Waltham Abbey (YH09858)																															●														
RUGGERY, Romford (YH12221)										●																																	●		
TALLY-HO RIDING SCHOOL, Grays (YH13844)																															●									●					
THORPE TACK ROOM, Clacton-on-Sea (YH14095)																															●														
UPMINSTER SADDLERY, Upminster (YH14604)																									●																				
GLOUCESTERSHIRE																																													
HENRY COLE, Cirencester (YH06681)							●																												●						●				
MORETON SADDLERY, Moreton In Marsh (YH09790)															●									●																			●		
STROUD SADDLERY, Stroud (YH13588)		●																																		●						●			
TEWKESBURY SADDLERY, Tewkesbury (YH13969)				●																																						●			
HAMPSHIRE																																													
COUNTRY RIDING WEAR, Hook (YH03424)																			●																										
DAVID CATLIN, Southampton (YH03916)																																										●			
HOPLANDS EQUESTRIAN, Stockbridge (YH07058)			●																																										
SADDLES, SADDLES, SADDLES, Portsmouth (YH12371)																																										●			
SCATS COUNTRYSTORE, Romsey (YH12497)																							●								●														
SCATS COUNTRYSTORE, Alton (YH12499)																							●								●														
SCATS COUNTRYSTORE, Andover (YH12500)																							●								●														
SCATS COUNTRYSTORE, Basingstoke (YH12501)																							●								●														

Brands Supplied
Q - Z

by Country by County	Quorn Sportswear	Rambo	Rectiligne	Regent	Renegade	Richardson Rice	Rockies	Rodney Powall	Ryder	Sabre	Saddle Master	Saddlecraft	San Giorgio	Saracen Horse Feeds	Sarm Hippique	Sergio Graso	Shayler	Shepherds	Shires	Silver Royal	Skin Rite	Small Tractors	Spillers	Stubben	Stylo	Tally Ho	Tedman	Thermatex	Thorowgood	Tiny Tack	Toggi	Top Score	Topspec	Tredstep	Triple Crown	Weatherbeeta	Webster	Wendals	Wessex	Westgates	Winergy	Wintec	Woof	World Beater	Zilco
SCATS COUNTRYSTORE, Lymington (YH12502)																															●														
SCATS COUNTRYSTORE, Winchester (YH12498)																							●								●														
TALLY HO, Whitchurch (YH13839)																										●																			
HEREFORDSHIRE																																													
COUNTRYWIDE, Hereford (YH03445)																							●																						
SHIRES EQUESTRIAN, Leominster (YH12755)																			●																										
TURNERS, Kington (YH14492)																							●																						
HERTFORDSHIRE																																													
PATCHETTS, Watford (YH10815)																	●							●							●												●		
ISLE OF WIGHT																																													
SCATS COUNTRYSTORE, Newport (YH12503)																							●								●														
KENT																																													
ARIZONAS, Tunbridge Wells (YH00527)					●															●																									
FROGPOOL MANOR SADDLERY, Chislehurst (YH05515)																								●							●					●						●			
SCATS COUNTRYSTORE, Canterbury (YH12504)																							●								●														
SCATS COUNTRYSTORE, Marden (YH12505)																							●								●														
LANCASHIRE																																													
EQUESTRIANA, Blackburn (YH04724)																			●																										
HORSE BITS SADDLERY, Bury (YH07106)										●															●																				
RICHARD BATTERSBY, Heywood (YH11802)																							●																						
LEICESTERSHIRE																																													
CLAYBROOKE, Lutterworth (YH02996)																							●																						
CLOTHES HORSE, Leicester (YH03062)																													●		●														
DTA, Leicester (YH04303)										●																					●														
LINCOLNSHIRE																																													
RICHARD GRICE TRAILERS, Market Rasen (YH11803)						●																																							
SHEEPGATE TACK & TOGS, Boston (YH12697)				●																				●	●						●														
TACK BOX, Lincoln (YH13785)																													●		●					●									
LINCOLNSHIRE (NORTH)																																													
CROWSTONS, Scunthorpe (YH03684)												●	●			●			●																	●									
MASON, D & M, Scunthorpe (YH09239)																									●																			●	
LONDON (GREATER)																																													

Brands Supplied
Q - Z

by Country by County	Quorn Sportswear	Rambo	Rectiligne	Regent	Renegade	Richardson Rice	Rockies	Rodney Powall	Ryder	Sabre	Saddle Master	Saddlecraft	San Giorgio	Saracen Horse Feeds	Sarm Hippique
HYDE PARK RIDING WEAR, London (YH07345)				●								●			
RIDGWAY STABLES, London (YH11870)															
MANCHESTER (GREATER)															
EQUITACK, Bolton (YH04823)															
MERSEYSIDE															
HAMMONDS, Huyton (YH06362)															
MIDLANDS (WEST)															
SABRE LEATHER, Walsall (YH12339)										●					
THOROWGOOD, Walsall (YH14089)															
NORFOLK															
DARROW FARM SUPPLIES, Diss (YH03899)															
G J L, Fakenham (YH05585)															
HORSES IN SPORT, Diss (YH07169)															●
HORSETALK, King's Lynn (YH07176)															
NORTHAMPTONSHIRE															
EDENGATE SADDLERY, Northampton (YH04550)															
STUBBEN, Corby (YH13600)															
NORTHUMBERLAND															
A C BURN, Berwick-upon-Tweed (YH00021)															
WILLOW WEAR, Hexham (YH15505)				●											
NOTTINGHAMSHIRE															
BRIDLE WAY & GAUNTLEYS, Newark (YH01892)										●					
SADDLE RACK, Nottingham (YH12346)												●			
SADDLECRAFT, Nottingham (YH12355)												●			
ST CLEMENTS LODGE, Nottingham (YH13274)															
OXFORDSHIRE															
JODS GALORE, Henley-on-Thames (YH07775)															
SANSOMS SADDLERY, Witney (YH12429)				●											
SCATS COUNTRYSTORE, Faringdon (YH12506)															
WEATHERBEETA, Banbury (YH15023)															
SHROPSHIRE															
HORSE SHOP, Telford (YH07140)															

by Country by County	Sergio Graso	Shayler	Shepherds	Shires	Silver Royal	Skin Rite	Small Tractors	Spillers	Stubben	Stylo	Tally Ho	Tedman	Thermatex	Thorowgood	Tiny Tack
HYDE PARK RIDING WEAR, London (YH07345)				●						●					
RIDGWAY STABLES, London (YH11870)										●	●				
MANCHESTER (GREATER)															
EQUITACK, Bolton (YH04823)				●						●					
MERSEYSIDE															
HAMMONDS, Huyton (YH06362)								●							
MIDLANDS (WEST)															
SABRE LEATHER, Walsall (YH12339)															
THOROWGOOD, Walsall (YH14089)														●	
NORFOLK															
DARROW FARM SUPPLIES, Diss (YH03899)															
G J L, Fakenham (YH05585)								●							
HORSES IN SPORT, Diss (YH07169)									●				●		
HORSETALK, King's Lynn (YH07176)															
NORTHAMPTONSHIRE															
EDENGATE SADDLERY, Northampton (YH04550)														●	
STUBBEN, Corby (YH13600)															
NORTHUMBERLAND															
A C BURN, Berwick-upon-Tweed (YH00021)								●							
WILLOW WEAR, Hexham (YH15505)															
NOTTINGHAMSHIRE															
BRIDLE WAY & GAUNTLEYS, Newark (YH01892)															
SADDLE RACK, Nottingham (YH12346)				●											
SADDLECRAFT, Nottingham (YH12355)															
ST CLEMENTS LODGE, Nottingham (YH13274)								●							
OXFORDSHIRE															
JODS GALORE, Henley-on-Thames (YH07775)															
SANSOMS SADDLERY, Witney (YH12429)														●	
SCATS COUNTRYSTORE, Faringdon (YH12506)								●							
WEATHERBEETA, Banbury (YH15023)															
SHROPSHIRE															
HORSE SHOP, Telford (YH07140)									●						

by Country by County	Toggi	Top Score	Topspec	Tredstep	Triple Crown	Weatherbeeta	Webster	Wendals	Wessex	Westgates	Winergy	Wintec	Woof	World Beater	Zilco
HYDE PARK RIDING WEAR, London (YH07345)	●														
RIDGWAY STABLES, London (YH11870)															
MANCHESTER (GREATER)															
EQUITACK, Bolton (YH04823)						●		●							
MERSEYSIDE															
HAMMONDS, Huyton (YH06362)															
MIDLANDS (WEST)															
SABRE LEATHER, Walsall (YH12339)															
THOROWGOOD, Walsall (YH14089)															
NORFOLK															
DARROW FARM SUPPLIES, Diss (YH03899)	●														
G J L, Fakenham (YH05585)		●													
HORSES IN SPORT, Diss (YH07169)						●									
HORSETALK, King's Lynn (YH07176)						●						●			
NORTHAMPTONSHIRE															
EDENGATE SADDLERY, Northampton (YH04550)								●							
STUBBEN, Corby (YH13600)				●											
NORTHUMBERLAND															
A C BURN, Berwick-upon-Tweed (YH00021)															
WILLOW WEAR, Hexham (YH15505)						●									
NOTTINGHAMSHIRE															
BRIDLE WAY & GAUNTLEYS, Newark (YH01892)															
SADDLE RACK, Nottingham (YH12346)													●		
SADDLECRAFT, Nottingham (YH12355)															
ST CLEMENTS LODGE, Nottingham (YH13274)	●					●									
OXFORDSHIRE															
JODS GALORE, Henley-on-Thames (YH07775)	●												●		
SANSOMS SADDLERY, Witney (YH12429)	●					●							●		
SCATS COUNTRYSTORE, Faringdon (YH12506)	●														
WEATHERBEETA, Banbury (YH15023)						●						●			
SHROPSHIRE															
HORSE SHOP, Telford (YH07140)															

Brands Supplied
Q - Z

by Country by County

by Country by County	Quorn Sportswear	Rambo	Rectiligne	Regent	Renegade	Richardson Rice	Rockies	Rodney Powall	Ryder	Sabre	Saddle Master	Saddlecraft	San Giorgio	Saracen Horse Feeds	Sarm Hippique
TOUCHDOWN LIVERIES, Whitchurch (YH14253)															
SOMERSET															
ROSE MILL FEEDS, Ilminster (YH12094)															
THORNEY COPSE, Wincanton (YH14066)								●							
W.E.S GARRETT MASTER SADDLERS, Cheddar (YH14803)			●												
SUFFOLK															
EQUISAVE HORSE AMBULANCES, Newmarket (YH04816)						●									
GIBSON SADDLERS, Newmarket (YH05746)															
GLADWELLS, Ipswich (YH05802)															
LINKWOOD EQUESTIAN, Bury St Edmunds (YH08665)															
MILL SADDLERY, Stowmarket (YH09587)															
RIDE AWAY SADDLERY, Ipswich (YH11846)															
WESTBRINK FARMS, Newmarket (YH15184)														●	
SURREY															
ANIMAL ALTERNATIVES, Richmond (YH00425)															
HASTILOW COMPETITION SADDLES, Godalming (YH06526)															
LINGFIELD TACK, Lingfield (YH08660)				●											
SCATS COUNTRYSTORE, Godalming (YH12507)															
SCATS COUNTRYSTORE, Redhill (YH12508)															
SUPERPET THE HORSE SHOP, Epsom (YH13654)				●											
SUSSEX (EAST)															
SCATS COUNTRYSTORE, Heathfield (YH12509)															
SUSSEX (WEST)															
BRENDON HORSE & RIDER, Brighton (YH01837)															
DRAGONFLY SADDLERY, Hassocks (YH04252)															
GEOFF DEAN SADDLERY, Worthing (YH05714)															
LIGHTS, Brighton (YH08616)														●	
PEPER HAROW HORSE TRAILERS, Horsham (YH10968)						●									
SCATS COUNTRYSTORE, Billingshurst (YH12510)															
WARWICKSHIRE															
A & J SADDLERY, Southam (YH00012)															
CREWE GARDENS, Kenilworth (YH03594)															

by Country by County	Sergio Graso	Shayler	Shepherds	Shires	Silver Royal	Skin Rite	Small Tractors	Spillers	Stubben	Stylo	Tally Ho	Tedman	Thermatex	Thorowgood	Tiny Tack
TOUCHDOWN LIVERIES, Whitchurch (YH14253)															
SOMERSET															
ROSE MILL FEEDS, Ilminster (YH12094)								●							
THORNEY COPSE, Wincanton (YH14066)				●									●	●	
W.E.S GARRETT MASTER SADDLERS, Cheddar (YH14803)										●					
SUFFOLK															
EQUISAVE HORSE AMBULANCES, Newmarket (YH04816)															
GIBSON SADDLERS, Newmarket (YH05746)			●										●		
GLADWELLS, Ipswich (YH05802)								●							
LINKWOOD EQUESTIAN, Bury St Edmunds (YH08665)				●					●					●	
MILL SADDLERY, Stowmarket (YH09587)															
RIDE AWAY SADDLERY, Ipswich (YH11846)				●											
WESTBRINK FARMS, Newmarket (YH15184)															
SURREY															
ANIMAL ALTERNATIVES, Richmond (YH00425)						●									
HASTILOW COMPETITION SADDLES, Godalming (YH06526)															
LINGFIELD TACK, Lingfield (YH08660)									●						
SCATS COUNTRYSTORE, Godalming (YH12507)								●							
SCATS COUNTRYSTORE, Redhill (YH12508)								●							
SUPERPET THE HORSE SHOP, Epsom (YH13654)															
SUSSEX (EAST)															
SCATS COUNTRYSTORE, Heathfield (YH12509)															
SUSSEX (WEST)															
BRENDON HORSE & RIDER, Brighton (YH01837)									●					●	
DRAGONFLY SADDLERY, Hassocks (YH04252)				●					●					●	
GEOFF DEAN SADDLERY, Worthing (YH05714)									●						
LIGHTS, Brighton (YH08616)								●							
PEPER HAROW HORSE TRAILERS, Horsham (YH10968)															
SCATS COUNTRYSTORE, Billingshurst (YH12510)								●							
WARWICKSHIRE															
A & J SADDLERY, Southam (YH00012)								●							
CREWE GARDENS, Kenilworth (YH03594)															

by Country by County	Toggi	Top Score	Topspec	Tredstep	Triple Crown	Weatherbeeta	Webster	Wendals	Wessex	Westgates	Winergy	Wintec	Woof	World Beater	Zilco
TOUCHDOWN LIVERIES, Whitchurch (YH14253)					●										
SOMERSET															
ROSE MILL FEEDS, Ilminster (YH12094)			●					●							
THORNEY COPSE, Wincanton (YH14066)						●									
W.E.S GARRETT MASTER SADDLERS, Cheddar (YH14803)	●		●												
SUFFOLK															
EQUISAVE HORSE AMBULANCES, Newmarket (YH04816)															
GIBSON SADDLERS, Newmarket (YH05746)	●												●		
GLADWELLS, Ipswich (YH05802)					●										
LINKWOOD EQUESTIAN, Bury St Edmunds (YH08665)															
MILL SADDLERY, Stowmarket (YH09587)						●						●			
RIDE AWAY SADDLERY, Ipswich (YH11846)						●				●		●			
WESTBRINK FARMS, Newmarket (YH15184)		●													
SURREY															
ANIMAL ALTERNATIVES, Richmond (YH00425)															
HASTILOW COMPETITION SADDLES, Godalming (YH06526)													●		
LINGFIELD TACK, Lingfield (YH08660)	●														
SCATS COUNTRYSTORE, Godalming (YH12507)	●														
SCATS COUNTRYSTORE, Redhill (YH12508)	●														
SUPERPET THE HORSE SHOP, Epsom (YH13654)															
SUSSEX (EAST)															
SCATS COUNTRYSTORE, Heathfield (YH12509)	●														
SUSSEX (WEST)															
BRENDON HORSE & RIDER, Brighton (YH01837)															
DRAGONFLY SADDLERY, Hassocks (YH04252)															
GEOFF DEAN SADDLERY, Worthing (YH05714)						●									
LIGHTS, Brighton (YH08616)															
PEPER HAROW HORSE TRAILERS, Horsham (YH10968)									●						
SCATS COUNTRYSTORE, Billingshurst (YH12510)	●														
WARWICKSHIRE															
A & J SADDLERY, Southam (YH00012)															
CREWE GARDENS, Kenilworth (YH03594)										●					

Brands Supplied
Q - Z

by Country by County

by Country by County	Quorn Sportswear	Rambo	Rectiligne	Regent	Renegade	Richardson Rice	Rockies	Rodney Powall	Ryder	Sabre	Saddle Master	Saddlecraft	San Giorgio	Saracen Horse Feeds	Sarm Hippique
WARWICKSHIRE TRAILERS, Solihull (YH14953)						●									
WAVERLEY EQUESTRIAN CTRE, Leamington Spa (YH15011)															
WILTSHIRE															
BEST BOOTS, Chippenham (YH01324)			●												
EQUIFOR, Marlborough (YH04746)															
HURDCOTT LIVERY STABLES, Salisbury (YH07311)															
SCATS COUNTRYSTORE, Devizes (YH12512)															
SCATS COUNTRYSTORE, Salisbury (YH12511)															
WORCESTERSHIRE															
BROMSGROVE SADDLERY, Bromsgrove (YH02026)		●								●					
COUNTRYWIDE, Worcester (YH03446)															
EQUIMIX, Stourport-on-Severn (YH04756)				●											
YORKSHIRE (EAST)															
PATRICK WILKINSON, Beverley (YH10825)															
YORKSHIRE (NORTH)															
HORSEFEEDSUK, Harrogate (YH07154)							●							●	
LANGTON HORSE WEAR, Northallerton (YH08416)															
RIDE-AWAY, York (YH11850)				●											
YORKSHIRE (SOUTH)															
DARKHORSE TINYTACK, Barnsley (YH03888)															
YORKSHIRE (WEST)															
BARDSEY MILLS, Otley (YH00927)							●								
CALDENE CLOTHING, Hebden Bridge (YH02430)	●										●				
DAYS PET SHOP, Bradford (YH03971)															
EQUITACK SADDLERY, Wakefield (YH04825)										●					
HILLAM TRAILERS, Cleckheaton (YH06837)															
MIDDLESTOWN SADDLERY, Wakefield (YH09540)															

by Country by County	Sergio Graso	Shayler	Shepherds	Shires	Silver Royal	Skin Rite	Small Tractors	Spillers	Stubben	Stylo	Tally Ho	Tedman	Thermatex	Thorowgood	Tiny Tack
WARWICKSHIRE TRAILERS, Solihull (YH14953)															
WAVERLEY EQUESTRIAN CTRE, Leamington Spa (YH15011)									●						
WILTSHIRE															
BEST BOOTS, Chippenham (YH01324)															
EQUIFOR, Marlborough (YH04746)												●			
HURDCOTT LIVERY STABLES, Salisbury (YH07311)				●											
SCATS COUNTRYSTORE, Devizes (YH12512)								●							
SCATS COUNTRYSTORE, Salisbury (YH12511)								●							
WORCESTERSHIRE															
BROMSGROVE SADDLERY, Bromsgrove (YH02026)				●										●	
COUNTRYWIDE, Worcester (YH03446)								●							
EQUIMIX, Stourport-on-Severn (YH04756)															
YORKSHIRE (EAST)															
PATRICK WILKINSON, Beverley (YH10825)									●						
YORKSHIRE (NORTH)															
HORSEFEEDSUK, Harrogate (YH07154)								●						●	
LANGTON HORSE WEAR, Northallerton (YH08416)				●											
RIDE-AWAY, York (YH11850)															
YORKSHIRE (SOUTH)															
DARKHORSE TINYTACK, Barnsley (YH03888)															●
YORKSHIRE (WEST)															
BARDSEY MILLS, Otley (YH00927)								●							
CALDENE CLOTHING, Hebden Bridge (YH02430)															
DAYS PET SHOP, Bradford (YH03971)															
EQUITACK SADDLERY, Wakefield (YH04825)									●					●	
HILLAM TRAILERS, Cleckheaton (YH06837)															
MIDDLESTOWN SADDLERY, Wakefield (YH09540)				●						●				●	

by Country by County	Toggi	Top Score	Topspec	Tredstep	Triple Crown	Weatherbeeta	Webster	Wendals	Wessex	Westgates	Winergy	Wintec	Woof	World Beater	Zilco
WARWICKSHIRE TRAILERS, Solihull (YH14953)															
WAVERLEY EQUESTRIAN CTRE, Leamington Spa (YH15011)															
WILTSHIRE															
BEST BOOTS, Chippenham (YH01324)															
EQUIFOR, Marlborough (YH04746)							●								●
HURDCOTT LIVERY STABLES, Salisbury (YH07311)															
SCATS COUNTRYSTORE, Devizes (YH12512)	●														
SCATS COUNTRYSTORE, Salisbury (YH12511)	●														
WORCESTERSHIRE															
BROMSGROVE SADDLERY, Bromsgrove (YH02026)										●					
COUNTRYWIDE, Worcester (YH03446)	●					●							●		
EQUIMIX, Stourport-on-Severn (YH04756)	●												●		
YORKSHIRE (EAST)															
PATRICK WILKINSON, Beverley (YH10825)	●					●									
YORKSHIRE (NORTH)															
HORSEFEEDSUK, Harrogate (YH07154)			●		●				●		●				
LANGTON HORSE WEAR, Northallerton (YH08416)	●					●							●		
RIDE-AWAY, York (YH11850)	●														
YORKSHIRE (SOUTH)															
DARKHORSE TINYTACK, Barnsley (YH03888)															
YORKSHIRE (WEST)															
BARDSEY MILLS, Otley (YH00927)			●		●										
CALDENE CLOTHING, Hebden Bridge (YH02430)															
DAYS PET SHOP, Bradford (YH03971)	●							●							
EQUITACK SADDLERY, Wakefield (YH04825)						●									
HILLAM TRAILERS, Cleckheaton (YH06837)															●
MIDDLESTOWN SADDLERY, Wakefield (YH09540)						●									

Brands Supplied
Q - Z

by Country by County	Quorn Sportswear	Rambo	Rectiligne	Regent	Renegade	Richardson Rice	Rockies	Rodney Powall	Ryder	Sabre	Saddle Master	Saddlecraft	San Giorgio	Saracen Horse Feeds	Sarm Hippique	Sergio Graso	Shayler	Shepherds	Shires	Silver Royal	Skin Rite	Small Tractors	Spillers	Stubben	Stylo	Tally Ho	Tedman	Thermatex	Thorowgood	Tiny Tack	Toggi	Top Score	Topspec	Tredstep	Triple Crown	Weatherbeeta	Webster	Wendals	Wessex	Westgates	Winergy	Wintec	Woof	World Beater	Zilco
IRELAND																																													
COUNTY DUBLIN																																													
COLEMANS OF SANDYFORD, Dublin (YH03166)												●												●										●		●						●			
COUNTY KERRY																																													
BRIDLES & BITS, Tralee (YH01893)				●																				●		●					●							●							
COUNTY KILKENNY																																													
EUROFARM, Kilkenny (YH04898)																			●																										
COUNTY WESTMEATH																																													
TALLY HO, Athlone (YH13838)																										●																			
NORTHERN IRELAND																																													
COUNTY DOWN																																													
HOLMESTEAD SADDLERY, Downpatrick (YH06981)																								●							●														
SCOTLAND																																													
ABERDEENSHIRE																																													
MILL OF URAS EQUESTRIAN, Stonehaven (YH09583)		●																																											
ARGYLL AND BUTE																																													
TACKLE & TACK, Oban (YH13818)																							●																						
WHAT EVERY HORSE WANTS, Helensburgh (YH15266)																									●											●									
AYRSHIRE (EAST)																																													
FERRIE, J & A, Newmilns (YH05169)																			●						●																				
AYRSHIRE (SOUTH)																																													
AYR TRAILER CTRE, Ayr (YH00701)						●																																							
DUMFRIES AND GALLOWAY																																													
DOUGLAS, JOHN L, Newton Stewart (YH04214)																						●																							
GEE GEE'S, Dumfries (YH05690)																									●				●							●							●		
ROBERT THORNE, Annan (YH11944)																							●																						
FALKIRK																																													
COUNTRY FEEDS LARBERT, Larbert (YH03408)																																						●							
GLASGOW (CITY OF)																																													
BUSBY EQUITATION CTRE, Busby (YH02302)																															●					●									
EVERYTHING EQUESTRIAN, Busby (YH04957)																															●					●									

www.hccyourhorse.com

Brands Supplied
Q - Z

by Country by County

by Country by County	Quorn Sportswear	Rambo	Rectiligne	Regent	Renegade	Richardson Rice	Rockies	Rodney Powall	Ryder	Sabre	Saddle Master	Saddlecraft	San Giorgio	Saracen Horse Feeds	Sarm Hippique	Sergio Graso	Shayler	Shepherds	Shires	Silver Royal	Skin Rite	Small Tractors	Spillers	Stubben	Stylo	Tally Ho	Tedman	Thermatex	Thorowgood	Tiny Tack	Toggi	Top Score	Topspec	Tredstep	Triple Crown	Weatherbeeta	Webster	Wendals	Wessex	Westgates	Winergy	Wintec	Woof	World Beater	Zilco
LOTHIAN (MID)																																													
R H MILLER, Dalkeith (YH11541)		●		●						●					●								●	●							●					●									
MORAY																																													
GREENFIELDS SADDLERY, Elgin (YH06085)																															●														
SHENVAL FARM, Ballindalloch (YH12709)						●																																							
PERTH AND KINROSS																																													
MCCASH'S, Perth (YH09326)																			●				●																						
SCOTTISH BORDERS																																													
A C BURN, Jedburgh (YH00022)																							●																						
WALES																																													
CARMARTHENSHIRE																																													
TACK EXCHANGE, Llanelli (YH13787)																													●																
THERMATEX, Cardigan (YH13986)																												●																	
FLINTSHIRE																																													
T F S, Buckley (YH13739)												●											●								●														
GWYNEDD																																													
BRONALLT, Caernarfon (YH02029)																			●						●				●							●									
PEMBROKESHIRE																																													
BOULSTON, Haverfordwest (YH01672)																															●														
PEMBROKESHIRE EQUESTRIAN, Haverfordwest (YH10919)												●																																	
POWYS																																													
LLWYNON, Brecon (YH08749)																								●					●							●				●		●	●		

SECTION 8A

A-Z of Manufacturers and Suppliers

An alphabetical listing of manufacturers and suppliers, with name, address, contact information and products supplied.

This section can be used to locate a manufacturer or supplier you already know the name of. Alternatively, it can be used to find out more information on a company you have located in Section 8B.

There is a key to identify whether the business is a manufacturer, supplier or both.

AERBORN EQUESTRIAN LTD

Pegasus House, 198 Sneinton Dale, Nottingham, **Nottinghamshire,** NG2 4HJ, **ENGLAND.**
(T) 0115 9505631 (F) 0115 9483273
(E) info@aerborn.u-net.com
(W) www.aerborn.co.uk
S
Products Supplied:
Rugs

AIR-O-WEAR

Aydon South Farm, Corbridge, **Northumberland,** NE45 5PL, **ENGLAND.**
(T) 01434 632816 (F) 01434 632849
(E) enquiries@airowear.co.uk
(W) www.airowear.co.uk
S
Products Supplied:
Protective Body Wear

ALBION SADDLEMAKERS CO LTD

Albion House, 55 Caldmore Road, Walsall, **Midlands (West),** WS1 3NR, **ENGLAND.**
(T) 01922 646210 (F) 01922 643777
(E) sales@albion-saddlemakers.co.uk
(W) www.albion-saddlemakers.co.uk
M
Products Supplied:
Saddles

ALLEN & PAGE LTD

Norfolk Mill, Shipdam, Thetford, **Norfolk,** IP25 7SD, **ENGLAND.**
(T) 01362 822900 (F) 01362 822910
(E) sales@allenandpage.com
(W) www.allenandpage.com
M
Products Supplied:
Feed & Buckets

ARMADILLO PRODUCTS LTD

18 Newton Tony, Salisbury, **Wiltshire,** SP4 0HA, **ENGLAND.**
(T) 01980 629796 (F) 01980 629250
(E) armadillo@horsetrading.co.uk
(W) www.armadillo-products.co.uk
M
Products Supplied:
Boot & Bandage

ATLANTIC EQUINE LTD

Calcutt House, Flecknoe, Rugby, **Warwickshire,** CV23 8AU, **ENGLAND.**
(T) 01788 891406 (F) 01788 890793
(E) sales@atlantic-equine.co.uk
(W) www.atlantic-equine.co.uk
M
Products Supplied:
Health Products

BADMINTON HORSE FEEDS

South St, Oakham, **Rutland,** LE15 6BG, **ENGLAND.**
(T) 01572 756091 (F) 01572 756021
(W) www.badmintonfeeds.co.uk
M
Products Supplied:
Feed & Buckets

BAILEYS HORSE FEEDS

Four Elms Mills, Bardfield Saling, Braintree, **Essex,** CM7 5EJ, **ENGLAND.**
(T) 01371 850247 (F) 01371 851269
(E) info@baileyshorsefeeds.co.uk
(W) www.baileyshorsefeeds.co.uk
M
Products Supplied:
Feed & Buckets

BERKELEY & CO LTD

Stafford Park 18, Telford, **Shropshire,** TF3 3AW, **ENGLAND.**
(T) 01952 290446 (F) 01952 290094
(E) adrian@berkeley.ltd.uk
(W) www.berkeley.ltd.uk
Contact: David Higgs
M
Products Supplied:
Bridlework

BEST BOOTS LTD

Nettleton, Chippenham, **Wiltshire,** SN14 7NS, **ENGLAND.**
(T) 01249 783530 (F) 01249 782058
(E) info@bestboots.co.uk
(W) www.bestboots.co.uk
S
Products Supplied:
Jackets
Riding Boots

BLACKMORE VALE SADDLERY

Four Winds, West Bourton, Gillingham, **Dorset,** SP8 5PE, **ENGLAND.**
(T) 01747 840741
(W) www.craft-fair.co.uk/BLACKMOREVALE.HTM
Contact: Sue Harvey
M
Products Supplied:
Bridlework

BRINDLE AND WHITE (RUG-TIDY)

Broad Carr, Strines, New Mills, **Derbyshire,** SK22 3BA, **ENGLAND.**
(T) 0161 427 0404 (F) 0161 427 0404
(E) info@rug-tidy.co.uk
(W) www.rug-tidy.co.uk
M
Products Supplied:
Rugs

CARR & DAY & MARTIN

Quay Equestrian Ltd, St Georges Quay, Lancaster, LA! 5QJ, **ENGLAND.**
(T) 0800 413136/ 01524 381821 (F) 01524 32080
(W) www.quayequestrian.com
M
Products Supplied:
Grooming

CHART STABLES LTD

Bridgend Farm, Hurtsford Lane, Charing, **Kent,** TN27 0ER, **ENGLAND.**
(T) 01233 713611/713778 (F) 01233 713598
(E) enquiries@chartstables.co.uk
(W) www.chartstables.co.uk
M S
Products Supplied:
Shelter & Stables

DAVIES & CO

Beatrice Rd, Kettering, **Northamptonshire,** NN16 9QS, **ENGLAND.**
(T) 01536 513456 (F) 01536 310080
(E) equimat@dinkie.com
(W) www.equimat.co.uk
M S
Products Supplied:
Shelter & Stables

DENGIE CROPS LIMITED

Heybridge Business Centre, 110 The Causeway, Maldon, **Essex,** CM9 4ND, **ENGLAND.**
(T) 0845 345 5115/ 01621 841188 (F) 01621 842111
(E) feeds@dengie.com
(W) www.dengie.com
M
Products Supplied:
Feed & Buckets

DODSON & HORRELL LIMITED

Ringstead Kettering, Northhampton, **Northamptonshire,** NN14 4BX, **ENGLAND.**
(T) 0870 4423322 (F) 01832 737303
(E) enquires@dosonandhorrell.com
(W) www.dodsonandhorrell.com
M
Products Supplied:
Feed & Buckets

EQUINE AMERICA

7 Lawson Hunt Business Park, Broadbridge Heath, **Sussex (West),** RH12 3JR, **ENGLAND.**
(T) 01403 255809/255511 (F) 01403 241083
(E) equine.america@virgin.net
(W) www.cortaflex.co.uk
M
Products Supplied:
Health Products

EQUINE PRODUCTS UK LTD

22 Riverside Court, Newburn Haugh Ind Est, Newcastle Upon Tyne, **Tyne and Wear,** NE15 8SG, **ENGLAND.**
(T) 0191 264 5536 (F) 0191 264 0487
(E) info@equine-camel.co.uk
(W) www.equine-camel.co.uk
M
Products Supplied:
Feed & Buckets

ESPRO LTD

Espro House, Clayton St, Wigan, **Lancashire,** WN3 4DA, **ENGLAND.**
(T) 01942 321999 (F) 01942 231188
(E) sales@espro.co.uk
(W) www.espro.co.uk
M S
Products Supplied:
Bridlework
Feed & Buckets
Girths
Grooming
Road Safety Wear
Saddles

FAL TEXTILE INDUSTRIES LTD

Unit12, Ennerdale Rd, Blyth, **Northumberland,** NE24 4RT, **ENGLAND.**
(T) 01670 357300 (F) 01670 357301
(E) sales@falpro.com
(W) www.falpro.com
M
Products Supplied:
Rugs

FEEDMARK

Church Farm, St Cross, Harleston, **Suffolk,** IP20 0NY, **ENGLAND.**
(T) 01986 782368 (F) 01986 782466
(E) ukoffice@feedmark.com
(W) www.feedmark.com
M
Products Supplied:
Feed & Buckets

FIELDGUARD LTD

Norley Farm, Horsham Rd, Cranleigh, **Surrey,** GU6 8EH, **ENGLAND.**
(T) 01483 275182 (F) 01483 275341
(E) info@fieldguard.com
(W) www.fieldguard.com
M
Products Supplied:
Fences

FRANK BAINES SADDLERY

Northcote St, Walsall, **Midlands (West),** WS2 8BQ, **ENGLAND.**
(T) 01922 640847 (F) 01922 616475
(E) enquiries@frankbaines-saddlery.com
(W) www.frankbaines-saddlery.com
M
Products Supplied:
Saddles

FURNASIA LTD
Kestrel, Burwash, **Sussex (East),** TN19 7JP, **ENGLAND.**
(T) 01435 883345 **(F)** 01435 883642
(E) furnasia@dialpipex.com
(W) www.greenguard.co.uk
M S
Products Supplied:
Feed & Buckets

GORRINGE SPORTSWEAR LTD
Arclive House, 2 Short St, Walsall, **Midlands (West),** WS2 9EB, **ENGLAND.**
(T) 01922 628131/2 **(F)** 01922 724336
(E) gorringeridingwear@btinternet.com
(W) www.gorringe.com
M
Products Supplied:
Jodhpurs
Show Jackets

GRIFFIN NUU MED
Pipers Farm, Ashcott, **Somerset,** TA7 9QN, **ENGLAND.**
(T) 01458 210324 **(F)** 01458 210396
(E) GriffinNuumed@numnah.co.uk
(W) www.numnah.co.uk
M
Products Supplied:
Girths
Grooming
Saddlecloths & Numnahs

GRO-WELL FEEDS LIMITED
Hercules Way, Bowerhill, Melksham, **Wiltshire,** SN12 6TS, **ENGLAND.**
(T) 01225 708482
(W) www.equilibra.co.uk
M
Products Supplied:
Feed & Buckets

H W DABBS SADDLEMAKERS LTD
William House, Marsh Lane, Walsall, **Midlands (West),** WS2 9LN, **ENGLAND.**
(T) 01922 612238 **(F)** 01922 647691
(E) sales@saddlery.co.uk
(W) www.saddlery.co.uk
M
Products Supplied:
Saddles

HORACE BATTEN (BOOTMAKER) LTD
2 Coton Rd, Ravensthorpe, **Northamptonshire,** NN6 8EG, **ENGLAND.**
(T) 01858 410069 **(F)** 01858 410069
(E) sales@horacebatten.co.uk
(W) www.horacebatten.co.uk
M
Products Supplied:
Jodhpur Boots
Riding Boots

HORSEWARE IRELAND
Quay St, Dundalk, **County Louth, IRELAND.**
(T) 042 9389000 **(F)** 042 9337671
(E) info@horseware.com
(W) www.horseware.com
M S
Products Supplied:
Rugs

J W WILKINSON & CO
Dockray Hall Rd, Kendal, **Cumbria,** LA9 4QY, **ENGLAND.**
(T) 01539 720013 **(F)** 01539 729119
(E) sales@kingshead-saddlery.co.uk
(W) www.kingshead-saddlery.co.uk
M S
Products Supplied:
Rugs

JACK ELLIS BODY PROTECTION
Marshall House, West St, Leicester, **Leicestershire,** LE3 8DT, **ENGLAND.**
(T) 0116 232 0022 **(F)** 0116 232 0032
(E) sales@jackellis.co.uk
(W) www.jackellis.co.uk
M
Products Supplied:
Protective Body Wear

JAMES LOCK & CO LTD
6 St James's St, London, **London (Greater),** SW1A 1EF, **ENGLAND.**
(T) 0207 9308874 / 0207 9305849 **(F)** 0207 9761908
(E) info@lockhatters.co.uk
(W) www.lockhatters.co.uk
M
Products Supplied:
Hats & Skulls

LENRYS ASSOCIATES LIMITED
Lenrys House, Maurice Gaymer Rd, Attleborough, **Norfolk,** NR17 2QZ, **ENGLAND.**
(T) 01953 457452
(E) lenrys.associates@netcom.co.uk
(W) www.lenrys.co.uk
M
Products Supplied:
Health Products

LISTER SHEARING EQUIPMENT LIMITED
Long St, Dursley, **Gloucestershire,** GL11 4HR, **ENGLAND.**
(T) 01453 544831/2/3 **(F)** 01453 544831
(E) info@lister-shearing.co.uk
(W) www.lister-shearing.co.uk
M S
Products Supplied:
Grooming

LOVESON
Station Rd, Irthlingborough, **Northamptonshire,** NN9 5QE, **ENGLAND.**
(T) 01933 652652 **(F)** 01933 650454
(E) thl@loveson.co.uk
(W) www.loveson.co.uk
M
Products Supplied:
Chaps
Gloves & Accessories
Jodhpur Boots
Jodhpurs
Rugs

MATCHMAKERS INTERNATIONAL LTD
Park View Mills, Wibsey Park Avenue, Bradford, **Yorkshire (West),** BD6 3SR, **ENGLAND.**
(T) 01274 711101 **(F)** 01274 711030
(W) www.masta.co.uk
M
Products Supplied:
Rugs

NATURAL ANIMAL FEEDS
High House, Penrhos, Raglan, **Monmouthshire,** NP15 2DJ, **WALES.**
(T) 01600 780256 **(F)** 01600 780536
(E) naf@nutri.org
(W) www.naf-uk.com
M
Products Supplied:
Feed & Buckets

NEW EQUINE WEAR
P O Box 823, Malmesbury, **Wiltshire,** SN16 0RT, **ENGLAND.**
(T) 07000 639266 **(F)** 07000 785020
(E) sales@newequinewear.co.uk
(W) www.newequinewear.co.uk
M
Products Supplied:
Boot & Bandage

OLD MILL WHIPS
Unit 9 C.E.A, 9 Meadowbank Rd, Carrickfergus, **County Antrim,** BT38 9, **IRELAND.**
(T) 028 9336 8599 **(F)** 028 9335 3111
(E) info@ridingwhips.com
(W) www.ridingwhips.com
M
Products Supplied:
Whips

PATEY (LONDON) LTD
1 Amelia St, London, **London (Greater),** SE17 3PY, **ENGLAND.**
(T) 020 7703 6528
(E) enquiries@pateyhats.co.uk
(W) www.pateyhats.co.uk
M
Products Supplied:
Hats & Skulls

PRETTY PONIES
Unit 9, The Sidings Industrial Est, Whalley, **Lancashire,** BB7 9SE, **ENGLAND.**
(T) 01254 822044
(E) clfanc@aol.com
(W) www.prettyponies.co.uk
M S
Products Supplied:
Gloves & Accessories
Jackets

PROLITE LTD
The Saddlery, Fryers Rd, Walsall, **Midlands (West),** WS3 2XJ, **ENGLAND.**
(T) 01922 711676 **(F)** 01922 711654
(E) enquiries@prolitepads.com
(W) www.prolite-equestrian.com
M
Products Supplied:
Rugs
Saddlecloths & Numnahs

QUALTEX
Bond Street Works, Off Hanging Lane, Hebden Bridge, **Yorkshire (West),** HX7 7OE, **ENGLAND.**
(T) 01422 844347 **(F)** 01422 845663
(E) sales@qualtex.co.uk
(W) www.qualtex.co.uk
M
Products Supplied:
Rugs
Saddlecloths & Numnahs

RADDERY EQUINE LTD
Raddery Park, Raddery Fortrose, Fortrose, **Highlands,** IV10 8SN, **SCOTLAND.**
(T) 01381 620615 **(F)** 01381 620615
(E) info@raddery.co.uk
(W) www.radderyequine.co.uk
M
Products Supplied:
Gloves & Accessories
Hats & Skulls

ROBINSON ANIMAL HEALTHCARE
Waterside, Goyt Side Road, Chesterfield, **Derbyshire,** S40 2YF, **ENGLAND.**
(T) 01246 505383/ 505450 **(F)** 01246 220671
(W) www.robinsoncare.com
S
Products Supplied:
Health Products

SABRE LEATHER COMPANY LTD
19 - 21 Sandwell St, Walsall, **Midlands (West),** WS1 3DR, **ENGLAND.**
(T) 01922 629925 **(F)** 01922 723463
(E) sales@sabreleather.co.uk
(W) www.sabreleather.co.uk
M
Products Supplied:
Boot & Bandage
Bridlework

SHIRES EQUESTRIAN PRODUCTS
15 Southern Avenue, Leominster, **Herefordshire,** HR6 0QF, **ENGLAND.**
(T) 01568 613600 **(F)** 01568 613599
(E) sales@shiresequestrian.co.uk
(W) www.shires-equestrian.co.uk
S
Products Supplied:
Jodhpur Boots

SPILLERS SPECIALITY FEEDS LTD
Old Wolverton Rd, Milton Keynes, **Buckinghamshire,** MK12 5PZ, **ENGLAND.**
(T) 01908 222888 **(F)** 01908 222800
(E) helpline@spillers-feeds.com
(W) www.spillers-feeds.com
M
Products Supplied:
Feed & Buckets

STUBBEN UK
1 & 2 Oakley Hay Lodge, Great Folds Rd, Northampton, **Northamptonshire,** NN18 9AS, **ENGLAND.**
(T) 01536 744554 **(F)** 01536 744664
(W) www.stuebben.com
M
Products Supplied:
Bridlework
Grooming
Riding Boots
Saddles

TALLY HO (UK) LTD
15 Kingsley Park, Whitchurch, **Hampshire,** RG28 7HA, **ENGLAND.**
(T) 01256 892815 **(F)** 01256 892815
(E) tallyho@aol.com
(W) www.tallyho.ie
M
Products Supplied:
Chaps
Jodhpurs

THE SMD GROUP LTD
Park Rd, Faringdon, **Oxfordshire,** SN7 8LA, **ENGLAND.**
(T) 01367 242818/0845 600 2701 **(F)** 01367 242819
(E) hac-tac@smdgroup.co.uk
(W) www.hac-tac.co.uk
M
Products Supplied:
Gloves & Accessories
Jodhpurs

THERMATEX MADE IN WALES (UK)
27 - 30 Pentwood Est, Cardigan, **Ceredigion,** SA43 3AD, **ENGLAND.**
(T) 01239 614648 **(F)** 01239 621234
(E) info@thermatex.co.uk
(W) www.thermatex.co.uk
M
Products Supplied:
Rugs

THOROWGOOD LTD
The Saddlery, Fryers Rd, Walsall, **Midlands (West),** WS3 2XJ, **ENGLAND.**
(T) 01922 711676 **(F)** 01922 711654
(E) enquiries@thorowgood.co.uk
(W) www.thorowgood.com
M
Products Supplied:
Saddles

TOPSPEC EQUINE LTD
Studley House, Baddiley, Nantwich, **Cheshire,** CW5 8PY, **ENGLAND.**
(T) 01270 624095
(E) info@topspec.com
(W) www.topspec.com
M
Products Supplied:
Feed & Buckets

TROJAN EQUESTRIAN
Newton-of-Conmay, Fraserburgh, **Aberdeenshire,** AB43 8UU, **SCOTLAND.**
(T) 01346 532971 **(F)** 01346 532961
(E) trojan@globalnet.co.uk
(W) www.users.globalnet.co.uk/~trojaneq/page2.html
M
Products Supplied:
Chaps
Rugs

VALE BROTHERS LIMITED
Long St, Walsall, **Midlands (West),** WS2 9OG, **ENGLAND.**
(T) 01922 624363 **(F)** 01922 720994
(W) www.valebrothers.co.uk
M
Products Supplied:
Grooming

WEATHERBEETA LTD
7 Riverside, Tramway Est, Banbury, **Oxfordshire,** OX16 5TU, **ENGLAND.**
(T) 01295 268123
(E) sales@weatherbeeta.com
(W) www.weatherbeeta.co.uk
Contact: Michael Mullavey
M
Products Supplied:
Jodhpur Boots
Rugs

WHITAKERS EQUESTRIAN SERVICES LTD
Unit 3, Hickers Way, Aylesbury, **Buckinghamshire,** HP18 9RW, **ENGLAND.**
(T) 01844 202151 **(F)** 01844 202152
(W) www.polyjumps.com
M
Products Supplied:
Jumps & Poles

W'UNDERWEAR
9 Station Rd, Morcott, Oakham, **Rutland,** LE15 9DX, **ENGLAND.**
(T) 01572 747595 **(F)** 01572 747595
(E) roger@wunderwear.co.uk
(W) www.insite-online.com/wunderwear/index.htm
M **S**
Products Supplied:
Protective Body Wear

SECTION 8B

A-Z Product Profile

An alphabetical listing of equestrian products, categorised under broad product headings. Contains details of the Recommended Retail Price, the manufacturer and/or supplier and a brief description of the product.

Once you have found the name of the manufacturer and/or supplier of the product you require, you can then refer back to Section 8A where their contact details will be listed.

BITS

ELICO PINCHLESS - FULL CHEEK EGGBUTT
Sizes available are 4 1/2" - 6".
RRP: £21.75
Supplier: B Jenkinson & Sons

ELICO PINCHLESS DRESSAGE EGGBUTT
Sizes available are 4", 4 1/2", 5".
RRP: £18.35
Supplier: B Jenkinson & Sons

ELICO PINCHLESS FRENCH CONTINETAL GAG
Sizes available are 4 1/2" - 6".
RRP: £24.50
Supplier: B Jenkinson & Sons

ELICO PINCHLESS JOINTED EGGBUTT
Sizes available 4" - 6".
RRP: £19.75
Supplier: B Jenkinson & Sons

ELICO PINCHLESS JOINTED PELHAM
Sizes available are 4 1/2" - 6".
RRP: £27.99
Supplier: B Jenkinson & Sons

BOOT & BANDAGE

ARMADILLO TENDON BOOTS
For the protection of the tendon, they also have tendon strips and fetlock cups incorporated.
RRP: £46.95
Manufacturer: Armadillo Products Ltd

N.E.W MAGNET THERAPY HOOF BOOT
Accelerates healing and condition in a natural way. Offers maximum comfort and protection and is easy to wash and fit. RRP quoted is for a small boot. Medium & large boots are £50.00.
RRP: £45.00
Manufacturer: New Equine Wear

SABRE OPEN FRONT TENDON BOOT
Jumping boot with tendon support. Brass roller and buckles on bridle butt straps.
RRP: £53.53
Manufacturer: Sabre Leather Company Ltd

BRIDLEWORK

BERKELEY BUCKLES
Make buckles for all equestrian needs, ie: girth buckles, head collar buckles etc.
Manufacturer: Berkeley & Co Ltd

BLACKMORE VALE WEYMOUTH BRIDLE
Hand made bridle with brass or stainless steel buckles and fittings.
Manufacturer: Blackmore Vale Saddlery

ESPRO FUR FABRIC NOSEBAND SLEEVE
Fastens easily with velcro, helps to prevent rubbing.
RRP: £0.99
Manufacturer: Espro Ltd
Supplier: Espro Ltd

SABRE BRAIDED FLASH SNAFFLE
Emboised head and cheeks, braided detail on the brow and cavesson. RRP quoted is based on full size, 5/8ths with metallic motif.
RRP: £85.00
Manufacturer: Sabre Leather Company Ltd

STUBBEN THOUSAND RANGE BRIDLE
Leather bridle with rubber reins. One of a range of eighteen bridles made by Stubben.
RRP: £130.00
Manufacturer: Stubben UK

CHAPS

LOVESON STUDLEY SUEDE CHAPS
Made from quality suede, with elastic and zip fastening.
RRP: £19.95
Manufacturer: Loveson

TALLY HO FULL CHAPS
Full suede and wax chaps, fully lined. Available in various colours.
Manufacturer: Tally Ho (Uk) Ltd

TALLY HO NAPPA PRO CHAPS
Leather with a suede patch, spur rest patch and plain toe. Available in black and brown.
Manufacturer: Tally Ho (Uk) Ltd

TALLY HO STANDARD HALF CHAPS
Suede with elasticated panels to ensure a good fit and prevent slipping.
Manufacturer: Tally Ho (Uk) Ltd

TROJAN FULL LEATHER CHAPS
Leather made to measure, also available in suede.
Manufacturer: Trojan Equestrian

FEED & BUCKETS

ALLEN & PAGE SLIM & HEALTHY
The slim & healthy range contains linseed & soya oils. It can help with skin and coat condition. It is low in starch and high in fibre, therefore, it can help to reduce digestive upsets.
RRP: £6.80
Manufacturer: Allen & Page Ltd

BADMINTON UNIVERSAL WORKING MIX
Universal Working Mix is fully balanced to meet the needs of a working horse. It provides highly digestible energy in a fast release form. Available in 20kg buckets.
RRP: £6.66
Manufacturer: Badminton Horse Feeds

BAILEYS ECONOMY CUBES
An excellent high fibre, low energy, non-heating feed, available in 20kg bags.
RRP: £4.30
Manufacturer: Baileys Horse Feeds

BAILEYS VITAMIN MINERAL SUPPLEMENT
A top quality, high specification, broad-spectrum vitamin and mineral supplement, available in 3kg buckets.
RRP: £7.50
Manufacturer: Baileys Horse Feeds

DENGIE ALFA EASY
This is the lightest energy feed of the Dengie range, ideal for light exercise. Available in 18kg bags.
RRP: £6.70
Manufacturer: Dengie Crops Limited

DENGIE ALFA EXTRA
A medium energy feed for improving condition of the coat. Available in 18kg bags.
RRP: £6.70
Manufacturer: Dengie Crops Limited

DODSON & HORRELL PASTURE MIX
Pasture Mix is an attractive muesli of micronised cereal and grass fibre pellets mixed in unique Dobson & Horrell syrup. Available in 20kg bags.
RRP: £6.50
Manufacturer: Dodson & Horrell Limited

DUBLIN HORSE HAGE NET
Available in a range of sizes and colours.
RRP: £3.99
Supplier: Ride-Away

EQUILIBRA FEED
Enables horse and ponies to thrive on forage based diet without the need of supplements. Highly digestable source of energy. Available in 20kg bags.
RRP: £30.50
Manufacturer: Gro-Well Feeds Limited

EQUINE PRODUCTS
EQUINE PRODUCTS PREMIER E SUPPLEMENT
Premier E is a high performance supplement to aid fertility and help build muscles. Available in 1.5kg tubs.
RRP: £14.80
Manufacturer: Equine Products UK Ltd

ESPRO BUCKET COVER
Made from PU coated nylon, fully elasticated to fit securley around the bucket brim.
RRP: £2.25
Manufacturer: Espro Ltd
Supplier: Espro Ltd

FEEDMARK CLARITY RESPIRATORY SUPPLEMENT
Clarity helps to maintain respiratory health. RRP quoted is for the 2kg buckets. Also available in 4kg and 8kg tubs at RRP £41.95 and £77.95 respectively.
RRP: £22.95
Manufacturer: Feedmark

FEEDMARK FIBRE CHOP
Ideal for horses and ponies as a sole forage or hay replacer. Available in 20kg bags.
RRP: £6.99
Manufacturer: Feedmark

FEEDMARK HARDY HOOF
Hardy Hoof is a feed supplement full of nutrients to produce healthy hooves. RRP quoted is for a 3kg bag.
RRP: £54.95
Manufacturer: Feedmark

FEEDMARK LOW ENERGY CUBES
High in fibre and low in starch, contains no oats, barley, maize or molasses. Ideal for resting or light working horses and ponies. Available in 20kg bags.
RRP: £5.99
Manufacturer: Feedmark

GREENGUARD GRAZING MASK
A small muzzle type attachment for head collars. Designed with slots that restrict grazing to help with excess weight, crib biting, wood chewing and bandage biting.
RRP: £35.99
Manufacturer: Furnasia Ltd
Supplier: Furnasia Ltd

LIVERY 14LT BUCKET AND LID
Bucket and lid, with the capacity of 14 litres.
RRP: £2.95
Supplier: Ride-Away

NAF MUD GARD
Mud Gard supports healthy skin and has a unique nutritional approach to tackle mud reaction. It also provides nutrients which target skin damage and helps to repair skin tissue.
RRP: £29.15
Manufacturer: Natural Animal Feeds

SPILLERS COOL MIX WITH BISCUITS
Cool Mix is a blend of nutrients concentrated in a diamond shape biscuit. It helps to improve and support the health of the horse. Available in 20kg bags.
RRP: £6.95
Manufacturer: Spillers Speciality Feeds Ltd

TOPSPEC TOPSPEC FEED BALANCER
TopSpec feed balancer is a nutrient-rich feed for horses with high quality protein. This is a non heating source of energy.
RRP: £29.50
Manufacturer: TopSpec Equine Ltd

WEATHERBEETA FEED SCOOP
Plastic feed scoop.
RRP: £2.50
Supplier: Ride-Away

FENCES

FIELDGUARD HORSE FENCING
Safe for both horses and stallions. RRP quoted is per metre for a four acre field.
RRP: £1.45
Manufacturer: Fieldguard Ltd

GIRTHS

AERBORN ELASTIC END GIRTH
The elastic girth gives up to 8% stretch which allows the girth to adapt, according to the horses activity. Available in a range of sizes 34 - 56, also in a range of colours.
RRP: £15.55
Supplier: Ride-Away

ESPRO FUR FABRIC GIRTH SLEEVE
30" long double thickness synthetic fleece designed to fit any girth, helps to prevent rubbing.
RRP: £1.75
Manufacturer: Espro Ltd
Supplier: Espro Ltd

NUUMED WOOL GIRTH SLEEVE
100% Wool. Available in two lengths 28" and 40", RRP quoted is for 28" girth, the 40" RRP is £21.00.
RRP: £16.95
Manufacturer: Griffin Nuu Med

THOROWGOOD DRESSAGE GIRTH
The Maxam girth is soft and breathable with roller buckles to make the adjustments easy and to extend the life of the girth.
RRP: £11.95
Supplier: Ride-Away

GLOVES & ACCESSORIES

HAC TAC DRESSAGE GLOVES
Suede and knitted back gloves with wrist protection.
RRP: £13.00
Manufacturer: The SMD Group Ltd

LOVESON LEATHER GLOVES
Leather with crochet cotton back and elasticated horseshoe design. Sizes available XS, S, M & L
RRP: £7.95
Manufacturer: Loveson

PRETTY PONIES VELCRO-WRIST GLOVES
Velcro-wrist gloves available for men, ladies and children in a variety of colours. RRP quoted is for adult sizes, children's gloves are £23.99.
RRP: £28.99
Manufacturer: Pretty Ponies

RADDERY GLOVES WOOF-WEAR
The gloves have neoprene backs and suedette palms. Keep hands warm with out restricting movement.
RRP: £16.98
Manufacturer: Raddery Equine Ltd

GROOMING

CARR & DAY & MARTIN VANNER PRESTS TRADITIONAL HOOF OIL
Vanner Prests Traditional Hoof Oil, a particularly effective remedy for dry hooves. Quickly absorbed and with a special blend of vegetable oil compounds, it protects and nourishes hooves, applied by brush. Available in 500ml, 1l, at £6.99 and 5l, at £23.99.
RRP: £3.85
Manufacturer: Carr & Day & Martin

DUBLIN DELUXE GROOMING KIT
Available in 3 colours. Contains small body brush, dandy brush, sponge, round plastic brush, kite scraper, mane comb with a rubber handle and a deluxe hoof pick.
RRP: £10.99
Supplier: Ride-Away

DUBLIN GROOMING BOX
Tough plastic grooming box with a hinged lid. 12 litre capacity. Available in 4 colours.
RRP: £14.95
Supplier: Ride-Away

ELICO SLICKA RAKE
A massaging and grooming brush. It has a curved head with deep penetrating, dual action teeth which groom through the outer coat, and open up the inner coat. Effective on wet or dry coats.
RRP: £2.99
Supplier: B Jenkinson & Sons

ESPRO FUR FABRIC GROOMING BUFFER
Made with a polycotton backing, used to remove the dust from a horses coat.
RRP: £3.75
Manufacturer: Espro Ltd

ESPRO TIDY TRAY COVER
PU coated nylon, elasticated and shaped to fit onto a standard size tidy tray.
RRP: £2.25
Manufacturer: Espro Ltd
Supplier: Espro Ltd

LISTER METEOR TRIMMING CLIPPER
Meteor is a small and stylish rechargable trimming clipper with easy to use "snap-on" blades. Ideal for the clipping of heads, faces and other sensitive areas. The charge lasts approx 45 minutes, it also comes with a set of 4 blades.
RRP: £63.45
Manufacturer: Lister Shearing Equipment Limited
Supplier: Lister Shearing Equipment Limited

LISTER NEON CLIPPERS
This all-mains, full-width clipper is incredibly light and easy to use with an advanced triangulated grip.
RRP: £269.66
Manufacturer: Lister Shearing Equipment Limited
Supplier: Lister Shearing Equipment Limited

NUUMED GROOMING MITT
100% wool, double sided grooming mitt.
RRP: £11.50
Manufacturer: Griffin Nuu Med

STUBBEN BODY BRUSHES
Standard Body Brush, wooden backed with pig bristles. Also available in a leather backed version.
RRP: £12.00
Manufacturer: Stubben UK

VALE BROTHERS BODY BRUSH 2H
Wooden backed, pure horse hair brush, densely filled to add a shine to the horses coat.
RRP: £8.99
Manufacturer: Vale Brothers Limited

WEATHERBEETA ALUMINIUM MANE COMB
RRP: £0.50
Supplier: Ride-Away

HATS & SKULLS

JAMES LOCK DRESAGE HAT
Low crown hat, available in black or navy.
RRP: £200.00
Manufacturer: James Lock & Co Ltd

JAMES LOCK HICKSTEAD RIDING HAT
BSI velvet riding hat with leather harness. Available in navy or black velvet with a flesh coloured strap.
RRP: £150.00
Manufacturer: James Lock & Co Ltd

JAMES LOCK RIDING TOP HAT
Reinforced heavy weight hat with quilted inside pads. Handmade to measure.
RRP: £700.00
Manufacturer: James Lock & Co Ltd

PATEY STANDARD RIDING HAT
Made to measure riding hats, for hunting, dressage and showing. Finished in velvet, available in a range of four styles and five colours.
RRP: £295.00
Manufacturer: Patey (London) Ltd

RADDERY TROXEL RIDING HELMET
Troxel helmets are of approved quality standard by BERA, BHS, SERC. The helmet also comes with a visor as an extra. Cost for the visor is £6.80.
RRP: £28.04
Manufacturer: Raddery Equine Ltd

HEALTH PRODUCTS

CORTAFLEX CORTAFLEX SOLUTION
Helps to maintain and promote healthy cartilage in horses. Available in 946ml, 3.8l and 19l bottles. The RRP quoted is for the 946ml bottle.
RRP: £53.99
Manufacturer: Equine America

EQUILOX HOOF REPAIR & RECONSTRUCTION SYSTEM
Manufacturer: Atlantic Equine Ltd

HORSEWISE ANTISEPTIC SPRAY
Formulated with 100% tea tree oil, to aid the healing of cuts and bites. RRP quoted is for 3,785ml spray
RRP: £30.88
Manufacturer: Lenrys Associates Limited

ROBINSON CARE ANIMALINTEX POULTICE
Impregnated multi-layered poultice and wound dressing for the treatment of equine and canine wounds. Absorbent dressings can be used as either a hot poultice, a cold poultice to reduce inflammation, or a dry dressing to stem bleeding and absorb fluids.
RRP: £4.80
Manufacturer: Robinson Animal Healthcare
Supplier: Robinson Animal Healthcare

JACKETS

LE CHAMEAU FORET JACKET
Kotkor coated jacket with a checked lining, 4 outer pockets and 1 security pocket. Mulitple use snap fastening back pocket.
RRP: £165.00
Manufacturer: Best Boots Ltd
Supplier: Best Boots Ltd

PRETTY PONIES VERONIQUE JACKET
Mens heavyweight wool, navy cutaway jacket, with velvet collar, pocket trims and fox buttons. Also available for ladies and children.
RRP: £230.00
Manufacturer: Pretty Ponies

JODHPUR BOOTS

HORACE BATTEN FIELD BOOT
Brown leather boots with seven eyelet laced instep which prevents the boot slipping when dismounting. RRP is a guide, boots can be made to personal specifications.
RRP: £600.00
Manufacturer: Horace Batten (Bootmaker) Ltd

LOVESON GROSVENOR JODHPUR BOOT
Leather upper square toe boot, available in tan and black. Available in sizes 11 - 11, RRP quoted for sizes 3.5 - 11.
RRP: £37.50
Manufacturer: Loveson

SHIRES WOODSTOCK JODHPUR BOOTS
Black leather jodhpur boots available in sizes 31 - 41, also available in brown.
RRP: £21.00
Manufacturer: Shires Equestrian Products
Supplier: Shires Equestrian Products

WEATHERBEETA DUBLIN MYERS JODHPUR BOOT
Leather upper with a non slip sole and elastic sides. RRP quoted is for adult size boots, childrens boots are £19.95.
RRP: £29.99
Manufacturer: Weatherbeeta Ltd

JODHPURS

GORRINGE GORRINGE JODHPUR
The Gorringe range are hard wearing and durable and cater for all riders.
RRP: £79.95
Manufacturer: Gorringe Sportswear Ltd

GORRINGE PRO SEAT JODHPURS
Jodhpurs and breeches with a synthetic grip seat panel and a zip pocket. Available for ladies and children.
Manufacturer: Gorringe Sportswear Ltd

HAC TAC ORIGINAL LADIES JODPURS
Ladies jodhpurs and breeches made for comfort, with suede knee patches. Fully washable.
RRP: £45.00
Manufacturer: The SMD Group Ltd

LOVESON RUSTLER JODHPUR BOOTS - RODEO
Leather upper with a soft padded collar and pvc foot. Sizes available 3 - 11.
RRP: £24.95
Manufacturer: Loveson

TALLY HO AACHEN BREECHES
Mens breeches, fitted with pleats and slant pockets.
Manufacturer: Tally Ho (Uk) Ltd

TALLY HO NOVA PRIX JODHPURS
Ladies Jodhpurs with a synthetic leather patch, and zip fob pocket.
Manufacturer: Tally Ho (Uk) Ltd

TALLY HO TRIGGA JODHPURS
Drawstring waist jodhpurs with mock fly and stud. Available in various colours.
Manufacturer: Tally Ho (Uk) Ltd

JUMPS & POLES

RUSTIC POLES, UPRIGHTS & WINGS
Supply poles, uprights, wings and many more. They cater for novice to advanced, designed with safety for both horse and rider in mind. They are maintenance free, rot proof, strong and durable. Prices vary from £50.00 - £200.00
Manufacturer: Whitakers Equestrian Services Ltd

PROTECTIVE BODY WEAR

AIR-O-WEAR REIVER 2000
Comfortable to wear, lightwear and flexible. Easy to adjust at the waist, covers are removable for washing.
Manufacturer: Air-O-Wear
Supplier: Air-O-Wear

AIR-O-WEAR ZIPPA PLUS
The body protector is comfortable to wear, light weight and flexible. The Zippa range is for both adults and juniors.
RRP: £129.95
Manufacturer: Air-O-Wear
Supplier: Air-O-Wear

JACK ELLIS EURO VEST PROTECTOR
The RRP quoted is the bottom of the scale, prices vary according to level (thickness) and size.
RRP: £45.00
Manufacturer: Jack Ellis Body Protection

WUNDERWEAR W'UNDERCOVER
W'undercover, protects the vunrable shoulder area from rubbing. RRP quoted is for the largest sized cover.
RRP: £70.50
Manufacturer: W'underwear
Supplier: W'underwear

RIDING BOOTS

HORACE BATTEN BOX CALF RIDING BOOT
Made in the traditional GOODYEAR WELTED way. Hand stitched uppers and innersoles. All boots have leather uppers, soles, insoles, heels and inside linings. RRP is a guide, boots can be made to personal specifications.
RRP: £450.00
Manufacturer: Horace Batten (Bootmaker) Ltd

LE CHAMEAU BELVOIR RIDING BOOTS
Made of natural rubber, are available in 7 calf fittings. Sizes available 35 - 47, in black. RRP quoted is for cotton lined boots.
RRP: £84.95
Manufacturer: Stubben UK

LE CHAMEAU NEWMARKET KHAKI RIDING BOOT
Tan leather and khaki canvas, rear fastening boots. Sizes available 35 - 46, also available in 4 different calf fittings.
RRP: £164.95
Manufacturer: Best Boots Ltd
Supplier: Best Boots Ltd

ROAD SAFETY WEAR

ESPRO FLUORESCENT BRUSHING BOOTS
Made from fluorescent lime neoprene, with a pvc padded striking pad. Velcro straps to hold the boots in place, with additional reflective tape for extra visability.
RRP: £17.95
Manufacturer: Espro Ltd

ESPRO FLUORESCENT HAT COVER
Features a reflective strip on the back for maximum day and night visability, elasticated for easy fit.
RRP: £3.95
Manufacturer: Espro Ltd
Supplier: Espro Ltd

ESPRO FLUORESCENT TAIL COVER
Hi-visability double thickness tail guard, fastens around the tail with velcro. Fits to the Espro exercise sheet also has a full length reflective tape, enhances day and night time visability.
RRP: £4.35
Manufacturer: Espro Ltd
Supplier: Espro Ltd

ESPRO LTD SAM BROWNE BELT
Traditional style Sam Browne with fluorescent waistband and shoulder strap.
RRP: £5.95
Manufacturer: Espro Ltd
Supplier: Espro Ltd

ESPRO REFLECTIVE BODY WARMER
Ideal for riding in poor conditions. Has a 4oz filling and cotton lining which will keep you warm while the fluorescent outer and reflective strips ensure maximum night visability.
RRP: £26.95
Manufacturer: Espro Ltd
Supplier: Espro Ltd

ESPRO REFLECTIVE TABARD
'Caution Horse & Rider' hi-visability polyester with reflective strips, front and back. Day and night visability.
RRP: £6.45
Manufacturer: Espro Ltd
Supplier: Espro Ltd

ESPRO WRAP ROUND EXERCISE SHEET.
Made from Yellow polyester, covers riders legs to ensure much higher visability. Also includes reflective tape on both sides.
RRP: £15.95
Manufacturer: Espro Ltd
Supplier: Espro Ltd

RUGS

AERBORN PEGASUS STABLE RUG
The Pegasus is a deep fitting stable rug, with adjustable front fastenings and leg straps.
RRP: £39.99
Manufacturer: Aerborn Equestrian Ltd

BRINDLE AND WHITE RUG-TIDY
Wall mounted rug rack, holds rugs horizontally, as your horse wears them.
Manufacturer: Brindle and White (Rug-Tidy)

BUCAS SMARTEX RUG
An all weather turnout rug, waterproof and breathable outer fabric with a stay dry lining.
RRP: £85.00
Manufacturer: Prolite Ltd

FAL GOLIATH ULTIMATE RUG
The Goliath Ultimate is waterproof, heavyweight, windproof and has a duvet interior, suitable for all weather conditions. Price quoted is for a 5'3" rug with fixed lining.
RRP: £201.00
Manufacturer: Fal Textile Industries Ltd

HORSEWARE RAMBO TURNOUT RUG
The Rambo rug is made of strong and breathable nylon, which reduces friction and polishes the coat. It's easy to wash and is also hygienic. RRP quoted is for a standard size, medium weight blanket.
RRP: £127.95
Manufacturer: Horseware Ireland

HORSEWARE RHINO PLUS STABLE RUG
Offers freedom of movement, front closure system with an intergrated neck cover.
RRP: £84.95
Manufacturer: Horseware Ireland

KINGSHEAD DRIMAX LITE TURNOUT RUG
Texturised polyester with Protex 2000, waterproof, breathable coating, available in black & colbalt.
RRP: £99.99
Manufacturer: J W Wilkinson & Co
Supplier: J W Wilkinson & Co

KINGSHEAD HONEYCOOL COOLER
100% Polyester, with 2 buckle breast straps, crossed surcingles, acrylic fur wither patch, fillet loops and is also darted at the rear for a cosy fit.
RRP: £29.99
Manufacturer: J W Wilkinson & Co
Supplier: J W Wilkinson & Co

KINGSHEAD KENDAL- DAY RUGS
100% Wool. The single breast strap is made of Havana leather with a brass buckle. Binding colour is optional.
RRP: £99.99
Manufacturer: J W Wilkinson & Co
Supplier: J W Wilkinson & Co

MASTA QUARTER SHEET WITH LIGHT
The quarter sheet is waterproof, it sits behind the saddle and has a detachable red light, which flashes and reflective strips for added safety.
RRP: £28.90
Manufacturer: Matchmakers International Ltd

QUALTEX COOLER - MULTI PURPOSE
Very versitile rug which means that it can be used as an anti sweat rug, travelling rug, summer sheet or as an under rug.
Manufacturer: Qualtex

QUALTEX FLY SHEET
Twin breasted straps, tail guard with adjustable leg straps.
Manufacturer: Qualtex

THERMATEX ORIGINAL THERMATEX RUG
Double front closure, lightweight, easy to fit, machine washable. Available in 13 colours, it is a multi purpose rug.
RRP: £88.00
Manufacturer: Thermatex Made in Wales (UK)

THERMATEX THERMATEX 2000 LIGHTWEIGHT
Made from a unique wool and acrylic blend with a polypropylene insulating layer. Easy to fit, machine washable. Rocco fitting as standard.
RRP: £112.00
Manufacturer: Thermatex Made in Wales (UK)

TREADSTONE TURNBERRY TURNOUT RUG
Made from fully waterproof and breathable materials.
RRP: £69.95
Manufacturer: Loveson

TROJAN COOLER RUG
Seamless waffle cooler with surcingles and adjustable chest straps. Available in navy or green and in three sizes. The RRP quoted is for rug upto 5'6", upto 6'6" RRP is £45.00 and over 6'6" RRp is £48.00.
RRP: £40.00
Manufacturer: Trojan Equestrian

TROJAN POLAR FLEECE
Cozy polar fleece rug, available in full or high neck, comes in a range of colours. Sizes available from upto 5'6" to over 6'6", the RRP quoted is for over 6'6". Upto 5'6" RRP is £45.00, upto 6'6" RRP is £48.00.
RRP: £53.00
Manufacturer: Trojan Equestrian

WEATHERBEETA ASPEN COMBO RUG
The Aspen Combo is 100% waterproof and breathable, it protects from all weather conditions. It has a seamless back and nylon shoulders to prevent rubbing.
RRP: £110.00
Manufacturer: Weatherbeeta Ltd

SADDLECLOTHS & NUMNAHS

NUUMED ALL PURPOSE ORIGINAL SEAT SAVER
100% wool seat saver, shaped to ensure comfort and a secure fit.
RRP: £33.95
Manufacturer: Griffin Nuu Med

NUUMED EVERY-DAY QUILT NUMNAH
Hard wearing and well cut numnah made of high density 5oz box quilt.
RRP: £13.00
Manufacturer: Griffin Nuu Med

NUUMED HIGH WITHER HALF WOOL LINED PAD
Shaped with a wool pad and wool lining for over the pressure points. Available in 5oz or 9oz quilting weight.
RRP: £45.00
Manufacturer: Griffin Nuu Med

NUUMED HIGH WITHER PRO PAD
A unique high wither pad which has been proven to benefit all shapes of horses. The pad, which is made in a smart 12oz quilt, is an ideal everyday pad giving a good level of protection, available self bound or with contrasting binding.
RRP: £29.50
Manufacturer: Griffin Nuu Med

PROLITE GP RELIEF PAD
Lightweight and contoured to fit the shape of the horses back. Designed to relieve pressure from the spine and other areas.
RRP: £49.00
Manufacturer: Prolite Ltd

PROLITE SADDLE PADS
The GP Relief Pad increases the bearing area of any saddle, it's lightweight with a spine clearance channel. RRP quoted is for a Standard GP saddle pad.
RRP: £14.00
Manufacturer: Prolite Ltd

QUALTEX GENERAL PURPOSE SADDLE PADS
Quilted cotton saddle pads.
Manufacturer: Qualtex

SADDLES

ALBION KONTROL SADDLE
The Kontrol is a show jumping saddle which gives the horse gymnastic freedom.
RRP: £1100.00
Manufacturer: Albion Saddlemakers Co Ltd

ESPRO FUR FABRIC SEAT COVER
Elasticated fur fabric seat cover, fits easily onto the saddle, providing comfort for the rider.
RRP: £6.95
Manufacturer: Espro Ltd
Supplier: Espro Ltd

FRANK BAINES THE ELAN CLOSE CONTACT SADDLE
This saddle is available in ten different tree widths, in a range of sizes 15" - 19", which enables the rider to maintain perfect balance and control of the horse.
RRP: £930.00
Manufacturer: Frank Baines Saddlery

FRANK BAINES THE ELEGANCE DRESSAGE SADDLE
Developed for maximum comfort for the horse, also allowing the rider to achieve perfect balance. Sizes range from 17" - 18.5", also available in a range of colours, tawny nut, mid havana, newmarket tan.
RRP: £930.00
Manufacturer: Frank Baines Saddlery

JAGUAR XJR EVENT SADDLE
Has padded forward flaps, pencil knee rolls and a deep comfortable seat. Ideal for three day events.
Manufacturer: H W Dabbs Saddlemakers Ltd

STUBBEN ARTUS CS SADDLE
High quality leather saddle with a deep seat for comfort and good grip. Available in various tree widths.
RRP: £790.00
Manufacturer: Stubben UK

THOROWGOOD MAXAM GENERAL PUPOSE SADDLE
Lightweight and comfortable saddle which gives the rider good balance and position.
RRP: £149.00
Manufacturer: Thorowgood Ltd

THOROWGOOD TEQNIC GPD SADDLE
The GPD is a more influenced show saddle with a deep seat and cut back that allows extra fitting clearance for high withered horses.
RRP: £199.00
Manufacturer: Thorowgood Ltd

SHELTER & STABLES

CHART STABLES SHELTERS
Field shelters and stores available with or without overhangs, can be totally open fronted or partly enclosed.
Manufacturer: Chart Stables Ltd
Supplier: Chart Stables Ltd

CHART STABLES STABLE RANGE
The Clipper, Chart and Chester ranges offer a variety of stabling that can be adapted to meet individual needs.
Manufacturer: Chart Stables Ltd
Supplier: Chart Stables Ltd

EQUIMAT MATTING
Wall, trailer and stable matting available. This helps to improve horses comfort, health and also provides cushioning and protection all round. RRP quoted is based on 12' x 12', 20mm thick locking mat.
RRP: £317.25
Manufacturer: Davies & Co
Supplier: Davies & Co

SHOW JACKETS

GORRINGE SHOW JACKET
Available in polyester or wool with a panelled back, single vent and a velvet collar. For ladies and children, in navy or black.
Manufacturer: Gorringe Sportswear Ltd

TACK ROOM

TIRUS SADDLE SAFE
Anti theft device, designed to secure all G.P saddles onto a standard metal saddle rack. RRP quoted includes a £1.00 UK Mainland carriage charge.
RRP: £12.50
Supplier: Tirus Equestrian Products

WHIPS

OLD MILL WHIPS DRESSAGE WHIP DRS10
The dressage whip has leather handles plaited top and middle fibreglass inner. Various lengths available.
RRP: £14.95
Manufacturer: Old Mill Whips

YARD

DUBLIN SHAVINGS FORK
A small shavings fork.
RRP: £7.99
Supplier: Ride-Away

ELICO EQUINE DECAHEDRON
A twenty sided equine activity toy. You can fill it with treats or dry food and let your horse play. RRP quoted is for an 8" decahedron, a 10" toy is available at £13.70.
RRP: £10.50
Supplier: B Jenkinson & Sons

ELICO PLASTIC SHOVEL
Plastic lightweight shovel.
RRP: £12.50
Supplier: B Jenkinson & Sons

TIRUS YARD KNIFE
Plastic safety knife designed to cut through things such as vacuum packed bags of shavings. RRP quoted includes £0.35 UK Mainland carriage charge.
RRP: £2.85
Supplier: Tirus Equestrian Products

WEATHERBEETA DELUXE STABLE RAKE
Stable rake with a wide metal handle.
RRP: £12.99
Supplier: Ride-Away

"...and to think I could be at home watching Eastenders"

Relax...
with the name
you can trust
Baileys®
Feeding from experience
aileys Horse Feeds
Telephone: 01371 850247
www.baileyshorsefeeds.co.uk